THE
Baseball
Encyclopedia

THE
Baseball
Encyclopedia

Sixth Edition/Revised, Updated and Expanded

THE COMPLETE AND OFFICIAL
RECORD OF MAJOR LEAGUE BASEBALL

Joseph L. Reichler, Editor

MACMILLAN PUBLISHING COMPANY
NEW YORK

COLLIER MACMILLAN PUBLISHERS
LONDON

SIXTH EDITION

EDITORIAL AND RESEARCH STAFF:

Jeffrey Neuman, *Editorial Director*
Scott Corngold
Jackie Dickens
Robert Keefe
Richard Kline

Casey Kwang-Chong Lee
Fred C. Richardson
David Shaw
Gene Waller

Special thanks to Pete Palmer, Frank J. Williams, and The Society for American Baseball Research.

Macmillan Publishing Company
866 Third Avenue, New York, N.Y. 10022
Collier Macmillan Canada, Inc.

Library of Congress Cataloging in Publication Data

Main entry under title:

The Baseball encyclopedia.

 Bibliography: p.
 1. Baseball—United States—Statistics.
I. Reichler, Joseph L, 1915-
GV877.B27   1985   796.357′0212   85-306
ISBN 0-02-601930-2

Sixth Edition 1985

10 9 8 7 6 5 4 3 2 1

Portions of this book appeared in different form in *The Baseball Trade Register,* Copyright © 1984 by Joseph L. Reichler.

Printed in the United States of America

Contents

THE
Baseball
Encyclopedia

PART ONE

Introduction

PREFACE

THE DEVELOPMENT OF BASEBALL

Preface

WHEN BOBBY THOMSON hit his game-winning home run in the last inning to give the Giants a 5–4 victory over the Dodgers and a pennant in 1951, there was a rookie waiting in the on-deck circle. It was Willie Mays. Although he was later to go on to greatness, Mays was then just another player with much promise. The same may be said of the first modern computer, which was also unveiled that year.

There seemed to be no relationship between baseball and computers until 1967, when it was decided to produce a complete and comprehensive baseball reference work. This was to be accomplished by building a data bank of major league baseball's existing statistics through the findings of a staff of skilled researchers.

The initial step in building the baseball data bank was to find out what kind of information was available and where it could best be found. Although baseball's official sheets were begun in 1903 and detailed day-by-day records of each player and team, it wasn't until 1920 that such items as runs batted in were first officially compiled. Since existing records were insufficient to build the data file, the only way to produce information from 1876, when major league baseball began, was to find other sources of data. A survey of newspapers was conducted in libraries around the country where major league teams played. A surprising amount of material was uncovered. There were scattered play-by-play accounts of the games, along with excellent box scores and stories. The newly found documented evidence left no doubt that the data file could be built.

To further ensure the value of the project, two of baseball's outstanding historians were called upon to join the staff. One was Lee Allen, the historian of the Baseball Hall of Fame in Cooperstown, New York, and the other was John Tattersall, an executive with a steamship firm in Philadelphia. Both men marveled at the idea of a complete reference work. Allen—long known as "the walking encyclopedia of baseball"—specialized in accumulating facts about the players. He had spent thirty years collecting the largest baseball demographic file in the country. A lot of that time had been spent visiting state record bureaus, speaking to ballplayers, corresponding with the descendants of ballplayers long dead, and even pursuing leads to graveyards to look at burial markers in search of information. Lee Allen suffered a fatal

7

heart attack on May 20, 1969, and did not live to see the final product of his efforts, the culmination of a lifelong dream. Historian, columnist, reporter, and author, Lee was our foremost authority on baseball history.

Tattersall's forty-year plunge into nineteenth-century baseball history made him an expert on that period. The original material he gathered over the years was housed in a basement library that contained boxes of the sports sections of different newspapers from the early 1900s until the sixties, a wide assortment of baseball publications, and a collection of scrapbooks from 1876 through 1900. There were box scores of every major league game played during that time, neatly preserved by year and league. By using these books, Tattersall was able to construct day-by-day playing records, which helped him to find or reconfirm past statistical achievements. The addition of Allen and Tattersall to the staff, and their invaluable collections, which would later supplement the other source material, gave the project a vital boost.

The steps to be taken were significant. They would include checking past performances and producing much new information on baseball before 1920 —such as double plays, earned run averages, and runs batted in. Because the accuracy of some existing records might be brought into question, it became necessary to get official sanction for the project from baseball. The presidents of the American and National Leagues both enthusiastically put their stamp of approval on the project after hearing the plan. In addition to the significance of the information, the technological phase of the project contained great challenges. Instead of manually handling the information through the usual typesetting method after it was processed by the computer, a new process was going to be used that would take the records from the computer and produce film of the actual book pages. These same baseball authorities also took comfort in the fact that existing official records, which were hand-posted, would be cross-checked by the computer. They were well aware that some of the tens of millions of entries would contain their allotted share of clerical bookkeeping errors. In order to verify the research findings and set up guidelines never before established, a special records committee was formed to discuss and vote upon the issues in question. The group consisted of representatives from the Commissioner's and both league offices, as well as a representative from the Hall of Fame and the Baseball Writer's Association of America (the committee members along with their rulings can be found in Appendix B).

A staff of researchers was assembled, and the relative calm of the past months became a frenzy of activity. While researchers mapped out the individual projects assigned to them, the source materials that were used for the research began to arrive. Included were baseball's official records—documents that record a man's day-by-day playing information—which were used as the basic source of entry. Along with these microfilmed records were hundreds of reels of microfilmed newspapers from the early 1870s until 1920, the collections of Allen and Tattersall, and baseball's trade papers, which included *The Sporting News, The Sporting Times,* and *The Sporting Life.* This amount of data, and the research staff, which increased as the project grew, made it necessary to keep tight controls. The flow of information over the coming months would continue to multiply. A basic file was established that contained the names of every man who had played major league baseball, along with the years he played and his team affiliations. Once this information was gathered and fed into the computer, rosters were produced for each year, league, and team; these rosters served as a form for entering the information. This meant that a man's yearly record could not be missed. It was also a method for eliminating players included on the roster by mistake. If, for instance, a man played for New York in the National League in 1917 and was erroneously placed on the roster of the 1917 New York American League club, the mistake would be caught when the yearly information was entered from the source material.

To complete the information on the roster forms, baseball's official sheets were the first source used. These data were supplemented by information researched from newspapers. For the years when official sheets did not exist, they were produced, for the first time, after careful study of over 19,000 games. This was accomplished by researching and transcribing the information in newspaper box scores and stories to obtain the necessary day-by-day tallies. The best sources for getting the information were usually the local newspapers of the city where the game was played and the city of the visiting team. Sometimes, however, ten sources were checked to re-create the game and accurately determine such items as runs batted in and earned runs. As research requirements increased, the original source material no longer proved sufficient, and researchers were sent across the country to ferret out information. Every source for untapped material was checked, and researchers traveled to large cities and small towns and spent days in libraries and historical societies digging through the newspaper stacks. Many times a team's runs batted in for one game had to be researched in two cities hundreds of miles apart. It was a gigantic puzzle, with the pieces falling slowly into place.

While the search for statistical information was being conducted, research on the demographic file was also in progress. This involved checking a player's height, weight, batting and throwing style, birth, death, relatives in the major leagues, nicknames, career interruptions, and managerial information.

This sometimes lead to the discovery of "phantoms," men who were originally included on baseball's all-time list because of typographical errors in the box scores. At the same time, "new" men were found, men who may have only pinch hit or pinch run and were never included in a box score.

Although a good portion of this information came from Lee Allen's files, the last two items—career interruptions and managers—were areas of original research. Interruptions, which accounted for gaps in a player's career, included injury, illness, military service, and suspensions. To dig out this information, stories of the game and the accompanying notes were read in detail. The results of the research helped to show why certain ballplayers retired early or why young players with promise never reached fulfillment. The research on managers meant finding the individual won-and-lost record of every man. This proved the most difficult research. A manager in early baseball was often designated as a field captain, not a manager, as he would be known today.

The last important step of the research phase began when the statistical information from the rosters was fed into the computer. Certain checks were built into the system to ensure the accuracy of the final material. If a team's hits did not equal the hits of the individuals on the team, a message was printed along with the information and the item in question was further researched. Although these procedures have helped to solve many of baseball's long-standing mysteries, there are questions still unanswered and research for the missing or incomplete information goes on.

In March of 1969 the initial work on this volume came to an end. But, in reality, it was just beginning. Since then, the official *Baseball Encyclopedia* has been updated five times—in 1974, 1976, 1979, 1982, and 1985. Joe Reichler, special assistant to the Commissioner of Baseball and a noted baseball author and historian, was engaged to do the work. In order to avoid bulkiness and to keep the book within a reasonable price range, it was decided to eliminate the pitchers from the Player Register, excepting those who were above-average hitters or who had performed at other positions as well.

However, new features have been added, such as the No-Hit Pitchers; consecutive game playing; Hall of Fame Roster; Triple Crown Winners; Most Valuable Player; and Cy Young and Rookie of the Year awards. And this year, for the first time, information on trades and performance at home and on the road have been added, along with inning-by-inning World Series, League Championship Series, and All-Star Game line scores. The editors are always on the lookout for more interesting and noteworthy features.

An enormous amount of mail comes in to Macmillan regarding this Encyclopedia. Much comes from readers who wish to correct errors that have slipped in along the way. We are grateful to those who take the time to write us, and apologize to anyone who may be waiting for a reply; every letter is read and every correction appreciated, but due to the backlog, we're sometimes a little slow in acknowledging your help. We would especially like to thank Frank J. Williams, who has been extraordinarily generous in sharing his research with us. Thanks to the efforts of Mr. Williams, the Society for American Baseball Research, and all those who have written us, this is the most complete and accurate Baseball Encyclopedia ever published. And the next one will be even better.

The Development of Baseball

THE FIRST SEEDS that led to organized baseball in the United States were planted on the Elysian Fields in Hoboken, New Jersey, on June 19, 1846. Two amateur teams met and played a form of baseball no one had ever seen before. Under the rules established by Alexander J. Cartwright, a surveyor and amateur athlete, who umpired the game, the Knickerbockers were beaten by the New York Nine 23–1. Cartwright's game, which included guidelines to the field as well as the playing rules, served to mark the only acceptable date of baseball's beginning.

Before that the origin is vague. Credit has been given to the Egyptians and every succeeding culture. It was in America that the English game of "rounders" finally evolved into baseball.

Although Cartwright's conception of the game as it was then played has changed somewhat, it served as the foundation on which organized amateur teams throughout the country were built. The amateurs flourished for twenty-three years before a group of Cincinnatians decided that their city needed a winner. . . .

It was 1869. . . . The territory of Wyoming was organized and woman suffrage was proudly proclaimed. . . . Dimitri Mendeleev devised the periodic table of elements. . . . A financial panic on Wall Street shook the economy of the country and the headline "Black Friday" became etched on the pages of American history.

Cincinnati also made news, although it affected few people at the time. Two years earlier a barnstorming team, the Washington Nationals, trounced the local favorites. For citizens of that Midwestern community it was an act of humiliation. They were determined to have a winning team even if it meant paying the players. And they did.

Harry Wright, a jeweler and head of a local amateur club, was paid the sum of $1200 to manage the team, the Red Stockings, and to play center field. The only man on the team from Cincinnati was Charlie Gould, the first baseman. The others included Harry's brother George, who played shortstop, Asa Brainard, pitcher, Fred Waterman, third base, Charlie Sweasy, second base, Doug Allison, catcher, Andy Leonard, left field, Cal McVey, right field, and Dick Hurley, substitute.

Those concerned with the game s sudden departure from amateur standing watched closely as Harry Wright led the rampaging Red Stockings as they traveled over 11,000 miles and achieved the phenomenal record of 56 victories and one tie. Aaron Champion, the club's president, declared in that triumphant season of 1869 that he would rather be president of the Cincinnati Baseball Club than of the United States. Champion's joy was not long-lasting, though. Still undefeated, the team walked onto the Capitoline Grounds in Brooklyn on June 14, 1870, and confidently presented their credentials to the Atlantics, a Brooklyn team. The afternoon ended in bitter disappointment for Cincinnati. In the bottom of the eleventh inning the Atlantics scored three times to win 8–7.

Other defeats later in the season, coupled with the team's mounting salaries and expenses, brought on the end of the Red Stockings—but not before they gave an important piece of heritage to American history. The Red Stockings were a revelation, uprooting the foundation of amateur baseball and replacing it with a caliber of play that paved the way for the first professional baseball league. . . .

The date was March 17, 1871. Amidst the noise and exuberance of St. Patrick's Day, ten men met in Collier's Cafe on Broadway and Thirteenth Street in New York and formed the National Association of Professional Baseball Players. James N. Kerns, a representative of the Philadelphia Athletics, was elected president.

Charter members of the association were the Boston Red Stockings, Chicago White Stockings, Cleveland Forest Citys, Fort Wayne Kekiongas, New York Mutuals, Philadelphia Athletics, Rockford Forest Citys, Washington Nationals, and the Washington Olympics. The Brooklyn Eckfords, one of the ten clubs represented at the meeting, did not start the first season. They thought the organ zation too precarious and would not risk the $10 admission fee. It wasn't until the Kekiongas franchise folded in August that the Eckfords joined. As things turned out, though, it wasn't the year for Brooklyn (a haunting cry—"Wait till next year"—was born, and would follow the Eckfords' namesakes well into the twentieth century); in a post-season convention, the league nullified Brooklyn's games on the basis of late entry and struck them from the record books for 1871.

The Philadelphia Athletics won the championship with a record of 22 wins and 7 losses, and Chicago came in second. The pre-season favorite, Boston, led by the Wright brothers, McVey and Gould, finished third. Injuries accounted for the team's failure that year, but Boston came back to win four consecutive pennants.

Gambling and bribery infiltrated the league over the years and by 1875 the public's confidence in this loosely knit association of teams faded. Boston remained above this corruption, yet unwittingly added to the demise of the

National Association through their constant domination of the competition.

But baseball had just begun. It was on February 2, 1876, at the Grand Central Hotel in New York that William A. Hulbert, along with other club delegates, created the National League. It was Hulbert, a businessman, who thought it wise to create a league with a tighter organization and a higher caliber of players than had previously existed. Yet the new league could not have survived without taking the best of the National Association players. Hulbert, owner of the Chicago club, realized this and first influenced one of the Boston regulars, Al Spalding, to come and play for him. Spalding brought along other star Boston players and a member of the Philadelphia Athletics, "Cap" Anson, whose feats are now history.

Hulbert had exerted a great deal of pressure on the eastern club representatives to get them to ratify the league constitution. To preserve peace among the clubs he proposed Morgan G. Bulkeley, a Hartford man, for league president. But after serving one year, largely as a figurehead, Bulkeley left the office and went on to become a United States senator. Hulbert took over the presidency in 1877. He ruled the league with an iron hand, seeing it through scandal, financial hardships, and an upheaval of franchises, until his death in 1882.

That year, while the National League began to find steady ground, an opposing league was born. Cincinnati had been expelled from the National League after the 1880 season for condoning Sunday baseball games and permitting liquor on the grounds. A year later they were back in the major leagues when Justus Thorner of Cincinnati and H. D. "Denny" Knight of Pittsburgh formed the American Association. The National League refused to recognize this new body, consequently bringing about a fierce battle. Player raids weakened franchises in both leagues, but the Association's willingness to cut ticket prices from 50 to 25 cents and their scheduling of Sunday baseball gave them the edge in the struggle for attendance.

Their superiority at the box office clearly reflected the thinking of the times. A. G. Mills, the National League president, realizing how suicidal it was to pursue the fight, brought about the National Agreement between the two leagues in 1883. This pact granted certain mutual protections, particularly over player contracts, and provided the cooperation which led to the first post-season series between the league champions in 1884, which was not, however, a banner year for the club owners.

A St. Louis millionaire, Henry V. Lucas, formed the Union Association, and baseball was at war again. He challenged the reserve rule, a clause in a player's contract which binds him permanently to a team until he is released, traded, or sold. By ignoring this clause—one of baseball's fundamental rules—Lucas was able to lure many players from the other leagues. Yet this very theft by the Unions caused their downfall; their own players were raided in turn by the other leagues, and of the twelve franchises that started the season, only five finished. The chief beneficiary of the Union Association's brief lifespan turned out to be Lucas. He joined the National League by buying what remained of the Cleveland franchise and moving them to St. Louis. A semblance of order remained for five years—then chaos erupted.

In 1885 a small organization established for the protection and promotion of players' rights, the Brotherhood of Professional Ball Players, was founded. The Brotherhood made some inroads over the years, but could not fully resolve the grievances that confronted them. The players were frustrated by a salary ceiling, the reserve clause rule, arbitrary fines, and other inequities thrust upon them by the club owners. The limit of endurance was reached in 1890 when they rebelled and formed the Players' League. The new league went through the 1890 season fighting the other two leagues for attendance, with the result that the season proved a financial disaster for all concerned.

Monte Ward, a New York Giant defector, was an able spokesman for the Players' League. He helped to bring it about and fought an uphill battle to maintain it, but he did not have the resources of the National League, which voiced itself through Al Spalding. Negotiations between the two leagues went on during the summer and winter months, until the inexperienced Brotherhood found itself no longer in existence. Wild and ill-founded rumors hurt them, and organizational weaknesses and high salaries marked their failure. Those who had jumped their contracts were allowed to go back to their old teams without penalty. Some advances were made on the part of the players, but the rebellion succeeded in bringing about an unfortunate circumstance it had never intended.

The American Association began the season of 1891 by withdrawing from the National Agreement following a dispute over reassignment of Players' League personnel who were left unprotected on the "reserve list." Unlike the earlier war with the senior league, the Association was not financially strong. Their 25-cent admission fee proved insufficient to meet the demands of expenses as competition decreased their gate revenues. By the season's end the American Association folded. Baltimore, St. Louis, Washington, and Louisville were absorbed by the National League, bringing its total to twelve clubs. The remaining franchises were bought out and peace and monopoly reigned once again.

The Association was gone, but it had introduced Sunday games and league control of umpires. For these and other reforms the Association will always be remembered. Yet it was inevitable that the giant of baseball could not remain long without competition.

Once again, it started in Cincinnati. There, in 1892, Ban Johnson, a sports writer, and Charlie Comiskey, manager of the Cincinnati Reds, first talked of a dream that was to see its fulfillment nine years later. Through Comiskey's efforts Johnson took over the reorganized Western Association, a minor league, in 1894, and worked hard for the day when his circuit could obtain major league status.

The time drew near in 1900. That year the Western Association changed its name to the American League and placed clubs in several eastern cities. Johnson had tried to speak with National League officials about the move to the East, but when his efforts were snubbed he abandoned the National Agreement—under which all organized baseball now operated—and declared open war. Johnson grabbed up enough National League talent so that, when the American League started the season of 1901, it was indeed a "major" league.

The skirmish lasted until 1903, when the National League saw the light of day and came to terms with its junior competitor. The first modern World Series marked their truce that year, but in 1904 the leagues fought again and the World Series was not held. The following year saw the reconciliation of a marriage that was made more from necessity than love. The leagues went contentedly on their way—enriching baseball's history with many great names—until 1914, when both baseball and the world were in trouble again.

The hostilities in Europe exploded into World War I, and the peace in baseball was broken when James A. Gilmore, president of the minor Federal League, brought his circuit into direct competition with the two major leagues. The new league had plenty of money to spend and they did so willingly, taking famous players such as Eddie Plank from the American League and Three Finger Brown from the National. It was a battle that was fought mostly in the courts, with the result that all parties concerned were financially hurt. Before the 1916 season began the National and American Leagues had reached a peaceful settlement with their rival, but not before assuming responsibility for $385,000 of Federal League contracts, permitting two franchises to be bought by the Federal League owners and guaranteeing payment to reimburse the investments of several others. Baseball had paid the price for peace, only to feel the pain of disorder again in 1920. This time, though, the disaster was internal.

Something was wrong with the 1919 World Series between the Chicago White Sox and the Cincinnati Reds. But this time Cincinnati could claim complete innocence. For once they were not the instigators in shaping baseball's history. Chicago was the culprit. Some of the White Sox players had thrown the Series.

An investigation was held by Ban Johnson and the case went to court. Before the court reached its decision in 1920 baseball had wisely selected its first commissioner, Judge Kenesaw Mountain Landis, who had gained prominence several years earlier through his handling of the Federal League case. His appointment marked the end of the National Commission, a three-man body set up in 1903 to govern baseball. The judge was a stern disciplinarian, bent on improving the conditions of the game—both on and off the field. This was quickly proven in his first decision. A lack of hard evidence prevented the court from convicting the individuals involved in the World Series "fix," but Landis barred them from baseball for life. Although many disagreed with his actions, baseball prospered because of him. He put the game on solid ground and made it a respected and admired sport. In this he was aided by baseball's great change in 1920.

To take advantage of the rising popularity of a young star named Babe Ruth, the ball was made much livelier. Ruth had broken the all-time home run record by hitting 29 for the Boston Red Sox in 1919. In 1920, after being sold to the New York Yankees, Ruth hit 54 home runs. This combination of Ruth, the lively ball, and the publicity generated by the New York City press took much of the glare of attention away from the scandal of the 1919 World Series and brought to baseball the beginning of an unprecedented era of prosperity and home runs.

Baseball had struggled for half a century, surviving league wars, scandal, and chaos before it began to take on a long-sought maturity. With the problem of organization no longer running into direct conflict with the playing of the game itself, it became possible to redirect much of the energy that had been squandered in past years. This was proven during the twenties, with the emergence of a brand of baseball that was colorful and exciting.

The home run ball brought the crowds in increasing number, changed the style of play, and set the pattern of baseball for the next fifty years. Pitchers could no longer fool with weaker hitters, who were now capable occasionally of hitting the home run, and old strategies had to be replaced.

The greatest stars baseball had known were all assembled during the twenties, but it could not lay sole claim to the public spotlight. Baseball contributed only part of the aura to what is called The Golden Age of Sports. It was a time when larger-than-life heroes emerged to capture the imagination: Red Grange and the immortal Four Horsemen, who streaked across endless football fields; Jack Dempsey and Gene Tunney and the remembered "long count" of boxing; Bobby Jones and Walter Hagan of golf, and Bill Tilden, who made tennis seem more than a rich man's game. Baseball's Ty Cobb, Tris Speaker, Walter Johnson, Eddie Collins, and Grover Alexander were at the twilight of their careers. And while Lou Gehrig and Lefty Grove were just getting established, Babe Ruth and Rogers Hornsby were at their prime, setting records at a blistering rate. The feats of these two men were amazing—Ruth's 467 home runs in the decade and Hornsby batting for a five-year average of .401 —but these were the kinds of achievement which marked the twenties.

During the Depression of the thirties baseball provided the public with a chance temporarily to forget the realities of a broken economy, and its popularity is best exemplified in the 1931 World Series when the St. Louis Cardinals, better known in those days as the "gas house gang" for their fiery style of play, met the Athletics. Herbert Hoover, President of the United States, attended the Series, but could not compete for applause with a .500 Series batting average of a brash Cardinal rookie named Pepper Martin. The President was met with a round of boos while screams of appreciation greeted Martin. But more important during this period were two innovations in the game which would prove to have a significance far beyond that time. In May of 1935 the first major league game was played at night. The event took place in Cincinnati and was met with great success. It was also during the thirties that radio began to be utilized, and by bringing live play-by-play accounts of a game into the home, new fans were brought into the ballparks.

Night games and a growing baseball audience slowly increased until the early forties, when all progress was stymied by World War II. Unlike the "work or fight" order of World War I, which curtailed the 1918 season, baseball was encouraged to continue by President Franklin Roosevelt, who felt that it could contribute greatly to the morale of the country. The ranks of baseball were drained by the call to arms, but the veterans too old for active military duty and the youngsters still not of age for the service provided the personnel necessary to keep the game going.

A year after the war, in 1946, baseball could not, however, return at once to the tranquillity it had enjoyed in the pre-war days. The players had become dissatisfied by their lack of financial security and formed a committee demanding a pension fund, a minimum salary of $5,000, shorter spring-training schedules, and a limitation of salary cuts. Baseball owners might have fought the demands under normal circumstances, but they willingly gave in when a players' union was near final organization and the outlaw Mexican League raided the majors of several star players, who were eventually suspended for three and a half years for having jumped their contracts.

Nineteen forty-six also saw the appearance of the first American Negro in organized baseball in this century when Branch Rickey, of the Brooklyn Dodgers, signed Jackie Robinson to a contract. Robinson spent the 1946 season with the Montreal Royals, a Dodger farm team, and broke into the lineup of the parent club in 1947. There was tension in many cities, but Robinson more than proved himself and won the Rookie of the Year Award. Many Negro and Latin American players soon entered the game, producing season totals that equalled or surpassed the records of many established players. Baseball was going through a lucrative period, but this was only an omen of the greater prosperity to come.

In the late 1940s television started to take over from radio and many people were given the opportunity to see major league baseball for the first time. Communications had improved, along with commercial air travel, and they would both have a far-reaching effect on baseball. Until the early fifties base-ball had no need to have franchises in any city except those clustered in the East and Midwest, where travel by train was not an expensive and time-consuming burden. Air travel brought on talk of franchise shifts to areas beyond the familiar playing grounds of the major leagues. The Boston Braves moved to Milwaukee in 1953, and although the move did not open wide vistas, it was an indication of the dramatic changes to come. Aside from the factor of even faster air transportation, the guarantee of large radio and tele-vision markets made it less hazardous to attempt new locations. Two of base-ball's oldest teams, the National League Brooklyn Dodgers and New York Giants, saw this opportunity and moved their franchises to California before the 1958 season started, satisfying one portion of the population and dis-appointing the other.

The change was not enough; the public started to demand growth. Baseball was reluctant to make any commitment until the proposed Continental League, backed by Branch Rickey, made an attempt to become the third major league. Although Rickey's idea failed while on the drawing board, it precipitated the first expansion of the major leagues in sixty years as the American League increased to ten teams in 1961, followed by a similar in-crease of the National League in 1962.

It was around this time that an internal change began to take place in baseball. The old sportsman type of owner was being replaced by corporate ownership, marking the transition toward big business. Television revenues increased, along with gate attendance, indicating the sweeping interest in the game. Other habits of baseball also began changing. Spring training, gen-erally restricted to Florida, was now taking place in the West as well. Winter baseball became increasingly popular in South American countries because of the growing number of Latins in the game, consequently serving as an aid to the development of young ballplayers.

In 1969 the growth of baseball reached new heights. Both leagues were increased to twelve clubs, consisting of two six-team divisions. The National League moved into Canada with its Montreal franchise to mark baseball's growth on an international level. The game, already extremely popular in the Latin American countries, reached new heights of interest in Puerto Rico, Nicaragua, and Venezuela and representatives of these lands began discreetly inquiring about big-league franchises in the near future. Japan, where base-ball reigns supreme as the No. 1 sport, expressed interest in a "true" World Series involving the championship teams of the United States and Japan.

The popularity of the sport in the United States was best revealed during a mammoth off-the-field publicity campaign to celebrate professional base-ball's one hundredth anniversary. The fans of the nation, through individual newspapers and radio stations, were asked to select an All-Time All-Star team in each of the major league cities. The contest generated considerable interest and reached its climax in Washington, D.C., on July 21, 1969, two nights before the Major League All-Star Game. Then, at a memorable banquet—the biggest in all sports history—two Major League All-Star teams were announced. One was the All-Time team, another was an All-Star team limited to living players. In the climax, Babe Ruth was acclaimed the greatest player ever, and Joe DiMaggio the greatest living player, barely edging out Willie Mays.

This unprecedented promotion emphasizing baseball's centennial was highlighted by a Centennial Dinner, attended by virtually all of Washington's dignitaries, prominent personalities in all walks of life, including the clergy, business, and entertainment as well as baseball luminaries of the past and present. It was followed by a visit to the White House the next afternoon where some 500 players, club executives, and newspapermen were hosted by President Nixon.

"I don't believe anything like this has ever happened before," said Ford Frick, a former baseball commissioner. It was, indeed, a remarkable coup for baseball and did much to solidify the game's image as the National Pastime.

Nineteen sixty-nine was also a year of unrest. The Major League Baseball Players' Association, formed in 1966, boycotted spring training because of a dispute involving the pension fund. An estimated 125 players, including many of the game's top stars, met in New York City on February 3, in the largest mass player meeting in history. They pledged not to sign their contracts or to report to spring training until the pension dispute was resolved. Agreement was finally reached through the intervention of Bowie Kuhn, who only weeks before had succeeded Gen. William D. Eckert as Commissioner of Baseball. In a meeting between the Player Relations Committee of the owners and the Executive Council of the Players' Association on February 25, a three-year agreement was finally hammered out which called for the owners to contribute $4,500,000 annually to the players' pension fund. This was an increase of $350,000 from the owners' original offer. The players also received increased across-the-board benefits. Among them was the lowering of the basic requirements from five to four years for eligibility and the lowering of minimum age for drawing pension benefits from 50 to 45.

Baseball was to pass through an even more turbulent time the next year when Curt Flood, a veteran outfielder, objected to his trade by St. Louis to Philadelphia and filed suit against baseball's reserve clause. This was to challenge the legality of the standard baseball contract and made headlines for months. The suit was filed January 16, 1970. In August of that year, Judge Irving Ben Cooper of the U.S. District Court in New York City upheld the defense argument that federal antitrust laws do not apply to baseball.

This dismissal was upheld first by a three-judge U.S. Circuit Court of Appeals on April 7, 1971 and finally by the Supreme Court. By a 5–3 majority, the Supreme Court, on June 19, upheld baseball's unique exemption from the antitrust laws and the controversial reserve rule which binds a player to the team that holds his contract.

Baseball rejoiced in this favorable decision but was given little time to celebrate. Nineteen seventy-two was the year the major league players staged a 13-day strike, the first general strike in baseball history, delaying the opening of the championship season by ten days and causing cancellation of 86 regular season games. The player strike came some 15 months after the umpires had refused to work the opening games of the 1970 American and National League Championship Series. All 12 umpires assigned to post season playoffs struck and had the support of the Major League Umpires Association. Minor league umpires and retired major league arbiters were used in the first two games before an agreement was reached. The settlement resulted in salary increases for umpires as well as increased pension benefits. The player strike, too, ended only after the owners had agreed to increase their contribution to the pension plan and the transfer of surplus pension funds.

Another player strike was narrowly averted in March of 1973 when the owners agreed to outside arbitration in salary negotiations. It was also agreed that a player with ten years of major league experience, the last five with the same club, could not be traded without his consent. The first player to publicly take advantage of the rule was Ron Santo of the Chicago Cubs, who rejected a trade that would have sent him to the California Angels.

Baseball's precious reserve clause which binds a player to one team unless he is traded, retires, or released, was shaken to its very foundation in a day-before-Christmas Eve decision handed down by an arbitrator who ruled that players who perform one season without a signed contract should become free agents at liberty to sell their services to the highest bidder.

Specifically, the arbitrator ruled that two pitchers, Andy Messersmith of the Los Angeles Dodgers and Dave McNally of the Montreal Expos, were both free agents and no longer bound by their contracts because their respective clubs had agreed to allow them to play a full season without being signed. Realizing that if this ruling were upheld in the courts it could topple the major league's legal right to own players indefinitely, the clubs immediately took steps to challenge the decision.

At the heart of the controversy was the fact that baseball has long enjoyed stricter control of its players than any other professional sport. Three times in the last fifty years the Supreme Court has reviewed the game's reserve clause and has allowed it to stand. In more recent years, however, the contract system has increasingly been challenged, especially in collective bargaining with the Major League Baseball Players' Association. In 1974 the same arbitrator who ruled in the Messersmith and McNally cases, Peter M. Seitz, declared Jim "Catfish" Hunter free of his contract with the Oakland A's after which Hunter auctioned himself to the New York Yankees for $3.25 million.

The Hunter and Oakland dispute involved an alleged breach of contract by the team, which owed $50,000 to the pitcher. In the Messersmith and McNally cases, the issue was more basic. Both refused to sign contracts for 1975, pitched without contracts, and then demanded their freedom in the open market. The clubs maintained that the wording in the contract gave them the right to renew a player's contract from year to year whether the player signed or not; the players felt that the renewal was good for one year only and could not be invoked indefinitely.

It was baseball's contention that the arbitrator's decision, if upheld, would have dire results, wreak great harm to the reserve system, and do serious damage to the sport by encouraging players to sign with the highest bidder. This would enable the rich clubs to corral the biggest stars and result in the diminishing or elimination of the competitive factor so important to the health and popularity of the sport.

In handing down the decision, Seitz stated: "I am not an Abraham Lincoln signing the Emancipation Proclamation. Involuntary servitude has nothing to do with this case. The decision does not destroy baseball. But if the club owners think it will ruin baseball, they have it in their power to prevent the damage."

Baseball's second expansion did not work out quite as well as its first, which had produced solid franchises in New York, Houston, Minnesota, and California. (Actually, the existing Washington franchise was moved to Minnesota, with a new club placed in the nation's capital.) Of the four clubs in the 1969 expansion—Montreal, Seattle, San Diego, and Kansas City—Seattle was sold and moved to Milwaukee after just one year and San Diego teetered at the edge before Ray Kroc, president of McDonald's, came to the rescue by purchasing the club from the beleaguered C. Arnhold Smith, thus preventing another shift. In 1972, Robert Short, owner of the expansion Washington Senators, was given permission by the American League to move his club to Arlington, Texas, where they became the Texas Rangers.

The American League expanded again in 1977, adding a club in Toronto and a new one in Seattle, which had completed a magnificent domed stadium. The American League thus became a fourteen-team circuit, while the National League held at twelve teams.

The years 1976 through 1981 saw enormous change. They were years of thrilling successes on the field and turmoil and strife off it. Attendance and TV revenue reached new highs, but player-owner relations hit an all-time low. The bad feelings between the players and owners culminated in the long and costly player strike that nearly ruined the 1981 season and left a bitter taste in the mouths of even the most devoted fans.

The balance of power, always weighted heavily in the owners' favor, was suddenly in the hands of the players with the modification of the reserve clause in 1976. Twenty-four players took advantage of the change in the first year to break with their clubs, becoming free agents by playing out their option year without signing new contracts. Through the complicated free-agent draft, a dozen of the more-established players attracted multimillion-dollar contracts. Reggie Jackson made the biggest splash, signing a five-year contract with the Yankees for $3 million, but it would soon be dwarfed in the gold rush to come.

The year 1976 also saw a seventeen-day spring training lockout by club owners, a new four-year agreement incorporating the players' unprecedented rights and privileges, and a multimillion-dollar damage suit brought by Oakland owner Charlie Finley against Commissioner Bowie Kuhn. Kuhn had voided Finley's sale of outfielder Joe Rudi and pitcher Rollie Fingers to the Boston Red Sox for $2 million and pitcher Vida Blue to the New York Yankees for $1.5 million. After a lengthy court battle, federal judge Frank McGarr of Chicago ruled in favor of Kuhn, holding that the commissioner had the authority to act "in the best interests" of baseball.

Activity in the free-agent market boomed in 1977 when no fewer than 89 players became eligible for the reentry draft. These included some who had played out their option year and others with six or more years of major league service who had refused 1978 contracts. The second draft made millionaires of another dozen players. In the next four years, from 1978 to 1981, 43 players would receive contracts worth over a million dollars. Dave Winfield topped them all when he signed a ten-year contract with the Yankees in November 1980 for a reported $13 million. The contract included a cost-of-living increase which could boost the ten-year total past the $20 million mark.

The free agents were not the only ones to receive enormous contracts. Players no longer had to accept what their clubs were offering and even used the threat of free agency to force their clubs to offer more-lucrative contracts. Some owners, in an attempt to get something in exchange for players who they knew would leave anyway, traded players—Fred Lynn, Rick Burleson, Ken Griffey, and Rod Carew for example—before they reached free-agent status. Even average players reaped benefits: The average salary jumped from $50,000 in 1976 to $200,000 in 1981. While the owners' wild spending was decried by impartial observers, the consensus was that they had no one to blame but themselves.

Finally, in 1980, the owners decided to do something about skyrocketing salaries. They insisted on a clause in the new standard player agreement that would guarantee a club losing a player through free agency a player from the club signing the free agent. The Players' Association refused. Director Marvin Miller maintained that the players would not give back rights they had won in the courts. As evidence of their solidarity, the players staged a walkout the last week of spring training and vowed to call a strike on May 23 if there was no signed pact. The strike was averted only minutes before the deadline when the 26 club owners and the Players' Association agreed to a contract settlement. The parties agreed to establish a player-management study committee on free agency and compensation. If they were unable to reach agreement, the owners could implement their compensation proposal in February 1981, and the players could get a strike deadline.

The owners implemented a system: for every "premium" player lost through free agency, a professional replacement was to be supplied by the club signing the free agent. The owners also presented their guidelines for determining who these premium players would be.

The Players' Association rejected the plan, arguing that it tended to punish clubs signing premium free agents and thus would restrict their freedom. On June 12, 1981, the players began the longest strike in sports history, a strike that shut down major league baseball for 50 days at the height of the season, and caused the cancellation of 714 games. The strike was finally settled on July 31, and the season resumed a week later.

The terms of the settlement were:

1. Teams losing premium free agents would receive compensation from a pool rather than directly from the signing club.
2. A team signing a premium free agent could keep 24 players out of the pool; all other teams could protect 26.
3. A team losing a player from the pool would receive $150,000 from an industry fund to which all clubs would contribute.
4. No club may lose more than one player per year from the pool.
5. Five clubs could choose to sit out the reentry draft for premium players for a three-year period and thus avoid exposing players to the pool.
6. Players would receive full credit for service time lost during the strike.
7. The Basic Agreement was extended through 1984.
8. The Players' Association agreed to drop an unfair labor practices charge against the owners.

When the strike began, baseball was enjoying a banner season. Attendance was at a record high, and there were tight races in all four divisions. Rookie sensations Fernando Valenzuela and Tim Raines had captured the imagination of the fans, but the shutdown cast an ominous cloud over the game. Disgruntled fans vowed to boycott the games once play resumed.

In the hope that it would create a new interest in the game, the owners adopted a controversial split-season format. Teams leading their divisions when the strike began automatically qualified for the playoffs. The winners of the second half of the season played the leaders of the first half in a new tier of divisional playoffs; the winners went on to the League Championship Series. An unfortunate consequence of this system was that the teams with the best overall records in each of the National League divisions, the Cincinnati Reds and St. Louis Cardinals, failed to qualify for the post-season tournament.

With a final Basic Agreement in hand until the end of 1984, the owners and players hoped that the spotlight could be put back onto the game as played on the field. Unfortunately, that proved to be difficult, and this time the owners had only themselves to blame. In an owners' meeting in August 1982, it became clear that the reelection of Bowie Kuhn as commissioner was in deep trouble. Voting rules required that the commissioner receive a three-fourths majority in each league; no-votes from four National League owners would be sufficient to deny Kuhn another term. Five National League owners were unalterably opposed to Kuhn's reelection. None had any questions about Kuhn's integrity or ability to govern the on-the-field elements of the game. The most frequently cited objection was that Kuhn was not a businessman, and didn't have the expertise to oversee intricate television rights negotiations or create and implement detailed marketing plans for baseball as a whole.

At that August meeting, some owners proposed the creation of a position with the extraterrestrial-sounding name COOBA—Chief Operating Officer for Baseball Affairs—to oversee the business end of the game. This idea could only rise so far before sinking under the weight of unanswered questions: would COOBA be above and/or independent of the commissioner, or would he report to him? Did COOBA represent a necessary step in the evolution of the commissioner's office, or was it merely a way of pacifying the Intractible Five and saving Kuhn's job?

Whatever the truth behind COOBA, it was a short-lived proposal. After twelve months of increasingly divisive debate, it became clear that there was no way Kuhn could survive in his job with his powers intact. In August 1983, he withdrew himself from consideration for another term. His tenure, scheduled to expire in that month, would be extended until year's end, at which time a yet-unnamed commissioner would take over. The search for a new commissioner was already underway; it had begun in March in order to present alternatives to Kuhn.

The search proved not to be so simple. The committee, headed by Bud Selig of the Milwaukee Brewers, spent over fifteen months interviewing candidates before settling on Peter Ueberroth, then serving as president of the Los Angeles Olympics Organizing Committee. The owners agreed to wait until Ueberroth was through with his duties on behalf of the 1984 Summer Olympics, and extended Kuhn's term once again, through October 1, 1984. More importantly, the owners had to accept a series of reforms which, had they existed during Kuhn's term, would have made the search for a replacement unnecessary. First and foremost, the commissioner was recognized as baseball's chief executive officer; all departments, including the Player Relations Committee and Major League Baseball Promotions, would report directly to him. Second, the voting rules for reelection were changed to require a simple majority of the twenty-six teams, with the one stipulation that he must receive at least five votes from each league. A third change increased the maximum fine the commissioner could charge a team from $5,000 to $250,000. The concessions amounted to a substantial rearming of the office of commissioner. Ueberroth was immediately tested by an umpires strike during the 1984 playoffs; he showed considerable skill as an arbitrator in settling the dispute in time for regular umps to work the fifth game of the National League playoffs. The generous settlement left high hopes that he would maintain the independence of the commissioner's office from his nominal employers, the owners.

The last years of Bowie Kuhn's reign were full of ironies. At the same time that owners were decrying the escalation of salaries, they were agreeing to pay them in alarming numbers. Where Pete Rose had once expressed a desire to be the first $100,000-a-year singles hitter, the going rate for utility infielders was approaching four times that amount. The million-dollar-a-year barrier was broken and then shattered; two million soon became the touchstone figure, with payments deferred far into the next century. Pulled up by free-agent salaries and arbitration awards, the average player salary rose to over $325,000 a year.

Free agency was here to stay, and yet this feared outcome had its own unanticipated twists. The overriding concern, voiced annually at baseball's winter meetings by Kuhn, was that free agency would destroy competitive balance by enabling the richest teams to corner the market on superstars. But baseball is not so easy a game to dominate; in today's age of unprecedented player movement, competitive balance is healthier than ever. From 1982 to 1984, twelve different teams reached the League Championship Series—as perfect a competitive balance as can be achieved. This new balance was underscored in every division in 1984. The Chicago Cubs and New York Mets rose from the depths of the National League East to battle for the pennant, and gave every indication that they were poised to do battle for years to come. The San Diego Padres finally won their first divisional title after years of effort and expenditures of millions of dollars. The Minnesota Twins stayed in the American League West race until the last weekend of the season, led by a strong crew of young hitters and pitchers with not a high-priced free agent among them. And the Detroit Tigers capped a long rebuilding program by winning 104 games and making Sparky Anderson the first manager to win either 100 games or a World Series crown in each league.

The other subsidiary benefit of the free-agent market is that it keeps baseball in the public eye all year long. The winter Hot Stove League has been greatly enlivened by the pursuit of free agents, and the willingness to sign them has become an important signal to fans that their team's ownership is willing to do whatever is necessary to bring them a winner.

All other questions aside, no one can deny that the years since the establishment of free agency have seen an extraordinary growth in the popularity of baseball. Regular-season attendance passed 45 million in 1983, and fourteen of the twenty-six major league teams topped the 2 million mark in at least one of the last three seasons. The latest television contract between Major League Baseball and NBC and ABC brought in 1.1 billion dollars to be divided by the teams in addition to their local rights money. By every conceivable measure, baseball has once again proven itself to be America's national pastime.

PART TWO

Special Achievements

MOST VALUABLE PLAYER AWARD

ROOKIE OF THE YEAR AWARD

CY YOUNG AWARD

TRIPLE CROWN WINNERS

CONSECUTIVE GAMES PLAYED

NO-HIT GAMES

BASEBALL HALL OF FAME

33

MOST VALUABLE PLAYERS

	NATIONAL LEAGUE		AMERICAN LEAGUE
		CHALMERS	
1911	Frank Schulte, Chicago (OF)	1911	Ty Cobb, Detroit (OF)
1912	Larry Doyle, New York (2B)	1912	Tris Speaker, Boston (OF)
1913	Jake Daubert, Brooklyn (1B)	1913	Walter Johnson, Washington (P)
1914	Johnny Evers, Boston (2B)	1914	Eddie Collins, Philadelphia (2B)
		LEAGUE	
1922	No Selection	1922	George Sisler, St. Louis (1B)
1923	No Selection	1923	Babe Ruth, New York (OF)
1924	Dazzy Vance, Brooklyn (P)	1924	Walter Johnson, Washington (P)
1925	Rogers Hornsby, St. Louis (2B)	1925	Roger Peckinpaugh, Washington (SS)
1926	Bob O'Farrell, St. Louis (C)	1926	George Burns, Cleveland (1B)
1927	Paul Waner, Pittsburgh (OF)	1927	Lou Gehrig, New York (1B)
1928	Jim Bottomley, St. Louis. (1B)	1928	Mickey Cochrane, Philadelphia (C)
1929	Rogers Hornsby, Chicago (2B)	1929	No Selection
		BASEBALL WRITERS ASSOCIATION OF AMERICA	
1931	Frankie Frisch, St. Louis (2B)	1931	Lefty Grove, Philadelphia (P)
1932	Chuck Klein, Philadelphia (OF)	1932	Jimmie Foxx, Philadelphia (1B)
1933	Carl Hubbell, New York (P)	1933	Jimmie Foxx, Philadelphia (1B)
1934	Dizzy Dean, St. Louis (P)	1934	Mickey Cochrane, Detroit (C)
1935	Gabby Hartnett, Chicago (C)	1935	Hank Greenberg, Detroit (1B)
1936	Carl Hubbell, New York (P)	1936	Lou Gehrig, New York (1B)
1937	Joe Medwick, St. Louis (OF)	1937	Charlie Gehringer, Detroit (2B)
1938	Ernie Lombardi, Cincinnati (C)	1938	Jimmie Foxx, Boston (1B)
1939	Bucky Walters, Cincinnati (P)	1939	Joe DiMaggio, New York (OF)
1940	Frank McCormick, Cincinnati (1B)	1940	Hank Greenberg, Detroit (1B)
1941	Dolph Camilli, Brooklyn (1B)	1941	Joe DiMaggio, New York (OF)
1942	Mort Cooper, St. Louis (P)	1942	Joe Gordon, New York (2B)
1943	Stan Musial, St. Louis (OF)	1943	Spud Chandler, New York (P)
1944	Marty Marion, St. Louis (SS)	1944	Hal Newhouser, Detroit (P)
1945	Phil Cavarretta, Chicago (1B)	1945	Hal Newhouser, Detroit (P)
1946	Stan Musial, St. Louis (1B)	1946	Ted Williams, Boston (OF)
1947	Bob Elliott, Boston (3B)	1947	Joe DiMaggio, New York (OF)
1948	Stan Musial, St. Louis (OF)	1948	Lou Boudreau, Cleveland (SS)
1949	Jackie Robinson, Brooklyn (2B)	1949	Ted Williams, Boston (OF)
1950	Jim Konstanty, Philadelphia (P)	1950	Phil Rizzuto, New York (SS)
1951	Roy Campanella, Brooklyn (C)	1951	Yogi Berra, New York (C)
1952	Hank Sauer, Chicago (OF)	1952	Bobby Shantz, Philadelphia (P)
1953	Roy Campanella, Brooklyn (C)	1953	Al Rosen, Cleveland (3B)
1954	Willie Mays, New York (OF)	1954	Yogi Berra, New York (C)
1955	Roy Campanella, Brooklyn (C)	1955	Yogi Berra, New York (C)
1956	Don Newcombe, Brooklyn (P)	1956	Mickey Mantle, New York (OF)
1957	Henry Aaron, Milwaukee (OF)	1957	Mickey Mantle, New York (OF)
1958	Ernie Banks, Chicago (SS)	1958	Jackie Jensen, Boston (OF)
1959	Ernie Banks, Chicago (SS)	1959	Nellie Fox, Chicago (2B)
1960	Dick Groat, Pittsburgh (SS)	1960	Roger Maris, New York (OF)
1961	Frank Robinson, Cincinnati (OF)	1961	Roger Maris, New York (OF)
1962	Maury Wills, Los Angeles (SS)	1962	Mickey Mantle, New York (OF)
1963	Sandy Koufax, Los Angeles (P)	1963	Elston Howard, New York (C)
1964	Ken Boyer, St. Louis (3B)	1964	Brooks Robinson, Baltimore (3B)
1965	Willie Mays, San Francisco (OF)	1965	Zoilo Versalles, Minnesota (SS)
1966	Roberto Clemente, Pittsburgh (OF)	1966	Frank Robinson, Baltimore (OF)
1967	Orlando Cepeda, St. Louis (1B)	1967	Carl Yastrzemski, Boston (OF)
1968	Bob Gibson, St. Louis (P)	1968	Denny McLain, Detroit (P)
1969	Willie McCovey, San Francisco (1B)	1969	Harmon Killebrew, Minnesota (3B)
1970	Johnny Bench, Cincinnati (C)	1970	Boog Powell, Baltimore (1B)
1971	Joe Torre, St. Louis (3B)	1971	Vida Blue, Oakland (P)
1972	Johnny Bench, Cincinnati (C)	1972	Richie Allen, Chicago (1B)
1973	Pete Rose, Cincinnati (OF)	1973	Reggie Jackson, Oakland (OF)
1974	Steve Garvey, Los Angeles (1B)	1974	Jeff Burroughs, Texas (OF)
1975	Joe Morgan, Cincinnati (2B)	1975	Fred Lynn, Boston (OF)
1976	Joe Morgan, Cincinnati (2B)	1976	Thurman Munson, New York (C)
1977	George Foster, Cincinnati (OF)	1977	Rod Carew, Minnesota (1B)
1978	Dave Parker, Pittsburgh (OF)	1978	Jim Rice, Boston (OF)
1979	Keith Hernandez, St. Louis (1B)	1979	Don Baylor, California (DH)
	Willie Stargell, Pittsburgh (1B)	1980	George Brett, Kansas City (3B)
1980	Mike Schmidt, Philadelphia (3B)	1981	Rollie Fingers, Milwaukee (P)
1981	Mike Schmidt, Philadelphia (3B)	1982	Robin Yount, Milwaukee (SS)
1982	Dale Murphy, Atlanta (OF)	1983	Cal Ripken, Baltimore (SS)
1983	Dale Murphy, Atlanta (OF)	1984	Willie Hernandez, Detroit (P)
1984	Ryne Sandberg, Chicago (2B)		

ROOKIE OF THE YEAR
(one selection 1947-48)

	NATIONAL LEAGUE		**AMERICAN LEAGUE**
1947	Jackie Robinson, Brooklyn (1B)	1949	Roy Sievers, St. Louis (OF)
1948	**Alvin Dark, Boston (SS)**	1950	Walt Dropo, Boston (1B)
1949	Don Newcombe, Brooklyn (P)	1951	Gil McDougald, New York (3B)
1950	Sam Jethroe, Boston (OF)	1952	Harry Byrd, Philadelphia (P)
1951	Willie Mays, New York (OF)	1953	Harvey Kuenn, Detroit (SS)
1952	Joe Black, Brooklyn (P)	1954	Bob Grim, New York (P)
1953	Junior Gilliam, Brooklyn (2B)	1955	Herb Score, Cleveland (P)
1954	Wally Moon, St. Louis (OF)	1956	Luis Aparicio, Chicago (SS)
1955	Bill Virdon, St. Louis (OF)	1957	**Tony Kubek. New York (SS)**
1956	Frank Robinson, Cincinnati (OF)	1958	Albie Pearson, Washington (OF)
1957	Jack Sanford, Philadelphia (P)	1959	Bob Allison, Washington (OF)
1958	Orlando Cepeda, San Francisco (1B)	1960	Ron Hansen, Baltimore (SS)
1959	Willie McCovey, San Francisco (1B)	1961	Don Schwall, Boston (P)
1960	Frank Howard, Los Angeles (OF)	1962	Tom Tresh, New York (SS)
1961	Billy Williams, Chicago (OF)	1963	Gary Peters, Chicago (P)
1962	Ken Hubbs, Chicago (2B)	1964	**Tony Oliva, Minnesota (OF)**
1963	Pete Rose, Cincinnati (2B)	1965	**Curt Blefary, Baltimore (OF)**
1964	Richie Allen, Philadelphia (3B)	1966	Tommie Agee, Chicago (OF)
1965	Jim Lefebvre, Los Angeles (2B)	1967	Rod Carew, Minnesota (2B)
1966	Tommy Helms, Cincinnati (2B)	1968	Stan Bahnsen, New York (P)
1967	Tom Seaver, New York (P)	1969	Lou Piniella, Kansas City (OF)
1968	Johnny Bench, Cincinnati (C)	1970	Thurman Munson, New York (C)
1969	Ted Sizemore, Los Angeles (2B)	1971	Chris Chambliss, Cleveland (1B)
1970	Carl Morton, Montreal (P)	1972	Carlton Fisk, Boston (C)
1971	Earl Williams, Atlanta (C)	1973	Al Bumbry, Baltimore (OF)
1972	Jon Matlack, New York (P)	1974	Mike Hargrove, Texas (1B)
1973	Gary Matthews, San Francisco (OF)	1975	Fred Lynn, Boston (OF)
1974	**Bake McBride, St. Louis (OF)**	1976	Mark Fidrych, Detroit (P)
1975	John Montefusco, San Francisco (P)	1977	**Eddie Murray, Baltimore (DH)**
1976	Pat Zachry, Cincinnati (P)	1978	**Lou Whitaker, Detroit (2B)**
	Butch Metzger, San Diego (P)	1979	**Alfredo Griffin, Toronto (SS)**
1977	Andre Dawson, Montreal (OF)		**John Castino, Minnesota (3B)**
1978	Bob Horner, Atlanta (3B)	1980	Joe Charboneau, Cleveland (OF)
1979	**Rick Sutcliffe, Los Angeles (P)**	1981	Dave Righetti, New York (P)
1980	Steve Howe. Los Angeles (P)	1982	Cal Ripken, Baltimore (SS)
1981	**Fernando Valenzuela, Los Angeles (P)**	1983	**Ron Kittle, Chicago (OF)**
1982	**Steve Sax, Los Angeles (2B)**	1984	**Alvin Davis, Seattle (1B)**
1983	Darryl Strawberry, New York (OF)		
1984	Dwight Gooden, New York (P)		

CY YOUNG AWARD WINNERS
(one selection 1956-66)

	NATIONAL LEAGUE		**AMERICAN LEAGUE**
1956	Don Newcombe, Brooklyn (RH)	1958	Bob Turley, New York (RH)
1957	Warren Spahn, Milwaukee (LH)	1959	Early Wynn, Chicago (RH)
1960	Vernon Law, Pittsburgh (RH)	1961	Whitey Ford, New York (LH)
1962	Don Drysdale, Los Angeles (RH)	1964	Dean Chance, Los Angeles (RH)
1963	Sandy Koufax, Los Angeles (LH)	1967	Jim Lonborg, Boston (RH)
1965	Sandy Koufax, Los Angeles (LH)	1968	Denny McLain, Detroit (RH)
1966	Sandy Koufax, Los Angeles (LH)	1969	Mike Cuellar, Baltimore (tie) (LH)
1967	Mike McCormick, San Francisco (LH)	1969	Denny McLain, Detroit (tie) (RH)
1968	Bob Gibson, St. Louis (RH)	1970	Jim Perry, Minnesota (RH)
1969	Tom Seaver, New York (RH)	1971	Vida Blue, Oakland (LH)
1970	Bob Gibson, St. Louis (RH)	1972	Gaylord Perry, Cleveland (RH)
1971	Ferguson Jenkins, Chicago (RH)	1973	Jim Palmer, Baltimore (RH)
1972	Steve Carlton, Philadelphia (LH)	1974	Jim (Catfish) Hunter, Oakland (RH)
1973	Tom Seaver, New York (RH)	1975	Jim Palmer, Baltimore (RH)
1974	Mike Marshall, Los Angeles (RH)	1976	Jim Palmer, Baltimore (RH)
1975	Tom Seaver, New York (RH)	1977	Sparky Lyle, New York (LH)
1976	Randy Jones, San Diego (LH)	1978	Ron Guidry, New York (LH)
1977	Steve Carlton, Philadelphia (LH)	1979	**Mike Flanagan, Baltimore (LH)**
1978	Gaylord Perry, San Diego (RH)	1980	**Steve Stone. Baltimore (RH)**
1979	Bruce Sutter, Chicago (RH)	1981	**Rollie Fingers, Milwaukee (RH)**
1980	**Steve Carlton, Philadelphia (LH)**	1982	Pete Vuckovich, Milwaukee (RH)
1981	**Fernando Valenzuela, Los Angeles (LH)**	1983	LaMarr Hoyt, Chicago (RH)
1982	Steve Carlton, Philadelphia (LH)	1984	Willie Hernandez, Detroit (LH)
1983	John Denny, Philadelphia (RH)		
1984	Rick Sutcliffe, Chicago (RH)		

TRIPLE CROWN WINNERS

NATIONAL LEAGUE

Paul Hines, Providence	1878
Hugh Duffy, Boston	1894
Heinie Zimmerman, Chicago	1912
Rogers Hornsby, St. Louis	1922
Rogers Hornsby, St. Louis	1925
Chuck Klein, Philadelphia	1933
Joe Medwick, St. Louis	1937

AMERICAN LEAGUE

Napoleon Lajoie, Philadelphia	1901
Ty Cobb, Detroit	1909
Jimmie Foxx, Philadelphia	1933
Lou Gehrig, New York	1934
Ted Williams, Boston	1942
Ted Williams, Boston	1947
Mickey Mantle, New York	1956
Frank Robinson, Baltimore	1966
Carl Yastrzemski, Boston	1967

CONSECUTIVE GAMES PLAYED

(500 or more games)

Lou Gehrig	2130	Eddie Brown	618
Everett Scott	1307	Roy McMillan	598
Steve Garvey	1207	George Pinckney	577
Billy Williams	1117	Steve Brodie	574
Joe Sewell	1103	Aaron Ward	565
Stan Musial	895	Candy LaChance	540
Eddie Yost	829	Buck Freeman	535
Gus Suhr	822	Fred Luderus	533
Nellie Fox	798	Clyde Milan	512
Pete Rose	745	Charlie Gehringer	511
Richie Ashburn	730	Vada Pinson	508
Ernie Banks	717	Charlie Gehringer	504
Earl Averill	673	Omar Moreno	503
Frank McCormick	652		
Sandy Alomar	648		

NO-HIT GAMES

(9 innings or more)

NATIONAL LEAGUE

1876
July 15 — George W. Bradley, St.L. vs Har. 2-0

1880
June 12 — John Richmond, Wor. vs Cle. 1-0 (perfect game)
June 17 — John M. Ward, Pro. vs Buf. 5-0 (perfect game)
Aug. 19 — Larry Corcoran, Chi. vs Bos. 6-0
Aug. 20 — Jim Galvin, Buf. at Wor. 1-0

1882
Sep. 20 — Larry Corcoran, Chi. vs Wor. 5-0
Sep. 22 — Tom Lovett, Bkn. vs N.Y. 4-0

1883
July 25 — Charles Radbourn, Pro. at Cle. 8-0
Sep. 13 — Hugh Daily, Cle. at Phi. 1-0

1884
June 27 — Larry Corcoran, Chi. vs Pro. 6-0
Aug. 4 — Jim Galvin, Buf. at Det. 18-0

1885
July 27 — John Clarkson, Chi. vs Pro. 6-0
Aug. 29 — Charles Ferguson, Phi. vs Pro. 1-0

1891
July 31 — Amos Rusie, N.Y. vs Bkn. 6-0

1892
Aug. 6 — John Stivetts, Bos. vs Bkn. 11-0
Aug. 22 — Alex Sanders, Lou. vs Bal. 6-2
Oct. 15 — Charlie Jones, Cin. vs Pit. 7-1

1893
Aug. 16 — Bill Hawke, Bal. vs Was. 5-0

1897
Sep. 18 — Cy Young, Cle. vs Cin. 6-0

1898
Apr. 22 — Ted Breitenstein, Cin. vs Pit. 11-0
Apr. 22 — Jim Hughes, Bal. vs Bos. 8-0
July 8 — Frank Donahue, Phi. vs Bos. 5-0
Aug. 21 — Walter Thornton, Chi. vs Bkn. 2-0

1899
May 25 — Deacon Phillippe, Lou. vs N.Y. 7-0
Aug. 7 — Vic Willis, Bos. vs Was. 7-1

1900
July 12 — Frank Hahn, Cin. vs Phi. 4-0

1901
July 15 — Christy Mathewson, N.Y. at St.L. 5-0

1903
Sep. 18 — Chick Fraser, Phi. at Chi. 10-0

1904
June 11 — Bob Wicker, Chi. at N.Y. 1-0 (hit in 10th; won in 12th)

1905
June 13 — Christy Mathewson, N.Y. at Chi. 1-0

1906
May 1 — John Lush, Phi. at Bkn 1-0
July 20 — Mal Eason, Bkn. at St.L. 2-0
Aug. 1 — Harry McIntyre, Bkn. vs Pit. 0-1 (hit in 11th; lost in 13th)

1907
May 8 — Frank Pfeffer, Bos. vs Cin. 6-0
Sep. 20 — Nick Maddox, Pit. vs Bkn. 2-1

1908
July 4 — George Wiltse, N.Y. vs Phi. 1-0 (10 innings)
Sep. 5 — Nap Rucker, Bkn. vs Bos 6-0

1909
Apr. 15 — Leon Ames, N.Y. vs Bkn. 0-3 (hit in 10th; lost in 13th)

1912
Sep. 6 — Jeff Tesreau, N.Y. at Phi. 3-0

1914
Sep. 9 — George Davis, Bos. vs Phi. 7-0

1915
Apr. 15 — Rube Marquard, N.Y. vs Bkn. 2-0
Aug. 31 — Jimmy Lavender, Chi. at N.Y. 2-0

1916
June 16 — Tom Hughes, Bos. vs Pit. 2-0

	1917
May 2	Jim Vaughn, Chi. vs Cin. 0-1 (hit in 10th; lost in 10th)
May 2	Fred Toney, Cin. at Chi. 1-0 (10 innings)
	1919
May 11	Hod Eller, Cin. at St.L. 6-0
	1922
May 7	Jesse Barnes, N.Y. vs Phi. 6-0
	1924
July 17	Jesse Haines, St.L. vs Bos. 5-0
	1925
Sep. 13	Dazzy Vance, Bkn. vs Phi. 10-1
	1929
May 8	Carl Hubbell, N.Y. vs Pit 11-0
	1934
Sep. 21	Paul Dean, St.L. vs Bkn. 3-0
	1938
June 11	Johnny Vander Meer, Cin. vs Bos. 3-0
June 15	Johnny Vander Meer, Cin. at Bkn. 6-0
	1940
Apr. 30	Tex Carleton, Bkn. at Cin. 3-0
	1941
Aug. 30	Lon Warneke, St.L at Cin. 2-0
	1944
Apr. 27	Jim Tobin, Bos. vs Bkn. 2-0
May 15	Clyde Shoun, Cin. vs Bos. 1-0
	1946
Apr. 23	Ed Head, Bkn. vs Bos. 5-0
	1947
June 18	Ewell Blackwell, Cin. vs Bos. 6-0
	1948
Sep. 9	Rex Barney, Bkn. at N.Y. 2-0
	1950
Aug. 11	Vern Bickford, Bos. vs Bkn. 7-0
	1951
May 6	Cliff Chambers, Pit. at Bos. 3-0
	1952
June 19	Carl Erskine, Bkn. vs Chi. 5-0
	1954
June 12	Jim Wilson, Mil. vs Phi. 2-0
	1955
May 12	Sam Jones, Chi. vs Pit. 4-0
	1956
May 12	Carl Erskine, Bkn. vs N.Y. 3-0
Sep. 25	Sal Maglie, Bkn. vs Phi. 5-0
	1959
May 26	Harvey Haddix, Pit. at Mil. 0-1 (hit in 13th; lost in 13th)
	1960
May 15	Don Cardwell, Chi. vs St.L. 4-0
Aug. 18	Lew Burdette, Mil. vs Phi. 1-0
Sep. 15	Warren Spahn, Mil. vs Phi. 4-0
	1961
Apr. 28	Warren Spahn, Mil. vs S.F. 1-0
	1962
June 30	Sandy Koufax, L.A. vs N.Y. 5-0

	1963
May 11	Sandy Koufax, L.A. vs S.F. 8-0
May 17	Don Nottebart, Hou. vs Phi. 4-1
June 15	Juan Marichal, S.F. vs Hou. 1-0
	1964
Apr. 23	Ken Johnson, Hou. vs Cin. 0-1
June 4	Sandy Koufax, L.A. at Phi. 3-0
June 21	Jim Bunning, Phi. at N.Y 6-0 (perfect game)
	1965
June 14	Jim Maloney, Cin. vs N.Y. 0-1 (hit in 10th; lost in 10th)
Aug. 9	Jim Maloney, Cin. at Chi. 1-0 (10 innings)
Sep. 9	Sandy Koufax, L.A. vs Chi. 1-0 (perfect game)
	1967
June 18	Don Wilson, Hou. vs Atl. 2-0
	1968
July 29	George Culver, Cin. at Phi. 6-1
Sep. 17	Gaylord Perry, S.F. vs St.L. 1-0
Sep. 18	Ray Washburn, St.L. at S.F. 2-0
	1969
Apr. 17	Bill Stoneman, Mon. at Phi. 7-0
Apr. 30	Jim Maloney, Cin. vs Hou. 1-0
May 1	Don Wilson, Hou. at Cin. 4-0
Aug. 19	Ken Holtzman, Chi. vs Atl. 3-0
Sep. 20	Bob Moose, Pit. at N.Y. 4-0
	1970
June 12	Dock Ellis, Pit. at S.D. 2-0
July 20	Bill Singer, L.A. vs Phi. 5-0
	1971
June 3	Ken Holtzman, Chi. at Cin. 1-0
June 23	Rick Wise, Phi. at Cin. 4-0
Aug. 14	Bob Gibson, St.L. at Pit. 11-0
	1972
Apr. 16	Burt Hooton, Chi. vs Phi. 4-0
Sep. 2	Milt Pappas, Chi. vs S.D. 8-0
Oct. 2	Bill Stoneman, Mon. vs N.Y. 7-0
	1973
Aug. 5	Phil Niekro, Atl. vs S.D. 9-0
	1975
Aug. 24	Ed Halicki, S.F. vs N.Y. 6-0
	1976
July 9	Larry Dierker, Hou. vs Mon. 6-0
Aug. 9	John Candelaria, Pit. vs L.A. 2-0
Sep. 29	John Montefusco, S.F. vs Atl. 9-0
	1978
Apr. 16	Bob Forsch, St.L. vs Phi. 5-0
June 16	Tom Seaver, Cin. vs St.L. 4-0
	1979
Apr. 7	Ken Forsch, Hou. vs Atl. 6-0
	1980
June 27	Jerry Reuss, L.A. at S.F. 8-0
	1981
May 10	Charlie Lea, Mon. vs S.F. 4-0
Sep. 26	Nolan Ryan, Hou. vs L.A. 5-0
	1983
Sep. 26	Bob Forsch, St. L. vs. Mon. 3-0

AMERICAN LEAGUE

1901
May 9   Earl Moore, Cle. vs Chi. 2-4 (hit in 10th; lost in 10th)

1902
Sep. 20   Jimmy Callahan, Chi. vs Det. 3-0

1904
May 5   Cy Young, Bos. vs Phi. 3-0 (perfect game)
Aug. 17   Jesse Tannehill, Bos. vs Chi. 6-0

1905
July 22   Weldon Henley, Phi. at St.L. 6-0
Sep. 6   Frank Smith, Chi. at Det. 15-0
Sep. 27   Bill Dinneen, Bos. vs Chi. 2-0

1908
June 30   Cy Young, Bos. at N.Y. 8-0
Sep. 18   Bob Rhoades, Cle. vs Chi. 2-0
Sep. 20   Frank Smith, Chi. vs Phi. 1-0
Oct. 2   Addie Joss, Cle. vs Chi. 1-0 (perfect game)

1910
Apr. 20   Addie Joss, Cle. at Chi. 1-0
May 12   Chief Bender, Phi. vs Cle. 4-0
Aug. 30   Tom Hughes, N.Y. vs Cle. 0-5 (hit in 10th; lost in 11th)

1911
July 29   Joe Wood, Bos. vs St.L. 5-0
Aug. 27   Ed Walsh, Chi. vs Bos. 5-0

1912
July 4   George Mullin, Det. vs St.L. 7-0
Aug. 30   Earl Hamilton, St.L at Det. 5-1

1914
May 14   Jim Scott, Chi. at Was. 0-1 (hit in 10th; lost in 10th)
May 31   Joe Benz, Chi. vs Cle. 6-1

1916
June 21   George Foster, Bos. vs N.Y. 2-0
Aug. 26   Joe Bush, Phi. vs Cle. 5-0
Aug. 30   Hub Leonard, Bos. vs St.L. 4-0

1917
Apr. 14   Ed Cicotte, Chi. at St.L. 11-0
Apr. 24   George Mogridge, N.Y at Bos. 2-1
May 5   Ernie Koob, St.L vs Chi. 1-0
May 6   Bob Groom, St.L vs Chi. 3-0
June 23   Ernie Shore, Bos. vs Was. 4-0 (perfect game)

1918
June 3   Hub Leonard, Bos. at Det. 5-0

1919
Sep. 10   Ray Caldwell, Bos. at N.Y. 3-0

1920
July 1   Walter Johnson, Was. at Bos. 1-0

1922
Apr. 30   Charlie Robertson, Chi. at Det. 2-0 (perfect game)

1923
Sep. 4   Sam Jones, N.Y. at Phi. 2-0
Sep. 7   Howard Ehmke, Bos. at Phi. 4-0

1926
Aug. 21   Ted Lyons, Chi. at Bos. 6-0

1931
Apr. 29   Wes Ferrell, Cle. vs St.L. 9-0
Aug. 8   Bob Burke, Was. vs Bos. 5-0

1934
Sep. 18   Bobo Newsom, St.L. vs Bos. 1-2 (hit in 10th; lost in 10th)

1935
Aug. 31   Vern Kennedy, Chi. vs St.L. 5-0

1937
June 1   Bill Dietrich, Chi. vs St.L. 8-0

1938
Aug. 27   Monte Pearson, N.Y. vs Cle. 13-0

1940
Apr. 16   Bob Feller, Cle. at Chi. 1-0 (opening day)

1945
Sep. 9   Dick Fowler, Phi. vs St.L. 1-0

1946
Apr. 30   Bob Feller, Cle. vs N.Y. 1-0

1947
July 10   Don Black, Cle. vs Phi. 3-0
Sep. 3   Bill McCahan, Phi. vs Was. 3-0

1948
June 30   Bob Lemon, Cle. vs Det. 2-0

1951
July 1   Bob Feller, Cle. vs Det. 2-1
July 12   Allie Reynolds, N.Y. at Cle. 1-0
Sep. 28   Allie Reynolds, N.Y. vs Bos. 8-0

1952
May 15   Virgil Trucks, Det. vs Was. 1-0
Aug. 25   Virgil Trucks, Det. at N.Y 1-0

1953
May 6   Bobo Holloman, St.L vs Phi. 6-0 (first major league start)

1956
July 14   Mel Parnell, Bos. vs Chi. 4-0

1957
Aug. 20   Bob Keegan, Chi. vs Was. 6-0

1958
July 20   Jim Bunning, Det. at Bos. 3-0
Sep. 2   Hoyt Wilhelm, Bal. vs N.Y. 1-0

1962
May 5   Bo Belinsky, L.A. vs Bal. 2-0
June 26   Earle Wilson, Bos. vs L.A. 2-0
Aug. 1   Bill Monbouquette, Bos. at Chi. 1-0
Aug. 26   Jack Kralick, Min. vs K.C. 1-0

1965
Sep. 16   Dave Morehead, Bos. vs Cle. 2-0

1966
June 10   Sonny Siebert, Cle. vs Was. 2-0

1967
Apr. 30   Steve Barber (8 $^2/_3$) and Stu Miller ($^1/_3$), Bal. vs Det. 1-2
Aug. 25   Dean Chance, Min. at Cle. 2-1
Sep. 10   Joel Horlen, Chi. vs Det. 6-0

1968
Apr. 27   Tom Phoebus, Bal. vs Bos. 6-0
May 8   Jim Hunter, Oak. vs Min. 4-0 (perfect game)

1969
Aug. 13   Jim Palmer, Bal. vs Oak. 8-0

1970
July 3   Clyde Wright, Cal. vs Oak. 4-0
Sep. 21   Vida Blue, Oak. vs Min. 6-0

1973
Apr. 27   Steve Busby, K.C. vs Det. 3-0
May 15   Nolan Ryan, Cal. at K.C. 3-0
July 15   Nolan Ryan, Cal. at Det. 6-0
July 30   Jim Bibby, Tex. at Oak. 6-0

1974
June 19   Steve Busby, K.C. at Mil. 2-0
July 19   Dick Bosman, Cle. vs Oak. 4-0
Sep. 28   Nolan Ryan, Cal. vs Min. 4-0

1975
Nolan Ryan, Cal. vs Bal. 1-0
Blue (5), Abbott & Lindblad (1), Fingers (2), Oak. vs Cal. 5-0

1976
John Odom (5) and Francisco Barrios (4), Chi. at Oak. 2-1

1977
Jim Colborn, K.C. vs Tex. 6-0
Dennis Eckersley, Cle. vs Cal. 1-0
Bert Blyleven, Tex. at Cal. 6-0

1981
Len Barker, Cle. vs Tor. 3-0 (perfect game)

1983
Dave Righetti, N.Y. vs. Bos. 4-0
Mike Warren, Oak. vs. Chi. 3-0

1984
Jack Morris, Det. at Chi. 4-0
Mike Witt, Cal. at Tex. 1-0 (perfect game)

AMERICAN ASSOCIATION

1882
Tony Mullane, Lou. at Cin. 2-0
Guy Hecker, Lou. at Pit. 3-1

1884
Al Atkisson, Phi. vs Pit. 10-1
Ed Morris, Col. at Pit. 5-0
Frank Mountain, Col. at Was. 12-0
Sam Kimber, Bkn. vs Tol. 0-0 (11 innings, game called due to darkness)

1886
Al Atkisson, Phi. vs N.Y. 3-2
Bill Terry, Bkn. vs St.L. 1-0
Matt Kilroy, Bal. vs Tol. 6-0

1888
May 27   Bill Terry, Bkn. vs Lou. 4-0
June 6   Henry Porter, K.C. at Bal. 4-0
July 26   Ed Seward, Phi. vs Cin. 12-2
July 31   Gus Weyhing, Phi. vs K.C. 4-0

1890
Sep. 15   Ledell Titcomb, Roc. vs Syr. 7-0

1891
Oct. 4   Ted Breitenstein, St.L. vs Lou. 8-0 (first major league start)

FEDERAL LEAGUE

1914
Sep. 19   Ed Lafitte, Bkn. vs K.C. 6-2

1915
Apr. 24   Frank Allen, Pit. vs St.L. 2-0
May 15   Claude Hendrix, Chi. vs Pit. 10-0
Aug. 16   Miles Main, K.C. vs Buf. 5-0
Sep. 7   Art Davenport, St.L. vs Cin. 3-0

UNION ASSOCIATION

1884
Aug. 26   Dick Burns, Cin. at K.C. 3-1
Sep. 28   Ed Cushman, Mil. vs Was. 5-0

NATIONAL ASSOCIATION

1875
July 28   Joe Borden, Phi. vs Chi. 4-0

BASEBALL HALL OF FAME

PLAYER	Position	Career Dates	Year Selected
Henry Aaron	OF	1954-1976	1982
Grover Alexander	P	1911-1930	1938
Cap Anson	1B	1876-1897	1939
Luis Aparicio	SS	1956-1973	1984
Luke Appling	SS	1930-1950	1964
Earl Averill	OF	1929-1941	1975
J. Frank Baker	3B	1908-1922	1955
Dave Bancroft	SS	1915-1930	1971
Ernie Banks	SS-1B	1953-1971	1977
Jake Beckley	1B	1888-1907	1971
James "Cool Papa" Bell*	OF		1974
Chief Bender	P	1903-1925	1938
Yogi Berra	C	1946-1965	1971
Jim Bottomley	1B	1922-1937	1974
Lou Boudreau	SS	1938-1952	1970
Roger Bresnahan	C	1897-1915	1945
Dan Brouthers	1B	1879-1904	1945
Mordecai Brown	P	1903-1916	1949
Jesse Burkett	OF	1890-1905	1946
Roy Campanella	C	1948-1957	1969
Max Carey	OF	1910-1929	1961
Frank Chance	1B	1898-1914	1946
Oscar Charleston*	OF		1976
Jack Chesbro	P	1899-1909	1946
Fred Clarke	OF	1894-1915	1945
John Clarkson	P	1882-1894	1963
Roberto Clemente	OF	1955-1972	1973
Ty Cobb	OF	1905-1928	1936
Mickey Cochrane	C	1925-1937	1947
Eddie Collins	2B	1906-1930	1939
Jimmy Collins	3B	1895-1908	1945
Earle Combs	OF	1924-1935	1970
Roger Connor	1B	1880-1897	1976

Career Dates indicate first and last appearances in the majors.
* Elected on the basis of his career in the Negro Leagues.

BASEBALL HALL OF FAME

PLAYER	Position	Career Dates	Year Selected
Stan Coveleski	P	1912-1928	1969
Sam Crawford	OF	1899-1917	1957
Joe Cronin	SS	1926-1945	1956
Candy Cummings	P	1872-1877	1939
Kiki Cuyler	OF	1921-1938	1968
Dizzy Dean	P	1930-1947	1953
Ed Delahanty	OF	1888-1903	1945
Bill Dickey	C	1928-1946	1954
Martin DiHigo*	P		1977
Joe DiMaggio	OF	1936-1951	1955
Don Drysdale	P	1956-1969	1984
Hugh Duffy	OF	1888-1906	1945
Johnny Evers	2B	1902-1929	1946
Buck Ewing	C	1880-1897	1946
Red Faber	P	1914-1933	1964
Bob Feller	P	1936-1956	1962
Rick Ferrell	C	1929-1947	1984
Elmer Flick	OF	1898-1910	1963
Whitey Ford	P	1950-1967	1974
Jimmie Foxx	1B	1925-1945	1951
Frankie Frisch	2B	1919-1937	1947
Pud Galvin	P	1879-1892	1965
Lou Gehrig	1B	1923-1939	1939
Charlie Gehringer	2B	1924-1942	1949
Bob Gibson	P	1959-1975	1981
Josh Gibson*	C		1972
Lefty Gomez	P	1930-1943	1972
Goose Goslin	OF	1921-1938	1968
Hank Greenberg	1B	1930-1947	1956
Burleigh Grimes	P	1916-1934	1964
Lefty Grove	P	1925-1941	1947
Chick Hafey	OF	1924-1937	1971
Jesse Haines	P	1918-1937	1970
Billy Hamilton	OF	1888-1901	1961
Gabby Hartnett	C	1922-1941	1955
Harry Heilmann	OF	1914-1932	1952
Billy Herman	2B	1931-1947	1975
Harry Hooper	OF	1909-1925	1971
Rogers Hornsby	2B	1915-1937	1942
Waite Hoyt	P	1918-1938	1969
Carl Hubbell	P	1928-1943	1947
Monte Irvin*	OF	1949-1956	1973
Travis Jackson	SS	1922-1936	1982
Hugh Jennings	SS	1891-1918	1945
Judy Johnson*	3B		1975
Walter Johnson	P	1907-1927	1936
Addie Joss	P	1902-1910	1978
Al Kaline	OF	1953-1974	1980
Tim Keefe	P	1880-1893	1964
Willie Keeler	OF	1892-1910	1939
George Kell	3B	1943-1957	1983
Joe Kelley	OF	1891-1908	1971
George Kelly	1B	1915-1932	1973
King Kelly	C	1878-1893	1945
Harmon Killebrew	1B-3B	1954-1975	1984
Ralph Kiner	OF	1946-1955	1975
Chuck Klein	OF	1928-1944	1979
Sandy Koufax	P	1955-1966	1971
Nap Lajoie	2B	1896-1916	1937
Bob Lemon	P	1941-1958	1976
Buck Leonard*	1B		1972
Fred Lindstrom	3B	1924-1936	1976
John Henry Lloyd	SS-1B		1976
Ted Lyons	P	1923-1946	1955
Mickey Mantle	OF	1951-1968	1974
Heinie Manush	OF	1923-1939	1964
Rabbit Maranville	SS-2B	1912-1935	1954
Juan Marichal	P	1960-1975	1983
Rube Marquard	P	1908-1925	1971
Eddie Mathews	3B	1952-1968	1978
Christy Mathewson	P	1900-1916	1936
Willie Mays	OF	1951-1973	1979
Tommy McCarthy	OF	1884-1896	1946
Joe McGinnity	P	1899-1908	1946
Joe Medwick	OF	1932-1948	1968
Johnny Mize	1B	1936-1953	1981
Stan Musial	OF-1B	1941-1963	1969

Career Dates indicate first and last appearances in the majors.
* Elected on the basis of his career in the Negro Leagues.

BASEBALL HALL OF FAME

PLAYER	Position	Career Dates	Year Selected
Kid Nichols	P	1890-1906	1949
Jim O'Rourke	OF	1876-1904	1945
Mel Ott	OF	1926-1947	1951
Satchel Paige*	P	1948-1965	1971
Herb Pennock	P	1912-1934	1948
Eddie Plank	P	1901-1917	1946
Hoss Radbourn	P	1880-1891	1939
Pee Wee Reese	SS	1940-1958	1984
Sam Rice	OF	1915-1935	1963
Eppa Rixey	P	1912-1933	1963
Robin Roberts	P	1948-1966	1976
Brooks Robinson	3B	1955-1977	1983
Frank Robinson	OF	1956-1976	1982
Jackie Robinson	2B	1947-1956	1962
Edd Roush	OF	1913-1931	1962
Red Ruffing	P	1924-1947	1967
Amos Rusie	P	1889-1901	1977
Babe Ruth	OF	1914-1935	1936
Ray Schalk	C	1912-1929	1955
Joe Sewell	SS	1920-1933	1977
Al Simmons	OF	1924-1944	1953
George Sisler	1B	1915-1930	1939
Duke Snider	OF	1947-1964	1980
Warren Spahn	P	1942-1965	1973
Al Spalding	P	1871-1878	1939
Tris Speaker	OF	1907-1928	1937
Bill Terry	1B	1923-1936	1954
Sam Thompson	OF	1885-1906	1974
Joe Tinker	SS	1902-1916	1946
Pie Traynor	3B	1920-1937	1948
Dazzy Vance	P	1915-1935	1955
Rube Waddell	P	1897-1910	1946
Honus Wagner	SS	1897-1917	1936
Bobby Wallace	SS	1894-1918	1953
Ed Walsh	P	1904-1917	1946
Lloyd Waner	OF	1927-1945	1967
Paul Waner	OF	1926-1945	1952
Monte Ward	2B-P	1878-1894	1964
Mickey Welch	P	1880-1892	1973
Zach Wheat	OF	1909-1927	1959
Ted Williams	OF	1939-1960	1966
Hack Wilson	OF	1923-1934	1979
Early Wynn	P	1939-1963	1971
Cy Young	P	1890-1911	1937
Ross Youngs	OF	1917-1926	1972

Career Dates indicate first and last appearances in the majors.
* Elected on the basis of his career in the Negro Leagues.

MANAGERS	Year Selected	MANAGERS	Year Selected
Walt Alston	1983	Joe McCarthy	1957
Charles Comiskey	1939	John McGraw	1937
Clark Griffith	1946	Bill McKechnie	1962
Bucky Harris	1974	Wilbert Robinson	1945
Miller Huggins	1964	Casey Stengel	1974
Al Lopez	1977	Harry Wright	1953
Connie Mack	1937	George Wright	1937

SELECTED FOR MERITORIOUS SERVICE

Edward Barrow (Manager-Executive)
Morgan G. Bulkeley (Executive)
Alexander J. Cartwright (Executive),
Henry Chadwick (Writer-Statistician)
John "Jocko" Conlan (Umpire)
Thomas Connolly (Umpire)
William G. Evans (Umpire-Executive)
Andrew "Rube" Foster (Player-Executive)
Ford C. Frick (Commissioner-Executive)

William Harridge (Executive)
Cal Hubbard (Umpire)
B. Bancroft Johnson (Executive)
William Klem (Umpire)
Kenesaw M. Landis (Commissioner)
Larry S. MacPhail (Executive)
W. Branch Rickey (Manager-Executive)
George M. Weiss (Executive)

PART THREE

National Association
Register

ALPHABETICAL LIST OF EVERY MAN WHO EVER

PLAYED IN THE NATIONAL ASSOCIATION

AND HIS RECORD IN THAT LEAGUE

National Association Register

This section contains an alphabetical listing of every man who played in the National Association, baseball's first professional league, which lasted from 1871 through 1875. In addition to the facts about the players and their year-by-year batting and pitching records, there are team and managerial records for each year. Information about the National Association is not as complete as the other data that appears in this book. This is because many statistical items are not available as a result of poor newspaper coverage.

The records of men who played in the National Association and in the major leagues are not combined because the National Association is not considered a major league. The reasons for this, as defined by the Special Baseball Records Committee, was because of the erratic schedule and procedures of the National Association. For men who played in the National Association and went on to play or manage in the major leagues, their major league records can be found in the appropriate sections of this book. Appearing last, after the alphabetical player listing, are the yearly league standings and team data. All information and abbreviations that may appear unfamiliar are explained in the sample format presented below.

	W	L	PCT	GB	R	AB	H	BA	Manager	W	L	Manager	W	L
1871														
Philadelphia Athletics	22	7	.759		367	1331	412	**.310**	Hicks Hayhurst	22	7			
Chicago White Stockings	20	9	.690	2	302	1250	316	.253	Tom Foley	20	9			
Boston Red Stockings	22	10	.688	1.5	**401**	**1438**	424	.295	Harry Wright	22	10			
Washington Olympics	16	15	.516	7	310	1400	371	.265	Nick Young	16	15			
Troy Haymakers	15	15	.500	7.5	353	1302	370	.284	Bill Craver	14	12	Lip Pike	1	3
New York Mutuals	17	18	.486	8	302	1428	392	.275	Bob Ferguson	17	18			
Cleveland Forest Citys	10	19	.345	12	249	1214	326	.269	Charlie Pabor	10	19			
Fort Wayne Kekiongas	7	21	.250	14.5	137	765	179	.234	Harry Deane	3	18	Bill Lennon	4	3
Rockford Forest Citys	6	21	.222	15	231	1081	273	.253	Hiram Waldo	6	21			

TEAM COLUMN HEADINGS AND
STATISTICAL INFORMATION

	W	L	PCT	GB	R	AB	H	BA	Manager	W	L	Manager	W	L

W	Wins
L	Losses
PCT	Winning Percentage
GB	Games Behind the League Leader
R	Runs Scored

AB   At Bats
H   Hits
BA   Batting Average
MGR   The name and record of the man who managed the team. Teams with more than one manager have the manager listed in the order of when they managed. The top listing indicates the first manager.

League Leaders. Statistics that appear in bold faced print indicate that the team led the league that year in a particular statistical category. The Boston Red Stockings, for example, led the league in hits with 424. When there is a tie for the league lead, the figures for all teams who tied are shown in bold face.

The following is the record of John Doe, a fictitious player used as an example to illustrate the information about the players:

		G	AB	H	R	BA	W	L	PCT	G by POS

John Doe

DOE, JOHN LEE (Slim)   BR TR 6'2" 165 lbs.
Played as John Cherry part of 1871
Born John Lee Doughnut Brother of Bill Doe
B. Jan. 1, 1850, New York, N. Y.   D. July 1, 1955, New York, N. Y.
1875 Broken hand
Hall of Fame 1946
Manager 1872
No-hit game vs. the Chicago White Stockings, July 26, 1873.

			G	AB	H	R	BA	W	L	PCT	G by POS
1871	Philadelphia Athletics		26	132	65	45	**.492**	2	2	.500	3B-22, P-4
1872	Boston Red Stockings		35	169	43	25	.254	6	4	.600	3B-20, P-15
1873			51	238	59	36	.248	7	3	.700	3B-36, P-15
1874	2 teams	New York Mutuals (25G. .314 W-2 L-2)			Lord Baltimores (25G. .296 W-3 L-0)						
"	total		50	196	60	36	.305	5	2	.714	3B-40, P-10
1875	Brooklyn Atlantics		1	0	0	0	–	0	0	–	P-1
	5 yrs.		163	735	227	142	.309	20	11	.645	3B-118, P-45

PLAYER INFORMATION

This shortened version of the player's full name is the name most familiar to the fans. All players in this section are alphabetically arranged by the last name part of this name.   John Doe

Player's full name. The arrangement is last name first, then first and middle name(s).   DOE, JOHN LEE

Player's nickname. Any name or names appearing in parentheses indicates a nickname.   (Slim)

The player's batting and throwing style. Doe, for instance, batted and threw right handed. A "BB" would mean Doe was a switch hitter, a "BL" would mean that he batted left handed, and a "TL" would mean that he threw left handed.   BR TR

Player's height.   6'2"

Player's average playing weight.   165 lbs.

The player at one time in his career played under another name and can be found in box scores or newspaper stories under that name. In the case of Doe, he was still an amateur athlete when he entered baseball in 1871, and in order to protect his amateur standing he adopted an alias.   Played as John Cherry part of 1871

Born John Lee Doughnut	The name the player was given at birth. (For the most part, the player never used this name while playing in the National Association, but, if he did, it would be listed as "played as," which is explained above under the heading "Played as John Cherry part of 1871.")
Brother of Bill Doe	The player's brother. (Relatives indicated here are fathers, sons, brothers, grandfathers, and grandsons who played or managed in the National Association and the major leagues.)
B. Jan. 1, 1850, New York, N.Y.	Date and place of birth.
D. July 1, 1955, New York, N.Y.	Date and place of death. (Since all men who played in the National Association are dead, the word "deceased" is shown if no information is presently available.)
1875 Broken hand	Career interruption. These interruptions are shown for all players who missed 30 consecutive days or more of play in the National Association due to such causes as illness, injury, or suspension. If an interruption is not fully explained, such as showing "injury" for a player instead of listing what the injury may have been, it means no other information was presently available; however, all types of illness are always shown under the general heading of "illness." This is because injuries are usually a direct result of playing baseball, while illnesses are not.
Hall of Fame 1946	Doe was elected to the Baseball Hall of Fame in 1946.
Manager 1872	Doe also served as a manager. All men who were managers, along with their managerial records, can also be found with the team information.
No-hit game vs. the Chicago White Stockings, July 26, 1873	Doe pitched a no-hitter against the Chicago White Stockings on July 26, 1873.

PLAYER COLUMN HEADINGS INFORMATION

G	Games Played
AB	At Bats
H	Hits
R	Runs Scored
BA	Batting Average
W	Wins as a Pitcher
L	Losses as a Pitcher
PCT	Pitcher's Winning Percentage
G by POS	Games by Position (All fielding positions that a man played within the given year are shown. The position where the most games were played is listed first.)

TEAM INFORMATION

1871	Philadelphia Athletics											
1872	Boston Red Stockings											
1873												
1874	2 teams	New York Mutuals	(25G.	.314	W-2 L-2)		Lord Baltimores	(25G.	.296	W-3 L-0)		
"	total		50	196		60	36	.305	5	2	.714	3B-40, P-10
1875	Brooklyn Atlantics											
	5 yrs.											

Blank space appearing beneath a team indicates that the team is the same. Doe, for example, played for the Boston Red Stockings from 1872 through 1873.

2 Teams Total. Indicates a player played for more than one team in the same year. Doe played for two teams in 1874. The number of games he played, his batting average, and pitching decisions for each team are also shown. Directly beneath this line, following the word "total," is Doe's combined record for both teams in 1874.

PLAYER STATISTICAL INFORMATION

	G	AB	H	R	BA	W	L	PCT	G by POS

John Doe

DOE, JOHN LEE (Slim)   BR TR   6'2" 165 lbs.
Played as John Cherry part of 1871
Born John Lee Doughnut Brother of Bill Doe
B. Jan. 1, 1850, New York, N. Y.   D. July 1, 1955, New York, N. Y.
1875 Broken hand
Hall of Fame 1946
Manager 1872
No-hit game vs. the Chicago White Stockings, July 26, 1873.

			G	AB	H	R	BA	W	L	PCT	G by POS
1871	Philadelphia Athletics		26	132	65	45	**.492**	2	2	.500	3B-22, P-4
1872	Boston Red Stockings		35	169	43	25	.254	6	4	.600	3B-20, P-15
1873			51	238	59	36	.248	7	3	.700	3B-36, P-15
1874	2 teams New York Mutuals (25G. .314 W-2 L-2)					Lord Baltimores	(25G.	.296	W-3 L-0)		
"	total		50	196	60	36	.305	5	2	.714	3B-40, P-10
1875	Brooklyn Atlantics		1	0	0	0	–	0	0	–	P-1
	5 yrs.		163	735	227	142	.309	20	11	.645	3B-118, P-45

Meaningless Averages. Indicated by the use of a dash (—). In the case of Doe, a dash is shown for his 1875 batting average. This means that although he played one game he had no official at bats. A batting average of .000 would mean he had at least one at bat with no hits. If a dash is shown in place of a pitcher's winning percentage, as it does in the case of Doe in 1875, it means that although he pitched in one game he never had a decision. A percentage of .000 would mean he had at least one loss.

League Leaders. Statistics that appear in bold faced print indicate the player led the league that year in a particular statistical category. Doe, for example, led the National Association in batting in 1871. When there is a tie for league lead, the figures for all the men who tied are shown in bold face.

	G	AB	H	R	BA	W	L	PCT	G by POS

John Abadie

ABADIE, JOHN
B. Nov. 4, 1854, Philadelphia, Pa.   D. May 17, 1905, Pemberton, N. J.

BR TR 6   192 lbs.

1875 2 teams Brooklyn Atlantics (1G .250) Philadelphia Centennials(11G .217)									
" total	12	50	11	4	.220				1B-12

Dave Abercrombie

ABERCROMBIE, DAVID
B. 1840, Falkirk, Scotland   D. Sept. 2, 1916, Baltimore Md.

1871 Troy Haymakers	1	4	0	0	.000				SS-1

Bob Addy

ADDY, ROBERT EDWARD (The Magnet)
B. 1838, Rochester, N. Y.   D. Apr. 10, 1910, Pocatello, Ida.

BL TL 5'8"   160 lbs

1871 Rockford Forest Citys	25	122	31	29	.254				SS-3, 2B-22
1873 2 teams Boston Red Stockings (31G .340) Philadelphias (10G .286)									
" total	41	218	71	49	.326				RF-31, 2B-10
1874 Hartfords	50	208	55	26	.264				2B-45, 3B-4, SS-1
1875 Philadelphias	69	308	81	60	.263				RF-66, 2B-3
4 yrs.	185	856	238	164	.278				RF-97, 2B-58, 3B-4, SS-4

Ham Allen

ALLEN, HOMER
Deceased.

1872 Middletown Mansfields	16	71	12	8	.169				RF-10, SS-6

Andy Allison

ALLISON, ANDREW K.
B. 1848, New York, N. Y.   Deceased.

5'10"   150 lbs.

1872 Brooklyn Eckfords	25	107	15	11	.140				1B-23, OF-2

Art Allison

ALLISON, ARTHUR ALGERNON
Brother of Doug Allison.
B. Jan. 29, 1849, Philadelphia, Pa.   D. Feb. 25, 1916, Washington, D. C.

5'8"   150 lbs.

1871 Cleveland Forest Citys	29	140	36	27	.257				CF-29
1872	18	88	23	13	.261				CF-18
1873 Elizabeth Resolutes	23	102	31	12	.304				RF-20, 1B-2, C-1
1875 2 teams Hartfords (35G .242) Washington Nationals (27G .169)									
" total	62	279	59	42	.211				RF-34, 1B-24, OF-2, C-1 2B-1
4 yrs.	132	609	149	94	.245				RF-54, CF-47, 1B-26, OF-2 C-2, 2B-1

Bill Allison

ALLISON, WILLIAM ANDREW
B. Sept. 17, 1848   D. June 12, 1923

1872 Brooklyn Eckfords	3	11	2	3	.182				OF-2, 2B-1

Doug Allison

ALLISON, DOUGLAS L.
Brother of Art Allison.
B. 1846, Philadelphia, Pa.   D. Dec. 19, 1916, Washington, D. C.

BR TR 5'10½" 160 lbs.

1871 Washington Olympics	27	132	44	28	.333				C-27
1872 2 teams Brooklyn Eckfords (18G .299) Troy Haymakers (23G .319)									
" total	41	206	64	41	.311				C-40, SS-1
1873 2 teams New York Mutuals (11G .245) Elizabeth Resolutes (18G .275)									
" total	29	144	38	17	.264				C-26, OF-3
1874 New York Mutuals	65	326	88	65	.270				RF-41, C-24
1875 Hartfords	61	293	68	38	.232				C-59, 1B-3
5 yrs.	223	1101	302	189	.274				C-176, RF-41, OF-3, 1B-3 SS-1

Cap Anson

ANSON, ADRIAN CONSTANTINE (Pop)
B. Apr. 17, 1851, Marshalltown, Iowa   D. Apr. 14, 1922, Chicago, Ill.
Hall of Fame 1939.

BR TR 6'   227 lbs.

1871 Rockford Forest Citys	25	122	43	30	.352				3B-20, C-3, 2B-2, OF-1
1872 Philadelphia Athletics	45	231	88	60	.381				3B-45
1873	51	272	96	52	.353				1B-36, 3B-10, 2B-4, C-1 CF-1
1874	55	267	98	51	.367				1B-22, 3B-20, OF-8, SS-5
1875	69	330	105	84	.318				1B-32, OF-22, C-11, 3B-4
5 yrs.	245	1222	430	277	.352				3B-99, 1B-90, OF-31, C-15 2B-6, SS-5, CF-1

Bob Armstrong

ARMSTRONG, ROBERT L.
B. 1850, Baltimore, Md.   Deceased.

6'2"   160 lbs.

1871 Fort Wayne Kekiongas	12	48	11	9	.229				CF-12

Billy Arnold

ARNOLD, WILLIS S.
B. Mar. 2, 1851, Middletown, Conn.   D. Jan. 18, 1899, Albany, N. Y.

1872 Middletown Mansfields	2	8	1	2	.125				OF-2

Harry Arundel

ARUNDEL, HARRY
Brother of Tug Arundel.
B. 1857, Philadelphia, Pa.   D. Apr. 7, 1904, Cleveland, Ohio

1875 Brooklyn Atlantics	1	4	0	0	.000				OF-1

	G	AB	H	R	BA	W	L	PCT	G by POS

Ed Atkinson

ATKINSON, EDWARD
B. Baltimore, Md.　Deceased.

	G	AB	H	R	BA				G by POS
1873　Washington Nationals	2	9	0	2	.000				OF-2

Henry Austin

AUSTIN, HENRY C.
B. Brooklyn, N. Y.　D. Sept. 3, 1895, Amityville, N. Y.

	G	AB	H	R	BA				G by POS
1873　Elizabeth Resolutes	23	106	24	11	.226				CF-23

Stud Bancker

BANCKER, JOHN
B. Philadelphia, Pa.　Deceased.

	G	AB	H	R	BA				G by POS
1875　New Havens	19	77	11	3	.143				C-12, 3B-3, 2B-3, SS-1

Al Barker

BARKER, ALFRED L
B. Jan. 18, 1839, Rockford, Ill.　D. Sept. 15, 1912, Rockford, Ill.

	G	AB	H	R	BA				G by POS
1871　Rockford Forest Cities	1	5	1	0	.200				OF-1

Tom Barlow

BARLOW, THOMAS H.
Deceased.

	G	AB	H	R	BA				G by POS
1872　Brooklyn Atlantics	35	174	48	31	.276				C-34, SS-2
1873	55	283	71	48	.251				C-55
1874　Hartfords	32	157	49	37	.312				SS-32
1875　2 teams　Brooklyn Atlantics (1G　.000)　New Havens (1G　.200)									
"　total	2	9	1	1	.111				SS-1, 2B-1
4 yrs.	124	623	169	117	.271				C-89, SS-35, 2B-1

Ross Barnes

BARNES, ROSCOE CONKLING　　BR　TR　5'8½"　145 lbs.
B. May 8, 1850, Mt. Morris, N. Y.　D. Feb. 8, 1915, Chicago, Ill.

	G	AB	H	R	BA				G by POS
1871　Boston Red Stockings	31	172	65	66	.378				2B-16, SS-15, 3B-1
1872	45	240	97	81	.404				2B-45
1873	60	338	136	126	.402				2B-47, 3B-13
1874	52	277	94	73	.339				2B-52
1875	78	398	148	116	.372				2B-78
5 yrs.	266	1425	540	462	.379				2B-238, SS-15, 3B-14

Billy Barnie

BARNIE, WILLIAM HARRISON (Bald Billy)　　5'7"　157 lbs.
B. Jan. 26, 1853, New York, N. Y.　D. July 15, 1900, Hartford, Conn.

	G	AB	H	R	BA				G by POS
1874　Hartfords	45	184	36	19	.196				C-23, RF-21, SS-1
1875　2 teams　New York Mutuals (10G　.150)　Keokuk Westerns (10G　.108)									
"　total	20	77	10	4	.130				OF-10, C-10
2 yrs.	65	261	46	23	.176				C-33, RF-21, OF-10, SS-1

Bill Barrett

BARRETT, WILLIAM
B. Washington, D. C.　Deceased.

	G	AB	H	R	BA				G by POS
1871　Fort Wayne Kekiongas	1	5	1	1	.200				C-1, 3B-1
1872　2 teams　Brooklyn Atlantics (7G　.267)　Washington Olympics (1G　.000)									
"　total	8	35	8	4	.229				OF-7, C-1
1873　Lord·Baltimores	1	4	1	0	.250				OF-1, SS-1
3 yrs.	10	44	10	5	.227				OF-8, C-2, 3B-1, SS-1

Barron

BARRON,
Deceased.

	G	AB	H	R	BA				G by POS
1874　Lord Baltimores	16	76	22	6	.289				OF-16

Frank Barrows

BARROWS, FRANK LEWIS
B. Boston, Mass.　D. Sept. 24, 1901, Boston, Mass.

	G	AB	H	R	BA				G by POS
1871　Boston Red Stockings	18	87	14	13	.161				OF-17, 2B-1

John Bass

BASS, JOHN E.　　5'6"　150 lbs.
B. 1850, Baltimore, Md.　Deceased.

	G	AB	H	R	BA				G by POS
1871　Cleveland Forest Cities	22	91	25	18	.275				SS-22
1872　Brooklyn Atlantics	1	4	1	0	.250				OF-1
2 yrs.	23	95	26	18	.274				SS-22, OF-1

Joe Battin

BATTIN, JOSEPH V.
B. Nov. 11, 1851, Philadelphia, Pa.　D. Dec. 11, 1937, Akron, Ohio

	G	AB	H	R	BA				G by POS
1871　Cleveland Forest Cities	1	4	0	0	.000				OF-1
1873　Philadelphia Athletics	1	6	3	4	.500				OF-1
1874	51	228	62	41	.272				2B-40, OF-7, SS-4
1875　St. Louis	66	278	73	32	.263				2B-60, 3B-6
4 yrs.	119	516	138	77	.267				2B-100, OF-9, 3B-6, SS-4

Tommy Beals

BEALS, THOMAS L.　　5'5"　144 lbs.
D. Nov. 9, 1911

	G	AB	H	R	BA				G by POS
1871　Washington Olympics	10	38	7	7	.184				OF-8, 2B-2
1872	9	39	11	8	.282				2B-5, OF-2, SS-2
1873　Washington Nationals	37	170	46	35	.271				2B-26, C-11, OF-1
1874　Boston Red Stockings	18	98	20	20	.204				2B-10, OF-8
1875	35	157	46	38	.293				OF-31, 2B-6
5 yrs.	109	502	130	108	.259				OF-50, 2B-49, C-11, SS-2

	G	AB	H	R	BA	W	L	PCT	G by POS

Charlie Bearman

BEARMAN, CHARLES S.
B. 1848, Hoboken, N. J. D. Feb., 1879   6' 180 lbs.

	G	AB	H	R	BA	W	L	PCT	G by POS
1871 Fort Wayne Kekiongas	1	3	0	0	.000				1B-1

George Bechtel

BECHTEL, GEORGE A.
B. 1848, Philadelphia, Pa. Deceased.   5'11" 165 lbs.

	G	AB	H	R	BA	W	L	PCT	G by POS
1871 Philadelphia Athletics	20	94	30	23	.319	1	2	.333	OF-15, P-3, 3B-2
1872 New York Mutuals	52	262	79	64	.302				RF-51, 1B-1
1873 Philadelphias	53	266	62	54	.233	0	3	.000	RF-50, P-3
1874	31	153	43	29	.281	1	3	.250	OF-27, P-4
1875 2 teams Philadelphia Athletics (34G	.292	W-3 L-1)	Philadelphia Centennials(14G			.266	W-2	L-12)	
" total	48	218	62	44	.284	5	13	.143	RF-30, P-18
5 yrs.	204	993	276	214	.278	7	21	.250	RF-131, OF-42, P-28, 3B-2, 1B-1

Steve Bellan

BELLAN, ESTEBAN ENRIQUE
B. 1850, Cuba D. Aug. 8, 1932   5'6" 154 lbs.

	G	AB	H	R	BA	W	L	PCT	G by POS
1871 Troy Haymakers	29	136	29	25	.213				3B-28, SS-1
1872	23	115	32	22	.278				SS-9, 3B-8, OF-6
1873 New York Mutuals	7	37	7	4	.189				3B-7
3 yrs.	59	288	68	51	.236				3B-43, SS-10, OF-6

Cy Bentley

BENTLEY, CYRUS G.
Deceased.

	G	AB	H	R	BA	W	L	PCT	G by POS
1872 Middletown Mansfields	23	113	27	26	.239	2	14	.125	P-16, OF-8

Nate Berkenstock

BERKENSTOCK, NATHAN
B. 1831, Pa. D. Feb. 23, 1900, Philadelphia, Pa.

	G	AB	H	R	BA	W	L	PCT	G by POS
1871 Philadelphia Athletics	1	4	0	0	.000				OF-1

Tom Berry

BERRY, THOMAS HANEY
B. Dec. 31, 1842, Chester, Pa. D. June 6, 1915, Chester, Pa.   5'6" 140 lbs.

	G	AB	H	R	BA	W	L	PCT	G by POS
1871 Philadelphia Athletics	1	4	1	0	.250				OF-1

Harry Berthrong

BERTHRONG, HARRY W.
B. Dec. 31, 1843, Munford, N. Y. D. Apr. 24, 1928, Chelsea, Mass.   5'6½" 140 lbs.

	G	AB	H	R	BA	W	L	PCT	G by POS
1871 Washington Olympics	17	78	17	17	.218				LF-12, 2B-4, 3B-1

Bestick

BESTICK,
Deceased.

	G	AB	H	R	BA	W	L	PCT	G by POS
1872 Brooklyn Eckfords	4	14	3	0	.214				C-4

E. P. Bevans

BEVANS, E. P.
B. 1848, N. Y. Deceased.   5'8" 138 lbs.

	G	AB	H	R	BA	W	L	PCT	G by POS
1871 Troy Haymakers	3	15	5	7	.333				2B-3
1872 Brooklyn Atlantics	10	44	9	7	.205				2B-8, OF-1, SS-1
2 yrs.	13	59	14	14	.237				2B-11, OF-1, SS-1

Oscar Bielaski

BIELASKI, OSCAR   BR TR
B. Mar. 21, 1847, Washington, D. C. D. Nov. 8, 1911, Washington, D. C.

	G	AB	H	R	BA	W	L	PCT	G by POS
1872 Washington Nationals	10	47	8	12	.170				RF-10
1873	38	187	49	35	.262				RF-38
1874 Lord Baltimores	28	126	26	18	.206				RF-26, 2B-1, 1B-1
1875 Chicago White Stockings	52	211	49	21	.232				RF-52
4 yrs.	128	571	132	86	.231				RF-126, 2B-1, 1B-1

George Bird

BIRD, GEORGE RAYMOND   BR TR 5'9" 150 lbs.
B. June 23, 1850, Stillman Valley, Ill. D. Nov. 9, 1940, Rockford, Ill.

	G	AB	H	R	BA	W	L	PCT	G by POS
1871 Rockford Forest Citys	25	112	24	18	.214				CF-25

Dave Birdsall

BIRDSALL, DAVID SOLOMON   5'9" 126 lbs.
B. July 16, 1838, New York, N. Y. D. Dec. 30, 1896, Boston, Mass.

	G	AB	H	R	BA	W	L	PCT	G by POS
1871 Boston Red Stockings	29	155	43	51	.277				RF-26, C-3
1872	14	78	14	10	.179				C-11, OF-5
1873	3	12	1	4	.083				OF-3
3 yrs.	46	245	58	65	.237				RF-26, C-14, OF-8

Joe Blong

BLONG, JOSEPH MYLES   BR TR
B. Sept. 17, 1853, St. Louis, Mo. D. Sept. 22, 1892, St. Louis, Mo.

	G	AB	H	R	BA	W	L	PCT	G by POS
1875 St. Louis Reds	16	70	10	3	.143	3	11	.214	P-14, OF-3

Boland

BOLAND,
Deceased.

	G	AB	H	R	BA	W	L	PCT	G by POS
1875 Brooklyn Atlantics	1	4	0	0	.000				OF-1

Tommy Bond

BOND, THOMAS HENRY   BR TR 5'7½" 160 lbs.
B. Apr. 2, 1856, Granard, Ireland D. Jan. 24, 1941, Boston, Mass.

	G	AB	H	R	BA	W	L	PCT	G by POS
1874 Brooklyn Atlantics	55	249	54	25	.217	22	**32**	.407	P-55
1875 Hartfords	71	297	78	30	.263	19	16	.543	P-39, OF-29, 2B-2, 1B-2
2 yrs.	126	546	132	55	.242	41	48	.461	P-94, OF-29, 2B-2, 1B-2

	G	AB	H	R	BA	W	L	PCT	G by POS

Eddie Booth

BOOTH, EDWARD H.
Deceased.

	G	AB	H	R	BA	W	L	PCT	G by POS
1872 2 teams Brooklyn Atlantics (14G .250) Middletown Mansfields (24G .336)									
" total	38	180	55	36	.306				2B-21, OF-17
1873 2 teams Brooklyn Atlantics (15G .171) Elizabeth Resolutes (18G .299)									
" total	33	147	35	17	.238				LF-16, OF-15, 2B-2
1874 Brooklyn Atlantics	44	194	46	24	.237				LF-44
1875 New York Mutuals	68	286	57	33	.199				RF-62, 2B-6
4 yrs.	183	807	193	110	.239				RF-62, LF-60, OF-32, 2B-29

Bill Boyd

BOYD, WILLIAM J.
Deceased.

	G	AB	H	R	BA	W	L	PCT	G by POS
1872 New York Mutuals	35	169	43	25	.254				3B-33, OF-1, SS-1
1873 Brooklyn Atlantics	48	233	63	31	.270				RF-43, 3B-5
1874 Hartfords	26	123	47	22	.382				3B-25, OF-21
1875 Brooklyn Atlantics	36	154	45	14	.292				2B-15, OF-11, 3B-9, 1B-1
4 yrs.	145	679	198	92	.292				3B-72, RF-43, OF-33, 2B-15, SS-1, 1B-1

George Bradley

BRADLEY, GEORGE WASHINGTON (Grin)   BR TR 5'10½" 175 lbs.
B. July 13, 1852, Reading, Pa.   D. Oct. 2, 1931, Philadelphia, Pa.

	G	AB	H	R	BA	W	L	PCT	G by POS
1875 St. Louis	61	250	67	28	.268	33	26	.559	P-60, OF-1, 3B-1

Brady

BRADY,
Deceased.

	G	AB	H	R	BA	W	L	PCT	G by POS
1875 Chicago White Stockings	1	4	1	1	.250				OF-1

Steve Brady

BRADY, STEPHEN A.
B. July 14, 1851, Worcester, Mass.   D. Nov. 2, 1917, Hartford, Conn.

	G	AB	H	R	BA	W	L	PCT	G by POS
1874 Hartfords	25	110	37	18	.336				3B-17, OF-8
1875 Washington Nationals	19	83	11	4	.133				2B-16, OF-2, 1B-1
2 yrs.	44	193	48	22	.249				3B-17, 2B-16, OF-10, 1B-1

Tom Brady

BRADY, THOMAS
B. Hartford, Conn.   Deceased.

	G	AB	H	R	BA	W	L	PCT	G by POS
1875 Hartfords	1	4	0	0	.000				OF-1

Asa Brainard

BRAINARD, ASA (Count)   5'8½" 150 lbs.
B. 1841, Albany, N.Y.   D. Dec. 29, 1888, Denver, Colo.

	G	AB	H	R	BA	W	L	PCT	G by POS
1871 Washington Olympics	30	140	28	24	.200	13	15	.464	P-30
1872 2 teams Middletown Mansfields (7G .161 W-0 L-3) Washington Olympics (9G .405 W-2 L-7)									
" total	16	73	22	10	.301	2	10	.222	P-12, 2B-4
1873 Lord Baltimores	15	64	16	16	.250	4	7	.364	P-13, OF-2
1874	47	209	50	19	.239	5	24	.172	P-29, 2B-17, OF-2
4 yrs.	108	486	116	69	.239	24	56	.300	P-84, 2B-21, OF-4

Mike Brannock

BRANNOCK, MICHAEL J
B. Chicago, Ill.   Deceased.

	G	AB	H	R	BA	W	L	PCT	G by POS
1871 Chicago White Stockings	3	13	1	2	.077				3B-3
1875	2	9	1	2	.111				3B-2
2 yrs.	5	22	2	4	.091				3B-5

Jim Britt

BRITT, JAMES E.
Deceased.

	G	AB	H	R	BA	W	L	PCT	G by POS
1872 Brooklyn Atlantics	35	155	34	24	.219	8	**27**	.229	P-35
1873	54	246	47	29	.191	17	**36**	.321	P-54
2 yrs.	89	401	81	53	.202	25	63	.284	P-89

Brown

BROWN,
Deceased.

	G	AB	H	R	BA	W	L	PCT	G by POS
1874 Lord Baltimores	1	5	0	0	.000				SS-1

Oliver Brown

BROWN, OLIVER E.
B. Brooklyn, N.Y.   Deceased.

	G	AB	H	R	BA	W	L	PCT	G by POS
1872 Brooklyn Atlantics	4	17	1	0	.059				OF-4
1875	3	14	1	0	.071				1B-4
2 yrs.	7	31	2	0	.065				OF-4, 1B-4

Jack Burdock

BURDOCK, JOHN JOSEPH (Black Jack)   BR TR 5'9½" 158 lbs.
B. 1851, Brooklyn, N.Y.   D. Nov. 28, 1931, Brooklyn, N.Y.

	G	AB	H	R	BA	W	L	PCT	G by POS
1872 Brooklyn Atlantics	35	176	44	27	.250				SS-33, C-2, 2B-1
1873	55	261	62	56	.238				2B-55
1874 New York Mutuals	61	284	78	46	.275				3B-61
1875 Hartfords	73	360	102	72	.283				2B-72, 3B-1
4 yrs.	224	1081	286	201	.265				2B-128, 3B-62, SS-33, C-2

Henry Burroughs

BURROUGHS, HENRY F.   5'8" 147 lbs.
B. 1845, Detroit, Mich.   Deceased.

	G	AB	H	R	BA	W	L	PCT	G by POS
1871 Washington Olympics	12	63	14	11	.222				OF-8, 3B-5
1872	2	8	1	1	.125				OF-2
2 yrs.	14	71	15	12	.211				OF-10, 3B-5

	G	AB	H	R	BA	W	L	PCT	G by POS

Doc Bushong

BUSHONG, ALBERT JOHN   BR   TR   5'11"   165 lbs.
B. Jan. 10, 1856, Philadelphia, Pa.   D. Aug. 19, 1908, Brooklyn, N. Y.

	G	AB	H	R	BA				G by POS
1875 Brooklyn Atlantics	1	5	3	0	.600				C-1

Frank Buttery

BUTTERY, FRANK
B. May 13, 1851, Silver Mine, Conn.   D. Dec. 16, 1902, Silver Mine, Conn.

	G	AB	H	R	BA	W	L	PCT	G by POS
1872 Middletown Mansfields	17	88	26	18	.295	3	2	.600	OF-6, P-6, 3B-6

Hugh Campbell

CAMPBELL, HUGH
D. 1881

	G	AB	H	R	BA	W	L	PCT	G by POS
1873 Elizabeth Resolutes	20	93	12	9	.129	2	16	.111	P-18, OF-1, 2B-1

Mike Campbell

CAMPBELL, MICHAEL
B. N. J.   Deceased.

	G	AB	H	R	BA				G by POS
1873 Elizabeth Resolutes	21	89	13	9	.146				1B-17, SS-3, OF-1

John Carbine

CARBINE, JOHN C.   6'   187 lbs.
B. 1852, Syracuse, N. Y.   Deceased.

	G	AB	H	R	BA				G by POS
1875 Keokuk Westerns	10	39	2	1	.051				1B-10

Tom Carey

CAREY, THOMAS JOHN   BR   TR   5'8"   145 lbs.
Born J. J. Norton.
B. 1849, Brooklyn, N. Y.   Deceased.
Manager 1873-74.

	G	AB	H	R	BA				G by POS
1871 Fort Wayne Kekiongas	19	85	20	15	.235				2B-18, SS-1
1872 Lord Baltimores	41	196	58	39	.296				2B-26, SS-8, OF-3, 3B-3
									1B-1
1873	55	292	95	72	.325				2B-51, 3B-3, SS-3
1874 New York Mutuals	64	292	83	55	.284				SS-51, 2B-13
1875 Hartfords	85	390	99	63	.254				SS-85
5 yrs.	264	1255	355	244	.283				SS-148, 2B-108, 3B-6, OF-3
									1B-1

Lew Carl

CARL, LEWIS
B. Baltimore, Md.   Deceased.

	G	AB	H	R	BA				G by POS
1874 Lord Baltimores	1	4	0	0	.000				C-1

Jim Carlton

CARLTON, JAMES   5'8"   155 lbs.
B. 1849, N. Y.   Deceased.

	G	AB	H	R	BA				G by POS
1871 Cleveland Forest Citys	29	136	32	31	.235				1B-29
1872	7	38	12	8	.316				1B-7
2 yrs.	36	174	44	39	.253				1B-36

John Cassidy

CASSIDY, JOHN P.   BR   TL   5'8"   168 lbs.
B. 1855, Brooklyn, N. Y.   D. July 3, 1891, Brooklyn, N. Y.

	G	AB	H	R	BA	W	L	PCT	G by POS
1875 2 teams Brooklyn Atlantics (40G		.168 W-1 L-25)		New Havens (6G	.125	)			
" total	46	191	31	16	.162	1	25	.038	P-27, 1B-13, OF-10

Jack Chapman

CHAPMAN, JOHN CURTIS   TR   5'11"   170 lbs.
B. May 8, 1843, Brooklyn, N. Y.   D. June 10, 1916, Brooklyn, N. Y.

	G	AB	H	R	BA				G by POS
1874 Brooklyn Atlantics	53	248	64	32	.258				RF-52, 1B-1
1875 St. Louis	43	187	46	27	.246				RF-43
2 yrs.	96	435	110	59	.253				RF-95, 1B-1

Bobby Clack

CLACK, ROBERT S. (Gentlemanly Bobby)   BR   TR   5'9"   153 lbs.
B. 1851, Brooklyn, N. Y.   D. Oct. 22, 1933, Danvers, Mass.

	G	AB	H	R	BA				G by POS
1874 Brooklyn Atlantics	32	134	21	22	.157				CF-30, 1B-2
1875	17	60	6	1	.100				RF-17
2 yrs.	49	194	27	23	.139				CF-30, RF-17, 1B-2

John Clapp

CLAPP, JOHN EDGAR   BR   TR   5'7"   175 lbs.
Brother of Aaron Clapp.
B. July 17, 1851, Ithaca, N. Y.   D. Dec. 17, 1904, Ithaca, N. Y.

	G	AB	H	R	BA				G by POS
1872 Middletown Mansfields	19	98	30	30	.306				C-19
1873 Philadelphia Athletics	45	219	63	35	.288				C-42, SS-2, 2B-1
1874	39	169	56	46	.331				C-26, OF-13, SS-1
1875	60	298	74	65	.248				C-60
4 yrs.	163	784	223	176	.284				C-147, OF-13, SS-3, 2B-1

Denny Clare

CLARE, DANIEL J.
B. Brooklyn, N. Y.   Deceased.

	G	AB	H	R	BA				G by POS
1872 Brooklyn Atlantics	2	7	1	1	.143				2B-2

	G	AB	H	R	BA	W	L	PCT	G by POS

Jim Clinton

CLINTON, JAMES LAWRENCE (Big Jim)   BR TR 5'8½"   174 lbs.
B. Aug. 10, 1850, New York, N. Y.   D. Sept. 3, 1921, Brooklyn, N. Y.
Manager 1872.

	G	AB	H	R	BA	W	L	PCT	G by POS
1872 Brooklyn Eckfords	24	101	19	11	.188				3B-9, OF-8, SS-4, 2B-3
1873 Elizabeth Resolutes	9	40	9	5	.225				3B-8, OF-1
1874 Brooklyn Atlantics	2	11	2	3	.182				OF-1, 2B-1
1875	22	83	10	3	.120	1	12	.077	P-14, OF-5, 1B-4, 2B-1
4 yrs.	57	235	40	22	.170	1	12	.077	3B-17, OF-15, P-14, 2B-5
									SS-4, 1B-4

Dan Collins

COLLINS, DANIEL THOMAS
B. July 12, 1854   Deceased.

	G	AB	H	R	BA	W	L	PCT	G by POS
1874 Chicago White Stockings	3	12	1	1	.083	1	1	.500	OF-2, P-2, SS-1

Fred Cone

CONE, JOSEPH FREDERICK   5'9½"   171 lbs.
B. May, 1848, Rockford, Ill.   D. Apr. 13, 1909, Chicago, Ill.

	G	AB	H	R	BA	W	L	PCT	G by POS
1871 Boston Red Stockings	18	85	20	17	.235				LF-18

Terry Connell

CONNELL, TERENCE G.
B. June 17, 1855, Philadelphia, Pa.   D. Mar. 25, 1924, Philadelphia, Pa.

	G	AB	H	R	BA	W	L	PCT	G by POS
1874 Chicago White Stockings	1	4	0	0	.000	0	0	.000	C-1

Ned Connors

CONNORS, JOSEPH P.   5'9"   156 lbs.
B. 1850, N. Y.   Deceased.

	G	AB	H	R	BA	W	L	PCT	G by POS
1871 Troy Haymakers	7	33	6	7	.182				1B-4, OF-2, 2B-1

Wilbur Coons

COONS, WILBUR K.
B. Philadelphia, Pa.   D. Aug. 30, 1915, Burlington, N. J.

	G	AB	H	R	BA	W	L	PCT	G by POS
1875 Philadelphia Athletics	4	14	2	1	.143				C-4

Dennis Coughlin

COUGHLIN, DENNIS F.
Deceased.

	G	AB	H	R	BA	W	L	PCT	G by POS
1872 Washington Nationals	8	37	12	5	.324				CF-5, SS-2, 2B-1

Fred Crane

CRANE, FRED
Deceased.

	G	AB	H	R	BA	W	L	PCT	G by POS
1873 Elizabeth Resolutes	1	4	1	0	.250				2B-1
1875 Brooklyn Atlantics	21	81	17	7	.210				1B-20, OF-1
2 yrs.	22	85	18	7	.212				1B-20, OF-1, 2B-1

Bill Craver

CRAVER, WILLIAM H.   BR TR 5'9"   160 lbs.
B. 1844, Troy, N. Y.   D. June 17, 1901, Troy, N. Y.
Manager 1871-72, 1874.

	G	AB	H	R	BA	W	L	PCT	G by POS
1871 Troy Haymakers	27	122	37	26	.303				2B-18, SS-4, C-3, 1B-2
1872 Lord Baltimores	33	180	50	52	.278				C-25, OF-5, 3B-2, 2B-2
1873	36	185	52	38	.281				C-20, SS-12, OF-3, 1B-1
1874 Philadelphias	55	275	95	71	.345				2B-53, C-3
1875 2 teams Philadelphia Athletics (54G .314) Philadelphia Centennials(14G .265)									
" total	68	332	101	79	.304				2B-53, SS-9, 3B-4, C-1
									1B-1
5 yrs.	219	1094	335	266	.306				2B-126, C-52, SS-25, OF-8
									3B-6, 1B-4

Art Croft

CROFT, ARTHUR F.
B. Jan. 23, 1855, St. Louis, Mo.   D. Mar. 16, 1884, St. Louis, Mo.

	G	AB	H	R	BA	W	L	PCT	G by POS
1875 St. Louis Reds	18	72	11	4	.153				LF-18

Bill Crowley

CROWLEY, WILLIAM MICHAEL   BR TR 5'9"   175 lbs.
B. Apr. 8, 1857, Philadelphia, Pa.   D. July 14, 1891, Gloucester, N. J.

	G	AB	H	R	BA	W	L	PCT	G by POS
1875 Philadelphias	9	37	4	4	.108				OF-4, 3B-3, 2B-1, 1B-1

Candy Cummings

CUMMINGS, WILLIAM ARTHUR   BR TR 5'9"   120 lbs.
B. Oct. 17, 1848, Ware, Mass.   D. May 16, 1924, Toledo, Ohio
Hall of Fame 1939.

	G	AB	H	R	BA	W	L	PCT	G by POS
1872 New York Mutuals	55	260	51	36	.196	33	20	.623	P-55, OF-1
1873 Lord Baltimores	42	200	50	31	.250	28	14	.667	P-42
1874 Philadelphias	54	240	50	30	.208	28	26	.519	P-54
1875 Hartfords	52	235	43	32	.183	35	12	.745	P-47, OF-6
4 yrs.	203	935	194	129	.207	124	72	.633	P-198, OF-7

Ned Cuthbert

CUTHBERT, EDGAR E.   BR TR 5'6"   140 lbs.
B. June 20, 1845, Philadelphia, Pa.   D. Feb. 6, 1905, St. Louis, Mo.

	G	AB	H	R	BA	W	L	PCT	G by POS
1871 Philadelphia Athletics	28	162	39	47	.241				LF-27, C-1
1872	46	265	87	80	.328				LF-46
1873 Philadelphias	51	284	75	79	.264				LF-51
1874 Chicago White Stockings	58	306	79	64	.258				LF-55, C-3
1875 St. Louis	68	308	82	69	.266				LF-67, C-2
5 yrs.	251	1325	362	339	.273				LF-246, C-6

	G	AB	H	R	BA	W	L	PCT	G by POS

John Dailey

DAILEY, JOHN J.
B. Brooklyn, N. Y. Deceased.

	G	AB	H	R	BA				G by POS
1875 2 teams Brooklyn Atlantics (2G .125) Washington Nationals (26G .208)									
" total	28	114	23	18	.202				SS-17, 3B-7, 2B-2, OF-1, 1B-1

Harry Deane

DEANE, JOHN HENRY   5'7"   150 lbs.
B. May 6, 1846, Trenton, N. J.   D. May 31, 1925, Indianapolis, Ind.
Manager 1871.

	G	AB	H	R	BA				G by POS
1871 Fort Wayne Kekiongas	5	24	4	3	.167				OF-5
1874 Lord Baltimores	47	212	49	29	.231				CF-45, 2B-2
2 yrs.	52	236	53	32	.225				CF-45, OF-5, 2B-2

Harmon Dehlman

DEHLMAN, HARMON J.
B. Catasauqua, Pa.   D. Mar. 13, 1885, Wilkes-Barre, Pa.

	G	AB	H	R	BA				G by POS
1872 Brooklyn Atlantics	35	164	33	26	.201				1B-35
1873	54	236	50	50	.212				1B-54
1874	53	232	51	40	.220				1B-53
1875 St. Louis	67	284	61	43	.215				1B-67
4 yrs.	209	916	195	159	.213				1B-209

Jim Devlin

DEVLIN, JAMES ALEXANDER   BR TR 5'11"   175 lbs.
B. 1849, Philadelphia, Pa.   D. Oct. 10, 1883, Philadelphia, Pa.

	G	AB	H	R	BA	W	L	PCT	G by POS
1873 Philadelphias	22	104	26	18	.250				1B-12, 3B-5, SS-3, OF-2
1874 Chicago White Stockings	44	215	59	28	.274				1B-22, OF-16, 3B-6
1875	70	336	95	60	.283	6	16	.273	1B-43, P-26, OF-3
3 yrs.	136	655	180	106	.275	6	16	.273	1B-77, P-26, OF-21, 3B-11, SS-3

Packy Dillon

DILLON, PACKARD ANDREW
B. St. Louis, Mo.   D. Jan. 9, 1890, Guelph, Ont., Canada

	G	AB	H	R	BA				G by POS
1875 St. Louis Reds	3	16	3	1	.188				C-3

W. C. Dole

DOLE, W. C.
Deceased.

	G	AB	H	R	BA				G by POS
1875 New Havens	1	4	2	1	.500				OF-1

T. J. Donnelly

DONNELLY, T. J.
Deceased.

	G	AB	H	R	BA				G by POS
1871 Fort Wayne Kekiongas	9	35	7	8	.200				OF-9, 3B-1
1873 Washington Nationals	30	141	35	15	.248				SS-13, 2B-11, OF-6
1874 Philadelphias	5	21	5	2	.238				OF-2, SS-2, 2B-1
3 yrs.	44	197	47	25	.239				OF-17, SS-15, 2B-12, 3B-1

Herm Doscher

DOSCHER, JOHN HENRY, SR.   5'10"   182 lbs.
Father of Jack Doscher.
B. Dec. 20, 1852, New York, N. Y.   D. Mar. 30, 1934, Buffalo, N. Y.

	G	AB	H	R	BA				G by POS
1872 Brooklyn Atlantics	6	26	9	4	.346				OF-6
1873	1	6	1	1	.167				OF-1
1875 Washington Nationals	21	75	12	3	.160				3B-19, SS-2
3 yrs.	28	107	22	8	.206				3B-19, OF-7, SS-2

Joe Doyle

DOYLE, JOSEPH
B. Cincinnati, Ohio   Deceased.

	G	AB	H	R	BA				G by POS
1872 Washington Nationals	8	36	8	4	.222				SS-6, 3B-1, 2B-1

Ed Duffy

DUFFY, EDWARD C   TR 5'7½"   152 lbs.
B. 1844, Ireland   D. June, 1889

	G	AB	H	R	BA				G by POS
1871 Chicago White Stockings	25	121	28	31	.231				SS-24, 3B-1

Edwards

EDWARDS,
Deceased.

	G	AB	H	R	BA	W	L	PCT	G by POS
1875 Brooklyn Atlantics	1	5	1	1	.200	0	0	.000	OF-1, P-1

Dave Eggler

EGGLER, DAVID DANIEL   BR TR 5'9"   165 lbs.
B. Apr. 30, 1851, Brooklyn, N. Y.   D. Apr. 5, 1902, Buffalo, N. Y.

	G	AB	H	R	BA				G by POS
1871 New York Mutuals	33	150	47	37	.313				CF-33
1872	56	295	102	95	.346				CF-56
1873	53	281	92	83	.327				CF-53
1874 Philadelphias	58	306	96	70	.314				CF-56, 2B-2
1875 Philadelphia Athletics	66	302	87	65	.288				CF-66
5 yrs.	266	1334	424	350	.318				CF-264, 2B-2

Eland

ELAND,
Deceased.

	G	AB	H	R	BA				G by POS
1873 Marylands	1	4	0	0	.000				OF-1

	G	AB	H	R	BA	W	L	PCT	G by POS

Joe Ellick

ELLICK, JOSEPH J.
B. 1856, Cincinnati, Ohio   Deceased.

	G	AB	H	R	BA				G by POS
1875 St. Louis Reds	6	24	5	1	.208				3B-3, OF-2, SS-1

G. Ewell

EWELL, G.
Deceased.

	G	AB	H	R	BA				G by POS
1871 Cleveland Forest Cities	1	4	0	0	.000				OF-1

Jack Farrell

FARRELL, JOHN (Hartford Jack)
D. Nov. 15, 1916, Hartford, Conn.

	G	AB	H	R	BA				G by POS
1874 Hartfords	3	15	5	3	.333				OF-3

John Farrow

FARROW, JOHN JACOB   TR
B. 1852, Verplanck's Point, N. Y.   D. Dec. 31, 1914, Perth Amboy, N. J.

	G	AB	H	R	BA				G by POS
1873 Elizabeth Resolutes	12	51	8	2	.157				C-7, OF-2, SS-2, 1B-1
1874 Brooklyn Atlantics	27	125	26	16	.208				C-15, 2B-12
2 yrs.	39	176	34	18	.193				C-22, 2B-12, OF-2, SS-2
									1B-1

Bob Ferguson

FERGUSON, ROBERT V. (Death to Flying Things)   BB TR 5'9½" 149 lbs.
B. 1845, Brooklyn, N. Y.   D. May 3, 1894, Brooklyn, N. Y.
Manager 1871-75.

	G	AB	H	R	BA	W	L	PCT	G by POS
1871 New York Mutuals	33	156	34	30	.218				3B-19, 2B-10, C-4
1872 Brooklyn Atlantics	35	164	43	34	.262				3B-35
1873	51	238	59	36	.248	0	1	.000	3B-50, P-1
1874	56	249	64	34	.257	0	1	.000	3B-55, C-2, P-1
1875 Hartfords	84	373	87	65	.233				3B-84
5 yrs.	259	1180	287	199	.243	0	2	.000	3B-243, 2B-10, C-6, P-2

Sam Field

FIELD, SAMUEL JAY   BR TR 5'9½" 182 lbs.
B. Oct. 12, 1848, Philadelphia, Pa.   D. Oct. 28, 1904, Sinking Spring, Pa.

	G	AB	H	R	BA				G by POS
1875 2 teams Philadelphia Centennials(3G .091) Washington Nationals (5G .235)									
" total	8	28	5	2	.179				C-6, OF-2

George Fields

FIELDS, GEORGE W.
Deceased.

	G	AB	H	R	BA				G by POS
1872 Middletown Mansfields	17	71	20	18	.282				3B-10, OF-6, SS-1

Cherokee Fisher

FISHER, WILLIAM CHARLES   BR TR 5'9" 164 lbs.
B. Dec., 1845, Philadelphia, Pa.   D. Sept. 26, 1912, New York, N. Y.

	G	AB	H	R	BA	W	L	PCT	G by POS
1871 Rockford Forest Citys	25	124	28	24	.226	4	20	.167	P-24, SS-1
1872 Lord Baltimores	44	234	48	39	.205	9	3	.750	3B-17, OF-16, P-13
1873 Philadelphia Athletics	51	259	66	51	.255	2	2	.500	RF-45, P-7, 1B-1
1874 Hartfords	52	231	53	29	.229	14	21	.400	P-35, OF-10, 3B-6, SS-1
1875 Philadelphias	41	169	39	26	.231	22	18	.550	P-40, OF-1
5 yrs.	213	1017	234	169	.230	51	64	.443	P-119, RF-45, OF-27, 3B-23
									SS-2, 1B-1

Wes Fisler

FISLER, WESTON DICKSON   5'6" 137 lbs.
B. July 5, 1841, Camden, N. J.   D. Dec. 25, 1922, Philadelphia, Pa.

	G	AB	H	R	BA				G by POS
1871 Philadelphia Athletics	28	150	44	43	.293				1B-26, 2B-2
1872	46	248	81	50	.327				2B-46
1873	43	227	71	42	.313				2B-35, 1B-8
1874	37	175	67	27	.383				1B-28, 2B-9
1875	57	272	75	54	.276				1B-44, OF-9, 2B-4
5 yrs.	211	1072	338	216	.315				1B-106, 2B-96, OF-9

Frank Fleet

FLEET, FRANK H.
B. 1848, New York, N. Y.   D. June 13, 1900, New York, N. Y.

	G	AB	H	R	BA	W	L	PCT	G by POS
1871 New York Mutuals	1	5	2	1	.400	0	1	.000	P-1
1872 Brooklyn Eckfords	13	58	11	10	.190				3B-10, 2B-2, OF-1
1873 Elizabeth Resolutes	22	96	22	11	.229	0	3	.000	2B-8, SS-7, P-3, 3B-3
									1B-1
1874 Brooklyn Atlantics	20	94	22	18	.234				C-12, 2B-7, OF-1
1875 2 teams Brooklyn Atlantics (26G .216 W-0 L-1) St. Louis (3G .083 W-2 L-1)									
" total	29	128	26	14	.203	2	2	.667	2B-11, C-10, SS-6, P-4
5 yrs.	85	381	83	54	.218	2	6	.250	2B-28, C-22, 3B-13, SS-13
									P-8, OF-2, 1B-1

Fletcher

FLETCHER,
Deceased.

	G	AB	H	R	BA				G by POS
1872 Brooklyn Eckfords	2	8	2	1	.250				OF-2

Silver Flint

FLINT, FRANK SYLVESTER   BR TR 5'10" 170 lbs.
B. Aug. 3, 1855, Philadelphia, Pa.   D. Jan. 14, 1892, Chicago, Ill.

	G	AB	H	R	BA				G by POS
1875 St. Louis Reds	16	58	5	3	.086				C-15, 3B-1

	G	AB	H	R	BA	W	L	PCT	G by POS

Dickie Flowers

FLOWERS, CHARLES RICHARD
B. 1850, Philadelphia, Pa.   D. Oct. 5, 1892, Philadelphia, Pa.

	G	AB	H	R	BA				G by POS
1871 Troy Haymakers	21	109	33	40	.303				SS-20, 2B-1
1872 Philadelphia Athletics	3	17	4	1	.235				SS-3
2 yrs.	24	126	37	41	.294				SS-23, 2B-1

Clipper Flynn

FLYNN, WILLIAM   TR 5'7"   140 lbs.
B. 1850, Troy, N. Y.   D. Nov. 5, 1881, Troy, N. Y.

	G	AB	H	R	BA				G by POS
1871 Troy Haymakers	29	148	46	44	.311				1B-19, OF-9, 3B-1
1872 Washington Olympics	9	41	9	4	.220				1B-9
2 yrs.	38	189	55	48	.291				1B-28, OF-9, 3B-1

Tom Foley

FOLEY, THOMAS J.   5'9½"   157 lbs.
B. Aug. 16, 1842, Cashel, Ireland   D. Nov. 3, 1926, Chicago, Ill.
Manager 1871.

	G	AB	H	R	BA				G by POS
1871 Chicago White Stockings	18	84	21	18	.250				CF-14, C-3, 3B-1

Will Foley

FOLEY, WILLIAM BROWN   BR TR 5'9½"   150 lbs.
B. Nov. 15, 1855, Chicago, Ill.   D. Nov. 15, 1916, Chicago, Ill.

	G	AB	H	R	BA				G by POS
1875 Chicago White Stockings	3	14	3	0	.214				3B-3

Jim Foran

FORAN, JAMES H.   5'6½"   159 lbs.
B. 1848, N. Y.   Deceased.

	G	AB	H	R	BA				G by POS
1871 Fort Wayne Kekiongas	19	90	31	20	.344				1B-15, OF-4

Davy Force

FORCE, DAVID W.   BR TR 5'4"   130 lbs.
B. July 27, 1849, New York, N. Y.   D. June 21, 1918, Englewood, N. J.

	G	AB	H	R	BA	W	L	PCT	G by POS
1871 Washington Olympics	32	166	44	45	.265				SS-31, 3B-1
1872 2 teams Lord Baltimores (18G .409) Troy Haymakers (25G .414)									
" total	43	226	93	69	.412				3B-34, SS-9
1873 Lord Baltimores	48	250	85	75	.340	1	1	.500	3B-32, SS-15, P-2
1874 Chicago White Stockings	59	305	92	61	.302				3B-38, SS-20, OF-1, P-1
1875 Philadelphia Athletics	77	391	122	77	.312				SS-77
5 yrs.	259	1338	436	327	.326	1	1	.500	SS-152, 3B-105, P-3, OF-1

Bill French

FRENCH, WILLIAM
B. Baltimore, Md.   Deceased.

	G	AB	H	R	BA	W	L	PCT	G by POS
1873 Marylands	5	19	4	3	.211	0	1	.000	RF-2, 1B-2, P-1

Fulmer

FULMER,
Deceased.

	G	AB	H	R	BA				G by POS
1875 Brooklyn Atlantics	1	4	2	1	.500				3B-1

Chick Fulmer

FULMER, CHARLES JOHN   BR TR 6'   158 lbs.
B. Feb. 12, 1851, Philadelphia, Pa.   D. Feb. 15, 1940, Philadelphia, Pa.

	G	AB	H	R	BA				G by POS
1871 Rockford Forest Citys	16	70	17	12	.243				SS-15, 1B-1
1872 New York Mutuals	36	169	51	29	.302				3B-23, SS-13
1873 Philadelphias	49	244	64	41	.262				SS-48, C-1
1874	57	265	70	49	.264				SS-31, 3B-26
1875	68	288	64	49	.222				SS-54, 3B-14
5 yrs.	226	1036	266	180	.257				SS-161, 3B-63, C-1, 1B-1

John Galvin

GALVIN, JOHN
D. May, 1904, Brooklyn, N. Y.

	G	AB	H	R	BA				G by POS
1872 Brooklyn Atlantics	1	4	0	0	.000				2B-1
1874	1	4	0	1	.000				2B-1
2 yrs.	2	8	0	1	.000				2B-2

Pud Galvin

GALVIN, JAMES FRANCIS (Gentle Jeems, The Little Steam Engine)
                                                                      BR TR 5'8"   190 lbs.
Brother of Lou Galvin.
B. Dec. 25, 1855, St. Louis, Mo.   D. Mar. 7, 1902, Pittsburgh, Pa.
Hall of Fame 1965.

	G	AB	H	R	BA	W	L	PCT	G by POS
1875 St. Louis	12	37	8	8	.216	4	2	.667	P-8, OF-5

Count Gedney

GEDNEY, ALFRED W.   5'9"   140 lbs.
B. May 10, 1849, Brooklyn, N. Y.   D. Mar. 26, 1922, Hackensack, N. J.

	G	AB	H	R	BA	W	L	PCT	G by POS
1872 2 teams Brooklyn Eckfords (18G .158) Troy Haymakers (9G .413)									
" total	27	122	31	23	.254				LF-18, CF-9
1873 New York Mutuals	53	236	60	41	.254				LF-53
1874 Philadelphia Athletics	54	235	76	48	.323				LF-50, 1B-4
1875 New York Mutuals	67	263	52	29	.198	1	0	.000	LF-66, P-1
4 yrs.	201	856	219	141	.256	1	0	.000	LF-187, CF-9, 1B-4, P-1

	G	AB	H	R	BA	W	L	PCT	G by POS

Billy Geer

GEER, WILLIAM HENRY HARRISON
B. Aug. 13, 1849, Syracuse, N. Y.   Deceased.

TR   5'8"   160 lbs.

	G	AB	H	R	BA				G by POS
1874 New York Mutuals	2	8	2	0	.250				OF-2
1875 New Havens	37	173	39	20	.225				OF-17, 2B-13, SS-5, 3B-1
									1B-1
2 yrs.	39	181	41	20	.227				OF-19, 2B-13, SS-5, 3B-1
									1B-1

Joe Gerhardt

GERHARDT, JOHN JOSEPH (Move Up Joe)
B. Feb. 14, 1855, Washington, D. C.   D. Mar. 11, 1922, Middletown, N. Y.

BR   TR   6'   160 lbs.

	G	AB	H	R	BA				G by POS
1873 Washington Nationals	13	56	11	6	.196				SS-13
1874 Lord Baltimores	14	65	20	10	.308				SS-14
1875 New York Mutuals	57	254	54	29	.213				3B-44, 2B-12, SS-1
3 yrs.	84	375	85	45	.227				3B-44, SS-28, 2B-12

Barney Gilligan

GILLIGAN, ANDREW BERNARD
B. Jan. 3, 1857, Cambridge, Mass.   D. Apr. 1, 1934, Lynn, Mass.

BR   TR   5'6½"   130 lbs.

	G	AB	H	R	BA				G by POS
1875 Brooklyn Atlantics	2	8	2	2	.250				OF-1, C-1

Jim Gilmore

GILMORE, JAMES
B. Baltimore, Md.   Deceased.

	G	AB	H	R	BA				G by POS
1875 Washington Nationals	4	15	5	4	.333				C-2, 3B-1, 2B-1

Gilroy

GILROY,
Deceased.

	G	AB	H	R	BA				G by POS
1874 Chicago White Stockings	8	39	8	4	.205				C-8
1875 Philadelphia Athletics	2	8	2	0	.250				OF-1, C-1
2 yrs.	10	47	10	4	.213				C-9, OF-1

John Glenn

GLENN, JOHN W.
B. 1849, Rochester, N. Y.   D. Nov. 10, 1888, Glens Falls, N. Y.

BR   TR   5'8½"   169 lbs.

	G	AB	H	R	BA				G by POS
1871 Washington Olympics	26	123	37	24	.301				RF-26
1872 2 teams Washington Nationals (1G	.500) Washington Olympics (9G			.150)					LF-9, OF-1
" total	10	44	8	5	.182				LF-9, OF-1
1873 Washington Nationals	39	194	49	39	.253				1B-39
1874 Chicago White Stockings	55	245	64	34	.261				1B-38, OF-17
1875	70	325	76	48	.234				LF-44, 1B-26
5 yrs.	200	931	234	150	.251				1B-103, LF-53, RF-26, OF-18

Mike Golden

GOLDEN, MICHAEL HENRY
B. Sept. 11, 1851, Shirley, Mass.   D. Jan. 11, 1929, Rockford, Ill.

BR   TR   5'7"   166 lbs.

	G	AB	H	R	BA	W	L	PCT	G by POS
1875 2 teams Chicago White Stockings (39G	.242 W-7 L-7) Keokuk Westerns (13G			.140 W-1 L-12)					P-28, OF-24, 1B-1
" total	52	211	46	21	.218	8	19	.077	P-28, OF-24, 1B-1

Wally Goldsmith

GOLDSMITH, WALLACE
B. 1849, Baltimore, Md.   Deceased.

5'7"   146 lbs.

	G	AB	H	R	BA				G by POS
1871 Fort Wayne Kekiongas	19	91	19	9	.209				SS-12, 3B-5, C-1, 2B-1
1872 Washington Olympics	9	40	9	4	.225				SS-5, 2B-4
1873 Marylands	1	4	0	0	.000				2B-1
1875 2 teams New Havens (1G .500) Keokuk Westerns (13G			.113)						3B-13, 2B-1
" total	14	57	8	3	.140				3B-13, 2B-1
4 yrs.	43	192	36	16	.188				3B-18, SS-17, 2B-7, C-1

Charlie Gould

GOULD, CHARLES HARVEY
B. Aug. 21, 1847, Cincinnati, Ohio   D. Apr. 10, 1917, Flushing, N. Y.
Manager 1875

BR   TR   6'   172 lbs.

	G	AB	H	R	BA				G by POS
1871 Boston Red Stockings	31	156	42	38	.269				1B-30, OF-1
1872	45	223	57	41	.256				1B-44, OF-2
1874 Lord Baltimores	33	151	34	20	.225				1B-32, C-1
1875 New Havens	27	115	29	9	.252				1B-26, OF-1
4 yrs.	136	645	162	108	.251				1B-132, OF-4, C-1

Greyson

GREYSON,
Deceased.

	G	AB	H	R	BA	W	L	PCT	G by POS
1873 Washington Nationals	8	35	5	4	.143	1	7	.125	P-8

Bill Hague

HAGUE, WILLIAM L.
Born William L. Haug.
B. 1852, Philadelphia, Pa.   Deceased.

BR   TR   5'9"   164 lbs.

	G	AB	H	R	BA				G by POS
1875 St. Louis	62	261	59	24	.226				3B-61, 1B-1

George Hall

HALL, GEORGE W.
B. 1849, Brooklyn, N. Y.   Deceased.

BL   5'7"   142 lbs.

	G	AB	H	R	BA				G by POS
1871 Washington Olympics	32	146	38	31	.260				CF-32
1872 Lord Baltimores	54	263	79	69	.300				CF-53, 1B-1
1873	34	169	54	43	.320				CF-34
1874 Boston Red Stockings	47	209	67	58	.321				CF-47
1875 Philadelphia Athletics	77	362	108	70	.298				LF-77
5 yrs.	244	1149	346	271	.301				CF-166, LF-77, 1B-1

	G	AB	H	R	BA	W	L	PCT	G by POS

Jim Hall

HALL, JAMES
D. Jan. 30, 1886, Brooklyn, N. Y.

	G	AB	H	R	BA				G by POS
1872 Brooklyn Atlantics	13	57	14	8	.246				2B-12, OF-1
1874	2	8	1	0	.125				2B-2
1875 Keokuk Westerns	1	4	1	0	.250				OF-1
3 yrs.	16	69	16	8	.232				2B-14, OF-2

Jimmy Hallinan

HALLINAN, JAMES H.   BL TL 5'9"   172 lbs.
B. May 27, 1849, Ireland   D. Oct. 28, 1879, Chicago, Ill.

	G	AB	H	R	BA				G by POS
1871 Fort Wayne Kekiongas	5	25	5	7	.200				SS-5
1875 2 teams New York Mutuals (44G	.299)	Keokuk Westerns (13G	.241)						
" total	57	262	75	42	.286				SS-56, 3B-1
2 yrs.	62	287	80	49	.279				SS-61, 3B-1

Ralph Ham

HAM, RALPH A.   5'8"   158 lbs.
B. 1850, Troy, N. Y.   D. Feb. 13, 1905, Troy, N. Y.

	G	AB	H	R	BA				G by POS
1871 Rockford Forest Citys	25	118	26	25	.220				LF-18, 2B-5, SS-2
1872 Middletown Mansfields	1	6	2	0	.333				SS-1
2 yrs.	26	124	28	25	.226				LF-18, 2B-5, SS-3

Bill Harbidge

HARBIDGE, WILLIAM ARTHUR   BL TL   162 lbs.
B. Mar. 29, 1855, Philadelphia, Pa.   D. Mar. 17, 1924, Philadelphia, Pa.

	G	AB	H	R	BA				G by POS
1875 Hartfords	51	227	49	32	.216				C-25, OF-13, 2B-10, 1B-3

Harrison

HARRISON,
Deceased.

	G	AB	H	R	BA				G by POS
1875 New Havens	1	4	2	0	.500				C-1

Scott Hastings

HASTINGS, WINFIELD SCOTT   TR 5'8"   161 lbs.
B. Aug. 10, 1847, Hillsboro, Ohio   D. Aug. 15, 1907, Sawtelle, Calif.
Manager 1872.

	G	AB	H	R	BA				G by POS
1871 Rockford Forest Citys	25	120	28	27	.233				C-23, 2B-2, OF-1
1872 2 teams Lord Baltimores (11G	.196)	Cleveland Forest Citys (21G	.422)						
" total	32	172	60	52	.349				C-20, OF-7, 2B-6
1873 Lord Baltimores	30	160	41	42	.256				C-19, OF-10, 2B-1
1874 Hartfords	52	237	88	60	.371				C-31, OF-20, 2B-1
1875 Chicago White Stockings	66	298	74	43	.248				C-39, OF-25, 2B-2
5 yrs.	205	987	291	224	.295				C-132, OF-63, 2B-12

John Hatfield

HATFIELD, JOHN VAN BUREN   5'10"   165 lbs.
Brother of Gil Hatfield.
B. 1847, New York, N. Y.   D. Feb. 20, 1909, Long Island City, N. Y.

	G	AB	H	R	BA	W	L	PCT	G by POS
1871 New York Mutuals	33	168	44	41	.262				LF-24, 2B-7, 3B-2
1872	56	**297**	90	75	.303				2B-56
1873	52	260	76	54	.292				3B-42, 2B-10
1874	63	299	67	47	.224	0	0	.000	LF-59, 3B-4, P-1, 1B-1
1875	2	9	4	2	.444				OF-2
5 yrs.	206	1033	281	219	.272	0	0	.000	LF-83, 2B-73, 3B-48, OF-2
									P-1, 1B-1

Hearn

HEARN,
Deceased.

	G	AB	H	R	BA				G by POS
1872 Washington Olympics	1	3	1	0	.333				SS-1

Frank Heifer

HEIFER, FRANKLIN (Heck)
B. Jan. 18, 1854, Reading, Pa.   D. Aug. 29, 1893, Reading, Pa.

	G	AB	H	R	BA	W	L	PCT	G by POS
1875 Boston Red Stockings	11	48	16	11	.333	0	0	.000	1B-7, OF-5, P-1

Hellings

HELLINGS,
Deceased.

	G	AB	H	R	BA				G by POS
1875 Brooklyn Atlantics	1	4	1	0	.250				2B-1

George Heuble

HEUBLE, GEORGE A.   5'11½"   178 lbs.
B. 1849, Paterson, N. J.   D. Feb., 1896, Philadelphia, Pa.

	G	AB	H	R	BA				G by POS
1871 Philadelphia Athletics	17	78	25	10	.321				RF-16, 1B-1
1872 Washington Olympics	5	24	3	2	.125				CF-5
2 yrs.	22	102	28	12	.275				RF-16, CF-5, 1B-1

Nat Hicks

HICKS, NATHAN WOODHULL   BR TR 6'1"   186 lbs.
B. Apr. 19, 1845, Hempstead, N. Y.   D. Apr. 21, 1907, Hoboken, N. J.
Manager 1875.

	G	AB	H	R	BA				G by POS
1872 New York Mutuals	56	276	85	54	.308				C-55, OF-2
1873	28	132	28	12	.212				C-28
1874 Philadelphias	58	284	73	51	.257				C-56, OF-2
1875 New York Mutuals	62	270	63	32	.233				C-59, OF-3
4 yrs.	204	962	249	149	.259				C-198, OF-7

Higby

HIGBY,
Deceased.

	G	AB	H	R	BA				G by POS
1872 Brooklyn Atlantics	1	4	0	0	.000				OF-1

	G	AB	H	R	BA	W	L	PCT	G by POS

Dick Higham

HIGHAM, RICHARD
B. 1852, England   D. Mar. 18, 1905, Chicago, Ill.
Manager 1874.

BL   TR

		G	AB	H	R	BA	G by POS
1871	New York Mutuals	21	97	32	21	.330	2B-11, OF-8, C-1, 3B-1
1872	Lord Baltimores	46	242	82	67	.339	C-21, OF-18, 2B-6, 1B-1
1873	New York Mutuals	49	247	75	57	.304	OF-18, 2B-16, C-14, 3B-1
1874		65	342	87	58	.254	C-41, OF-23, 2B-1
1875	2 teams Chicago White Stockings (43G .234) New York Mutuals (15G .333)						
"	total	58	280	72	55	.257	C-30, 2B-19, OF-7, 1B-2
	5 yrs.	239	1208	348	258	.288	C-107, OF-74, 2B-53, 1B-3 3B-2

Paul Hines

HINES, PAUL A.
B. Mar. 1, 1852, Washington, D. C.   D. July 10, 1935, Hyattsville, Md.

BR   TR   5'9½"   173 lbs.

		G	AB	H	R	BA	G by POS
1872	Washington Nationals	11	49	14	10	.286	1B-10, 3B-1
1873		39	186	61	33	.328	LF-36, 2B-2, C-1
1874	Chicago White Stockings	59	283	78	47	.276	CF-46, 2B-12, SS-2
1875		69	322	101	42	.314	CF-41, 2B-28
	4 yrs.	178	840	254	132	.302	CF-87, 2B-42, LF-36, 1B-10 SS-2, C-1, 3B-1

Charlie Hodes

HODES, CHARLES
B. 1848, New York, N. Y.   D. Feb. 14, 1875, Brooklyn, N. Y.

TR   5'11½"   175 lbs.

		G	AB	H	R	BA	G by POS
1871	Chicago White Stockings	28	138	34	32	.246	C-18, 3B-7, OF-2, SS-1
1872	Troy Haymakers	13	65	15	17	.231	SS-5, OF-4, C-3, 3B-1
1874	Brooklyn Atlantics	21	84	12	8	.143	OF-19, 2B-2
	3 yrs.	62	287	61	57	.213	OF-25, C-21, 3B-8, SS-6 2B-2

Jim Holdsworth

HOLDSWORTH, JAMES (Long Jim)
Deceased.

BR   TR

		G	AB	H	R	BA	G by POS
1872	2 teams Cleveland Forest Citys (21G .321) Brooklyn Eckfords (2G .250)						
"	total	23	117	37	19	.316	SS-23
1873	New York Mutuals	53	232	71	45	.306	SS-53
1874	Philadelphias	58	302	99	59	.328	3B-31, SS-23, OF-4
1875	New York Mutuals	71	339	92	47	.271	CF-45, SS-26
	4 yrs.	205	990	299	170	.302	SS-125, CF-45, 3B-31, OF-4

Holly Hollingshead

HOLLINGSHEAD, JOHN SAMUEL
Also appeared in box score as Holly
B. Jan. 17, 1853, Washington, D. C.   D. Oct. 6, 1926, Washington, D. C.

		G	AB	H	R	BA	G by POS
1872	Washington Nationals	9	45	14	12	.311	2B-9
1873		30	137	35	25	.255	CF-30, 2B-1
1875		19	88	20	8	.227	CF-19
	3 yrs.	58	270	69	45	.256	CF-49, 2B-10

Mike Hooper

HOOPER, MICHAEL H.
B. 1845, Baltimore, Md.   Deceased.

5'6"   165 lbs.

		G	AB	H	R	BA	G by POS
1873	Marylands	2	9	0	0	.000	OF-1, C-1

Charlie Houtz

HOUTZ, CHARLES
B. St. Louis, Mo.   Deceased.

5'7"   150 lbs.

		G	AB	H	R	BA	G by POS
1875	St. Louis Reds	18	75	23	5	.307	1B-18

Dick Hunt

HUNT, RICHARD M.
B. 1847, N. Y.   Deceased.

5'9"   145 lbs.

		G	AB	H	R	BA	G by POS
1872	Brooklyn Eckfords	11	52	15	11	.288	RF-8, 2B-3

Dick Hurley

HURLEY, WILLIAM F.
B. 1847   Deceased.

BL   5'7"   160 lbs.

		G	AB	H	R	BA	G by POS
1872	Washington Olympics	2	8	0	0	.000	OF-2

Sam Jackson

JACKSON, SAMUEL
B. Mar. 24, 1849, Ripon Yorkshire, England   D. Aug. 4, 1893, Clifton Springs, N. Y.

BR   TR   5'5½"   160 lbs.

		G	AB	H	R	BA	G by POS
1871	Boston Red Stockings	15	77	15	15	.195	2B-14, OF-1
1872	Brooklyn Atlantics	3	13	2	0	.154	OF-3
	2 yrs.	18	90	17	15	.189	2B-14, OF-4

Nat Jewett

JEWETT, NATHAN W.
B. 1842   Deceased.

5'6"   137 lbs.

		G	AB	H	R	BA	G by POS
1872	Brooklyn Eckfords	2	8	1	1	.125	C-2

Tom Johns

JOHNS, THOMAS P.
B. Baltimore, Md.   Deceased.

		G	AB	H	R	BA	G by POS
1873	Marylands	1	5	0	0	.000	OF-1

Caleb Johnson

JOHNSON, CALEB CLARK
B. May 23, 1844, Fulton, Ill.   D. Mar. 7, 1925, Sterling, Ill.

		G	AB	H	R	BA	G by POS
1871	Cleveland Forest Citys	16	65	16	10	.246	2B-8, OF-7, SS-1

		G	AB	H	R	BA	W	L	PCT	G by POS

Jones

JONES,
Deceased.

		G	AB	H	R	BA				G by POS
1873	Marylands	1	5	3	0	.600				OF-1
1874	Lord Baltimores	2	7	1	0	.143				OF-1, C-1
1875	Hartfords	1	5	0	1	.000				OF-1
3 yrs.		4	17	4	1	.235				OF-3, C-1

Charley Jones

JONES, CHARLES WESLEY   BR TR 5'11½ " 202 lbs.
Born Benjamin Wesley Rippay.
B. Apr. 3, 1850, Alamance County, N. C.   Deceased.

		G	AB	H	R	BA				G by POS
1875	Keokuk Westerns	12	52	13	4	.250				LF-12

Joe Josephs

JOSEPHS, JOSEPH   BR TR 5'10"   140 lbs.
Born Joseph Borden
B. May 9, 1854, Jacobstown, N. J.   D. Oct. 14, 1929, Yeadon, Pa.
No-hit game vs. Chicago White Stockings July 28, 1875.

		G	AB	H	R	BA	W	L	PCT	G by POS
1875	Philadelphias	7	29	3	3	.103	2	4	.333	P-7

Kavanaugh

KAVANAUGH,
Deceased.

		G	AB	H	R	BA				G by POS
1872	Brooklyn Eckfords	5	22	4	5	.182				1B-4, OF-1

Jim Keenan

KEENAN, JAMES W.   BR TR 5'10"   186 lbs.
B. Feb. 10, 1858, New Haven, Conn.   D. Sept. 21, 1926, Cincinnati, Ohio

		G	AB	H	R	BA				G by POS
1875	New Havens	3	12	1	1	.083				3B-2, C-1

George Keerl

KEERL, GEORGE HENRY (Cap)   BR TR 5'7"   145 lbs.
B. Apr. 10, 1847, Baltimore, Md.   D. Sept. 13, 1923, Menominee, Mich.

		G	AB	H	R	BA				G by POS
1875	Chicago White Stockings	6	26	3	2	.115				2B-6

Bill Kelley

KELLEY, WILLIAM J.
B. New York, N. Y.   Deceased.

		G	AB	H	R	BA				G by POS
1871	Fort Wayne Kekiongas	18	71	15	17	.211				RF-17, 1B-1

John Kenney

KENNEY, JOHN
Deceased.

		G	AB	H	R	BA				G by POS
1872	Brooklyn Atlantics	5	21	0	0	.000				2B-3, OF-2

Joe Kernan

KERNAN, JOSEPH
B. Baltimore, Md.   Deceased.

		G	AB	H	R	BA				G by POS
1873	Marylands	2	8	3	1	.375				OF-1, 2B-1

Henry Kessler

KESSLER, HENRY (Lucky)   BR TR 5'10"   144 lbs.
B. 1847, Brooklyn, N. Y.   D. Jan. 9, 1900, Franklin, Pa.

		G	AB	H	R	BA				G by POS
1873	Brooklyn Atlantics	1	6	1	0	.167				1B-1
1874		14	57	16	8	.281				C-8, 2B-4, OF-2, 3B-1
1875		25	108	26	17	.241				SS-18, OF-6, C-1, 2B-1
3 yrs.		40	171	43	25	.251				SS-18, C-9, OF-8, 2B-5 3B-1, 1B-1

Gene Kimball

KIMBALL, EUGENE   5'10"   160 lbs.
B. Aug. 31, 1850, Rochester, N. Y.   D. Aug. 2, 1882, Rochester, N. Y.

		G	AB	H	R	BA				G by POS
1871	Cleveland Forest Citys	29	136	25	18	.184				2B-17, OF-6, SS-6

Mart King

KING, MARSHAL NEY   TR 5'9½ " 176 lbs.
B. Dec., 1848, Troy, N. Y.   D. Oct. 19, 1911, Troy, N. Y.

		G	AB	H	R	BA				G by POS
1871	Chicago White Stockings	20	109	16	23	.147				OF-10, C-7, SS-3
1872	Troy Haymakers	3	12	0	0	.000				OF-3
2 yrs.		23	121	16	23	.132				OF-13, C-7, SS-3

Steve King

KING, STEPHEN   5'9"   175 lbs.
B. 1845, Troy, N. Y.   D. July 8, 1895, Troy, N. Y.

		G	AB	H	R	BA				G by POS
1871	Troy Haymakers	29	144	57	45	.396				LF-29
1872		25	128	38	31	.297				LF-25
2 yrs.		54	272	95	76	.349				LF-54

George Knight

KNIGHT, GEORGE HENRY
B. Nov. 24, 1855, Lakeville, Conn.   D. Oct. 4, 1912, Lakeville, Conn.

		G	AB	H	R	BA	W	L	PCT	G by POS
1875	New Havens	1	4	0	0	.000	1	0	.000	P-1

Lon Knight

KNIGHT, ALONZO P.   BR TR 5'11½ " 165 lbs.
B. June 16, 1853, Philadelphia, Pa.   D. Apr. 23, 1932, Philadelphia, Pa.

		G	AB	H	R	BA	W	L	PCT	G by POS
1875	Philadelphia Athletics	13	51	6	5	.118	6	5	.545	P-13

	G	AB	H	R	BA	W	L	PCT	G by POS

Jake Knowdell

KNOWDELL, JACOB AUGUSTUS
B. Brooklyn, N. Y. Deceased.

5'7½" 148 lbs.

	G	AB	H	R	BA	G by POS
1874 Brooklyn Atlantics	23	90	12	8	.133	C-20, OF-3
1875	43	165	32	17	.194	C-33, SS-8, OF-3
2 yrs.	66	255	44	25	.173	C-53, SS-8, OF-6

Henry Kohler

KOHLER, HENRY C.
B. Baltimore, Md. Deceased.

	G	AB	H	R	BA	G by POS
1871 Fort Wayne Kekiongas	3	12	2	0	.167	1B-2, 3B-1
1873 Marylands	5	22	3	2	.136	3B-5, C-1
1874 Lord Baltimores	1	4	0	0	.000	1B-1
3 yrs.	9	38	5	2	.132	3B-6, 1B-3, C-1

Juice Latham

LATHAM, GEORGE WARREN
B. Sept. 6, 1852, Utica, N. Y.   D. May 26, 1914, Utica, N. Y.

	G	AB	H	R	BA	G by POS
1875 2 teams Boston Red Stockings (16G .321) New Havens (20G .183)						
" total	36	160	40	28	.250	1B-29, SS-4, 3B-3

Ben Laughlin

LAUGHLIN, BENJAMIN
Deceased.

	G	AB	H	R	BA	G by POS
1873 Elizabeth Resolutes	12	54	12	3	.222	2B-10, 3B-1, 1B-1

Mike Ledwith

LEDWITH, MICHAEL
B. Brooklyn, N. Y. Deceased.

	G	AB	H	R	BA	G by POS
1874 Brooklyn Atlantics	1	4	1	0	.250	C-1

Bill Lennon

LENNON, WILLIAM F.
B. 1848, Brooklyn, N. Y. Deceased.
Manager 1871.

5'7" 145 lbs.

	G	AB	H	R	BA	G by POS
1871 Fort Wayne Kekiongas	12	48	11	4	.229	C-12
1872 Washington Nationals	11	52	12	11	.231	C-11
1873 Marylands	4	15	3	1	.200	1B-3, C-1, 3B-1
3 yrs.	27	115	26	16	.226	C-24, 1B-3, 3B-1

Lentz

LENTZ,
Deceased.

	G	AB	H	R	BA	G by POS
1872 Brooklyn Eckfords	4	15	2	3	.133	C-4

Andy Leonard

LEONARD, ANDREW JACKSON
B. June 1, 1846, County Cavan, Ireland   D. Aug. 22, 1903, Roxbury, Mass.

BR TR 5'7" 155 lbs.

	G	AB	H	R	BA	G by POS
1871 Washington Olympics	31	151	43	34	.285	2B-20, OF-10, SS-1
1872 Boston Red Stockings	46	252	86	60	.341	LF-37, 3B-6, 2B-3
1873	58	319	95	83	.298	LF-45, 2B-12, SS-1
1874	71	350	119	71	.340	LF-51, SS-11, 2B-9
1875	80	396	128	87	.323	LF-73, 3B-3, SS-3, 2B-1
5 yrs.	286	1468	471	335	.321	LF-206, 2B-45, SS-16, OF-10
						3B-9

Marshall Locke

LOCKE, MARSHALL
B. Indianapolis, Ind. Deceased.

	G	AB	H	R	BA	G by POS
1874 Lord Baltimores	1	5	0	0	.000	SS-1

Len Lovett

LOVETT, LEONARD WALKER
B. July 17, 1852, Lancaster County, Pa.   D. Nov. 18, 1922, Newark, Del.

BR TR

	G	AB	H	R	BA	W	L	PCT	G by POS
1873 Elizabeth Resolutes	1	5	2	1	.400	0	1	.000	P-1
1875 Philadelphia Centennials	5	22	4	2	.182				OF-5
2 yrs.	6	27	6	3	.222	0	1	.000	OF-5, P-1

Charlie Lowe

LOWE, CHARLES
B. Baltimore, Md. Deceased.

	G	AB	H	R	BA	G by POS
1872 Brooklyn Atlantics	6	27	4	1	.148	2B-6

John Lowry

LOWRY, JOHN D.
B. Baltimore, Md. Deceased.

	G	AB	H	R	BA	G by POS
1875 Washington Nationals	5	17	3	1	.176	OF-5

Henry Luff

LUFF, HENRY T.
B. Sept. 14, 1856, Philadelphia, Pa.   D. Oct. 11, 1916, Philadelphia, Pa.

	G	AB	H	R	BA	W	L	PCT	G by POS
1875 New Havens	38	172	45	15	.262	1	7	.125	3B-26, P-8, OF-4

Denny Mack

MACK, DENNIS JOSEPH
Born Dennis Joseph McCrohan.
B. 1851, Easton, Pa.   D. Apr. 10, 1888, Wilkes-Barre, Pa.

5'7" 164 lbs.

	G	AB	H	R	BA	W	L	PCT	G by POS
1871 Rockford Forest Citys	25	130	31	34	.238	0	1	.000	2B-23, P-1, SS-1
1872 Philadelphia Athletics	46	227	56	66	.247				1B-24, SS-22
1873 Philadelphias	46	218	61	54	.280				1B-40, OF-4, SS-1, 2B-1
1874	56	261	53	47	.203				1B-56
4 yrs.	173	836	201	201	.240	0	1	.000	1B-120, SS-24, 2B-24, OF-4
									P-1

Malone

MALONE,
Deceased.

	G	AB	H	R	BA	W	L	PCT	G by POS
1872 Brooklyn Eckfords	4	16	4	1	.250	0	3	.000	P-3, OF-1

	G	AB	H	R	BA	W	L	PCT	G by POS

Fergy Malone

MALONE, FERGUSON G.
B. 1842, Ireland   D. Jan. 18, 1905, Seattle, Wash.   BL TL 5'8"   156 lbs.

1871 Philadelphia Athletics	27	145	46	33	.317				C-27
1872	39	216	58	46	.269				C-21, 1B-18
1873 Philadelphias	53	284	76	59	.268				C-52, SS-1
1874 Chicago White Stockings	47	238	53	33	.223				C-47
1875 Philadelphias	27	114	26	15	.228				1B-21, C-4, OF-2
5 yrs.	193	997	259	186	.260				C-151, 1B-39, OF-2, SS-1

Jack Manning

MANNING, JOHN E.
B. Dec. 20, 1853, Braintree, Mass.   D. Aug. 15, 1929, Boston, Mass.   BR TR 5'8½" 158 lbs.

1873 Boston Red Stockings	33	169	44	30	.260				1B-28, OF-5
1874 2 teams Lord Baltimores (42G .299 W-4 L-14) Hartfords (1G .250)									
" total	43	188	56	36	.298	4	14	.222	2B-20, P-19, SS-5, 3B-1
1875 Boston Red Stockings	77	351	100	71	.285	13	3	.813	RF-58, P-17, 3B-2, 1B-2
3 yrs.	153	708	200	137	.282	17	17	.500	RF-58, P-36, 1B-30, 2B-20, OF-5, SS-5, 3B-3

Al Martin

MARTIN, ALBERT
Deceased.

1872 Brooklyn Eckfords	4	19	5	2	.263				2B-4
1874 Brooklyn Atlantics	7	35	4	1	.114				2B-6, OF-1
1875	6	26	3	1	.115				OF-6
3 yrs.	17	80	12	4	.150				2B-10, OF-7

Phoney Martin

MARTIN, ALPHONSE CASE
B. Aug. 4, 1845, New York, N. Y.   D. May 24, 1933, Hollis, N. Y.   5'7"   148 lbs.

1872 2 teams Brooklyn Eckfords (18G .183 W-2 L-8) Troy Haymakers (25G .287 W-1 L-2)									
" total	43	204	50	37	.245	3	10	.333	RF-23, P-13, OF-8
1873 New York Mutuals	29	139	29	12	.209	0	2	.000	RF-27, P-2
2 yrs.	72	343	79	49	.230	3	12	.200	RF-50, P-15, OF-8

Charlie Mason

MASON, CHARLES E.
B. June 25, 1853, Ark.   D. Oct. 21, 1936, Philadelphia, Pa.

1875 2 teams Philadelphia Centennials(12G .229) Washington Nationals (7G .100)									
" total	19	78	14	6	.179				RF-10, OF-7, 1B-2

Bobby Mathews

MATHEWS, ROBERT T.
B. Nov. 21, 1851, Baltimore, Md.   D. Apr. 17, 1898, Baltimore, Md.   BR TR 5'5½" 145 lbs.

1871 Fort Wayne Kekiongas	19	89	25	17	.281	7	12	.368	P-19
1872 Lord Baltimores	47	218	50	30	.229	25	16	.610	P-45, OF-3, 3B-2
1873 New York Mutuals	52	235	43	39	.183	29	22	.569	P-51, OF-1
1874	65	303	71	46	.234	42	23	.646	P-65
1875	70	278	49	23	.176	29	38	.433	P-70
5 yrs.	253	1123	238	155	.212	132	111	.543	P-250, OF-4, 3B-2

Bub McAtee

McATEE, MICHAEL JAMES
B. Mar., 1845, Troy, N. Y.   D. Oct. 18, 1876, Troy, N. Y.   TR 5'9"   160 lbs.

1871 Chicago White Stockings	26	141	39	34	.277				1B-26
1872 Troy Haymakers	25	129	27	31	.209				1B-25
2 yrs.	51	270	66	65	.244				1B-51

Dick McBride

McBRIDE, JAMES DICKSON
B. 1845, Philadelphia, Pa.   D. Oct. 10, 1916, Philadelphia, Pa.   TR 5'9"   150 lbs.

1871 Philadelphia Athletics	25	141	30	36	.213	20	5	.800	P-25
1872	46	262	72	58	.275	30	14	.682	P-46
1873	49	267	68	42	.255	25	21	.543	P-46, OF-5
1874	55	268	72	31	.269	33	22	.600	P-55
1875	60	275	73	43	.265	44	14	.759	P-60
5 yrs.	235	1213	315	210	.260	152	76	.667	P-232, OF-5

Frank McCartin

McCARTIN, FRANK
B. Middletown, Conn.   Deceased.

1872 Middletown Mansfields	19	85	23	17	.271				CF-19

McCloskey

McCLOSKEY,
Deceased.

1875 Washington Nationals	10	38	5	1	.132				C-10

Joe McDermott

McDERMOTT, JOSEPH
Deceased.

1871 Fort Wayne Kekiongas	2	9	1	3	.111				OF-2
1872 Brooklyn Eckfords	7	33	9	3	.273	0	7	.000	P-7
2 yrs.	9	42	10	6	.238	0	7	.000	P-7, OF-2

Jack McDonald

McDONALD, DANIEL
B. 1847, Brooklyn, N. Y.   D. Nov. 23, 1880, Brooklyn, N. Y.

1872 2 teams Brooklyn Atlantics (14G .214) Brooklyn Eckfords (1G .000)									
" total	15	61	12	8	.197				RF-14, SS-1

	G	AB	H	R	BA	W	L	PCT	G by POS

McDoolan

McDOOLAN,
Deceased.

	G	AB	H	R	BA	W	L	PCT	G by POS
1873 Marylands	1	4	0	1	.000	0	1	.000	P-1

Mike McGeary

McGEARY, MICHAEL HENRY　　　　　　　5'7"　138 lbs.
B. 1851, Philadelphia, Pa. Deceased.

	G	AB	H	R	BA	G by POS
1871 Troy Haymakers	29	156	38	42	.244	C-26, SS-3
1872 Philadelphia Athletics	46	227	78	67	.344	C-25, SS-20, OF-1
1873	52	286	81	63	.283	SS-43, C-10
1874	54	276	100	61	.362	SS-26, C-24, OF-4
1875 Philadelphias	69	313	92	71	.294	3B-24, 2B-23, SS-18, OF-3 C-1
5 yrs.	250	1258	389	304	.309	SS-110, C-86, 3B-24, 2B-23 OF-8

F. McGee

McGEE, F.
Deceased.

	G	AB	H	R	BA	G by POS
1874 Brooklyn Atlantics	16	66	10	4	.152	OF-15, SS-2, 2B-1
1875 2 teams Brooklyn Atlantics (18G .134) New York Mutuals (25G .158)						
" total	43	168	25	7	.149	OF-25, CF-13, 2B-5
2 yrs.	59	234	35	11	.150	OF-40, CF-13, 2B-6, SS-2

Tim McGinley

McGINLEY, TIMOTHY S.　　　　　　　5'9½"　155 lbs.
B. Philadelphia, Pa. D. Nov. 2, 1899, Oakland, Calif.

	G	AB	H	R	BA	G by POS
1875 2 teams Philadelphia Centennials(13G .226) New Havens (33G .255)						
" total	46	194	48	19	.247	C-45, OF-1

John McKelvey

McKELVEY, JOHN WELLINGTON　　　BR TR 5'7½" 175 lbs.
B. Aug. 27, 1847, Rochester, N. Y. D. May 31, 1944, Rochester, N. Y.

	G	AB	H	R	BA	G by POS
1875 New Havens	43	202	42	26	.208	RF-39, 3B-4

Ed McKenna

McKENNA, EDWARD
B. St. Louis, Mo. Deceased.

	G	AB	H	R	BA	G by POS
1874 Philadelphias	1	4	0	0	.000	1B-1

John McMullen

McMULLEN, JOHN F. (Lefty)　　　　　BR TL 5'9" 160 lbs.
B. 1849, Philadelphia, Pa. D. Apr. 11, 1881, Philadelphia, Pa.

	G	AB	H	R	BA	W	L	PCT	G by POS
1871 Troy Haymakers	29	145	38	38	.262	13	15	.464	P-29
1872 New York Mutuals	54	256	60	49	.234	1	0	.000	LF-53, P-2
1873 Philadelphia Athletics	52	240	61	54	.254	1	0	.000	LF-51, P-1
1874	55	271	105	61	**.387**				CF-54, C-1
1875 Philadelphias	54	225	56	34	.249	0	1	.000	CF-53, P-1
5 yrs.	244	1137	320	236	.281	15	16	.484	CF-107, LF-104, P-33, C-1

Trick McSorley

McSORLEY, JOHN BERNARD　　　　　5'4" 142 lbs.
B. Dec. 6, 1858, St. Louis, Mo. D. Feb. 9, 1936, St. Louis, Mo.

	G	AB	H	R	BA	G by POS
1875 St. Louis Reds	14	51	9	4	.176	3B-8, OF-6

Cal McVey

McVEY, CALVIN ALEXANDER　　　　BR TR 5'9" 170 lbs.
B. Aug. 30, 1850, Montrose Lee County, Iowa D. Aug. 20, 1926, San Francisco, Calif.
Manager 1873.

	G	AB	H	R	BA	W	L	PCT	G by POS
1871 Boston Red Stockings	29	**155**	65	43	.419				C-28, OF-1
1872	46	242	74	56	.306				C-40, OF-9
1873 Lord Baltimores	35	187	69	47	.369				C-17, OF-6, SS-5, 2B-3 1B-3, 3B-1
1874 Boston Red Stockings	70	343	**131**	**90**	.382				RF-55, C-15
1875	82	392	138	90	.352	1	0	.000	1B-54, OF-17, C-11, P-2
5 yrs.	262	1319	477	326	.362	1	0	.000	C-111, 1B-57, RF-55, OF-33 SS-5, 2B-3, P-2, 3B-1

Bob Metcalf

METCALF, ROBERT
B. Brooklyn, N. Y. Deceased.

	G	AB	H	R	BA	G by POS
1875 New York Mutuals	7	31	6	1	.194	3B-4, OF-2, SS-1

Levi Meyerle

MEYERLE, LEVI SAMUEL (Long Levi)　　　BR TR 6'1" 177 lbs.
B. 1849, Philadelphia, Pa. D. Nov. 4, 1921, Philadelphia, Pa.

	G	AB	H	R	BA	G by POS
1871 Philadelphia Athletics	26	132	**65**	45	**.492**	3B-26
1872	27	154	49	30	.318	RF-25, 3B-1, SS-1
1873 Philadelphias	48	248	82	52	.331	3B-48
1874 Chicago White Stockings	52	263	97	63	.369	2B-26, 3B-14, OF-7, SS-5
1875 Philadelphias	68	296	93	55	.314	2B-32, 3B-21, 1B-15
5 yrs.	221	1093	386	245	.353	3B-110, 2B-58, RF-25, 1B-15 OF-7, SS-6

Joe Miller

MILLER, JOSEPH WICK　　　　　　5'10½" 169 lbs.
B. July 24, 1850, Germany D. Aug. 30, 1891, White Bear Lake, Minn.

	G	AB	H	R	BA	G by POS
1872 Washington Nationals	1	4	1	0	.250	1B-1
1875 2 teams Chicago White Stockings (16G .138) Keokuk Westerns (13G .111)						
" total	29	119	15	6	.126	2B-27, OF-2
2 yrs.	30	123	16	6	.130	2B-27, OF-2, 1B-1

	G	AB	H	R	BA	W	L	PCT	G by POS

Tom Miller

MILLER, THOMAS P.
B. Philadelphia, Pa.   D. May 29, 1876, Philadelphia, Pa.

5'10½" 160 lbs.

	G	AB	H	R	BA				G by POS
1874 Philadelphia Athletics	4	16	8	1	.500				C-4
1875 St. Louis	54	211	35	17	.166				C-52, 3B-3
2 yrs.	58	227	43	18	.189				C-56, 3B-3

Charlie Mills

MILLS, CHARLES
B. Brooklyn, N. Y.   D. Apr. 10, 1874, Brooklyn, N. Y.

6'

	G	AB	H	R	BA				G by POS
1871 New York Mutuals	32	149	37	27	.248				C-28, OF-3, 2B-1
1872	6	30	4	6	.133				OF-5, C-2
2 yrs.	38	179	41	33	.229				C-30, OF-8, 2B-1

Everett Mills

MILLS, EVERETT
B. 1845, Newark, N. J.   D. June 22, 1908, Newark, N. J.

6'1"   174 lbs.

	G	AB	H	R	BA				G by POS
1871 Washington Olympics	32	161	44	38	.273				1B-32
1872 Lord Baltimores	53	259	71	52	.274				1B-53
1873	53	262	83	62	.317				1B-52, OF-1
1874 Hartfords	53	242	69	40	.285				1B-53
1875	78	353	92	58	.261				1B-78
5 yrs.	269	1277	359	250	.281				1B-268, OF-1

Ed Mincher

MINCHER, EDWARD JOHN
B. Baltimore, Md.   Deceased.

	G	AB	H	R	BA				G by POS
1871 Fort Wayne Kekiongas	9	36	8	4	.222				LF-9
1872 Washington Nationals	11	51	6	5	.118				LF-11
2 yrs.	20	87	14	9	.161				LF-20

Maury Moore

MOORE, MAURICE
D. Feb. 24, 1881, New York, N. Y.

	G	AB	H	R	BA				G by POS
1875 Brooklyn Atlantics	23	90	20	6	.222				SS-14, 1B-6, 3B-3

Dan Morgan

MORGAN, DANIEL
Deceased.

	G	AB	H	R	BA	W	L	PCT	G by POS
1875 St. Louis Reds	18	73	15	11	.205	1	3	.250	CF-8, 3B-6, P-5

Mullen

MULLEN,
Deceased.

	G	AB	H	R	BA				G by POS
1872 Cleveland Forest Citys	1	6	4	1	.667				OF-1

Munn

MUNN,
Deceased.

	G	AB	H	R	BA				G by POS
1875 Brooklyn Atlantics	1	4	0	0	.000				2B-1

Tim Murnane

MURNANE, TIMOTHY HAYES
B. June 4, 1852, Naugatuck, Conn.   D. Feb. 13, 1917, Boston, Mass.

BL TR 5'9½" 172 lbs.

	G	AB	H	R	BA				G by POS
1872 Middletown Mansfields	24	115	34	29	.296				1B-24
1873 Philadelphia Athletics	42	201	43	54	.214				CF-29, 1B-8, 2B-6
1874	19	84	21	9	.250				OF-12, 2B-6, 1B-1
1875 Philadelphias	69	316	90	71	.285				1B-31, OF-26, 2B-12
4 yrs.	154	716	188	163	.263				1B-64, OF-38, CF-29, 2B-24

Jack Nelson

NELSON, JACKSON W.
B. Mar. 14, 1849, Brooklyn, N. Y.   D. Sept. 5, 1910, Brooklyn, N. Y.

BL TR 5'6" 145 lbs.

	G	AB	H	R	BA				G by POS
1872 2 teams Brooklyn Eckfords (18G .235) Troy Haymakers (4G .368)									
" total	22	100	26	14	.260				CF-8, 2B-8, OF-3, 3B-2, SS-1
1873 New York Mutuals	36	177	54	27	.305				2B-27, OF-6, 3B-3
1874	65	313	69	57	.220				2B-51, SS-14
1875	70	300	56	28	.187				2B-47, 3B-22, OF-1
4 yrs.	193	890	205	126	.230				2B-133, 3B-27, SS-15, OF-10, CF-8

Nevins

NEVINS,
Deceased.

	G	AB	H	R	BA				G by POS
1873 Elizabeth Resolutes	13	56	11	7	.196				3B-11, OF-1, 2B-1

Al Nichols

NICHOLS, ALFRED H.
B. Brooklyn, N. Y.   Deceased.

5'11" 180 lbs.

	G	AB	H	R	BA				G by POS
1875 Brooklyn Atlantics	32	132	21	4	.159				3B-32

Tricky Nichols

NICHOLS, FREDERICK C.
B. Bridgeport, Conn.   Deceased.

BR TR 5'7½" 150 lbs.

	G	AB	H	R	BA	W	L	PCT	G by POS
1875 New Havens	33	126	22	12	.175	4	28	.125	P-32, OF-1

Frank Norton

NORTON, FRANK
B. June 19, 1850, Wis.   D. Feb. 8, 1923, Chicago, Ill.

	G	AB	H	R	BA				G by POS
1871 Washington Olympics	1		0	0	.000				OF-1

	G	AB	H	R	BA	W	L	PCT	G by POS

Fancy O'Neal

O'NEAL,
B. Hartford, Conn.   Deceased.

	G	AB	H	R	BA				
1874 Hartfords	1	3	0	0	.000				OF-1

O'Neill

O'NEILL,
B. Bedford, Pa.   Deceased.

	G	AB	H	R	BA	W	L	PCT	G by POS
1875 Brooklyn Atlantics	7	26	3	3	.115	0	4	.000	P-4, OF-3

Tom Oran

ORAN, THOMAS
D. Sept. 21, 1886, St. Louis, Mo.

	G	AB	H	R	BA				
1875 St. Louis Reds	18	79	14	8	.177				RF-18

O'Rourke

O'ROURKE,
Deceased.

	G	AB	H	R	BA	W	L	PCT	G by POS
1872 Brooklyn Eckfords	1	4	2	0	.500	0	1	.000	P-1

Jim O'Rourke

O'ROURKE, JAMES HENRY (Orator Jim)   BR TR 5'8"   185 lbs.
Brother of John O'Rourke.
B. Aug. 24, 1852, Bridgeport, Conn.   D. Jan. 8, 1919, Bridgeport, Conn.
Hall of Fame 1945.

	G	AB	H	R	BA				G by POS
1872 Middletown Mansfields	23	101	29	23	.287				SS-16, C-5, 3B-2
1873 Boston Red Stockings	57	300	99	79	.330				1B-32, OF-20, C-5
1874	70	334	115	80	.344				1B-70
1875	75	374	108	96	.289				CF-45, 3B-27, 1B-3
4 yrs.	225	1109	351	278	.317				1B-105, CF-45, 3B-29, OF-20 SS-16, C-10

Charlie Pabor

PABOR, CHARLES HENRY (The Old Woman In The Red Cap) BL TL 5'8"   155 lbs.
B. Sept. 24, 1846, Brooklyn, N. Y.   D. Apr. 22, 1913, New Haven, Conn.
Manager 1871, 1875.

	G	AB	H	R	BA	W	L	PCT	G by POS
1871 Cleveland Forest Citys	29	142	44	24	.310	0	1	.000	LF-28, P-1
1872	20	93	25	12	.269	1	0	.000	LF-19, P-1
1873 Brooklyn Atlantics	55	237	82	36	.346				LF-55
1874 Philadelphias	17	83	18	11	.217				OF-17
1875 2 teams Brooklyn Atlantics (42G .229 W-0 L-0) New Havens (6G .320)									
" total	48	182	44	19	.242	0	0	.000	LF-41, OF-6, P-2
5 yrs.	169	737	213	102	.289	1	1	.500	LF-143, OF-23, P-4

Bill Parks

PARKS, WILLIAM ROBERT   BR TR 5'8"   150 lbs.
B. June 4, 1849, Easton, Pa.   D. Oct. 10, 1911, Easton, Pa.
Manager 1875.

	G	AB	H	R	BA	W	L	PCT	G by POS
1875 2 teams Washington Nationals (26G .183 W-3 L-9) Philadelphias (2G .125)									
" total	28	123	22	12	.179	3	9	.250	LF-15, P-12, OF-2

Dan Patterson

PATTERSON, DANIEL THOMAS   TL 5'9"   143 lbs.
B. 1846, New York, N. Y.   Deceased.

	G	AB	H	R	BA				G by POS
1871 New York Mutuals	32	151	31	31	.205				RF-31, 2B-1
1872 Brooklyn Eckfords	12	50	8	5	.160				CF-11, 1B-1
1874 New York Mutuals	1	5	2	1	.400				OF-1, 1B-1
1875 Brooklyn Atlantics	10	38	8	3	.211				OF-5, 2B-5
4 yrs.	55	244	49	40	.201				RF-31, CF-11, OF-6, 2B-6 1B-2

Dickey Pearce

PEARCE, RICHARD J.   5'3½"   161 lbs.
B. Jan. 2, 1836, Brooklyn, N. Y.   D. Oct. 12, 1908, Onset. Mass.
Manager 1872, 1875.

	G	AB	H	R	BA				G by POS
1871 New York Mutuals	33	165	44	31	.267				SS-33
1872	43	208	39	28	.188				SS-42, OF-1
1873 Brooklyn Atlantics	55	279	72	42	.258				SS-55
1874	56	262	76	49	.290				SS-56, 3B-2
1875 St. Louis	70	293	75	49	.256				SS-70
5 yrs.	257	1207	306	199	.254				SS-256, 3B-2, OF-1

Johnny Peters

PETERS, JOHN PAUL   BR TR   180 lbs.
B. Apr. 8, 1850, Louisiana, Mo.   D. Jan. 3, 1924, St. Louis, Mo.

	G	AB	H	R	BA				G by POS
1874 Chicago White Stockings	54	248	69	39	.278				SS-32, 2B-21, 3B-1
1875	70	314	87	40	.277				SS-66, 2B-4
2 yrs.	124	562	156	79	.278				SS-98, 2B-25, 3B-1

Neal Phelps

PHELPS, CORNELIUS CARMAN
B. Nov. 19, 1840, New York, N. Y.   D. Feb. 12, 1885, New York, N. Y.

	G	AB	H	R	BA				G by POS
1871 Fort Wayne Kekiongas	1	4	0	0	.000				1B-1
1873 New York Mutuals	1	6	0	0	.000				OF-1
1874	6	23	3	5	.130				OF-6
1875	2	6	2	1	.333				OF-2
4 yrs.	10	39	5	6	.128				OF-9, 1B-1

	G	AB	H	R	BA	W	L	PCT	G by POS

Lip Pike

PIKE, LIPMAN EMANUEL   BL TL 5'8"   158 lbs.
Brother of Jay Pike.
B. May 25, 1845, New York, N. Y.   D. Oct. 10, 1893, Brooklyn, N. Y.
Manager 1871, 1874.

	G	AB	H	R	BA				G by POS
1871 Troy Haymakers	28	134	47	42	.351				RF-18, 2B-6, 1B-4
1872 Lord Baltimores	54	278	80	69	.288				RF-24, 2B-21, 3B-9
1873	56	301	89	73	.296				RF-56, 2B-1
1874 Hartfords	52	228	79	58	.346				CF-27, SS-18, 2B-7
1875 St. Louis	70	313	107	61	.342				CF-62, 2B-8
5 yrs.	260	1254	402	303	.321				RF-98, CF-89, 2B-43, SS-18
									3B-9, 1B-4

Ed Pinkham

PINKHAM, EDWARD   TL 5'7"   142 lbs.
B. 1849, Brooklyn, N. Y.   Deceased.

	G	AB	H	R	BA	W	L	PCT	G by POS
1871 Chicago White Stockings	24	110	25	27	.227	1	0	.000	3B-16, OF-7, P-1

Al Pratt

PRATT, ALBERT G. (Uncle Al)   TR 5'7"   140 lbs.
B. Nov. 19, 1847, Pittsburgh, Pa.   D. Nov. 21, 1937, Pittsburgh, Pa.

	G	AB	H	R	BA	W	L	PCT	G by POS
1871 Cleveland Forest Citys	29	130	33	32	.254	10	18	.357	P-28, OF-1
1872	15	69	18	10	.261	3	9	.250	P-13, OF-3
2 yrs.	44	199	51	42	.256	13	27	.325	P-41, OF-4

Tom Pratt

PRATT, THOMAS J.   5'7½"   150 lbs.
B. 1840, Chelsea, Mass.   D. Sept. 28, 1908, Philadelphia, Pa.

	G	AB	H	R	BA	W	L	PCT	G by POS
1871 Philadelphia Athletics	1	6	2	2	.333				1B-1

Joe Quest

QUEST, JOSEPH L.   5'6"   150 lbs.
B. 1852, New Castle, Pa.   Deceased.

	G	AB	H	R	BA	W	L	PCT	G by POS
1871 Cleveland Forest Citys	3	16	3	1	.188				2B-2, SS-1

Joe Quinn

QUINN, JOSEPH C.   5'8½"   148 lbs.
B. 1851, Chicago, Ill.   D. Jan. 2, 1909, Chicago, Ill.

	G	AB	H	R	BA				G by POS
1871 Fort Wayne Kekiongas	5	21	4	8	.190				C-5
1875 3 teams Chicago White Stockings (17G .194) Keokuk Westerns (11G .298) Hartford Mutuals (3G .100)									
" total	31	124	28	16	.226				C-19, OF-13
2 yrs.	36	145	32	24	.221				C-24, OF-13

Paddy Quinn

QUINN, PATRICK
B. Boston, Mass.   Deceased.

	G	AB	H	R	BA	W	L	PCT	G by POS
1875 Brooklyn Atlantics	2	8	1	2	.125				OF-2

John Radcliff

RADCLIFF, JOHN J.   5'6"   140 lbs.
B. 1846, Camden, N. J.   D. July 26, 1911, Ocean City, N. J.

	G	AB	H	R	BA				G by POS
1871 Philadelphia Athletics	28	153	40	47	.261				SS-28
1872 Lord Baltimores	54	293	83	71	.283				SS-48, 3B-5, 2B-1
1873	44	246	69	57	.280				3B-22, SS-22
1874 Philadelphias	23	102	21	19	.206				OF-16, 2B-3, SS-2, 3B-1
									1B-1
1875 Philadelphia Centennials	5	25	4	2	.160				SS-5
5 yrs.	154	819	217	196	.265				SS-105, 3B-28, OF-16, 2B-4
									1B-1

Al Reach

REACH, ALFRED JAMES   BL TL 5'6"   155 lbs.
B. May 25, 1840, London, England   D. Jan. 14, 1928, Atlantic City, N. J.
Manager 1874-75.

	G	AB	H	R	BA	W	L	PCT	G by POS
1871 Philadelphia Athletics	26	135	47	43	.348				2B-26
1872	23	115	22	21	.191				OF-19, 1B-4
1873	13	64	15	13	.234				OF-8, 2B-5
1874	14	53	9	8	.170				RF-14
1875	5	22	5	4	.227				OF-3, 2B-2
5 yrs.	81	389	98	89	.252				2B-33, OF-30, RF-14, 1B-4

Bob Reach

REACH, ROBERT   5'5"   155 lbs.
B. Aug. 28, 1843, Brooklyn, N. Y.   D. May 19, 1922, Springfield, Mass.

	G	AB	H	R	BA	W	L	PCT	G by POS
1872 Washington Olympics	1	5	1	1	.200				SS-1
1873 Washington Nationals	1	5	1	1	.200				SS-1
2 yrs.	2	10	2	2	.200				SS-2

Billy Redmond

REDMOND, WILLIAM T.   BL TL
B. Brooklyn, N. Y.   Deceased.

	G	AB	H	R	BA	W	L	PCT	G by POS
1875 St. Louis Reds	18	80	14	10	.175				SS-17, 3B-1

Hugh Reed

REED, HUGH
B. Chicago, Ill.   Deceased.

	G	AB	H	R	BA	W	L	PCT	G by POS
1874 Lord Baltimores	1	4	0	0	.000				OF-1

	G	AB	H	R	BA	W	L	PCT	G by POS

Jack Remsen

REMSEN, JOHN J.
B. 1851, Brooklyn, N. Y. Deceased.

BR TR 5'11" 189 lbs.

	G	AB	H	R	BA				G by POS
1872 Brooklyn Atlantics	35	166	34	22	.205				CF-35
1873	51	215	63	29	.293				CF-51
1874 New York Mutuals	64	286	64	51	.224				CF-63, 1B-1
1875 Hartfords	85	371	95	71	.256				CF-85
4 yrs.	235	1038	256	173	.247				CF-234, 1B-1

Larry Ressler

RESSLER, LAWRENCE P.
Deceased.

	G	AB	H	R	BA				G by POS
1875 Washington Nationals	26	106	20	15	.189				RF-19, 2B-7

Revels

REVELS,
Deceased.

	G	AB	H	R	BA				G by POS
1874 Lord Baltimores	1	4	0	0	.000				OF-1

Rexter

REXTER,
Deceased.

	G	AB	H	R	BA				G by POS
1875 Brooklyn Atlantics	1	5	0	0	.000				OF-1

John Richmond

RICHMOND, JOHN H.
B. Philadelphia, Pa. Deceased.

	G	AB	H	R	BA				G by POS
1875 Philadelphia Athletics	29	122	26	30	.213				2B-16, OF-11, C-2

Billy Riley

RILEY, WILLIAM JAMES (Pigtail Billy)
B. 1857, Cincinnati, Ohio D. Nov. 9, 1887, Cincinnati, Ohio

BR TR 5'10" 160 lbs.

	G	AB	H	R	BA				G by POS
1875 Keokuk Westerns	8	34	5	4	.147				RF-8

Tom Roberts

ROBERTS, THOMAS
B. Baltimore, Md. Deceased.

	G	AB	H	R	BA				G by POS
1874 Brooklyn Atlantics	1	4	0	0	.000				OF-1

A. V. Robinson

ROBINSON, A. V.
Deceased.

	G	AB	H	R	BA				G by POS
1872 Washington Olympics	7	32	6	6	.188				RF-7

Adam Rocap

ROCAP, ADAM
B. 1854, Philadelphia, Pa. D. Mar. 29, 1892, Philadelphia, Pa.

5'9" 170 lbs.

	G	AB	H	R	BA				G by POS
1875 Philadelphia Athletics	14	70	12	13	.171				OF-11, 2B-3

Fraley Rogers

ROGERS, FRALEY W.
B. Brooklyn, N. Y. D. May 10, 1881, New York, N. Y.

	G	AB	H	R	BA				G by POS
1872 Boston Red Stockings	46	201	59	40	.294				RF-42, 1B-6

Johnny Ryan

RYAN, JOHN JOSEPH
B. Philadelphia, Pa. D. Mar. 22, 1902, Philadelphia, Pa.

5'7½" 150 lbs.

	G	AB	H	R	BA	W	L	PCT	G by POS
1873 Philadelphias	2	9	2	1	.222				OF-1, 1B-1
1874 Lord Baltimores	47	196	35	28	.179				LF-47
1875 New Havens	37	153	23	17	.150	1	5	.167	LF-29, P-6, 3B-1, SS-1
3 yrs.	86	358	60	46	.168	1	5	.167	LF-76, P-6, OF-1, 3B-1
									SS-1, 1B-1

Pony Sager

SAGER, SAMUEL B.
B. 1847, Marshalltown, Iowa Deceased.

	G	AB	H	R	BA				G by POS
1871 Rockford Forest Citys	8	40	12	9	.300				OF-4, SS-4

Lew Say

SAY, LEWIS I.
Brother of Jimmy Say.
B. Feb. 4, 1854, Baltimore, Md. D. June 5, 1930, Fallston, Md.

BR TR 5'7" 145 lbs.

	G	AB	H	R	BA				G by POS
1873 Marylands	3	12	2	1	.167				SS-2, LF-1
1874 Lord Baltimores	18	71	12	3	.169				SS-18
1875 Washington Nationals	10	38	9	4	.237				SS-8, OF-1, 2B-1
3 yrs.	31	121	23	8	.190				SS-28, OF-1, LF-1, 2B-1

Harry Schafer

SCHAFER, HARRY C. (Silk Stocking)
B. Aug. 14, 1846, Philadelphia, Pa. D. Feb. 28, 1935, Philadelphia, Pa.

BR TR 5'9½" 143 lbs.

	G	AB	H	R	BA				G by POS
1871 Boston Red Stockings	31	151	41	38	.272				3B-31, 2B-1
1872	48	225	59	50	.262				3B-43, OF-5
1873	60	301	79	64	.262				3B-47, OF-13
1874	71	324	86	71	.265				3B-71
1875	51	224	66	50	.295				3B-50, OF-1
5 yrs.	261	1225	331	273	.270				3B-242, OF-19, 2B-1

Frank Selman

SELMAN, FRANK C.
Played as Frank Williams 1871-73, Part Of 1874. Also known as Frank C. Williams.
B. Baltimore, Md. D. Oct. 14, 1890, New York, N. Y.

	G	AB	H	R	BA	W	L	PCT	G by POS
1871 Fort Wayne Kekiongas	14	69	15	12	.217				3B-13, C-2, SS-1
1872 Washington Olympics	8	40	11	3	.275				C-6, 3B-2
1873 Marylands	1	5	1	1	.200	0	1	.000	P-1
1874 Lord Baltimores	12	58	16	9	.276				SS-7, C-6, OF-1
4 yrs.	35	172	43	25	.250	0	1	.000	3B-15, C-14, SS-8, OF-1, P-1

	G	AB	H	R	BA	W	L	PCT	G by POS

Count Sensenderfer

SENSENDERFER, JOHN PHILLIPS JENKINS (Sen-Sen)   5'9"   170 lbs.
B. Dec. 28, 1847, Philadelphia, Pa.   D. May 3, 1903, Philadelphia, Pa.

	G	AB	H	R	BA				G by POS
1871 Philadelphia Athletics	25	127	43	38	.339				CF-25
1872	1	5	2	2	.400				OF-1
1873	19	88	22	12	.250				OF-19
1874	4	16	4	3	.250				OF-4
4 yrs.	49	236	71	55	.301				CF-25, OF-24

George Seward

SEWARD, GEORGE E.   5'7½"   145 lbs.
B. St. Louis, Mo.   Deceased.

	G	AB	H	R	BA				G by POS
1875 St. Louis	24	95	20	12	.211				C-17, OF-5, 2B-2

Shaffer

SHAFFER,
Deceased.

	G	AB	H	R	BA				G by POS
1875 Brooklyn Atlantics	1	4	0	0	.000				OF-1

Orator Shaffer

SHAFFER, GEORGE   BL TR 5'9"   165 lbs.
Brother of Taylor Shaffer.
B. 1852, Philadelphia, Pa.   Deceased.

	G	AB	H	R	BA				G by POS
1874 2 teams Hartfords (9G .200) New York Mutuals (1G .167)									
" total	10	41	8	7	.195				OF-10
1875 Philadelphias	18	79	19	11	.241				OF-10, 3B-6, 1B-2
2 yrs.	28	120	27	18	.225				OF-20, 3B-6, 1B-2

John Sheppard

SHEPPARD, JOHN
B. Baltimore, Md.   Deceased.

	G	AB	H	R	BA				G by POS
1873 Marylands	2	7	0	0	.000				OF-1, C-1

Sheridan

SHERIDAN,
Deceased.

	G	AB	H	R	BA				G by POS
1875 Brooklyn Atlantics	1	4	0	0	.000				OF-1

Joe Simmons

SIMMONS, JOSEPH S.   5'9½"   166 lbs.
B. June 13, 1845, New York, N. Y.   Deceased.
Manager 1875.

	G	AB	H	R	BA				G by POS
1871 Chicago White Stockings	27	134	27	29	.201				RF-25, 1B-2
1872 Cleveland Forest Citys	17	87	20	11	.230				1B-14, OF-3
1875 Keokuk Westerns	13	56	9	5	.161				CF-10, 1B-3
3 yrs.	57	277	56	45	.202				RF-25, 1B-19, CF-10, OF-3

Marty Simpson

SIMPSON, MARTIN
B. Baltimore, Md.   Deceased.

	G	AB	H	R	BA				G by POS
1873 Marylands	3	11	0	2	.000				2B-2, C-1

Bill Smiley

SMILEY, WILLIAM B.
B. 1856, Baltimore, Md.   D. July 11, 1884, Baltimore, Md.

	G	AB	H	R	BA				G by POS
1874 Lord Baltimores	2	7	0	0	.000				3B-2

Bill Smith

SMITH, WILLIAM J..
B. Baltimore, Md.   Deceased.
Manager 1873.

	G	AB	H	R	BA				G by POS
1873 Marylands	4	16	1	1	.063				CF-3, C-1

Charlie Smith

SMITH, CHARLES J.   5'10½"   150 lbs.
B. Dec. 11, 1840, Brooklyn, N. Y.   D. Nov. 15, 1897, Great Neck, N. Y.

	G	AB	H	R	BA				G by POS
1871 New York Mutuals	14	72	17	15	.236				3B-11, 2B-3

John Smith

SMITH, JOHN
B. Baltimore, Md.   Deceased.

	G	AB	H	R	BA				G by POS
1873 Marylands	5	21	4	1	.190				OF-2, SS-2, 2B-1
1874 Lord Baltimores	5	19	3	1	.158				SS-5, OF-1
1875 New Havens	1	4	0	0	.000				SS-1
3 yrs.	11	44	7	2	.159				SS-8, OF-3, 2B-1

Tom Smith

SMITH, THOMAS N.
B. Baltimore, Md.   Deceased.

	G	AB	H	R	BA				G by POS
1875 Brooklyn Atlantics	3	14	1	0	.071				2B-3

Snow

SNOW,
B. Boston, Mass.   Deceased.

	G	AB	H	R	BA				G by POS
1874 Brooklyn Atlantics	1	1	0	0	.000				OF-1

Jim Snyder

SNYDER, JAMES   5'7"   130 lbs.
B. 1851, N. Y.   D. 1881

	G	AB	H	R	BA				G by POS
1872 Brooklyn Eckfords	26	109	30	15	.275				SS-22, OF-3, C-1

Josh Snyder

SNYDER, JOSHUA
D. May, 1881

	G	AB	H	R	BA				G by POS
1872 Brooklyn Eckfords	9	41	7	3	.171				OF-9

	G	AB	H	R	BA	W	L	PCT	G by POS

Pop Snyder

SNYDER, CHARLES N.
B. Oct. 6, 1854, Washington, D. C.   D. Oct. 29, 1924, Washington, D. C.
BR TR 5'11½ " 184 lbs.

		G	AB	H	R	BA				G by POS
1873	Washington Nationals	28	118	18	16	.153				C-28, OF-1
1874	Lord Baltimores	39	168	32	23	.190				C-39
1875	Philadelphias	66	206	62	39	.301				C-65, OF-1
	3 yrs.	133	492	112	78	.228				C-132, OF-2

Ed Somerville

SOMERVILLE, EDWARD
B. Philadelphia, Pa.   D. Sept. 30, 1877, Hamilton, Ont., Canada

		G	AB	H	R	BA				G by POS
1875	2 teams	Philadelphia Centennials(14G .220)	New Havens (33G .207)							
"	total	47	204	43	21	.211				2B-44, 3B-1, SS-1, 1B-1

Al Spalding

SPALDING, ALBERT GOODWILL
B. Sept. 2, 1850, Byron, Ill.   D. Sept. 9, 1915, Point Loma, Calif.
Hall of Fame 1939.
BR TR 6'1"   170 lbs.

		G	AB	H	R	BA	W	L	PCT	G by POS
1871	Boston Red Stockings	31	151	40	43	.265	**20**	10	.667	P-31, OF-2
1872		48	248	84	59	.339	**37**	8	**.822**	P-48, OF-2
1873		60	331	105	85	.317	**41**	15	**.732**	P-57, OF-3
1874		71	**363**	121	80	.333	**52**	18	**.743**	P-71
1875		74	352	112	67	.318	**57**	5	**.919**	P-66, OF-10, 1B-2
	5 yrs.	284	1445	462	334	.320	207	56	.787	P-273, OF-17, 1B-2

Spencer

SPENCER,
Deceased.

		G	AB	H	R	BA				G by POS
1872	Washington Nationals	2	10	2	3	.200				SS-2

Joe Start

START, JOSEPH (Old Reliable)
B. Oct. 14, 1842, New York, N. Y.   D. Mar. 27, 1927, Providence, R. I.
BL TL 5'9"   165 lbs.

		G	AB	H	R	BA				G by POS
1871	New York Mutuals	33	165	56	35	.339				1B-33
1872		55	281	77	62	.274				1B-55
1873		53	262	66	44	.252				1B-53
1874		63	321	93	68	.290				1B-63
1875		69	324	90	57	.278				1B-69
	5 yrs.	273	1353	382	266	.282				1B-273

Bill Stearns

STEARNS, WILLIAM E.
B. Washington, D. C.   Deceased.
TR

		G	AB	H	R	BA	W	L	PCT	G by POS
1871	Washington Olympics	2	11	0	1	.000	2	0	.000	P-2
1872	Washington Nationals	11	47	12	7	.255	0	11	.000	P-11
1873		31	140	24	22	.171	7	24	.226	P-31
1874	Hartfords	32	130	25	16	.192	2	16	.111	P-18, OF-14
1875	Washington Nationals	21	78	20	9	.256	1	14	.067	P-16, OF-6
	5 yrs.	97	406	81	55	.200	12	65	.156	P-78, OF-20

Gat Stires

STIRES, GARRETT
B. Oct. 13, 1849, Hunterdon County, N. J.   D. June 13, 1933, Byron, Ill.
BL TR 5'8"   180 lbs.

		G	AB	H	R	BA				G by POS
1871	Rockford Forest Citys	25	118	32	23	.271				RF-25

Stoddard

STODDARD,
Deceased.

		G	AB	H	R	BA				G by POS
1875	Brooklyn Atlantics	2	9	1	1	.111				OF-2

Ed Stratton

STRATTON, EDWARD
B. Baltimore, Md.   Deceased.

		G	AB	H	R	BA	W	L	PCT	G by POS
1873	Marylands	3	12	2	1	.167	0	2	.000	P-2, OF-1

Sy Studley

STUDLEY, SEYMOUR L. (Warhorse)
B. Washington, D. C.   Deceased.

		G	AB	H	R	BA				G by POS
1872	Washington Nationals	5	22	3	3	.136				OF-5

Sullivan

SULLIVAN,
Deceased.

		G	AB	H	R	BA				G by POS
1875	New Havens	2	10	3	3	.300				OF-2

Ezra Sutton

SUTTON, EZRA BALLOU
B. Sept. 17, 1850, Seneca Falls, N. Y.   D. June 20, 1907, Braintree, Mass.
BR TR 5'8½ " 153 lbs.

		G	AB	H	R	BA				G by POS
1871	Cleveland Forest Citys	29	130	45	35	.346				3B-29
1872		21	110	31	30	.282				3B-21
1873	Philadelphia Athletics	51	258	82	52	.318				3B-44, SS-7, 2B-1
1874		55	246	85	54	.346				3B-36, SS-20
1875		75	357	117	85	.328				3B-73, OF-1, 1B-1
	5 yrs.	231	1101	360	256	.327				3B-203, SS-27, OF-1, 2B-1
										1B-1

	G	AB	H	R	BA	W	L	PCT	G by POS

Marty Swandell

SWANDELL, JOHN MARTIN
B. 1845, Brooklyn, N. Y.   Deceased.

TL   5'10½ " 146 lbs.

		G	AB	H	R	BA				G by POS
1872	Brooklyn Eckfords	14	58	12	6	.207				3B-8, OF-4, 2B-1, 1B-1
1873	Elizabeth Resolutes	2	10	1	1	.100				OF-1, 1B-1
	2 yrs.	16	68	13	7	.191				3B-8, OF-5, 1B-2, 2B-1

Charlie Sweasy

SWEASY, CHARLES JAMES
Born Charles James Swasey.
B. Nov. 2, 1847, Newark, N. J.   D. Mar. 30, 1908, Newark, N. J.
Manager 1875.

BR   TR   5'9"   172 lbs.

		G	AB	H	R	BA				G by POS
1871	Washington Olympics	5	20	4	4	.200				2B-5
1872	Cleveland Forest Citys	11	54	12	8	.222				2B-10, OF-1
1873	Boston Red Stockings	1	5	1	0	.200				2B-1
1874	2 teams Brooklyn Atlantics (10G	.128)	Lord Baltimores (8G	.235)						
"	total	18	73	13	6	.178				2B-17, OF-1
1875	St. Louis Reds	18	72	12	5	.167				2B-18
	5 yrs.	53	224	42	23	.188				2B-51, OF-2

Taylor

TAYLOR,
Deceased.

		G	AB	H	R	BA				G by POS
1874	Lord Baltimores	13	51	10	3	.196				1B-13

Terry

TERRY,
Deceased.

		G	AB	H	R	BA				G by POS
1875	Washington Nationals	6	24	2	0	.083				OF-4, 1B-2

Al Thake

THAKE, ALBERT
B. Oct. 1, 1849, England   D. Sept. 1, 1872, Ft. Hamilton, N. Y.

6

		G	AB	H	R	BA				G by POS
1872	Brooklyn Atlantics	17	73	20	12	.274				LF-16, 2B-1

A. M. Thompson

THOMPSON, A. M.
B. St. Paul, Minn.   Deceased.

		G	AB	H	R	BA				G by POS
1875	2 teams Brooklyn Atlantics (1G	.400)	Washington Nationals (11G	.095)						
"	total	12	47	6	4	.128				C-10, OF-2

Jim Tipper

TIPPER, JAMES
B. June 18, 1849, Middletown, Conn.   D. Apr. 19, 1895, New Haven, Conn.

		G	AB	H	R	BA				G by POS
1872	Middletown Mansfields	24	110	29	23	.264				LF-18, 3B-6
1874	Hartfords	45	196	60	36	.306				LF-45
1875	New Havens	41	170	25	9	.147				CF-41
	3 yrs.	110	476	114	68	.239				LF-63, CF-41, 3B-6

Fred Treacey

TREACEY, FREDERICK S.
Brother of P. Treacey.
B. 1847, Brooklyn, N. Y.   Deceased.

TR   5'9½ "   145 lbs.

		G	AB	H	R	BA				G by POS
1871	Chicago White Stockings	25	125	43	39	.344				LF-25
1872	Philadelphia Athletics	46	242	62	53	.256				CF-46
1873	Philadelphias	51	246	62	49	.252				CF-51
1874	Chicago White Stockings	35	160	28	18	.175				RF-35
1875	2 teams Philadelphia Centennials(11G	.271)	Philadelphias (42G	.207)						
"	total	53	227	50	28	.220				LF-53
	5 yrs.	210	1000	245	187	.245				CF-97, LF-78, RF-35

George Trenwith

TRENWITH, GEORGE
B. Philadelphia, Pa.   D. Feb. 1, 1890, Philadelphia, Pa.

		G	AB	H	R	BA				G by POS
1875	2 teams Philadelphia Centennials(10G	.174)	New Havens (6G	.200)						
"	total	16	71	13	6	.183				3B-16

Charlie Waitt

WAITT, CHARLES C.
B. Oct. 14, 1853, Hallowell, Me.   Deceased.

5'11"   165 lbs.

		G	AB	H	R	BA				G by POS
1875	St. Louis	31	122	26	14	.213				OF-29, 1B-2

Oscar Walker

WALKER, OSCAR
B. Mar. 18, 1854, Brooklyn, N. Y.   D. May 20, 1889, Brooklyn, N. Y.

BL   TL   5'10"   166 lbs.

		G	AB	H	R	BA				G by POS
1875	Brooklyn Atlantics	1	3	0	0	.000				OF-1

Wall

WALL,
Deceased.

		G	AB	H	R	BA				G by POS
1873	Washington Nationals	1	4	1	1	.250				SS-1

Fred Warner

WARNER, FREDERICK JOHN RODNEY
B. 1855, Philadelphia, Pa.   D. Feb. 13, 1886, Philadelphia, Pa.

5'7"   155 lbs.

		G	AB	H	R	BA				G by POS
1875	Philadelphia Centennials	14	59	14	11	.237				CF-14

	G	AB	H	R	BA	W	L	PCT	G by POS

Fred Waterman

WATERMAN, FREDERICK A.   5'7½"   148 lbs.
  B. 1845, New York, N. Y.   D. Dec. 16, 1899, Cincinnati, Ohio

	G	AB	H	R	BA				G by POS
1871 Washington Olympics	32	167	51	46	.305				3B-27, C-6
1872	9	45	18	13	.400				3B-7, C-2
1873 Washington Nationals	15	81	27	20	.333				SS-9, OF-4, 3B-2
1875 Chicago White Stockings	5	23	6	2	.261				3B-4, 2B-1
4 yrs.	61	316	102	81	.323				3B-40, SS-9, C-8, OF-4 2B-1

Sam Weaver

WEAVER, SAMUEL H.   TR
  B. July 20, 1855, Philadelphia, Pa.   D. Feb. 1, 1914, Philadelphia, Pa.

	G	AB	H	R	BA	W	L	PCT	G by POS
1875 Philadelphias	1	4	1	1	.250	1	0	.000	P-1

Billy West

WEST, WILLIAM NELSON
  B. Aug. 21, 1840, Philadelphia, Pa.   D. Aug. 18, 1891, Philadelphia, Pa.

	G	AB	H	R	BA				G by POS
1874 Brooklyn Atlantics	10	43	8	4	.186				2B-10

Deacon White

WHITE, JAMES LAURIE   BL TR 5'11"   175 lbs.
  Brother of Will White.
  B. Dec. 7, 1847, Caton, N. Y.   D. July 7, 1939, Aurora, Ill.

	G	AB	H	R	BA				G by POS
1871 Cleveland Forest Citys	29	149	47	40	.315				C-27, 2B-2
1872	21	110	37	21	.336				C-13, 2B-6, OF-3
1873 Boston Red Stockings	60	325	124	76	.382				C-55, OF-5
1874	69	349	112	73	.321				C-55, OF-12, 2B-1, 1B-1
1875	80	383	136	77	.355				C-72, OF-7, 1B-1
5 yrs.	259	1316	456	287	.347				C-222, OF-27, 2B-9, 1B-2

Elmer White

WHITE, ELMER
  B. Dec. 7, 1850, Caton, N. Y.   D. Mar. 17, 1872, Caton, N. Y.

	G	AB	H	R	BA				G by POS
1871 Cleveland Forest Citys	15	71	20	13	.282				RF-13, C-2

Warren White

WHITE, WILLIAM WARREN
  D. Mar. 3, 1898
  Manager 1872, 1874.

	G	AB	H	R	BA				G by POS
1871 Washington Olympics	1	4	0	0	.000				2B-1
1872 Washington Nationals	10	44	14	8	.318				3B-9, SS-1
1873	39	166	44	29	.265				3B-37, SS-2
1874 Lord Baltimores	45	224	57	21	.254				3B-45
1875 Chicago White Stockings	70	304	72	37	.237				3B-61, SS-4, OF-3, 2B-2
5 yrs.	165	742	187	95	.252				3B-152, SS-7, OF-3, 2B-3

Rynie Wolters

WOLTERS, REINDER ALBERTUS   6'   165 lbs.
  B. Mar. 17, 1842, Schantz, Netherlands   D. Jan. 3, 1917, Newark, N. J.

	G	AB	H	R	BA	W	L	PCT	G by POS
1871 New York Mutuals	32	150	48	33	.320	16	16	.500	P-32
1872 Cleveland Forest Citys	15	77	17	7	.221	2	6	.250	P-8, RF-8
1873 Elizabeth Resolutes	1	4	0	1	.000	0	1	.000	P-1
3 yrs.	48	231	65	41	.281	18	23	.439	P-41, RF-8

Wood

WOOD,
  Deceased.

	G	AB	H	R	BA				G by POS
1874 Lord Baltimores	1	6	0	0	.000				2B-1

Jimmy Wood

WOOD, JAMES LEON   TR 5'8½"   150 lbs.
  B. Dec. 1, 1844, Brooklyn, N. Y.   Deceased.
  1873 Leg amputated.
  Manager 1872-75.

	G	AB	H	R	BA				G by POS
1871 Chicago White Stockings	28	145	51	44	.352				2B-28
1872 2 teams Brooklyn Eckfords (7G .176) Troy Haymakers (25G .322)									2B-32
" total	32	152	44	49	.289				2B-32
1873 Philadelphias	42	224	66	67	.295				2B-42
3 yrs.	102	521	161	160	.309				2B-102

Red Woodhead

WOODHEAD, JAMES
  B. 1851, England   D. Sept. 7, 1881, Boston, Mass.

	G	AB	H	R	BA				G by POS
1873 Marylands	1	5	0	1	.000				SS-1

Favel Wordsworth

WORDSWORTH, FAVEL PERRY (Red)
  B. Jan., 1851, New York, N. Y.   D. Aug. 12, 1888, New York, N. Y.

	G	AB	H	R	BA				G by POS
1873 Elizabeth Resolutes	11	45	10	6	.222				SS-11

Herb Worth

WORTH, HERBERT
  Deceased.

	G	AB	H	R	BA				G by POS
1872 Brooklyn Atlantics	1	6	1	1	.167				OF-1

		G	AB	H	R	BA	W	L	PCT	G by POS

George Wright

WRIGHT, GEORGE   BR   TR   5'9½"   150 lbs.
Brother of Harry Wright.   Brother of Sam Wright.
B. Jan. 28, 1847, Yonkers, N. Y.   D. Aug. 21, 1937, Boston, Mass.
Hall of Fame 1937.

		G	AB	H	R	BA	W	L	PCT	G by POS
1871	Boston Red Stockings	16	88	36	35	.409				SS-15, 1B-1
1872		48	253	85	86	.336				SS-48
1873		59	333	126	98	.378				SS-59
1874		60	319	110	75	.345				SS-60
1875		79	407	137	105	.337				SS-79
	5 yrs.	262	1400	494	399	.353				SS-261, 1B-1

Harry Wright

WRIGHT, WILLIAM HENRY   BR   TR   5'9½"   157 lbs.
Brother of Sam Wright.   Brother of George Wright.
B. Jan. 10, 1835, Sheffield, England   D. Oct. 3, 1895, Atlantic City, N. J.
Manager 1871-75.
Hall of Fame 1953.

		G	AB	H	R	BA	W	L	PCT	G by POS
1871	Boston Red Stockings	31	161	43	42	.267	0	0	.000	CF-30, P-2, SS-1
1872		48	214	56	38	.262	2	0	.000	CF-48, P-2
1873		58	283	66	57	.233	2	1	.667	CF-55, P-3
1874		41	189	58	44	.307				OF-40, C-1
1875		1	4	1	1	.250				OF-1
	5 yrs.	179	851	224	182	.263	4	1	.800	CF-133, OF-41, P-7, C-1 SS-1

Sam Wright

WRIGHT, SAMUEL   BR   TR   5'7½"   146 lbs.
Brother of Harry Wright.   Brother of George Wright.
B. Nov. 25, 1848, New York, N. Y.   D. May 6, 1928, Boston, Mass.

		G	AB	H	R	BA	W	L	PCT	G by POS
1875	New Havens	33	137	24	11	.175				SS-33

Yeatman

YEATMAN,
Deceased.

		G	AB	H	R	BA	W	L	PCT	G by POS
1872	Washington Nationals	1	3	0	0	.000				OF-2

Tom York

YORK, THOMAS J.   BL   5'9"   165 lbs.
B. July 13, 1848, Brooklyn, N. Y.   D. Feb. 17, 1936, New York, N. Y.

		G	AB	H	R	BA	W	L	PCT	G by POS
1871	Troy Haymakers	29	156	34	37	.218				CF-29
1872	Lord Baltimores	49	249	67	60	.269				LF-49
1873		56	279	79	68	.283				LF-56
1874	Philadelphias	50	241	60	37	.249				LF-50
1875	Hartfords	85	387	110	66	.284				LF-85
	5 yrs.	269	1312	350	268	.267				LF-240, CF-29

George Zettlein

ZETTLEIN, GEORGE (The Charmer)   BR   TR   5'9"   162 lbs.
B. July 18, 1844, Brooklyn, N. Y.   D. May 23, 1905, Patchogue, N. Y.

		G	AB	H	R	BA	W	L	PCT	G by POS
1871	Chicago White Stockings	28	130	31	23	.238	18	9	.667	P-27, OF-1
1872	2 teams Brooklyn Eckfords (9G	.059 W-1 L-7) Troy Haymakers (25G			.248	W-14 L-8)			
"	total	34	151	31	26	.205	15	15	.636	P-31, OF-4
1873	Philadelphias	50	235	49	40	.209	36	14	.720	P-50
1874	Chicago White Stockings	57	247	46	26	.186	27	30	.474	P-57
1875	2 teams Chicago White Stockings (32G	.216 W-17 L-14) Philadelphias (21G			.203	W-12 L-8)			
"	total	53	213	45	19	.211	29	22	.569	P-52, 1B-2
	5 yrs.	222	976	202	134	.207	125	90	.581	P-217, OF-5, 1B-2

	W	L	PCT	GB	R	AB	H	BA	Manager	W	L	Manager	W	L

1871

	W	L	PCT	GB	R	AB	H	BA	Manager	W	L	Manager	W	L
Philadelphia Athletics	22	7	.759		367	1331	412	**.310**	Hicks Hayhurst	22	7			
Chicago White Stockings	20	9	.690	2	302	1250	316	.253	Tom Foley	20	9			
Boston Red Stockings	22	10	.688	1.5	**401**	**1438**	**424**	.295	Harry Wright	22	10			
Washington Olympics	16	15	.516	7	310	1400	371	.265	Nick Young	16	15			
Troy Haymakers	15	15	.500	7.5	353	1302	370	.284	Bill Craver	14	12	Lip Pike	1	3
New York Mutuals	17	18	.486	8	302	1428	392	.275	Bob Ferguson	17	18			
Cleveland Forest Citys	10	19	.345	12	249	1214	326	.269	Charlie Pabor	10	19			
Fort Wayne Kekiongas	7	21	.250	14.5	137	765	179	.234	Harry Deane	3	18	Bill Lennon	4	3
Rockford Forest Citys	6	21	.222	15	231	1081	273	.253	Hiram Waldo	6	21			

1872

	W	L	PCT	GB	R	AB	H	BA	Manager	W	L	Manager	W	L
Boston Red Stockings	39	8	.830		521	2176	671	**.308**	Harry Wright	39	8			
Philadelphia Athletics	30	14	.682	7.5	534	2209	659	.298	Hicks Hayhurst	30	14			
Lord Baltimores	34	19	.642	8	**597**	**2561**	**717**	.280	Bill Craver	34	19			
New York Mutuals	34	20	.630	8.5	523	2503	681	.272	Dickey Pearce	34	20			
Troy Haymakers	15	10	.600	13	272	1123	333	.297	Jimmy Wood	15	10			
Cleveland Forest Citys	6	15	.286	20	171	957	283	.296	Scott Hastings	6	15			
Brooklyn Atlantics	8	27	.229	25	220	1452	334	.230	Bob Ferguson	8	27			
Washington Olympics	2	7	.222	18	54	372	93	.250	Nick Young	2	7			
Middletown Mansfields	5	19	.208	22.5	223	1013	277	.273	Ben Douglas	5	19			
Brooklyn Eckfords	3	26	.103	27	151	1133	233	.206	Jim Clinton	0	11	Jimmy Wood	3	15
Washington Nationals	0	11	.000	21	80	449	107	.238	Joe Miller	0	11			

1873

	W	L	PCT	GB	R	AB	H	BA	Manager	W	L	Manager	W	L
Boston Red Stockings	43	16	.729		**739**	**2878**	**931**	**.323**	Harry Wright	43	16			
Philadelphias	36	17	.679	4	526	2418	641	.265	Jimmy Wood	36	17			
Lord Baltimores	33	22	.600	8	624	2599	783	.301	Tom Carey	10	8	Cal McVey	23	14
Philadelphia Athletics	28	23	.549	11	474	2387	671	.281	Hicks Hayhurst	28	23			
New York Mutuals	29	24	.547	11	424	2297	614	.267	Bill Cammeyer	29	24			
Brooklyn Atlantics	17	37	.315	23.5	366	2310	583	.252	Bob Ferguson	17	37			
Washington Nationals	8	31	.205	25	283	1629	406	.249	Nick Young	8	31			
Elizabeth Resolutes	2	21	.087	23	98	923	204	.221	John Benjamin	2	21			
Marylands	0	5	.000	27	15	169	23	.136	John Smith	0	5			

1874

	W	L	PCT	GB	R	AB	H	BA	Manager	W	L	Manager	W	L
Boston Red Stockings	52	18	.743		**735**	**3155**	**1033**	**.327**	Harry Wright	52	18			
New York Mutuals	42	23	.646	7.5	500	2808	708	.252	Tom Carey	19	16	Dick Higham	23	7
Philadelphia Athletics	33	23	.589	12	441	2304	763	.331	Al Reach	33	23			
Philadelphias	29	29	.500	17	475	2537	683	.269	Bill Craver	29	29			
Chicago White Stockings	28	31	.475	18.5	418	2565	674	.263	Jimmy Wood	28	31			
Brooklyn Atlantics	22	33	.400	22.5	301	2233	495	.222	Bob Ferguson	22	33			
Hartfords	17	37	.315	27	371	2103	611	.291	Lip Pike	17	37			
Lord Baltimores	9	38	.191	31.5	227	1890	430	.228	Warren White	9	38			

1875

	W	L	PCT	GB	R	AB	H	BA	Manager	W	L	Manager	W	L
Boston Red Stockings	71	8	.899		**832**	**3564**	**1161**	**.326**	Harry Wright	71	8			
Philadelphia Athletics	53	20	.726	15	699	3292	942	.286	Al Reach	53	20			
Hartfords	54	28	.659	18.5	554	3466	863	.249	Bob Ferguson	54	28			
St. Louis	39	29	.574	26.5	385	2651	660	.249	Dickey Pearce	39	29			
Philadelphias	37	31	.544	28.5	469	2645	683	.258	George Young	37	31			
Chicago White Stockings	30	37	.448	35	380	2832	709	.250	Jimmy Wood	30	37			
New York Mutuals	30	38	.441	35.5	328	2771	630	.227	Nat Hicks	30	38			
St. Louis Reds	4	14	.222	36.5	55	670	121	.181	Charlie Sweasy	4	14			
New Havens	7	40	.149	48	170	1814	368	.203	Charlie Gould	7	40			
Washington Nationals	4	23	.148	41	96	990	181	.183	Bill Parks	4	23			
Philadelphia Centennials	2	12	.143	36.5	70	549	125	.228	Hicks Hayhurst	2	12			
Keokuk Westerns	1	12	.077	37	45	484	81	.167	Joe Simmons	1	12			
Brooklyn Atlantics	2	42	.045	51.5	132	1590	306	.192	Charlie Pabor	2	42			

PART FOUR

All-Time Leaders

INDIVIDUAL BATTING, SINGLE SEASON

INDIVIDUAL PITCHING, SINGLE SEASON

INDIVIDUAL FIELDING, SINGLE SEASON

INDIVIDUAL BATTING, LIFETIME

INDIVIDUAL PITCHING, LIFETIME

INDIVIDUAL FIELDING, LIFETIME

All-Time Leaders

The All-Time Leaders section provides information on individual all-time single season and lifetime leaders for all major leagues from 1876 through today. Included for all the various categories are leaders in batting, fielding, and pitching.

Much of the information has never been compiled, especially for the period 1876 through 1919. For certain other years some statistics are still missing or incomplete.

When teams in this section are listed by an abbreviation of the city in which the team played, the abbreviations are as follows:

ALT	Altoona	NWK	Newark
ATL	Atlanta	NY	New York
BAL	Baltimore	OAK	Oakland
BKN	Brooklyn	PHI	Philadelphia
BOS	Boston	PIT	Pittsburgh
BUF	Buffalo	PRO	Providence
CAL	California	RIC	Richmond
CHI	Chicago	ROC	Rochester
CIN	Cincinnati	SD	San Diego
CLE	Cleveland	SEA	Seattle
COL	Columbus	SF	San Francisco
DET	Detroit	STL	St. Louis
HAR	Hartford	STP	St. Paul
HOU	Houston	SYR	Syracuse
IND	Indianapolis	TEX	Texas
KC	Kansas City	TOL	Toledo
LA	Los Angeles	TOR	Toronto
LOU	Louisville	TRO	Troy
MIL	Milwaukee	WAS	Washington
MIN	Minnesota	WIL	Wilmington
MON	Montreal	WOR	Worcester

Three franchises in the history of major league baseball changed their location during the season. These teams are designated by the first letter of the two cities they represented. They are:

B-B Brooklyn-Baltimore (American Association, 1890)
C-M Cincinnati-Milwaukee (American Association, 1891)
C-P Chicago-Pittsburgh (Union Association, 1884)

INDIVIDUAL ALL-TIME
SINGLE SEASON LEADERS

The top 20 men are shown in batting and base running, the top 15 in pitching and relief pitching. If required by ties, 1 additional player is shown. If ties would require more than 1 additional man to be shown, none of the last tied group is included. All the information is self-explanatory, with the possible exception of Home Run Percentage, which is the number of home runs per 100 times at bat.

Stolen Bases. As shown here, stolen bases start in 1898. Although stolen bases were first considered a statistical item in 1886, they were known as "bases advanced," which credited a stolen base to a man taking an extra base on another player's hit or out, until 1898.

Pitching Categories. Pitching information appears for two separate periods: 1876 through 1892; 1893 through today, except for relief pitching information which is shown only from 1893. The reason for these separate categories is because of the pitching distance, which was not moved to its present distance of 60 feet 6 inches until 1893.

Estimated Earned Run Averages (applies to all parts of this section). Any time an earned run average appears in italics it indicates that not all the earned runs allowed by the pitcher are known, and the information had to be estimated. For example, it is known that a team allowed 560 runs in 112 games. Of these games, it is known that in 90 of them the team allowed 420 runs of which 315 or 75% were earned. The man pitched 207⅔ innings in 40 games and allowed 134 runs. In 35 of these games, it is known that he allowed 118 runs of which 83 were earned. By multiplying the team's known ratio of earned runs to total runs (75%) by the pitcher's 16 (134 minus 118) remaining runs allowed, a figure of 12 additional estimated earned runs is calculated. This means that the pitcher allowed an estimated total of 95 earned runs in 207⅔ innings for an estimated earned run average of 4.12. In all cases at least 50% of the runs allowed by the team were "known" as a basis for estimating earned run averages.

League Leader Qualifications. Throughout baseball there have been different rules used to determine the minimum appearances necessary to qualify for league leader in categories concerning averages (Batting Average, Earned Run Average, etc.). For the rules and the years they were in effect, see Appendix C.

INDIVIDUAL LIFETIME LEADERS

The ranking of the batting, base running, pitching, and fielding leaders is based on calculation to 5 decimal points, although no more than the first 3 decimal points are shown. Players with *identical* ranking (through 5 decimal points) are listed with the same rank number. The following minimum criteria were used to establish the lifetime leaders:

BATTING

Batting average, all players .300, 4,000 times at bat

Slugging average, .500, 4,000 at bat
Total bases, 4,000
Games played, 2,000
At bats, 9,000
Hits, 2,000
Doubles, 400
Triples, 150
Home runs, 300
Home run percentage, top 35 players, 4,000 at bat
Extra base hits, 800
Runs batted in, 1,000
RBI per game, top 35 players, 4,000 at bat
Runs, 1,000
Runs per game, top 35 players, 4,000 at bat
Bases on balls, 1,000
Bases on balls average, top 35 players, 4,000 at bat
Stolen bases, 300
Pinch hits, 50
Pinch hit batting average, top 35 players, 150 pinch hit at bat
Fewest strikeouts per game, top 35 players, 4,000 at bat
Most strikeouts per game, top 35 players, 4,000 at bat
Strikeouts, 1,000

PITCHING

Wins, 200 or more
Winning percentage, top 35 players, 300 games pitched
Earned run average, 2.50, 1,500 innings pitched
Games, 500
Completed games, 300
Innings pitched, 3,500
Strikeouts, 1,500
Strikeouts per nine innings, top 35 players, 1,500 innings
Shutouts, 30
Least hits per nine innings, top 35 players, 1,500 innings
Most bases on balls, top 35 players
Least bases on balls per nine innings, top 35 players,
    1,500 innings
Most losses, top 35 players

RELIEF PITCHING

Wins, 50
Winning percentage, top 35 players, 500 innings pitched
Saves, 75
Wins plus saves, 125
Games, 400

FIELDING

The top 15 players in each category are shown for each position. A minimum 1,000 games played at the indicated position is required, except for pitchers, where 1,500 innings or more pitched is the criteria.

BATTING AVERAGE

1. Hugh Duffy, 1894 438
2. Tip O'Neill, 1887 435
3. Willie Keeler, 1897 432
4. Ross Barnes, 1876 429
5. Rogers Hornsby, 1924 424
6. Jesse Burkett, 1895 423
7. Nap Lajoie, 1901 422
8. George Sisler, 1922 420
9. Ty Cobb, 1911 420
10. Tuck Turner, 1894 416
11. Fred Dunlap, 1884 412
12. Ty Cobb, 1912 410
13. Jesse Burkett, 1896 410
14. Ed Delahanty, 1899 408
15. Joe Jackson, 1911 408
16. George Sisler, 1920 407
17. Fred Clarke, 1897 406
18. Ted Williams, 1941 406
19. Harry Stovey, 1884 404
20. Sam Thompson, 1894 404

SLUGGING AVERAGE

1. Babe Ruth, 1920 847
2. Babe Ruth, 1921 846
3. Babe Ruth, 1927 772
4. Lou Gehrig, 1927 765
5. Babe Ruth, 1923 764
6. Rogers Hornsby, 1925 756
7. Jimmie Foxx, 1932 749
8. Babe Ruth, 1924 739
9. Babe Ruth, 1926 737
10. Ted Williams, 1941 735
11. Babe Ruth, 1930 732
12. Ted Williams, 1957 731
13. Hack Wilson, 1930 723
14. Rogers Hornsby, 1922 722
15. Lou Gehrig, 1930 721
16. Babe Ruth, 1928 709
17. Al Simmons, 1930 708
18. Lou Gehrig, 1934 706
19. Mickey Mantle, 1956 705
20. Jimmie Foxx, 1938 704

TOTAL BASES

1. Babe Ruth, 1921 457
2. Rogers Hornsby, 1922 450
3. Lou Gehrig, 1927 447
4. Chuck Klein, 1930 445
5. Jimmie Foxx, 1932 438
6. Stan Musial, 1948 429
7. Hack Wilson, 1930 423
8. Chuck Klein, 1932 420
9. Lou Gehrig, 1930 419
10. Joe DiMaggio, 1937 418
11. Babe Ruth, 1927 417
12. Babe Herman, 1930 416
13. Lou Gehrig, 1931 410
14. Rogers Hornsby, 1929 409
15. Lou Gehrig, 1934 409
16. Joe Medwick, 1937 406
16. Jim Rice, 1978 406
18. Chuck Klein, 1929 405
18. Hal Trosky, 1936 405
20. Jimmie Foxx, 1933 403
20. Lou Gehrig, 1936 403

AT BATS

1. Willie Wilson, 1980 705
2. Juan Samuel, 1984 701
3. Dave Cash, 1975 699
4. Matty Alou, 1969 698
5. Woody Jensen, 1936 696
6. Omar Moreno, 1979 695
6. Maury Wills, 1962 695
8. Bobby Richardson, 1962 . . . 692
9. Lou Brock, 1967 689
9. Sandy Alomar, 1971 689
11. Dave Cash, 1974 687
12. Horace Clarke, 1970 686
13. Lloyd Waner, 1931 681
13. Joe Moore, 1935 681
15. Pete Rose, 1973 680
15. Frank Taveras, 1979 680
17. Harvey Kuenn, 1953 679
17. Bobby Richardson, 1964 . . . 679
17. Curt Flood, 1964 679
20. Dick Groat, 1962 678

HITS

1. George Sisler, 1920 257
2. Bill Terry, 1930 254
2. Lefty O'Doul, 1929 254
4. Al Simmons, 1925 253
5. Rogers Hornsby, 1922 250
5. Chuck Klein, 1930 250
7. Ty Cobb, 1911 248
8. George Sisler, 1922 246
9. Willie Keeler, 1897 243
10. Babe Herman, 1930 241
10. Heinie Manush, 1928 241
12. Jesse Burkett, 1896 240
13. Rod Carew, 1977 239
14. Harry Heilmann, 1921 237
14. Paul Waner, 1927 237
14. Joe Medwick, 1937 237
17. Hugh Duffy, 1894 236
17. Jack Tobin, 1921 236
19. Jesse Burkett, 1895 235
19. Rogers Hornsby, 1921 235

DOUBLES

1. Earl Webb, 1931 67
2. George Burns, 1926 64
2. Joe Medwick, 1936 64
4. Hank Greenberg, 1934 63
5. Paul Waner, 1932 62
6. Charlie Gehringer, 1936 60
7. Tris Speaker, 1923 59
7. Chuck Klein, 1930 59
9. Billy Herman, 1936 57
9. Billy Herman, 1935 57
11. Ed Delahanty, 1899 56
11. Joe Medwick, 1937 56
11. George Kell, 1950 56
14. Gee Walker, 1936 55
15. Hal McRae, 1977 54
16. Tris Speaker, 1912 53
16. Al Simmons, 1926 53
16. Paul Waner, 1936 53
16. Stan Musial, 1953 53

TRIPLES

1. Owen Wilson, 1912 36
2. Heinie Reitz, 1894 31
2. Dave Orr, 1886 31
4. Perry Werden, 1893 29
5. Harry Davis, 1897 28
6. Sam Thompson, 1894 27
6. George Davis, 1893 27
6. Jimmy Williams, 1899 27
9. George Treadway, 1894 26
9. Long John Reilly, 1890 26
9. Joe Jackson, 1912 26
9. Sam Crawford, 1914 26
9. Kiki Cuyler, 1925 26
14. Harry Stovey, 1884 25
14. Roger Connor, 1894 25
14. Tommy Long, 1915 25
14. Larry Doyle, 1911 25
14. Sam Crawford, 1903 25
14. Buck Freeman, 1899 25
20. Ed McKean, 1893 24
20. Ty Cobb, 1911 24

HOME RUNS

1. Roger Maris, 1961 61
2. Babe Ruth, 1927 60
3. Babe Ruth, 1921 59
4. Hank Greenberg, 1938 58
4. Jimmie Foxx, 1932 58
6. Hack Wilson, 1930 56
7. Babe Ruth, 1920 54
7. Mickey Mantle, 1961 54
7. Babe Ruth, 1928 54
7. Ralph Kiner, 1949 54
11. Mickey Mantle, 1956 52
11. Willie Mays, 1965 52
11. George Foster, 1977 52
14. Ralph Kiner, 1947 51
14. Willie Mays, 1955 51
14. Johnny Mize, 1947 51
17. Jimmie Foxx, 1938 50

HOME RUN PERCENTAGE

1. Babe Ruth, 1920 . . . . 11.8
2. Babe Ruth, 1927 . . . . 11.1
3. Babe Ruth, 1921 . . . . 10.9
4. Mickey Mantle, 1961 . . . . . . 10.5
5. Hank Greenberg, 1938 . . . . . 10.4
6. Roger Maris, 1961 . . . . 10.3
7. Babe Ruth, 1928 . . . . 10.1
8. Jimmie Foxx, 1932 . . . . 9.9
9. Ralph Kiner, 1949 . . . . 9.8
10. Mickey Mantle, 1956 . . . . . 9.8
11. Hack Wilson, 1930 . . . . 9.6
12. Hank Aaron, 1971 . . . . 9.5
12. Babe Ruth, 1926 . . . . 9.5
14. Jim Gentile, 1961 . . . . 9.5
15. Babe Ruth, 1923 . . . . 9.5
16. Willie Stargell, 1971 . . . . . . 9.4
17. Rudy York, 1937 . . . . 9.3
18. Willie Mays, 1965 . . . . 9.3
19. Babe Ruth, 1929 . . . . 9.2
20. Willie McCovey, 1969 . . . . . 9.2

EXTRA BASE HITS

1. Babe Ruth, 1921 119
2. Lou Gehrig, 1927 117
3. Chuck Klein, 1930 107
4. Hank Greenberg, 1937 103
4. Stan Musial, 1948 103
4. Chuck Klein, 1932 103
7. Rogers Hornsby, 1922 102
8. Lou Gehrig, 1930 100
8. Jimmie Foxx, 1932 100
10. Babe Ruth, 1920 99
10. Babe Ruth, 1923 99
10. Hank Greenberg, 1940 99
13. Hank Greenberg, 1935 98
14. Babe Ruth, 1927 97
14. Hack Wilson, 1930 97
14. Joe Medwick, 1937 97
17. Hank Greenberg, 1934 96
17. Joe DiMaggio, 1937 96
17. Hal Trosky, 1936 96
20. Lou Gehrig, 1934 95
20. Joe Medwick, 1936 95

RUNS BATTED IN

1. Hack Wilson, 1930 190
2. Lou Gehrig, 1931 184
3. Hank Greenberg, 1937 183
4. Jimmie Foxx, 1938 175
4. Lou Gehrig, 1927 175
6. Lou Gehrig, 1930 174
7. Babe Ruth, 1921 171
8. Hank Greenberg, 1935 170
8. Chuck Klein, 1930 170
10. Jimmie Foxx, 1932 169
11. Joe DiMaggio, 1937 167
12. Sam Thompson, 1887 166
13. Sam Thompson, 1895 165
13. Al Simmons, 1930 165
13. Lou Gehrig, 1934 165
16. Babe Ruth, 1927 164
17. Babe Ruth, 1931 163
17. Jimmie Foxx, 1933 163
19. Hal Trosky, 1936 162

RUNS BATTED IN PER GAME

1. Sam Thompson, 1894 . . . . . 1.42
2. Sam Thompson, 1895 . . . . . 1.39
3. Sam Thompson, 1887 . . . . . 1.31
4. Hack Wilson, 1930 . . . . 1.23
5. Al Simmons, 1930 . . . . 1.20
6. Cap Anson, 1894 . . . . 1.19
7. Hank Greenberg, 1937 . . . . . 1.19
8. Lou Gehrig, 1931 . . . . 1.19
9. Cap Anson, 1886 . . . . 1.18
10. Jimmie Foxx, 1938 . . . . . . 1.17
11. Hugh Duffy, 1894 . . . . 1.16
12. Dave Orr, 1890 . . . . 1.16
13. Ed Delahanty, 1894 . . . . . . 1.15
14. Babe Ruth, 1929 . . . . 1.14
15. Lou Gehrig, 1930 . . . . 1.13
16. Lou Gehrig, 1927 . . . . 1.13
17. Babe Ruth, 1921 . . . . 1.12
18. Babe Ruth, 1931 . . . . 1.12
19. Hank Greenberg, 1935 . . . . 1.12
20. Ed Delahanty, 1893 . . . . . . 1.11

RUNS

1. Billy Hamilton, 1894	196
2. Babe Ruth, 1921	177
2. Tom Brown, 1891	177
4. Joe Kelley, 1894	167
4. Tip O'Neill, 1887	167
4. Lou Gehrig, 1936	167
7. Billy Hamilton, 1895	166
8. Willie Keeler, 1894	165
9. Babe Ruth, 1928	163
9. Lou Gehrig, 1931	163
9. Arlie Latham, 1887	163
12. Willie Keeler, 1895	162
13. Hugh Duffy, 1890	161
14. Hugh Duffy, 1894	160
14. Fred Dunlap, 1884	160
14. Jesse Burkett, 1896	160
17. Hughie Jennings, 1895	159
18. Babe Ruth, 1920	158
18. Babe Ruth, 1927	158
18. Bobby Lowe, 1894	158
18. Chuck Klein, 1930	158

RUNS PER GAME

1. Ross Barnes, 1876	1.91
2. Fred Dunlap, 1884	1.58
3. Billy Hamilton, 1894	1.50
4. George Gore, 1890	1.42
5. Billy Hamilton, 1895	1.35
6. Tip O'Neill, 1887	1.35
7. Billy Hamilton, 1893	1.34
8. Herman Long, 1894	1.32
9. King Kelly, 1886	1.31
10. Joe Kelley, 1894	1.29
11. Tom Brown, 1891	1.29
12. Ed Delahanty, 1894	1.29
13. Ed Delahanty, 1895	1.28
14. Hugh Duffy, 1894	1.28
15. Willie Keeler, 1894	1.28
16. George Gore, 1886	1.27
17. John McGraw, 1894	1.26
18. Dan Brouthers, 1887	1.24
19. Bill Dahlen, 1894	1.24
20. Willie Keeler, 1895	1.24

BASES ON BALLS

1. Babe Ruth, 1923	170
2. Ted Williams, 1947	162
2. Ted Williams, 1949	162
4. Ted Williams, 1946	156
5. Eddie Yost, 1956	151
6. Eddie Joost, 1949	149
7. Babe Ruth, 1920	148
7. Jimmy Wynn, 1969	148
7. Eddie Stanky, 1945	148
10. Jimmy Sheckard, 1911	147
11. Mickey Mantle, 1957	146
12. Ted Williams, 1941	145
12. Ted Williams, 1942	145
12. Harmon Killebrew, 1969	145
15. Babe Ruth, 1926	144
15. Eddie Stanky, 1950	144
15. Babe Ruth, 1921	144
18. Ted Williams, 1951	143
19. Babe Ruth, 1924	142
20. Eddie Yost, 1950	141

STOLEN BASES

1. Rickey Henderson, 1982	130
2. Lou Brock, 1974	118
3. Rickey Henderson, 1983	108
4. Maury Wills, 1962	104
5. Rickey Henderson, 1980	100
6. Ron LeFlore, 1980	97
7. Ty Cobb, 1915	96
7. Omar Moreno, 1980	96
9. Maury Wills, 1965	94
10. Tim Raines, 1983	90
11. Clyde Milan, 1912	88
12. Willie Wilson, 1979	83
12. Ty Cobb, 1911	83
14. Bob Bescher, 1911	81
14. Eddie Collins, 1910	81
16. Dave Collins, 1980	79
16. Willie Wilson, 1980	79
18. Ron LeFlore, 1979	78
18. Tim Raines, 1982	78

PINCH HITS

1. Jose Morales, 1976	25
2. Dave Philley, 1961	24
2. Vic Davalillo, 1970	24
2. Rusty Staub, 1983	24
5. Peanuts Lowrey, 1953	22
5. Sam Leslie, 1932	22
5. Red Schoendienst, 1962	22
8. Smoky Burgess, 1966	21
8. Merv Rettenmund, 1977	21
10. Frenchy Bordagaray, 1938	20
10. Jerry Turner, 1978	20
10. Doc Miller, 1913	20
10. Ed Coleman, 1936	20
10. Joe Frazier, 1954	20
10. Smoky Burgess, 1965	20
10. Ken Boswell, 1976	20

PINCH HIT BATTING AVERAGE

1. Ed Kranepool, 1974	.486
2. Smead Jolley, 1931	.467
3. Frenchy Bordagaray, 1938	.465
4. Gates Brown, 1968	.462
5. Rick Miller, 1983	.457
6. Jose Pagan, 1969	.452
7. Elmer Valo, 1955	.452
8. Ted Easterly, 1912	.433
9. Don Dillard, 1961	.429
9. Joe Cronin, 1943	.429
11. Richie Ashburn, 1962	.419
11. Bob Bowman, 1958	.419
11. Dick Williams, 1962	.419
14. Merritt Ranew, 1963	.415
15. Kurt Bevacqua, 1983	.412
15. Bob Hansen, 1974	.412
17. Dave Philley, 1958	.409
18. Frankie Baumholtz, 1955	.405
19. Jerry Lynch, 1961	.404

MOST STRIKEOUTS PER GAME

1. Jim Davis, 1954	.690
2. Bill Hands, 1967	.680
3. Clem Labine, 1953	.640
4. Dean Chance, 1967	.630
5. Ray Washburn, 1967	.620
6. Billy McCool, 1967	.620
7. Joe Coleman, 1967	.610
8. Steve Barber, 1967	.610
9. Jim Nash, 1967	.600
10. Dean Stone, 1954	.580
11. Dave Koslo, 1952	.570
12. Ray Culp, 1967	.570
13. Wade Blasingame, 1967	.550
13. Lou Kretlow, 1953	.550
15. Gary Nolan, 1967	.540
16. Jim Lonborg, 1967	.530
17. Bob Veale, 1967	.520
18. Bob Feller, 1952	.520
19. Bill Dillman, 1967	.520
20. Dick Ellsworth, 1967	.510

STRIKEOUTS

1. Bobby Bonds, 1970	189
2. Bobby Bonds, 1969	187
3. Mike Schmidt, 1975	180
4. Dave Nicholson, 1963	175
4. Gorman Thomas, 1979	175
6. Reggie Jackson, 1968	171
7. Gorman Thomas, 1980	170
8. Juan Samuel, 1984	168
9. Gary Alexander, 1978	166
10. Donn Clendenon, 1968	163
11. Butch Hobson, 1977	162
12. Richie Allen, 1968	161
12. Reggie Jackson, 1971	161
14. Reggie Jackson, 1982	156
14. Dave Kingman, 1982	156
14. Tommie Agee, 1970	156
14. Tony Armas, 1984	156
18. Frank Howard, 1967	155
18. Jeff Burroughs, 1975	155
20. Willie Stargell, 1971	154

WINS

1. Jack Chesbro, 1904 41
2. Ed Walsh, 1908 40
3. Christy Mathewson, 1908 . . . 37
4. Walter Johnson, 1913 36
4. Jouett Meekin, 1894 36
4. Amos Rusie, 1894 36
7. Joe McGinnity, 1904 35
7. Cy Young, 1895 35
9. Frank Killen, 1893 34
9. Joe Wood, 1912 34
11. Christy Mathewson, 1904 . . . 33
11. Kid Nichols, 1893 33
11. Cy Young, 1901 33
11. Grover Alexander, 1916 33
15. Cy Young, 1893 32
15. Pink Hawley, 1895 32

WINNING PERCENTAGE

1. Roy Face, 1959 947
2. Johnny Allen, 1937 938
3. Ron Guidry, 1978 893
4. Freddie Fitzsimmons, 1940 . .889
5. Lefty Grove, 1931 886
6. Bob Stanley, 1978 882
7. Preacher Roe, 1951 880
8. Tom Seaver, 1981 875
9. Joe Wood, 1912 872
10. Wild Bill Donovan, 1907 862
11. Whitey Ford, 1961 862
12. Chief Bender, 1914 850
13. Lefty Grove, 1930 848

EARNED RUN AVERAGE

1. Dutch Leonard, 1914 . . . . 1.01
2. Three Finger Brown, 1906 . 1.04
3. Walter Johnson, 1913 . . . . 1.09
4. Bob Gibson, 1968 . . . . . . 1.12
5. Christy Mathewson, 1909 . 1.14
6. Jack Pfiester, 1907 . . . . . 1.15
7. Addie Joss, 1908 . . . . . . 1.16
8. Carl Lundgren, 1907 . . . . 1.17
9. Grover Alexander, 1915 . . . 1.22
10. Cy Young, 1908 . . . . 1.26
11. Ed Walsh, 1910 . . . . 1.27
12. Walter Johnson, 1918 . . . . 1.27
13. Christy Mathewson, 1905 . 1.27
14. Jack Coombs, 1910 . . . . . 1.30
15. Three Finger Brown, 1909 . 1.31

GAMES

1. Mike Marshall, 1974 106
2. Kent Tekulve, 1979 94
3. Mike Marshall, 1973 92
4. Kent Tekulve, 1978 91
5. Wayne Granger, 1969 90
5. Mike Marshall, 1979 90
7. Wilbur Wood, 1968 88
8. Kent Tekulve, 1982 85
9. Ted Abernathy, 1965 84
9. Enrique Romo, 1979 84
9. Dick Tidrow, 1980 84
12. Ken Sanders, 1971 83
13. Eddie Fisher, 1965 82
13. Bill Campbell, 1983 82
15. John Wyatt, 1964 81
15. Dale Murray, 1976 81

GAMES STARTED

1. Amos Rusie, 1893 52
2. Jack Chesbro, 1904 51
3. Frank Killen, 1896 50
3. Amos Rusie, 1894 50
3. Pink Hawley, 1895 50
3. Ted Breitenstein, 1894 50
3. Ted Breitenstein, 1895 50
8. Ed Walsh, 1908 49
8. Wilbur Wood, 1972 49
10. Joe McGinnity, 1903 48
10. Jouett Meekin, 1894 48
10. Frank Killen, 1893 48
10. Wilbur Wood, 1973 48
14. Cy Young, 1894 47
14. Jack Taylor, 1898 47
14. Amos Rusie, 1895 47

COMPLETE GAMES

1. Amos Rusie, 1893 50
2. Jack Chesbro, 1904 48
3. Ted Breitenstein, 1894 46
3. Ted Breitenstein, 1895 46
5. Vic Willis, 1902 45
5. Amos Rusie, 1894 45
7. Kid Nichols, 1893 44
7. Cy Young, 1894 44
7. Joe McGinnity, 1903 44
7. Pink Hawley, 1895 44
7. Frank Killen, 1896 44

INNINGS PITCHED

1. Amos Rusie, 1893 482
2. Ed Walsh, 1908 464
3. Jack Chesbro, 1904 455
4. Ted Breitenstein, 1894 447
5. Pink Hawley, 1895 444
6. Amos Rusie, 1894 444
7. Joe McGinnity, 1903 434
8. Frank Killen, 1896 432
9. Ted Breitenstein, 1895 430
10. Kid Nichols, 1893 425
11. Cy Young, 1893 423
12. Ed Walsh, 1907 422
13. Frank Killen, 1893 415
14. Cy Young, 1896 414
15. Vic Willis, 1902 410

STRIKEOUTS

1. Nolan Ryan, 1973 383
2. Sandy Koufax, 1965 382
3. Nolan Ryan, 1974 367
4. Rube Waddell, 1904 349
5. Bob Feller, 1946 348
6. Nolan Ryan, 1977 341
7. Nolan Ryan, 1972 329
8. Nolan Ryan, 1976 327
9. Sam McDowell, 1965 325
10. Sandy Koufax, 1966 317
11. J. R. Richard, 1979 313
11. Walter Johnson, 1910 313
13. Steve Carlton, 1972 310
14. Mickey Lolich, 1971 308
15. Sandy Koufax, 1963 306

STRIKEOUTS PER 9 INNINGS

1. Dwight Gooden, 1984 . . . . 11.39
2. Sam McDowell, 1965 . . . 10.71
3. Nolan Ryan, 1973 . . . . . 10.57
4. Sandy Koufax, 1962 . . . . 10.55
5. Nolan Ryan, 1972 . . . . . 10.43
6. Sam McDowell, 1966 . . . 10.42
7. Nolan Ryan, 1976 . . . . . 10.36
8. Sandy Koufax, 1965 . . . . 10.24
9. Sandy Koufax, 1960 . . . . 10.13
10. Nolan Ryan, 1978 . . . . . 9.96
11. Nolan Ryan, 1974 . . . . . 9.92
12. J. R. Richard, 1978 . . . . 9.92
13. Herb Score, 1955 . . . . . 9.70
14. Nolan Ryan, 1984 . . . . . 9.65
15. J. R. Richard, 1979 . . . . 9.65

SHUTOUTS

1. Grover Alexander, 1916 16
2. Bob Gibson, 1968 13
2. Jack Coombs, 1910 13
4. Christy Mathewson, 1908 . . . 12
4. Grover Alexander, 1915 12
6. Walter Johnson, 1913 11
6. Ed Walsh, 1908 11
6. Dean Chance, 1964 11
6. Sandy Koufax, 1963 11

HITS PER 9 INNINGS

1. Nolan Ryan, 1972 . . . . 5.26
2. Luis Tiant, 1968 . . . . 5.30
3. Ed Reulbach, 1906 . . . . 5.33
4. Jim Hearn, 1950 . . . . 5.64
5. Carl Lundgren, 1907 . . . . 5.65
6. Dutch Leonard, 1914 . . . . . . 5.70
7. Tommy Byrne, 1949 . . . . 5.74
8. Dave McNally, 1968 . . . . 5.77
9. Sandy Koufax, 1965 . . . . 5.79
10. Russ Ford, 1910 . . . . 5.83
11. Al Downing, 1963 . . . . 5.84
12. Herb Score, 1956 . . . . 5.85
13. Bob Gibson, 1968 . . . . 5.85
14. Sam McDowell, 1965 . . . . . . 5.87
15. Ed Walsh, 1910 . . . . 5.89

BASES ON BALLS

1. Amos Rusie, 1893 218
2. Cy Seymour, 1898 213
3. Bob Feller, 1938 208
4. Nolan Ryan, 1977 204
5. Nolan Ryan, 1974 202
6. Amos Rusie, 1894 200
7. Bob Feller, 1941 194
8. Bobo Newsom, 1938 192
9. Ted Breitenstein, 1894 191
10. Tony Mullane, 1893 189
11. Kid Gleason, 1893 187
12. Sam Jones, 1955 185
13. Nolan Ryan, 1976 183
14. Bob Turley, 1954 181
14. Willie McGill, 1893 181
14. Bob Harmon, 1911 181

BASES ON BALLS PER 9 INNINGS

1. Babe Adams, 1920 62
2. Christy Mathewson, 1913 .62
3. Christy Mathewson, 1914 .66
4. Cy Young, 1904 69
5. Red Lucas, 1933 74
6. Cy Young, 1906 78
7. Babe Adams, 1919 79
8. Babe Adams, 1922 79
9. Slim Sallee, 1919 79
10. Slim Sallee, 1918 82
11. Addie Joss, 1908 83
12. Cy Young, 1905 84
13. Deacon Phillippe, 1902 86
14. Grover Alexander, 1923 . .89
15. Cy Young, 1901 90

LOSSES

1. Red Donahue, 1897 33
2. Jim Hughey, 1899 30
2. Ted Breitenstein, 1895 30
4. Vic Willis, 1905 29
4. Bill Hart, 1896 29
4. Jack Taylor, 1898 29
7. Still Bill Hill, 1896 28
7. Duke Esper, 1893 28
9. George Bell, 1910 27
9. Paul Derringer, 1933 27
9. Bill Hart, 1897 27
9. Willie Sudhoff, 1898 27
9. Dummy Taylor, 1901 27
9. Pink Hawley, 1894 27
15. Bill Carrick, 1899 26

RELIEF PITCHING

WINS

1. Roy Face, 1959	18
2. Bill Campbell, 1976	17
2. John Hiller, 1974	17
4. Ron Perranoski, 1963	16
4. Jim Konstanty, 1950	16
4. Tom Johnson, 1977	16
4. Dick Radatz, 1964	16
8. Hoyt Wilhelm, 1952	15
8. Luis Arroyo, 1961	15
8. Dick Radatz, 1963	15
8. Eddie Fisher, 1965	15
8. Mace Brown, 1938	15
8. Dale Murray, 1975	15
8. Mike Marshall, 1974	15

SAVES

1. Bruce Sutter, 1984	45
1. Dan Quisenberry, 1983	45
3. Dan Quisenberry, 1984	44
4. John Hiller, 1973	38
5. Clay Carroll, 1972	37
5. Rollie Fingers, 1978	37
5. Bruce Sutter, 1979	37
8. Bruce Sutter, 1982	36
8. Bill Caudill, 1984	36
10. Sparky Lyle, 1972	35
10. Dan Quisenberry, 1982	35
10. Rollie Fingers, 1977	35
10. Wayne Granger, 1970	35
14. Ron Perranoski, 1970	34

GAMES

1. Mike Marshall, 1974	106
2. Kent Tekulve, 1979	94
3. Mike Marshall, 1973	92
4. Kent Tekulve, 1978	91
5. Wayne Granger, 1969	90
6. Mike Marshall, 1979	89
7. Wilbur Wood, 1968	86
8. Kent Tekulve, 1982	85
9. Ted Abernathy, 1965	84
9. Enrique Romo, 1979	84
9. Dick Tidrow, 1980	84
12. Ken Sanders, 1971	83
13. Eddie Fisher, 1965	82
13. Bill Campbell, 1983	82
15. John Wyatt, 1964	81
15. Dale Murray, 1976	81

WINNING PERCENTAGE

1. Tom Hughes, 1915	1.000
1. Joe Pate, 1926	1.000
1. Lew Burdette, 1953	1.000
1. Sandy Consuegra, 1954	1.000
1. Nig Cuppy, 1894	1.000
1. Bob Grim, 1954	1.000
1. Grant Jackson, 1973	1.000
1. Emil Kush, 1946	1.000
1. George Mullin, 1914	1.000
1. Charlie Root, 1937	1.000
11. Roy Face, 1959	.947
12. Phil Regan, 1966	.933
13. Eddie Yuhas, 1952	.917
14. Ellis Kinder, 1951	.909
14. Stan Williams, 1970	.909
14. Aurelio Lopez, 1984	.909

WINS PLUS SAVES

1. Dan Quisenberry, 1984	50
1. Bruce Sutter, 1984	50
1. Dan Quisenberry, 1983	50
4. John Hiller, 1973	48
5. Dick Radatz, 1964	45
5. Mike Marshall, 1973	45
5. Dan Quisenberry, 1980	45
5. Bruce Sutter, 1982	45
5. Bill Caudill, 1984	45
10. Luis Arroyo, 1961	44
10. Bill Campbell, 1977	44
10. Sparky Lyle, 1972	44
10. Dan Quisenberry, 1982	44

LOSSES

1. Gene Garber, 1979	16
2. Darold Knowles, 1970	14
2. Mike Marshall, 1975	14
2. Mike Marshall, 1979	14
2. John Hiller, 1974	14
6. Rollie Fingers, 1978	13
6. Skip Lockwood, 1978	13
6. Wilbur Wood, 1970	13

PITCHING BEFORE 1893

WINS

1. Old Hoss Radbourn, 1884	60
2. John Clarkson, 1885	53
3. Guy Hecker, 1884	52
4. Old Hoss Radbourn, 1883	49
4. John Clarkson, 1889	49
6. Charlie Buffinton, 1884	48
7. Al Spalding, 1876	47
7. Monte Ward, 1879	47
9. Matt Kilroy, 1887	46
9. Pud Galvin, 1884	46
9. Pud Galvin, 1883	46

COMPLETE GAMES

1. Will White, 1879	75
2. Old Hoss Radbourn, 1884	73
3. Guy Hecker, 1884	72
3. Jim McCormick, 1880	72
3. Pud Galvin, 1883	72
6. Pud Galvin, 1884	71
7. Tim Keefe, 1883	68
7. John Clarkson, 1885	68
7. John Clarkson, 1889	68
10. Bill Hutchison, 1892	67

SHUTOUTS

1. George Bradley, 1876	16
2. Ed Morris, 1886	12
2. Tommy Bond, 1879	12
2. Pud Galvin, 1884	12
5. Dave Foutz, 1886	11
5. Old Hoss Radbourn, 1884	11
7. John Clarkson, 1885	10
8. Monte Ward, 1880	9
8. Cy Young, 1892	9
8. George Derby, 1881	9
8. Tommy Bond, 1878	9

WINNING PERCENTAGE

1. Jim McCormick, 1884	.875
1. Fred Goldsmith, 1880	.875
3. Billy Taylor, 1884	.862
4. Old Hoss Radbourn, 1884	.833
5. Mickey Welch, 1885	.800
5. Jocko Flynn, 1886	.800
7. Bob Caruthers, 1889	.784
8. Al Spalding, 1876	.783
9. Jack Manning, 1876	.783
10. Charlie Sweeney, 1884	.774

INNINGS PITCHED

1. Will White, 1879	680
2. Old Hoss Radbourn, 1884	679
3. Guy Hecker, 1884	671
4. Jim McCormick, 1880	658
5. Pud Galvin, 1883	656
6. Pud Galvin, 1884	636
7. Old Hoss Radbourn, 1883	632
8. Bill Hutchison, 1892	627
9. John Clarkson, 1885	623
10. Jim Devlin, 1876	622

HITS PER 9 INNINGS

1. Tim Keefe, 1880	6.09
2. Charlie Sweeney, 1884	6.23
3. Jim McCormick, 1884	6.47
4. Dupee Shaw, 1884	6.47
5. Jim Handiboe, 1886	6.47
6. Guy Hecker, 1882	6.49
7. Tim Keefe, 1888	6.55
8. Adonis Terry, 1888	6.69
9. Silver King, 1888	6.72
10. Tim Keefe, 1885	6.72

EARNED RUN AVERAGE

1. Tim Keefe, 1880	.86
2. Denny Driscoll, 1882	1.21
3. George Bradley, 1876	1.23
4. Guy Hecker, 1882	1.30
5. George Bradley, 1880	1.38
6. Old Hoss Radbourn, 1884	1.38
7. Monte Ward, 1878	1.51
8. Harry McCormick, 1882	1.52
9. Will White, 1882	1.54
10. Jim McCormick, 1884	1.54

STRIKEOUTS

1. Matt Kilroy, 1886	513
2. Toad Ramsey, 1886	499
3. One Arm Daily, 1884	483
4. Old Hoss Radbourn, 1884	441
5. Charlie Buffinton, 1884	417
6. Guy Hecker, 1884	385
7. Bill Sweeney, 1884	374
8. Pud Galvin, 1884	369
9. Mark Baldwin, 1889	368
10. Tim Keefe, 1883	361

BASES ON BALLS PER 9 INNINGS

1. George Zettlein, 1876	.23
2. Cherokee Fisher, 1876	.24
3. George Bradley, 1880	.28
4. Tommy Bond, 1876	.29
5. Tommy Bond, 1879	.39
6. Bobby Mathews, 1876	.42
7. Charlie Sweeney, 1884	.43
8. Guy Hecker, 1882	.43
9. Al Spalding, 1876	.44
10. Pud Galvin, 1879	.47

GAMES

1. Guy Hecker, 1884	76
1. Will White, 1879	76
1. Pud Galvin, 1883	76
1. Old Hoss Radbourn, 1883	76
5. Old Hoss Radbourn, 1884	75
5. Bill Hutchison, 1892	75
7. Jim McCormick, 1880	74
7. Lee Richmond, 1880	74
9. John Clarkson, 1889	73
10. Pud Galvin, 1884	72

STRIKEOUTS PER 9 INNINGS

1. Dupee Shaw, 1884	8.81
2. One Arm Daily, 1884	8.68
3. Matt Kilroy, 1886	7.92
4. Charlie Gagus, 1884	7.92
5. John Clarkson, 1884	7.78
6. Toad Ramsey, 1886	7.63
7. Tony Mullane, 1890	7.51
8. Jim Whitney, 1884	7.23
9. Mike Dorgan, 1884	7.17
10. Walter Burke, 1884	7.13

LOSSES

1. John Coleman, 1883	48
2. Will White, 1880	42
3. Larry McKeon, 1884	41
4. George Bradley, 1879	40
4. Jim McCormick, 1879	40
6. Pud Galvin, 1880	37
6. George Cobb, 1892	37
6. Kid Carsey, 1891	37
6. Henry Porter, 1888	37
10. Stump Weidman, 1886	36

PUTOUTS	ASSISTS	FIELDING AVERAGE

1B

PUTOUTS	ASSISTS	FIELDING AVERAGE
1. Jiggs Donahue, 1907 1846	1. Bill Buckner, 1983 161	1. Steve Garvey, 1984.... 1.000
2. George Kelly, 1920 1759	2. Bill Buckner, 1982 159	2. Stuffy McInnis, 1921.... .999
3. Phil Todt, 1926 1755	3. Mickey Vernon, 1949.... 155	3. Frank McCormick, 1946. .999
4. Wally Pipp, 1926 1710	4. Fred Tenney, 1905.... 152	4. Steve Garvey, 1981.... .999
5. Jiggs Donahue, 1906 1697	5. Ferris Fain, 1952 150	4. Jim Spencer, 1973.... .999
6. Candy LaChance, 1904.... 1691	6. Rudy York, 1943 149	6. Wes Parker, 1968 .... .999
7. Tom Jones, 1907 1687	7. Keith Hernandez, 1983.... 147	7. Eddie Murray, 1981.... .999
8. Ernie Banks, 1965 1682	8. Rudy York, 1942 146	8. Jim Spencer, 1976.... .998
9. Wally Pipp, 1922 1667	8. Keith Hernandez, 1979.... 146	9. Jim Spencer, 1981.... .998
10. Lou Gehrig, 1927 1662	10. Vic Power, 1960.... 145	10. Joe Judge, 1930 .... .998

2B

PUTOUTS	ASSISTS	FIELDING AVERAGE
1. Bid McPhee, 1886 529	1. Frankie Frisch, 1927 641	1. Rob Wilfong, 1980.... .995
2. Bobby Grich, 1974.... 484	2. Hughie Critz, 1926 588	2. Bobby Grich, 1973.... .995
3. Bucky Harris, 1922 479	3. Rogers Hornsby, 1927 582	3. Jerry Adair, 1964.... .994
4. Nellie Fox, 1956.... 478	4. Oscar Melillo, 1930 572	4. Tim Cullen, 1970.... .994
5. Lou Bierbauer, 1889 472	5. Ryne Sandberg, 1983 571	5. Manny Trillo, 1982 .... .994
6. Billy Herman, 1933 466	6. Rabbit Maranville, 1924 568	6. Red Schoendienst, 1956. .993
7. Cub Stricker, 1887 461	7. Frank Parkinson, 1922 562	7. Tito Fuentes, 1973.... .993
8. Buddy Myer, 1935.... 460	8. Tony Cuccinello, 1936.... 559	7. Ryne Sandberg, 1984.... .993
9. Bill Sweeney, 1912 459	9. Johnny Hodapp, 1930.... 557	9. Joe Morgan, 1977.... .993
9. Bill Wambsganss, 1924 459	10. Lou Bierbauer, 1892 555	9. Snuffy Stirnweiss, 1948 . .993

3B

PUTOUTS	ASSISTS	FIELDING AVERAGE
1. Denny Lyons, 1887 255	1. Graig Nettles, 1971.... 412	1. Don Money, 1974 .... .989
2. Jimmy Collins, 1900 251	2. Brooks Robinson, 1974.... 410	2. Hank Majeski, 1947 .... .988
2. Jimmy Williams, 1899.... 251	2. Graig Nettles, 1973.... 410	3. Aurelio Rodriguez, 1978. .987
4. Jimmy Collins, 1898 243	4. Harlond Clift, 1937 405	4. Willie Kamm, 1933 .... .984
4. Willie Kamm, 1928 243	4. Brooks Robinson, 1967.... 405	5. George Kell, 1946 .... .983
6. Willie Kamm, 1927 236	6. Mike Schmidt, 1974 404	6. Heinie Groh, 1924.... .983
7. Frank Baker, 1913.... 233	7. Doug DeCinces, 1982 399	7. Carney Lansford, 1979. .982
8. Bill Coughlin, 1901 232	8. Buddy Bell, 1982 396	8. George Kell, 1950 .... .982
9. Ernie Courtney, 1905 229	8. Mike Schmidt, 1977 396	9. Pinky Whitney, 1937.... .982
10. Jimmy Austin, 1911 228	8. Clete Boyer, 1962 396	10. Buddy Bell, 1980 .... .980

SS

PUTOUTS	ASSISTS	FIELDING AVERAGE
1. Hughie Jennings, 1895 425	1. Ozzie Smith, 1980.... 621	1. Larry Bowa, 1979 .... .991
1. Donie Bush, 1914 425	2. Glenn Wright, 1924.... 601	2. Ed Brinkman, 1972.... .990
3. Rabbit Maranville, 1914.... 407	3. Dave Bancroft, 1920 598	3. Larry Bowa, 1972 .... .987
4. Eddie Miller, 1940 405	4. Tommy Thevenow, 1926 597	4. Larry Bowa, 1971 .... .986
4. Dave Bancroft, 1922 405	5. Ivan DeJesus, 1977.... 595	5. Larry Bowa, 1978 .... .986
6. Monte Cross, 1898 404	6. Cal Ripken, 1984.... 583	6. Frank Duffy, 1973 .... .986
7. Dave Bancroft, 1921 396	7. Whitey Wietelmann, 1943 581	7. Roger Metzger, 1976 .... .986
8. Mickey Doolan, 1906 395	8. Dave Bancroft, 1922 579	8. Dave Concepcion, 1977.... .985
9. Buck Weaver, 1913 392	9. Rabbit Maranville, 1914.... 574	9. Tim Foli, 1982 .... .985
10. Rabbit Maranville, 1915 391	10. Don Kessinger, 1968.... 573	10. Robin Yount, 1981.... .985
10. Buck Herzog, 1915 391		

OF

PUTOUTS	ASSISTS	FIELDING AVERAGE
1. Taylor Douthit, 1928 547	1. Tom Dolan, 1883 62	
2. Richie Ashburn, 1951 538	2. Orator Shaffer, 1879.... 50	
3. Richie Ashburn, 1949 514	3. Hugh Nicol, 1884.... 48	
4. Chet Lemon, 1977.... 512	4. Hardy Richardson, 1881.... 45	
5. Dwayne Murphy, 1980 507	5. Pete Gillespie, 1887 44	Many players tied with 1.000
6. Richie Ashburn, 1956 503	5. Tommy McCarthy, 1888.... 44	
6. Dom DiMaggio, 1948 503	5. Chuck Klein, 1930.... 44	
8. Richie Ashburn, 1957 502	8. Jimmy Bannon, 1894 43	
9. Richie Ashburn, 1953 496	8. Charlie Duffee, 1889 43	
10. Richie Ashburn, 1958 495	10. Jim Fogarty, 1889 42	

C

PUTOUTS	ASSISTS	FIELDING AVERAGE
1. Johnny Edwards, 1969.... 1135	1. Bill Rariden, 1915 238	1. Buddy Rosar, 1946 .... 1.000
2. Johnny Edwards, 1963 1008	2. Bill Rariden, 1914 215	1. Yogi Berra, 1958 .... 1.000
3. Randy Hundley, 1969.... 978	3. Pat Moran, 1903 214	1. Lou Berberet, 1957 .... 1.000
4. Tony Pena, 1983 976	4. Art Wilson, 1914 212	1. Pete Daley, 1957.... 1.000
5. Bill Freehan, 1968 971	4. Oscar Stanage, 1911 212	5. Joe Azcue, 1967 .... .999
6. Gary Carter, 1982 954	6. Gabby Street, 1909 210	6. Wes Westrum, 1950 .... .999
7. Bill Freehan, 1967 950	7. Frank Snyder, 1915 204	7. Thurman Munson, 1971. .998
8. Johnny Bench, 1968 942	8. George Gibson, 1910 203	8. Gus Triandos, 1963.... .998
9. Elston Howard, 1964.... 939	9. Bill Bergen, 1909 202	9. Ellie Hendricks, 1969 .... .998
10. Tim McCarver, 1969.... 925	9. Claude Berry, 1914 202	10. Sherm Lollar, 1961.... .998

P

PUTOUTS	ASSISTS	FIELDING AVERAGE
1. Dave Foutz, 1886 57	1. Ed Walsh, 1907 227	
2. Tony Mullane, 1882 54	2. Will White, 1882 223	
3. George Bradley, 1876 50	3. Ed Walsh, 1908 190	
3. Guy Hecker, 1884 50	4. Harry Howell, 1905 178	
5. Mike Boddicker, 1984.... 49	5. Tony Mullane, 1882 177	Many players tied with 1.000
6. Larry Corcoran, 1884 47	6. John Clarkson, 1885 174	
7. Ted Breitenstein, 1895 45	7. John Clarkson, 1889 172	
7. Al Spalding, 1876 45	8. Matt Kilroy, 1887 167	
9. Dave Foutz, 1887 44	9. Jack Chesbro, 1904 166	
9. Jim Devlin, 1876 44	10. George Mullin, 1904 163	
9. Bill Hutchison, 1890 44		

All-Time Single Season Leaders - Individual Fielding

TOTAL CHANCES	TOTAL CHANCES/GAME	DOUBLE PLAYS

1B

TOTAL CHANCES		TOTAL CHANCES/GAME		DOUBLE PLAYS	
1. Jiggs Donahue, 1907	1998	1. Joe Gerhardt, 1876	13.3	1. Ferris Fain, 1949	194
2. Phil Todt, 1926	1903	2. Jiggs Donahue, 1907	12.7	2. Ferris Fain, 1950	192
3. George Kelly, 1920	1873	3. Gene Paulette, 1917	12.7	3. Donn Clendenon, 1966	182
4. Jiggs Donahue, 1906	1837	4. Frank Isbell, 1909	12.7	4. Ron Jackson, 1979	175
5. Tom Jones, 1907	1821	5. Cap Anson, 1879	12.6	5. Gil Hodges, 1951	171
6. Wally Pipp, 1926	1817	6. Oscar Walker, 1879	12.6	6. Mickey Vernon, 1949	168
7. Ernie Banks, 1965	1790	7. Joe Start, 1878	12.5	7. Ted Kluszewski, 1954	166
8. Jiggs Donahue, 1905	1780	8. Tim Murnane, 1878	12.5	8. Rudy York, 1944	163
9. Earl Sheely, 1921	1778	9. Joe Start, 1879	12.5	9. Rod Carew, 1977	161
10. Fred Tenney, 1908	1769	10. Jake Goodman, 1878	12.5	9. Donn Clendenon, 1965	161

2B

TOTAL CHANCES		TOTAL CHANCES/GAME		DOUBLE PLAYS	
1. Frankie Frisch, 1927	1059	1. Thorny Hawkes, 1879	8.4	1. Bill Mazeroski, 1966	161
2. Bid McPhee, 1886	1058	2. Chick Fulmer, 1879	8.3	2. Gerry Priddy, 1950	150
3. Burgess Whitehead, 1936	1026	3. Jack Burdock, 1878	8.3	3. Bill Mazeroski, 1961	144
4. Nap Lajoie, 1908	1025	3. Ed Somerville, 1876	8.3	4. Nellie Fox, 1957	141
5. Billy Herman, 1933	1023	5. Joe Gerhardt, 1877	8.1	4. Dave Cash, 1974	141
6. Oscar Melillo, 1931	1003	6. Fred Pfeffer, 1884	8.1	6. Buddy Myer, 1935	138
7. Jimmy Dykes, 1921	1002	7. Davy Force, 1881	8.1	6. Bill Mazeroski, 1962	138
8. Gerry Priddy, 1950	1001	8. Jack Burdock, 1879	7.9	8. Red Schoendienst, 1954	137
9. Bucky Harris, 1922	992	9. Joe Quest, 1878	7.8	8. Jerry Coleman, 1950	137
10. Fred Pfeffer, 1889	991	10. Pop Smith, 1885	7.7	8. Jackie Robinson, 1951	137

3B

TOTAL CHANCES		TOTAL CHANCES/GAME		DOUBLE PLAYS	
1. Jimmy Williams, 1899	671	1. Al Nichols, 1876	5.8	1. Graig Nettles, 1971	54
2. Bill Shindle, 1892	660	2. Bob Ferguson, 1877	5.6	2. Harlond Clift, 1937	50
3. Tommy Leach, 1904	643	3. Arthur Irwin, 1882	5.4	3. Johnny Pesky, 1949	48
4. Harlond Clift, 1937	637	4. Jumbo Davis, 1888	5.1	3. Paul Molitor, 1982	48
5. Bill Shindle, 1889	636	4. John Shetzline, 1882	5.1	5. Sammy Hale, 1929	46
6. Jimmy Collins, 1899	629	6. Cap Anson, 1876	5.0	5. Clete Boyer, 1965	46
7. Charlie Reilly, 1890	626	7. Bill Shindle, 1892	4.9	5. Gary Gaetti, 1983	46
8. Arlie Latham, 1891	622	8. Jack Gleason, 1882	4.9	8. Frank Malzone, 1961	45
9. Jimmy Collins, 1900	620	9. Bill Bradley, 1900	4.9	8. Eddie Yost, 1950	45
10. Jimmy Collins, 1898	617	10. George Bradley, 1880	4.8	8. Darrell Evans, 1974	45

SS

TOTAL CHANCES		TOTAL CHANCES/GAME		DOUBLE PLAYS	
1. Dave Bancroft, 1922	1046	1. Herman Long, 1889	7.3	1. Rick Burleson, 1980	147
2. Rabbit Maranville, 1914	1046	2. Hughie Jennings, 1895	7.2	2. Roy Smalley, 1979	144
3. Donie Bush, 1914	1027	3. Dave Bancroft, 1918	7.1	3. Bobby Wine, 1970	137
4. Tommy Thevenow, 1926	1013	4. Phil Tomney, 1889	7.1	4. Lou Boudreau, 1944	134
5. Dave Bancroft, 1920	1005	5. George Davis, 1899	7.1	5. Rafael Ramirez, 1982	130
6. Monte Cross, 1898	1003	5. Hughie Jennings, 1896	7.1	6. Roy McMillan, 1954	129
6. Donie Bush, 1911	1003	7. Hughie Jennings, 1897	7.0	7. Gene Alley, 1966	128
6. Heinie Wagner, 1908	1003	7. Bobby Wallace, 1901	7.0	7. Hod Ford, 1928	128
9. George McBride, 1908	992	7. Monte Cross, 1897	7.0	7. Vern Stephens, 1949	128
10. Monte Cross, 1899	989	10. Bill Dahlen, 1895	6.9	10. Dick Groat, 1958	127
				10. Zoilo Versalles, 1962	127

OF

TOTAL CHANCES		TOTAL CHANCES/GAME		DOUBLE PLAYS	
1. Taylor Douthit, 1928	566	1. Fred Treacey, 1876	4.4	1. Jack Tobin, 1919	15
2. Richie Ashburn, 1951	560	2. Tom Dolan, 1883	4.3	1. Happy Felsch, 1919	15
3. Richie Ashburn, 1949	538	3. Redleg Snyder, 1876	3.8	3. Jimmy Sheckard, 1899	14
4. Chet Lemon, 1977	536	3. Charley Jones, 1877	3.8	4. Tom Brown, 1893	13
5. Richie Ashburn, 1957	527	5. Taylor Douthit, 1928	3.7		
6. Dom DiMaggio, 1948	526	6. Mike Mansell, 1879	3.6		
7. Dwayne Murphy, 1980	525	7. Richie Ashburn, 1951	3.6		
8. Richie Ashburn, 1956	523	8. Chet Lemon, 1977	3.6		
9. Richie Ashburn, 1953	519	9. Thurman Tucker, 1944	3.6		
10. Lloyd Waner, 1931	515	10. Kirby Puckett, 1984	3.6		

C

TOTAL CHANCES		TOTAL CHANCES/GAME		DOUBLE PLAYS	
1. Johnny Edwards, 1969	1221	1. Bill Holbert, 1883	10.6	1. Steve O'Neill, 1916	36
2. Johnny Edwards, 1963	1101	2. Sam Trott, 1884	10.4	2. Frankie Hayes, 1945	29
3. Tony Pena, 1983	1075	3. Bill Holbert, 1884	9.7	3. Ray Schalk, 1916	25
4. Gary Carter, 1982	1068	4. Jocko Milligan, 1884	9.4	3. Yogi Berra, 1951	25
5. Randy Hundley, 1969	1065	4. Mert Hackett, 1884	9.4	5. Jack Lapp, 1915	23
6. Johnny Bench, 1968	1053	6. Barney Gilligan, 1884	9.3	5. Tom Haller, 1968	23
7. Bill Freehan, 1968	1050	6. Mike Hines, 1883	9.3	5. Muddy Ruel, 1924	23
7. Bill Freehan, 1967	1021	8. George Baker, 1884	9.0	8. Steve O'Neill, 1914	22
9. Bo Diaz, 1983	1014	9. Jocko Milligan, 1885	8.8	8. Bob O'Farrell, 1922	22
10. Elston Howard, 1964	1008	10. Lew Brown, 1877	8.7		

P

TOTAL CHANCES		TOTAL CHANCES/GAME		DOUBLE PLAYS	
1. Ed Walsh, 1907	266	1. Guy Bush, 1933	6.5	1. Lefty Gomez, 1938	15
2. Will White, 1882	257	2. Harry Howell, 1905	5.4	1. Howie Fox, 1948	15
3. Tony Mullane, 1882	241	3. Harry Howell, 1904	5.1	1. Bob Lemon, 1953	15
4. Tim Keefe, 1883	238	4. Harry Arundel, 1882	5.1	4. Randy Jones, 1976	12
5. Ed Walsh, 1908	237	5. Will White, 1882	4.8	4. Eddie Rommel, 1924	12
6. John Clarkson, 1889	235	6. Ed Walsh, 1907	4.8	4. Curt Davis, 1934	12
7. Matt Kilroy, 1887	224	7. George Mullin, 1904	4.5		
8. John Clarkson, 1885	220	8. Tony Mullane, 1882	4.4		
9. Harry Howell, 1905	206	9. Red Donahue, 1902	4.4		
10. Guy Hecker, 1884	205	10. Nick Altrock, 1905	4.4		

BATTING AVERAGE

1. Ty Cobb	.367
2. Rogers Hornsby	.358
3. Joe Jackson	.356
4. Ed Delahanty	.345
5. Willie Keeler	.345
6. Ted Williams	.344
7. Tris Speaker	.344
8. Billy Hamilton	.344
9. Dan Brouthers	.343
10. Pete Browning	.343
11. Babe Ruth	.342
12. Harry Heilmann	.342
13. Bill Terry	.341
14. Jesse Burkett	.341
15. George Sisler	.340
16. Lou Gehrig	.340
17. Nap Lajoie	.339
18. Riggs Stephenson	.336
19. Al Simmons	.334
20. Cap Anson	.334
21. Paul Waner	.333
22. Eddie Collins	.333
23. Stan Musial	.331
24. Sam Thompson	.331
25. Rod Carew	.330
26. Heinie Manush	.330
27. Honus Wagner	.329
28. Hugh Duffy	.328
29. Tip O'Neill	.326
30. Jimmie Foxx	.325
31. Earle Combs	.325
32. Joe DiMaggio	.325
33. Babe Herman	.324
34. Joe Medwick	.324
35. Edd Roush	.323
36. Sam Rice	.322
37. Ross Youngs	.322
38. Kiki Cuyler	.321
39. Charlie Gehringer	.320
40. Chuck Klein	.320
41. Pie Traynor	.320
42. Mickey Cochrane	.320
43. Joe Kelley	.319
44. Ken Williams	.319
45. Roger Connor	.318
46. Earl Averill	.318
47. Arky Vaughan	.318
48. Roberto Clemente	.317
49. Chick Hafey	.317
50. Zack Wheat	.317
51. Lloyd Waner	.316
52. George Van Haltren	.316
53. Frankie Frisch	.316
54. Goose Goslin	.316
55. Elmer Flick	.315
56. Fred Clarke	.315
57. Bibb Falk	.314
58. Cecil Travis	.314
59. George Brett	.314
60. Hank Greenberg	.313
61. Jack Fournier	.313
62. Bill Dickey	.313
63. Hughie Jennings	.312
63. Bill Madlock	.312
65. Johnny Mize	.312
66. Joe Sewell	.312
67. Barney McCosky	.312
68. Bing Miller	.312
69. Freddie Lindstrom	.311
70. Jackie Robinson	.311
71. Baby Doll Jacobson	.311
72. Rip Radcliff	.311
73. Elmer Smith	.311
74. Ginger Beaumont	.311
75. Mike Tiernan	.311
76. Denny Lyons	.310
77. Irish Meusel	.310
78. Luke Appling	.310
79. Bobby Veach	.310
80. Jim O'Rourke	.310
81. John Stone	.310
82. Jim Bottomley	.310
83. Sam Crawford	.309
84. Jimmy Ryan	.309
85. Bob Meusel	.309
86. Jack Tobin	.309
87. Spud Davis	.308
88. Richie Ashburn	.308
89. Jake Beckley	.308
90. Stuffy McInnis	.308
91. Joe Vosmik	.307
92. King Kelly	.307
93. Frank Baker	.307
94. George Burns	.307
95. Matty Alou	.307
96. Hack Wilson	.307
97. Chick Stahl	.307
98. Johnny Pesky	.307
99. George Kell	.306
100. Cupid Childs	.306
101. Dixie Walker	.306
102. Ernie Lombardi	.306
103. Ralph Garr	.306
104. Pete Rose	.305
105. Hank Aaron	.305
106. Al Oliver	.305
107. Cecil Cooper	.305
108. Billy Herman	.304
109. Tony Oliva	.304
110. Mel Ott	.304
111. Curt Walker	.304
112. Deacon White	.303
113. Cy Seymour	.303
114. Charlie Jamieson	.303
115. Jake Daubert	.303
116. Henry Larkin	.303
117. Buck Ewing	.303
118. Steve Brodie	.303
119. Dave Parker	.303
120. Buddy Myer	.303
121. Harvey Kuenn	.303
122. Jim Rice	.303
123. Hal Trosky	.302
124. Ed McKean	.302
125. George Grantham	.302
126. Ben Chapman	.302
127. Carl Reynolds	.302
128. Tommy Holmes	.302
129. Ken Griffey	.302
130. Willie Mays	.302
131. Joe Cronin	.301
132. Stan Hack	.301
133. Jack Doyle	.301
134. Oyster Burns	.301
135. George Gore	.301
136. Paul Hines	.301
137. Harry Stovey	.301
138. Keith Hernandez	.300
139. Wally Berger	.300
140. Patsy Donovan	.300
141. Ethan Allen	.300
142. Enos Slaughter	.300
143. Earl Sheely	.300
144. Billy Goodman	.300

SLUGGING AVERAGE

1. Babe Ruth	.690
2. Ted Williams	.634
3. Lou Gehrig	.632
4. Jimmie Foxx	.609
5. Hank Greenberg	.605
6. Joe DiMaggio	.579
7. Rogers Hornsby	.577
8. Johnny Mize	.562
9. Stan Musial	.559
10. Willie Mays	.557
11. Mickey Mantle	.557
12. Hank Aaron	.557
13. Ralph Kiner	.548
14. Hack Wilson	.545
15. Chuck Klein	.543
16. Duke Snider	.540
17. Frank Robinson	.537
18. Mike Schmidt	.535
19. Al Simmons	.535
20. Richie Allen	.534
21. Earl Averill	.533
22. Mel Ott	.533
23. Babe Herman	.532
24. Ken Williams	.531
25. Willie Stargell	.529
26. Chick Hafey	.526
27. Jim Rice	.524
28. Hal Trosky	.522
29. Wally Berger	.522
30. Harry Heilmann	.520
31. Dan Brouthers	.520
32. Joe Jackson	.518
33. Willie McCovey	.515
34. Ty Cobb	.513
35. Eddie Mathews	.509
36. Jeff Heath	.509
37. Harmon Killebrew	.509
38. Eddie Murray	.507
39. Bob Johnson	.506
40. Bill Terry	.506
41. Sam Thompson	.505
42. Joe Medwick	.505
43. Ed Delahanty	.504
44. Jim Bottomley	.500
45. Tris Speaker	.500
46. Fred Lynn	.500
47. Goose Goslin	.500
48. Roy Campanella	.500
48. George Brett	.500
50. Ernie Banks	.500

TOTAL BASES

1. Hank Aaron	6856
2. Stan Musial	6134
3. Willie Mays	6066
4. Ty Cobb	5863
5. Babe Ruth	5793
6. Pete Rose	5559
7. Carl Yastrzemski	5539
8. Frank Robinson	5373
9. Tris Speaker	5105
10. Lou Gehrig	5059
11. Mel Ott	5041
12. Jimmie Foxx	4956
13. Honus Wagner	4888
14. Ted Williams	4884
15. Al Kaline	4852
16. Rogers Hornsby	4712
17. Ernie Banks	4706
18. Al Simmons	4685
19. Billy Williams	4599
20. Mickey Mantle	4511
21. Roberto Clemente	4492
22. Paul Waner	4471
22. Nap Lajoie	4471
24. Tony Perez	4375
25. Eddie Mathews	4349
26. Sam Crawford	4336
27. Goose Goslin	4325
28. Reggie Jackson	4304
29. Brooks Robinson	4270
30. Vada Pinson	4264
31. Eddie Collins	4263
32. Charlie Gehringer	4257
33. Lou Brock	4238
34. Willie McCovey	4219
35. Willie Stargell	4190
36. Rusty Staub	4167
37. Jake Beckley	4158
38. Harmon Killebrew	4143
39. Cap Anson	4109
40. Zack Wheat	4100
41. Harry Heilmann	4053

GAMES

1. Pete Rose	3371
2. Carl Yastrzemski	3308
3. Hank Aaron	3298
4. Ty Cobb	3034
5. Stan Musial	3026
6. Willie Mays	2992
7. Rusty Staub	2897
8. Brooks Robinson	2896
9. Al Kaline	2834
10. Eddie Collins	2826
11. Frank Robinson	2808
12. Tris Speaker	2789
13. Honus Wagner	2786
14. Mel Ott	2732
15. Rabbit Maranville	2670
16. Joe Morgan	2650
17. Tony Perez	2628
18. Lou Brock	2616
19. Luis Aparicio	2599
20. Willie McCovey	2588
21. Paul Waner	2549
22. Ernie Banks	2528
23. Sam Crawford	2517
24. Babe Ruth	2503
25. Billy Williams	2488
26. Max Carey	2476
27. Nap Lajoie	2475
28. Vada Pinson	2469
29. Bill Dahlen	2443
30. Ron Fairly	2442
31. Harmon Killebrew	2435
32. Roberto Clemente	2433
33. Reggie Jackson	2430
34. Willie Davis	2429
35. Luke Appling	2422
36. Zack Wheat	2410
37. Mickey Vernon	2409
38. Sam Rice	2404
39. Mickey Mantle	2401

40. Eddie Mathews	2388
41. Jake Beckley	2386
41. Bobby Wallace	2386
43. Enos Slaughter	2380
44. George Davis	2377
45. Nellie Fox	2367
46. Willie Stargell	2360
47. Rod Carew	2342
48. Bert Campaneris	2328
49. Charlie Gehringer	2323
50. Jimmie Foxx	2317
51. Frankie Frisch	2311
52. Harry Hooper	2308
53. Ted Williams	2292
54. Goose Goslin	2287
55. Jimmy Dykes	2282
56. Cap Anson	2276
57. Lave Cross	2275
58. Al Oliver	2272
59. Rogers Hornsby	2259
60. Fred Clarke	2245
60. Graig Nettles	2245
62. Ron Santo	2243
63. Doc Cramer	2239
64. Red Schoendienst	2216
65. Al Simmons	2215
66. Joe Torre	2209
67. Tommy Corcoran	2201
68. Tony Taylor	2195
69. Richie Ashburn	2189
70. Joe Judge	2170
71. Pee Wee Reese	2166
72. Lou Gehrig	2164
72. Charlie Grimm	2164
74. Bill Mazeroski	2163
75. Larry Bowa	2161
76. Johnny Bench	2158
77. Tommy Leach	2155
78. Harry Heilmann	2146
79. Duke Snider	2143
80. Bid McPhee	2138
81. Stuffy McInnis	2128
82. Orlando Cepeda	2124
82. Joe Cronin	2124
82. Willie Keeler	2124
85. Jimmy Sheckard	2121
86. Yogi Berra	2120
87. Eddie Yost	2109
88. Joe Kuhel	2105
89. Roy McMillan	2093
90. Norm Cash	2089
91. Ted Simmons	2086
92. Sherry Magee	2085
93. Ed Konetchy	2083
94. Felipe Alou	2082
94. Ken Singleton	2082
96. Don Kessinger	2078
97. Jesse Burkett	2072
98. Gil Hodges	2071
98. Lee May	2071
100. George Sisler	2055
100. Dave Concepcion	2055
102. Boog Powell	2042
103. Ken Boyer	2034
103. George Scott	2034
105. Phil Cavarretta	2030
106. Willie Horton	2028
107. Sal Bando	2019
108. Jose Cardenal	2017
108. Aurelio Rodriguez	2017
110. Dick Bartell	2016
110. Mark Belanger	2016
112. Jake Daubert	2014
113. Wally Moses	2012
113. Roger Peckinpaugh	2012
113. Jimmy Ryan	2012
116. Heinie Manush	2009
117. Cy Williams	2002
118. Bill Russell	2000

AT BATS

1. Pete Rose	13411
2. Hank Aaron	12364
3. Carl Yastrzemski	11988
4. Ty Cobb	11429
5. Stan Musial	10972
6. Willie Mays	10881
7. Brooks Robinson	10654
8. Honus Wagner	10427
9. Lou Brock	10332
10. Luis Aparicio	10230
11. Tris Speaker	10208
12. Al Kaline	10116
13. Rabbit Maranville	10078

14. Frank Robinson	10006
15. Eddie Collins	9949
16. Rusty Staub	9675
17. Vada Pinson	9645
18. Nap Lajoie	9589
19. Sam Crawford	9580
20. Jake Beckley	9527
21. Paul Waner	9459
22. Mel Ott	9456
23. Roberto Clemente	9454
24. Ernie Banks	9421
25. Tony Perez	9395
26. Max Carey	9363
27. Billy Williams	9350
28. Joe Morgan	9281
29. Sam Rice	9269
30. Nellie Fox	9232
31. Willie Davis	9174
32. Doc Cramer	9140
33. Frankie Frisch	9112
34. Cap Anson	9108
35. Zack Wheat	9106
36. Lave Cross	9064
37. George Davis	9060
38. Bill Dahlen	9046

HITS

1. Ty Cobb	4191
2. Pete Rose	4097
3. Hank Aaron	3771
4. Stan Musial	3630
5. Tris Speaker	3515
6. Honus Wagner	3430
7. Carl Yastrzemski	3419
8. Eddie Collins	3311
9. Willie Mays	3283
10. Nap Lajoie	3251
11. Paul Waner	3152
12. Cap Anson	3041
13. Lou Brock	3023
14. Al Kaline	3007
15. Roberto Clemente	3000
16. Sam Rice	2987
17. Sam Crawford	2964
18. Willie Keeler	2962
19. Frank Robinson	2943
20. Jake Beckley	2931
21. Rogers Hornsby	2930
22. Rod Carew	2929
23. Al Simmons	2927
24. Zack Wheat	2884
25. Frankie Frisch	2880
26. Mel Ott	2876
27. Babe Ruth	2873
27. Jesse Burkett	2873
29. Brooks Robinson	2848
30. Charlie Gehringer	2839
31. George Sisler	2812
32. Vada Pinson	2757
33. Luke Appling	2749
34. Goose Goslin	2735
35. Lou Gehrig	2721
36. Billy Williams	2711
37. Fred Clarke	2708
38. Doc Cramer	2705
39. Rusty Staub	2704
40. George Davis	2688
41. Luis Aparicio	2677
42. Al Oliver	2676
43. Max Carey	2665
44. Nellie Fox	2663
45. Harry Heilmann	2660
46. Ted Williams	2654
47. Jimmie Foxx	2646
48. Lave Cross	2644
49. Tony Perez	2621
50. Rabbit Maranville	2605
51. Ed Delahanty	2591
52. Ernie Banks	2583
53. Richie Ashburn	2574
54. Willie Davis	2561
55. George Van Haltren	2536
56. Jimmy Ryan	2529
57. Heinie Manush	2524
58. Joe Morgan	2518
59. Mickey Vernon	2495
60. Bill Dahlen	2482
61. Roger Connor	2480
62. Joe Medwick	2471
63. Harry Hooper	2466
64. Lloyd Waner	2459
65. Red Schoendienst	2449
66. Pie Traynor	2416
67. Mickey Mantle	2415

68. Stuffy McInnis	2406
69. Enos Slaughter	2383
70. Edd Roush	2376
71. Orlando Cepeda	2351
72. Joe Judge	2350
73. Billy Herman	2345
74. Joe Torre	2342
75. Jake Daubert	2326
76. Eddie Mathews	2315
77. Hugh Duffy	2314
77. Bobby Wallace	2314
79. Jim Bottomley	2313
80. Dan Brouthers	2304
80. Jim O'Rourke	2304
82. Kiki Cuyler	2299
82. Charlie Grimm	2299
84. Reggie Jackson	2293
85. Bid McPhee	2291
86. Joe Cronin	2285
87. Tommy Corcoran	2264
88. Steve Garvey	2257
89. Jimmy Dykes	2256
90. Ron Santo	2254
91. Patsy Donovan	2249
91. Bert Campaneris	2249
93. Joe Kelley	2242
94. Fred Tenney	2239
95. Willie Stargell	2232
96. Joe Sewell	2226
96. Ted Simmons	2226
98. Joe DiMaggio	2214
99. Joe Kuhel	2212
100. Willie McCovey	2211
101. Bill Terry	2193
101. Stan Hack	2193
103. Pee Wee Reese	2170
104. Sherry Magee	2169
105. Dick Bartell	2165
106. Billy Hamilton	2163
107. Hal Chase	2158
108. Yogi Berra	2150
109. Ed Konetchy	2148
110. Herman Long	2145
111. Tommy Leach	2144
112. Ken Boyer	2143
113. Larry Bowa	2141
114. Wally Moses	2138
114. Dick Groat	2138
116. Maury Wills	2134
117. Buddy Myer	2131
118. Monte Ward	2123
119. Tommy Davis	2121
120. Duke Snider	2116
121. Arky Vaughan	2103
122. Felipe Alou	2101
123. Clyde Milan	2100
124. Bill Buckner	2095
124. Jimmy Sheckard	2095
126. Harvey Kuenn	2092
127. Alvin Dark	2089
128. Harmon Killebrew	2086
129. Ed McKean	2083
130. George Burns	2077
131. Chuck Klein	2076
132. Bobby Veach	2064
132. Dixie Walker	2064
134. Del Ennis	2063
135. Bob Elliott	2061
136. George Kell	2054
136. Dummy Hoy	2054
138. Bob Johnson	2051
139. Johnny Bench	2048
140. Bobby Doerr	2042
141. Jack Glasscock	2040
142. Chris Chambliss	2031
142. Lee May	2031
144. Ken Singleton	2029
145. Earl Averill	2020
145. Reggie Smith	2020
145. Amos Otis	2020
148. George Burns	2018
149. Bill Mazeroski	2016
150. Johnny Mize	2011
151. Tony Taylor	2007
152. Dave Bancroft	2004

DOUBLES

1. Tris Speaker	793
2. Pete Rose	726
3. Stan Musial	725
4. Ty Cobb	724
5. Honus Wagner	651
6. Nap Lajoie	648
7. Carl Yastrzemski	646

8. Hank Aaron	624
9. Paul Waner	603
10. Charlie Gehringer	574
11. Harry Heilmann	542
12. Rogers Hornsby	541
13. Joe Medwick	540
14. Al Simmons	539
15. Lou Gehrig	535
16. Cap Anson	532
17. Frank Robinson	528
18. Ted Williams	525
19. Willie Mays	523
20. Ed Delahanty	521
21. Al Oliver	518
22. Joe Cronin	515
23. Babe Ruth	506
24. Goose Goslin	500
25. Al Kaline	498
26. Sam Rice	497
27. Rusty Staub	496
28. Heinie Manush	491
29. Mickey Vernon	490
30. Mel Ott	488
31. Billy Herman	486
31. Lou Brock	486
33. Tony Perez	485
33. Vada Pinson	485
35. Brooks Robinson	482
36. Zack Wheat	476
37. Jake Beckley	475
38. Frankie Frisch	466
39. Jim Bottomley	465
40. Dan Brouthers	461
41. Jimmie Foxx	458
42. Sam Crawford	457
43. George Davis	454
44. Jimmy Dykes	453
45. Jimmy Ryan	451
46. Joe Morgan	449
47. Hal McRae	448
48. George Burns	444
49. Dick Bartell	442
49. Roger Connor	442
51. Luke Appling	440
51. Roberto Clemente	440
53. Eddie Collins	437
54. Joe Sewell	436
54. Ted Simmons	436
56. Wally Moses	435
57. Billy Williams	434
58. Joe Judge	433
59. Rod Carew	428
60. Red Schoendienst	427
61. Sherry Magee	425
61. George Sisler	425
63. Willie Stargell	423
64. Max Carey	419
65. Cesar Cedeno	418
66. Orlando Cepeda	417
67. Bill Dahlen	416
68. Jim O'Rourke	414
69. Enos Slaughter	413
70. Joe Kuhel	412
71. Lave Cross	411
72. Reggie Jackson	410
73. Ben Chapman	407
73. Ernie Banks	407
75. Earl Averill	401
75. Marty McManus	401

TRIPLES

1. Sam Crawford	312
2. Ty Cobb	297
3. Honus Wagner	252
4. Jake Beckley	244
5. Roger Connor	233
6. Fred Clarke	223
6. Tris Speaker	223
8. Dan Brouthers	206
9. Joe Kelley	194
10. Paul Waner	190
11. Bid McPhee	189
12. Eddie Collins	187
13. Harry Stovey	185
13. Jesse Burkett	185
15. Sam Rice	184
16. Ed Delahanty	183
17. Edd Roush	182
18. Ed Konetchy	181
19. Buck Ewing	178
20. Rabbit Maranville	177
20. Stan Musial	177
22. Goose Goslin	173
23. Tommy Leach	172

23. Zack Wheat	172
25. Elmer Flick	170
26. Rogers Hornsby	169
27. Joe Jackson	168
28. Sherry Magee	166
28. George Davis	166
28. Roberto Clemente	166
31. Jake Daubert	165
31. George Sisler	165
33. Pie Traynor	164
34. Bill Dahlen	163
34. Nap Lajoie	163
36. Mike Tiernan	162
36. Lou Gehrig	162
36. George Van Haltren	162
39. Sam Thompson	160
39. Heinie Manush	160
39. Harry Hooper	160
42. Joe Judge	159
42. Max Carey	159
44. Ed McKean	158
45. Kiki Cuyler	157
45. Jimmy Ryan	157
47. Tommy Corcoran	155
48. Earle Combs	154
49. Willie Keeler	153
49. Bobby Wallace	153
51. Jim Bottomley	151
51. Harry Heilmann	151

HOME RUNS

1. Hank Aaron	755
2. Babe Ruth	714
3. Willie Mays	660
4. Frank Robinson	586
5. Harmon Killebrew	573
6. Mickey Mantle	536
7. Jimmie Foxx	534
8. Ted Williams	521
8. Willie McCovey	521
10. Eddie Mathews	512
10. Ernie Banks	512
12. Mel Ott	511
13. Reggie Jackson	503
14. Lou Gehrig	493
15. Willie Stargell	475
15. Stan Musial	475
17. Carl Yastrzemski	452
18. Billy Williams	426
19. Mike Schmidt	425
20. Duke Snider	407
21. Al Kaline	399
22. Johnny Bench	389
23. Frank Howard	382
24. Orlando Cepeda	379
25. Dave Kingman	377
25. Norm Cash	377
27. Rocky Colavito	374
28. Tony Perez	371
29. Gil Hodges	370
30. Ralph Kiner	369
31. Joe DiMaggio	361
32. Johnny Mize	359
33. Yogi Berra	358
34. Lee May	354
35. Graig Nettles	353
36. Richie Allen	351
37. Ron Santo	342
38. Boog Powell	339
39. Joe Adcock	336
40. Bobby Bonds	332
41. Hank Greenberg	331
42. Willie Horton	325
43. Roy Sievers	318
44. Reggie Smith	314
45. George Foster	313
46. Greg Luzinski	307
46. Al Simmons	307
48. Jim Rice	304
49. Rogers Hornsby	301
50. Chuck Klein	300

HOME RUN PERCENTAGE

1. Babe Ruth	8.5
2. Ralph Kiner	7.1
3. Harmon Killebrew	7.0
4. Mike Schmidt	6.9
5. Dave Kingman	6.8
6. Ted Williams	6.8
7. Mickey Mantle	6.6
8. Jimmie Foxx	6.6

9. Hank Greenberg	6.4
10. Willie McCovey	6.4
11. Lou Gehrig	6.2
12. Hank Aaron	6.1
13. Willie Mays	6.1
14. Hank Sauer	6.0
15. Eddie Mathews	6.0
16. Willie Stargell	6.0
17. Frank Howard	5.9
18. Frank Robinson	5.9
19. Reggie Jackson	5.8
20. Roy Campanella	5.8
21. Rocky Colavito	5.8
22. Gus Zernial	5.7
23. Duke Snider	5.7
24. Norm Cash	5.6
25. Johnny Mize	5.6
26. Richie Allen	5.5
27. Ernie Banks	5.4
28. Mel Ott	5.4
29. Roger Maris	5.4
30. Joe DiMaggio	5.3
31. Gil Hodges	5.3
32. Wally Post	5.2
33. Hack Wilson	5.1
34. Jim Rice	5.1
35. Bob Allison	5.1

EXTRA BASE HITS

1. Hank Aaron	1477
2. Stan Musial	1377
3. Babe Ruth	1356
4. Willie Mays	1323
5. Lou Gehrig	1190
6. Frank Robinson	1186
7. Carl Yastrzemski	1157
8. Ty Cobb	1139
9. Tris Speaker	1133
10. Ted Williams	1117
10. Jimmie Foxx	1117
12. Mel Ott	1071
13. Pete Rose	1015
14. Rogers Hornsby	1011
15. Ernie Banks	1009
16. Honus Wagner	1004
17. Al Simmons	995
18. Al Kaline	972
19. Reggie Jackson	959
20. Willie Stargell	953
21. Mickey Mantle	952
22. Billy Williams	948
23. Eddie Mathews	938
24. Tony Perez	934
25. Goose Goslin	921
26. Willie McCovey	920
27. Paul Waner	905
28. Charlie Gehringer	904
29. Nap Lajoie	893
30. Harmon Killebrew	887
31. Joe DiMaggio	881
32. Harry Heilmann	876
33. Vada Pinson	868
34. Sam Crawford	866
35. Joe Medwick	858
36. Duke Snider	850
37. Roberto Clemente	846
38. Jim Bottomley	835
39. Rusty Staub	834
40. Orlando Cepeda	823
41. Brooks Robinson	818
42. Joe Morgan	813
43. Roger Connor	811
44. Johnny Mize	809
45. Al Oliver	808
46. Jake Beckley	807
47. Ed Delahanty	804
48. Joe Cronin	803

RUNS BATTED IN

1. Hank Aaron	2297
2. Babe Ruth	2211
3. Lou Gehrig	1990
4. Ty Cobb	1961
5. Stan Musial	1951
6. Jimmie Foxx	1921
7. Willie Mays	1903
8. Mel Ott	1860
9. Carl Yastrzemski	1844
10. Ted Williams	1839
11. Al Simmons	1827
12. Frank Robinson	1812

13. Honus Wagner	1732
14. Cap Anson	1715
15. Ernie Banks	1636
16. Goose Goslin	1609
17. Nap Lajoie	1599
18. Tony Perez	1590
19. Rogers Hornsby	1584
19. Harmon Killebrew	1584
21. Al Kaline	1583
22. Jake Beckley	1575
23. Tris Speaker	1559
24. Willie McCovey	1555
25. Harry Heilmann	1551
26. Willie Stargell	1540
27. Joe DiMaggio	1537
28. Sam Crawford	1525
29. Reggie Jackson	1516
30. Mickey Mantle	1509
31. Billy Williams	1475
32. Ed Delahanty	1464
33. Rusty Staub	1458
34. Eddie Mathews	1453
35. George Davis	1435
36. Yogi Berra	1430
37. Charlie Gehringer	1427
38. Joe Cronin	1424
39. Jim Bottomley	1422
40. Joe Medwick	1383
41. Johnny Bench	1376
42. Orlando Cepeda	1365
43. Brooks Robinson	1357
44. Lave Cross	1345
45. Johnny Mize	1337
46. Duke Snider	1333
47. Ron Santo	1331
48. Mickey Vernon	1311
49. Paul Waner	1309
50. Roberto Clemente	1305
51. Enos Slaughter	1304
52. Sam Thompson	1299
52. Hugh Duffy	1299
52. Eddie Collins	1299
55. Al Oliver	1295
56. Del Ennis	1284
57. Bob Johnson	1283
58. Hank Greenberg	1276
59. Gil Hodges	1274
60. Pie Traynor	1273
61. Zack Wheat	1261
62. Bobby Doerr	1247
62. Ted Simmons	1247
64. Lee May	1244
64. Frankie Frisch	1244
66. Pete Rose	1243
67. Bill Dahlen	1233
68. Bill Dickey	1209
69. Chuck Klein	1201
70. Bob Elliott	1195
71. Joe Kelley	1193
72. Tony Lazzeri	1191
73. Boog Powell	1187
74. Joe Torre	1185
75. Sherry Magee	1182
76. Mike Schmidt	1180
77. Gabby Hartnett	1179
78. Vic Wertz	1178
79. George Sisler	1175
80. Vern Stephens	1174
81. Heinie Manush	1173
82. Vada Pinson	1170
83. Bobby Veach	1166
84. Earl Averill	1165
85. Willie Horton	1163
86. Rocky Colavito	1159
87. Rudy York	1152
88. Graig Nettles	1151
89. Roy Sievers	1147
90. Ken Boyer	1141
91. Steve Garvey	1137
92. Tommy Corcoran	1135
93. Joe Morgan	1134
94. Greg Luzinski	1128
95. Joe Adcock	1122
96. Bobby Wallace	1121
97. George Foster	1120
98. Richie Allen	1119
98. Frank Howard	1119
100. Luke Appling	1116
101. Norm Cash	1103
102. Jimmy Ryan	1093
103. Reggie Smith	1092
104. Bill Terry	1078
104. Roger Connor	1078
104. Charlie Grimm	1078
104. Sam Rice	1078
108. Jim Rice	1076
109. Pinky Higgins	1075

110. Jimmy Dykes	1071
111. Ed McKean	1070
112. Bob Meusel	1067
113. Kiki Cuyler	1065
113. Ken Singleton	1065
115. Hack Wilson	1062
116. Stuffy McInnis	1060
117. Carl Furillo	1058
118. Dan Brouthers	1056
119. Willie Davis	1053
120. Herman Long	1052
120. Tommy Davis	1052
122. Joe Sewell	1051
122. George Scott	1051
124. Joe Kuhel	1049
125. Ron Fairly	1044
126. Bobby Murcer	1043
127. Sal Bando	1039
128. Joe Judge	1037
129. Ron Cey	1029
130. Ted Kluszewski	1028
131. Bobby Thomson	1026
132. Dave Kingman	1025
133. Bobby Bonds	1024
134. Minnie Minoso	1023
134. Dixie Walker	1023
136. George Kelly	1020
137. Dave Winfield	1016
138. Ralph Kiner	1015
138. Fred Clarke	1015
140. George Van Haltren	1014
141. Frank Baker	1013
142. Hal Trosky	1012
143. Amos Otis	1007
144. Cy Williams	1005

RBI PER GAME

1. Sam Thompson	.92
2. Lou Gehrig	.92
3. Hank Greenberg	.92
4. Joe DiMaggio	.89
5. Babe Ruth	.88
6. Jimmie Foxx	.83
7. Al Simmons	.82
8. Ted Williams	.80
9. Ed Delahanty	.80
10. Hack Wilson	.79
11. Bob Meusel	.76
12. Cap Anson	.75
13. Hal Trosky	.75
14. Hugh Duffy	.75
15. Harry Heilmann	.72
16. Jim Rice	.72
17. Rudy York	.72
18. Jim Bottomley	.71
19. Johnny Mize	.71
20. Roy Campanella	.70
21. Goose Goslin	.70
22. Rogers Hornsby	.70
23. Earl Averill	.70
24. Joe Medwick	.70
25. Hank Aaron	.70
26. Ralph Kiner	.69
27. Bob Johnson	.69
28. Chuck Klein	.69
29. Tony Lazzeri	.68
30. Vern Stephens	.68
31. Mel Ott	.68
32. Bill Dickey	.68
33. Del Ennis	.67
34. Yogi Berra	.67
35. Joe Cronin	.67

RUNS

1. Ty Cobb	2245
2. Babe Ruth	2174
2. Hank Aaron	2174
4. Pete Rose	2090
5. Willie Mays	2062
6. Stan Musial	1949
7. Lou Gehrig	1888
8. Tris Speaker	1881
9. Mel Ott	1859
10. Frank Robinson	1829
11. Eddie Collins	1818
12. Carl Yastrzemski	1816
13. Ted Williams	1798
14. Charlie Gehringer	1774
15. Jimmie Foxx	1751
16. Honus Wagner	1740
17. Willie Keeler	1722

18. Cap Anson	1719
19. Jesse Burkett	1713
20. Billy Hamilton	1692
21. Bid McPhee	1684
22. Mickey Mantle	1677
23. Joe Morgan	1651
24. Jimmy Ryan	1643
25. George Van Haltren	1639
26. Fred Clarke	1626
26. Paul Waner	1626
28. Al Kaline	1622
29. Roger Connor	1621
30. Bill Dahlen	1611
31. Lou Brock	1610
32. Jake Beckley	1600
33. Ed Delahanty	1599
34. Rogers Hornsby	1579
35. Hugh Duffy	1553
36. Max Carey	1545
37. George Davis	1544
38. Frankie Frisch	1532
39. Dan Brouthers	1523
40. Tom Brown	1521
41. Sam Rice	1515
42. Eddie Mathews	1509
43. Al Simmons	1507
44. Nap Lajoie	1504
45. Harry Stovey	1494
46. Goose Goslin	1483
47. Arlie Latham	1478
48. Herman Long	1460
49. Jim O'Rourke	1446
50. Harry Hooper	1429
51. Dummy Hoy	1426
51. Joe Kelley	1426
53. Roberto Clemente	1416
54. Billy Williams	1410
55. Monte Ward	1408
56. Mike Griffin	1406
57. Sam Crawford	1393
58. Joe DiMaggio	1390
59. Reggie Jackson	1380
60. Vada Pinson	1366
61. King Kelly	1363
62. Doc Cramer	1357
63. Tommy Leach	1355
63. Rod Carew	1355
65. Pee Wee Reese	1338
66. Luis Aparicio	1335
67. Lave Cross	1333
68. George Gore	1327
69. Richie Ashburn	1322
70. Luke Appling	1319
71. Patsy Donovan	1318
72. Mike Tiernan	1313
73. Kiki Cuyler	1305
73. Ernie Banks	1305
75. Jimmy Sheckard	1296
76. Harry Heilmann	1291
77. Zack Wheat	1289
78. Heinie Manush	1287
79. George Sisler	1284
80. Harmon Killebrew	1283
81. Donie Bush	1280
82. Nellie Fox	1279
83. Fred Tenney	1278
84. Sam Thompson	1263
85. Duke Snider	1259
86. Bobby Bonds	1258
87. Rabbit Maranville	1255
88. Enos Slaughter	1247
89. Bob Johnson	1239
89. Stan Hack	1239
91. Joe Kuhel	1236
92. Joe Cronin	1233
92. Tony Perez	1233
94. Brooks Robinson	1232
95. Willie McCovey	1229
96. Ed McKean	1227
97. Earl Averill	1224
98. Red Schoendienst	1223
99. Cupid Childs	1218
100. Willie Davis	1217
101. Eddie Yost	1215
102. Lloyd Waner	1201
103. Joe Medwick	1198
104. Mickey Vernon	1196
105. Willie Stargell	1195
106. George Burns	1188
106. Tommy Corcoran	1188
108. Rusty Staub	1187
109. Earle Combs	1186
110. Fielder Jones	1184
110. Joe Judge	1184
112. Pie Traynor	1183
113. Bert Campaneris	1181
114. Jim Bottomley	1177

115. Yogi Berra	1175
116. Buddy Myer	1174
117. Arky Vaughan	1173
118. Chuck Klein	1168
118. Al Oliver	1168
120. Jack Glasscock	1163
120. Billy Herman	1163
120. Jim Gilliam	1163
123. Mike Schmidt	1161
124. Lu Blue	1151
125. Ben Chapman	1144
126. Joe Sewell	1141
127. Ron Santo	1138
128. Minnie Minoso	1136
129. Bobby Lowe	1135
130. Orlando Cepeda	1131
131. Dick Bartell	1130
132. Buck Ewing	1129
133. Reggie Smith	1123
134. Hardy Richardson	1120
134. Bill Terry	1120
136. Johnny Mize	1118
137. Jake Daubert	1117
138. Wally Moses	1114
139. Sherry Magee	1112
140. Jimmy Dykes	1108
141. Jimmy Wynn	1105
141. Gil Hodges	1105
143. Ken Boyer	1104
144. Richie Allen	1099
144. Edd Roush	1099
146. Fred Pfeffer	1094
146. Bobby Doerr	1094
148. Amos Otis	1092
149. Johnny Bench	1091
150. Tommy Tucker	1084
151. Paul Hines	1083
152. Billy Nash	1072
153. Harland Clift	1070
153. Graig Nettles	1070
155. Tommy McCarthy	1069
156. Maury Wills	1067
157. Kip Selbach	1064
157. Alvin Dark	1064
157. Bob Elliott	1064
160. Charlie Jamieson	1062
161. Bobby Wallace	1057
162. Jimmy Collins	1055
163. Hank Greenberg	1051
164. Dave Bancroft	1048
165. Dom DiMaggio	1046
165. Norm Cash	1046
167. Mickey Cochrane	1041
167. Cesar Cedeno	1041
169. Dixie Walker	1037
170. John McGraw	1026
171. Tom Daly	1024
171. Cy Williams	1024
173. Kid Gleason	1020
174. Darrell Evans	1016
175. Toby Harrah	1014
176. Roy Thomas	1013
177. Marty McManus	1008
178. Frankie Crosetti	1006
178. Roger Peckinpaugh	1006
180. Tony Taylor	1005
181. Augie Galan	1004
181. Clyde Milan	1004
183. Vern Stephens	1001
184. Steve Garvey	1000

RUNS PER 9 INNINGS

1. Billy Hamilton	1.06
2. George Gore	1.01
3. Harry Stovey	1.00
4. King Kelly	.93
5. Mike Griffin	.93
6. Dan Brouthers	.91
7. Arlie Latham	.91
8. Sam Thompson	.90
9. Hugh Duffy	.89
10. Mike Tiernan	.89
11. Lou Gehrig	.87
12. Ed Delahanty	.87
13. Babe Ruth	.87
14. Buck Ewing	.86
15. Abner Dalrymple	.85
16. Tom Brown	.85
17. Hardy Richardson	.84
18. Tommy McCarthy	.84
19. Tip O'Neill	.83
20. Denny Lyons	.83
21. Cupid Childs	.83
22. Jesse Burkett	.83

23. Curt Welch	.83
24. George Van Haltren	.83
25. Jimmy Ryan	.82
26. Earle Combs	.82
27. Jim O'Rourke	.82
28. Roger Connor	.81
29. Willie Keeler	.81
30. Pete Browning	.81
31. Red Rolfe	.80
32. Joe DiMaggio	.80
33. Dummy Hoy	.79
34. Bid McPhee	.79
35. Long John Reilly	.79

BASES ON BALLS

1. Babe Ruth	2056
2. Ted Williams	2019
3. Joe Morgan	1865
4. Carl Yastrzemski	1845
5. Mickey Mantle	1734
6. Mel Ott	1708
7. Eddie Yost	1614
8. Stan Musial	1599
9. Harmon Killebrew	1559
10. Lou Gehrig	1508
11. Eddie Collins	1503
12. Willie Mays	1463
13. Jimmie Foxx	1452
14. Pete Rose	1450
15. Eddie Mathews	1444
16. Frank Robinson	1420
17. Hank Aaron	1402
18. Tris Speaker	1381
19. Willie McCovey	1345
20. Luke Appling	1302
21. Al Kaline	1277
22. Ken Singleton	1263
23. Ty Cobb	1249
24. Rusty Staub	1245
25. Jimmy Wynn	1224
26. Pee Wee Reese	1210
27. Darrell Evans	1204
28. Richie Ashburn	1198
29. Billy Hamilton	1187
30. Charlie Gehringer	1185
31. Mike Schmidt	1178
32. Reggie Jackson	1172
33. Donie Bush	1158
34. Max Bishop	1153
35. Harry Hooper	1136
36. Jimmy Sheckard	1135
37. Ron Santo	1108
38. Lu Blue	1092
38. Stan Hack	1092
40. Paul Waner	1091
41. Bob Johnson	1073
42. Harland Clift	1070
43. Bill Dahlen	1064
44. Joe Cronin	1059
45. Ron Fairly	1052
46. Billy Williams	1045
47. Norm Cash	1043
48. Roy Thomas	1042
49. Eddie Joost	1041
50. Max Carey	1040
51. Rogers Hornsby	1038
52. Jim Gilliam	1036
53. Sal Bando	1031
54. Jesse Burkett	1029
55. Enos Slaughter	1019
56. Ralph Kiner	1011
57. Dummy Hoy	1004
58. Miller Huggins	1002
58. Roger Connor	1002
60. Boog Powell	1001

BB AVERAGE

1. Ted Williams	.208
2. Max Bishop	.204
3. Babe Ruth	.197
4. Eddie Stanky	.188
5. Gene Tenace	.183
6. Eddie Yost	.180
7. Mickey Mantle	.176
8. Joe Morgan	.167
9. Earl Torgeson	.165
10. Roy Thomas	.164
11. Ralph Kiner	.163
12. Harmon Killebrew	.161
13. Mike Schmidt	.160
14. Billy Hamilton	.159

15. Lou Gehrig	.159
16. Elmer Valo	.158
17. Harlond Clift	.157
18. Eddie Joost	.157
19. Lu Blue	.156
20. Jimmy Wynn	.155
21. Mel Ott	.153
22. Miller Huggins	.153
23. Jimmie Foxx	.151
24. Darrell Evans	.151
25. Dolf Camilli	.150
26. Ken Singleton	.149
27. Cupid Childs	.149
28. Mike Hargrove	.149
29. Elbie Fletcher	.149
30. Andre Thornton	.148
31. Topsy Hartsel	.147
32. Eddie Mathews	.145
33. Mickey Cochrane	.142
34. Augie Galan	.142
35. Gene Woodling	.141

STOLEN BASES

1. Lou Brock	938
2. Ty Cobb	892
3. Eddie Collins	743
4. Max Carey	738
5. Honus Wagner	703
6. Joe Morgan	689
7. Bert Campaneris	649
8. Maury Wills	586
9. Cesar Cedeno	535
10. Luis Aparicio	506
11. Clyde Milan	495
12. Rickey Henderson	493
13. Davey Lopes	483
14. Omar Moreno	469
15. Bobby Bonds	461
16. Jimmy Sheckard	460
17. Ron LeFlore	455
18. Sherry Magee	441
19. Tris Speaker	433
20. Bob Bescher	428
21. Frankie Frisch	419
22. Tommy Harper	408
23. Frank Chance	405
24. Donie Bush	403
25. Willie Davis	398
26. Billy North	395
27. Willie Wilson	393
28. Freddie Patek	385
29. George Burns	383
30. Sam Mertes	377
31. George Sisler	375
31. Harry Hooper	375
33. Nap Lajoie	367
34. Sam Crawford	366
35. Hal Chase	363
36. Tommy Leach	361
37. Sam Rice	351
38. Fred Clarke	350
39. George Case	349
40. Rod Carew	348
41. Amos Otis	341
42. Willie Mays	338
43. Joe Tinker	336
44. Elmer Flick	334
45. Jose Cardenal	329
46. Julio Cruz	328
46. Kiki Cuyler	328
48. Miller Huggins	324
48. Johnny Evers	324
50. Tim Raines	321
50. Red Murray	321
52. Hans Lobert	316
53. Dave Collins	313
53. Larry Bowa	313
55. Buck Herzog	312
56. Vada Pinson	305
57. Frank Taveras	300

PINCH HITS

1. Manny Mota	150
2. Smoky Burgess	145
3. Jose Morales	123
4. Jerry Lynch	116
5. Red Lucas	114
6. Terry Crowley	108
7. Gates Brown	107
8. Mike Lum	103
9. Steve Braun	102

10. Vic Davalillo	95
10. Larry Biittner	95
12. Dave Philley	93
13. Ed Kranepool	90
13. Elmer Valo	90
13. Jay Johnstone	90
16. Rusty Staub	89
17. Greg Gross	88
18. Jesus Alou	82
18. Tim McCarver	82
20. Dalton Jones	81
20. Tito Francona	81
22. Tom Hutton	79
23. Kurt Bevacqua	77
23. Enos Slaughter	77
25. Bob Fothergill	76
25. George Crowe	76
27. Jerry Turner	73
28. Ed Kirkpatrick	71
28. Jimmy Stewart	71
30. Bob Skinner	69
30. Mike Jorgensen	69
32. Champ Summers	68
32. Ron Fairly	68
34. Merv Rettenmund	66
34. Bob Johnson	66
34. Willie McCovey	66
34. Ernie Lombardi	66
34. Ken Boswell	66
39. Gene Woodling	65
40. Oscar Gamble	64
41. Tommy Davis	63
41. Tony Taylor	63
41. Julio Becquer	63
41. Jim King	63
45. Peanuts Lowrey	62
45. Bob Bailey	62
45. Vic Wertz	62
45. Bob Hale	62
49. Mike Vail	61
50. Cliff Johnson	60
50. Ty Cline	60
52. Ron Northey	59
52. Sam Leslie	59
52. Russ Nixon	59
52. Duke Snider	59
52. Clarence Gaston	59
52. Gene Clines	59
52. Jim Dwyer	59
59. Red Ruffing	58
60. Denny Walling	57
60. Jerry Hairston	57
60. Ham Hyatt	57
60. Wes Covington	57
60. Lee Maye	57
65. Red Schoendienst	56
65. Jose Pagan	56
65. Fred Whitfield	56
65. Lee Lacy	56
65. Charlie Maxwell	56
65. Walker Cooper	56
71. Billy Sullivan	55
71. Earl Torgeson	55
71. Bob Cerv	55
71. Len Gabrielson	55
71. John Lowenstein	55
71. Willie Stargell	55
71. Dusty Rhodes	55
71. Phil Gagliano	55
79. Frenchy Bordagaray	54
79. Debs Garms	54
79. Willie Smith	54
79. Del Unser	54
83. Johnny Mize	53
83. Ted Kluszewski	53
83. Lenny Green	53
86. Dane Iorg	52
86. Dom Dallessandro	52
86. Walt Williams	52
86. Irv Noren	52
86. Jim Wohlford	52
86. Larry Stahl	52
92. Harvey Hendrick	51
92. Glenn Adams	51
92. Pat Kelly	51
92. Dick Williams	51
92. John Milner	51
97. Jose Cardenal	50

PH BATTING AVERAGE

1. Tommy Davis	.320
2. Frenchy Bordagaray	.312
3. Frankie Baumholtz	.307
4. Red Schoendienst	.303
5. Bob Fothergill	.300
6. Dave Philley	.299
7. Rick Miller	.297
8. Manny Mota	.297
9. Ted Easterly	.296
10. Harvey Hendrick	.295
11. Manny Sanguillen	.288
11. Johnny Grubb	.288
13. Smoky Burgess	.286
14. Steve Braun	.286
15. Johnny Mize	.283
16. Rusty Staub	.282
17. Bubba Morton	.281
18. Don Mueller	.280
19. Mickey Vernon	.279
20. Gene Woodling	.278
21. Bobby Adams	.277
22. Oscar Gamble	.277
23. Ed Kranepool	.277
24. Tom Paciorek	.276
25. Jose Morales	.276
26. Ron Northey	.276
27. Glenn Adams	.276
28. Kurt Bevacqua	.274
29. Merv Rettenmund	.274
30. Dane Iorg	.274
31. Sam Leslie	.273
32. Pat Kelly	.273
32. Debs Garms	.273
34. Jesus Alou	.272
35. Bob Johnson	.272

FEWEST STRIKEOUTS PER AT BAT

1. Joe Sewell	.016
2. Willie Keeler	.019
3. Lloyd Waner	.022
4. Nellie Fox	.023
5. Tommy Holmes	.024
6. Lave Cross	.028
7. Tris Speaker	.028
8. Stuffy McInnis	.028
9. Andy High	.030
10. Sam Rice	.030
11. Doggie Miller	.030
12. Frankie Frisch	.030
13. Jack Glasscock	.031
14. Lou Bierbauer	.032
15. Edd Roush	.032
16. Charlie Comiskey	.033
17. Frank McCormick	.033
18. Don Mueller	.033
19. Cap Anson	.034
20. Billy Southworth	.034
21. Jack Tobin	.034
22. Rip Radcliff	.035
23. Dan Brouthers	.035
24. Ed McKean	.036
25. Jack McCarthy	.036
26. Pie Traynor	.037
27. Fielder Jones	.038
28. Patsy Donovan	.038
29. Doc Cramer	.038
30. Sam Thompson	.038
31. Carson Bigbee	.038
32. Cupid Childs	.039
33. Eddie Collins	.039
34. Steve Brodie	.039
35. Hank Severeid	.039

MOST STRIKEOUTS PER AT BAT

1. Dave Kingman	.285
2. Reggie Jackson	.260
3. Bobby Bonds	.249
4. Mike Schmidt	.249
5. Rick Monday	.247
6. Richie Allen	.246
7. Donn Clendenon	.245
8. Willie Stargell	.244
9. Woodie Held	.235
10. Greg Luzinski	.230
11. Gene Tenace	.227
12. Frank Howard	.225
13. Larry Hisle	.224
14. Deron Johnson	.222
15. Jimmy Wynn	.214

16. Mickey Mantle	.211
17. Harmon Killebrew	.209
18. Lee May	.206
19. Jeff Burroughs	.206
20. Bob Allison	.205
21. Doug Rader	.204
22. Wally Post	.203
23. George Foster	.202
24. Ron LeFlore	.199
25. Dick Green	.196
26. Tony Perez	.194
27. Dwight Evans	.193
28. George Scott	.191
29. John Briggs	.191
30. Willie McCovey	.189
31. Larry Doby	.189
32. Bobby Grich	.188
33. Bill Robinson	.188
34. Claudell Washington	.188
35. Sixto Lezcano	.187

STRIKEOUTS

1. Reggie Jackson	2247
2. Willie Stargell	1936
3. Tony Perez	1820
4. Bobby Bonds	1757
5. Lou Brock	1730
6. Mickey Mantle	1710
7. Harmon Killebrew	1699
8. Dave Kingman	1576
9. Lee May	1570
10. Richie Allen	1556
11. Willie McCovey	1550
12. Mike Schmidt	1543
13. Frank Robinson	1532
14. Willie Mays	1526
15. Rick Monday	1513
16. Greg Luzinski	1495
17. Eddie Mathews	1487
18. Frank Howard	1460
19. Jimmy Wynn	1427
20. George Scott	1418
21. Carl Yastrzemski	1393
22. Hank Aaron	1383
23. Ron Santo	1343
24. Babe Ruth	1330
25. Deron Johnson	1318
26. Willie Horton	1313
27. Jimmie Foxx	1311
28. Johnny Bench	1278
29. George Foster	1271
30. Ken Singleton	1246
31. Duke Snider	1237
32. Ernie Banks	1236
33. Roberto Clemente	1230
34. Boog Powell	1226
35. Vada Pinson	1196
36. Orlando Cepeda	1169
37. Bobby Grich	1147
38. Bert Campaneris	1142
39. Donn Clendenon	1140
40. Gil Hodges	1137
41. Leo Cardenas	1135
42. Bob Bailey	1126
43. Gorman Thomas	1108
44. Jeff Burroughs	1099
45. Jim Fregosi	1097
46. Joe Torre	1094
47. Norm Cash	1091
48. Tony Taylor	1083
49. Tommy Harper	1080
50. Pete Rose	1077
51. Dwight Evans	1067
52. Jim Rice	1065
53. Johnny Callison	1064
54. Joe Adcock	1059
55. Doug Rader	1057
56. Billy Williams	1046
57. Graig Nettles	1044
58. Bob Allison	1033
59. Ron Cey	1031
60. Reggie Smith	1030
61. Dave Concepcion	1029
62. Al Kaline	1020
63. Ken Boyer	1017
64. Joe Morgan	1015
65. Larry Doby	1011
66. Amos Otis	1008
67. Darrell Evans	1001

WINS

1.	Cy Young	511
2.	Walter Johnson	416
3.	Christy Mathewson	373
3.	Grover Alexander	373
5.	Warren Spahn	363
6.	Pud Galvin	361
7.	Kid Nichols	360
8.	Tim Keefe	344
9.	Eddie Plank	327
10.	John Clarkson	326
11.	Gaylord Perry	314
12.	Steve Carlton	313
13.	Mickey Welch	311
14.	Old Hoss Radbourn	308
15.	Lefty Grove	300
15.	Early Wynn	300
17.	Tom Seaver	288
18.	Robin Roberts	286
19.	Tony Mullane	285
20.	Ferguson Jenkins	284
20.	Phil Niekro	284
22.	Jim Kaat	283
23.	Don Sutton	280
24.	Red Ruffing	273
25.	Burleigh Grimes	270
26.	Jim Palmer	268
27.	Bob Feller	266
27.	Eppa Rixey	266
29.	Jim McCormick	264
29.	Gus Weyhing	264
31.	Ted Lyons	260
32.	Tommy John	255
33.	Red Faber	254
34.	Carl Hubbell	253
35.	Bob Gibson	251
36.	Joe McGinnity	247
36.	Vic Willis	247
36.	Jack Quinn	247
39.	Jack Powell	246
40.	Amos Rusie	243
40.	Juan Marichal	243
42.	Clark Griffith	240
42.	Herb Pennock	240
44.	Three Finger Brown	239
45.	Waite Hoyt	237
46.	Whitey Ford	236
47.	Charlie Buffinton	231
47.	Nolan Ryan	231
49.	Will White	229
49.	Luis Tiant	229
49.	Sad Sam Jones	229
52.	George Mullin	228
53.	Catfish Hunter	224
53.	Jim Bunning	224
55.	Paul Derringer	223
55.	Mel Harder	223
57.	Hooks Dauss	221
58.	Bob Caruthers	218
58.	Earl Whitehill	218
60.	Freddie Fitzsimmons	217
60.	Mickey Lolich	217
62.	Wilbur Cooper	216
62.	Jerry Koosman	216
64.	Stan Coveleski	215
64.	Jim Perry	215
66.	Billy Pierce	211
66.	Bobo Newsom	211
68.	Chief Bender	210
68.	Jesse Haines	210
70.	Don Drysdale	209
70.	Milt Pappas	209
72.	Carl Mays	208
72.	Eddie Cicotte	208
74.	Jack Stivetts	207
74.	Bob Lemon	207
74.	Hal Newhouser	207
77.	Silver King	206
78.	Lew Burdette	203
79.	Al Orth	202
80.	Rube Marquard	201
80.	Charlie Root	201
82.	George Uhle	200

WINNING PERCENTAGE

1.	Bob Caruthers	.692
2.	Dave Foutz	.690
3.	Whitey Ford	.690
4.	Ron Guidry	.680
5.	Lefty Grove	.680
6.	Vic Raschi	.667
7.	Christy Mathewson	.665
8.	Larry Corcoran	.663
9.	Sal Maglie	.657
10.	Sam Leever	.656
11.	Sandy Koufax	.655
12.	Johnny Allen	.654
13.	Lefty Gomez	.649
14.	Three Finger Brown	.649
15.	John Clarkson	.648
16.	Dizzy Dean	.644
17.	Grover Alexander	.642
18.	Kid Nichols	.641
19.	Jim Palmer	.638
20.	Ed Reulbach	.633
21.	Deacon Phillippe	.633
22.	Joe McGinnity	.632
23.	Juan Marichal	.631
24.	Mort Cooper	.631
25.	Clark Griffith	.630
26.	Allie Reynolds	.630
27.	Jesse Tannehill	.629
28.	Eddie Plank	.629
29.	Ray Kremer	.627
30.	Tommy Bond	.627
31.	Fred Goldsmith	.626
32.	Don Newcombe	.623
33.	Chief Bender	.623
34.	Nig Cuppy	.623
35.	Jeff Tesreau	.623

EARNED RUN AVERAGE

1.	Ed Walsh	1.82
2.	Addie Joss	1.88
3.	Three Finger Brown	2.06
4.	Monte Ward	*2.10*
5.	Christy Mathewson	2.13
6.	Rube Waddell	2.16
7.	Walter Johnson	2.17
8.	Orval Overall	2.24
9.	Tommy Bond	*2.25*
10.	Will White	*2.28*
11.	Ed Reulbach	2.28
12.	Jim Scott	2.32
13.	Eddie Plank	2.34
14.	Larry Corcoran	*2.36*
15.	Eddie Cicotte	2.37
16.	George McQuillan	2.38
17.	Ed Killian	2.38
18.	Doc White	2.38
19.	Nap Rucker	2.42
20.	Jeff Tesreau	2.43
21.	Jim McCormick	*2.43*
22.	Terry Larkin	2.43
23.	Chief Bender	2.46
24.	Hooks Wiltse	2.47
25.	Sam Leever	2.47
26.	Lefty Leifield	2.47
27.	Hippo Vaughn	2.49

GAMES

1.	Hoyt Wilhelm	1070
2.	Lindy McDaniel	987
3.	Cy Young	906
4.	Sparky Lyle	899
5.	Jim Kaat	898
6.	Rollie Fingers	897
7.	Don McMahon	874
8.	Roy Face	848
9.	Tug McGraw	824
10.	Walter Johnson	802
11.	Gaylord Perry	777
12.	Phil Niekro	771
13.	Darold Knowles	765
14.	Jack Quinn	755
15.	Ron Reed	751
16.	Warren Spahn	750
17.	Tom Burgmeier	745
18.	Ron Perranoski	737
19.	Ron Kline	736
20.	Clay Carroll	731
21.	Mike Marshall	723
21.	Gene Garber	723
23.	Kent Tekulve	719
24.	Johnny Klippstein	711
25.	Stu Miller	704
26.	Pud Galvin	697
27.	Grover Alexander	696
28.	Bob Miller	694
29.	Grant Jackson	692
29.	Eppa Rixey	692
31.	Early Wynn	691
32.	Eddie Fisher	690
33.	Ted Abernathy	681

34.	Robin Roberts	676
35.	Waite Hoyt	674
36.	Red Faber	669
37.	Dave Giusti	668
38.	Ferguson Jenkins	664
39.	Steve Carlton	657
40.	Paul Lindblad	655
40.	Don Sutton	655
42.	Wilbur Wood	651
43.	Sad Sam Jones	647
43.	Gary Lavelle	647
43.	Dave LaRoche	647
46.	Tommy John	646
47.	Dutch Leonard	640
47.	Gerry Staley	640
49.	Diego Segui	639
50.	Christy Mathewson	636
51.	Charlie Root	632
52.	Jim Perry	630
52.	Goose Gossage	630
54.	Lew Burdette	626
55.	Murry Dickson	625
55.	Woodie Fryman	625
57.	Red Ruffing	624
58.	Eddie Plank	622
59.	Kid Nichols	621
60.	Dick Tidrow	620
61.	Burleigh Grimes	617
61.	Herb Pennock	617
63.	Lefty Grove	616
64.	Joe Niekro	610
65.	Bill Campbell	609
66.	Bob Friend	602
66.	Al Worthington	602
68.	Tim Keefe	601
68.	Elias Sosa	601
70.	Bobo Newsom	600
71.	Ted Lyons	594
72.	Jerry Koosman	593
72.	Tom Seaver	593
72.	Pedro Borbon	593
75.	Jim Bunning	591
76.	Dick Farrell	590
77.	Moe Drabowsky	589
78.	Mickey Lolich	586
79.	Billy Pierce	585
80.	Jim Brewer	584
81.	Mel Harder	582
81.	Pedro Ramos	582
83.	Paul Derringer	579
84.	Jack Powell	577
85.	Bob Locker	576
86.	Stan Bahnsen	574
87.	Luis Tiant	573
88.	Mudcat Grant	571
89.	Bob Feller	570
89.	Larry French	570
91.	Curt Simmons	569
92.	Mickey Welch	564
93.	Ray Sadecki	563
94.	Larry Jackson	558
94.	Jim Palmer	558
96.	Jack Russell	557
97.	Tony Mullane	556
98.	Jesse Haines	555
99.	Firpo Marberry	551
99.	Phil Regan	551
101.	Dolf Luque	550
102.	Bruce Sutter	549
103.	Nolan Ryan	546
104.	John Hiller	545
104.	Al Hrabosky	545
106.	Rube Walberg	544
107.	Guy Bush	542
107.	Syl Johnson	542
107.	Charlie Hough	542
110.	Claude Osteen	541
110.	Earl Whitehill	541
112.	Hooks Dauss	538
112.	Gus Weyhing	538
114.	Bobby Shantz	537
115.	Rube Marquard	536
116.	Carl Hubbell	535
116.	Rudy May	535
118.	Randy Moffitt	534
119.	Red Ames	533
119.	Tom Zachary	533
121.	John Clarkson	531
122.	Camilo Pascual	529
123.	Bob Gibson	528
123.	Bump Hadley	528
123.	Old Hoss Radbourn	528
126.	Bill Henry	527
126.	Terry Forster	527
128.	Joe Nuxhall	526
129.	Dizzy Trout	521
130.	Milt Pappas	520

131. Gary Bell	519
131. Dick Drago	519
133. Don Drysdale	518
134. Wilbur Cooper	517
134. Virgil Trucks	517
136. Frank Linzy	516
137. Bill Sherdel	514
137. Dale Murray	514
139. Freddie Fitzsimmons	513
139. Clem Labine	513
139. George Uhle	513
139. Vic Willis	513
143. Ken Forsch	511
144. Harry Gumbert	508
145. Rick Wise	506
146. Billy Hoeft	505
147. Turk Lown	504
147. Dan Spillner	504
149. Eddie Cicotte	502
150. Chris Short	501
151. Catfish Hunter	500
151. Eddie Rommel	500

COMPLETE GAMES

1. Cy Young	751
2. Pud Galvin	639
3. Tim Keefe	558
4. Kid Nichols	533
5. Walter Johnson	531
6. Mickey Welch	525
7. Old Hoss Radbourn	489
8. John Clarkson	485
9. Tony Mullane	469
10. Jim McCormick	466
11. Gus Weyhing	448
12. Grover Alexander	439
13. Christy Mathewson	435
14. Jack Powell	422
15. Eddie Plank	412
16. Will White	394
17. Amos Rusie	392
18. Vic Willis	388
19. Warren Spahn	382
20. Jim Whitney	377
21. Adonis Terry	368
22. Ted Lyons	356
23. George Mullin	353
24. Charlie Buffinton	351
25. Chick Fraser	342
26. Clark Griffith	337
27. Red Ruffing	335
28. Silver King	329
29. Al Orth	324
30. Bill Hutchison	319
31. Guy Hecker	314
31. Joe McGinnity	314
31. Burleigh Grimes	314
34. Red Donahue	312
35. Bill Dinneen	306
36. Robin Roberts	305
37. Gaylord Perry	303
38. Ted Breitenstein	300
38. Lefty Grove	300

INNINGS PITCHED

1. Cy Young	7356
2. Pud Galvin	5941
3. Walter Johnson	5924
4. Gaylord Perry	5351
5. Warren Spahn	5244
6. Grover Alexander	5189
7. Kid Nichols	5084
8. Tim Keefe	5072
9. Phil Niekro	4834
10. Mickey Welch	4802
11. Steve Carlton	4787
12. Christy Mathewson	4782
13. Robin Roberts	4689
14. Don Sutton	4568
15. Early Wynn	4564
16. Tony Mullane	4540
17. John Clarkson	4536
18. Old Hoss Radbourn	4535
19. Jim Kaat	4528
20. Eddie Plank	4505
21. Ferguson Jenkins	4500
22. Eppa Rixey	4495
23. Jack Powell	4388
24. Tom Seaver	4368
25. Red Ruffing	4344
26. Gus Weyhing	4324

27. Jim McCormick	4276
28. Burleigh Grimes	4180
29. Ted Lyons	4161
30. Tommy John	4124
31. Red Faber	4088
32. Vic Willis	3996
33. Jim Palmer	3948
34. Lefty Grove	3941
35. Jack Quinn	3935
36. Bob Gibson	3885
37. Sad Sam Jones	3883
38. Bob Feller	3827
39. Amos Rusie	3770
40. Waite Hoyt	3763
41. Jim Bunning	3760
42. Bobo Newsom	3759
43. Jerry Koosman	3740
44. Nolan Ryan	3706
45. George Mullin	3687
46. Paul Derringer	3645
47. Mickey Lolich	3639
48. Bob Friend	3611
49. Carl Hubbell	3589
50. Earl Whitehill	3566
51. Herb Pennock	3558
52. Will White	3543
53. Adonis Terry	3523
54. Juan Marichal	3509

STRIKEOUTS

1. Nolan Ryan	3874
2. Steve Carlton	3872
3. Gaylord Perry	3534
4. Walter Johnson	3508
5. Tom Seaver	3403
6. Don Sutton	3208
7. Ferguson Jenkins	3192
8. Bob Gibson	3117
9. Phil Niekro	3048
10. Jim Bunning	2855
11. Mickey Lolich	2832
12. Cy Young	2799
13. Bert Blyleven	2669
14. Warren Spahn	2583
15. Bob Feller	2581
16. Tim Keefe	2533
17. Christy Mathewson	2502
18. Jerry Koosman	2496
19. Don Drysdale	2486
20. Jim Kaat	2461
21. Sam McDowell	2453
22. Luis Tiant	2416
23. Sandy Koufax	2396
24. Robin Roberts	2357
25. Early Wynn	2334
26. Rube Waddell	2316
27. Juan Marichal	2303
28. Lefty Grove	2266
29. Eddie Plank	2246
30. Jim Palmer	2212
31. Grover Alexander	2199
32. Camilo Pascual	2167
33. Bobo Newsom	2082
34. Dazzy Vance	2045
35. Tommy John	2030
36. John Clarkson	2015
37. Catfish Hunter	2012
38. Billy Pierce	1999
39. Red Ruffing	1987
40. Vida Blue	1972
41. Amos Rusie	1957
42. Whitey Ford	1956
43. Kid Nichols	1885
44. Mickey Welch	1850
45. Old Hoss Radbourn	1830
46. Tony Mullane	1812
47. Pud Galvin	1799
48. Hal Newhouser	1796
49. Rudy May	1760
50. Ed Walsh	1736
51. Bob Friend	1734
52. Joe Coleman	1728
52. Milt Pappas	1728
54. Chief Bender	1711
55. Larry Jackson	1709
56. Jim McCormick	1704
57. Bob Veale	1703
58. Red Ames	1702
59. Charlie Buffinton	1700
60. Curt Simmons	1697
61. Carl Hubbell	1678
62. Tommy Bridges	1674
63. Gus Weyhing	1665
64. Vic Willis	1651

65. Frank Tanana	1647
65. Rick Wise	1647
67. Al Downing	1639
68. Mike Cuellar	1632
69. Jerry Reuss	1631
70. Chris Short	1629
71. Andy Messersmith	1625
72. Jack Powell	1621
73. Ray Sadecki	1614
74. Claude Osteen	1612
75. Hoyt Wilhelm	1610
76. Jim Maloney	1605
77. Steve Rogers	1603
78. Ken Holtzman	1601
79. Rube Marquard	1593
80. Woodie Fryman	1587
81. Jim Perry	1576
82. Harvey Haddix	1575
83. Jim Whitney	1571
84. Adonis Terry	1555
85. Wild Bill Donovan	1552
86. Dean Chance	1534
86. Virgil Trucks	1534
88. Juan Pizarro	1522
89. Jon Matlack	1516
90. Toad Ramsey	1515
90. Bill Singer	1515
92. Sonny Siebert	1512
92. Dave McNally	1512
92. Burleigh Grimes	1512
95. Paul Derringer	1507

STRIKEOUTS PER 9 INNINGS

1. Nolan Ryan	9.41
2. Sandy Koufax	9.28
3. Sam McDowell	8.86
4. J. R. Richard	8.37
5. Bob Veale	7.96
6. Jim Maloney	7.81
7. Sam Jones	7.54
8. Steve Carlton	7.28
9. Bob Gibson	7.22
10. Rube Waddell	7.04
11. Bert Blyleven	7.02
12. Tom Seaver	7.01
13. Mickey Lolich	7.00
14. Rollie Fingers	6.97
15. Ron Guidry	6.96
16. Jim Bunning	6.83
17. Juan Pizarro	6.73
18. Bobby Bolin	6.71
19. Ray Culp	6.69
20. Stan Williams	6.66
21. Camilo Pascual	6.66
22. Bob Turley	6.65
23. Don Wilson	6.60
24. Tug McGraw	6.58
25. Denny Lemaster	6.57
26. Andy Messersmith	6.56
27. Don Drysdale	6.52
28. Al Downing	6.50
29. Toad Ramsey	6.49
30. Diego Segui	6.46
31. Hoyt Wilhelm	6.43
32. Dean Chance	6.43
33. Ferguson Jenkins	6.38
34. Moe Drabowsky	6.37
35. Earl Wilson	6.37

SHUTOUTS

1. Walter Johnson	110
2. Grover Alexander	90
3. Christy Mathewson	80
4. Cy Young	76
5. Eddie Plank	69
6. Warren Spahn	63
7. Tom Seaver	60
8. Ed Walsh	57
8. Three Finger Brown	57
8. Pud Galvin	57
11. Don Sutton	56
11. Bob Gibson	56
13. Steve Carlton	55
14. Nolan Ryan	54
15. Jim Palmer	53
15. Gaylord Perry	53
17. Juan Marichal	52
18. Rube Waddell	50
18. Vic Willis	50
20. Don Drysdale	49
20. Luis Tiant	49

20.	Ferguson Jenkins	49
20.	Early Wynn	49
24.	Red Ruffing	48
24.	Kid Nichols	48
26.	Babe Adams	47
26.	Jack Powell	47
28.	Bert Blyleven	46
28.	Addie Joss	46
28.	Doc White	46
28.	Bob Feller	46
32.	Whitey Ford	45
32.	Tommy John	45
32.	Robin Roberts	45
35.	Phil Niekro	44
36.	Milt Pappas	43
37.	Catfish Hunter	42
37.	Bucky Walters	42
39.	Mickey Lolich	41
39.	Hippo Vaughn	41
39.	Chief Bender	41
42.	Sandy Koufax	40
42.	Claude Osteen	40
42.	Jim Bunning	40
42.	Mel Stottlemyre	40
42.	Larry French	40
42.	Ed Reulbach	40
42.	Mickey Welch	40
42.	Tim Keefe	40
50.	Sam Leever	39
50.	Eppa Rixey	39
52.	Nap Rucker	38
52.	Billy Pierce	38
52.	Stan Coveleski	38
55.	Steve Rogers	37
55.	Vida Blue	37
55.	Larry Jackson	37
55.	John Clarkson	37
59.	Camilo Pascual	36
59.	Allie Reynolds	36
59.	Bill Doak	36
59.	Bob Friend	36
59.	Curt Simmons	36
59.	Mike Cuellar	36
59.	Eddie Cicotte	36
59.	Sad Sam Jones	36
59.	Carl Hubbell	36
59.	Wilbur Cooper	36
59.	Tommy Bond	36
59.	Will White	36
71.	Virgil Trucks	35
71.	Jack Coombs	35
71.	Joe Bush	35
71.	Herb Pennock	35
71.	Jack Chesbro	35
71.	Wild Bill Donovan	35
71.	Lefty Grove	35
71.	Burleigh Grimes	35
71.	George Mullin	35
71.	Old Hoss Radbourn	35
81.	Earl Moore	34
81.	Jesse Tannehill	34
83.	Dean Chance	33
83.	Jerry Reuss	33
83.	Dave McNally	33
83.	Mort Cooper	33
83.	Lew Burdette	33
83.	Lefty Tyler	33
83.	Bob Shawkey	33
83.	Tommy Bridges	33
83.	Hal Newhouser	33
83.	Charlie Buffinton	33
83.	Jim McCormick	33
94.	Jim Perry	32
94.	Jerry Koosman	32
94.	Lefty Leifield	32
94.	Dutch Leonard	32
94.	Paul Derringer	32
94.	Joe McGinnity	32
100.	Ken Holtzman	31
100.	Ken Raffensberger	31
100.	Jim Kaat	31
100.	Bob Lemon	31
100.	Lon Warneke	31
100.	Bobo Newsom	31
100.	Al Orth	31
100.	Tony Mullane	31
108.	Jim Maloney	30
108.	Jon Matlack	30
108.	Johnny Vander Meer	30
108.	Orval Overall	30
108.	Rick Wise	30
108.	Art Nehf	30
108.	Dutch Leonard	30
108.	Rube Marquard	30
108.	Dazzy Vance	30
108.	Red Faber	30
108.	Amos Rusie	30

HITS PER 9 INNINGS

1.	Nolan Ryan	6.47
2.	Sandy Koufax	6.79
3.	J. R. Richard	6.88
4.	Andy Messersmith	6.94
5.	Hoyt Wilhelm	7.02
6.	Sam McDowell	7.03
7.	Ed Walsh	7.12
8.	Bob Turley	7.18
9.	Orval Overall	7.22
10.	Jeff Tesreau	7.24
11.	Ed Reulbach	7.24
12.	Addie Joss	7.30
13.	Tom Seaver	7.35
14.	Jim Maloney	7.39
15.	Rube Waddell	7.48
16.	Walter Johnson	7.48
17.	Bob Gibson	7.60
18.	Don Wilson	7.61
19.	Jim Palmer	7.63
20.	Larry Cheney	7.68
21.	Three Finger Brown	7.68
22.	Sam Jones	7.68
23.	Bob Feller	7.69
24.	Johnny Vander Meer	7.69
25.	Catfish Hunter	7.72
26.	Al Downing	7.72
27.	Rollie Fingers	7.74
28.	Charlie Hough	7.75
29.	Stan Williams	7.79
29.	Bobby Bolin	7.79
31.	Barney Pelty	7.80
32.	Jim Scott	7.81
33.	Dean Chance	7.81
34.	Frank Smith	7.82
35.	Tug McGraw	7.82

BASES ON BALLS

1.	Nolan Ryan	2091
2.	Early Wynn	1775
3.	Bob Feller	1764
4.	Bobo Newsom	1732
5.	Amos Rusie	1716
6.	Steve Carlton	1603
7.	Gus Weyhing	1566
8.	Red Ruffing	1541
9.	Phil Niekro	1528
10.	Bump Hadley	1442
11.	Warren Spahn	1434
12.	Earl Whitehill	1431
13.	Tony Mullane	1409
14.	Walter Johnson	1405
15.	Sad Sam Jones	1396
16.	Gaylord Perry	1379
17.	Mike Torrez	1371
18.	Bob Gibson	1336
19.	Chick Fraser	1332
20.	Sam McDowell	1312
21.	Jim Palmer	1311
22.	Mark Baldwin	1307
23.	Adonis Terry	1301
24.	Mickey Welch	1297
25.	Burleigh Grimes	1295
26.	Kid Nichols	1282
27.	Tom Seaver	1265
28.	Joe Bush	1263
29.	Allie Reynolds	1261
30.	Bob Lemon	1251
31.	Hal Newhouser	1249
32.	George Mullin	1238
33.	Tim Keefe	1231
34.	Cy Young	1217
35.	Red Faber	1213

BASES ON BALLS PER 9 INNINGS

1.	Tommy Bond	.58
2.	George Bradley	.67
3.	Terry Larkin	.71
4.	Monte Ward	.92
5.	Fred Goldsmith	.96
6.	Jim Whitney	1.06
7.	Bobby Mathews	1.11
8.	Pud Galvin	1.13
9.	Deacon Phillippe	1.25
10.	Will White	1.26
11.	Babe Adams	1.29
12.	Jack Lynch	1.39
13.	Addie Joss	1.43
14.	Cy Young	1.49
15.	Guy Hecker	1.51

16.	Lee Richmond	1.53
17.	Jesse Tannehill	1.55
18.	Jim McCormick	1.58
19.	Christy Mathewson	1.59
20.	Red Lucas	1.61
21.	Nick Altrock	1.62
22.	Grover Alexander	1.65
23.	Jumbo McGinnis	1.65
24.	Ernie Bonham	1.67
25.	Ed Morris	1.67
26.	Noodles Hahn	1.70
27.	Charlie Ferguson	1.72
28.	Fritz Peterson	1.73
29.	Robin Roberts	1.73
30.	Old Hoss Radbourn	1.74
31.	Dick Rudolph	1.77
32.	Al Orth	1.77
33.	Stump Weidman	1.78
34.	Pete Donohue	1.80
35.	Jesse Barnes	1.80

LOSSES

1.	Cy Young	313
2.	Pud Galvin	310
3.	Walter Johnson	279
4.	Gaylord Perry	265
5.	Jack Powell	255
6.	Eppa Rixey	251
7.	Robin Roberts	245
7.	Warren Spahn	245
9.	Early Wynn	244
10.	Phil Niekro	238
11.	Jim Kaat	237
12.	Gus Weyhing	236
13.	Ted Lyons	230
13.	Bob Friend	230
15.	Ferguson Jenkins	226
16.	Tim Keefe	225
16.	Red Ruffing	225
18.	Bobo Newsom	222
19.	Don Sutton	218
20.	Sad Sam Jones	217
20.	Jack Quinn	217
22.	Tony Mullane	215
23.	Jim McCormick	214
24.	Chick Fraser	212
24.	Paul Derringer	212
24.	Burleigh Grimes	212
24.	Red Faber	212
28.	Grover Alexander	208
29.	Jim Whitney	207
29.	Mickey Welch	207
29.	Steve Carlton	207
32.	Vic Willis	206
32.	Nolan Ryan	206
34.	Jerry Koosman	205
35.	Kid Nichols	202

RELIEF WINS

1.	Hoyt Wilhelm	123
2.	Lindy McDaniel	119
3.	Rollie Fingers	106
4.	Sparky Lyle	99
5.	Roy Face	96
6.	Mike Marshall	92
7.	Don McMahon	90
8.	Tug McGraw	89
9.	Clay Carroll	88
10.	Goose Gossage	82
11.	Stu Miller	79
11.	Ron Perranoski	79
11.	Tom Burgmeier	79
14.	Gene Garber	75
15.	Johnny Murphy	73
15.	Gary Lavelle	73
17.	John Hiller	72
17.	Bill Campbell	72
19.	Dick Hall	71
20.	Kent Tekulve	70
21.	Pedro Borbon	69
22.	Al Hrabosky	64
23.	Clem Labine	63
23.	Darold Knowles	63
25.	Dick Farrell	62
25.	Frank Linzy	62
25.	Jim Brewer	62
25.	Grant Jackson	62
25.	Dave LaRoche	62
30.	Bob Stanley	61
30.	Paul Lindblad	61
32.	Joe Heving	60

33. Johnny Klippstein	59
33. Elias Sosa	59
35. Phil Regan	58
35. Bruce Sutter	58
37. Bob Locker	57
37. Ted Abernathy	57
39. Mark Clear	56
39. Mace Brown	56
39. Gerry Staley	56
39. Eddie Fisher	56
43. Dave Giusti	55
44. Jack Quinn	54
44. Ron Reed	54
44. Ron Kline	54
44. Al Worthington	54
48. Firpo Marberry	53
48. Dale Murray	53
50. Dick Radatz	52
50. Ed Roebuck	52
50. Tippy Martinez	52
53. Eddie Rommel	51
53. Hugh Casey	51
53. Jim Konstanty	51
53. Dick Tidrow	51
57. Aurelio Lopez	50

RELIEF WINNING PERCENTAGE

1. Hugh Casey .718
2. Aurelio Lopez .685
3. Guy Bush .683
4. Doug Bird .672
5. Eddie Rommel .662
6. Grant Jackson .653
7. Mace Brown .651
8. Pedro Borbon .651
9. Al Hrabosky .646
10. Al Brazle .641
11. Hooks Dauss .635
12. Johnny Murphy .635
13. Ed Roebuck .634
14. Dick Hall .634
15. Joe Heving .632
16. Clyde Shoun .621
17. Charlie Root .618
18. Tom Morgan .615
19. Willie Hernandez .614
20. Harry Gumbert .611
21. Bob Stanley .610
22. Mark Clear .609
23. Jack Quinn .607
24. Tom Burgmeier .598
25. Dave Giusti .598
26. Johnny Klippstein .596
27. Ellis Kinder .595
28. Bob Locker .594
29. Jim Konstanty .593
30. Phil Regan .592
31. Tippy Martinez .591
32. Goose Gossage .590
33. Firpo Marberry .589
34. Fred Gladding .585
35. Moe Drabowsky .584
35. Sid Monge .584

SAVES

1. Rollie Fingers 324
2. Bruce Sutter 260
3. Sparky Lyle 238
4. Goose Gossage 231
5. Hoyt Wilhelm 227
6. Roy Face 193
7. Mike Marshall 188
8. Dan Quisenberry 180
8. Tug McGraw 180
10. Ron Perranoski 179
11. Lindy McDaniel 172
12. Gene Garber 169
13. Kent Tekulve 158
14. Stu Miller 154
15. Don McMahon 153
16. Ted Abernathy 148
17. Dave Giusti 145
18. Clay Carroll 143
18. Darold Knowles 143
20. Jim Brewer 132
21. Gary Lavelle 127
22. Dave LaRoche 126
23. John Hiller 125
24. Jack Aker 123
25. Dick Radatz 122
26. Terry Forster 121

27. Bill Campbell 119
28. Greg Minton 115
29. Frank Linzy 111
30. Tippy Martinez 110
30. Al Worthington 110
32. Fred Gladding 109
33. Wayne Granger 108
33. Ron Kline 108
35. Johnny Murphy 107
36. Ron Davis 103
36. John Wyatt 103
36. Ron Reed 103
39. Ellis Kinder 102
39. Tom Burgmeier 102
41. Firpo Marberry 101
42. Joe Hoerner 99
43. Bob Stanley 97
43. Al Hrabosky 97
45. Clem Labine 96
45. Randy Moffitt 96
47. Bob Locker 95
48. Phil Regan 92
49. Bill Henry 90
50. Bill Caudill 89
51. Jim Kern 88
52. Jeff Reardon 86
52. Cecil Upshaw 86
52. Ken Sanders 86
55. Tom Hume 85
56. Claude Raymond 83
56. Dick Farrell 83
56. Elias Sosa 83
59. Larry Sherry 82
60. Eddie Fisher 81
61. Lee Smith 80
61. Aurelio Lopez 80
61. Eddie Watt 80
61. Pedro Borbon 80
65. Grant Jackson 79
66. Joe Page 76
66. Doug Bair 76
68. Ed Farmer 75

WINS PLUS SAVES

1. Rollie Fingers 430
2. Hoyt Wilhelm 350
3. Sparky Lyle 337
4. Bruce Sutter 318
5. Goose Gossage 313
6. Lindy McDaniel 291
7. Roy Face 289
8. Mike Marshall 280
9. Tug McGraw 269
10. Ron Perranoski 258
11. Gene Garber 244
12. Don McMahon 243
13. Stu Miller 233
14. Clay Carroll 231
15. Kent Tekulve 228
16. Dan Quisenberry 216
17. Darold Knowles 206
18. Ted Abernathy 205
19. Dave Giusti 200
19. Gary Lavelle 200
21. John Hiller 197
22. Jim Brewer 194
23. Bill Campbell 191
24. Dave LaRoche 188
25. Tom Burgmeier 181
26. Johnny Murphy 180
27. Dick Radatz 174
28. Frank Linzy 173
29. Jack Aker 170
30. Al Worthington 164
31. Tippy Martinez 162
31. Terry Forster 162
31. Ron Kline 162
34. Al Hrabosky 161
35. Clem Labine 159
36. Bob Stanley 158
37. Fred Gladding 157
37. Ron Reed 157
39. Firpo Marberry 154
40. Bob Locker 152
41. Phil Regan 150
42. Pedro Borbon 149
43. Greg Minton 147
44. Ellis Kinder 146
45. Ron Davis 145
45. Dick Farrell 145
47. Wayne Granger 143
48. John Wyatt 142
48. Elias Sosa 142
50. Grant Jackson 141

51. Dick Hall 139
51. Randy Moffitt 139
53. Joe Hoerner 138
54. Jim Kern 137
54. Eddie Fisher 137
56. Aurelio Lopez 130
57. Larry Sherry 129
58. Jim Konstanty 125
58. Claude Raymond 125
58. Johnny Klippstein 125
58. Paul Lindblad 125

RELIEF GAMES

1. Hoyt Wilhelm 1018
2. Lindy McDaniel 913
3. Sparky Lyle 899
4. Don McMahon 872
5. Rollie Fingers 860
6. Roy Face 821
7. Tug McGraw 785
8. Darold Knowles 757
9. Tom Burgmeier 742
10. Ron Perranoski 736
11. Kent Tekulve 719
12. Gene Garber 714
13. Clay Carroll 703
14. Mike Marshall 699
15. Ted Abernathy 647
16. Gary Lavelle 644
17. Dave LaRoche 632
18. Eddie Fisher 627
19. Paul Lindblad 623
20. Stu Miller 611
21. Grant Jackson 609
22. Bill Campbell 600
23. Elias Sosa 598
24. Bob Miller 595
25. Goose Gossage 593
26. Pedro Borbon 589
27. Bob Locker 576
28. Jim Brewer 549
28. Johnny Klippstein 549
28. Bruce Sutter 549
31. Al Hrabosky 544
32. Dave Giusti 535
33. Ron Kline 533
33. Al Worthington 533
33. Randy Moffitt 533
36. Ron Reed 515
37. Frank Linzy 514
38. Dale Murray 513
39. John Hiller 502
40. Jack Aker 495
41. Joe Hoerner 493
42. Terry Forster 488
43. Bill Henry 483
44. Dick Tidrow 482
45. Tippy Martinez 478
46. Clem Labine 475
47. Ron Taylor 474
48. Diego Segui 468
49. Ed Roebuck 459
50. Jack Baldschun 457
51. Dick Farrell 456
52. Turk Lown 455
52. Willie Hernandez 455
54. Gerry Staley 454
55. Wayne Granger 451
56. Fred Gladding 449
57. Phil Regan 446
58. Claude Raymond 442
59. Doug Bair 441
60. Moe Drabowsky 435
60. Don Elston 435
62. John Wyatt 426
63. Dick Hall 421
64. Sid Monge 418
65. Charlie Hough 416
66. Greg Minton 414
67. Ken Sanders 407
68. Steve Hamilton 404
69. Larry Sherry 400
69. Dave Tomlin 400

GAMES		GAMES		FIELDING AVERAGE	

1B

1. Jake Beckley	2377
2. Mickey Vernon	2237
3. Lou Gehrig	2136
4. Charlie Grimm	2129
5. Joe Judge	2084
6. Ed Konetchy	2071
7. Cap Anson	2058
8. Joe Kuhel	2057
9. Willie McCovey	2054
10. Jake Daubert	2001
11. Stuffy McInnis	1995
12. George Sisler	1970
13. Norm Cash	1946
14. Chris Chambliss	1927
15. Lee May	1921

C

1. Al Lopez	1918
2. Rick Ferrell	1805
3. Gabby Hartnett	1790
4. Johnny Bench	1744
5. Ray Schalk	1726
6. Ted Simmons	1722
7. Bill Dickey	1712
8. Yogi Berra	1696
9. Jim Hegan	1629
10. Deacon McGuire	1611
11. Bill Freehan	1581
12. Sherm Lollar	1571
13. Luke Sewell	1561
14. Ernie Lombardi	1542
15. Steve O'Neill	1528

3B

1. Brooks Robinson	.971
2. Ken Reitz	.970
3. George Kell	.969
4. Don Money	.968
5. Don Wert	.968
6. Willie Kamm	.967
7. Heinie Groh	.967
8. Clete Boyer	.965
9. Ken Keltner	.965
10. Buddy Bell	.964
11. Jim Davenport	.964
12. Aurelio Rodriguez	.964
13. Willie Jones	.963
14. Ron Cey	.963
15. Toby Harrah	.963

2B

1. Eddie Collins	2650
2. Joe Morgan	2527
3. Nellie Fox	2295
4. Charlie Gehringer	2206
5. Bid McPhee	2125
6. Bill Mazeroski	2094
7. Nap Lajoie	2036
8. Bobby Doerr	1852
9. Red Schoendienst	1834
10. Billy Herman	1829
11. Frankie Frisch	1775
12. Johnny Evers	1736
13. Larry Doyle	1730
14. Del Pratt	1685
15. Kid Gleason	1584

P

1. Hoyt Wilhelm	1070
2. Lindy McDaniel	987
3. Cy Young	906
4. Sparky Lyle	899
5. Jim Kaat	898
6. Don McMahon	874
7. Roy Face	848
8. Tug McGraw	824
9. Rollie Fingers	823
10. Walter Johnson	802
11. Gaylord Perry	777
12. Phil Niekro	771
13. Darold Knowles	765
14. Jack Quinn	755
15. Ron Reed	751

SS

1. Larry Bowa	.980
2. Mark Belanger	.977
3. Ozzie Smith	.977
4. Bucky Dent	.976
5. Roger Metzger	.976
6. Dal Maxvill	.973
7. Tim Foli	.973
8. Lou Boudreau	.973
9. Eddie Miller	.972
10. Luis Aparicio	.972
11. Roy McMillan	.972
12. Dave Concepcion	.971
13. Bobby Wine	.971
14. Leo Cardenas	.971
15. Ed Brinkman	.970

3B

1. Brooks Robinson	2870
2. Eddie Mathews	2181
3. Ron Santo	2130
4. Graig Nettles	2116
5. Eddie Yost	2008
6. Aurelio Rodriguez	1983
7. Sal Bando	1896
8. Pie Traynor	1864
9. Stan Hack	1836
10. Ken Boyer	1785
11. Ron Cey	1769
12. Pinky Higgins	1768
13. Mike Schmidt	1751
14. Lave Cross	1721
15. George Kell	1692

FIELDING AVERAGE

OF

1. Pete Rose	.991
2. Amos Otis	.991
3. Joe Rudi	.991
4. Mickey Stanley	.991
5. Jimmy Piersall	.990
6. Jim Landis	.989
7. Ken Berry	.989
8. Tommy Holmes	.989
9. Gene Woodling	.989
10. Cesar Geronimo	.988
11. Paul Blair	.988
12. George Hendrick	.988
13. Roy White	.988
14. Jim Busby	.988
15. Dwight Evans	.987

SS

1. Luis Aparicio	2581
2. Luke Appling	2218
3. Rabbit Maranville	2154
4. Larry Bowa	2147
5. Bill Dahlen	2132
6. Bert Campaneris	2097
7. Tommy Corcoran	2073
8. Roy McMillan	2028
9. Pee Wee Reese	2014
10. Roger Peckinpaugh	1983
11. Don Kessinger	1955
12. Dave Concepcion	1952
13. Mark Belanger	1942
14. Honus Wagner	1888
15. Dick Groat	1877

1B

1. Steve Garvey	.996
2. Wes Parker	.996
3. Jim Spencer	.995
4. Eddie Murray	.995
5. Dan Driessen	.995
6. Frank McCormick	.995
7. Vic Power	.994
8. Carl Yastrzemski	.994
9. Joe Adcock	.994
10. Ernie Banks	.994
11. Mike Jorgensen	.994
12. John Mayberry	.994
13. Lee May	.994
14. Ed Kranepool	.994
15. Keith Hernandez	.994

C

1. Bill Freehan	.993
2. Elston Howard	.993
3. Jim Sundberg	.992
4. Sherm Lollar	.992
5. Tom Haller	.992
6. Johnny Edwards	.992
7. Gary Carter	.991
8. Jerry Grote	.991
9. Johnny Bench	.990
10. Randy Hundley	.990
11. Earl Battey	.990
12. Tim McCarver	.990
13. Jim Hegan	.990
14. Johnny Roseboro	.989
15. Del Crandall	.989

OF

1. Ty Cobb	2943
2. Willie Mays	2843
3. Hank Aaron	2760
4. Tris Speaker	2700
5. Lou Brock	2507
6. Al Kaline	2488
7. Max Carey	2422
8. Vada Pinson	2403
9. Roberto Clemente	2370
10. Zack Wheat	2350
11. Willie Davis	2323
12. Mel Ott	2313
13. Sam Crawford	2297
14. Harry Hooper	2292
15. Paul Waner	2288

2B

1. Jerry Lumpe	.984
2. Cookie Rojas	.984
3. Dave Cash	.984
4. Nellie Fox	.984
5. Bobby Grich	.983
6. Tommy Helms	.983
7. Dick Green	.983
8. Red Schoendienst	.983
9. Frank White	.983
10. Bill Mazeroski	.983
11. Horace Clarke	.983
12. Frank Bolling	.982
13. Joe Morgan	.981
14. Manny Trillo	.981
15. Jerry Remy	.981

P

1. Don Mossi	.990
2. Gary Nolan	.990
3. Lon Warneke	.988
4. Jim Wilson	.988
5. Woodie Fryman	.988
6. Rick Rhoden	.986
7. Larry Gura	.985
8. Grover Alexander	.985
9. General Crowder	.984
10. Bill Monbouquette	.984
11. Harry Brecheen	.983
12. Rick Wise	.982
13. Scott McGregor	.982
14. Ron Guidry	.981

PUTOUTS		PUTOUTS		PUTOUTS/GAME	
1B		**C**		**3B**	
1. Jake Beckley	23709	1. Bill Freehan	9941	1. Jerry Denny	1.6
2. Ed Konetchy	21361	2. Johnny Roseboro	9291	2. Denny Lyons	1.5
3. Cap Anson	20761	3. Johnny Bench	9260	3. Billy Nash	1.5
4. Charlie Grimm	20711	4. Johnny Edwards	8925	4. Bill Shindle	1.4
5. Stuffy McInnis	20119	5. Ted Simmons	8725	5. Jimmy Austin	1.4
6. Mickey Vernon	19808	6. Yogi Berra	8711	6. Jimmy Collins	1.4
7. Jake Daubert	19634	7. Tim McCarver	8206	7. Frank Baker	1.4
8. Lou Gehrig	19510	8. Jerry Grote	8081	8. Hick Carpenter	1.4
9. Joe Kuhel	19386	9. Bill Dickey	7965	9. Lave Cross	1.3
10. Joe Judge	19277	10. Jim Sundberg	7654	10. Hans Lobert	1.3
11. George Sisler	18814	11. Bob Boone	7593	11. Willie Kamm	1.3
12. Wally Pipp	18779	12. Jim Hegan	7506	12. Harry Steinfeldt	1.3
13. Jim Bottomley	18337	13. Del Crandall	7352	13. Bobby Byrne	1.3
14. Hal Chase	18177	14. Carlton Fisk	7350	14. Willie Jones	1.3
15. Fred Tenney	17919	15. Gabby Hartnett	7292	15. George Pinckney	1.3

2B		**P**		**SS**	
1. Eddie Collins	6526	1. Ferguson Jenkins	363	1. Dave Bancroft	2.5
2. Bid McPhee	6300	2. Phil Niekro	353	2. Honus Wagner	2.4
3. Nellie Fox	6090	3. Gaylord Perry	349	3. Rabbit Maranville	2.4
4. Joe Morgan	5742	4. Tony Mullane	327	4. Monte Cross	2.4
5. Nap Lajoie	5407	5. Pud Galvin	324	5. Herman Long	2.4
6. Charlie Gehringer	5369	6. Robin Roberts	316	6. George Davis	2.3
7. Bill Mazeroski	4974	7. Chick Fraser	315	7. Dick Bartell	2.3
8. Bobby Doerr	4928	8. Kid Nichols	311	8. Bill Dahlen	2.3
9. Billy Herman	4780	9. Don Sutton	295	9. Bobby Wallace	2.3
10. Fred Pfeffer	4711	10. Jim Palmer	292	10. Ivy Olson	2.3
11. Red Schoendienst	4616	11. Juan Marichal	291	11. George McBride	2.2
12. Frankie Frisch	4348	11. Bob Gibson	291	12. Mickey Doolan	2.2
		11. Tom Seaver	291	13. Tommy Corcoran	2.2
		14. Christy Mathewson	281	14. Doc Lavan	2.2
				15. Travis Jackson	2.2

3B				**OF**	
1. Brooks Robinson	2697			1. Taylor Douthit	3.0
2. Jimmy Collins	2372			2. Richie Ashburn	2.9
3. Eddie Yost	2356			3. Mike Kreevich	2.8
4. Lave Cross	2304			4. Dom DiMaggio	2.8
5. Pie Traynor	2291			5. Chet Lemon	2.8
6. Billy Nash	2219			6. Sammy West	2.7
7. Frank Baker	2154			7. Sam Chapman	2.7
8. Willie Kamm	2151	**PUTOUTS/GAME**		8. Rick Manning	2.7
9. Eddie Mathews	2049			9. Garry Maddox	2.7
10. Willie Jones	2045			10. Fred Schulte	2.7
11. Jimmy Austin	2042			11. Andre Dawson	2.7
12. Arlie Latham	1975			12. Omar Moreno	2.7
13. Ron Santo	1955			13. Lloyd Waner	2.7
14. Stan Hack	1944			14. Billy North	2.6
15. Pinky Higgins	1849			15. Vince DiMaggio	2.6

SS		**1B**		**C**	
1. Rabbit Maranville	5139	1. Tom Jones	10.5	1. Johnny Edwards	6.4
2. Bill Dahlen	4850	2. Candy LaChance	10.5	2. Johnny Roseboro	6.3
3. Dave Bancroft	4623	3. George Stovall	10.4	3. Bill Freehan	6.3
4. Honus Wagner	4576	4. George Kelly	10.4	4. Jerry Grote	6.0
5. Tommy Corcoran	4550	5. Wally Pipp	10.3	5. Tim McCarver	5.9
6. Luis Aparicio	4548	6. Ed Konetchy	10.3	6. Tom Haller	5.8
7. Luke Appling	4398	7. Bill Phillips	10.2	7. Earl Battey	5.7
8. Herman Long	4219	8. Walter Holke	10.2	8. Elston Howard	5.7
9. Bobby Wallace	4142	9. Charlie Comiskey	10.1	9. Randy Hundley	5.6
10. Pee Wee Reese	4040	10. Long John Reilly	10.1	10. Clay Dalrymple	5.5
11. Donie Bush	4038	11. George Burns	10.1	11. Roy Campanella	5.5
12. Monte Cross	3974	12. Cap Anson	10.1	12. Gary Carter	5.5
13. Roger Peckinpaugh	3919	13. Stuffy McInnis	10.1	13. Manny Sanguillen	5.4
14. Dick Bartell	3872	14. Bill Terry	10.1	14. Johnny Bench	5.3
15. Joe Tinker	3758	15. Hal Chase	10.0	15. Yogi Berra	5.1

OF		**2B**		**P**	
1. Willie Mays	7095	1. Fred Pfeffer	3.1	1. Dave Foutz	.8
2. Tris Speaker	6791	2. Cub Stricker	3.0	2. Nick Altrock	.8
3. Max Carey	6363	3. Bid McPhee	3.0	3. Chick Fraser	.7
4. Ty Cobb	6361	4. Gerry Priddy	2.7	4. Carl Morton	.7
5. Richie Ashburn	6089	5. Lou Bierbauer	2.7	5. Mel Stottlemyre	.7
6. Hank Aaron	5539	6. Bucky Harris	2.7	6. Jack Morris	.7
7. Willie Davis	5449	7. Bobby Doerr	2.7	7. Nixey Callahan	.7
8. Doc Cramer	5412	8. Cupid Childs	2.7	8. Ted Breitenstein	.6
9. Vada Pinson	5097	9. Nap Lajoie	2.7	9. Larry Corcoran	.6
10. Al Kaline	5035	10. Nellie Fox	2.7	10. Rick Reuschel	.6
11. Zack Wheat	4996	11. Eddie Stanky	2.6	11. Juan Marichal	.6
12. Al Simmons	4988	12. Billy Herman	2.6	12. Harry Howell	.6
13. Amos Otis	4936	13. Oscar Melillo	2.6	13. Guy Hecker	.6
14. Paul Waner	4881	14. Buddy Myer	2.6	14. Steve Rogers	.6
15. Lloyd Waner	4860	15. Joe Quinn	2.5		

ASSISTS		ASSISTS		ASSISTS/GAME	
1B		**C**		**3B**	
1. George Sisler	1528	1. Deacon McGuire	1859	1. Buddy Bell	2.4
2. Mickey Vernon	1448	2. Ray Schalk	1811	2. Mike Schmidt	2.3
3. Fred Tenney	1363	3. Steve O'Neill	1698	3. Graig Nettles	2.3
4. Chris Chambliss	1320	4. Red Dooin	1590	4. Bill Shindle	2.3
5. Norm Cash	1317	5. Chief Zimmer	1580	5. Arlie Latham	2.3
6. Jake Beckley	1315	6. Johnny Kling	1552	6. Clete Boyer	2.2
7. Joe Judge	1300	7. Ivy Wingo	1487	7. Jimmy Collins	2.2
8. Ed Konetchy	1292	8. Wilbert Robinson	1454	8. George Brett	2.2
9. Gil Hodges	1281	9. Bill Bergen	1444	9. Doug DeCinces	2.2
10. Stuffy McInnis	1238	10. Duke Farrell	1417	10. Darrell Evans	2.2
11. Jimmie Foxx	1222	10. Wally Schang	1417	11. Brooks Robinson	2.2
11. Willie McCovey	1222	12. George Gibson	1386	12. Lave Cross	2.2
13. Charlie Grimm	1214	13. Oscar Stanage	1379	13. Ron Santo	2.2
14. Joe Kuhel	1163	14. Malachi Kittredge	1363	14. Doug Rader	2.1
15. Wally Pipp	1152	15. Lou Criger	1342	15. Billy Nash	2.1

2B		**P**		**SS**	
1. Eddie Collins	7630	1. Cy Young	2013	1. Germany Smith	3.7
2. Charlie Gehringer	7068	2. Christy Mathewson	1503	2. Ozzie Smith	3.6
3. Joe Morgan	6967	3. Grover Alexander	1419	3. Art Fletcher	3.6
4. Bill Mazeroski	6685	4. Pud Galvin	1390	4. Bill Dahlen	3.5
5. Bid McPhee	6593	5. Walter Johnson	1348	5. Dave Bancroft	3.5
6. Nellie Fox	6373	6. Burleigh Grimes	1252	6. Bones Ely	3.5
7. Nap Lajoie	6259	7. George Mullin	1244	7. Travis Jackson	3.5
8. Frankie Frisch	6026	8. Jack Quinn	1240	8. George Davis	3.5
9. Bobby Doerr	5710	9. Ed Walsh	1210	9. Jack Glasscock	3.5
10. Billy Herman	5681	10. Eppa Rixey	1195	10. Bobby Wallace	3.5
11. Red Schoendienst	5243	11. John Clarkson	1143	11. Tommy Corcoran	3.4
12. Rogers Hornsby	5166	12. Carl Mays	1138	12. Herman Long	3.4
13. Hughie Critz	5138	13. Hooks Dauss	1128	13. Rabbit Maranville	3.4
14. Johnny Evers	5124	14. Vic Willis	1124	14. Freddy Parent	3.4
15. Fred Pfeffer	5104	15. Eddie Plank	1108	15. Joe Tinker	3.4
		15. Red Faber	1108		

3B				**OF**	
1. Brooks Robinson	6205			1. Tommy McCarthy	.2
2. Graig Nettles	4837			2. Chicken Wolf	.2
3. Ron Santo	4581			3. Pop Corkhill	.2
4. Eddie Mathews	4323			4. Sam Thompson	.2
5. Aurelio Rodriguez	4150			5. Tom Brown	.2
6. Mike Schmidt	4108			6. Curt Welch	.2
7. Buddy Bell	3947	**ASSISTS/GAME**		7. Jimmy Ryan	.2
8. Sal Bando	3720			8. George Van Haltren	.2
9. Lave Cross	3703			9. George Gore	.2
10. Jimmy Collins	3702			10. Ed Delahanty	.2
11. Eddie Yost	3659			11. Paul Hines	.2
12. Ken Boyer	3652			12. Ned Hanlon	.2
13. Ron Cey	3624			13. Tris Speaker	.2
14. Arlie Latham	3545			14. Tilly Walker	.2
15. Pie Traynor	3525			15. George Wood	.2

SS		**1B**		**C**	
1. Luis Aparicio	8016	1. Ferris Fain	.8	1. Duke Farrell	1.4
2. Bill Dahlen	7500	2. Vic Power	.8	2. Red Dooin	1.3
3. Rabbit Maranville	7354	3. Bill Buckner	.8	3. Johnny Kling	1.3
4. Luke Appling	7218	4. Keith Hernandez	.8	4. Bill Killefer	1.3
5. Tommy Corcoran	7106	5. George Sisler	.8	5. Oscar Stanage	1.3
6. Larry Bowa	6654	6. Rudy York	.8	6. Chief Zimmer	1.3
7. Dave Bancroft	6561	7. Fred Tenney	.8	7. Jack Warner	1.3
8. Roger Peckinpaugh	6334	8. Dick Stuart	.7	8. Ivy Wingo	1.2
9. Bobby Wallace	6303	9. Elbie Fletcher	.7	9. Billy Sullivan	1.2
10. Don Kessinger	6212	10. George McQuinn	.7	10. George Gibson	1.2
11. Roy McMillan	6191	11. Mike Hargrove	.7	11. Deacon McGuire	1.2
12. Germany Smith	6154	12. Bill Terry	.7	12. Malachi Kittredge	1.1
13. Herman Long	6130	13. George Stovall	.7	13. Steve O'Neill	1.1
14. Donie Bush	6119	14. Frank McCormick	.7	14. Wilbert Robinson	1.1
15. Bert Campaneris	6064	15. Chris Chambliss	.7	15. Frank Snyder	1.1

OF		**2B**		**P**	
1. Tris Speaker	448	1. Hughie Critz	3.5	1. Addie Joss	3.0
2. Ty Cobb	392	2. Frankie Frisch	3.4	2. Harry Howell	2.8
3. Jimmy Ryan	375	3. Oscar Melillo	3.4	3. Ed Walsh	2.8
4. Tom Brown	348	4. Lou Bierbauer	3.3	4. Nick Altrock	2.8
4. George Van Haltren	348	5. Fred Pfeffer	3.3	5. Willie Sudhoff	2.7
6. Harry Hooper	344	6. Rogers Hornsby	3.3	6. Nixey Callahan	2.6
7. Max Carey	339	7. Tony Cuccinello	3.2	7. George Mullin	2.5
8. Jimmy Sheckard	307	8. Cupid Childs	3.2	8. Ed Willett	2.5
9. Clyde Milan	294	9. Charlie Gehringer	3.2	9. Barney Pelty	2.5
10. King Kelly	290	10. Bill Mazeroski	3.2	10. Red Donahue	2.5
11. Orator Shaffer	289	11. Bobby Lowe	3.2	11. Bill Bernhard	2.4
12. Sam Thompson	283	12. Manny Trillo	3.1	12. Jack Taylor	2.4
13. Sam Rice	278	13. Max Bishop	3.1	13. Christy Mathewson	2.4
14. Dummy Hoy	273	14. Billy Herman	3.1	14. Jesse Tannehill	2.3
15. Jesse Burkett	270	15. Bid McPhee	3.1	15. Bob Rhoads	2.3

PART FIVE

The Teams and Their Players

YEAR-BY-YEAR ORDER OF FINISH

THE LINEUPS, INCLUDING PITCHERS

INDIVIDUAL BATTING, PITCHING, AND FIELDING

THE MANAGERS

TEAM STATISTICS

LEAGUE LEADERS

The Teams and Their Players

The Teams and Their Players is a chronological listing of team standings, league leaders, basic team rosters, and player records for every major league from 1876 through today. This section, which serves as a cross-reference to the Player and Pitcher Registers, makes it possible to find out such information as who played second base for the Brooklyn Dodgers in 1924, or who were the top pitchers for the Detroit Tigers in 1917. It also gives the yearly league leaders in many statistical categories and includes the names and records of the men who managed the teams. The information is presented on a year-by-year basis starting with the National League in 1876.

All information and abbreviations that may appear unfamiliar are explained in the sample format presented below. The National League team rosters of 1876 would normally appear first, but for the purpose of using an example to illustrate the information only the Chicago team is shown. They finished first in 1876, and all teams are presented in the order of final standing.

	POS	Player	AB	BA	HR	RBI	PO	A	E	DP	TC/G	FA	Pitcher	G	IP	W	L	SV	ERA
Chi.	1B	C. McVey	308	.347	1	53	485	10	21	21	9.4	.959	A. Spalding	61	529	46	12	0	1.75
W-52 L-14	2B	R. Barnes	322	.429	1	59	167	199	36	22	6.1	.910	C. McVey	11	59	6	2	2	1.52
Al Spalding	SS	J. Peters	316	.351	1	47	95	193	21	16	4.7	.932							
	3B	C. Anson	309	.356	1	59	135	147	50	8	5.0	.849							
	RF	B. Addy	142	.282	0	16	46	6	13	0	2.0	.800							
	CF	P. Hines	305	.331	2	59	159	8	14	4	2.8	.923							
	LF	J. Glenn	276	.304	0	32	128	5	18	1	2.7	.881							
	C	D. White	303	.343	1	60	295	50	64	3	6.5	.844							
	P	A. Spalding	292	.312	0	44	45	92	7	7	2.4	.951							
	OF	O. Bielaski	139	.209	0	10	41	4	14	1	1.8	.763							

ROSTER COLUMN HEADINGS INFORMATION

POS	Fielding Position
AB	At Bats
BA	Batting Average
HR	Home Runs
RBI	Runs Batted In
PO	Put Outs
A	Assists
E	Errors
DP	Double Plays
TC/G	Total Fielding Chances per Game
FA	Fielding Average
G	Games Pitched In
IP	Innings Pitched (rounded off to the nearest inning)
W	Wins
L	Losses
SV	Saves
ERA	Earned Run Average

TEAM INFORMATION EXPLANATION

The abbreviations for the team rosters appear as listed below.

ALT.	Altoona	NWK.	Newark
ATL.	Atlanta	N.Y.	New York
BAL.	Baltimore	OAK.	Oakland
BOS.	Boston	PHI.	Philadelphia
BKN.	Brooklyn	PIT.	Pittsburgh
BUF.	Buffalo	PRO.	Providence
CAL.	California	RIC.	Richmond
CHI.	Chicago	ROC.	Rochester
CIN.	Cincinnati	S. D.	San Diego
CLE.	Cleveland	SEA.	Seattle
COL.	Columbus	S. F.	San Francisco
DET.	Detroit	ST. L.	St. Louis
HAR.	Hartford	ST. P.	St. Paul
HOU.	Houston	SYR.	Syracuse
IND.	Indianapolis	TEX.	Texas
K. C.	Kansas City	TOL.	Toledo
L. A.	Los Angeles	TOR.	Toronto
LOU.	Louisville	TRO.	Troy
MIL.	Milwaukee	WAS.	Washington
MIN.	Minnesota	WIL.	Wilmington
MON.	Montreal	WOR.	Worcester

Three franchises in the history of major league baseball changed their location during the season. These teams are designated by the first letter of the two cities they represented. They are:

B-B   Brooklyn-Baltimore (American Association, 1890)
C-M   Cincinnati-Milwaukee (American Association, 1891)
C-P   Chicago-Pittsburgh (Union Association, 1884)

Directly beneath the city abbreviation is the team won and lost record and name of the man who managed the team. (Teams with more than one manager have the managers listed in the order of when they managed. The top listing would indicate the first manager.)

Multiple Team Players. If a man played for more than one team in the same year, the information shown is only his record for the indicated team.

Regulars. The men who appear first on the team roster are considered the regulars for that team at the positions indicated. There are several factors for determining regulars of which "most games played at a position" and "most fielding chances at a position," are the two prime considerations. Fielding information applies only to the position indicated. For regular outfielders the fielding information is for all the outfield positions.

Substitutes. Appearing directly beneath the regulars are the substitutes for the team. Substitutes listed here must have a total of at least one at bat per scheduled game, or 20 or more runs batted in for the season. Substitutes are listed in order of most at bats, and can be someone who played most of the team's games as a regular, but not at one position. The rules for determining the listed positions of substitutes are as follows:

One Position Substitutes. If a man played at least 70% of his games in the field at one position, then he is listed only at that position, except for outfielders, where all three outfield positions are included under one category. Fielding information applies only to the position indicated.

Two Position Substitutes. If a man did not play at least 70% of his games in the field at one position, but did play more than 90% of his total games at two positions, then he is shown with a combination fielding position. For example, a player who has an "S2" shown in his position column, would mean that he played at least 90% of his games between shortstop and second base. These combinations are always indicated by the first letter or number of the position. Fielding information applies only to the two positions indicated. The position listed first is where the most games were played.

Utility Players. If a player has a "UT" shown in his position column, it means that he did not meet the above 70% or 90% requirement and is listed as a utility player. The fielding information is his total for all positions.

Pinch Hitters. Men who played less than 15 games in the field, but who had 20 runs batted in or more, are considered pinch hitters and are listed as "PH" and no fielding information is shown.

Total Chances per Game. This statistic is not shown for men who were two position substitutes or utility players, because total chances per game is only meaningful in reference to a specific fielding position.

Pitchers. A pitcher is included if he pitched 100 or more innings, or had ten decisions (a decision being a win, loss, or save). Pitchers are listed in order of innings pitched.

League Leader Qualifications (also applies for Yearly League Leaders Information). Throughout baseball, there have been different rules used to determine the minimum appearances necessary to qualify for league leader in categories concerning averages. (Batting Average, Earned Run Average, etc.) For the rules and the years they were in effect, see Appendix C.

League Batting Leaders. Batting statistics that appear in bold faced print indicate that the player led his league in a particular batting category. When there is a tie for league lead, the figures for all the men who tied are shown in bold face.

League Fielding Leaders. Fielding statistics that appear in bold faced print indicate that the player led his league in a particular fielding category at his position. For the purpose of determining league leaders, all outfield positions are combined into one position. When there is a tie for league lead, the figures for all the men who tied are shown in bold face.

League Pitching Leaders. Pitching statistics that appear in bold faced print indicate that the pitcher led his league in a particular pitching category. When there is a tie for league lead, the figures for all the men who tied are shown in bold face.

Traded League Leaders. An asterisk (*) next to a particular figure indicates that the player led the league that year in the particular statistical category, but since he played for more than one team, the figure does not necessarily represent his league leading total or average.

Unavailable Information. Any time a blank space is shown in a particular statistical column it indicates that the information was unavailable or incomplete. This, however, does not apply for *Total Chances per Game,* which is explained above.

Estimated Earned Run Averages (also applies for Yearly League Leaders Information). Any time an earned run average appears in italics it indicates that not all the earned runs allowed by the pitcher are known, and the information had to be estimated. For example, it is known that a pitcher's team allowed 560 runs in 112 games. Of these games, it is known that in 90 of them the team allowed 420 of which 315 or 75% were earned. The man is known to have pitched 207⅔ innings in 40 games and allowed 134 runs. In 35 of these games it is known that he allowed 118 runs of which 83 were earned. By multiplying the team's known ratio of earned runs to total runs (75%) by the pitcher's 16 (134 minus 118) remaining runs allowed, a figure of 12 additional estimated earned runs is calculated. This means that the pitcher allowed an estimated total of 95 earned runs in 207⅔ innings, for an estimated earned run average of 4.12. In all cases at least 50% of the runs allowed by the team were "known" as a basis for estimating earned run averages.

YEARLY LEAGUE LEADERS INFORMATION

Appearing directly after the roster information are yearly league leaders. The categories generally include the top three and the top five players. However, there can be exceptions to the number of men included in the various categories depending on ties for a position. The exceptions are explained below if there are ties for any position other than first. The rule used for first place ties is that if more than six men tied for first (in a category that lists five), then the information in the categories show only the number of players tied, along with the appropriate statistic. For

	POS	Player	AB	BA	HR	RBI	PO	A	E	DP	TC/G	FA	Pitcher	G	IP	W	L	SV	ERA
Cin.	1B	C. Gould	258	.252	0	11	584	13	39	28	10.4	.939	D. Dean	30	263	4	26	0	3.73
	2B	C. Sweasy	225	.204	0	10	167	158	51	30	6.8	.864	C. Fisher	28	229	4	20	0	3.02
W-9 L-56	SS	H. Kessler	248	.258	0	11	57	118	47	11	4.8	.788							
Charlie Gould	3B	W. Foley	221	.226	0	9	67	101	41	4	4.5	.804							
	RF	D. Pearson	233	.236	0	13	46	9	9	2	2.1	.859							
	CF	C. Jones	276	.286	4	38	151	11	27	2	3.0	.857							
	LF	R. Snyder	205	.151	0	12	168	6	37	1	3.8	.825							
	C	A. Booth	272	.261	0	14	77	29	38	3	6.0	.736							
	P	D. Dean	138	.261	0	4	22	38	13	2	2.4	.822							
	PO	C. Fisher	129	.248	0	4	31	28	13	0		.819							
	UT	B. Clack	118	.161	0	5	105	33	26	1		.841							

BATTING AND BASE RUNNING LEADERS

Batting Average

R. Barnes, CHI	.429
G. Hall, PHI	.366
C. Anson, CHI	.356
J. Peters, CHI	.351
C. McVey, CHI	.347

Slugging Average

R. Barnes, CHI	.590
G. Hall, PHI	.545
L. Pike, STL	.472
C. Anson, CHI	.453
L. Meyerle, PHI	.449

Home Runs

G. Hall, PHI	5
C. Jones, CIN	4

Total Bases

R. Barnes, CHI	190
G. Hall, PHI	146
C. Anson, CHI	140
P. Hines, CHI	134
L. Pike, STL	133
G. Wright, BOS	133

Runs Batted In

D. White, CHI	60
P. Hines, CHI	59
C. Anson, CHI	59
R. Barnes, CHI	59
C. McVey, CHI	53

Stolen Bases

(not available)

Hits

R. Barnes, CHI	138
J. Peters, CHI	111
C. Anson, CHI	110

Base on Balls

R. Barnes, CHI	20
J. O'Rourke, BOS	15
J. Burdock, HAR	13

Home Run Percentage

G. Hall, PHI	1.9
C. Jones, CIN	1.4
L. Brown, BOS	1.0

Runs Scored

R. Barnes, CHI	126
G. Wright, BOS	72
J. Peters, CHI	70

Doubles

P. Hines, CHI	21
D. Higham, HAR	21
R. Barnes, CHI	21

Triples

R. Barnes, CHI	14
G. Hall, PHI	13
L. Pike, STL	10
L. Meyerle, PHI	8

PITCHING LEADERS

Winning Percentage

A. Spalding, CHI	.783
J. Manning, BOS	.783
T. Bond, HAR	.705
G. Bradley, STL	.703
C. Cummings, HAR	.667

Earned Run Average

G. Bradley, STL	1.23
J. Devlin, LOU	1.56
C. Cummings, HAR	1.67
T. Bond, HAR	1.68
A. Spalding, CHI	1.75

Wins

A. Spalding, CHI	47
G. Bradley, STL	45
T. Bond, HAR	31
J. Devlin, LOU	30
B. Mathews, NY	21

Saves

J. Manning, BOS	5
C. McVey, CHI	2
G. Zettlein, PHI	2

Strikeouts

J. Devlin, LOU	122
G. Bradley, STL	103
T. Bond, HAR	88
A. Spalding, CHI	39
B. Mathews, NY	37

Complete Games

J. Devlin, LOU	66
G. Bradley, STL	63
B. Mathews, NY	55
A. Spalding, CHI	53
T. Bond, HAR	45

Fewest Hits per 9 Innings

G. Bradley, STL	7.38
T. Bond, HAR	7.83
J. Devlin, LOU	8.19

Shutouts

G. Bradley, STL	16
A. Spalding, CHI	8
T. Bond, HAR	6

Fewest Walks per 9 Innings

G. Zettlein, PHI	0.23
C. Fisher, CIN	0.24
T. Bond, HAR	0.29

Most Strikeouts per 9 Inn.

T. Bond, HAR	1.94
J. Devlin, LOU	1.77
G. Bradley, STL	1.62

Innings

J. Devlin, LOU	622
G. Bradley, STL	573
A. Spalding, CHI	529

Games Pitched

J. Devlin, LOU	68
G. Bradley, STL	64
A. Spalding, CHI	61

	W	L	PCT	GB	R	OR	Batting 2B	3B	HR	BA	SA	SB	Fielding E	DP	FA	CG	BB	Pitching SO	ShO	SV	ERA
CHI	52	14	.788		624	257	131	32	7	.337	.416	0	282	33	.899	58	29	51	8	4	1.76
STL	45	19	.703	6	386	229	73	27	2	.259	.313	0	268	33	.902	63	39	103	16	0	1.22
HAR	47	21	.691	6	429	261	96	22	2	.267	.322	0	337	27	.888	69	27	114	11	0	1.67
BOS	39	31	.557	15	471	450	96	24	9	.266	.328	0	442	42	.860	49	104	77	3	7	2.51
LOU	30	36	.455	22	280	344	68	14	6	.249	.294	0	397	44	.875	67	38	125	5	0	1.69
NY	21	35	.375	26	260	412	39	15	2	.227	.261	0	473	18	.825	56	24	37	2	0	2.94
PHI	14	45	.237	34.5	378	534	79	35	7	.271	.342	0	456	32	.839	53	41	22	1	2	3.22
CIN	9	56	.138	42.5	238	579	51	12	4	.234	.271	0	469	45	.841	57	34	60		0	3.62
					3066	3066	633	181	39	.265	.321	0	3124	274	.866	472	336	589	46	13	2.31

	POS	Player	AB	BA	HR	RBI	PO	A	E	DP	TC/G	FA	Pitcher	G	IP	W	L	SV	ERA
Bos. W-42 L-18 Harry Wright	1B	D. White	266	.387	2	49	324	13	13	16	10.0	.963	T. Bond	58	521	40	17	0	2.11
	2B	G. Wright	290	.276	0	35	171	209	53	28	7.5	.878							
	SS	E. Sutton	253	.292	0	39	66	91	21	8	4.9	.882							
	3B	J. Morrill	242	.302	0	28	33	43	12	1	2.9	.864							
	RF	H. Schafer	141	.277	0	13	17	1	11	0	1.3	.621							
	CF	J. O'Rourke	265	.362	0	23	112	9	22	0	2.4	.846							
	LF	A. Leonard	272	.287	0	27	79	5	12	2	2.6	.875							
	C	L. Brown	221	.253	1	31	360	67	49	5	8.7	.897							
	P	T. Bond	259	.228	0	30	29	104	9	2	2.4	.937							
	OF	T. Murnane	140	.279	1	15	39	5	10	2	1.8	.815							
Lou. W-35 L-25 Jack Chapman	1B	J. Latham	278	.291	0	22	659	24	36	28	12.2	.950	J. Devlin	61	559	35	25	0	2.25
	2B	J. Gerhardt	250	.304	1	35	167	244	52	30	8.1	.888							
	SS	B. Craver	238	.265	0	29	71	175	26	15	4.8	.904							
	3B	B. Hague	263	.266	1	24	78	78	29	4	3.1	.843							
	RF	O. Shaffer	260	.285	3	34	121	21	28	1	2.8	.835							
	CF	B. Crowley	238	.282	1	23	109	20	23	2	2.6	.849							
	LF	G. Hall	269	.323	0	26	92	7	11	1	1.8	.900							
	C	P. Snyder	248	.258	2	28	292	102	39	8	7.1	.910							
	P	J. Devlin	268	.269	1	27	30	110	10	2	2.5	.933							
Har. W-31 L-27 Bob Ferguson	1B	J. Start	271	.332	1	21	704	10	27	25	12.4	.964	T. Larkin	56	501	29	25	0	2.14
	2B	J. Burdock	277	.260	0	9	185	189	40	25	7.5	.903							
	SS	T. Carey	274	.255	1	20	49	203	53	11	5.1	.826							
	3B	B. Ferguson	254	.256	0	35	109	155	50	6	5.6	.841							
	RF	J. Cassidy	251	.378	0	27	41	16	22	2	1.4	.722							
	CF	J. Holdsworth	260	.254	0	20	79	11	18	1	2.0	.833							
	LF	T. York	237	.283	1	37	130	5	21	1	2.8	.865							
	C	B. Harbidge	167	.222	0	8	143	27	23	2	6.0	.881							
	P	T. Larkin	228	.228	1	18	26	89	15	0	2.3	.885							
	C	D. Allison	115	.148	0	6	127	36	19	4	6.3	.896							
St. L. W-28 L-32 John Lucas W-14 L-12 George McManus W-14 L-20	1B	H. Dehlman	119	.185	0	11	306	4	23	14	10.7	.931	T. Nichols	42	350	18	23	0	2.60
	2B	M. McGeary	258	.252	0	20	125	140	35	12	7.7	.883	J. Blong	25	187	10	9	0	2.74
	SS	D. Force	225	.262	0	22	75	160	22	9	5.1	.914							
	3B	J. Battin	226	.199	1	22	58	77	29	6	5.1	.823							
	RF	J. Blong	218	.216	0	13	60	6	13	0	2.0	.835							
	CF	J. Remsen	123	.260	0	13	73	4	8	0	2.6	.906							
	LF	M. Dorgan	266	.308	0	23	70	5	16	3	1.8	.824							
	C	J. Clapp	255	.318	0	34	269	44	40	2	6.7	.887							
	1O	A. Croft	220	.232	0	27	338	10	22	10		.941							
	P	T. Nichols	186	.167	0	9	14	62	4	1	1.9	.950							
Chi. W-26 L-33 Al Spalding	1B	A. Spalding	254	.256	0	35	472	21	21	23	11.4	.959	G. Bradley	50	394	18	23	0	3.31
	2B	R. Barnes	92	.272	0	5	49	70	23	5	6.5	.838	C. McVey	17	92	4	8	2	4.50
	SS	J. Peters	265	.317	0	41	124	215	45	23	6.4	.883							
	3B	C. Anson	255	.337	0	32	74	77	20	9	4.3	.883							
	RF	P. Hines	261	.280	0	23	75	4	19	1	2.0	.806							
	CF	D. Eggler	136	.265	0	20	60	8	11	3	2.4	.861							
	LF	J. Glenn	202	.228	0	20	66	7	4	1	2.1	.948							
	C	C. McVey	266	.368	0	36	137	34	28	3	5.0	.859							
	P	G. Bradley	214	.243	0	12	25	71	5	1	2.0	.950							
	2O	H. Smith	94	.202	0	3	47	32	18	2		.814							
	OF	J. Hallinan	89	.281	0	11	27	1	7	1	1.8	.800							
Cin. W-15 L-42 Lip Pike W-3 L-11 Bob Addy W-12 L-31	1B	C. Gould	91	.275	0	13	229	9	20	13	10.8	.922	C. Cummings	19	156	5	14	0	4.34
	2B	J. Hallinan	73	.370	0	7	52	36	15	8	6.4	.854	B. Mathews	15	129	3	12	0	4.04
	SS	J. Manning	252	.317	0	36	30	62	32	2	4.8	.742	B. Mitchell	12	100	6	5	0	3.51
	3B	W. Foley	216	.190	0	18	94	130	44	9	4.8	.836							
	RF	B. Addy	245	.278	0	31	74	17	22	5	2.0	.805							
	CF	L. Pike	262	.298	4	23	79	10	22	1	2.9	.802							
	LF	C. Jones	69	.304	1	16	104*	11	23*	1	3.6*	.833							
	C	S. Hastings	71	.141	0	3	63	24	23	1	5.5	.791							
	PH	C. Jones	163	.313	1	20													
	UT	A. Booth	157	.172	0	13	77	101	36	6		.832							
	S2	L. Meyerle	107	.327	0	15	54	86	24	5		.854							
	P	C. Cummings	70	.200	0	4	6	31	3	0	2.1	.925							

BATTING AND BASE RUNNING LEADERS

Batting Average
D. White, BOS	.387
J. Cassidy, HAR	.378
C. McVey, CHI	.368
J. O'Rourke, BOS	.362
C. Anson, CHI	.337

Slugging Average
D. White, BOS	.545
C. Jones, CHI, CIN	.471
J. Cassidy, HAR	.458
C. McVey, CHI	.455
J. O'Rourke, BOS	.445

Home Runs
L. Pike, CIN	4
O. Shaffer, LOU	3
C. Jones, CHI, CIN	2
P. Snyder, LOU	2
D. White, BOS	2

Total Bases
D. White, BOS	145
C. McVey, CHI	121
J. O'Rourke, BOS	118
G. Hall, LOU	118
J. Cassidy, HAR	115

PITCHING LEADERS

Winning Percentage
T. Bond, BOS	.702
J. Devlin, LOU	.583
T. Larkin, HAR	.537
J. Blong, STL	.526
G. Bradley, CHI	.439
T. Nichols, STL	.439

Earned Run Average
T. Bond, BOS	2.11
T. Larkin, HAR	2.14
J. Devlin, LOU	2.25
T. Nichols, STL	2.60
J. Blong, STL	2.74

Wins
T. Bond, BOS	40
J. Devlin, LOU	35
T. Larkin, HAR	29
G. Bradley, CHI	18
T. Nichols, STL	18

Saves
C. McVey, CHI	2
J. Manning, CIN	1
A. Spalding, CHI	1

BATTING AND BASE RUNNING LEADERS

Runs Batted In			Stolen Bases
D. White, BOS	49		(not available)
J. Peters, CHI	41		
E. Sutton, BOS	39		
C. Jones, CHI, CIN	38		
T. York, HAR	37		

Hits			Base on Balls	
D. White, BOS	103		J. O'Rourke, BOS	20
C. McVey, CHI	98		C. Jones, CHI, CIN	15
J. O'Rourke, BOS	96		A. Booth, CIN	12
			G. Hall, LOU	12

Home Run Percentage			Runs Scored	
L. Pike, CIN	1.5		J. O'Rourke, BOS	68
O. Shaffer, LOU	1.2		C. McVey, CHI	58
C. Jones, CHI, CIN	0.8		G. Wright, BOS	58

Doubles			Triples	
C. Anson, CHI	19		D. White, BOS	11
T. York, HAR	16		C. Jones, CHI, CIN	10
J. Manning, CIN	16		L. Brown, BOS	8
			G. Hall, LOU	8

PITCHING LEADERS

Strikeouts			Complete Games	
T. Bond, BOS	170		J. Devlin, LOU	61
J. Devlin, LOU	141		T. Bond, BOS	58
T. Larkin, HAR	96		T. Larkin, HAR	55
T. Nichols, STL	80		T. Nichols, STL	35
G. Bradley, CHI	59		G. Bradley, CHI	35

Fewest Hits per 9 Innings			Shutouts	
T. Bond, BOS	9.16		T. Bond, BOS	6
T. Larkin, HAR	9.16		T. Larkin, HAR	4
T. Nichols, STL	9.67		J. Devlin, LOU	4
			G. Bradley, CHI	2

Fewest Walks per 9 Innings			Most Strikeouts per 9 Inn.	
T. Bond, BOS	0.62		B. Mitchell, CIN	3.69
J. Devlin, LOU	0.66		T. Bond, BOS	2.94
C. Cummings, CIN	0.75		J. Blong, STL	2.45

Innings			Games Pitched	
J. Devlin, LOU	559		J. Devlin, LOU	61
T. Bond, BOS	521		T. Bond, BOS	58
T. Larkin, HAR	501		T. Larkin, HAR	56

	W	L	PCT	GB	R	OR	2B	3B	Batting HR	BA	SA	SB	E	Fielding DP	FA	CG	BB	Pitching SO	ShO	SV	ERA
BOS	42	18	.700		419	263	91	37	4	.296	.370	0	290	36	.889	61	38	177	7	0	2.15
LOU	35	25	.583	7	339	288	75	36	9	.280	.354	0	267	37	.904	61	41	141	4	0	2.25
HAR	31	27	.534	10	341	311	63	31	4	.270	.328	0	313	32	.885	59	56	99	4	0	2.32
STL	28	32	.467	14	284	318	51	36	1	.244	.302	0	281	29	.892	52	92	132	1	0	2.66
CHI	26	33	.441	15.5	366	375	79	30		.278	.340	0	313	43	.883	45	58	92	3	3	3.37
CIN	15	42	.263	25.5	291	485	72	34	6	.255	.329	0	394	33	.852	48	61	85	1	1	4.19
					2040	2040	431	204	24	.271	.338	0	1858	210	.884	326	346	726	20	4	2.81

National League 1878

	POS	Player	AB	BA	HR	RBI	PO	A	E	DP	TC/G	FA	Pitcher	G	IP	W	L	SV	ERA
Bos. W-41 L-19 Harry Wright	1B	J. Morrill	233	.240	0	23	606	22	28	36	11.1	.957	T. Bond	59	533	40	19	0	2.06
	2B	J. Burdock	246	.260	0	25	245	212	41	34	8.3	.918							
	SS	G. Wright	267	.225	0	12	72	197	15	24	4.8	.947							
	3B	E. Sutton	239	.226	1	29	80	118	25	8	3.8	.888							
	RF	J. Manning	248	.254	0	23	61	9	23	1	1.6	.753							
	CF	J. O'Rourke	255	.278	1	29	102	15	19	4	2.4	.860							
	LF	A. Leonard	262	.260	0	16	65	8	21	1	1.6	.777							
	C	P. Snyder	226	.212	0	14	344	92	42	2	8.2	.912							
	P	T. Bond	236	.212	0	23	27	117	9	4	2.6	.941							
Cin. W-37 L-23 Cal McVey	1B	C. Sullivan	244	.258	0	20	680	23	18	33	11.8	.975	W. White	52	468	30	21	0	1.79
	2B	J. Gerhardt	259	.297	0	28	159	206	38	26	6.7	.906							
	SS	B. Geer	237	.219	0	20	58	177	36	15	4.5	.867							
	3B	C. McVey	271	.306	2	28	78	106	42	6	3.7	.814							
	RF	K. Kelly	237	.283	0	27	51	24	23	2	2.1	.765							
	CF	L. Pike	145	.324	0	11	38	4	9	1	1.6	.824							
	LF	C. Jones	261	.310	3	39	120	9	15	1	2.4	.896							
	C	D. White	258	.314	0	29	262	66	33	4	7.5	.909							
	P	W. White	197	.142	0	9	13	90	15	2	2.3	.873							
	OF	B. Dickerson	123	.309	0	9	56	1	8	0	2.2	.877							
Pro. W-33 L-27 George Ware	1B	T. Murnane	188	.239	0	14	543	22	36	25	12.5	.940	M. Ward	37	334	22	13	0	1.51
	2B	C. Sweasy	212	.175	0	8	141	183	59	20	7.0	.846	T. Nichols	11	98	4	7	0	4.22
	SS	T. Carey	253	.237	0	24	56	207	38	8	4.9	.874							
	3B	B. Hague	250	.204	0	25	81	177	21	5	4.5	.925							
	RF	D. Higham	281	.320	1	29	76	27	24	4	2.0	.811							
	CF	P. Hines	257	.358	4	50	109	15	22	4	2.4	.849							
	LF	T. York	269	.309	1	26	89	14	15	3	1.9	.873							
	C	L. Brown	243	.305	1	43	232	84	43	11	8.0	.880							
	P	M. Ward	138	.196	1	15	23	74	15	4	3.0	.866							
	C	D. Allison	76	.289	0	7	96	27	12	1	7.1	.911							

	POS	Player	AB	BA	HR	RBI	PO	A	E	DP	TC/G	FA	Pitcher	G	IP	W	L	SV	ERA
Chi.	1B	J. Start	285	.351	1	27	719	13	33	28	12.5	.957	T. Larkin	56	506	29	26	0	2.24
W-30 L-30	2B	B. McClellan	205	.224	0	29	87	139	35	15	6.2	.866							
Bob Ferguson	SS	B. Ferguson	259	.351	0	39	71	226	40	17	5.9	.881							
	3B	F. Hankinson	240	.267	1	27	94	138	33	9	4.6	.875							
	RF	J. Cassidy	256	.266	0	29	89	30	28	6	2.5	.810							
	CF	J. Remsen	224	.232	1	19	103	14	7	5	2.2	.944							
	LF	C. Anson	261	.341	0	40	60	6	14	0	1.7	.825							
	C	B. Harbidge	240	.296	0	37	257	66	45	1	7.4	.878							
	P	T. Larkin	226	.288	0	32	19	90	18	0	2.3	.858							
	O2	J. Hallinan	67	.284	0	2	26	14	12	1		.769							
Ind.	1B	A. Croft	222	.158	0	16	534	8	21	19	11.0	.963	T. Nolan	38	347	13	22	0	2.57
W-24 L-36	2B	J. Quest	278	.205	0	13	228	196	60	27	7.8	.876	J. McCormick	14	117	5	8	0	1.69
John Clapp	SS	F. Warner	165	.248	0	10	41	124	17	9	4.4	.907	T. Healey	11	89	6	4	1*	2.22
	3B	N. Williamson	250	.232	1	19	88	128	33	6	4.0	.867							
	RF	O. Shaffer	266	.338	0	30	105	28	25	2	2.5	.842							
	CF	R. McKelvey	253	.225	2	36	119	18	25	2	2.6	.846							
	LF	J. Clapp	263	.304	0	29	60	5	8	0	1.7	.890							
	C	S. Flint	254	.224	0	18	285	102	39	7	7.2	.908							
	P	T. Nolan	152	.243	0	16	19	80	11	5	2.9	.900							
	SS	C. Nelson	84	.131	0	5	19	50	13	1	4.3	.841							
Mil.	1B	J. Goodman	252	.246	1	27	693	12	42	15	12.5	.944	S. Weaver	45	383	12	31	0	1.95
W-15 L-45	2B	J. Peters	246	.309	0	22	97	136	40	14	8.0	.853	M. Golden	22	161	3	13	0	4.14
Jack Chapman	SS	B. Redmond	187	.230	0	21	31	97	35	5	4.2	.785							
	3B	W. Foley	229	.271	0	22	68	87	36	8	3.6	.812							
	RF	B. Holbert	173	.185	0	12	35	19	12	1	2.2	.818							
	CF	M. Golden	214	.206	0	20	50	9	12	2	1.8	.831							
	LF	A. Dalrymple	271	.354	0	15	128	11	28	3	2.7	.832							
	C	C. Bennett	184	.245	1	12	176	31	42	4	7.1	.831							
	UT	G. Creamer	193	.212	0	15	82	117	37	7		.843							
	P	S. Weaver	170	.200	0	3	31	78	16	1	2.8	.872							

BATTING AND BASE RUNNING LEADERS

Batting Average

P. Hines, PRO	.358
A. Dalrymple, MIL	.354
B. Ferguson, CHI	.351
J. Start, CHI	.351
C. Anson, CHI	.341

Slugging Average

P. Hines, PRO	.486
T. York, PRO	.465
O. Shaffer, IND	.455
L. Brown, PRO	.453
C. Jones, CIN	.441

Home Runs

P. Hines, PRO	4
C. Jones, CIN	3
R. McKelvey, IND	2
C. McVey, CIN	2

Total Bases

P. Hines, PRO	125
T. York, PRO	125
J. Start, CHI	125
O. Shaffer, IND	121
D. Higham, PRO	117

Runs Batted In

P. Hines, PRO	50
L. Brown, PRO	43
C. Anson, CHI	40
B. Ferguson, CHI	39
C. Jones, CIN	39

Stolen Bases

(not available)

Hits

J. Start, CHI	100
A. Dalrymple, MIL	96
P. Hines, PRO	92

Base on Balls

J. Remsen, CHI	17
T. Larkin, CHI	17

Home Run Percentage

P. Hines, PRO	1.6
C. Jones, CIN	1.1
R. McKelvey, IND	0.8

Runs Scored

D. Higham, PRO	60
J. Start, CHI	58
T. York, PRO	56

Doubles

D. Higham, PRO	22
L. Brown, PRO	21
O. Shaffer, IND	19
T. York, PRO	19

Triples

T. York, PRO	10
J. O'Rourke, BOS	7
C. Jones, CIN	7

PITCHING LEADERS

Winning Percentage

T. Bond, BOS	.678
M. Ward, PRO	.629
W. White, CIN	.588
T. Larkin, CHI	.527
T. Nolan, IND	.371

Earned Run Average

M. Ward, PRO	1.51
J. McCormick, IND	1.69
W. White, CIN	1.79
S. Weaver, MIL	1.95
T. Bond, BOS	2.06

Wins

T. Bond, BOS	40
W. White, CIN	30
T. Larkin, CHI	29
M. Ward, PRO	22
T. Nolan, IND	13

Saves

T. Healey, IND, PRO	1

Strikeouts

T. Bond, BOS	182
W. White, CIN	169
T. Larkin, CHI	163
T. Nolan, IND	125
M. Ward, PRO	116

Complete Games

T. Bond, BOS	57
T. Larkin, CHI	56
W. White, CIN	52
S. Weaver, MIL	39
M. Ward, PRO	37
T. Nolan, IND	37

Fewest Hits per 9 Innings

M. Ward, PRO	8.30
S. Weaver, MIL	8.72
T. Larkin, CHI	9.09

Shutouts

T. Bond, BOS	9
M. Ward, PRO	6
W. White, CIN	5

Fewest Walks per 9 Innings

S. Weaver, MIL	0.49
T. Larkin, CHI	0.55
T. Bond, BOS	0.56

Most Strikeouts per 9 Inn.

W. White, CIN	3.25
T. Nolan, IND	3.24
M. Ward, PRO	3.13

Innings

T. Bond, BOS	533
T. Larkin, CHI	506
W. White, CIN	468

Games Pitched

T. Bond, BOS	59
T. Larkin, CHI	56
W. White, CIN	52

	W	L	PCT	GB	R	OR	Batting 2B	3B	HR	BA	SA	SB	Fielding E	DP	FA	CG	BB	Pitching SO	ShO	SV	ERA
BOS	41	19	.683		298	241	75	25	2	.241	.300	0	228	48	.914	58	38	184	9	0	2.32
CIN	37	23	.617	4	333	281	67	22	5	.276	.331	0	269	37	.900	61	63	220	6	0	1.84
PRO	33	27	.550	8	353	337	107	30	8	.263	.346	0	311	42	.892	59	86	173	6	0	2.38
CHI	30	30	.500	11	371	331	91	20	3	.290	.350	0	304	37	.891	61	35	175	1	0	2.37
IND	24	36	.400	17	293	328	76	15	3	.236	.286	0	290	37	.898	59	87	182	2	1	2.32
MIL	15	45	.250	26	256	386	65	20	2	.250	.300	0	376	32	.866	54	55	147	1	0	2.60
					1904	1904	481	132	23	.259	.319	0	1778	233	.893	352	364	1081	25	1	2.30

National League 1879

	POS	Player	AB	BA	HR	RBI	PO	A	E	DP	TC/G	FA	Pitcher	G	IP	W	L	SV	ERA
Pro. W-59 L-25 George Wright	1B	J. Start	317	.319	2	37	779	11	22	24	12.5	.973	M. Ward	70	587	47	17	1	2.15
	2B	M. McGeary	374	.275	0	35	218	255	62	21	7.3	.884	B. Mathews	27	189	12	8	1	2.29
	SS	G. Wright	388	.276	1	42	96	319	34	17	5.3	.924							
	3B	B. Hague	209	.225	0	21	54	122	38	2	4.2	.822							
	RF	J. O'Rourke	362	.348	1	46	51	11	17	2	1.4	.785							
	CF	P. Hines	409	.357	2	52	146	24	26	3	2.3	.867							
	LF	T. York	342	.310	1	50	114	9	14	2	1.7	.898							
	C	L. Brown	229	.258	2	40	286	63	63*	5	8.6*	.847							
	P	M. Ward	364	.286	2	41	31	134	11	2	2.5	.938							
	PO	B. Mathews	173	.202	1	10	21	44	9	1		.878							
	C	E. Gross	132	.348	0	24	152	39	22	1	7.1	.897							
Bos. W-54 L-30 Harry Wright	1B	E. Cogswell	236	.322	1	18	539	10	19	24	11.6	.967	T. Bond	64	555	43	19	0	1.96
	2B	J. Burdock	359	.240	0	36	303	300	59	43	7.9	.911	C. Foley	21	162	9	9	1	2.51
	SS	E. Sutton	339	.248	0	34	53	167	29	15	4.9	.884							
	3B	J. Morrill	348	.282	0	49	70	96	23	2	3.7	.878							
	RF	S. Houck	356	.267	2	49	62	17	18	2	2.1	.814							
	CF	J. O'Rourke	317	.341	6	62	147	10	21	2	2.5	.882							
	LF	C. Jones	355	.315	9	62	162	20	13	1	2.3	.933							
	C	P. Snyder	329	.237	2	35	398	142	44	10	7.3	.925							
	P	T. Bond	257	.241	0	21	33	144	8	7	2.9	.957							
	OF	B. Hawes	155	.200	0	9	38	10	10	2	1.7	.828							
	PO	C. Foley	146	.315	0	17	13	28	12	0		.774							
Buf. W-46 L-32 John Clapp	1B	O. Walker	287	.275	1	35	828	30	49	52	12.6	.946	P. Galvin	66	593	37	27	0	2.28
	2B	C. Fulmer	306	.268	0	28	273	301	60	46	8.3	.905	McGunnigle	14	120	9	5	0	2.63
	SS	D. Force	316	.209	0	8	74	264	26	26	4.7	.929							
	3B	H. Richardson	336	.283	0	37	83	153	44	13	3.6	.843							
	RF	B. Crowley	261	.287	0	30	62	14	18	4	2.2	.809							
	CF	D. Eggler	317	.208	0	27	114	11	11	2	1.7	.919							
	LF	J. Hornung	319	.266	0	38	128	12	26	1	2.2	.844							
	C	J. Clapp	292	.264	1	36	286	60	36	4	6.1	.906							
	P	P. Galvin	265	.249	0	27	35	141	26	8	3.1	.871							
	OF	McGunnigle	171	.175	0	5	61	6	6	0	2.1	.918							
Chi. W-46 L-33 Cap Anson	1B	C. Anson	227	.396	0	34	620	8	16	26	12.6	.975	T. Larkin	58	513	31	23	0	2.44
	2B	J. Quest	334	.207	0	22	263	331	48	30	7.7	.925	F. Hankinson	26	231	15	10	0	2.50
	SS	J. Peters	379	.245	1	31	94	271	71	14	5.3	.837							
	3B	N. Williamson	320	.294	1	36	84	193	41	13	4.5	.871							
	RF	O. Shaffer	316	.304	0	35	99	50	37	3	2.6	.801							
	CF	G. Gore	266	.263	0	32	93	9	15	0	2.2	.872							
	LF	A. Dalrymple	333	.291	0	23	103	4	40	1	2.1	.728							
	C	S. Flint	324	.284	1	41	341	109	42	6	6.3	.915							
	P	T. Larkin	228	.219	0	18	10	79	8	1	1.7	.918							
	UT	F. Hankinson	171	.181	0	8	42	87	14	1		.902							
	OF	J. Remsen	152	.217	0	8	52	4	9	1	2.1	.862							
Cin. W-43 L-37 Deacon White W-8 L-8 Cal McVey W-35 L-29	1B	C. McVey	354	.297	0	55	736	5	42	33	10.9	.946	W. White	76	680	43	31	0	1.99
	2B	J. Gerhardt	313	.198	1	39	191	192	39	23	7.7	.908							
	SS	R. Barnes	323	.266	1	30	93	211	48	14	5.8	.864							
	3B	K. Kelly	345	.348	2	47	36	88	25	3	4.5	.832							
	RF	W. Foley	218	.211	0	25	38	9	8	0	2.2	.855							
	CF	P. Hotaling	369	.279	1	27	118	16	25	2	2.3	.843							
	LF	B. Dickerson	350	.291	2	57	144	9	38	1	2.4	.801							
	C	D. White	333	.330	1	52	307	92	44	3	7.5	.901							
	P	W. White	294	.136	0	17	20	114	20	0	2.0	.870							
	UT	M. Burke	117	.222	0	8	36	62	32	3		.754							

	POS	Player	AB	BA	HR	RBI	PO	A	E	DP	TC/G	FA	Pitcher	G	IP	W	L	SV	ERA
Cle.	1B	B. Phillips	365	.271	0	29	726	22	36	23	10.5	.954	J. McCormick	62	546	20	**40**	0	2.42
W-27 L-55	2B	J. Glasscock	325	.209	0	29	201	208	36	18	6.7	.919	B. Mitchell	23	195	7	15	0	3.28
Jim McCormick	SS	T. Carey	335	.239	0	32	79	263	54	13	5.0	.864							
	3B	F. Warner	316	.244	0	22	78	109	39	5	4.2	.827							
	RF	C. Eden	353	.272	3	34	101	21	29	3	1.9	.808							
	CF	G. Strief	264	.174	0	15	104	8	10	0	2.2	.918							
	LF	B. Riley	165	.145	0	9	79	12	16	1	2.5	.850							
	C	D. Kennedy	193	.290	1	18	277	50	40	2	8.0	.891							
	P	J. McCormick	282	.220	0	20	**39**	119	9	4	2.7	.946							
	CO	B. Gilligan	205	.171	0	11	179	47	36	0		.863							
	P	B. Mitchell	109	.147	0	6	11	24	14	0	2.1	.714							
Syr.	1B	H. Carpenter	261	.203	0	20	298	10	17	12	9.6	.948	H. McCormick	54	457	18	33	0	2.99
W-22 L-48	2B	J. Farrell	241	.303	1	22	162	186	52	16	7.4	.870	B. Purcell	22	180	4	15	0	3.76
Mike Dorgan	SS	J. Macullar	246	.211	0	13	61	111	27	9	5.4	.864							
	3B	R. Woodhead	131	.160	0	2	52	51	27	4	3.8	.792							
	RF	B. Purcell	277	.260	0	24	64	4	20	0	1.9	.773							
	CF	J. Richmond	254	.213	1	23	76	7	12	1	2.7	.874							
	LF	M. Mansell	242	.215	1	13	**204**	11	29	2	**3.6**	.881							
	C	B. Holbert	229	.201	0	21	277	64	39	4	6.8	.897							
	UT	M. Dorgan	270	.267	1	17	275	60	46	10		.879							
	P	H. McCormick	230	.222	1	21	13	68	8	0	1.6	.910							
Tro.	1B	D. Brouthers	168	.274	4	17	406	6	33	11	12.0	.926	G. Bradley	54	487	13	**40**	0	2.85
W-19 L-56	2B	T. Hawkes	250	.208	0	20	220	264	56	26	**8.4**	.896	H. Salisbury	10	89	4	6	0	2.22
Horace Phillips	SS	E. Caskin	304	.257	0	21	42	169	23	10	5.6	.902							
W-12 L-46	3B	H. Doscher	191	.220	0	18	49	96	35	7	3.8	.806							
Bob Ferguson	RF	J. Evans	280	.232	0	17	153	30	24	**4**	2.9	.884							
W-7 L-10	CF	A. Hall	306	.258	0	14	126	18	27	3	2.6	.842							
	LF	T. Mansell	177	.243	0	11	63	3	23	1	2.2	.742							
	C	C. Reilley	236	.229	0	19	231	49	43	2	6.6	.867							
	P	G. Bradley	251	.247	0	23	24	132	24	0	3.3	.867							
	1O	A. Clapp	146	.267	0	18	279	7	25	10		.920							
	3B	B. Ferguson	123	.252	0	4	29	55	20	5	4.3	.808							
	SS	C. Nelson	106	.264	0	10	37	89	25	8	6.3	.834							
	OF	S. Taylor	97	.216	0	8	37	2	12	0	2.1	.765							

BATTING AND BASE RUNNING LEADERS

Batting Average

C. Anson, CHI	.396
P. Hines, PRO	.357
J. O'Rourke, PRO	.348
K. Kelly, CIN	.348
J. O'Rourke, BOS	.341

Slugging Average

J. O'Rourke, BOS	.521
C. Jones, BOS	.510
C. Anson, CHI	.493
K. Kelly, CIN	.493
P. Hines, PRO	.482

Home Runs

C. Jones, BOS	9
J. O'Rourke, BOS	6
D. Brouthers, TRO	4
C. Eden, CLE	3

Total Bases

P. Hines, PRO	197
C. Jones, BOS	181
K. Kelly, CIN	170
J. O'Rourke, PRO	166
J. O'Rourke, BOS	165

Runs Batted In

J. O'Rourke, BOS	62
C. Jones, BOS	62
B. Dickerson, CIN	57
C. McVey, CIN	55
D. White, CIN	52
P. Hines, PRO	52

Stolen Bases

(not available)

Hits

P. Hines, PRO	146
J. O'Rourke, PRO	126
K. Kelly, CIN	120

Base on Balls

C. Jones, BOS	29
N. Williamson, CHI	24
T. York, PRO	19

Home Run Percentage

C. Jones, BOS	2.5
J. O'Rourke, BOS	1.9
C. Eden, CLE	0.8

Runs Scored

C. Jones, BOS	85
P. Hines, PRO	81
G. Wright, PRO	79

Doubles

C. Eden, CLE	31
A. Dalrymple, CHI	25
T. York, PRO	25
P. Hines, PRO	25

Triples

B. Dickerson, CIN	14
N. Williamson, CHI	13
K. Kelly, CIN	12
J. O'Rourke, BOS	11

PITCHING LEADERS

Winning Percentage

M. Ward, PRO	.734
T. Bond, BOS	.694
B. Mathews, PRO	.667
F. Hankinson, CHI	.600
W. White, CIN	.581

Wins

M. Ward, PRO	47
T. Bond, BOS	43
W. White, CIN	43
P. Galvin, BUF	37
T. Larkin, CHI	31

Strikeouts

M. Ward, PRO	239
W. White, CIN	232
J. McCormick, CLE	197
T. Bond, BOS	155
T. Larkin, CHI	142

Fewest Hits per 9 Innings

McGunnigle, BUF	8.47
M. Ward, PRO	8.75
T. Bond, BOS	8.80

Fewest Walks per 9 Innings

T. Bond, BOS	0.39
P. Galvin, BUF	0.47
G. Bradley, TRO	0.48

Innings

W. White, CIN	680
P. Galvin, BUF	593
M. Ward, PRO	587

Earned Run Average

T. Bond, BOS	1.96
W. White, CIN	1.99
M. Ward, PRO	2.15
P. Galvin, BUF	2.28
B. Mathews, PRO	2.29

Saves

M. Ward, PRO	1
C. Foley, BOS	1
B. Mathews, PRO	1

Complete Games

W. White, CIN	75
P. Galvin, BUF	65
J. McCormick, CLE	59
T. Bond, BOS	59
M. Ward, PRO	58

Shutouts

T. Bond, BOS	12
P. Galvin, BUF	6
H. McCormick, SYR	5
W. White, CIN	4

Most Strikeouts per 9 Inn.

McGunnigle, BUF	4.65
B. Mathews, PRO	4.29
B. Mitchell, CLE	4.16

Games Pitched

W. White, CIN	76
M. Ward, PRO	70
P. Galvin, BUF	66

	W	L	PCT	GB	R	OR	2B	3B	Batting HR	BA	SA	SB	E	Fielding DP	FA	CG	BB	Pitching SO	ShO	SV	ERA
PRO	59	25	.702		612	355	142	55	12	.296	.381	0	382	41	.902	73	62	329	2	2	2.18
BOS	54	30	.643	5	562	348	138	51	20	.274	.368	0	319	58	.913	79	46	230	12	1	2.19
BUF	46	32	.590	10	394	365	105	54	2	.252	.328	0	331	62	.906	78	47	198	8	0	2.34
CHI	46	33	.582	10.5	437	411	167	32	3	.259	.336	0	381	52	.900	82	57	211	5	0	2.46
CIN	43	37	.538	14	485	464	127	53	8	.264	.347	0	454	48	.877	79	81	246	4	0	2.29
CLE	27	55	.329	31	322	461	116	29	4	.223	.285	0	406	42	.889	79	116	287	3	0	2.65
SYR	22	48	.314	30	276	462	61	19	5	.227	.270	0	398	37	.872	64	52	132	5	0	3.19
TRO	19	56	.253	35.5	321	543	102	24	4	.237	.294	0	460	44	.875	75	47	210	3	0	2.80
					3409	3409	958	317	58	.255	.329	0	3131	384	.892	609	508	1843	42	3	2.50

National League 1880

	POS	Player	AB	BA	HR	RBI	PO	A	E	DP	TC/G	FA	Pitcher	G	IP	W	L	SV	ERA
Chi. W-67 L-17 Cap Anson	1B	C. Anson	356	.337	1	74	833	15	20	28	10.7	.977	L. Corcoran	63	536	43	14	2	1.95
	2B	J. Quest	300	.237	0	27	223	270	58	26	6.9	.895	F. Goldsmith	26	210	21	3	1	1.75
	SS	T. Burns	333	.309	0	43	62	186	39	9	3.6	.864							
	3B	N. Williamson	311	.251	0	31	83	143	27	5	4.0	.893							
	RF	K. Kelly	344	.291	1	60	49	32	23	1	1.6	.779							
	CF	G. Gore	322	.360	2	47	124	18	21	4	2.2	.871							
	LF	A. Dalrymple	382	.330	0	36	157	19	29	4	2.4	.859							
	C	S. Flint	284	.162	0	17	388	117	37	4	8.1	.932							
	P	L. Corcoran	286	.231	0	25	34	122	7	2	2.6	.957							
	PO	F. Goldsmith	142	.261	0	15	21	53	8	0		.902							
Pro. W-52 L-32 Jim Bullock	1B	J. Start	345	.278	0	27	954	10	29	30	12.1	.971	M. Ward	70	595	40	23	1	1.74
	2B	J. Farrell	339	.271	3	36	207	274	61	26	6.8	.887	G. Bradley	28	196	12	9	1	1.38
	SS	J. Peters	359	.228	0	24	111	268	42	26	4.9	.900							
	3B	G. Bradley	309	.227	0	23	71	165	40	8	4.8	.855							
	RF	M. Dorgan	321	.246	0	31	96	25	20	4	1.8	.858							
	CF	P. Hines	374	.307	3	35	148	17	13	7	2.4	.927							
	LF	T. York	203	.212	0	18	94	5	7	1	2.0	.934							
	C	E. Gross	347	.259	1	24	429	126	86	5	7.4	.866							
	P	M. Ward	356	.228	0	27	43	133	3	1	2.6	.983							
	OF	S. Houck	184	.201	1	22	86	10	14	0	2.2	.873							
Cle. W-47 L-37 Jim McCormick	1B	B. Phillips	334	.254	1		842	25	33	37	10.6	.963	J. McCormick	74	658	45	28	0	1.85
	2B	F. Dunlap	373	.276	4		252	290	53	44	7.0	.911							
	SS	J. Glasscock	296	.243	0		107	252	44	21	5.2	.891							
	3B	F. Hankinson	263	.209	1		68	89	29	7	3.3	.844							
	RF	O. Shaffer	338	.266	0		128	35	18	5	2.2	.901							
	CF	P. Hotaling	325	.240	0		115	14	15	4	1.8	.896							
	LF	N. Hanlon	280	.246	0		135	9	35	4	2.6	.804							
	C	D. Kennedy	250	.200	0		397	68	52	9	8.0	.899							
	P	J. McCormick	289	.246	0		36	135	22	3	2.6	.886							
	3B	M. McGeary	111	.252	0		37	49	11	4	3.3	.887							
	C	B. Gilligan	99	.172	1		124	33	5	4	7.0	.969							
Tro. W-41 L-42 Bob Ferguson	1B	E. Cogswell	209	.301	0		475	15	20	18	10.9	.961	M. Welch	65	574	34	30	0	2.54
	2B	B. Ferguson	332	.262	0		294	255	58	38	7.4	.904	T. Keefe	12	105	6	6	0	0.86
	SS	E. Caskin	333	.225	0		97	297	51	16	5.4	.885							
	3B	R. Connor	340	.332	3		116	159	60	10	4.0	.821							
	RF	J. Evans	180	.256	0		68	9	8	4	1.8	.906							
	CF	J. Cassidy	352	.253	0		128	18	20	1	2.0	.880							
	LF	P. Gillespie	346	.243	2		185	14	21	5	2.7	.905							
	C	B. Holbert	212	.189	0		261	107	36	6	7.0	.911							
	P	M. Welch	251	.287	4		35	86	21	4	2.2	.947							
	1B	B. Tobin	136	.162	0		297	8	16	25	9.7	.950							
	OF	B. Dickerson	119	.193	0		77	7	9	3	3.1	.903							
Wor. W-40 L-43 Frank Bancroft	1B	C. Sullivan	166	.259	0		447	12	8	19	10.9	.983	L. Richmond	74	591	32	32	3	2.15
	2B	G. Creamer	306	.199	0		238	274	68	34	6.8	.883	F. Corey	25	148	8	9	2	2.43
	SS	A. Irwin	352	.259	1		95	339	51	27	5.9	.895							
	3B	A. Whitney	302	.222	1		83	162	40	6	3.8	.860							
	RF	L. Knight	201	.239	0		47	22	11	1	1.6	.863							
	CF	H. Stovey	355	.265	6		68	6	12	1	1.9	.860							
	LF	G. Wood	327	.245	0		123	10	17	0	1.9	.887							
	C	C. Bennett	193	.228	0		280	45	31	3	7.7	.913							
	P	L. Richmond	309	.227	0		13	97	23	1	1.8	.827							
	C	D. Bushong	146	.171	0		261	76	30	6	9.2	.918							
	OP	F. Corey	138	.174	0		25	19	13	2		.772							
	OF	B. Dickerson	133	.293	0		48	4	9	2	2.0	.852							

	POS	Player	AB	BA	HR	RBI	PO	A	E	DP	TC/G	FA	Pitcher	G	IP	W	L	SV	ERA
Bos.	1B	J. Morrill	342	.237	2	44	434	26	16	26	10.3	.966	T. Bond	63	493	26	29	0	2.67
W-40 L-44	2B	J. Burdock	356	.253	2	35	328	275	50	39	7.6	.923	C. Foley	36	238	14	14	0	3.89
Harry Wright	SS	E. Sutton	288	.250	0	25	50	122	20	14	4.9	.896							
	3B	J. O'Rourke	363	.275	6	45	17	15	3	2	3.5	.914							
	RF	C. Foley	332	.292	2	31	35	6	8	1	1.4	.837							
	CF	J. O'Rourke	313	.275	3	36	156	19	26	0	2.5	.871							
	LF	C. Jones	280	.300	5	37	108	11	25	3	2.2	.826							
	C	P. Powers	126	.143	0	10	152	59	37	6	6.7	.851							
	PO	T. Bond	282	.220	0	24	60	152	16	8		.930							
	SS	J. Richmond	129	.248	0	9	30	73	19	14	3.9	.844							
	C	S. Trott	125	.208	0	9	170	56	27	0	7.0	.893							
Buf.	1B	D. Esterbrook	253	.241	0	35	463	17	31	20	10.9	.939	P. Galvin	58	459	20	37	0	2.71
W-24 L-58	2B	D. Force	290	.169	0	17	163	206	24	27	7.4	.939	S. Weidman	17	114	1	9	0	3.40
Bill McGunnigle	SS	M. Moynahan	100	.330	0	14	30	70	16	7	4.3	.862	T. Poorman	11	85	1	8	1	4.13
W-4 L-13	3B	H. Richardson	343	.259	0	17	108	154	47	6	3.8	.848							
Sam Crane	RF	D. Stearns	104	.183	0	13	21	3	7	1	1.6	.774							
W-20 L-45	CF	B. Crowley	354	.268	0	20	131	23	33	3	2.5	.824							
	LF	J. Hornung	342	.266	1	42	127	12	20	2	2.4	.874							
	C	J. Rowe	326	.252	1	36	231	56	33	3	5.3	.897							
	P	P. Galvin	241	.212	0	12	24	97	13	1	2.3	.903							
	1O	O. Walker	126	.230	1	15	267	10	27	17		.911							
Cin.	1B	L. Reilly	272	.206	0	16	615	13	35	36	9.2	.947	W. White	62	517	18	42	0	2.14
W-21 L-59	2B	P. Smith	334	.207	0	27	282	243	89	32	7.4	.855	B. Purcell	25	196	3	17	0	3.21
John Clapp	SS	L. Say	191	.199	0	15	54	164	44	11	5.5	.832							
	3B	H. Carpenter	300	.240	0	23	136	126	45	9	4.6	.853							
	RF	J. Manning	190	.216	2	17	59	12	18	1	1.9	.798							
	CF	B. Purcell	325	.292	1	24	78	14	21	1	2.1	.814							
	LF	M. Mansell	187	.193	2	12	147	13	25	5	3.5	.865							
	C	J. Clapp	323	.282	1	20	420	121	62	5	8.3	.897							
	P	W. White	207	.169	0	14	17	68	10	2	1.5	.895							
	OF	D. White	141	.298	0	7	36	9	16	1	1.8	.738							
	S3	A. Leonard	133	.211	1	17	29	75	21	4		.832							
	UT	C. Reilley	103	.204	0	9	68	16	14	0		.857							
	OF	J. Sommer	88	.182	0	6	38	4	4	1	2.1	.913							

BATTING AND BASE RUNNING LEADERS

Batting Average

G. Gore, CHI	.360
C. Anson, CHI	.337
R. Connor, TRO	.332
A. Dalrymple, CHI	.330
T. Burns, CHI	.309

Slugging Average

G. Gore, CHI	.463
R. Connor, TRO	.459
A. Dalrymple, CHI	.458
H. Stovey, WOR	.454
J. O'Rourke, BOS	.441

Home Runs

H. Stovey, WOR	6
J. O'Rourke, BOS	6
C. Jones, BOS	5
F. Dunlap, CLE	4

Total Bases

A. Dalrymple, CHI	175
H. Stovey, WOR	161
J. O'Rourke, BOS	160
F. Dunlap, CLE	160
R. Connor, TRO	156

Runs Batted In

(not available)

Stolen Bases

(not available)

Hits

A. Dalrymple, CHI	126
C. Anson, CHI	120
G. Gore, CHI	116

Base on Balls

B. Ferguson, TRO	24
G. Gore, CHI	21
J. Clapp, CIN	21
J. O'Rourke, BOS	21

Home Run Percentage

C. Jones, BOS	1.8
H. Stovey, WOR	1.7
J. O'Rourke, BOS	1.7

Runs Scored

A. Dalrymple, CHI	91
H. Stovey, WOR	76
K. Kelly, CHI	72

Doubles

F. Dunlap, CLE	27
A. Dalrymple, CHI	25
C. Anson, CHI	24

Triples

H. Stovey, WOR	14
A. Dalrymple, CHI	12
J. Hornung, BUF	11
J. O'Rourke, BOS	11

PITCHING LEADERS

Winning Percentage

F. Goldsmith, CHI	.875
L. Corcoran, CHI	.754
G. Bradley, PRO	.636
M. Ward, PRO	.635
J. McCormick, CLE	.616

Earned Run Average

T. Keefe, TRO	0.86
G. Bradley, PRO	1.38
M. Ward, PRO	1.74
F. Goldsmith, CHI	1.75
J. McCormick, CLE	1.85

Wins

J. McCormick, CLE	45
L. Corcoran, CHI	43
M. Ward, PRO	40
M. Welch, TRO	34
L. Richmond, WOR	32

Saves

L. Richmond, WOR	3
F. Corey, WOR	2
L. Corcoran, CHI	2

Strikeouts

L. Corcoran, CHI	268
J. McCormick, CLE	260
L. Richmond, WOR	243
M. Ward, PRO	230
W. White, CIN	161

Complete Games

J. McCormick, CLE	72
M. Welch, TRO	64
M. Ward, PRO	59
W. White, CIN	58
L. Corcoran, CHI	57
L. Richmond, WOR	57

Fewest Hits per 9 Innings

T. Keefe, TRO	6.09
L. Corcoran, CHI	6.78
G. Bradley, PRO	7.26

Shutouts

M. Ward, PRO	9
J. McCormick, CLE	7

Fewest Walks per 9 Innings

G. Bradley, PRO	0.28
P. Galvin, BUF	0.63
M. Ward, PRO	0.68

Most Strikeouts per 9 Inn.

L. Corcoran, CHI	4.50
F. Goldsmith, CHI	3.85
L. Richmond, WOR	3.70

Innings

J. McCormick, CLE	658
M. Ward, PRO	595
L. Richmond, WOR	591

Games Pitched

J. McCormick, CLE	74
L. Richmond, WOR	74
M. Ward, PRO	70

	W	L	PCT	GB	R	OR	2B	3B	HR	BA	SA	SB	E	DP	FA	CG	BB	SO	ShO	SV	ERA
CHI	67	17	.798		**538**	317	**164**	39	4	**.279**	**.360**	0	**329**	41	**.911**	80	129	**367**	9	3	1.93
PRO	52	32	.619	15	419	**299**	114	34	8	.248	.313	0	357	53	.910	75	**51**	286	**12**	2	**1.64**
CLE	47	37	.560	20	387	337	130	**52**	7	.242	.327	0	330	52	.910	**83**	98	289	7	1	1.90
TRO	41	42	.494	25.5	392	438	114	37	5	.251	.319	0	366	**58**	.900	81	113	173	4	0	2.74
WOR	40	43	.482	26.5	412	370	129	**52**	8	.231	.316	0	355	49	.905	68	97	297	5	**5**	2.27
BOS	40	44	.476	27	416	456	134	41	**20**	.253	.343	0	367	54	.901	70	86	187	3	0	3.08
BUF	24	58	.293	42	331	502	104	37	3	.226	.289	0	408	55	.890	72	78	186	6	1	3.09
CIN	21	59	.263	44	296	472	91	36	7	.224	.288	0	437	49	.877	79	88	208	3	0	2.44
					3191	3191	980	328	62	.245	.320	0	2949	411	.901	608	740	1993	51	12	2.37

National League 1881

	POS	Player	AB	BA	HR	RBI	PO	A	E	DP	TC/G	FA	Pitcher	G	IP	W	L	SV	ERA
Chi. W-56 L-28 Cap Anson	1B	C. Anson	343	**.399**	1	82	892	43	24	48	**11.4**	**.975**	L. Corcoran	45	397	**31**	14	0	2.31
	2B	J. Quest	293	.246	1	26	238	249	37	28	6.8	.929	F. Goldsmith	39	330	24	13	0	2.59
	SS	T. Burns	342	.278	4	42	100	249	52	20	5.0	.870							
	3B	N. Williamson	343	.268	1	48	117	**194**	31	10	4.5	**.909**							
	RF	K. Kelly	353	.323	2	55	85	31	22	2	1.9	.841							
	CF	G. Gore	309	.298	1	44	146	21	24	3	2.7	.874							
	LF	A. Dalrymple	362	.323	1	37	143	14	**31**	1	2.3	.835							
	C	S. Flint	306	.310	1	34	319	92	27	6	5.5	.938							
	P	L. Corcoran	189	.222	0	9	29	63	11	0	2.3	.893							
	P	F. Goldsmith	158	.241	0	16	18	95	18	2	**3.4**	.863							
	OF	H. Nicol	108	.204	0	7	44	11	4	1	2.3	.932							
Pro. W-47 L-37 Jim Bullock W-17 L-17 Bob Morrow W-30 L-20	1B	J. Start	348	.328	0	29	837	17	33	50	11.2	.963	M. Ward	39	330	18	18	0	*2.13*
	2B	J. Farrell	345	.238	5	36	214	**271**	**64**	40	6.7	.883	O. Radbourn	41	325	25	11	0	*2.43*
	SS	B. McClellan	259	.166	0	16	59	147	35	18	4.8	.855	B. Mathews	14	102	4	8	0*	3.17
	3B	J. Denny	320	.241	1	24	144	181	62	12	**4.6**	.840							
	RF	M. Ward	357	.244	0	53	64	14	9	0	2.2	.897							
	CF	P. Hines	361	.285	2	31	178	14	22	2	2.7	.897							
	LF	T. York	316	.304	2	47	159	17	29	1	2.4	.859							
	C	E. Gross	182	.275	1	24	240	70	37	5	6.9	.893							
	UT	O. Radbourn	270	.219	0	28	57	121	30	8		.856							
	C	B. Gilligan	183	.219	0	20	184	41	17	9	6.7	.930							
Buf. W-45 L-38 Jim O'Rourke	1B	D. Brouthers	270	.319	**8**	45	321	11	17	17	11.6	.951	P. Galvin	56	474	29	24	0	*2.37*
	2B	D. Force	278	.180	0	15	168	218	26	19	**8.1**	**.937**	J. Lynch	20	166	10	9	0	*3.59*
	SS	J. Peters	229	.214	0	25	102	183	43	17	**6.2**	.869							
	3B	J. O'Rourke	348	.302	0	30	85	80	36	8	3.6	.821							
	RF	C. Foley	**375**	.256	1	25	79	14	24	5	2.1	.795							
	CF	H. Richardson	344	.291	2	53	179	**45**	21	3	**3.1**	.914							
	LF	D. White	319	.310	0	53	19	8	11	0	2.2	.711							
	C	J. Rowe	246	.333	1	43	187	39	25	5	5.5	.900							
	P	P. Galvin	236	.212	0	21	**36**	**123**	19	**7**	3.2	.893							
	C	S. Sullivan	121	.190	0	15	108	31	24	1	5.3	.853							
	OF	B. Purcell	113	.292	0	17	32	4	15	0	2.0	.706							
Det. W-41 L-43 Frank Bancroft	1B	M. Powell	219	.338	1	38	513	17	31	47	10.2	.945	G. Derby	56	495	29	26	0	2.20
	2B	J. Gerhardt	297	.242	0	36	259	242	51	**62**	7.0	.908	S. Weidman	13	115	8	5	0	**1.80**
	SS	S. Houck	308	.279	1	36	88	241	50	**40**	5.1	.868							
	3B	A. Whitney	214	.182	0	9	73	141	38	10	4.3	.849							
	RF	L. Knight	340	.271	1	52	116	21	17	6	1.9	.890							
	CF	N. Hanlon	305	.279	2	28	141	15	18	4	2.4	.897							
	LF	G. Wood	337	.297	2	32	132	18	24	4	2.2	.862							
	C	C. Bennett	299	.301	7	64	**418**	85	20	6	7.5	**.962**							
	P	G. Derby	236	.186	0	12	25	97	9	4	2.3	.931							
	1B	L. Brown	108	.241	3	14	252	8	11	20	10.0	.959							
Tro. W-39 L-45 Bob Ferguson	1B	R. Connor	367	.292	2	31	836	40	**46**	51	10.8	.950	T. Keefe	46	413	19	27	0	*3.16*
	2B	B. Ferguson	339	.283	1	35	**263**	254	55	47	6.7	.904	M. Welch	40	368	20	18	0	*2.67*
	SS	E. Caskin	234	.226	0	21	85	205	30	18	5.1	.906							
	3B	F. Hankinson	321	.193	1	19	151	169	33	**21**	4.2	.907							
	RF	J. Evans	315	.241	0	28	145	31	14	5	2.3	.926							
	CF	J. Cassidy	370	.222	1	11	143	20	24	0	2.2	.872							
	LF	P. Gillespie	348	.276	0	41	180	16	14	5	2.3	.933							
	C	B. Ewing	272	.250	0	25	211	89	28	9	7.5	.915							
	C	B. Holbert	180	.272	0	14	201	69	24	**10**	6.8	.918							
	P	T. Keefe	152	.230	0	19	23	79	17	5	2.6	.857							
	P	M. Welch	148	.203	0	11	20	39	7	3	1.7	.894							

POS	Player	AB	BA	HR	RBI	PO	A	E	DP	TC/G	FA	Pitcher	G	IP	W	L	SV	ERA
Bos. W-38 L-45 Harry Wright																		
1B	J. Morrill	311	.289	1	39	743	37	25	32	10.9	.969	J. Whitney	66	552	31	33	0	2.48
2B	J. Burdock	282	.238	1	24	202	207	40	35	6.2	.911	J. Fox	17	124	6	8	0	3.33
SS	R. Barnes	295	.271	0	17	91	214	52	17	5.7	.854							
3B	E. Sutton	333	.291	0	31	114	157	38	10	3.8	.877							
RF	F. Lewis	114	.219	0	9	35	6	8	1	1.8	.837							
CF	B. Crowley	279	.254	0	31	130	17	20	5	2.3	.880							
LF	J. Hornung	324	.241	2	25	198	19	12	5	2.8	.948							
C	P. Snyder	219	.228	0	16	261	105	42	0	6.8	.897							
P	J. Whitney	282	.255	0	32	19	99	28	3	2.2	.808							
UT	P. Deasley	147	.238	0	8	159	48	21	6		.908							
UT	J. Fox	118	.178	0	4	68	29	10	4		.907							
OF	J. Richmond	98	.276	1	12	59	4	2	1	2.6	.969							
Cle. W-36 L-48 Mike McGeary																		
1B	B. Phillips	357	.272	1	44	806	24	29	51	10.1	.966	J. McCormick	59	526	26	30	0	2.45
2B	F. Dunlap	351	.325	3	24	258	254	51	41	7.1	.909	T. Nolan	22	180	8	14	0	3.05
SS	J. Glasscock	335	.257	0	33	105	274	37	29	5.3	.911							
3B	G. Bradley	241	.249	2	18	78	76	24	6	3.7	.865							
RF	O. Shaffer	343	.257	1	34	122	24	20	4	2.0	.880							
CF	J. Remsen	172	.174	0	13	117	7	18	1	3.0	.873							
LF	M. Moynahan	135	.230	0	8	65	3	9	2	2.4	.883							
C	J. Clapp	261	.253	0	25	211	73	35	8	6.6	.890							
P	J. McCormick	309	.256	0	26	34	81	13	4	2.2	.898							
UT	T. Nolan	168	.244	0	18	32	37	9	2		.885							
C	D. Kennedy	150	.313	0	15	207	36	21	4	7.5	.920							
OF	B. Taylor	103	.243	0	12	51	4	9	1	2.8	.859							
Wor. W-32 L-50 Freeman Brown																		
1B	H. Stovey	341	.270	2	30	562	16	28	26	10.6	.954	L. Richmond	53	462	25	26	0	3.39
2B	G. Creamer	309	.207	0	25	230	248	51	39	6.6	.904	F. Corey	23	189	6	15	0	3.72
SS	A. Irwin	206	.267	0	24	50	155	36	11	4.8	.851							
3B	H. Carpenter	347	.216	2	31	141	172	56	14	4.4	.848							
RF	M. Dorgan	220	.277	0	18	41	7	7	1	2.4	.873							
CF	P. Hotaling	317	.309	1	35	142	21	26	2	2.6	.862							
LF	B. Dickerson	367	.316	1	31	153	28	22	6	2.5	.892							
C	D. Bushong	275	.233	0	21	368	124	44	10	7.1	.918							
P	L. Richmond	252	.250	0	28	18	100	8	3	2.4	.937							
UT	F. Corey	203	.222	0	10	55	71	15	3		.894							
SS	C. Nelson	103	.282	1	15	20	94	13	6	5.3	.898							

BATTING AND BASE RUNNING LEADERS

Batting Average
C. Anson, CHI	.399
M. Powell, DET	.338
J. Rowe, BUF	.333
J. Start, PRO	.328
F. Dunlap, CLE	.325

Slugging Average
D. Brouthers, BUF	.541
C. Anson, CHI	.510
J. Rowe, BUF	.480
C. Bennett, DET	.478
F. Dunlap, CLE	.444

Home Runs
D. Brouthers, BUF	8
C. Bennett, DET	7
J. Farrell, PRO	5
T. Burns, CHI	4
L. Brown, DET, PRO	3
F. Dunlap, CLE	3

Total Bases
C. Anson, CHI	175
F. Dunlap, CLE	156
K. Kelly, CHI	153
A. Dalrymple, CHI	150
B. Dickerson, WOR	149

Runs Batted In
C. Anson, CHI	82
C. Bennett, DET	64
K. Kelly, CHI	55
D. White, BUF	53
H. Richardson, BUF	53
M. Ward, PRO	53

Stolen Bases
(not available)

Hits
C. Anson, CHI	137
A. Dalrymple, CHI	117
B. Dickerson, WOR	116

Base on Balls
J. Clapp, CLE	35
T. York, PRO	29
B. Ferguson, TRO	29
J. Farrell, PRO	29

Home Run Percentage
D. Brouthers, BUF	3.0
C. Bennett, DET	2.3
J. Farrell, PRO	1.4

Runs Scored
G. Gore, CHI	86
K. Kelly, CHI	84
A. Dalrymple, CHI	72

Doubles
K. Kelly, CHI	27
P. Hines, PRO	27
H. Stovey, WOR	25
F. Dunlap, CLE	25

Triples
J. Rowe, BUF	11
B. Phillips, CLE	10

PITCHING LEADERS

Winning Percentage
O. Radbourn, PRO	.694
L. Corcoran, CHI	.689
F. Goldsmith, CHI	.649
P. Galvin, BUF	.547
G. Derby, DET	.527

Earned Run Average
S. Weidman, DET	1.80
M. Ward, PRO	2.13
G. Derby, DET	2.20
L. Corcoran, CHI	2.31
P. Galvin, BUF	2.37

Wins
L. Corcoran, CHI	31
J. Whitney, BOS	31
P. Galvin, BUF	29
G. Derby, DET	29
J. McCormick, CLE	26

Saves
B. Mathews, BOS, PRO	2
J. Morrill, BOS	1

Strikeouts
G. Derby, DET	212
J. McCormick, CLE	178
J. Whitney, BOS	162
L. Richmond, WOR	156
L. Corcoran, CHI	150

Complete Games
J. McCormick, CLE	57
J. Whitney, BOS	57
G. Derby, DET	55
L. Richmond, WOR	50
P. Galvin, BUF	48

Fewest Hits per 9 Innings
J. McCormick, CLE	8.28
S. Weidman, DET	8.45
O. Radbourn, PRO	8.55

Shutouts
G. Derby, DET	9
J. Whitney, BOS	6
F. Goldsmith, CHI	5
P. Galvin, BUF	5

Fewest Walks per 9 Innings
P. Galvin, BUF	0.87
S. Weidman, DET	0.94
F. Goldsmith, CHI	1.20

Most Strikeouts per 9 Inn.
G. Derby, DET	3.86
L. Corcoran, CHI	3.40
M. Ward, PRO	3.25

Innings
J. Whitney, BOS	552
J. McCormick, CLE	526
G. Derby, DET	495

Games Pitched
J. Whitney, BOS	66
J. McCormick, CLE	59
G. Derby, DET	56
P. Galvin, BUF	56

	W	L	PCT	GB	R	OR	Batting 2B	3B	HR	BA	SA	SB	Fielding E	DP	FA	CG	BB	Pitching SO	ShO	SV	ERA
CHI	56	28	.667		550	379	157	36	12	.295	.380	0	309	54	.916	81	122	228	9	0	2.43
PRO	47	37	.560	9	447	426	144	37	11	.253	.335	0	390	66	.896	76	138	264	7	0	2.40
BUF	45	38	.542	10.5	440	447	157	50	12	.264	.361	0	408	48	.891	72	89	185	5	0	2.84
DET	41	43	.488	15	439	429	131	53	17	.260	.357	0	338	80	.905	83	137	265	10	0	2.65
TRO	39	45	.464	17	399	429	124	31	5	.248	.314	0	311	70	.905	85	159	207	7	0	2.97
BOS	38	45	.458	17.5	349	410	121	27	5	.251	.317	0	325	54	.909	72	143	199	6	3	2.71
CLE	36	48	.429	20	392	414	120	39	7	.255	.326	0	348	68	.904	82	126	240	2	0	2.68
WOR	32	50	.390	23	410	492	114	31	7	.253	.316	0	353	50	.903	80	120	196	5	0	3.54
					3426	3426	1068	304	76	.260	.338	0	2782	490	.905	631	1034	1784	51	3	2.77

National League 1882

Team	POS	Player	AB	BA	HR	RBI	PO	A	E	DP	TC/G	FA	Pitcher	G	IP	W	L	SV	ERA
Chi. W-55 L-29 Cap Anson	1B	C. Anson	348	.362	1	83	810	27	45	42	10.8	.949	F. Goldsmith	44	405	28	16	0	2.42
	2B	T. Burns	355	.248	0	48	129	127	25	21	6.5	.911	L. Corcoran	40	356	27	13	0	1.95
	SS	K. Kelly	377	.305	1	55	66	117	43	9	5.4	.810							
	3B	N. Williamson	348	.282	3	60	108	210	43	16	4.3	.881							
	RF	H. Nicol	186	.199	1	16	59	27	11	1	2.1	.887							
	CF	G. Gore	367	.319	3	51	153	23	33	5	2.5	.842							
	LF	A. Dalrymple	397	.295	1	36	185	8	27	4	2.6	.877							
	C	S. Flint	331	.251	4	44	440	91	37	3	7.0	.935							
	P	F. Goldsmith	183	.230	0	19	26	67	6	0	2.2	.939							
	P	L. Corcoran	169	.207	1	24	22	64	8	1	2.4	.915							
	2B	J. Quest	159	.201	0	15	113	127	33	18	6.7	.879							
Pro. W-52 L-32 Harry Wright	1B	J. Start	356	.329	0		905	21	25	54	11.6	.974	O. Radbourn	55	474	31	19	0	2.09
	2B	J. Farrell	366	.254	2		212	283	71	41	6.7	.875	M. Ward	33	278	19	13	1	2.59
	SS	G. Wright	185	.162	0		46	133	26	16	4.5	.873							
	3B	J. Denny	329	.246	2		136	206	55	7	4.7	.861							
	RF	M. Ward	355	.245	0		69	20	19	3	2.2	.824							
	CF	P. Hines	379	.309	4		151	16	27	4	2.4	.861							
	LF	T. York	321	.268	1		159	11	24	3	2.4	.876							
	C	B. Gilligan	201	.224	0		287	82	27	8	7.3	.932							
	PO	O. Radbourn	326	.239	1		71	97	16	4		.913							
	C	S. Nava	97	.206	0		112	31	22	6	6.1	.867							
Bos. W-45 L-39 John Morrill	1B	J. Morrill	349	.289	2	54	741	16	28	22	10.3	.964	J. Whitney	49	420	24	21	0	2.64
	2B	H. Burdock	319	.238	0	27	223	256	35	28	6.2	.932	B. Mathews	34	285	19	15	0	2.87
	SS	S. Wise	298	.221	4	34	84	197	49	13	4.6	.852							
	3B	E. Sutton	319	.251	2	38	98	146	41	6	3.7	.856							
	RF	E. Rowen	327	.248	1	43	47	7	7	2	1.3	.885							
	CF	P. Hotaling	378	.259	0	28	150	16	26	5	2.3	.865							
	LF	J. Hornung	388	.302	1	50	191	14	15	4	2.6	.932							
	C	P. Deasley	264	.265	0	29	357	54	18	0	7.7	.958							
	P	J. Whitney	251	.323	5	48	13	88	13	3	2.3	.886							
	P	B. Mathews	169	.225	0	13	5	34	6	1	1.3	.867							
Buf. W-45 L-39 Jim O'Rourke	1B	D. Brouthers	351	.368	6		882	19	24	35	11.0	.974	P. Galvin	52	445	28	23	0	3.17
	2B	H. Richardson	354	.271	2		275	280	63	28	7.4	.898	O. Daily	29	256	15	14	0	2.99
	SS	D. Force	278	.241	1		66	209	28	13	5.0	.908							
	3B	D. White	337	.282	1		59	111	33	6	3.2	.837							
	RF	C. Foley	341	.305	3		118	22	28	7	2.0	.833							
	CF	J. O'Rourke	370	.281	2		140	15	24	3	2.2	.866							
	LF	B. Purcell	380	.276	2		144	11	34	0	2.3	.820							
	C	J. Rowe	308	.266	1		246	41	15	5	6.6	.950							
	P	P. Galvin	206	.214	0		20	85	8	1	2.2	.929							
	P	O. Daily	110	.164	0		1	28	4	0	1.1	.879							
	C	T. Dolan	89	.157	0		70	26	6	1	5.7	.941							
Cle. W-42 L-40 Ford Evans	1B	B. Phillips	335	.260	4	47	827	24	25	55	11.2	.971	J. McCormick	68	596	36	29	0	2.37
	2B	F. Dunlap	364	.280	0	28	268	297	63	62	7.5	.900	G. Bradley	18	147	7	10	0	3.73
	SS	J. Glasscock	358	.291	4	46	111	311	47	40	5.7	.900							
	3B	M. Muldoon	341	.246	6	45	86	133	30	12	4.1	.880							
	RF	O. Shaffer	313	.214	3	28	111	17	31	2	1.9	.805							
	CF	J. Richmond	140	.171	0	11	65	12	7	0	2.0	.917							
	LF	D. Esterbrook	179	.246	0	19	102	15	14	6	2.9	.893							
	C	F. Briody	194	.258	0	13	251	89	37	6	7.1	.902							
	P	J. McCormick	262	.218	2	15	43	100	13	1	2.3	.917							
	UT	G. Bradley	115	.183	0	6	82	47	13	8		.908							
	C	K. Kelly	104	.135	0	5	113	35	37	2	6.2	.800							
	3B	H. Doscher	104	.240	0	10	33	45	13	2	4.1	.857							
	OF	D. Rowe	97	.258	1	17	33	3	7	1	1.9	.837							

	POS	Player	AB	BA	HR	RBI	PO	A	E	DP	TC/G	FA	Pitcher	G	IP	W	L	SV	ERA
Det.	1B	M. Powell	338	.240	1	29	680	14	44	27	9.2	.940	S. Weidman	46	411	25	20	0	2.63
W-42 L-41	2B	D. Troy	152	.243	0	14	74	76	27	9	5.7	.847	G. Derby	40	362	17	20	0	3.26
Frank Bancroft	SS	M. McGeary	133	.143	0	2	56	112	13	5	5.5	.928							
	3B	J. Farrell	283	.247	1	24	50	65	26	8	3.4	.816							
	RF	L. Knight	347	.207	0	24	112	25	21	2	1.9	.867							
	CF	N. Hanlon	347	.231	5	38	**194**	19	27	8	**2.9**	.888							
	LF	G. Wood	375	.269	**7**	29	161	14	23	8	2.4	.884							
	C	C. Bennett	342	.301	5	51	**446**	70	30	8	**8.4**	.945							
	P	S. Weidman	193	.218	0	20	35	71	11	2	2.5	.906							
	P	G. Derby	149	.195	0	8	19	69	4	1	2.3	**.957**							
	UT	S. Trott	129	.240	0	12	207	53	33	6		.887							
	3S	A. Whitney	115	.183	0	4	58	66	21	7		.855							
Tro.	1B	J. Smith	149	.242	0	14	352	9	15	19	10.7	.960	T. Keefe	43	375	17	26	0	*2.50*
W-35 L-48	2B	B. Ferguson	319	.257	0	33	247	221	44	38	6.5	.914	M. Welch	33	281	14	16	0	*3.46*
Bob Ferguson	SS	F. Pfeffer	330	.218	1	31	161	276	73	35	**6.1**	.857	J. Egan	12	100	4	6	0	*4.14*
	3B	B. Ewing	328	.271	2	29	76	112	24	11	4.8	.887							
	RF	C. Roseman	331	.236	1	43	107	21	22	6	1.8	.853							
	CF	R. Connor	349	.330	4	42	52	2	11	0	2.7	.831							
	LF	P. Gillespie	298	.275	2	32	144	9	32	1	2.5	.827							
	C	B. Holbert	251	.183	0	23	247	**124**	45	**13**	7.2	.892							
	P	T. Keefe	189	.228	1	19	32	89	11	4	3.1	.917							
	P	M. Welch	151	.245	1	17	10	46	10	4	2.0	.848							
	OF	B. Harbidge	123	.187	0	13	43	3	9	1	2.4	.836							
	O3	J. Cassidy	121	.174	0	9	35	23	25	1		.699							
	OP	J. Egan	115	.200	0	10	23	13	20	3		.643							
Wor.	1B	H. Stovey	360	.289	5	26	469	13	22	25	11.7	.956	L. Richmond	48	411	14	**33**	0	*3.74*
W-18 L-66	2B	G. Creamer	286	.227	1	29	241	283	54	50	7.1	.907	F. Corey	21	139	1	13	0	*3.56*
Freeman Brown	SS	F. Corey	255	.247	0	29	29	76	19	5	4.8	.847	F. Mountain	13	102	2	11	0	*3.97*
W-4 L-19	3B	A. Irwin	333	.219	0	30	84	147	45	8	**5.4**	.837							
Tommy Bond	RF	J. Evans	334	.213	0	25	131	**31**	16	2	2.6	.910							
W-5 L-22	CF	J. Hayes	326	.270	4	54	93	13	18	2	2.1	.855							
Jack Chapman	LF	J. Clinton	98	.163	0	3	43	4	17	1	2.5	.734							
W-9 L-25	C	D. Bushong	253	.158	1	15	308	101	43	8	6.6	.897							
	P	L. Richmond	228	.281	2	28	15	97	14	2	2.6	.889							
	OF	T. O'Brien	89	.202	0	7	41	4	12	0	2.9	.789							

BATTING AND BASE RUNNING LEADERS

Batting Average
D. Brouthers, BUF	.368
C. Anson, CHI	.362
R. Connor, TRO	.330
J. Start, PRO	.329
J. Whitney, BOS	.323

Slugging Average
D. Brouthers, BUF	.547
R. Connor, TRO	.530
J. Whitney, BOS	.510
C. Anson, CHI	.500
P. Hines, PRO	.467

Home Runs
G. Wood, DET	7
M. Muldoon, CLE	6
D. Brouthers, BUF	6

Total Bases
D. Brouthers, BUF	192
R. Connor, TRO	185
P. Hines, PRO	177
C. Anson, CHI	174
A. Dalrymple, CHI	167

Runs Batted In
(not available)

Stolen Bases
(not available)

Hits
D. Brouthers, BUF	129
C. Anson, CHI	126

Base on Balls
G. Gore, CHI	29
O. Shaffer, CLE	27
N. Williamson, CHI	27

Home Run Percentage
J. Whitney, BOS	2.0
G. Wood, DET	1.9
M. Muldoon, CLE	1.8

Runs Scored
G. Gore, CHI	99
A. Dalrymple, CHI	96
H. Stovey, WOR	90

Doubles
K. Kelly, CHI	37
C. Anson, CHI	29
P. Hines, PRO	28

Triples
R. Connor, TRO	18
F. Corey, WOR	12
G. Wood, DET	12

PITCHING LEADERS

Winning Percentage
L. Corcoran, CHI	.675
F. Goldsmith, CHI	.636
O. Radbourn, PRO	.620
M. Ward, PRO	.594
B. Mathews, BOS	.559

Earned Run Average
L. Corcoran, CHI	1.95
O. Radbourn, PRO	2.09
J. McCormick, CLE	2.37
F. Goldsmith, CHI	2.42
T. Keefe, TRO	2.50

Wins
J. McCormick, CLE	36
O. Radbourn, PRO	31
F. Goldsmith, CHI	28
P. Galvin, BUF	28
L. Corcoran, CHI	27

Saves
M. Ward, PRO	1

Strikeouts
O. Radbourn, PRO	201
J. McCormick, CLE	200
G. Derby, DET	182
J. Whitney, BOS	180
L. Corcoran, CHI	170

Complete Games
J. McCormick, CLE	65
O. Radbourn, PRO	51
P. Galvin, BUF	48
J. Whitney, BOS	46
F. Goldsmith, CHI	44

Fewest Hits per 9 Innings
L. Corcoran, CHI	7.11
O. Radbourn, PRO	8.15
J. McCormick, CLE	8.31

Shutouts
O. Radbourn, PRO	6
M. Welch, TRO	5

Fewest Walks per 9 Innings
B. Mathews, BOS	0.69
P. Galvin, BUF	0.81
F. Goldsmith, CHI	0.84

Most Strikeouts per 9 Inn.
B. Mathews, BOS	4.83
G. Derby, DET	4.52
L. Corcoran, CHI	4.30

Innings
J. McCormick, CLE	596
O. Radbourn, PRO	474
P. Galvin, BUF	445

Games Pitched
J. McCormick, CLE	68
O. Radbourn, PRO	55
P. Galvin, BUF	52

	W	L	PCT	GB	R	OR	2B	3B	HR	BA	SA	SB	E	DP	FA	CG	BB	SO	ShO	SV	ERA
CHI	55	29	.655		604	353	209	54	15	.277	.389	0	376	54	.898	83	102	279	7	0	2.22
PRO	52	32	.619	3	463	356	121	54	10	.250	.333	0	371	67	.901	80	87	273	9	1	2.27
BOS	45	39	.536	10	472	414	114	50	15	.264	.347	0	314	37	.910	81	77	352	4	0	2.80
BUF	45	39	.536	10	500	461	146	47	18	.274	.368	0	315	42	.910	79	114	287	3	0	3.25
CLE	42	40	.512	12	402	411	139	40	20	.238	.331	0	358	41	.905	81	132	232	4	0	2.75
DET	42	41	.506	12.5	488		117	44	20	.230	.315	0	396	44	.893	82	129	354	7	0	2.98
TRO	35	48	.422	19.5	430	522	116	44	59	.244	.333	0	432	70	.887	81	168	189	6	0	3.08
WOR	18	66	.214	37	379	652	109	57	16	.231	.322	0	468	66	.877	75	151	195		0	3.75
					3657	3657	1071	405	126	.251	.343	0	3030	451	.897	642	960	2161	40	1	2.89

American Association 1882

Cin.
W-55 L-25
Pop Snyder

POS	Player	AB	BA	HR	RBI	PO	A	E	DP	TC/G	FA	Pitcher	G	IP	W	L	SV	ERA
1B	D. Stearns	214	.257	0		305	5	23	16	9.5	.931	W. White	54	480	40	12	0	1.54
2B	B. McPhee	311	.228	1		274	207	42	36	6.7	.920	H. McCormick	25	220	14	11	0	1.52
SS	C. Fulmer	324	.281	0		130	243	43	14	5.3	.897							
3B	H. Carpenter	351	.342	1		137	167	60	7	4.6	.835							
RF	H. Wheeler	344	.250	1		94	11	25	1	2.0	.808							
CF	J. Macullar	299	.234	0		141	13	13	2	2.1	.922							
LF	J. Sommer	354	.288	1		188	9	16	2	2.7	.925							
C	P. Snyder	309	.291	1		358	92	41	3	7.0	.916							
P	W. White	207	.266	0		23	223	11	3	4.8	.957							
1B	H. Luff	120	.233	0		266	7	23	12	11.0	.922							
P	H. McCormick	93	.129	0		12	76	5	0	3.7	.946							

Phi.
W-41 L-34
Lew Simmons
W-20 L-19
Charlie Mason
W-21 L-15

POS	Player	AB	BA	HR	RBI	PO	A	E	DP	TC/G	FA	Pitcher	G	IP	W	L	SV	ERA
1B	J. Latham	323	.285	0		792	12	23	28	11.2	.972	S. Weaver	42	371	26	15	0	2.74
2B	C. Stricker	272	.217	0		239	251	52	29	7.5	.904	B. Sweeney	20	170	9	11	0	2.91
SS	L. Say	199	.226	1		69	192	40	7	6.1	.867							
3B	F. Mann	121	.231	0		32	39	18	3	3.1	.798							
RF	B. Blakiston	281	.228	0		52	13	11	0	2.0	.855							
CF	J. Mansell	126	.238	0		49	4	14	0	2.2	.791							
LF	J. Birchall	338	.263	0		134	14	24	0	2.3	.860							
C	J. O'Brien	241	.303	3		205	66	22	1	6.5	.925							
CO	J. Dorgan	181	.282	0		158	30	30	0		.862							
P	S. Weaver	155	.232	0		16	127	9	1	3.6	.941							
P	B. Sweeney	88	.159	0		9	51	6	0	3.3	.909							
SS	J. Say	82	.207	0		31	76	14	10	5.5	.884							

Lou.
W-42 L-38
John Dyler
W-6 L-7
Bill Reccius
W-24 L-18
Leech Maskrey
W-12 L-13

POS	Player	AB	BA	HR	RBI	PO	A	E	DP	TC/G	FA	Pitcher	G	IP	W	L	SV	ERA
1B	G. Hecker	349	.278	3		689	22	31	43	11.2	.958	T. Mullane	55	460	30	24	0	1.88
2B	P. Browning	288	.382	5		157	127	35	19	7.6	.890	G. Hecker	13	104	6	6	0	1.30
SS	D. Mack	264	.182	0		51	161	24	9	4.8	.898	J. Reccius	13	95	6	6	0	3.03
3B	B. Schenck	231	.260	0		70	110	41	4	3.8	.814							
RF	C. Wolf	318	.299	0		71	21	10	2	1.5	.902							
CF	J. Reccius	266	.237	1		87	15	17	3	1.8	.857							
LF	L. Maskrey	288	.226	0		136	11	16	1	2.1	.902							
C	D. Sullivan	286	.273	0		294	95	54	3	8.2	.878							
UT	T. Mullane	303	.257	0		187	191	24	10		.940							
UT	J. Strike	110	.164	0		110	45	22	6		.876							

Pit.
W-39 L-39
Al Pratt

POS	Player	AB	BA	HR	RBI	PO	A	E	DP	TC/G	FA	Pitcher	G	IP	W	L	SV	ERA
1B	C. Lane	214	.178	3		480	12	13	19	11.7	.974	H. Salisbury	38	335	20	18	0	2.63
2B	G. Strief	297	.195	2		241	200	40	28	6.2	.917	D. Driscoll	23	201	13	9	0	1.21
SS	J. Peters	333	.288	0		90	280	49	21	5.4	.883	H. Arundel	14	120	4	10	0	4.65
3B	J. Battin	133	.211	1		62	108	24	5	5.7	.876							
RF	E. Swartwood	325	.329	5		99	9	25	2	1.9	.788							
CF	J. Leary	257	.292	2		26	2	9	0	1.4	.757							
LF	M. Mansell	347	.277	2		159	16	36	1	2.7	.829							
C	B. Taylor	299	.281	4		116	40	25	0	6.7	.862							
P	H. Salisbury	145	.152	0		10	96	11	1	3.1	.906							
OF	C. Morton	103	.282	0		31	9	9	0	2.0	.816							
C	R. Kemmler	99	.253	0		123	37	14	1	7.6	.920							
C	J. Keenan	96	.219	1		142	21	17	3	8.2	.906							
P	D. Driscoll	80	.138	1		4	50	7	1	2.7	.885							

St. L.
W-37 L-43
Ned Cuthbert
W-27 L-32
Ed Brown
W-10 L-11

POS	Player	AB	BA	HR	RBI	PO	A	E	DP	TC/G	FA	Pitcher	G	IP	W	L	SV	ERA
1B	C. Comiskey	329	.243	1		860	14	30	25	11.7	.967	J. McGinnis	44	379	25	18	0	2.47
2B	B. Smiley	240	.213	0		145	155	39	20	5.9	.885	J. Schappert	15	128	8	7	0	3.52
SS	B. Gleason	347	.288	1		131	294	85	23	6.5	.833							
3B	J. Gleason	331	.254	2		107	168	83	11	4.9	.768							
RF	G. Seward	144	.215	0		40	12	15	1	1.9	.776							
CF	O. Walker	318	.239	7		158	18	32	4	2.8	.846							
LF	N. Cuthbert	233	.223	0		74	12	10	0	1.6	.896							
C	S. Sullivan	188	.181	0		231	46	50	4	6.5	.847							
P	J. McGinnis	203	.217	0		13	97	11	2	2.8	.909							
UT	H. McCaffrey	153	.275	0		71	49	17	5		.876							
UT	E. Fusselbach	136	.228	0		92	54	25	4		.854							

	POS	Player	AB	BA	HR	RBI	PO	A	E	DP	TC/G	FA	Pitcher	G	IP	W	L	SV	ERA
Bal.	1B	Householder	307	.254	1		749	20	23	30	10.7	.971	D. Landis	42	341	11	27*	0	*3.33*
W-19 L-54	2B	G. Pierce	151	.199	0		123	99	57*	17	7.3	.796	T. Nichols	16	118	1	12	0	*5.02*
Henry Myers	SS	H. Myers	294	.180	0		66	257	70	15	5.8	.822	E. Geiss	13	96	4	9	0	4.80
	3B	J. Shetzline	282	.220	0		91	121	53	9	5.1	.800							
	RF	T. Brown	181	.304	1		59	16	28	1	2.3	.728							
	CF	M. Cline	172	.221	0		78	16	20	1	2.9	.825							
	LF	C. Waitt	250	.156	0		142	11	22	2	2.4	.874							
	C	E. Whiting	308	.260	0		299	**108**	81	6	6.8	.834							
	P	D. Landis	175	.166	0		19	101	11*	2	3.1	.916							
	3O	H. Jacoby	121	.174	1		46	59	26	3		.802							
	PO	T. Nichols	95	.158	0		26	36	13	0		.827							

BATTING AND BASE RUNNING LEADERS

Batting Average

P. Browning, LOU	.382
H. Carpenter, CIN	.342
E. Swartwood, PIT	.329
J. O'Brien, PHI	.303
C. Wolf, LOU	.299

Home Runs

O. Walker, STL	7
P. Browning, LOU	5
E. Swartwood, PIT	5
B. Taylor, PIT	4

Runs Batted In

(not available)

Hits

H. Carpenter, CIN	120
P. Browning, LOU	110
E. Swartwood, PIT	107

Home Run Percentage

O. Walker, STL	2.2
P. Browning, LOU	1.7
E. Swartwood, PIT	1.5

Doubles

P. Browning, LOU	19
E. Swartwood, PIT	18
M. Mansell, PIT	18

Slugging Average

P. Browning, LOU	.521
E. Swartwood, PIT	.498
B. Taylor, PIT	.455
M. Mansell, PIT	.438
H. Carpenter, CIN	.422

Total Bases

E. Swartwood, PIT	162
M. Mansell, PIT	152
P. Browning, LOU	150
H. Carpenter, CIN	148
B. Taylor, PIT	136

Stolen Bases

(not available)

Base on Balls

J. Gleason, STL	27
P. Browning, LOU	26
J. Sommer, CIN	24

Runs Scored

E. Swartwood, PIT	86
J. Sommer, CIN	82
H. Carpenter, CIN	78

Triples

M. Mansell, PIT	16
B. Taylor, PIT	12
E. Swartwood, PIT	11
H. Wheeler, CIN	11

PITCHING LEADERS

Winning Percentage

W. White, CIN	.769
S. Weaver, PHI	.634
J. McGinnis, STL	.581
H. McCormick, CIN	.560
T. Mullane, LOU	.556

Wins

W. White, CIN	40
T. Mullane, LOU	30
S. Weaver, PHI	26
J. McGinnis, STL	25
H. Salisbury, PIT	20

Strikeouts

T. Mullane, LOU	170
H. Salisbury, PIT	135
J. McGinnis, STL	134
W. White, CIN	122
S. Weaver, PHI	104

Fewest Hits per 9 Innings

G. Hecker, LOU	6.49
H. McCormick, CIN	7.25
D. Driscoll, PIT	7.25

Fewest Walks per 9 Innings

G. Hecker, LOU	0.43
D. Driscoll, PIT	0.54
S. Weaver, PHI	0.85

Innings

W. White, CIN	480
T. Mullane, LOU	460
J. McGinnis, STL	379

Earned Run Average

D. Driscoll, PIT	1.21
G. Hecker, LOU	1.30
H. McCormick, CIN	1.52
W. White, CIN	1.54
T. Mullane, LOU	1.88

Saves

E. Fusselbach, STL	1

Complete Games

W. White, CIN	52
T. Mullane, LOU	51
J. McGinnis, STL	42
S. Weaver, PHI	41
H. Salisbury, PIT	38

Shutouts

W. White, CIN	8
T. Mullane, LOU	5
H. McCormick, CIN	3
J. McGinnis, STL	3

Most Strikeouts per 9 Inn.

H. Salisbury, PIT	3.63
H. Arundel, PIT	3.52
T. Mullane, LOU	3.32

Games Pitched

T. Mullane, LOU	55
W. White, CIN	54
J. McGinnis, STL	44
D. Landis, BAL, PHI	44

	W	L	PCT	GB	R	OR	2B	3B	HR	BA	SA	SB	E	DP	FA	CG	BB	SO	ShO	SV	ERA
CIN	55	25	.688		489	268	95	47	5	.264	.332	0	332	41	**.907**	77	125	165	11	0	*1.67*
PHI	41	34	.547	11.5	406	389	89	21	4	.244	.297	0	361	36	.895	72	99	190	2	0	*2.99*
LOU	42	38	.525	13	443	352	**110**	28	9	.259	.328	0	385	**57**	.893	73	112	240	6	0	*2.87*
PIT	39	39	.500	15	428	418	**110**	58	21	.251	**.351**	0	397	40	.889	77	82	252	2	0	*2.95*
STL	37	43	.463	18	399	496	87	41	11	.231	.302	0	446	41	.875	75	103	225	3	1	*3.87*
BAL	19	54	.260	32.5	273	515	60	24	4	.207	.254	0	490	41	.859	64	108	113	1	0	*2.72*
					2438	2438	551	219	54	.244	.312	0	2411	256	.886	438	629	1185	25	1	*2.72*

	POS	Player	AB	BA	HR	RBI	PO	A	E	DP	TC/G	FA	Pitcher	G	IP	W	L	SV	ERA
Bos. W-63 L-35 Jack Burdock W-31 L-26 John Morrill W-32 L-9	1B	J. Morrill	404	.319	6	68	794	20	22	33	10.3	.974	J. Whitney	62	514	37	21	2	2.24
	2B	J. Burdock	400	.330	5	88	224	290	44	39	5.8	.921	C. Buffinton	43	333	24	13	1	3.03
	SS	S. Wise	406	.271	4	58	134	274	88	21	5.2	.823							
	3B	E. Sutton	414	.324	3	73	120	152	42	14	3.4	.866							
	RF	P. Radford	258	.205	0	14	86	16	20	2	1.7	.836							
	CF	E. Smith	115	.217	0	16	54	3	6	3	2.1	.905							
	LF	J. Hornung	446	.278	8	66	175	15	13	3	2.1	.936							
	C	M. Hines	231	.225	0	16	382	103	62	5	9.3	.887							
	PO	J. Whitney	409	.281	5	57	67	100	25	2		.870							
	OP	C. Buffinton	341	.238	1	26	67	68	33	6		.804							
	C	M. Hackett	179	.235	2	24	254	57	31	2	7.8	.909							
Chi. W-59 L-39 Cap Anson	1B	C. Anson	413	.308	0		1031	41	40	59	11.3	.964	L. Corcoran	56	474	34	20	0	2.49
	2B	F. Pfeffer	371	.235	1		264	264	67	49	7.5	.887	F. Goldsmith	46	383	25	19	0	3.15
	SS	T. Burns	405	.294	2		121	260	56	25	5.5	.872							
	3B	N. Williamson	402	.276	2		111	252	87	20	4.6	.807							
	RF	K. Kelly	428	.255	3		101	38	32	5	2.1	.813							
	CF	G. Gore	392	.334	2		195	27	34	4	2.8	.867							
	LF	A. Dalrymple	363	.298	2		149	12	34	3	2.4	.826							
	C	S. Flint	332	.265	0		301	104	57	4	5.6	.877							
	P	L. Corcoran	263	.209	0		37	88	13	3	2.5	.906							
	P	F. Goldsmith	235	.221	1		23	86	17	3	2.7	.865							
Pro. W-58 L-40 Harry Wright	1B	J. Start	370	.284	1		923	29	43	48	11.4	.957	O. Radbourn	76	632	49	25	1	2.05
	2B	J. Farrell	420	.305	3		258	365	51	51	7.1	.924	C. Sweeney	20	147	7	7	0	3.13
	SS	A. Irwin	406	.286	0		93	293	65	29	4.8	.856	L. Richmond	12	92	3	7	0	3.33
	3B	J. Denny	393	.275	8		178	188	52	13	4.3	.876							
	RF	J. Cassidy	366	.238	0		120	26	23	2	1.9	.864							
	CF	P. Hines	442	.299	4		169	21	20	2	2.4	.905							
	LF	C. Carroll	238	.265	1		109	11	13	4	2.3	.902							
	C	B. Gilligan	263	.198	0		379	108	54	10	7.3	.900							
	P	O. Radbourn	381	.283	3		33	139	15	3	2.5	.920							
	OF	L. Richmond	194	.284	1		47	3	20	0	1.7	.714							
	C	S. Nava	100	.240	0		98	41	32	4	6.3	.813							
Cle. W-55 L-42 Frank Bancroft	1B	B. Phillips	382	.246	2		953	22	33	53	10.4	.967	O. Daily	45	379	23	19	1	2.42
	2B	F. Dunlap	396	.326	4		304	290	58	49	7.0	.911	J. McCormick	43	342	27	13	1	1.84
	SS	J. Glasscock	383	.287	0		134	313	38	28	5.2	.922	W. Sawyer	17	141	4	10	0	2.36
	3B	M. Muldoon	378	.228	0		122	170	62	9	3.6	.825							
	RF	J. Evans	332	.238	0		119	29	16	1	1.9	.902							
	CF	P. Hotaling	417	.259	0		181	23	42	5	2.5	.829							
	LF	T. York	381	.260	2		176	15	30	3	2.2	.864							
	C	D. Bushong	215	.172	0		370	88	46	5	8.0	.909							
	P	J. McCormick	157	.236	0		18	101	14	2	3.2	.895							
	C	O. Briody	145	.234	0		171	46	24	5	7.3	.900							
	P	O. Daily	142	.127	0		6	71	5	1	1.8	.939							
Buf. W-52 L-45 Jim O'Rourke	1B	D. Brouthers	425	.374	3		1040	35	44	40	11.5	.961	P. Galvin	76	656	46	29	0	2.72
	2B	H. Richardson	399	.311	1		289	344	68	33	7.6	.903	G. Derby	14	108	2	10	1	5.85
	SS	D. Force	378	.217	0		79	240	42	22	4.6	.884							
	3B	D. White	391	.292	0		84	128	54	8	3.5	.797							
	RF	O. Shaffer	401	.292	0		182	41	36	3	2.7	.861							
	CF	D. Eggler	153	.248	0		83	4	16	1	2.7	.845							
	LF	J. O'Rourke	436	.328	1		89	8	15	0	1.8	.866							
	C	J. Rowe	374	.278	1		234	50	32	3	6.4	.899							
	P	P. Galvin	322	.220	1		20	127	10	4	2.1	.936							
	OF	J. Lillie	201	.234	1		73	8	16	2	2.1	.835							
	OF	C. Foley	111	.270	0		44	2	6	0	2.3	.885							
N. Y. W-46 L-50 John Clapp	1B	R. Connor	409	.357	1		958	40	44	37	10.6	.958	M. Welch	54	426	27	21	0	2.73
	2B	D. Troy	316	.215	0		187	226	57	23	6.4	.879	M. Ward	33	277	12	14	0	2.70
	SS	E. Caskin	383	.238	1		146	250	67	14	5.7	.855	T. O'Neill	19	148	5	12	0	4.07
	3B	F. Hankinson	337	.220	2		122	166	43	9	3.6	.870							
	RF	M. Dorgan	261	.234	0		104	7	20	1	2.2	.847							
	CF	M. Ward	380	.255	7		118	28	24	2	3.0	.859							
	LF	P. Gillespie	411	.314	1		216	11	26	6	2.6	.897							
	C	B. Ewing	376	.303	10		270	96	31	8	6.3	.922							
	PO	M. Welch	320	.234	3		71	63	38	4		.779							
	CO	J. Humphries	107	.112	0		84	31	26	0		.816							
Det. W-40 L-58 Jack Chapman	1B	M. Powell	421	.273	1		995	32	54	62	10.7	.950	S. Weidman	52	402	20	24	2	3.53
	2B	S. Trott	295	.244	0		102	92	26	16	5.2	.882	D. Shaw	26	247	10	15	0	2.50
	SS	S. Houck	416	.252	0		162	328	85	36	5.7	.852	D. Burns	17	128	2	12	0	4.51
	3B	J. Farrell	444	.243	0		111	248	66	13	4.2	.845	J. Jones	12	93	6	5	0	3.50
	RF	T. Mansell	131	.221	0		35	12	15	1	1.8	.758							
	CF	N. Hanlon	413	.242	1		216	13	30	6	2.9	.884							
	LF	G. Wood	441	.302	5		226	15	34	3	2.8	.876							
	C	C. Bennett	371	.305	5		333	88	25	11	6.2	.944							
	PO	S. Weidman	313	.185	1		73	81	18	2		.895							
	PO	D. Shaw	141	.206	0		21	50	7	5		.910							
	OP	D. Burns	140	.186	0		22	32	14	2		.794							
	2B	J. Quest	137	.234	0		114	112	26	25	6.8	.897							

POS	Player	AB	BA	HR	RBI	PO	A	E	DP	TC/G	FA	Pitcher	G	IP	W	L	SV	ERA
1B	S. Farrar	377	.233	1		1038	31	39	45	11.2	.965	J. Coleman	65	538	12	**48**	0	*4.87*
2B	B. Ferguson	329	.258	0		261	287	**88**	38	7.4	.862	A. Hagan	17	137	1	14	0	*5.45*
SS	B. McClellan	326	.230	1		152	254	72	25	**6.1**	.849							
3B	F. Warner	141	.227	0		46	54	29	4	3.4	.775							
RF	J. Manning	420	.267	0		155	37	33	5	2.3	.853							
CF	F. Lewis	160	.250	0		84	8	21	1	3.0	.814							
LF	B. Purcell	425	.268	1		60	14	14	2	2.0	.841							
C	E. Gross	231	.307	1		207	70	**74**	1	6.4	.789							
PO	J. Coleman	354	.234	0		91	132	31	6		.878							
UT	B. Harbidge	280	.221	0		138	79	62	3		.778							
UT	F. Ringo	221	.190	0		197	98	64	9		.822							

Phi.
W-17 L-81
Bob Ferguson
W-4 L-13
Blondie Purcell
W-13 L-68

BATTING AND BASE RUNNING LEADERS

Batting Average

D. Brouthers, BUF	.374
R. Connor, NY	.357
G. Gore, CHI	.334
J. Burdock, BOS	.330
J. O'Rourke, BUF	.328

Home Runs

B. Ewing, NY	10
J. Denny, PRO	8
J. Hornung, BOS	8
M. Ward, NY	7
J. Morrill, BOS	6

Runs Batted In

(not available)

Hits

D. Brouthers, BUF	159
R. Connor, NY	146
J. O'Rourke, BUF	143

Home Run Percentage

B. Ewing, NY	2.7
J. Denny, PRO	2.0
M. Ward, NY	1.8

Doubles

N. Williamson, CHI	49
D. Brouthers, BUF	41
T. Burns, CHI	37
C. Anson, CHI	36

Slugging Average

D. Brouthers, BUF	.572
J. Morrill, BOS	.525
R. Connor, NY	.506
E. Sutton, BOS	.486
B. Ewing, NY	.481

Total Bases

D. Brouthers, BUF	243
J. Morrill, BOS	212
R. Connor, NY	207
E. Sutton, BOS	201
J. Hornung, BOS	199

Stolen Bases

(not available)

Base on Balls

T. York, CLE	37
N. Hanlon, DET	34
M. Powell, DET	28

Runs Scored

J. Hornung, BOS	107
G. Gore, CHI	105
J. O'Rourke, BUF	102

Triples

D. Brouthers, BUF	17
J. Morrill, BOS	16
R. Connor, NY	15
E. Sutton, BOS	15

PITCHING LEADERS

Winning Percentage

J. McCormick, CLE	.675
O. Radbourn, PRO	.662
C. Buffinton, BOS	.649
J. Whitney, BOS	.638
L. Corcoran, CHI	.630

Wins

O. Radbourn, PRO	49
P. Galvin, BUF	46
J. Whitney, BOS	37
L. Corcoran, CHI	34
J. McCormick, CLE	27
M. Welch, NY	27

Strikeouts

J. Whitney, BOS	345
O. Radbourn, PRO	315
P. Galvin, BUF	279
L. Corcoran, CHI	216
C. Buffinton, BOS	188

Fewest Hits per 9 Innings

W. Sawyer, CLE	7.60
O. Radbourn, PRO	8.01
J. McCormick, CLE	8.32

Fewest Walks per 9 Innings

J. Whitney, BOS	0.61
P. Galvin, BUF	0.69
O. Radbourn, PRO	0.80

Innings

P. Galvin, BUF	656
O. Radbourn, PRO	632
J. Coleman, PHI	538

Earned Run Average

J. McCormick, CLE	1.84
O. Radbourn, PRO	2.05
J. Whitney, BOS	2.24
W. Sawyer, CLE	2.36
O. Daily, CLE	2.42

Saves

J. Whitney, BOS	2
S. Weidman, DET	2

Complete Games

P. Galvin, BUF	72
O. Radbourn, PRO	66
J. Coleman, PHI	59
J. Whitney, BOS	54
L. Corcoran, CHI	51

Shutouts

C. Buffinton, BOS	5
P. Galvin, BUF	5

Most Strikeouts per 9 Inn.

J. Whitney, BOS	6.04
C. Buffinton, BOS	5.08
W. Sawyer, CLE	4.85

Games Pitched

P. Galvin, BUF	76
O. Radbourn, PRO	76
J. Coleman, PHI	65

	W	L	PCT	GB	R	OR	Batting 2B	3B	HR	BA	SA	SB	Fielding E	DP	FA	CG	BB	Pitching SO	ShO	SV	ERA
BOS	63	35	.643		669	456	209	**86**	34	.276	**.408**	0	409	58	.901	89	**90**	538	**5**	**3**	2.55
CHI	59	39	.602	4	**679**	540	**277**	61	13	.273	.393	0	543	76	.879	91	123	299	**5**	1	2.78
PRO	58	40	.592	5	636	**436**	189	59	21	.272	.372	0	419	75	.903	88	111	376	4	1	2.37
CLE	55	42	.567	7.5	476	443	184	38	8	.246	.329	0	**389**	69	**.909**	**92**	217	402	**5**	2	**2.22**
BUF	52	45	.536	10.5	614	576	184	59	8	**.284**	.371	0	445	52	.896	90	101	362	**5**	2	3.32
NY	46	50	.479	16	530	577	138	69	25	.255	.355	0	468	52	.889	87	170	323	**5**	0	2.94
DET	40	58	.408	23	524	650	164	48	13	.250	.330	0	470	**77**	.893	89	184	324	4	2	3.56
PHI	17	81	.173	46	437	**887**	181	47	4	.240	.320	0	639	62	.858	91	125	253	3	0	5.33
					4565	4565	1526	467	126	.262	.360	0	3782	521	.891	717	1121	2877	36	11	3.13

	POS	Player	AB	BA	HR	RBI	PO	A	E	DP	TC/G	FA	Pitcher	G	IP	W	L	SV	ERA
Phi.	1B	H. Stovey	421	.352	14		984	22	37	31	11.2	.965	B. Mathews	44	381	30	13	0	*2.46*
W-66 L-32	2B	C. Stricker	330	.273	1		253	223	93	23	6.5	.837	G. Bradley	26	214	16	7	0	*3.15*
Lew Simmons	SS	M. Moynahan	400	.308	1		105	268	75	14	4.7	.833	F. Corey	18	148	10	7	0	*3.40*
	3B	G. Bradley	312	.234	1		46	106	43	6	4.4	.779							
	RF	L. Knight	429	.252	1		123	22	24	5	1.8	.858							
	CF	B. Blakiston	167	.246	0		51	5	10	0	1.8	.848							
	LF	J. Birchall	**449**	.241	1		168	22	45	0	2.4	.809							
	C	J. O'Brien	390	.290	0		301	58	51	3	7.1	.876							
	UT	F. Corey	298	.258	1		86	150	57	7		.805							
	C	E. Rowen	196	.219	0		266	52	54	2	8.5	.855							
	P	B. Mathews	167	.186	0		15	68	12	2	2.2	.874							
St. L.	1B	C. Comiskey	401	.294	2		**1085**	20	43	49	**12.0**	.963	T. Mullane	53	461	35	15	1	*2.19*
W-65 L-33	2B	G. Strief	302	.225	1		205	214	47	28	7.0	.899	J. McGinnis	45	383	28	16	0	*2.33*
Ted Sullivan	SS	B. Gleason	425	.287	2		120	257	56	22	4.4	.871							
W-53 L-27	3B	A. Latham	406	.236	0		120	256	58	14	4.4	.866							
Charlie Comiskey	RF	H. Nicol	368	.288	0		133	31	15	4	2.1	.916							
W-12 L-6	CF	F. Lewis	209	.301	1		89	6	17	0	2.3	.848							
	LF	T. Dolan	295	.214	1		**214**	**51**	12	4	**6.6**	**.957**							
	C	P. Deasley	206	.257	0		301	59	27	6	6.9	**.930**							
	PO	T. Mullane	307	.225	0		58	104	25	5		.866							
	P	J. McGinnis	180	.200	0		14	80	21	3	2.6	.817							
	OF	T. Mansell	112	.402	0		32	1	9	0	1.5	.786							
Cin.	1B	L. Reilly	437	.311	9		959	19	40	**50**	10.4	.961	W. White	65	577	**43**	22	0	**2.09**
W-61 L-37	2B	B. McPhee	367	.245	2		**314**	**277**	46	**48**	6.6	**.928**	R. Deagle	18	148	10	8	0	*2.31*
Pop Snyder	SS	C. Fulmer	361	.258	5		**134**	243	60	**26**	4.8	.863	H. McCormick	15	129	8	6	0	*2.87*
	3B	H. Carpenter	436	.296	3		133	181	47	6	3.8	.870							
	RF	P. Corkhill	375	.216	2		162	10	13	0	2.2	.930							
	CF	C. Jones	391	.294	11		172	12	26	1	2.3	.876							
	LF	J. Sommer	413	.278	3		171	11	31	1	2.3	.854							
	C	P. Snyder	250	.256	0		283	71	31	4	6.8	.919							
	P	W. White	240	.225	0		23	106	23	1	2.3	.849							
	CO	P. Powers	114	.246	0		74	20	12	0		.887							
	C	B. Traffley	105	.200	0		121	33	27	2	6.2	.851							
N. Y.	1B	S. Brady	432	.271	0		824	29	35	31	11.0	.961	T. Keefe	**68**	**619**	41	27	0	*2.41*
W-54 L-42	2B	S. Crane	349	.235	0		283	249	87	26	6.4	.859	J. Lynch	29	255	13	15	0	*4.09*
Jim Mutrie	SS	C. Nelson	417	.305	0		98	232	47	18	3.9	.875							
	3B	D. Esterbrook	407	.253	0		110	173	42	8	3.4	.871							
	RF	C. Roseman	398	.251	0		105	19	21	3	1.6	.855							
	CF	J. O'Rourke	315	.270	2		95	12	18	2	1.6	.856							
	LF	E. Kennedy	356	.219	2		112	10	16	0	1.5	.884							
	C	B. Holbert	299	.237	0		**527**	**138**	58	8	10.6	.920							
	P	T. Keefe	259	.220	0		31	**148**	59	3	**3.5**	.752							
	C	Reipschlager	145	.186	0		202	46	17	1	9.1	.936							
	P	J. Lynch	107	.187	0		18	46	20	0	2.9	.762							
Lou.	1B	J. Latham	368	.250	0		625	21	30	40	10.1	.956	G. Hecker	55	451	28	25	0	*3.33*
W-52 L-45	2B	J. Gerhardt	319	.263	0		278	263	56	42	7.7	.906	S. Weaver	46	419	24	20	0	*3.70*
Bill Reccius	SS	J. Leary	165	.188	3		62	106	38	11	5.2	.816							
W-12 L-10	3B	J. Gleason	355	.296	2		83	107	49	6	2.9	.795							
Leech Maskrey	RF	C. Wolf	389	.262	1		157	29	23	6	2.7	.890							
W-24 L-16	CF	L. Maskrey	361	.202	1		193	19	20	1	2.4	.914							
Joe Gerhardt	LF	P. Browning	360	.336	4		94	5	16	1	2.4	.861							
W-16 L-19	C	E. Whiting	240	.292	2		244	62	40	5	6.9	.884							
	UT	G. Hecker	334	.269	1		144	100	24	7		.910							
	P	S. Weaver	203	.192	0		21	81	6	3	2.3	**.944**							
	C	D. Sullivan	147	.211	0		149	34	21	2	6.4	.897							
	UT	McLaughlin	146	.192	0		105	72	27	8		.868							
Col.	1B	J. Field	295	.254	1		781	10	52	44	11.1	.938	F. Mountain	59	503	26	**33**	0	*3.60*
W-32 L-65	2B	P. Smith	405	.262	4		250	247	62	38	**7.7**	.889	E. Dundon	20	167	3	16	0	*4.48*
Horace Phillips	SS	J. Richmond	385	.283	0		122	**304**	60	19	5.3	**.877**	J. Valentine	13	102	2	10	0	*3.53*
	3B	W. Kuehne	374	.227	1		61	133	39	11	3.4	.833							
	RF	T. Brown	420	.274	5		151	22	42	3	2.2	.805							
	CF	F. Mann	394	.249	1		124	16	24	4	2.0	.854							
	LF	H. Wheeler	371	.226	0		131	15	35	2	2.2	.807							
	C	R. Kemmler	318	.208	0		388	97	71	10	6.8	.872							
	P	F. Mountain	276	.217	3		31	105	24	3	2.7	.850							
	C1	J. Straub	100	.130	0		182	22	21	8		.907							
Pit.	1B	E. Swartwood	413	**.356**	3		632	23	45	28	11.7	.936	D. Driscoll	41	336	18	21	0	*3.99*
W-31 L-67	2B	G. Creamer	369	.255	0		310	274	67	42	7.2	.897	B. Barr	26	203	6	18	1	*4.38*
Al Pratt	SS	D. Mack	224	.196	0		29	106	25	7	4.2	.844	B. Taylor	19	127	4	7	0	*5.39*
W-12 L-20	3B	J. Battin	388	.214	1		151	**258**	50	12	**4.7**	**.891**	J. Neagle	16	114	3	12	0	*5.84*
Ormond Butler	RF	B. Dickerson	355	.248	0		106	28	34	2	2.2	.798							
W-17 L-36	CF	B. Taylor	369	.260	2		49	10	20	0	2.1	.747							
Joe Battin	LF	M. Mansell	412	.257	3		186	11	26	1	2.3	.883							
W-2 L-11	C	J. Hayes	351	.262	3		277	70	34	2	6.1	.911							
	P	D. Driscoll	148	.182	0		14	99	14	2	3.1	.890							
	UT	B. Barr	142	.246	0		62	43	17	2		.861							
	UT	C. Morgan	114	.158	0		59	72	25	4		.840							
	SS	McLaughlin	114	.219	1		19	78	24	4	4.8	.802							
	PO	J. Neagle	101	.188	0		23	22	10	0		.818							

	POS	Player	AB	BA	HR	RBI	PO	A	E	DP	TC/G	FA	Pitcher	G	IP	W	L	SV	ERA
Bal.	1B	D. Stearns	382	.246	1		984	38	57	38	11.7	.947	H. Henderson	45	358	10	32	0	4.02
W-28 L-68	2B	T. Manning	121	.215	0		105	106	20	8	6.6	.913	B. Emslie	24	201	9	13	0	3.17
Billy Barnie	SS	L. Say	324	.256	1		76	241	82	13	5.4	.794	J. Fox	20	165	6	13	0	4.03
	3B	J. McCormick	389	.262	0		138	196	84	10	4.5	.799							
	RF	D. Rowe	256	.313	0		70	5	19	0	1.9	.798							
	CF	D. Eggler	202	.188	0		92	6	9	1	2.0	.916							
	LF	J. Clinton	399	.313	0		158	18	33	2	2.3	.842							
	C	K. Kelly	202	.228	0		169	35	50	3	6.7	.803							
	P	H. Henderson	191	.162	1		23	59	22	3	2.3	.788							
	OF	G. Gardner	161	.273	1		62	5	13	0	2.3	.838							
	2B	T. O'Brien	138	.268	0		77	93	36	8	7.1	.825							
	CO	P. Baker	121	.273	1		113	14	21	2		.858							
	C	R. Sweeney	101	.208	0		97	40	19	2	6.8	.878							

BATTING AND BASE RUNNING LEADERS
PITCHING LEADERS

Batting Average
E. Swartwood, PIT	.356
H. Stovey, PHI	.352
P. Browning, LOU	.336
J. Clinton, BAL	.313
D. Rowe, BAL	.313

Slugging Average
H. Stovey, PHI	.565
L. Reilly, CIN	.485
E. Swartwood, PIT	.475
C. Jones, CIN	.473
P. Browning, LOU	.469

Winning Percentage
T. Mullane, STL	.700
B. Mathews, PHI	.698
G. Bradley, PHI	.696
W. White, CIN	.662
J. McGinnis, STL	.636

Earned Run Average
W. White, CIN	2.09
T. Mullane, STL	2.19
R. Deagle, CIN	2.31
J. McGinnis, STL	2.33
T. Keefe, NY	2.41

Home Runs
H. Stovey, PHI	14
C. Jones, CIN	11
L. Reilly, CIN	9
C. Fulmer, CIN	5
T. Brown, COL	5

Total Bases
H. Stovey, PHI	238
L. Reilly, CIN	212
E. Swartwood, PIT	196
C. Jones, CIN	185
P. Browning, LOU	169

Wins
W. White, CIN	43
T. Keefe, NY	41
T. Mullane, STL	35
B. Mathews, PHI	30
J. McGinnis, STL	28
G. Hecker, LOU	28

Saves
T. Mullane, STL	1
B. Barr, PIT	1

Runs Batted In
(not available)

Stolen Bases
(not available)

Strikeouts
T. Keefe, NY	361
B. Mathews, PHI	203
T. Mullane, STL	191
F. Mountain, COL	159
G. Hecker, LOU	153

Complete Games
T. Keefe, NY	68
W. White, CIN	64
F. Mountain, COL	57
G. Hecker, LOU	53
T. Mullane, STL	49

Hits
H. Stovey, PHI	148
E. Swartwood, PIT	147
L. Reilly, CIN	136

Base on Balls
D. Stearns, BAL	34
C. Nelson, NY	31
M. Moynahan, PHI	30

Fewest Hits per 9 Innings
T. Keefe, NY	7.07
T. Mullane, STL	7.27
W. White, CIN	7.38

Shutouts
J. McGinnis, STL	6
W. White, CIN	6
T. Keefe, NY	5

Home Run Percentage
H. Stovey, PHI	3.3
C. Jones, CIN	2.8
L. Reilly, CIN	2.1

Runs Scored
H. Stovey, PHI	110
L. Reilly, CIN	103
H. Carpenter, CIN	99

Fewest Walks per 9 Innings
B. Mathews, PHI	0.73
S. Weaver, LOU	0.82
J. Lynch, NY	0.88

Most Strikeouts per 9 Inn.
T. Keefe, NY	5.25
B. Mathews, PHI	4.80
J. Lynch, NY	4.20

Doubles
H. Stovey, PHI	32
E. Swartwood, PIT	24
J. Hayes, PIT	23
L. Knight, PHI	23

Triples
P. Smith, COL	17
W. Kuehne, COL	14
L. Reilly, CIN	14

Innings
T. Keefe, NY	619
W. White, CIN	577
F. Mountain, COL	503

Games Pitched
T. Keefe, NY	68
W. White, CIN	65
F. Mountain, COL	59

	W	L	PCT	GB	R	OR	2B	3B	HR	BA	SA	SB	E	DP	FA	CG	BB	SO	ShO	SV	ERA
PHI	66	32	.673		720	547	149	50	20	.262	.345	0	584	40	.865	92	95	347	1	0	2.87
STL	65	33	.663	1	549	409	118	46	7	.255	.321	0	388	62	.909	93	150	325	9	1	2.23
CIN	61	37	.622	5	662	413	122	73	35	.262	.364	0	383	57	.905	96	168	213	8	0	2.26
NY	54	42	.563	11	498	405	111	58	6	.250	.319	0	439	45	.895	97	123	480	6	0	2.90
LOU	52	45	.536	13.5	564	562	114	66	12	.251	.330	0	488	67	.884	96	110	269	7	0	3.50
COL	32	65	.330	33.5	476	659	101	78	16	.240	.326	0	540	69	.873	90	211	222	4	0	3.97
PIT	31	67	.316	35	525	728	120	58	13	.247	.323	0	506	55	.884	82	151	271	1	1	4.62
BAL	28	68	.292	37	471	742	125	49	5	.246	.314	0	624	44	.855	86	190	290	1	0	4.08
					4465	4465	960	478	114	.252	.331	0	3952	439	.884	732	1198	2417	37	2	3.30

POS	Player	AB	BA	HR	RBI	PO	A	E	DP	TC/G	FA	Pitcher	G	IP	W	L	SV	ERA
Pro. W-84 L-28 Frank Bancroft																		
1B	J. Start	381	.276	2		939	21	20	31	10.5	**.980**	O. Radbourn	**75**	679	**60**	12	1	*1.38*
2B	J. Farrell	469	.217	1		249	351	51	36	6.0	.922	C. Sweeney	27	221	17	8	1	*1.55*
SS	A. Irwin	404	.240	2		99	307	55	20	4.5	.881							
3B	J. Denny	439	.248	6		144	168	45	5	3.6	.874							
RF	P. Radford	355	.197	1		146	26	23	4	2.0	.882							
CF	P. Hines	490	.302	3		202	20	26	5	2.3	.895							
LF	C. Carroll	452	.261	3		206	11	23	1	2.1	.904							
C	B. Gilligan	294	.245	1		**605**	94	54	7	9.3	.928							
P	O. Radbourn	361	.230	1		21	119	17	1	2.1	.892							
PO	C. Sweeney	168	.298	1		31	49	6	1		.930							
C	S. Nava	116	.095	0		172	40	27	1	8.9	.887							
Bos. W-73 L-38 John Morrill																		
1B	J. Morrill	438	.260	3		953	34	30	33	11.2	.971	C. Buffinton	67	587	47	16	0	*2.15*
2B	J. Burdock	361	.269	6		183	278	39	23	5.7	**.922**	J. Whitney	41	336	24	17	0	*2.09*
SS	S. Wise	426	.214	4		156	307	61	16	4.9	.884							
3B	E. Sutton	468	.346	3		119	186	31	7	3.1	**.908**							
RF	B. Crowley	407	.270	6		125	22	22	5	1.6	.870							
CF	J. Manning	345	.241	2		115	15	18	2	2.0	.878							
LF	J. Hornung	518	.268	7		182	14	18	1	1.9	.916							
C	M. Hackett	268	.205	1		512	104	48	2	**9.4**	.928							
P	C. Buffinton	352	.267	1		40	118	9	2	2.5	.946							
UT	J. Whitney	270	.259	3		135	80	10	3		.956							
C	M. Hines	132	.174	0		255	64	28	7	9.9	.919							
Buf. W-64 L-47 Jim O'Rourke																		
1B	D. Brouthers	398	.327	14		958	30	37	38	11.0	.964	P. Galvin	72	636	46	22	0	*1.99*
2B	H. Richardson	439	.301	6		191	243	50	18	6.8	.897	B. Serad	37	308	16	20	0	*4.27*
SS	D. Force	403	.206	0		110	312	48	21	4.5	**.898**							
3B	D. White	452	.325	5		113	198	66	11	3.5	.825							
RF	J. Lillie	471	.223	3		190	**41**	**40**	**7**	2.4	.852							
CF	D. Eggler	241	.195	0		104	14	15	1	2.1	.887							
LF	J. O'Rourke	467	.347	5		112	6	14	2	1.5	.894							
C	J. Rowe	400	.315	4		373	60	26	3	7.1	**.943**							
CO	G. Myers	325	.182	2		320	61	78	5		.830							
P	P. Galvin	274	.179	0		32	**154**	7	3	2.7	.964							
2B	C. Collins	169	.178	0		108	137	23	15	6.4	.914							
P	B. Serad	137	.175	0		4	57	14	1	2.0	.813							
Chi. W-62 L-50 Cap Anson																		
1B	C. Anson	475	.335	21		**1211**	40	**58**	**86**	**11.7**	.956	L. Corcoran	60	517	35	23	0	*2.40*
2B	F. Pfeffer	467	.289	**25**		**395**	**422**	**88**	**85**	8.1	.903	F. Goldsmith	21	188	9	11	0	*4.26*
SS	T. Burns	343	.245	7		99	254	68	21	5.3	.838	J. Clarkson	14	118	10	3	0	*2.14*
3B	N. Williamson	417	.278	**27**		121	**250**	60	**25**	4.4	.861							
RF	K. Kelly	452	**.354**	13		69	31	26	1	2.0	.794							
CF	G. Gore	422	.318	5		185	25	32	5	2.3	.868							
LF	A. Dalrymple	**521**	.309	22		176	18	26	5	2.0	.882							
C	S. Flint	279	.204	9		354	110	61	9	7.2	.884							
P	L. Corcoran	251	.243	1		**47**	132	**24**	5	3.4	.882							
OF	B. Sunday	176	.222	4		45	8	27	1	1.9	.663							
N. Y. W-62 L-50 James Price W-56 L-42 Monte Ward W-6 L-8																		
1B	A. McKinnon	470	.272	4		1097	31	53	57	10.2	.955	M. Welch	65	557	39	21	0	*2.50*
2B	R. Connor	477	.317	4		230	205	71	30	7.6	.860	E. Begley	31	266	12	18	0	*4.16*
SS	S. Caskin	351	.231	2		121	278	53	**28**	4.7	.883	M. Dorgan	14	113	8	6	0	*3.50*
3B	F. Hankinson	389	.231	2		135	182	47	8	3.5	.871							
RF	M. Dorgan	341	.276	1		101	13	20	3	2.1	.851							
CF	M. Ward	482	.253	2		103	13	21	2	2.3	.847							
LF	P. Gillespie	413	.264	2		159	8	20	1	1.9	.893							
C	B. Ewing	382	.277	3		445	**127**	41	10	7.7	.933							
OF	D. Richardson	277	.253	1		77	20	10	3	1.9	.907							
P	M. Welch	249	.241	3		25	78	14	**6**	1.8	.880							
P	E. Begley	121	.182	0		16	46	9	2	2.3	.873							
Phi. W-39 L-73 Harry Wright																		
1B	S. Farrar	428	.245	1		1142	**42**	42	41	11.0	.966	C. Ferguson	50	417	21	25	1	*3.54*
2B	E. Andrews	420	.221	0		239	326	69	37	5.8	.891	B. Vinton	21	182	10	10	0	*2.23*
SS	B. McClellan	450	.258	3		**165**	313	**83**	22	5.1	.852	J. Coleman	21	154	5	15	0	*4.90*
3B	J. Mulvey	401	.229	2		151	216	**73**	20	4.4	.834	J. McElroy	13	111	1	12	0	*4.86*
RF	J. Manning	424	.271	5		140	26	30	**7**	1.9	.847							
CF	J. Fogarty	378	.212	1		193	12	19	3	**2.9**	.915							
LF	B. Purcell	428	.252	1		182	12	28	1	2.2	.874							
C	J. Crowley	168	.244	0		198	49	50	2	6.2	.832							
P	C. Ferguson	203	.246	0		23	72	12	4	2.1	.888							
OP	J. Coleman	171	.246	0	·	61	44	13	2		.890							
Cle. W-35 L-77 Charlie Hackett																		
1B	B. Phillips	464	.276	3	46	1107	30	48	59	10.7	.959	J. Harkins	46	391	12	**32**	0	*3.68*
2B	G. Smith	291	.254	4	26	111	136	34	23	6.7	.879	J. McCormick	42	359	19	22	0	*2.86*
SS	J. Glasscock	281	.249	1	22	118	267	46	16	**6.2**	.893	S. Moffett	24	198	3	19	0	*3.87*
3B	M. Muldoon	422	.239	2	38	126	204	66	15	3.6	.835							
RF	J. Evans	313	.259	1	39	136	19	14	3	2.2	**.917**							
CF	P. Hotaling	408	.243	3	27	174	23	35	5	2.3	.849							
LF	W. Murphy	168	.226	1	9	60	7	26	0	2.2	.720							
C	D. Bushong	203	.236	0	10	355	98	58	**11**	8.2	.886							
OP	S. Moffett	256	.184	0	14	78	65	23	2		.861							
P	J. Harkins	229	.205	0	20	15	81	17	3	2.5	.850							
P	J. McCormick	190	.263	0	23	18	67	0	4	2.0	**1.000**							
C	F. Briody	148	.169	1	12	243	74	27	5	8.2	.922							
2S	G. Pinckney	144	.313	0	16	73	110	32	11		.851							
OF	E. Burch	124	.210	0	7	52	10	7	1	2.2	.899							

	POS	Player	AB	BA	HR	RBI	PO	A	E	DP	TC/G	FA	Pitcher	G	IP	W	L	SV	ERA
Det.	1B	M. Scott	438	.247	3		1120	26	38	37	10.8	.968	F. Meinke	35	289	8	22	0	3.18
	2B	B. Geis	283	.177	2		190	217	65	27	6.5	.862	D. Shaw	28	228	9	18	0	3.04
W-28 L-84	SS	F. Meinke	341	.164	6		57	146	39	16	4.7	.839	S. Weidman	26	213	4	21	0	3.72
Jack Chapman	3B	J. Farrell	461	.226	3		126	198	61	12	3.5	.842	C. Getzien	17	147	5	12	0	1.95
	RF	S. Weidman	300	.163	0		76	12	16	2	2.0	.846	J. Brill	12	103	2	10	0	5.50
	CF	N. Hanlon	450	.264	5		241	30	39	5	2.0	.874							
	LF	G. Wood	473	.252	8		190	17	24	1	2.0	.896							
	C	C. Bennett	341	.264	3		454	97	50	9	7.5	.917							
	P	D. Shaw	136	.191	1		10	55	11	2	2.7	.855							
	UT	H. Jones	129	.209	0		52	90	17	1		.893							

BATTING AND BASE RUNNING LEADERS

Batting Average

K. Kelly, CHI	.354
J. O'Rourke, BUF	.347
E. Sutton, BOS	.346
C. Anson, CHI	.335
D. Brouthers, BUF	.327

Slugging Average

D. Brouthers, BUF	.568
N. Williamson, CHI	.554
C. Anson, CHI	.543
K. Kelly, CHI	.524
F. Pfeffer, CHI	.514

PITCHING LEADERS

Winning Percentage

O. Radbourn, PRO	.833
C. Buffinton, BOS	.746
C. Sweeney, PRO	.680
P. Galvin, BUF	.676
M. Welch, NY	.650

Earned Run Average

O. Radbourn, PRO	1.38
C. Sweeney, PRO	1.55
C. Getzien, DET	1.95
P. Galvin, BUF	1.99
J. Whitney, BOS	2.09

Home Runs

N. Williamson, CHI	27
F. Pfeffer, CHI	25
A. Dalrymple, CHI	22
C. Anson, CHI	21
D. Brouthers, BUF	14

Total Bases

A. Dalrymple, CHI	263
C. Anson, CHI	258
F. Pfeffer, CHI	240
K. Kelly, CHI	237
N. Williamson, CHI	231

Wins

O. Radbourn, PRO	60
C. Buffinton, BOS	47
P. Galvin, BUF	46
M. Welch, NY	39
L. Corcoran, CHI	35

Saves

J. Morrill, BOS	2
O. Radbourn, PRO	1
J. O'Rourke, BUF	1
C. Ferguson, PHI	1
C. Sweeney, PRO	1

Runs Batted In

(not available)

Stolen Bases

(not available)

Strikeouts

O. Radbourn, PRO	441
C. Buffinton, BOS	417
P. Galvin, BUF	369
M. Welch, NY	345
L. Corcoran, CHI	272

Complete Games

O. Radbourn, PRO	73
P. Galvin, BUF	71
C. Buffinton, BOS	63
M. Welch, NY	62
L. Corcoran, CHI	57

Hits

J. O'Rourke, BUF	162
E. Sutton, BOS	162
A. Dalrymple, CHI	161

Base on Balls

G. Gore, CHI	61
K. Kelly, CHI	46
P. Hines, PRO	44

Fewest Hits per 9 Innings

C. Sweeney, PRO	6.23
O. Radbourn, PRO	7.00
J. Clarkson, CHI	7.17

Shutouts

P. Galvin, BUF	12
O. Radbourn, PRO	11
C. Buffinton, BOS	8

Home Run Percentage

N. Williamson, CHI	6.5
F. Pfeffer, CHI	5.4
C. Anson, CHI	4.4

Runs Scored

K. Kelly, CHI	120
J. O'Rourke, BUF	119
J. Hornung, BOS	119

Fewest Walks per 9 Innings

J. Whitney, BOS	0.72
P. Galvin, BUF	0.89
C. Buffinton, BOS	1.17

Most Strikeouts per 9 Inn.

J. Clarkson, CHI	7.78
J. Whitney, BOS	7.23
M. Dorgan, NY	7.17

Doubles

P. Hines, PRO	36
J. O'Rourke, BUF	33
C. Anson, CHI	30
J. Manning, PHI	29

Triples

B. Ewing, NY	20
D. Brouthers, BUF	16
J. Rowe, BUF	14

Innings

O. Radbourn, PRO	679
P. Galvin, BUF	636
C. Buffinton, BOS	587

Games Pitched

O. Radbourn, PRO	75
P. Galvin, BUF	72
C. Buffinton, BOS	67

	W	L	PCT	GB	R	OR	Batting 2B	3B	HR	BA	SA	SB	Fielding E	DP	FA	CG	BB	Pitching SO	ShO	SV	ERA
PRO	84	28	.750		665	388	153	43	21	.241	.315	0	398	50	.918	107	172	639	16	2	1.59
BOS	73	38	.658	10.5	684	468	179	60	36	.254	.351	0	384	46	.922	109	135	742	14	2	2.47
BUF	64	47	.577	19.5	700	626	163	69	39	.262	.361	0	462	71	.905	108	189	534	14	1	2.95
CHI	62	50	.554	22	834	647	162	50	142	.281	.446	0	595	107	.886	106	231	472	9	0	3.03
NY	62	50	.554	22	693	623	148	67	24	.255	.341	0	514	69	.895	111	326	567	4	0	3.12
PHI	39	73	.348	45	549	824	149	39	14	.234	.301	0	536	67	.888	106	254	411	3	1	3.93
CLE	35	77	.313	49	458	716	147	49	16	.237	.312	0	512	75	.897	107	269	482	7	0	3.43
DET	28	84	.250	56	445	736	114	47	31	.208	.284	0	549	60	.886	109	245	488	3	0	3.38
					5028	5028	1215	424	323	.247	.340	0	3950	545	.900	863	1821	4335	70	6	2.98

	POS	Player	AB	BA	HR	RBI	PO	A	E	DP	TC/G	FA	Pitcher	G	IP	W	L	SV	ERA
N. Y. W-75 L-32 Jim Mutrie	1B	D. Orr	458	.354	9		1161	24	49	29	11.2	.960	T. Keefe	58	492	37	17	0	2.29
	2B	D. Troy	421	.264	2		224	314	74	25	5.7	.879	J. Lynch	54	487	37	14	0	2.64
	SS	C. Nelson	432	.255	1		113	292	56	16	4.2	.879							
	3B	D. Esterbrook	477	.314	1		126	208	43	11	3.4	.886							
	RF	S. Brady	485	.252	0		154	26	16	1	1.8	.918							
	CF	C. Roseman	436	.298	4		157	12	22	0	1.8	.885							
	LF	E. Kennedy	378	.190	1		138	13	14	4	1.7	.915							
	C	B. Holbert	255	.208	0		374	142	54	7	9.7	.905							
	C	Reipschlager	233	.240	0		369	109	39	3	10.1	.925							
	P	T. Keefe	213	.235	3		18	95	30	2	2.5	.790							
	P	J. Lynch	195	.154	0		24	80	37	3	2.6	.738							
Col. W-69 L-39 Gus Schmelz	1B	J. Field	417	.233	4		1150	27	52	58	11.7	.958	E. Morris	52	430	34	13	0	2.18
	2B	P. Smith	445	.238	6		324	394	75	55	7.3	.905	F. Mountain	42	361	23	17	1	2.45
	SS	J. Richmond	398	.251	3		96	306	62	26	4.4	.866	E. Dundon	11	81	6	4	0	3.78
	3B	W. Kuehne	415	.236	5		117	218	46	13	3.5	.879							
	RF	T. Brown	451	.273	5		164	18	33	5	2.0	.847							
	CF	F. Mann	366	.276	7		120	12	22	2	1.6	.857							
	LF	J. Cahill	210	.219	0		1	3	2	0	3.0	.667							
	C	R. Kemmler	211	.199	0		268	77	36	3	6.6	.906							
	C	F. Carroll	252	.278	6		379	89	28	3	9.2	.944							
	P	F. Mountain	210	.238	4		14	88	9	0	2.6	.919							
	P	E. Morris	199	.186	0		19	88	23	3	2.5	.823							
Lou. W-68 L-40 Joe Gerhardt W-39 L-18 Mike Walsh W-29 L-22	1B	J. Latham	308	.169	0		788	32	33	48	11.2	.961	G. Hecker	76	671	52	20	0	1.80
	2B	J. Gerhardt	404	.220	0		334	389	64	64	7.5	.919	P. Reccius	18	129	6	7	0	2.71
	SS	McLaughlin	335	.200	1		121	330	55	34	5.4	.891	D. Driscoll	13	102	6	6	0	3.44
	3B	P. Browning	454	.330	4		79	66	35	4	3.5	.806	R. Deagle	12	87	4	6	0	2.58
	RF	C. Wolf	486	.300	3		173	26	26	4	2.2	.884							
	CF	M. Cline	396	.290	2		143	25	24	1	2.1	.875							
	LF	L. Maskrey	412	.250	0		138	17	18	2	1.7	.896							
	C	D. Sullivan	247	.239	0		340	61	30	2	6.8	.930							
	P	G. Hecker	321	.296	4		50	145	10	3	2.7	.951							
	UT	P. Reccius	263	.240	3		56	147	31	7		.868							
	C	E. Whiting	157	.223	0		199	54	31	6	7.1	.891							
St. L. W-67 L-40 Jimmy Williams	1B	C. Comiskey	460	.239	2		1193	38	40	56	11.8	.969	J. McGinnis	40	354	24	16	0	2.84
	2B	J. Quest	310	.206	0		232	242	56	39	6.6	.894	D. Foutz	25	207	15	6	0	2.18
	SS	B. Gleason	472	.269	1		119	316	67	23	4.6	.867	D. Davis	25	198	10	12	0	2.90
	3B	A. Latham	474	.274	1		142	302	70	16	4.7	.864	T. O'Neill	17	141	11	4	0	2.68
	RF	H. Nicol	442	.260	0		144	48	28	3	2.5	.873							
	CF	F. Lewis	300	.323	0		118	15	23	1	2.1	.853							
	LF	T. O'Neill	297	.276	3		67	6	17	1	1.4	.811							
	C	P. Deasley	254	.205	0		428	120	48	3	7.9	.919							
	OF	G. Strief	184	.201	2		50	5	10	0	1.5	.846							
	P	J. McGinnis	146	.233	0		8	71	12	1	2.3	.868							
	C	T. Dolan	137	.263	0		188	45	34	2	7.9	.873							
	PO	D. Foutz	119	.227	0		26	45	6	6		.922							
Cin. W-68 L-41 Will White W-43 L-25 Pop Snyder W-25 L-16	1B	L. Reilly	448	.339	11		977	26	30	60	10.0	.971	W. White	52	456	34	18	0	3.32
	2B	B. McPhee	462	.292	5		415	365	64	74	7.5	.924	B. Mountjoy	33	289	19	12	0	2.93
	SS	J. Peoples	267	.169	0		54	140	40	19	5.0	.829	G. Shallix	23	200	11	10	0	3.70
	3B	H. Carpenter	474	.255	4		157	168	44	16	3.4	.881							
	RF	P. Corkhill	452	.274	4		169	29	14	5	2.3	.934							
	CF	T. Mansell	266	.248	0		88	3	30	0	1.8	.752							
	LF	C. Jones	472	.314	7		207	12	28	0	2.2	.887							
	C	P. Snyder	268	.257	0		341	135	40	5	7.9	.922							
	P	W. White	184	.190	1		8	72	18	2	1.9	.816							
	OF	B. West	131	.244	0		46	1	10	0	1.7	.825							
	C	P. Powers	130	.138	0		152	53	25	2	7.4	.891							
	SS	F. Fennelly	122	.352	2		25	84	25	12	4.8	.813							
	P	B. Mountjoy	119	.151	0		13	64	6	2	2.5	.928							
	SS	C. Fulmer	114	.175	0		22	66	24	7	3.9	.786							
Bal. W-63 L-43 Billy Barnie	1B	D. Stearns	396	.237	3		959	48	54	36	10.6	.949	B. Emslie	50	455	32	17	0	2.75
	2B	T. Manning	341	.205	2		228	277	52	28	6.1	.907	H. Henderson	52	439	27	23	0	2.62
	SS	J. Macullar	358	.204	4		119	317	67	23	4.7	.867							
	3B	J. Sommer	479	.269	4		118	168	54	10	3.5	.841							
	RF	G. Gardner	173	.214	2		62	12	12	0	2.2	.860							
	CF	J. Clinton	433	.273	3		133	17	35	5	1.8	.811							
	LF	T. York	314	.223	1		100	7	20	1	1.5	.843							
	C	S. Trott	284	.257	2		491	87	43	10	10.4	.931							
	C	B. Traffley	210	.176	0		321	57	30	6	8.7	.926							
	P	H. Henderson	203	.227	0		27	78	22	3	2.4	.827							
	P	B. Emslie	195	.190	0		27	83	22	0	2.6	.833							
	OF	D. Casey	149	.248	3		48	5	6	2	1.6	.898							
	O2	O. Burns	131	.298	6		49	34	13	2		.865							

POS	Player	AB	BA	HR	RBI	PO	A	E	DP	TC/G	FA	Pitcher	G	IP	W	L	SV	ERA
Phi.												B. Mathews	49	431	30	18	0	3.32
1B	H. Stovey	443	.404	11		1061	32	45	46	10.9	.960	B. Taylor	30	260	18	12	0	2.53
2B	C. Stricker	399	.231	1		280	257	80	40	5.8	.870	A. Atkisson	22	184	11	11	0	4.20
SS	S. Houck	472	.297	0		122	379	60	30	5.2	.893							
3B	F. Corey	439	.276	5		121	209	42	10	3.6	.887							
RF	L. Knight	484	.271	1		158	36	19	6	2.0	.911							
CF	H. Larkin	326	.276	3		106	7	19	0	1.6	.856							
LF	J. Birchall	221	.258	0		81	7	17	1	2.0	.838							
C	J. Milligan	268	.287	3		474	100	37	5	9.4	.939							
P	B. Mathews	184	.185	0		8	78	25	1	2.3	.775							
C	J. O'Brien	138	.283	1		169	43	16	6	7.6	.930							
OF	B. Blakiston	128	.258	0		48	7	6	1	2.2	.902							
P	B. Taylor	111	.252	0		12	64	21	1	3.2	.784							
Tol.												T. Mullane	68	576	35	25	0	2.48
1B	C. Lane	215	.228	1		474	20	27	17	11.3	.948	H. O'Day	39	309	7	28	1	3.97
2B	S. Barkley	435	.306	1		318	358	51	46	7.1	.930							
SS	J. Miller	423	.239	1		125	320	70	26	4.9	.864							
3B	E. Brown	153	.176	0		41	54	22	1	3.0	.812							
RF	T. Poorman	382	.233	0		129	29	29	5	2.0	.845							
CF	C. Welch	425	.224	0		206	24	29	3	2.4	.888							
LF	F. Olin	86	.256	1		22	6	4	0	1.2	.875							
C	F. Walker	152	.263	0		220	70	37	4	8.0	.887							
UT	T. Mullane	352	.276	3		139	161	41	10		.880							
PO	H. O'Day	242	.211	0		38	90	17	2		.883							
UT	J. Moffett	204	.201	0		421	42	33	23		.933							
C	D. McGuire	151	.185	1		224	56	29	1	7.5	.906							
3B	G. Meister	119	.193	0		27	40	15	3	2.4	.817							
UT	C. Morton	111	.162	0		33	26	8	1		.881							
Bkn.												A. Terry	57	485	20	35	0	3.49
1B	Householder	273	.242	3		426	18	19	17	11.6	.959	S. Kimber	40	352	17	20	0	3.91
2B	B. Greenwood	385	.216	3		230	300	59	40	6.4	.900	J. Conway	13	105	3	9	0	4.44
SS	B. Geer	391	.210	0		176	360	81	34	5.8	.869							
3B	F. Warner	352	.222	1		94	147	52	13	3.5	.823							
RF	J. Cassidy	433	.252	2		124	25	26	5	1.8	.851							
CF	J. Remsen	301	.223	3		152	7	15	2	2.1	.914							
LF	O. Walker	382	.270	2		87	12	15	0	1.9	.868							
C	J. Corcoran	185	.211	0		191	57	36	4	7.5	.873							
P	A. Terry	240	.233	0		32	81	34	0	2.6	.769							
OF	I. Benners	189	.201	1		64	1	13	0	1.6	.833							
1B	J. Knowles	153	.235	1		304	17	16	18	11.6	.953							
P	S. Kimber	138	.145	0		32	67	30	0	3.2	.767							
Ric.												E. Dugan	20	166	5	14	0	4.49
1B	J. Powell	151	.245	0		380	18	24	15	10.3	.943	P. Meegan	17	140	5	9	0	4.37
2B	T. Larkin	139	.201	0		94	129	23	14	6.2	.907							
SS	B. Schenck	151	.205	3		32	121	30	8	4.6	.836							
3B	B. Nash	166	.199	1		77	87	34	8	4.4	.828							
RF	M. Mansell	113	.301	0		24	5	9	1	1.3	.763							
CF	D. Johnston	146	.281	2		86	10	15	3	3.0	.865							
LF	E. Glenn	175	.246	1		85	5	18	2	2.5	.833							
C	J. Hanna	67	.194	0		108	38	12	2	7.5	.924							
CO	M. Quinton	94	.234	0		62	20	12	3		.872							
P	E. Dugan	70	.114	0		13	23	13	0	2.5	.735							
P	P. Meegan	59	.136	0		6	34	9	0	2.9	.816							
Pit.												F. Sullivan	51	441	16	35	0	4.20
1B	J. Knowles	182	.231	0		499	15	21	20	11.6	.961	J. Neagle	38	326	11	26	0	3.73
2B	G. Creamer	339	.183	0		308	336	43	47	7.0	.937							
SS	B. White	291	.227	0		58	185	58	12	5.0	.807							
3B	J. Battin	158	.177	0		53	95	13	4	3.7	.919							
RF	E. Swartwood	399	.288	0		109	22	32	2	2.1	.804							
CF	G. Taylor	152	.211	0		68	7	19	0	2.3	.798							
LF	D. Miller	347	.225	0		74	13	22	1	2.2	.798							
C	B. Colgan	161	.155	0		228	71	31	5	7.5	.906							
P	F. Sullivan	189	.153	0		24	90	24	2	2.7	.826							
P	J. Neagle	148	.149	0		19	57	24	1	2.6	.760							
3O	J. McDonald	145	.159	0		43	38	19	2		.810							
SS	T. Forster	126	.222	0		45	103	17	8	5.9	.897							
C	J. Hayes	124	.226	0		135	30	16	2	7.5	.912							
OF	C. Eden	122	.270	1		40	4	14	0	1.9	.759							
1B	J. Faatz	112	.241	0		283	6	11	16	10.3	.963							
Ind.												L. McKeon	61	512	18	41	0	3.50
1B	J. Kerins	361	.216	6		887	41	27	20	11.0	.972	B. Barr	16	132	3	11	0	4.99
2B	E. Merrill	196	.179	0		144	162	34	15	6.2	.900	J. Aydelott	12	106	5	7	0	4.92
SS	M. Phillips	413	.269	0		108	335	71	16	5.3	.862							
3B	P. Callahan	258	.260	2		66	94	37	5	3.2	.812							
RF	P. Weihe	256	.254	4		90	14	17	2	2.1	.860							
CF	J. Morrison	182	.264	1		78	9	24	4	2.5	.784							
LF	J. Peltz	393	.219	3		155	16	38	1	2.0	.818							
C	J. Keenan	249	.293	3		399	71	39	5	8.6	.923							
P	L. McKeon	247	.215	0		35	124	20	1	2.9	.888							
OF	J. Dorgan	141	.298	0		37	9	12	1	2.0	.793							
2B	C. Collins	138	.225	0		97	105	26	10	6.0	.886							
UT	J. Donnelly	134	.254	0		33	62	21	2		.819							
32	B. Watkins	127	.205	0		44	57	14	4		.878							

Phi. W-61 L-46, Charlie Mason, W-28 L-23, Bill Sharsig, W-33 L-23

Tol. W-46 L-58, Charlie Morton

Bkn. W-40 L-64, George Taylor

Ric. W-12 L-30, Felix Moses

Pit. W-30 L-78, Joe Battin, W-1 L-3, George Creamer, W-2 L-7, Denny McKnight, W-12 L-17, Bob Ferguson, W-5 L-21, Horace Phillips, W-10 L-30

Ind. W-29 L-78, Jim Gifford, W-25 L-59, Bill Watkins, W-4 L-19

	POS	Player	AB	BA	HR	RBI	PO	A	E	DP	TC/G	FA	Pitcher	G	IP	W	L	SV	ERA
	1B	W. Prince	166	.217	0		405	4	26	19	10.1	.940	B. Barr	32	281	9	23	0	3.45
Was.	2B	T. Hawkes	151	.278	0		124	103	20	10	6.5	.919	J. Hamill	19	157	2	17	0	4.48
W-12 L-51	SS	F. Fennelly	257	.292	2		88	215	48	14	5.9	.863	E. Trumbull	10	84	1	9	0	4.71
Holly Hollingshead	3B	B. Gladman	224	.156	1		62	90	39	5	3.6	.796							
	RF	B. Morgan	162	.173	0		46	4	14	1	2.1	.781							
	CF	H. Mullin	120	.142	0		47	6	8	0	1.8	.869							
	LF	T. Farley	52	.212	0		24	2	4	1	2.1	.867							
	C	J. Humphries	193	.176	0		198	52	31	6	8.0	.890							
	P	B. Barr	135	.148	2		13	57	24	1	2.9	.745							
	UT	E. Yewell	93	.247	0		40	55	17	7		.848							
	OP	E. Trumbull	86	.116	0		24	24	14	1		.774							
	2O	F. Olin	83	.386	0		45	27	20	3		.783							
	C	J. Hanna	76	.066	0		94	31	18	1	7.9	.874							
	P	J. Hamill	71	.099	0		14	31	17	0	3.3	.726							

BATTING AND BASE RUNNING LEADERS

Batting Average

H. Stovey, PHI	.404
D. Orr, NY	.354
L. Reilly, CIN	.339
P. Browning, LOU	.330
F. Lewis, STL	.323

Slugging Average

H. Stovey, PHI	.648
L. Reilly, CIN	.551
D. Orr, NY	.539
F. Fennelly, CIN, WAS	.480
C. Jones, CIN	.470

Home Runs

H. Stovey, PHI	11
L. Reilly, CIN	11
D. Orr, NY	9
F. Mann, COL	7
C. Jones, CIN	7

Total Bases

H. Stovey, PHI	287
L. Reilly, CIN	247
D. Orr, NY	247
C. Jones, CIN	222
P. Browning, LOU	212

Runs Batted In

(not available)

Stolen Bases

(not available)

Hits

H. Stovey, PHI	179
D. Orr, NY	162
L. Reilly, CIN	152

Base on Balls

C. Nelson, NY	74
B. Geer, BKN	38
C. Jones, CIN	37

Home Run Percentage

H. Stovey, PHI	2.5
L. Reilly, CIN	2.5
F. Carroll, COL	2.4

Runs Scored

H. Stovey, PHI	126
C. Jones, CIN	117
A. Latham, STL	115

Doubles

S. Barkley, TOL	39
P. Browning, LOU	34
D. Orr, NY	32

Triples

H. Stovey, PHI	25
L. Reilly, CIN	19
F. Mann, COL	18

PITCHING LEADERS

Winning Percentage

J. Lynch, NY	.725
E. Morris, COL	.723
G. Hecker, LOU	.722
D. Foutz, STL	.714
T. Keefe, NY	.685

Earned Run Average

G. Hecker, LOU	1.80
D. Foutz, STL	2.18
E. Morris, COL	2.18
T. Keefe, NY	2.29
F. Mountain, COL	2.45

Wins

G. Hecker, LOU	52
J. Lynch, NY	37
T. Keefe, NY	37
T. Mullane, TOL	35
E. Morris, COL	34
W. White, CIN	34

Saves

O. Burns, BAL	1
F. Mountain, COL	1
H. O'Day, TOL	1

Strikeouts

G. Hecker, LOU	385
H. Henderson, BAL	346
T. Mullane, TOL	334
T. Keefe, NY	323
L. McKeon, IND	308

Complete Games

G. Hecker, LOU	72
T. Mullane, TOL	65
L. McKeon, IND	59
T. Keefe, NY	57
A. Terry, BKN	55

Fewest Hits per 9 Innings

E. Morris, COL	7.02
G. Hecker, LOU	7.06
T. Keefe, NY	7.10

Shutouts

T. Mullane, TOL	8
W. White, CIN	7
G. Hecker, LOU	6

Fewest Walks per 9 Innings

D. Driscoll, LOU	0.62
G. Hecker, LOU	0.75
J. Lynch, NY	0.78

Most Strikeouts per 9 Inn.

H. Henderson, BAL	7.09
D. Davis, STL	6.49
E. Morris, COL	6.33

Innings

G. Hecker, LOU	671
T. Mullane, TOL	576
L. McKeon, IND	512

Games Pitched

G. Hecker, LOU	76
T. Mullane, TOL	68
L. McKeon, IND	61

	W	L	PCT	GB	R	OR	2B	3B	Batting HR	BA	SA	SB	E	Fielding DP	FA	CG	BB	Pitching SO	ShO	SV	ERA
NY	75	32	.701		734	423	155	64	21	.262	.348	0	450	42	.905	111	119	611	9	0	2.46
COL	69	39	.639	6.5	585	459	107	96	40	.240	.351	0	433	74	.908	102	172	526	8	1	2.68
LOU	68	40	.630	7.5	573	425	152	68	18	.254	.340	0	426	84	.912	101	97	470	6	0	2.17
STL	67	40	.626	8	658	539	151	60	11	.249	.326	0	490	65	.900	99	172	477	8	0	2.67
CIN	68	41	.624	8	754	512	109	98	34	.254	.353	0	430	82	.900	111	181	308	11	0	3.33
BAL	63	43	.594	11.5	636	515	133	84	30	.233	.335	0	459	61	.900	105	219	635	8	1	2.71
PHI	61	46	.570	14	700	546	167	100	26	.267	.379	0	457	63	.901	105	127	530	5	0	3.40
TOL	46	58	.442	27.5	463	571	153	48	8	.231	.305	0	469	67	.900	103	169	501	9	1	3.07
BKN	40	64	.385	33.5	476	644	112	47	16	.225	.292	0	520	68	.889	105	163	378	6	0	3.79
RIC	12	30	.286	30.5	194	294	40	33	7	.221	.308	0	239	27	.874	45	52	167	1	0	4.54
PIT	30	78	.278	45.5	406	725	105	50	2	.211	.268	0	524	71	.889	108	216	338	4	0	4.35
IND	29	78	.271	46	462	755	129	62	20	.234	.316	0	514	45	.889	107	199	479	2	0	4.21
WAS	12	51	.190	41	248	481	61	24	5	.200	.258	0	400	40	.858	62	110	235	3	0	4.00
					6889	6889	1574	834	238	.240	.325	0	5811	789	.897	1264	1996	5655	80	3	3.24

	POS	Player	AB	BA	HR	RBI	PO	A	E	DP	TC/G	FA	Pitcher	G	IP	W	L	SV	ERA
St. L. W-94 L-19 Henry Lucas	1B	J. Quinn	429	.270	0		1033	33	62	55	11.3	.945	C. Sweeney	33	271	24	7	0	1.83
	2B	F. Dunlap	449	.412	13		341	300	51	54	6.9	.926	B. Taylor	33	263	25	4	4	1.68
	SS	M. Whitehead	393	.211	1		85	269	87	19*	4.7	.803	H. Boyle	19	150	15	3	1	1.74
	3B	J. Gleason	395	.324	3		95	170	80	11	3.8	.768	P. Werden	16	141	12	1	0	1.97
	RF	O. Shaffer	467	.360	2		110	24	20	3	1.5	.870	C. Hodnett	14	121	12	2	0	2.01
	CF	D. Rowe	485	.293	3		146	15	9	5	1.8	.947							
	LF	B. Dickerson	211	.365	0		65	12	9	2	2.0	.895							
	C	G. Baker	317	.164	0		435	113	63	11	9.0	.897							
	UT	H. Boyle	262	.260	4		85	49	19	7		.876							
	UT	J. Brennan	231	.216	0		172	92	40	4		.868							
	P	B. Taylor	186	.366	3		17	51	10	2	2.4	.872							
	P	C. Sweeney	171	.316	1		23	76	6	4	3.2	.943							
Mil. W-8 L-4 Tom Loftus	1B	T. Griffin	41	.220	0		100	1	9	0	10.0	.918	H. Porter	6	51	3	3	0	3.00
	2B	A. Myers	46	.326	0		26	30	10	1	5.5	.848	E. Cushman	4	36	4	0	0	1.00
	SS	T. Sexton	47	.234	0		8	21	5	1	2.8	.853							
	3B	T. Morrissey	47	.170	0		7	15	9	1	2.6	.710							
	RF	E. Hogan	37	.081	0		16	9	6	1	2.8	.806							
	CF	L. Baldwin	27	.222	0		6	1	2	1	1.8	.778							
	LF	S. Behel	33	.242	0		4	1	0	0	.6	1.000							
	C	C. Broughton	39	.308	0		65	9	5	0	11.3	.937							
	PO	H. Porter	40	.275	0		2	10	0	0		1.000							
Cin. W-69 L-36 Dan O'Leary W-33 L-29 Sam Crane W-36 L-7	1B	M. Powell	185	.319	1		463	11	30	19	11.7	.940	G. Bradley	41	342	25	15	0	2.71
	2B	S. Crane	309	.233	1		224	217	73	27	6.4	.858	D. Burns	40	330	23	15	0	2.46
	SS	J. Jones	272	.261	2		54	140	32	9	5.5	.858	J. McCormick	26	210	21	3	0	1.54
	3B	C. Barber	204	.201	0		68	112	35	4	3.9	.837							
	RF	B. Hawes	349	.278	4		74	7	17	0	1.7	.827							
	CF	B. Harbidge	341	.279	2		101	24	13	2	1.7	.906							
	LF	L. Sylvester	333	.267	2		110	23	35	2	2.1	.792							
	C	K. Kelly	142	.282	1		210	60	42	3	8.4	.865							
	OP	D. Burns	350	.306	4		87	81	26	1		.866							
	UT	G. Bradley	226	.190	0		82	94	24	4		.880							
	SS	J. Glasscock	172	.419	2		45	107	19	4	4.8	.889							
	OF	D. O'Leary	132	.258	1		48	8	9	0	2.0	.862							
	1B	M. McQuery	132	.280	2		340	8	8	9	10.2	.978							
	3B	E. Cleveland	115	.322	1		48	54	19	0	4.2	.843							
Bal. W-58 L-47 Charlie Levis W-53 L-35 Bill Henderson W-5 L-12	1B	C. Levis	373	.228	6		923	24	45	33	11.4*	.955	B. Sweeney	62	538	40	21	0	2.59
	2B	D. Phelan	402	.246	3		272	251	77	33	6.0	.872	T. Lee	15	122	5	8	0	3.39
	SS	L. Say	339	.239	2		103*	234*	87*	16*	5.4*	.795							
	3B	Y. Robinson	415	.267	2		98	163	53	10	4.4	.831							
	RF	B. Graham	167	.269	0		60	10	16	2	2.2	.814							
	CF	N. Cuthbert	168	.202	0		41	10	17	0	1.5	.750							
	LF	E. Seery	463	.311	2		157*	26*	38	3	2.1	.828							
	C	E. Fusselbach	303	.284	1		378	137	50	5	10.5	.912							
	P	B. Sweeney	296	.240	0		25	133	34	3	3.1	.823							
	CO	R. Sweeney	186	.226	0		218	60	35	1		.888							
	OF	H. Oberbeck	125	.184	0		33	10	6	1	1.8	.878							
Bos. W-58 L-51 Tim Murnane W-8 L-17 Tom Furniss W-4 L-6 Jake Morse W-46 L-28	1B	T. Murnane	311	.235	0		588	7	31	8	9.9	.951	W. Burke	38	322	19	15	0	2.85
	2B	T. O'Brien	449	.263	4		257	267	90	23	6.2	.853	D. Shaw	39	316	21	15	0	1.77
	SS	W. Hackett	415	.243	1		126	294	71	12	4.8	.855	T. Bond	23	189	13	9	0	3.00
	3B	J. Irwin	432	.234	1		117	191	87	7	3.8	.780							
	RF	C. Crane	428	.285	12		74	21	20	3	2.0	.826							
	CF	M. Slattery	413	.208	0		140	26	41	3	2.2	.802							
	LF	F. Butler	255	.169	0		56	8	15	1	1.5	.810							
	C	L. Brown	325	.231	1		414	117	50	6	10.8	.914							
	OF	T. McCarthy	209	.215	0		39	11	13	1	1.3	.794							
	P	W. Burke	184	.223	0		13	45	11	2	1.8	.841							
	PO	T. Bond	162	.296	0		22	57	12	2		.868							
	P	D. Shaw	153	.242	0		18	59	17	1	2.4	.819							
Chi.-Pit. W-41 L-50 Ed Hengle W-34 L-39 Joe Battin W-1 L-5 Joe Ellick W-6 L-6	1B	J. Schoeneck	366	.317	2		916*	24	43	27	10.9	.956*	O. Daily	56	485	27	29	0	2.36
	2B	M. Hengle	74	.203	0		40	39	15	2	4.9	.840	A. Atkisson	16	140	6	10	0	1.48
	SS	S. Matthias	142	.275	0		30	101	25	5	4.3	.840							
	3B	W. Foley	71	.282	0		18	23	10	2	2.7	.804							
	RF	J. Ellick	394	.236	0		43	13	6	1	1.1	.903							
	CF	C. Briggs	182	.170	1		42	6	11	1	1.6	.814							
	LF	Householder	310	.239	1		41	3	9	2	1.3	.830							
	C	B. Krieg	279	.247	0		429	115	40	3	11.2	.932							
	P	O. Daily	196	.219	0		12	105	20	2	2.4	.854							
	UT	T. Suck	188	.149	0		217	85	46	4		.868							
	OF	H. Wheeler	158	.228	1		45	3	14	0	1.7	.774							
	OF	G. Gardner	149	.255	0		32	2	5	0	1.3	.872							

POS	Player	AB	BA	HR	RBI	PO	A	E	DP	TC/G	FA	Pitcher	G	IP	W	L	SV	ERA
Phi. W-56 L-54 Harry Wright																		
1B	S. Farrar	420	.245	3		1153	41	31	50	11.0	.975	E. Daily	50	440	26	23	0	2.21
2B	A. Myers	357	.204	1		201	287	64	31	5.9	.884	C. Ferguson	48	405	26	20	0	*2.22*
SS	C. Bastian	389	.167	4		164	337	62	34	5.5	.890							
3B	J. Mulvey	443	.269	6		144	201	62	12	3.8	.848							
RF	J. Manning	445	.256	3		134	21	18	3	1.6	.896							
CF	J. Fogarty	427	.232	0		227	26	16	5	3.1	.941							
LF	E. Andrews	421	.266	0		175	11	16	1	2.0	.921							
C	J. Clements	188	.191	1		181	47	28	2	6.2	.891							
P	C. Ferguson	235	.306	1		27	87	9	3	2.6	.927							
P	E. Daily	184	.207	1		11	87	12	2	2.2	.891							
C	T. Cusick	141	.177	0		180	60	57	2	7.8	.808							
C	C. Ganzel	125	.168	0		175	39	27	3	7.3	.888							
Pro. W-53 L-57 Frank Bancroft																		
1B	J. Start	374	.275	0	41	1036	35	31	42	10.9	.972	O. Radbourn	49	446	26	20	0	*2.20*
2B	J. Farrell	257	.206	1	19	158	194	39	16	5.8	.900	D. Shaw	49	400	23	26	0	*2.57*
SS	A. Irwin	218	.179	0	14	70	209	40	17	5.5	.875							
3B	J. Denny	318	.223	3	25	128	157	43	10	4.0	.869							
RF	P. Radford	371	.243	0	32	141	26	29	7	2.2	.852							
CF	P. Hines	411	.270	1	35	199	18	34	3	2.7	.865							
LF	C. Carroll	426	.232	1	40	207	10	28	2	2.4	.886							
C	B. Gilligan	252	.214	0	12	305	84	57	13	6.9	.872							
UT	C. Bassett	285	.144	0	16	141	248	39	24		.909							
P	O. Radbourn	249	.233	0	22	18	115	9	7	2.9	.937							
C	C. Daily	223	.260	0	19	220	70	41	8	6.9	.876							
P	D. Shaw	165	.133	0	9	11	76	8	2	1.9	.916							
Bos. W-46 L-66 John Morrill																		
1B	J. Morrill	394	.226	4	44	952	32	31	53	11.0	.969	J. Whitney	51	441	18	**32**	0	*2.98*
2B	J. Burdock	169	.142	0	7	99	134	21	16	5.6	.917	C. Buffinton	51	434	22	27	0	*2.88*
SS	S. Wise	424	.283	4	46	135	270	67	29	**6.0**	.858	D. Davis	11	94	5	6	0	*4.29*
3B	E. Sutton	457	.313	4	47	132	168	43	**18**	3.8	.875							
RF	T. Poorman	227	.238	3	25	82	9	14	1	1.9	.867							
CF	J. Manning	306	.206	2	27	164	21	21	3	2.5	.898							
LF	T. McCarthy	148	.182	0	11	69	8	12	0	2.2	.865							
C	T. Gunning	174	.184	0	15	252	68	45	4	7.6	.877							
UT	C. Buffinton	338	.240	1	33	196	121	27	11		.922							
PO	J. Whitney	290	.234	0	36	49	130	20	1		.899							
OF	G. Whiteley	135	.185	1	7	42	8	14	2	2.0	.781							
C	P. Dealy	130	.223	1	9	162	42	22	8	7.8	.903							
2S	W. Hackett	125	.184	0	9	59	86	22	9		.868							
C	M. Hackett	115	.183	0	4	194	53	27	6	8.1	.901							
OF	D. Johnston	111	.234	1	23	40	8	9	2	2.2	.842							
Det. W-41 L-67 Charlie Morton W-18 L-39 Bill Watkins W-23 L-28																		
1B	M. McQuery	278	.273	3	30	707	28	18	32	10.9	.976	S. Weidman	38	330	14	24	0	*3.14*
2B	S. Crane	245	.192	2	20	179	197	38	21	6.1	.908	C. Getzien	37	330	12	25	0	*3.03*
SS	M. Phillips	139	.209	0	17	35	120	21	6	5.3	.881	L. Baldwin	21	179	11	9	1	*1.86*
3B	J. Donnelly	211	.232	1	22	73	102	31	3	3.7	.850	D. Casey	12	104	4	8	0	*3.29*
RF	S. Thompson	254	.303	7	44	84	24	14	0	2.0	.885							
CF	N. Hanlon	424	.302	1	29	220	19	38	2	2.6	.863							
LF	G. Wood	362	.290	5	28	112	11	16	1	2.0	.885							
C	C. Bennett	349	.269	5	60	347	87	38	10	7.6	.919							
2B	J. Quest	200	.195	0	21	107	122	26	10	6.5	.898							
OF	J. Dorgan	161	.286	0	24	55	5	10	2	1.8	.857							
OP	S. Weidman	153	.157	1	14	19	60	17	1		.823							
1B	M. Scott	148	.264	0	12	394	18	14	17	11.2	.967							
P	C. Getzien	137	.212	0	16	17	66	8	0	2.5	.912							
PO	L. Baldwin	124	.242	0	18	29	44	10	1		.880							
C	D. McGuire	121	.190	0	9	249	52	26	2	10.5	.920							
Buf. W-38 L-74 Jack Chapman W-12 L-19 George Hughson W-18 L-33 Pud Galvin W-8 L-22																		
1B	D. Brouthers	407	.359	7	60	996	25	26	54	10.7	.975	P. Galvin	33	284	13	19	1	*4.09*
2B	D. Force	253	.225	0	17	113	134	33	23	6.7	.882	B. Serad	30	241	7	21	0	*4.10*
SS	J. Rowe	421	.290	2	51	71	186	51	26	4.7	.834	P. Conway	27	210	10	17	0	*4.67*
3B	D. White	404	.292	0	57	118	198	40	12	3.6	.888	P. Wood	24	199	8	15	0	*4.44*
RF	J. Lillie	430	.249	2	30	183	23	33	4	2.1	.862							
CF	H. Richardson	426	.319	6	44	120	6	14	2	2.9	.900							
LF	B. Crowley	344	.241	1	36	152	8	23	1	2.0	.874							
C	G. Myers	326	.206	0	19	305	95	45	4	6.4	.899							
P	P. Galvin	122	.189	1	10	17	83	13	3	3.4	.885							
St. L. W-36 L-72 Henry Lucas																		
1B	A. McKinnon	411	.294	1	44	1102	26	25	50	11.5	.978	H. Boyle	42	367	16	24	0	2.75
2B	F. Dunlap	423	.270	2	25	314	374	49	53	7.0	.934	C. Sweeney	35	275	11	21	0	3.93
SS	J. Glasscock	446	.280	1	40	156	397	50	33	5.5	.917	J. Kirby	14	129	5	8	0	3.55
3B	E. Caskin	262	.179	0	12	82	139	29	5	3.6	.884	O. Daily	11	91	3	8	0	3.94
RF	O. Shaffer	257	.195	0	18	106	28	12	0	2.1	.918							
CF	J. Quinn	343	.213	0	15	83	8	13	0	1.8	.875							
LF	E. Seery	216	.162	0	14	95	16	16	1	2.2	.874							
C	F. Briody	215	.195	1	17	243	83	39	3	6.1	.893							
OP	C. Sweeney	267	.206	0	24	81	67	27	3		.846							
PO	H. Boyle	258	.202	1	21	88	73	15	4		.915							
OF	F. Lewis	181	.293	1	27	71	18	4	2	2.1	.957							
C	G. Baker	131	.122	0	5	148	31	28	1	6.5	.865							

BATTING AND BASE RUNNING LEADERS

Batting Average

R. Connor, NY	.371
D. Brouthers, BUF	.359
M. Dorgan, NY	.326
H. Richardson, BUF	.319
G. Gore, CHI	.313

Slugging Average

D. Brouthers, BUF	.543
R. Connor, NY	.495
B. Ewing, NY	.471
C. Anson, CHI	.461
H. Richardson, BUF	.458

Home Runs

A. Dalrymple, CHI	11
K. Kelly, CHI	9
S. Thompson, DET	7
D. Brouthers, BUF	7
T. Burns, CHI	7
C. Anson, CHI	7

Total Bases

R. Connor, NY	225
D. Brouthers, BUF	221
A. Dalrymple, CHI	219
C. Anson, CHI	214
J. O'Rourke, NY	211

Runs Batted In

(not available)

Stolen Bases

(not available)

Hits

R. Connor, NY	169
D. Brouthers, BUF	146
C. Anson, CHI	144

Base on Balls

N. Williamson, CHI	75
G. Gore, CHI	68
J. Morrill, BOS	64

Home Run Percentage

A. Dalrymple, CHI	2.2
K. Kelly, CHI	2.1
B. Ewing, NY	1.8

Runs Scored

K. Kelly, CHI	124
J. O'Rourke, NY	119
G. Gore, CHI	115

Doubles

C. Anson, CHI	35
D. Brouthers, BUF	32
J. Rowe, BUF	28

Triples

J. O'Rourke, NY	16
R. Connor, NY	15
C. Bennett, DET	13
G. Gore, CHI	13

PITCHING LEADERS

Winning Percentage

M. Welch, NY	.800
J. Clarkson, CHI	.768
J. McCormick, CHI, PRO	.750
T. Keefe, NY	.711
C. Ferguson, PHI	.565
O. Radbourn, PRO	.565

Earned Run Average

T. Keefe, NY	1.58
M. Welch, NY	1.66
J. Clarkson, CHI	1.85
L. Baldwin, DET	1.86
O. Radbourn, PRO	2.20

Wins

J. Clarkson, CHI	53
M. Welch, NY	44
T. Keefe, NY	32
O. Radbourn, PRO	26
C. Ferguson, PHI	26
E. Daily, PHI	26

Saves

F. Pfeffer, CHI	2
N. Williamson, CHI	2

Strikeouts

J. Clarkson, CHI	318
M. Welch, NY	258
C. Buffinton, BOS	242
T. Keefe, NY	230
J. Whitney, BOS	200

Complete Games

J. Clarkson, CHI	68
M. Welch, NY	55
J. Whitney, BOS	50
O. Radbourn, PRO	49
C. Buffinton, BOS	49
E. Daily, PHI	49

Fewest Hits per 9 Innings

T. Keefe, NY	6.72
M. Welch, NY	6.80
L. Baldwin, DET	6.88

Shutouts

J. Clarkson, CHI	10
T. Keefe, NY	7
M. Welch, NY	7

Fewest Walks per 9 Innings

J. Whitney, BOS	0.75
P. Galvin, BUF	1.17
J. Clarkson, CHI	1.40

Most Strikeouts per 9 Inn.

D. Casey, DET	6.84
L. Baldwin, DET	6.78
T. Keefe, NY	5.20

Innings

J. Clarkson, CHI	623
M. Welch, NY	492
O. Radbourn, PRO	446

Games Pitched

J. Clarkson, CHI	70
M. Welch, NY	56
J. Whitney, BOS	51
C. Buffinton, BOS	51

	W	L	PCT	GB	R	OR	Batting 2B	3B	HR	BA	SA	SB	E	Fielding DP	FA	CG	BB	Pitching SO	ShO	SV	ERA
CHI	87	25	.777		834	470	184	74	55	.264	.385	0	496	80	.903	108	202	458	14	4	2.23
NY	85	27	.759	2	691	370	150	82	16	.269	.359	0	331	85	.929	109	266	519	15	1	1.72
PHI	56	54	.509	30	513	511	156	35	20	.229	.302	0	447	66	.905	108	218	378	9	0	2.39
PRO	53	57	.482	33	442	531	114	30	6	.220	.272	0	459	70	.903	111	188	480	10	0	3.03
BOS	46	66	.411	41	528	589	144	53	22	.232	.312	0	478	79	.901	105	224	475	6	1	2.88
DET	41	67	.380	44	514	582	149	65	26	.243	.338	0	463	61	.901	105	234	320	3	1	4.30
BUF	38	74	.339	49	495	761	149	50	23	.251	.333	0	464	65	.901	107	234	320	3	1	4.30
STL	36	72	.333	49	390	593	121	21	8	.221	.270	0	398	67	.916	107	278	337	4	0	3.37
					4407	4407	1167	410	176	.241	.322	0	3536	573	.908	863	1845	3338	69	7	2.82

American Association 1885

	POS	Player	AB	BA	HR	RBI	PO	A	E	DP	TC/G	FA	Pitcher	G	IP	W	L	SV	ERA
St. L.	1B	C. Comiskey	340	.256	2		879	24	29	34	11.2	.969	B. Caruthers	53	482	**40**	13	0	*2.07*
W-79 L-33	2B	S. Barkley	418	.268	2		286	328	53	38	6.9	.921	D. Foutz	47	408	33	14	0	*2.63*
Charlie Comiskey	SS	B. Gleason	472	.252	3		115	303	63	18	4.3	.869	J. McGinnis	13	112	6	6	0	*3.38*
	3B	A. Latham	485	.206	1		112	**217**	47	16	3.4	.875							
	RF	H. Nicol	425	.207	0		213	33	31	2	2.5	.888							
	CF	C. Welch	432	.271	2		**236**	25	15	5	2.5	**.946**							
	LF	T. O'Neill	206	.350	3		83	6	12	1	1.9	.881							
	C	D. Bushong	300	.267	0		**429**	**122**	40	10	7.0	.932							
	UT	Y. Robinson	287	.261	0		155	76	32	7		.878							
	P	D. Foutz	238	.248	0		24	104	14	3	3.0	.901							
	P	B. Caruthers	222	.225	1		24	84	11	4	2.2	.908							

	POS	Player	AB	BA	HR	RBI	PO	A	E	DP	TC/G	FA	Pitcher	G	IP	W	L	SV	ERA
Cin.	1B	L. Reilly	482	.297	5		1034	22	41	59	10.3	.963	W. White	34	293	18	15	0	3.53
W-63 L-49	2B	B. McPhee	440	.275	0		339	354	47	57	6.7	.936	L. McKeon	33	290	20	13	0	2.86
O. P. Caylor	SS	F. Fennelly	454	.273	10		151	359	74	46	5.2	.873	B. Mountjoy	17	154	10	7	0	3.16
	3B	H. Carpenter	473	.277	2		153	191	56	17	3.6	.860	G. Pechiney	11	98	7	4	0	2.02
	RF	P. Corkhill	440	.252	1		208	38	16	5	2.4	.939	G. Shallix	13	91	6	4	0	3.25
	CF	J. Clinton	408	.238	0		215	14	32	4	2.5	.877							
	LF	C. Jones	487	.322	4		214	22	29	6	2.4	.891							
	C	P. Snyder	152	.237	1		185	64	34	3	7.4	.880							
	C	J. Keenan	132	.265	1		164	37	16	1	6.6	.926							
	UT	K. Baldwin	126	.135	1		142	37	34	4		.840							
	P	L. McKeon	121	.165	0		18	41	1	0	1.8	.983							
	P	W. White	118	.169	0		10	35	6	0	1.5	.882							
Pit.	1B	J. Field	209	.239	1		622	15*	23	33	11.8	.965	E. Morris	63	581	39	24	0	2.35
W-56 L-55	2B	P. Smith	453	.249	0		372	384	64	53	7.7	.922	P. Meegan	18	146	7	8	0	3.39
Horace Phillips	SS	A. Whitney	373	.233	0		95	219	28	21	4.6	.918	H. O'Day	12	103	5	7	0	3.67
	3B	W. Kuehne	411	.226	0		102	187	45	14	3.4	.865	P. Galvin	11	88	3	7	0	3.67
	RF	T. Brown	437	.307	4		186	21	43	2	2.3	.828							
	CF	F. Mann	391	.253	0		157	10	17	2	1.9	.908							
	LF	C. Eden	405	.254	0		111	7	27	2	1.5	.814							
	C	F. Carroll	280	.268	0		328	99	38	3	7.8	.918							
	P	E. Morris	237	.186	0		24	93	20	4	2.2	.854							
	1B	M. Scott	210	.248	0		623	16	9	28	11.8	.986							
	C	D. Miller	166	.163	0		177	49	27	4	7.7	.893							
	SO	J. Richmond	131	.206	0		27	66	17	6		.845							
Phi.	1B	H. Stovey	486	.337	13		877	28	31	47	11.4	.967	B. Mathews	48	422	30	17	0	2.43
W-55 L-57	2B	C. Stricker	398	.234	1		284	304	81	41	6.3	.879	T. Lovett	16	139	7	8	0	3.70
Lon Knight	SS	S. Houck	388	.255	0		121	362	77	34	6.0	.863	E. Knouff	14	106	7	6	0	3.65
W-16 L-19	3B	F. Corey	384	.245	1		102	184	42	14	3.6	.872	E. Cushman	10	87	3	7	0	3.52
Charlie Mason	RF	J. Coleman	398	.299	2		128	23	28	5	1.9	.844							
W-17 L-21	CF	H. Larkin	453	.329	8		208	23	31	9	2.4	.882							
Bill Sharsig	LF	B. Purcell	304	.296	0		78	13	15	1	1.6	.858							
W-22 L-17	C	J. Milligan	265	.268	2		419	84	35	11	8.8	.935							
	UT	J. O'Brien	225	.267	2		276	95	38	10		.907							
	P	B. Mathews	179	.168	0		7	67	10	1	1.8	.881							
	UT	G. Strief	175	.274	0		62	82	19	10		.883							
	OF	L. Knight	119	.210	0		49	9	5	3	2.2	.921							
Bkn.	1B	B. Phillips	391	.302	3		1109	24	32	40	11.8	.973	H. Porter	54	482	33	21	0	2.78
W-53 L-59	2B	G. Pinckney	447	.277	0		147	173	34	15	6.2	.904	J. Harkins	34	293	14	20	0	3.75
Joe Doyle	SS	G. Smith	419	.258	4		161	455	81	23	6.5	.884	A. Terry	25	209	6	17	1	4.26
W-13 L-20	3B	B. McClellan	464	.267	0		65	84	29	9	3.1	.837							
Charlie Hackett	RF	J. Cassidy	221	.213	1		62	7	12	3	1.5	.852							
W-15 L-25	CF	P. Hotaling	370	.257	1		159	17	21	3	2.1	.893							
Charlie Byrne	LF	E. Swartwood	399	.266	0		140	8	26	0	1.8	.851							
W-25 L-14	C	J. Hayes	137	.131	0		209	53	29	4	6.9	.900							
	OP	A. Terry	264	.170	1		89	46	13	2		.912							
	P	H. Porter	195	.205	0		13	93	7	0	2.1	.938							
	P	J. Harkins	159	.264	1		36	63	16	0	3.4	.861							
	C	J. Peoples	151	.199	1		173	57	27	3	6.9	.905							
	OF	J. McTamany	131	.275	1		43	0	5	0	1.4	.896							
Lou.	1B	J. Kerins	456	.243	3		966	28	56	47	10.9	.947	G. Hecker	54	480	30	24	0	2.18
W-53 L-59	2B	McLaughlin	411	.212	2		320	266	78	43	7.1	.883	N. Baker	25	217	13	12	0	3.40
Jim Hart	SS	J. Miller	339	.183	0		94	266	44	23	5.1	.891	A. Mays	17	150	6	11	0	2.76
	3B	P. Reccius	402	.241	1		105	183	59	17	3.6	.830							
	RF	C. Wolf	483	.292	1		180	19	18	4	2.0	.917							
	CF	P. Browning	481	.362	9		214	20	26	4	2.3	.900							
	LF	L. Maskrey	423	.229	1		169	9	20	2	1.8	.899							
	C	J. Crotty	129	.155	0		190	51	21	2	6.9	.920							
	P	G. Hecker	299	.271	2		30	105	10	1	2.7	.931							
	C	A. Cross	130	.285	0		173	48	18	1	6.8	.925							
N. Y.	1B	D. Orr	444	.342	6		1089	20	39	48	10.7	.966	J. Lynch	44	379	23	21	0	3.61
W-44 L-64	2B	T. Forster	213	.221	0		127	143	29	21	5.8	.903	E. Cushman	22	191	8	14	0	2.78
Jim Gifford	SS	C. Nelson	420	.255	1		153	370	63	33	5.5	.892	D. Crothers	18	154	7	11	0	5.08
	3B	F. Hankinson	362	.224	2		106	212	33	9	3.7	.906	E. Begley	15	115	4	9	0	4.93
	RF	S. Brady	434	.295	3		178	10	26	3	2.0	.865	B. Becannon	10	85	2	8	0	6.25
	CF	C. Roseman	410	.278	3		177	9	29	1	2.1	.865							
	LF	E. Kennedy	349	.203	2		154	15	32	1	2.1	.841							
	C	Reipschlager	268	.243	0		262	117	52	6	7.3	.879							
	CO	B. Holbert	202	.173	0		250	85	34	5		.908							
	2B	D. Troy	177	.220	2		124	103	35	17	6.2	.866							
	P	J. Lynch	153	.196	0		11	34	4	0	1.1	.918							

	POS	Player	AB	BA	HR	RBI	PO	A	E	DP	TC/G	FA	Pitcher	G	IP	W	L	SV	ERA
	1B	D. Stearns	253	.186	1		605	19	17	35	10.2	.973	H. Henderson	61	539	25	**35**	0	3.19
	2B	T. Manning	157	.204	0		118	132	22	19	6.6	.919	B. Emslie	13	107	3	10	0	4.28
	SS	J. Macullar	320	.191	3		175	311	68	28	5.7	.877	O. Burns	15	106	7	4	**3**	3.58
Bal.	3B	M. Muldoon	410	.251	2		103	184	43	16	3.3	.870							
W-41 L-68	RF	E. Greer	211	.199	0		93	6	10	1	2.3	.908							
Billy Barnie	CF	D. Casey	264	.288	3		100	10	24	0	2.1	.821							
	LF	J. Sommer	471	.251	1		230	14	21	2	2.5	.921							
	C	B. Traffley	254	.154	1		357	105	28	6	8.0	**.943**							
	UT	O. Burns	321	.231	5		121	83	27	12		.883							
	P	H. Henderson	229	.223	1		28	81	14	**4**	2.0	.886							
	2B	G. Gardner	170	.218	0		113	132	30	16	7.1	.891							
	1B	J. Field	144	.208	0		373	13*	15	15	10.6	.963							

BATTING AND BASE RUNNING LEADERS

Batting Average
P. Browning, LOU	.362
D. Orr, NY	.342
H. Stovey, PHI	.337
H. Larkin, PHI	.329
C. Jones, CIN	.322

Slugging Average
D. Orr, NY	.543
P. Browning, LOU	.530
H. Larkin, PHI	.525
H. Stovey, PHI	.519
C. Jones, CIN	.456

Home Runs
H. Stovey, PHI	13
F. Fennelly, CIN	10
P. Browning, LOU	9
H. Larkin, PHI	8
D. Orr, NY	6

Total Bases
P. Browning, LOU	255
H. Stovey, PHI	252
D. Orr, NY	241
H. Larkin, PHI	238
C. Jones, CIN	222

Runs Batted In
(not available)

Stolen Bases
(not available)

Hits
P. Browning, LOU	174
H. Stovey, PHI	164
C. Jones, CIN	157

Base on Balls
C. Nelson, NY	61
J. Macullar, BAL	49
P. Hotaling, BKN	49

Home Run Percentage
H. Stovey, PHI	2.7
F. Fennelly, CIN	2.2
P. Browning, LOU	1.9

Runs Scored
H. Stovey, PHI	130
H. Larkin, PHI	114
C. Jones, CIN	108

Doubles
H. Larkin, PHI	37
P. Browning, LOU	34
D. Orr, NY	29

Triples
D. Orr, NY	21
W. Kuehne, PIT	19

PITCHING LEADERS

Winning Percentage
B. Caruthers, STL	.755
D. Foutz, STL	.702
B. Mathews, PHI	.638
E. Morris, PIT	.619
H. Porter, BKN	.611

Earned Run Average
B. Caruthers, STL	2.07
G. Hecker, LOU	2.18
E. Morris, PIT	2.35
B. Mathews, PHI	2.43
D. Foutz, STL	2.63

Wins
B. Caruthers, STL	40
E. Morris, PIT	39
D. Foutz, STL	33
H. Porter, BKN	33
B. Mathews, PHI	30
G. Hecker, LOU	30

Saves
O. Burns, BAL	3
P. Corkhill, CIN	1
P. Reccius, LOU	1
J. Sommer, BAL	1
A. Terry, BKN	1

Strikeouts
E. Morris, PIT	298
B. Mathews, PHI	286
H. Henderson, BAL	263
G. Hecker, LOU	209
H. Porter, BKN	197

Complete Games
E. Morris, PIT	63
H. Henderson, BAL	59
B. Caruthers, STL	53
H. Porter, BKN	53
G. Hecker, LOU	51

Fewest Hits per 9 Innings
E. Morris, PIT	7.11
A. Mays, LOU	7.74
D. Foutz, STL	7.75

Shutouts
B. Caruthers, STL	6
E. Morris, PIT	6
J. McGinnis, STL	3

Fewest Walks per 9 Innings
J. Lynch, NY	1.00
G. Hecker, LOU	1.01
B. Caruthers, STL	1.06

Most Strikeouts per 9 Inn.
B. Mathews, PHI	6.09
E. Cushman, NY, PHI	5.50
E. Morris, PIT	4.62

Innings
E. Morris, PIT	581
H. Henderson, BAL	539
B. Caruthers, STL	482

Games Pitched
E. Morris, PIT	63
H. Henderson, BAL	61
G. Hecker, LOU	54
H. Porter, BKN	54

	W	L	PCT	GB	R	OR	2B	3B	Batting HR	BA	SA	SB	E	Fielding DP	FA	CG	BB	Pitching SO	ShO	SV	ERA
STL	79	33	.705		677	461	132	57	14	.246	.319	0	381	64	**.920**	111	168	378	11	0	2.43
CIN	63	49	.563	16	642	575	108	77	25	.258	.341	0	426	**86**	.910	102	250	330	7	1	3.27
PIT	56	55	.505	22.5	547	539	123	79	5	.240	.315	0	426	77	.912	104	201	454	7	0	2.92
PHI	55	57	.491	24	**764**	691	169	77	**29**	**.265**	**.364**	0	483	79	.901	105	212	**506**	5	0	3.22
BKN	53	59	.473	26	624	650	121	65	14	.245	.319	0	447	56	.908	110	211	436	3	1	3.45
LOU	53	59	.473	26	564	598	126	**83**	19	.248	.336	0	466	75	.904	109	217	462	3	1	2.68
NY	44	64	.407	33	526	688	123	58	20	.247	.327	0	452	62	.901	103	204	408	2	0	4.15
BAL	41	68	.376	36.5	541	683	124	59	17	.219	.296	0	419	71	.909	104	222	395	2	**4**	3.89
					4885	4885	1026	555	143	.246	.328	0	3500	570	.908	848	1685	3369	40	7	3.24

	W	L	PCT	GB	R	OR	Batting 2B	3B	HR	BA	SA	SB	Fielding E	DP	FA	CG	BB	Pitching SO	ShO	SV	ERA
STL	93	46	.669		944	592	206	85	20	.273	.360	0	494	96	.915	134	329	583	14	2	2.52
PIT	80	57	.584	12	810	647	187	96	15	.241	.329	0	487	90	.917	137	299	515	15	1	2.84
BKN	76	61	.555	16	832	832	196	80	16	.250	.330	0	611	87	.900	138	464	540	6	0	3.41
LOU	66	70	.485	25.5	833	805	182	88	20	.263	.348	0	593	89	.901	131	432	720	5	2	3.07
CIN	65	73	.471	27.5	883	865	145	97	40	.249	.342	0	588	122	.904	129	481	495	3	0	4.18
PHI	63	72	.467	28	772	942	192	82	21	.235	.321	0	637	99	.894	134	388	513	4	0	3.98
NY	53	82	.393	38	628	766	108	72	18	.224	.289	0	546	81	.907	134	386	559	5	0	3.50
BAL	48	83	.366	41	625	878	124	51	8	.204	.258	0	536	59	.908	134	403	805	5	0	4.08
					6327	6327	1340	651	158	.243	.323	0	4492	723	.906	1071	3182	4730	57	5	3.45

National League 1887

Det.
W-79 L-45
Bill Watkins

POS	Player	AB	BA	HR	RBI	PO	A	E	DP	TC/G	FA	Pitcher	G	IP	W	L	SV	ERA
1B	D. Brouthers	500	.338	12	101	1141	35	38	67	9.9	.969	C. Getzien	43	367	29	13	0	3.73
2B	F. Dunlap	272	.265	5	45	212	225	24	44	7.1	.948	L. Baldwin	24	211	13	10	0	3.84
SS	J. Rowe	537	.318	6	96	119	378	51	36	4.4	.907	S. Weidman	21	183	13	7	0	5.36
3B	D. White	449	.303	3	75	133	225	64	18	4.0	.848	P. Conway	17	146	8	9	0	2.90
RF	S. Thompson	545	.372	11	166	217	24	24	7	2.1	.909	L. Twitchell	15	112	11	1	1	4.33
CF	N. Hanlon	471	.274	4	69	264	18	30	4	2.6	.904							
LF	L. Twitchell	264	.333	0	51	84	4	13	1	1.9	.871							
C	C. Ganzel	227	.260	0	20	275	71	33	5	7.4	.913							
2O	H. Richardson	543	.328	11	94	328	223	37	28		.937							
C	C. Bennett	160	.244	3	20	197	57	13	9	5.9	.951							
P	C. Getzien	156	.186	1	14	23	58	3	1	2.0	.964							
C	F. Briody	128	.227	2	26	144	61	21	4	6.8	.907							

Phi.
W-75 L-48
Harry Wright

POS	Player	AB	BA	HR	RBI	PO	A	E	DP	TC/G	FA	Pitcher	G	IP	W	L	SV	ERA
1B	S. Farrar	443	.282	4	72	1149	46	28	55	10.5	.977	D. Casey	45	390	28	13	0	2.86
2B	McLaughlin	205	.220	1	26	106	156	36	15	6.0	.879	C. Buffinton	40	332	21	17	0	3.66
SS	A. Irwin	374	.254	2	56	119	358	58	30	5.4	.892	C. Ferguson	37	297	22	10	1	3.00
3B	J. Mulvey	474	.287	2	78	123	197	50	18	3.3	.865							
RF	J. Fogarty	495	.261	8	50	273	39	27	9	2.8	.920							
CF	E. Andrews	464	.325	4	67	203	18	24	1	2.5	.902							
LF	G. Wood	491	.289	14	66	155	10	24	2	1.8	.873							
C	J. Clements	246	.280	1	47	328	79	26	8	7.3	.940							
UT	C. Buffinton	269	.268	1	46	124	93	23	8		.904							
UT	C. Ferguson	264	.337	3	85	93	130	22	11		.910							
2S	D. Bastian	221	.213	1	21	101	165	25	19		.914							
P	D. Casey	164	.165	1	17	10	66	9	0	1.9	.894							
C	D. McGuire	150	.307	2	23	214	52	35	6	7.3	.884							

Chi.
W-71 L-50
Cap Anson

POS	Player	AB	BA	HR	RBI	PO	A	E	DP	TC/G	FA	Pitcher	G	IP	W	L	SV	ERA
1B	C. Anson	472	.347	7	102	1232	70	36	75	11.0	.973	J. Clarkson	60	523	38	21	0	3.08
2B	F. Pfeffer	479	.278	16	89	393	402	72	68	7.0	.917	M. Baldwin	40	334	18	17	1	3.40
SS	N. Williamson	439	.267	9	78	133	361	61	31	4.4	.890	Van Haltren	20	161	11	7	1	3.86
3B	T. Burns	424	.264	3	60	168	246	61	23	4.4	.872							
RF	B. Sunday	199	.291	3	32	78	4	25	2	2.1	.766							
CF	J. Ryan	508	.285	11	74	164	33	33	7	1.9	.857							
LF	M. Sullivan	472	.284	7	77	189	10	36	0	2.0	.847							
C	T. Daly	256	.207	2	17	354	148	35	12	8.4	.935							
P	J. Clarkson	215	.242	6	25	34	125	7	5	2.8	.958							
C	S. Flint	187	.267	3	21	255	73	33	3	7.7	.909							
OP	Van Haltren	172	.203	3	17	47	26	8	2		.901							
OC	D. Darling	141	.319	3	20	132	45	23	3		.885							
P	M. Baldwin	139	.187	4	17	7	45	6	0	1.5	.897							
OF	B. Pettit	138	.261	2	12	34	8	5	0	1.5	.894							

N.Y.
W-68 L-55
Jim Mutrie

POS	Player	AB	BA	HR	RBI	PO	A	E	DP	TC/G	FA	Pitcher	G	IP	W	L	SV	ERA
1B	R. Connor	471	.285	17	104	1325	44	10	67	10.9	.993	T. Keefe	56	479	35	19	0	3.10
2B	D. Richardson	450	.278	3	62	257	384	50	46	6.4	.928	M. Welch	40	346	23	15	0	3.36
SS	M. Ward	545	.338	1	53	226	469	61	53	5.9	.919	B. George	13	108	3	9	0	5.25
3B	B. Ewing	318	.305	6	44	76	101	28	6	4.0	.863							
RF	M. Dorgan	283	.258	0	34	128	6	20	0	2.2	.870							
CF	G. Gore	459	.290	1	49	221	20	30	7	2.4	.889							
LF	M. Tiernan	407	.287	10	62	150	10	25	3	1.8	.865							
C	W. Brown	170	.218	0	25	229	69	28	5	7.1	.914							
UT	J. O'Rourke	397	.285	3	88	248	127	48	7		.887							
OF	P. Gillespie	295	.264	3	37	91	44	6	1	1.9	.957							
P	T. Keefe	191	.220	2	23	17	102	15	1	2.4	.888							
P	M. Welch	148	.243	2	15	17	51	12	0	2.0	.850							
C	P. Deasley	118	.314	0	23	86	31	18	0	5.6	.867							

POS	Player	AB	BA	HR	RBI	PO	A	E	DP	TC/G	FA	Pitcher	G	IP	W	L	SV	ERA
1B	J. Morrill	504	.280	12	81	1231	50	21	**76**	10.3	.984	O. Radbourn	50	425	24	23	0	4.55
2B	J. Burdock	237	.257	0	29	117	188	41	34	5.3	.882	K. Madden	37	321	22	14	0	3.79
SS	S. Wise	467	.334	9	92	152	233	58	22	6.2	.869	D. Conway	26	222	9	15	0	4.66
3B	B. Nash	475	.295	7	94	207	242	59	19	4.3	.884	B. Stemmyer	15	119	6	8	1	5.20
RF	K. Kelly	484	.322	8	63	78	11	15	2	1.7	.856							
CF	D. Johnston	507	.258	5	77	**339**	34	27	**9**	**3.1**	.933							
LF	J. Hornung	437	.270	5	49	192	23	15	3	2.3	.935							
C	P. Tate	231	.260	0	27	209	109	26	6	6.5	.924							
UT	E. Sutton	326	.304	3	46	178	234	58	12		.877							
P	O. Radbourn	175	.229	1	24	15	69	15	3	2.0	.848							
OS	B. Wheelock	166	.253	2	15	68	69	19	5		.878							
PO	D. Conway	145	.248	0	10	25	53	13	0		.857							
P	K. Madden	132	.242	1	10	4	59	13	1	2.1	.829							

Bos.
W-61 L-60
John Morrill

POS	Player	AB	BA	HR	RBI	PO	A	E	DP	TC/G	FA	Pitcher	G	IP	W	L	SV	ERA
1B	S. Barkley	340	.224	1	35	552	15	12	24	10.9	.979	P. Galvin	49	441	28	21	0	3.29
2B	P. Smith	456	.215	2	54	225	298	49	32	6.4	.914	J. McCormick	36	322	13	23	0	4.30
SS	W. Kuehne	402	.299	1	41	136	310	59	29	5.5	.883	E. Morris	38	318	14	22	0	4.31
3B	A. Whitney	431	.260	0	51	166	237	33	13	3.7	**.924**							
RF	J. Coleman	475	.293	2	54	214	17	26	3	2.2	.899							
CF	T. Brown	192	.245	0	6	130	10	21*	0	3.4	.870							
LF	A. Dalrymple	358	.212	2	31	184	14	22	1	2.4	.900							
C	D. Miller	342	.243	1	34	266	58	25	1	4.8	.928							
UT	F. Carroll	421	.328	6	54	451	56	62	9		.891							
1B	A. McKinnon	200	.340	1	30	483	25	12	27	10.8	.977							
P	P. Galvin	193	.212	2	22	22	123	11	2	**3.2**	.929							
OF	E. Beecher	169	.243	2	22	85	12	9	1	2.6	.915							
UT	J. Fields	164	.268	0	17	141	29	18	2		.904							
P	J. McCormick	136	.243	0	18	13	88	8	1	3.0	.927							
P	E. Morris	126	.198	0	10	5	52	5	1	1.6	.919							

Pit.
W-55 L-69
Horace Phillips

POS	Player	AB	BA	HR	RBI	PO	A	E	DP	TC/G	FA	Pitcher	G	IP	W	L	SV	ERA
1B	B. O'Brien	453	.278	**19**	73	1159	26	32	53	**11.7**	.974	J. Whitney	47	405	24	21	0	3.22
2B	A. Myers	362	.232	2	36	193	248	44	23	6.2	.909	H. O'Day	30	255	8	20	0	4.17
SS	J. Farrell	339	.221	0	41	91	156	35	14	5.9	.876	F. Gilmore	28	235	7	20	0	3.87
3B	J. Donnelly	425	.200	1	46	136	**275**	63	21	4.1	.867	D. Shaw	21	181	7	13	0	6.45
RF	E. Daily	311	.251	2	36	116	8	21	1	1.9	.855							
CF	P. Hines	478	.308	10	72	180	14	25	5	2.0	.886							
LF	C. Carroll	420	.248	4	37	146	19	18	6	1.8	.902							
C	C. Mack	314	.201	0	20	**391**	119	53	**15**	7.4	.906							
UT	P. Dealy	312	.272	1	18	171	105	34	9		.890							
OF	G. Shoch	264	.239	1	18	115	15	15	3	2.3	.897							
P	J. Whitney	201	.264	2	22	13	92	11	5	2.5	.905							

Was.
W-46 L-76
John Gaffney

POS	Player	AB	BA	HR	RBI	PO	A	E	DP	TC/G	FA	Pitcher	G	IP	W	L	SV	ERA
1B	O. Schomberg	419	.308	5	83	1216	28	**55**	**76**	11.6	.958	E. Healy	41	341	12	**29**	0	5.17
2B	C. Bassett	452	.230	1	47	273	**444**	53	62	6.5	**.931**	H. Boyle	39	328	13	24	0	3.65
SS	J. Glasscock	483	.294	0	40	241	**493**	73	58	6.4	.906	L. Shreve	14	122	5	9	0	4.72
3B	J. Denny	510	.324	11	97	201	262	58	21	**4.5**	.889							
RF	J. Cahill	263	.205	0	26	84	11	20	1	2.1	.826							
CF	J. McGeachy	405	.269	1	56	231	22	30	3	2.9	.894							
LF	E. Seery	465	.224	4	28	220	25	30	2	2.3	.891							
C	G. Myers	235	.217	1	20	176	58	18	8	5.0	.929							
C	T. Arundel	157	.197	0	13	153	64	34	5	6.0	.865							
C	M. Hackett	147	.238	2	10	128	52	12	4	4.8	.938							
P	H. Boyle	141	.191	2	13	11	41	5	2	1.5	.912							
OF	T. Brown	140	.179	2	9	58	7	15*	2	2.2	.813							
P	E. Healy	138	.174	3	14	7	51	12	0	1.7	.829							

Ind.
W-37 L-89
Watch Burnham
W-6 L-22
Fred Thomas
W-11 L-18
Horace Fogel
W-20 L-49

BATTING AND BASE RUNNING LEADERS

Batting Average

S. Thompson, DET	.372
C. Anson, CHI	.347
D. Brouthers, DET	.338
M. Ward, NY	.338
S. Wise, BOS	.334

Slugging Average

S. Thompson, DET	.571
D. Brouthers, DET	.562
R. Connor, NY	.541
S. Wise, BOS	.522
C. Anson, CHI	.517

Home Runs

B. O'Brien, WAS	19
R. Connor, NY	17
F. Pfeffer, CHI	16
G. Wood, PHI	14
D. Brouthers, DET	12
J. Morrill, BOS	12

Total Bases

S. Thompson, DET	311
D. Brouthers, DET	281
H. Richardson, DET	272
J. Denny, IND	256
R. Connor, NY	255

Runs Batted In

S. Thompson, DET	166
R. Connor, NY	104
C. Anson, CHI	102
D. Brouthers, DET	101
J. Denny, IND	97

Stolen Bases

M. Ward, NY	111
J. Fogarty, PHI	102
K. Kelly, BOS	84
N. Hanlon, DET	69
J. Glasscock, IND	62

PITCHING LEADERS

Winning Percentage

C. Getzien, DET	.690
C. Ferguson, PHI	.688
D. Casey, PHI	.683
T. Keefe, NY	.648
J. Clarkson, CHI	.644

Earned Run Average

D. Casey, PHI	2.86
P. Conway, DET	2.90
C. Ferguson, PHI	3.00
J. Clarkson, CHI	3.08
T. Keefe, NY	3.10

Wins

J. Clarkson, CHI	38
T. Keefe, NY	35
C. Getzien, DET	29
D. Casey, PHI	28
P. Galvin, PIT	28

Saves

8 tied with	1

Strikeouts

J. Clarkson, CHI	237
T. Keefe, NY	186
M. Baldwin, CHI	164
C. Buffinton, PHI	160
J. Whitney, WAS	146

Complete Games

J. Clarkson, CHI	56
T. Keefe, NY	54
O. Radbourn, BOS	48
P. Galvin, PIT	47
J. Whitney, WAS	46

BATTING AND BASE RUNNING LEADERS

Hits
S. Thompson, DET	203
M. Ward, NY	184
H. Richardson, DET	178

Base on Balls
J. Fogarty, PHI	82
R. Connor, NY	75
N. Williamson, CHI	73

Home Run Percentage
B. O'Brien, WAS	4.2
R. Connor, NY	3.6
F. Pfeffer, CHI	3.3

Runs Scored
D. Brouthers, DET	153
J. Rowe, DET	135
H. Richardson, DET	131

Doubles
D. Brouthers, DET	36
K. Kelly, BOS	34
J. Denny, IND	34

Triples
S. Thompson, DET	23
R. Connor, NY	22
D. Brouthers, DET	20
D. Johnston, BOS	20

PITCHING LEADERS

Fewest Hits per 9 Innings
P. Conway, DET	8.14
T. Keefe, NY	8.40
D. Casey, PHI	8.69

Shutouts
D. Casey, PHI	4

Fewest Walks per 9 Innings
J. Whitney, WAS	0.93
P. Galvin, PIT	1.37
C. Ferguson, PHI	1.42

Most Strikeouts per 9 Inn.
M. Baldwin, CHI	4.42
F. Gilmore, WAS	4.37
C. Buffinton, PHI	4.33

Innings
J. Clarkson, CHI	523
T. Keefe, NY	479
P. Galvin, PIT	441

Games Pitched
J. Clarkson, CHI	60
T. Keefe, NY	56
O. Radbourn, BOS	50

	W	L	PCT	GB	R	OR	2B	3B	HR	BA	SA	SB	E	DP	FA	CG	BB	SO	ShO	SV	ERA
DET	79	45	.637		969	714	213	126	59	.299	.436	267	394	92	.925	122	344	337	3	1	3.95
PHI	75	48	.610	3.5	901	702	213	89	47	.274	.389	355	471	76	.912	119	305	435	7	1	3.47
CHI	71	50	.587	6.5	813	716	178	98	80	.271	.412	382	472	99	.914	117	338	510	4	3	3.46
NY	68	55	.553	10.5	816	723	167	93	48	.279	.389	415	431	83	.921	123	373	412	5	1	3.57
BOS	61	60	.504	16.5	831	792	185	94	54	.277	.395	373	522	94	.905	123	396	254	4	1	4.41
PIT	55	69	.444	24	621	750	183	78	20	.258	.349	221	425	70	.921	123	246	248	3	0	4.12
WAS	46	76	.377	32	601	818	149	63	47	.242	.336	334	483	77	.910	124	299	396	4	0	4.19
IND	37	89	.294	43	628	965	162	70	33	.247	.339	334	479	105	.912	119	431	245	4	1	5.25
					6180	6180	1450	711	388	.269	.381	2681	3677	696	.915	970	2732	2837	34	8	4.05

American Association 1887

St. L. — W-95 L-40 — Charlie Comiskey

POS	Player	AB	BA	HR	RBI	PO	A	E	DP	TC/G	FA	Pitcher	G	IP	W	L	SV	ERA
1B	C. Comiskey	538	.335	4		1135	51	29	60	10.5	.976	S. King	46	390	34	11	1	3.78
2B	Y. Robinson	430	.305	1		320	355	76	52	6.4	.899	B. Caruthers	39	341	29	9	0	3.30
SS	B. Gleason	598	.288	0		169	411	83	27	4.9	.875	D. Foutz	40	339	25	12	0	3.87
3B	A. Latham	627	.316	2		155	288	62	17	3.8	.877							
RF	B. Caruthers	364	.357	8		91	11	11	1	2.1	.903							
CF	C. Welch	544	.278	3		336	29	23	7	3.2	.941							
LF	T. O'Neill	517	.435	14		247	8	30	2	2.3	.895							
C	J. Boyle	350	.189	2		339	114	56	7	5.9	.890							
UT	D. Foutz	423	.357	4		282	65	23	11		.938							
P	S. King	222	.207	0		16	69	6	0	2.0	.934							
C	D. Bushong	201	.254	0		201	93	23	3	6.1	.927							

Cin. — W-81 L-54 — Gus Schmelz

POS	Player	AB	BA	HR	RBI	PO	A	E	DP	TC/G	FA	Pitcher	G	IP	W	L	SV	ERA
1B	L. Reilly	551	.309	10		1267	33	26	84	10.4	.980	E. Smith	52	447	33	18	0	2.94
2B	B. McPhee	540	.289	2		442	434	72	76	7.3	.924	T. Mullane	48	416	31	17	0	3.24
SS	F. Fennelly	526	.266	8		161	421	99	31	5.1	.855	B. Serad	22	187	10	11	1	4.08
3B	H. Carpenter	498	.249	1		144	242	70	17	3.6	.846							
RF	H. Nicol	475	.215	1		194	20	19	1	1.9	.918							
CF	P. Corkhill	541	.311	5		310	29	17	7	2.8	.952							
LF	W. Tebeau	318	.296	4		175	14	24	2	2.5	.887							
C	K. Baldwin	388	.253	1		381	165	79	9	6.5	.874							
P	T. Mullane	199	.221	3		29	72	6	5	2.2	.944							
P	E. Smith	186	.253	0		7	67	13	2	1.7	.851							
C	J. Keenan	174	.253	0		161	67	20	8	6.5	.919							
OF	C. Jones	153	.314	2		74	7	9	2*	2.2	.900							

Bal. — W-77 L-58 — Billy Barnie

POS	Player	AB	BA	HR	RBI	PO	A	E	DP	TC/G	FA	Pitcher	G	IP	W	L	SV	ERA
1B	T. Tucker	524	.275	6		1346	50	35	49	10.5	.976	M. Kilroy	69	589	46	20	0	3.07
2B	B. Greenwood	495	.263	0		357	360	56	33	6.6	.928	P. Smith	58	491	25	30	0	3.79
SS	O. Burns	551	.341	10		136	245	72	20	4.6	.841							
3B	J. Davis	485	.309	8		91	199	61	7	4.0	.826							
RF	B. Purcell	567	.250	4		203	18	18	5	1.7	.925							
CF	M. Griffin	532	.301	3		256	13	22	1	2.1	.924							
LF	J. Sommer	463	.266	0		191	20	22	4	2.1	.906							
C	S. Trott	300	.257	0		373	102	44	6	7.5	.915							
P	M. Kilroy	239	.247	0		37	167	20	2	3.2	.911							
P	P. Smith	205	.234	1		9	108	20	1	2.4	.854							
C	C. Fulmer	201	.269	0		201	73	28	5	6.3	.907							
UT	L. Daniels	165	.248	0		188	44	45	5		.838							

	POS	Player	AB	BA	HR	RBI	PO	A	E	DP	TC/G	FA	Pitcher	G	IP	W	L	SV	ERA
Lou. W-76 L-60 John Kelly	1B	J. Kerins	476	.294	5		695	18	22	26	9.9	.970	T. Ramsey	65	561	37	27	0	3.43
	2B	R. Mack	478	.308	1		366	395	73	48	6.5	.912	Chamberlain	36	309	18	16	0	3.79
	SS	B. White	512	.252	2		**204**	**431**	96	**45**	5.5	.869	G. Hecker	33	285	19	12	1	4.16
	3B	J. Werrick	533	.285	7		153	286	89	12	3.9	.831							
	RF	C. Wolf	569	.281	1		207	27	15	5	1.9	.940							
	CF	P. Browning	547	.402	4		281	21	46	7	2.6	.868							
	LF	H. Collins	559	.290	1		192	19	27	1	2.2	.887							
	C	P. Cook	223	.247	0		220	95	29	4	6.3	.916							
	UT	G. Hecker	370	.319	4		429	82	29	27		.946							
	P	T. Ramsey	225	.191	0		7	88	31	0	1.9	.754							
	C	L. Cross	203	.266	0		251	66	31	7	7.9	.911							
Phi. W-64 L-69 Frank Bancroft W-22 L-25 Bill Sharsig W-42 L-44	1B	J. Milligan	377	.302	2		436	13	16	21	9.3	.966	E. Seward	55	471	25	25	0	4.13
	2B	L. Bierbauer	530	.272	1		332	378	61	45	6.1	.921	G. Weyhing	55	466	26	28	0	4.27
	SS	C. McGarr	536	.295	1		198	402	86	42	5.0	.875	A. Atkisson	15	125	6	8	0	5.92
	3B	D. Lyons	570	.367	6		**255**	215	73	**29**	4.0	.866							
	RF	T. Poorman	585	.265	4		237	18	25	6	2.1	.911							
	CF	H. Stovey	497	.286	4		195	16	23	1	2.9	.902							
	LF	H. Larkin	497	.310	3		183	14	23	0	2.4	.895							
	C	W. Robinson	264	.227	1		281	137	46	9	6.9	.901							
	P	E. Seward	266	.188	5		21	79	11	1	2.0	.901							
	OF	F. Mann	229	.275	0		103	7	10	2	2.2	.917							
	P	G. Weyhing	209	.201	0		18	88	24	**5**	2.4	.815							
Bkn. W-60 L-74 Charlie Byrne	1B	B. Phillips	533	.266	2		1299	46	24	62	10.4	**.982**	H. Porter	40	340	15	24	0	4.21
	2B	B. McClellan	548	.263	1		366	397	105	52	6.4	.879	A. Terry	40	318	16	16	**3**	4.02
	SS	G. Smith	435	.294	4		157	387	70	23	**6.1**	**.886**	J. Harkins	24	199	10	14	0	6.02
	3B	G. Pinckney	580	.267	3		196	**290**	60	26	4.0	**.890**	S. Toole	24	194	14	10	0	4.31
	RF	E. Swartwood	363	.253	1		129	23	30	5	2.0	.835	H. Henderson	13	112	5	8	0	3.95
	CF	J. McTamany	520	.258	1		281	**32**	28	**8**	2.5	.918							
	LF	E. Greer	327	.254	2		155	8	14	1	2.3	.921							
	C	J. Peoples	268	.254	1		226	106	59	3	6.9	.849							
	OP	A. Terry	352	.293	3		124	86	23	1		.901							
	OF	E. Burch	188	.293	2		90	8	11	1	2.2	.899							
	C	B. Clark	177	.266	0		197	66	40	7	6.7	.868							
	P	H. Porter	146	.199	1		8	66	12	1	2.2	.860							
N. Y. W-44 L-89 Bob Ferguson W-6 L-24 Dave Orr W-28 L-36 O. P. Caylor W-10 L-29	1B	D. Orr	345	.368	2		806	28	27	41	10.6	.969	A. Mays	52	441	17	**34**	0	4.73
	2B	J. Gerhardt	307	.221	0		288	271	65	48	7.4	.896	E. Cushman	26	220	10	14	0	5.97
	SS	P. Radford	486	.254	4		121	229	70	28	5.5	.833	J. Lynch	21	187	7	14	0	5.10
	3B	F. Hankinson	512	.268	1		161	276	69	26	4.0	.864	J. Shaffer	13	112	2	11	0	6.19
	RF	C. Roseman	241	.228	0		99	6	16	2	2.1	.868	S. Weidman	12	97	4	8	0	4.64
	CF	C. Jones	247	.255	3		114	18	12	6*	2.3	.917							
	LF	D. O'Brien	522	.301	5		244	20	25	4	2.4	.913							
	C	B. Holbert	255	.227	0		237	102	43	9	6.4	.887							
	OS	C. Nelson	257	.245	0		120	111	27	18		.895							
	P	A. Mays	221	.204	2		21	144	24	4	**3.6**	.873							
	C	J. Donahue	220	.282	1		208	90	42	3	6.7	.876							
	O2	J. Meister	158	.222	1		66	38	10	8		.912							
Cle. W-39 L-92 Jimmy Williams	1B	J. Toy	423	.222	1		707	30	19	54	9.2	.975	B. Crowell	45	389	14	31	0	4.88
	2B	C. Stricker	534	.264	2		**461**	365	80	61	7.2	.912	M. Morrison	40	317	12	25	0	4.92
	SS	E. McKean	539	.286	2		195	351	**99**	32	5.2	.847	O. Daily	16	140	4	12	0	3.67
	3B	P. Reccius	229	.205	0		85	137	31	18	4.1	.877	B. Gilks	13	108	7	5	0	3.08
	RF	F. Mann	259	.309	2		112	11	17	4	2.2	.879	G. Pechiney	10	86	1	9	0	7.12
	CF	P. Hotaling	505	.299	3		267	23	31	5	2.5	.903							
	LF	M. Allen	463	.276	4		222	22	29	6	2.4	.894							
	C	P. Snyder	282	.255	0		314	143	53	8	8.1	.896							
	C	Reipschlager	231	.212	0		196	105	43	9	7.2	.875							
	OF	S. Carroll	216	.199	0		79	7	16	1	1.9	.843							
	P	B. Crowell	156	.141	0		5	65	5	4	1.7	.933							
	P	M. Morrison	141	.191	0		14	109	11	4	3.4	.918							

BATTING AND BASE RUNNING LEADERS

Batting Average

T. O'Neill, STL	.435
P. Browning, LOU	.402
D. Orr, NY	.368
D. Lyons, PHI	.367
B. Caruthers, STL	.357

Slugging Average

T. O'Neill, STL	.691
P. Browning, LOU	.556
B. Caruthers, STL	.547
O. Burns, BAL	.525
D. Lyons, PHI	.523

Home Runs

T. O'Neill, STL	14
O. Burns, BAL	10
L. Reilly, CIN	10
B. Caruthers, STL	8
J. Davis, BAL	8
F. Fennelly, CIN	8

Total Bases

T. O'Neill, STL	357
P. Browning, LOU	304
D. Lyons, PHI	298
O. Burns, BAL	289
L. Reilly, CIN	263

Runs Batted In

(not available)

Stolen Bases

H. Nicol, CIN	138
A. Latham, STL	129
C. Comiskey, STL	117
P. Browning, LOU	103
B. McPhee, CIN	95

PITCHING LEADERS

Winning Percentage

B. Caruthers, STL	.763
S. King, STL	.756
M. Kilroy, BAL	.697
D. Foutz, STL	.676
E. Smith, CIN	.647

Earned Run Average

E. Smith, CIN	2.94
M. Kilroy, BAL	3.07
B. Gilks, CLE	3.08
T. Mullane, CIN	3.24
B. Caruthers, STL	3.30

Wins

M. Kilroy, BAL	46
T. Ramsey, LOU	37
S. King, STL	34
E. Smith, CIN	33
T. Mullane, CIN	31

Saves

A. Terry, BKN	3

Strikeouts

T. Ramsey, LOU	355
M. Kilroy, BAL	217
P. Smith, BAL	206
G. Weyhing, PHI	193
E. Smith, CIN	176

Complete Games

M. Kilroy, BAL	66
T. Ramsey, LOU	61
P. Smith, BAL	54
G. Weyhing, PHI	53
E. Seward, PHI	52

BATTING AND BASE RUNNING LEADERS

Hits			Base on Balls	
T. O'Neill, STL	225		P. Radford, NY	106
P. Browning, LOU	220		Y. Robinson, STL	92
D. Lyons, PHI	209		H. Nicol, CIN	86

Home Run Percentage			Runs Scored	
T. O'Neill, STL	2.7		T. O'Neill, STL	167
B. Caruthers, STL	2.2		A. Latham, STL	163
L. Reilly, CIN	1.8		M. Griffin, BAL	142

Doubles			Triples	
T. O'Neill, STL	52		J. Kerins, LOU	19
D. Lyons, PHI	43		J. Davis, BAL	19
P. Browning, LOU	36		T. O'Neill, STL	19
			B. McPhee, CIN	19

PITCHING LEADERS

Fewest Hits per 9 Innings			Shutouts	
E. Smith, CIN	8.05		T. Mullane, CIN	6
E. Seward, PHI	8.51		M. Kilroy, BAL	6
S. Toole, BKN	8.63		E. Seward, PHI	3
			E. Smith, CIN	3

Fewest Walks per 9 Innings			Most Strikeouts per 9 Inn.	
G. Hecker, LOU	1.58		T. Ramsey, LOU	5.70
B. Caruthers, STL	1.61		M. Morrison, CLE	4.49
J. Lynch, NY	1.73		A. Terry, BKN	3.91

Innings			Games Pitched	
M. Kilroy, BAL	589		M. Kilroy, BAL	69
T. Ramsey, LOU	561		T. Ramsey, LOU	65
P. Smith, BAL	491		P. Smith, BAL	58

	W	L	PCT	GB	R	OR	Batting 2B	3B	HR	BA	SA	SB	Fielding E	DP	FA	CG	BB	Pitching SO	ShO	SV	ERA
STL	95	40	.704		1131	761	261	78	39	.307	.413	581	485	86	.916	132	323	334	6	2	3.78
CIN	81	54	.600	14	892	745	179	102	37	.268	.371	527	488	106	.915	129	396	330	11	1	3.59
BAL	77	58	.570	18	975	861	202	100	31	.277	.380	545	558	66	.906	132	418	470	8	0	3.87
LOU	76	60	.559	19.5	956	854	195	98	26	.289	.384	466	576	83	.903	133	357	544	3	1	3.82
PHI	64	69	.481	30	893	890	231	84	29	.277	.375	476	528	95	.907	131	433	417	5	1	4.59
BKN	60	74	.448	34.5	904	918	200	82	25	.261	.350	409	565	88	.904	132	454	332	3	3	4.46
NY	44	89	.331	50	754	1093	193	66	20	.248	.328	305	643	102	.893	132	406	316	1	0	5.30
CLE	39	92	.298	54	729	1112	178	77	14	.252	.332	355	589	97	.897	127	533	332	2	1	4.99
					7234	7234	1639	687	221	.273	.367	3664	4432	723	.905	1048	3320	3075	39	9	4.29

National League 1888

	POS	Player	AB	BA	HR	RBI	PO	A	E	DP	TC/G	FA	Pitcher	G	IP	W	L	SV	ERA
N. Y. W-84 L-47 Jim Mutrie	1B	R. Connor	481	.291	14	71	1337	43	26	57	10.6	.982	T. Keefe	51	434	35	12	0	1.74
	2B	D. Richardson	561	.226	8	61	321	423	46	43	5.9	.942	M. Welch	47	425	26	19	0	1.93
	SS	M. Ward	510	.251	2	49	185	331	86	39	4.9	.857	C. Titcomb	23	197	14	8	0	2.24
	3B	A. Whitney	328	.220	1	28	90	184	35	11	3.4	.887	C. Crane	12	93	5	6	1	2.43
	RF	M. Tiernan	443	.293	9	52	174	16	8	2	1.8	.960							
	CF	M. Slattery	391	.246	1	35	187	16	18	3	2.1	.919							
	LF	J. O'Rourke	409	.274	4	50	130	13	6	1	1.7	.960							
	C	B. Ewing	415	.306	6	58	480	143	35	12	8.4	.947							
	OF	G. Gore	254	.220	2	17	88	4	18	0	1.7	.836							
	P	T. Keefe	181	.127	2	8	29	79	10	1	2.3	.915							
	P	M. Welch	169	.189	2	10	16	75	17	1	2.3	.843							
Chi. W-77 L-58 Cap Anson	1B	C. Anson	515	.344	12	84	1314	65	20	85	10.4	.986	G. Krock	39	340	24	14	0	2.44
	2B	F. Pfeffer	517	.250	8	57	421	457	65	78	7.0	.931	M. Baldwin	30	251	13	15	0	2.76
	SS	N. Williamson	452	.250	8	73	120	375	65	48	4.2	.884	Van Haltren	30	246	13	13	1	3.52
	3B	T. Burns	483	.238	3	70	194	273	49	16	3.9	.905	J. Tener	12	102	7	5	0	2.74
	RF	H. Duffy	298	.282	7	64	103	19	12	5	2.0	.910							
	CF	J. Ryan	549	.332	16	64	217	34	35	5	2.2	.878							
	LF	M. Sullivan	314	.236	7	39	114	13	10	7	1.8	.927							
	C	T. Daly	219	.192	0	29	400	107	33	10	8.7	.939							
	OP	Van Haltren	318	.283	4	34	98	62	17	0		.904							
	CO	D. Farrell	241	.232	3	19	221	53	39	4		.875							
	OF	B. Pettit	169	.254	4	23	46	8	4	3	1.3	.931							
Phi. W-69 L-61 Harry Wright	1B	S. Farrar	508	.244	1	53	1345	53	30	57	10.9	.979	C. Buffinton	46	400	28	17	0	1.91
	2B	C. Bastian	275	.193	1	17	145	253	23	14	6.5	.945	D. Casey	33	286	14	18	0	3.15
	SS	A. Irwin	448	.219	0	28	204	374	64	31	5.3	.900	B. Sanders	31	275	19	10	0	1.90
	3B	J. Mulvey	398	.216	0	39	87	174	32	9	2.9	.891	K. Gleason	24	200	7	16	0	2.84
	RF	J. Fogarty	454	.236	1	35	239	26	20	9	2.4	.930							
	CF	E. Andrews	528	.239	3	44	210	23	25	5	2.1	.903							
	LF	G. Wood	433	.229	6	15	175	15	20	3	2.0	.905							
	C	J. Clements	326	.245	1	32	494	104	47	6	7.6	.927							
	2B	E. Delahanty	290	.228	1	31	129	170	44	20	6.1	.872							
	PO	B. Sanders	236	.246	1	31	55	79	9	1		.937							
	P	C. Buffinton	160	.181	0	12	31	122	10	3	3.5	.939							
	UT	P. Schriver	134	.194	1	23	156	63	36	3		.859							

	POS	Player	AB	BA	HR	RBI	PO	A	E	DP	TC/G	FA	Pitcher	G	IP	W	L	SV	ERA
Bos. W-70 L-64 John Morrill	1B	J. Morrill	486	.198	4	39	1398	72	31	67	11.3	.979	J. Clarkson	54	483	33	20	0	2.76
	2B	J. Quinn	156	.301	4	29	97	115	20	11	6.1	.914	B. Sowders	36	317	19	15	0	2.07
	SS	S. Wise	417	.240	4	40	179	271	57	34	5.7	.888	O. Radbourn	24	207	7	16	0	2.87
	3B	B. Nash	526	.283	4	75	139	250	37	20	4.1	.913	K. Madden	20	165	7	11	0	2.95
	RF	T. Brown	420	.248	9	49	172	18	22	3	2.0	.896							
	CF	D. Johnston	585	.296	12	68	286	30	36	3	2.6	.898							
	LF	J. Hornung	431	.239	3	53	151	10	9	0	1.6	.947							
	C	K. Kelly	440	.318	9	71	367	146	54	8	7.5	.905							
	SS	I. Ray	206	.248	2	26	58	130	26	6	4.5	.879							
	P	J. Clarkson	205	.195	1	17	22	117	19	3	2.9	.880							
	C	P. Tate	148	.230	1	6	188	64	43	6	7.2	.854							
Det. W-68 L-63 Bill Watkins W-49 L-45 Bob Leadley W-19 L-18	1B	D. Brouthers	522	.307	9	66	1345	48	42	56	11.1	.971	C. Getzien	46	404	19	25	0	3.05
	2B	H. Richardson	266	.289	7	32	173	185	29	21	6.7	.925	P. Conway	45	391	30	14	0	2.26
	SS	J. Rowe	451	.277	2	74	133	312	72	24	4.9	.861	H. Gruber	27	240	11	14	0	2.29
	3B	D. White	527	.298	4	71	146	244	65	19	3.6	.857	E. Beatin	12	107	5	7	0	2.86
	RF	C. Campau	251	.203	1	18	101	10	8	3	1.7	.933							
	CF	N. Hanlon	459	.266	5	39	230	7	21	3	2.4	.919							
	LF	L. Twitchell	524	.244	5	67	195	13	27	4	1.8	.885							
	C	C. Bennett	258	.264	5	29	424	94	18	10	7.3	.966							
	UT	C. Ganzel	386	.249	1	46	288	241	52	24		.910							
	OF	S. Thompson	238	.282	6	40	86	4	12	0	1.8	.882							
	UT	S. Sutcliffe	191	.257	0	23	172	127	39	13		.885							
	P	C. Getzien	167	.246	1	10	29	70	16	5	2.5	.861							
	P	P. Conway	167	.275	3	23	10	96	7	4	2.5	.938							
Pit. W-66 L-68 Horace Phillips	1B	J. Beckley	283	.343	0	27	744	19	16	38	11.0	.979	E. Morris	55	480	29	24	0	2.31
	2B	F. Dunlap	321	.262	1	36	240	279	33	44	6.7	.940	P. Galvin	50	437	23	25	0	2.63
	SS	P. Smith	481	.206	4	52	91	247	37	18	5.0	.901	H. Staley	25	207	12	12	0	2.69
	3B	W. Kuehne	524	.235	3	62	96	168	26	10	3.9	.910							
	RF	J. Coleman	438	.231	0	26	160	20	14	2	2.1	.928							
	CF	B. Sunday	505	.236	0	15	297	27	21	5	2.9	.939							
	LF	A. Dalrymple	227	.220	0	14	81	9	9	0	1.7	.909							
	C	D. Miller	404	.277	0	36	268	76	35	6	5.6	.908							
	CO	F. Carroll	366	.249	2	48	314	63	48	10		.887							
	1O	A. Maul	259	.208	0	31	449	16	14	22		.971							
	P	E. Morris	189	.101	0	6	20	106	8	3	2.4	.940							
	P	P. Galvin	175	.143	1	3	23	113	10	2	2.9	.932							
	OC	J. Fields	169	.195	1	15	103	22	23	2		.845							
Ind. W-50 L-85 Harry Spence	1B	D. Esterbrook	246	.220	0	17	628	20	16	32	10.9	.976	H. Boyle	37	323	15	22	0	3.26
	2B	C. Bassett	481	.241	2	60	250	423	57	44	5.7	.922	E. Healy	37	321	12	24	0	3.89
	SS	J. Glasscock	442	.269	1	45	201	334	59	36	5.4	.901	L. Shreve	35	298	11	24	0	4.63
	3B	J. Denny	524	.261	12	63	158	214	44	14	4.3	.894	B. Burdick	20	176	10	10	0	2.81
	RF	J. McGeachy	452	.219	0	30	194	27	16	5	2.0	.932							
	CF	P. Hines	513	.281	4	58	255	13	26	3	2.4	.912							
	LF	E. Seery	500	.220	5	50	258	19	18	6	2.2	.939							
	C	D. Buckley	260	.273	5	22	213	60	31	5	6.0	.898							
	UT	G. Myers	248	.238	2	16	235	85	32	6		.909							
	C	C. Daily	202	.218	0	14	215	69	34	6	7.6	.893							
	1B	J. Schoeneck	169	.237	0	20	501	16	14	19	11.1	.974							
Was. W-48 L-86 Walter Hewett W-12 L-29 Ted Sullivan W-36 L-57	1B	B. O'Brien	528	.225	9	66	1272	38	33	55	10.2	.975	H. O'Day	46	403	16	29	0	3.10
	2B	A. Myers	502	.207	2	46	271	399	60	37	5.5	.918	J. Whitney	39	325	18	21	0	3.05
	SS	G. Shoch	317	.183	2	24	84	168	28	6	5.4	.900	W. Widner	13	115	5	7	0	2.82
	3B	J. Donnelly	428	.201	0	23	126	230	51	15	3.5	.875	G. Keefe	13	114	6	7	0	2.84
	RF	E. Daily	453	.225	8	39	179	19	19	4	2.2	.912	F. Gilmore	12	96	1	9	0	6.59
	CF	D. Hoy	503	.274	2	29	296	26	37	7	2.6	.897							
	LF	W. Wilmot	473	.224	4	43	260	19	41	4	2.7	.872							
	C	C. Mack	300	.187	3	29	361	152	47	8	7.1	.916							
	SS	S. Fuller	170	.182	0	12	67	140	38	14	5.2	.845							
	P	H. O'Day	166	.139	0	6	19	64	7	1	2.0	.922							
	P	J. Whitney	141	.170	1	17	15	67	11	2	2.4	.882							

BATTING AND BASE RUNNING LEADERS

Batting Average

C. Anson, CHI	.344
J. Ryan, CHI	.332
K. Kelly, BOS	.318
D. Brouthers, DET	.307
B. Ewing, NY	.306

Home Runs

J. Ryan, CHI	16
R. Connor, NY	14
C. Anson, CHI	12
J. Denny, IND	12
D. Johnston, BOS	12

Slugging Average

J. Ryan, CHI	.515
C. Anson, CHI	.499
R. Connor, NY	.480
K. Kelly, BOS	.480
D. Johnston, BOS	.472

Total Bases

J. Ryan, CHI	283
D. Johnston, BOS	276
C. Anson, CHI	257
D. Brouthers, DET	242
R. Connor, NY	231

PITCHING LEADERS

Winning Percentage

T. Keefe, NY	.745
P. Conway, DET	.682
B. Sanders, PHI	.655
G. Krock, CHI	.632
J. Clarkson, BOS	.623

Wins

T. Keefe, NY	35
J. Clarkson, BOS	33
P. Conway, DET	30
E. Morris, PIT	29
C. Buffinton, PHI	28

Earned Run Average

T. Keefe, NY	1.74
B. Sanders, PHI	1.90
C. Buffinton, PHI	1.91
M. Welch, NY	1.93
B. Sowders, BOS	2.07

Saves

G. Wood, PHI	2

BATTING AND BASE RUNNING LEADERS

Runs Batted In

C. Anson, CHI	84
B. Nash, BOS	75
J. Rowe, DET	74
N. Williamson, CHI	73

Stolen Bases

D. Hoy, WAS	82
E. Seery, IND	80
B. Sunday, PIT	71
F. Pfeffer, CHI	64
J. Ryan, CHI	60

Hits

J. Ryan, CHI	182
C. Anson, CHI	177
D. Johnston, BOS	173

Base on Balls

R. Connor, NY	73
D. Hoy, WAS	69
D. Brouthers, DET	68

Home Run Percentage

J. Ryan, CHI	2.9
R. Connor, NY	2.9
C. Anson, CHI	2.3

Runs Scored

D. Brouthers, DET	118
J. Ryan, CHI	115
D. Johnston, BOS	102

Doubles

D. Brouthers, DET	33
J. Ryan, CHI	33
D. Johnston, BOS	31

Triples

D. Johnston, BOS	18
R. Connor, NY	17
B. Ewing, NY	15
B. Nash, BOS	15

PITCHING LEADERS

Strikeouts

T. Keefe, NY	333
J. Clarkson, BOS	223
C. Getzien, DET	202
C. Buffinton, PHI	199
H. O'Day, WAS	186

Complete Games

E. Morris, PIT	54
J. Clarkson, BOS	53
T. Keefe, NY	51
P. Galvin, PIT	49
M. Welch, NY	47

Fewest Hits per 9 Innings

T. Keefe, NY	6.55
C. Titcomb, NY	6.81
G. Keefe, WAS	6.87

Shutouts

T. Keefe, NY	8
C. Buffinton, PHI	6
P. Galvin, PIT	6

Fewest Walks per 9 Innings

B. Sanders, PHI	1.08
P. Galvin, PIT	1.09
G. Krock, CHI	1.19

Most Strikeouts per 9 Inn.

T. Keefe, NY	6.90
C. Titcomb, NY	5.89
M. Baldwin, CHI	5.63

Innings

J. Clarkson, BOS	483
E. Morris, PIT	480
P. Galvin, PIT	437

Games Pitched

E. Morris, PIT	55
J. Clarkson, BOS	54
T. Keefe, NY	51

	W	L	PCT	GB	R	OR	2B	3B	HR	BA	SA	SB	E	DP	FA	CG	BB	SO	ShO	SV	ERA
NY	84	47	.641		659	479	130	76	55	.242	.336	314	432	76	.924	136	308	724	19	1	1.96
CHI	77	58	.570	9	734	659	147	95	77	.260	.383	287	417	112	.927	123	308	588	13	1	2.96
PHI	69	61	.531	14.5	535	509	151	46	16	.225	.290	246	424	70	.923	125	196	519	9	3	2.38
BOS	70	64	.522	15.5	669	619	167	89	56	.245	.351	293	494	91	.917	134	269	484	7	0	2.61
DET	68	63	.519	16	721	629	177	71	52	.263	.361	193	463	83	.919	130	183	522	9	1	2.74
PIT	66	68	.493	19.5	534	580	150	49	14	.227	.289	287	416	88	.927	135	223	367	13	0	2.67
IND	50	85	.370	36	603	731	180	33	33	.238	.313	350	449	84	.921	132	308	388	6	0	3.81
WAS	48	86	.358	37.5	482	731	98	49	31	.208	.271	331	494	69	.912	133	298	406	6	0	3.54
					4937	4937	1200	508	334	.239	.325	2301	3589	673	.921	1048	2093	3998	82	6	2.83

American Association 1888

	POS	Player	AB	BA	HR	RBI	PO	A	E	DP	TC/G	FA	Pitcher	G	IP	W	L	SV	ERA
St. L. W-92 L-43 Charlie Comiskey	1B	C. Comiskey	576	.273	6	83	1293	46	42	52	10.4	.970	S. King	66	586	45	21	0	1.64
	2B	Y. Robinson	455	.231	3	53	197	256	53	18	5.0	.895	N. Hudson	39	333	25	10	0	2.54
	SS	B. White	275	.175	2	30	132*	205	41	10	5.1	.892	Chamberlain	14	112	11	2	0	1.61
	3B	A. Latham	570	.265	2	31	178	287	62	19	4.0	.882	J. Devlin	11	90	6	5	0	3.19
	RF	T. McCarthy	511	.274	1	68	243	44	21	12	2.4	.932							
	CF	H. Lyons	499	.194	4	63	237	32	33	4	2.5	.891							
	LF	T. O'Neill	529	.335	5	98	231	8	16	1	2.0	.937							
	C	J. Boyle	257	.241	1	23	381	123	37	11	7.7	.932							
	C	J. Milligan	219	.251	5	37	317	85	25	11	7.4	.941							
	P	S. King	207	.208	1	14	32	119	12	4	2.5	.926							
	PO	N. Hudson	196	.255	2	28	72	55	9	4		.934							
	SO	E. Herr	172	.267	3	43	63	71	19	4		.876							
Bkn. W-88 L-52 Bill McGunnigle	1B	D. Orr	394	.305	1	59	976	44	22	41	10.5	.979	B. Caruthers	44	392	29	15	0	2.39
	2B	J. Burdock	246	.122	1	8	172	223	42	23	6.2	.904	M. Hughes	40	363	25	13	0	2.13
	SS	G. Smith	402	.214	3	61	155	352	94	29	5.8	.844	A. Terry	23	195	13	8	0	2.03
	3B	G. Pinckney	575	.271	4	52	189	234	48	14	3.3	.898	D. Foutz	23	176	12	7	0	2.51
	RF	D. Foutz	563	.277	3	99	115	13	15	3	1.8	.895	A. Mays	18	161	9	9	0	2.80
	CF	P. Radford	308	.218	2	29	180	22	12	2	2.4	.944							
	LF	D. O'Brien	532	.280	2	65	231	15	11	1	1.9	.932							
	C	D. Bushong	253	.209	0	16	347	105	42	8	7.2	.915							
	OP	B. Caruthers	335	.230	5	53	127	97	26	5		.896							
	2B	B. McClellan	278	.205	0	21	145	149	31	23	5.8	.905							
	SO	O. Burns	220	.286	2	27	72	98	31	6		.846							
	C	B. Clark	150	.240	1	20	197	61	36	6	8.2	.878							

POS	Player	AB	BA	HR	RBI	PO	A	E	DP	TC/G	FA	Pitcher	G	IP	W	L	SV	ERA
Phi. W-81 L-52 Bill Sharsig																		
1B	H. Larkin	546	.269	7	101	1218	36	**42**	44	10.6	.968	E. Seward	57	519	35	19	0	2.01
2B	L. Bierbauer	535	.267	0	80	342	**399**	**68**	39	6.7	.916	G. Weyhing	47	404	28	18	0	2.25
SS	B. Gleason	499	.224	0	61	112	370	80	32	4.6	.858	M. Mattimore	26	221	15	10	0	3.38
3B	D. Lyons	456	.296	6	83	159	193	49	11	3.6	.878							
RF	T. Poorman	383	.227	2	44	115	8	14	1	1.4	.898							
CF	C. Welch	549	.282	1	61	272	23	15	6	2.3	.952							
LF	H. Stovey	530	.287	9	65	204	12	13	4	1.9	.943							
C	W. Robinson	254	.244	1	31	**428**	**143**	38	5	9.4	.938							
P	E. Seward	225	.142	2	14	24	125	19	4	2.9	.887							
P	G. Weyhing	184	.217	1	14	42	93	17	1	2.8	.871							
C	G. Townsend	161	.155	0	12	225	76	31	2	7.9	.907							
PO	M. Mattimore	142	.268	0	12	32	71	10	6		.912							
Cin. W-80 L-54 Gus Schmelz																		
1B	L. Reilly	527	.321	**13**	**103**	1264	42	31	**73**	11.4	.977	L. Viau	42	388	27	14	0	2.65
2B	B. McPhee	458	.240	4	51	369	365	47	**65**	7.2	**.940**	T. Mullane	44	380	26	16	1	2.84
SS	F. Fennelly	448	.196	2	56	150	419*	94*	37*	5.9	.858	E. Smith	40	348	22	17	0	2.74
3B	H. Carpenter	551	.267	3	67	142	286	66	15	3.6	.866							
RF	H. Nicol	548	.239	1	35	188	17	9	4	1.7	.958							
CF	P. Corkhill	490	.271	1	74	255*	17	12	5	2.4*	.958*							
LF	W. Tebeau	411	.229	3	51	195	20	21	3	2.0	.911							
C	J. Keenan	313	.233	1	40	356	114	29	7	7.2	.942							
C	K. Baldwin	271	.218	1	25	350	107	41	6	7.7	.918							
P	T. Mullane	175	.251	1	16	22	81	13	1	2.6	.888							
P	L. Viau	149	.087	0	8	18	78	9	0	2.5	.914							
S2	H. Kappel	143	.259	1	15	47	89	38	9		.782							
Bal. W-57 L-80 Billy Barnie																		
1B	T. Tucker	520	.287	6	61	1354	**59**	36	64	11.2	.975	B. Cunningham	51	453	22	29	0	3.39
2B	B. Greenwood	409	.191	0	29	158	243	38	17	5.1	.913	M. Kilroy	40	321	17	21	0	4.04
SS	J. Farrell	398	.204	3	36	75	173	27	11	5.1	.902	P. Smith	35	292	14	19	0	3.61
3B	B. Shindle	514	.208	1	53	**218**	**340**	47	26	4.5	**.922**							
RF	B. Purcell	406	.236	2	39	145	9	16	3	1.7	.906							
CF	M. Griffin	542	.260	0	46	274	27	20	6	2.3	.938							
LF	O. Burns	308	.308	4	40	97	3	17	1	2.1	.855							
C	C. Fulmer	166	.187	0	10	237	42	30	5	6.9	.903							
OS	J. Sommer	297	.219	0	35	107	105	29	13		.880							
UT	J. O'Brien	196	.224	0	18	286	43	26	9		.927							
P	B. Cunningham	177	.186	1	9	20	106	**25**	3	3.0	.834							
OF	W. Goldsby	165	.236	0	14	53	3	6	0	1.4	.903							
P	M. Kilroy	145	.179	0	19	17	60	6	2	2.1	.928							
C	S. Trott	108	.278	0	22	156	32	19	4	7.7	.908							
Cle. W-50 L-82 Jimmy Williams W-19 L-41 Tom Loftus W-31 L-41																		
1B	J. Faatz	470	.264	0	51	1171	39	13	50	10.2	**.989**	J. Bakely	61	533	25	33	0	2.97
2B	C. Stricker	493	.233	1	33	**387**	361	57	58	6.6	.929	D. O'Brien	30	259	11	19	0	3.30
SS	E. McKean	548	.299	6	68	120	240	36	13	5.1	.909	B. Crowell	18	151	5	13	0	5.79
3B	G. Alberts	364	.216	1	48	68	103	20	9	3.9	.895							
RF	E. Hogan	269	.227	0	24	104	8	13	1	1.6	.896							
CF	P. Hotaling	403	.251	0	55	170	10	25	7	2.1	.878							
LF	B. Gilks	484	.229	1	63	136	15	16	2	1.9	.904							
C	C. Zimmer	212	.241	0	22	311	111	40	6	7.8	.913							
OF	M. Goodfellow	269	.245	0	29	93	8	16	1	1.9	.863							
C	P. Snyder	237	.215	0	14	308	130	**48**	**11**	8.4	.901							
3B	J. McGlone	203	.182	1	22	70	93	44	5	4.3	.787							
P	J. Bakely	194	.134	1	9	21	114	18	3	2.5	.882							
Lou. W-48 L-87 John Kerins W-11 L-32 Mordecai Davidson W-37 L-55																		
1B	S. Smith	206	.238	1	31	568	22	18	15	10.5	.970	T. Ramsey	40	342	8	30	0	3.42
2B	R. Mack	446	.217	3	34	307	344	67	35	6.4	.907	S. Stratton	33	270	10	17	0	3.64
SS	B. White	198	.278	1	30	52*	130	41	5	5.9	.816	G. Hecker	28	223	8	17	0	3.39
3B	J. Werrick	413	.215	0	51	96	170	62	9	3.7	.811	Chamberlain	24	196	14	9	0	2.53
RF	C. Wolf	538	.286	0	67	113	19	17	4	1.8	.886	J. Ewing	21	191	8	13	0	2.83
CF	P. Browning	383	.313	3	72	174	16	24	8	2.2	.888							
LF	H. Collins	485	.307	2	50	175	20	24	4	2.7	.890							
C	P. Cook	185	.184	0	13	221	81	35	7	6.4	.896							
OC	J. Kerins	319	.235	2	41	308	65	47	5		.888							
OP	S. Stratton	249	.257	1	29	66	70	17	1		.889							
1P	G. Hecker	211	.251	0	29	289	5	20	11		.936							
OC	F. Vaughn	189	.196	1	21	164	49	28	6		.884							
C	L. Cross	181	.227	0	15	202	60	20	3	7.6	.929							
P	T. Ramsey	142	.120	0	9	8	57	18	1	2.1	.783							
K. C. W-43 L-89 Dave Rowe W-14 L-35 Sam Barkley W-26 L-43 Bill Watkins W-3 L-11																		
1B	B. Phillips	509	.236	1	56	**1476**	55	32	66	12.1	.980	H. Porter	55	474	18	**37**	0	4.16
2B	S. Barkley	482	.216	3	51	341	314	43	44	6.0	.938	T. Sullivan	24	215	8	16	0	3.40
SS	H. Easterday	401	.190	3	37	120	459	73	30	5.7	**.888**	B. Fagan	17	142	5	11	0	5.69
3B	J. Davis	491	.267	3	61	155	334	**91**	**27**	5.1	.843	F. Hoffman	12	104	3	9	0	2.77
RF	M. Cline	293	.235	0	19	91	22	15	4	1.8	.883	S. Toole	12	92	5	6	0	6.68
CF	J. McTamany	516	.246	4	41	245	27	26	5	2.3	.913							
LF	M. Allen	136	.213	0	10	72	9	6	1	2.5	.931							
C	J. Donahue	337	.234	1	28	282	106	42	9	6.4	.902							
OC	L. Daniels	218	.202	1	28	159	67	34	7		.869							
P	H. Porter	195	.144	0	10	11	**133**	16	3	2.9	.900							
UT	F. Hankinson	155	.174	1	20	72	84	18	12		.897							

BATTING AND BASE RUNNING LEADERS

Batting Average

T. O'Neill, STL	.335
L. Reilly, CIN	.321
P. Browning, LOU	.313
H. Collins, BKN, LOU	.307
D. Orr, BKN	.305

Slugging Average

L. Reilly, CIN	.501
H. Stovey, PHI	.460
T. O'Neill, STL	.446
O. Burns, BAL, BKN	.441
P. Browning, LOU	.439

Home Runs

L. Reilly, CIN	13
H. Stovey, PHI	9
H. Larkin, PHI	7

Total Bases

L. Reilly, CIN	264
H. Stovey, PHI	244
T. O'Neill, STL	236
O. Burns, BAL, BKN	233
E. McKean, CLE	233

Runs Batted In

L. Reilly, CIN	103
H. Larkin, PHI	101
D. Foutz, BKN	99
T. O'Neill, STL	98
P. Corkhill, BKN, CIN	93

Stolen Bases

A. Latham, STL	109
H. Nicol, CIN	103
C. Welch, PHI	95
T. McCarthy, STL	93
H. Stovey, PHI	87

Hits

T. O'Neill, STL	177
L. Reilly, CIN	169
E. McKean, CLE	164

Base on Balls

Y. Robinson, STL	116
F. Fennelly, CIN, PHI	72
J. McTamany, KC	67
H. Nicol, CIN	67

Home Run Percentage

L. Reilly, CIN	2.5
H. Stovey, PHI	1.7
B. Caruthers, BKN	1.5

Runs Scored

G. Pinckney, BKN	134
H. Collins, BKN, LOU	133
H. Stovey, PHI	127

Doubles

H. Collins, BKN, LOU	31
L. Reilly, CIN	28
C. Wolf, LOU	28
H. Larkin, PHI	28

Triples

H. Stovey, PHI	20
O. Burns, BAL, BKN	15
E. McKean, CLE	15

PITCHING LEADERS

Winning Percentage

N. Hudson, STL	.714
Chamberlain, LOU, STL	.694
S. King, STL	.682
B. Caruthers, BKN	.659
L. Viau, CIN	.659

Earned Run Average

S. King, STL	1.64
E. Seward, PHI	2.01
A. Terry, BKN	2.03
M. Hughes, BKN	2.13
Chamberlain, LOU, STL	2.19

Wins

S. King, STL	45
E. Seward, PHI	35
B. Caruthers, BKN	29
G. Weyhing, PHI	28
L. Viau, CIN	27

Saves

T. Mullane, CIN	1
P. Corkhill, BKN, CIN	1
B. Gilks, CLE	1

Strikeouts

E. Seward, PHI	272
S. King, STL	258
T. Ramsey, LOU	228
J. Bakely, CLE	212
G. Weyhing, PHI	204

Complete Games

S. King, STL	64
J. Bakely, CLE	60
E. Seward, PHI	57
H. Porter, KC	53
B. Cunningham, BAL	50

Fewest Hits per 9 Innings

A. Terry, BKN	6.69
S. King, STL	6.72
E. Seward, PHI	6.73

Shutouts

E. Seward, PHI	6
S. King, STL	6
N. Hudson, STL	5
E. Smith, CIN	5

Fewest Walks per 9 Innings

S. King, STL	1.17
B. Caruthers, BKN	1.22
N. Hudson, STL	1.59

Most Strikeouts per 9 Inn.

A. Terry, BKN	6.37
T. Ramsey, LOU	5.99
Chamberlain, LOU, STL	5.14

Innings

S. King, STL	586
J. Bakely, CLE	533
E. Seward, PHI	519

Games Pitched

S. King, STL	66
J. Bakely, CLE	61
E. Seward, PHI	57

	W	L	PCT	GB	R	OR	2B	3B	HR	BA	SA	SB	E	DP	FA	CG	BB	SO	ShO	SV	ERA
							Batting							Fielding				Pitching			
STL	92	43	.681		789	501	149	47	36	.250	.324	468	430	73	.924	132	225	517	12	0	2.09
BKN	88	52	.629	6.5	758	584	172	70	25	.242	.321	334	507	88	.917	138	285	577	9	0	2.33
PHI	81	52	.609	10	827	594	183	89	31	.250	.344	434	477	73	.918	133	324	596	13	0	2.41
CIN	80	54	.597	11.5	745	628	132	82	32	.242	.323	469	458	100	.923	132	310	539	10	2	2.73
BAL	57	80	.416	36	653	799	162	70	18	.229	.306	326	461	88	.920	130	419	525	3	0	3.78
CLE	50	82	.379	40.5	651	839	128	59	12	.234	.295	353	490	87	.915	131	389	500	6	1	3.72
LOU	48	87	.356	44	689	870	183	67	14	.241	.315	318	611	75	.900	133	281	599	6	0	3.25
KC	43	89	.326	47.5	579	896	142	61	17	.218	.285	257	507	95	.914	128	401	381	4	0	4.29
					5691	5691	1251	545	185	.238	.315	2959	3941	679	.916	1057	2634	4234	63	3	3.06

National League 1889

	POS	Player	AB	BA	HR	RBI	PO	A	E	DP	TC/G	FA	Pitcher	G	IP	W	L	SV	ERA
N. Y.	1B	R. Connor	496	.317	13	130	1265	32	30	68	10.1	.977	M. Welch	45	375	27	12	2	3.02
W-83 L-43	2B	D. Richardson	497	.280	7	100	332	416	53	60	6.4	.934	T. Keefe	47	364	28	13	1	3.31
Jim Mutrie	SS	M. Ward	479	.299	1	67	229	319	68	38	5.7	.890	C. Crane	29	230	14	10	0	3.68
	3B	A. Whitney	473	.218	1	59	160	265	57	27	3.7	.882	H. O'Day	10	78	9	1	0	4.27
	RF	M. Tiernan	499	.335	11	73	179	19	23	2	1.8	.896							
	CF	G. Gore	488	.305	7	54	239	21	41	5	2.5	.864							
	LF	J. O'Rourke	502	.321	3	81	165	18	22	2	1.6	.893							
	C	B. Ewing	407	.327	4	87	524	149	45	10	7.4	.937							
	P	M. Welch	156	.192	0	12	13	59	4	2	1.7	.947							
	P	T. Keefe	149	.154	0	8	10	78	8	3	2.0	.917							
	C	W. Brown	139	.259	1	29	138	38	32	3	5.6	.846							

	POS	Player	AB	BA	HR	RBI	PO	A	E	DP	TC/G	FA	Pitcher	G	IP	W	L	SV	ERA
Bos. W-83 L-45 Jim Hart	1B	D. Brouthers	485	.373	7	118	1243	58	35	78	10.6	.974	J. Clarkson	73	620	49	19	1	2.73
	2B	H. Richardson	536	.304	7	79	246	310	46	44	7.0	.924	O. Radbourn	33	277	20	11	0	3.67
	SS	J. Quinn	444	.261	2	69	67	167	38	19	4.3	.860	K. Madden	22	178	10	10	1	4.40
	3B	B. Nash	481	.274	3	76	205	274	50	25	4.1	.905							
	RF	K. Kelly	507	.294	9	78	155	24	32	4	1.9	.848							
	CF	D. Johnston	539	.228	5	67	267	22	26	6	2.4	.917							
	LF	T. Brown	362	.232	2	24	169	13	20	1	2.2	.901							
	C	C. Bennett	247	.231	4	28	419	74	23	9	6.3	**.955**							
	UT	C. Ganzel	275	.265	1	43	292	87	30	19		.927							
	P	J. Clarkson	262	.206	2	23	36	172	27	8	3.2	.885							
	SS	P. Smith	208	.260	0	32	121	170	36*	23	5.5	.890							
Chi. W-67 L-65 Cap Anson	1B	C. Anson	518	.342	7	117	**1409**	**79**	27	73	11.3	.982	B. Hutchison	37	318	16	17	0	3.54
	2B	F. Pfeffer	531	.228	7	77	**452**	**483**	56	69	7.4	.943	J. Tener	35	287	15	15	0	3.64
	SS	N. Williamson	173	.237	1	30	48	130	33	7	4.5	.844	F. Dwyer	32	276	16	13	0	3.59
	3B	T. Burns	525	.242	4	66	**225**	**301**	72	30	4.4	.880	A. Gumbert	31	246	16	13	0	3.62
	RF	H. Duffy	**584**	.312	12	89	184	19	24	2	1.8	.894							
	CF	J. Ryan	576	.325	17	72	252	36	23	9	2.9	.926							
	LF	Van Haltren	543	.309	9	81	222	25	28	3	2.1	.898							
	C	D. Farrell	407	.248	11	75	344	119	46	3	6.7	.910							
	SS	C. Bastian	155	.135	0	10	63	153	19	9	5.2	.919							
	P	A. Gumbert	153	.288	7	29	17	44	6	1	2.2	.910							
	P	J. Tener	150	.273	1	19	22	69	7	1	2.8	.929							
Phi. W-63 L-64 Harry Wright	1B	S. Farrar	477	.268	3	58	1265	42	30	66	10.3	.978	C. Buffinton	47	380	27	17	0	3.24
	2B	A. Myers	305	.269	0	28	192	261	78*	33	7.1	.853	B. Sanders	44	350	19	18	1	3.55
	SS	B. Hallman	462	.253	2	60	237	337	67	39	6.0	.895	K. Gleason	29	205	9	15	1	5.58
	3B	J. Mulvey	544	.289	6	77	165	284	54	20	3.9	.893	D. Casey	20	153	6	10	0	3.77
	RF	S. Thompson	533	.296	20	111	173	19	21	7	1.7	.901							
	CF	J. Fogarty	499	.259	3	54	**302**	**42**	14	6	2.8	**.961**							
	LF	G. Wood	422	.251	5	53	164	9	16	1	2.1	.915							
	C	J. Clements	310	.284	4	35	380	77	42	7	6.4	.916							
	O2	E. Delahanty	246	.293	0	27	116	61	17	11		.912							
	C	P. Schriver	211	.265	1	19	233	76	27	4	7.0	.920							
	P	B. Sanders	169	.278	0	21	22	58	11	1	2.1	.879							
	P	C. Buffinton	154	.208	0	21	18	80	9	4	2.3	.916							
Pit. W-61 L-71 Horace Phillips Fred Dunlap W-28 L-43 Ned Hanlon W-7 L-9 W-26 L-19	1B	J. Beckley	522	.301	9	97	1236	53	24	73	10.8	.982	H. Staley	49	420	21	**26**	1	3.51
	2B	F. Dunlap	451	.235	2	65	342	393	39	51	6.4	**.950**	P. Galvin	41	341	23	16	0	4.17
	SS	J. Rowe	317	.259	2	32	108	228	39	26	5.0	.896	E. Morris	21	170	6	13	0	4.13
	3B	W. Kuehne	390	.246	5	57	89	157	32	14	3.7	.885	B. Sowders	13	53	6	5	0*	7.35
	RF	B. Sunday	321	.240	2	25	157	17	10	2	2.3	.946							
	CF	N. Hanlon	461	.239	2	37	277	18	26	2	2.8	.919							
	LF	A. Maul	257	.276	4	44	123	17	8	4	2.3	.946							
	C	D. Miller	422	.268	6	56	299	87	**48**	8	5.7	.889							
	CO	F. Carroll	318	.330	2	51	228	56	27	4		.913							
	OF	J. Fields	289	.311	2	43	97	7	17	2	2.0	.860							
	SS	P. Smith	258	.209	5	27	93	187	32*	21	5.4	.897							
	3B	D. White	225	.253	0	26	68	95	24	7	3.6	.872							
	P	H. Staley	186	.161	0	8	19	89	5	3	2.3	.956							
	P	P. Galvin	150	.187	0	16	20	72	11	6	2.5	.893							
Cle. W-61 L-72 Tom Loftus	1B	J. Faatz	442	.231	2	38	1145	62	24	67	10.5	.981	D. O'Brien	41	347	22	17	0	4.15
	2B	C. Stricker	566	.251	1	47	434	429	63	65	6.9	.932	E. Beatin	36	318	20	15	0	3.57
	SS	E. McKean	500	.318	4	75	206	398	62	42	5.5	.907	J. Bakely	36	304	12	22	0	2.96
	3B	P. Tebeau	521	.282	8	76	185	287	54	26	3.9	.897	H. Gruber	25	205	7	16	1	3.64
	RF	P. Radford	487	.238	1	46	205	24	14	6	1.8	.942							
	CF	J. McAleer	447	.235	1	35	247	29	13	9	2.6	.955							
	LF	L. Twitchell	549	.275	4	95	220	10	21	0	1.9	.916							
	C	C. Zimmer	259	.259	1	21	315	131	33	10	5.9	.931							
	UT	B. Gilks	210	.238	0	18	172	54	9	9		.962							
	C	S. Sutcliffe	161	.248	1	21	179	70	30	3	7.5	.892							
	P	D. O'Brien	140	.250	0	18	25	70	7	3	2.5	.931							
Ind. W-59 L-75 Frank Bancroft W-25 L-42 Jack Glasscock W-34 L-33	1B	P. Hines	486	.305	6	72	1090	57	**43**	66	10.9	.964	H. Boyle	46	379	21	23	0	3.92
	2B	C. Bassett	477	.245	4	68	322	451	52	67	6.5	.937	C. Getzien	45	349	18	22	1	4.54
	SS	J. Glasscock	582	.352	7	85	**246**	**478**	67	**60**	6.0	.915	A. Rusie	33	225	13	10	0	5.32
	3B	J. Denny	578	.282	18	112	199	276	45	12	4.2	.913							
	RF	J. McGeachy	532	.267	2	63	189	36	20	8	1.9	.918							
	CF	M. Sullivan	256	.285	4	35	133	9	14	4	2.4	.910							
	LF	E. Seery	526	.314	8	60	220	20.	24	4	2.1	.909							
	C	D. Buckley	260	.258	8	41	182	53	33	2	4.9	.877							
	C	C. Daily	219	.251	0	26	225	49	35	1	6.1	.887							
	OF	E. Andrews	173	.306	0	22	67	10	10	1	2.2	.910							
	P	H. Boyle	155	.245	1	17	17	51	3	0	1.5	.958							
	OC	G. Myers	149	.195	0	12	106	36	18	1		.888							

POS	Player	AB	BA	HR	RBI	PO	A	E	DP	TC/G	FA	Pitcher	G	IP	W	L	SV	ERA
1B	J. Carney	273	.231	1	29	521	16	24	29	10.6	.957	A. Ferson	36	288	17	17	0	3.90
2B	S. Wise	472	.250	4	62	170	225	36	26	6.0	.916	G. Haddock	33	276	11	19	0	4.20
SS	A. Irwin	313	.233	0	32	165	279	52	36	5.8	.895	G. Keefe	30	230	8	18	0	5.13
3B	J. Irwin	228	.289	0	25	82	129	32	14	4.2	.868	H. O'Day	13	108	2	10	0	4.33
RF	E. Beecher	179	.296	0	30	61	7	11	1	2.0	.861	E. Healy	13	101	1	11	0	6.24
CF	D. Hoy	507	.274	0	39	255	29	35	4	2.5	.890							
LF	W. Wilmot	432	.289	9	57	232	22	20	4	2.5	.927							
C	T. Daly	250	.300	1	40	268	86	32	5	6.8	.917							
UT	C. Mack	386	.293	0	42	432	100	42	4		.903							
3B	P. Sweeney	193	.228	1	23	67	83	37	6	4.0	.802							
2B	A. Myers	176	.261	0	20	147	148	18*	26	6.8	.942							
1B	J. Morrill	146	.185	2	16	369	18	8	15	9.9	.980							
UT	S. Clark	145	.255	3	22	101	75	26	10		.871							

Was.
W-41 L-83
John Morrill
W-13 L-39
Arthur Irwin
W-28 L-44

BATTING AND BASE RUNNING LEADERS

Batting Average
D. Brouthers, BOS	.373
J. Glasscock, IND	.352
C. Anson, CHI	.342
M. Tiernan, NY	.335
F. Carroll, PIT	.330

Slugging Average
R. Connor, NY	.528
J. Ryan, CHI	.516
D. Brouthers, BOS	.507
M. Tiernan, NY	.501
S. Thompson, PHI	.492

Home Runs
S. Thompson, PHI	20
J. Denny, IND	18
J. Ryan, CHI	17
R. Connor, NY	13
H. Duffy, CHI	12

Total Bases
J. Ryan, CHI	297
J. Glasscock, IND	272
R. Connor, NY	262
S. Thompson, PHI	262
H. Duffy, CHI	253

Runs Batted In
R. Connor, NY	130
D. Brouthers, BOS	118
C. Anson, CHI	117
J. Denny, IND	112
S. Thompson, PHI	111

Stolen Bases
J. Fogarty, PHI	99
K. Kelly, BOS	68
T. Brown, BOS	63
M. Ward, NY	62
J. Glasscock, IND	57

Hits
J. Glasscock, IND	205
J. Ryan, CHI	187
H. Duffy, CHI	182

Base on Balls
M. Tiernan, NY	96
R. Connor, NY	93
P. Radford, CLE	91

Home Run Percentage
S. Thompson, PHI	3.8
J. Denny, IND	3.1
J. Ryan, CHI	3.0

Runs Scored
M. Tiernan, NY	147
H. Duffy, CHI	144
J. Ryan, CHI	140

Doubles
K. Kelly, BOS	41
J. Glasscock, IND	40
J. O'Rourke, NY	36
S. Thompson, PHI	36

Triples
W. Wilmot, WAS	19
R. Connor, NY	17
J. Fogarty, PHI	17

PITCHING LEADERS

Winning Percentage
J. Clarkson, BOS	.721
M. Welch, NY	.692
T. Keefe, NY	.683
O. Radbourn, BOS	.645
C. Buffinton, PHI	.614

Earned Run Average
J. Clarkson, BOS	2.73
J. Bakely, CLE	2.96
M. Welch, NY	3.02
C. Buffinton, PHI	3.24
T. Keefe, NY	3.31

Wins
J. Clarkson, BOS	49
T. Keefe, NY	28
C. Buffinton, PHI	27
M. Welch, NY	27
P. Galvin, PIT	23

Saves
B. Sowders, BOS, PIT	2
B. Bishop, CHI	2
M. Welch, NY	2

Strikeouts
J. Clarkson, BOS	284
T. Keefe, NY	209
H. Staley, PIT	159
C. Buffinton, PHI	153
C. Getzien, IND	139

Complete Games
J. Clarkson, BOS	68
H. Staley, PIT	46
D. O'Brien, CLE	39
M. Welch, NY	39

Fewest Hits per 9 Innings
T. Keefe, NY	7.66
M. Welch, NY	8.16
J. Clarkson, BOS	8.55

Shutouts
J. Clarkson, BOS	8
P. Galvin, PIT	4

Fewest Walks per 9 Innings
P. Galvin, PIT	2.06
H. Boyle, IND	2.26
O. Radbourn, BOS	2.34

Most Strikeouts per 9 Inn.
T. Keefe, NY	5.17
C. Crane, NY	5.09
A. Rusie, IND	4.36

Innings
J. Clarkson, BOS	620
H. Staley, PIT	420
C. Buffinton, PHI	380

Games Pitched
J. Clarkson, BOS	73
H. Staley, PIT	49
C. Buffinton, PHI	47
T. Keefe, NY	47

	W	L	PCT	GB	R	OR	Batting					SB	Fielding			Pitching					
							2B	3B	HR	BA	SA		E	DP	FA	CG	BB	SO	ShO	SV	ERA
NY	83	43	.659		935	708	207	77	53	.282	.394	292	437	90	.920	118	523	542	6	3	3.47
BOS	83	45	.648	1	826	626	196	53	43	.270	.363	331	413	105	.926	121	413	497	10	4	3.36
CHI	67	65	.508	19	867	814	184	66	79	.263	.377	243	463	91	.923	123	408	434	6	2	3.73
PHI	63	64	.496	20.5	742	748	215	52	44	.266	.362	269	466	92	.915	106	428	443	4	2	4.00
PIT	61	71	.462	25	726	801	209	65	42	.253	.351	231	385	94	.931	125	374	345	5	1	4.51
CLE	61	72	.459	25.5	656	720	131	59	25	.250	.319	237	365	108	.936	132	519	435	6	1	3.66
IND	59	75	.440	28	819	894	228	35	62	.278	.377	252	420	102	.926	109	420	408	3	2	4.85
WAS	41	83	.331	41	632	892	151	57	25	.251	.329	232	519	91	.904	113	527	388	1	0	4.68
					6203	6203	1521	464	373	.264	.359	2087	3468	773	.923	947	3612	3492	41	15	4.02

POS	Player	AB	BA	HR	RBI	PO	A	E	DP	TC/G	FA	Pitcher	G	IP	W	L	SV	ERA
Bkn.												B. Caruthers	56	445	**40**	11	1	3.13
W-93 L-44												A. Terry	41	326	22	15	0	3.29
Bill McGunnigle												T. Lovett	29	229	17	10	0	4.32
1B	D. Foutz	553	.277	7	113	1371	33	30	65	10.7	.979	M. Hughes	20	153	9	8	0	4.35
2B	H. Collins	560	.266	2	73	385	410	61	56	6.2	.929							
SS	G. Smith	446	.231	3	53	182	417	67	37	5.6	.899							
3B	G. Pinckney	545	.246	4	82	183	278	53	19	3.7	**.897**							
RF	O. Burns	504	.304	5	100	139	23	14	5	1.6	.920							
CF	P. Corkhill	537	.250	8	78	317	35	19	8	2.7	**.949**							
LF	D. O'Brien	567	.300	5	80	255	14	28	5	2.2	.906							
C	J. Visner	295	.258	8	68	198	72	40	7	5.8	.871							
C	B. Clark	182	.275	0	22	275	86	**54**	4	7.8	.870							
P	B. Caruthers	172	.250	2	31	29	95	4	4	2.3	.969							
P	A. Terry	160	.300	2	26	24	86	4	2	2.8	.965							
St. L.												S. King	56	458	33	17	1	3.14
W-90 L-45												Chamberlain	53	422	32	15	1	2.97
Charlie Comiskey												J. Stivetts	26	192	13	7	1	**2.25**
1B	C. Comiskey	587	.286	3	102	1225	45	39	71	9.8	.970							
2B	Y. Robinson	452	.208	5	70	305	333	81	53	5.4	.887							
SS	S. Fuller	517	.226	0	51	240	459	67	46	5.5	.913							
3B	A. Latham	512	.246	4	49	197	249	59	22	4.4	.883							
RF	T. McCarthy	**604**	.291	2	63	229	38	32	11	2.1	.893							
CF	C. Duffee	509	.244	15	86	296	**43**	23	7	**2.7**	.936							
LF	T. O'Neill	534	.335	9	110	264	12	19	3	2.2	.936							
C	J. Boyle	347	.245	4	42	378	108	27	11	6.4	.947							
C	J. Milligan	273	.366	12	76	370	105	34	7	7.7	.933							
P	S. King	189	.228	0	30	19	91	5	2	2.1	.957							
P	Chamberlain	171	.199	2	31	15	67	7	0	1.7	.921							
Phi.												G. Weyhing	54	449	30	21	0	2.95
W-75 L-58												E. Seward	39	320	21	15	0	3.97
Bill Sharsig												S. McMahon	30	255	16	12	0	3.35
1B	H. Larkin	516	.318	3	74	1230	37	35	**88**	9.9	.973							
2B	L. Bierbauer	549	.304	7	105	**472**	406	55	80	**7.2**	.941							
SS	F. Fennelly	513	.257	1	64	181	453	93	53	5.3	.872							
3B	D. Lyons	510	.329	9	82	202	291	80	29	4.4	.860							
RF	B. Purcell	507	.316	0	85	172	15	20	3	1.6	.903							
CF	C. Welch	516	.271	0	39	282	29	26	10	2.7	.923							
LF	H. Stovey	556	.308	19	119	287	38	37	9	2.6	.898							
C	W. Robinson	264	.231	0	28	290	106	24	8	6.1	.943							
C	L. Cross	199	.221	0	23	278	102	27	7	7.4	.934							
P	G. Weyhing	191	.131	0	12	12	71	8	2	1.7	.912							
P	E. Seward	143	.217	2	17	13	67	9	1	2.3	.899							
Cin.												J. Duryea	53	401	32	19	1	2.56
W-76 L-63												L. Viau	47	373	22	20	1	3.79
Gus Schmelz												T. Mullane	33	220	11	9	**5**	2.99
1B	L. Reilly	427	.260	5	66	1143	30	19	76	10.9	**.984**	E. Smith	29	203	9	12	0	4.88
2B	B. McPhee	543	.269	5	57	429	**446**	50	**85**	6.9	**.946**							
SS	O. Beard	558	.285	1	77	214	**537**	87	63	5.9	.896							
3B	H. Carpenter	486	.261	0	63	143	207	69	18	3.5	.835							
RF	H. Nicol	474	.255	2	58	168	22	17	4	1.8	.918							
CF	B. Holliday	563	.343	19	104	234	29	22	6	2.1	.923							
LF	W. Tebeau	496	.252	7	70	241	18	33	3	2.2	.887							
C	J. Keenan	300	.287	6	60	319	91	16	11	6.5	.962							
C	K. Baldwin	223	.247	1	34	274	89	35	5	7.2	.912							
UT	T. Mullane	196	.296	0	29	78	80	22	10		.878							
OC	B. Earle	169	.266	4	31	157	31	34	5		.847							
P	J. Duryea	162	.272	0	17	15	80	11	1	2.0	.896							
P	L. Viau	147	.143	0	9	9	61	4	2	1.6	.946							
Bal.												M. Kilroy	59	481	29	25	0	2.85
W-70 L-65												F. Foreman	51	414	23	21	0	3.52
Billy Barnie												B. Cunningham	39	279	16	19	1	4.87
1B	T. Tucker	527	.372	5	99	1144	45	44	63	10.0	.964							
2B	R. Mack	519	.241	1	87	367	358	**83**	70	6.0	.897							
SS	J. Farrell	157	.210	1	26	65	131	24	13	5.2	.891							
3B	B. Shindle	567	.314	3	64	**225**	323	88	25	4.6	.862							
RF	J. Sommer	386	.220	1	36	172	24	15	7	2.0	.929							
CF	M. Griffin	533	.280	4	48	246	17	26	5	2.7	.910							
LF	J. Hornung	533	.229	1	78	250	32	27	10	2.3	.913							
C	P. Tate	253	.182	1	27	306	75	25	3	6.5	.938							
P	M. Kilroy	208	.274	1	26	25	139	**17**	4	3.1	.906							
C	T. Quinn	194	.175	1	15	290	81	30	10	7.3	.925							
P	F. Foreman	181	.144	1	11	9	72	14	1	1.9	.853							
SS	W. Holland	143	.189	0	16	37	102	24	9	4.2	.853							
Col.												M. Baldwin	63	514	27	**34**	1	3.61
W-60 L-78												W. Widner	41	294	12	20	1	5.20
Al Buckenberger												H. Gastright	32	223	10	16	0	4.57
1B	D. Orr	560	.327	4	87	1291	**61**	23	64	10.3	.983	A. Mays	21	140	10	7	0	4.82
2B	B. Greenwood	414	.225	3	49	313	322	60	50	5.9	.914							
SS	H. Easterday	324	.173	4	34	134	326	57	27	5.8	.890							
3B	L. Marr	546	.306	1	75	111	151	44	13	4.6	.856							
RF	S. Johnson	459	.283	2	79	75	12	12	2	1.4	.879							
CF	J. McTamany	529	.276	4	52	247	28	30	8	2.2	.902							
LF	E. Daily	578	.256	3	70	212	27	**41**	4	2.1	.854							
C	J. O'Connor	398	.269	4	60	**423**	128	26	7	**6.9**	.955							
P	M. Baldwin	208	.188	2	25	**33**	91	13	1	2.2	.905							
S3	H. Kappel	173	.272	3	21	69	128	40	7		.831							

POS	Player	AB	BA	HR	RBI	PO	A	E	DP	TC/G	FA	Pitcher	G	IP	W	L	SV	ERA
K. C.												P. Swartzel	48	410	19	27	1	4.32
W-55 L-82												J. Conway	41	335	19	19	0	3.25
Bill Watkins												J. Sowders	25	185	6	16	1	4.82
1B	D. Stearns	560	.286	2	87	1398	56	49	75	11.1	.967	J. McCarty	15	120	8	6	0	3.91
2B	S. Barkley	176	.284	0	23	90	103	16	20	5.1	.923	T. Sullivan	10	87	2	8	0	5.67
SS	H. Long	574	.279	3	60	335	479	117	55	7.3	.874							
3B	J. Davis	241	.266	0	30	93	140	57	14	4.7	.803							
RF	B. Hamilton	534	.301	3	77	202	20	37	6	1.9	.857							
CF	J. Burns	579	.304	5	97	323	11	32	4	2.7	.913							
LF	J. Manning	506	.204	3	68	119	20	11	2	2.2	.927							
C	C. Hoover	258	.248	1	25	266	105	34	8	6.1	.916							
UT	J. Donahue	252	.234	0	32	187	100	46	7		.862							
UT	J. Pickett	201	.224	0	12	77	44	23	4		.840							
UT	B. Alvord	186	.231	0	18	66	140	43	17		.827							
P	P. Swartzel	174	.144	0	20	19	145	11	6	3.6	.937							
P	J. Conway	149	.208	0	12	10	85	7	2	2.5	.931							
Lou.												R. Ehret	45	364	10	29	0	4.80
W-27 L-111												J. Ewing	40	331	6	30	0	4.87
Dude Esterbrook W-2 L-8												G. Hecker	17	151	5	11	0	5.59
Chicken Wolf W-15 L-51												T. Ramsey	18	140	1	16	0	5.59
Dan Shannon W-9 L-43												S. Stratton	19	134	3	13	1	3.23
Jack Chapman W-1 L-9																		
1B	G. Hecker	327	.284	1	36	609	23	20	43	10.0	.969							
2B	D. Shannon	498	.257	4	48	307	391	69	59	6.3	.910							
SS	P. Tomney	376	.213	4	38	229	454	114	57	7.1	.857							
3B	H. Raymond	515	.239	0	47	206	261	60	23	4.1	.886							
RF	C. Wolf	546	.291	3	57	159	16	10	2	2.1	.946							
CF	F. Weaver	499	.291	0	60	249	30	25	4	2.5	.918							
LF	P. Browning	324	.256	2	32	152	12	22	4	2.2	.882							
C	P. Cook	286	.227	0	15	293	138	35	6	6.3	.925							
UT	F. Vaughn	360	.239	3	45	441	121	51	18		.917							
PO	R. Ehret	258	.252	1	31	36	101	22	3		.862							
UT	S. Stratton	229	.288	4	34	198	57	21	15		.924							

BATTING AND BASE RUNNING LEADERS

Batting Average
T. Tucker, BAL	.372
B. Holliday, CIN	.343
T. O'Neill, STL	.335
D. Lyons, PHI	.329
D. Orr, COL	.327

Slugging Average
H. Stovey, PHI	.527
B. Holliday, CIN	.519
T. Tucker, BAL	.484
T. O'Neill, STL	.478
D. Lyons, PHI	.469

Home Runs
H. Stovey, PHI	19
B. Holliday, CIN	19
C. Duffee, STL	15
J. Milligan, STL	12
D. Lyons, PHI	9
T. O'Neill, STL	9

Total Bases
H. Stovey, PHI	293
B. Holliday, CIN	292
T. Tucker, BAL	255
T. O'Neill, STL	255
D. Orr, COL	250

Runs Batted In
H. Stovey, PHI	119
D. Foutz, BKN	113
T. O'Neill, STL	110
L. Bierbauer, PHI	105
B. Holliday, CIN	104

Stolen Bases
B. Hamilton, KC	117
D. O'Brien, BKN	91
H. Long, KC	89
H. Nicol, CIN	80
A. Latham, STL	69

Hits
T. Tucker, BAL	196
B. Holliday, CIN	193
D. Orr, COL	183

Base on Balls
Y. Robinson, STL	118
J. McTamany, COL	116
M. Griffin, BAL	91

Home Run Percentage
H. Stovey, PHI	3.4
B. Holliday, CIN	3.4
C. Duffee, STL	2.9

Runs Scored
M. Griffin, BAL	152
H. Stovey, PHI	152
D. O'Brien, BKN	146

Doubles
C. Welch, PHI	39
H. Stovey, PHI	37
D. Lyons, PHI	36

Triples
L. Marr, COL	15
H. Stovey, PHI	14
M. Griffin, BAL	14
O. Beard, CIN	14

PITCHING LEADERS

Winning Percentage
B. Caruthers, BKN	.784
Chamberlain, STL	.681
S. King, STL	.660
J. Stivetts, STL	.650
T. Lovett, BKN	.630

Earned Run Average
J. Stivetts, STL	2.25
J. Duryea, CIN	2.56
M. Kilroy, BAL	2.85
G. Weyhing, PHI	2.95
Chamberlain, STL	2.97

Wins
B. Caruthers, BKN	40
S. King, STL	33
Chamberlain, STL	32
J. Duryea, CIN	32
G. Weyhing, PHI	30

Saves
T. Mullane, CIN	5

Strikeouts
M. Baldwin, COL	368
M. Kilroy, BAL	217
G. Weyhing, PHI	213
Chamberlain, STL	202
S. King, STL	188

Complete Games
M. Kilroy, BAL	55
M. Baldwin, COL	54
G. Weyhing, PHI	50
S. King, STL	47
B. Caruthers, BKN	46

Fewest Hits per 9 Innings
J. Stivetts, STL	7.18
G. Weyhing, PHI	7.66
A. Terry, BKN	7.87

Shutouts
B. Caruthers, BKN	7
M. Baldwin, COL	6
F. Foreman, BAL	5
M. Kilroy, BAL	5

Fewest Walks per 9 Innings
B. Caruthers, BKN	2.10
J. Conway, KC	2.42
S. King, STL	2.46

Most Strikeouts per 9 Inn.
J. Stivetts, STL	6.71
M. Baldwin, COL	6.45
A. Terry, BKN	5.13

Innings
M. Baldwin, COL	514
M. Kilroy, BAL	481
S. King, STL	458

Games Pitched
M. Baldwin, COL	63
M. Kilroy, BAL	59
S. King, STL	56
B. Caruthers, BKN	56

	W	L	PCT	GB	R	OR	2B	3B	Batting HR	BA	SA	SB	E	Fielding DP	FA	CG	BB	Pitching SO	ShO	SV	ERA
BKN	93	44	.679		**995**	706	188	79	48	.263	.365	389	**421**	92	**.928**	120	**400**	471	**10**	1	3.61
STL	90	45	.667	2	957	**680**	211	64	**58**	.266	.370	336	438	100	.925	121	413	**617**	7	3	**3.00**
PHI	75	58	.564	16	880	787	**239**	65	43	**.275**	.377	252	465	120	.921	**130**	509	479	9	1	3.53
CIN	76	63	.547	18	897	769	197	**96**	52	.270	**.382**	462	440	**121**	.907	128	424	540	**10**	1	3.56
BAL	70	65	.519	22	791	795	155	68	20	.254	.328	311	536	104	.907	128	551	610	9	4	4.39
COL	60	78	.435	33.5	779	924	171	95	36	.259	.356	304	497	92	.916	114	551	457		2	4.36
KC	55	82	.401	38	852	1031	162	77	17	.254	.328	**472**	611	109	.900	128	457	447	2	1	4.81
LOU	27	111	.196	66.5	632	1091	170	75	22	.252	.330	203	584	117	.907	127	475	451		1	4.81
					6783	6783	1493	619	296	.262	.354	2729	3992	855	.916	982	3704	4177	50	21	3.84

National League 1890

	POS	Player	AB	BA	HR	RBI	PO	A	E	DP	TC/G	FA	Pitcher	G	IP	W	L	SV	ERA
Bkn. W-86 L-43 Bill McGunnigle	1B	D. Foutz	509	.303	5	98	1192	39	28	63	11.1	.978	T. Lovett	44	372	30	11	0	2.78
	2B	H. Collins	510	.278	3	69	298	420	42	56	5.9	.945	A. Terry	46	370	26	16	0	2.94
	SS	G. Smith	481	.191	1	47	232	468	74	49	6.0	.904	B. Caruthers	37	300	23	11	0	3.09
	3B	G. Pinckney	485	.309	7	83	179	222	29	15	3.4	.933							
	RF	O. Burns	472	.284	13	**128**	137	23	10	4	1.5	.941							
	CF	D. O'Brien	350	.314	2	63	176	14	8	2	2.3	**.960**							
	LF	P. Corkhill	204	.225	1	21	122	6	3	1	2.7	.977							
	C	T. Daly	292	.243	5	43	332	72	20	7	6.1	.953							
	OP	A. Terry	363	.278	4	59	123	79	19	6		.914							
	OP	B. Caruthers	238	.265	1	29	65	83	20	2		.881							
	P	T. Lovett	164	.201	1	20	10	79	10	3	2.3	.899							
	C	B. Clark	151	.219	0	15	164	40	40	5	5.8	.836							
Chi. W-84 L-53 Cap Anson	1B	C. Anson	504	.312	7	107	1345	**49**	31	61	10.6	.978	B. Hutchison	71	**603**	**42**	25	**2**	2.70
	2B	B. Glenalvin	250	.268	4	26	128	194	25	20	5.3	.928	P. Luby	34	268	20	9	1	3.19
	SS	J. Cooney	574	.272	4	52	237	452	47	50	5.5	**.936**	E. Stein	20	161	12	6	0	3.81
	3B	T. Burns	538	.277	6	86	188	290	54	25	3.8	.898	M. Sullivan	12	96	5	6	0	4.59
	RF	J. Andrews	202	.188	3	17	80	10	10	1	1.9	.900							
	CF	W. Wilmot	571	.278	**14**	99	**320**	26	23	4	2.7	.938							
	LF	C. Carroll	**582**	.285	7	65	265	28	20	7	2.3	.936							
	C	M. Kittredge	333	.201	3	35	458	113	34	9	6.3	.944							
	O2	H. Earl	384	.247	6	51	144	145	42	11		.873							
	P	B. Hutchison	261	.203	2	27	**44**	128	14	5	2.6	.925							
	C	T. Nagle	144	.271	1	11	161	25	12	0	6.0	.939							
	OF	E. Foster	105	.248	5	23	69	2	1	0	2.7	.986							
Phi. W-78 L-54 Harry Wright	1B	A. McCauley	418	.244	1	42	1053	26	30	68	9.9	.973	K. Gleason	60	506	38	17	**2**	2.63
	2B	A. Myers	487	.277	2	81	347	352	38	**62**	6.3	.948	T. Vickery	46	382	24	22	0	3.44
	SS	B. Allen	456	.226	2	57	337	**500**	69	**68**	6.8	.924	P. Smith	24	204	8	12	0	4.28
	3B	E. Mayer	484	.242	1	70	173	224	55	22	3.9	.878							
	RF	S. Thompson	549	.313	4	102	170	29	13	5	1.6	.939							
	CF	E. Burke	430	.263	4	50	202	23	24	4	2.6*	.904							
	LF	B. Hamilton	496	.325	2	49	232	23	**34**	4	2.3	.882							
	C	J. Clements	381	.315	7	74	**503**	92	35	12	6.9	.944							
	P	K. Gleason	224	.210	0	17	24	95	8	4	2.1	.937							
	UT	P. Schriver	223	.274	0	35	272	63	33	12		.910							
	P	T. Vickery	159	.208	0	11	17	71	**20**	3	2.3	.815							
	UT	B. Grey	128	.242	0	21	69	42	18	4		.860							
Cin. W-77 L-55 Tom Loftus	1B	L. Reilly	553	.300	6	86	**1392**	38	**33**	**77**	11.1	.977	B. Rhines	46	401	28	17	0	**1.95**
	2B	B. McPhee	528	.256	3	39	**404**	**431**	51	62	6.7	.942	J. Duryea	33	274	16	12	0	2.92
	SS	O. Beard	492	.268	3	72	145	419	65	43	5.6	.897	T. Mullane	25	209	12	10	1	2.24
	3B	A. Latham	164	.250	0	15	54	103	27	10	4.5	.853	F. Foreman	25	198	13	10	0	3.95
	RF	L. Marr	527	.300	2	73	68	12	6	3	1.3	.930	L. Viau	13	90	7	5	0	4.50
	CF	B. Holliday	518	.270	4	75	253	20	15	5	2.2	.948							
	LF	J. Knight	481	.312	4	67	224	11	19	0	2.0	.925							
	C	J. Harrington	236	.246	1	23	345	73	19	3	6.7	.957							
	UT	T. Mullane	286	.276	0	34	114	116	37	7		.861							
	C	J. Keenan	202	.139	3	19	244	63	16	5	6.5	.950							
	OF	H. Nicol	186	.210	0	19	62	8	6	3	1.7	.921							
	P	B. Rhines	154	.188	0	11	23	77	7	3	2.3	.935							
Bos. W-76 L-57 Frank Selee	1B	T. Tucker	539	.295	1	62	1341	39	29	53	10.7	**.979**	K. Nichols	48	427	27	19	0	2.21
	2B	P. Smith	463	.229	1	53	234	401	**57**	41	5.2	.918	J. Clarkson	44	383	25	18	0	3.27
	SS	H. Long	431	.251	8	52	230	352	66	40	6.4	.898	C. Getzien	40	350	23	17	0	3.19
	3B	C. McGarr	487	.236	1	51	151	228	27	13	3.5	**.933**							
	RF	S. Brodie	514	.296	0	67	225	19	12	6	1.9	.953							
	CF	P. Hines	273	.264	2	48	114	4	16	2	1.9	.881							
	LF	M. Sullivan	505	.285	6	61	241	13	13	1	2.2	.951							
	C	C. Bennett	281	.214	3	40	448	90	23	8	6.6	**.959**							
	UT	B. Lowe	207	.280	2	21	103	82	11	2		.944							
	UT	L. Hardie	185	.227	3	17	171	49	28	5		.887							
	P	K. Nichols	174	.247	0	23	14	85	13	1	2.3	.884							
	P	J. Clarkson	173	.249	2	26	21	72	14	3	2.4	.869							
	CO	C. Ganzel	163	.270	0	24	144	28	7	4		.961							
	P	C. Getzien	147	.231	2	25	14	63	19	2	2.4	.802							
	OF	P. Donovan	140	.179	0	9	45	4	6	1	1.7	.891							

	POS	Player	AB	BA	HR	RBI	PO	A	E	DP	TC/G	FA	Pitcher	G	IP	W	L	SV	ERA
N. Y.	1B	L. Whistler	170	.288	2	29	490	10	9	28	11.3	.982	A. Rusie	67	549	29	30	1	2.56
W-63 L-68	2B	C. Bassett	410	.239	0	54	201	332	27	43	5.6	.952	M. Welch	37	292	18	13	0	2.99
Jim Mutrie	SS	J. Glasscock	512	.336	1	66	275	421	69	46	6.2	.910	J. Sharrott	25	184	11	10	0	2.89
	3B	J. Denny	437	.213	3	42	165	210	47	16	4.0	.889	J. Burkett	21	118	3	10	0	5.57
	RF	J. Burkett	401	.309	4	60	108	23	28	4	1.8	.824							
	CF	M. Tiernan	553	.304	13	59	210	13	26	5	1.9	.896							
	LF	J. Hornung	513	.238	0	65	110	12	9	3	1.7	.931							
	C	D. Buckley	266	.256	2	26	365	93	34	4	7.9	.931							
	UT	A. Clarke	395	.225	0	49	288	138	55	11		.886							
	P	A. Rusie	284	.278	0	28	25	129	20	5	2.6	.885							
	1B	D. Esterbrook	197	.289	0	29	430	13	7	24	10.0	.984							
	OF	J. Henry	144	.243	0	16	56	4	9	1	1.9	.870							
Cle.	1B	P. Veach	238	.235	0	32	634	40	20	37	10.8	.971	E. Beatin	54	474	22	31	0	3.83
W-44 L-88	2B	J. Ardner	323	.223	0	35	205	257	40	42	6.0	.920	J. Wadsworth	20	170	2	16	0	5.20
Gus Schmelz	SS	E. McKean	530	.296	7	61	266	433	75	46	5.8	.903	C. Young	17	148	9	7	0	3.47
W-21 L-55	3B	W. Smalley	502	.213	0	42	221	327	64	27	4.5	.895	E. Lincoln	15	118	3	11	0	4.42
Bob Leadley	RF	V. Daily	246	.289	0	32	103	13	19	2	2.1	.859	L. Viau	13	107	4	9	0	3.36
W-23 L-33	CF	G. Davis	526	.264	6	73	282	35	18	9	2.5	.946							
	LF	B. Gilks	544	.213	0	41	237	20	16	2	2.2	.941							
	C	C. Zimmer	444	.214	2	57	480	188	45	14	5.7	.937							
	1B	J. Virtue	223	.305	2	25	633	21	12	33	10.7	.982							
	P	E. Beatin	191	.141	1	21	30	101	8	7	2.6	.942							
	O1	T. Dowse	159	.208	0	9	140	10	8	10		.949							
	OF	B. West	151	.245	2	29	50	9	12	1	1.9	.831							
Pit.	1B	G. Hecker	340	.226	0	38	610	31	25	26	9.7	.962	K. Baker	25	178	3	19	0	5.60
W-23 L-113	2B	S. LaRoque	434	.242	1	40	227	244	38	32	6.5	.925	G. Hecker	14	120	2	12	0	5.11
Guy Hecker	SS	E. Sales	189	.228	1	23	85	151	35	10	5.3	.871	D. Anderson	13	108	2	11	0	4.67
	3B	D. Miller	549	.273	4	66	127	213	60	18	4.5	.850	B. Sowders	15	106	3	8	0	4.42
	RF	B. Sunday	358	.257	1	33	181	23	27	9*	2.7	.883	C. Schmit	11	83	1	9	0	5.83
	CF	T. Berger	391	.266	0	40	72	11	8	1	2.2	.912	B. Phillips	10	82	1	9	0	7.57
	LF	J. Kelty	207	.237	1	27	100	6	12	1	2.0	.898	B. Gumbert	10	79	4	6	0	5.22
	C	H. Decker	354	.274	5	38	267	72	34	5	5.3	.909							
	UT	B. Wilson	304	.214	0	21	409	90	60	22		.893							
	3B	F. Roat	215	.223	2	17	64	102	30	9	4.5	.847							
	OF	F. Osborne	168	.238	1	14	64	8	15	0	2.5	.828							

BATTING AND BASE RUNNING LEADERS

Batting Average

J. Glasscock, NY	.336
B. Hamilton, PHI	.325
J. Clements, PHI	.315
D. O'Brien, BKN	.314
S. Thompson, PHI	.313

Slugging Average

M. Tiernan, NY	.495
J. Clements, PHI	.472
L. Reilly, CIN	.472
O. Burns, BKN	.468
J. Burkett, NY	.461

Home Runs

W. Wilmot, CHI	14
O. Burns, BKN	13
M. Tiernan, NY	13
H. Long, BOS	8

Total Bases

M. Tiernan, NY	274
L. Reilly, CIN	261
S. Thompson, PHI	243
W. Wilmot, CHI	240
J. Glasscock, NY	225

Runs Batted In

O. Burns, BKN	128
C. Anson, CHI	107
S. Thompson, PHI	102
W. Wilmot, CHI	99
D. Foutz, BKN	98

Stolen Bases

B. Hamilton, PHI	102
H. Collins, BKN	85
B. Sunday, PHI, PIT	84
W. Wilmot, CHI	76
M. Tiernan, NY	56

Hits

J. Glasscock, NY	172
S. Thompson, PHI	172
M. Tiernan, NY	168

Base on Balls

C. Anson, CHI	113
B. Allen, PHI	87
E. McKean, CLE	87

Home Run Percentage

O. Burns, BKN	2.8
W. Wilmot, CHI	2.5
M. Tiernan, NY	2.4

Runs Scored

H. Collins, BKN	148
C. Carroll, CHI	134
B. Hamilton, PHI	133

Doubles

S. Thompson, PHI	41
H. Collins, BKN	32
J. Glasscock, NY	32

Triples

L. Reilly, CIN	26
B. McPhee, CIN	22
M. Tiernan, NY	21

PITCHING LEADERS

Winning Percentage

T. Lovett, BKN	.732
K. Gleason, PHI	.691
P. Luby, CHI	.690
B. Caruthers, BKN	.676
B. Hutchison, CHI	.627

Earned Run Average

B. Rhines, CIN	1.95
K. Nichols, BOS	2.21
A. Rusie, NY	2.56
K. Gleason, PHI	2.63
B. Hutchison, CHI	2.70

Wins

B. Hutchison, CHI	42
K. Gleason, PHI	38
T. Lovett, BKN	30
A. Rusie, NY	29
B. Rhines, CIN	28

Saves

D. Foutz, BKN	2
K. Gleason, PHI	2
B. Hutchison, CHI	2

Strikeouts

A. Rusie, NY	345
B. Hutchison, CHI	289
K. Nichols, BOS	222
K. Gleason, PHI	222
A. Terry, BKN	185

Complete Games

B. Hutchison, CHI	65
A. Rusie, NY	56
K. Gleason, PHI	54
E. Beatin, CLE	53
K. Nichols, BOS	47

Fewest Hits per 9 Innings

A. Rusie, NY	7.15
B. Hutchison, CHI	7.54
B. Rhines, CIN	7.56

Shutouts

K. Nichols, BOS	7
B. Rhines, CIN	6
K. Gleason, PHI	6
B. Hutchison, CHI	5

Fewest Walks per 9 Innings

C. Young, CLE	1.83
J. Duryea, CIN	1.97
C. Getzien, BOS	2.11

Most Strikeouts per 9 Inn.

T. Mullane, CIN	7.51
A. Rusie, NY	5.59
K. Nichols, BOS	4.68

Innings

B. Hutchison, CHI	603
A. Rusie, NY	549
K. Gleason, PHI	506

Games Pitched

B. Hutchison, CHI	71
A. Rusie, NY	67
K. Gleason, PHI	60

	W	L	PCT	GB	R	OR	2B	3B	HR	BA	SA	SB	E	DP	FA	CG	BB	SO	ShO	SV	ERA
									Batting					**Fielding**				**Pitching**			
BKN	86	43	.667		**884**	620	184	75	43	.264	**.369**	349	320	92	.940	115	401	403	6	2	3.05
CHI	84	53	.613	6	847	692	146	59	**68**	.260	.356	329	344	89	.940	126	481	504	6	**3**	3.24
PHI	78	54	.591	9.5	823	707	**220**	78	23	**.269**	.364	334	398	122	.929	122	486	507	8	2	3.32
CIN	77	55	.583	10.5	753	633	150	**120**	28	.259	.361	312	382	106	.932	124	407	488	9	1	3.05
BOS	76	57	.571	12	763	**593**	175	62	31	.258	.341	285	359	77	.934	**132**	**354**	506	**13**	1	**2.93**
NY	63	68	.481	24	713	698	208	89	25	.259	.354	289	449	104	.921	115	607	**612**	6	1	3.06
CLE	44	88	.333	43.5	630	832	132	59	21	.232	.299	152	405	108	.929	129	462	306	2	0	4.13
PIT	23	113	.169	66.5	597	1235	160	43	20	.230	.294	208	607	94	.896	119	573	381	3	0	*5.97*
					6010	6010	1375	585	259	.254	.342	2258	3264	792	.927	982	3771	3707	53	10	*3.60*

American Association 1890

Lou.
W-88 L-44
Jack Chapman

POS	Player	AB	BA	HR	RBI	PO	A	E	DP	TC/G	FA	Pitcher	G	IP	W	L	SV	ERA
1B	H. Taylor	553	.306	0		1301	51	25	54	11.7	.982	S. Stratton	50	431	34	14	0	*2.36*
2B	T. Shinnick	493	.256	1		288	351	52	42	5.3	.925	R. Ehret	43	359	25	14	2	*2.53*
SS	P. Tomney	386	.277	1		180	406	64	31	6.0	.902	G. Meakim	28	192	12	7	1	*2.91*
3B	H. Raymond	521	.259	2		182	241	61	18	4.1	.874	H. Goodall	18	109	8	5	4	*3.39*
RF	C. Wolf	543	.363	4		199	16	14	5	1.9	.939							
CF	F. Weaver	557	.289	3		227	23	18	4	2.1	.933							
LF	C. Hamburg	485	.272	3		229	16	14	3	1.9	.946							
C	J. Ryan	337	.217	0		415	148	41	5	6.8	.932							
P	S. Stratton	189	.323	0		18	111	3	2	2.6	.977							
P	R. Ehret	146	.212	0		9	64	12	2	2.0	.859							

Col.
W-79 L-55
Al Buckenberger
W-42 L-42
Gus Schmelz
W-37 L-13

POS	Player	AB	BA	HR	RBI	PO	A	E	DP	TC/G	FA	Pitcher	G	IP	W	L	SV	ERA
1B	M. Lehane	512	.211	0		1430	73	27	80	10.9	.982	H. Gastright	48	401	30	14	0	*2.94*
2B	J. Crooks	485	.221	1		348	345	46	57	5.6	.938	F. Knauss	37	276	17	12	2	*2.81*
SS	H. Easterday	197	.157	0		82	202	39	20	5.6	.879	J. Easton	37	256	15	14	1	*3.52*
3B	C. Reilly	530	.266	4		205	354	67	26	4.6	.893	Chamberlain	25	175	12	6	0	*2.21*
RF	J. Sneed	484	.291	2		161	20	24	5	1.6	.883	W. Widner	13	96	4	8	0	*3.28*
CF	J. McTamany	466	.258	1		232	17	16	8	2.1	.940							
LF	S. Johnson	538	.346	1		164	12	14	1	1.4	.926							
C	J. O'Connor	457	.324	2		539	146	27	13	6.7	.962							
UT	J. Doyle	298	.268	2		231	153	54	14		.877							
SS	B. Wheelock	190	.237	1		92	162	33	12	5.5	.885							
P	H. Gastright	169	.213	0		12	55	5	2	1.5	.931							

St. L.
W-78 L-58
Tommy McCarthy
W-13 L-13
Chief Roseman
W-32 L-19
Count Campau
W-33 L-26

POS	Player	AB	BA	HR	RBI	PO	A	E	DP	TC/G	FA	Pitcher	G	IP	W	L	SV	ERA
1B	E. Cartwright	300	.300	8		706	25	18	37	10.0	.976	J. Stivetts	54	419	29	20	0	*3.52*
2B	B. Higgins	258	.252	0		168	204	19	34	5.8	.951	T. Ramsey	44	349	24	17	0	*3.69*
SS	S. Fuller	526	.278	1		222	389	91	39	5.4	.870	J. Hart	26	201	12	8	0	*3.67*
3B	P. Sweeney	190	.179	0		40	28	16	3	4.0	.810	B. Whitrock	16	105	5	6	1	*3.51*
RF	T. McCarthy	548	.350	6		159	19	21	5	2.0	.894							
CF	C. Duffee	378	.275	3		120	16	7	8	2.2	.951							
LF	C. Campau	314	.322	10		113	14	9	1	1.8	.934							
C	J. Munyan	342	.266	4		452	115	37	8	7.3	.939							
OF	C. Roseman	302	.341	2		61	7	15	2	1.4	.819							
OF	T. Gettinger	227	.238	3		62	8	9	1	1.4	.886							
P	J. Stivetts	226	.288	7		24	86	13	3	2.3	.894							
P	T. Ramsey	145	.228	0		12	31	16	2	1.3	.729							

Tol.
W-68 L-64
Charlie Morton

POS	Player	AB	BA	HR	RBI	PO	A	E	DP	TC/G	FA	Pitcher	G	IP	W	L	SV	ERA
1B	P. Werden	498	.295	6		1178	59	35	57	10.3	.972	E. Healy	46	389	22	21	0	*2.89*
2B	P. Nicholson	523	.268	4		294	385	52	45	5.5	.929	E. Cushman	40	316	17	21	1	*4.19*
SS	F. Scheibeck	485	.241	1		282	412	92	35	5.9	.883	F. Smith	35	286	19	13	0	*3.27*
3B	B. Alvord	495	.273	2		203	252	67	13	4.5	.872	C. Sprague	19	123	9	5	0	*3.89*
RF	E. Swartwood	462	.327	3		224	23	20	2	2.1	.925							
CF	W. Tebeau	381	.268	1		182	14	10	1	2.2	.951							
LF	B. Van Dyke	502	.257	2		172	17	16	0	1.9	.922							
C	H. Sage	275	.149	2		336	153	27	3	6.5	.948							
OP	C. Sprague	199	.236	1		60	18	8	1		.907							
P	E. Healy	156	.218	1		24	62	14	2	2.2	.860							

Roc.
W-63 L-63
Pat Powers

POS	Player	AB	BA	HR	RBI	PO	A	E	DP	TC/G	FA	Pitcher	G	IP	W	L	SV	ERA
1B	T. O'Brien	273	.190	0		675	20	21	40	10.5	.971	B. Barr	57	493	28	**24**	0	*3.25*
2B	B. Greenwood	437	.222	2		331	343	59	59	6.0	.920	W. Calihan	37	296	18	15	0	*3.28*
SS	M. Phillips	257	.206	0		101	222	29	24	5.5	.918	C. Titcomb	20	169	10	9	0	*3.74*
3B	J. Knowles	491	.281	5		162	303	63	19	4.3	.881	B. Miller	13	92	3	7	1	*4.29*
RF	T. Scheffler	445	.245	3		196	29	22	6	2.1	.911	J. Fitzgerald	11	78	3	8	0	*4.04*
CF	S. Griffin	407	.307	5		159	7	28	1	1.8	.856							
LF	H. Lyons	**584**	.260	3		264	25	25	4	2.4	.920							
C	D. McGuire	331	.299	4		389	99	32	9	**7.3**	.938							
C	D. McKeough	218	.225	0		186	76	20	4	6.0	.929							
P	B. Barr	201	.179	2		20	111	10	2	2.5	.929							
UT	J. Grim	192	.266	2		151	99	27	15		.903							
1B	J. Field	188	.202	4		486	12	18	24	10.1	.965							
P	W. Calihan	159	.145	1		14	71	9	6	2.5	.904							

POS	Player	AB	BA	HR	RBI	PO	A	E	DP	TC/G	FA	Pitcher	G	IP	W	L	SV	ERA
Syr.																		
1B	M. McQuery	461	.308	2		1146	45	34	63	10.0	.972	D. Casey	45	361	19	22	0	4.14
2B	C. Childs	493	.345	2		372	367	57	59	6.4	.928	J. Keefe	43	352	17	24	0	4.32
SS	McLaughlin	329	.264	2		120	258	41	22	4.9	.902	M. Morrison	17	127	6	9	0	5.88
3B	T. O'Rourke	332	.283	1		117	168	44	9	3.8	.866	E. Mars	16	121	9	5	0	4.67
RF	P. Friel	261	.249	3		77	7	8	2	1.5	.913							
CF	R. Wright	348	.305	0		170	15	19	7	2.3	.907							
LF	B. Ely	496	.262	0		179	14	18	1	2.7	.915							
C	G. Briggs	316	.180	0		200	71	21	6	6.3	.928							
P	D. Casey	160	.163	0		22	78	14	4	2.5	.877							
P	J. Keefe	157	.191	0		14	71	4	2	2.1	.955							
OF	H. Simon	156	.301	2		62	2	4	1	1.8	.941							
C	T. O'Rourke	153	.216	0		187	48	24	6	6.5	.907							
Phi.																		
1B	J. O'Brien	433	.261	4		1018	52	26	61	10.1	.976	S. McMahon	48*	410*	29*	18	1	3.34
2B	T. Shaffer	261	.172	0		214	195	35	39	6.4	.921	E. Green	25	191	7	15	1	5.80
SS	B. Conroy	404	.171	1		119	257	45	26	5.7	.893	E. Seward	21	154	6	12	0	4.73
3B	D. Lyons	339	.354	7		147	203	35	14	4.4	**.909**	D. Esper	18	144	8	9	0	4.89
RF	O. Shaffer	390	.282	1		143	17	7	6	1.7	**.958**	C. Stecher	10	68	0	10	0	0.32
CF	C. Welch	396	.268	2		225	23	22	8*	2.6*	.919							
LF	B. Purcell	463	.276	2		170	17	10	3	1.8	.949							
C	W. Robinson	329	.237	4		412	103	39	10*	6.8	.930							
UT	J. Kappel	208	.240	1		75	92	31	8		.843							
P	S. McMahon	175	.229	2		29*	112*	8	6*	3.1	.946							
Bkn.-Bal.																		
1B	B. O'Brien	388	.278	4		1015	35	29	66	11.2	.973	E. Daily	27	236	10	15	0	4.05
2B	J. Gerhardt	369	.203	3		359*	348*	47	67*	7.6*	.938*	McCullough	26	216	4	21	0	4.59
SS	C. Nelson	223	.251	0		60	198	40	20	5.2	.866	M. Mattimore	19	178	6	14	0	4.54
3B	J. Davis	142	.303	2		49	87	25	9	4.2	.845	L. German	17	132	5	11	0	4.83
RF	E. Daily	394	.239	1		107	17	15	3	2.2	.892	S. McMahon	12*	99*	7*	3	0	3.00
CF	J. Peltz	384	.227	1		207	18	24*	6	2.5	.904	C. Murphy	12	96	3	9	0	5.72
LF	H. Simon	373	.257	0		176	16	10	4	2.3	.950							
C	J. Toy	160	.181	0		148	86	36	4	6.1	.867							
UT	F. Bowes	232	.220	0		164	67	35	8		.868							
UT	H. Pitz	189	.138	0		161	100	45	11		.853							
SS	F. Fennelly	178	.247	2		70	135	34	8	6.3	.858							

Syr. W-55 L-72 George Frazer

Phi. W-54 L-78 Bill Sharsig

Bkn.-Bal. W-41 L-92 Jim Kennedy W-26 L-73 Billy Barnie W-15 L-19

BATTING AND BASE RUNNING LEADERS

Batting Average

C. Wolf, LOU	.363
D. Lyons, PHI	.354
T. McCarthy, STL	.350
S. Johnson, COL	.346
C. Childs, SYR	.345

Home Runs

C. Campau, STL	10
E. Cartwright, STL	8
J. Stivetts, STL	7
D. Lyons, PHI	7
P. Werden, TOL	6
T. McCarthy, STL	6

Runs Batted In

(not available)

Hits

C. Wolf, LOU	197
T. McCarthy, STL	192
S. Johnson, COL	186

Home Run Percentage

D. Lyons, PHI	2.1
S. Griffin, ROC	1.2
D. McGuire, ROC	1.2

Doubles

C. Childs, SYR	33
D. Lyons, PHI	29
C. Wolf, LOU	29

Slugging Average

D. Lyons, PHI	.531
C. Childs, SYR	.481
C. Wolf, LOU	.479
T. McCarthy, STL	.467
S. Johnson, COL	.461

Total Bases

C. Wolf, LOU	260
T. McCarthy, STL	256
S. Johnson, COL	248
C. Childs, SYR	237
P. Werden, TOL	227

Stolen Bases

T. McCarthy, STL	83
T. Scheffler, ROC	77
B. Van Dyke, TOL	73
C. Welch, B-B, PHI	72
E. Daily, B-B, LOU	62
T. Shinnick, LOU	62

Base on Balls

J. McTamany, COL	112
J. Crooks, COL	96
E. Swartwood, TOL	80

Runs Scored

J. McTamany, COL	140
T. McCarthy, STL	137
S. Fuller, STL	118

Triples

P. Werden, TOL	20
S. Johnson, COL	18
B. Alvord, TOL	16
J. Sneed, COL, TOL	15

PITCHING LEADERS

Winning Percentage

S. Stratton, LOU	.708
H. Gastright, COL	.682
Chamberlain, COL, STL	.682
R. Ehret, LOU	.641
S. McMahon, B-B, PHI	.632
G. Meakim, LOU	.632

Wins

S. McMahon, B-B, PHI	36
S. Stratton, LOU	34
H. Gastright, COL	30
J. Stivetts, STL	29
B. Barr, ROC	28

Strikeouts

S. McMahon, B-B, PHI	291
J. Stivetts, STL	289
T. Ramsey, STL	257
E. Healy, TOL	225
B. Barr, ROC	209

Fewest Hits per 9 Innings

F. Knauss, COL	6.73
H. Gastright, COL	7.00
J. Easton, COL	7.50

Fewest Walks per 9 Innings

S. Stratton, LOU	1.27
R. Ehret, LOU	1.98
T. Ramsey, STL	2.63

Innings

S. McMahon, B-B, PHI	509
B. Barr, ROC	493
S. Stratton, LOU	431

Earned Run Average

S. Stratton, LOU	2.36
R. Ehret, LOU	2.53
F. Knauss, COL	2.81
Chamberlain, COL, STL	2.83
E. Healy, TOL	2.89

Saves

H. Goodall, LOU	4
R. Ehret, LOU	2
F. Knauss, COL	2

Complete Games

S. McMahon, B-B, PHI	55
B. Barr, ROC	52
E. Healy, TOL	44
S. Stratton, LOU	44
H. Gastright, COL	41
J. Stivetts, STL	41

Shutouts

Chamberlain, COL, STL	6
R. Ehret, LOU	4
H. Gastright, COL	4
S. Stratton, LOU	4

Most Strikeouts per 9 Inn.

T. Ramsey, STL	6.63
J. Stivetts, STL	6.20
G. Meakim, LOU	5.77

Games Pitched

S. McMahon, B-B, PHI	60
B. Barr, ROC	57
J. Stivetts, STL	54

	W	L	PCT	GB	R	OR	2B	3B	Batting HR	BA	SA	SB	E	Fielding DP	FA	CG	BB	Pitching SO	ShO	SV	ERA
LOU	88	44	.667		819	**588**	156	65	15	**.279**	.350	341	**380**	79	**.933**	114	293	587	13	**7**	**2.58**
COL	79	55	.590	10	831	617	159	78	15	.258	.334	353	401	101	.931	120	471	624	**14**	3	2.99
STL	78	58	.574	12	**870**	736	178	72	**49**	.273	**.370**	307	478	93	.916	118	447	**733**	4	1	3.67
TOL	68	64	.515	20	739	689	152	**108**	24	.252	.348	**421**	419	75	.925	122	429	533	4	2	3.56
ROC	63	63	.500	22	709	711	131	64	31	.239	.316	310	416	95	.926	122	530	477	5	2	3.56
SYR	55	72	.433	30.5	698	831	151	59	14	.259	.329	292	391	90	.925	115	518	454	5	0	4.98
PHI	54	78	.409	34	702	945	**181**	51	24	.235	.314	305	452	93	.918	119	514	461	3	2	5.22
B-B	41	92	.308	47.5	674	925	150	62	16	.223	.292	283	522	**113**	.912	**132**	545	364	1	0	4.52
					6042	6042	1258	559	188	.253	.332	2612	3459	739	.923	962	3747	4233	49	17	3.86

Players' League 1890

	POS	Player	AB	BA	HR	RBI	PO	A	E	DP	TC/G	FA	Pitcher	G	IP	W	L	SV	ERA
Bos. W-81 L-48 King Kelly	1B	D. Brouthers	464	.345	1	97	1187	73	**49**	78	10.6	.963	O. Radbourn	41	343	27	12	0	3.31
	2B	J. Quinn	509	.301	7	82	431	395	51	70	6.7	**.942**	A. Gumbert	39	277	22	11	0	3.96
	SS	A. Irwin	354	.260	0	45	137	331	65	44	5.6	.878	B. Daley	34	235	18	8	2	3.60
	3B	B. Nash	488	.266	5	90	198	**307**	78	**37**	4.5	.866	M. Kilroy	30	218	10	15	0	4.26
	RF	H. Stovey	481	.297	11	83	186	24	18	3	1.9	.921							
	CF	T. Brown	543	.276	4	61	276	32	30	8	2.6	.911							
	LF	H. Richardson	555	.326	11	**143**	235	13	13	3	2.1	.950							
	C	M. Murphy	246	.228	2	32	257	59	34	8	5.2	.903							
	UT	K. Kelly	340	.326	4	66	274	145	55	12		.884							
	P	O. Radbourn	154	.253	0	16	16	99	8	4	3.0	.935							
	P	A. Gumbert	145	.241	3	20	15	83	13	0	2.8	.883							
Bkn. W-76 L-56 Monte Ward	1B	D. Orr	464	.373	6	124	1009	42	30	67	10.1	.972	G. Weyhing	49	390	30	16	0	3.60
	2B	L. Bierbauer	589	.306	7	99	372	**468**	62	**77**	6.8	.931	J. Sowders	39	309	19	16	0	3.82
	SS	M. Ward	561	.369	4	60	**303**	450	105	59	**6.7**	.878	Van Haltren	28	223	15	10	2	4.28
	3B	B. Joyce	489	.252	1	78	176	284	**107**	22	4.3	.811	C. Murphy	20	139	4	10	2	4.79
	RF	J. McGeachy	443	.244	1	65	206	16	23	1	2.4	.906	G. Hemming	19	123	8	4	3*	3.80
	CF	E. Andrews	395	.253	3	38	220	17	23	3	2.8	.912							
	LF	E. Seery	394	.223	1	50	216	21	28	3	2.5	.894							
	C	T. Kinslow	242	.264	4	46	298	72	37	7	6.4	.909							
	OP	Van Haltren	376	.335	5	54	138	84	21	6		.914							
	C1	P. Cook	218	.252	0	31	319	57	30	20		.926							
	C	C. Daily	168	.250	0	35	141	34	24	5	5.0	.879							
	P	G. Weyhing	165	.164	1	15	12	55	12	2	1.6	.848							
	P	J. Sowders	132	.189	1	20	7	75	7	1	2.3	.921							
N. Y. W-74 L-57 Buck Ewing	1B	R. Connor	484	.372	13	103	**1335**	80	21	79	11.7	**.985**	C. Crane	43	330	16	18	0	4.63
	2B	D. Shannon	324	.216	3	44	162	262	43	35	6.1	.908	H. O'Day	43	329	23	15	3	4.21
	SS	D. Richardson	528	.256	4	80	153	263	46	33	6.8	.900	J. Ewing	35	267	18	12	2	4.24
	3B	A. Whitney	442	.219	0	45	129	172	47	11	4.0	.865	T. Keefe	30	229	17	11	0	3.38
	RF	J. O'Rourke	478	.360	9	115	175	25	15	3	1.9	.930							
	CF	G. Gore	399	.318	10	55	146	11	22	3	1.9	.877							
	LF	M. Slattery	411	.307	5	67	175	5	19	1	2.1	.905							
	C	B. Ewing	352	.338	8	72	372	107	26	7	6.2	**.949**							
	OF	D. Johnston	306	.242	1	43	164	18	21	3	2.7	.897							
	3S	G. Hatfield	287	.279	1	37	79	156	54	13		.813							
	UT	W. Brown	230	.278	4	43	241	49	26	5		.918							
	CO	F. Vaughn	166	.265	1	22	112	21	18	3		.881							
	P	H. O'Day	150	.227	1	23	11	71	7	0	2.1	.921							
	P	C. Crane	146	.315	0	16	17	71	16	0	2.4	.846							
Chi. W-75 L-62 Charlie Comiskey	1B	C. Comiskey	377	.244	0	59	882	41	33	52	10.9	.965	M. Baldwin	**59**	**501**	**32**	24	0	3.31
	2B	F. Pfeffer	499	.257	5	80	441	387	**76**	73	**7.3**	.916	S. King	56	461	**32**	22	0	**2.69**
	SS	C. Bastian	283	.191	0	29	85	202	39	24	5.1	.880	C. Bartson	25	188	8	10	1	4.26
	3B	N. Williamson	261	.195	1	26	53	91	34	6	3.4	.809	F. Dwyer	12	69	3	6	1	6.23
	RF	H. Duffy	**596**	.326	7	82	255	34	26	5	2.3	.917							
	CF	J. Ryan	486	.340	6	89	257	25	25	5	2.6	.919							
	LF	T. O'Neill	577	.302	3	75	231	8	19	1	1.9	.926							
	C	D. Farrell	451	.290	2	84	428	132	43	12	**6.7**	.929							
	UT	J. Boyle	369	.260	1	49	335	154	61	16		.889							
	UT	D. Darling	221	.258	2	39	296	72	37	24		.909							
	P	M. Baldwin	215	.209	1	25	26	**146**	15	2	3.2	.920							
	3B	A. Latham	214	.229	1	20	65	119	25	9	4.0	.880							
	P	S. King	185	.168	1	16	22	139	6	**5**	3.0	.964							

	POS	Player	AB	BA	HR	RBI	PO	A	E	DP	TC/G	FA	Pitcher	G	IP	W	L	SV	ERA
Phi.	1B	S. Farrar	481	.254	1	69	1238	58	36	**79**	10.5	.973	B. Sanders	43	347	20	17	1	3.76
W-68 L-63	2B	J. Pickett	407	.280	4	64	236	284	62	46	5.8	.893	P. Knell	35	287	22	11	0	3.83
Ben Hilt	SS	B. Shindle	584	.322	10	90	266	442	119	67	6.4	.856	C. Buffinton	36	283	19	14	1	3.81
W-17 L-19	3B	J. Mulvey	519	.287	6	87	144	227	62	15	3.6	.857	B. Husted	18	129	5	12	0	4.88
Jim Fogarty	RF	J. Fogarty	347	.239	4	58	192	17	8	3	2.4	**.963**	B. Cunningham	14	109	3	9	0	5.22
W-30 L-19	CF	M. Griffin	492	.291	6	54	278	33	15	10	2.8	.954							
Charlie Buffinton	LF	G. Wood	539	.289	9	102	254	**35**	34	9	2.4	.895							
W-21 L-25	C	J. Milligan	234	.295	3	57	260	66	39	**13**	6.2	.893							
	UT	B. Hallman	356	.267	1	37	194	103	36	15		.892							
	C	L. Cross	245	.298	3	47	191	70	34	7	6.0	.885							
	P	B. Sanders	189	.312	0	30	17	93	9	5*	2.8	.924							
	P	C. Buffinton	150	.273	1	24	12	77	14	5	2.9	.864							
Pit.	1B	J. Beckley	516	.324	10	120	1256	58	32	61	11.1	.976	H. Staley	46	388	21	25	0	3.23
W-60 L-68	2B	Y. Robinson	306	.229	0	38	226	286	65	46	5.9	.887	A. Maul	30	247	16	12	0	3.79
Ned Hanlon	SS	T. Corcoran	505	.240	1	61	210	431	84	36	5.9	.884	P. Galvin	26	217	12	13	0	4.35
	3B	W. Kuehne	528	.239	5	73	159	304	82	18	4.3	.850	E. Morris	18	144	8	7	0	4.86
	RF	J. Visner	521	.265	3	71	198	18	26	4	1.9	.893	J. Tener	14	117	3	11	0	7.31
	CF	N. Hanlon	472	.278	1	44	291	15	30	4	2.8	.911							
	LF	J. Fields	526	.283	9	86	153	21	24	3	2.5	.879							
	C	F. Carroll	416	.298	2	71	206	50	43	1	5.3	.856							
	C	T. Quinn	207	.213	1	15	203	58	33	3	5.3	.888							
	P	H. Staley	164	.207	1	25	11	86	6	**5**	2.2	.942							
	PO	A. Maul	162	.259	0	21	49	83	15	5		.898							
Cle.	1B	H. Larkin	506	.332	5	112	1268	40	30	63	10.7	.978	H. Gruber	48	383	21	23	1	4.27
W-55 L-75	2B	C. Stricker	544	.244	2	65	295	353	68	57	6.6	.905	J. Bakely	43	326	13	25	0	4.47
Jay Faatz	SS	E. Delahanty	517	.298	3	64	143	244	79	33	6.1	.830	D. O'Brien	25	206	8	16	0	3.40
W-10 L-25	3B	P. Tebeau	450	.300	5	74	**204**	246	66	25	**4.7**	**.872**	W. McGill	24	184	11	9	0	4.12
Henry Larkin	RF	H. Radford	466	.292	2	62	137	16	18	5	2.1	.895							
W-27 L-33	CF	J. McAleer	341	.267	1	42	249	15	17	4	**3.3**	.940							
Patsy Tebeau	LF	P. Browning	493	**.387**	5	93	248	18	32	4	2.5	.893							
W-18 L-17	C	S. Sutcliffe	386	.329	2	60	264	115	**50**	9	5.1	.883							
	OF	L. Twitchell	233	.223	2	36	61	8	15	1	1.5	.821							
	C3	J. Brennan	233	.253	0	26	147	73	42	7		.840							
	P	H. Gruber	163	.221	0	9	8	109	14	3	2.7	.893							
	OF	J. Carney	89	.348	0	21	21	3	4	0	1.5	.857							
Buf.	1B	D. White	439	.260	0	47	582	40	19	33	11.2	.970	G. Haddock	35	291	9	**26**	0	5.76
W-36 L-96	2B	S. Wise	505	.293	6	102	328	375	73	58	6.5	.906	B. Cunningham	25	211	9	15	0	5.84
Jack Rowe	SS	J. Rowe	504	.250	2	76	228	381	67	56	5.4	.901	G. Keefe	25	196	6	16	0	6.52
	3B	J. Irwin	308	.234	0	34	79	139	29	13	3.9	.883	L. Twitchell	12	104	5	7	0	4.57
	RF	J. Halligan	211	.251	3	33	73	11	18	1	2.4	.824	B. Stafford	12	98	3	9	0	5.14
	CF	D. Hoy	493	.298	1	53	289	23	30	9	2.8	.912							
	LF	E. Beecher	536	.297	3	90	211	24	**55**	4	2.3	.810							
	C	C. Mack	503	.266	0	53	**449**	140	48	**13**	5.7	.925							
	UT	S. Clark	260	.265	1	25	168	63	19	14		.924							
	OP	L. Twitchell	172	.221	2	17	49	37	7	1		.925							
	UT	J. Rainey	166	.235	1	20	72	42	17	8		.870							
	P	G. Haddock	146	.247	0	24	20	86	8	2	3.3	.930							

BATTING AND BASE RUNNING LEADERS

Batting Average

P. Browning, CLE	.387
D. Orr, BKN	.373
R. Connor, NY	.372
M. Ward, BKN	.369
J. O'Rourke, NY	.360

Home Runs

R. Connor, NY	13
H. Stovey, BOS	11
H. Richardson, BOS	11
G. Gore, NY	10
J. Beckley, PIT	10
B. Shindle, PHI	10

Runs Batted In

H. Richardson, BOS	143
D. Orr, BKN	124
J. Beckley, PIT	120
J. O'Rourke, NY	115
H. Larkin, CLE	112

Hits

M. Ward, BKN	207
H. Duffy, CHI	194
P. Browning, CLE	191

Slugging Average

R. Connor, NY	.566
J. Beckley, PIT	.541
D. Orr, BKN	.537
P. Browning, CLE	.531
J. O'Rourke, NY	.515

Total Bases

H. Duffy, CHI	283
B. Shindle, PHI	281
J. Beckley, PIT	279
R. Connor, NY	274
H. Richardson, BOS	268

Stolen Bases

H. Stovey, BOS	97
H. Duffy, CHI	79
T. Brown, BOS	79
N. Hanlon, PIT	65
M. Ward, BKN	63

Base on Balls

B. Joyce, BKN	123
Y. Robinson, PIT	101
D. Brouthers, BOS	99

PITCHING LEADERS

Winning Percentage

O. Radbourn, BOS	.692
B. Daley, BOS	.692
A. Gumbert, BOS	.667
P. Knell, PHI	.667
G. Weyhing, BKN	.652

Wins

S. King, CHI	32
M. Baldwin, CHI	32
G. Weyhing, BKN	30
O. Radbourn, BOS	27
H. O'Day, NY	23

Strikeouts

M. Baldwin, CHI	211
S. King, CHI	185
G. Weyhing, BKN	177
J. Ewing, NY	145
H. Staley, PIT	145

Fewest Hits per 9 Innings

S. King, CHI	8.20
C. Crane, NY	8.80
G. Hemming, BKN, CLE	8.87

Earned Run Average

S. King, CHI	2.69
H. Staley, PIT	3.23
M. Baldwin, CHI	3.31
O. Radbourn, BOS	3.31
T. Keefe, NY	3.38

Saves

G. Hemming, BKN, CLE	3
H. O'Day, NY	3
B. Daley, BOS	2
J. Ewing, NY	2
C. Murphy, BKN	2
Van Haltren, BKN	2

Complete Games

M. Baldwin, CHI	54
S. King, CHI	48
H. Staley, PIT	44
H. Gruber, CLE	39
G. Weyhing, BKN	38

Shutouts

S. King, CHI	4
H. Staley, PIT	3
G. Weyhing, BKN	3

BATTING AND BASE RUNNING LEADERS

Home Run Percentage
R. Connor, NY	2.7
G. Gore, NY	2.5
H. Stovey, BOS	2.3

Runs Scored
H. Duffy, CHI	161
T. Brown, BOS	146
H. Stovey, BOS	142

Doubles
P. Browning, CLE	40
J. Beckley, PIT	38
J. O'Rourke, NY	37

Triples
J. Beckley, PIT	22
J. Visner, PIT	22
B. Shindle, PHI	21

PITCHING LEADERS

Fewest Walks per 9 Innings
H. Staley, PIT	1.72
B. Sanders, PHI	1.79
P. Galvin, PIT	2.03

Most Strikeouts per 9 Inn.
J. Ewing, NY	4.88
B. Daley, BOS	4.21
G. Weyhing, BKN	4.08

Innings
M. Baldwin, CHI	501
S. King, CHI	461
G. Weyhing, BKN	390

Games Pitched
M. Baldwin, CHI	59
S. King, CHI	56
G. Weyhing, BKN	49

	W	L	PCT	GB	R	OR	2B	3B	HR	BA	SA	SB	E	DP	FA	CG	BB	SO	ShO	SV	ERA
							Batting						Fielding					Pitching			
BOS	81	48	.628		992	767	223	77	51	.282	.397	412	460	109	.918	105	467	345	6	2	3.79
BKN	76	56	.576	6.5	964	893	186	93	34	.277	.374	272	531	114	.909	111	570	377	4	7	3.95
NY	74	57	.565	8	1018	875	204	97	64	.284	.404	231	450	94	.921	111	569	449	3	6	4.17
CHI	75	62	.547	10	886	770	200	96	30	.264	.361	276	492	107	.918	124	503	460	5	2	3.39
PHI	68	63	.519	14	941	855	187	113	49	.278	.393	203	510	118	.910	118	495	361	4	2	4.05
PIT	60	68	.469	20.5	835	892	168	113	36	.260	.370	249	512	80	.907	121	334	318	7	0	4.22
CLE	55	75	.423	26.5	849	1027	213	94	27	.286	.386	180	533	103	.907	115	571	325	1	1	4.23
BUF	36	96	.273	46.5	793	1199	180	64	20	.260	.337	160	491	116	.914	125	673	351	2	0	6.11
					7278	7278	1561	747	311	.274	.378	1983	3979	841	.913	930	4182	2986	32	20	4.23

National League 1891

	POS	Player	AB	BA	HR	RBI	PO	A	E	DP	TC/G	FA	Pitcher	G	IP	W	L	SV	ERA
Bos. W-87 L-51 Frank Selee	1B	T. Tucker	548	.270	2	69	1313	55	34	66	10.0	.976	J. Clarkson	55	461	33	19	3	2.79
	2B	J. Quinn	508	.240	3	63	275	364	42	44	5.5	.938	K. Nichols	52	426	30	17	3	2.39
	SS	H. Long	577	.288	10	74	345	444	85	60	6.3	.902	H. Staley	31	252	20	8	0	2.50
	3B	B. Nash	537	.276	5	95	213	264	53	20	3.8	.900							
	RF	H. Stovey	544	.279	16	95	232	22	25	4	2.1	.910							
	CF	S. Brodie	523	.260	2	78	268	25	15	9	2.3	.951							
	LF	B. Lowe	497	.260	6	74	186	16	16	2	2.0	.927							
	C	C. Bennett	256	.215	5	39	383	75	19	10	6.4	.960							
	C	C. Ganzel	263	.259	1	29	288	59	16	3	6.2	.956							
	P	J. Clarkson	187	.225	0	26	27	114	13	2	2.8	.916							
	P	K. Nichols	183	.197	0	27	30	100	7	5	2.6	.949							
Chi. W-82 L-53 Cap Anson	1B	C. Anson	540	.291	8	120	1407	79	29	86	11.1	.981	B. Hutchison	66	561	43	19	1	2.81
	2B	F. Pfeffer	498	.247	7	77	429	474	77	78	7.2	.921	A. Gumbert	32	256	17	11	0	3.58
	SS	J. Cooney	465	.245	0	42	145	433	52	39	5.3	.917	P. Luby	30	206	8	11	1	4.76
	3B	B. Dahlen	551	.263	9	76	120	211	42	13	4.4	.887	E. Stein	14	101	7	6	0	3.74
	RF	C. Carroll	515	.256	7	80	168	15	17	5	1.5	.915	T. Vickery	14	80	5	5	0	4.07
	CF	J. Ryan	505	.287	9	66	231	25	27	3	2.4	.905							
	LF	W. Wilmot	498	.279	11	71	223	15	20	0	2.1	.922							
	C	M. Kittredge	296	.209	2	27	384	87	30	5	6.3	.940							
	P	B. Hutchison	243	.185	2	25	22	103	13	0	2.1	.906							
	3B	T. Burns	243	.226	1	17	92	107	24	11	4.2	.892							
	P	P. Luby	98	.245	2	24	8	42	2	2	1.7	.962							
	C	P. Schriver	90	.333	1	21	135	27	6	3	6.2	.964							
N. Y. W-71 L-61 Jim Mutrie	1B	R. Connor	479	.290	6	94	1362	56	25	77	11.2	.983	A. Rusie	61	500	33	20	1	2.55
	2B	D. Richardson	516	.269	5	51	323	429	38	60	6.9	.952	J. Ewing	33	269	21	8	0	2.27
	SS	J. Glasscock	369	.241	0	55	164	274	42	39	4.9	.913	M. Welch	22	160	6	9	1	4.28
	3B	C. Bassett	524	.260	4	68	143	270	42	18	3.8	.908	J. Sharrott	10	69	4	5	1	2.60
	RF	M. Tiernan	542	.306	17	73	138	16	17	4	1.3	.901							
	CF	G. Gore	528	.284	2	48	234	16	25	3	2.1	.909							
	LF	J. O'Rourke	555	.295	5	95	195	18	22	1	1.9	.906							
	C	D. Buckley	253	.217	4	31	446	83	23	7	7.5	.958							
	UT	L. Whistler	265	.245	4	38	143	128	49	11		.847							
	P	A. Rusie	220	.245	0	15	10	106	14	4	2.1	.892							
	C	A. Clarke	174	.190	0	21	189	50	22	6	6.2	.916							
Phi. W-68 L-69 Harry Wright	1B	W. Brown	441	.243	0	50	997	48	12	60	10.9	.989	K. Gleason	53	418	24	22	1	3.51
	2B	A. Myers	514	.230	2	69	354	438	53	67	6.3	.937	D. Esper	39	296	20	15	1	3.56
	SS	B. Allen	438	.221	1	51	258	426	79	50	6.5	.896	J. Thornton	37	269	15	16	2	3.68
	3B	B. Shindle	415	.210	0	38	153	248	58	24	4.4	.874	T. Keefe	11	78	3	6	1	3.91
	RF	S. Thompson	554	.294	8	90	234	32	18	6	2.1	.937							
	CF	E. Delahanty	543	.243	4	86	199	22	22	3	2.5	.909							
	LF	B. Hamilton	527	.340	2	60	287	17	31	7	2.5	.907							
	C	J. Clements	423	.310	4	75	415	108	41	10	5.3	.927							
	UT	E. Mayer	268	.187	0	31	100	105	29	4		.876							
	P	K. Gleason	214	.248	0	17	22	73	11	2	2.0	.896							

	POS	Player	AB	BA	HR	RBI	PO	A	E	DP	TC/G	FA	Pitcher	G	IP	W	L	SV	ERA
Cle.	1B	J. Virtue	517	.261	2	72	**1465**	44	**44**	70	11.2	.972	C. Young	55	424	27	20	2	2.85
	2B	C. Childs	551	.281	2	83	371	455	**82**	54	6.4	.910	H. Gruber	44	349	17	22	0	4.13
W-65 L-74	SS	E. McKean	603	.282	6	69	248	463	**91**	42	5.7	.887	L. Viau	45	344	18	17	0	3.01
Bob Leadley	3B	P. Tebeau	249	.261	1	41	102	150	33	13	4.7	.884							
W-31 L-34	RF	S. Johnson	327	.257	1	46	99	10	16	1	1.6	.872							
Patsy Tebeau	CF	G. Davis	571	.292	1	89	257	27	21	1	2.6	.931							
W-34 L-40	LF	J. McAleer	565	.237	2	61	284	19	25	1	2.4	.924							
	C	C. Zimmer	440	.255	3	69	**476**	**181**	45	7	6.1	.936							
	UT	J. Doyle	250	.276	0	43	178	73	38	5		.869							
	P	C. Young	174	.167	1	18	10	89	9	0	2.0	.917							
	OF	J. Burkett	167	.269	0	13	53	5	7	1	1.5	.892							
	P	L. Viau	144	.160	0	6	12	79	**14**	2	2.3	.867							
	P	H. Gruber	141	.163	1	20	8	90	10	**5**	2.5	.907							
	3B	J. Denny	138	.225	0	21	39	60	13	1	3.9	.884							
Bkn.	1B	D. Foutz	521	.257	2	73	1235	47	31	50	10.6	.976	T. Lovett	44	366	23	19	0	3.69
	2B	H. Collins	435	.276	3	31	180	222	40	19	6.1	.910	B. Caruthers	38	297	18	14	1	3.12
W-61 L-76	SS	M. Ward	441	.277	0	39	180	296	66	28	6.2	.878	G. Hemming	27	200	8	15	1	4.96
Monte Ward	3B	G. Pinckney	501	.273	2	71	146	261	43	10	3.5	.904	A. Terry	25	194	6	16	1	4.22
	RF	O. Burns	470	.285	4	83	173	16	16	5	1.8	.922	B. Inks	13	96	3	10	0	4.02
	CF	M. Griffin	521	.271	3	65	**353**	31	16	7	**3.0**	**.960**							
	LF	D. O'Brien	395	.253	5	57	203	11	11	1	2.2	.951							
	C	T. Kinslow	228	.237	0	33	252	54	26	6	5.4	.922							
	C	C. Daily	206	.320	0	30	230	65	24	2	5.8	.925							
	UT	T. Daly	200	.250	2	27	289	58	38	8		.901							
	PO	B. Caruthers	171	.281	2	23	29	68	10	2		.907							
	2B	J. O'Brien	167	.246	0	26	85	102	32	13	5.1	.854							
	P	T. Lovett	153	.163	0	17	23	59	6	2	2.0	.932							
Cin.	1B	L. Reilly	546	.242	4	64	1104	26	21	60	**11.5**	.982	T. Mullane	51	426	24	25	0	3.23
	2B	B. McPhee	562	.256	6	38	389	**492**	42	72	6.7	**.954**	B. Rhines	48	373	17	24	1	2.87
W-56 L-81	SS	G. Smith	512	.201	3	53	240	**507**	75	40	6.0	.909	O. Radbourn	26	218	12	12	0	4.25
Tom Loftus	3B	A. Latham	533	.272	7	53	177	**370**	75	**24**	4.6	.879	C. Crane	15	117	4	8	0	4.09
	RF	L. Marr	286	.259	0	32	75	6	16	2	1.3	.835	J. Duryea	10	77	1	9	0	5.38
	CF	B. Holliday	442	.319	9	84	186	13	13	3	1.9	.939							
	LF	P. Browning	216	.343	0	33	103	6	9	2	2.1	.924							
	C	J. Harrington	333	.228	2	41	388	106	**50**	6	5.9	.908							
	1C	J. Keenan	252	.202	4	33	587	51	30	22		.955							
	OF	J. Halligan	247	.312	3	44	89	6	16	1	1.8	.856							
	P	T. Mullane	209	.148	0	10	22	93	5	2	2.4	.958							
	OF	M. Slattery	158	.209	1	16	91	4	6	1	2.5	.941							
	P	B. Rhines	148	.122	0	5	8	95	7	3	2.3	.936							
Pit.	1B	J. Beckley	554	.292	4	73	1250	**87**	24	63	10.2	.982	M. Baldwin	53	438	22	28	0	2.76
	2B	L. Bierbauer	500	.206	1	47	331	384	55	42	6.4	.929	S. King	48	384	14	**29**	1	3.11
W-55 L-80	SS	F. Shugart	320	.275	2	33	172	235	44	34	6.0	.902	P. Galvin	33	247	14	13	0	2.88
Ned Hanlon	3B	C. Reilly	415	.219	3	44	128	232	60	8	4.2	.857							
W-31 L-47	RF	F. Carroll	353	.218	4	48	160	12	16	2	2.1	.915							
Bill McGunnigle	CF	N. Hanlon	455	.266	0	60	219	25	**33**	1	2.3	.881							
W-24 L-33	LF	P. Browning	203	.291	4	28	115	8	13	0	2.7	.904							
	C	C. Mack	280	.214	0	29	359	79	35	1	6.6	.926							
	UT	D. Miller	548	.285	4	57	339	238	80	13		.878							
	P	M. Baldwin	177	.153	1	12	**37**	80	13	4	2.5	.900							
	OF	A. Maul	149	.188	0	14	58	7	9	2	1.9	.878							
	P	S. King	148	.169	0	9	19	67	10	**5**	2.0	.896							
	OF	P. Corkhill	145	.228	3	20	77	9	6	3	2.2	.935							
	OF	B. Lally	143	.224	1	17	45	2	9	0	1.4	.839							

BATTING AND BASE RUNNING LEADERS

Batting Average

B. Hamilton, PHI	.340
B. Holliday, CIN	.319
P. Browning, CIN, PIT	.317
J. Clements, PHI	.310
M. Tiernan, NY	.306

Slugging Average

M. Tiernan, NY	.500
H. Stovey, BOS	.498
B. Holliday, CIN	.473
J. Ryan, CHI	.444
R. Connor, NY	.443

Home Runs

M. Tiernan, NY	17
H. Stovey, BOS	16
W. Wilmot, CHI	11
H. Long, BOS	10

Total Bases

M. Tiernan, NY	271
H. Stovey, BOS	271
H. Long, BOS	241
G. Davis, CLE	235
J. Beckley, PIT	234

Runs Batted In

C. Anson, CHI	120
B. Nash, BOS	95
H. Stovey, BOS	95
J. O'Rourke, NY	95
R. Connor, NY	94

Stolen Bases

B. Hamilton, PHI	115
A. Latham, CIN	87
M. Griffin, BKN	65
H. Long, BOS	60
M. Ward, BKN	57
H. Stovey, BOS	57

PITCHING LEADERS

Winning Percentage

J. Ewing, NY	.724
B. Hutchison, CHI	.694
H. Staley, BOS, PIT	.649
K. Nichols, BOS	.638
J. Clarkson, BOS	.635

Earned Run Average

J. Ewing, NY	2.27
K. Nichols, BOS	2.39
A. Rusie, NY	2.55
H. Staley, BOS, PIT	2.58
M. Baldwin, PIT	2.76

Wins

B. Hutchison, CHI	43
J. Clarkson, BOS	33
A. Rusie, NY	33
K. Nichols, BOS	30
C. Young, CLE	27

Saves

J. Clarkson, BOS	3
K. Nichols, BOS	3
C. Young, CLE	2
J. Thornton, PHI	2

Strikeouts

A. Rusie, NY	337
B. Hutchison, CHI	261
K. Nichols, BOS	240
M. Baldwin, PIT	197
S. King, PIT	160

Complete Games

B. Hutchison, CHI	56
A. Rusie, NY	52
M. Baldwin, PIT	48
J. Clarkson, BOS	47
K. Nichols, BOS	45

BATTING AND BASE RUNNING LEADERS

Hits		Base on Balls		Fewest Hits per 9 Innings		Shutouts	
B. Hamilton, PHI	179	B. Hamilton, PHI	102	A. Rusie, NY	7.03	A. Rusie, NY	6
E. McKean, CLE	170	C. Childs, CLE	97	M. Baldwin, PIT	7.92	J. Ewing, NY	5
G. Davis, CLE	167	R. Connor, NY	83	J. Ewing, NY	7.92	K. Nichols, BOS	5
						B. Hutchison, CHI	4

PITCHING LEADERS

Home Run Percentage		Runs Scored		Fewest Walks per 9 Innings		Most Strikeouts per 9 Inn.	
M. Tiernan, NY	3.1	B. Hamilton, PHI	141	K. Nichols, BOS	2.18	A. Rusie, NY	6.06
H. Stovey, BOS	2.9	H. Long, BOS	129	H. Staley, BOS, PIT	2.22	K. Nichols, BOS	5.07
W. Wilmot, CHI	2.2	C. Childs, CLE	120	P. Galvin, PIT	2.26	J. Ewing, NY	4.61

Doubles		Triples		Innings		Games Pitched	
M. Griffin, BKN	36	J. Beckley, PIT	20	B. Hutchison, CHI	561	B. Hutchison, CHI	66
G. Davis, CLE	35	H. Stovey, BOS	20	A. Rusie, NY	500	A. Rusie, NY	61
H. Stovey, BOS	31	B. McPhee, CIN	16	J. Clarkson, BOS	461	J. Clarkson, BOS	55
						C. Young, CLE	55

	W	L	PCT	GB	R	OR	2B	3B	Batting HR	BA	SA	SB	E	Fielding DP	FA	CG	BB	Pitching SO	ShO	SV	ERA
BOS	87	51	.630		847	658	181	82	51	.255	.356	289	358	96	.938	126	364	525	9	6	2.76
CHI	82	53	.607	3.5	832	730	159	87	61	.253	.359	238	397	119	.932	114	475	477	6	3	3.47
NY	71	61	.538	13	754	711	189	72	48	.263	.362	224	384	104	.933	117	593	651	11	3	2.99
PHI	68	69	.496	18.5	756	773	180	51	21	.252	.322	232	443	108	.925	105	505	343	3	5	3.73
CLE	65	74	.468	22.5	835	888	183	87	23	.255	.339	242	485	86	.920	118	476	400	1	3	3.50
BKN	61	76	.445	25.5	765	820	200	69	23	.260	.345	337	432	73	.924	121	459	407	8	3	3.86
CIN	56	81	.409	30.5	646	790	148	90	40	.242	.335	244	409	101	.931	125	465	393	6	1	3.55
PIT	55	80	.407	30.5	679	744	148	71	28	.239	.317	205	475	76	.917	122	465	446	7	2	2.89
					6114	6114	1388	609	295	.252	.342	2011	3383	763	.928	948	3802	3642	51	26	3.34

American Association 1891

	POS	Player	AB	BA	HR	RBI	PO	A	E	DP	TC/G	FA	Pitcher	G	IP	W	L	SV	ERA
Bos. W-93 L-42 Arthur Irwin	1B	D. Brouthers	486	.350	5	108	1313	34	30	82	10.6	.978	G. Haddock	51	380	34	11	1	2.49
	2B	C. Stricker	514	.216	0	46	405	418	51	78	6.3	.942	C. Buffinton	48	364	28	9	3	2.55
	SS	P. Radford	456	.259	0	65	230	453	71	51	5.8	.906	D. O'Brien	40	269	19	13	1	3.65
	3B	D. Farrell	473	.302	12	110	87	160	22	8	4.1	.918	B. Daley	19	127	8	6	2	2.98
	RF	H. Duffy	536	.336	8	108	166	23	17	3	1.7	.917							
	CF	T. Brown	589	.321	5	71	228	23	35	7	2.1	.878							
	LF	H. Richardson	278	.255	7	51	101	5	5	2	1.9	.955							
	C	M. Murphy	402	.216	4	54	532	118	31	8	6.5	.954							
	3B	B. Joyce	243	.309	3	51	82	149	41	12	4.3	.849							
	P	G. Haddock	185	.243	3	23	21	116	12	2	2.9	.919							
	P	C. Buffinton	181	.188	1	16	10	117	9	3	2.8	.934							
	OF	J. McGeachy	178	.253	1	21	57	4	6	0	1.6	.910							
St. L. W-86 L-52 Charlie Comiskey	1B	C. Comiskey	580	.262	3	93	1433	62	31	78	10.8	.980	J. Stivetts	64	440	33	22	1	2.86
	2B	B. Eagan	302	.215	4	43	177	278	35	29	5.9	.929	W. McGill	35	249	18	10	1	2.93
	SS	S. Fuller	586	.217	2	63	168	309	80	36	5.4	.856	C. Griffith	27	186	14	6	0	3.33
	3B	D. Lyons	451	.315	11	84	151	246	59	16	3.8	.871	J. Neal	15	110	8	4	1	4.24
	RF	T. McCarthy	578	.310	8	95	164	24	22	5	1.9	.895	G. Rettger	14	93	7	3	1	3.40
	CF	D. Hoy	567	.291	5	66	255	26	28	3	2.2	.909							
	LF	T. O'Neill	521	.321	10	95	197	5	14	0	1.7	.935							
	C	J. Boyle	439	.280	5	79	428	88	35	11	6.1	.936							
	P	J. Stivetts	302	.305	7	54	22	110	15	2	2.3	.898							
	UT	J. Munyan	182	.231	0	20	207	55	25	4		.913							
Bal. W-72 L-63 Billy Barnie W-68 L-61 George Van Haltren W-4 L-2	1B	P. Werden	552	.290	6	104	1422	58	30	79	10.9	.980	S. McMahon	61	503	34	25	1	2.81
	2B	S. Wise	388	.247	1	48	225	299	66	30	6.0	.888	B. Cunningham	30	238	11	14	0	4.01
	SS	I. Ray	418	.278	0	58	71	103	28	9	5.1	.861	K. Madden	32	224	13	12	1	4.10
	3B	P. Gilbert	513	.230	3	72	201	324	84	34	4.4	.862	E. Healy	23	170	9	10	0	3.75
	RF	B. Johnson	480	.271	2	79	235	28	37	5	2.3	.877							
	CF	C. Welch	514	.268	3	55	258	25	16	4	2.6	.946							
	LF	Van Haltren	566	.318	9	83	143	21	22	7	2.3	.882							
	C	W. Robinson	334	.216	2	46	415	80	24	11	5.6	.954							
	P	S. McMahon	210	.205	1	15	14	141	11	4	2.7	.934							
	C	G. Townsend	204	.191	0	18	191	68	26	5	4.9	.909							

POS	Player	AB	BA	HR	RBI	PO	A	E	DP	TC/G	FA	Pitcher	G	IP	W	L	SV	ERA
Phi. W-73 L-66 Bill Sharsig W-15 L-17 George Wood W-54 L-46 Billy Barnie W-4 L-3																		
1B	H. Larkin	526	.279	10	93	987	33	27	56	9.4	.974	G. Weyhing	52	450	31	20	0	3.18
2B	B. Hallman	587	.283	6	69	327	399	55	53	5.5	.930	Chamberlain	49	406	22	23	0	4.22
SS	T. Corcoran	511	.254	7	71	300	434	72	5	6.1	.911	B. Sanders	19	145	11	5	0	3.79
3B	J. Mulvey	453	.254	5	66	172	241	49	18	4.1	.894	W. Calihan	13	112	6	6	0	6.43
RF	J. McGeachy	201	.229	2	13	82	10	8	0	2.0	.920							
CF	P. Corkhill	349	.209	0	31	182	14	9	3	2.5	.956							
LF	G. Wood	528	.309	3	61	221	25	16	10	2.1	.939							
C	J. Milligan	455	.303	11	106	470	101	37	9	7.0	.939							
UT	L. Cross	402	.301	5	52	297	103	28	12		.935							
OF	J. McTamany	218	.225	3	21	118	10	14	1	2.4	.901							
P	G. Weyhing	198	.111	0	11	27	73	8	2	2.1	.926							
P	Chamberlain	176	.188	2	19	20	89	10	2	2.4	.916							
OP	B. Sanders	156	.250	1	19	32	31	8	1		.887							
Cin-Mil. W-64 L-72 King Kelly W-43 L-57 Charlie Cushman W-21 L-15																		
1B	J. Carney	477	.283	6	66	1308	65	33	58	10.8	.977	F. Dwyer	45	375	19	23	0	3.98
2B	Y. Robinson	342	.178	1	37	222	287	78*	33	6.1	.867	C. Crane	32	250	14	14	0	2.45
SS	J. Canavan	568	.238	10	87	231	339	93	32	5.9	.860	W. Mains	32	214	12	14	0	3.07
3B	A. Whitney	347	.199	3	33	129	198	35	12	3.9	.903*	G. Davies	12	102	7	5	0	2.65
RF	E. Seery	372	.285	4	36	160	17	20	3	2.0	.898	F. Killen	11	97	7	4	0	1.68
CF	D. Johnston	376	.221	6	51	193	20	25	4	2.4	.895							
LF	E. Andrews	356	.211	0	26	173	25	8	4	2.5	.961							
C	K. Kelly	283	.297	1	53	214	99	33	10	5.3	.905							
C	F. Vaughn	274	.285	1	23	273	77	29	11	5.9	.923							
P	F. Dwyer	181	.271	0	20	22	94	11	1	2.8	.913							
OF	E. Burke	144	.236	1	21	70	8	7	3	2.4	.918							
OF	A. Dalrymple	135	.311	1	22	44	6	5	1	1.7	.909							
Col. W-61 L-76 Gus Schmelz																		
1B	M. Lehane	511	.215	1	52	1362	71	28	98	10.7	.981	P. Knell	58	462	28	27	0	2.92
2B	J. Crooks	519	.245	0	46	399	404	36	72	6.1	.957	H. Gastright	35	284	12	19	0	3.78
SS	B. Wheelock	498	.229	0	39	248	474	81	65	5.9	.899	J. Dolan	27	203	12	11	0	4.16
3B	W. Kuehne	261	.215	2	22	85	146	30	15	3.8	.885	J. Easton	20	150	5	12	0	4.43
RF	J. Sneed	366	.257	1	61	142	10	18	4	1.7	.894							
CF	J. McTamany	304	.250	3	35	161	10	13	4	2.3	.929							
LF	C. Duffee	552	.301	10	90	235	33	21	7	2.3	.927							
C	J. Donahue	280	.218	0	35	343	108	28	11	6.4	.942							
OC	J. O'Connor	229	.266	0	37	135	37	11	5		.940							
OF	L. Twitchell	224	.277	2	35	67	4	9	0	1.4	.888							
P	P. Knell	215	.158	0	19	40	119	10	1	2.9	.941							
C	T. Dowse	201	.224	0	22	254	52	27	6	6.5	.919							
Lou. W-55 L-84 Jack Chapman																		
1B	H. Taylor	356	.295	2	37	927	45	21	56	10.8	.979	J. Fitzgerald	33	276	14	18	0	3.59
2B	T. Shinnick	443	.221	1	54	226	332	52	45	5.1	.915	J. Meekin	29	228	10	16	0	4.30
SS	H. Jennings	360	.292	1	58	187	225	49	28	6.6	.894	R. Ehret	26	221	13	13	0	3.47
3B	O. Beard	257	.241	0	24	84	149	32	16	4.3	.879	S. Stratton	20	172	6	13	0	4.08
RF	C. Wolf	537	.253	1	82	185	28	19	5	1.7	.918	J. Doran	15	126	5	10	0	5.43
CF	F. Weaver	565	.283	1	55	294	33	15	7	2.6	.956	E. Daily	15	111	4	8	0	5.74
LF	P. Donovan	439	.321	2	53	214	15	22	0	2.4	.912							
C	J. Ryan	253	.225	2	25	223	83	23	10	5.9	.930							
UT	T. Cahill	433	.256	3	47	389	242	69	32		.901							
3B	W. Kuehne	159	.277	1	18	56	95	16	8	4.1	.904							
C	P. Cook	153	.229	0	23	120	39	16	0	5.0	.909							
Was. W-43 L-92 Sam Trott W-4 L-8 Pop Snyder W-23 L-46 Dan Shannon W-12 L-25 Sandy Griffin W-4 L-13																		
1B	M. McQuery	261	.241	2	37	701	30	17	39	11.0	.977	K. Carsey	54	415	14	37	0	4.99
2B	T. Dowd	464	.259	1	44	230	287	67	38	5.5	.885	F. Foreman	43	345	18	21	1	3.73
SS	G. Hatfield	500	.256	1	48	211	334	82	40	6.0	.869	J. Bakely	13	104	2	10	0	5.35
3B	B. Alvord	312	.234	0	30	147	210	57	10	5.1	.862							
RF	L. Murphy	400	.265	1	35	164	10	25	3	2.0	.874							
CF	P. Hines	206	.282	0	31	81	8	15	4	2.2	.856							
LF	E. Beecher	235	.243	2	28	109	13	26	4	2.6	.824							
C	D. McGuire	413	.303	3	66	442	130	56	8	6.4	.911							
1B	A. McCauley	206	.282	1	31	541	22	18	27	9.8	.969							
OC	S. Sutcliffe	201	.353	2	33	115	36	15	4		.910							
P	K. Carsey	187	.150	0	15	22	120	12	5	2.9	.922							
P	F. Foreman	153	.222	4	19	13	66	4	4	1.9	.952							

BATTING AND BASE RUNNING LEADERS

Batting Average

D. Brouthers, BOS	.350
H. Duffy, BOS	.336
T. Brown, BOS	.321
T. O'Neill, STL	.321
Van Haltren, BAL	.318

Slugging Average

D. Brouthers, BOS	.512
J. Milligan, PHI	.505
D. Farrell, BOS	.474
T. Brown, BOS	.469
L. Cross, PHI	.458

Home Runs

D. Farrell, BOS	12
D. Lyons, STL	11
J. Milligan, PHI	11

Total Bases

T. Brown, BOS	276
Van Haltren, BAL	251
D. Brouthers, BOS	249
H. Duffy, BOS	240
T. McCarthy, STL	236

PITCHING LEADERS

Winning Percentage

C. Buffinton, BOS	.757
G. Haddock, BOS	.756
C. Griffith, BOS, STL	.708
G. Weyhing, PHI	.608
J. Stivetts, STL	.600

Earned Run Average

C. Crane, C-M	2.45
G. Haddock, BOS	2.49
C. Buffinton, BOS	2.55
G. Davies, C-M	2.65
S. McMahon, BAL	2.81

Wins

S. McMahon, BAL	34
G. Haddock, BOS	34
J. Stivetts, STL	33
G. Weyhing, PHI	31
C. Buffinton, BOS	28
P. Knell. COL	28

Saves

C. Buffinton, BOS	3
B. Daley, BOS	2

BATTING AND BASE RUNNING LEADERS

Runs Batted In
D. Farrell, BOS	110
D. Brouthers, BOS	108
H. Duffy, BOS	108
J. Milligan, PHI	106
P. Werden, BAL	104

Stolen Bases
T. Brown, BOS	106
H. Duffy, BOS	85
Van Haltren, BAL	75
D. Hoy, STL	59
P. Radford, BOS	55

PITCHING LEADERS

Strikeouts
J. Stivetts, STL	259
P. Knell, COL	228
G. Weyhing, PHI	219
S. McMahon, BAL	219
Chamberlain, PHI	204

Complete Games
S. McMahon, BAL	53
G. Weyhing, PHI	51
P. Knell, COL	47
K. Carsey, WAS	46
Chamberlain, PHI	44

Hits
T. Brown, BOS	189
H. Duffy, BOS	180
Van Haltren, BAL	180

Base on Balls
D. Hoy, STL	119
J. Crooks, COL	103
J. McTamany, COL, PHI	101

Fewest Hits per 9 Innings
P. Knell, COL	7.07
J. Stivetts, STL	7.30
C. Buffinton, BOS	7.50

Shutouts
G. Haddock, BOS	5
P. Knell, COL	5
S. McMahon, BAL	5

Home Run Percentage
D. Farrell, BOS	2.5
D. Lyons, STL	2.4
J. Milligan, PHI	2.4

Runs Scored
T. Brown, BOS	177
Van Haltren, BAL	136
D. Hoy, STL	136

Fewest Walks per 9 Innings
S. Stratton, LOU	1.78
B. Sanders, PHI	2.30
S. McMahon, BAL	2.67

Most Strikeouts per 9 Inn.
J. Meekin, LOU	5.68
G. Davies, C-M	5.38
J. Stivetts, STL	5.30

Doubles
J. Milligan, PHI	35
T. Brown, BOS	30
T. O'Neill, STL	28
C. Duffee, COL	28

Triples
T. Brown, BOS	21
D. Brouthers, BOS	19
P. Werden, BAL	18
J. Canavan, C-M	18

Innings
S. McMahon, BAL	503
P. Knell, COL	462
G. Weyhing, PHI	450

Games Pitched
J. Stivetts, STL	64
S. McMahon, BAL	61
P. Knell, COL	58

	W	L	PCT	GB	R	OR	2B	3B	HR	BA	SA	SB	E	DP	FA	CG	BB	SO	ShO	SV	ERA
BOS	93	42	.689		1028	675	163	100	51	**.274**	**.380**	447	392	115	.934	108	497	524	9	8	3.03
STL	86	52	.623	8.5	976	753	169	51	58	.266	.355	283	468	91	.920	103	576	621	8	5	3.27
BAL	72	63	.533	21	850	798	142	99	30	.255	.345	342	503	103	.915	118	472	408	6	2	3.43
PHI	73	66	.525	22	817	794	**182**	**123**	55	.258	.376	149	389	109	.933	**135**	520	533	3	0	4.01
C-M	64	72	.471	29.5	776	799	163	73	40	.241	.330	211	505	88	.915	121	566	468	5	1	3.19
COL	61	76	.445	33	702	777	154	61	20	.237	.308	280	379	126	**.935**	118	588	502	6	0	3.75
LOU	55	84	.396	40	713	890	130	69	17	.258	.324	230	458	113	.922	128	**464**	485	9	1	4.27
WAS	43	92	.319	50	691	1067	147	84	19	.251	.330	219	589	95	.900	123	566	486	2	2	4.83
					6553	6553	1250	660	290	.255	.344	2161	3683	840	.922	954	4249	4027	48	19	3.72

National League 1892

	POS	Player	AB	BA	HR	RBI	PO	A	E	DP	TC/G	FA	Pitcher	G	IP	W	L	SV	ERA
Bos. W-102 L-48 Frank Selee	1B	T. Tucker	542	.282	1	62	1484	51	45	96	10.6	.972	K. Nichols	53	454	35	16	0	2.83
	2B	J. Quinn	532	.218	1	59	356	426	40	75	5.7	.951	J. Stivetts	53	415	35	16	1	3.04
	SS	H. Long	647	.286	6	77	297	497	99	65	6.3	.889	H. Staley	37	300	22	10	0	3.03
	3B	B. Nash	526	.260	4	95	197	351	62	23	4.5	.898	J. Clarkson	16	146	8	6	0	2.35
	RF	T. McCarthy	603	.242	4	63	219	29	33	4	1.8	.883							
	CF	H. Duffy	612	.301	5	81	259	17	17	4	2.0	.942							
	LF	B. Lowe	475	.242	3	57	175	17	15	2	2.3	.928							
	C	K. Kelly	281	.189	2	41	319	98	40	11	6.3	.912							
	P	J. Stivetts	240	.296	3	36	17	96	12	5	2.4	.904							
	C	C. Ganzel	198	.268	0	25	202	50	18	1	5.3	.933							
	P	K. Nichols	197	.198	2	21	25	88	4	4	2.2	.966							
Cle. W-93 L-56 Patsy Tebeau	1B	J. Virtue	557	.282	2	89	1500	61	26	61	10.8	.984	C. Young	53	453	36	11	0	**1.93**
	2B	C. Childs	558	.317	3	53	357	441	53	51	5.9	.938	N. Cuppy	47	376	28	13	1	2.51
	SS	E. McKean	531	.262	0	93	207	369	92	29	5.2	.862	J. Clarkson	29	243	17	10	1	2.55
	3B	G. Davis	597	.253	5	82	100	166	25	8	3.7	.914	G. Davies	26	216	10	16	0	2.59
	RF	J. O'Connor	572	.248	1	58	152	21	12	4	1.7	.935							
	CF	J. McAleer	571	.238	4	70	367	25	16	2	7.1	.961							
	LF	J. Burkett	608	.275	6	66	271	20	31	7	2.2	.904							
	C	C. Zimmer	413	.262	1	64	514	122	42	11	6.1	.938							
	3B	P. Tebeau	340	.244	2	49	99	156	25	17	3.8	.911							
	P	C. Young	196	.158	1	15	19	122	8	**7**	2.8	.946							
	P	N. Cuppy	168	.214	0	24	10	103	6	3	2.5	.950							
Bkn. W-95 L-59 Monte Ward	1B	D. Brouthers	588	**.335**	5	**124**	1498	105	29	69	10.7	.982	G. Haddock	46	381	29	13	1	3.14
	2B	M. Ward	614	.265	2	47	377	472	**74**	48	6.2	.920	E. Stein	48	377	27	16	1	2.84
	SS	T. Corcoran	615	.237	1	74	291	495	64	49	5.6	.925	D. Foutz	27	203	13	8	1	3.41
	3B	B. Joyce	372	.245	6	45	141	164	49	8	3.8	.862	B. Hart	28	195	9	12	1	3.28
	RF	O. Burns	542	.315	4	96	162	16	12	4	1.5	.937	B. Kennedy	26	191	13	9	1	3.86
	CF	M. Griffin	459	.277	3	66	267	25	4	7	2.3	**.986**							
	LF	D. O'Brien	490	.243	1	56	222	16	11	3	2.0	.956							
	C	C. Daily	278	.234	0	28	342	85	26	9	6.7	.943							
	UT	T. Daly	446	.256	4	51	260	170	33	16		.929							
	C	T. Kinslow	246	.305	2	40	355	89	32	6	7.2	.933							
	OP	D. Foutz	220	.186	1	26	50	60	14	2		.887							
	P	G. Haddock	158	.177	0	11	21	80	11	5	2.4	.902							

Phi.
W-87 L-66
Harry Wright

POS	Player	AB	BA	HR	RBI	PO	A	E	DP	TC/G	FA	Pitcher	G	IP	W	L	SV	ERA
1B	R. Connor	564	.294	12	73	1483	59	23	99	10.1	.985	G. Weyhing	59	470	32	21	3	2.66
2B	B. Hallman	586	.292	2	84	335	379	49	60	5.5	.936	K. Carsey	43	318	19	16	1	3.12
SS	B. Allen	563	.227	2	64	331	537	77	67	6.2	.919	T. Keefe	39	313	20	16	0	2.36
3B	C. Reilly	331	.196	1	24	106	169	29	13	4.3	.905	D. Esper	21	160	12	6	1	3.42
RF	S. Thompson	609	.305	9	104	223	28	17	7	1.8	.937	P. Knell	11	80	5	5	0	4.05
CF	E. Delahanty	477	.306	6	91	261	25	17	6	2.5	.944							
LF	B. Hamilton	554	.330	3	53	291	26	28	7	2.5	.919							
C	J. Clements	402	.264	8	76	557	107	35	12	6.4	.950							
UT	L. Cross	541	.275	4	69	327	236	35	17		.941							
P	G. Weyhing	214	.136	0	13	20	63	20	2	1.7	.806							

Cin.
W-82 L-68
Charlie Comiskey

POS	Player	AB	BA	HR	RBI	PO	A	E	DP	TC/G	FA	Pitcher	G	IP	W	L	SV	ERA
1B	C. Comiskey	551	.227	3	71	1469	73	25	103	11.1	.984	Chamberlain	52	406	19	23	0	3.39
2B	B. McPhee	573	.291	4	60	451	471	51	86	6.8	.948	T. Mullane	37	295	21	10	1	2.59
SS	G. Smith	506	.239	8	63	239	561	70	55	6.3	.920	F. Dwyer	33	259	19	10	1	2.33
3B	A. Latham	622	.238	0	44	167	329	66	26	4.0	.883	M. Sullivan	21	166	12	4	0	3.08
RF	B. Holliday	602	.292	13	91	271	20	21	6	2.1	.933	B. Rhines	12	84	4	7	0	5.06
CF	P. Browning	307	.303	3	52	152	13	15	0	2.2	.917							
LF	T. O'Neill	419	.251	2	52	188	13	17	3	2.0	.922							
C	M. Murphy	234	.197	2	24	315	67	18	6	5.4	.955							
UT	F. Vaughn	346	.254	2	50	394	80	33	22		.935							
P	Chamberlain	160	.225	2	15	16	67	9	0	1.8	.902							

Pit.
W-80 L-73
Tom Burns
W-25 L-30
Al Buckenberger
W-55 L-43

POS	Player	AB	BA	HR	RBI	PO	A	E	DP	TC/G	FA	Pitcher	G	IP	W	L	SV	ERA
1B	J. Beckley	614	.236	10	96	1523	132	38	88	11.2	.978	M. Baldwin	56	440	26	27	0	3.47
2B	L. Bierbauer	649	.236	8	65	385	555	49	66	6.5	.950	R. Ehret	39	316	16	20	0	2.65
SS	F. Shugart	554	.267	0	62	303	466	99	43	6.5	.886	A. Terry	30	240	17	7	1	2.51
3B	D. Farrell	605	.215	8	77	180	286	64	20	4.0	.879	E. Smith	17	134	6	7	0	3.63
RF	P. Donovan	388	.294	2	26	111	18	19	4	1.6	.872	P. Galvin	12	96	5	6	0	2.63
CF	J. Kelley	205	.239	0	28	101	13	10	4	2.2	.919							
LF	E. Smith	511	.274	4	63	223	15	31	0	2.2	.885							
C	C. Mack	346	.243	1	31	404	143	28	11	6.3	.951							
UT	D. Miller	623	.254	2	59	413	145	44	22		.927							
OF	P. Corkhill	256	.184	0	25	148	13	8	4	2.5	.953							
P	M. Baldwin	178	.101	1	13	37	86	18	2	2.5	.872							

Chi.
W-70 L-76
Cap Anson

POS	Player	AB	BA	HR	RBI	PO	A	E	DP	TC/G	FA	Pitcher	G	IP	W	L	SV	ERA
1B	C. Anson	559	.272	1	74	1491	67	44	62	11.0	.973	B. Hutchison	75	627	37	34	0	2.74
2B	J. Canavan	439	.166	0	32	282	349	53	40	6.1	.923	A. Gumbert	46	383	22	19	0	3.41
SS	B. Dahlen	587	.295	5	58	178	232	41	29	6.3	.909	P. Luby	31	247	10	17	1	3.13
3B	J. Parrott	335	.215	2	22	115	164	34	7	4.0	.891							
RF	S. Dungan	433	.284	0	53	183	8	20	2	1.9	.905							
CF	J. Ryan	505	.293	10	65	241	26	23	5	2.4	.921							
LF	W. Wilmot	380	.216	2	35	197	8	22	0	2.5	.903							
C	P. Schriver	326	.224	1	34	367	102	36	5	6.2	.929							
OF	G. Decker	291	.227	1	28	73	12	12	3	1.6	.876							
P	B. Hutchison	263	.217	1	22	21	156	13	4	2.5	.932							
SS	J. Cooney	238	.172	0	20	101	211	30	15	5.3	.912							
C	M. Kittredge	229	.179	0	10	359	87	26	5	6.8	.945							
P	A. Gumbert	178	.236	1	8	10	97	9	1	2.5	.922							
PO	P. Luby	163	.190	2	20	28	62	9	3		.909							

N. Y.
W-71 L-80
Pat Powers

POS	Player	AB	BA	HR	RBI	PO	A	E	DP	TC/G	FA	Pitcher	G	IP	W	L	SV	ERA
1B	B. Ewing	393	.310	7	76	669	49	19	35	10.1	.974	A. Rusie	64	532	32	28	0	2.88
2B	E. Burke	363	.259	6	41	149	181	55	19	6.5	.857	S. King	52	419	22	24	0	3.24
SS	S. Fuller	508	.226	1	48	294	434	92	44	5.8	.888	C. Crane	47	364	16	24	1	3.80
3B	D. Lyons	389	.257	8	51	152	206	53	13	3.8	.871							
RF	M. Tiernan	450	.287	5	66	155	15	19	2	1.6	.899							
CF	H. Lyons	411	.238	0	57	186	16	20	1	2.3	.910							
LF	J. O'Rourke	448	.304	0	56	146	11	15	1	1.5	.913							
C	J. Boyle	436	.183	0	32	418	126	46	9	7.5	.922							
UT	J. Doyle	366	.298	5	55	231	154	60	13		.865							
P	A. Rusie	252	.210	1	26	27	132	21	5	2.8	.883							
UT	H. Richardson	248	.214	2	34	218	136	24	16		.937							
OF	G. Gore	193	.254	0	11	102	8	8	2	2.2	.932							
P	S. King	167	.210	2	23	22	81	11	4	2.2	.904							
P	C. Crane	163	.245	0	14	27	69	22	4	2.5	.814							
1B	J. McMahon	147	.224	1	24	312	13	9	13	9.3	.973							

Lou.
W-63 L-89
Jack Chapman
W-23 L-35
Fred Pfeffer
W-40 L-54

POS	Player	AB	BA	HR	RBI	PO	A	E	DP	TC/G	FA	Pitcher	G	IP	W	L	SV	ERA
1B	L. Whistler	285	.235	5	34	773	32	18	52	11.4*	.978	S. Stratton	42	352	21	19	0	2.92
2B	F. Pfeffer	470	.257	2	76	313	377	50	72	6.4	.932	B. Sanders	31	268	12	19	0	3.22
SS	H. Jennings	594	.222	2	61	343	537	90	59	6.4	.907	F. Clausen	24	200	9	13	0	3.06
3B	W. Kuehne	287	.167	0	36	104	160	38	16	4.0	.874	J. Meekin	19	156	7	10	0	4.03
RF	E. Seery	154	.201	0	15	65	10	3	1	1.9	.964	A. Jones	18	147	5	11	0	3.31
CF	T. Brown	660	.227	2	45	351	37	34	8	2.8	.919	L. Viau	16	131	4	11	0	3.99
LF	F. Weaver	551	.254	0	57	185	18	22	3	1.8	.902							
C	J. Grim	370	.243	1	36	262	85	22	7	5.3	.940							
UT	H. Taylor	493	.260	0	34	498	74	29	29		.952							
3B	C. Bassett	313	.214	2	35	76	179	41	13	4.1	.861							
PO	S. Stratton	219	.256	0	23	35	91	14	4		.900							
UT	B. Sanders	198	.273	3	18	172	61	12	7		.951							
C	B. Merritt	168	.196	1	13	175	58	15	6	5.4	.940							

	POS	Player	AB	BA	HR	RBI	PO	A	E	DP	TC/G	FA	Pitcher	G	IP	W	L	SV	ERA
Was.	1B	H. Larkin	464	.280	8	96	1121	69	38	77	10.5	.969	F. Killen	60	460	29	26	0	3.31
W-58 L-93	2B	T. Dowd	584	.243	1	50	208	264	58	33	5.4	.891	B. Abbey	27	196	5	18	1	3.45
Billy Barnie	SS	D. Richardson	551	.240	3	58	225	355	43	45	6.7	.931	P. Knell	22	170	9	13	0	3.65
W-13 L-21	3B	Y. Robinson	218	.179	0	19	70	125	34	11	3.9	.852	J. Duryea	18	127	3	10	2	2.41
Arthur Irwin	CF	D. Hoy	593	.280	3	75	275	16	38	3	2.2	.884	J. Meekin	14	112	3	10	0	3.46
W-34 L-46	LF	C. Duffee	492	.248	6	51	230	34	25	8	2.3	.913							
Danny Richardson	C	D. McGuire	315	.232	4	43	381	100	33	8	5.8	.936							
W-11 L-26	C1	J. Milligan	323	.276	5	43	522	99	24	22		.963							
	OF	L. Twitchell	192	.219	0	20	73	5	9	1	1.8	.897							
	P	F. Killen	186	.199	4	23	20	121	22	2	2.7	.865							
	OF	P. Donovan	163	.239	0	12	56	9	12	3	1.9	.844							
St. L.	1B	P. Werden	598	.258	8	84	1467	102	28	81	10.7	.982	K. Gleason	47	400	16	24	0	3.33
W-56 L-94	2B	J. Crooks	445	.213	7	38	286	300	44	43	6.2	.930	Breitenstein	39	282	14	20	0	4.69
Chris Von Der Ahe	SS	J. Glasscock	566	.267	3	72	280	472	69	46	5.9	.916	P. Hawley	20	166	6	14	0	3.19
	3B	G. Pinckney	290	.172	0	25	84	161	31	12	3.5	.888	C. Getzien	13	108	5	8	0	5.67
	RF	B. Caruthers	513	.277	3	69	159	14	21	2	1.6	.892	B. Caruthers	16	102	2	8	1	5.84
	CF	S. Brodie	602	.252	4	60	296	21	19	4	2.5	.943	P. Galvin	12	92	5	7	0	3.23
	LF	C. Carroll	407	.273	4	49	181	19	22	1	2.2	.901	F. Dwyer	10	64	2	8	0	5.63
	C	D. Buckley	410	.227	5	52	513	123	43	14	5.7	.937							
	UT	K. Gleason	233	.215	3	25													
	OF	G. Moriarity	177	.175	3	19	96	9	23	0	2.7	.820							
Bal.	1B	S. Sutcliffe	276	.279	1	27	678	24	31	39	11.1	.958	S. McMahon	48	397	20	25	0	3.24
W-46 L-101	2B	C. Stricker	269	.264	3	37	212	224	39	31	6.3	.918	G. Cobb	53	394	10	37	0	4.86
George Van Haltren	SS	T. O'Rourke	239	.310	0	35	104	180	43	17	5.0	.869	T. Vickery	24	176	8	10	0	3.53
W-1 L-14	3B	B. Shindle	619	.252	3	50	200	382	78	27	4.9	.882	C. Buffinton	13	97	5	8	0	4.92
John Waltz	RF	Van Haltren	556	.302	7	57	217	27	43*	5	2.2	.850							
W-0 L-2	CF	C. Welch	237	.236	1	22	129	4	14	1	2.3	.905							
Ned Hanlon	LF	H. Stovey	283	.272	2	55	109	6	11	2	2.0	.913							
W-45 L-85	C	W. Robinson	330	.267	2	57	332	86	36	8	5.2	.921							
	C	J. Gunson	314	.213	0	32	281	92	32	3	6.0	.921							
	SS	G. Shoch	308	.276	1	50	96	197	43	17	5.9	.872							
	UT	J. McGraw	286	.269	1	26	165	144	28	16		.917							
	1B	L. Whistler	209	.225	2	21	540	26	16	21	11.4*	.973							
	OF	P. Ward	186	.290	1	33	53	13	8	4	1.7	.892							
	UT	J. Halligan	178	.270	2	43	220	13	19	10		.925							
	P	S. McMahon	177	.141	0	18	7	94	12	2	2.4	.894							
	P	G. Cobb	172	.209	1	13	12	96	14	0	2.3	.885							

BATTING AND BASE RUNNING LEADERS

Batting Average
D. Brouthers, BKN	.335
B. Hamilton, PHI	.330
C. Childs, CLE	.317
O. Burns, BKN	.315
B. Ewing, NY	.310

Slugging Average
E. Delahanty, PHI	.495
D. Brouthers, BKN	.480
B. Ewing, NY	.466
R. Connor, PHI	.463
O. Burns, BKN	.454

Home Runs
B. Holliday, CIN	13
R. Connor, PHI	12
J. Ryan, CHI	10
J. Beckley, PIT	10
S. Thompson, PHI	9

Total Bases
D. Brouthers, BKN	282
B. Holliday, CIN	270
S. Thompson, PHI	263
R. Connor, PHI	261
H. Duffy, BOS	251

Runs Batted In
D. Brouthers, BKN	124
S. Thompson, PHI	104
H. Larkin, WAS	96
O. Burns, BKN	96
J. Beckley, PIT	96

Stolen Bases
M. Ward, BKN	88
T. Brown, LOU	78
A. Latham, CIN	66
H. Duffy, BOS	61
B. Dahlen, CHI	60
D. Hoy, WAS	60

Hits
D. Brouthers, BKN	197
S. Thompson, PHI	186
H. Long, BOS	185

Base on Balls
J. Crooks, STL	136
C. Childs, CLE	117
R. Connor, PHI	116
T. McCarthy, BOS	93

Home Run Percentage
B. Holliday, CIN	2.2
R. Connor, PHI	2.1
D. Lyons, NY	2.1

Runs Scored
C. Childs, CLE	136
B. Hamilton, PHI	132
H. Duffy, BOS	125

Doubles
R. Connor, PHI	37
H. Long, BOS	33
E. Delahanty, PHI	30
D. Brouthers, BKN	30

Triples
E. Delahanty, PHI	21
J. Virtue, CLE	20
D. Brouthers, BKN	20

PITCHING LEADERS

Winning Percentage
C. Young, CLE	.766
G. Haddock, BKN	.690
H. Staley, BOS	.688
K. Nichols, BOS	.686
J. Stivetts, BOS	.686

Earned Run Average
C. Young, CLE	1.93
T. Keefe, PHI	2.36
J. Clarkson, BOS, CLE	2.48
N. Cuppy, CLE	2.51
A. Terry, BAL, PIT	2.57

Wins
B. Hutchison, CHI	37
C. Young, CLE	36
K. Nichols, BOS	35
J. Stivetts, BOS	35
G. Weyhing, PHI	32
A. Rusie, NY	32

Saves
G. Weyhing, PHI	3
J. Duryea, CIN, WAS	2

Strikeouts
B. Hutchison, CHI	316
A. Rusie, NY	303
G. Weyhing, PHI	202
E. Stein, BKN	190
K. Nichols, BOS	187

Complete Games
B. Hutchison, CHI	67
A. Rusie, NY	58
K. Nichols, BOS	50
C. Young, CLE	48

Fewest Hits per 9 Innings
T. Mullane, CIN	6.77
A. Rusie, NY	6.85
A. Terry, BAL, PIT	6.94

Shutouts
C. Young, CLE	9
E. Stein, BKN	6
G. Weyhing, PHI	6

Fewest Walks per 9 Innings
S. Stratton, LOU	1.79
F. Dwyer, CIN, STL	2.03
B. Sanders, LOU	2.08

Most Strikeouts per 9 Inn.
B. Kennedy, BKN	5.09
A. Rusie, NY	4.87
B. Hutchison, CHI	4.54

Innings
B. Hutchison, CHI	627
A. Rusie, NY	532
G. Weyhing, PHI	470

Games Pitched
B. Hutchison, CHI	75
A. Rusie, NY	64
F. Killen, WAS	60

	W	L	PCT	GB	R	OR	Batting					SB	Fielding			Pitching					
							2B	3B	HR	BA	SA		E	DP	FA	CG	BB	SO	ShO	SV	ERA
BOS	102	48	.680		862	649	203	51	34	.250	.327	338	454	128	.929	143	460	509	15	1	2.86
CLE	93	56	.624	8.5	855	**613**	196	96	26	.254	.340	225	407	95	.935	140	472	**413**	11	2	**2.41**
BKN	95	59	.617	9	**935**	733	183	105	30	.262	.350	**409**	398	98	**.940**	132	600	597	12	5	3.25
PHI	87	66	.569	16.5	860	690	**225**	95	50	.262	.367	216	**393**	128	.939	131	492	502	10	5	2.93
CIN	82	68	.547	20	766	731	155	75	44	.241	.322	270	402	**140**	.939	131	535	437	8	2	3.17
PIT	80	73	.523	23.5	802	796	143	108	38	.236	.322	222	483	113	.927	130	537	455	3	1	3.10
CHI	70	76	.479	30	635	735	149	92	26	.235	.316	233	424	85	.932	133	424	518	6	1	3.16
NY	71	80	.470	31.5	811	826	173	85	38	.251	.337	301	565	97	.912	139	635	**641**	5	1	3.29
LOU	63	89	.414	40	649	804	133	61	18	.226	.284	275	471	133	.928	**147**	447	430	9	0	3.34
WAS	58	93	.384	44.5	731	869	148	78	38	.239	.320	276	547	122	.916	129	556	479	5	3	3.46
STL	56	94	.373	46	703	922	138	53	45	.226	.298	209	452	100	.929	139	543	478	4	1	4.20
BAL	46	101	.313	54.5	779	1020	160	**111**	30	.254	.343	227	584	100	.910	131	536	437	2	1	4.28
					9388	9388	2006	1010	417	.245	.327	3201	5580	1339	.928	1625	6178	5955	90	23	3.28

First Half	W	L	PCT	GB		Second Half	W	L	PCT	GB
BOS*	52	22	.702			CLE	53	23	.697	
BKN	51	26	.662	2.5		BOS	50	26	.658	3
PHI	46	30	.605	7		BKN	44	33	.571	9.5
CIN	44	31	.587	8.5		PIT	43	34	.558	10.5
CLE	40	33	.548	11.5		PHI	41	36	.532	12.5
PIT	37	39	.487	16		NY	40	37	.519	13.5
WAS	35	41	.461	18		CHI	39	37	.513	14
CHI	31	39	.443	21		CIN	38	37	.507	14.5
STL	31	42	.425	22.5		LOU	33	42	.440	19.5
NY	31	43	.419	23		BAL	26	46	.361	25
LOU	30	47	.390	25.5		STL	25	52	.325	28.5
BAL	20	55	.267	34.5		WAS	23	52	.307	29.5

*Defeated Cleveland in playoff 5 games to 0 (1 tie).

National League 1893

	POS	Player	AB	BA	HR	RBI	PO	A	E	DP	TC/G	FA	Pitcher	G	IP	W	L	SV	ERA
Bos. W-86 L-43 Frank Selee	1B	T. Tucker	486	.284	7	91	1252	39	27	89	10.9	.980	K. Nichols	52	425	33	13	1	3.52
	2B	B. Lowe	526	.298	13	89	308	409	49	58	6.3	.936	J. Stivetts	37	284	19	13	1	4.41
	SS	H. Long	552	.288	6	58	271	469	98	67	6.8	.883	H. Staley	36	263	18	10	0	5.13
	3B	B. Nash	485	.291	10	123	189	300	41	23	4.1	.923	H. Gastright	19	156	12	4	0	5.13
	RF	C. Carroll	438	.224	4	54	226	18	22	5	2.2	.917							
	CF	H. Duffy	560	.363	6	118	313	15	16	6	2.6	.953							
	LF	T. McCarthy	462	.346	5	111	202	28	25	4	2.4	.902							
	C	C. Bennett	191	.209	4	27	204	40	12	1	4.3	.953							
	UT	C. Ganzel	281	.267	1	48	278	49	15	14		.956							
	P	K. Nichols	177	.220	2	26	21	81	5	5	2.1	.953							
	P	J. Stivetts	172	.297	3	25	13	50	3	2	1.8	.955							
	C	B. Merritt	141	.348	3	26	129	25	9	6	4.4	.945							
	P	H. Staley	113	.265	2	21	3	60	9	2	2.0	.875							
Pit. W-81 L-48 Al Buckenberger	1B	J. Beckley	542	.303	5	106	1360	95	21	83	11.3	.986	F. Killen	55	415	**34**	10	0	3.64
	2B	L. Bierbauer	528	.284	4	94	352	441	34	71	6.5	.959	R. Ehret	39	314	18	18	0	3.44
	SS	J. Glasscock	293	.341	1	74	155	239	28	40	6.4	.934	A. Terry	26	170	12	8	0	4.45
	3B	D. Lyons	490	.306	3	105	214	303	46	23	4.3	.918	A. Gumbert	22	163	11	7	0	5.15
	RF	P. Donovan	499	.317	2	56	178	16	13	5	1.8	.937							
	CF	Van Haltren	529	.338	3	79	227	24	38	3	2.6	.869							
	LF	E. Smith	518	.346	7	103	271	20	25	7	2.5	.921							
	C	D. Miller	154	.182	0	17	141	45	17	3	5.1	.916							
	OF	J. Stenzel	224	.362	4	37	82	4	9	2	2.1	.905							
	SS	F. Shugart	210	.262	1	32	98	178	37	15	6.1	.882							
	P	F. Killen	171	.275	4	30	16	103	14	2	2.4	.895							
	P	R. Ehret	136	.176	1	17	12	80	11	0	2.6	.893							
	C	C. Mack	133	.286	0	15	128	47	11	5	5.0	.941							
Cle. W-73 L-55 Patsy Tebeau	1B	J. Virtue	378	.265	1	60	777	47	21	48	11.6	.975	C. Young	53	423	32	16	1	3.36
	2B	C. Childs	485	.326	3	65	348	424	62	56	6.8	.926	J. Clarkson	36	295	16	17	0	4.45
	SS	E. McKean	545	.310	4	133	247	431	74	55	6.0	.902	N. Cuppy	31	244	17	10	0	4.47
	3B	C. McGarr	249	.309	0	28	93	147	31	7	4.3	.886	C. Hastings	15	92	4	5	1	4.70
	RF	B. Ewing	500	.344	6	122	201	14	17	3	2.1	.927							
	CF	J. McAleer	350	.237	2	41	230	16	19	3	2.9	.928							
	LF	J. Burkett	511	.348	6	82	239	19	**46**	5	2.4	.849							
	C	C. Zimmer	227	.308	2	41	169	73	8	10	4.5	.968							
	13	P. Tebeau	486	.329	2	102	652	177	41	35		.953							
	CO	J. O'Connor	384	.286	3	75	252	70	19	2		.944							
	P	C. Young	187	.235	1	27	27	112	8	1	2.8	.946							

Phi.
W-72 L-57 — Harry Wright

POS	Player	AB	BA	HR	RBI	PO	A	E	DP	TC/G	FA	Pitcher	G	IP	W	L	SV	ERA
1B	J. Boyle	504	.286	4	81	1066	74	14	71	10.3	.988	G. Weyhing	42	345	23	16	0	4.74
2B	B. Hallman	596	.307	4	76	281	370	34	54	5.7	.950	K. Carsey	39	318	20	15	0	4.81
SS	B. Allen	471	.268	8	90	302	447	66	65	6.6	.919	T. Keefe	22	178	10	7	0	4.40
3B	C. Reilly	416	.245	4	56	164	235	47	21	4.3	.895	J. Taylor	25	170	10	9	1	4.24
RF	S. Thompson	600	.370	11	126	171	17	14	3	1.5	.931							
CF	B. Hamilton	355	.380	5	44	228	8	16	6	3.1	.937							
LF	E. Delahanty	595	.368	19	146	318	31	19	8	3.1	.948							
C	J. Clements	376	.285	17	80	329	75	25	5	4.7	.942							
UT	L. Cross	415	.299	4	78	291	182	27	27		.946							
OF	T. Turner	155	.323	1	13	79	5	6	2	2.5	.933							
OF	J. Sharrott	152	.250	1	22	51	5	12	0	2.1	.824							
P	G. Weyhing	147	.150	0	11	31	56	5	3	2.2	.946							
P	K. Carsey	145	.186	0	10	17	81	8	1	2.7	.925							

N. Y.
W-68 L-64 — Monte Ward

POS	Player	AB	BA	HR	RBI	PO	A	E	DP	TC/G	FA	Pitcher	G	IP	W	L	SV	ERA
1B	R. Connor	511	.309	11	105	1423	83	40	70	11.5	.974	A. Rusie	56	482	29	18	1	3.23
2B	M. Ward	588	.328	2	77	348	464	73	41	6.6	.918	M. Baldwin	45	331	16	20	2*	4.10
SS	S. Fuller	474	.236	0	51	260	464	71	48	6.1	.911	L. German	20	152	8	8	0	4.14
3B	G. Davis	549	.362	11	119	181	305	64	27	4.1	.884							
RF	M. Tiernan	511	.309	15	102	178	12	15	2	1.6	.927							
CF	B. Stafford	281	.281	5	27	129	8	15	4	2.3	.901							
LF	E. Burke	537	.279	9	80	278	19	29	2	2.4	.911							
C	J. Doyle	318	.321	1	51	186	62	22	7	5.6	.919							
P	A. Rusie	212	.269	3	27	23	114	15	5	2.7	.901							
OF	H. Lyons	187	.273	0	21	113	9	11	3	2.8	.917							
C	J. Milligan	147	.231	1	25	188	67	18	5	6.5	.934							
P	M. Baldwin	134	.127	0	9	24	52	6	1	1.8	.927							
C	P. Wilson	114	.246	2	21	106	20	4	1	4.2	.969							

Bkn.
W-65 L-63 — Dave Foutz

POS	Player	AB	BA	HR	RBI	PO	A	E	DP	TC/G	FA	Pitcher	G	IP	W	L	SV	ERA
1B	D. Brouthers	282	.337	2	59	736	47	11	51	10.3	.986	B. Kennedy	46	383	26	20	1	3.72
2B	T. Daly	470	.289	8	70	207	265	44	22	6.3	.915	E. Stein	37	298	19	15	0	3.77
SS	T. Corcoran	459	.275	2	58	218	444	68	44	6.3	.907	G. Haddock	23	151	8	9	0	5.60
3B	G. Shoch	327	.263	2	54	48	66	9	5	3.3	.927	D. Daub	12	103	6	6	0	3.84
RF	O. Burns	415	.270	7	60	159	19	13	5	1.8	.932	G. Sharrott	13	95	4	6	1	5.87
CF	M. Griffin	362	.293	5	59	232	19	9	8	2.8	.965							
LF	D. Foutz	557	.246	7	67	157	10	16	1	2.4	.913							
C	T. Kinslow	312	.244	4	45	290	80	27	11	5.2	.932							
C	C. Daily	215	.265	1	32	215	46	18	2	5.5	.935							
2B	D. Richardson	206	.223	0	27	115	107	12	18	5.1	.949							
OF	H. Stovey	175	.251	1	29	115	3	13	0	2.7	.901							
P	B. Kennedy	157	.248	0	16	12	109	10	6	2.8	.924							

Cin.
W-65 L-63 — Charlie Comiskey

POS	Player	AB	BA	HR	RBI	PO	A	E	DP	TC/G	FA	Pitcher	G	IP	W	L	SV	ERA
1B	C. Comiskey	259	.220	0	26	675	21	15	57	11.1	.979	F. Dwyer	37	287	18	15	2	4.13
2B	B. McPhee	491	.281	3	66	396	445	30	101	7.0	.954	Chamberlain	34	241	16	12	0	3.73
SS	G. Smith	500	.236	3	56	250	500	53	67	6.2	.934	M. Sullivan	27	184	8	11	1	5.05
3B	A. Latham	531	.282	2	49	172	281	55	23	4.0	.892	T. Parrott	22	154	10	7	0	4.09
RF	J. McCarthy	195	.282	0	22	87	7	12	0	2.3	.887	T. Mullane	15	122	6	6	1*	4.41
CF	B. Holliday	500	.310	5	89	270	14	17	4	2.4	.944	S. King	17	105	5	6	1	4.89
LF	J. Canavan	461	.226	5	64	243	15	19	0	2.4	.931							
C	F. Vaughn	483	.280	1	108	270	77	11	10	4.5	.969							
C	M. Murphy	200	.235	1	19	162	45	15	6	4.0	.932							
1B	F. Motz	156	.256	2	25	426	38	9	27	11.0	.981							
OF	P. Ward	150	.280	0	10	54	8	13	4	1.9	.827							

Bal.
W-60 L-70 — Ned Hanlon

POS	Player	AB	BA	HR	RBI	PO	A	E	DP	TC/G	FA	Pitcher	G	IP	W	L	SV	ERA
1B	H. Taylor	360	.283	1	54	882	43	23	58	10.8	.976	S. McMahon	43	346	24	16	1	4.37
2B	H. Reitz	490	.286	1	76	315	421	48	62	6.0	.939	T. Mullane	34	245	13	16	1*	4.45
SS	S. McGraw	480	.321	5	64	218	350	67	40	5.4	.894	B. Hawke	29	225	11	16	0	4.76
3B	B. Shindle	521	.261	1	75	176	308	63	24	4.4	.885	E. McNabb	21	142	8	7	0	4.12
RF	G. Treadway	458	.260	1	67	192	27	24	4	2.1	.901	K. Baker	15	92	3	8	0	8.44
CF	J. Kelley	502	.305	9	76	307	22	21	4	2.8	.940							
LF	J. Long	226	.212	2	25	109	8	14	1	2.4	.893							
C	W. Robinson	359	.334	3	57	349	70	26	8	4.8	.942							
C	B. Clarke	183	.175	1	24	135	45	18	3	5.2	.909							
P	S. McMahon	148	.243	0	22	16	75	18	2	2.5	.835							
OF	T. O'Rourke	135	.363	0	19	48	1	1	0	2.0	.980							

Chi.
W-56 L-71 — Cap Anson

POS	Player	AB	BA	HR	RBI	PO	A	E	DP	TC/G	FA	Pitcher	G	IP	W	L	SV	ERA
1B	C. Anson	398	.314	0	91	997	44	20	59	10.5	.981	B. Hutchison	44	348	16	23	0	4.75
2B	B. Lange	469	.281	8	88	151	181	42	21	6.6	.888	W. McGill	39	303	17	18	0	4.61
SS	B. Dahlen	485	.301	5	64	229	306	65	33	6.8	.892	H. Mauck	23	143	8	10	0	4.41
3B	J. Parrott	455	.244	1	65	145	251	42	21	4.4	.904							
RF	S. Dungan	465	.297	2	64	175	20	17	3	2.0	.920							
CF	J. Ryan	341	.299	3	30	162	16	18	2	2.7	.908							
LF	W. Wilmot	392	.301	3	61	198	16	31	1	2.6	.873							
C	M. Kittredge	255	.231	2	30	260	81	22	4	5.2	.939							
UT	G. Decker	328	.271	2	48	333	79	33	25		.926							
C	P. Schriver	229	.284	4	34	215	62	22	8	5.3	.926							
P	B. Hutchison	162	.253	0	25	13	62	7	3	1.9	.915							
UT	L. Camp	156	.263	2	17	55	66	18	7		.871							

	POS	Player	AB	BA	HR	RBI	PO	A	E	DP	TC/G	FA	Pitcher	G	IP	W	L	SV	ERA
St. L.	1B	P. Werden	500	.276	1	94	1194	81	**42**	75	10.6	.968	Breitenstein	48	383	19	20	1	**3.18**
W-57 L-75	2B	J. Quinn	547	.230	0	71	354	366	44	63	5.7	.942	K. Gleason	48	380	21	25	1	4.61
Bill Watkins	SS	J. Glasscock	195	.287	1	26	85	159	25	19	5.6	.907	P. Hawley	31	227	5	12	1	4.60
	3B	J. Crooks	448	.237	1	48	210	286	50	19	**4.4**	.908	D. Clarkson	24	186	12	9	0	3.48
	RF	T. Dowd	581	.282	1	54	225	27	15	9	2.0	.944							
	CF	S. Brodie	469	.318	2	79	273	21	15	7	2.9	.951							
	LF	C. Frank	164	.335	1	17	84	9	7	1	2.5	.930							
	C	H. Peitz	362	.254	1	45	296	86	21	7	5.4	.948							
	UT	F. Shugart	246	.280	0	28	107	101	34	11		.860							
	P	K. Gleason	199	.256	0	20	30	87	12	3	2.7	.907							
	SS	B. Ely	178	.253	0	16	98	139	25	16	6.0	.905							
	P	Breitenstein	160	.181	1	14	**42**	82	8	4	2.8	.939							
	C	J. Gunson	151	.272	0	15	130	36	13	4	5.1	.927							
	UT	D. Cooley	107	.346	0	21	46	12	4	2		.935							
Lou.	1B	W. Brown	461	.304	1	85	1082	51	13	76	10.3	.989*	G. Hemming	41	332	18	17	1	5.18
W-50 L-75	2B	F. Pfeffer	508	.254	3	75	355	398	49	74	6.4	.939	S. Stratton	38	324	12	24	0	5.45
Billy Barnie	SS	T. O'Rourke	352	.281	0	53	118	176	46	26	5.7	.865	B. Rhodes	20	152	5	12	0	7.60
	3B	G. Pinckney	446	.235	1	62	126	279	34	26	3.7	.923	J. Menefee	15	129	8	7	0	4.24
	RF	F. Weaver	439	.292	2	49	151	17	16	2	2.2	.913							
	CF	T. Brown	529	.240	5	54	**339**	**39**	29	**13**	3.3	.929							
	LF	P. Browning	220	.355	1	37	114	5	16	1	2.4	.881							
	C	J. Grim	415	.267	3	54	281	112	20	**15**	4.5	.952							
	PO	S. Stratton	221	.226	0	16	59	96	8	4		.951							
	OF	L. Twitchell	187	.310	1	31	91	6	14	0	2.5	.874							
	SS	J. Denny	175	.246	1	22	91	139	20	16	6.0	.920							
	P	G. Hemming	158	.203	0	19	19	80	7	2	2.6	.934							
Was.	1B	H. Larkin	319	.317	4	73	781	29	31	48	10.4	.963	D. Esper	42	334	12	**28**	0	4.71
W-40 L-89	2B	S. Wise	521	.311	5	77	315	302	51	45	**7.3**	.924	A. Maul	37	297	12	21	0	5.30
Jim O'Rourke	SS	J. Sullivan	508	.266	2	64	233	396	**102**	34	5.7	.860	J. Meekin	31	245	10	15	0	4.96
	3B	J. Mulvey	226	.235	0	19	76	140	31	10	4.5	.874	J. Duryea	17	117	4	10	0	7.54
	RF	P. Radford	464	.228	2	34	198	29	25	4	2.0	.901	O. Stockdale	11	69	2	8	0	8.22
	CF	D. Hoy	564	.245	0	45	281	26	37	8	2.6	.892							
	LF	J. O'Rourke	547	.287	3	95	174	16	15	2	2.4	.927							
	C	D. Farrell	511	.280	4	75	304	**140**	**37**	5	5.9	.923							
	C	D. McGuire	237	.262	1	26	172	45	27	3	4.9	.889							
	UT	C. Stricker	218	.183	0	20	168	146	36	23		.897							
	P	D. Esper	143	.287	0	24	14	79	9	0	2.4	.912							
	P	A. Maul	134	.254	0	12	11	69	10	1	2.4	.889							
	P	J. Meekin	113	.257	3	20	12	53	7	3	2.3	.903							

BATTING AND BASE RUNNING LEADERS

Batting Average

B. Hamilton, PHI	.380
S. Thompson, PHI	.370
E. Delahanty, PHI	.368
H. Duffy, BOS	.363
G. Davis, NY	.362

Slugging Average

E. Delahanty, PHI	.583
G. Davis, NY	.561
S. Thompson, PHI	.530
E. Smith, PIT	.525
B. Hamilton, PHI	.524

Home Runs

E. Delahanty, PHI	19
J. Clements, PHI	17
M. Tiernan, NY	15
B. Lowe, BOS	13

Total Bases

E. Delahanty, PHI	347
S. Thompson, PHI	318
G. Davis, NY	308
E. Smith, PIT	272
E. McKean, CLE	258
H. Duffy, BOS	258

Runs Batted In

E. Delahanty, PHI	146
E. McKean, CLE	133
S. Thompson, PHI	126
B. Nash, BOS	123
B. Ewing, CLE	122

Stolen Bases

T. Brown, LOU	66
T. Dowd, STL	59
A. Latham, CIN	57
E. Burke, NY	54
H. Duffy, BOS	50

Hits

S. Thompson, PHI	222
E. Delahanty, PHI	219
H. Duffy, BOS	203

Base on Balls

J. Crooks, STL	121
C. Childs, CLE	120
P. Radford, WAS	105

Home Run Percentage

J. Clements, PHI	4.5
E. Delahanty, PHI	3.2
M. Tiernan, NY	2.9

Runs Scored

H. Long, BOS	149
H. Duffy, BOS	147

Doubles

S. Thompson, PHI	37
E. Delahanty, PHI	35
P. Tebeau, CLE	32
J. Beckley, PIT	32

Triples

P. Werden, STL	29
G. Davis, NY	27
E. McKean, CLE	24

PITCHING LEADERS

Winning Percentage

H. Gastright, BOS, PIT	.750
F. Killen, PIT	.733
K. Nichols, BOS	.717
C. Young, CLE	.667
H. Staley, BOS	.643

Earned Run Average

Breitenstein, STL	3.18
A. Rusie, NY	3.23
C. Young, CLE	3.36
R. Ehret, PIT	3.44
D. Clarkson, STL	3.48

Wins

F. Killen, PIT	34
K. Nichols, BOS	33
C. Young, CLE	32
A. Rusie, NY	29
B. Kennedy, BKN	26

Saves

T. Mullane, BAL, CIN	2
M. Baldwin, NY, PIT	2
F. Dwyer, CIN	2
F. Donnelly, CHI	2

Strikeouts

A. Rusie, NY	208
B. Kennedy, BKN	107
Breitenstein, STL	102
C. Young, CLE	102
G. Weyhing, PHI	101

Complete Games

A. Rusie, NY	50
K. Nichols, BOS	44
C. Young, CLE	42
B. Kennedy, BKN	40

Fewest Hits per 9 Innings

A. Rusie, NY	8.42
Breitenstein, STL	8.44
F. Killen, PIT	8.70

Shutouts

R. Ehret, PIT	4
A. Rusie, NY	4

Fewest Walks per 9 Innings

C. Young, CLE	2.19
K. Nichols, BOS	2.50
N. Cuppy, CLE	2.77

Most Strikeouts per 9 Inn.

A. Rusie, NY	3.88
J. Meekin, WAS	3.34
P. Hawley, STL	2.89

Innings

A. Rusie, NY	482
K. Nichols, BOS	425
C. Young, CLE	423

Games Pitched

A. Rusie, NY	56
F. Killen, PIT	55
C. Young, CLE	53

	W	L	PCT	GB	R	OR	Batting					SB	Fielding			CG	BB	Pitching			
							2B	3B	HR	BA	SA		E	DP	FA			SO	ShO	SV	ERA
BOS	86	43	.667		1008	795	178	50	64	.290	.391	243	353	118	.936	**115**	402	253	2	2	4.43
PIT	81	48	.628	5	970	**766**	176	**127**	37	.299	.411	210	347	112	.938	104	504	280	**8**	1	4.08
CLE	73	55	.570	12.5	976	839	222	98	31	.300	.408	252	395	92	.929	110	**356**	242	2	2	4.20
PHI	72	57	.558	14	**1011**	841	**246**	90	79	**.301**	**.430**	202	**318**	121	**.944**	107	521	283	4	2	4.68
NY	68	64	.515	19.5	941	845	182	101	62	.293	.410	**299**	432	95	.927	111	581	**395**	6	4	4.29
BKN	65	63	.508	20.5	775	845	173	83	44	.266	.370	213	385	88	.930	109	547	297	3	3	4.55
CIN	65	63	.508	20.5	759	814	161	65	28	.259	.340	238	321	**138**	.943	97	549	258	4	**5**	4.54
BAL	60	70	.462	26.5	820	893	164	86	27	.275	.365	233	384	95	.929	104	534	275	1	2	4.97
CHI	56	71	.441	29	829	874	186	93	32	.279	.379	255	421	92	.922	101	553	273	4	**5**	4.81
STL	57	75	.432	30.5	745	829	152	98	10	.264	.341	250	398	110	.930	114	542	301	3	4	**4.06**
LOU	50	75	.400	34	759	942	178	73	18	.260	.342	203	330	111	.937	114	479	190	4	1	5.90
WAS	40	89	.310	46	722	1032	180	83	24	.266	.354	154	497	96	.912	110	574	292	2	0	5.56
					10315	10315	2198	1047	456	.280	.379	2752	4581	1268	.931	1296	6142	3339	43	31	4.66

National League 1894

	POS	Player	AB	BA	HR	RBI	PO	A	E	DP	TC/G	FA	Pitcher	G	IP	W	L	SV	ERA
Bal. W-89 L-39 Ned Hanlon	1B	D. Brouthers	525	.347	9	128	1184	65	31	83	10.4	.976	S. McMahon	35	276	25	8	0	4.21
	2B	H. Reitz	446	.303	2	105	264	336	20	50	6.4	**.968**	B. Hawke	32	205	16	9	3	5.84
	SS	H. Jennings	501	.335	4	109	**307**	499	63	69	**6.8**	.928	K. Gleason	21	172	15	5	0	4.45
	3B	J. McGraw	512	.340	1	92	131	247	46	17	3.6	.892	B. Inks	22	133	9	4	1	5.55
	RF	W. Keeler	590	.371	5	94	215	25	16	4	2.0	.938	T. Mullane	21	123	8	9	4*	6.31
	CF	S. Brodie	573	.366	3	113	310	14	17	4	2.6	.950	D. Esper	16	102	10	2	2	3.88
	LF	J. Kelley	507	.393	6	111	276	16	15	3	2.4	.951							
	C	W. Robinson	414	.353	1	98	370	84	27	8	4.4	.944							
	P	S. McMahon	126	.286	0	25	17	62	5	2	2.4	.940							
	2B	F. Bonner	118	.322	0	24	60	62	13	8	5.0	.940							
N. Y. W-88 L-44 Monte Ward	1B	J. Doyle	425	.369	3	100	981	59	**38**	51	**10.9**	.965	A. Rusie	54	444	**36**	13	1	**2.78**
	2B	M. Ward	540	.265	0	77	331	446	64	52	6.2	.924	J. Meekin	52	409	**36**	10	2	3.70
	SS	S. Fuller	368	.283	2	46	205	291	65	39	6.3	.884	H. Westervelt	23	141	7	10	0	5.04
	3B	G. Davis	492	.346	9	91	150	247	40	18	3.5	.908	L. German	23	134	9	8	1	5.78
	RF	M. Tiernan	424	.276	5	77	169	9	15	1	1.7	.922							
	CF	Van Haltren	519	.331	7	104	299	29	31	5	2.6	.914							
	LF	E. Burke	566	.304	5	77	260	17	20	3	2.2	.933							
	C	D. Farrell	401	.284	4	66	**460**	**140**	**48**	9	**6.2**	.926							
	SO	Y. Murphy	280	.271	0	28	142	149	34	14		.895							
	P	A. Rusie	186	.280	3	26	28	113	14	4	2.9	.910							
	C1	P. Wilson	175	.331	1	32	246	28	31	9		.898							
	P	J. Meekin	170	.282	5	29	15	60	4	3	1.5	.949							
Bos. W-83 L-49 Frank Selee	1B	T. Tucker	500	.330	3	100	1108	68	18	82	9.7	.985	K. Nichols	50	407	32	13	0	4.75
	2B	B. Lowe	**613**	.346	17	115	345	402	59	62	6.2	.927	J. Stivetts	45	338	28	13	0	4.90
	SS	H. Long	475	.324	12	79	217	359	75	52	6.6	.885	H. Staley	27	209	13	10	0	6.81
	3B	B. Nash	512	.289	8	87	**204**	**267**	34	24	3.8	**.933**	T. Lovett	15	104	8	6	0	5.97
	RF	J. Bannon	494	.336	13	114	240	**43**	41	12	2.5	.873							
	CF	H. Duffy	539	**.438**	**18**	**145**	315	27	27	5	3.0	.927							
	LF	T. McCarthy	539	.349	13	126	291	28	34	10	2.8	.904							
	C	C. Ganzel	266	.278	3	56	184	52	27	6	4.5	.897							
	PO	J. Stivetts	244	.328	8	64	49	49	12	2		.891							
	C	J. Ryan	201	.269	1	29	168	46	21	7	4.6	.911							
	SS	Connaughton	171	.345	2	33	62	111	21	11	5.9	.892							
	P	K. Nichols	170	.294	0	34	34	67	7	3	2.2	.935							
	C	F. Tenney	86	.395	2	21	55	20	9	3	4.2	.893							
	P	H. Staley	85	.235	2	25	5	28	6	0	1.4	.846							
Phi. W-71 L-57 Arthur Irwin	1B	J. Boyle	495	.301	4	88	950	61	18	76	9.0	.983	J. Taylor	41	298	23	13	1	4.08
	2B	B. Hallman	505	.309	0	66	318	320	48	62	5.8	.930	K. Carsey	35	277	18	12	0	5.56
	SS	J. Sullivan	304	.352	3	63	169	224	50	32	5.9	.887	G. Weyhing	38	266	16	14	1	5.81
	3B	L. Cross	529	.386	7	125	177	234	36	24	4.5	.919	G. Harper	12	86	6	6	0	5.32
	RF	S. Thompson	458	.404	13	141	159	12	4	2	1.7	**.977**							
	CF	B. Hamilton	559	.399	4	87	**361**	15	14	4	3.0	.964							
	LF	E. Delahanty	497	.400	4	131	212	23	19	4	2.9	.925							
	C	J. Clements	159	.346	3	36	178	32	12	4	4.9	.946							
	OF	T. Turner	339	.416	1	82	134	7	13	1	2.0	.916							
	C	M. Grady	190	.363	0	40	101	29	18	7	3.4	.878							
	C	D. Buckley	160	.294	1	26	157	39	7	2	4.8	.966							
	SS	B. Allen	149	.255	0	19	87	129	20	15	5.9	.915							
	P	J. Taylor	144	.333	0	22	13	68	12	3	2.3	.871							
	3B	C. Reilly	135	.296	0	19	34	56	13	3	3.7	.874							

	POS	Player	AB	BA	HR	RBI	PO	A	E	DP	TC/G	FA	Pitcher	G	IP	W	L	SV	ERA
Bkn. W-70 L-61 Dave Foutz	1B	D. Foutz	293	.307	0	51	658	33	17	37	9.8	.976	B. Kennedy	48	361	22	19	2	4.92
	2B	T. Daly	492	.341	8	82	317	354	68	52	6.0	.908	E. Stein	45	359	27	14	1	4.54
	SS	T. Corcoran	576	.300	5	92	280	439	76	45	6.2	.904	D. Daub	33	215	9	12	0	6.32
	3B	B. Shindle	476	.296	4	96	192	226	48	12	4.0	.897	H. Gastright	16	93	2	6	2	6.39
	RF	O. Burns	513	.361	5	109	208	15	12	4	1.9	.949							
	CF	M. Griffin	405	.365	5	75	297	14	10	5	3.0	.969							
	LF	G. Treadway	479	.328	4	102	274	16	35	2	2.7	.892							
	C	T. Kinslow	223	.305	2	41	217	47	27	4	4.8	.907							
	1B	C. LaChance	257	.323	5	52	508	16	11	26	9.6	.979							
	UT	G. Shoch	239	.322	1	37	130	77	17	6		.924							
	C	C. Daily	234	.256	0	32	218	61	21	7	5.0	.930							
	P	B. Kennedy	161	.304	0	23	7	82	8	4	2.0	.918							
	PH	E. Stein	146	.260	2	28													
Cle. W-68 L-61 Patsy Tebeau	1B	P. Tebeau	523	.302	3	89	1077	46	26	66	10.0	.977	C. Young	52	409	25	22	1	3.94
	2B	C. Childs	479	.353	2	52	313	374	63	51	6.4	.916	N. Cuppy	43	316	24	15	0	4.56
	SS	E. McKean	554	.357	8	128	269	411	71	43	5.8	.905	J. Clarkson	22	151	8	9	0	4.42
	3B	C. McGarr	523	.275	2	74	170	242	45	17	3.6	.902	M. Sullivan	13	91	6	5	0	6.35
	RF	H. Blake	296	.264	1	51	120	16	10	4	2.0	.932							
	CF	J. McAleer	253	.289	2	40	175	9	9	3	3.0	.953							
	LF	J. Burkett	523	.358	8	94	242	17	24	5	2.3	.915							
	C	C. Zimmer	341	.284	4	65	289	100	15	16	4.5	.963							
	CO	J. O'Connor	330	.315	2	51	249	43	20	4		.936							
	OF	B. Ewing	211	.251	2	39	86	7	9	2	2.0	.912							
	P	C. Young	186	.215	2	26	16	108	7	4	2.5	.947							
	O1	W. Tebeau	150	.313	0	25	172	2	13	13		.930							
	P	N. Cuppy	135	.259	0	19	17	60	2	5	1.8	.975							
Pit. W-65 L-65 Al Buckenberger W-53 L-55 Connie Mack W-12 L-10	1B	J. Beckley	533	.343	8	120	1227	84	30	80	10.2	.978	R. Ehret	46	347	19	21	0	5.14
	2B	L. Bierbauer	525	.303	3	107	309	453	50	58	6.2	.938	A. Gumbert	37	269	15	14	0	6.02
	SS	J. Glasscock	332	.280	1	63	189	295	35	46	6.1	.933	F. Killen	28	204	14	11	0	4.50
	3B	D. Lyons	254	.323	4	50	119	155	31	11	4.3	.898	T. Colcolough	22	149	8	5	0	7.08
	RF	P. Donovan	576	.302	4	76	267	22	21	5	2.3	.932	J. Menefee	13	112	5	8	0	5.40
	CF	J. Stenzel	522	.354	13	121	311	23	27	6	2.8	.925							
	LF	E. Smith	489	.356	6	72	275	18	21	8	2.5	.933							
	C	C. Mack	228	.250	1	21	274	67	19	6	5.2	.947							
	3B	F. Hartman	182	.319	2	20	65	97	23	6	3.8	.876							
	C	J. Sugden	139	.331	2	23	105	27	13	4	4.7	.910							
	P	R. Ehret	135	.170	0	11	12	61	12	2	1.8	.859							
	UT	F. Weaver	115	.348	0	24	73	47	15	6		.889							
Chi. W-57 L-75 Cap Anson	1B	C. Anson	347	.395	5	99	739	47	8	52	9.7	.990	B. Hutchison	36	278	14	15	0	6.06
	2B	J. Parrott	532	.261	3	64	285	379	49	56	5.8	.931	C. Griffith	36	261	21	11	0	4.92
	SS	B. Dahlen	508	.362	15	107	186	253	50	43	7.4	.898	W. McGill	27	208	7	19	0	5.84
	3B	C. Irwin	498	.289	8	95	89	123	46	15	3.9	.822	A. Terry	23	163	5	11	0	5.84
	RF	J. Ryan	481	.360	3	62	221	22	24	3	2.5	.910	S. Stratton	15	119	8	5	0	6.03
	CF	B. Lange	442	.328	6	90	267	25	29	10	2.9	.910							
	LF	W. Wilmot	597	.330	5	130	264	16	41	5	2.4	.872							
	C	P. Schriver	349	.275	3	47	290	91	32	12	4.7	.923							
	UT	G. Decker	384	.313	8	92	497	39	32	32		.944							
	C	M. Kittredge	168	.315	0	23	209	36	20	4	5.2	.925							
	P	C. Griffith	142	.232	0	15	20	45	4	1	1.9	.942							
	P	B. Hutchison	136	.309	6	16	10	45	5	1	1.7	.917							
	PO	S. Stratton	96	.375	3	23	16	21	2	2		.949							
St. L. W-56 L-76 George Miller	1B	R. Connor	380	.321	7	79	897	68	26	72*	10.0	.974	Breitenstein	56	447	27	25	0	4.79
	2B	J. Quinn	405	.286	4	61	341	339	34	74	6.7	.952	P. Hawley	53	393	19	26	0	4.90
	SS	B. Ely	510	.326	12	89	273	442	79	51	6.3	.901	D. Clarkson	32	233	8	17	0	6.36
	3B	D. Miller	481	.339	8	86	68	96	33	6	3.8	.832							
	RF	T. Dowd	524	.271	4	62	199	14	16	4	2.0	.930							
	CF	F. Shugart	527	.292	7	72	276	26	29	2	2.7	.912							
	LF	C. Frank	319	.279	4	42	161	11	26	4	2.6	.869							
	C	H. Peitz	338	.263	3	49	146	51	13	3	5.4	.938							
	OF	D. Cooley	206	.296	1	21	74	1	15	1	2.3	.833							
	P	Breitenstein	182	.220	0	13	42	83	9	4	2.4	.933							
	P	P. Hawley	163	.264	2	23	29	77	12	2	2.2	.898							
Cin. W-55 L-75 Charlie Comiskey	1B	C. Comiskey	220	.264	0	33	536	24	16	36	9.6	.972	F. Dwyer	45	348	19	22	1	5.07
	2B	B. McPhee	481	.320	5	88	389	446	49	72	7.0	.945	T. Parrott	41	309	17	19	1	5.60
	SS	G. Smith	482	.263	3	76	233	501	72	75	6.3	.911	Chamberlain	23	178	10	9	0	5.77
	3B	A. Latham	524	.313	4	60	158	248	66	20	3.7	.860	C. Fisher	11	91	2	8	0	7.32
	RF	J. Canavan	356	.272	13	70	188	9	21	6	2.3	.904							
	CF	D. Hoy	506	.312	5	70	314	29	40	3	3.0	.896							
	LF	B. Holliday	519	.383	13	119	243	22	25	5	2.4	.914							
	C	M. Murphy	255	.275	1	37	194	70	29	5	4.0	.901							
	UT	F. Vaughn	284	.310	7	64	362	64	26	19		.942							
	UT	T. Parrott	229	.323	4	40	143	87	22	10		.913							
	P	F. Dwyer	172	.267	2	28	31	62	5	2	2.2	.949							
	O1	J. McCarthy	167	.269	0	21	193	19	13	12		.942							
	C	B. Merritt	113	.327	1	21	55	26	4	0	3.5	.953							

POS	Player	AB	BA	HR	RBI	PO	A	E	DP	TC/G	FA	Pitcher	G	IP	W	L	SV	ERA
1B	E. Cartwright	507	.294	12	106	1219	71	36	63	10.0	.973	W. Mercer	49	333	17	23	3	3.76
2B	P. Ward	347	.303	0	36	167	237	45	21	5.7	.900	A. Maul	28	202	11	15	0	5.98
SS	F. Scheibeck	196	.230	0	17	108	204	44	15	6.8	.876	D. Esper	19	122	5	10	0	7.50
3B	B. Joyce	355	.355	17	89	152	183	52	20	3.9	.866	M. Sullivan	20	118	2	10	1	6.58
RF	B. Hassamaer	494	.322	4	90	109	11	11	4	1.9	.916	O. Stockdale	18	117	5	9	0	5.06
CF	C. Abbey	523	.314	7	101	344	26	37	6	3.2	.909	C. Petty	16	103	3	8	0	5.59
LF	K. Selbach	372	.306	7	71	153	8	15	2	2.2	.915							
C	D. McGuire	425	.306	6	78	288	114	36	8	4.2	.918							
UT	P. Radford	325	.240	0	49	219	247	73	23		.865							
OF	W. Tebeau	222	.225	0	28	118	8	21	1	2.4	.857							
P	W. Mercer	162	.284	2	29	14	68	5	1	1.8	.943							
C	D. Dugdale	134	.239	0	16	72	32	15	0	3.6	.874							
P	A. Maul	124	.242	2	20	8	49	8	0	2.3	.877							

Was. W-45 L-87 Gus Schmelz

POS	Player	AB	BA	HR	RBI	PO	A	E	DP	TC/G	FA	Pitcher	G	IP	W	L	SV	ERA
1B	L. Lutenberg	250	.192	0	23	593	38	15	54	9.6	.977	G. Hemming	35	294	13	19	1	4.37
2B	F. Pfeffer	409	.308	5	59	255	284	36	58	6.4	.937	P. Knell	32	247	7	21	0	5.32
SS	D. Richardson	430	.253	1	40	232	360	54	59	6.0	.916	J. Menefee	28	212	8	17	0	4.29
3B	J. Denny	221	.276	0	32	85	124	30	12	4.0	.874	J. Wadsworth	22	173	4	18	0	7.60
RF	O. Smith	134	.299	3	20	63	5	9	0	2.0	.883							
CF	T. Brown	536	.254	9	57	331	21	34	8	3.0	.912							
LF	F. Clarke	316	.275	7	48	162	15	23	2	2.6	.885							
C	J. Grim	410	.298	7	70	262	100	27	9	5.1	.931							
UT	F. Weaver	244	.221	3	24	191	28	11	9		.952							
UT	T. O'Rourke	220	.277	0	27	316	41	22	36		.942							
OF	L. Twitchell	210	.267	2	32	103	15	12	4	2.5	.908							
3B	P. Flaherty	145	.297	0	15	42	70	19	7	3.4	.855							

Lou. W-36 L-94 Billy Barnie

BATTING AND BASE RUNNING LEADERS

Batting Average

H. Duffy, BOS	.438
T. Turner, PHI	.416
S. Thompson, PHI	.404
E. Delahanty, PHI	.400
B. Hamilton, PHI	.399

Slugging Average

H. Duffy, BOS	.679
S. Thompson, PHI	.670
B. Joyce, WAS	.648
J. Kelley, BAL	.602
J. Stenzel, PIT	.580

Home Runs

H. Duffy, BOS	18
B. Joyce, WAS	17
B. Lowe, BOS	17
B. Dahlen, CHI	15

Total Bases

H. Duffy, BOS	366
B. Lowe, BOS	319
S. Thompson, PHI	307
J. Kelley, BAL	305
W. Keeler, BAL	305

Runs Batted In

H. Duffy, BOS	145
S. Thompson, PHI	141
E. Delahanty, PHI	131
W. Wilmot, CHI	130
D. Brouthers, BAL	128
E. McKean, CLE	128

Stolen Bases

B. Hamilton, PHI	99
J. McGraw, BAL	78
W. Wilmot, CHI	74
T. Brown, LOU	66
B. Lange, CHI	65

Hits

H. Duffy, BOS	236
B. Hamilton, PHI	223
W. Keeler, BAL	219

Base on Balls

B. Hamilton, PHI	126
C. Childs, CLE	107
J. Kelley, BAL	107

Home Run Percentage

B. Joyce, WAS	4.8
J. Canavan, CIN	3.7
H. Duffy, BOS	3.3

Runs Scored

B. Hamilton, PHI	196
J. Kelley, BAL	167
W. Keeler, BAL	165

Doubles

H. Duffy, BOS	50
J. Kelley, BAL	48
W. Wilmot, CHI	45

Triples

H. Reitz, BAL	31
S. Thompson, PHI	27
G. Treadway, BKN	26

PITCHING LEADERS

Winning Percentage

J. Meekin, NY	.786
S. McMahon, BAL	.758
A. Rusie, NY	.735
K. Nichols, BOS	.711
J. Stivetts, BOS	.683

Earned Run Average

A. Rusie, NY	2.78
J. Meekin, NY	3.70
W. Mercer, WAS	3.76
C. Young, CLE	3.94
J. Taylor, PHI	4.08

Wins

J. Meekin, NY	36
A. Rusie, NY	36
K. Nichols, BOS	32
J. Stivetts, BOS	28
E. Stein, BKN	27
Breitenstein, STL	27

Saves

T. Mullane, BAL, CLE	4
B. Hawke, BAL	3
W. Mercer, WAS	3

Strikeouts

A. Rusie, NY	195
Breitenstein, STL	140
J. Meekin, NY	133
P. Hawley, STL	120
K. Nichols, BOS	113

Complete Games

Breitenstein, STL	46
A. Rusie, NY	45
C. Young, CLE	44
K. Nichols, BOS	40
J. Meekin, NY	40

Fewest Hits per 9 Innings

A. Rusie, NY	8.64
J. Meekin, NY	8.89
E. Stein, BKN	9.93

Shutouts

N. Cuppy, CLE	3
K. Nichols, BOS	3
A. Rusie, NY	3

Fewest Walks per 9 Innings

C. Young, CLE	2.33
J. Menefee, LOU, PIT	2.48
K. Gleason, BAL, STL	2.54

Most Strikeouts per 9 Inn.

A. Rusie, NY	3.95
B. Hawke, BAL	2.99
J. Wadsworth, LOU	2.97

Innings

Breitenstein, STL	447
A. Rusie, NY	444
J. Meekin, NY	409

Games Pitched

Breitenstein, STL	56
A. Rusie, NY	54
P. Hawley, STL	53

	W	L	PCT	GB	R	OR	Batting 2B	3B	HR	BA	SA	SB	Fielding E	DP	FA	CG	Pitching BB	SO	ShO	SV	ERA
BAL	89	39	.695		1171	820	271	**150**	33	.343	.483	324	**293**	105	**.944**	97	472	275	1	**11**	5.00
NY	88	44	.667	3	940	**789**	197	96	44	.301	.409	319	443	101	.924	111	539	**395**	5	5	**3.83**
BOS	83	49	.629	8	**1222**	1002	**272**	93	**103**	.331	**.484**	241	415	120	.925	108	**411**	262	3	1	5.41
PHI	71	57	.555	18	1143	966	252	131	40	**.349**	.476	273	338	111	.935	102	469	262	3	4	5.63
BKN	70	61	.534	20.5	1021	1007	228	130	42	.313	.440	282	390	85	.928	105	555	285	3	5	5.51
CLE	68	61	.527	21.5	932	896	241	90	37	.303	.414	220	344	107	.935	107	435	254	**6**	1	4.97
PIT	65	65	.500	25	955	972	222	123	49	.312	.443	256	354	106	.936	106	457	304	2	0	5.60
CHI	57	75	.432	34	1041	1066	265	86	65	.314	.441	**327**	452	113	.918	**117**	557	281		0	5.68
STL	56	76	.424	35	771	954	171	113	54	.286	.408	190	426	109	.923	114	500	319	2	0	5.29
CIN	55	75	.423	35	910	1085	224	68	60	.294	.410	215	423	119	.925	110	491	219	4	3	5.99
WAS	45	87	.341	46	882	1122	218	118	59	.287	.425	249	499	81	.908	102	446	190	1	4	5.51
LOU	36	94	.277	54	692	1001	173	88	42	.269	.375	217	428	**130**	.920	113	475	258	2	1	5.45
					11680	11680	2734	1286	628	.309	.435	3113	4805	1287	.927	1292	5807	3304	32	35	5.32

National League 1895

	POS	Player	AB	BA	HR	RBI	PO	A	E	DP	TC/G	FA	Pitcher	G	IP	W	L	SV	ERA
Bal. W-87 L-43 Ned Hanlon	1B	S. Carey	490	.261	1	75	1132	43	15	73	9.7	**.987**	B. Hoffer	41	314	30	7	0	3.21
	2B	K. Gleason	421	.309	0	74	205	250	51	32	6.0	.899	G. Hemming	34	262	20	13	0	4.05
	SS	H. Jennings	529	.386	4	125	**425**	457	56	**71**	7.2	**.940**	D. Esper	34	218	10	12	1	3.92
	3B	J. McGraw	388	.369	2	48	100	239	47	19	4.1	.878	D. Clarkson	20	142	12	3	0	3.87
	RF	W. Keeler	565	.391	4	78	244	21	10	5	2.1	.964	S. McMahon	15	122	10	4	0	2.94
	CF	S. Brodie	528	.348	2	134	307	23	12	2	2.6	.965							
	LF	J. Kelley	518	.365	10	134	260	20	16	5	2.3	.946							
	C	W. Robinson	282	.262	0	48	243	78	7	6	4.4	**.979**							
	2B	H. Reitz	245	.294	0	29	120	137	17	25	5.7	.938							
	C	B. Clarke	241	.290	0	35	176	67	16	8	4.3	.938							
Cle. W-84 L-46 Patsy Tebeau	1B	P. Tebeau	264	.318	2	52	473	19	4	28	10.1	.992	C. Young	47	370	**35**	10	0	3.24
	2B	C. Childs	462	.288	4	90	337	394	**63**	42	**6.7**	.921	N. Cuppy	47	353	26	14	2	3.54
	SS	E. McKean	**565**	.342	8	119	246	424	67	42	5.6	.909	B. Wallace	30	229	12	14	1	4.09
	3B	C. McGarr	419	.265	2	59	125	217	51	13	3.6	.870	P. Knell	20	117	7	5	0	5.40
	RF	H. Blake	315	.276	3	45	119	13	15	3	1.8	.898							
	CF	J. McAleer	531	.286	2	68	341	14	25	1	2.9	.934							
	LF	J. Burkett	555	**.423**	5	83	273	17	38	4	2.5	.884							
	C	C. Zimmer	315	.340	5	56	318	77	10	2	4.8	.975							
	C1	J. O'Connor	340	.291	0	58	520	66	16	24		.973							
	O1	W. Tebeau	337	.326	0	68	480	25	17	12		.967							
	P	C. Young	140	.214	0	13	15	**120**	6	2	3.0	.957							
	P	N. Cuppy	140	.286	0	25	30	90	4	2	2.6	.968							
Phi. W-78 L-53 Arthur Irwin	1B	J. Boyle	**565**	.253	0	67	1245	61	**36**	69	10.1	.973	K. Carsey	44	342	24	16	1	4.92
	2B	B. Hallman	539	.314	1	91	299	392	42	57	6.0	.943	J. Taylor	41	335	26	14	1	4.49
	SS	J. Sullivan	373	.338	2	50	182	270	62	32	5.8	.879	W. McGill	20	146	10	8	0	5.55
	3B	L. Cross	535	.271	2	101	191	**308**	32	23	**4.2**	**.940**	A. Orth	11	88	9	1	1	3.89
	RF	S. Thompson	538	.392	**18**	**165**	186	31	13	2	1.9	.943							
	CF	B. Hamilton	517	.389	7	74	313	11	31	5	2.9	.913							
	LF	E. Delahanty	481	.399	11	106	237	16	15	4	2.6	.944							
	C	J. Clements	322	.394	13	75	280	69	11	7	4.1	.969							
	OF	T. Turner	210	.386	2	43	89	5	17	0	2.0	.847							
	S3	C. Reilly	179	.268	0	25	70	123	23	14		.894							
	P	J. Taylor	155	.290	3	35	19	89	5	3	2.8	.956							
	P	K. Carsey	141	.291	0	20	9	77	12	2	2.2	.878							
	C	M. Grady	123	.325	1	23	103	10	9	2	3.2	.926							
Chi. W-72 L-58 Cap Anson	1B	C. Anson	474	.335	2	91	1176	60	19	**82**	10.3	.985	C. Griffith	42	353	25	13	0	3.93
	2B	A. Stewart	365	.241	8	76	252	281	52	53	6.0	.911	A. Terry	38	311	21	14	0	4.80
	SS	B. Dahlen	509	.273	7	62	281	**527**	**86**	70	6.9	.904	B. Hutchison	38	291	13	21	0	4.73
	3B	B. Everett	550	.358	3	88	174	263	75	12	3.9	.854							
	RF	J. Ryan	443	.323	6	49	161	18	12	6	1.8	.937							
	CF	B. Lange	478	.389	10	98	298	28	27	6	2.9	.924							
	LF	W. Wilmot	466	.283	8	72	226	19	23	5	2.5	.914							
	C	T. Donahue	219	.269	2	36	234	45	26	8	4.8	.915							
	OF	G. Decker	297	.276	2	41	98	3	10	0	1.9	.910							
	C	M. Kittredge	212	.226	3	29	197	48	6	4	4.3	.976							
	P	C. Griffith	144	.319	1	27	27	81	9	2	2.8	.923							
	P	A. Terry	137	.219	1	10	13	81	11	3	2.8	.895							

	POS	Player	AB	BA	HR	RBI	PO	A	E	DP	TC/G	FA	Pitcher	G	IP	W	L	SV	ERA
Bkn. W-71 L-60 Dave Foutz	1B	C. LaChance	536	.312	8	108	1286	53	23	68	10.9	.983	B. Kennedy	39	280	18	13	1	5.12
	2B	T. Daly	455	.281	2	68	318	346	30	42	6.0	.930	E. Stein	32	255	15	13	1	4.72
	SS	T. Corcoran	541	.277	2	69	293	488	64	49	6.7	.924	A. Gumbert	33	234	11	16	1	5.08
	3B	B. Shindle	486	.278	3	69	142	257	46	16	3.8	.897	D. Daub	25	185	10	10	0	4.29
	RF	G. Treadway	339	.257	7	54	117	7	16	4	1.6	.886	C. Lucid	21	137	10	7	0	5.52
	CF	M. Griffin	522	.335	4	65	349	23	12	12	2.9	.969							
	LF	J. Anderson	419	.286	9	87	205	11	29	4	2.4	.882							
	C	J. Grim	329	.280	0	44	253	103	20	10	4.1	.947							
	UT	G. Shoch	216	.259	0	29	98	63	14	6		.920							
	C	C. Daily	142	.211	1	11	127	25	7	7	4.1	.956							
	P	B. Kennedy	127	.307	0	21	5	66	5	1	1.9	.934							
	OF	D. Foutz	115	.296	0	21	26	3	4	1	1.7	.879							
Bos. W-71 L-60 Frank Selee	1B	T. Tucker	462	.249	3	73	1159	82	28	78	10.2	.978	K. Nichols	48	394	30	14	3	3.29
	2B	B. Lowe	412	.296	7	62	265	336	29	50	6.4	.954	J. Stivetts	38	291	17	17	0	4.64
	SS	H. Long	540	.319	9	75	280	409	84	48	6.3	.891	C. Dolan	25	198	11	7	1	4.27
	3B	B. Nash	508	.289	10	108	193	246	59	26	3.8	.882	J. Sullivan	21	179	11	9	0	4.82
	RF	J. Bannon	489	.350	6	74	209	30	33	3	2.2	.879							
	CF	H. Duffy	540	.352	9	100	322	20	20	7	2.8	.945							
	LF	T. McCarthy	452	.290	2	73	199	16	28	2	2.2	.885							
	C	C. Ganzel	277	.264	1	52	345	65	16	9	5.6	.962							
	C	J. Ryan	189	.291	0	18	167	46	11	2	5.2	.951							
	OC	F. Tenney	174	.276	1	21	109	24	7	2		.950							
	P	J. Stivetts	158	.190	0	24	24	50	3	1	2.0	.961							
	P	K. Nichols	157	.236	0	18	29	73	4	2	2.2	.962							
Pit. W-71 L-61 Connie Mack	1B	J. Beckley	530	.328	5	110	1340	54	31	76	11.0	.978	P. Hawley	56	444	32	21	1	3.18
	2B	L. Bierbauer	466	.258	0	69	284	400	39	52	6.2	.946	B. Hart	36	262	14	17	1	4.75
	SS	M. Cross	393	.257	3	54	254	327	77	42	6.1	.883	B. Foreman	19	140	8	6	2	3.22
	3B	B. Clingman	382	.259	0	45	137	256	50	16	4.2	.887	F. Killen	13	95	5	5	0	5.49
	RF	P. Donovan	519	.308	1	58	187	11	8	2	1.6	.961	J. Gardner	11	85	8	2	0	2.64
	CF	J. Stenzel	514	.374	7	97	257	23	27	6	2.4	.912							
	LF	E. Smith	492	.297	1	81	250	16	31	2	2.4	.896							
	C	B. Merritt	239	.285	0	27	245	58	21	7	5.1	.935							
	UT	F. Genins	252	.250	2	24	127	99	29	7		.886							
	P	P. Hawley	185	.308	5	42	16	110	13	2	2.5	.906							
	C	J. Sugden	155	.310	1	17	176	57	25	4	5.3	.903							
Cin. W-66 L-64 Buck Ewing	1B	B. Ewing	434	.318	5	94	957	79	26	69	10.1	.976	F. Dwyer	37	280	18	15	0	4.24
	2B	B. McPhee	432	.299	1	75	355	366	34	57	6.6	.955	B. Rhines	38	268	19	10	0	4.81
	SS	G. Smith	503	.300	4	74	251	457	59	58	6.0	.923	T. Parrott	41	263	11	18	3	5.47
	3B	A. Latham	460	.311	2	69	126	197	52	13	3.5	.861	F. Foreman	32	219	11	14	1	4.11
	RF	D. Miller	529	.335	8	112	243	25	18	8	2.2	.937	B. Phillips	18	109	6	7	2	6.03
	CF	G. Hogriever	239	.272	2	34	174	10	13	3	3.0	.934							
	LF	D. Hoy	429	.277	3	55	235	14	33	6	2.6	.883							
	C	F. Vaughn	334	.305	0	48	262	78	24	10	4.7	.934							
	OF	E. Burke	228	.268	1	28	135	8	16	2	2.8	.899							
	UT	T. Parrott	201	.343	3	41	151	70	13	12		.944							
	UT	B. Grey	181	.304	1	29	89	108	24	13		.891							
	OF	B. Holliday	127	.299	0	20	60	3	4	1	2.1	.940							
	P	B. Rhines	113	.221	0	23	17	56	9	3	2.2	.890							
N. Y. W-66 L-65 George Davis W-17 L-17 Jack Doyle W-31 L-31 Harvey Watkins W-18 L-17	1B	J. Doyle	319	.313	1	66	599	34	21	27	11.3	.968	A. Rusie	49	393	22	21	0	3.73
	2B	B. Stafford	463	.279	3	73	242	329	56	44	5.7	.911	D. Clarke	37	282	18	15	1	3.39
	SS	S. Fuller	458	.225	0	32	270	499	73	59	6.7	.913	J. Meekin	29	226	16	11	0	5.30
	3B	G. Davis	433	.330	5	101	122	175	40	18	4.2	.881	L. German	25	178	7	11	0	5.96
	RF	M. Tiernan	476	.347	7	70	184	8	11	2	1.7	.946							
	CF	Van Haltren	521	.340	8	103	252	26	26	3	2.3	.914							
	LF	E. Burke	167	.251	1	12	77	8	8	2	2.4	.914							
	C	D. Farrell	312	.288	1	58	269	67	21	11	5.8	.941							
	C	P. Wilson	238	.235	0	30	214	56	18	8	5.4	.938							
	UT	Y. Murphy	184	.201	0	16	82	39	18	4		.871							
	P	A. Rusie	179	.246	1	19	19	93	11	4	2.5	.911							
	O1	T. Bannon	159	.270	0	8	198	18	19	16		.919							
	OF	O. Burns	114	.307	1	25	42	5	7	0	1.7	.870							
Was. W-43 L-85 Gus Schmelz	1B	E. Cartwright	472	.331	3	90	1102	95	19	69	10.0	.984	W. Mercer	43	311	13	23	2	4.46
	2B	J. Crooks	409	.279	6	57	327	364	32	43	6.2	.956	V. Anderson	29	205	9	16	0	5.89
	SS	F. Scheibeck	167	.186	0	25	95	142	30	17	6.1	.888	O. Stockdale	20	136	6	11	1	6.09
	3B	B. Joyce	474	.312	17	95	186	232	77	16	3.9	.844	A. Maul	16	136	10	5	0	2.45
	RF	B. Hassamaer	358	.279	1	60	104	4	4	1	1.5	.964	J. Malarkey	22	101	0	8	2	5.99
	CF	C. Abbey	511	.296	8	84	275	32	33	7	2.6	.903	J. Boyd	14	85	2	11	0	7.07
	LF	K. Selbach	516	.322	6	55	289	21	30	4	2.9	.912							
	C	D. McGuire	533	.336	10	97	408	179	40	11	4.8	.936							
	P	W. Mercer	196	.255	1	26	25	58	12	2	2.2	.874							
	UT	J. Boyd	157	.268	1	16	50	55	24	5		.814							
	OF	T. Brown	134	.239	2	16	59	1	6	0	1.9	.909							

	POS	Player	AB	BA	HR	RBI	PO	A	E	DP	TC/G	FA	Pitcher	G	IP	W	L	SV	ERA
St. L.	1B	R. Connor	402	.326	8	77	953	62	14	60	10.0	.986	Breitenstein	54	430	18	**30**	1	4.44
W-39 L-92	2B	J. Quinn	543	.311	2	74	**359**	390	43	**63**	5.9	.946	R. Ehret	37	232	6	19	0	6.02
Al Buckenberger	SS	B. Ely	467	.259	1	46	247	407	53	52	6.0	.925	H. Staley	23	159	6	13	0	5.22
W-16 L-32	3B	D. Miller	490	.292	5	74	54	72	26	5	3.3	.829	B. Kissinger	24	141	4	12	0	6.72
Joe Quinn	RF	T. Dowd	505	.323	6	74	218	11	18	3	2.1	.927	J. McDougal	18	115	4	10	0	8.32
W-13 L-27	CF	T. Brown	350	.217	1	31	215	15	12	3	2.9	.950							
Lew Phelan	LF	D. Cooley	563	.339	6	75	320	17	23	1	2.9	.936							
W-8 L-21	C	H. Peitz	334	.284	2	65	260	80	23	10	5.1	.937							
	P	Breitenstein	218	.193	0	18	**45**	98	**14**	1	2.9	.911							
Chris Von Der Ahe	OF	B. Sheehan	180	.317	1	18	56	7	4	1	1.6	.940							
W-2 L-12	3B	D. Lyons	129	.295	2	25	61	49	13	2	3.7	.894							
Lou.	1B	H. Spies	276	.268	2	35	439	22	9	30	10.0	.981	B. Cunningham	31	231	11	16	0	4.75
W-35 L-96	2B	J. O'Brien	539	.256	1	50	304	396	46	56	6.0	.938	G. Weyhing	28	213	7	19	0	5.41
John McCloskey	SS	F. Shugart	473	.264	4	70	178	258	63	39	5.7	.874	M. McDermott	33	207	4	19	0	5.99
	3B	J. Collins	373	.279	6	49	131	181	25	12	4.4	.926	B. Inks	28	205	7	20	0	6.40
	RF	T. Gettinger	260	.269	2	32	127	5	13	1	2.3	.910							
	CF	J. Wright	228	.276	1	30	127	4	5	1	2.3	.963							
	LF	F. Clarke	556	.354	4	82	344	20	**49**	4	**3.1**	.881							
	C	J. Warner	232	.267	1	20	195	47	18	4	4.1	.931							
	O3	W. Preston	197	.279	1	24	71	54	33	5		.791							
	UT	D. Holmes	161	.373	3	20	49	32	21	2		.794							
	C1	T. Welsh	153	.242	1	8	254	41	21	17		.934							

BATTING AND BASE RUNNING LEADERS

Batting Average
J. Burkett, CLE .423
E. Delahanty, PHI .399
J. Clements, PHI .394
S. Thompson, PHI .392
W. Keeler, BAL .391

Slugging Average
S. Thompson, PHI .654
J. Clements, PHI .612
E. Delahanty, PHI .611
B. Lange, CHI .575
J. Kelley, BAL .546

Home Runs
S. Thompson, PHI 18
B. Joyce, WAS 17
J. Clements, PHI 13
E. Delahanty, PHI 11

Total Bases
S. Thompson, PHI 352
J. Burkett, CLE 301
E. Delahanty, PHI 294
J. Kelley, BAL 283
E. McKean, CLE 283

Runs Batted In
S. Thompson, PHI 165
J. Kelley, BAL 134
S. Brodie, BAL 134
H. Jennings, BAL 125
E. McKean, CLE 119

Stolen Bases
B. Hamilton, PHI 95
B. Lange, CHI 67
J. McGraw, BAL 61
J. Kelley, BAL 54
J. Stenzel, PIT 53
H. Jennings, BAL 53

Hits
J. Burkett, CLE 235
W. Keeler, BAL 211
S. Thompson, PHI 211

Base on Balls
B. Joyce, WAS 96
B. Hamilton, PHI 96
M. Griffin, BKN 93

Home Run Percentage
J. Clements, PHI 4.0
B. Joyce, WAS 3.6
S. Thompson, PHI 3.3

Runs Scored
B. Hamilton, PHI 166
W. Keeler, BAL 162
H. Jennings, BAL 159

Doubles
E. Delahanty, PHI 49
S. Thompson, PHI 45
H. Jennings, BAL 41

Triples
K. Selbach, WAS 22
M. Tiernan, NY 21
S. Thompson, PHI 21
D. Cooley, STL 21

PITCHING LEADERS

Winning Percentage
B. Hoffer, BAL .811
C. Young, CLE .778
K. Nichols, BOS .682
C. Griffith, CHI .658
B. Rhines, CIN .655

Earned Run Average
A. Maul, WAS 2.45
S. McMahon, BAL 2.94
P. Hawley, PIT 3.18
B. Hoffer, BAL 3.21
B. Foreman, PIT 3.22

Wins
C. Young, CLE 35
P. Hawley, PIT 32
B. Hoffer, BAL 30
K. Nichols, BOS 30

Saves
T. Parrott, CIN 3
E. Beam, PHI 3
K. Nichols, BOS 3

Strikeouts
A. Rusie, NY 201
K. Nichols, BOS 146
P. Hawley, PIT 142
Breitenstein, STL 127
C. Young, CLE 121

Complete Games
Breitenstein, STL 46
P. Hawley, PIT 44
K. Nichols, BOS 42
A. Rusie, NY 42
C. Griffith, CHI 39

Fewest Hits per 9 Innings
S. McMahon, BAL 8.09
B. Foreman, PIT 8.44
B. Hoffer, BAL 8.48

Shutouts
5 tied with 4

Fewest Walks per 9 Innings
C. Young, CLE 1.83
D. Clarke, NY 1.92
K. Nichols, BOS 2.04

Most Strikeouts per 9 Inn.
A. Rusie, NY 4.60
W. McGill, PHI 4.32
B. Foreman, PIT 3.48

Innings
P. Hawley, PIT 444
Breitenstein, STL 430
K. Nichols, BOS 394

Games Pitched
P. Hawley, PIT 56
Breitenstein, STL 54
A. Rusie, NY 49

	W	L	PCT	GB	R	OR	Batting						Fielding			Pitching					
							2B	3B	HR	BA	SA	SB	E	DP	FA	CG	BB	SO	ShO	SV	ERA
BAL	87	43	.669		1009	**646**	235	89	25	.324	.427	310	**288**	108	**.946**	104	430	244	10	4	**3.80**
CLE	84	46	.646	3	917	720	194	67	29	.305	.395	187	348	77	.936	108	**346**	326	6	3	3.90
PHI	78	53	.595	9.5	**1068**	957	**272**	73	**61**	.330	.450	276	369	93	.933	106	485	330	2	7	5.47
CHI	72	58	.554	15	866	854	171	85	55	.298	.405	260	401	**113**	.928	119	432	297	3	1	4.67
BKN	71	60	.542	16.5	867	834	189	77	39	.282	.379	183	325	96	.941	103	395	216	5	6	4.94
BOS	71	60	.542	16.5	907	826	197	57	54	.290	.391	199	364	104	.934	115	363	370	4	4	4.27
PIT	71	61	.538	17	811	787	190	89	26	.290	.386	257	392	95	.930	106	500	382	4	6	4.05
CIN	66	64	.508	21	903	854	235	**107**	33	.298	.415	**326**	377	112	.931	97	362	245	2	6	4.81
NY	66	65	.504	21.5	852	834	191	90	32	.288	.389	292	438	106	.922	115	415	**409**	6	1	4.51
WAS	43	85	.336	43	837	1048	207	101	55	.287	.412	237	447	96	.917	99	465	258		5	5.28
STL	39	92	.298	48.5	747	1032	155	89	36	.281	.373	205	380	94	.930	105	439	280	1	1	5.76
LOU	35	96	.267	52.5	698	1090	171	73	34	.279	.368	156	477	104	.913	104	469	245	3	1	5.90
					10482	10482	2407	997	479	.296	.399	2888	4606	1198	.930	1281	5101	3602	46	45	4.78

	POS	Player	AB	BA	HR	RBI	PO	A	E	DP	TC/G	FA	Pitcher	G	IP	W	L	SV	ERA
Bal.	1B	J. Doyle	487	.345	1	101	1173	42	32	85	10.6	.974	B. Hoffer	35	309	25	7	0	3.38
W-90 L-39	2B	H. Reitz	464	.287	4	106	256	335	30	54	5.3	.952	A. Pond	28	214	16	8	0	3.49
Ned Hanlon	SS	H. Jennings	523	.398	0	121	377	476	66	70	7.1	.928	G. Hemming	25	202	15	6	0	4.19
	3B	J. Donnelly	396	.328	0	71	140	217	47	15	3.8	.884	S. McMahon	22	176	12	9	0	3.48
	RF	W. Keeler	546	.392	4	82	227	20	8	6	2.0	.969	D. Esper	20	156	14	5	0	3.58
	CF	S. Brodie	516	.297	2	87	320	22	10	6	2.7	.972							
	LF	J. Kelley	519	.364	8	100	280	20	13	3	2.4	.958							
	C	W. Robinson	245	.347	2	38	260	48	17	5	4.9	.948							
	C	B. Clarke	300	.297	2	71	203	53	14	5	4.0	.948							
Cle.	1B	P. Tebeau	543	.269	2	94	1340	75	21	88	11.8	.985	C. Young	51	414	29	16	3	3.24
W-80 L-48	2B	C. Childs	498	.355	1	106	375	487	53	73	6.9	.942	N. Cuppy	46	358	25	14	1	3.12
Patsy Tebeau	SS	E. McKean	571	.338	7	112	214	400	57	57	5.0	.915	Z. Wilson	33	240	17	9	1	4.01
	3B	C. McGarr	455	.268	1	53	123	228	29	20	3.4	.924	B. Wallace	22	145	10	7	0	3.34
	RF	H. Blake	383	.240	1	43	184	17	12	5	2.1	.944							
	CF	J. McAleer	455	.288	1	54	278	18	13	5	2.7	.958							
	LF	J. Burkett	586	.410	6	72	269	18	23	4	2.3	.926							
	C	C. Zimmer	336	.277	3	46	338	81	12	9	4.7	.972							
	UT	J. O'Connor	256	.297	1	43	242	40	7	13		.976							
	P	C. Young	180	.289	3	28	8	145	12	3	3.2	.927							
	OP	B. Wallace	149	.235	1	17	42	35	5	4		.939							
	P	N. Cuppy	141	.270	1	20	14	106	4	3	2.7	.968							
Cin.	1B	B. Ewing	263	.278	1	38	669	49	15	41	10.6	.980	F. Dwyer	36	289	24	11	1	3.15
W-77 L-50	2B	B. McPhee	433	.305	1	87	297	357	15	56	5.7	.978	R. Ehret	34	277	18	14	0	3.42
Buck Ewing	SS	G. Smith	456	.287	2	71	207	407	49	47	5.5	.915	F. Foreman	27	191	15	6	1	3.68
	3B	C. Irwin	476	.296	1	67	200	262	34	28	3.9	.931	C. Fisher	27	160	10	7	2	4.45
	RF	D. Miller	504	.321	4	93	199	21	24	7	2.0	.902	B. Rhines	19	143	8	6	0	2.45
	CF	D. Hoy	443	.298	4	57	303	14	18	3	2.8	.946							
	LF	E. Burke	521	.340	1	52	290	13	21	3	2.7	.935							
	C	H. Peitz	211	.299	2	34	201	42	8	6	3.7	.968							
	C1	F. Vaughn	433	.293	2	66	740	82	21	41		.975							
	P	R. Ehret	102	.196	1	20	15	69	7	3	2.7	.923							
Bos.	1B	T. Tucker	474	.304	2	72	1214	72	20	72	10.7	.985	K. Nichols	49	375	30	15	1	2.81
W-74 L-57	2B	B. Lowe	305	.321	2	48	193	280	17	31	6.7	.965	J. Stivetts	42	329	21	13	0	4.10
Frank Selee	SS	H. Long	508	.339	6	100	311	415	83	52	6.7	.897	J. Sullivan	31	225	11	12	1	4.03
	3B	J. Collins	304	.296	1	46	134	207	34	16	4.7	.909	F. Klobedanz	10	81	6	4	0	3.01
	RF	J. Bannon	343	.251	0	50	132	13	16	2	2.1	.901							
	CF	B. Hamilton	523	.365	3	52	276	8	20	2	2.3	.934							
	LF	H. Duffy	533	.302	5	112	250	15	12	2	2.2	.957							
	C	M. Bergen	245	.269	4	37	207	70	24	6	4.8	.920							
	OC	F. Tenney	348	.336	2	49	183	40	14	4		.941							
	P	J. Stivetts	221	.344	3	49	30	57	5	3	2.2	.946							
	3B	J. Harrington	198	.197	1	25	56	102	35	7	3.9	.819							
	C	C. Ganzel	179	.263	1	18	139	47	2	4	4.6	.989							
	2B	D. McGann	171	.322	2	30	88	111	21	10	5.1	.905							
	P	K. Nichols	147	.190	1	24	19	92	0	3	5.8	1.000							
Chi.	1B	C. Anson	402	.331	2	90	880	54	16	67	9.7	.983	C. Griffith	36	318	22	13	0	3.54
W-71 L-57	2B	F. Pfeffer	360	.244	2	52	227	307	30	43	6.0	.947	D. Friend	36	291	18	14	0	4.74
Cap Anson	SS	B. Dahlen	476	.361	9	74	310	456	71	66	6.7	.915	A. Terry	30	235	15	13	0	4.28
	3B	B. Everett	575	.320	2	46	148	180	44	10	3.8	.882	B. Briggs	26	194	12	8	1	4.31
	RF	J. Ryan	490	.312	3	86	207	21	22	4	2.0	.912							
	CF	B. Lange	469	.326	4	92	313	18	24	3	2.9	.932							
	LF	G. Decker	421	.280	5	61	131	10	11	0	2.1	.928							
	C	M. Kittredge	215	.223	1	19	251	56	12	12	5.0	.962							
	C	T. Donahue	188	.218	0	20	235	60	20	7	5.5	.937							
	3B	B. McCormick	168	.220	1	23	34	72	21	5	3.6	.835							
	P	C. Griffith	135	.267	1	16	20	79	9	3	3.0	.917							
	2B	H. Truby	109	.257	2	31	76	82	11	17	6.0	.935							
Pit.	1B	J. Beckley	217	.253	3	32	558	31	11	42	10.7	.982	F. Killen	52	432	29	15	0	3.41
W-66 L-63	2B	D. Padden	219	.242	2	24	176	149	24	14	5.7	.931	P. Hawley	49	378	22	21	0	3.57
Connie Mack	SS	B. Ely	537	.285	3	77	258	432	62	52	5.9	.918	J. Hughey	25	155	6	8	0	4.99
	3B	D. Lyons	436	.307	4	71	165	201	44	15	3.5	.893	C. Hastings	17	104	5	10	1	5.88
	RF	P. Donovan	573	.319	3	59	224	24	12	8	2.0	.954							
	CF	J. Stenzel	479	.361	2	82	247	13	22	5	2.5	.922							
	LF	E. Smith	484	.362	6	94	302	14	18	6	2.7	.946							
	C	J. Sugden	301	.296	0	36	284	70	18	12	5.3	.952							
	C	B. Merritt	282	.291	1	42	242	75	20	5	5.4	.941							
	2B	L. Bierbauer	258	.287	0	39	140	206	12	32	6.1	.966							
	P	F. Killen	173	.231	2	25	15	115	10	1	2.7	.929							
	1B	H. Davis	168	.190	0	23	325	18	12	17	10.1	.966							
	P	P. Hawley	163	.239	1	21	12	108	10	2	2.7	.923							

	POS	Player	AB	BA	HR	RBI	PO	A	E	DP	TC/G	FA	Pitcher	G	IP	W	L	SV	ERA
N. Y.	1B	W. Clark	247	.291	0	33	634	25	17	40	10.4	.975	D. Clarke	48	351	17	24	1	4.26
W-64 L-67	2B	K. Gleason	541	.299	4	89	329	397	48	38	6.0	.938	J. Meekin	42	334	26	14	0	3.82
Arthur Irwin	SS	Connaughton	315	.260	2	43	89	199	35	19	6.0	.892	M. Sullivan	25	185	10	13	0	4.66
W-38 L-53	3B	G. Davis	494	.320	6	99	117	169	26	11	4.2	.917	E. Doheny	17	108	6	7	0	4.49
Bill Joyce	RF	M. Tiernan	521	.369	7	89	213	15	7	4	1.8	.970							
W-26 L-14	CF	Van Haltren	562	.351	5	74	272	25	15	4	2.3	.952							
	LF	B. Stafford	230	.287	0	40	78	9	10	2	1.8	.897							
	C	P. Wilson	253	.237	0	23	256	64	22	4	4.8	.936							
	O1	H. Davis	233	.275	2	50	307	13	15	14		.955							
	UT	D. Farrell	191	.283	1	37	144	83	26	13		.897							
	1B	J. Beckley	182	.302	5	38	418	22	8	18	10.0	.982							
	3B	B. Joyce	165	.370	5*	43	71	103	23	4	4.0	.883							
	P	D. Clarke	147	.204	0	10	12	72	8	1	1.9	.913							
	P	J. Meekin	144	.299	2	16	17	62	8	3	2.1	.908							
Phi.	1B	D. Brouthers	218	.344	1	41	566	23	10	44	10.5	.983	J. Taylor	45	359	20	21	1	4.79
W-62 L-68	2B	B. Hallman	469	.320	2	83	304	368	39	62	5.9	.945	A. Orth	25	196	15	7	0	4.41
Billy Nash	SS	B. Hulen	339	.265	0	38	149	205	51	33	5.5	.874	K. Carsey	27	187	11	11	1	5.62
	3B	B. Nash	227	.247	3	30	87	148	23	12	4.0	.911	H. Keener	16	113	3	11	0	5.88
	RF	S. Thompson	517	.298	12	100	231	28	7	11	2.2	.974							
	CF	D. Cooley	287	.307	2	22	130	6	15	2	2.4	.901							
	LF	E. Delahanty	499	.397	13	126	262	18	14	4	3.0	.952							
	C	M. Grady	242	.318	1	44	167	60	14	12	4.0	.942							
	3S	L. Cross	406	.256	1	73	165	270	28	26		.940							
	OF	J. Sullivan	191	.251	2	24	99	3	4	0	2.4	.962							
	C	J. Clements	184	.359	5	45	149	51	7	3	3.9	.966							
	1B	N. Lajoie	174	.328	4	42	363	11	2	27	9.6	.995							
	P	J. Taylor	157	.185	0	18	19	107	11	3	3.0	.920							
	C	J. Boyle	145	.297	1	28	83	21	9	3	4.0	.920							
	OF	S. Mertes	143	.238	0	14	85	3	9	0	2.8	.907							
Bkn.	1B	C. LaChance	348	.284	7	58	956	37	14	62	11.3	.986	B. Kennedy	42	306	15	20	1	4.42
W-58 L-73	2B	T. Daly	224	.281	3	29	168	190	36	31	6.0	.909	H. Payne	34	242	14	16	0	3.39
Dave Foutz	SS	T. Corcoran	532	.289	3	73	323	477	64	69	6.5	.926	D. Daub	32	225	12	11	0	3.60
	3B	B. Shindle	516	.279	1	61	144	251	38	20	3.3	.912	B. Abbey	25	164	8	8	0	5.15
	RF	F. Jones	399	.353	3	46	171	10	14	6	1.9	.928	G. Harper	16	86	4	8	0	5.55
	CF	M. Griffin	493	.314	4	51	316	8	13	1	2.8	.961							
	LF	T. McCarthy	377	.249	3	47	175	20	17	6	2.1	.920							
	C	J. Grim	281	.267	2	35	242	82	21	7	4.5	.939							
	O1	J. Anderson	430	.314	1	55	538	28	16	30		.973							
	2B	G. Shoch	250	.292	1	28	103	184	18	16	4.9	.941							
	C	B. Burrell	206	.301	0	23	176	42	17	3	3.9	.928							
Was.	1B	E. Cartwright	499	.277	1	62	1276	71	30	76	10.4	.978	W. Mercer	46	366	25	18	0	4.13
W-58 L-73	2B	J. O'Brien	270	.267	4	33	166	228	20	33	5.7	.952	D. McJames	37	280	12	20	1	4.27
Gus Schmelz	SS	DeMontreville	533	.343	8	77	305	479	97	53	6.6	.890	L. German	28	167	2	20	1	6.32
	3B	B. Joyce	310	.313	9*	51	50	108	20	6	3.7	.888	S. King	22	145	10	7	1	4.09
	RF	B. Lush	352	.247	4	45	142	19	21	4	2.0	.885							
	CF	T. Brown	435	.294	2	59	262	7	21	2	2.5	.928							
	LF	K. Selbach	487	.304	5	100	303	13	18	3	2.7	.946							
	C	D. McGuire	389	.321	2	70	349	87	30	14	4.8	.936							
	OF	C. Abbey	301	.262	1	49	105	10	16		1.7	.878							
	P	W. Mercer	156	.244	1	14	36	89	21	3	3.2	.856							
	3B	J. Rogers	154	.279	1	30	27	70	13	2	3.4	.882							
	C3	D. Farrell	130	.300	1	30	75	47	5	1		.961							
	2B	J. Crooks	84	.286	3	20	49	49	9	5	5.4	.916							
St. L.	1B	R. Connor	483	.284	11	72	1217	94	16	48	10.5	.988	Breitenstein	44	340	18	26	0	4.48
W-40 L-90	2B	T. Dowd	521	.265	5	46	182	220	35	22	5.6	.920	B. Hart	42	336	12	29	0	5.12
Harry Diddlebock	SS	M. Cross	427	.244	6	52	298	394	84	31	6.2	.892	R. Donahue	32	267	7	24	0	5.80
W-7 L-11	RF	T. Turner	203	.246	1	27	69	4	3	1	1.5	.961	B. Kissinger	20	136	2	9	1	6.49
Arlie Latham	CF	T. Parrott	474	.291	7	70	276	16	15	7	2.8	.951							
W-0 L-2	LF	K. Douglass	296	.264	1	28	105	13	14	3	1.8	.894							
Chris Von Der Ahe	C	E. McFarland	290	.241	3	36	276	117	16	6	5.1	.961							
W-0 L-2	OF	J. Sullivan	212	.292	2	21	81	4	4	1	2.0	.955							
Roger Connor	2B	J. Quinn	191	.209	1	17	92	167	12	7	5.6	.956							
W-9 L-37	C	M. Murphy	175	.257	0	11	178	48	18	5	5.1	.926							
Tommy Dowd	OF	D. Cooley	166	.307	0	13	91	2	4	0	2.4	.959							
W-24 L-38	P	Breitenstein	162	.259	0	12	34	89	7	4	3.0	.946							
	P	B. Hart	161	.186	0	15	29	106	8	3	3.4	.944							
Lou.	1B	J. Rogers	290	.259	0	38	591	37	19	42	10.8	.971	C. Fraser	43	349	13	25	1	4.87
W-38 L-93	2B	J. O'Brien	186	.339	2	24	125	147	24	19	6.0	.919	S. Hill	43	320	9	28	2	4.31
John McCloskey	SS	J. Dolan	165	.212	3	18	92	159	16	25	6.1	.940	B. Cunningham	27	189	7	14	1	5.09
W-9 L-34	3B	B. Clingman	423	.234	2	37	188	281	38	21	4.2	.925	A. Herman	14	94	4	6	0	5.63
Bill McGunnigle	RF	T. McCreery	441	.351	7	65	177	20	18	4	1.9	.916							
W-29 L-59	CF	O. Pickering	165	.303	1	22	97	12	12	4	2.7	.901							
	LF	F. Clarke	517	.327	9	79	277	18	30	2	2.5	.908							
	C	C. Dexter	402	.279	3	37	179	63	26	9	4.9	.903							
	UT	D. Miller	324	.275	1	33	202	130	31	14		.915							
	1B	P. Cassidy	184	.212	0	12	348	17	10	14	9.9	.973							
	P	C. Fraser	146	.151	0	6	39	95	25	5	3.7	.843							
	OF	D. Holmes	141	.270	0	18	43	6	13	1	1.9	.790							

BATTING AND BASE RUNNING LEADERS

Batting Average

J. Burkett, CLE	.410
H. Jennings, BAL	.398
E. Delahanty, PHI	.397
W. Keeler, BAL	.392
M. Tiernan, NY	.369

Slugging Average

E. Delahanty, PHI	.631
B. Dahlen, CHI	.561
T. McCreery, LOU	.546
J. Kelley, BAL	.543
J. Burkett, CLE	.541

Home Runs

B. Joyce, NY, WAS	14
E. Delahanty, PHI	13
S. Thompson, PHI	12
R. Connor, STL	11
B. Dahlen, CHI	9
F. Clarke, LOU	9

Total Bases

J. Burkett, CLE	317
E. Delahanty, PHI	315
J. Kelley, BAL	282
W. Keeler, BAL	274
Van Haltren, NY	273

Runs Batted In

E. Delahanty, PHI	126
H. Jennings, BAL	121
H. Duffy, BOS	112
E. McKean, CLE	112
H. Reitz, BAL	106
C. Childs, CLE	106

Stolen Bases

B. Hamilton, BOS	93
J. Kelley, BAL	87
B. Lange, CHI	84
D. Miller, CIN	76
J. Doyle, BAL	73

Hits

J. Burkett, CLE	240
W. Keeler, BAL	214
H. Jennings, BAL	208

Base on Balls

B. Hamilton, BOS	110
B. Joyce, NY, WAS	101
C. Childs, CLE	100

Home Run Percentage

B. Joyce, NY, WAS	2.9
E. Delahanty, PHI	2.6
S. Thompson, PHI	2.3

Runs Scored

J. Burkett, CLE	160
B. Dahlen, CHI	153
W. Keeler, BAL	153

Doubles

E. Delahanty, PHI	44
D. Miller, CIN	38
J. Kelley, BAL	31

Triples

T. McCreery, LOU	21
Van Haltren, NY	21
B. Dahlen, CHI	19
J. Kelley, BAL	19

PITCHING LEADERS

Winning Percentage

B. Hoffer, BAL	.781
F. Foreman, CIN	.714
G. Hemming, BAL	.714
F. Dwyer, CIN	.686
A. Orth, PHI	.682

Earned Run Average

B. Rhines, CIN	2.45
K. Nichols, BOS	2.81
N. Cuppy, CLE	3.12
F. Dwyer, CIN	3.15
C. Young, CLE	3.24

Wins

K. Nichols, BOS	30
C. Young, CLE	29
F. Killen, PIT	29
J. Meekin, NY	26

Saves

C. Young, CLE	3
C. Fisher, CIN	2
S. Hill, LOU	2

Strikeouts

C. Young, CLE	137
P. Hawley, PIT	137
F. Killen, PIT	134
Breitenstein, STL	114
J. Meekin, NY	110

Complete Games

F. Killen, PIT	44
C. Young, CLE	42
W. Mercer, WAS	38

Fewest Hits per 9 Innings

B. Rhines, CIN	8.06
P. Hawley, PIT	9.10
M. Sullivan, NY	9.13

Shutouts

C. Young, CLE	5
F. Killen, PIT	5

Fewest Walks per 9 Innings

C. Young, CLE	1.35
D. Clarke, NY	1.54
F. Dwyer, CIN	1.87

Most Strikeouts per 9 Inn.

B. Briggs, CHI	3.90
A. Pond, BAL	3.36
D. McJames, WAS	3.31

Innings

F. Killen, PIT	432
C. Young, CLE	414
P. Hawley, PIT	378

Games Pitched

F. Killen, PIT	52
C. Young, CLE	51
P. Hawley, PIT	49
K. Nichols, BOS	49

	W	L	PCT	GB	R	OR	2B	3B	HR	BA	SA	SB	E	DP	FA	CG	BB	SO	ShO	SV	ERA
BAL	90	39	.698		995	662	207	100	23	.328	.429	441	296	114	.945	115	339	302	9	1	3.67
CLE	80	48	.625	9.5	840	650	207	72	28	.301	.391	175	288	117	.949	113	280	336	9	5	3.46
CIN	77	50	.606	12	783	620	205	73	19	.294	.388	350	252	107	.951	105	310	219	12	4	3.67
BOS	74	57	.565	17	860	761	175	74	36	.300	.392	241	368	94	.934	110	397	277	6	3	3.78
CHI	71	57	.555	18.5	815	799	182	97	34	.286	.390	332	366	115	.934	118	467	353	2	1	4.41
PIT	66	63	.512	24	787	741	169	94	27	.292	.385	217	317	103	.941	108	439	362	8	1	4.30
NY	64	67	.489	27	829	821	159	87	40	.297	.394	274	365	90	.933	104	403	312	1	2	4.54
PHI	62	68	.477	28.5	890	891	234	84	49	.295	.413	191	313	112	.941	107	387	243	3	2	5.20
BKN	58	73	.443	33	692	764	174	87	28	.284	.379	198	297	104	.945	97	400	259	3	1	4.25
WAS	58	73	.443	33	818	920	179	79	45	.286	.388	258	398	99	.927	106	435	292	2	3	4.61
STL	40	90	.308	50.5	593	929	134	78	37	.257	.346	185	345	73	.936	115	456	279	1	1	5.33
LOU	38	93	.290	53	653	997	142	80	37	.261	.351	195	475	110	.916	108	541	288	1	4	5.12
					9555	9555	2167	1005	403	.290	.387	3057	4080	1238	.938	1306	4854	3522	57	28	4.36

National League 1897

		POS	Player	AB	BA	HR	RBI	PO	A	E	DP	TC/G	FA	Pitcher	G	IP	W	L	SV	ERA
Bos.		1B	F. Tenney	566	.325	1	85	1248	81	16	69	10.5	.988	K. Nichols	46	368	30	11	3	2.64
W-93 L-39		2B	B. Lowe	499	.309	5	106	270	404	34	33	5.8	.952	F. Klobedanz	38	309	26	7	0	4.60
Frank Selee		SS	H. Long	452	.327	3	69	274	353	66	40	6.5	.905	T. Lewis	38	290	21	12	1	3.85
		3B	J. Collins	529	.346	6	132	214	303	47	20	4.2	.917	J. Stivetts	18	129	12	5	0	3.41
		RF	C. Stahl	469	.358	4	97	164	17	14	4	1.8	.928	J. Sullivan	13	89	4	5	2	3.94
		CF	B. Hamilton	507	.343	3	61	296	10	12	0	2.5	.962							
		LF	H. Duffy	554	.341	11	129	266	12	7	2	2.2	.975							
		C	M. Bergen	327	.248	2	45	351	66	16	4	5.1	.963							
		OP	J. Stivetts	199	.367	2	37	50	39	6	1		.937							
		P	F. Klobedanz	148	.324	1	20	8	47	2	4	1.5	.965							
		P	K. Nichols	147	.265	3	28	29	62	3	1	2.0	.968							
		SS	B. Allen	119	.319	1	24	78	117	16	12	6.6	.924							

	POS	Player	AB	BA	HR	RBI	PO	A	E	DP	TC/G	FA	Pitcher	G	IP	W	L	SV	ERA
Bal. W-90 L-40 Ned Hanlon	1B	J. Doyle	463	.356	1	87	1105	75	25	72	10.6	.979	J. Corbett	37	313	24	8	0	3.11
	2B	H. Reitz	477	.289	2	84	280	449	29	62	5.9	.962	B. Hoffer	38	303	22	11	0	4.30
	SS	H. Jennings	439	.355	2	79	335	425	55	54	7.0	.933	A. Pond	32	248	18	9	0	3.52
	3B	J. McGraw	391	.325	0	48	112	182	38	16	3.2	.886	J. Nops	30	221	20	6	0	2.81
	RF	W. Keeler	562	.432	1	74	217	12	7	2	1.8	.970							
	CF	J. Stenzel	536	.353	5	116	264	12	20	2	2.3	.932							
	LF	J. Kelley	505	.388	1	118	240	15	11	3	2.0	.959							
	C	B. Clarke	241	.270	1	38	191	38	15	2	4.1	.939							
	UT	J. Quinn	285	.260	1	45	142	176	16	22		.952							
	C	W. Robinson	181	.315	0	23	184	36	8	2	4.8	.965							
	P	J. Corbett	150	.247	0	22	21	76	16	1	3.1	.858							
	1O	T. O'Brien	147	.252	0	32	243	15	9	9		.966							
	P	B. Hoffer	139	.237	1	16	22	64	4	4	2.4	.956							
	C	F. Bowerman	130	.315	1	21	155	29	10	1	5.4	.948							
N. Y. W-83 L-48 Bill Joyce	1B	W. Clark	431	.283	1	75	1038	64	18	69	10.5	.984	A. Rusie	38	322	29	8	0	**2.54**
	2B	K. Gleason	540	.319	1	106	309	395	53	43	5.9	.930	J. Meekin	37	304	20	11	0	3.76
	SS	G. Davis	525	.358	9	134	337	434	62	67	6.4	.926	C. Seymour	38	292	20	14	1	3.21
	3B	B. Joyce	396	.306	3	64	165	199	63	17	4.0	.852	M. Sullivan	23	149	8	7	2	5.09
	RF	M. Tiernan	528	.330	5	72	178	11	14	2	1.6	.931							
	CF	Van Haltren	564	.330	3	64	267	31	20	4	2.5	.937							
	LF	D. Holmes	306	.268	1	44	113	9	13	2	1.8	.904							
	C	J. Warner	397	.275	2	51	513	127	32	17	6.1	.952							
	OF	T. McCreery	177	.299	1	28	53	10	7*	1	1.6	.900							
	UT	P. Wilson	154	.299	0	22	222	26	13	9		.950							
	P	A. Rusie	144	.278	0	22	19	77	8	3	2.7	.923							
	P	C. Seymour	137	.241	2	14	15	98	20	5	3.5	.850							
	P	J. Meekin	137	.299	0	10	14	56	11	2	2.2	.864							
Cin. W-76 L-56 Buck Ewing	1B	J. Beckley	365	.345	7	76	830	45	19	56	9.2	.979	Breitenstein	40	320	23	12	0	3.62
	2B	B. McPhee	282	.301	1	39	209	267	17	34	6.1	**.966**	B. Rhines	41	289	21	15	0	4.08
	SS	C. Ritchey	337	.282	0	41	144	204	40	21	5.5	.897	F. Dwyer	37	247	18	13	0	3.78
	3B	C. Irwin	505	.289	0	74	186	236	27	19	3.4	.940	R. Ehret	34	184	8	10	2	4.78
	RF	D. Miller	440	.316	4	70	203	18	17	2	2.0	.929	B. Damman	16	95	6	4	0	4.74
	CF	D. Hoy	497	.292	2	42	359	10	26	5	3.1	.934							
	LF	E. Burke	387	.266	1	41	224	11	15	4	2.6	.940							
	C	H. Peitz	266	.293	1	44	260	67	7	8	4.7	**.979**							
	S2	T. Corcoran	445	.288	3	57	286	360	48	51		.931							
	1B	F. Vaughn	199	.291	0	30	342	17	5	19	10.4	.986							
	OF	B. Holliday	195	.313	2	20	76	2	5	0	2.0	.940							
	C	P. Schriver	178	.303	1	30	147	42	8	3	3.7	.959							
	P	Breitenstein	124	.266	0	23	16	65	3	3	2.1	.964							
Cle. W-69 L-62 Patsy Tebeau	1B	P. Tebeau	412	.267	0	59	912	44	6	47	10.5	.994	C. Young	46	335	21	18	0	3.79
	2B	C. Childs	444	.338	1	61	319	384	42	42	6.5	.944	Z. Wilson	34	264	16	11	0	4.16
	SS	E. McKean	523	.273	2	78	226	385	53	36	5.3	.920	J. Powell	27	225	15	9	0	3.16
	3B	B. Wallace	522	.339	4	112	190	249	34	10	3.6	.928	N. Cuppy	19	139	10	6	0	3.18
	RF	L. Sockalexis	278	.338	3	42	117	10	16	3	2.2	.888							
	CF	O. Pickering	182	.352	1	22	110	5	6	1	2.6	.950							
	LF	J. Burkett	519	.383	2	60	226	18	13	3	2.0	.949							
	C	C. Zimmer	294	.316	0	40	278	81	9	10	4.6	.976							
	UT	J. O'Connor	397	.290	2	69	477	23	16	10		.969							
	P	C. Young	153	.222	0	19	16	88	9	0	2.5	.920							
	C	L. Criger	138	.225	0	22	129	35	11	1	4.7	.937							
	UT	McAllister	137	.219	0	11	74	21	9	1		.913							
Bkn. W-61 L-71 Billy Barnie	1B	C. LaChance	520	.308	4	90	1289	64	30	**76**	11.0	.978	B. Kennedy	44	343	19	22	1	3.91
	2B	G. Shoch	284	.278	0	38	188	240	27	25	6.7	.941	H. Payne	40	280	14	17	0	4.63
	SS	G. Smith	428	.201	0	29	201	399	61	36	5.9	.908	J. Dunn	25	217	14	9	0	4.57
	3B	B. Shindle	542	.284	3	105	185	241	45	13	3.5	.904	C. Fisher	20	149	9	7	1	4.23
	RF	F. Jones	553	.322	2	49	233	22	16	8	2.0	.941	D. Daub	19	138	6	11	0	6.08
	CF	M. Griffin	534	.318	2	56	353	13	17	6	2.9	.956							
	LF	J. Anderson	492	.325	4	85	253	11	18	2	2.5	.936							
	C	J. Grim	290	.248	0	25	241	98	19	8	4.6	.947							
	2B	J. Canavan	240	.217	2	34	157	162	32	18	5.6	.909							
	CO	B. Smith	237	.300	1	39	138	51	19	8		.909							
	P	B. Kennedy	147	.272	1	18	14	87	4	4	2.4	.962							
Was. W-61 L-71 Gus Schmelz W-9 L-25 Tom Brown W-52 L-46	1B	T. Tucker	352	.338	5	61	856	42	15	58	9.8	.984	W. Mercer	45	332	20	20	2	3.25
	2B	J. O'Brien	320	.244	3	45	223	260	30	43	6.0	.942	D. McJames	44	324	15	23	2	3.61
	SS	DeMontreville	**566**	.348	3	93	254	352	78	47	6.9	.886	C. Swaim	27	194	10	11	0	4.41
	3B	C. Reilly	351	.276	2	60	149	224	39	17	4.1	.905	S. King	23	154	7	8	1	4.79
	RF	C. Abbey	300	.260	3	34	126	14	8	1	1.9	.946							
	CF	T. Brown	469	.292	5	45	252	17	21	5	2.5	.928							
	LF	K. Selbach	486	.313	5	59	305	14	15	2	2.7	.955							
	C	D. McGuire	327	.343	4	53	290	88	21	6	5.5	.947							
	UT	Z. Wrigley	388	.284	3	64	175	209	50	18		.885							
	C	D. Farrell	261	.322	0	53	220	91	18	10	5.2	.945							
	OF	J. Gettman	143	.315	3	29	49	3	1	0	1.5	.981							
	PH	W. Mercer	135	.319	0	19													

POS	Player	AB	BA	HR	RBI	PO	A	E	DP	TC/G	FA	Pitcher	G	IP	W	L	SV	ERA
Pit. W-60 L-71 Patsy Donovan																		
1B	H. Davis	429	.305	2	63	570	29	22	26	9.7	.965	F. Killen	42	337	17	23	0	4.46
2B	D. Padden	517	.282	2	58	**369**	402	48	36	6.1	.941	P. Hawley	40	311	18	18	0	4.80
SS	B. Ely	516	.283	2	74	308	451	60	41	6.2	.927	J. Hughey	25	149	6	10	1	5.06
3B	Hoffmeister	188	.309	3	36	48	70	31	7	3.1	.792	J. Tannehill	21	142	9	9	1	4.25
RF	P. Donovan	479	.322	0	57	186	17	11	5	1.8	.949	C. Hastings	16	118	5	4	0	4.58
CF	S. Brodie	370	.292	2	53	218	11	4	1	2.3	**.983**	J. Gardner	14	95	5	5	0	5.19
LF	E. Smith	467	.310	6	54	245	19	28	1	2.4	.904							
C	J. Sugden	288	.222	0	38	317	82	25	6	5.2	.941							
C	B. Merritt	209	.263	1	26	202	43	14	6	4.9	.946							
OP	J. Tannehill	184	.266	0	22	89	53	13	1		.916							
3B	J. Donnelly	161	.193	0	14	51	87	12	1	3.4	.920							
Chi. W-59 L-73 Cap Anson																		
1B	C. Anson	424	.302	3	75	933	62	25	67	9.9	.975	C. Griffith	41	344	21	19	1	3.72
2B	J. Connor	285	.291	3	38	176	293	32	40	6.6	.936	D. Friend	24	203	12	11	0	4.52
SS	B. Dahlen	277	.296	6	40	215	291	38	48	7.3	.930	N. Callahan	23	190	12	9	0	4.03
3B	B. Everett	379	.314	5	39	119	147	42	9	3.7	.864	B. Briggs	22	187	4	17	0	5.26
RF	J. Ryan	520	.308	5	85	211	28	14	7	1.9	.945	W. Thornton	16	130	6	7	0	4.70
CF	B. Lange	479	.340	5	83	264	17	16	4	2.5	.946	R. Denzer	12	95	2	8	0	5.13
LF	G. Decker	428	.290	5	63	112	12	10	1	1.8	.925							
C	M. Kittredge	262	.202	1	30	324	75	20	6	5.3	.952							
3S	B. McCormick	419	.267	2	55	171	268	59	26		.882							
UT	N. Callahan	360	.292	3	47	147	201	42	25		.892							
OF	W. Thornton	265	.321	0	55	74	8	23	0	1.8	.781							
C	T. Donahue	188	.239	0	21	218	64	15	2	5.4	.949							
P	C. Griffith	162	.235	0	21	23	85	6	3	2.8	.947							
Phi. W-55 L-77 George Stallings																		
1B	N. Lajoie	545	.363	10	127	1079	37	18	45	10.5	.984	J. Taylor	40	317	16	20	2	4.23
2B	L. Cross	344	.259	3	51	68	120	7	10	5.1	.964	A. Orth	36	282	14	19	0	4.62
SS	S. Gillen	270	.259	0	27	129	197	38	6	5.3	.896	J. Fifield	27	211	5	18	0	5.51
3B	B. Nash	337	.258	0	39	114	146	23	10	3.6	.919	G. Wheeler	26	191	11	10	0	3.96
RF	T. Dowd	391	.292	0	43	116	9	11	3	1.9	.919							
CF	D. Cooley	**566**	.329	4	40	322	16	14	6	2.7	.960							
LF	E. Delahanty	530	.377	5	96	266	23	9	2	2.3	.970							
C	J. Boyle	288	.253	2	36	215	4	4	3	4.5	.982							
O2	P. Geier	316	.278	1	35	158	129	18	6		.941							
C	J. Clements	185	.238	6	36	163	40	8	3	4.3	.962							
SS	F. Shugart	163	.252	5	25	104	128	34	15	6.7	.872							
P	A. Orth	152	.329	1	17	9	69	6	1	2.3	.929							
P	J. Taylor	139	.252	1	17	12	89	16	2	2.9	.863							
Lou. W-52 L-78 Jim Rogers W-17 L-26 Fred Clarke W-35 L-52																		
1B	P. Werden	506	.302	5	83	**1318**	**116**	23	70	11.1	.984	C. Fraser	35	286	15	17	0	4.09
2B	J. Rogers	150	.147	2	22	86	120	15	12	5.7	.932	B. Cunningham	29	235	14	13	0	4.14
SS	B. Stafford	432	.278	7	53	197	353	70	33	6.0	.887	S. Hill	27	199	7	17	0	3.62
3B	B. Clingman	395	.228	2	47	176	269	25	16	4.2	.947	B. Magee	22	155	4	12	0	5.39
RF	T. McCreery	338	.284	4	40	130	13	24*	2	1.9	.856							
CF	O. Pickering	246	.252	1	21	134	15	10	2	2.6	.937							
LF	F. Clarke	525	.406	6	67	282	18	24	0	2.5	.926							
C	B. Wilson	381	.213	1	41	338	113	29	7	4.7	.940							
UT	C. Dexter	257	.280	2	46	132	68	27	8		.881							
OF	H. Wagner	241	.344	2	39	101	17	12	5	2.5	.908							
2B	A. Johnson	161	.242	0	23	68	92	22	8	5.5	.879							
S2	J. Dolan	133	.211	0	7	84	113	26	14		.883							
St. L. W-29 L-102 Tommy Dowd W-6 L-25 Hugh Nicol W-9 L-29 Bill Hallman W-13 L-46 Chris Von Der Ahe W-1 L-2																		
1B	M. Grady	322	.280	7	55	797	48	23	54	10.5	.974	R. Donahue	**46**	348	11	**33**	1	6.13
2B	B. Hallman	298	.221	0	26	189	244	28	35	6.0	.939	B. Hart	39	295	9	27	0	6.26
SS	M. Cross	462	.286	4	55	327	**513**	73	47	7.0	.920	K. Carsey	12	99	3	8	0	6.00
3B	F. Hartman	516	.306	2	67	159	253	**63**	14	3.8	.867							
RF	T. Turner	416	.291	2	41	146	10	9	3	1.6	.945							
CF	D. Harley	330	.291	3	35	186	19	23	3	2.6	.899							
LF	B. Lally	355	.279	2	42	192	9	23	2	2.7	.897							
C	K. Douglass	516	.329	6	50	171	64	13	4	4.1	.948							
2O	J. Houseman	278	.245	0	21	168	131	24	10		.926							
C	M. Murphy	207	.169	0	12	145	62	11	3	4.1	.950							
P	B. Hart	156	.250	2	14	21	76	8	4	2.7	.924							
P	R. Donahue	155	.213	1	14	24	97	3	1	2.7	.976							
OF	T. Dowd	145	.262	0	9	65	0	6	0	2.4	.915							

BATTING AND BASE RUNNING LEADERS

Batting Average		Slugging Average	
W. Keeler, BAL	.432	N. Lajoie, PHI	.578
F. Clarke, LOU	.406	W. Keeler, BAL	.553
J. Kelley, BAL	.388	F. Clarke, LOU	.550
J. Burkett, CLE	.383	E. Delahanty, PHI	.538
E. Delahanty, PHI	.377	G. Davis, NY	.516

Home Runs		Total Bases	
H. Duffy, BOS	11	N. Lajoie, PHI	315
N. Lajoie, PHI	10	W. Keeler, BAL	311
G. Davis, NY	9	F. Clarke, LOU	289
J. Beckley, CIN, NY	8	E. Delahanty, PHI	285
M. Grady, PHI, STL	7	G. Davis, NY	264
B. Stafford, LOU, NY	7		

PITCHING LEADERS

Winning Percentage		Earned Run Average	
F. Klobedanz, BOS	.788	A. Rusie, NY	2.54
A. Rusie, NY	.784	K. Nichols, BOS	2.64
J. Nops, BAL	.769	J. Nops, BAL	2.81
J. Corbett, BAL	.750	J. Corbett, BAL	3.11
K. Nichols, BOS	.732	J. Powell, CLE	3.16

Wins		Saves	
K. Nichols, BOS	30	K. Nichols, BOS	3
A. Rusie, NY	29		
F. Klobedanz, BOS	26		
J. Corbett, BAL	24		
Breitenstein, CIN	23		

BATTING AND BASE RUNNING LEADERS

Runs Batted In

G. Davis, NY	134
J. Collins, BOS	132
H. Duffy, BOS	129
N. Lajoie, PHI	127
J. Kelley, BAL	118

Hits

W. Keeler, BAL	243
F. Clarke, LOU	213
E. Delahanty, PHI	200

Home Run Percentage

M. Grady, PHI, STL	2.1
H. Duffy, BOS	2.0
G. Davis, NY	1.9

Doubles

J. Stenzel, BAL	43
E. Delahanty, PHI	40
N. Lajoie, PHI	40

Stolen Bases

B. Lange, CHI	73
B. Hamilton, BOS	70
J. Stenzel, BAL	69
G. Davis, NY	65
W. Keeler, BAL	64

Base on Balls

B. Hamilton, BOS	105
J. McGraw, BAL	99
M. Griffin, BKN	81

Runs Scored

B. Hamilton, BOS	152
W. Keeler, BAL	145
M. Griffin, BKN	136

Triples

H. Davis, PIT	28
N. Lajoie, PHI	23
B. Wallace, CLE	21

PITCHING LEADERS

Strikeouts

C. Seymour, NY	157
D. McJames, WAS	156
J. Corbett, BAL	149
K. Nichols, BOS	136
A. Rusie, NY	135

Fewest Hits per 9 Innings

C. Seymour, NY	8.23
A. Rusie, NY	8.77
K. Nichols, BOS	8.85

Fewest Walks per 9 Innings

C. Young, CLE	1.32
J. Tannehill, PIT	1.52
K. Nichols, BOS	1.66

Innings

K. Nichols, BOS	368
R. Donahue, STL	348
C. Griffith, CHI	344

Complete Games

C. Griffith, CHI	38
F. Killen, PIT	38
R. Donahue, STL	38
K. Nichols, BOS	37
B. Kennedy, BKN	36

Shutouts

D. McJames, WAS	3
W. Mercer, WAS	3

Most Strikeouts per 9 Inn.

C. Seymour, NY	4.83
D. McJames, WAS	4.34
J. Corbett, BAL	4.28

Games Pitched

K. Nichols, BOS	46
R. Donahue, STL	46
C. Young, CLE	46

	W	L	PCT	GB	R	OR	2B	3B	HR	BA	SA	SB	E	DP	FA	CG	BB	SO	ShO	SV	ERA
BOS	93	39	.705		1025	665	230	83	**45**	.319	**.426**	233	272	80	.951	115	393	329	**8**	**7**	3.65
BAL	90	40	.692	2	964	674	**243**	66	20	**.325**	.414	**401**	277	110	.951	118	382	361	3	0	3.55
NY	83	48	.634	9.5	895	695	188	84	31	.299	.392	328	397	109	.930	118	486	**456**	8	3	**3.47**
CIN	76	56	.576	17	763	705	219	69	22	.290	.383	194	273	100	.948	100	329	270	4	2	4.09
CLE	69	62	.527	23.5	773	680	192	88	16	.298	.389	181	**261**	74	.950	111	**289**	277	6	0	3.95
BKN	61	71	.462	32	802	845	202	72	22	.279	.365	187	364	99	.936	114	410	256	4	2	4.60
WAS	61	71	.462	32	781	793	194	77	36	.297	.395	208	369	103	.933	103	400	348	7	5	4.01
PIT	60	71	.458	32.5	676	835	140	**108**	25	.276	.370	170	346	70	.936	112	318	342	2	2	4.67
CHI	59	73	.447	34	832	894	189	97	38	.282	.386	264	393	**112**	.932	**131**	433	361	2	1	4.53
PHI	55	77	.417	38	752	792	213	83	40	.293	.398	163	296	72	.944	115	364	253	4	2	4.60
LOU	52	78	.400	40	669	859	160	70	40	.265	.358	195	395	85	.929	114	459	267	2	0	4.42
STL	29	102	.221	63.5	588	1083	149	67	31	.275	.356	172	375	84	.933	109	453	207	1	1	6.21
					9520	9520	2319	964	366	.292	.386	2696	4018	1098	.939	1360	4716	3727	51	25	4.31

National League 1898

	POS	Player	AB	BA	HR	RBI	PO	A	E	DP	TC/G	FA	Pitcher	G	IP	W	L	SV	ERA
Bos. W-102 L-47 Frank Selee	1B	F. Tenney	488	.334	0	62	1090	66	23	71	10.1	.980	K. Nichols	50	388	**29**	12	**3**	2.13
	2B	B. Lowe	566	.272	4	94	397	457	37	63	6.1	.958	T. Lewis	41	313	26	8	2	2.90
	SS	H. Long	589	.265	6	99	326	472	67	65	6.1	.923	V. Willis	41	311	24	13	0	2.84
	3B	J. Collins	597	.328	**15**	111	243	332	42	20	4.1	.932	F. Klobedanz	35	271	19	10	0	3.89
	RF	C. Stahl	469	.311	3	52	199	14	7	4	1.8	.968							
	CF	B. Hamilton	417	.369	3	50	189	8	21	2	2.0	.904							
	LF	H. Duffy	568	.315	8	108	332	18	16	2	2.4	.956							
	C	M. Bergen	446	.280	3	60	496	109	**24**	4	5.4	.962							
	UT	G. Yeager	221	.267	3	24	303	40	19	6		.948							
	P	K. Nichols	158	.241	2	23	21	78	4	1	2.1	.961							
Bal. W-96 L-53 Ned Hanlon	1B	D. McGann	535	.301	5	106	1416	68	26	78	10.4	.983	D. McJames	45	374	27	15	0	2.36
	2B	DeMontreville	567	.328	0	86	303	386	41	35	5.9	.944	J. Hughes	38	301	23	12	0	3.20
	SS	H. Jennings	534	.328	1	87	289	368	50	41	6.1	.929	A. Maul	28	240	20	6	0	2.10
	3B	J. McGraw	515	.342	0	53	142	271	46	16	3.4	.900	J. Nops	33	235	16	9	0	3.56
	RF	W. Keeler	564	**.379**	1	44	210	14	9	2	1.8	.961	F. Kitson	17	119	8	6	0	3.24
	CF	J. Kelley	467	.328	2	110	235	18	8	4	2.1	.969							
	LF	D. Holmes	442	.285	1	64	247	13	18	4	2.5	.935							
	C	W. Robinson	289	.277	0	38	288	72	13	4	4.8	.965							
	C	B. Clarke	285	.242	0	27	289	69	14	6	5.3	.962							
	P	J. Hughes	164	.226	2	20	**29**	78	11	1	3.1	.907							
	OF	J. Stenzel	138	.254	0	22	57	6	5	1	1.9	.926							

	POS	Player	AB	BA	HR	RBI	PO	A	E	DP	TC/G	FA	Pitcher	G	IP	W	L	SV	ERA
Cin. W-92 L-60 Buck Ewing	1B	J. Beckley	459	.294	4	72	1167	53	21	76	10.5	.983	P. Hawley	43	331	27	11	0	3.37
	2B	B. McPhee	486	.249	1	60	299	396	32	74	5.6	.956	Breitenstein	39	316	21	14	0	3.42
	SS	T. Corcoran	619	.250	2	87	353	561	67	76	6.4	.932	S. Hill	33	262	13	14	0	3.98
	3B	C. Irwin	501	.240	3	55	223	305	34	20	4.1	.940	F. Dwyer	31	240	16	10	0	3.04
	RF	D. Miller	586	.299	3	90	292	23	24	4	2.2	.929	B. Damman	35	225	16	10	2	3.61
	CF	A. McBride	486	.302	2	43	288	18	13	3	2.7	.959							
	LF	E. Smith	486	.342	1	66	280	15	16	5	2.5	.949							
	C	H. Peitz	330	.273	1	43	323	90	24	12	4.3	.945							
	UT	H. Steinfeldt	308	.295	0	43	202	158	41	17		.898							
	1C	F. Vaughn	275	.305	1	46	462	50	17	28		.968							
Chi. W-85 L-65 Tom Burns	1B	B. Everett	596	.319	0	69	1519	70	42	123	10.9	.974	C. Griffith	38	326	26	10	0	**1.88**
	2B	J. Connor	505	.226	0	67	330	437	44	75	5.9	.946	N. Callahan	31	274	20	10	0	2.46
	SS	B. Dahlen	524	.290	1	79	369	511	76	77	6.7	.921	W. Woods	27	215	9	13	0	3.14
	3B	B. McCormick	530	.247	2	78	152	322	60	31	3.9	.888	W. Thornton	28	215	13	10	0	3.34
	RF	S. Mertes	269	.297	1	47	97	13	15	6	2.1	.880	M. Kilroy	13	100	6	7	0	4.31
	CF	B. Lange	442	.319	6	69	269	19	9	4	2.7	.970	F. Isbell	13	81	4	7	0	3.56
	LF	J. Ryan	572	.323	4	79	267	20	27	2	2.2	.914							
	C	T. Donahue	396	.220	0	39	450	107	22	16	4.7	.962							
	OP	W. Thornton	210	.295	0	14	74	53	17	5		.882							
	OF	D. Green	188	.314	4	27	87	10	3	5	2.1	.970							
	P	N. Callahan	164	.262	0	22	27	63	5	3	3.1	.947							
	UT	F. Isbell	159	.233	0	8	54	43	19	5		.836							
	UT	W. Woods	154	.175	0	8	42	87	15	3		.896							
Cle. W-81 L-68 Patsy Tebeau	1B	P. Tebeau	477	.258	1	63	956	43	16	43	11.2	.984	C. Young	46	378	25	14	0	2.53
	2B	C. Childs	422	.289	1	31	273	370	48	37	6.3	.931	J. Powell	42	342	24	15	0	3.00
	SS	E. McKean	604	.285	9	94	304	425	53	47	5.2	.932	Z. Wilson	33	255	13	18	0	3.60
	3B	B. Wallace	593	.270	3	99	201	329	36	19	4.0	.936	N. Cuppy	18	128	9	8	0	3.30
	RF	H. Blake	474	.245	0	58	234	25	13	3	2.0	.952							
	CF	J. McAleer	366	.238	0	48	239	10	9	4	2.5	.965							
	LF	J. Burkett	624	.345	0	42	268	17	19	3	2.0	.938							
	C	L. Criger	287	.279	1	32	322	105	19	9	5.4	.957							
	UT	J. O'Connor	478	.249	1	56	761	92	20	36		.977							
	P	C. Young	154	.253	2	13	12	122	4	2	3.0	.971							
Phi. W-78 L-71 George Stallings W-19 L-27 Bill Shettsline W-59 L-44	1B	K. Douglass	582	.258	2	48	1236	73	32	74	9.2	.976	W. Piatt	39	306	24	14	0	3.18
	2B	N. Lajoie	610	.328	5	127	442	406	46	59	6.1	.949	R. Donahue	35	284	17	17	0	3.55
	SS	M. Cross	525	.257	1	50	404	506	93	65	6.7	.907	A. Orth	32	250	15	12	0	3.02
	3B	B. Lauder	361	.263	2	67	132	171	47	6	3.6	.866	J. Fifield	21	171	11	9	0	3.31
	RF	E. Flick	453	.313	7	81	237	21	19	4	2.1	.931	G. Wheeler	15	112	6	8	0	4.17
	CF	D. Cooley	629	.312	4	55	352	15	22	2	2.6	.943							
	LF	E. Delahanty	548	.334	4	92	302	20	12	5	2.3	.964							
	C	E. McFarland	429	.282	3	71	420	136	23	7	4.8	.960							
N. Y. W-77 L-73 Bill Joyce W-23 L-21 Cap Anson W-9 L-13 Bill Joyce W-45 L-39	1B	B. Joyce	508	.258	10	91	1252	87	47	73	10.7	.966	C. Seymour	45	357	25	17	0	3.18
	2B	K. Gleason	570	.221	0	62	366	468	55	57	6.2	.938	J. Meekin	38	320	16	18	0	3.77
	SS	G. Davis	486	.307	2	86	349	421	55	61	6.8	.933	A. Rusie	37	300	20	11	1	3.03
	3B	F. Hartman	475	.272	2	88	146	280	57	16	3.9	.882	E. Doheny	28	213	7	19	0	3.68
	RF	J. Doyle	297	.283	1	43	39	10	8	2	1.5	.860	C. Gettig	17	115	6	3	0	3.83
	CF	Van Haltren	654	.312	2	68	299	22	29	5	2.2	.917							
	LF	M. Tiernan	415	.280	4	49	130	12	4	2	1.4	.973							
	C	J. Warner	373	.257	0	42	536	139	22	10	6.4	.968							
	PO	C. Seymour	297	.276	4	23	71	119	25	9		.884							
	UT	M. Grady	287	.296	3	49	321	74	34	7		.921							
	UT	C. Gettig	196	.250	0	26	70	103	21	6		.892							
	OF	W. Wilmot	138	.239	2	22	35	4	5	0	1.3	.886							
Pit. W-72 L-76 Bill Watkins	1B	W. Clark	209	.306	1	31	601	27	10	29	11.2	.984	J. Tannehill	43	327	25	13	2	2.95
	2B	D. Padden	463	.257	2	43	301	407	40	46	5.8	.947	B. Rhines	31	258	12	16	0	3.52
	SS	B. Ely	519	.212	2	44	311	527	51	58	6.0	**.943**	J. Gardner	25	185	10	13	0	3.21
	3B	B. Grey	528	.229	0	67	172	258	59	16	3.6	.879	F. Killen	23	178	10	11	0	3.75
	RF	P. Donovan	610	.302	0	37	238	21	20	4	1.9	.928	C. Hastings	19	137	4	10	0	3.41
	CF	T. O'Brien	413	.259	1	45	144	15	13	4*	2.5	.924	B. Hart	16	125	5	9	1	4.82
	LF	J. McCarthy	537	.289	4	78	296	19	22	4	2.5	.935							
	C	P. Schriver	315	.229	0	32	302	95	18	6	4.5	.957							
	C	F. Bowerman	241	.274	0	29	204	76	16	8	5.0	.946							
	1B	H. Davis	222	.293	1	24	556	22	12	30	11.1	.980							
	OF	T. McCreery	190	.311	2	20	107	6	8	1	2.4	.934							
	OF	S. Brodie	156	.263	0	21	110	4	5	1	2.8	.958							
Lou. W-70 L-81 Fred Clarke	1B	H. Wagner	591	.305	10	105	729	41	22	44	10.6	.972	B. Cunningham	44	362	28	15	0	3.16
	2B	H. Smith	121	.190	0	13	74	87	16	8	5.4	.910	B. Magee	38	295	16	15	0	4.05
	SS	C. Ritchey	558	.260	5	51	194	228	37	32	5.7	.919	P. Dowling	36	286	13	20	0	4.16
	3B	B. Clingman	538	.257	0	50	119	191	29	12	4.3	.914	C. Fraser	26	203	7	19	0	5.32
	RF	C. Dexter	421	.314	1	66	148	13	7	2	1.8	.958	R. Ehret	12	89	3	7	0	5.76
	CF	D. Hoy	582	.304	6	66	348	19	21	6	2.6	.940							
	LF	F. Clarke	599	.317	3	47	344	19	23	3	2.6	.940							
	C	M. Kittredge	287	.244	1	31	258	80	20	10	4.2	.944							
	2O	B. Stafford	181	.298	1	25	91	82	17	9		.911							

Bkn. — W-54 L-91 · Billy Barnie W-15 L-20 · Mike Griffin W-1 L-3 · Charlie Ebbets W-38 L-68

POS	Player	AB	BA	HR	RBI	PO	A	E	DP	TC/G	FA	Pitcher	G	IP	W	L	SV	ERA
1B	C. LaChance	526	.247	5	65	807	20	10	53	11.3	.988	B. Kennedy	40	339	16	21	0	3.37
2B	F. Hallman	509	.244	2	63	268	419	41	46	5.9	.944	J. Dunn	41	323	16	21	0	3.60
SS	G. Magoon	343	.224	1	39	199	357	45	38	6.5	.925	J. Yeager	36	291	12	22	0	3.65
3B	B. Shindle	466	.225	1	41	154	278	42	23	4.0	.911	R. Miller	23	152	4	14	0	5.34
RF	F. Jones	599	.302	1	69	229	17	14	7	1.8	.946	K. McKenna	14	101	2	6	0	5.63
CF	M. Griffin	544	.296	2	40	314	20	9	7	2.6	.974							
LF	J. Sheckard	409	.291	4	64	213	12	18	2	2.3	.926							
C	J. Ryan	301	.189	0	24	289	93	16	13	4.7	.960							
1B	T. Tucker	283	.279	1	34	797*	49	8	44	11.7*	.991							
OC	B. Smith	199	.261	0	23	103	24	13	5		.907							
C	J. Grim	178	.281	0	11	155	56	11	6	4.3	.950							
P	J. Dunn	167	.246	0	19	22	70	6	2	2.4	.939							

Was. — W-51 L-101 · Tom Brown W-3 L-13 · Jack Doyle W-20 L-24 · Deacon McGuire W-19 L-49 · Arthur Irwin W-9 L-15

POS	Player	AB	BA	HR	RBI	PO	A	E	DP	TC/G	FA	Pitcher	G	IP	W	L	SV	ERA
1B	J. Doyle	177	.305	2	26	344	17	14	23	9.9	.963	G. Weyhing	45	361	15	26	0	4.51
2B	H. Reitz	489	.303	2	47	323	401	31	56	5.7	.959	W. Mercer	33	234	12	18	0	4.81
SS	Z. Wrigley	400	.245	2	39	252	326	68	42	6.7	.895	B. Dinneen	29	218	9	16	0	4.00
3B	J. Smith	234	.303	3	28	65	74	15	6	3.3	.903	F. Killen	17	128	6	9	0	3.58
RF	J. Gettman	567	.277	5	47	234	18	20	4	2.0	.926	C. Swaim	16	101	3	11	1	4.26
CF	J. Anderson	430	.305	9	71	200	20	12	3	2.5	.948							
LF	K. Selbach	515	.303	3	60	320	24	19	6	2.8	.948							
C	D. McGuire	489	.268	1	57	371	93	16	11	5.2	.967							
C1	D. Farrell	338	.314	1	53	434	96	27	22		.952							
UT	W. Mercer	249	.321	2	25	91	116	29	8		.877							
UT	B. Wagner	223	.224	1	31	82	102	37	8		.833							
OF	B. Freeman	107	.364	3	21	39	5	1	2	1.6	.978							

St. L. — W-39 L-111 · Tim Hurst

POS	Player	AB	BA	HR	RBI	PO	A	E	DP	TC/G	FA	Pitcher	G	IP	W	L	SV	ERA
1B	G. Decker	286	.259	1	45	772	17	16	31	10.7	.980*	J. Taylor	50	397	15	29	1	3.90
2B	J. Crooks	225	.231	1	20	192	209	17	23	6.3	.959	W. Sudhoff	41	315	11	27	1	4.34
SS	G. Smith	157	.159	1	9	79	167	26	14	5.3	.904	J. Hughey	35	284	7	24	0	3.93
3B	L. Cross	602	.317	3	79	215	351	33	20	4.0	.945	K. Carsey	20	124	2	12	0	6.33
RF	T. Dowd	586	.244	0	32	208	11	19	3	1.8	.920							
CF	J. Stenzel	404	.282	1	33	257	8	16	2	2.6	.943							
LF	D. Harley	549	.246	0	42	311	26	27	3	2.6	.926							
C	J. Clements	335	.257	3	41	287	81	11	8	4.4	.971							
2S	J. Quinn	375	.251	0	36	218	340	31	30		.947							
C	J. Sugden	289	.253	0	34	181	88	18	8	4.8	.937							
1B	T. Tucker	252	.238	0	20	755*	36	22	40	11.3*	.973							
P	J. Taylor	157	.242	1	18	18	144	22	2	3.7	.880							

BATTING AND BASE RUNNING LEADERS

Batting Average
W. Keeler, BAL	.379
B. Hamilton, BOS	.369
J. Burkett, CLE	.345
J. McGraw, BAL	.342
E. Smith, CIN	.342

Slugging Average
J. Anderson, BKN, WAS	.494
J. Collins, BOS	.479
E. Flick, PHI	.457
E. Delahanty, PHI	.454
B. Hamilton, BOS	.453

Home Runs
J. Collins, BOS	15
B. Joyce, NY	10
H. Wagner, LOU	10
J. Anderson, BKN, WAS	9
E. McKean, CLE	9

Total Bases
J. Collins, BOS	286
N. Lajoie, PHI	275
Van Haltren, NY	270
J. Anderson, BKN, WAS	257
D. Cooley, PHI	256

Runs Batted In
N. Lajoie, PHI	127
J. Collins, BOS	111
J. Kelley, BAL	110
H. Duffy, BOS	108
D. McGann, BAL	106

Stolen Bases
B. Hamilton, BOS	59
E. Delahanty, PHI	58
DeMontreville, BAL	49
C. Dexter, LOU	44
J. McGraw, BAL	43

Hits
J. Burkett, CLE	215
W. Keeler, BAL	214
Van Haltren, NY	204

Base on Balls
J. McGraw, BAL	112
B. Joyce, NY	88
B. Hamilton, BOS	87

Home Run Percentage
J. Collins, BOS	2.5
B. Joyce, NY	2.0
E. Flick, PHI	1.8

Runs Scored
J. McGraw, BAL	143
H. Jennings, BAL	135
Van Haltren, NY	129

Doubles
N. Lajoie, PHI	40
E. Delahanty, PHI	36
B. Dahlen, CHI	35
J. Collins, BOS	35

Triples
J. Anderson, BKN, WAS	22
D. Hoy, LOU	16
Van Haltren, NY	16

PITCHING LEADERS

Winning Percentage
A. Maul, BAL	.769
T. Lewis, BOS	.765
C. Griffith, CHI	.722
P. Hawley, CIN	.711
K. Nichols, BOS	.707

Earned Run Average
C. Griffith, CHI	1.88
A. Maul, BAL	2.10
K. Nichols, BOS	2.13
D. McJames, BAL	2.36
N. Callahan, CHI	2.46

Wins
K. Nichols, BOS	29
B. Cunningham, LOU	28
P. Hawley, CIN	27
D. McJames, BAL	27
T. Lewis, BOS	26
C. Griffith, CHI	26

Saves
K. Nichols, BOS	3
B. Damman, CIN	2
T. Lewis, BOS	2
J. Tannehill, PIT	2
P. Hickman, BOS	2

Strikeouts
C. Seymour, NY	244
D. McJames, BAL	178
V. Willis, BOS	160
K. Nichols, BOS	138
W. Piatt, PHI	121

Complete Games
J. Taylor, STL	42
B. Cunningham, LOU	41
C. Young, CLE	40
D. McJames, BAL	40
K. Nichols, BOS	40

Fewest Hits per 9 Innings
K. Nichols, BOS	7.33
V. Willis, BOS	7.64
T. Lewis, BOS	7.67

Shutouts
W. Piatt, PHI	6
J. Powell, CLE	6

Fewest Walks per 9 Innings
C. Young, CLE	0.98
F. Dwyer, CIN	1.58
B. Cunningham, LOU	1.62

Most Strikeouts per 9 Inn.
C. Seymour, NY	6.03
V. Willis, BOS	4.63
D. McJames, BAL	4.28

Innings
J. Taylor, STL	397
K. Nichols, BOS	388
C. Young, CLE	378

Games Pitched
J. Taylor, STL	50
K. Nichols, BOS	50
C. Young, CLE	46

	W	L	PCT	GB	R	OR	Batting 2B	3B	HR	BA	SA	SB	Fielding E	DP	FA	Pitching CG	BB	SO	ShO	SV	ERA
BOS	102	47	.685		872	614	190	55	**53**	.290	**.377**	172	310	102	.950	127	470	432	9	**7**	2.98
BAL	96	53	.644	6	**933**	623	154	77	12	**.302**	.368	**250**	326	105	.947	138	400	422	12	0	2.90
CIN	92	60	.605	11.5	831	740	207	**101**	19	.271	.359	165	325	128	.950	131	449	294	10	2	3.50
CHI	85	65	.567	17.5	828	679	175	83	19	.274	.350	220	412	**149**	.936	137	364	323	**13**	0	**2.83**
CLE	81	68	.544	21	730	683	162	56	18	.263	.325	93	**301**	95	**.952**	**142**	**309**	339	9	0	3.20
PHI	78	71	.523	24	823	784	**238**	81	33	.280	.377	182	379	102	.937	129	399	325	10	0	3.72
NY	77	73	.513	25.5	837	800	190	86	33	.266	.352	214	447	113	.932	141	587	**558**	9	1	3.44
PIT	72	76	.486	29.5	634	694	140	88	14	.258	.328	107	340	105	.946	131	346	330	10	3	3.41
LOU	70	81	.464	33	728	833	150	71	32	.267	.342	235	382	114	.939	137	470	271	4	0	4.24
BKN	54	91	.372	46	638	811	156	66	17	.256	.322	130	334	125	.947	134	476	294	1	0	4.01
WAS	51	101	.336	52.5	704	939	177	81	35	.271	.355	197	443	119	.929	129	450	371		1	4.52
STL	39	111	.260	63.5	571	929	149	55	13	.247	.305	104	388	97	.939	133	372	288		2	4.53
					9129	9129	2088	900	298	.271	.347	2069	4387	1354	.942	1609	5092	4247	87	16	3.60

National League 1899

	POS	Player	AB	BA	HR	RBI	PO	A	E	DP	TC/G	FA	Pitcher	G	IP	W	L	SV	ERA
Bkn. W-101 L-47 Ned Hanlon	1B	D. McGann	214	.243	2	32	645	31	10	49	11.2	.985*	J. Dunn	41	299	23	13	2	3.70
	2B	T. Daly	498	.313	5	88	377	453	63	69	6.3	.929	J. Hughes	35	292	**28**	6	0	2.68
	SS	B. Dahlen	428	.283	4	76	256	377	40	48	6.1	.941	B. Kennedy	40	277	22	8	2	2.79
	3B	D. Casey	525	.269	1	43	162	258	51	20	3.5	.892	D. McJames	37	275	19	15	1	3.50
	RF	W. Keeler	571	.377	1	61	208	21	5	4	1.7	.979							
	CF	F. Jones	365	.285	2	38	199	11	12	2	2.3	.946							
	LF	J. Kelley	540	.330	6	93	307	26	8	7	2.4	.977							
	C	D. Farrell	254	.299	2	55	251	111	20	9	4.9	.948							
	O1	J. Anderson	439	.269	3	92	537	30	19	27		.968							
	1B	H. Jennings	216	.296	0	40	446	25	7	24	9.6	.985							
	C	D. McGuire	157	.318	0	23	144	58*	6	2	4.5	.971							
Bos. W-95 L-57 Frank Selee	1B	F. Tenney	603	.347	1	67	1474	**99**	35	**107**	10.7	.978	K. Nichols	42	349	21	17	1	2.94
	2B	B. Lowe	559	.272	4	88	361	461	40	66	5.8	.954	V. Willis	41	343	27	10	2	2.50
	SS	H. Long	578	.265	6	100	351	435	60	**68**	5.9	.929	T. Lewis	29	235	17	11	0	3.49
	3B	J. Collins	599	.277	4	91	217	**376**	36	23	4.2	.943	J. Meekin	13	108	7	6	0	2.83
	RF	C. Stahl	576	.351	8	53	253	26	9	6	1.9	.969	F. Killen	12	99	7	5	0	4.26
	CF	B. Hamilton	297	.310	1	33	166	11	9	2	2.3	.952	H. Bailey	12	87	6	4	0	3.95
	LF	H. Duffy	588	.279	3	102	344	9	11	1	2.5	.970							
	C	M. Bergen	260	.258	1	34	253	89	16	4	5.0	.955							
	C	B. Clarke	223	.224	2	32	213	69	18	4	5.0	.940							
	OF	B. Stafford	182	.302	3	40	86	0	4	0	2.2	.956							
	OF	C. Frisbee	152	.329	0	20	68	9	11	1	2.2	.875							
Phi. W-94 L-58 Bill Shettsline	1B	D. Cooley	406	.276	1	31	756	34	24	56	10.3	.971	W. Piatt	39	305	23	15	0	3.45
	2B	N. Lajoie	308	.380	5	70	224	231	22	39	7.1	.954	R. Donahue	35	279	21	8	0	3.39
	SS	M. Cross	557	.257	3	65	**370**	**529**	**90**	55	6.4	.909	C. Fraser	35	271	21	13	0	3.36
	3B	B. Lauder	583	.268	3	90	210	307	62	22	3.8	.893	A. Orth	21	145	13	3	1	**2.49**
	RF	E. Flick	485	.342	2	98	234	24	19	7	2.2	.931	B. Bernhard	21	132	6	6	0	2.65
	CF	R. Thomas	547	.325	0	47	313	22	17	8	2.6	.952	J. Fifield	14	93	3	8	1	4.08
	LF	E. Delahanty	573	**.408**	9	**137**	284	26	10	4	2.2	.969							
	C	E. McFarland	324	.333	1	57	305	125	14	**14**	4.7	.968							
	UT	P. Chiles	338	.320	2	76	330	44	25	18		.937							
	C	K. Douglass	275	.255	0	27	179	76	8	7	4.0	.970							
	2B	J. Dolan	222	.257	1	30	113	190	28	10	5.4	.915							
Bal. W-86 L-62 John McGraw	1B	C. LaChance	472	.307	1	75	1272	40	21	72	10.7	.984	J. McGinnity	48	**380**	**28**	17	-2	2.58
	2B	DeMontreville	240	.279	1	36	174	197	15	16	6.4	.961	F. Kitson	40	330	22	16	0	2.76
	SS	B. Keister	523	.329	3	75	169	283	53	25	5.6	.895	J. Nops	33	259	17	11	0	4.03
	3B	J. McGraw	399	.391	1	33	142	270	24	14	3.7	.945	H. Howell	28	209	13	8	1	3.91
	RF	J. Sheckard	536	.295	3	75	298	33	20	14	2.4	.943							
	CF	S. Brodie	531	.309	3	87	310	15	7	5	2.4	**.979**							
	LF	D. Holmes	553	.320	4	66	321	24	**27**	5	2.7	.927							
	C	W. Robinson	356	.284	0	47	286	83	20	2	3.7	.949							
	O3	D. Fultz	210	.295	0	18	94	41	16	1		.894							
	SS	G. Magoon	207	.256	0	31	143	215	30	19	6.3	.923							
	1C	P. Crisham	172	.291	0	20	282	23	8	3		.974							
	C	B. Smith	120	.383	0	25	109	26	7	3	3.9	.951							
St. L. W-84 L-67 Patsy Tebeau	1B	P. Tebeau	281	.246	1	26	648	22	14	33	10.5	.980	J. Powell	48	373	23	21	0	3.52
	2B	C. Childs	465	.267	1	48	323	355	48	45	5.8	.934	C. Young	44	369	26	15	1	2.58
	SS	B. Wallace	577	.302	12	108	238	386	55	40	6.8	.919	W. Sudhoff	26	189	13	10	0	3.61
	3B	L. Cross	403	.303	4	64	157	277	18	25*	4.4	.960*	N. Cuppy	21	172	11	8	0	3.15
	RF	E. Heidrick	591	.328	2	82	211	**34**	20	6	1.8	.925	C. Jones	12	85	6	5	0	3.59
	CF	H. Blake	292	.240	2	41	176	10	4	3	2.2	.979							
	LF	J. Burkett	567	.402	7	71	296	20	21	3	2.4	.938							
	C	L. Criger	258	.256	2	44	228	91	17	6	4.5	.949							
	C1	J. O'Connor	289	.253	0	43	427	76	18	20		.965							
	1C	Schreckengost	277	.278	2	37	516	49	23	35		.961							
	UT	E. McKean	277	.260	3	40	254	156	34	25		.923							
	OF	M. Donlin	267	.330	6	27	96	7	15	2	2.3	.873							

	POS	Player	AB	BA	HR	RBI	PO	A	E	DP	TC/G	FA	Pitcher	G	IP	W	L	SV	ERA
Cin.	1B	J. Beckley	513	.333	3	99	1291	72	19	74	10.3	.986	N. Hahn	38	309	23	7	0	2.68
W-83 L-67	2B	B. McPhee	373	.279	1	65	245	312	26	41	5.6	.955	P. Hawley	34	250	14	17	1	4.24
Buck Ewing	SS	T. Corcoran	537	.277	0	81	281	416	52	52	6.1	.931	B. Phillips	33	228	17	9	1	3.32
	3B	C. Irwin	314	.232	1	52	108	142	25	5	3.5	.909	Breitenstein	26	211	14	10	0	3.59
	RF	D. Miller	323	.251	0	37	148	18	13	4	2.2	.927	J. Taylor	24	168	9	10	2	4.12
	CF	E. Smith	339	.298	1	24	178	12	16	3	2.4	.922							
	LF	K. Selbach	521	.296	3	87	355	27	19	10	2.9	.953							
	C	H. Peitz	290	.272	1	43	329	89	10	12	4.7	.977							
	32	H. Steinfeldt	386	.244	0	43	175	239	41	17		.910							
	OF	A. McBride	251	.347	1	23	124	8	7	2	2.2	.950							
	C	B. Wood	194	.314	0	24	160	49	14	3	4.2	.937							
	S3	K. Elberfeld	138	.261	0	22	74	108	25	9		.879							
	OF	S. Crawford	127	.307	1	20	56	9	2	2	2.2	.970							
Pit.	1B	W. Clark	298	.285	0	44	837	36	10	37	11.3	.989	S. Leever	51	379	20	23	3	3.18
W-76 L-73	2B	J. O'Brien	279	.226	1	33	211	243	26	32	6.1	.946	J. Tannehill	41	333	24	14	1	2.57
Bill Watkins	SS	B. Ely	522	.278	3	72	274	472	58	45	6.1	.928	T. Sparks	28	170	8	6	0	3.86
W-8 L-16	3B	J. Williams	617	.355	9	116	251	354	66	14	4.4	.902	B. Hoffer	23	164	8	10	0	3.63
Patsy Donovan	RF	P. Donovan	531	.294	1	55	184	9	12	3	1.7	.941	J. Chesbro	19	149	6	10	0	4.11
W-68 L-57	CF	G. Beaumont	437	.352	3	38	235	20	21	6	2.7	.924							
	LF	J. McCarthy	560	.305	3	47	281	18	12	5	2.3	.961							
	C	F. Bowerman	424	.259	3	53	276	128	22	7	5.4	.948							
	OF	T. McCreery	455	.323	2	64	198	16	21	2	2.4	.911							
	C	P. Schriver	301	.282	1	49	275	94	16	6	4.9	.958							
	1B	P. Dillon	121	.256	0	20	301	17	4	16	10.7	.988							
Chi.	1B	B. Everett	536	.310	1	74	1491	95	47	103	12.0	.971	J. Taylor	41	355	18	21	0	3.76
W-75 L-73	2B	B. McCormick	376	.258	2	52	200	344	34	47	5.8	.941	C. Griffith	38	320	22	13	0	2.79
Tom Burns	SS	DeMontreville	310	.281	0	40	192	306	54	38	6.7	.902	N. Callahan	35	294	21	12	0	3.06
	3B	H. Wolverton	389	.285	1	49	123	227	57	12	4.2	.860	N. Garvin	24	199	9	13	0	2.85
	RF	D. Green	475	.295	6	56	175	22	11	11	1.8	.947	B. Phyle	10	84	1	8	1	4.20
	CF	B. Lange	416	.325	1	58	224	22	6	11	2.7	.971							
	LF	J. Ryan	525	.301	3	68	266	18	13	6	2.4	.956							
	C	T. Donahue	278	.248	0	29	304	100	21	13	4.7	.951							
	OF	S. Mertes	426	.298	9	81	197	20	18	4	2.2	.923							
	23	J. Connor	234	.205	0	24	101	211	26	25		.923							
	C	F. Chance	192	.286	1	22	166	64	12	6	4.2	.950							
	SS	G. Magoon	189	.228	0	21	138	216	41	34	6.7	.896							
Lou.	1B	M. Kelley	282	.241	3	33	745	38	21	37	10.6	.974	B. Cunningham	39	324	17	17	0	3.84
W-75 L-77	2B	C. Ritchey	540	.309	4	71	352	414	51	54	6.0	.938	D. Phillippe	42	321	20	17	1	3.17
Fred Clarke	SS	B. Clingman	366	.262	2	44	195	381	53	43	5.8	.916	P. Dowling	34	290	13	17	0	3.11
	3B	T. Leach	406	.288	5	57	135	200	34	13	4.6	.908	W. Woods	26	186	9	13	0	3.28
	RF	C. Dexter	295	.258	1	33	131	16	9	2	2.2	.942	R. Waddell	10	79	7	2	1	3.08
	CF	D. Hoy	633	.306	5	49	321	21	27	8	2.4	.927	B. Magee	12	71	3	7	0	5.20
	LF	F. Clarke	601	.348	5	70	327	20	13	2	2.5	.964							
	C	C. Zimmer	262	.298	2	29	184	77	4	6	4.3	.985*							
	3O	H. Wagner	549	.359	7	113	197	182	24	15		.940							
	C	M. Powers	169	.207	0	22	118	27	9	5	4.1	.942							
	P	B. Cunningham	154	.260	2	17	35	100	8	2	3.7	.944							
N. Y.	1B	J. Doyle	454	.308	3	76	1110	69	29	76	10.7	.976	B. Carrick	44	362	16	26	0	4.65
W-60 L-90	2B	K. Gleason	576	.264	0	59	403	465	50	60	6.3	.946	C. Seymour	32	268	14	17	0	3.56
John Day	SS	G. Davis	416	.346	1	57	311	412	42	57	7.1	.945	E. Doheny	35	265	14	17	0	4.51
W-30 L-40	3B	F. Hartman	174	.236	1	16	56	100	20	11	3.5	.886	J. Meekin	18	148	5	11	0	4.37
Fred Hoey	RF	P. Foster	301	.296	3	57	103	8	6	3	1.4	.949	C. Gettig	18	128	7	8	0	4.43
W-30 L-50	CF	Van Haltren	604	.301	2	58	284	31	23	8	2.2	.932							
	LF	T. O'Brien	573	.297	6	77	243	21	19	7	2.2	.933							
	C	J. Warner	293	.266	0	19	312	123	22	8	5.6	.952							
	UT	P. Wilson	328	.268	0	42	416	140	49	34		.919							
	C3	M. Grady	311	.334	2	54	147	137	26	9		.916							
	P	C. Seymour	159	.327	2	27	16	88	20	1	3.9	.839							
Was.	1B	D. McGann	280	.343	5	58	667	36	7	37	9.3	.990*	G. Weyhing	43	335	17	23	0	4.54
W-54 L-98	2B	F. Bonner	347	.274	2	44	192	264	29	34	5.7	.940	B. Dinneen	37	291	14	18	0	3.93
Arthur Irwin	SS	D. Padden	451	.277	2	61	201	281	46	33	6.2	.913	D. McFarlan	32	212	8	18	0	4.76
	3B	C. Atherton	242	.248	0	23	91	119	26	7	3.7	.890	W. Mercer	23	186	7	14	0	4.60
	RF	B. Freeman	588	.318	25	122	220	14	14	3	1.6	.944							
	CF	J. Slagle	599	.272	0	41	407	20	21	8	3.1	.953							
	LF	J. O'Brien	468	.282	6	51	266	21	23	5	2.6	.926							
	C	D. McGuire	199	.271	1	12	178	71*	7	3	4.6	.973							
	UT	W. Mercer	375	.299	1	35	109	156	40	8		.869							
	UT	S. Barry	247	.287	1	33	254	65	19	13		.944							
	1B	P. Cassidy	178	.315	3	32	337	16	11	26	9.8	.970							

	POS	Player	AB	BA	HR	RBI	PO	A	E	DP	TC/G	FA	Pitcher	G	IP	W	L	SV	ERA
Cle.	1B	T. Tucker	456	.241	0	40	1229	58	30	71	10.4	.977	J. Hughey	36	283	4	30	0	5.41
W-20 L-134	2B	J. Quinn	615	.286	0	72	350	440	31	61	5.6	.962	C. Knepper	27	220	4	22	0	5.78
Lave Cross	SS	H. Lochhead	541	.238	1	43	319	490	81	54	6.1	.909	F. Bates	20	153	1	18	0	7.24
W-8 L-30	3B	S. Sullivan	473	.245	0	55	110	237	23	21	3.7	.938	C. Schmit	20	138	2	17	0	5.86
Joe Quinn	RF	McAllister	418	.237	1	31	106	10	7	4	1.6	.943	Colliflower	14	98	1	11	0	8.17
W-12 L-104	CF	T. Dowd	605	.278	2	35	341	10	17	2	2.5	.954	W. Sudhoff	11	86	3	8	0	6.98
	LF	D. Harley	567	.250	1	50	299	27	27	7	2.5	.924							
	C	J. Sugden	250	.276	0	14	196	108	21	11	4.9	.935							
	OF	C. Hemphill	202	.277	2	23	61	6	11	1	1.4	.859							
	3B	L. Cross	154	.286	1	20	66	81	7	7*	4.1	.955*							

BATTING AND BASE RUNNING LEADERS

Batting Average

E. Delahanty, PHI	.408
J. Burkett, STL	.402
J. McGraw, BAL	.391
W. Keeler, BKN	.377
H. Wagner, LOU	.359

Slugging Average

E. Delahanty, PHI	.585
B. Freeman, WAS	.563
J. Williams, PIT	.532
H. Wagner, LOU	.530
J. Burkett, STL	.504

Home Runs

B. Freeman, WAS	25
B. Wallace, STL	12
S. Mertes, CHI	9
E. Delahanty, PHI	9
J. Williams, PIT	9

Total Bases

E. Delahanty, PHI	335
B. Freeman, WAS	331
J. Williams, PIT	328
H. Wagner, LOU	291
J. Burkett, STL	286

Runs Batted In

E. Delahanty, PHI	137
B. Freeman, WAS	122
J. Williams, PIT	116
H. Wagner, LOU	113
B. Wallace, STL	108

Stolen Bases

J. Sheckard, BAL	77
J. McGraw, BAL	73
E. Heidrick, STL	55
D. Holmes, BAL	50
F. Clarke, LOU	49

Hits

E. Delahanty, PHI	234
J. Burkett, STL	228
J. Williams, PIT	219

Base on Balls

J. McGraw, BAL	124
R. Thomas, PHI	115
C. Childs, STL	74
Van Haltren, NY	74

Home Run Percentage

B. Freeman, WAS	4.3
S. Mertes, CHI	2.1
B. Wallace, STL	2.1

Runs Scored

J. McGraw, BAL	140
W. Keeler, BKN	140
R. Thomas, PHI	137

Doubles

E. Delahanty, PHI	56
H. Wagner, LOU	47
D. Holmes, BAL	31

Triples

J. Williams, PIT	27
B. Freeman, WAS	25
C. Stahl, BOS	18

PITCHING LEADERS

Winning Percentage

J. Hughes, BKN	.824
N. Hahn, CIN	.767
B. Kennedy, BKN	.733
V. Willis, BOS	.730
R. Donahue, PHI	.724

Earned Run Average

A. Orth, PHI	2.49
V. Willis, BOS	2.50
J. Tannehill, PIT	2.57
J. McGinnity, BAL	2.58
C. Young, STL	2.58

Wins

J. Hughes, BKN	28
J. McGinnity, BAL	28
V. Willis, BOS	27
C. Young, STL	26
J. Tannehill, PIT	24

Saves

S. Leever, PIT	3
J. McGinnity, BAL	2
J. Dunn, BKN	2
B. Kennedy, BKN	2
J. Taylor, CIN	2
V. Willis, BOS	2

Strikeouts

N. Hahn, CIN	145
C. Seymour, NY	142
S. Leever, PIT	121
V. Willis, BOS	120
E. Doheny, NY	115

Complete Games

C. Young, STL	40
B. Carrick, NY	40
J. Powell, STL	40
J. Taylor, CHI	39
J. McGinnity, BAL	38

Fewest Hits per 9 Innings

V. Willis, BOS	7.28
J. Hughes, BKN	7.71
N. Hahn, CIN	8.16

Shutouts

V. Willis, BOS	5

Fewest Walks per 9 Innings

C. Young, STL	1.07
A. Orth, PHI	1.18
N. Cuppy, STL	1.36

Most Strikeouts per 9 Inn.

C. Seymour, NY	4.76
N. Hahn, CIN	4.22
E. Doheny, NY	3.90

Innings

J. McGinnity, BAL	380
S. Leever, PIT	379
J. Powell, STL	373

Games Pitched

S. Leever, PIT	51
J. Powell, STL	48
J. McGinnity, BAL	48

	W	L	PCT	GB	R	OR	2B	3B	Batting HR	BA	SA	SB	E	Fielding DP	FA	CG	BB	Pitching SO	ShO	SV	ERA
BKN	101	47	.682		892	658	178	97	26	.291	.382	271	314	125	.948	121	463	331	9	9	3.25
BOS	95	57	.625	8	858	645	178	89	40	.287	.377	185	303	124	.952	138	432	385	13	4	3.26
PHI	94	58	.618	9	916	743	241	84	30	.301	.395	212	379	110	.940	129	370	281	15	2	3.47
BAL	86	62	.581	15	827	691	204	71	17	.297	.376	364	308	96	.949	133	349	294	9	4	3.31
STL	84	67	.556	18.5	819	739	172	89	46	.285	.377	210	397	117	.939	134	321	331	7	1	3.36
CIN	83	67	.553	19	856	770	194	105	13	.275	.360	228	339	111	.947	130	370	360	8	5	3.70
PIT	76	73	.510	25.5	834	765	196	121	27	.289	.384	179	361	98	.945	117	437	334	9	4	3.45
LOU	75	77	.493	28	827	775	192	68	40	.280	.364	233	394	102	.939	134	323	287	5	2	3.45
CHI	75	73	.507	26	812	763	173	82	27	.277	.359	247	428	145	.935	147	330	313	8	1	3.37
NY	60	90	.400	42	734	863	161	65	23	.281	.352	234	433	140	.932	138	628	397	4	0	4.29
WAS	54	98	.355	49	743	983	162	87	47	.272	.363	176	403	99	.935	131	422	328	3	0	4.93
CLE	20	134	.130	84	529	1252	142	50	12	.253	.305	127	388	121	.937	138	527	215		0	6.37
					9647	9647	2193	1008	348	.282	.366	2666	4447	1388	.942	1590	4972	3856	90	32	3.85

	POS	Player	AB	BA	HR	RBI	PO	A	E	DP	TC/G	FA	Pitcher	G	IP	W	L	SV	ERA
Bkn. W-82 L-54 Ned Hanlon	1B	H. Jennings	441	.272	1	69	1050	76	21	71	10.2	.982	J. McGinnity	45	347	29	9	0	2.90
	2B	T. Daly	343	.312	4	55	233	234	40	39	5.5	.921	B. Kennedy	42	292	20	13	0	3.91
	SS	B. Dahlen	483	.259	1	69	321	517	55	59	6.7	.938	F. Kitson	40	253	15	13	4	4.19
	3B	L. Cross	461	.293	4	67	162	282	27	10	4.0	.943*	H. Howell	21	110	6	5	0	3.75
	RF	W. Keeler	565	.368	4	68	227	22	16	4	1.9	.940							
	CF	F. Jones	556	.309	4	54	315	15	15	3	2.5	.957							
	LF	J. Kelley	454	.319	6	91	174	12	8	2	2.5	.959							
	C	D. Farrell	273	.275	0	39	252	88	20	8	4.9	.944							
	OF	J. Sheckard	273	.300	1	39	171	13	15	3	2.6	.925							
	C	D. McGuire	241	.286	0	34	218	77	15	7	4.5	.952							
	UT	DeMontreville	234	.244	0	28	159	176	25	19		.931							
	P	J. McGinnity	145	.193	0	16	15	75	12	4	2.3	.882							
Pit. W-79 L-60 Fred Clarke	1B	D. Cooley	249	.201	0	22	683	20	8	39	10.8	.989	D. Phillippe	38	279	18	14	0	2.84
	2B	C. Ritchey	476	.292	1	67	303	357	33	51	5.6	.952	J. Tannehill	29	234	20	6	0	2.88
	SS	B. Ely	475	.244	0	51	242	503	52	62	6.1	.935	S. Leever	30	233	15	13	0	2.71
	3B	J. Williams	416	.264	5	68	153	254	51	21	4.4	.889	J. Chesbro	32	216	14	13	1	3.67
	RF	H. Wagner	528	.381	4	100	181	11	7	4	1.7	.965	R. Waddell	29	209	8	13	0	2.37
	CF	G. Beaumont	567	.279	4	50	274	10	17	3	2.2	.944							
	LF	F. Clarke	399	.281	3	32	263	8	16	2	2.8	.944							
	C	C. Zimmer	271	.295	0	35	318	100	17	8	5.6	.961							
	1O	T. O'Brien	376	.290	3	61	718	27	31	37		.960							
	UT	T. Leach	160	.213	1	16	74	117	24	9		.888							
	C	J. O'Connor	147	.238	0	19	108	44	9	2	4.0	.944							
Phi. W-75 L-63 Bill Shettsline	1B	E. Delahanty	539	.323	2	109	1299	66	27	86	10.7	.981	A. Orth	33	262	12	13	1	3.78
	2B	N. Lajoie	451	.346	7	92	287	341	30	69	6.5	.954	R. Donahue	32	240	15	10	0	3.60
	SS	M. Cross	466	.202	3	62	339	459	62	68	6.6	.928	C. Fraser	29	223	16	10	0	3.14
	3B	H. Wolverton	383	.282	3	58	122	234	48	16	4.0	.881	B. Bernhard	32	219	15	10	2	4.77
	RF	E. Flick	547	.378	11	110	232	23	24	6	2.0	.914	W. Piatt	22	161	9	10	0	4.65
	CF	R. Thomas	531	.316	0	33	303	19	14	6	2.4	.958	J. Dunn	10	80	5	5	0	4.84
	LF	J. Slagle	574	.287	0	45	320	22	29	5	2.6	.922							
	C	E. McFarland	344	.305	0	38	278	137	16	9	4.6	.963							
	UT	J. Dolan	257	.198	1	27	136	198	26	17		.928							
	C	K. Douglass	160	.300	0	25	138	59	14	4	4.5	.934							
	P	A. Orth	129	.310	1	21	15	68	5	3	2.7	.943							
	12	P. Chiles	111	.216	1	23	165	42	6	14		.972							
Bos. W-66 L-72 Frank Selee	1B	F. Tenney	437	.279	1	56	1021	82	21	50	10.1	.981	B. Dinneen	40	321	20	14	0	3.12
	2B	B. Lowe	474	.278	3	71	323	335	34	38	5.4	.951	V. Willis	32	236	10	17	0	4.19
	SS	H. Long	486	.261	12	66	257	454	48	34	6.1	.937	K. Nichols	29	231	13	15	0	3.07
	3B	J. Collins	586	.304	6	95	251	329	40	21	4.4	.935	T. Lewis	30	209	13	12	0	4.13
	RF	B. Freeman	418	.301	6	65	130	3	7	1	1.5	.950	T. Pittinger	18	114	2	9	0	5.13
	CF	B. Hamilton	520	.333	1	47	326	14	19	6	2.6	.947	N. Cuppy	17	105	8	4	1	3.08
	LF	C. Stahl	553	.295	5	82	277	22	10	4	2.3	.968							
	C	B. Clarke	270	.315	1	30	246	104	27	8	5.6	.928							
	UT	S. Barry	254	.260	1	37	199	82	23	13		.924							
	C	B. Sullivan	238	.273	8	41	227	71	8	10	4.6	.974							
	OF	H. Duffy	181	.304	2	31	107	5	5	2	2.4	.957							
Chi. W-65 L-75 Tom Loftus	1B	J. Ganzel	284	.275	4	32	817	34	17	40	11.1	.980	N. Callahan	32	285	13	16	0	3.82
	2B	C. Childs	538	.243	0	44	323	431	52	57	5.9	.935	C. Griffith	30	248	14	13	0	3.05
	SS	B. McCormick	379	.219	3	48	161	307	48	32	6.1	.907	N. Garvin	30	246	10	18	0	2.41
	3B	B. Bradley	444	.282	5	49	164	291	61	11	4.9	.882	J. Taylor	28	222	10	17	1	2.55
	RF	J. Ryan	415	.277	5	59	177	12	18	3	2.0	.913	J. Menefee	16	117	9	4	0	3.85
	CF	D. Green	389	.298	5	49	218	10	15	2	2.4	.938							
	LF	J. McCarthy	503	.294	0	48	233	20	15	4	2.2	.944							
	C	T. Donahue	216	.236	0	17	232	63	23	6	4.8	.928							
	O1	S. Mertes	481	.295	7	60	520	30	26	20		.955							
	SS	B. Clingman	159	.208	0	11	81	150	34	19	5.6	.872							
	C	F. Chance	151	.305	0	13	155	65	16	2	4.6	.932							
	CO	C. Dexter	125	.200	2	20	98	36	6	4		.957							
St. L. W-65 L-75 Patsy Tebeau W-48 L-55 Louie Heilbroner W-17 L-20	1B	D. McGann	450	.302	4	58	1212	58	13	41	10.6	.990	C. Young	41	321	20	18	0	3.00
	2B	B. Keister	497	.300	1	72	206	315	41	26	4.8	.927	C. Jones	39	293	13	19	0	3.54
	SS	B. Wallace	489	.272	4	70	327	447	55	31	6.6	.934	J. Powell	38	288	17	17	0	4.44
	3B	J. McGraw	334	.344	2	33	106	213	32	7	3.5	.909	W. Sudhoff	16	127	6	8	0	2.76
	RF	P. Donovan	503	.316	0	61	180	13	10	4	1.6	.951	J. Hughey	20	113	5	7	0	5.19
	CF	E. Heidrick	339	.301	2	45	215	21	10	4	3.0	.959							
	LF	J. Burkett	560	.363	7	68	337	17	25	6	2.7	.934							
	C	L. Criger	288	.271	2	38	282	105	19	8	5.4	.953							
	O1	M. Donlin	276	.326	10	48	308	11	21	14		.938							
	C	W. Robinson	210	.248	0	28	189	72	7	3	5.0	.974							
	O3	P. Dillard	183	.230	0	12	74	47	14	2		.896							

	POS	Player	AB	BA	HR	RBI	PO	A	E	DP	TC/G	FA	Pitcher	G	IP	W	L	SV	ERA
Cin.	1B	J. Beckley	558	.341	2	94	**1389**	93	30	91	**10.8**	.980	E. Scott	43	323	17	21	1	3.82
W-62 L-77	2B	J. Quinn	266	.274	0	25	154	169	17	24	4.6	.950	N. Hahn	38	303	16	19	0	3.29
Bob Allen	SS	T. Corcoran	523	.245	1	54	262	436	60	56	6.1	.921	D. Newton	35	235	9	15	0	4.14
	3B	H. Steinfeldt	513	.248	2	66	107	175	24	11	4.6	.922	B. Phillips	29	208	9	11	0	4.28
	RF	A. McBride	436	.275	4	59	163	10	16	5	1.7	.915	Breitenstein	24	192	10	10	0	3.65
	CF	J. Barrett	545	.316	5	42	287	25	24	6	2.5	.929							
	LF	S. Crawford	389	.267	7	59	237	18	14	2	**2.9**	.948							
	C	H. Peitz	294	.255	2	34	310	125	19	13	**5.7**	.958							
	3B	C. Irwin	333	.273	1	44	74	128	15	11	3.6	.931							
	C	M. Kahoe	175	.189	1	9	207	79	11	5	5.8	.963							
	C3	B. Wood	139	.266	0	22	68	56	12	5		.912							
N. Y.	1B	J. Doyle	505	.273	1	66	1269	**96**	**41**	**92**	10.6	.971	B. Carrick	45	342	19	**22**	0	3.53
W-60 L-78	2B	K. Gleason	523	.248	1	29	321	326	48	51	6.3	.931	P. Hawley	41	329	18	18	0	3.53
Buck Ewing	SS	G. Davis	426	.324	3	61	279	450	43	**94**	6.8	**.944**	W. Mercer	32	242	13	17	0	3.86
W-21 L-41	3B	P. Hickman	473	.313	9	91	183	276	**86**	19	4.5	.842	E. Doheny	20	134	4	14	0	5.45
George Davis	RF	E. Smith	321	.277	2	39	91	10	5	2	1.3	.953							
W-39 L-37	CF	Van Haltren	571	.315	1	51	325	**28**	23	7	2.7	.939							
	LF	K. Selbach	523	.337	4	68	327	25	18	**8**	2.6	.951							
	C	F. Bowerman	270	.241	1	42	232	136	**28**	**15**	5.3	.929							
	UT	M. Grady	251	.219	0	27	247	106	37	18		.905							
	UT	W. Mercer	248	.294	0	27	75	149	32	11		.875							

BATTING AND BASE RUNNING LEADERS

Batting Average
H. Wagner, PIT	.381
E. Flick, PHI	.378
W. Keeler, BKN	.368
J. Burkett, STL	.363
N. Lajoie, PHI	.346

Home Runs
H. Long, BOS	12
E. Flick, PHI	11
M. Donlin, STL	10
P. Hickman, NY	9
B. Sullivan, BOS	8

Runs Batted In
E. Flick, PHI	110
E. Delahanty, PHI	109
H. Wagner, PIT	100
J. Collins, BOS	95
J. Beckley, CIN	94

Hits
W. Keeler, BKN	208
E. Flick, PHI	207
J. Burkett, STL	203

Home Run Percentage
H. Long, BOS	2.5
E. Flick, PHI	2.0
P. Hickman, NY	1.9

Doubles
H. Wagner, PIT	45
E. Flick, PHI	33
N. Lajoie, PHI	32
E. Delahanty, PHI	32

Slugging Average
H. Wagner, PIT	.573
E. Flick, PHI	.545
N. Lajoie, PHI	.517
J. Kelley, BKN	.485
P. Hickman, NY	.482

Total Bases
E. Flick, PHI	305
H. Wagner, PIT	302
J. Burkett, STL	262
W. Keeler, BKN	259
J. Beckley, CIN	242

Stolen Bases
P. Donovan, STL	45
Van Haltren, NY	45
J. Barrett, CIN	44
W. Keeler, BKN	41
S. Mertes, CHI	38
H. Wagner, PIT	38

Base on Balls
R. Thomas, PHI	115
B. Hamilton, BOS	107
J. McGraw, STL	85

Runs Scored
R. Thomas, PHI	134
J. Slagle, PHI	115
J. Barrett, CIN	114
Van Haltren, NY	114

Triples
H. Wagner, PIT	22
J. Kelley, BKN	17
P. Hickman, NY	17

PITCHING LEADERS

Winning Percentage
J. Tannehill, PIT	.769
J. McGinnity, BKN	.763
C. Fraser, PHI	.615
B. Kennedy, BKN	.606
B. Bernhard, PHI	.600
R. Donahue, PHI	.600

Wins
J. McGinnity, BKN	29
C. Young, STL	20
J. Tannehill, PIT	20
B. Kennedy, BKN	20
B. Dinneen, BOS	20

Strikeouts
R. Waddell, PIT	130
N. Hahn, CIN	127
C. Young, STL	119
N. Garvin, CHI	107
B. Dinneen, BOS	107

Fewest Hits per 9 Innings
R. Waddell, PIT	7.59
N. Garvin, CHI	8.22
K. Nichols, BOS	8.36

Fewest Walks per 9 Innings
C. Young, STL	1.01
D. Phillippe, PIT	1.35
J. Tannehill, PIT	1.65

Innings
J. McGinnity, BKN	347
B. Carrick, NY	342
P. Hawley, NY	329

Earned Run Average
R. Waddell, PIT	2.37
N. Garvin, CHI	2.41
J. Taylor, CHI	2.55
S. Leever, PIT	2.71
W. Sudhoff, STL	2.76

Saves
F. Kitson, BKN	4
B. Bernhard, PHI	2

Complete Games
P. Hawley, NY	34
B. Dinneen, BOS	33
C. Young, STL	32
J. McGinnity, BKN	32

Shutouts
K. Nichols, BOS	4
C. Griffith, CHI	4
C. Young, STL	4
N. Hahn, CIN	4

Most Strikeouts per 9 Inn.
R. Waddell, PIT	5.61
N. Garvin, CHI	3.91
N. Hahn, CIN	3.77

Games Pitched
J. McGinnity, BKN	45
B. Carrick, NY	45
E. Scott, CIN	43

	W	L	PCT	GB	R	OR	Batting 2B	3B	HR	BA	SA	SB	Fielding E	DP	FA	Pitching CG	BB	SO	ShO	SV	ERA
BKN	82	54	.603		816	722	199	81	26	**.293**	**.383**	**274**	303	102	.948	104	405	300	8	**4**	3.89
PIT	79	60	.568	4.5	733	**612**	185	**100**	25	.272	.368	174	322	106	.945	114	**295**	**415**	11	1	**3.06**
PHI	75	63	.543	8	810	792	187	82	29	.290	.378	205	330	**125**	.945	116	402	284	7	3	4.12
BOS	66	72	.478	17	778	739	163	68	**48**	.283	.373	182	**273**	86	**.953**	116	463	340	8	2	3.72
CHI	65	75	.464	19	635	751	**202**	51	33	.260	.342	189	418	98	.933	**137**	324	357	9	1	3.23
STL	65	75	.464	19	744	748	141	81	36	.291	.375	243	331	73	.943	117	299	325	**12**	0	3.75
CIN	62	77	.446	21.5	703	745	178	83	23	.266	.354	183	341	120	.945	118	404	399	9	1	3.83
NY	60	78	.435	23	713	823	177	61	23	.279	.357	236	439	124	.928	114	442	277	4	0	3.96
					5932	5932	1432	607	253	.279	.366	1686	2757	834	.942	936	3034	2697	68	12	3.69

Pit. — W-90 L-49 — Fred Clarke

POS	Player	AB	BA	HR	RBI	PO	A	E	DP	TC/G	FA	Pitcher	G	IP	W	L	SV	ERA
1B	K. Bransfield	566	.295	0	91	1374	52	28	72	10.5	.981	D. Phillippe	37	296	22	12	2	2.22
2B	C. Ritchey	540	.296	1	74	340	**392**	**46**	**53**	5.6	.941	J. Chesbro	36	288	21	10	1	2.38
SS	B. Ely	240	.208	0	28	112	215	30	23	5.6	.916	J. Tannehill	32	252	18	10	1	**2.18**
3B	T. Leach	374	.299	1	44	122	196	34	9	3.8	.903	S. Leever	21	176	14	5	0	2.86
RF	L. Davis	335	.313	2	33	140	18	4	7	1.9	.975							
CF	G. Beaumont	558	.332	8	72	289	8	18	2	2.4	.943							
LF	F. Clarke	527	.324	6	60	282	13	9	0	2.4	.970							
C	C. Zimmer	236	.220	0	21	285	69	9	4	5.3	.975							
UT	H. Wagner	556	.353	6	**126**	297	280	48	35		.923							
C	J. O'Connor	202	.193	0	22	256	59	7	5	5.5	.978							

Phi. — W-83 L-57 — Bill Shettsline

POS	Player	AB	BA	HR	RBI	PO	A	E	DP	TC/G	FA	Pitcher	G	IP	W	L	SV	ERA
1B	H. Jennings	302	.275	1	39	745	38	17	20	10.0	.979	R. Donahue	35	304	21	13	0	2.60
2B	B. Hallman	445	.184	0	38	177	261	13	20	5.0	**.971**	A. Orth	35	282	20	12	0	2.27
SS	M. Cross	483	.197	1	44	**343**	445	65	31	6.1	.924	B. Duggleby	34	276	19	12	0	2.87
3B	H. Wolverton	379	.309	0	43	114	190	26	9	3.5	**.921**	D. White	31	237	14	13	0	3.19
RF	E. Flick	542	.336	8	88	278	23	12	7	2.3	.962	J. Townsend	19	144	9	6	0	3.45
CF	R. Thomas	479	.309	1	28	283	9	10	2	2.3	.967							
LF	E. Delahanty	538	.357	8	108	179	9	10	2	2.4	.949							
C	E. McFarland	295	.285	1	32	316	102	13	2	5.8	.970							
UT	S. Barry	252	.246	1	22	122	123	31	8		.888							
OF	J. Slagle	183	.202	1	20	108	12*	9	3	2.7	.930							
C	K. Douglass	173	.324	0	23	201	29	5	2	5.7	.979							
C	F. Jacklitsch	120	.250	0	24	126	39	5	3	5.7	.971							

Bkn. — W-79 L-57 — Ned Hanlon

POS	Player	AB	BA	HR	RBI	PO	A	E	DP	TC/G	FA	Pitcher	G	IP	W	L	SV	ERA
1B	J. Kelley	492	.309	4	65	984	82	27	63	9.5	.975	W. Donovan	**45**	351	**25**	15	1	2.77
2B	T. Daly	520	.315	3	90	370	357	43	46	**5.8**	.944	F. Kitson	38	281	19	11	2	2.98
SS	B. Dahlen	513	.261	4	82	301	450	57	49	6.3	.929	J. Hughes	31	251	17	12	0	3.27
3B	C. Irwin	242	.215	0	20	88*	106	9	5	3.1	.956	D. Newton	13	105	6	5	0	2.83
RF	W. Keeler	589	.355	2	43	181	17	3	4	1.6	**.985**	D. McJames	13	91	5	6	0	4.75
CF	T. McCreery	335	.290	3	53	189	9	11	2	2.5	.947							
LF	J. Sheckard	558	.353	11	104	287	15	18	5	2.6	.944							
C	D. McGuire	301	.296	0	40	415	94	21	4	6.5	.960							
C	D. Farrell	284	.296	1	31	285	90	8	8	6.5	.979							
OF	C. Dolan	253	.261	0	29	108	9	4	2	1.9	.967							
3B	F. Gatins	197	.228	1	21	56	58	10	5	2.7	.919							

St. L. — W-76 L-64 — Patsy Donovan

POS	Player	AB	BA	HR	RBI	PO	A	E	DP	TC/G	FA	Pitcher	G	IP	W	L	SV	ERA
1B	D. McGann	426	.289	6	56	1030	50	18	64	10.7	.984	J. Powell	45	338	19	19	**3**	3.54
2B	D. Padden	488	.256	2	62	286	336	33	47	5.7	.950	J. Harper	39	309	23	13	0	3.62
SS	B. Wallace	556	.322	2	91	326	542	60	67	7.0	.929	W. Sudhoff	38	276	17	11	2	3.52
3B	O. Krueger	520	.275	2	79	171	275	60	11	3.6	.881	E. Murphy	23	165	10	9	0	4.20
RF	P. Donovan	527	.292	1	73	215	19	5	8	1.9	.979							
CF	E. Heidrick	502	.339	6	67	258	15	16	2	2.4	.945							
LF	J. Burkett	597	**.382**	10	75	307	17	27	4	2.5	.923							
C	J. Ryan	300	.197	0	31	292	84	7	7	5.9	.982							
CO	A. Nichols	308	.244	1	33	256	60	13	9		.960							
C1	P. Schriver	166	.271	1	23	273	61	10	13		.971							

Bos. — W-69 L-69 — Frank Selee

POS	Player	AB	BA	HR	RBI	PO	A	E	DP	TC/G	FA	Pitcher	G	IP	W	L	SV	ERA
1B	F. Tenney	457	.278	1	22	1059	**86**	28	58	10.4	.976	K. Nichols	38	321	18	15	0	3.22
2B	DeMontreville	570	.304	5	72	272	344	30	35	5.4	.954	B. Dinneen	37	309	16	19	0	2.94
SS	H. Long	518	.228	3	68	304	468	44	55	5.9	**.946**	T. Pittinger	34	281	13	16	0	3.01
3B	B. Lowe	491	.255	3	47	149	192	33	12	3.4	.912							
RF	J. Slagle	255	.271	0	7	89	11*	7	3	1.6	.935							
CF	B. Hamilton	349	.292	3	38	232	7	14	4	2.6	.945							
LF	D. Cooley	240	.258	0	27	127	5	8	1	2.6	.943							
C	M. Kittredge	381	.252	2	40	**581**	136	12	7	6.5	.984							
OF	F. Crolius	200	.240	1	13	65	3	12	1	1.6	.850							
UT	P. Moran	180	.211	2	18	299	37	14	8		.960							
OF	F. Murphy	176	.261	1	18	97	10	7	1	2.5	.939							
P	K. Nichols	163	.282	4	28	27	69	4	1	2.6	.960							
P	B. Dinneen	147	.211	1	6	14	72	7	2	2.5	.925							

Chi. — W-53 L-86 — Tom Loftus

POS	Player	AB	BA	HR	RBI	PO	A	E	DP	TC/G	FA	Pitcher	G	IP	W	L	SV	ERA
1B	J. Doyle	285	.232	0	39	698	60	21	32	10.4	.973	L. Hughes	37	308	11	21	0	3.24
2B	C. Childs	237	.257	0	21	146	192	22	34	5.8	.939	J. Taylor	33	276	13	19	0	3.36
SS	B. McCormick	427	.234	1	32	202	405	59	47	5.9	.911	R. Waddell	29	244	13	15	0	2.81
3B	F. Raymer	463	.233	0	43	79	143	30	5	3.1	.881	V. Willis	27	221	8	17	0	3.59
RF	F. Chance	241	.278	0	36	61	7	5	0	1.5	.932	M. Eason	21	182	8	13	0	3.80
CF	D. Green	537	.313	6	60	312	17	24	7	**2.7**	.932	J. Menefee						
LF	T. Hartsel	558	.335	7	54	273	16	15	3	2.2	.951							
C	J. Kling	253	.277	0	21	319	75	20	7	6.0	.952							
UT	C. Dexter	460	.267	1	66	618	125	27	32		.965							
C	M. Kahoe	237	.224	1	21	368	74	12	8	7.2	.974							
2B	P. Childs	213	.225	0	14	128	198	14	19	5.6	.959							
OF	C. Dolan	171	.263	0	16	63	9	10	3	2.0	.878							
OP	J. Menefee	152	.257	0	13	52	47	8	1		.925							

	POS	Player	AB	BA	HR	RBI	PO	A	E	DP	TC/G	FA	Pitcher	G	IP	W	L	SV	ERA
N. Y.	1B	J. Ganzel	526	.215	2	66	1421	77	21	59	11.0	.986	D. Taylor	45	353	18	27	0	3.18
W-52 L-85	2B	R. Nelson	130	.200	0	7	44	125	22	10	4.9	.885	C. Mathewson	40	336	20	17	0	2.41
George Davis	SS	G. Davis	495	.309	7	65	296	396	45	42	6.5	.939	B. Phyle	24	169	7	10	1	4.27
	3B	S. Strang	493	.282	1	34	127	194	45	16	4.0	.877							
	RF	A. McBride	264	.280	2	29	84	8	5	3	1.5	.948							
	CF	Van Haltren	544	.342	1	47	263	23	18	5	2.3	.941							
	LF	K. Selbach	502	.289	1	56	215	11	14	2	1.9	.942							
	C	J. Warner	291	.241	0	20	361	107	16	11	5.8	.967							
	UT	P. Hickman	401	.282	4	62	154	154	35	10		.898							
	C	F. Bowerman	191	.199	0	14	256	67	17	6	7.4	.950							
Cin.	1B	J. Beckley	580	.307	3	79	1366	71	34	79	10.5	.977	N. Hahn	42	375	22	19	0	2.71
W-52 L-87	2B	H. Steinfeldt	382	.249	6	47	138	142	18	23	6.0	.940	B. Phillips	37	281	14	20	0	4.64
Bid McPhee	SS	G. Magoon	460	.252	1	53	253	345	53	36	5.8	.919	D. Newton	20	168	4	14	0	4.12
	3B	C. Irwin	260	.238	0	25	87*	139	27	10	3.8	.893	A. Stimmel	20	153	4	14	0	4.11
	RF	S. Crawford	515	.330	16	104	209	20	19	6	2.0	.923							
	CF	J. Dobbs	435	.274	2	27	189	11	11	4	2.1	.948							
	LF	D. Harley	535	.273	4	27	245	20	30	2	2.2	.898							
	C	B. Bergen	308	.179	1	17	406	117	16	8	6.2	.970							
	UT	H. Peitz	269	.305	1	24	321	127	9	14		.980							
	2B	B. Fox	163	.178	0	7	104	136	13	19	5.8	.949							
	OF	H. Bay	157	.210	1	3	78	3	4	3	2.1	.953							
	P	N. Hahn	141	.170	0	7	14	85	6	4	2.5	.943							

BATTING AND BASE RUNNING LEADERS

Batting Average
J. Burkett, STL	.382
E. Delahanty, PHI	.357
W. Keeler, BKN	.355
H. Wagner, PIT	.353
J. Sheckard, BKN	.353

Slugging Average
J. Sheckard, BKN	.536
E. Delahanty, PHI	.533
S. Crawford, CIN	.528
J. Burkett, STL	.524
E. Flick, PHI	.500

Home Runs
S. Crawford, CIN	16
J. Sheckard, BKN	11
J. Burkett, STL	10
E. Flick, PHI	8
E. Delahanty, PHI	8
G. Beaumont, PIT	8

Total Bases
J. Burkett, STL	313
J. Sheckard, BKN	299
E. Delahanty, PHI	287
H. Wagner, PIT	273
E. Flick, PHI	272
S. Crawford, CIN	272

Runs Batted In
H. Wagner, PIT	126
E. Delahanty, PHI	108
S. Crawford, CIN	104
J. Sheckard, BKN	104
B. Wallace, STL	91
K. Bransfield, PIT	91

Stolen Bases
H. Wagner, PIT	49
T. Hartsel, PHI	41
S. Strang, NY	40
D. Harley, CIN	37
G. Beaumont, PIT	36

Hits
J. Burkett, STL	228
W. Keeler, BKN	209
J. Sheckard, BKN	197

Base on Balls
R. Thomas, PHI	100
T. Hartsel, CHI	74
L. Davis, BKN, PIT	66

Home Run Percentage
S. Crawford, CIN	3.1
J. Sheckard, BKN	2.0
J. Burkett, STL	1.7

Runs Scored
J. Burkett, STL	139
W. Keeler, BKN	123
G. Beaumont, PIT	120

Doubles
E. Delahanty, PHI	39
H. Wagner, PIT	39
J. Beckley, CIN	39

Triples
J. Sheckard, BKN	19
E. Flick, PHI	17
K. Bransfield, PIT	17
J. Burkett, STL	17

PITCHING LEADERS

Winning Percentage
J. Chesbro, PIT	.677
J. Harper, STL	.657
D. Phillippe, PIT	.647
J. Tannehill, PIT	.643
R. Donahue, PHI	.629

Earned Run Average
J. Tannehill, PIT	2.18
D. Phillippe, PIT	2.22
A. Orth, PHI	2.27
V. Willis, BOS	2.36
J. Chesbro, PIT	2.38

Wins
W. Donovan, BKN	25
J. Harper, STL	23
D. Phillippe, PIT	22
N. Hahn, CIN	22
J. Chesbro, PIT	21
R. Donahue, PHI	21

Saves
J. Powell, STL	3
F. Kitson, BKN	2
D. Phillippe, PIT	2
W. Sudhoff, STL	2

Strikeouts
N. Hahn, CIN	239
W. Donovan, BKN	226
L. Hughes, CHI	225
C. Mathewson, NY	221
R. Waddell, CHI, PIT	172

Complete Games
N. Hahn, CIN	41
D. Taylor, NY	37
W. Donovan, BKN	36
C. Mathewson, NY	36
R. Donahue, PHI	34

Fewest Hits per 9 Innings
J. Townsend, PHI	7.39
C. Mathewson, NY	7.71
V. Willis, BOS	7.72

Shutouts
J. Chesbro, PIT	6
A. Orth, PHI	6
V. Willis, BOS	6

Fewest Walks per 9 Innings
A. Orth, PHI	1.02
D. Phillippe, PIT	1.16
J. Tannehill, PIT	1.28

Most Strikeouts per 9 Inn.
L. Hughes, CHI	6.57
R. Waddell, CHI, PIT	6.16
C. Mathewson, NY	5.92

Innings
N. Hahn, CIN	375
D. Taylor, NY	353
W. Donovan, BKN	351

Games Pitched
D. Taylor, NY	45
W. Donovan, BKN	45
J. Powell, STL	45

	W	L	PCT	GB	R	OR	2B	3B	HR	BA	SA	SB	E	DP	FA	CG	BB	SO	ShO	SV	ERA
PIT	90	49	.647		776	534	185	92	28	.286	.378	203	287	97	.950	119	244	505	15	4	2.58
PHI	83	57	.593	7.5	668	543	194	58	24	.267	.347	199	262	65	.954	125	259	480	16	0	2.87
BKN	79	57	.581	9.5	744	600	206	97	32	.288	.390	178	281	99	.950	111	435	583	7	3	3.14
STL	76	64	.543	14.5	792	689	187	97	39	.258	.383	190	305	108	.949	118	332	445	5	5	3.68
BOS	69	69	.500	20.5	530	556	135	36	28	.250	.312	157	282	89	.952	128	349	558	11	0	2.90
CHI	53	86	.381	37	578	698	153	61	18	.258	.326	203	336	87	.943	131	324	586	2	0	3.33
NY	52	85	.380	37	544	755	166	47	19	.255	.321	133	348	81	.941	118	377	542	11	1	3.87
CIN	52	87	.374	38	561	818	179	70	38	.251	.339	137	355	102	.940	126	365	542	4	0	4.17
					5193	5193	1405	558	226	.268	.350	1400	2456	728	.947	976	2685	4241	71	13	3.32

POS	Player	AB	BA	HR	RBI	PO	A	E	DP	TC/G	FA	Pitcher	G	IP	W	L	SV	ERA
Chi. W-83 L-53 Clark Griffith																		
1B	F. Isbell	556	.257	3	70	1387	101	31	79	11.1	.980	R. Patterson	41	312	20	16	0	3.37
2B	S. Mertes	545	.277	5	98	337	396	47	54	5.9	.940	C. Griffith	35	267	24	7	1	2.67
SS	F. Shugart	415	.251	2	47	223	338	73	32	5.9	.885	N. Callahan	27	215	15	8	0	2.42
3B	F. Hartman	473	.309	3	89	151	263	49	15	3.9	.894	J. Katoll	27	208	11	10	0	2.81
RF	F. Jones	521	.311	2	65	216	20	16	5	1.9	.937	E. Harvey	16	92	3	6	1	3.62
CF	D. Hoy	527	.294	2	60	278	16	13	6	2.3	.958							
LF	H. McFarland	473	.275	4	59	283	14	17	3	2.4	.946							
C	B. Sullivan	367	.245	4	56	396	104	17	13	5.3	.967							
C	J. Sugden	153	.275	0	19	179	47	7	4	5.5	.970							
SS	J. Burke	148	.264	0	21	56	94	23	10	5.6	.867							
Bos. W-79 L-57 Jimmy Collins																		
1B	B. Freeman	490	.345	12	114	1278	55	36	71	10.7	.974	C. Young	43	371	33	10	0	1.62
2B	H. Ferris	523	.250	2	63	359	450	61	68	6.3	.930	T. Lewis	39	316	16	17	1	3.53
SS	F. Parent	517	.306	4	59	260	446	63	52	5.6	.918	G. Winter	28	241	16	12	0	2.80
3B	J. Collins	564	.332	6	94	203	328	50	24	4.2	.914	F. Mitchell	17	109	6	6	0	3.81
RF	C. Hemphill	545	.261	3	62	188	22	17	4	1.7	.925	N. Cuppy	13	93	4	6	0	4.15
CF	C. Stahl	515	.309	6	72	277	12	13	3	2.3	.957							
LF	T. Dowd	594	.268	3	52	288	11	20	3	2.3	.937							
C	Schreckengost	280	.304	0	38	273	102	30	8	5.6	.926							
C	L. Criger	268	.231	0	24	300	109	14	11	6.2	.967							
P	C. Young	153	.209	0	17	12	105	3	3	2.8	.975							
Det. W-74 L-61 George Stallings																		
1B	P. Dillon	281	.288	1	42	777	44	18	57	11.3	.979	R. Miller	38	332	23	13	1	2.95
2B	K. Gleason	547	.274	3	75	334	457	64	67	6.3	.925	E. Siever	38	289	18	15	0	3.24
SS	K. Elberfeld	436	.310	3	76	332	411	76	62	6.8	.907	J. Cronin	30	220	13	15	0	3.89
3B	D. Casey	540	.283	2	46	133	324	58	25	4.1	.887	J. Yeager	26	200	12	11	1	2.61
RF	D. Holmes	537	.294	4	62	217	18	24	5	2.0	.907							
CF	J. Barrett	542	.293	4	65	300	31	21	7	2.6	.940							
LF	D. Nance	461	.280	3	66	240	20	19	6	2.1	.932							
C	F. Buelow	231	.225	2	29	213	84	10	4	4.4	.967							
UT	McAllister	306	.301	3	57	381	66	42	19		.914							
C	A. Shaw	171	.269	1	23	134	46	12	5	4.6	.938							
Phi. W-74 L-62 Connie Mack																		
1B	H. Davis	496	.306	8	76	1265	83	33	67	11.8	.976	C. Fraser	40	331	22	16	0	3.81
2B	N. Lajoie	543	.422	14	125	395	381	32	60	6.8	.960	E. Plank	33	261	17	13	0	3.31
SS	J. Dolan	338	.216	1	38	88	223	42	30	5.8	.881	B. Bernhard	31	257	17	10	0	4.52
3B	L. Cross	420	.331	2	73	140	236	33	7	4.1	.919	S. Wiltse	19	166	13	5	0	3.58
RF	S. Seybold	457	.333	8	90	157	10	8	2	1.8	.954	W. Piatt	18	140	5	12	1	4.63
CF	D. Fultz	561	.292	0	52	216	13	16	0	2.3	.935							
LF	M. McIntyre	308	.276	0	46	155	8	14	0	2.2	.921							
C	M. Powers	431	.251	1	47	400	137	27	6	5.1	.952							
OF	J. Hayden	211	.265	0	17	63	11	14	0	1.8	.841							
OF	P. Geier	211	.232	0	23	80	5	6	1	1.8	.934							
SS	B. Ely	171	.216	0	16	85	156	23	19	5.9	.913							
Bal. W-68 L-65 John McGraw																		
1B	J. Hart	206	.311	0	23	561	9	14	28	10.1	.976	J. McGinnity	48	382	26	20	1	3.56
2B	J. Williams	501	.317	7	96	339	412	52	47	6.2	.935	H. Howell	37	295	14	21	0	3.67
SS	B. Keister	442	.328	2	93	231	322	97	30	5.8	.851	F. Foreman	24	191	12	6	1	3.67
3B	J. McGraw	230	.352	0	28	80	107	23	5	3.0	.890	J. Nops	27	177	12	10	1	4.08
RF	C. Seymour	552	.303	1	77	271	23	17	4	2.3	.945							
CF	S. Brodie	306	.310	2	41	178	4	7	0	2.3	.963							
LF	M. Donlin	481	.341	5	67	179	12	17	2	2.8	.918							
C	R. Bresnahan	293	.263	1	32	199	63	23	3	4.1	.919							
OF	J. Jackson	364	.250	2	50	234	4	7	1	2.6	.971							
UT	J. Dunn	362	.249	0	36	157	206	53	14		.873							
OF	S. Brodie	309	.311	2	41	178	4	7	0	2.3	.963							
C	W. Robinson	241	.299	0	26	235	61	16	4	4.7	.949							
UT	H. Howell	188	.218	2	26	59	93	16	6		.905							
P	J. McGinnity	148	.209	0	6	15	104	9	2	2.7	.930							
Was. W-61 L-73 Jimmy Manning																		
1B	M. Grady	347	.285	9	56	575	52	16	34	10.9	.975	B. Carrick	42	324	14	23	0	3.75
2B	J. Farrell	555	.272	3	96	176	246	39	43	6.4	.915	W. Lee	36	262	16	16	0	4.40
SS	B. Clingman	480	.242	2	55	290	462	55	56	5.9	.932	C. Patten	32	254	18	10	0	3.93
3B	B. Coughlin	506	.275	6	68	232	275	43	16	4.0	.922	W. Mercer	24	180	9	13	1	4.56
RF	S. Dungan	559	.320	1	73	145	15	9	4	1.6	.947	D. Gear	24	163	4	11	0	4.03
CF	I. Waldron	332*	.322	0	22	140	7	7	0	2.0	.955							
LF	P. Foster	392	.278	6	53	200	9	17	1	2.2	.925							
C	B. Clarke	422	.280	3	54	358	122	24	11	4.7	.952							
2B	J. Quinn	266	.252	3	36	158	177	16	17	5.3	.954							
OP	D. Gear	199	.236	0	20	56	59	6	3		.950							
UT	W. Mercer	140	.300	0	16	92	57	15	10		.909							
Cle. W-55 L-82 Jimmy McAleer																		
1B	C. LaChance	548	.303	1	75	1342	58	30	73	10.8	.979	P. Dowling	33	256	11	22*	0	3.86
2B	E. Beck	539	.289	6	79	310	404	56	44	5.8	.927	E. Moore	31	251	16	14	0	2.90
SS	F. Scheibeck	329	.213	0	38	176	268	51	26	5.4	.897	B. Hart	20	158	7	11	0	3.77
3B	B. Bradley	516	.293	1	55	192	298	37	25	4.0	.930	E. Scott	17	125	7	6	1	4.40
RF	J. O'Brien	375	.283	0	39	150	9	10	4	1.8	.941	J. Bracken	12	100	4	8	0	6.21
CF	O. Pickering	547	.309	0	40	315	22	18	9	2.6	.949	B. Hoffer	16	99	3	8	3	4.55
LF	J. McCarthy	343	.321	0	32	157	9	9	5	2.0	.949	H. McNeal	12	85	5	5	0	4.43
C	B. Wood	346	.292	1	49	307	106	21	11	5.2	.952							
OF	E. Harvey	170	.353	1	24	82	7	11	4	2.2	.890							

	POS	Player	AB	BA	HR	RBI	PO	A	E	DP	TC/G	FA	Pitcher	G	IP	W	L	SV	ERA
Mil.	1B	J. Anderson	576	.330	8	99	1310	66	25	81	11.2	.982	B. Reidy	37	301	16	20	0	4.21
	2B	B. Gilbert	492	.270	0	43	319	395	49	66	6.0	.936	N. Garvin	37	257	7	20	2	3.46
W-48 L-89	SS	W. Conroy	503	.256	5	64	285	408	59	46	6.4	.922	B. Husting	34	217	10	15	1	4.27
Hugh Duffy	3B	J. Burke	233	.206	0	26	83	132	35	5	3.9	.860	T. Sparks	29	210	7	16	0	3.51
	RF	B. Hallman	549	.246	2	47	226	22	26	6	2.0	.905	P. Hawley	26	182	7	14	0	4.59
	CF	H. Duffy	286	.308	2	45	141	5	5	0	2.0	.967							
	LF	G. Hogriever	221	.235	0	16	134	3	15	1	2.8	.901							
	C	B. Maloney	290	.293	0	22	284	111	20	6	5.8	.952							
	UT	B. Friel	376	.266	4	35	142	183	46	16		.876							
	OF	I. Waldron	266*	.297	0	29	97	9	14	0	1.9	.883							

BATTING AND BASE RUNNING LEADERS

Batting Average

N. Lajoie, PHI	.422
B. Freeman, BOS	.345
M. Donlin, BAL	.341
S. Seybold, PHI	.333
J. Collins, BOS	.332

Slugging Average

N. Lajoie, PHI	.635
B. Freeman, BOS	.527
S. Seybold, PHI	.499
J. Williams, BAL	.495
J. Collins, BOS	.495

Home Runs

N. Lajoie, PHI	13
B. Freeman, BOS	12
M. Grady, WAS	9
S. Seybold, PHI	8
H. Davis, PHI	8
J. Anderson, MIL	8

Total Bases

N. Lajoie, PHI	342
J. Collins, BOS	279
J. Anderson, MIL	274
B. Freeman, BOS	258
J. Williams, BAL	248

Runs Batted In

N. Lajoie, PHI	125
B. Freeman, BOS	114
J. Anderson, MIL	99
S. Mertes, CHI	98
J. Williams, BAL	96

Stolen Bases

F. Isbell, CHI	52
S. Mertes, CHI	46
F. Jones, CHI	38
C. Seymour, BAL	38
O. Pickering, CLE	36
D. Fultz, PHI	36

Hits

N. Lajoie, PHI	229
J. Anderson, MIL	190
J. Collins, BOS	187

Base on Balls

D. Hoy, BOS	86
F. Jones, CHI	84
J. Barrett, DET	76

Home Run Percentage

M. Grady, WAS	2.6
B. Freeman, BOS	2.4
N. Lajoie, PHI	2.4

Runs Scored

N. Lajoie, PHI	145
F. Jones, CHI	120
J. Williams, BAL	113

Doubles

N. Lajoie, PHI	48
J. Anderson, MIL	46
J. Collins, BOS	42
J. Farrell, WAS	32

Triples

B. Keister, BAL	21
J. Williams, BAL	21
S. Mertes, CHI	17

PITCHING LEADERS

Winning Percentage

C. Griffith, CHI	.774
C. Young, BOS	.767
N. Callahan, CHI	.652
C. Patten, WAS	.643
R. Miller, DET	.639

Earned Run Average

C. Young, BOS	1.62
N. Callahan, CHI	2.42
J. Yeager, DET	2.61
C. Griffith, CHI	2.67
G. Winter, BOS	2.80

Wins

C. Young, BOS	33
J. McGinnity, BAL	26
C. Griffith, CHI	24
R. Miller, DET	23
C. Fraser, PHI	22

Saves

B. Hoffer, CLE	3
J. McGinnity, BAL	3
N. Garvin, MIL	2

Strikeouts

C. Young, BOS	158
R. Patterson, CHI	127
P. Dowling, CLE, MIL	124
N. Garvin, MIL	122
C. Fraser, PHI	110

Complete Games

J. McGinnity, BAL	39
C. Young, BOS	38
R. Miller, DET	35
C. Fraser, PHI	35
B. Carrick, WAS	34

Fewest Hits per 9 Innings

C. Young, BOS	7.85
N. Callahan, CHI	8.15
E. Moore, CLE	8.38

Shutouts

C. Griffith, CHI	5
C. Young, BOS	5

Fewest Walks per 9 Innings

C. Young, BOS	0.90
D. Gear, WAS	1.21
W. Lee, WAS	1.55

Most Strikeouts per 9 Inn.

N. Garvin, MIL	4.27
C. Patten, WAS	3.86
C. Young, BOS	3.83

Innings

J. McGinnity, BAL	382
C. Young, BOS	371
R. Miller, DET	332

Games Pitched

J. McGinnity, BAL	48
C. Young, BOS	43
P. Dowling, CLE, MIL	43

	W	L	PCT	GB	R	OR	Batting						Fielding			Pitching					
							2B	3B	HR	BA	SA	SB	E	DP	FA	CG	BB	SO	ShO	SV	ERA
CHI	83	53	.610	—	819	632	173	89	32	.276	.370	280	345	100	.941	110	312	394	11	2	2.98
BOS	79	57	.581	4	759	608	183	104	37	.279	.382	157	337	104	.943	123	294	396	7	1	3.04
DET	74	61	.548	8.5	742	696	180	80	29	.279	.370	205	410	127	.930	118	313	307	9	2	3.30
PHI	74	62	.544	9	805	760	239	86	35	.288	.394	173	337	93	.942	124	374	350	6	1	4.00
BAL	68	65	.511	13.5	761	750	179	111	24	.293	.396	207	401	76	.926	115	344	271	4	3	3.73
WAS	61	73	.455	21	683	771	191	83	34	.269	.365	127	323	97	.943	118	284	308	8	1	4.09
CLE	55	82	.401	28.5	666	831	197	68	12	.271	.348	125	329	99	.942	122	464	334	7	4	4.12
MIL	48	89	.350	35.5	641	828	192	66	26	.261	.345	176	393	106	.934	107	395	376	3	4	4.06
					5876	5876	1534	687	229	.277	.371	1450	2875	802	.938	937	2780	2736	55	18	3.66

POS	Player	AB	BA	HR	RBI	PO	A	E	DP	TC/G	FA	Pitcher	G	IP	W	L	SV	ERA
Pit. W-103 L-36 Fred Clarke																		
1B	K. Bransfield	417	.305	1	69	1064	41	18	40	11.1	.984	J. Chesbro	35	286	**28**	6	1	2.17
2B	C. Ritchey	405	.277	2	55	275	341	22	48	5.6	**.966**	D. Phillippe	31	272	20	9	0	2.05
SS	W. Conroy	365	.244	1	47	192	327	42	39	5.9	.925	J. Tannehill	26	231	20	6	0	1.95
3B	T. Leach	514	.280	6	85	170	**316**	39	10	3.9	.926	S. Leever	28	222	16	7	2	2.39
RF	L. Davis	232	.280	0	20	80	6	5	1	1.5	.945	E. Doheny	22	188	16	4	0	2.53
CF	G. Beaumont	544	**.357**	0	67	260	15	7	8	2.2	.975							
LF	F. Clarke	461	.321	2	53	215	13	10	2	2.1	.958							
C	H. Smith	185	.189	0	12	265	49	9	3	6.5	.972							
UT	H. Wagner	538	.329	3	**91**	532	176	32	33		.957							
UT	J. Burke	203	.296	0	26	90	120	23	8		.901							
C	J. O'Connor	170	.294	1	28	187	49	5	2	5.7	.979							
PO	J. Tannehill	148	.291	1	17	25	57	4	3		.953							
C	C. Zimmer	142	.268	0	17	202	48	8	8	6.3	.969							
Bkn. W-75 L-63 Ned Hanlon																		
1B	T. McCreery	430	.244	4	57	1032	59	**23**	53	10.3	.979	W. Donovan	35	298	17	15	1	2.78
2B	T. Flood	476	.218	3	50	297	374	**41**	33	5.4	.942	D. Newton	31	264	15	14	0	2.42
SS	B. Dahlen	527	.264	2	74	278	440	66	34	5.7	.916	F. Kitson	31	260	19	12	0	2.84
3B	C. Irwin	458	.273	2	43	173	244	33	21	3.5	.927	J. Hughes	31	254	15	11	0	2.87
RF	W. Keeler	556	.338	0	38	208	14	5	4	1.7	**.978**	R. Evans	13	97	5	6*	0	2.68
CF	C. Dolan	**592**	.280	1	54	283	10	20	2	2.2	.936							
LF	J. Sheckard	486	.270	4	37	**284**	12	11	6	2.5	.964							
C	H. Hearne	231	.281	0	28	298	67	13	7	5.8	.966							
C1	D. Farrell	264	.242	0	24	469	90	12	8		.979							
P	W. Donovan	161	.168	1	16	20	71	5	2	2.7	.948							
Bos. W-73 L-64 Al Buckenberger																		
1B	F. Tenney	489	.315	2	30	1251	**105**	21	75	10.3	**.985**	V. Willis	**51**	**410**	27	**19**	**3**	2.20
2B	DeMontreville	481	.268	0	53	271	294	36	24	5.4	.940	T. Pittinger	46	389	27	15	0	2.52
SS	H. Long	429	.228	2	44	279	360	37	46	6.4	.945	M. Eason	27	206	9	14	0	2.75
3B	E. Gremminger	522	.257	1	66	**222**	282	26	15	3.8	.951	J. Malarkey	21	170	8	11	1	2.59
RF	P. Carney	522	.270	2	65	153	19	13	7	1.4	.930							
CF	B. Lush	413	.223	2	19	251	24	14	5	2.5	.952							
LF	D. Cooley	548	.296	0	58	250	7	13	2	2.1	.952							
C	M. Kittredge	255	.235	2	30	363	99	9	5	6.5	.981							
C	P. Moran	251	.239	1	24	332	95	8	5	6.1	**.982**							
UT	C. Dexter	183	.257	1	18	111	113	19	12		.922							
OF	E. Courtney	165	.218	0	17	71	5	2	0	2.0	.974							
P	V. Willis	150	.153	0	7	**37**	105	4	5	2.9	.973							
P	T. Pittinger	147	.136	0	10	20	83	6	2	2.4	.945							
Cin. W-70 L-70 Bid McPhee W-27 L-37 Frank Bancroft W-10 L-7 Joe Kelley W-33 L-26																		
1B	J. Beckley	532	.331	5	69	**1262**	64	**23**	84	10.5	.983	N. Hahn	36	312	22	12	0	1.76
2B	H. Peitz	387	.315	1	60	124	126	22	23	5.7	.919	B. Phillips	33	263	16	15	0	2.50
SS	T. Corcoran	537	.251	0	54	292	412	56	49	5.5	.926	H. Thielman	25	211	8	15	1	3.24
3B	H. Steinfeldt	479	.278	1	49	190	315	**49**	29	4.3	.932	E. Poole	16	138	12	4	0	2.15
RF	S. Crawford	555	.333	3	78	208	24	17	5	1.8	.932	B. Ewing	15	118	6	6	0	2.98
CF	D. Hoy	279	.290	2	20	149	4	11	1	2.3	.933							
LF	J. Dobbs	256	.297	0	16	146	11	6	2	2.6	.963							
C	B. Bergen	322	.180	0	36	406	137	23	13	6.4	.959							
OF	C. Seymour	235	.349	2	37	139	10	13	3	2.7	.920							
2B	E. Beck	187	.305	1	20	70	92	11	11	5.4	.936							
2B	G. Magoon	162	.272	0	23	83	144	17	16	6.0	.930							
UT	J. Kelley	156	.321	1	12	78	59	6	9		.958							
OF	M. Donlin	143	.294	0	9	59	5	9	1	2.3	.877							
Chi. W-68 L-69 Frank Selee																		
1B	F. Chance	236	.284	1	31	391	20	13	21	11.2	.969	J. Taylor	36	325	22	11	1	**1.33**
2B	B. Lowe	472	.246	0	31	326	406	33	59	**6.5**	.957	P. Williams	31	254	12	16	0	2.51
SS	J. Tinker	501	.273	2	54	243	**453**	**72**	47	6.2	.906	J. Menefee	22	197	12	10	0	2.42
3B	G. Schaefer	291	.196	0	14	103	152	40	11	3.9	.864	C. Lundgren	18	160	9	9	0	1.97
RF	D. Jones	243	.305	0	14	146	3	7	1	2.4	.955	B. Rhoads	16	118	4	8	1	3.20
CF	J. Dobbs	235	.302	0	35	122	8	3	5	2.3	.977	J. St. Vrain	12	95	4	6	0	2.08
LF	J. Slagle	454	.315	0	28	262	15	10	5	2.5	.965							
C	J. Kling	434	.286	0	57	**471**	158	17	**16**	5.8	.974							
UT	C. Dexter	266	.226	2	26	303	71	27	20		.933							
UT	J. Menefee	216	.231	0	15	230	57	13	7		.957							
OF	D. Miller	187	.246	0	13	97	9	5	0	2.2	.955							
UT	J. Taylor	186	.237	0	17	42	133	9	5		.951							
OF	B. Congalton	179	.223	1	24	71	6	1	1	1.7	.987							
O1	A. Williams	160	.231	0	14	226	15	11	10		.956							
St. L. W-56 L-78 Patsy Donovan																		
1B	K. Brashear	388	.276	1	40	751	36	16	49	12.0	.980	M. O'Neill	36	288	18	14	0	2.93
2B	J. Farrell	565	.250	0	25	297	**422**	40	**72**	6.4	.947	S. Yerkes	39	273	11	**20**	0	3.66
SS	O. Krueger	467	.266	0	46	184	390	66	47	6.0	.897	E. Murphy	23	164	9	7	1	3.02
3B	F. Hartman	416	.216	0	52	138	229	37	9	3.8	.908	B. Wicker	22	152	5	13	0	3.19
RF	P. Donovan	502	.315	0	35	179	**30**	9	6	1.7	.931	C. Currie	15	118	6	5	0	2.75
CF	H. Smoot	518	.311	3	48	**284**	14	22	5	2.5	.931							
LF	G. Barclay	543	.300	3	53	247	16	28	3	2.1	.904							
C	J. Ryan	267	.180	0	14	258	86	12	8	5.4	.926							
1B	A. Nichols	251	.267	1	31	577	24	10	26	10.9	.984							
C	J. O'Neill	192	.141	0	12	246	79	9	5	5.7	.973							

	POS	Player	AB	BA	HR	RBI	PO	A	E	DP	TC/G	FA	Pitcher	G	IP	W	L	SV	ERA
Phi.	1B	H. Jennings	289	.277	1	32	659	46	12	32	10.4	.983	D. White	36	306	16	**20**	1	2.53
W-56 L-81	2B	P. Childs	403	.194	0	25	271	349	36	26	5.3	.945	B. Duggleby	33	259	11	17	0	3.38
Bill Shettsline	SS	R. Hulswitt	497	.272	0	38	**318**	400	65	37	6.3	.917	H. Iburg	30	236	11	18	0	3.89
	3B	B. Hallman	254	.248	0	35	71	147	16	3	3.3	.932	C. Fraser	27	224	12	13	0	3.42
	RF	S. Barry	543	.287	3	57	185	15	13	3	1.6	.939							
	CF	R. Thomas	500	.286	0	24	277	23	8	3	2.2	.974							
	LF	G. Browne	281	.260	0	26	158	14	17*	2	2.7*	.910							
	C	R. Dooin	333	.231	0	35	433	117	**29**	10	**6.9**	.950							
	1C	K. Douglass	408	.233	0	37	792	63	18	28		.979							
	UT	H. Krug	198	.227	0	14	116	62	12	10		.937							
	PO	D. White	179	.263	1	15	35	84	12	0		.908							
N. Y.	1B	D. McGann	227	.300	0	21	634	39	13	38	11.2	.981	C. Mathewson	34	277	14	17	0	2.11
W-48 L-88	2B	H. Smith	511	.252	0	33	**347**	403	37	58	5.7	.953	D. Taylor	26	201	7	15	0	2.29
Horace Fogel	SS	J. Bean	176	.222	0	5	71	153	28	19	5.3	.889	R. Evans	23	176	8	13*	0	3.17
W-18 L-23	3B	B. Lauder	482	.237	1	44	189	251	45	17	4.0	.907	J. McGinnity	19	153	8	8	0	2.06
Heinie Smith	RF	J. Dunn	342	.211	0	14	47	4	2	2	1.2	.962	T. Sparks	15	115	4	10	1	3.76
W-5 L-27	CF	S. Brodie	416	.281	3	42	219	22	12	7	2.3	.953	J. Cronin	13	114	5	6	0	2.45
John McGraw	LF	J. Jones	249	.237	0	19	122	9	15	2	2.2	.897							
W-25 L-38	C	F. Bowerman	367	.253	0	26	428	143	26	10	6.1	.956							
	OF	G. Browne	216	.319	0	14	104	7	13*	1	2.3*	.895							
	1B	J. Doyle	186	.301	1	19	490	34	5	28	10.8	.991							
	UT	R. Bresnahan	178	.292	1	22	164	40	13	8		.940							

BATTING AND BASE RUNNING LEADERS

Batting Average
G. Beaumont, PIT	.357
W. Keeler, BKN	.338
S. Crawford, CIN	.333
J. Beckley, CIN	.331
H. Wagner, PIT	.329

Slugging Average
H. Wagner, PIT	.467
S. Crawford, CIN	.461
F. Clarke, PIT	.453
T. Leach, PIT	.442
J. Beckley, CIN	.429

Home Runs
T. Leach, PIT	6
J. Beckley, CIN	5
T. McCreery, BKN	4
J. Sheckard, BKN	4

Total Bases
S. Crawford, CIN	256
H. Wagner, PIT	251
J. Beckley, CIN	228
T. Leach, PIT	227
G. Beaumont, PIT	226

Runs Batted In
H. Wagner, PIT	91
T. Leach, PIT	85
S. Crawford, CIN	78
B. Dahlen, BKN	74
K. Bransfield, PIT	69
J. Beckley, CIN	69

Stolen Bases
H. Wagner, PIT	42
J. Slagle, CHI	40
P. Donovan, STL	34
G. Beaumont, PIT	33
H. Smith, NY	32

Hits
G. Beaumont, PIT	194
W. Keeler, BKN	188
S. Crawford, CIN	185

Base on Balls
R. Thomas, PHI	107
B. Lush, BOS	76
F. Tenney, BOS	73

Home Run Percentage
T. Leach, PIT	1.2
J. Beckley, CIN	0.9
T. McCreery, BKN	0.9

Runs Scored
H. Wagner, PIT	105
F. Clarke, PIT	104
G. Beaumont, PIT	100

Doubles
H. Wagner, PIT	33
F. Clarke, PIT	27
D. Cooley, BOS	26

Triples
S. Crawford, CIN	23
T. Leach, PIT	22
H. Wagner, PIT	16

PITCHING LEADERS

Winning Percentage
J. Chesbro, PIT	.824
E. Doheny, PIT	.800
J. Tannehill, PIT	.769
S. Leever, PIT	.696
D. Phillippe, PIT	.690

Earned Run Average
J. Taylor, CHI	1.33
N. Hahn, CIN	1.76
J. Tannehill, PIT	1.95
C. Lundgren, CHI	1.97
D. Phillippe, PIT	2.05

Wins
J. Chesbro, PIT	28
T. Pittinger, BOS	27
V. Willis, BOS	27
J. Taylor, CHI	22
N. Hahn, CIN	22

Saves
V. Willis, BOS	3
S. Leever, PIT	2

Strikeouts
V. Willis, BOS	225
D. White, PHI	185
T. Pittinger, BOS	174
W. Donovan, BKN	170
C. Mathewson, NY	159

Complete Games
V. Willis, BOS	45
T. Pittinger, BOS	36
N. Hahn, CIN	34
D. White, PHI	34
J. Taylor, CHI	33

Fewest Hits per 9 Innings
D. Newton, BKN	7.08
J. McGinnity, NY	7.18
J. Taylor, CHI	7.51

Shutouts
J. Taylor, CHI	8
C. Mathewson, NY	8
J. Chesbro, PIT	8

Fewest Walks per 9 Innings
D. Phillippe, PIT	0.86
J. Tannehill, PIT	0.97
J. Menefee, CHI	1.19

Most Strikeouts per 9 Inn.
D. White, PHI	5.44
C. Mathewson, NY	5.17
W. Donovan, BKN	5.14

Innings
V. Willis, BOS	410
T. Pittinger, BOS	389
J. Taylor, CHI	325

Games Pitched
V. Willis, BOS	51
T. Pittinger, BOS	46
S. Yerkes, STL	39

	W	L	PCT	GB	R	OR	2B	3B	HR	BA	SA	SB	E	DP	FA	CG	BB	SO	ShO	SV	ERA
PIT	103	36	.741		**775**	440	199	94	19	**.287**	**.377**	222	247	87	.958	131	**250**	564	21	3	2.30
BKN	75	63	.543	27.5	564	519	147	50	19	.257	.320	145	275	79	.952	131	363	536	15	1	2.69
BOS	73	64	.533	29	571	515	142	39	14	.250	.305	189	**240**	90	**.959**	124	372	523	14	**4**	2.61
CIN	70	70	.500	33.5	632	566	188	77	18	.282	.363	131	322	**118**	.945	130	352	430	9	1	2.67
CHI	68	69	.496	34	530	501	131	40	6	.251	.299	**222**	327	111	.946	**132**	279	437	18	2	**2.21**
STL	56	78	.418	44.5	517	695	116	37	10	.258	.304	158	336	107	.944	112	338	400	7	2	3.47
PHI	56	81	.409	46	484	649	113	42	5	.247	.293	108	305	81	.946	118	334	504	8	2	3.50
NY	48	88	.353	53.5	401	589	149	34	8	.238	.291	187	330	104	.943	118	332	501	11	1	2.82
					4474	4474	1185	413	99	.259	.320	1362	2382	777	.949	996	2620	3895	103	16	2.78

POS	Player	AB	BA	HR	RBI	PO	A	E	DP	TC/G	FA	Pitcher	G	IP	W	L	SV	ERA

Phi. W-83 L-53 Connie Mack

POS	Player	AB	BA	HR	RBI	PO	A	E	DP	TC/G	FA	Pitcher	G	IP	W	L	SV	ERA
1B	H. Davis	561	.307	6	92	1247	87	22	58	10.6	.984	E. Plank	36	300	20	15	0	3.30
2B	D. Murphy	291	.313	1	48	167	197	14	22	5.0	.963	R. Waddell	33	276	24	7	0	2.05
SS	M. Cross	497	.231	3	59	373	466	66	37	6.6	.927	B. Husting	32	204	14	5	0	3.79
3B	L. Cross	559	.342	0	108	185	306	30	18	3.8	.942	S. Wiltse	19	138	8	8	1	5.15
RF	S. Seybold	522	.316	**16**	97	246	11	10	3	2.0	.963	F. Mitchell	18	108	5	7	1	3.59
CF	D. Fultz	506	.302	1	49	231	18	10	1	2.3	.961	H. Wilson	13	96	7	5	0	2.43
LF	T. Hartsel	545	.283	5	58	238	18	12	2	2.0	.955							
C	Schreckengost	284	.324	2	43	367*	108	20*	3	7.0*	.960							
C	M. Powers	246	.264	2	39	229	110	18	5	5.3	.950							
2B	L. Castro	143	.245	1	15	71	85	14	10	4.7	.918							

St. L. W-78 L-58 Jimmy McAleer

POS	Player	AB	BA	HR	RBI	PO	A	E	DP	TC/G	FA	Pitcher	G	IP	W	L	SV	ERA
1B	J. Anderson	524	.284	4	85	1361	47	22	78	11.3	.985	J. Powell	42	328	22	17	**2**	3.21
2B	D. Padden	413	.264	1	40	288	363	22	64	5.8	.967	R. Donahue	35	316	22	11	0	2.76
SS	B. Wallace	495	.287	1	63	299	474	42	64	6.2	.948	J. Harper	29	222	15	11	0	4.13
3B	L. Cross	504	.246	3	51	147	271	44	**26**	3.5	.905	W. Sudhoff	30	220	13	13	0	2.86
RF	C. Hemphill	416	.317	6	58	164	15	9	6	1.9	.952							
CF	E. Heidrick	447	.289	3	56	264	16	18	4	**2.7**	.940							
LF	J. Burkett	549	.306	5	52	300	17	**26**	5	2.5	.924							
C	J. Sugden	203	.246	0	15	192	67	12	**9**	4.4	.956							
UT	B. Friel	267	.240	2	20	194	94	15	17		.950							
C	M. Kahoe	197	.244	2	28	214	52	9	4	5.2	.967							

Bos. W-77 L-60 Jimmy Collins

POS	Player	AB	BA	HR	RBI	PO	A	E	DP	TC/G	FA	Pitcher	G	IP	W	L	SV	ERA
1B	C. LaChance	541	.279	6	56	**1544**	46	27	80	11.7	.983	C. Young	**45**	**385**	**32**	11	0	2.15
2B	H. Ferris	499	.244	8	63	312	**461**	39	59	6.1	.952	B. Dinneen	42	371	21	21	0	2.93
SS	F. Parent	**567**	.275	3	62	287	**496**	58	60	6.1	.931	G. Winter	20	168	11	9	0	2.99
3B	J. Collins	429	.322	6	61	143	255	19	14	3.9	**.954**	T. Sparks	17	143	7	9	0	3.47
RF	B. Freeman	564	.309	11	**121**	222	15	14	3	1.8	.944							
CF	C. Stahl	508	.323	2	58	244	15	12	2	2.2	.956							
LF	P. Dougherty	438	.342	0	34	170	8	20	1	1.9	.899							
C	L. Criger	266	.256	0	28	330	117	16	6	5.8	.965							
3O	H. Gleason	240	.225	2	25	91	67	11	7		.935							
C	J. Warner	222	.234	0	12	252	81	7	8	5.3	.979							
P	C. Young	148	.230	1	12	10	82	7	4	2.2	.929							
P	B. Dinneen	141	.128	0	9	7	77	4	1	2.1	.955							

Chi. W-74 L-60 Clark Griffith

POS	Player	AB	BA	HR	RBI	PO	A	E	DP	TC/G	FA	Pitcher	G	IP	W	L	SV	ERA
1B	F. Isbell	515	.252	4	59	1401	**93**	21	**97**	11.4	.986	N. Callahan	35	282	16	14	0	3.60
2B	T. Daly	489	.225	1	54	312	370	31	**70**	5.2	.957	R. Patterson	34	268	19	14	0	3.06
SS	G. Davis	485	.299	3	93	289	427	37	**72**	5.8	**.951**	W. Piatt	32	246	12	12	0	3.51
3B	S. Strang	536	.295	3	46	170	**334**	62	21	**4.1**	.890	C. Griffith	28	213	15	9	0	4.19
RF	D. Green	481	.312	0	62	217	11	14	4	1.9	.942	N. Garvin	23	175	10	10	0	2.21
CF	F. Jones	532	.321	0	54	323	25	10	**11**	2.7	.972							
LF	S. Mertes	497	.282	1	79	223	**26**	21	5	2.3	.922							
C	B. Sullivan	263	.243	1	26	242	81	11	8	4.8	.967							
C	E. McFarland	244	.230	1	25	282	71	12	7	5.3	.967							
PO	N. Callahan	218	.234	0	13	54	107	9	7		.947							

Cle. W-69 L-67 Bill Armour

POS	Player	AB	BA	HR	RBI	PO	A	E	DP	TC/G	FA	Pitcher	G	IP	W	L	SV	ERA
1B	P. Hickman	426	.380	8	94	1079	47	40*	63	11.9*	.966	E. Moore	36	293	17	17	1	2.95
2B	N. Lajoie	348	.368	7	64	270	283	15	49	**6.6***	**.974***	A. Joss	32	269	17	13	0	2.77
SS	J. Gochnaur	459	.185	0	37	289	447	48	59	5.7	.933	B. Bernhard	27	217	17	5	1	2.20
3B	B. Bradley	550	.340	11	77	**188**	324	43	21	4.1	.923	C. Wright	21	148	7	11	1	3.95
RF	E. Flick	424	.297	2	61	156	13	13	2	1.7	.929							
CF	H. Bay	455	.290	0	23	242	13	7	3	2.4	**.973**							
LF	J. McCarthy	359	.284	0	41	178	6	11	0	2.1	.944							
C	H. Bemis	317	.312	1	29	333	**120**	17	2	5.4	.964							
OF	O. Pickering	293	.256	3	26	138	5	3	1	2.3	.979							
C	B. Wood	258	.295	0	40	169	53	14	4	4.5	.941							

Was. W-61 L-75 Tom Loftus

POS	Player	AB	BA	HR	RBI	PO	A	E	DP	TC/G	FA	Pitcher	G	IP	W	L	SV	ERA
1B	S. Carey	452	.314	0	60	1190	69	14	54	10.6	**.989**	A. Orth	38	324	19	18	0	3.97
2B	J. Doyle	312	.247	1	20	145	197	26	17	5.4	.929	C. Patten	36	300	17	16	1	4.05
SS	B. Ely	381	.262	1	46	238	350	49	31	6.1	.923	B. Carrick	31	258	11	17	0	4.86
3B	B. Coughlin	469	.301	6	71	104	157	21	6	4.3	.926	J. Townsend	27	220	9	16	0	4.45
RF	W. Lee	391	.256	4	45	171	14	17	1	2.1	.916	W. Lee	13	98	5	7	0	5.05
CF	J. Ryan	484	.320	6	44	280	16	16	0	2.6	.949							
LF	E. Delahanty	473	**.376**	10	93	236	11	10	0	2.3	.961							
C	B. Clarke	291	.268	7	42	288	97	11	8	4.6	**.972**							
UT	B. Keister	483	.300	9	90	229	166	34	14		.921							
3B	H. Wolverton	249	.249	1	23	86	139	24	8	4.2	.904							
C	L. Drill	221	.262	1	29	175	51	19	2	4.6	.922							
P	A. Orth	175	.217	2	10	25	95	10	3	3.4	.923							

Det. W-52 L-83 Frank Dwyer

POS	Player	AB	BA	HR	RBI	PO	A	E	DP	TC/G	FA	Pitcher	G	IP	W	L	SV	ERA
1B	P. Dillon	243	.206	0	22	709	52	19	45	11.8	.976	W. Mercer	35	282	15	18	1	3.04
2B	K. Gleason	441	.247	1	38	**320**	349	**42**	66	6.0	.941	G. Mullin	35	260	13	16	0	3.67
SS	K. Elberfeld	488	.260	1	64	326	459	67	63	6.6	.921	E. Siever	25	188	8	11	1	**1.91**
3B	D. Casey	520	.273	3	55	174	309	51	17	4.0	.904	R. Miller	20	149	6	12	1	3.69
RF	D. Holmes	362	.257	2	33	155	16	9	5	2.0	.950	J. Yeager	19	140	6	12	0	4.82
CF	J. Barrett	509	.303	4	44	**326**	22	14	6	2.7	.961							
LF	D. Harley	491	.281	2	44	238	15	19	1	2.2	.930							
C	D. McGuire	229	.227	2	23	210	65	14	6	4.1	.952							
UT	McAllister	229	.210	1	32	301	67	14	19		.963							
C	F. Buelow	224	.223	2	29	174	81	**20**	5	4.4	.927							
1B	E. Beck	162	.296	2	22	343	26	11	24	10.6	.971							
UT	J. Yeager	161	.242	1	23	59	94	9	3		.944							

POS	Player	AB	BA	HR	RBI	PO	A	E	DP	TC/G	FA	Pitcher	G	IP	W	L	SV	ERA
1B	D. McGann	250	.316	0	42	658	41	9	52	10.4	.987	H. Howell	26	199	9	15	0	4.12
2B	J. Williams	498	.313	8	83	248	332	34	46	5.9	.945	J. McGinnity	25	199	13	10	0	3.44
SS	B. Gilbert	445	.245	2	38	349	410	78	72	6.5	.907	S. Wiltse	19	164	7	11	0	5.10
3B	R. Bresnahan	235	.272	4	34	33	55	12	4	3.3	.880	C. Shields	23	142	4	11	1	4.24
RF	C. Seymour	280	.268	3	41	121	9	6	2	1.9	.956	J. Katoll	15	123	5	10	0	4.02
CF	H. McFarland	242	.322	3	36	152	12	6	1	2.8	.965	I. Butler	16	116	1	10	0	5.34
LF	K. Selbach	503	.320	3	60	286	17	19	3	2.5	.941	L. Hughes	13	108	7	6	0	3.90
C	W. Robinson	335	.293	1	57	262	75	18	4	4.1	.949							
UT	H. Howell	347	.268	2	42	152	208	26	10		.933							
OF	H. Arndt	248	.254	2	28	106	10	17	1	2.1	.872							
OF	J. Kelley	222	.311	1	34	101	7	3	2	2.3	.973							
1B	T. Jones	159	.283	0	14	341	22	17	23	10.3	.955							
UT	B. Smith	145	.234	0	21	135	34	7	5		.960							
UT	S. Wiltse	132	.295	2	24	160	44	10	8		.953							

Bal.
W-50 L-88
John McGraw
W-28 L-34
Wilbert Robinson
W-22 L-54

BATTING AND BASE RUNNING LEADERS

Batting Average
E. Delahanty, WAS	.376
N. Lajoie, CLE, PHI	.366
P. Hickman, BOS, CLE	.363
P. Dougherty, BOS	.342
L. Cross, PHI	.342

Slugging Average
E. Delahanty, WAS	.590
N. Lajoie, CLE, PHI	.551
P. Hickman, BOS, CLE	.541
B. Bradley, CLE	.515
S. Seybold, PHI	.506

Home Runs
S. Seybold, PHI	16
P. Hickman, BOS, CLE	11
B. Bradley, CLE	11
B. Freeman, BOS	11
E. Delahanty, WAS	10

Total Bases
P. Hickman, BOS, CLE	289
B. Bradley, CLE	283
B. Freeman, BOS	283
E. Delahanty, WAS	279
S. Seybold, PHI	264

Runs Batted In
B. Freeman, BOS	121
P. Hickman, BOS, CLE	110
L. Cross, PHI	108
S. Seybold, PHI	97
E. Delahanty, WAS	93
G. Davis, CHI	93

Stolen Bases
T. Hartsel, PHI	47
S. Mertes, CHI	46
D. Fultz, PHI	44
B. Gilbert, BAL	38
F. Isbell, CHI	38
S. Strang, CHI	38

Hits
P. Hickman, BOS, CLE	195
L. Cross, PHI	191
B. Bradley, CLE	187

Base on Balls
T. Hartsel, PHI	87
S. Strang, CHI	76
J. Barrett, DET	74

Home Run Percentage
S. Seybold, PHI	3.1
B. Clarke, WAS	2.4
E. Delahanty, WAS	2.1

Runs Scored
D. Fultz, PHI	109
T. Hartsel, PHI	109
S. Strang, CHI	108

Doubles
E. Delahanty, WAS	43
H. Davis, PHI	43
B. Bradley, CLE	39
L. Cross, PHI	39

Triples
J. Williams, BAL	21
B. Freeman, BOS	19
E. Delahanty, WAS	14
H. Ferris, BOS	14

PITCHING LEADERS

Winning Percentage
B. Bernhard, CLE, PHI	.783
R. Waddell, PHI	.774
C. Young, BOS	.744
R. Donahue, STL	.667
C. Griffith, CHI	.625

Earned Run Average
E. Siever, DET	1.91
R. Waddell, PHI	2.05
B. Bernhard, CLE, PHI	2.15
C. Young, BOS	2.15
N. Garvin, CHI	2.21

Wins
C. Young, BOS	32
R. Waddell, PHI	24
J. Powell, STL	22
R. Donahue, STL	22
B. Dinneen, BOS	21

Saves
J. Powell, STL	3

Strikeouts
R. Waddell, PHI	210
C. Young, BOS	160
J. Powell, STL	137
B. Dinneen, BOS	136
E. Plank, PHI	107

Complete Games
C. Young, BOS	41
B. Dinneen, BOS	39
A. Orth, WAS	36
J. Powell, STL	36
R. Donahue, STL	33
C. Patten, WAS	33

Fewest Hits per 9 Innings
B. Bernhard, CLE, PHI	7.01
R. Waddell, PHI	7.30
A. Joss, CLE	7.52

Shutouts
A. Joss, CLE	5
E. Siever, DET	4
W. Mercer, DET	4
E. Moore, CLE	4

Fewest Walks per 9 Innings
A. Orth, WAS	1.11
C. Young, BOS	1.24
B. Bernhard, CLE, PHI	1.47

Most Strikeouts per 9 Inn.
R. Waddell, PHI	6.84
J. Powell, STL	3.76
C. Young, BOS	3.74

Innings
C. Young, BOS	385
B. Dinneen, BOS	371
J. Powell, STL	328

Games Pitched
C. Young, BOS	45
B. Dinneen, BOS	42
J. Powell, STL	42

	W	L	PCT	GB	R	OR	Batting 2B	3B	HR	BA	SA	SB	Fielding E	DP	FA	CG	BB	Pitching SO	ShO	SV	ERA
PHI	83	53	.610		775	636	235	67	38	.287	.389	201	270	75	.953	114	368	455	5	2	3.29
STL	78	58	.574	5	619	607	208	61	29	.265	.353	137	274	122	.953	120	343	348	8	2	3.34
BOS	77	60	.562	6.5	664	600	195	95	42	.278	.383	132	263	101	.955	123	326	431	6	1	3.02
CHI	74	60	.552	8	675	602	170	50	14	.268	.335	265	257	125	.955	116	331	346	11	0	3.41
CLE	69	67	.507	14	686	667	248	68	33	.289	.389	140	287	96	.950	116	411	361	16	3	3.28
WAS	61	75	.449	22	709	790	261	66	48	.283	.396	121	316	70	.945	130	312	300	2	1	4.36
DET	52	83	.385	30.5	566	657	141	55	22	.251	.320	130	332	111	.943	116	370	245	9	3	3.56
BAL	50	88	.362	34	715	850	202	107	33	.277	.385	189	357	109	.938	119	354	258	3	1	4.33
					5409	5409	1660	569	259	.275	.369	1315	2356	809	.949	954	2815	2744	60	13	3.57

	POS	Player	AB	BA	HR	RBI	PO	A	E	DP	TC/G	FA	Pitcher	G	IP	W	L	SV	ERA
Pit.	1B	K. Bransfield	505	.265	2	57	1347	88	28	**82**	**11.5**	.981	D. Phillippe	36	289	24	7	2	2.43
W-91 L-49	2B	C. Ritchey	506	.287	0	59	281	**460**	30	45	5.6	**.961**	S. Leever	36	284	25	7	1	**2.06**
Fred Clarke	SS	H. Wagner	512	**.355**	5	101	303	397	50	**51**	6.8	.933	E. Doheny	27	223	16	8	2	3.19
	3B	T. Leach	507	.298	7	87	178	292	**65**	16	**4.2**	.879	B. Kennedy	18	125	9	6	0	3.45
	RF	J. Sebring	506	.277	4	64	208	20	18	11	2.0	.927							
	CF	G. Beaumont	**613**	.341	7	68	258	15	15	2	2.0	.948							
	LF	F. Clarke	427	.351	5	70	168	10	7	3	1.8	.962							
	C	E. Phelps	273	.282	2	31	315	81	8	7	5.3	.980							
	UT	O. Krueger	256	.246	1	28	109	113	20	17		.917							
	C	H. Smith	212	.175	0	19	259	75	9	2	5.7	.974							
N. Y.	1B	D. McGann	482	.270	3	50	1188	64	15	58	9.8	**.988**	J. McGinnity	**55**	**434**	**31**	20	2	2.43
W-84 L-55	2B	B. Gilbert	413	.252	1	40	314	366	47	42	5.7	.935	C. Mathewson	45	366	30	13	2	2.26
John McGraw	SS	C. Babb	424	.248	0	46	238	343	56	35	5.6	.912	D. Taylor	33	245	13	13	0	4.23
	3B	B. Lauder	395	.281	0	53	140	194	34	10	3.4	.908	J. Cronin	20	116	6	4	1	3.81
	RF	G. Browne	591	.313	3	45	212	13	20	4	1.7	.918	R. Miller	15	85	2	5	**3**	4.13
	CF	R. Bresnahan	406	.350	4	55	150	14	6	6	2.0	.965							
	LF	S. Mertes	517	.280	7	**104**	265	24	8	5	2.2	**.973**							
	C	J. Warner	285	.284	0	34	450	123	8	9	**6.8**	**.986**							
	OF	Van Haltren	280	.257	0	28	136	3	6	1	1.9	.959							
	UT	J. Dunn	257	.241	0	37	101	173	26	24		.913							
	C	F. Bowerman	210	.276	1	31	316	66	9	9	7.1	.977							
	P	J. McGinnity	165	.206	0	11	**31**	94	**16**	3	2.6	.887							
	P	C. Mathewson	124	.226	1	20	18	93	3	0	2.5	.974							
Chi.	1B	F. Chance	441	.327	2	81	1204	68	**36**	49	10.8	.972	J. Taylor	37	312	21	14	1	2.45
W-82 L-56	2B	J. Evers	464	.293	0	52	245	306	37	39	5.3	.937	J. Weimer	35	282	21	9	0	2.30
Frank Selee	SS	J. Tinker	460	.291	2	70	229	362	61	37	6.1	.906	B. Wicker	32	247	19	10	1	3.02
	3B	D. Casey	435	.290	1	40	143	190	31	5	3.3	.915	C. Lundgren	27	193	10	9	**3**	2.94
	RF	D. Harley	386	.231	0	33	162	18	15	2	1.9	.923	J. Menefee	20	147	8	8	0	3.00
	CF	D. Jones	497	.282	1	62	249	14	8	3	2.1	.970							
	LF	J. Slagle	543	.298	0	44	292	16	21	8	2.4	.936							
	C	J. Kling	491	.297	3	68	**565**	189	24	13	5.9	.969							
Cin.	1B	J. Beckley	459	.327	2	81	1127	78	30	56	10.4	.976	N. Hahn	34	296	22	12	0	2.52
W-74 L-65	2B	T. Daly	307	.293	1	38	151	221	25	22	5.0	.937	B. Ewing	29	247	14	13	1	2.77
Joe Kelley	SS	T. Corcoran	459	.246	2	73	263	367	38	42	5.8	.943	J. Sutthoff	30	225	16	10	0	2.80
	3B	H. Steinfeldt	439	.312	6	83	159	212	25	11	3.8	.937	E. Poole	25	184	8	13	0	3.28
	RF	C. Dolan	385	.288	0	58	107	11	8	2	1.4	.937	J. Harper	17	135	6	8	0	4.33
	CF	C. Seymour	558	.342	7	72	**318**	14	**36**	2	**2.7**	.902	B. Phillips	16	118	8	6	0	3.35
	LF	M. Donlin	496	.351	7	67	209	15	25	4	2.1	.900							
	C	H. Peitz	358	.260	0	42	365	93	14	7	6.1	.970							
	UT	J. Kelley	383	.316	3	45	239	86	22	11		.937							
	C	B. Bergen	207	.227	0	19	251	85	7	3	5.9	.980							
Bkn.	1B	J. Doyle	524	.313	0	91	**1418**	83	29	74	11.0	.981	O. Jones	38	324	20	16	0	2.94
W-70 L-66	2B	T. Flood	309	.249	0	32	195	216	34	37	5.3	.924	H. Schmidt	40	301	21	13	2	3.83
Ned Hanlon	SS	B. Dahlen	474	.262	1	64	296	**477**	42	48	5.9	**.948**	N. Garvin	38	298	15	18	2	3.08
	3B	S. Strang	508	.272	0	38	147	245	37	13	3.5	.914	R. Evans	15	110	4	8	0	3.27
	RF	J. McCreedie	213	.324	0	20	68	6	6	3	1.4	.925	B. Reidy	15	104	7	6	0	3.46
	CF	J. Dobbs	414	.237	2	59	241	11	9	4	2.4	.966							
	LF	J. Sheckard	515	.332	**9**	75	314	**36**	18	7	2.6	.951							
	C	L. Ritter	259	.236	0	37	309	80	**25**	6	5.6	.940							
	2B	D. Jordan	267	.236	0	21	101	132	18	12	4.6	.928							
	C	F. Jacklitsch	176	.267	1	21	201	71	7	7	5.3	.975							
	OF	D. Gessler	154	.247	0	18	56	4	1	1	1.4	.984							
	OF	T. McCreery	141	.262	0	10	54	4	7	2	1.7	.892							
Bos.	1B	F. Tenney	447	.313	3	41	1145	**93**	33	60	10.4	.974	T. Pittinger	44	352	19	**23**	0	3.48
W-58 L-80	2B	Abbaticchio	489	.227	1	46	**316**	325	45	35	5.9	.934	V. Willis	33	278	12	18	0	2.98
Al Buckenberger	SS	H. Aubrey	325	.212	0	27	185	301	74	20	6.0	.868	J. Malarkey	32	253	11	16	0	3.09
	3B	E. Gremminger	511	.264	5	56	**217**	**300**	36	**20**	4.0	.935	W. Piatt	25	181	8	13	0	3.18
	RF	P. Carney	392	.240	1	49	112	10	6	4	1.4	.953							
	CF	C. Dexter	457	.223	3	34	177	13	12	6	1.9	.941							
	LF	D. Cooley	553	.289	1	70	246	11	13	4	2.1	.952							
	C	P. Moran	389	.262	7	54	400	**214**	24	17	6.0	.962							
	OF	J. Stanley	308	.250	1	47	117	21	15	2	2.0	.902							
	2S	F. Bonner	173	.220	1	10	104	116	15	19		.936							
Phi.	1B	K. Douglass	377	.255	1	36	902	51	15	41	10.0	.985	B. Duggleby	36	264	13	18	1	3.75
W-49 L-86	2B	K. Gleason	412	.284	1	49	236	280	22	30	5.3	.959	C. Fraser	31	250	12	17	1	4.50
Chief Zimmer	SS	R. Hulswitt	519	.247	1	58	**354**	430	**81**	43	6.3	.906	T. Sparks	28	248	11	15	0	2.72
	3B	H. Wolverton	494	.308	0	53	182	247	27	8	3.7	**.941**	F. Mitchell	28	227	11	15	0	4.48
	RF	B. Keister	400	.320	3	63	133	22	10	1	1.7	.939	McFetridge	14	103	0	11	0	4.91
	CF	R. Thomas	477	.327	1	27	**318**	19	13	3	2.7	.963							
	LF	S. Barry	550	.276	1	60	211	14	7	2	2.2	.970							
	C	F. Roth	220	.273	0	22	235	82	22	9	5.7	.935							
	OF	J. Titus	280	.286	2	34	126	13	7	2	2.0	.952							
	UT	B. Hallman	198	.212	0	17	148	101	16	6		.940							
	C	R. Dooin	188	.218	0	14	186	82	17	1	5.6	.940							

	POS	Player	AB	BA	HR	RBI	PO	A	E	DP	TC/G	FA	Pitcher	G	IP	W	L	SV	ERA
St. L.	1B	J. Hackett	351	.228	0	36	947	40	28	63	11.4	.972	C. McFarland	28	229	9	18	0	3.07
W-43 L-94	2B	J. Farrell	519	.272	1	32	281	394	53	52	6.2	.927	T. Brown	26	201	9	13	0	2.60
Patsy Donovan	SS	D. Brain	464	.231	1	60	163	244	41	34	6.2	.908	C. Currie	22	148	4	12	1	4.01
	3B	J. Burke	431	.285	0	42	139	199	33	14	4.0	.911	B. Rhoads	17	129	5	8	0	4.60
	RF	P. Donovan	410	.327	0	39	142	16	8	5	1.6	.952	M. O'Neill	19	115	4	13	0	4.77
	CF	H. Smoot	500	.296	4	49	231	14	15	3	2.0	.942	E. Murphy	15	106	4	8	0	3.31
	LF	G. Barclay	419	.248	0	42	187	13	22	0	2.1	.901	J. Dunleavy	14	102	6	8	0	4.06
	C	J. O'Neill	246	.236	0	27	348	135	14	8	6.7	.972							
	C	J. Ryan	227	.238	1	10	168	65	7	4	5.1	.971							
	OF	J. Dunleavy	193	.249	0	10	58	10	2	5	1.9	.972							
	SS	O. Williams	187	.203	0	9	94	161	33	16	5.5	.885							

BATTING AND BASE RUNNING LEADERS

Batting Average
H. Wagner, PIT	.355
F. Clarke, PIT	.351
M. Donlin, CIN	.351
R. Bresnahan, NY	.350
C. Seymour, CIN	.342

Slugging Average
F. Clarke, PIT	.532
H. Wagner, PIT	.518
M. Donlin, CIN	.516
R. Bresnahan, NY	.493
H. Steinfeldt, CIN	.481

Home Runs
J. Sheckard, BKN	9

Total Bases
G. Beaumont, PIT	272
C. Seymour, CIN	267
H. Wagner, PIT	265
M. Donlin, CIN	256
J. Sheckard, BKN	245

Runs Batted In
S. Mertes, NY	104
H. Wagner, PIT	101
J. Doyle, BKN	91
T. Leach, PIT	87
H. Steinfeldt, CIN	83

Stolen Bases
F. Chance, CHI	67
J. Sheckard, BKN	67
S. Strang, BKN	46
H. Wagner, PIT	46
S. Mertes, NY	45

Hits
G. Beaumont, PIT	209
C. Seymour, CIN	191
G. Browne, NY	185

Base on Balls
R. Thomas, PHI	107
B. Dahlen, BKN	82
J. Slagle, CHI	81

Home Run Percentage
P. Moran, BOS	1.8
J. Sheckard, BKN	1.7
M. Donlin, CIN	1.4

Runs Scored
G. Beaumont, PIT	137
M. Donlin, CIN	110
G. Browne, NY	105

Doubles
F. Clarke, PIT	32
H. Steinfeldt, CIN	32
S. Mertes, NY	32

Triples
H. Wagner, PIT	19
M. Donlin, CIN	18
T. Leach, PIT	17

PITCHING LEADERS

Winning Percentage
S. Leever, PIT	.781
D. Phillippe, PIT	.774
J. Weimer, CHI	.700
C. Mathewson, NY	.698
E. Doheny, PIT	.667

Earned Run Average
S. Leever, PIT	2.06
C. Mathewson, NY	2.26
J. Weimer, CHI	2.30
J. McGinnity, NY	2.43
D. Phillippe, PIT	2.43

Wins
J. McGinnity, NY	31
C. Mathewson, NY	30
S. Leever, PIT	25
D. Phillippe, PIT	24
N. Hahn, CIN	22

Saves
C. Lundgren, CHI	3
R. Miller, NY	3

Strikeouts
C. Mathewson, NY	267
J. McGinnity, NY	171
N. Garvin, BKN	154
T. Pittinger, BOS	140
J. Weimer, CHI	128

Complete Games
J. McGinnity, NY	44
C. Mathewson, NY	37
T. Pittinger, BOS	35
N. Hahn, CIN	34
J. Taylor, CHI	33

Fewest Hits per 9 Innings
J. Weimer, CHI	7.69
C. Mathewson, NY	7.89
J. Taylor, CHI	7.98

Shutouts
S. Leever, PIT	7
N. Hahn, CIN	5
H. Schmidt, BKN	5

Fewest Walks per 9 Innings
D. Phillippe, PIT	0.90
B. Reidy, BKN	1.21
N. Hahn, CIN	1.43

Most Strikeouts per 9 Inn.
C. Mathewson, NY	6.56
W. Piatt, BOS	4.97
N. Garvin, BKN	4.65

Innings
J. McGinnity, NY	434
C. Mathewson, NY	366
T. Pittinger, BOS	352

Games Pitched
J. McGinnity, NY	55
C. Mathewson, NY	45
T. Pittinger, BOS	44

	W	L	PCT	GB	R	OR	Batting					SB	Fielding			CG	BB	Pitching			
							2B	3B	HR	BA	SA		E	DP	FA			SO	ShO	SV	ERA
PIT	91	49	.650		792	613	208	110	34	.287	.393	172	295	100	.951	117	384	454	16	5	2.91
NY	84	55	.604	6.5	729	548	181	49	20	.272	.344	264	287	87	.951	115	371	628	8	8	2.95
CHI	82	56	.594	8	695	594	191	62	9	.275	.347	259	338	78	.942	117	354	451	6	6	2.77
CIN	74	65	.532	16.5	764	749	228	92	28	.288	.390	144	312	84	.946	126	378	480	11	1	3.07
BKN	70	66	.515	19	666	674	177	56	15	.265	.339	273	284	98	.951	125	377	438	11	4	3.44
BOS	58	80	.420	32	575	661	176	47	25	.245	.318	159	361	89	.937	125	460	516	5	0	3.34
PHI	49	86	.363	39.5	618	743	186	62	12	.268	.341	120	300	76	.947	126	425	381	5	2	3.97
STL	43	94	.314	46.5	505	762	138	65	8	.251	.313	171	354	111	.940	111	430	419	4	2	3.76
					5344	5344	1485	543	151	.269	.349	1562	2531	723	.946	955	3179	3767	66	28	3.27

	POS	Player	AB	BA	HR	RBI	PO	A	E	DP	TC/G	FA	Pitcher	G	IP	W	L	SV	ERA
Bos. W-91 L-47 Jimmy Collins	1B	C. LaChance	522	.257	1	53	1471	57	25	68	11.0	.984	C. Young	40	342	28	9	2	2.08
	2B	H. Ferris	525	.251	9	66	313	434	39	50	5.7	.950	B. Dinneen	37	299	21	13	2	2.26
	SS	F. Parent	560	.304	4	80	296	456	57	36	5.8	.930	L. Hughes	33	245	20	7	0	2.57
	3B	J. Collins	540	.296	5	72	178	260	22	19	3.5	.952	N. Gibson	24	183	13	9	0	3.19
	RF	B. Freeman	567	.287	13	104	195	13	15	2	1.6	.933	G. Winter	24	178	9	8	0	3.08
	CF	C. Stahl	299	.274	2	44	135	11	6	2	2.1	.961							
	LF	P. Dougherty	590	.331	4	59	259	16	14	3	2.1	.952							
	C	L. Criger	317	.192	3	31	491	156	14	10	6.9	.979							
	OF	J. O'Brien	338	.210	3	38	128	9	6	2	2.0	.958							
Phi. W-75 L-60 Connie Mack	1B	H. Davis	420	.298	5	55	942	63	29	38	9.9	.972	E. Plank	43	336	23	16	0	2.38
	2B	D. Murphy	513	.273	1	60	241	349	32	34	4.7	.949	R. Waddell	39	324	21	16	0	2.44
	SS	M. Cross	470	.247	3	45	305	396	45	36	5.4	.940	C. Bender	36	270	17	15	0	3.07
	3B	L. Cross	559	.292	2	90	152	228	20	14	2.9	.950	W. Henley	29	186	12	9	0	3.91
	RF	S. Seybold	522	.299	8	84	177	9	7	4	1.6	.964							
	CF	O. Pickering	512	.281	1	36	272	17	9	5	2.2	.970							
	LF	T. Hartsel	373	.311	5	26	144	6	5	0	1.6	.968							
	C	Schreckengost	306	.255	3	30	514	106	16	4	8.3	.975							
	OF	D. Hoffman	248	.246	2	22	111	4	6	0	2.0	.950							
	C	M. Powers	247	.227	0	23	349	86	8	3	6.7	.982							
Cle. W-77 L-63 Bill Armour	1B	P. Hickman	518	.330	12	97	1310	66	40	67	11.3	.972	A. Joss	32	293	18	13	0	2.15
	2B	N. Lajoie	488	.355	7	93	366	402	36	61	6.5	.955	E. Moore	29	239	19	9	1	1.77
	SS	J. Gochnaur	438	.185	0	48	236	414	98	45	5.6	.869	B. Bernhard	20	166	14	6	0	2.12
	3B	B. Bradley	543	.315	6	68	151	299	37	18	3.6	.924	R. Donahue	16	137	7	9	0	2.44
	RF	E. Flick	529	.299	2	51	219	15	11	3	1.8	.955	C. Wright	15	102	3	9	0	5.75
	CF	H. Bay	579	.292	1	35	293	13	16	3	2.3	.950							
	LF	J. McCarthy	415	.265	0	43	178	10	7	5	1.8	.964							
	C	H. Bemis	314	.261	1	41	315	82	5	6	5.4	.988							
	C	F. Abbott	255	.235	1	25	337	97	19	9	6.4	.958							
N. Y. W-72 L-62 Clark Griffith	1B	J. Ganzel	476	.277	3	71	1385	94	18	68	11.6	.988	J. Chesbro	40	325	21	15	0	2.77
	2B	J. Williams	502	.267	3	82	266	438	32	59	5.6	.957	J. Tannehill	32	240	15	15	0	3.27
	SS	K. Elberfeld	349	.287	0	45	221	291	48	40	6.2*	.914	C. Griffith	25	213	14	11	0	2.70
	3B	W. Conroy	503	.272	1	45	164	243	36	11	3.6	.919	H. Howell	25	156	9	6	0	3.53
	RF	W. Keeler	515	.318	0	32	177	10	13	4	1.6	.935	B. Wolfe	20	148	6	9	0	2.97
	CF	H. McFarland	362	.243	5	45	207	9	14	2	2.2	.939							
	LF	L. Davis	372	.237	0	25	176	7	19	1	2.0	.906							
	C	M. Beville	258	.194	0	29	296	66	15	4	5.0	.960							
	OF	D. Fultz	295	.224	0	15	156	11	12	2	2.3	.933							
	C	J. O'Connor	212	.203	0	12	282	56	4	6	5.4	.988							
Det. W-65 L-71 Ed Barrow	1B	C. Carr	548	.281	2	79	1276	111	25	60	10.5	.982	G. Mullin	41	321	19	15	2	2.25
	2B	H. Smith	336	.223	1	22	200	267	36	30	5.4	.928	W. Donovan	35	307	17	16	0	2.29
	SS	McAllister	265	.260	0	22	77	129	26	12	5.0	.888	F. Kitson	31	258	15	16	0	2.58
	3B	J. Yeager	402	.256	0	45	126	176	26	9	3.1	.921	R. Kisinger	16	119	7	9	0	2.96
	RF	S. Crawford	550	.335	4	89	225	16	10	3	1.8	.960							
	CF	J. Barrett	517	.315	2	31	303	19	15	7	2.5	.955							
	LF	B. Lush	423	.274	1	33	227	17	8	4	2.5	.968							
	C	D. McGuire	248	.250	0	21	330	73	17	9	6.1	.960							
	S2	H. Long	239	.222	0	23	161	198	32	18		.918							
	C	F. Buelow	192	.214	1	13	254	66	13	6	5.6	.961							
St. L. W-65 L-74 Jimmy McAleer	1B	J. Anderson	550	.284	2	78	1416	91	22	71	11.5	.986	J. Powell	38	306	15	19	2	2.91
	2B	B. Friel	351	.228	0	25	108	171	26	15	4.8	.915	W. Sudhoff	38	294	21	15	0	2.27
	SS	B. Wallace	519	.245	1	54	282	468	62	53	6.0	.923	E. Siever	31	254	13	14	0	2.48
	3B	H. Hill	317	.243	0	25	110	165	23	10	3.5	.923	R. Donahue	16	131	8	7	0	2.75
	RF	C. Hemphill	383	.245	3	29	155	17	7	4	1.7	.961							
	CF	E. Heidrick	461	.280	1	42	252	17	13	5	2.4	.954							
	LF	J. Burkett	514	.296	3	40	230	10	15	4	1.9	.941							
	C	M. Kahoe	244	.189	0	23	333	64	12	8	5.8	.971							
	C	J. Sugden	241	.216	0	22	321	81	7	6	6.2	.983							
	32	B. McCormick	207	.217	1	16	79	131	10	14		.955							
	OF	J. Martin	173	.214	0	7	53	6	1	3	1.6	.983							
Chi. W-60 L-77 Nixey Callahan	1B	F. Isbell	546	.242	2	59	1180	87	20	57	11.0	.984	D. White	37	300	17	16	0	2.13
	2B	G. Magoon	334	.228	0	25	198	253	31	28	5.1	.936	R. Patterson	34	293	15	15	1	2.70
	SS	L. Tannehill	503	.225	2	50	291	457	76	58	6.0	.908	P. Flaherty	40	294	11	25	1	3.74
	3B	N. Callahan	439	.292	2	56	113	203	37	5	3.5	.895	F. Owen	26	167	8	12	1	3.50
	RF	D. Green	499	.309	6	62	219	16	17	8	1.9	.933							
	CF	F. Jones	530	.287	0	45	324	11	5	3	2.5	.985							
	LF	D. Holmes	344	.279	0	18	151	14*	6	0	2.1	.965							
	C	J. Slattery	211	.218	0	20	215	44	7	0	4.8	.974							
	OF	B. Hallman	207	.208	0	18	114	7	6	0	2.2	.953							
	C	E. McFarland	201	.209	1	19	240	65	10	7	5.6	.968							
	2B	T. Daly	150	.207	0	19	96	103	11	12	4.9	.948							

POS	Player	AB	BA	HR	RBI	PO	A	E	DP	TC/G	FA	Pitcher	G	IP	W	L	SV	ERA
Was. W-43 L-94 Tom Loftus																		
1B	B. Clarke	465	.239	2	38	891	44	14	44	10.8	.985	C. Patten	36	300	11	22	1	3.60
2B	B. McCormick	219	.215	1	24	130	205	14	27	5.5	.960*	A. Orth	36	280	10	22	2	4.34
SS	C. Moran	373	.225	1	24	216	300	31	37	5.7	.943	H. Wilson	30	242	7	18	0	3.31
3B	B. Coughlin	470	.251	1	31	170	224	20	13	3.5	.952	W. Lee	22	167	8	12	0	3.08
RF	W. Lee	231	.208	0	13	100	6	8	2	2.4	.930	J. Townsend	20	127	2	11	0	4.76
CF	J. Ryan	437	.245	7	46	288	7	9	1	2.7	.970	D. Dunkle	14	108	5	9	0	4.24
LF	K. Selbach	536	.250	3	49	251	10	12	2	2.0	.956							
C	M. Kittredge	192	.214	0	16	238	76	7	2	5.4	.978							
UT	R. Robinson	373	.212	1	20	185	248	43	27		.910							
1B	S. Carey	183	.202	0	23	435	23	11	18	10.0	.977							
P	A. Orth	162	.302	0	11	17	86	9	0	3.1	.920							
OF	E. Delahanty	156	.333	1	21	69	6	3	1	2.0	.962							
C	L. Drill	154	.253	0	23	208	47	9	5	5.6	.966							

BATTING AND BASE RUNNING LEADERS

Batting Average
N. Lajoie, CLE	.355
S. Crawford, DET	.335
P. Dougherty, BOS	.331
P. Hickman, CLE	.330
W. Keeler, NY	.318

Slugging Average
N. Lajoie, CLE	.533
P. Hickman, CLE	.502
B. Freeman, BOS	.496
B. Bradley, CLE	.495
S. Crawford, DET	.489

Home Runs
B. Freeman, BOS	13
P. Hickman, CLE	12
H. Ferris, BOS	9
S. Seybold, PHI	8
J. Ryan, WAS	7
N. Lajoie, CLE	7

Total Bases
B. Freeman, BOS	281
B. Bradley, CLE	269
S. Crawford, DET	269
N. Lajoie, CLE	260
P. Hickman, CLE	260

Runs Batted In
B. Freeman, BOS	104
P. Hickman, CLE	97
N. Lajoie, CLE	93
L. Cross, PHI	90
S. Crawford, DET	89

Stolen Bases
H. Bay, CLE	45
O. Pickering, PHI	40
D. Holmes, CHI, WAS	35
P. Dougherty, BOS	35
W. Conroy, NY	33

Hits
P. Dougherty, BOS	195
S. Crawford, DET	184
N. Lajoie, CLE	173

Base on Balls
J. Barrett, DET	74
B. Lush, DET	70
O. Pickering, PHI	53

Home Run Percentage
P. Hickman, CLE	2.3
B. Freeman, BOS	2.3
H. Ferris, BOS	1.7

Runs Scored
P. Dougherty, BOS	108
B. Bradley, CLE	103
W. Keeler, NY	95
J. Barrett, DET	95

Doubles
S. Seybold, PHI	45
N. Lajoie, CLE	40
B. Freeman, BOS	39

Triples
S. Crawford, DET	25
B. Bradley, CLE	22
B. Freeman, BOS	20

PITCHING LEADERS

Winning Percentage
C. Young, BOS	.757
L. Hughes, BOS	.741
E. Moore, CLE	.679
B. Dinneen, BOS	.636
E. Plank, PHI	.590

Earned Run Average
E. Moore, CLE	1.77
C. Young, BOS	2.08
B. Bernhard, CLE	2.12
D. White, CHI	2.13
A. Joss, CLE	2.15

Wins
C. Young, BOS	28
E. Plank, PHI	23
W. Sudhoff, STL	21
R. Waddell, PHI	21
B. Dinneen, BOS	21
J. Chesbro, NY	21

Saves
C. Young, BOS	2
A. Orth, WAS	2
J. Powell, STL	2
B. Dinneen, BOS	2
G. Mullin, DET	2

Strikeouts
R. Waddell, PHI	302
W. Donovan, DET	187
C. Young, BOS	176
E. Plank, PHI	176
G. Mullin, DET	170

Complete Games
W. Donovan, DET	34
C. Young, BOS	34
R. Waddell, PHI	34
J. Powell, STL	33
J. Chesbro, NY	33
E. Plank, PHI	33

Fewest Hits per 9 Innings
E. Moore, CLE	7.13
W. Donovan, DET	7.24
A. Joss, CLE	7.35

Shutouts
C. Young, BOS	7
B. Dinneen, BOS	6
G. Mullin, DET	6

Fewest Walks per 9 Innings
C. Young, BOS	0.97
B. Bernhard, CLE	1.14
R. Donahue, CLE, STL	1.14

Most Strikeouts per 9 Inn.
R. Waddell, PHI	8.39
W. Donovan, DET	5.48
E. Moore, CLE	5.35

Innings
C. Young, BOS	342
E. Plank, PHI	336
J. Chesbro, NY	325

Games Pitched
E. Plank, PHI	43
G. Mullin, DET	41

	W	L	PCT	GB	R	OR	Batting 2B	3B	HR	BA	SA	SB	Fielding E	DP	FA	Pitching CG	BB	SO	ShO	SV	ERA
BOS	91	47	.659		707	505	222	113	48	.272	.392	141	239	86	.959	123	269	579	20	4	2.57
PHI	75	60	.556	14.5	597	519	228	68	31	.264	.362	157	217	66	.960	112	315	728	10	1	2.97
CLE	77	63	.550	15	639	578	230	95	31	.270	.378	176	322	99	.946	125	271	521	20	1	2.66
NY	72	62	.537	17	579	573	193	62	18	.250	.331	160	264	87	.953	123	336	463	8	2	3.08
DET	65	71	.478	25	567	539	162	91	12	.268	.351	128	281	82	.950	123	336	554	15	2	2.75
STL	65	74	.468	26.5	500	525	166	78	12	.242	.319	101	268	94	.953	111	245	511	12	4	2.77
CHI	60	77	.438	30.5	516	613	176	49	14	.247	.314	180	297	85	.949	114	287	391	9	4	3.02
WAS	43	94	.314	47.5	438	691	172	72	18	.231	.311	131	260	86	.954	122	306	452	6	2	3.82
					4543	4543	1549	628	184	.256	.345	1174	2148	685	.953	954	2266	4199	100	20	2.95

POS	Player	AB	BA	HR	RBI	PO	A	E	DP	TC/G	FA	Pitcher	G	IP	W	L	SV	ERA
N. Y. W-106 L-47 John McGraw																		
1B	D. McGann	517	.286	6	71	1481	94	15	62	11.3	.991	J. McGinnity	51	408	35	8	5	1.61
2B	B. Gilbert	478	.253	1	54	305	466	44	48	5.6	.946	C. Mathewson	48	368	33	12	0	2.03
SS	B. Dahlen	523	.268	2	80	316	494	61	61	6.0	.930	D. Taylor	37	296	21	15	0	2.34
3B	A. Devlin	474	.281	1	66	126	285	42	10	3.5	.907	H. Wiltse	24	165	13	3	3	2.84
RF	G. Browne	596	.284	4	39	201	20	18	7	1.6	.925	R. Ames	16	115	4	6	3	2.27
CF	R. Bresnahan	402	.284	5	33	151	14	8	9	1.9	.954							
LF	S. Mertes	532	.276	4	78	244	17	12	1	1.9	.956							
C	J. Warner	287	.199	1	15	427	115	10	7	6.4	**.982**							
C	F. Bowerman	289	.232	2	27	413	96	12	11	**6.6**	.977							
OF	M. McCormick	203	.266	1	26	95	3	9	2	1.9	.916							
UT	J. Dunn	181	.309	1	19	61	89	15	7		.909							
Chi. W-93 L-60 Frank Selee																		
1B	F. Chance	451	.310	6	49	1205	106	13	48	10.8	.990	J. Weimer	37	307	20	14	0	1.91
2B	J. Evers	532	.265	0	47	381	518	54	53	6.3	.943	B. Briggs	34	277	19	11	2	2.05
SS	J. Tinker	488	.221	3	41	327	465	64	54	6.1	.925	C. Lundgren	31	242	17	10	1	2.60
3B	D. Casey	548	.268	1	43	157	241	39	11	3.3	.911	B. Wicker	30	229	17	8	0	2.67
RF	D. Jones	336	.244	3	39	128	8	10	0	1.5	.932	T. Brown	26	212	15	10	1	1.86
CF	J. McCarthy	432	.264	0	51	213	8	9	0	2.0	.961	F. Corridon	12	100	5	5	0	3.05
LF	J. Slagle	481	.260	1	31	194	15	18	7	1.9	.921							
C	J. Kling	452	.243	2	46	499	135	17	6	6.3	.974							
UT	S. Barry	263	.262	1	26	270	73	21	16		.942							
UT	O. Williams	185	.200	0	8	161	67	9	3		.962							
C	J. O'Neill	168	.214	1	19	256	62	6	5	6.6	.981							
PO	B. Wicker	155	.219	0	9	48	34	7	1		.921							
Cin. W-88 L-65 Joe Kelley																		
1B	J. Kelley	449	.281	0	63	1049	76	14	48	9.7	.988	N. Hahn	35	298	16	18	0	2.06
2B	M. Huggins	491	.263	2	30	337	448	46	32	5.9	.945	J. Harper	35	285	23	9	0	2.37
SS	T. Corcoran	578	.230	2	74	353	471	56	54	5.9	**.936**	W. Kellum	31	225	15	10	2	2.60
3B	H. Steinfeldt	349	.244	1	52	153	168	41	13	3.7	.887	T. Walker	24	217	15	8	0	2.24
RF	C. Dolan	465	.284	6	51	157	13	11	0	1.8	.939	B. Ewing	26	212	11	13	0	2.46
CF	C. Seymour	531	.313	5	58	308	20	17	4	2.7	.951	J. Sutthoff	12	90	5	6	0	2.30
LF	F. Odwell	468	.284	1	58	284	18	14	6	2.5	.956							
C	A. Schlei	291	.237	0	32	384	123	12	5	5.5	.977							
3B	O. Woodruff	306	.190	0	20	75	116	14	4	3.4	.932							
C	H. Peitz	272	.243	1	30	255	89	9	10	5.5	.975							
OF	M. Donlin	236	.356	1	38	87	8	14	1	2.1	.872							
OF	J. Sebring	222	.225	0	24	88	11*	0	3	1.8	1.000							
Pit. W-87 L-66 Fred Clarke																		
1B	K. Bransfield	520	.223	0	60	1454	89	30	70	11.3	.981	S. Leever	34	253	18	11	0	2.17
2B	C. Ritchey	544	.263	0	51	330	482	36	48	5.4	.958	P. Flaherty	29	242	19	9	0	2.05
SS	H. Wagner	490	.349	4	75	274	367	49	46	5.7	.929	M. Lynch	27	223	15	11	0	2.71
3B	T. Leach	579	.257	2	56	212	371	60	18	4.4	.907	D. Phillippe	21	167	10	10	1	3.24
RF	J. Sebring	305	.269	0	32	146	16*	7	5	2.1	.959	C. Case	18	141	10	5	0	2.94
CF	G. Beaumont	615	.301	3	54	287	14	10	6	2.0	.968	R. Miller	19	134	7	8	0	3.35
LF	F. Clarke	278	.306	0	25	135	4	3	2	2.0	.979							
C	E. Phelps	302	.242	0	28	360	97	17	8	5.2	.964							
UT	O. Krueger	268	.194	1	26	115	117	23	10		.910							
OF	M. McCormick	238	.290	2	23	87	7	6	0	1.5	.940							
St. L. W-75 L-79 Kid Nichols																		
1B	J. Beckley	551	.325	1	67	1526	64	20	65	11.3	.988	J. Taylor	41	352	21	19	1	2.22
2B	J. Farrell	509	.255	0	20	297	450	53	55	6.2	.934	K. Nichols	36	317	21	13	1	2.02
SS	D. Shay	340	.256	1	18	153	319	46	30	5.3	.911	C. McFarland	32	269	14	17	0	3.21
3B	J. Burke	406	.227	0	37	148	217	42	10	3.4	.897	M. O'Neill	25	220	10	14	0	2.09
RF	S. Shannon	500	.280	1	26	246	18	6	10	2.0	**.978**	J. Corbett	14	109	5	9	0	4.39
CF	H. Smoot	520	.281	3	66	270	17	10	6	2.2	.966							
LF	G. Barclay	375	.200	1	28	170	7	10	2	1.8	.947							
C	M. Grady	323	.313	5	43	323	77	19	7	5.4	.955							
UT	D. Brain	488	.266	7	72	259	308	45	26		.926							
OF	J. Dunleavy	172	.233	1	14	68	6	1	2	1.7	.987							
Bkn. W-56 L-97 Ned Hanlon																		
1B	P. Dillon	511	.258	0	31	1304	99	25	56	10.7	.982	O. Jones	46	377	17	**25**	0	2.75
2B	D. Jordan	252	.179	0	19	142	176	14	17	4.7	.958	J. Cronin	40	307	12	23	0	2.70
SS	C. Babb	521	.265	0	53	370	459	65	44	5.9	.927	N. Garvin	23	182	5	15	0	1.68
3B	M. McCormick	347	.184	0	27	138	190	31	**21**	3.5	.914	E. Poole	25	178	8	13	1	3.39
RF	H. Lumley	577	.279	**9**	78	228	26	12	8	1.8	.955	D. Scanlan	13	104	7	6	0	2.16
CF	J. Dobbs	363	.248	0	30	200	6	14	0	2.4	.936							
LF	J. Sheckard	507	.239	1	46	291	16	14	5	2.3	.956							
C	B. Bergen	329	.182	0	12	414	151	24	10	6.3	.959							
OF	D. Gessler	341	.290	2	28	170	15	16	2	2.3	.920							
2B	S. Strang	271	.192	1	9	100	164	26	13	4.6	.910							
C	L. Ritter	214	.248	0	19	249	88	12	7	6.1	.966							
Bos. W-55 L-98 Al Buckenberger																		
1B	F. Tenney	533	.270	1	37	1451	115	23	66	11.0	.986	V. Willis	43	350	18	**25**	0	2.85
2B	F. Raymer	419	.210	1	27	272	351	27	38	5.7	**.958**	T. Pittinger	38	335	15	21	0	2.66
SS	Abbaticchio	579	.256	3	54	367	473	78	47	6.0	.915	K. Wilhelm	39	288	14	22	0	3.69
3B	J. Delahanty	499	.285	3	60	158	223	48	12	3.8	.888	T. Fisher	31	214	6	15	0	4.25
RF	R. Cannell	346	.234	0	18	135	5	16	1	1.7	.897	E. McNichol	17	122	2	12	0	4.28
CF	P. Geier	580	.243	1	27	243	20	19	11	2.1	.933							
LF	D. Cooley	467	.272	5	70	201	3	5	4	1.8	.976							
C	T. Needham	269	.260	4	19	326	140	27	8	6.4	.945							
C3	P. Moran	398	.226	4	34	373	197	36	16		.941							
OF	P. Carney	279	.204	0	11	89	12	5	5	1.5	.953							

	POS	Player	AB	BA	HR	RBI	PO	A	E	DP	TC/G	FA	Pitcher	G	IP	W	L	SV	ERA
Phi.	1B	J. Doyle	236	.220	1	22	585	52	15	27	10.0	.977	C. Fraser	42	302	14	24	1	3.25
	2B	K. Gleason	587	.274	0	42	379	463	52	44	5.9	.942	B. Duggleby	32	224	12	13	1	3.78
W-52 L-100	SS	R. Hulswitt	406	.244	1	36	273	310	56	42	5.7	.912	T. Sparks	26	201	7	18	0	2.65
Hugh Duffy	3B	H. Wolverton	398	.266	0	49	143	191	27	15	3.5	**.925**	J. Sutthoff	19	164	6	13	0	3.68
	RF	S. Magee	364	.277	3	57	146	19	14	3	1.9	.922	J. McPherson	15	128	1	10	0	3.66
	CF	R. Thomas	496	.290	3	29	**321**	21	9	4	2.5	.974	F. Mitchell	13	109	4	7	0	3.40
	LF	J. Titus	504	.294	4	55	258	21	14	7	2.1	.952	F. Corridon	12	94	6	5	0	2.19
	C	R. Dooin	355	.242	6	36	411	149	**37**	**12**	6.2	.938							
	1O	J. Lush	369	.276	2	42	580	31	34	27		.947							
	C	F. Roth	229	.258	1	20	241	76	14	8	4.9	.958							
	S3	S. Donahue	200	.215	0	14	83	106	33	10		.851							
	UT	B. Hall	163	.160	0	17	149	80	31	13		.881							

BATTING AND BASE RUNNING LEADERS

Batting Average

H. Wagner, PIT	.349
M. Donlin, CIN, NY	.329
J. Beckley, STL	.325
M. Grady, STL	.313
C. Seymour, CIN	.313

Slugging Average

H. Wagner, PIT	.520
M. Grady, STL	.474
M. Donlin, CIN, NY	.457
C. Seymour, CIN	.439
F. Chance, CHI	.430

Home Runs

H. Lumley, BKN	9
D. Brain, STL	7
R. Dooin, PHI	6
F. Chance, CHI	6
C. Dolan, CIN	6
D. McGann, NY	6

Total Bases

H. Wagner, PIT	255
H. Lumley, BKN	247
C. Seymour, CIN	233
G. Beaumont, PIT	230
J. Beckley, STL	222

Runs Batted In

B. Dahlen, NY	80
S. Mertes, NY	78
H. Lumley, BKN	78
H. Wagner, PIT	75
T. Corcoran, CIN	74

Stolen Bases

H. Wagner, PIT	53
B. Dahlen, NY	47
S. Mertes, NY	47
F. Chance, CHI	42
D. McGann, NY	42

Hits

G. Beaumont, PIT	185
J. Beckley, STL	179
H. Wagner, PIT	171

Base on Balls

R. Thomas, PHI	102
M. Huggins, CIN	88
A. Devlin, NY	62

Home Run Percentage

R. Dooin, PHI	1.7
H. Lumley, BKN	1.6
M. Grady, STL	1.5

Runs Scored

G. Browne, NY	99
H. Wagner, PIT	97
G. Beaumont, PIT	97

Doubles

H. Wagner, PIT	44
S. Mertes, NY	28
J. Delahanty, BOS	27

Triples

H. Lumley, BKN	18
H. Wagner, PIT	14

PITCHING LEADERS

Winning Percentage

J. McGinnity, NY	.814
C. Mathewson, NY	.733
J. Harper, CIN	.719
B. Wicker, CHI	.680
P. Flaherty, PIT	.679

Earned Run Average

J. McGinnity, NY	1.61
N. Garvin, BKN	1.68
T. Brown, CHI	1.86
J. Weimer, CHI	1.91
K. Nichols, STL	2.02

Wins

J. McGinnity, NY	35
C. Mathewson, NY	33
J. Harper, CIN	23
K. Nichols, STL	21
D. Taylor, NY	21
J. Taylor, STL	21

Saves

J. McGinnity, NY	5
R. Ames, NY	3
H. Wiltse, NY	3
W. Kellum, CIN	2
B. Briggs, CHI	2
B. Milligan, NY	2

Strikeouts

C. Mathewson, NY	212
V. Willis, BOS	196
J. Weimer, CHI	177
T. Pittinger, BOS	146
J. McGinnity, NY	144

Complete Games

J. Taylor, STL	39
V. Willis, BOS	39
O. Jones, BKN	38
J. McGinnity, NY	38
K. Nichols, STL	35
T. Pittinger, BOS	35

Fewest Hits per 9 Innings

T. Brown, CHI	6.57
J. Weimer, CHI	6.71
J. McGinnity, NY	6.77

Shutouts

J. McGinnity, NY	9
J. Harper, CIN	6

Fewest Walks per 9 Innings

N. Hahn, CIN	1.06
D. Phillippe, PIT	1.40
K. Nichols, STL	1.42

Most Strikeouts per 9 Inn.

R. Ames, NY	7.28
H. Wiltse, NY	5.74
J. Corbett, STL	5.63

Innings

J. McGinnity, NY	408
O. Jones, BKN	377
C. Mathewson, NY	368

Games Pitched

J. McGinnity, NY	51
C. Mathewson, NY	48
O. Jones, BKN	46

	W	L	PCT	GB	R	OR	2B	3B	Batting HR	BA	SA	SB	E	Fielding DP	FA	CG	BB	Pitching SO	ShO	SV	ERA
NY	106	47	.693		744	476	202	65	31	.262	.344	283	294	93	.956	127	349	707	21	14	2.17
CHI	93	60	.608	13	597	517	157	62	22	.248	.315	227	298	89	.954	139	402	618	18	5	2.30
CIN	88	65	.575	18	692	547	189	92	21	.255	.338	179	301	81	.954	142	343	502	12	2	2.35
PIT	87	66	.569	19	675	586	164	102	15	.258	.338	178	**291**	93	.955	133	379	455	15	1	2.89
STL	75	79	.487	31.5	602	595	175	66	24	.253	.327	199	307	83	.952	**146**	319	529	7	2	2.64
BKN	56	97	.366	50	497	614	159	53	15	.232	.295	205	343	87	.945	135	414	453	12	2	2.70
BOS	55	98	.359	51	491	752	153	50	24	.237	.300	143	348	91	.946	136	500	544	14	0	3.43
PHI	52	100	.342	53.5	571	782	170	54	23	.248	.316	159	403	93	.937	131	425	469	10	2	3.39
					4869	4869	1369	544	175	.249	.322	1573	2585	710	.950	1089	3131	4277	109	28	2.73

Bos. — W-95 L-59 — Jimmy Collins

POS	Player	AB	BA	HR	RBI	PO	A	E	DP	TC/G	FA
1B	C. LaChance	573	.227	1	47	1691	59	14	65	11.2	.992
2B	H. Ferris	563	.213	3	63	366	460	33	42	5.5	.962
SS	F. Parent	591	.291	6	77	327	493	63	44	5.7	.929
3B	J. Collins	631	.266	3	67	191	320	30	15	3.5	.945
RF	B. Freeman	597	.280	7	84	216	14	11	4	1.5	.954
CF	C. Stahl	587	.295	3	67	293	6	12	0	2.0	.961
LF	K. Selbach	376	.258	0	30	190	8	8	2	2.1	.961
C	L. Criger	299	.211	2	34	502	112	12	7	6.6	.981
C	D. Farrell	198	.212	0	15	234	62	13	6	5.5	.958
OF	P. Dougherty	195*	.272	0	4	95	4	8*	3	2.2	.925

Pitcher	G	IP	W	L	SV	ERA
C. Young	43	380	26	16	1	1.97
B. Dinneen	37	336	23	14	0	2.20
J. Tannehill	33	282	21	11	0	2.04
N. Gibson	33	273	17	14	0	2.21
G. Winter	20	136	8	4	0	2.32

N. Y. — W-92 L-59 — Clark Griffith

POS	Player	AB	BA	HR	RBI	PO	A	E	DP	TC/G	FA
1B	J. Ganzel	465	.260	6	48	1243	63	16	49	11.2	.988
2B	J. Williams	559	.263	2	74	315	465	40	52	5.6	.951
SS	K. Elberfeld	445	.263	2	46	237	432	48	44	5.9	.933
3B	W. Conroy	489	.243	1	52	137	231	22	8	3.5	.944
RF	W. Keeler	543	.343	2	40	186	16	14	7	1.5	.935
CF	D. Fultz	339	.274	2	32	194	8	5	2	2.3	.976
LF	P. Dougherty	452*	.283	6	22	135	14	12*	1	1.5	.925
C	D. McGuire	322	.208	0	20	530	120	20	11	6.9	.970
OF	J. Anderson	558	.278	3	82	186	9	9	1	1.8	.956
C	R. Kleinow	209	.206	0	16	276	66	12	5	5.7	.966
P	J. Chesbro	174	.236	1	17	24	166	12	7	3.7	.941

Pitcher	G	IP	W	L	SV	ERA
J. Chesbro	55	455	41	12	0	1.82
J. Powell	47	390	23	19	0	2.44
A. Orth	20	138	11	6	0	2.68
L. Hughes	19	136	7	11	0	3.70
C. Griffith	16	100	7	5	0	2.87

Chi. — W-89 L-65 Nixey Callahan W-22 L-18 / Fielder Jones W-67 L-47

POS	Player	AB	BA	HR	RBI	PO	A	E	DP	TC/G	FA
1B	J. Donahue	367	.248	1	48	1067	85	25	49	11.7	.979
2B	G. Dundon	373	.228	0	36	186	282	13	25	4.7	.973
SS	G. Davis	563	.252	1	69	347	514	58	62	6.0	.937
3B	L. Tannehill	547	.229	0	61	180	369	31	22	3.8	.947
RF	D. Green	536	.265	2	62	231	13	9	5	1.7	.964
CF	F. Jones	564	.243	3	43	325	15	8	4	2.3	.977
LF	N. Callahan	482	.261	0	54	158	9	4	0	1.6	.977
C	B. Sullivan	371	.229	1	44	463	130	22	10	5.7	.964
12	F. Isbell	314	.210	1	34	652	128	20	28		.975
OF	D. Holmes	251	.311	1	19	111	8	3	3	1.9	.975
C	E. McFarland	160	.275	0	20	195	39	6	2	4.9	.975

Pitcher	G	IP	W	L	SV	ERA
F. Owen	37	315	21	15	1	1.94
N. Altrock	38	307	19	14	1	2.96
F. White	30	228	16	12	0	1.78
F. Smith	26	202	16	9	0	2.09
R. Patterson	22	165	9	9	0	2.29
E. Walsh	18	111	6	3	1	2.60

Cle. — W-86 L-65 — Bill Armour

POS	Player	AB	BA	HR	RBI	PO	A	E	DP	TC/G	FA
1B	P. Hickman	337	.288	4	45	391	22	14	17	10.7	.967
2B	N. Lajoie	554	.381	6	102	272	255	21	42	5.8	.962
SS	T. Turner	404	.235	1	45	191	376	36	28	5.4	.940
3B	B. Bradley	607	.300	5	83	178	308	23	18	3.3	.955
RF	E. Flick	579	.306	6	56	234	19	12	5	1.8	.955
CF	H. Bay	506	.261	3	36	281	15	4	6	2.3	.987
LF	B. Lush	477	.258	1	50	269	11	12	4	2.1	.959
C	H. Bemis	336	.226	0	25	393	86	21	8	6.3	.958
1B	G. Stovall	182	.297	1	31	376	22	9	18	10.7	.978

Pitcher	G	IP	W	L	SV	ERA
B. Bernhard	38	321	23	13	0	2.13
R. Donahue	35	277	19	14	0	2.40
E. Moore	26	228	12	11	0	2.25
A. Joss	25	192	14	10	0	1.59
B. Rhoads	22	175	10	9	0	2.87
O. Hess	21	151	8	7	0	1.67

Phi. — W-81 L-70 — Connie Mack

POS	Player	AB	BA	HR	RBI	PO	A	E	DP	TC/G	FA
1B	H. Davis	404	.309	10	62	1011	57	19	33	10.7	.983
2B	D. Murphy	557	.287	7	77	280	455	46	35	5.2	.941
SS	M. Cross	503	.189	1	38	276	424	47	26	4.9	.937
3B	L. Cross	607	.290	1	71	164	247	28	15	2.8	.936
RF	S. Seybold	510	.292	3	64	180	12	5	5	1.5	.975
CF	O. Pickering	455	.226	0	30	217	13	15	2	2.0	.939
LF	T. Hartsel	534	.253	2	25	216	15	10	2	1.6	.959
C	Schreckengost	311	.186	1	21	589	76	14	5	8.1	.979
OF	D. Hoffman	204	.299	3	24	83	5	6	1	1.8	.936
C	M. Powers	184	.190	0	11	338	52	14	6	7.2	.965

Pitcher	G	IP	W	L	SV	ERA
R. Waddell	46	383	25	19	0	1.62
E. Plank	43	357	26	16	0	2.14
W. Henley	36	296	15	17	0	2.53
C. Bender	29	204	10	11	0	2.87

St. L. — W-65 L-87 — Jimmy McAleer

POS	Player	AB	BA	HR	RBI	PO	A	E	DP	TC/G	FA
1B	T. Jones	625	.243	2	68	1443	92	19	51	11.6	.988
2B	D. Padden	453	.238	0	36	288	373	28	31	5.2	.959
SS	B. Wallace	550	.273	2	69	303	482	44	37	6.0	.947
3B	C. Moran	272	.173	0	14	69	169	16	2	3.1	.937
RF	C. Hemphill	438	.256	2	45	177	12	15	5	1.9	.926
CF	E. Heidrick	538	.273	1	36	291	22	12	6	2.5	.963
LF	J. Burkett	576	.273	2	27	266	24	18	4	2.1	.942
C	J. Sugden	347	.262	0	30	370	94	5	11	5.9	.989
OF	P. Hynes	254	.236	0	15	72	1	8	0	1.3	.901
C	M. Kahoe	236	.216	0	12	307	91	13	3	6.0	.968
3B	H. Hill	219	.215	0	14	78	79	33*	3	3.4	.826
UT	H. Gleason	155	.213	0	6	66	108	15	11		.921

Pitcher	G	IP	W	L	SV	ERA
B. Pelty	39	301	15	18	0	2.84
H. Howell	34	300	13	21	0	2.19
F. Glade	35	289	18	15	1	2.27
W. Sudhoff	27	222	8	15	0	3.76
E. Siever	29	217	10	15	0	2.65

Det. — W-62 L-90 Ed Barrow / W-32 L-46 Bobby Lowe / W-30 L-44

POS	Player	AB	BA	HR	RBI	PO	A	E	DP	TC/G	FA
1B	C. Carr	360	.214	0	40	901	99*	17	46	11.1	.983
2B	B. Lowe	506	.208	0	40	328	402	27	44	5.4	.964
SS	C. O'Leary	456	.213	1	16	308	439	54	48	5.9	.933
3B	E. Gremminger	309	.214	1	28	103	123	12	3	2.9	.950
RF	S. Crawford	571	.250	2	73	230	18	7	8	1.7	.973
CF	J. Barrett	624	.268	0	31	339	29	11	6	2.3	.971
LF	M. McIntyre	578	.253	2	46	334	16	15	4	2.4	.959
C	L. Drill	160	.244	0	13	195	51	13*	6*	5.3	.950
UT	R. Robinson	320	.241	0	37	151	216	22	17		.943
3B	B. Coughlin	206	.228	0	17	53	104	12	2	3.0	.929
C	B. Wood	175	.246	1	17	232	69	8	5	6.6	.974
C1	M. Beville	174	.207	0	13	354	41	16	11		.961
1B	P. Hickman	144	.243	2	22	396	23	13	18	11.1	.970

Pitcher	G	IP	W	L	SV	ERA
G. Mullin	45	382	17	23	0	2.40
E. Killian	40	332	14	20	1	2.44
W. Donovan	34	293	17	16	0	2.46
F. Kitson	26	200	8	13	1	3.07
J. Stovall	22	147	3	13	0	4.42

	POS	Player	AB	BA	HR	RBI	PO	A	E	DP	TC/G	FA	Pitcher	G	IP	W	L	SV	ERA
	1B	J. Stahl	520	.262	3	50	1202	85	**29**	52	11.1	.978	C. Patten	45	358	14	23	**3**	3.07
Was.	2B	B. McCormick	404	.218	0	39	204	355	37	39	5.3	.938	J. Townsend	36	291	5	**26**	0	3.58
W-38 L-113	SS	J. Cassidy	581	.241	1	33	249	301	37	38	5.9	.937	B. Jacobson	33	254	6	23	0	3.55
Malachi Kittredge	3B	H. Hill	290	.197	0	17	86	126	25*	4	3.3	.895	B. Wolfe	17	127	6	9	0	3.27
W-1 L-16	RF	P. Donovan	436	.229	0	19	217	15	9	4	2.0	.963	L. Hughes	16	124	2	13	1	3.47
Patsy Donovan	CF	B. O'Neill	365	.244	1	16	141	9	18	1	1.8	.893	D. Dunkle	12	74	2	9	0	4.96
W-37 L-97	LF	F. Huelsman	303	.248	2	30	138	7	6	2	1.8	.960							
	C	M. Kittredge	265	.242	0	24	346	99	8	4	5.7	.982							
	C1	B. Clarke	275	.211	0	17	517	86	13	24		.979							
	3B	B. Coughlin	265	.275	0	17	95	121	14	7	3.6	.939							
	SS	C. Moran	243	.222	0	7	114	171	25	17	5.1	.919							
	OF	K. Selbach	178	.275	0	14	103	5	8	1	2.4	.931							

BATTING AND BASE RUNNING LEADERS

Batting Average

N. Lajoie, CLE	.381
W. Keeler, NY	.343
H. Davis, PHI	.309
E. Flick, CLE	.306
B. Bradley, CLE	.300

Slugging Average

N. Lajoie, CLE	.554
H. Davis, PHI	.490
E. Flick, CLE	.453
D. Murphy, PHI	.437
P. Hickman, CLE, DET	.416

Home Runs

H. Davis, PHI	10
D. Murphy, PHI	7
B. Freeman, BOS	7

Total Bases

N. Lajoie, CLE	307
E. Flick, CLE	262
C. Stahl, BOS	247
B. Freeman, BOS	246
P. Dougherty, BOS, NY	245
D. Murphy, PHI	245

Runs Batted In

N. Lajoie, CLE	102
B. Freeman, BOS	84
B. Bradley, CLE	83
J. Anderson, NY	82
D. Murphy, PHI	77
F. Parent, BOS	77

Stolen Bases

E. Flick, CLE	42
H. Bay, CLE	38
E. Heidrick, STL	35
G. Davis, CHI	32
W. Conroy, NY	30

Hits

N. Lajoie, CLE	211
W. Keeler, NY	186
B. Bradley, CLE	182

Base on Balls

J. Barrett, DET	79
J. Burkett, STL	78
T. Hartsel, PHI	75

Home Run Percentage

H. Davis, PHI	2.5
J. Ganzel, NY	1.3
D. Murphy, PHI	1.3

Runs Scored

P. Dougherty, BOS, NY	113
E. Flick, CLE	97
B. Bradley, CLE	94

Doubles

N. Lajoie, CLE	50
J. Collins, BOS	33

Triples

J. Cassidy, WAS	19
C. Stahl, BOS	19
B. Freeman, BOS	19

PITCHING LEADERS

Winning Percentage

J. Chesbro, NY	.774
J. Tannehill, BOS	.656
F. Smith, CHI	.640
B. Bernhard, CLE	.639
B. Dinneen, BOS	.622

Earned Run Average

A. Joss, CLE	1.59
R. Waddell, PHI	1.62
O. Hess, CLE	1.67
D. White, CHI	1.78
J. Chesbro, NY	1.82

Wins

J. Chesbro, NY	41
C. Young, BOS	26
E. Plank, PHI	26
R. Waddell, PHI	25

Saves

C. Patten, WAS	3

Strikeouts

R. Waddell, PHI	349
J. Chesbro, NY	239
C. Young, BOS	203
J. Powell, NY	202
E. Plank, PHI	201

Complete Games

J. Chesbro, NY	48
G. Mullin, DET	42
C. Young, BOS	40
R. Waddell, PHI	39
J. Powell, NY	38

Fewest Hits per 9 Innings

J. Chesbro, NY	6.69
F. Owen, CHI	6.94
F. Smith, CHI	6.98

Shutouts

C. Young, BOS	10
R. Waddell, PHI	8

Fewest Walks per 9 Innings

C. Young, BOS	0.69
J. Tannehill, BOS	1.05
R. Patterson, CHI	1.31

Most Strikeouts per 9 Inn.

R. Waddell, PHI	8.20
C. Bender, PHI	6.58
E. Moore, CLE	5.49

Innings

J. Chesbro, NY	455
J. Powell, NY	390
R. Waddell, PHI	383

Games Pitched

J. Chesbro, NY	55
J. Powell, NY	47
R. Waddell, PHI	46

	W	L	PCT	GB	R	OR	2B	3B	Batting HR	BA	SA	SB	E	Fielding DP	FA	CG	BB	Pitching SO	ShO	SV	ERA
BOS	95	59	.617		608	**466**	194	**105**	26	.247	.340	101	242	83	.962	**148**	**233**	612	21	1	**2.12**
NY	92	59	.609	1.5	598	526	195	91	27	.259	.347	163	275	90	.958	123	311	684	15	1	2.57
CHI	89	65	.578	6	600	482	193	68	14	.242	.316	**216**	**238**	95	**.964**	134	303	550	**26**	3	2.30
CLE	86	65	.570	7.5	**647**	482	**225**	90	26	**.262**	**.356**	189	255	86	.959	141	285	627	20	0	2.22
PHI	81	70	.536	12.5	557	503	197	77	**31**	.249	.336	137	250	67	.959	137	366	**887**	**26**	0	2.35
STL	65	87	.428	29	481	604	153	53	10	.239	.293	150	267	78	.960	135	333	577	13	1	2.83
DET	62	90	.408	32	505	627	154	70	11	.231	.293	112	273	92	.959	143	556	556	15	2	2.77
WAS	38	113	.252	55.5	437	743	171	57	10	.227	.288	150	314	**97**	.951	137	347	533	8	**4**	3.62
					4433	4433	1482	611	155	.245	.321	1218	2114	688	.959	1098	2611	5026	144	12	2.60

POS	Player	AB	BA	HR	RBI	PO	A	E	DP	TC/G	FA	Pitcher	G	IP	W	L	SV	ERA
N. Y. W-105 L-48 John McGraw																		
1B	D. McGann	491	.299	5	75	1350	86	13	59	10.7	.991	C. Mathewson	43	339	31	8	2	1.27
2B	B. Gilbert	376	.247	0	24	245	367	34	41	5.6	.947	J. McGinnity	46	320	21	15	3	2.87
SS	B. Dahlen	520	.242	7	81	313	501	45	58	5.8	.948	R. Ames	34	263	22	8	0	2.74
3B	A. Devlin	525	.246	2	61	156	299	33	14	3.2	.932	D. Taylor	32	213	15	9	0	2.66
RF	G. Browne	536	.293	4	43	175	9	17	1	1.6	.915	H. Wiltse	32	197	15	6	3	2.47
CF	M. Donlin	606	.356	7	80	250	17	19	4	1.9	.934							
LF	S. Mertes	551	.279	5	108	230	10	10	3	1.7	.960							
C	R. Bresnahan	331	.302	0	46	492	114	19	15	7.2	.970							
C	F. Bowerman	297	.269	3	41	383	66	8	4	6.3	.982							
UT	S. Strang	294	.259	3	29	123	144	25	11		.914							
Pit. W-96 L-57 Fred Clarke																		
1B	D. Howard	435	.292	2	63	912	48	22	57	10.9	.978	D. Phillippe	38	279	22	13	0	2.19
2B	C. Ritchey	533	.255	0	52	279	478	31	59	5.2	.961	S. Leever	33	230	19	6	0	2.70
SS	H. Wagner	548	.363	6	101	353	517	60	64	6.4	.935	C. Case	31	217	12	10	1	2.57
3B	D. Brain	307	.257	3	46	82	170	21	13	3.5	.923	M. Lynch	33	206	17	8	2	3.80
RF	O. Clymer	365	.296	0	23	136	7	2	5	1.6	.986	P. Flaherty	27	188	9	10	1	3.49
CF	G. Beaumont	384	.328	3	40	200	12	6	5	2.2	.972	C. Robitaille	17	120	8	5	0	2.93
LF	F. Clarke	525	.299	2	51	270	16	7	4	2.1	.976							
C	H. Peitz	278	.223	0	27	337	105	16	14	5.3	.965							
O3	T. Leach	499	.257	2	53	238	134	16	15		.959							
1B	B. Clancey	227	.229	2	34	551	27	10	30	11.3	.983							
Chi. W-92 L-61 Frank Selee W-52 L-38 Frank Chance W-40 L-23																		
1B	F. Chance	392	.316	2	70	1165	75	13	54	10.9	.990	E. Reulbach	34	292	18	13	1	1.42
2B	J. Evers	340	.276	1	37	249	290	36	38	5.8	.937	J. Weimer	33	250	18	12	1	2.27
SS	J. Tinker	547	.247	2	66	345	527	56	67	6.2	.940	T. Brown	30	249	18	12	0	2.17
3B	D. Casey	526	.232	1	56	160	252	22	7	3.1	.949	B. Wicker	22	178	13	7	0	2.02
RF	B. Maloney	558	.260	2	56	251	18	13	4	1.9	.954	C. Lundgren	23	169	13	4	0	2.24
CF	J. Slagle	568	.269	0	37	306	27	13	6	2.2	.962	B. Briggs	20	168	8	8	0	2.14
LF	W. Schulte	493	.274	1	47	189	14	4	0	1.7	.981	B. Pfeffer	15	101	4	5	0	2.50
C	J. Kling	380	.218	1	52	538	136	24	12	6.6	.966							
2B	S. Hofman	287	.237	1	38	138	178	15	13	5.6	.955							
C	J. O'Neill	172	.198	0	12	276	63	9	8	7.0	.974							
OF	J. McCarthy	170	.276	0	14	63	9	1	4	2.0	.986							
Phi. W-83 L-69 Hugh Duffy																		
1B	K. Bransfield	580	.259	3	76	1398	92	23	75	10.0	.985	T. Pittinger	46	337	23	14	2	3.10
2B	K. Gleason	608	.247	1	50	365	457	46	49	5.6	.947	B. Duggleby	38	289	18	17	0	2.46
SS	M. Doolan	492	.254	1	48	299	432	51	45	5.8	.935	T. Sparks	34	260	14	11	1	2.18
3B	E. Courtney	601	.275	2	77	229	249	40	13	3.3	.923	F. Corridon	35	212	10	13	1	3.48
RF	J. Titus	548	.308	2	89	255	24	11	4	2.0	.962	K. Nichols	17	139	10	6	0	2.27
CF	R. Thomas	562	.317	0	31	373	27	7	6	2.8	.983							
LF	S. Magee	603	.299	5	98	341	19	14	6	2.4	.963							
C	R. Dooin	380	.250	0	36	505	152	24	9	6.4	.965							
Cin. W-79 L-74 Joe Kelley																		
1B	S. Barry	494	.324	1	56	1216	61	23	7	10.6	.982	O. Overall	42	318	17	22	0	2.86
2B	M. Huggins	564	.273	1	38	346	525	51	55	6.2	.945	B. Ewing	40	312	20	11	0	2.51
SS	T. Corcoran	605	.248	2	85	344	531	44	67	6.1	.952	C. Chech	39	268	14	15	0	2.89
3B	H. Steinfeldt	384	.271	1	39	152	221	33	16	3.9	.919	J. Harper	26	179	10	13	0	3.87
RF	F. Odwell	468	.241	9	65	216	18	8	5	1.9	.967	T. Walker	23	145	9	7	0	3.23
CF	C. Seymour	581	.377	8	121	347	25	21	12	2.6	.947							
LF	J. Kelley	321	.277	1	37	137	11	4	0	1.8	.974							
C	A. Schlei	314	.226	1	36	398	153	22	16	6.4	.962							
UT	A. Bridwell	254	.252	0	17	104	118	17	15		.929							
OF	J. Sebring	217	.286	2	28	63	6	9	2	1.4	.885							
C	E. Phelps	156	.231	0	18	189	55	13	5	5.8	.949							
St. L. W-58 L-96 Kid Nichols W-19 L-29 Jimmy Burke W-17 L-32 Matt Robison W-22 L-35																		
1B	J. Beckley	514	.286	1	57	1442	69	28	56	11.5	.982	J. Taylor	37	309	15	21	1	3.44
2B	H. Arndt	415	.243	2	36	173	254	22	25	5.0	.951	C. McFarland	31	250	8	18	1	3.82
SS	G. McBride	281	.217	2	34	147	273	28	29	5.6	.938	J. Thielman	32	242	15	16	0	3.50
3B	J. Burke	431	.225	1	30	174	238	34	13	3.7	.924	B. Brown	23	179	8	11	0	2.97
RF	J. Dunleavy	435	.241	1	25	177	25	8	7	1.8	.962	W. Egan	23	171	6	15	0	3.58
CF	H. Smoot	534	.311	4	58	295	18	8	6	2.3	.975							
LF	S. Shannon	544	.268	0	41	299	7	5	3	2.2	.984							
C	M. Grady	311	.286	4	41	288	79	17	7	5.4	.956							
S2	D. Shay	281	.238	0	28	172	230	35	22		.920							
O2	J. Clarke	167	.257	3	18	74	49	12	3		.911							
SS	D. Brain	158	.228	1	17	58	74	13	4	5.0	.910							
Bos. W-51 L-103 Fred Tenney																		
1B	F. Tenney	549	.288	0	28	1556	152	32	68	11.8	.982	I. Young	43	378	20	21	0	2.90
2B	F. Raymer	498	.211	0	31	256	381	34	33	5.0	.949	V. Willis	41	342	11	29	0	3.21
SS	A. Abbaticchio	610	.279	3	41	386	468	53	53	6.1	.919	C. Fraser	39	334	14	21	0	3.29
3B	H. Wolverton	463	.225	2	55	139	256	28	12	3.5	.934	K. Wilhelm	34	242	4	23	0	4.54
RF	C. Dolan	433	.275	3	48	175	19	11	2	1.8	.946							
CF	R. Cannell	567	.247	0	36	315	14	23	6	2.3	.935							
LF	J. Delahanty	461	.258	5	55	186	16	8	1	1.7	.962							
C	P. Moran	267	.240	2	22	389	113	7	5	6.5	.986							
C	T. Needham	271	.218	2	17	292	134	23	6	5.8	.949							
32	B. Lauterborn	200	.185	0	9	82	127	27	3		.886							
OF	B. Sharpe	170	.182	0	11	55	11	7	3	1.7	.904							
P	C. Fraser	156	.224	0	10	36	80	9	1	3.2	.928							

	POS	Player	AB	BA	HR	RBI	PO	A	E	DP	TC/G	FA	Pitcher	G	IP	W	L	SV	ERA
Bkn.	1B	D. Gessler	431	.290	3	46	1017	79	**33**	54	10.6	.971	H. McIntyre	40	309	8	25	1	3.70
W-48 L-104	2B	C. Malay	349	.252	1	31	138	216	26	17	5.1	.932	D. Scanlan	33	250	14	12	0	2.92
Ned Hanlon	SS	P. Lewis	433	.254	3	33	253	371	66	63	5.8	.904	E. Stricklett	33	237	9	18	1	3.34
	3B	E. Batch	568	.252	5	49	203	246	**57**	**22**	3.5	.887	M. Eason	27	207	5	21	0	4.30
	RF	H. Lumley	505	.293	7	47	177	21	19	4	1.7	.912	O. Jones	29	174	8	15	1	4.66
	CF	J. Dobbs	460	.254	2	36	246	11	17	1	2.2	.938	F. Mitchell	12	96	3	7	0	4.78
	LF	J. Sheckard	480	.292	3	41	266	24	10	6	2.3	.967							
	C	L. Ritter	311	.219	1	28	397	106	**26**	4	6.3	.951							
	C	B. Bergen	247	.190	0	22	371	127	24	8	6.9	.954							
	S1	C. Babb	235	.187	0	17	388	132	24	32		.956							
	OF	B. Hall	203	.236	2	15	101	6	7	2	2.7	.939							
	2B	R. Owens	168	.214	1	20	102	132	18	19	5.9	.929							

BATTING AND BASE RUNNING LEADERS

Batting Average
C. Seymour, CIN	.377
H. Wagner, PIT	.363
M. Donlin, NY	.356
G. Beaumont, PIT	.328
R. Thomas, PHI	.317

Slugging Average
C. Seymour, CIN	.559
H. Wagner, PIT	.505
M. Donlin, NY	.495
J. Titus, PHI	.436
M. Grady, STL	.434

PITCHING LEADERS

Winning Percentage
C. Mathewson, NY	.795
S. Leever, PIT	.760
R. Ames, NY	.733
H. Wiltse, NY	.714
M. Lynch, PIT	.680

Earned Run Average
C. Mathewson, NY	1.27
E. Reulbach, CHI	1.42
B. Wicker, CHI	2.02
B. Briggs, CHI	2.14
T. Brown, CHI	2.17

Home Runs
F. Odwell, CIN	9
C. Seymour, CIN	8
H. Lumley, BKN	7
B. Dahlen, NY	7
M. Donlin, NY	7

Total Bases
C. Seymour, CIN	325
M. Donlin, NY	300
H. Wagner, PIT	277
S. Magee, PHI	253
J. Titus, PHI	239

Wins
C. Mathewson, NY	31
T. Pittinger, PHI	23
D. Phillippe, PIT	22
R. Ames, NY	22
J. McGinnity, NY	21

Saves
C. Elliott, NY	6
H. Wiltse, NY	3
J. McGinnity, NY	3
M. Lynch, PIT	2
C. Mathewson, NY	2
T. Pittinger, PHI	2

Runs Batted In
C. Seymour, CIN	121
S. Mertes, NY	108
H. Wagner, PIT	101
S. Magee, PHI	98
J. Titus, PHI	89

Stolen Bases
A. Devlin, NY	59
B. Maloney, CHI	59
H. Wagner, PIT	57
S. Mertes, NY	52
S. Magee, PHI	48

Strikeouts
C. Mathewson, NY	206
R. Ames, NY	198
O. Overall, CIN	173
B. Ewing, CIN	164
I. Young, BOS	156

Complete Games
I. Young, BOS	41
V. Willis, BOS	36
C. Fraser, BOS	35
J. Taylor, STL	34
C. Mathewson, NY	33

Hits
C. Seymour, CIN	219
M. Donlin, NY	216
H. Wagner, PIT	199

Base on Balls
M. Huggins, CIN	103
J. Slagle, CHI	97
R. Thomas, PHI	93

Fewest Hits per 9 Innings
E. Reulbach, CHI	6.41
C. Mathewson, NY	6.69
B. Wicker, CHI	7.03

Shutouts
C. Mathewson, NY	8
I. Young, BOS	7

Home Run Percentage
F. Odwell, CIN	1.9
H. Lumley, BKN	1.4
C. Seymour, CIN	1.4

Runs Scored
M. Donlin, NY	124
R. Thomas, PHI	118
M. Huggins, CIN	117

Fewest Walks per 9 Innings
D. Phillippe, PIT	1.55
T. Brown, CHI	1.59
I. Young, BOS	1.69

Most Strikeouts per 9 Inn.
R. Ames, NY	6.78
H. Wiltse, NY	5.48
C. Mathewson, NY	5.47

Doubles
C. Seymour, CIN	40
J. Titus, PHI	36
H. Wagner, PIT	32

Triples
C. Seymour, CIN	21
S. Mertes, NY	17
S. Magee, PHI	17

Innings
I. Young, BOS	378
V. Willis, BOS	342
C. Mathewson, NY	339

Games Pitched
T. Pittinger, PHI	46
J. McGinnity, NY	46
I. Young, BOS	43
C. Mathewson, NY	43

	W	L	PCT	GB	R	OR	Batting 2B	3B	HR	BA	SA	SB	Fielding E	DP	FA	Pitching CG	BB	SO	ShO	SV	ERA
NY	105	48	.686		**780**	504	**191**	88	**39**	**.273**	**.368**	**291**	258	93	.960	118	**364**	**760**	18	**14**	2.39
PIT	96	57	.627	9	692	569	190	91	22	.266	.350	202	255	112	.961	113	389	512	12	4	2.86
CHI	92	61	.601	13	667	**442**	157	82	12	.245	.314	267	**248**	99	**.962**	133	385	627	**23**	2	**2.04**
PHI	83	69	.546	21.5	708	603	187	82	16	.260	.336	180	275	99	.957	119	411	516	12	5	2.81
CIN	79	74	.516	26	736	691	160	**101**	27	.269	.354	181	310	**122**	.953	119	439	547	10	1	3.01
STL	58	96	.377	47.5	534	741	140	85	20	.248	.321	162	274	83	.957	135	367	411	10	2	3.59
BOS	51	103	.331	54.5	467	733	148	52	17	.234	.293	132	325	89	.951	139	433	533	14	0	3.52
BKN	48	104	.316	56.5	506	807	154	60	29	.246	.317	186	411	101	.936	125	476	556	7	3	3.76
					5090	5090	1327	641	182	.255	.332	1601	2356	798	.954	1001	3264	4462	106	31	2.99

	POS	Player	AB	BA	HR	RBI	PO	A	E	DP	TC/G	FA	Pitcher	G	IP	W	L	SV	ERA
Phi. W-92 L-56 Connie Mack	1B	H. Davis	602	.284	8	83	1621	91	24	43	11.7	.986	E. Plank	41	347	25	12	0	2.26
	2B	D. Murphy	533	.278	6	71	287	387	31	29	4.7	.956	R. Waddell	46	329	26	11	0	**1.48**
	SS	J. Knight	325	.203	3	29	143	188	39	9	4.6	.895	A. Coakley	35	255	20	7	0	1.84
	3B	L. Cross	583	.266	0	77	161	249	32	6	3.0	.928	C. Bender	35	229	16	10	0	2.83
	RF	S. Seybold	488	.270	6	59	213	13	4	5	1.7	.983	W. Henley	25	184	4	12	0	2.60
	CF	D. Hoffman	454	.262	1	35	214	12	14	4	2.0	.942							
	LF	T. Hartsel	533	.276	0	28	253	6	17	1	1.9	.938							
	C	Schreckengost	416	.272	0	45	**790**	114	15	**11**	**8.2**	.984							
	SS	M. Cross	248	.270	0	24	159	195	27	22	5.0	.929							
	OF	B. Lord	238	.239	0	13	94	9	4	3	1.8	.963							
Chi. W-92 L-60 Fielder Jones	1B	J. Donahue	533	.287	1	76	**1645**	114	21	**77**	11.9	.988	F. Owen	42	334	21	13	0	2.10
	2B	G. Dundon	364	.192	0	22	218	321	12	23	5.3	.978	N. Altrock	38	316	22	12	0	1.88
	SS	G. Davis	550	.278	1	55	330	501	46	**56**	5.6	.948	F. Smith	39	292	19	13	0	2.13
	3B	L. Tannehill	480	.200	0	39	168	**358**	**39**	17	4.0	.931	D. White	36	260	18	14	0	1.76
	RF	D. Green	379	.243	0	44	119	9	12	3	1.3	.914	E. Walsh	22	137	8	3	0	2.17
	CF	F. Jones	568	.245	2	38	**337**	21	11	5	2.4	.970							
	LF	D. Holmes	328	.201	0	22	150	11	11	1	1.9	.936							
	C	B. Sullivan	323	.201	2	26	389	104	13	8	5.4	.974							
	OF	N. Callahan	345	.272	1	43	120	10	6	0	1.5	.956							
	UT	F. Isbell	341	.296	2	45	219	136	13	18		.965							
	C	E. McFarland	250	.280	0	31	343	88	12	8	6.3	.973							
Det. W-79 L-74 Bill Armour	1B	P. Lindsay	329	.267	0	31	761	57	18	40	9.5	.978	G. Mullin	44	**348**	21	21	0	2.51
	2B	G. Schaefer	554	.244	2	47	**403**	389	37	35	5.5	.955	E. Killian	39	313	23	14	0	2.27
	SS	C. O'Leary	512	.213	1	33	358	411	55	40	5.6	.933	W. Donovan	34	281	18	15	0	2.60
	3B	B. Coughlin	489	.252	0	44	137	255	37	12	3.1	.914	F. Kitson	33	226	12	14	1	3.47
	RF	S. Crawford	575	.297	6	75	152	18	2	3	1.7	**.988**							
	CF	D. Cooley	377	.247	1	32	223	12	10	5	**2.5**	.959							
	LF	M. McIntyre	495	.263	0	30	286	18	10	6	2.4	.968							
	C	L. Drill	211	.261	0	24	345	73	13	10	6.2	.970							
	OF	P. Hickman	213	.221	2	20	72	7	5	3	1.8	.940							
	UT	B. Lowe	181	.193	0	9	93	54	4	1		.974							
Bos. W-78 L-74 Jimmy Collins	1B	M. Grimshaw	285	.239	4	35	768	35	16	35	11.1	.980	C. Young	38	321	18	19	0	1.82
	2B	H. Ferris	523	.220	6	59	320	**424**	30	38	5.5	.961	J. Tannehill	37	272	22	9	0	2.48
	SS	F. Parent	602	.234	0	33	294	461	**66**	48	5.4	.920	G. Winter	35	264	16	16	0	2.96
	3B	J. Collins	508	.276	4	65	164	268	36	12	3.6	.923	B. Dinneen	31	244	12	15	1	3.73
	RF	K. Selbach	418	.246	4	47	186	8	15	1	1.8	.928	N. Gibson	23	134	4	7	0	3.69
	CF	C. Stahl	500	.258	0	47	249	11	6	4	2.0	.977							
	LF	J. Burkett	573	.257	4	47	276	11	**22**	2	1.9	.929							
	C	L. Criger	313	.198	1	36	539	**147**	20	5	6.5	.972							
	1O	B. Freeman	455	.240	3	49	647	25	19	20		.973							
Cle. W-76 L-78 Nap Lajoie	1B	C. Carr	306	.235	1	31	940	50	9	33	11.5	.991	A. Joss	33	286	20	12	0	2.01
	2B	N. Lajoie	249	.329	2	41	148	177	3	25	5.6	.991	E. Moore	31	269	15	15	0	2.64
	SS	T. Turner	582	.263	4	72	285	430	41	49	4.9	.946	B. Rhoads	28	235	16	9	0	2.83
	3B	B. Bradley	537	.268	0	51	**187**	312	29	**17**	3.6	**.945**	O. Hess	26	214	10	15	0	3.16
	RF	E. Flick	496	**.306**	4	64	177	18	13	3	1.6	.938	B. Bernhard	22	174	7	13	0	3.36
	CF	H. Bay	550	.298	0	22	303	14	10	4	2.3	.969	R. Donahue	20	138	6	12	0	3.40
	LF	J. Jackson	421	.257	2	31	191	16	11	3	2.1	.950							
	C	F. Buelow	236	.174	1	18	262	72	13	4	5.9	.963							
	12	G. Stovall	419	.272	1	47	745	160	30	35		.968							
	C	H. Bemis	226	.292	0	28	256	52	9	4	5.5	.972							
	OP	O. Hess	175	.251	2	13	74	67	9	2		.940							
	2B	N. Kahl	131	.221	0	21	60	94	9	3	5.3	.945							
N. Y. W-71 L-78 Clark Griffith	1B	H. Chase	465	.249	3	49	1171	61	**31**	63	10.4	.975	A. Orth	40	305	18	16	0	2.86
	2B	B. Williams	470	.228	6	60	335	332	25	**51**	5.4	.964	J. Chesbro	41	303	19	15	0	2.20
	SS	K. Elberfeld	390	.262	0	53	244	317	57	35	5.7	.908	B. Hogg	39	205	9	13	1	3.20
	3B	J. Yeager	401	.267	0	42	103	173	23	6	3.3	.923	J. Powell	36	202	8	13	1	3.52
	RF	W. Keeler	560	.302	4	38	194	17	7	1	1.6	.968	C. Griffith	25	103	9	6	1	1.67
	CF	D. Fultz	422	.232	0	42	252	14	9	2	2.3	.967	A. Puttmann	17	86	2	7	1	4.27
	LF	P. Dougherty	418	.263	3	29	173	11	21	2	1.9	.898							
	C	R. Kleinow	253	.221	1	24	361	82	10	4	5.5	.978							
	UT	W. Conroy	385	.273	2	25	287	142	24	14		.947							
	C	D. McGuire	228	.219	0	33	366	69	11	4	6.3	.975							
	OF	E. Hahn	160	.319	0	11	83	5	4	1	2.1	.957							
Was. W-64 L-87 Jake Stahl	1B	J. Stahl	501	.244	5	66	1593	94	21	51	**12.2**	.988	C. Patten	42	310	14	21	0	3.14
	2B	P. Hickman	360	.311	2	46	170	281	38*	19	5.8	.922	L. Hughes	39	291	16	20	1	2.35
	SS	J. Cassidy	576	.215	1	49	308	**520**	**66**	50	5.9	.926	J. Townsend	34	263	7	16	0	2.63
	3B	H. Hill	374	.209	1	24	130	206	34	10	3.6	.908	B. Wolfe	28	182	8	14	2	2.57
	RF	J. Anderson	400	.290	1	38	161	7	7	1	2.0	.960	B. Jacobson	22	144	9	9	0	3.30
	CF	C. Jones	544	.208	2	41	240	**24**	11	6	1.9	.960							
	LF	F. Huelsman	421	.271	3	62	189	7	15	2	1.7	.929							
	C	M. Heydon	245	.192	1	26	368	125	**23**	7	6.7	.955							
	32	R. Nill	319	.182	3	31	138	188	28	15		.921							
	OF	P. Knoll	244	.213	0	29	101	8	8	1	1.7	.932							
	C	M. Kittredge	238	.164	0	14	323	113	10	8	5.9	.978							
	2B	J. Mullin	163	.190	0	13	83	97	14	8	5.0	.928							

	POS	Player	AB	BA	HR	RBI	PO	A	E	DP	TC/G	FA	Pitcher	G	IP	W	L	SV	ERA
St. L.	1B	T. Jones	504	.242	0	48	1502	105	25	52	12.1	.985	H. Howell	38	323	15	22	0	1.98
W-54 L-99	2B	I. Rockenfeld	322	.217	0	16	210	255	37	19	5.3	.926	F. Glade	32	275	6	25	0	2.81
Jimmy McAleer	SS	B. Wallace	587	.271	1	59	**385**	506	62	40	6.1	.935	B. Pelty	31	259	14	14	0	2.75
	3B	H. Gleason	535	.217	1	57	118	271	38	8	3.0	.911	W. Sudhoff	32	244	10	19	0	2.99
	RF	E. Frisk	429	.261	3	36	117	15	11	2	1.2	.923	J. Buchanan	22	141	5	10	2	3.50
	CF	B. Koehler	536	.237	2	47	227	24	8	11	2.0	.969							
	LF	G. Stone	632	.296	7	52	278	15	14	5	2.0	.954							
	C	J. Sugden	266	.173	0	23	407	112	9	6	7.4	.983							
	OF	I. Van Zandt	322	.233	1	20	69	7	11	0	1.2	.874							

BATTING AND BASE RUNNING LEADERS

Batting Average
E. Flick, CLE	.306
W. Keeler, NY	.302
H. Bay, CLE	.298
S. Crawford, DET	.297
F. Isbell, CHI	.296

Slugging Average
E. Flick, CLE	.466
F. Isbell, CHI	.440
S. Crawford, DET	.433
H. Davis, PHI	.422
G. Stone, STL	.410

Home Runs
H. Davis, PHI	8
G. Stone, STL	7

Total Bases
G. Stone, STL	259
H. Davis, PHI	254
S. Crawford, DET	249
P. Hickman, DET, WAS	232
E. Flick, CLE	229

Runs Batted In
H. Davis, PHI	83
L. Cross, PHI	77
J. Donahue, CHI	76
S. Crawford, DET	75
T. Turner, CLE	72

Stolen Bases
D. Hoffman, PHI	46
D. Fultz, NY	44
J. Stahl, WAS	41
T. Hartsel, PHI	36
H. Bay, CLE	36
H. Davis, PHI	36

Hits
G. Stone, STL	187
S. Crawford, DET	171
H. Davis, PHI	171

Base on Balls
T. Hartsel, PHI	121
F. Jones, CHI	73
K. Selbach, BOS	67
J. Burkett, BOS	67

Home Run Percentage
H. Davis, PHI	1.3
S. Seybold, PHI	1.2
H. Ferris, BOS	1.1

Runs Scored
H. Davis, PHI	92
F. Jones, CHI	91
H. Bay, CLE	90

Doubles
H. Davis, PHI	47
S. Crawford, DET	40
S. Seybold, PHI	37
P. Hickman, DET, WAS	37

Triples
E. Flick, CLE	19
H. Ferris, BOS	16
T. Turner, CLE	14

PITCHING LEADERS

Winning Percentage
A. Coakley, PHI	.741
J. Tannehill, BOS	.710
R. Waddell, PHI	.703
E. Plank, PHI	.676
N. Altrock, CHI	.647

Earned Run Average
R. Waddell, PHI	1.48
D. White, CHI	1.76
C. Young, BOS	1.82
A. Coakley, PHI	1.84
N. Altrock, CHI	1.88

Wins
R. Waddell, PHI	26
E. Plank, PHI	25
E. Killian, DET	23
J. Tannehill, BOS	22
N. Altrock, CHI	22

Saves
R. Waddell, PHI	4
C. Griffith, NY	3
C. Bender, PHI	3
B. Wolfe, WAS	2
J. Buchanan, STL	2

Strikeouts
R. Waddell, PHI	287
E. Plank, PHI	210
C. Young, BOS	208
H. Howell, STL	198
F. Smith, CHI	171

Complete Games
E. Plank, PHI	36
H. Howell, STL	35
G. Mullin, DET	35
E. Killian, DET	33
C. Young, BOS	32
F. Owen, CHI	32

Fewest Hits per 9 Innings
R. Waddell, PHI	6.33
F. Smith, CHI	6.63
C. Young, BOS	6.96

Shutouts
E. Killian, DET	8
R. Waddell, PHI	7
A. Orth, NY	6
J. Tannehill, BOS	6

Fewest Walks per 9 Innings
C. Young, BOS	0.84
A. Joss, CLE	1.45
F. Owen, CHI	1.51

Most Strikeouts per 9 Inn.
R. Waddell, PHI	7.86
C. Young, BOS	5.89
C. Bender, PHI	5.58

Innings
G. Mullin, DET	348
E. Plank, PHI	347
F. Owen, CHI	334

Games Pitched
R. Waddell, PHI	46
G. Mullin, DET	44
F. Owen, CHI	42
C. Patten, WAS	42

	W	L	PCT	GB	R	OR	2B	3B	HR	BA	SA	SB	E	DP	FA	CG	BB	SO	ShO	SV	ERA
PHI	92	56	.622		617	486	**256**	51	24	.255	**.339**	189	264	64	.958	117	409	**895**	**20**	0	2.19
CHI	92	60	.605	2	613	443	200	55	11	.237	.304	194	**217**	95	**.968**	131	329	613	17	0	**1.99**
DET	79	74	.516	15.5	511	608	190	54	14	.243	.312	129	265	80	.957	124	474	578	17	1	2.83
BOS	78	74	.513	16	583	557	165	69	**29**	.234	.311	131	294	75	.953	125	**292**	652	15	1	2.84
CLE	76	78	.494	19	559	582	211	**72**	18	**.255**	.335	188	229	84	.963	**139**	334	555	16	0	2.85
NY	71	78	.477	21.5	587	644	163	61	23	.248	.319	**200**	293	88	.952	88	396	642	19	**7**	2.93
WAS	64	87	.424	29.5	560	613	193	68	22	.223	.302	169	318	76	.951	118	385	539	11	3	2.87
STL	54	99	.353	40.5	509	606	153	49	16	.232	.289	130	295	78	.955	133	389	633	11	2	2.74
					4539	4539	1531	479	157	.241	.314	1330	2175	640	.957	975	3008	5107	126	14	2.65

Chi. — W-116 L-36 — Frank Chance

POS	Player	AB	BA	HR	RBI	PO	A	E	DP	TC/G	FA
1B	F. Chance	474	.319	3	71	1376	82	16	71	10.8	.989
2B	J. Evers	533	.255	1	51	344	441	44	51	5.4	.947
SS	J. Tinker	523	.233	1	64	288	472	45	55	5.5	.944
3B	H. Steinfeldt	539	.327	3	83	160	253	20	13	2.9	.954
RF	W. Schulte	563	.281	7	60	218	18	6	7	1.7	.975
CF	J. Slagle	498	.239	0	33	276	9	7	5	2.3	.976
LF	J. Sheckard	549	.262	1	45	264	13	4	1	1.9	.986
C	J. Kling	343	.312	2	46	520	126	12	7	6.9	.982
C	P. Moran	226	.252	0	35	335	78	9	6	6.9	.979
UT	S. Hofman	195	.256	2	20	253	52	7	18		.978

Pitcher	G	IP	W	L	SV	ERA
T. Brown	36	277	26	6	3	**1.04**
J. Pfiester	31	242	20	8	0	1.56
E. Reulbach	33	218	19	4	2	1.65
C. Lundgren	27	208	17	6	2	2.21
J. Taylor	17	147	12	3	0	1.83
O. Overall	18	144	12	3	1	1.88

N. Y. — W-96 L-56 — John McGraw

POS	Player	AB	BA	HR	RBI	PO	A	E	DP	TC/G	FA
1B	D. McGann	451	.237	0	37	1391	83	8	61	11.1	.995
2B	B. Gilbert	307	.231	1	27	223	324	35	32	5.9	.940
SS	B. Dahlen	471	.240	1	49	287	454	49	36	5.5	.938
3B	A. Devlin	498	.299	2	65	171	355	31	22	3.8	.944
RF	G. Browne	477	.264	0	38	153	17	12	3	1.5	.934
CF	C. Seymour	269	.320	4	42	129	7	3	3	1.9	.978
LF	S. Shannon	287	.254	0	25	109	4	5	2	1.6	.958
C	R. Bresnahan	405	.281	0	43	407	125	14	6	6.7	.974
2O	S. Strang	313	.319	4	49	176	175	21	13		.944
C	F. Bowerman	285	.228	1	42	300	80	6	8	5.8	.984
OF	S. Mertes	253	.237	1	33	119	10	4	0	1.9	.970

Pitcher	G	IP	W	L	SV	ERA
J. McGinnity	45	340	**27**	12	2	2.25
C. Mathewson	38	267	22	12	1	2.97
H. Wiltse	38	249	16	11	5	2.27
D. Taylor	31	213	17	9	0	2.20
R. Ames	31	203	12	10	1	2.66

Pit. — W-93 L-60 — Fred Clarke

POS	Player	AB	BA	HR	RBI	PO	A	E	DP	TC/G	FA
1B	J. Nealon	556	.255	3	**83**	1592	102	23	**90**	11.1	.987
2B	C. Ritchey	484	.269	1	62	326	439	27	59	5.2	**.966**
SS	H. Wagner	516	**.339**	2	71	334	473	51	**57**	6.3	.941
3B	T. Sheehan	315	.241	1	34	104	166	15	11	3.2	.947
RF	B. Ganley	511	.258	0	31	207	16	8	5	1.7	.965
CF	G. Beaumont	310	.265	2	32	148	6	9	2	2.1	.945
LF	F. Clarke	417	.309	1	39	209	15	6	3	2.1	.974
C	G. Gibson	259	.178	0	20	336	97	13	10	5.5	.971
3O	T. Leach	476	.286	1	39	204	141	20	4		.945
OF	D. Meier	273	.256	0	16	73	5	2	2	1.5	.975
C	H. Peitz	125	.240	0	20	186	45	5	2	6.2	.979

Pitcher	G	IP	W	L	SV	ERA
V. Willis	41	322	22	13	1	1.73
S. Leever	36	260	22	7	0	2.32
L. Leifield	37	256	18	13	1	1.87
D. Phillippe	33	219	15	10	0	2.47
M. Lynch	18	119	6	5	0	2.42

Phi. — W-71 L-82 — Hugh Duffy

POS	Player	AB	BA	HR	RBI	PO	A	E	DP	TC/G	FA
1B	K. Bransfield	524	.275	1	60	1318	88	29	57	10.3	.980
2B	K. Gleason	494	.227	0	34	215	358	32	39	4.5	.947
SS	M. Doolan	535	.230	1	55	395	480	66	51	6.1	.930
3B	E. Courtney	398	.236	0	42	113	163	23	9	3.1	.923
RF	J. Titus	484	.267	1	57	236	23	7	7	1.9	.974
CF	R. Thomas	493	.254	0	16	340	12	5	5	2.5	.986
LF	S. Magee	563	.282	6	67	316	18	6	2	2.2	.982
C	R. Dooin	351	.245	0	32	475	111	32	9	5.8	.948
PO	J. Lush	212	.264	0	15	59	92	12	3		.926
32	P. Sentelle	192	.229	1	14	70	105	19	4		.902
C	J. Donovan	166	.199	0	15	222	52	13	4	5.5	.955

Pitcher	G	IP	W	L	SV	ERA
T. Sparks	42	317	19	16	3	2.16
J. Lush	37	281	18	15	0	2.37
B. Duggleby	42	280	13	19	2	2.25
L. Richie	33	206	9	11	0	2.41
T. Pittinger	20	130	8	10	0	3.40

Bkn. — W-66 L-86 — Patsy Donovan

POS	Player	AB	BA	HR	RBI	PO	A	E	DP	TC/G	FA
1B	T. Jordan	450	.262	12	78	1240	64	30	44	10.6	.978
2B	W. Alperman	441	.252	3	46	245	308	35	25	5.7	.940
SS	P. Lewis	452	.243	0	37	244	393	54	35	5.1	.922
3B	D. Casey	571	.233	0	34	172	272	39	11	3.2	.919
RF	H. Lumley	484	.324	9	61	231	13	13	5	2.0	.949
CF	B. Maloney	566	.221	0	32	355	19	13	6	2.6	.966
LF	J. McCarthy	322	.304	0	35	158	13	14	1	2.2	.924
C	B. Bergen	353	.159	0	19	485	149	15	9	6.3	.977
UT	J. Hummel	286	.199	1	21	310	156	18	25		.963
C	L. Ritter	226	.208	0	15	211	61	6	4	5.2	.978
OF	E. Batch	203	.256	0	11	101	5	4	0	2.2	.964

Pitcher	G	IP	W	L	SV	ERA
E. Stricklett	41	292	14	18	5	2.72
D. Scanlan	38	288	18	13	1	3.19
H. McIntyre	39	276	13	21	3	2.97
M. Eason	34	227	10	17	0	3.25
J. Pastorius	29	212	10	14	0	3.61

Cin. — W-64 L-87 — Ned Hanlon

POS	Player	AB	BA	HR	RBI	PO	A	E	DP	TC/G	FA
1B	S. Deal	231	.208	0	21	624	46	10	25	10.5	.985
2B	M. Huggins	545	.292	0	26	344	458	44	62	5.8	.948
SS	T. Corcoran	430	.207	1	33	263	379	40	51	5.8	.941
3B	J. Delahanty	379	.280	1	39	136	170	33	4	3.2	.903
RF	F. Jude	308	.208	1	31	95	14	4	1	1.4	.965
CF	C. Seymour	307	.257	4	38	202	10	7	3	2.8	.968
LF	J. Kelley	465	.228	1	53	184	13	7	5	1.7	.966
C	A. Schlei	388	.245	4	54	455	139	24	8	6.8	.961
1O	S. Barry	279	.287	1	33	481	32	8	24		.985
UT	H. Lobert	268	.310	0	19	118	178	20	8		.937
OF	H. Smoot	220	.259	1	17	109	10	7	0	2.1	.944
OF	F. Odwell	202	.223	0	21	94	10	4	0	1.9	.963

Pitcher	G	IP	W	L	SV	ERA
J. Weimer	41	305	20	14	1	2.22
B. Ewing	33	288	13	14	0	2.38
C. Fraser	31	236	10	20	0	2.67
B. Wicker	20	150	6	14	0	2.70
C. Hall	14	95	4	6	1	3.32

St. L. — W-52 L-98 — John McCloskey

POS	Player	AB	BA	HR	RBI	PO	A	E	DP	TC/G	FA
1B	J. Beckley	320	.247	0	44	928	43	13	38	11.6	.987
2B	P. Bennett	595	.262	1	34	295	447	41	43	5.1	.948
SS	G. McBride	313	.169	0	13	194	310	30	33	5.9	.944
3B	H. Arndt	256	.270	2	26	108	139	9	15	3.9	.965
RF	A. Burch	335	.266	0	11	155	15	12	6	2.0	.934
CF	H. Smoot	343	.248	0	34	174	8	9	4	2.2	.953
LF	S. Shannon	302	.258	0	25	165	9	5	3	2.2	.972
C	M. Grady	280	.250	3	27	115	67	5	5	3.1	.973
UT	Hoelskoetter	317	.224	0	14	109	173	19	10		.937
O1	S. Barry	237	.249	0	12	261	16	11	9		.962
OF	S. Mertes	191	.246	0	19	77	4	10	0	1.7	.890
OF	J. Himes	155	.271	0	14	76	10	2	2	2.2	.977

Pitcher	G	IP	W	L	SV	ERA
B. Brown	32	238	8	16	0	2.64
E. Karger	25	192	5	16	1	2.72
F. Beebe	20	161	9	9	0	3.02
J. Taylor	17	155	8	9	0	2.15
C. Druhot	15	130	6	7	0	2.62
G. Thompson	17	103	2	11	0	4.28
W. Egan	16	86	2	9	0	4.59

	POS	Player	AB	BA	HR	RBI	PO	A	E	DP	TC/G	FA	Pitcher	G	IP	W	L	SV	ERA
Bos.	1B	F. Tenney	544	.283	1	28	1456	118	28	78	11.2	.983	I. Young	43	358	16	25	0	2.91
W-49 L-102	2B	A. Strobel	317	.202	1	24	181	259	25	32	5.0	.946	V. Lindaman	39	307	12	23	0	2.43
Fred Tenney	SS	A. Bridwell	459	.227	0	22	322	390	54	43	6.4	.930	B. Pfeffer	35	302	13	22	0	2.95
	3B	D. Brain	525	.250	5	45	208	321	48	26	4.2	.917	G. Dorner	34	257	8	25*	0	3.88
	RF	C. Dolan	549	.248	0	39	207	26	18	4	1.7	.928							
	CF	J. Bates	504	.252	6	54	238	12	11	4	1.9	.958							
	LF	D. Howard	545	.261	1	54	118	14	13	3	1.7	.910							
	C	T. Needham	285	.189	1	12	317	114	17	9	5.9	.962							
	UT	S. Brown	231	.208	0	20	235	88	13	5		.961							
	C	J. O'Neill	167	.180	0	4	259	72	10	6	7.1	.971							
	P	B. Pfeffer	158	.196	1	11	13	91	4	0	3.1	.963							

BATTING AND BASE RUNNING LEADERS

Batting Average

H. Wagner, PIT	.339
H. Steinfeldt, CHI	.327
H. Lumley, BKN	.324
S. Strang, NY	.319
F. Chance, CHI	.319

Slugging Average

H. Lumley, BKN	.477
H. Wagner, PIT	.459
S. Strang, NY	.435
H. Steinfeldt, CHI	.430
F. Chance, CHI	.430

Home Runs

T. Jordan, BKN	12
H. Lumley, BKN	9
C. Seymour, CIN, NY	8
W. Schulte, CHI	7
J. Bates, BOS	6
S. Magee, PHI	6

Total Bases

H. Wagner, PIT	237
H. Steinfeldt, CHI	232
H. Lumley, BKN	231
S. Magee, PHI	229
W. Schulte, CHI	223

Runs Batted In

H. Steinfeldt, CHI	83
J. Nealon, PIT	83
C. Seymour, CIN, NY	80
T. Jordan, BKN	78
F. Chance, CHI	71
H. Wagner, PIT	71

Stolen Bases

F. Chance, CHI	57
S. Magee, PHI	55
A. Devlin, NY	54
H. Wagner, PIT	53
J. Evers, CHI	49

Hits

H. Steinfeldt, CHI	176
H. Wagner, PIT	175
C. Seymour, CIN, NY	165

Base on Balls

R. Thomas, PHI	107
R. Bresnahan, NY	81
J. Titus, PHI	78

Home Run Percentage

T. Jordan, BKN	2.7
H. Lumley, BKN	1.9
C. Seymour, CIN, NY	1.4

Runs Scored

F. Chance, CHI	103
H. Wagner, PIT	103
J. Sheckard, CHI	90
J. Nealon, PIT	82

Doubles

H. Wagner, PIT	38
S. Magee, PHI	36
K. Bransfield, PHI	28

Triples

F. Clarke, PIT	13
W. Schulte, CHI	13
H. Lumley, BKN	12
J. Nealon, PIT	12

PITCHING LEADERS

Winning Percentage

E. Reulbach, CHI	.826
T. Brown, CHI	.813
S. Leever, PIT	.759
C. Lundgren, CHI	.739
J. Pfiester, CHI	.714

Earned Run Average

T. Brown, CHI	1.04
J. Pfiester, CHI	1.56
E. Reulbach, CHI	1.65
V. Willis, PIT	1.73
L. Leifield, PIT	1.87

Wins

J. McGinnity, NY	27
T. Brown, CHI	26
C. Mathewson, NY	22
S. Leever, PIT	22
V. Willis, PIT	22

Saves

G. Ferguson, NY	6
H. Wiltse, NY	5
E. Stricklett, BKN	5

Strikeouts

F. Beebe, CHI, STL	171
B. Pfeffer, BOS	158
R. Ames, NY	156
J. Pfiester, CHI	153
J. Lush, PHI	151
I. Young, BOS	151

Complete Games

I. Young, BOS	37
B. Pfeffer, BOS	33
J. Taylor, CHI, STL	32
V. Lindaman, BOS	32
V. Willis, PIT	32
J. McGinnity, NY	32

Fewest Hits per 9 Innings

E. Reulbach, CHI	5.33
T. Brown, CHI	6.43
J. Pfiester, CHI	6.44

Shutouts

T. Brown, CHI	10
L. Leifield, PIT	8
J. Weimer, CIN	7

Fewest Walks per 9 Innings

D. Phillippe, PIT	1.07
S. Leever, PIT	1.66
T. Sparks, PHI	1.76

Most Strikeouts per 9 Inn.

R. Ames, NY	6.90
F. Beebe, CHI, STL	6.67
J. Pfiester, CHI	5.70

Innings

I. Young, BOS	358
J. McGinnity, NY	340
V. Willis, PIT	322

Games Pitched

J. McGinnity, NY	45
I. Young, BOS	43
T. Sparks, PHI	42
B. Duggleby, PHI	42

	W	L	PCT	GB	R	OR	Batting 2B	3B	HR	BA	SA	SB	Fielding E	DP	FA	CG	BB	Pitching SO	ShO	SV	ERA
CHI	116	36	.763		704	381	181	71	20	.262	.339	283	194	100	.969	125	446	702	31	9	1.76
NY	96	56	.632	20	625	508	162	53	15	.255	.321	288	233	84	.963	105	394	639	19	16	2.49
PIT	93	60	.608	23.5	622	464	164	67	12	.261	.327	162	228	109	.964	116	309	532	27	2	2.21
PHI	71	82	.464	45.5	530	568	197	47	12	.241	.307	180	271	83	.956	108	436	500	21	5	2.58
BKN	66	86	.434	50	495	620	141	68	25	.236	.308	175	283	73	.955	119	453	476	22	9	3.13
CIN	64	87	.424	51.5	530	582	140	71	16	.238	.304	170	262	97	.959	126	470	567	11	5	2.69
STL	52	98	.347	63	475	620	137	69	10	.235	.296	110	272	92	.957	118	479	559	4	2	3.04
BOS	49	102	.325	66.5	408	646	136	43	16	.226	.281	93	337	102	.947	137	436	562	10	0	3.17
					4389	4389	1258	489	126	.244	.310	1461	2080	740	.959	954	3423	4537	145	48	2.63

	POS	Player	AB	BA	HR	RBI	PO	A	E	DP	TC/G	FA	Pitcher	G	IP	W	L	SV	ERA
Chi.	1B	J. Donahue	556	.257	1	57	1697	118	22	62	11.9	.988	F. Owen	42	293	22	13	2	2.33
W-93 L-58	2B	F. Isbell	549	.279	0	57	292	363	35	36	5.2	.949	N. Altrock	38	288	20	13	0	2.06
Fielder Jones	SS	G. Davis	484	.277	0	80	263	475	42	44	6.0	.946	E. Walsh	41	278	17	13	1	1.88
	3B	L. Tannehill	378	.183	0	33	131	278	21	12	4.3	.951	D. White	28	219	18	6	0	**1.52**
	RF	B. O'Neill	330	.248	1	21	118	12	7	1	1.5	.949	R. Patterson	21	142	10	7	1	2.09
	CF	F. Jones	496	.230	2	34	312	23	4	5	2.4	**.988**	F. Smith	20	122	5	5	1	3.39
	LF	E. Hahn	484	.227	0	27	164	21	10	3	1.5	.949							
	C	B. Sullivan	387	.214	2	33	475	134	16	7	5.3	.974							
	OF	P. Dougherty	253	.233	1	27	118	10	2	1	1.8	.985							
	3B	G. Rohe	225	.258	0	25	66	122	15	6	3.6	.926							
N. Y.	1B	H. Chase	597	.323	0	76	1504	89	33	54	10.8	.980	A. Orth	45	**339**	**27**	17	0	2.34
W-90 L-61	2B	J. Williams	501	.277	3	77	336	412	32	34	5.6	.959	J. Chesbro	49	325	24	16	1	2.96
Clark Griffith	SS	K. Elberfeld	346	.306	2	31	200	317	42	18	5.7	.925	B. Hogg	28	206	14	13	0	2.93
	3B	F. LaPorte	454	.264	2	54	118	210	35	11	3.2	.904	W. Clarkson	32	151	9	4	0	2.32
	RF	W. Keeler	592	.304	2	33	213	16	3	3	1.5	.987	D. Newton	21	125	6	5	0	3.17
	CF	D. Hoffman	320	.256	0	23	176	7	12	1	2.0	.938							
	LF	F. Delahanty	307	.238	2	41	180	7	9	1	2.1	.954							
	C	R. Kleinow	268	.220	0	31	381	102	13	8	5.2	.974							
	OS	W. Conroy	567	.245	4	54	295	154	21	15		.955							
	3O	G. Moriarty	197	.234	0	23	78	79	15	3		.913							
Cle.	1B	C. Rossman	396	.308	1	53	1145	45	19	47	11.5	.984	O. Hess	43	334	20	17	**3**	1.83
W-89 L-64	2B	N. Lajoie	602	.355	0	91	**354**	**415**	21	**76**	6.1	**.973**	B. Rhoads	38	315	22	10	1	1.80
Nap Lajoie	SS	T. Turner	584	.291	2	54	287	570	36	61	6.1	**.960**	A. Joss	34	282	21	9	1	1.72
	3B	B. Bradley	302	.275	2	25	107	177	10	6	3.6	.966	B. Bernhard	31	255	16	15	0	2.54
	RF	B. Congalton	419	.320	2	50	174	6	8	0	1.6	.957	J. Townsend	17	93	3	7	0	2.91
	CF	E. Flick	**624**	.311	1	62	248	13	5	4	1.8	.981							
	LF	J. Jackson	374	.214	0	38	189	5	5	2	1.9	.975							
	C	H. Bemis	297	.276	2	30	340	73	16	7	5.3	.963							
	UT	G. Stovall	443	.273	0	37	666	153	21	53		.975							
	OF	H. Bay	280	.275	0	14	131	8	3	2	2.1	.979							
	C	N. Clarke	179	.358	1	21	211	58	5	4	5.1	.982							
	P	O. Hess	154	.201	0	11	25	86	6	4	2.7	.949							
Phi.	1B	H. Davis	551	.292	**12**	**96**	1352	91	**37**	**66**	10.2	.975	R. Waddell	43	273	15	17	0	2.21
W-78 L-67	2B	D. Murphy	448	.301	2	60	239	308	26	38	4.8	.955	C. Bender	36	238	15	10	**3**	2.53
Connie Mack	SS	M. Cross	445	.200	1	40	305	411	47	48	5.7	.938	J. Dygert	35	214	11	13	0	2.70
	3B	J. Knight	253	.194	3	20	71	130	17	6	3.3	.922	E. Plank	26	212	19	6	0	2.25
	RF	S. Seybold	411	.316	5	59	150	10	13	3	1.5	.925	J. Coombs	23	173	10	10	0	2.50
	CF	B. Lord	434	.233	1	44	212	13	14	4	2.1	.941	A. Coakley	22	149	7	8	0	3.14
	LF	T. Hartsel	533	.255	1	30	238	15	8	5	1.8	.969							
	C	Schreckengost	338	.284	1	41	**532**	110	19	7	**7.4**	.971							
	OF	H. Armbruster	265	.238	2	24	124	9	4	1	1.9	.971							
	C	M. Powers	185	.157	0	7	297	79	10	2	6.8	.974							
	3B	R. Oldring	174	.241	0	19	53	87	16	5	3.2	.897							
St. L.	1B	T. Jones	539	.252	0	30	1476	116	25	55	11.3	.985	H. Howell	35	277	15	14	1	2.11
W-76 L-73	2B	P. O'Brien	524	.233	2	57	254	274	**38**	31	4.7	.933	F. Glade	35	267	15	14	1	2.36
Jimmy McAleer	SS	B. Wallace	476	.258	2	67	309	461	41	47	5.9	.949	B. Pelty	34	261	16	11	2	1.59
	3B	R. Hartzell	404	.213	0	24	119	209	41	11	3.6	.889	J. Powell	28	244	13	14	1	1.77
	RF	H. Niles	541	.229	2	31	140	**34**	6	5	1.7	.967	B. Jacobson	24	155	9	9	0	2.50
	CF	C. Hemphill	585	.289	4	62	304	17	13	1	2.2	.961	E. Smith	19	155	8	11	0	3.72
	LF	G. Stone	581	**.358**	6	71	295	10	10	3	2.0	.968							
	C	T. Spencer	188	.176	0	17	226	60	**20**	3	5.7	.935							
	C	B. Rickey	201	.284	3	24	233	58	14	2	5.6	.954							
	OF	B. Koehler	186	.220	0	15	81	8	4	4	1.8	.957							
	C	J. O'Connor	174	.190	0	11	248	64	3	2	5.8	.990							
Det.	1B	P. Lindsay	499	.224	0	33	1122	66	28	55	10.0	.977	G. Mullin	40	330	21	18	0	2.78
W-71 L-78	2B	G. Schaefer	446	.238	2	42	348	328	37	42	**6.3**	.948	R. Donahue	38	241	13	14	0	2.73
Bill Armour	SS	C. O'Leary	443	.219	2	34	**326**	398	**58**	37	6.2	.926	E. Siever	30	223	14	11	0	2.71
	3B	B. Coughlin	498	.235	2	60	**188**	265	29	**16**	3.3	.940	W. Donovan	25	212	9	15	0	3.15
	RF	S. Crawford	563	.295	2	72	171	19	3	2	1.7	.964	E. Killian	21	150	10	6	2	3.43
	CF	T. Cobb	350	.320	1	41	208	14	9	4	2.4	.961	J. Eubank	24	135	4	10	2	3.53
	LF	M. McIntyre	493	.260	0	39	254	25	5	8	2.1	.982							
	C	B. Schmidt	216	.218	0	10	257	104	16	4	5.6	.958							
	OF	D. Jones	323	.260	0	24	193	10	4	3	2.5	.981							
	C	F. Payne	222	.270	0	20	177	49	8	3	5.0	.966							
Was.	1B	J. Stahl	482	.222	0	51	1322	78	24	51	10.5	.983	C. Falkenberg	40	299	14	20	1	2.86
W-55 L-95	2B	L. Schlafly	426	.246	2	30	341	358	28	42	5.9	.961	C. Patten	38	283	19	16	0	2.17
Jake Stahl	SS	D. Altizer	433	.256	1	27	257	323	43	31	5.5	.931	C. Smith	33	235	9	16	0	2.91
	3B	L. Cross	494	.263	1	46	157	242	20	9	3.2	**.952**	L. Hughes	30	204	7	17	0	3.62
	RF	P. Hickman	451	.284	9	57	137	12	7	2	1.6	.955	F. Kitson	30	197	6	14	0	3.65
	CF	C. Jones	497	.241	0	42	279	20	12	7	2.4	.961							
	LF	J. Anderson	583	.271	3	70	286	19	**15**	2	2.1	.953							
	C	H. Wakefield	211	.280	1	21	237	59	17	5	5.2	.946							
	UT	R. Nill	315	.235	0	15	148	211	36	21		.909							
	OF	J. Stanley	221	.163	0	9	78	7	6	0	1.4	.934							

	POS	Player	AB	BA	HR	RBI	PO	A	E	DP	TC/G	FA	Pitcher	G	IP	W	L	SV	ERA
Bos.	1B	M. Grimshaw	428	.290	0	48	1165	64	16	39	11.3	.987	C. Young	39	288	13	**21**	2	3.19
W-49 L-105	2B	H. Ferris	495	.244	2	44	316	375	29	41	5.7	.960	J. Harris	30	235	2	**21**	2	3.52
Jimmy Collins	SS	F. Parent	600	.235	1	49	312	472	56	48	5.9	.933	B. Dinneen	28	219	8	19	0	2.92
W-44 L-92	3B	R. Morgan	307	.215	1	21	126	139	41	8	3.5	.866	G. Winter	29	208	6	18	2	4.12
Chick Stahl	RF	J. Hayden	322	.280	1	13	136	7	4	1	1.7	.973	J. Tannehill	27	196	13	11	0	3.16
W-5 L-13	CF	C. Stahl	595	.286	4	51	344	24	15	9	2.5	.961	R. Glaze	19	123	4	6	0	3.59
	LF	J. Hoey	361	.244	0	24	155	7	15	0	1.9	.915							
	C	C. Armbruster	201	.144	0	6	262	99	17	6	5.7	.955							
	O1	B. Freeman	392	.250	1	30	467	47	8	22		.985							
	OF	K. Selbach	228	.211	0	23	109	6	4	2	2.1	.966							
	UT	J. Godwin	193	.187	0	15	79	115	26	11		.882							

BATTING AND BASE RUNNING LEADERS

PITCHING LEADERS

Batting Average
- G. Stone, STL .358
- N. Lajoie, CLE .355
- H. Chase, NY .323
- B. Congalton, CLE .320
- S. Seybold, PHI .316

Slugging Average
- G. Stone, STL .501
- N. Lajoie, CLE .460
- H. Davis, PHI .459
- E. Flick, CLE .439
- P. Hickman, WAS .421

Winning Percentage
- E. Plank, PHI .760
- D. White, CHI .750
- A. Joss, CLE .700
- B. Rhoads, CLE .688
- F. Owen, CHI .629

Earned Run Average
- D. White, CHI 1.52
- B. Pelty, STL 1.59
- A. Joss, CLE 1.72
- J. Powell, STL 1.77
- B. Rhoads, CLE 1.80

Home Runs
- H. Davis, PHI 12
- P. Hickman, WAS 9
- G. Stone, STL 6
- S. Seybold, PHI 5

Total Bases
- G. Stone, STL 291
- N. Lajoie, CLE 277
- E. Flick, CLE 275
- H. Davis, PHI 253
- H. Chase, NY 236

Wins
- A. Orth, NY 27
- J. Chesbro, NY 24
- B. Rhoads, CLE 22
- F. Owen, CHI 22
- A. Joss, CLE 21
- G. Mullin, DET 21

Saves
- C. Bender, PHI 3
- O. Hess, CLE 3

Runs Batted In
- H. Davis, PHI 96
- N. Lajoie, CLE 91
- G. Davis, CHI 80
- J. Williams, NY 77
- H. Chase, NY 76

Stolen Bases
- J. Anderson, WAS 39
- E. Flick, CLE 39
- D. Altizer, WAS 37
- F. Isbell, CHI 37
- J. Donahue, CHI 36

Strikeouts
- R. Waddell, PHI 196
- C. Falkenberg, WAS 178
- E. Walsh, CHI 171
- O. Hess, CLE 167
- C. Bender, PHI 159

Complete Games
- A. Orth, NY 36
- G. Mullin, DET 35
- O. Hess, CLE 33
- B. Rhoads, CLE 31
- H. Howell, STL 30
- C. Falkenberg, WAS 30

Hits
- N. Lajoie, CLE 214
- G. Stone, STL 208
- E. Flick, CLE 194

Base on Balls
- T. Hartsel, PHI 88
- F. Jones, CHI 83
- E. Hahn, CHI, NY 72

Fewest Hits per 9 Innings
- B. Pelty, STL 6.53
- D. White, CHI 6.57
- E. Walsh, CHI 6.95

Shutouts
- E. Walsh, CHI 10
- A. Joss, CLE 9
- R. Waddell, PHI 8

Home Run Percentage
- H. Davis, PHI 2.2
- P. Hickman, WAS 2.0
- S. Seybold, PHI 1.2

Runs Scored
- E. Flick, CLE 98
- T. Hartsel, PHI 96
- W. Keeler, NY 96

Fewest Walks per 9 Innings
- C. Young, BOS 0.78
- R. Patterson, CHI 1.08
- N. Altrock, CHI 1.31

Most Strikeouts per 9 Inn.
- R. Waddell, PHI 6.47
- C. Bender, PHI 6.00
- E. Walsh, CHI 5.53

Doubles
- N. Lajoie, CLE 49
- H. Davis, PHI 42
- E. Flick, CLE 34

Triples
- E. Flick, CLE 22
- G. Stone, STL 20
- S. Crawford, DET 16

Innings
- A. Orth, NY 339
- O. Hess, CLE 334
- G. Mullin, DET 330

Games Pitched
- J. Chesbro, NY 49
- A. Orth, NY 45
- O. Hess, CLE 44

	W	L	PCT	GB	R	OR	2B	3B	Batting HR	BA	SA	SB	E	Fielding DP	FA	CG	BB	Pitching SO	ShO	SV	ERA
CHI	93	58	.616		570	**460**	152	52	7	.230	.286	214	243	80	.963	117	**255**	543	**32**	5	2.13
NY	90	61	.596	3	643	544	166	**77**	17	.266	.339	192	272	69	.957	99	351	605	18	4	2.78
CLE	89	64	.582	5	**663**	482	**240**	73	11	**.279**	**.357**	203	**216**	**111**	**.967**	133	365	530	27	4	**2.09**
PHI	78	67	.538	12	561	536	213	49	**32**	.247	.330	166	267	86	.956	107	425	**749**	19	4	2.60
STL	76	73	.510	16	565	501	145	60	20	.247	.312	221	267	86	.956	**133**	314	558	17	5	2.23
DET	71	78	.477	21	518	596	154	66	10	.242	.306	206	260	86	.959	128	389	469	7	4	3.06
WAS	55	95	.367	37.5	518	670	144	65	26	.238	.309	**233**	279	78	.955	115	451	558	12	1	3.25
BOS	49	105	.318	45.5	462	711	160	75	13	.239	.306	99	335	84	.949	124	285	549	6	**6**	3.41
					4500	4500	1374	517	136	.249	.319	1534	2162	674	.958	956	2835	4561	138	33	2.69

Det. — W-92 L-58 — Hughie Jennings

POS	Player	AB	BA	HR	RBI	PO	A	E	DP	TC/G	FA
1B	C. Rossman	571	.277	0	69	1478	62	30	57	10.3	.981
2B	R. Downs	374	.219	1	42	149	207	27	10	4.8	.930
SS	C. O'Leary	465	.241	0	34	353	448	44	35	6.1	.948
3B	B. Coughlin	519	.243	0	46	163	236	30	9	3.2	.930
RF	T. Cobb	605	**.350**	5	**116**	238	30	11	12	1.9	.961
CF	S. Crawford	582	.323	4	81	311	22	12	2	2.4	.965
LF	D. Jones	491	.273	0	27	282	15	9	2	**2.4**	.971
C	B. Schmidt	349	.244	0	23	446	132	34	14	5.9	.944
UT	G. Schaefer	372	.258	1	32	239	286	23	23		.958
C	F. Payne	169	.166	0	14	205	55	5	4	5.8	.981
P	G. Mullin	157	.217	0	13	15	133	6	1	3.3	.961

Pitcher	G	IP	W	L	SV	ERA
G. Mullin	46	357	20	20	3	2.59
E. Killian	41	314	25	13	1	1.78
E. Siever	39	275	18	11	1	2.16
W. Donovan	32	271	25	4	1	2.19

Phi. — W-88 L-57 — Connie Mack

POS	Player	AB	BA	HR	RBI	PO	A	E	DP	TC/G	FA
1B	H. Davis	582	.266	**8**	87	1475	103	**38**	50	10.8	.976
2B	D. Murphy	469	.271	2	57	271	386	24	28	5.6	.965
SS	S. Nicholls	460	.302	0	23	178	258	33	12	5.7	.930
3B	J. Collins	365	.274	0	35	97	185	30	11	3.1	.904
RF	S. Seybold	564	.271	5	92	201	19	6	7	1.5	.973
CF	R. Oldring	441	.286	1	40	180	10	5	0	1.7	.974
LF	T. Hartsel	507	.280	3	29	191	11	7	2	1.5	.967
C	Schreckengost	356	.272	0	38	**640**	145	12	4	**8.1**	**.985**
SS	M. Cross	248	.206	0	18	169	226	19	17	5.6	.954
OF	B. Lord	170	.182	1	11	91	6	5	0	1.9	.951
C	M. Powers	159	.182	0	9	313	80	7	8	6.8	.983

Pitcher	G	IP	W	L	SV	ERA
E. Plank	43	344	24	16	0	2.20
R. Waddell	44	285	19	13	0	2.15
J. Dygert	42	262	21	8	1	2.34
C. Bender	33	219	16	8	3	2.05
J. Coombs	23	133	6	9	2	3.12

Chi. — W-87 L-64 — Fielder Jones

POS	Player	AB	BA	HR	RBI	PO	A	E	DP	TC/G	FA
1B	J. Donahue	**609**	.259	1	68	**1846**	140	12	78	**12.7**	**.994**
2B	F. Isbell	486	.243	0	41	276	384	30	41	5.8	.957
SS	G. Davis	466	.238	1	52	223	485	38	53	5.7	.949
3B	G. Rohe	494	.213	2	51	58	161	25	14	3.2	.898
RF	E. Hahn	592	.255	0	45	182	24	2	6	1.3	**.990**
CF	F. Jones	559	.261	0	47	307	18	9	6	2.2	.973
LF	P. Dougherty	533	.270	1	59	209	19	13	4	1.6	.946
C	B. Sullivan	339	.174	0	36	477	117	10	12	5.6	.983
P	E. Walsh	154	.162	1	10	35	**227**	4	2	4.8	.985

Pitcher	G	IP	W	L	SV	ERA
E. Walsh	**56**	**422**	24	18	**4**	**1.60**
F. Smith	41	310	23	10	0	2.47
D. White	46	291	**27**	13	1	2.26
N. Altrock	30	214	7	13	2	2.57
R. Patterson	19	96	4	6	0	2.63

Cle. — W-85 L-67 — Nap Lajoie

POS	Player	AB	BA	HR	RBI	PO	A	E	DP	TC/G	FA
1B	G. Stovall	466	.236	1	36	1381	68	25	**90**	12.1	.983
2B	N. Lajoie	509	.299	2	63	314	461	25	**86**	6.3	.969
SS	T. Turner	524	.242	0	46	258	477	39	**67**	5.3	.950
3B	B. Bradley	498	.223	0	34	164	278	29	**18**	3.4	**.938**
RF	E. Flick	549	.302	3	58	219	22	11	7	1.7	.956
CF	J. Birmingham	476	.235	1	33	273	**33**	17	8	2.4	.947
LF	B. Hinchman	514	.228	1	50	231	18	11	3	1.7	.958
C	N. Clarke	390	.269	3	33	470	119	24	9	5.3	.961
C	H. Bemis	172	.250	0	19	180	42	10	3	4.5	.957

Pitcher	G	IP	W	L	SV	ERA
A. Joss	42	339	**27**	11	2	1.83
G. Liebhardt	38	280	18	14	1	2.05
B. Rhoads	35	275	15	14	1	2.29
J. Thielman	20	166	11	8	0	2.33
O. Hess	17	93	6	6	1	2.89
W. Clarkson	17	91	4	6	0	1.99

N. Y. — W-70 L-78 — Clark Griffith

POS	Player	AB	BA	HR	RBI	PO	A	E	DP	TC/G	FA
1B	H. Chase	498	.287	2	68	1144	77	34	50	10.4	.973
2B	J. Williams	504	.270	2	63	357	393	26	45	5.6	.966
SS	K. Elberfeld	447	.271	0	51	295	400	52	31	6.3	.930
3B	G. Moriarty	437	.277	0	43	115	160	31	8	3.4	.899
RF	W. Keeler	423	.234	0	17	144	13	5	5	1.5	.969
CF	D. Hoffman	517	.253	4	46	286	20	15	4	2.4	.953
LF	W. Conroy	530	.234	3	51	204	10	10	2	2.2	.955
C	R. Kleinow	269	.264	0	26	318	97	14	5	5.0	.967
3O	F. LaPorte	470	.270	0	48	149	125	30	4		.901
C	I. Thomas	208	.192	1	24	257	90	17	7	5.5	.953

Pitcher	G	IP	W	L	SV	ERA
A. Orth	36	249	14	**21**	0	2.61
J. Chesbro	30	206	10	10	0	2.53
S. Doyle	29	194	11	11	1	2.65
B. Hogg	25	167	10	8	0	3.08
D. Newton	19	133	7	10	0	3.18
B. Keefe	19	58	3	5	3	2.50

St. L. — W-69 L-83 — Jimmy McAleer

POS	Player	AB	BA	HR	RBI	PO	A	E	DP	TC/G	FA
1B	T. Jones	549	.250	0	34	1687	103	31	69	11.7	.983
2B	H. Niles	492	.289	2	35	280	352	**34**	41	5.7	.949
SS	B. Wallace	538	.257	0	70	338	**517**	54	54	6.2	.941
3B	J. Yeager	436	.239	1	44	108	194	20	12	3.5	.938
RF	O. Pickering	576	.259	0	60	210	14	12	5	1.6	.949
CF	C. Hemphill	603	.259	0	38	**320**	12	15	2	2.3	.957
LF	G. Stone	596	.320	4	59	276	12	9	5	1.9	.970
C	T. Spencer	230	.265	0	24	250	80	15	6	5.5	.957
32	R. Hartzell	220	.236	0	13	85	114	14	6		.934
C	J. Stephens	173	.202	0	11	200	63	9	4	4.9	.967

Pitcher	G	IP	W	L	SV	ERA
H. Howell	42	316	16	15	3	1.93
B. Pelty	36	273	12	**21**	1	2.57
J. Powell	32	256	13	16	1	2.68
F. Glade	24	202	13	9	0	2.67
B. Dinneen	24	155	7	10	4*	2.43

Bos. — W-59 L-90
Cy Young W-3 L-4
George Huff W-3 L-5
Bob Unglaub W-8 L-20
Deacon McGuire W-45 L-61

POS	Player	AB	BA	HR	RBI	PO	A	E	DP	TC/G	FA
1B	B. Unglaub	544	.254	1	62	1504	84	22	71	11.6	.986
2B	H. Ferris	561	.241	4	60	**424**	459	30	43	6.1	.967
SS	H. Wagner	385	.213	2	21	283	387	50	31	6.6	.931
3B	J. Knight	364	.212	2	29	129*	211*	28*	15*	3.8*	.924
RF	B. Congalton	496	.286	2	47	169	18	6	4	1.5	.969
CF	D. Sullivan	551	.245	1	26	296	16	8	3	2.2	.975
LF	J. Barrett	390	.244	1	28	183	14	7	5	2.1	.966
C	L. Criger	226	.181	0	14	288	109	9	12	5.4	.978
UT	F. Parent	409	.276	1	26	195	191	25	20		.939
C	A. Shaw	198	.192	0	7	294	106	12	10	5.6	.971
O1	M. Grimshaw	181	.204	0	33	163	8	5	10		.972
3B	J. Collins	158	.291	0	10	46	72	17	2	3.3	.874

Pitcher	G	IP	W	L	SV	ERA
C. Young	43	343	22	15	1	1.99
G. Winter	35	257	12	15	1	2.07
R. Glaze	32	182	8	13	0	2.32
T. Pruiett	35	174	3	11	3	3.11
J. Tannehill	18	131	6	7	1	2.47
C. Morgan	16	114	6	6	0	1.97

	POS	Player	AB	BA	HR	RBI	PO	A	E	DP	TC/G	FA	Pitcher	G	IP	W	L	SV	ERA
Was.	1B	J. Anderson	333	.288	0	44	615	32	11	13	10.8	.983	C. Smith	36	259	10	20	0	2.61
W-49 L-102	2B	J. Delahanty	404	.292	2	54	172	180	22	18	5.5	.941	C. Patten	36	237	12	16	0	3.56
Joe Cantillon	SS	D. Altizer	540	.269	1	42	157	251	32	23	6.2	.927	C. Falkenberg	32	234	6	17	0	2.35
	3B	B. Shipke	189	.196	1	9	57	127	11	2	3.1	.944	L. Hughes	34	211	7	14	4	3.11
	RF	B. Ganley	605	.276	1	35	276	23	19	5	2.1	.940	W. Johnson	14	111	5	9	0	1.87
	CF	C. Jones	437	.265	0	37	226	6	8	2	2.2	.967	O. Graham	20	104	4	9	0	3.98
	LF	O. Clymer	206	.316	1	16	79	4	8	0	1.8	.912	H. Gehring	15	87	3	7	0	3.31
	C	J. Warner	207	.256	0	17	271	64	10	4	5.4	.971							
	2O	R. Nill	215	.219	0	25	113	106	8	9		.965							
	1O	P. Hickman	193	.285	1	23	306	20	13	13		.962							
	OF	C. Milan	183	.279	0	9	80	12	7	1	2.1	.929							
	C	M. Heydon	164	.183	0	9	247	52	12	4	5.5	.961							
	3B	L. Cross	161	.199	0	10	38	98	3	2	3.4	.978							

BATTING AND BASE RUNNING LEADERS

Batting Average

T. Cobb, DET	.350
S. Crawford, DET	.323
G. Stone, STL	.320
E. Flick, CLE	.302
S. Nicholls, PHI	.302

Slugging Average

T. Cobb, DET	.473
S. Crawford, DET	.460
E. Flick, CLE	.412
G. Stone, STL	.399
H. Davis, PHI	.397

Home Runs

H. Davis, PHI	8
S. Seybold, PHI	5
T. Cobb, DET	5

Total Bases

T. Cobb, DET	286
S. Crawford, DET	268
G. Stone, STL	238
H. Davis, PHI	231
E. Flick, CLE	226

Runs Batted In

T. Cobb, DET	116
S. Seybold, PHI	92
H. Davis, PHI	87
S. Crawford, DET	81
B. Wallace, STL	70

Stolen Bases

T. Cobb, DET	49
W. Conroy, NY	41
E. Flick, CLE	41
B. Ganley, WAS	40
D. Altizer, WAS	38

Hits

T. Cobb, DET	212
G. Stone, STL	191
S. Crawford, DET	188

Base on Balls

T. Hartsel, PHI	106
E. Hahn, CHI	84
F. Jones, CHI	67

Home Run Percentage

H. Davis, PHI	1.4
S. Seybold, PHI	0.9
T. Cobb, DET	0.8

Runs Scored

S. Crawford, DET	102
D. Jones, DET	101
T. Cobb, DET	97

Doubles

H. Davis, PHI	36
S. Crawford, DET	34
N. Lajoie, CLE	30
J. Collins, BOS, PHI	30

Triples

E. Flick, CLE	18
S. Crawford, DET	17
T. Cobb, DET	15
B. Unglaub, BOS	13

PITCHING LEADERS

Winning Percentage

W. Donovan, DET	.862
J. Dygert, PHI	.724
A. Joss, CLE	.711
C. Bender, PHI	.708
F. Smith, CHI	.697

Earned Run Average

E. Walsh, CHI	1.60
E. Killian, DET	1.78
A. Joss, CLE	1.83
W. Johnson, WAS	1.87
H. Howell, STL	1.93

Wins

A. Joss, CLE	27
D. White, CHI	27
W. Donovan, DET	25
E. Killian, DET	25
E. Plank, PHI	24
E. Walsh, CHI	24

Saves

L. Hughes, WAS	4
B. Dinneen, BOS, STL	4
E. Walsh, CHI	4

Strikeouts

R. Waddell, PHI	232
E. Walsh, CHI	206
E. Plank, PHI	183
J. Dygert, PHI	151
C. Young, BOS	147

Complete Games

E. Walsh, CHI	37
G. Mullin, DET	35
A. Joss, CLE	34
C. Young, BOS	33
E. Plank, PHI	33

Fewest Hits per 9 Innings

J. Dygert, PHI	6.88
G. Winter, BOS	6.94
E. Walsh, CHI	7.27

Shutouts

E. Plank, PHI	8
R. Waddell, PHI	7
D. White, CHI	7

Fewest Walks per 9 Innings

D. White, CHI	1.18
N. Altrock, CHI	1.31
C. Young, BOS	1.34

Most Strikeouts per 9 Inn.

R. Waddell, PHI	7.33
W. Johnson, WAS	5.53
J. Dygert, PHI	5.19

Innings

E. Walsh, CHI	422
G. Mullin, DET	357
E. Plank, PHI	344

Games Pitched

E. Walsh, CHI	56
D. White, CHI	47
G. Mullin, DET	46

	W	L	PCT	GB	R	OR	Batting 2B	3B	HR	BA	SA	SB	Fielding E	DP	FA	CG	BB	Pitching SO	ShO	SV	ERA
DET	92	58	.613		696	519	180	76	11	.266	.336	192	260	79	.959	120	380	512	15	7	2.33
PHI	88	57	.607	1.5	582	509	220	45	22	.255	.330	138	263	67	.958	106	378	789	27	6	2.35
CHI	87	64	.576	5.5	584	475	148	34	6	.237	.283	175	233	101	.966	112	305	604	17	9	2.22
CLE	85	67	.559	8	528	523	182	68	11	.241	.310	193	264	137	.960	127	362	513	20	5	2.26
NY	70	78	.473	21	604	671	150	67	14	.249	.314	206	334	79	.947	93	428	511	9	5	3.03
STL	69	83	.454	24	538	560	154	63	9	.253	.312	144	266	97	.959	129	352	463	15	9	2.61
BOS	59	90	.396	32.5	466	556	155	48	18	.234	.292	124	274	103	.959	100	337	517	17	6	2.45
WAS	49	102	.325	43.5	505	690	137	57	12	.243	.300	223	311	69	.952	106	341	569	11	5	3.11
					4503	4503	1326	458	103	.247	.310	1395	2205	732	.958	893	2883	4478	131	52	2.54

Chi.
W-99 L-55
Frank Chance

POS	Player	AB	BA	HR	RBI	PO	A	E	DP	TC/G	FA	Pitcher	G	IP	W	L	SV	ERA
1B	F. Chance	452	.272	2	55	1291	86	15	56	11.0	.989	T. Brown	44	312	29	9	5	1.47
2B	J. Evers	416	.300	0	37	237	361	25	39	5.1	.960	E. Reulbach	46	298	24	7	1	2.03
SS	J. Tinker	548	.266	6	68	314	570	39	48	5.9	.958	J. Pfiester	33	252	12	10	0	2.00
3B	H. Steinfeldt	539	.241	1	62	166	275	28	15	3.1	.940	O. Overall	37	225	15	11	2	1.92
RF	W. Schulte	386	.236	1	43	148	11	1	3	1.6	.994	C. Fraser	26	163	11	9	2	2.27
CF	J. Slagle	352	.222	0	26	199	6	5	2	2.1	.976	C. Lundgren	23	139	6	9	0	4.22
LF	J. Sheckard	403	.231	2	22	201	13	10	3	1.9	.955							
C	J. Kling	424	.276	4	59	596	149	16	11	6.5	.979							
UT	S. Hofman	411	.243	2	42	532	97	23	16		.965							
OF	D. Howard	315	.279	1	26	129	10	5	1	1.8	.965							

N. Y.
W-98 L-56
John McGraw

POS	Player	AB	BA	HR	RBI	PO	A	E	DP	TC/G	FA	Pitcher	G	IP	W	L	SV	ERA
1B	F. Tenney	583	.256	2	49	1634	117	18	68	11.3	.990	C. Mathewson	56	391	37	11	5	1.43
2B	L. Doyle	377	.308	0	33	180	291	33	28	4.9	.935	H. Wiltse	44	330	23	14	2	2.24
SS	A. Bridwell	467	.285	0	46	277	486	39	39	5.6	.933	D. Crandall	32	215	12	10	0	2.93
3B	A. Devlin	534	.253	2	45	203	331	30	19	3.6	.947	J. McGinnity	37	186	11	7	4	2.27
RF	M. Donlin	593	.334	6	106	239	21	6	1	1.7	.977	D. Taylor	27	128	8	5	2	2.33
CF	C. Seymour	587	.267	5	92	340	29	20	9	2.5	.949	R. Ames	18	114	7	4	0	1.81
LF	S. Shannon	268	.224	1	21	114	8	3	3	1.7	.976							
C	R. Bresnahan	449	.283	1	54	657	140	12	12	5.8	.985							
OF	M. McCormick	252	.302	0	32	97	3	11	2	1.7	.901							
2B	B. Herzog	160	.300	0	11	61	125	16	19	4.8	.921							

Pit.
W-98 L-56
Fred Clarke

POS	Player	AB	BA	HR	RBI	PO	A	E	DP	TC/G	FA	Pitcher	G	IP	W	L	SV	ERA
1B	H. Swacina	176	.216	0	13	501	19	9	19	10.6	.983	V. Willis	41	305	23	11	0	2.07
2B	A. Abbaticchio	500	.250	1	61	268	423	22	42	5.0	.969	N. Maddox	36	261	23	8	1	2.28
SS	H. Wagner	568	.354	10	109	354	469	50	47	5.8	.943	H. Camnitz	38	237	16	9	2	1.56
3B	T. Leach	583	.259	5	41	199	293	33	19	3.5	.937	L. Leifield	34	219	15	14	2	2.10
RF	O. Wilson	529	.227	3	43	258	20	13	3	2.0	.955	S. Leever	38	193	15	7	2	2.10
CF	R. Thomas	386	.256	1	24	269	7	7	4	2.8*	.975							
LF	F. Clarke	551	.265	2	53	350	15	10	2	2.5	.973							
C	G. Gibson	486	.228	2	45	607	136	21	10	5.5	.973							
1B	A. Storke	202	.252	1	12	481	17	6	19	10.3	.988							
1B	J. Kane	145	.241	0	22	378	24	14	19	10.4	.966							

Phi.
W-83 L-71
Billy Murray

POS	Player	AB	BA	HR	RBI	PO	A	E	DP	TC/G	FA	Pitcher	G	IP	W	L	SV	ERA
1B	K. Bransfield	527	.304	3	71	1472	89	22	67	11.1	.986	G. McQuillan	48	360	23	17	2	1.53
2B	O. Knabe	555	.218	0	27	344	470	26	42	5.6	.969	T. Sparks	33	263	16	15	2	2.60
SS	M. Doolan	445	.234	2	49	269	419	45	32	5.7	.939	F. Corridon	27	208	14	10	1	2.51
3B	E. Grant	598	.244	0	32	197	271	35	22	3.8	.930	L. Richie	25	158	7	10	1	1.83
RF	J. Titus	539	.286	2	48	215	22	9	3	1.7	.963	L. Moren	28	154	8	9	0	2.92
CF	F. Osborn	555	.267	2	44	359	14	12	3	2.5	.969	B. Foxen	22	147	7	7	0	1.95
LF	S. Magee	508	.283	2	57	279	15	9	5	2.1	.970							
C	R. Dooin	435	.248	0	41	554	191	26	17	5.8	.966							
UT	E. Courtney	160	.181	0	6	157	61	6	7		.973							

Cin.
W-73 L-81
John Ganzel

POS	Player	AB	BA	HR	RBI	PO	A	E	DP	TC/G	FA	Pitcher	G	IP	W	L	SV	ERA
1B	J. Ganzel	388	.250	1	53	1116	61	12	52	11.0	.990	B. Ewing	37	294	17	15	3	2.21
2B	M. Huggins	498	.239	0	23	302	406	30	45	5.5	.959	B. Spade	35	249	17	12	1	2.74
SS	R. Hulswitt	386	.228	1	28	242	368	42	37	5.5	.936	A. Coakley	35	242	8	18	2	1.86
3B	H. Lobert	570	.293	4	63	121	181	26	11	3.3	.921	B. Campbell	35	221	12	13	1	2.60
RF	M. Mitchell	406	.222	1	37	193	16	9	2	1.8	.959	J. Weimer	15	117	8	7	0	2.39
CF	J. Kane	455	.213	3	23	292	15	6	2	2.5	.981	J. Dubuc	15	85	5	6	0	2.74
LF	D. Paskert	395	.243	1	36	251	15	13	3	2.4	.953							
C	A. Schlei	300	.220	1	22	355	96	18	10	5.3	.962							
C	L. McLean	309	.217	1	28	280	82	14	9	5.4	.963							
3B	M. Mowrey	227	.220	0	23	51	110	11	6	3.1	.936							

Bos.
W-63 L-91
Joe Kelley

POS	Player	AB	BA	HR	RBI	PO	A	E	DP	TC/G	FA	Pitcher	G	IP	W	L	SV	ERA
1B	D. McGann	475	.240	2	55	1229	93	16	66	11.1	.988	V. Lindaman	43	271	12	16	1	2.36
2B	C. Ritchey	421	.273	2	36	325	368	24	46	6.0	.967	P. Flaherty	31	244	12	18	0	3.25
SS	B. Dahlen	524	.239	3	48	291	553	43	58	6.2	.952	G. Dorner	38	216	8	19	0	3.54
3B	B. Sweeney	418	.244	0	40	174	277	34	14	3.9	.930	G. Ferguson	37	208	12	11	0	2.47
RF	G. Browne	536	.228	1	34	248	20	14	8	2.0	.950	I. Young	16	85	4	8	0	2.86
CF	G. Beaumont	476	.267	2	52	259	17	10	3	2.4	.965							
LF	J. Bates	445	.258	1	29	205	15	12	2	2.0	.948							
C	F. Bowerman	254	.228	1	25	228	69	9	12	4.9	.971							
UT	J. Hannifin	257	.206	2	22	152	179	19	15		.946							
OF	J. Kelley	228	.259	2	17	71	5	5	1	2.1	.938							
C	P. Graham	215	.274	0	22	242	75	15	6	5.4	.955							
OF	B. Becker	171	.275	0	7	40	8	3	1	1.2	.941							

Bkn.
W-53 L-101
Patsy Donovan

POS	Player	AB	BA	HR	RBI	PO	A	E	DP	TC/G	FA	Pitcher	G	IP	W	L	SV	ERA
1B	T. Jordan	515	.247	12	60	1462	55	28	52	10.6	.982	N. Rucker	42	333	17	19	0	2.08
2B	H. Pattee	264	.216	0	9	158	246	15	15	5.7	.964	K. Wilhelm	42	332	16	22	0	1.87
SS	P. Lewis	415	.219	1	30	227	352	35	33	5.3	.943	H. McIntyre	40	288	11	20	2	2.69
3B	T. Sheehan	468	.214	0	29	174	280	34	13	3.4	.930	J. Pastorius	28	214	4	20	0	2.44
RF	H. Lumley	440	.216	4	39	157	13	8	6	1.5	.955	G. Bell	29	155	4	15	1	3.59
CF	B. Maloney	359	.195	3	17	238	11	14	4	2.6	.947							
LF	A. Burch	456	.243	2	18	242	24	8	6	2.4	.971							
C	B. Bergen	302	.175	0	15	470	137	7	9	6.2	.989							
UT	J. Hummel	594	.241	4	41	367	182	18	25		.968							
2B	W. Alperman	213	.197	1	15	74	110	13	8	4.7	.934							

POS	Player	AB	BA	HR	RBI	PO	A	E	DP	TC/G	FA	Pitcher	G	IP	W	L	SV	ERA
1B	E. Konetchy	545	.248	5	50	1610	**122**	24	61	**11.4**	.986	B. Raymond	48	324	15	**25**	2	2.03
2B	B. Gilbert	276	.214	0	10	222	254	24	23	5.6	.952	J. Lush	38	251	11	18	1	2.12
SS	P. O'Rourke	164	.195	0	16	80	171	41	10	5.5	.860	F. Beebe	29	174	5	13	0	2.63
3B	B. Byrne	439	.191	0	14	183	248	**35**	14	3.8	.925	E. Karger	22	141	4	9	0	3.06
RF	R. Murray	593	.282	7	62	274	22	**28**	4	2.1	.914	S. Sallee	25	129	3	8	0	3.15
CF	A. Shaw	367	.264	1	19	179	23	15	7	2.4	.931	A. Fromme	20	116	5	13	0	2.72
LF	J. Delahanty	499	.255	1	44	243	11	6	1	1.9	.977	Higginbotham	19	107	3	8	0	3.20
C	B. Ludwig	187	.182	0	8	227	87	16	2	5.3	.952							
UT	C. Charles	454	.205	1	17	215	322	49	25		.916							
OF	S. Barry	268	.228	0	11	109	10	4	0	1.8	.967							
C	Hoelskoetter	155	.232	0	6	182	56	13	6	6.1	.948							

St. L.
W-49 L-105
John McCloskey

BATTING AND BASE RUNNING LEADERS

Batting Average

H. Wagner, PIT	.354
M. Donlin, NY	.334
L. Doyle, NY	.308
K. Bransfield, PHI	.304
J. Evers, CHI	.300

Slugging Average

H. Wagner, PIT	.542
M. Donlin, NY	.452
S. Magee, PHI	.417
H. Lobert, CIN	.407
R. Murray, STL	.400

Home Runs

T. Jordan, BKN	12
H. Wagner, PIT	10
R. Murray, STL	7
J. Tinker, CHI	6
M. Donlin, NY	6

Total Bases

H. Wagner, PIT	308
M. Donlin, NY	268
R. Murray, STL	237
H. Lobert, CIN	232
T. Leach, PIT	222

Runs Batted In

H. Wagner, PIT	109
M. Donlin, NY	106
C. Seymour, NY	92
K. Bransfield, PHI	71
J. Tinker, CHI	68

Stolen Bases

H. Wagner, PIT	53
R. Murray, STL	48
H. Lobert, CIN	47
S. Magee, PHI	40
J. Evers, CHI	36

Hits

H. Wagner, PIT	201
M. Donlin, NY	198
H. Lobert, CIN	167
R. Murray, STL	167

Base on Balls

R. Bresnahan, NY	83
F. Tenney, NY	72
J. Evers, CHI	66

Home Run Percentage

T. Jordan, BKN	2.3
H. Wagner, PIT	1.8
R. Murray, STL	1.2

Runs Scored

F. Tenney, NY	101
H. Wagner, PIT	100
T. Leach, PIT	93

Doubles

H. Wagner, PIT	39
S. Magee, PHI	30
F. Chance, CHI	27

Triples

H. Wagner, PIT	19
H. Lobert, CIN	18
S. Magee, PHI	16
T. Leach, PIT	16

PITCHING LEADERS

Winning Percentage

E. Reulbach, CHI	.774
C. Mathewson, NY	.771
T. Brown, CHI	.763
N. Maddox, PIT	.742
V. Willis, PIT	.676

Earned Run Average

C. Mathewson, NY	1.43
T. Brown, CHI	1.47
G. McQuillan, PHI	1.53
H. Camnitz, PIT	1.56
A. Coakley, CHI, CIN	1.78

Wins

C. Mathewson, NY	37
T. Brown, CHI	29
E. Reulbach, CHI	24

Saves

T. Brown, CHI	5
C. Mathewson, NY	5
J. McGinnity, NY	4
B. Ewing, CIN	3

Strikeouts

C. Mathewson, NY	259
N. Rucker, BKN	199
O. Overall, CHI	167
B. Raymond, STL	145
E. Reulbach, CHI	133

Complete Games

C. Mathewson, NY	34
K. Wilhelm, BKN	33
G. McQuillan, PHI	32
N. Rucker, BKN	30
H. Wiltse, NY	30

Fewest Hits per 9 Innings

T. Brown, CHI	6.17
B. Raymond, STL	6.55
C. Mathewson, NY	6.57

Shutouts

C. Mathewson, NY	12
T. Brown, CHI	9

Fewest Walks per 9 Innings

C. Mathewson, NY	0.97
T. Brown, CHI	1.41
T. Sparks, PHI	1.74

Most Strikeouts per 9 Inn.

O. Overall, CHI	6.68
C. Mathewson, NY	5.97
N. Rucker, BKN	5.37

Innings

C. Mathewson, NY	391
G. McQuillan, PHI	360
N. Rucker, BKN	333

Games Pitched

C. Mathewson, NY	56
G. McQuillan, PHI	48
B. Raymond, STL	48

	W	L	PCT	GB	R	OR	Batting 2B	3B	HR	BA	SA	SB	Fielding E	DP	FA	Pitching CG	BB	SO	ShO	SV	ERA
CHI	99	55	.643		625	457	**197**	56	19	.249	.321	**212**	**206**	76	**.969**	108	437	**668**	**28**	10	2.14
NY	98	56	.636	1	**652**	458	182	43	20	**.267**	**.333**	181	250	79	.962	95	**288**	656	25	**15**	2.14
PIT	98	56	.636	1	585	474	162	**98**	25	.247	.332	186	226	74	.964	100	406	468	24	8	2.12
PHI	83	71	.539	16	503	**446**	194	68	11	.244	.316	200	238	75	.963	116	379	476	22	6	**2.10**
CIN	73	81	.474	26	488	542	129	77	14	.227	.294	196	255	72	.959	110	415	433	17	7	2.37
BOS	63	91	.409	36	537	621	137	43	17	.239	.293	134	252	**90**	.962	92	423	416	14	1	2.79
BKN	53	101	.344	46	375	515	110	60	**28**	.213	.277	113	247	66	.961	**118**	444	535	20	3	2.47
STL	49	105	.318	50	372	624	134	57	17	.223	.283	150	348	68	.946	97	430	528	13	4	2.64
					4137	4137	1245	502	151	.239	.306	1372	2022	600	.961	836	3222	4180	163	54	2.35

Det. W-90 L-63 — Hughie Jennings

POS	Player	AB	BA	HR	RBI	PO	A	E	DP	TC/G	FA	Pitcher	G	IP	W	L	SV	ERA
1B	C. Rossman	524	.294	2	71	1429	102	29	70	11.3	.981	E. Summers	40	301	24	12	1	1.64
2B	R. Downs	289	.221	1	35	180	265	36	24	5.9	.925	G. Mullin	39	291	17	13	0	3.10
SS	G. Schaefer	584	.259	3	52	162	254	37	35	6.7	.918	W. Donovan	29	243	18	7	0	2.08
3B	B. Coughlin	405	.215	0	23	129	214	21	12	3.1	.942	E. Willett	30	197	15	8	1	2.28
RF	T. Cobb	581	.324	4	108	212	23	14	5	1.7	.944	E. Killian	27	181	12	9	1	2.99
CF	S. Crawford	591	.311	7	80	252	9	8	2	2.0	.970							
LF	M. McIntyre	569	.295	0	28	329	17	8	4	2.3	.977							
C	B. Schmidt	419	.265	1	38	541	184	37	12	6.3	.951							
SS	C. O'Leary	211	.251	0	17	130	179	27	15	5.3	.920							

Cle. W-90 L-64 — Nap Lajoie

POS	Player	AB	BA	HR	RBI	PO	A	E	DP	TC/G	FA	Pitcher	G	IP	W	L	SV	ERA
1B	G. Stovall	534	.292	2	45	1509	87	16	79	12.2	.990	A. Joss	42	325	24	11	2	1.16
2B	N. Lajoie	581	.289	2	74	450	538	37	78	6.6	.964	B. Rhoads	37	270	18	12	0	1.77
SS	G. Perring	310	.216	0	19	74	159	18	15	5.2	.928	G. Liebhardt	39	262	15	16	0	2.20
3B	B. Bradley	548	.243	1	46	142	209	23	13	3.2	.939	H. Berger	29	199	13	8	0	2.12
RF	B. Hinchman	464	.231	6	59	106	13	3	1	1.6	.975	C. Chech	27	166	11	7	0	1.74
CF	J. Birmingham	413	.213	2	38	250	20	12	6	2.3	.957							
LF	J. Clarke	492	.242	1	21	220	13	9	1	1.8	.963							
C	N. Clarke	290	.241	1	27	327	108	14	6	5.0	.969							
C	H. Bemis	277	.224	0	33	326	74	15	5	5.5	.964							
OS	T. Turner	201	.239	0	19	65	68	6	4		.957							
O1	P. Hickman	197	.234	2	16	248	20	12	7		.957							
OF	W. Good	154	.279	1	14	62	0	11	0	1.7	.849							

Chi. W-88 L-64 — Fielder Jones

POS	Player	AB	BA	HR	RBI	PO	A	E	DP	TC/G	FA	Pitcher	G	IP	W	L	SV	ERA
1B	J. Donahue	304	.204	0	22	968	57	6	30	12.4	.994	E. Walsh	66	464	40	15	6	1.42
2B	G. Davis	419	.217	0	26	191	314	21	25	5.5	.960	F. Smith	41	298	16	17	1	2.03
SS	F. Parent	391	.207	0	35	212	442	49	33	6.0	.930	D. White	41	296	18	13	0	2.55
3B	L. Tannehill	482	.216	0	35	135	341	33	15	3.7	.935	F. Owen	25	140	6	7	0	3.41
RF	E. Hahn	447	.251	0	21	160	4	6	2	1.4	.965	N. Altrock	23	136	5	7	2	2.71
CF	F. Jones	529	.253	1	50	288	17	10	5	2.1	.968							
LF	P. Dougherty	482	.278	0	45	173	7	10	1	1.4	.947							
C	B. Sullivan	430	.191	0	29	553	156	11	11	5.3	.985							
OF	J. Anderson	355	.262	0	47	96	9	4	7	1.2	.963							
1B	F. Isbell	320	.247	1	49	824	46	9	30	13.5	.990							
2B	J. Atz	206	.194	0	27	82	137	15	12	5.1	.936							
P	E. Walsh	157	.172	1	10	41	190	6	9	3.6	.975							

St. L. W-83 L-69 — Jimmy McAleer

POS	Player	AB	BA	HR	RBI	PO	A	E	DP	TC/G	FA	Pitcher	G	IP	W	L	SV	ERA
1B	T. Jones	549	.246	1	50	1616	90	24	79	11.2	.986	H. Howell	41	324	18	18	1	1.89
2B	J. Williams	539	.236	4	53	352	445	31	50	5.6	.963	R. Waddell	43	286	19	14	3	1.89
SS	B. Wallace	487	.253	1	60	286	510	41	45	6.1	.951	J. Powell	33	256	16	13	1	2.11
3B	H. Ferris	555	.270	2	74	222	316	27	27	3.8	.952	B. Dinneen	27	167	14	7	0	2.10
RF	R. Hartzell	422	.265	2	32	117	15	8	5	1.7	.943	B. Pelty	20	122	7	4	0	1.99
CF	D. Hoffman	363	.251	1	25	185	19	8	8	2.1	.962	B. Graham	21	117	6	7	0	2.30
LF	G. Stone	588	.281	5	31	274	11	16	3	2.0	.947	B. Bailey	22	107	3	5	0	3.04
C	T. Spencer	286	.210	0	28	398	109	9	9	5.8	.983							
OF	C. Jones	263	.232	0	17	116	13	5	2	1.9	.963							
OF	A. Schweitzer	182	.291	1	14	86	14	5	3	1.9	.952							

Bos. W-75 L-79 — Deacon McGuire / Fred Lake   W-53 L-62   W-22 L-17

POS	Player	AB	BA	HR	RBI	PO	A	E	DP	TC/G	FA	Pitcher	G	IP	W	L	SV	ERA
1B	J. Stahl	258	.248	0	23	830	45	12	34	11.2	.986	C. Young	36	299	21	11	2	1.26
2B	A. McConnell	502	.279	2	43	237	349	38	32	5.0	.939	E. Cicotte	39	207	11	12	2	2.43
SS	H. Wagner	526	.247	1	46	373	569	61	51	6.6	.939	C. Morgan	30	205	14	13	1	2.46
3B	H. Lord	558	.260	2	37	181	271	47	13	3.5	.906	F. Burchell	31	180	10	8	0	2.96
RF	D. Gessler	435	.308	3	63	162	8	9	4	1.4	.950	G. Winter	22	148	4	14	0	3.05
CF	D. Sullivan	353	.241	0	25	193	18	4	4	2.2	.981*	E. Steele	16	118	5	7	0	1.83
LF	J. Thoney	416	.255	0	30	208	12	12	2	2.3	.948	T. Pruiett	13	59	1	7	2	1.99
C	L. Criger	237	.190	0	25	380	120	10	11	6.1	.980							
OF	G. Cravath	277	.256	1	34	128	7	11	3	1.9	.925							
1B	B. Unglaub	266	.263	1	25	744	50	16	22	11.3	.980							
UT	F. LaPorte	156	.237	0	15	67	115	10	7		.948							

Phi. W-68 L-85 — Connie Mack

POS	Player	AB	BA	HR	RBI	PO	A	E	DP	TC/G	FA	Pitcher	G	IP	W	L	SV	ERA
1B	H. Davis	513	.248	5	62	1410	86	22	44	10.3	.986	R. Vickers	53	300	18	19	1	2.34
2B	E. Collins	330	.273	1	40	111	127	14	5	5.4	.944	E. Plank	34	245	14	16	1	2.17
SS	S. Nicholls	550	.216	4	31	221	370	56	26	5.4	.913	J. Dygert	41	239	11	15	1	2.87
3B	J. Collins	433	.217	0	30	117	216	26	14	3.1	.928	J. Coombs	26	153	7	5	0	2.00
RF	D. Murphy	525	.265	4	66	145	11	6	4	1.9	.963	C. Bender	18	139	8	9	1	1.75
CF	R. Oldring	434	.221	1	39	246	9	16	3	2.3	.941	B. Schlitzer	24	131	6	8	0	3.16
LF	T. Hartsel	460	.243	4	29	211	6	9	2	1.8	.960							
C	Schreckengost	207	.222	0	16	352	91	10	3	6.9	.978							
OP	J. Coombs	220	.255	1	23	102	48	4	4		.974							
C	M. Powers	172	.180	0	7	303	74	13	3	6.5	.967							

Was. W-67 L-85 — Joe Cantillon

POS	Player	AB	BA	HR	RBI	PO	A	E	DP	TC/G	FA	Pitcher	G	IP	W	L	SV	ERA
1B	J. Freeman	531	.252	1	45	1548	66	41	69	10.7	.975	L. Hughes	43	276	18	15	4	2.21
2B	J. Delahanty	287	.317	1	30	181	232	16	25	5.4	.963	W. Johnson	36	257	14	14	1	1.64
SS	G. McBride	518	.232	0	34	372	568	52	58	6.4	.948	C. Smith	26	184	9	13	1	2.40
3B	B. Shipke	341	.208	0	20	111	190	22	11	2.9	.932	B. Keeley	28	170	6	11	1	2.97
RF	O. Clymer	368	.253	1	35	81	16	7	7	1.3	.933	B. Burns	23	165	6	11	0	1.69
CF	C. Milan	485	.239	1	32	265	18	12	6	2.4	.959	E. Cates	19	115	4	8	0	2.51
LF	B. Ganley	549	.239	1	36	280	13	11	1	2.0	.964							
C	G. Street	394	.206	1	32	578	167	21	14	6.0	.973							
OF	O. Pickering	373	.225	2	30	135	6	9	1	1.5	.940							
32	B. Unglaub	276	.308	0	29	111	178	15	12		.951							
23	D. Altizer	205	.224	0	18	87	145	13	13		.947							

	POS	Player	AB	BA	HR	RBI	PO	A	E	DP	TC/G	FA	Pitcher	G	IP	W	L	SV	ERA
N. Y.	1B	H. Chase	405	.257	1	36	1020	54	22	35	11.4	.980	J. Chesbro	45	289	14	20	0	2.93
W-51 L-103	2B	H. Niles	361	.249	4	24	166	220	30	15	4.9	.928	J. Lake	38	269	9	22	0	3.17
Clark Griffith	SS	N. Ball	446	.247	0	38	268	438	80	28	6.0	.898	R. Manning	41	245	13	16	1	2.94
W-24 L-32	3B	W. Conroy	531	.237	1	39	179	249	28	12	3.8	.939	B. Hogg	24	152	4	16	0	3.01
Kid Elberfeld	RF	W. Keeler	323	.263	1	14	123	9	9	2	1.6	.936	A. Orth	21	139	2	13	0	3.42
W-27 L-71	CF	C. Hemphill	505	.297	0	44	285	13	20	2	2.2	.937	D. Newton	23	88	4	5	1	2.95
	LF	J. Stahl	274	.255	2	42	111	14	9	3	2.0	.933							
	C	R. Kleinow	279	.168	1	13	281	116	14	5	4.6	.966							
	UT	G. Moriarty	348	.236	0	27	609	117	24	30		.968							
	C	W. Blair	211	.190	1	13	225	58	12	4	1.9	.959							
	OF	I. McIlveen	169	.213	0	8	70	4	4	0	1.8	.949							

BATTING AND BASE RUNNING LEADERS

Batting Average
T. Cobb, DET	.324
S. Crawford, DET	.311
D. Gessler, BOS	.308
C. Hemphill, NY	.297
M. McIntyre, DET	.295

Slugging Average
T. Cobb, DET	.475
S. Crawford, DET	.457
D. Gessler, BOS	.423
C. Rossman, DET	.418
M. McIntyre, DET	.383

Home Runs
S. Crawford, DET	7
B. Hinchman, CLE	6
H. Niles, BOS, NY	5
H. Davis, PHI	5
G. Stone, STL	5

Total Bases
T. Cobb, DET	276
S. Crawford, DET	270
C. Rossman, DET	219
M. McIntyre, DET	218
N. Lajoie, CLE	218

Runs Batted In
T. Cobb, DET	108
S. Crawford, DET	80
H. Ferris, STL	74
N. Lajoie, CLE	74
C. Rossman, DET	71

Stolen Bases
P. Dougherty, CHI	47
C. Hemphill, NY	42
G. Schaefer, DET	40
T. Cobb, DET	39
J. Clarke, CLE	37

Hits
T. Cobb, DET	188
S. Crawford, DET	184
M. McIntyre, DET	168
N. Lajoie, CLE	168

Base on Balls
T. Hartsel, PHI	93
F. Jones, CHI	86
M. McIntyre, DET	83

Home Run Percentage
B. Hinchman, CLE	1.3
H. Niles, BOS, NY	1.3
S. Crawford, DET	1.2

Runs Scored
M. McIntyre, DET	105
S. Crawford, DET	102
G. Schaefer, DET	96

Doubles
T. Cobb, DET	36
C. Rossman, DET	33
S. Crawford, DET	33

Triples
T. Cobb, DET	20
J. Stahl, BOS, NY	16
S. Crawford, DET	16

PITCHING LEADERS

Winning Percentage
E. Walsh, CHI	.727
W. Donovan, DET	.720
A. Joss, CLE	.686
E. Summers, DET	.667
C. Young, BOS	.656

Earned Run Average
A. Joss, CLE	1.16
C. Young, BOS	1.26
E. Walsh, CHI	1.42
W. Johnson, WAS	1.64
E. Summers, DET	1.64

Wins
E. Walsh, CHI	40
A. Joss, CLE	24
E. Summers, DET	24
C. Young, BOS	21

Saves
E. Walsh, CHI	6
L. Hughes, WAS	4
J. Chesbro, NY	3
R. Waddell, STL	3

Strikeouts
E. Walsh, CHI	269
R. Waddell, STL	232
L. Hughes, WAS	165
J. Dygert, PHI	164
W. Johnson, WAS	160

Complete Games
E. Walsh, CHI	42
C. Young, BOS	30
A. Joss, CLE	29
H. Howell, STL	27
G. Mullin, DET	26

Fewest Hits per 9 Innings
A. Joss, CLE	6.42
F. Smith, CHI	6.44
E. Walsh, CHI	6.65

Shutouts
E. Walsh, CHI	11
A. Joss, CLE	9

Fewest Walks per 9 Innings
A. Joss, CLE	0.83
B. Burns, WAS	0.98
E. Walsh, CHI	1.09

Most Strikeouts per 9 Inn.
R. Waddell, STL	7.31
J. Dygert, PHI	6.18
W. Johnson, WAS	5.60

Innings
E. Walsh, CHI	464
A. Joss, CLE	325
H. Howell, STL	324

Games Pitched
E. Walsh, CHI	66
R. Vickers, PHI	53
J. Chesbro, NY	45

	W	L	PCT	GB	R	OR	2B	3B	HR	BA	SA	SB	E	DP	FA	CG	BB	SO	ShO	SV	ERA
DET	90	63	.588		645	552	199	86	19	.264	.347	165	305	95	.953	120	318	553	15	5	2.40
CLE	90	64	.584	.5	570	471	188	58	18	.239	.309	169	257	95	.962	108	328	548	18	5	2.02
CHI	88	64	.579	1.5	535	480	145	41	3	.224	.271	209	232	82	.966	107	284	623	23	10	2.22
STL	83	69	.546	6.5	543	478	173	56	21	.245	.312	126	237	97	.964	107	387	607	16	5	2.15
BOS	75	79	.487	15.5	563	515	116	88	14	.246	.312	168	297	71	.955	102	366	624	12	7	2.27
PHI	68	85	.444	22	487	554	183	49	21	.223	.291	116	272	68	.957	102	409	740	23	4	2.57
WAS	67	85	.441	22.5	479	530	131	74	8	.235	.295	170	275	89	.958	105	348	649	14	7	2.34
NY	51	103	.331	39.5	458	700	142	51	12	.236	.291	230	337	78	.947	91	457	584	11	3	3.16
					4280	4280	1277	503	116	.239	.304	1353	2212	675	.958	842	2897	4928	132	46	2.39

Pit. W-110 L-42 Fred Clarke

POS	Player	AB	BA	HR	RBI	PO	A	E	DP	TC/G	FA
1B	B. Abstein	512	.260	1	70	1412	65	27	70	11.1	.982
2B	D. Miller	560	.279	3	87	260	426	34	50	4.8	.953
SS	H. Wagner	495	.339	5	100	344	430	49	58	6.1	.940
3B	J. Barbeau	350	.220	0	25	99	139	29*	8	3.1	.891
RF	O. Wilson	569	.272	4	59	292	19	14	7	2.1	.957
CF	T. Leach	587	.261	6	43	333	12	11	3	2.6	.969
LF	F. Clarke	550	.287	3	68	362	17	5	2	2.5	.987
C	G. Gibson	510	.265	2	52	655	192	15	9	5.7	.983
3B	B. Byrne	168	.256	0	7	50*	107*	2	3	3.5*	.987

Pitcher	G	IP	W	L	SV	ERA
V. Willis	39	290	22	11	0	2.24
H. Camnitz	41	283	25	6	3	1.62
N. Maddox	31	203	13	8	0	2.21
L. Leifield	32	202	19	8	0	2.37
D. Phillippe	22	132	8	3	0	2.32
B. Adams	25	130	12	3	2	1.11
S. Leever	19	70	8	1	2	2.83

Chi. W-104 L-49 Frank Chance

POS	Player	AB	BA	HR	RBI	PO	A	E	DP	TC/G	FA
1B	F. Chance	324	.272	0	46	901	40	6	43	10.3	.994
2B	J. Evers	463	.263	1	24	262	354	38	29	5.2	.942
SS	J. Tinker	516	.256	4	57	320	470	50	49	5.9	.940
3B	H. Steinfeldt	528	.252	2	59	183	299	31	16	3.4	.940
RF	W. Schulte	538	.264	4	60	169	14	6	1	1.4	.968
CF	S. Hofman	527	.285	2	58	347	16	13	5	2.5	.965
LF	J. Sheckard	525	.255	1	43	277	18	10	5	2.1	.967
C	J. Archer	261	.230	1	30	408	97	21	7	6.6	.960
C	P. Moran	246	.220	1	23	181	97	8	3	3.9	.972
1B	D. Howard	203	.197	1	24	593	32	13	29	11.2	.980
UT	H. Zimmerman	183	.273	0	21	100	93	19	12		.910

Pitcher	G	IP	W	L	SV	ERA
T. Brown	50	343	27	9	7	1.31
O. Overall	38	285	20	11	2	1.42
E. Reulbach	35	263	19	10	0	1.78
J. Pfiester	29	197	17	6	0	2.43
R. Kroh	17	120	9	4	0	1.65

N. Y. W-92 L-61 John McGraw

POS	Player	AB	BA	HR	RBI	PO	A	E	DP	TC/G	FA
1B	F. Tenney	375	.235	3	30	1046	72	16	53	11.6	.986
2B	L. Doyle	570	.302	6	49	292	322	39	51	4.6	.940
SS	A. Bridwell	476	.294	0	55	268	439	45	55	5.2	.940
3B	A. Devlin	491	.265	0	55	191	317	36	21	3.8	.934
RF	R. Murray	570	.263	7	91	222	30	14	1	1.8	.947
CF	B. O'Hara	360	.236	1	30	202	19	5	4	2.0	.978
LF	M. McCormick	413	.291	3	27	144	13	13	6	1.6	.924
C	A. Schlei	279	.244	0	30	493	127	24	9	7.2	.963
OF	C. Seymour	280	.311	1	30	138	11	5	3	2.1	.968
1B	F. Merkle	236	.191	0	20	621	27	16	29	9.6	.976
C	C. Meyers	220	.277	1	30	376	71	17	4	7.3	.963

Pitcher	G	IP	W	L	SV	ERA
C. Mathewson	37	275	25	6	2	1.14
B. Raymond	39	270	18	12	0	2.47
H. Wiltse	37	269	20	11	3	2.00
R. Ames	34	240	15	10	1	2.70
R. Marquard	29	173	5	13	0	2.60
D. Crandall	30	122	6	4	4	2.88

Cin. W-77 L-76 Clark Griffith

POS	Player	AB	BA	HR	RBI	PO	A	E	DP	TC/G	FA
1B	D. Hoblitzell	517	.308	4	67	1444	74	28	80	10.9	.982
2B	D. Egan	480	.275	2	53	271	376	34	45	5.9	.950
SS	T. Downey	416	.231	1	32	260	363	62	54	5.8	.909
3B	H. Lobert	425	.212	4	52	182	204	33	16	3.4	.921
RF	M. Mitchell	523	.310	4	86	262	20	11	3	2.0	.962
CF	R. Oakes	415	.270	3	31	218	15	5	3	2.1	.979
LF	B. Bescher	446	.240	1	34	247	14	13	4	2.3	.953
C	L. McLean	324	.256	2	36	379	119	11	16	5.4	.978
OF	D. Paskert	322	.252	0	33	172	11	6	3	2.3	.968
23	M. Huggins	159	.214	0	6	95	125	16	14		.932

Pitcher	G	IP	W	L	SV	ERA
A. Fromme	37	279	19	13	2	1.90
H. Gaspar	44	260	18	11	2	2.01
J. Rowan	38	226	11	12	0	2.79
B. Ewing	31	218	11	12	0	2.43
B. Campbell	30	148	7	11	2	2.67
B. Spade	14	98	5	5	0	2.85
J. Dubuc	19	71	3	5	2	3.66

Phi. W-74 L-79 Billy Murray

POS	Player	AB	BA	HR	RBI	PO	A	E	DP	TC/G	FA
1B	K. Bransfield	527	.292	1	59	1377	89	16	71	10.7	.989
2B	O. Knabe	402	.234	0	33	237	312	36	38	5.4	.938
SS	M. Doolan	493	.219	1	35	352	484	54	58	6.1	.939
3B	E. Grant	631	.269	1	37	184	310	22	18	3.4	.957
RF	J. Titus	540	.270	3	46	241	23	8	6	1.8	.971
CF	J. Bates	266	.293	1	15	130	12	6	3	2.0	.959
LF	S. Magee	522	.270	2	66	283	11	9	0	1.7	.970
C	R. Dooin	468	.224	2	38	517	199	40	14	5.4	.947
OF	F. Osborn	189	.185	0	19	126	14	3	3	2.6	.979
2B	J. Ward	184	.266	0	23	58	77	8	12	3.0	.944
OF	P. Deininger	169	.260	0	16	83	5	1	0	2.0	.989

Pitcher	G	IP	W	L	SV	ERA
E. Moore	38	300	18	12	0	2.10
L. Moren	39	254	16	15	1	2.66
G. McQuillan	41	248	13	16	2	2.14
F. Corridon	27	171	11	7	0	2.11
T. Sparks	24	122	6	11	0	2.96
H. Coveleski	24	122	6	10	1	2.74
B. Foxen	18	83	3	7	0	3.35

Bkn. W-55 L-98 Harry Lumley

POS	Player	AB	BA	HR	RBI	PO	A	E	DP	TC/G	FA
1B	T. Jordan	330	.273	3	36	937	29	17	36	10.3	.983
2B	W. Alperman	420	.248	1	41	266	297	42	32	5.3	.931
SS	T. McMillan	373	.212	0	24	190	310	47	32	5.2	.914
3B	E. Lennox	435	.262	2	44	167	210	16	18	3.2	.959
RF	H. Lumley	172	.250	0	14	83	9	5	1	1.9	.948
CF	A. Burch	601	.271	1	30	320	23	16	4	2.4	.955
LF	W. Clement	340	.256	0	17	179	14	7	4	2.3	.965
C	B. Bergen	346	.139	1	15	436	202	18	18	5.9	.973
UT	J. Hummel	542	.280	4	52	728	207	35	38		.964
UT	P. McElveen	258	.198	3	25	147	107	14	11		.948
OF	J. Kustus	173	.145	1	11	92	6	5	1	2.1	.951

Pitcher	G	IP	W	L	SV	ERA
N. Rucker	38	309	13	19	1	2.24
G. Bell	33	256	16	15	1	2.71
H. McIntyre	32	228	7	17	0	3.63
K. Wilhelm	22	163	3	13	0	3.26
D. Scanlan	19	141	8	7	0	2.93
G. Hunter	16	113	4	10	0	2.46
J. Pastorius	12	80	1	9	0	5.76

St. L. W-54 L-98 Roger Bresnahan

POS	Player	AB	BA	HR	RBI	PO	A	E	DP	TC/G	FA
1B	E. Konetchy	576	.286	4	80	1584	97	26	71	11.2	.985
2B	C. Charles	339	.236	0	29	162	186	31	28	5.3	.918
SS	R. Hulswitt	289	.280	0	29	147	200	26	16	5.7	.930
3B	B. Byrne	421	.214	1	33	164*	252*	35	11	4.3*	.922
RF	S. Evans	498	.259	2	56	212	19	13	10	1.7	.947
CF	A. Shaw	331	.248	2	34	189	14	13	1	2.3	.940
LF	R. Ellis	575	.268	3	46	332	28	17	9	2.6	.955
C	E. Phelps	306	.248	0	22	330	87	20	11	5.3	.954
O2	J. Delahanty	411	.214	2	54	203	121	22	11		.936
C	R. Bresnahan	234	.244	0	23	211	78	12	3	5.1	.960
3B	J. Barbeau	175	.251	0	5	56	72	14*	7	3.1	.901
SS	A. Storke	174	.282	0	10	93	135	10	14	5.4	.958

Pitcher	G	IP	W	L	SV	ERA
F. Beebe	44	288	15	21	1	2.82
J. Lush	34	221	11	18	0	3.13
S. Sallee	32	219	10	11	0	2.42
B. Harmon	21	159	6	11	0	3.68
L. Backman	21	128	3	11	0	4.14
J. Raleigh	15	81	1	10	0	3.79

	POS	Player	AB	BA	HR	RBI	PO	A	E	DP	TC/G	FA	Pitcher	G	IP	W	L	SV	ERA
Bos.	1B	F. Stem	245	.208	0	11	656	62	8	31	10.7	.989	A. Mattern	47	316	16	20	3	2.85
W-45 L-108	2B	D. Shean	267	.247	1	29	164	209	17	34	5.4	.956	G. Ferguson	36	227	5	23	0	3.73
Frank Bowerman	SS	J. Coffey	257	.187	0	20	133	213	40	18	5.3	.896	K. White	23	148	6	13	0	3.22
W-23 L-55	3B	B. Sweeney	493	.243	1	36	156	243	43	14	3.9	.903	L. Richie	22	132	7	7	2	2.32
Harry Smith	RF	B. Becker	562	.246	6	24	222	26	18	8	1.8	.932	B. Brown	18	123	4	10	0	3.14
W-22 L-53	CF	G. Beaumont	407	.263	0	60	234	15	8	3	2.3	.969							
	LF	R. Thomas	281	.263	0	11	155	9	4	1	2.4	.976							
	C	P. Graham	267	.240	0	17	193	111	22	14	4.3	.933							
	O1	F. Beck	334	.198	3	27	464	26	14	18		.972							
	OF	J. Bates	236	.288	1	23	123	15	8	0	2.4	.945							
	2B	C. Starr	216	.222	0	6	103	140	18	19	4.8	.931							
	1B	C. Autry	199	.196	0	13	605	38	4	27	10.6	.994							
	SS	B. Dahlen	197	.234	2	16	101	184	29	20	6.4	.908							

BATTING AND BASE RUNNING LEADERS

Batting Average
H. Wagner, PIT	.339
M. Mitchell, CIN	.310
D. Hoblitzell, CIN	.308
L. Doyle, NY	.301
A. Bridwell, NY	.294

Slugging Average
H. Wagner, PIT	.489
M. Mitchell, CIN	.430
L. Doyle, NY	.419
D. Hoblitzell, CIN	.418
M. McCormick, NY	.402

Home Runs
R. Murray, NY	7
B. Becker, BOS	6
L. Doyle, NY	6
T. Leach, PIT	6
H. Wagner, PIT	5

Total Bases
H. Wagner, PIT	242
L. Doyle, NY	238
E. Konetchy, STL	228
M. Mitchell, CIN	225
D. Miller, PIT	222

Runs Batted In
H. Wagner, PIT	100
R. Murray, NY	91
D. Miller, PIT	87
M. Mitchell, CIN	86
E. Konetchy, STL	80

Stolen Bases
B. Bescher, CIN	54
R. Murray, NY	48
D. Egan, CIN	39
S. Magee, PHI	38
A. Burch, BKN	38

Hits
L. Doyle, NY	172
E. Grant, PHI	170
H. Wagner, PIT	168

Base on Balls
F. Clarke, PIT	80
B. Byrne, PIT, STL	78
J. Evers, CHI	73

Home Run Percentage
R. Murray, NY	1.2
B. Becker, BOS	1.1
L. Doyle, NY	1.1

Runs Scored
T. Leach, PIT	126
F. Clarke, PIT	97
H. Wagner, PIT	92
B. Byrne, PIT, STL	92

Doubles
H. Wagner, PIT	39
S. Magee, PHI	33
D. Miller, PIT	31

Triples
M. Mitchell, CIN	17
S. Magee, PHI	14
E. Konetchy, STL	14
D. Miller, PIT	13

PITCHING LEADERS

Winning Percentage
H. Camnitz, PIT	.806
C. Mathewson, NY	.806
T. Brown, CHI	.750
J. Pfiester, CHI	.739
L. Leifield, PIT	.704

Earned Run Average
C. Mathewson, NY	1.14
T. Brown, CHI	1.31
O. Overall, CHI	1.42
H. Camnitz, PIT	1.62
R. Kroh, CHI	1.65

Wins
T. Brown, CHI	27
H. Camnitz, PIT	25
C. Mathewson, NY	25
V. Willis, PIT	22
O. Overall, CHI	20
H. Wiltse, NY	20

Saves
T. Brown, CHI	7
D. Crandall, NY	4
H. Camnitz, PIT	3
A. Mattern, BOS	3
L. Richie, BOS, PHI	3
H. Wiltse, NY	3

Strikeouts
O. Overall, CHI	205
N. Rucker, BKN	201
E. Moore, PHI	173
T. Brown, CHI	172
R. Ames, NY	156

Complete Games
T. Brown, CHI	32
G. Bell, BKN	29
N. Rucker, BKN	28
C. Mathewson, NY	26

Fewest Hits per 9 Innings
C. Mathewson, NY	6.28
A. Fromme, CIN	6.28
O. Overall, CHI	6.44

Shutouts
O. Overall, CHI	9
C. Mathewson, NY	8
T. Brown, CHI	8

Fewest Walks per 9 Innings
C. Mathewson, NY	1.18
T. Brown, CHI	1.39
H. Wiltse, NY	1.70

Most Strikeouts per 9 Inn.
O. Overall, CHI	6.47
R. Ames, NY	5.85
N. Rucker, BKN	5.85

Innings
T. Brown, CHI	343
A. Mattern, BOS	316
N. Rucker, BKN	309

Games Pitched
T. Brown, CHI	50
A. Mattern, BOS	47
F. Beebe, STL	44
H. Gaspar, CIN	44

	W	L	PCT	GB	R	OR	Batting 2B	3B	HR	BA	SA	SB	Fielding E	DP	FA	CG	BB	Pitching SO	ShO	SV	ERA
PIT	110	42	.724		701	448	218	92	25	.260	.353	185	227	100	.964	94	320	490	20	9	2.07
CHI	104	49	.680	6.5	632	376	203	60	20	.245	.322	187	244	95	.961	111	364	680	32	9	1.75
NY	92	61	.601	18.5	621	546	173	68	26	.255	.329	230	307	99	.954	105	397	735	16	12	2.27
CIN	77	76	.503	33.5	603	599	159	72	22	.250	.323	280	308	120	.952	91	510	477	10	9	2.52
PHI	74	79	.484	36.5	514	518	185	53	12	.244	.309	185	241	97	.961	89	470	610	17	6	2.44
BKN	55	98	.359	55.5	442	627	176	59	16	.229	.296	141	282	86	.954	84	483	435	4	2	3.10
STL	54	98	.355	56	583	728	148	56	15	.243	.303	161	322	90	.950	126	528	594	18	2	3.41
BOS	45	108	.294	65.5	427	681	124	43	15	.223	.274	135	340	101	.947	98	543	414	12	6	3.20
					4523	4523	1386	503	151	.244	.314	1504	2271	788	.955	798	3615	4435	129	55	2.59

POS	Player	AB	BA	HR	RBI	PO	A	E	DP	TC/G	FA	Pitcher	G	IP	W	L	SV	ERA
Det. W-98 L-54 Hughie Jennings																		
1B	C. Rossman	287	.261	0	39	913	36	18	30	12.9	.981	G. Mullin	40	304	**29**	8	1	2.22
2B	G. Schaefer	280	.250	0	22	180	273	16	26	5.5	.966	E. Willett	41	293	21	10	1	2.34
SS	D. Bush	532	.273	0	33	308	**567**	71	38	6.0	.925	E. Summers	35	282	19	9	1	2.24
3B	G. Moriarty	473	.273	1	39	117	253	24	11	3.7	**.939**	E. Killian	25	173	11	9	1	1.71
RF	T. Cobb	573	**.377**	**9**	**107**	222	24	14	7	1.7	.946	W. Donovan	21	140	8	7	2	2.31
CF	S. Crawford	589	.314	6	97	297	7	11	2	2.3	.965							
LF	M. McIntyre	476	.244	1	34	217	14	6	1	1.9	.975							
C	B. Schmidt	253	.209	1	28	315	107	**20**	7	5.5	.955							
3B	C. O'Leary	261	.203	0	13	59	118	15	4	3.6	.922							
C	O. Stanage	252	.262	0	21	324	80	15	12	5.4	.964							
OF	D. Jones	204	.279	0	10	103	4	2	1	1.9	.982							
2B	J. Delahanty	150	.253	0	20	88	127	13*	13	5.0	.943							
Phi. W-95 L-58 Connie Mack																		
1B	H. Davis	530	.268	4	75	1432	74	19	65	10.2	.988	E. Plank	34	275	19	10	0	1.70
2B	E. Collins	572	.346	3	56	373	**406**	27	**55**	5.3	**.967**	C. Bender	34	250	18	8	1	1.66
SS	J. Barry	409	.215	1	23	196	351	43	40	4.8	.927	C. Morgan	28	229	16	11	0	1.65
3B	F. Baker	541	.305	4	85	**209**	**277**	**42**	16	3.6	.920	H. Krause	32	213	18	8	0	**1.39**
RF	D. Murphy	541	.281	5	69	191	17	5	5	1.4	.977	J. Coombs	31	206	12	11	1	2.32
CF	R. Oldring	326	.230	1	28	174	7	7	1	2.1	.963	J. Dygert	32	137	9	5	0	2.42
LF	B. Ganley	274	.197	0	9	185	9	4	2	2.6	.980*							
C	I. Thomas	256	.223	0	31	479	112	9	5	**7.1**	**.985**							
OF	T. Hartsel	267	.270	0	18	140	0	5	0	2.0	.966							
OF	H. Heitmuller	210	.286	0	15	111	4	9	2	2.1	.927							
C	P. Livingston	175	.234	0	15	306	106	13	6	6.6	.969							
Bos. W-88 L-63 Fred Lake																		
1B	J. Stahl	435	.294	6	60	1353	50	20	57	11.3	.986	F. Arellanes	45	231	16	12	**8**	2.18
2B	A. McConnell	453	.238	0	36	251	389	**31**	43	**5.5**	.954	E. Cicotte	27	160	13	5	2	1.97
SS	H. Wagner	430	.256	1	49	282	413	50	40	**6.1**	.934	J. Wood	24	159	11	7	0	2.21
3B	H. Lord	534	.311	0	31	180	268	34	10	3.6	.929	C. Chech	17	107	7	5	0	2.95
RF	D. Gessler	386	.298	0	46	135	18	11	1	1.5	.933	C. Hall	11	60	6	4	0	2.56
CF	T. Speaker	544	.309	7	77	**319**	**35**	10	**12**	2.6	.973							
LF	H. Niles	546	.245	1	38	197	20	11	3	1.9	.952							
C	B. Carrigan	280	.296	1	36	347	110	13	9	6.1	.972							
OF	H. Hooper	255	.282	0	12	124	14	7	3	1.7	.952							
C	P. Donahue	176	.239	2	25	249	71	6	3	5.6	.982							
2S	C. French	167	.251	0	13	86	140	24	14		.904							
Chi. W-78 L-74 Billy Sullivan																		
1B	F. Isbell	433	.224	0	33	1204	66	8	48	**12.7**	**.994**	F. Smith	**51**	**365**	25	17	1	1.80
2B	J. Atz	381	.236	0	22	202	311	25	40	4.6	.954	J. Scott	36	250	12	12	0	2.30
SS	F. Parent	472	.261	0	30	182	357	41	34	5.9	.929	E. Walsh	31	230	15	11	2	1.41
3B	L. Tannehill	531	.222	0	47	103	168	17	11	3.2	.941	D. White	24	178	11	9	0	1.72
RF	E. Hahn	287	.181	1	16	93	3	1	1	1.3	.990	B. Burns	22	174	7	13	0	1.96
CF	D. Altizer	382	.233	1	20	99	12	6	1	1.9	.949							
LF	P. Dougherty	491	.285	1	55	184	10	12	0	1.5	.942							
C	B. Sullivan	265	.162	0	16	452	119	10	6	6.0	.983							
32	B. Purtell	361	.258	0	40	162	248	24	24		.945							
OP	D. White	192	.234	0	7	71	54	8	1		.940							
C	F. Owens	174	.201	0	17	266	62	14	2	6.0	.959							
OF	W. Cole	165	.236	0	16	83	5	11	1	2.2	.889							
P	F. Smith	127	.173	0	20	**26**	**154**	4	3	3.6	.978							
N. Y. W-74 L-77 George Stallings																		
1B	H. Chase	474	.283	4	63	1202	71	**28**	53	11.0	.978	J. Warhop	36	243	13	15	2	2.40
2B	F. LaPorte	309	.298	0	31	142	208	23	30	4.5	.938	J. Lake	31	215	14	11	1	1.88
SS	J. Knight	360	.236	0	40	141	204	38	19	4.9	.901	R. Manning	26	173	7	11	1	3.17
3B	J. Austin	437	.231	1	39	176	236	32	**19**	**4.0**	.928	L. Brockett	26	152	10	8	1	2.37
RF	W. Keeler	360	.264	1	32	111	9	4	2	1.3	.968	S. Doyle	17	126	8	6	0	2.58
CF	R. Demmitt	427	.246	4	30	185	22	**21**	7	2.1	.908	J. Quinn	23	119	9	5	1	1.97
LF	C. Engle	492	.278	3	71	299	17	18	5	2.5	.946	T. Hughes	24	119	7	8	1	2.65
C	R. Kleinow	206	.228	0	15	343	83	15	6	5.7	.966	P. Wilson	14	94	6	5	0	3.17
S3	K. Elberfeld	379	.237	0	26	196	269	26	30		.947							
OF	B. Cree	343	.262	2	27	121	9	7	2	1.8	.949							
OF	C. Hemphill	181	.243	0	10	75	6	2	1	1.8	.976							
C	J. Sweeney	176	.267	0	21	274	83	**20**	7	6.1	.947							
Cle. W-71 L-82 Nap Lajoie W-57 L-57 Deacon McGuire W-14 L-25																		
1B	G. Stovall	565	.246	2	49	**1478**	**109**	19	**80**	11.1	.988	C. Young	35	295	19	15	0	2.26
2B	N. Lajoie	469	.324	1	47	193	370	28	**55**	4.9	.953	H. Berger	34	257	13	14	1	2.63
SS	N. Ball	324	.256	1	25	198	289	46	42	5.6	.914	A. Joss	33	243	14	13	0	1.71
3B	B. Bradley	334	.186	0	22	89	157	11	16	3.0	.957	C. Falkenberg	24	165	10	9	0	2.40
RF	W. Good	318	.214	0	17	110	12	6	2	1.6	.953	B. Rhoads	20	133	5	9	0	2.90
CF	J. Birmingham	343	.289	1	38	203	15	12	2	2.3	.948							
LF	B. Hinchman	457	.258	2	53	233	0	20	1	1.9	.921							
C	T. Easterly	287	.261	1	27	335	110	16	9	6.1	.965							
3B	G. Perring	283	.223	0	20	83	151	17	6	3.8	.932							
OF	B. Lord	249	.269	1	25	110	13	1	4	1.8	.992							
OF	E. Flick	235	.255	0	15	87	4	4	1	1.6	.958							
S2	T. Turner	208	.250	0	16	112	176	11	21		.963							
C	N. Clarke	164	.274	0	14	192	65	13	2	6.1	.952							

	POS	Player	AB	BA	HR	RBI	PO	A	E	DP	TC/G	FA	Pitcher	G	IP	W	L	SV	ERA
St. L.	1B	T. Jones	337	.249	0	29	950	70	11	57	10.9	.989	J. Powell	34	239	12	16	3	2.11
W-61 L-89	2B	J. Williams	374	.195	0	22	221	280	20	42	4.8	.962	R. Waddell	31	220	11	14	0	2.37
Jimmy McAleer	SS	B. Wallace	403	.238	1	35	193	279	27	34	5.7	.946	B. Pelty	27	199	11	11	0	2.30
	3B	H. Ferris	556	.216	3	58	157	242	27	15	3.7	.937	B. Bailey	32	199	9	10	0	2.44
	RF	R. Hartzell	595	.271	0	32	120	21	9	5	1.8	.940	B. Graham	34	187	8	14	1	3.12
	CF	D. Hoffman	387	.269	2	26	230	10	8	6	2.3	.968	B. Dinneen	17	112	6	7	0	3.46
	LF	G. Stone	310	.287	1	15	147	8	12	4	2.1	.928							
	C	L. Criger	212	.170	0	9	387	98	7	16	6.7	.986							
	1O	A. Griggs	364	.280	0	43	504	38	14	22		.975							
	OF	J. McAleese	267	.213	0	12	120	11	13	2	1.8	.910							
	C	J. Stephens	223	.220	3	18	335	103	9	9	6.2	.980							
Was.	1B	J. Donahue	283	.237	0	28	766	36	13	28	10.1	.984	W. Johnson	40	297	13	25	1	2.21
W-42 L-110	2B	J. Delahanty	302	.222	1	21	177	211	18*	26	4.8	.956	B. Groom	44	261	7	26	0	2.87
Joe Cantillon	SS	G. McBride	504	.234	0	34	341	499	58	56	5.8	.935	D. Gray	36	218	5	19	0	3.59
	3B	W. Conroy	488	.244	1	20	136	239	25	14	3.3	.938	C. Smith	23	146	3	12	0	3.27
	RF	J. Lelivelt	318	.292	0	24	179	14	6	3	2.2	.970	L. Hughes	22	120	4	7	1	2.69
	CF	C. Milan	400	.200	1	15	222	19	7	3	2.1	.972							
	LF	G. Browne	393	.272	1	16	147	12	11	3	1.7	.935							
	C	G. Street	407	.211	0	29	714	210	18	18	6.9	.981							
	UT	B. Unglaub	480	.265	3	41	669	121	13	39		.984							

BATTING AND BASE RUNNING LEADERS

Batting Average
T. Cobb, DET	.377
E. Collins, PHI	.346
N. Lajoie, CLE	.324
S. Crawford, DET	.314
H. Lord, BOS	.311

Slugging Average
T. Cobb, DET	.517
S. Crawford, DET	.452
E. Collins, PHI	.449
F. Baker, PHI	.447
T. Speaker, BOS	.443

Home Runs
T. Cobb, DET	9
T. Speaker, BOS	7
J. Stahl, BOS	6
S. Crawford, DET	6
D. Murphy, PHI	5

Total Bases
T. Cobb, DET	296
S. Crawford, DET	266
E. Collins, PHI	257
F. Baker, PHI	242
T. Speaker, BOS	241

Runs Batted In
T. Cobb, DET	107
S. Crawford, DET	97
F. Baker, PHI	85
T. Speaker, BOS	77
H. Davis, PHI	75

Stolen Bases
T. Cobb, DET	76
E. Collins, PHI	67
D. Bush, DET	53
P. Dougherty, CHI	36
H. Lord, BOS	36

Hits
T. Cobb, DET	216
E. Collins, PHI	198
S. Crawford, DET	185

Base on Balls
D. Bush, DET	88
E. Collins, PHI	62
R. Demmitt, NY	55

Home Run Percentage
T. Cobb, DET	1.6
J. Stahl, BOS	1.4
T. Speaker, BOS	1.3

Runs Scored
T. Cobb, DET	116
D. Bush, DET	114
E. Collins, PHI	104

Doubles
S. Crawford, DET	35
N. Lajoie, CLE	33
T. Cobb, DET	33

Triples
F. Baker, PHI	19
D. Murphy, PHI	14
S. Crawford, DET	14

PITCHING LEADERS

Winning Percentage
G. Mullin, DET	.784
C. Bender, PHI	.692
H. Krause, PHI	.692
E. Summers, DET	.679
E. Willett, DET	.677

Earned Run Average
H. Krause, PHI	1.39
E. Walsh, CHI	1.41
C. Bender, PHI	1.66
E. Plank, PHI	1.70
A. Joss, CLE	1.71

Wins
G. Mullin, DET	29
F. Smith, CHI	25
E. Willett, DET	21

Saves
F. Arellanes, BOS	8
J. Warhop, NY	4
J. Powell, STL	3
T. Hughes, NY	3

Strikeouts
F. Smith, CHI	177
W. Johnson, WAS	164
H. Berger, CLE	162
C. Bender, PHI	161
R. Waddell, STL	141

Complete Games
F. Smith, CHI	37
C. Young, CLE	30
G. Mullin, DET	29
W. Johnson, WAS	27
C. Morgan, BOS, PHI	26

Fewest Hits per 9 Innings
C. Morgan, BOS, PHI	6.26
H. Krause, PHI	6.38
E. Walsh, CHI	6.49

Shutouts
E. Walsh, CHI	8
H. Krause, PHI	7
F. Smith, CHI	7
J. Coombs, PHI	6

Fewest Walks per 9 Innings
A. Joss, CLE	1.15
D. White, CHI	1.57
J. Powell, STL	1.58

Most Strikeouts per 9 Inn.
H. Krause, PHI	5.87
C. Bender, PHI	5.80
R. Waddell, STL	5.76

Innings
F. Smith, CHI	365
G. Mullin, DET	304
W. Johnson, WAS	297

Games Pitched
F. Smith, CHI	51
F. Arellanes, BOS	45
B. Groom, WAS	44
E. Willett, DET	41

	W	L	PCT	GB	R	OR	Batting 2B	3B	HR	BA	SA	SB	Fielding E	DP	FA	Pitching CG	BB	SO	ShO	SV	ERA
DET	98	54	.645		**666**	493	**209**	58	19	**.267**	.342	**280**	276	87	.959	**117**	359	528	17	12	2.26
PHI	95	58	.621	3.5	600	**414**	186	**89**	**20**	.257	**.343**	205	**245**	92	.961	111	386	**728**	**27**	3	**1.92**
BOS	88	63	.583	9.5	590	561	151	69	**20**	.263	.333	215	292	95	.955	75	384	555	11	**15**	2.60
CHI	78	74	.513	20	494	465	145	56	4	.221	.275	211	246	101	**.964**	112	**341**	671	26	4	2.04
NY	74	77	.490	23.5	591	580	143	61	16	.248	.311	187	329	94	.948	94	422	597	18	7	2.68
CLE	71	82	.464	27.5	519	543	173	81	10	.241	.313	174	275	**110**	.957	110	349	569	15	2	2.39
STL	61	89	.407	36	443	574	116	45	11	.232	.280	136	267	107	.958	105	383	620	21	4	2.88
WAS	42	110	.276	56	382	655	148	41	9	.223	.275	136	280	100	.957	99	424	653	11	2	3.04
					4285	4285	1271	500	109	.244	.309	1544	2210	786	.957	823	3048	4921	146	49	2.47

Chi.
W-104 L-50 — Frank Chance

POS	Player	AB	BA	HR	RBI	PO	A	E	DP	TC/G	FA
1B	F. Chance	295	.298	0	36	773	38	3	48	9.4	.996
2B	J. Evers	433	.263	0	28	282	347	33	55	5.3	.950
SS	J. Tinker	473	.288	3	69	277	411	42	54	5.6	.942
3B	H. Steinfeldt	448	.252	2	58	137	246	22	16	3.2	.946
RF	W. Schulte	559	.301	10	68	221	18	8	5	1.6	.968
CF	S. Hofman	477	.325	3	86	249	19	7	4	2.5	.975
LF	J. Sheckard	507	.256	5	51	308	21	8	3	2.4	.976
C	J. Kling	297	.269	2	32	407	118	11	10	6.2	.979
UT	H. Zimmerman	335	.284	3	38	164	181	33	28		.913
C1	J. Archer	313	.259	2	41	620	97	20	31		.973
OF	G. Beaumont	172	.267	2	22	107	5	5	0	2.1	.957

Pitcher	G	IP	W	L	SV	ERA
T. Brown	46	295	25	13	7	1.86
K. Cole	33	240	20	4	0	1.80
H. McIntyre	28	176	13	9	0	3.07
E. Reulbach	24	173	12	8	0	3.12
O. Overall	23	145	12	6	1	2.68
L. Richie	30	130	11	4	3	2.70
J. Pfiester	14	100	6	3	0	1.79

N. Y.
W-91 L-63 — John McGraw

POS	Player	AB	BA	HR	RBI	PO	A	E	DP	TC/G	FA
1B	F. Merkle	506	.292	4	70	1390	84	29	87	10.4	.981
2B	L. Doyle	575	.285	8	69	313	388	53	62	5.0	.930
SS	A. Bridwell	492	.276	0	48	304	417	41	52	5.4	.946
3B	A. Devlin	493	.260	2	67	179	284	33	20	3.4	.933
RF	R. Murray	553	.277	4	87	246	26	15	3	1.9	.948
CF	F. Snodgrass	396	.321	2	44	214	12	7	1	2.3	.970
LF	J. Devore	490	.304	2	27	191	18	16	3	1.7	.929
C	C. Meyers	365	.285	1	62	638	154	25	16	7.0	.969
OF	C. Seymour	287	.265	1	40	137	9	10	1	2.1	.936
OF	B. Becker	126	.286	3	24	63	7	2	0	1.6	.972

Pitcher	G	IP	W	L	SV	ERA
C. Mathewson	39	318	27	9	0	1.90
H. Wiltse	36	235	14	12	1	2.72
L. Drucke	34	215	12	10	0	2.47
D. Crandall	42	208	17	4	4	2.56
R. Ames	33	190	12	11	0	2.22
B. Raymond	19	99	4	11	0	3.81

Pit.
W-86 L-67 — Fred Clarke

POS	Player	AB	BA	HR	RBI	PO	A	E	DP	TC/G	FA
1B	J. Flynn	332	.274	6	52	869	49	22	54	10.1	.977
2B	D. Miller	444	.227	1	48	263	318	33	45	5.2	.946
SS	H. Wagner	556	.320	4	81	337	413	51	62	5.8	.936
3B	B. Byrne	602	.296	2	52	167	289	35	11	3.3	.929
RF	O. Wilson	536	.276	4	50	255	23	8	5	2.0	.972
CF	T. Leach	529	.270	4	52	352	14	13	4	2.9	.966
LF	F. Clarke	429	.263	2	63	284	10	10	4	2.6	.967
C	G. Gibson	482	.259	3	44	633	203	14	8	5.9	.984
OF	V. Campbell	282	.326	4	21	145	8	18	2	2.3	.895
UT	B. McKechnie	212	.217	0	12	146	166	12	20		.963
1B	H. Hyatt	175	.263	1	30	323	19	5	19	9.1	.986

Pitcher	G	IP	W	L	SV	ERA
H. Camnitz	38	260	12	13	2	3.22
B. Adams	34	245	18	9	0	2.24
L. Leifield	40	218	15	12	1	2.64
K. White	30	153	10	9	2	3.46
D. Phillippe	31	122	14	2	4	2.29
S. Leever	26	111	6	5	2	2.76
B. Powell	12	75	4	6	0	2.40

Phi.
W-78 L-75 — Red Dooin

POS	Player	AB	BA	HR	RBI	PO	A	E	DP	TC/G	FA
1B	K. Bransfield	427	.239	3	52	1026	51	20	82	10.0	.982
2B	O. Knabe	510	.261	1	44	383	381	37	72	5.9	.954
SS	M. Doolan	536	.263	2	57	283	500	43	71	5.6	.948
3B	E. Grant	579	.268	1	67	193	256	31	22	3.2	.935
RF	J. Titus	535	.241	3	35	226	22	6	4	1.8	.976
CF	J. Bates	498	.305	3	61	308	24	16	8	2.7	.954
LF	S. Magee	519	.331	6	123	285	9	8	2	2.0	.974
C	R. Dooin	331	.242	0	30	472	131	28	14	6.9	.956
UT	J. Walsh	242	.248	3	31	122	101	23	11		.907
C	P. Moran	199	.236	0	11	278	83	4	5	6.5	.989

Pitcher	G	IP	W	L	SV	ERA
E. Moore	46	283	22	15	0	2.58
B. Ewing	34	255	16	14	0	3.00
L. Moren	34	205	13	14	1	3.55
G. McQuillan	24	152	9	6	1	1.60
E. Stack	20	117	6	7	0	4.00
L. Schettler	27	107	2	6	1	3.20
B. Foxen	16	78	5	5	0	2.55

Cin.
W-75 L-79 — Clark Griffith

POS	Player	AB	BA	HR	RBI	PO	A	E	DP	TC/G	FA
1B	D. Hoblitzell	611	.278	4	70	1454	67	24	64	10.4	.984
2B	D. Egan	474	.245	0	46	264	381	26	49	5.1	.961
SS	T. McMillan	248	.185	0	13	162	270	34	32	5.7	.927
3B	H. Lobert	314	.309	3	40	123	164	21	11	3.4	.932
RF	M. Mitchell	583	.286	5	88	257	19	12	4	1.9	.958
CF	D. Paskert	506	.300	2	46	355	25	17	4	2.9	.957
LF	B. Bescher	589	.250	4	48	339	16	20	4	2.5	.947
C	L. McLean	423	.298	2	71	485	158	11	18	5.5	.983
S3	T. Downey	378	.270	2	32	201	281	60	26		.889
C	T. Clarke	151	.278	1	20	217	52	8	3	4.9	.971

Pitcher	G	IP	W	L	SV	ERA
H. Gaspar	48	275	15	17	5	2.59
G. Suggs	35	266	19	11	3	2.40
J. Rowan	42	261	14	13	1	2.93
F. Beebe	35	214	12	15	0	3.07
B. Burns	31	179	8	13	0	3.48

Bkn.
W-64 L-90 — Bill Dahlen

POS	Player	AB	BA	HR	RBI	PO	A	E	DP	TC/G	FA
1B	J. Daubert	552	.264	8	50	1418	72	16	81	10.5	.989
2B	J. Hummel	578	.244	5	74	344	424	28	67	5.2	.965
SS	T. Smith	321	.181	1	16	254	318	36	57	6.0	.941
3B	E. Lennox	367	.259	3	42	135	149	15	14	3.0	.950
RF	J. Dalton	273	.227	1	21	129	12	5	3	2.0	.966
CF	B. Davidson	509	.238	0	34	283	11	12	3	2.3	.961
LF	Z. Wheat	606	.284	2	55	354	21	15	6	2.5	.962
C	B. Bergen	249	.161	0	14	373	151	10	15	6.0	.981
OF	A. Burch	352	.236	1	20	124	11	6	6	2.0	.957
3B	P. McElveen	213	.225	1	26	72	78	9	12	2.9	.943
C	T. Erwin	202	.188	1	10	259	114	20	10	5.8	.949

Pitcher	G	IP	W	L	SV	ERA
N. Rucker	41	320	17	18	0	2.58
G. Bell	44	310	10	27	1	2.64
C. Barger	35	272	15	15	1	2.88
D. Scanlan	34	217	9	11	2	2.61
E. Knetzer	20	133	7	5	0	3.19
K. Wilhelm	15	68	3	7	0	4.74

St. L.
W-63 L-90 — Roger Bresnahan

POS	Player	AB	BA	HR	RBI	PO	A	E	DP	TC/G	FA
1B	E. Konetchy	520	.302	3	78	1499	98	15	81	11.2	.991
2B	M. Huggins	547	.265	1	36	325	452	30	58	5.3	.963
SS	A. Hauser	375	.205	2	36	212	345	41	31	5.1	.931
3B	M. Mowrey	489	.282	2	70	171	301	37	30	3.6	.927
RF	S. Evans	506	.241	2	73	226	16	8	3	1.8	.968
CF	R. Oakes	468	.252	0	43	266	12	18	3	2.3	.939
LF	R. Ellis	550	.258	4	54	268	25	18	4	2.2	.942
C	E. Phelps	270	.263	0	37	320	84	10	10	5.2	.976
C	R. Bresnahan	234	.278	0	27	295	100	16	11	5.3	.961

Pitcher	G	IP	W	L	SV	ERA
B. Harmon	43	236	13	15	2	4.46
J. Lush	36	225	14	13	1	3.20
V. Willis	33	212	9	12	3	3.35
F. Corridon	30	156	6	14	2	3.81
L. Backman	26	116	6	7	1	3.03
S. Sallee	18	115	7	8	2	2.97

	POS	Player	AB	BA	HR	RBI	PO	A	E	DP	TC/G	FA	Pitcher	G	IP	W	L	SV	ERA
Bos.	1B	B. Sharpe	439	.239	0	29	1122	81	16	72	10.8	.987	A. Mattern	51	305	16	19	1	2.98
W-53 L-100	2B	D. Shean	543	.239	3	36	408	493	44	92	6.4	.953	B. Brown	46	263	9	23	2	2.67
Fred Lake	SS	B. Sweeney	499	.267	5	46	232	300	57	52	5.4	.903	S. Frock	45	255	11	19	2	3.21
	3B	B. Herzog	380	.250	3	32	110	223	31	17	3.5	.915	C. Curtis	43	251	6	24	2	3.55
	RF	D. Miller	482	.286	3	55	203	9	11	3	1.7	.951	G. Ferguson	26	123	8	7	0	3.80
	CF	F. Beck	571	.275	10	64	293	19	12	6	2.4	.963							
	LF	B. Collins	584	.241	3	40	355	23	9	2	2.6	.977							
	C	P. Graham	291	.282	0	21	318	132	16	11	5.4	.966							
	SS	Abbaticchio	178	.247	0	10	73	149	22	19	5.3	.910							

BATTING AND BASE RUNNING LEADERS

Batting Average
S. Magee, PHI	.331
V. Campbell, PIT	.326
S. Hofman, CHI	.325
F. Snodgrass, NY	.321
H. Wagner, PIT	.320

Slugging Average
S. Magee, PHI	.507
S. Hofman, CHI	.461
W. Schulte, CHI	.460
F. Merkle, NY	.441
V. Campbell, PIT	.436

Home Runs
W. Schulte, CHI	10
F. Beck, BOS	10
J. Daubert, BKN	8
L. Doyle, NY	8
J. Flynn, PIT	6
S. Magee, PHI	6

Total Bases
S. Magee, PHI	263
W. Schulte, CHI	257
B. Byrne, PIT	251
Z. Wheat, BKN	244
H. Wagner, PIT	240

Runs Batted In
S. Magee, PHI	123
M. Mitchell, CIN	88
R. Murray, NY	87
S. Hofman, CHI	86
H. Wagner, PIT	81

Stolen Bases
B. Bescher, CIN	70
R. Murray, NY	57
D. Paskert, CIN	51
S. Magee, PHI	49
J. Devore, NY	43

Hits
H. Wagner, PIT	178
B. Byrne, PIT	178
S. Magee, PHI	172
Z. Wheat, BKN	172

Base on Balls
M. Huggins, STL	116
J. Evers, CHI	108
S. Magee, PHI	94

Home Run Percentage
J. Flynn, PIT	1.8
W. Schulte, CHI	1.8
F. Beck, BOS	1.8

Runs Scored
S. Magee, PHI	110
M. Huggins, STL	101
B. Byrne, PIT	101

Doubles
B. Byrne, PIT	43
S. Magee, PHI	39
Z. Wheat, BKN	36

Triples
M. Mitchell, CIN	18
S. Magee, PHI	17
S. Hofman, CHI	16
E. Konetchy, STL	16

PITCHING LEADERS

Winning Percentage
K. Cole, CHI	.833
D. Crandall, NY	.810
C. Mathewson, NY	.750
B. Adams, PIT	.667
T. Brown, CHI	.658

Earned Run Average
G. McQuillan, PHI	1.60
K. Cole, CHI	1.80
T. Brown, CHI	1.86
C. Mathewson, NY	1.89
R. Ames, NY	2.22

Wins
C. Mathewson, NY	27
T. Brown, CHI	25
K. Cole, CHI	20
E. Moore, PHI	20

Saves
T. Brown, CHI	7
H. Gaspar, CIN	5
D. Crandall, NY	4
D. Phillippe, PIT	4

Strikeouts
E. Moore, PHI	185
C. Mathewson, NY	184
S. Frock, BOS, PIT	171
L. Drucke, NY	151
N. Rucker, BKN	147

Complete Games
T. Brown, CHI	27
C. Mathewson, NY	27
N. Rucker, BKN	27
C. Barger, BKN	25
G. Bell, BKN	25

Fewest Hits per 9 Innings
G. McQuillan, PHI	6.44
K. Cole, CHI	6.53
O. Overall, CHI	6.59

Shutouts
T. Brown, CHI	7
E. Moore, PHI	6
A. Mattern, BOS	6
N. Rucker, BKN	6

Fewest Walks per 9 Innings
G. Suggs, CIN	1.62
C. Mathewson, NY	1.70
D. Crandall, NY	1.86

Most Strikeouts per 9 Inn.
L. Drucke, NY	6.31
S. Frock, BOS, PIT	5.98
E. Moore, PHI	5.88

Innings
N. Rucker, BKN	320
C. Mathewson, NY	318
G. Bell, BKN	310

Games Pitched
A. Mattern, BOS	51
H. Gaspar, CIN	48

	W	L	PCT	GB	R	OR	2B	3B	HR	BA	SA	SB	E	DP	FA	CG	BB	SO	ShO	SV	ERA
CHI	104	50	.675		711	497	219	84	34	.268	.366	173	230	110	.963	99	474	609	27	11	2.51
NY	91	63	.591	13	715	545	204	83	31	.275	.366	282	291	117	.955	96	397	717	9	8	2.68
PIT	86	67	.562	17.5	655	576	214	83	33	.266	.360	148	245	102	.961	73	392	479	13	11	2.83
PHI	78	75	.510	25.5	674	682	223	71	22	.255	.338	199	258	132	.960	84	547	657	16	7	3.05
CIN	75	79	.487	29	620	665	150	79	23	.259	.333	310	291	103	.955	86	528	497	16	9	3.08
BKN	64	90	.416	40	497	622	166	73	25	.229	.305	151	235	125	.964	103	545	555	15	4	3.07
STL	63	90	.412	40.5	637	717	167	70	15	.248	.319	179	261	109	.959	83	541	466	3	12	3.78
BOS	53	100	.346	50.5	495	700	173	49	31	.246	.317	152	305	137	.954	74	599	531	12	7	3.22
					5004	5004	1516	592	214	.256	.338	1594	2116	935	.959	698	4023	4511	111	69	3.02

	POS	Player	AB	BA	HR	RBI	PO	A	E	DP	TC/G	FA	Pitcher	G	IP	W	L	SV	ERA
Phi. W-102 L-48 Connie Mack	1B	H. Davis	492	.248	1	41	1353	64	20	**74**	10.3	.986	J. Coombs	**45**	353	**31**	9	1	1.30
	2B	E. Collins	583	.322	3	81	**402**	**451**	25	**67**	**5.7**	**.972**	C. Morgan	36	291	18	12	0	1.55
	SS	J. Barry	487	.259	3	60	279	406	63	54	5.2	.916	E. Plank	38	250	16	10	2	2.01
	3B	F. Baker	561	.283	2	74	**207**	313	45	**35**	3.9	.920	C. Bender	30	250	23	5	0	1.58
	RF	D. Murphy	560	.300	4	64	209	15	6	5	1.5	.974	H. Krause	16	112	6	6	0	2.88
	CF	R. Oldring	546	.308	4	57	249	14	6	6	2.0	**.978**							
	LF	T. Hartsel	285	.221	0	22	113	8	7	2	1.5	.945							
	C	J. Lapp	192	.234	0	17	361	88	9	6	7.3	.980							
	OF	B. Lord	288	.278	1	20	142	6	3	2	2.1	.980							
	C	I. Thomas	180	.278	0	19	324	86	14	8	7.1	.967							
N. Y. W-88 L-63 George Stallings Hal Chase W-9 L-2	1B	H. Chase	524	.290	3	73	1373	65	28	68	11.3	.981	R. Ford	36	300	26	6	1	1.65
	2B	F. LaPorte	432	.264	2	67	127	220	15	21	4.6	.959	J. Warhop	37	254	14	14	2	2.87
	SS	J. Knight	414	.312	3	45	169	247	32	39	5.7	.929	J. Quinn	35	237	18	12	0	2.36
	3B	J. Austin	432	.218	2	36	204	284	30	10	**3.9**	.942	H. Vaughn	30	222	13	11	1	1.83
	RF	H. Wolter	479	.267	4	42	192	11	13	3	1.7	.940	T. Hughes	23	152	7	9	1	3.50
	CF	C. Hemphill	351	.239	0	21	159	10	5	2	1.9	.971							
	LF	B. Cree	467	.287	4	73	202	11	10	3	1.7	.955							
	C	J. Sweeney	215	.200	0	13	388	106	13	3	6.5	.974							
	OF	B. Daniels	356	.253	1	17	170	9	8	2	2.2	.957							
	2B	E. Gardner	271	.244	1	24	169	199	25	36	5.6	.936							
	SS	R. Roach	220	.214	0	20	112	173	27	27	5.4	.913							
	C	F. Mitchell	196	.230	0	18	262	69	11	2	5.0	.968							
Det. W-86 L-68 Hughie Jennings	1B	T. Jones	432	.255	0	45	1405	67	23	50	11.1	.985	G. Mullin	38	289	21	12	0	2.87
	2B	J. Delahanty	378	.294	2	45	246	267	33	36	5.2	.940	E. Summers	30	220	13	12	0	2.53
	SS	D. Bush	496	.262	3	34	310	487	51	31	6.0	.940	W. Donovan	26	209	17	7	0	2.42
	3B	G. Moriarty	490	.251	2	60	165	302	37	17	3.8	.927	E. Willett	37	147	16	11	0	3.60
	RF	S. Crawford	588	.289	5	**120**	223	10	9	2	1.6	.963	S. Stroud	28	130	5	9	1	3.25
	CF	T. Cobb	509	**.385**	8	91	305	18	14	4	2.5	.958	R. Works	18	86	3	6	1	3.57
	LF	D. Jones	377	.265	0	24	181	13	9	2	2.0	.956							
	C	O. Stanage	275	.207	2	25	344	148	25	6	6.2	.952							
	OF	M. McIntyre	305	.236	0	25	147	12	9	2	2.2	.946							
	2S	C. O'Leary	211	.242	0	9	116	153	16	12		.944							
	C	B. Schmidt	197	.259	1	23	239	80	9	1	5.0	.973							
Bos. W-81 L-72 Patsy Donovan	1B	J. Stahl	531	.271	10	77	**1488**	60	23	46	11.1	.985	E. Cicotte	36	250	15	11	0	2.74
	2B	L. Gardner	413	.283	2	36	222	320	32	28	5.1	.944	R. Collins	35	245	13	11	1	1.62
	SS	H. Wagner	491	.273	1	52	303	424	57	40	5.6	.927	J. Wood	35	198	12	13	0	1.68
	3B	H. Lord	288	.250	1	32	90	138	18	10	3.5	.927	C. Hall	35	189	12	9	2	1.91
	RF	H. Hooper	584	.267	2	27	241	**30**	18	7	1.9	.944	E. Karger	27	183	11	7	1	3.19
	CF	T. Speaker	538	.340	7	65	**337**	20	16	7	**2.7**	.957	C. Smith	24	156	11	6	1	2.30
	LF	D. Lewis	541	.283	8	68	261	28	17	9	2.1	.944	F. Arellanes	18	100	4	7	0	2.88
	C	B. Carrigan	342	.249	3	53	**495**	134	25	12	5.9	.962							
	UT	C. Engle	363	.264	2	38	129	223	29	17		.924							
	3B	F. Purtell	168	.208	1	15	41	87*	13*	2	3.4	.908							
Cle. W-71 L-81 Deacon McGuire	1B	G. Stovall	521	.261	0	52	1404	**91**	18	60	**11.5**	**.988**	C. Falkenberg	37	257	14	13	1	2.95
	2B	N. Lajoie	591	.384	4	76	387	419	28	60	5.6	.966	W. Mitchell	35	184	12	8	0	2.60
	SS	T. Turner	574	.230	0	33	194	320	14	42	5.6	**.973**	C. Young	21	163	7	10	0	2.53
	3B	B. Bradley	214	.196	0	12	89	126	10	8	3.7	.956	E. Koestner	27	145	5	10	2	3.04
	RF	J. Graney	454	.236	1	31	209	14	12	5	2.1	.949	S. Harkness	26	136	10	7	1	3.04
	CF	J. Birmingham	364	.231	0	35	223	24	10	8	2.5	.961	F. Link	22	123	5	6	1	3.30
	LF	A. Krueger	223	.170	0	14	116	10	6	3	2.1	.955	A. Joss	13	107	5	5	0	2.26
	C	T. Easterly	363	.306	0	55	200	104	15	7	4.8	.953	G. Kahler	12	95	6	4	0	1.60
	OF	H. Niles	240	.213	1	18	70	7	2	1	1.4	.975	H. Fanwell	17	92	2	9	0	3.62
	OF	B. Lord	201	.219	0	17	77	14	4	4	1.7	.958							
	C	H. Bemis	167	.216	1	16	186	63	10	4	5.6	.961							
Chi. W-68 L-85 Hugh Duffy	1B	C. Gandil	275	.193	2	21	854	57	10	34	12.4	.989	E. Walsh	**45**	370	18	**20**	5	**1.27**
	2B	R. Zeider	498	.217	0	31	205	242	33	31	5.5	.931	D. White	33	246	15	13	1	2.56
	SS	L. Blackburne	242	.174	0	10	173	265	43	29	6.5	.911	J. Scott	41	230	8	18	1	2.43
	3B	B. Purtell	368	.234	1	36	117	233*	36*	16	3.8	.907	F. Olmstead	32	184	10	12	0	1.95
	RF	S. Collins	315	.197	1	24	101	11	6	6	1.8	.949	I. Young	27	136	4	8	0	2.72
	CF	P. Meloan	222	.243	0	23	76	16	5	1	1.5	.948	F. Lange	23	131	9	4	0	1.65
	LF	P. Dougherty	443	.248	1	43	158	9	14	2	1.5	.923	F. Smith	19	129	4	9	0	2.03
	C	F. Payne	257	.218	0	19	409	106	14	11	**6.8**	.974							
	OF	F. Parent	258	.178	1	16	92	5	3	1	1.6	.970							
	S1	L. Tannehill	230	.222	1	21	258	144	12	21		.971							
	2O	C. French	170	.165	0	4	69	54	10	6		.925							
	3B	H. Lord	165	.297	0	10	44	75	6	4	2.8	.952							
Was. W-66 L-85 Jimmy McAleer	1B	B. Unglaub	431	.234	0	44	1230	79	20	51	10.7	.985	W. Johnson	**45**	**373**	25	17	1	1.35
	2B	R. Killefer	345	.229	0	24	173	231	26	27	4.9	.940	B. Groom	34	258	12	17	0	2.76
	SS	G. McBride	514	.230	1	55	**370**	**518**	58	**57**	6.1	.939	D. Gray	34	229	8	19	0	2.63
	3B	K. Elberfeld	455	.251	2	42	139	223	22	15	3.4	**.943**	D. Walker	29	199	11	11	0	3.30
	RF	D. Gessler	487	.259	2	50	161	23	9	3	1.3	.953	D. Reisling	30	191	10	10	1	2.54
	CF	C. Milan	531	.279	0	16	267	**30**	17	**10**	2.2	.946							
	LF	J. Lelivelt	347	.265	0	33	149	13	6	5	1.9	.964							
	C	G. Street	257	.202	1	16	417	151	13	8	6.8	**.978**							
	3O	W. Conroy	351	.254	1	27	151	91	10	6		.960							
	2O	G. Schaefer	229	.275	0	14	89	108	11	16		.947							

	POS	Player	AB	BA	HR	RBI	PO	A	E	DP	TC/G	FA	Pitcher	G	IP	W	L	SV	ERA
St. L.	1B	P. Newnam	384	.216	2	26	1041	56	32	53	11.0	.972	J. Lake	35	261	11	17	2	2.20
W-47 L-107	2B	F. Truesdale	415	.219	1	25	279	313	56	41	5.3	.914	B. Bailey	34	192	3	18	0	3.32
Jack O'Connor	SS	B. Wallace	508	.258	0	37	258	344	33	37	6.5	.948	B. Pelty	27	165	5	11	0	3.48
	3B	R. Hartzell	542	.218	2	30	123	203	25	19	3.9	.929	F. Ray	21	141	4	10	0	3.58
	RF	A. Schweitzer	379	.230	2	37	149	15	11	3	1.6	.937	J. Powell	21	129	7	11	0	2.30
	CF	D. Hoffman	380	.237	0	27	202	14	9	5	2.1	.960							
	LF	G. Stone	562	.256	0	40	220	20	7	2	1.7	.972							
	C	J. Stephens	299	.241	0	23	418	156	17	18	6.2	.971							
	UT	A. Griggs	416	.236	2	30	322	120	32	29		.932							
	C	B. Killefer	193	.124	0	7	311	124	29	16	6.4	.938							

BATTING AND BASE RUNNING LEADERS

Batting Average
T. Cobb, DET	.385
N. Lajoie, CLE	.384
T. Speaker, BOS	.340
E. Collins, PHI	.322
J. Knight, NY	.312

Slugging Average
T. Cobb, DET	.554
N. Lajoie, CLE	.514
T. Speaker, BOS	.468
D. Murphy, PHI	.436
R. Oldring, PHI	.430

Home Runs
J. Stahl, BOS	10
T. Cobb, DET	8
D. Lewis, BOS	8
T. Speaker, BOS	7
S. Crawford, DET	5

Total Bases
N. Lajoie, CLE	304
T. Cobb, DET	282
T. Speaker, BOS	252
S. Crawford, DET	249
D. Murphy, PHI	244

Runs Batted In
S. Crawford, DET	120
T. Cobb, DET	91
E. Collins, PHI	81
J. Stahl, BOS	77
N. Lajoie, CLE	76

Stolen Bases
E. Collins, PHI	81
T. Cobb, DET	65
D. Bush, DET	49
R. Zeider, CHI	49
C. Milan, WAS	44

Hits
N. Lajoie, CLE	227
T. Cobb, DET	196
E. Collins, PHI	188

Base on Balls
D. Bush, DET	78
C. Milan, WAS	71
H. Wolter, NY	66
T. Cobb, DET	64

Home Run Percentage
J. Stahl, BOS	1.9
T. Cobb, DET	1.6
D. Lewis, BOS	1.5

Runs Scored
T. Cobb, DET	106
T. Speaker, BOS	92
N. Lajoie, CLE	92

Doubles
N. Lajoie, CLE	51
T. Cobb, DET	36
D. Lewis, BOS	29

Triples
S. Crawford, DET	19
B. Lord, CLE, PHI	18
D. Murphy, PHI	18

PITCHING LEADERS

Winning Percentage
C. Bender, PHI	.821
R. Ford, NY	.813
J. Coombs, PHI	.775
W. Donovan, DET	.708
G. Mullin, DET	.636

Earned Run Average
E. Walsh, CHI	1.27
J. Coombs, PHI	1.30
W. Johnson, WAS	1.35
C. Morgan, PHI	1.55
C. Bender, PHI	1.58

Wins
J. Coombs, PHI	31
R. Ford, NY	26
W. Johnson, WAS	25
C. Bender, PHI	23
G. Mullin, DET	21

Saves
C. Hall, BOS	5
E. Walsh, CHI	5
F. Browning, DET	3

Strikeouts
W. Johnson, WAS	313
E. Walsh, CHI	258
J. Coombs, PHI	224
R. Ford, NY	209
C. Bender, PHI	155

Complete Games
W. Johnson, WAS	38
J. Coombs, PHI	35
E. Walsh, CHI	33
R. Ford, NY	29
G. Mullin, DET	27

Fewest Hits per 9 Innings
R. Ford, NY	5.83
E. Walsh, CHI	5.89
J. Coombs, PHI	6.32

Shutouts
J. Coombs, PHI	13
R. Ford, NY	8
W. Johnson, WAS	8

Fewest Walks per 9 Innings
E. Walsh, CHI	1.49
C. Young, CLE	1.49
R. Collins, BOS	1.51

Most Strikeouts per 9 Inn.
W. Johnson, WAS	7.55
J. Wood, BOS	6.60
E. Walsh, CHI	6.28

Innings
W. Johnson, WAS	373
E. Walsh, CHI	370
J. Coombs, PHI	353

Games Pitched
W. Johnson, WAS	45
E. Walsh, CHI	45
J. Coombs, PHI	45

	W	L	PCT	GB	R	OR	Batting 2B	3B	HR	BA	SA	SB	Fielding E	DP	FA	CG	BB	SO	ShO	SV	ERA
PHI	102	48	.680		672	439	194	106	19	.266	.356	207	230	117	.965	123	450	789	24	5	1.79
NY	88	63	.583	14.5	629	502	163	75	20	.248	.322	288	284	95	.956	110	364	532	17	8	3.00
DET	86	68	.558	18	679	580	192	73	26	.261	.344	249	288	79	.956	108	460	670	13	5	2.46
BOS	81	72	.529	22.5	637	564	175	87	43	.259	.351	194	309	80	.954	100	414	614	13	6	2.89
CLE	71	81	.467	32	539	654	185	63	9	.244	.308	189	247	112	.964	92	487	614	13	5	2.01
CHI	68	85	.444	35.5	456	495	115	58	7	.211	.261	183	314	100	.954	103	381	785	23	7	2.01
WAS	66	85	.437	36.5	498	552	145	46	9	.236	.289	192	264	99	.959	119	374	675	19	3	2.46
STL	47	107	.305	57	454	778	131	60	12	.220	.276	169	377	113	.944	100	532	557	9	3	3.09
					4564	4564	1300	568	145	.243	.314	1671	2313	795	.956	855	3462	5276	132	42	2.53

	POS	Player	AB	BA	HR	RBI	PO	A	E	DP	TC/G	FA	Pitcher	G	IP	W	L	SV	ERA
N. Y. W-99 L-54 John McGraw	1B	F. Merkle	541	.283	12	84	1375	**117**	**22**	73	10.2	.985	C. Mathewson	45	307	26	13	3	**1.99**
	2B	L. Doyle	526	.310	13	77	272	340	36	46	4.6	.944	R. Marquard	45	278	24	7	2	2.50
	SS	A. Bridwell	263	.270	0	31	129	249	34	26	5.4	.917	R. Ames	34	205	11	10	1	2.68
	3B	A. Devlin	260	.273	0	25	75	144	13	3	2.9	.944	D. Crandall	41	199	15	5	5	2.63
	RF	R. Murray	488	.291	3	78	196	12	10	1	1.7	.944	H. Wiltse	30	187	12	9	0	3.27
	CF	F. Snodgrass	534	.294	1	77	293	31	9	8	2.2	.973	B. Raymond	17	82	6	4	0	3.31
	LF	J. Devore	565	.280	3	50	241	29	19	5	1.9	.934							
	C	C. Meyers	391	.332	1	61	**729**	108	18	11	6.7	.979							
	UT	A. Fletcher	326	.319	1	37	153	285	32	27		.932							
	3B	B. Herzog	247	.267	1	26	88	138	18	7	3.8	.926							
	OF	B. Becker	172	.262	1	20	72	7	2	0	1.5	.975							
	P	D. Crandall	113	.239	2	21	9	59	3	2	1.7	.958							
Chi. W-92 L-62 Frank Chance	1B	V. Saier	259	.259	1	37	715	33	15	44	10.5	.980	T. Brown	**53**	270	21	11	**13**	2.80
	2B	H. Zimmerman	535	.307	9	85	256	304	32	42	5.5	.946	L. Richie	36	253	15	11	1	2.31
	SS	J. Tinker	536	.278	4	69	**333**	**486**	55	56	6.1	**.937**	E. Reulbach	33	222	16	9	0	2.96
	3B	J. Doyle	472	.282	5	62	134	278	**35**	25	3.5	.922	K. Cole	32	221	18	7	0	3.13
	RF	W. Schulte	577	.300	**21**	**121**	246	19	8	8	1.8	.971	H. McIntyre	25	149	11	7	0	4.11
	CF	S. Hofman	512	.252	2	70	230	11	8	5	2.3	.968							
	LF	J. Sheckard	539	.276	4	50	332	**32**	14	**12**	2.4	.963							
	C	J. Archer	387	.253	4	41	476	124	14	11	6.0	.977							
	2B	J. Evers	155	.226	0	7	66	90	4	17	4.8	.975							
	OF	W. Good	145	.269	2	21	74	3	6	1	2.1	.928							
Pit. W-85 L-69 Fred Clarke	1B	N. Hunter	209	.254	2	24	504	26	6	44	8.8	.989	L. Leifield	42	318	16	16	1	2.63
	2B	D. Miller	470	.268	6	78	273	357	38	65	5.2	.943	B. Adams	40	293	22	12	0	2.33
	SS	H. Wagner	473	**.334**	9	89	221	312	39	55	5.7	.932	H. Camnitz	40	268	20	15	0	3.13
	3B	B. Byrne	598	.259	2	52	181	**282**	35	21	3.3	.930	E. Steele	31	166	9	9	2	2.60
	RF	O. Wilson	544	.300	12	107	273	20	7	10	2.1	.977	C. Hendrix	22	119	4	6	1	2.73
	CF	M. Carey	427	.258	5	43	304	11	8	5	2.6	.975	J. Ferry	26	86	6	4	3	3.15
	LF	F. Clarke	392	.324	5	49	216	8	7	3	2.3	.970							
	C	G. Gibson	311	.209	0	19	452	117	12	16	5.9	.979							
	OF	T. Leach	386	.238	3	43	208	15	3	3	2.5	.987							
	UT	B. McKechnie	321	.227	2	37	598	109	21	49		.971							
	C	M. Simon	215	.228	0	22	320	75	13	6	6.0	.968							
	SS	A. McCarthy	150	.240	2	31	70	88	3	12	4.9	.981							
Phi. W-79 L-73 Red Dooin	1B	F. Luderus	551	.301	16	99	1373	77	**22**	85	10.1	.985	G. Alexander	48	**367**	**28**	13	3	2.57
	2B	O. Knabe	528	.237	1	42	310	412	38	54	5.4	.950	E. Moore	42	308	15	19	1	2.63
	SS	M. Doolan	512	.238	1	49	295	474	53	**68**	5.7	.936	G. Chalmers	38	209	13	10	4	3.11
	3B	H. Lobert	541	.285	9	72	**202**	213	20	13	3.0	.954	B. Burns	21	121	6	10	0	3.42
	RF	J. Titus	236	.284	8	26	85	10	2	3	1.6	.979	E. Stack	13	78	5	5	0	3.59
	CF	D. Paskert	560	.273	4	47	361	20	8	6	2.5	.979							
	LF	S. Magee	445	.288	15	94	248	14	5	3	2.2	**.981**							
	C	R. Dooin	247	.328	1	16	436	97	18	5	7.4	.967							
	UT	J. Walsh	289	.270	1	31	148	79	12	14		.950							
	OF	F. Beck	210	.281	3	25	81	7	4	4	1.5	.957							
St. L. W-75 L-74 Roger Bresnahan	1B	E. Konetchy	571	.289	6	88	**1652**	71	16	85	**11.0**	**.991**	B. Harmon	51	348	23	16	4	3.13
	2B	M. Huggins	509	.261	1	24	281	439	29	62	5.5	.961	B. Steele	43	287	18	**19**	3	3.73
	SS	A. Hauser	515	.241	3	46	223	400	**56**	51	5.1	.918	S. Sallee	36	245	15	9	2	2.76
	3B	M. Mowrey	471	.268	0	61	174	267	26	19	3.5	.944	R. Golden	30	149	4	9	0	5.02
	RF	S. Evans	547	.294	5	71	258	17	8	5	1.9	.972	R. Geyer	29	149	9	6	0	3.27
	CF	R. Oakes	551	.263	2	59	**364**	26	16	8	**2.7**	.961							
	LF	R. Ellis	555	.250	3	66	297	21	**21**	3	2.3	.938							
	C	J. Bliss	258	.229	1	27	332	103	22	9	5.4	.952							
	C	R. Bresnahan	227	.278	3	41	323	100	13	9	5.7	.970							
	UT	W. Smith	194	.216	2	19	63	139	14	7		.935							
Cin. W-70 L-83 Clark Griffith	1B	D. Hoblitzell	**622**	.289	11	97	1442	91	16	81	9.8	.990	G. Suggs	36	261	15	13	0	3.00
	2B	D. Egan	558	.249	1	56	341	**480**	44	**67**	5.4	.949	H. Gaspar	44	254	10	17	3	3.30
	SS	T. Downey	360	.261	0	36	198	267	48	26	5.5	.906	B. Keefe	39	234	12	13	3	2.69
	3B	E. Grant	458	.223	1	53	158	208	18	21	3.1	.953	A. Fromme	38	208	10	11	0	3.46
	RF	M. Mitchell	529	.291	2	84	280	23	9	8	2.2	.971	F. Smith	34	176	10	14	1	3.98
	CF	J. Bates	518	.292	1	41	352	21	13	4	2.6	.966							
	LF	B. Bescher	599	.275	1	45	267	21	14	2	2.0	.954							
	C	L. McLean	328	.287	0	34	414	138	18	**16**	5.8	.968							
	C	T. Clarke	203	.241	1	25	313	74	12	10	4.9	.970							
	SS	J. Esmond	198	.273	1	11	110	104	19	19	5.3	.918							
	OF	F. Beck	87	.184	2	20	25	2	0	0	1.7	1.000							
Bkn. W-64 L-86 Bill Dahlen	1B	J. Daubert	573	.307	5	45	1485	88	18	**91**	10.7	.989	N. Rucker	48	316	22	18	4	2.71
	2B	J. Hummel	477	.270	5	58	296	352	19	58	5.3	**.972**	C. Barger	30	217	11	15	0	3.52
	SS	B. Tooley	433	.206	1	29	226	340	46	42	5.4	.925	E. Knetzer	35	204	11	12	0	3.49
	3B	E. Zimmerman	417	.185	3	36	167	229	16	24	3.4	**.961**	B. Schardt	39	195	5	15	4	3.59
	RF	B. Coulson	521	.234	0	50	253	21	9	5	2.0	.968	D. Scanlan	22	114	3	10	1	3.64
	CF	B. Davidson	292	.233	1	26	168	4	8	1	2.4	.956	G. Bell	19	101	5	6	0	4.28
	LF	Z. Wheat	534	.287	5	76	287	14	14	0	2.3	.955							
	C	B. Bergen	227	.132	0	10	346	121	9	10	5.7	**.981**							
	C	T. Erwin	218	.271	7	34	273	98	11	6	5.2	.971							
	S2	D. Stark	193	.295	0	19	111	134	19	20		.928							
	OF	A. Burch	167	.228	0	7	98	6	3	3	2.5	.972							

POS	Player	AB	BA	HR	RBI	PO	A	E	DP	TC/G	FA	Pitcher	G	IP	W	L	SV	ERA
1B	F. Tenney	369	.263	1	36	901	64	15	47	10.5	.985	B. Brown	42	241	8	18	2	4.29
2B	B. Sweeney	523	.314	3	63	372	410	46	61	6.1	.944	A. Mattern	33	186	4	15	0	4.97
SS	B. Herzog	294	.310	5	41	149	248	28	31	5.7	.934	L. Tyler	28	165	7	10	0	5.06
3B	S. Ingerton	521	.250	5	61	92	119	13	6	3.9	.942	H. Perdue	24	137	6	10	1	4.98
RF	D. Miller	577	.333	7	91	243	26	11	4	1.9	.961	O. Weaver	27	121	3	12	0	6.47
CF	M. Donlin	222	.315	2	34	117	8	12	2	2.4	.912	B. Pfeffer	26	97	7	5	2	4.73
LF	A. Kaiser	197	.203	2	15	101	6	9	3	2.0	.922	C. Curtis	12	77	1	8	1	4.44
C	J. Kling	241	.224	2	24	302	106*	21*	6	6.0	.951							
C	B. Rariden	246	.228	0	21	291	110	20	12	6.5	.952							
SS	A. Bridwell	182	.291	0	10	78	149	12	19	4.7	.950							
3B	E. McDonald	175	.206	1	21	63	86	7	10	2.9	.955							
OF	W. Good	165	.267	0	15	108	13	7	1	3.0	.945							
UT	H. Spratt	154	.240	2	13	82	75	19	9		.892							
OF	G. Jackson	147	.347	0	25	74	4	6	1	2.2	.929							
OF	P. Flaherty	94	.287	2	20	26	2	2	0	1.6	.933							

Bos. W-44 L-107 Fred Tenney

BATTING AND BASE RUNNING LEADERS

Batting Average
H. Wagner, PIT	.334
D. Miller, BOS	.333
C. Meyers, NY	.332
F. Clarke, PIT	.324
A. Fletcher, NY	.319

Slugging Average
W. Schulte, CHI	.534
L. Doyle, NY	.527
H. Wagner, PIT	.507
F. Clarke, PIT	.492
S. Magee, PHI	.483

Home Runs
W. Schulte, CHI	21
F. Luderus, PHI	16
S. Magee, PHI	15
L. Doyle, NY	13
F. Merkle, NY	12
O. Wilson, PIT	12

Total Bases
W. Schulte, CHI	308
L. Doyle, NY	277
F. Luderus, PHI	260
D. Hoblitzell, CIN	258
O. Wilson, PIT	257

Runs Batted In
W. Schulte, CHI	121
O. Wilson, PIT	107
F. Luderus, PHI	99
D. Hoblitzell, CIN	97
S. Magee, PHI	94

Stolen Bases
B. Bescher, CIN	81
J. Devore, NY	61
F. Snodgrass, NY	51
F. Merkle, NY	49
R. Murray, NY	48
B. Herzog, BOS, NY	48

Hits
D. Miller, BOS	192
D. Hoblitzell, CIN	180
J. Daubert, BKN	176

Base on Balls
J. Sheckard, CHI	147
J. Bates, CIN	103
B. Bescher, CIN	102

Home Run Percentage
W. Schulte, CHI	3.6
S. Magee, PHI	3.4
F. Luderus, PHI	2.9

Runs Scored
J. Sheckard, CHI	121
M. Huggins, STL	106
B. Bescher, CIN	106

Doubles
E. Konetchy, STL	38
D. Miller, BOS	36
O. Wilson, PIT	34

Triples
L. Doyle, NY	25
M. Mitchell, CIN	22
W. Schulte, CHI	21

PITCHING LEADERS

Winning Percentage
R. Marquard, NY	.774
D. Crandall, NY	.750
K. Cole, CHI	.720
G. Alexander, PHI	.683
C. Mathewson, NY	.667

Earned Run Average
C. Mathewson, NY	1.99
L. Richie, CHI	2.31
B. Adams, PIT	2.33
R. Marquard, NY	2.50
G. Alexander, PHI	2.57

Wins
G. Alexander, PHI	28
C. Mathewson, NY	26
R. Marquard, NY	24
B. Harmon, STL	23
B. Adams, PIT	22
N. Rucker, BKN	22

Saves
T. Brown, CHI	13
D. Crandall, NY	5
N. Rucker, BKN	4
G. Chalmers, PHI	4
B. Schardt, BKN	4
B. Harmon, STL	4

Strikeouts
R. Marquard, NY	237
G. Alexander, PHI	227
N. Rucker, BKN	190
E. Moore, PHI	174
B. Harmon, STL	144

Complete Games
G. Alexander, PHI	31
C. Mathewson, NY	29
B. Harmon, STL	28
L. Leifield, PIT	26
B. Adams, PIT	24

Fewest Hits per 9 Innings
G. Alexander, PHI	6.99
R. Marquard, NY	7.16
N. Rucker, BKN	7.27

Shutouts
B. Adams, PIT	7
G. Alexander, PHI	7

Fewest Walks per 9 Innings
C. Mathewson, NY	1.11
B. Adams, PIT	1.29
T. Brown, CHI	1.83

Most Strikeouts per 9 Inn.
R. Marquard, NY	7.68
G. Alexander, PHI	5.57
N. Rucker, BKN	5.42

Innings
G. Alexander, PHI	367
B. Harmon, STL	348
L. Leifield, PIT	318

Games Pitched
T. Brown, CHI	53
B. Harmon, STL	51
G. Alexander, PHI	48
N. Rucker, BKN	48

	W	L	PCT	GB	R	OR	2B	3B	HR	BA	SA	SB	E	DP	FA	CG	BB	SO	ShO	SV	ERA
NY	99	54	.647		756	542	225	105	41	**.279**	**.391**	347	255	86	.959	95	**369**	771	19	**16**	**2.69**
CHI	92	62	.597	7.5	**757**	607	218	101	54	.260	.374	214	260	114	.963	91	375	605	14	10	2.84
PIT	85	69	.552	14.5	744	560	206	**106**	48	.262	.371	160	232	**131**	.963	90	598	697	**20**	9	3.30
PHI	79	73	.520	19.5	658	673	214	56	**60**	.259	.359	153	**231**	113	**.963**	88	701	561	6	9	3.68
STL	75	74	.503	22	671	745	199	85	27	.252	.340	175	261	106	.960	77	476	557	4	10	3.26
CIN	70	83	.458	29	682	700	180	105	21	.261	.346	290	295	108	.955	81	566	533	14	10	3.39
BKN	64	86	.427	33.5	539	659	151	71	28	.237	.311	184	243	112	.947	73	672	486	5	6	5.08
BOS	44	107	.291	54	699	1020	**249**	54	37	.267	.355	169	347	110	.947						3.39
					5506	5506	1642	683	316	.260	.356	1692	2124	880	.958	680	4282	4792	94	81	3.39

Phi.
W-101 L-50 Connie Mack

POS	Player	AB	BA	HR	RBI	PO	A	E	DP	TC/G	FA	Pitcher	G	IP	W	L	SV	ERA
1B	S. McInnis	468	.321	3	77	1048	55	17	55	11.5	.985	J. Coombs	47	337	28	12	2	3.53
2B	E. Collins	493	.365	3	73	348	349	24	49	5.5	.967	E. Plank	40	257	23	8	4	2.10
SS	J. Barry	442	.265	1	63	268	384	39	49	5.4	.944	C. Morgan	38	250	15	7	1	2.70
3B	F. Baker	592	.334	11	115	217	274	30	26	3.5	.942	C. Bender	31	216	17	5	3	2.16
RF	D. Murphy	508	.329	6	66	162	34	8	6	1.5	.961	H. Krause	27	169	12	8	2	3.04
CF	R. Oldring	495	.297	3	59	225	13	5	2	2.0	.979							
LF	B. Lord	574	.310	3	55	271	17	11	5	2.3	.963							
C	I. Thomas	297	.273	0	39	499	150	17	12	6.5	.974							
OF	A. Strunk	215	.256	1	21	127	11	3	4	2.3	.979							
1B	H. Davis	183	.197	1	22	427	36	11	21	8.9	.977							
C	J. Lapp	167	.353	1	26	270	47	9	8	5.7	.972							
P	J. Coombs	141	.319	2	23	24	71	9	3	2.2	.913							

Det.
W-89 L-65 Hughie Jennings

POS	Player	AB	BA	HR	RBI	PO	A	E	DP	TC/G	FA	Pitcher	G	IP	W	L	SV	ERA
1B	J. Delahanty	542	.339	3	94	744	21	17	17	10.9	.978	G. Mullin	30	234	18	10	0	3.07
2B	C. O'Leary	256	.266	0	25	169	201	13	19	5.7	.966	E. Willett	38	231	13	14	1	3.66
SS	D. Bush	561	.232	1	36	372	556	75	42	6.7	.925	E. Summers	30	179	11	11	1	3.66
3B	G. Moriarty	478	.243	1	60	157	273	33	11	3.6	.929	E. Lafitte	29	172	11	8	1	3.92
RF	S. Crawford	574	.378	7	115	181	16	5	3	1.4	.975	W. Donovan	20	168	10	9	0	3.31
CF	T. Cobb	591	.420	8	144	376	24	18	10	2.9	.957	R. Works	30	167	11	5	1	3.87
LF	D. Jones	341	.273	0	19	156	15	9	3	2.0	.950	J. Lively	18	114	7	5	0	4.59
C	O. Stanage	503	.264	3	51	599	212	41	13	6.0	.952							
OF	D. Drake	315	.279	1	36	141	4	9	1	1.9	.942							
1B	D. Gainor	248	.302	2	25	671	38	18	36	10.5	.975							

Cle.
W-80 L-73 Deacon McGuire
W-6 L-11 George Stovall
W-74 L-62

POS	Player	AB	BA	HR	RBI	PO	A	E	DP	TC/G	FA	Pitcher	G	IP	W	L	SV	ERA
1B	G. Stovall	458	.271	0	79	1073	87	17	56	10.0	.986	V. Gregg	34	244	23	7	0	1.81
2B	N. Ball	412	.296	3	45	206	289	29	38	5.5	.945	G. Krapp	34	215	13	9	1	3.44
SS	I. Olson	545	.261	1	50	293	428	72	51	5.7	.909	W. Mitchell	30	177	7	14	0	3.76
3B	T. Turner	417	.252	0	28	114	208	10	10	3.5	.970	F. Blanding	29	176	7	11	2	3.68
RF	J. Jackson	571	.408	7	83	242	32	12	8	1.9	.958	G. Kahler	30	154	9	8	1	3.27
CF	J. Birmingham	447	.304	2	51	231	19	7	6	2.5	.973	C. Falkenberg	15	107	8	5	1	3.29
LF	J. Graney	527	.269	1	45	258	22	22	5	2.1	.927							
C	G. Fisher	203	.261	0	12	298	96	18	11	7.1	.956							
12	N. Lajoie	315	.365	2	60	479	109	14	33		.977							
OF	T. Easterly	287	.324	1	37	67	7	7	3	1.5	.914							
C	S. Smith	154	.299	1	21	270	62	7	10	7.1	.979							

Chi.
W-77 L-74 Hugh Duffy

POS	Player	AB	BA	HR	RBI	PO	A	E	DP	TC/G	FA	Pitcher	G	IP	W	L	SV	ERA
1B	S. Collins	370	.262	4	48	878	67	19	46	9.9	.980	E. Walsh	56	369	27	18	4	2.22
2B	A. McConnell	396	.280	1	34	189	280	13	31	4.7	.973	D. White	34	214	10	14	2	2.98
SS	L. Tannehill	516	.254	0	49	262	380	29	37	6.6	.957	J. Scott	39	202	14	11	0	2.63
3B	H. Lord	561	.321	3	61	175	226	25	21	3.1	.941	F. Lange	29	162	8	8	0	3.23
RF	M. McIntyre	569	.323	1	52	235	18	14	5	1.8	.948	F. Olmstead	25	118	6	6	2	4.21
CF	P. Bodie	551	.289	4	97	256	24	9	9	2.3	.948	J. Baker	22	94	2	7	1	3.93
LF	N. Callahan	466	.281	3	60	173	10	7	2	1.7	.963	I. Young	24	93	5	6	2	4.37
C	B. Sullivan	256	.215	0	31	447	114	8	13	6.4	.986							
UT	R. Zeider	217	.253	2	21	358	92	15	16		.968							
OF	P. Dougherty	211	.289	0	32	78	6	6	1	1.6	.933							
P	E. Walsh	155	.206	0	9	27	159	8	5	3.5	.959							

Bos.
W-78 L-75 Patsy Donovan

POS	Player	AB	BA	HR	RBI	PO	A	E	DP	TC/G	FA	Pitcher	G	IP	W	L	SV	ERA
1B	C. Engle	514	.270	2	48	550	43	14	24	9.3	.977	J. Wood	44	277	23	17	3	2.02
2B	H. Wagner	261	.257	1	48	106	104	12	11	5.6	.946	E. Cicotte	35	221	11	15	0	2.81
SS	S. Yerkes	502	.279	1	57	232	337	47	37	5.3	.924	R. Collins	31	204	11	12	1	2.39
3B	L. Gardner	492	.285	4	44	92	161	10	3	3.7	.962	L. Pape	27	176	10	8	0	2.45
RF	H. Hooper	524	.311	4	45	181	27	10	1	1.7	.954	C. Hall	32	147	8	7	4	3.73
CF	T. Speaker	510	.327	8	80	297	26	15	5	2.4	.956	E. Karger	25	131	5	8	0	3.37
LF	D. Lewis	469	.307	7	86	203	27	15	4	2.0	.939							
C	B. Carrigan	232	.289	1	30	326	94	12	11	7.0	.972							
1C	B. Williams	284	.239	0	31	727	73	20	28		.976							
C	L. Nunamaker	183	.257	0	19	309	79	11	8	6.8	.972							

N. Y.
W-76 L-76 Hal Chase

POS	Player	AB	BA	HR	RBI	PO	A	E	DP	TC/G	FA	Pitcher	G	IP	W	L	SV	ERA
1B	H. Chase	527	.315	3	62	1255	81	36	62	11.1	.974	R. Ford	37	281	22	11	0	2.27
2B	E. Gardner	357	.263	0	39	181	290	20	44	4.9	.959	R. Caldwell	41	255	14	14	1	3.35
SS	J. Knight	470	.268	3	62	200	247	46	30	6.0	.907	J. Warhop	31	210	12	13	0	4.16
3B	R. Hartzell	527	.296	3	91	158	221	26	18	3.3	.936	J. Quinn	40	175	8	10	2	3.76
RF	H. Wolter	434	.304	4	36	178	18	10	8	1.8	.951	R. Fisher	29	172	10	11	0	3.25
CF	B. Daniels	462	.286	2	31	256	15	17	6	2.4	.941	H. Vaughn	26	146	8	10	0	4.39
LF	B. Cree	520	.348	4	88	245	19	10	2	2.0	.964							
C	W. Blair	222	.194	0	26	379	101	15	12	5.9	.970							
C	J. Sweeney	229	.231	0	18	394	94	18	8	6.1	.964							
SS	O. Johnson	209	.234	3	36	78	126	21	17	4.8	.907							
OF	C. Hemphill	201	.284	1	15	95	4	5	0	1.9	.952							

Was.
W-64 L-90 Jimmy McAleer

POS	Player	AB	BA	HR	RBI	PO	A	E	DP	TC/G	FA	Pitcher	G	IP	W	L	SV	ERA
1B	G. Schaefer	440	.334	0	45	1038	71	23	57	10.5	.980	W. Johnson	40	323	25	13	1	1.89
2B	B. Cunningham	331	.190	3	37	168	244	30	18	4.8	.932	B. Groom	37	255	13	17	2	3.82
SS	G. McBride	557	.235	0	59	353	546	56	60	6.2	.941	L. Hughes	34	223	11	17	0	3.47
3B	W. Conroy	349	.232	2	28	87	177	20	11	3.3	.930	D. Walker	32	186	8	13	0	3.39
RF	D. Gessler	450	.282	4	78	130	19	9	2	1.3	.943	D. Gray	28	121	2	13	0	5.06
CF	C. Milan	616	.315	3	35	347	33	17	2	2.6	.957							
LF	T. Walker	356	.278	2	39	163	14	16	1	2.1	.917							
C	G. Street	216	.222	0	14	362	102	13	10	6.7	.973							
23	K. Elberfeld	404	.272	0	47	233	297	31	34		.945							
C1	J. Henry	261	.203	0	21	549	123	21	15		.970							
OF	J. Lelivelt	225	.320	0	22	82	11	6	1	2.0	.939							

	POS	Player	AB	BA	HR	RBI	PO	A	E	DP	TC/G	FA	Pitcher	G	IP	W	L	SV	ERA
St. L.	1B	J. Black	186	.151	0	7	519	37	16	31	10.6	.972	J. Lake	30	215	10	15	0	3.30
	2B	F. LaPorte	507	.314	2	82	287	398	36	59	5.4	.950	J. Powell	31	208	8	19	1	3.29
W-45 L-107	SS	B. Wallace	410	.232	0	31	280	417	42	47	6.0	.943	B. Pelty	28	207	7	15	0	2.83
Bobby Wallace	3B	J. Austin	541	.261	2	45	228	337	42	27	4.1	.931	E. Hamilton	32	177	5	12	0	3.97
	RF	A. Schweitzer	237	.215	0	34	100	13	8	4	1.8	.934	R. Mitchell	28	134	4	8	0	3.84
	CF	B. Shotton	572	.255	0	36	356	21	20	2	2.9	.950	L. George	27	116	4	9	0	4.18
	LF	H. Hogan	443	.260	2	62	263	26	22*	3	2.7	.929	R. Nelson	16	81	3	9	0	5.22
	C	N. Clarke	256	.215	0	18	251	111	29	15	5.4	.926							
	C	J. Stephens	212	.231	0	17	223	94	17	7	5.1	.949							
	OF	P. Meloan	206	.262	3	14	69	6	8	1	1.5	.904							
	S2	E. Hallinan	169	.207	0	14	118	133	24	24		.913							

BATTING AND BASE RUNNING LEADERS

Batting Average

T. Cobb, DET	.420
J. Jackson, CLE	.408
S. Crawford, DET	.378
E. Collins, PHI	.365
B. Cree, NY	.348

Slugging Average

T. Cobb, DET	.621
J. Jackson, CLE	.590
S. Crawford, DET	.526
B. Cree, NY	.513
F. Baker, PHI	.505

Home Runs

F. Baker, PHI	11
T. Speaker, BOS	8
T. Cobb, DET	8
D. Lewis, BOS	7
J. Jackson, CLE	7
S. Crawford, DET	7

Total Bases

T. Cobb, DET	367
J. Jackson, CLE	337
S. Crawford, DET	302
F. Baker, PHI	299
B. Cree, NY	267

Runs Batted In

T. Cobb, DET	144
S. Crawford, DET	115
F. Baker, PHI	115
P. Bodie, CHI	97
J. Delahanty, DET	94

Stolen Bases

T. Cobb, DET	83
C. Milan, WAS	58
B. Cree, NY	48
N. Callahan, CHI	45
H. Lord, CHI	43

Hits

T. Cobb, DET	248
J. Jackson, CLE	233
S. Crawford, DET	217

Base on Balls

D. Bush, DET	98
D. Gessler, WAS	74
C. Milan, WAS	74

Home Run Percentage

F. Baker, PHI	1.9
T. Speaker, BOS	1.6
D. Lewis, BOS	1.5

Runs Scored

T. Cobb, DET	147
D. Bush, DET	126
J. Jackson, CLE	126

Doubles

T. Cobb, DET	47
J. Jackson, CLE	45
F. Baker, PHI	40

Triples

T. Cobb, DET	24
B. Cree, NY	22
J. Jackson, CLE	19

PITCHING LEADERS

Winning Percentage

C. Bender, PHI	.773
V. Gregg, CLE	.767
E. Plank, PHI	.742
J. Coombs, PHI	.700
C. Morgan, PHI	.682

Earned Run Average

V. Gregg, CLE	1.81
W. Johnson, WAS	1.89
J. Wood, BOS	2.02
E. Plank, PHI	2.10
C. Bender, PHI	2.16

Wins

J. Coombs, PHI	28
E. Walsh, CHI	27
W. Johnson, WAS	25
E. Plank, PHI	23
V. Gregg, CLE	23
J. Wood, BOS	23

Saves

E. Plank, PHI	5
C. Hall, BOS	4
E. Walsh, CHI	4
J. Wood, BOS	3
C. Bender, PHI	3

Strikeouts

E. Walsh, CHI	255
J. Wood, BOS	231
W. Johnson, WAS	207
J. Coombs, PHI	185
R. Ford, NY	158

Complete Games

W. Johnson, WAS	36
E. Walsh, CHI	33
R. Ford, NY	26
J. Coombs, PHI	26
J. Wood, BOS	25
G. Mullin, DET	25

Fewest Hits per 9 Innings

V. Gregg, CLE	6.34
J. Wood, BOS	7.35
G. Krapp, CLE	7.63

Shutouts

E. Plank, PHI	6
W. Johnson, WAS	6

Fewest Walks per 9 Innings

D. White, CHI	1.47
J. Lake, STL	1.67
E. Walsh, CHI	1.76

Most Strikeouts per 9 Inn.

J. Wood, BOS	7.51
E. Walsh, CHI	6.23
W. Johnson, WAS	5.76

Innings

E. Walsh, CHI	369
J. Coombs, PHI	337
W. Johnson, WAS	323

Games Pitched

E. Walsh, CHI	56
J. Coombs, PHI	47
J. Wood, BOS	44
R. Caldwell, NY	41

	W	L	PCT	GB	R	OR	2B	3B	Batting HR	BA	SA	SB	E	Fielding DP	FA	CG	BB	Pitching SO	ShO	SV	ERA
PHI	101	50	.669		861	601	235	93	35	.296	.397	226	225	100	.965	97	487	739	13	13	3.01
DET	89	65	.578	13.5	831	777	230	96	30	.292	.388	276	318	78	.951	108	460	538	8	3	3.73
CLE	80	73	.523	22	691	709	238	81	20	.282	.369	209	302	108	.954	93	550	673	6	6	3.37
CHI	77	74	.510	24	717	627	179	92	20	.269	.350	201	252	98	.961	87	384	752	16	11	3.01
BOS	78	75	.510	24	680	647	203	66	35	.274	.362	190	323	93	.949	87	475	713	10	8	2.73
NY	76	76	.500	25.5	686	726	190	96	26	.272	.363	270	328	99	.949	91	406	667	5	3	3.54
WAS	64	90	.416	38.5	624	760	159	53	16	.258	.320	215	305	90	.953	106	410	628	13	3	3.52
STL	45	107	.296	56.5	567	810	187	63	17	.239	.312	125	358	104	.945	92	463	383	8	1	3.83
					5657	5657	1621	640	199	.273	.358	1712	2411	770	.953	761	3635	5093	79	48	3.34

N. Y. — W-103 L-48 — John McGraw

POS	Player	AB	BA	HR	RBI	PO	A	E	DP	TC/G	FA
1B	F. Merkle	479	.309	11	84	1229	72	27	77	10.3	.980
2B	L. Doyle	558	.330	10	90	313	379	38	68	5.1	.948
SS	A. Fletcher	419	.282	1	57	237	428	52	60	5.7	.927
3B	B. Herzog	482	.263	2	47	159	308	29	21	3.5	.942
RF	R. Murray	549	.277	3	92	255	20	9	7	2.0	.968
CF	B. Becker	402	.264	6	58	230	20	11	4	2.2	.958
LF	F. Snodgrass	535	.269	3	69	229	25	14	4	2.3	.948
C	C. Meyers	371	.358	6	54	576	111	19	10	5.8	.973
OF	J. Devore	327	.275	2	37	155	14	15	3	1.9	.918
UT	T. Shafer	163	.288	0	23	80	119	22	10		.900

Pitcher	G	IP	W	L	SV	ERA
C. Mathewson	43	310	23	12	4	2.12
R. Marquard	43	295	26	11	0	2.57
J. Tesreau	36	243	17	7	1	1.96
R. Ames	33	179	11	5	2	2.46
D. Crandall	37	162	13	7	2	3.61
H. Wiltse	28	134	9	6	2	3.16

Pit. — W-93 L-58 — Fred Clarke

POS	Player	AB	BA	HR	RBI	PO	A	E	DP	TC/G	FA
1B	D. Miller	567	.275	4	87	1385	85	23	93	10.2	.985
2B	A. McCarthy	401	.277	1	41	237	320	22	52	5.5	.962
SS	H. Wagner	558	.324	7	102	341	462	32	74	5.8	.962
3B	B. Byrne	528	.288	3	35	144	187	18	14	2.7	.948
RF	M. Donlin	244	.316	2	35	102	8	2	1	1.8	.982
CF	O. Wilson	583	.300	11	95	324	20	14	5	2.4	.961
LF	M. Carey	587	.302	5	66	369	19	13	10	2.7	.968
C	G. Gibson	300	.240	2	35	484	101	6	11	6.3	.990
2B	A. Butler	154	.273	1	17	71	99	7	12	4.1	.960
OF	H. Hyatt	97	.289	0	22	20	1	1	0	1.5	.955

Pitcher	G	IP	W	L	SV	ERA
C. Hendrix	39	289	24	9	1	2.59
H. Camnitz	41	277	22	12	2	2.83
M. O'Toole	37	275	15	17	0	2.71
H. Robinson	33	175	12	7	2	2.26
B. Adams	28	170	11	8	0	2.91

Chi. — W-91 L-59 — Frank Chance

POS	Player	AB	BA	HR	RBI	PO	A	E	DP	TC/G	FA
1B	V. Saier	451	.288	2	61	1165	52	10	67	10.2	.992
2B	J. Evers	478	.341	1	63	319	439	32	71	5.5	.959
SS	J. Tinker	550	.282	0	75	354	470	50	73	6.2	.943
3B	H. Zimmerman	557	.372	14	103	142	242	35	16	3.5	.916
RF	W. Schulte	553	.264	13	70	219	19	12	6	1.8	.952
CF	T. Leach	265	.242	2	32	181	11	5	4	2.7*	.975*
LF	J. Sheckard	523	.245	3	47	332	26	14	4	2.5	.962
C	J. Archer	385	.283	5	58	504	149	23	15	5.7	.966
OF	W. Miller	241	.307	0	22	109	6	7	2	1.9	.943

Pitcher	G	IP	W	L	SV	ERA
L. Cheney	42	303	26	10	0	2.85
J. Lavender	42	252	16	13	3	3.04
L. Richie	39	238	16	8	0	2.95
E. Reulbach	39	169	10	6	3	3.78
C. Smith	21	94	7	4	1	4.21
T. Brown	15	89	5	6	0	2.64

Cin. — W-75 L-78 — Hank O'Day

POS	Player	AB	BA	HR	RBI	PO	A	E	DP	TC/G	FA
1B	D. Hoblitzell	558	.294	2	85	1326	87	21	73	9.8	.985
2B	D. Egan	507	.247	0	52	345	452	22	55	5.5	.973
SS	J. Esmond	231	.195	1	40	154	180	25	22	4.9	.930
3B	A. Phelan	461	.243	3	54	153	250	33	18	3.4	.924
RF	M. Mitchell	552	.283	4	78	251	18	15	8	2.0	.947
CF	A. Marsans	416	.317	1	38	222	11	6	2	2.4	.975
LF	B. Bescher	548	.281	4	38	347	15	14	4	2.6	.963
C	L. McLean	333	.243	1	27	425	124	15	16	5.8	.973
SS	E. Grant	255	.239	2	20	102	171	15	20	5.1	.948
OF	J. Bates	239	.289	1	29	157	15	9	4	2.8	.950
C	T. Clarke	146	.281	0	22	239	58	5	7	4.8	.983

Pitcher	G	IP	W	L	SV	ERA
G. Suggs	42	303	19	16	3	2.94
R. Benton	50	302	18	21	2	3.10
A. Fromme	43	296	16	18	0	2.74
B. Humphries	30	159	9	11	2	3.23

Phi. — W-73 L-79 — Red Dooin

POS	Player	AB	BA	HR	RBI	PO	A	E	DP	TC/G	FA
1B	F. Luderus	572	.257	10	69	1421	104	15	77	10.5	.990
2B	O. Knabe	426	.282	0	46	258	342	30	45	5.1	.952
SS	M. Doolan	532	.258	1	62	289	476	40	49	5.5	.950
3B	H. Lobert	257	.327	2	33	80	86	4	3	2.7	.976
RF	G. Cravath	436	.284	11	70	200	26	8	5	2.1	.966
CF	D. Paskert	540	.315	2	43	336	19	12	4	2.6	.967
LF	S. Magee	464	.306	6	72	251	8	10	2	2.2	.963
C	B. Killefer	268	.224	1	22	407	134	15	17	6.5	.973
C	R. Dooin	184	.234	0	22	254	69	14	2	5.8	.958
OF	D. Miller	177	.288	0	21	61	9	1	1	1.8	.986
3B	T. Downey	171	.292	1	22	57	76	16	3	3.2	.893
OF	J. Titus	157	.274	3	22	53	2	5	1	1.4	.917

Pitcher	G	IP	W	L	SV	ERA
G. Alexander	46	310	19	17	2	2.81
T. Seaton	44	255	16	12	2	3.28
E. Moore	31	182	9	14	0	3.31
A. Brennan	27	174	11	9	2	3.57
E. Rixey	23	162	10	10	0	2.50

St. L. — W-63 L-90 — Roger Bresnahan

POS	Player	AB	BA	HR	RBI	PO	A	E	DP	TC/G	FA
1B	E. Konetchy	538	.314	8	82	1392	90	13	77	10.5	.991
2B	M. Huggins	431	.304	0	29	272	337	37	50	5.7	.943
SS	A. Hauser	479	.259	0	42	262	446	50	54	5.7	.934
3B	M. Mowrey	408	.255	2	50	131	220	26	22	3.5	.931
RF	S. Evans	491	.283	6	72	219	24	15	2	1.9	.942
CF	R. Oakes	495	.281	3	58	324	15	19	5	2.6	.947
LF	L. Magee	458	.290	0	40	198	18	10	2	2.7	.956
C	I. Wingo	310	.265	2	44	360	148	23	11	5.8	.957
OF	R. Ellis	305	.269	4	33	173	10	14	5	2.6	.929
3S	W. Smith	219	.256	0	26	81	126	10	10		.954

Pitcher	G	IP	W	L	SV	ERA
S. Sallee	48	294	16	17	6	2.60
B. Harmon	43	268	18	18	0	3.93
B. Steele	40	194	9	13	1	4.69
R. Geyer	41	181	7	14	0	3.28
J. Willis	31	130	4	9	2	4.44

Bkn. — W-58 L-95 — Bill Dahlen

POS	Player	AB	BA	HR	RBI	PO	A	E	DP	TC/G	FA
1B	J. Daubert	559	.308	3	66	1373	76	10	68	10.2	.993
2B	G. Cutshaw	357	.280	0	28	192	290	21	31	5.5	.958
SS	B. Tooley	265	.234	2	37	147	214	47	23	5.4	.885
3B	R. Smith	486	.286	4	57	156	251	27	16	3.5	.938
RF	H. Northen	412	.282	2	46	178	11	10	3	2.0	.950
CF	H. Moran	508	.276	1	40	273	24	12	5	2.4	.961
LF	Z. Wheat	453	.305	8	65	285	13	10	2	2.5	.968
C	O. Miller	316	.278	1	31	455	141	15	11	6.5	.975
2O	J. Hummel	411	.282	5	54	175	161	11	17		.968
SS	B. Fisher	257	.233	0	26	121	200	29	23	4.7	.917
OF	J. Daley	199	.256	2	13	116	10	7	3	2.4	.947
C	E. Phelps	111	.288	0	23	130	35	4	4	5.3	.976

Pitcher	G	IP	W	L	SV	ERA
N. Rucker	45	298	18	21	4	2.21
P. Ragan	36	208	7	18	1	3.63
E. Yingling	25	163	6	11	0	3.59
E. Stack	28	142	7	5	1	3.36
E. Knetzer	33	140	7	9	0	4.55
F. Allen	20	109	3	9	0	3.63
C. Barger	16	94	1	9	0	5.46
M. Kent	20	93	5	5	0	4.84
C. Curtis	19	80	4	7	0	3.94

	POS	Player	AB	BA	HR	RBI	PO	A	E	DP	TC/G	FA	Pitcher	G	IP	W	L	SV	ERA
Bos.	1B	B. Houser	332	.286	8	52	759	37	11	48	9.7	.986	L. Tyler	42	256	12	**22**	0	4.18
W-52 L-101	2B	B. Sweeney	593	.344	1	100	**459**	**475**	**40**	**76**	**6.4**	.959	O. Hess	33	254	12	17	0	3.76
Johnny Kling	SS	F. O'Rourke	196	.122	0	16	92	167	24	16	4.8	.915	H. Perdue	37	249	13	16	3	3.80
	3B	E. McDonald	459	.259	2	34	147	216	23	18	3.3	.940	W. Dickson	36	189	3	19	0	3.86
	RF	J. Titus	345	.325	2	48	152	12	6	1	1.8	.965	E. Donnelly	37	184	5	10	0	4.35
	CF	V. Campbell	**624**	.296	3	48	340	20	**24**	6	2.7	.938	B. Brown	31	168	4	15	0	4.01
	LF	G. Jackson	397	.262	4	48	230	20	15	3	2.5	.943							
	C	J. Kling	252	.317	2	30	322	108	19	**20**	6.1	.958							
	UT	A. Devlin	436	.289	0	54	768	140	15	52		.984							
	O3	J. Kirke	359	.320	4	62	99	45	23	4		.862							
	C	B. Rariden	247	.223	1	14	297	103	15	6	5.7	.964							
	OF	D. Miller	201	.234	2	24	79	12	5	4	1.9	.948							

BATTING AND BASE RUNNING LEADERS

Batting Average

H. Zimmerman, CHI	.372
C. Meyers, NY	.358
B. Sweeney, BOS	.344
J. Evers, CHI	.341
L. Doyle, NY	.330

Slugging Average

H. Zimmerman, CHI	.571
O. Wilson, PIT	.513
H. Wagner, PIT	.496
C. Meyers, NY	.477
L. Doyle, NY	.471

Home Runs

H. Zimmerman, CHI	14
W. Schulte, CHI	13
G. Cravath, PHI	11
F. Merkle, NY	11
O. Wilson, PIT	11

Total Bases

H. Zimmerman, CHI	318
O. Wilson, PIT	299
H. Wagner, PIT	277
B. Sweeney, BOS	264
L. Doyle, NY	263

Runs Batted In

H. Zimmerman, CHI	103
H. Wagner, PIT	102
B. Sweeney, BOS	100
O. Wilson, PIT	95
R. Murray, NY	92

Stolen Bases

B. Bescher, CIN	67
M. Carey, PIT	45
F. Snodgrass, NY	43
R. Murray, NY	38
F. Merkle, NY	37
B. Herzog, NY	37

Hits

H. Zimmerman, CHI	207
B. Sweeney, BOS	204
V. Campbell, BOS	185

Base on Balls

J. Sheckard, CHI	122
D. Paskert, PHI	91
M. Huggins, STL	87

Home Run Percentage

G. Cravath, PHI	2.5
H. Zimmerman, CHI	2.5
W. Schulte, CHI	2.4

Runs Scored

B. Bescher, CIN	120
M. Carey, PIT	114
D. Paskert, PHI	102
V. Campbell, BOS	102

Doubles

H. Zimmerman, CHI	41
D. Paskert, PHI	37
H. Wagner, PIT	35

Triples

O. Wilson, PIT	36
R. Murray, NY	20
H. Wagner, PIT	20

PITCHING LEADERS

Winning Percentage

C. Hendrix, PIT	.727
L. Cheney, CHI	.722
J. Tesreau, NY	.708
R. Marquard, NY	.703
L. Richie, CHI	.667

Earned Run Average

J. Tesreau, NY	1.96
C. Mathewson, NY	2.12
N. Rucker, BKN	2.21
H. Robinson, PIT	2.26
E. Rixey, PHI	2.50

Wins

R. Marquard, NY	26
L. Cheney, CHI	26
C. Hendrix, PIT	24
C. Mathewson, NY	23
H. Camnitz, PIT	22

Saves

S. Sallee, STL	6
N. Rucker, BKN	4
C. Mathewson, NY	4

Strikeouts

G. Alexander, PHI	195
C. Hendrix, PIT	176
R. Marquard, NY	175
R. Benton, CIN	162
N. Rucker, BKN	151

Complete Games

L. Cheney, CHI	28
C. Mathewson, NY	27
G. Alexander, PHI	26
C. Hendrix, PIT	25
G. Suggs, CIN	25

Fewest Hits per 9 Innings

J. Tesreau, NY	6.56
H. Robinson, PIT	7.51
M. O'Toole, PIT	7.75

Shutouts

M. O'Toole, PIT	6
N. Rucker, BKN	6
G. Suggs, CIN	5

Fewest Walks per 9 Innings

C. Mathewson, NY	0.99
H. Robinson, PIT	1.54
G. Suggs, CIN	1.66

Most Strikeouts per 9 Inn.

G. Alexander, PHI	5.66
C. Hendrix, PIT	5.49
R. Marquard, NY	5.35

Innings

G. Alexander, PHI	310
C. Mathewson, NY	310
L. Cheney, CHI	303

Games Pitched

R. Benton, CIN	50
S. Sallee, STL	48
G. Alexander, PHI	46

	W	L	PCT	GB	R	OR	2B	3B	Batting HR	BA	SA	SB	E	Fielding DP	FA	CG	BB	Pitching SO	ShO	SV	ERA
NY	103	48	.682		**823**	571	231	89	**47**	.286	.395	**319**	280	123	.956	93	**338**	652	8	**13**	**2.58**
PIT	93	58	.616	10	751	565	222	**129**	39	.284	**.398**	177	**169**	125	**.972**	**94**	497	**664**	**18**	6	2.85
CHI	91	59	.607	11.5	756	666	**245**	91	43	.277	.387	164	249	125	.960	80	493	554	14	8	3.42
CIN	75	78	.490	29	656	722	183	89	21	.256	.339	248	247	102	.960	86	452	561	12	10	3.42
PHI	73	79	.480	30.5	670	689	244	68	43	.267	.367	159	231	98	.963	82	515	616	10	8	3.25
STL	63	90	.412	41	659	825	190	77	27	.268	.352	193	274	113	.957	62	560	487	6	11	3.85
BKN	58	95	.379	46	651	748	220	73	32	.268	.358	179	255	96	.959	71	510	553	10	7	3.64
BOS	52	101	.340	52	693	873	227	68	35	.273	.360	137	295	**129**	.954	92	521	542	5	3	4.17
					5659	5659	1762	684	287	.272	.369	1576	2000	911	.960	660	3886	4629	83	66	3.40

Bos. W-105 L-47 Jake Stahl

POS	Player	AB	BA	HR	RBI	PO	A	E	DP	TC/G	FA	Pitcher	G	IP	W	L	SV	ERA
1B	J. Stahl	326	.301	3	60	853	49	18	37	10.0	.980	J. Wood	43	344	34	5	1	1.91
2B	S. Yerkes	523	.252	0	42	244	323	34	39	4.6	.943	B. O'Brien	37	276	20	13	0	2.58
SS	H. Wagner	504	.274	2	68	332	391	61	43	5.4	.922	H. Bedient	41	231	20	9	2	2.92
3B	L. Gardner	517	.315	3	86	167	296	35	16	3.5	.930	R. Collins	27	199	13	8	0	2.53
RF	H. Hooper	590	.242	2	53	220	22	9	6	1.7	.964	C. Hall	34	191	15	8	2	3.02
CF	T. Speaker	580	.383	10	98	372	35	18	9	2.8	.958							
LF	D. Lewis	581	.284	6	109	301	23	18	4	2.2	.947							
C	B. Carrigan	266	.263	0	24	413	102	16	7	6.1	.970							
UT	C. Engle	171	.234	0	18	248	60	13	15		.960							

Was. W-91 L-61 Clark Griffith

POS	Player	AB	BA	HR	RBI	PO	A	E	DP	TC/G	FA	Pitcher	G	IP	W	L	SV	ERA
1B	C. Gandil	443	.305	2	81	1106	68	12	49	10.1	.990	W. Johnson	50	368	32	12	2	1.39
2B	R. Morgan	273	.238	1	30	150	173	21	21	4.6	.939	B. Groom	43	316	24	13	1	2.62
SS	G. McBride	521	.226	1	52	349	498	53	55	5.9	.941	L. Hughes	31	196	13	10	2	2.94
3B	E. Foster	618	.285	2	70	168	348	45	22	3.6	.920	J. Cashion	26	170	10	6	1	3.17
RF	D. Moeller	519	.276	6	46	227	25	15	5	2.0	.944							
CF	C. Milan	601	.306	1	79	326	31	25	6	2.5	.935							
LF	H. Shanks	399	.231	1	47	189	14	8	2	1.9	.962							
C	J. Henry	191	.194	0	9	347	113	11	7	7.5	.977							
C	E. Ainsmith	186	.226	0	22	415	85	22	5	9.0	.958							
UT	G. Schaefer	166	.247	0	19	169	30	8	7		.961							
C	B. Williams	157	.318	0	22	234	74	7	6	7.0	.978							
P	W. Johnson	144	.264	2	20	15	93	4	4	2.2	.964							

Phi. W-90 L-62 Connie Mack

POS	Player	AB	BA	HR	RBI	PO	A	E	DP	TC/G	FA	Pitcher	G	IP	W	L	SV	ERA
1B	S. McInnis	568	.327	3	101	1533	100	27	88	10.8	.984	J. Coombs	40	262	21	10	2	3.29
2B	E. Collins	543	.348	0	64	387	426	38	63	5.6	.955	E. Plank	37	260	26	6	2	2.22
SS	J. Barry	483	.261	0	55	238	438	55	55	5.3	.925	B. Brown	34	199	13	11	1	3.66
3B	F. Baker	577	.347	10	133	217	321	34	25	3.8	.941	B. Houck	30	181	8	8	0	2.94
RF	B. Lord	378	.238	0	25	148	15	10	5	1.8	.942	C. Bender	27	171	13	8	2	2.74
CF	R. Oldring	395	.301	1	24	214	8	6	1	2.4	.974	C. Morgan	16	94	3	8	0	3.75
LF	A. Strunk	412	.289	3	63	278	16	3	3	2.5	.990							
C	J. Lapp	281	.292	1	35	354	105	20	10	5.8	.958							
OF	H. Maggert	242	.256	1	13	103	5	7	0	1.9	.939							
OF	D. Murphy	130	.323	2	20	39	2	5	2	1.3	.891							

Chi. W-78 L-76 Nixey Callahan

POS	Player	AB	BA	HR	RBI	PO	A	E	DP	TC/G	FA	Pitcher	G	IP	W	L	SV	ERA
1B	R. Zeider	420	.245	1	42	682	54	16	28	11.4	.979	E. Walsh	62	393	27	17	10	2.15
2B	M. Rath	591	.272	1	19	353	463	31	46	5.4	.963	J. Benz	41	238	13	17	0	2.92
SS	B. Weaver	523	.224	1	43	342	425	71	53	5.7	.915	D. White	32	172	8	10	0	3.24
3B	H. Lord	570	.267	5	54	127	172	35	11	3.2	.895	F. Lange	31	165	10	10	3	3.27
RF	S. Collins	575	.292	2	81	177	11	6	0	1.8	.969	E. Cicotte	20	152	9	7	0	2.84
CF	P. Bodie	472	.294	5	72	208	11	7	3	1.7	.969	R. Peters	28	109	5	6	0	4.14
LF	N. Callahan	408	.272	1	52	166	3	11	0	1.7	.939	G. Mogridge	17	65	3	4	3	4.04
C	W. Kuhn	178	.202	0	10	318	104	15	8	5.8	.966							
OF	W. Mattick	285	.260	1	35	154	8	3	1	2.1	.982							
C	B. Block	136	.257	0	26	222	65	6	4	6.4	.980							

Cle. W-75 L-78 Harry Davis / W-54 L-71 Joe Birmingham / W-21 L-7

POS	Player	AB	BA	HR	RBI	PO	A	E	DP	TC/G	FA	Pitcher	G	IP	W	L	SV	ERA
1B	A. Griggs	273	.304	0	39	661	43	10	33	10.1	.986	V. Gregg	37	271	20	13	2	2.59
2B	N. Lajoie	448	.368	0	90	241	249	21	49	5.3	.959	F. Blanding	39	262	18	14	1	2.92
SS	Peckinpaugh	236	.212	1	22	127	188	26	16	5.1	.924	G. Kahler	41	246	12	19	1	3.69
3B	T. Turner	370	.308	0	33	129	199	17	21	3.3	.951	W. Mitchell	29	164	5	8	1	2.80
RF	J. Jackson	572	.395	3	90	273	30	16	2	2.1	.950	B. Steen	26	143	9	8	0	3.77
CF	J. Birmingham	369	.255	0	45	198	18	11	8	2.4	.952	J. Baskette	29	116	8	4	1	3.18
LF	B. Ryan	328	.271	1	31	167	11	7	2	2.1	.962							
C	S. O'Neill	215	.228	0	14	316	108	17	9	6.6	.961							
UT	I. Olson	467	.253	0	33	230	318	44	18		.926							
OF	J. Graney	264	.242	0	20	148	11	7	5	2.2	.958							
C	T. Easterly	186	.296	1	21	226	69	13	11*	2.2	.958							
1B	D. Johnston	164	.280	1	11	330	17	3	27	8.5	.991							

Det. W-69 L-84 Hughie Jennings

POS	Player	AB	BA	HR	RBI	PO	A	E	DP	TC/G	FA	Pitcher	G	IP	W	L	SV	ERA
1B	G. Moriarty	375	.248	0	54	800	27	11	19	11.8	.987	E. Willett	37	284	17	15	0	3.29
2B	B. Louden	403	.241	1	36	200	288	25	25	6.0	.951	J. Dubuc	37	250	17	10	3	2.77
SS	D. Bush	511	.231	2	38	317	547	66	45	6.5	.929	G. Mullin	30	226	12	17	0	3.54
3B	C. Deal	142	.225	0	11	48	113	10	3	4.2	.942	J. Lake	26	163	9	11	1	3.10
RF	S. Crawford	581	.325	4	109	169	16	3	5	1.3	.984	R. Works	27	157	5	10	1	4.24
CF	T. Cobb	553	.410	7	90	324	21	22	5	2.6	.940							
LF	D. Jones	316	.294	0	24	141	13	6	4	2.0	.963							
C	O. Stanage	394	.261	0	41	440	168	32	14	5.4	.950							
UT	O. Vitt	273	.245	0	19	109	99	11	8		.950							
2O	J. Delahanty	266	.286	0	41	148	120	23	19		.921							
1B	D. Gainor	179	.240	0	20	547	22	8	25	11.5	.986							

St. L. W-53 L-101 Bobby Wallace / W-12 L-27 George Stovall / W-41 L-74

POS	Player	AB	BA	HR	RBI	PO	A	E	DP	TC/G	FA	Pitcher	G	IP	W	L	SV	ERA
1B	G. Stovall	398	.254	0	45	845	68	16	64	9.9	.983	E. Hamilton	41	250	11	14	2	3.24
2B	D. Pratt	570	.302	5	69	273	326	36	49	5.2	.943	J. Powell	32	235	9	16	0	3.10
SS	B. Wallace	323	.241	0	31	185	271	28	29	5.6	.942	Baumgardner	30	218	11	14	0	3.38
3B	J. Austin	536	.252	2	44	219	292	50	29	3.8	.911	M. Allison	31	169	6	17	1	3.62
RF	P. Compton	268	.280	2	30	139	9	12	1	2.2	.925	E. Brown	23	120	5	8	0	2.99
CF	B. Shotton	580	.290	2	40	381	20	25	7	2.8	.941							
LF	H. Hogan	360	.214	1	36	229	14	7	6	2.5	.972							
C	J. Stephens	205	.249	0	22	262	110	18	10	5.9	.954							
2O	F. LaPorte	266	.312	1	38	123	107	16	24		.935							
OF	G. Williams	216	.292	2	32	94	12	8	3	1.8	.930							
1B	J. Kutina	205	.205	1	18	489	24	8	28	10.2	.985							
C	P. Krichell	161	.217	0	8	255	72	14	9	6.0	.959							

	POS	Player	AB	BA	HR	RBI	PO	A	E	DP	TC/G	FA	Pitcher	G	IP	W	L	SV	ERA
	1B	H. Chase	522	.274	4	58	1162	79	27	49	10.5	.979	R. Ford	36	292	13	21	0	3.55
N. Y.	2B	H. Simmons	401	.239	0	41	162	207	21	23	4.4	.946	J. Warhop	39	258	10	19	3	2.86
W-50 L-102	SS	J. Martin	231	.225	0	17	123	201	36	18	5.6	.900	R. Caldwell	30	183	8	16	0	4.47
Harry Wolverton	3B	D. Paddock	156	.288	1	14	49	69	14	4	3.2	.894	G. McConnell	23	177	8	12	0	2.75
	RF	G. Zinn	401	.262	6	55	158	9	20	1	1.8	.893	J. Quinn	18	103	5	7	0	5.79
	CF	R. Hartzell	416	.272	1	38	101	9	7	2	2.1	.940	R. Fisher	17	90	2	8	0	5.88
	LF	B. Daniels	496	.274	2	41	277	13	17	1	2.3	.945	H. Vaughn	15	63	2	8	0	5.14
	C	J. Sweeney	351	.268	0	30	548	167	34	9	6.9	.955							
	UT	D. Sterrett	230	.265	1	32	259	22	5	4		.983							
	OF	B. Cree	190	.332	0	22	123	5	7	1	2.7	.948							
	2B	E. Gardner	160	.281	0	26	93	107	17	11	5.0	.922							
	OF	J. Lelivelt	149	.362	2	23	75	4	3	2	2.3	.963							

BATTING AND BASE RUNNING LEADERS

Batting Average

T. Cobb, DET	.410
J. Jackson, CLE	.395
T. Speaker, BOS	.383
N. Lajoie, CLE	.368
E. Collins, PHI	.348

Slugging Average

T. Cobb, DET	.586
J. Jackson, CLE	.579
T. Speaker, BOS	.567
F. Baker, PHI	.541
S. Crawford, DET	.470

Home Runs

T. Speaker, BOS	10
F. Baker, PHI	10
T. Cobb, DET	7
G. Zinn, NY	6
D. Moeller, WAS	6
D. Lewis, BOS	6

Total Bases

J. Jackson, CLE	331
T. Speaker, BOS	329
T. Cobb, DET	324
F. Baker, PHI	312
S. Crawford, DET	273

Runs Batted In

F. Baker, PHI	133
S. Crawford, DET	109
D. Lewis, BOS	109
S. McInnis, PHI	101
T. Speaker, BOS	98

Stolen Bases

C. Milan, WAS	88
E. Collins, PHI	63
T. Cobb, DET	61
T. Speaker, BOS	52
R. Zeider, CHI	47

Hits

T. Cobb, DET	227
J. Jackson, CLE	226
T. Speaker, BOS	222

Base on Balls

D. Bush, DET	117
E. Collins, PHI	101
M. Rath, CHI	95

Home Run Percentage

F. Baker, PHI	1.7
T. Speaker, BOS	1.6
G. Zinn, NY	1.5

Runs Scored

E. Collins, PHI	137
T. Speaker, BOS	136
J. Jackson, CLE	121

Doubles

T. Speaker, BOS	53
J. Jackson, CLE	44
F. Baker, PHI	40
D. Lewis, BOS	36

Triples

J. Jackson, CLE	26
T. Cobb, DET	23
F. Baker, PHI	21
S. Crawford, DET	21

PITCHING LEADERS

Winning Percentage

J. Wood, BOS	.872
E. Plank, PHI	.813
W. Johnson, WAS	.727
J. Coombs, PHI	.677
H. Bedient, BOS	.667

Earned Run Average

W. Johnson, WAS	1.39
J. Wood, BOS	1.91
E. Walsh, CHI	2.15
E. Plank, PHI	2.22
R. Collins, BOS	2.53

Wins

J. Wood, BOS	34
W. Johnson, WAS	32
E. Walsh, CHI	27
E. Plank, PHI	26
B. Groom, WAS	24

Saves

E. Walsh, CHI	10

Strikeouts

W. Johnson, WAS	303
J. Wood, BOS	258
E. Walsh, CHI	254
V. Gregg, CLE	184
B. Groom, WAS	179

Complete Games

J. Wood, BOS	35
W. Johnson, WAS	34
R. Ford, NY	32
E. Walsh, CHI	32
E. Willett, DET	28
B. Groom, WAS	28

Fewest Hits per 9 Innings

W. Johnson, WAS	6.33
J. Wood, BOS	6.99
B. Houck, PHI	7.37

Shutouts

J. Wood, BOS	10
W. Johnson, WAS	7
E. Walsh, CHI	6
R. Collins, BOS	4

Fewest Walks per 9 Innings

C. Bender, PHI	1.74
W. Johnson, WAS	1.86
R. Collins, BOS	1.90

Most Strikeouts per 9 Inn.

W. Johnson, WAS	7.24
J. Wood, BOS	6.75
V. Gregg, CLE	6.10

Innings

E. Walsh, CHI	393
W. Johnson, WAS	368
J. Wood, BOS	344

Games Pitched

E. Walsh, CHI	62
W. Johnson, WAS	50
J. Wood, BOS	43
B. Groom, WAS	43

	W	L	PCT	GB	R	OR	Batting 2B	3B	HR	BA	SA	SB	Fielding E	DP	FA	CG	BB	Pitching SO	ShO	SV	ERA
BOS	105	47	.691		800	544	269	84	29	.277	.380	185	267	88	.957	108	385	712	18	6	2.76
WAS	91	61	.599	14	698	581	202	86	20	.256	.341	274	297	92	.954	98	525	828	11	6	2.69
PHI	90	62	.592	15	780	656	204	108	22	.282	.377	258	263	115	.959	100	518	601	11	9	3.32
CHI	78	76	.506	28	640	647	174	80	17	.255	.329	205	291	102	.956	85	426	697	14	16	3.06
CLE	75	78	.490	30.5	680	681	218	77	10	.273	.352	194	287	124	.954	94	523	622	7	7	3.30
DET	69	84	.451	36.5	720	768	189	86	19	.267	.349	270	338	91	.950	107	517	506	7	5	3.78
STL	53	101	.344	53	556	790	166	71	19	.249	.320	176	341	127	.947	85	442	547	8	5	3.71
NY	50	102	.329	55	632	839	168	79	18	.259	.334	247	382	77	.940	105	436	637	4	3	4.13
					5506	5506	1590	671	154	.265	.348	1809	2466	816	.952	782	3772	5150	80	57	3.34

	POS	Player	AB	BA	HR	RBI	PO	A	E	DP	TC/G	FA	Pitcher	G	IP	W	L	SV	ERA
N. Y.	1B	F. Merkle	563	.261	3	69	1463	76	22	86	10.2	.986	C. Mathewson	40	306	25	11	2	**2.06**
W-101 L-51	2B	L. Doyle	482	.280	5	73	315	345	31	55	5.3	.955	R. Marquard	42	288	23	10	2	2.50
John McGraw	SS	A. Fletcher	538	.297	4	71	245	435	50	42	5.4	.932	J. Tesreau	41	282	22	13	0	2.17
	3B	B. Herzog	290	.286	3	31	95	139	13	18	2.9	.947	A. Demaree	31	200	13	4	2	2.21
	RF	R. Murray	520	.267	2	59	279	24	11	3	2.1	.965	A. Fromme	26	112	11	6	0	4.01
	CF	F. Snodgrass	457	.291	3	49	312	19	11	1	2.6	.968	D. Crandall	35	98	4	4	6	2.86
	LF	G. Burns	605	.286	2	54	321	22	13	2	2.4	.963							
	C	C. Meyers	378	.312	3	47	579	143	25	12	6.4	.967							
	UT	T. Shafer	508	.287	5	52	220	254	43	26		.917							
Phi.	1B	F. Luderus	588	.262	18	86	1533	92	26	76	10.7	.984	T. Seaton	52	**322**	**27**	12	1	2.60
W-88 L-63	2B	O. Knabe	571	.263	2	53	311	**466**	33	58	5.5	.959	G. Alexander	47	306	22	8	2	2.79
Red Dooin	SS	M. Doolan	518	.218	1	43	**338**	**482**	51	63	5.9	.941	A. Brennan	40	207	14	12	1	2.39
	3B	H. Lobert	573	.300	7	55	181	225	11	13	2.9	**.974**	E. Mayer	39	171	9	9	1	3.11
	RF	G. Cravath	525	.341	19	128	208	20	10	1	1.7	.958	E. Rixey	35	156	9	5	2	3.12
	CF	D. Paskert	454	.262	4	29	330	19	10	8	3.0	.972	G. Chalmers	26	116	3	10	1	4.81
	LF	S. Magee	470	.306	11	70	236	7	8	2	2.0	.968							
	C	B. Killefer	360	.244	0	24	569	**166**	9	**16**	6.3	.988							
	OF	B. Becker	306	.324	9	44	172	6	3	1	2.4	.983							
Chi.	1B	V. Saier	518	.288	14	92	1469	71	26	79	10.6	.983	L. Cheney	**54**	305	21	14	**11**	2.57
W-88 L-65	2B	J. Evers	444	.284	3	49	303	426	30	70	5.6	.960	J. Lavender	40	204	10	14	2	3.66
Johnny Evers	SS	A. Bridwell	405	.240	1	37	282	399	37	46	5.3	.948	B. Humphries	28	181	16	4	0	2.69
	3B	H. Zimmerman	447	.313	9	95	139	232	**36**	18	3.3	.912	G. Pearce	25	163	13	5	0	2.31
	RF	W. Schulte	495	.279	9	72	180	13	9	2	1.6	.955	C. Smith	20	138	7	9	0	2.55
	CF	T. Leach	454	.289	6	32	270	15	3	5	2.4	**.990**							
	LF	M. Mitchell	278	.259	4	35	176	14	12*	0	2.5	.941							
	C	J. Archer	367	.267	2	44	454	138	19	6	5.9	.969							
	23	A. Phelan	259	.251	2	35	102	147	19	12		.929							
	OF	W. Miller	203	.236	1	16	136	9	3	5	2.3	.980							
	C	R. Bresnahan	161	.230	1	21	194	67	10	2	4.7	.963							
	OF	C. Williams	156	.224	4	32	77	4	2	0	1.9	.976							
Pit.	1B	D. Miller	580	.272	7	90	1400	78	22	67	10.0	.985	B. Adams	43	314	21	10	0	2.15
W-78 L-71	2B	J. Viox	492	.317	2	65	223	314	23	29	4.5	.959	C. Hendrix	42	241	14	15	3	2.84
Fred Clarke	SS	H. Wagner	413	.300	3	56	289	323	24	47	**6.1**	.962	H. Robinson	43	196	14	9	2	2.38
	3B	B. Byrne	448	.270	1	47	154	176	21	14	3.2	.940	H. Camnitz	36	192	6	17	2	3.74
	RF	O. Wilson	580	.266	10	73	301	14	10	3	2.1	.969	M. O'Toole	26	145	6	8	1	3.30
	CF	M. Mitchell	199	.271	1	16	150	9	9*	0	3.1	.946	G. McQuillan	25	142	8	6	1	3.43
	LF	M. Carey	**620**	.277	5	49	**363**	**28**	16	6	2.6	.961							
	C	M. Simon	255	.247	1	17	393	151	14	6	6.1	.975							
	2S	A. Butler	214	.280	0	20	126	144	25	14		.915							
	OF	F. Kommers	155	.232	0	22	94	1	2	0	2.4	.979							
Bos.	1B	H. Myers	524	.273	2	50	1344	85	19	57	10.7	.987	L. Tyler	39	290	16	17	2	2.79
W-69 L-82	2B	B. Sweeney	502	.257	4	40	301	391	**45**	42	5.4	.939	D. Rudolph	33	249	14	13	0	2.92
George Stallings	SS	R. Maranville	571	.247	2	48	317	475	43	49	5.8	.949	O. Hess	29	218	7	17	0	3.83
	3B	A. Devlin	210	.229	0	12	83	134	6	4	3.2	.973	H. Perdue	38	212	16	13	1	3.26
	RF	J. Titus	269	.297	5	38	94	8	9	1	1.5	.919	B. James	24	136	6	10	0	2.79
	CF	L. Mann	407	.253	3	51	250	14	11	2	2.3	.960	W. Dickson	19	128	6	7	0	3.23
	LF	J. Connolly	427	.281	5	57	214	16	11	2	1.9	.954							
	C	B. Rariden	246	.236	3	30	377	111	12	6	5.7	.976							
	UT	F. Smith	285	.228	0	27	104	150	27	11		.904							
	OF	B. Lord	235	.251	6	26	81	4	8	0	1.5	.914							
	C	B. Whaling	211	.242	0	25	328	84	4	4	5.4	**.990**							
Bkn.	1B	J. Daubert	508	**.350**	2	52	1279	80	13	**91**	9.9	.991	P. Ragan	44	265	15	18	0	3.77
W-65 L-84	2B	G. Cutshaw	592	.267	7	80	**402**	448	38	**79**	**6.0**	.957	N. Rucker	41	260	14	15	3	2.87
Bill Dahlen	SS	B. Fisher	474	.262	4	54	263	364	**52**	60	5.2	.923	F. Allen	34	175	4	18	2	2.83
	3B	R. Smith	540	.296	6	76	175	**295**	34	13	3.3	.933	C. Curtis	30	152	8	9	1	3.26
	RF	H. Moran	515	.266	0	26	231	15	13	7	2.0	.950	E. Yingling	26	147	8	8	0	2.58
	CF	C. Stengel	438	.272	7	43	270	16	12	1	2.5	.960	E. Reulbach	15	110	7	6	0	2.05
	LF	Z. Wheat	535	.301	7	71	338	13	8	7	2.7	.978							
	C	O. Miller	320	.272	0	26	448	148	18	13	6.0	.971							
	UT	J. Hummel	198	.242	2	24	126	66	8	24		.960							
	C	B. Fischer	165	.267	1	12	193	65	7	2	5.2	.974							
Cin.	1B	D. Hoblitzell	502	.285	3	68	1373	60	17	76	10.8	.988	C. Johnson	44	269	14	16	0	3.01
W-64 L-89	2B	H. Groh	397	.282	3	48	249	358	23	43	5.6	.963	G. Suggs	36	199	8	15	2	4.03
Joe Tinker	SS	J. Tinker	382	.317	1	57	223	320	18	34	5.6	**.968**	G. Packard	39	191	7	11	0	2.97
	3B	J. Dodge	323	.241	4	45	96	170	27	10	3.2	.908	R. Ames	31	187	11	13	2	2.88
	RF	J. Bates	407	.278	6	51	192	19	12	6	2.0	.946	T. Brown	39	173	11	12	6	2.91
	CF	A. Marsans	435	.297	0	38	170	12	7	2	2.4	.963	R. Benton	23	144	11	7	0	3.49
	LF	B. Bescher	511	.258	1	27	283	22	10	2	2.3	.968							
	C	T. Clarke	330	.264	1	38	378	131	11	5	5.2	.979							
	OF	J. Devore	217	.267	3	14	106	9	10	3	2.2	.920							
	C	J. Kling	209	.273	0	23	259	94	9	3	5.7	.975							
	2S	D. Egan	195	.282	0	22	115	150	12	20		.957							
	SS	M. Berghammer	188	.218	1	13	97	143	24	16	5.0	.909							
	3B	R. Almeida	130	.262	3	21	42	71	10	6	3.3	.919							

	POS	Player	AB	BA	HR	RBI	PO	A	E	DP	TC/G	FA	Pitcher	G	IP	W	L	SV	ERA
St. L.	1B	E. Konetchy	502	.273	7	68	1432	91	7	71	11.0	.995	S. Sallee	49	273	18	15	5	2.70
	2B	M. Huggins	381	.286	0	27	266	339	14	44	5.5	.977	B. Harmon	42	273	8	21	1	3.92
W-51 L-99	SS	C. O'Leary	404	.218	0	31	193	297	25	22	5.0	.951	D. Griner	34	225	10	22	0	5.08
Miller Huggins	3B	M. Mowrey	449	.258	0	33	143	284	21	23	3.4	.953	P. Perritt	36	175	6	14	0	5.25
	RF	S. Evans	245	.249	1	31	111	5	2	0	1.6	.983	B. Doak	15	93	2	8	1	3.10
	CF	R. Oakes	537	.291	0	49	321	16	11	2	2.4	.968							
	LF	L. Magee	529	.265	2	31	250	21	5	5	2.6	.982							
	C	I. Wingo	305	.256	2	35	346	132	28	12	5.2	.945							
	UT	P. Whitted	402	.221	0	38	225	207	27	27		.941							
	OF	T. Cather	183	.213	0	12	67	8	7	0	1.4	.915							

BATTING AND BASE RUNNING LEADERS

Batting Average
J. Daubert, BKN	.350
G. Cravath, PHI	.341
J. Viox, PIT	.317
J. Tinker, CIN	.317
B. Becker, CIN, PHI	.316

Slugging Average
G. Cravath, PHI	.568
B. Becker, CIN, PHI	.502
H. Zimmerman, CHI	.490
S. Magee, PHI	.479
V. Saier, CHI	.477

Home Runs
G. Cravath, PHI	19
F. Luderus, PHI	18
V. Saier, CHI	14
S. Magee, PHI	11
O. Wilson, PIT	10

Total Bases
G. Cravath, PHI	298
F. Luderus, PHI	254
V. Saier, CHI	247
H. Lobert, PHI	243
D. Miller, PIT	243

Runs Batted In
G. Cravath, PHI	128
H. Zimmerman, CHI	95
V. Saier, CHI	92
D. Miller, PIT	90
F. Luderus, PHI	86

Stolen Bases
M. Carey, PIT	61
H. Myers, BOS	57
H. Lobert, PHI	41
G. Burns, NY	40
G. Cutshaw, BKN	39

Hits
G. Cravath, PHI	179
J. Daubert, BKN	178
G. Burns, NY	173

Base on Balls
B. Bescher, CIN	94
M. Huggins, STL	91
T. Leach, CHI	77

Home Run Percentage
G. Cravath, PHI	3.6
F. Luderus, PHI	3.1
V. Saier, CHI	2.7

Runs Scored
T. Leach, CHI	99
M. Carey, PIT	99
H. Lobert, PHI	98

Doubles
R. Smith, BKN	40
G. Burns, NY	37
S. Magee, PHI	36

Triples
V. Saier, CHI	21
D. Miller, PIT	20
E. Konetchy, STL	17

PITCHING LEADERS

Winning Percentage
B. Humphries, CHI	.800
G. Alexander, PHI	.733
R. Marquard, NY	.697
C. Mathewson, NY	.694
T. Seaton, PHI	.692

Earned Run Average
C. Mathewson, NY	2.06
B. Adams, PIT	2.15
J. Tesreau, NY	2.17
A. Demaree, NY	2.21
G. Pearce, CHI	2.31

Wins
T. Seaton, PHI	27
C. Mathewson, NY	25
R. Marquard, NY	23
G. Alexander, PHI	22
J. Tesreau, NY	22

Saves
L. Cheney, CHI	11
T. Brown, CIN	6
D. Crandall, NY, STL	6
S. Sallee, STL	5

Strikeouts
T. Seaton, PHI	168
J. Tesreau, NY	167
G. Alexander, PHI	159
R. Marquard, NY	151
B. Adams, PIT	144

Complete Games
L. Tyler, BOS	28
C. Mathewson, NY	25
L. Cheney, CHI	25
B. Adams, PIT	24
G. Alexander, PHI	23

Fewest Hits per 9 Innings
J. Tesreau, NY	7.09
T. Seaton, PHI	7.32
F. Allen, BKN	7.42

Shutouts
G. Alexander, PHI	9
T. Seaton, PHI	6

Fewest Walks per 9 Innings
C. Mathewson, NY	0.62
B. Humphries, CHI	1.19
B. Adams, PIT	1.41

Most Strikeouts per 9 Inn.
J. Tesreau, NY	5.33
C. Hendrix, PIT	5.15
B. James, BOS	4.84

Innings
T. Seaton, PHI	322
B. Adams, PIT	314
G. Alexander, PHI	306

Games Pitched
L. Cheney, CHI	54
T. Seaton, PHI	52
S. Sallee, STL	49

	W	L	PCT	GB	R	OR	2B	3B	Batting HR	BA	SA	SB	E	Fielding DP	FA	CG	BB	Pitching SO	ShO	SV	ERA
NY	101	51	.664		684	502	226	70	31	**.273**	.361	**296**	254	107	.961	82	**315**	651	12	**16**	**2.43**
PHI	88	63	.583	12.5	693	636	**257**	78	**73**	.265	**.382**	156	**214**	112	**.968**	77	512	**667**	**20**	11	3.15
CHI	88	65	.575	13.5	**720**	640	194	**96**	59	.257	.369	181	259	106	.959	89	478	556	12	14	3.13
PIT	78	71	.523	21.5	673	585	210	86	35	.263	.356	181	226	94	.964	74	434	590	9	7	2.90
BOS	69	82	.457	31.5	641	690	191	60	39	.270	.363	188	273	82	.957	70	439	548	9	3	3.19
BKN	65	84	.436	34.5	595	613	193	86	**96**	.261	.347	226	251	**125**	.961	71	456	522	10	6	3.46
CIN	64	89	.418	37.5	607	714	170	72	14	.247	.315	171	219	113	**.965**	73	476	464	6	10	4.24
STL	51	99	.340	49	523	756	152	72	27	.261	.347										3.20
					5136	5136	1593	644	310	.262	.354	1576	1939	843	.962	641	3529	4595	90	77	

	POS	Player	AB	BA	HR	RBI	PO	A	E	DP	TC/G	FA	Pitcher	G	IP	W	L	SV	ERA
Phi. W-96 L-57 Connie Mack	1B	S. McInnis	543	.326	4	90	1504	80	12	85	10.8	.992	E. Plank	41	243	18	10	4	2.60
	2B	E. Collins	534	.345	3	73	314	449	28	54	5.3	.965	C. Bender	48	237	21	10	3	2.21
	SS	J. Barry	455	.275	3	85	248	403	32	60	5.1	.953	B. Brown	43	235	17	11	1	2.94
	3B	F. Baker	565	.336	12	126	233	280	44	19	3.7	.921	J. Bush	39	200	14	6	3	3.82
	RF	E. Murphy	508	.295	1	30	166	14	11	2	1.4	.942	B. Houck	41	176	14	6	0	4.14
	CF	J. Walsh	303	.254	0	27	184	11	8	4	2.3	.961	B. Shawkey	18	111	6	5	0	2.34
	LF	R. Oldring	538	.283	5	71	236	9	8	3	1.9	.968							
	C	J. Lapp	238	.227	1	20	313	110	14	3	5.7	.968							
	OF	A. Strunk	292	.305	0	46	168	9	7	3	2.3	.962							
	C	W. Schang	207	.266	3	30	317	97	14	9	6.0	.967							
Was. W-90 L-64 Clark Griffith	1B	C. Gandil	550	.318	1	72	1436	103	15	89	10.7	.990	W. Johnson	47	346	36	7	2	1.09
	2B	R. Morgan	481	.272	0	57	254	359	32	61	4.8	.950	B. Groom	37	264	16	16	0	3.23
	SS	G. McBride	499	.214	1	52	316	490	34	62	5.6	.960	J. Boehling	38	235	17	7	4	2.14
	3B	E. Foster	409	.247	1	41	112	217	36	20	3.5	.901	J. Engel	36	165	8	9	0	3.06
	RF	D. Moeller	589	.236	5	42	249	27	22	4	1.9	.926	L. Hughes	36	130	4	12	6	4.30
	CF	J. Milan	579	.301	3	54	296	20	23	7	2.2	.932							
	LF	H. Shanks	390	.254	1	37	207	13	5	3	2.1	.978							
	C	J. Henry	273	.223	1	26	476	127	11	9	6.4	.982							
	UT	F. LaPorte	242	.252	0	18	83	114	9	13		.956							
	C	E. Ainsmith	229	.214	2	20	418	82	17	10	6.5	.967							
Cle. W-86 L-66 Joe Birmingham	1B	D. Johnston	530	.255	2	39	1319	76	15	76	10.6	.989	V. Gregg	44	286	20	13	3	2.24
	2B	N. Lajoie	465	.335	1	68	279	363	20	59	5.3	.970	C. Falkenberg	39	276	23	10	0	2.22
	SS	R. Chapman	508	.258	3	39	299	408	48	59	5.5	.936	W. Mitchell	34	217	14	8	0	1.74
	3B	I. Olson	370	.249	0	32	97	145	12	7	3.5	.953	F. Blanding	41	215	15	10	0	2.55
	RF	J. Jackson	528	.373	7	71	211	28	18	5	1.7	.930	B. Steen	22	128	4	5	2	2.45
	CF	N. Leibold	286	.259	0	12	142	12	9	1	2.3	.945	G. Kahler	24	118	5	9	0	3.14
	LF	J. Graney	517	.267	3	68	275	16	9	5	2.0	.970	N. Cullop	23	98	3	7	0	4.42
	C	F. Carisch	222	.216	0	26	391	114	15	10	6.6	.971							
	UT	T. Turner	388	.247	0	44	188	279	18	35		.963							
	OF	B. Ryan	243	.296	0	32	138	7	2	2	2.2	.986							
	C	S. O'Neill	234	.295	0	29	353	119	13	9	6.2	.973							
Bos. W-79 L-71 Jake Stahl W-39 L-41 Bill Carrigan W-40 L-30	1B	C. Engle	498	.289	2	50	1239	57	17	55	9.9	.987	D. Leonard	42	259	14	16	1	2.39
	2B	S. Yerkes	487	.267	1	48	220	341	25	31	4.5	.957	H. Bedient	43	259	15	14	5	2.78
	SS	H. Wagner	365	.227	2	34	274	311	39	36	5.9	.938	R. Collins	30	247	19	8	0	2.63
	3B	L. Gardner	473	.281	0	63	126	220	21	13	2.8	.943	J. Wood	23	146	11	5	2	2.29
	RF	H. Hooper	586	.288	4	40	248	25	9	7	1.9	.968	E. Moseley	24	121	9	5	3	3.13
	CF	T. Speaker	520	.365	3	81	374	30	25	7	3.1	.942	C. Hall	35	105	4	4	3	3.43
	LF	D. Lewis	551	.298	0	90	262	29	12	3	2.1	.960	B. O'Brien	15	90	4	9	0	3.69
	C	B. Carrigan	256	.242	0	28	383	127	11	8	6.4	.979							
	UT	H. Janvrin	276	.207	3	25	172	177	26	17		.931							
Chi. W-78 L-74 Nixey Callahan	1B	H. Chase	384	.286	2	39	1009	71	27*	53	10.9	.976	R. Russell	51	316	22	16	4	1.91
	2B	M. Rath	295	.200	0	12	159	251	16	32	5.0	.962	J. Scott	48	312	20	20	1	1.90
	SS	B. Weaver	533	.272	4	52	392	520	70	73	6.5	.929	E. Cicotte	41	268	18	12	1	1.58
	3B	H. Lord	547	.263	1	42	142	221	30	13	2.6	.924	J. Benz	33	151	7	10	1	2.74
	RF	S. Collins	535	.239	1	47	244	19	14	3	1.9	.949	D. White	19	103	2	4	0	3.50
	CF	P. Bodie	406	.264	8	48	226	14	8	1	2.1	.968	E. Walsh	16	98	8	3	1	2.58
	LF	W. Mattick	207	.188	0	11	116	14	3	2	2.1	.977							
	C	R. Schalk	401	.244	1	38	599	154	15	18	6.1	.980							
	2B	J. Berger	223	.215	2	20	111	214	14	18	4.9	.959							
	OF	L. Chappell	208	.231	0	15	114	5	6	1	2.1	.952							
	1O	J. Fournier	172	.233	1	23	306	23	5	10		.985							
Det. W-66 L-87 Hughie Jennings	1B	D. Gainor	363	.267	2	25	1118	50	14	55	11.6	.988	E. Willett	34	242	13	14	0	3.09
	2B	O. Vitt	359	.240	2	33	151	234	16	24	5.1	.960	J. Dubuc	36	243	15	14	2	2.89
	SS	D. Bush	593	.251	1	40	331	510	56	61	5.9	.938	H. Dauss	33	225	13	12	1	2.68
	3B	G. Moriarty	347	.239	0	30	122	183	20	9	3.5	.938	M. Hall	30	165	10	12	2	3.27
	RF	S. Crawford	610	.316	9	83	201	14	8	5	1.6	.964	J. Lake	28	137	8	7	1	3.28
	CF	T. Cobb	428	.390	4	67	262	22	16	8	2.5	.947							
	LF	B. Veach	494	.269	0	64	250	16	24	3	2.1	.917							
	C	O. Stanage	241	.224	0	21	277	106	16	6	5.2	.960							
	UT	B. Louden	191	.241	0	23	76	146	17	11		.929							
	2B	P. Baumann	191	.298	1	22	97	136	14	15	5.0	.943							
	C	R. McKee	187	.283	1	22	237	84	17	5	5.5	.950							
	OF	H. High	183	.230	0	16	104	8	2	0	2.3	.982							
N. Y. W-57 L-94 Frank Chance	1B	J. Knight	250	.236	0	24	494	45	11	26	11.0	.980	R. Fisher	43	246	12	16	1	3.18
	2B	R. Hartzell	490	.259	0	38	203	234	27	29	5.7	.942	R. Ford	33	237	12	18	2	2.66
	SS	R. Peckinpaugh	340	.268	1	32	184	303	36	30	5.6	.931	A. Schulz	38	193	7	13	0	3.73
	3B	E. Midkiff	284	.197	0	14	102	185	13	12	3.9	.957	G. McConnell	35	180	4	15	3	3.20
	RF	B. Daniels	320	.216	0	22	128	15	5	3	1.7	.966	R. Caldwell	27	164	9	8	1	2.41
	CF	H. Wolter	425	.254	2	43	228	15	14	1	2.1	.946	R. Keating	28	151	6	12	0	3.21
	LF	B. Cree	534	.272	1	63	239	17	3	5	1.8	.988	J. Warhop	15	62	4	6	0	3.75
	C	J. Sweeney	351	.265	2	40	511	180	26	9	6.4	.964							
	3B	F. Maisel	187	.257	0	12	70	83	8	3	3.2	.950							
	UT	R. Zeider	159	.233	0	12	138	102	17	13		.934							

	POS	Player	AB	BA	HR	RBI	PO	A	E	DP	TC/G	FA	Pitcher	G	IP	W	L	SV	ERA
	1B	G. Stovall	303	.287	1	24	751	65	10	38	10.9	.988	Baumgardner	38	253	10	19	1	3.13
St. L.	2B	D. Pratt	592	.296	2	87	364	425	41	56	5.7	.951	C. Weilman	39	252	10	**20**	0	3.40
W-57 L-96	SS	M. Balenti	211	.180	0	11	107	169	23	25	5.3	.923	R. Mitchell	33	245	13	16	1	3.01
George Stovall	3B	J. Austin	489	.266	2	42	216	**288**	30	21	3.8	**.944**	E. Hamilton	31	217	13	12	1	2.57
W-50 L-84	RF	G. Williams	538	.273	5	53	225	26	13	7	1.8	.951	W. Leverenz	30	203	6	17	1	2.58
Jimmy Austin	CF	B. Shotton	549	.297	1	28	357	29	20	**11**	2.8	.951							
W-2 L-6	LF	J. Johnston	380	.224	2	27	222	23	9	3	2.4	.965							
Branch Rickey	C	S. Agnew	307	.208	2	24	383	170	**28**	17	5.6	.952							
W-5 L-6																			
	1B	B. Brief	258	.217	1	26	622	34	9	41	10.7	.986							
	SS	B. Wallace	147	.211	0	21	67	96	12	8	4.6	.931							

BATTING AND BASE RUNNING LEADERS

Batting Average
T. Cobb, DET	.390
J. Jackson, CLE	.373
T. Speaker, BOS	.365
E. Collins, PHI	.345
F. Baker, PHI	.336

Slugging Average
J. Jackson, CLE	.551
T. Speaker, BOS	.535
T. Cobb, DET	.535
F. Baker, PHI	.492
S. Crawford, DET	.489

Home Runs
F. Baker, PHI	12
S. Crawford, DET	9
P. Bodie, CHI	8
J. Jackson, CLE	7

Total Bases
S. Crawford, DET	298
J. Jackson, CLE	291
T. Speaker, BOS	278
F. Baker, PHI	278
E. Collins, PHI	242

Runs Batted In
F. Baker, PHI	126
S. McInnis, PHI	90
D. Lewis, BOS	90
D. Pratt, STL	87
J. Barry, PHI	85

Stolen Bases
C. Milan, WAS	75
D. Moeller, WAS	62
E. Collins, PHI	55
T. Cobb, DET	51
T. Speaker, BOS	46

Hits
J. Jackson, CLE	197
S. Crawford, DET	193
F. Baker, PHI	190
T. Speaker, BOS	190

Base on Balls
B. Shotton, STL	99
E. Collins, PHI	85

Home Run Percentage
F. Baker, PHI	2.1
P. Bodie, CHI	2.0
S. Crawford, DET	1.5

Runs Scored
E. Collins, PHI	125
F. Baker, PHI	116
J. Jackson, CLE	109

Doubles
J. Jackson, CLE	39
T. Speaker, BOS	35
F. Baker, PHI	34

Triples
S. Crawford, DET	23
T. Speaker, BOS	22
J. Jackson, CLE	17

PITCHING LEADERS

Winning Percentage
W. Johnson, WAS	.837
R. Collins, BOS	.714
J. Boehling, WAS	.708
C. Falkenberg, CLE	.697
C. Bender, PHI	.677

Earned Run Average
W. Johnson, WAS	1.09
E. Cicotte, CHI	1.58
W. Mitchell, CLE	1.74
J. Scott, CHI	1.90
R. Russell, CHI	1.91

Wins
W. Johnson, WAS	36
C. Falkenberg, CLE	23
R. Russell, CHI	22
C. Bender, PHI	21

Saves
C. Bender, PHI	12
L. Hughes, WAS	6

Strikeouts
W. Johnson, WAS	243
C. Falkenberg, CLE	166
V. Gregg, CLE	166
J. Scott, CHI	158
B. Groom, WAS	156

Complete Games
W. Johnson, WAS	29
R. Russell, CHI	26
J. Scott, CHI	25
Baumgardner, STL	23
V. Gregg, CLE	23
C. Falkenberg, CLE	23

Fewest Hits per 9 Innings
W. Johnson, WAS	5.98
W. Mitchell, CLE	6.35
W. Leverenz, STL	7.06

Shutouts
W. Johnson, WAS	11
R. Russell, CHI	8
E. Plank, PHI	7
C. Falkenberg, CLE	6

Fewest Walks per 9 Innings
W. Johnson, WAS	0.99
R. Collins, BOS	1.35
R. Mitchell, STL	1.72

Most Strikeouts per 9 Inn.
J. Wood, BOS	7.60
W. Johnson, WAS	6.32
W. Mitchell, CLE	5.85

Innings
W. Johnson, WAS	346
R. Russell, CHI	316
J. Scott, CHI	312

Games Pitched
R. Russell, CHI	51
J. Scott, CHI	48
C. Bender, PHI	48

	W	L	PCT	GB	R	OR	2B	3B	HR	BA	SA	SB	E	DP	FA	CG	BB	SO	ShO	SV	ERA
PHI	96	57	.627		794	593	223	80	33	.280	.376	221	212	108	.966	69	532	630	17	22	3.19
WAS	90	64	.584	6.5	596	566	156	80	20	.252	.327	287	261	122	.960	78	465	757	23	20	2.72
CLE	86	66	.566	9.5	631	529	205	74	16	.268	.348	191	242	124	.962	95	502	689	18	5	2.52
BOS	79	71	.527	15.5	630	607	221	101	17	.269	.364	189	237	84	.961	87	442	710	11	11	2.93
CHI	78	74	.513	17.5	486	492	157	66	23	.236	.310	156	255	104	.960	86	438	602	17	8	2.33
DET	66	87	.431	30	624	720	180	101	24	.265	.355	203	300	105	.954	90	504	468	4	7	3.41
NY	57	94	.377	38	529	669	154	45	9	.237	.293	203	293	94	.954	75	455	530	8	7	3.27
STL	57	96	.373	39	528	642	179	73	18	.237	.312	209	301	125	.954	104	454	476	14	5	3.06
					4818	4818	1475	620	160	.256	.336	1675	2101	866	.959	684	3792	4862	112	85	2.93

POS	Player	AB	BA	HR	RBI	PO	A	E	DP	TC/G	FA	Pitcher	G	IP	W	L	SV	ERA
Bos. W-94 L-59 George Stallings																		
1B	B. Schmidt	537	.285	1	71	1485	88	16	**109**	10.8	.990	D. Rudolph	42	336	**27**	10	0	2.35
2B	J. Evers	491	.279	1	40	301	397	17	73	5.1	**.976**	B. James	46	332	26	7	2	1.90
SS	R. Maranville	586	.246	4	78	**407**	574	65	92	**6.7**	.938	L. Tyler	38	271	16	14	2	2.69
3B	C. Deal	257	.210	0	23	86	133	12	8	3.1	.948	D. Crutcher	33	159	5	6	0	3.46
RF	L. Gilbert	224	.268	5	25	79	14	2	2	1.6	.979	O. Hess	14	89	5	6	1	3.03
CF	L. Mann	389	.247	4	40	273	24	15	8	2.5	.952							
LF	J. Connolly	399	.306	9	65	168	19	5	1	1.6	.974							
C	H. Gowdy	366	.243	3	46	475	151	**21**	11	5.6	.968							
UT	P. Whitted	218	.261	2	31	161	61	12	9		.949							
3B	R. Smith	207	.314	3	37	84*	139*	15	12*	4.0*	.937							
C	B. Whaling	172	.209	0	12	272	91	7	7	6.3	.981							
OF	H. Moran	154	.266	0	4	59	4	4	0	1.6	.940							
OF	T. Cather	145	.297	0	27	57	4	3	1	1.3	.953							
N. Y. W-84 L-70 John McGraw																		
1B	F. Merkle	512	.258	7	63	1463	88	16	80	10.7	.990	J. Tesreau	42	322	26	10	1	2.37
2B	L. Doyle	539	.260	5	63	307	379	29	61	4.9	.959	C. Mathewson	41	312	24	13	2	3.00
SS	A. Fletcher	514	.286	2	79	299	446	63	0	6.0	.922	R. Marquard	39	268	12	22	2	3.06
3B	M. Stock	365	.263	3	41	95	261	23	17	3.4	.939	A. Demaree	38	224	10	17	0	3.09
RF	F. Snodgrass	392	.263	0	44	200	11	5	4	2.3	.977	A. Fromme	38	138	9	5	2	3.20
CF	B. Bescher	512	.270	6	35	298	14	13	7	2.6	.960							
LF	G. Burns	561	.303	3	60	326	19	18	5	2.4	.950							
C	C. Meyers	381	.286	1	55	**487**	150	20	**16**	5.2	.970							
UT	E. Grant	282	.277	0	29	97	191	23	16		.926							
OF	D. Robertson	256	.266	2	32	101	13	6	2	1.7	.950							
C	L. McLean	154	.260	0	14	211	42	7	8	3.5	.973							
OF	R. Murray	139	.223	0	23	56	2	0	0	1.2	1.000							
St. L. W-81 L-72 Miller Huggins																		
1B	D. Miller	573	.290	4	88	1019	57	8	46	**11.1**	.993	P. Perritt	41	286	16	13	2	2.36
2B	M. Huggins	509	.263	1	24	328	428	28	58	5.3	.964	S. Sallee	46	282	18	17	**6**	2.10
SS	A. Butler	274	.201	1	24	155	228	30	24	4.9	.927	B. Doak	36	256	20	6	0	**1.72**
3B	Z. Beck	457	.232	3	45	141	264	28	24	3.5	.935	D. Griner	37	179	9	13	2	2.51
RF	O. Wilson	580	.259	9	73	312	**34**	6	**11**	2.3	**.983**	H. Perdue	22	153	8	8	1	2.82
CF	L. Magee	529	.284	2	40	210	14	7	4	2.3	.970	H. Robinson	26	126	6	8	0	3.00
LF	C. Dolan	421	.240	4	32	182	10	9	2	2.1	.955							
C	F. Snyder	326	.230	1	25	419	130	12	12	5.7	**.979**							
OF	W. Cruise	256	.227	4	28	158	6	4	1	2.1	.976							
C	I. Wingo	237	.300	4	26	276	93	16	7	5.5	.958							
Chi. W-78 L-76 Hank O'Day																		
1B	V. Saier	537	.240	18	72	1521	59	22	62	10.5	.986	L. Cheney	**50**	311	20	18	5	2.54
2B	B. Sweeney	463	.218	1	38	301	426	35	40	5.7	.954	H. Vaughn	42	294	21	13	1	2.05
SS	R. Corriden	318	.230	3	29	174	212	46	29	4.5	.894	J. Lavender	37	214	11	11	0	3.07
3B	H. Zimmerman	564	.296	4	87	141	197	**39**	13	3.2	.897	B. Humphries	34	171	10	11	0	2.68
RF	W. Good	580	.272	2	43	242	25	**20**	10	1.9	.930	G. Pearce	30	141	8	12	1	3.51
CF	T. Leach	577	.263	7	46	321	16	11	5	2.5	.968	Z. Zabel	29	128	4	4	1	2.18
LF	W. Schulte	465	.241	5	61	217	9	11	2	1.8	.954							
C	R. Bresnahan	248	.278	0	24	365	113	11	6	5.8	.978							
C	J. Archer	248	.258	0	19	367	105	13	8	6.4	.973							
Bkn. W-81 L-79 Wilbert Robinson																		
1B	J. Daubert	474	**.329**	6	45	1097	48	8	68	9.2	.993	J. Pfeffer	43	315	23	12	4	1.97
2B	G. Cutshaw	583	.257	2	78	**455**	444	38	**74**	6.1	.959	E. Reulbach	44	256	11	18	3	2.64
SS	D. Egan	337	.226	1	21	150	232	36	21	5.0	.914	P. Ragan	38	208	10	15	3	2.98
3B	R. Smith	330	.245	4	48	136*	193*	22	16*	3.9*	.937	R. Aitchison	26	172	12	7	0	2.66
RF	C. Stengel	412	.316	4	60	173	15	7	3	1.6	.964	F. Allen	36	171	8	14	0	3.10
CF	J. Dalton	442	.319	1	45	240	7	9	2	2.2	.965	N. Rucker	16	104	7	6	0	3.39
LF	Z. Wheat	533	.319	9	89	**331**	21	14	5	2.5	.962							
C	L. McCarty	284	.254	1	30	398	110	16	9	6.3	.970							
SS	O. O'Mara	247	.263	1	7	110	183	26	17	5.1	.918							
OF	H. Myers	227	.286	0	17	102	4	4	0	1.8	.964							
3B	G. Getz	210	.248	0	20	69	134	11	12	3.9	.949							
1O	J. Hummel	208	.264	0	20	338	21	6	13		.984							
C	O. Miller	169	.231	0	9	236	66	11	5	6.3	.965							
Phi. W-74 L-80 Red Dooin																		
1B	F. Luderus	443	.248	12	55	1102	76	**30**	49	10.0	.975	G. Alexander	46	**355**	**27**	15	1	2.38
2B	B. Byrne	467	.272	0	26	187	312	35	19	5.3	.934	E. Mayer	48	321	21	19	2	2.58
SS	J. Martin	292	.253	0	21	185	251	33	24	5.7	.930	B. Tincup	28	155	7	10	1	2.61
3B	H. Lobert	505	.275	1	52	188	174	22	10	2.9	**.943**	R. Marshall	27	134	6	7	1	3.75
RF	G. Cravath	499	.299	**19**	100	205	**34**	14	7	1.8	.930	J. Oeschger	32	124	4	8	1	3.77
CF	D. Paskert	451	.264	3	44	303	19	14	4	**2.6**	.958	E. Rixey	24	103	2	11	0	4.37
LF	B. Becker	514	.325	9	66	270	17	16	3	2.4	.947							
C	B. Killefer	299	.234	0	27	464	**154**	14	11	**7.0**	.978							
UT	S. Magee	544	.314	15	**103**	549	187	37	20		.952							
2B	H. Irelan	165	.236	1	16	98	142	24	12	6.0	.909							

POS	Player	AB	BA	HR	RBI	PO	A	E	DP	TC/G	FA	Pitcher	G	IP	W	L	SV	ERA
	Pit. W-69 L-85 Fred Clarke																	
1B	E. Konetchy	563	.249	4	51	**1576**	**93**	8	70	10.9	.995	B. Adams	40	283	13	16	1	2.51
2B	J. Viox	506	.265	1	57	250	400	42	43	5.0	.939	W. Cooper	40	267	16	15	0	2.13
SS	H. Wagner	552	.252	1	50	322	424	39	45	5.9	.950	G. McQuillan	45	259	13	17	4	2.98
3B	M. Mowrey	284	.254	1	25	83	156	10	8	3.2	.960	B. Harmon	37	245	13	17	3	2.53
RF	M. Mitchell	273	.234	2	23	174	11	3	6	2.5	.984	J. Conzelman	33	101	5	6	1	2.94
CF	J. Kelly	508	.222	1	48	319	15	19	3	2.6	.946							
LF	M. Carey	593	.243	1	31	318	23	12	3	2.3	.966							
C	G. Gibson	274	.285	0	30	358	126	13	8	4.9	.974							
OF	Z. Collins	182	.242	0	15	92	8	4	2	2.1	.962							
UT	A. McCarthy	173	.150	1	14	63	136	11	10		.948							
	Cin. W-60 L-94 Buck Herzog																	
1B	D. Hoblitzell	248	.210	0	29	802	31	10	43	11.2	.988	R. Ames	47	297	15	**23**	6	2.64
2B	H. Groh	455	.288	2	32	252	394	44	56	5.1	.936	R. Benton	41	271	17	18	2	2.96
SS	B. Herzog	498	.281	1	40	324	474	52	58	6.2	.939	P. Douglas	45	239	11	18	1	2.56
3B	B. Niehoff	484	.242	4	49	154	272	35	15	3.4	.924	E. Yingling	34	198	8	13	0	3.45
RF	H. Moran	395	.235	1	35	175	11	9	4	1.8	.954	P. Schneider	29	144	5	13	1	2.81
CF	B. Daniels	269	.219	0	19	144	7	4	2	2.2	.974							
LF	G. Twombly	240	.233	0	19	111	11	4	2	1.9	.968							
C	T. Clarke	313	.262	2	25	448	132	16	12	5.5	.973							
OF	D. Miller	192	.255	0	33	79	2	2	1	1.8	.976							
C	M. Gonzalez	176	.233	0	10	252	101	17	5	4.5	.954							
OF	J. Bates	163	.245	2	15	91	4	9	1	1.8	.913							
OF	A. Marsans	124	.298	0	22	72	4	7	1	2.3	.916							

BATTING AND BASE RUNNING LEADERS

Batting Average
- J. Daubert, BKN .329
- B. Becker, PHI .325
- J. Dalton, BKN .319
- Z. Wheat, BKN .319
- C. Stengel, BKN .316

Slugging Average
- S. Magee, PHI .509
- G. Cravath, PHI .499
- J. Connolly, BOS .494
- Z. Wheat, BKN .452
- B. Becker, PHI .446

Home Runs
- G. Cravath, PHI 19
- V. Saier, CHI 18
- S. Magee, PHI 15
- F. Luderus, PHI 12

Total Bases
- S. Magee, PHI 277
- G. Cravath, PHI 249
- Z. Wheat, BKN 241
- H. Zimmerman, CHI 239
- G. Burns, NY 234

Runs Batted In
- S. Magee, PHI 103
- G. Cravath, PHI 100
- Z. Wheat, BKN 89
- D. Miller, STL 88
- H. Zimmerman, CHI 87

Stolen Bases
- G. Burns, NY 62
- B. Herzog, CIN 46
- C. Dolan, STL 42
- M. Carey, PIT 38
- B. Bescher, NY 36
- L. Magee, STL 36

Hits
- S. Magee, PHI 171
- Z. Wheat, BKN 170
- G. Burns, NY 170

Base on Balls
- M. Huggins, STL 105
- V. Saier, CHI 94
- G. Burns, NY 89

Home Run Percentage
- G. Cravath, PHI 3.8
- V. Saier, CHI 3.4
- S. Magee, PHI 2.8

Runs Scored
- G. Burns, NY 100
- S. Magee, PHI 96
- J. Daubert, BKN 89

Doubles
- S. Magee, PHI 39
- H. Zimmerman, CHI 36
- G. Burns, NY 35
- J. Connolly, BOS 28

Triples
- M. Carey, PIT 17
- H. Zimmerman, CHI 12
- O. Wilson, STL 12
- G. Cutshaw, BKN 12

PITCHING LEADERS

Winning Percentage
- B. James, BOS .788
- B. Doak, STL .769
- D. Rudolph, BOS .730
- J. Tesreau, NY .722
- J. Pfeffer, BKN .657

Earned Run Average
- B. Doak, STL 1.72
- B. James, BOS 1.90
- J. Pfeffer, BKN 1.97
- H. Vaughn, CHI 2.05
- S. Sallee, STL 2.10

Wins
- D. Rudolph, BOS 27
- G. Alexander, PHI 27
- B. James, BOS 26
- J. Tesreau, NY 26
- C. Mathewson, NY 24

Saves
- S. Sallee, STL 6
- R. Ames, CIN 6
- L. Cheney, CHI 5
- G. McQuillan, PIT 4
- J. Pfeffer, BKN 4

Strikeouts
- G. Alexander, PHI 214
- J. Tesreau, NY 189
- H. Vaughn, CHI 165
- L. Cheney, CHI 157
- B. James, BOS 156

Complete Games
- G. Alexander, PHI 32
- D. Rudolph, BOS 31
- B. James, BOS 30
- C. Mathewson, NY 29
- J. Pfeffer, BKN 27

Fewest Hits per 9 Innings
- J. Tesreau, NY 6.65
- B. Doak, STL 6.79
- L. Cheney, CHI 6.91

Shutouts
- J. Tesreau, NY 8
- B. Doak, STL 7

Fewest Walks per 9 Innings
- C. Mathewson, NY 0.66
- B. Adams, PIT 1.24
- R. Marquard, NY 1.58

Most Strikeouts per 9 Inn.
- G. Alexander, PHI 5.43
- J. Tesreau, NY 5.28
- H. Vaughn, CHI 5.06

Innings
- G. Alexander, PHI 355
- D. Rudolph, BOS 336
- B. James, BOS 332

Games Pitched
- L. Cheney, CHI 50
- E. Mayer, PHI 48
- R. Ames, CIN 47

	W	L	PCT	GB	R	OR	Batting 2B	3B	HR	BA	SA	SB	Fielding E	DP	FA	Pitching CG	BB	SO	ShO	SV	ERA
BOS	94	59	.614		657	548	213	60	35	.251	.335	139	246	143	.963	104	477	606	19	5	2.74
NY	84	70	.545	10.5	672	576	222	59	30	.265	.348	239	254	119	.961	88	367	563	20	9	2.94
STL	81	72	.529	13	558	540	203	65	33	.248	.333	204	239	109	.964	83	422	531	16	11	**2.38**
CHI	78	76	.506	16.5	605	638	199	74	42	.269	.355	162	310	87	.951	80	528	651	14	9	2.71
BKN	75	79	.487	19.5	622	612	172	90	31	.263	.361	173	324	81	.950	85	452	650	14	6	3.06
PHI	74	80	.481	20.5	651	673	211	52	62	.243	.337	147	239	96	.966	86	392	488	10	9	2.70
PIT	69	85	.448	25.5	503	540	148	79	18	.233	.303	147	314	113	.952	74	489	607	15	**14**	2.94
CIN	60	94	.390	34.5	530	671	142	64	16	.236	.299	224	232	112	.961	70	466	605	11	10	2.82
					4798	4798	1510	543	267	.251	.334	1435	2158	860	.958	670	3593	4701	119	73	2.78

	POS	Player	AB	BA	HR	RBI	PO	A	E	DP	TC/G	FA	Pitcher	G	IP	W	L	SV	ERA
Phi. W-99 L-53 Connie Mack	1B	S. McInnis	576	.314	1	95	1423	85	7	89	10.2	.995	B. Shawkey	38	237	16	8	2	2.73
	2B	E. Collins	526	.344	2	85	354	387	23	55	5.0	.970	J. Bush	38	206	16	12	3	3.06
	SS	J. Barry	467	.242	0	42	244	447	39	61	5.2	.947	J. Wyckoff	32	185	11	7	2	3.02
	3B	F. Baker	570	.319	9	97	221	292	24	20	3.6	.955	E. Plank	34	185	15	7	3	2.87
	RF	E. Murphy	573	.272	3	43	194	15	13	4	1.5	.941	C. Bender	28	179	17	3	2	2.26
	CF	A. Strunk	404	.275	2	45	280	14	4	3	2.5	.987	H. Pennock	28	152	11	4	3	2.79
	LF	R. Oldring	466	.277	3	49	215	7	8	5	2.0	.965	R. Bressler	29	148	10	4	2	1.77
	C	W. Schang	307	.287	3	45	498	154	30	11	6.8	.956							
	OF	J. Walsh	216	.236	3	36	107	7	4	3	2.1	.966							
	C	J. Lapp	199	.231	0	19	330	88	10	4	6.4	.977							
Bos. W-91 L-62 Bill Carrigan	1B	D. Hoblitzell	229	.319	0	33	627	30	14	22	9.9	.979	R. Collins	39	272	20	13	0	2.51
	2B	S. Yerkes	293	.218	1	23	177	241	12	38	4.7	.972	D. Leonard	36	223	19	5	3	1.01
	SS	E. Scott	539	.239	2	37	324	408	39	50	5.4	.949	R. Foster	32	213	14	8	0	1.65
	3B	L. Gardner	553	.259	3	68	187	312	31	18	3.5	.942	H. Bedient	42	177	8	12	2	3.60
	RF	H. Hooper	530	.258	1	41	231	23	7	5	1.9	.973	E. Shore	20	148	10	4	1	1.89
	CF	T. Speaker	571	.338	4	90	423	29	15	12	3.0	.968	J. Wood	18	113	9	3	1	2.62
	LF	D. Lewis	510	.278	2	79	254	22	14	2	2.0	.952	A. Johnson	16	99	4	9	0	3.08
	C	B. Carrigan	178	.253	1	22	350	84	7	8	5.7	.984							
	UT	H. Janvrin	492	.238	1	51	669	237	43	50		.955							
	C	H. Cady	159	.258	0	8	217	80	9	1	5.3	.971							
Was. W-81 L-73 Clark Griffith	1B	C. Gandil	526	.259	3	75	1284	143	13	84	9.9	.991	W. Johnson	51	372	28	18	1	1.72
	2B	R. Morgan	491	.257	1	49	290	379	37	58	4.8	.948	D. Ayers	49	265	12	15	3	2.54
	SS	G. McBride	503	.203	0	24	367	460	36	72	5.5	.958	J. Shaw	48	257	15	17	4	2.70
	3B	E. Foster	616	.282	2	50	200	247	34	25	3.1	.929	J. Boehling	27	196	12	8	1	3.03
	RF	D. Moeller	571	.250	1	45	208	19	17	4	1.6	.930	J. Bentley	30	125	5	7	4	2.37
	CF	J. Milan	437	.295	1	39	230	10	13	0	2.2	.949	J. Engel	35	124	7	5	3	2.97
	LF	H. Shanks	500	.224	4	64	276	14	14	3	2.2	.954							
	C	J. Henry	261	.169	0	20	513	124	13	9	7.1	.980							
	OF	M. Mitchell	193	.285	1	20	99	11	5	0	2.2	.957							
	C	B. Williams	169	.278	1	22	181	54	6	0	5.5	.975							
Det. W-80 L-73 Hughie Jennings	1B	G. Burns	478	.291	5	57	1576	79	30	72	12.3	.982	H. Coveleski	44	303	22	12	2	2.49
	2B	M. Kavanagh	439	.248	4	35	228	333	43	30	5.3	.929	H. Dauss	45	302	18	15	4	2.86
	SS	D. Bush	596	.252	0	32	425	544	58	64	6.5	.944	J. Dubuc	36	224	13	14	1	3.46
	3B	G. Moriarty	465	.254	1	40	125	312	20	16	3.6	.956	P. Cavet	31	151	7	7	2	2.44
	RF	S. Crawford	582	.314	8	104	193	18	5	4	1.4	.977	A. Main	32	138	6	6	3	2.67
	CF	T. Cobb	345	.368	2	57	177	8	10	0	2.0	.949	M. Hall	25	90	4	6	0	2.69
	LF	B. Veach	531	.275	1	72	282	22	11	6	2.2	.965							
	C	O. Stanage	400	.193	0	25	532	190	30	11	6.2	.960							
	23	O. Vitt	195	.251	0	8	63	154	9	13		.960							
	OF	H. High	184	.266	0	17	92	2	4	1	1.8	.959							
	UT	H. Heilmann	182	.225	2	22	209	31	11	11		.956							
St. L. W-71 L-82 Branch Rickey	1B	J. Leary	533	.265	0	45	1256	75	17	64	10.4	.987	E. Hamilton	44	302	17	18	2	2.50
	2B	D. Pratt	584	.283	5	65	358	423	46	48	5.4	.944	C. Weilman	44	299	18	13	1	2.08
	SS	D. Lavan	239	.264	1	21	178	193	34	17	5.5	.916	B. James	44	284	15	14	1	2.85
	3B	J. Austin	466	.238	0	34	183	249	30	18	3.6	.935	Baumgardner	45	184	14	13	3	2.79
	RF	G. Williams	499	.253	4	47	200	24	16	2	1.7	.933	W. Leverenz	27	111	1	12	0	3.80
	CF	B. Shotton	579	.269	0	38	359	15	24	4	2.6	.940	R. Mitchell	28	103	4	5	4	4.35
	LF	T. Walker	517	.298	6	78	311	30	10	5	2.4	.972							
	C	S. Agnew	311	.212	0	16	451	163	25	10	5.7	.961							
	SS	B. Wares	215	.209	0	23	128	196	35	23	5.3	.903							
	31	I. Howard	209	.244	0	20	252	63	9	5		.972							
Chi. W-70 L-84 Nixey Callahan	1B	J. Fournier	379	.311	6	44	1025	78	25	30	11.6	.978	J. Benz	48	283	14	19	2	2.26
	2B	L. Blackburne	474	.222	1	35	239	433	26	28	4.9	.963	E. Cicotte	45	269	11	16	3	2.04
	SS	B. Weaver	541	.246	2	28	367	389	59	50	6.1	.928	J. Scott	43	253	14	18	1	2.84
	3B	J. Breton	231	.212	0	24	84	159	24	6	3.4	.910	R. Faber	40	181	10	9	4	2.68
	RF	S. Collins	598	.274	3	65	268	21	19	5	2.0	.938	R. Russell	38	167	8	12	1	2.90
	CF	P. Bodie	327	.229	3	29	175	14	8	2	2.1	.959	M. Wolfgang	24	119	9	5	0	1.89
	LF	R. Demmitt	515	.258	2	46	217	24	12	3	1.8	.953							
	C	R. Schalk	392	.270	0	36	613	183	21	20	6.6	.974							
	1B	H. Chase	206	.267	0	20	632	43	13	27	11.9	.981							
	3B	S. Alcock	156	.173	0	7	57	95	16	10	3.5	.905							
N. Y. W-70 L-84 Frank Chance W-61 L-76 Roger Peckinpaugh W-9 L-8	1B	C. Mullen	323	.260	0	44	898	62	6	54	10.4	.994	J. Warhop	37	217	8	15	0	2.37
	2B	L. Boone	370	.222	0	21	238	294	22	32	6.2	.960	R. Caldwell	31	213	17	9	1	1.94
	SS	Peckinpaugh	570	.223	3	51	356	500	39	45	5.7	.956	R. Keating	34	210	7	11	1	2.96
	3B	F. Maisel	548	.239	2	47	206	245	35	17	3.3	.928	R. Fisher	29	209	10	12	1	2.28
	RF	D. Cook	470	.283	1	40	171	15	10	2	1.6	.949	M. McHale	31	191	7	16	1	2.97
	CF	B. Cree	275	.309	0	40	190	10	5	4	2.7	.976	K. Cole	33	142	11	9	0	3.30
	LF	R. Hartzell	481	.233	1	32	241	15	7	2	2.1	.973	B. Brown	20	122	5	5	1	3.24
	C	J. Sweeney	258	.213	1	22	369	120	10	7	6.4	.980							
	C	L. Nunamaker	257	.265	2	29	304	126	13	12	6.3	.971							
	2B	F. Truesdale	217	.212	0	13	121	185	17	19	4.8	.947							
	OF	T. Daley	191	.251	0	9	26	12	6	2	.8	.864							
	1B	H. Williams	178	.163	1	17	577	25	15	19	10.6	.976							
	OF	B. Holden	165	.182	0	12	98	3	2	0	2.3	.981							

	POS	Player	AB	BA	HR	RBI	PO	A	E	DP	TC/G	FA	Pitcher	G	IP	W	L	SV	ERA
Cle.	1B	D. Johnston	340	.244	0	23	847	36	12	43	10.1	.987	W. Mitchell	39	257	12	17	1	3.19
W-51 L-102	2B	N. Lajoie	419	.258	0	50	187	215	17	45	5.2	.959	B. Steen	30	201	9	14	0	2.60
	SS	R. Chapman	375	.275	2	42	161	187	33	24	5.3	.913	R. Hagerman	37	198	9	15	0	3.09
Joe Birmingham	3B	T. Turner	428	.245	1	33	138	229	14	23	**3.7**	**.963**	G. Morton	25	128	1	13	1	3.02
	RF	J. Jackson	453	.338	3	53	195	13	7	4	1.8	.967	F. Blanding	29	116	3	9	1	3.96
	CF	N. Leibold	402	.264	0	32	221	22	8	4	2.4	.931	A. Collamore	27	105	3	7	0	3.25
	LF	J. Graney	460	.265	1	39	274	15	20	0	2.4	.935	V. Gregg	17	97	9	3	0	3.07
	C	S. O'Neill	269	.253	0	20	393	134	24	**22**	6.8	.956							
	UT	I. Olson	310	.242	1	20	197	197	17	20		.959							
	OF	J. Kirke	242	.273	1	25	73	3	2	1	1.9	.974							
	O1	R. Wood	220	.236	1	15	209	16	7	13		.970							

BATTING AND BASE RUNNING LEADERS

Batting Average
T. Cobb, DET .368
E. Collins, PHI .344
T. Speaker, BOS .338
J. Jackson, CLE .338
F. Baker, PHI .319

Slugging Average
T. Cobb, DET .513
T. Speaker, BOS .503
S. Crawford, DET .483
J. Jackson, CLE .464
E. Collins, PHI .452

Home Runs
F. Baker, PHI 9
S. Crawford, DET 8
J. Fournier, CHI 6
T. Walker, STL 6
G. Burns, DET 5
D. Pratt, STL 5

Total Bases
T. Speaker, BOS 287
S. Crawford, DET 281
F. Baker, PHI 252
D. Pratt, STL 240
E. Collins, PHI 238

Runs Batted In
S. Crawford, DET 104
F. Baker, PHI 97
S. McInnis, PHI 95
T. Speaker, BOS 90
E. Collins, PHI 85

Stolen Bases
F. Maisel, NY 74
E. Collins, PHI 58
T. Speaker, BOS 42
B. Shotton, STL 40
C. Milan, WAS 38
Peckinpaugh, NY 38

Hits
T. Speaker, BOS 193
S. Crawford, DET 183
F. Baker, PHI 182

Base on Balls
D. Bush, DET 112
E. Collins, PHI 97
E. Murphy, PHI 87

Home Run Percentage
J. Fournier, CHI 1.6
F. Baker, PHI 1.6
S. Crawford, DET 1.4

Runs Scored
E. Collins, PHI 122
E. Murphy, PHI 101
T. Speaker, BOS 100

Doubles
T. Speaker, BOS 46
D. Lewis, BOS 37
D. Pratt, STL 34
S. Collins, CHI 34

Triples
S. Crawford, DET 26
L. Gardner, BOS 19
T. Speaker, BOS 18

PITCHING LEADERS

Winning Percentage
C. Bender, PHI .850
D. Leonard, BOS .783
E. Plank, PHI .682
B. Shawkey, PHI .667
R. Caldwell, NY .654

Earned Run Average
D. Leonard, BOS 1.01
R. Foster, BOS 1.65
W. Johnson, WAS 1.72
E. Shore, BOS 1.89
R. Caldwell, NY 1.94

Wins
W. Johnson, WAS 28
H. Coveleski, DET 22
R. Collins, BOS 20
D. Leonard, BOS 19
C. Weilman, STL 18
H. Dauss, DET 18

Saves
D. Leonard, BOS 4
J. Shaw, WAS 4
H. Dauss, DET 4
R. Faber, CHI 4
R. Mitchell, STL 4
J. Bentley, WAS 4

Strikeouts
W. Johnson, WAS 225
W. Mitchell, CLE 179
D. Leonard, BOS 174
J. Shaw, WAS 164
H. Dauss, DET 150

Complete Games
W. Johnson, WAS 33
H. Coveleski, DET 23
R. Caldwell, NY 22
H. Dauss, DET 22

Fewest Hits per 9 Innings
D. Leonard, BOS 5.70
R. Caldwell, NY 6.46
E. Shore, BOS 6.77

Shutouts
W. Johnson, WAS 9
C. Bender, PHI 7
D. Leonard, BOS 7

Fewest Walks per 9 Innings
M. McHale, NY 1.55
W. Johnson, WAS 1.79
J. Warhop, NY 1.83

Most Strikeouts per 9 Inn.
D. Leonard, BOS 7.03
W. Mitchell, CLE 6.27
J. Shaw, WAS 5.74

Innings
W. Johnson, WAS 372
H. Coveleski, DET 303
E. Hamilton, STL 302

Games Pitched
W. Johnson, WAS 51
D. Ayers, WAS 49
J. Benz, CHI 48
J. Shaw, WAS 48

	W	L	PCT	GB	R	OR	Batting 2B	3B	HR	BA	SA	SB	E	Fielding DP	FA	CG	BB	Pitching SO	ShO	SV	ERA
PHI	99	53	.651		749	520	165	80	**29**	**.272**	**.352**	231	**213**	116	**.966**	89	521	720	24	17	2.78
BOS	91	62	.595	8.5	588	511	**226**	85	18	.250	.338	177	242	99	.963	88	397	605	24	8	**2.35**
WAS	81	73	.526	19	572	519	176	81	18	.244	.320	220	254	116	.961	75	520	**784**	25	**20**	2.54
DET	80	73	.523	19.5	615	618	195	84	25	.258	.344	211	286	101	.958	81	498	567	14	12	2.86
STL	71	82	.464	28.5	523	614	185	75	17	.243	.319	233	317	114	.952	81	540	553	15	11	2.85
CHI	70	84	.455	30	487	568	161	71	19	.239	.311	167	299	90	.955	**98**	**390**	660	17	11	2.48
NY	70	84	.455	30	536	550	149	52	12	.229	.287	251	238	93	.963	69	666	688	10	3	3.21
CLE	51	102	.333	48.5	538	708	178	70	10	.245	.312	167	300	**119**	.953	69	666	688	10	3	3.21
					4608	4608	1435	598	148	.248	.323	1657	2149	848	.959	655	3933	5140	138	87	2.73

POS	Player	AB	BA	HR	RBI	PO	A	E	DP	TC/G	FA	Pitcher	G	IP	W	L	SV	ERA
Ind. W-88 L-65 Bill Phillips																		
1B	C. Carr	441	.293	3	69	1088	59	11	67	10.1	.991	C. Falkenberg	49	377	25	18	3	2.22
2B	F. LaPorte	505	.311	4	107	300	373	31	61	5.3	.956	E. Moseley	43	317	18	18	1	3.47
SS	J. Esmond	542	.295	2	49	317	448	67	54	5.5	.919	G. Kaiserling	37	275	17	9	0	3.11
3B	B. McKechnie	570	.304	2	38	195	327	34	28	3.7	.939	G. Mullin	36	203	14	10	2	2.70
RF	B. Kauff	571	.370	8	95	310	31	17	5	2.3	.953	H. Billiard	32	126	9	8	1	3.72
CF	V. Campbell	544	.318	7	44	218	18	19	6	1.9	.925							
LF	A. Scheer	363	.306	3	45	150	13	13	2	1.7	.926							
C	B. Rariden	396	.235	0	47	714	215	18	14	7.3	.981							
OF	A. Kaiser	187	.230	1	16	98	3	9	0	2.2	.918							
OF	E. Roush	166	.325	1	30	85	5	1	1	2.1	.989							
P	G. Mullin	77	.312	0	21	9	45	5	1	1.6	.915							
Chi. W-87 L-67 Joe Tinker																		
1B	F. Beck	555	.279	11	77	1614	55	31	86	10.8	.982	C. Hendrix	49	362	29	11	5	1.69
2B	J. Farrell	524	.235	0	35	354	457	39	54	5.5	.954	M. Fiske	38	198	12	9	0	3.14
SS	J. Tinker	438	.256	2	46	271	408	38	48	5.7	.947	E. Lange	36	190	12	10	2	2.23
3B	R. Zeider	452	.274	1	36	151	217	25	27	3.4	.936	D. Watson	26	172	9	11	1	2.04
RF	A. Wickland	536	.276	6	68	252	23	11	3	1.8	.962	Prendergast	30	136	5	9	0	2.38
CF	D. Zwilling	592	.313	15	95	340	15	14	3	2.4	.962	T. McGuire	24	131	5	7	0	3.70
LF	M. Flack	502	.247	2	39	232	18	7	2	1.9	.973	A. Johnson	16	120	9	5	0	1.58
C	A. Wilson	440	.291	10	64	674	212	24	19	6.9	.974							
3B	H. Fritz	174	.213	0	13	34	59	9	7	2.2	.912							
Bal. W-84 L-70 Otto Knabe																		
1B	H. Swacina	617	.280	0	90	1616	104	26	74	11.1	.985	J. Quinn	46	343	26	14	1	2.60
2B	O. Knabe	469	.226	2	42	287	389	31	49	4.9	.956	G. Suggs	46	319	25	12	3	2.90
SS	M. Doolan	486	.245	1	53	305	476	42	55	5.7	.949	K. Wilhelm	47	244	13	17	4	4.03
3B	J. Walsh	428	.308	10	65	125	217	25	18	3.2	.932	F. Smith	39	175	9	8	2	2.99
RF	B. Meyer	500	.304	5	40	172	14	17	6	1.5	.916	B. Bailey	19	129	6	9	0	3.08
CF	V. Duncan	557	.287	2	53	255	20	26	8	2.0	.914	S. Conley	35	125	5	8	0	2.52
LF	H. Simmons	352	.270	1	38	91	10	12	2	1.5	.894							
C	F. Jacklitsch	337	.276	2	48	580	167	9	13	6.4	.988							
OF	G. Zinn	225	.280	3	25	82	5	6	1	1.6	.935							
OF	J. Bates	190	.305	1	29	108	7	6	0	2.1	.950							
3B	Kirkpatrick	174	.253	2	16	28	40	5	1	2.0	.932							
C	H. Russell	168	.232	0	13	193	44	11	2	5.3	.956							
Buf. W-80 L-71 Larry Schlafly																		
1B	J. Agler	463	.272	0	20	734	49	12	44	10.5	.985	F. Anderson	37	260	13	16	0	3.08
2B	T. Downey	541	.218	2	42	265	388	26	49	5.3	.962	G. Krapp	36	253	14	14	0	2.49
SS	B. Louden	431	.313	6	63	299	285	43	34	5.5	.931	R. Ford	35	247	20	6	6	1.82
3B	F. Smith	473	.220	2	45	170	229	30	14	3.4	.930	E. Moore	36	195	10	14	2	4.30
RF	T. McDonald	250	.296	3	32	94	7	5	2	1.7	.953	A. Schulz	27	171	10	11	1	3.37
CF	C. Hanford	597	.291	13	90	331	24	10	5	2.4	.973	H. Moran	34	154	11	8	1	4.27
LF	F. Delahanty	274	.201	2	27	116	8	3	1	1.6	.976*							
C	W. Blair	378	.243	0	33	604	194	13	17	6.3	.984							
1B	H. Chase	291	.347	3	48	690	38	15	33	10.2	.980							
OF	E. Booe	241	.224	0	14	86	8	4	2	1.7	.959							
OF	D. Young	174	.276	4	22	49	2	3	2	1.3	.944							
Bkn. W-77 L-77 Bill Bradley																		
1B	H. Myers	305	.220	1	29	784	44	9	47	9.5	.989	T. Seaton	44	303	25	13	2	3.03
2B	S. Hofman	515	.287	5	83	232	289	27	39	5.1	.951	E. Lafitte	42	291	16	16	2	2.63
SS	E. Gagnier	337	.187	0	25	219	244	33	37	5.6	.933	H. Finneran	27	175	12	11	1	3.18
3B	T. Wisterzil	534	.257	0	66	207	294	23	24	3.5	.956	R. Sommers	23	82	4	7	0	4.06
RF	S. Evans	514	.348	12	96	163	13	11	2	1.7	.941	J. Bluejacket	17	67	4	5	1	3.76
CF	A. Shaw	376	.324	5	49	198	14	10	4	2.2	.955							
LF	G. Anderson	364	.316	3	24	176	15	11	2	2.2	.946							
C	G. Land	335	.275	0	29	490	147	20	11	6.8	.970							
OF	C. Cooper	399	.241	2	25	188	12	16	4	2.1	.926							
SS	A. Halt	261	.234	3	25	164	184	43	30	5.5	.890							
2B	J. Delahanty	214	.290	0	15	104	117	10	15	4.2	.957							
C	F. Owens	184	.277	2	20	228	67	10	10	5.3	.967							
OF	D. Murphy	161	.304	4	32	65	8	1	2	1.6	.986							
K. C. W-67 L-84 George Stovall																		
1B	G. Stovall	450	.284	7	75	1201	70	14	82	11.1	.989	G. Packard	42	302	21	13	4	2.89
2B	D. Kenworthy	545	.317	15	91	437	407	43	79	6.1	.952	N. Cullop	44	296	14	17	1	2.34
SS	P. Goodwin	374	.235	1	32	85	208	30	21	4.8	.907	D. Stone	39	187	7	14	0	4.34
3B	G. Perring	496	.278	2	69	100	223	23	20	3.4	.934	B. Harris	31	154	7	8	1	4.09
RF	E. Gilmore	530	.287	1	32	196	24	6	7	1.7	.973	P. Henning	28	138	6	12	1	4.83
CF	A. Krueger	441	.259	4	47	249	14	10	1	2.3	.963	D. Adams	36	136	3	9	3	3.51
LF	C. Chadbourne	581	.277	1	37	238	34	10	6	1.9	.965	C. Johnson	20	134	9	10	0	3.16
C	T. Easterly	436	.335	1	67	570	173	24	16	6.0	.969							
OF	C. Coles	194	.253	1	25	52	4	7	0	1.6	.889							
SS	J. Rawlings	193	.212	0	15	121	222	23	25	6.0	.937							
UT	C. Daringer	160	.263	0	16	70	142	19	16		.918							

POS	Player	AB	BA	HR	RBI	PO	A	E	DP	TC/G	FA	Pitcher	G	IP	W	L	SV	ERA
Pit.												E. Knetzer	37	272	19	11	1	2.88
1B	H. Bradley	427	.307	0	61	1132	60	12	52	10.2	.990	H. Camnitz	36	262	14	18	1	3.23
2B	J. Lewis	394	.234	1	48	304	332	34	33	5.8	.949	W. Dickson	40	257	9	**21**	1	3.16
SS	E. Holly	350	.246	0	26	238	263	31	30	5.7	.942	C. Barger	33	228	10	16	1	4.34
3B	E. Lennox	430	.312	11	84	136	193	16	12	2.8	.954	M. Walker	35	169	3	16	0	4.31
RF	H. Savage	479	.284	1	26	141	15	6	3	1.7	.963	G. LaClaire	22	103	5	2	0	4.01
CF	R. Oakes	571	.312	7	75	313	23	14	2	2.4	.960							
LF	D. Jones	352	.273	2	24	216	11	7	1	2.5	.970							
C	C. Berry	411	.238	2	36	550	202	23	18	6.4	.970							
O2	T. McDonald	223	.318	3	29	77	83	13	10		.925							
UT	C. Rheam	214	.210	0	20	431	55	16	16		.968							
OF	F. Delahanty	159	.239	1	7	57	5	1	0	1.8	.984*							
SS	S. Yerkes	142	.338	1	25	89	139	6	13	6.0	.974							
St. L.												B. Groom	42	281	13	**20**	1	3.24
1B	H. Miller	490	.222	0	46	1256	65	14	48	10.3	.990	D. Davenport	33	216	8	13	4	3.46
2B	D. Crandall	278	.309	2	41	98	152	20	10	4.3	.926	H. Keupper	42	213	8	20	0	4.27
SS	A. Bridwell	381	.236	1	33	217	291	30	36	5.2	.944	D. Crandall	27	196	12	9	0	3.54
3B	A. Boucher	516	.231	2	49	193	263	42	18	3.4	.916	E. Willett	27	175	4	16	0	4.22
RF	J. Tobin	529	.270	7	35	185	31	11	3	1.7	.952	T. Brown	26	175	12	6	0	3.30
CF	D. Drake	514	.251	3	42	207	16	10	2	2.0	.957							
LF	W. Miller	402	.294	4	50	248	15	13	3	2.5	.953							
C	M. Simon	276	.207	0	21	433	132	9	9	**7.4**	.984							
2S	J. Misse	306	.196	0	22	229	279	43	29		.922							
OF	F. Kommers	244	.307	3	41	107	11	12	1	1.9	.908							
UT	G. Hartley	212	.288	1	25	249	79	11	12		.968							
OF	L. Kirby	195	.246	2	18	100	7	3	2	2.2	.973							
C	H. Chapman	181	.210	0	14	247	77	9	8	6.5	.973							

Pit. record: W-64 L-86 — Doc Gessler W-6 L-12 — Rebel Oakes W-58 L-74

St. L. record: W-62 L-89 — Three Finger Brown W-50 L-63 — Fielder Jones W-12 L-26

BATTING AND BASE RUNNING LEADERS

Batting Average
B. Kauff, IND	.370
S. Evans, BKN	.348
T. Easterly, KC	.335
A. Shaw, BKN	.324
V. Campbell, IND	.318

Slugging Average
S. Evans, BKN	.556
B. Kauff, IND	.534
D. Kenworthy, KC	.525
E. Lennox, PIT	.493
D. Zwilling, CHI	.480

Home Runs
D. Kenworthy, KC	15
D. Zwilling, CHI	15
C. Hanford, BUF	13
S. Evans, BKN	12
E. Lennox, PIT	11
F. Beck, CHI	11

Total Bases
B. Kauff, IND	305
S. Evans, BKN	286
D. Kenworthy, KC	286
D. Zwilling, CHI	284
C. Hanford, BUF	267

Runs Batted In
F. LaPorte, IND	107
S. Evans, BKN	96
B. Kauff, IND	95
D. Zwilling, CHI	95
D. Kenworthy, KC	91

Stolen Bases
B. Kauff, IND	75
B. McKechnie, IND	47
H. Myers, BKN	43
C. Chadbourne, KC	42

Hits
B. Kauff, IND	211
D. Zwilling, CHI	185
S. Evans, BKN	179

Base on Balls
A. Wickland, CHI	81
J. Agler, BUF	77
B. Kauff, IND	72

Home Run Percentage
D. Kenworthy, KC	2.8
E. Lennox, PIT	2.6
D. Zwilling, CHI	2.5

Runs Scored
B. Kauff, IND	120
B. McKechnie, IND	107
V. Duncan, BAL	99

Doubles
B. Kauff, IND	44
S. Evans, BKN	41
D. Kenworthy, KC	40

Triples
S. Evans, BKN	15
J. Esmond, IND	15
D. Kenworthy, KC	14

PITCHING LEADERS

Winning Percentage
R. Ford, BUF	.769
C. Hendrix, CHI	.725
G. Suggs, BAL	.676
T. Seaton, BKN	.658
G. Kaiserling, IND	.654

Earned Run Average
A. Johnson, CHI	1.58
C. Hendrix, CHI	1.69
R. Ford, BUF	1.82
D. Watson, CHI, STL	2.01
C. Falkenberg, IND	2.22

Wins
C. Hendrix, CHI	29
J. Quinn, BAL	26
G. Suggs, BAL	25
T. Seaton, BKN	25
C. Falkenberg, IND	25

Saves
R. Ford, BUF	6
C. Hendrix, CHI	5
K. Wilhelm, BAL	4
G. Packard, KC	4
D. Davenport, STL	4

Strikeouts
C. Falkenberg, IND	236
E. Moseley, IND	205
C. Hendrix, CHI	189
T. Seaton, BKN	172
B. Groom, STL	167

Complete Games
C. Hendrix, CHI	34
C. Falkenberg, IND	33
E. Moseley, IND	29
J. Quinn, BAL	27
T. Seaton, BKN	26
G. Suggs, BAL	26

Fewest Hits per 9 Innings
C. Hendrix, CHI	6.51
A. Johnson, CHI	6.60
R. Ford, BUF	6.91

Shutouts
C. Falkenberg, IND	9
T. Seaton, BKN	7
C. Hendrix, CHI	6
G. Suggs, BAL	6

Fewest Walks per 9 Innings
R. Ford, BUF	1.49
G. Suggs, BAL	1.61
J. Quinn, BAL	1.71

Most Strikeouts per 9 Inn.
B. Bailey, BAL	9.16
D. Davenport, STL	5.93
E. Moseley, IND	5.83

Innings
C. Falkenberg, IND	377
C. Hendrix, CHI	362
J. Quinn, BAL	343

Games Pitched
C. Falkenberg, IND	49
C. Hendrix, CHI	49
K. Wilhelm, BAL	47

	W	L	PCT	GB	R	OR	2B	3B	Batting HR	BA	SA	SB	E	Fielding DP	FA	CG	BB	Pitching SO	ShO	SV	ERA
IND	88	65	.575		762	622	230	90	33	.285	.383	273	289	113	.956	104	476	664	15	8	3.06
CHI	87	67	.565	1.5	621	517	227	50	51	.258	.352	171	249	113	.962	93	393	650	17	8	2.44
BAL	84	70	.545	4.5	645	628	222	67	32	.268	.357	152	263	105	.960	88	392	732	15	10	3.13
BUF	80	71	.530	7	620	602	177	74	38	.250	.336	228	228	109	.962	89	505	662	15	13	3.16
BKN	77	77	.500	11.5	662	677	225	85	42	.269	.368	220	283	120	.956	91	559	636	11	7	3.33
KC	67	84	.444	20	644	683	226	77	39	.267	.364	171	279	135	.957	82	445	600	10	10	3.41
PIT	64	86	.427	22.5	605	698	180	90	34	.262	.352	153	253	92	.960	97	444	510	9	4	3.56
STL	62	89	.411	25	565	697	193	65	26	.247	.326	113	273	94	.957	97	409	661	9	6	3.59
					5124	5124	1680	598	295	.263	.355	1481	2131	881	.959	741	3623	5115	101	66	3.20

National League 1915

POS	Player	AB	BA	HR	RBI	PO	A	E	DP	TC/G	FA	Pitcher	G	IP	W	L	SV	ERA
Phi. W-90 L-62 Pat Moran																		
1B	F. Luderus	499	.315	7	62	1409	99	11	76	10.8	.993	G. Alexander	49	376	31	10	3	1.22
2B	B. Niehoff	529	.238	2	49	307	411	41	55	5.1	.946	E. Mayer	43	275	21	15	2	2.36
SS	D. Bancroft	563	.254	7	30	336	492	64	60	5.8	.928	A. Demaree	32	210	14	11	1	3.05
3B	B. Byrne	387	.209	0	21	98	183	9	9	2.8	.969	E. Rixey	29	177	11	12	1	2.39
RF	G. Cravath	522	.285	24	115	233	28	15	2	1.8	.946	G. Chalmers	26	170	8	9	1	2.48
CF	D. Paskert	328	.244	3	39	181	10	6	2	1.9	.970							
LF	B. Becker	338	.246	11	35	177	5	11	0	2.0	.943							
C	B. Killefer	320	.238	0	24	539	126	19	6	6.5	.972							
OF	P. Whitted	448	.281	1	43	266	7	6	2	2.6	.978							
3B	M. Stock	227	.260	1	15	62	106	5	7	3.1	.971							
C	E. Burns	174	.241	0	16	241	61	6	6	4.6	.981							
Bos. W-83 L-69 George Stallings																		
1B	B. Schmidt	458	.251	2	60	1221	60	17	80	10.2	.987	D. Rudolph	44	341	22	19	1	2.37
2B	J. Evers	278	.263	1	22	170	209	16	33	4.8	.959	T. Hughes	50	280	16	14	5	2.12
SS	R. Maranville	509	.244	2	43	391	486	55	63	6.3	.941	P. Ragan	33	227	15	12	0	2.46
3B	R. Smith	549	.264	2	65	170	292	26	26	3.1	.947	L. Tyler	32	205	10	9	0	2.86
RF	H. Moran	419	.200	0	21	168	17	7	3	1.6	.964							
CF	S. Magee	571	.280	2	87	346	16	7	4	2.8	.981							
LF	J. Connolly	305	.298	0	23	158	10	5	2	1.9	.971							
C	H. Gowdy	316	.247	2	30	460	148	16	11	5.3	.974							
2B	Fitzpatrick	303	.221	0	24	135	160	10	23	4.3	.967							
UT	D. Egan	220	.259	0	21	179	92	16	20		.944							
C	B. Whaling	190	.221	0	13	292	68	5	2	5.1	.986							
Bkn. W-80 L-72 Wilbert Robinson																		
1B	J. Daubert	544	.301	2	47	1441	102	11	73	10.4	.993	J. Pfeffer	40	292	19	14	3	2.10
2B	G. Cutshaw	566	.246	0	62	397	473	26	53	5.8	.971	W. Dell	40	215	11	10	1	2.34
SS	O. O'Mara	577	.244	0	31	319	431	78	44	5.6	.906	J. Coombs	29	196	15	10	0	2.58
3B	J. Getz	477	.258	2	46	140	290	22	14	3.5	.951	S. Smith	29	174	14	8	2	2.59
RF	C. Stengel	459	.237	3	50	220	13	10	2	1.9	.959	E. Appleton	34	138	4	10	0	3.32
CF	H. Myers	605	.248	2	46	352	23	14	5	2.5	.964	N. Rucker	19	123	9	4	1	2.42
LF	Z. Wheat	528	.258	5	66	345	18	18	4	2.6	.953	P. Douglas	20	117	5	5	0	2.62
C	O. Miller	254	.224	0	25	363	91	9	8	5.5	.981							
C	L. McCarty	276	.239	0	19	310	101	13	5	5.0	.969							
Chi. W-73 L-80 Roger Bresnahan																		
1B	V. Saier	497	.264	11	64	1348	65	21	71	10.3	.985	H. Vaughn	41	270	20	12	1	2.87
2B	H. Zimmerman	520	.265	3	62	211	267	29	30	5.1	.943	J. Lavender	41	220	10	16	3	2.58
SS	B. Fisher	568	.287	5	53	277	434	51	35	5.2	.933	G. Pearce	36	176	13	9	0	3.32
3B	A. Phelan	448	.219	3	35	136	203	22	14	3.3	.939	B. Humphries	31	172	8	13	2	2.31
RF	W. Good	498	.253	2	27	192	13	14	4	1.8	.936	Z. Zabel	36	163	7	10	0	3.20
CF	C. Williams	518	.257	13	64	347	14	12	2	2.5	.968	L. Cheney	25	131	8	9	0	3.56
LF	W. Schulte	550	.249	12	69	280	24	12	3	2.1	.962	P. Standridge	29	112	4	1	0	3.61
C	J. Archer	309	.243	1	27	447	126	13	11	6.7	.978	K. Adams	26	107	1	9	0	4.71
C	R. Bresnahan	221	.204	1	19	345	95	8	9	6.6	.982							
Pit. W-73 L-81 Fred Clarke																		
1B	D. Johnston	543	.265	5	64	1453	48	13	65	10.3	.991	B. Harmon	37	270	16	17	1	2.50
2B	J. Viox	503	.256	2	45	239	362	29	35	4.7	.954	A. Mamaux	38	252	21	8	0	2.04
SS	H. Wagner	566	.274	6	78	298	395	38	53	5.6	.948	B. Adams	40	245	14	14	2	2.87
3B	D. Baird	512	.219	1	53	142	226	24	13	3.0	.939	W. Cooper	38	186	5	16	4	3.30
RF	B. Hinchman	577	.307	5	77	261	17	9	5	1.8	.969	E. Kantlehner	29	163	5	12	2	2.26
CF	Z. Collins	354	.294	1	23	217	11	14	3	2.4	.942	G. McQuillan	30	149	8	10	1	2.84
LF	M. Carey	564	.254	3	27	307	21	6	5	2.4	.982							
C	G. Gibson	351	.251	1	30	551	134	25	14	5.9	.965							
St. L. W-72 L-81 Miller Huggins																		
1B	D. Miller	553	.264	2	72	1000	50	10	54	12.8	.991	B. Doak	38	276	16	18	1	2.64
2B	M. Huggins	353	.241	2	24	194	315	23	44	5.0	.957	S. Sallee	46	275	13	17	3	2.84
SS	A. Butler	469	.254	1	31	235	351	53	43	4.9	.917	L. Meadows	39	244	13	11	0	2.99
3B	B. Betzel	367	.251	0	27	105	221	22	10	3.3	.937	D. Griner	37	150	5	11	3	2.81
RF	T. Long	507	.294	2	61	236	18	20	1	2.0	.927	H. Robinson	32	143	7	8	0	2.45
CF	O. Wilson	348	.276	3	39	234	20	4	3	2.4	.984	H. Perdue	31	115	6	12	1	4.21
LF	B. Bescher	486	.263	4	34	257	12	8	1	2.1	.971	R. Ames	15	113	9	3	1	2.46
C	F. Snyder	473	.298	2	55	592	204	14	9	5.6	.983							
OF	C. Dolan	322	.280	2	18	179	4	14	0	2.0	.929							
1B	H. Hyatt	295	.268	2	46	616	21	6	31	7.9	.991							
3B	Z. Beck	223	.233	0	15	59	127	13	10	3.3	.935							

	POS	Player	AB	BA	HR	RBI	PO	A	E	DP	TC/G	FA	Pitcher	G	IP	W	L	SV	ERA
Cin. W-71 L-83 Buck Herzog	1B	F. Mollwitz	525	.259	1	51	1545	79	7	107	10.7	.996	G. Dale	49	297	18	17	3	2.46
	2B	B. Rodgers	213	.239	0	12	96	170	15	30	5.0	.947	P. Schneider	48	276	13	19	2	2.48
	SS	B. Herzog	579	.264	1	42	391	513	53	90	6.3	.945	F. Toney	36	223	15	6	2	1.58
	3B	H. Groh	587	.290	3	50	153	280	14	34	3.4	.969	R. Benton	35	176	9	13	4*	3.32
	RF	T. Griffith	583	.307	4	85	225	11	12	1	1.6	.952	K. Lear	40	168	6	10	0	3.01
	CF	R. Killefer	555	.272	1	41	334	17	9	5	2.4	.975	L. McKenry	21	110	5	5	0	2.94
	LF	K. Williams	219	.242	0	16	117	11	7	4	2.2	.948							
	C	I. Wingo	339	.221	3	29	413	124	19	15	5.7	.966							
	OF	T. Leach	335	.224	0	17	200	9	9	2	2.3	.959							
	C	T. Clarke	226	.288	0	21	294	71	7	7	5.2	.981							
	UT	I. Olson	207	.232	0	14	170	166	19	20		.946							
	2B	J. Wagner	197	.178	0	13	99	122	9	28	5.0	.961							
N. Y. W-69 L-83 John McGraw	1B	F. Merkle	505	.299	4	62	1123	53	13	62	10.7	.989	J. Tesreau	43	306	19	16	3	2.29
	2B	L. Doyle	591	.320	4	70	313	396	40	66	5.0	.947	P. Perritt	35	220	12	18	0	2.66
	SS	A. Fletcher	562	.254	3	74	302	544	58	76	6.1	.936	C. Mathewson	27	186	8	14	0	3.58
	3B	H. Lobert	386	.251	0	38	109	192	16	9	3.0	.950	S. Stroud	32	184	11	9	1	2.79
	RF	D. Robertson	544	.294	3	58	225	13	11	4	1.8	.956	R. Marquard	27	169	9	8	2	3.73
	CF	F. Snodgrass	252	.194	0	20	160	12	12	2	1.8	.935	R. Schauer	32	105	2	8	0	3.50
	LF	G. Burns	622	.272	3	51	278	13	12	4	2.0	.960	R. Benton	10	61	4	5	1*	2.82
	C	C. Meyers	289	.232	1	26	464	90	8	15	5.1	**.986**							
	UT	F. Brainerd	249	.201	1	21	443	94	18	37		.968							
	3B	E. Grant	192	.208	0	10	39	57	3	3	1.8	.970							

BATTING AND BASE RUNNING LEADERS

Batting Average

L. Doyle, NY	.320
F. Luderus, PHI	.315
T. Griffith, CIN	.307
B. Hinchman, PIT	.307
J. Daubert, BKN	.301

Slugging Average

G. Cravath, PHI	.510
F. Luderus, PHI	.457
T. Long, STL	.446
V. Saier, CHI	.445
L. Doyle, NY	.442

Home Runs

G. Cravath, PHI	24
C. Williams, CHI	13
W. Schulte, CHI	12
B. Becker, PHI	11
V. Saier, CHI	11

Total Bases

G. Cravath, PHI	266
L. Doyle, NY	261
T. Griffith, CIN	254
B. Hinchman, PIT	253
H. Wagner, PIT	239

Runs Batted In

G. Cravath, PHI	115
S. Magee, BOS	87
T. Griffith, CIN	85
H. Wagner, PIT	78
B. Hinchman, PIT	77

Stolen Bases

M. Carey, PIT	36
B. Herzog, CIN	35
V. Saier, CHI	29
D. Baird, PIT	29
G. Cutshaw, BKN	28

Hits

L. Doyle, NY	189
T. Griffith, CIN	179
B. Hinchman, PIT	177

Base on Balls

G. Cravath, PHI	86
D. Bancroft, PHI	77
J. Viox, PIT	75

Home Run Percentage

G. Cravath, PHI	4.6
B. Becker, PHI	3.3
C. Williams, CHI	2.5

Runs Scored

G. Cravath, PHI	89
L. Doyle, NY	86
D. Bancroft, PHI	85

Doubles

L. Doyle, NY	40
F. Luderus, PHI	36
V. Saier, CHI	35

Triples

T. Long, STL	25
H. Wagner, PIT	17
T. Griffith, CIN	16

PITCHING LEADERS

Winning Percentage

G. Alexander, PHI	.756
A. Mamaux, PIT	.724
F. Toney, CIN	.714
H. Vaughn, CHI	.625
J. Coombs, BKN	.600

Earned Run Average

G. Alexander, PHI	1.22
F. Toney, CIN	1.58
A. Mamaux, PIT	2.04
J. Pfeffer, BKN	2.10
T. Hughes, BOS	2.12

Wins

G. Alexander, PHI	31
D. Rudolph, BOS	22
A. Mamaux, PIT	21
E. Mayer, PHI	21
H. Vaughn, CHI	20

Saves

T. Hughes, BOS	5
R. Benton, CIN, NY	5
W. Cooper, PIT	4

Strikeouts

G. Alexander, PHI	241
J. Tesreau, NY	176
T. Hughes, BOS	171
A. Mamaux, PIT	152
H. Vaughn, CHI	148

Complete Games

G. Alexander, PHI	36
D. Rudolph, BOS	30
J. Pfeffer, BKN	26
B. Harmon, PIT	25
J. Tesreau, NY	24

Fewest Hits per 9 Innings

G. Alexander, PHI	6.05
F. Toney, CIN	6.47
A. Mamaux, PIT	6.51

Shutouts

G. Alexander, PHI	12
A. Mamaux, PIT	8
J. Tesreau, NY	8

Fewest Walks per 9 Innings

C. Mathewson, NY	0.97
B. Humphries, CHI	1.21
B. Adams, PIT	1.25

Most Strikeouts per 9 Inn.

G. Alexander, PHI	5.76
T. Hughes, BOS	5.49
A. Mamaux, PIT	5.44

Innings

G. Alexander, PHI	376
D. Rudolph, BOS	341
J. Tesreau, NY	306

Games Pitched

T. Hughes, BOS	50
G. Alexander, PHI	49
G. Dale, CIN	49

	W	L	PCT	GB	R	OR	2B	3B	HR	BA	SA	SB	E	DP	FA	CG	BB	SO	ShO	SV	ERA
PHI	90	62	.592		589	**463**	202	39	**58**	.247	.340	121	216	99	.966	**98**	342	652	**20**	8	**2.17**
BOS	83	69	.546	7	582	545	**231**	57	17	.240	.319	121	**213**	115	**.966**	87	366	630	15	9	2.57
BKN	80	72	.526	10	536	560	165	75	14	.248	.317	131	238	96	.963	91	473	499	16	7	2.66
CHI	73	80	.477	17.5	570	620	212	66	53	.244	**.342**	166	268	94	.958	91	384	544	18	10	2.60
PIT	73	81	.474	18	557	520	197	91	24	.246	.334	**182**	214	100	.966	79	402	538	13	9	2.89
STL	72	81	.471	18.5	**590**	601	159	**92**	20	**.254**	.333	162	235	109	.964	79	480	572	19	**12**	2.84
CIN	71	83	.461	20	516	585	194	84	15	.253	.331	156	256	119	.960	78	**325**	637	15	8	3.11
NY	69	83	.454	21	582	628	195	68	24	.251	.329	155									
					4522	4522	1555	572	225	.248	.331	1194	1862	880	.964	679	3269	4729	134	69	2.75

POS	Player	AB	BA	HR	RBI	PO	A	E	DP	TC/G	FA	Pitcher	G	IP	W	L	SV	ERA
Bos. W-101 L-50 Bill Carrigan																		
1B	D. Hoblitzell	399	.283	2	61	1095	63	15	51	10.0	.987	R. Foster	37	255	19	8	1	2.11
2B	H. Wagner	267	.240	0	29	161	195	28	18	4.9	.927	E. Shore	38	247	19	8	0	1.64
SS	E. Scott	359	.201	0	28	198	298	20	31	5.2	.961	B. Ruth	32	218	18	8	2	2.44
3B	L. Gardner	430	.258	1	55	134	227	26	16	3.0	.933	D. Leonard	32	183	15	7	0	2.36
RF	H. Hooper	566	.235	2	51	255	23	8	7	1.9	.972	J. Wood	25	157	15	5	1	1.49
CF	T. Speaker	547	.322	0	69	378	21	10	8	2.7	.976	C. Mays	38	132	6	5	7	2.60
LF	D. Lewis	557	.291	2	76	263	15	14	3	1.9	.952	R. Collins	25	105	4	7	2	4.30
C	P. Thomas	203	.236	0	21	325	81	13	7	5.1	.969							
S3	H. Janvrin	316	.269	0	37	122	191	31	16		.910							
2B	J. Barry	248	.262	0	26	143	216	14	19	4.8	.962							
C	H. Cady	205	.278	0	17	313	79	8	12	5.2	.980							
1B	D. Gainor	200	.295	1	29	457	33	6	22	8.9	.988							
P	B. Ruth	92	.315	4	21	17	63	2	3	2.6	.976							
Det. W-100 L-54 Hughie Jennings																		
1B	G. Burns	392	.253	5	50	1155	57	17	65	11.8	.986	H. Coveleski	50	313	22	13	4	2.45
2B	R. Young	378	.243	0	31	233	371	32	44	5.3	.950	H. Dauss	46	310	24	13	2	2.50
SS	D. Bush	561	.228	1	44	340	504	57	61	5.8	.937	J. Dubuc	39	258	17	12	2	3.21
3B	O. Vitt	560	.250	1	48	191	324	19	19	3.5	.964	B. Boland	45	203	13	7	2	3.11
RF	S. Crawford	612	.299	4	112	219	8	6	1	1.5	.974	B. Steen	20	79	5	1	4	2.72
CF	T. Cobb	563	.369	3	99	328	22	18	7	2.4	.951	B. James	11	67	7	3	0	2.42
LF	B. Veach	569	.313	3	112	297	19	8	4	2.1	.975							
C	O. Stanage	300	.223	1	31	395	111	19	0	5.3	.964							
12	M. Kavanagh	332	.295	4	49	559	119	19	23		.973							
Chi. W-93 L-61 Pants Rowland																		
1B	J. Fournier	422	.322	5	77	674	41	10	31	11.2	.986	R. Faber	50	300	24	14	2	2.55
2B	E. Collins	521	.332	4	77	344	487	22	54	5.5	.974	J. Scott	48	296	24	11	2	2.03
SS	B. Weaver	563	.268	3	49	281	470	49	54	5.4	.939	J. Benz	39	238	15	11	0	2.11
3B	L. Blackburne	283	.216	0	25	88	134	12	13	2.8	.949	R. Russell	41	229	11	10	2	2.59
RF	E. Murphy	273	.315	0	26	113	7	6	0	1.8	.952	E. Cicotte	39	223	13	12	3	3.02
CF	H. Felsch	427	.248	3	53	247	9	11	1	2.3	.959							
LF	S. Collins	576	.257	2	33	197	13	8	2	2.1	.963							
C	R. Schalk	413	.266	1	54	655	159	13	8	6.2	.984							
3O	B. Roth	240	.250	3*	35	79	48	18	1		.876							
OF	J. Jackson	162	.265	2	36	84	6	5	1	2.1	.947							
1B	B. Brief	154	.214	2	17	458	23	7	21	10.6	.986							
Was. W-85 L-68 Clark Griffith																		
1B	C. Gandil	485	.291	2	64	1237	77	19	65	9.9	.986	W. Johnson	47	337	27	13	4	1.55
2B	R. Morgan	193	.233	0	21	102	175	10	23	5.0	.965	B. Gallia	43	260	17	11	1	2.29
SS	G. McBride	476	.204	1	30	326	422	25	47	5.3	.968	J. Boehling	40	229	14	13	0	3.22
3B	E. Foster	618	.275	0	52	92	147	21	14	3.3	.919	D. Ayers	40	211	14	9	3	2.21
RF	D. Moeller	438	.226	2	23	167	13	9	6	1.6	.952	J. Shaw	25	133	6	11	1	2.50
CF	C. Milan	573	.288	2	66	352	13	21	3	2.6	.946	H. Harper	19	86	4	4	2	1.77
LF	H. Shanks	492	.250	0	47	151	13	3	1	2.1	.982							
C	J. Henry	277	.220	1	22	478	122	17	4	6.6	.972							
C	B. Williams	197	.244	0	31	213	51	9	4	6.8	.967							
OF	M. Acosta	163	.209	0	18	75	4	3	2	1.5	.963							
N.Y. W-69 L-83 Wild Bill Donovan																		
1B	W. Pipp	479	.246	4	60	1396	85	12	85	11.1	.992	R. Caldwell	36	305	19	16	0	2.89
2B	L. Boone	431	.204	5	43	249	392	23	59	5.8	.965	R. Fisher	30	248	18	11	0	2.11
SS	Peckinpaugh	540	.220	5	44	291	468	47	60	5.7	.942	J. Warhop	21	143	7	9	0	3.96
3B	F. Maisel	530	.281	4	46	184	223	26	20	3.2	.940	B. Shawkey	16	86	4	7	0	3.26
RF	D. Cook	476	.271	2	33	188	20	9	4	1.7	.959	M. McHale	13	78	3	7	0	4.25
CF	H. High	427	.258	1	43	254	10	5	1	2.3	.981							
LF	R. Hartzell	387	.251	3	60	200	10	8	2	2.0	.963							
C	L. Nunamaker	249	.225	0	17	324	99	16	9	5.7	.964							
23	P. Baumann	219	.292	2	28	129	140	6	20		.978							
OF	B. Cree	196	.214	0	15	97	6	6	1	2.1	.945							
P	R. Caldwell	144	.243	4	20	12	72	1	5	2.4	.988							
St. L. W-63 L-91 Branch Rickey																		
1B	J. Leary	227	.242	0	15	433	32	7	41	8.9	.985	C. Weilman	47	296	18	19	4	2.34
2B	D. Pratt	602	.291	3	78	417	441	31	82	5.6	.965	G. Lowdermilk	38	222	9	17	0	3.12
SS	D. Lavan	514	.218	1	48	313	475	75	81	5.5	.913	E. Hamilton	35	204	9	17	0	2.87
3B	J. Austin	477	.266	1	30	188	264	41	32	3.5	.917	B. James	34	170	7	10	1	3.59
RF	D. Walsh	150	.220	0	6	66	11	4	0	1.8	.951	E. Koob	28	134	4	5	0	2.36
CF	T. Walker	510	.269	5	49	333	27	23	5	2.8	.940							
LF	B. Shotton	559	.283	1	30	295	15	23	4	2.2	.931							
C	S. Agnew	295	.203	0	19	398	153	39	16	5.8	.934							
UT	I. Howard	324	.278	1	43	488	90	12	33		.980							
UT	G. Sisler	274	.285	3	29	413	38	7	21		.985							
C	H. Severeid	203	.222	1	22	247	66	11	2	5.1	.966							
Cle. W-57 L-95 Joe Birmingham W-12 L-16 Lee Fohl W-45 L-79																		
1B	J. Kirke	339	.310	2	40	886	52	13	37	10.9	.986	G. Morton	34	240	16	15	1	2.14
2B	B. Wambsganss	375	.195	0	21	138	237	25	24	5.1	.938	W. Mitchell	36	236	11	14	1	2.82
SS	R. Chapman	570	.270	3	67	396	508	50	38	5.8	.944	R. Hagerman	29	151	6	14	0	3.52
3B	W. Barbare	246	.191	0	11	99	141	10	12	3.7	.960	S. Jones	48	146	4	9	3	3.65
RF	E. Smith	476	.248	3	67	202	15	18	4	1.9	.923	R. Walker	25	131	4	9	1	3.98
CF	N. Leibold	207	.256	0	4	147	10	5	0	3.1	.969	F. Coumbe	30	114	4	7	2	3.47
LF	J. Graney	404	.260	1	56	227	17	7	1	2.2	.972							
C	S. O'Neill	386	.236	2	34	556	175	24	17	6.6	.968							
O1	J. Jackson	299	.331	3	45	352	21	10	12		.974							
2B	T. Turner	262	.252	0	14	82	136	8	11		.965							
OF	B. Southworth	177	.220	0	8	90	7	6	3	4.4	.942							
OF	B. Roth	144	.299	4*	20	60	5	9	1	2.3 / 1.9	.878							

Phi. — W-43 L-109 — Connie Mack

POS	Player	AB	BA	HR	RBI	PO	A	E	DP	TC/G	FA	Pitcher	G	IP	W	L	SV	ERA
1B	S. McInnis	456	.314	0	49	1123	83	13	63	10.2	.989	J. Wyckoff	43	276	10	**22**	0	3.52
2B	N. Lajoie	490	.280	1	61	251	332	23	61	5.5	.962	R. Bressler	32	178	4	17	0	5.20
SS	L. Kopf	386	.225	1	33	152	205	31	24	5.2	.920	J. Bush	25	146	5	15	0	4.14
3B	W. Schang	359	.248	1	44	64	81	18	9	3.8	.890	T. Sheehan	15	102	4	9	0	4.15
RF	J. Walsh	417	.206	1	20	231	15	6	1	2.3	.976	B. Shawkey	17	100	6	6	0	4.05
CF	A. Strunk	485	.297	1	45	225	24	5	4	2.3	.980	T. Knowlson	18	101	4	6	0	3.49
LF	R. Oldring	408	.248	6	42	212	9	4	3	2.3	**.982**	H. Pennock	11	44	3	6	1	5.32
C	J. Lapp	312	.272	2	31	376	115	17	23	5.7	.967							
OF	E. Murphy	260	.231	0	17	55	7	7	0	1.2	.899							
2B	L. Malone	201	.204	1	17	117	109	20	9	5.7	.919							
SS	J. Barry	194	.222	0	15	106	150	13	21	5.0	.952							
C	W. McAvoy	184	.190	0	6	235	130	25	8	6.1	.936							

BATTING AND BASE RUNNING LEADERS

Batting Average
- T. Cobb, DET .369
- E. Collins, CHI .332
- J. Fournier, CHI .322
- T. Speaker, BOS .322
- S. McInnis, PHI .314

Slugging Average
- J. Fournier, CHI .491
- T. Cobb, DET .487
- M. Kavanagh, DET .452
- J. Jackson, CHI, CLE .445
- B. Roth, CHI, CLE .438

Home Runs
- B. Roth, CHI, CLE 7
- R. Oldring, PHI 6

Total Bases
- T. Cobb, DET 274
- S. Crawford, DET 264
- B. Veach, DET 247
- D. Pratt, STL 237
- E. Collins, CHI 227

Runs Batted In
- B. Veach, DET 112
- S. Crawford, DET 112
- T. Cobb, DET 99
- S. Collins, CHI 85
- J. Jackson, CHI, CLE 81

Stolen Bases
- T. Cobb, DET 96
- F. Maisel, NY 51
- E. Collins, CHI 46
- B. Shotton, STL 43
- C. Milan, WAS 40

Hits
- T. Cobb, DET 208
- S. Crawford, DET 183
- B. Veach, DET 178

Base on Balls
- E. Collins, CHI 119
- B. Shotton, STL 118
- D. Bush, DET 118
- T. Cobb, DET 118

Home Run Percentage
- B. Roth, CHI, CLE 1.8
- R. Oldring, PHI 1.5
- G. Burns, DET 1.3

Runs Scored
- T. Cobb, DET 144
- E. Collins, CHI 118
- O. Vitt, DET 116

Doubles
- B. Veach, DET 40

Triples
- S. Crawford, DET 19
- J. Fournier, CHI 18

PITCHING LEADERS

Winning Percentage
- J. Wood, BOS .750
- R. Foster, BOS .704
- B. Ruth, BOS .692
- E. Shore, BOS .692
- J. Scott, CHI .686

Earned Run Average
- J. Wood, BOS 1.49
- W. Johnson, WAS 1.55
- E. Shore, BOS 1.64
- J. Scott, CHI 2.03
- R. Fisher, NY 2.11

Wins
- W. Johnson, WAS 28
- H. Dauss, DET 24
- J. Scott, CHI 24
- R. Faber, CHI 24
- H. Coveleski, DET 22

Saves
- C. Mays, BOS 5

Strikeouts
- W. Johnson, WAS 203
- R. Faber, CHI 182
- J. Wyckoff, PHI 157
- H. Coveleski, DET 150
- W. Mitchell, CLE 149

Complete Games
- W. Johnson, WAS 35
- R. Caldwell, NY 31
- H. Dauss, DET 27
- J. Scott, CHI 23

Fewest Hits per 9 Innings
- D. Leonard, BOS 6.38
- B. Ruth, BOS 6.86
- J. Wood, BOS 6.86

Shutouts
- J. Scott, CHI 7
- W. Johnson, WAS 7
- G. Morton, CLE 6

Fewest Walks per 9 Innings
- W. Johnson, WAS 1.50
- J. Benz, CHI 1.62
- R. Russell, CHI 1.84

Most Strikeouts per 9 Inn.
- D. Leonard, BOS 5.69
- W. Mitchell, CLE 5.68
- R. Faber, CHI 5.47

Innings
- W. Johnson, WAS 337
- H. Coveleski, DET 313
- H. Dauss, DET 310

Games Pitched
- H. Coveleski, DET 50
- R. Faber, CHI 50
- J. Scott, CHI 48
- S. Jones, CLE 48

	W	L	PCT	GB	R	OR	2B	3B	HR	BA	SA	SB	E	DP	FA	CG	BB	SO	ShO	SV	ERA
BOS	101	50	.669		668	499	202	76	14	.260	.339	118	226	95	.964	82	446	634	19	15	2.39
DET	100	54	.649	2.5	778	573	**207**	94	23	**.268**	**.358**	**241**	258	107	.961	86	489	550	9	**19**	2.86
CHI	93	61	.604	9.5	717	509	163	**102**	25	.258	.348	186	230	101	.964	87	455	635	17	9	2.43
WAS	85	68	.556	17	571	492	152	79	**31**	.244	.312	233	222	95	.965	92	**350**	**715**	21	13	**2.31**
NY	69	83	.454	32.5	583	596	167	50	19	.233	.305	202	335	144	.949	76	612	566	6	7	3.09
STL	63	91	.409	39.5	521	693	166	65	19	.246	.315	138	280	82	.957	62	518	610	11	10	3.07
CLE	57	95	.375	44.5	539	670	169	79	20	.241	.317	127	338	118	.947	78	517	588	6	2	3.13
PHI	43	109	.283	58.5	545	890	183	72	16	.237	.311	127	217	118	**.966**	101	827	559	12	2	4.33
					4922	4922	1409	617	160	.248	.326	1443	2106	860	.959	664	4214	4857	101	77	2.94

	POS	Player	AB	BA	HR	RBI	PO	A	E	DP	TC/G	FA	Pitcher	G	IP	W	L	SV	ERA
Chi. W-86 L-66 Joe Tinker	1B	F. Beck	373	.223	5	38	1073	42	9	57	9.6	.992	G. McConnell	44	303	**25**	10	1	2.20
	2B	R. Zeider	494	.227	0	34	208	240	28	39	5.7	.941	C. Hendrix	40	285	16	15	4	3.00
	SS	J. Smith	318	.217	4	30	187	246	46*	28	5.2	.904	Prendergast	42	254	14	12	0	2.48
	3B	H. Fritz	236	.250	3	26	79	106	7	8	2.7	.964	T. Brown	35	236	17	8	3	2.09
	RF	M. Flack	523	.314	3	45	226	24	8	5	1.9	.969	D. Black	25	121	6	7	0	2.45
	CF	D. Zwilling	548	.286	13	**94**	**356**	20	8	6	2.6	.979	A. Brennan	19	106	3	9	0	3.74
	LF	L. Mann	470	.306	4	58	269	17	9	3	2.3	.969							
	C	A. Wilson	269	.305	7	31	391	96	10	6	5.7	.980							
	C	B. Fischer	292	.329	4	50	324	100	12	9	5.5	.972							
	2B	J. Farrell	222	.216	0	14	138	182	20	26	4.9	.941							
	OF	C. Hanford	179	.240	0	22	66	2	2	0	1.6	.971							
	3B	T. Wisterzil	164	.244	0	14	65	109	6	6	3.8	.967							
St. L. W-87 L-67 Fielder Jones	1B	B. Borton	549	.286	3	83	1571	58	12	91	10.3	.993	D. Davenport	55	**393**	22	18	1	2.20
	2B	B. Vaughn	521	.280	0	32	249	357	30	43	5.0	.953	D. Crandall	51	313	21	15	0	2.59
	SS	E. Johnson	512	.240	7	67	348	477	51	64	5.8	.942	E. Plank	42	268	21	11	2	2.08
	3B	C. Deal	223	.323	1	27	76	136	11	9	3.4	.951	B. Groom	37	209	12	11	1	3.27
	RF	J. Tobin	**625**	.294	6	51	279	21	11	3	2.0	.965	D. Watson	33	136	7	10	0	3.98
	CF	D. Drake	343	.265	1	41	180	10	5	2	2.0	.974							
	LF	W. Miller	536	.306	1	63	299	16	12	3	2.1	.963							
	C	G. Hartley	394	.274	1	50	565	151	**21**	11	6.5	.972							
	3B	A. Kores	201	.234	1	22	80	161	10	12	4.2	.960							
	C	H. Chapman	186	.199	1	29	293	79	4	6	7.1	.989							
	OF	L. Kirby	178	.213	0	16	87	8	3	2	1.9	.969							
	2B	A. Bridwell	175	.229	0	9	60	98	8	9	4.0	.952							
Pit. W-86 L-67 Rebel Oakes	1B	E. Konetchy	576	.314	10	93	1536	81	10	83	10.7	**.994**	F. Allen	41	283	23	12	0	2.51
	2B	S. Yerkes	434	.288	1	49	242	322	19	38	5.1	.967	E. Knetzer	41	279	18	15	3	2.58
	SS	M. Berghammer	469	.243	0	33	286	359	39	55	5.2	**.943**	C. Rogge	37	254	17	12	0	2.55
	3B	M. Mowrey	521	.280	1	49	174	**268**	19	15	3.1	**.959**	B. Hearn	29	176	6	11	0	3.38
	RF	R. Kelly	524	.294	4	50	292	27	**16**	5	2.3	.952	C. Barger	34	153	10	7	5	2.29
	CF	R. Oakes	580	.278	0	82	348	12	10	2	2.4	.973	W. Dickson	27	97	6	5	0	4.19
	LF	A. Wickland	389	.301	1	30	234	11	8	0	2.3	.968							
	C	C. Berry	292	.192	1	26	384	144	11	8	5.4	.980							
	UT	J. Lewis	231	.264	0	26	150	152	11	20		.965							
	C	P. O'Connor	219	.228	0	16	275	112	5	4	5.9	.987							
K. C. W-81 L-72 George Stovall	1B	G. Stovall	480	.231	0	44	1417	**87**	20	61	**11.8**	.987	N. Cullop	44	302	22	11	2	2.44
	2B	D. Kenworthy	396	.298	3	52	230	283	35	35	5.1	.936	G. Packard	42	282	20	11	2	2.68
	SS	J. Rawlings	399	.216	2	24	209	366	46	36	5.2	.926	C. Johnson	46	281	18	17	1	2.75
	3B	G. Perring	553	.259	6	67	135	226	16	14	3.7	.958	A. Main	35	230	13	14	3	2.54
	RF	E. Gilmore	411	.285	1	47	215	17	5	4	2.0	**.979**	P. Henning	40	207	8	16	3	3.17
	CF	C. Chadbourne	587	.227	1	35	308	24	7	7	2.2	.979							
	LF	A. Shaw	448	.281	6	67	184	11	12	0	1.7	.942							
	C	T. Easterly	309	.272	3	32	398	132	17	11	6.2	.969							
	OF	A. Krueger	240	.238	2	26	116	8	2	2	1.9	.984							
	S2	P. Goodwin	229	.236	0	16	106	180	24	17		.923							
	C	D. Brown	227	.242	1	26	270	104	15	4	6.0	.961							
	3B	B. Bradley	203	.187	0	9	55	95	8	4	2.6	.949							
Nwk. W-80 L-72 Bill Phillips W-26 L-27 Bill McKechnie W-54 L-45	1B	E. Huhn	415	.227	1	41	1001	53	16	68	10.6	.985	E. Reulbach	33	270	20	10	1	2.23
	2B	F. LaPorte	550	.253	2	56	**330**	**431**	32	**69**	5.4	.960	E. Moseley	38	268	16	16	0	**1.91**
	SS	J. Esmond	569	.258	5	62	**353**	**482**	54	67	5.7	.939	G. Kaiserling	41	261	13	14	2	2.24
	3B	B. McKechnie	451	.251	1	43	184	226	19	17	3.7	.956	H. Moran	34	206	13	10	0	2.54
	RF	V. Campbell	525	.310	1	44	200	15	12	3	1.8	.947	C. Falkenberg	25	172	9	11	3	3.24
	CF	E. Roush	551	.298	3	60	331	20	10	3	2.5	.972	T. Seaton	12	75	3	6	1	2.28
	LF	A. Scheer	546	.267	2	60	287	16	9	5	2.0	.971							
	C	B. Rariden	444	.270	0	40	709	**238**	**21**	18	**6.8**	.978							
	UT	G. Schaefer	154	.214	0	8	146	31	7	12		.962							
Buf. W-74 L-78 Larry Schlafly W-14 L-29 Walter Blair W-1 L-1 Harry Lord W-59 L-48	1B	H. Chase	567	.291	**17**	89	1460	83	**26**	84	11.0	.983	A. Schulz	42	310	21	14	0	3.08
	2B	B. Louden	469	.281	4	48	191	262	10	36	5.3	.978	H. Bedient	53	269	15	18	**10**	3.17
	SS	R. Roach	346	.269	2	31	212	297	22	38	5.8	.959	F. Anderson	36	240	19	13	0	2.51
	3B	H. Lord	359	.270	1	21	85	158	14	13	2.8	.946	G. Krapp	38	231	9	19	0	3.51
	RF	T. McDonald	251	.271	6	39	93	4	8	1	1.6	.924	R. Ford	21	127	5	9	0	4.52
	CF	C. Engle	501	.261	3	71	211	8	7	2	2.3	.969							
	LF	B. Meyer	333	.231	1	29	134	9	8	1	1.7	.947							
	C	W. Blair	290	.224	2	20	404	150	11	15	5.8	**.981**							
	OF	J. Dalton	437	.293	2	46	218	11	8	4	2.0	.966							
	OF	S. Hofman	346	.234	0	27	132	16	6	5	1.9	.961							
	23	T. Downey	282	.199	1	19	165	193	22	25		.942							
	C	N. Allen	215	.205	0	17	347	110	**21**	8	6.0	.956							

	POS	Player	AB	BA	HR	RBI	PO	A	E	DP	TC/G	FA	Pitcher	G	IP	W	L	SV	ERA
Bkn.	1B	H. Myers	341	.287	1	36	961	56	10	52	9.6	.990	H. Finneran	37	215	12	13	0	2.80
W-70 L-82	2B	L. Magee	452	.323	4	49	271	321	40	46	5.5	.937	D. Marion	35	208	10	9	0	3.20
Lee Magee	SS	F. Smith	385	.247	5	58	203	281	42	24	5.6	.920	T. Seaton	32	189	12	11	3	4.56
W-53 L-64	3B	A. Halt	524	.250	3	64	174	224	30	23	3.9	.930	J. Bluejacket	24	163	9	11	0	3.15
John Ganzel	RF	G. Anderson	511	.264	2	39	200	16	10	5	1.7	.956	B. Upham	33	121	7	8	4	3.05
W-17 L-18	CF	B. Kauff	483	.342	12	83	317	32	15	7	2.7	.959	E. Lafitte	17	118	6	9	0	3.98
	LF	C. Cooper	527	.294	2	63	274	26	13	3	2.6	.958	F. Wilson	18	102	1	7	0	3.78
	C	G. Land	290	.259	0	22	314	114	18	13	5.5	.960	H. Wiltse	18	59	3	5	5	2.28
	OF	S. Evans	216	.296	3	30	89	8	4	2	1.7	.960							
	3B	T. Wisterzil	106	.311	0	21	45	67	6	7	3.8	.949							
Bal.	1B	H. Swacina	301	.246	1	38	735	57	11	50	10.7	.986	J. Quinn	44	274	9	22	1	3.45
W-47 L-107	2B	O. Knabe	320	.253	1	25	203	264	12	52	5.1	.975	G. Suggs	35	233	13	17	1	4.14
Otto Knabe	SS	M. Doolan	404	.186	2	21	303	400	40	67*	6.2*	.946	B. Bailey	36	190	5	19	0	4.63
	3B	J. Walsh	401	.302	9	60	131	190	22	15	3.2	.936	C. Bender	26	178	4	16	1	3.99
	RF	S. Evans	340	.315	1	37	111	12	10	4	1.5	.925	A. Johnson	23	151	7	11	1	3.35
	CF	V. Duncan	531	.267	2	43	257	19	10	6	2.3	.965	G. LaClaire	18	84	2	8	0	2.46
	LF	G. Zinn	312	.269	5	43	139	11	8	4	1.8	.949							
	C	F. Owens	334	.251	3	28	462	146	15	19	6.3	.976							
	OF	McCandless	406	.214	5	34	209	16	13	8	2.3	.945							
	1B	J. Agler	214	.215	0	14	573	44	12	42	10.8	.981							
	UT	Kirkpatrick	171	.240	0	19	101	108	20	11		.913							

BATTING AND BASE RUNNING LEADERS

Batting Average
B. Kauff, BKN	.342
B. Fischer, CHI	.329
L. Magee, BKN	.323
E. Konetchy, PIT	.314
M. Flack, CHI	.314

Slugging Average
B. Kauff, BKN	.509
E. Konetchy, PIT	.483
H. Chase, BUF	.471
B. Fischer, CHI	.449
D. Zwilling, CHI	.442

Home Runs
H. Chase, BUF	17
D. Zwilling, CHI	13
B. Kauff, BKN	12
E. Konetchy, PIT	10
J. Walsh, BAL, STL	9

Total Bases
E. Konetchy, PIT	278
H. Chase, BUF	267
J. Tobin, STL	254
B. Kauff, BKN	246
D. Zwilling, CHI	242

Runs Batted In
D. Zwilling, CHI	94
E. Konetchy, PIT	93
H. Chase, BUF	89
B. Kauff, BKN	83
B. Borton, STL	83

Stolen Bases
B. Kauff, BKN	55
M. Mowrey, PIT	40
R. Kelly, PIT	38
M. Flack, CHI	37
L. Magee, BKN	34

Hits
J. Tobin, STL	184
E. Konetchy, PIT	181
S. Evans, BAL, BKN	171

Base on Balls
B. Borton, STL	92
B. Kauff, BKN	85
M. Berghammer, PIT	83

Home Run Percentage
H. Chase, BUF	3.0
A. Wilson, CHI	2.6
B. Kauff, BKN	2.5

Runs Scored
B. Borton, STL	97
M. Berghammer, PIT	96
S. Evans, BAL, BKN	94

Doubles
S. Evans, BAL, BKN	34
D. Zwilling, CHI	32
H. Chase, BUF	31
E. Konetchy, PIT	31

Triples
L. Mann, CHI	19
E. Konetchy, PIT	18
R. Kelly, PIT	17
E. Gilmore, KC	15

PITCHING LEADERS

Winning Percentage
G. McConnell, CHI	.714
T. Brown, CHI	.680
N. Cullop, KC	.667
E. Reulbach, NWK	.667
F. Allen, PIT	.657

Earned Run Average
E. Moseley, NWK	1.91
E. Plank, STL	2.08
T. Brown, CHI	2.09
G. McConnell, CHI	2.20
D. Davenport, STL	2.20

Wins
G. McConnell, CHI	25
F. Allen, PIT	23
N. Cullop, KC	22
D. Davenport, STL	22
D. Crandall, STL	21

Saves
H. Bedient, BUF	10
C. Barger, PIT	5
H. Wiltse, BKN	5
B. Upham, BKN	4
C. Hendrix, CHI	4
T. Seaton, BKN, NWK	4

Strikeouts
D. Davenport, STL	229
A. Schulz, BUF	160
G. McConnell, CHI	151
E. Plank, STL	147
F. Anderson, BUF	142
E. Moseley, NWK	142

Complete Games
D. Davenport, STL	30
C. Hendrix, CHI	26
A. Schulz, BUF	25
F. Allen, PIT	24

Fewest Hits per 9 Innings
D. Davenport, STL	6.88
A. Main, KC	7.08
E. Plank, STL	7.11

Shutouts
D. Davenport, STL	10
E. Plank, STL	6
F. Allen, PIT	6

Fewest Walks per 9 Innings
E. Plank, STL	1.81
C. Bender, BAL	1.87
N. Cullop, KC	1.99

Most Strikeouts per 9 Inn.
F. Anderson, BUF	5.32
D. Davenport, STL	5.25
E. Plank, STL	4.93

Innings
D. Davenport, STL	393
D. Crandall, STL	313
A. Schulz, BUF	310

Games Pitched
D. Davenport, STL	55
H. Bedient, BUF	53
D. Crandall, STL	51
C. Johnson, KC	46

	W	L	PCT	GB	R	OR	Batting 2B	3B	HR	BA	SA	SB	Fielding E	DP	FA	Pitching CG	BB	SO	ShO	SV	ERA
CHI	86	66	.566		641	538	185	77	50	.257	.352	161	233	102	.964	97	402	576	21	9	2.64
STL	87	67	.565		634	528	199	81	23	.261	.345	195	212	111	.967	94	396	698	24	7	2.73
PIT	86	67	.562	.5	592	524	180	80	20	.262	.341	224	182	98	.971	88	441	517	16	11	2.79
KC	81	72	.529	5.5	547	551	200	66	27	.244	.328	144	246	96	.962	95	390	526	16	10	2.82
NWK	80	72	.526	6	585	562	210	80	17	.252	.334	184	239	124	.963	79	553	594	14	11	3.38
BUF	74	78	.487	12	574	634	193	68	40	.249	.338	249	290	103	.955	78	536	467	10	13	3.37
BKN	70	82	.461	16	647	673	205	75	36	.268	.360	128	273	140	.957	85	466	570	5	4	3.96
BAL	47	107	.305	40	550	760	196	53	36	.244	.325	128									
					4770	4770	1568	580	249	.255	.340	1469	1907	886	.963	716	3637	4529	122	70	3.03

Bkn. W-94 L-60 Wilbert Robinson

POS	Player	AB	BA	HR	RBI	PO	A	E	DP	TC/G	FA	Pitcher	G	IP	W	L	SV	ERA
1B	J. Daubert	478	.316	3	33	1195	66	9	56	10.1	.993	J. Pfeffer	41	329	25	11	1	1.92
2B	G. Cutshaw	581	.260	2	63	361	467	36	51	5.6	.958	L. Cheney	41	253	18	12	0	1.92
SS	I. Olson	351	.254	1	38	234	303	47	28	5.7	.920	S. Smith	36	219	14	10	1	2.34
3B	M. Mowrey	495	.244	0	60	154	291	16	17	3.2	.965	R. Marquard	36	205	13	6	5	1.58
RF	J. Johnston	425	.252	1	26	224	16	9	3	2.3	.964	J. Coombs	27	159	13	8	0	2.66
CF	H. Myers	412	.262	3	36	242	11	8	5	2.5	.969	W. Dell	32	155	8	9	1	2.26
LF	Z. Wheat	568	.312	9	73	333	14	9	0	2.4	.975							
C	C. Meyers	239	.247	0	21	389	95	8	9	6.6	.984							
OF	C. Stengel	462	.279	8	53	206	14	8	4	1.9	.965							
C	O. Miller	216	.255	1	17	311	85	13	6	5.9	.968							
SS	O. O'Mara	193	.202	0	15	117	148	30	13	5.8	.898							

Phi. W-91 L-62 Pat Moran

POS	Player	AB	BA	HR	RBI	PO	A	E	DP	TC/G	FA	Pitcher	G	IP	W	L	SV	ERA
1B	F. Luderus	508	.281	5	53	1499	71	28	83	10.9	.982	G. Alexander	48	389	33	12	3	1.55
2B	B. Niehoff	548	.243	4	61	285	437	49	65	5.3	.936	E. Rixey	38	287	22	10	0	1.85
SS	D. Bancroft	477	.212	3	33	326	510	60	64	6.3	.933	A. Demaree	39	285	19	14	1	2.62
3B	M. Stock	509	.281	1	43	128	213	16	22	3.1	.955	E. Mayer	28	140	7	7	0	3.15
RF	G. Cravath	448	.283	11	70	182	17	7	2	1.6	.966	C. Bender	27	123	7	7	3	3.74
CF	D. Paskert	555	.279	8	46	332	14	6	4	2.4	.983	G. McQuillan	21	62	1	7	2	2.76
LF	P. Whitted	526	.281	6	68	285	13	11	3	2.3	.964							
C	B. Killefer	286	.217	3	27	443	89	8	15	5.9	.985							
C	E. Burns	219	.233	0	14	283	87	7	5	5.0	.981							

Bos. W-89 L-63 George Stallings

POS	Player	AB	BA	HR	RBI	PO	A	E	DP	TC/G	FA	Pitcher	G	IP	W	L	SV	ERA
1B	E. Konetchy	566	.260	3	70	1626	96	18	96	11.0	.990	D. Rudolph	41	312	19	12	3	2.16
2B	B. Evers	241	.216	0	15	98	175	14	29	4.0	.951	L. Tyler	34	249	17	10	1	2.02
SS	R. Maranville	604	.235	4	38	386	515	50	79	6.1	.947	P. Ragan	28	182	9	9	0	2.08
3B	R. Smith	509	.259	3	60	166	299	36	15	3.3	.928	J. Barnes	33	163	6	14	1	2.37
RF	J. Wilhoit	383	.230	2	38	177	12	4	3	1.8	.979	T. Hughes	40	161	16	3	5	2.35
CF	F. Snodgrass	382	.249	1	32	274	19	5	5	2.7	.983	A. Nehf	22	121	7	5	0	2.01
LF	S. Magee	419	.241	3	54	220	6	5	0	1.9	.978	F. Allen	19	113	8	2	1	2.07
C	H. Gowdy	349	.252	1	34	533	158	14	19	6.1	.980	E. Reulbach	21	109	7	6	0	2.47
OF	Z. Collins	268	.209	1	18	114	10	7	3	1.7	.947							
2B	D. Egan	238	.223	0	16	81	125	11	11	4.1	.949							
2O	Fitzpatrick	216	.213	1	18	114	96	9	14		.959							
P	L. Tyler	93	.204	3	20	9	72	3	3	2.5	.964							

N. Y. W-86 L-66 John McGraw

POS	Player	AB	BA	HR	RBI	PO	A	E	DP	TC/G	FA	Pitcher	G	IP	W	L	SV	ERA
1B	F. Merkle	401	.237	7	44	1183	58	20	61	11.3	.984	J. Tesreau	40	268	18	14	1	2.92
2B	L. Doyle	441	.268	2	47	270	352	26	53	5.7	.960	P. Perritt	42	251	18	11	2	2.62
SS	A. Fletcher	500	.286	3	66	253	497	48	56	6.0	.940	R. Benton	38	239	16	8	2	2.87
3B	B. McKechnie	260	.246	0	17	70	134	13	8	3.1	.940	F. Anderson	38	188	9	13	2	3.40
RF	D. Robertson	587	.307	12	69	248	17	11	5	1.9	.960	F. Schupp	30	140	9	3	1	0.90
CF	B. Kauff	552	.264	9	74	329	22	14	6	2.4	.962	S. Sallee	15	112	9	4	0	1.37
LF	G. Burns	623	.279	5	41	289	19	12	3	2.1	.963							
C	B. Rariden	351	.222	1	29	576	144	21	10	6.2	.972							
UT	B. Herzog	280	.261	0	25	140	238	17	28		.957							

Chi. W-67 L-86 Joe Tinker

POS	Player	AB	BA	HR	RBI	PO	A	E	DP	TC/G	FA	Pitcher	G	IP	W	L	SV	ERA
1B	V. Saier	498	.253	7	50	1622	74	27	78	11.7	.984	H. Vaughn	44	294	17	14	1	2.20
2B	O. Knabe	145	.276	0	7	72	128	13	17	5.1	.939	C. Hendrix	36	218	8	16	2	2.68
SS	C. Wortman	234	.201	2	16	124	191	32	24	5.0	.908	J. Lavender	36	188	10	14	2	2.82
3B	H. Zimmerman	398	.291	6	64*	88	198	21	11	4.1*	.932	G. McConnell	28	171	4	12	0	2.57
RF	M. Flack	465	.258	3	20	193	22	2	4	1.6	.989	G. Packard	37	155	10	6	5	2.78
CF	C. Williams	405	.279	12	66	260	7	3	0	2.3	.989	Prendergast	35	152	6	11	2	2.31
LF	L. Mann	415	.272	2	29	200	9	6	1	1.9	.972	T. Seaton	31	121	6	6	1	3.27
C	J. Archer	205	.220	1	30	236	84	7	5	5.0	.979							
UT	R. Zeider	345	.235	1	22	140	199	21	19		.942							
OF	W. Schulte	230	.296	5	27	108	8	6	0	1.9	.951							
SS	E. Mulligan	189	.153	0	9	116	200	40	27	6.1	.888							
C	B. Fischer	179	.196	1	14	246	73	9	3	5.9	.973							
OF	J. Kelly	169	.254	2	15	98	4	5	0	2.3	.953							

Pit. W-65 L-89 Nixey Callahan

POS	Player	AB	BA	HR	RBI	PO	A	E	DP	TC/G	FA	Pitcher	G	IP	W	L	SV	ERA
1B	D. Johnston	404	.213	0	39	1042	47	14	44	10.0	.987	A. Mamaux	45	310	21	15	2	2.53
2B	J. Farmer	166	.271	0	14	53	77	10	6	4.5	.929	W. Cooper	42	246	12	11	2	1.87
SS	H. Wagner	432	.287	1	39	226	261	30	32	5.6	.942	F. Miller	30	173	7	10	1	2.29
3B	D. Baird	430	.216	1	28	90	145	17	12	3.2	.933	B. Harmon	31	173	8	11	0	2.81
RF	B. Hinchman	555	.315	4	76	222	8	9	2	1.9	.962	E. Kantlehner	34	165	5	15	2	3.16
CF	M. Carey	599	.264	7	42	419	32	8	10	3.0	.983	E. Jacobs	34	153	6	10	0	2.94
LF	D. Costello	159	.239	0	8	82	0	2	0	2.0	.976	B. Adams	16	72	2	9	0	5.72
C	W. Schmidt	184	.190	2	15	232	88	8	6	5.8	.976							
UT	J. Schultz	204	.260	0	22	75	86	22	3		.880							
OF	W. Schulte	177	.254	0	14	89	2	3	0	2.0	.968							
3B	H. Warner	168	.238	2	14	60	56	13	5	3.1	.899							
2O	C. Bigbee	164	.250	0	3	81	54	9	7		.938							

Cin. W-60 L-93 Buck Herzog / W-34 L-49 Ivy Wingo / W-1 L-1 Christy Mathewson / W-25 L-43

POS	Player	AB	BA	HR	RBI	PO	A	E	DP	TC/G	FA	Pitcher	G	IP	W	L	SV	ERA
1B	H. Chase	542	.339	4	82	932	37	14	66	10.0	.986	F. Toney	41	300	14	17	1	2.28
2B	B. Louden	439	.219	1	32	238	345	19	48	5.6	.968	P. Schneider	44	274	10	19	1	2.69
SS	B. Herzog	281	.267	1	24	162	203	27	30	6.0	.931	A. Schulz	44	215	8	19	2	3.14
3B	H. Groh	553	.269	2	28	123	252	17	32	3.6	.957	C. Mitchell	29	195	11	10	0	3.14
RF	T. Griffith	595	.266	2	61	238	28	9	5	1.8	.964	E. Knetzer	36	171	5	12	1	2.89
CF	E. Roush	272	.287	0	15	192	7	6	1	3.0	.971	E. Moseley	31	150	7	10	1	3.89
LF	G. Neale	530	.262	0	20	307	20	9	6	2.5	.973							
C	I. Wingo	347	.245	2	40	463	170	28	15	6.2	.958							
OF	R. Killefer	234	.244	1	18	138	6	5	2	2.2	.966							
1B	F. Mollwitz	183	.224	0	16	482	23	10	29	9.5	.981							
C	T. Clarke	177	.237	0	17	187	58	9	3	5.0	.965							

	POS	Player	AB	BA	HR	RBI	PO	A	E	DP	TC/G	FA	Pitcher	G	IP	W	L	SV	ERA
St. L.	1B	D. Miller	505	.238	1	46	948	43	7	60	10.7	.993	L. Meadows	51	289	12	23	2	2.58
	2B	B. Betzel	510	.233	1	37	275	366	27	64	5.9	.960	R. Ames	45	228	11	16	7	2.64
W-60 L-93	SS	R. Corhan	295	.210	0	18	153	278	39	35	5.6	.917	B. Doak	29	192	12	8	0	2.63
Miller Huggins	3B	R. Hornsby	495	.313	6	65	82	174	20	7	3.3	.928	B. Steele	29	148	5	15	0	3.41
	RF	T. Long	403	.293	1	33	143	13	9	2	1.6	.945	H. Jasper	21	107	5	6	1	3.28
	CF	J. Smith	357	.244	6	34	212	12	12	4	2.0	.949	S. Williams	36	105	6	7	1	4.20
	LF	B. Bescher	561	.235	6	43	284	18	15	2	2.1	.953	M. Watson	18	103	4	6	0	3.06
	C	M. Gonzalez	331	.239	0	29	367	136	10	8	5.5	.981	S. Sallee	16	70	5	5	1	3.47
	C1	F. Snyder	406	.259	0	39	731	138	19	35		.979							
	OF	O. Wilson	355	.239	3	32	181	11	9	3	1.8	.955							
	3B	Z. Beck	184	.223	0	10	45	86	13	7	2.8	.910							

BATTING AND BASE RUNNING LEADERS

Batting Average

H. Chase, CIN	.339
J. Daubert, BKN	.316
B. Hinchman, PIT	.315
R. Hornsby, STL	.313
Z. Wheat, BKN	.312

Slugging Average

Z. Wheat, BKN	.461
H. Chase, CIN	.459
C. Williams, CHI	.459
R. Hornsby, STL	.444
G. Cravath, PHI	.440

Home Runs

C. Williams, CHI	12
D. Robertson, NY	12
G. Cravath, PHI	11
B. Kauff, NY	9
Z. Wheat, BKN	9

Total Bases

Z. Wheat, BKN	262
D. Robertson, NY	250
H. Chase, CIN	249
B. Hinchman, PIT	237
G. Burns, NY	229

Runs Batted In

H. Zimmerman, CHI, NY	83
H. Chase, CIN	82
B. Hinchman, PIT	76
B. Kauff, NY	74
Z. Wheat, BKN	73

Stolen Bases

M. Carey, PIT	63
B. Kauff, NY	40
B. Bescher, STL	39
G. Burns, NY	37
B. Herzog, CIN, NY	34

Hits

H. Chase, CIN	184
D. Robertson, NY	180
Z. Wheat, BKN	177

Base on Balls

H. Groh, CIN	84
V. Saier, CHI	79
D. Bancroft, PHI	74

Home Run Percentage

C. Williams, CHI	3.0
G. Cravath, PHI	2.5
D. Robertson, NY	2.0

Runs Scored

G. Burns, NY	105
M. Carey, PIT	90
D. Robertson, NY	88

Doubles

B. Niehoff, PHI	42
Z. Wheat, BKN	32
D. Paskert, PHI	30

Triples

B. Hinchman, PIT	16
E. Roush, CIN, NY	15
R. Hornsby, STL	15
B. Kauff, NY	15

PITCHING LEADERS

Winning Percentage

T. Hughes, BOS	.842
G. Alexander, PHI	.733
J. Pfeffer, BKN	.694
E. Rixey, PHI	.688
R. Benton, NY	.667

Earned Run Average

G. Alexander, PHI	1.55
R. Marquard, BKN	1.58
E. Rixey, PHI	1.85
W. Cooper, PIT	1.87
J. Pfeffer, BKN	1.92

Wins

G. Alexander, PHI	33
J. Pfeffer, BKN	25
E. Rixey, PHI	22
A. Mamaux, PIT	21
D. Rudolph, BOS	19
A. Demaree, PHI	19

Saves

R. Ames, STL	7
R. Marquard, BKN	5
T. Hughes, BOS	5
G. Packard, CHI	5

Strikeouts

G. Alexander, PHI	167
L. Cheney, BKN	166
A. Mamaux, PIT	163
F. Toney, CIN	146
H. Vaughn, CHI	144

Complete Games

G. Alexander, PHI	38
J. Pfeffer, BKN	30
D. Rudolph, BOS	27
A. Mamaux, PIT	26
A. Demaree, PHI	25

Fewest Hits per 9 Innings

L. Cheney, BKN	6.33
W. Cooper, PIT	6.91
F. Miller, PIT	7.02

Shutouts

G. Alexander, PHI	16
L. Tyler, BOS	6
J. Pfeffer, BKN	6

Fewest Walks per 9 Innings

D. Rudolph, BOS	1.10
G. Alexander, PHI	1.16
A. Demaree, PHI	1.52

Most Strikeouts per 9 Inn.

L. Cheney, BKN	5.91
C. Hendrix, CHI	4.83
A. Mamaux, PIT	4.73

Innings

G. Alexander, PHI	389
J. Pfeffer, BKN	329
D. Rudolph, BOS	312

Games Pitched

L. Meadows, STL	51
G. Alexander, PHI	48
A. Mamaux, PIT	45
R. Ames, STL	45

	W	L	PCT	GB	R	OR	Batting 2B	3B	HR	BA	SA	SB	Fielding E	DP	FA	Pitching CG	BB	SO	ShO	SV	ERA
BKN	94	60	.610		585	467	195	80	28	.261	.345	187	224	90	.965	96	372	634	22	9	2.12
PHI	91	62	.595	2.5	581	489	223	53	42	.250	.341	149	234	119	.963	97	325	601	26	9	2.36
BOS	89	63	.586	4	542	453	166	73	22	.233	.307	141	212	124	.967	97	310	644	21	11	2.19
NY	86	66	.566	7	597	503	188	74	42	.253	.343	133	286	104	.957	72	365	616	17	13	2.65
CHI	67	86	.438	26.5	520	541	194	56	46	.239	.325	173	260	97	.959	88	443	596	10	7	2.76
PIT	65	89	.422	29	484	586	147	91	20	.240	.316	157	228	126	.965	86	458	569	7	6	3.10
CIN	60	93	.392	33.5	505	622	187	88	14	.254	.331	182	278	124	.957	58	445	529	11	14	3.14
STL	60	93	.392	33.5	476	629	155	74	25	.243	.318	182	278	124	.957	58	445	529	11	14	3.14
					4290	4290	1455	589	239	.247	.328	1328	1939	892	.963	682	3013	4827	136	80	2.61

Bos. W-91 L-63 — Bill Carrigan

POS	Player	AB	BA	HR	RBI	PO	A	E	DP	TC/G	FA	Pitcher	G	IP	W	L	SV	ERA
1B	D. Hoblitzell	417	.259	0	50	1225	67	15	64	10.4	.989	B. Ruth	44	324	23	12	1	**1.75**
2B	J. Barry	330	.203	0	20	200	282	13	30	5.3	.974	D. Leonard	48	274	18	12	6	2.36
SS	E. Scott	366	.232	0	27	217	339	19	36	4.8	.967	C. Mays	44	245	18	13	3	2.39
3B	L. Gardner	493	.308	2	62	149	278	21	24	3.0	.953	E. Shore	38	226	16	10	1	2.63
RF	H. Hooper	575	.271	1	37	266	19	10	5	2.0	.966	R. Foster	33	182	14	7	2	3.06
CF	T. Walker	467	.266	3	46	290	12	13	4	2.5	.959							
LF	D. Lewis	563	.268	1	56	306	16	10	4	2.2	.970							
C	P. Thomas	216	.264	1	21	321	86	8	7	4.6	.981							
S2	H. Janvrin	310	.223	0	26	166	225	27	37		.935							
C	H. Cady	162	.191	0	13	188	49	8	4	3.9	.967							

Chi. W-89 L-65 — Pants Rowland

POS	Player	AB	BA	HR	RBI	PO	A	E	DP	TC/G	FA	Pitcher	G	IP	W	L	SV	ERA
1B	J. Fournier	313	.240	3	44	855	49	20	47	10.9	.978	R. Russell	56	264	18	11	3	2.42
2B	E. Collins	545	.308	0	52	346	415	19	75	5.0	.976	L. Williams	43	224	13	7	1	2.89
SS	Z. Terry	269	.190	0	17	148	243	27	36	4.5	.935	R. Faber	35	205	17	9	1	2.02
3B	B. Weaver	582	.227	3	38	124	193	20	22	4.0	.941	E. Cicotte	44	187	15	7	5	1.78
RF	S. Collins	527	.243	0	42	238	20	11	6	2.0	.959	J. Scott	32	165	7	14	3	2.72
CF	H. Felsch	546	.300	7	70	340	19	7	5	2.6	.981	J. Benz	28	142	9	5	0	2.03
LF	J. Jackson	592	.341	3	78	290	17	8	5	2.0	.975	M. Wolfgang	27	127	4	6	0	1.98
C	R. Schalk	410	.232	0	41	**653**	**166**	10	25	**6.7**	**.988**	D. Danforth	28	94	6	5	2	3.27
1B	J. Ness	258	.267	1	34	655	31	15	45	10.2	.979							
3B	F. McMullin	187	.257	0	10	74	115	10	11	3.2	.950							

Det. W-87 L-67 — Hughie Jennings

POS	Player	AB	BA	HR	RBI	PO	A	E	DP	TC/G	FA	Pitcher	G	IP	W	L	SV	ERA
1B	G. Burns	479	.286	4	73	1355	54	22	71	11.5	.985	H. Coveleski	44	324	21	11	2	1.97
2B	R. Young	528	.263	1	45	352	417	27	55	5.5	.966	H. Dauss	39	239	19	12	4	3.21
SS	D. Bush	550	.225	0	34	278	435	34	41	5.2	.954	J. Dubuc	36	170	10	10	1	2.96
3B	O. Vitt	597	.226	0	42	**208**	**385**	22	**32**	**4.1**	**.964**	B. James	30	152	8	12	1	3.68
RF	H. Heilmann	451	.282	2	76	110	10	6	0	1.6	.952	G. Cunningham	35	150	7	10	2	2.75
CF	T. Cobb	542	.371	5	68	325	18	17	9	2.5	.953	B. Boland	46	130	10	3	3	3.94
LF	B. Veach	566	.306	3	91	342	14	12	4	2.5	.967	W. Mitchell	23	128	7	5	0	3.31
C	O. Stanage	291	.237	0	30	387	108	15	11	5.4	.971							
OF	S. Crawford	322	.286	0	42	85	6	2	2	1.2	.978							

N. Y. W-80 L-74 — Wild Bill Donovan

POS	Player	AB	BA	HR	RBI	PO	A	E	DP	TC/G	FA	Pitcher	G	IP	W	L	SV	ERA
1B	W. Pipp	545	.262	12	93	1513	99	13	**89**	11.0	.992	B. Shawkey	53	277	24	14	**8**	2.21
2B	J. Gedeon	435	.211	0	27	235	341	27	55	4.9	.955	G. Mogridge	30	195	6	12	0	2.31
SS	Peckinpaugh	552	.255	4	58	285	**468**	43	50	5.5	.946	R. Fisher	31	179	11	8	2	3.17
3B	F. Baker	360	.269	10	52	133	210	22	16	3.8	.940	A. Russell	34	171	6	10	6	3.20
RF	F. Gilhooley	223	.278	1	10	93	9	3	3	1.8	.971	N. Cullop	28	167	13	6	1	2.05
CF	L. Magee	510	.257	3	45	301	17	8	3	2.5	.975	R. Caldwell	21	166	5	12	0	2.99
LF	H. High	377	.263	1	28	216	14	12	2	2.2	.950	R. Keating	14	91	5	6	0	3.07
C	L. Nunamaker	260	.296	0	28	353	102	8	13	5.9	.983							
UT	P. Baumann	237	.287	1	25	93	64	8	8		.952							
C	R. Walters	203	.266	0	23	346	102	12	13	7.1	.974							
OF	R. Oldring	158	.234	1	12	66	1	3	3	1.6	.957							
O3	F. Maisel	158	.228	0	7	60	26	4	4		.956							

St. L. W-79 L-75 — Fielder Jones

POS	Player	AB	BA	HR	RBI	PO	A	E	DP	TC/G	FA	Pitcher	G	IP	W	L	SV	ERA
1B	G. Sisler	580	.305	4	76	1507	83	**24**	85	**11.6**	.985	D. Davenport	**59**	291	12	11	2	2.85
2B	D. Pratt	596	.267	5	**103**	438	491	**33**	74	**6.1**	.966	C. Weilman	46	276	17	18	2	2.15
SS	D. Lavan	343	.236	0	19	217	386	32	52	**6.0**	.950	E. Plank	37	236	16	15	3	2.33
3B	J. Austin	411	.207	1	28	128	274	26	21	3.5	.939	B. Groom	41	217	13	9	4	2.57
RF	W. Miller	485	.266	1	50	215	12	14	0	1.8	.942	E. Koob	33	167	11	8	2	2.54
CF	A. Marsans	528	.254	1	60	351	25	9	7	2.6	.977	E. Hamilton	22	91	5	7	0	3.05
LF	B. Shotton	**618**	.282	1	36	357	25	**20**	6	2.6	.950							
C	H. Severeid	293	.273	0	34	313	99	10	6	4.7	.976							
SS	E. Johnson	236	.229	0	19	115	192	21	19	5.5	.936							
C	G. Hartley	222	.225	0	12	263	98	12	10	5.0	.968							

Cle. W-77 L-77 — Lee Fohl

POS	Player	AB	BA	HR	RBI	PO	A	E	DP	TC/G	FA	Pitcher	G	IP	W	L	SV	ERA
1B	C. Gandil	533	.259	0	72	**1557**	**105**	9	84	11.5	**.995**	J. Bagby	48	279	16	16	5	2.55
2B	I. Howard	246	.187	0	23	108	219	10	17	5.2	.970	S. Coveleski	45	232	15	13	3	3.41
SS	B. Wambsganss	475	.246	0	45	208	325	43	38	5.4	.925	G. Morton	27	150	12	8	0	2.89
3B	T. Turner	428	.262	0	38	87	173	10	10	3.5	.963	E. Klepfer	31	143	6	6	2	2.52
RF	B. Roth	409	.286	4	72	166	20	9	6	1.7	.954	F. Coumbe	29	120	7	5	0	2.02
CF	T. Speaker	546	**.386**	2	83	359	25	10	**10**	2.6	.975	A. Gould	30	107	5	7	1	2.53
LF	J. Graney	589	.241	5	54	309	22	14	5	2.2	.959	F. Beebe	20	101	5	3	2	2.41
C	S. O'Neill	378	.235	0	29	540	154	**21**	**36**	5.6	.971							
UT	R. Chapman	346	.231	0	27	207	310	32	35		.942							
OF	E. Smith	213	.277	3	40	77	7	3	3	1.5	.966							

Was. W-77 L-77 — Clark Griffith

POS	Player	AB	BA	HR	RBI	PO	A	E	DP	TC/G	FA	Pitcher	G	IP	W	L	SV	ERA
1B	J. Judge	336	.220	0	31	935	69	14	53	9.9	.986	W. Johnson	48	**371**	**25**	20	1	1.89
2B	R. Morgan	315	.267	1	29	133	222	16	34	4.5	.957	B. Gallia	49	284	17	12	2	2.76
SS	G. McBride	466	.227	1	36	282	438	32	53	5.4	.957	H. Harper	36	250	14	10	0	2.45
3B	E. Foster	606	.252	1	44	104	143	19	14	3.2	.929	D. Ayers	43	157	5	9	2	3.78
RF	D. Moeller	240	.246	1	23	94	11	4	3	1.7	.963	J. Boehling	27	140	9	11	0	3.09
CF	C. Milan	565	.273	1	45	**372**	27	16	8	**2.8**	.961	J. Shaw	26	106	3	8	1	2.62
LF	H. Shanks	471	.253	1	48	203	19	3	4	2.6	.987							
C	J. Henry	305	.249	0	46	538	124	13	17	5.8	.981							
1C	B. Williams	202	.267	0	20	388	30	6	21		.986							
OF	S. Rice	197	.299	1	17	83	5	4	1	2.0	.957							
OF	E. Smith	168	.214	2	27	75	5	1	1	1.8	.988							
3B	J. Leonard	168	.274	0	14	53	65	6	6	3.0	.952							
OF	H. Rondeau	162	.222	1	28	110	4	5	0	2.5	.958							

	POS	Player	AB	BA	HR	RBI	PO	A	E	DP	TC/G	FA	Pitcher	G	IP	W	L	SV	ERA
Phi.	1B	S. McInnis	512	.295	1	60	1404	96	12	87	10.8	.992	E. Myers	44	315	14	23	1	3.66
W-36 L-117	2B	N. Lajoie	426	.246	2	35	254	325	16	61	5.7	.973	J. Bush	40	287	15	24	0	2.57
Connie Mack	SS	W. Witt	563	.245	2	36	299	423	78	59	5.6	.903	J. Nabors	40	213	1	20	1	3.47
	3B	C. Pick	398	.241	0	20	143	230	42	25	3.8	.899	T. Sheehan	38	188	1	16	0	3.69
	RF	J. Walsh	390	.233	1	27	172	-13	12	4	1.7	.939	J. Johnson	12	84	2	8	0	3.74
	CF	A. Strunk	544	.316	3	49	291	20	7	5	2.2	.978							
	LF	R. Oldring	146	.247	0	14	64	6	8	2	2.0	.897							
	C	B. Meyer	138	.232	1	12	217	79	12	5	6.4	.961							
	OC	W. Schang	338	.266	7	38	266	77	19	6		.948							
	3O	L. McElwee	155	.265	0	10	52	61	13	7		.897							

BATTING AND BASE RUNNING LEADERS

Batting Average

T. Speaker, CLE	.386
T. Cobb, DET	.371
J. Jackson, CHI	.341
A. Strunk, PHI	.316
L. Gardner, BOS	.308

Slugging Average

T. Speaker, CLE	.502
J. Jackson, CHI	.495
T. Cobb, DET	.493
B. Veach, DET	.433
F. Baker, NY	.428

Home Runs

W. Pipp, NY	12
F. Baker, NY	10
W. Schang, PHI	7
H. Felsch, CHI	7

Total Bases

J. Jackson, CHI	293
T. Speaker, CLE	274
T. Cobb, DET	267
B. Veach, DET	245
H. Felsch, CHI	233
D. Pratt, STL	233

Runs Batted In

D. Pratt, STL	103
W. Pipp, NY	93
B. Veach, DET	91
T. Speaker, CLE	83
J. Jackson, CHI	78

Stolen Bases

T. Cobb, DET	68
A. Marsans, STL	46
B. Shotton, STL	41
E. Collins, CHI	40
T. Speaker, CLE	35

Hits

T. Speaker, CLE	211
J. Jackson, CHI	202
T. Cobb, DET	201

Base on Balls

B. Shotton, STL	111
J. Graney, CLE	102
E. Collins, CHI	86

Home Run Percentage

F. Baker, NY	2.8
W. Pipp, NY	2.2
W. Schang, PHI	2.1

Runs Scored

T. Cobb, DET	113
J. Graney, CLE	106
T. Speaker, CLE	102

Doubles

T. Speaker, CLE	41
J. Graney, CLE	41
J. Jackson, CHI	40

Triples

J. Jackson, CHI	21
E. Collins, CHI	17
W. Witt, PHI	15
B. Veach, DET	15

PITCHING LEADERS

Winning Percentage

E. Cicotte, CHI	.682
B. Ruth, BOS	.657
H. Coveleski, DET	.656
R. Faber, CHI	.654
B. Shawkey, NY	.632

Earned Run Average

B. Ruth, BOS	1.75
E. Cicotte, CHI	1.78
W. Johnson, WAS	1.89
H. Coveleski, DET	1.97
R. Faber, CHI	2.02

Wins

W. Johnson, WAS	25
B. Shawkey, NY	24
B. Ruth, BOS	23
H. Coveleski, DET	21
H. Dauss, DET	19
C. Mays, BOS	19

Saves

B. Shawkey, NY	8
A. Russell, NY	6
E. Cicotte, CHI	5
J. Bagby, CLE	5
D. Leonard, BOS	5

Strikeouts

W. Johnson, WAS	228
E. Myers, PHI	182
B. Ruth, BOS	170
J. Bush, PHI	157
H. Harper, WAS	149

Complete Games

W. Johnson, WAS	36
E. Myers, PHI	31
J. Bush, PHI	25
B. Ruth, BOS	23
H. Coveleski, DET	22

Fewest Hits per 9 Innings

B. Ruth, BOS	6.40
B. Shawkey, NY	6.64
E. Cicotte, CHI	6.64

Shutouts

B. Ruth, BOS	9
J. Bush, PHI	8
D. Leonard, BOS	6

Fewest Walks per 9 Innings

R. Russell, CHI	1.43
H. Coveleski, DET	1.75
E. Shore, BOS	1.95

Most Strikeouts per 9 Inn.

L. Williams, CHI	5.54
W. Johnson, WAS	5.53
H. Harper, WAS	5.37

Innings

W. Johnson, WAS	371
H. Coveleski, DET	324
B. Ruth, BOS	324

Games Pitched

D. Davenport, STL	59
R. Russell, CHI	56
B. Shawkey, NY	53
B. Gallia, WAS	49

	W	L	PCT	GB	R	OR	2B	3B	Batting HR	BA	SA	SB	E	Fielding DP	FA	CG	BB	Pitching SO	ShO	SV	ERA
BOS	91	63	.591		548	**480**	196	56	14	.248	.318	129	**183**	108	**.972**	76	463	584	**24**	16	2.48
CHI	89	65	.578	2	601	500	194	**100**	17	.251	.339	190	197	134	.968	73	**405**	644	20	15	**2.36**
DET	87	67	.565	4	**673**	573	202	96	17	**.264**	**.350**	190	211	110	.968	81	578	531	8	13	2.97
NY	80	74	.519	11	575	561	194	59	**35**	.246	.326	179	219	119	.967	84	476	616	12	17	2.77
STL	79	75	.513	12	591	545	181	50	13	.245	.307	**234**	248	120	.963	72	478	505	9	13	2.58
CLE	77	77	.500	14	630	621	**233**	66	16	.250	.331	160	232	130	.965	65	467	537	9	16	2.89
WAS	76	77	.497	14.5	534	543	170	60	12	.242	.306	151	185	231	119	.964	84	540	**706**	11	8	2.66
PHI	36	117	.235	54.5	447	776	169	65	19	.242	.313	151	314	126	.951	**94**	715	575	11	3	3.84
					4599	4599	1539	552	143	.248	.324	1425	1841	966	.965	629	4122	4698	104	101	2.81

	POS	Player	AB	BA	HR	RBI	PO	A	E	DP	TC/G	FA	Pitcher	G	IP	W	L	SV	ERA
N. Y. W-98 L-56 John McGraw	1B	W. Holke	527	.277	2	55	1635	70	19	104	11.3	.989	F. Schupp	36	272	21	7	0	1.95
	2B	B. Herzog	417	.235	2	31	251	327	32	60	5.4	.948	S. Sallee	34	216	18	7	4	2.17
	SS	A. Fletcher	557	.260	4	56	276	565	39	71	5.8	.956	P. Perritt	35	215	17	7	1	1.88
	3B	H. Zimmerman	585	.297	5	102	148	349	28	22	3.5	.947	R. Benton	35	215	15	9	3	2.72
	RF	D. Robertson	532	.259	12	54	266	12	17	1	2.1	.942	J. Tesreau	33	184	13	8	2	3.09
	CF	B. Kauff	559	.308	5	68	357	12	9	4	2.5	.976	F. Anderson	38	162	8	8	3	1.44
	LF	G. Burns	597	.302	5	45	325	16	9	4	2.3	.974							
	C	B. Rariden	266	.271	0	25	354	74	13	7	4.4	.971							
	C	L. McCarty	162	.247	2	19	235	43	6	0	5.3	.979							
Phi. W-87 L-65 Pat Moran	1B	F. Luderus	522	.261	5	72	1597	91	16	91	11.1	.991	G. Alexander	45	388	30	13	0	1.86
	2B	B. Niehoff	361	.255	2	42	203	326	31	37	5.8	.945	E. Rixey	39	281	16	21	1	2.27
	SS	D. Bancroft	478	.243	4	43	274	439	49	56	6.4	.936	J. Oeschger	42	262	16	14	0	2.75
	3B	M. Stock	564	.264	3	53	132	255	24	16	3.1	.942	E. Mayer	28	160	11	6	0	2.76
	RF	G. Cravath	503	.280	12	83	209	17	13	3	1.7	.946	J. Lavender	28	129	5	8	1	3.55
	CF	D. Paskert	546	.251	4	43	286	19	5	4	2.2	.984	C. Bender	20	113	8	2	2	1.67
	LF	F. Whitted	553	.280	3	70	275	19	7	0	2.1	.977							
	C	B. Killefer	409	.274	0	31	617	138	12	14	6.4	.984							
	2B	J. Evers	183	.224	1	12	83	145	4	15	4.7	.983							
St. L. W-82 L-70 Miller Huggins	1B	G. Paulette	332	.265	0	34	1130	45	8	82	12.7	.993	B. Doak	44	281	16	20	2	3.10
	2B	D. Miller	544	.248	2	45	219	308	22	56	6.0	.960	L. Meadows	43	265	15	9	2	3.09
	SS	R. Hornsby	523	.327	8	66	268	527	52	82	5.9	.939	R. Ames	43	209	15	10	3	2.71
	3B	D. Baird	364	.253	0	24	110	259	23	24	3.8*	.941	M. Watson	41	161	10	13	0	3.51
	RF	T. Long	530	.232	3	41	173	9	16	2	1.4	.919	G. Packard	34	153	9	6	2	2.47
	CF	J. Smith	462	.297	3	34	233	12	10	6	2.0	.961	O. Horstmann	35	138	9	4	1	3.45
	LF	W. Cruise	529	.295	5	59	285	15	11	6	2.0	.965	M. Goodwin	14	85	6	4	0	2.21
	C	F. Snyder	313	.236	1	33	341	134	12	10	5.2	.975							
	2B	B. Betzel	328	.216	1	17	159	217	15	40	5.2	.962							
	C	M. Gonzalez	290	.262	1	28	241	97	8	8	5.1	.977							
	3B	F. Smith	165	.182	1	17	62	110	9	5	3.5	.950							
Cin. W-78 L-76 Christy Mathewson	1B	H. Chase	602	.277	4	86	1499	80	28	100	10.6	.983	P. Schneider	46	342	20	19	0	1.98
	2B	D. Shean	442	.210	2	35	332	412	30	69	5.9	.961	F. Toney	43	340	24	16	1	2.20
	SS	L. Kopf	573	.255	2	26	276	470	68	59	5.6	.916	M. Regan	32	216	11	10	0	2.71
	3B	H. Groh	599	.304	1	53	178	331	18	28	3.4	.966	C. Mitchell	32	159	9	15	1	3.22
	RF	T. Griffith	363	.270	1	45	165	19	5	3	1.9	.974	H. Eller	37	152	10	5	1	2.36
	CF	E. Roush	522	.341	4	67	335	15	14	0	2.7	.962	J. Ring	24	88	3	7	2	4.40
	LF	G. Neale	385	.294	3	33	216	13	5	1	2.0	.979							
	C	I. Wingo	399	.266	2	39	459	151	21	12	5.3	.967							
	OF	J. Thorpe	251	.247	4	36	143	7	6	2	2.3	.962							
	OF	S. Magee	137	.321	0	23	83	7	1	1	2.2	.989							
Chi. W-74 L-80 Fred Mitchell	1B	F. Merkle	549	.266	3	57	1415	66	26	84	10.8	.983	H. Vaughn	41	296	23	13	0	2.01
	2B	L. Doyle	476	.254	6	61	300	348	33	54	5.3	.952	P. Douglas	51	293	14	20	1	2.55
	SS	C. Wortman	190	.174	0	9	85	162	22	26	4.1	.918	C. Hendrix	40	215	10	12	1	2.60
	3B	C. Deal	449	.254	0	47	151	254	18	31	3.3	.957	A. Demaree	24	141	5	9	1	2.55
	RF	M. Flack	447	.248	0	21	199	14	12	3	1.9	.947	P. Carter	23	113	5	8	2	3.26
	CF	C. Williams	468	.241	5	42	340	23	15	4	2.8	.960	V. Aldridge	30	107	6	6	2	3.12
	LF	L. Mann	444	.273	1	44	203	20	11	2	2.0	.953	Prendergast	35	99	3	6	1	3.35
	C	A. Wilson	211	.213	2	25	361	92	15	5	6.2	.968	T. Seaton	16	75	5	4	1	2.53
	UT	R. Zeider	354	.243	0	27	151	226	28	35		.931							
	OF	H. Wolter	353	.249	0	28	131	14	9	5	1.6	.942							
	C	R. Elliott	223	.251	0	28	307	93	13	9	5.7	.969							
	SS	P. Kilduff	202	.277	0	15	91	128	19	19	4.7	.920							
Bos. W-72 L-81 George Stallings	1B	E. Konetchy	474	.272	2	54	1351	70	8	65	11.1	.994	J. Barnes	50	295	13	21	1	2.68
	2B	J. Rawlings	371	.256	2	31	177	290	11	40	5.0	.977	D. Rudolph	32	243	13	13	0	3.41
	SS	R. Maranville	561	.260	3	43	341	474	46	67	6.1	.947	L. Tyler	32	239	14	12	1	2.52
	3B	R. Smith	505	.295	2	62	141	264	33	27	3.0	.925	A. Nehf	38	233	17	8	0	2.16
	RF	W. Rehg	341	.270	1	31	122	9	6	2	1.6	.956	P. Ragan	30	148	6	9	1	2.93
	CF	R. Powell	357	.272	4	30	231	14	6	2	2.9	.976	F. Allen	29	112	3	11	0	3.94
	LF	J. Kelly	445	.222	3	36	284	16	17	8	2.7	.946							
	C	W. Tragesser	297	.222	0	25	433	105	16	11	5.7	.971							
	OF	S. Magee	246	.256	1	29	137	7	7	3	2.3	.954							
	OF	J. Wilhoit	186	.274	1	10	70	7	6	1	1.6	.928							
	UT	Fitzpatrick	178	.253	0	17	71	67	15	5		.902							
	C	H. Gowdy	154	.214	0	14	204	75	9	3	5.9	.969							
Bkn. W-70 L-81 Wilbert Robinson	1B	J. Daubert	468	.261	2	30	1188	82	12	59	10.3	.991	J. Pfeffer	30	266	11	15	0	2.23
	2B	G. Cutshaw	487	.259	4	49	319	377	27	43	5.4	.963	L. Cadore	37	264	13	13	3	2.45
	SS	I. Olson	580	.269	2	38	283	431	45	53	5.7	.941	R. Marquard	37	233	19	12	0	2.55
	3B	M. Mowrey	271	.214	0	25	73	164	12	13	3.1	.952	S. Smith	38	211	12	12	3	3.32
	RF	C. Stengel	549	.257	6	73	256	30	9	9	2.0	.969	L. Cheney	35	210	8	12	2	2.35
	CF	J. Hickman	370	.259	6	36	222	22	15	6	2.6	.942	J. Coombs	31	141	7	11	0	3.96
	LF	Z. Wheat	362	.312	1	41	216	12	5	5	2.1	.979							
	C	O. Miller	274	.230	1	17	412	95	11	8	5.7	.979							
	UT	H. Myers	471	.268	1	41	410	102	19	15		.964							
	OF	J. Johnston	330	.270	0	25	150	8	7	1	1.8	.958							
	3B	F. O'Rourke	198	.237	0	15	72	134	10	6	3.7	.954							

	POS	Player	AB	BA	HR	RBI	PO	A	E	DP	TC/G	FA	Pitcher	G	IP	W	L	SV	ERA
Pit.	1B	H. Wagner	230	.265	0	24	433	22	7	27	9.8	.985	W. Cooper	40	298	17	11	1	2.36
W-51 L-103	2B	J. Pitler	382	.233	0	23	283	277	20	46	5.5	.966	E. Jacobs	38	227	6	19	2	2.81
Nixey Callahan	SS	C. Ward	423	.236	0	43	206	312	50	49	5.1	.912	F. Miller	38	224	10	19	1	3.13
W-20 L-40	3B	T. Boeckel	219	.265	0	23	71	116	13	9	3.2	.935	B. Grimes	37	194	3	16	0	3.53
Honus Wagner	RF	L. King	381	.249	1	35	198	16	7	6	2.2	.968	B. Steele	27	180	5	11	1	2.76
W-1 L-4	CF	M. Carey	588	.296	1	51	440	28	10	8	3.1	.979	H. Carlson	34	161	7	11	1	2.90
Hugo Bezdek	LF	C. Bigbee	469	.239	0	21	235	9	10	2	2.4	.961	A. Mamaux	16	86	2	11	0	5.25
W-30 L-59	C	B. Fischer	245	.286	3	25	272	77	14	8	5.3	.961							
	OF	B. Hinchman	244	.189	2	29	99	5	6	0	2.3	.945							
	C	W. Schmidt	183	.246	0	17	229	84	7	9	5.2	.978							

BATTING AND BASE RUNNING LEADERS

Batting Average

E. Roush, CIN	.341
R. Hornsby, STL	.327
Z. Wheat, BKN	.312
B. Kauff, NY	.308
H. Groh, CIN	.304

Slugging Average

R. Hornsby, STL	.484
G. Cravath, PHI	.473
E. Roush, CIN	.454
Z. Wheat, BKN	.423
G. Burns, NY	.412

Home Runs

G. Cravath, PHI	12
D. Robertson, NY	12
R. Hornsby, STL	8
J. Hickman, BKN	6
L. Doyle, CHI	6
C. Stengel, BKN	6

Total Bases

R. Hornsby, STL	253
G. Burns, NY	246
H. Groh, CIN	246
G. Cravath, PHI	238
E. Roush, CIN	237
H. Chase, CIN	237

Runs Batted In

H. Zimmerman, NY	102
H. Chase, CIN	86
G. Cravath, PHI	83
C. Stengel, BKN	73
F. Luderus, PHI	72

Stolen Bases

M. Carey, PIT	46
G. Burns, NY	40
B. Kauff, NY	30
R. Maranville, BOS	27
D. Baird, PIT, STL	26

Hits

H. Groh, CIN	182
G. Burns, NY	180
E. Roush, CIN	178

Base on Balls

G. Burns, NY	75
H. Groh, CIN	71
G. Cravath, PHI	70

Home Run Percentage

G. Cravath, PHI	2.4
D. Robertson, NY	2.3
J. Hickman, BKN	1.6

Runs Scored

G. Burns, NY	103
H. Groh, CIN	91
B. Kauff, NY	89

Doubles

H. Groh, CIN	39
R. Smith, BOS	31
F. Merkle, BKN, CHI	31

Triples

R. Hornsby, STL	17
G. Cravath, PHI	16
H. Chase, CIN	15

PITCHING LEADERS

Winning Percentage

F. Schupp, NY	.750
S. Sallee, NY	.720
P. Perritt, NY	.708
G. Alexander, PHI	.698
A. Nehf, BOS	.680

Earned Run Average

G. Alexander, PHI	1.86
P. Perritt, NY	1.88
F. Schupp, NY	1.95
P. Schneider, CIN	1.98
H. Vaughn, CHI	2.01

Wins

G. Alexander, PHI	30
F. Toney, CIN	24
H. Vaughn, CHI	23
F. Schupp, NY	21
P. Schneider, CIN	20

Saves

S. Sallee, NY	4
R. Ames, STL	3
F. Anderson, NY	3
S. Smith, BKN	3
R. Benton, NY	3
L. Cadore, BKN	3

Strikeouts

G. Alexander, PHI	201
H. Vaughn, CHI	195
P. Douglas, CHI	151
F. Schupp, NY	147
P. Schneider, CIN	142

Complete Games

G. Alexander, PHI	35
F. Toney, CIN	31
J. Barnes, BOS	27
H. Vaughn, CHI	27
F. Schupp, NY	25
P. Schneider, CIN	25

Fewest Hits per 9 Innings

F. Schupp, NY	6.68
A. Nehf, BOS	7.60
J. Pfeffer, BKN	7.61

Shutouts

G. Alexander, PHI	8
W. Cooper, PIT	7
F. Toney, CIN	7
F. Schupp, NY	6

Fewest Walks per 9 Innings

G. Alexander, PHI	1.35
S. Sallee, NY	1.42
A. Nehf, BOS	1.50

Most Strikeouts per 9 Inn.

H. Vaughn, CHI	5.94
F. Schupp, NY	4.86
G. Alexander, PHI	4.67

Innings

G. Alexander, PHI	388
P. Schneider, CIN	342
F. Toney, CIN	340

Games Pitched

P. Douglas, CHI	51
J. Barnes, BOS	50
P. Schneider, CIN	46

	W	L	PCT	GB	R	OR	Batting 2B	3B	HR	BA	SA	SB	Fielding E	DP	FA	Pitching CG	BB	SO	ShO	SV	ERA
NY	98	56	.636		635	457	170	71	39	.261	.343	162	208	122	.968	92	327	551	18	14	2.27
PHI	87	65	.572	10	578	501	225	60	38	.248	.339	109	212	112	.967	103	327	617	22	4	2.46
STL	82	70	.539	15	531	568	159	93	26	.250	.333	159	221	153	.967	66	421	502	16	10	3.03
CIN	78	76	.506	20	601	611	196	100	26	.264	.354	153	247	120	.962	95	404	492	12	6	2.66
CHI	74	80	.481	24	552	553	194	67	17	.239	.313	127	267	121	.959	79	374	654	15	9	2.62
BOS	72	81	.471	25.5	536	558	169	75	22	.246	.320	155	224	122	.966	105	371	593	21	3	2.77
BKN	70	81	.464	26.5	511	566	159	78	25	.247	.322	130	245	102	.962	99	405	582	7	9	2.78
PIT	51	103	.331	47	464	594	160	61	9	.238	.298	150	251	119	.961	84	432	509	17	6	3.01
					4408	4408	1432	605	202	.249	.328	1145	1875	971	.964	723	3061	4500	128	61	2.70

POS	Player	AB	BA	HR	RBI	PO	A	E	DP	TC/G	FA	Pitcher	G	IP	W	L	SV	ERA
Chi. W-100 L-54 Pants Rowland																	
1B	C. Gandil	553	.273	0	57	1405	77	8	84	10.0	.995	E. Cicotte	49	347	28	12	4	1.53
2B	E. Collins	564	.289	0	67	353	388	24	68	4.9	.969	R. Faber	41	248	16	13	3	1.92
SS	S. Risberg	474	.203	1	45	291	352	61	57	4.8	.913	L. Williams	45	230	17	8	1	2.97
3B	B. Weaver	447	.284	3	32	154	218	20	18	3.7	.949	R. Russell	35	189	15	5	3	1.95
RF	N. Leibold	428	.236	0	29	204	18	9	3	1.9	.961	D. Danforth	50	173	11	6	9	2.65
CF	H. Felsch	575	.308	6	102	440	24	7	5	3.1	.985	J. Scott	24	125	6	7	1	1.87
LF	J. Jackson	538	.301	5	75	341	18	6	4	2.5	.984	J. Benz	19	95	7	3	0	2.47
C	R. Schalk	424	.226	3	51	624	148	15	13	5.7	.981							
OF	S. Collins	252	.234	1	14	125	6	1	4	1.8	.992							
3B	F. McMullin	194	.237	0	12	61	90	11	4	3.1	.932							
Bos. W-90 L-62 Jack Barry																	
1B	D. Hoblitzell	420	.257	1	47	1274	52	14	58	11.4	.990	B. Ruth	41	326	24	13	2	2.01
2B	J. Barry	388	.214	2	30	196	339	14	40	4.7	.974	D. Leonard	37	294	16	17	1	2.17
SS	E. Scott	528	.241	0	50	315	483	39	64	5.3	.953	C. Mays	35	289	22	9	0	1.74
3B	L. Gardner	501	.265	1	65	148	315	31	18	3.4	.937	E. Shore	29	227	13	10	1	2.22
RF	H. Hooper	559	.256	3	45	245	20	8	3	1.8	.971	R. Foster	17	125	8	7	0	2.53
CF	T. Walker	337	.246	2	37	225	20	7	7	2.6	.972	H. Pennock	24	101	5	5	1	3.31
LF	D. Lewis	553	.302	1	65	324	20	10	6	2.4	.972							
C	S. Agnew	260	.208	0	16	297	88	14	5	4.7	.965							
C	P. Thomas	202	.238	0	24	296	69	5	4	4.8	.986							
OF	J. Walsh	185	.265	0	12	103	8	2	0	2.4	.982							
1B	D. Gainor	172	.308	2	19	490	27	6	29	10.5	.989							
OF	C. Shorten	168	.179	0	16	82	2	2	0	2.0	.977							
Cle. W-88 L-66 Lee Fohl																	
1B	J. Harris	369	.304	0	65	1019	86	17	58	11.8	.985	J. Bagby	49	321	23	13	7	1.96
2B	B. Wambsganss	499	.255	0	43	316	442	38	70	5.8	.952	S. Coveleski	45	298	19	14	4	1.81
SS	R. Chapman	563	.302	3	36	360	528	59	71	6.1	.938	E. Klepfer	41	213	14	4	1	2.37
3B	J. Evans	385	.190	2	33	138	279	27	20	3.5	.939	G. Morton	35	161	10	10	2	2.74
RF	B. Roth	495	.285	1	72	228	18	11	6	1.9	.957	F. Coumbe	34	134	8	6	5	2.14
CF	T. Speaker	523	.352	2	60	365	23	8	5	2.8	.980	O. Lambeth	26	97	7	6	2	3.14
LF	J. Graney	535	.228	3	35	288	14	13	6	2.2	.959							
C	S. O'Neill	370	.184	0	29	446	145	12	19	4.7	.980							
1B	L. Guisto	200	.185	0	29	611	33	7	45	11.0	.989							
32	T. Turner	180	.206	0	15	86	119	4	7		.981							
OF	E. Smith	161	.261	3	22	64	5	1	2	1.8	.986							
Det. W-78 L-75 Hughie Jennings																	
1B	G. Burns	407	.226	1	40	1127	57	12	44	11.5	.990	H. Dauss	37	271	17	14	2	2.43
2B	R. Young	503	.231	1	35	300	449	33	46	5.5	.958	B. Boland	43	238	16	11	6	2.68
SS	D. Bush	581	.281	0	24	281	423	51	41	5.1	.932	H. Ehmke	35	206	10	15	2	2.97
3B	O. Vitt	512	.254	0	47	164	260	27	18	3.2	.940	B. James	34	198	13	10	1	2.09
RF	H. Heilmann	556	.281	5	86	200	17	9	4	1.8	.960	W. Mitchell	30	185	12	8	0	2.19
CF	T. Cobb	588	.383	7	102	373	27	11	9	2.7	.973	G. Cunningham	44	139	2	7	4	2.91
LF	B. Veach	571	.319	8	103	356	17	17	5	2.5	.956	H. Coveleski	16	69	4	6	0	2.61
C	O. Stanage	297	.205	0	30	385	88	11	13	5.1	.977							
C	T. Spencer	192	.240	0	22	250	57	7	10	5.1	.978							
Was. W-74 L-79 Clark Griffith																	
1B	J. Judge	393	.285	2	30	906	60	12	59	9.8	.988	W. Johnson	47	328	23	16	3	2.30
2B	R. Morgan	338	.266	1	30	206	243	18	45	4.9	.961	J. Shaw	47	266	15	14	1	3.21
SS	H. Shanks	430	.202	0	28	205	255	35	44	5.5	.929	B. Gallia	42	208	9	13	1	2.99
3B	E. Foster	554	.235	0	43	95	178	19	15	3.4	.935	D. Ayers	40	208	11	10	1	2.17
RF	S. Rice	586	.302	0	69	265	26	12	5	2.0	.962	G. Dumont	37	205	5	14	2	2.55
CF	C. Milan	579	.294	0	48	339	18	14	3	2.4	.962	H. Harper	31	179	11	12	0	3.01
LF	M. Menosky	322	.258	1	34	208	15	4	3	2.4	.982							
C	E. Ainsmith	350	.191	0	42	580	154	22	15	6.4	.971							
3B	J. Leonard	297	.192	0	23	78	119	16	15	3.2	.925							
1B	P. Gharrity	176	.284	0	18	371	29	8	18	9.9	.980							
C	J. Henry	163	.190	0	18	274	54	4	6	5.6	.988							
N. Y. W-71 L-82 Wild Bill Donovan																	
1B	W. Pipp	587	.244	9	70	1609	109	17	97	11.2	.990	B. Shawkey	32	236	13	15	0	2.44
2B	F. Maisel	404	.198	0	20	219	280	17	37	5.2	.967	R. Caldwell	32	236	13	16	0	2.86
SS	R. Peckinpaugh	543	.260	0	41	292	467	54	84	5.5	.934	G. Mogridge	29	196	9	11	0	2.98
3B	F. Baker	553	.282	6	71	202	317	28	21	3.7	.949	N. Cullop	30	146	5	9	1	3.32
RF	E. Miller	379	.251	0	35	204	16	9	2	2.0	.961	U. Shocker	26	145	8	5	1	2.61
CF	T. Hendryx	393	.249	5	44	215	17	11	1	2.3	.955	R. Fisher	23	144	8	9	0	2.19
LF	H. High	365	.236	1	19	188	16	3	3	2.1	.986	S. Love	33	130	6	5	1	2.35
C	L. Nunamaker	310	.261	0	33	372	113	12	15	5.5	.976	A. Russell	25	104	7	8	2	2.24
OF	L. Magee	173	.220	0	8	84	6	6	1	1.9	.938							
C	R. Walters	171	.263	0	14	263	73	11	6	6.1	.968							
OF	F. Gilhooley	165	.242	0	8	78	5	6	1	1.9	.933							
St. L. W-57 L-97 Fielder Jones																	
1B	G. Sisler	539	.353	2	52	1384	101	22	97	11.3	.985	D. Davenport	47	281	17	17	2	3.08
2B	D. Pratt	450	.247	1	53	324	353	29	64	5.9	.959	A. Sothoron	48	277	14	19	4	2.83
SS	D. Lavan	355	.239	0	30	229	338	47	67	5.6	.923	B. Groom	38	233	8	19	3	2.94
3B	J. Austin	455	.240	0	19	159	248	23	22	3.6	.947	E. Koob	39	134	6	14	1	3.91
RF	B. Jacobson	529	.248	4	55	292	18	8	6	2.4	.975	E. Plank	20	131	5	6	1	1.79
CF	A. Marsans	257	.230	0	20	155	3	6	1	2.4	.963	T. Rogers	24	109	3	6	0	3.89
LF	B. Shotton	398	.224	1	20	182	10	16	6	1.9	.923	E. Hamilton	27	83	0	9	1	3.14
C	H. Severeid	501	.265	1	57	529	156	24	10	5.1	.966							
OF	T. Sloan	313	.230	2	25	120	10	5	4	1.8	.963							
OF	E. Smith	199	.281	0	10	114	12	3	5	2.5	.977							
UT	E. Johnson	199	.246	2	20	122	197	25	19		.927							

	POS	Player	AB	BA	HR	RBI	PO	A	E	DP	TC/G	FA	Pitcher	G	IP	W	L	SV	ERA
Phi. W-55 L-98 Connie Mack	1B	S. McInnis	567	.303	0	44	**1658**	95	12	81	11.8	.993	J. Bush	37	233	11	17	2	2.47
	2B	R. Grover	482	.224	0	34	279	425	29	51	5.3	.960	R. Schauer	33	215	7	16	1	3.14
	SS	W. Witt	452	.252	0	28	190	354	38	41	5.2	.935	E. Myers	38	202	9	16	3	4.42
	3B	R. Bates	485	.237	2	66	168	267	**31**	17	**3.8**	.933	J. Johnson	34	191	9	12	0	2.78
	RF	C. Jamieson	347	.265	0	27	121	12	9	4	1.7	.937	W. Noyes	27	171	10	10	1	2.95
	CF	A. Strunk	540	.281	1	45	346	13	5	5	2.5	**.986**	S. Seibold	33	160	4	16	1	3.94
	LF	P. Bodie	557	.291	7	74	258	**32**	11	7	2.1	.963							
	C	W. Schang	316	.285	3	36	260	102	17	11	4.8	.955							
	C	B. Meyer	162	.235	0	9	235	66	12	2	5.7	.962							

BATTING AND BASE RUNNING LEADERS

Batting Average
T. Cobb, DET .383
G. Sisler, STL .353
T. Speaker, CLE .352
B. Veach, DET .319
H. Felsch, CHI .308

Slugging Average
T. Cobb, DET .571
T. Speaker, CLE .486
B. Veach, DET .457
G. Sisler, STL .453
J. Jackson, CHI .429

Home Runs
W. Pipp, NY 9
B. Veach, DET 8
P. Bodie, PHI 7
T. Cobb, DET 7
F. Baker, NY 6
H. Felsch, CHI 6

Total Bases
T. Cobb, DET 336
B. Veach, DET 261
T. Speaker, CLE 254
G. Sisler, STL 244
P. Bodie, PHI 233

Runs Batted In
B. Veach, DET 103
H. Felsch, CHI 102
T. Cobb, DET 102
H. Heilmann, DET 86
J. Jackson, CHI 75

Stolen Bases
T. Cobb, DET 55
E. Collins, CHI 53
R. Chapman, CLE 52
B. Roth, CLE 51
G. Sisler, STL 37

Hits
T. Cobb, DET 225
G. Sisler, STL 190
T. Speaker, CLE 184

Base on Balls
J. Graney, CLE 94
E. Collins, CHI 89
H. Hooper, BOS 80
D. Bush, DET 80

Home Run Percentage
W. Pipp, NY 1.5
B. Veach, DET 1.4
T. Hendryx, NY 1.3

Runs Scored
D. Bush, DET 112
T. Cobb, DET 107
R. Chapman, CLE 98

Doubles
T. Cobb, DET 44
T. Speaker, CLE 42
B. Veach, DET 31

Triples
T. Cobb, DET 23
J. Jackson, CHI 17
J. Judge, WAS 15

PITCHING LEADERS

Winning Percentage
R. Russell, CHI .750
D. Danforth, CHI .714
C. Mays, BOS .710
E. Cicotte, CHI .700
L. Williams, CHI .680

Earned Run Average
E. Cicotte, CHI 1.53
C. Mays, BOS 1.74
S. Coveleski, CLE 1.81
R. Faber, CHI 1.92
R. Russell, CHI 1.95

Wins
E. Cicotte, CHI 28
B. Ruth, BOS 24
J. Bagby, CLE 23
W. Johnson, WAS 23
C. Mays, BOS 22

Saves
D. Danforth, CHI 9
J. Bagby, CLE 7
B. Boland, DET 6

Strikeouts
W. Johnson, WAS 188
E. Cicotte, CHI 150
D. Leonard, BOS 144
S. Coveleski, CLE 133
B. Ruth, BOS 128

Complete Games
B. Ruth, BOS 35
W. Johnson, WAS 30
E. Cicotte, CHI 29
C. Mays, BOS 27
D. Leonard, BOS 26
J. Bagby, CLE 26

Fewest Hits per 9 Innings
S. Coveleski, CLE 6.09
E. Cicotte, CHI 6.39
B. Ruth, BOS 6.73

Shutouts
S. Coveleski, CLE 9
J. Bagby, CLE 8
W. Johnson, WAS 8

Fewest Walks per 9 Innings
R. Russell, CHI 1.52
G. Mogridge, NY 1.79
E. Cicotte, CHI 1.82

Most Strikeouts per 9 Inn.
W. Johnson, WAS 5.16
H. Harper, WAS 4.97
J. Bush, PHI 4.67

Innings
E. Cicotte, CHI 347
W. Johnson, WAS 328
B. Ruth, BOS 326

Games Pitched
D. Danforth, CHI 50
E. Cicotte, CHI 49
J. Bagby, CLE 49
A. Sothoron, STL 48

	W	L	PCT	GB	R	OR	Batting 2B	3B	HR	BA	SA	SB	Fielding E	DP	FA	Pitching CG	BB	SO	ShO	SV	ERA
CHI	100	54	.649		657	464	152	**80**	19	.253	.326	219	204	117	.967	78	**413**	517	**22**	21	**2.16**
BOS	90	62	.592	9	556	**453**	198	64	14	.246	.319	105	**183**	116	**.972**	115	**413**	509	15	7	2.20
CLE	88	66	.571	12	584	543	**218**	63	14	.245	.322	210	242	136	.964	73	438	451	20	**22**	2.52
DET	78	75	.510	21.5	639	577	204	76	26	**.259**	.344	163	234	95	.964	78	504	516	20	15	2.56
WAS	74	79	.484	25.5	543	566	173	70	4	.241	.304	166	251	127	.961	84	536	**637**	21	10	2.77
NY	71	82	.464	28.5	524	560	172	52	**27**	.239	.308	136	225	129	.957	65	537	429	12	12	3.20
STL	57	97	.370	43	511	687	183	63	15	.245	.315	157	281	**139**	.957	87	427	571	10	6	2.66
PHI	55	98	.359	44.5	527	691	177	62	17	.254	.322	112	251	106	.961	80	562	516	8	8	3.27
					4541	4541	1477	530	136	.248	.320	1268	1871	965	.964	660	3830	4146	128	101	2.66

	POS	Player	AB	BA	HR	RBI	PO	A	E	DP	TC/G	FA	Pitcher	G	IP	W	L	SV	ERA
Chi. W-84 L-45 Fred Mitchell	1B	F. Merkle	482	.297	3	65	**1388**	82	15	69	11.5	.990	H. Vaughn	35	**290**	**22**	10	0	**1.74**
	2B	R. Zeider	251	.223	0	26	142	207	16	22	4.6	.956	L. Tyler	33	269	19	9	1	2.00
	SS	C. Hollocher	**509**	.316	2	38	278	418	53	39	5.7	.929	C. Hendrix	32	233	19	7	0	2.78
	3B	C. Deal	414	.239	2	34	144	247	24	21	3.5	.942	P. Douglas	25	157	9	9	2	2.13
	RF	M. Flack	478	.257	4	41	199	20	5	5	1.9	.978							
	CF	D. Paskert	461	.286	3	59	283	12	6	1	2.5	.980							
	LF	L. Mann	489	.288	2	55	229	15	10	3	2.0	.961							
	C	B. Killefer	331	.233	0	22	**487**	110	11	12	5.8	**.982**							
N. Y. W-71 L-53 John McGraw	1B	W. Holke	326	.252	1	27	938	68	10	50	11.5	.990	P. Perritt	35	233	18	13	0	2.74
	2B	L. Doyle	257	.261	3	36	121	221	11	24	4.8	.969	R. Causey	29	158	11	6	2	2.79
	SS	A. Fletcher	468	.263	0	47	268	**484**	32	54	6.3	**.959**	A. Demaree	26	142	8	6	1	2.47
	3B	H. Zimmerman	463	.272	1	56	128	209	16	8	3.5	.955	S. Sallee	18	132	8	8	2	2.25
	RF	R. Youngs	474	.302	1	25	197	22	12	3	1.9	.948							
	CF	B. Kauff	270	.315	2	39	147	11	8	4	2.5	.952							
	LF	G. Burns	465	.290	4	51	292	10	11	1	2.6	.965							
	C	L. McCarty	257	.268	0	24	288	67	9	3	4.9	.975							
	C	B. Rariden	183	.224	0	17	195	45	4	3	3.9	.984							
Cin. W-68 L-60 Christy Mathewson W-61 L-57 Heinie Groh W-7 L-3	1B	H. Chase	259	.301	2	38	607	38	13	59	9.8	.980	P. Schneider	33	218	10	15	0	3.51
	2B	L. Magee	459	.290	0	28	275	361	**29**	**73**	5.8	.956	H. Eller	37	218	16	12	1	2.36
	SS	L. Blackburne	435	.228	1	45	319	413	48	69	6.2	.938	J. Ring	21	142	9	5	0	2.85
	3B	H. Groh	493	.320	1	37	**180**	253	14	**37**	3.5	.969	F. Toney	21	137	6	10	2*	2.90
	RF	T. Griffith	427	.265	2	48	201	18	7	3	1.9	.969	R. Bressler	17	128	8	5	0	2.46
	CF	E. Roush	435	.333	5	62	320	13	14	2	3.1	.960	M. Regan	22	80	5	5	2	3.26
	LF	G. Neale	371	.270	1	32	249	11	5	2	2.6	**.981**							
	C	I. Wingo	323	.254	0	31	315	111	**12**	13	4.7	.973							
	1O	S. Magee	400	.298	2	**76**	685	41	14	40		.981							
Pit. W-65 L-60 Hugo Bezdek	1B	F. Mollwitz	432	.269	0	45	1252	73	13	67	11.2	.990	W. Cooper	38	273	19	14	**3**	2.11
	2B	G. Cutshaw	463	.285	5	68	**323**	**366**	26	60	5.7	**.964**	F. Miller	23	170	11	8	0	2.38
	SS	B. Caton	303	.234	0	17	136	276	32	35	5.6	.928	R. Sanders	28	156	7	9	1	2.60
	3B	B. McKechnie	435	.255	2	43	162	261	15	26	3.5	.966	E. Mayer	15	123	9	3	0	2.26
	RF	B. Southworth	246	.341	2	43	137	12	3	4	2.4	.980	R. Comstock	15	81	5	6	1	3.00
	CF	M. Carey	468	.274	3	48	**359**	25	**17**	**9**	**3.2**	.958							
	LF	C. Bigbee	310	.255	1	19	168	13	8	1	2.1	.958							
	C	W. Schmidt	323	.238	0	27	373	**153**	10	**19**	5.2	.981							
Bkn. W-57 L-69 Wilbert Robinson	1B	J. Daubert	396	.308	2	47	1069	63	10	43	10.9	**.991**	B. Grimes	**41**	270	19	9	1	2.14
	2B	M. Doolan	308	.179	0	18	230	283	17	37	5.8	.968	R. Marquard	34	239	9	**18**	0	2.64
	SS	I. Olson	506	.239	1	17	265	388	58	42	5.6	.918	L. Cheney	32	201	11	13	1	3.00
	3B	O. O'Mara	450	.213	1	24	126	262	20	15	3.4	.951	J. Coombs	27	189	8	14	0	3.81
	RF	J. Johnston	484	.281	0	27	178	18	9	4	2.1	.956							
	CF	H. Myers	407	.256	4	40	294	17	8	7	3.0	.975							
	LF	Z. Wheat	409	**.335**	0	51	219	11	5	2	2.2	.979							
	C	O. Miller	228	.193	0	8	276	77	10	6	5.9	.972							
	OF	J. Hickman	167	.234	1	16	76	9	8	1	2.0	.914							
	C	M. Wheat	157	.217	1	3	151	50	7	1	5.5	.966							
Phi. W-55 L-68 Pat Moran	1B	F. Luderus	468	.288	5	67	1307	**98**	17	**74**	11.4	.988	Prendergast	33	252	13	14	1	2.89
	2B	McGaffigan	192	.203	1	8	100	155	14	19	5.1	.948	B. Hogg	29	228	13	13	1	2.53
	SS	D. Bancroft	499	.265	0	26	**371**	457	**64**	57	7.1	.928	J. Oeschger	30	184	6	**18**	**3**	3.03
	3B	M. Stock	481	.274	1	42	132	273	23	16	3.5	.946	E. Jacobs	18	123	9	5	1	2.41
	RF	G. Cravath	426	.232	**8**	54	184	19	15	3	1.8	.931	M. Watson	23	113	5	7	0	3.43
	CF	C. Williams	351	.276	6	39	229	10	8	4	2.7	.968	E. Mayer	13	104	7	4	0	3.12
	LF	I. Meusel	473	.279	4	62	296	14	9	2	2.7	.972							
	C	B. Adams	227	.176	0	12	261	69	8	8	4.4	.976							
	C	E. Burns	184	.207	0	9	184	77	5	3	3.9	.981							
	2B	H. Pearce	164	.244	0	18	97	157	15	18	5.8	.944							
Bos. W-53 L-71 George Stallings	1B	E. Konetchy	437	.236	2	56	1226	61	11	69	11.6	**.992**	A. Nehf	32	284	15	15	0	2.69
	2B	B. Herzog	473	.228	0	26	240	322	23	43	**5.9**	.961	P. Ragan	30	206	8	17	0	3.23
	SS	J. Rawlings	410	.207	0	21	137	256	16	27	5.8	.956	D. Rudolph	21	154	9	10	0	2.57
	3B	R. Smith	429	.298	2	65	123	**291**	**35**	16	**3.8**	.922	B. Hearn	17	126	5	6	0	2.49
	RF	A. Wickland	332	.262	4	32	183	11	5	2	2.1	.975	D. Fillingim	14	113	7	6	0	2.23
	CF	R. Powell	188	.213	0	20	121	8	7	2	2.6	.949							
	LF	R. Massey	203	.291	0	18	75	4	3	2	1.8	.963							
	C	A. Wilson	280	.246	0	19	292	96	9	7	4.7	.977							
	OF	J. Kelly	155	.232	0	15	93	4	7	0	2.3	.933							
St. L. W-51 L-78 Jack Hendricks	1B	G. Paulette	461	.273	0	52	1093	59	**20**	64	12.1	.983	B. Doak	31	211	9	15	1	2.43
	2B	B. Fisher	246	.317	2	20	147	232	8	34	6.1	.979	R. Ames	27	207	9	14	1	2.31
	SS	R. Hornsby	416	.281	5	60	208	434	46	55	6.3	.933	B. Sherdel	35	182	6	12	0	2.71
	3B	D. Baird	316	.247	2	25	99	219	11	12	4.1	.967	G. Packard	30	182	12	12	2	3.50
	RF	W. Cruise	240	.271	6	39	103	4	4	0	1.7	.964	L. Meadows	30	165	8	14	1	3.59
	CF	C. Heathcote	348	.259	4	32	222	6	16	0	2.8	.934	J. May	29	153	5	6	0	3.83
	LF	A. McHenry	272	.261	1	29	145	14	8	3	2.1	.952							
	C	M. Gonzalez	349	.252	3	20	362	124	11	17	5.0	.978							
	UT	B. Betzel	230	.222	0	13	100	103	17	10		.923							
	OF	J. Smith	166	.211	0	4	87	9	6	6	2.4	.941							

BATTING AND BASE RUNNING LEADERS

Batting Average
Z. Wheat, BKN	.335
E. Roush, CIN	.333
H. Groh, CIN	.320
C. Hollocher, CHI	.316
J. Daubert, BKN	.308

Slugging Average
E. Roush, CIN	.455
J. Daubert, BKN	.429
R. Hornsby, STL	.416
S. Magee, CIN	.415
A. Wickland, BOS	.398

Home Runs
G. Cravath, PHI	8
W. Cruise, STL	6
C. Williams, PHI	6

Total Bases
C. Hollocher, CHI	202
E. Roush, CIN	198
H. Groh, CIN	195
L. Mann, CHI	188
F. Merkle, CHI	187

Runs Batted In
S. Magee, CIN	76
G. Cutshaw, PIT	68
F. Luderus, PHI	67
R. Smith, BOS	65
F. Merkle, CHI	65

Stolen Bases
M. Carey, PIT	58
G. Burns, NY	40
C. Hollocher, CHI	26
D. Baird, STL	25
G. Cutshaw, PIT	25

Hits
C. Hollocher, CHI	161
H. Groh, CIN	158
E. Roush, CIN	145

Base on Balls
M. Carey, PIT	62
M. Flack, CHI	56

Home Run Percentage
G. Cravath, PHI	1.9
C. Williams, PHI	1.7
A. Wickland, BOS	1.2

Runs Scored
H. Groh, CIN	88
G. Burns, NY	80
M. Flack, CHI	74

Doubles
H. Groh, CIN	28
G. Cravath, PHI	27
L. Mann, CHI	27

Triples
J. Daubert, BKN	15
A. Wickland, BOS	13
S. Magee, CIN	13
L. Magee, CIN	13

PITCHING LEADERS

Winning Percentage
C. Hendrix, CHI	.731
E. Mayer, PHI, PIT	.696
H. Vaughn, CHI	.688
B. Grimes, BKN	.679
L. Tyler, CHI	.679

Earned Run Average
H. Vaughn, CHI	1.74
L. Tyler, CHI	2.00
W. Cooper, PIT	2.11
P. Douglas, CHI	2.13
B. Grimes, BKN	2.14

Wins
H. Vaughn, CHI	22
C. Hendrix, CHI	19
B. Grimes, BKN	19
L. Tyler, CHI	19
W. Cooper, PIT	19

Saves
W. Cooper, PIT	3
F. Anderson, NY	3
J. Oeschger, PHI	3
F. Toney, CIN, NY	3

Strikeouts
H. Vaughn, CHI	148
W. Cooper, PIT	117
B. Grimes, BKN	113
L. Tyler, CHI	102
A. Nehf, BOS	96

Complete Games
A. Nehf, BOS	28
H. Vaughn, CHI	27
W. Cooper, PIT	26
L. Tyler, CHI	22
C. Hendrix, CHI	21

Fewest Hits per 9 Innings
H. Vaughn, CHI	6.70
B. Grimes, BKN	7.01
W. Cooper, PIT	7.21

Shutouts
L. Tyler, CHI	8
H. Vaughn, CHI	8
B. Grimes, BKN	7
P. Perritt, NY	6

Fewest Walks per 9 Innings
S. Sallee, NY	0.82
P. Perritt, NY	1.47
F. Toney, CIN, NY	1.54

Most Strikeouts per 9 Inn.
H. Vaughn, CHI	4.59
W. Cooper, PIT	3.85
B. Grimes, BKN	3.77

Innings
H. Vaughn, CHI	290
A. Nehf, BOS	284
W. Cooper, PIT	273

Games Pitched
B. Grimes, BKN	40
W. Cooper, PIT	38
H. Eller, CIN	37

	W	L	PCT	GB	R	OR	2B	3B	HR	BA	SA	SB	E	DP	FA	CG	BB	SO	ShO	SV	ERA
CHI	84	45	.651		538	391	164	53	21	.265	.342	159	188	91	.966	92	296	472	25	6	2.18
NY	71	53	.573	10.5	480	423	150	53	13	.260	.330	130	152	78	.970	74	228	330	18	11	2.64
CIN	68	60	.531	15.5	538	496	165	84	15	.278	.366	128	192	127	.964	84	381	367	14	6	3.00
PIT	65	60	.520	17	466	411	107	72	15	.248	.321	200	179	108	.966	85	299	367	12	7	2.48
BKN	57	69	.452	25.5	360	459	121	62	10	.250	.315	113	193	74	.963	85	320	395	17	2	2.81
PHI	55	68	.447	26	430	507	158	28	25	.244	.313	97	211	91	.961	78	369	312	10	6	3.15
BOS	53	71	.427	28.5	424	469	107	59	13	.244	.307	83	184	89	.965	96	277	340	13	0	2.90
STL	51	78	.395	33	454	534	147	64	27	.244	.325	119	220	116	.962	72	352	361	3	5	2.96
					3690	3690	1119	475	139	.254	.328	1029	1519	774	.965	666	2522	2898	112	43	2.76

American League 1918

	POS	Player	AB	BA	HR	RBI	PO	A	E	DP	TC/G	FA	Pitcher	G	IP	W	L	SV	ERA
Bos.	1B	S. McInnis	423	.272	0	56	1066	71	9	45	12.2	.992	C. Mays	35	293	21	13	0	2.21
W-75 L-51	2B	D. Shean	425	.264	0	34	241	341	20	38	5.2	.967	J. Bush	36	273	15	15	2	2.11
Ed Barrow	SS	E. Scott	443	.221	0	43	270	419	17	38	5.6	.976	S. Jones	24	184	16	5	0	2.25
	3B	F. Thomas	144	.257	1	11	54	97	5	4	3.8	.968	B. Ruth	20	166	13	7	0	2.22
	RF	H. Hooper	474	.289	1	44	221	16	9	8	2.0	.963	D. Leonard	16	126	8	6	0	2.72
	CF	A. Strunk	413	.257	0	35	230	13	3	4	2.2	.988							
	LF	B. Ruth	317	.300	11	66	121	8	7	3	2.3	.949							
	C	S. Agnew	199	.166	0	6	254	104	13	10	5.2	.965							
	C	W. Schang	225	.244	0	20	188	49	9	4	4.3	.963							
	OF	G. Whiteman	214	.266	1	28	95	5	7	1	1.6	.935							

POS	Player	AB	BA	HR	RBI	PO	A	E	DP	TC/G	FA	Pitcher	G	IP	W	L	SV	ERA
Cle. W-73 L-54 Lee Fohl																		
1B	D. Johnston	273	.227	0	25	738	40	9	25	10.8	.989	S. Coveleski	38	311	22	13	1	1.82
2B	B. Wambsganss	315	.295	0	40	204	251	23	35	5.5	.952	J. Bagby	45	271	17	16	6	2.69
SS	R. Chapman	446	.267	1	32	321	398	49	42	6.0	.936	G. Morton	30	215	14	8	0	2.64
3B	J. Evans	243	.263	1	22	91	155	18	17	3.6	.932	F. Coumbe	30	150	13	7	3	3.00
RF	B. Roth	375	.283	1	59	175	16	13	3	1.9	.936	J. Enzmann	30	137	5	7	2	2.37
CF	T. Speaker	471	.318	0	61	352	15	10	6	3.0	.973							
LF	J. Wood	422	.296	5	66	193	10	8	4	2.2	.962							
C	S. O'Neill	359	.242	1	35	409	154	10	10	5.1	.983							
32	T. Turner	233	.249	0	23	77	170	5	6		.980							
OF	J. Graney	177	.237	0	9	77	2	2	0	1.8	.975							
Was. W-72 L-56 Clark Griffith																		
1B	J. Judge	502	.261	1	46	1304	92	21	71	10.9	.985	W. Johnson	39	325	23	13	3	1.27
2B	R. Morgan	300	.233	0	30	172	251	18	29	5.5	.959	H. Harper	35	244	11	10	1	2.18
SS	D. Lavan	464	.278	0	45	275	354	57	43	5.9	.917	J. Shaw	41	241	16	12	1	2.42
3B	E. Foster	519	.283	0	29	156	281	30	31	3.7	.936	D. Ayers	39	220	10	12	3	2.83
RF	W. Schulte	267	.288	0	44	145	10	5	4	2.1	.969							
CF	C. Milan	503	.290	0	56	299	17	9	3	2.6	.972							
LF	B. Shotton	505	.261	0	21	277	15	18	6	2.5	.942							
C	E. Ainsmith	292	.212	0	20	413	131	14	13	6.3	.975							
O2	H. Shanks	436	.257	1	56	279	143	21	21		.953							
N. Y. W-60 L-63 Miller Huggins																		
1B	W. Pipp	349	.304	2	44	918	61	12	75	10.9	.988	G. Mogridge	45	230	16	13	7	2.27
2B	D. Pratt	477	.275	2	55	340	386	23	82	5.9	.969	S. Love	38	229	13	12	1	3.07
SS	R. Peckinpaugh	446	.231	0	43	260	439	28	75	6.0	.961	R. Caldwell	24	177	9	8	1	3.06
3B	F. Baker	504	.306	6	68	175	282	13	30	3.7	.972	A. Russell	27	141	7	11	4	3.26
RF	F. Gilhooley	427	.276	1	23	206	15	9	8	2.1	.961	H. Finneran	23	114	3	6	0	3.78
CF	E. Miller	202	.243	1	20	149	13	9	0	2.8	.947	H. Thormahlen	16	113	7	3	0	2.48
LF	P. Bodie	324	.256	3	46	181	17	6	3	2.3	.971							
C	T. Hannah	250	.220	2	21	343	111	12	16	5.3	.974							
C	R. Walters	191	.199	0	12	199	47	12	6	5.2	.953							
St. L. W-58 L-64 Fielder Jones W-23 L-24 Jimmy Austin W-6 L-8 Jimmy Burke W-29 L-32																		
1B	G. Sisler	452	.341	2	41	1244	95	13	64	11.9	.990	A. Sothoron	29	209	12	12	0	1.94
2B	J. Gedeon	441	.213	1	41	309	409	17	45	6.0	.977	D. Davenport	31	180	10	11	1	3.25
SS	J. Austin	367	.264	0	20	117	158	18	13	5.1	.939	T. Rogers	29	154	8	10	2	3.27
3B	F. Maisel	284	.232	0	16	108	154	14	10	3.5	.949	B. Gallia	19	124	8	6	0	3.48
RF	R. Demmitt	405	.281	1	61	206	25	12	8	2.1	.951	R. Wright	18	111	8	2	0	2.51
CF	J. Tobin	480	.277	0	36	244	20	8	8	2.2	.971	U. Shocker	14	95	6	5	2	1.81
LF	E. Smith	286	.269	0	32	164	14	9	4	2.3	.952							
C	L. Nunamaker	274	.259	0	22	315	108	9	10	5.3	.979							
OF	T. Hendryx	219	.279	0	33	108	4	2	1	1.8	.982							
SS	W. Gerber	171	.240	0	10	109	174	24	20	5.5	.922							
Chi. W-57 L-67 Pants Rowland																		
1B	C. Gandil	439	.271	0	55	1123	64	10	70	10.5	.992	E. Cicotte	38	266	12	19	2	2.64
2B	E. Collins	330	.276	2	30	231	285	14	53	5.5	.974	Shellenback	28	183	9	12	2	2.66
SS	B. Weaver	420	.300	0	29	191	319	32	50	5.5	.941	J. Benz	29	154	8	8	0	2.51
3B	F. McMullin	235	.277	1	16	74	151	14	9	3.5	.941	D. Danforth	39	139	6	15	3	3.43
RF	H. Felsch	206	.252	1	20	149	7	7	5	3.1	.957	R. Russell	19	125	7	5	0	2.60
CF	S. Collins	365	.274	1	56	230	20	7	1	2.8	.973	L. Williams	15	106	6	4	1	2.73
LF	N. Leibold	440	.250	1	31	259	16	6	5	2.5	.979							
C	R. Schalk	333	.219	0	22	422	114	12	15	5.2	.978							
OF	E. Murphy	286	.297	0	23	111	3	5	1	1.9	.958							
UT	S. Risberg	273	.256	1	27	168	160	21	27		.940							
OF	J. Jackson	65	.354	1	20	36	1	0	0	2.2	1.000							
Det. W-55 L-71 Hughie Jennings																		
1B	H. Heilmann	286	.276	5	44	367	18	5	11	10.5	.987	H. Dauss	33	250	12	16	3	2.99
2B	R. Young	298	.188	0	21	190	271	30	28	5.4	.939	B. Boland	29	204	14	10	0	2.65
SS	D. Bush	500	.234	0	22	280	364	48	29	5.4	.931	R. Kallio	30	181	8	14	0	3.62
3B	O. Vitt	267	.240	0	17	106	137	12	15	3.9	.953	G. Cunningham	27	140	6	7	1	3.15
RF	G. Harper	227	.242	0	16	125	5	6	2	2.1	.956	B. James	19	122	6	11	0	3.76
CF	T. Cobb	421	.382	3	64	225	12	6	1	2.6	.975	E. Erickson	12	94	4	5	1	2.48
LF	B. Veach	499	.279	3	78	277	14	7	3	2.3	.977							
C	A. Yelle	144	.174	0	7	172	81	14	5	5.1	.948							
3B	B. Jones	287	.275	0	21	81	83	11	6	2.8	.937							
C	O. Stanage	186	.253	1	14	188	54	5	9	5.3	.980							
OF	F. Walker	167	.198	1	20	102	5	9	1	2.6	.922							
C	T. Spencer	155	.219	0	8	153	46	7	3	4.3	.966							
Phi. W-52 L-76 Connie Mack																		
1B	G. Burns	505	.352	6	70	1384	104	26	109	11.8	.983	S. Perry	44	332	21	19	1	1.98
2B	R. Dykes	186	.188	0	13	139	189	21	33	6.2	.940	V. Gregg	30	199	8	14	2	3.12
SS	J. Dugan	406	.195	3	34	211	281	37	46	6.2	.930	W. Adams	32	169	5	12	0	4.42
3B	L. Gardner	463	.285	1	52	158	291	17	33	3.7	.940	M. Watson	21	142	7	10	0	3.37
RF	C. Jamieson	416	.202	0	11	182	15	6	4	2.0	.970	E. Myers	18	95	4	8	1	4.63
CF	T. Walker	414	.295	11	48	242	25	13	4	2.6	.954	B. Geary	16	87	2	5	4	2.69
LF	M. Kopp	363	.234	0	18	221	20	7	6	2.6	.972							
C	W. McAvoy	271	.244	0	32	235	123	15	15	5.0	.960							
S2	R. Shannon	225	.240	0	16	155	223	39	40		.906							
C	C. Perkins	218	.188	1	14	201	103	3	11	5.1	.990							
OF	M. Acosta	169	.302	0	14	77	7	5	2	2.0	.944							

BATTING AND BASE RUNNING LEADERS

Batting Average

T. Cobb, DET	.382
G. Burns, PHI	.352
G. Sisler, STL	.341
T. Speaker, CLE	.318
F. Baker, NY	.306

Slugging Average

B. Ruth, BOS	.555
T. Cobb, DET	.515
G. Burns, PHI	.467
G. Sisler, STL	.440
T. Speaker, CLE	.435

Home Runs

B. Ruth, BOS	11
T. Walker, PHI	11
F. Baker, NY	6
G. Burns, PHI	6
H. Heilmann, DET	5
J. Wood, CLE	5

Total Bases

G. Burns, PHI	236
T. Cobb, DET	217
F. Baker, NY	206
T. Speaker, CLE	205
G. Sisler, STL	199

Runs Batted In

B. Veach, DET	78
G. Burns, PHI	70
F. Baker, NY	68
B. Ruth, BOS	66
J. Wood, CLE	66

Stolen Bases

G. Sisler, STL	45
B. Roth, CLE	35
T. Cobb, DET	34
R. Chapman, CLE	30
T. Speaker, CLE	27

Hits

G. Burns, PHI	178
T. Cobb, DET	161
G. Sisler, STL	154
F. Baker, NY	154

Base on Balls

R. Chapman, CLE	84
D. Bush, DET	79
H. Hooper, BOS	75

Home Run Percentage

B. Ruth, BOS	3.5
T. Walker, PHI	2.7
F. Baker, NY	1.2

Runs Scored

R. Chapman, CLE	84
T. Cobb, DET	83
H. Hooper, BOS	81

Doubles

T. Speaker, CLE	33
B. Ruth, BOS	26
H. Hooper, BOS	26

Triples

T. Cobb, DET	14
H. Hooper, BOS	13
B. Veach, DET	13
B. Roth, CLE	12

PITCHING LEADERS

Winning Percentage

S. Jones, BOS	.762
W. Johnson, WAS	.639
S. Coveleski, CLE	.629
C. Mays, BOS	.618
J. Shaw, WAS	.571

Earned Run Average

W. Johnson, WAS	1.27
S. Coveleski, CLE	1.82
A. Sothoron, STL	1.94
S. Perry, PHI	1.98
J. Bush, BOS	2.11

Wins

W. Johnson, WAS	23
S. Coveleski, CLE	22
C. Mays, BOS	21
S. Perry, PHI	21
J. Bagby, CLE	17

Saves

G. Mogridge, NY	7
J. Bagby, CLE	6

Strikeouts

W. Johnson, WAS	162
J. Shaw, WAS	129
J. Bush, BOS	125
G. Morton, CLE	123
C. Mays, BOS	114

Complete Games

C. Mays, BOS	30
S. Perry, PHI	30
W. Johnson, WAS	29
J. Bush, BOS	26
S. Coveleski, CLE	25

Fewest Hits per 9 Innings

A. Sothoron, STL	6.55
W. Johnson, WAS	6.67
H. Harper, WAS	6.71

Shutouts

W. Johnson, WAS	8
C. Mays, BOS	8
J. Bush, BOS	7
S. Jones, BOS	5

Fewest Walks per 9 Innings

E. Cicotte, CHI	1.35
J. Benz, CHI	1.64
G. Mogridge, NY	1.68

Most Strikeouts per 9 Inn.

G. Morton, CLE	5.16
J. Shaw, WAS	4.81
W. Johnson, WAS	4.49

Innings

S. Perry, PHI	332
W. Johnson, WAS	325
S. Coveleski, CLE	311

Games Pitched

J. Bagby, CLE	45
G. Mogridge, NY	45
S. Perry, PHI	44

	W	L	PCT	GB	R	OR	2B	3B	HR	BA	SA	SB	E	DP	FA	CG	BB	SO	ShO	SV	ERA
BOS	75	51	.595		473	381	159	54	15	.249	.327	110	149	89	.971	105	380	392	26	2	2.31
CLE	73	54	.575	2.5	510	447	176	67	9	.260	.341	165	207	82	.962	78	343	364	5	13	2.63
WAS	72	56	.563	4	461	392	156	48	5	.256	.316	137	226	95	.960	75	395	505	19	8	2.14
NY	60	63	.488	13.5	491	474	160	45	20	.257	.330	88	161	87	.970	59	463	369	8	13	3.03
STL	58	64	.475	15	426	448	152	40	5	.259	.320	138	190	86	.963	67	402	346	8	8	2.75
CHI	57	67	.460	17	457	443	136	54	9	.256	.321	116	169	98	.967	76	300	349	9	8	2.69
DET	55	71	.437	20	473	555	141	56	13	.249	.318	123	211	77	.960	74	437	374	8	5	3.40
PHI	52	76	.406	24	412	563	124	44	22	.243	.308	83	228	136	.959	80	479	279	13	8	3.22
					3703	3703	1204	408	98	.254	.323	960	1541	800	.964	614	3199	2978	96	65	2.77

National League 1919

	POS	Player	AB	BA	HR	RBI	PO	A	E	DP	TC/G	FA	Pitcher	G	IP	W	L	SV	ERA
Cin. W-96 L-44 Pat Moran	1B	J. Daubert	537	.276	2	44	1437	80	17	75	11.0	.989	H. Eller	38	248	20	9	2	2.39
	2B	M. Rath	537	.264	1	29	345	452	21	59	5.9	.974	D. Ruether	33	243	19	6	0	1.82
	SS	L. Kopf	503	.270	0	58	273	407	41	39	5.3	.943	S. Sallee	29	228	21	7	0	2.06
	3B	H. Groh	448	.310	5	63	171	226	12	22	3.4	.971	J. Ring	32	183	10	9	3	2.26
	RF	G. Neale	500	.242	1	54	285	16	13	4	2.3	.959	R. Fisher	26	174	14	5	1	2.17
	CF	E. Roush	504	.321	4	71	335	22	4	5	2.7	.989	D. Luque	30	106	9	3	3	2.63
	LF	R. Bressler	165	.206	2	17	105	4	4	1	2.4	.965							
	C	I. Wingo	245	.273	0	27	266	106	12	6	5.1	.969							
	C	B. Rariden	218	.216	1	24	283	67	6	5	5.1	.983							
	OF	S. Magee	163	.215	0	21	98	2	1	0	2.1	.990							

N. Y. — W-87 L-53 — John McGraw

POS	Player	AB	BA	HR	RBI	PO	A	E	DP	TC/G	FA
1B	H. Chase	408	.284	5	45	1205	65	21	62	12.1	.984
2B	L. Doyle	381	.289	7	52	214	311	24	48	5.5	.956
SS	A. Fletcher	488	.277	3	54	265	521	47	49	6.6	.944
3B	H. Zimmerman	444	.255	4	58	122	268	25	16	3.4	.940
RF	R. Youngs	489	.311	2	43	235	23	16	7	2.1	.942
CF	B. Kauff	491	.277	10	67	306	18	17	3	2.5	.950
LF	G. Burns	534	.303	2	46	290	15	3	4	2.2	.990
C	L. McCarty	210	.281	2	21	203	56	8	1	4.5	.970
23	F. Frisch	190	.226	2	24	100	130	6	7		.975
C	M. Gonzalez	158	.190	0	8	179	49	9	3	4.6	.962

Pitcher	G	IP	W	L	SV	ERA
J. Barnes	38	296	25	9	1	2.40
R. Benton	35	209	17	11	2	2.63
F. Toney	24	181	13	6	1	1.84
J. Dubuc	36	132	6	4	3	2.66
R. Causey	19	105	9	3	0	3.69
A. Nehf	13	102	9	2	0	1.50

Chi. — W-75 L-65 — Fred Mitchell

POS	Player	AB	BA	HR	RBI	PO	A	E	DP	TC/G	FA
1B	F. Merkle	498	.267	3	62	1494	56	23	66	11.9	.985
2B	C. Pick	269	.242	0	18	135	253	22*	31	5.8	.946
SS	C. Hollocher	430	.270	3	26	219	418	40	49	5.9	.941
3B	C. Deal	405	.289	2	52	157	233	11	14	3.5	.973
RF	M. Flack	469	.294	6	35	194	18	3	1	1.9	.986
CF	D. Paskert	270	.196	2	29	146	12	5	1	2.0	.969
LF	L. Mann	299	.227	1	22	155	10	3	2	2.2	.982
C	B. Killefer	315	.286	0	22	478	124	8	7	6.1	.987
UT	L. Magee	267	.292	1	17	130	88	13	5		.944
OF	T. Barber	230	.313	0	21	123	7	7	1	2.0	.949
2B	B. Herzog	193	.275	0	17	81	151	3	14	4.5	.987

Pitcher	G	IP	W	L	SV	ERA
H. Vaughn	38	307	21	14	1	1.79
G. Alexander	30	235	16	11	1	1.72
C. Hendrix	33	206	10	14	0	2.62
S. Martin	35	164	8	8	2	2.47
P. Douglas	25	162	10	6	0	2.00
P. Carter	28	85	5	4	1	2.65

Pit. — W-71 L-68 — Hugo Bezdek

POS	Player	AB	BA	HR	RBI	PO	A	E	DP	TC/G	FA
1B	F. Mollwitz	168	.173	0	12	478	19	3	21	9.6	.994
2B	G. Cutshaw	512	.242	3	51	344	392	15	56	5.4	.980
SS	Z. Terry	472	.227	0	27	207	395	25	41	4.9	.960
3B	W. Barbare	293	.273	1	34	109	136	10	11	3.2	.961
RF	C. Stengel	321	.293	4	43	195	7	9	3	2.4	.957
CF	C. Bigbee	478	.276	2	27	343	21	11	5	3.0	.971
LF	B. Southworth	453	.280	4	61	253	17	9	5	2.3	.968
C	W. Schmidt	267	.251	0	29	315	110	8	8	5.1	.982
OF	M. Carey	244	.307	0	9	173	5	10	1	3.0	.947
1B	V. Saier	166	.223	2	17	493	17	8	18	10.2	.985
1B	P. Whitted	131	.389	0	21	311	27	4	21	10.4	.988

Pitcher	G	IP	W	L	SV	ERA
W. Cooper	35	287	19	13	1	2.67
B. Adams	34	263	17	10	1	1.98
F. Miller	32	202	13	12	0	3.03
E. Hamilton	28	160	8	11	1	3.31
H. Carlson	22	141	8	10	0	2.23

Bkn. — W-69 L-71 — Wilbert Robinson

POS	Player	AB	BA	HR	RBI	PO	A	E	DP	TC/G	FA
1B	E. Konetchy	486	.298	1	47	1288	89	9	62	10.5	.994
2B	J. Johnston	405	.281	1	23	157	294	19	31	5.4	.960
SS	I. Olson	590	.278	1	38	349	445	44	57	6.0	.934
3B	L. Malone	162	.204	0	11	52	75	9	4	2.9	.934
RF	T. Griffith	484	.281	6	57	210	20	11	3	1.9	.954
CF	H. Myers	512	.307	5	73	358	13	8	5	2.9	.979
LF	Z. Wheat	536	.297	5	62	297	9	9	2	2.3	.971
C	E. Krueger	226	.248	5	36	305	88	15	2	6.2	.963
2B	L. Magee	181	.238	0	7	74	124	13	10	5.9	.938
C	O. Miller	164	.226	0	5	223	58	10	5	5.7	.966

Pitcher	G	IP	W	L	SV	ERA
J. Pfeffer	30	267	17	.13	0	2.66
L. Cadore	35	251	14	12	0	2.37
A. Mamaux	30	199	10	12	0	2.66
B. Grimes	25	181	10	11	0	3.47
S. Smith	30	173	7	12	1	2.24
C. Mitchell	23	109	7	5	0	3.06

Bos. — W-57 L-82 — George Stallings

POS	Player	AB	BA	HR	RBI	PO	A	E	DP	TC/G	FA
1B	W. Holke	518	.292	0	48	1474	95	11	86	11.6	.993
2B	B. Herzog	275	.280	1	25	130	191	16	23	4.8	.953
SS	R. Maranville	480	.267	5	43	361	446	53	74	6.9	.941
3B	T. Boeckel	365	.249	1	24	98	188	12	11	3.2	.960
RF	R. Powell	470	.236	2	33	213	21	12	7	2.0	.950
CF	J. Riggert	240	.283	4	17	165	6	9	2	3.0	.950
LF	W. Cruise	241	.216	1	21	124	7	3	1	2.0	.978
C	H. Gowdy	219	.279	1	22	230	105	8	11	4.6	.977
2B	J. Rawlings	275	.255	1	16	105	169	11	20	4.9	.961
O3	R. Smith	241	.245	1	25	128	64	9	5		.955
C	A. Wilson	191	.257	0	16	213	82	7	4	4.7	.977
OF	J. Thorpe	156	.327	1	25	73	2	6	0	2.1	.926
OF	L. Mann	145	.283	3	20	82	9	7	1	2.5	.929

Pitcher	G	IP	W	L	SV	ERA
D. Rudolph	37	274	13	18	2	2.17
D. Fillingim	32	186	6	13	2	3.38
A. Nehf	22	169	8	9	0	3.09
R. Keating	22	136	7	11	0	2.98
A. Demaree	25	128	6	6	3	3.80
J. Scott	19	104	6	6	1	3.13

St. L. — W-54 L-83 — Branch Rickey

POS	Player	AB	BA	HR	RBI	PO	A	E	DP	TC/G	FA
1B	D. Miller	346	.231	1	24	687	40	14	34	10.9	.981
2B	M. Stock	492	.307	0	52	168	254	15	32	5.7	.966
SS	D. Lavan	356	.242	1	15	207	352	43	49	6.1	.929
3B	R. Hornsby	512	.318	8	71	73	151	16	11	3.3	.933
RF	J. Smith	408	.223	0	15	197	19	9	6	2.0	.960
CF	C. Heathcote	401	.279	1	29	225	10	8	3	2.4	.967
LF	A. McHenry	371	.286	1	47	183	20	3	3	2.0	.985
C	V. Clemons	239	.264	2	22	289	89	7	8	5.1	.982
OF	B. Shotton	270	.285	1	20	104	10	9	2	1.8	.927
OF	J. Schultz	229	.253	2	21	75	6	0	1	1.7	1.000
C	F. Snyder	154	.182	0	14	149	80	4	4	4.9	.983

Pitcher	G	IP	W	L	SV	ERA
B. Doak	31	203	13	14	0	3.11
M. Goodwin	33	179	11	9	0	2.51
O. Tuero	45	155	5	7	4	3.20
B. Sherdel	36	137	5	9	1	3.47
J. May	28	126	3	12	0	3.22
L. Meadows	22	92	4	10*	0	3.03
E. Jacobs	17	85	3	6	1	2.53

Phi. — W-47 L-90 — Jack Coombs — W-18 L-44 — Gavvy Cravath — W-29 L-46

POS	Player	AB	BA	HR	RBI	PO	A	E	DP	TC/G	FA
1B	F. Luderus	509	.293	5	54	1385	108	22	82	11.0	.985
2B	G. Paulette	243	.259	1	31	141	173	14	28	6.2	.957
SS	D. Bancroft	335	.272	0	25	242	306	28	43	6.5	.951
3B	L. Blackburne	291	.199	2	9	85	167	18	11	3.8*	.933
RF	L. Callahan	235	.230	1	9	102	13	6	1	2.1	.940
CF	C. Williams	435	.278	9	39	278	13	9	2	2.8	.970
LF	I. Meusel	521	.305	5	59	256	14	9	4	2.2	.968
C	B. Adams	232	.233	1	17	249	90	12	15	4.8	.966
O2	P. Whitted	289	.249	3	32	169	74	9	8		.964
2S	H. Pearce	244	.180	0	9	129	198	17	30		.951
3B	D. Baird	242	.252	2	30	100	147	13	17	3.9	.950
OF	G. Cravath	214	.341	12	45	89	7	9	2	1.9	.914
S2	E. Sicking	185	.216	0	15	117	157	15	37		.948

Pitcher	G	IP	W	L	SV	ERA
G. Smith	31	185	5	11	0	3.22
E. Rixey	23	154	6	12	0	3.97
B. Hogg	22	150	5	12	0	4.43
L. Meadows	18	149	8	10*	0	2.47
G. Packard	21	134	6	8	0	4.15
E. Jacobs	17	129	6	10	0	3.85
F. Woodward	17	101	6	9	0	4.74

BATTING AND BASE RUNNING LEADERS

Batting Average

E. Roush, CIN	.321
R. Hornsby, STL	.318
R. Youngs, NY	.311
H. Groh, CIN	.310
M. Stock, STL	.307

Slugging Average

H. Myers, BKN	.436
L. Doyle, NY	.433
H. Groh, CIN	.431
E. Roush, CIN	.431
R. Hornsby, STL	.430

Home Runs

G. Cravath, PHI	12
B. Kauff, NY	10
C. Williams, PHI	9
R. Hornsby, STL	8
L. Doyle, NY	7

Total Bases

H. Myers, BKN	223
R. Hornsby, STL	220
Z. Wheat, BKN	219
E. Roush, CIN	217
G. Burns, NY	216

Runs Batted In

H. Myers, BKN	73
E. Roush, CIN	71
R. Hornsby, STL	71
B. Kauff, NY	67
H. Groh, CIN	63

Stolen Bases

G. Burns, NY	40
G. Cutshaw, PIT	36
C. Bigbee, PIT	31
J. Smith, STL	30
B. Herzog, BOS, CHI	28
G. Neale, CIN	28

Hits

I. Olson, BKN	164
R. Hornsby, STL	163
E. Roush, CIN	162
G. Burns, NY	162

Base on Balls

G. Burns, NY	82
M. Rath, CIN	64
H. Groh, CIN	56

Home Run Percentage

C. Williams, PHI	2.1
B. Kauff, NY	2.0
L. Doyle, NY	1.8

Runs Scored

G. Burns, NY	86
H. Groh, CIN	79
J. Daubert, CIN	79
M. Rath, CIN	77

Doubles

R. Youngs, NY	31
F. Luderus, PHI	30
G. Burns, NY	30

Triples

B. Southworth, PIT	14
H. Myers, BKN	14
E. Roush, CIN	13

PITCHING LEADERS

Winning Percentage

D. Ruether, CIN	.760
S. Sallee, CIN	.750
J. Barnes, NY	.735
H. Eller, CIN	.690
B. Adams, PIT	.630

Earned Run Average

G. Alexander, CHI	1.72
H. Vaughn, CHI	1.79
D. Ruether, CIN	1.82
F. Toney, NY	1.84
B. Adams, PIT	1.98

Wins

J. Barnes, NY	25
S. Sallee, CIN	21
H. Vaughn, CHI	21
H. Eller, CIN	20
D. Ruether, CIN	19
W. Cooper, PIT	19

Saves

O. Tuero, STL	4
A. Demaree, BOS	3
J. Dubuc, NY	3
D. Luque, CIN	3
J. Ring, CIN	3

Strikeouts

H. Vaughn, CHI	141
H. Eller, CIN	137
G. Alexander, CHI	121
L. Meadows, PHI, STL	116
W. Cooper, PIT	106

Complete Games

W. Cooper, PIT	27
J. Pfeffer, BKN	26
H. Vaughn, CHI	25
D. Rudolph, BOS	24
B. Adams, PIT	23
J. Barnes, NY	23

Fewest Hits per 9 Innings

G. Alexander, CHI	6.89
W. Cooper, PIT	7.19
D. Ruether, CIN	7.23

Shutouts

G. Alexander, CHI	9
B. Adams, PIT	7
H. Eller, CIN	7
R. Fisher, CIN	5

Fewest Walks per 9 Innings

B. Adams, PIT	0.79
S. Sallee, CIN	0.79
J. Barnes, NY	1.07

Most Strikeouts per 9 Inn.

H. Eller, CIN	4.97
G. Alexander, CHI	4.63
L. Meadows, PHI, STL	4.33

Innings

H. Vaughn, CHI	307
J. Barnes, NY	296
W. Cooper, PIT	287

Games Pitched

O. Tuero, STL	45
L. Meadows, PHI, STL	40

	W	L	PCT	GB	R	OR	Batting 2B	3B	HR	BA	SA	SB	Fielding E	DP	FA	CG	BB	Pitching SO	ShO	SV	ERA
CIN	96	44	.686		578	402	135	83	20	.263	.342	143	152	98	.974	89	298	407	23	9	2.23
NY	87	53	.621	9	605	470	204	64	40	.269	.366	157	216	96	.964	72	305	340	11	13	2.70
CHI	75	65	.536	21	454	407	166	58	21	.256	.332	150	186	87	.969	80	294	495	21	5	2.21
PIT	71	68	.511	24.5	472	466	130	82	17	.249	.325	196	166	89	.970	92	263	391	16	4	2.88
BKN	69	71	.493	27	525	513	167	66	25	.263	.340	112	166	84	.972	98	292	476	12	1	2.73
BOS	57	82	.410	38.5	465	552	142	62	24	.253	.324	145	204	111	.966	79	337	374	5	9	3.17
STL	54	83	.394	40.5	463	552	163	52	18	.256	.326	148	217	112	.963	55	415	414	6	8	3.23
PHI	47	90	.343	47.5	510	699	208	50	42	.251	.342	114	219	112	.963	93	408	397	6	2	4.17
					4072	4072	1315	517	207	.258	.337	1165	1578	789	.968	658	2612	3294	100	51	2.91

American League 1919

	POS	Player	AB	BA	HR	RBI	PO	A	E	DP	TC/G	FA	Pitcher	G	IP	W	L	SV	ERA
Chi.	1B	C. Gandil	441	.290	1	60	1116	60	3	71	10.3	.997	E. Cicotte	40	307	29	7	1	1.82
W-88 L-52	2B	E. Collins	518	.319	4	80	347	401	20	66	5.5	.974	L. Williams	41	297	23	11	1	2.64
Kid Gleason	SS	S. Risberg	414	.256	2	38	175	278	32	39	5.0	.934	D. Kerr	39	212	13	7	0	2.88
	3B	B. Weaver	571	.296	3	75	113	200	12	14	3.4	.963	R. Faber	25	162	11	9	0	3.83
	RF	N. Leibold	434	.302	0	26	218	26	9	4	2.2	.928	G. Lowdermilk	20	97	5	5	0	2.79
	CF	H. Felsch	502	.275	7	86	360	32	13	15	3.0	.968							
	LF	J. Jackson	516	.351	7	96	252	15	9	4	2.0	.967							
	C	R. Schalk	394	.282	0	34	551	130	13	14	5.4	.981							
	OF	S. Collins	179	.279	1	16	82	7	4	5	2.0	.957							
	3B	F. McMullin	170	.294	0	19	45	90	10	10	3.2	.931							

	POS	Player	AB	BA	HR	RBI	PO	A	E	DP	TC/G	FA	Pitcher	G	IP	W	L	SV	ERA
Cle. W-84 L-55 Lee Fohl W-45 L-34 Tris Speaker W-39 L-21	1B	D. Johnston	331	.305	1	33	957	57	16	57	10.5	.984	S. Coveleski	43	296	24	12	4	2.52
	2B	B. Wambsganss	526	.278	2	60	342	436	30	60	5.8	.963	J. Bagby	35	241	17	11	3	2.80
	SS	R. Chapman	433	.300	3	53	255	347	36	44	5.5	.944	G. Morton	26	147	9	9	0	2.81
	3B	L. Gardner	524	.300	2	79	143	291	25	23	3.3	.946	E. Myers	23	135	8	7	1	3.74
	RF	E. Smith	395	.278	9	54	167	12	8	8	1.7	.957	G. Uhle	26	127	10	5	0	2.91
	CF	T. Speaker	494	.296	2	63	375	25	7	6	3.0	.983							
	LF	J. Graney	461	.234	1	30	281	13	12	2	2.4	.961							
	C	S. O'Neill	398	.289	2	47	472	125	14	13	5.0	.977							
	OF	J. Wood	192	.255	1	27	90	6	7	1	1.6	.932							
	1B	J. Harris	184	.375	1	46	451	38	6	22	10.8	.988							
N. Y. W-80 L-59 Miller Huggins	1B	W. Pipp	523	.275	7	50	**1488**	94	15	77	11.6	.991	J. Quinn	38	264	15	14	0	2.63
	2B	D. Pratt	527	.292	4	56	315	491	26	64	5.9	.969	B. Shawkey	41	261	20	11	4	2.72
	SS	Peckinpaugh	453	.305	7	33	271	434	43	57	6.2	.943	H. Thormahlen	30	189	12	10	1	2.62
	3B	F. Baker	567	.293	10	83	176	286	22	28	3.4	.955	G. Mogridge	35	187	10	7	0	2.50
	RF	S. Vick	407	.248	2	27	166	11	9	2	1.9	.952	C. Mays	13	120	9	3	0	1.65
	CF	P. Bodie	475	.278	6	59	293	19	13	6	2.4	.960	E. Shore	20	95	5	8	0	4.17
	LF	D. Lewis	559	.272	7	89	254	13	4	4	1.9	.985	A. Russell	23	91	5	5	1*	3.47
	C	M. Ruel	233	.240	0	31	340	90	11	6	5.4	.975							
	OS	C. Fewster	244	.283	1	15	118	80	17	8		.921							
	C	T. Hannah	227	.238	1	20	298	66	6	12	5.1	.984							
Det. W-80 L-60 Hughie Jennings	1B	H. Heilmann	537	.320	8	95	1402	78	**31**	61	10.8	.979	H. Dauss	34	256	21	9	0	3.55
	2B	R. Young	456	.211	1	25	300	389	22	38	5.9	.969	H. Ehmke	33	249	17	10	1	3.18
	SS	D. Bush	509	.244	0	26	**290**	376	40	38	5.5	.943	B. Boland	35	243	14	16	1	3.04
	3B	B. Jones	439	.260	1	57	134	219	21	14	2.9	.944	D. Leonard	29	217	14	13	0	2.77
	RF	I. Flagstead	287	.331	5	41	140	15	8	4	2.0	.951	S. Love	22	90	6	4	1	3.01
	CF	T. Cobb	497	**.384**	1	70	272	19	8	3	2.4	.973							
	LF	B. Veach	538	.355	3	101	338	14	12	3	2.6	.967							
	C	E. Ainsmith	364	.272	3	32	456	107	**22**	7	5.5	.962							
	OF	C. Shorten	270	.315	0	22	143	2	4	2	2.0	.973							
St. L. W-67 L-72 Jimmy Burke	1B	G. Sisler	511	.352	10	83	1249	**120**	13	62	10.5	.991	A. Sothoron	40	270	20	13	3	2.20
	2B	J. Gedeon	437	.254	0	27	290	345	16	44	5.5	**.975**	B. Gallia	34	222	11	14	2	3.60
	SS	W. Gerber	462	.227	1	37	287	422	**45**	42	5.4	.940	U. Shocker	30	211	13	11	0	2.69
	3B	J. Austin	396	.237	1	21	161	207	24	15	**4.0**	.939	C. Weilman	20	148	10	6	0	2.07
	RF	E. Smith	252	.250	1	36	155	13	5	4	2.5	.971	D. Davenport	24	123	3	11	0	3.94
	CF	B. Jacobson	455	.323	4	51	270	9	15	2	2.8	.949	L. Leifield	19	92	6	4	0	2.93
	LF	J. Tobin	486	.327	6	57	247	16	13	15	2.2	.953							
	C	H. Severeid	351	.248	0	36	401	106	9	12	5.0	**.983**							
	OF	K. Williams	227	.300	6	35	168	10	12	3	3.0	.937							
	OF	R. Demmitt	202	.238	1	19	60	6	10	0	1.6	.868							
	32	H. Bronkie	196	.255	0	14	75	113	11	13		.945							
Bos. W-66 L-71 Ed Barrow	1B	S. McInnis	440	.305	1	58	1236	82	7	**84**	11.2	.995	S. Jones	35	245	12	20	1	3.75
	2B	R. Shannon	290	.259	0	17	171	228	11	40	5.2	.973	H. Pennock	32	219	16	8	0	2.71
	SS	E. Scott	507	.278	0	38	276	423	17	63	5.7	**.976**	C. Mays	21	145	5	11	2	2.48
	3B	O. Vitt	469	.243	0	40	129	254	13	24	3.0	**.967**	B. Ruth	17	133	9	5	1	2.97
	RF	H. Hooper	491	.267	3	49	262	19	6	2	2.2	.979	A. Russell	10	120	10	4	4*	2.54
	CF	B. Roth	227	.256	0	23	125	7	8	1	2.5	.943	W. Hoyt	13	105	4	6	0	3.25
	LF	B. Ruth	432	.322	29	114	230	16	2	6	2.2	**.992**	R. Caldwell	18	86	7	4	0	3.75
	C	W. Schang	330	.306	0	55	359	131	14	15	4.9	.972							
	OF	A. Strunk	184	.272	0	17	118	4	4	1	2.6	.968							
Was. W-56 L-84 Clark Griffith	1B	J. Judge	521	.288	2	33	1177	78	15	66	9.5	.988	J. Shaw	**45**	**307**	16	17	4	2.73
	2B	H. Janvrin	208	.178	1	13	108	120	18	14	4.4	.927	W. Johnson	39	290	20	14	2	**1.49**
	SS	H. Shanks	491	.248	1	54	238	260	42	2	5.7	.922	H. Harper	35	208	6	**21**	0	3.72
	3B	E. Foster	478	.264	0	26	120	267	22	16	3.6	.946	E. Erickson	20	132	6	12	0	3.95
	RF	S. Rice	557	.321	3	71	285	18	12	3	2.2	.962							
	CF	C. Milan	321	.287	0	37	195	9	10	2	2.5	.953							
	LF	M. Menosky	342	.287	6	39	222	7	5	1	2.3	.979							
	C	V. Picinich	212	.274	3	22	303	92	9	5	5.9	.978							
	CO	P. Gharrity	347	.271	2	43	329	72	15	7		.964							
	OF	B. Murphy	252	.262	0	28	177	8	8	2	2.6	.959							
	23	J. Leonard	198	.258	2	20	81	98	8	14		.957							
Phi. W-36 L-104 Connie Mack	1B	G. Burns	470	.296	8	57	918	71	20	44	11.7	.980	R. Naylor	31	205	5	18	0	3.34
	2B	R. Shannon	155	.271	0	14	66	116	10	10	5.2	.948	W. Kinney	43	203	9	15	2	3.64
	SS	J. Dugan	387	.271	1	30	228	307	42	39	5.9	.927	J. Johnson	34	202	9	15	0	3.61
	3B	F. Thomas	453	.212	2	23	168	242	24	14	3.5	.924	S. Perry	25	184	4	17	1	3.58
	RF	M. Kopp	235	.226	1	12	127	7	11	0	2.2	.924	T. Rogers	23	140	4	12	0	4.31
	CF	T. Walker	456	.292	10	64	253	13	**19**	4	2.5	.933							
	LF	W. Witt	460	.267	0	33	134	3	4	0	2.4	.972							
	C	C. Perkins	305	.252	2	29	340	**134**	14	15	5.6	.971							
	OF	B. Roth	195	.323	5	29	78	1	2	2	1.7	.975							
	OF	A. Strunk	194	.211	0	13	98	7	2	0	2.1	.981							
	1B	D. Burrus	194	.258	0	8	337	21	5	15	9.6	.986							
	C	W. McAvoy	170	.141	0	11	182	73	7	6	4.6	.973							

BATTING AND BASE RUNNING LEADERS

PITCHING LEADERS

Batting Average

T. Cobb, DET	.384
B. Veach, DET	.355
G. Sisler, STL	.352
J. Jackson, CHI	.351
I. Flagstead, DET	.331

Slugging Average

B. Ruth, BOS	.657
G. Sisler, STL	.530
B. Veach, DET	.519
T. Cobb, DET	.515
J. Jackson, CHI	.506

Winning Percentage

E. Cicotte, CHI	.806
H. Dauss, DET	.700
L. Williams, CHI	.676
S. Coveleski, CLE	.667
H. Pennock, BOS	.667

Earned Run Average

W. Johnson, WAS	1.49
E. Cicotte, CHI	1.82
C. Weilman, STL	2.07
C. Mays, BOS, NY	2.11
A. Sothoron, STL	2.20

Home Runs

B. Ruth, BOS	29
T. Walker, PHI	10
G. Sisler, STL	10
F. Baker, NY	10
E. Smith, CLE	9

Total Bases

B. Ruth, BOS	284
B. Veach, DET	279
G. Sisler, STL	271
J. Jackson, CHI	261
T. Cobb, DET	256
H. Heilmann, DET	256

Wins

E. Cicotte, CHI	29
S. Coveleski, CLE	24
L. Williams, CHI	23
H. Dauss, DET	21

Saves

A. Russell, BOS, NY	5
S. Coveleski, CLE	4
B. Shawkey, NY	4
J. Shaw, WAS	4
A. Sothoron, STL	3
J. Bagby, CLE	3

Runs Batted In

B. Ruth, BOS	114
B. Veach, DET	101
J. Jackson, CHI	96
H. Heilmann, DET	95
D. Lewis, NY	89

Stolen Bases

E. Collins, CHI	33
T. Cobb, DET	28
G. Sisler, STL	28
S. Rice, WAS	26
H. Hooper, BOS	23
J. Judge, WAS	23

Strikeouts

W. Johnson, WAS	147
J. Shaw, WAS	128
L. Williams, CHI	125
B. Shawkey, NY	122
S. Coveleski, CLE	118

Complete Games

E. Cicotte, CHI	30
W. Johnson, WAS	27
L. Williams, CHI	27
S. Coveleski, CLE	24
C. Mays, BOS, NY	23
J. Shaw, WAS	23

Hits

T. Cobb, DET	191
B. Veach, DET	191
J. Jackson, CHI	181

Base on Balls

J. Graney, CLE	105
B. Ruth, BOS	101
J. Judge, WAS	81

Fewest Hits per 9 Innings

W. Johnson, WAS	7.28
H. Thormahlen, NY	7.39
B. Shawkey, NY	7.51

Shutouts

W. Johnson, WAS	7

Home Run Percentage

B. Ruth, BOS	6.7
E. Smith, CLE	2.3
T. Walker, PHI	2.2

Runs Scored

B. Ruth, BOS	103
G. Sisler, STL	96
T. Cobb, DET	92

Fewest Walks per 9 Innings

E. Cicotte, CHI	1.44
W. Johnson, WAS	1.58
J. Bagby, CLE	1.64

Most Strikeouts per 9 Inn.

A. Russell, BOS, NY	4.82
W. Johnson, WAS	4.56
W. Kinney, PHI	4.31

Doubles

B. Veach, DET	45
T. Speaker, CLE	38
T. Cobb, DET	36

Triples

B. Veach, DET	17
G. Sisler, STL	15
H. Heilmann, DET	15

Innings

J. Shaw, WAS	307
E. Cicotte, CHI	307
L. Williams, CHI	297

Games Pitched

J. Shaw, WAS	45
A. Russell, BOS, NY	44
S. Coveleski, CLE	43
W. Kinney, PHI	43

	W	L	PCT	GB	R	OR	2B	3B	Batting HR	BA	SA	SB	E	Fielding DP	FA	CG	BB	Pitching SO	ShO	SV	ERA
CHI	88	52	.629		668	534	218	70	25	.287	.380	150	176	116	.969	88	342	468	14	3	3.04
CLE	84	55	.604	3.5	634	535	254	71	25	.278	.381	113	201	102	.965	80	362	432	10	10	2.92
NY	80	59	.576	7.5	582	514	193	49	45	.267	.356	101	192	108	.968	85	433	500	14	6	2.78
DET	80	60	.571	8	620	582	222	84	23	.283	.381	121	205	81	.964	85	431	428	10	4	3.30
STL	67	72	.482	20.5	535	567	187	73	31	.264	.355	74	216	98	.963	77	421	415	14	5	3.13
BOS	66	71	.482	20.5	565	552	181	49	33	.261	.344	108	141	118	.975	89	420	380	15	8	3.30
WAS	56	84	.400	32	533	570	177	63	24	.260	.339	142	227	86	.960	69	451	536	12	8	3.01
PHI	36	104	.257	52	459	742	175	71	35	.244	.334	103	259	96	.956	72	503	417	1	3	4.26
					4596	4596	1607	530	241	.268	.359	912	1617	805	.965	645	3363	3576	90	47	3.21

National League 1920

	POS	Player	AB	BA	HR	RBI	PO	A	E	DP	TC/G	FA	Pitcher	G	IP	W	L	SV	ERA
Bkn.	1B	E. Konetchy	497	.308	5	63	1332	79	14	70	11.0	.990	B. Grimes	40	304	23	11	2	2.22
W-93 L-61	2B	P. Kilduff	478	.272	0	58	316	454	26	69	5.9	.967	L. Cadore	35	254	15	14	0	2.62
Wilbert Robinson	SS	I. Olson	637	.254	1	46	275	404	47	48	5.8	.935	J. Pfeffer	30	215	16	9	0	3.01
	3B	J. Johnston	635	.291	1	52	159	282	31	21	3.2	.934	A. Mamaux	41	191	12	8	4	2.69
	RF	T. Griffith	334	.260	2	30	132	7	4	1	1.6	.972	R. Marquard	28	190	10	7	0	3.23
	CF	H. Myers	582	.304	4	80	386	17	9	5	2.7	.978	S. Smith	33	136	11	9	3	1.85
	LF	Z. Wheat	583	.328	9	73	287	10	9	5	2.1	.971							
	C	O. Miller	301	.289	0	33	418	65	7	8	5.5	.986							
	OF	B. Neis	249	.253	2	22	145	11	7	4	2.0	.957							

POS	Player	AB	BA	HR	RBI	PO	A	E	DP	TC/G	FA	Pitcher	G	IP	W	L	SV	ERA
N. Y. W-86 L-68 John McGraw																		
1B	G. Kelly	590	.266	11	**94**	**1759**	**103**	11	**115**	12.1	.994	J. Barnes	43	293	20	15	0	2.64
2B	L. Doyle	471	.285	4	50	278	389	23	61	5.2	.967	A. Nehf	40	281	21	12	0	3.08
SS	D. Bancroft	442	.299	0	31	256*	445*	40	67*	6.9*	.946*	F. Toney	42	278	21	11	1	2.65
3B	F. Frisch	440	.280	4	77	104	251	12	23	3.3	.967	P. Douglas	46	226	14	10	2	2.71
RF	R. Youngs	581	.351	6	78	288	**26**	**22**	7	2.2	.935	R. Benton	33	193	9	16	2	3.03
CF	L. King	261	.276	7	42	167	8	9	1	2.2	.951							
LF	G. Burns	631	.287	6	46	336	11	6	5	2.3	.983							
C	F. Snyder	264	.250	3	27	269	92	8	6	4.4	.978							
C	E. Smith	262	.294	1	30	252	73	8	12	4.1	.976							
SS	A. Fletcher	171	.257	0	24	79	154	22	16	6.2	.914							
OF	B. Kauff	157	.274	3	26	111	10	5	0	2.5	.960							
Cin. W-82 L-71 Pat Moran																		
1B	J. Daubert	553	.304	4	48	1358	63	15	90	10.3	.990	J. Ring	42	293	17	16	1	3.23
2B	M. Rath	506	.267	2	28	310	399	17	60	5.8	**.977**	D. Ruether	37	266	16	12	3	2.47
SS	L. Kopf	458	.245	0	59	249	363	47	0	5.4	.929	H. Eller	35	210	13	12	0	2.95
3B	H. Groh	550	.298	0	49	179	252	14	**30**	3.1	.969	D. Luque	37	208	13	9	1	2.51
RF	G. Neale	530	.255	3	46	347	19	5	7	2.5	.987	R. Fisher	33	201	10	11	1	2.73
CF	E. Roush	579	.339	4	90	**410**	18	11	6	**3.2**	.975	S. Sallee	21	116	5	6	2	3.34
LF	P. Duncan	576	.295	2	83	334	15	13	4	2.4	.964							
C	I. Wingo	364	.264	2	38	368	115	21	**14**	4.7	.958							
Pit. W-79 L-75 George Gibson																		
1B	C. Grimm	533	.227	2	54	1496	95	8	95	10.8	**.995**	W. Cooper	44	327	24	15	2	2.39
2B	G. Cutshaw	488	.252	0	47	336	423	25	62	**6.1**	.968	B. Adams	35	263	17	13	2	2.16
SS	B. Caton	352	.236	0	27	191	296	37	40	5.5	.929	H. Carlson	39	247	14	13	3	3.36
3B	P. Whitted	494	.261	1	74	166	229	16	16	3.3	.961	E. Hamilton	39	231	10	13	3	3.24
RF	B. Southworth	546	.284	2	53	337	12	3	3	2.5	**.991**	E. Ponder	33	196	11	15	0	2.62
CF	M. Carey	485	.289	1	35	345	10	12	0	2.8	.967							
LF	C. Bigbee	550	.280	4	32	289	16	9	4	2.4	.971							
C	W. Schmidt	310	.277	0	20	323	109	13	10	4.8	.971							
OF	F. Nicholson	247	.360	4	30	125	9	6	2	2.4	.957							
S2	W. Barbare	186	.274	0	12	75	151	13	20		.946							
C	B. Haeffner	175	.194	0	14	192	48	7	1	4.8	.972							
Chi. W-75 L-79 Fred Mitchell																		
1B	F. Merkle	330	.285	3	38	906	54	15	52	11.5	.985	G. Alexander	46	**363**	**27**	14	5	**1.91**
2B	Z. Terry	496	.280	0	52	138	222	9	30	5.9	.976	H. Vaughn	40	301	19	16	0	2.54
SS	C. Hollocher	301	.319	0	22	196	280	23	34	6.2	.954	C. Hendrix	27	204	9	12	0	3.58
3B	C. Deal	450	.240	3	39	129	268	11	22	3.2	**.973**	L. Tyler	27	193	11	12	0	3.31
RF	M. Flack	520	.302	4	49	216	16	8	2	1.8	.967	S. Martin	35	136	4	15	2	4.83
CF	D. Paskert	487	.279	5	71	306	23	15	3	2.5	.956	P. Carter	31	106	3	6	2	4.67
LF	D. Robertson	500	.300	10	75	230	10	8	1	1.9	.968							
C	B. O'Farrell	270	.248	3	19	317	100	19	6	5.1	.956							
1B	T. Barber	340	.265	0	50	739	30	9	40	11.3	.988							
23	B. Herzog	305	.193	0	19	153	241	29	32		.931							
C	B. Killefer	191	.220	0	16	304	80	9	6	6.4	.977							
OF	B. Twombly	183	.235	2	14	91	6	3	0	2.2	.970							
St. L. W-75 L-79 Branch Rickey																		
1B	J. Fournier	530	.306	3	61	1373	88	**25**	100	10.8	.983	J. Haines	**47**	302	13	20	2	2.98
2B	R. Hornsby	589	**.370**	9	**94**	**343**	**524**	34	**76**	6.0	.962	B. Doak	39	270	20	12	1	2.53
SS	S. Lavan	516	.289	1	63	327	489	**50**	77	6.3	.942	F. Schupp	38	251	16	13	0	3.52
3B	M. Stock	**639**	.319	0	76	158	**300**	30	23	3.1	.939	B. Sherdel	43	170	11	10	**6**	3.28
RF	J. Schultz	320	.263	0	32	147	7	9	3	2.0	.945	M. Goodwin	32	116	3	8	1	4.95
CF	C. Heathcote	489	.284	3	56	296	**26**	12	3	2.6	.964	E. Jacobs	23	78	4	8	1	5.21
LF	A. McHenry	504	.282	10	65	297	21	16	1	2.5	.952							
C	V. Clemons	338	.281	1	36	408	111	12	11	5.2	.977							
OF	J. Smith	313	.332	1	28	144	12	6	1	2.0	.963							
UT	H. Janvrin	270	.274	1	28	307	93	13	33		.969							
C	P. Dillhoefer	224	.263	0	13	291	72	18	6	5.2	.953							
OF	B. Shotton	180	.228	1	12	85	9	4	2	1.9	.959							
Bos. W-62 L-90 George Stallings																		
1B	W. Holke	551	.294	3	64	1528	81	14	97	11.3	.991	J. Oeschger	38	299	15	13	0	3.46
2B	C. Pick	383	.274	2	28	219	333	28	45	6.2	.952	J. Scott	44	291	10	21	1	3.53
SS	R. Maranville	493	.266	1	43	354	462	45	62	6.5	.948	D. Fillingim	37	272	12	21	0	3.11
3B	T. Boeckel	582	.268	3	62	219	266	**33**	30	3.4	.936	H. McQuillan	38	226	11	15	5	3.55
RF	W. Cruise	288	.278	1	21	122	10	7	3	1.7	.950	D. Rudolph	18	89	4	8	0	4.04
CF	R. Powell	609	.225	6	29	370	25	18	5	2.8	.956							
LF	L. Mann	424	.276	3	32	228	13	5	1	2.2	.980							
C	M. O'Neil	304	.283	0	28	304	153	18	10	4.5	.962							
2B	H. Ford	257	.241	1	30	122	219	10	21	5.9	.972							
OF	J. Sullivan	250	.296	1	28	115	10	3	2	1.9	.977							
OF	E. Eayrs	244	.328	1	24	108	6	6	2	1.9	.950							
C	H. Gowdy	214	.243	0	18	231	104	7	12	4.6	.980							
Phi. W-62 L-91 Gavvy Cravath																		
1B	G. Paulette	562	.288	1	36	1428	99	18	94	11.1	.988	E. Rixey	41	284	11	**22**	2	3.48
2B	J. Rawlings	384	.234	3	30	221	321	17	53	5.8	.970	G. Smith	43	251	13	18	2	3.45
SS	A. Fletcher	379	.296	4	38	223	368	26	47	6.1	.948	L. Meadows	35	247	16	14	0	2.84
3B	R. Miller	338	.219	0	28	89	179	17	15	3.1	.940	R. Causey	35	181	7	14	3	4.32
RF	C. Stengel	445	.292	9	50	212	16	11	1	2.0	.954	B. Hubbell	24	150	9	9	2	3.84
CF	C. Williams	590	.325	15	72	388	22	12	4	2.9	.972	B. Gallia	18	72	2	6	2	4.50
LF	I. Meusel	518	.309	14	69	260	16	21	6	2.3	.929							
C	M. Wheat	230	.226	3	20	262	105	15	8	5.2	.961							
UT	D. Miller	343	.254	1	27	254	234	27	48		.948							
OF	LeBourveau	261	.257	3	12	133	16	8	1	2.2	.940							
3B	Wrightstone	206	.262	3	17	75	109	13	7	3.5	.934							
C	W. Tragesser	176	.210	6	26	157	46	12	4	4.1	.944							
SS	D. Bancroft	171	.298	0	5	106*	153*	5	28*	6.3*	.981*							

BATTING AND BASE RUNNING LEADERS

Batting Average
R. Hornsby, STL .370
R. Youngs, NY .351
E. Roush, CIN .339
Z. Wheat, BKN .328
C. Williams, PHI .325

Slugging Average
R. Hornsby, STL .559
C. Williams, PHI .497
R. Youngs, NY .477
I. Meusel, PHI .473
Z. Wheat, BKN .463

Home Runs
C. Williams, PHI 15
I. Meusel, PHI 14
G. Kelly, NY 11
D. Robertson, CHI 10
A. McHenry, STL 10

Total Bases
R. Hornsby, STL 329
C. Williams, PHI 293
R. Youngs, NY 277
Z. Wheat, BKN 270
H. Myers, BKN 269

Runs Batted In
R. Hornsby, STL 94
G. Kelly, NY 94
E. Roush, CIN 90
P. Duncan, CIN 83
H. Myers, BKN 80

Stolen Bases
M. Carey, PIT 52
E. Roush, CIN 36
F. Frisch, NY 34
C. Bigbee, PIT 31
G. Neale, CIN 29

Hits
R. Hornsby, STL 218
R. Youngs, NY 204
M. Stock, STL 204

Base on Balls
G. Burns, NY 76
R. Youngs, NY 75
D. Paskert, CHI 64

Home Run Percentage
I. Meusel, PHI 2.7
C. Williams, PHI 2.5
C. Stengel, PHI 2.0

Runs Scored
G. Burns, NY 115
D. Bancroft, NY, PHI 102
J. Daubert, CIN 97

Doubles
R. Hornsby, STL 44
H. Myers, BKN 36
C. Williams, PHI 36
D. Bancroft, NY, PHI 36

Triples
H. Myers, BKN 22
R. Hornsby, STL 20
E. Roush, CIN 16

PITCHING LEADERS

Winning Percentage
B. Grimes, BKN .676
G. Alexander, CHI .659
F. Toney, NY .656
J. Pfeffer, BKN .640
A. Nehf, NY .636

Earned Run Average
G. Alexander, CHI 1.91
B. Adams, PIT 2.16
B. Grimes, BKN 2.22
W. Cooper, PIT 2.39
D. Ruether, CIN 2.47

Wins
G. Alexander, CHI 27
W. Cooper, PIT 24
B. Grimes, BKN 23
F. Toney, NY 21
A. Nehf, NY 21

Saves
B. Sherdel, STL 6
G. Alexander, CHI 5
H. McQuillan, BOS 5
A. Mamaux, BKN 4
B. Hubbell, NY, PHI 4

Strikeouts
G. Alexander, CHI 173
H. Vaughn, CHI 131
B. Grimes, BKN 131
J. Haines, STL 120
F. Schupp, STL 119

Complete Games
G. Alexander, CHI 33
W. Cooper, PIT 28
B. Grimes, BKN 25
E. Rixey, PHI 25
H. Vaughn, CHI 24

Fewest Hits per 9 Innings
D. Luque, CIN 7.28
D. Ruether, CIN 7.96
B. Grimes, BKN 8.03

Shutouts
B. Adams, PIT 8
G. Alexander, CHI 7

Fewest Walks per 9 Innings
B. Adams, PIT 0.62
W. Cooper, PIT 1.43
A. Nehf, NY 1.44

Most Strikeouts per 9 Inn.
G. Alexander, CHI 4.29
F. Schupp, STL 4.27
R. Marquard, BKN 4.22

Innings
G. Alexander, CHI 363
W. Cooper, PIT 327
B. Grimes, BKN 304

Games Pitched
J. Haines, STL 47
G. Alexander, CHI 46
P. Douglas, NY 46

	W	L	PCT	GB	R	OR	Batting					SB	Fielding			CG	BB	Pitching			ERA
							2B	3B	HR	BA	SA		E	DP	FA			SO	ShO	SV	
BKN	93	61	.604		660	528	205	99	28	.277	.367	70	226	118	.966	89	327	553	17	10	2.62
NY	86	68	.558	7	682	543	210	76	46	.269	.363	131	210	137	.969	86	297	380	18	9	2.80
CIN	82	71	.536	10.5	639	569	169	76	18	.277	.349	158	200	125	.968	90	393	435	12	9	2.84
PIT	79	75	.513	14	530	552	162	90	16	.257	.332	181	186	119	.971	92	280	444	17	10	2.89
CHI	75	79	.487	18	619	635	223	67	34	.264	.354	115	225	112	.965	95	382	508	13	9	3.27
STL	75	79	.487	18	675	682	238	96	32	.289	.385	126	256	136	.961	72	479	529	9	12	3.43
BOS	62	90	.408	30	523	670	168	86	23	.260	.339	88	239	125	.964	93	415	368	13	6	3.54
PHI	62	91	.405	30.5	565	714	229	54	64	.263	.364	100	232	135	.964	77	444	419	8	11	3.63
					4893	4893	1604	644	261	.270	.357	969	1774	1007	.966	694	3017	3636	107	76	3.13

American League 1920

	POS	Player	AB	BA	HR	RBI	PO	A	E	DP	TC/G	FA	Pitcher	G	IP	W	L	SV	ERA
Cle. W-98 L-56 Tris Speaker	1B	D. Johnston	535	.292	2	71	1427	91	12	83	10.4	.992	J. Bagby	48	340	31	12	0	2.89
	2B	B. Wambsganss	565	.244	1	55	414	489	38	75	6.2	.960	S. Coveleski	41	315	24	14	2	2.49
	SS	R. Chapman	435	.303	3	49	243	371	26	43	5.8	.959	R. Caldwell	34	238	20	10	0	3.86
	3B	L. Gardner	597	.310	3	118	156	362	13	32	3.4	.976	G. Morton	29	137	8	6	1	4.47
	RF	E. Smith	456	.316	12	103	217	8	7	1	1.8	.970	G. Uhle	27	85	4	5	1	5.21
	CF	T. Speaker	552	.388	8	107	363	24	9	8	2.7	.977							
	LF	C. Jamieson	370	.319	1	40	185	14	7	0	2.1	.966							
	C	S. O'Neill	489	.321	3	55	576	128	17	1	4.9	.976							
	OF	J. Evans	172	.349	0	23	79	6	3	0	2.0	.966							
	OF	J. Wood	137	.270	1	30	71	6	1	0	1.4	.987							

Chi. W-96 L-58 Kid Gleason

POS	Player	AB	BA	HR	RBI	PO	A	E	DP	TC/G	FA
1B	S. Collins	495	.303	1	63	1146	63	15	69	10.5	.988
2B	E. Collins	601	.369	3	75	**449**	471	23	76	6.2	**.976**
SS	S. Risberg	458	.266	2	65	238	400	45	59	5.5	.934
3B	B. Weaver	630	.333	2	75	153	276	31	15	3.7	.933
RF	N. Leibold	413	.220	1	28	190	18	5	5	2.0	.977
CF	H. Felsch	556	.338	14	115	385	25	8	10	2.9	.981
LF	J. Jackson	570	.382	12	121	314	14	12	2	2.3	.965
C	R. Schalk	485	.270	1	61	**581**	138	10	19	4.8	**.986**
OF	A. Strunk	183	.230	1	14	96	3	2		2.1	.980*

Pitcher	G	IP	W	L	SV	ERA
R. Faber	40	319	23	13	1	2.99
E. Cicotte	37	303	21	10	2	3.26
L. Williams	39	299	22	14	0	3.91
D. Kerr	45	254	21	9	5	3.37
R. Wilkinson	34	145	7	9	2	4.03

N. Y. W-95 L-59 Miller Huggins

POS	Player	AB	BA	HR	RBI	PO	A	E	DP	TC/G	FA
1B	W. Pipp	610	.280	11	76	**1649**	100	15	**101**	**11.5**	.991
2B	D. Pratt	574	.314	4	97	354	515	26	77	5.8	.971
SS	Peckinpaugh	534	.270	8	54	263	441	28	56	5.3	.962
3B	A. Ward	496	.256	11	54	132	303	16	23	4.0	.965
RF	B. Ruth	458	.376	54	**137**	259	21	19	3	2.2	.936
CF	P. Bodie	471	.295	7	79	264	12	9	2	2.2	.968
LF	D. Lewis	365	.271	4	61	182	14	8	1	2.1	.961
C	M. Ruel	261	.268	1	15	317	62	6	2	4.8	.984
O3	B. Meusel	460	.328	11	83	150	85	20	6		.922
C	T. Hannah	259	.247	2	25	308	64	15	1	5.0	.961

Pitcher	G	IP	W	L	SV	ERA
C. Mays	45	312	26	11	2	3.06
B. Shawkey	38	268	20	13	2	**2.45**
J. Quinn	41	253	18	10	3	3.20
R. Collins	36	187	14	8	1	3.17
H. Thormahlen	29	143	9	6	1	4.14
G. Mogridge	26	125	5	9	1	4.31

St. L. W-76 L-77 Jimmy Burke

POS	Player	AB	BA	HR	RBI	PO	A	E	DP	TC/G	FA
1B	G. Sisler	**631**	**.407**	19	122	1477	**140**	16	87	10.6	.990
2B	J. Gedeon	606	.292	0	61	365	421	29	75	5.3	.964
SS	W. Gerber	584	.279	2	60	288	**513**	52	65	5.5	.939
3B	J. Austin	280	.271	1	32	108	171	17	14	3.9	.943
RF	J. Tobin	593	.341	4	62	293	18	13	1	2.2	.960
CF	B. Jacobson	609	.355	9	122	394	18	9	5	2.7	.979
LF	K. Williams	521	.307	10	72	331	17	14	6	2.6	.961
C	H. Severeid	422	.277	2	49	480	111	10	11	5.1	.983
3B	E. Smith	353	.306	3	55	73	146	20	2	3.4	.916
C	J. Billings	155	.277	0	11	138	36	6	1	4.5	.967

Pitcher	G	IP	W	L	SV	ERA
D. Davis	38	269	18	12	0	3.17
U. Shocker	38	246	20	10	5	2.71
A. Sothoron	36	218	8	15	2	4.70
C. Weilman	30	183	9	13	2	4.47
B. Burwell	33	113	6	4	4	3.65
E. Vangilder	24	105	3	8	0	5.50
B. Bayne	18	100	5	6	0	3.70

Bos. W-72 L-81 Ed Barrow

POS	Player	AB	BA	HR	RBI	PO	A	E	DP	TC/G	FA
1B	S. McInnis	559	.297	2	71	1586	91	7	**101**	11.4	**.996**
2B	M. McNally	312	.256	0	23	168	233	30	38	5.7	.930
SS	E. Scott	569	.269	4	61	**330**	496	23	64	5.5	**.973**
3B	E. Foster	386	.259	0	41	99	233	15	20	3.9	.957
RF	M. Menosky	532	.297	3	64	281	17	12	2	2.2	.961
CF	T. Hendryx	363	.328	0	73	208	6	8	1	2.3	.964
LF	H. Hooper	536	.312	7	53	263	22	11	2	2.1	.963
C	R. Walters	258	.198	0	28	351	94	9	15	**5.3**	.980
CO	W. Schang	387	.305	4	51	377	83	18	8		.962
3B	O. Vitt	296	.220	1	28	61	148	3	5	3.3	.986
2B	C. Brady	180	.228	0	12	111	193	8	21	5.9	.974

Pitcher	G	IP	W	L	SV	ERA
S. Jones	37	274	13	16	0	3.94
J. Bush	35	244	15	15	1	4.25
H. Pennock	27	242	16	13	2	3.68
H. Harper	27	163	5	14	0	3.04
W. Hoyt	22	121	6	6	1	4.38
A. Russell	16	108	5	6	1	3.01
E. Myers	12	97	9	1	0	2.13
B. Karr	26	92	3	8	1	4.81

Was. W-68 L-84 Clark Griffith

POS	Player	AB	BA	HR	RBI	PO	A	E	DP	TC/G	FA
1B	J. Judge	493	.333	5	51	1194	62	10	67	10.2	.992
2B	B. Harris	506	.300	1	68	345	401	33	59	5.8	.958
SS	J. O'Neill	294	.289	1	40	130	251	23	22	5.1	.943
3B	F. Ellerbe	336	.292	0	36	101	167	19	8	3.8	.934
RF	B. Roth	468	.291	9	92	184	15	10	0	1.6	.952
CF	S. Rice	624	.338	3	80	**454**	24	20	5	**3.3**	.960
LF	C. Milan	506	.322	3	41	291	15	9	1	2.6	.971
C	P. Gharrity	428	.245	3	44	409	148	20	13	4.8	.965
UT	H. Shanks	444	.268	4	37	294	154	17	12		.963
UT	R. Shannon	222	.288	0	30	89	148	18	14		.929

Pitcher	G	IP	W	L	SV	ERA
T. Zachary	44	263	15	16	2	3.77
E. Erickson	39	239	12	16	1	3.84
J. Shaw	38	236	11	18	1	4.27
H. Courtney	37	188	8	11	0	4.74
W. Johnson	21	144	8	10	3	3.13
A. Schacht	22	99	6	4	1	4.44
J. Acosta	17	83	5	4	1	4.03

Det. W-61 L-93 Hughie Jennings

POS	Player	AB	BA	HR	RBI	PO	A	E	DP	TC/G	FA
1B	H. Heilmann	543	.309	9	89	1207	80	19	52	10.7	.985
2B	R. Young	594	.291	0	33	405	436	27	46	5.8	.969
SS	D. Bush	506	.263	1	33	258	421	45	39	5.2	.938
3B	B. Pinelli	284	.229	0	21	110	183	14	20	4.1	.954
RF	C. Shorten	364	.288	1	40	168	14	2	3	1.9	.989
CF	T. Cobb	428	.334	2	63	246	8	9	2	2.3	.966
LF	B. Veach	612	.307	11	113	357	26	13	4	2.6	.967
C	O. Stanage	238	.231	0	17	248	75	14	4	4.3	.958
OF	I. Flagstead	311	.235	3	35	164	13	6	4	2.2	.967
3B	B. Jones	265	.249	1	35	80	146	14	7	3.6	.942
C	E. Ainsmith	186	.231	1	19	219	55	13	4	4.7	.955
1B	B. Ellison	155	.219	0	21	363	26	1	4	10.3	.997

Pitcher	G	IP	W	L	SV	ERA
H. Dauss	38	270	13	21	0	3.56
H. Ehmke	38	268	15	18	3	3.29
R. Oldham	39	215	8	13	1	3.85
D. Ayers	46	209	7	14	1	3.88
D. Leonard	28	191	10	17	0	4.33

Phi. W-48 L-106 Connie Mack

POS	Player	AB	BA	HR	RBI	PO	A	E	DP	TC/G	FA
1B	I. Griffin	467	.238	0	20	1252	96	13	77	10.8	.990
2B	R. Dykes	546	.256	0	35	305	373	32	38	**6.6**	.955
SS	C. Galloway	298	.201	0	18	184	252	34	22	5.6	.928
3B	F. Thomas	255	.231	1	10	78	140	9	3	3.7	.960
RF	W. Witt	218	.321	1	25	68	2	3	0	1.5	.959
CF	F. Welch	360	.258	4	40	194	14	14	4	2.3	.937
LF	T. Walker	585	.304	17	82	318	26	22	5	2.5	.940
C	C. Perkins	493	.260	5	52	524	179	15	15	4.9	.979
UT	J. Dugan	491	.322	3	60	225	328	35	48		.940
OF	A. Strunk	202	.297	0	20	97	2	1	0	1.9	.990*
OC	G. Myatt	196	.250	0	18	83	22	10	3		.913

Pitcher	G	IP	W	L	SV	ERA
S. Perry	42	264	11	**25**	1	3.62
R. Naylor	42	251	10	23	0	3.47
S. Harriss	31	192	9	14	0	4.08
E. Rommel	33	174	7	7	1	2.85
R. Moore	24	133	1	13	0	4.68
D. Keefe	31	130	6	7	0	2.97

BATTING AND BASE RUNNING LEADERS

PITCHING LEADERS

Batting Average

G. Sisler, STL	.407
T. Speaker, CLE	.388
J. Jackson, CHI	.382
B. Ruth, NY	.376
E. Collins, CHI	.369

Slugging Average

B. Ruth, NY	.847
G. Sisler, STL	.632
J. Jackson, CHI	.589
T. Speaker, CLE	.562
H. Felsch, CHI	.540

Winning Percentage

J. Bagby, CLE	.721
C. Mays, NY	.703
D. Kerr, CHI	.700
E. Cicotte, CHI	.677
R. Caldwell, CLE	.667
U. Shocker, STL	.667

Earned Run Average

B. Shawkey, NY	2.45
S. Coveleski, CLE	2.49
U. Shocker, STL	2.71
J. Bagby, CLE	2.89
R. Faber, CHI	2.99

Home Runs

B. Ruth, NY	54
G. Sisler, STL	19
T. Walker, PHI	17
H. Felsch, CHI	14
E. Smith, CLE	12
J. Jackson, CHI	12

Total Bases

G. Sisler, STL	399
B. Ruth, NY	388
J. Jackson, CHI	336
T. Speaker, CLE	310
B. Jacobson, STL	305

Wins

J. Bagby, CLE	31
C. Mays, NY	26
S. Coveleski, CLE	24
R. Faber, CHI	23
L. Williams, CHI	22

Saves

D. Kerr, CHI	5
U. Shocker, STL	5
B. Burwell, STL	4
W. Johnson, WAS	3
J. Quinn, NY	3
H. Ehmke, DET	3

Runs Batted In

B. Ruth, NY	137
B. Jacobson, STL	122
G. Sisler, STL	122
J. Jackson, CHI	121
L. Gardner, CLE	118

Stolen Bases

S. Rice, WAS	63
G. Sisler, STL	42
B. Roth, WAS	24
M. Menosky, BOS	23
J. Tobin, STL	21

Strikeouts

S. Coveleski, CLE	133
L. Williams, CHI	128
B. Shawkey, NY	126
R. Faber, CHI	108
U. Shocker, STL	107

Complete Games

J. Bagby, CLE	30
E. Cicotte, CHI	28
R. Faber, CHI	28
S. Coveleski, CLE	26
C. Mays, NY	26
L. Williams, CHI	26

Hits

G. Sisler, STL	257
E. Collins, CHI	222
J. Jackson, CHI	218

Base on Balls

B. Ruth, NY	148
T. Speaker, CLE	97
H. Hooper, BOS	88

Fewest Hits per 9 Innings

S. Coveleski, CLE	8.11
U. Shocker, STL	8.21
R. Collins, NY	8.22

Shutouts

C. Mays, NY	6
U. Shocker, STL	5
B. Shawkey, NY	5

Home Run Percentage

B. Ruth, NY	11.8
G. Sisler, STL	3.0
T. Walker, PHI	2.9

Runs Scored

B. Ruth, NY	158
G. Sisler, STL	137
T. Speaker, CLE	137

Fewest Walks per 9 Innings

W. Johnson, WAS	1.69
J. Quinn, NY	1.71
S. Coveleski, CLE	1.86

Most Strikeouts per 9 Inn.

W. Johnson, WAS	4.89
B. Shawkey, NY	4.24
H. Harper, BOS	3.93

Doubles

T. Speaker, CLE	50
G. Sisler, STL	49
J. Jackson, CHI	42

Triples

J. Jackson, CHI	20
G. Sisler, STL	18
H. Hooper, BOS	17

Innings

J. Bagby, CLE	340
R. Faber, CHI	319
S. Coveleski, CLE	315

Games Pitched

J. Bagby, CLE	48
D. Ayers, DET	46
C. Mays, NY	45
D. Kerr, CHI	45

	W	L	PCT	GB	R	OR	2B	3B	HR	BA	SA	SB	E	DP	FA	CG	BB	SO	ShO	SV	ERA
							Batting						Fielding					Pitching			
CLE	98	56	.636		857	642	301	95	35	.303	.417	73	185	124	.971	93	401	466	10	7	3.41
CHI	96	58	.623	2	794	666	263	97	37	.295	.402	108	198	142	.968	112	405	440	9	10	3.59
NY	95	59	.617	3	839	629	268	71	115	.280	.426	64	193	129	.970	88	420	480	16	11	3.31
STL	76	77	.497	21.5	797	766	278	84	50	.308	.419	121	232	119	.963	84	578	444	9	14	4.03
BOS	72	81	.471	25.5	651	699	216	71	22	.269	.351	98	183	131	.972	91	461	481	11	6	3.82
WAS	68	84	.447	29	723	802	232	81	36	.290	.386	161	232	95	.963	80	520	418	10	10	4.17
DET	61	93	.396	37	651	832	228	72	30	.270	.358	75	229	95	.965	76	561	483	9	7	4.04
PHI	48	106	.312	50	555	831	218	49	44	.252	.337	51	267	126	.959	81	461	423	5	2	3.93
					5867	5867	2004	620	369	.283	.387	751	1719	961	.966	705	3807	3635	79	67	3.79

National League 1921

		POS	Player	AB	BA	HR	RBI	PO	A	E	DP	TC/G	FA	Pitcher	G	IP	W	L	SV	ERA
N. Y.		1B	G. Kelly	587	.308	23	122	1552	115	17	132	11.3	.990	A. Nehf	41	261	20	10	1	3.63
W-94 L-59		2B	J. Rawlings	307	.267	1	30	204*	280*	15*	61*	5.8	.970	J. Barnes	42	259	15	9	6	3.10
John McGraw		SS	D. Bancroft	606	.318	6	67	396	546	39	105	6.4	.960	F. Toney	42	249	18	11	3	3.61
		3B	F. Frisch	618	.341	8	100	79	200	19	16	3.2	.936	P. Douglas	40	222	15	10	2	4.22
		RF	R. Youngs	504	.327	3	102	122	11	3	3	1.0	.978	R. Ryan	36	147	7	10	3	3.73
		CF	G. Burns	605	.299	4	61	360	16	11	2	2.6	.972	S. Sallee	37	96	6	4	2	3.64
		LF	I. Meusel	243	.329	2	36	122	10	4	0	2.2	.971							
		C	F. Snyder	309	.320	8	45	299	98	6	7	4.0	.985							
		C	E. Smith	229	.336	10	51	195	56	9	4	3.3	.965							
		OF	C. Walker	192	.286	3	35	247	16	6	5	4.6	.978							
		3B	G. Rapp	181	.215	0	15	55	135	12	12	3.6*	.941							

Pit. W-90 L-63 — George Gibson

POS	Player	AB	BA	HR	RBI	PO	A	E	DP	TC/G	FA	Pitcher	G	IP	W	L	SV	ERA
1B	C. Grimm	562	.274	7	71	1517	67	9	93	10.6	.994	W. Cooper	38	327	22	14	0	3.25
2B	G. Cutshaw	350	.340	0	53	196	253	23	36	5.6	.951	W. Glazner	36	234	14	5	1	2.77
SS	R. Maranville	612	.294	1	70	325	529	34	72	5.8	.962	E. Hamilton	35	225	13	15	0	3.36
3B	C. Barnhart	449	.258	3	62	101	204	14	19	2.7	.956	B. Adams	25	160	14	5	0	2.64
RF	P. Whitted	403	.283	7	63	247	9	3	6	2.5	.988	J. Morrison	21	144	9	7	0	2.88
CF	M. Carey	521	.309	7	56	431	15	20	6	3.4	.957	J. Zinn	32	127	7	6	4	3.68
LF	C. Bigbee	632	.323	3	42	351	27	9	6	2.7	.977	H. Carlson	31	110	4	8	4	4.27
C	W. Schmidt	393	.282	0	38	438	120	8	15	5.1	.986							
23	C. Tierney	442	.299	3	52	191	237	18	37		.960							
OF	D. Robertson	230	.322	6	48	117	2	5	0	2.1	.960							

St. L. W-87 L-66 — Branch Rickey

POS	Player	AB	BA	HR	RBI	PO	A	E	DP	TC/G	FA	Pitcher	G	IP	W	L	SV	ERA
1B	J. Fournier	574	.343	16	86	1416	73	19	91	10.1	.987	J. Haines	37	244	18	12	0	3.50
2B	R. Hornsby	592	.397	21	126	305	477	25	59	5.7	.969	B. Pertica	38	208	14	10	2	3.37
SS	D. Lavan	560	.259	2	82	382	540	49	88	6.5	.950	B. Doak	32	209	15	6	1	2.59
3B	M. Stock	587	.307	3	84	148	243	25	21	2.8	.940	R. Walker	38	171	11	12	3	4.22
RF	J. Smith	411	.328	7	33	179	11	9	3	1.9	.955	B. Sherdel	38	144	9	8	1	3.18
CF	L. Mann	256	.328	7	30	174	11	6	2	2.4	.969	J. Pfeffer	19	99	9	3	0	4.29
LF	A. McHenry	574	.350	17	102	371	13	14	3	2.6	.965	L. North	40	86	4	4	7	3.54
C	V. Clemons	341	.320	2	48	357	101	7	12	4.3	.985							
OF	J. Schultz	275	.309	6	45	120	7	3	4	1.9	.977							
OF	H. Mueller	176	.352	1	34	117	5	3	1	2.3	.976							
C	P. Dillhoefer	162	.241	0	15	170	52	11	0	3.4	.953							
OF	C. Heathcote	156	.244	0	9	83	5	7	0	1.9	.926							

Bos. W-79 L-74 — Fred Mitchell

POS	Player	AB	BA	HR	RBI	PO	A	E	DP	TC/G	FA	Pitcher	G	IP	W	L	SV	ERA
1B	W. Holke	579	.261	3	63	1471	86	4	100	10.4	.997	J. Oeschger	46	299	20	14	0	3.52
2B	H. Ford	555	.279	2	61	297	417	20	48	6.2	.973	M. Watson	44	259	14	13	2	3.85
SS	W. Barbare	550	.302	0	49	294	393	31	58	5.9	.957	H. McQuillan	45	250	13	17	5	4.00
3B	T. Boeckel	592	.313	10	84	184	276	33	19	3.2	.933	D. Fillingim	44	240	15	10	1	3.45
RF	B. Southworth	569	.308	7	79	288	25	8	6	2.3	.975	J. Scott	47	234	15	13	3	3.70
CF	R. Powell	624	.306	12	74	377	21	19	3	2.8	.954							
LF	W. Cruise	344	.346	8	55	232	2	9	3	2.4	.963							
C	M. O'Neil	277	.249	2	29	276	117	13	8	4.3	.968							
OF	F. Nicholson	245	.327	5	41	112	4	2	0	2.0	.983							
C	H. Gowdy	164	.299	2	17	162	50	4	3	4.1	.981							

Bkn. W-77 L-75 — Wilbert Robinson

POS	Player	AB	BA	HR	RBI	PO	A	E	DP	TC/G	FA	Pitcher	G	IP	W	L	SV	ERA
1B	R. Schmandt	350	.306	1	43	941	52	11	74	10.9	.989	B. Grimes	37	302	22	13	0	2.83
2B	P. Kilduff	372	.288	3	45	243	379	24	57	6.2	.963	D. Ruether	36	211	10	13	2	4.26
SS	I. Olson	652	.267	3	35	343	465	49	77	6.4	.943	L. Cadore	35	212	13	14	0	4.17
3B	J. Johnston	624	.325	5	56	162	312	33	34	3.4	.935	C. Mitchell	37	190	11	9	2	2.89
RF	T. Griffith	455	.312	12	71	215	27	7	5	2.0	.972	S. Smith	35	175	7	11	4	3.90
CF	H. Myers	549	.288	4	68	278	25	10	5	2.5	.968	J. Miljus	28	94	6	3	1	4.23
LF	Z. Wheat	568	.320	14	85	283	18	11	3	2.1	.965							
C	O. Miller	286	.234	1	27	338	107	13	10	5.0	.972							
OF	B. Neis	230	.257	4	34	126	13	8	1	1.9	.946							
1B	E. Konetchy	197	.269	3	23	564	28	8*	41	11.1*	.987							
C	E. Krueger	163	.264	3	20	179	39	7	4	4.3	.969							

Cin. W-70 L-83 — Pat Moran

POS	Player	AB	BA	HR	RBI	PO	A	E	DP	TC/G	FA	Pitcher	G	IP	W	L	SV	ERA
1B	J. Daubert	516	.306	2	64	1290	78	10	98	10.1	.993	D. Luque	41	304	17	19	3	3.38
2B	S. Bohne	613	.285	3	44	256	327	16	56	5.9	.973	E. Rixey	40	301	19	18	1	2.78
SS	L. Kopf	367	.218	1	25	195	304	28	39	5.7	.947	R. Marquard	39	266	17	14	0	3.39
3B	H. Groh	357	.331	0	48	97	188	15	27	3.1	.950	P. Donohue	21	118	7	6	1	3.35
RF	R. Bressler	323	.307	1	54	155	6	8	2	2.0	.953	L. Brenton	17	60	1	8	1	4.05
CF	E. Roush	418	.352	4	71	286	9	6	0	2.8	.980							
LF	P. Duncan	532	.308	2	60	349	19	11	2	2.6	.971							
C	I. Wingo	295	.268	3	38	318	101	18	11	4.8	.959							
UT	L. Fonseca	297	.276	1	41	307	155	14	30		.971							
C	B. Hargrave	263	.289	1	38	270	50	9	2	4.5	.973							
OF	G. Neale	241	.241	0	12	128	7	5	2	2.3	.964							
SS	S. Crane	215	.233	0	16	129	173	15	32	5.0	.953							

Chi. W-64 L-89 — Johnny Evers W-42 L-56 / Bill Killefer W-22 L-33

POS	Player	AB	BA	HR	RBI	PO	A	E	DP	TC/G	FA	Pitcher	G	IP	W	L	SV	ERA
1B	R. Grimes	530	.321	6	79	1544	68	12	93	11.0	.993	G. Alexander	31	252	15	13	1	3.39
2B	Z. Terry	488	.275	2	45	272	413	20	57	5.7	.972	S. Martin	37	217	11	15	1	4.35
SS	C. Hollocher	558	.289	3	37	282	491	30	72	5.9	.963	B. Freeman	38	177	9	10	3	4.11
3B	C. Deal	422	.289	3	66	122	239	10	19	3.3	.973	V. Cheeves	37	163	11	12	0	4.64
RF	M. Flack	572	.301	6	37	244	19	3	2	2.0	.989	L. York	40	139	5	9	1	4.73
CF	G. Maisel	393	.310	0	43	259	12	6	2	2.6	.978	H. Vaughn	17	109	3	11	0	6.01
LF	T. Barber	452	.314	1	54	234	23	8	4	2.2	.970							
C	B. O'Farrell	260	.250	4	32	269	87	12	8	4.1	.967							
UT	J. Kelleher	301	.309	4	47	192	194	15	31		.963							
OF	J. Sullivan	240	.329	4	41	122	3	5	0	2.0	.962							
OF	B. Twombly	175	.377	1	18	81	11	3	0	2.1	.968							
C	T. Daly	143	.238	0	22	171	48	6	10	4.8	.973							

	POS	Player	AB	BA	HR	RBI	PO	A	E	DP	TC/G	FA	Pitcher	G	IP	W	L	SV	ERA
Phi.	1B	E. Konetchy	268	.321	8	59	771	55	12*	38	11.8*	.986	J. Ring	34	246	10	19	1	4.24
W-51 L-103	2B	J. Smith	247	.231	4	22	125	239	11	19	5.7	.971	G. Smith	39	221	4	**20**	1	4.76
Wild Bill Donovan	SS	F. Parkinson	391	.253	5	32	233	404	47	55	6.5	.931	B. Hubbell	36	220	9	16	2	4.33
W-31 L-71	3B	Wrightstone	372	.296	9	51	58	108	14	6	3.3	.922	L. Meadows	28	194	11	16	0	4.31
Kaiser Wilhelm	RF	LeBourveau	281	.295	6	35	126	7	13	2	1.9	.911	J. Winters	18	114	5	10	0	3.63
W-20 L-32	CF	C. Williams	562	.320	18	75	382	29	9	5	2.9	.979	H. Betts	32	101	3	7	4	4.47
	LF	I. Meusel	343	.353	12	58	153	18	13	4	2.2	.929							
	C	F. Bruggy	277	.310	5	28	231	73	15	14	3.7	.953							
	3 1	D. Miller	320	.297	0	23	433	96	18	35		.967							
	1 O	C. Lee	286	.308	4	29	542	22	10	35		.983							
	2B	J. Rawlings	254	.291	1	16	138*	215*	17*	32*	6.2	.954							
	OF	L. King	216	.269	4	32	115	8	12	0	2.4	.911							
	SS	R. Miller	204	.304	3	26	91	132	22	20	5.3	.910							
	3B	G. Rapp	202	.277	1	10	62	90	8	7	3.2*	.950							
	C	J. Peters	155	.290	3	23	116	24	10	0	3.4	.933							

BATTING AND BASE RUNNING LEADERS

Batting Average
R. Hornsby, STL	.397
E. Roush, CIN	.352
A. McHenry, STL	.350
W. Cruise, BOS	.346
J. Fournier, STL	.343

Slugging Average
R. Hornsby, STL	.639
A. McHenry, STL	.531
G. Kelly, NY	.528
I. Meusel, NY, PHI	.515
J. Fournier, STL	.505

Home Runs
G. Kelly, NY	23
R. Hornsby, STL	21
C. Williams, PHI	18
A. McHenry, STL	17
J. Fournier, STL	16

Total Bases
R. Hornsby, STL	378
G. Kelly, NY	310
A. McHenry, STL	305
I. Meusel, NY, PHI	302
F. Frisch, NY	300

Runs Batted In
R. Hornsby, STL	126
G. Kelly, NY	122
R. Youngs, NY	102
A. McHenry, STL	102
F. Frisch, NY	100

Stolen Bases
F. Frisch, NY	49
M. Carey, PIT	37
J. Johnston, BKN	28
S. Bohne, CIN	26
R. Maranville, PIT	25

Hits
R. Hornsby, STL	235
F. Frisch, NY	211
C. Bigbee, PIT	204

Base on Balls
G. Burns, NY	80
R. Youngs, NY	71
M. Carey, PIT	70
R. Grimes, CHI	70

Home Run Percentage
G. Kelly, NY	3.9
R. Hornsby, STL	3.5
C. Williams, PHI	3.2

Runs Scored
R. Hornsby, STL	131
D. Bancroft, NY	121
F. Frisch, NY	121

Doubles
R. Hornsby, STL	44
G. Kelly, NY	42
J. Johnston, BKN	41

Triples
R. Hornsby, STL	18
R. Powell, BOS	18

PITCHING LEADERS

Winning Percentage
B. Doak, STL	.714
A. Nehf, NY	.667
B. Grimes, BKN	.629
J. Barnes, NY	.625
F. Toney, NY	.621

Earned Run Average
B. Doak, STL	2.59
B. Adams, PIT	2.64
W. Glazner, PIT	2.77
E. Rixey, CIN	2.78
B. Grimes, BKN	2.83

Wins
B. Grimes, BKN	22
W. Cooper, PIT	22
A. Nehf, NY	20
J. Oeschger, BOS	20
E. Rixey, CIN	19

Saves
L. North, STL	7
J. Barnes, NY	6
H. McQuillan, BOS	5

Strikeouts
B. Grimes, BKN	136
W. Cooper, PIT	134
D. Luque, CIN	102
H. McQuillan, BOS	94

Complete Games
B. Grimes, BKN	30
W. Cooper, PIT	29
D. Luque, CIN	25
G. Alexander, CHI	21
J. Ring, PHI	21
E. Rixey, CIN	21

Fewest Hits per 9 Innings
J. Morrison, PIT	8.19
W. Glazner, PIT	8.23
B. Adams, PIT	8.72

Shutouts
7 tied with	3

Fewest Walks per 9 Innings
B. Adams, PIT	1.01
G. Alexander, CHI	1.18
J. Barnes, NY	1.53

Most Strikeouts per 9 Inn.
B. Grimes, BKN	4.05
W. Cooper, PIT	3.69
B. Doak, STL	3.58

Innings
W. Cooper, PIT	327
D. Luque, CIN	304
B. Grimes, BKN	302

Games Pitched
J. Scott, BOS	47
J. Oeschger, BOS	46
H. McQuillan, BOS	45

	W	L	PCT	GB	R	OR	2B	3B	HR	BA	SA	SB	E	DP	FA	CG	BB	SO	ShO	SV	ERA
NY	94	59	.614		**840**	637	237	93	75	.298	.421	**137**	187	**155**	.971	71	**295**	357	9	**18**	3.55
PIT	90	63	.588	4	692	**595**	231	**104**	37	.285	.387	134	172	129	.973	**88**	322	**500**	10	10	**3.17**
STL	87	66	.569	7	809	681	**260**	88	83	**.308**	**.437**	94	219	130	.965	71	399	464	10	16	3.62
BOS	79	74	.516	15	721	697	209	100	61	.290	.400	94	199	122	.969	74	420	382	**11**	12	3.62
BKN	77	75	.507	16.5	667	681	209	85	59	.280	.386	91	232	142	.964	82	361	471	8	12	3.90
CIN	70	83	.458	24	618	649	221	94	20	.278	.370	117	193	139	.969	83	305	408	7	9	3.70
CHI	64	89	.418	30	668	773	234	56	37	.292	.378	70	**166**	129	**.974**	73	409	441	7	7	3.46
PHI	51	103	.331	43.5	617	919	238	50	**88**	.284	.397	66	295	127	.955	82	371	333	5	8	4.48
					5632	5632	1839	670	460	.289	.397	803	1663	1073	.967	624	2882	3356	67	92	3.78

N. Y. — W-98 L-55 — Miller Huggins

POS	Player	AB	BA	HR	RBI	PO	A	E	DP	TC/G	FA
1B	W. Pipp	588	.296	8	97	1624	89	16	116	11.3	.991
2B	A. Ward	556	.306	5	75	262	409	26	35	5.7	.963
SS	Peckinpaugh	577	.288	8	71	318	443	42	75	5.4	.948
3B	F. Baker	330	.294	9	71	84	173	11	16	3.2	.959
RF	B. Meusel	598	.318	24	135	253	28	20	8	2.0	.934
CF	E. Miller	242	.298	4	36	134	10	8	2	2.7	.947
LF	B. Ruth	540	.378	59	171	348	17	13	6	2.5	.966
C	W. Schang	424	.316	6	55	500	101	19	13	4.7	.969
3B	M. McNally	215	.260	1	24	54	131	5	5	4.0	.974
OF	C. Fewster	207	.280	1	19	71	5	2	1	1.8	.974
P	C. Mays	143	.343	2	22	8	104	2	4	2.3	.982

Pitcher	G	IP	W	L	SV	ERA
C. Mays	49	337	27	9	7	3.05
W. Hoyt	43	282	19	13	3	3.09
B. Shawkey	38	245	18	12	2	4.08
R. Collins	28	137	11	5	0	5.44
J. Quinn	33	129	8	7	0	3.48

Cle. — W-94 L-60 — Tris Speaker

POS	Player	AB	BA	HR	RBI	PO	A	E	DP	TC/G	FA
1B	D. Johnston	384	.297	2	44	960	62	12	72	8.9	.988
2B	B. Wambsganss	410	.285	2	46	268	255	20	51	5.3	.963
SS	J. Sewell	572	.318	4	91	319	480	47	75	5.5	.944
3B	L. Gardner	586	.319	3	115	179	335	27	23	3.6	.950
RF	E. Smith	431	.290	16	84	183	16	6	1	1.6	.971
CF	T. Speaker	506	.362	3	74	345	15	6	2	2.9	.984
LF	C. Jamieson	536	.310	1	45	277	17	8	3	2.2	.974
C	S. O'Neill	335	.322	1	50	393	92	9	8	4.7	.982
1B	G. Burns	244	.361	0	48	534	41	6	40	8.0	.990
2B	R. Stephenson	206	.330	2	34	122	153	17	30	5.4	.942
OF	J. Wood	194	.366	4	60	105	3	3	1	1.7	.973
OF	J. Evans	153	.333	0	21	90	8	7	2	2.2	.933
C	L. Nunamaker	131	.359	0	24	166	31	6	3	4.4	.970

Pitcher	G	IP	W	L	SV	ERA
S. Coveleski	43	316	23	13	2	3.36
G. Uhle	41	238	16	13	2	4.01
D. Mails	34	194	14	8	2	3.94
J. Bagby	40	192	14	12	4	4.70
R. Caldwell	37	147	6	6	4	4.90
A. Sothoron	22	145	12	4	0	3.24
G. Morton	30	108	8	3	0	2.76

St. L. — W-81 L-73 — Lee Fohl

POS	Player	AB	BA	HR	RBI	PO	A	E	DP	TC/G	FA
1B	G. Sisler	582	.371	11	104	1267	108	10	86	10.0	.993
2B	M. McManus	412	.260	3	64	212	269	24	44	5.3	.952
SS	W. Gerber	436	.278	2	48	269	331	36	60	5.6	.943
3B	F. Ellerbe	430	.288	2	48	158	226	19	9	3.8	.953
RF	J. Tobin	671	.352	8	59	277	28	14	5	2.1	.956
CF	B. Jacobson	599	.352	5	90	375	7	7	1	2.8	.982
LF	K. Williams	547	.347	24	117	331	24	26	3	2.6	.932
C	H. Severeid	472	.324	2	78	481	117	17	11	4.9	.972
S2	D. Lee	180	.167	0	11	138	151	19	30		.938

Pitcher	G	IP	W	L	SV	ERA
U. Shocker	47	327	27	12	4	3.55
D. Davis	40	265	16	16	0	4.44
E. Vangilder	31	180	11	12	0	3.94
R. Kolp	37	167	8	7	0	4.97
B. Bayne	47	164	11	5	3	4.72
E. Palmero	24	90	4	7	0	5.00

Was. — W-80 L-73 — George McBride

POS	Player	AB	BA	HR	RBI	PO	A	E	DP	TC/G	FA
1B	J. Judge	622	.301	7	72	1417	89	6	109	9.9	.996
2B	B. Harris	584	.289	0	54	407	481	38	91	6.0	.959
SS	F. O'Rourke	444	.234	3	54	272	378	55	52	5.8	.922
3B	H. Shanks	562	.302	7	69	218	330	23	35	3.7	.960
RF	C. Milan	406	.288	1	40	196	19	16	2	2.4	.931
CF	S. Rice	561	.330	4	79	380	18	15	3	2.9	.964
LF	B. Miller	420	.288	9	71	247	13	15	4	2.5	.945
C	P. Gharrity	387	.310	7	55	408	110	12	14	4.6	.977
OF	F. Brower	203	.261	1	35	88	10	9	3	2.3	.916
OF	E. Smith	180	.217	2	12	84	10	5	2	2.3	.949

Pitcher	G	IP	W	L	SV	ERA
G. Mogridge	38	288	18	14	0	3.00
W. Johnson	35	264	17	14	1	3.51
T. Zachary	39	250	18	16	1	3.96
E. Erickson	32	179	8	10	0	3.62
H. Courtney	30	133	6	9	1	5.63
J. Acosta	33	116	5	4	3	4.36
A. Schacht	29	83	6	6	1	4.90

Bos. — W-75 L-79 — Hugh Duffy

POS	Player	AB	BA	HR	RBI	PO	A	E	DP	TC/G	FA
1B	S. McInnis	584	.307	0	74	1549	102	1	109	10.9	.999
2B	D. Pratt	521	.324	5	100	283	408	28	90	5.4	.961
SS	E. Scott	576	.262	1	60	380	528	26	94	6.1	.972
3B	E. Foster	412	.284	0	30	74	189	16	18	3.0	.943
RF	S. Collins	542	.286	4	65	264	22	10	8	2.1	.966
CF	N. Leibold	467	.306	0	30	283	15	16	9	2.7	.949
LF	M. Menosky	477	.300	3	43	278	12	9	3	2.2	.970
C	M. Ruel	358	.277	1	43	375	86	11	7	4.3	.977
3B	O. Vitt	232	.190	0	12	63	138	8	14	2.9	.962
C	R. Walters	169	.201	0	13	232	53	3	11	5.3	.990
OF	T. Hendryx	137	.241	0	21	66	2	3	0	1.7	.958

Pitcher	G	IP	W	L	SV	ERA
S. Jones	40	299	23	16	1	3.22
J. Bush	37	254	16	9	1	3.50
H. Pennock	32	223	12	14	0	4.04
A. Russell	39	173	7	11	3	4.11
E. Myers	30	172	8	12	0	4.87
B. Karr	26	118	8	7	0	3.67

Det. — W-71 L-82 — Ty Cobb

POS	Player	AB	BA	HR	RBI	PO	A	E	DP	TC/G	FA
1B	L. Blue	585	.308	5	75	1478	85	16	75	10.4	.990
2B	R. Young	401	.299	0	29	285	270	31	44	5.5	.947
SS	D. Bush	402	.281	0	27	172	260	23	35	5.6	.949
3B	B. Jones	554	.303	1	72	194	324	27	12	3.9	.950
RF	H. Heilmann	602	.394	19	139	233	10	10	1	1.8	.960
CF	T. Cobb	507	.389	12	101	301	27	10	2	2.8	.970
LF	B. Veach	612	.338	16	128	384	21	11	4	2.8	.974
C	J. Bassler	388	.307	0	56	433	113	14	7	4.9	.975
SS	I. Flagstead	259	.305	0	31	111	139	27	8	5.0	.903
OF	C. Shorten	217	.272	0	23	101	3	2	2	2.0	.981
UT	J. Sargent	178	.253	2	22	112	134	21	21		.921

Pitcher	G	IP	W	L	SV	ERA
D. Leonard	36	245	11	13	1	3.75
H. Dauss	32	233	10	15	1	4.33
R. Oldham	40	229	11	14	1	4.24
H. Ehmke	30	196	13	14	0	4.54
C. Holling	35	136	3	7	4	4.30
J. Middleton	38	122	6	11	7	5.03
B. Cole	20	110	7	4	1	4.27

Chi. — W-62 L-92 — Kid Gleason

POS	Player	AB	BA	HR	RBI	PO	A	E	DP	TC/G	FA
1B	E. Sheely	563	.304	11	95	1637	119	22	121	11.5	.988
2B	E. Collins	526	.337	2	58	376	458	28	84	6.3	.968
SS	E. Johnson	613	.295	1	51	291	494	44	80	5.9	.947
3B	E. Mulligan	609	.251	1	45	162	307	22	28	3.2	.955
RF	H. Hooper	419	.327	8	58	182	12	5	3	1.8	.975
CF	A. Strunk	401	.332	3	69	214	10	7	2	2.1	.970
LF	B. Falk	585	.285	5	82	288	9	13	5	2.1	.958
C	R. Schalk	416	.252	0	47	453	129	9	19	4.7	.985
OF	J. Mostil	326	.301	3	42	215	12	13	1	2.6	.946
UT	H. McClellan	196	.179	1	14	112	141	8	23		.969

Pitcher	G	IP	W	L	SV	ERA
R. Faber	43	331	25	15	1	2.48
D. Kerr	44	309	19	17	1	4.72
R. Wilkinson	36	198	4	20	3	5.13
S. Hodge	36	143	6	8	2	6.56
D. McWeeny	27	98	3	6	2	6.08
D. Mulrenan	12	56	2	8	0	7.23

	POS	Player	AB	BA	HR	RBI	PO	A	E	DP	TC/G	FA	Pitcher	G	IP	W	L	SV	ERA
Phi.	1B	J. Walker	423	.258	2	45	1008	49	12	71	10.8	.989	E. Rommel	46	285	16	23	3	3.94
W-53 L-100	2B	J. Dykes	613	.274	17	77	434	522	46	88	6.5	.954	S. Harriss	39	228	11	16	2	4.27
Connie Mack	SS	C. Galloway	465	.265	3	47	205	305	43	52	5.0	.922	R. Moore	29	192	10	10	0	4.51
	3B	J. Dugan	461	.295	10	58	118	208	16	19	2.9	.953	B. Hasty	35	179	5	16	0	4.87
	RF	W. Witt	629	.315	4	45	288	15	13	3	2.1	.959	D. Keefe	44	173	2	9	1	4.68
	CF	F. Welch	403	.285	7	45	251	16	16	1	2.7	.943	R. Naylor	32	169	3	13	0	4.84
	LF	T. Walker	556	.304	23	101	337	24	17	3	2.7	.955	S. Perry	12	70	3	6	1	4.11
	C	C. Perkins	538	.288	12	73	540	137	20	16	4.9	.971							
	1B	F. Brazill	177	.271	0	19	340	22	6	28	10.2	.984							
	SS	E. McCann	157	.223	0	15	55	93	8	12	4.9	.949							

BATTING AND BASE RUNNING LEADERS

Batting Average

H. Heilmann, DET	.394
T. Cobb, DET	.389
B. Ruth, NY	.378
G. Sisler, STL	.371
T. Speaker, CLE	.362

Home Runs

B. Ruth, NY	59
K. Williams, STL	24
B. Meusel, NY	24
T. Walker, PHI	23
H. Heilmann, DET	19

Runs Batted In

B. Ruth, NY	171
H. Heilmann, DET	139
B. Meusel, NY	135
B. Veach, DET	128
K. Williams, STL	117

Hits

H. Heilmann, DET	237
J. Tobin, STL	236
G. Sisler, STL	216

Home Run Percentage

B. Ruth, NY	10.9
K. Williams, STL	4.4
T. Walker, PHI	4.1

Doubles

T. Speaker, CLE	52
B. Ruth, NY	44
H. Heilmann, DET	43
B. Veach, DET	43

Slugging Average

B. Ruth, NY	.846
H. Heilmann, DET	.606
T. Cobb, DET	.596
K. Williams, STL	.561
B. Meusel, NY	.559

Total Bases

B. Ruth, NY	457
H. Heilmann, DET	365
B. Meusel, NY	334
J. Tobin, STL	327
B. Veach, DET	324

Stolen Bases

G. Sisler, STL	35
B. Harris, WAS	29
S. Rice, WAS	25
T. Cobb, DET	22
E. Johnson, CHI	22

Base on Balls

B. Ruth, NY	144
L. Blue, DET	103
Peckinpaugh, NY	84

Runs Scored

B. Ruth, NY	177
J. Tobin, STL	132
Peckinpaugh, NY	128

Triples

H. Shanks, WAS	19
G. Sisler, STL	18
J. Tobin, STL	18

PITCHING LEADERS

Winning Percentage

C. Mays, NY	.750
U. Shocker, STL	.692
J. Bush, BOS	.640
S. Coveleski, CLE	.639
R. Faber, CHI	.625

Wins

C. Mays, NY	27
U. Shocker, STL	27
R. Faber, CHI	25
S. Coveleski, CLE	23
S. Jones, BOS	23

Strikeouts

W. Johnson, WAS	143
U. Shocker, STL	132
B. Shawkey, NY	126
R. Faber, CHI	124
D. Leonard, DET	120

Fewest Hits per 9 Innings

R. Faber, CHI	7.97
J. Bush, BOS	8.63
C. Mays, NY	8.88

Fewest Walks per 9 Innings

C. Mays, NY	2.03
G. Mogridge, WAS	2.06
J. Bagby, CLE	2.07

Innings

C. Mays, NY	337
R. Faber, CHI	331
U. Shocker, STL	327

Earned Run Average

R. Faber, CHI	2.48
G. Mogridge, WAS	3.00
C. Mays, NY	3.05
W. Hoyt, NY	3.09
S. Jones, BOS	3.22

Saves

J. Middleton, DET	7
C. Mays, NY	7
J. Bagby, CLE	4
R. Caldwell, CLE	4
U. Shocker, STL	4
C. Holling, DET	4

Complete Games

R. Faber, CHI	32
U. Shocker, STL	31
C. Mays, NY	30
S. Coveleski, CLE	29

Shutouts

S. Jones, BOS	5
G. Mogridge, WAS	4
R. Faber, CHI	4
U. Shocker, STL	4

Most Strikeouts per 9 Inn.

W. Johnson, WAS	4.87
B. Shawkey, NY	4.63
D. Leonard, DET	4.41

Games Pitched

C. Mays, NY	49
U. Shocker, STL	47
B. Bayne, STL	47

	W	L	PCT	GB	R	OR	2B	3B	Batting HR	BA	SA	SB	E	Fielding DP	FA	CG	BB	Pitching SO	ShO	SV	ERA
NY	98	55	.641		948	708	285	87	134	.300	.464	89	222	138	.965	92	470	481	7	15	3.79
CLE	94	60	.610	4.5	925	712	355	90	42	.308	.430	58	204	124	.967	81	430	475	11	14	3.90
STL	81	73	.526	17.5	835	845	246	106	66	.304	.425	92	224	127	.964	79	557	478	9	9	4.62
WAS	80	73	.523	18	704	738	240	96	42	.277	.383	111	235	153	.963	80	442	452	8	10	3.97
BOS	75	79	.487	23.5	668	696	248	69	17	.277	.361	83	157	151	.975	88	452	446	9	5	3.98
DET	71	82	.464	27	883	852	268	100	58	.316	.433	95	232	107	.963	73	495	452	4	17	4.40
CHI	62	92	.403	36.5	683	858	242	82	35	.283	.379	97	200	155	.969	86	549	392	7	9	4.94
PHI	53	100	.346	45	657	894	256	64	83	.274	.390	68	274	144	.958	75	548	431	1	7	4.60
					6303	6303	2140	694	477	.292	.408	693	1748	1099	.965	654	3943	3607	56	86	4.28

POS	Player	AB	BA	HR	RBI	PO	A	E	DP	TC/G	FA	Pitcher	G	IP	W	L	SV	ERA
N. Y. W-93 L-61 John McGraw																		
1B	G. Kelly	592	.328	17	107	1642	103	13	123	11.6	.993	A. Nehf	37	268	19	13	1	3.29
2B	F. Frisch	514	.327	5	51	176	288	12	40	5.6	.975	J. Barnes	37	213	13	8	0	3.51
SS	D. Bancroft	651	.321	4	60	405	579	62	93	6.7	.941	R. Ryan	46	192	17	12	3	3.01
3B	H. Groh	426	.265	3	51	100	207	11	25	2.9	.965	P. Douglas	24	158	11	4	0	2.63
RF	R. Youngs	559	.331	7	86	280	28	19	6	2.2	.942	C. Jonnard	33	96	6	1	5	3.84
CF	C. Stengel	250	.368	7	48	179	7	6	2	2.5	.969	H. McQuillan	15	94	6	5	1	3.82
LF	I. Meusel	617	.331	16	132	279	15	6	1	1.9	.980	F. Toney	13	86	5	6	0	4.17
C	F. Snyder	318	.343	5	51	272	74	7	10	3.6	.980	J. Scott	17	80	8	2	2	4.41
2B	J. Rawlings	308	.282	1	30	166	252	7	44	5.5	.984							
C	E. Smith	234	.278	9	39	214	56	6	3	3.7	.978							
OF	B. Cunningham	229	.328	2	33	155	7	2	3	2.3	.988							
Cin. W-86 L-68 Pat Moran																		
1B	J. Daubert	610	.336	12	66	1652	79	11	127	11.2	.994	E. Rixey	40	313	25	13	0	3.53
2B	S. Bohne	383	.274	3	51	183	320	22	50	6.2	.958	J. Couch	43	264	16	9	1	3.89
SS	I. Caveney	394	.239	3	54	256	404	47	74	6.0	.934	D. Luque	39	261	13	23	0	3.31
3B	B. Pinelli	547	.305	1	72	204	350	32	19	3.8	.945	P. Donohue	33	242	18	9	1	3.12
RF	G. Harper	430	.340	2	68	220	15	11	2	2.3	.955	C. Keck	27	131	7	6	1	3.37
CF	G. Burns	631	.285	1	53	386	20	10	3	2.7	.976							
LF	P. Duncan	607	.328	8	94	316	19	10	4	2.3	.971							
C	B. Hargrave	320	.316	7	57	261	60	6	5	3.8	.982							
2B	L. Fonseca	291	.361	4	45	197	251	14	40	6.5	.970							
C	I. Wingo	260	.285	3	45	211	81	11	6	3.9	.964							
OF	E. Roush	165	.352	1	24	96	8	1	0	2.4	.990							
Pit. W-85 L-69 George Gibson W-32 L-33 Bill McKechnie W-53 L-36																		
1B	C. Grimm	593	.292	0	76	1478	68	10	104	10.1	.994	W. Cooper	41	295	23	14	0	3.18
2B	C. Tierney	441	.345	7	86	179	302	18	52	4.8	.964	J. Morrison	45	286	17	11	1	3.43
SS	R. Maranville	672	.295	0	63	359	453	33	81	6.1	.961	W. Glazner	34	193	11	12	1	4.38
3B	P. Traynor	571	.282	4	81	147	216	21	19	3.1	.945	B. Adams	27	171	8	11	0	3.57
RF	R. Russell	220	.368	12	75	115	5	4	2	2.1	.969	E. Hamilton	33	160	11	7	2	3.99
CF	M. Carey	629	.329	10	70	449	22	15	4	3.1	.969	H. Carlson	39	145	9	12	2	5.70
LF	C. Bigbee	614	.350	5	99	345	27	17	5	2.6	.956							
C	J. Gooch	353	.329	1	42	382	102	15	10	4.8	.970							
3O	C. Barnhart	209	.330	1	38	76	34	8	4		.932							
C	W. Schmidt	152	.329	0	22	159	22	1	1	4.6	.995							
OF	R. Rohwer	129	.295	3	22	56	5	4	1	2.2	.938							
St. L. W-85 L-69 Branch Rickey																		
1B	J. Fournier	404	.295	10	61	902	60	18	63	9.0	.982	J. Pfeffer	44	261	19	12	2	3.58
2B	R. Hornsby	623	.401	42	152	398	473	30	81	5.9	.967	B. Sherdel	47	241	17	13	2	3.88
SS	S. Toporcer	352	.324	3	36	168	246	27	31	4.8	.939	J. Haines	29	183	11	9	0	3.84
3B	M. Stock	581	.305	5	79	172	245	22	22	2.9	.950	B. Doak	37	180	11	13	2	5.54
RF	M. Flack	267	.292	2	21	116	5	4	3	1.9	.968	L. North	53	150	10	3	4	4.45
CF	J. Smith	510	.310	8	46	282	11	15	3	2.3	.951	B. Pertica	34	117	8	8	0	5.91
LF	J. Schultz	344	.314	2	64	195	7	5	1	2.3	.976	C. Barfoot	42	118	4	5	2	4.21
C	E. Ainsmith	379	.293	13	59	428	99	20	14	4.7	.963							
SS	D. Lavan	264	.227	0	27	169	246	28	40	5.4	.937							
OF	A. McHenry	238	.303	5	43	132	13	10	3	2.5	.935							
C	V. Clemons	160	.256	0	15	172	50	1	2	3.5	.996							
OF	H. Mueller	159	.270	3	26	83	6	5	2	2.1	.947							
1B	J. Bottomley	151	.325	5	35	346	12	5	20	10.7	.986							
OF	L. Mann	147	.347	2	20	87	3	2	1	1.6	.978							
OF	R. Blades	130	.300	3	21	61	6	5	0	2.5	.931							
1B	D. Gainor	97	.268	2	23	175	9	4	6	7.2	.979							
Chi. W-80 L-74 Bill Killefer																		
1B	R. Grimes	509	.354	14	99	1378	68	19	106	10.6	.987	V. Aldridge	36	258	16	15	0	3.52
2B	Z. Terry	496	.286	0	67	298	442	28	75	6.1	.964	G. Alexander	33	246	16	13	1	3.63
SS	C. Hollocher	592	.340	3	69	332	502	30	89	5.7	.965	T. Osborne	41	184	9	5	3	4.50
3B	M. Krug	450	.276	4	60	129	184	21	19	3.2	.937	V. Cheeves	39	183	12	11	2	4.09
RF	B. Friberg	296	.311	0	23	126	13	4	5	1.9	.972	P. Jones	44	164	8	9	3	4.72
CF	J. Statz	462	.297	1	34	309	16	14	4	3.1	.959	T. Kaufmann	37	153	7	13	3	4.06
LF	H. Miller	466	.352	12	78	219	15	10	3	2.1	.959	G. Stueland	34	111	9	4	0	5.92
C	B. O'Farrell	392	.324	4	60	446	143	14	22	4.8	.977							
OF	C. Heathcote	243	.280	1	34	131	5	2	1	2.3	.986							
OF	T. Barber	226	.310	0	29	78	4	4	2	1.8	.953							
3B	J. Kelleher	193	.259	0	20	44	93	10	9	3.2	.932							
OF	M. Callaghan	175	.257	0	20	85	2	5	0	1.7	.946							
Bkn. W-76 L-78 Wilbert Robinson																		
1B	R. Schmandt	396	.268	2	44	1017	65	12	83	9.9	.989	D. Ruether	35	267	21	12	0	3.53
2B	I. Olson	551	.272	1	47	193	283	20	43	5.8	.960	B. Grimes	36	259	17	14	1	4.76
SS	J. Johnston	567	.319	4	49	102	189	16	33	6.1	.948	D. Vance	36	246	18	12	0	3.70
3B	A. High	579	.283	6	65	131	257	17	23	3.1	.958	L. Cadore	29	190	8	15	0	4.35
RF	T. Griffith	329	.316	4	49	167	13	9	4	2.3	.974	S. Smith	28	109	4	8	2	4.56
CF	H. Myers	618	.317	6	89	399	16	11	2	2.8	.974	H. Shriver	25	108	4	6	0	2.99
LF	Z. Wheat	600	.335	16	112	317	14	3	1	2.2	.991							
C	H. DeBerry	259	.301	3	35	309	64	11	5	4.7	.971							
OF	B. Griffith	325	.308	2	35	148	7	3	3	2.1	.981							
C	O. Miller	180	.261	1	23	216	56	9	3	4.9	.968							
1B	C. Mitchell	155	.290	3	28	365	27	3	32	9.4	.992							
P	D. Ruether	125	.208	2	20	9	56	0	6	1.9	1.000							

	POS	Player	AB	BA	HR	RBI	PO	A	E	DP	TC/G	FA	Pitcher	G	IP	W	L	SV	ERA
Phi.	1B	R. Leslie	513	.271	6	50	1517	63	16	110	11.5	.990	J. Ring	40	249	12	18	1	4.58
W-57 L-96	2B	F. Parkinson	545	.275	15	70	323	562	34	78	6.6	.963	L. Meadows	33	237	12	18	0	4.03
Kaiser Wilhelm	SS	A. Fletcher	396	.280	7	53	202	379	38	63	5.8	.939	G. Smith	42	194	5	14	0	4.78
	3B	G. Rapp	502	.253	0	38	117	249	20	20	3.3	.948	B. Hubbell	35	189	7	15	1	5.00
	RF	C. Walker	581	.337	12	89	295	24	15	8	2.3	.955	L. Weinert	34	167	8	11	1	3.40
	CF	C. Williams	584	.308	26	92	376	19	11	2	2.7	.973	J. Winters	34	138	6	6	2	5.33
	LF	C. Lee	422	.322	17	77	167	10	6	2	2.1	.967	J. Singleton	22	93	1	10	0	5.90
	C	B. Henline	430	.316	14	64	400	113	9	13	4.4	**.983**							
	3S	Wrightstone	331	.305	5	33	109	227	11	25		.968							
	OF	LeBourveau	167	.269	2	20	77	4	7	1	2.1	.920							
	OF	J. Mokan	151	.252	3	27	62	5	7	1	2.4	.905							
	C	J. Peters	143	.245	4	24	118	24	7	3	3.8	.953							
Bos.	1B	W. Holke	395	.291	0	46	1017	44	8	65	10.2	.993	M. Watson	41	201	8	14	1	4.70
W-53 L-100	2B	L. Kopf	466	.266	1	37	175	243	25	35	5.7	.944	F. Miller	31	200	11	13	1	3.51
Fred Mitchell	SS	H. Ford	515	.272	2	60	267	387	32	57	6.0	.953	R. Marquard	39	198	11	15	1	5.09
	3B	T. Boeckel	402	.289	6	47	128	168	15	13	2.9	.952	J. Oeschger	46	196	6	21	1	5.06
	RF	W. Cruise	352	.278	4	46	212	9	12	3	2.3	.948	H. McQuillan	28	136	5	10	0	4.24
	CF	R. Powell	550	.296	6	37	377	18	8	2	3.0	.980	D. Fillingim	25	117	5	9	2	4.54
	LF	A. Nixon	318	.264	2	22	189	6	5	0	2.5	.975							
	C	M. O'Neil	251	.223	0	26	239	70	7	3	4.0	.978							
	UT	W. Barbare	373	.231	0	40	241	238	14	44		.972							
	OF	F. Nicholson	222	.252	2	29	125	5	12	0	2.3	.915							
	C	H. Gowdy	221	.317	1	27	204	63	8	6	3.8	.971							
	C1	F. Gibson	164	.299	3	20	245	28	5	14		.982							
	OF	B. Southworth	158	.323	4	18	100	7	5	0	2.7	.955							

BATTING AND BASE RUNNING LEADERS

Batting Average

R. Hornsby, STL	.401
R. Grimes, CHI	.354
H. Miller, CHI	.352
C. Bigbee, PIT	.350
C. Tierney, PIT	.345

Slugging Average

R. Hornsby, STL	.722
R. Grimes, CHI	.572
C. Lee, PHI	.540
C. Tierney, PIT	.515
C. Williams, PHI	.514

Home Runs

R. Hornsby, STL	42
C. Williams, PHI	26
C. Lee, PHI	17
G. Kelly, NY	17
Z. Wheat, BKN	16
I. Meusel, NY	16

Total Bases

R. Hornsby, STL	450
I. Meusel, NY	314
Z. Wheat, BKN	302
C. Williams, PHI	300
J. Daubert, CIN	300

Runs Batted In

R. Hornsby, STL	152
I. Meusel, NY	132
Z. Wheat, BKN	112
G. Kelly, NY	107
R. Grimes, CHI	99
C. Bigbee, PIT	99

Stolen Bases

M. Carey, PIT	51
F. Frisch, NY	31
G. Burns, CIN	30
C. Bigbee, PIT	24
R. Maranville, PIT	24

Hits

R. Hornsby, STL	250
C. Bigbee, PIT	215
D. Bancroft, NY	209

Base on Balls

M. Carey, PIT	80
B. O'Farrell, CHI	79
D. Bancroft, NY	79

Home Run Percentage

R. Hornsby, STL	6.7
C. Williams, PHI	4.5
C. Lee, PHI	4.0

Runs Scored

R. Hornsby, STL	141
M. Carey, PIT	140
J. Smith, STL	117
D. Bancroft, NY	117

Doubles

R. Hornsby, STL	46
R. Grimes, CHI	45
P. Duncan, CIN	44

Triples

J. Daubert, CIN	22
I. Meusel, NY	17
C. Bigbee, PIT	15
R. Maranville, PIT	15

PITCHING LEADERS

Winning Percentage

P. Donohue, CIN	.667
E. Rixey, CIN	.658
J. Couch, CIN	.640
D. Ruether, BKN	.636
W. Cooper, PIT	.622

Earned Run Average

R. Ryan, NY	3.01
P. Donohue, CIN	3.12
W. Cooper, PIT	3.18
A. Nehf, NY	3.29
D. Luque, CIN	3.31

Wins

E. Rixey, CIN	25
W. Cooper, PIT	23
D. Ruether, BKN	21
J. Pfeffer, STL	19
A. Nehf, NY	19

Saves

C. Jonnard, NY	5
L. North, STL	4
R. Ryan, NY	3
T. Osborne, CHI	3
T. Kaufmann, CHI	3
A. Mamaux, BKN	3

Strikeouts

D. Vance, BKN	134
W. Cooper, PIT	129
J. Ring, PHI	116
J. Morrison, PIT	104
B. Grimes, BKN	99

Complete Games

W. Cooper, PIT	27
D. Ruether, BKN	26
E. Rixey, CIN	26

Fewest Hits per 9 Innings

R. Ryan, NY	9.11
D. Luque, CIN	9.17
D. Vance, BKN	9.49

Shutouts

D. Vance, BKN	5
J. Morrison, PIT	5
B. Adams, PIT	4
W. Cooper, PIT	4

Fewest Walks per 9 Innings

B. Adams, PIT	0.79
G. Alexander, CHI	1.25
E. Rixey, CIN	1.29

Most Strikeouts per 9 Inn.

D. Vance, BKN	4.91
J. Ring, PHI	4.19
W. Cooper, PIT	3.94

Innings

E. Rixey, CIN	313
W. Cooper, PIT	295
J. Morrison, PIT	286

Games Pitched

L. North, STL	53
B. Sherdel, STL	47
J. Oeschger, BOS	46
R. Ryan, NY	46

	W	L	PCT	GB	R	OR	2B	3B	Batting HR	BA	SA	SB	E	Fielding DP	FA	CG	BB	Pitching SO	ShO	SV	ERA
NY	93	61	.604		852	**658**	253	90	80	.305	.428	116	194	145	**.970**	73	393	388	7	**15**	**3.45**
CIN	86	68	.558	7	766	677	226	99	45	.296	.401	130	205	147	.968	**88**	326	357	8	3	3.53
PIT	85	69	.552	8	**865**	736	239	**110**	52	**.308**	.419	**145**	187	126	.970	**88**	358	490	**15**	7	3.98
STL	85	69	.552	8	863	819	**280**	88	107	.301	**.444**	73	239	122	.961	60	447	465	8	12	4.44
CHI	80	74	.519	13	771	808	248	71	42	.293	.390	79	204	**154**	.968	74	475	402	12	8	4.34
BKN	76	78	.494	17	743	754	235	76	56	.290	.392	79	208	139	.967	82	490	**499**	12	8	4.05
PHI	57	96	.373	35.5	738	920	268	55	**116**	.282	.415	48	225	152	.965	73	460	394	6	5	4.64
BOS	53	100	.346	39.5	596	822	162	73	32	.263	.341	67	215	121	.965	62	489	360	7	6	4.37
					6194	6194	1911	662	530	.292	.404	755	1677	1106	.967	600	3438	3355	71	68	4.10

American League 1922

	POS	Player	AB	BA	HR	RBI	PO	A	E	DP	TC/G	FA	Pitcher	G	IP	W	L	SV	ERA
N. Y. W-94 L-60 Miller Huggins	1B	W. Pipp	577	.329	9	90	**1667**	88	13	106	11.6	.993	B. Shawkey	39	300	20	12	1	2.91
	2B	A. Ward	558	.267	7	68	358	**489**	23	73	5.7	.974	W. Hoyt	37	265	19	12	0	3.43
	SS	E. Scott	557	.269	3	45	302	**538**	31	74	5.7	**.964**	S. Jones	45	260	13	13	**8**	3.67
	3B	J. Dugan	252	.286	3	25	59	117	6	10	3.0	.967	J. Bush	39	255	26	7	3	3.31
	RF	B. Meusel	473	.319	16	84	202	24	12	0	2.4	.976	C. Mays	34	240	13	14	2	3.60
	CF	W. Witt	528	.297	4	40	312	9	8	1	2.3	.964							
	LF	B. Ruth	406	.315	35	99	225	14	9	3	2.6	.976							
	C	W. Schang	408	.319	1	53	456	102	14	12	4.6	.976							
	3B	F. Baker	234	.278	7	36	68	108	7	7	3.1	.962							
	OF	E. Miller	172	.267	3	18	101	7	2	0	2.2	.982							
St. L. W-93 L-61 Lee Fohl	1B	G. Sisler	586	**.420**	8	105	1293	125	17	116	10.2	.988	U. Shocker	48	348	24	17	3	2.97
	2B	M. McManus	606	.312	11	109	398	467	**32**	103	5.9	.944	E. Vangilder	43	245	19	13	4	3.42
	SS	W. Gerber	604	.267	1	51	**322**	470	47	**93**	5.5	.944	D. Davis	25	174	11	6	0	4.08
	3B	F. Ellerbe	342	.246	1	33	137	224	17	20	4.2	.955	R. Kolp	32	170	14	4	0	3.93
	RF	J. Tobin	625	.331	13	66	221	15	15	5	1.7	.940	R. Wright	31	154	9	7	5	2.92
	CF	B. Jacobson	555	.317	9	102	367	9	12	3	**2.8**	.969	H. Pruett	39	120	7	7	7	2.33
	LF	K. Williams	585	.332	**39**	**155**	372	16	12	4	2.6	.970	B. Bayne	26	93	4	5	2	4.56
	C	H. Severeid	517	.321	3	78	552	123	11	10	5.1	.984							
	C	P. Collins	127	.307	8	23	129	19	3	4	5.6	.980							
Det. W-79 L-75 Ty Cobb	1B	L. Blue	584	.300	6	45	1506	75	15	107	11.1	.991	H. Ehmke	45	280	17	17	1	4.22
	2B	G. Cutshaw	499	.267	2	61	334	390	21	69	5.6	.972	H. Pillette	40	275	19	12	1	2.85
	SS	T. Rigney	536	.300	2	63	262	493	**50**	74	5.2	.938	H. Dauss	39	219	13	13	4	4.20
	3B	B. Jones	455	.257	3	44	161	267	17	22	**3.7**	**.962**	R. Oldham	43	212	10	13	3	4.67
	RF	H. Heilmann	455	.356	21	92	175	6	10	2	1.7	.948	O. Olsen	37	137	7	6	3	4.53
	CF	T. Cobb	526	.401	4	99	330	14	7	3	2.6	.980	S. Johnson	29	97	7	3	1	3.71
	LF	B. Veach	618	.327	9	126	375	16	7	3	2.6	.982							
	C	J. Bassler	372	.323	0	41	421	113	11	12	4.6	.980							
	3B	F. Haney	213	.352	0	25	43	105	10	11	3.8	.937							
	2B	D. Clark	185	.292	3	26	72	99	10	16	4.8	.945							
	OF	B. Fothergill	152	.322	0	29	50	2	3	1	1.4	.945							
Cle. W-78 L-76 Tris Speaker	1B	S. McInnis	537	.305	1	78	1376	73	5	96	10.4	**.997**	G. Uhle	50	287	22	16	3	4.07
	2B	W. Wambsganss	538	.262	0	47	297	376	27	72	5.6	.961	S. Coveleski	35	277	17	14	2	3.32
	SS	J. Sewell	558	.299	2	83	295	462	49	72	**5.8**	.939	G. Morton	38	203	14	9	0	4.00
	3B	L. Gardner	470	.285	2	68	133	259	20	**24**	3.2	.951	D. Mails	26	104	4	7	0	5.28
	RF	J. Wood	505	.297	8	92	247	18	11	5	2.0	.960	J. Bagby	25	98	4	5	1	6.32
	CF	T. Speaker	426	.378	11	71	285	13	5	6	2.8	**.983**	J. Edwards	25	88	3	8	0	4.70
	LF	C. Jamieson	567	.323	3	57	289	18	7	5	2.2	.978	J. Lindsey	29	84	4	5	1	6.02
	C	S. O'Neill	392	.311	2	65	450	116	**15**	9	4.5	.974	D. Boone	11	75	4	6	0	4.06
	32	R. Stephenson	233	.339	2	32	75	135	12	11		.946							
	OF	J. Evans	145	.269	0	22	92	1	3	0	2.0	.969							
Chi. W-77 L-77 Kid Gleason	1B	E. Sheely	526	.317	6	80	1512	103	12	101	10.9	.993	R. Faber	43	353	21	17	2	**2.80**
	2B	E. Collins	598	.324	1	69	406	451	21	73	5.7	.976	C. Robertson	37	272	14	15	0	3.64
	SS	E. Johnson	603	.254	0	56	259	468	37	74	5.4	.952	D. Leverett	33	225	13	10	2	3.32
	3B	E. Mulligan	372	.234	0	31	94	200	11	14	3.5	.964	S. Hodge	35	139	7	6	1	4.14
	RF	H. Hooper	602	.304	11	80	288	19	12	**7**	2.1	.962	Blankenship	24	128	8	10	1	3.81
	CF	J. Mostil	458	.303	7	70	333	9	12	2	2.7	.966	H. Courtney	18	88	5	6	0	4.93
	LF	B. Falk	483	.298	12	79	253	10	10	2	2.1	.963							
	C	R. Schalk	442	.281	4	60	**591**	150	8	16	**5.3**	**.989**							
	OF	A. Strunk	311	.289	0	33	170	9	2	2	2.4	.989							
	3B	H. McClellan	301	.226	2	28	77	158	7	15	3.4	.971							

	POS	Player	AB	BA	HR	RBI	PO	A	E	DP	TC/G	FA	Pitcher	G	IP	W	L	SV	ERA
Was. W-69 L-85 Clyde Milan	1B	J. Judge	591	.294	10	81	1413	101	6	131	10.3	.996	W. Johnson	41	280	15	16	4	2.99
	2B	B. Harris	602	.269	2	40	479	483	30	116	6.4	.970	G. Mogridge	34	252	18	13	0	3.58
	SS	Peckinpaugh	520	.254	2	48	265	524	41	93	5.6	.951	R. Francis	39	225	7	18	2	4.28
	3B	B. LaMotte	214	.252	1	23	90	138	11	10	3.9	.954	T. Zachary	32	185	15	10	1	3.12
	RF	F. Brower	471	.293	9	71	208	9	5	1	1.8	.977	E. Erickson	30	142	4	12	2	4.96
	CF	S. Rice	633	.295	6	69	385	23	21	3	2.8	.951	J. Brillheart	31	120	4	6	1	3.61
	LF	G. Goslin	358	.324	3	53	197	8	15	1	2.4	.932	T. Phillips	17	70	3	7	0	4.89
	C	P. Gharrity	273	.256	5	45	282	85	7	9	4.3	.981							
	3O	H. Shanks	272	.283	1	32	125	112	16	16		.937							
	C	V. Picinich	210	.229	0	19	273	55	8	4	4.4	.976							
	OF	E. Smith	205	.259	1	23	88	12	9	3	2.2	.917							
Phi. W-65 L-89 Connie Mack	1B	J. Hauser	368	.323	9	43	936	55	14	61	10.7	.986	E. Rommel	51	294	27	13	2	3.28
	2B	R. Young	470	.223	1	35	302	350	27	53	5.7	.960	S. Harriss	47	230	9	20	3	5.02
	SS	C. Galloway	571	.324	6	69	321	493	41	76	5.5	.952	B. Hasty	28	193	9	14	0	4.25
	3B	J. Dykes	501	.275	12	68	186	295	28	21	3.6	.945	R. Naylor	35	171	10	15	0	4.73
	RF	F. Welch	375	.259	11	49	191	12	11	2	2.1	.949	F. Heimach	37	172	7	11	1	5.03
	CF	B. Miller	535	.336	21	90	314	19	8	3	2.5	.977							
	LF	T. Walker	565	.283	37	99	309	19	15	4	2.3	.956							
	C	C. Perkins	505	.267	6	60	432	130	9	10	4.0	.984							
	OF	F. McGowan	300	.230	1	20	210	13	8	2	2.8	.965							
	1B	D. Johnston	260	.250	1	29	641	31	7	34	10.4	.990							
Bos. W-61 L-93 Hugh Duffy	1B	G. Burns	558	.306	12	73	1412	94	20	103	10.9	.987	J. Quinn	40	256	13	15	0	3.48
	2B	D. Pratt	607	.301	6	86	362	484	30	80	5.7	.966	R. Collins	32	211	14	11	0	3.76
	SS	J. Mitchell	203	.251	1	8	98	184	11	31	5.1	.962	H. Pennock	32	202	10	17	1	4.32
	3B	J. Dugan	341	.287	3	38	72	143	13	13	3.6	.943	A. Ferguson	39	198	9	16	2	4.31
	RF	S. Collins	472	.271	1	52	245	6	13	1	2.3	.951	B. Karr	41	183	5	12	1	4.47
	CF	J. Harris	408	.316	6	54	186	15	10	2	2.5	.953	A. Russell	34	126	6	7	2	5.01
	LF	M. Menosky	406	.283	3	32	240	14	6	3	2.5	.977	B. Piercy	29	121	3	9	0	4.67
	C	M. Ruel	361	.255	0	28	359	96	10	17	4.2	.978							
	OF	N. Leibold	271	.258	1	18	190	10	7	3	2.9	.966							
	OF	E. Smith	231	.286	6	32	117	7	7	3	2.2	.947							
	SS	F. O'Rourke	216	.264	1	17	86	134	22	17	5.0	.909							
	3S	P. Pittenger	186	.258	0	7	88	148	22	19		.915							

BATTING AND BASE RUNNING LEADERS

Batting Average

G. Sisler, STL	.420
T. Cobb, DET	.401
T. Speaker, CLE	.378
H. Heilmann, DET	.356
B. Miller, PHI	.336

Slugging Average

B. Ruth, NY	.672
K. Williams, STL	.627
T. Speaker, CLE	.606
H. Heilmann, DET	.598
G. Sisler, STL	.594

Home Runs

K. Williams, STL	39
T. Walker, PHI	37
B. Ruth, NY	35
H. Heilmann, DET	21
B. Miller, PHI	21

Total Bases

K. Williams, STL	367
G. Sisler, STL	348
T. Walker, PHI	310
T. Cobb, DET	297
B. Miller, PHI	296
J. Tobin, STL	296

Runs Batted In

K. Williams, STL	155
B. Veach, DET	126
M. McManus, STL	109
G. Sisler, STL	105
B. Jacobson, STL	102

Stolen Bases

G. Sisler, STL	51
K. Williams, STL	37
B. Harris, WAS	25
E. Johnson, CHI	21
E. Collins, CHI	20
S. Rice, WAS	20

Hits

G. Sisler, STL	246
T. Cobb, DET	211
J. Tobin, STL	207

Base on Balls

W. Witt, NY	89
B. Ruth, NY	84
L. Blue, DET	82

Home Run Percentage

B. Ruth, NY	8.6
K. Williams, STL	6.7
T. Walker, PHI	6.5

Runs Scored

G. Sisler, STL	134
L. Blue, DET	131
K. Williams, STL	128

Doubles

T. Speaker, CLE	48
D. Pratt, BOS	44
T. Cobb, DET	42
G. Sisler, STL	42

Triples

G. Sisler, STL	18
T. Cobb, DET	16
B. Jacobson, STL	16

PITCHING LEADERS

Winning Percentage

J. Bush, NY	.788
E. Rommel, PHI	.675
B. Shawkey, NY	.625
W. Hoyt, NY	.613
H. Pillette, DET	.613

Earned Run Average

R. Faber, CHI	2.80
H. Pillette, DET	2.85
B. Shawkey, NY	2.91
U. Shocker, STL	2.97
W. Johnson, WAS	2.99

Wins

E. Rommel, PHI	27
J. Bush, NY	26
U. Shocker, STL	24
G. Uhle, CLE	22
R. Faber, CHI	21

Saves

S. Jones, NY	8
H. Pruett, STL	7
R. Wright, STL	5
H. Dauss, DET	4
E. Vangilder, STL	4
W. Johnson, WAS	4

Strikeouts

U. Shocker, STL	149
R. Faber, CHI	148
B. Shawkey, NY	130
H. Ehmke, DET	108
W. Johnson, WAS	105

Complete Games

R. Faber, CHI	31
U. Shocker, STL	29
W. Johnson, WAS	23
G. Uhle, CLE	23
E. Rommel, PHI	22

Fewest Hits per 9 Innings

U. Shocker, STL	6.85
J. Bush, NY	8.46
R. Faber, CHI	8.52

Shutouts

G. Uhle, CLE	5

Fewest Walks per 9 Innings

U. Shocker, STL	1.53
E. Vangilder, STL	1.76
C. Mays, NY	1.87

Most Strikeouts per 9 Inn.

G. Morton, CLE	4.53
S. Harriss, PHI	4.00
B. Shawkey, NY	3.90

Innings

R. Faber, CHI	353
U. Shocker, STL	348
B. Shawkey, NY	300

Games Pitched

E. Rommel, PHI	51
G. Uhle, CLE	50
U. Shocker, STL	48

	W	L	PCT	GB	R	OR	2B	3B (Batting) HR	BA	SA	SB	E	DP (Fielding)	FA	CG	BB	SO	ShO (Pitching)	SV	ERA
NY	94	60	.610	–	758	618	220	75	95	.287	.412	62	157	122	.975	98	423	458	7	14	3.39
STL	93	61	.604	1	867	643	291	94	98	.313	.455	132	201	158	.968	79	421	534	8	22	3.38
DET	79	75	.513	15	828	791	250	87	54	.305	.414	78	191	135	.970	67	473	461	7	15	4.27
CLE	78	76	.506	16	768	817	320	73	32	.292	.398	89	202	140	.968	76	464	489	14	7	4.60
CHI	77	77	.500	17	691	691	243	62	45	.278	.373	106	155	161	.969	86	529	484	13	8	3.93
WAS	69	85	.448	25	650	706	229	76	45	.268	.367	94	196	132	.975	84	500	422	11	10	3.81
PHI	65	89	.422	29	705	830	229	63	111	.269	.400	60	215	119	.966	73	469	373	4	6	4.59
BOS	61	93	.396	33	598	769	250	55	45	.263	.357	60	224	139	.965	71	503	359	10	6	4.30
					5865	5865	2032	585	525	.284	.397	681	1541	1106	.969	634	3782	3580	74	88	4.03

National League 1923

Team	POS	Player	AB	BA	HR	RBI	PO	A	E	DP	TC/G	FA	Pitcher	G	IP	W	L	SV	ERA
N. Y. W-95 L-58 John McGraw	1B	G. Kelly	560	.307	16	103	1568	60	12	111	11.3	.993	H. McQuillan	38	230	15	14	0	3.41
	2B	F. Frisch	641	.348	12	111	307	451	21	79	5.8	.973	J. Scott	40	220	16	7	1	3.89
	SS	D. Bancroft	444	.304	1	31	246	381	43	53	7.0	.936	A. Nehf	34	196	13	10	2	4.50
	3B	H. Groh	465	.290	4	48	117	233	9	18	3.0	.975	J. Bentley	31	183	13	8	3	4.48
	RF	R. Youngs	596	.336	3	87	282	22	13	7	2.1	.994	R. Ryan	45	173	16	5	4	3.49
	CF	J. O'Connell	252	.250	6	39	145	2	3	1	2.3	.980	M. Watson	17	108	8	5	0	3.43
	LF	I. Meusel	595	.297	19	125	268	10	15	2	2.0	.949	C. Jonnard	45	96	4	3	5	3.28
	C	F. Snyder	402	.256	5	63	428	90	5	12	4.7	.990							
	S3	T. Jackson	327	.275	4	37	103	257	23	29		.940							
	OF	C. Stengel	218	.339	5	43	115	4	2	1	2.1	.983							
	OF	B. Cunningham	203	.271	5	27	123	8	1	2	1.9	.992							
Cin. W-91 L-63 Pat Moran	1B	J. Daubert	500	.292	2	54	1224	77	9	95	10.8	.993	D. Luque	41	322	27	8	2	1.93
	2B	S. Bohne	539	.252	3	47	243	333	15	46	6.2	.975	E. Rixey	42	309	20	15	1	2.80
	SS	I. Caveney	488	.277	4	63	313	477	49	86	6.1	.942	P. Donohue	42	274	21	15	3	3.38
	3B	B. Pinelli	423	.277	0	51	131	250	25	17	3.5	.938	R. Benton	33	219	14	10	1	3.66
	RF	G. Burns	614	.274	3	45	327	11	14	3	2.3	.960	C. Keck	35	87	3	6	2	3.72
	CF	E. Roush	527	.351	6	88	337	14	11	3	2.6	.970							
	LF	P. Duncan	566	.327	7	83	291	11	2	2	2.1	.993							
	C	B. Hargrave	378	.333	10	78	404	90	6	12	4.6	.988							
	2B	L. Fonseca	237	.278	3	28	123	169	13	27	6.8	.957							
	C	I. Wingo	171	.263	1	24	172	44	7	2	3.9	.969							
Pit. W-87 L-67 Bill McKechnie	1B	C. Grimm	563	.345	7	99	1453	81	8	130	10.1	.995	J. Morrison	42	302	25	13	2	3.49
	2B	J. Rawlings	461	.284	1	45	294	388	30	68	6.0	.958	W. Cooper	39	295	17	19	0	3.57
	SS	R. Maranville	581	.277	1	41	332	505	30	94	6.1	.965	L. Meadows	31	227	16	10	0	3.01
	3B	P. Traynor	616	.338	12	101	191	310	26	30	3.4	.951	B. Adams	26	159	13	7	1	4.42
	RF	C. Barnhart	327	.324	9	72	179	14	3	1	2.1	.985	E. Hamilton	28	141	7	9	1	3.77
	CF	M. Carey	610	.308	6	63	450	28	19	4	3.2	.962							
	LF	C. Bigbee	499	.299	0	54	283	12	3	3	2.4	.990							
	C	W. Schmidt	335	.248	0	37	279	88	7	10	3.9	.981							
	OF	R. Russell	291	.289	9	58	156	4	5	0	2.2	.970							
	C	J. Gooch	202	.277	1	20	217	56	7	7	4.2	.975							
	2B	C. Tierney	120	.292	2	23	65	94	10	22*	5.8	.941							
	OF	W. Mueller	111	.306	0	20	62	2	4	0	2.6	.941							
Chi. W-83 L-71 Bill Killefer	1B	R. Grimes	216	.329	2	36	629	30	6	46	10.7	.991	G. Alexander	39	305	22	12	2	3.19
	2B	G. Grantham	570	.281	8	70	374	518	55	90	6.3	.942	V. Aldridge	30	217	16	9	0	3.48
	SS	S. Adams	311	.289	4	35	153	248	28	45	5.4	.955	T. Kaufmann	33	206	14	10	3	3.10
	3B	M. Stock	547	.318	12	88	168	294	22	33	3.3	.955	T. Osborne	37	180	8	15	1	4.56
	RF	C. Heathcote	393	.249	1	27	231	14	5	1	2.2	.980	V. Keen	35	177	12	8	1	3.00
	CF	J. Statz	655	.319	10	70	438	26	12	7	3.1	.975	F. Fussell	28	76	3	5	3	5.54
	LF	H. Miller	485	.301	20	88	256	17	6	4	2.2	.978							
	C	B. O'Farrell	452	.319	12	84	418	118	13	11	4.4	.976							
	SS	C. Hollocher	260	.342	1	28	124	212	13	35	5.4	.963							
	C1	G. Hartnett	231	.268	8	39	413	39	5	25		.989							
	UT	J. Kelleher	193	.306	6	21	228	84	22	21		.934							
	1B	A. Elliott	168	.250	2	29	450	19	4	36	9.1	.992							
St. L. W-79 L-74 Branch Rickey	1B	J. Bottomley	523	.371	8	94	1264	43	18	95	10.2	.986	J. Haines	37	266	20	13	0	3.11
	2B	R. Hornsby	424	.384	17	83	192	283	19	47	5.1	.962	B. Sherdel	39	225	15	13	2	4.32
	SS	H. Freigau	358	.263	1	35	193	290	37	42	6.0	.929	F. Toney	29	197	11	12	0	3.84
	3B	M. Stock	603	.289	2	96	165	261	20	24	3.0	.955	B. Doak	30	185	8	13	0	3.26
	RF	M. Flack	505	.291	3	28	242	8	13	4	2.2	.951	J. Pfeffer	26	152	8	9	0	4.02
	CF	H. Myers	330	.300	2	48	239	15	6	0	3.0	.977	J. Stuart	37	150	9	5	3	4.27
	LF	J. Smith	407	.310	5	41	247	11	7	3	2.5	.974	C. Barfoot	33	101	3	3	1	3.73
	C	E. Ainsmith	263	.213	3	34	235	57	6	3	3.7	.980							
	OF	R. Blades	317	.246	5	44	194	11	7	1	2.6	.967							
	2S	S. Toporcer	303	.254	3	35	192	239	24	57		.947							
	OF	H. Mueller	265	.343	5	41	197	9	8	3	2.9	.963							
	C	H. McCurdy	185	.265	0	15	157	30	6	4	3.3	.969							

	POS	Player	AB	BA	HR	RBI	PO	A	E	DP	TC/G	FA	Pitcher	G	IP	W	L	SV	ERA
Bkn. W-76 L-78 Wilbert Robinson	1B	J. Fournier	515	.351	22	102	1281	82	21	90	10.4	.985	B. Grimes	39	**327**	21	18	0	3.58
	2B	J. Johnston	625	.325	4	60	221	291	28	25	6.4	.948	D. Vance	37	280	18	15	0	3.50
	SS	A. High	426	.270	3	37	94	122	15	23	5.1	.935	D. Ruether	34	275	15	14	0	4.22
	3B	B. McCarren	216	.245	3	27	72	106	14	11	2.9	.927	L. Dickerman	35	166	8	12	0	3.59
	RF	T. Griffith	481	.293	8	66	215	14	18	4	1.9	.927	A. Decatur	36	105	3	3	3	2.67
	CF	B. Neis	445	.274	5	37	268	20	18	3	2.8	.941	D. Henry	17	94	4	6	0	3.91
	LF	G. Bailey	411	.265	1	42	245	10	11	0	2.7	.959	G. Smith	25	91	3	6	1	3.66
	C	Z. Taylor	337	.288	0	46	354	118	16	6	5.8	.967							
	OF	Z. Wheat	349	.375	8	65	135	4	14	1	1.8	.908							
	2B	I. Olson	292	.260	1	35	161	244	11	36	5.8	.974							
	OF	B. Griffith	248	.294	2	37	111	1	6	0	1.9	.949							
	C	H. DeBerry	235	.285	1	48	273	65	10	8	5.8	.971							
Bos. W-54 L-100 Fred Mitchell	1B	S. McInnis	607	.315	2	95	1500	89	14	136	10.4	.991	R. Marquard	38	239	11	14	0	3.73
	2B	H. Ford	380	.271	2	50	213	300	16	61	5.6	.970	J. Genewich	43	227	13	14	1	3.72
	SS	B. Smith	375	.251	0	40	234	360	35	69	6.2	.944	J. Barnes	31	195	10	14	2	2.76
	3B	T. Boeckel	568	.298	7	79	169	265	28	27	3.1	.939	J. Oeschger	44	166	5	15	2	5.68
	RF	B. Southworth	611	.319	6	78	326	22	21	6	2.4	.943	T. McNamara	32	139	3	13	0	4.91
	CF	R. Powell	338	.302	4	38	214	8	14	0	2.8	.941	L. Benton	35	128	5	9	0	4.99
	LF	G. Felix	506	.273	6	44	276	11	15	2	2.5	.950	D. Fillingim	35	100	1	9	0	5.20
	C	M. O'Neil	306	.212	0	20	298	104	11	5	4.3	.973							
	OF	A. Nixon	321	.274	0	19	214	14	3	4	2.9	.987							
	C	E. Smith	191	.288	3	19	141	51	5	7	5.8	.975							
Phi. W-50 L-104 Art Fletcher	1B	W. Holke	562	.311	7	70	1425	69	13	136	10.3	.991	J. Ring	39	313	18	16	0	3.76
	2B	C. Tierney	480	.317	11	65	249	416	17	82*	6.0	.975	W. Glazner	28	161	7	14	1	4.69
	SS	H. Sand	470	.228	4	32	277	411	49	91	6.1	.934	L. Weinert	38	156	4	17	1	5.42
	3B	Wrightstone	392	.273	7	57	73	121	12	12	2.9	.942	C. Mitchell	29	139	9	10	0	4.72
	RF	C. Walker	527	.281	5	66	284	19	17	5	2.3	.947	R. Head	35	132	2	9	0	6.66
	CF	C. Williams	535	.293	41	114	350	9	7	3	2.7	.981	P. Behan	31	131	3	12	2	5.50
	LF	J. Mokan	400	.313	10	48	235	16	8	0	2.5	.969							
	C	B. Henline	330	.324	7	46	288	71	8	8	3.8	.978							
	OF	C. Lee	355	.321	11	47	136	4	6	3	1.8	.959							
	C	J. Wilson	252	.262	1	25	235	50	12	10	4.3	.960							
	UT	F. Parkinson	219	.242	3	28	118	175	18	36		.942							
	3B	G. Rapp	179	.263	1	10	58	84	8	9	3.3	.947							

BATTING AND BASE RUNNING LEADERS

Batting Average
R. Hornsby, STL	.384
J. Bottomley, STL	.371
J. Fournier, BKN	.351
E. Roush, CIN	.351
F. Frisch, NY	.348

Slugging Average
R. Hornsby, STL	.627
J. Fournier, BKN	.588
C. Williams, PHI	.576
C. Barnhart, PIT	.563
J. Bottomley, STL	.535

Home Runs
C. Williams, PHI	41
J. Fournier, BKN	22
H. Miller, CHI	20
I. Meusel, NY	19
R. Hornsby, STL	17

Total Bases
F. Frisch, NY	311
C. Williams, PHI	308
J. Fournier, BKN	303
P. Traynor, PIT	301
J. Statz, CHI	288

Runs Batted In
I. Meusel, NY	125
C. Williams, PHI	114
F. Frisch, NY	111
G. Kelly, NY	103
J. Fournier, BKN	102

Stolen Bases
M. Carey, PIT	51
G. Grantham, CHI	43
C. Heathcote, CHI	32
J. Smith, STL	32
F. Frisch, NY	29
J. Statz, CHI	29

Hits
F. Frisch, NY	223
J. Statz, CHI	209
P. Traynor, PIT	208

Base on Balls
G. Burns, CIN	101
H. Sand, PHI	82
R. Youngs, NY	73
M. Carey, PIT	73

Home Run Percentage
C. Williams, PHI	7.7
J. Fournier, BKN	4.3
H. Miller, CHI	4.1

Runs Scored
R. Youngs, NY	121
M. Carey, PIT	120
F. Frisch, NY	116

Doubles
E. Roush, CIN	41
G. Grantham, CHI	36
C. Tierney, PHI, PIT	36
J. Bottomley, STL	34

Triples
M. Carey, PIT	19
P. Traynor, PIT	19
E. Roush, CIN	18

PITCHING LEADERS

Winning Percentage
D. Luque, CIN	.771
R. Ryan, NY	.762
J. Scott, NY	.696
J. Morrison, PIT	.658
G. Alexander, CHI	.647

Earned Run Average
D. Luque, CIN	1.93
E. Rixey, CIN	2.80
V. Keen, CHI	3.00
T. Kaufmann, CHI	3.10
J. Haines, STL	3.11

Wins
D. Luque, CIN	27
J. Morrison, PIT	25
G. Alexander, CHI	22
P. Donohue, CIN	21
B. Grimes, BKN	21

Saves
C. Jonnard, NY	5
R. Ryan, NY	4

Strikeouts
D. Vance, BKN	197
D. Luque, CIN	151
B. Grimes, BKN	119
J. Morrison, PIT	114
J. Ring, PHI	112

Complete Games
B. Grimes, BKN	33
D. Luque, CIN	28
J. Morrison, PIT	27
G. Alexander, CHI	26
W. Cooper, PIT	26

Fewest Hits per 9 Innings
D. Luque, CIN	7.80
D. Vance, BKN	8.44
J. Morrison, PIT	8.56

Shutouts
D. Luque, CIN	6
J. Barnes, BOS, NY	5
H. McQuillan, NY	5

Fewest Walks per 9 Innings
G. Alexander, CHI	0.89
B. Adams, PIT	1.42
J. Genewich, BOS	1.82

Most Strikeouts per 9 Inn.
D. Vance, BKN	6.32
D. Luque, CIN	4.22
J. Bentley, NY	3.93

Innings
B. Grimes, BKN	327
D. Luque, CIN	322
J. Ring, PHI	313

Games Pitched
R. Ryan, NY	45
C. Jonnard, NY	45
J. Oeschger, BOS	44

	W	L	PCT	GB	R	OR	2B	3B	HR	BA	SA	SB	E	DP	FA	CG	BB	SO	ShO	SV	ERA
NY	95	58	.621		**854**	679	248	76	85	**.295**	.415	106	**176**	141	.972	62	424	453	10	**18**	3.90
CIN	91	63	.591	4.5	708	**629**	237	95	45	.285	.392	96	202	144	.969	88	**359**	450	11	9	**3.21**
PIT	87	67	.565	8.5	786	696	224	**111**	49	.295	.404	154	179	157	.971	92	402	414	5	9	3.87
CHI	83	71	.539	12.5	756	704	243	52	90	.288	.406	**181**	208	144	.967	80	435	408	8	11	3.82
STL	79	74	.516	16	746	732	**274**	76	63	.286	.398	89	232	141	.963	77	456	398	9	7	3.87
BKN	76	78	.494	19.5	753	741	214	81	62	.285	.387	71	293	137	.955	**94**	477	**549**	8	5	3.73
BOS	54	100	.351	41.5	636	798	213	58	32	.273	.353	57	230	157	.964	55	394	351	**13**	7	4.22
PHI	50	104	.325	45.5	748	1008	259	39	**112**	.278	.401	70	217	**172**	.966	68	549	385	3	8	5.30
					5987	5987	1912	588	538	.286	.395	824	1737	1193	.966	616	3496	3408	67	74	3.99

Batting columns: 2B, 3B, HR, BA, SA. Fielding columns: E, DP, FA. Pitching columns: CG, BB, SO, ShO, SV, ERA.

American League 1923

N. Y. — W-98 L-54 — Miller Huggins

POS	Player	AB	BA	HR	RBI	PO	A	E	DP	TC/G	FA
1B	W. Pipp	569	.304	6	108	1461	81	12	97	10.8	.992
2B	A. Ward	567	.284	10	82	387	493	18	86	5.9	**.980**
SS	E. Scott	533	.246	6	60	245	414	27	65	4.5	**.961**
3B	J. Dugan	**644**	.283	7	67	155	300	12	28	3.2	**.974**
RF	B. Ruth	522	**.393**	**41**	**131**	378	20	11	2	2.8	.973
CF	W. Witt	596	.314	6	56	357	14	8	4	2.6	**.979**
LF	B. Meusel	460	.313	9	91	206	17	11	2	1.9	.953
C	W. Schang	272	.276	2	29	292	60	11	6	4.5	.970
C	F. Hofmann	238	.290	3	26	292	34	7	7	4.8	.979
OF	E. Smith	183	.306	7	35	86	5	5	2	2.0	.948

Pitcher	G	IP	W	L	SV	ERA
J. Bush	37	276	19	15	0	3.43
B. Shawkey	36	259	16	11	1	3.51
S. Jones	39	243	21	8	4	3.63
W. Hoyt	37	239	17	9	1	3.02
H. Pennock	35	224	19	6	3	3.33

Det. — W-83 L-71 — Ty Cobb

POS	Player	AB	BA	HR	RBI	PO	A	E	DP	TC/G	FA
1B	L. Blue	504	.284	1	46	1347	93	12	74	**11.3**	.992
2B	F. Haney	503	.282	4	67	162	178	16	29	5.2	.955
SS	T. Rigney	470	.315	1	74	209	383	35	46	4.9	.944
3B	B. Jones	372	.250	1	40	109	224	16	17	3.6	.954
RF	H. Heilmann	524	**.403**	18	115	272	13	12	2	2.3	.960
CF	T. Cobb	556	.340	6	88	362	14	12	2	2.8	.969
LF	H. Manush	308	.334	4	54	158	6	8	0	2.2	.953
C	J. Bassler	383	.298	0	49	447	133	7	8	4.6	.988
UT	D. Pratt	297	.310	0	40	281	179	18	32		.962
OF	B. Veach	293	.321	2	39	127	6	8	0	1.7	.943
OF	B. Fothergill	241	.315	1	49	121	4	3	0	1.9	.977

Pitcher	G	IP	W	L	SV	ERA
H. Dauss	50	316	21	13	3	3.62
H. Pillette	47	250	14	**19**	1	3.85
K. Holloway	42	194	11	10	1	4.45
S. Johnson	37	176	12	7	0	3.98
B. Cole	52	163	13	5	5	4.14
R. Collins	17	92	3	7	0	4.87
R. Francis	33	79	5	8	1	4.42

Cle. — W-82 L-71 — Tris Speaker

POS	Player	AB	BA	HR	RBI	PO	A	E	DP	TC/G	FA
1B	F. Brower	397	.285	16	66	1047	66	13	87	10.1	.988
2B	B. Wambsganss	345	.290	1	59	252	275	20	46	6.2	.963
SS	J. Sewell	553	.353	3	109	286	497	**59**	82	5.6	.930
3B	R. Lutzke	511	.256	3	65	**186**	**358**	35	23	**4.0**	.940
RF	H. Summa	525	.328	3	69	216	15	11	5	1.8	.955
CF	T. Speaker	574	.380	17	**130**	369	26	13	7	2.7	.968
LF	C. Jamieson	**644**	.345	2	51	360	18	10	1	2.6	.974
C	S. O'Neill	330	.248	0	50	354	68	14	3	3.9	.968
2B	R. Stephenson	301	.319	5	65	205	214	13	49	6.5	.970
C	G. Myatt	220	.286	3	40	188	37	16	3	3.5	.934
P	G. Uhle	144	.361	0	22	18	89	2	9	2.0	.982
OF	J. Connolly	109	.303	3	25	42	2	2	0	1.2	.957

Pitcher	G	IP	W	L	SV	ERA
G. Uhle	54	**358**	**26**	16	5	3.77
S. Coveleski	33	228	13	14	2	**2.76**
J. Edwards	38	179	10	10	1	3.71
J. Shaute	33	172	10	8	0	3.51
G. Morton	33	129	6	6	1	4.24
S. Smith	30	124	9	6	1	3.27
D. Boone	27	70	4	6	0	6.01

Was. — W-75 L-78 — Donie Bush

POS	Player	AB	BA	HR	RBI	PO	A	E	DP	TC/G	FA
1B	J. Judge	405	.314	2	63	1070	88	8	**113**	10.4	**.993**
2B	B. Harris	532	.282	2	70	418	449	35	**120**	6.3	.961
SS	Peckinpaugh	568	.264	2	62	311	**510**	45	105	5.6	.948
3B	O. Bluege	379	.245	2	42	126	247	25	30	3.7	.937
RF	S. Rice	595	.316	3	75	307	21	10	8	2.3	.970
CF	N. Leibold	315	.305	1	22	186	13	4	2	2.4	.980
LF	G. Goslin	600	.300	9	99	310	26	15	5	2.4	.957
C	M. Ruel	449	.316	0	54	**528**	146	14	14	5.2	.980
OF	J. Evans	372	.263	0	38	159	5	3	2	2.3	.982
C1	P. Gharrity	251	.207	3	33	417	47	8	27		.983

Pitcher	G	IP	W	L	SV	ERA
W. Johnson	43	262	17	12	4	3.54
G. Mogridge	33	211	13	13	1	3.11
T. Zachary	35	204	10	16	0	4.49
A. Russell	52	181	10	8	**9**	3.03
P. Zahniser	33	177	9	10	0	3.86
C. Warmoth	21	105	7	4	0	4.29
Hollingsworth	17	73	3	7	0	4.09

St. L. — W-74 L-78 Lee Fohl, W-51 L-49 Jimmy Austin, W-23 L-29

POS	Player	AB	BA	HR	RBI	PO	A	E	DP	TC/G	FA
1B	D. Schliebner	444	.275	4	52	1141	79	13	102	9.7	.989
2B	M. McManus	582	.309	15	94	386	373	32	86	5.9	.960
SS	W. Gerber	605	.281	1	62	**334**	461	42	86	5.4	.950
3B	G. Robertson	251	.247	0	17	86	117	14	6	2.9	.935
RF	J. Tobin	637	.317	13	73	269	14	9	3	1.9	.969
CF	B. Jacobson	592	.309	8	81	409	10	11	4	2.9	.974
LF	K. Williams	555	.357	29	91	333	23	12	5	2.5	.967
C	H. Severeid	432	.308	3	51	513	88	4	9	**5.2**	**.993**
3B	H. Ezzell	279	.244	0	14	88	159	10	13	3.5	.961
C	P. Collins	181	.177	3	30	161	31	4	4	4.2	.980

Pitcher	G	IP	W	L	SV	ERA
E. Vangilder	41	282	16	17	1	3.06
U. Shocker	43	277	20	12	5	3.41
D. Danforth	38	226	16	14	1	3.94
R. Kolp	34	171	5	12	1	3.89
D. Davis	19	109	4	6	0	3.62
H. Pruett	32	104	4	7	2	4.31
R. Wright	20	83	7	4	0	6.42

	POS	Player	AB	BA	HR	RBI	PO	A	E	DP	TC/G	FA	Pitcher	G	IP	W	L	SV	ERA
Phi.	1B	J. Hauser	537	.307	16	94	1475	86	15	109	10.8	.990	E. Rommel	56	298	18	19	5	3.27
W-69 L-83	2B	J. Dykes	416	.252	4	43	245	315	21	55	5.7	.964	B. Hasty	44	243	13	15	1	4.44
Connie Mack	SS	C. Galloway	504	.278	2	62	285	408	41	73	5.5	.944	S. Harriss	46	209	10	16	6	4.00
	3B	S. Hale	434	.288	3	51	85	222	28	17	3.1	.916	F. Heimach	40	208	6	12	0	4.32
	RF	F. Welch	421	.297	4	55	253	13	9	4	2.4	.967	R. Naylor	26	143	12	7	0	3.46
	CF	W. Matthews	485	.274	1	25	316	3	18	0	2.7	.947	R. Walberg	26	115	4	8	0	5.32
	LF	B. Miller	458	.299	12	64	262	10	6	0	2.3	.978							
	C	C. Perkins	500	.270	2	65	475	102	17	12	4.3	.971							
	OF	F. McGowan	287	.254	1	19	154	12	5	1	2.2	.971							
	2B	H. Scheer	210	.238	2	21	147	156	9	30	5.1	.971							
	3B	H. Riconda	175	.263	0	12	45	114	15	9	3.7	.914							
Chi.	1B	E. Sheely	570	.296	4	88	1563	96	14	113	10.7	.992	C. Robertson	38	255	13	18	0	3.81
W-69 L-85	2B	E. Collins	505	.360	5	67	347	430	20	77	5.6	.975	R. Faber	32	232	14	11	0	3.41
Kid Gleason	SS	H. McClellan	550	.235	1	41	217	394	27	63	4.6	.958	M. Cvengros	41	215	12	13	3	4.39
	3B	W. Kamm	544	.292	6	87	173	352	22	29	3.7	.960	Blankenship	44	209	9	14	0	4.27
	RF	H. Hooper	576	.288	10	65	272	15	12	3	2.1	.960	D. Leverett	38	193	10	13	0	4.06
	CF	J. Mostil	546	.291	3	64	422	21	12	5	3.2	.974	S. Thurston	44	192	7	8	4	3.05
	LF	B. Falk	274	.307	5	38	148	6	8	3	2.0	.951							
	C	R. Schalk	382	.228	1	44	481	93	10	20	4.8	.983							
	OF	R. Elsh	209	.249	0	24	127	7	6	1	2.5	.957							
	OF	B. Barrett	162	.272	2	23	89	5	6	1	2.5	.940							
Bos.	1B	G. Burns	551	.328	7	82	1485	92	16	103	10.9	.990	H. Ehmke	43	317	20	17	3	3.78
W-61 L-91	2B	C. Fewster	284	.236	0	15	103	140	16	21	5.4	.938	J. Quinn	42	243	13	17	7	3.89
Frank Chance	SS	J. Mitchell	347	.225	0	19	184	264	18	40	5.4	.961	A. Ferguson	34	198	9	13	0	4.04
	3B	H. Shanks	464	.254	3	57	89	169	17	16	3.2	.938	B. Piercy	30	187	8	17	0	3.41
	RF	I. Flagstead	382	.312	8	53	218	33*	16	8*	2.6	.962	G. Murray	39	178	7	11	0	4.91
	CF	D. Reichle	361	.258	1	39	190	10	5	2	2.2	.976	C. Fullerton	37	143	2	15	1	5.09
	LF	J. Harris	483	.335	13	76	289	13	10	2	2.4	.968							
	C	V. Picinich	268	.276	2	31	247	89	15	7	4.3	.957							
	UT	N. McMillan	459	.253	0	42	261	327	35	48		.944							
	OF	S. Collins	342	.231	0	18	164	17	9	2	2.1	.953							
	C	A. DeVormer	209	.258	0	18	181	48	5	3	4.3	.979							
	OF	M. Menosky	188	.229	0	25	103	12	10	1	2.6	.920							
	2B	P. Pittenger	177	.215	0	15	77	86	7	12	4.0	.959							

BATTING AND BASE RUNNING LEADERS

Batting Average
H. Heilmann, DET	.403
B. Ruth, NY	.393
T. Speaker, CLE	.380
E. Collins, CHI	.360
K. Williams, STL	.357

Slugging Average
B. Ruth, NY	.764
H. Heilmann, DET	.632
K. Williams, STL	.623
T. Speaker, CLE	.610
J. Harris, BOS	.520

Home Runs
B. Ruth, NY	41
K. Williams, STL	29
H. Heilmann, DET	18
T. Speaker, CLE	17
F. Brower, CLE	16
J. Hauser, PHI	16

Total Bases
B. Ruth, NY	399
T. Speaker, CLE	350
K. Williams, STL	346
H. Heilmann, DET	331
J. Tobin, STL	303

Runs Batted In
B. Ruth, NY	130
T. Speaker, CLE	130
H. Heilmann, DET	115
J. Sewell, CLE	109
W. Pipp, NY	108

Stolen Bases
E. Collins, CHI	47
J. Mostil, CHI	41
B. Harris, WAS	23
S. Rice, WAS	20
C. Jamieson, CLE	19

Hits
C. Jamieson, CLE	222
T. Speaker, CLE	218
H. Heilmann, DET	211

Base on Balls
B. Ruth, NY	170
J. Sewell, CLE	98
L. Blue, DET	96

Home Run Percentage
B. Ruth, NY	7.9
K. Williams, STL	5.2
F. Brower, CLE	4.0

Runs Scored
B. Ruth, NY	151
T. Speaker, CLE	133
C. Jamieson, CLE	130

Doubles
T. Speaker, CLE	59
G. Burns, BOS	47
B. Ruth, NY	45

Triples
S. Rice, WAS	18
G. Goslin, WAS	18
J. Mostil, CHI	15
J. Tobin, STL	15

PITCHING LEADERS

Winning Percentage
H. Pennock, NY	.760
S. Jones, NY	.724
W. Hoyt, NY	.654
U. Shocker, STL	.625
G. Uhle, CLE	.619

Earned Run Average
S. Coveleski, CLE	2.76
W. Hoyt, NY	3.02
E. Vangilder, STL	3.06
G. Mogridge, WAS	3.11
E. Rommel, PHI	3.27

Wins
G. Uhle, CLE	26
S. Jones, NY	21
H. Dauss, DET	21
U. Shocker, STL	20
H. Ehmke, BOS	20

Saves
A. Russell, WAS	9
J. Quinn, BOS	7
S. Harriss, PHI	6

Strikeouts
W. Johnson, WAS	130
B. Shawkey, NY	125
J. Bush, NY	125
H. Ehmke, BOS	121
U. Shocker, STL	109
G. Uhle, CLE	109

Complete Games
G. Uhle, CLE	29
H. Ehmke, BOS	28
U. Shocker, STL	24
J. Bush, NY	23
H. Dauss, DET	22

Fewest Hits per 9 Innings
B. Shawkey, NY	8.07
W. Hoyt, NY	8.56
J. Bush, NY	8.59

Shutouts
S. Coveleski, CLE	5
W. Johnson, WAS	4
E. Vangilder, STL	4
H. Dauss, DET	4

Fewest Walks per 9 Innings
U. Shocker, STL	1.59
S. Coveleski, CLE	1.66
J. Quinn, BOS	1.96

Most Strikeouts per 9 Inn.
W. Johnson, WAS	4.47
B. Shawkey, NY	4.35
J. Bush, NY	4.08

Innings
G. Uhle, CLE	358
H. Ehmke, BOS	317
H. Dauss, DET	316

Games Pitched
E. Rommel, PHI	56
G. Uhle, CLE	54
A. Russell, WAS	52
B. Cole, DET	52

	W	L	PCT	GB	R	OR	2B	3B	Batting HR	BA	SA	SB	E	Fielding DP	FA	CG	BB	Pitching SO	ShO	SV	ERA
NY	98	54	.645		823	**622**	231	79	**105**	.291	**.422**	69	**144**	131	**.977**	**102**	491	**506**	9	10	**3.66**
DET	83	71	.539	16	831	741	270	69	41	**.300**	.401	87	200	103	.968	61	**459**	447	9	12	4.09
CLE	82	71	.536	16.5	**888**	746	**301**	75	59	**.301**	.420	79	226	143	.964	76	466	407	**10**	11	3.91
WAS	75	78	.490	23.5	720	747	224	**93**	26	.274	.367	102	216	**182**	.966	70	559	474	8	**16**	3.99
STL	74	78	.487	24	688	720	248	62	82	.281	.398	64	177	145	.971	83	528	488	**10**	10	3.93
PHI	69	83	.454	29	661	761	229	65	52	.271	.370	72	221	127	.965	65	550	400	6	12	4.08
CHI	69	85	.448	30	692	741	254	57	42	.279	.373	**191**	184	138	.971	74	534	467	5	11	4.03
BOS	61	91	.401	37	584	809	253	54	34	.261	.351	77	232	126	.963	78	520	412	3	11	4.20
					5887	5887	2010	554	441	.282	.388	741	1600	1095	.968	609	4107	3601	60	93	3.99

National League 1924

	POS	Player	AB	BA	HR	RBI	PO	A	E	DP	TC/G	FA	Pitcher	G	IP	W	L	SV	ERA
N. Y. W-93 L-60 John McGraw	1B	G. Kelly	571	.324	21	**136**	1309	60	10	105	11.0	.993	V. Barnes	35	229	16	10	3	3.06
	2B	F. Frisch	603	.328	7	69	**391**	537	27	100	**6.7**	.937	J. Bentley	28	188	16	5	1	3.78
	SS	T. Jackson	596	.302	11	76	332	534	58	101	6.1	.937	H. McQuillan	27	184	14	8	3	2.69
	3B	H. Groh	559	.281	2	46	121	286	7	13	2.9	**.983**	A. Nehf	30	172	14	4	2	3.62
	RF	R. Youngs	526	.356	10	74	236	17	12	3	2.0	.955	W. Dean	26	126	6	12	0	5.01
	CF	H. Wilson	383	.295	10	57	230	8	8	2	2.4	.967	R. Ryan	37	125	8	6	5	4.26
	LF	I. Meusel	549	.310	6	102	287	4	10	0	2.2	.967	M. Watson	22	100	7	4	0	3.79
	C	F. Snyder	354	.302	5	53	308	79	5	8	3.6	.987	C. Jonnard	34	90	4	5	5	2.41
	OF	B. Southworth	281	.256	3	36	167	5	12	2	2.5	.935							
	C	H. Gowdy	191	.325	4	37	223	51	5	8	3.6	.982							
	1B	B. Terry	163	.239	5	24	325	14	4	30	8.2	.988							
Bkn. W-92 L-62 Wilbert Robinson	1B	J. Fournier	563	.334	**27**	116	1388	99	22	102	9.9	.985	B. Grimes	38	**311**	22	13	1	3.82
	2B	A. High	582	.328	6	61	295	437	27	52	5.7	.964	D. Vance	35	309	**28**	6	0	**2.16**
	SS	J. Mitchell	243	.263	1	16	131	216	18	30	5.7	.951	D. Ruether	30	167	8	13	3	3.94
	3B	M. Stock	561	.242	2	52	139	200	**25**	14	2.6	.931	B. Doak	21	149	11	5	0	3.07
	RF	T. Griffith	482	.251	3	67	210	9	8	3	1.6	.965	A. Decatur	31	128	10	9	1	4.07
	CF	E. Brown	455	.308	5	74	311	3	8	0	2.8	.975	T. Osborne	21	104	6	5	0	5.09
	LF	Z. Wheat	566	.375	14	97	288	13	11	4	2.2	.965							
	C	Z. Taylor	345	.290	1	39	388	96	6	13	**5.3**	**.988**							
	SS	J. Johnston	315	.298	2	29	136	203	22	32	5.7	.939							
	C	H. DeBerry	218	.243	3	26	394	57	3	8	7.2	.993							
	OF	B. Neis	211	.303	4	26	114	5	8	1	2.0	.937							
Pit. W-90 L-63 Bill McKechnie	1B	C. Grimm	542	.288	2	63	**1596**	72	8	**139**	11.1	**.995**	W. Cooper	38	269	20	14	1	3.28
	2B	R. Maranville	594	.266	2	71	365	**568**	26	109	6.3	**.973**	R. Kremer	41	259	18	10	1	3.19
	SS	G. Wright	**616**	.287	7	111	310	**601**	52	102	6.3	.946	J. Morrison	41	238	11	16	2	3.75
	3B	P. Traynor	545	.294	5	82	179	268	15	**31**	3.3	.968	L. Meadows	36	229	13	12	0	3.26
	RF	C. Barnhart	344	.276	3	51	186	8	6	3	2.3	.970	E. Yde	33	194	16	3	0	2.83
	CF	M. Carey	599	.297	7	55	**428**	16	16	3	3.1	.965							
	LF	K. Cuyler	466	.354	9	85	246	19	16	4	2.5	.943							
	C	J. Gooch	224	.290	0	25	198	47	3	12	3.6	.988							
	OF	C. Bigbee	282	.262	0	15	155	9	10	2	2.3	.943							
	O3	E. Moore	209	.359	2	13	92	30	1	2		.992							
	C	W. Schmidt	177	.243	1	20	166	51	3	6	3.9	.986							
	C	E. Smith	111	.369	4	21	127	23	4	3	4.4	.974							
Cin. W-83 L-70 Jack Hendricks	1B	J. Daubert	405	.281	1	31	1128	74	12	84	**11.9**	.990	E. Rixey	35	238	15	14	1	2.76
	2B	H. Critz	413	.322	3	35	229	357	27	58	6.4	.956	C. Mays	37	226	20	9	0	3.15
	SS	S. Caveney	337	.273	4	32	200	310	42	59	6.1	.924	P. Donohue	35	222	16	9	0	3.60
	3B	B. Pinelli	510	.306	0	70	**182**	318	23	21	**3.7**	.954	D. Luque	31	219	10	15	0	3.16
	RF	C. Walker	397	.300	4	46	213	14	5	4	2.1	.959	T. Sheehan	39	167	9	11	1	3.24
	CF	E. Roush	483	.348	3	72	270	10	12	4	2.5	.959	R. Benton	32	163	7	9	1	2.77
	LF	P. Duncan	319	.270	2	37	124	3	10	0	1.7	.927	J. May	38	99	3	3	**6**	3.00
	C	B. Hargrave	312	.301	3	33	322	80	7	7	4.5	.983							
	1O	R. Bressler	383	.347	4	49	561	35	9	36		.985							
	UT	S. Bohne	349	.255	4	46	194	294	23	40		.955							
	OF	G. Burns	336	.256	2	33	168	13	7	4	2.1	.963							
	C	I. Wingo	192	.286	1	23	215	50	3	7	4.1	.989							
Chi. W-81 L-72 Bill Killefer	1B	H. Cotter	310	.261	4	33	873	59	10	72	10.5	.989	V. Aldridge	32	244	15	12	0	3.50
	2B	G. Grantham	469	.316	12	60	273	426	**44**	78	6.3	.941	V. Keen	40	235	15	14	3	3.80
	SS	S. Adams	418	.280	1	27	169	277	28	62	5.4	.941	T. Kaufmann	34	208	16	11	0	4.02
	3B	B. Friberg	495	.279	5	82	163	268	21	21	3.2	.954	E. Jacobs	38	190	11	12	1	3.74
	RF	C. Heathcote	392	.309	3	30	228	7	5	3	2.2	.979	G. Alexander	21	169	12	5	0	3.03
	CF	J. Statz	549	.277	3	49	373	**22**	16	5	**3.1**	.974	S. Blake	29	106	6	6	1	4.57
	LF	D. Grigsby	411	.299	3	48	244	16	7	4	2.2	.974	R. Wheeler	29	101	3	6	0	3.91
	C	G. Hartnett	354	.299	16	67	369	97	**18**	12	4.6	.963							
	SS	C. Hollocher	286	.245	2	21	156	248	13	42	5.9	.969							
	C	B. O'Farrell	183	.240	3	28	204	40	4	5	4.4	.984							
	1B	R. Grimes	177	.299	5	34	530	12	10	40	11.0	.982							
	OF	O. Vogel	172	.267	1	7	101	7	5	2	2.1	.956							
	OF	B. Weis	133	.278	0	23	81	6	8	2	2.5	.978							
	UT	B. Barrett	133	.241	5	21	123	80	13	20		.940							
	OF	H. Miller	131	.336	4	25	54	1	3	0	1.8	.948							

	POS	Player	AB	BA	HR	RBI	PO	A	E	DP	TC/G	FA	Pitcher	G	IP	W	L	SV	ERA
St. L.	1B	J. Bottomley	528	.316	14	111	1297	48	24	110	10.3	.982	J. Haines	35	223	8	19	0	4.41
W-65 L-89	2B	R. Hornsby	536	.424	25	94	301	517	30	102	5.9	.965	A. Sothoron	29	197	10	16	0	3.57
Branch Rickey	SS	J. Cooney	383	.295	1	57	242	322	18	68	5.9	.969	B. Sherdel	35	169	8	9	1	3.42
	3B	H. Freigau	376	.269	2	39	127	171	13	24	3.2	.958	J. Stuart	28	159	9	11	0	4.75
	RF	J. Smith	459	.283	2	33	251	18	9	8	2.4	.968	E. Dyer	29	137	8	11	0	4.61
	CF	W. Holm	293	.294	0	23	162	9	2	1	2.5	.988	L. Dickerman	18	120	7	4	0	2.41
	LF	R. Blades	456	.311	11	68	256	6	12	1	2.7	.988	H. Bell	28	113	3	8	1	4.92
	C	M. Gonzalez	402	.296	3	53	413	96	7	15	4.3	.986							
	O1	H. Mueller	296	.264	2	37	335	15	9	17		.975							
	OF	M. Flack	209	.263	2	21	90	9	3	0	2.0	.971							
	3S	S. Toporcer	198	.313	1	24	54	103	7	8		.957							
	OF	T. Douthit	173	.277	0	13	118	5	3	2	2.5	.976							
	OF	C. Hafey	91	.253	2	22	48	3	4	1	2.3	.927							
Phi.	1B	W. Holke	563	.300	6	64	1516	90	12	134	10.9	.993	J. Ring	32	215	10	12	0	3.97
W-55 L-96	2B	H. Ford	530	.272	3	53	337	543	27	96	6.3	.970	H. Carlson	38	204	8	17	2	4.86
Art Fletcher	SS	H. Sand	539	.245	6	40	333	460	34	95	6.0	.959	B. Hubbell	36	179	10	9	2	4.83
	3B	Wrightstone	388	.307	7	58	114	154	16	19	2.9	.944	C. Mitchell	30	165	6	13	1	5.62
	RF	G. Harper	411	.294	16	55	219	13	2	4	2.1	.991*	W. Glazner	35	157	7	16	0	5.92
	CF	C. Williams	558	.328	24	93	368	13	15	0	2.7	.962	H. Betts	37	144	7	10	2	4.30
	LF	J. Mokan	366	.260	9	44	195	9	3	1	2.2	.986	J. Couch	37	137	4	8	3	4.73
	C	B. Henline	289	.284	5	35	248	76	9	12	4.0	.973							
	OF	J. Schultz	284	.282	5	29	137	7	6	0	2.0	.960							
	C	J. Wilson	280	.279	6	39	240	93	11	14	4.2	.968							
	UT	F. Parkinson	156	.212	1	19	63	127	7	23		.964							
Bos.	1B	S. McInnis	581	.291	1	59	1435	95	10	129	10.5	.994	J. Barnes	37	268	15	20	0	3.23
W-53 L-100	2B	C. Tierney	505	.259	6	58	235	399	24	83	5.7	.964	J. Genewich	34	200	10	19	1	5.21
Dave Bancroft	SS	B. Smith	347	.228	2	38	180	273	20	54	5.9	.958	J. Cooney	34	181	8	9	2	3.18
	3B	E. Padgett	502	.255	1	46	95	194	10	23	2.6	.967	T. McNamara	35	179	8	12	0	5.18
	RF	C. Stengel	461	.280	5	39	211	12	5	4	1.8	.978	J. Yeargin	32	141	1	11	0	5.09
	CF	F. Wilson	215	.237	1	15	140	5	4	1	2.7	.973	L. Benton	30	128	5	7	1	4.15
	LF	B. Cunningham	437	.272	1	40	243	16	8	3	2.4	.970	D. Stryker	20	73	3	8	0	6.01
	C	M. O'Neil	362	.246	0	22	362	108	7	8	4.5	.985							
	SS	D. Bancroft	319	.279	2	21	186	259	18	57	5.9	.961							
	C	F. Gibson	229	.310	1	30	159	52	6	4	4.7	.972							
	OF	G. Felix	204	.211	1	10	147	6	8	1	3.2	.950							
	OF	R. Powell	188	.261	1	15	117	9	7	3	2.9	.947							

BATTING AND BASE RUNNING LEADERS

Batting Average
R. Hornsby, STL	.424
Z. Wheat, BKN	.375
R. Youngs, NY	.356
K. Cuyler, PIT	.354
E. Roush, CIN	.348

Slugging Average
R. Hornsby, STL	.696
C. Williams, PHI	.552
Z. Wheat, BKN	.549
K. Cuyler, PIT	.539
G. Kelly, NY	.531

Home Runs
J. Fournier, BKN	27
R. Hornsby, STL	25
C. Williams, PHI	24
G. Kelly, NY	21
G. Hartnett, CHI	16
G. Harper, CIN, PHI	16

Total Bases
R. Hornsby, STL	373
Z. Wheat, BKN	311
C. Williams, PHI	308
G. Kelly, NY	303
J. Fournier, BKN	302

Runs Batted In
G. Kelly, NY	136
J. Fournier, BKN	116
J. Bottomley, STL	111
G. Wright, PIT	111
I. Meusel, NY	102

Stolen Bases
M. Carey, PIT	49
K. Cuyler, PIT	32
C. Heathcote, CHI	26
J. Smith, STL	24
P. Traynor, PIT	24

Hits
R. Hornsby, STL	227
Z. Wheat, BKN	212
F. Frisch, NY	198

Base on Balls
R. Hornsby, STL	89
J. Fournier, BKN	83
R. Youngs, NY	77

Home Run Percentage
R. Hornsby, STL	4.7
G. Hartnett, CHI	4.5
C. Williams, PHI	4.3

Runs Scored
R. Hornsby, STL	121
F. Frisch, NY	121
M. Carey, PIT	113

Doubles
R. Hornsby, STL	43
Z. Wheat, BKN	41
G. Kelly, NY	37

Triples
E. Roush, CIN	21
R. Maranville, PIT	20
G. Wright, PIT	18

PITCHING LEADERS

Winning Percentage
E. Yde, PIT	.842
D. Vance, BKN	.824
J. Bentley, NY	.762
C. Mays, CIN	.690
R. Kremer, PIT	.643

Earned Run Average
D. Vance, BKN	2.16
H. McQuillan, NY	2.69
E. Rixey, CIN	2.76
E. Yde, PIT	2.83
G. Alexander, CHI	3.03

Wins
D. Vance, BKN	28
B. Grimes, BKN	22
C. Mays, CIN	20
W. Cooper, PIT	20
R. Kremer, PIT	18

Saves
J. May, CIN	6
R. Ryan, NY	5
C. Jonnard, NY	5

Strikeouts
D. Vance, BKN	262
B. Grimes, BKN	135
D. Luque, CIN	86
J. Morrison, PIT	85
T. Kaufmann, CHI	79

Complete Games
D. Vance, BKN	30
B. Grimes, BKN	30
W. Cooper, PIT	25
J. Barnes, BOS	21
V. Aldridge, CHI	20

Fewest Hits per 9 Innings
D. Vance, BKN	6.94
E. Yde, PIT	7.93
J. Morrison, PIT	8.07

Shutouts
5 tied with	4

Fewest Walks per 9 Innings
G. Alexander, CHI	1.33
W. Cooper, PIT	1.34
C. Mays, CIN	1.43

Most Strikeouts per 9 Inn.
D. Vance, BKN	7.64
B. Grimes, BKN	3.91
A. Nehf, NY	3.77

Innings
B. Grimes, BKN	311
D. Vance, BKN	309
W. Cooper, PIT	269

Games Pitched
R. Kremer, PIT	41
J. Morrison, PIT	41
V. Keen, CHI	40
T. Sheehan, CIN	39

	W	L	PCT	GB	R	OR	2B	3B	HR	BA	SA	SB	E	DP	FA	CG	BB	SO	ShO	SV	ERA
NY	93	60	.608		857	641	269	81	95	.300	.432	82	186	160	.971	71	392	406	4	21	3.62
BKN	92	62	.597	1.5	717	675	227	54	72	.287	.391	34	196	121	.968	98	403	640	10	5	3.64
PIT	90	63	.588	3	724	588	222	122	43	.287	.399	181	183	161	.971	85	323	364	15	5	3.27
CIN	83	70	.542	10	649	579	236	111	36	.290	.397	103	217	142	.966	77	293	451	14	9	3.12
CHI	81	72	.529	12	698	698	207	59	66	.276	.378	137	218	153	.966	85	438	416	4	6	3.83
STL	65	89	.422	28.5	740	750	270	87	67	.290	.411	86	191	162	.969	79	486	393	7	6	4.15
PHI	55	96	.364	37	676	849	256	56	94	.275	.397	57	175	168	.972	59	469	349	7	10	4.87
BOS	53	100	.346	40	520	800	194	52	25	.256	.327	74	168	154	.973	66	402	364	10	4	4.46
					5581	5581	1881	622	498	.283	.392	754	1534	1221	.970	620	3206	3383	71	66	3.87

American League 1924

Was. — W-92 L-62 — Bucky Harris

POS	Player	AB	BA	HR	RBI	PO	A	E	DP	TC/G	FA	Pitcher	G	IP	W	L	SV	ERA
1B	J. Judge	516	.324	3	79	1276	86	8	108	9.8	.994	W. Johnson	38	278	23	7	0	2.72
2B	B. Harris	544	.268	1	58	393	386	26	100	5.6	.968	G. Mogridge	30	213	16	11	0	3.76
SS	Peckinpaugh	523	.272	2	73	278	487	29	81	5.1	.963	T. Zachary	33	203	15	9	2	2.75
3B	O. Bluege	402	.281	2	49	88	195	16	11	2.9	.946	F. Marberry	50	195	11	12	15	3.09
RF	S. Rice	646	.334	1	76	331	18	12	4	2.3	.967	J. Martina	24	125	6	8	0	4.67
CF	N. Leibold	246	.293	0	20	148	7	1	0	2.2	.994	C. Ogden	16	108	9	5	0	2.59
LF	G. Goslin	579	.344	12	129	369	12	16	4	2.6	.960	P. Zahniser	24	92	5	7	0	4.40
C	M. Ruel	501	.283	0	57	612	112	15	23	5.0	.980	A. Russell	37	82	5	1	8	4.37
OF	E. McNeely	179	.330	0	15	105	3	3	1	2.6	.973							
OF	W. Matthews	169	.302	0	13	121	7	2	2	3.0	.985							
3B	D. Prothro	159	.333	0	24	40	68	10	6	2.6	.915							

N. Y. — W-89 L-63 — Miller Huggins

POS	Player	AB	BA	HR	RBI	PO	A	E	DP	TC/G	FA	Pitcher	G	IP	W	L	SV	ERA
1B	W. Pipp	589	.295	9	113	1447	106	9	106	10.2	.994	H. Pennock	40	286	21	9	3	2.83
2B	A. Ward	400	.253	8	66	303	385	19	60	5.9	.973	J. Bush	39	252	17	16	1	3.57
SS	E. Scott	548	.250	4	64	322	455	27	80	5.3	.966	W. Hoyt	46	247	18	13	4	3.79
3B	J. Dugan	610	.302	3	56	177	250	17	22	3.0	.962	B. Shawkey	38	208	16	11	0	4.12
RF	B. Ruth	529	.378	46	121	340	18	14	4	2.4	.962	S. Jones	36	179	9	6	3	3.63
CF	W. Witt	600	.297	1	36	362	11	9	1	2.7	.976							
LF	B. Meusel	579	.325	12	120	252	17	14	4	2.0	.951							
C	W. Schang	356	.292	5	52	423	89	15	9	4.8	.972							
C	F. Hofmann	166	.175	1	11	179	45	2	2	4.2	.991							

Det. — W-86 L-68 — Ty Cobb

POS	Player	AB	BA	HR	RBI	PO	A	E	DP	TC/G	FA	Pitcher	G	IP	W	L	SV	ERA
1B	L. Blue	395	.311	2	50	1099	85	17	72	11.1	.986	E. Whitehill	35	233	17	9	0	3.86
2B	D. Pratt	429	.303	1	77	133	192	18	38	5.4	.948	R. Collins	34	216	14	7	0	3.21
SS	T. Rigney	499	.289	4	93	273	463	25	72	5.2	.967	L. Stoner	36	216	11	11	0	4.72
3B	B. Jones	393	.272	0	47	108	196	14	12	3.0	.956	K. Holloway	49	181	14	6	3	4.07
RF	H. Heilmann	570	.346	10	113	263	31	9	6	2.1	.970	H. Dauss	40	131	12	11	6	4.59
CF	T. Cobb	625	.338	4	74	417	12	6	8	2.8	.986	B. Cole	28	109	3	9	2	4.69
LF	H. Manush	422	.289	9	68	224	4	5	1	2.2	.979	S. Johnson	29	104	5	4	3	4.93
C	J. Bassler	379	.346	1	68	402	103	11	11	4.2	.979	E. Wells	29	102	6	8	4	4.06
3B	F. Haney	256	.309	1	30	48	146	14	9	3.5	.933							
2B	L. Burke	241	.253	0	17	125	167	13	30	5.3	.957							
2B	F. O'Rourke	181	.276	0	19	115	140	8	27	6.6	.970							
OF	B. Fothergill	166	.301	0	15	89	2	3	1	2.1	.968							
C	L. Woodall	165	.309	0	24	174	41	3	5	3.5	.986							
OF	A. Wingo	150	.287	1	26	59	3	5	2	1.6	.925							

St. L. — W-74 L-78 — George Sisler

POS	Player	AB	BA	HR	RBI	PO	A	E	DP	TC/G	FA	Pitcher	G	IP	W	L	SV	ERA
1B	G. Sisler	636	.305	9	74	1319	111	23	114	9.6	.984	U. Shocker	39	239	16	13	1	4.17
2B	M. McManus	442	.333	5	80	324	365	20	67	6.0	.972	D. Danforth	41	220	15	12	4	4.51
SS	W. Gerber	496	.272	0	55	317	422	42	77	5.3	.946	E. Wingard	36	218	13	12	1	3.51
3B	G. Robertson	439	.319	4	52	112	203	14	22	3.0	.957	D. Davis	29	160	11	13	0	4.10
RF	J. Tobin	569	.299	2	48	248	19	12	5	2.1	.957	E. Vangilder	43	145	5	10	1	5.76
CF	B. Jacobson	579	.318	19	97	484	7	7	4	3.3	.986	R. Kolp	25	97	5	7	0	5.68
LF	K. Williams	398	.324	18	84	257	13	9	2	2.6	.968							
C	H. Severeid	432	.308	4	48	436	104	6	12	4.2	.989							
OF	J. Evans	209	.254	0	18	118	3	4	1	2.6	.968							
UT	N. McMillan	201	.279	0	27	132	122	11	19		.958							

Phi. — W-71 L-81 — Connie Mack

POS	Player	AB	BA	HR	RBI	PO	A	E	DP	TC/G	FA	Pitcher	G	IP	W	L	SV	ERA
1B	J. Hauser	562	.288	27	115	1513	94	12	131	11.1	.993	E. Rommel	43	278	18	15	1	3.95
2B	M. Bishop	294	.255	2	21	189	273	15	50	6.0	.969	F. Heimach	40	198	14	12	0	4.73
SS	C. Galloway	464	.276	2	48	285	389	34	71	5.5	.952	Baumgartner	36	181	13	6	4	2.88
3B	H. Riconda	281	.253	1	21	95	147	19	14	3.6	.927	D. Burns	37	154	6	8	1	5.08
RF	B. Miller	398	.342	6	62	172	11	5	4	2.0	.973	S. Gray	34	152	8	7	2	3.98
CF	A. Simmons	594	.308	8	102	390	17	10	4	2.7	.976	R. Meeker	30	146	5	12	0	4.68
LF	B. Lamar	367	.330	7	48	184	13	6	4	2.3	.970	S. Harriss	36	123	6	10	2	4.68
C	C. Perkins	392	.242	0	32	415	102	9	9	4.1	.983							
2B	J. Dykes	410	.312	3	50	213	253	19	46	6.2	.961							
OF	F. Welch	293	.290	5	31	120	15	2	2	1.9	.985							
3B	S. Hale	261	.318	2	17	39	108	8	10	2.8	.948							
OF	P. Strand	167	.228	0	13	80	3	1	0	1.9	.988							

POS	Player	AB	BA	HR	RBI	PO	A	E	DP	TC/G	FA	Pitcher	G	IP	W	L	SV	ERA
Cle. W-67 L-86 Tris Speaker																		
1B	G. Burns	462	.310	4	66	1227	110	18	85	10.7	.987	J. Shaute	46	283	20	17	2	3.75
2B	C. Fewster	322	.267	0	36	194	229	17	36	4.7	.961	S. Smith	39	248	12	14	1	3.02
SS	J. Sewell	594	.316	4	104	349	514	36	76	5.9	.960	S. Coveleski	37	240	15	16	0	4.04
3B	R. Lutzke	341	.243	0	42	154	238	22	25	4.0	.947	G. Uhle	28	196	9	15	1	4.77
RF	H. Summa	390	.290	2	38	167	10	11	2	2.0	.941							
CF	T. Speaker	486	.344	9	65	323	20	13	3	2.8	.963							
LF	C. Jamieson	594	.359	3	53	330	11	9	6	2.5	.974							
C	G. Myatt	342	.342	8	73	248	63	7	7	3.3	.978							
OF	P. McNulty	291	.268	0	26	137	9	6	2	2.0	.961							
2B	R. Stephenson	240	.371	4	44	114	179	12	20	5.3	.946							
C	L. Sewell	165	.291	0	17	171	42	9	5	4.0	.959							
1B	F. Brower	107	.280	3	20	187	17	2	11	7.9	.990							
Bos. W-67 L-87 Lee Fohl																		
1B	J. Harris	491	.301	3	77	1266	101	10	100	10.8	.993	H. Ehmke	45	315	19	17	4	3.46
2B	B. Wambsganss	636	.274	0	49	459	490	37	98	6.4	.962	A. Ferguson	40	235	14	17	2	3.79
SS	D. Lee	288	.253	0	29	198	246	30	43	5.3	.937	J. Quinn	43	228	12	13	7	3.20
3B	D. Clark	325	.277	2	54	88	173	15	8	3.0	.946	C. Fullerton	33	152	7	12	2	4.32
RF	I. Boone	486	.333	13	96	189	17	5	3	1.7	.976	B. Piercy	22	115	5	7	0	6.20
CF	I. Flagstead	560	.305	5	43	370	9	10	2	2.7	.974	G. Murray	28	80	2	9	0	6.72
LF	B. Veach	519	.295	5	99	268	15	13	2	2.3	.956							
C	S. O'Neill	307	.238	0	38	342	75	13	2	4.7	.970							
3B	H. Ezzell	273	.275	0	32	59	127	2	6	3.0	.989							
OF	S. Collins	240	.292	0	28	85	4	4	0	1.7	.957							
UT	H. Shanks	193	.259	0	25	118	129	9	23		.965							
C	V. Picinich	158	.266	1	24	155	36	10	2	3.9	.950							
Chi. W-66 L-87 Johnny Evers																		
1B	E. Sheely	535	.320	3	103	1423	79	14	97	10.4	.991	S. Thurston	38	291	20	14	1	3.80
2B	E. Collins	556	.349	6	86	396	446	20	83	5.7	.977	T. Lyons	41	216	12	11	3	4.87
SS	B. Barrett	406	.271	2	56	167	199	39	36	5.3	.904	R. Faber	21	161	9	11	0	3.85
3B	W. Kamm	528	.254	6	93	190	312	15	31	3.6	.971	S. Connally	44	160	7	13	6	4.05
RF	H. Hooper	476	.328	10	62	251	22	4	8	2.3	.986	Blankenship	25	125	7	6	1	5.17
CF	J. Mostil	385	.325	4	49	281	13	8	2	3.0	.974	M. Cvengros	26	106	3	12	0	5.88
LF	B. Falk	526	.352	6	99	292	26	10	4	2.4	.970	C. Robertson	17	97	4	10	0	4.99
C	B. Crouse	305	.259	1	44	298	97	23	9	4.6	.945							
OF	M. Archdeacon	288	.319	0	25	173	8	8	2	2.5	.958							

BATTING AND BASE RUNNING LEADERS

Batting Average
B. Ruth, NY	.378
C. Jamieson, CLE	.359
B. Falk, CHI	.352
E. Collins, CHI	.349
J. Bassler, DET	.346

Slugging Average
B. Ruth, NY	.739
H. Heilmann, DET	.533
K. Williams, STL	.533
B. Jacobson, STL	.528
G. Myatt, CLE	.518

Home Runs
B. Ruth, NY	46
J. Hauser, PHI	27
B. Jacobson, STL	19
K. Williams, STL	18
I. Boone, BOS	13

Total Bases
B. Ruth, NY	391
B. Jacobson, STL	306
H. Heilmann, DET	304
G. Goslin, WAS	299
J. Hauser, PHI	290

Runs Batted In
G. Goslin, WAS	129
B. Ruth, NY	121
B. Meusel, NY	120
J. Hauser, PHI	115
H. Heilmann, DET	113
W. Pipp, NY	113

Stolen Bases
E. Collins, CHI	42
B. Meusel, NY	26
S. Rice, WAS	24
T. Cobb, DET	23
C. Jamieson, CLE	21

Hits
S. Rice, WAS	216
C. Jamieson, CLE	213
T. Cobb, DET	211

Base on Balls
B. Ruth, NY	142
T. Rigney, DET	102
E. Sheely, CHI	95

Home Run Percentage
B. Ruth, NY	8.7
J. Hauser, PHI	4.8
K. Williams, STL	4.5

Runs Scored
B. Ruth, NY	143
T. Cobb, DET	115
E. Collins, CHI	108

Doubles
H. Heilmann, DET	45
J. Sewell, CLE	45
B. Jacobson, STL	41
B. Wambsganss, BOS	41

Triples
W. Pipp, NY	19
G. Goslin, WAS	17
H. Heilmann, DET	16

PITCHING LEADERS

Winning Percentage
W. Johnson, WAS	.767
H. Pennock, NY	.700
E. Whitehill, DET	.654
T. Zachary, WAS	.625
G. Mogridge, WAS	.593
B. Shawkey, NY	.593

Earned Run Average
W. Johnson, WAS	2.72
T. Zachary, WAS	2.75
H. Pennock, NY	2.83
Baumgartner, PHI	2.88
S. Smith, CLE	3.02

Wins
W. Johnson, WAS	23
H. Pennock, NY	21
S. Thurston, CHI	20
J. Shaute, CLE	20
H. Ehmke, BOS	19

Saves
F. Marberry, WAS	15
A. Russell, WAS	8
J. Quinn, BOS	7
H. Dauss, DET	6
S. Connally, CHI	6

Strikeouts
W. Johnson, WAS	158
H. Ehmke, BOS	119
B. Shawkey, NY	114
H. Pennock, NY	101
U. Shocker, STL	84

Complete Games
S. Thurston, CHI	28
H. Ehmke, BOS	26
H. Pennock, NY	25
E. Rommel, PHI	21
J. Shaute, CLE	21

Fewest Hits per 9 Innings
W. Johnson, WAS	7.55
R. Collins, DET	8.29
T. Zachary, WAS	8.79

Shutouts
W. Johnson, WAS	6
D. Davis, STL	5

Fewest Walks per 9 Innings
S. Smith, CLE	1.53
U. Shocker, STL	1.84
S. Thurston, CHI	1.86

Most Strikeouts per 9 Inn.
W. Johnson, WAS	5.12
B. Shawkey, NY	4.94
H. Ehmke, BOS	3.40

Innings
H. Ehmke, BOS	315
S. Thurston, CHI	291
H. Pennock, NY	286

Games Pitched
F. Marberry, WAS	50
K. Holloway, DET	49
J. Shaute, CLE	46
W. Hoyt, NY	46

	W	L	PCT	GB	R	OR	2B	3B	Batting HR	BA	SA	SB	E	Fielding DP	FA	CG	BB	Pitching SO	ShO	SV	ERA
WAS	92	62	.597		755	**613**	255	**88**	22	.294	.387	115	171	149	.972	74	505	469	12	**25**	**3.35**
NY	89	63	.586	2	798	667	248	86	**98**	.289	**.426**	69	**156**	131	**.974**	76	522	**487**	**13**	13	3.86
DET	86	68	.558	6	**849**	796	**315**	76	35	**.298**	.404	100	187	142	.971	60	**466**	441	5	20	4.19
STL	74	78	.487	17	764	797	265	62	67	.294	.408	85	183	141	.969	66	512	382	11	7	4.55
PHI	71	81	.467	20	685	778	251	59	63	.281	.389	79	180	**157**	.971	68	597	371	7	10	4.39
CLE	67	86	.438	24.5	755	814	306	59	41	.296	.399	84	205	130	.967	**87**	503	315	7	7	4.40
BOS	67	87	.435	25	725	801	300	61	30	.277	.374	79	210	124	.967	73	519	414	8	16	4.36
CHI	66	87	.431	25.5	793	858	254	58	41	.288	.382	**138**	229	136	.963	76	512	360	1	11	4.75
					6124	6124	2194	549	397	.290	.396	749	1521	1110	.969	580	4136	3239	64	109	4.23

National League 1925

	POS	Player	AB	BA	HR	RBI	PO	A	E	DP	TC/G	FA	Pitcher	G	IP	W	L	SV	ERA
Pit. W-95 L-58 Bill McKechnie	1B	G. Grantham	359	.326	8	52	925	44	11	96	9.6	.989	L. Meadows	35	255	19	10	1	3.67
	2B	E. Moore	547	.298	6	77	307	401	**36**	82	6.1	.952	R. Kremer	40	215	17	8	2	3.69
	SS	G. Wright	614	.308	18	121	338	**530**	56	**109**	6.0	.939	V. Aldridge	30	213	15	7	0	3.63
	3B	P. Traynor	591	.320	6	106	**226**	**303**	24	**41**	**3.7**	**.957**	J. Morrison	**44**	211	17	14	**4**	3.88
	RF	K. Cuyler	617	.357	17	102	362	21	13	4	2.6	.967	E. Yde	33	207	17	9	0	4.13
	CF	M. Carey	542	.343	5	44	363	20	**20**	2	**3.1**	.950	B. Adams	33	101	6	5	3	5.42
	LF	C. Barnhart	539	.325	4	114	295	11	12	2	2.3	.962							
	C	E. Smith	329	.313	8	64	317	77	13	**15**	4.2	.968							
	C	J. Gooch	215	.298	0	30	172	39	7	8	2.9	.968							
	1B	S. McInnis	155	.368	0	24	377	24	3	40	8.8	.993							
N. Y. W-86 L-66 John McGraw	1B	B. Terry	489	.319	11	70	1270	77	14	83	**10.8**	.990	J. Scott	36	240	14	15	3	3.15
	2B	G. Kelly	586	.309	20	99	273	394	13	68	6.3	.981	V. Barnes	32	222	15	11	2	3.53
	SS	T. Jackson	411	.285	9	59	277	366	40	64	6.2	.941	K. Greenfield	29	172	12	8	0	3.88
	3B	F. Lindstrom	356	.287	4	33	123	147	12	9	2.9	.957	J. Bentley	28	157	11	9	1	5.04
	RF	R. Youngs	500	.264	6	53	214	24	12	2	2.0	.952	A. Nehf	29	155	11	9	1	3.77
	CF	B. Southworth	473	.292	6	44	289	7	11	1	2.6	.964	W. Dean	33	151	10	7	1	4.64
	LF	I. Meusel	516	.328	21	111	244	16	11	2	2.2	.959							
	C	F. Snyder	325	.240	11	50	336	71	6	7	4.3	**.985**							
	UT	F. Frisch	502	.331	11	48	215	393	37	45		.943							
	OF	H. Wilson	180	.239	6	30	75	3	2	2	1.6	.975							
Cin. W-80 L-73 Jack Hendricks	1B	W. Holke	232	.280	1	20	642	35	2	60	10.4	.997	P. Donohue	42	**301**	21	14	2	3.08
	2B	H. Critz	541	.277	2	51	340	542	27	**96**	6.3	.941	D. Luque	36	291	16	18	0	**2.63**
	SS	I. Caveney	358	.249	2	47	209	349	35	72	5.3	.941	E. Rixey	39	287	21	11	1	2.88
	3B	B. Pinelli	492	.283	2	49	113	265	22	21	3.7	.945	R. Benton	33	147	9	10	1	4.05
	RF	C. Walker	509	.318	6	71	332	12	6	4	2.5	**.983**	J. May	36	137	8	9	2	3.87
	CF	E. Roush	540	.339	8	83	343	15	8	3	2.7	.978	C. Mays	12	52	3	5	2	3.31
	LF	B. Zitzmann	301	.252	0	21	135	5	6	0	1.6	.959							
	C	B. Hargrave	273	.300	2	33	283	42	7	1	4.0	.979							
	1O	R. Bressler	319	.348	4	61	602	23	12	46		.981							
	OF	E. Smith	284	.271	8	46	139	8	5	5	1.9	.967							
	3B	C. Dressen	215	.274	3	19	40	95	7	8	3.0	.951							
	SS	S. Bohne	214	.257	2	24	84	138	16	24	4.9	.933							
St. L. W-77 L-76 Branch Rickey W-13 L-25 Rogers Hornsby W-64 L-51	1B	J. Bottomley	619	.367	21	128	**1466**	74	**21**	**133**	10.2	.987	J. Haines	29	207	13	14	0	4.57
	2B	R. Hornsby	504	**.403**	**39**	**143**	287	416	34	95	5.4	.954	B. Sherdel	32	200	15	6	1	3.11
	SS	S. Toporcer	268	.284	2	26	141	215	15	40	5.6	.960	F. Rhem	30	170	8	13	1	4.92
	3B	L. Bell	586	.285	11	88	151	284	**36**	39	3.1	.924	A. Sothoron	28	156	10	10	0	4.05
	RF	C. Hafey	358	.302	5	57	180	9	9	2	2.3	.955	D. Reinhart	20	145	11	5	0	3.05
	CF	H. Mueller	243	.313	1	26	165	6	8	5	2.5	.955	D. Mails	21	131	7	7	0	4.60
	LF	R. Blades	462	.342	12	57	266	13	6	4	2.5	.979	L. Dickerman	29	131	4	11	1	5.58
	C	B. O'Farrell	317	.278	3	32	324	67	10	5	4.4	.975	E. Dyer	27	82	4	3	3	4.15
	OF	R. Shinners	251	.295	7	36	161	2	3	1	2.5	.982							
	OF	J. Smith	243	.251	4	31	152	7	7	2	2.6	.958							
	OF	M. Flack	241	.249	0	28	103	8	1	1	1.9	.991							
	S2	J. Cooney	187	.273	0	18	97	137	6	31		.975							
	SS	T. Thevenow	175	.269	0	17	98	169	14	18	5.6	.950							
Bos. W-70 L-83 Dave Bancroft	1B	D. Burrus	588	.340	5	87	1416	**85**	15	110	10.0	**.990**	J. Cooney	31	246	14	14	0	3.48
	2B	D. Gautreau	279	.262	0	23	171	231	10	39	6.1	.976	J. Barnes	32	216	11	16	0	4.53
	SS	D. Bancroft	479	.319	2	49	300	459	44	81	**6.4**	**.945**	L. Benton	31	183	14	7	1	3.09
	3B	B. Marriott	370	.268	1	40	96	187	22	13	3.4	.928	J. Genewich	34	169	12	10	1	3.99
	RF	J. Welsh	484	.312	7	63	237	**27**	11	7	2.4	.960	K. Graham	34	157	7	12	1	4.41
	CF	G. Felix	459	.307	2	66	328	15	10	3	3.1	.972	R. Ryan	37	123	2	8	6	6.31
	LF	B. Neis	355	.285	5	45	282	8	9	1	3.4	.970	R. Marquard	26	72	2	8	0	5.75
	C	F. Gibson	316	.278	2	50	271	60	11	7	3.9	.968							
	OF	D. Harris	340	.265	5	36	217	12	9	3	2.6	.962							
	2S	E. Padgett	256	.305	0	29	118	152	11	29		.961							
	C	M. O'Neil	222	.257	2	30	208	31	7	3	3.6	.972							
	3B	A. High	219	.288	4	28	47	93	3	7	2.4	.979							
	OF	L. Mann	184	.342	2	20	116	7	1	1	2.2	.992							
	UT	B. Smith	174	.282	0	23	78	145	17	20		.929							

Bkn. — W-68 L-85 — Wilbert Robinson

POS	Player	AB	BA	HR	RBI	PO	A	E	DP	TC/G	FA	Pitcher	G	IP	W	L	SV	ERA
1B	J. Fournier	545	.350	22	130	1317	82	15	105	9.8	.989	D. Vance	31	265	22	9	0	3.53
2B	M. Stock	615	.328	1	62	305	477	18	74	5.7	.978	B. Grimes	33	247	12	19	0	5.04
SS	J. Mitchell	336	.250	0	18	184	266	25	49	5.3	.947	R. Ehrhardt	36	208	10	14	1	5.03
3B	J. Johnston	431	.297	2	43	76	110	24	10	2.6	.886	T. Osborne	41	175	8	15	1	4.94
RF	D. Cox	434	.329	7	64	197	14	7	4	2.0	.968	J. Petty	28	153	9	9	0	4.88
CF	E. Brown	618	.306	5	99	**449**	7	13	3	3.1	.972	B. Hubbell	33	87	3	6	1	5.30
LF	Z. Wheat	616	.359	14	103	320	7	13	2	2.3	.962							
C	Z. Taylor	352	.310	3	44	294	102	17	12	4.3	.959							
3B	C. Tierney	265	.257	2	39	54	102	6	6	2.7	.963							
SS	H. Ford	216	.273	1	15	126	185	11	33	4.9	.966							
C	H. DeBerry	193	.259	2	24	309	50	7	4	6.7	.981							

Phi. — W-68 L-85 — Art Fletcher

POS	Player	AB	BA	HR	RBI	PO	A	E	DP	TC/G	FA	Pitcher	G	IP	W	L	SV	ERA
1B	C. Hawks	320	.322	5	45	775	45	12	64	9.2	.986	J. Ring	38	270	14	16	0	4.37
2B	B. Friberg	304	.270	5	22	181	257	16	37	5.9	.965	H. Carlson	35	234	13	14	0	4.23
SS	H. Sand	496	.278	3	55	352	420	60	91	5.8	.928	C. Mitchell	32	199	10	17	1	5.28
3B	C. Huber	436	.284	5	54	107	199	17	16	2.7	.947	A. Decatur	25	128	4	13	2	5.27
RF	C. Williams	314	.331	13	60	173	12	2	3	1.9	.989	J. Knight	33	105	7	6	3	6.84
CF	G. Harper	495	.349	18	97	319	16	10	5	2.7	.971	H. Betts	35	97	4	5	1	5.55
LF	G. Burns	349	.292	1	22	189	9	2	2	2.3	.990	J. Couch	34	94	5	6	2	5.44
C	J. Wilson	335	.328	3	54	275	50	6	9	3.7	.982							
21	L. Fonseca	467	.319	7	60	648	245	20	68		.978							
OF	F. Leach	292	.312	5	28	178	2	9	1	2.9	.952							
UT	Wrightstone	286	.346	14	61	152	62	16	11		.930							
C	B. Henline	263	.304	8	48	209	53	12	9	4.0	.956							
OF	J. Mokan	209	.330	6	42	120	1	2	0	1.8	.984							

Chi. — W-68 L-86 Bill Killefer / W-33 L-42 Rabbit Maranville / W-23 L-30 George Gibson / W-12 L-14

POS	Player	AB	BA	HR	RBI	PO	A	E	DP	TC/G	FA	Pitcher	G	IP	W	L	SV	ERA
1B	C. Grimm	519	.306	10	76	1317	73	15	125	10.1	.989	G. Alexander	32	236	15	11	0	3.39
2B	S. Adams	627	.287	2	48	354	551	16	90	6.4	**.983**	S. Blake	36	231	10	18	2	4.86
SS	R. Maranville	266	.233	0	23	162	261	20	51	6.0	.955	W. Cooper	32	212	12	14	2	4.28
3B	H. Freigau	476	.307	8	71	98	185	27	20	3.2	.913	T. Kaufmann	31	196	13	13	2	4.50
RF	C. Heathcote	380	.263	5	39	241	21	8	8	2.7	.970	G. Bush	42	182	6	13	4	4.30
CF	M. Brooks	349	.281	13	72	249	9	6	2	3.0	.977	P. Jones	28	124	6	6	0	4.65
LF	A. Jahn	226	.301	0	37	124	5	2	3	2.3	.985							
C	G. Hartnett	398	.289	24	67	**409**	114	23	15	5.0	.958							
OF	T. Griffith	235	.285	7	27	109	9	8	1	2.1	.937							
C	M. Gonzalez	197	.264	3	18	155	31	2	7	3.8	.989							
OF	B. Weis	180	.267	2	25	78	3	3	0	1.8	.964							
S3	P. Pittenger	173	.312	0	15	71	127	11	13		.947							
OF	D. Grigsby	137	.255	0	20	81	4	3	2	2.3	.966							

BATTING AND BASE RUNNING LEADERS

Batting Average

R. Hornsby, STL	.403
J. Bottomley, STL	.367
Z. Wheat, BKN	.359
K. Cuyler, PIT	.357
J. Fournier, BKN	.350

Slugging Average

R. Hornsby, STL	.756
K. Cuyler, PIT	.593
J. Bottomley, STL	.578
J. Fournier, BKN	.569
G. Harper, PHI	.558

Home Runs

R. Hornsby, STL	39
G. Hartnett, CHI	24
J. Fournier, BKN	22
I. Meusel, NY	21
J. Bottomley, STL	21

Total Bases

R. Hornsby, STL	381
K. Cuyler, PIT	366
J. Bottomley, STL	358
Z. Wheat, BKN	333
J. Fournier, BKN	310

Runs Batted In

R. Hornsby, STL	143
J. Fournier, BKN	130
J. Bottomley, STL	128
G. Wright, PIT	121
C. Barnhart, PIT	114

Stolen Bases

M. Carey, PIT	46
K. Cuyler, PIT	41
S. Adams, CHI	26
E. Roush, CIN	22
F. Frisch, NY	21

Hits

J. Bottomley, STL	227
Z. Wheat, BKN	221
K. Cuyler, PIT	220

Base on Balls

J. Fournier, BKN	86
R. Hornsby, STL	83
E. Moore, PIT	73

Home Run Percentage

R. Hornsby, STL	7.7
G. Hartnett, CHI	6.0
C. Williams, PHI	4.1

Runs Scored

K. Cuyler, PIT	144
R. Hornsby, STL	133
Z. Wheat, BKN	125

Doubles

J. Bottomley, STL	44
K. Cuyler, PIT	43
Z. Wheat, BKN	42

Triples

K. Cuyler, PIT	26
C. Walker, CIN	16
E. Roush, CIN	16
J. Fournier, BKN	16

PITCHING LEADERS

Winning Percentage

B. Sherdel, STL	.714
D. Vance, BKN	.710
V. Aldridge, PIT	.682
R. Kremer, PIT	.680
E. Rixey, CIN	.656

Earned Run Average

D. Luque, CIN	2.63
E. Rixey, CIN	2.88
A. Reinhart, STL	3.05
P. Donohue, CIN	3.08
L. Benton, BOS	3.09

Wins

D. Vance, BKN	22
E. Rixey, CIN	21
P. Donohue, CIN	21
L. Meadows, PIT	19

Saves

J. Morrison, PIT	4
G. Bush, CHI	4

Strikeouts

D. Vance, BKN	221
D. Luque, CIN	140
S. Blake, CHI	93
J. Ring, PHI	93
V. Aldridge, PIT	88

Complete Games

P. Donohue, CIN	27
D. Vance, BKN	26
D. Luque, CIN	22
E. Rixey, CIN	22
J. Ring, PHI	21

Fewest Hits per 9 Innings

D. Luque, CIN	8.13
L. Benton, BOS	8.35
D. Vance, BKN	8.38

Shutouts

D. Vance, BKN	4
H. Carlson, PHI	4
D. Luque, CIN	4
P. Donohue, CIN	3

Fewest Walks per 9 Innings

G. Alexander, CHI	1.11
P. Donohue, CIN	1.47
E. Rixey, CIN	1.47

Most Strikeouts per 9 Inn.

D. Vance, BKN	7.50
D. Luque, CIN	4.33
V. Aldridge, PIT	3.71

Innings

P. Donohue, CIN	301
D. Luque, CIN	291
E. Rixey, CIN	287

Games Pitched

J. Morrison, PIT	44
P. Donohue, CIN	42
G. Bush, CHI	42

	W	L	PCT	GB	R	OR	2B	3B	Batting HR	BA	SA	SB	E	Fielding DP	FA	CG	BB	Pitching SO	ShO	SV	ERA
PIT	95	58	.621		912	715	316	105	77	.307	.448	159	224	171	.964	77	387	386	2	13	3.87
NY	86	66	.566	8.5	736	702	239	61	114	.283	.415	79	199	129	.968	80	408	446	6	8	3.94
CIN	80	73	.523	15	690	643	221	90	44	.285	.387	108	203	161	.968	92	324	437	11	12	3.38
STL	77	76	.503	18	828	764	292	80	109	.299	.445	70	204	156	.966	82	470	428	8	7	4.36
BOS	70	83	.458	25	708	802	260	70	41	.292	.390	47	221	145	.964	77	458	351	5	4	4.39
BKN	68	85	.444	27	786	866	250	80	64	.296	.406	37	210	130	.966	82	477	518	4	4	4.77
PHI	68	85	.444	27	812	930	288	58	100	.295	.425	48	211	147	.966	69	444	371	8	9	5.02
CHI	68	86	.442	27.5	723	773	254	70	85	.275	.396	94	198	161	.969	75	485	435	5	10	4.41
					6195	6195	2120	614	634	.292	.414	672	1670	1200	.966	634	3453	3372	49	67	4.27

American League 1925

	POS	Player	AB	BA	HR	RBI	PO	A	E	DP	TC/G	FA	Pitcher	G	IP	W	L	SV	ERA
Was. W-96 L-55 Bucky Harris	1B	J. Judge	376	.314	8	66	901	71	7	92	9.0	.993	S. Coveleski	32	241	20	5	0	2.84
	2B	B. Harris	551	.287	1	66	402	429	26	107	6.0	.970	W. Johnson	30	229	20	7	0	3.07
	SS	Peckinpaugh	422	.294	4	64	215	345	28	71	4.7	.952	D. Ruether	30	223	18	7	0	3.87
	3B	O. Bluege	522	.287	4	79	158	285	22	29	3.2	.953	T. Zachary	38	218	12	15	2	3.85
	RF	S. Rice	649	.350	1	87	339	20	12	7	2.4	.968	F. Marberry	55	93	8	6	15	3.47
	CF	E. McNeely	385	.286	3	37	259	13	7	3	2.5	.975							
	LF	G. Goslin	601	.334	18	113	385	24	12	1	2.8	.971							
	C	M. Ruel	393	.310	0	54	491	103	11	18	4.8	.982							
	1O	J. Harris	300	.323	12	59	461	41	6	40		.988							
	P	W. Johnson	97	.433	2	20	5	37	0	2	1.4	1.000							
Phi. W-88 L-64 Connie Mack	1B	J. Poole	480	.298	5	67	1166	65	23	102	10.2	.982	E. Rommel	52	261	21	10	3	3.69
	2B	M. Bishop	368	.280	4	27	233	352	26	53	5.9	.957	S. Harriss	46	252	19	12	1	3.50
	SS	C. Galloway	481	.241	3	71	296	431	35	89	5.1	.954	L. Grove	45	197	10	13	1	4.75
	3B	S. Hale	391	.345	8	63	98	173	24	19	3.1	.919	S. Gray	32	196	16	8	3	3.40
	RF	B. Miller	474	.319	10	81	158	7	5	1	1.5	.971	R. Walberg	53	192	8	14	7	3.99
	CF	A. Simmons	658	.384	24	129	447	8	16	2	3.1	.966	Baumgartner	37	113	6	3	3	3.57
	LF	B. Lamar	568	.356	3	77	283	18	15	4	2.4	.953							
	C	M. Cochrane	420	.331	6	55	419	79	8	9	3.8	.984							
	32	J. Dykes	465	.323	5	55	225	302	21	45		.962							
	OF	F. Welch	202	.277	4	41	85	6	3	1	1.6	.968							
St. L. W-82 L-71 George Sisler	1B	G. Sisler	649	.345	12	105	1330	131	26	120	9.9	.983	M. Gaston	42	239	15	14	1	4.41
	2B	M. McManus	587	.288	13	90	430	479	31	93	6.1	.967	J. Bush	33	214	14	14	0	4.97
	SS	B. LaMotte	356	.272	2	51	220	270	39	57	5.7	.926	E. Vangilder	52	193	14	8	6	4.70
	3B	G. Robertson	582	.271	14	76	201	287	32	41	3.4	.938	D. Davis	35	180	12	7	1	4.59
	RF	H. Rice	354	.359	11	47	175	13	3	1	2.2	.984	J. Giard	30	161	10	5	0	5.04
	CF	B. Jacobson	540	.341	15	76	383	18	13	9	3.0	.969	D. Danforth	38	159	7	9	2	4.36
	LF	K. Williams	411	.331	25	105	242	11	12	4	2.6	.955	E. Wingard	32	153	9	10	0	5.06
	C	L. Dixon	205	.224	1	19	233	70	6	8	4.1	.981							
	OF	H. Bennett	298	.279	2	37	140	12	14	1	2.3	.916							
	SS	W. Gerber	246	.272	0	19	144	206	19	39	5.2	.949							
	C	P. Hargrave	225	.284	8	43	211	44	5	4	4.2	.981							
	OF	J. Tobin	193	.301	2	27	61	1	0	0	1.6	1.000							
	OF	J. Evans	159	.314	0	20	96	3	0	2	2.1	1.000							
	C	H. Severeid	109	.367	1	21	114	24	1	3	4.5	.993							
Det. W-81 L-73 Ty Cobb	1B	L. Blue	532	.306	3	94	1480	101	19	115	10.8	.988	E. Whitehill	35	239	11	11	2	4.66
	2B	F. O'Rourke	482	.293	5	57	309	382	21	67	6.0	.971	H. Dauss	35	228	16	11	1	3.16
	SS	J. Tavener	453	.245	0	47	229	398	24	73	4.9	.963	K. Holloway	38	158	13	4	2	4.62
	3B	F. Haney	398	.279	0	40	115	207	16	22	3.2	.953	L. Stoner	34	152	10	9	1	4.26
	RF	H. Heilmann	573	.393	13	133	278	9	9	1	2.0	.970	R. Collins	26	140	6	11	0	4.56
	CF	T. Cobb	415	.378	12	102	267	9	15	1	2.8	.948	E. Wells	35	134	6	9	2	6.23
	LF	A. Wingo	440	.370	5	68	282	16	9	6	2.5	.971	D. Leonard	18	126	11	4	0	4.51
	C	J. Bassler	344	.279	0	52	375	87	8	14	4.0	.983	J. Doyle	45	118	4	7	8	5.93
	OF	H. Manush	277	.303	5	47	153	7	3	0	2.2	.982							
	OF	B. Fothergill	204	.353	2	28	120	6	3	2	2.2	.977							
	2B	L. Burke	180	.289	0	24	100	130	9	27	4.6	.962							
	C	L. Woodall	171	.205	0	13	165	38	7	4	2.8	.967							
Chi. W-79 L-75 Eddie Collins	1B	E. Sheely	600	.315	9	111	1565	95	20	136	11.0	.988	T. Lyons	43	263	21	11	3	3.26
	2B	E. Collins	425	.346	3	80	290	346	20	74	5.7	.970	R. Faber	34	238	12	11	0	3.78
	SS	I. Davis	562	.240	0	61	313	472	53	97	5.8	.937	Blankenship	40	222	17	8	1	3.16
	3B	W. Kamm	509	.279	6	83	182	310	22	32	3.4	.957	S. Thurston	36	175	10	14	1	6.17
	RF	H. Hooper	442	.265	6	55	231	16	6	4	2.0	.976	C. Robertson	24	137	8	12	0	5.26
	CF	J. Mostil	605	.299	2	50	446	11	7	5	3.0	.985	M. Cvengros	22	105	3	9	0	4.30
	LF	B. Falk	602	.301	4	99	306	18	14	4	2.2	.959	S. Connally	40	105	6	7	8	4.64
	C	R. Schalk	343	.274	0	52	368	99	8	15	3.8	.983							
	UT	B. Barrett	245	.363	3	40	132	131	19	24		.933							
	C	B. Crouse	131	.351	2	25	104	36	7	5	3.1	.952							

POS	Player	AB	BA	HR	RBI	PO	A	E	DP	TC/G	FA	Pitcher	G	IP	W	L	SV	ERA
Cle.																		
1B	G. Burns	488	.336	6	79	1195	82	14	94	10.2	.989	S. Smith	31	237	11	14	1	4.86
2B	C. Fewster	294	.248	1	38	222	237	30	41	5.7	.939	G. Uhle	29	211	13	11	0	4.10
W-70 L-84	SS	J. Sewell	608	.336	1	98	314	529	29	80	5.7	**.967**	B. Karr	32	198	11	12	0	4.78
Tris Speaker	3B	R. Lutzke	238	.218	1	16	61	129	13	9	2.9	.936	J. Miller	32	190	10	13	2	3.31
	RF	P. McNulty	373	.314	6	43	206	16	8	2	2.1	.965	G. Buckeye	30	153	13	8	0	3.65
	CF	T. Speaker	429	.389	12	87	311	16	11	**9**	3.1	.967	J. Shaute	26	131	4	12	4	5.43
	LF	C. Jamieson	557	.296	4	42	324	16	**16**	4	2.6	.955							
	C	G. Myatt	358	.271	11	54	273	53	9	2	3.4	.973							
	32	F. Spurgeon	376	.287	0	32	155	250	21	30		.951							
	OF	C. Lee	230	.322	4	42	129	7	7	2	2.0	.951							
	OF	H. Summa	224	.330	0	25	83	2	3	0	1.6	.966							
	C	L. Sewell	220	.232	0	18	216	54	8	13	4.2	.971							
N. Y.																		
1B	L. Gehrig	437	.295	20	68	1126	53	13	72	10.5	.989	H. Pennock	47	**277**	16	17	2	2.96
2B	A. Ward	439	.246	4	38	246	317	20	57	5.2	.966	S. Jones	43	247	15	**21**	2	4.63
W-69 L-85	SS	P. Wanninger	403	.236	1	22	214	296	30	59	4.9	.944	U. Shocker	41	244	12	12	2	3.65
Miller Huggins	3B	J. Dugan	404	.292	0	31	118	202	10	19	3.4	.970	W. Hoyt	46	243	11	14	6	4.00
	RF	B. Ruth	359	.290	25	66	207	15	6	3	2.3	.974	B. Shawkey	33	186	6	14	0	4.11
	CF	E. Combs	593	.342	3	61	401	12	9	2	2.8	.979							
	LF	B. Meusel	624	.290	**33**	**138**	249	9	4	6	2.0	.985							
	C	B. Bengough	283	.258	0	23	325	83	3	12	4.4	**.993**							
	OF	B. Paschal	247	.360	12	56	117	6	6	0	2.0	.953							
	1B	W. Pipp	178	.230	3	24	399	38	4	40	9.4	.991							
	2S	E. Johnson	170	.282	5	17	87	107	9	21		.956							
	C	W. Schang	167	.240	2	24	172	55	6	8	4.0	.974							
	32	H. Shanks	155	.258	1	18	64	87	6	13		.962							
Bos.																		
1B	P. Todt	544	.278	11	75	1408	100	13	126	10.9	.991	H. Ehmke	34	261	9	20	1	3.73
2B	B. Wambsganss	360	.231	1	41	254	326	26	60	5.9	.957	T. Wingfield	41	254	12	19	2	3.96
W-47 L-105	SS	D. Lee	255	.224	0	19	188	260	37	64	5.8	.924	R. Ruffing	37	217	9	18	1	5.01
Lee Fohl	3B	D. Prothro	415	.313	0	51	115	211	19	16	3.2	.945	P. Zahniser	37	177	5	12	1	5.15
	RF	I. Boone	476	.330	9	68	198	9	13	1	1.9	.941	J. Quinn	19	105	7	8	0	4.37
	CF	I. Flagstead	572	.280	6	61	429	**24**	11	6	**3.2**	.976	B. Ross	33	94	3	8	0	6.20
	LF	R. Carlyle	276	.326	7	49	122	5	13	0	2.1	.907							
	C	V. Picinich	251	.255	1	25	222	53	9	3	3.8	.968							
	OF	T. Vache	252	.313	3	48	87	2	9	0	1.8	.908							
	OF	D. Williams	218	.229	0	13	117	4	6	1	2.4	.953							
	3B	H. Ezzell	186	.285	0	15	53	89	13	5	3.3	.916							
	2B	B. Rogell	169	.195	0	17	98	145	17	29	5.3	.935							
	SS	B. Connally	107	.262	0	21	60	72	7	13	4.1	.950							

BATTING AND BASE RUNNING LEADERS

Batting Average

H. Heilmann, DET	.393
T. Speaker, CLE	.389
A. Simmons, PHI	.384
T. Cobb, DET	.378
A. Wingo, DET	.370

Slugging Average

K. Williams, STL	.613
T. Cobb, DET	.598
A. Simmons, PHI	.596
T. Speaker, CLE	.578
H. Heilmann, DET	.569

Home Runs

B. Meusel, NY	33
B. Ruth, NY	25
K. Williams, STL	25
A. Simmons, PHI	24
L. Gehrig, NY	20

Total Bases

A. Simmons, PHI	392
B. Meusel, NY	338
G. Goslin, WAS	329
H. Heilmann, DET	326
G. Sisler, STL	311

Runs Batted In

B. Meusel, NY	138
H. Heilmann, DET	133
A. Simmons, PHI	129
G. Goslin, WAS	113
E. Sheely, CHI	111

Stolen Bases

J. Mostil, CHI	43
G. Goslin, WAS	26
S. Rice, WAS	26
E. Collins, CHI	19
L. Blue, DET	19
I. Davis, CHI	19

Hits

A. Simmons, PHI	253
S. Rice, WAS	227
H. Heilmann, DET	225

Base on Balls

W. Karnm, CHI	90
J. Mostil, CHI	90
M. Bishop, PHI	87
E. Collins, CHI	87

Home Run Percentage

K. Williams, STL	6.1
B. Meusel, NY	5.3
L. Gehrig, NY	4.6

Runs Scored

J. Mostil, CHI	135
A. Simmons, PHI	122
E. Combs, NY	117

Doubles

M. McManus, STL	44
E. Sheely, CHI	43
A. Simmons, PHI	43

Triples

G. Goslin, WAS	20
J. Mostil, CHI	16
G. Sisler, STL	15

PITCHING LEADERS

Winning Percentage

S. Coveleski, WAS	.800
W. Johnson, WAS	.741
D. Ruether, WAS	.720
Blankenship, CHI	.680
E. Rommel, PHI	.677

Earned Run Average

S. Coveleski, WAS	2.84
H. Pennock, NY	2.96
W. Johnson, WAS	3.07
H. Dauss, DET	3.16
Blankenship, CHI	3.16

Wins

E. Rommel, PHI	21
T. Lyons, CHI	21
S. Coveleski, WAS	20
W. Johnson, WAS	20
S. Harriss, PHI	19

Saves

F. Marberry, WAS	15
S. Connally, CHI	8
J. Doyle, DET	8
R. Walberg, PHI	7
E. Vangilder, STL	6
W. Hoyt, NY	6

Strikeouts

L. Grove, PHI	116
W. Johnson, WAS	108
S. Harriss, PHI	95
H. Ehmke, BOS	95
S. Jones, NY	92

Complete Games

S. Smith, CLE	22
H. Ehmke, BOS	22
H. Pennock, NY	21
T. Lyons, CHI	19
T. Wingfield, BOS	18

Fewest Hits per 9 Innings

W. Johnson, WAS	8.29
S. Coveleski, WAS	8.59
H. Pennock, NY	8.68

Shutouts

T. Lyons, CHI	5
J. Giard, STL	4
S. Gray, PHI	4

Fewest Walks per 9 Innings

S. Smith, CLE	1.82
J. Quinn, BOS, PHI	1.85
U. Shocker, NY	2.14

Most Strikeouts per 9 Inn.

W. Johnson, WAS	4.24
S. Gray, PHI	3.68
S. Harriss, PHI	3.39

Innings

H. Pennock, NY	277
T. Lyons, CHI	263
E. Rommel, PHI	261

Games Pitched

F. Marberry, WAS	55
R. Walberg, PHI	53
E. Rommel, PHI	52
E. Vangilder, STL	52

	W	L	PCT	GB	R	OR	2B	3B	HR	BA	SA	SB	E	DP	FA	CG	BB	SO	ShO	SV	ERA
WAS	96	55	.636		829	**669**	251	71	56	.303	.411	**134**	170	**166**	.972	69	543	464	9	**21**	**3.67**
PHI	88	64	.579	8.5	830	714	298	79	76	**.307**	.434	67	211	148	.966	61	544	**495**	8	18	3.89
STL	82	71	.536	15	897	909	**304**	68	110	.298	**.439**	85	226	164	.964	67	675	419	7	10	4.85
DET	81	73	.526	16.5	**903**	829	277	**84**	50	.302	.413	97	173	143	.972	66	556	419	2	18	4.61
CHI	79	75	.513	18.5	811	771	299	59	38	.284	.385	129	200	162	.968	71	**489**	374	**12**	13	4.34
CLE	70	84	.455	27.5	782	810	285	58	52	.297	.399	90	210	146	.967	**93**	493	345	6	9	4.49
NY	69	85	.448	28.5	706	774	247	74	110	.275	.410	67	**160**	150	**.974**	80	505	492	8	13	4.33
BOS	47	105	.309	49.5	639	921	257	64	41	.266	.364	42	271	150	.957	68	510	310	6	6	4.97
					6397	6397	2218	557	533	.292	.407	711	1621	1229	.968	575	4315	3318	58	108	4.39

National League 1926

POS	Player	AB	BA	HR	RBI	PO	A	E	DP	TC/G	FA		Pitcher	G	IP	W	L	SV	ERA
St. L. W-89 L-65 Rogers Hornsby																			
1B	J. Bottomley	603	.299	19	**120**	1607	54	**19**	118	10.9	.989		F. Rhem	34	258	**20**	7	0	3.21
2B	R. Hornsby	527	.317	11	93	245	433	27	73	5.3	.962		B. Sherdel	34	235	16	12	0	3.49
SS	T. Thevenow	563	.256	2	63	**371**	**597**	45	98	**6.5**	.956		J. Haines	33	183	13	4	1	3.25
3B	L. Bell	581	.325	17	100	165	254	22	25	2.8	.950		V. Keen	26	152	10	9	0	4.56
RF	B. Southworth	391	.317	11	69	228	5	7	0	2.4	.971		G. Alexander	23	148	9	7	2	2.91
CF	T. Douthit	530	.308	3	52	**440**	14	**20**	2	**3.4**	.958		A. Reinhart	27	143	10	5	0	4.22
LF	R. Blades	416	.305	8	43	229	10	5	1	2.3	.980		H. Bell	27	85	6	6	2	3.18
C	B. O'Farrell	492	.293	7	68	**466**	117	10	12	4.1	**.983**								
OF	C. Hafey	225	.271	4	38	106	6	3	1	2.1	.974								
OF	H. Mueller	191	.267	3	28	106	7	6	3	2.3	.950								
OF	W. Holm	144	.285	0	21	75	1	3	1	2.0	.962								
Cin. W-87 L-67 Jack Hendricks																			
1B	W. Pipp	574	.291	6	99	**1710**	92	15	**140**	**11.7**	.992		P. Donohue	47	**286**	**20**	14	2	3.37
2B	H. Critz	607	.270	3	79	357	**588**	18	**107**	6.2	**.981**		C. Mays	39	281	19	12	1	3.14
SS	F. Emmer	224	.196	0	18	141	242	34	40	5.3	.918		E. Rixey	34	233	14	8	0	3.40
3B	C. Dressen	474	.266	4	48	108	**284**	14	19	**3.3**	.966		D. Luque	34	234	13	16	0	3.43
RF	C. Walker	571	.306	6	78	325	21	14	8	2.4	.961		J. May	45	168	13	9	3	3.22
CF	E. Roush	563	.323	7	79	304	12	15	2	2.3	.978		R. Lucas	39	154	8	5	2	3.68
LF	Christensen	329	.350	0	41	170	6	4	2	1.9	.978								
C	B. Hargrave	326	**.353**	6	62	276	50	4	7	3.5	**.988**								
OF	R. Bressler	297	.357	1	51	155	4	5	1	2.1	.970								
C	V. Picinich	240	.263	2	31	240	52	10	6	3.5	.967								
3S	B. Pinelli	207	.222	0	24	52	141	11	9		.946								
SS	H. Ford	197	.279	0	18	152	190	13	57	6.2	.963								
Pit. W-84 L-69 Bill McKechnie																			
1B	G. Grantham	449	.318	8	70	1203	66	13	106	9.7	.990		R. Kremer	37	231	**20**	6	5	**2.61**
2B	H. Rhyne	366	.251	2	39	167	220	13	46	6.1	.968		L. Meadows	36	227	**20**	9	0	3.97
SS	G. Wright	458	.308	8	77	242	382	49	82	5.8	.927		V. Aldridge	37	190	10	13	1	4.07
3B	P. Traynor	574	.317	3	92	**182**	279	**23**	**39**	3.3	.952		E. Yde	37	187	8	7	0	3.65
RF	P. Waner	536	.336	8	79	307	21	8	3	2.4	.976		D. Songer	35	126	7	8	2	3.13
CF	M. Carey	324	.222	0	28	225	8	14	3	3.0	.943		J. Morrison	26	122	6	8	2	3.38
LF	K. Cuyler	614	.321	9	92	405	19	14	4	2.8	.968		J. Bush	19	111	6	6	3	3.01
C	E. Smith	292	.346	2	46	307	63	14	10	3.9	.964								
C	J. Gooch	218	.271	1	52	202	38	5	6	3.1	.980								
OF	C. Barnhart	203	.192	0	10	101	5	1	1	1.8	.991								
2B	J. Rawlings	181	.232	0	20	126	164	9	25	5.1	.970								
Chi. W-82 L-72 Joe McCarthy																			
1B	C. Grimm	524	.277	8	82	1416	68	18	139	10.2	.988		C. Root	42	271	18	**17**	2	2.82
2B	S. Adams	**624**	.309	0	39	324	485	**29**	93	6.2	.965		S. Blake	39	198	11	12	1	3.60
SS	J. Cooney	513	.251	1	47	344	492	24	**107**	6.1	**.972**		T. Kaufmann	26	170	9	7	2	3.02
3B	H. Freigau	508	.270	3	51	133	242	13	22	2.9	.966		P. Jones	30	160	12	7	2	3.09
RF	C. Heathcote	510	.276	10	53	306	22	5	8	2.5	**.985**		G. Bush	35	157	13	9	2	2.86
CF	H. Wilson	529	.321	**21**	109	348	11	10	5	2.6	.973		B. Osborn	31	136	6	5	1	3.63
LF	R. Stephenson	281	.338	3	44	126	7	7	0	1.9	.978		B. Piercy	19	90	6	5	0	4.48
C	G. Hartnett	284	.275	8	41	307	86	9	6	4.6	.978								
C	M. Gonzalez	253	.249	1	23	306	53	4	5	4.7	.989								
OF	P. Scott	189	.286	3	34	114	7	4	2	2.1	.968								
OF	J. Kelly	176	.335	0	32	58	3	3	0	1.6	.953								
N. Y. W-74 L-77 John McGraw																			
1B	G. Kelly	499	.303	13	80	1196	79	9	89	11.3	**.993**		J. Scott	**50**	226	13	15	5	4.34
2B	F. Frisch	545	.314	5	44	261	471	19	69	5.9	.975		K. Greenfield	39	223	13	12	1	3.96
SS	T. Jackson	385	.327	8	51	256	351	24	71	5.8	.962		Fitzsimmons	37	219	14	10	0	2.88
3B	F. Lindstrom	543	.302	9	76	151	251	16	23	3.0	.962		V. Barnes	31	185	8	13	1	2.87
RF	R. Youngs	372	.306	4	43	170	18	5	5	2.1	.980		J. Ring	33	183	11	10	2	4.57
CF	T. Tyson	335	.293	3	35	232	9	5	5	2.7	.980		H. McQuillan	33	167	11	10	0	3.72
LF	I. Meusel	449	.292	6	65	197	10	9	1	1.9	.958		C. Davies	38	89	2	4	**6**	3.94
C	P. Florence	188	.229	2	14	212	41	**17**	7	3.6	.937								
OF	H. Mueller	305	.249	4	29	194	13	11	2	2.7	.950								
1B	B. Terry	225	.289	5	43	391	31	9	36	11.3	.979								
SS	D. Farrell	171	.287	2	23	106	124	12	22	4.6	.950								
OF	B. Southworth	116	.328	5	30	62	2		1	2.4	.950								

POS	Player	AB	BA	HR	RBI	PO	A	E	DP	TC/G	FA	Pitcher	G	IP	W	L	SV	ERA
Bkn. W-71 L-82 Wilbert Robinson																		
1B	B. Herman	496	.319	11	81	918	60	14	55	9.8	.986	J. Petty	38	276	17	17	1	2.84
2B	C. Fewster	337	.243	2	24	225	297	26	38	5.3	.953	B. Grimes	30	225	12	13	0	3.71
SS	J. Butler	501	.269	1	68	243	317	30	43	5.8	.949	D. McWeeny	42	216	11	13	1	3.04
3B	B. Marriott	360	.267	3	42	80	173	20	6	2.6	.927	B. McGraw	33	174	9	13	1	4.59
RF	D. Cox	398	.296	1	45	201	12	8	2	1.9	.964	D. Vance	24	169	9	10	1	3.89
CF	G. Felix	432	.280	3	53	270	11	13	2	2.4	.956	J. Barnes	31	158	10	11	1	5.24
LF	Z. Wheat	411	.290	5	35	202	9	10	3	2.2	.955	R. Ehrhardt	44	97	2	5	4	3.90
C	M. O'Neil	201	.209	0	20	247	53	11	5	4.2	.965							
OF	M. Jacobson	288	.247	0	23	191	5	5	2	2.3	.975							
1B	J. Fournier	243	.284	11	48	548	28	8	19	9.1	.986							
SS	R. Maranville	234	.235	0	24	138	192	18	28	5.8	.948							
C	C. Hargreaves	208	.250	2	23	224	65	4	6	4.2	.986							
Bos. W-66 L-86 Dave Bancroft																		
1B	D. Burrus	486	.270	3	61	1153	103	12	97	9.8	.991	L. Benton	43	232	14	14	1	3.85
2B	D. Gautreau	266	.267	0	8	170	205	23	42	5.4	.942	J. Genewich	37	216	8	16	2	3.88
SS	D. Bancroft	453	.311	1	44	317	398	33	75	6.1	.956	B. Smith	33	193	10	13	1	3.91
3B	A. High	476	.296	2	66	99	155	10	15	3.3	.962	J. Wertz	32	189	11	9	0	3.28
RF	J. Welsh	490	.278	3	57	283	23	11	8	2.5	.965	G. Mogridge	39	142	6	10	3	4.50
CF	J. Smith	322	.311	2	25	206	8	6	0	2.7	.973	B. Hearn	34	117	4	9	2	4.22
LF	E. Brown	612	.328	4	84	401	10	15	2	2.8	.965	H. Goldsmith	19	101	5	7	0	4.37
C	Z. Taylor	432	.255	0	42	394	123	8	17	4.3	.985							
3S	E. Taylor	272	.268	0	33	117	174	13	28		.957							
OF	F. Wilson	236	.237	0	23	121	6	9	1		.934							
2B	E. Moore	184	.266	0	15	90	123	6	27	2.4	.973							
OF	L. Mann	129	.302	1	20	79	5	3	0	5.8	.966							
										1.9								
Phi. W-58 L-93 Art Fletcher																		
1B	J. Bentley	240	.258	2	27	516	28	4	41	9.8	.993	H. Carlson	35	267	17	12	0	3.23
2B	B. Friberg	478	.268	1	51	**381**	512	22	89	6.4	.976	C. Mitchell	28	179	9	14	1	4.58
SS	H. Sand	567	.272	4	37	358	495	**55**	88	6.1	.939	C. Willoughby	47	168	8	12	1	5.95
3B	C. Huber	376	.245	1	34	110	214	15	22	2.9	.956	W. Dean	33	164	8	16	0	6.10
RF	C. Williams	336	.345	18	53	143	14	6	3	1.8	.963	D. Ulrich	45	148	8	13	1	4.08
CF	F. Leach	492	.329	11	71	313	15	7	2	2.7	.979	J. Knight	35	143	3	12	2	6.62
LF	J. Mokan	456	.303	6	62	221	16	8	4	2.0	.967							
C	J. Wilson	279	.305	4	32	228	78	16	5	4.1	.950							
UT	Wrightstone	368	.307	7	57	549	125	19	64		.973							
OF	A. Nixon	311	.293	4	41	206	7	5	3	2.5	.977							
C	B. Henline	283	.283	2	30	217	46	8	9	3.5	.970							
OF	G. Harper	194	.314	7	38	111	2	7	1	2.2	.942							

BATTING AND BASE RUNNING LEADERS

Batting Average

B. Hargrave, CIN	.353
Christensen, CIN	.350
E. Smith, PIT	.346
C. Williams, PHI	.345
P. Waner, PIT	.336

Slugging Average

C. Williams, PHI	.568
H. Wilson, CHI	.539
P. Waner, PIT	.528
B. Hargrave, CIN	.525
L. Bell, STL	.518

Home Runs

H. Wilson, CHI	21
J. Bottomley, STL	19
C. Williams, PHI	18
L. Bell, STL	17
B. Southworth, NY, STL	16

Total Bases

J. Bottomley, STL	305
L. Bell, STL	301
H. Wilson, CHI	285
P. Waner, PIT	283
K. Cuyler, PIT	282

Runs Batted In

J. Bottomley, STL	120
H. Wilson, CHI	109
L. Bell, STL	100
B. Southworth, NY, STL	99
W. Pipp, CIN	99

Stolen Bases

K. Cuyler, PIT	35
S. Adams, CHI	27
T. Douthit, STL	23
F. Frisch, NY	23
R. Youngs, NY	21

Hits

E. Brown, BOS	201
K. Cuyler, PIT	197
S. Adams, CHI	193

Base on Balls

H. Wilson, CHI	69
P. Waner, PIT	66
H. Sand, PHI	66

Home Run Percentage

C. Williams, PHI	5.4
H. Wilson, CHI	4.0
B. Southworth, NY, STL	3.2

Runs Scored

K. Cuyler, PIT	113
P. Waner, PIT	101
B. Southworth, NY, STL	99
H. Sand, PHI	99

Doubles

J. Bottomley, STL	40
E. Roush, CIN	37
H. Wilson, CHI	36

Triples

P. Waner, PIT	22
C. Walker, CIN	20
P. Traynor, PIT	17

PITCHING LEADERS

Winning Percentage

R. Kremer, PIT	.769
F. Rhem, STL	.741
L. Meadows, PIT	.690
C. Mays, CIN	.613
P. Donohue, CIN	.588

Earned Run Average

R. Kremer, PIT	2.61
C. Root, CHI	2.82
J. Petty, BKN	2.84
Fitzsimmons, NY	2.88
T. Kaufmann, CHI	3.02

Wins

R. Kremer, PIT	20
F. Rhem, STL	20
L. Meadows, PIT	20
P. Donohue, CIN	20
C. Mays, CIN	19

Saves

C. Davies, NY	6
J. Scott, NY	5
R. Kremer, PIT	5
R. Ehrhardt, BKN	4

Strikeouts

D. Vance, BKN	140
C. Root, CHI	127
J. May, CIN	103
L. Benton, BOS	103
J. Petty, BKN	101

Complete Games

C. Mays, CIN	24
J. Petty, BKN	23
C. Root, CHI	21
H. Carlson, PHI	20
F. Rhem, STL	20

Fewest Hits per 9 Innings

J. Petty, BKN	8.03
F. Rhem, STL	8.41
P. Jones, CHI	8.48

Shutouts

P. Donohue, CIN	5
B. Smith, BOS	4
S. Blake, CHI	4

Fewest Walks per 9 Innings

P. Donohue, CIN	1.23
G. Alexander, CHI, STL	1.39
H. Carlson, PHI	1.58

Most Strikeouts per 9 Inn.

D. Vance, BKN	7.46
P. Jones, CHI	4.49
S. Blake, CHI	4.33

Innings

P. Donohue, CIN	286
C. Mays, CIN	281
J. Petty, BKN	276

Games Pitched

J. Scott, NY	50
P. Donohue, CIN	47
C. Willoughby, PHI	47

	W	L	PCT	GB	R	OR	2B	3B	Batting HR	BA	SA	SB	E	Fielding DP	FA	CG	BB	Pitching SO	ShO	SV	ERA
STL	89	65	.578		**817**	678	259	82	**90**	.286	**.415**	83	198	141	.969	**90**	397	365	10	6	3.67
CIN	87	67	.565	2	747	651	242	**120**	35	.290	.400	51	183	160	.972	88	**324**	424	**14**	8	3.42
PIT	84	69	.549	4.5	769	689	243	106	44	.285	.396	91	220	161	.965	83	455	387	12	**18**	3.67
CHI	82	72	.532	7	682	**602**	**291**	49	66	.278	.390	85	**162**	**174**	**.974**	77	486	508	13	14	**3.26**
NY	74	77	.490	13.5	663	668	214	58	73	.278	.384	94	186	150	.970	61	427	419	4	15	3.77
BKN	71	82	.464	17.5	623	705	246	62	40	.263	.358	76	229	95	.963	83	472	**517**	5	9	3.82
BOS	66	86	.434	22	624	719	209	62	16	.277	.350	81	208	150	.967	60	455	408	9	9	4.03
PHI	58	93	.384	29.5	687	900	244	50	75	.281	.390	47	224	153	.964	68	454	331	5	5	5.19
					5612	5612	1948	589	439	.280	.386	608	1610	1184	.968	610	3470	3359	72	84	3.84

American League 1926

	POS	Player	AB	BA	HR	RBI	PO	A	E	DP	TC/G	FA	Pitcher	G	IP	W	L	SV	ERA
N. Y. W-91 L-63 Miller Huggins	1B	L. Gehrig	572	.313	16	107	1566	73	15	87	10.7	.991	H. Pennock	40	266	23	11	2	3.62
	2B	T. Lazzeri	589	.275	18	114	298	461	31	72	5.3	.961	U. Shocker	41	258	19	11	2	3.38
	SS	M. Koenig	617	.271	5	62	281	422	**52**	66	5.4	.931	W. Hoyt	40	218	16	12	4	3.85
	3B	J. Dugan	434	.288	1	64	122	221	16	10	2.9	.955	S. Jones	39	161	9	8	5	4.98
	RF	B. Ruth	495	.372	**47**	**145**	308	11	7	5	2.2	.979	M. Thomas	33	140	6	6	0	4.23
	CF	E. Combs	606	.299	8	56	375	8	12	2	2.7	.970	B. Shawkey	29	104	8	7	3	3.62
	LF	B. Meusel	413	.315	12	81	211	4	9	1	2.1	.960							
	C	P. Collins	290	.286	7	35	394	76	14	**14**	4.8	.971							
	OF	B. Paschal	258	.287	7	33	134	10	10	0	2.1	.935							
	3B	M. Gazella	168	.232	0	21	37	78	11	5	2.8	.913							
Cle. W-88 L-66 Tris Speaker	1B	G. Burns	603	.358	4	114	1499	99	19	122	10.7	.988	G. Uhle	39	**318**	**27**	11	1	2.83
	2B	F. Spurgeon	614	.295	0	49	341	**479**	32	93	5.7	.962	D. Levsen	33	237	16	13	0	3.41
	SS	J. Sewell	578	.324	4	85	326	463	37	86	5.4	.955	J. Shaute	34	207	14	10	1	3.53
	3B	R. Lutzke	475	.261	0	59	160	302	19	27	3.4	.960	S. Smith	27	188	11	10	0	3.73
	RF	H. Summa	581	.308	4	76	328	18	9	5	2.3	.975	G. Buckeye	32	166	6	9	0	3.10
	CF	T. Speaker	540	.304	7	86	394	20	8	7	2.8	.981	B. Karr	30	113	5	6	1	5.00
	LF	C. Jamieson	555	.299	2	45	293	15	13	5	2.2	.960	J. Miller	18	83	7	4	1	3.27
	C	L. Sewell	433	.238	0	46	437	**91**	9	3	4.3	.983							
Phi. W-83 L-67 Connie Mack	1B	J. Poole	361	.294	8	63	887	55	8	71	9.4	.992	L. Grove	45	258	13	13	6	**2.51**
	2B	M. Bishop	400	.265	0	33	235	365	8	55	5.1	**.987**	E. Rommel	37	219	11	11	0	3.08
	SS	C. Galloway	408	.240	0	49	274	315	41	49	4.7	.935	J. Quinn	31	164	10	11	1	3.41
	3B	S. Hale	327	.281	4	43	82	152	13	16	3.2	.947	R. Walberg	40	151	12	10	2	2.80
	RF	W. French	397	.305	1	36	186	12	6	7	2.1	.971	S. Gray	38	151	11	12	0	3.64
	CF	A. Simmons	581	.343	19	109	333	11	9	5	2.4	.975	H. Ehmke	20	147	12	4	0	2.81
	LF	B. Lamar	419	.284	5	50	199	10	10	2	2.1	.954	J. Pate	47	113	9	0	6	2.71
	C	M. Cochrane	370	.273	8	47	502	90	15	**5**	5.3	.975							
	32	J. Dykes	429	.287	1	44	197	322	20	42		.963							
	1B	J. Hauser	229	.192	8	36	630	35	3	39	10.3	.996							
	OF	F. Welch	174	.282	4	23	75	4	2	1	1.7	.975							
Was. W-81 L-69 Bucky Harris	1B	J. Judge	453	.291	7	92	1145	95	8	90	9.8	.994	W. Johnson	33	262	15	16	0	3.61
	2B	B. Harris	537	.283	1	63	**356**	427	30	74	5.8	.963	S. Coveleski	36	245	14	11	1	3.12
	SS	B. Myer	434	.304	1	62	215	297	40	47	4.7	.928	D. Ruether	23	169	12	6	0	4.84
	3B	O. Bluege	487	.271	3	65	139	256	20	15	3.1	.952	F. Marberry	**64**	138	12	7	**22**	3.00
	RF	S. Rice	**641**	.337	3	76	342	**25**	15	5	2.5	.961	G. Crowder	19	100	7	4	1	3.96
	CF	E. McNeely	442	.303	0	48	274	9	9	3	2.4	.969							
	LF	G. Goslin	567	.354	17	108	373	25	15	**8**	2.8	.964							
	C	M. Ruel	368	.299	1	53	452	81	6	13	4.6	**.989**							
	1O	J. Harris	257	.307	5	55	354	20	3	20		.992							
Chi. W-81 L-72 Eddie Collins	1B	E. Sheely	525	.299	6	89	1380	84	8	87	10.2	**.995**	T. Lyons	39	284	18	16	2	3.01
	2B	E. Collins	375	.344	1	62	228	307	15	53	5.4	.973	T. Thomas	44	249	15	12	2	3.80
	SS	B. Hunnefield	470	.274	3	48	185	259	32	44	4.9	.933	Blankenship	29	209	13	10	1	3.61
	3B	W. Kamm	480	.294	0	62	**177**	**323**	11	16	**3.6**	**.978**	R. Faber	27	185	15	9	0	3.56
	RF	B. Barrett	368	.307	6	61	179	8	6	2	1.9	.969	J. Edwards	32	142	6	9	1	4.18
	CF	J. Mostil	600	.328	4	42	**440**	15	15	**4**	**3.2**	.969	S. Thurston	31	134	6	8	3	5.02
	LF	B. Falk	566	.345	8	108	338	16	3	4	2.3	**.992**	S. Connally	31	108	6	5	3	3.16
	C	R. Schalk	226	.265	0	32	251	45	7	6	3.8	.977							
	OF	S. Harris	222	.252	2	27	106	6	6	2	1.9	.949							
	2B	R. Morehart	192	.318	0	21	71	136	11	13	4.5	.950							
Det. W-79 L-75 Ty Cobb	1B	L. Blue	429	.287	1	52	1153	56	17	95	11.2	.986	E. Whitehill	36	252	16	13	0	3.99
	2B	C. Gehringer	459	.277	1	48	255	323	16	56	5.3	.973	S. Gibson	35	196	12	9	2	3.48
	SS	J. Tavener	532	.265	1	58	300	470	39	**92**	5.2	.952	E. Wells	36	178	12	10	0	4.15
	3B	J. Warner	311	.251	0	34	105	175	13	9	3.1	.956	L. Stoner	32	160	7	10	0	5.47
	RF	H. Heilmann	502	.367	9	103	228	18	7	4	1.9	.972	K. Holloway	36	139	4	4	2	5.12
	CF	H. Manush	498	**.378**	14	86	283	7	10	3	2.5	.967	H. Dauss	35	124	11	7	4	4.20
	LF	B. Fothergill	387	.367	3	73	245	3	10	0	2.5	.961	R. Collins	30	122	8	8	1	2.73
	C	C. Manion	176	.199	0	14	227	48	8	2	3.8	.972	A. Johns	35	113	6	4	1	5.35
	32	F. O'Rourke	363	.242	1	41	181	256	23	42		.950							
	OF	A. Wingo	298	.282	1	45	155	13	14	2	2.5	.923							
	1B	J. Neun	242	.298	0	15	433	22	3	34	9.3	.993							
	OF	T. Cobb	233	.339	4	62	109	4	6	2	2.2	.950							
	C	J. Bassler	174	.305	0	22	223	61	0	6	4.5	1.000							

POS	Player	AB	BA	HR	RBI	PO	A	E	DP	TC/G	FA	Pitcher	G	IP	W	L	SV	ERA
St. L. W-62 L-92 George Sisler																		
1B	G. Sisler	613	.290	7	71	1467	87	21	**141**	10.6	.987	T. Zachary	34	247	14	15	0	3.60
2B	O. Melillo	385	.255	1	30	225	297	19	65	6.1	.965	M. Gaston	32	214	10	**18**	0	4.33
SS	W. Gerber	411	.270	0	42	261	358	37	**92**	5.1	.944	E. Vangilder	42	181	9	11	1	5.17
3B	M. McManus	549	.284	9	68	119	197	14	17	3.9	.958	E. Wingard	39	169	5	8	3	3.57
RF	B. Miller	353	.331	4	50	219	12	15*	2	2.6	.939	W. Ballou	43	154	11	10	2	4.79
CF	H. Rice	578	.313	9	59	300	22	10	4	2.5	.970	J. Giard	22	90	3	10	0	7.00
LF	K. Williams	347	.280	17	74	189	12	11	2	2.3	.948	D. Davis	27	83	3	8	1	4.66
C	W. Schang	285	.330	8	50	224	75	10	7	3.8	.968							
3B	G. Robertson	247	.251	1	19	58	112	14	9	3.3	.924							
C	P. Hargrave	235	.281	7	37	165	50	5	7	3.7	.977							
OF	H. Bennett	225	.267	1	26	106	9	6	3	2.4	.950							
OF	C. Durst	219	.237	3	16	143	5	3	0	2.6	.980							
OF	B. Jacobson	182	.286	2	21	105	2	4	0	2.2	.964							
Bos. W-46 L-107 Lee Fohl																		
1B	P. Todt	599	.255	7	69	1755	126	22	114	12.4	.988	H. Wiltse	37	196	8	15	0	4.22
2B	B. Regan	403	.263	4	34	264	392	24	66	6.4	.965	T. Wingfield	43	191	11	16	3	4.44
SS	T. Rigney	525	.270	4	53	286	492	25	80	5.5	.969	P. Zahniser	30	172	6	18	0	4.97
3B	F. Haney	462	.221	0	52	149	322	21	30	3.6	.957	R. Ruffing	37	166	6	15	2	4.39
RF	B. Jacobson	394	.305	6	69	193	7	4	1	2.1	.980	T. Welzer	40	141	4	3	0	4.79
CF	I. Flagstead	415	.299	3	31	264	14	5	4	2.9	.982	S. Harriss	21	113	6	10	0	4.46
LF	S. Rosenthal	285	.267	4	34	100	0	4	0	1.6	.962	F. Heimach	20	102	2	9	0	5.65
C	A. Gaston	301	.223	0	21	284	69	7	5	3.7	.981	H. Ehmke	14	97	3	10	0	5.46
2B	M. Herrera	237	.257	0	19	112	168	11	23	6.1	.962							
OF	J. Tobin	209	.273	1	14	79	7	3	1	1.7	.966							
OF	W. Shaner	191	.283	0	21	106	3	4	2	2.4	.965							
OF	F. Bratchi	167	.275	0	19	55	1	3	0	1.6	.949							
OF	R. Carlyle	164	.287	2	16	62	4	7	0	2.0	.904							

BATTING AND BASE RUNNING LEADERS

Batting Average

H. Manush, DET	.378
B. Ruth, NY	.372
B. Fothergill, DET	.367
H. Heilmann, DET	.367
G. Burns, CLE	.358

Slugging Average

B. Ruth, NY	.737
A. Simmons, PHI	.566
H. Manush, DET	.564
L. Gehrig, NY	.549
G. Goslin, WAS	.543

Home Runs

B. Ruth, NY	47
A. Simmons, PHI	19
T. Lazzeri, NY	18
K. Williams, STL	17
G. Goslin, WAS	17

Total Bases

B. Ruth, NY	365
A. Simmons, PHI	329
L. Gehrig, NY	314
G. Goslin, WAS	308
G. Burns, CLE	298

Runs Batted In

B. Ruth, NY	145
T. Lazzeri, NY	114
G. Burns, CLE	114
A. Simmons, PHI	109
B. Falk, CHI	108
G. Goslin, WAS	108

Stolen Bases

J. Mostil, CHI	35
S. Rice, WAS	25
B. Hunnefield, CHI	24
E. McNeely, WAS	18
J. Sewell, CLE	17

Hits

G. Burns, CLE	216
S. Rice, WAS	216
G. Goslin, WAS	201

Base on Balls

B. Ruth, NY	144
M. Bishop, PHI	116
T. Rigney, BOS	108

Home Run Percentage

B. Ruth, NY	9.5
K. Williams, STL	4.9
A. Simmons, PHI	3.3

Runs Scored

B. Ruth, NY	139
L. Gehrig, NY	135
J. Mostil, CHI	120

Doubles

G. Burns, CLE	64
A. Simmons, PHI	53
T. Speaker, CLE	52

Triples

L. Gehrig, NY	20
C. Gehringer, DET	17
G. Goslin, WAS	15
J. Mostil, CHI	15

PITCHING LEADERS

Winning Percentage

G. Uhle, CLE	.711
H. Pennock, NY	.676
R. Faber, CHI	.652
U. Shocker, NY	.633
W. Hoyt, NY	.571

Earned Run Average

L. Grove, PHI	2.51
G. Uhle, CLE	2.83
T. Lyons, CHI	3.01
E. Rommel, PHI	3.08
S. Coveleski, WAS	3.12

Wins

G. Uhle, CLE	27
H. Pennock, NY	23
U. Shocker, NY	19
T. Lyons, CHI	18

Saves

F. Marberry, WAS	22
H. Dauss, DET	9
J. Pate, PHI	6
L. Grove, PHI	6
S. Jones, NY	5

Strikeouts

L. Grove, PHI	194
G. Uhle, CLE	159
T. Thomas, CHI	127
W. Johnson, WAS	125
E. Whitehill, DET	109

Complete Games

G. Uhle, CLE	32
T. Lyons, CHI	24
W. Johnson, WAS	22
L. Grove, PHI	20
H. Pennock, NY	19
U. Shocker, NY	19

Fewest Hits per 9 Innings

L. Grove, PHI	7.92
T. Thomas, CHI	8.13
G. Uhle, CLE	8.48

Shutouts

E. Wells, DET	4

Fewest Walks per 9 Innings

H. Pennock, NY	1.45
S. Smith, CLE	1.48
E. Rommel, PHI	2.22

Most Strikeouts per 9 Inn.

L. Grove, PHI	6.77
T. Thomas, CHI	4.59
G. Uhle, CLE	4.50

Innings

G. Uhle, CLE	318
T. Lyons, CHI	284
H. Pennock, NY	266

Games Pitched

F. Marberry, WAS	64
J. Pate, PHI	47
L. Grove, PHI	45

	W	L	PCT	GB	R	OR	Batting 2B	3B	HR	BA	SA	SB	Fielding E	DP	FA	Pitching CG	BB	SO	ShO	SV	ERA
NY	91	63	.591		**847**	713	262	75	121	.289	**.437**	79	210	117	.966	64	478	486	4	20	3.86
CLE	88	66	.571	3	738	612	**333**	49	27	.289	.386	88	173	153	.972	**96**	**450**	381	**11**	4	3.40
PHI	83	67	.553	6	677	**570**	259	65	61	.269	.383	56	171	131	.972	62	451	**571**	10	16	**3.00**
WAS	81	69	.540	8	802	761	244	**97**	43	**.292**	.401	**122**	184	129	.969	65	566	418	5	**26**	4.34
CHI	81	72	.529	9.5	730	665	314	60	32	.289	.390	121	**165**	122	**.973**	85	506	458	11	12	3.74
DET	79	75	.513	12	793	830	281	90	36	.291	.398	88	193	151	.969	57	555	469	10	18	4.41
STL	62	92	.403	29	682	845	253	78	72	.276	.394	62	235	**167**	.963	64	654	337	5	9	4.66
BOS	46	107	.301	44.5	562	835	249	54	32	.256	.343	48	193	143	.970	53	546	336	6	5	4.72
					5831	5831	2195	568	424	.281	.392	664	1524	1113	.969	546	4206	3456	62	110	4.02

National League 1927

POS	Player	AB	BA	HR	RBI	PO	A	E	DP	TC/G	FA	Pitcher	G	IP	W	L	SV	ERA
Pit. W-94 L-60 Donie Bush																		
1B	J. Harris	411	.326	5	73	1056	78	11	84	9.9	.990	L. Meadows	40	299	19	10	0	3.40
2B	G. Grantham	531	.305	8	66	279	363	32	65	5.4	.953	C. Hill	43	278	22	11	3	3.24
SS	G. Wright	570	.281	9	105	**296**	430	**45**	82	5.4	.942	V. Aldridge	35	239	15	10	1	4.25
3B	P. Traynor	573	.342	5	106	**212**	265	19	**23**	3.5	.962	R. Kremer	35	226	19	8	2	**2.47**
RF	P. Waner	623	**.380**	9	**131**	326	20	7	4	2.5	.980	J. Dawson	20	81	3	7	0	4.46
CF	L. Waner	629	.355	2	27	396	9	10	0	2.8	.976	J. Miljus	19	76	8	3	0	1.90
LF	C. Barnhart	360	.319	3	54	222	5	5	2	2.5	.978							
C	J. Gooch	291	.258	2	48	285	57	9	7	3.9	.974							
OF	K. Cuyler	285	.309	3	31	195	6	4	0	2.8	.980							
C	E. Smith	189	.270	5	25	187	32	3	2	3.6	.986							
2B	H. Rhyne	168	.274	0	17	105	101	8	19	4.8	.963							
St. L. W-92 L-61 Bob O'Farrell																		
1B	J. Bottomley	574	.303	19	124	**1656**	70	20	**149**	11.5	.989	J. Haines	38	301	24	10	1	2.72
2B	F. Frisch	617	.337	10	78	396	**641**	22	**104**	6.9	.979	G. Alexander	37	268	21	10	3	2.52
SS	H. Schuble	218	.257	4	28	120	192	29	36	5.2	.915	B. Sherdel	39	232	17	12	**6**	3.53
3B	L. Bell	390	.259	9	65	85	142	**24**	13	2.5	.904	F. Rhem	27	169	10	12	0	4.41
RF	W. Holm	419	.286	3	66	201	3	7	0	2.2	.967							
CF	T. Douthit	488	.262	5	50	396	8	**15**	4	**3.4**	.964							
LF	C. Hafey	346	.329	18	63	179	19	4	7	2.1	.980							
C	F. Snyder	194	.258	1	30	174	37	4	5	3.5	.981							
OF	B. Southworth	306	.301	2	39	153	6	5	2	2.0	.970							
3S	S. Toporcer	290	.248	0	19	86	157	12	21		.953							
SS	T. Thevenow	191	.194	0	4	111	199	18	38	5.6	.945							
OF	R. Blades	180	.317	2	29	64	0	6	0	1.4	.914							
C	B. O'Farrell	178	.264	0	18	141	45	4	5	3.6	.979							
C	J. Schulte	156	.288	9	32	172	45	10	6	3.8	.956							
N. Y. W-92 L-62 John McGraw																		
1B	B. Terry	580	.326	20	121	1621	**105**	12	135	**11.6**	.993	B. Grimes	39	260	19	8	2	3.54
2B	R. Hornsby	568	.361	26	125	299	582	25	98	5.8	.972	Fitzsimmons	42	245	17	10	3	3.72
SS	T. Jackson	469	.318	14	98	287	**444**	37	85	6.2	.972	V. Barnes	35	229	14	11	2	3.98
3B	F. Lindstrom	562	.306	7	58	93	178	9	12	3.2	.968	L. Benton	29	173	13	5	2	3.95
RF	G. Harper	483	.331	16	87	299	13	8	5	2.3	.975	D. Henry	45	164	11	6	4	4.23
CF	E. Roush	570	.304	7	58	327	19	9	4	2.6	.975	B. Clarkson	26	87	3	9	2	4.36
LF	H. Mueller	190	.289	3	19	100	1	6	0	1.9	.944							
C	Z. Taylor	258	.233	0	21	267	51	9	8	4.0	.972							
3B	A. Reese	355	.265	4	21	50	126	17	14	3.0	.912							
OF	M. Ott	163	.282	1	19	52	2	1	1	1.7	.982							
OF	T. Tyson	159	.264	1	17	73	5	6	1	2.0	.929							
SS	D. Farrell	142	.387	3	34	77	116	17	19	5.8	.919							
C	A. DeVormer	141	.248	2	21	115	27	7	0	2.8	.953							
Chi. W-85 L-68 Joe McCarthy																		
1B	C. Grimm	543	.311	2	74	1437	99	15	117	10.6	.990	C. Root	**48**	**309**	**26**	15	2	3.76
2B	C. Beck	391	.258	2	44	238	358	19	62	6.2	.969	S. Blake	32	224	13	14	0	3.29
SS	W. English	334	.290	1	28	177	281	29	47	5.8	.940	G. Bush	36	193	10	10	2	3.03
3B	S. Adams	647	.292	0	49	45	107	6	12	3.0	.967	H. Carlson	27	184	12	8	0	3.17
RF	E. Webb	332	.301	14	52	171	14	8	5	2.2	.959	J. Brillheart	32	129	4	2	0	4.13
CF	H. Wilson	551	.318	30	129	**400**	13	14	3	2.9	.960	P. Jones	30	113	7	8	0	4.07
LF	R. Stephenson	579	.344	7	82	297	18	8	5	2.2	.975	B. Osborn	24	108	5	5	0	4.18
C	G. Hartnett	449	.294	10	80	479	99	16	21	**4.8**	.973							
OF	C. Heathcote	228	.294	2	25	136	13	2	7	2.6	.987							
3B	E. Pick	181	.171	2	21	60	71	13	9	2.9	.910							
OF	P. Scott	156	.314	0	21	70	3	1	1	2.1	.986							
Cin. W-75 L-78 Jack Hendricks																		
1B	W. Pipp	443	.260	2	41	1145	66	5	86	10.7	**.996**	R. Lucas	37	240	18	11	2	3.38
2B	H. Critz	396	.278	4	49	239	388	20	69	5.7	.969	J. May	44	236	15	12	1	3.51
SS	H. Ford	409	.274	1	46	218	323	27	75	5.5	.952	D. Luque	29	231	13	12	0	3.20
3B	C. Dressen	548	.292	2	55	131	**315**	15	20	3.2	.957	E. Rixey	34	220	12	10	1	3.48
RF	C. Walker	527	.292	6	80	316	15	15	8	2.5	.967	P. Donohue	33	191	6	16	0	4.11
CF	E. Allen	359	.295	2	20	250	6	3	3	2.6	.988	C. Mays	14	82	3	7	0	3.51
LF	R. Bressler	467	.291	3	77	261	15	8	5	2.4	.972	A. Nehf	21	45	3	5	4	5.56
C	B. Hargrave	305	.308	0	35	261	57	4	10	3.5	**.988**							
OF	B. Zitzmann	232	.284	0	24	135	2	6	0	2.4	.958							
1B	G. Kelly	222	.270	5	21	456	32	4	46	10.0	.992							
OF	Christensen	185	.254	0	16	106	6	5	3	2.3	.957							
C	V. Picinich	173	.254	0	12	218	31	5	8	4.2	.980							
P	R. Lucas	150	.313	0	28	7	51	1	2	1.6	.983							

	POS	Player	AB	BA	HR	RBI	PO	A	E	DP	TC/G	FA	Pitcher	G	IP	W	L	SV	ERA
Bkn.	1B	B. Herman	412	.272	14	73	968	68	21	64	10.1	.980	D. Vance	34	273	16	15	1	2.70
W-65 L-88	2B	J. Partridge	572	.260	7	40	330	454	52	63	6.0	.938	J. Petty	42	272	13	18	1	2.98
Wilbert Robinson	SS	J. Butler	521	.238	2	57	214	251	20	49	5.4	.959	J. Elliott	30	188	6	13	3	3.30
	3B	B. Barrett	355	.259	5	38	76	167	21	12	2.8	.920	D. McWeeny	34	164	4	8	1	3.56
	RF	M. Carey	538	.266	1	54	331	19	11	6	2.6	.970	B. Doak	27	145	11	8	0	3.48
	CF	J. Statz	507	.274	1	21	371	14	4	5	3.2	.990	R. Ehrhardt	46	96	3	7	2	3.57
	LF	G. Felix	445	.265	0	57	221	13	13	1	2.1	.947	J. Barnes	18	79	2	10	0	5.72
	C	H. DeBerry	201	.234	1	21	339	59	5	8	6.0	.988	W. Clark	27	74	7	2	2	2.32
	O1	H. Hendrick	458	.310	4	50	556	37	10	37		.983							
	SS	J. Flowers	231	.234	2	20	137	184	19	29	5.2	.944							
	C	B. Henline	177	.266	1	18	216	50	15	6	4.7	.947							
Bos.	1B	J. Fournier	374	.283	10	53	901	63	11	63	9.6	.989	B. Smith	41	261	10	18	3	3.76
W-60 L-94	2B	D. Gautreau	236	.246	0	20	136	196	12	22	6.0	.965	K. Greenfield	27	190	11	14	0	3.84
Dave Bancroft	SS	D. Bancroft	375	.243	1	31	275	329	39	66	6.2	.939	J. Genewich	40	181	11	8	1	3.83
	3B	A. High	384	.302	4	46	93	122	20	9	2.6	.915	J. Wertz	42	164	4	10	1	4.55
	RF	L. Richbourg	450	.309	2	34	233	10	12	0	2.3	.953	C. Robertson	28	154	7	17	0	4.72
	CF	J. Welsh	497	.288	9	54	377	24	13	6	3.2	.969	F. Edwards	29	92	2	8	0	4.99
	LF	E. Brown	558	.306	2	75	335	10	7	1	2.3	.980	G. Mogridge	20	49	6	4	5	3.70
	C	S. Hogan	229	.288	3	32	215	54	4	3	4.5	.985							
	UT	D. Farrell	424	.292	1	58	252	335	37	47		.941							
	UT	E. Moore	411	.302	1	32	200	223	16	36		.964							
	1B	D. Burrus	220	.318	0	32	505	44	16	51	9.3	.972							
	OF	J. Smith	183	.317	1	24	106	7	6	1	2.5	.950							
	C	F. Gibson	167	.222	0	19	130	35	6	3	3.6	.965							
Phi.	1B	Wrightstone	533	.306	6	75	1268	90	15	114	10.1	.989	J. Scott	48	233	9	21	1	5.09
W-51 L-103	2B	F. Thompson	597	.303	1	70	424	485	35	97	6.2	.963	A. Ferguson	31	227	8	16	0	4.84
Stuffy McInnis	SS	H. Sand	535	.299	1	49	201	247	24	36	5.5	.949	D. Ulrich	32	193	8	11	1	3.17
	3B	B. Friberg	335	.233	1	28	124	226	15	23	3.5	.959	H. Pruett	31	186	7	17	1	6.05
	RF	C. Williams	492	.274	30	98	241	22	8	8	2.1	.970	L. Sweetland	21	104	2	10	0	6.16
	CF	F. Leach	536	.306	12	83	385	26	8	10	3.0	.981	C. Willoughby	35	98	3	7	2	6.54
	LF	D. Spalding	442	.296	0	25	250	7	2	1	2.3	.992	H. Carlson	11	64	4	5	1	5.23
	C	J. Wilson	443	.275	2	45	377	82	12	12	3.8	.975							
	SS	J. Cooney	259	.270	0	15	155	238	8	51	5.4	.980*							
	OF	J. Mokan	213	.286	0	33	97	5	4	0	1.7	.962							
	OF	A. Nixon	154	.312	0	18	121	3	4	0	2.9	.969							

BATTING AND BASE RUNNING LEADERS

Batting Average

P. Waner, PIT	.380
R. Hornsby, NY	.361
L. Waner, PIT	.355
R. Stephenson, CHI	.344
P. Traynor, PIT	.342

Home Runs

C. Williams, PHI	30
H. Wilson, CHI	30
R. Hornsby, NY	26
B. Terry, NY	20
J. Bottomley, STL	19

Runs Batted In

P. Waner, PIT	131
H. Wilson, CHI	129
R. Hornsby, NY	125
J. Bottomley, STL	124
B. Terry, NY	121

Hits

P. Waner, PIT	237
L. Waner, PIT	223
F. Frisch, STL	208

Home Run Percentage

C. Williams, PHI	6.1
H. Wilson, CHI	5.4
C. Hafey, STL	5.2

Doubles

R. Stephenson, CHI	46
P. Waner, PIT	40
C. Dressen, CIN	36
F. Lindstrom, NY	36

Slugging Average

C. Hafey, STL	.590
R. Hornsby, NY	.586
H. Wilson, CHI	.579
P. Waner, PIT	.543
B. Terry, NY	.529

Total Bases

P. Waner, PIT	338
R. Hornsby, NY	333
H. Wilson, CHI	319
B. Terry, NY	307
J. Bottomley, STL	292

Stolen Bases

F. Frisch, STL	48
M. Carey, BKN	32
H. Hendrick, BKN	29
S. Adams, CHI	26
L. Richbourg, BOS	24

Base on Balls

R. Hornsby, NY	86
G. Harper, NY	84
G. Grantham, PIT	74
J. Bottomley, STL	74

Runs Scored

R. Hornsby, NY	133
L. Waner, PIT	133
H. Wilson, CHI	119

Triples

P. Waner, PIT	17
J. Bottomley, STL	15
F. Thompson, PHI	14

PITCHING LEADERS

Winning Percentage

L. Benton, BOS, NY	.708
J. Haines, STL	.706
B. Grimes, NY	.704
R. Kremer, PIT	.704
G. Alexander, STL	.677

Wins

C. Root, CHI	26
J. Haines, STL	24
C. Hill, PIT	22
G. Alexander, STL	21

Strikeouts

D. Vance, BKN	184
C. Root, CHI	145
J. May, CIN	121
B. Grimes, NY	102
J. Petty, BKN	101

Fewest Hits per 9 Innings

D. Vance, BKN	7.97
R. Kremer, PIT	8.16
J. Haines, STL	8.17

Fewest Walks per 9 Innings

G. Alexander, STL	1.28
R. Lucas, CIN	1.46
P. Donohue, CIN	1.51

Innings

C. Root, CHI	309
J. Haines, STL	301
L. Meadows, PIT	299

Earned Run Average

R. Kremer, PIT	2.47
G. Alexander, STL	2.52
D. Vance, BKN	2.70
J. Haines, STL	2.72
J. Petty, BKN	2.98

Saves

B. Sherdel, STL	6
G. Mogridge, BOS	5
A. Nehf, CHI, CIN	5
D. Henry, NY	4

Complete Games

D. Vance, BKN	25
J. Haines, STL	25
L. Meadows, PIT	25
G. Alexander, STL	22
C. Hill, PIT	22

Shutouts

J. Haines, STL	6
R. Lucas, CIN	4
C. Root, CHI	4
R. Kremer, PIT	3

Most Strikeouts per 9 Inn.

D. Vance, BKN	6.06
J. Elliott, BKN	4.73
J. May, CIN	4.62

Games Pitched

C. Root, CHI	48
J. Scott, PHI	48
R. Ehrhardt, BKN	46

	W	L	PCT	GB	R	OR	2B	3B	Batting HR	BA	SA	SB	E	Fielding DP	FA	CG	BB	Pitching SO	ShO	SV	ERA
PIT	94	60	.610		817	659	258	78	54	.305	.412	65	187	130	.969	90	418	435	10	10	3.66
STL	92	61	.601	1.5	754	665	264	79	84	.278	.408	110	213	170	.966	89	363	394	14	11	3.57
NY	92	62	.597	2	817	720	251	62	109	.297	.427	73	195	160	.969	65	453	442	7	16	3.97
CHI	85	68	.556	8.5	750	661	266	63	74	.284	.400	65	181	152	.971	75	514	465	11	5	3.65
CIN	75	78	.490	18.5	643	653	222	77	29	.278	.367	62	165	160	.973	87	316	407	12	12	3.54
BKN	65	88	.425	28.5	541	619	195	74	39	.253	.342	106	229	117	.963	74	418	574	7	10	3.36
BOS	60	94	.390	34	651	771	216	61	37	.279	.363	100	231	130	.963	52	468	402	3	11	4.22
PHI	51	103	.331	43	678	903	216	46	57	.280	.370	68	169	152	.972	81	462	377	5	6	5.35
					5651	5651	1888	540	483	.282	.386	649	1570	1171	.969	613	3412	3496	69	81	3.91

American League 1927

	POS	Player	AB	BA	HR	RBI	PO	A	E	DP	TC/G	FA
N. Y. W-110 L-44 Miller Huggins	1B	L. Gehrig	584	.373	47	175	1662	88	15	108	11.4	.992
	2B	T. Lazzeri	570	.309	18	102	213	398	18	60	5.6	.971
	SS	M. Koenig	526	.285	3	62	262	423	47	76	6.0	.936
	3B	J. Dugan	387	.269	2	43	93	196	19	15	2.8	.938
	RF	B. Ruth	540	.356	60	164	328	14	13	4	2.4	.963
	CF	E. Combs	648	.356	6	64	411	6	14	4	2.8	.968
	LF	B. Meusel	516	.337	8	103	249	15	14	1	2.1	.950
	C	P. Collins	251	.275	7	36	267	56	8	1	3.7	.976
	2B	R. Morehart	195	.256	1	20	101	175	16	27	5.5	.945
	C	J. Grabowski	195	.277	0	25	197	47	4	3	3.6	.984
	OF	C. Durst	129	.248	0	25	47	1	1	0	1.4	.980
Phi. W-91 L-63 Connie Mack	1B	J. Dykes	417	.324	5	60	816	49	10	59	10.7	.989
	2B	M. Bishop	372	.277	0	22	211	342	19	48	5.4	.967
	SS	J. Boley	370	.311	1	52	182	318	26	49	4.6	.951
	3B	S. Hale	501	.313	5	81	152	247	16	46	3.2	.961
	RF	T. Cobb	490	.357	5	93	243	9	8	2	2.1	.969
	CF	A. Simmons	406	.392	15	108	247	10	4	2	2.5	.985
	LF	W. French	326	.304	0	41	190	6	9	2	2.2	.956
	C	M. Cochrane	432	.338	12	80	559	85	9	11	5.3	.986
	OF	B. Lamar	324	.299	4	47	148	9	8	1	2.1	.952
	OF	Z. Wheat	247	.324	1	38	105	8	2	1	1.9	.983
	2B	E. Collins	225	.338	1	15	124	150	10	31	5.1	.965
	SS	C. Galloway	181	.265	0	22	115	150	15	20	4.6	.946
	1B	J. Foxx	130	.323	3	20	258	15	7	10	8.8	.975
Was. W-85 L-69 Bucky Harris	1B	J. Judge	522	.308	2	71	1309	71	6	79	10.2	.996
	2B	B. Harris	475	.267	1	55	316	413	21	48	5.9	.972
	SS	B. Reeves	380	.255	1	39	194	296	41	36	5.5	.923
	3B	O. Bluege	503	.274	1	66	185	337	21	20	3.7	.961
	RF	S. Rice	603	.297	2	65	258	12	7	2	2.0	.975
	CF	T. Speaker	523	.327	2	73	278	12	10	5	2.5	.967
	LF	G. Goslin	581	.334	13	120	356	8	17	3	2.6	.955
	C	M. Ruel	428	.308	1	52	495	100	7	8	4.7	.988
	OF	E. McNeely	185	.276	0	16	81	3	2	1	1.8	.977
	C	B. Tate	131	.313	1	24	148	24	4	4	4.5	.977
Det. W-82 L-71 George Moriarty	1B	L. Blue	365	.260	1	42	1019	68	18	99	10.6	.984
	2B	C. Gehringer	508	.317	4	61	304	438	27	84	6.4	.965
	SS	J. Tavener	419	.274	5	59	246	356	33	79	5.6	.948
	3B	J. Warner	559	.267	1	45	156	277	24	34	3.3	.947
	RF	H. Heilmann	505	.398	14	120	218	11	8	5	1.8	.966
	CF	H. Manush	593	.298	6	80	361	9	11	3	2.5	.971
	LF	B. Fothergill	527	.359	9	64	315	3	13	1	2.4	.961
	C	L. Woodall	246	.280	0	39	265	72	1	6	3.9	.997
	UT	M. McManus	369	.268	9	69	245	263	17	54		.968
	1B	J. Neun	204	.324	0	27	548	30	12	45	11.1	.980
	C	J. Bassler	200	.285	0	24	206	56	7	8	4.0	.974
	OF	A. Wingo	137	.234	0	20	43	6	6	2	1.6	.891
Chi. W-70 L-83 Ray Schalk	1B	B. Clancy	464	.300	3	53	1184	81	11	76	10.4	.991
	2B	A. Ward	463	.270	5	56	275	437	27	66	5.4	.963
	SS	B. Hunnefield	365	.285	2	36	150	210	26	38	4.9	.933
	3B	W. Kamm	540	.270	0	59	236	279	15	21	3.6	.972
	RF	B. Barrett	556	.286	4	83	289	22	12	6	2.2	.963
	CF	A. Metzler	543	.319	3	61	397	16	15	6	3.2	.965
	LF	B. Falk	535	.327	3	83	372	22	9	9	2.8	.978
	C	H. McCurdy	262	.286	1	27	261	55	9	8	4.0	.972
	C	B. Crouse	222	.239	0	20	202	79	8	10	3.6	.972
	SS	Peckinpaugh	217	.295	0	23	101	170	10	30	4.7	.964

Pitcher	G	IP	W	L	SV	ERA
W. Hoyt	36	256	22	7	1	2.63
W. Moore	50	213	19	7	13	2.28
H. Pennock	34	210	19	8	2	3.00
U. Shocker	31	200	18	6	0	2.84
D. Ruether	27	184	13	6	0	3.38
G. Pipgras	29	166	10	3	0	4.11
M. Thomas	21	89	7	4	0	4.87
L. Grove	51	262	20	12	9	3.19
R. Walberg	46	249	16	12	4	3.97
J. Quinn	34	207	15	10	1	3.17
H. Ehmke	30	190	12	10	0	4.22
E. Rommel	30	147	11	3	1	4.36
S. Gray	38	141	9	6	3	4.60
H. Lisenbee	39	242	18	9	0	3.57
S. Thurston	29	205	13	13	0	4.47
B. Hadley	30	199	14	6	0	2.85
F. Marberry	56	155	10	7	9	4.64
G. Braxton	58	155	10	9	13	2.95
T. Zachary	15	110	4	7	0	3.67
W. Johnson	18	108	5	6	0	5.10
B. Burke	36	100	3	2	0	3.96
G. Crowder	15	67	4	7	0	4.54
E. Whitehill	41	236	16	14	3	3.36
L. Stoner	38	215	10	13	5	3.98
S. Gibson	33	190	11	12	0	3.69
K. Holloway	36	183	11	12	6	4.07
R. Collins	30	173	13	7	0	4.69
O. Carroll	31	172	10	6	0	3.98
T. Thomas	40	308	19	16	1	2.98
T. Lyons	39	308	22	14	2	2.84
Blankenship	37	237	12	17	0	5.06
S. Connally	43	198	10	15	5	4.08
R. Faber	18	111	4	7	0	4.55

POS	Player	AB	BA	HR	RBI	PO	A	E	DP	TC/G	FA	Pitcher	G	IP	W	L	SV	ERA
Cle. W-66 L-87 Jack McCallister																		
1B	G. Burns	549	.319	3	78	1362	102	15	111	10.6	.990	W. Hudlin	43	265	18	12	0	4.01
2B	L. Fonseca	428	.311	2	40	229	304	15	51	5.7	.973	J. Shaute	45	230	9	16	2	4.22
SS	J. Sewell	569	.316	1	92	361	480	33	80	5.7	**.962**	G. Buckeye	35	205	10	17	1	3.96
3B	R. Lutzke	311	.251	0	41	120	199	21	24	3.5	.938	J. Miller	34	185	10	8	0	3.21
RF	H. Summa	574	.286	4	74	242	12	12	3	1.8	.955	G. Uhle	25	153	8	9	1	4.34
CF	F. Eichrodt	267	.221	0	25	170	13	4	6	2.3	.979	D. Levsen	25	80	3	7	0	5.49
LF	C. Jamieson	489	.309	0	36	300	13	10	2	2.5	.969	G. Grant	25	75	4	6	1	4.46
C	L. Sewell	470	.294	0	53	402	119	20	14	4.3	.963							
3B	J. Hodapp	240	.304	5	40	69	132	14	15	3.2	.935							
2B	F. Spurgeon	179	.251	1	19	124	150	18	28	5.6	.938							
St. L. W-59 L-94 Dan Howley																		
1B	G. Sisler	614	.327	5	97	1374	131	24	138	10.3	.984	M. Gaston	37	254	13	17	1	5.00
2B	O. Melillo	356	.225	0	26	229	293	36	72	5.5	.935	E. Vangilder	44	203	10	12	1	4.79
SS	W. Gerber	438	.224	0	45	290	427	41	91	5.4	.946	S. Jones	30	190	8	14	0	4.32
3B	F. O'Rourke	538	.268	1	39	183	244	20	27	3.7	.955	E. Wingard	38	156	2	13	0	6.56
RF	H. Rice	520	.287	7	68	277	26	20	7	2.5	.938	L. Stewart	27	156	8	11	1	4.28
CF	B. Miller	492	.325	5	75	309	9	10	3	2.6	.970	E. Nevers	27	95	3	8	2	4.94
LF	K. Williams	421	.323	17	74	260	15	10	4	2.5	.965	W. Ballou	21	90	5	6	0	4.78
C	W. Schang	263	.319	5	42	213	73	7	10	3.9	.976	T. Zachary	13	78	4	6	0	4.37
23	S. Adams	259	.266	0	29	159	190	21	35		.943	G. Crowder	21	74	3	5	3	5.01
OF	H. Bennett	256	.266	3	30	118	5	7	1	2.4	.946							
C	S. O'Neill	191	.230	1	22	180	57	4	8	4.0	.983							
OF	F. Schulte	189	.317	3	34	117	3	11	0	2.7	.916							
Bos. W-51 L-103 Bill Carrigan																		
1B	P. Todt	516	.236	6	52	1401	112	13	121	11.0	.991	H. Wiltse	36	219	10	18	1	5.10
2B	B. Regan	468	.274	2	66	283	397	28	76	5.9	.960	S. Harriss	44	218	14	21	1	4.18
SS	B. Myer	469	.288	1	47	239	311	35	64	5.8	.940	T. Welzer	37	182	6	11	1	4.46
3B	B. Rogell	207	.266	2	28	49	123	6	8	3.4	.966	MacFayden	34	160	5	8	2	4.27
RF	J. Tobin	374	.310	2	40	152	10	9	4	1.8	.947	R. Ruffing	26	158	5	13	2	4.66
CF	I. Flagstead	466	.285	4	69	326	19	5	4	2.7	**.986**	J. Russell	34	147	4	9	0	4.10
LF	W. Shaner	406	.273	3	49	220	13	11	1	2.3	.955	D. Lundgren	30	136	5	12	0	6.27
C	G. Hartley	244	.275	1	31	214	51	9	5	3.2	.967							
UT	J. Rothrock	428	.259	1	36	323	284	26	63		.959							
OF	C. Carlyle	278	.234	1	28	127	10	5	0	1.7	.965							
C	F. Hofmann	217	.272	0	24	241	59	18	4	3.9	.943							
3B	R. Rollings	184	.266	0	9	39	66	7	2	2.5	.938							
OF	B. Jacobson	155	.245	0	24	90	4	2	0	2.5	.979							

BATTING AND BASE RUNNING LEADERS

Batting Average

H. Heilmann, DET	.398
A. Simmons, PHI	.392
L. Gehrig, NY	.373
B. Fothergill, DET	.359
T. Cobb, PHI	.357

Slugging Average

B. Ruth, NY	.772
L. Gehrig, NY	.765
A. Simmons, PHI	.645
H. Heilmann, DET	.616
K. Williams, STL	.527

Home Runs

B. Ruth, NY	60
L. Gehrig, NY	47
T. Lazzeri, NY	18
K. Williams, STL	17
A. Simmons, PHI	15

Total Bases

L. Gehrig, NY	447
B. Ruth, NY	417
E. Combs, NY	331
H. Heilmann, DET	311
G. Goslin, WAS	300

Runs Batted In

L. Gehrig, NY	175
B. Ruth, NY	164
H. Heilmann, DET	120
G. Goslin, WAS	120
B. Fothergill, DET	114

Stolen Bases

G. Sisler, STL	27
B. Meusel, NY	24
J. Neun, DET	22
T. Cobb, PHI	22
T. Lazzeri, NY	22

Hits

E. Combs, NY	231
L. Gehrig, NY	218
H. Heilmann, DET	201
G. Sisler, STL	201

Base on Balls

B. Ruth, NY	138
L. Gehrig, NY	109
M. Bishop, PHI	105

Home Run Percentage

B. Ruth, NY	11.1
L. Gehrig, NY	8.0
K. Williams, STL	4.0

Runs Scored

B. Ruth, NY	158
L. Gehrig, NY	149
E. Combs, NY	137

Doubles

L. Gehrig, NY	52
G. Burns, CLE	51
H. Heilmann, DET	50

Triples

E. Combs, NY	23
L. Gehrig, NY	18
H. Manush, DET	18

PITCHING LEADERS

Winning Percentage

W. Hoyt, NY	.759
U. Shocker, NY	.750
W. Moore, NY	.731
H. Pennock, NY	.704
H. Lisenbee, WAS	.667

Earned Run Average

W. Hoyt, NY	2.63
U. Shocker, NY	2.84
T. Lyons, CHI	2.84
B. Hadley, WAS	2.85
T. Thomas, CHI	2.98

Wins

W. Hoyt, NY	22
T. Lyons, CHI	22
L. Grove, PHI	20
W. Moore, NY	19
H. Pennock, NY	19
T. Thomas, CHI	19

Saves

W. Moore, NY	13
G. Braxton, WAS	13
F. Marberry, WAS	9
L. Grove, PHI	9
K. Holloway, DET	6
J. Pate, PHI	6

Strikeouts

L. Grove, PHI	174
R. Walberg, PHI	136
T. Thomas, CHI	107
H. Lisenbee, WAS	105
G. Braxton, WAS	95
E. Whitehill, DET	95

Complete Games

T. Lyons, CHI	30
T. Thomas, CHI	24
W. Hoyt, NY	23
M. Gaston, STL	21
H. Pennock, NY	18
W. Hudlin, CLE	18

Fewest Hits per 9 Innings

T. Thomas, CHI	7.93
B. Hadley, WAS	8.02
H. Lisenbee, WAS	8.22

Shutouts

H. Lisenbee, WAS	4

Fewest Walks per 9 Innings

J. Quinn, PHI	1.61
U. Shocker, NY	1.85
W. Hoyt, NY	1.90

Most Strikeouts per 9 Inn.

L. Grove, PHI	5.97
R. Walberg, PHI	4.91
R. Ruffing, BOS	4.38

Innings

T. Thomas, CHI	308
T. Lyons, CHI	308
W. Hudlin, CLE	265

Games Pitched

G. Braxton, WAS	58
F. Marberry, WAS	56
L. Grove, PHI	51

	W	L	PCT	GB	R	OR	2B	Batting 3B HR	BA	SA	SB	E	Fielding DP	FA	CG	BB	Pitching SO	ShO	SV	ERA
NY	110	44	.714		975	599	291	103 158	.307	.489	90	195	123	.969	82	409	431	11	20	3.20
PHI	91	63	.591	19	841	726	281	70 56	.303	.414	98	190	124	.970	66	442	553	8	24	3.95
WAS	85	69	.552	25	782	730	268	87 29	.287	.386	133	195	125	.969	62	491	497	10	23	3.95
DET	82	71	.536	27.5	845	805	282	100 51	.289	.409	141	206	173	.968	75	577	421	5	17	4.12
CHI	70	83	.458	39.5	662	708	285	61 36	.278	.378	90	178	131	.971	85	440	365	10	8	3.91
CLE	66	87	.431	43.5	668	766	321	52 26	.283	.379	63	201	146	.968	72	508	366	5	8	4.27
STL	59	94	.386	50.5	724	904	262	59 55	.276	.380	91	248	166	.960	80	604	385	4	8	4.95
BOS	51	103	.331	59	597	856	271	78 28	.259	.357	82	228	162	.964	63	558	381	6	7	4.68
					6094	6094	2261	610 439	.285	.399	788	1641	1150	.967	585	4029	3399	59	115	4.12

National League 1928

	POS	Player	AB	BA	HR	RBI	PO	A	E	DP	TC/G	FA	Pitcher	G	IP	W	L	SV	ERA
St. L. W-95 L-59 Bill McKechnie	1B	J. Bottomley	576	.325	31	136	1454	52	20	113	10.3	.987	B. Sherdel	38	249	21	10	5	2.86
	2B	F. Frisch	547	.300	10	86	383	474	21	80	6.3	.969	G. Alexander	34	244	16	9	2	3.36
	SS	R. Maranville	366	.240	1	34	236	362	19	57	5.5	.969	J. Haines	33	240	20	8	0	3.18
	3B	W. Holm	386	.277	3	47	100	145	22	9	3.2	.918	F. Rhem	28	170	11	8	3	4.14
	RF	G. Harper	272	.305	17	58	156	13	2	2	2.0	.988	C. Mitchell	19	150	8	9	0	3.30
	CF	T. Douthit	648	.295	3	43	547	10	9	4	3.7	.984	S. Johnson	34	120	8	4	3	3.90
	LF	C. Hafey	520	.337	27	111	287	13	11	3	2.3	.965	A. Reinhart	23	75	4	6	2	2.87
	C	J. Wilson	411	.258	2	50	394*	82*	8	13*	4.0	.983							
	3B	A. High	368	.285	6	37	56	117	12	10	2.5	.935							
	OF	W. Roettger	261	.341	6	44	152	2	3	1	2.4	.981							
	SS	T. Thevenow	171	.205	0	13	100	158	19	29	4.3	.931							
N. Y. W-93 L-61 John McGraw	1B	B. Terry	568	.326	17	101	1584	78	12	148	11.2	.993	L. Benton	42	310	25	9	4	2.73
	2B	A. Cohen	504	.274	9	59	304	434	24	90	6.0	.969	Fitzsimmons	40	261	20	9	1	3.68
	SS	T. Jackson	537	.270	14	77	354	547	45	112	6.3	.958	J. Genewich	26	158	11	4	3	3.18
	3B	F. Lindstrom	646	.358	14	107	145	340	21	34	3.3	.958	C. Hubbell	20	124	10	6	1	2.83
	RF	M. Ott	435	.322	18	77	214	14	7	4	2.0	.970	V. Aldridge	22	119	4	7	2	4.83
	CF	J. Welsh	476	.307	9	54	310	8	6	3	2.8	.981	J. Faulkner	38	117	9	8	2	3.53
	LF	L. O'Doul	354	.319	8	46	149	4	6	0	1.7	.962	D. Henry	17	64	3	6	1	3.80
	C	S. Hogan	411	.333	10	71	389	57	10	11	3.7	.978							
	UT	A. Reese	406	.308	6	44	232	136	16	21		.958							
	OF	L. Mann	193	.264	2	25	97	3	5	1	1.5	.952							
	OF	E. Roush	163	.252	2	13	100	7	5	0	2.9	.955							
	C	B. O'Farrell	133	.195	2	20	138	27	2	1	2.7	.988							
Chi. W-91 L-63 Joe McCarthy	1B	C. Grimm	547	.294	5	62	1458	70	10	147	10.5	.993	P. Malone	42	251	18	13	2	2.84
	2B	F. Maguire	574	.279	1	41	410	524	23	126	6.9	.976	S. Blake	34	241	17	11	1	2.47
	SS	W. English	475	.299	2	34	245	382	36	85	5.8	.946	C. Root	40	237	14	18	2	3.57
	3B	C. Beck	483	.257	3	52	74	156	10	24	2.8	.958	G. Bush	42	204	15	6	2	3.83
	RF	K. Cuyler	499	.285	17	79	257	18	5	3	2.2	.982	A. Nehf	31	177	13	7	0	2.65
	CF	H. Wilson	520	.313	31	120	321	11	14	2	2.4	.960	P. Jones	39	154	10	6	3	4.03
	LF	R. Stephenson	512	.324	8	90	268	10	5	1	2.1	.982							
	C	G. Hartnett	388	.302	14	57	455	103	6	14	4.8	.989							
	3B	J. Butler	174	.270	0	16	51	120	9	9	3.1	.950							
	C	M. Gonzalez	158	.272	1	21	198	35	4	8	5.3	.983							
	OF	E. Webb	140	.250	3	23	65	4	1	0	2.3	.986							
Pit. W-85 L-67 Donie Bush	1B	G. Grantham	440	.323	10	85	1117	71	17	83	10.1	.986	B. Grimes	48	331	25	14	3	2.99
	2B	S. Adams	539	.276	0	38	265	343	18	54	5.9	.971	C. Hill	36	237	16	10	2	3.53
	SS	G. Wright	407	.310	8	66	194	301	39	59	5.3	.927	R. Kremer	34	219	15	13	0	4.64
	3B	P. Traynor	569	.337	3	124	175	296	27	15	3.5	.946	F. Fussell	28	160	8	9	1	3.61
	RF	P. Waner	602	.370	6	86	299	14	8	0	2.5	.975	J. Dawson	31	129	7	7	3	3.29
	CF	L. Waner	659	.335	5	61	418	15	9	4	2.9	.980	E. Brame	24	96	7	4	0	5.08
	LF	F. Brickell	202	.322	3	41	107	6	5	1	2.4	.958	J. Miljus	21	70	5	7	1	5.30
	C	C. Hargreaves	260	.285	1	32	230	47	11*	7	3.7	.962							
	2S	D. Bartell	233	.305	1	36	158	199	16	40		.957							
	OF	C. Barnhart	196	.296	4	30	96	3	3	0	2.1	.971							
	OF	P. Scott	177	.311	5	33	90	5	2	5	2.3	.979							
	OF	A. Comorosky	176	.295	2	34	118	2	4	1	2.5	.968							
Cin. W-78 L-74 Jack Hendricks	1B	G. Kelly	402	.296	3	58	894	69	9	99	9.8	.991	E. Rixey	43	291	19	18	2	3.43
	2B	H. Critz	641	.296	5	52	333	497	25	124	5.6	.971	D. Luque	33	234	11	10	1	3.57
	SS	H. Ford	506	.241	0	54	355	508	25	128	6.0	.972	R. Kolp	44	209	13	10	3	3.19
	3B	C. Dressen	498	.291	1	59	122	283	27	27	3.2	.938	R. Lucas	27	167	13	9	1	3.39
	RF	C. Walker	427	.279	6	73	289	9	14	3	2.6	.955	P. Donohue	23	150	7	11	0	4.74
	CF	E. Allen	485	.305	1	62	348	12	7	4	2.8	.981							
	LF	B. Zitzmann	266	.297	3	35	313	5	4	2	2.1	.958							
	C	V. Picinich	324	.302	7	35	279	65	6	6	3.8	.983							
	1B	W. Pipp	272	.283	2	26	673	40	8	69	10.0	.989							
	OF	M. Callaghan	238	.290	0	24	140	5	3	2	2.1	.980							
	OF	P. Purdy	223	.309	0	25	137	3	5	1	2.4	.966							
	C	B. Hargrave	190	.295	0	23	181	37	2	2	3.9	.991							

	POS	Player	AB	BA	HR	RBI	PO	A	E	DP	TC/G	FA	Pitcher	G	IP	W	L	SV	ERA
Bkn.	1B	D. Bissonette	587	.320	25	106	1482	77	**20**	95	10.2	.987	D. Vance	38	280	22	10	2	**2.09**
W-77 L-76	2B	J. Flowers	339	.274	2	44	260	270	16	46	5.8	.971	D. McWeeny	42	244	14	14	1	3.17
Wilbert Robinson	SS	D. Bancroft	515	.247	0	51	350	484	46	66	5.9	.948	J. Petty	40	234	15	15	1	4.04
	3B	H. Hendrick	425	.318	11	59	74	200	26	19	3.3	.913	W. Clark	40	195	12	9	3	2.68
	RF	B. Herman	486	.340	12	91	225	12	**16**	2	2.0	.937	J. Elliott	41	192	9	14	1	3.89
	CF	M. Carey	296	.247	2	19	202	8	3	1	2.2	.986	B. Doak	28	99	3	8	3	3.26
	LF	R. Bressler	501	.295	4	70	254	7	4	0	1.9	**.985**							
	C	H. DeBerry	258	.252	0	23	377	56	10	5	5.5	.977							
	UT	H. Riconda	281	.224	3	35	181	222	20	25		.953							
	OF	T. Tyson	210	.271	1	21	130	6	5	3	2.6	.965							
	OF	J. Statz	171	.234	0	16	107	3	4	2	1.5	.965							
Bos.	1B	G. Sisler	491	.340	4	68	1188	**86**	15	100	10.9	.988	B. Smith	38	244	13	17	2	3.87
W-50 L-103	2B	R. Hornsby	486	**.387**	21	94	295	450	21	85	5.5	.973	E. Brandt	38	225	9	**21**	0	5.07
Jack Slattery	SS	D. Farrell	483	.215	3	43	289	418	**51**	73	5.7	.933	A. Delaney	39	192	9	17	2	3.79
W-11 L-20	3B	L. Bell	591	.277	10	91	**177**	314	**27**	**37**	3.4	.948	K. Greenfield	32	144	3	11	0	5.32
Rogers Hornsby	RF	L. Richbourg	612	.337	2	52	367	8	11	1	2.6	.972	J. Cooney	24	90	3	7	1	4.32
W-39 L-83	CF	J. Smith	254	.280	1	32	165	4	2	0	2.6	.988	J. Genewich	13	81	3	7	0	4.13
	LF	E. Brown	523	.268	2	59	302	6	13	3	2.5	.960							
	C	Z. Taylor	399	.251	2	30	367	83	7	8	3.7	.985							
	OF	E. Moore	215	.237	2	18	131	7	6	3	2.7	.958							
Phi.	1B	D. Hurst	396	.285	19	64	964	68	12	92	10.0	.989	R. Benge	40	202	8	18	1	4.55
W-43 L-109	2B	F. Thompson	634	.287	3	50	409	509	**32**	109	6.3	.966	J. Ring	35	173	4	17	1	6.40
Burt Shotton	SS	H. Sand	426	.211	0	38	290	410	36	94	5.4	.951	L. Sweetland	37	135	3	15	2	6.58
	3B	P. Whitney	585	.301	10	103	171	293	22	27	3.3	.955	B. McGraw	39	132	7	8	1	4.64
	RF	C. Klein	253	.360	11	34	128	7	3	0	2.2	.978	A. Ferguson	34	132	5	10	2	5.67
	CF	D. Sothern	579	.285	5	38	358	**19**	14	**7**	2.9	.964	C. Willoughby	35	131	6	5	1	5.30
	LF	F. Leach	588	.304	13	96	296	11	7	5	2.6	.978	A. Walsh	38	122	4	9	2	6.18
	C	W. Lerian	239	.272	2	25	239	61	7	12	4.1	.977	R. Miller	33	108	0	12	1	5.42
	OF	C. Williams	238	.256	12	37	118	9	0	0	1.8	1.000							
	C	S. Davis	163	.282	3	18	149	46	4	7	4.1	.980							

BATTING AND BASE RUNNING LEADERS

Batting Average

R. Hornsby, BOS	.387
P. Waner, PIT	.370
F. Lindstrom, NY	.358
G. Sisler, BOS	.340
B. Herman, BKN	.340

Slugging Average

R. Hornsby, BOS	.632
J. Bottomley, STL	.628
C. Hafey, STL	.604
H. Wilson, CHI	.588
P. Waner, PIT	.547

Home Runs

H. Wilson, CHI	31
J. Bottomley, STL	31
C. Hafey, STL	27
D. Bissonette, BKN	25
R. Hornsby, BOS	21

Total Bases

J. Bottomley, STL	362
F. Lindstrom, NY	330
P. Waner, PIT	329
D. Bissonette, BKN	319
C. Hafey, STL	314

Runs Batted In

J. Bottomley, STL	136
P. Traynor, PIT	124
H. Wilson, CHI	120
C. Hafey, STL	111
F. Lindstrom, NY	107

Stolen Bases

K. Cuyler, CHI	37
F. Frisch, STL	29
C. Walker, CIN	19
F. Thompson, PHI	19
M. Carey, BKN	18
H. Critz, CIN	18

Hits

F. Lindstrom, NY	231
P. Waner, PIT	223
L. Waner, PIT	221

Base on Balls

R. Hornsby, BOS	107
T. Douthit, STL	84
R. Bressler, BKN	80

Home Run Percentage

H. Wilson, CHI	6.0
G. Harper, NY, STL	5.8
J. Bottomley, STL	5.4

Runs Scored

P. Waner, PIT	142
J. Bottomley, STL	123
L. Waner, PIT	121

Doubles

P. Waner, PIT	50
C. Hafey, STL	46
R. Hornsby, BOS	42
J. Bottomley, STL	42

Triples

J. Bottomley, STL	20
P. Waner, PIT	19
L. Waner, PIT	14

PITCHING LEADERS

Winning Percentage

L. Benton, NY	.735
J. Haines, STL	.714
G. Bush, CHI	.714
Fitzsimmons, NY	.690
D. Vance, BKN	.688

Earned Run Average

D. Vance, BKN	2.09
S. Blake, CHI	2.47
A. Nehf, CHI	2.65
W. Clark, BKN	2.68
L. Benton, NY	2.73

Wins

L. Benton, NY	25
B. Grimes, PIT	25
D. Vance, BKN	22
B. Sherdel, STL	21
J. Haines, STL	20
Fitzsimmons, NY	20

Saves

B. Sherdel, STL	5
H. Haid, STL	5
H. Carlson, CHI	4
L. Benton, NY	4

Strikeouts

D. Vance, BKN	200
P. Malone, CHI	155
C. Root, CHI	122
B. Grimes, PIT	97
L. Benton, NY	90

Complete Games

L. Benton, NY	28
B. Grimes, PIT	28
D. Vance, BKN	24
B. Sherdel, STL	20
J. Haines, STL	20

Fewest Hits per 9 Innings

D. Vance, BKN	7.26
S. Blake, CHI	7.82
P. Malone, CHI	7.83

Shutouts

5 tied with	4

Fewest Walks per 9 Innings

G. Alexander, STL	1.37
B. Sherdel, STL	2.03
L. Benton, NY	2.06

Most Strikeouts per 9 Inn.

D. Vance, BKN	6.42
P. Malone, CHI	5.57
C. Root, CHI	4.63

Innings

B. Grimes, PIT	331
L. Benton, NY	310
E. Rixey, CIN	291

Games Pitched

B. Grimes, PIT	48
R. Kolp, CIN	44
E. Rixey, CIN	43

	W	L	PCT	GB	R	OR	2B	3B	HR	BA	SA	SB	E	DP	FA	CG	BB	SO	ShO	SV	ERA
STL	95	59	.617		807	636	**292**	70	113	.281	.425	82	160	134	.974	**83**	**399**	422	4	**21**	3.38
NY	93	61	.604	2	807	653	276	59	**118**	.293	**.430**	62	178	175	.972	79	405	399	7	16	3.67
CHI	91	63	.591	4	714	**615**	251	64	92	.278	.402	**83**	**156**	176	**.975**	75	508	531	12	14	3.40
PIT	85	67	.559	9	**837**	704	246	**100**	52	**.309**	.421	64	201	123	.967	82	446	385	8	11	3.95
CIN	78	74	.513	16	648	686	229	67	32	.280	.368	**83**	162	**194**	.974	68	410	355	11	11	3.94
BKN	77	76	.503	17.5	665	640	229	70	66	.266	.374	81	217	113	.965	75	468	**551**	16	15	**3.25**
BOS	50	103	.327	44.5	631	878	241	41	52	.275	.367	60	193	141	.969	54	524	343	1	6	4.83
PHI	43	109	.283	51	660	957	257	47	85	.267	.382	53	181	171	.971	42	671	403	4	11	5.52
					5769	5769	2021	518	610	.281	.397	568	1448	1227	.971	558	3831	3389	63	105	3.98

American League 1928

	POS	Player	AB	BA	HR	RBI	PO	A	E	DP	TC/G	FA	Pitcher	G	IP	W	L	SV	ERA
N. Y. W-101 L-53 Miller Huggins	1B	L. Gehrig	562	.374	27	**142**	**1488**	79	18	112	10.3	.989	G. Pipgras	46	**301**	**24**	13	3	3.38
	2B	T. Lazzeri	404	.332	10	82	236	331	26	56	5.1	.956	W. Hoyt	42	273	23	7	**8**	3.36
	SS	M. Koenig	533	.319	4	63	260	328	49	69	5.1	.923	H. Pennock	28	211	17	6	3	2.56
	3B	J. Dugan	312	.276	6	34	87	129	11	13	2.5	.952	H. Johnson	31	199	14	9	0	4.30
	RF	B. Ruth	536	.323	**54**	**142**	304	9	8	0	2.1	.975	A. Shealy	23	96	8	6	2	5.06
	CF	E. Combs	626	.310	7	56	**424**	11	9	7	3.0	.980	W. Moore	35	60	4	4	2	4.18
	LF	B. Meusel	518	.297	11	113	259	16	7	6	2.2	.975							
	C	J. Grabowski	202	.238	1	21	265	32	4	8	4.0	.987							
	2S	L. Durocher	296	.270	0	31	158	274	18	42		.960							
	3B	G. Robertson	251	.291	1	36	75	112	15	5	2.9	.926							
	C	B. Bengough	161	.267	0	9	206	37	2	7	4.2	.992							
Phi. W-98 L-55 Connie Mack	1B	J. Hauser	300	.260	16	59	811	41	12	51	9.8	.986	L. Grove	39	262	**24**	8	4	2.58
	2B	M. Bishop	472	.316	6	50	284	371	15	62	5.4	.978	R. Walberg	38	236	17	12	1	3.55
	SS	J. Boley	425	.264	0	49	244	320	30	51	4.5	.949	J. Quinn	31	211	18	7	1	2.90
	3B	S. Hale	314	.309	4	58	86	189	20	17	3.7	.932	E. Rommel	43	174	13	5	4	3.06
	RF	T. Cobb	353	.323	1	40	154	7	6	0	1.8	.964	G. Earnshaw	26	158	7	7	1	3.81
	CF	B. Miller	510	.329	8	85	298	8	10	2	2.4	.968	H. Ehmke	23	139	9	8	0	3.62
	LF	A. Simmons	464	.351	15	107	231	10	3	2	2.1	.988	O. Orwoll	27	106	6	5	2	4.58
	C	M. Cochrane	468	.293	10	57	**645**	71	25	8	**5.7**	.966							
	UT	J. Foxx	400	.328	13	79	412	154	17	32		.971							
	OF	M. Haas	332	.280	6	39	175	9	5	1	2.3	.974							
	UT	J. Dykes	242	.277	5	30	166	164	9	21		.973							
	OF	T. Speaker	191	.267	3	29	111	8	3	1	2.4	.975							
	1P	O. Orwoll	170	.306	0	22	328	41	7	32		.981							
St. L. W-82 L-72 Dan Howley	1B	L. Blue	549	.281	14	80	1472	**107**	17	121	10.4	.989	S. Gray	35	263	20	12	3	3.19
	2B	O. Brannan	483	.244	10	66	272	434	26	74	5.4	.964	G. Crowder	41	244	21	5	2	3.69
	SS	R. Kress	560	.273	3	81	**318**	400	55	99	5.2	.929	J. Ogden	38	243	15	16	2	4.15
	3B	F. O'Rourke	391	.263	1	62	149	160	15	13	3.4	.954	G. Blaeholder	38	214	10	15	3	4.37
	RF	E. McNeely	496	.236	0	44	229	19	4	2	2.1	.984	L. Stewart	29	143	7	9	3	4.67
	CF	F. Schulte	556	.286	7	85	419	21	12	6	3.2	.973	D. Coffman	29	86	4	5	1	6.09
	LF	H. Manush	638	.378	13	108	355	6	3	2	2.4	.992							
	C	W. Schang	245	.286	3	39	263	46	5	5	3.8	.984							
	C	C. Manion	243	.226	2	31	302	49	7	10	5.0	.980							
	OF	F. McGowan	168	.363	2	18	99	3	4	1	2.3	.962							
	3B	Bettencourt	159	.283	4	24	38	68	6	4	2.7	.946							
Was. W-75 L-79 Bucky Harris	1B	J. Judge	542	.306	3	93	1412	92	6	118	10.1	.996	B. Hadley	33	232	12	13	0	3.54
	2B	B. Harris	358	.204	0	28	251	326	18	61	6.2	.970	S. Jones	30	225	17	7	0	2.84
	SS	B. Reeves	353	.303	3	42	159	190	35	32	5.8	.909	G. Braxton	38	218	13	11	6	**2.51**
	3B	O. Bluege	518	.297	2	75	150	**330**	20	34	**3.5**	.960	F. Marberry	**48**	161	13	13	3	3.85
	RF	S. Rice	616	.328	2	55	240	11	7	5	1.8	.973	M. Gaston	28	149	6	12	0	5.51
	CF	R. Barnes	417	.302	6	51	255	16	6	2	2.7	.978	L. Brown	27	107	4	4	1	4.04
	LF	G. Goslin	456	**.379**	17	102	266	14	11	4	2.3	.962	T. Zachary	20	103	6	9	0	5.44
	C	M. Ruel	350	.257	0	55	397	73	5	5	4.7	**.989**							
	OF	S. West	378	.302	3	40	210	13	1	0	1.9	**.996**							
	SS	J. Cronin	227	.242	0	25	133	190	16	42	5.4	.953							
	2B	J. Hayes	210	.257	0	22	101	123	6	26	5.6	.974							
	C	E. Kenna	118	.297	1	20	104	26	8	3	4.1	.942							
Chi. W-72 L-82 Ray Schalk W-32 L-42 Lena Blackburne W-40 L-40	1B	B. Clancy	487	.271	2	37	1175	93	12	104	10.0	.991	T. Thomas	36	283	17	16	2	3.08
	2B	B. Hunnefield	333	.294	2	24	160	239	14	47	5.0	.966	T. Lyons	39	240	15	14	6	3.98
	SS	B. Cissell	443	.260	1	60	255	360	41	77	5.3	.938	G. Adkins	36	225	10	16	1	3.73
	3B	W. Kamm	552	.308	1	84	**243**	278	12	33	3.4	**.977**	R. Faber	27	201	13	9	0	3.75
	RF	A. Metzler	464	.304	3	55	288	11	10	3	2.3	.968	Blankenship	27	158	9	11	0	4.61
	CF	J. Mostil	503	.270	0	51	394	16	10	3	**3.2**	.976	E. Walsh	14	78	4	7	0	4.96
	LF	B. Falk	286	.290	1	37	164	9	5	0	2.3	.972							
	C	B. Crouse	218	.252	2	20	196	61	11	3	3.5	.959							
	OF	C. Reynolds	291	.323	2	36	135	6	3	2	1.9	.979							
	2S	B. Redfern	261	.234	0	35	166	223	24	39		.942							
	O2	B. Barrett	235	.277	3	26	122	62	5	7		.974							
	C	M. Berg	224	.246	0	29	256	52	3	8	4.3	.990							

POS	Player	AB	BA	HR	RBI	PO	A	E	DP	TC/G	FA	Pitcher	G	IP	W	L	SV	ERA
Det. W-68 L-86 George Moriarty																		
1B	B. Sweeney	309	.252	0	19	675	55	5	51	9.8	.993	O. Carroll	34	231	16	12	2	3.27
2B	C. Gehringer	603	.320	6	74	377	**507**	35	101	6.0	.962	E. Whitehill	31	196	11	16	0	4.31
SS	J. Tavener	473	.260	5	52	302	405	42	81	5.7	.944	V. Sorrell	29	171	8	11	0	4.79
3B	M. McManus	500	.288	8	73	114	183	14	12	3.4	.955	E. Vangilder	38	156	11	10	5	3.91
RF	H. Heilmann	558	.328	14	107	215	17	7	2	1.9	.971	L. Stoner	36	126	5	8	4	4.35
CF	H. Rice	510	.302	6	81	346	9	14	0	2.9	.962	K. Holloway	30	120	4	8	2	4.34
LF	B. Fothergill	347	.317	3	63	179	6	8	0	2.1	.959	S. Gibson	20	120	5	8	0	5.42
C	P. Hargrave	321	.274	10	63	301	35	8	5	3.9	.977	H. Billings	21	111	5	10	0	5.12
OF	A. Wingo	242	.285	2	30	144	5	5	1	2.2	.968	G. Smith	39	106	1	1	3	4.42
3B	J. Warner	206	.214	0	13	62	107	10	6	3.4	.944							
C	L. Woodall	186	.210	0	13	218	44	2	3	4.3	.992							
OF	J. Stone	113	.354	2	21	49	2	2	0	2.0	.962							
Cle. W-62 L-92 Roger Peckinpaugh																		
1B	L. Fonseca	263	.327	3	36	541	41	0	65	10.4	1.000	J. Shaute	36	254	13	17	2	4.04
2B	C. Lind	**650**	.294	1	54	**390**	505	37	**116**	**6.1**	.960	W. Hudlin	42	220	14	14	7	4.04
SS	J. Sewell	588	.323	4	70	297	**438**	28	**103**	5.6	.963	G. Uhle	31	214	12	17	1	4.07
3B	J. Hodapp	449	.323	2	73	103	220	19	20	3.4	.944	J. Miller	25	158	8	9	0	4.44
RF	H. Summa	504	.284	3	57	223	12	7	5	1.8	.971	G. Grant	28	155	10	8	0	5.04
CF	S. Langford	427	.276	4	50	239	5	7	2	2.3	.972	B. Bayne	37	109	2	5	3	5.13
LF	C. Jamieson	433	.307	1	37	282	**22**	5	1	2.8	.984							
C	L. Sewell	411	.270	3	52	430	117	16	**13**	4.8	.972							
UT	E. Morgan	265	.313	4	54	387	69	18	41		.962							
1B	G. Burns	209	.249	5	30	470	38	8	44	9.7	.984							
Bos. W-57 L-96 Bill Carrigan																		
1B	P. Todt	539	.252	12	73	1486	94	5	96	**11.0**	.997	R. Ruffing	42	289	10	**25**	2	3.89
2B	B. Regan	511	.264	7	75	294	467	29	87	5.8	.963	E. Morris	47	258	19	15	5	3.53
SS	W. Gerber	300	.213	0	28	201	328	25	50	5.4	.955	J. Russell	32	201	11	14	0	3.84
3B	B. Myer	536	.313	1	44	137	306	14	**35**	3.2	.969	MacFayden	33	195	9	15	0	4.75
RF	D. Taitt	482	.299	3	61	251	19	7	8	2.0	.975	S. Harriss	27	128	8	11	1	4.63
CF	I. Flagstead	510	.290	1	39	346	18	10	4	2.8	.973							
LF	K. Williams	462	.303	8	67	253	10	8	0	2.1	.970							
C	F. Hofmann	199	.226	0	16	223	44	5	7	3.8	.982							
UT	J. Rothrock	344	.267	3	22	242	61	12	14		.962							
S2	B. Rogell	296	.233	0	29	150	232	23	34		.943							
C	C. Berry	177	.260	1	19	153	34	8	2	3.1	.959							
C	J. Heving	158	.259	0	11	153	25	6	2	3.0	.967							

BATTING AND BASE RUNNING LEADERS

Batting Average
G. Goslin, WAS	.379
H. Manush, STL	.378
L. Gehrig, NY	.374
A. Simmons, PHI	.351
T. Lazzeri, NY	.332

Slugging Average
B. Ruth, NY	.709
L. Gehrig, NY	.648
G. Goslin, WAS	.614
H. Manush, STL	.575
A. Simmons, PHI	.558

Home Runs
B. Ruth, NY	54
L. Gehrig, NY	27
G. Goslin, WAS	17
J. Hauser, PHI	16
A. Simmons, PHI	15

Total Bases
B. Ruth, NY	380
H. Manush, STL	367
L. Gehrig, NY	364
E. Combs, NY	290
H. Heilmann, DET	283

Runs Batted In
B. Ruth, NY	142
L. Gehrig, NY	142
B. Meusel, NY	113
H. Manush, STL	108
A. Simmons, PHI	107
H. Heilmann, DET	107

Stolen Bases
B. Myer, BOS	30
J. Mostil, CHI	23
H. Rice, DET	20
B. Cissell, CHI	18
O. Bluege, WAS	18

Hits
H. Manush, STL	241
L. Gehrig, NY	210
S. Rice, WAS	202

Base on Balls
B. Ruth, NY	135
L. Blue, STL	105
M. Bishop, PHI	97

Home Run Percentage
B. Ruth, NY	10.1
L. Gehrig, NY	4.8
G. Goslin, WAS	3.7

Runs Scored
B. Ruth, NY	163
L. Gehrig, NY	139
E. Combs, NY	118

Doubles
L. Gehrig, NY	47
H. Manush, STL	47
B. Meusel, NY	45

Triples
E. Combs, NY	21
H. Manush, STL	20
C. Gehringer, DET	16

PITCHING LEADERS

Winning Percentage
G. Crowder, STL	.808
W. Hoyt, NY	.767
L. Grove, PHI	.750
H. Pennock, NY	.739
J. Quinn, PHI	.720

Earned Run Average
G. Braxton, WAS	2.51
H. Pennock, NY	2.56
L. Grove, PHI	2.58
S. Jones, WAS	2.84
J. Quinn, PHI	2.90

Wins
L. Grove, PHI	24
G. Pipgras, NY	24
W. Hoyt, NY	23
G. Crowder, STL	21
S. Gray, STL	20

Saves
W. Hoyt, NY	8
W. Hudlin, CLE	7
T. Lyons, CHI	6
G. Braxton, WAS	6
E. Vangilder, DET	5
E. Morris, BOS	5

Strikeouts
L. Grove, PHI	183
G. Pipgras, NY	139
T. Thomas, CHI	129
R. Ruffing, BOS	118
G. Earnshaw, PHI	117

Complete Games
R. Ruffing, BOS	25
L. Grove, PHI	24
T. Thomas, CHI	24
G. Pipgras, NY	22

Fewest Hits per 9 Innings
G. Braxton, WAS	7.30
L. Grove, PHI	7.84
S. Jones, WAS	8.37

Shutouts
H. Pennock, NY	5

Fewest Walks per 9 Innings
J. Quinn, PHI	1.45
H. Pennock, NY	1.71
G. Braxton, WAS	1.81

Most Strikeouts per 9 Inn.
L. Grove, PHI	6.29
H. Johnson, NY	4.97
R. Walberg, PHI	4.28

Innings
G. Pipgras, NY	301
R. Ruffing, BOS	289
T. Thomas, CHI	283

Games Pitched
F. Marberry, WAS	48
E. Morris, BOS	47
G. Pipgras, NY	46
E. Rommel, PHI	43

	W	L	PCT	GB	R	OR	2B	3B	Batting HR	BA	SA	SB	E	Fielding DP	FA	CG	BB	Pitching SO	ShO	SV	ERA
NY	101	53	.656		894	685	269	79	133	.296	.450	51	194	136	.968	83	452	487	13	21	3.74
PHI	98	55	.641	2.5	829	615	323	75	89	.295	.436	59	181	124	.970	81	424	607	15	16	3.36
STL	82	72	.532	19	772	742	276	76	63	.274	.393	76	189	146	.969	80	454	456	6	15	4.17
WAS	75	79	.487	26	718	705	277	93	40	.284	.393	110	178	146	.972	77	466	462	15	10	3.88
CHI	72	82	.468	29	656	725	231	77	24	.270	.358	139	186	149	.970	88	501	418	6	11	3.98
DET	68	86	.442	33	744	804	265	97	62	.279	.401	113	218	140	.965	65	567	451	5	16	4.32
CLE	62	92	.403	39	674	830	299	61	34	.285	.382	50	221	187	.965	71	511	416	4	15	4.47
BOS	57	96	.373	43.5	589	770	260	62	38	.264	.361	99	178	139	.971	70	452	407	5	9	4.39
					5876	5876	2200	620	483	.281	.397	697	1545	1167	.969	615	3827	3704	69	113	4.04

National League 1929

	POS	Player	AB	BA	HR	RBI	PO	A	E	DP	TC/G	FA	Pitcher	G	IP	W	L	SV	ERA
Chi. W-98 L-54 Joe McCarthy	1B	C. Grimm	463	.298	10	91	1228	74	10	114	10.9	.992	C. Root	43	272	19	6	5	3.47
	2B	R. Hornsby	602	.380	39	149	286	547	23	106	5.5	.973	G. Bush	50	271	18	7	8	3.66
	SS	W. English	608	.276	1	52	332	497	39	107	6.0	.955	P. Malone	40	267	22	10	2	3.57
	3B	N. McMillan	495	.271	5	55	131	226	21	21	3.2	.944	S. Blake	35	218	14	13	1	4.29
	RF	K. Cuyler	509	.360	15	102	288	15	8	6	2.4	.974	A. Nehf	32	121	8	5	1	5.59
	CF	H. Wilson	574	.345	39	159	380	14	12	4	2.7	.970	H. Carlson	31	112	11	5	2	5.16
	LF	R. Stephenson	495	.362	17	110	245	9	4	4	2.0	.984	M. Cvengros	32	64	5	4	2	4.64
	C	Z. Taylor	215	.274	1	31	247	36	6	4	4.5*	.979							
	OF	C. Heathcote	224	.313	2	31	131	4	2	2	2.6	.985							
	3B	C. Beck	190	.211	0	9	18	70	2	5	2.7	.978							
	C	M. Gonzalez	167	.240	0	18	212	34	2	7	4.1	.992							
Pit. W-88 L-65 Donie Bush W-67 L-51 Jewel Ens W-21 L-14	1B	E. Sheely	485	.293	6	88	1292	83	5	102	9.9	.996	B. Grimes	33	233	17	7	2	3.13
	2B	G. Grantham	349	.307	12	90	205	239	15	54	6.0	.967	E. Brame	37	230	16	11	0	4.55
	SS	D. Bartell	610	.302	2	57	179	246	21	21	4.6	.953	R. Kremer	34	222	18	10	0	4.26
	3B	P. Traynor	540	.356	4	108	148	238	20	23	3.1	.951	J. Petty	36	184	11	10	0	3.71
	RF	P. Waner	596	.336	15	100	328	15	5	5	2.4	.986	S. Swetonic	41	144	8	10	5	4.82
	CF	L. Waner	662	.353	5	74	450	22	6	6	3.2	.987	L. French	30	123	7	5	1	4.90
	LF	A. Comorosky	473	.321	6	97	256	6	10	3	2.2	.963	H. Meine	22	108	7	6	1	4.50
	C	C. Hargreaves	328	.268	1	44	308	56	7	7	3.6	.981							
	C	R. Hemsley	235	.289	0	37	240	48	14	7	3.8	.954							
	UT	S. Adams	196	.260	0	11	75	130	17	14		.923							
	SS	S. Clarke	178	.264	2	21	73	132	18	19	5.4	.919							
	P	E. Brame	116	.310	4	25	7	36	3	0	1.2	.935							
N. Y. W-84 L-67 John McGraw	1B	B. Terry	607	.372	14	117	1575	111	11	146	11.4	.994	C. Hubbell	39	268	18	11	1	3.69
	2B	A. Cohen	347	.294	5	47	227	315	20	52	6.0	.964	L. Benton	39	237	11	17	3	4.14
	SS	T. Jackson	551	.294	21	94	329	552	28	110	6.1	.969	Fitzsimmons	37	222	15	11	1	4.10
	3B	F. Lindstrom	549	.319	15	91	134	258	14	24	3.2	.966	B. Walker	29	178	14	7	0	3.09
	RF	M. Ott	545	.328	42	151	335	26	10	12	2.5	.973	C. Mays	37	123	7	2	4	4.32
	CF	E. Roush	450	.324	8	52	248	18	5	5	2.5	.982	D. Henry	27	101	5	6	1	3.82
	LF	F. Leach	411	.290	8	47	149	2	4	0	1.6	.974	J. Scott	30	92	7	6	1	3.53
	C	S. Hogan	317	.300	5	45	286	47	7	5	3.7	.979	J. Genewich	21	85	3	7	1	6.78
	OF	C. Fullis	274	.288	7	29	151	3	6	0	2.1	.963							
	C	B. O'Farrell	248	.306	4	42	254	22	6	2	3.4	.979							
	2B	A. Reese	209	.263	0	21	104	163	11	24	6.3	.960							
	32	D. Farrell	178	.213	0	16	87	114	13	18		.939							
	PH	P. Crawford	57	.298	3	24													
St. L. W-78 L-74 Billy Southworth W-43 L-45 Gabby Street W-2 L-0 Bill McKechnie W-33 L-29	1B	J. Bottomley	560	.314	29	137	1347	75	13	122	9.9	.991	B. Sherdel	33	196	10	15	0	5.93
	2B	F. Frisch	527	.334	5	74	295	374	21	66	5.7	.970	S. Johnson	42	182	13	7	3	3.60
	SS	C. Gelbert	512	.262	3	65	338	499	46	95	6.0	.948	J. Haines	28	180	13	10	0	5.71
	3B	A. High	603	.295	10	63	91	204	10	17	2.5	.967	C. Mitchell	25	173	8	11	0	4.27
	RF	E. Orsatti	346	.332	3	39	176	12	5	5	2.5	.974	H. Haid	38	155	9	9	4	4.07
	CF	T. Douthit	613	.336	9	62	442	8	12	1	3.1	.974	F. Frankhouse	30	133	7	2	1	4.12
	LF	C. Hafey	517	.338	29	125	278	8	10	1	2.3	.966	G. Alexander	22	132	9	8	0	3.89
	C	J. Wilson	394	.325	4	71	410	80	14	16	4.2	.972							
	OF	W. Roettger	269	.253	2	42	137	4	1	0	2.1	.993							
	OF	W. Holm	176	.233	0	14	115	4	7	2	2.9	.944							
	C	E. Smith	145	.345	1	22	131	21	6	1	3.2	.962							
Phi. W-71 L-82 Burt Shotton	1B	D. Hurst	589	.304	31	125	1509	112	24	125	10.7	.985	C. Willoughby	49	243	15	14	4	4.99
	2B	F. Thompson	623	.324	4	53	395	512	33	103	6.4	.965	L. Sweetland	43	204	13	11	2	5.11
	SS	T. Thevenow	317	.227	0	35	188	296	24	56	5.6	.953	R. Benge	38	199	11	15	4	6.29
	3B	P. Whitney	612	.327	8	115	168	333	17	29	3.4	.967	P. Collins	43	153	9	7	5	5.75
	RF	C. Klein	616	.356	43	145	321	18	12	3	2.4	.966	H. Elliott	40	114	3	7	2	6.06
	CF	D. Sothern	294	.306	5	27	193	9	7	2	2.9	.967	B. McGraw	41	86	5	5	5	5.73
	LF	L. O'Doul	638	.398	32	122	320	14	10	5	2.2	.971	L. Koupal	15	87	5	5	2	4.78
	C	W. Lerian	273	.223	7	25	271	69	5	13	3.3	.986	H. Smythe	19	69	4	6	1	5.24
	SO	B. Friberg	455	.301	7	55	234	195	28	33		.939							
	C	S. Davis	263	.342	7	48	198	47	10	7	2.6	.961							
	OF	H. Peel	156	.269	0	19	94	2	1	1	2.5	.990							
	PH	C. Williams	65	.292	5	21													

	POS	Player	AB	BA	HR	RBI	PO	A	E	DP	TC/G	FA	Pitcher	G	IP	W	L	SV	ERA
Bkn.	1B	D. Bissonette	431	.281	12	75	1093	47	15	70	10.2	.987	W. Clark	41	279	16	19	1	3.74
	2B	E. Moore	402	.296	0	48	135	228	17	31	5.1	.955	D. Vance	31	231	14	13	0	3.89
W-70 L-83	SS	D. Bancroft	358	.277	1	44	224	309	25	45	5.5	.955	R. Moss	39	182	11	6	0	5.04
Wilbert Robinson	3B	W. Gilbert	569	.304	3	58	137	271	19	16	3.0	.956	C. Dudley	35	157	6	14	0	5.69
	RF	B. Herman	569	.381	21	113	244	10	16	2	1.9	.941	D. McWeeny	36	146	4	10	1	6.10
	CF	J. Frederick	628	.328	24	75	410	13	11	1	3.0	.975	J. Morrison	39	137	13	7	8	4.48
	LF	R. Bressler	456	.318	9	77	263	7	13	0	2.3	.954							
	C	V. Picinich	273	.260	4	31	311	62	8	8	4.5	.979							
	UT	H. Hendrick	384	.354	14	82	467	62	16	29		.971							
	C	H. DeBerry	210	.262	1	25	304	36	3	3	5.0	.991							
	2B	B. Rhiel	205	.278	4	25	94	137	5	16	5.0	.979							
Cin.	1B	G. Kelly	577	.293	5	103	1537	103	11	127	11.2	.993	R. Lucas	32	270	19	12	0	3.60
	2B	H. Critz	425	.247	1	50	210	395	16	72	5.9	.974	E. Rixey	35	201	10	13	1	4.16
W-66 L-88	SS	H. Ford	529	.276	3	50	239	368	30	86	5.9	.953	J. May	41	199	10	14	3	4.61
Jack Hendricks	3B	C. Dressen	401	.244	1	36	77	157	17	9	2.6	.932	P. Donohue	32	178	10	13	0	5.42
	RF	C. Walker	492	.313	7	83	298	11	10	2	2.3	.969	D. Luque	32	176	5	16	0	4.50
	CF	E. Allen	538	.292	6	64	393	12	5	2	3.0	.988	R. Kolp	30	145	8	10	0	4.03
	LF	E. Swanson	574	.300	4	43	317	9	10	2	2.4	.970							
	C	J. Gooch	287	.300	0	34	251	61	8	7	3.7	.975							
	C	C. Sukeforth	237	.354	1	33	171	40	4	4	2.8	.981							
	SS	P. Pittenger	210	.295	0	27	107	153	12	37	5.4	.956							
	3B	J. Stripp	187	.214	3	20	49	120	7	4	3.2	.960							
	OF	P. Purdy	181	.271	1	16	84	3	2	0	2.1	.978							
Bos.	1B	G. Sisler	629	.326	1	79	1398	111	28	131	10.0	.982	B. Smith	34	231	11	17	3	4.68
	2B	F. Maguire	496	.252	0	41	334	437	23	94	5.8	.971	S. Seibold	33	206	12	17	1	4.73
W-56 L-98	SS	R. Maranville	560	.284	0	55	319	536	35	104	6.1	.961	P. Jones	35	188	7	15	0	4.64
Judge Fuchs	3B	L. Bell	483	.298	9	72	107	198	15	15	2.5	.953	E. Brandt	26	168	8	13	0	5.53
	RF	L. Richbourg	557	.305	3	56	323	14	10	2	2.6	.971	B. Cantwell	27	157	4	13	2	4.47
	CF	E. Clark	279	.315	1	30	216	7	5	3	3.1	.978	D. Leverett	24	98	3	7	1	6.36
	LF	G. Harper	457	.291	10	68	266	7	8	2	2.2	.972	B. Cunningham	17	92	4	6	1	4.52
	C	A. Spohrer	342	.272	2	48	314	57	18	5	3.6	.954							
	OF	J. Welsh	186	.290	2	16	177	6	4	1	3.7	.979							

BATTING AND BASE RUNNING LEADERS

Batting Average
L. O'Doul, PHI	.398
B. Herman, BKN	.381
R. Hornsby, CHI	.380
B. Terry, NY	.372
R. Stephenson, CHI	.362

Slugging Average
R. Hornsby, CHI	.679
C. Klein, PHI	.657
M. Ott, NY	.635
C. Hafey, STL	.632
L. O'Doul, PHI	.622

Home Runs
C. Klein, PHI	43
M. Ott, NY	42
R. Hornsby, CHI	39
H. Wilson, CHI	39
L. O'Doul, PHI	32

Total Bases
R. Hornsby, CHI	409
C. Klein, PHI	405
L. O'Doul, PHI	397
H. Wilson, CHI	355
B. Herman, BKN	348

Runs Batted In
H. Wilson, CHI	159
M. Ott, NY	151
R. Hornsby, CHI	149
C. Klein, PHI	145
J. Bottomley, STL	137

Stolen Bases
K. Cuyler, CHI	43
E. Swanson, CIN	33
F. Frisch, STL	24
E. Allen, CIN	21
B. Herman, BKN	21

Hits
L. O'Doul, PHI	254
L. Waner, PIT	234
R. Hornsby, CHI	229

Base on Balls
M. Ott, NY	113
G. Grantham, PIT	93
P. Waner, PIT	89

Home Run Percentage
M. Ott, NY	7.7
C. Klein, PHI	7.0
H. Wilson, CHI	6.8

Runs Scored
R. Hornsby, CHI	156
L. O'Doul, PHI	152
M. Ott, NY	138

Doubles
J. Frederick, BKN	52
C. Hafey, STL	47
R. Hornsby, CHI	47

Triples
L. Waner, PIT	20
C. Walker, CIN	15
P. Waner, PIT	15
P. Whitney, PHI	14

PITCHING LEADERS

Winning Percentage
C. Root, CHI	.760
G. Bush, CHI	.720
B. Grimes, PIT	.708
P. Malone, CHI	.688
R. Kremer, PIT	.643

Earned Run Average
B. Walker, NY	3.09
B. Grimes, PIT	3.13
C. Root, CHI	3.47
P. Malone, CHI	3.57
R. Lucas, CIN	3.60

Wins
P. Malone, CHI	22
C. Root, CHI	19
R. Lucas, CIN	19
G. Bush, CHI	18
R. Kremer, PIT	18
C. Hubbell, NY	18

Saves
J. Morrison, BKN	8
G. Bush, CHI	8
L. Koupal, BKN, PHI	6
P. Collins, PHI	5
S. Swetonic, PIT	5
C. Root, CHI	5

Strikeouts
P. Malone, CHI	166
W. Clark, BKN	140
D. Vance, BKN	126
C. Root, CHI	124
C. Hubbell, NY	106

Complete Games
R. Lucas, CIN	28

Fewest Hits per 9 Innings
R. Lucas, CIN	8.90
C. Hubbell, NY	9.17
R. Kremer, PIT	9.18

Shutouts
P. Malone, CHI	5
Fitzsimmons, NY	4
C. Root, CHI	4

Fewest Walks per 9 Innings
D. Vance, BKN	1.83
R. Lucas, CIN	1.93
J. Petty, PIT	2.05

Most Strikeouts per 9 Inn.
P. Malone, CHI	5.60
D. Vance, BKN	4.90
W. Clark, BKN	4.52

Innings
W. Clark, BKN	279
C. Root, CHI	272
G. Bush, CHI	271

Games Pitched
G. Bush, CHI	50
C. Willoughby, PHI	49

	W	L	PCT	GB	R	OR	2B	3B	HR	BA	SA	SB	E	DP	FA	CG	BB	SO	ShO	SV	ERA
								Batting					Fielding					Pitching			
CHI	98	54	.645		**982**	758	**310**	45	140	.303	.452	103	154	**169**	**.975**	79	537	548	**14**	21	4.16
PIT	88	65	.575	10.5	904	780	285	**116**	60	.303	.430	94	181	136	.970	79	439	409	5	13	**3.97**
NY	84	67	.556	13.5	897	**709**	251	47	136	.296	.436	85	158	163	.975	68	**387**	431	9	13	4.66
STL	78	74	.513	20	831	806	**310**	84	100	.293	.438	72	174	149	.971	**83**	474	453	6	8	4.66
PHI	71	82	.464	27.5	897	1032	305	51	**153**	**.309**	**.467**	59	191	153	.969	45	616	369	5	**24**	6.13
BKN	70	83	.458	28.5	755	888	282	69	99	.291	.427	80	192	113	.968	59	549	**549**	7	16	4.92
CIN	66	88	.429	33	686	760	258	79	34	.281	.379	**134**	162	148	.974	75	413	347	5	8	4.41
BOS	56	98	.364	43	657	876	252	78	32	.280	.375	65	204	146	.967	78	530	366	4	12	5.12
					6609	6609	2253	569	754	.294	.426	692	1416	1177	.971	566	3945	3472	55	115	4.71

American League 1929

Team	POS	Player	AB	BA	HR	RBI	PO	A	E	DP	TC/G	FA	Pitcher	G	IP	W	L	SV	ERA
Phi. W-104 L-46 Connie Mack	1B	J. Foxx	517	.354	33	117	1226	74	6	98	9.2	.995	L. Grove	42	275	20	6	4	**2.81**
	2B	M. Bishop	475	.232	3	36	301	371	21	58	5.4	.970	R. Walberg	40	268	18	11	4	3.60
	SS	J. Boley	303	.251	2	47	161	229	15	50	4.6	.963	G. Earnshaw	44	255	**24**	8	1	3.29
	3B	S. Hale	379	.277	1	40	90	171	12	13	2.8	.956	J. Quinn	35	161	11	9	2	3.97
	RF	B. Miller	556	.335	8	93	311	10	10	4	2.3	.970	B. Shores	39	153	11	6	7	3.60
	CF	M. Haas	578	.313	16	82	373	10	7	2	2.8	.982	E. Rommel	32	114	12	2	4	2.85
	LF	A. Simmons	581	.365	34	**157**	349	19	4	2	2.6	.989							
	C	M. Cochrane	514	.331	7	95	**659**	77	13	9	5.5	**.983**							
	UT	J. Dykes	401	.327	13	79	203	273	33	41		.935							
N.Y. W-88 L-66 Miller Huggins W-82 L-61 Art Fletcher W-6 L-5	1B	L. Gehrig	553	.300	35	126	1458	82	9	134	10.1	.994	G. Pipgras	39	225	18	12	0	4.23
	2B	T. Lazzeri	545	.354	18	106	368	467	**27**	**101**	5.9	.969	W. Hoyt	30	202	10	9	1	4.24
	SS	L. Durocher	341	.246	0	32	197	299	22	59	5.6	.958	E. Wells	31	193	13	9	0	4.33
	3B	G. Robertson	309	.298	0	35	80	116	7	6	2.6	.966	H. Sherid	33	160	6	6	1	3.49
	RF	B. Ruth	499	.345	**46**	154	240	5	4	2	1.9	.984	H. Pennock	27	158	9	11	2	4.90
	CF	E. Combs	586	.345	3	65	358	10	13	5	2.7	.966	F. Heimach	35	135	11	6	4	4.01
	LF	B. Meusel	391	.261	10	57	206	9	7	2	2.3	.968	T. Zachary	26	120	12	0	2	2.48
	C	B. Dickey	447	.324	10	65	476	**95**	12	**13**	4.6	.979	W. Moore	41	62	6	4	8	4.06
	S3	M. Koenig	373	.292	3	41	137	216	32	34		.917							
	3B	L. Lary	236	.309	5	26	38	95	8	10	2.6	.943							
	OF	C. Durst	202	.257	4	31	151	5	2	1	2.2	.987							
	OF	S. Byrd	170	.312	5	28	108	6	6	2	2.2	.950							
Cle. W-81 L-71 Roger Peckinpaugh	1B	L. Fonseca	566	**.369**	6	103	1486	**107**	8	**141**	**10.9**	.995	W. Hudlin	40	280	17	15	1	3.34
	2B	J. Hodapp	294	.327	4	51	162	271	10	32	6.2	.977	W. Ferrell	43	243	21	10	5	3.60
	SS	J. Tavener	250	.212	2	27	158	275	25	59	5.1	.945	J. Miller	29	206	14	12	0	3.58
	3B	J. Sewell	578	.315	7	73	163	**336**	13	28	3.4	.975	J. Shaute	26	162	8	8	0	4.28
	RF	B. Falk	430	.309	13	94	219	15	14	4	2.0	.944	J. Miljus	34	128	8	8	2	5.19
	CF	E. Averill	602	.331	18	97	**388**	14	14	3	2.7	.966	K. Holloway	25	119	6	5	0	3.03
	LF	C. Jamieson	364	.291	0	26	192	8	4	1	2.2	.980	J. Zinn	18	105	4	6	2	5.04
	C	L. Sewell	406	.236	1	39	433	81	**18**	11	4.3	.966							
	OF	E. Morgan	318	.318	3	37	100	8	11	1	1.5	.908							
	SS	R. Gardner	256	.262	1	24	175	240	21	50	5.3	.952							
	2B	C. Lind	224	.241	0	13	190	209	18	60	6.5	.957							
	O2	D. Porter	192	.328	1	24	95	63	8	8		.952							
St. L. W-79 L-73 Dan Howley	1B	L. Blue	573	.293	6	61	**1491**	88	10	127	10.5	.994	S. Gray	43	**305**	18	15	1	3.72
	2B	O. Melillo	494	.296	5	67	342	**519**	24	98	6.3	.973	G. Crowder	40	267	17	15	4	3.92
	SS	R. Kress	557	.305	9	107	312	441	43	**94**	5.5	**.946**	G. Blaeholder	42	222	14	15	2	4.18
	3B	F. O'Rourke	585	.251	2	62	171	242	25	**30**	2.9	.943	R. Collins	26	155	11	6	1	4.00
	RF	F. McGowan	441	.254	2	51	257	16	7	5	2.4	.975	L. Stewart	23	149	9	6	0	3.25
	CF	F. Schulte	446	.307	3	71	361	12	4	3	**3.3**	**.989**	J. Ogden	34	131	4	8	0	4.93
	LF	H. Manush	574	.355	6	81	293	11	4	3	2.2	.987	C. Kimsey	24	64	3	6	1	5.04
	C	W. Schang	249	.237	5	36	268	56	4	6	3.9	.988							
	OF	E. McNeely	230	.243	1	18	96	4	2	0	1.6	.980							
	C	R. Ferrell	144	.229	0	24	140	35	7	3	4.0	.962							
Was. W-71 L-81 Walter Johnson	1B	J. Judge	543	.315	6	71	1323	88	6	116	10.0	**.996**	F. Marberry	**49**	250	19	12	**11**	3.06
	2B	B. Myer	563	.300	3	82	205	271	21	51	5.6	.958	B. Hadley	37	194	6	16	0	5.65
	SS	J. Cronin	494	.281	8	61	285	**459**	**62**	92	5.6	.923	G. Braxton	37	182	12	10	4	4.85
	3B	J. Hayes	424	.276	2	57	56	132	11	15	3.2	.945	L. Brown	40	168	8	7	0	4.18
	RF	S. Rice	616	.323	1	62	272	20	9	**8**	2.0	.978	S. Jones	24	154	9	9	0	3.92
	CF	S. West	510	.267	3	75	376	**25**	9	4	2.9	.978	B. Burke	37	141	6	8	0	4.79
	LF	G. Goslin	553	.288	18	91	299	7	10	1	2.2	.968	M. Thomas	22	125	7	8	2	3.52
	C	B. Tate	265	.294	0	30	291	49	10	10	4.7	.971	A. Liska	24	94	3	9	0	4.77
	UT	O. Bluege	220	.295	5	31	74	145	6	24		.973							
	C	M. Ruel	188	.245	0	20	247	52	3	6	4.8	.990							

	POS	Player	AB	BA	HR	RBI	PO	A	E	DP	TC/G	FA	Pitcher	G	IP	W	L	SV	ERA
Det.	1B	D. Alexander	626	.343	25	137	1443	90	**18**	129	10.0	.988	G. Uhle	32	249	15	11	0	4.08
W-70 L-84	2B	C. Gehringer	634	.339	13	106	**404**	501	23	93	6.0	**.975**	E. Whitehill	38	245	14	15	1	4.62
Bucky Harris	SS	H. Schuble	258	.233	2	28	141	216	46	43	4.7	.886	V. Sorrell	36	226	14	15	1	5.18
	3B	M. McManus	599	.280	18	90	206	289	14	29	3.4	.972	O. Carroll	34	202	9	17	1	4.63
	RF	H. Heilmann	453	.344	15	120	193	8	7	3	1.8	.966	E. Yde	29	87	7	3	0	5.30
	CF	H. Rice	536	.304	6	69	345	16	15	6	3.0	.960	L. Stoner	24	53	3	3	4	5.26
	LF	R. Johnson	640	.314	10	69	377	**25**	**31**	5	3.0	.928							
	C	E. Phillips	221	.235	2	21	255	34	10	4	4.7	.967							
	OF	B. Fothergill	277	.354	6	62	116	2	4	1	2.1	.967							
	C	P. Hargrave	185	.330	3	26	175	38	6	7	4.6	.973							
	C	M. Shea	162	.290	3	24	157	32	7	4	3.9	.964							
Chi.	1B	A. Shires	353	.312	3	41	815	58	8	78	10.0	.991	T. Thomas	36	260	14	18	1	3.19
W-59 L-93	2B	J. Kerr	419	.258	1	39	307	459	23	84	**6.5**	.971	T. Lyons	37	259	14	20	2	4.10
Lena Blackburne	SS	B. Cissell	618	.280	5	62	**357**	**459**	55	90	**5.7**	.937	R. Faber	31	234	13	13	0	3.88
	3B	W. Kamm	523	.268	3	63	**221**	270	11	27	**3.5**	**.978**	H. McKain	34	158	6	9	1	3.65
	RF	C. Reynolds	517	.317	11	67	268	13	15	5	2.3	.949	G. Adkins	31	138	2	11	0	5.33
	CF	D. Hoffman	337	.258	3	37	237	4	4	2	2.8	.984	E. Walsh	24	129	6	11	0	5.65
	LF	A. Metzler	568	.275	2	49	316	16	14	3	2.5	.960							
	C	M. Berg	351	.288	0	47	290	86	7	12	3.6	.982							
	1B	B. Clancy	290	.283	3	45	647	49	6	47	9.5	.991							
	OF	C. Watwood	278	.302	2	18	188	7	12	2	2.7	.942							
Bos.	1B	P. Todt	534	.262	4	64	1467	102	14	128	10.3	.991	R. Ruffing	35	244	9	**22**	1	4.86
W-58 L-96	2B	B. Regan	371	.288	1	54	193	282	19	66	5.4	.962	M. Gaston	39	244	12	19	2	3.73
Bill Carrigan	SS	H. Rhyne	346	.251	0	38	220	297	36	71	4.9	.935	J. Russell	35	226	6	18	0	3.94
	3B	B. Reeves	460	.248	2	28	152	242	**38**	27	3.3	.912	MacFayden	32	221	10	18	0	3.62
	RF	B. Barrett	370	.270	3	35	204	16	6	4	2.1	.973	E. Morris	33	208	14	14	1	4.45
	CF	J. Rothrock	473	.300	6	59	342	12	11	3	2.9	.970	B. Bayne	27	84	5	5	0	6.72
	LF	R. Scarritt	540	.294	1	71	302	16	19	6	2.3	.944							
	C	C. Berry	207	.242	1	21	236	51	5	8	4.1	.983							
	UT	B. Narleski	260	.277	0	25	146	200	15	41		.958							
	OF	E. Bigelow	211	.284	1	26	63	5	4	1	1.2	.944							
	C	J. Heving	188	.319	0	23	207	40	3	4	4.5	.988							
	OF	K. Williams	139	.345	3	21	75	3	3	2	2.3	.963							

BATTING AND BASE RUNNING LEADERS

Batting Average

L. Fonseca, CLE	.369
A. Simmons, PHI	.365
H. Manush, STL	.355
T. Lazzeri, NY	.354
J. Foxx, PHI	.354

Slugging Average

B. Ruth, NY	.697
A. Simmons, PHI	.642
J. Foxx, PHI	.625
L. Gehrig, NY	.582
D. Alexander, DET	.580

Home Runs

B. Ruth, NY	46
L. Gehrig, NY	35
A. Simmons, PHI	34
J. Foxx, PHI	33
D. Alexander, DET	25

Total Bases

A. Simmons, PHI	373
D. Alexander, DET	363
B. Ruth, NY	348
C. Gehringer, DET	337
J. Foxx, PHI	323

Runs Batted In

A. Simmons, PHI	157
B. Ruth, NY	154
D. Alexander, DET	137
L. Gehrig, NY	126
H. Heilmann, DET	120

Stolen Bases

C. Gehringer, DET	28
B. Cissell, CHI	26
B. Miller, PHI	24
J. Rothrock, BOS	23
R. Johnson, DET	20

Hits

D. Alexander, DET	215
C. Gehringer, DET	215
A. Simmons, PHI	212

Base on Balls

M. Bishop, PHI	128
L. Blue, STL	126
L. Gehrig, NY	122

Home Run Percentage

B. Ruth, NY	9.2
J. Foxx, PHI	6.4
L. Gehrig, NY	6.3

Runs Scored

C. Gehringer, DET	131
R. Johnson, DET	128
L. Gehrig, NY	127

Doubles

H. Manush, STL	45
C. Gehringer, DET	45
R. Johnson, DET	45

Triples

C. Gehringer, DET	19
R. Scarritt, BOS	17
B. Miller, PHI	16

PITCHING LEADERS

Winning Percentage

L. Grove, PHI	.769
G. Earnshaw, PHI	.750
W. Ferrell, CLE	.677
R. Walberg, PHI	.621
F. Marberry, WAS	.613

Earned Run Average

L. Grove, PHI	2.81
F. Marberry, WAS	3.06
T. Thomas, CHI	3.19
G. Earnshaw, PHI	3.29
W. Hudlin, CLE	3.34

Wins

G. Earnshaw, PHI	24
W. Ferrell, CLE	21
L. Grove, PHI	20
F. Marberry, WAS	19

Saves

F. Marberry, WAS	11
W. Moore, NY	8
B. Shores, PHI	7
W. Ferrell, CLE	5

Strikeouts

L. Grove, PHI	170
G. Earnshaw, PHI	149
G. Pipgras, NY	125
F. Marberry, WAS	121
R. Ruffing, BOS	109
S. Gray, STL	109

Complete Games

T. Thomas, CHI	24
G. Uhle, DET	23
S. Gray, STL	23
W. Hudlin, CLE	22
T. Lyons, CHI	21
L. Grove, PHI	21

Fewest Hits per 9 Innings

G. Earnshaw, PHI	8.23
E. Wells, NY	8.33
F. Marberry, WAS	8.38

Shutouts

G. Blaeholder, STL	4
MacFayden, BOS	4
G. Crowder, STL	4
S. Gray, STL	4

Fewest Walks per 9 Innings

J. Russell, BOS	1.59
T. Thomas, CHI	2.08
G. Uhle, DET	2.10

Most Strikeouts per 9 Inn.

L. Grove, PHI	5.56
G. Earnshaw, PHI	5.27
G. Pipgras, NY	4.99

Innings

S. Gray, STL	305
W. Hudlin, CLE	280
L. Grove, PHI	275

Games Pitched

F. Marberry, WAS	49
G. Earnshaw, PHI	44
S. Gray, STL	43
W. Ferrell, CLE	43

	W	L	PCT	GB	R	OR	2B	3B	HR	BA	SA	SB	E	DP	FA	CG	BB	SO	ShO	SV	ERA
							|←	Batting	→|				|←	Fielding	→|	|←		Pitching			→|
PHI	104	46	.693		901	**615**	288	76	122	.296	.451	61	**146**	117	**.975**	72	487	**573**	8	**24**	**3.44**
NY	88	66	.571	18	899	775	262	74	**142**	.295	.450	51	178	152	.971	64	485	484	12	18	4.17
CLE	81	71	.533	24	717	736	294	79	62	.294	.417	75	198	**162**	.968	80	488	389	8	10	4.05
STL	79	73	.520	26	733	713	276	63	46	.276	.380	72	156	148	.975	83	**462**	415	**15**	10	4.08
WAS	71	81	.467	34	730	776	244	66	48	.276	.375	86	195	156	.968	61	496	494	3	17	4.34
DET	70	84	.455	36	**926**	928	**339**	**97**	110	.299	.453	95	242	149	.961	82	646	467	5	9	4.96
CHI	59	93	.388	46	627	792	240	74	37	.268	.363	**106**	188	153	.970	78	505	328	5	7	4.41
BOS	58	96	.377	48	605	803	285	69	28	.267	.365	85	218	159	.965	**84**	496	416	9	5	4.43
					6138	6138	2228	598	595	.284	.407	631	1521	1196	.969	604	4065	3566	65	100	4.24

National League 1930

St. L.   W-92 L-62   Gabby Street

POS	Player	AB	BA	HR	RBI	PO	A	E	DP	TC/G	FA	Pitcher	G	IP	W	L	SV	ERA
1B	J. Bottomley	487	.304	15	97	1164	41	12	127	9.8	.990	B. Hallahan	35	237	15	9	2	4.66
2B	F. Frisch	540	.346	10	114	307	473	25	93	**6.5**	.969	S. Johnson	32	188	12	10	2	4.65
SS	C. Gelbert	513	.304	3	72	322	472	44	104	6.0	.947	J. Haines	29	182	13	8	1	4.30
3B	S. Adams	570	.314	0	55	66	159	8	18	2.2	**.966**	B. Grimes	22	152	13	6	0	3.01
RF	G. Watkins	391	.373	17	87	163	10	8	4	2.0	.956	F. Rhem	26	140	12	8	0	4.45
CF	T. Douthit	**664**	.303	7	93	**425**	8	16	3	2.9	.964	H. Bell	39	115	4	3	8	3.90
LF	C. Hafey	446	.336	26	107	189	11	5	0	1.8	.976	A. Grabowski	33	106	6	4	1	4.84
C	J. Wilson	362	.318	1	58	456	67	7	11	5.0	.987	J. Lindsey	39	106	7	5	5	4.43
OF	S. Fisher	254	.374	8	61	122	6	5	0	2.0	.962							
C	G. Mancuso	227	.366	7	59	277	33	10	2	5.2	.969							
3B	A. High	215	.279	2	29	34	68	1	5	2.1	.990							
OF	R. Blades	101	.396	4	25	66	1	3	0	2.2	.957							

Chi.   W-90 L-64 Joe McCarthy   W-86 L-64 Rogers Hornsby   W-4 L-0

POS	Player	AB	BA	HR	RBI	PO	A	E	DP	TC/G	FA	Pitcher	G	IP	W	L	SV	ERA
1B	C. Grimm	429	.289	6	66	1040	68	6	103	9.9	**.995**	P. Malone	45	272	**20**	9	4	3.94
2B	F. Blair	578	.273	6	59	257	429	30	83	6.2	.958	G. Bush	46	225	15	10	3	6.20
SS	C. Beck	244	.213	6	34	97	165	13	36	4.8	.953	C. Root	37	220	16	14	3	4.33
3B	W. English	638	.335	14	59	83	135	6	19	2.7	.973	S. Blake	34	187	10	14	0	4.82
RF	K. Cuyler	642	.355	13	134	377	21	8	7	2.6	.980	B. Teachout	40	153	11	4	0	4.06
CF	H. Wilson	585	.356	**56**	**190**	357	9	**19**	2	2.5	.951	B. Osborn	35	127	10	6	1	4.97
LF	R. Stephenson	341	.367	5	68	132	5	6	1	1.8	.958							
C	G. Hartnett	508	.339	37	122	646	68	8	11	5.3	.989							
3B	L. Bell	248	.278	5	47	63	102	9	14	2.5	.948							
OF	D. Taylor	219	.283	2	37	97	3	3	0	2.0	.971							
1B	G. Kelly	166	.331	3	19	414	32	1	31	11.5	.998							

N. Y.   W-87 L-67   John McGraw

POS	Player	AB	BA	HR	RBI	PO	A	E	DP	TC/G	FA	Pitcher	G	IP	W	L	SV	ERA
1B	B. Terry	633	**.401**	23	129	**1538**	128	17	128	**10.9**	.990	B. Walker	39	245	17	15	1	3.93
2B	H. Critz	558	.265	4	50	346*	413*	22	88*	6.3	.972*	C. Hubbell	37	242	17	12	2	3.76
SS	T. Jackson	431	.339	13	82	218	441	30	72	6.0	.956	Fitzsimmons	41	224	19	7	1	4.25
3B	F. Lindstrom	609	.379	22	106	132	291	21	24	3.0	.953	H. Pruett	45	136	5	4	3	4.78
RF	M. Ott	521	.349	25	119	320	23	11	6	2.4	.949	C. Mitchell	24	129	10	3	0	3.98
CF	W. Roettger	420	.283	5	51	233	9	2	1	2.1	.992	J. Heving	41	90	7	5	6	5.22
LF	F. Leach	544	.327	13	71	208	11	5	4	1.8	.978	P. Donohue	18	87	7	6	1	6.13
C	S. Hogan	389	.339	13	75	386	46	8	5	4.6	.982	J. Genewich	18	61	2	5	3	5.61
C	B. O'Farrell	249	.301	4	54	259	34	8	0	4.4	.973							
OF	E. Allen	238	.307	7	31	122	6	2	0	2.1	.985							
S2	D. Marshall	223	.309	0	21	106	175	12	28		.959							
OF	A. Reese	172	.273	4	25	66	1	3	0	2.2	.957							

Bkn.   W-86 L-68   Wilbert Robinson

POS	Player	AB	BA	HR	RBI	PO	A	E	DP	TC/G	FA	Pitcher	G	IP	W	L	SV	ERA
1B	D. Bissonette	572	.336	16	113	1427	72	**20**	**142**	10.4	.987	D. Vance	35	259	17	15	0	**2.61**
SS	G. Wright	532	.321	22	126	297	462	28	97	5.9	.964	W. Clark	44	200	13	13	6	4.19
3B	W. Gilbert	623	.294	3	67	130	312	26	27	3.1	.944	D. Luque	31	199	14	8	2	4.30
RF	B. Herman	614	.393	35	130	260	10	6	1	1.8	.978	J. Elliott	35	198	10	7	1	3.95
CF	J. Frederick	616	.334	17	76	394	12	4	3	2.9	.990	R. Phelps	36	180	14	7	0	4.11
LF	R. Bressler	335	.299	3	52	200	5	1	1	2.3	.995	R. Moss	36	118	9	6	1	5.10
C	A. Lopez	421	.309	6	57	465	66	9	9	4.3	.983	S. Thurston	24	106	6	4	1	3.40
2B	J. Flowers	253	.320	2	50	153	200	19	42	5.7	.949							
UT	E. Moore	196	.281	1	20	117	115	10	23		.959							
OF	H. Hendrick	167	.257	5	28	68	4	4	2	1.8	.947							

Pit.   W-80 L-74   Jewel Ens

POS	Player	AB	BA	HR	RBI	PO	A	E	DP	TC/G	FA	Pitcher	G	IP	W	L	SV	ERA
1B	G. Suhr	542	.286	17	107	1445	79	13	**142**	10.2	.992	R. Kremer	39	**276**	**20**	12	0	5.02
2B	G. Grantham	552	.324	18	99	324	488	**36**	84	6.0	.958	L. French	42	275	17	18	1	4.36
SS	D. Bartell	475	.320	4	75	304	458	48	111	6.4	.941	E. Brame	32	236	17	8	1	4.70
3B	P. Traynor	497	.366	9	119	130	268	25	18	3.3	.941	G. Spencer	41	157	8	9	4	5.40
RF	P. Waner	589	.368	8	77	344	9	15	4	2.6	.959	H. Meine	20	117	6	8	1	6.14
CF	L. Waner	260	.362	1	36	165	6	3	1	2.7	.983	S. Swetonic	23	97	6	5	5	4.47
LF	A. Comorosky	597	.313	12	119	337	12	11	2	2.4	.969							
C	R. Hemsley	324	.253	2	45	325	50	8	11	3.9	.979							
OF	F. Brickell	219	.297	1	14	134	3	7	1	2.4	.951							
UT	C. Engle	216	.264	0	15	113	161	15	18	3.7	.948							
C	A. Bool	216	.259	7	46	190	42	8	1	3.7	.967							
OF	I. Flagstead	156	.250	2	21	70	4	3	1	1.9	.961							
P	E. Brame	116	.353	3	22	1	39	2	0	1.3	.952							

POS	Player	AB	BA	HR	RBI	PO	A	E	DP	TC/G	FA	Pitcher	G	IP	W	L	SV	ERA
Bos. W-70 L-84 Bill McKechnie																		
1B	G. Sisler	431	.309	3	67	915	81	13	103	9.4	.987	S. Seibold	36	251	15	16	2	4.12
2B	F. Maguire	516	.267	0	52	387	476	28	104	6.1	.969	B. Smith	38	220	10	14	5	4.26
SS	R. Maranville	558	.281	2	43	343	445	29	98	5.9	.965	B. Cantwell	31	173	9	15	2	4.88
3B	B. Chatham	404	.267	5	56	89	152	21	26	2.8	.920	T. Zachary	24	151	11	5	0	4.58
RF	L. Richbourg	529	.304	3	54	294	9	9	4	2.4	.971	E. Brandt	41	147	4	11	1	5.01
CF	J. Welsh	422	.275	3	36	329	8	7	2	3.1	.980	B. Sherdel	21	119	6	5	1	4.75
LF	W. Berger	555	.310	38	119	307	10	11	3	2.3	.966	F. Frankhouse	27	111	7	6	0	5.61
C	A. Spohrer	356	.317	2	37	322	36	16	4	3.5	.957	B. Cunningham	36	107	5	6	0	5.48
OF	E. Clark	233	.296	3	28	165	3	4	0	2.7	.977							
1B	J. Neun	212	.325	2	23	431	31	4	46	8.5	.991							
OF	R. Moore	191	.288	2	34	70	3	1	0	2.2	.986							
C	B. Cronin	178	.253	0	17	203	31	4	5	3.7	.983							
Cin. W-59 L-95 Dan Howley																		
1B	J. Stripp	464	.306	3	64	722	38	3	76	10.2	.996	B. Frey	44	245	11	**18**	1	4.70
2B	H. Ford	424	.231	1	34	152	217	6	45	5.7	.984	R. Lucas	33	211	14	16	1	5.38
SS	L. Durocher	354	.243	3	32	216	350	24	77	5.7	.959	L. Benton	35	178	7	12	1	5.12
3B	T. Cuccinello	443	.312	10	78	85	181	23	15	2.7	.920	R. Kolp	37	168	7	12	3	4.22
RF	H. Heilmann	459	.333	19	91	279	16	14	5	2.9	.955	E. Rixey	32	164	9	13	0	5.10
CF	B. Meusel	443	.289	10	62	223	8	9	3	2.1	.963	J. May	26	112	3	11	0	5.77
LF	C. Walker	472	.307	8	51	241	5	9	2	2.1	.965	A. Campbell	23	58	2	4	4	5.43
C	C. Sukeforth	296	.284	1	19	234	46	7	8	3.5	.976							
OF	E. Swanson	301	.309	2	22	178	5	7	1	2.7	.963							
C	J. Gooch	276	.243	2	30	233	42	13	4	3.6	.955							
OF	M. Callaghan	225	.276	0	16	142	3	2	1	2.7	.986							
2B	P. Crawford	224	.290	3	26	94	153	8	23	4.7	.969							
1B	G. Kelly	188	.287	5	35	503	35	4	44	10.8	.993							
Phi. W-52 L-102 Burt Shotton																		
1B	D. Hurst	391	.327	17	78	845	59	15	92	9.6	.984	P. Collins	47	239	16	11	3	4.78
2B	F. Thompson	478	.282	4	46	287	386	32	95	6.3	.955	R. Benge	38	226	11	15	1	5.70
SS	T. Thevenow	573	.286	0	78	344	554	56	113	6.1	.941	L. Sweetland	34	167	7	15	0	7.71
3B	P. Whitney	606	.342	8	117	186	313	18	29	3.5	.965	C. Willoughby	41	153	4	17	1	7.59
RF	C. Klein	648	.386	40	170	362	44	17	10	2.7	.960	H. Collard	30	127	6	12	0	6.80
CF	D. Sothern	347	.280	5	36	217	15	8	3	2.9	.967	H. Elliott	**48**	117	6	11	0	7.67
LF	L. O'Doul	528	.383	22	97	262	3	13	1	2.1	.953							
C	S. Davis	329	.313	14	65	307	50	5	5	3.8	.986							
UT	B. Friberg	331	.341	4	42	185	175	21	29		.945							
1B	M. Sherlock	299	.324	0	38	623	51	7	57	9.7	.990							
OF	F. Brickell	240	.246	0	17	151	6	6	0	3.1	.963							
C	T. Rensa	172	.285	3	31	131	20	11	5	3.3	.932							
C	H. McCurdy	148	.331	1	25	97	16	4	1	2.9	.966							

BATTING AND BASE RUNNING LEADERS   PITCHING LEADERS

Batting Average
B. Terry, NY	.401
B. Herman, BKN	.393
C. Klein, PHI	.386
L. O'Doul, PHI	.383
F. Lindstrom, NY	.379

Slugging Average
H. Wilson, CHI	.723
C. Klein, PHI	.687
B. Herman, BKN	.678
C. Hafey, STL	.652
G. Hartnett, CHI	.630

Winning Percentage
Fitzsimmons, NY	.731
P. Malone, CHI	.690
E. Brame, PIT	.680
R. Kremer, PIT	.625
B. Hallahan, STL	.625

Earned Run Average
D. Vance, BKN	2.61
C. Hubbell, NY	3.76
B. Walker, NY	3.93
P. Malone, CHI	3.94
B. Grimes, BOS, STL	4.07

Home Runs
H. Wilson, CHI	56
C. Klein, PHI	40
W. Berger, BOS	38
G. Hartnett, CHI	37
B. Herman, BKN	35

Total Bases
C. Klein, PHI	445
H. Wilson, CHI	423
B. Herman, BKN	416
B. Terry, NY	392
K. Cuyler, CHI	351

Wins
P. Malone, CHI	20
R. Kremer, PIT	20
Fitzsimmons, NY	19

Saves
H. Bell, STL	8
J. Heving, NY	6
W. Clark, BKN	6
J. Lindsey, STL	5
S. Swetonic, PIT	5
B. Smith, BOS	5

Runs Batted In
H. Wilson, CHI	190
C. Klein, PHI	170
K. Cuyler, CHI	134
B. Herman, BKN	130
B. Terry, NY	129

Stolen Bases
K. Cuyler, CHI	37
P. Waner, PIT	18
B. Herman, BKN	18
J. Stripp, CIN	15
F. Frisch, STL	15
F. Lindstrom, NY	15

Strikeouts
B. Hallahan, STL	177
D. Vance, BKN	173
P. Malone, CHI	142
C. Root, CHI	124
C. Hubbell, NY	117

Complete Games
E. Brame, PIT	22
P. Malone, CHI	22
L. French, PIT	21
D. Vance, BKN	20
S. Seibold, BOS	20

Hits
B. Terry, NY	254
C. Klein, PHI	250
B. Herman, BKN	241

Base on Balls
H. Wilson, CHI	105
M. Ott, NY	103
W. English, CHI	100

Fewest Hits per 9 Innings
D. Vance, BKN	8.39
B. Hallahan, STL	8.84
Fitzsimmons, NY	9.23

Shutouts
C. Root, CHI	4
D. Vance, BKN	4
C. Hubbell, NY	3
L. French, PIT	3

Home Run Percentage
H. Wilson, CHI	9.6
G. Hartnett, CHI	7.3
W. Berger, BOS	6.8

Runs Scored
C. Klein, PHI	158
K. Cuyler, CHI	155
W. English, CHI	152

Fewest Walks per 9 Innings
R. Lucas, CIN	1.88
D. Vance, BKN	1.91
R. Kremer, PIT	2.05

Most Strikeouts per 9 Inn.
B. Hallahan, STL	6.71
D. Vance, BKN	6.02
C. Root, CHI	5.07

Doubles
C. Klein, PHI	59
K. Cuyler, CHI	50
B. Herman, BKN	48

Triples
A. Comorosky, PIT	23
P. Waner, PIT	18
W. English, CHI	17
K. Cuyler, CHI	17

Innings
R. Kremer, PIT	276
L. French, PIT	275
P. Malone, CHI	272

Games Pitched
H. Elliott, PHI	48
P. Collins, PHI	47
G. Bush, CHI	46

	W	L	PCT	GB	R	OR	2B	3B	Batting HR	BA	SA	SB	E	Fielding DP	FA	CG	BB	Pitching SO	ShO	SV	ERA
STL	92	62	.597		1004	784	373	89	104	.314	.471	72	183	176	.970	63	477	641	5	21	4.40
CHI	90	64	.584	2	998	870	305	72	171	.309	.481	70	170	167	.973	67	528	601	6	12	4.80
NY	87	67	.565	5	959	814	264	83	143	.319	.473	59	164	164	.974	64	439	522	6	19	4.59
BKN	86	68	.558	6	871	738	303	73	122	.304	.454	53	174	167	.972	74	394	526	13	15	4.03
PIT	80	74	.519	12	891	928	285	119	86	.303	.449	76	216	164	.965	80	438	393	7	13	5.24
BOS	70	84	.455	22	693	835	246	78	66	.281	.393	69	178	167	.971	71	475	424	6	11	4.91
CIN	59	95	.383	33	665	857	265	67	74	.281	.400	48	161	164	.973	61	394	361	6	11	5.08
PHI	52	102	.338	40	944	1199	345	44	126	.315	.458	34	239	169	.962	54	543	384	3	7	6.71
					7025	7025	2386	625	892	.303	.448	481	1485	1338	.970	534	3688	3852	52	109	4.97

American League 1930

	POS	Player	AB	BA	HR	RBI	PO	A	E	DP	TC/G	FA	Pitcher	G	IP	W	L	SV	ERA
Phi. W-102 L-52 Connie Mack	1B	J. Foxx	562	.335	37	156	1362	79	14	101	9.5	.990	G. Earnshaw	49	296	22	13	2	4.44
	2B	M. Bishop	441	.252	10	38	267	418	17	61	5.5	.976	L. Grove	50	291	28	5	9	2.54
	SS	J. Boley	420	.276	4	55	221	296	16	62	4.4	.970	R. Walberg	38	205	13	12	1	4.69
	3B	J. Dykes	435	.301	6	73	124	191	13	18	2.7	.960	B. Shores	31	159	12	4	0	4.19
	RF	B. Miller	585	.303	9	100	309	10	8	3	2.1	.976	R. Mahaffey	33	153	9	5	0	5.01
	CF	M. Haas	532	.299	2	68	360	11	9	5	2.9	.976	E. Rommel	35	130	9	4	3	4.28
	LF	A. Simmons	554	.381	36	165	275	10	3	1	2.1	.990	J. Quinn	35	90	9	7	6	4.42
	C	M. Cochrane	487	.357	10	85	654	69	5	11	5.6	.993							
	S3	E. McNair	237	.266	0	34	93	104	17	12		.921							
	2S	D. Williams	191	.262	3	22	108	149	12	23		.955							
Was. W-94 L-60 Walter Johnson	1B	J. Judge	442	.326	10	80	1050	67	2	95	9.6	.998	B. Hadley	42	260	15	11	2	3.73
	2B	B. Myer	541	.303	2	61	330	405	27	89	5.7	.965	G. Crowder	27	202	15	9	1	3.60
	SS	J. Cronin	587	.346	13	126	336	509	35	95	5.7	.960	L. Brown	38	197	16	12	0	4.25
	3B	O. Bluege	476	.290	3	69	138	258	15	20	3.1	.964	F. Marberry	33	185	15	5	1	4.09
	RF	S. Rice	593	.349	1	73	297	13	12	4	2.2	.963	S. Jones	25	183	15	7	0	4.07
	CF	S. West	411	.328	6	67	310	8	9	1	2.8	.972	A. Liska	32	151	9	7	1	3.29
	LF	H. Manush	356	.362	7	65	159	5	2	0	1.9	.988	B. Burke	24	74	3	4	3	3.63
	C	R. Spencer	321	.255	0	36	395	44	5	3	4.8	.989	G. Braxton	15	27	3	2	5	3.29
	OF	D. Harris	205	.317	4	44	106	8	2	3	2.0	.983							
	C	M. Ruel	198	.253	0	26	243	32	4	5	4.7	.986							
	OF	G. Goslin	188	.271	7	38	72	2	5	1	1.7	.937							
	UT	J. Hayes	166	.283	1	20	149	110	5	33		.981							
N. Y. W-86 L-68 Bob Shawkey	1B	L. Gehrig	581	.379	41	174	1298	89	15	109	9.2	.989	G. Pipgras	44	221	15	15	4	4.11
	2B	T. Lazzeri	571	.303	9	121	184	245	13	39	5.7	.971	R. Ruffing	34	198	15	5	1	4.14
	SS	L. Lary	464	.289	3	52	224	324	35	58	5.2	.940	R. Sherid	37	184	12	13	4	5.23
	3B	B. Chapman	513	.316	10	81	100	149	24	11	3.0	.912	H. Johnson	44	175	14	11	2	4.67
	RF	B. Ruth	518	.359	49	153	266	10	10	0	2.2	.965	H. Pennock	25	156	11	7	0	4.32
	CF	H. Rice	346	.298	7	74	244	7	8	2	3.0	.969	E. Wells	27	151	12	3	0	5.20
	LF	E. Combs	532	.344	7	82	275	5	9	1	2.1	.969							
	C	B. Dickey	366	.339	5	65	418	51	11	5	4.8	.977							
	OF	S. Byrd	218	.284	6	31	119	2	1	0	1.4	.992							
	OF	D. Cooke	216	.255	6	29	133	2	3	1	1.9	.978							
	2B	J. Reese	188	.346	3	18	86	99	5	26	4.0	.969							
	P	R. Ruffing	99	.374	4	21	3	27	2	0	.9	.938							
Cle. W-81 L-73 Roger Peckinpaugh	1B	E. Morgan	584	.349	26	136	1275	80	18	116	9.2	.987	W. Ferrell	43	297	25	13	3	3.31
	2B	J. Hodapp	635	.354	9	121	403	557	30	103	6.4	.970	W. Hudlin	37	217	13	16	1	4.57
	SS	J. Goldman	306	.242	1	44	203	246	26	54	5.1	.945	C. Brown	35	214	11	12	1	4.97
	3B	J. Sewell	353	.289	0	48	83	184	14	16	2.9	.950	M. Harder	36	175	11	10	2	4.21
	RF	D. Porter	480	.350	4	57	189	12	8	4	1.8	.962	P. Appleton	39	119	8	7	1	4.02
	CF	E. Averill	534	.339	19	119	345	11	19	5	2.8	.949							
	LF	C. Jamieson	366	.301	1	52	162	7	8	0	1.9	.955							
	C	L. Sewell	292	.257	1	43	283	49	9	5	4.5	.974							
	OF	B. Seeds	277	.285	3	32	156	6	8	0	2.4	.953							
	C	G. Myatt	265	.294	2	37	214	43	6	8	3.7	.977							
	OF	B. Falk	191	.325	4	36	84	4	3	3	2.2	.967							
	SS	E. Montague	179	.263	1	16	84	104	17	19	4.5	.917							
	3S	J. Burnett	170	.312	0	20	44	105	11	14		.931							
Det. W-75 L-79 Bucky Harris	1B	D. Alexander	602	.326	20	135	1338	71	22	132	9.3	.985	G. Uhle	33	239	12	12	3	3.65
	2B	C. Gehringer	610	.330	16	98	399	501	19	97	6.0	.979	V. Sorrell	35	233	16	11	1	3.86
	SS	M. Koenig	267	.240	1	16	115	181	25	40	4.6	.922	E. Whitehill	34	221	17	13	1	4.24
	3B	M. McManus	484	.320	9	89	152	241	14	23	3.1	.966	C. Hogsett	33	146	9	8	1	5.42
	RF	R. Johnson	462	.275	2	35	218	15	16	4	2.1	.936	W. Hoyt	26	136	9	8	4	4.78
	CF	L. Funk	527	.275	4	65	354	8	13	4	2.9	.965	C. Sullivan	40	94	1	5	6	6.53
	LF	J. Stone	422	.313	3	56	222	5	8	1	2.2	.966	W. Wyatt	21	86	4	5	2	3.57
	C	R. Hayworth	227	.278	0	22	277	27	7	4	4.1	.977							
	S3	B. Akers	233	.279	9	40	119	184	20	43		.938							
	OF	H. Rice	128	.305	2	24	66	2	4	0	2.1	.944							
	P	G. Uhle	117	.308	2	21	10	29	1	2	1.2	.975							

	POS	Player	AB	BA	HR	RBI	PO	A	E	DP	TC/G	FA	Pitcher	G	IP	W	L	SV	ERA
St. L.	1B	L. Blue	425	.235	4	42	1110	68	16	91	10.8	.987	L. Stewart	35	271	20	12	0	3.45
W-64 L-90	2B	O. Melillo	574	.256	5	59	384	572	21	107	6.6	.979	D. Coffman	38	196	8	18	1	5.14
Bill Killefer	SS	R. Kress	614	.313	16	112	271	349	41	83	5.4	.938	G. Blaeholder	37	191	11	13	4	4.61
	3B	F. O'Rourke	400	.268	1	41	116	150	14	16	3.3	.950	R. Collins	35	172	9	7	2	4.35
	RF	T. Gullic	308	.250	4	44	136	12	5	3	1.9	.967	S. Gray	27	168	4	15	0	6.28
	CF	F. Schulte	392	.278	5	62	250	5	9	2	2.7	.966	C. Kimsey	42	113	6	10	1	6.35
	LF	G. Goslin	396	.326	30	100	237	13	7	0	2.5	.973	R. Stiles	20	102	3	6	0	5.89
	C	R. Ferrell	314	.268	1	41	336	66	7	5	4.0	.983	G. Crowder	13	77	3	7	1	4.66
	O1	E. McNeely	235	.272	0	20	302	18	8	30		.976							
	OF	R. Badgro	234	.239	1	27	112	8	6	3	2.1	.952							
	OF	A. Metzler	209	.258	1	23	114	2	6	0	2.2	.951							
	OF	H. Manush	198	.328	2	29	96	5	1	0	2.1	.990							
	3B	S. Hale	190	.274	2	25	46	80	7	5	2.8	.947							
Chi.	1B	B. Clancy	234	.244	3	27	583	24	3	38	9.7	.995	T. Lyons	42	298	22	15	1	3.78
W-62 L-92	2B	B. Cissell	561	.271	2	48	251	336	32	60	5.8	.948	P. Caraway	38	193	10	10	1	3.86
Donie Bush	SS	G. Mulleavy	289	.263	0	28	137	219	32	41	5.3	.918	T. Thomas	34	169	5	13	0	5.22
	3B	W. Kamm	331	.269	3	47	142	209	23	17	3.6	.939	R. Faber	29	169	8	13	1	4.21
	RF	S. Jolley	616	.313	16	114	249	17	14	4	1.9	.950	D. Henry	35	155	2	17	0	4.88
	CF	R. Barnes	266	.248	1	31	179	6	12	3	2.7	.939	E. Walsh	37	104	1	4	0	5.38
	LF	C. Reynolds	563	.359	22	100	336	11	9	1	2.7	.975	G. Braxton	19	91	4	10	1	6.45
	C	B. Tate	230	.317	0	27	219	40	5	5	3.8	.981	H. McKain	32	89	6	4	5	5.56
	1O	C. Watwood	427	.302	2	51	707	46	11	59		.986							
	2B	J. Kerr	266	.289	3	27	130	166	6	33	5.9	.980							
	OF	B. Fothergill	131	.305	0	24	49	2	7	0	1.9	.879							
Bos.	1B	P. Todt	383	.269	11	62	1001	65	8	84	10.3	.993	M. Gaston	38	273	13	20	2	3.92
W-52 L-102	2B	B. Regan	507	.266	3	53	308	439	29	92	6.1	.963	MacFayden	36	269	11	14	2	4.21
Heinie Wagner	SS	H. Rhyne	296	.203	0	23	188	284	28	63	4.7	.944	H. Lisenbee	37	237	10	17	0	4.40
	3B	O. Miller	370	.286	0	40	78	160	13	13	3.0	.948	J. Russell	35	230	9	20	0	5.45
	RF	E. Webb	449	.323	16	66	200	8	9	4	1.9	.959	E. Durham	33	140	4	15	1	4.69
	CF	T. Oliver	646	.293	0	46	477	9	9	3	3.2	.982	E. Morris	18	65	4	9	0	4.13
	LF	R. Scarritt	447	.289	2	48	256	5	9	0	2.5	.967							
	C	C. Berry	256	.289	6	35	279	56	4	4	4.0	.988							
	OF	C. Durst	302	.245	1	24	145	4	5	1	2.1	.968							
	3B	B. Reeves	272	.217	2	18	63	125	22	21	3.4	.895							
	1B	B. Sweeney	243	.309	4	30	541	30	2	49	10.2	.997							
	C	J. Heving	220	.277	0	17	195	37	3	7	3.3	.987							
	SS	R. Warstler	162	.185	1	13	100	149	14	30	4.9	.947							

BATTING AND BASE RUNNING LEADERS

Batting Average

A. Simmons, PHI	.381
L. Gehrig, NY	.379
B. Ruth, NY	.359
C. Reynolds, CHI	.359
M. Cochrane, PHI	.357

Slugging Average

B. Ruth, NY	.732
L. Gehrig, NY	.721
A. Simmons, PHI	.708
J. Foxx, PHI	.637
G. Goslin, STL, WAS	.601
E. Morgan, CLE	.601

Home Runs

B. Ruth, NY	49
L. Gehrig, NY	41
J. Foxx, PHI	37
G. Goslin, STL, WAS	37
A. Simmons, PHI	36

Total Bases

L. Gehrig, NY	419
A. Simmons, PHI	392
B. Ruth, NY	379
J. Foxx, PHI	358
G. Goslin, STL, WAS	351
E. Morgan, CLE	351

Runs Batted In

L. Gehrig, NY	174
A. Simmons, PHI	165
J. Foxx, PHI	156
B. Ruth, NY	153
G. Goslin, STL, WAS	138

Stolen Bases

M. McManus, DET	23
C. Gehringer, DET	19
R. Johnson, DET	17
G. Goslin, STL, WAS	17
J. Cronin, WAS	17

Hits

J. Hodapp, CLE	225
L. Gehrig, NY	220
A. Simmons, PHI	211

Base on Balls

B. Ruth, NY	136
M. Bishop, PHI	128
L. Gehrig, NY	101

Home Run Percentage

B. Ruth, NY	9.5
L. Gehrig, NY	7.1
J. Foxx, PHI	6.6

Runs Scored

A. Simmons, PHI	152
B. Ruth, NY	150
C. Gehringer, DET	144

Doubles

J. Hodapp, CLE	51
H. Manush, STL, WAS	49
E. Morgan, CLE	47
C. Gehringer, DET	47

Triples

E. Combs, NY	22
C. Reynolds, CHI	18
L. Gehrig, NY	17

PITCHING LEADERS

Winning Percentage

L. Grove, PHI	.848
F. Marberry, WAS	.750
S. Jones, WAS	.682
W. Ferrell, CLE	.658
R. Ruffing, BOS, NY	.652

Earned Run Average

L. Grove, PHI	2.54
W. Ferrell, CLE	3.31
L. Stewart, STL	3.45
G. Uhle, DET	3.65
B. Hadley, WAS	3.73

Wins

L. Grove, PHI	28
W. Ferrell, CLE	25
G. Earnshaw, PHI	22
T. Lyons, CHI	22
L. Stewart, STL	20

Saves

L. Grove, PHI	9
J. Quinn, PHI	6
G. Braxton, CHI, WAS	6
C. Sullivan, DET	5
H. McKain, CHI	5

Strikeouts

L. Grove, PHI	209
G. Earnshaw, PHI	193
B. Hadley, WAS	162
W. Ferrell, CLE	143
R. Ruffing, BOS, NY	131

Complete Games

T. Lyons, CHI	29
G. Crowder, STL, WAS	25
W. Ferrell, CLE	25
L. Stewart, STL	23
L. Grove, PHI	22

Fewest Hits per 9 Innings

B. Hadley, WAS	8.37
L. Grove, PHI	8.44
G. Crowder, STL, WAS	8.88

Shutouts

G. Pipgras, NY	3
G. Earnshaw, PHI	3

Fewest Walks per 9 Innings

H. Pennock, NY	1.15
T. Lyons, CHI	1.72
L. Grove, PHI	1.86

Most Strikeouts per 9 Inn.

L. Grove, PHI	6.46
G. Earnshaw, PHI	5.87
B. Hadley, WAS	5.60

Innings

T. Lyons, CHI	298
W. Ferrell, CLE	297
G. Earnshaw, PHI	296

Games Pitched

L. Grove, PHI	50
G. Earnshaw, PHI	49
G. Pipgras, NY	44
H. Johnson, NY	44

	W	L	PCT	GB	R	OR	2B	Batting 3B	HR	BA	SA	SB	Fielding E	DP	FA	CG	BB	Pitching SO	ShO	SV	ERA
PHI	102	52	.662		951	751	319	74	125	.294	.452	48	**145**	121	**.975**	72	488	**672**	**8**	**21**	4.28
WAS	94	60	.610	8	892	**689**	300	98	57	.302	.426	**101**	159	150	.974	**78**	504	524	4	14	**3.96**
NY	86	68	.558	16	**1062**	898	298	**110**	**152**	**.309**	**.488**	91	207	132	.965	65	524	572	6	15	4.88
CLE	81	73	.526	21	890	915	**358**	59	72	.304	.431	51	237	156	.962	69	528	441	4	14	4.88
DET	75	79	.487	27	783	833	298	90	82	.284	.421	98	192	156	.967	68	570	574	3	17	4.70
STL	64	90	.416	38	751	886	289	67	75	.268	.391	93	188	152	.970	68	449	470	5	10	5.07
CHI	62	92	.403	40	729	884	255	90	63	.276	.391	74	235	136	.962	67	**407**	471	2	10	4.71
BOS	52	102	.338	50	612	814	257	68	47	.264	.365	42	196	**161**	.968	**78**	488	356	4	5	4.70
					6670	6670	2374	656	673	.288	.421	598	1559	1164	.968	565	3958	4080	36	106	4.65

National League 1931

	POS	Player	AB	BA	HR	RBI	PO	A	E	DP	TC/G	FA	Pitcher	G	IP	W	L	SV	ERA
St. L. W-101 L-53 Gabby Street	1B	J. Bottomley	382	.348	9	75	897	43	12	95	10.2	.987	B. Hallahan	37	249	**19**	9	4	3.29
	2B	F. Frisch	518	.311	4	82	290	424	19	93	5.7	.974	B. Grimes	29	212	17	9	0	3.65
	SS	C. Gelbert	447	.289	1	62	281	435	31	91	5.7	.959	P. Derringer	35	212	18	8	2	3.36
	3B	S. Adams	608	.293	1	40	118	223	13	**29**	2.6	**.963**	F. Rhem	33	207	11	10	1	3.56
	RF	G. Watkins	503	.288	13	51	263	12	12	4	2.2	.958	S. Johnson	32	186	11	9	2	3.00
	CF	P. Martin	413	.300	7	75	282	10	10	2	2.7	.967	J. Haines	19	122	12	3	0	3.02
	LF	C. Hafey	450	**.349**	16	95	226	4	4	1	2.0	.983	J. Lindsey	35	75	6	4	7	2.77
	C	J. Wilson	383	.274	0	51	**498**	75	9	15	**5.3**	.985							
	1B	R. Collins	279	.301	4	59	563	42	3	54	8.9	.995							
	C	G. Mancuso	187	.262	1	23	239	40	8	6	5.1	.972							
	OF	E. Orsatti	158	.291	0	19	83	0	1	0	1.9	.988							
	OF	T. Douthit	133	.331	1	21	105	0	3	0	3.0	.972							
N. Y. W-87 L-65 John McGraw	1B	B. Terry	611	.349	9	112	1411	**105**	6	108	10.0	.990	Fitzsimmons	35	254	18	11	0	3.05
	2B	B. Hunnefield	196	.270	1	17	112	140	13	27	4.7	.951	C. Hubbell	36	247	14	12	3	2.66
	SS	T. Jackson	555	.310	5	71	303	**496**	25	79	5.7	**.970**	B. Walker	37	239	17	9	3	**2.26**
	3B	J. Vergez	565	.278	13	81	146	268	30	23	2.9	.932	C. Mitchell	27	190	13	11	0	4.07
	RF	F. Lindstrom	303	.300	5	36	150	4	4	1	2.2	.975	J. Berly	27	111	7	8	0	3.88
	CF	M. Ott	497	.292	29	115	332	20	7	4	2.6	.981	J. Heving	22	42	1	6	3	4.89
	LF	F. Leach	515	.309	6	36	239	6	6	1	2.0	.976							
	C	S. Hogan	396	.301	12	65	469	54	2	10	4.6	**.996**							
	OF	C. Fullis	302	.328	3	28	154	5	2	4	2.4	.988							
	OF	E. Allen	298	.329	5	43	151	2	4	1	2.0	.975							
	2B	H. Critz	238	.290	4	17	139	164	5	27	5.7	.984							
	2B	D. Marshall	194	.201	0	10	102	135	11	26	5.3	.956							
	C	B. O'Farrell	174	.224	1	19	223	27	5	1	3.2	.980							
Chi. W-84 L-70 Rogers Hornsby	1B	C. Grimm	531	.331	4	66	1357	79	10	107	10.0	**.993**	C. Root	39	251	17	14	2	3.48
	2B	R. Hornsby	357	.331	16	90	107	205	16	24	4.8	.951	B. Smith	36	240	15	12	2	3.22
	SS	W. English	634	.319	2	53	**322**	441	28	75	5.7	.965	P. Malone	36	228	16	9	0	3.90
	3B	L. Bell	252	.282	4	32	66	118	11	18	2.8	.944	G. Bush	39	180	16	8	2	4.49
	RF	K. Cuyler	613	.330	9	88	347	11	11	4	2.4	.970	L. Sweetland	26	130	8	7	0	5.04
	CF	H. Wilson	395	.261	13	61	210	9	5	1	2.2	.978	J. May	31	79	5	5	2	3.87
	LF	R. Stephenson	263	.319	1	52	134	1	2	1	1.7	.965							
	C	G. Hartnett	380	.282	8	70	444	68	10	**16**	5.0	.981							
	32	B. Jurges	293	.201	0	23	108	198	11	32		.965							
	OF	D. Taylor	270	.300	5	41	170	3	2	0	2.6	.989							
	21	F. Blair	240	.258	2	29	245	120	12	28		.968							
	OF	V. Barton	239	.238	13	50	133	2	5	0	2.3	.964							
	C	R. Hemsley	204	.309	3	31	236	40	7	5	4.3	.975							
Bkn. W-79 L-73 Wilbert Robinson	1B	D. Bissonette	587	.290	12	87	**1460**	66	16	136	10.1	.990	W. Clark	34	233	14	10	1	3.20
	2B	M. Finn	413	.274	0	45	260	331	15	65	5.4	.975	D. Vance	30	219	11	13	0	3.38
	SS	G. Slade	272	.239	1	29	173	274	25	54	5.8	.947	R. Phelps	28	149	7	9	0	5.00
	3B	W. Gilbert	552	.266	0	46	125	**295**	23	14	3.1	.948	S. Thurston	24	143	9	9	0	3.97
	RF	B. Herman	610	.313	18	97	287	24	13	7	2.2	.960	F. Heimach	31	135	9	7	1	3.46
	CF	J. Frederick	611	.270	17	71	398	10	**15**	2	2.9	.965	J. Shaute	35	129	11	8	0	4.83
	LF	L. O'Doul	512	.336	7	75	285	4	14	0	2.3	.954	D. Luque	19	103	7	6	0	4.56
	C	A. Lopez	360	.269	0	40	390	69	11	6	4.5	.977	J. Quinn	39	64	5	4	**15**	2.66
	SS	G. Wright	268	.284	9	32	151	255	25	52	5.7	.942							
	C	E. Lombardi	182	.297	4	23	218	23	4	5	4.9	.984							
	2B	F. Thompson	181	.265	1	21	89	120	12	36	5.1	.946							
	OF	R. Bressler	153	.281	0	26	54	1	1	0	1.6	.982							

	POS Player	AB	BA	HR	RBI	PO	A	E	DP	TC/G	FA	Pitcher	G	IP	W	L	SV	ERA
Pit. W-75 L-79 Jewel Ens	1B G. Suhr	270	.211	4	32	684	39	5	72	9.6	.993	H. Meine	36	284	19	13	0	2.98
	2B G. Grantham	465	.305	10	46	114	142	23	34	5.5	.918	L. French	39	276	15	13	1	3.26
	SS T. Thevenow	404	.213	0	38	245	432	25	92	5.9	.964	R. Kremer	30	230	11	15	0	3.33
	3B P. Traynor	615	.298	2	103	172	284	37	21	3.2	.925	G. Spencer	38	187	11	12	3	3.42
	RF P. Waner	559	.322	6	70	342	28	9	8	2.7	.976	E. Brame	26	180	9	13	0	4.21
	CF L. Waner	681	.314	4	57	484	20	11	5	3.4	.979							
	LF A. Comorosky	350	.243	1	48	214	4	5	2	2.5	.978							
	C E. Phillips	353	.232	7	44	293	49	5	12	3.4	.986							
	OF W. Jensen	267	.243	3	17	182	2	5	1	2.8	.974							
	2B T. Piet	167	.299	0	24	103	133	3	17	5.4	.987							
	2B H. Grosskloss	161	.280	0	20	92	115	4	35	5.4	.981							
	C E. Grace	150	.280	1	20	128	23	4	5	3.4	.974							
Phi. W-66 L-88 Burt Shotton	1B D. Hurst	489	.305	11	91	1206	104	18	117	9.8	.986	J. Elliott	52	249	19	14	5	4.27
	2B L. Mallon	375	.309	1	45	231	290	24	57	5.6	.956	R. Benge	38	247	14	18	2	3.17
	SS D. Bartell	554	.289	0	34	315	432	41	96	5.9	.948	P. Collins	42	240	12	16	4	3.86
	3B P. Whitney	501	.287	9	74	131	217	19	1	2.9	.948	C. Dudley	30	179	8	14	0	3.52
	RF B. Arlett	418	.313	18	72	196	14	10	6	2.3	.955	F. Watt	38	123	5	5	2	4.84
	CF F. Brickell	514	.253	1	31	341	8	8	2	2.9	.978	S. Bolen	28	99	3	12	0	6.39
	LF C. Klein	594	.337	31	121	292	13	9	0	2.1	.971	S. Blake	14	71	4	5	1	5.58
	C S. Davis	393	.326	4	51	420	78	3	10	4.4	.994							
	23 B. Friberg	353	.261	1	26	180	252	20	43		.956							
	C H. McCurdy	150	.287	1	25	157	27	6	1	4.2	.968							
Bos. W-64 L-90 Bill McKechnie	1B E. Sheely	538	.273	1	77	1374	70	12	108	10.2	.992	E. Brandt	33	250	18	11	2	2.92
	2B F. Maguire	492	.228	0	26	372	478	21	94	5.9	.976	T. Zachary	33	229	11	15	2	3.10
	SS R. Maranville	562	.260	0	33	271	432	38	93	5.4	.949	S. Seibold	33	206	10	18	0	4.67
	3B B. Urbanski	303	.238	0	17	76	145	9	15	3.4	.961	B. Cantwell	33	156	7	9	2	3.63
	RF Schulmerich	327	.309	2	43	190	6	7	0	2.3	.966	B. Sherdel	27	138	6	10	0	4.25
	CF W. Berger	617	.323	19	84	457	16	11	5	3.1	.977	B. Cunningham	33	137	3	12	1	4.48
	LF Worthington	491	.291	4	44	242	8	3	1	2.0	.988	F. Frankhouse	26	127	8	8	1	4.03
	C A. Spohrer	350	.240	0	27	392	54	8	5	4.1	.982							
	OF L. Richbourg	286	.287	2	29	154	3	3	2	2.3	.981							
	O3 R. Moore	192	.260	3	34	71	39	6	3		.948							
	3B B. Dreesen	180	.222	1	10	28	83	11	1	2.6	.910							
Cin. W-58 L-96 Dan Howley	1B H. Hendrick	530	.315	1	75	1348	67	18*	147*	10.5*	.987	S. Johnson	42	262	11	19	0	3.77
	2B T. Cuccinello	575	.315	2	93	376	499	28	128	5.9	.969	R. Lucas	29	238	14	13	0	3.59
	SS L. Durocher	361	.227	1	29	212	344	20	86	4.8	.965	L. Benton	38	204	10	15	2	3.35
	3B J. Stripp	426	.324	3	42	101	191	13	22	3.2	.957	B. Frey	34	134	8	12	2	4.92
	RF E. Crabtree	443	.269	4	37	240	19	7	6	2.6	.974	E. Rixey	22	127	4	7	0	3.91
	CF T. Douthit	374	.262	0	24	286	6	5	3	3.1	.983	R. Kolp	30	107	4	9	1	4.96
	LF E. Roush	376	.271	1	41	197	5	4	1	2.3	.981	O. Carroll	29	107	3	9	0	5.53
	C C. Sukeforth	351	.256	0	25	300	59	13	9	3.5	.965	J. Ogden	22	89	4	8	1	2.93
	OF N. Cullop	334	.263	8	48	177	5	6	3	2.3	.968							
	OF C. Heathcote	252	.258	0	28	164	13	2	4	3.0	.989							
	OF W. Roettger	185	.351	1	20	95	3	1	1	2.3	.990							
	SS H. Ford	175	.229	0	13	107	162	13	41	3.9	.954							
	C A. Asbjornson	118	.305	0	22	82	24	2	2	3.5	.981							

BATTING AND BASE RUNNING LEADERS

Batting Average
C. Hafey, STL	.349
B. Terry, NY	.349
J. Bottomley, STL	.348
C. Klein, PHI	.337
L. O'Doul, BKN	.336

Slugging Average
C. Klein, PHI	.584
R. Hornsby, CHI	.574
C. Hafey, STL	.569
M. Ott, NY	.545
B. Arlett, PHI	.538

Home Runs
C. Klein, PHI	31
M. Ott, NY	29
W. Berger, BOS	19
B. Arlett, PHI	18
B. Herman, BKN	18

Total Bases
C. Klein, PHI	347
B. Terry, NY	323
B. Herman, BKN	320
W. Berger, BOS	316
K. Cuyler, CHI	290

Runs Batted In
C. Klein, PHI	121
M. Ott, NY	115
B. Terry, NY	112
P. Traynor, PIT	103
B. Herman, BKN	97

Stolen Bases
F. Frisch, STL	28
B. Herman, BKN	17
P. Martin, STL	16
S. Adams, STL	16
G. Watkins, STL	15

Hits
L. Waner, PIT	214
B. Terry, NY	213
K. Cuyler, CHI	202
W. English, CHI	202

Base on Balls
M. Ott, NY	80
P. Waner, PIT	73
K. Cuyler, CHI	72

PITCHING LEADERS

Winning Percentage
P. Derringer, STL	.692
B. Hallahan, STL	.679
G. Bush, CHI	.667
B. Grimes, STL	.654
B. Walker, NY	.654

Earned Run Average
B. Walker, NY	2.26
C. Hubbell, NY	2.66
E. Brandt, BOS	2.92
H. Meine, PIT	2.98
S. Johnson, STL	3.00

Wins
B. Hallahan, STL	19
H. Meine, PIT	19
J. Elliott, PHI	19
P. Derringer, STL	18
E. Brandt, BOS	18
Fitzsimmons, NY	18

Saves
J. Quinn, BKN	15
J. Lindsey, STL	7
J. Elliott, PHI	5
B. Hallahan, STL	4
P. Collins, PHI	4

Strikeouts
B. Hallahan, STL	159
C. Hubbell, NY	156
D. Vance, BKN	150
P. Derringer, STL	134
C. Root, CHI	131

Complete Games
R. Lucas, CIN	24
E. Brandt, BOS	23
H. Meine, PIT	22
C. Hubbell, NY	21
L. French, PIT	20

Fewest Hits per 9 Innings
C. Hubbell, NY	7.76
B. Walker, NY	7.97
E. Brandt, BOS	8.21

Shutouts
B. Walker, NY	6
P. Derringer, STL	4
C. Hubbell, NY	4
Fitzsimmons, NY	4

BATTING AND BASE RUNNING LEADERS

Home Run Percentage		Runs Scored		Fewest Walks per 9 Innings		Most Strikeouts per 9 Inn.	
M. Ott, NY	5.8	C. Klein, PHI	121	S. Johnson, STL	1.40	D. Vance, BKN	6.17
C. Klein, PHI	5.2	B. Terry, NY	121	R. Lucas, CIN	1.47	B. Hallahan, STL	5.75
R. Hornsby, CHI	4.5	W. English, CHI	117	W. Clark, BKN	2.01	P. Derringer, STL	5.70

PITCHING LEADERS

Doubles		Triples		Innings		Games Pitched	
S. Adams, STL	46	B. Terry, NY	20	H. Meine, PIT	284	J. Elliott, PHI	52
W. Berger, BOS	44	B. Herman, BKN	16	L. French, PIT	276	S. Johnson, CIN	42
		P. Traynor, PIT	15	S. Johnson, CIN	262	P. Collins, PHI	42

	W	L	PCT	GB	R	OR	2B	3B	HR	BA	SA	SB	E	DP	FA	CG	BB	SO	ShO	SV	ERA
							Batting						**Fielding**				**Pitching**				
STL	101	53	.656		815	614	353	74	60	.286	.411	114	160	169	.974	80	449	626	17	20	3.45
NY	87	65	.572	13	768	599	251	64	101	.289	.416	83	159	126	.974	90	421	571	17	12	3.30
CHI	84	70	.545	17	828	710	340	67	83	.289	.422	49	169	141	.973	80	524	541	8	8	3.97
BKN	79	73	.520	21	681	673	240	77	71	.276	.390	45	187	154	.969	64	351	546	9	18	3.84
PIT	75	79	.487	26	636	691	243	70	41	.266	.360	59	194	167	.968	89	442	345	9	5	3.66
PHI	66	88	.429	35	684	828	299	52	81	.279	.400	42	210	149	.966	60	511	499	4	16	4.58
BOS	64	90	.416	37	533	680	221	59	34	.258	.341	46	170	141	.973	78	406	419	12	9	3.90
CIN	58	96	.377	43	592	742	241	70	21	.269	.352	24	165	194	.973	70	399	317	4	6	4.22
					5537	5537	2188	533	492	.277	.387	462	1414	1241	.971	611	3503	3864	80	94	3.86

American League 1931

	POS	Player	AB	BA	HR	RBI	PO	A	E	DP	TC/G	FA	Pitcher	G	IP	W	L	SV	ERA
Phi. W-107 L-45 Connie Mack	1B	J. Foxx	515	.291	30	120	964	49	7	89	9.1	.993	R. Walberg	44	291	20	12	3	3.74
	2B	M. Bishop	497	.294	5	37	314	414	12	84	5.7	.984	L. Grove	41	289	31	4	5	2.06
	SS	D. Williams	294	.269	6	40	152	214	27	59	5.5	.931	G. Earnshaw	43	282	21	7	6	3.67
	3B	J. Dykes	355	.273	3	46	105	153	7	19	3.0	.974	R. Mahaffey	30	162	15	4	2	4.21
	RF	B. Miller	534	.281	8	77	305	7	4	1	2.3	.987	E. Rommel	25	118	7	5	0	2.97
	CF	M. Haas	440	.323	8	56	272	6	3	4	2.8	.989	W. Hoyt	16	111	10	5	0	4.22
	LF	A. Simmons	513	.390	22	128	287	10	4	0	2.4	.987							
	C	M. Cochrane	459	.349	17	89	560	63	9	9	5.4	.986							
	UT	E. McNair	280	.271	5	33	97	155	19	36		.930							
	SS	J. Boley	224	.228	0	20	102	149	12	31	4.2	.954							
	OF	D. Cramer	223	.260	2	20	133	5	3	1	2.6	.979							
	1B	P. Todt	197	.244	5	44	403	13	2	36	8.0	.995							
	OF	J. Moore	143	.224	2	21	70	3	2	2	2.1	.973							
N. Y. W-94 L-59 Joe McCarthy	1B	L. Gehrig	619	.341	46	184	1352	58	13	120	9.2	.991	L. Gomez	40	243	21	9	3	2.63
	2B	T. Lazzeri	484	.267	8	83	216	288	22	52	5.8	.958	R. Ruffing	37	237	16	14	2	4.41
	SS	L. Lary	610	.280	10	107	321	484	46	85	5.5	.946	H. Johnson	40	196	13	8	4	4.72
	3B	J. Sewell	484	.302	6	64	131	227	18	14	3.1	.952	H. Pennock	25	189	11	6	0	4.28
	RF	B. Ruth	534	.373	46	163	237	5	7	2	1.8	.972	G. Pipgras	36	138	7	6	3	3.79
	CF	E. Combs	563	.318	5	58	335	5	9	2	2.7	.974	E. Wells	27	117	9	5	2	4.32
	LF	B. Chapman	600	.315	17	122	300	14	12	1	2.4	.963	R. Sherid	17	74	5	5	2	5.69
	C	B. Dickey	477	.327	6	78	670	78	3	6	6.0	.996							
	OF	S. Byrd	248	.270	3	32	148	3	4	1	1.8	.974							
	2B	J. Reese	245	.241	3	26	173	168	10	44	5.8	.972							
Was. W-92 L-62 Walter Johnson	1B	J. Kuhel	524	.269	8	85	1255	57	12	119	9.5	.991	L. Brown	42	259	15	14	0	3.20
	2B	B. Myer	591	.293	4	56	333	398	12	87	5.4	.984	G. Crowder	44	234	18	11	2	3.88
	SS	J. Cronin	611	.306	12	126	323	488	43	94	5.5	.950	F. Marberry	45	219	16	4	7	3.45
	3B	O. Bluege	570	.272	8	98	151	286	18	24	3.0	.960	C. Fischer	46	191	13	9	3	4.38
	RF	S. Rice	413	.310	0	42	221	7	7	2	2.2	.970	B. Hadley	55	180	11	10	8	3.06
	CF	S. West	526	.333	9	91	402	13	4	3	3.3	.990	S. Jones	25	148	9	10	1	4.32
	LF	H. Manush	616	.307	6	70	245	5	6	1	1.8	.977	B. Burke	30	129	8	3	2	4.27
	C	R. Spencer	483	.275	1	60	642	69	11	9	5.0	.985							
	OF	D. Harris	231	.312	5	50	111	4	6	1	2.0	.950							
	OF	H. Rice	162	.265	0	15	89	3	3	0	2.3	.968							
Cle. W-78 L-76 Roger Peckinpaugh	1B	E. Morgan	462	.351	11	86	1114	72	19	102	10.3	.984	W. Ferrell	40	276	22	12	3	3.75
	2B	J. Hodapp	468	.295	2	56	274	413	22	73	5.9	.969	W. Hudlin	44	254	15	14	4	4.60
	SS	J. Cronin	193	.285	1	26	127	202	27	30	5.6	.924	C. Brown	39	233	11	15	0	4.71
	3B	W. Kamm	410	.295	0	66	129*	208	19	29*	3.1*	.947	M. Harder	40	194	13	14	1	4.36
	RF	D. Porter	414	.312	1	38	184	7	6	0	1.8	.970	S. Connally	17	86	5	5	1	4.20
	CF	E. Averill	627	.333	32	143	398	9	10	3	2.7	.976							
	LF	J. Vosmik	591	.320	7	117	315	12	10	2	2.3	.970							
	C	L. Sewell	375	.275	1	53	384	61	9	5	4.3	.980							
	UT	J. Burnett	427	.300	1	52	194	296	34	52		.935							
	C	G. Myatt	195	.246	1	29	176	34	2	2	3.7	.991							
	OF	B. Falk	161	.304	2	28	55	1	3	0	1.8	.949							
	P	W. Ferrell	116	.319	9	30	19	74	3	3	2.4	.969							

	POS	Player	AB	BA	HR	RBI	PO	A	E	DP	TC/G	FA	Pitcher	G	IP	W	L	SV	ERA
St. L. W-63 L-91 Bill Killefer	1B	J. Burns	570	.260	4	70	1346	125	11	131	10.4	.993	L. Stewart	36	258	14	17	0	4.40
	2B	O. Melillo	617	.306	2	75	428	543	32	118	6.6	.968	S. Gray	43	258	11	24	2	5.09
	SS	J. Levey	498	.209	5	38	269	398	58	92	5.2	.920	G. Blaeholder	35	226	11	15	0	4.53
	3B	R. Kress	605	.311	16	114	92	141	16	12	3.0	.936	D. Coffman	32	169	9	13	1	3.88
	RF	T. Jenkins	230	.265	3	25	93	6	5	1	1.8	.952	R. Collins	17	107	5	5	0	3.79
	CF	F. Schulte	553	.304	9	65	361	13	11	4	2.9	.971	W. Hebert	23	103	6	7	0	5.07
	LF	G. Goslin	591	.328	24	105	319	14	14	1	2.3	.960	C. Kimsey	42	94	4	6	7	4.39
	C	R. Ferrell	386	.306	3	57	412	86	14	11	4.7	.973							
	3B	L. Storti	273	.220	3	26	78	134	17	20	3.4	.926							
	OF	Bettencourt	206	.257	3	26	99	6	4	1	1.9	.963							
Bos. W-62 L-90 Shano Collins	1B	B. Sweeney	498	.295	1	58	1283	92	9	89	11.2	.993	J. Russell	36	232	10	18	0	5.16
	2B	R. Warstler	181	.243	0	10	74	135	15	20	5.3	.933	MacFayden	35	231	16	12	0	4.02
	SS	H. Rhyne	565	.273	0	51	295	502	31	74	5.6	.963	W. Moore	53	185	11	13	10	3.88
	3B	O. Miller	389	.272	0	43	75	147	11	12	3.1	.953	E. Durham	38	165	8	10	0	4.25
	RF	E. Webb	589	.333	14	103	270	21	16	5	2.0	.948	H. Lisenbee	41	165	5	12	0	5.19
	CF	T. Oliver	586	.276	0	70	433	15	3	4	3.0	.993	E. Morris	37	131	5	7	0	4.75
	LF	J. Rothrock	475	.278	4	42	153	9	3	1	2.1	.982	M. Gaston	23	119	2	13	0	4.46
	C	C. Berry	357	.283	6	49	312	78	6	8	3.9	.985	B. Kline	28	98	5	5	0	4.41
	3B	U. Pickering	341	.252	9	52	90	143	8	8	3.3	.967							
	OF	A. Van Camp	324	.275	0	33	107	3	3	0	1.9	.973							
Det. W-61 L-93 Bucky Harris	1B	D. Alexander	517	.325	3	87	1197	53	16	91	10.0	.987	E. Whitehill	34	272	13	16	0	4.06
	2B	C. Gehringer	383	.311	4	53	224	236	10	54	6.0	.979	V. Sorrell	35	247	13	14	1	4.12
	SS	B. Rogell	185	.303	2	24	91	182	12	26	5.9	.958	G. Uhle	29	193	11	12	2	3.50
	3B	M. McManus	362	.271	3	53	92	172	14	18	3.5	.950	T. Bridges	35	173	8	16	0	4.99
	RF	R. Johnson	621	.279	8	55	332	25	15	8	2.5	.960	A. Herring	35	165	7	13	1	4.31
	CF	H. Walker	252	.286	0	16	170	4	7	1	2.7	.961	C. Hogsett	22	112	3	9	2	5.93
	LF	J. Stone	584	.327	10	76	319	11	14	6	2.3	.959	W. Hoyt	16	92	3	8	0	5.87
	C	R. Hayworth	273	.256	0	25	334	61	11	5	4.6	.973							
	UT	M. Owen	377	.223	3	39	308	220	24	46		.957							
	2S	M. Koenig	364	.253	1	39	191	236	28	41		.938							
	OF	G. Walker	189	.296	1	28	99	2	5	1	2.4	.953							
	OF	F. Doljack	187	.278	4	20	140	8	12	1	3.0	.925							
Chi. W-56 L-97 Donie Bush	1B	L. Blue	589	.304	1	62	1452	81	16	105	10.0	.990	V. Frazier	46	254	13	15	4	4.46
	2B	J. Kerr	444	.268	2	50	297	366	22	78	5.9	.968	T. Thomas	42	242	10	14	2	4.80
	SS	B. Cissell	409	.220	1	46	168	233	24	47	5.1	.944	P. Caraway	51	220	10	24	2	6.22
	3B	B. Sullivan	363	.275	2	33	96	152	24	9	3.3	.912	R. Faber	44	184	10	14	1	3.82
	RF	C. Reynolds	462	.290	6	77	233	10	13	3	2.3	.949	H. McKain	27	112	6	9	0	5.71
	CF	C. Watwood	367	.283	1	47	259	13	16	2	2.8	.944	T. Lyons	22	101	4	6	0	4.01
	LF	L. Fonseca	465	.299	2	71	183	4	5	1	2.0	.974							
	C	B. Tate	273	.267	0	22	310	69	5	11	4.5	.987							
	OF	B. Fothergill	312	.282	3	56	169	2	5	0	2.4	.972							
	SS	L. Appling	297	.232	1	28	147	232	42	37	5.5	.900							
	C	F. Grube	265	.219	1	24	248	50	7	3	3.8	.977							
	3B	I. Jeffries	223	.224	2	16	69	100	9	4	2.9	.949							
	OF	M. Simons	189	.275	0	12	112	3	6	0	2.1	.950							
	OF	S. Jolley	110	.300	3	28	29	1	5	1	1.5	.857							

BATTING AND BASE RUNNING LEADERS

Batting Average

A. Simmons, PHI	.390
B. Ruth, NY	.373
E. Morgan, CLE	.351
M. Cochrane, PHI	.349
L. Gehrig, NY	.341

Slugging Average

B. Ruth, NY	.700
L. Gehrig, NY	.662
A. Simmons, PHI	.641
E. Averill, CLE	.576
J. Foxx, PHI	.567

Home Runs

B. Ruth, NY	46
L. Gehrig, NY	46
E. Averill, CLE	32
J. Foxx, PHI	30
G. Goslin, STL	24

Total Bases

L. Gehrig, NY	410
B. Ruth, NY	374
E. Averill, CLE	361
A. Simmons, PHI	329
G. Goslin, STL	328

Runs Batted In

L. Gehrig, NY	184
B. Ruth, NY	163
E. Averill, CLE	143
A. Simmons, PHI	128
J. Cronin, WAS	126

Stolen Bases

B. Chapman, NY	61
R. Johnson, DET	33
J. Burns, STL	19
B. Cissell, CHI	18
T. Lazzeri, NY	18

Hits

L. Gehrig, NY	211
E. Averill, CLE	209
A. Simmons, PHI	200

Base on Balls

B. Ruth, NY	128
L. Blue, CHI	127
L. Gehrig, NY	117

PITCHING LEADERS

Winning Percentage

L. Grove, PHI	.886
F. Marberry, WAS	.800
R. Mahaffey, PHI	.789
G. Earnshaw, PHI	.750
L. Gomez, NY	.700

Earned Run Average

L. Grove, PHI	2.06
L. Gomez, NY	2.63
L. Brown, WAS	3.20
F. Marberry, WAS	3.45
G. Uhle, DET	3.50

Wins

L. Grove, PHI	31
W. Ferrell, CLE	22
G. Earnshaw, PHI	21
L. Gomez, NY	21
R. Walberg, PHI	20

Saves

W. Moore, BOS	10
B. Hadley, WAS	8
C. Kimsey, STL	7
F. Marberry, WAS	7
G. Earnshaw, PHI	6

Strikeouts

L. Grove, PHI	175
G. Earnshaw, PHI	152
L. Gomez, NY	150
R. Ruffing, NY	132
B. Hadley, WAS	124

Complete Games

L. Grove, PHI	27
W. Ferrell, CLE	27
G. Earnshaw, PHI	23
E. Whitehill, DET	22
L. Stewart, STL	20

Fewest Hits per 9 Innings

L. Gomez, NY	7.63
L. Grove, PHI	7.76
G. Earnshaw, PHI	8.15

Shutouts

L. Grove, PHI	4
G. Earnshaw, PHI	3

BATTING AND BASE RUNNING LEADERS

Home Run Percentage		Runs Scored	
B. Ruth, NY	8.6	L. Gehrig, NY	163
L. Gehrig, NY	7.4	B. Ruth, NY	149
J. Foxx, PHI	5.8	E. Averill, CLE	140

Doubles		Triples	
E. Webb, BOS	67	R. Johnson, DET	19
D. Alexander, DET	47	L. Blue, CHI	15
R. Kress, STL	46	L. Gehrig, NY	15

PITCHING LEADERS

Fewest Walks per 9 Innings		Most Strikeouts per 9 Inn.	
H. Pennock, NY	1.43	L. Gomez, NY	5.56
S. Gray, STL	1.88	T. Bridges, DET	5.46
L. Grove, PHI	1.93	L. Grove, PHI	5.46

Innings		Games Pitched	
R. Walberg, PHI	291	B. Hadley, WAS	55
L. Grove, PHI	289	W. Moore, BOS	53
G. Earnshaw, PHI	282	P. Caraway, CHI	51

	W	L	PCT	GB	R	OR	2B	3B	HR	BA	SA	SB	E	DP	FA	CG	BB	SO	ShO	SV	ERA
PHI	107	45	.704		858	626	311	64	118	.287	.435	27	141	151	.976	97	457	574	12	16	3.47
NY	94	59	.614	13.5	1067	760	277	78	155	.297	.457	138	169	131	.972	78	543	686	4	17	4.20
WAS	92	62	.597	16	843	691	308	93	49	.285	.400	72	142	148	.976	60	498	582	6	24	3.76
CLE	78	76	.506	30	885	833	321	69	71	.296	.419	63	232	143	.963	76	561	470	6	9	4.63
STL	63	91	.409	45	722	870	287	62	76	.271	.390	73	232	160	.963	65	448	436	4	10	4.76
BOS	62	90	.408	45	625	800	289	34	37	.262	.349	43	188	127	.970	61	473	365	5	10	4.60
DET	61	93	.396	47	651	836	292	69	43	.268	.371	117	220	139	.964	93	597	511	5	6	4.56
CHI	56	97	.366	51.5	704	939	238	69	27	.260	.343	94	245	131	.961	54	588	420	6	10	5.05
					6355	6355	2323	538	576	.278	.396	627	1569	1130	.968	584	4165	4044	48	102	4.38

National League 1932

	POS	Player	AB	BA	HR	RBI	PO	A	E	DP	TC/G	FA	Pitcher	G	IP	W	L	SV	ERA
Chi.	1B	C. Grimm	570	.307	7	80	1429	123	11	127	10.5	.993	L. Warneke	35	277	22	6	0	2.37
W-90 L-64	2B	B. Herman	656	.314	1	51	401	527	38	102	6.3	.961	G. Bush	40	239	19	11	0	3.21
Rogers Hornsby	SS	B. Jurges	396	.253	2	52	223	394	23	69	6.2	.964	P. Malone	37	237	15	17	0	3.38
W-53 L-44	3B	W. English	522	.272	3	47	96	173	12	13	3.0	.957	C. Root	39	216	15	10	3	3.58
Charlie Grimm	RF	K. Cuyler	446	.291	10	77	239	7	8	1	2.3	.969	B. Grimes	30	141	6	11	1	4.78
W-37 L-20	CF	J. Moore	443	.305	13	64	272	12	5	2	2.7	.983	B. Smith	34	119	4	3	2	4.61
	LF	R. Stephenson	583	.324	4	85	298	7	5	2	2.1	.984							
	C	G. Hartnett	406	.271	12	52	484	75	10	8	4.9	.982							
	3B	S. Hack	178	.236	2	19	36	90	12	5	2.7	.913							
	C	R. Hemsley	151	.238	4	20	173	17	5	3	4.1	.974							
	OF	L. Richbourg	148	.257	1	21	70	2	1	1	2.2	.986							
Pit.	1B	G. Suhr	581	.263	5	81	1388	84	18	111	9.7	.988	L. French	47	274	18	16	4	3.02
W-86 L-68	2B	T. Piet	574	.282	7	85	378	454	26	80	5.6	.970	B. Swift	39	214	14	10	4	3.61
George Gibson	SS	A. Vaughan	497	.318	4	61	247	403	46	74	5.4	.934	H. Meine	28	172	12	9	1	3.86
	3B	P. Traynor	513	.329	2	68	173	222	27	14	3.3	.936	B. Harris	34	168	10	9	2	3.64
	RF	P. Waner	630	.341	7	82	367	13	10	3	2.5	.974	S. Swetonic	24	163	11	6	0	2.82
	CF	L. Waner	565	.333	3	38	426	9	6	0	3.4	.986	G. Spencer	39	138	4	8	1	4.97
	LF	A. Comorosky	370	.286	4	46	255	4	5	2	2.9	.981	L. Chagnon	30	128	9	6	0	3.94
	C	E. Grace	390	.274	7	55	364	48	1	10	3.6	.998							
	OF	D. Barbee	327	.257	5	55	190	5	5	2	2.6	.975							
	S3	T. Thevenow	194	.237	0	26	82	126	14	24		.937							
Bkn.	1B	G. Kelly	202	.243	4	22	575	36	10	48	10.0	.984	W. Clark	40	273	20	12	0	3.49
W-81 L-73	2B	T. Cuccinello	597	.281	12	77	385	525	25	113	6.1	.973	V. Mungo	39	223	13	11	2	4.43
Max Carey	SS	G. Wright	446	.274	10	60	231	386	40	83	5.4	.939	D. Vance	27	176	12	11	1	4.20
	3B	J. Stripp	534	.303	6	64	92	201	14	22	3.3	.954	F. Heimach	36	168	9	4	0	3.97
	RF	H. Wilson	481	.297	23	123	220	14	11	4	2.0	.955	S. Thurston	28	153	12	8	0	4.06
	CF	D. Taylor	395	.324	11	48	271	8	3	1	2.9	.989	J. Shaute	34	117	7	7	4	4.62
	LF	L. O'Doul	595	.368	21	90	317	4	7	0	2.2	.979	J. Quinn	42	87	3	7	8	3.30
	C	A. Lopez	404	.275	1	43	456	82	13	10	4.4	.976							
	OF	J. Frederick	384	.299	16	56	201	6	5	2	2.4	.976							
	SS	G. Slade	250	.240	1	23	101	148	15	30	4.8	.943							
	1B	B. Clancy	196	.306	0	16	524	40	2	55	10.7	.996							
	3B	M. Finn	189	.238	0	14	34	92	9	7	2.7	.933							
Phi.	1B	D. Hurst	579	.339	24	143	1341	94	10	105	9.6	.993	E. Holley	34	228	11	14	0	3.95
W-78 L-76	2B	L. Mallon	347	.259	5	31	199	228	20	42	5.1	.955	R. Benge	41	222	13	12	6	4.05
Burt Shotton	SS	D. Bartell	614	.308	1	53	359	529	34	83	6.0	.963	S. Hansen	39	191	10	10	2	3.72
	3B	P. Whitney	624	.298	13	124	177	276	19	31	3.1	.960	P. Collins	43	184	14	12	3	5.27
	RF	C. Klein	650	.348	38	137	331	29	15	3	2.4	.960	F. Rhem	26	169	11	7	1	3.74
	CF	K. Davis	576	.309	5	57	411	15	11	6	3.3	.975	J. Elliott	39	166	11	10	0	5.42
	LF	H. Lee	595	.303	18	85	380	11	14	3	2.7	.965							
	C	S. Davis	402	.336	14	70	408	54	6	15	3.9	.987							
	2B	B. Friberg	154	.240	0	14	107	137	11	22	4.6	.957							

POS	Player	AB	BA	HR	RBI	PO	A	E	DP	TC/G	FA	Pitcher	G	IP	W	L	SV	ERA
Bos. 1B	A. Shires	298	.238	5	30	715	48	9	61	9.4	.988	E. Brandt	35	254	16	16	1	3.97
2B	R. Maranville	571	.235	0	37	**402**	473	22	91	6.0	**.975**	H. Betts	31	222	13	11	1	2.80
W-77 L-77 SS	S. Urbanski	563	.272	8	46	316	461	44	91	6.0	.946	B. Brown	35	213	14	7	1	3.30
Bill McKechnie 3B	F. Knothe	344	.238	1	36	81	168	14	7	3.0	.947	T. Zachary	32	212	12	11	0	3.10
RF	Schulmerich	404	.260	11	57	232	11	8	5	2.5	.968	B. Cantwell	37	146	13	11	5	2.96
CF	W. Berger	602	.307	17	73	396	10	3	3	3.1	**.993**	S. Seibold	28	137	3	10	0	4.68
LF	Worthington	435	.303	8	61	216	8	3	2	2.2	.987	F. Frankhouse	37	109	4	6	0	3.56
C	A. Spohrer	335	.269	0	33	374	62	4	2	4.4	.991							
UT	R. Moore	351	.293	3	43	258	67	5	34		.985							
OF	F. Leach	223	.247	1	29	126	2	3	0	2.6	.977							
C	P. Hargrave	217	.263	4	33	206	39	8	4	3.5	.968							
1B	B. Jordan	212	.321	2	29	514	31	5	48	11.2	.991							
OF	D. Holland	156	.295	1	18	94	3	1	0	2.5	.990							
N. Y. 1B	B. Terry	643	.350	28	117	**1493**	137	14	125	**10.7**	.991	C. Hubbell	40	284	18	11	2	2.50
2B	H. Critz	**659**	.276	2	50	392	471	23	94	5.9	.974	Fitzsimmons	35	238	11	11	0	4.43
W-72 L-82 SS	D. Marshall	226	.248	0	28	119	199	27	37	5.5	.922	B. Walker	31	163	8	12	2	4.14
John McGraw 3B	J. Vergez	376	.261	6	43	94	208	21	22	2.9	.935	J. Mooney	29	125	6	10	0	5.05
W-17 L-23 RF	M. Ott	566	.318	**38**	123	347	11	6	5	2.4	.984	H. Bell	35	120	8	4	2	3.68
Bill Terry CF	F. Lindstrom	595	.271	15	92	315	18	6	2	2.6	.982	D. Luque	38	110	6	7	5	4.01
W-55 L-59 LF	J. Moore	361	.305	2	27	160	6	3	10	2.0	.982	H. Schumacher	27	101	5	6	0	3.55
C	S. Hogan	502	.287	8	77	**522**	71	10	11	4.4	.983	W. Hoyt	18	97	5	7	0	3.42
OF	C. Fullis	235	.298	1	21	97	1	1	0	1.8	.990	S. Gibson	41	82	4	8	3	4.85
3S	G. English	204	.225	2	19	77	133	14	18		.938							
SS	T. Jackson	195	.256	4	38	106	166	22	31	5.7	.925							
St. L. 1B	R. Collins	549	.279	21	91	701	46	1	72	9.2	.999	D. Dean	46	**286**	18	15	2	3.30
2B	J. Reese	309	.265	2	26	209	220	9	48	5.7	.979	P. Derringer	39	233	11	14	0	4.05
W-72 L-82 SS	C. Gelbert	455	.268	1	45	246	389	37	69	5.5	.945	T. Carleton	44	196	10	13	0	4.08
Gabby Street 3B	J. Flowers	247	.255	2	18	59	91	3	10	2.8	.980	B. Hallahan	25	176	12	7	1	3.11
RF	G. Watkins	458	.312	9	63	267	11	15	1	2.4	.949	S. Johnson	32	165	5	14	2	4.92
CF	P. Martin	323	.238	4	34	151	10	4	3	2.4	.976	A. Stout	36	74	4	5	1	4.40
LF	E. Orsatti	375	.336	2	44	197	3	5	0	2.1	.976							
C	G. Mancuso	310	.284	5	43	454	53	12	7	6.3	.977							
23	F. Frisch	486	.292	3	60	252	309	14	58		.976							
1B	J. Bottomley	311	.296	11	48	662	41	10	67	9.6	.986							
C	J. Wilson	274	.248	2	28	326	55	7	9	5.2	.982							
OF	R. Blades	201	.229	3	29	117	2	3	0	2.0	.975							
Cin. 1B	H. Hendrick	398	.302	4	40	922	60	14	72	10.6	.986	R. Lucas	31	269	13	17	0	2.94
2B	G. Grantham	493	.292	6	39	258	347	26	45	5.5	.959	S. Johnson	42	245	13	15	2	3.27
W-60 L-94 SS	L. Durocher	457	.217	1	33	283	429	30	76	5.2	.960	O. Carroll	32	210	10	19	1	4.50
Dan Howley 3B	W. Gilbert	420	.214	1	40	90	198	22	16	2.8	.929	L. Benton	35	180	6	13	2	4.31
RF	B. Herman	577	.326	16	87	392	18	13	6	2.9	.969	R. Kolp	32	160	6	10	1	3.89
CF	E. Crabtree	402	.274	2	35	288	9	3	3	3.2	.990	B. Frey	28	131	4	10	0	4.32
LF	W. Roettger	347	.277	3	43	214	3	2	2	2.3	.991	E. Rixey	25	112	5	5	0	2.66
C	E. Lombardi	413	.303	11	68	288	76	14	6	3.5	.963							
OF	T. Douthit	333	.243	0	25	251	6	4	2	3.0	.985							
UT	J. Morrissey	269	.242	0	13	144	240	8	38		.980							
OF	C. Hafey	253	.344	2	36	131	5	5	0	1.7	.965							
3B	A. High	191	.188	0	12	34	62	5	2	2.2	.950							

BATTING AND BASE RUNNING LEADERS

Batting Average
L. O'Doul, BKN	.368
B. Terry, NY	.350
C. Klein, PHI	.348
P. Waner, PIT	.341
D. Hurst, PHI	.339

Home Runs
M. Ott, NY	38
C. Klein, PHI	38
B. Terry, NY	28
D. Hurst, PHI	24
H. Wilson, BKN	23

Runs Batted In
D. Hurst, PHI	143
C. Klein, PHI	137
P. Whitney, PHI	124
H. Wilson, BKN	123
M. Ott, NY	123

Hits
C. Klein, PHI	226
B. Terry, NY	225
L. O'Doul, BKN	219

Slugging Average
C. Klein, PHI	.646
M. Ott, NY	.601
B. Terry, NY	.580
L. O'Doul, BKN	.555
D. Hurst, PHI	.547

Total Bases
C. Klein, PHI	420
B. Terry, NY	373
M. Ott, NY	340
L. O'Doul, BKN	330
P. Waner, PIT	318

Stolen Bases
C. Klein, PHI	20
T. Piet, PIT	19
G. Watkins, STL	18
F. Frisch, STL	18
K. Davis, PHI	16

Base on Balls
M. Ott, NY	100
D. Hurst, PHI	65
D. Bartell, PHI	64

PITCHING LEADERS

Winning Percentage
L. Warneke, CHI	.786
G. Bush, CHI	.633
W. Clark, BKN	.625
F. Rhem, PHI, STL	.625
C. Hubbell, NY	.621

Wins
L. Warneke, CHI	22
W. Clark, BKN	20
G. Bush, CHI	19
C. Hubbell, NY	18
D. Dean, STL	18
L. French, PIT	18

Strikeouts
D. Dean, STL	191
C. Hubbell, NY	137
P. Malone, CHI	120
T. Carleton, STL	113
B. Brown, BOS	110

Fewest Hits per 9 Innings
S. Swetonic, PIT	7.41
L. Warneke, CHI	8.03
C. Hubbell, NY	8.24

Earned Run Average
L. Warneke, CHI	2.37
C. Hubbell, NY	2.50
H. Betts, BOS	2.80
S. Swetonic, PIT	2.82
R. Lucas, CIN	2.94

Saves
J. Quinn, BKN	8
R. Benge, PHI	6
B. Cantwell, BOS	5
D. Luque, NY	5

Complete Games
R. Lucas, CIN	28
L. Warneke, CHI	25
C. Hubbell, NY	22
L. French, PIT	20
E. Brandt, BOS	19
W. Clark, BKN	19

Shutouts
S. Swetonic, PIT	4
L. Warneke, CHI	4
D. Dean, STL	4

BATTING AND BASE RUNNING LEADERS			**PITCHING LEADERS**	

Home Run Percentage		Runs Scored		Fewest Walks per 9 Innings		Most Strikeouts per 9 Inn.	
M. Ott, NY	6.7	C. Klein, PHI	152	B. Swift, PIT	1.09	D. Dean, STL	6.01
C. Klein, PHI	5.8	B. Terry, NY	124	R. Lucas, CIN	1.17	B. Hallahan, STL	5.51
H. Wilson, BKN	4.8	L. O'Doul, BKN	120	C. Hubbell, NY	1.27	P. Malone, CHI	4.56

Doubles		Triples		Innings		Games Pitched	
P. Waner, PIT	62	B. Herman, CIN	19	D. Dean, STL	286	L. French, PIT	47
C. Klein, PHI	50	G. Suhr, PIT	16	C. Hubbell, NY	284	D. Dean, STL	46
R. Stephenson, CHI	49	C. Klein, PHI	15	L. Warneke, CHI	277	T. Carleton, STL	44
D. Bartell, PHI	48						

	W	L	PCT	GB	R	OR	2B	3B	HR	BA	SA	SB	E	DP	FA	CG	BB	SO	ShO	SV	ERA
									Batting					**Fielding**				**Pitching**			
CHI	90	64	.584		720	633	296	60	69	.278	.392	48	173	146	.973	79	409	527	9	7	3.44
PIT	86	68	.558	4	701	711	274	90	47	.285	.394	71	185	124	.969	72	338	377	12	12	3.75
BKN	81	73	.526	9	752	747	296	59	109	.283	.419	61	183	169	.971	61	403	499	7	16	4.28
PHI	78	76	.506	12	844	796	330	67	122	.292	.442	71	194	133	.968	59	450	459	4	17	4.47
BOS	77	77	.500	13	649	655	262	53	63	.265	.366	36	152	145	.976	72	420	440	8	8	3.53
NY	72	82	.468	18	755	706	263	54	116	.276	.406	31	191	143	.969	57	387	506	3	16	3.83
STL	72	82	.468	18	684	717	307	51	76	.269	.385	92	175	155	.971	70	455	681	13	9	3.97
CIN	60	94	.390	30	575	715	265	68	47	.263	.362	35	178	129	.971	83	276	359	6	6	3.79
					5680	5680	2293	502	649	.276	.396	445	1431	1144	.971	553	3138	3848	62	91	3.88

American League 1932

	POS	Player	AB	BA	HR	RBI	PO	A	E	DP	TC/G	FA	Pitcher	G	IP	W	L	SV	ERA
N. Y. W-107 L-47 Joe McCarthy	1B	L. Gehrig	596	.349	34	151	1293	75	18	101	8.9	.987	L. Gomez	37	265	24	7	1	4.21
	2B	T. Lazzeri	510	.300	15	113	362	405	17	70	5.9	.978	R. Ruffing	35	259	18	7	2	3.09
	SS	F. Crosetti	398	.241	5	57	155	216	25	49	4.8	.937	G. Pipgras	32	219	16	9	0	4.19
	3B	J. Sewell	503	.272	11	68	122	221	9	15	2.9	.974	J. Allen	33	192	17	4	4	3.70
	RF	B. Ruth	457	.341	41	137	209	10	9	1	1.8	.961	H. Pennock	22	147	9	5	0	4.60
	CF	E. Combs	591	.321	9	65	343	6	12	3	2.6	.967	MacFayden	17	121	7	5	1	3.93
	LF	B. Chapman	581	.299	10	107	303	13	17	2	2.2	.949							
	C	B. Dickey	423	.310	15	84	639	53	9	6	6.5	.987							
	SS	L. Lary	280	.232	3	39	152	218	23	39	4.9	.941							
	OF	S. Byrd	209	.297	8	30	129	4	5	1	1.5	.964							
Phi. W-94 L-60 Connie Mack	1B	J. Foxx	585	.364	58	169	1328	79	9	115	10.0	.994	L. Grove	44	292	25	10	7	2.84
	2B	M. Bishop	409	.254	5	37	232	340	7	68	5.5	.988	R. Walberg	41	272	17	10	1	4.73
	SS	E. McNair	554	.285	18	95	242	391	31	89	5.0	.953	G. Earnshaw	36	245	19	13	0	4.77
	3B	J. Dykes	558	.265	7	90	142	251	8	20	2.8	.980	R. Mahaffey	37	223	13	13	0	5.09
	RF	D. Cramer	384	.336	3	46	233	7	6	2	2.9	.976	T. Freitas	23	150	12	5	0	3.83
	CF	M. Haas	558	.305	6	65	372	6	5	2	2.8	.987							
	LF	A. Simmons	670	.322	35	151	290	9	6	4	2.0	.980							
	C	M. Cochrane	518	.293	23	112	652	94	5	15	5.5	.993							
	OF	B. Miller	305	.295	8	58	180	3	4	0	2.2	.979							
	2B	D. Williams	215	.251	4	24	122	175	15	30	5.9	.952							
Was. W-93 L-61 Walter Johnson	1B	J. Kuhel	347	.291	4	52	761	45	5	64	9.5	.994	G. Crowder	50	327	26	13	1	3.33
	2B	B. Myer	577	.279	5	52	352	426	20	97	5.7	.975	M. Weaver	43	234	22	10	2	4.08
	SS	J. Cronin	557	.318	6	116	306	448	32	95	5.6	.959	L. Brown	46	203	15	12	5	4.44
	3B	O. Bluege	507	.258	5	64	158	295	14	28	3.1	.970	F. Marberry	54	198	8	4	13	4.01
	RF	C. Reynolds	406	.305	9	63	229	3	4	0	2.5	.983	T. Thomas	18	117	8	7	0	3.54
	CF	S. West	554	.287	6	83	450	15	10	7	3.3	.979							
	LF	H. Manush	625	.342	14	116	318	6	4	3	2.2	.988							
	C	R. Spencer	317	.246	1	41	313	44	8	9	3.7	.978							
	1B	J. Judge	291	.258	3	29	668	46	2	71	9.2	.997							
	OF	S. Rice	288	.323	1	34	132	7	4	2	2.1	.972							
	C	M. Berg	195	.236	1	26	229	35	0	9	3.5	1.000							
	OF	D. Harris	156	.327	6	29	66	3	5	0	2.2	.932							
Cle. W-87 L-65 Roger Peckinpaugh	1B	E. Morgan	532	.293	4	64	1430	74	23	100	10.8	.985	W. Ferrell	38	288	23	13	1	3.66
	2B	B. Cissell	541	.320	6	93	329	475	30*	82	6.5*	.964	C. Brown	37	263	15	12	1	4.08
	SS	J. Burnett	512	.297	4	53	184	304	28	52	5.0	.946	M. Harder	39	255	15	13	0	3.75
	3B	W. Kamm	524	.286	3	83	164	299	16	20	3.2	.967	W. Hudlin	33	182	12	8	2	4.71
	RF	D. Porter	621	.308	4	62	269	2	5	0	1.9	.982	O. Hildebrand	27	129	8	6	0	3.69
	CF	E. Averill	631	.314	32	124	412	12	16	3	2.9	.964	J. Russell	18	113	5	7	1	4.70
	LF	J. Vosmik	621	.312	10	97	432	12	5	4	2.9	.989	S. Connally	35	112	8	6	3	4.33
	C	L. Sewell	300	.253	2	52	306	50	8	8	4.3	.978							
	C	G. Myatt	252	.246	8	46	211	32	3	3	3.8	.988							
	SS	E. Montague	192	.245	0	24	91	129	27	22	4.3	.891							

POS	Player	AB	BA	HR	RBI	PO	A	E	DP	TC/G	FA	Pitcher	G	IP	W	L	SV	ERA
1B	H. Davis	590	.269	4	74	1327	75	16	123	10.1	.989	E. Whitehill	33	244	16	12	0	4.54
2B	C. Gehringer	618	.298	19	107	**396**	495	**30**	**110**	6.1	.967	V. Sorrell	32	234	14	14	0	4.03
SS	B. Rogell	554	.271	9	61	275	433	42	88	5.4	.944	W. Wyatt	43	206	9	13	1	5.03
3B	H. Schuble	340	.271	5	52	70	152	14	10	3.1	.941	T. Bridges	34	201	14	12	1	3.36
RF	E. Webb	338	.287	3	51	163	8	8	0	2.1	.955	C. Hogsett	47	178	11	9	7	3.54
CF	G. Walker	480	.323	8	78	309	9	17	1	2.9	.949	G. Uhle	33	147	6	6	5	4.48
LF	J. Stone	582	.297	17	108	334	11	14	2	2.5	.961							
C	R. Hayworth	338	.293	2	44	399	59	4	8	4.4	.991							
UT	B. Rhiel	250	.280	3	38	150	65	5	21		.977							
OF	J. White	208	.260	2	21	96	6	4	2	2.3	.962							
OF	R. Johnson	195	.251	3	22	102	3	8	0	2.4	.929							
3B	N. Richardsen	155	.219	0	12	51	92	2	8	2.2	.986							
1B	J. Burns	617	.305	11	70	1399	**101**	12	**130**	10.1	.992	L. Stewart	41	260	14	19	1	4.61
2B	O. Melillo	612	.242	3	66	393	**526**	18	**110**	6.1	.981	G. Blaeholder	42	258	14	14	0	4.70
SS	J. Levey	568	.280	4	63	284	439	**47**	83	5.1	.939	B. Hadley	40	230	13	20*	1	5.53
3B	A. Scharein	303	.304	0	42	100	172	10	22	3.7	.965	S. Gray	52	207	8	12	4	4.53
RF	B. Campbell	585	.289	14	85	297	12	20*	4	2.4	.939	W. Hebert	35	108	1	12	1	6.48
CF	F. Schulte	565	.294	9	73	331	9	5	1	2.7	.986	C. Fischer	24	97	3	7	0	5.57
LF	G. Goslin	572	.299	17	104	330	**16**	18	5	2.4	.951							
C	R. Ferrell	438	.315	2	65	486	78	8	9	4.8	.986							
3B	L. Storti	193	.259	3	26	50	81	6	8	2.7	.956							
1B	L. Blue	373	.249	0	43	1014	88	16	106	10.6	.986	T. Lyons	33	231	10	15	2	3.28
2B	J. Hayes	475	.257	2	54	241	346	20	78	6.3	.967	S. Jones	30	200	10	15	0	4.22
SS	L. Appling	489	.274	3	63	195	287	37	66	6.1	.929	M. Gaston	28	167	7	17	1	4.00
3B	C. Selph	396	.283	0	51	83	120	20	14	3.1	.910	V. Frazier	29	146	3	13	0	6.23
RF	B. Seeds	434	.290	2	45	234	7	9	1	2.2	.964	P. Gregory	33	118	5	3	0	4.51
CF	L. Funk	440	.259	2	40	318	15	7	4	2.8	.979	R. Faber	42	106	2	11	6	3.74
LF	B. Fothergill	346	.295	7	50	136	4	7	0	1.7	.952							
C	F. Grube	277	.282	0	31	303	55	**16**	5	4.1	.957							
UT	R. Kress	515	.285	9	57	281	201	32	41		.938							
1B	B. Sullivan	307	.316	1	45	485	35	5	42	10.1	.990							
C	C. Berry	226	.305	4	31	212	52	5	5	3.8	.981							
OF	J. Hodapp	176	.227	3	20	58	0	2	0	1.9	.967							
1B	D. Alexander	376	.372*	8	56	1051	67	9	93	11.2*	.992	B. Weiland	43	196	6	16	1	4.51
2B	M. Olson	403	.248	0	25	266	324	28	68	5.8	.955	E. Durham	34	175	6	13	0	3.80
SS	R. Warstler	388	.211	0	34	254	373	41	84	**6.2**	.939	B. Kline	47	172	11	13	2	5.28
3B	U. Pickering	457	.260	2	40	110	222	**21**	22	2.8	.941	I. Andrews	25	142	8	6	0	3.81
RF	R. Johnson	348	.299	11	47	167	6	13	0	2.2	.930	W. Moore	37	84	4	10	4	5.23
CF	T. Oliver	455	.264	0	37	328	12	6	4	3.0	.983	MacFayden	12	78	1	10	0	5.10
LF	S. Jolley	531	.309	18	99	234	12	15	3	2.1	.943	J. Welch	20	72	4	6	0	5.23
C	B. Tate	273	.245	2	26	244	50	8	7	4.0	.974							
23	M. McManus	302	.235	5	24	147	227	17	28		.957							
OF	C. Watwood	266	.248	0	30	101	3	6	0	2.4	.945							
C	E. Connolly	222	.225	0	21	233	55	13	0	4.0	.957							
SS	H. Rhyne	207	.227	0	14	92	161	9	31	4.8	.966							
OF	E. Webb	192	.281	5	27	74	7	3	2	1.7	.964							
OF	G. Stumpf	169	.201	1	18	78	2	4	0	1.6	.952							

Det.
W-76 L-75
Bucky Harris

St. L.
W-63 L-91
Bill Killefer

Chi.
W-49 L-102
Lew Fonseca

Bos.
W-43 L-111
Shano Collins
W-11 L-46
Marty McManus
W-32 L-65

BATTING AND BASE RUNNING LEADERS

Batting Average
D. Alexander, BOS, DET	.367
J. Foxx, PHI	.364
L. Gehrig, NY	.349
H. Manush, WAS	.342
B. Ruth, NY	.341

Slugging Average
J. Foxx, PHI	.749
B. Ruth, NY	.661
L. Gehrig, NY	.621
E. Averill, CLE	.569
A. Simmons, PHI	.548

Home Runs
J. Foxx, PHI	58
B. Ruth, NY	41
A. Simmons, PHI	35
L. Gehrig, NY	34
E. Averill, CLE	32

Total Bases
J. Foxx, PHI	438
L. Gehrig, NY	370
A. Simmons, PHI	367
E. Averill, CLE	359
H. Manush, WAS	325

Runs Batted In
J. Foxx, PHI	169
L. Gehrig, NY	151
A. Simmons, PHI	151
B. Ruth, NY	137
E. Averill, CLE	124

Stolen Bases
B. Chapman, NY	38
G. Walker, DET	30
R. Johnson, BOS, DET	20
B. Cissell, CHI, CLE	18

Hits
A. Simmons, PHI	216
H. Manush, WAS	214
J. Foxx, PHI	213

Base on Balls
B. Ruth, NY	130
J. Foxx, PHI	116
M. Bishop, PHI	110

PITCHING LEADERS

Winning Percentage
J. Allen, NY	.810
L. Gomez, NY	.774
R. Ruffing, NY	.720
L. Grove, PHI	.714
M. Weaver, WAS	.688

Earned Run Average
L. Grove, PHI	2.84
R. Ruffing, NY	3.09
T. Lyons, CHI	3.28
G. Crowder, WAS	3.33
T. Bridges, DET	3.36

Wins
G. Crowder, WAS	26
L. Grove, PHI	25
L. Gomez, NY	24
W. Ferrell, CLE	23
M. Weaver, WAS	22

Saves
F. Marberry, WAS	13
W. Moore, BOS, NY	8
C. Hogsett, DET	7
L. Grove, PHI	7
R. Faber, CHI	6

Strikeouts
R. Ruffing, NY	190
L. Grove, PHI	188
L. Gomez, NY	176
B. Hadley, CHI, STL	145
G. Pipgras, NY	111

Complete Games
L. Grove, PHI	27
W. Ferrell, CLE	26
R. Ruffing, NY	22

Fewest Hits per 9 Innings
J. Allen, NY	7.59
R. Ruffing, NY	7.61
T. Bridges, DET	7.79

Shutouts
T. Bridges, DET	4
L. Grove, PHI	4

BATTING AND BASE RUNNING LEADERS

Home Run Percentage
J. Foxx, PHI 9.9
B. Ruth, NY 9.0
L. Gehrig, NY 5.7

Runs Scored
J. Foxx, PHI 151
A. Simmons, PHI 144
E. Combs, NY 143

Doubles
E. McNair, PHI 47
C. Gehringer, DET 44
J. Cronin, WAS 43

Triples
J. Cronin, WAS 18
T. Lazzeri, NY 16
B. Myer, WAS 16

PITCHING LEADERS

Fewest Walks per 9 Innings
C. Brown, CLE 1.71
G. Crowder, WAS 2.12
M. Harder, CLE 2.40

Most Strikeouts per 9 Inn.
R. Ruffing, NY 6.60
L. Gomez, NY 5.97
L. Grove, PHI 5.80

Innings
G. Crowder, WAS 327
L. Grove, PHI 292
W. Ferrell, CLE 288

Games Pitched
F. Marberry, WAS 54
S. Gray, STL 52
G. Crowder, WAS 50

	W	L	PCT	GB	R	OR	2B	3B	HR	BA	SA	SB	E	DP	FA	CG	BB	SO	ShO	SV	ERA
NY	107	47	.695		1002	724	279	82	160	.286	.454	77	188	124	.969	95	561	770	11	15	3.98
PHI	94	60	.610	13	981	752	303	51	173	.290	.457	38	124	142	.979	95	511	595	10	10	4.45
WAS	93	61	.604	14	840	716	303	100	61	.284	.408	70	125	157	.979	66	526	437	10	22	4.16
CLE	87	65	.572	19	845	747	310	74	78	.285	.413	52	191	129	.969	94	446	439	6	8	4.12
DET	76	75	.503	29.5	799	787	291	80	80	.273	.401	103	187	154	.969	67	592	521	9	17	4.30
STL	63	91	.409	44	736	898	274	69	67	.276	.388	69	188	156	.969	63	574	496	8	11	5.01
CHI	49	102	.325	56.5	667	897	274	56	36	.267	.360	89	264	170	.958	50	580	379	2	12	4.82
BOS	43	111	.279	64	566	915	253	57	53	.251	.351	46	233	165	.963	42	612	365	2	7	5.02
					6436	6436	2287	569	708	.277	.404	544	1500	1197	.969	572	4402	4002	58	102	4.48

National League 1933

	POS	Player	AB	BA	HR	RBI	PO	A	E	DP	TC/G	FA	Pitcher	G	IP	W	L	SV	ERA
N. Y. W-91 L-61 Bill Terry	1B	B. Terry	475	.322	6	58	1246	76	11	103	11.4	.992	C. Hubbell	45	309	23	12	5	1.66
	2B	H. Critz	558	.246	2	33	316	541	16	87	6.6	.982	H. Schumacher	35	259	19	12	1	2.16
	SS	B. Ryan	525	.238	3	48	296	494	42	95	5.7	.950	Fitzsimmons	36	252	16	11	0	2.90
	3B	J. Vergez	458	.271	16	72	101	222	25	17	2.8	.928	R. Parmelee	32	218	13	8	0	3.17
	RF	M. Ott	580	.283	23	103	283	12	5	3	2.0	.983	H. Bell	38	105	6	5	5	2.05
	CF	K. Davis	434	.258	7	37	248	7	3	3	2.2	.988	D. Luque	35	80	8	2	4	2.69
	LF	J. Moore	524	.292	0	42	266	19	10	6	2.2	.966							
	C	G. Mancuso	481	.264	6	56	580	83	19	15	4.8	.972							
	OF	L. O'Doul	229	.306	9	35	109	4	3	0	1.8	.974							
	1B	S. Leslie	137	.321	3	27	371	21	4	28	11.3	.990							
Pit. W-87 L-67 George Gibson	1B	G. Suhr	566	.267	10	75	1451	90	14	151	10.1	.991	L. French	47	291	18	13	1	2.72
	2B	T. Piet	362	.323	1	42	241	305	26	61	5.9	.955	B. Swift	37	218	14	10	0	3.13
	SS	A. Vaughan	573	.314	9	97	310	487	46	95	5.5	.945	H. Meine	32	207	15	8	0	3.65
	3B	P. Traynor	624	.304	1	82	176	300	27	16	3.3	.946	S. Swetonic	31	165	12	12	0	3.50
	RF	P. Waner	618	.309	7	70	346	16	7	2	2.4	.981	H. Smith	28	145	8	7	1	2.86
	CF	F. Lindstrom	538	.310	5	55	388	7	5	2	3.1	.988	W. Hoyt	36	117	5	7	4	2.92
	LF	L. Waner	500	.276	0	26	267	9	5	5	2.5	.982	L. Chagnon	39	100	6	4	1	3.69
	C	E. Grace	291	.289	3	44	305	37	7	7	4.0	.980	B. Harris	31	59	4	4	5	3.22
	2B	T. Thevenow	253	.312	0	34	137	172	8	31	5.2	.975							
	OF	W. Jensen	196	.296	0	15	95	1	2	0	2.5	.980							
	OF	A. Comorosky	162	.284	1	15	66	1	0	0	2.2	1.000							
Chi. W-86 L-68 Charlie Grimm	1B	C. Grimm	384	.247	3	37	979	84	4	94	10.3	.996	L. Warneke	36	287	18	13	1	2.00
	2B	B. Herman	619	.279	0	44	466	512	46	114	6.7	.956	G. Bush	41	259	20	12	2	2.75
	SS	B. Jurges	487	.269	5	50	298	476	34	95	5.7	.958	C. Root	35	242	15	10	0	2.60
	3B	W. English	398	.261	3	41	80	173	7	9	2.5	.973	P. Malone	31	186	10	14	0	3.91
	RF	B. Herman	508	.289	16	93	252	12	12	1	2.1	.957	B. Tinning	32	175	13	6	1	3.18
	CF	F. Demaree	515	.272	6	51	321	12	12	1	2.6	.965	L. Nelson	24	76	5	5	1	3.21
	LF	R. Stephenson	346	.329	4	51	187	5	3	2	2.1	.985	B. Grimes	17	70	3	6	3	3.49
	C	G. Hartnett	490	.276	16	88	550	77	7	17	4.5	.989							
	OF	K. Cuyler	262	.317	5	35	130	2	3	0	2.0	.978							
	3S	M. Koenig	218	.284	3	25	65	132	14	24		.934							
	1B	H. Hendrick	189	.291	4	23	328	23	6	31	9.4	.983							
Bos. W-83 L-71 Bill McKechnie	1B	B. Jordan	588	.286	4	46	1513	88	14	117	10.8	.991	E. Brandt	41	288	18	14	4	2.60
	2B	R. Maranville	478	.218	0	38	362	384	22	82	5.4	.971	B. Cantwell	40	255	20	10	2	2.62
	SS	B. Urbanski	566	.251	0	35	299	473	38	91	5.7	.953	F. Frankhouse	43	245	16	15	2	3.16
	3B	P. Whitney	382	.246	8	49	77	187	8	23*	2.2	.971	H. Betts	35	242	11	11	4	2.79
	RF	R. Moore	497	.302	8	70	275	11	6	1	2.4	.977	T. Zachary	26	125	7	9	2	3.53
	CF	W. Berger	528	.313	27	106	382	6	9	4	2.9	.977							
	LF	H. Lee	312	.221	1	28	207	6	5	2	2.5	.977							
	C	S. Hogan	328	.253	3	30	280	56	1	11	3.5	.997							
	OF	J. Mowry	249	.221	0	20	155	2	1	0	2.5	.990							
	C	A. Spohrer	184	.250	1	12	150	26	5	4	2.8	.972							
	3B	F. Knothe	158	.228	1	6	34	56	2	6	2.8	.978							
	3B	D. Gyselman	155	.239	0	12	45	93	11	4	3.5	.926							

	POS	Player	AB	BA	HR	RBI	PO	A	E	DP	TC/G	FA	Pitcher	G	IP	W	L	SV	ERA
St. L.	1B	R. Collins	493	.310	10	68	1054	79	7	82	9.3	.994	D. Dean	48	293	20	18	4	3.04
W-82 L-71	2B	F. Frisch	585	.303	4	66	371	378	14	71	5.8	.982	T. Carleton	44	277	17	11	3	3.38
Gabby Street	SS	L. Durocher	395	.258	2	41	238	358	24	64	5.0	.961*	B. Hallahan	36	244	16	13	0	3.50
W-46 L-45	3B	P. Martin	599	.316	8	57	139	273	25	14	3.0	.943	B. Walker	29	158	9	10	0	3.42
Frankie Frisch	RF	G. Watkins	525	.278	5	62	295	9	15	3	2.4	.953	J. Haines	32	115	9	6	1	2.50
W-36 L-26	CF	E. Orsatti	436	.298	0	38	274	5	4	1	2.8	.986	D. Vance	28	99	6	2	3	3.55
	LF	J. Medwick	595	.306	18	98	318	17	7	2	2.3	.980							
	C	J. Wilson	369	.255	1	45	498	58	10	13	5.3	.982							
	OF	E. Allen	261	.241	0	36	179	8	3	1	2.8	.984							
	UT	P. Crawford	224	.268	0	21	287	62	6	25		.983							
	C	B. O'Farrell	163	.239	2	20	211	19	7	1	4.7	.970							
	2B	R. Hornsby	83	.325	2	21	24	35	2	7	3.6	.967							
Bkn.	1B	S. Leslie	364	.286	5	46	855	49	17	44	9.7	.982	B. Beck	43	257	12	20	1	3.54
W-65 L-88	2B	T. Cuccinello	485	.252	9	65	311	334	15	64	5.5	.977	V. Mungo	41	248	16	15	1	2.72
Max Carey	SS	G. Wright	192	.255	1	18	95	124	15	29	4.6	.936	R. Benge	37	229	10	17	1	3.42
	3B	J. Stripp	537	.277	1	51	170	264	15	17	3.2	.967	O. Carroll	33	226	13	15	0	3.78
	RF	J. Frederick	556	.308	7	64	289	8	9	1	2.2	.971	S. Thurston	32	131	6	8	3	4.52
	CF	D. Taylor	358	.285	9	40	247	4	6	1	2.8	.977	J. Shaute	41	108	3	4	2	3.49
	LF	H. Wilson	360	.267	9	54	181	3	7	0	2.1	.963							
	C	A. Lopez	372	.301	3	41	449	84	5	14	4.3	.991							
	OF	B. Boyle	338	.299	0	31	195	2	5	0	2.2	.975							
	SS	J. Jordan	211	.256	0	17	104	182	9	25	5.8	.969							
	UT	J. Flowers	210	.233	2	22	130	158	11	21		.963							
	OF	J. Hutcheson	184	.234	6	21	84	8	1	2	2.1	.989							
	OF	L. O'Doul	159	.252	5	21	88	1	5	0	2.3	.947							
Phi.	1B	D. Hurst	550	.267	8	76	1355	114	23	132	10.5	.985	E. Holley	30	207	13	15	0	3.53
W-60 L-92	2B	J. Warner	340	.224	0	22	177	224	11	45	5.8	.973	S. Hansen	32	168	6	14	1	4.44
Burt Shotton	SS	D. Bartell	587	.271	1	37	381	493	45	100	6.0	.951	C. Moore	36	161	8	9	1	3.74
	3B	J. McLeod	232	.194	0	15	60	120	17	8	2.9	.914	J. Elliott	35	162	6	10	2	3.84
	RF	C. Klein	606	.368	28	120	339	21	5	5	2.4	.985	P. Collins	42	151	8	13	6	4.11
	CF	C. Fullis	647	.309	1	45	410	15	10	3	2.9	.977	F. Rhem	28	126	5	14	2	6.57
	LF	Schulmerich	365	.334	8	59	210	6	5	0	2.3	.977							
	C	S. Davis	495	.349	9	65	395	69	8	9	3.6	.983							
	2B	M. Finn	169	.237	0	13	107	164	10	34	5.5	.964							
	OF	H. Lee	167	.287	0	12	97	5	2	0	2.3	.981							
Cin.	1B	J. Bottomley	549	.250	13	83	1511	72	15	112	11.0	.991	P. Derringer	33	231	7	25*	1	3.23
W-58 L-94	2B	J. Morrissey	534	.230	0	26	187	295	18	46	5.7	.964	R. Lucas	29	220	10	16	0	3.40
Donie Bush	SS	O. Bluege	291	.213	0	18	162	256	28	48	4.7	.937	S. Johnson	34	211	7	18	1	3.49
	3B	S. Adams	538	.262	1	22	121	272	15	15	3.1	.963	L. Benton	34	153	10	11	2	3.71
	RF	H. Rice	510	.261	0	54	315	14	3	3	2.4	.991	R. Kolp	30	150	6	9	3	3.53
	CF	C. Hafey	568	.303	7	62	364	16	5	5	2.7	.987	B. Frey	37	132	6	4	0	3.82
	LF	J. Moore	514	.263	1	44	329	12	9	4	2.7	.974							
	C	E. Lombardi	350	.283	4	47	223	52	8	3	3.0	.972							
	2B	G. Grantham	260	.204	4	28	160	189	19	33	5.1	.948							
	OF	W. Roettger	209	.239	1	17	124	4	3	2	2.4	.977							

BATTING AND BASE RUNNING LEADERS

Batting Average

C. Klein, PHI	.368
S. Davis, PHI	.349
T. Piet, PIT	.323
B. Terry, NY	.322
Schulmerich, BOS, PHI	.318

Slugging Average

C. Klein, PHI	.602
W. Berger, BOS	.566
B. Herman, CHI	.502
J. Medwick, STL	.497
A. Vaughan, PIT	.478

Home Runs

C. Klein, PHI	28
W. Berger, BOS	27
M. Ott, NY	23
J. Medwick, STL	18

Total Bases

C. Klein, PHI	365
W. Berger, BOS	299
J. Medwick, STL	296
P. Waner, PIT	282
A. Vaughan, PIT	274

Runs Batted In

C. Klein, PHI	120
W. Berger, BOS	106
M. Ott, NY	103
J. Medwick, STL	98
A. Vaughan, PIT	97

Stolen Bases

P. Martin, STL	26
F. Frisch, PIT	18
C. Fullis, PHI	18
C. Klein, PHI	15
E. Orsatti, STL	14

Hits

C. Klein, PHI	223
C. Fullis, PHI	200
P. Waner, PIT	191

Base on Balls

M. Ott, NY	75
G. Suhr, PIT	72
P. Martin, STL	67

Home Run Percentage

W. Berger, BOS	5.1
C. Klein, PHI	4.6
M. Ott, NY	4.0

Runs Scored

P. Martin, STL	122
C. Klein, PHI	101
P. Waner, PIT	101

PITCHING LEADERS

Winning Percentage

B. Cantwell, BOS	.667
C. Hubbell, NY	.657
H. Meine, PIT	.652
G. Bush, CHI	.625
H. Schumacher, NY	.613

Earned Run Average

C. Hubbell, NY	1.66
L. Warneke, CHI	2.00
H. Schumacher, NY	2.16
E. Brandt, BOS	2.60
C. Root, CHI	2.60

Wins

C. Hubbell, NY	23
B. Cantwell, BOS	20
G. Bush, CHI	20
D. Dean, STL	20
H. Schumacher, NY	19

Saves

P. Collins, PHI	6
H. Bell, NY	5
B. Harris, PIT	5
C. Hubbell, NY	5

Strikeouts

D. Dean, STL	199
C. Hubbell, NY	156
T. Carleton, STL	147
L. Warneke, CHI	133
R. Parmelee, NY	132

Complete Games

D. Dean, STL	26
L. Warneke, CHI	26
E. Brandt, BOS	23
C. Hubbell, NY	22

Fewest Hits per 9 Innings

H. Schumacher, NY	6.92
C. Hubbell, NY	7.46
R. Parmelee, NY	7.87

Shutouts

C. Hubbell, NY	10
H. Schumacher, NY	7
L. French, PIT	5

Fewest Walks per 9 Innings

R. Lucas, CIN	0.74
C. Hubbell, NY	1.37
B. Swift, PIT	1.48

Most Strikeouts per 9 Inn.

D. Dean, STL	6.11
R. Parmelee, NY	5.44
T. Carleton, STL	4.78

BATTING AND BASE RUNNING LEADERS

Doubles		Triples	
C. Klein, PHI	44	A. Vaughan, PIT	19
J. Medwick, STL	40	P. Waner, PIT	16
F. Lindstrom, PIT	39	B. Herman, CHI	12
		P. Martin, STL	12

PITCHING LEADERS

Innings		Games Pitched	
C. Hubbell, NY	309	D. Dean, STL	48
D. Dean, STL	293	L. French, PIT	47
L. French, PIT	291	C. Hubbell, NY	45
		A. Liska, PHI	45

	W	L	PCT	GB	R	OR	2B	3B	HR	BA	SA	SB	E	DP	FA	CG	BB	SO	ShO	SV	ERA
NY	91	61	.599		636	515	204	41	82	.263	.361	31	178	156	.973	75	400	555	22	15	2.71
PIT	87	67	.565	5	667	619	249	84	39	.285	.383	34	166	133	.972	70	313	401	16	12	3.27
CHI	86	68	.558	6	646	536	256	51	72	.271	.380	52	168	163	.973	95	413	488	16	9	2.93
BOS	83	71	.539	9	552	531	217	56	54	.252	.345	25	138	148	.978	85	355	383	14	16	2.96
STL	82	71	.536	9.5	687	609	256	61	57	.276	.378	99	162	119	.973	73	452	635	10	16	3.37
BKN	65	88	.425	26.5	617	695	224	51	62	.263	.359	82	177	120	.971	71	374	415	9	10	3.73
PHI	60	92	.395	31	607	760	240	41	60	.274	.369	55	183	156	.970	52	410	341	10	13	4.34
CIN	58	94	.382	33	496	643	208	37	34	.246	.320	30	177	139	.971	74	257	310	13	8	3.42
					4908	4908	1854	422	460	.266	.362	408	1349	1134	.973	595	2974	3528	110	99	3.34

American League 1933

	POS	Player	AB	BA	HR	RBI	PO	A	E	DP	TC/G	FA	Pitcher	G	IP	W	L	SV	ERA
Was. W-99 L-53 Joe Cronin	1B	J. Kuhel	602	.322	11	107	1498	61	7	126	10.2	.996	G. Crowder	52	299	24	15	4	3.97
	2B	B. Myer	530	.302	4	61	356	417	17	92	6.1	.978	E. Whitehill	39	270	22	8	1	3.33
	SS	J. Cronin	602	.309	5	118	297	528	34	95	5.7	.960	L. Stewart	34	231	15	6	0	3.82
	3B	O. Bluege	501	.261	6	71	116	247	13	25	2.7	.965	M. Weaver	23	152	10	5	0	3.25
	RF	G. Goslin	549	.297	10	64	261	17	10	7	2.3	.965	T. Thomas	35	135	7	7	3	4.80
	CF	F. Schulte	550	.295	5	87	433	10	9	4	3.2	.980	J. Russell	50	124	12	6	13	2.69
	LF	H. Manush	658	.336	5	95	325	10	6	1	2.3	.982	B. McAfee	27	53	3	2	5	6.62
	C	L. Sewell	474	.264	2	61	516	61	6	12	4.1	.990							
	OF	D. Harris	177	.260	5	38	79	1	3	0	1.8	.964							
	UT	B. Boken	133	.278	3	26	72	91	7	13		.959							
N. Y. W-91 L-59 Joe McCarthy	1B	L. Gehrig	593	.334	32	139	1290	64	9	102	9.0	.993	R. Ruffing	35	235	9	14	3	3.91
	2B	T. Lazzeri	523	.294	18	104	338	407	25	71	5.6	.968	L. Gomez	35	235	16	10	2	3.18
	SS	F. Crosetti	451	.253	9	60	245	384	43	58	5.1	.936	J. Allen	25	185	15	7	1	4.39
	3B	J. Sewell	524	.273	2	54	123	224	13	27	2.7	.964	R. Van Atta	26	157	12	4	1	4.18
	RF	B. Ruth	459	.301	34	103	215	9	7	4	1.8	.970	J. Brown	21	74	7	5	0	5.23
	CF	E. Combs	419	.298	5	60	227	3	6	1	2.3	.975	H. Pennock	23	65	7	4	4	5.54
	LF	B. Chapman	565	.312	9	98	288	24	8	4	2.2	.975	W. Moore	35	62	5	6	8	5.52
	C	B. Dickey	478	.318	14	97	721	82	6	15	6.4	.993							
	OF	D. Walker	328	.274	15	51	194	7	8	1	2.7	.962							
Phi. W-79 L-72 Connie Mack	1B	J. Foxx	573	.356	48	163	1402	93	15	98	10.1	.990	L. Grove	45	275	24	8	6	3.20
	2B	M. Bishop	391	.294	4	42	254	359	16	52	5.6	.975	S. Cain	38	218	13	12	1	4.25
	SS	D. Williams	408	.289	11	73	199	243	38	34	5.7	.921	R. Walberg	40	201	9	13	4	4.88
	3B	P. Higgins	567	.314	14	99	159	270	24	23	3.0	.947	R. Mahaffey	33	179	13	10	0	5.17
	RF	E. Coleman	388	.281	6	68	178	5	10	2	2.2	.948	G. Earnshaw	21	118	5	10	0	5.97
	CF	D. Cramer	661	.295	8	75	387	13	12	2	2.7	.971							
	LF	B. Johnson	535	.290	21	93	298	16	16	3	2.3	.952							
	C	M. Cochrane	429	.322	15	60	476	67	6	8	4.3	.989							
	S2	E. McNair	310	.261	7	48	169	216	17	39		.958							
	OF	L. Finney	240	.267	3	32	136	6	8	1	2.4	.947							
Cle. W-75 L-76 Roger Peckinpaugh W-26 L-25 Walter Johnson W-49 L-51	1B	H. Boss	438	.269	1	53	1062	71	7	89	10.4	.994	M. Harder	43	253	15	17	4	2.95
	2B	O. Hale	351	.276	10	64	213	259	23	45	6.8	.954	O. Hildebrand	36	220	16	11	0	3.76
	SS	Knickerbocker	279	.226	2	32	151	233	25	37	5.1	.939	W. Ferrell	28	201	11	12	0	4.21
	3B	W. Kamm	447	.282	1	47	153	221	6	16	2.9	.984	C. Brown	33	185	11	12	1	3.41
	RF	D. Porter	499	.267	0	41	236	9	1	3	2.0	.996	W. Hudlin	34	147	5	13	1	3.97
	CF	E. Averill	599	.301	11	92	390	8	12	3	2.8	.971	M. Pearson	19	135	10	5	0	2.33
	LF	J. Vosmik	438	.263	4	56	242	15	4	3	2.3	.985	S. Connally	41	103	5	3	1	4.89
	C	R. Spencer	227	.203	0	23	258	42	3	4	4.2	.990							
	2S	B. Cissell	409	.230	6	33	238	351	28	47		.955							
	UT	J. Burnett	261	.272	1	29	124	198	23	31		.933							
	C	F. Pytlak	248	.310	2	33	246	57	0	11	4.4	1.000							
	OF	M. Galatzer	160	.238	1	17	74	4	2	0	2.0	.975							
	PO	W. Ferrell	140	.271	7	26	43	49	0	5		1.000							

	POS	Player	AB	BA	HR	RBI	PO	A	E	DP	TC/G	FA	Pitcher	G	IP	W	L	SV	ERA
Det. W-75 L-79 Bucky Harris W-73 L-79 Del Baker W-2 L-0	1B	H. Greenberg	449	.301	12	87	1133	63	14	111	10.3	.988	F. Marberry	37	238	16	11	2	3.29
	2B	C. Gehringer	628	.325	12	105	358	542	17	111	5.9	.981	T. Bridges	33	233	14	12	2	3.09
	SS	B. Rogell	587	.295	0	57	326	526	51	116	5.8	.944	V. Sorrell	36	233	11	15	1	3.79
	3B	M. Owen	550	.262	2	65	143	226	22	19	2.9	.944	C. Fischer	35	183	11	15	3	3.55
	RF	J. Stone	574	.280	11	80	280	11	9	1	2.1	.970	S. Rowe	19	123	7	4	0	3.58
	CF	P. Fox	535	.288	7	57	313	5	7	0	2.6	.978	C. Hogsett	45	116	6	10	9	4.50
	LF	G. Walker	483	.280	9	64	234	10	15	3	2.3	.942	V. Frazier	20	104	5	5	0	6.64
	C	R. Hayworth	425	.245	1	45	546	79	4	14	4.7	.994							
	OF	J. White	234	.252	2	34	122	4	3	1	2.4	.977							
	1B	H. Davis	173	.214	0	14	433	13	10	33	10.4	.978							
	OF	F. Doljack	147	.286	0	22	74	6	5	3	2.3	.941							
Chi. W-67 L-83 Lew Fonseca	1B	R. Kress	467	.248	10	78	1169	60	28	83	11.3	.978	T. Lyons	36	228	10	21	1	4.38
	2B	J. Hayes	535	.258	2	47	344	497	16	89	6.2	.981	S. Jones	27	177	10	12	0	3.36
	SS	L. Appling	612	.322	6	85	314	534	55	107	6.0	.939	M. Gaston	30	167	8	12	0	4.85
	3B	J. Dykes	554	.260	1	68	132	296	21	22	3.0	.953	E. Durham	24	139	10	6	0	4.48
	RF	E. Swanson	539	.306	1	63	281	7	8	0	2.1	.973	J. Heving	40	118	7	5	6	2.67
	CF	M. Haas	585	.287	1	51	347	9	6	2	2.5	.983	J. Miller	26	106	5	6	0	5.62
	LF	A. Simmons	605	.331	14	119	372	15	4	1	2.7	.990	P. Gregory	23	104	4	11	0	4.95
	C	F. Grube	256	.230	0	23	266	44	5	5	3.8	.984	R. Faber	36	86	3	4	5	3.44
	C	C. Berry	271	.255	2	28	260	39	4	1	3.7	.987							
Bos. W-63 L-86 Marty McManus	1B	D. Alexander	313	.281	5	40	728	47	6	51	9.9	.992	G. Rhodes	34	232	12	15	0	4.03
	2B	J. Hodapp	413	.312	3	54	273	334	25	65	6.3	.960	B. Weiland	39	216	8	14	3	3.87
	SS	R. Warstler	322	.217	1	17	150	275	22	40	5.1	.951	L. Brown	33	163	8	11	1	4.02
	3B	M. McManus	366	.284	3	36	79	123	9	9	2.8	.957	H. Johnson	25	155	8	6	1	4.06
	RF	R. Johnson	483	.313	10	95	280	14	25	3	2.6	.922	I. Andrews	34	140	7	13	1	4.95
	CF	D. Cooke	454	.291	5	54	257	6	12	5	2.3	.956	J. Welch	47	129	4	9	3	4.60
	LF	S. Jolley	411	.282	9	65	178	12	9	3	2.0	.955	G. Pipgras	22	128	9	8	1	4.07
	C	R. Ferrell	421	.297	3	72	500	76*	6*	9	5.1	.990	B. Kline	46	127	7	8	4	4.54
	S3	B. Werber	425	.259	3	39	167	257	39	43		.916							
	OF	T. Oliver	244	.258	0	23	187	9	3	3	2.3	.985							
	1O	B. Seeds	230	.243	0	23	422	22	8	33		.982							
	3B	B. Walters	195	.256	4	28	42	84	8	11	3.1	.940							
	1B	J. Judge	104	.288	0	22	259	12	0	21	9.7	1.000							
St. L. W-55 L-96 Bill Killefer W-34 L-59 Allen Sothoron W-1 L-3 Rogers Hornsby W-20 L-34	1B	J. Burns	556	.288	7	71	1336	81	12	129	10.0	.992	B. Hadley	45	317	15	20	3	3.92
	2B	O. Melillo	496	.292	3	79	362	451	7	110	6.3	.991	G. Blaeholder	38	256	15	19	0	4.72
	SS	J. Levey	529	.195	2	36	298	428	42	73	5.6	.945	E. Wells	36	204	6	14	1	4.20
	3B	A. Scharein	471	.204	0	26	113	208	17	31	3.6	.950	R. Stiles	31	115	3	7	1	5.01
	RF	B. Campbell	567	.277	16	106	250	18	14	4	2.0	.950	S. Gray	38	112	7	4	4	4.10
	CF	S. West	517	.300	11	48	329	14	4	3	2.7	.988	W. Hebert	33	88	4	6	0	5.30
	LF	C. Reynolds	475	.286	8	71	269	8	10	3	2.3	.965	D. Coffman	21	81	3	7	1	5.89
	C	M. Shea	279	.262	1	27	328	60	2	15*	4.6	.995*							
	UT	T. Gullic	304	.243	5	35	229	74	5	8		.984							
	32	L. Storti	210	.195	3	21	105	113	8	26		.965							
	OF	D. Garms	189	.317	4	24	91	5	4	1	2.1	.960							

BATTING AND BASE RUNNING LEADERS

Batting Average
J. Foxx, PHI	.356
H. Manush, WAS	.336
L. Gehrig, NY	.334
A. Simmons, CHI	.331
C. Gehringer, DET	.325

Slugging Average
J. Foxx, PHI	.703
L. Gehrig, NY	.605
B. Ruth, NY	.582
M. Cochrane, PHI	.515
B. Johnson, PHI	.505

Home Runs
J. Foxx, PHI	48
B. Ruth, NY	34
L. Gehrig, NY	32
B. Johnson, PHI	21
T. Lazzeri, NY	18

Total Bases
J. Foxx, PHI	403
L. Gehrig, NY	359
H. Manush, WAS	302
C. Gehringer, DET	294
A. Simmons, CHI	291

Runs Batted In
J. Foxx, PHI	163
L. Gehrig, NY	139
A. Simmons, CHI	119
J. Cronin, WAS	118
J. Kuhel, WAS	107

Stolen Bases
B. Chapman, NY	27
G. Walker, DET	26
E. Swanson, CHI	19
J. Kuhel, WAS	17
B. Werber, BOS, NY	15
T. Lazzeri, NY	15

Hits
H. Manush, WAS	221
J. Foxx, PHI	204
C. Gehringer, DET	204

Base on Balls
B. Ruth, NY	114
M. Bishop, PHI	106
M. Cochrane, PHI	106

Home Run Percentage
J. Foxx, PHI	8.4
B. Ruth, NY	7.4
L. Gehrig, NY	5.4

Runs Scored
L. Gehrig, NY	138
J. Foxx, PHI	125
H. Manush, WAS	115

PITCHING LEADERS

Winning Percentage
L. Grove, PHI	.750
E. Whitehill, WAS	.733
L. Stewart, WAS	.714
J. Allen, NY	.682
G. Crowder, WAS	.615
L. Gomez, NY	.615

Earned Run Average
M. Pearson, CLE	2.33
M. Harder, CLE	2.95
T. Bridges, DET	3.09
L. Gomez, NY	3.18
L. Grove, PHI	3.20

Wins
L. Grove, PHI	24
G. Crowder, WAS	24
E. Whitehill, WAS	22
L. Gomez, NY	16
O. Hildebrand, CLE	16
F. Marberry, DET	16

Saves
J. Russell, WAS	13
C. Hogsett, DET	9
W. Moore, NY	8
L. Grove, PHI	6
J. Heving, CHI	6

Strikeouts
L. Gomez, NY	163
B. Hadley, STL	149
R. Ruffing, NY	122
T. Bridges, DET	120
J. Allen, NY	119

Complete Games
L. Grove, PHI	21
B. Hadley, STL	19
E. Whitehill, WAS	19
R. Ruffing, NY	18
T. Bridges, DET	17
G. Crowder, WAS	17

Fewest Hits per 9 Innings
M. Pearson, CLE	7.38
T. Bridges, DET	7.42
B. Weiland, BOS	8.20

Shutouts
O. Hildebrand, CLE	6
L. Gomez, NY	4
G. Blaeholder, STL	3

Fewest Walks per 9 Innings
C. Brown, CLE	1.65
F. Marberry, DET	2.30
L. Stewart, WAS	2.34

Most Strikeouts per 9 Inn.
L. Gomez, NY	6.25
J. Allen, NY	5.80
R. Ruffing, NY	4.67

BATTING AND BASE RUNNING LEADERS   PITCHING LEADERS

Doubles		Triples		Innings		Games Pitched	
J. Cronin, WAS	45	H. Manush, WAS	17	B. Hadley, STL	317	G. Crowder, WAS	52
B. Johnson, PHI	44	E. Combs, NY	16	G. Crowder, WAS	299	J. Russell, WAS	50
J. Burns, STL	43	E. Averill, CLE	16	L. Grove, PHI	275	J. Welch, BOS	47
						B. Kline, BOS	46

	W	L	PCT	GB	R	OR	2B	3B	HR	BA	SA	SB	E	DP	FA	CG	BB	SO	ShO	SV	ERA
WAS	99	53	.651	—	850	**665**	281	**86**	60	**.287**	.402	65	**131**	149	**.979**	68	452	447	5	**26**	3.82
NY	91	59	.607	7	**927**	768	241	75	**144**	.283	.440	**74**	165	122	.972	70	612	**711**	8	22	4.36
PHI	79	72	.523	19.5	875	853	**297**	56	140	.285	**.441**	33	203	121	.966	69	644	423	6	14	4.81
CLE	75	76	.497	23.5	654	669	218	77	50	.261	.360	36	156	127	.974	**74**	465	437	**12**	7	**3.71**
DET	75	79	.487	25	722	733	283	78	57	.269	.380	68	178	**167**	.971	69	561	575	6	17	3.96
CHI	67	83	.447	31	683	814	231	53	43	.272	.360	43	186	143	.970	53	519	423	8	13	4.45
BOS	63	86	.423	34.5	700	758	294	56	50	.271	.377	62	204	133	.966	60	591	473	4	14	4.35
STL	55	96	.364	43.5	669	820	244	64	64	.253	.360	70	149	162	.976	55	531	426	7	10	4.82
					6080	6080	2089	545	608	.273	.390	451	1372	1124	.972	518	4375	3915	56	123	4.28

National League 1934

	POS	Player	AB	BA	HR	RBI	PO	A	E	DP	TC/G	FA	Pitcher	G	IP	W	L	SV	ERA
St. L. W-95 L-58 Frankie Frisch	1B	R. Collins	600	.333	**35**	128	1289	**110**	13	**115**	9.2	.991	D. Dean	50	312	**30**	7	7	2.66
	2B	F. Frisch	550	.305	3	75	294	351	15	74	5.7	.977	T. Carleton	40	241	16	11	2	4.26
	SS	L. Durocher	500	.260	3	70	320	407	33	86	5.2	.957	P. Dean	39	233	19	11	2	3.43
	3B	P. Martin	454	.289	5	49	85	195	**19**	7	2.8	.936	B. Hallahan	32	163	8	12	0	4.26
	RF	J. Rothrock	**647**	.284	11	72	343	10	9	4	2.4	.975	B. Walker	24	153	12	4	0	3.12
	CF	E. Orsatti	337	.300	0	31	207	5	3	0	2.4	.986							
	LF	J. Medwick	620	.319	18	106	322	10	**14**	1	2.3	.960							
	C	S. Davis	347	.300	9	65	459	42	6	7	5.4	.988							
	UT	B. Whitehead	332	.277	1	24	158	220	16	38		.959							
	C	B. DeLancey	253	.316	13	40	363	35	8	5	5.3	.980							
	OF	C. Fullis	199	.261	0	26	124	2	4	1	2.3	.969							
N. Y. W-93 L-60 Bill Terry	1B	B. Terry	602	.354	8	83	**1592**	105	10	**131**	11.2	**.994**	C. Hubbell	49	313	21	12	**8**	**2.30**
	2B	B. Critz	571	.242	6	40	353	**510**	19	**90**	6.4	.978	H. Schumacher	41	297	23	10	0	3.18
	SS	T. Jackson	523	.268	16	101	283	458	**43**	60	6.0	.945	Fitzsimmons	38	263	18	14	1	3.04
	3B	J. Vergez	320	.200	7	27	86	195	17	11	2.9	.943	R. Parmelee	22	153	10	6	0	3.42
	RF	M. Ott	582	.326	**35**	**135**	286	12	8	1	2.0	.974	J. Bowman	30	107	5	4	3	3.61
	CF	G. Watkins	296	.247	6	33	165	3	10	1	2.2	.944	A. Smith	30	67	3	5	5	4.32
	LF	J. Moore	580	.331	15	61	242	8	12	1	2.0	.954	H. Bell	22	54	4	3	5	3.67
	C	G. Mancuso	383	.245	7	46	448	67	**12**	7	4.3	.977	D. Luque	26	42	4	3	7	3.83
	UT	B. Ryan	385	.242	2	41	159	283	26	33		.944							
	OF	H. Leiber	187	.241	2	25	99	3	3	1	2.1	.971							
	OF	L. O'Doul	177	.316	9	46	60	1	2	0	1.7	.968							
Chi. W-86 L-65 Charlie Grimm	1B	C. Grimm	267	.296	5	47	683	43	4	39	9.9	.995	L. Warneke	43	291	22	10	3	3.21
	2B	B. Herman	456	.303	3	42	278	385	17	64	6.1	.975	B. Lee	35	214	13	14	1	3.40
	SS	B. Jurges	358	.246	8	33	205	334	19	63	5.7	.966	G. Bush	40	209	18	10	2	3.83
	3B	S. Hack	402	.289	1	21	102	198	16	10	2.9	.949	P. Malone	34	191	14	7	0	3.53
	RF	B. Herman	467	.304	14	84	192	7	6	2	1.8	.971	J. Weaver	27	159	11	9	0	3.91
	CF	K. Cuyler	559	.338	6	69	319	15	10	1	2.4	.971	B. Tinning	39	129	4	6	3	3.34
	LF	C. Klein	435	.301	20	80	222	6	9	2	2.2	.962	C. Root	34	118	4	7	0	4.28
	C	G. Hartnett	438	.299	22	90	**605**	86	3	11	5.4	**.996**							
	S3	W. English	421	.278	3	31	72	126	8	27		.961							
	OF	T. Stainback	359	.306	2	46	185	4	9	1	2.1	.955							
	2B	A. Galan	192	.260	5	22	90	106	8	16	4.7	.961							
Bos. W-78 L-73 Bill McKechnie	1B	B. Jordan	489	.311	2	58	1165	66	14	85	10.6	.989	E. Brandt	40	255	16	14	5	3.53
	2B	M. McManus	435	.276	8	47	156	247	15	39	5.7	.964	F. Frankhouse	37	234	17	9	1	3.20
	SS	B. Urbanski	605	.293	7	53	298	457	31	84	5.4	**.961**	H. Betts	40	213	17	10	3	4.06
	3B	P. Whitney	563	.259	12	79	105	**227**	11	11	3.1	**.968**	F. Rhem	25	153	8	8	0	3.60
	RF	T. Thompson	343	.265	0	37	205	12	8	3	2.7	.964	B. Cantwell	27	143	5	11	5	4.33
	CF	W. Berger	615	.298	34	121	385	9	9	2	2.7	.978	B. Smith	39	122	6	9	5	4.66
	LF	H. Lee	521	.292	8	79	317	5	5	1	2.6	.985							
	C	A. Spohrer	265	.223	0	17	296	45	8	5	3.6	.977							
	O1	R. Moore	422	.284	7	64	496	23	12	24		.977							
	C	S. Hogan	279	.262	4	34	291	53	5	8	3.9	.986							
	2B	L. Mallon	166	.295	0	18	92	145	8	17	5.8	.967							

POS	Player	AB	BA	HR	RBI	PO	A	E	DP	TC/G	FA	Pitcher	G	IP	W	L	SV	ERA
Pit.																		
1B	G. Suhr	573	.283	13	103	1326	75	9	108	9.3	.994	L. French	49	264	12	18	1	3.58
2B	C. Lavagetto	304	.220	3	46	214	234	18	39	5.6	.961	B. Swift	37	213	11	13	0	3.98
SS	A. Vaughan	558	.333	12	94	329	480	41	77	5.7	.952	R. Birkofer	41	204	11	12	1	4.10
3B	P. Traynor	444	.309	1	61	116	176	14	16	2.8	.954	W. Hoyt	48	191	15	6	5	2.93
RF	P. Waner	599	.362	14	90	323	15	5	1	2.4	.985	R. Lucas	29	173	10	9	0	4.38
CF	L. Waner	611	.283	1	48	**405**	8	9	1	3.0	.979	H. Meine	26	106	7	6	0	4.32
LF	F. Lindstrom	383	.290	4	49	181	8	2	1	2.1	.990							
C	E. Grace	289	.270	4	24	304	26	6	4	4.0	.982							
23	T. Thevenow	446	.271	0	54	214	280	19	37		.963							
OF	W. Jensen	283	.290	0	27	143	1	1	0	2.2	.993							
C	T. Padden	237	.321	0	22	297	20	7	3	4.3	.978							
Bkn.																		
1B	S. Leslie	546	.332	9	102	1262	93	9	104	9.9	.993	V. Mungo	45	**315**	18	16	3	3.37
2B	T. Cuccinello	528	.261	14	94	246	347	16	54	6.0	.974	R. Benge	36	227	14	12	0	4.32
SS	L. Frey	490	.284	8	57	232	375	35	81	5.9	.945	D. Leonard	44	184	14	11	5	3.28
3B	J. Stripp	384	.315	1	40	93	147	15	**20**	2.7	.941	J. Babich	25	135	7	11	1	4.20
RF	B. Boyle	472	.305	7	48	275	**20**	9	1	2.5	.970	T. Zachary	22	102	5	6	2	4.43
CF	L. Koenecke	460	.320	14	73	310	6	2	0	2.6	**.994**	L. Munns	33	99	3	7	0	4.71
LF	D. Taylor	405	.299	7	57	188	8	5	1	1.9	.975							
C	A. Lopez	439	.273	7	54	542	62	11	4	4.5	.982							
S2	J. Jordan	369	.266	0	43	157	246	19	40		.955							
OF	J. Frederick	307	.296	4	35	121	11	6	3	1.8	.957							
OF	H. Wilson	172	.262	6	27	71	3	2	3*	1.8	.974							
Phi.																		
1B	D. Camilli	378	.265	12	68	882	55	14*	102	9.3	.985	C. Davis	51	274	19	17	5	2.95
2B	L. Chiozza	484	.304	0	44	215	257	**31**	37	5.9	.938	P. Collins	45	254	13	18	1	4.18
SS	D. Bartell	604	.310	0	37	**350**	**483**	40	**93**	6.0	.954	S. Hansen	50	151	6	12	3	5.42
3B	B. Walters	300	.260	4	38	74	136	11	12	2.8	.950	S. Johnson	42	134	5	9	3	3.50
RF	J. Moore	458	.343	11	93	244	18	5	2	2.3	.981	C. Moore	35	127	4	9	0	6.47
CF	K. Davis	393	.293	3	48	304	13	3	3	3.2*	.991	E. Moore	20	122	5	7	1	4.05
LF	E. Allen	581	.330	10	85	337	19	8	3	2.5	.978							
C	A. Todd	302	.318	4	41	291	32	8	7	4.0	.976							
C	J. Wilson	277	.292	3	35	265	42	4	7	4.0	.987							
2B	I. Jeffries	175	.246	4	19	122	157	11	42	5.6	.962							
32	M. Haslin	166	.265	1	11	61	89	8	9		.949							
1B	D. Hurst	130	.262	2	21	317	17	2	30	8.4	.994							
Cin.																		
1B	J. Bottomley	556	.284	11	78	1303	77	15	106	10.0	.989	P. Derringer	47	261	15	21	4	3.59
2B	T. Piet	421	.259	1	38	126	149	15	27	5.9	.948	B. Frey	39	245	11	16	2	3.52
SS	G. Slade	555	.285	4	52	200	315	26	60	5.6	.952	S. Johnson	46	216	7	**22**	3	5.22
3B	M. Koenig	633	.272	1	67	57	130	14	1	3.1	.930	T. Freitas	30	153	6	12	1	4.01
RF	A. Comorosky	446	.258	0	40	285	5	7	1	2.5	.970	A. Stout	41	141	6	8	1	4.86
CF	C. Hafey	535	.293	18	67	380	7	13	1	2.9	.968							
LF	H. Pool	358	.327	2	50	196	8	10	1	2.3	.953							
C	E. Lombardi	417	.305	9	62	383	61	5	8	4.0	.989							
32	S. Adams	278	.252	0	14	92	156	8	21		.969							
OF	Schulmerich	209	.263	5	19	121	1	3	1	2.2	.976							

Pit.
W-74 L-76
George Gibson
W-27 L-24
Pie Traynor
W-47 L-52

Bkn.
W-71 L-81
Casey Stengel

Phi.
W-56 L-93
Jimmie Wilson

Cin.
W-52 L-99
Bob O'Farrell
W-26 L-58
Burt Shotton
W-1 L-0
Chuck Dressen
W-25 L-41

BATTING AND BASE RUNNING LEADERS

Batting Average
P. Waner, PIT	.362
B. Terry, NY	.354
K. Cuyler, CHI	.338
R. Collins, STL	.333
A. Vaughan, PIT	.333

Slugging Average
R. Collins, STL	.615
M. Ott, NY	.591
W. Berger, BOS	.546
P. Waner, PIT	.539
J. Medwick, STL	.529

Home Runs
M. Ott, NY	35
R. Collins, STL	35
W. Berger, BOS	34
G. Hartnett, CHI	22
C. Klein, CHI	20

Total Bases
R. Collins, STL	369
M. Ott, NY	344
W. Berger, BOS	336
J. Medwick, STL	328
P. Waner, PIT	323

Runs Batted In
M. Ott, NY	135
R. Collins, STL	128
W. Berger, BOS	121
J. Medwick, STL	106
G. Suhr, PIT	103

Stolen Bases
P. Martin, STL	23
K. Cuyler, CHI	15
D. Bartell, PHI	13
D. Taylor, BKN	12

Hits
P. Waner, PIT	217
B. Terry, NY	213
R. Collins, STL	200

Base on Balls
A. Vaughan, PIT	94
M. Ott, NY	85
L. Koenecke, BKN	70

Home Run Percentage
M. Ott, NY	6.0
R. Collins, STL	5.8
W. Berger, BOS	5.5

Runs Scored
P. Waner, PIT	122
M. Ott, NY	119
R. Collins, STL	116

PITCHING LEADERS

Winning Percentage
D. Dean, STL	.811
W. Hoyt, PIT	.714
H. Schumacher, NY	.697
L. Warneke, CHI	.688
F. Frankhouse, BOS	.654

Earned Run Average
C. Hubbell, NY	2.30
D. Dean, STL	2.66
C. Davis, PHI	2.95
Fitzsimmons, NY	3.04
B. Walker, STL	3.12

Wins
D. Dean, STL	30
H. Schumacher, NY	23
L. Warneke, CHI	22
C. Hubbell, NY	21
P. Dean, STL	19
C. Davis, PHI	19

Saves
C. Hubbell, NY	8
D. Dean, STL	7
D. Luque, NY	7
H. Bell, NY	6

Strikeouts
D. Dean, STL	195
V. Mungo, BKN	184
P. Dean, STL	150
L. Warneke, CHI	143
P. Derringer, CIN	122

Complete Games
D. Dean, STL	24
C. Hubbell, NY	23
L. Warneke, CHI	23
V. Mungo, BKN	22
E. Brandt, BOS	20

Fewest Hits per 9 Innings
C. Hubbell, NY	8.22
D. Dean, STL	8.32
L. Warneke, CHI	8.43

Shutouts
D. Dean, STL	7
P. Dean, STL	5
C. Hubbell, NY	5
B. Lee, CHI	4

Fewest Walks per 9 Innings
C. Hubbell, NY	1.06
B. Frey, CIN	1.54
D. Leonard, BKN	1.67

Most Strikeouts per 9 Inn.
P. Dean, STL	5.79
D. Dean, STL	5.63
V. Mungo, BKN	5.25

BATTING AND BASE RUNNING LEADERS

Doubles		Triples		Innings		Games Pitched	
K. Cuyler, CHI	42	J. Medwick, STL	18	V. Mungo, BKN	315	C. Davis, PHI	51
E. Allen, PHI	42	P. Waner, PIT	16	C. Hubbell, NY	313	D. Dean, STL	50
A. Vaughan, PIT	41	G. Suhr, PIT	13	D. Dean, STL	312	S. Hansen, PHI	50
		R. Collins, STL	12				

PITCHING LEADERS

	W	L	PCT	GB	R	OR	2B	3B	Batting HR	BA	SA	SB	E	Fielding DP	FA	CG	BB	Pitching SO	ShO	SV	ERA
STL	95	58	.621		799	656	294	75	104	.288	.425	69	166	141	.972	78	411	689	15	16	3.69
NY	93	60	.608	2	760	583	240	41	126	.275	.405	19	179	141	.972	66	351	499	12	30	3.19
CHI	86	65	.570	8	705	639	263	44	101	.279	.402	59	137	135	.977	73	417	633	11	9	3.76
BOS	78	73	.517	16	683	714	233	44	83	.272	.378	30	169	120	.972	62	405	462	11	20	4.11
PIT	74	76	.493	19.5	735	713	281	77	52	.287	.398	44	145	118	.975	61	354	487	8	8	4.20
BKN	71	81	.467	23.5	748	795	284	52	79	.281	.396	55	180	141	.970	66	476	520	6	12	4.48
PHI	56	93	.376	37	675	794	286	35	56	.284	.384	52	197	140	.966	52	437	416	8	15	4.76
CIN	52	99	.344	42	590	801	227	65	55	.266	.364	34	181	136	.970	51	389	438	3	19	4.37
					5695	5695	2108	433	656	.279	.394	362	1354	1072	.972	509	3240	4144	74	129	4.06

American League 1934

	POS	Player	AB	BA	HR	RBI	PO	A	E	DP	TC/G	FA	Pitcher	G	IP	W	L	SV	ERA
Det. W-101 L-53 Mickey Cochrane	1B	H. Greenberg	593	.339	26	139	1454	84	16	124	10.2	.990	T. Bridges	36	275	22	11	1	3.67
	2B	C. Gehringer	601	.356	11	127	355	516	17	100	5.8	.981	S. Rowe	45	266	24	8	1	3.45
	SS	B. Rogell	592	.296	3	100	259	518	31	99	5.2	.962	E. Auker	43	205	15	7	1	3.42
	3B	M. Owen	565	.317	8	96	202	253	21	33	3.1	.956	F. Marberry	38	156	15	5	3	4.57
	RF	P. Fox	516	.285	2	45	245	13	7	4	2.2	.974	V. Sorrell	28	130	6	9	2	4.79
	CF	J. White	384	.313	0	44	225	9	10	2	2.4	.959	C. Fischer	20	95	6	4	1	4.37
	LF	G. Goslin	614	.305	13	100	290	15	15	2	2.1	.953							
	C	M. Cochrane	437	.320	2	76	517	69	7	7	4.8	.988							
	OF	G. Walker	347	.300	6	39	191	5	11	2	2.6	.947							
	C	R. Hayworth	167	.293	0	27	226	23	4	3	4.7	.984							
	P	S. Rowe	109	.303	2	22	9	46	0	3	1.2	**1.000**							
N. Y. W-94 L-60 Joe McCarthy	1B	L. Gehrig	579	**.363**	49	165	1284	80	8	126	9.0	.994	L. Gomez	38	**282**	**26**	5	1	**2.33**
	2B	T. Lazzeri	438	.267	14	67	218	265	12	52	5.4	.976	R. Ruffing	36	256	19	11	0	3.93
	SS	F. Crosetti	554	.265	11	67	242	356	35	77	5.3	.945	J. Murphy	40	208	14	10	4	3.12
	3B	J. Saltzgaver	350	.271	6	36	71	130	10	10	2.5	.953	J. Broaca	26	177	12	9	0	4.16
	RF	B. Ruth	365	.288	22	84	197	3	8	0	1.9	.962	J. DeShong	31	134	6	7	3	4.11
	CF	B. Chapman	588	.308	5	86	368	12	13	2	2.6	.967							
	LF	S. Byrd	191	.246	3	23	156	2	2	1	1.5	**.988**							
	C	B. Dickey	395	.322	12	72	527	49	8	13	**5.6**	.986							
	S3	R. Rolfe	279	.287	0	18	121	159	19	31		.936							
	OF	M. Hoag	251	.267	3	34	142	7	4	2	1.8	.974							
	OF	E. Combs	251	.319	2	25	145	1	1	0	2.4	.993							
	2B	D. Heffner	241	.261	0	25	158	179	10	46	5.1	.971							
	C	A. Jorgens	183	.208	0	20	288	20	5	7	5.6	.984							
	OF	G. Selkirk	176	.313	5	38	90	3	1	1	2.0	.989							
Cle. W-85 L-69 Walter Johnson	1B	H. Trosky	625	.330	35	142	**1487**	**86**	**22**	**145**	10.4	.986	M. Harder	44	255	20	12	4	2.61
	2B	O. Hale	563	.302	13	101	408	480	41	107	**6.8**	.956	M. Pearson	39	255	18	13	2	4.52
	SS	Knickerbocker	593	.317	4	67	262	451	28	106	5.1	.962	O. Hildebrand	33	198	11	9	1	4.50
	3B	W. Kamm	386	.269	0	42	109	248	8	24	3.1	**.978**	W. Hudlin	36	195	15	10	4	4.75
	RF	S. Rice	335	.293	1	33	129	2	5	0	1.7	.963	L. Brown	38	117	5	10	6	3.85
	CF	E. Averill	598	.313	31	113	**410**	12	13	3	**2.8**	.970							
	LF	J. Vosmik	405	.341	6	78	199	7	5	2	2.0	.976							
	C	F. Pytlak	289	.260	0	35	325	38	4	4	4.2	.989							
	3B	J. Burnett	208	.293	3	30	43	59	2	6	2.5	.981							
	OF	M. Galatzer	196	.270	0	15	91	7	2	0	2.0	.980							
	OF	B. Seeds	186	.247	0	18	83	2	2	0	1.8	.977							
Bos. W-76 L-76 Bucky Harris	1B	E. Morgan	528	.267	3	79	1283	56	16	111	9.9	.988	G. Rhodes	44	219	12	12	2	4.56
	2B	B. Cissell	416	.267	4	44	280	281	24	62	6.1	.959	J. Welch	41	206	13	15	0	4.49
	SS	L. Lary	419	.241	2	54	260	396	24	66	5.3	.965*	Ostermueller	33	199	10	13	3	3.49
	3B	B. Werber	623	.321	11	67	136	**323**	29	25	**3.8**	.941	W. Ferrell	26	181	14	5	1	3.63
	RF	M. Solters	365	.299	7	58	197	11	15	1	2.5	.933	H. Johnson	31	124	6	8	1	5.36
	CF	C. Reynolds	413	.303	4	86	244	6	6	3	2.6	.977	L. Grove	22	109	8	8	0	6.50
	LF	R. Johnson	569	.320	7	119	260	12	15	1	2.1	.948	R. Walberg	30	105	6	7	1	4.04
	C	R. Ferrell	437	.297	1	48	531	72	6	7	4.8	**.990**							
	OF	D. Porter	265	.302	0	56	109	1	7	1	1.6	.940							
	2B	M. Bishop	253	.261	1	22	147	155	3	37	5.4	.990							
	OF	D. Cooke	168	.244	1	26	79	1	2	0	1.9	.976							

	POS	Player	AB	BA	HR	RBI	PO	A	E	DP	TC/G	FA	Pitcher	G	IP	W	L	SV	ERA
Phi. W-68 L-82 Connie Mack	1B	J. Foxx	539	.334	44	130	1378	85	10	133	10.5	.993	J. Marcum	37	232	14	11	0	4.50
	2B	R. Warstler	419	.236	1	36	228	392	20	87	6.0	.969	S. Cain	36	231	9	17	0	4.41
	SS	E. McNair	599	.280	17	82	305	489	41	109	5.5	.951	B. Dietrich	39	208	11	12	3	4.68
	3B	P. Higgins	543	.330	16	90	147	247	37	34	3.0	.914	J. Cascarella	42	194	12	15	1	4.68
	RF	E. Coleman	329	.280	14	60	140	8	3	2	1.8	.980	A. Benton	32	155	7	9	1	4.88
	CF	D. Cramer	649	.311	6	46	385	12	6	0	2.7	.985	R. Mahaffey	37	129	6	7	2	5.37
	LF	B. Johnson	547	.307	34	92	304	17	11	3	2.4	.967							
	C	C. Berry	269	.268	0	34	339	48	5	9	4.0	.987							
	OF	L. Finney	272	.279	1	28	112	3	7	1	2.3	.943							
	C	F. Hayes	248	.226	6	30	279	36	15	4	3.7	.955							
	2B	D. Williams	205	.273	2	17	110	171	13	31	5.5	.956							
	OF	B. Miller	177	.243	1	22	72	2	0	1	1.6	1.000							
St. L. W-67 L-85 Rogers Hornsby	1B	J. Burns	612	.257	13	73	1365	81	12	132	9.5	.992	B. Newsom	47	262	16	20	5	4.01
	2B	O. Melillo	552	.241	2	55	412	462	17	110	6.3	.981	G. Blaeholder	39	234	14	18	3	4.22
	SS	A. Strange	430	.233	1	45	260	392	31	84	5.5	.955	B. Hadley	39	213	10	16	1	4.35
	3B	H. Clift	572	.260	14	56	150	245	30	28	3.0	.929	D. Coffman	40	173	9	10	3	4.53
	RF	B. Campbell	481	.279	9	74	230	14	17	3	2.1	.935	I. Andrews	43	139	4	11	3	4.66
	CF	S. West	482	.326	9	55	303	14	9	3	2.7	.972	J. Knott	45	138	10	3	4	4.96
	LF	R. Pepper	564	.298	7	101	299	15	12	4	2.4	.963							
	C	R. Hemsley	431	.309	2	52	487	92	16	15	5.2	.973							
	UT	O. Bejma	262	.271	2	29	129	145	11	27		.961							
	OF	D. Garms	232	.293	0	31	111	2	7	0	2.1	.942							
	C	F. Grube	170	.288	0	11	186	21	8	4	3.9	.963							
Was. W-66 L-86 Joe Cronin	1B	J. Kuhel	263	.289	3	25	618	23	4	62	10.2	.994	E. Whitehill	32	235	14	11	0	4.52
	2B	B. Myer	524	.305	3	57	367	420	20	101	6.0	.975	M. Weaver	31	205	11	15	0	4.79
	SS	J. Cronin	504	.284	7	101	246	486	38	86	6.1	.951	B. Burke	37	168	8	8	0	3.21
	3B	C. Travis	392	.319	1	53	88	210	20	23	3.2	.937	J. Russell	54	158	5	10	7	4.17
	RF	J. Stone	419	.315	7	67	245	13	9	3	2.4	.966	L. Stewart	24	152	7	11	0	4.03
	CF	F. Schulte	524	.298	3	73	351	5	5	0	2.7	.986	T. Thomas	33	133	8	9	1	5.47
	LF	H. Manush	556	.349	11	89	293	5	6	2	2.3	.980	A. McColl	42	112	3	4	1	3.86
	C	E. Phillips	169	.195	2	16	162	21	3	4	3.5	.984	G. Crowder	29	101	4	10	3	6.79
	UT	O. Bluege	285	.246	0	11	114	202	10	28		.969							
	OF	D. Harris	235	.251	2	37	103	7	3	1	1.8	.973							
	1B	P. Susko	224	.286	2	25	608	40	8	58	11.3	.988							
	C	L. Sewell	207	.237	2	21	143	23	1	6	3.3	.994							
	UT	R. Kress	171	.228	4	24	327	32	2	21		.994							
Chi. W-53 L-99 Lew Fonseca W-4 L-13 Jimmy Dykes W-49 L-86	1B	Z. Bonura	510	.302	27	110	1239	77	5	94	10.4	.996	G. Earnshaw	33	227	14	11	0	4.52
	2B	J. Hayes	226	.257	1	31	147	188	7	35	5.6	.980	T. Lyons	30	205	11	13	1	4.87
	SS	L. Appling	452	.303	2	61	243	341	34	55	5.6	.945	M. Gaston	29	194	6	19	0	5.85
	3B	J. Dykes	456	.268	7	82	74	160	14	9	3.4	.944	S. Jones	27	183	8	12	0	5.11
	RF	E. Swanson	426	.298	0	34	193	4	4	1	1.9	.980	L. Tietje	34	176	5	14	0	4.81
	CF	M. Haas	351	.268	2	22	204	5	2	1	2.4	.991	P. Gallivan	35	127	4	7	1	5.61
	LF	A. Simmons	558	.344	18	104	286	14	4	3	2.2	.987	J. Heving	33	88	1	7	4	7.26
	C	E. Madjeski	281	.221	5	32	348	49	11	11	5.2	.973	W. Wyatt	23	68	4	11	2	7.18
	2B	B. Boken	297	.236	3	40	121	165	22	28	5.4	.929							
	OF	J. Conlan	225	.249	0	16	122	5	6	1	2.5	.955							
	3B	M. Hopkins	210	.214	2	28	63	136	9	4	3.3	.957							
	C	M. Shea	176	.159	0	5	240	35	8	4	4.7	.972							
	OF	F. Uhalt	165	.242	0	16	85	2	6	1	2.3	.935							

BATTING AND BASE RUNNING LEADERS

Batting Average

L. Gehrig, NY	.363
C. Gehringer, DET	.356
H. Manush, WAS	.349
A. Simmons, CHI	.344
J. Vosmik, CLE	.341

Slugging Average

L. Gehrig, NY	.706
J. Foxx, PHI	.653
H. Greenberg, DET	.600
H. Trosky, CLE	.598
E. Averill, CLE	.569

Home Runs

L. Gehrig, NY	49
J. Foxx, PHI	44
H. Trosky, CLE	35
B. Johnson, PHI	34
E. Averill, CLE	31

Total Bases

L. Gehrig, NY	409
H. Trosky, CLE	374
H. Greenberg, DET	356
J. Foxx, PHI	352
E. Averill, CLE	340

Runs Batted In

L. Gehrig, NY	165
H. Trosky, CLE	142
H. Greenberg, DET	139
J. Foxx, PHI	130
C. Gehringer, DET	127

Stolen Bases

B. Werber, BOS	40
J. White, DET	28
B. Chapman, NY	26
P. Fox, DET	25
G. Walker, DET	20

Hits

C. Gehringer, DET	214
L. Gehrig, NY	210
H. Trosky, CLE	206

Base on Balls

J. Foxx, PHI	111
L. Gehrig, NY	109
B. Ruth, NY	103

PITCHING LEADERS

Winning Percentage

L. Gomez, NY	.839
S. Rowe, DET	.750
F. Marberry, DET	.750
E. Auker, DET	.682
T. Bridges, DET	.667

Earned Run Average

L. Gomez, NY	2.33
M. Harder, CLE	2.61
J. Murphy, NY	3.12
E. Auker, DET	3.42
S. Rowe, DET	3.45

Wins

L. Gomez, NY	26
S. Rowe, DET	24
T. Bridges, DET	22
M. Harder, CLE	20
R. Ruffing, NY	19

Saves

J. Russell, WAS	7
L. Brown, CLE	6
B. Newsom, STL	5

Strikeouts

L. Gomez, NY	158
T. Bridges, DET	151
R. Ruffing, NY	149
S. Rowe, DET	149
M. Pearson, CLE	140

Complete Games

L. Gomez, NY	25
T. Bridges, DET	23
T. Lyons, CHI	21
S. Rowe, DET	20
R. Ruffing, NY	19
M. Pearson, CLE	19

Fewest Hits per 9 Innings

L. Gomez, NY	7.13
R. Ruffing, NY	8.15
T. Bridges, DET	8.15

Shutouts

M. Harder, CLE	6
L. Gomez, NY	6
R. Ruffing, NY	5

BATTING AND BASE RUNNING LEADERS

Home Run Percentage

L. Gehrig, NY	8.5
J. Foxx, PHI	8.2
B. Johnson, PHI	6.2

Runs Scored

C. Gehringer, DET	134
B. Werber, BOS	129
L. Gehrig, NY	128
E. Averill, CLE	128

Doubles

H. Greenberg, DET	63
C. Gehringer, DET	50
E. Averill, CLE	48

Triples

B. Chapman, NY	13
H. Manush, WAS	11

PITCHING LEADERS

Fewest Walks per 9 Innings

W. Ferrell, BOS	2.44
E. Auker, DET	2.46
G. Blaeholder, STL	2.61

Most Strikeouts per 9 Inn.

R. Ruffing, NY	5.23
L. Gomez, NY	5.05
S. Rowe, DET	5.04

Innings

L. Gomez, NY	282
T. Bridges, DET	275
S. Rowe, DET	266

Games Pitched

J. Russell, WAS	54
B. Newsom, STL	47
S. Rowe, DET	45
J. Knott, STL	45

	W	L	PCT	GB	R	OR	2B	3B	HR	BA	SA	SB	E	DP	FA	CG	BB	SO	ShO	SV	ERA
DET	101	53	.656		958	708	349	53	74	.300	.424	124	159	150	.974	74	488	640	10	14	4.06
NY	94	60	.610	7	842	669	226	61	135	.278	.419	71	157	151	.973	83	542	656	13	10	3.76
CLE	85	69	.552	16	814	763	340	46	100	.287	.423	52	172	164	.972	72	582	554	8	19	4.28
BOS	76	76	.500	24	820	775	287	70	51	.274	.383	116	188	141	.969	68	543	538	8	9	4.32
PHI	68	82	.453	31	764	838	236	50	144	.280	.425	57	196	166	.967	68	693	480	8	8	5.01
STL	67	85	.441	33	674	800	252	59	62	.268	.373	42	187	160	.969	50	632	499	6	20	4.49
WAS	66	86	.434	34	729	806	278	70	51	.278	.382	49	162	167	.974	61	503	412	3	12	4.68
CHI	53	99	.349	47	704	946	237	40	71	.263	.363	36	207	126	.966	72	628	506	4	8	5.41
					6305	6305	2205	449	688	.279	.399	547	1428	1225	.970	548	4611	4285	60	100	4.50

National League 1935

	POS	Player	AB	BA	HR	RBI	PO	A	E	DP	TC/G	FA	Pitcher	G	IP	W	L	SV	ERA
Chi. W-100 L-54 Charlie Grimm	1B	P. Cavarretta	589	.275	8	82	1347	98	20	129	10.1	.986	L. Warneke	42	262	20	13	4	3.06
	2B	B. Herman	666	.341	7	83	416	520	35	109	6.3	.964	B. Lee	39	252	20	6	1	2.96
	SS	B. Jurges	519	.241	1	59	348	484	31	99	5.9	.964	L. French	42	246	17	10	2	2.96
	3B	S. Hack	427	.311	4	64	87	237	20	21	3.1	.942	C. Root	38	201	15	8	2	3.08
	RF	C. Klein	434	.293	21	73	215	11	10	7	2.1	.958	T. Carleton	31	171	11	8	1	3.89
	CF	F. Demaree	385	.325	2	66	204	13	6	3	2.3	.973	R. Henshaw	31	143	13	5	1	3.28
	LF	A. Galan	646	.314	12	79	351	12	8	4	2.4	.978							
	C	G. Hartnett	413	.344	13	91	477	77	9	11	5.1	.984							
	O3	F. Lindstrom	342	.275	3	62	167	40	7	7		.967							
	C	K. O'Dea	202	.257	6	38	213	27	9	3	4.0	.964							
	OF	K. Cuyler	157	.268	4	18	98	5	2	1	2.5	.981							
St. L. W-96 L-58 Frankie Frisch	1B	R. Collins	578	.313	23	122	1269	95	18	107	9.2	.987	D. Dean	50	324	28	12	5	3.11
	2B	F. Frisch	354	.294	1	55	193	252	8	48	5.1	.982	P. Dean	46	270	19	12	5	3.37
	SS	L. Durocher	513	.265	8	78	313	420	28	81	5.4	.963	B. Walker	37	193	13	8	1	3.82
	3B	P. Martin	539	.299	9	54	113	171	30	17	2.8	.904	B. Hallahan	40	181	15	8	1	3.42
	RF	J. Rothrock	502	.273	3	56	283	5	6	1	2.3	.980	E. Heusser	33	123	5	5	2	2.92
	CF	T. Moore	456	.287	6	53	354	11	6	3	3.2	.984	J. Haines	30	115	6	5	2	3.59
	LF	J. Medwick	634	.353	23	126	352	8	13	0	2.4	.965	P. Collins	26	83	7	6	2	4.57
	C	B. DeLancey	301	.279	6	41	372	29	12	6	5.0	.971							
	2B	B. Whitehead	338	.263	0	33	172	218	8	43	5.0	.980							
	C	S. Davis	315	.317	1	60	335	34	3	2	4.6	.992							
	OF	E. Orsatti	221	.240	1	24	115	3	3	2	2.0	.975							
	3S	C. Gelbert	168	.292	2	21	62	95	5	16		.969							
	P	D. Dean	128	.234	2	21	13	42	2	0	1.1	.965							
N. Y. W-91 L-62 Bill Terry	1B	B. Terry	596	.341	6	64	1379	99	6	105	10.4	.996	C. Hubbell	42	303	23	12	0	3.27
	2B	M. Koenig	396	.283	3	37	123	206	11	20	5.3	.968	H. Schumacher	33	262	19	9	0	2.89
	SS	D. Bartell	539	.262	14	53	339	424	37	71	5.8	.954	R. Parmelee	34	226	14	10	0	4.22
	3B	T. Jackson	511	.301	9	80	139	220	20	13	3.0	.947	S. Castleman	29	174	15	6	0	4.09
	RF	M. Ott	593	.322	31	114	285	17	3	7	2.2	.990	A. Smith	40	124	10	8	5	3.41
	CF	H. Leiber	613	.331	22	107	357	5	13	2	2.4	.965	Fitzsimmons	18	94	4	8	0	4.02
	LF	J. Moore	681	.295	15	71	342	11	10	2	2.3	.972	A. Stout	40	88	1	4	5	4.91
	C	G. Mancuso	447	.298	5	56	484	71	16	4	4.5	.972							
	2B	H. Critz	219	.187	2	14	140	175	11	31	5.5	.966							
	2B	A. Cuccinello	165	.248	4	20	113	140	13	26	5.5	.951							
	C	H. Danning	152	.243	2	20	153	22	4	6	4.1	.978							
	P	H. Schumacher	107	.196	2	21	14	89	0	4	3.1	1.000							

	POS	Player	AB	BA	HR	RBI	PO	A	E	DP	TC/G	FA	Pitcher	G	IP	W	L	SV	ERA
Pit.	1B	G. Suhr	529	.272	10	81	1315	73	15	83	9.4	.989	C. Blanton	35	254	18	13	1	**2.58**
W-86 L-67	2B	P. Young	494	.265	7	82	282	315	30	47	5.9	.952	G. Bush	41	204	11	11	2	4.32
Pie Traynor	SS	A. Vaughan	499	.385	19	99	249	422	35	55	5.2	.950	B. Swift	39	204	15	8	1	2.70
	3B	T. Thevenow	408	.238	0	47	94	161	13	11	3.3	.951	J. Weaver	33	176	14	8	0	3.42
	RF	P. Waner	549	.321	11	78	283	13	5	2	2.2	.983	W. Hoyt	39	164	7	11	6	3.40
	CF	L. Waner	537	.309	0	46	350	5	4	1	3.0	.989	R. Birkofer	37	150	9	7	1	4.07
	LF	W. Jensen	627	.324	8	62	290	6	7	1	2.1	.977	R. Lucas	20	126	8	6	0	3.44
	C	T. Padden	302	.272	1	30	425	64	17	2	5.4	.966							
	2B	C. Lavagetto	231	.290	0	19	92	120	11	10	5.3	.951							
	C	E. Grace	224	.263	3	29	269	35	3	9	4.4	.990							
	3B	P. Traynor	204	.279	1	36	59	84	18	2	3.3	.888							
	OF	B. Hafey	184	.228	6	16	125	5	4	3	2.9	.970							
Bkn.	1B	S. Leslie	520	.308	5	93	1233	81	14	106	9.6	.989	V. Mungo	37	214	16	10	2	3.65
W-70 L-83	2B	T. Cuccinello	360	.292	8	53	158	186	8	48	5.5	.977	W. Clark	33	207	13	8	0	3.30
Casey Stengel	SS	L. Frey	515	.262	11	77	264	388	44	72	5.5	.937	G. Earnshaw	25	166	8	12	0	4.12
	3B	J. Stripp	373	.306	3	43	63	162	9	17	2.7	.962	T. Zachary	25	158	7	12	4	3.59
	RF	B. Boyle	475	.272	4	44	244	18	10	5	2.2	.963	J. Babich	37	143	7	14	0	6.66
	CF	F. Bordagaray	422	.282	1	39	227	14	5	2	2.3	.980	D. Leonard	43	138	2	9	8	3.92
	LF	D. Taylor	352	.290	7	59	193	4	6	0	2.1	.970	R. Benge	23	125	9	9	1	4.48
	C	A. Lopez	379	.251	3	39	472	65	11	8	4.3	.980							
	UT	J. Bucher	473	.302	7	58	194	188	18	29		.955							
	OF	L. Koenecke	325	.283	4	27	222	3	8	0	2.6	.966							
	2S	J. Jordan	295	.278	0	30	174	273	12	39		.974							
	C	B. Phelps	121	.364	5	22	118	16	6	4	4.1	.957							
Cin.	1B	J. Bottomley	399	.258	1	49	934	53	8	74	10.3	.992	P. Derringer	45	277	22	13	2	3.51
W-68 L-85	2B	A. Kampouris	499	.246	7	62	367	411	35	88	5.8	.957	Hollingsworth	38	173	6	13	0	3.89
Chuck Dressen	SS	B. Myers	445	.267	5	36	230	335	37	77	5.4	.939	G. Schott	33	159	8	11	0	3.91
	3B	L. Riggs	532	.278	5	46	132	**269**	31	21	**3.2**	.928	T. Freitas	31	144	5	10	2	4.57
	RF	I. Goodman	592	.269	12	72	322	17	14	4	2.4	.960	S. Johnson	30	130	5	11	0	6.23
	CF	S. Byrd	416	.262	9	52	284	10	9	1	2.6	.970	B. Frey	38	114	6	10	2	6.85
	LF	B. Herman	349	.335	10	58	156	5	4	0	2.2	.976	D. Brennan	38	114	5	5	3	3.15
	C	E. Lombardi	332	.343	12	64	298	49	6	4	4.3	.983	L. Herrmann	29	108	3	5	0	3.58
	13	B. Sullivan	241	.266	2	36	368	61	4	40		.991							
	OF	K. Cuyler	223	.251	2	22	123	5	2	2	2.3	.985							
	C	G. Campbell	218	.257	3	30	238	36	4	1	4.2	.986							
	UT	G. Slade	196	.281	1	14	91	115	11	20		.949							
Phi.	1B	D. Camilli	602	.261	25	83	**1442**	96	**20**	118	10.0	.987	C. Davis	44	231	16	14	2	3.66
W-64 L-89	2B	L. Chiozza	472	.284	3	47	296	405	39	54	6.2	.947	O. Jorgens	53	188	10	15	2	4.83
Jimmie Wilson	SS	M. Haslin	407	.265	3	52	212	249	34	52	5.7	.931	S. Johnson	37	175	10	8	6	3.56
	3B	J. Vergez	546	.249	9	63	**188**	222	20	**25**	2.9	**.953**	J. Bivin	47	162	2	9	1	5.79
	RF	J. Moore	600	.323	19	93	233	18	7	6	1.7	.973	B. Walters	24	151	9	9	0	4.17
	CF	E. Allen	645	.307	8	63	412	**26**	9	6	2.9	.980	J. Bowman	33	148	7	10	1	4.25
	LF	G. Watkins	600	.270	17	76	325	18	15	4	2.4	.958							
	C	A. Todd	328	.290	3	42	292	37	11	5	3.9	.968							
	C	J. Wilson	290	.279	1	37	329	44	7	9	4.9	.982							
	S2	C. Gomez	222	.230	0	16	150	216	19	36		.951							
Bos.	1B	B. Jordan	470	.279	5	35	857	66	16	59	9.9	.983	F. Frankhouse	40	231	11	15	0	4.76
W-38 L-115	2B	J. Mallon	412	.274	2	25	166	219	10	31	5.4	.975	B. Cantwell	39	211	4	**25**	0	4.61
Bill McKechnie	SS	B. Urbanski	514	.230	4	30	258	356	40	52	5.1	.939	B. Smith	46	203	8	18	5	3.94
	3B	P. Whitney	458	.240	4	60	83	144	10	8	3.2	.958	E. Brandt	29	175	5	19	0	5.00
	RF	R. Moore	407	.275	4	42	161	10	9	3	2.3	.950	H. Betts	44	160	2	9	0	5.47
	CF	W. Berger	589	.295	34	130	458	8	17	1	3.2	.965	MacFayden	28	152	5	13	0	5.10
	LF	H. Lee	422	.303	0	39	273	7	11	0	2.6	.962							
	C	A. Spohrer	260	.242	1	16	230	45	12	4	3.2	.958							
	OF	T. Thompson	297	.243	4	30	184	9	7	3	2.4	.965							
	UT	J. Coscarart	284	.236	1	29	115	177	14	20		.954							
	C	S. Hogan	163	.301	2	25	175	25	2	2	3.6	.990							

BATTING AND BASE RUNNING LEADERS

Batting Average
A. Vaughan, PIT	.385
J. Medwick, STL	.353
G. Hartnett, CHI	.344
E. Lombardi, CIN	.343
B. Herman, CHI	.341

Slugging Average
A. Vaughan, PIT	.607
J. Medwick, STL	.576
M. Ott, NY	.555
W. Berger, BOS	.548
G. Hartnett, CHI	.545

Home Runs
W. Berger, BOS	34
M. Ott, NY	31
D. Camilli, PHI	25
R. Collins, STL	23
J. Medwick, STL	23

Total Bases
J. Medwick, STL	365
M. Ott, NY	329
W. Berger, BOS	323
B. Herman, CHI	317
H. Leiber, NY	314

Runs Batted In
W. Berger, BOS	130
J. Medwick, STL	126
R. Collins, STL	122
M. Ott, NY	114
H. Leiber, NY	107

Stolen Bases
A. Galan, CHI	22
P. Martin, STL	20
F. Bordagaray, BKN	18
S. Hack, CHI	14
I. Goodman, CIN	14

PITCHING LEADERS

Winning Percentage
B. Lee, CHI	.769
S. Castleman, NY	.714
D. Dean, STL	.700
H. Schumacher, NY	.679
C. Hubbell, NY	.657

Earned Run Average
C. Blanton, PIT	2.58
B. Swift, PIT	2.70
H. Schumacher, NY	2.89
L. French, CHI	2.96
B. Lee, CHI	2.96

Wins
D. Dean, STL	28
C. Hubbell, NY	23
P. Derringer, CIN	22
B. Lee, CHI	20
L. Warneke, CHI	20

Saves
D. Leonard, BKN	8
W. Hoyt, PIT	6
S. Johnson, PHI	6

Strikeouts
D. Dean, STL	182
C. Hubbell, NY	150
V. Mungo, BKN	143
P. Dean, STL	143
C. Blanton, PIT	142

Complete Games
D. Dean, STL	29
C. Hubbell, NY	24
C. Blanton, PIT	23
L. Warneke, CHI	20
P. Derringer, CIN	20

BATTING AND BASE RUNNING LEADERS

Hits
B. Herman, CHI	227
J. Medwick, STL	224

Base on Balls
A. Vaughan, PIT	97
A. Galan, CHI	87
M. Ott, NY	82

Home Run Percentage
W. Berger, BOS	5.8
M. Ott, NY	5.2
C. Klein, CHI	4.8

Runs Scored
A. Galan, CHI	133
J. Medwick, STL	132
P. Martin, STL	121

Doubles
B. Herman, CHI	57
J. Medwick, STL	46
E. Allen, PHI	46

Triples
I. Goodman, CIN	18
L. Waner, PIT	14
J. Medwick, STL	13

PITCHING LEADERS

Fewest Hits per 9 Innings
C. Blanton, PIT	7.79
H. Schumacher, NY	8.08
R. Parmelee, NY	8.52

Shutouts
5 tied with	4

Fewest Walks per 9 Innings
W. Clark, BKN	1.22
C. Hubbell, NY	1.46
P. Derringer, CIN	1.59

Most Strikeouts per 9 Inn.
V. Mungo, BKN	6.00
D. Dean, STL	5.05
C. Blanton, PIT	5.02

Innings
D. Dean, STL	324
C. Hubbell, NY	303
P. Derringer, CIN	277

Games Pitched
O. Jorgens, PHI	53
D. Dean, STL	50
J. Bivin, PHI	47

	W	L	PCT	GB	R	OR	2B	3B	HR	BA	SA	SB	E	DP	FA	CG	BB	SO	ShO	SV	ERA
CHI	100	54	.649		847	597	303	62	88	.288	.414	66	186	163	.970	81	400	589	12	14	3.26
STL	96	58	.623	4	829	625	286	59	86	.284	.405	71	164	133	.972	73	382	594	9	18	3.54
NY	91	62	.595	8.5	770	675	248	56	123	.286	.416	32	174	129	.972	76	411	524	10	11	3.78
PIT	86	67	.562	13.5	743	647	255	90	66	.285	.402	30	190	94	.968	76	312	549	15	11	3.42
BKN	70	83	.458	29.5	711	767	235	62	59	.277	.376	60	188	146	.969	62	436	480	11	20	4.22
CIN	68	85	.444	31.5	646	772	244	68	73	.265	.378	72	204	139	.966	59	438	500	9	12	4.30
PHI	64	89	.418	35.5	685	871	249	32	92	.269	.378	52	228	145	.963	53	505	475	8	15	4.76
BOS	38	115	.248	61.5	575	852	233	33	75	.263	.362	20	197	101	.967	54	404	355	6	5	4.93
					5806	5806	2053	462	662	.277	.391	403	1531	1050	.968	534	3288	4066	80	106	4.02

American League 1935

	POS	Player	AB	BA	HR	RBI	PO	A	E	DP	TC/G	FA	Pitcher	G	IP	W	L	SV	ERA
Det.	1B	H. Greenberg	619	.328	36	170	1437	99	13	142	10.2	.992	S. Rowe	42	276	19	13	3	3.69
W-93 L-58	2B	C. Gehringer	610	.330	19	108	349	489	13	99	5.7	.985	T. Bridges	36	274	21	10	1	3.51
Mickey Cochrane	SS	B. Rogell	560	.275	6	71	280	512	24	104	5.4	.971	G. Crowder	33	241	16	10	0	4.26
	3B	M. Owen	483	.263	2	71	148	215	16	19	2.9	.958	E. Auker	36	195	18	7	0	3.83
	RF	P. Fox	517	.321	15	73	244	9	3	1	2.0	.988	J. Sullivan	25	126	6	6	0	3.51
	CF	J. White	412	.240	2	32	247	7	10	1	2.7	.962	C. Hogsett	40	97	6	6	5	3.54
	LF	G. Goslin	590	.292	9	109	326	6	12	2	2.4	.965							
	C	M. Cochrane	411	.319	5	47	504	50	6	6	5.1	.989							
	OF	G. Walker	362	.301	7	53	204	2	10	1	2.5	.954							
	C	R. Hayworth	175	.309	0	22	211	35	1	4	5.1	.996							
	P	S. Rowe	109	.312	3	28	11	42	1	1	1.3	.981							
N. Y.	1B	L. Gehrig	535	.329	30	119	1337	82	15	96	9.6	.990	L. Gomez	34	246	12	15	1	3.18
W-89 L-60	2B	T. Lazzeri	477	.273	13	83	285	329	19	72	5.4	.970	R. Ruffing	30	222	16	11	0	3.12
Joe McCarthy	SS	F. Crosetti	305	.256	8	50	153	261	16	42	4.9	.963	J. Broaca	29	201	15	7	0	3.58
	3B	R. Rolfe	639	.300	5	67	166	239	15	16	3.1	.964	J. Allen	23	167	13	6	0	3.61
	RF	G. Selkirk	491	.312	11	94	269	9	7	1	2.2	.975	V. Tamulis	30	161	10	5	1	4.09
	CF	B. Chapman	553	.289	8	74	372	25	15	7	3.0	.964	J. Murphy	40	117	10	5	0	4.08
	LF	J. Hill	392	.293	4	33	203	9	11	1	2.4	.951	J. Brown	20	87	6	5	0	3.61
	C	B. Dickey	448	.279	14	81	536	62	3	7	5.1	.995	P. Malone	29	56	3	5	3	5.43
	OF	E. Combs	298	.282	3	35	143	2	1	0	2.1	.993							
Cle.	1B	H. Trosky	632	.271	26	113	1567	88	11	129	10.9	.993	M. Harder	42	287	22	11	2	3.29
W-82 L-71	2B	B. Berger	461	.258	5	43	309	419	27	91	6.3	.964	W. Hudlin	36	232	15	11	5	3.69
Walter Johnson	SS	Knickerbocker	540	.298	0	55	247	453	32	82	5.7	.956	M. Pearson	30	182	8	13	0	4.90
Steve O'Neill	3B	O. Hale	589	.304	16	101	160	312	31	17	3.4	.938	T. Lee	32	181	7	10	1	4.04
W-46 L-48	RF	B. Campbell	308	.325	7	54	129	2	1	1	1.8	.992	O. Hildebrand	34	171	9	8	5	3.94
W-36 L-23	CF	E. Averill	563	.288	19	79	371	6	7	2	2.8	.982	L. Brown	42	122	8	7	3	3.61
	LF	J. Vosmik	620	.348	10	110	347	5	5	3	2.4	.986	L. Stewart	24	91	6	6	2	5.44
	C	E. Phillips	220	.273	1	41	233	18	5	3	3.7	.980							
	2S	R. Hughes	266	.293	0	14	151	215	13	44		.966							
	OF	M. Galatzer	259	.301	0	19	134	7	10	0	1.9	.934							
	OF	A. Wright	160	.238	2	18	56	4	1	0	1.3	.984							

POS	Player	AB	BA	HR	RBI	PO	A	E	DP	TC/G	FA	Pitcher	G	IP	W	L	SV	ERA
Bos.																		
1B	B. Dahlgren	525	.263	9	63	1433	69	**18**	109	10.2	.988	W. Ferrell	41	**322**	**25**	14	0	3.52
2B	O. Melillo	399	.261	1	39	286	372	18	85	6.4*	.973	L. Grove	35	273	20	12	1	**2.70**
SS	J. Cronin	556	.295	9	95	264	431	37	86	5.3	.949	G. Rhodes	34	146	2	10	2	5.41
3B	B. Werber	462	.255	14	61	**174**	264	27	20	**3.8**	.942	J. Welch	31	143	10	9	2	4.47
RF	D. Cooke	294	.306	3	34	172	4	5	1	2.2	.972	R. Walberg	44	143	5	9	3	3.91
CF	M. Almada	607	.290	3	59	337	22	12	3	2.5	.968	Ostermueller	22	138	7	8	1	3.92
LF	R. Johnson	553	.315	3	66	267	21	17	1	2.1	.944							
C	R. Ferrell	458	.301	3	61	520	79	13	12	4.7	.979							
UT	D. Williams	251	.251	3	25	122	154	12	21		.958							
OF	C. Reynolds	244	.270	6	35	146	7	4	0	2.5	.975							
P	W. Ferrell	150	.347	7	32	9	76	2	1	2.1	.977							
OF	B. Miller	138	.304	3	26	48	2	2	0	1.8	.962							
Chi.																		
1B	Z. Bonura	550	.295	21	92	1421	83	9	109	**11.0**	.994	J. Whitehead	28	222	13	13	0	3.72
2B	J. Hayes	329	.267	4	45	202	275	17	48	5.8	.966	V. Kennedy	31	212	11	11	1	3.91
SS	L. Appling	525	.307	1	71	**335**	**556**	39	93	**6.1**	.958	T. Lyons	23	191	15	8	0	3.02
3B	J. Dykes	403	.288	4	61	100	166	13	12	2.8	.953	L. Tietje	30	170	9	15	0	4.30
RF	M. Haas	327	.291	2	40	183	4	2	1	2.3	.989	S. Jones	21	140	8	7	0	4.05
CF	A. Simmons	525	.267	16	79	349	5	7	1	2.9	.981	R. Phelps	27	125	4	8	1	4.82
LF	R. Radcliff	623	.286	10	68	231	8	8	1	1.7	.968	C. Fischer	24	89	5	5	0	6.19
C	L. Sewell	421	.285	2	67	399	83	6	10	4.4	.988	W. Wyatt	30	52	4	3	5	6.75
OF	G. Washington	339	.283	8	47	137	10	4	2	1.9	.974							
2B	T. Piet	292	.298	3	27	129	216	9	32	6.0	.975							
Was.																		
1B	J. Kuhel	633	.261	2	74	1425	87	14	**150**	10.1	.991	E. Whitehill	34	279	14	13	0	4.29
2B	B. Myer	616	**.349**	5	100	**460**	473	20	**138**	6.3	.979	B. Hadley	35	230	10	15	0	4.92
SS	O. Bluege	320	.263	0	34	117	177	10	32	5.2	.967	B. Newsom	28	198	11	12*	2	4.45
3B	C. Travis	534	.318	0	61	136	254	15	29	3.6	.963	E. Linke	40	178	11	7	3	5.01
RF	J. Stone	454	.315	1	78	224	12	11	4	2.2	.955	J. Russell	43	126	4	9	3	5.71
CF	J. Powell	551	.312	6	98	361	10	9	4	2.8	.976	L. Pettit	41	109	8	5	3	4.95
LF	H. Manush	479	.273	4	56	251	8	4	5	2.4	.985							
C	C. Bolton	375	.304	2	55	356	52	12	8	4.0	.971							
SS	R. Kress	252	.298	2	42	118	204	12	53	6.3	.964							
OF	F. Schulte	224	.268	2	23	96	2	2	0	1.8	.980							
OF	D. Miles	216	.264	0	29	92	5	3	1	2.2	.970							
C	S. Holbrook	135	.259	2	25	145	12	8	0	3.5	.952							
St. L.																		
1B	J. Burns	549	.286	5	67	1239	57	11	115	9.3	.992	I. Andrews	50	213	13	7	1	3.54
2B	T. Carey	296	.291	0	42	189	253	18	52	6.1	.961	J. Knott	48	188	11	8	**7**	4.60
SS	L. Lary	371	.288	2	35	258	306	22	66	6.3	.962	J. Walkup	55	181	6	9	0	6.25
3B	H. Clift	475	.287	11	69	130	240	26	12	3.1	.934	R. Van Atta	53*	170	9	16	3	5.34
RF	E. Coleman	397	.287	17	71	173	11	5	1	1.9	.974	S. Cain	31	168	9	8	0	5.26
CF	S. West	527	.300	10	70	**449**	7	5	5	**3.4**	**.989**	F. Thomas	49	147	7	15	1	4.78
LF	M. Solters	552	.330	18	104	328	18	4	1	2.8	.989	D. Coffman	41	144	5	11	2	6.14
C	R. Hemsley	504	.290	0	48	510	105	13	10	4.5	.979							
OF	R. Pepper	261	.253	4	37	103	5	2	1	1.9	.982							
O1	B. Bell	220	.250	3	17	187	8	9	11		.956							
UT	J. Burnett	206	.223	0	26	71	136	13	18		.941							
2B	O. Bejma	198	.192	2	26	105	153	13	32	5.8	.952							
Phi.																		
1B	J. Foxx	535	.346	**36**	115	1109	77	3	107	9.8	**.997**	J. Marcum	39	243	17	12	3	4.08
2B	R. Warstler	496	.250	3	59	308	482	34	94	6.1	.959	B. Dietrich	43	185	7	13	3	5.39
SS	E. McNair	526	.270	4	57	232	346	27	78	5.0	.955	G. Blaeholder	23	149	6	10	0	3.99
3B	P. Higgins	524	.296	23	94	162	214	21	15	3.0	.947	W. Wilshere	27	142	9	9	1	4.05
RF	W. Moses	345	.325	5	35	157	7	10	1	2.2	.943	R. Mahaffey	27	136	8	4	0	3.90
CF	D. Cramer	**644**	.332	3	70	429	6	11	1	3.0	.975							
LF	B. Johnson	582	.299	28	109	337	13	20	4	2.5	.946							
C	P. Richards	257	.245	4	29	293	40	8	5	4.3	.977							
OF	L. Finney	410	.273	0	31	145	5	9	1	2.1	.943							
C	C. Berry	190	.253	3	29	189	37	3	7	4.1	.987							

Team records (left margin):
- **Bos.** W-78 L-75 Joe Cronin
- **Chi.** W-74 L-78 Jimmy Dykes
- **Was.** W-67 L-86 Bucky Harris
- **St. L.** W-65 L-87 Rogers Hornsby
- **Phi.** W-58 L-91 Connie Mack

BATTING AND BASE RUNNING LEADERS

Batting Average

B. Myer, WAS	.349
J. Vosmik, CLE	.348
J. Foxx, PHI	.346
D. Cramer, PHI	.332
C. Gehringer, DET	.330

Slugging Average

J. Foxx, PHI	.636
H. Greenberg, DET	.628
L. Gehrig, NY	.583
J. Vosmik, CLE	.537
P. Fox, DET	.513

Home Runs

J. Foxx, PHI	36
H. Greenberg, DET	36
L. Gehrig, NY	30
B. Johnson, PHI	28
H. Trosky, CLE	26

Total Bases

H. Greenberg, DET	389
J. Foxx, PHI	340
J. Vosmik, CLE	333
M. Solters, BOS, STL	314
L. Gehrig, NY	312

Runs Batted In

H. Greenberg, DET	170
L. Gehrig, NY	119
J. Foxx, PHI	115
H. Trosky, CLE	113
M. Solters, BOS, STL	112

Stolen Bases

B. Werber, BOS	29
L. Lary, STL, WAS	28
M. Almada, BOS	20
J. White, DET	19
B. Chapman, NY	17

PITCHING LEADERS

Winning Percentage

E. Auker, DET	.720
J. Broaca, NY	.682
T. Bridges, DET	.677
M. Harder, CLE	.667
T. Lyons, CHI	.652

Earned Run Average

L. Grove, BOS	2.70
T. Lyons, CHI	3.02
R. Ruffing, NY	3.12
L. Gomez, NY	3.18
M. Harder, CLE	3.29

Wins

W. Ferrell, BOS	25
M. Harder, CLE	22
T. Bridges, DET	21
L. Grove, BOS	20
S. Rowe, DET	19

Saves

J. Knott, STL	7
C. Hogsett, DET	5
J. Murphy, NY	5
W. Wyatt, CHI	5
O. Hildebrand, CLE	5
W. Hudlin, CLE	5

Strikeouts

T. Bridges, DET	163
S. Rowe, DET	140
L. Gomez, NY	138
L. Grove, BOS	121
J. Allen, NY	113

Complete Games

W. Ferrell, BOS	31
L. Grove, BOS	23
T. Bridges, DET	23
S. Rowe, DET	21

BATTING AND BASE RUNNING LEADERS

Hits
J. Vosmik, CLE	216
B. Myer, WAS	215
D. Cramer, PHI	214

Base on Balls
L. Gehrig, NY	132
L. Appling, CHI	122
J. Foxx, PHI	114

Home Run Percentage
J. Foxx, PHI	6.7
H. Greenberg, DET	5.8
L. Gehrig, NY	5.6

Runs Scored
L. Gehrig, NY	125
C. Gehringer, DET	123
H. Greenberg, DET	121

Doubles
J. Vosmik, CLE	47
H. Greenberg, DET	46
M. Solters, BOS, STL	45

Triples
J. Vosmik, CLE	20
J. Stone, WAS	18
H. Greenberg, DET	16

PITCHING LEADERS

Fewest Hits per 9 Innings
J. Allen, NY	8.03
R. Ruffing, NY	8.15
L. Gomez, NY	8.16

Shutouts
S. Rowe, DET	6
M. Harder, CLE	4
T. Bridges, DET	4

Fewest Walks per 9 Innings
M. Harder, CLE	1.66
L. Grove, BOS	2.14
S. Rowe, DET	2.22

Most Strikeouts per 9 Inn.
J. Allen, NY	6.09
T. Bridges, DET	5.35
L. Gomez, NY	5.05

Innings
W. Ferrell, BOS	322
M. Harder, CLE	287
E. Whitehill, WAS	279

Games Pitched
R. Van Atta, NY, STL	58
J. Walkup, STL	55
I. Andrews, STL	50

	W	L	PCT	GB	R	OR	2B	3B	HR	BA	SA	SB	E	DP	FA	CG	BB	SO	ShO	SV	ERA
DET	93	58	.616		919	665	301	83	106	.290	.435	70	128	154	.978	87	522	584	16	11	3.82
NY	89	60	.597	3	818	632	255	70	104	.280	.416	68	151	114	.974	76	516	594	12	13	3.60
CLE	82	71	.536	12	776	739	324	77	93	.284	.421	63	177	147	.972	67	457	498	11	21	4.15
BOS	78	75	.510	16	718	732	281	63	69	.276	.392	89	194	136	.969	82	520	470	6	11	4.05
CHI	74	78	.487	19.5	738	750	262	42	74	.275	.382	46	146	133	.976	80	574	436	8	8	4.38
WAS	67	86	.438	27	823	903	255	95	32	.285	.381	54	171	186	.972	67	613	456	5	12	5.25
STL	65	87	.428	28.5	718	930	291	51	73	.270	.384	45	187	138	.970	42	640	435	4	15	5.26
PHI	58	91	.389	34	710	869	243	44	112	.279	.406	42	190	150	.968	58	704	469	7	10	5.12
					6220	6220	2212	525	663	.280	.402	477	1344	1158	.972	559	4546	3942	69	101	4.45

National League 1936

	POS	Player	AB	BA	HR	RBI	PO	A	E	DP	TC/G	FA	Pitcher	G	IP	W	L	SV	ERA
N. Y. W-92 L-62 Bill Terry	1B	S. Leslie	417	.295	6	54	1030	68	10	81	11.2	.991	C. Hubbell	42	304	26	6	3	2.31
	2B	B. Whitehead	632	.278	4	47	442	552	32	107	6.7	.969	H. Schumacher	35	214	11	13	1	3.49
	SS	D. Bartell	510	.298	8	42	317	559	40	106	6.4	.956	A. Smith	43	209	14	13	2	3.78
	3B	T. Jackson	465	.230	7	53	99	196	15	8	2.7	.952	F. Gabler	43	162	9	8	6	3.12
	RF	M. Ott	534	.328	33	135	250	20	4	3	1.9	.985	Fitzsimmons	28	141	10	7	2	3.32
	CF	H. Leiber	337	.279	9	67	165	9	7	3	2.1	.961	H. Gumbert	39	141	11	3	0	3.90
	LF	J. Moore	649	.316	7	63	291	25	6	3	2.2	.981	S. Castleman	29	112	4	7	1	5.64
	C	G. Mancuso	519	.301	9	63	524	104	15	15	4.7	.977	D. Coffman	42	102	7	5	7	3.90
	OF	J. Ripple	311	.305	7	47	190	5	4	10	2.6	.980							
	1B	B. Terry	229	.310	2	39	525	41	2	55	10.1	.996							
Chi. W-87 L-67 Charlie Grimm	1B	P. Cavarretta	458	.273	9	56	980	71	14	93	9.3	.987	B. Lee	43	259	18	11	1	3.31
	2B	B. Herman	632	.334	5	93	457	492	24	110	6.4	.975	L. French	43	252	18	9	3	3.39
	SS	B. Jurges	429	.280	1	42	249	379	26	80	5.6	.960	L. Warneke	40	241	16	13	1	3.44
	3B	S. Hack	561	.298	6	78	121	202	17	13	2.4	.950	T. Carleton	35	197	14	10	1	3.65
	RF	F. Demaree	605	.350	16	96	285	16	10	1	2.0	.968	C. Davis	24	153	11	9	1	3.00
	CF	A. Galan	575	.264	8	81	381	9	5	3	2.7	.987	R. Henshaw	39	129	6	5	1	3.97
	LF	E. Allen	373	.295	3	39	191	2	4	2	2.2	.980	C. Root	33	74	3	6	1	4.15
	C	G. Hartnett	424	.307	7	64	504	75	5	8	5.1	.991							
	C	K. O'Dea	189	.307	2	38	211	27	5	1	4.4	.979							
	SS	W. English	182	.247	0	20	75	127	5	27	4.9	.976							
	OF	J. Gill	174	.253	7	28	72	3	5	1	2.0	.938							
St. L. W-87 L-67 Frankie Frisch	1B	J. Mize	414	.329	19	93	897	66	6	63	10.0	.994	D. Dean	51	315	24	13	11	3.17
	2B	S. Martin	332	.298	6	41	169	242	22	50	5.2	.949	R. Parmelee	37	221	11	11	2	4.56
	SS	L. Durocher	510	.286	1	58	300	392	21	80	5.2	.971	J. Winford	39	192	11	10	3	3.80
	3B	C. Gelbert	280	.229	3	27	60	104	6	11	2.8	.965	E. Heusser	42	104	7	3	3	5.43
	RF	P. Martin	572	.309	11	76	226	13	6	5	1.9	.976	J. Haines	25	99	7	5	1	3.90
	CF	T. Moore	590	.264	5	47	418	14	10	7	3.3	.977	P. Dean	17	92	5	5	1	4.60
	LF	J. Medwick	636	.351	18	138	367	16	6	4	2.5	.985	B. Walker	21	80	5	6	1	5.87
	C	S. Davis	363	.273	4	59	390	59	7	7	4.4	.985							
	2B	F. Frisch	303	.274	1	26	124	176	11	27	5.1	.965							
	1B	R. Collins	277	.292	13	48	475	37	5	48	8.5	.990							
	C	B. Ogrodowski	237	.228	1	20	314	32	4	6	4.1	.989							
	32	A. Garibaldi	232	.276	1	20	97	119	11	7		.952							

Pit. W-84 L-70 — Pie Traynor

POS	Player	AB	BA	HR	RBI	PO	A	E	DP	TC/G	FA	Pitcher	G	IP	W	L	SV	ERA
1B	G. Suhr	583	.312	11	118	1432	93	10	100	9.8	.993	B. Swift	45	262	16	16	2	4.01
2B	P. Young	475	.248	6	77	318	361	24	39	5.7	.966	C. Blanton	44	236	13	15	3	3.51
SS	A. Vaughan	568	.335	9	78	327	477	47	86	5.5	.945	J. Weaver	38	226	14	8	0	4.31
3B	B. Brubaker	554	.289	6	102	134	209	22	8	2.5	.940	R. Lucas	27	176	15	4	0	3.18
RF	P. Waner	585	.373	5	94	323	15	14	7	2.4	.960	M. Brown	47	165	10	11	3	3.87
CF	L. Waner	414	.321	1	31	245	2	4	2	2.7	.984	W. Hoyt	22	117	7	5	1	2.70
LF	W. Jensen	696	.283	10	58	338	6	9	1	2.3	.975	R. Birkofer	34	109	7	5	0	4.69
C	T. Padden	281	.249	1	31	342	62	10	6	4.8	.976							
C	A. Todd	267	.273	2	28	332	39	9	2	5.4	.976							
OF	F. Schulte	238	.261	1	17	129	1	3	1	2.4	.977							
2B	C. Lavagetto	197	.244	2	26	85	110	10	24	5.5	.951							

Cin. W-74 L-80 — Chuck Dressen

POS	Player	AB	BA	HR	RBI	PO	A	E	DP	TC/G	FA	Pitcher	G	IP	W	L	SV	ERA
1B	L. Scarsella	485	.313	3	65	1109	84	13	90	10.5	.989	P. Derringer	51	282	19	19	5	4.02
2B	A. Kampouris	355	.239	5	46	270	376	21	71	5.6	.969	Hollingsworth	29	184	9	10	0	4.16
SS	B. Myers	323	.269	6	27	225	304	35	73	5.8	.938	G. Schott	31	180	11	11	1	3.80
3B	L. Riggs	538	.257	6	57	122	267	13	19	2.9	.968	B. Hallahan	23	135	5	9	0	4.33
RF	I. Goodman	489	.284	17	71	274	6	8	2	2.4	.972	B. Frey	31	131	10	8	0	4.25
CF	K. Cuyler	567	.326	7	74	322	9	9	3	2.4	.974	P. Davis	26	126	8	8	5	3.58
LF	B. Herman	380	.279	13	71	175	3	6	0	2.0	.967	L. Stine	40	122	3	8	2	5.03
C	E. Lombardi	387	.333	12	68	330	54	15	10	3.8	.962	D. Brennan	41	94	5	2	9	4.39
UT	T. Thevenow	321	.234	0	36	178	248	23	49		.949							
OF	H. Walker	258	.275	4	23	158	4	5	2	2.3	.970							
C	G. Campbell	235	.268	1	40	257	49	5	9	4.4	.984							
O2	C. Chapman	219	.247	1	22	85	49	4	6		.971							

Bos. W-71 L-83 — Bill McKechnie

POS	Player	AB	BA	HR	RBI	PO	A	E	DP	TC/G	FA	Pitcher	G	IP	W	L	SV	ERA
1B	B. Jordan	555	.323	3	66	1307	96	10	137	10.4	.993	MacFayden	37	267	17	13	0	2.87
2B	T. Cuccinello	565	.308	7	86	383	559	28	128	6.5	.971	T. Chaplin	40	231	10	15	2	4.12
SS	B. Urbanski	494	.261	0	26	188	211	27	56	5.3	.937	J. Lanning	28	153	7	11	0	3.65
3B	J. Coscarart	367	.245	2	44	91	168	18	16	2.9	.935	B. Reis	35	139	6	5	0	4.48
RF	G. Moore	637	.290	13	67	314	32	8	0	2.3	.977	B. Smith	35	136	6	7	8	3.77
CF	W. Berger	534	.288	25	91	384	10	14	1	3.1	.966	B. Cantwell	34	133	9	9	2	3.04
LF	H. Lee	565	.253	3	64	319	5	9	1	2.2	.973	R. Benge	21	115	7	9	0	5.79
C	A. Lopez	426	.242	8	50	447	107	14	9	4.5	.975							
SS	R. Warstler	304	.211	0	17	157	278	24	59	6.2	.948							
O1	T. Thompson	266	.286	4	36	359	20	5	19		.987							

Bkn. W-67 L-87 — Casey Stengel

POS	Player	AB	BA	HR	RBI	PO	A	E	DP	TC/G	FA	Pitcher	G	IP	W	L	SV	ERA
1B	B. Hassett	635	.310	3	82	1401	121	26	89	9.9	.983	V. Mungo	45	312	18	19	3	3.35
2B	J. Jordan	398	.234	2	28	209	247	14	41	4.8	.970	F. Frankhouse	41	234	13	10	2	3.65
SS	L. Frey	524	.279	4	60	238	331	51	52	5.3	.918	E. Brandt	38	234	11	13	2	3.50
3B	J. Stripp	439	.317	1	60	132	174	10	13	3.0	.968	M. Butcher	38	148	6	6	2	3.96
RF	F. Bordagaray	372	.315	4	31	207	8	2	0	2.4	.991	W. Clark	33	120	7	11	2	4.43
CF	J. Cooney	507	.282	0	30	336	11	2	3	2.7	.994	G. Jeffcoat	40	96	5	6	3	4.52
LF	G. Watkins	364	.255	4	43	183	5	6	1	2.0	.969	G. Earnshaw	19	93	4	9	1	5.32
C	R. Berres	267	.240	1	13	436	59	6	7	4.8	.988	T. Baker	35	88	1	8	2	4.72
UT	J. Bucher	370	.251	2	41	145	138	19	15		.937							
C	B. Phelps	319	.367	5	57	334	49	9	6	4.0	.977							
OF	E. Wilson	173	.347	3	25	72	3	6	0	1.7	.926							

Phi. W-54 L-100 — Jimmie Wilson

POS	Player	AB	BA	HR	RBI	PO	A	E	DP	TC/G	FA	Pitcher	G	IP	W	L	SV	ERA
1B	D. Camilli	530	.315	28	102	1446	79	18	122	10.3	.988	B. Walters	40	258	11	21	0	4.26
2B	C. Gomez	332	.232	0	28	137	229	20	33	5.4	.948	C. Passeau	49	217	11	15	3	3.48
SS	L. Norris	581	.265	11	76	317	345	45	70	5.8	.936	J. Bowman	40	204	9	20	1	5.04
3B	P. Whitney	411	.294	6	59	106	212	15	15	3.0*	.955	O. Jorgens	39	167	8	8	0	4.79
RF	C. Klein	492	.309	20	86	213	13	17*	2	2.1	.930	S. Johnson	39	111	5	7	7	4.30
CF	L. Chiozza	572	.297	1	48	235	7	7	10	2.8	.972							
LF	J. Moore	472	.328	16	68	214	5	12	1	2.1	.948							
C	E. Grace	221	.249	4	32	217	29	6	3	3.9	.976							
OF	E. Sulik	404	.287	6	36	227	6	7	1	2.3	.971							
C	J. Wilson	230	.278	1	27	187	31	9	5	3.6	.960							
C	B. Atwood	192	.302	2	29	184	27	6	3	4.1	.972							

BATTING AND BASE RUNNING LEADERS

Batting Average

P. Waner, PIT	.373
B. Phelps, BKN	.367
J. Medwick, STL	.351
F. Demaree, CHI	.350
A. Vaughan, PIT	.335

Slugging Average

M. Ott, NY	.588
D. Camilli, PHI	.577
J. Mize, STL	.577
J. Medwick, STL	.577
P. Waner, PIT	.520

Home Runs

M. Ott, NY	33
D. Camilli, PHI	28
W. Berger, BOS	25
C. Klein, CHI, PHI	25
J. Mize, STL	19

Total Bases

J. Medwick, STL	367
M. Ott, NY	314
C. Klein, CHI, PHI	308
D. Camilli, PHI	306
P. Waner, PIT	304

Runs Batted In

J. Medwick, STL	138
M. Ott, NY	135
G. Suhr, PIT	118
C. Klein, CHI, PHI	104
D. Camilli, PHI	102
B. Brubaker, PIT	102

Stolen Bases

P. Martin, STL	23
S. Martin, STL	17
S. Hack, CHI	17
L. Chiozza, PHI	17

PITCHING LEADERS

Winning Percentage

C. Hubbell, NY	.813
R. Lucas, PIT	.789
L. French, CHI	.667
D. Dean, STL	.649
B. Lee, CHI	.621

Earned Run Average

C. Hubbell, NY	2.31
MacFayden, BOS	2.87
D. Dean, STL	3.17
R. Lucas, PIT	3.18
B. Lee, CHI	3.31

Wins

C. Hubbell, NY	26
D. Dean, STL	24
P. Derringer, CIN	19
L. French, CHI	18
B. Lee, CHI	18
V. Mungo, BKN	18

Saves

D. Dean, STL	11
D. Brennan, CIN	9
B. Smith, BOS	8
D. Coffman, NY	7
S. Johnson, PHI	7

Strikeouts

V. Mungo, BKN	238
D. Dean, STL	195
C. Blanton, PIT	127
C. Hubbell, NY	123
P. Derringer, CIN	121

Complete Games

D. Dean, STL	28
C. Hubbell, NY	25
V. Mungo, BKN	22
MacFayden, BOS	21
B. Lee, CHI	20

BATTING AND BASE RUNNING LEADERS

Hits		Base on Balls	
J. Medwick, STL	223	A. Vaughan, PIT	118
P. Waner, PIT	218	D. Camilli, PHI	116
F. Demaree, CHI	212	M. Ott, NY	111

Home Run Percentage		Runs Scored	
M. Ott, NY	6.2	A. Vaughan, PIT	122
D. Camilli, PHI	5.3	P. Martin, STL	121
R. Collins, STL	4.7	M. Ott, NY	120

Doubles		Triples	
J. Medwick, STL	64	I. Goodman, CIN	14
B. Herman, CHI	57	D. Camilli, PHI	13
P. Waner, PIT	53	J. Medwick, STL	13

PITCHING LEADERS

Fewest Hits per 9 Innings		Shutouts	
C. Hubbell, NY	7.85	7 tied with	4
V. Mungo, BKN	7.94		
B. Lee, CHI	8.28		

Fewest Walks per 9 Innings		Most Strikeouts per 9 Inn.	
R. Lucas, PIT	1.33	V. Mungo, BKN	6.87
P. Derringer, CIN	1.34	D. Dean, STL	5.57
D. Dean, STL	1.51	C. Blanton, PIT	4.85

Innings		Games Pitched	
D. Dean, STL	315	D. Dean, STL	51
V. Mungo, BKN	312	P. Derringer, CIN	51
C. Hubbell, NY	304	C. Passeau, PHI	49

	W	L	PCT	GB	R	OR	2B	3B	Batting HR	BA	SA	SB	E	Fielding DP	FA	CG	BB	Pitching SO	ShO	SV	ERA
NY	92	62	.597		742	621	237	48	97	.281	.395	31	168	164	.974	58	401	500	12	22	3.46
CHI	87	67	.565	5	755	603	275	36	76	.286	.392	68	146	156	.976	77	434	597	18	10	3.53
STL	87	67	.565	5	795	794	332	60	88	.281	.410	69	156	134	.974	65	477	561	5	24	4.48
PIT	84	70	.545	8	804	718	283	80	60	.286	.397	37	199	113	.967	67	379	559	5	12	3.89
CIN	74	80	.481	18	722	760	224	73	82	.274	.388	68	191	150	.969	50	418	459	6	23	4.22
BOS	71	83	.461	21	631	715	207	44	68	.265	.356	23	189	175	.971	60	451	421	7	13	3.94
BKN	67	87	.435	25	662	752	263	43	33	.272	.353	55	208	107	.966	59	528	654	7	18	3.98
PHI	54	100	.351	38	726	874	250	46	103	.281	.401	50	252	144	.959	51	515	454	7	14	4.64
					5837	5837	2071	430	607	.278	.386	401	1509	1143	.969	487	3603	4205	67	136	4.02

American League 1936

	POS	Player	AB	BA	HR	RBI	PO	A	E	DP	TC/G	FA	Pitcher	G	IP	W	L	SV	ERA
N. Y. W-102 L-51 Joe McCarthy	1B	L. Gehrig	579	.354	49	152	1377	82	9	128	9.5	.994	R. Ruffing	33	271	20	12	0	3.85
	2B	T. Lazzeri	537	.287	14	109	346	414	22	88	5.3	.968	M. Pearson	33	223	19	7	1	3.71
	SS	F. Crosetti	632	.288	15	78	320	463	43	95	5.5	.948	J. Broaca	37	206	12	7	3	4.24
	3B	R. Rolfe	568	.319	10	70	162	265	19	20	3.4	.957	L. Gomez	31	189	13	7	0	4.39
	RF	G. Selkirk	493	.308	18	107	290	10	8	3	2.3	.974	B. Hadley	31	174	14	4	1	4.35
	CF	J. Powell	324	.306	7	48	196	6	5	2	2.5	.976	P. Malone	35	135	12	4	9	3.81
	LF	J. DiMaggio	637	.323	29	125	339	22	8	2	2.7	.978	J. Murphy	27	88	9	3	5	3.38
	C	B. Dickey	423	.362	22	107	499	61	14	10	5.4	.976							
	OF	M. Hoag	156	.301	3	34	82	2	4	1	2.3	.955							
	OF	B. Chapman	139	.266	1	21	106	3	4	0	3.1	.965							
	C	J. Glenn	129	.271	1	20	167	24	6	2	4.5	.970							
	P	R. Ruffing	127	.291	5	22	13	56	1	6	2.1	.986							
	P	M. Pearson	91	.253	1	20	12	39	1	3	1.6	.981							
Det. W-83 L-71 Mickey Cochrane	1B	J. Burns	558	.283	4	63	1280	73	8	126	9.9	.994	T. Bridges	39	295	23	11	0	3.60
	2B	C. Gehringer	641	.354	15	116	397	524	25	116	6.1	.974	S. Rowe	41	245	19	10	3	4.51
	SS	B. Rogell	585	.274	6	68	286	462	20	98	5.3	.965	E. Auker	35	215	13	16	0	4.89
	3B	M. Owen	583	.295	9	105	190	281	24	28	3.2	.952	V. Sorrell	30	131	6	7	3	5.28
	RF	G. Walker	550	.353	12	93	280	14	16	5	2.5	.948	R. Lawson	41	128	8	6	3	5.48
	CF	A. Simmons	568	.327	13	112	352	8	5	1	2.6	.986							
	LF	G. Goslin	572	.315	24	125	266	11	13	1	2.0	.955							
	C	R. Hayworth	250	.240	1	30	305	28	4	5	4.2	.988							
	OF	P. Fox	220	.305	4	26	118	3	4	0	2.3	.968							
Chi. W-81 L-70 Jimmy Dykes	1B	Z. Bonura	587	.330	12	138	1500	107	7	150	11.1	.996	V. Kennedy	35	274	21	9	0	4.63
	2B	J. Hayes	417	.312	5	84	216	334	12	70	6.3	.979	J. Whitehead	34	231	13	13	1	4.64
	SS	L. Appling	526	.388	6	128	320	471	41	119	6.1	.951	S. Cain	30	195	14	10	0	4.75
	3B	J. Dykes	435	.267	7	60	108	240	18	14	2.9	.951	T. Lyons	26	182	10	13	0	5.14
	RF	M. Haas	408	.284	0	46	176	7	2	2	1.9	.989	M. Stratton	16	95	5	7	0	5.21
	CF	M. Kreevich	550	.307	5	69	300	17	12	5	2.5	.964	C. Brown	38	83	6	2	5	4.99
	LF	R. Radcliff	618	.335	8	82	213	6	15	2	1.8	.936	R. Phelps	15	69	4	6	0	6.03
	C	L. Sewell	451	.251	5	73	461	87	9	12	4.4	.984							
	23	T. Piet	352	.273	7	42	167	317	18	49		.964							
	OF	L. Rosenthal	317	.281	3	46	243	7	6	3	3.2	.977							

POS	Player	AB	BA	HR	RBI	PO	A	E	DP	TC/G	FA	Pitcher	G	IP	W	L	SV	ERA
Was.												B. Newsom	43	286	17	15	2	4.32
W-82 L-71												J. DeShong	34	224	18	10	2	4.63
Bucky Harris												E. Whitehill	28	212	14	11	0	4.87
1B	J. Kuhel	588	.321	16	118	1452	73	10	138	10.3	.993	P. Appleton	38	202	14	9	3	3.53
2B	O. Bluege	319	.288	1	55	128	158	2	35	5.5	.993	J. Cascarella	22	139	9	8	1	4.07
SS	C. Travis	517	.317	2	92	135	213	23	53	5.2	.938	M. Weaver	26	91	6	4	1	4.35
3B	B. Lewis	601	.291	6	67	152	297	32	24	3.5	.933							
RF	C. Reynolds	293	.276	4	41	142	8	5	0	2.2	.968							
CF	B. Chapman	401	.332	4	60	271	10	12	4	3.0	.959							
LF	J. Stone	437	.341	15	90	249	12	9	5	2.4	.967							
C	C. Bolton	289	.291	2	51	287	44	7	4	4.1	.979							
S2	R. Kress	391	.284	8	51	229	312	29	73		.949							
OF	J. Hill	233	.305	0	34	83	5	3	1	1.5	.967							
C	W. Millies	215	.312	0	25	205	40	8	3	3.5	.968							
OF	J. Powell	214	.290	1	30	115	2	6	1	2.3	.951							
2B	B. Myer	156	.269	0	15	120	143	4	31	6.2	.985							
OF	F. Sington	94	.319	1	28	52	1	3	0	2.2	.946							
Cle.												J. Allen	36	243	20	10	1	3.44
W-80 L-74												M. Harder	36	225	15	15	1	5.17
Steve O'Neill												O. Hildebrand	36	175	10	11	4	4.90
1B	H. Trosky	629	.343	42	**162**	1367	85	**22**	126	9.8	.985	D. Galehouse	36	148	8	7	1	4.85
2B	R. Hughes	638	.295	0	63	**421**	466	**25**	98	6.0	.973	L. Brown	24	140	8	10	1	4.17
SS	Knickerbocker	618	.294	8	73	313	486	40	97	5.4	.952	G. Blaeholder	35	134	8	4	0	5.09
3B	O. Hale	620	.316	14	87	169	**323**	28	26	3.5	.946	T. Lee	43	127	3	5	3	4.89
RF	R. Weatherly	349	.335	8	53	164	15	5	2	2.2	.973							
CF	E. Averill	614	.378	28	126	369	11	12	2	2.6	.969							
LF	J. Vosmik	506	.287	7	94	258	11	6	1	2.0	.978							
C	B. Sullivan	319	.351	2	48	324	40	12	8	5.2	.968							
C	F. Pytlak	224	.321	0	31	224	35	1	6	4.5	.996							
OF	B. Campbell	172	.372	6	30	68	4	3	2	1.6	.960							
Bos.												W. Ferrell	39	**301**	20	15	0	4.19
W-74 L-80												L. Grove	35	253	17	12	2	**2.81**
Joe Cronin												Ostermueller	43	181	10	16	2	4.87
1B	J. Foxx	585	.338	41	143	1226	76	12	108	9.5	.991	J. Marcum	31	174	8	13	1	4.81
2B	O. Melillo	327	.226	0	32	239	242	10	59	5.3	.980	J. Wilson	43	136	6	8	3	4.42
SS	E. McNair	494	.285	4	74	171	230	14	47	4.9	.966	R. Walberg	24	100	5	4	0	4.40
3B	B. Werber	535	.275	10	67	112	161	19	16	2.9	.935							
RF	M. Almada	320	.253	1	21	144	9	2	2	1.9	.987							
CF	D. Cramer	643	.292	0	41	**443**	20	12	**6**	3.1	.975							
LF	D. Cooke	341	.273	6	47	207	3	6	2	2.4	.972							
C	R. Ferrell	410	.312	8	55	**556**	55	8	5	5.1	**.987**							
OF	H. Manush	313	.291	0	45	110	3	4	1	1.6	.966							
UT	J. Kroner	298	.292	4	62	146	211	18	36		.952							
SS	J. Cronin	295	.281	2	43	115	191	23	34	5.5	.930							
P	W. Ferrell	135	.267	5	24	9	42	2	1	1.4	.962							
St. L.												C. Hogsett	39	215	13	15	1	5.52
W-57 L-95												J. Knott	47	193	9	17	6	7.29
Rogers Hornsby												I. Andrews	36	191	7	12	1	4.84
1B	J. Bottomley	544	.298	12	95	1250	47	10	103	9.3	.992	E. Caldwell	41	189	7	16	2	6.00
2B	T. Carey	488	.273	1	57	308	434	**25**	82	6.0	.967	T. Thomas	36	180	11	9	0	5.26
SS	L. Lary	620	.289	2	52	**339**	495	38	88	5.6	.956	R. Van Atta	**52**	123	4	7	2	6.60
3B	H. Clift	576	.302	20	73	158	310	24	27	3.2	.951							
RF	B. Bell	616	.344	11	123	291	11	8	**6**	2.2	.974							
CF	S. West	533	.278	7	70	442	10	8	2	3.1	.983							
LF	M. Solters	628	.291	17	134	356	16	17	5	2.6	.956							
C	R. Hemsley	377	.263	2	39	340	68	13	**16**	3.7	.969							
C	T. Giuliani	198	.217	0	13	226	29	9	7	4.0	.966							
OF	E. Coleman	137	.292	2	34	31	0	2	0	1.8	.939							
OF	R. Pepper	124	.282	2	23	31	1	2	0	1.9	.941							
Phi.												H. Kelley	35	235	15	12	3	3.86
W-53 L-100												G. Rhodes	35	216	9	**20**	1	5.74
Connie Mack												B. Ross	30	201	9	14	0	5.83
1B	L. Finney	**653**	.302	1	41	782	34	8	70	10.6	.990	H. Fink	34	189	8	16	3	5.39
2B	R. Warstler	236	.250	1	24	139	265	11	45	6.3	.973	B. Dietrich	21	72	4	6	3	6.53
SS	S. Newsome	471	.225	0	46	273	417	31	87	5.9	.957							
3B	P. Higgins	550	.289	12	80	151	266	26	24	3.1	.941							
RF	G. Puccinelli	457	.278	11	78	245	11	14	1	2.3	.948							
CF	W. Moses	585	.345	7	66	396	12	11	3	2.9	.974							
LF	B. Johnson	566	.292	25	121	289	13	12	3	2.4	.962							
C	F. Hayes	505	.271	10	67	489	69	16	8	4.0	.972							
1B	C. Dean	342	.287	1	48	680	37	8	62	9.4	.989							
2B	A. Niemiec	203	.197	1	20	134	180	9	32	6.2	.972							

BATTING AND BASE RUNNING LEADERS

PITCHING LEADERS

Batting Average		Slugging Average		Winning Percentage		Earned Run Average	
L. Appling, CHI	.388	L. Gehrig, NY	.696	M. Pearson, NY	.731	L. Grove, BOS	2.81
E. Averill, CLE	.378	H. Trosky, CLE	.644	V. Kennedy, CHI	.700	J. Allen, CLE	3.44
B. Dickey, NY	.362	J. Foxx, BOS	.631	T. Bridges, DET	.676	P. Appleton, WAS	3.53
C. Gehringer, DET	.354	E. Averill, CLE	.627	J. Allen, CLE	.667	T. Bridges, DET	3.60
L. Gehrig, NY	.354	B. Dickey, NY	.617	S. Rowe, DET	.655	M. Pearson, NY	3.71

Home Runs		Total Bases		Wins		Saves	
L. Gehrig, NY	49	H. Trosky, CLE	405	T. Bridges, DET	23	P. Malone, NY	9
H. Trosky, CLE	42	L. Gehrig, NY	403	V. Kennedy, CHI	21	J. Knott, STL	6
J. Foxx, BOS	41	E. Averill, CLE	385	J. Allen, CLE	20	C. Brown, CHI	5
J. DiMaggio, NY	29	J. Foxx, BOS	369	R. Ruffing, NY	20	J. Murphy, NY	5
E. Averill, CLE	28	J. DiMaggio, NY	367	W. Ferrell, BOS	20	O. Hildebrand, CLE	4

Runs Batted In		Stolen Bases		Strikeouts		Complete Games	
H. Trosky, CLE	162	L. Lary, STL	37	T. Bridges, DET	175	W. Ferrell, BOS	28
L. Gehrig, NY	152	J. Powell, NY, WAS	26	J. Allen, CLE	165	T. Bridges, DET	26
J. Foxx, BOS	143	B. Werber, BOS	23	B. Newsom, WAS	156	R. Ruffing, NY	25
Z. Bonura, CHI	138	B. Chapman, NY, WAS	20	L. Grove, BOS	130	B. Newsom, WAS	24
M. Solters, STL	134	R. Hughes, CLE	20	M. Pearson, NY	118	L. Grove, BOS	22

BATTING AND BASE RUNNING LEADERS

Hits		Base on Balls	
E. Averill, CLE	232	L. Gehrig, NY	130
C. Gehringer, DET	227	L. Lary, STL	117
H. Trosky, CLE	216	H. Clift, STL	115

Home Run Percentage		Runs Scored	
L. Gehrig, NY	8.5	L. Gehrig, NY	167
J. Foxx, BOS	7.0	H. Clift, STL	145
H. Trosky, CLE	6.7	C. Gehringer, DET	144

Doubles		Triples	
C. Gehringer, DET	60	R. Rolfe, NY	15
G. Walker, DET	55	E. Averill, CLE	15
B. Chapman, NY, WAS	50	J. DiMaggio, NY	15
O. Hale, CLE	50		

PITCHING LEADERS

Fewest Hits per 9 Innings		Shutouts	
M. Pearson, NY	7.71	L. Grove, BOS	6
L. Grove, BOS	8.42	T. Bridges, DET	5
J. Allen, CLE	8.67		

Fewest Walks per 9 Innings		Most Strikeouts per 9 Inn.	
T. Lyons, CHI	2.23	J. Allen, CLE	6.11
L. Grove, BOS	2.31	T. Bridges, DET	5.35
S. Rowe, DET	2.35	L. Gomez, NY	5.01

Innings		Games Pitched	
W. Ferrell, BOS	301	R. Van Atta, STL	52
T. Bridges, DET	295	J. Knott, STL	47
B. Newsom, WAS	286		

	W	L	PCT	GB	R	OR	2B	3B	HR	BA	SA	SB	E	DP	FA	CG	BB	SO	ShO	SV	ERA
NY	102	51	.667		1065	731	315	83	182	.300	.483	76	163	148	.973	77	663	624	6	21	4.17
DET	83	71	.539	19.5	921	871	326	55	94	.300	.431	72	153	159	.975	76	562	526	13	13	5.00
CHI	81	70	.536	20	920	873	282	56	60	.292	.397	66	168	174	.973	80	578	414	5	8	5.06
WAS	82	71	.536	20	889	799	293	84	62	.295	.414	103	182	163	.970	78	588	462	8	14	4.58
CLE	80	74	.519	22.5	921	862	357	82	123	.304	.461	66	178	154	.971	80	607	619	6	12	4.83
BOS	74	80	.481	28.5	775	764	288	62	86	.276	.400	54	165	139	.972	78	552	584	11	9	4.39
STL	57	95	.375	44.5	804	1064	299	66	79	.279	.403	62	188	143	.969	54	609	399	3	13	6.24
PHI	53	100	.346	49	714	1045	240	60	72	.269	.376	59	209	152	.965	68	696	405	3	12	6.08
					7009	7009	2400	548	758	.289	.421	558	1406	1232	.971	591	4855	4033	55	102	5.04

National League 1937

	POS	Player	AB	BA	HR	RBI	PO	A	E	DP	TC/G	FA	Pitcher	G	IP	W	L	SV	ERA
N. Y. W-95 L-57 Bill Terry	1B	J. McCarthy	420	.279	10	65	1123	82	16	89	11.1	.987	C. Hubbell	39	262	22	8	4	3.20
	2B	B. Whitehead	574	.286	5	52	394	514	24	106	6.1	.974	C. Melton	46	248	20	9	7	2.61
	SS	D. Bartell	516	.306	14	62	281	476	33	96	6.2	.958	H. Schumacher	38	218	13	12	1	3.60
	3B	L. Chiozza	439	.232	4	29	90	171	17	9	3.0	.939	H. Gumbert	34	200	10	11	1	3.68
	RF	M. Ott	545	.294	31	95	156	13	0	1	1.9	1.000	S. Castleman	23	160	11	6	0	3.31
	CF	J. Ripple	426	.317	5	66	193	6	4	1	1.8	.980	D. Coffman	42	80	8	3	3	3.04
	LF	J. Moore	580	.310	6	57	226	12	6	0	1.7	.975							
	C	H. Danning	292	.288	8	51	332	57	7	7	4.6	.982							
	C	G. Mancuso	287	.279	4	39	410	69	9	4	6.0	.982							
	OF	W. Berger	199	.291	12	43	107	4	4	0	2.2	.965							
	1B	S. Leslie	191	.309	3	30	444	38	5	45	11.1	.990							
	OF	H. Leiber	184	.293	4	32	78	1	1	0	1.7	.988							
Chi. W-93 L-61 Charlie Grimm	1B	R. Collins	456	.274	16	71	1068	80	11	94	10.4	.991	B. Lee	42	272	14	15	3	3.54
	2B	B. Herman	564	.335	8	65	384	468	41	97	6.5	.954	L. French	42	208	16	10	0	3.98
	SS	B. Jurges	450	.298	1	65	258	370	16	74	5.0	.975	T. Carleton	32	208	16	8	0	3.15
	3B	S. Hack	582	.297	2	63	151	247	13	25	2.7	.968	C. Root	43	179	13	5	5	3.38
	RF	F. Demaree	615	.324	17	115	283	17	6	6	2.0	.980	R. Parmelee	33	146	7	8	0	5.13
	CF	J. Marty	290	.290	5	44	196	4	5	0	2.4	.976	C. Bryant	38	135	9	3	3	4.26
	LF	A. Galan	611	.252	18	98	328	9	7	3	2.5	.980	C. Davis	28	124	10	5	1	4.08
	C	G. Hartnett	356	.354	12	82	436	65	2	7	5.0	.996	C. Shoun	37	93	7	7	0	5.61
	O1	P. Cavarretta	329	.286	5	56	454	40	10	28		.980							
	C	K. O'Dea	219	.301	4	32	234	29	4	4	4.2	.985							
	UT	L. Frey	198	.278	1	22	90	101	10	18		.950							
	OF	T. Stainback	160	.231	0	14	99	4	2	1	2.1	.981							
Pit. W-86 L-68 Pie Traynor	1B	G. Suhr	575	.278	5	97	1452	91	11	108	10.3	.993	C. Blanton	36	243	14	12	0	3.30
	2B	L. Handley	480	.250	3	37	296	375	35	67	5.6	.950	R. Bauers	34	188	13	6	1	2.88
	SS	A. Vaughan	469	.322	5	72	231	335	26	58	5.5	.956	E. Brandt	33	176	11	10	2	3.11
	3B	B. Brubaker	413	.254	6	48	98	216	16	16	2.9	.952	B. Swift	36	164	9	10	3	3.95
	RF	P. Waner	619	.354	2	74	271	16	9	3	2.0	.970	J. Bowman	30	128	8	8	1	4.57
	CF	L. Waner	537	.330	1	45	312	8	4	0	2.6	.988	R. Lucas	20	126	8	10	0	4.27
	LF	W. Jensen	509	.279	5	45	256	5	10	1	2.3	.963	J. Weaver	32	110	8	5	0	3.20
	C	A. Todd	514	.307	8	86	603	89	20	15	5.6	.972	M. Brown	50	108	7	2	7	4.18
	UT	P. Young	408	.260	9	54	195	328	24	52		.956	J. Tobin	20	87	6	3	1	3.00
	OF	J. Dickshot	264	.254	3	33	109	5	6	2	1.9	.950							

	POS	Player	AB	BA	HR	RBI	PO	A	E	DP	TC/G	FA	Pitcher	G	IP	W	L	SV	ERA
St. L.	1B	J. Mize	560	.364	25	113	1308	67	17	104	9.7	.988	B. Weiland	41	264	15	14	0	3.54
W-81 L-73	2B	J. Brown	525	.276	2	53	235	360	22	57	5.5	.964	L. Warneke	36	239	18	11	0	4.53
Frankie Frisch	SS	L. Durocher	477	.203	1	47	279	381	28	72	5.1	.959	D. Dean	27	197	13	10	1	2.69
	3B	D. Gutteridge	447	.271	7	61	133	176	7	18	3.0	.978	S. Johnson	38	192	12	12	1	3.32
	RF	D. Padgett	446	.314	10	74	225	9	11	5	2.2	.955	M. Ryba	38	135	9	6	0	4.13
	CF	T. Moore	461	.267	5	43	307	9	4	2	3.0	.988	R. Harrell	35	97	3	7	1	5.87
	LF	J. Medwick	633	**.374**	**31**	**154**	329	9	4	1	2.2	**.988**							
	C	B. Ogrodowski	279	.233	3	31	387	50	7	2	5.1	.984							
	OF	P. Martin	339	.304	5	38	204	12	6	3	2.7	.973							
	3O	F. Bordagaray	300	.293	1	37	105	72	9	2		.952							
	C	M. Owen	234	.231	0	20	287	49	9	6	4.4	.974							
	2B	S. Martin	223	.260	1	17	93	134	13	27	5.0	.946							
Bos.	1B	E. Fletcher	539	.247	1	38	**1587**	108	12	**117**	**11.5**	.993	L. Fette	35	259	20	10	0	2.88
W-79 L-73	2B	T. Cuccinello	575	.271	11	80	330	**524**	29	92	5.8	.967	J. Turner	33	257	20	11	1	**2.38**
Bill McKechnie	SS	R. Warstler	555	.223	3	36	298	**493**	**49**	85	5.6	.942	MacFayden	32	246	14	14	0	2.93
	3B	G. English	269	.290	2	37	61	121	8	9	2.7	.958	G. Bush	32	181	8	15	1	3.54
	RF	G. Moore	561	.283	16	70	340	**21**	8	1	2.5	.978	J. Lanning	32	117	5	7	2	3.93
	CF	V. DiMaggio	493	.256	13	69	351	21	7	2	2.9	.982	I. Hutchinson	31	92	4	6	0	3.73
	LF	D. Garms	478	.259	2	37	168	1	4	0	2.1	.977	F. Gabler	19	76	4	7	2	5.09
	C	A. Lopez	334	.204	3	38	342	83	7	5	4.2	.984							
	OF	R. Johnson	260	.277	3	22	131	5	5	0	2.2	.965							
	C	R. Mueller	187	.251	2	26	169	44	1	6	3.8	.995							
	3B	E. Mayo	172	.227	1	18	57	73	6	2	2.7	.956							
	OF	W. Berger	113	.274	5	22	51	1	0	0	1.9	1.000							
Bkn.	1B	B. Hassett	556	.304	1	53	1125	**116**	**20**	96	9.6	.984	M. Butcher	39	192	11	15	0	4.27
W-62 L-91	2B	C. Lavagetto	503	.282	8	70	229	294	28	56	5.5	.949	L. Hamlin	39	186	11	13	1	3.59
Burleigh Grimes	SS	W. English	378	.238	1	42	220	303	24	51	4.7	.956	F. Frankhouse	33	179	10	13	0	4.27
	3B	J. Stripp	300	.243	1	26	75	91	5	4	2.6	.971	W. Hoyt	27	167	7	7	0	3.23
	RF	H. Manush	466	.333	4	73	187	7	6	1	1.6	.970	V. Mungo	25	161	9	11	3	2.91
	CF	J. Cooney	430	.293	0	37	279	9	7	2	2.7	.976	R. Henshaw	42	156	5	12	2	5.07
	LF	T. Winsett	350	.237	5	42	209	6	9	1	2.2	.960	Fitzsimmons	13	91	4	8	0	4.27
	C	B. Phelps	409	.313	7	58	465	76	16	10	5.0	.971							
	23	J. Bucher	380	.253	4	37	165	192	23	35		.939							
	OF	G. Brack	372	.274	5	38	208	10	7	0	2.2	.969							
Phi.	1B	D. Camilli	475	.339	27	80	1256	99	8	104	10.4	**.994**	C. Passeau	50	**292**	14	18	2	4.34
W-61 L-92	2B	D. Young	360	.194	0	24	200	333	28	63	5.2	.950	B. Walters	37	246	14	15	0	4.75
Jimmie Wilson	SS	G. Scharein	511	.241	0	57	**335**	456	44	**98**	5.7	.947	W. LaMaster	50	220	15	**19**	4	5.31
	3B	P. Whitney	487	.341	8	79	136	238	7	17	2.9	**.982**	H. Mulcahy	**56**	216	8	18	3	5.13
	RF	C. Klein	406	.325	15	57	175	11	10	3	1.9	.949	O. Jorgens	52	141	3	4	3	4.41
	CF	H. Martin	579	.283	8	49	**353**	9	8	1	2.7	.978	S. Johnson	32	138	4	10	3	5.02
	LF	M. Arnovich	410	.290	10	60	237	10	7	5	2.4	.972							
	C	B. Atwood	279	.244	2	32	290	48	11	5	4.4	.968							
	UT	L. Norris	381	.257	9	36	212	264	22	43		.956							
	OF	E. Browne	332	.292	6	52	92	7	2	1	1.9	.980							
	OF	J. Moore	307	.319	9	59	124	9	8	1	2.0	.943							
	C	E. Grace	223	.211	6	29	275	30	3	10	4.8	.990							
Cin.	1B	B. Jordan	316	.282	1	28	669	46	8	55	9.5	.989	L. Grissom	50	224	12	17	6	3.26
W-56 L-98	2B	A. Kampouris	458	.249	17	71	367	439	33	87	5.7	.961	P. Derringer	43	223	10	14	1	4.04
Chuck Dressen	SS	B. Myers	335	.251	7	43	190	360	30	67	4.8	.948	P. Davis	42	218	11	13	3	3.59
W-51 L-78	3B	L. Riggs	384	.242	6	45	112	223	21	16	**3.6**	.941	Hollingsworth	43	202	9	15	5	3.91
Bobby Wallace	RF	I. Goodman	549	.273	12	55	291	13	8	0	2.2	.974	G. Schott	37	154	4	13	1	2.97
W-5 L-20	CF	C. Hafey	257	.261	9	41	128	5	4	0	2.1	.971	B. Hallahan	21	63	3	9	0	6.14
	LF	K. Cuyler	406	.271	0	32	174	8	5	1	1.8	.973							
	C	E. Lombardi	368	.334	9	59	333	58	11	3	4.5	.973							
	1B	L. Scarsella	329	.246	3	34	589	37	10	55	9.8	.984							
	OF	H. Walker	221	.249	1	19	135	5	1	3	2.4	.993							
	C	S. Davis	209	.268	3	33	300	40	7	3	5.9	.980							
	OF	P. Weintraub	177	.271	3	20	78	3	2	1	1.8	.976							
	3B	J. Outlaw	165	.273	0	11	41	87	12	4	3.4	.914							

BATTING AND BASE RUNNING LEADERS

Batting Average
J. Medwick, STL	.374
J. Mize, STL	.364
G. Hartnett, CHI	.354
P. Waner, PIT	.354
P. Whitney, PHI	.341

Slugging Average
J. Medwick, STL	.641
J. Mize, STL	.595
D. Camilli, PHI	.587
G. Hartnett, CHI	.548
M. Ott, NY	.523

Home Runs
M. Ott, NY	31
J. Medwick, STL	31
D. Camilli, PHI	27
J. Mize, STL	25
A. Galan, CHI	18

Total Bases
J. Medwick, STL	406
J. Mize, STL	333
F. Demaree, CHI	298
M. Ott, NY	285
D. Camilli, PHI	279

PITCHING LEADERS

Winning Percentage
C. Hubbell, NY	.733
C. Melton, NY	.690
L. Fette, BOS	.667
T. Carleton, CHI	.667
J. Turner, BOS	.645

Earned Run Average
J. Turner, BOS	2.38
C. Melton, NY	2.61
D. Dean, STL	2.69
R. Bauers, PIT	2.88
L. Fette, BOS	2.88

Wins
C. Hubbell, NY	22
C. Melton, NY	20
L. Fette, BOS	20
J. Turner, BOS	20
L. Warneke, STL	18

Saves
M. Brown, PIT	7
C. Melton, NY	7
L. Grissom, CIN	6
C. Root, CHI	5
Hollingsworth, CIN	5

BATTING AND BASE RUNNING LEADERS

Runs Batted In

J. Medwick, STL	154
F. Demaree, CHI	115
J. Mize, STL	113
G. Suhr, PIT	97
M. Ott, NY	95

Stolen Bases

A. Galan, CHI	23
S. Hack, CHI	16
T. Moore, STL	13
C. Lavagetto, BKN	13
G. Scharein, PHI	13
B. Hassett, BKN	13

Hits

J. Medwick, STL	237
P. Waner, PIT	219
J. Mize, STL	204

Base on Balls

M. Ott, NY	102
D. Camilli, PHI	90
G. Suhr, PIT	83
S. Hack, CHI	83

Home Run Percentage

M. Ott, NY	5.7
D. Camilli, PHI	5.7
J. Medwick, STL	4.9

Runs Scored

J. Medwick, STL	111
B. Herman, CHI	106
S. Hack, CHI	106

Doubles

J. Medwick, STL	56
J. Mize, STL	40
D. Bartell, NY	38

Triples

A. Vaughan, PIT	17
G. Suhr, PIT	14
L. Handley, PIT	12
I. Goodman, CIN	12

PITCHING LEADERS

Strikeouts

C. Hubbell, NY	159
L. Grissom, CIN	149
C. Blanton, PIT	143
C. Melton, NY	142
W. LaMaster, PHI	135
C. Passeau, PHI	135

Complete Games

J. Turner, BOS	24
L. Fette, BOS	23
B. Weiland, STL	21

Fewest Hits per 9 Innings

V. Mungo, BKN	7.60
L. Grissom, CIN	7.77
C. Melton, NY	7.84

Shutouts

L. Grissom, CIN	5
J. Turner, BOS	5
L. Fette, BOS	5

Fewest Walks per 9 Innings

D. Dean, STL	1.51
W. Hoyt, BKN, PIT	1.66
J. Turner, BOS	1.82

Most Strikeouts per 9 Inn.

V. Mungo, BKN	6.82
L. Grissom, CIN	6.00
R. Bauers, PIT	5.66

Innings

C. Passeau, PHI	292
B. Lee, CHI	272
B. Weiland, STL	264

Games Pitched

H. Mulcahy, PHI	56
O. Jorgens, PHI	52

	W	L	PCT	GB	R	OR	Batting 2B	3B	HR	BA	SA	SB	Fielding E	DP	FA	CG	BB	Pitching SO	ShO	SV	ERA
NY	95	57	.625		732	602	251	41	111	.278	.403	45	159	143	.974	67	404	653	11	17	3.43
CHI	93	61	.604	3	811	682	253	74	96	.287	.416	71	151	141	.975	73	502	596	11	13	3.97
PIT	86	68	.558	10	704	646	223	86	47	.285	.384	32	181	135	.970	67	428	643	12	17	3.56
STL	81	73	.526	15	789	733	264	67	94	.282	.406	78	164	127	.973	81	448	573	10	4	3.95
BOS	79	73	.520	16	579	556	200	41	63	.247	.339	45	157	128	.975	63	476	592	5	8	4.13
BKN	62	91	.405	33.5	616	772	258	53	37	.265	.354	69	217	127	.964	59	501	529	6	15	5.06
PHI	61	92	.399	34.5	724	869	258	37	103	.273	.391	66	184	157	.970	64	533	581	10	18	3.94
CIN	56	98	.364	40	612	707	215	59	73	.254	.360	53	208	139	.966	64	533	581	10	18	3.91
					5567	5567	1922	458	624	.272	.382	459	1421	1097	.971	559	3664	4554	81	102	3.91

American League 1937

	POS	Player	AB	BA	HR	RBI	PO	A	E	DP	TC/G	FA	Pitcher	G	IP	W	L	SV	ERA
N. Y. W-102 L-52 Joe McCarthy	1B	L. Gehrig	569	.351	37	159	1370	74	16	113	9.3	.989	L. Gomez	34	278	21	11	0	2.33
	2B	T. Lazzeri	446	.244	14	70	251	382	22	64	5.2	.966	R. Ruffing	31	256	20	7	0	2.98
	SS	F. Crosetti	611	.234	11	49	313	467	43	86	5.6	.948	B. Hadley	29	178	11	8	0	5.30
	3B	R. Rolfe	648	.276	4	62	195	309	20	27	3.4	.962	M. Pearson	22	145	9	3	1	3.17
	RF	M. Hoag	362	.301	3	46	181	8	9	2	2.0	.955	J. Murphy	39	110	13	4	10	4.17
	CF	J. DiMaggio	621	.346	46	167	413	21	17	4	3.0	.962	P. Malone	28	92	4	4	6	5.48
	LF	J. Powell	365	.263	3	45	201	5	4	2	2.2	.981	K. Wicker	16	88	7	3	0	4.40
	C	B. Dickey	530	.332	29	133	692	80	7	11	5.7	.991	S. Chandler	12	82	7	4	0	2.84
	OF	G. Selkirk	256	.328	18	68	140	9	2	1	2.2	.987	F. Makosky	26	58	5	2	3	4.97
	OF	T. Henrich	206	.320	8	42	90	6	3	1	1.7	.970							
	2S	D. Heffner	201	.249	0	21	123	126	6	30		.976							
Det. W-89 L-65 Mickey Cochrane	1B	H. Greenberg	594	.337	40	183	1477	102	13	133	10.3	.992	E. Auker	39	253	17	9	1	3.88
	2B	C. Gehringer	564	.371	14	96	331	485	12	102	5.8	.986	T. Bridges	34	245	15	12	0	4.07
	SS	B. Rogell	536	.276	8	64	323	451	26	103	5.5	.968	R. Lawson	37	217	18	7	1	5.26
	3B	M. Owen	396	.288	1	45	108	219	10	17	3.2	.970	J. Wade	33	165	7	10	0	5.39
	RF	P. Fox	628	.331	12	82	321	6	8	0	2.3	.976	Poffenberger	29	137	10	5	3	4.65
	CF	J. White	305	.246	0	21	216	4	6	0	2.8	.973	G. Gill	31	128	11	4	1	4.51
	LF	G. Walker	635	.335	18	113	316	9	15	2	2.3	.956	S. Coffman	28	101	7	5	0	4.37
	C	R. York	375	.307	35	103	190	27	9	6	4.2	.960	J. Russell	25	40	2	5	4	7.59
	OF	C. Laabs	242	.240	8	37	133	2	4	0	2.2	.971							
	OF	G. Goslin	181	.238	4	35	81	2	4	1	2.2	.954							
	C	B. Tebbetts	162	.191	2	16	155	25	7	1	3.9	.963							
Chi. W-86 L-68 Jimmy Dykes	1B	Z. Bonura	447	.345	19	100	1114	63	13	123	10.3	.989	V. Kennedy	32	221	14	13	0	5.09
	2B	J. Hayes	573	.229	2	79	353	490	14	115	6.0	.984	T. Lee	30	205	12	10	0	3.52
	SS	L. Appling	574	.317	4	77	280	541	49	111	5.6	.944	T. Lyons	22	169	12	7	0	4.15
	3B	T. Piet	332	.235	4	38	83	163	16	12	3.0	.939	J. Whitehead	26	166	11	8	0	4.07
	RF	D. Walker	593	.302	9	95	270	10	14	1	1.9	.952	M. Stratton	22	165	15	5	0	2.40
	CF	M. Kreevich	583	.302	12	73	401	13	5	4	3.0	.988	B. Dietrich	29	143	8	10	1	4.90
	LF	R. Radcliff	584	.325	4	79	273	9	10	5	2.1	.966	C. Brown	53	100	7	7	18	3.42
	C	L. Sewell	412	.269	1	61	502	72	9	11	4.9	.985							
	13	J. Dykes	85	.306	1	23	152	27	1	15		.994							

	POS	Player	AB	BA	HR	RBI	PO	A	E	DP	TC/G	FA	Pitcher	G	IP	W	L	SV	ERA
Cle. W-83 L-71 Steve O'Neill	1B	H. Trosky	601	.298	32	128	1403	76	10	131	9.8	.993	M. Harder	38	234	15	12	2	4.28
	2B	J. Kroner	283	.237	2	26	155	189	11	45	5.5	.969	D. Galehouse	36	201	9	14	3	4.57
	SS	L. Lary	644	.290	8	77	325	489	31	95	5.4	.963	W. Hudlin	35	176	12	11	2	4.10
	3B	O. Hale	561	.267	6	82	96	199	11	24	3.4	.964	J. Allen	24	173	15	1	0	2.55
	RF	B. Campbell	448	.301	4	61	204	14	5	5	1.8	.978	B. Feller	26	149	9	7	1	3.39
	CF	E. Averill	609	.299	21	92	362	11	9	3	2.4	.976	E. Whitehill	33	147	8	8	2	6.49
	LF	M. Solters	589	.323	20	109	283	19	15	3	2.1	.953	J. Heving	40	73	8	4	5	4.83
	C	F. Pytlak	397	.315	1	44	559	80	9	13	5.6	.986							
	32	R. Hughes	346	.277	1	40	157	233	13	32		.968							
	C	B. Sullivan	168	.286	3	22	146	20	9	1	4.6	.949							
Bos. W-80 L-72 Joe Cronin	1B	J. Foxx	569	.285	36	127	1287	106	8	122	9.3	**.994**	L. Grove	32	262	17	9	0	3.02
	2B	E. McNair	455	.292	12	76	242	316	18	67	5.4	.969	J. Wilson	51	221	16	10	7	3.70
	SS	J. Cronin	570	.307	18	110	300	414	31	89	5.0	.958	B. Newsom	30	208	13	10	0	4.38
	3B	P. Higgins	570	.302	9	106	161	258	29	29	2.9	.935	J. Marcum	37	184	13	11	3	4.85
	RF	B. Chapman	423	.307	7	57	262	9	4	1	2.5	.985	A. McKain	36	137	8	8	2	4.66
	CF	D. Cramer	560	.305	0	51	365	12	12	4	2.9	.969	R. Walberg	32	105	5	7	1	5.59
	LF	B. Mills	505	.295	7	58	239	8	14	0	2.2	.946	Ostermueller	25	87	3	7	1	4.98
	C	G. Desautels	305	.243	0	27	491	44	4	4	5.7	.993							
	OF	F. Gaffke	184	.288	6	34	80	3	3	0	1.7	.965							
	C	M. Berg	141	.255	0	20	208	24	5	2	5.0	.979							
Was. W-73 L-80 Bucky Harris	1B	J. Kuhel	547	.283	6	61	1242	85	9	**141**	9.8	.993	J. DeShong	37	264	14	15	1	4.90
	2B	B. Myer	430	.293	1	65	308	338	23	90	5.6	.966	W. Ferrell	25	208*	11	13	0	3.94
	SS	C. Travis	526	.344	3	66	229	396	23	99	5.0	.965	M. Weaver	30	189	12	9	0	4.39
	3B	B. Lewis	668	.314	10	79	146	293	29	32	3.0	.938	P. Appleton	35	168	8	15	2	4.39
	RF	J. Stone	542	.330	6	88	300	15	5	3	2.3	.984	E. Linke	36	129	6	1	3	5.60
	CF	M. Almada	433	.309	4	33	308	16	12	3	3.4	.964	C. Fischer	17	72	4	5	2	4.38
	LF	A. Simmons	419	.279	8	84	240	7	4	5	2.5	.984	S. Cohen	33	55	2	4		3.11
	C	R. Ferrell	279	.229	1	32	341	42	5	5	4.6	.987							
	OF	F. Sington	228	.237	3	36	120	4	5	0	2.0	.961							
	C	W. Millies	179	.223	0	28	199	33	7	7	4.3	.971							
Phi. W-54 L-97 Connie Mack	1B	C. Dean	309	.262	2	31	705	38	7	55	9.6	.991	G. Caster	34	232	12	19	0	4.43
	2B	R. Peters	339	.260	3	43	138	170	11	34	4.6	.966	H. Kelley	41	205	13	21	0	5.36
	SS	S. Newsome	438	.253	1	30	256	408	32	76	5.7	.954	E. Smith	38	197	4	17	5	3.94
	3B	B. Werber	493	.292	7	70	132	260	17	25	3.3	.958	B. Thomas	35	170	8	15	0	4.99
	RF	W. Moses	649	.320	25	86	323	16	15	4	2.3	.958	B. Ross	28	147	5	10	0	4.89
	CF	J. Hill	242	.293	1	37	163	4	8	0	2.6	.954	L. Nelson	30	116	4	9	2	5.90
	LF	B. Johnson	477	.306	25	108	313	14	8	3	2.5	.976							
	C	E. Brucker	317	.259	6	37	323	48	11	13	4.2	.971							
	1O	L. Finney	379	.251	1	20	519	30	12	39		.979							
	OF	J. Rothrock	232	.267	0	21	130	2	1	0	2.3	.992							
	C	F. Hayes	188	.261	10	38	208	23	7	4	4.3	.971							
	2B	W. Ambler	162	.216	0	11	107	149	12	34	4.8	.955							
	P	L. Nelson	113	.354	4	29	3	14	0	0	.6	1.000							
St. L. W-46 L-108 Rogers Hornsby W-25 L-50 Jim Bottomley W-21 L-58	1B	H. Davis	450	.276	3	35	1065	54	10	108	10.1	.991	O. Hildebrand	30	201	8	17	1	5.14
	2B	T. Carey	487	.275	1	40	202	253	8	58	5.3	.983	J. Knott	38	191	8	18	2	4.89
	SS	Knickerbocker	491	.261	4	61	205	368	25	59	5.2	.958	C. Hogsett	37	177	6	19	2	6.29
	3B	H. Clift	571	.306	29	118	198	405	34	50	4.1	.947	J. Walkup	27	150	9	12	0	7.36
	RF	B. Bell	642	.340	14	117	222	22	4	6	1.9	.984	J. Bonetti	28	143	4	11	1	5.84
	CF	S. West	457	.328	7	58	298	17	4	6	3.0	.987	B. Trotter	34	122	2	9	1	5.81
	LF	J. Vosmik	594	.325	4	93	333	12	10	4	2.5	.972	L. Koupal	26	106	4	9	0	6.56
	C	R. Hemsley	334	.222	3	28	332	70	13	13	4.4	.969							
	OF	E. Allen	320	.316	0	31	186	8	4	1	2.5	.980							
	C	B. Huffman	176	.273	1	24	140	20	5	4	3.9	.970							

BATTING AND BASE RUNNING LEADERS

Batting Average
C. Gehringer, DET	.371
L. Gehrig, NY	.351
J. DiMaggio, NY	.346
Z. Bonura, CHI	.345
C. Travis, WAS	.344

Slugging Average
J. DiMaggio, NY	.673
H. Greenberg, DET	.668
R. York, DET	.651
L. Gehrig, NY	.643
Z. Bonura, CHI	.573

Home Runs
J. DiMaggio, NY	46
H. Greenberg, DET	40
L. Gehrig, NY	37
J. Foxx, BOS	36
R. York, DET	35

Total Bases
J. DiMaggio, NY	418
H. Greenberg, DET	397
L. Gehrig, NY	366
W. Moses, PHI	357
H. Trosky, CLE	329

Runs Batted In
H. Greenberg, DET	183
J. DiMaggio, NY	167
L. Gehrig, NY	159
B. Dickey, NY	133
H. Trosky, CLE	128

Stolen Bases
B. Werber, PHI	35
B. Chapman, BOS, WAS	35
G. Walker, DET	23
J. Hill, PHI, WAS	18
L. Appling, CHI	18
L. Lary, CLE	18

PITCHING LEADERS

Winning Percentage
J. Allen, CLE	.938
M. Stratton, CHI	.750
R. Ruffing, NY	.741
R. Lawson, DET	.720
L. Gomez, NY	.656

Earned Run Average
L. Gomez, NY	2.33
M. Stratton, CHI	2.40
J. Allen, CLE	2.55
R. Ruffing, NY	2.98
L. Grove, BOS	3.02

Wins
L. Gomez, NY	21
R. Ruffing, NY	20
R. Lawson, DET	18
E. Auker, DET	17
L. Grove, BOS	17

Saves
C. Brown, CHI	18
J. Murphy, NY	10
J. Wilson, BOS	7
P. Malone, NY	6
J. Heving, CLE	5
E. Smith, PHI	5

Strikeouts
L. Gomez, NY	194
B. Newsom, BOS, WAS	166
L. Grove, BOS	153
B. Feller, CLE	150
T. Bridges, DET	138

Complete Games
W. Ferrell, BOS, WAS	26
L. Gomez, NY	25
R. Ruffing, NY	22
L. Grove, BOS	21
J. DeShong, WAS	20

BATTING AND BASE RUNNING LEADERS

Hits

B. Bell, STL	218
J. DiMaggio, NY	215
G. Walker, DET	213

Base on Balls

L. Gehrig, NY	127
H. Greenberg, DET	102
J. Foxx, BOS	99

Home Run Percentage

R. York, DET	9.3
J. DiMaggio, NY	7.4
H. Greenberg, DET	6.7

Runs Scored

J. DiMaggio, NY	151
R. Rolfe, NY	143
L. Gehrig, NY	138

Doubles

B. Bell, STL	51
H. Greenberg, DET	49
W. Moses, PHI	48

Triples

M. Kreevich, CHI	16
D. Walker, CHI	16
J. Stone, WAS	15
J. DiMaggio, NY	15

PITCHING LEADERS

Fewest Hits per 9 Innings

L. Gomez, NY	7.53
M. Stratton, CHI	7.76
E. Smith, PHI	8.15

Shutouts

L. Gomez, NY	6
M. Stratton, CHI	5

Fewest Walks per 9 Innings

M. Stratton, CHI	2.02
W. Hudlin, CLE	2.05
R. Ruffing, NY	2.39

Most Strikeouts per 9 Inn.

L. Gomez, NY	6.27
J. Wilson, BOS	5.57
B. Newsom, BOS, WAS	5.43

Innings

W. Ferrell, BOS, WAS	281
L. Gomez, NY	278
B. Newsom, BOS, WAS	275

Games Pitched

C. Brown, CHI	53
J. Wilson, BOS	51
B. Newsom, BOS, WAS	41
H. Kelley, PHI	41

	W	L	PCT	GB	R	OR	2B	3B	HR	BA	SA	SB	E	DP	FA	CG	BB	SO	ShO	SV	ERA
NY	102	52	.662		979	671	282	73	174	.283	.456	60	170	134	.972	82	506	652	15	21	3.65
DET	89	65	.578	13	935	841	309	62	150	.292	.452	89	147	149	.976	70	635	485	6	11	4.87
CHI	86	68	.558	16	780	730	280	76	67	.280	.400	70	174	173	.971	70	532	533	15	21	4.17
CLE	83	71	.539	19	817	768	304	76	103	.280	.423	76	159	153	.974	64	563	630	4	15	4.39
BOS	80	72	.526	21	821	775	269	64	100	.281	.411	79	177	139	.970	74	597	682	6	14	4.48
WAS	73	80	.477	28.5	757	841	245	84	47	.279	.379	95	170	181	.972	75	676	535	5	14	4.58
PHI	54	97	.358	46.5	699	854	278	60	94	.267	.397	30	198	150	.967	65	613	469	6	9	4.85
STL	46	108	.299	56	715	1023	327	44	71	.285	.399	30	173	166	.972	55	653	468	2	8	6.00
					6503	6503	2294	539	806	.281	.415	560	1368	1245	.972	555	4775	4454	59	113	4.62

National League 1938

	POS	Player	AB	BA	HR	RBI	PO	A	E	DP	TC/G	FA	Pitcher	G	IP	W	L	SV	ERA
Chi. W-89 L-63 Charlie Grimm W-45 L-36 Gabby Hartnett W-44 L-27	1B	R. Collins	490	.267	13	61	1264	111	6	118	10.2	.996	B. Lee	44	291	22	9	2	2.66
	2B	B. Herman	624	.277	1	56	404	517	18	111	6.2	.981	C. Bryant	44	270	19	11	2	3.10
	SS	B. Jurges	465	.245	1	47	277	417	34	82	5.4	.953	L. French	43	201	10	19	0	3.80
	3B	S. Hack	609	.320	4	67	178	300	23	26	3.3	.954	T. Carleton	33	168	10	9	0	5.42
	RF	F. Demaree	476	.273	8	62	199	12	6	1	1.7	.972	C. Root	44	161	8	7	8	2.86
	CF	C. Reynolds	497	.302	3	67	328	10	6	4	2.8	.983	J. Russell	42	102	6	1	3	3.34
	LF	A. Galan	395	.286	6	69	211	10	3	3	2.2	.987	V. Page	13	68	5	4	1	3.84
	C	G. Hartnett	299	.274	10	59	358	40	2	8	4.8	.995							
	O1	P. Cavarretta	268	.239	1	28	277	21	4	14		.987							
	C	K. O'Dea	247	.263	3	33	294	32	10	3	4.7	.970							
	OF	J. Marty	235	.243	7	35	143	6	2	1	2.2	.987							
	UT	T. Lazzeri	120	.267	5	23	49	75	7	12		.947							
Pit. W-86 L-64 Pie Traynor	1B	G. Suhr	530	.294	3	64	1512	81	12	150	11.1	.993	R. Bauers	40	243	13	14	3	3.07
	2B	P. Young	562	.278	4	79	370	554	26	120	6.4	.973	J. Tobin	40	241	14	12	0	3.47
	SS	A. Vaughan	541	.322	7	68	306	507	33	107	5.8	.961	C. Blanton	29	173	11	7	0	3.70
	3B	L. Handley	570	.268	6	51	119	304	23	26	3.3	.948	B. Klinger	28	159	12	5	1	2.99
	RF	P. Waner	625	.280	6	69	284	11	7	0	2.1	.977	B. Swift	36	150	7	5	4	3.24
	CF	L. Waner	619	.313	5	57	341	15	5	5	2.5	.986	M. Brown	51	133	15	9	5	3.80
	LF	J. Rizzo	555	.301	23	111	284	5	15	1	2.2	.951							
	C	A. Todd	491	.265	7	75	574	89	10	7	5.1	.985							
N. Y. W-83 L-67 Bill Terry	1B	J. McCarthy	470	.272	8	59	1315	77	10	111	11.2	.993	C. Melton	36	243	14	14	0	3.89
	2B	A. Kampouris	268	.246	5	37	198	255	13	52	5.9	.972	H. Gumbert	38	236	15	13	0	4.01
	SS	D. Bartell	481	.262	9	49	288	447	37	85	6.1	.952	H. Schumacher	28	185	13	8	0	3.50
	3B	M. Ott	527	.311	36	116	98	238	15	14	3.1	.957	C. Hubbell	24	179	13	10	1	3.07
	RF	J. Ripple	501	.261	10	60	236	13	6	2	1.9	.976	B. Lohrman	31	152	9	6	0	3.32
	CF	H. Leiber	360	.269	12	65	181	6	5	3	2.2	.974	D. Coffman	51	111	8	4	12	3.48
	LF	J. Moore	506	.302	11	56	214	8	5	1	2.0	.978	J. Brown	43	90	5	3	5	1.80
	C	H. Danning	448	.306	9	60	449	50	8	7	4.4	.984							
	OF	B. Seeds	296	.291	9	52	147	6	2	2	2.0	.987							
	2O	L. Chiozza	179	.235	3	17	80	111	11	9		.946							
	S3	G. Myatt	170	.306	3	10	77	128	17	24		.923							
	C	G. Mancuso	158	.348	2	15	184	24	5	5	4.8	.977							
	1B	S. Leslie	154	.253	1	16	304	15	4	21	10.1	.988							

	POS	Player	AB	BA	HR	RBI	PO	A	E	DP	TC/G	FA	Pitcher	G	IP	W	L	SV	ERA
Cin. W-82 L-68 Bill McKechnie	1B	F. McCormick	640	.327	5	106	1441	95	7	127	10.2	.995	P. Derringer	41	307	21	14	3	2.93
	2B	L. Frey	501	.265	4	36	278	390	25	80	5.7	.964	Vander Meer	32	225	15	10	0	3.12
	SS	B. Myers	442	.253	12	47	255	380	41	74	5.5	.939	B. Walters	27	168	11	6	1	3.69
	3B	L. Riggs	531	.252	2	55	146	280	24	18	3.2	.947	P. Davis	29	168	7	12	1	3.97
	RF	I. Goodman	568	.292	30	92	306	10	4	1	2.3	.988	J. Weaver	30	129	6	4	3	3.13
	CF	H. Craft	612	.270	15	83	436	15	8	3	3.0	.983	W. Moore	19	90	6	4	0	3.49
	LF	W. Berger	407	.307	16	56	192	7	7	2	2.1	.966	G. Schott	31	83	5	5	2	4.45
	C	E. Lombardi	489	.342	19	95	512	73	9	8	4.8	.985	J. Cascarella	33	61	4	7	4	4.57
	OF	D. Cooke	233	.275	2	33	126	4	5	1	2.6	.963							
Bos. W-77 L-75 Casey Stengel	1B	E. Fletcher	529	.272	6	48	1424	126	15	108	10.7	.990	J. Turner	35	268	14	18	0	3.46
	2B	T. Cuccinello	555	.265	9	76	323	458	21	84	5.5	.974	L. Fette	33	240	11	13	1	3.15
	SS	R. Warstler	467	.231	0	40	285	428	48	76	5.6	.937	MacFayden	29	220	14	9	0	2.95
	3B	J. Stripp	229	.275	1	19	61	111	6	12	3.1	.966*	I. Hutchinson	36	151	9	8	4	2.74
	RF	J. Cooney	432	.271	0	17	209	6	4	2	2.0	.982	M. Shoffner	26	140	8	7	1	3.54
	CF	V. DiMaggio	540	.228	14	61	415	19	12	10	3.0	.973	J. Lanning	32	138	8	7	0	3.72
	LF	M. West	418	.234	10	63	205	6	3	2	2.0	.986	D. Errickson	34	123	9	7	6	3.15
	C	R. Mueller	274	.237	4	35	239	47	2	4	3.8	.993							
	O3	D. Garms	428	.315	0	47	174	104	11	8		.962							
	C	A. Lopez	236	.267	1	14	240	42	3	4	4.0	.989							
	OF	G. Moore	180	.272	3	19	97	4	2	0	2.2	.981							
	3B	G. English	165	.248	2	21	33	75	5	3	2.6	.956							
St. L. W-71 L-80 Frankie Frisch W-62 L-72 Mike Gonzalez W-9 L-8	1B	J. Mize	531	.337	27	102	1297	93	15	117	10.0	.989	B. Weiland	35	228	16	11	1	3.59
	2B	S. Martin	417	.278	1	27	225	301	18	59	5.5	.967	B. McGee	47	216	7	12	5	3.21
	SS	L. Myers	227	.242	1	19	110	195	18	36	4.7	.944	L. Warneke	31	197	13	8	0	3.97
	3B	D. Gutteridge	552	.255	9	64	94	148	14	17	3.5	.945	C. Davis	40	173	12	8	3	3.63
	RF	E. Slaughter	395	.276	8	58	189	7	6	0	2.2	.970	R. Henshaw	27	130	5	11	0	4.02
	CF	T. Moore	312	.272	4	21	219	5	3	1	3.0	.987	M. Macon	38	129	4	11	2	4.11
	LF	J. Medwick	590	.322	21	122	330	12	9	6	2.4	.974	C. Shoun	40	117	6	6	1	4.14
	C	M. Owen	397	.267	4	36	463	67	11	8	4.7	.980							
	OF	D. Padgett	388	.271	8	65	140	14	6	3	2.3	.963							
	UT	J. Brown	382	.301	0	38	195	264	21	55		.956							
	OF	P. Martin	269	.294	2	38	138	1	2	1	2.3	.986							
	3B	J. Stripp	199	.286	0	18	53	76	3	9	2.6	.977*							
	OF	F. Bordagaray	156	.282	0	21	67	3	3	0	2.5	.959							
Bkn. W-69 L-80 Burleigh Grimes	1B	D. Camilli	509	.251	24	100	1356	95	8	129	10.1	.995	L. Hamlin	44	237	12	15	6	3.68
	2B	J. Hudson	498	.261	2	37	304	395	27	79	5.5	.963	Fitzsimmons	27	203	11	8	0	3.02
	SS	L. Durocher	479	.219	1	56	287	399	24	90	5.0	.966	T. Pressnell	43	192	11	14	3	3.56
	3B	C. Lavagetto	487	.273	6	79	136	229	28	26	3.0	.929	V. Tamulis	38	160	12	6	2	3.83
	RF	G. Rosen	473	.281	4	51	263	19	3	4	2.5	.989	B. Posedel	33	140	8	9	1	5.66
	CF	E. Koy	521	.299	11	76	306	7	5	4	2.4	.984	V. Mungo	24	133	4	11	0	3.92
	LF	B. Hassett	335	.293	0	40	154	0	9	0	2.3	.945	M. Butcher	24	73	5	4	2	6.56
	C	B. Phelps	208	.308	5	46	218	25	5	5	4.5	.980							
	OF	K. Cuyler	253	.273	2	23	125	9	1	1	2.0	.993							
	OF	T. Stainback	104	.327	0	20	52	1	1	0	2.3	.981							
Phi. W-45 L-105 Jimmie Wilson W-45 L-103 Hans Lobert W-0 L-2	1B	P. Weintraub	351	.311	4	45	913	75	12	70	10.2	.988	H. Mulcahy	46	267	10	20	1	4.61
	2B	E. Mueller	444	.250	4	34	229	266	17	44	4.6	.967	C. Passeau	44	239	11	18	1	4.52
	SS	D. Young	340	.229	0	31	156	263	30	44	5.2	.933	Hollingsworth	24	174	5	16	0	3.82
	3B	P. Whitney	300	.277	3	38	68	131	14	8	2.8	.934	P. Sivess	39	116	3	6	3	5.51
	RF	F. Klein	458	.247	8	61	229	8	10	1	2.1	.960	M. Butcher	12	98	4	8	0	2.93
	CF	H. Martin	466	.298	3	39	298	7	11	2	2.7	.965	B. Walters	12	83	4	8	0	5.23
	LF	M. Arnovich	502	.275	4	72	327	18	6	0	2.6	.983	W. LaMaster	18	64	4	7	0	7.77
	C	B. Atwood	281	.196	3	28	350	53	13	12	4.4	.969							
	S2	G. Scharein	390	.238	1	29	246	327	37	57		.939							
	3B	B. Jordan	310	.300	0	18	42	103	4	13	2.6	.973							
	OF	G. Brack	282	.287	4	28	156	5	6	2	2.5	.964							
	C	S. Davis	215	.247	2	23	217	27	5	5	4.0	.980							

BATTING AND BASE RUNNING LEADERS

Batting Average
E. Lombardi, CIN	.342
J. Mize, STL	.337
F. McCormick, CIN	.327
J. Medwick, STL	.322
A. Vaughan, PIT	.322

Slugging Average
J. Mize, STL	.614
M. Ott, NY	.583
J. Medwick, STL	.536
I. Goodman, CIN	.533
E. Lombardi, CIN	.524

Home Runs
M. Ott, NY	36
I. Goodman, CIN	30
J. Mize, STL	27
D. Camilli, BKN	24
J. Rizzo, PIT	23

Total Bases
J. Mize, STL	326
J. Medwick, STL	316
M. Ott, NY	307
I. Goodman, CIN	303
J. Rizzo, PIT	285

Runs Batted In
J. Medwick, STL	122
M. Ott, NY	116
J. Rizzo, PIT	111
F. McCormick, CIN	106
J. Mize, STL	102

Stolen Bases
S. Hack, CHI	16
C. Lavagetto, BKN	15
E. Koy, BKN	15
A. Vaughan, PIT	14
D. Gutteridge, STL	14

PITCHING LEADERS

Winning Percentage
B. Lee, CHI	.710
C. Bryant, CHI	.633
M. Brown, PIT	.625
P. Derringer, CIN	.600
Vander Meer, CIN	.600

Earned Run Average
B. Lee, CHI	2.66
P. Derringer, CIN	2.93
MacFayden, BOS	2.95
B. Klinger, PIT	2.99
Fitzsimmons, BKN	3.02

Wins
B. Lee, CHI	22
P. Derringer, CIN	21
C. Bryant, CHI	19
B. Weiland, STL	16

Saves
D. Coffman, NY	12
C. Root, CHI	8
D. Errickson, BOS	6
L. Hamlin, BKN	6

Strikeouts
C. Bryant, CHI	135
P. Derringer, CIN	132
Vander Meer, CIN	125
B. Lee, CHI	121
B. Weiland, STL	117
R. Bauers, PIT	117

Complete Games
P. Derringer, CIN	26
J. Turner, BOS	22
B. Walters, CIN, PHI	20
MacFayden, BOS	19
B. Lee, CHI	19

BATTING AND BASE RUNNING LEADERS

PITCHING LEADERS

Hits			Base on Balls	
F. McCormick, CIN	209		D. Camilli, BKN	119
S. Hack, CHI	195		M. Ott, NY	118
L. Waner, PIT	194		A. Vaughan, PIT	104

Fewest Hits per 9 Innings			Shutouts	
Vander Meer, CIN	7.07		B. Lee, CHI	9
R. Bauers, PIT	7.67		MacFayden, BOS	5
C. Bryant, CHI	7.82			

Home Run Percentage			Runs Scored	
M. Ott, NY	6.8		M. Ott, NY	116
I. Goodman, CIN	5.3		S. Hack, CHI	109
J. Mize, STL	5.1		D. Camilli, BKN	106

Fewest Walks per 9 Innings			Most Strikeouts per 9 Inn.	
P. Derringer, CIN	1.44		C. Hubbell, NY	5.23
C. Hubbell, NY	1.66		Vander Meer, CIN	4.99
J. Turner, BOS	1.81		B. Weiland, STL	4.61

Doubles			Triples	
J. Medwick, STL	47		J. Mize, STL	16
F. McCormick, CIN	40		D. Gutteridge, STL	15
H. Martin, PHI	36		G. Suhr, PIT	14
P. Young, PIT	36			

Innings			Games Pitched	
P. Derringer, CIN	307		M. Brown, PIT	51
B. Lee, CHI	291		D. Coffman, NY	51
C. Bryant, CHI	270		B. McGee, STL	47
			H. Mulcahy, PHI	46

	W	L	PCT	GB	R	OR	Batting 2B	3B	HR	BA	SA	SB	Fielding E	DP	FA	CG	BB	Pitching SO	ShO	SV	ERA
CHI	89	63	.586		713	598	242	70	65	.269	.377	49	135	151	.978	67	454	583	16	18	3.37
PIT	86	64	.573	2	707	630	265	66	65	.279	.388	47	163	168	.974	57	432	557	8	15	3.46
NY	83	67	.553	5	705	637	210	36	125	.271	.396	31	168	147	.973	59	389	497	8	18	3.62
CIN	82	68	.547	6	723	634	251	57	110	.277	.406	19	172	133	.971	72	463	542	11	16	3.62
BOS	77	75	.507	12	561	618	199	39	54	.250	.333	49	173	136	.972	83	465	413	15	12	3.40
STL	71	80	.470	17.5	725	721	288	74	91	.279	.407	55	199	145	.967	58	474	534	10	16	3.84
BKN	69	80	.463	18.5	704	710	225	79	61	.257	.367	66	157	148	.973	56	446	469	12	14	4.07
PHI	45	105	.300	43	550	840	233	29	40	.254	.333	38	201	135	.966	68	582	492	3	6	4.93
					5388	5388	1913	450	611	.267	.376	354	1368	1163	.972	520	3705	4087	83	115	3.78

American League 1938

	POS	Player	AB	BA	HR	RBI	PO	A	E	DP	TC/G	FA	Pitcher	G	IP	W	L	SV	ERA
N. Y. W-99 L-53 Joe McCarthy	1B	L. Gehrig	576	.295	29	114	1483	100	14	157	10.2	.991	R. Ruffing	31	247	21	7	0	3.31
	2B	J. Gordon	458	.255	25	97	290	450	31	98	6.1	.960	L. Gomez	32	239	18	12	0	3.35
	SS	F. Crosetti	631	.263	9	55	352	506	47	120	5.8	.948	M. Pearson	28	202	16	7	0	3.97
	3B	R. Rolfe	631	.311	10	80	151	294	19	26	3.1	.959	S. Chandler	23	172	14	5	0	4.03
	RF	T. Henrich	471	.270	22	91	239	14	4	1	2.0	.984	B. Hadley	29	167	9	8	1	3.60
	CF	J. DiMaggio	599	.324	32	140	366	20	15	4	2.8	.963	S. Sundra	25	94	6	4	0	4.80
	LF	G. Selkirk	335	.254	10	62	176	7	5	5	2.0	.973	J. Murphy	32	91	8	2	11	4.24
	C	B. Dickey	454	.313	27	115	518	94	8	7	4.9	.987							
	OF	M. Hoag	267	.277	0	48	132	5	5	5	3.0	.965							
	OF	J. Powell	164	.256	2	20	86	1	2	0	2.1	.978							
	2B	Knickerbocker	128	.250	1	21	78	86	3	23	4.9	.982							
	C	J. Glenn	123	.260	0	25	134	15	4	3	3.8	.974							
Bos. W-88 L-61 Joe Cronin	1B	J. Foxx	565	.349	50	175	1282	116	19	153	9.5	.987	J. Bagby	43	199	15	11	2	4.21
	2B	B. Doerr	509	.289	5	80	372	420	26	118	5.6	.968	J. Wilson	37	195	15	15	1	4.30
	SS	J. Cronin	530	.325	17	94	304	449	36	110	5.6	.954	Ostermueller	31	177	13	5	2	4.58
	3B	P. Higgins	524	.303	5	106	140	272	39	28	3.3	.914	L. Grove	24	164	14	4	1	3.08
	RF	B. Chapman	480	.340	6	80	267	15	10	5	2.3	.966	E. Dickman	32	104	5	5	0	5.28
	CF	D. Cramer	658	.301	0	71	417	15	6	3	3.0	.986	A. McKain	37	100	5	4	6	4.52
	LF	J. Vosmik	621	.324	9	86	302	14	7	4	2.2	.978	J. Marcum	15	92	5	6	0	4.09
	C	G. Desautels	333	.291	2	48	423	52	7	7	4.5	.985	J. Heving	16	82	8	1	2	3.73
	C	J. Peacock	195	.303	1	39	177	12	3	2	3.4	.984	B. Harris	13	80	5	5	1	4.03
	OF	R. Nonnenkamp	180	.283	0	18	85	5	3	1	2.4	.968							
Cle. W-86 L-66 Ossie Vitt	1B	H. Trosky	554	.334	19	110	1232	102	10	124	9.1	.993	B. Feller	39	278	17	11	1	4.08
	2B	O. Hale	496	.278	8	69	304	343	25	72	5.3	.963	M. Harder	38	240	17	10	4	3.83
	SS	L. Lary	568	.268	3	51	296	399	26	88	5.1	.964	J. Allen	30	200	14	8	0	4.19
	3B	K. Keltner	576	.276	26	113	141	271	19	19	2.9	.956	E. Whitehill	26	160	9	8	0	5.56
	RF	B. Campbell	511	.290	12	72	220	13	8	3	2.0	.967	W. Hudlin	29	127	8	8	1	4.89
	CF	E. Averill	482	.330	14	93	331	14	9	2	2.7	.975	D. Galehouse	36	114	7	8	3	4.34
	LF	J. Heath	502	.343	21	112	254	5	7	2	2.2	.974	J. Humphries	45	103	9	8	6	5.23
	C	F. Pytlak	364	.308	1	43	475	56	7	11	5.4	.987							
	OF	R. Weatherly	210	.262	2	18	110	7	3	3	2.2	.975							
	C	R. Hemsley	203	.296	2	28	358	38	8	5	7.0	.980							
	OF	M. Solters	199	.201	2	22	91	4	3	3	2.1	.969							

	POS	Player	AB	BA	HR	RBI	PO	A	E	DP	TC/G	FA	Pitcher	G	IP	W	L	SV	ERA
Det. W-84 L-70 Mickey Cochrane W-47 L-50 Del Baker W-37 L-20	1B	H. Greenberg	556	.315	58	146	1484	120	14	146	10.4	.991	V. Kennedy	33	190	12	9	2	5.06
	2B	C. Gehringer	568	.306	20	107	393	455	21	115	5.7	.976	G. Gill	24	164	12	9	0	4.12
	SS	B. Rogell	501	.259	3	55	291	431	31	101	5.6	.959	E. Auker	27	161	11	10	0	5.27
	3B	D. Ross	265	.260	1	30	90	157	14	15	3.5	.946	T. Bridges	25	151	13	9	1	4.59
	RF	P. Fox	634	.293	7	96	301	13	2	2	2.1	.994	R. Lawson	27	127	8	9	1	5.46
	CF	C. Morgan	306	.284	0	27	192	6	4	2	2.7	.980	Poffenberger	25	125	6	7	1	4.82
	LF	D. Walker	454	.308	6	43	224	8	5	1	2.1	.979	H. Eisenstat	32	125	9	6	4	3.73
	C	R. York	463	.298	33	127	406	70	5	10	4.1	.990	S. Coffman	39	96	4	2	6	6.02
	3B	M. Christman	318	.248	1	44	86	146	4	14	3.4	.983							
	OF	C. Laabs	211	.237	7	37	128	4	4	1	2.6	.971							
	OF	J. White	206	.262	0	15	141	4	5	0	2.7	.967							
	C	B. Tebbetts	143	.294	1	25	108	20	2	4	2.5	.985							
Was. W-75 L-76 Bucky Harris	1B	Z. Bonura	540	.289	22	114	1209	93	9	132	10.2	.993	D. Leonard	33	223	12	15	0	3.43
	2B	B. Myer	437	.336	6	71	308	355	12	91	5.6	.982	P. Appleton	43	164	7	9	5	4.60
	SS	C. Travis	567	.335	5	67	304	457	40	113	5.6	.950	K. Chase	32	150	9	10	1	5.58
	3B	B. Lewis	656	.296	12	91	161	329	47	32	3.6	.912	W. Ferrell	23	149	13	8	0	5.92
	RF	G. Case	433	.305	2	40	207	7	8	2	2.2	.964	H. Kelley	38	148	9	8	1	4.49
	CF	S. West	344	.302	5	47	221	4	4	3	2.7	.983	M. Weaver	31	139	7	6	0	5.24
	LF	A. Simmons	470	.302	21	95	232	4	4	1	2.1	.983	J. DeShong	31	131	5	8	0	6.58
	C	R. Ferrell	411	.292	1	58	512	69	11	15	4.5	.981	J. Krakauskas	29	121	7	5	0	3.12
	OF	T. Wright	263	.350	2	36	107	3	2	3	1.9	.982	C. Hogsett	31	91	5	6	3	6.03
	OF	J. Stone	213	.244	3	28	107	5	3	0	2.2	.974							
	OF	M. Almada	197	.244	1	15	147	7	5	1	3.4	.969							
	2B	O. Bluege	184	.261	0	21	85	110	2	26	5.2	.990							
Chi. W-65 L-83 Jimmy Dykes	1B	J. Kuhel	412	.267	8	51	1136	59	14	97	10.9	.988	T. Lee	33	245	13	12	1	3.49
	2B	J. Hayes	238	.328	1	20	146	183	8	51	5.5	.976	T. Lyons	23	195	9	11	0	3.70
	SS	L. Appling	294	.303	0	44	149	258	20	37	5.5	.953	M. Stratton	26	186	15	9	2	4.01
	3B	M. Owen	577	.281	6	55	136	305	24	29	3.3	.948	J. Whitehead	32	183	10	11	2	4.76
	RF	Steinbacher	399	.331	4	61	202	7	8	2	2.1	.963	J. Rigney	38	167	9	9	1	3.56
	CF	M. Kreevich	489	.297	6	73	379	7	10	2	3.1	.975	J. Knott	20	131	5	10	0	4.05
	LF	G. Walker	442	.305	16	87	197	9	9	2	2.0	.958							
	C	L. Sewell	211	.213	0	27	205	55	4	7	4.1	.985							
	OF	R. Radcliff	503	.330	5	81	230	5	5	0	2.4	.979							
	S2	B. Berger	470	.217	3	36	230	341	36	78		.941							
	C	T. Rensa	165	.248	3	19	185	36	4	4	3.9	.982							
St. L. W-55 L-97 Gabby Street	1B	G. McQuinn	602	.324	12	82	1207	90	10	134	8.8	.992	B. Newsom	44	330	20	16	1	5.08
	2B	D. Heffner	473	.245	2	69	365	363	22	103	5.3	.971	L. Mills	30	210	10	12	0	5.31
	SS	R. Kress	566	.302	7	79	321	388	26	100	4.9	.965	O. Hildebrand	23	163	8	10	0	5.69
	3B	H. Clift	534	.290	34	118	176	306	19	31	3.4	.962	R. Van Atta	25	104	4	7	0	6.06
	RF	B. Bell	526	.262	13	84	266	12	6	3	2.2	.979	J. Walkup	18	94	1	12	0	6.80
	CF	M. Almada	436	.342	3	37	247	9	9	1	2.6	.966	F. Johnson	17	69	3	7	3	5.61
	LF	B. Mills	466	.285	3	46	235	9	9	2	2.2	.964							
	C	B. Sullivan	375	.277	7	49	441	65	5	10	5.2	.990							
	OF	M. Mazzera	204	.279	6	29	74	7	2	1	1.8	.976							
	C	T. Heath	194	.227	2	22	315	42	5	5	5.6	.986							
	OF	S. West	165	.309	1	27	101	0	3	0	2.5	.971							
Phi. W-53 L-99 Connie Mack	1B	L. Finney	454	.275	10	48	574	24	6	35	9.4	.990	G. Caster	42	280	16	20	1	4.37
	2B	D. Lodigiani	325	.280	6	44	193	233	21	45	5.6	.953	B. Thomas	42	212	9	14	0	4.92
	SS	W. Ambler	393	.234	0	38	209	310	32	54	4.8	.942	L. Nelson	32	191	10	11	2	5.65
	3B	B. Werber	499	.259	11	69	168	266	30	21	3.5	.935	B. Ross	29	184	9	16	0	5.32
	RF	W. Moses	589	.307	8	49	304	11	11	3	2.3	.966	E. Smith	43	131	3	10	4	5.92
	CF	B. Johnson	563	.313	30	113	400	21	16	3	2.9	.963	N. Potter	35	111	2	12	5	6.47
	LF	S. Chapman	406	.259	17	63	229	8	12	0	2.2	.952							
	C	F. Hayes	316	.291	11	55	319	38	9	2	4.1	.975							
	2B	S. Sperry	253	.273	0	27	121	185	13	26	5.3	.959							
	1B	D. Siebert	194	.284	0	28	403	41	0	35	9.7	1.000							
	C	E. Brucker	171	.374	3	35	188	20	3	1	4.8	.986							

BATTING AND BASE RUNNING LEADERS

Batting Average

J. Foxx, BOS	.349
J. Heath, CLE	.343
B. Chapman, BOS	.340
B. Myer, WAS	.336
C. Travis, WAS	.335

Slugging Average

J. Foxx, BOS	.704
H. Greenberg, DET	.683
J. Heath, CLE	.602
J. DiMaggio, NY	.581
R. York, DET	.579

Home Runs

H. Greenberg, DET	58
J. Foxx, BOS	50
H. Clift, STL	34
R. York, DET	33
J. DiMaggio, NY	32

Total Bases

J. Foxx, BOS	398
H. Greenberg, DET	380
J. DiMaggio, NY	348
B. Johnson, PHI	311
J. Heath, CLE	302

Runs Batted In

J. Foxx, BOS	175
H. Greenberg, DET	146
J. DiMaggio, NY	140
R. York, DET	127
H. Clift, STL	118

Stolen Bases

F. Crosetti, NY	27
L. Lary, CLE	23
B. Werber, PHI	19
B. Lewis, WAS	17
P. Fox, DET	16

PITCHING LEADERS

Winning Percentage

R. Ruffing, NY	.750
M. Pearson, NY	.696
M. Harder, CLE	.630
M. Stratton, CHI	.625
B. Feller, CLE	.607

Earned Run Average

L. Grove, BOS	3.08
R. Ruffing, NY	3.31
L. Gomez, NY	3.35
D. Leonard, WAS	3.43
T. Lee, CHI	3.49

Wins

R. Ruffing, NY	21
B. Newsom, STL	20
L. Gomez, NY	18
M. Harder, CLE	17
B. Feller, CLE	17

Saves

J. Murphy, NY	11
J. Humphries, CLE	6
A. McKain, BOS	6
P. Appleton, WAS	5
N. Potter, PHI	5

Strikeouts

B. Feller, CLE	240
B. Newsom, STL	226
L. Mills, STL	134
L. Gomez, NY	129
R. Ruffing, NY	127

Complete Games

B. Newsom, STL	31
R. Ruffing, NY	22
L. Gomez, NY	20
B. Feller, CLE	20
G. Caster, PHI	20

BATTING AND BASE RUNNING LEADERS

Hits		Base on Balls	
J. Vosmik, BOS	201	H. Greenberg, DET	119
D. Cramer, BOS	198	J. Foxx, BOS	119
J. Foxx, BOS	197	H. Clift, STL	118
M. Almada, STL, WAS	197		

Home Run Percentage		Runs Scored	
H. Greenberg, DET	10.4	H. Greenberg, DET	144
J. Foxx, BOS	8.8	J. Foxx, BOS	139
R. York, DET	7.1	C. Gehringer, DET	133

Doubles		Triples	
J. Cronin, BOS	51	J. Heath, CLE	18
G. McQuinn, STL	42	E. Averill, CLE	15
B. Chapman, BOS	40	J. DiMaggio, NY	13
H. Trosky, CLE	40		

PITCHING LEADERS

Fewest Hits per 9 Innings		Shutouts	
B. Feller, CLE	7.29	R. Ruffing, NY	4
J. Allen, CLE	8.51	L. Gomez, NY	4
M. Pearson, NY	8.82	J. Wilson, BOS	3
		D. Leonard, WAS	3

Fewest Walks per 9 Innings		Most Strikeouts per 9 Inn.	
D. Leonard, WAS	2.14	B. Feller, CLE	7.78
M. Harder, CLE	2.32	B. Newsom, STL	6.17
T. Lyons, CHI	2.40	T. Bridges, DET	6.02

Innings		Games Pitched	
B. Newsom, STL	330	J. Humphries, CLE	45
G. Caster, PHI	280	B. Newsom, STL	44
B. Feller, CLE	278		

	W	L	PCT	GB	R	OR	2B	3B	HR	BA	SA	SB	E	DP	FA	CG	BB	SO	ShO	SV	ERA
NY	99	53	.651		**966**	710	283	63	**174**	.274	**.446**	91	169	169	.973	**91**	566	567	**10**	13	**3.91**
BOS	88	61	.591	9.5	902	751	298	56	98	**.299**	.434	55	190	172	.968	67	**528**	484	**10**	15	4.46
CLE	86	66	.566	13	847	782	**300**	89	113	.281	.434	83	151	145	.974	68	681	**717**	5	**17**	4.60
DET	84	70	.545	16	862	795	219	52	137	.272	.411	76	147	172	**.976**	75	608	435	2	11	4.79
WAS	75	76	.497	23.5	814	873	278	72	85	.293	.416	65	180	**179**	.970	59	655	515	6	11	4.94
CHI	65	83	.439	32	709	752	239	55	67	.277	.383	56	196	155	.967	83	550	432	5	9	4.36
STL	55	97	.362	44	755	962	273	36	92	.281	.397	51	**145**	163	.975	71	737	632	3	7	5.80
PHI	53	99	.349	46	726	956	243	62	98	.270	.396	65	206	119	.965	56	599	473	4	12	5.48
					6581	6581	2133	485	864	.281	.415	542	1384	1274	.971	570	4924	4255	45	95	4.79

National League 1939

	POS	Player	AB	BA	HR	RBI	PO	A	E	DP	TC/G	FA	Pitcher	G	IP	W	L	SV	ERA
Cin. W-97 L-57 Bill McKechnie	1B	F. McCormick	630	.332	18	**128**	**1518**	100	7	**153**	10.4	**.996**	B. Walters	39	**319**	**27**	11	0	**2.29**
	2B	L. Frey	484	.291	11	55	324	412	18	83	6.1	.976	P. Derringer	38	301	25	7	0	2.93
	SS	B. Myers	509	.281	9	56	309	512	42	110	5.7	.951	W. Moore	42	188	13	12	3	3.45
	3B	B. Werber	599	.289	5	57	165	**308**	34	32	3.4	.933	L. Grissom	33	154	9	7	0	4.10
	RF	I. Goodman	470	.323	7	84	246	16	5	4	2.2	.981	J. Thompson	42	152	13	5	2	2.54
	CF	H. Craft	502	.257	13	67	300	13	6	4	2.4	.981	Vander Meer	30	129	5	9	0	4.67
	LF	W. Berger	329	.258	14	44	158	6	5	0	1.8	.970							
	C	E. Lombardi	450	.287	20	85	536	63	10	7	5.1	.984							
	OF	L. Gamble	221	.267	0	14	87	5	1	0	1.7	.989							
	C	Hershberger	174	.345	0	32	204	21	3	2	3.8	.987							
	OF	Bongiovanni	159	.258	0	16	89	1	1	1	2.3	.989							
St. L. W-92 L-61 Ray Blades	1B	J. Mize	564	**.349**	28	108	1348	90	19	123	9.6	.987	C. Davis	49	248	22	16	7	3.63
	2B	S. Martin	425	.268	3	30	242	304	13	62	5.2	**.977**	M. Cooper	45	211	12	6	4	3.25
	SS	J. Brown	**645**	.298	3	51	208	349	25	67	5.6	.957	B. Bowman	51	169	13	5	**9**	2.60
	3B	D. Gutteridge	524	.269	7	54	136	203	24	24	2.5	.934	L. Warneke	34	162	13	7	2	3.78
	RF	E. Slaughter	604	.320	12	86	**348**	18	12	5	2.5	.968	B. McGee	43	156	12	5	0	3.81
	CF	T. Moore	417	.295	17	77	291	16	2	1	2.6	**.994**	B. Weiland	32	146	10	12	1	3.57
	LF	J. Medwick	606	.332	14	117	313	10	8	1	2.2	.976	C. Shoun	**53**	103	3	1	**9**	3.76
	C	M. Owen	344	.259	3	35	452	52	9	7	4.1	.982							
	O3	P. Martin	281	.306	3	37	128	34	7	2		.959							
	C	D. Padgett	233	.399	5	53	249	18	6	5	4.5	.978							
Bkn. W-84 L-69 Leo Durocher	1B	D. Camilli	565	.290	26	104	1515	**129**	17	**138**	10.6	.990	L. Hamlin	40	270	20	13	0	3.64
	2B	P. Coscarart	419	.277	4	43	256	338	25	69	5.8	.960	H. Casey	40	227	15	10	1	2.93
	SS	L. Durocher	390	.277	1	34	228	322	25	73	5.1	.957	V. Tamulis	39	159	9	8	4	4.37
	3B	C. Lavagetto	587	.300	10	87	163	278	24	28	3.1	.948	T. Pressnell	31	157	9	7	2	4.02
	RF	A. Parks	239	.272	1	19	125	2	3	0	2.0	.977	Fitzsimmons	27	151	7	9	3	3.87
	CF	G. Moore	306	.225	3	39	140	8	6	3	1.8	.961	W. Wyatt	16	109	8	3	0	2.31
	LF	E. Koy	425	.278	8	67	252	4	10	1	2.3	.962	I. Hutchinson	41	106	5	2	1	4.34
	C	B. Phelps	323	.285	6	42	361	40	8	6	4.4	.980	R. Evans	24	64	1	8	1	5.18
	S2	J. Hudson	343	.254	2	32	175	259	18	56		.960							
	C	A. Todd	245	.278	5	32	284	35	5	5	4.4	.985							
	OF	D. Walker	225	.280	2	38	144	5	5	3	2.6	.968							
	OF	T. Stainback	201	.269	3	19	121	0	8	0	2.3	.938							
	OF	G. Rosen	183	.251	1	12	106	0	0	0	2.3	1.000							
	OF	J. Ripple	106	.330	0	28	55	0	0	0	2.0	1.000							

POS	Player	AB	BA	HR	RBI	PO	A	E	DP	TC/G	FA	Pitcher	G	IP	W	L	SV	ERA
Chi.																		
1B	R. Russell	542	.273	9	79	1383	83	18	109	10.4	.988	B. Lee	37	282	19	15	0	3.44
2B	B. Herman	623	.307	7	70	377	485	29	95	5.7	.967	C. Passeau	34	221	13	9	3	3.05
SS	D. Bartell	336	.238	3	34	241	307	33	62	5.8	.943	L. French	36	194	15	8	1	3.29
3B	S. Hack	641	.298	8	56	177	278	21	15	3.1	.956	C. Root	35	167	8	8	4	4.03
RF	J. Gleeson	332	.223	4	45	175	5	8	1	2.1	.957	V. Page	27	139	7	7	1	3.88
CF	H. Leiber	365	.310	24	88	249	5	6	0	2.7	.977	D. Dean	19	96	6	4	0	3.36
LF	A. Galan	549	.304	6	71	290	6	9	0	2.1	.970	E. Whitehill	24	89	4	7	1	5.14
C	G. Hartnett	306	.278	12	59	336	47	3	3	4.5	.992	J. Russell	39	69	4	3	3	3.67
OF	C. Reynolds	281	.246	4	44	168	5	5	1	2.5	.972							
C	G. Mancuso	251	.231	2	17	333	36	7	6	4.9	.981							
OF	B. Nicholson	220	.295	5	38	123	5	6	0	2.3	.955							
SS	B. Mattick	178	.287	0	23	102	179	22	28	6.3	.927							
N. Y.																		
1B	Z. Bonura	455	.321	11	85	1205	90	11	110	10.7	.992	H. Gumbert	36	244	18	11	0	4.32
2B	B. Whitehead	335	.239	2	24	232	320	17	60	6.3	.970	C. Melton	41	207	12	15	5	3.56
SS	B. Jurges	543	.285	6	43	295	482	28	95	5.9	.965	B. Lohrman	38	186	12	13	1	4.07
3B	T. Hafey	256	.242	6	26	61	130	8	10	2.8	.960	H. Schumacher	29	182	13	10	0	4.81
RF	M. Ott	396	.308	27	80	175	6	5	2	1.9	.973	C. Hubbell	29	154	11	9	2	2.75
CF	F. Demaree	560	.304	11	79	329	11	5	2	2.3	.986	M. Salvo	32	136	4	10	1	4.63
LF	J. Moore	562	.269	10	47	260	13	4	2	2.0	.986	J. Brown	31	56	4	0	7	4.15
C	H. Danning	520	.313	16	74	550	80	6	13	4.8	.991							
2B	A. Kampouris	201	.249	5	29	146	179	9	34	5.4	.973							
OF	B. Seeds	173	.266	5	26	77	2	2	0	1.6	.975							
Pit.																		
1B	E. Fletcher	370	.303	12	71	1010	56	8	97	10.6*	.993	B. Klinger	37	225	14	17	0	4.36
2B	P. Young	293	.276	3	29	202	270	16	61	5.8	.967	M. Brown	47	200	9	13	7	3.37
SS	A. Vaughan	595	.306	6	62	330	531	34	103	5.9	.962	J. Bowman	37	185	10	14	1	4.48
3B	L. Handley	376	.285	1	42	83	180	18	14	2.8	.936	R. Sewell	52	176	10	9	2	4.08
RF	P. Waner	461	.328	3	45	206	12	5	4	2.1	.978	J. Tobin	25	145	9	9	0	4.52
CF	L. Waner	379	.285	0	24	225	9	2	1	2.6	.992	B. Swift	36	130	5	7	4	3.89
LF	J. Rizzo	330	.261	6	55	186	2	5	0	2.2	.974							
C	R. Mueller	180	.233	2	18	203	32	7	5	3.0	.971							
23	B. Brubaker	345	.232	7	43	183	286	26	47		.947							
OF	C. Klein	270	.300	11	47	133	4	7	0	2.2	.951							
OF	F. Bell	262	.286	2	34	152	6	4	0	2.4	.975							
C	R. Berres	231	.229	0	16	269	36	2	4	3.8	.993							
1B	G. Suhr	204	.289	1	31	521	23	4	42	10.5	.993							
Bos.																		
1B	B. Hassett	590	.308	2	60	1143	112	19	127	10.0	.985	B. Posedel	33	221	15	13	0	3.92
2B	T. Cuccinello	310	.306	2	40	208	246	14	66	5.9	.970	MacFayden	33	192	8	14	2	3.90
SS	E. Miller	296	.267	4	31	183	275	14	76	6.1	.970	J. Turner	25	158	4	11	0	4.28
3B	H. Majeski	367	.272	7	54	111	196	18	19	3.3	.945	L. Fette	27	146	10	10	0	2.96
RF	D. Garms	513	.298	2	37	183	6	7	2	2.0	.964	M. Shoffner	25	132	4	6	1	3.13
CF	J. Cooney	368	.274	2	27	236	10	2	2	2.1	.992	J. Lanning	37	129	5	6	4	3.42
LF	M. West	449	.285	19	82	287	8	8	2	2.4	.974	D. Errickson	28	128	6	9	1	4.00
C	A. Lopez	412	.252	8	49	424	72	7	11	3.9	.986	J. Sullivan	31	114	6	9	2	3.64
UT	R. Warstler	342	.243	0	24	194	301	20	75		.961							
OF	A. Simmons	330	.282	7	43	158	7	3	2	2.0	.982							
UT	S. Sisti	215	.228	1	11	136	152	8	8		.973							
Phi.																		
1B	G. Suhr	198	.318	3	24	520	37	3	50	9.3	.995	H. Mulcahy	38	226	9	16	4	4.99
2B	R. Hughes	237	.228	1	16	183	184	6	30	5.7	.984	K. Higbe	34	187	10	14	2	4.85
SS	G. Scharein	399	.238	1	33	258	331	26	69	5.3	.958	B. Beck	34	183	7	14	3	4.73
3B	P. May	464	.287	2	62	153	263	19	28	3.3	.956	I. Pearson	26	125	2	13	0	5.76
RF	J. Marty	299	.254	9	44	176	9	5	3	2.4	.974	S. Johnson	22	111	8	8	2	3.81
CF	H. Martin	393	.282	1	22	276	5	7	1	3.0	.976	M. Butcher	19	104	2	13*	0	5.61
LF	M. Arnovich	491	.324	5	67	335	10	6	0	2.7	.983	R. Harrell	22	95	3	7	0	5.42
C	S. Davis	202	.307	0	23	260	40	0	1	3.5	1.000	Hollingsworth	15	60	1	9	0	5.85
UT	E. Mueller	341	.279	9	43	163	166	11	38		.968							
OF	G. Brack	270	.289	6	41	89	4	4	1	2.0	.959							
OF	L. Scott	232	.280	1	26	109	7	5	1	2.2	.959							
SS	D. Young	217	.263	3	20	70	104	10	16	3.3	.946							
1B	J. Bolling	211	.289	3	13	392	38	8	35	9.1	.982							
C	W. Millies	205	.234	0	12	229	37	10	3	3.3	.964							

BATTING AND BASE RUNNING LEADERS

Batting Average

J. Mize, STL	.349
F. McCormick, CIN	.332
J. Medwick, STL	.332
P. Waner, PIT	.328
M. Arnovich, PHI	.324

Slugging Average

J. Mize, STL	.626
M. Ott, NY	.581
H. Leiber, CHI	.556
D. Camilli, BKN	.524
I. Goodman, CIN	.515

Home Runs

J. Mize, STL	28
M. Ott, NY	27
D. Camilli, BKN	26
H. Leiber, CHI	24
E. Lombardi, CIN	20

Total Bases

J. Mize, STL	353
F. McCormick, CIN	312
J. Medwick, STL	307
D. Camilli, BKN	296
E. Slaughter, STL	291

PITCHING LEADERS

Winning Percentage

P. Derringer, CIN	.781
B. Walters, CIN	.711
L. French, CHI	.652
H. Gumbert, NY	.621
L. Hamlin, BKN	.606

Earned Run Average

B. Walters, CIN	2.29
C. Hubbell, NY	2.75
H. Casey, BKN	2.93
P. Derringer, CIN	2.93
L. Fette, BOS	2.96

Wins

B. Walters, CIN	27
P. Derringer, CIN	25
C. Davis, STL	22
L. Hamlin, BKN	20
B. Lee, CHI	19

Saves

B. Bowman, STL	9
C. Shoun, STL	9
J. Brown, NY	7
C. Davis, STL	7
M. Brown, PIT	7

BATTING AND BASE RUNNING LEADERS

Runs Batted In
F. McCormick, CIN	128
J. Medwick, STL	117
J. Mize, STL	108
D. Camilli, BKN	104
H. Leiber, CHI	88

Stolen Bases
L. Handley, PIT	17
S. Hack, CHI	17
B. Werber, CIN	15
C. Lavagetto, BKN	14
B. Hassett, BOS	13

Hits
F. McCormick, CIN	209
J. Medwick, STL	201
J. Mize, STL	197

Base on Balls
D. Camilli, BKN	110
M. Ott, NY	100
J. Mize, STL	92

Home Run Percentage
M. Ott, NY	6.8
H. Leiber, CHI	6.6
J. Mize, STL	5.0

Runs Scored
B. Werber, CIN	115
S. Hack, CHI	112
B. Herman, CHI	111

Doubles
E. Slaughter, STL	52
J. Medwick, STL	48
J. Mize, STL	44

Triples
B. Herman, CHI	18
I. Goodman, CIN	16
J. Mize, STL	14

PITCHING LEADERS

Strikeouts
C. Passeau, CHI, PHI	137
B. Walters, CIN	137
M. Cooper, STL	130
P. Derringer, CIN	128
B. Lee, CHI	105

Complete Games
B. Walters, CIN	31
P. Derringer, CIN	28
B. Lee, CHI	20
L. Hamlin, BKN	19
B. Posedel, BOS	18

Fewest Hits per 9 Innings
B. Walters, CIN	7.05
L. Fette, BOS	7.58
L. Hamlin, BKN	8.51

Shutouts
L. Fette, BOS	6
B. Posedel, BOS	5
P. Derringer, CIN	5
B. McGee, STL	4

Fewest Walks per 9 Innings
P. Derringer, CIN	1.05
C. Hubbell, NY	1.40
C. Davis, STL	1.74

Most Strikeouts per 9 Inn.
L. French, CHI	4.55
C. Passeau, CHI, PHI	4.49
K. Higbe, CHI, PHI	4.07

Innings
B. Walters, CIN	319
P. Derringer, CIN	301
B. Lee, CHI	282

Games Pitched
C. Shoun, STL	53
R. Sewell, PIT	52
B. Bowman, STL	51

	W	L	PCT	GB	R	OR	Batting 2B	3B	HR	BA	SA	SB	Fielding E	DP	FA	Pitching CG	BB	SO	ShO	SV	ERA
CIN	97	57	.630		767	595	269	60	98	.278	.405	46	162	170	.974	86	499	637	13	9	3.27
STL	92	61	.601	4.5	779	633	332	62	98	.294	.432	44	177	140	.971	45	498	603	18	32	3.59
BKN	84	69	.549	12.5	708	645	265	57	78	.265	.380	59	176	157	.972	69	399	528	9	13	3.64
CHI	84	70	.545	13	724	678	263	62	91	.266	.391	61	186	126	.970	72	430	584	8	13	3.80
NY	77	74	.510	18.5	703	685	211	38	116	.272	.396	26	153	142	.975	55	478	505	6	20	4.07
PIT	68	85	.444	28.5	666	721	261	60	63	.276	.384	44	168	153	.972	53	423	524	10	15	4.15
BOS	63	88	.417	32.5	572	659	199	39	56	.264	.348	41	181	178	.971	68	513	430	11	15	3.71
PHI	45	106	.298	50.5	553	856	232	40	49	.261	.351	47	171	133	.970	67	579	447	3	12	5.17
					5472	5472	2032	418	649	.272	.386	368	1374	1209	.972	515	3819	4258	78	129	3.92

American League 1939

	POS	Player	AB	BA	HR	RBI	PO	A	E	DP	TC/G	FA	Pitcher	G	IP	W	L	SV	ERA
N.Y. W-106 L-45 Joe McCarthy	1B	B. Dahlgren	531	.235	15	89	1303	68	13	140	9.6	.991	R. Ruffing	28	233	21	7	0	2.93
	2B	J. Gordon	567	.284	28	111	370	461	28	116	5.7	.967	L. Gomez	26	198	12	8	0	3.41
	SS	F. Crosetti	656	.233	10	56	323	460	26	118	5.3	.968	B. Hadley	26	154	12	6	2	2.98
	3B	R. Rolfe	648	.329	14	80	151	282	19	22	3.0	.958	A. Donald	24	153	13	3	1	3.71
	RF	C. Keller	398	.334	11	83	213	5	7	1	2.1	.969	M. Pearson	22	146	12	5	0	4.49
	CF	J. DiMaggio	462	.381	30	126	328	13	5	2	3.0	.986	O. Hildebrand	21	127	10	4	2	3.06
	LF	G. Selkirk	418	.306	21	101	254	4	3	1	2.1	.989	S. Sundra	24	121	11	1	0	2.76
	C	B. Dickey	480	.302	24	105	571	57	7	8	5.0	.989	M. Russo	21	116	8	3	2	2.41
	OF	T. Henrich	347	.277	9	57	205	7	2	1	2.4	.991	J. Murphy	38	61	3	6	19	4.40
	P	R. Ruffing	114	.307	1	20	8	32	2	2	1.5	.952							
Bos. W-89 L-62 Joe Cronin	1B	J. Foxx	467	.360	35	105	1101	91	10	104	9.8	.992	L. Grove	23	191	15	4	0	2.54
	2B	B. Doerr	525	.318	12	73	336	431	19	95	6.2	.976	J. Wilson	36	177	11	11	2	4.67
	SS	J. Cronin	520	.308	19	107	306	437	32	93	5.5	.959	Ostermueller	34	159	11	7	4	4.24
	3B	J. Tabor	577	.289	14	95	144	338	40	32	3.5	.923	E. Auker	31	151	9	10	0	5.36
	RF	T. Williams	565	.327	31	145	318	11	19	3	2.3	.945	D. Galehouse	30	147	9	10	0	4.54
	CF	D. Cramer	589	.311	0	56	356	12	6	0	2.8	.984	E. Dickman	48	114	8	3	5	4.43
	LF	J. Vosmik	554	.276	7	84	296	9	8	0	2.2	.974	J. Heving	46	107	11	3	7	3.70
	C	J. Peacock	274	.277	0	36	314	33	10	6	4.3	.972	J. Bagby	21	80	5	5	0	7.09
	1O	L. Finney	249	.325	1	46	328	12	6	28		.983							
	C	G. Desautels	226	.243	0	21	310	48	2	5	4.9	.994							
	2B	T. Carey	161	.242	0	20	75	87	0	19	4.6	1.000							
Cle. W-87 L-67 Ossie Vitt	1B	H. Trosky	448	.335	25	104	1004	97	9	97	9.4	.992	B. Feller	39	297	24	9	1	2.85
	2B	O. Hale	253	.312	4	48	141	146	10	31	4.1	.966	A. Milnar	37	209	14	12	3	3.79
	SS	S. Webb	269	.264	2	26	165	203	27	40	4.9	.932	M. Harder	29	208	15	9	1	3.50
	3B	K. Keltner	587	.325	13	97	187	297	13	40	3.2	.974	J. Allen	28	175	9	7	0	4.58
	RF	B. Campbell	450	.287	8	72	200	12	13	3	2.0	.942	W. Hudlin	27	143	9	10	3	4.91
	CF	B. Chapman	545	.290	6	82	356	12	11	0	2.6	.971	H. Eisenstat	26	104	6	7	2	3.30
	LF	J. Heath	431	.292	14	69	263	7	10	2	2.6	.964							
	C	R. Hemsley	395	.263	2	36	499	58	9	7	5.3	.984							
	UT	O. Grimes	364	.269	4	56	501	192	22	75		.969							
	OF	R. Weatherly	323	.310	1	32	146	3	6	1	2.0	.961							
	SS	L. Boudreau	225	.258	0	19	103	184	14	31	5.7	.953							
	C	F. Pytlak	183	.268	0	14	227	24	0	5	4.9	1.000							

	POS	Player	AB	BA	HR	RBI	PO	A	E	DP	TC/G	FA	Pitcher	G	IP	W	L	SV	ERA
Chi. W-85 L-69 Jimmy Dykes	1B	J. Kuhel	546	.300	15	56	1256	72	11	113	9.8	.992	T. Lee	33	235	15	11	3	4.21
	2B	O. Bejma	307	.251	8	44	170	199	7	36	4.6	.981	J. Rigney	35	219	15	8	0	3.70
	SS	L. Appling	516	.314	0	56	289	461	39	78	5.3	.951	E. Smith	29	177	9	11	0	3.67
	3B	E. McNair	479	.324	7	82	90	194	19	23	2.9	.937	T. Lyons	21	173	14	6	0	2.76
	RF	L. Rosenthal	324	.265	10	51	193	5	2	1	2.2	.990	J. Knott	25	150	11	6	0	4.15
	CF	M. Kreevich	541	.323	5	77	419	18	11	4	3.2	.975	B. Dietrich	25	128	7	8	0	5.22
	LF	G. Walker	598	.291	13	111	365	11	13	3	2.6	.967	C. Brown	61	118	11	10	18	3.88
	C	M. Tresh	352	.259	0	38	480	59	8	7	4.6	.985							
	OF	R. Radcliff	397	.264	2	53	130	1	4	0	1.7	.970							
	2B	J. Hayes	269	.249	0	23	172	201	10	51	5.6	.974							
	3B	M. Owen	194	.237	0	15	63	99	8	11	3.1	.953							
Det. W-81 L-73 Del Baker	1B	H. Greenberg	500	.312	33	112	1205	75	9	108	9.5	.993	B. Newsom	35	246	17	10	2	3.37
	2B	C. Gehringer	406	.325	16	86	245	312	13	67	5.3	.977	T. Bridges	29	198	17	7	2	3.50
	SS	F. Croucher	324	.269	5	40	139	256	28	47	4.5	.934	S. Rowe	28	164	10	12	0	4.99
	3B	P. Higgins	489	.276	8	76	140	241	36	22	3.2	.914	D. Trout	33	162	9	10	2	3.61
	RF	P. Fox	519	.295	7	66	275	12	9	3	2.3	.970	A. Benton	37	150	6	8	5	4.56
	CF	B. McCosky	611	.311	4	58	428	7	6	2	3.0	.986	A. McKain	32	130	5	6	4	3.68
	LF	E. Averill	309	.262	10	58	157	3	4	0	2.1	.976							
	C	B. Tebbetts	341	.261	4	53	449	64	16	10	5.3	.970							
	C	R. York	329	.307	20	68	283	38	5	5	4.9	.985							
	2S	B. McCoy	192	.302	1	33	108	150	11	25		.959							
	OF	R. Cullenbine	179	.240	6	23	81	2	9	1	2.0	.902							
	S3	B. Rogell	174	.230	2	23	76	130	15	24		.932							
	S2	R. Kress	157	.242	1	22	77	116	11	28		.946							
	OF	D. Walker	154	.305	4	19	93	4	3	1	2.7	.970							
	OF	B. Bell	134	.239	0	24	73	4	0	1	2.1	1.000							
Was. W-65 L-87 Bucky Harris	1B	M. Vernon	276	.257	1	30	690	40	11	75	9.9	.985	D. Leonard	34	269	20	8	0	3.54
	2B	J. Bloodworth	318	.289	4	40	226	219	13	66	6.3	.972	K. Chase	32	232	10	19	0	3.80
	SS	C. Travis	476	.292	5	63	194	359	24	74	4.9	.958	J. Krakauskas	39	217	11	17	1	4.60
	3B	B. Lewis	536	.319	10	75	122	326	32	31	3.6	.933	J. Haynes	27	173	8	12	0	5.36
	RF	G. Case	530	.302	2	35	332	7	16	2	2.9	.955	A. Carrasquel	40	159	5	9	2	4.69
	CF	S. West	390	.282	3	52	232	7	2	3	2.7	.992	P. Appleton	40	103	5	10	6	4.56
	LF	T. Wright	499	.309	4	93	236	10	13	4	2.1	.950							
	C	R. Ferrell	274	.281	0	31	327	46	9	9	4.6	.976							
	OF	B. Estalella	280	.275	8	41	157	3	6	1	2.2	.964							
	2B	B. Myer	258	.302	1	32	175	188	12	48	5.8	.968							
	OF	J. Welaj	201	.274	1	33	113	2	3	1	2.1	.975							
	S3	C. Gelbert	188	.255	3	29	60	122	7	20		.963							
	C	T. Giuliani	172	.250	0	18	201	28	5	3	4.7	.979							
Phi. W-55 L-97 Connie Mack	1B	D. Siebert	402	.294	6	47	874	74	9	73	9.7	.991	L. Nelson	35	198	10	13	1	4.78
	2B	J. Gantenbein	348	.290	4	36	165	179	19	26	4.8	.948	N. Potter	41	196	8	12	2	6.60
	SS	S. Newsome	248	.222	0	17	176	221	21	44	4.5	.950	B. Ross	29	174	6	14	0	6.00
	3B	D. Lodigiani	393	.260	6	44	103	181	17	8	3.4	.944	B. Beckmann	27	155	7	11	0	5.39
	RF	W. Moses	437	.307	3	35	209	10	8	2	2.2	.965	G. Caster	28	136	9	9	0	4.90
	CF	S. Chapman	498	.269	15	64	350	11	17	2	3.2	.955	C. Pippen	25	119	4	11	1	5.99
	LF	B. Johnson	544	.338	23	114	369	15	13	3	2.6	.967	C. Dean	54	117	5	8	7	5.25
	C	F. Hayes	431	.283	20	83	380	60	10	12	3.9	.978	B. Joyce	30	108	3	5	0	6.69
	23	B. Nagel	341	.252	12	39	134	218	21	32		.944							
	OF	D. Miles	320	.300	1	37	146	4	5	1	2.0	.968							
	SS	W. Ambler	227	.211	0	24	126	184	15	31	4.2	.954							
	C	E. Brucker	172	.291	3	31	150	18	0	5	3.6	1.000							
	1B	N. Etten	155	.252	3	29	376	19	4	29	9.7	.990							
St. L. W-43 L-111 Fred Haney	1B	G. McQuinn	617	.316	20	94	1377	116	11	122	9.8	.993	J. Kramer	40	212	9	16	0	5.83
	2B	J. Berardino	468	.256	5	58	315	339	29	67	6.0	.958	V. Kennedy	33	192	9	17*	0	5.73
	SS	D. Heffner	375	.267	1	35	138	218	21	33	5.2	.944	B. Trotter	41	157	6	13	0	5.34
	3B	H. Clift	526	.270	15	84	184	324	25	34	3.6	.953	R. Lawson	36	151	3	7	0	5.32
	RF	M. Hoag	482	.295	10	75	218	13	7	2	2.0	.971	L. Mills	34	144	4	11	2	6.55
	CF	C. Laabs	317	.300	10	62	199	7	6	0	2.7	.944	B. Harris	28	126	3	12	0	5.71
	LF	J. Gallagher	266	.246	9	40	143	8	9	1	2.4	.944	G. Gill	27	95	1	12	0	7.11
	C	J. Glenn	286	.273	4	29	280	48	11	4	4.1	.968							
	OF	B. Sullivan	332	.289	5	50	139	7	7	3	2.6	.954							
	SS	M. Christman	222	.216	0	20	151	209	15	45	5.9	.960							
	OF	J. Grace	207	.304	3	22	83	9	3	0	1.8	.968							
	OF	M. Mazzera	111	.297	3	22	56	1	1	0	2.3	.983							

BATTING AND BASE RUNNING LEADERS

Batting Average		Slugging Average	
J. DiMaggio, NY	.381	J. Foxx, BOS	.694
J. Foxx, BOS	.360	J. DiMaggio, NY	.671
B. Johnson, PHI	.338	H. Greenberg, DET	.622
H. Trosky, CLE	.335	T. Williams, BOS	.609
C. Keller, NY	.334	H. Trosky, CLE	.589

Home Runs		Total Bases	
J. Foxx, BOS	35	T. Williams, BOS	344
H. Greenberg, DET	33	J. Foxx, BOS	324
T. Williams, BOS	31	R. Rolfe, NY	321
J. DiMaggio, NY	30	G. McQuinn, STL	318
J. Gordon, NY	28	H. Greenberg, DET	311

PITCHING LEADERS

Winning Percentage		Earned Run Average	
L. Grove, BOS	.789	L. Grove, BOS	2.54
R. Ruffing, NY	.750	T. Lyons, CHI	2.76
B. Feller, CLE	.727	B. Feller, CLE	2.85
D. Leonard, WAS	.714	R. Ruffing, NY	2.93
T. Bridges, DET	.708	L. Gomez, NY	3.41

Wins		Saves	
B. Feller, CLE	24	J. Murphy, NY	19
R. Ruffing, NY	21	C. Brown, CHI	18
D. Leonard, WAS	20	J. Heving, BOS	7
B. Newsom, DET, STL	20	C. Dean, PHI	7
T. Bridges, DET	17	P. Appleton, WAS	6

BATTING AND BASE RUNNING LEADERS

Runs Batted In

T. Williams, BOS	145
J. DiMaggio, NY	126
B. Johnson, PHI	114
H. Greenberg, DET	112
J. Gordon, NY	111
G. Walker, CHI	111

Hits

R. Rolfe, NY	213
G. McQuinn, STL	195
K. Keltner, CLE	191

Home Run Percentage

J. Foxx, BOS	7.5
H. Greenberg, DET	6.6
J. DiMaggio, NY	6.5

Doubles

R. Rolfe, NY	46
T. Williams, BOS	44
H. Greenberg, DET	42

Stolen Bases

G. Case, WAS	51
P. Fox, DET	23
M. Kreevich, CHI	23
B. McCosky, DET	20
B. Chapman, CLE	18
J. Kuhel, CHI	18

Base on Balls

H. Clift, STL	111
T. Williams, BOS	107
L. Appling, CHI	105

Runs Scored

R. Rolfe, NY	139
T. Williams, BOS	131
J. Foxx, BOS	130

Triples

B. Lewis, WAS	16
B. McCosky, DET	14
B. Campbell, CLE	13
G. McQuinn, STL	13

PITCHING LEADERS

Strikeouts

B. Feller, CLE	246
B. Newsom, DET, STL	192
T. Bridges, DET	129
J. Rigney, CHI	119
K. Chase, WAS	118

Fewest Hits per 9 Innings

B. Feller, CLE	6.89
L. Gomez, NY	7.86
R. Ruffing, NY	8.14

Fewest Walks per 9 Innings

T. Lyons, CHI	1.36
D. Leonard, WAS	1.97
T. Lee, CHI	2.68

Innings

B. Feller, CLE	297
B. Newsom, DET, STL	292
D. Leonard, WAS	269

Complete Games

B. Feller, CLE	24
B. Newsom, DET, STL	24
R. Ruffing, NY	22
D. Leonard, WAS	21
L. Grove, BOS	17

Shutouts

R. Ruffing, NY	5
B. Feller, CLE	4

Most Strikeouts per 9 Inn.

B. Feller, CLE	7.46
B. Newsom, DET, STL	5.92
T. Bridges, DET	5.86

Games Pitched

C. Brown, CHI	61
C. Dean, PHI	54
E. Dickman, BOS	48
J. Heving, BOS	46

	W	L	PCT	GB	R	OR	2B	3B	HR	BA	SA	SB	E	DP	FA	CG	BB	SO	ShO	SV	ERA
NY	106	45	.702		967	556	259	55	166	.287	.451	72	126	159	.978	87	567	565	12	26	3.31
BOS	89	62	.589	17	890	795	287	57	124	.291	.436	42	180	147	.970	52	543	539	4	20	4.56
CLE	87	67	.565	20.5	797	700	291	79	85	.280	.413	72	180	148	.970	69	602	614	9	13	4.08
CHI	85	69	.552	22.5	755	737	220	56	64	.275	.374	113	167	140	.972	62	454	535	5	21	4.31
DET	81	73	.526	26.5	849	762	277	67	124	.279	.426	88	198	147	.967	64	574	633	6	16	4.29
WAS	65	87	.428	41.5	702	797	249	79	44	.278	.379	94	205	167	.966	72	602	521	4	10	4.60
PHI	55	97	.362	51.5	711	1022	282	55	98	.271	.400	60	210	131	.964	50	579	397	5	12	5.79
STL	43	111	.279	64.5	733	1035	242	50	91	.268	.381	48	199	144	.968	56	739	516	3	3	6.01
					6404	6404	2107	498	796	.279	.407	589	1465	1183	.969	512	4660	4320	48	121	4.62

National League 1940

	POS	Player	AB	BA	HR	RBI	PO	A	E	DP	TC/G	FA	Pitcher	G	IP	W	L	SV	ERA
Cin. W-100 L-53 Bill McKechnie	1B	F. McCormick	618	.309	19	127	1587	98	8	146	10.9	.995	B. Walters	36	305	22	10	0	2.48
	2B	L. Frey	563	.266	8	54	366	512	21	111	6.0	.977	P. Derringer	37	297	20	12	0	3.06
	SS	B. Myers	282	.202	5	30	155	269	17	62	5.0	.961	J. Thompson	33	225	16	9	0	3.32
	3B	B. Werber	584	.277	12	48	139	287	17	24	3.1	.962	J. Turner	24	187	14	7	0	2.89
	RF	I. Goodman	519	.258	12	63	252	6	8	0	2.0	.970	W. Moore	25	117	8	8	1	3.63
	CF	H. Craft	422	.244	6	48	284	7	1	2	2.7	.997	J. Beggs	37	77	12	3	7	2.00
	LF	M. McCormick	417	.300	1	30	266	9	4	2	2.6	.986							
	C	E. Lombardi	376	.319	14	74	397	46	5	5	4.4	.989							
	SS	E. Joost	278	.216	1	24	145	240	16	48	5.1	.960							
	OF	M. Arnovich	211	.284	0	21	129	5	0	0	2.2	1.000							
	C	Hershberger	123	.309	0	26	121	11	2	0	3.6	.985							
	OF	J. Ripple	101	.307	4	20	45	0	0	0	1.5	1.000							
Bkn. W-88 L-65 Leo Durocher	1B	D. Camilli	512	.287	23	96	1299	79	11	85	9.9	.992	W. Wyatt	37	239	15	14	0	3.46
	2B	P. Coscarart	506	.237	9	58	326	379	31	58	5.3	.958	L. Hamlin	33	182	9	8	0	3.06
	SS	P. Reese	312	.272	5	28	190	238	18	41	5.4	.960	V. Tamulis	41	154	8	5	2	3.09
	3B	C. Lavagetto	448	.257	4	43	137	191	24	12	3.0	.932	H. Casey	44	154	11	8	2	3.62
	RF	J. Vosmik	404	.282	1	42	193	9	5	1	2.1	.976	T. Carleton	34	149	6	6	2	3.81
	CF	D. Walker	556	.308	6	66	360	6	10	3	2.8	.973	C. Davis	22	137	8	7	2	3.81
	LF	J. Medwick	423	.300	14	66	240	7	5	0	2.4	.980	Fitzsimmons	20	134	16	2	1	2.81
	C	B. Phelps	370	.295	13	61	428	35	11	3	4.8	.977	T. Pressnell	24	68	6	5	2	3.69
	OF	J. Wasdell	230	.278	3	37	70	1	4	0	1.8	.947							
	3O	P. Reiser	225	.293	3	20	59	58	5	7		.959							
	S2	J. Hudson	179	.218	0	19	94	145	15	20		.941							
	SS	L. Durocher	160	.231	1	14	102	131	10	22	4.6	.959							

	POS	Player	AB	BA	HR	RBI	PO	A	E	DP	TC/G	FA	Pitcher	G	IP	W	L	SV	ERA
St. L.	1B	J. Mize	579	.314	43	137	1376	80	14	105	9.6	.990	L. Warneke	33	232	16	10	0	3.14
W-84 L-69	2B	J. Orengo	415	.287	7	56	204	216	21	45	5.7	.952	M. Cooper	38	231	11	12	3	3.63
Ray Blades	SS	M. Marion	435	.278	3	46	245	366	33	76	5.2	.949	B. McGee	38	218	16	10	0	3.80
W-15 L-24	3B	S. Martin	369	.238	4	32	52	89	4	2	2.0	.972	C. Shoun	54	197	13	11	5	3.92
Mike Gonzalez	RF	E. Slaughter	516	.306	17	73	267	8	3	5	2.1	.989	B. Bowman	28	114	7	5	0	4.33
W-0 L-5	CF	T. Moore	537	.304	17	64	383	11	5	4	3.0	.987	M. Lanier	35	105	9	6	3	3.34
Billy Southworth	LF	E. Koy	348	.310	8	52	192	2	6	0	2.2	.970							
W-69 L-40	C	M. Owen	307	.264	0	27	378	56	9	8	3.9	.980							
	UT	J. Brown	454	.280	0	30	198	243	22	42		.952							
	C	D. Padgett	240	.242	6	41	243	34	11	5	4.0	.962							
	OF	P. Martin	228	.316	3	39	103	8	3	0	1.8	.974							
	OF	J. Medwick	158	.304	3	20	81	1	1	0	2.2	.988							
Pit.	1B	E. Fletcher	510	.273	16	104	1512	**104**	11	128	**11.1**	.993	R. Sewell	33	190	16	5	1	2.80
W-78 L-76	2B	F. Gustine	524	.281	1	55	288	402	**43**	92	5.6	.941	J. Bowman	32	188	9	10	2	4.46
Frankie Frisch	SS	A. Vaughan	594	.300	7	95	308	**542**	**52**	94	5.8	.942	M. Brown	48	173	10	9	7	3.49
	3B	L. Handley	302	.281	1	19	84	139	18	12	3.0	.925	Heintzelman	39	165	8	8	3	4.47
	RF	B. Elliott	551	.292	5	64	302	12	7	0	2.2	.978	B. Klinger	39	142	8	13	3	5.39
	CF	V. DiMaggio	356	.289	19	54	220	13	5	3	2.2	.979	M. Butcher	35	136	8	9	2	6.01
	LF	M. Van Robays	572	.273	11	116	276	10	11	3	2.1	.963	J. Lanning	38	116	4	4	2	4.05
	C	S. Davis	285	.326	5	39	288	61	12	11	4.1	.967	D. Lanahan	40	108	6	8	2	4.25
	3B	D. Garms	358	**.355**	5	57	65	123	7	15	3.0	.964	MacFadyen	35	91	5	4	2	3.55
	OF	P. Waner	238	.290	1	32	62	3	1	0	1.5	.985							
	C	A. Lopez	174	.259	1	24	224	29	2	7	4.3	.992*							
	OF	L. Waner	166	.259	0	3	90	3	1	1	2.2	.989							
	2B	P. Young	136	.250	2	20	51	79	13	9	4.3	.909							
Chi.	1B	P. Cavarretta	193	.280	2	22	524	30	5	57	10.8	.991	C. Passeau	46	281	20	13	5	2.50
W-75 L-79	2B	B. Herman	558	.292	5	57	366	448	22	94	**6.2**	.974	L. French	40	246	14	14	2	3.29
Gabby Hartnett	SS	B. Mattick	441	.218	0	33	233	431	38	76	5.6	.946	B. Lee	37	211	9	17	0	5.03
	3B	S. Hack	603	**.317**	8	40	**175**	**302**	23	**27**	3.4	.954	V. Olsen	34	173	13	9	0	2.97
	RF	B. Nicholson	491	.297	25	98	235	10	13	2	2.1	.950	Raffensberger	43	115	7	9	3	3.38
	CF	H. Leiber	440	.302	17	86	187	8	3	0	1.9	.985	J. Mooty	20	114	6	6	1	2.92
	LF	J. Gleeson	485	.313	5	41	273	14	5	3	2.4	.983	C. Root	36	113	2	4	1	3.82
	C	A. Todd	381	.255	6	42	418	59	8	11	4.7	.984							
	OF	Dallessandro	287	.268	1	36	156	1	5	0	2.2	.969							
	1B	R. Russell	215	.247	5	33	518	18	10	22	10.7	.982							
	OF	A. Galan	209	.230	3	22	114	6	2	2	2.3	.984							
	1B	Z. Bonura	182	.264	4	20	408	40	4	34	10.3	.991							
	S2	R. Warstler	159	.226	1	18	90	141	14	20		.943							
N. Y.	1B	B. Young	556	.286	17	101	1505	86	13	112	10.9	.992	H. Gumbert	35	237	12	14	2	3.76
W-72 L-80	2B	T. Cuccinello	307	.208	5	36	106	130	3	17	5.1	.987	H. Schumacher	34	227	13	13	1	3.25
Bill Terry	SS	M. Witek	453	.256	3	31	192	307	22	46	5.9	.958	C. Hubbell	31	214	11	12	0	3.65
	3B	B. Whitehead	568	.282	4	36	68	130	11	5	2.8	.947	B. Lohrman	31	195	10	15	1	3.78
	RF	M. Ott	536	.289	19	79	210	9	4	2	2.0	.982	C. Melton	37	167	10	11	2	4.91
	CF	F. Demaree	460	.302	7	61	233	6	5	5	2.1	.980	J. Brown	41	55	2	4	7	3.42
	LF	J. Moore	543	.276	6	46	259	9	5	1	2.1	.982	R. Lynn	33	42	4	3	3	3.83
	C	H. Danning	524	.300	13	91	634	91	15	13	5.6	.980							
	OF	J. Rucker	277	.296	4	23	121	3	6	0	2.3	.954							
	SS	B. Jurges	214	.252	2	36	123	196	11	36	5.2	.967							
	OF	B. Seeds	155	.290	4	16	64	3	1	0	1.7	.985							
Bos.	1B	B. Hassett	458	.234	0	27	877	91	21	102	10.1	.979	D. Errickson	34	236	12	13	4	3.16
W-65 L-87	2B	B. Rowell	486	.305	3	58	251	360	30	81	5.6	.953	B. Posedel	35	233	12	17	1	4.13
Casey Stengel	SS	E. Miller	569	.276	14	79	**405**	487	28	**122**	**6.1**	**.970**	J. Sullivan	36	177	10	14	1	3.55
	3B	S. Sisti	459	.251	6	34	117	192	21	21	3.2	.936	M. Salvo	21	161	10	9	0	3.08
	RF	M. West	524	.261	7	72	220	16	6	1	2.4	.975	Strincevich	32	129	4	8	1	5.53
	CF	J. Cooney	365	.318	0	21	238	5	2	0	2.5	.992	J. Tobin	15	96	7	3	0	3.83
	LF	C. Ross	569	.281	17	89	347	12	14	2	2.5	.962							
	C	R. Berres	229	.192	0	14	254	56	6	6	3.7	.981							
	OF	G. Moore	363	.292	5	39	198	11	3	3	2.3	.986							
Phi.	1B	A. Mahan	544	.244	2	39	1380	102	12	120	10.3	.992	K. Higbe	41	283	14	19	1	3.72
W-50 L-103	2B	H. Schulte	436	.236	1	21	282	317	12	70	5.1	.980	H. Mulcahy	36	280	13	**22**	0	3.60
Doc Prothro	SS	B. Bragan	474	.222	7	44	268	443	49	83	5.8	.936	I. Pearson	29	145	3	14	1	5.45
	3B	P. May	501	.293	1	48	139	297	21	12	**3.4**	.954	S. Johnson	37	138	5	14	1	4.88
	RF	C. Klein	354	.218	7	37	180	4	3	2	1.6	.984	B. Beck	29	129	4	9	0	4.31
	CF	J. Marty	455	.270	13	50	296	7	8	0	2.6	.974	L. Smoll	33	109	2	8	0	5.37
	LF	J. Rizzo	367	.292	20	53	207	6	7	2	2.4	.968							
	C	B. Warren	289	.246	12	34	326	63	10	9	4.1	.975							
	UT	E. Mueller	263	.247	3	28	146	96	5	13		.980							
	C	B. Atwood	203	.192	0	22	238	43	3	3	4.1	.989							
	OF	M. Mazzera	156	.237	0	13	62	5	1	2	1.6	.985							

BATTING AND BASE RUNNING LEADERS

Batting Average		Slugging Average	
D. Garms, PIT	.355	J. Mize, STL	.636
E. Lombardi, CIN	.319	B. Nicholson, CHI	.534
J. Cooney, BOS	.318	D. Camilli, BKN	.529
S. Hack, CHI	.317	V. DiMaggio, CIN, PIT	.519
J. Mize, STL	.314	E. Slaughter, STL	.504

PITCHING LEADERS

Winning Percentage		Earned Run Average	
Fitzsimmons, BKN	.889	B. Walters, CIN	2.48
R. Sewell, PIT	.762	C. Passeau, CHI	2.50
B. Walters, CIN	.688	R. Sewell, PIT	2.80
J. Thompson, CIN	.640	Fitzsimmons, BKN	2.81
P. Derringer, CIN	.625	J. Turner, CIN	2.89

BATTING AND BASE RUNNING LEADERS

Home Runs

J. Mize, STL	43
B. Nicholson, CHI	25
J. Rizzo, CIN, PHI, PIT	24
D. Camilli, BKN	23

Total Bases

J. Mize, STL	368
F. McCormick, CIN	298
J. Medwick, BKN, STL	280
D. Camilli, BKN	271
A. Vaughan, PIT	269

Runs Batted In

J. Mize, STL	137
F. McCormick, CIN	127
M. Van Robays, PIT	116
E. Fletcher, PIT	104
B. Young, NY	101

Stolen Bases

L. Frey, CIN	22
S. Hack, CHI	21
T. Moore, STL	18
B. Werber, CIN	16
P. Reese, BKN	15

Hits

S. Hack, CHI	191
F. McCormick, CIN	191
J. Mize, STL	182

Base on Balls

E. Fletcher, PIT	119
M. Ott, NY	100
D. Camilli, BKN	89

Home Run Percentage

J. Mize, STL	7.4
V. DiMaggio, CIN, PIT	5.3
B. Nicholson, CHI	5.1

Runs Scored

A. Vaughan, PIT	113
J. Mize, STL	111
B. Werber, CIN	105

Doubles

F. McCormick, CIN	44
A. Vaughan, PIT	40
J. Gleeson, CHI	39

Triples

A. Vaughan, PIT	15
C. Ross, BOS	14

PITCHING LEADERS

Wins

B. Walters, CIN	22
P. Derringer, CIN	20
C. Passeau, CHI	20

Saves

J. Beggs, CIN	7
M. Brown, PIT	7
J. Brown, NY	7
C. Passeau, CHI	5
C. Shoun, STL	5

Strikeouts

K. Higbe, PHI	137
W. Wyatt, BKN	124
C. Passeau, CHI	124
H. Schumacher, NY	123
P. Derringer, CIN	115
B. Walters, CIN	115

Complete Games

B. Walters, CIN	29
P. Derringer, CIN	26
H. Mulcahy, PHI	21
C. Passeau, CHI	20
K. Higbe, PHI	20

Fewest Hits per 9 Innings

B. Walters, CIN	7.11
K. Higbe, PHI	7.70
J. Thompson, CIN	7.87

Shutouts

M. Salvo, BOS	5
B. Lohrman, NY	5
W. Wyatt, BKN	5

Fewest Walks per 9 Innings

P. Derringer, CIN	1.46
J. Turner, CIN	1.54
Fitzsimmons, BKN	1.67

Most Strikeouts per 9 Inn.

H. Schumacher, NY	4.88
W. Wyatt, BKN	4.66
K. Higbe, PHI	4.36

Innings

B. Walters, CIN	305
P. Derringer, CIN	297
K. Higbe, PHI	283

Games Pitched

C. Shoun, STL	54
M. Brown, PIT	48
C. Passeau, CHI	46

	W	L	PCT	GB	R	OR	2B	3B	Batting HR	BA	SA	SB	E	Fielding DP	FA	CG	BB	Pitching SO	ShO	SV	ERA
CIN	100	53	.654		707	**528**	264	38	89	.266	.379	72	**117**	158	**.981**	**91**	445	557	10	11	**3.05**
BKN	88	65	.575	12	697	621	256	**70**	93	.260	.383	56	183	110	.970	65	393	**634**	**17**	14	3.50
STL	84	69	.549	16	747	699	266	61	**119**	.275	**.411**	**97**	174	134	.971	71	488	550	10	14	3.83
PIT	78	76	.506	22.5	**809**	783	**276**	68	76	**.276**	.394	69	217	160	.966	69	492	491	8	**24**	4.36
CHI	75	79	.487	25.5	681	636	272	48	86	.267	.384	63	199	143	.968	69	430	564	12	14	3.54
NY	72	80	.474	27.5	663	659	201	46	91	.267	.374	45	184	**169**	.970	76	573	435	9	12	4.36
BOS	65	87	.428	34.5	623	745	219	50	59	.256	.349	48	184	136	.970	66	475	485	5	8	4.40
PHI	50	103	.327	50	494	750	180	35	75	.238	.331	25	181	136	.972	66	475	485	5	8	3.85
					5421	5421	1934	416	688	.264	.376	475	1394	1142	.972	544	3769	4322	82	115	3.85

American League 1940

	POS	Player	AB	BA	HR	RBI	PO	A	E	DP	TC/G	FA	Pitcher	G	IP	W	L	SV	ERA
Det. W-90 L-64 Del Baker	1B	R. York	588	.316	33	134	1390	107	15	101	9.8	.990	B. Newsom	36	264	21	5	0	2.83
	2B	C. Gehringer	515	.313	10	81	276	374	19	72	4.8	.972	T. Bridges	29	198	12	9	0	3.37
	SS	D. Bartell	528	.233	7	53	295	394	34	74	5.2	.953	S. Rowe	27	169	16	3	0	3.46
	3B	P. Higgins	480	.271	13	76	133	239	29	16	3.1	.928	J. Gorsica	29	160	7	7	0	4.33
	RF	P. Fox	350	.289	5	48	169	6	6	0	2.1	.967	H. Newhouser	28	133	9	9	0	4.86
	CF	B. McCosky	589	.340	4	57	349	7	6	2	2.6	.983	D. Trout	33	101	3	7	2	4.47
	LF	H. Greenberg	573	.340	41	150	298	14	15	1	2.2	.954	A. Benton	42	79	6	10	17	4.42
	C	B. Tebbetts	379	.296	4	46	572	89	17	10	6.3	.975	F. Hutchinson	17	76	3	7	0	5.68
	OF	B. Campbell	297	.283	8	44	133	6	6	0	2.0	.959							
	C	B. Sullivan	220	.309	3	41	292	29	8	4	5.8	.976							
	OF	E. Averill	118	.280	2	20	23	2	1	0	1.2	.962							
Cle. W-89 L-65 Ossie Vitt	1B	H. Trosky	522	.295	25	93	1207	70	11	129	9.3	.991	B. Feller	**43**	**320**	**27**	11	4	2.61
	2B	R. Mack	530	.283	12	69	323	417	27	109	5.3	.965	A. Milnar	37	242	18	10	3	3.27
	SS	L. Boudreau	627	.295	9	101	277	**454**	24	**116**	4.9	**.968**	M. Harder	31	186	12	11	0	4.06
	3B	K. Keltner	543	.254	15	77	170	277	22	27	3.2	.953	A. Smith	31	183	15	7	2	3.44
	RF	B. Bell	444	.279	4	58	193	5	6	1	2.1	.971	J. Allen	32	139	9	8	5	3.44
	CF	R. Weatherly	578	.303	12	59	370	10	12	3	2.9	.969	J. Dobson	40	100	3	7	3	4.95
	LF	B. Chapman	548	.286	4	50	307	10	12	3	2.4	.964							
	C	R. Hemsley	416	.267	4	42	591	65	4	8	5.6	**.994**							
	OF	J. Heath	356	.219	14	50	197	6	6	1	2.3	.971							

	POS	Player	AB	BA	HR	RBI	PO	A	E	DP	TC/G	FA	Pitcher	G	IP	W	L	SV	ERA
N. Y. W-88 L-66 Joe McCarthy	1B	B. Dahlgren	568	.264	12	73	**1488**	75	15	143	10.2	.990	R. Ruffing	30	226	15	12	0	3.38
	2B	J. Gordon	616	.281	30	103	374	**505**	23	116	5.8	.975	M. Russo	30	189	14	8	1	3.28
	SS	F. Crosetti	546	.194	4	31	246	396	31	73	4.6	.954	S. Chandler	27	172	8	7	0	4.60
	3B	R. Rolfe	588	.250	10	53	161	288	24	24	3.4	.949	M. Breuer	27	164	8	9	0	4.55
	RF	C. Keller	500	.286	21	93	317	5	11	2	2.4	.967	A. Donald	24	119	8	3	0	3.03
	CF	J. DiMaggio	508	**.352**	31	133	359	5	8	2	2.9	.978	M. Pearson	16	110	7	5	0	3.69
	LF	G. Selkirk	379	.269	19	71	220	9	9	6	2.1	.962	S. Sundra	27	99	4	6	2	5.53
	C	B. Dickey	372	.247	9	54	425	55	3	9	4.7	.994	E. Bonham	12	99	9	3	0	**1.90**
	OF	T. Henrich	293	.307	10	53	147	10	5	2	2.1	.969	B. Hadley	25	80	3	5	2	5.74
	C	B. Rosar	228	.298	4	37	258	30	5	8	4.7	.983	J. Murphy	35	63	8	4	9	3.69
Bos. W-82 L-72 Joe Cronin	1B	J. Foxx	515	.297	36	119	844	79	9	87	9.8	.990	J. Bagby	36	183	10	16	2	4.73
	2B	B. Doerr	595	.291	22	105	**401**	480	21	**118**	6.0	.977	J. Wilson	41	158	12	6	5	5.08
	SS	J. Cronin	548	.285	24	111	252	443	**38**	89	5.0	.948	L. Grove	22	153	7	6	0	3.99
	3B	J. Tabor	459	.285	21	81	143	267	**33**	25	3.7	.926	Ostermueller	31	144	5	9	0	4.95
	RF	D. DiMaggio	418	.301	8	46	239	**16**	6	5	2.8	.977	H. Hash	34	120	7	3	4	4.95
	CF	D. Cramer	**661**	.303	1	51	333	11	11	2	2.4	.969	D. Galehouse	25	120	6	6	0	5.18
	LF	T. Williams	561	.344	23	113	302	13	13	2	2.3	.960	J. Heving	39	119	12	7	3	4.01
	C	G. Desautels	222	.225	0	17	325	27	3	8	5.1	.992	E. Dickman	35	100	8	6	3	6.03
	O1	L. Finney	534	.320	5	73	652	33	7	41		.990							
Chi. W-82 L-72 Jimmy Dykes	1B	J. Kuhel	603	.280	27	94	1395	91	18	112	9.7	.988	J. Rigney	39	281	14	18	3	3.11
	2B	S. Webb	334	.237	1	29	143	229	12	44	5.2	.969	T. Lee	28	228	12	13	0	3.47
	SS	L. Appling	566	.348	0	79	**307**	436	37	83	5.2	.953	E. Smith	32	207	14	9	0	3.21
	3B	B. Kennedy	606	.252	3	52	**178**	322	**33**	25	3.5	.938	T. Lyons	22	186	12	8	0	3.24
	RF	T. Wright	581	.337	5	88	278	11	11	2	2.1	.963	J. Knott	25	158	11	9	0	4.56
	CF	M. Kreevich	582	.265	8	55	**428**	12	8	3	3.1	.982	B. Dietrich	23	150	10	6	0	4.03
	LF	M. Solters	428	.308	12	80	266	6	8	2	2.6	.971	C. Brown	37	66	4	6	10	3.68
	C	M. Tresh	480	.281	1	64	**619**	69	12	7	5.2	.983							
	OF	L. Rosenthal	276	.301	6	42	208	4	5	0	2.4	.977							
	2B	E. McNair	251	.227	7	31	128	170	13	27	4.8	.958							
St. L. W-67 L-87 Fred Haney	1B	G. McQuinn	594	.279	16	84	1436	**124**	13	**157**	**10.5**	**.992**	E. Auker	38	264	16	11	0	3.96
	2B	D. Heffner	487	.236	3	53	311	426	17	102	**6.0**	.977	V. Kennedy	34	222	12	17	0	5.59
	SS	J. Berardino	523	.258	16	85	250	336	**38**	83	5.6	.939	B. Harris	35	194	11	15	1	4.93
	3B	H. Clift	523	.273	20	87	161	**329**	21	**32**	3.5	.959	J. Niggeling	28	154	7	11	0	4.45
	RF	C. Laabs	218	.271	10	40	124	3	4	1	2.1	.969	B. Trotter	36	98	7	6	2	3.77
	CF	W. Judnich	519	.303	24	89	356	7	4	4	2.8	**.989**	R. Lawson	30	72	5	3	4	5.13
	LF	R. Radcliff	584	.342	7	81	282	8	8	2	2.1	.973	J. Kramer	16	65	3	7	0	6.26
	C	B. Swift	398	.244	0	39	389	55	9	8	3.5	.980							
	OF	R. Cullenbine	257	.230	7	31	114	5	3	2	2.1	.975							
	OF	J. Grace	229	.258	5	25	86	6	4	0	1.9	.958							
	OF	M. Hoag	191	.262	3	26	64	4	2	0	1.5	.971							
	SS	A. Strange	167	.186	0	6	65	112	7	24	5.3	.962							
Was. W-64 L-90 Bucky Harris	1B	Z. Bonura	311	.273	3	45	712	42	14	70	9.7	.982	D. Leonard	35	289	14	**19**	0	3.49
	2B	J. Bloodworth	469	.245	11	70	260	274	12	74	5.7	.978	K. Chase	35	262	15	17	0	3.23
	SS	J. Pofahl	406	.234	2	36	191	302	25	69	4.6	.952	S. Hudson	38	252	17	16	1	4.57
	3B	C. Travis	528	.322	2	76	116	265	27	30	3.6	.934	W. Masterson	31	130	3	13	2	4.90
	RF	B. Lewis	600	.317	6	63	206	11	9	1	2.0	.960	J. Krakauskas	32	109	1	6	2	6.44
	CF	G. Case	656	.293	5	56	384	10	12	0	2.6	.970	R. Monteagudo	27	101	2	6	2	6.08
	LF	G. Walker	595	.294	13	96	285	10	10	2	2.2	.967							
	C	R. Ferrell	326	.273	0	28	427	67	10	5	5.1	.980							
	OF	J. Welaj	215	.256	3	21	132	1	3	0	2.6	.978							
	2B	B. Myer	210	.290	0	29	119	176	10	34	5.6	.967							
	C	J. Early	206	.257	5	14	276	41	10	5	5.8	.969							
Phi. W-54 L-100 Connie Mack	1B	D. Siebert	595	.286	5	77	1322	119	**22**	112	9.5	.985	J. Babich	31	229	14	13	0	3.73
	2B	B. McCoy	490	.257	7	62	261	392	**34**	82	5.3	.951	N. Potter	31	201	9	14	0	4.44
	SS	A. Brancato	298	.191	1	23	136	180	17	35	4.2	.949	G. Caster	36	178	4	**19**	2	6.56
	3B	A. Rubeling	376	.245	4	38	96	184	20	13	3.1	.933	C. Dean	30	159	6	13	1	6.61
	RF	W. Moses	537	.309	9	50	295	10	8	1	2.4	.974	B. Ross	24	156	5	10	1	4.38
	CF	S. Chapman	508	.276	23	85	348	13	14	2	2.9	.963	B. Beckmann	34	127	8	4	1	4.17
	LF	B. Johnson	512	.288	31	103	310	15	13	4	2.5	.962	E. Heusser	41	110	6	13	5	4.99
	C	F. Hayes	465	.308	16	70	515	63	**17**	9	4.4	.971	P. Vaughan	18	99	2	9	2	5.35
	OF	D. Miles	236	.301	1	23	117	3	7	0	2.5	.945							
	SS	B. Lillard	206	.238	1	21	112	157	23	28	4.2	.921							
	3B	J. Gantenbein	197	.239	4	23	31	75	8	11	2.5	.930							

BATTING AND BASE RUNNING LEADERS

Batting Average

J. DiMaggio, NY	.352
L. Appling, CHI	.348
T. Williams, BOS	.344
R. Radcliff, STL	.342
H. Greenberg, DET	.340

Slugging Average

H. Greenberg, DET	.670
J. DiMaggio, NY	.626
T. Williams, BOS	.594
R. York, DET	.583
J. Foxx, BOS	.581

Home Runs

H. Greenberg, DET	41
J. Foxx, BOS	36
R. York, DET	33
J. DiMaggio, NY	31
B. Johnson, PHI	31

Total Bases

H. Greenberg, DET	384
R. York, DET	343
T. Williams, BOS	333
J. DiMaggio, NY	318
J. Gordon, NY	315

PITCHING LEADERS

Winning Percentage

S. Rowe, DET	.842
B. Newsom, DET	.808
B. Feller, CLE	.711
A. Smith, CLE	.682
A. Milnar, CLE	.643

Earned Run Average

E. Bonham, NY	1.90
B. Feller, CLE	2.61
B. Newsom, DET	2.83
J. Rigney, CHI	3.11
E. Smith, CHI	3.21

Wins

B. Feller, CLE	27
B. Newsom, DET	21
A. Milnar, CLE	18
S. Hudson, WAS	17
S. Rowe, DET	16
E. Auker, STL	16

Saves

A. Benton, DET	17
C. Brown, CHI	10
J. Murphy, NY	9

BATTING AND BASE RUNNING LEADERS

Runs Batted In
H. Greenberg, DET	150
R. York, DET	134
J. DiMaggio, NY	133
J. Foxx, BOS	119
T. Williams, BOS	113

Stolen Bases
G. Case, WAS	35
G. Walker, WAS	21
J. Gordon, NY	18
M. Kreevich, CHI	15
B. Lewis, WAS	15

Hits
R. Radcliff, STL	200
B. McCosky, DET	200
D. Cramer, BOS	200

Base on Balls
C. Keller, NY	106
H. Clift, STL	104
J. Foxx, BOS	101
C. Gehringer, DET	101

Home Run Percentage
H. Greenberg, DET	7.2
J. Foxx, BOS	7.0
J. DiMaggio, NY	6.1

Runs Scored
T. Williams, BOS	134
H. Greenberg, DET	129
B. McCosky, DET	123

Doubles
H. Greenberg, DET	50
R. York, DET	46
L. Boudreau, CLE	46

Triples
B. McCosky, DET	19
C. Keller, NY	15
L. Finney, BOS	15

PITCHING LEADERS

Strikeouts
B. Feller, CLE	261
B. Newsom, DET	164
J. Rigney, CHI	141
T. Bridges, DET	133
K. Chase, WAS	129

Complete Games
B. Feller, CLE	31
T. Lee, CHI	24
D. Leonard, WAS	23

Fewest Hits per 9 Innings
B. Feller, CLE	6.88
E. Bonham, NY	7.52
J. Rigney, CHI	7.70

Shutouts
T. Lyons, CHI	4
A. Milnar, CLE	4
B. Feller, CLE	4

Fewest Walks per 9 Innings
E. Bonham, NY	1.18
T. Lyons, CHI	1.79
T. Lee, CHI	2.21

Most Strikeouts per 9 Inn.
B. Feller, CLE	7.33
T. Bridges, DET	6.06
B. Newsom, DET	5.59

Innings
B. Feller, CLE	320
D. Leonard, WAS	289
J. Rigney, CHI	281

Games Pitched
B. Feller, CLE	43
A. Benton, DET	42
J. Wilson, BOS	41
E. Heusser, PHI	41

	W	L	PCT	GB	R	OR	2B	3B	Batting HR	BA	SA	SB	E	Fielding DP	FA	CG	BB	Pitching SO	ShO	SV	ERA
DET	90	64	.584		888	717	312	65	134	.286	.442	66	194	116	.968	59	570	752	10	23	4.01
CLE	89	65	.578	1	710	637	287	61	101	.265	.398	53	149	164	.975	72	512	686	13	22	3.63
NY	88	66	.571	2	817	671	243	66	155	.259	.418	59	152	158	.975	76	511	559	10	14	3.89
BOS	82	72	.532	8	872	825	301	80	145	.286	.449	55	173	156	.972	51	625	613	4	18	3.74
CHI	82	72	.532	8	735	672	238	63	73	.278	.387	52	185	125	.969	83	480	574	10	9	5.12
STL	67	87	.435	23	757	882	278	58	118	.263	.401	51	158	179	.974	64	646	439	4	59	4.59
WAS	64	90	.416	26	665	811	266	67	52	.271	.374	94	194	166	.968	74	618	618	6	7	4.59
PHI	54	100	.351	36	703	932	242	53	105	.262	.387	48	238	131	.960	72	534	488	4	12	5.22
					6147	6147	2167	513	883	.271	.407	478	1443	1195	.970	551	4496	4729	61	121	4.38

National League 1941

	POS	Player	AB	BA	HR	RBI	PO	A	E	DP	TC/G	FA	Pitcher	G	IP	W	L	SV	ERA
Bkn. W-100 L-54 Leo Durocher	1B	D. Camilli	529	.285	34	120	1379	98	16	107	10.1	.989	K. Higbe	48	298	22	9	3	3.14
	2B	B. Herman	536	.291	3	41	297	354	20	64	5.0	.970	W. Wyatt	38	288	22	10	1	2.34
	SS	P. Reese	595	.229	2	46	346	473	47	76	5.7	.946	H. Casey	45	162	14	11	7	3.89
	3B	C. Lavagetto	441	.277	1	78	117	215	22	17	3.0	.938	C. Davis	28	154	13	7	2	2.97
	RF	D. Walker	531	.311	9	71	309	19	8	8	2.3	.976	L. Hamlin	30	136	8	8	1	4.24
	CF	P. Reiser	536	.343	14	76	356	14	7	0	2.8	.981							
	LF	J. Medwick	538	.318	18	88	270	11	5	2	2.2	.983							
	C	M. Owen	386	.231	1	44	530	64	3	7	4.7	.995							
	OF	J. Wasdell	265	.298	4	48	84	2	4	0	1.7	.956							
	3B	L. Riggs	197	.305	5	36	48	75	9	4	3.1	.932							
	P	W. Wyatt	109	.239	3	22	11	47	2	5	1.6	.967							
St. L. W-97 L-56 Billy Southworth	1B	J. Mize	473	.317	16	100	1157	82	8	104	10.2	.994	L. Warneke	37	246	17	9	0	3.15
	2B	C. Crespi	560	.279	4	46	382	421	32	94	5.8	.962	E. White	32	210	17	7	2	2.40
	SS	M. Marion	547	.252	3	58	299	489	38	85	5.3	.954	M. Cooper	29	187	13	9	0	3.91
	3B	J. Brown	549	.306	3	56	135	276	15	22	3.5	.965	M. Lanier	35	153	10	8	3	2.82
	RF	E. Slaughter	425	.311	13	76	173	5	10	1	1.7	.947	H. Gumbert	33	144	11	5	1	2.74
	CF	T. Moore	493	.294	6	68	293	14	5	3	2.6	.984	H. Krist	37	114	10	0	2	4.03
	LF	J. Hopp	445	.303	4	50	213	4	4	1	2.4	.982	I. Hutchinson	29	47	1	5	5	3.86
	C	G. Mancuso	328	.229	2	37	482	58	6	6	5.2	.989							
	OF	D. Padgett	324	.247	5	44	115	1	5	0	2.0	.959							
	C	W. Cooper	200	.245	1	20	247	39	10	11	4.7	.966							
	OF	C. Triplett	185	.286	3	21	78	4	3	0	1.8	.965							
	OF	E. Crabtree	167	.341	5	28	71	2	0	0	1.5	1.000							

POS	Player	AB	BA	HR	RBI	PO	A	E	DP	TC/G	FA	Pitcher	G	IP	W	L	SV	ERA
Cin. W-88 L-66 Bill McKechnie																		
1B	F. McCormick	603	.269	17	97	**1464**	92	8	**130**	10.2	.995	B. Walters	37	**302**	19	15	2	2.83
2B	L. Frey	543	.254	6	59	340	432	24	93	5.5	.970	P. Derringer	29	228	12	14	1	3.31
SS	E. Joost	537	.253	4	40	310	415	45	85	5.2	.942	Vander Meer	33	226	16	13	0	2.82
3B	B. Werber	418	.239	4	46	120	256	16	30	3.7	.959	E. Riddle	33	217	19	4	1	**2.24**
RF	J. Gleeson	301	.233	3	34	153	1	3	0	1.9	.981	J. Turner	23	113	6	4	0	3.11
CF	H. Craft	413	.249	10	59	280	6	5	1	2.5	.983	J. Thompson	27	109	6	6	1	4.87
LF	M. McCormick	369	.287	4	31	240	9	6	2	2.5	.976	J. Beggs	37	57	4	3	5	3.79
C	E. Lombardi	398	.264	10	60	496	70	10	9	5.0	.983							
OF	E. Koy	204	.250	2	27	92	3	1	1	2.0	.990							
C	D. West	172	.215	1	17	209	21	7	3	3.7	.970							
3B	C. Aleno	169	.243	1	18	41	77	3	6	3.0	.975							
OF	L. Waner	164	.256	0	6	68	3	1	1	1.6	.986							
Pit. W-81 L-73 Frankie Frisch																		
1B	E. Fletcher	521	.288	11	74	1444	**118**	14	113	**10.4**	.991	R. Sewell	39	249	14	**17**	2	3.72
2B	F. Gustine	463	.270	1	46	269	317	28	45	5.9	.954	M. Butcher	33	236	17	12	0	3.05
SS	A. Vaughan	374	.316	6	38	172	289	20	42	5.0	.958	Heintzelman	35	196	11	11	0	3.44
3B	L. Handley	459	.288	0	33	125	247	21	19	3.4	.947	J. Lanning	34	176	11	11	1	3.13
RF	B. Elliott	527	.273	3	76	281	9	9	2	2.2	.970	B. Klinger	35	117	9	4	4	3.93
CF	V. DiMaggio	528	.267	21	100	391	11	10	3	2.7	.976	D. Dietz	33	100	7	2	1	2.33
LF	M. Van Robays	457	.282	4	78	292	9	8	3	2.6	.974							
C	A. Lopez	317	.265	5	43	345	54	8	5	3.6	.980							
2B	S. Martin	233	.305	0	19	127	154	8	26	5.5	.972							
SS	A. Anderson	223	.215	1	10	97	161	19	29	4.8	.931							
3O	D. Garms	220	.264	3	42	73	44	9	1		.929							
OF	B. Stewart	172	.267	0	10	71	5	3	2	1.9	.962							
N. Y. W-74 L-79 Bill Terry																		
1B	B. Young	574	.265	25	104	1395	87	21	124	10.0	.986	H. Schumacher	30	206	12	10	1	3.36
2B	B. Whitehead	403	.228	1	23	288	285	18	60	5.7	.970	C. Melton	42	194	8	11	1	3.01
SS	B. Jurges	471	.293	5	61	230	432	30	82	5.2	.957	C. Hubbell	26	164	11	9	1	3.57
3B	D. Bartell	373	.303	5	35	91	169	11	16	3.2	.959	B. Lohrman	33	159	9	10	3	4.02
RF	M. Ott	525	.286	27	90	256	**19**	9	3	2.0	.968	B. Carpenter	29	132	11	6	2	3.83
CF	J. Rucker	**622**	.288	1	42	344	13	12	5	2.6	.967	B. McGee	22	106	2	9	0	4.91
LF	J. Moore	428	.273	7	40	237	5	7	0	2.1	.972	B. Bowman	29	80	6	7	1	5.71
C	H. Danning	459	.244	7	56	**530**	77	4	8	**5.3**	.993	J. Brown	31	57	1	5	**8**	3.32
3B	J. Orengo	252	.214	4	25	74	132	9	12	3.6	.958							
OF	M. Arnovich	207	.280	2	22	103	5	2	0	1.8	.982							
C	G. Hartnett	150	.300	5	26	138	15	1	1	4.5	.994							
Chi. W-70 L-84 Jimmie Wilson																		
1B	B. Dahlgren	359	.281	16	59	957	38	9	84	10.2	.991	C. Passeau	34	231	14	14	0	3.35
2B	L. Stringer	512	.246	5	53	356	**455**	34	84	**6.2**	.960	V. Olsen	37	186	10	8	1	3.15
SS	B. Sturgeon	433	.245	0	25	215	366	27	68	4.8	.956	B. Lee	28	167	8	14	1	3.76
3B	S. Hack	586	.317	7	45	138	295	21	22	3.0	.954	J. Mooty	33	153	8	9	4	3.35
RF	B. Nicholson	532	.254	26	98	293	10	9	2	2.2	.971	P. Erickson	32	141	5	7	1	3.70
CF	P. Cavarretta	346	.286	6	40	128	3	1	2	2.0	.992	L. French	26	138	5	14	0	4.63
LF	Dallessandro	486	.272	6	85	292	4	4	0	2.3	.987	C. Root	19	107	8	7	0	5.40
C	McCullough	418	.227	9	53	481	64	10	6	4.7	.982							
OF	L. Novikoff	203	.241	5	24	92	3	0	0	1.8	1.000							
O1	H. Leiber	162	.216	7	25	192	8	5	13		.976							
C	B. Scheffing	132	.242	1	20	126	17	5	1	4.4	.966							
Bos. W-62 L-92 Casey Stengel																		
1B	B. Hassett	405	.296	1	33	895	78	9	92	9.9	.991	J. Tobin	33	238	12	12	0	3.10
2B	B. Rowell	483	.267	7	60	265	312	**40**	81	5.5	.935	M. Salvo	35	195	7	16	0	4.06
SS	E. Miller	585	.239	6	68	336	485	29	**112**	5.5	.966	A. Johnson	43	183	7	15	1	3.53
3B	S. Sisti	541	.259	1	45	162	287	**41**	28	3.6	.916	D. Errickson	38	166	6	12	1	4.78
RF	G. Moore	397	.272	5	43	229	13	8	2	2.3	.968	A. Javery	34	161	10	11	1	4.31
CF	J. Cooney	442	.319	0	29	274	9	1	3	2.6	**.996**	T. Earley	33	139	6	8	3	2.53
LF	M. West	484	.277	12	68	302	13	6	5	2.4	.981	F. Lamanna	35	73	5	4	1	5.33
C	R. Berres	279	.201	1	19	356	64	2	3	3.5	**.995**							
OF	P. Waner	294	.279	2	46	129	7	5	3	1.8	.965							
C	P. Masi	180	.222	3	18	194	31	5	3	2.8	.978							
2B	S. Roberge	167	.216	0	15	95	132	5	31	5.0	.978							
1B	B. Dahlgren	166	.235	7	30	379	28	3	45	10.5	.993							
Phi. W-43 L-111 Doc Prothro																		
1B	N. Etten	540	.311	14	79	1286	89	**23**	124	9.3	.984	J. Podgajny	34	181	9	12	0	4.62
2B	D. Murtaugh	347	.219	0	11	233	247	11	49	5.8	.978	T. Hughes	34	170	9	14	0	4.45
SS	B. Bragan	557	.251	4	69	322	437	45	86	5.2	.944	S. Johnson	39	163	5	12	2	4.52
3B	P. May	490	.267	0	39	**194**	**324**	15	**31**	**3.8**	**.972**	C. Blanton	28	164	6	13	0	4.51
RF	S. Benjamin	480	.235	3	27	185	11	4	3	1.8	.980	I. Pearson	46	136	4	14	6	3.57
CF	J. Marty	477	.268	8	39	286	7	11	0	2.3	.964	L. Grissom	29	131	2	13	0	3.97
LF	D. Litwhiler	590	.305	18	66	**393**	12	**15**	3	2.8	.964	F. Hoerst	37	106	3	10	0	5.20
C	B. Warren	345	.214	9	35	412	**84**	**14**	16	4.6	.973	B. Beck	34	95	1	9	0	4.63
OF	J. Rizzo	235	.217	4	24	114	8	4	2	2.0	.968							
UT	E. Mueller	233	.227	1	22	114	107	6	21		.974							
C	M. Livingston	207	.203	0	18	263	34	8	5	4.3	.974							
2S	H. Marnie	158	.241	0	11	129	103	2	24		.991							

BATTING AND BASE RUNNING LEADERS

Batting Average		Slugging Average	
P. Reiser, BKN	.343	P. Reiser, BKN	.558
J. Cooney, BOS	.319	D. Camilli, BKN	.556
J. Medwick, BKN	.318	J. Mize, STL	.535
S. Hack, CHI	.317	J. Medwick, BKN	.517
J. Mize, STL	.317	E. Slaughter, STL	.496

PITCHING LEADERS

Winning Percentage		Earned Run Average	
E. Riddle, CIN	.826	E. Riddle, CIN	2.24
K. Higbe, BKN	.710	W. Wyatt, BKN	2.34
E. White, STL	.708	E. White, STL	2.40
W. Wyatt, BKN	.688	Vander Meer, CIN	2.82
L. Warneke, STL	.654	B. Walters, CIN	2.83

BATTING AND BASE RUNNING LEADERS

Home Runs

D. Camilli, BKN	34
M. Ott, NY	27
B. Nicholson, CHI	26
B. Young, NY	25
B. Dahlgren, BOS, CHI	23

Total Bases

P. Reiser, BKN	299
D. Camilli, BKN	294
J. Medwick, BKN	278
D. Litwhiler, PHI	275
B. Young, NY	265

Runs Batted In

D. Camilli, BKN	120
B. Young, NY	104
J. Mize, STL	100
V. DiMaggio, PIT	100
B. Nicholson, CHI	98

Stolen Bases

D. Murtaugh, PHI	18
S. Benjamin, PHI	17
L. Handley, PIT	16
L. Frey, CIN	16
J. Hopp, STL	15

Hits

S. Hack, CHI	186
P. Reiser, BKN	184
D. Litwhiler, PHI	180

Base on Balls

E. Fletcher, PIT	118
D. Camilli, BKN	104
M. Ott, NY	100

Home Run Percentage

D. Camilli, BKN	6.4
M. Ott, NY	5.1
B. Nicholson, CHI	4.9

Runs Scored

P. Reiser, BKN	117
S. Hack, CHI	111
J. Medwick, BKN	100

Doubles

J. Mize, STL	39
P. Reiser, BKN	39
J. Rucker, NY	38

Triples

P. Reiser, BKN	17
E. Fletcher, PIT	13
J. Hopp, STL	11

PITCHING LEADERS

Wins

K. Higbe, BKN	22
W. Wyatt, BKN	22
E. Riddle, CIN	19
B. Walters, CIN	19

Saves

J. Brown, NY	8
H. Casey, BKN	7
B. Crouch, PHI, STL	7
I. Pearson, PHI	6
J. Beggs, CIN	5
I. Hutchinson, STL	5

Strikeouts

Vander Meer, CIN	202
W. Wyatt, BKN	176
B. Walters, CIN	129
K. Higbe, BKN	121
M. Cooper, STL	118

Complete Games

B. Walters, CIN	27
W. Wyatt, BKN	23
J. Tobin, BOS	20
C. Passeau, CHI	20
M. Butcher, PIT	19
K. Higbe, BKN	19

Fewest Hits per 9 Innings

Vander Meer, CIN	6.84
W. Wyatt, BKN	6.96
E. White, STL	7.24

Shutouts

W. Wyatt, BKN	7
Vander Meer, CIN	6
C. Davis, BKN	5
B. Walters, CIN	5

Fewest Walks per 9 Innings

C. Davis, BKN	1.57
C. Passeau, CHI	2.03
P. Derringer, CIN	2.13

Most Strikeouts per 9 Inn.

Vander Meer, CIN	8.03
M. Cooper, STL	5.69
W. Wyatt, BKN	5.49

Innings

B. Walters, CIN	302
K. Higbe, BKN	298
W. Wyatt, BKN	288

Games Pitched

K. Higbe, BKN	48
I. Pearson, PHI	46
H. Casey, BKN	45

	W	L	PCT	GB	R	OR	2B	3B	HR	BA	SA	SB	E	DP	FA	CG	BB	SO	ShO	SV	ERA
BKN	100	54	.649		800	581	286	69	101	.272	.405	36	162	125	.974	66	495	603	17	22	3.14
STL	97	56	.634	2.5	734	589	254	56	70	.272	.377	47	172	146	.973	64	502	659	15	20	3.19
CIN	88	66	.571	12	616	564	213	33	64	.247	.337	68	152	147	.975	89	510	627	19	10	3.17
PIT	81	73	.526	19	690	643	233	65	56	.268	.368	59	196	130	.968	71	492	410	8	12	3.48
NY	74	79	.484	25.5	667	706	248	35	95	.260	.371	36	160	144	.974	55	539	566	12	18	3.94
CHI	70	84	.455	30	666	670	239	25	99	.253	.365	39	180	139	.970	74	449	548	8	9	3.72
BOS	62	92	.403	38	592	720	231	38	48	.251	.334	61	191	146	.969	62	554	546	10	9	3.95
PHI	43	111	.279	57	501	793	188	38	64	.244	.331	65	187	147	.969	35	606	552	4	9	4.50
					5266	5266	1892	359	597	.258	.361	411	1400	1152	.972	516	4147	4411	93	109	3.63

American League 1941

	POS	Player	AB	BA	HR	RBI	PO	A	E	DP	TC/G	FA	Pitcher	G	IP	W	L	SV	ERA
N. Y. W-101 L-53 Joe McCarthy	1B	J. Sturm	524	.239	3	36	1099	85	12	117	9.6	.990	M. Russo	28	210	14	10	1	3.09
	2B	J. Gordon	588	.276	24	87	332	397	32	109	5.8	.958	R. Ruffing	23	186	15	6	0	3.54
	SS	P. Rizzuto	515	.307	3	46	252	399	29	109	5.3	.957	S. Chandler	28	164	10	4	4	3.19
	3B	R. Rolfe	561	.264	8	42	140	263	23	28	3.2	.946	A. Donald	22	159	9	5	0	3.57
	RF	T. Henrich	538	.277	31	85	280	13	6	4	2.2	.980	L. Gomez	23	156	15	5	0	3.74
	CF	J. DiMaggio	541	.357	30	125	385	16	9	5	2.9	.978	M. Breuer	26	141	9	7	2	4.09
	LF	C. Keller	507	.298	33	122	328	7	7	2	2.5	.980	E. Bonham	23	127	9	6	2	2.98
	C	B. Dickey	348	.284	7	71	422	45	3	11	4.5	.994	J. Murphy	35	77	8	3	15	1.98
	C	B. Rosar	209	.287	1	36	246	24	1	6	4.5	.996							
	UT	G. Priddy	174	.213	1	26	167	119	8	46		.973							
	OF	G. Selkirk	164	.220	6	25	84	4	3	2	1.9	.967							
	SS	F. Crosetti	148	.223	1	22	80	89	10	20	5.6	.944							
	P	R. Ruffing	89	.303	2	22	7	21	0	3	1.2	1.000							
Bos. W-84 L-70 Joe Cronin	1B	J. Foxx	487	.300	19	105	1155	112	10	105	10.3	.992	D. Newsome	36	214	19	10	0	4.13
	2B	B. Doerr	500	.282	16	93	290	389	20	85	5.3	.971	M. Harris	35	194	8	14	1	3.25
	SS	J. Cronin	518	.311	16	95	225	324	24	64	4.8	.958	C. Wagner	29	187	12	8	0	3.07
	3B	J. Tabor	498	.279	16	101	123	277	30	24	3.4	.930	L. Grove	21	134	7	7	0	4.37
	RF	L. Finney	497	.288	4	53	181	7	11	2	2.2	.945	J. Dobson	27	134	12	5	0	4.49
	CF	D. DiMaggio	584	.283	8	58	386	16	15	2	2.9	.964	M. Ryba	40	121	7	3	6	4.46
	LF	T. Williams	456	.406	37	120	262	11	11	2	2.1	.961	J. Wilson	27	116	4	13	1	5.03
	C	F. Pytlak	336	.271	2	39	416	41	4	7	5.1	.991							
	OF	P. Fox	268	.302	0	31	123	5	3	2	2.1	.977							
	C	J. Peacock	261	.284	0	27	298	33	4	7	4.8	.988							
	SS	S. Newsome	227	.225	2	17	95	133	10	28	3.4	.958							
	OF	S. Spence	203	.232	2	28	97	6	0	2	2.0	1.000							

	POS	Player	AB	BA	HR	RBI	PO	A	E	DP	TC/G	FA	Pitcher	G	IP	W	L	SV	ERA
Chi. W-77 L-77 Jimmy Dykes	1B	J. Kuhel	600	.250	12	63	**1444**	108	10	113	10.3	.994	T. Lee	35	300	22	11	1	**2.37**
	2B	Knickerbocker	343	.245	7	29	204	221	13	58	5.0	.970	E. Smith	34	263	13	17	1	3.18
	SS	L. Appling	592	.314	1	57	294	**473**	42	95	5.3	.948	J. Rigney	30	237	13	13	0	3.84
	3B	D. Lodigiani	322	.239	4	40	120	187	12	22	3.7	.962	T. Lyons	22	187	12	10	0	3.70
	RF	T. Wright	513	.322	10	97	279	8	8	3	2.2	.973	B. Dietrich	19	109	5	8	0	5.35
	CF	M. Kreevich	436	.232	0	37	302	7	2	2	2.8	**.994**	B. Ross	20	108	3	8	0	3.16
	LF	M. Hoag	380	.255	1	44	215	6	10	1	2.3	.957	J. Hallett	22	75	5	5	0	6.03
	C	M. Tresh	390	.251	0	33	**488**	81	11	12	5.0	.981							
	2B	D. Kolloway	280	.271	3	24	118	181	14	23	5.0	.955							
	3B	B. Kennedy	257	.206	1	29	88	153	17	12	3.6	.934							
	OF	M. Solters	251	.259	4	43	135	7	5	1	2.3	.966							
	OF	B. Chapman	190	.226	2	19	122	4	1	1	2.6	.992							
Cle. W-75 L-79 Roger Peckinpaugh	1B	H. Trosky	310	.294	11	51	727	54	9	77	9.3	.989	B. Feller	**44**	**343**	**25**	13	2	3.15
	2B	R. Mack	501	.228	9	44	363	386	23	**109**	5.3	.970	A. Milnar	35	229	12	19	0	4.36
	SS	L. Boudreau	579	.257	10	56	**296**	444	26	97	5.2	**.966**	A. Smith	29	207	12	13	0	3.83
	3B	K. Keltner	581	.269	23	84	181	**346**	16	**36**	**3.6**	.971	J. Bagby	33	201	9	15	2	4.04
	RF	J. Heath	585	.340	24	123	259	20	15	1	1.9	.949	C. Brown	41	74	3	3	5	3.27
	CF	R. Weatherly	363	.289	3	37	208	1	7	1	2.5	.968	J. Heving	27	71	5	2	5	2.29
	LF	G. Walker	445	.283	6	48	257	9	5	0	2.6	.982	M. Harder	15	69	5	4	1	5.24
	C	R. Hemsley	288	.240	2	24	401	42	9	8	4.7	.980							
	OF	S. Campbell	328	.250	3	35	202	6	4	0	2.7	.981							
	1B	O. Grimes	244	.238	4	24	544	31	3	53	9.3	.995							
	C	G. Desautels	189	.201	1	17	300	32	1	5	5.0	.997							
Det. W-75 L-79 Del Baker	1B	R. York	590	.259	27	111	1393	110	**21**	111	9.8	.986	B. Newsom	43	250	12	**20**	2	4.60
	2B	C. Gehringer	436	.220	3	46	279	324	11	59	5.3	**.982**	H. Newhouser	33	173	9	11	0	4.79
	SS	F. Croucher	489	.254	2	39	270	361	44	85	5.0	.935	J. Gorsica	33	171	9	11	2	4.47
	3B	P. Higgins	540	.298	11	73	153	304	26	14	3.3	.946	A. Benton	38	158	15	6	7	2.97
	RF	B. Campbell	512	.275	15	93	241	5	6	1	1.9	.976	D. Trout	37	152	9	9	2	3.74
	CF	R. McCosky	494	.324	3	55	328	6	5	2	2.8	.985	T. Bridges	25	148	9	12	0	3.41
	LF	R. Radcliff	379	.317	3	39	155	6	5	1	1.9	.970	S. Rowe	27	139	8	6	1	4.14
	C	B. Tebbetts	359	.284	2	47	461	**83**	13	11	**5.7**	.977							
	C	B. Sullivan	234	.282	3	29	339	33	9	7	6.0	.976							
	OF	P. Mullin	220	.345	5	23	117	2	7	0	2.5	.944							
	OF	T. Stainback	200	.245	2	10	107	3	6	0	1.5	.948							
St. L. W-70 L-84 Fred Haney W-15 L-29 Luke Sewell W-55 L-55	1B	G. McQuinn	495	.297	18	80	1138	109	6	**109**	10.0	**.995**	E. Auker	34	216	14	15	0	5.50
	2B	D. Heffner	399	.233	0	17	224	307	14	52	5.2	.974	B. Muncrief	36	214	13	9	1	3.65
	SS	J. Berardino	469	.271	5	89	261	305	27	81	4.8	.954	D. Galehouse	30	190	9	10	0	3.64
	3B	H. Clift	584	.255	17	84	**195**	316	22	27	3.5	.959	B. Harris	34	187	12	14	1	5.21
	RF	C. Laabs	392	.278	15	59	217	6	4	2	2.3	.982	J. Niggeling	24	168	7	9	0	3.80
	CF	W. Judnich	546	.284	14	83	383	11	8	3	2.9	.980	G. Caster	32	104	3	7	3	5.00
	LF	F. Cullenbine	501	.317	9	98	258	12	10	3	2.3	.964							
	C	R. Ferrell	321	.252	2	23	340	51	2	11	4.0	.995							
	OF	J. Grace	362	.309	6	60	164	13	3	1	2.0	.983							
	2B	J. Lucadello	351	.279	2	31	147	185	13	36	4.9	.962							
	C	B. Swift	170	.259	0	21	180	22	3	3	3.5	.985							
Was. W-70 L-84 Bucky Harris	1B	M. Vernon	531	.299	9	93	1186	80	10	**122**	9.7	.992	D. Leonard	34	256	18	13	0	3.45
	2B	J. Bloodworth	506	.245	7	66	**380**	436	24	107	**6.4**	.971	S. Hudson	33	250	13	14	0	3.46
	SS	C. Travis	608	.359	7	101	279	388	25	99	5.1	.964	K. Chase	33	206	6	18	0	5.08
	3B	G. Archie	379	.269	3	48	71	150	15	12	3.2	.936	S. Sundra	28	168	9	13	0	5.29
	RF	B. Lewis	569	.297	9	72	229	16	7	3	2.6	.972	R. Anderson	32	112	4	6	0	4.18
	CF	D. Cramer	**660**	.273	2	66	369	9	6	1	2.5	.984	B. Zuber	36	96	6	4	2	5.42
	LF	G. Case	649	.271	2	53	362	**21**	10	3	2.6	.975	A. Carrasquel	35	97	6	2	3	3.44
	C	J. Early	355	.287	10	54	385	52	**16**	**13**	4.5	.965	W. Masterson	34	78	4	3	3	5.97
	C	A. Evans	159	.277	1	19	195	24	7	6	4.4	.969							
Phi. W-64 L-90 Connie Mack	1B	D. Siebert	467	.334	5	79	1102	106	12	95	9.9	.990	P. Marchildon	30	204	10	15	0	3.57
	2B	B. McCoy	517	.271	8	61	285	423	27	87	5.4	.963	J. Knott	27	194	13	11	0	4.40
	SS	A. Brancato	530	.234	2	49	263	395	**61**	80	5.2	.915	L. McCrabb	26	157	9	13	2	5.49
	3B	P. Suder	531	.245	4	52	175	271	20	25	3.4	.957	L. Harris	33	132	4	4	2	4.78
	RF	W. Moses	438	.301	4	35	263	12	7	5	2.6	.975	B. Beckmann	22	130	5	9	1	4.57
	CF	S. Chapman	552	.322	25	106	**416**	**21**	15	5	**3.2**	.967	T. Ferrick	36	119	8	10	7	3.77
	LF	B. Johnson	552	.275	22	107	287	17	3	0	2.5	.990	B. Hadley	25	102	4	6	3	5.01
	C	F. Hayes	439	.280	12	63	403	65	8	11	3.9	.983							
	OF	E. Collins	219	.242	0	12	119	3	4	1	2.5	.968							
	OF	D. Miles	170	.312	0	15	79	2	0	1	2.3	1.000							

BATTING AND BASE RUNNING LEADERS

Batting Average

T. Williams, BOS	.406
C. Travis, WAS	.359
J. DiMaggio, NY	.357
J. Heath, CLE	.340
D. Siebert, PHI	.334

Slugging Average

T. Williams, BOS	.735
J. DiMaggio, NY	.643
J. Heath, CLE	.586
C. Keller, NY	.580
S. Chapman, PHI	.543

Home Runs

T. Williams, BOS	37
C. Keller, NY	33
T. Henrich, NY	31
J. DiMaggio, NY	30
R. York, DET	27

Total Bases

J. DiMaggio, NY	348
J. Heath, CLE	343
T. Williams, BOS	335
C. Travis, WAS	316
S. Chapman, PHI	300

PITCHING LEADERS

Winning Percentage

L. Gomez, NY	.750
A. Benton, DET	.714
R. Ruffing, NY	.714
T. Lee, CHI	.667
B. Feller, CLE	.658

Earned Run Average

T. Lee, CHI	2.37
C. Wagner, BOS	3.07
M. Russo, NY	3.09
B. Feller, CLE	3.15
E. Smith, CHI	3.18

Wins

B. Feller, CLE	25
T. Lee, CHI	22
D. Newsome, BOS	19
D. Leonard, WAS	18

Saves

J. Murphy, NY	15
A. Benton, DET	7
T. Ferrick, PHI	7
M. Ryba, BOS	6
C. Brown, CLE	5
J. Heving, CLE	5

BATTING AND BASE RUNNING LEADERS

Runs Batted In
J. DiMaggio, NY	125
J. Heath, CLE	123
C. Keller, NY	122
T. Williams, BOS	120
R. York, DET	111

Stolen Bases
G. Case, WAS	33
J. Kuhel, CHI	20
J. Heath, CLE	18
M. Kreevich, CHI	17
J. Tabor, BOS	17

Hits
C. Travis, WAS	218
J. Heath, CLE	199
J. DiMaggio, NY	193

Base on Balls
T. Williams, BOS	145
R. Cullenbine, STL	121
H. Clift, STL	113
C. Keller, NY	102

Home Run Percentage
T. Williams, BOS	8.1
C. Keller, NY	6.5
T. Henrich, NY	5.8

Runs Scored
T. Williams, BOS	135
J. DiMaggio, NY	122
D. DiMaggio, BOS	117
H. Clift, STL	108

Doubles
L. Boudreau, CLE	45
J. DiMaggio, NY	43
W. Judnich, STL	40

Triples
J. Heath, CLE	20
C. Travis, WAS	19
K. Keltner, CLE	13

PITCHING LEADERS

Strikeouts
B. Feller, CLE	260
B. Newsom, DET	175
T. Lee, CHI	130
J. Rigney, CHI	119
M. Harris, BOS	111
E. Smith, CHI	111

Complete Games
T. Lee, CHI	30
B. Feller, CLE	28
E. Smith, CHI	21
T. Lyons, CHI	19
D. Leonard, WAS	19

Fewest Hits per 9 Innings
B. Feller, CLE	7.45
T. Lee, CHI	7.73
T. Bridges, DET	7.80

Shutouts
B. Feller, CLE	6
J. Humphries, CHI	4
S. Chandler, NY	4
D. Leonard, WAS	4

Fewest Walks per 9 Innings
T. Lyons, CHI	1.78
D. Leonard, WAS	1.90
B. Muncrief, STL	2.23

Most Strikeouts per 9 Inn.
B. Feller, CLE	6.82
B. Newsom, DET	6.29
T. Bridges, DET	5.49

Innings
B. Feller, CLE	343
T. Lee, CHI	300
E. Smith, CHI	263

Games Pitched
B. Feller, CLE	44
B. Newsom, DET	43
C. Brown, CLE	41

	W	L	PCT	GB	R	OR	2B	3B	HR	BA	SA	SB	E	DP	FA	CG	BB	SO	ShO	SV	ERA
NY	101	53	.656		830	631	243	60	151	.269	.419	51	165	196	.973	75	598	589	13	26	3.53
BOS	84	70	.545	17	865	750	304	55	124	.283	.430	67	172	139	.972	70	611	574	8	11	4.19
CHI	77	77	.500	24	638	649	245	47	47	.255	.343	91	180	145	.971	106	521	564	14	4	3.52
CLE	75	79	.487	26	677	668	249	84	103	.256	.393	63	142	158	.976	68	660	617	10	19	3.90
DET	75	79	.487	26	686	743	247	55	91	.263	.375	43	186	129	.969	52	645	697	8	16	4.18
STL	70	84	.455	31	765	823	281	58	91	.266	.390	50	151	156	.975	65	549	454	7	10	4.72
WAS	70	84	.455	31	728	798	257	80	52	.272	.376	79	187	169	.969	69	603	544	8	7	4.35
PHI	64	90	.416	37	713	840	240	69	85	.268	.387	27	200	150	.967	64	557	386	3	18	4.83
					5902	5902	2066	508	734	.266	.389	471	1383	1242	.972	569	4744	4425	71	111	4.15

National League 1942

	POS	Player	AB	BA	HR	RBI	PO	A	E	DP	TC/G	FA	Pitcher	G	IP	W	L	SV	ERA
St. L. W-106 L-48 Billy Southworth	1B	J. Hopp	314	.258	3	37	746	44	14	68	9.1	.983	M. Cooper	37	279	**22**	7	0	**1.78**
	2B	C. Crespi	292	.243	0	35	219	190	14	42	5.1	.967	J. Beazley	43	215	21	6	3	2.13
	SS	M. Marion	485	.276	0	54	296	448	31	87	5.3	.960	H. Gumbert	38	163	9	5	5	3.26
	3B	W. Kurowski	366	.254	9	42	124	194	19	19	3.2	.944	M. Lanier	34	160	13	8	2	2.98
	RF	E. Slaughter	591	.318	13	98	287	15	4	2	2.0	.987	E. White	26	128	7	5	2	2.52
	CF	T. Moore	489	.288	6	49	271	9	4	0	2.3	.986	M. Dickson	36	121	6	3	2	2.91
	LF	S. Musial	467	.315	10	72	296	6	5	0	2.3	.984	H. Krist	34	118	13	3	1	2.51
	C	W. Cooper	438	.281	7	65	519	62	**17**	6	**5.2**	.972	H. Pollet	27	109	7	5	0	2.88
	23	J. Brown	**606**	.256	1	71	296	326	24	65		.963	L. Warneke	12	82	6	4	0	3.29
	1B	R. Sanders	282	.252	5	39	626	35	6	54	8.7	.991							
	C	K. O'Dea	192	.234	5	32	247	37	6	6	5.9	.979							
	OF	H. Walker	191	.314	0	16	115	6	4	0	2.2	.968							
	OF	C. Triplett	154	.273	1	23	82	2	3	0	1.9	.966							
Bkn. W-104 L-50 Leo Durocher	1B	D. Camilli	524	.252	26	109	**1334**	85	12	**123**	9.5	.992	K. Higbe	38	222	16	11	0	3.25
	2B	B. Herman	571	.256	2	65	**383**	402	22	**97**	5.3	.973	W. Wyatt	31	217	19	7	0	2.73
	SS	P. Reese	564	.255	3	53	**337**	482	35	**99**	5.7	.959	C. Davis	32	206	15	6	2	2.36
	3B	A. Vaughan	495	.277	2	49	118	208	14	18	2.9	.959	L. French	38	148	15	4	0	1.83
	RF	D. Walker	393	.290	6	54	207	8	3	2	2.0	.986	E. Head	36	137	10	6	4	3.56
	CF	P. Reiser	480	.310	10	64	277	9	9	2	2.4	.990	J. Allen	27	118	10	6	3	3.20
	LF	J. Medwick	553	.300	4	96	287	5	3	1	2.1	.990	H. Casey	50	112	6	3	**13**	2.25
	C	M. Owen	421	.259	0	44	**595**	66	9	12	5.0	.987							
	OF	J. Rizzo	217	.230	4	27	124	6	3	1	1.9	.977							
	OF	A. Galan	209	.263	0	22	101	2	1	0	1.9	.990							
	3B	L. Riggs	180	.278	3	22	36	65	6	7	2.3	.944							

	POS	Player	AB	BA	HR	RBI	PO	A	E	DP	TC/G	FA	Pitcher	G	IP	W	L	SV	ERA
N. Y. W-85 L-67 Mel Ott	1B	J. Mize	541	.305	26	110	1393	74	8	98	10.7	.995	H. Schumacher	29	216	12	13	0	3.04
	2B	M. Witek	553	.260	5	48	371	441	18	72	5.6	.978	B. Carpenter	28	186	11	10	0	3.15
	SS	B. Jurges	464	.256	2	30	251	401	15	67	5.4	.978	B. Lohrman	26	158	13	4	0	2.56
	3B	B. Werber	370	.205	1	13	79	227	24	14	3.5	.927	C. Hubbell	24	157	11	8	0	3.95
	RF	M. Ott	549	.295	30	93	269	15	3	3	1.9	.990	C. Melton	23	144	11	5	1	2.63
	CF	W. Marshall	401	.257	11	59	222	13	6	4	2.3	.975	H. Feldman	31	114	7	1	0	3.16
	LF	B. Barna	331	.257	6	58	169	4	3	0	2.0	.983	B. McGee	31	104	6	3	1	2.93
	C	H. Danning	408	.279	1	34	459	55	11	7	4.5	.979	A. Adams	61	88	7	4	11	1.84
	3S	D. Bartell	316	.244	5	24	135	191	14	27		.959							
	OF	B. Young	287	.279	11	59	101	4	3	2	2.0	.972							
	OF	B. Maynard	190	.247	4	32	103	6	2	2	1.9	.982							
	OF	H. Leiber	147	.218	4	23	93	2	1	1	2.3	.990							
Cin. W-76 L-76 Bill McKechnie	1B	F. McCormick	564	.277	13	89	1403	101	10	132	10.5	.993	R. Starr	37	277	15	13	0	2.67
	2B	L. Frey	523	.266	2	39	340	424	18	95	5.6	.977	B. Walters	34	254	15	14	0	2.66
	SS	E. Joost	562	.224	6	41	248	380	45	79	5.2	.933	Vander Meer	33	244	18	12	0	2.43
	3B	B. Haas	585	.239	6	54	160	273	35	33	3.2	.925	P. Derringer	29	209	10	11	0	3.06
	RF	M. Marshall	530	.255	7	43	245	3	6	2	2.0	.976	E. Riddle	29	158	7	11	0	3.69
	CF	G. Walker	422	.230	5	50	277	7	8	2	2.7	.973	J. Thompson	29	102	4	7	0	3.36
	LF	E. Tipton	207	.222	4	18	126	3	3	0	2.3	.977	J. Beggs	38	89	6	5	8	2.13
	C	R. Lamanno	371	.264	12	43	421	59	11	7	4.7	.978							
	OF	I. Goodman	226	.243	0	15	101	7	1	2	1.9	.991							
Pit. W-66 L-81 Frankie Frisch	1B	E. Fletcher	506	.289	7	57	1379	118	12	104	10.5	.992	R. Sewell	40	248	17	15	2	3.41
	2B	F. Gustine	388	.229	2	35	227	312	26	53	5.2	.954	B. Klinger	37	153	8	11	1	3.24
	SS	P. Coscarart	487	.228	3	29	203	315	26	50	5.0	.952	M. Butcher	24	151	5	8	1	2.93
	3B	B. Elliott	560	.296	9	89	173	285	36	22	3.5	.927	D. Dietz	40	134	6	9	3	3.95
	RF	J. Barrett	332	.247	0	26	202	11	6	4	2.3	.973	Heintzelman	27	130	8	11	0	4.57
	CF	V. DiMaggio	496	.238	15	75	383	20	5	3	5.0	.978	J. Lanning	34	119	6	8	1	3.32
	LF	J. Wasdell	409	.259	3	38	191	8	9	1	2.1	.957	L. Hamlin	23	112	4	4	0	3.94
	C	A. Lopez	289	.256	1	26	327	53	2	14	3.9	.995	H. Gornicki	25	112	5	6	2	2.57
	OF	M. Van Robays	328	.232	1	46	199	6	3	3	2.5	.986	L. Wilkie	35	107	6	7	1	4.19
	C	B. Phelps	257	.284	9	41	244	40	12	5	4.1	.959							
	UT	B. Stewart	183	.219	0	20	87	23	3	0		.973							
	SS	A. Anderson	166	.271	0	7	77	103	11	17	4.0	.942							
Chi. W-68 L-86 Jimmie Wilson	1B	P. Cavarretta	482	.270	3	54	567	44	5	48	10.1	.992	C. Passeau	35	278	19	14	0	2.68
	2B	L. Stringer	406	.236	9	41	268	343	29	59	5.7	.955	B. Lee	32	220	13	13	0	3.85
	SS	L. Merullo	515	.256	2	37	299	438	42	80	5.4	.946	H. Bithorn	38	171	9	14	2	3.68
	3B	S. Hack	553	.300	6	39	154	261	15	21	3.1	.965	V. Olsen	32	140	6	9	1	4.49
	RF	B. Nicholson	588	.294	21	78	327	18	5	2	2.3	.986	B. Fleming	33	134	5	6	2	3.01
	CF	Dallessandro	264	.261	4	43	134	6	2	1	2.2	.986	L. Warneke	15	99	5	7	2	2.27
	LF	L. Novikoff	483	.300	7	64	232	11	9	2	2.1	.964	J. Schmitz	23	87	3	7	2	3.43
	C	McCullough	337	.282	5	31	386	61	9	10	4.7	.980							
	UT	R. Russell	302	.242	8	41	392	90	14	40		.972							
	1B	J. Foxx	205	.205	3	19	489	24	9	32	10.0	.983							
	OF	C. Gilbert	179	.184	0	7	99	6	2	2	2.3	.981							
	2S	B. Sturgeon	162	.247	0	7	112	163	4	33		.986							
Bos. W-59 L-89 Casey Stengel	1B	M. West	452	.254	16	56	807	47	8	66	10.1	.991	J. Tobin	37	288	12	21	0	3.97
	2B	S. Sisti	407	.211	4	35	304	351	20	66	5.4	.970	A. Javery	42	261	12	16	0	3.03
	SS	E. Miller	534	.243	6	47	285	450	13	78	5.2	.983	L. Tost	35	148	10	10	0	3.53
	3B	N. Fernandez	577	.255	6	55	123	206	31	16	3.7	.914	M. Salvo	25	131	7	8	0	3.03
	RF	P. Waner	333	.258	1	39	150	6	5	3	1.7	.969	T. Earley	27	113	6	11	1	4.71
	CF	T. Holmes	558	.278	4	41	373	16	4	4	2.8	.990	J. Sain	40	97	4	7	6	3.90
	LF	C. Ross	220	.195	5	19	123	2	1	0	2.2	.992							
	C	E. Lombardi	309	.330	11	46	251	41	6	3	3.5	.980							
	C	C. Kluttz	210	.267	1	31	200	29	5	5	4.1	.979							
	1B	B. Gremp	207	.217	3	19	504	33	5	45	8.7	.991							
	OF	J. Cooney	198	.207	0	7	59	2	1	0	1.1	.984							
	OF	F. Demaree	187	.225	3	24	114	4	0	1	2.4	1.000							
	23	S. Roberge	172	.215	1	12	87	127	6	19		.973							
Phi. W-42 L-109 Hans Lobert	1B	N. Etten	459	.264	8	41	1152	83	19	99	9.3	.985	T. Hughes	40	253	12	18	1	3.06
	2B	A. Glossop	454	.225	4	40	322	351	27	79	5.9	.961	R. Melton	42	209	9	20	4	3.70
	SS	B. Bragan	335	.218	2	15	161	238	26	49	5.4	.939	S. Johnson	39	195	8	19	0	3.69
	3B	P. May	345	.238	0	18	109	227	13	23	3.3	.963	J. Podgajny	43	187	6	14	0	3.91
	RF	R. Northey	402	.251	5	31	206	12	11	2	2.1	.952	F. Hoerst	33	151	4	16	1	5.20
	CF	L. Waner	287	.261	0	10	170	6	6	0	2.4	.967							
	LF	D. Litwhiler	591	.271	9	56	308	9	0	0	2.1	1.000							
	C	B. Warren	225	.209	7	20	264	50	9	4	4.1	.972							
	UT	D. Murtaugh	506	.241	0	27	302	377	43	61		.940							
	OF	E. Koy	258	.244	4	26	149	4	3	1	2.0	.981							
	C	M. Livingston	239	.205	2	22	275	36	4	8	4.0	.987							
	OF	S. Benjamin	210	.224	2	8	75	7	2	1	1.9	.976							
	OP	E. Naylor	168	.196	0	14	66	11	1	0		.987							

BATTING AND BASE RUNNING LEADERS

Batting Average		Slugging Average	
E. Lombardi, BOS	.330	J. Mize, NY	.521
E. Slaughter, STL	.318	M. Ott, NY	.497
S. Musial, STL	.315	E. Slaughter, STL	.494
P. Reiser, BKN	.310	S. Musial, STL	.490
J. Mize, NY	.305	E. Lombardi, BOS	.482

PITCHING LEADERS

Winning Percentage		Earned Run Average	
L. French, BKN	.789	M. Cooper, STL	1.78
J. Beazley, STL	.778	J. Beazley, STL	2.13
M. Cooper, STL	.759	C. Davis, BKN	2.36
W. Wyatt, BKN	.731	Vander Meer, CIN	2.43
C. Davis, BKN	.714	B. Lohrman, NY, STL	2.48

BATTING AND BASE RUNNING LEADERS

Home Runs
M. Ott, NY	30
D. Camilli, BKN	26
J. Mize, NY	26
B. Nicholson, CHI	21
M. West, BOS	16

Total Bases
E. Slaughter, STL	292
J. Mize, NY	282
B. Nicholson, CHI	280
M. Ott, NY	273
D. Camilli, BKN	247

Runs Batted In
J. Mize, NY	110
D. Camilli, BKN	109
E. Slaughter, STL	98
J. Medwick, BKN	96
M. Ott, NY	93

Stolen Bases
P. Reiser, BKN	20
P. Reese, BKN	15
N. Fernandez, BOS	15
J. Hopp, STL	14
L. Merullo, CHI	14

Hits
E. Slaughter, STL	188
B. Nicholson, CHI	173

Base on Balls
M. Ott, NY	109
E. Fletcher, PIT	105
D. Camilli, BKN	97

Home Run Percentage
M. Ott, NY	5.5
D. Camilli, BKN	5.0
J. Mize, NY	4.8

Runs Scored
M. Ott, NY	118
E. Slaughter, STL	100
J. Mize, NY	97

Doubles
M. Marion, STL	38
J. Medwick, BKN	37
S. Hack, CHI	36

Triples
E. Slaughter, STL	17
B. Nicholson, CHI	11
S. Musial, STL	10
D. Litwhiler, PHI	9

PITCHING LEADERS

Wins
M. Cooper, STL	22
J. Beazley, STL	21
W. Wyatt, BKN	19
C. Passeau, CHI	19
Vander Meer, CIN	18

Saves
H. Casey, BKN	13
A. Adams, NY	11
J. Beggs, CIN	8
J. Sain, BOS	6
H. Gumbert, STL	5

Strikeouts
Vander Meer, CIN	186
M. Cooper, STL	152
K. Higbe, BKN	115
B. Walters, CIN	109
R. Melton, PHI	107

Complete Games
J. Tobin, BOS	28
C. Passeau, CHI	24
M. Cooper, STL	22
B. Walters, CIN	21
Vander Meer, CIN	21

Fewest Hits per 9 Innings
M. Cooper, STL	6.69
Vander Meer, CIN	6.93
K. Higbe, BKN	7.31

Shutouts
M. Cooper, STL	10
C. Davis, BKN	5
R. Sewell, PIT	5
A. Javery, BOS	5

Fewest Walks per 9 Innings
L. Warneke, CHI, STL	1.79
B. Lohrman, NY, STL	1.85
C. Hubbell, NY	1.94

Most Strikeouts per 9 Inn.
Vander Meer, CIN	6.86
M. Cooper, STL	4.91
K. Higbe, BKN	4.67

Innings
J. Tobin, BOS	288
M. Cooper, STL	279
C. Passeau, CHI	278

Games Pitched
A. Adams, NY	61
H. Casey, BKN	50
J. Beazley, STL	43
J. Podgajny, PHI	43

	W	L	PCT	GB	R	OR	2B	3B	Batting HR	BA	SA	SB	E	Fielding DP	FA	CG	BB	SO	Pitching ShO	SV	ERA
STL	106	48	.688		755	482	282	69	60	.268	.379	71	169	137	.972	70	473	651	18	15	2.55
BKN	104	50	.675	2	742	510	263	34	62	.265	.362	79	138	150	.977	67	493	612	16	24	2.84
NY	85	67	.559	20	675	600	162	35	109	.254	.361	39	138	128	.977	70	493	497	12	13	3.31
CIN	76	76	.500	29	527	545	198	39	66	.231	.321	42	177	158	.971	80	526	616	12	8	2.82
PIT	66	81	.449	36.5	585	631	173	49	54	.245	.330	41	184	129	.969	64	435	426	13	11	3.58
CHI	68	86	.442	38	591	665	224	41	75	.254	.353	61	170	169	.973	71	525	507	10	14	3.60
BOS	59	89	.399	44	515	645	210	19	68	.240	.329	49	142	138	.976	68	518	414	9	8	3.76
PHI	42	109	.278	62.5	394	706	168	37	44	.232	.306	37	194	147	.968	51	605	472	2	6	4.12
					4784	4784	1680	323	538	.249	.343	419	1312	1156	.973	541	4068	4195	92	99	3.31

American League 1942

	POS	Player	AB	BA	HR	RBI	PO	A	E	DP	TC/G	FA	Pitcher	G	IP	W	L	SV	ERA
N. Y. W-103 L-51 Joe McCarthy	1B	B. Hassett	538	.284	5	48	1128	118	11	130	9.5	.991	E. Bonham	28	226	21	5	0	2.27
	2B	J. Gordon	538	.322	18	103	354	442	28	121	5.6	.966	S. Chandler	24	201	16	5	0	2.38
	SS	P. Rizzuto	553	.284	4	68	324	445	30	114	5.5	.962	R. Ruffing	24	194	14	7	0	3.21
	3B	F. Crosetti	285	.242	4	23	70	105	9	14	3.0	.951	H. Borowy	25	178	15	4	1	2.52
	RF	T. Henrich	483	.267	13	67	219	10	3	5	1.9	.987	M. Breuer	27	164	8	9	1	3.07
	CF	J. DiMaggio	610	.305	21	114	409	10	8	3	2.8	.981	A. Donald	20	148	11	3	0	3.11
	LF	C. Keller	544	.292	26	108	321	10	5	1	2.2	.985	L. Gomez	13	80	6	4	0	4.28
	C	B. Dickey	268	.295	2	37	322	44	9	7	4.7	.976	J. Murphy	31	58	4	10	11	3.41
	3B	R. Rolfe	265	.219	8	25	57	132	8	16	3.3	.959							
	C	B. Rosar	209	.230	2	34	249	26	1	7	4.8	.996							
	UT	G. Priddy	189	.280	2	28	146	114	9	26		.967							
Bos. W-93 L-59 Joe Cronin	1B	T. Lupien	463	.281	3	70	1091	68	9	99	9.7	.992	T. Hughson	38	281	22	6	4	2.59
	2B	B. Doerr	545	.290	15	102	376	453	21	105	6.0	.975	C. Wagner	29	205	14	11	0	3.29
	SS	J. Pesky	620	.331	2	51	320	465	37	94	5.6	.955	J. Dobson	30	183	11	9	0	3.30
	3B	J. Tabor	508	.252	12	75	168	236	33	24	3.2	.924	D. Newsome	24	158	8	10	0	5.01
	RF	L. Finney	397	.285	3	61	199	8	5	1	2.2	.976	O. Judd	31	150	8	10	2	3.89
	CF	D. DiMaggio	622	.286	14	48	439	19	6	7	3.1	.987	B. Butland	23	111	7	1	1	2.51
	LF	T. Williams	522	.356	36	137	313	15	4	4	2.2	.988	Y. Terry	20	85	6	5	1	3.92
	C	B. Conroy	250	.200	4	20	324	40	11	6	4.5	.971	M. Brown	34	60	9	3	6	3.43
	C	J. Peacock	286	.266	0	25	280	44	4	8	4.0	.988							
	OF	P. Fox	256	.262	3	42	111	2	4	0	1.6	.966							
	31	J. Cronin	79	.304	4	24	46	26	6	7		.923							

	POS	Player	AB	BA	HR	RBI	PO	A	E	DP	TC/G	FA	Pitcher	G	IP	W	L	SV	ERA
St. L.	1B	G. McQuinn	554	.262	12	78	1384	105	13	116	10.4	.991	E. Auker	35	249	14	13	0	4.08
W-82 L-69	2B	D. Gutteridge	616	.255	1	50	377	454	23	94	5.9	.973	J. Niggeling	28	206	15	11	0	2.66
Luke Sewell	SS	V. Stephens	575	.294	14	92	290	415	42	82	5.2	.944	D. Galehouse	32	191	12	12	1	3.62
	3B	H. Clift	541	.274	7	55	160	287	28	28	3.4	.941	Hollingsworth	33	161	10	6	4	2.96
	RF	C. Laabs	520	.275	27	99	276	13	9	3	2.1	.970	B. Muncrief	24	134	6	8	0	3.89
	CF	W. Judnich	457	.313	17	82	330	4	3	0	2.8	.991	S. Sundra	20	111	8	3	0	3.82
	LF	G. McQuillen	339	.283	3	47	156	2	5	0	2.1	.969	G. Caster	39	80	8	2	5	2.81
	C	R. Ferrell	273	.223	0	26	356	57	6	7	4.4	.986							
	OF	M. Chartak	237	.249	9	43	142	10	4	3	2.4	.974							
	C	F. Hayes	159	.252	2	17	175	25	6	2	4.0	.971							
	OF	T. Criscola	158	.297	1	13						.0							
Cle.	1B	L. Fleming	548	.292	14	82	1503	90	12	152	10.3	.993	J. Bagby	38	271	17	9	1	2.96
W-75 L-79	2B	R. Mack	481	.225	2	45	340	434	25	105	5.6	.969	M. Harder	29	199	13	14	0	3.44
Lou Boudreau	SS	L. Boudreau	506	.283	2	58	281	426	26	107	5.0	.965	C. Dean	27	173	8	11	1	3.81
	3B	K. Keltner	624	.287	6	78	166	353	30	38	3.6	.945	A. Smith	30	168	10	15	0	3.96
	RF	O. Hockett	601	.250	7	48	284	12	6	3	2.1	.980	A. Milnar	28	157	6	8	0	4.13
	CF	R. Weatherly	473	.258	5	39	324	7	3	4	2.9	.991	V. Kennedy	28	108	4	8	1	4.08
	LF	J. Heath	568	.278	10	76	326	12	7	3	2.4	.980	J. Heving	27	46	5	3	3	4.86
	C	O. Denning	214	.210	1	19	213	36	2	6	3.2	.992							
	OF	B. Mills	195	.277	1	26	142	4	4	2	2.8	.973							
	C	J. Hegan	170	.194	0	11	227	32	6	7	4.0	.977							
	C	G. Desautels	162	.247	0	9	180	16	5	0	3.3	.975							
Det.	1B	R. York	577	.260	21	90	1413	146	19	117	10.4	.988	A. Benton	35	227	7	13	2	2.90
W-73 L-81	2B	J. Bloodworth	533	.242	13	57	334	431	22	66	5.9	.972	D. Trout	35	223	12	18	0	3.43
Del Baker	SS	B. Hitchcock	280	.211	0	29	157	199	21	39	4.7	.944	H. White	34	217	12	12	1	2.91
	3B	P. Higgins	499	.267	11	79	134	243	30	24	3.0	.926	H. Newhouser	38	184	8	14	5	2.45
	RF	B. Harris	398	.271	9	45	164	5	10	2	1.7	.944	T. Bridges	23	174	9	7	1	2.74
	CF	D. Cramer	630	.263	0	43	352	15	7	6	2.5	.981	V. Trucks	28	168	14	8	0	2.74
	LF	B. McCosky	600	.293	7	50	351	7	7	2	2.4	.981							
	C	B. Tebbetts	308	.247	1	27	446	69	12	10	5.4	.977							
	O3	D. Ross	226	.274	3	30	94	30	7	4		.947							
	C	D. Parsons	188	.197	2	11	274	44	6	6	5.2	.981							
	SS	M. Franklin	154	.260	2	16	67	79	5	14	4.7	.967							
	OF	R. Radcliff	144	.250	1	20	43	1	1	1	1.9	.978							
Chi.	1B	J. Kuhel	413	.249	4	52	1085	70	11	94	10.4	.991	J. Humphries	28	228	12	12	0	2.68
W-66 L-82	2B	D. Kolloway	601	.273	3	60	308	345	23	80	5.8	.966	E. Smith	29	215	7	20	1	3.98
Jimmy Dykes	SS	L. Appling	543	.262	3	53	269	418	38	77	5.1	.948	T. Lyons	20	180	14	6	0	2.10
	3B	B. Kennedy	412	.231	0	38	99	207	14	17	3.3	.956	B. Dietrich	26	160	6	11	0	4.89
	RF	W. Moses	577	.270	7	49	323	14	7	3	2.4	.980	B. Ross	22	113	5	7	1	5.00
	CF	M. Hoag	412	.240	2	37	266	12	8	4	2.6	.972	J. Haynes	40	103	8	5	6	2.62
	LF	T. Wright	300	.333	0	47	176	6	6	1	2.3	.968	J. Wade	15	86	5	5	0	4.10
	C	M. Tresh	233	.232	0	15	258	37	7	2	4.2	.977	O. Grove	12	66	4	6	0	5.16
	C	T. Turner	182	.242	3	21	199	35	7	5	4.5	.971							
	3B	D. Lodigiani	168	.280	0	15	40	96	8	4	3.3	.944							
	OF	S. West	151	.232	0	25	112	1	2	1	2.6	.983							
Was.	1B	M. Vernon	621	.271	9	86	1360	95	26	109	9.8	.982	S. Hudson	35	239	10	17	2	4.36
W-62 L-89	2B	E. Clary	240	.275	0	16	162	181	11	37	5.1	.969	B. Newsom	30	214	11	17	0	4.93
Bucky Harris	SS	J. Sullivan	357	.235	0	42	217	235	31	51	5.3	.936	E. Wynn	30	190	10	16	0	5.12
	3B	B. Estalella	429	.277	8	65	89	134	14	4	3.0	.941	A. Carrasquel	35	152	7	7	3	3.43
	RF	B. Campbell	378	.278	5	63	188	4	9	1	2.3	.955	W. Masterson	25	143	5	9	2	3.34
	CF	S. Spence	629	.323	4	79	395	7	11	0	2.8	.973	B. Zuber	37	127	9	9	1	3.84
	LF	G. Case	513	.320	5	43	270	4	14	1	2.4	.951							
	C	J. Early	353	.204	3	46	392	71	2	11	4.8	.981							
	UT	J. Pofahl	283	.208	0	28	166	204	18	45		.954							
	UT	B. Repass	259	.239	2	17	142	178	12	21		.964							
	O3	R. Cullenbine	241	.286	2	35	125	69	11	5		.946							
	C	A. Evans	223	.229	0	10	254	42	12	5	4.6	.961							
Phi.	1B	D. Siebert	612	.260	2	74	1345	104	16	109	9.6	.989	P. Marchildon	38	244	17	14	1	4.20
W-55 L-99	2B	W. Knickerbocker	289	.253	1	19	178	220	15	45	5.1	.964	R. Wolff	32	214	12	15	3	3.32
Connie Mack	SS	P. Suder	476	.256	4	54	141	193	16	31	5.1	.954	L. Harris	26	166	11	15	0	3.74
	3B	B. Blair	484	.279	5	66	143	234	28	21	3.2	.931	Christopher	30	165	4	13	1	3.82
	RF	E. Valo	459	.251	2	40	264	5	10	0	2.3	.964	D. Fowler	31	140	6	11	1	4.95
	CF	M. Kreevich	444	.255	1	30	314	4	6	0	3.0	.981	H. Besse	30	133	2	9	1	6.50
	LF	B. Johnson	550	.291	13	80	318	18	13	1	2.3	.963	J. Knott	20	95	2	10	0	5.57
	C	H. Wagner	288	.236	1	30	371	47	6	7	4.5	.986							
	OF	D. Miles	346	.272	0	22	177	6	3	0	2.3	.984							
	2S	C. Davis	272	.224	2	26	175	210	19	30		.953							
	C	B. Swift	192	.229	0	15	253	39	9	3	5.0	.970							

BATTING AND BASE RUNNING LEADERS

Batting Average		Slugging Average	
T. Williams, BOS	.356	T. Williams, BOS	.648
J. Pesky, BOS	.331	C. Keller, NY	.513
S. Spence, WAS	.323	W. Judnich, STL	.499
J. Gordon, NY	.322	J. DiMaggio, NY	.498
G. Case, WAS	.320	C. Laabs, STL	.498

PITCHING LEADERS

Winning Percentage		Earned Run Average	
E. Bonham, NY	.808	T. Lyons, CHI	2.10
H. Borowy, NY	.789	E. Bonham, NY	2.27
T. Hughson, BOS	.786	S. Chandler, NY	2.38
S. Chandler, NY	.762	H. Newhouser, DET	2.45
J. Bagby, CLE	.654	H. Borowy, NY	2.52

BATTING AND BASE RUNNING LEADERS

Home Runs

T. Williams, BOS	36
C. Laabs, STL	27
C. Keller, NY	26
R. York, DET	21
J. DiMaggio, NY	21

Total Bases

T. Williams, BOS	338
J. DiMaggio, NY	304
C. Keller, NY	279
D. DiMaggio, BOS	272
S. Spence, WAS	272

Runs Batted In

T. Williams, BOS	137
J. DiMaggio, NY	114
C. Keller, NY	108
J. Gordon, NY	103
B. Doerr, BOS	102

Stolen Bases

G. Case, WAS	44
M. Vernon, WAS	25
J. Kuhel, CHI	22
P. Rizzuto, NY	22
M. Hoag, CHI	17
L. Appling, CHI	17

Hits

J. Pesky, BOS	205
S. Spence, WAS	203
T. Williams, BOS	186
J. DiMaggio, NY	186

Base on Balls

T. Williams, BOS	145
C. Keller, NY	114
H. Clift, STL	106
L. Fleming, CLE	106

Home Run Percentage

T. Williams, BOS	6.9
C. Laabs, STL	5.2
C. Keller, NY	4.8

Runs Scored

T. Williams, BOS	141
J. DiMaggio, NY	123
D. DiMaggio, BOS	110

Doubles

D. Kolloway, CHI	40
H. Clift, STL	39
J. Heath, CLE	37

Triples

S. Spence, WAS	15
J. Heath, CLE	13
J. DiMaggio, NY	13

PITCHING LEADERS

Wins

T. Hughson, BOS	22
E. Bonham, NY	21
J. Bagby, CLE	17
P. Marchildon, PHI	17
S. Chandler, NY	16

Saves

J. Murphy, NY	11
M. Brown, BOS	6
J. Haynes, CHI	6
G. Caster, STL	5
H. Newhouser, DET	5

Strikeouts

B. Newsom, WAS	113
T. Hughson, BOS	113
A. Benton, DET	110
P. Marchildon, PHI	110
J. Niggeling, STL	107

Complete Games

E. Bonham, NY	22
T. Hughson, BOS	22
T. Lyons, CHI	20
S. Hudson, WAS	19
E. Smith, CHI	18
P. Marchildon, PHI	18

Fewest Hits per 9 Innings

H. Newhouser, DET	6.71
J. Niggeling, STL	7.55
J. Dobson, BOS	7.64

Shutouts

E. Bonham, NY	6
T. Hughson, BOS	4

Fewest Walks per 9 Innings

F. Bonham, NY	0.96
T. Lyons, CHI	1.30
R. Ruffing, NY	1.91

Most Strikeouts per 9 Inn.

H. Newhouser, DET	5.05
T. Bridges, DET	5.02
B. Newsom, WAS	4.76

Innings

T. Hughson, BOS	281
J. Bagby, CLE	271
E. Auker, STL	249

Games Pitched

J. Haynes, CHI	40
G. Caster, STL	39

	W	L	PCT	GB	R	OR	2B	3B	Batting HR	BA	SA	SB	Fielding E	DP	FA	CG	BB	Pitching SO	ShO	SV	ERA
NY	103	51	.669		801	507	223	57	108	.269	.394	69	142	190	.976	88	431	558	18	17	2.91
BOS	93	59	.612	9	761	594	244	55	103	.276	.403	68	157	156	.974	84	553	500	11	17	3.44
STL	82	69	.543	19.5	730	637	239	62	98	.259	.385	37	167	143	.972	68	505	488	12	13	3.59
CLE	75	79	.487	28	590	659	223	58	50	.253	.345	69	163	175	.974	61	560	448	12	11	3.59
DET	73	81	.474	30	589	587	217	37	76	.246	.344	39	194	142	.969	65	598	671	12	14	3.13
CHI	66	82	.446	34	538	609	214	36	25	.246	.318	114	173	144	.970	86	473	432	8	8	3.58
WAS	62	89	.411	39.5	653	817	224	49	40	.258	.341	98	222	133	.962	68	558	496	12	11	4.58
PHI	55	99	.357	48	549	801	213	46	33	.249	.325	44	188	124	.969	67	639	546	5	9	4.48
					5211	5211	1797	400	533	.257	.357	538	1406	1207	.971	587	4317	4139	90	100	3.66

National League 1943

	POS	Player	AB	BA	HR	RBI	PO	A	E	DP	TC/G	FA	Pitcher	G	IP	W	L	SV	ERA
St. L. W-105 L-49 Billy Southworth	1B	R. Sanders	478	.280	11	73	1302	71	7	142	9.8	.995	M. Cooper	37	274	21	8	3	2.30
	2B	L. Klein	627	.287	7	62	301	356	18	99	5.4	.973	M. Lanier	32	213	15	7	3	1.90
	SS	M. Marion	418	.280	1	52	232	424	20	93	5.3	.970	H. Krist	34	164	11	5	3	2.90
	3B	W. Kurowski	522	.287	13	70	166	255	21	29	3.2	.952	H. Brecheen	29	135	9	6	4	2.26
	RF	S. Musial	617	.357	13	81	376	15	7	4	2.6	.982	H. Gumbert	21	133	10	5	0	2.84
	CF	H. Walker	564	.294	2	53	321	14	12	4	2.4	.965	H. Pollet	16	118	8	4	0	1.75
	LF	D. Litwhiler	258	.279	7	31	139	7	0	1	2.1	1.000*	M. Dickson	31	116	8	2	0	3.58
	C	W. Cooper	449	.318	9	81	504	49	14	5	5.1	.975	G. Munger	32	93	9	5	2	3.95
	O3	D. Garms	249	.257	0	22	111	25	9	5		.938	A. Brazle	13	88	8	2	0	1.53
	O1	J. Hopp	241	.224	2	25	286	17	12	23		.962	E. White	14	79	5	5	0	3.78
	C	K. O'Dea	203	.281	3	25	237	32	3	6	4.9	.989							
Cin. W-87 L-67 Bill McKechnie	1B	F. McCormick	472	.303	8	59	1156	85	6	116	10.4	.995	Vander Meer	36	289	15	16	0	2.87
	2B	L. Frey	586	.263	2	43	399	461	13	112	6.1	.985	E. Riddle	36	260	21	11	3	2.63
	SS	E. Miller	576	.224	2	71	335	543	19	123	5.8	.979	B. Walters	34	246	15	15	0	3.54
	3B	S. Mesner	504	.272	0	52	132	274	24	29	3.3	.944	R. Starr	36	217	11	10	1	3.64
	RF	M. Marshall	508	.236	4	39	240	12	5	4	2.0	.981	C. Shoun	45	147	14	5	7	3.06
	CF	G. Walker	429	.245	3	54	231	8	5	3	2.3	.980	J. Beggs	39	115	7	6	6	2.34
	LF	E. Tipton	493	.288	9	49	298	5	5	2	2.2	.984							
	C	R. Mueller	427	.260	8	52	579	100	8	17	4.9	.988							
	UT	B. Haas	332	.262	4	44	432	97	9	52		.983							
	OF	E. Crabtree	254	.276	2	26	135	4	9	2	2.3	.939							

Bkn.
W-81 L-72
Leo Durocher

POS	Player	AB	BA	HR	RBI	PO	A	E	DP	TC/G	FA	Pitcher	G	IP	W	L	SV	ERA
1B	D. Camilli	353	.246	6	43	853	60	7	78	9.7	.992	K. Higbe	35	185	13	10	0	3.70
2B	B. Herman	585	.330	2	100	291	322	18	69	5.4	.971	W. Wyatt	26	181	14	5	0	2.49
SS	A. Vaughan	610	.305	5	66	175	291	17	55	4.9	.965	E. Head	47	170	9	10	6	3.66
3B	F. Bordagaray	268	.302	0	19	28	26	7	0	2.4	.885	C. Davis	31	164	10	13	3	3.78
RF	D. Walker	540	.302	5	71	262	20	9	2	2.1	.969	B. Newsom	22	125	9	4	1	3.02
CF	A. Galan	495	.287	9	67	347	12	7	1	3.0	.981	R. Melton	30	119	5	8	0	3.92
LF	L. Olmo	238	.303	4	37	128	6	6	0	2.5	.957	L. Webber	54	116	2	2	10	3.81
C	M. Owen	365	.260	0	54	414	47	6	11	4.7	.987	M. Macon	25	77	7	5	0	5.96
OF	P. Waner	225	.311	1	26	116	4	5	1	2.2	.960							
C	B. Bragan	220	.264	2	24	253	34	8	6	5.2	.973							
UT	A. Glossop	217	.171	3	21	102	161	24	24		.916							
1B	H. Schultz	182	.269	1	34	386	33	6	27	9.4	.986							
OF	J. Medwick	173	.272	0	25	65	2	2	0	1.6	.971							

Pit.
W-80 L-74
Frankie Frisch

POS	Player	AB	BA	HR	RBI	PO	A	E	DP	TC/G	FA	Pitcher	G	IP	W	L	SV	ERA
1B	E. Fletcher	544	.283	9	70	1541	108	6	141	10.7	.996	R. Sewell	35	265	21	9	3	2.54
2B	P. Coscarart	491	.242	0	48	186	263	18	54	5.5	.961	B. Klinger	33	195	11	8	0	2.72
SS	F. Gustine	414	.290	0	43	135	230	24	41	5.7	.938	H. Bithorn	33	194	10	8	1	2.60
3B	B. Elliott	581	.315	7	101	149	294	24	34	3.1	.949	W. Hebert	34	184	10	11	0	2.98
RF	J. Barrett	290	.231	1	32	165	6	2	0	1.7	.988	H. Gornicki	42	147	9	13	4	3.98
CF	V. DiMaggio	580	.248	15	88	457	16	7	3	3.1	.985	X. Rescigno	37	133	6	9	2	3.05
LF	J. Russell	533	.259	4	44	285	16	3	3	2.3	.990							
C	A. Lopez	372	.263	1	39	378	66	4	9	3.9	.991							
OF	M. Van Robays	236	.288	1	35	120	5	8	1	2.2	.940							
OF	T. O'Brien	232	.310	2	26	76	4	3	0	1.7	.964							
C	B. Baker	172	.273	1	26	157	29	4	3	3.4	.979							
2B	A. Rubeling	168	.262	0	9	87	138	6	27	5.3	.974							
SS	H. Geary	166	.151	1	13	92	127	10	25	5.0	.956							

Chi.
W-74 L-79
Jimmie Wilson

POS	Player	AB	BA	HR	RBI	PO	A	E	DP	TC/G	FA	Pitcher	G	IP	W	L	SV	ERA
1B	P. Cavarretta	530	.291	8	73	1290	67	18	103	10.3	.987	C. Passeau	35	257	15	12	1	2.91
2B	E. Stanky	510	.245	0	47	362	416	27	78	6.1	.966	H. Bithorn	39	250	18	12	2	2.60
SS	L. Merullo	453	.254	1	25	218	396	39	68	5.2	.940	P. Derringer	32	174	10	14	3	3.57
3B	S. Hack	533	.289	3	35	149	264	17	11	3.2	.960	H. Wyse	38	156	9	7	5	2.94
RF	B. Nicholson	608	.309	29	128	340	16	8	2	2.4	.978	E. Hanyzewski	33	130	8	7	0	2.56
CF	P. Lowrey	480	.292	1	63	315	13	6	4	3.0	.982	B. Lee	13	78	3	7	0	3.56
LF	I. Goodman	225	.320	3	45	120	2	4	1	2.1	.968							
C	McCullough	266	.237	2	23	271	25	7	2	3.7	.977							
OF	L. Novikoff	233	.279	0	28	96	2	2	1	1.6	.980							
OF	Dallessandro	176	.222	1	31	87	2	3	0	2.0	.967							

Bos.
W-68 L-85
Casey Stengel

POS	Player	AB	BA	HR	RBI	PO	A	E	DP	TC/G	FA	Pitcher	G	IP	W	L	SV	ERA
1B	J. McCarthy	313	.304	2	33	839	53	4	51	11.5	.996	A. Javery	41	303	17	16	0	3.21
2B	C. Ryan	457	.212	1	24	224	306	21	41	5.5	.962	N. Andrews	36	284	14	20	0	2.57
SS	W. Wietelmann	534	.215	0	29	307	581	40	91	6.1	.957	R. Barrett	38	255	12	18	0	3.18
3B	E. Joost	421	.185	2	20	104	171	16	15	4.3	.945	J. Tobin	33	250	14	14	0	2.66
RF	C. Workman	615	.249	10	67	310	22	4	7	2.3	.988	M. Salvo	20	93	5	6	0	3.28
CF	T. Holmes	629	.270	5	41	408	18	3	3	2.8	.993							
LF	B. Nieman	335	.251	7	46	195	12	8	1	2.3	.963							
C	P. Masi	238	.273	2	28	192	40	2	1	3.2	.991							
OF	C. Ross	285	.218	7	32	165	8	4	1	2.3	.977							
1B	K. Farrell	280	.268	0	21	740	50	3	61	11.5	.996							
C	C. Kluttz	207	.246	0	20	176	43	6	5	4.1	.973							

Phi.
W-64 L-90
Bucky Harris
W-40 L-53
Freddie
Fitzsimmons
W-24 L-37

POS	Player	AB	BA	HR	RBI	PO	A	E	DP	TC/G	FA	Pitcher	G	IP	W	L	SV	ERA
1B	J. Wasdell	522	.261	4	67	749	56	10	62	9.9	.988	A. Gerheauser	38	215	10	19	0	3.60
2B	D. Murtaugh	451	.273	1	35	321	345	18	76	6.1	.974	S. Rowe	27	199	14	8	1	2.94
SS	G. Stewart	336	.211	2	24	128	232	20	41	4.9	.947	T. Kraus	34	200	9	15	2	3.16
3B	P. May	415	.282	1	48	142	280	16	20	3.3	.963	D. Barrett	23	169	10	9	1	2.39
RF	R. Northey	586	.278	16	68	292	19	7	6	2.2	.978	S. Johnson	21	113	8	3	2	3.27
CF	B. Adams	418	.256	4	38	298	6	5	8*	2.9	.984	C. Fuchs	17	78	2	7	1	4.29
LF	C. Triplett	360	.272	14	52	184	11	6	0	2.2	.970							
C	M. Livingston	265	.249	3	18	268	49	4	5	3.8	.988*							
UT	B. Dahlgren	508	.287	5	56	800	151	24	81		.975							
2B	R. Hamrick	160	.200	0	9	67	78	6	9	4.9	.960							
SS	C. Brewster	159	.220	0	12	73	110	20	18	4.4	.901							

N. Y.
W-55 L-98
Mel Ott

POS	Player	AB	BA	HR	RBI	PO	A	E	DP	TC/G	FA	Pitcher	G	IP	W	L	SV	ERA
1B	J. Orengo	266	.218	6	29	730	61	6	49	9.7	.992	C. Melton	34	186	9	13	0	3.19
2B	M. Witek	622	.314	6	55	401	505	31	90	6.1	.967	J. Wittig	40	164	5	15	4	4.23
SS	B. Jurges	481	.229	4	29	209	303	24	44	5.4	.955	V. Mungo	45	154	3	7	2	3.91
3B	D. Bartell	337	.270	5	28	62	131	4	9	3.6	.980	A. Adams	70	140	11	7	9	2.82
RF	M. Ott	380	.234	18	47	219	12	6	1	2.1	.975	R. Fischer	22	131	5	10	1	4.61
CF	J. Rucker	505	.273	2	46	300	9	10	3	2.7	.969	K. Chase	21	129	4	12	0	4.11
LF	J. Medwick	324	.281	5	45	130	9	5	2	1.9	.965	H. Feldman	31	105	4	5	0	4.30
C	G. Mancuso	252	.198	2	20	336	40	10	1	5.0	.974	B. Lohrman	17	80	5	6	1	5.15
UT	S. Gordon	474	.251	9	63	551	148	17	59		.976							
OF	B. Maynard	393	.206	9	32	157	10	2	0	2.3	.988							
C	E. Lombardi	295	.305	10	51	296	36	10	8	4.7	.971							

BATTING AND BASE RUNNING LEADERS

Batting Average		Slugging Average	
S. Musial, STL	.357	S. Musial, STL	.562
B. Herman, BKN	.330	B. Nicholson, CHI	.531
W. Cooper, STL	.318	W. Cooper, STL	.463
B. Elliott, PIT	.315	B. Elliott, PIT	.444
M. Witek, NY	.314	C. Triplett, PHI, STL	.439

PITCHING LEADERS

Winning Percentage		Earned Run Average	
M. Cooper, STL	.724	H. Pollet, STL	1.75
R. Sewell, PIT	.700	M. Lanier, STL	1.90
M. Lanier, STL	.682	M. Cooper, STL	2.30
E. Riddle, CIN	.656	W. Wyatt, BKN	2.49
H. Bithorn, CHI	.600	R. Sewell, PIT	2.54

BATTING AND BASE RUNNING LEADERS

Home Runs

B. Nicholson, CHI	29
M. Ott, NY	18
R. Northey, PHI	16
C. Triplett, PHI, STL	15
V. DiMaggio, PIT	15

Total Bases

S. Musial, STL	347
B. Nicholson, CHI	323
B. Elliott, PIT	258
L. Klein, STL	257
R. Northey, PHI	252
A. Vaughan, BKN	252

Runs Batted In

B. Nicholson, CHI	128
B. Elliott, PIT	101
B. Herman, BKN	100
V. DiMaggio, PIT	88
W. Cooper, STL	81
S. Musial, STL	81

Stolen Bases

A. Vaughan, BKN	20
P. Lowrey, CHI	13
F. Gustine, PIT	12
J. Russell, PIT	12
C. Workman, BOS	12

Hits

S. Musial, STL	220
M. Witek, NY	195
B. Herman, BKN	193

Base on Balls

A. Galan, BKN	103
M. Ott, NY	95
E. Fletcher, PIT	95

Home Run Percentage

B. Nicholson, CHI	4.8
M. Ott, NY	4.7
C. Triplett, PHI, STL	3.9

Runs Scored

A. Vaughan, BKN	112
S. Musial, STL	108
B. Nicholson, CHI	95

Doubles

S. Musial, STL	48
V. DiMaggio, PIT	41
B. Herman, BKN	41

Triples

S. Musial, STL	20
L. Klein, STL	14
P. Lowrey, CHI	12
B. Elliott, PIT	12

PITCHING LEADERS

Wins

M. Cooper, STL	21
R. Sewell, PIT	21
E. Riddle, CIN	21
H. Bithorn, CHI	18
A. Javery, BOS	17

Saves

L. Webber, BKN	10
A. Adams, NY	9
C. Shoun, CIN	7
J. Beggs, CIN	6
E. Head, BKN	6

Strikeouts

Vander Meer, CIN	174
M. Cooper, STL	141
A. Javery, BOS	134
M. Lanier, STL	123
K. Higbe, BKN	108

Complete Games

R. Sewell, PIT	25
J. Tobin, BOS	24
M. Cooper, STL	24
N. Andrews, BOS	23
B. Walters, CIN	21
Vander Meer, CIN	21

Fewest Hits per 9 Innings

H. Pollet, STL	6.31
W. Wyatt, BKN	6.92
Vander Meer, CIN	7.10

Shutouts

H. Bithorn, CHI	7
M. Cooper, STL	6

Fewest Walks per 9 Innings

S. Rowe, PHI	1.31
P. Derringer, CHI	2.02
W. Wyatt, BKN	2.14

Most Strikeouts per 9 Inn.

Vander Meer, CIN	5.42
M. Lanier, STL	5.19
H. Pollet, STL	4.64

Innings

A. Javery, BOS	303
Vander Meer, CIN	289
N. Andrews, BOS	284

Games Pitched

A. Adams, NY	70
L. Webber, BKN	54
E. Head, BKN	47

	W	L	PCT	GB	R	OR	Batting 2B	3B	HR	BA	SA	SB	Fielding E	DP	FA	Pitching CG	BB	SO	ShO	SV	ERA
STL	105	49	.682		679	475	259	72	70	**.279**	**.391**	40	151	183	.976	**94**	477	**639**	21	15	**2.57**
CIN	87	67	.565	18	608	543	229	47	43	.256	.340	49	**125**	**193**	**.980**	78	581	498	18	17	3.13
BKN	81	72	.529	23.5	**716**	674	**263**	35	39	.272	.357	58	168	137	.972	50	585	588	12	**22**	3.88
PIT	80	74	.519	25	669	605	240	**73**	42	.262	.357	**64**	170	159	.973	74	421	396	11	12	3.06
CHI	74	79	.484	30.5	632	600	207	56	52	.261	.351	53	168	138	.973	67	**394**	513	12	14	3.24
BOS	68	85	.444	36.5	465	612	202	36	39	.233	.309	56	176	139	.972	87	440	409	13	4	3.25
PHI	64	90	.416	41	571	676	186	36	66	.249	.335	29	189	143	.969	66	456	431	11	14	3.79
NY	55	98	.359	49.5	558	713	153	33	**81**	.247	.335	35	166	140	.973	35	626	588	6	19	4.08
					4898	4898	1739	388	432	.258	.347	384	1313	1232	.974	551	3980	4062	104	117	3.37

American League 1943

	POS	Player	AB	BA	HR	RBI	PO	A	E	DP	TC/G	FA	Pitcher	G	IP	W	L	SV	ERA
N. Y. W-98 L-56 Joe McCarthy	1B	N. Etten	583	.271	14	107	1410	79	17	148	9.8	.989	S. Chandler	30	253	**20**	4	0	**1.64**
	2B	J. Gordon	543	.249	17	69	407	**490**	29	114	**6.1**	.969	E. Bonham	28	226	15	8	1	2.27
	SS	F. Crosetti	348	.233	2	20	194	260	26	58	5.3	.946	B. Wensloff	29	223	13	11	1	2.54
	3B	B. Johnson	592	.280	5	94	**183**	326	18	**32**	3.4	.966	H. Borowy	29	217	14	9	0	2.82
	RF	B. Metheny	360	.261	9	36	156	1	6	0	1.8	.963	A. Donald	22	119	6	4	0	4.60
	CF	J. Lindell	441	.245	4	51	269	11	10	1	2.4	.966	B. Zuber	20	118	8	4	1	3.89
	LF	C. Keller	512	.271	31	86	338	8	2	0	2.5	.994	M. Russo	24	102	5	10	1	3.72
	C	B. Dickey	242	.351	4	33	322	37	2	5	5.1	.994	J. Murphy	37	68	12	4	8	2.51
	OF	R. Weatherly	280	.264	7	28	174	2	3	0	2.6	.983							
	SS	S. Stirnweiss	274	.219	1	25	110	192	20	50	4.7	.938							
	OF	T. Stainback	231	.260	0	14	141	3	1	2	2.4	.993							
	C	K. Sears	187	.278	2	22	233	31	7	5	5.4	.974							
	C	R. Hemsley	180	.239	2	24	234	31	5	3	5.2	.981							
Was. W-84 L-69 Ossie Bluege	1B	M. Vernon	553	.268	7	70	1351	75	14	125	10.1	.990	E. Wynn	37	257	18	12	0	2.91
	2B	G. Priddy	560	.271	4	62	364	411	23	105	6.0	.971	D. Leonard	31	220	11	13	1	3.28
	SS	J. Sullivan	456	.208	1	55	276	445	41	89	**5.7**	.946	M. Candini	28	166	11	7	1	2.49
	3B	E. Clary	254	.256	0	19	86	119	12	6	3.2	.945	M. Haefner	36	165	11	5	6	2.29
	RF	G. Case	613	.294	1	52	318	8	5	2	2.4	.985	A. Carrasquel	39	144	11	7	5	3.68
	CF	S. Spence	570	.267	12	88	396	12	7	1	2.8	.983	J. Mertz	33	117	5	7	3	4.63
	LF	B. Johnson	438	.265	7	63	212	11	1	1	2.5	.996	Scarborough	24	86	4	4	3	2.83
	C	J. Early	423	.258	5	60	443	83	11	10	4.4	.980	E. Pyle	18	73	4	8	1	4.09
	OF	G. Moore	254	.268	2	39	125	5	2	0	2.3	.985							
	C	T. Giuliani	133	.226	0	20	154	24	7	1	3.8	.962							
	OF	J. Powell	132	.265	0	20	83	4	2	0	2.7	.978							

Cle. — W-82 L-71 — Lou Boudreau

POS	Player	AB	BA	HR	RBI	PO	A	E	DP	TC/G	FA	Pitcher	G	IP	W	L	SV	ERA
1B	M. Rocco	405	.240	5	46	1012	61	5	111	10.0	.995	J. Bagby	36	273	17	14	1	3.10
2B	R. Mack	545	.220	7	62	381	444	28	123	5.6	.967	A. Smith	29	208	17	7	1	2.55
SS	L. Boudreau	539	.286	3	67	328	488	25	122	5.5	.970	A. Reynolds	34	199	11	12	3	2.99
3B	K. Keltner	427	.260	4	39	113	228	11	24	3.3	.969	V. Kennedy	28	147	10	7	0	2.45
RF	R. Cullenbine	488	.289	8	56	245	14	5	6	2.2	.981	M. Harder	19	135	8	7	0	3.06
CF	O. Hockett	601	.276	2	51	347	13	15	3	2.7	.960	J. Salveson	23	86	5	3	3	3.35
LF	J. Heath	424	.274	18	79	264	4	9	1	2.5	.968	C. Dean	17	76	5	5	0	4.50
C	B. Rosar	382	.283	1	41	480	91	10	11	5.1	.983	J. Heving	30	72	1	1	9	2.75
OF	H. Edwards	297	.276	3	28	173	4	3	0	2.4	.983	M. Naymick	29	63	4	4	2	2.30
UT	R. Peters	215	.219	1	19	66	98	11	17		.937							
C	G. Desautels	185	.205	0	19	251	28	5	4	4.3	.982							

Chi. — W-82 L-72 — Jimmy Dykes

POS	Player	AB	BA	HR	RBI	PO	A	E	DP	TC/G	FA	Pitcher	G	IP	W	L	SV	ERA
1B	J. Kuhel	531	.213	5	46	1471	106	8	143	10.4	.995	O. Grove	32	216	15	9	2	2.75
2B	D. Kolloway	348	.216	1	33	246	240	16	71	5.9	.968	J. Humphries	28	188	11	11	0	3.30
SS	L. Appling	585	.328	3	80	300	500	36	115	5.4	.957	E. Smith	25	188	11	11	0	3.69
3B	R. Hodgin	407	.314	1	50	34	120	9	7	2.9	.945	B. Dietrich	26	187	12	10	0	2.80
RF	W. Moses	599	.245	3	48	370	12	8	2	2.6	.979	B. Ross	21	149	11	7	0	3.19
CF	T. Tucker	528	.235	3	39	399	14	5	1	3.2	.988	T. Lee	19	127	5	9	0	4.18
LF	G. Curtright	488	.291	3	48	301	7	9	1	2.5	.972	J. Haynes	35	109	7	2	3	2.96
C	M. Tresh	279	.215	0	20	321	62	7	4	4.6	.982	Maltzberger	37	99	7	4	14	2.46
2B	S. Webb	213	.235	0	22	118	169	14	35	5.6	.953	J. Wade	21	84	3	7	0	3.01
3B	J. Grant	197	.259	4	22	43	115	19	11	3.5	.893							
C	T. Turner	154	.240	2	11	186	34	5	5	4.6	.978							

Det. — W-78 L-76 — Steve O'Neill

POS	Player	AB	BA	HR	RBI	PO	A	E	DP	TC/G	FA	Pitcher	G	IP	W	L	SV	ERA
1B	R. York	571	.271	34	118	1349	149	15	105	9.8	.990	D. Trout	44	247	20	12	6	2.48
2B	J. Bloodworth	474	.241	6	52	349	393	21	74	5.9	.972	V. Trucks	33	203	16	10	2	2.84
SS	J. Hoover	575	.243	4	38	301	393	41	84	5.1	.944	H. Newhouser	37	196	8	17	1	3.04
3B	P. Higgins	523	.277	10	84	156	253	26	22	3.2	.940	T. Bridges	25	192	12	7	0	2.39
RF	B. Harris	354	.254	6	32	192	6	8	2	2.1	.961	H. White	32	178	7	12	2	3.39
CF	D. Cramer	606	.300	1	43	346	9	4	3	2.6	.989	S. Overmire	29	147	7	6	1	3.18
LF	D. Wakefield	633	.316	7	79	314	11	14	1	2.2	.959	J. Gorsica	35	96	4	5	5	3.36
C	P. Richards	313	.220	5	33	537	86	9	12	6.3	.986							
UT	D. Ross	247	.267	0	18	106	65	9	10		.950							
23	J. Wood	164	.323	1	17	70	64	12	6		.918							

St. L. — W-72 L-80 — Luke Sewell

POS	Player	AB	BA	HR	RBI	PO	A	E	DP	TC/G	FA	Pitcher	G	IP	W	L	SV	ERA
1B	G. McQuinn	449	.243	12	74	1072	86	9	88	9.6	.992	D. Galehouse	31	224	11	11	1	2.77
2B	D. Gutteridge	538	.273	1	36	328	331	29	64	5.2	.958	S. Sundra	32	208	15	11	0	3.25
SS	V. Stephens	512	.289	22	91	220	339	34	51	4.8	.943	B. Muncrief	35	205	13	12	1	2.81
3B	H. Clift	379	.232	3	25	126	252	20	20	3.8*	.950	N. Potter	33	168	10	5	1	2.78
RF	M. Chartak	344	.256	10	37	160	4	5	2	2.2	.970	Hollingsworth	35	154	6	13	3	4.21
CF	M. Byrnes	429	.280	4	50	289	13	1	3	2.7	.997	J. Niggeling	20	150	6	8	0	3.17
LF	C. Laabs	580	.250	17	85	346	16	9	4	2.5	.976	G. Caster	35	76	6	8	8	2.12
C	F. Hayes	250	.188	5	30	301	40	6	8	4.6	.983							
UT	M. Christman	336	.271	2	35	279	172	3	41		.993							
OF	A. Zarilla	228	.254	2	17	123	5	5	2	2.2	.962							
C	R. Ferrell	209	.239	0	20	327	52	5	7	5.5	.987							
OF	M. Kreevich	161	.255	0	10	146	5	1	1	3.0	.993							

Bos. — W-68 L-84 — Joe Cronin

POS	Player	AB	BA	HR	RBI	PO	A	E	DP	TC/G	FA	Pitcher	G	IP	W	L	SV	ERA
1B	T. Lupien	608	.255	4	47	1487	118	12	149	10.6	.993	T. Hughson	35	266	12	15	2	2.64
2B	B. Doerr	604	.270	16	75	415	490	9	132	5.9	.990	J. Dobson	25	164	7	11	0	3.12
SS	S. Newsome	449	.265	1	22	222	310	21	69	5.6	.962	Y. Terry	30	164	7	9	1	3.52
3B	J. Tabor	537	.242	13	85	135	261	26	32	3.2	.938	O. Judd	23	155	11	6	0	2.90
RF	P. Fox	489	.288	2	44	261	10	11	2	2.3	.961	D. Newsome	25	154	8	13	0	4.49
CF	C. Metkovich	321	.246	5	27	183	6	9	3	2.6	.955	M. Ryba	40	144	7	5	3	3.26
LF	L. Culberson	312	.272	3	34	211	10	5	2	2.9	.978	P. Woods	23	101	5	6	1	4.92
C	R. Partee	299	.281	0	31	349	57	7	11	4.5	.983	M. Brown	49	93	6	6	9	2.12
SS	E. Lake	216	.199	3	16	128	195	13	43	5.3	.961							
OF	J. Lazor	208	.226	0	13	135	7	3	0	2.3	.979							
PH	J. Cronin	77	.312	5	29													

Phi. — W-49 L-105 — Connie Mack

POS	Player	AB	BA	HR	RBI	PO	A	E	DP	TC/G	FA	Pitcher	G	IP	W	L	SV	ERA
1B	D. Siebert	558	.251	1	72	1332	111	15	117	10.1	.990	J. Flores	31	231	12	14	0	3.11
2B	P. Suder	475	.221	3	41	231	269	15	58	5.4	.971	R. Wolff	41	221	10	15	6	3.54
SS	I. Hall	544	.256	0	54	298	435	40	91	5.2	.948	L. Harris	32	216	7	21	1	4.20
3B	E. Mayo	471	.219	0	28	176	223	10	18	3.3	.976	D. Black	33	208	6	16	1	4.20
RF	J. Welaj	281	.242	0	15	187	3	8	0	2.8	.960	O. Arntzen	32	164	4	13	0	4.22
CF	J. White	500	.240	1	30	335	8	12	2	2.7	.966	Christopher	24	133	5	8	2	3.45
LF	B. Estalella	367	.259	11	63	225	5	6	1	2.4	.975	E. Fagan	18	37	2	6	3	6.27
C	H. Wagner	289	.239	1	26	340	56	8	3	4.1	.980							
OF	E. Valo	249	.221	3	18	134	4	2	0	2.6	.986							
C	B. Swift	224	.192	1	11	278	53	8	9	4.4	.976							
2B	D. Heffner	178	.208	0	8	98	127	5	27	4.9	.978							
OF	J. Tyack	155	.258	0	23	82	4	2	0	2.3	.977							

BATTING AND BASE RUNNING LEADERS

Batting Average		Slugging Average	
L. Appling, CHI	.328	R. York, DET	.527
D. Wakefield, DET	.316	C. Keller, NY	.525
R. Hodgin, CHI	.314	V. Stephens, STL	.482
D. Cramer, DET	.300	J. Heath, CLE	.481
G. Case, WAS	.294	D. Wakefield, DET	.434

PITCHING LEADERS

Winning Percentage		Earned Run Average	
S. Chandler, NY	.833	S. Chandler, NY	1.64
A. Smith, CLE	.708	E. Bonham, NY	2.27
E. Bonham, NY	.652	T. Bridges, DET	2.39
D. Trout, DET	.625	D. Trout, DET	2.48
O. Grove, CHI	.625	B. Wensloff, NY	2.54

BATTING AND BASE RUNNING LEADERS

Home Runs
R. York, DET	34
C. Keller, NY	31
V. Stephens, STL	22
J. Heath, CLE	18
J. Gordon, NY	17
C. Laabs, STL	17

Total Bases
R. York, DET	301
D. Wakefield, DET	275
C. Keller, NY	269
B. Doerr, BOS	249
V. Stephens, STL	247

Runs Batted In
R. York, DET	118
N. Etten, NY	107
B. Johnson, NY	94
V. Stephens, STL	91
S. Spence, WAS	88

Stolen Bases
G. Case, WAS	61
W. Moses, CHI	56
T. Tucker, CHI	29
L. Appling, CHI	27
M. Vernon, WAS	24

Hits
D. Wakefield, DET	200
L. Appling, CHI	192
D. Cramer, DET	182

Base on Balls
C. Keller, NY	106
J. Gordon, NY	98
R. Cullenbine, CLE	96

Home Run Percentage
C. Keller, NY	6.1
R. York, DET	6.0
V. Stephens, STL	4.3

Runs Scored
G. Case, WAS	102
C. Keller, NY	97
D. Wakefield, DET	91

Doubles
D. Wakefield, DET	38
G. Case, WAS	36
D. Gutteridge, STL	35
N. Etten, NY	35

Triples
J. Lindell, NY	12
W. Moses, CHI	12
C. Keller, NY	11
R. York, DET	11

PITCHING LEADERS

Wins
S. Chandler, NY	20
D. Trout, DET	20
E. Wynn, WAS	18
A. Smith, CLE	17
J. Bagby, CLE	17

Saves
Maltzberger, CHI	14
M. Brown, BOS	9
J. Heving, CLE	9
J. Murphy, NY	8
G. Caster, STL	8

Strikeouts
A. Reynolds, CLE	151
H. Newhouser, DET	144
S. Chandler, NY	134
T. Bridges, DET	124
V. Trucks, DET	118

Complete Games
S. Chandler, NY	20
T. Hughson, BOS	20
O. Grove, CHI	18
B. Wensloff, NY	18
D. Trout, DET	18

Fewest Hits per 9 Innings
A. Reynolds, CLE	6.34
J. Niggeling, STL, WAS	6.66
S. Chandler, NY	7.01

Shutouts
S. Chandler, NY	5
D. Trout, DET	5
E. Bonham, NY	4
T. Hughson, BOS	4

Fewest Walks per 9 Innings
D. Leonard, WAS	1.88
S. Chandler, NY	1.92
E. Bonham, NY	2.07

Most Strikeouts per 9 Inn.
A. Reynolds, CLE	6.84
H. Newhouser, DET	6.62
T. Bridges, DET	5.82

Innings
J. Bagby, CLE	273
T. Hughson, BOS	266
E. Wynn, WAS	257

Games Pitched
M. Brown, BOS	49
D. Trout, DET	44
R. Wolff, PHI	41

	W	L	PCT	GB	R	OR	2B	3B	HR	BA	SA	SB	E	DP	FA	CG	BB	SO	ShO	SV	ERA
NY	98	56	.636		669	542	218	59	100	.256	.376	46	160	166	.974	83	489	653	14	13	2.93
WAS	84	69	.549	13.5	666	595	245	50	47	.254	.347	142	179	145	.971	61	540	495	16	21	3.18
CLE	82	71	.536	15.5	600	577	246	45	55	.255	.350	47	157	183	.975	64	606	585	14	20	3.15
CHI	82	72	.532	16	573	594	193	46	33	.247	.320	173	166	167	.973	70	501	476	12	19	3.20
DET	78	76	.506	20	632	560	200	47	77	.261	.359	40	177	130	.971	67	549	706	18	20	3.00
STL	72	80	.474	25	596	604	229	36	78	.245	.349	37	152	127	.975	64	488	572	10	14	3.41
BOS	68	84	.447	29	563	607	223	42	57	.244	.332	86	153	179	.976	62	615	513	13	16	3.45
PHI	49	105	.318	49	497	717	174	44	26	.232	.297	55	162	148	.973	73	536	503	5	13	4.05
					4796	4796	1728	369	473	.249	.341	626	1306	1245	.973	544	4324	4503	102	136	3.30

National League 1944

	POS	Player	AB	BA	HR	RBI	PO	A	E	DP	TC/G	FA	Pitcher	G	IP	W	L	SV	ERA
St. L. W-105 L-49 Billy Southworth	1B	R. Sanders	601	.295	12	102	1370	64	8	142	9.5	.994	M. Cooper	34	252	22	7	1	2.46
	2B	E. Verban	498	.257	0	43	319	380	23	105	4.9	.968	M. Lanier	33	224	17	12	0	2.65
	SS	M. Marion	506	.267	6	63	268	461	21	90	5.2	.972	T. Wilks	36	207	17	4	0	2.65
	3B	W. Kurowski	555	.270	20	87	188	281	17	20	3.3	.965	H. Brecheen	30	189	16	5	0	2.85
	RF	S. Musial	568	.347	12	94	353	16	5	2	2.6	.987	A. Jurisich	30	130	7	9	1	3.39
	CF	J. Hopp	527	.336	11	72	316	2	1	1	2.4	.997	G. Munger	21	121	11	3	2	1.34
	LF	D. Litwhiler	492	.264	15	82	294	6	8	1	2.3	.974	F. Schmidt	37	114	7	3	5	3.15
	C	W. Cooper	397	.317	13	72	442	40	10	7	5.1	.980							
	C	K. O'Dea	265	.249	6	37	326	34	2	4	5.2	.994							
	OF	A. Bergamo	192	.286	2	19	83	0	1	0	1.7	.988							
Pit. W-90 L-63 Frankie Frisch	1B	B. Dahlgren	599	.289	12	101	1440	128	20	105	10.1	.987	R. Sewell	38	286	21	12	2	3.18
	2B	P. Coscarart	554	.264	4	42	371	389	26	71	5.8	.967	Ostermueller	28	205	11	7	1	2.73
	SS	F. Gustine	405	.230	2	42	183	330	34	52	4.7	.938	M. Butcher	35	199	13	11	1	3.12
	3B	B. Elliott	538	.297	10	108	169	285	27	22	3.4	.944	Strincevich	40	190	14	7	2	3.08
	RF	J. Barrett	568	.269	7	83	373	12	11	4	2.7	.972	P. Roe	39	185	13	11	1	3.11
	CF	V. DiMaggio	342	.240	9	50	234	8	4	4	2.4	.984	X. Rescigno	48	124	10	8	5	4.35
	LF	J. Russell	580	.312	8	66	345	20	5	7	2.5	.986	C. Cuccurullo	32	106	2	1	4	4.06
	C	A. Lopez	331	.230	1	34	372	52	7	6	3.7	.984	R. Starr	27	90	6	5	3	5.02
	OF	F. Colman	226	.270	6	53	102	4	4	0	2.1	.964							
	UT	A. Rubeling	184	.245	4	30	70	56	2	7		.984							
	SS	F. Zak	160	.300	0	11	93	162	14	24	4.0	.948							
	OF	T. O'Brien	156	.250	3	20	50	5	2	1	1.2	.965							

Cin. — W-89 L-65 — Bill McKechnie

POS	Player	AB	BA	HR	RBI	PO	A	E	DP	TC/G	FA	Pitcher	G	IP	W	L	SV	ERA
1B	F. McCormick	581	.305	20	102	1508	135	13	130	10.8	.992	B. Walters	34	285	23	8	1	2.40
2B	W. Williams	653	.240	1	35	377	542	27	97	6.1	.971	C. Shoun	38	203	13	10	2	3.02
SS	E. Miller	536	.209	4	55	357	544	27	100	6.0	.971	E. Heusser	30	193	13	11	2	2.38
3B	S. Mesner	414	.242	1	47	120	246	19	21	3.2	.951	de la Cruz	34	191	9	9	1	3.25
RF	G. Walker	478	.278	5	62	293	3	10	0	2.6	.967	H. Gumbert	24	155	10	8	2	3.30
CF	D. Clay	356	.250	0	17	272	4	2	0	2.8	.993	A. Carter	33	148	11	7	3	2.61
LF	E. Tipton	479	.301	3	36	329	8	6	1	2.5	.983	J. Konstanty	20	113	6	4	0	2.80
C	R. Mueller	555	.286	10	73	471	65	9	5	3.5	.983							
OF	M. Marshall	229	.245	4	23	131	6	5	3	2.4	.965							
OF	T. Criscola	157	.229	0	14	80	4	2	0	2.5	.977							

Chi. — W-75 L-79 — Jimmie Wilson W-1 L-9, Roy Johnson W-0 L-1, Charlie Grimm W-74 L-69

POS	Player	AB	BA	HR	RBI	PO	A	E	DP	TC/G	FA	Pitcher	G	IP	W	L	SV	ERA
1B	P. Cavarretta	614	.321	5	82	1337	77	11	121	10.3	.992	H. Wyse	41	257	16	15	1	3.15
2B	D. Johnson	608	.278	2	71	385	462	47	85	5.8	.947	C. Passeau	34	227	15	9	3	2.89
SS	L. Merullo	193	.212	1	16	115	167	19	26	5.4	.937	P. Derringer	42	180	7	13	4	4.15
3B	S. Hack	383	.282	3	32	96	164	17	7	3.7	.939	B. Fleming	39	158	9	10	0	3.13
RF	B. Nicholson	582	.287	33	122	305	18	7	4	2.1	.979	B. Chipman	26	129	9	9	2	3.49
CF	A. Pafko	469	.269	6	62	333	24	6	4	3.0	.983	H. Vandenberg	35	126	7	4	2	3.63
LF	Dallessandro	381	.304	8	74	212	9	4	2	2.1	.982	P. Erickson	33	124	5	9	1	3.55
C	D. Williams	262	.240	0	27	317	50	7	7	4.9	.981	R. Lynn	22	84	5	4	1	4.06
3S	R. Hughes	478	.287	1	28	220	303	20	54		.963							
2S	B. Schuster	154	.221	1	14	71	109	9	21		.952							

N. Y. — W-67 L-87 — Mel Ott

POS	Player	AB	BA	HR	RBI	PO	A	E	DP	TC/G	FA	Pitcher	G	IP	W	L	SV	ERA
1B	P. Weintraub	361	.316	13	77	928	72	8	72	10.2	.992	B. Voiselle	43	313	21	16	0	3.02
2B	G. Hausmann	466	.266	1	30	301	350	27	66	5.6	.960	H. Feldman	40	205	11	13	2	4.16
SS	B. Kerr	548	.266	9	63	328	507	40	81	5.9	.954	E. Pyle	31	164	7	10	0	4.34
3B	H. Luby	323	.254	2	35	83	134	13	14	3.5	.943	A. Adams	65	138	8	11	13	4.25
RF	M. Ott	399	.288	26	82	199	6	3	0	2.0	.986	R. Fischer	38	129	6	14	2	5.18
CF	J. Rucker	587	.244	6	39	310	14	5	0	2.4	.985	J. Allen	18	84	4	7	0	4.07
LF	J. Medwick	490	.337	7	85	290	8	2	2	2.5	.993							
C	E. Lombardi	373	.255	10	58	350	47	13	11	4.1	.968							
13	N. Reyes	374	.289	8	53	580	120	12	49		.983							
3B	B. Jurges	246	.211	1	23	48	124	7	7	2.9	.961							
C	G. Mancuso	195	.251	1	25	249	37	7	4	4.1	.976							
OF	R. Treadway	170	.300	0	5	87	3	4	0	2.5	.957							

Bos. — W-65 L-89 — Bob Coleman

POS	Player	AB	BA	HR	RBI	PO	A	E	DP	TC/G	FA	Pitcher	G	IP	W	L	SV	ERA
1B	B. Etchison	308	.214	8	33	757	48	6	64	9.5	.993	J. Tobin	43	299	18	19	3	3.01
2B	C. Ryan	332	.295	4	25	210	272	13	57	6.2	.974	N. Andrews	37	257	16	15	2	3.22
SS	W. Wietelmann	417	.240	2	32	215	287	24	60	5.1	.954	A. Javery	40	254	10	19	3	3.54
3B	D. Phillips	489	.258	1	53	84	177	19	22	3.1	.932	R. Barrett	42	230	9	16	2	4.06
RF	C. Workman	418	.208	11	53	161	16	3	3	1.7	.983	I. Hutchinson	40	120	9	7	1	4.21
CF	T. Holmes	631	.309	13	73	426	14	4	7	2.9	.991							
LF	B. Nieman	468	.265	16	65	261	13	7	2	2.2	.975							
C	P. Masi	251	.275	3	23	180	34	5	3	3.5	.977							
1B	M. Macon	366	.273	3	36	625	49	16	62	9.6	.977							
C	C. Kluttz	229	.279	2	19	199	40	5	5	4.2	.980							
OF	A. Wright	195	.256	7	35	88	2	3	1	2.0	.968							
C	S. Hofferth	180	.200	1	26	158	22	3	3	3.9	.984							
OF	C. Ross	154	.227	5	26	75	8	0	2	2.2	1.000							

Bkn. — W-63 L-91 — Leo Durocher

POS	Player	AB	BA	HR	RBI	PO	A	E	DP	TC/G	FA	Pitcher	G	IP	W	L	SV	ERA
1B	H. Schultz	526	.255	11	83	1091	85	14	90	8.8	.988	H. Gregg	39	198	9	16	2	5.46
2B	E. Stanky	261	.276	0	16	132	138	11	28	4.8	.961	C. Davis	31	194	10	11	4	3.34
SS	B. Bragan	266	.267	0	17	77	109	9	16	3.8	.954	R. Melton	37	187	9	13	0	3.46
3B	F. Bordagaray	501	.281	6	51	107	150	15	14	2.8	.945	L. Webber	48	140	7	8	3	4.94
RF	D. Walker	535	.357	13	91	260	17	11	4	2.1	.962	C. McLish	23	84	3	10	0	7.82
CF	G. Rosen	264	.261	0	23	199	12	2	0	3.3	.991							
LF	A. Galan	547	.318	12	93	323	10	4	3	2.3	.988							
C	M. Owen	461	.273	1	42	506	57	12	8	4.6	.979							
UT	L. Olmo	520	.258	9	85	316	138	27	18		.944							
1B	J. Bolling	131	.351	1	25	206	20	2	7	8.4	.991							

Phi. — W-61 L-92 — Freddie Fitzsimmons

POS	Player	AB	BA	HR	RBI	PO	A	E	DP	TC/G	FA	Pitcher	G	IP	W	L	SV	ERA
1B	T. Lupien	597	.283	5	52	1453	103	13	114	10.4	.992	Raffensberger	37	259	13	20	0	3.06
2B	M. Mullen	464	.267	0	31	291	316	23	52	5.5	.963	C. Schanz	40	241	13	16	3	3.32
SS	R. Hamrick	292	.205	1	23	160	293	25	55	6.5	.948	D. Barrett	37	221	12	18	0	3.86
3B	G. Stewart	377	.220	0	29	77	181	10	12	3.2	.963	B. Lee	31	208	10	11	1	3.15
RF	R. Northey	570	.288	22	104	286	24	6	7	2.1	.981	A. Gerheauser	30	183	8	16	0	4.58
CF	B. Adams	584	.283	17	64	449	14	10	1	3.1	.979							
LF	J. Wasdell	451	.277	3	40	243	6	5	0	2.1	.980							
C	B. Finley	281	.249	1	21	289	34	11	7	4.5	.967							
UT	C. Letchas	396	.237	0	33	219	300	16	54		.970							
C	J. Peacock	253	.225	0	21	274	38	3	4	4.3	.990							
3B	T. Cieslak	220	.245	2	11	35	72	15	1	2.5	.877							
OF	C. Triplett	184	.234	1	25	90	3	1	1	2.1	.989							

BATTING AND BASE RUNNING LEADERS

Batting Average		Slugging Average	
D. Walker, BKN	.357	S. Musial, STL	.549
S. Musial, STL	.347	B. Nicholson, CHI	.545
J. Medwick, NY	.337	M. Ott, NY	.544
J. Hopp, STL	.336	D. Walker, BKN	.529
P. Cavarretta, CHI	.321	P. Weintraub, NY	.524

PITCHING LEADERS

Winning Percentage		Earned Run Average	
T. Wilks, STL	.810	E. Heusser, CIN	2.38
H. Brecheen, STL	.762	B. Walters, CIN	2.40
M. Cooper, STL	.759	M. Cooper, STL	2.46
B. Walters, CIN	.742	M. Lanier, STL	2.65
R. Sewell, PIT	.636	T. Wilks, STL	2.65

BATTING AND BASE RUNNING LEADERS

Home Runs
B. Nicholson, CHI	33
M. Ott, NY	26
R. Northey, PHI	22
W. Kurowski, STL	20
F. McCormick, CIN	20

Total Bases
B. Nicholson, CHI	317
S. Musial, STL	312
T. Holmes, BOS	288
D. Walker, BKN	283
R. Northey, PHI	283

Runs Batted In
B. Nicholson, CHI	122
B. Elliott, PIT	108
R. Northey, PHI	104
F. McCormick, CIN	102
R. Sanders, STL	102

Stolen Bases
J. Barrett, PIT	28
T. Lupien, PHI	18
R. Hughes, CHI	16
J. Hopp, STL	15
B. Kerr, NY	14

Hits
S. Musial, STL	197
P. Cavarretta, CHI	197
T. Holmes, BOS	195

Base on Balls
A. Galan, BKN	101
B. Nicholson, CHI	93
M. Ott, NY	90
S. Musial, STL	90

Home Run Percentage
M. Ott, NY	6.5
B. Nicholson, CHI	5.7
R. Northey, PHI	3.9

Runs Scored
B. Nicholson, CHI	116
S. Musial, STL	112
J. Russell, PIT	109

Doubles
S. Musial, STL	51
A. Galan, BKN	43
T. Holmes, BOS	42

Triples
J. Barrett, PIT	19
B. Elliott, PIT	16
P. Cavarretta, CHI	15

PITCHING LEADERS

Wins
B. Walters, CIN	23
M. Cooper, STL	22
R. Sewell, PIT	21
B. Voiselle, NY	21
J. Tobin, BOS	18

Saves
A. Adams, NY	13
X. Rescigno, PIT	5
F. Schmidt, STL	5
C. Cuccurullo, PIT	4
C. Davis, BKN	4

Strikeouts
B. Voiselle, NY	161
M. Lanier, STL	141
A. Javery, BOS	137
Raffensberger, PHI	136
Ostermueller, BKN, PIT	97
M. Cooper, STL	97

Complete Games
J. Tobin, BOS	28
B. Walters, CIN	27
B. Voiselle, NY	25
R. Sewell, PIT	24
M. Cooper, STL	22

Fewest Hits per 9 Innings
B. Walters, CIN	7.36
T. Wilks, STL	7.51
M. Lanier, STL	7.70

Shutouts
M. Cooper, STL	7
B. Walters, CIN	6

Fewest Walks per 9 Innings
Raffensberger, PHI	1.57
Strincevich, PIT	1.75
C. Davis, BKN	1.81

Most Strikeouts per 9 Inn.
M. Lanier, STL	5.66
A. Javery, BOS	4.85
Raffensberger, PHI	4.73

Innings
B. Voiselle, NY	313
J. Tobin, BOS	299
R. Sewell, PIT	286

Games Pitched
A. Adams, NY	65
L. Webber, BKN	48
X. Rescigno, PIT	48

	W	L	PCT	GB	R	OR	2B	3B	Batting HR	BA	SA	SB	E	Fielding DP	FA	CG	BB	Pitching SO	ShO	SV	ERA
STL	105	49	.682		772	490	274	59	100	.275	.402	37	112	162	.982	89	468	637	26	12	2.67
PIT	90	63	.588	14.5	744	662	248	80	70	.265	.379	87	191	122	.970	77	435	452	10	19	3.44
CIN	89	65	.578	16	573	537	229	31	51	.254	.338	51	137	153	.978	93	384	359	17	12	2.97
CHI	75	79	.487	30	702	669	236	46	71	.261	.360	53	186	151	.970	70	452	535	11	13	3.59
NY	67	87	.435	38	682	773	191	47	93	.263	.370	38	179	128	.971	47	587	499	4	21	4.29
BOS	65	89	.422	40	593	674	250	39	79	.246	.353	37	182	160	.971	70	527	454	13	12	3.67
BKN	63	91	.409	42	690	832	255	51	56	.269	.366	43	197	112	.966	50	660	487	4	13	4.68
PHI	61	92	.399	43.5	539	658	199	42	55	.251	.336	32	177	138	.972	66	459	496	11	6	3.64
					5295	5295	1882	395	575	.261	.363	378	1361	1126	.972	562	3972	3919	96	108	3.61

American League 1944

	POS	Player	AB	BA	HR	RBI	PO	A	E	DP	TC/G	FA	Pitcher	G	IP	W	L	SV	ERA
St. L. W-89 L-65 Luke Sewell	1B	G. McQuinn	516	.250	11	72	1332	72	9	116	9.7	.994	J. Kramer	33	257	17	13	0	2.49
	2B	D. Gutteridge	603	.245	3	36	368	407	35	95	5.5	.957	N. Potter	32	232	19	7	0	2.83
	SS	V. Stephens	559	.293	20	109	239	480	35	71	5.3	.954	B. Muncrief	33	219	13	8	1	3.08
	3B	M. Christman	547	.271	6	83	172	316	14	34	3.5	.972	S. Jakucki	35	198	13	9	3	3.55
	RF	G. Moore	390	.238	6	58	208	5	7	2	2.2	.968	D. Galehouse	24	153	9	10	0	3.12
	CF	M. Byrnes	407	.295	4	45	282	7	7	1	2.4	.976	Hollingsworth	26	93	5	7	1	4.47
	LF	M. Kreevich	402	.301	5	44	282	4	4	0	2.9	.986	G. Caster	42	81	6	6	12	2.44
	C	F. Mancuso	244	.205	1	24	311	35	17	9	4.2	.953							
	OF	A. Zarilla	288	.299	6	45	167	4	4	1	2.2	.977							
	C	R. Hayworth	269	.223	1	25	336	39	13	4	4.5	.966							
	OF	C. Laabs	201	.234	5	23	108	3	0	2	2.0	1.000							
Det. W-88 L-66 Steve O'Neill	1B	R. York	583	.276	18	98	1453	107	17	163	10.4	.989	D. Trout	49	352	27	14	0	2.12
	2B	E. Mayo	607	.249	5	63	384	458	19	120	6.0	.978	H. Newhouser	47	312	29	9	2	2.22
	SS	J. Hoover	441	.236	0	29	256	405	48	102	6.0	.932	R. Gentry	37	204	12	14	0	4.24
	3B	P. Higgins	543	.297	7	76	146	311	22	21	3.3	.954	S. Overmire	32	200	11	11	1	3.07
	RF	J. Outlaw	535	.273	3	57	254	14	10	2	2.0	.964	J. Gorsica	34	162	6	14	4	4.11
	CF	D. Cramer	578	.292	2	42	337	13	7	2	2.5	.980							
	LF	D. Wakefield	276	.355	12	53	155	3	6	1	2.1	.963							
	C	P. Richards	300	.237	3	37	413	60	10	13	5.4	.979							
	OF	C. Hostetler	265	.298	0	20	129	5	2	1	2.1	.985							
	C	B. Swift	247	.255	1	19	288	48	6	4	4.5	.982							
	OF	D. Ross	167	.210	2	15	67	2	3	1	1.9	.958							
	UT	J. Orengo	154	.201	0	10	124	124	20	24		.925							
	P	D. Trout	133	.271	5	24	21	94	4	8	2.4	.966							

	POS	Player	AB	BA	HR	RBI	PO	A	E	DP	TC/G	FA	Pitcher	G	IP	W	L	SV	ERA
N. Y.	1B	N. Etten	573	.293	**22**	91	1382	106	16	144	9.8	.989	H. Borowy	35	253	17	12	2	2.64
W-83 L-71	2B	S. Stirnweiss	643	.319	8	43	**433**	**481**	17	113	**6.0**	**.982**	M. Dubiel	30	232	13	13	0	3.38
Joe McCarthy	SS	M. Milosevich	312	.247	0	32	176	281	22	68	5.3	.954	E. Bonham	26	214	12	9	0	2.99
	3B	O. Grimes	387	.279	5	46	105	189	17	14	3.2	.945	A. Donald	30	159	13	10	0	3.34
	RF	B. Metheny	518	.239	14	67	232	8	11	2	1.9	.956	B. Zuber	22	107	5	7	0	4.21
	CF	J. Lindell	594	.300	18	103	468	9	7	3	3.2	.986	J. Page	19	103	5	7	0	4.56
	LF	H. Martin	328	.302	9	47	177	8	7	4	2.4	.964	J. Turner	35	42	4	4	7	3.46
	C	M. Garbark	299	.261	1	33	372	47	5	9	5.0	.988							
	C	R. Hemsley	284	.268	2	26	298	41	6	7	4.5	.983							
	3B	D. Savage	239	.264	4	24	66	109	10	11	3.1	.946							
	SS	F. Crosetti	197	.239	5	30	115	150	11	33	5.0	.960							
	OF	E. Levy	153	.242	4	29	75	2	3	0	2.2	.963							
Bos.	1B	L. Finney	251	.287	0	32	521	23	7	53	9.3	.987	T. Hughson	28	203	18	5	5	2.26
W-77 L-77	2B	B. Doerr	468	.325	15	81	341	363	17	96	5.8	.976	P. Woods	38	171	4	8	0	3.27
Joe Cronin	SS	S. Newsome	472	.242	0	41	249	421	26	79	5.5	.963	J. Bowman	26	168	12	8	0	4.81
	3B	J. Tabor	438	.285	13	72	125	258	20	14	3.5	.950	E. O'Neill	28	152	6	11	0	4.63
	RF	P. Fox	496	.315	1	64	228	7	3	1	2.0	.987	M. Ryba	42	138	12	7	2	3.33
	CF	C. Metkovich	549	.277	9	59	242	8	10	2	3.2	.962	C. Hausmann	32	137	4	7	3	3.42
	LF	B. Johnson	525	.324	17	106	270	23	7	3	2.1	.977	Y. Terry	27	133	6	10	0	4.21
	C	R. Partee	280	.243	2	41	326	40	4	5	4.4	.989	F. Barrett	38	90	8	7	8	3.69
	OF	L. Culberson	282	.238	2	21	182	6	4	2	2.7	.979							
	32	J. Bucher	277	.274	4	31	99	138	11	25		.956							
	C	H. Wagner	223	.332	1	38	299	29	10	4	5.3	.970							
	OF	T. McBride	216	.245	0	24	113	8	1	1	2.1	.992							
	1B	J. Cronin	191	.241	5	28	428	27	9	39	9.5	.981							
Cle.	1B	M. Rocco	**653**	.266	13	70	**1467**	138	11	158	10.4	.993	S. Gromek	35	204	10	9	1	2.56
W-72 L-82	2B	R. Mack	284	.232	0	29	226	243	24	73	5.9	.951	M. Harder	30	196	12	10	0	3.71
Lou Boudreau	SS	L. Boudreau	584	**.327**	3	67	339	516	19	134	5.9	**.978**	A. Smith	28	182	7	13	0	3.42
	3B	K. Keltner	573	.295	13	91	168	369	18	37	3.7	.968	E. Klieman	47	178	11	13	5	3.38
	RF	R. Cullenbine	571	.284	16	80	275	15	10	6	2.0	.967	A. Reynolds	28	158	11	8	1	3.30
	CF	O. Hockett	457	.289	1	50	275	6	5	1	2.6	.983	J. Heving	**63**	119	8	3	10	1.96
	LF	P. Seerey	342	.234	15	39	196	8	3	1	2.4	.986	R. Poat	36	81	4	8	1	5.13
	C	B. Rosar	331	.263	0	30	409	59	5	**13**	4.8	**.989**							
	2B	R. Peters	282	.223	1	24	151	181	8	45	5.4	.976							
	OF	M. Hoag	277	.285	1	27	171	9	10*	3	2.9	.947							
	OF	P. O'Dea	173	.318	0	13	72	2	4	1	1.9	.949							
	OF	J. Heath	151	.331	5	33	76	4	4	2	2.3	.952							
Phi.	1B	B. McGhee	287	.289	1	19	701	46	8	51	10.1	.989	B. Newsom	37	265	13	15	1	2.82
W-72 L-82	2B	I. Hall	559	.268	0	45	248	286	11	40	5.6	.980	Christopher	35	215	14	14	1	2.97
Connie Mack	SS	E. Busch	484	.271	0	40	204	330	34	50	5.1	.940	L. Hamlin	29	190	6	12	0	3.74
	3B	G. Kell	514	.268	0	44	167	289	20	25	3.4	.958	J. Flores	27	186	9	11	0	3.39
	RF	J. White	267	.221	1	21	162	5	9	2	2.4	.949	D. Black	29	177	10	12	0	4.06
	CF	B. Estalella	506	.298	7	60	318	12	4	4	2.6	.988	L. Harris	23	174	10	9	0	3.30
	LF	F. Garrison	449	.269	4	37	289	6	4	0	2.5	.987	J. Berry	53	111	10	8	**12**	1.94
	C	F. Hayes	581	.248	13	78	636	89	13	10	4.8	.982							
	1O	D. Siebert	468	.306	6	52	759	53	10	60		.988							
	OF	H. Epps	229	.262	0	13	141	4	4	1	2.5	.973							
Chi.	1B	H. Trosky	497	.241	10	70	1310	57	9	122	**10.6**	.993	B. Dietrich	36	246	16	**17**	0	3.62
W-71 L-83	2B	R. Schalk	587	.220	1	44	360	391	28	109	5.5	.964	O. Grove	34	235	14	15	0	3.72
Jimmy Dykes	SS	S. Webb	513	.211	0	30	202	461	39	81	5.2	.944	E. Lopat	27	210	11	10	0	3.26
	3B	R. Hodgin	465	.295	1	51	77	215	18	22	3.8	.942	J. Humphries	30	169	8	10	1	3.67
	RF	W. Moses	535	.280	3	34	267	7	7	2	2.1	.975	J. Haynes	33	154	5	6	2	2.57
	CF	T. Tucker	446	.287	2	46	414	12	4	2	**3.6**	**.991**	T. Lee	15	113	3	9	0	3.02
	LF	E. Carnett	457	.276	1	60	199	7	11	0	2.5	.949	Maltzberger	46	91	10	5	**12**	2.96
	C	M. Tresh	312	.260	0	25	370	47	8	5	4.6	.981							
	OF	G. Curtright	198	.253	2	23	101	8	6	3	2.3	.948							
	3B	D. Clarke	169	.260	0	27	36	107	9	6	3.4	.941							
	OF	J. Dickshot	162	.253	0	15	72	3	2	1	1.9	.974							
Was.	1B	J. Kuhel	518	.278	4	51	1251	83	**17**	119	9.8	.987	D. Leonard	32	229	14	14	0	3.06
W-64 L-90	2B	G. Myatt	538	.284	0	40	341	299	29	81	5.5	.957	M. Haefner	31	228	12	15	1	3.04
Ossie Bluege	SS	J. Sullivan	471	.251	0	30	276	426	**50**	89	5.4	.934	E. Wynn	33	208	8	**17**	2	3.38
	3B	G. Torres	524	.267	0	58	120	297	21	25	3.6	.952	J. Niggeling	24	206	10	8	0	2.32
	RF	J. Powell	367	.240	1	37	196	5	4	0	2.3	.980	R. Wolff	33	155	4	15	2	4.99
	CF	S. Spence	592	.316	18	100	434	29	5	9	3.1	.989	A. Carrasquel	43	134	8	7	2	3.43
	LF	G. Case	465	.249	2	32	288	7	9	2	2.7	.970	M. Candini	28	103	6	7	1	4.11
	C	R. Ferrell	339	.277	0	25	403	71	9	8	5.0	.981							
	OF	R. Ortiz	316	.253	5	35	165	2	9	1	2.2	.949							
	C	M. Guerra	210	.281	1	29	211	32	10	8	4.4	.960							
	2B	F. Vaughn	109	.257	1	21	61	70	8	16	5.3	.942							

BATTING AND BASE RUNNING LEADERS

Batting Average		Slugging Average	
L. Boudreau, CLE	.327	B. Doerr, BOS	.528
B. Doerr, BOS	.325	B. Johnson, BOS	.528
B. Johnson, BOS	.324	J. Lindell, NY	.500
S. Stirnweiss, NY	.319	S. Spence, WAS	.486
S. Spence, WAS	.316	N. Etten, NY	.466
		K. Keltner, CLE	.466

PITCHING LEADERS

Winning Percentage		Earned Run Average	
T. Hughson, BOS	.783	D. Trout, DET	2.12
H. Newhouser, DET	.763	H. Newhouser, DET	2.22
N. Potter, STL	.731	T. Hughson, BOS	2.26
D. Trout, DET	.659	J. Niggeling, WAS	2.32
H. Borowy, NY	.586	J. Kramer, STL	2.49

BATTING AND BASE RUNNING LEADERS

Home Runs
N. Etten, NY	22
V. Stephens, STL	20
R. York, DET	18
S. Spence, WAS	18
J. Lindell, NY	18

Total Bases
J. Lindell, NY	297
S. Stirnweiss, NY	296
S. Spence, WAS	288
B. Johnson, BOS	277
N. Etten, NY	267
K. Keltner, CLE	267

Runs Batted In
V. Stephens, STL	109
B. Johnson, BOS	106
J. Lindell, NY	103
S. Spence, WAS	100
R. York, DET	98

Stolen Bases
S. Stirnweiss, NY	55
G. Case, WAS	49
G. Myatt, WAS	26
W. Moses, CHI	21
D. Gutteridge, STL	20

Hits
S. Stirnweiss, NY	205
L. Boudreau, CLE	191
S. Spence, WAS	187

Base on Balls
N. Etten, NY	97
B. Johnson, BOS	95
R. Cullenbine, CLE	87

Home Run Percentage
P. Seerey, CLE	4.4
N. Etten, NY	3.8
V. Stephens, STL	3.6

Runs Scored
S. Stirnweiss, NY	125
B. Johnson, BOS	106
R. Cullenbine, CLE	98

Doubles
L. Boudreau, CLE	45
K. Keltner, CLE	41
B. Johnson, BOS	40

Triples
J. Lindell, NY	16
S. Stirnweiss, NY	16
D. Gutteridge, STL	11
B. Doerr, BOS	10

PITCHING LEADERS

Wins
H. Newhouser, DET	29
D. Trout, DET	27
N. Potter, STL	19
T. Hughson, BOS	18
H. Borowy, NY	17
J. Kramer, STL	17

Saves
J. Berry, PHI	12
Maltzberger, CHI	12
G. Caster, STL	12
J. Heving, CLE	10
F. Barrett, BOS	8

Strikeouts
H. Newhouser, DET	187
D. Trout, DET	144
B. Newsom, PHI	142
J. Kramer, STL	124
J. Niggeling, WAS	121

Complete Games
D. Trout, DET	33
H. Newhouser, DET	25
T. Hughson, BOS	19
E. Wynn, WAS	19
M. Dubiel, NY	19
H. Borowy, NY	19

Fewest Hits per 9 Innings
S. Gromek, CLE	7.07
J. Niggeling, WAS	7.16
H. Newhouser, DET	7.61

Shutouts
D. Trout, DET	7
H. Newhouser, DET	6
R. Gentry, DET	4
S. Jakucki, STL	4

Fewest Walks per 9 Innings
L. Harris, PHI	1.34
D. Leonard, WAS	1.45
E. Bonham, NY	1.73

Most Strikeouts per 9 Inn.
H. Newhouser, DET	5.39
J. Niggeling, WAS	5.29
S. Gromek, CLE	5.08

Innings
D. Trout, DET	352
H. Newhouser, DET	312
B. Newsom, PHI	265

Games Pitched
J. Heving, CLE	63
J. Berry, PHI	53
D. Trout, DET	49

	W	L	PCT	GB	R	OR	2B	3B	HR	BA	SA	SB	E	DP	FA	CG	BB	SO	ShO	SV	ERA
STL	89	65	.578		684	587	223	45	72	.252	.352	44	171	142	.972	71	469	581	16	17	3.17
DET	88	66	.571	1	658	581	220	44	60	.263	.354	61	190	184	.970	87	452	568	20	8	3.09
NY	83	71	.539	6	674	617	216	74	96	.264	.387	91	156	170	.974	78	532	529	9	13	3.39
BOS	77	77	.500	12	739	676	277	56	69	.270	.380	60	171	154	.972	58	592	524	5	17	3.82
CLE	72	82	.468	17	643	677	270	50	70	.266	.372	48	165	192	.974	48	621	524	7	18	3.65
PHI	72	82	.468	17	525	594	169	47	23	.247	.327	42	176	127	.971	72	390	534	9	14	3.26
CHI	71	83	.461	18	543	662	210	55	23	.247	.320	66	183	154	.970	64	420	481	5	17	3.58
WAS	64	90	.416	25	592	664	186	42	33	.261	.330	127	218	156	.964	83	475	503	12	11	3.49
					5058	5058	1771	413	459	.260	.353	539	1430	1279	.971	561	3951	4244	83	115	3.43

National League 1945

	POS	Player	AB	BA	HR	RBI	PO	A	E	DP	TC/G	FA	Pitcher	G	IP	W	L	SV	ERA
Chi. W-98 L-56 Charlie Grimm	1B	P. Cavarretta	498	.355	6	97	1149	77	9	83	10.3	.993	H. Wyse	38	278	22	10	0	2.68
	2B	D. Johnson	557	.302	2	58	309	440	19	74	5.6	.975	C. Passeau	34	227	17	9	1	2.46
	SS	L. Merullo	394	.239	2	37	209	336	30	49	4.9	.948	P. Derringer	35	214	16	11	4	3.45
	3B	S. Hack	597	.323	2	43	195	312	13	27	3.6	.975	R. Prim	34	165	13	8	2	2.40
	RF	B. Nicholson	559	.243	13	88	300	12	3	4	2.1	.990	H. Borowy	15	122	11	2	1	2.13
	CF	A. Pafko	534	.298	12	110	371	11	2	0	2.7	.995	P. Erickson	28	108	7	4	3	3.32
	LF	P. Lowrey	523	.283	7	89	280	17	4	1	2.2	.987	H. Vandenberg	30	95	6	3	2	3.49
	C	M. Livingston	224	.254	2	23	263	27	3	2	4.3	.990							
	UT	R. Hughes	222	.261	0	8	120	157	13	28		.955							
	C	P. Gillespie	163	.288	3	25	161	20	2	1	4.1	.989							
	1B	H. Becker	133	.286	2	27	222	12	0	21	8.4	1.000							
St. L. W-95 L-59 Billy Southworth	1B	R. Sanders	537	.276	8	78	1259	90	19	113	9.6	.986	R. Barrett	36	247*	21*	9	0	2.74
	2B	E. Verban	597	.278	0	72	398	406	18	95	5.3	.978	K. Burkhart	42	217	19	8	2	2.90
	SS	M. Marion	430	.277	1	59	237	372	21	70	5.2	.967	B. Donnelly	31	166	8	10	2	3.52
	3B	W. Kurowski	511	.323	21	102	172	235	15	28	3.2	.964	H. Brecheen	24	157	14	4	2	2.52
	RF	J. Hopp	446	.289	3	44	244	5	5	2	2.4	.980	G. Dockins	31	126	8	6	0	3.21
	CF	B. Adams	578	.292	20	101	382	9	9	3	2.9	.978	T. Wilks	18	98	4	7	0	2.93
	LF	Schoendienst	565	.278	1	47	286	10	5	1	2.6	.983	J. Creel	26	87	5	4	2	4.14
	C	K. O'Dea	307	.254	4	43	321	50	2	14	4.1	.995							
	OF	A. Bergamo	304	.316	3	44	146	9	5	3	2.1	.969							
	C	D. Rice	253	.261	1	28	284	39	2	6	4.2	.994							

POS	Player	AB	BA	HR	RBI	PO	A	E	DP	TC/G	FA	Pitcher	G	IP	W	L	SV	ERA
Bkn. W-87 L-67 Leo Durocher																		
1B	A. Galan	576	.307	9	92	558	34	7	53	9.1	.988	H. Gregg	42	254	18	13	2	3.47
2B	E. Stanky	555	.258	1	39	**429**	441	34	**101**	5.9	.962	V. Lombardi	38	204	10	11	4	3.31
SS	E. Basinski	336	.262	0	33	166	262	34	59	4.6	.926	C. Davis	24	150	10	10	0	3.25
3B	F. Bordagaray	273	.256	2	49	54	93	19	7	2.9	.886	A. Herring	22	124	7	4	2	3.48
RF	D. Walker	607	.300	8	124	346	18	3	4	2.4	.992	T. Seats	31	122	10	7	0	4.36
CF	G. Rosen	606	.325	12	75	392	7	3	1	2.9	.993	C. King	42	112	5	5	3	4.09
LF	L. Olmo	556	.313	10	110	225	8	7	2	2.3	.971	R. Branca	16	110	5	6	1	3.04
C	M. Sandlock	195	.282	2	17	196	20	2	3	4.6	.991	C. Buker	42	87	7	2	5	3.30
1B	E. Stevens	201	.274	4	29	478	38	7	40	9.5	.987	L. Webber	17	75	7	3	0	3.58
SS	T. Brown	196	.245	2	19	93	164	23	27	5.1	.918							
3B	B. Hart	161	.230	3	27	54	62	11	8	3.3	.913							
Pit. W-82 L-72 Frankie Frisch																		
1B	B. Dahlgren	531	.250	5	75	1373	93	6	**115**	10.4	**.996**	P. Roe	33	235	14	13	1	2.87
2B	P. Coscarart	392	.242	8	38	257	361	14	74	5.2	.978	Strincevich	36	228	16	10	2	3.31
SS	F. Gustine	478	.280	2	66	177	291	**35**	52	4.8	.930	R. Sewell	33	188	11	9	1	4.07
3B	B. Elliott	541	.290	8	108	94	178	21	18	3.6	.928	M. Butcher	28	169	10	8	0	3.03
RF	J. Barrett	507	.256	15	67	318	8	8	0	2.5	.976	A. Gerheauser	32	140	5	10	1	3.91
CF	A. Gionfriddo	409	.284	2	42	235	6	9	2	2.4	.964	K. Gables	29	139	11	7	1	4.15
LF	J. Russell	510	.284	12	77	313	9	9	1	2.4	.973	X. Rescigno	44	79	3	5	9	5.72
C	A. Lopez	243	.218	0	18	326	38	3	7	4.0	.992							
3B	L. Handley	312	.298	1	32	85	183	15	13	3.6	.947							
C	B. Salkeld	267	.311	15	52	279	40	9	8	3.8	.973							
SS	V. Barnhart	201	.269	0	19	104	166	21	31	4.9	.928							
OF	T. O'Brien	161	.335	0	18	72	2	3	0	1.7	.961							
1O	F. Colman	153	.209	4	30	143	14	1	10		.994							
N. Y. W-78 L-74 Mel Ott																		
1B	P. Weintraub	283	.272	10	42	774	60	6	49	10.9	.993	B. Voiselle	41	232	14	14	0	4.49
2B	G. Hausmann	623	.279	2	45	376	489	29	65	5.8	.968	H. Feldman	35	218	12	13	1	3.27
SS	B. Kerr	546	.249	4	40	**333**	515	32	81	5.9	.964	V. Mungo	26	183	14	7	0	3.20
3B	N. Reyes	431	.288	5	44	111	232	14	12	3.1	.961	J. Brewer	28	160	8	6	0	3.83
RF	M. Ott	451	.308	21	79	217	11	4	1	2.0	.983	A. Adams	65	113	11	9	15	3.42
CF	J. Rucker	429	.273	7	51	256	6	6	2	2.7	.978	S. Emmerich	31	100	4	4	0	4.86
LF	D. Gardella	430	.272	18	71	182	6	9	1	2.1	.954	A. Hansen	23	93	4	3	3	4.66
C	E. Lombardi	368	.307	19	70	**425**	49	8	8	5.0	.983	R. Fischer	31	77	3	8	1	5.63
OF	R. Treadway	224	.241	4	23	107	3	7	0	2.0	.940							
C	C. Kluttz	222	.279	4	21	195	32	5	5	4.1	.978							
3B	B. Jurges	176	.324	3	24	40	94	9	3	3.3	.937							
Bos. W-67 L-85 Bob Coleman W-42 L-49 Del Bissonette W-25 L-36																		
1B	V. Shupe	283	.269	0	15	650	53	8	81	9.2	.989	J. Tobin	27	197	9	14	0	3.84
2B	W. Wietelmann	428	.271	4	33	222	232	13	58	5.4	.972	B. Logan	34	187	7	11	1	3.18
SS	D. Culler	527	.262	2	30	252	386	31	71	5.3	.954	J. Hutchings	57	185	7	6	3	3.75
3B	C. Workman	514	.274	25	87	97	205	**30**	18	3.1	.910	N. Andrews	21	138	7	12	0	4.58
RF	T. Holmes	636	.352	28	117	334	13	6	4	2.3	.983	E. Wright	15	111	8	3	0	2.51
CF	Gillenwater	517	.288	7	72	**451**	24	10	5	3.5	.979	B. Lee	16	106	6	3	0	2.79
LF	B. Nieman	247	.247	14	56	132	4	10	1	2.6	.932	M. Cooper	20	78	7	4	1	3.35
C	P. Masi	371	.272	7	46	335	**52**	8	7	4.2	.980	Hendrickson	37	73	4	8	5	4.91
1B	J. Mack	260	.231	3	44	635	48	6	48	10.6	.991							
OF	J. Medwick	218	.284	0	26	78	7	0	2	2.2	1.000							
C	S. Hofferth	170	.235	3	15	168	31	4	7	4.5	.980							
Cin. W-61 L-93 Bill McKechnie																		
1B	F. McCormick	580	.276	10	81	**1469**	**118**	9	104	**10.6**	.994	E. Heusser	31	223	11	16	1	3.71
2B	W. Williams	482	.237	0	27	295	393	22	61	5.3	.969	J. Bowman	25	186	11	13	0	3.59
SS	E. Miller	421	.238	13	49	245	382	16	61	5.6	**.975**	B. Walters	22	168	10	10	2	2.68
3B	S. Mesner	540	.254	1	52	170	**326**	15	**35**	3.5	.971	H. Fox	45	164	8	13	0	4.93
RF	A. Libke	449	.283	4	53	223	13	9	**6**	2.3	.963	V. Kennedy	24	158	5	12	1	4.00
CF	D. Clay	**656**	.280	1	50	446	10	5	3	3.0	.989							
LF	E. Tipton	331	.242	5	34	192	2	6	1	2.4	.970							
C	A. Lakeman	258	.256	8	31	226	31	10	4	3.6	.963							
OF	G. Walker	316	.253	2	21	123	4	5	1	2.0	.962							
C	A. Unser	204	.265	3	21	207	30	11	5	4.1	.956							
2S	K. Wahl	194	.201	0	10	135	170	15	22		.953							
OF	D. Sipek	156	.244	0	13	68	2	2	0	2.3	.972							
OF	H. Sauer	116	.293	5	20	69	0	2	0	2.5	.972							
Phi. W-46 L-108 Freddie Fitzsimmons W-17 L-50 Ben Chapman W-29 L-58																		
1B	J. Wasdell	500	.300	7	60	597	43	7	51	10.3	.989	D. Barrett	36	191	7	**20**	1	5.43
2B	F. Daniels	230	.200	0	10	171	215	18	41	5.4	.955	A. Karl	**67**	181	9	8	15	2.99
SS	B. Mott	289	.221	0	22	134	189	19	41	5.4	.944	C. Schanz	35	145	4	15	5	4.35
3B	J. Antonelli	504	.256	1	28	129	201	14	24	3.2	.959	C. Sproull	34	130	4	11	1	5.94
RF	V. Dinges	397	.287	4	36	132	10	2	5	2.2	.986	D. Mauney	20	123	6	10	1	3.08
CF	V. DiMaggio	452	.257	19	84	337	16	2	4	2.9	.994	O. Judd	23	83	5	4	2	3.81
LF	C. Triplett	363	.240	7	46	202	3	**12**	1	2.4	.945	T. Kraus	19	82	4	9	0	5.40
C	A. Seminick	188	.239	6	26	198	30	5	3	3.3	.979							
UT	G. Crawford	302	.295	2	24	152	148	17	18		.946							
UT	J. Foxx	224	.268	7	38	304	54	8	19		.978							
OF	R. Monteagudo	193	.301	0	15	61	6	6	2	2.1	.918							
C	G. Mancuso	176	.199	0	16	215	34	3	4	3.6	.988							
OF	J. Powell	173	.231	1	14	67	5	1	2	1.7	.986							
SS	W. Flager	168	.250	2	15	98	145	14	25	5.4	.946							

BATTING AND BASE RUNNING LEADERS

Batting Average
P. Cavarretta, CHI	.355
T. Holmes, BOS	.352
G. Rosen, BKN	.325
S. Hack, CHI	.323
W. Kurowski, STL	.323

Slugging Average
T. Holmes, BOS	.577
W. Kurowski, STL	.511
P. Cavarretta, CHI	.500
M. Ott, NY	.499
L. Olmo, BKN	.462

PITCHING LEADERS

Winning Percentage
K. Burkhart, STL	.704
H. Wyse, CHI	.688
R. Barrett, BOS, STL	.657
C. Passeau, CHI	.654
Strincevich, PIT	.615

Earned Run Average
H. Borowy, CHI	2.13
C. Passeau, CHI	2.46
H. Brecheen, STL	2.52
B. Walters, CIN	2.68
H. Wyse, CHI	2.68

Home Runs
T. Holmes, BOS	28
C. Workman, BOS	25
B. Adams, PHI, STL	22
M. Ott, NY	21
W. Kurowski, STL	21

Total Bases
T. Holmes, BOS	367
G. Rosen, BKN	279
B. Adams, PHI, STL	279
D. Walker, BKN	266
W. Kurowski, STL	261

Wins
R. Barrett, BOS, STL	23
H. Wyse, CHI	22
K. Burkhart, STL	19
H. Gregg, BKN	18
C. Passeau, CHI	17

Saves
A. Adams, NY	15
A. Karl, PHI	15
X. Rescigno, PIT	9
Hendrickson, BOS	5
C. Buker, BKN	5
C. Schanz, PHI	5

Runs Batted In
D. Walker, BKN	124
T. Holmes, BOS	117
A. Pafko, CHI	110
L. Olmo, BKN	110
B. Adams, PHI, STL	109

Stolen Bases
Schoendienst, STL	26
J. Barrett, PIT	25
D. Clay, CIN	19
J. Russell, PIT	15
L. Olmo, BKN	15
T. Holmes, BOS	15

Strikeouts
P. Roe, PIT	148
H. Gregg, BKN	139
B. Voiselle, NY	115
V. Mungo, NY	101
J. Hutchings, BOS	99

Complete Games
R. Barrett, BOS, STL	24
H. Wyse, CHI	23
C. Passeau, CHI	19
Strincevich, PIT	18
E. Heusser, CIN	18

Hits
T. Holmes, BOS	224
G. Rosen, BKN	197
S. Hack, CHI	193

Base on Balls
E. Stanky, BKN	148
A. Galan, BKN	114
S. Hack, CHI	99

Fewest Hits per 9 Innings
H. Borowy, CHI	7.72
H. Brecheen, STL	7.78
H. Gregg, BKN	7.82

Shutouts
C. Passeau, CHI	5

Home Run Percentage
C. Workman, BOS	4.9
M. Ott, NY	4.7
T. Holmes, BOS	4.4

Runs Scored
E. Stanky, BKN	128
G. Rosen, BKN	126
T. Holmes, BOS	125

Fewest Walks per 9 Innings
C. Davis, BKN	1.26
R. Barrett, BOS, STL	1.71
P. Roe, PIT	1.76

Most Strikeouts per 9 Inn.
P. Roe, PIT	5.67
H. Gregg, BKN	4.92
B. Voiselle, NY	4.45

Doubles
T. Holmes, BOS	47
D. Walker, BKN	42
B. Elliott, PIT	36
A. Galan, BKN	36

Triples
L. Olmo, BKN	13
A. Pafko, CHI	12
J. Rucker, NY	11
G. Rosen, BKN	11

Innings
R. Barrett, BOS, STL	285
H. Wyse, CHI	278
H. Gregg, BKN	254

Games Pitched
A. Karl, PHI	67
A. Adams, NY	65
J. Hutchings, BOS	57

	W	L	PCT	GB	R	OR	2B	3B	HR	BA	SA	SB	E	DP	FA	CG	BB	SO	ShO	SV	ERA
CHI	98	56	.636		735	532	229	52	57	**.277**	.372	69	**121**	124	**.980**	86	385	541	15	14	**2.98**
STL	95	59	.617	3	756	583	256	44	64	.273	.371	55	137	150	.977	77	497	510	**18**	9	3.24
BKN	87	67	.565	11	**795**	724	257	**71**	57	.271	.376	75	230	144	.962	61	586	**557**	7	18	3.70
PIT	82	72	.532	16	753	686	259	56	72	.267	.377	81	178	141	.971	73	455	518	8	16	3.76
NY	78	74	.513	19	668	700	175	35	114	.269	**.379**	38	166	112	.973	53	529	530	13	21	4.06
BOS	67	85	.441	30	721	728	229	25	101	.267	.374	**82**	193	**160**	.969	57	557	404	7	13	4.04
CIN	61	93	.396	37	536	694	221	26	56	.249	.333	71	146	138	.976	77	534	372	11	6	4.00
PHI	46	108	.299	52	548	865	197	27	56	.246	.326	54	234	150	.962	31	608	433	4	**26**	4.64
					5512	5512	1823	336	577	.265	.364	525	1405	1119	.971	515	4151	3865	83	123	3.80

American League 1945

	POS	Player	AB	BA	HR	RBI	PO	A	E	DP	TC/G	FA	Pitcher	G	IP	W	L	SV	ERA
Det.	1B	R. York	595	.264	18	87	**1464**	113	19	142	10.3	.988	H. Newhouser	40	**313**	**25**	9	2	**1.81**
W-88 L-65	2B	E. Mayo	501	.285	10	54	326	393	15	91	5.9	**.980**	D. Trout	41	246	18	15	2	3.14
Steve O'Neill	SS	S. Webb	407	.199	0	21	215	343	25	71	5.6	.957	A. Benton	31	192	13	8	3	2.02
	3B	B. Maier	486	.263	1	34	142	226	25	19	3.2	.936	S. Overmire	31	162	9	9	4	3.88
	RF	R. Cullenbine	523	.277	18	93	321	23*	7	3	2.4	.980	L. Mueller	26	135	6	8	1	3.68
	CF	D. Cramer	541	.275	6	58	314	7	3	4	2.3	**.991**	J. Tobin	14	58	4	5	1	3.55
	LF	J. Outlaw	446	.271	0	34	192	13	7	6	2.0	.967							
	C	B. Swift	279	.233	0	24	358	60	5	12	4.5	.988							
	OF	H. Greenberg	270	.311	13	60	129	3	0	0	1.8	1.000							
	C	P. Richards	234	.256	3	32	361	44	2	7	4.9	.995							
	SS	J. Hoover	222	.257	1	17	126	163	17	35	4.5	.944							

	POS	Player	AB	BA	HR	RBI	PO	A	E	DP	TC/G	FA	Pitcher	G	IP	W	L	SV	ERA
Was. W-87 L-67 Ossie Bluege	1B	J. Kuhel	533	.285	2	75	1323	94	16	101	10.2	.989	R. Wolff	33	250	20	10	2	2.12
	2B	G. Myatt	490	.296	1	39	228	231	13	48	5.0	.972	M. Haefner	37	238	16	14	3	3.47
	SS	G. Torres	562	.237	0	48	272	437	35	65	5.1	.953	M. Pieretti	44	233	14	13	2	3.32
	3B	H. Clift	375	.211	8	53	111	214	23	18	3.1	.934	D. Leonard	31	216	17	7	1	2.13
	RF	B. Lewis	258	.333	2	37	151	8	3	3	2.3	.981	J. Niggeling	26	177	7	12	0	3.16
	CF	G. Binks	550	.278	6	81	321	13	8	4	2.7	.977	A. Carrasquel	35	123	7	5	1	2.71
	LF	G. Case	504	.294	1	31	316	17	7	3	2.8	.979							
	C	R. Ferrell	286	.266	1	38	331	64	4	3	4.8	.990							
	2B	F. Vaughn	268	.235	1	25	177	189	21	35	5.1	.946							
	OF	M. Kreevich	158	.278	1	23	98	2	3	0	2.6*	.971							
St. L. W-81 L-70 Luke Sewell	1B	G. McQuinn	483	.277	7	61	1143	105	11	87	9.3	.991	N. Potter	32	255	15	11	0	2.47
	2B	D. Gutteridge	543	.238	2	49	334	334	21	66	5.4	.970	J. Kramer	29	193	10	15	2	3.36
	SS	V. Stephens	571	.289	24	89	256	439	28	69	5.0	.961	S. Jakucki	30	192	12	10	2	3.51
	3B	M. Christman	289	.277	4	34	79	137	6	12	2.9	.973	T. Shirley	32	184	8	12	0	3.63
	RF	G. Moore	354	.260	5	50	184	10	6	0	2.0	.970	Hollingsworth	26	173	12	9	1	2.70
	CF	M. Kreevich	295	.237	2	21	230	4	2	0	3.0*	.992	B. Muncrief	27	146	13	4	1	2.72
	LF	M. Byrnes	442	.249	8	59	319	12	4	0	2.7	.988							
	C	F. Mancuso	365	.268	1	38	467	55	6	10	4.6	.989							
	UT	L. Schulte	430	.247	0	36	167	245	23	24		.947							
	OF	P. Gray	234	.218	0	13	162	3	7	1	2.8	.959							
	O1	L. Finney	213	.277	2	22	233	18	2	14		.992							
	OF	B. Martin	185	.200	2	16	116	7	1	2	2.6	.992							
	C	R. Hayworth	160	.194	0	17	216	23	2	5	4.4	.992							
N. Y. W-81 L-71 Joe McCarthy	1B	N. Etten	565	.285	18	111	1401	94	17	149	9.9	.989	B. Bevens	29	184	13	9	0	3.67
	2B	S. Stirnweiss	632	.309	10	64	432	492	29	119	6.3	.970	E. Bonham	23	181	8	11	0	3.29
	SS	F. Crosetti	441	.238	4	48	264	380	37	86	5.4	.946	A. Gettel	27	155	9	8	3	3.90
	3B	O. Grimes	480	.265	4	45	162	296	31	35	3.5	.937	M. Dubiel	26	151	10	9	0	4.64
	RF	B. Metheny	509	.248	8	53	227	12	4	2	1.9	.984	H. Borowy	18	132	10	5	0	3.13
	CF	T. Stainback	327	.257	5	32	233	10	8	6	3.0	.968	B. Zuber	21	127	5	11	1	3.19
	LF	H. Martin	408	.267	7	53	233	8	4	1	2.4	.984	J. Page	20	102	6	3	0	2.82
	C	M. Garbark	176	.216	1	26	202	41	7	10	4.2	.972	R. Ruffing	11	87	7	3	0	2.89
	OF	R. Derry	253	.225	13	45	170	4	4	2	2.6	.978	J. Turner	30	54	3	4	10	3.64
	OF	C. Keller	163	.301	10	34	110	4	0	0	2.6	1.000							
	C	A. Robinson	160	.281	8	24	186	16	0	3	4.5	1.000							
	OF	J. Lindell	159	.283	1	20	108	2	2	0	2.7	.982							
Cle. W-73 L-72 Lou Boudreau	1B	M. Rocco	565	.264	10	56	1203	115	10	112	9.4	.992	S. Gromek	33	251	19	9	1	2.55
	2B	D. Meyer	524	.292	7	48	317	313	14	66	5.0	.978	A. Reynolds	44	247	18	12	4	3.20
	SS	L. Boudreau	346	.306	3	48	217	289	9	73	5.3	.983	J. Bagby	25	159	8	11	1	3.73
	3B	D. Ross	363	.262	2	43	119	175	13	14	2.9	.958	A. Smith	21	134	5	12	1	3.84
	RF	P. Seerey	414	.237	14	56	227	7	6	3	2.1	.975	E. Klieman	38	126	5	8	4	3.85
	CF	F. Mackiewicz	359	.273	2	37	288	11	4	4	2.7	.987	P. Center	31	86	6	3	1	3.99
	LF	J. Heath	370	.305	15	61	214	3	6	1	2.2	.973	M. Harder	11	76	3	7	0	3.67
	C	F. Hayes	385	.236	6	43	508*	63	7	23*	4.9*	.988*							
	UT	A. Cihocki	283	.212	0	24	154	208	15	42		.960							
	OF	P. O'Dea	221	.235	1	21	118	4	1	2	2.3	.992							
	OF	L. Fleming	140	.329	3	22	59	2	4	2	2.0	.938							
Chi. W-71 L-78 Jimmy Dykes	1B	K. Farrell	396	.258	0	34	913	74	11	76	10.3	.989	T. Lee	29	228	15	12	0	2.44
	2B	R. Schalk	513	.248	1	65	380	389	18	90	5.9	.977	O. Grove	33	217	14	12	1	3.44
	SS	C. Michaels	445	.245	2	54	259	426	47	74	5.8	.936	E. Lopat	26	199	10	13	1	4.11
	3B	T. Cuccinello	402	.308	2	49	73	221	20	22	2.8	.936	J. Humphries	22	153	6	14	1	4.24
	RF	W. Moses	569	.295	2	50	329	12	8	1	2.5	.977	B. Dietrich	18	122	7	10	0	4.19
	CF	O. Hockett	417	.293	2	55	273	7	5	3	2.7	.982	E. Caldwell	27	105	6	7	4	3.59
	LF	J. Dickshot	486	.302	4	58	253	13	8	3	2.2	.971	J. Haynes	14	104	5	5	1	3.55
	C	M. Tresh	458	.249	0	47	575	102	11	7	4.6	.984							
	OF	G. Curtright	324	.281	4	32	196	8	3	0	2.5	.986							
	1B	B. Nagel	220	.209	3	27	503	34	9	42	9.6	.984							
	3B	F. Baker	208	.250	0	19	36	99	4	6	2.4	.971							
Bos. W-71 L-83 Joe Cronin	1B	C. Metkovich	539	.260	5	62	935	76	15	96	10.6	.985	B. Ferriss	35	265	21	10	2	2.96
	2B	S. Newsome	438	.290	1	48	206	231	17	54	5.5	.963	J. Wilson	23	144	6	8	0	3.30
	SS	E. Lake	473	.279	11	51	265	459	40	112	5.9	.948	E. O'Neill	24	142	8	11	0	5.15
	3B	J. Tobin	278	.252	0	41	82	151	12	17	3.4	.951	C. Hausmann	31	125	5	7	2	5.04
	RF	J. Lazor	335	.310	5	45	141	6	6	0	1.9	.961	M. Ryba	34	123	7	6	2	2.49
	CF	L. Culberson	331	.275	6	45	219	14	8	6	2.6	.967	P. Woods	24	107	4	7	2	4.19
	LF	B. Johnson	529	.280	12	74	296	15	8	4	2.3	.975	W. Heflin	20	102	4	10	0	4.06
	C	B. Garbark	199	.261	0	17	249	31	2	9	4.2	.993	F. Barrett	37	86	4	3	3	2.62
	OF	T. McBride	344	.305	1	47	180	10	3	4	2.4	.984	V. Johnson	26	85	6	4	2	4.01
	2B	B. Steiner	304	.252	3	20	202	213	14	63	5.6	.967							
	OF	P. Fox	208	.245	0	20	84	5	1	1	1.6	.989							
	3B	T. LaForest	204	.250	2	16	45	97	5	11	3.3	.966							
	1B	D. Camilli	198	.212	2	19	505	44	5	62	10.3	.991							

	POS	Player	AB	BA	HR	RBI	PO	A	E	DP	TC/G	FA	Pitcher	G	IP	W	L	SV	ERA
Phi.	1B	D. Siebert	573	.267	7	51	1427	**135**	14	129	**10.7**	.991	B. Newsom	36	257	8	**20**	0	3.29
W-52 L-98	2B	I. Hall	616	.261	0	50	422	**498**	21	108	6.2	.978	Christopher	33	227	13	13	2	3.17
Connie Mack	SS	E. Busch	416	.250	0	35	209	370	29	67	5.2	.952	J. Flores	29	191	7	10	1	3.43
	3B	G. Kell	567	.272	4	56	**186**	**345**	20	32	**3.7**	**.964**	L. Knerr	27	130	5	11	0	4.22
	RF	H. Peck	449	.276	5	39	190	9	**12**	3	1.9	.943	J. Berry	**52**	130	8	7	5	2.35
	CF	B. Estalella	451	.299	8	52	314	10	4	3	2.6	.988	D. Black	26	125	5	11	0	5.17
	LF	C. Metro	200	.210	3	15	100	5	3	0	1.9	.972	C. Gassaway	24	118	4	7	0	3.74
	C	B. Rosar	300	.210	1	25	338	54	5	6	4.7	.987	S. Gerkin	21	102	0	12	0	3.62
	OF	B. McGhee	250	.252	0	19	84	2	1	0	1.8	.989							
	OF	M. Smith	203	.212	0	11	120	4	3	0	2.0	.976							
	SS	B. Wilkins	154	.260	0	4	74	118	16	23	5.2	.923							

BATTING AND BASE RUNNING LEADERS   PITCHING LEADERS

Batting Average
S. Stirnweiss, NY	.309
T. Cuccinello, CHI	.308
J. Dickshot, CHI	.302
B. Estalella, PHI	.299
G. Myatt, WAS	.296

Slugging Average
S. Stirnweiss, NY	.476
V. Stephens, STL	.473
R. Cullenbine, CLE, DET	.444
N. Etten, NY	.437
B. Estalella, PHI	.435

Winning Percentage
H. Newhouser, DET	.735
D. Leonard, WAS	.708
S. Gromek, CLE	.679
B. Ferriss, BOS	.677
R. Wolff, WAS	.667

Earned Run Average
H. Newhouser, DET	1.81
A. Benton, DET	2.02
R. Wolff, WAS	2.12
D. Leonard, WAS	2.13
T. Lee, CHI	2.44

Home Runs
V. Stephens, STL	24
R. Cullenbine, CLE, DET	18
N. Etten, NY	18
R. York, DET	18
J. Heath, CLE	15

Total Bases
S. Stirnweiss, NY	301
V. Stephens, STL	270
N. Etten, NY	247
R. York, DET	246
W. Moses, CHI	239

Wins
H. Newhouser, DET	25
B. Ferriss, BOS	21
R. Wolff, WAS	20
S. Gromek, CLE	19
A. Reynolds, CLE	18
D. Trout, DET	18

Saves
J. Turner, NY	10
J. Berry, PHI	5

Runs Batted In
N. Etten, NY	111
R. Cullenbine, CLE, DET	93
V. Stephens, STL	89
R. York, DET	87
G. Binks, WAS	81

Stolen Bases
S. Stirnweiss, NY	33
G. Myatt, WAS	30
G. Case, WAS	30
C. Metkovich, BOS	19
J. Dickshot, CHI	18

Strikeouts
H. Newhouser, DET	212
N. Potter, STL	129
B. Newsom, PHI	127
A. Reynolds, CLE	112
T. Lee, CHI	108
R. Wolff, WAS	108

Complete Games
H. Newhouser, DET	29
B. Ferriss, BOS	26
R. Wolff, WAS	21
S. Gromek, CLE	21
N. Potter, STL	21

Hits
S. Stirnweiss, NY	195
W. Moses, CHI	168
V. Stephens, STL	165

Base on Balls
R. Cullenbine, CLE, DET	112
E. Lake, BOS	106
O. Grimes, NY	97

Fewest Hits per 9 Innings
H. Newhouser, DET	6.86
R. Wolff, WAS	7.20
N. Potter, STL	7.47

Shutouts
H. Newhouser, DET	8
A. Benton, DET	5
B. Ferriss, BOS	5

Home Run Percentage
V. Stephens, STL	4.2
P. Seerey, CLE	3.4
R. Cullenbine, CLE, DET	3.4

Runs Scored
S. Stirnweiss, NY	107
V. Stephens, STL	90
R. Cullenbine, CLE, DET	83

Fewest Walks per 9 Innings
E. Bonham, NY	1.10
D. Leonard, WAS	1.46
R. Wolff, WAS	1.91

Most Strikeouts per 9 Inn.
H. Newhouser, DET	6.09
J. Kramer, STL	4.62
N. Potter, STL	4.55

Doubles
W. Moses, CHI	35
G. Binks, WAS	32
S. Stirnweiss, NY	32

Triples
S. Stirnweiss, NY	22
W. Moses, CHI	15
J. Kuhel, WAS	13

Innings
H. Newhouser, DET	313
B. Ferriss, BOS	265
B. Newsom, PHI	257

Games Pitched
J. Berry, PHI	52
A. Reynolds, CLE	44
M. Pieretti, WAS	44

	W	L	PCT	GB	R	OR	Batting 2B	3B	HR	BA	SA	SB	Fielding E	DP	FA	Pitching CG	BB	SO	ShO	SV	ERA
DET	88	65	.575		633	565	**227**	47	77	.256	.361	60	158	173	.975	78	538	**588**	19	16	2.99
WAS	87	67	.565	1.5	622	562	197	**63**	27	.258	.334	**110**	183	124	.970	82	**440**	550	19	11	**2.92**
STL	81	70	.536	6	597	548	215	37	63	.249	.341	25	143	123	.976	91	506	570	10	8	3.14
NY	81	71	.533	6.5	**676**	606	189	61	**93**	.259	**.373**	64	175	170	.971	78	485	474	9	14	3.45
CLE	73	72	.503	11	557	548	216	48	65	.255	.359	19	**126**	149	**.977**	76	501	497	14	12	3.31
CHI	71	78	.477	15	596	633	204	55	22	**.262**	.337	78	180	139	.970	84	448	486	13	13	3.69
BOS	71	83	.461	17.5	599	674	225	44	50	.260	.346	72	169	**198**	.973	71	656	490	15	13	3.80
PHI	52	98	.347	34.5	494	638	201	37	33	.245	.316	25	168	160	.973	65	571	531	11	8	3.62
					4774	4774	1674	392	430	.255	.346	453	1302	1236	.973	625	4145	4186	110	95	3.36

	POS	Player	AB	BA	HR	RBI	PO	A	E	DP	TC/G	FA	Pitcher	G	IP	W	L	SV	ERA
St. L.	1B	S. Musial	**624**	**.365**	16	103	1056	65	13	119	9.9	.989	H. Pollet	40	**266**	**21**	10	5	**2.10**
W-98 L-58	2B	Schoendienst	606	.281	0	34	340	354	11	87	5.5	**.984**	H. Brecheen	36	231	15	15	3	2.49
Eddie Dyer	SS	M. Marion	498	.233	3	46	**290**	**480**	21	**105**	5.5	.973	M. Dickson	47	184	15	6	1	2.88
	3B	W. Kurowski	519	.301	14	89	**175**	**249**	15	**17**	3.2	**.966**	A. Brazle	37	153	11	10	0	3.29
	RF	E. Slaughter	609	.300	18	**130**	284	23	6	6	2.0	.981	J. Beazley	19	103	7	5	0	4.46
	CF	H. Walker	346	.237	3	27	215	11	6	2	2.5	.974	K. Burkhart	25	100	6	3	2	2.88
	LF	E. Dusak	275	.240	9	42	139	12	1	1	2.0	.993							
	C	J. Garagiola	211	.237	3	22	260	25	3	6	4.1	.990							
	OF	T. Moore	278	.263	3	28	158	5	3	0	2.5	.982							
	1O	D. Sisler	235	.260	3	42	334	31	6	31		.990							
	OF	B. Adams	173	.185	5	22	95	1	1	1	1.7	.990							
Bkn.	1B	E. Stevens	310	.242	10	60	716	48	11	59	7.8	.986	J. Hatten	42	222	14	11	2	2.84
W-96 L-60	2B	E. Stanky	483	.273	0	36	**356**	359	17	**88**	5.2	.977	K. Higbe	42	211	17	8	1	3.03
Leo Durocher	SS	P. Reese	542	.284	5	60	285	463	26	104	5.1	.966	V. Lombardi	41	193	13	10	3	2.89
	3B	C. Lavagetto	242	.236	3	27	70	108	14	11	2.9	.927	H. Behrman	47	151	11	5	4	2.93
	RF	D. Walker	576	.319	9	116	237	15	8	3	1.7	.969	H. Gregg	26	117	6	4	2	2.99
	CF	C. Furillo	335	.284	3	35	292	9	5	4	2.7	.984	R. Melton	24	100	6	3	1	1.99
	LF	P. Reiser	423	.277	11	73	205	14	5	2	2.3	.978	H. Casey	46	100	11	5	5	1.99
	C	B. Edwards	292	.267	1	25	431	53	9	9	**5.4**	.982	A. Herring	35	86	7	2	5	3.35
	UT	A. Galan	274	.310	3	38	211	44	16	3		.941							
	OF	D. Whitman	265	.260	2	31	178	5	0	0	2.2	1.000							
	1B	H. Schultz	249	.253	3	27	576	58	7	65	7.4	.989							
	C	F. Anderson	199	.256	2	14	258	35	11	5	4.3	.964							
	32	B. Herman	184	.288	0	28	73	91	5	13		.970							
Chi.	1B	E. Waitkus	441	.304	4	55	992	81	4	76	10.2	.996	J. Schmitz	41	224	11	11	2	2.61
W-82 L-71	2B	D. Johnson	314	.242	1	19	192	228	8	34	5.2	.981	H. Wyse	40	201	14	12	1	2.68
Charlie Grimm	SS	B. Jurges	221	.222	0	17	119	204	8	26	4.5	.976	H. Borowy	32	201	12	10	0	3.76
	3B	S. Hack	323	.285	0	26	102	168	9	6	3.1	.968	P. Erickson	32	137	9	7	0	2.43
	RF	P. Cavarretta	510	.294	8	78	196	7	7	2	2.4	.967	C. Passeau	21	129	9	8	0	3.13
	CF	P. Lowrey	540	.257	4	54	308	15	7	3	2.6	.979	E. Kush	40	130	9	2	2	3.05
	LF	M. Rickert	392	.263	7	47	200	5	6	1	2.0	.972	B. Chipman	34	109	6	5	2	3.13
	C	McCullough	307	.287	4	34	390	40	4	4	4.9	.991	H. Bithorn	26	87	6	5	1	3.84
	OF	B. Nicholson	296	.220	8	41	179	4	5	1	2.4	.973							
	SS	B. Sturgeon	294	.296	1	21	109	158	19	31	4.0	.934							
	OF	A. Pafko	234	.282	3	39	165	13	4	4	2.8	.978							
	2B	L. Stringer	209	.244	3	19	135	150	13	17	4.8	.956							
	C	M. Livingston	176	.256	2	20	239	25	5	3	4.8	.981							
	3B	J. Ostrowski	160	.213	3	12	33	80	8	5	2.4	.934							
Bos.	1B	R. Sanders	259	.243	6	35	659	61	9	57	9.5	.988	J. Sain	37	265	20	14	2	2.21
W-81 L-72	2B	C. Ryan	502	.241	1	48	285	317	20	53	5.2	.948	M. Cooper	28	199	13	11	1	3.12
Billy Southworth	SS	D. Culler	482	.255	0	33	279	380	36	68	5.3	.948	E. Wright	36	176	12	9	0	3.52
	3B	N. Fernandez	372	.255	2	42	83	150	15	10	3.1	.940	B. Lee	25	140	10	9	0	4.18
	RF	T. Holmes	568	.310	6	79	294	17	4	7	2.2	.987	S. Johnson	28	127	6	5	1	2.76
	LF	B. Rowell	293	.280	3	31	168	8	4	2	2.1	.978	W. Spahn	24	126	8	5	1	2.94
	C	P. Masi	397	.267	3	62	**470**	56	10	5	4.3	.981							
	1O	J. Hopp	445	.333	3	48	670	45	11	45		.985							
	UT	B. Herman	252	.306	3	22	279	116	11	48		.973							
	OF	D. Litwhiler	247	.291	8	38	128	2	2	0	2.0	.985							
	3B	S. Roberge	169	.231	2	20	63	80	4	11	3.1	.973							
	OF	M. McCormick	164	.262	1	16	109	1	3	0	2.4	.973							
	C	D. Padgett	98	.255	2	21	65	12	5	1	3.2	.939							
Phi.	1B	F. McCormick	504	.284	11	66	1185	98	1	92	9.6	**.999**	Raffensberger	39	196	8	15	**6**	3.63
W-69 L-85	2B	E. Verban	473	.275	0	34	353	381*	28*	83	5.5	.963	O. Judd	30	173	11	12	2	3.53
Ben Chapman	SS	S. Newsome	375	.232	1	23	179	310	23	53	4.8	.955	S. Rowe	17	136	11	4	0	2.12
	3B	J. Tabor	463	.268	10	50	156	221	18	17	3.2	.954	C. Schanz	32	116	6	6	4	5.80
	RF	R. Northey	438	.249	16	62	194	7	6	3	1.9	.971	T. Hughes	29	111	6	9	1	4.38
	CF	J. Wyrostek	545	.281	6	45	**388**	18	8	4	**2.9**	.981	D. Mauney	24	90	6	4	2	2.70
	LF	D. Ennis	540	.313	17	73	332	16	9	4	2.6	.975	A. Karl	39	65	3	7	5	4.96
	C	A. Seminick	406	.264	12	52	461	61	**14**	12	4.5	.974							
	UT	R. Hughes	276	.236	0	22	123	144	11	27		.960							
	OF	C. Gilbert	260	.242	1	17	154	9	0	4	2.4	1.000							
Cin.	1B	B. Haas	535	.264	3	50	1346	91	9	**140**	11.0	.994	Vander Meer	29	204	10	12	0	3.17
W-67 L-87	2B	B. Adams	311	.244	4	24	190	251	15	67	6.2	.967	E. Blackwell	33	194	9	13	0	2.45
Bill McKechnie	SS	E. Miller	299	.194	6	36	184	297	15	79	5.6	.970	J. Beggs	28	190	12	10	1	2.32
	3B	G. Hatton	436	.271	14	69	108	194	**19**	14	2.8	.941	E. Heusser	29	168	7	14	2	3.22
	RF	A. Libke	431	.253	5	42	191	14	6	4	1.8	.972	B. Walters	22	151	10	7	0	2.56
	CF	D. Clay	435	.228	2	22	312	10	4	3	2.7	.988	J. Hetki	32	126	6	6	1	2.99
	LF	E. Lukon	312	.250	12	34	190	5	3	1	2.4	.985	H. Gumbert	36	119	6	8	4	3.24
	C	R. Mueller	378	.254	8	48	405	**65**	3	12	4.7	**.994**							
	2O	L. Frey	333	.246	3	24	210	176	15	33		.963							
	23	B. Zientara	280	.289	0	16	114	219	11	38		.968							
	SS	C. Corbitt	274	.248	1	16	126	229	20	45	4.9	.947							
	C	R. Lamanno	239	.243	1	30	222	37	7	6	4.4	.974							
	OF	M. West	202	.213	5	18	112	6	6	3	2.1	.952							

POS	Player	AB	BA	HR	RBI	PO	A	E	DP	TC/G	FA	Pitcher	G	IP	W	L	SV	ERA
Pit. 1B	E. Fletcher	532	.256	4	66	1356	106	8	97	10.0	.995	Ostermueller	27	193	13	10	0	2.84
W-63 L-91 2B	F. Gustine	495	.259	8	52	290	328	21	61	5.7	.967	Strincevich	32	176	10	15	1	3.58
Frankie Frisch SS	B. Cox	411	.290	2	36	235	323	39	59	5.2	.935	Heintzelman	32	158	8	12	1	3.77
W-62 L-89 3B	L. Handley	416	.238	1	28	107	237	15	13	3.5	.958	R. Sewell	25	149	8	12	0	3.68
Spud Davis RF	B. Elliott	486	.263	5	68	188	8	1	5	2.1	.995	E. Bahr	27	137	8	6	0	2.63
W-1 L-2 CF	J. Russell	516	.277	8	50	308	7	11	1	2.4	.966	J. Hallett	35	115	5	7	0	3.29
LF	R. Kiner	502	.247	23	81	339	6	11	0	2.5	.969	K. Gables	32	101	2	4	1	5.27
C	A. Lopez	150	.307	1	12	173	30	3	4	3.7	.985	J. Lanning	27	91	4	5	1	3.07
UT	J. Brown	241	.241	0	12	127	168	16	28		.949	P. Roe	21	70	3	8	2	5.14
C	B. Salkeld	160	.294	3	19	176	31	6	3	4.2	.972							
N. Y. 1B	J. Mize	377	.337	22	70	928	83	11	80	10.1	.989	D. Koslo	40	265	14	19	1	3.63
W-61 L-93 2B	B. Blattner	420	.255	11	49	285	315	15	62	5.4	.976	M. Kennedy	38	187	9	10	1	3.42
Mel Ott SS	B. Kerr	497	.249	6	40	240	400	12	66	5.2	.982	B. Voiselle	36	178	9	15	0	3.74
3B	B. Rigney	360	.236	3	31	77	143	8	8	3.1	.965	K. Trinkle	48	151	7	14	2	3.87
RF	G. Rosen	310	.281	5	30	200	3	5	0	2.5	.976	J. Thompson	39	63	4	6	4	1.29
CF	W. Marshall	510	.282	13	48	253	14	6	2	2.2	.978							
LF	S. Gordon	450	.293	5	45	197	8	1	0	2.0	.995							
C	W. Cooper	280	.268	8	46	277	38	9	3	4.4	.972							
1O	B. Young	291	.278	7	33	492	24	7	25		.987							
23	M. Witek	284	.264	4	29	138	150	20	23		.935							
OF	J. Graham	270	.219	14	47	105	7	6	0	1.9	.949							
C	E. Lombardi	238	.290	12	39	272	36	7	7	5.0	.978							
OF	J. Rucker	197	.264	1	13	91	1	5	0	1.8	.948							

BATTING AND BASE RUNNING LEADERS

Batting Average
S. Musial, STL	.365
J. Hopp, BOS	.333
D. Walker, BKN	.319
D. Ennis, PHI	.313
T. Holmes, BOS	.310

Slugging Average
S. Musial, STL	.587
D. Ennis, PHI	.485
E. Slaughter, STL	.465
W. Kurowski, STL	.462
D. Walker, BKN	.448

Home Runs
R. Kiner, PIT	23
J. Mize, NY	22
E. Slaughter, STL	18
D. Ennis, PHI	17
R. Northey, PHI	16
S. Musial, STL	16

Total Bases
S. Musial, STL	366
E. Slaughter, STL	283
D. Ennis, PHI	262
D. Walker, BKN	258
T. Holmes, BOS	241

Runs Batted In
E. Slaughter, STL	130
D. Walker, BKN	116
S. Musial, STL	103
W. Kurowski, STL	89
R. Kiner, PIT	81

Stolen Bases
P. Reiser, BKN	34
B. Haas, CIN	22
J. Hopp, BOS	21
B. Adams, CIN	16
D. Walker, BKN	14

Hits
S. Musial, STL	228
D. Walker, BKN	184
E. Slaughter, STL	183

Base on Balls
E. Stanky, BKN	137
E. Fletcher, PIT	111
P. Cavarretta, CHI	88

Home Run Percentage
R. Kiner, PIT	4.6
R. Northey, PHI	3.7
G. Hatton, CIN	3.2

Runs Scored
S. Musial, STL	124
E. Slaughter, STL	100
E. Stanky, BKN	98

Doubles
S. Musial, STL	50
T. Holmes, BOS	35
W. Kurowski, STL	32
B. Herman, BKN, BOS	31

Triples
S. Musial, STL	20
P. Cavarretta, CHI	10
P. Reese, BKN	10
D. Walker, BKN	9

PITCHING LEADERS

Winning Percentage
M. Dickson, STL	.714
K. Higbe, BKN	.680
H. Pollet, STL	.677
J. Sain, BOS	.588
H. Brecheen, STL	.500

Earned Run Average
H. Pollet, STL	2.10
J. Sain, BOS	2.21
J. Beggs, CIN	2.32
E. Blackwell, CIN	2.45
H. Brecheen, STL	2.49

Wins
H. Pollet, STL	21
J. Sain, BOS	20
K. Higbe, BKN	17
M. Dickson, STL	15
H. Brecheen, STL	15

Saves
Raffensberger, PHI	6
H. Casey, BKN	5
A. Herring, BKN	5
A. Karl, PHI	5
H. Pollet, STL	5

Strikeouts
J. Schmitz, CHI	135
K. Higbe, BKN	134
J. Sain, BOS	129
D. Koslo, NY	121
H. Brecheen, STL	117

Complete Games
J. Sain, BOS	24
H. Pollet, STL	22
D. Koslo, NY	17
Ostermueller, PIT	16
M. Cooper, BOS	15

Fewest Hits per 9 Innings
M. Kennedy, NY	7.38
J. Schmitz, CHI	7.38
E. Blackwell, CIN	7.41

Shutouts
E. Blackwell, CIN	6
Vander Meer, CIN	5
H. Brecheen, STL	5

Fewest Walks per 9 Innings
M. Cooper, BOS	1.76
Raffensberger, PHI	1.79
J. Beggs, CIN	1.85

Most Strikeouts per 9 Inn.
K. Higbe, BKN	5.72
J. Schmitz, CHI	5.42
E. Blackwell, CIN	4.63

Innings
H. Pollet, STL	266
D. Koslo, NY	265
J. Sain, BOS	265

Games Pitched
K. Trinkle, NY	48
M. Dickson, STL	47
H. Behrman, BKN	47

	W	L	PCT	GB	R	OR	Batting 2B	3B	HR	BA	SA	SB	Fielding E	DP	FA	Pitching CG	BB	SO	ShO	SV	ERA
STL*	98	58	.628		**712**	545	**265**	56	81	**.265**	**.381**	58	124	167	**.980**	75	493	607	**18**	15	3.01
BKN	96	60	.615	2	701	570	233	**66**	55	.260	.361	**100**	174	154	.972	52	671	**647**	14	**28**	3.05
CHI	82	71	.536	14.5	626	581	223	50	56	.254	.346	43	146	119	.976	59	527	609	14	11	3.24
BOS	81	72	.529	15.5	630	592	238	48	44	.264	.353	60	169	129	.972	74	478	531	10	12	3.37
PHI	69	85	.448	28	560	705	209	40	80	.258	.359	41	148	144	.975	55	542	490	11	23	3.99
CIN	67	87	.435	30	523	570	206	33	65	.239	.327	82	155	**192**	.975	69	**467**	506	16	11	3.07
PIT	63	91	.409	34	552	668	202	52	60	.250	.344	48	184	127	.970	61	541	458	10	6	3.72
NY	61	93	.396	36	612	685	176	37	**121**	.255	.374	46	159	121	.973	48	660	581	8	13	3.92
					4916	4916	1752	382	562	.256	.355	478	1259	1153	.974	493	4379	4429	101	119	3.42

* Defeated Brooklyn in a playoff 2 games to 0.

	POS	Player	AB	BA	HR	RBI	PO	A	E	DP	TC/G	FA	Pitcher	G	IP	W	L	SV	ERA
Bos.	1B	R. York	579	.276	17	119	**1327**	116	8	**154**	9.4	.994	T. Hughson	39	278	20	11	3	2.75
W-104 L-50	2B	B. Doerr	583	.271	18	116	420	483	13	129	6.1	**.986**	B. Ferriss	40	274	25	6	3	3.25
Joe Cronin	SS	J. Pesky	621	.335	2	55	296	479	25	96	5.2	.969	M. Harris	34	223	17	9	0	3.64
	3B	R. Russell	274	.208	6	35	59	137	12	24	3.0	.942	J. Dobson	32	167	13	7	0	3.24
	RF	C. Metkovich	281	.246	4	25	125	3	7	0	1.7	.948	J. Bagby	21	107	7	6	0	3.71
	CF	D. DiMaggio	534	.316	7	73	390	9	6	2	2.9	.985	E. Johnson	29	80	5	4	3	3.71
	LF	T. Williams	514	.342	38	123	325	7	10	2	2.3	.971	B. Klinger	28	57	3	2	9	2.37
	C	H. Wagner	370	.230	6	52	**553**	39	10	3	5.2	.983							
	3B	P. Higgins	200	.275	2	28	52	109	9	14	2.9	.947							
	OF	L. Culberson	179	.313	3	18	87	1	3	0	1.9	.967							
	OF	W. Moses	175	.206	2	17	92	3	2	1	2.2	.979							
Det.	1B	H. Greenberg	523	.277	**44**	**127**	1272	93	15	110	**9.9**	.989	H. Newhouser	37	292	**26**	9	1	**1.94**
W-92 L-62	2B	J. Bloodworth	249	.245	5	36	157	184	9	46	4.9	.974	D. Trout	38	276	17	13	3	2.34
Steve O'Neill	SS	E. Lake	587	.254	8	31	232	391	35	85	4.2	.947	V. Trucks	32	237	14	9	0	3.23
	3B	G. Kell	434	.327	4	41	105*	210*	5	22*	3.0*	.984*	F. Hutchinson	28	207	14	11	2	3.09
	RF	R. Cullenbine	328	.335	15	56	125	12	5	1	1.8	.965	A. Benton	28	141	11	7	1	3.65
	CF	H. Evers	304	.266	4	33	196	2	5	0	2.7	.975	S. Overmire	24	97	5	7	1	4.62
	LF	D. Wakefield	396	.268	12	59	210	6	8	1	2.2	.964							
	C	B. Tebbetts	280	.243	1	34	486	53	10	4	6.3	.982							
	O3	J. Outlaw	299	.261	2	31	101	64	7	4		.959							
	OF	P. Mullin	276	.246	3	35	121	8	7	1	1.8	.949							
	OF	D. Cramer	204	.294	1	26	89	2	0	0	1.8	1.000							
	2B	E. Mayo	202	.252	0	22	96	125	8	28	4.7	.965							
	2B	S. Webb	169	.219	0	17	97	143	7	28	4.9	.972							
N. Y.	1B	N. Etten	323	.232	9	49	717	55	7	80	9.3	.991	S. Chandler	34	257	20	8	2	2.10
W-87 L-67	2B	J. Gordon	376	.210	11	47	281	346	17	87	6.0	.974	B. Bevens	31	250	16	13	0	2.23
Joe McCarthy	SS	P. Rizzuto	471	.257	2	38	267	378	26	97	**5.4**	.961	J. Page	31	136	9	8	3	3.57
W-22 L-13	3B	S. Stirnweiss	487	.251	0	37	66	152	2	18	2.8	.991	R. Gumpert	33	133	11	3	1	2.31
Bill Dickey	RF	T. Henrich	565	.251	19	83	224	10	2	2	5	.992	E. Bonham	18	105	5	8	3	3.70
W-57 L-48	CF	J. DiMaggio	503	.290	25	95	314	15	6	3	2.6	.982	A. Gettel	26	103	6	7	0	2.97
Johnny Neun	LF	C. Keller	538	.275	30	101	324	4	7	0	2.2	.979	J. Murphy	27	45	4	2	7	3.40
W-8 L-6	C	A. Robinson	330	.297	16	64	410	50	8	5	4.9	.983							
	OF	J. Lindell	332	.259	10	40	159	8	3	3	2.3	.982							
	3B	B. Johnson	296	.260	4	35	71	163	11	15	3.3	.955							
Was.	1B	M. Vernon	587	**.353**	8	85	1320	101	15	133	9.8	.990	M. Haefner	33	228	14	11	1	2.85
W-76 L-78	2B	G. Priddy	511	.254	6	58	378	428	**32**	105	6.1	.962	B. Newsom	24	178	11	8	1	2.78
Ossie Bluege	SS	C. Travis	465	.252	1	56	133	196	14	45	4.6	.959	D. Leonard	26	162	10	10	0	3.56
	3B	B. Hitchcock	354	.212	0	25	53	87	12	7	3.3	.921	Scarborough	32	156	7	11	1	4.05
	RF	B. Lewis	582	.292	7	45	304	16	10	5	2.3	.970	S. Hudson	31	142	8	11	1	3.60
	CF	S. Spence	578	.292	16	87	412	15	8	3	2.9	.982	R. Wolff	21	122	5	8	0	2.58
	LF	J. Grace	321	.302	2	31	185	4	8	2	2.7	.959	E. Wynn	17	107	8	5	0	3.11
	C	A. Evans	272	.254	2	30	336	30	13	5	4.7	.966	W. Masterson	29	91	5	6	1	6.01
	UT	S. Robertson	230	.200	6	19	88	132	19	22		.921							
	C	J. Early	189	.201	4	18	246	45	12	7	4.7	.960							
	UT	G. Torres	185	.254	0	13	82	137	11	20		.952							
	OF	J. Heath	166	.283	4	27	92	3	3	0	2.1	.969							
Chi.	1B	H. Trosky	299	.254	2	31	729	33	7	63	9.6	.991	E. Lopat	29	231	13	13	0	2.73
W-74 L-80	2B	D. Kolloway	482	.280	3	53	235	281	15	74	5.9	.972	O. Grove	33	205	8	13	0	3.02
Jimmy Dykes	SS	L. Appling	582	.309	1	55	252	**505**	39	99	5.3	.951	J. Haynes	32	177	7	9	2	3.76
W-10 L-20	3B	D. Lodigiani	155	.245	0	13	41	88	9	4	3.1	.935	E. Smith	24	145	8	11	1	2.85
Ted Lyons	RF	T. Wright	422	.275	7	52	217	5	2	0	2.1	.991	F. Papish	31	138	7	5	0	2.74
W-64 L-60	CF	T. Tucker	438	.288	1	36	276	11	3	1	2.6	.990	E. Caldwell	39	91	13	4	8	2.08
	LF	B. Kennedy	411	.258	5	34	157	10	6	1	2.3	.965	J. Rigney	15	83	5	5	0	4.03
	C	M. Tresh	217	.217	0	21	330	48	2	**13**	4.8	.995	R. Hamner	25	71	2	7	1	4.42
	2B	C. Michaels	291	.268	2	22	185	195	17	51	6.0	.957							
	OF	R. Hodgin	258	.252	0	25	114	3	2	0	2.1	.983							
	OF	W. Platt	247	.251	3	32	130	4	4	1	2.3	.971							
	1B	J. Kuhel	238	.273	4	20	596	38	4	65	10.3	.994							
	C	F. Hayes	179	.212	2	16	199	32	5	4	4.7*	.979							
	OF	W. Moses	168	.274	4	16	84	2	0	0	2.4	1.000							

	POS	Player	AB	BA	HR	RBI	PO	A	E	DP	TC/G	FA	Pitcher	G	IP	W	L	SV	ERA
Cle. W-68 L-86 Lou Boudreau	1B	L. Fleming	306	.278	8	42	607	62	11	60	8.5	.984	B. Feller	48	371	26	15	4	2.18
	2B	D. Meyer	207	.232	0	16	110	150	6	26	4.2	.977	R. Embree	28	200	8	12	0	3.47
	SS	L. Boudreau	515	.293	6	62	315	405	22	94	5.3	.970	A. Reynolds	31	183	11	15	0	3.88
	3B	K. Keltner	398	.241	13	45	112	195	11	18	2.8	.965	S. Gromek	29	154	5	15	4	4.33
	RF	H. Edwards	458	.301	10	54	226	13	8	1	2.0	.968	B. Lemon	32	94	4	5	1	2.49
	CF	P. Seerey	404	.225	26	62	248	4	5	1	2.2	.981	J. Berry	21	37	3	6	1	3.38
	LF	G. Case	484	.225	1	22	226	5	4	0	2.0	.983							
	C	J. Hegan	271	.236	0	17	486	47	5	11	6.2	.991							
	OF	F. Mackiewicz	258	.260	0	16	172	2	3	1	2.5	.983							
	2B	J. Conway	258	.225	0	18	125	131	12	27	5.4	.955							
	2B	R. Mack	171	.205	1	9	118	142	8	37	4.4	.970							
	C	F. Hayes	156	.256	3	18	302	16	6	2	6.5*	.981							
St. L. W-66 L-88 Luke Sewell W-53 L-71 Zack Taylor W-13 L-17	1B	C. Stevens	432	.248	3	27	1020	86	6	98	9.3	.995	J. Kramer	31	195	13	11	0	3.19
	2B	J. Berardino	582	.265	5	68	374	414	23	96	5.7	.972	D. Galehouse	30	180	8	12	0	3.65
	SS	V. Stephens	450	.307	14	64	224	343	30	71	5.3	.950	S. Zoldak	35	170	9	11	2	3.43
	3B	M. Christman	458	.258	1	41	61	171	6	21	3.1	.975	N. Potter	23	145	8	9	0	3.72
	RF	A. Zarilla	371	.259	4	43	236	13	7	6	2.4	.973	T. Shirley	27	140	6	12	0	4.96
	CF	W. Judnich	511	.262	15	72	409	6	2	2	3.0	.995	B. Muncrief	29	115	3	12	0	4.99
	LF	J. Heath	316	.275	12	57	147	5	6	1	1.9	.962	S. Ferens	34	88	2	9	0	4.50
	C	F. Mancuso	262	.240	3	23	298	31	9	3	4.0	.973	T. Ferrick	25	32	4	1	5	2.78
	OF	C. Laabs	264	.261	16	52	151	5	2	2	2.2	.987							
	3B	B. Dillinger	225	.280	0	11	56	98	13	11	3.1	.922							
	32	J. Lucadello	210	.248	1	15	84	102	7	14		.964							
	C	H. Helf	182	.192	6	21	251	51	11	7	4.5	.965							
	OF	G. McQuillen	166	.241	1	12	77	8	2	0	1.8	.977							
	OF	J. Grace	161	.230	1	13	82	6	3	1	2.1	.967							
Phi. W-49 L-105 Connie Mack	1B	G. McQuinn	484	.225	3	35	1098	99	15	107	9.0	.988	P. Marchildon	36	227	13	16	1	3.49
	2B	G. Handley	251	.251	0	21	159	146	17	32	4.7	.947	D. Fowler	32	206	9	16	0	3.28
	SS	P. Suder	455	.281	2	50	151	204	15	39	5.5	.959	B. Savage	40	164	3	15	2	4.06
	3B	H. Majeski	264	.250	1	25	78	159	8	22	3.4	.967	J. Flores	29	155	9	7	1	2.32
	RF	E. Valo	348	.307	1	31	182	7	5	0	2.2	.974	L. Knerr	30	148	3	16	0	5.40
	CF	B. McCosky	308	.354	1	34	207	2	4	0	2.5	.981	L. Harris	34	125	3	14	0	5.24
	LF	S. Chapman	545	.261	20	67	369	13	12	4	2.7	.970	Christopher	30	119	5	7	0	4.30
	C	B. Rosar	424	.283	2	47	532	73	0	9	5.2	1.000							
	OF	T. Stainback	291	.244	0	20	153	5	6	1	2.5	.963							
	SS	J. Wallaesa	194	.196	5	11	111	130	22	31	4.5	.916							
	2B	O. Grimes	191	.262	1	20	98	105	9	30	4.9	.958							
	2B	I. Hall	185	.249	0	19	105	113	6	20	5.6	.973							
	OF	R. Derry	184	.207	0	14	127	3	2	2	2.6	.985							

BATTING AND BASE RUNNING LEADERS

Batting Average
M. Vernon, WAS	.353
T. Williams, BOS	.342
J. Pesky, BOS	.335
G. Kell, DET, PHI	.322
D. DiMaggio, BOS	.316

Slugging Average
T. Williams, BOS	.667
H. Greenberg, DET	.604
C. Keller, NY	.533
J. DiMaggio, NY	.511
H. Edwards, CLE	.509

Home Runs
H. Greenberg, DET	44
T. Williams, BOS	38
C. Keller, NY	30
P. Seerey, CLE	26
J. DiMaggio, NY	25

Total Bases
T. Williams, BOS	343
H. Greenberg, DET	316
M. Vernon, WAS	298
C. Keller, NY	287
S. Spence, WAS	287

Runs Batted In
H. Greenberg, DET	127
T. Williams, BOS	123
R. York, BOS	119
B. Doerr, BOS	116
C. Keller, NY	101

Stolen Bases
G. Case, CLE	28
S. Stirnweiss, NY	18
E. Lake, DET	15
P. Rizzuto, NY	14
D. Kolloway, CHI	14
M. Vernon, WAS	14

Hits
J. Pesky, BOS	208
M. Vernon, WAS	207
L. Appling, CHI	180

Base on Balls
T. Williams, BOS	156
C. Keller, NY	113
E. Lake, DET	103

Home Run Percentage
H. Greenberg, DET	8.4
T. Williams, BOS	7.4
P. Seerey, CLE	6.4

Runs Scored
T. Williams, BOS	142
J. Pesky, BOS	115
E. Lake, DET	105

Doubles
M. Vernon, WAS	51
S. Spence, WAS	50
J. Pesky, BOS	43

Triples
H. Edwards, CLE	16
B. Lewis, WAS	13

PITCHING LEADERS

Winning Percentage
B. Ferriss, BOS	.806
H. Newhouser, DET	.743
S. Chandler, NY	.714
M. Harris, BOS	.654
T. Hughson, BOS	.645

Earned Run Average
H. Newhouser, DET	1.94
S. Chandler, NY	2.10
B. Feller, CLE	2.18
B. Bevens, NY	2.23
D. Trout, DET	2.34

Wins
H. Newhouser, DET	26
B. Feller, CLE	26
B. Ferriss, BOS	25
S. Chandler, NY	20
T. Hughson, BOS	20

Saves
B. Klinger, BOS	9
E. Caldwell, CHI	8
J. Murphy, NY	7
T. Ferrick, CLE, STL	6

Strikeouts
B. Feller, CLE	348
H. Newhouser, DET	275
T. Hughson, BOS	172
V. Trucks, DET	161
D. Trout, DET	151

Complete Games
B. Feller, CLE	36
H. Newhouser, DET	29
B. Ferriss, BOS	26
D. Trout, DET	23
T. Hughson, BOS	21

Fewest Hits per 9 Innings
H. Newhouser, DET	6.62
B. Feller, CLE	6.71
S. Chandler, NY	6.99

Shutouts
B. Feller, CLE	10

Fewest Walks per 9 Innings
T. Hughson, BOS	1.65
E. Lopat, CHI	1.87
B. Ferriss, BOS	2.33

Most Strikeouts per 9 Inn.
H. Newhouser, DET	8.47
B. Feller, CLE	8.43
V. Trucks, DET	6.12

Innings
B. Feller, CLE	371
H. Newhouser, DET	292
T. Hughson, BOS	278

Games Pitched
B. Feller, CLE	48
B. Ferriss, BOS	40
B. Savage, PHi	40

	W	L	PCT	GB	R	OR	2B	3B	HR	BA	SA	SB	E	DP	FA	CG	BB	SO	ShO	SV	ERA
								Batting						Fielding			Pitching				
BOS	104	50	.675		792	594	268	50	109	.271	.402	45	139	165	.977	79	501	667	15	20	3.38
DET	92	62	.597	12	704	567	212	41	108	.258	.374	65	155	138	.974	94	497	896	18	15	3.22
NY	87	67	.565	17	684	547	208	50	136	.248	.387	48	150	174	.975	68	552	653	17	17	3.13
WAS	76	78	.494	28	608	706	260	63	60	.260	.366	51	211	162	.966	71	547	537	8	10	3.74
CHI	74	80	.481	30	562	595	206	44	37	.257	.333	78	175	170	.972	62	508	550	9	16	3.10
CLE	68	86	.442	36	537	637	233	56	79	.245	.356	57	147	147	.975	63	649	789	16	13	3.62
STL	66	88	.429	38	621	711	220	46	84	.251	.356	23	159	157	.974	63	573	574	13	12	3.95
PHI	49	105	.318	55	529	680	220	51	40	.253	.338	39	167	141	.971	61	577	562	10	5	3.90
					5037	5037	1827	401	653	.256	.364	406	1303	1254	.973	561	4404	5228	106	108	3.50

National League 1947

	POS	Player	AB	BA	HR	RBI	PO	A	E	DP	TC/G	FA	Pitcher	G	IP	W	L	SV	ERA
Bkn.	1B	J. Robinson	590	.297	12	48	1323	92	16	144	9.5	.989	R. Branca	43	280	21	12	1	2.67
W-94 L-60	2B	E. Stanky	559	.252	3	53	402	406	12	123	5.6	.985	J. Hatten	42	225	17	8	0	3.63
Clyde Sukeforth	SS	P. Reese	476	.284	12	73	266	441	25	99	5.2	.966	V. Lombardi	33	175	12	11	3	2.99
W-1 L-0	3B	S. Jorgensen	441	.274	5	67	116	235	19	26	2.9	.949	H. Taylor	33	162	10	5	1	3.11
Burt Shotton	RF	D. Walker	529	.306	9	94	261	9	10	0	1.9	.964	H. Gregg	37	104	4	5	1	5.87
W-93 L-60	CF	C. Furillo	437	.295	8	88	287	9	7	3	2.5	.977	H. Behrman	40	92	5	3	8	5.48
	LF	P. Reiser	388	.309	5	46	240	3	3	0	2.3	.988	C. King	29	88	6	5	0	2.77
	C	B. Edwards	471	.295	9	80	592	58	11	11	5.2	.983	H. Casey	46	77	10	4	18	3.99
	OF	G. Hermanski	189	.275	7	39	105	5	2	0	1.7	.982							
	O3	A. Vaughan	126	.325	2	25	56	20	0	3		1.000							
St. L.	1B	S. Musial	587	.312	19	95	1360	77	8	138	9.7	.994	M. Dickson	47	232	13	16	3	3.07
W-89 L-65	2B	Schoendienst	659	.253	3	48	357	404	19	109	5.5	.976	G. Munger	40	224	16	5	3	3.37
Eddie Dyer	SS	M. Marion	540	.272	4	74	329	452	15	104	5.3	.981	H. Brecheen	29	223	16	11	1	3.30
	3B	W. Kurowski	513	.310	27	104	140	250	19	17	2.9	.954	H. Pollet	37	176	9	11	2	4.34
	RF	E. Dusak	328	.284	6	28	178	13	6	2	2.2	.970	A. Brazle	44	168	14	8	4	2.84
	CF	T. Moore	460	.283	7	45	292	6	5	2	2.5	.983	J. Hearn	37	162	12	7	1	3.22
	LF	E. Slaughter	551	.294	10	86	306	15	6	5	2.3	.982	K. Burkhart	34	95	3	6	1	5.21
	C	D. Rice	261	.218	12	44	380	33	8	7	4.5	.981							
	OF	R. Northey	311	.293	15	63	122	8	7	1	1.5	.949							
	C	J. Garagiola	183	.257	5	25	281	23	4	2	4.2	.987							
	OF	J. Medwick	150	.307	4	28	56	3	0	2	1.4	1.000							
Bos.	1B	E. Torgeson	399	.281	16	78	1033	76	18	83	9.6	.984	W. Spahn	40	290	21	10	3	2.33
W-86 L-68	2B	B. Ryan	544	.265	5	69	393	432	23	88	5.7	.973	J. Sain	38	266	21	12	1	3.52
Billy Southworth	SS	D. Culler	214	.248	0	19	106	212	11	31	4.4	.967	R. Barrett	36	211	11	12	1	3.55
	3B	B. Elliott	555	.317	22	113	129	302	20	25	3.0	.956	B. Voiselle	22	131	8	7	0	4.32
	RF	T. Holmes	618	.309	9	53	336	12	4	4	2.4	.989	S. Johnson	36	113	6	8	2	4.23
	CF	J. Hopp	430	.288	2	32	296	2	6	0	2.4	.980							
	LF	B. Rowell	384	.276	5	40	202	4	12	0	2.2	.945							
	C	P. Masi	411	.304	9	50	411	58	5	1	3.9	.989							
	OF	M. McCormick	284	.285	3	36	155	4	3	0	2.1	.981							
	OF	D. Litwhiler	226	.261	7	31	119	2	3	0	1.9	.976							
	1B	F. McCormick	212	.354	2	43	428	26	2	31	9.5	.996							
	SS	N. Fernandez	209	.206	2	21	89	146	17	22	4.1	.933							
N. Y.	1B	J. Mize	586	.302	51	138	1380	117	6	120	9.8	.996	L. Jansen	42	248	21	5	1	3.16
W-81 L-73	2B	B. Rigney	531	.267	17	59	184	229	11	41	5.9	.974	D. Koslo	39	217	15	10	0	4.39
Mel Ott	SS	B. Kerr	547	.287	7	49	270	460	17	77	5.4	.977	M. Kennedy	34	148	9	12	0	4.85
	3B	L. Lohrke	329	.240	11	35	118	187	20	20	2.9	.938	C. Hartung	23	138	9	7	0	4.57
	RF	W. Marshall	587	.291	36	107	334	19	10	6	2.3	.972	K. Trinkle	62	94	8	4	10	3.75
	CF	B. Thomson	545	.283	29	85	330	12	7	2	2.7	.980	H. Iott	20	71	3	8	0	5.93
	LF	S. Gordon	437	.272	13	57	254	12	8	0	2.2	.971							
	C	W. Cooper	515	.305	35	122	560	51	13	8	4.7	.979							
	OF	L. Gearhart	179	.246	6	17	94	4	4	1	2.3	.961							
	2B	M. Witek	160	.219	3	17	102	125	4	27	5.8	.983							
	C	E. Lombardi	110	.282	4	21	86	11	2	2	4.1	.980							
Cin.	1B	B. Young	364	.283	14	79	730	56	8	66	8.5	.990	E. Blackwell	33	273	22	8	0	2.47
W-73 L-81	2B	B. Zientara	418	.258	2	24	243	247	12	53	5.0	.976	Vander Meer	30	186	9	14	0	4.40
Johnny Neun	SS	E. Miller	545	.268	19	87	295	445	21	88	5.0	.972	K. Peterson	37	152	6	13	2	4.25
	3B	G. Hatton	524	.281	16	77	143	248	26	18	3.1	.938	B. Lively	38	123	4	7	0	4.68
	RF	F. Baumholtz	643	.283	5	45	282	18	7	2	2.0	.977	B. Walters	20	122	8	8	0	5.75
	CF	B. Haas	482	.286	3	67	170	2	8	0	2.6	.956	E. Erautt	36	119	4	9	0	5.07
	LF	A. Galan	392	.314	6	61	246	2	3	0	2.1	.988	Raffensberger	19	107	6	5	1	4.13
	C	R. Lamanno	413	.257	5	50	556	62	9	6	5.8	.986	H. Gumbert	46	90	10	10	10	3.89
	2B	B. Adams	217	.272	4	20	172	177	12	46	5.2	.967							
	OF	E. Lukon	200	.205	11	33	103	4	0	2	1.0	1.000							
	C	R. Mueller	192	.250	6	33	221	28	4	2	4.6	.984							
	OF	T. Tatum	176	.273	1	16	117	6	0	3	2.5	1.000							
	OF	C. Vollmer	155	.219	1	13	125	2	2	0	2.0	.984							

	POS	Player	AB	BA	HR	RBI	PO	A	E	DP	TC/G	FA	Pitcher	G	IP	W	L	SV	ERA
Chi.	1B	E. Waitkus	514	.292	2	35	1161	101	8	109	10.1	.994	J. Schmitz	38	207	13	18	4	3.22
	2B	D. Johnson	402	.259	3	26	255	291	17	65	5.2	.970	D. Lade	34	187	11	10	0	3.94
W-69 L-85	SS	L. Merullo	373	.241	0	29	219	322	29	77	5.3	.949	H. Borowy	40	183	8	12	2	4.38
Charlie Grimm	3B	P. Lowrey	448	.281	5	37	83	194	16	21	3.2	.945	P. Erickson	40	174	7	12	1	4.34
	RF	B. Nicholson	487	.244	26	75	281	7	3	1	2.1	.990	H. Wyse	37	142	6	9	1	4.31
	CF	A. Pafko	513	.302	13	66	327	9	5	3	2.7	.985	B. Chipman	32	135	7	6	0	3.68
	LF	P. Cavarretta	459	.314	2	63	203	11	5	3	2.2	.977	E. Kush	47	91	8	3	5	3.36
	C	B. Scheffing	363	.264	5	50	379	52	7	4	4.5	.984	C. Passeau	19	63	2	6	2	6.25
	3B	S. Hack	240	.271	0	12	64	136	8	11	3.2	.962							
	C	McCullough	234	.252	3	30	280	35	5	3	5.0	.984							
	S2	B. Sturgeon	232	.254	0	21	135	192	6	42		.982							
	OF	C. Aberson	140	.279	4	20	62	7	6	1	1.9	.920							
Phi.	1B	H. Schultz	403	.223	6	35	986	67	7	92	9.3	.993	D. Leonard	32	235	17	12	0	2.68
	2B	E. Verban	540	.285	0	42	450	453	17	111	5.9	.982	S. Rowe	31	196	14	10	1	4.32
W-62 L-92	SS	S. Newsome	310	.229	2	22	131	247	12	60	4.6	.969	O. Judd	32	147	4	15	0	4.60
Ben Chapman	3B	L. Handley	277	.253	0	42	87	144	6	8	2.9	.975	Heintzelman	24	136	7	10	1	4.04
	RF	J. Wyrostek	454	.273	5	51	261	11	8	2	2.2	.971	T. Hughes	29	127	4	11	1	3.47
	CF	H. Walker	488	.371*	1	41	350	15	13*	2	3.0	.966	B. Donnelly	38	121	4	6	5	2.98
	LF	D. Ennis	541	.275	12	81	320	12	7	2	2.5	.979	A. Jurisich	34	118	1	7	3	4.94
	C	A. Seminick	337	.252	13	50	438	53	11	6	4.7	.978	C. Schanz	34	102	2	4	2	4.16
	3B	J. Tabor	251	.235	4	31	68	96	15	8	2.7	.916	F. Schmidt	29	77	5	8	0	4.70
	SS	R. LaPointe	211	.308	1	15	82	158	11	25	4.6	.956							
	1C	A. Lakeman	182	.159	6	19	286	18	4	16		.987							
	OF	B. Adams	182	.247	2	15	78	5	4	2	1.7	.954							
	C	D. Padgett	158	.316	0	24	111	16	5	1	3.4	.962							
Pit.	1B	H. Greenberg	402	.249	25	74	983	79	9	85	9.0	.992	K. Higbe	46	225	11	17	5	3.72
	2B	J. Bloodworth	316	.250	7	48	222	206	9	56	5.0	.979	Ostermueller	26	183	12	10	0	3.84
W-62 L-92	SS	B. Cox	529	.274	15	54	220	388	20	63	4.9	.968	E. Bonham	33	150	11	8	3	3.85
Billy Herman	3B	F. Gustine	616	.297	9	67	198	330	31	35	3.6	.945	P. Roe	38	144	4	15	2	5.25
W-61 L-92	RF	W. Westlake	407	.273	17	69	239	8	3	0	2.3	.988	R. Sewell	24	121	6	4	0	3.57
Bill Burwell	CF	J. Russell	478	.253	8	51	343	6	7	3	3.0	.980	J. Bagby	37	116	5	4	0	4.67
W-1 L-0	LF	R. Kiner	565	.313	51	127	390	8	7	1	2.7	.983	M. Queen	14	74	3	7	0	4.01
	C	D. Howell	214	.276	4	25	272	30	8	2	4.2	.974							
	OF	C. Rikard	324	.287	4	32	177	2	4	0	2.3	.978							
	C	C. Kluttz	232	.302	6	42	247	55	4	7	4.4	.987							
	2B	E. Basinski	161	.199	4	17	116	130	7	34	4.5	.972							
	1B	E. Fletcher	157	.242	1	22	324	25	5	28	7.1	.986							

BATTING AND BASE RUNNING LEADERS

Batting Average
H. Walker, PHI, STL	.363
B. Elliott, BOS	.317
P. Cavarretta, CHI	.314
R. Kiner, PIT	.313
S. Musial, STL	.312

Slugging Average
R. Kiner, PIT	.639
J. Mize, NY	.614
W. Cooper, NY	.586
W. Kurowski, STL	.544
W. Marshall, NY	.528

Home Runs
R. Kiner, PIT	51
J. Mize, NY	51
W. Marshall, NY	36
W. Cooper, NY	35
B. Thomson, NY	29

Total Bases
R. Kiner, PIT	361
J. Mize, NY	360
W. Marshall, NY	310
W. Cooper, NY	302
S. Musial, STL	296

Runs Batted In
J. Mize, NY	138
R. Kiner, PIT	127
W. Cooper, NY	122
B. Elliott, BOS	113
W. Marshall, NY	107

Stolen Bases
J. Robinson, BKN	29
P. Reiser, BKN	14
J. Hopp, BOS	13
H. Walker, PHI, STL	13
E. Torgeson, BOS	11

Hits
T. Holmes, BOS	191
H. Walker, PHI, STL	186
S. Musial, STL	183
F. Gustine, PIT	183

Base on Balls
H. Greenberg, PIT	104
P. Reese, BKN	104
E. Stanky, BKN	103

Home Run Percentage
R. Kiner, PIT	9.0
J. Mize, NY	8.7
W. Cooper, NY	6.8

Runs Scored
J. Mize, NY	137
J. Robinson, BKN	125
R. Kiner, PIT	118

Doubles
E. Miller, CIN	38
B. Elliott, BOS	35
C. Ryan, BOS	33
T. Holmes, BOS	33

Triples
H. Walker, PHI, STL	16
E. Slaughter, STL	13
S. Musial, STL	13

PITCHING LEADERS

Winning Percentage
L. Jansen, NY	.808
G. Munger, STL	.762
E. Blackwell, CIN	.733
J. Hatten, BKN	.680
W. Spahn, BOS	.677

Earned Run Average
W. Spahn, BOS	2.33
E. Blackwell, CIN	2.47
R. Branca, BKN	2.67
D. Leonard, PHI	2.68
M. Dickson, STL	3.07

Wins
E. Blackwell, CIN	22
L. Jansen, NY	21
W. Spahn, BOS	21
R. Branca, BKN	21
J. Sain, BOS	21

Saves
H. Casey, BKN	18
H. Gumbert, CIN	10
K. Trinkle, NY	10
H. Behrman, BKN, PIT	8

Strikeouts
E. Blackwell, CIN	193
R. Branca, BKN	148
J. Sain, BOS	132
G. Munger, STL	123
W. Spahn, BOS	123

Complete Games
E. Blackwell, CIN	23
J. Sain, BOS	22
W. Spahn, BOS	22
L. Jansen, NY	20
D. Leonard, PHI	19

Fewest Hits per 9 Innings
H. Taylor, BKN	7.22
E. Blackwell, CIN	7.48
W. Spahn, BOS	7.61

Shutouts
W. Spahn, BOS	7
G. Munger, STL	6
E. Blackwell, CIN	6

Fewest Walks per 9 Innings
L. Jansen, NY	2.07
S. Rowe, PHI	2.07
D. Leonard, PHI	2.18

Most Strikeouts per 9 Inn.
E. Blackwell, CIN	6.36
G. Munger, STL	4.93
R. Branca, BKN	4.76

Innings
W. Spahn, BOS	290
R. Branca, BKN	280
E. Blackwell, CIN	273

Games Pitched
K. Trinkle, NY	62
K. Higbe, BKN, PIT	50
H. Behrman, BKN, PIT	50

	W	L	PCT	GB	R	OR	2B	3B	Batting HR	BA	SA	SB	E	Fielding DP	FA	CG	BB	Pitching SO	ShO	SV	ERA
BKN	94	60	.610		774	668	241	50	83	.272	.384	88	129	164	.978	47	626	592	14	34	3.82
STL	89	65	.578	5	780	634	235	65	115	.270	.401	28	128	169	.979	65	495	642	13	20	3.53
BOS	86	68	.558	8	701	622	265	42	85	.275	.390	58	153	124	.974	74	453	486	14	13	3.62
NY	81	73	.526	13	830	761	220	48	221	.271	.454	29	155	136	.974	58	590	553	6	14	4.44
CIN	73	81	.474	21	681	755	242	43	95	.259	.375	46	138	134	.977	54	589	633	13	13	4.41
CHI	69	85	.448	25	567	722	231	48	71	.259	.361	22	150	159	.975	46	618	571	8	15	4.10
PHI	62	92	.403	32	589	687	210	52	60	.258	.352	60	152	140	.974	70	501	514	8	14	3.96
PIT	62	92	.403	32	744	817	216	44	156	.261	.406	30	149	131	.975	44	592	501	9	13	4.68
					5666	5666	1860	392	886	.265	.390	361	1154	1157	.976	458	4464	4492	85	136	4.07

American League 1947

	POS	Player	AB	BA	HR	RBI	PO	A	E	DP	TC/G	FA	Pitcher	G	IP	W	L	SV	ERA
N. Y. W-97 L-57 Bucky Harris	1B	G. McQuinn	517	.304	13	80	1198	93	8	120	9.1	.994	A. Reynolds	34	242	19	8	2	3.20
	2B	S. Stirnweiss	571	.256	5	41	337	402	13	107	5.1	.983	S. Shea	27	179	14	5	1	3.07
	SS	P. Rizzuto	549	.273	2	60	340	450	25	111	5.4	.969	B. Bevens	28	165	7	13	0	3.82
	3B	B. Johnson	494	.285	10	95	136	204	17	12	2.7	.952	J. Page	56	141	14	8	17	2.48
	RF	T. Henrich	550	.287	16	98	278	13	5	2	2.2	.983	S. Chandler	17	128	9	5	0	2.46
	CF	J. DiMaggio	534	.315	20	97	316	2	1	0	2.3	.997	B. Newsom	17	116	7	5	0	2.80
	LF	J. Lindell	476	.275	11	67	308	6	7	1	2.7	.978	V. Raschi	15	105	7	2	0	3.87
	C	A. Robinson	252	.270	5	36	346	38	1	3	5.2	.997	K. Drews	30	92	6	6	1	4.91
	CO	Y. Berra	293	.280	11	54	307	18	9	5		.973							
	OF	C. Keller	151	.238	13	36	85	2	3	0	2.1	.967							
Det. W-85 L-69 Steve O'Neill	1B	R. Cullenbine	464	.224	24	78	1184	139	15	111	9.7	.989	H. Newhouser	40	285	17	17	2	2.87
	2B	E. Mayo	535	.279	6	48	326	365	12	80	5.0	.983	F. Hutchinson	33	220	18	10	2	3.03
	SS	E. Lake	602	.211	12	46	268	441	43	94	4.8	.943	D. Trout	32	186	10	11	2	3.48
	3B	G. Kell	588	.320	5	93	167	333	20	25	3.4	.962	V. Trucks	36	181	10	12	4	4.53
	RF	P. Mullin	398	.256	15	62	229	10	3	2	2.3	.988	S. Overmire	28	141	11	5	0	3.77
	CF	H. Evers	460	.296	10	67	354	10	8	2	3.0	.978	A. Benton	31	133	6	7	7	4.40
	LF	D. Wakefield	368	.283	8	51	197	10	11	2	2.2	.950	A. Houtteman	23	111	7	2	0	3.42
	C	B. Swift	279	.251	1	21	401	45	5	6	4.6	.989	H. White	35	85	4	5	2	3.61
	OF	V. Wertz	333	.288	6	44	160	6	6	0	2.1	.965							
	C	H. Wagner	191	.288	5	33	275	25	3	3	4.3	.990							
	OF	D. Cramer	157	.268	2	30	79	3	3	0	2.4	.965							
Bos. W-83 L-71 Joe Cronin	1B	J. Jones	404	.235	16	76	1018*	73	10	11	10.1*	.991	J. Dobson	33	229	18	8	1	2.95
	2B	B. Doerr	561	.258	17	95	376	466	16	118	5.9	.981	B. Ferriss	33	218	12	11	0	4.04
	SS	J. Pesky	638	.324	0	39	251	391	16	90	4.9	.976	T. Hughson	29	189	12	11	0	3.33
	3B	S. Dente	168	.232	0	11	40	83	8	11	2.8	.939	D. Galehouse	21	149	11	7	0	3.32
	RF	S. Mele	453	.302	12	73	233	10	2	1	2.1	.992	E. Johnson	45	142	12	11	8	2.97
	CF	D. DiMaggio	513	.283	8	71	413	19	10	4	3.3	.977	H. Dorish	41	136	7	8	2	4.70
	LF	T. Williams	528	.343	32	114	347	10	9	2	2.3	.975							
	C	B. Tebbetts	291	.299	1	28	332	50	10*	6	4.4	.974							
	OF	W. Moses	255	.275	2	27	109	2	3	0	2.0	.974							
	3S	E. Pellagrini	231	.203	4	19	73	142	14	17		.939							
	1B	R. York	184	.212	6	27	395	36	2	45*	9.0	.995*							
	C	R. Partee	169	.231	0	16	207	26	6	4	4.4	.975							
Cle. W-80 L-74 Lou Boudreau	1B	E. Robinson	318	.245	14	52	800	55	5	79	9.9	.994	B. Feller	42	299	20	11	3	2.68
	2B	J. Gordon	562	.272	29	93	341	466	18	110	5.3	.978	D. Black	30	191	10	12	0	3.92
	SS	L. Boudreau	538	.307	4	67	305	475	14	120	5.4	.982	B. Lemon	37	167	11	5	3	3.44
	3B	K. Keltner	541	.257	11	76	156	266	12	29	2.9	.972	R. Embree	27	163	8	10	0	3.15
	RF	H. Edwards	393	.260	15	59	199	3	2	0	2.0	.990	A. Gettel	31	149	11	10	0	4.01
	CF	C. Metkovich	473	.254	5	40	349	2	4	2	3.0	.989	B. Stephens	31	92	5	10	1	4.01
	LF	D. Mitchell	493	.316	1	34	252	8	6	1	2.3	.977	E. Klieman	58	92	5	4	17	3.03
	C	J. Hegan	378	.249	4	42	566	54	7	14	4.7	.989	S. Gromek	29	84	3	5	4	3.74
	OF	H. Peck	392	.293	8	44	166	5	3	3	1.8	.983	M. Harder	15	80	6	4	0	4.50
	1B	L. Fleming	281	.242	4	43	662	63	8	78	9.5	.989							
	OF	P. Seerey	216	.171	11	29	105	7	5	1	1.7	.957							
Phi. W-78 L-76 Connie Mack	1B	F. Fain	461	.291	7	71	1141	101	19	118	9.6	.985	P. Marchildon	35	277	19	9	0	3.22
	2B	P. Suder	528	.241	5	60	304	413	10	94	5.2	.986	D. Fowler	36	227	12	11	0	2.81
	SS	E. Joost	540	.206	13	64	370	452	38	100	5.7	.956	B. McCahan	29	165	10	5	0	3.32
	3B	H. Majeski	479	.280	8	72	160	263	5	28	3.2	.988	J. Coleman	32	160	6	12	1	4.32
	RF	E. Valo	370	.300	5	36	205	9	6	0	2.1	.973	J. Flores	28	151	4	13	0	3.39
	CF	S. Chapman	551	.252	14	83	428	16	6	2	3.1	.987	B. Savage	44	146	8	10	2	3.76
	LF	B. McCosky	546	.328	1	52	346	8	6	2	2.6	.983	C. Scheib	21	116	4	6	0	5.04
	C	B. Rosar	359	.259	1	33	406	70	2	12	4.7	.996	Christopher	44	81	10	7	12	2.90
	OF	G. Binks	333	.258	2	34	157	8	6	1	2.3	.965							
	C	M. Guerra	209	.215	0	18	203	36	9	5	4.0	.964							

POS	Player	AB	BA	HR	RBI	PO	A	E	DP	TC/G	FA	Pitcher	G	IP	W	L	SV	ERA
Chi. W-70 L-84 Ted Lyons																		
1B	R. York	400	.243	15	64	932	71	5	104*	9.9	.995*	E. Lopat	31	253	16	13	0	2.81
2B	D. Kolloway	485	.278	2	35	274	306	23	76	6.1	.962	F. Papish	38	199	12	12	3	3.26
SS	L. Appling	503	.306	8	49	232	422	35	86	5.3	.949	J. Haynes	29	182	14	6	0	2.42
3B	F. Baker	371	.264	0	22	84	253	7	28	3.4	.980	O. Grove	25	136	6	8	0	4.44
RF	B. Kennedy	428	.262	6	48	204	8	7	3	2.1	.968	B. Gillespie	25	118	5	8	0	4.73
CF	D. Philley	551	.258	2	45	355	9	5	2	2.8	.986	E. Harrist	33	94	3	8	5	3.56
LF	T. Wright	401	.324	4	54	198	6	6	1	2.1	.971	T. Lee	21	87	3	7	1	4.47
C	M. Tresh	274	.241	0	20	313	38	9	10	4.0	.975	P. Gebrian	27	66	2	3	5	4.48
23	C. Michaels	355	.273	3	34	208	264	15	61		.969	Maltzberger	33	64	1	4	5	3.39
OF	T. Tucker	254	.236	1	17	171	5	4	2	2.8	.978	E. Caldwell	40	54	1	4	8	3.64
C	G. Dickey	211	.223	1	27	285	35	5	5	4.1	.985							
SO	J. Wallaesa	205	.195	7	32	129	95	5	22		.978							
OF	R. Hodgin	180	.294	1	24	99	2	1	0	2.5	.990							
1B	J. Jones	171	.240	3	20	444*	31	6	49	11.2*	.988							
Was. W-64 L-90 Ossie Bluege																		
1B	M. Vernon	600	.265	7	85	1299	105	19	123	9.2	.987	W. Masterson	35	253	12	16	1	3.13
2B	G. Priddy	505	.214	3	49	382	405	16	89	5.5	.980	E. Wynn	33	247	17	15	0	3.64
SS	M. Christman	374	.222	1	33	203	291	11	75	4.8	.978	M. Haefner	31	193	10	14	1	3.64
3B	E. Yost	428	.238	0	14	125	198	14	11	3.0	.958	Scarborough	33	161	6	13	0	3.41
RF	B. Lewis	506	.261	6	48	259	11	9	2	2.1	.968	S. Hudson	20	106	6	9	0	5.60
CF	S. Spence	506	.279	16	73	404	12	7	3	3.0	.984	B. Newsom	14	84	4	6	0	4.09
LF	J. Grace	234	.248	3	17	162	4	4	0	2.5	.976	T. Ferrick	31	60	1	7	9	3.15
C	A. Evans	319	.241	2	23	389	48	5	14	4.7	.989							
OF	S. Robertson	266	.233	1	23	126	5	7	1	2.5	.949							
3B	C. Travis	204	.216	1	10	28	68	7	6	2.6	.932							
OF	T. McBride	166	.271	0	15	103	2	3	0	2.1	.972							
St. L. W-59 L-95 Muddy Ruel																		
1B	W. Judnich	500	.258	18	64	1067	76	13	118	9.0	.989	J. Kramer	33	199	11	16	1	4.97
2B	J. Berardino	306	.261	1	20	242	221	11	61	5.5	.977	E. Kinder	34	194	8	15	1	4.49
SS	V. Stephens	562	.279	15	83	283	494	24	113	5.4	.958	F. Sanford	34	187	7	16	4	3.71
3B	B. Dillinger	571	.294	3	37	169	265	19	21	3.3	.958	B. Muncrief	31	176	8	14	0	4.90
RF	A. Zarilla	380	.224	3	38	209	6	3	0	2.0	.986	S. Zoldak	35	171	9	10	1	3.47
CF	P. Lehner	483	.248	7	48	344	1	7	0	2.8	.980	C. Fannin	26	146	6	8	1	3.58
LF	J. Heath	491	.251	27	85	297	7	4	4	2.2	.987	N. Potter	32	123	4	10	2	4.04
C	L. Moss	274	.157	6	27	362	43	7	6	4.3	.983							
OF	R. Coleman	343	.259	2	30	174	7	3	4	2.0	.984							
UT	B. Hitchcock	275	.222	1	28	209	190	14	45		.966							
C	J. Early	214	.224	3	19	301	43	4	5	4.1	.989							

BATTING AND BASE RUNNING LEADERS

Batting Average
T. Williams, BOS	.343
B. McCosky, PHI	.328
J. Pesky, BOS	.324
T. Wright, CHI	.324
G. Kell, DET	.320

Slugging Average
T. Williams, BOS	.634
J. DiMaggio, NY	.522
J. Gordon, CLE	.496
T. Henrich, NY	.485
J. Heath, STL	.485

Home Runs
T. Williams, BOS	32
J. Gordon, CLE	29
J. Heath, STL	27
R. Cullenbine, DET	24
R. York, BOS, CHI	21

Total Bases
T. Williams, BOS	335
J. DiMaggio, NY	279
J. Gordon, CLE	279
T. Henrich, NY	267
J. Pesky, BOS	250

Runs Batted In
T. Williams, BOS	114
T. Henrich, NY	98
J. DiMaggio, NY	97
J. Jones, BOS, CHI	96
B. Johnson, NY	95
B. Doerr, BOS	95

Stolen Bases
B. Dillinger, STL	34
D. Philley, CHI	21
M. Vernon, WAS	12
J. Pesky, BOS	12

Hits
J. Pesky, BOS	207
G. Kell, DET	188
T. Williams, BOS	181

Base on Balls
T. Williams, BOS	162
R. Cullenbine, DET	137
E. Lake, DET	120

Home Run Percentage
T. Williams, BOS	6.1
J. Heath, STL	5.5
R. Cullenbine, DET	5.2

Runs Scored
T. Williams, BOS	125
T. Henrich, NY	109
J. Pesky, BOS	106

Doubles
L. Boudreau, CLE	45
T. Williams, BOS	40
T. Henrich, NY	35
J. DiMaggio, NY	31

Triples
T. Henrich, NY	13
M. Vernon, WAS	12
D. Philley, CHI	11

PITCHING LEADERS

Winning Percentage
A. Reynolds, NY	.704
J. Dobson, BOS	.692
P. Marchildon, PHI	.679
B. Feller, CLE	.645
F. Hutchinson, DET	.643

Earned Run Average
S. Chandler, NY	2.46
B. Feller, CLE	2.68
D. Fowler, PHI	2.81
E. Lopat, CHI	2.81
H. Newhouser, DET	2.87

Wins
B. Feller, CLE	20
A. Reynolds, NY	19
P. Marchildon, PHI	19
J. Dobson, BOS	18
F. Hutchinson, DET	18

Saves
J. Page, NY	17
E. Klieman, CLE	17
Christopher, PHI	12
T. Ferrick, WAS	9
E. Johnson, BOS	8
E. Caldwell, CHI	8

Strikeouts
B. Feller, CLE	196
H. Newhouser, DET	176
W. Masterson, WAS	135
A. Reynolds, NY	129
P. Marchildon, PHI	128

Complete Games
H. Newhouser, DET	24
E. Lopat, CHI	22
E. Wynn, WAS	22
P. Marchildon, PHI	21
B. Feller, CLE	20

Fewest Hits per 9 Innings
S. Shea, NY	6.40
B. Feller, CLE	6.92
S. Chandler, NY	7.03

Shutouts
B. Feller, CLE	5
M. Haefner, WAS	4
A. Reynolds, NY	4
W. Masterson, WAS	4

Fewest Walks per 9 Innings
D. Galehouse, BOS, STL	2.48
F. Hutchinson, DET	2.50
E. Lopat, CHI	2.60

Most Strikeouts per 9 Inn.
B. Feller, CLE	5.90
T. Hughson, BOS	5.66
H. Newhouser, DET	5.56

Innings
B. Feller, CLE	299
H. Newhouser, DET	285
P. Marchildon, PHI	277

Games Pitched
E. Klieman, CLE	58
J. Page, NY	56
E. Johnson, BOS	45

	W	L	PCT	GB	R	OR	Batting 2B	3B	HR	BA	SA	SB	Fielding E	DP	FA	Pitching CG	BB	SO	ShO	SV	ERA
NY	97	57	.630		**794**	**568**	230	**72**	**115**	**.271**	**.407**	27	109	151	.981	73	628	**691**	14	21	**3.39**
DET	85	69	.552	12	714	642	**234**	42	103	.258	.377	52	155	142	.975	**77**	**531**	648	**15**	18	3.57
BOS	83	71	.539	14	720	669	206	54	103	.265	.382	41	137	172	.977	64	575	586	13	19	3.81
CLE	80	74	.519	17	687	588	**234**	51	112	.259	.385	29	**104**	178	**.983**	55	628	590	13	**29**	3.44
PHI	78	76	.506	19	633	614	218	52	61	.252	.349	37	143	161	.976	70	597	493	12	15	3.51
CHI	70	84	.455	27	553	661	211	41	53	.256	.342	**91**	155	**180**	.975	47	603	522	11	27	3.64
WAS	64	90	.416	33	496	675	186	48	42	.241	.321	53	143	151	.976	67	579	551	**15**	12	3.97
STL	59	95	.383	38	564	744	189	52	90	.241	.350	69	134	169	.977	50	604	552	7	13	4.33
					5161	5161	1708	412	679	.256	.364	399	1080	1304	.977	503	4745	4633	100	154	3.71

National League 1948

	POS	Player	AB	BA	HR	RBI	PO	A	E	DP	TC/G	FA	Pitcher	G	IP	W	L	SV	ERA
Bos. W-91 L-62 Billy Southworth	1B	E. Torgeson	438	.253	10	67	1069	81	8	85	9.0	.993	J. Sain	42	315	24	15	1	2.60
	2B	E. Stanky	247	.320	2	29	168	202	7	45	5.7	.981	W. Spahn	36	257	15	12	1	3.71
	SS	A. Dark	543	.322	3	48	253	393	25	66	5.0	.963	B. Voiselle	37	216	13	13	2	3.63
	3B	B. Elliott	540	.283	23	100	**146**	298	26	18	3.1	.945	V. Bickford	33	146	11	5	1	3.27
	RF	T. Holmes	585	.325	6	61	283	8	5	4	2.2	.983	R. Barrett	34	128	7	8	0	3.65
	CF	M. McCormick	343	.303	1	39	187	7	5	3	2.0	.975	B. Hogue	40	86	8	2	2	3.23
	LF	J. Heath	364	.319	20	76	223	6	2	2	2.2	**.991**	C. Shoun	36	74	5	1	4	4.01
	C	P. Masi	376	.253	5	44	458	39	6	5	4.6	.988							
	OF	J. Russell	322	.264	9	54	246	3	2	0	3.0	.992							
	OF	C. Conatser	224	.277	3	23	146	3	4	1	2.0	.974							
	2S	S. Sisti	221	.244	0	21	140	173	14	32		.957							
	C	B. Salkeld	198	.242	8	28	254	32	3	5	4.9	.990							
	1B	F. McCormick	180	.250	4	34	343	33	5	30	7.6	.987							
St. L. W-85 L-69 Eddie Dyer	1B	N. Jones	481	.254	10	81	1148	63	17	98	9.6	.986	M. Dickson	42	252	12	16	1	4.14
	2B	R. Schoendienst	408	.272	4	36	230	269	10	57	5.3	.980	H. Brecheen	33	233	20	7	1	**2.24**
	SS	M. Marion	567	.252	4	43	263	445	19	80	5.1	**.974**	H. Pollet	36	186	13	8	0	4.54
	3B	D. Lang	323	.269	4	31	81	188	10	13	2.9	.964	G. Munger	39	166	10	11	0	4.50
	RF	E. Slaughter	549	.321	11	90	330	9	10	1	2.4	.971	A. Brazle	42	156	10	6	1	3.80
	CF	T. Moore	207	.232	4	18	131	2	1	0	1.9	.993	T. Wilks	57	131	6	6	13	2.62
	LF	S. Musial	611	.376	39	131	347	10	7	3	2.3	.981	J. Hearn	34	90	8	6	1	4.22
	C	D. Rice	290	.197	4	34	447	46	2	5	5.0	**.996**							
	UT	E. Dusak	311	.209	6	19	191	80	5	14		.982							
	OF	R. Northey	246	.321	13	64	85	2	1	0	1.3	.989							
	2S	R. LaPointe	222	.225	0	15	142	158	12	36		.962							
	3B	W. Kurowski	220	.214	2	33	55	100	10	7	2.5	.939							
Bkn. W-84 L-70 Leo Durocher W-37 L-38 Burt Shotton W-47 L-32	1B	G. Hodges	481	.249	11	70	830	60	13	85	9.4	.986	R. Barney	44	247	15	13	0	3.10
	2B	J. Robinson	574	.296	12	85	308	315	13	80	5.5	**.980**	R. Branca	36	216	14	9	1	3.51
	SS	P. Reese	566	.274	9	75	**335**	453	31	93	5.5	.962	J. Hatten	42	209	13	10	0	3.58
	3B	B. Cox	237	.249	3	15	51	107	7	7	2.4	.958	P. Roe	34	178	12	8	2	2.63
	RF	G. Hermanski	400	.290	15	60	225	13	7	1	2.1	.971	E. Palica	41	125	6	6	3	4.45
	CF	C. Furillo	364	.297	4	44	274	13	5	2	2.8	.983	H. Behrman	34	91	5	4	7	4.05
	LF	M. Rackley	281	.327	0	15	143	7	8	1	2.1	.949	W. Ramsdell	27	50	4	4	4	5.19
	C	R. Campanella	279	.258	9	45	413	45	9	12	6.0	.981							
	UT	B. Edwards	286	.276	8	54	264	43	12	2		.962							
	23	E. Miksis	221	.213	2	16	122	143	9	19		.967							
	OF	D. Whitman	165	.291	0	20	93	3	1	0	2.0	.990							
	OF	G. Shuba	161	.267	4	32	87	1	6	1	1.7	.936							
	OF	D. Snider	160	.244	5	21	87	5	1	0	2.0	.989							
	1B	P. Ward	146	.260	1	21	268	20	3	21	7.7	.990							
	3B	T. Brown	145	.241	2	20	43	60	7	7	2.6	.962							
	OF	A. Vaughan	123	.244	3	22	47	4	0	0	2.0	1.000							
Pit. W-83 L-71 Billy Meyer	1B	E. Stevens	429	.254	10	69	1021	83	4	94	9.5	**.996**	B. Chesnes	25	194	14	6	0	3.57
	2B	D. Murtaugh	514	.290	1	71	**375**	412	17	**95**	5.5	.979	E. Riddle	28	191	12	10	1	3.49
	SS	S. Rojek	641	.290	4	51	262	**475**	29	91	4.9	.962	V. Lombardi	38	163	10	9	4	3.70
	3B	F. Gustine	449	.267	9	42	119	256	21	21	3.3	.947	K. Higbe	56	158	8	7	10	3.36
	RF	D. Walker	408	.316	2	54	168	4	4	0	1.6	.977	E. Bonham	23	136	6	3	4	3.80
	CF	W. Westlake	428	.285	17	65	274	8	7	2	2.3	.976	Ostermueller	23	134	8	11	0	4.42
	LF	R. Kiner	555	.265	**40**	123	382	6	10	1	2.6	.975	R. Sewell	21	122	13	3	0	3.48
	C	Fitz Gerald	262	.267	1	35	338	36	15	4	4.1	.961	E. Singleton	38	92	4	6	2	4.97
	OF	J. Hopp	392	.278	1	31	192	3	0	1	2.4	1.000							
	C	C. Kluttz	271	.221	4	20	298	54	8	8	4.0	.978							
	3B	E. Bockman	176	.239	4	23	50	100	6	9	3.1	.962							
	1O	M. West	146	.178	8	21	209	20	2	14		.991							

	POS	Player	AB	BA	HR	RBI	PO	A	E	DP	TC/G	FA	Pitcher	G	IP	W	L	SV	ERA
N. Y. W-78 L-76 Mel Ott W-37 L-38 Leo Durocher W-41 L-38	1B	J. Mize	560	.289	40	125	1359	111	13	114	9.8	.991	L. Jansen	42	277	18	12	2	3.61
	2B	B. Rigney	424	.264	10	43	258	275	18	48	5.2	.967	S. Jones	55	201	16	8	5	3.35
	SS	B. Kerr	496	.240	0	46	269	456	25	72	5.2	.967	R. Poat	39	158	11	10	0	4.34
	3B	S. Gordon	521	.299	30	107	126	220	19	19	3.2	.948	C. Hartung	36	153	8	8	1	4.75
	RF	W. Marshall	537	.272	14	86	266	16	5	2	2.0	.983	D. Koslo	35	149	8	10	3	3.87
	CF	W. Lockman	584	.286	18	59	388	6	5	0	2.8	.987	M. Kennedy	25	114	3	9	0	4.01
	LF	B. Thomson	471	.248	16	63	313	10	10	2	2.7	.970	A. Hansen	36	100	5	3	1	2.97
	C	W. Cooper	290	.266	16	54	307	21	7	3	4.2	.979	K. Trinkle	53	71	4	5	7	3.18
	32	L. Lohrke	280	.250	5	31	125	170	22	21		.931							
Phi. W-66 L-88 Ben Chapman W-37 L-42 Dusty Cooke W-6 L-5 Eddie Sawyer W-23 L-41	1B	D. Sisler	446	.274	11	56	986	73	18	88	9.0	.983	D. Leonard	34	226	12	17	0	2.51
	2B	G. Hamner	446	.260	3	48	210	224	15	46	5.2	.967	C. Simmons	31	170	7	13	0	4.87
	SS	E. Miller	468	.246	14	61	229	341	20	63	4.8	.966	M. Dubiel	37	150	8	10	4	3.89
	3B	P. Caballero	351	.245	0	19	105	147	10	14	3.3	.962	S. Rowe	30	148	10	10	2	4.07
	RF	D. Ennis	589	.290	30	95	297	15	14	4	2.2	.957	R. Roberts	20	147	7	9	0	3.19
	CF	R. Ashburn	463	.333	2	40	344	14	7	2	3.1	.981	B. Donnelly	26	132	5	7	2	3.69
	LF	J. Blatnik	415	.260	6	45	220	9	13	1	2.3	.946	Heintzelman	27	130	6	11	2	4.29
	C	A. Seminick	391	.225	13	44	541	74	22	8	5.1	.965							
	31	B. Haas	333	.282	4	34	366	107	24	26		.952							
	OF	H. Walker	332	.292	2	23	198	6	4	1	2.6	.981							
	UT	B. Rowell	196	.240	1	22	76	42	12	7		.908							
	2B	E. Verban	169	.231	0	11	104	126	6	25	4.4	.975							
Cin. W-64 L-89 Johnny Neun W-44 L-56 Bucky Walters W-20 L-33	1B	T. Kluszewski	379	.274	12	57	833	65	9	60	9.3	.990	Vander Meer	33	232	17	14	0	3.41
	2B	B. Adams	262	.298	1	21	160	143	11	33	4.9	.965	Raffensberger	40	180	11	12	0	3.84
	SS	V. Stallcup	539	.228	3	65	264	433	32	84	4.9	.956	H. Fox	34	171	6	9	1	4.53
	3B	G. Hatton	458	.240	9	44	141	243	28	21	3.3	.932	H. Wehmeier	33	147	11	8	0	5.86
	RF	F. Baumholtz	415	.296	4	30	216	11	3	2	2.1	.987	E. Blackwell	22	139	7	9	1	4.54
	CF	J. Wyrostek	512	.273	14	76	331	8	8	1	2.7	.977	K. Peterson	43	137	2	15	1	4.60
	LF	H. Sauer	530	.260	35	97	270	14	8	6	2.2	.973	H. Gumbert	61	106	10	8	17	3.47
	C	R. Lamanno	385	.242	0	27	537	49	13	11	4.8	.978							
	OF	D. Litwhiler	338	.275	14	44	165	3	2	2	2.0	.988							
	UT	C. Corbitt	258	.256	0	18	138	160	7	24		.977							
	2B	B. Zientara	187	.187	0	7	143	140	3	32	4.8	.990							
Chi. W-64 L-90 Charlie Grimm	1B	E. Waitkus	562	.295	7	44	1064	92	9	77	10.0	.992	J. Schmitz	34	242	18	13	1	2.64
	2B	H. Schenz	337	.261	1	14	184	190	10	45	4.9	.974	R. Meyer	29	165	10	10	0	3.66
	SS	R. Smalley	361	.216	4	36	189	351	34	70	4.6	.941	D. McCall	30	151	4	13	0	4.82
	3B	A. Pafko	548	.312	26	101	125	314	29	29	3.4	.938	B. Rush	36	133	5	11	0	3.92
	RF	B. Nicholson	494	.261	19	67	244	7	5	1	1.9	.980	H. Borowy	39	127	5	10	1	4.89
	CF	H. Jeffcoat	473	.279	4	42	307	12	8	3	2.7	.976	R. Hamner	27	111	5	9	0	4.69
	LF	P. Lowrey	435	.294	2	54	225	9	4	2	2.3	.983	C. Chambers	29	104	2	9	0	4.43
	C	B. Scheffing	293	.300	5	45	332	36	4	5	4.8	.989	D. Lade	19	87	5	6	0	4.02
	1O	P. Cavarretta	334	.278	3	40	446	32	3	46		.994	J. Dobernic	54	86	7	2	1	3.15
	2B	E. Verban	248	.294	1	16	134	164	11	47	5.5	.964							
	OF	C. Maddern	214	.252	4	27	98	6	2	0	1.9	.981							
	C	McCullough	172	.209	1	7	225	25	7	5	5.0	.973							
	C	R. Walker	171	.275	5	26	178	22	4	3	4.6	.980							

BATTING AND BASE RUNNING LEADERS

Batting Average		Slugging Average	
S. Musial, STL	.376	S. Musial, STL	.702
R. Ashburn, PHI	.333	J. Mize, NY	.564
T. Holmes, BOS	.325	S. Gordon, NY	.537
A. Dark, BOS	.322	R. Kiner, PIT	.533
E. Slaughter, STL	.321	D. Ennis, PHI	.525

Home Runs		Total Bases	
R. Kiner, PIT	40	S. Musial, STL	429
J. Mize, NY	40	J. Mize, NY	316
S. Musial, STL	39	D. Ennis, PHI	309
H. Sauer, CIN	35	R. Kiner, PIT	296
S. Gordon, NY	30	A. Pafko, CHI	283
D. Ennis, PHI	30		

Runs Batted In		Stolen Bases	
S. Musial, STL	131	R. Ashburn, PHI	32
J. Mize, NY	125	P. Reese, BKN	25
R. Kiner, PIT	123	S. Rojek, PIT	24
S. Gordon, NY	107	J. Robinson, BKN	22
A. Pafko, CHI	101	E. Torgeson, BOS	19

Hits		Base on Balls	
S. Musial, STL	230	B. Elliott, BOS	131
T. Holmes, BOS	190	R. Kiner, PIT	112
S. Rojek, PIT	186	J. Mize, NY	94

Home Run Percentage		Runs Scored	
R. Kiner, PIT	7.2	S. Musial, STL	135
J. Mize, NY	7.1	W. Lockman, NY	117
H. Sauer, CIN	6.6	J. Mize, NY	110

PITCHING LEADERS

Winning Percentage		Earned Run Average	
H. Brecheen, STL	.741	H. Brecheen, STL	2.24
S. Jones, NY	.667	D. Leonard, PHI	2.51
J. Sain, BOS	.615	J. Sain, BOS	2.60
L. Jansen, NY	.600	J. Schmitz, CHI	2.64
J. Schmitz, CHI	.581	R. Barney, BKN	3.10

Wins		Saves	
J. Sain, BOS	24	H. Gumbert, CIN	17
H. Brecheen, STL	20	T. Wilks, STL	13
L. Jansen, NY	18	K. Higbe, PIT	10
J. Schmitz, CHI	18	K. Trinkle, NY	7
Vander Meer, CIN	17	H. Behrman, BKN	7

Strikeouts		Complete Games	
H. Brecheen, STL	149	J. Sain, BOS	28
R. Barney, BKN	138	H. Brecheen, STL	21
J. Sain, BOS	137	J. Schmitz, CHI	18
L. Jansen, NY	126	D. Leonard, PHI	16
R. Branca, BKN	122	W. Spahn, BOS	16

Fewest Hits per 9 Innings		Shutouts	
J. Schmitz, CHI	6.92	H. Brecheen, STL	7
R. Barney, BKN	7.04		
H. Brecheen, STL	7.44		

Fewest Walks per 9 Innings		Most Strikeouts per 9 Inn.	
L. Jansen, NY	1.75	H. Brecheen, STL	5.75
H. Brecheen, STL	1.89	R. Branca, BKN	5.09
D. Leonard, PHI	2.15	R. Barney, BKN	5.04

BATTING AND BASE RUNNING LEADERS

PITCHING LEADERS

Doubles		Triples		Innings		Games Pitched	
S. Musial, STL	46	S. Musial, STL	18	J. Sain, BOS	315	H. Gumbert, CIN	61
D. Ennis, PHI	40	J. Hopp, PIT	12	L. Jansen, NY	277	T. Wilks, STL	57
A. Dark, BOS	39	E. Slaughter, STL	11	W. Spahn, BOS	257	K. Higbe, PIT	56

	W	L	PCT	GB	R	OR	Batting 2B	3B	HR	BA	SA	SB	Fielding E	DP	FA	CG	BB	Pitching SO	ShO	SV	ERA
BOS	91	62	.595		739	584	272	49	95	.275	.399	43	143	132	.976	70	430	579	10	17	3.38
STL	85	69	.552	6.5	742	646	238	58	105	.263	.389	24	119	138	.980	60	476	635	13	18	3.91
BKN	84	70	.545	7.5	744	667	256	54	91	.261	.381	114	161	151	.973	52	633	670	9	22	3.75
PIT	83	71	.539	8.5	706	699	191	54	108	.263	.380	68	137	150	.977	65	564	519	5	19	4.15
NY	78	76	.506	13.5	780	704	210	49	164	.256	.408	51	156	134	.974	54	551	527	15	21	3.93
PHI	66	88	.429	25.5	591	729	227	39	91	.259	.368	68	210	126	.964	61	561	552	6	15	4.08
CIN	64	89	.418	27	588	752	221	37	104	.247	.365	42	158	135	.973	40	572	599	9	20	4.47
CHI	64	90	.416	27.5	597	706	225	44	87	.262	.369	39	172	152	.972	51	609	636	7	10	4.00
					5487	5487	1840	384	845	.261	.383	449	1256	1118	.974	453	4396	4717	74	142	3.95

American League 1948

	POS	Player	AB	BA	HR	RBI	PO	A	E	DP	TC/G	FA	Pitcher	G	IP	W	L	SV	ERA
Cle. W-97 L-58 Lou Boudreau	1B	E. Robinson	493	.254	16	83	1213	79	7	123	9.9	.995	B. Lemon	43	294	20	14	2	2.82
	2B	J. Gordon	550	.280	32	124	330	436	23	97	5.5	.971	B. Feller	44	280	19	15	3	3.56
	SS	L. Boudreau	560	.355	18	106	297	483	20	119	5.3	.975	G. Bearden	37	230	20	7	1	2.43
	3B	K. Keltner	558	.297	31	119	123	312	14	27	2.9	.969	S. Gromek	38	130	9	3	2	2.84
	RF	L. Doby	439	.301	14	66	287	12	14	3	2.7	.955	S. Zoldak	23	106	9	6	0	2.81
	CF	T. Tucker	242	.260	1	19	172	5	0	2	2.7	1.000	Christopher	45	59	3	2	17	2.90
	LF	D. Mitchell	608	.336	4	56	307	12	3	3	2.3	.991							
	C	J. Hegan	472	.248	14	61	637	76	7	17	5.1	.990							
	OF	A. Clark	271	.310	9	38	108	4	2	1	1.8	.982							
	OF	W. Judnich	218	.257	2	29	93	4	3	0	2.0	.970							
	OF	H. Edwards	160	.269	3	18	76	1	1	0	1.9	.987							
	P	B. Lemon	119	.286	5	21	23	86	4	8	2.6	.965							
Bos. W-96 L-59 Joe McCarthy	1B	B. Goodman	445	.310	1	66	1101	69	8	118	10.1	.993	J. Dobson	38	245	16	10	2	3.56
	2B	B. Doerr	527	.285	27	111	366	430	6	119	5.8	.993	M. Parnell	35	212	15	8	0	3.14
	SS	V. Stephens	635	.269	29	137	269	540	24	113	5.4	.971	J. Kramer	29	205	18	5	0	4.35
	3B	J. Pesky	565	.281	3	55	121	303	22	35	3.2	.951	E. Kinder	28	178	10	7	0	3.74
	RF	S. Spence	391	.235	12	61	206	4	5	1	2.3	.977	D. Galehouse	27	137	8	8	3	4.00
	CF	D. DiMaggio	648	.285	9	87	503	13	10	4	3.4	.981	B. Ferriss	31	115	7	3	5	5.23
	LF	T. Williams	509	.369	25	127	289	9	5	2	2.3	.983	M. Harris	20	114	7	10	0	5.30
	C	B. Tebbetts	446	.280	5	68	470	56	10	8	4.3	.981	E. Johnson	35	91	10	4	5	4.53
	OF	W. Moses	189	.259	2	29	101	2	2	1	2.3	.981							
	OF	S. Mele	180	.233	2	25	99	2	3	0	1.9	.971							
	32	B. Hitchcock	124	.298	1	20	54	82	4	15	2.3	.971							
	C	M. Batts	118	.314	1	24	118	18	2	3	3.4	.986							
N. Y. W-94 L-60 Bucky Harris	1B	G. McQuinn	302	.248	11	41	693	48	5	79	8.3	.993	A. Reynolds	39	236	16	7	3	3.77
	2B	S. Stirnweiss	515	.252	3	32	346	364	5	103	5.1	.993	E. Lopat	33	227	17	11	0	3.65
	SS	P. Rizzuto	464	.252	6	50	259	348	17	85	4.9	.973	V. Raschi	36	223	19	8	1	3.84
	3B	B. Johnson	446	.294	12	64	147	213	20	25	3.2	.947	S. Shea	28	156	9	10	1	3.41
	RF	T. Henrich	588	.308	25	100	216	8	5	4	2.2	.978	T. Byrne	31	134	8	5	2	3.30
	CF	J. DiMaggio	594	.320	39	155	441	8	13	1	3.0	.972	J. Page	55	108	7	8	16	4.26
	LF	J. Lindell	309	.317	13	55	165	7	1	1	2.2	.994							
	C	G. Niarhos	228	.268	0	19	376	33	4	7	5.0	.990							
	CO	Y. Berra	469	.305	14	98	390	40	9	7		.979							
	UT	B. Brown	363	.300	3	48	130	173	18	33		.944							
	OF	C. Keller	247	.267	6	44	126	1	3	0	2.0	.977							
Phi. W-84 L-70 Connie Mack	1B	F. Fain	520	.281	7	88	1284	120	16	148	9.8	.989	P. Marchildon	33	226	9	15	0	4.53
	2B	P. Suder	519	.241	7	60	342	461	10	114	5.5	.988	J. Coleman	33	216	14	13	0	4.09
	SS	E. Joost	509	.250	16	55	325	409	20	115	5.6	.973	D. Fowler	29	205	15	8	2	3.78
	3B	H. Majeski	590	.310	12	120	163	268	11	19	3.1	.975	C. Scheib	32	199	14	8	0	3.94
	RF	E. Valo	383	.305	3	46	231	4	4	1	2.2	.983	L. Brissie	39	194	14	10	5	4.13
	CF	S. Chapman	445	.258	13	70	368	8	7	2	3.2	.982	C. Harris	45	94	5	2	5	4.13
	LF	B. McCosky	515	.326	0	46	277	9	3	1	2.2	.990	B. McCahan	17	87	4	7	0	5.71
	C	B. Rosar	302	.255	4	41	335	39	1	10	4.2	.997	B. Savage	33	75	5	1	5	6.21
	OF	D. White	253	.245	1	28	108	3	5	5	2.1	.957							
	OF	R. Coleman	210	.243	0	21	126	7	3	3	2.6	.978							
	C	M. Guerra	142	.211	1	23	163	20	5	1	4.0	.973							
	P	C. Scheib	104	.298	2	21	14	36	1	5	1.6	.980							

	POS	Player	AB	BA	HR	RBI	PO	A	E	DP	TC/G	FA	Pitcher	G	IP	W	L	SV	ERA
Det. W-78 L-76 Steve O'Neill	1B	G. Vico	521	.267	8	58	1169	85	15	112	8.9	.988	H. Newhouser	39	272	21	12	1	3.01
	2B	E. Mayo	370	.249	2	42	202	223	11	48	5.1	.975	F. Hutchinson	33	221	13	11	0	4.32
	SS	J. Lipon	458	.290	5	52	211	346	17	63	4.9	.970	V. Trucks	43	212	14	13	2	3.78
	3B	G. Kell	368	.304	2	44	108	146	8	15	2.8	.969	D. Trout	32	184	10	14	2	3.43
	RF	P. Mullin	496	.288	23	80	274	7	8	0	2.2	.972	A. Houtteman	43	164	2	16	10	4.66
	CF	H. Evers	538	.314	10	103	392	8	11	0	3.0	.973	S. Overmire	37	66	3	4	3	5.97
	LF	V. Wertz	391	.248	7	67	196	11	10	3	2.2	.954							
	C	B. Swift	292	.223	4	33	476	55	5	13	4.8	.991							
	OF	D. Wakefield	322	.276	11	53	198	3	11	1	2.5	.948							
	S2	N. Berry	256	.266	0	16	138	199	17	46		.952							
	3B	J. Outlaw	198	.283	0	25	39	87	11	8	2.9	.920							
	2B	E. Lake	198	.263	2	18	110	132	7	31	5.5	.972							
St. L. W-59 L-94 Zack Taylor	1B	C. Stevens	288	.260	1	26	737	56	7	89	9.4	.991	F. Sanford	42	227	12	21	2	4.64
	2B	G. Priddy	560	.296	8	79	407	471	29	132	6.2	.968	C. Fannin	34	214	10	14	1	4.17
	SS	E. Pellagrini	290	.238	2	27	194	292	18	85	5.1	.964	N. Garver	38	198	7	11	5	3.41
	3B	B. Dillinger	644	.321	2	44	187	242	20	30	2.9	.955	B. Kennedy	26	132	7	8	0	4.70
	RF	A. Zarilla	529	.329	12	74	322	5	13	0	2.5	.962	B. Stephens	43	123	3	6	3	6.02
	CF	P. Lehner	333	.276	2	46	223	4	6	2	2.6	.974	F. Biscan	47	99	6	7	2	6.11
	LF	W. Platt	454	.271	7	82	230	5	13	2	2.2	.948	J. Ostrowski	26	78	4	6	3	5.97
	C	L. Moss	335	.257	14	46	357	52	5	8	4.0	.988							
	SS	S. Dente	267	.270	0	22	138	207	15	46	4.7	.958							
	OF	D. Kokos	258	.298	4	40	126	8	5	2	2.0	.964							
	1B	H. Arft	248	.238	5	38	598	43	3	81	9.3	.995							
	C	R. Partee	231	.203	0	17	297	22	6	7	4.3	.982							
	OF	D. Lund	161	.248	3	25	72	3	0	0	1.7	1.000							
Was. W-56 L-97 Joe Kuhel	1B	M. Vernon	558	.242	3	48	1297	113	15	128	9.5	.989	E. Wynn	33	198	8	19	0	5.82
	2B	A. Kozar	577	.250	1	58	348	444	27	89	5.5	.969	W. Masterson	33	188	8	15	2	3.83
	SS	M. Christman	409	.259	1	40	207	259	15	59	4.7	.969	Scarborough	31	185	15	8	1	2.82
	3B	E. Yost	555	.249	2	50	189	240	15	21	3.1	.966	S. Hudson	39	182	4	16	1	5.88
	RF	B. Stewart	401	.279	7	69	265	5	7	1	2.4	.977	M. Haefner	28	148	5	13	0	4.02
	CF	Gillenwater	221	.244	3	21	186	4	5	0	2.9	.974	D. Thompson	46	131	6	10	4	3.84
	LF	G. Coan	513	.232	7	60	341	11	11	3	2.8	.970	T. Ferrick	37	74	2	5	10	4.15
	C	J. Early	246	.220	1	28	268	51	3	7	3.5	.991							
	OF	E. Wooten	258	.256	1	23	178	9	4	2	2.6	.979							
	C	A. Evans	228	.259	2	28	245	38	5	6	3.4	.983							
	OF	T. McBride	206	.257	1	29	108	7	2	3	2.1	.983							
	OF	S. Robertson	187	.246	2	22	105	3	7	0	2.3	.939							
	SS	J. Sullivan	173	.208	0	12	94	138	12	33	4.3	.951							
Chi. W-51 L-101 Ted Lyons	1B	T. Lupien	617	.246	6	54	1436	92	11	155	10.0	.993	B. Wight	34	223	9	20	1	4.80
	2B	D. Kolloway	417	.273	6	38	241	276	18	62	6.4	.966	J. Haynes	27	150	9	10	0	3.97
	SS	C. Michaels	484	.248	5	56	164	285	20	65	5.5	.957	A. Gettel	22	148	8	10	1	4.01
	3B	L. Appling	497	.314	0	47	84	163	15	13	3.6	.943	M. Pieretti	21	120	8	10	1	4.95
	RF	T. Wright	455	.279	4	61	227	9	3	3	2.1	.987	H. Judson	40	107	4	5	8	4.78
	CF	D. Philley	488	.287	5	42	381	22	9	6	3.2	.978	F. Papish	32	95	2	8	4	5.00
	LF	P. Seerey	340	.229	18	64	198	9	4	5	2.3	.981	O. Grove	32	88	2	10	1	6.16
	C	A. Robinson	326	.252	8	39	303	50	4	4	3.9	.989	G. Moulder	33	86	3	6	2	6.41
	3B	F. Baker	335	.215	0	18	78	170	10	17	3.6	.961							
	OF	R. Hodgin	331	.266	1	34	184	9	6	0	2.5	.970							
	C	R. Weigel	163	.233	0	26	108	19	4	4	3.4	.969							

BATTING AND BASE RUNNING LEADERS

Batting Average

T. Williams, BOS	.369
L. Boudreau, CLE	.355
D. Mitchell, CLE	.336
A. Zarilla, STL	.329
B. McCosky, PHI	.326

Slugging Average

T. Williams, BOS	.615
J. DiMaggio, NY	.598
T. Henrich, NY	.554
L. Boudreau, CLE	.534
K. Keltner, CLE	.522

Home Runs

J. DiMaggio, NY	39
J. Gordon, CLE	32
K. Keltner, CLE	31
V. Stephens, BOS	29
B. Doerr, BOS	27

Total Bases

J. DiMaggio, NY	355
T. Henrich, NY	326
T. Williams, BOS	313
L. Boudreau, CLE	299
V. Stephens, BOS	299

Runs Batted In

J. DiMaggio, NY	155
V. Stephens, BOS	137
T. Williams, BOS	127
J. Gordon, CLE	124
H. Majeski, PHI	120

Stolen Bases

B. Dillinger, STL	28
G. Coan, WAS	23
M. Vernon, WAS	15
D. Mitchell, CLE	13

Hits

B. Dillinger, STL	207
D. Mitchell, CLE	204
L. Boudreau, CLE	199

Base on Balls

T. Williams, BOS	126
E. Joost, PHI	119
F. Fain, PHI	113

PITCHING LEADERS

Winning Percentage

J. Kramer, BOS	.783
G. Bearden, CLE	.741
V. Raschi, NY	.704
A. Reynolds, NY	.696

Earned Run Average

G. Bearden, CLE	2.43
B. Lemon, CLE	2.82
H. Newhouser, DET	3.01
M. Parnell, BOS	3.14
D. Trout, DET	3.43

Wins

H. Newhouser, DET	21
G. Bearden, CLE	20
B. Lemon, CLE	20
V. Raschi, NY	19
B. Feller, CLE	19

Saves

Christopher, CLE	17
J. Page, NY	16
T. Ferrick, WAS	10
A. Houtteman, DET	10
H. Judson, CHI	8

Strikeouts

B. Feller, CLE	164
B. Lemon, CLE	147
H. Newhouser, DET	143
L. Brissie, PHI	127
V. Raschi, NY	124

Complete Games

B. Lemon, CLE	20
H. Newhouser, DET	19
V. Raschi, NY	18
B. Feller, CLE	18

Fewest Hits per 9 Innings

B. Lemon, CLE	7.08
G. Bearden, CLE	7.33
B. Feller, CLE	8.19

Shutouts

B. Lemon, CLE	10
G. Bearden, CLE	6
V. Raschi, NY	6
J. Dobson, BOS	5

BATTING AND BASE RUNNING LEADERS

Home Run Percentage

J. DiMaggio, NY	6.6
J. Gordon, CLE	5.8
K. Keltner, CLE	5.6

Runs Scored

T. Henrich, NY	138
D. DiMaggio, BOS	127
T. Williams, BOS	124
J. Pesky, BOS	124

Doubles

T. Williams, BOS	44
T. Henrich, NY	42
H. Majeski, PHI	41

Triples

T. Henrich, NY	14
B. Stewart, NY, WAS	13

PITCHING LEADERS

Fewest Walks per 9 Innings

F. Hutchinson, DET	1.95
E. Lopat, NY	2.62
J. Kramer, BOS	2.81

Most Strikeouts per 9 Inn.

L. Brissie, PHI	5.89
B. Feller, CLE	5.27
V. Raschi, NY	5.01

Innings

B. Lemon, CLE	294
B. Feller, CLE	280
H. Newhouser, DET	272

Games Pitched

J. Page, NY	55
A. Widmar, STL	49
F. Biscan, STL	47

	W	L	PCT	GB	R	OR	2B	3B	HR	BA	SA	SB	E	DP	FA	CG	BB	SO	ShO	SV	ERA
CLE*	97	58	.626		840	568	242	54	155	.282	.431	54	114	183	.982	66	628	595	26	30	3.22
BOS	96	59	.619	1	907	720	277	40	121	.274	.409	38	116	174	.981	70	592	513	11	13	4.20
NY	94	60	.610	2.5	857	633	251	75	139	.278	.432	24	120	161	.979	62	641	654	16	24	3.75
PHI	84	70	.545	12.5	729	735	231	47	68	.260	.362	39	113	180	.981	74	638	486	7	18	4.43
DET	78	76	.506	18.5	700	726	219	58	78	.267	.375	22	155	143	.974	60	589	678	5	22	4.15
STL	59	94	.386	37	671	849	251	62	63	.271	.378	63	168	190	.972	35	737	531	4	20	5.01
WAS	56	97	.366	40	578	796	203	75	31	.244	.331	76	154	144	.974	42	734	446	4	22	4.65
CHI	51	101	.336	44.5	559	814	172	39	55	.251	.331	46	160	176	.974	35	673	403	2	23	4.89
					5841	5841	1846	450	710	.266	.382	362	1100	1351	.977	444	5232	4306	75	172	4.28

* Defeated Boston in a 1 game playoff.

National League 1949

	POS	Player	AB	BA	HR	RBI	PO	A	E	DP	TC/G	FA	Pitcher	G	IP	W	L	SV	ERA
Bkn. W-97 L-57 Burt Shotton	1B	G. Hodges	596	.285	23	115	1336	80	7	142	9.1	.995	D. Newcombe	38	244	17	8	1	3.17
	2B	J. Robinson	593	.342	16	124	395	421	16	119	5.3	.981	P. Roe	30	213	15	6	1	2.79
	SS	P. Reese	617	.279	16	73	316	454	18	93	5.1	.977	J. Hatten	37	187	12	8	2	4.18
	3B	B. Cox	390	.233	8	40	104	213	12	28	3.3	.964	R. Branca	34	187	13	5	1	4.39
	RF	C. Furillo	549	.322	18	106	286	13	11	2	2.2	.965	J. Banta	48	152	10	6	3	3.37
	CF	D. Snider	552	.292	23	92	355	12	6	2	2.6	.984	R. Barney	38	141	9	8	1	4.41
	LF	G. Hermanski	224	.299	8	42	140	7	3	1	1.9	.980	E. Palica	49	97	8	9	6	3.62
	C	R. Campanella	436	.287	22	82	684	55	11	5	5.9	.985	
	C	B. Edwards	148	.209	8	25	184	13	2	0	4.9	.990	
St. L. W-96 L-58 Eddie Dyer	1B	N. Jones	380	.300	8	62	876	40	15	85	9.5	.984	H. Pollet	39	231	20	9	1	2.77
	2B	Schoendienst	640	.297	3	54	399	424	11	105	6.0	.987	H. Brecheen	32	215	14	11	1	3.35
	SS	M. Marion	515	.272	5	70	242	441	17	74	5.2	.976	A. Brazle	39	206	14	8	0	3.18
	3B	E. Kazak	326	.304	6	42	64	175	19	20	3.2	.926	G. Munger	35	188	15	8	2	3.87
	RF	S. Musial	612	.338	36	123	326	10	3	5	2.2	.991	G. Staley	45	171	10	10	6	2.73
	CF	D. Diering	369	.263	3	38	300	7	4	1	2.5	.987	T. Wilks	59	118	10	3	9	3.73
	LF	E. Slaughter	568	.336	13	96	330	10	6	1	2.3	.983	
	C	D. Rice	284	.236	4	29	355	29	3	4	4.2	.992	
	OF	R. Northey	265	.260	7	50	93	4	2	2	1.4	.980	
	3B	T. Glaviano	258	.267	6	36	67	181	19	15	3.7	.929	
	1B	R. Nelson	244	.221	4	32	564	24	0	48	8.4	1.000	
	C	J. Garagiola	241	.261	3	26	332	35	6	1	4.7	.984	
Phi. W-81 L-73 Eddie Sawyer	1B	D. Sisler	412	.289	7	50	815	40	11	93	9.0	.987	Heintzelman	33	250	17	10	0	3.02
	2B	E. Miller	266	.207	6	29	240	189	6	54	5.3	.986	R. Roberts	43	227	15	15	4	3.69
	SS	G. Hamner	662	.263	6	53	280	506	32	101	5.3	.961	R. Meyer	37	213	17	8	1	3.08
	3B	W. Jones	532	.244	19	77	181	308	27	19	3.6	.948	H. Borowy	28	193	12	12	0	4.19
	RF	B. Nicholson	299	.234	11	40	185	10	1	1	2.2	.995	C. Simmons	38	131	4	10	1	4.59
	CF	R. Ashburn	662	.284	1	37	514	11	3	3	3.5	.980	J. Konstanty	53	97	9	5	7	3.25
	LF	D. Ennis	610	.302	25	110	359	16	13	1	2.5	.966	S. Rowe	23	65	3	7	0	4.82
	C	A. Seminick	334	.243	24	68	411	54	12	6	4.9	.975	
	OF	S. Hollmig	251	.255	2	26	108	5	5	1	1.8	.958	
	C	S. Lopata	240	.271	8	27	236	19	7	2	4.5	.973	
	1B	E. Waitkus	209	.306	1	28	452	36	3	51	9.1	.994	
	2B	M. Goliat	189	.212	3	19	140	143	9	31	5.8	.969	
	3B	B. Blattner	97	.247	5	21	11	11	1	2	.4	.957	
Bos. W-75 L-79 Billy Southworth	1B	E. Fletcher	413	.262	11	51	965	71	9	96	8.6	.991	W. Spahn	38	302	21	14	0	3.07
	2B	E. Stanky	506	.285	1	42	357	354	15	92	5.4	.979	J. Sain	37	243	10	17	0	4.81
	SS	A. Dark	529	.276	3	53	232	387	25	76	5.2	.961	V. Bickford	37	231	16	11	0	4.25
	3B	B. Elliott	482	.280	17	76	141	300	17	27	3.5	.963	B. Voiselle	30	169	7	8	1	4.04
	RF	T. Holmes	380	.266	8	59	210	10	3	4	2.2	.987	N. Potter	41	97	6	11	7	4.19
	CF	J. Russell	415	.231	9	54	269	3	7	3	2.3	.975	J. Antonelli	22	96	3	7	0	3.56
	LF	M. Rickert	277	.292	6	49	149	9	3	2	2.1	.981	B. Hall	31	74	6	4	0	4.36
	C	B. Salkeld	161	.255	5	25	230	21	5	3	4.1	.980	
	UT	S. Sisti	268	.257	5	22	156	80	7	11		.971	
	C	D. Crandall	228	.263	4	34	287	39	6	5	5.3	.982	
	OF	P. Reiser	221	.271	8	40	139	5	3	2	2.3	.980	
	OF	E. Sauer	214	.266	3	31	134	3	4	1	2.0	.972	
	UT	C. Ryan	208	.250	6	20	118	131	8	24		.969	
	OF	J. Heath	111	.306	9	23	56	2	1	1	1.9	.983	

	POS	Player	AB	BA	HR	RBI	PO	A	E	DP	TC/G	FA	Pitcher	G	IP	W	L	SV	ERA
N. Y. W-73 L-81 Leo Durocher	1B	J. Mize	388	.263	18	62	906	65	6	77	**9.7**	.994	L. Jansen	37	260	15	16	0	3.85
	2B	H. Thompson	275	.280	9	34	197	175	15	44	5.6	.961	M. Kennedy	38	223	12	14	1	3.43
	SS	B. Kerr	220	.209	0	19	125	224	15	33	4.1	.959	D. Koslo	38	212	11	14	4	**2.50**
	3B	S. Gordon	489	.284	26	90	112	206	14	18	2.7	.958	S. Jones	42	207	15	12	0	3.34
	RF	W. Marshall	499	.307	12	70	292	13	8	3	2.3	.974	C. Hartung	33	155	9	11	0	5.00
	CF	B. Thomson	641	.309	27	109	488	10	9	4	3.3	.982							
	LF	W. Lockman	617	.301	11	65	353	10	10	1	2.5	.973							
	C	W. Westrum	169	.243	7	28	224	18	5	4	4.0	.980							
	UT	B. Rigney	389	.278	6	47	185	317	32	46		.940							
	UT	L. Lohrke	180	.267	5	22	86	143	9	13		.962							
	C	R. Mueller	170	.224	5	23	197	21	4	2	4.0	.982							
	C	W. Cooper	147	.211	4	21	148	18*	3	2	4.2	.982							
Pit. W-71 L-83 Billy Meyer	1B	J. Hopp	371	.318	5	39	642	44	7	69	9.0	.990	M. Dickson	44	224	12	14	0	3.29
	2B	M. Basgall	308	.218	2	26	224	224	13	58	4.7	.972	B. Werle	35	221	12	13	0	4.24
	SS	S. Rojek	557	.244	0	31	240	461	25	92	5.0	.966	C. Chambers	34	177	13	7	0	3.96
	3B	Castiglione	448	.268	6	43	100	213	14	26	3.3	.957	B. Chesnes	27	145	7	13	1	5.88
	RF	W. Westlake	525	.282	23	104	319	12	6	4	2.4	.982	V. Lombardi	34	134	5	5	1	4.57
	CF	D. Restelli	232	.250	12	40	167	4	7	2	2.9	.961	E. Bonham	18	89	7	4	0	4.25
	LF	R. Kiner	549	.310	**54**	**127**	311	12	7	3	2.2	.979	E. Riddle	16	74	1	8	1	5.33
	C	McCullough	241	.237	4	21	363	39	6	8*	4.5	.985	H. Casey	33	39	4	1	5	4.66
	2B	D. Murtaugh	236	.203	2	24	202	182	10	58	5.3	.975							
	1B	E. Stevens	221	.262	4	32	533	58	3	65	10.2	.995							
	3B	E. Bockman	220	.223	6	19	59	127	8	14	2.9	.959							
	OF	T. Saffell	205	.322	2	25	122	2	1	1	2.4	.992							
	OF	D. Walker	181	.282	1	18	58	2	1	0	1.6	.984							
	C	Fitz Gerald	160	.263	2	18	163	22	5	5	3.4	.974							
Cin. W-62 L-92 Bucky Walters W-61 L-90 Luke Sewell W-1 L-2	1B	T. Kluszewski	531	.309	8	68	1140	65	14	109	9.1	.989	Raffensberger	41	284	18	17	0	3.39
	2B	J. Bloodworth	452	.261	9	59	229	234	9	56	5.1	.981	H. Fox	38	215	6	**19**	0	3.98
	SS	V. Stallcup	575	.254	3	45	256	437	27	87	5.1	.963	H. Wehmeier	33	213	11	12	0	4.68
	3B	G. Hatton	537	.263	11	69	143	290	11	**29**	3.3	.975	Vander Meer	28	160	5	10	0	4.90
	RF	J. Wyrostek	474	.249	9	46	293	10	9	1	2.4	.971	E. Erautt	39	113	4	11	1	3.36
	CF	L. Merriman	287	.230	4	26	214	7	7	1	2.7	.969	B. Lively	31	103	4	6	1	3.92
	LF	P. Lowrey	309	.275	2	25	202	7	1	2	2.7	.995	E. Blackwell	30	77	5	5	1	4.23
	C	W. Cooper	307	.280	16	62	316	43*	8	3	4.8	.978							
	OF	H. Walker	314	.318	1	23	177	7	7	1	2.5	.963							
	OF	D. Litwhiler	292	.291	11	48	143	6	2	1	1.8	.987							
	2B	B. Adams	277	.253	0	25	162	138	5	29	4.8	.984							
	C	D. Howell	172	.244	2	18	191	35	3	2	4.1	.987							
Chi. W-61 L-93 Charlie Grimm W-19 L-31 Frankie Frisch W-42 L-62	1B	H. Reich	386	.280	3	34	759	**83**	9	57	10.0	.989	J. Schmitz	36	207	11	13	3	4.35
	2B	E. Verban	343	.289	0	22	218	249	**17**	60	5.5	.965	B. Rush	35	201	10	18	4	4.07
	SS	R. Smalley	477	.245	8	35	265	438	**39**	91	5.6	.947	D. Leonard	33	180	7	16	0	4.15
	3B	F. Gustine	261	.226	4	27	52	110	12	13	3.2	.931	M. Dubiel	32	148	6	9	4	4.14
	RF	H. Jeffcoat	363	.245	2	26	250	12	10	2	2.7	.963	D. Lade	36	130	4	5	1	5.00
	CF	A. Pafko	519	.281	18	69	217	8	3	2	2.3	.987	W. Hacker	30	126	5	8	0	4.23
	LF	H. Sauer	357	.291	27	83	199	10*	4	2	2.2	.981	B. Chipman	38	113	7	8	1	3.97
	C	M. Owen	198	.273	2	18	219	35	8	5	4.4	.969	B. Muncrief	34	75	5	6	2	4.56
	1B	P. Cavarretta	360	.294	8	49	673	63	5	58	10.6	.993							
	3S	B. Ramazzotti	190	.179	0	6	48	112	3	15		.982							
	OF	H. Edwards	176	.290	7	21	80	4	1	2	1.7	.988							
	C	R. Walker	172	.244	3	22	166	23	7	2	4.6	.964							
	OF	F. Baumholtz	164	.226	1	15	67	3	1	3	1.7	.986							
	OF	H. Walker	159	.264	1	14	69	3	4	0	1.9	.947							

BATTING AND BASE RUNNING LEADERS

Batting Average
J. Robinson, BKN .342
S. Musial, STL .338
E. Slaughter, STL .336
C. Furillo, BKN .322
R. Kiner, PIT .310

Slugging Average
R. Kiner, PIT .658
S. Musial, STL .624
J. Robinson, BKN .528
D. Ennis, PHI .525
B. Thomson, NY .518

Home Runs
R. Kiner, PIT 54
S. Musial, STL 36
H. Sauer, CHI, CIN 31
B. Thomson, NY 27
S. Gordon, NY 26

Total Bases
S. Musial, STL 382
R. Kiner, PIT 361
B. Thomson, NY 332
D. Ennis, PHI 320
J. Robinson, BKN 313

Runs Batted In
R. Kiner, PIT 127
J. Robinson, BKN 124
S. Musial, STL 123
G. Hodges, BKN 115
D. Ennis, PHI 110

Stolen Bases
J. Robinson, BKN 37
P. Reese, BKN 26
G. Hermanski, BKN 12
H. Jeffcoat, CHI 12
D. Snider, BKN 12
W. Lockman, NY 12

PITCHING LEADERS

Winning Percentage
P. Roe, BKN .714
H. Pollet, STL .690
R. Meyer, PHI .680
D. Newcombe, BKN .680
G. Munger, STL .652

Earned Run Average
D. Koslo, NY 2.50
H. Pollet, STL 2.77
P. Roe, BKN 2.79
Heintzelman, PHI 3.02
W. Spahn, BOS 3.07

Wins
W. Spahn, BOS 21
H. Pollet, STL 20
Raffensberger, CIN 18
R. Meyer, PHI 17
D. Newcombe, BKN 17
Heintzelman, PHI 17

Saves
T. Wilks, STL 9
J. Konstanty, PHI 7
N. Potter, BOS 7
G. Staley, STL 6
E. Palica, BKN 6

Strikeouts
W. Spahn, BOS 151
D. Newcombe, BKN 149
L. Jansen, NY 113
R. Branca, BKN 109
P. Roe, BKN 109

Complete Games
W. Spahn, BOS 25
Raffensberger, CIN 20
D. Newcombe, BKN 19
H. Pollet, STL 17
L. Jansen, NY 17

BATTING AND BASE RUNNING LEADERS

Hits

S. Musial, STL	207
J. Robinson, BKN	203
B. Thomson, NY	198

Base on Balls

R. Kiner, PIT	117
P. Reese, BKN	116
E. Stanky, BOS	113

PITCHING LEADERS

Fewest Hits per 9 Innings

D. Koslo, NY	8.19
D. Newcombe, BKN	8.21
M. Kennedy, NY	8.38

Shutouts

H. Pollet, STL	5
D. Newcombe, BKN	5
Heintzelman, PHI	5
Raffensberger, CIN	5

Home Run Percentage

R. Kiner, PIT	9.8
H. Sauer, CHI, CIN	6.1
S. Musial, STL	5.9

Runs Scored

P. Reese, BKN	132
S. Musial, STL	128
J. Robinson, BKN	122

Fewest Walks per 9 Innings

D. Koslo, NY	1.83
P. Roe, BKN	1.86
B. Werle, PIT	2.08

Most Strikeouts per 9 Inn.

D. Newcombe, BKN	5.49
C. Chambers, PIT	4.72
P. Roe, BKN	4.61

Doubles

S. Musial, STL	41
D. Ennis, PHI	39
G. Hatton, CIN	38
J. Robinson, BKN	38

Triples

E. Slaughter, STL	13
S. Musial, STL	13
J. Robinson, BKN	12

Innings

W. Spahn, BOS	302
Raffensberger, CIN	284
L. Jansen, NY	260

Games Pitched

T. Wilks, STL	59
J. Konstanty, PHI	53
E. Palica, BKN	49

	W	L	PCT	GB	R	OR	2B	3B	HR	BA	SA	SB	E	DP	FA	CG	BB	SO	ShO	SV	ERA
BKN	97	57	.630		**879**	651	236	47	**152**	.274	**.419**	**117**	**122**	162	**.980**	62	582	**743**	15	17	3.80
STL	96	58	.623	1	766	**616**	**281**	54	102	**.277**	.404	17	146	149	.976	64	506	606	13	19	**3.45**
PHI	81	73	.526	16	662	668	232	**55**	122	.254	.388	27	156	141	.974	58	**502**	495	12	15	3.89
BOS	75	79	.487	22	706	719	246	33	103	.258	.374	28	148	144	.976	**68**	520	591	12	11	3.99
NY	73	81	.474	24	736	693	203	52	147	.261	.401	43	161	134	.973	**68**	544	516	10	9	3.82
PIT	71	83	.461	26	681	760	191	41	126	.259	.384	48	132	**173**	.978	53	535	556	9	15	4.57
CIN	62	92	.403	35	627	770	264	35	86	.260	.368	31	138	150	.977	55	640	538	10	6	4.33
CHI	61	93	.396	36	593	773	212	53	97	.256	.373	53	186	160	.970	44	564	532	8	17	4.50
					5650	5650	1865	370	935	.262	.389	364	1189	1213	.975	472	4393	4577	89	109	4.04

American League 1949

	POS	Player	AB	BA	HR	RBI	PO	A	E	DP	TC/G	FA	Pitcher	G	IP	W	L	SV	ERA
N. Y. W-97 L-57 Casey Stengel	1B	T. Henrich	411	.287	24	85	445	28	2	64	9.1	.996	V. Raschi	38	275	21	10	0	3.34
	2B	J. Coleman	447	.275	2	42	298	315	12	102	5.1	.981	E. Lopat	31	215	15	10	1	3.26
	SS	P. Rizzuto	614	.275	5	64	329	440	23	118	5.2	.971	A. Reynolds	35	214	17	6	1	4.00
	3B	B. Brown	343	.283	6	61	84	158	13	17	3.0	.949	T. Byrne	32	196	15	7	0	3.72
	RF	H. Bauer	301	.272	10	45	156	11	4	3	1.8	.977	J. Page	60	135	13	8	27	2.59
	CF	C. Mapes	304	.247	7	38	228	14	6	4	2.3	.976	F. Sanford	29	95	7	3	0	3.87
	LF	G. Woodling	296	.270	5	44	163	5	3	1	1.7	.982							
	C	Y. Berra	415	.277	20	91	544	60	7	**18**	**5.6**	.989							
	3B	B. Johnson	329	.249	8	56	77	136	11	16	2.8	.951							
	OF	J. DiMaggio	272	.346	14	67	195	1	3	0	2.6	.985							
	OF	J. Lindell	211	.242	6	27	114	4	2	1	1.8	.983							
	1B	D. Kryhoski	177	.294	1	27	363	31	7	39	7.9	.983							
	2B	S. Stirnweiss	157	.261	0	11	121	106	6	34	4.6	.974							
Bos. W-96 L-58 Joe McCarthy	1B	B. Goodman	443	.298	0	56	1069	79	9	148	9.9	**.992**	M. Parnell	39	**295**	**25**	7	2	**2.77**
	2B	B. Doerr	541	.309	18	109	395	439	17	134	**6.1**	.980	E. Kinder	43	252	23	6	4	3.36
	SS	V. Stephens	610	.290	39	**159**	257	**508**	27	**128**	5.1	.966	J. Dobson	33	213	14	12	2	3.85
	3B	J. Pesky	604	.306	2	69	**184**	**333**	16	**48**	3.6	.970	C. Stobbs	26	152	11	6	0	4.03
	RF	A. Zarilla	474	.281	9	71	241	6	4	4	2.1	.984	J. Kramer	21	112	6	8	1	5.16
	CF	D. DiMaggio	605	.307	8	60	420	13	10	1	**3.1**	.977	W. Masterson	18	55	3	4	4	4.25
	LF	T. Williams	566	.343	**43**	**159**	337	12	6	3	2.3	.983							
	C	B. Tebbetts	404	.270	5	48	481	51	11	13	4.6	.980							
	C	M. Batts	157	.242	3	31	193	23	5	2	4.4	.977							
Cle. W-89 L-65 Lou Boudreau	1B	M. Vernon	584	.291	18	83	**1438**	155	14	168	**10.5**	.991	B. Lemon	37	280	22	10	1	2.99
	2B	J. Gordon	541	.251	20	84	297	430	15	123	5.1	.980	B. Feller	36	211	15	14	0	3.75
	SS	L. Boudreau	475	.284	4	60	176	272	8	78	5.2	.982	M. Garcia	41	176	14	5	2	2.36
	3B	K. Keltner	246	.232	8	30	51	145	4	11	2.9	.980	E. Wynn	26	165	11	7	0	4.15
	RF	B. Kennedy	424	.276	9	57	190	12	2	4	2.1	.990	A. Benton	40	136	9	6	10	2.12
	CF	L. Doby	547	.280	24	85	355	7	9	2	2.5	.976	G. Bearden	32	127	8	8	0	5.10
	LF	D. Mitchell	**640**	.317	3	56	337	10	2	2	2.3	**.994**	S. Gromek	27	92	4	6	0	3.33
	C	J. Hegan	468	.224	8	55	651	73	7	16	4.8	.990	S. Paige	31	83	4	7	5	3.04
	SS	R. Boone	258	.252	4	26	162	210	21	58	5.2	.947							
	OF	T. Tucker	197	.244	0	14	119	2	2	0	2.4	.984							

	POS	Player	AB	BA	HR	RBI	PO	A	E	DP	TC/G	FA	Pitcher	G	IP	W	L	SV	ERA
Det. W-87 L-67 Red Rolfe	1B	P. Campbell	255	.278	3	30	461	38	7	67	6.8	.986	H. Newhouser	38	292	18	11	1	3.36
	2B	N. Berry	329	.237	0	18	225	234	14	56	5.0	.970	V. Trucks	41	275	19	11	4	2.81
	SS	J. Lipon	439	.251	3	59	240	364	22	92	5.2	.965	A. Houtteman	34	204	15	10	0	3.71
	3B	G. Kell	522	.343	3	59	154	271	11	23	3.3	.975	T. Gray	34	195	10	10	1	3.51
	RF	V. Wertz	608	.304	20	133	302	14	6	4	2.1	.981	F. Hutchinson	33	189	15	7	1	2.96
	CF	J. Groth	348	.293	11	73	247	8	9	3	2.7	.966	D. Trout	33	59	3	6	3	4.40
	LF	H. Evers	432	.303	7	72	319	12	2	2	2.7	.994							
	C	A. Robinson	331	.269	13	56	458	44	7	9	4.7	.986							
	21	D. Kolloway	483	.294	2	47	607	184	18	93		.978							
	OF	P. Mullin	310	.268	12	59	169	4	2	0	2.2	.989							
	UT	E. Lake	240	.196	1	15	113	167	10	37		.966							
	C	B. Swift	189	.238	2	18	232	26	3	6	3.8	.989							
Phi. W-81 L-73 Connie Mack	1B	F. Fain	525	.263	3	78	1275	122	22	194	9.5	.984	A. Kellner	38	245	20	12	1	3.75
	2B	P. Suder	445	.267	10	75	203	259	12	85	5.3	.975	J. Coleman	33	240	13	14	1	3.86
	SS	E. Joost	525	.263	23	81	352	442	25	126	5.7	.969	L. Brissie	34	229	16	11	3	4.28
	3B	H. Majeski	448	.277	9	67	117	219	15	37	3.1	.957	D. Fowler	31	214	15	11	1	3.75
	RF	W. Moses	308	.276	1	25	169	7	3	3	1.9	.983	C. Scheib	38	183	9	12	0	5.12
	CF	S. Chapman	589	.278	24	108	450	11	10	3	3.1	.975	B. Shantz	33	127	6	8	2	3.40
	LF	E. Valo	547	.283	5	85	395	8	8	0	2.7	.981							
	C	M. Guerra	298	.265	3	31	328	48	7	3	4.0	.982							
	2B	N. Fox	247	.255	0	21	191	196	7	68	5.1	.982							
	OF	D. White	169	.213	0	10	89	4	1	0	2.0	.989							
	OF	T. Wright	149	.235	2	25	60	5	2	0	1.9	.970							
Chi. W-63 L-91 Jack Onslow	1B	C. Kress	353	.278	1	44	907	66	6	103	10.3	.994	B. Wight	35	245	15	13	1	3.31
	2B	C. Michaels	561	.308	6	83	392	484	22	135	5.8	.976	R. Gumpert	34	234	13	16	1	3.81
	SS	L. Appling	492	.301	5	58	253	450	26	95	5.2	.964	B. Pierce	32	172	7	15	0	3.88
	3B	F. Baker	388	.260	1	40	106	269	9	31	3.1	.977	B. Kuzava	29	157	10	6	0	4.02
	RF	D. Philley	598	.286	0	44	282	16	7	3	2.1	.977	M. Pieretti	39	116	4	6	4	5.51
	CF	M. Metkovich	338	.237	5	45	212	1	7	0	2.5	.968	H. Judson	26	108	1	14	4	4.58
	LF	H. Adams	208	.293	0	16	112	4	3	1	2.5	.975	M. Surkont	44	96	3	5	4	4.78
	C	D. Wheeler	192	.240	1	22	210	36	6	4	4.3	.976	M. Haefner	14	80	4	6	1	4.37
	O1	S. Souchock	252	.234	7	37	346	21	6	30		.984							
	OF	G. Zernial	198	.318	5	38	73	4	0	0	1.7	1.000							
	C	J. Tipton	191	.204	3	19	203	32	2	4	4.5	.992							
	C	E. Malone	170	.271	1	16	186	22	2	2	4.1	.990							
	OF	J. Ostrowski	158	.266	5	31	81	3	5	0	2.2	.944							
St. L. W-53 L-101 Zack Taylor	1B	J. Graham	500	.238	2	79	1118	87	19	120	9.0	.984	N. Garver	41	224	12	17	3	3.98
	2B	G. Priddy	544	.290	11	63	407	415	27	96	5.9	.968	B. Kennedy	48	154	4	11	1	4.69
	SS	E. Pellagrini	235	.238	2	15	164	227	16	52	5.4	.961	C. Fannin	30	143	8	14	1	6.17
	3B	B. Dillinger	544	.324	1	51	166	209	25	22	3.0	.938	A. Papai	42	142	4	11	2	5.06
	RF	D. Kokos	501	.261	23	77	290	16	6	5	2.3	.981	J. Ostrowski	40	141	8	8	2	4.79
	CF	S. Spence	314	.245	13	45	205	10	1	2	2.5	.975	K. Drews	31	140	4	12	0	6.64
	LF	R. Sievers	471	.306	16	91	314	14	9	1	2.7	.973	R. Embree	35	127	3	13	1	5.37
	C	S. Lollar	284	.261	8	49	279	39	4	3	3.5	.988	T. Ferrick	50	104	6	4	6	3.88
	OF	P. Lehner	297	.229	3	37	153	1	2	0	2.8	.987							
	C	L. Moss	278	.291	10	39	283	41	10	9	4.0	.970							
	OF	W. Platt	244	.258	3	29	135	3	2	0	2.4	.986							
	SS	J. Sullivan	243	.226	0	18	117	144	16	35	3.9	.942							
Was. W-50 L-104 Joe Kuhel	1B	E. Robinson	527	.294	18	78	1299	100	18	133	9.9	.987	S. Hudson	40	209	8	17	1	4.22
	2B	A. Kozar	350	.269	4	31	232	235	11	57	4.7	.977	Scarborough	34	200	13	11	0	4.60
	SS	S. Dente	590	.273	1	53	314	462	35	106	5.3	.957	P. Calvert	34	161	6	17	1	5.43
	3B	E. Yost	435	.253	9	45	158	232	19	23	3.4	.954	M. Harris	23	129	2	12	0	5.16
	RF	B. Stewart	388	.284	8	43	207	8	4	3	2.1	.982	L. Hittle	36	109	5	7	0	4.21
	CF	C. Vollmer	443	.253	14	59	324	3	6	1	2.9	.982	J. Haynes	37	96	2	9	2	6.26
	LF	G. Coan	358	.218	3	25	225	8	6	3	2.5	.975	D. Weik	27	95	3	12	1	5.38
	C	A. Evans	321	.271	2	42	322	47	3	2	3.5	.992	M. Haefner	19	92	5	5	0	4.42
	UT	S. Robertson	374	.251	11	42	185	253	25	43		.946							
	OF	S. Mele	264	.242	3	25	108	5	4	3	1.9	.966							
	OF	B. Lewis	257	.245	3	28	136	4	3	1	2.1	.979							

BATTING AND BASE RUNNING LEADERS

Batting Average		Slugging Average	
G. Kell, DET	.343	T. Williams, BOS	.650
T. Williams, BOS	.343	V. Stephens, BOS	.539
B. Dillinger, STL	.324	T. Henrich, NY	.526
D. Mitchell, CLE	.317	B. Doerr, BOS	.497
B. Doerr, BOS	.309	Y. Berra, NY	.480

Home Runs		Total Bases	
T. Williams, BOS	43	T. Williams, BOS	368
V. Stephens, BOS	39	V. Stephens, BOS	329
T. Henrich, NY	24	V. Wertz, DET	283
J. Graham, STL	24	D. Mitchell, CLE	274
L. Doby, CLE	24	B. Doerr, BOS	269
S. Chapman, PHI	24		

PITCHING LEADERS

Winning Percentage		Earned Run Average	
E. Kinder, BOS	.793	M. Parnell, BOS	2.77
M. Parnell, BOS	.781	V. Trucks, DET	2.81
A. Reynolds, NY	.739	B. Lemon, CLE	2.99
B. Lemon, CLE	.688	E. Lopat, NY	3.26
T. Byrne, NY	.682	B. Wight, CHI	3.31
F. Hutchinson, DET	.682		

Wins		Saves	
M. Parnell, BOS	25	J. Page, NY	27
E. Kinder, BOS	23	A. Benton, CLE	10
B. Lemon, CLE	22	T. Ferrick, STL	6
V. Raschi, NY	21	S. Paige, CLE	5
A. Kellner, PHI	20		

BATTING AND BASE RUNNING LEADERS

Runs Batted In

T. Williams, BOS	159
V. Stephens, BOS	159
V. Wertz, DET	133
B. Doerr, BOS	109
S. Chapman, PHI	108

Stolen Bases

B. Dillinger, STL	20
P. Rizzuto, NY	18
E. Valo, PHI	14
D. Philley, CHI	13

Hits

D. Mitchell, CLE	203
T. Williams, BOS	194
D. DiMaggio, BOS	186

Base on Balls

T. Williams, BOS	162
E. Joost, PHI	149
F. Fain, PHI	136

Home Run Percentage

T. Williams, BOS	7.6
V. Stephens, BOS	6.4
T. Henrich, NY	5.8

Runs Scored

T. Williams, BOS	150
E. Joost, PHI	128
D. DiMaggio, BOS	126

Doubles

T. Williams, BOS	39
G. Kell, DET	38
D. DiMaggio, BOS	34

Triples

D. Mitchell, CLE	23
B. Dillinger, STL	13
E. Valo, PHI	12

PITCHING LEADERS

Strikeouts

V. Trucks, DET	153
H. Newhouser, DET	144
E. Kinder, BOS	138
B. Lemon, CLE	138
T. Byrne, NY	129

Complete Games

M. Parnell, BOS	27
B. Lemon, CLE	22
H. Newhouser, DET	22
V. Raschi, NY	21
A. Kellner, PHI	19
E. Kinder, BOS	19

Fewest Hits per 9 Innings

T. Byrne, NY	5.74
B. Lemon, CLE	6.79
V. Trucks, DET	6.84

Shutouts

E. Kinder, BOS	6
V. Trucks, DET	6
M. Garcia, CLE	5

Fewest Walks per 9 Innings

A. Houtteman, DET	2.61
E. Lopat, NY	2.88
R. Gumpert, CHI	3.19

Most Strikeouts per 9 Inn.

T. Byrne, NY	5.92
V. Trucks, DET	5.01
E. Kinder, BOS	4.93

Innings

M. Parnell, BOS	295
H. Newhouser, DET	292
B. Lemon, CLE	280

Games Pitched

J. Page, NY	60
D. Welteroth, WAS	52
T. Ferrick, STL	50

	W	L	PCT	GB	R	OR	2B	3B	Batting HR	BA	SA	SB	E	Fielding DP	FA	CG	BB	Pitching SO	ShO	SV	ERA
NY	97	57	.630		829	637	215	60	115	.269	.400	58	138	195	.977	59	812	**671**	12	**36**	3.69
BOS	96	58	.623	1	**896**	667	272	36	**131**	**.282**	**.420**	43	120	207	.980	84	661	598	16	16	3.97
CLE	89	65	.578	8	675	**574**	194	58	112	.260	.384	44	**103**	192	**.983**	65	611	594	10	19	**3.36**
DET	87	67	.565	10	751	655	215	51	88	.267	.378	39	131	174	.978	70	628	631	**19**	12	3.77
PHI	81	73	.526	16	726	725	214	49	82	.260	.369	36	140	**217**	.976	**85**	758	490	9	11	4.23
CHI	63	91	.409	34	648	737	207	**66**	43	.257	.347	**62**	141	180	.977	57	693	502	10	17	4.30
STL	53	101	.344	44	667	913	213	30	117	.254	.377	38	166	154	.971	43	685	432	3	16	5.21
WAS	50	104	.325	47	584	868	207	41	81	.254	.356	46	161	168	.973	44	779	451	9	9	5.10
					5776	5776	1737	391	769	.263	.379	366	1100	1487	.977	507	5627	4369	88	136	4.20

National League 1950

	POS	Player	AB	BA	HR	RBI	PO	A	E	DP	TC/G	FA	Pitcher	G	IP	W	L	SV	ERA
Phi. W-91 L-63 Eddie Sawyer	1B	E. Waitkus	641	.284	2	44	**1387**	99	10	142	9.7	.993	R. Roberts	40	304	20	11	1	3.02
	2B	M. Goliat	483	.234	13	64	345	393	21	89	5.5	.972	C. Simmons	31	215	17	8	1	3.40
	SS	G. Hamner	637	.270	11	82	293	513	48	100	5.4	.944	B. Miller	35	174	11	6	1	3.57
	3B	W. Jones	610	.267	25	88	190	323	25	30	3.4	.954	R. Meyer	32	160	9	11	1	5.30
	RF	D. Ennis	595	.311	31	126	279	10	9	3	2.0	.970	J. Konstanty	**74**	152	16	7	**22**	2.66
	CF	R. Ashburn	594	.303	2	41	**405**	8	5	2	**2.8**	.988	B. Church	31	142	8	6	1	2.73
	LF	D. Sisler	523	.296	13	83	293	9	4	0	2.2	.987	Heintzelman	23	125	3	9	0	4.09
	C	A. Seminick	393	.288	24	68	551	54	**15**	9	5.0	.976							
Bkn. W-89 L-65 Burt Shotton	1B	G. Hodges	561	.283	32	113	1273	100	8	**159**	9.0	**.994**	D. Newcombe	40	267	19	11	3	3.70
	2B	J. Robinson	518	.328	14	81	359	390	11	**133**	5.3	**.986**	P. Roe	36	251	19	11	1	3.30
	SS	P. Reese	531	.260	11	52	282	398	26	94	5.3	.963	E. Palica	43	201	13	8	1	3.58
	3B	B. Cox	451	.257	8	44	102	233	15	35	3.3	**.957**	R. Branca	43	142	7	9	7	4.69
	RF	C. Furillo	620	.305	18	106	246	**18**	8	2	1.8	.971	D. Bankhead	41	129	9	4	3	5.50
	CF	D. Snider	620	.321	31	107	378	15	7	1	2.6	.983	C. Erskine	22	103	7	6	1	4.72
	LF	G. Hermanski	289	.298	7	34	172	5	2	0	2.3	.989	B. Podbielan	20	73	5	4	1	5.33
	C	R. Campanella	437	.281	31	89	**683**	54	11	14	6.1	.985	J. Banta	16	41	4	4	2	4.35
	OF	J. Russell	214	.229	10	32	131	3	1	0	2.5	.993							
	3B	B. Morgan	199	.226	7	21	33	121	5	15	3.1	.969							
	OF	T. Brown	86	.291	8	20	31	2	3	0	2.3	.917							
N. Y. W-86 L-68 Leo Durocher	1B	T. Gilbert	322	.220	4	32	784	65	10	80	7.7	.988	L. Jansen	40	275	19	13	3	3.01
	2B	E. Stanky	527	.300	8	51	**407**	418	20	128	5.6	.976	S. Maglie	47	206	18	4	1	2.71
	SS	A. Dark	587	.279	16	67	288	465	30	101	5.1	.962	S. Jones	40	199	13	16	2	4.61
	3B	H. Thompson	512	.289	20	91	136	303	**26**	**43**	3.4	.944	D. Koslo	40	187	13	15	3	3.91
	RF	D. Mueller	525	.291	7	84	205	7	3	2	1.7	.986	J. Hearn	16	125	11	3	0	1.94*
	CF	B. Thomson	563	.252	25	85	394	15	9	5	2.8	.978	M. Kennedy	36	114	5	4	2	4.72
	LF	W. Lockman	532	.295	6	52	305	11	7	3	2.5	.978	J. Kramer	35	87	3	6	1	3.53
	C	W. Westrum	437	.236	23	71	608	**71**	1	**21**	4.9	**.999**							
	1O	M. Irvin	374	.299	15	66	568	50	12	62		.981							

	POS	Player	AB	BA	HR	RBI	PO	A	E	DP	TC/G	FA	Pitcher	G	IP	W	L	SV	ERA
Bos. W-83 L-71 Billy Southworth	1B	E. Torgeson	576	.290	23	87	1365	110	21	126	9.6	.986	V. Bickford	40	312	19	14	0	3.47
	2B	R. Hartsfield	419	.277	7	24	236	247	26	53	5.3	.949	W. Spahn	41	293	21	17	1	3.16
	SS	B. Kerr	507	.227	2	46	310	471	28	97	5.2	.965	J. Sain	37	278	20	13	0	3.94
	3B	B. Elliott	531	.305	24	107	141	256	20	26	3.0	.952	B. Chipman	27	124	7	7	1	4.43
	RF	T. Holmes	322	.298	9	51	151	6	0	0	1.8	1.000	B. Hogue	36	63	3	5	7	5.03
	CF	S. Jethroe	582	.273	18	58	355	17	12	6	2.7	.969							
	LF	S. Gordon	481	.304	27	103	278	8	3	1	2.3	.990							
	C	W. Cooper	337	.329	14	60	386	47	12	9	5.1	.973							
	OF	W. Marshall	298	.235	5	40	150	11	7	2	2.0	.958							
	C	D. Crandall	255	.220	4	37	311	41	12	7	4.9	.967							
	OF	L. Olmo	154	.227	5	22	74	1	2	0	1.4	.974							
St. L. W-78 L-75 Eddie Dyer	1B	R. Nelson	235	.247	1	20	596	51	5	66	9.3	.992	H. Pollet	37	232	14	13	2	3.29
	2B	Schoendienst	642	.276	7	63	393	403	12	124	5.7	.985	M. Lanier	27	181	11	9	0	3.13
	SS	M. Marion	372	.247	4	40	180	313	11	73	5.0	.978	G. Staley	42	170	13	13	3	4.99
	3B	T. Glaviano	410	.285	11	44	103	255	25	16	3.6	.935	A. Brazle	46	165	11	9	6	4.10
	RF	E. Slaughter	556	.290	10	101	260	9	6	1	1.9	.978	H. Brecheen	27	163	8	11	1	3.80
	CF	C. Diering	204	.250	3	18	178	8	2	2	2.3	.989	G. Munger	32	155	7	8	0	3.90
	LF	B. Howerton	313	.281	10	59	183	2	6	0	2.0	.969	C. Boyer	36	120	7	7	1	3.52
	C	D. Rice	414	.244	9	54	572	63	10	12	5.0	.984							
	O1	S. Musial	555	**.346**	28	109	760	39	8	67		.990							
	3B	E. Kazak	207	.256	5	23	36	95	9	7	2.9	.936							
	SS	E. Miller	172	.227	3	22	72	173	5	29	4.9	.980							
	C	J. Garagiola	88	.318	2	20	99	8	0	2	3.6	1.000							
Cin. W-66 L-87 Luke Sewell	1B	T. Kluszewski	538	.307	25	111	1123	61	15	101	9.2	.987	E. Blackwell	40	261	17	15	4	2.97
	2B	C. Ryan	367	.259	3	43	304	283	16	13	5.9*	.973	Raffensberger	38	239	14	19	0	4.26
	SS	V. Stallcup	483	.251	8	54	253	389	18	79	4.9	.973	H. Wehmeier	41	230	10	18	4	5.67
	3B	G. Hatton	438	.260	11	54	145	230	18	19	3.1	.954	H. Fox	34	187	11	8	1	4.33
	RF	J. Wyrostek	509	.285	8	76	238	8	5	0	1.9	.980	W. Ramsdell	27	157	7	12	0	3.72
	CF	L. Merriman	298	.258	2	31	181	4	2	1	2.2	.989	F. Smith	38	91	2	7	3	3.87
	LF	B. Usher	321	.259	6	35	190	7	3	1	2.1	.985							
	C	D. Howell	224	.223	2	22	338	26	5	4	4.6	.986							
	OF	J. Adcock	372	.293	8	55	177	6	6	3	2.5	.968							
	23	B. Adams	348	.282	3	25	170	200	14	34		.964							
	OF	P. Lowrey	264	.227	1	11	153	4	2	1	2.2	.987							
	C	J. Pramesa	228	.307	5	30	328	37	7	2	5.1	.981							
Chi. W-64 L-89 Frankie Frisch	1B	P. Ward	285	.253	6	33	734	73	4	78	10.7	.995	B. Rush	39	255	13	**20**	1	3.71
	2B	Terwilliger	480	.242	10	32	314	380	24	80	5.7	.967	J. Schmitz	39	193	10	16	0	4.99
	SS	R. Smalley	557	.230	21	85	**332**	541	51	115	**6.0**	.945	P. Minner	39	190	8	13	4	4.11
	3B	B. Serena	435	.239	17	61	122	274	23	24	3.4	.945	F. Hiller	38	153	12	5	1	3.53
	RF	B. Borkowski	256	.273	4	29	150	3	4	1	2.4	.975	M. Dubiel	39	143	6	10	2	4.16
	CF	A. Pafko	514	.304	36	92	342	12	8	1	2.5	.978	D. Lade	34	118	5	6	2	4.74
	LF	H. Sauer	540	.274	32	103	236	12	9	1	2.1	.965	J. Klippstein	33	105	2	9	1	5.25
	C	M. Owen	259	.243	2	21	318	39	8	8	4.2	.978	D. Leonard	35	74	5	1	6	3.77
	1B	P. Cavarretta	256	.273	10	31	606	47	9	55	9.9	.986							
	C	R. Walker	213	.230	6	16	240	34	7	6	4.5	.975							
	OF	C. Mauro	185	.227	1	10	86	2	5	0	1.9	.946							
	OF	H. Jeffcoat	179	.235	2	18	83	6	3	0	1.7	.967							
	OF	R. Northey	114	.281	4	20	38	3	1	2	1.6	.976							
	OF	H. Edwards	110	.364	2	21	38	2	1	0	1.4	.976							
Pit. W-57 L-96 Billy Meyer	1B	J. Hopp	318	.340	8	47	534	32	6	61	8.2	.990	C. Chambers	37	249	12	15	0	4.30
	2B	D. Murtaugh	367	.294	2	37	273	292	14	84	5.4	.976	M. Dickson	51	225	10	15	3	3.80
	SS	S. Rojek	230	.257	0	17	102	160	9	39	4.0	.967	B. Werle	48	215	8	16	8	4.60
	3B	B. Dillinger	222	.288	1	9	60	116	8	13	3.6	.957	B. Macdonald	32	153	8	10	1	4.29
	RF	G. Bell	422	.282	8	53	203	10	5	3	2.1	.977	V. Law	27	128	7	9	0	4.92
	CF	W. Westlake	477	.285	24	95	329	4	3	3	2.7	**.991**	M. Queen	33	120	5	14	0	5.98
	LF	R. Kiner	547	.272	**47**	118	287	13	11	2	2.1	.965							
	C	McCullough	279	.254	6	34	362	45	6	3	4.1	.985							
	SS	D. O'Connell	315	.292	8	32	147	228	9	47	5.9	.977							
	UT	Castiglione	263	.255	3	22	116	125	10	23		.960							
	1B	J. Phillips	208	.293	5	34	450	39	7	46	9.2	.986							
	3B	N. Fernandez	198	.258	6	27	48	101	12	6	3.1	.925							
	OF	T. Saffell	182	.203	2	6	128	5	1	0	3.1	.993							
	OF	T. Beard	177	.232	4	12	112	4	2	0	2.4	.983							
	C	R. Mueller	156	.269	6	24	204	30	1	3	3.7	.996							

BATTING AND BASE RUNNING LEADERS

Batting Average
S. Musial, STL	.346
J. Robinson, BKN	.328
D. Snider, BKN	.321
D. Ennis, PHI	.311
T. Kluszewski, CIN	.307

Slugging Average
S. Musial, STL	.596
A. Pafko, CHI	.591
R. Kiner, PIT	.590
S. Gordon, BOS	.557
D. Snider, BKN	.553

Home Runs
R. Kiner, PIT	47
A. Pafko, CHI	36
H. Sauer, CHI	32
G. Hodges, BKN	32

Total Bases
D. Snider, BKN	343
S. Musial, STL	331
D. Ennis, PHI	328
R. Kiner, PIT	323
A. Pafko, CHI	304

PITCHING LEADERS

Winning Percentage
S. Maglie, NY	.818
J. Konstanty, PHI	.696
C. Simmons, PHI	.680
R. Roberts, PHI	.645
D. Newcombe, BKN	.633
P. Roe, BKN	.633

Earned Run Average
J. Hearn, NY, STL	2.49
S. Maglie, NY	2.71
E. Blackwell, CIN	2.97
L. Jansen, NY	3.01
R. Roberts, PHI	3.02

Wins
W. Spahn, BOS	21
R. Roberts, PHI	20
J. Sain, BOS	20

Saves
J. Konstanty, PHI	22
B. Werle, PIT	8
B. Hogue, BOS	7
R. Branca, BKN	7
A. Brazle, STL	6
D. Leonard, CHI	6

BATTING AND BASE RUNNING LEADERS

PITCHING LEADERS

Runs Batted In		Stolen Bases	
D. Ennis, PHI	126	S. Jethroe, BOS	35
R. Kiner, PIT	118	P. Reese, BKN	17
G. Hodges, BKN	113	D. Snider, BKN	16
T. Kluszewski, CIN	111	E. Torgeson, BOS	15
S. Musial, STL	109	R. Ashburn, PHI	14

Strikeouts		Complete Games	
W. Spahn, BOS	191	V. Bickford, BOS	27
E. Blackwell, CIN	188	J. Sain, BOS	25
L. Jansen, NY	161	W. Spahn, BOS	25
C. Simmons, PHI	146	L. Jansen, NY	21
R. Roberts, PHI	146	R. Roberts, PHI	21

Hits		Base on Balls	
D. Snider, BKN	199	E. Stanky, NY	144
S. Musial, STL	192	R. Kiner, PIT	122
C. Furillo, BKN	189	E. Torgeson, BOS	119

Fewest Hits per 9 Innings		Shutouts	
J. Hearn, NY, STL	5.64	J. Hearn, NY, STL	5
E. Blackwell, CIN	7.00	S. Maglie, NY	5
S. Maglie, NY	7.38	L. Jansen, NY	5
		R. Roberts, PHI	5

Home Run Percentage		Runs Scored	
R. Kiner, PIT	8.6	E. Torgeson, BOS	120
R. Campanella, BKN	7.1	E. Stanky, NY	115
A. Pafko, CHI	7.0	R. Kiner, PIT	112

Fewest Walks per 9 Innings		Most Strikeouts per 9 Inn.	
Raffensberger, CIN	1.51	E. Blackwell, CIN	6.48
L. Jansen, NY	1.80	C. Simmons, PHI	6.12
J. Sain, BOS	2.26	W. Spahn, BOS	5.87

Doubles		Triples	
Schoendienst, STL	43	R. Ashburn, PHI	14
S. Musial, STL	41	G. Bell, PIT	11
J. Robinson, BKN	39	D. Snider, BKN	10

Innings		Games Pitched	
V. Bickford, BOS	312	J. Konstanty, PHI	74
R. Roberts, PHI	304	M. Dickson, PIT	51
W. Spahn, BOS	293	B. Werle, PIT	48

	W	L	PCT	GB	R	OR	2B	3B	HR	BA	SA	SB	E	DP	FA	CG	BB	SO	ShO	SV	ERA
PHI	91	63	.591		722	624	225	55	125	.265	.396	33	151	155	.975	57	530	620	13	27	3.50
BKN	89	65	.578	2	847	724	247	46	194	.272	.444	77	127	183	.979	62	591	772	10	21	4.28
NY	86	68	.558	5	735	643	204	50	133	.258	.392	42	137	181	.977	70	536	596	19	15	3.71
BOS	83	71	.539	8	785	736	246	36	148	.263	.405	71	182	146	.970	88	554	615	7	10	4.14
STL	78	75	.510	12.5	693	670	255	50	102	.259	.386	23	130	172	.978	57	535	603	10	14	3.97
CIN	66	87	.431	24.5	654	734	257	27	99	.260	.376	37	140	132	.976	67	582	686	7	13	4.32
CHI	64	89	.418	26.5	643	772	224	47	161	.248	.401	46	201	169	.968	55	593	559	9	19	4.28
PIT	57	96	.373	33.5	681	857	227	59	138	.264	.406	43	136	165	.977	42	616	556	6	16	4.96
					5760	5760	1885	370	1100	.261	.401	372	1204	1303	.975	498	4537	5007	81	135	4.14

American League 1950

	POS	Player	AB	BA	HR	RBI	PO	A	E	DP	TC/G	FA	Pitcher	G	IP	W	L	SV	ERA
N. Y. W-98 L-56 Casey Stengel	1B	J. Collins	205	.234	8	28	480	36	7	62	5.3	.987	V. Raschi	33	257	21	8	1	4.00
	2B	J. Coleman	522	.287	6	69	384	384	18	137	5.2	.977	A. Reynolds	35	241	16	12	2	3.74
	SS	P. Rizzuto	617	.324	7	66	301	452	14	123	4.9	.982	E. Lopat	35	236	18	8	1	3.47
	3B	B. Johnson	327	.260	6	40	82	169	11	20	2.6	.958	T. Byrne	31	203	15	9	0	4.74
	RF	H. Bauer	415	.320	13	70	228	8	3	3	2.2	.987	F. Sanford	26	113	5	4	0	4.55
	CF	J. DiMaggio	525	.301	32	122	363	9	9	1	2.8	.976	W. Ford	20	112	9	1	1	2.81
	LF	G. Woodling	449	.283	6	60	263	16	2	3	2.4	.993	T. Ferrick	30	57	8	4	9	3.65
	C	Y. Berra	597	.322	28	124	777	64	13	16	5.8	.985	J. Page	37	55	3	7	13	5.04
	OF	C. Mapes	356	.247	12	61	183	8	10	4	2.0	.950							
	3B	B. Brown	277	.267	4	37	63	140	9	13	2.6	.958							
	1B	J. Mize	274	.277	25	72	490	31	2	73	7.3	.996							
	1B	T. Henrich	151	.272	6	34	224	7	3	23	6.9	.987							
Det. W-95 L-59 Red Rolfe	1B	D. Kolloway	467	.289	6	62	1087	85	13	133	10.0	.989	A. Houtteman	41	275	19	12	4	3.54
	2B	G. Priddy	618	.277	11	75	440	542	19	150	6.4	.981	F. Hutchinson	39	232	17	8	0	3.96
	SS	J. Lipon	601	.293	2	63	273	483	33	126	5.4	.958	H. Newhouser	35	214	15	13	3	4.34
	3B	G. Kell	641	.340	8	101	186	315	9	30	3.2	.982	D. Trout	34	185	13	5	4	3.75
	RF	V. Wertz	559	.308	27	123	286	5	10	3	2.1	.967	T. Gray	27	149	10	7	1	4.40
	CF	J. Groth	566	.306	12	85	374	9	6	0	2.5	.985	H. White	42	111	9	6	1	4.54
	LF	H. Evers	526	.323	21	103	325	15	1	3	2.5	.997							
	C	A. Robinson	283	.226	9	37	355	42	3	4	3.9	.993							
	1B	D. Kryhoski	169	.219	4	19	409	27	4	44	9.4	.991							
	OF	P. Mullin	142	.218	6	23	62	4	0	1	2.1	1.000							
	P	F. Hutchinson	95	.326	0	20	17	50	4	6	1.8	.944							

Bos.
W-94 L-60
Joe McCarthy
W-32 L-30
Steve O'Neill
W-62 L-30

POS	Player	AB	BA	HR	RBI	PO	A	E	DP	TC/G	FA
1B	W. Dropo	559	.322	34	**144**	1142	77	15	147	9.2	.988
2B	B. Doerr	586	.294	27	120	**443**	431	11	130	5.9	**.988**
SS	V. Stephens	628	.295	30	**144**	258	431	13	115	4.8	.981
3B	J. Pesky	490	.312	1	49	160	257	11	29	**3.7**	.974
RF	A. Zarilla	471	.325	9	74	230	12	6	1	1.9	.976
CF	D. DiMaggio	588	.328	7	70	390	15	7	2	2.9	.983
LF	T. Williams	334	.317	28	97	165	7	8	0	2.1	.956
C	B. Tebbetts	268	.310	8	45	285	44	4	5	4.5	.988
UT	B. Goodman	424	**.354**	4	68	344	89	9	28		.980
C	M. Batts	238	.273	4	34	306	29	2	3	4.6	.994
OF	C. Vollmer	169	.284	7	37	80	3	4	0	2.2	.954
OF	T. Wright	107	.318	0	20	40	1	2	1	1.8	.953

Pitcher	G	IP	W	L	SV	ERA
M. Parnell	40	249	18	10	3	3.61
E. Kinder	48	207	14	12	9	4.26
J. Dobson	39	207	15	10	4	4.18
C. Stobbs	32	169	12	7	1	5.10
M. McDermott	38	130	7	3	5	5.19
W. Masterson	33	129	8	6	1	5.64
W. Nixon	22	101	8	6	2	6.04

Cle.
W-92 L-62
Lou Boudreau

POS	Player	AB	BA	HR	RBI	PO	A	E	DP	TC/G	FA
1B	L. Easter	540	.280	28	107	1100	82	11	114	9.3	.991
2B	J. Gordon	368	.236	19	57	224	283	16	69	5.0	.969
SS	R. Boone	365	.301	7	58	178	267	26	64	4.6	.945
3B	A. Rosen	554	.287	**37**	116	151	**322**	15	24	3.2	.969
RF	B. Kennedy	540	.291	9	54	294	13	4	3	2.2	.987
CF	L. Doby	503	.326	25	102	367	2	5	1	2.7	.987
LF	D. Mitchell	506	.308	3	49	236	3	7	1	1.9	.972
C	J. Hegan	415	.219	14	58	656	**64**	5	14	5.6	.993
SS	L. Boudreau	260	.269	1	29	118	170	4	44	4.8	.986
2B	B. Avila	201	.299	1	21	153	135	5	46	4.7	.983
OF	A. Clark	163	.215	6	21	75	2	1	0	1.9	.987
P	B. Lemon	136	.272	6	26	22	66	4	6	2.1	.957

Pitcher	G	IP	W	L	SV	ERA
B. Lemon	44	**288**	**23**	11	3	3.84
B. Feller	35	247	16	11	0	3.43
E. Wynn	32	214	18	8	0	**3.20**
M. Garcia	33	184	11	11	0	3.86
S. Gromek	31	113	10	7	0	3.65
S. Zoldak	33	64	4	2	4	3.96
A. Benton	36	63	4	2	4	3.57
J. Flores	28	53	3	3	4	3.74

Was.
W-67 L-87
Bucky Harris

POS	Player	AB	BA	HR	RBI	PO	A	E	DP	TC/G	FA
1B	M. Vernon	327	.306	9	65	743	61	8	93	9.6	.990*
2B	C. Michaels	388	.250	4	47	298	323	16*	91	6.1	.975
SS	S. Dente	603	.239	2	59	225	406	32	88	5.2	.952
3B	E. Yost	573	.295	11	58	205	307	30	45	3.5	.945
RF	B. Stewart	378	.267	4	35	202	10	2	3	2.1	.991
CF	I. Noren	542	.295	14	98	357	20	6	5	3.2	.984
LF	G. Coan	366	.303	7	50	220	4	7	1	2.4	.970
C	A. Evans	289	.235	2	30	289	23	4	8	3.6	.987
OF	S. Mele	435	.274	12	86	192	8	2	0	2.0	.990
C	M. Grasso	195	.287	1	22	238	38	17	6	4.2	.942
OF	J. Ostrowski	141	.227	4	23	105	3	6	1	2.5	.947

Pitcher	G	IP	W	L	SV	ERA
S. Hudson	30	238	14	14	0	4.09
B. Kuzava	22	155	8	7	0	3.95
C. Marrero	27	152	6	10	1	4.50
S. Consuegra	21	125	7	8	2	4.40
J. Haynes	27	102	7	5	0	5.84
M. Harris	53	98	5	9	**15**	4.78

Chi.
W-60 L-94
Jack Onslow
W-8 L-22
Red Corriden
W-52 L-72

POS	Player	AB	BA	HR	RBI	PO	A	E	DP	TC/G	FA
1B	E. Robinson	428	.311	20	73	982*	60	14	105	8.9	.987
2B	N. Fox	457	.247	0	30	340	344	18	100	5.8	.974
SS	C. Carrasquel	524	.282	4	46	234	458	28	113	5.1	.961
3B	H. Majeski	414	.309	6	46	115	246	11	31	3.3	.970
RF	M. Rickert	278	.237	4	27	150	3	5	1	2.0	.968
CF	D. Philley	619	.242	14	80	367	19	8	8	2.6	.980
LF	G. Zernial	543	.280	29	93	306	9	10	2	2.4	.969
C	P. Masi	377	.279	7	55	440	52	2	9	4.3	**.996**
3B	F. Baker	186	.317	0	11	50	102	2	7	2.9	.987
1B	G. Goldsberry	127	.268	2	25	235	29	3	37	6.7	.989

Pitcher	G	IP	W	L	SV	ERA
B. Pierce	33	219	12	16	1	3.98
B. Wight	30	206	10	16	0	3.58
B. Cain	34	172	9	12	2	3.93
R. Gumpert	40	155	5	12	0	4.75
Scarborough	27	149	10	13	1	5.30
H. Judson	46	112	2	3	0	3.94
K. Holcombe	24	96	3	10	1	4.59
L. Aloma	42	88	7	2	4	3.80

St. L.
W-58 L-96
Zack Taylor

POS	Player	AB	BA	HR	RBI	PO	A	E	DP	TC/G	FA
1B	D. Lenhardt	480	.273	22	81	618	39	8	77	7.7	.988
2B	O. Friend	372	.237	8	50	244	302	22	62	6.1	.961
SS	T. Upton	389	.237	2	30	198	328	30	65	4.8	.946
3B	B. Sommers	137	.255	0	14	25	52	7	5	2.3	.917
RF	K. Wood	369	.225	13	62	162	16	9	2	2.0	.952
CF	R. Coleman	384	.271	8	55	253	7	4	1	2.7	.985
LF	D. Kokos	490	.261	18	67	342	8	11	2	2.8	.970
C	S. Lollar	396	.280	13	65	367	48	8	9	3.9	.981
OF	R. Sievers	370	.238	10	57	222	12	4	3	3.1	.983
23	S. Stirnweiss	326	.218	1	24	191	206	12	51		.971
1B	H. Arft	280	.268	1	32	701	51	4	59	9.0	.995
C	L. Moss	222	.266	8	34	204	20	10	4	3.9	.957
OF	J. Delsing	209	.263	0	15	150	4	1	3	2.9	.994
SS	B. DeMars	178	.247	0	13	113	123	17	32	4.7	.933

Pitcher	G	IP	W	L	SV	ERA
N. Garver	37	260	13	18	0	3.39
A. Widmar	36	195	7	15	4	4.76
S. Overmire	31	161	9	12	0	4.19
D. Starr	32	124	7	5	2	5.02
H. Dorish	29	109	4	9	0	6.44
C. Fannin	25	102	5	9	1	6.53
D. Johnson	25	96	5	6	1	6.09
D. Pillette	24	74	3	5	2	7.09

Phi.
W-52 L-102
Connie Mack

POS	Player	AB	BA	HR	RBI	PO	A	E	DP	TC/G	FA
1B	F. Fain	522	.282	10	83	1286	**124**	19	**192**	9.5	.987
2B	B. Hitchcock	399	.273	1	54	297	319	21	105	6.0	.967
SS	E. Joost	476	.233	18	58	241	389	29	117	5.0	.966
3B	B. Dillinger	356	.309	3	41	92	173	12	18	3.3	.957
RF	E. Valo	446	.280	10	46	264	9	5	3	2.4	.982
CF	S. Chapman	553	.251	23	95	**428**	11	10	4	**3.2**	.978
LF	P. Lehner	427	.309	9	52	247	10	5	1	2.6	.981
C	M. Guerra	252	.282	2	26	253	33	3	8	3.7	.990
3B	K. Wahl	280	.257	2	27	70	141	12	11	3.7	.946
OF	W. Moses	265	.264	2	21	147	7	2	2	2.5	.987
UT	P. Suder	248	.246	8	35	167	181	9	55		.975
C	J. Tipton	184	.266	6	20	201	24	3	3	3.9	.987
OF	B. McCosky	179	.240	0	11	73	1	1	1	1.8	.987

Pitcher	G	IP	W	L	SV	ERA
L. Brissie	46	246	7	19	8	4.02
A. Kellner	36	225	8	**20**	2	5.47
B. Shantz	36	215	8	14	0	4.61
H. Wyse	41	171	9	14	0	5.85
B. Hooper	45	170	15	10	5	5.02
C. Scheib	43	106	3	10	3	7.22

BATTING AND BASE RUNNING LEADERS

Batting Average

B. Goodman, BOS	.354
G. Kell, DET	.340
D. DiMaggio, BOS	.328
L. Doby, CLE	.326
A. Zarilla, BOS	.325

Slugging Average

J. DiMaggio, NY	.585
W. Dropo, BOS	.583
H. Evers, DET	.551
L. Doby, CLE	.545
A. Rosen, CLE	.543

Home Runs

A. Rosen, CLE	37
W. Dropo, BOS	34
J. DiMaggio, NY	32
V. Stephens, BOS	30
G. Zernial, CHI	29

Total Bases

W. Dropo, BOS	326
V. Stephens, BOS	321
Y. Berra, NY	318
G. Kell, DET	310
J. DiMaggio, NY	307

Runs Batted In

W. Dropo, BOS	144
V. Stephens, BOS	144
Y. Berra, NY	124
V. Wertz, DET	123
J. DiMaggio, NY	122

Stolen Bases

D. DiMaggio, BOS	15
E. Valo, PHI	12
P. Rizzuto, NY	12
G. Coan, WAS	10
J. Lipon, DET	9

Hits

G. Kell, DET	218
P. Rizzuto, NY	200
D. DiMaggio, BOS	193

Base on Balls

E. Yost, WAS	141
F. Fain, PHI	132
J. Pesky, BOS	104

Home Run Percentage

A. Rosen, CLE	6.7
J. DiMaggio, NY	6.1
W. Dropo, BOS	6.1

Runs Scored

D. DiMaggio, BOS	131
P. Rizzuto, NY	125
V. Stephens, BOS	125
Y. Berra, NY	116

Doubles

G. Kell, DET	56
V. Wertz, DET	37
P. Rizzuto, NY	36

Triples

H. Evers, DET	11
B. Doerr, BOS	11
D. DiMaggio, BOS	11

PITCHING LEADERS

Winning Percentage

V. Raschi, NY	.724
E. Lopat, NY	.692
E. Wynn, CLE	.692
F. Hutchinson, DET	.680
B. Lemon, CLE	.676

Earned Run Average

E. Wynn, CLE	3.20
N. Garver, STL	3.39
B. Feller, CLE	3.43
E. Lopat, NY	3.47
A. Houtteman, DET	3.54

Wins

B. Lemon, CLE	23
V. Raschi, NY	21
A. Houtteman, DET	19
E. Lopat, NY	18
E. Wynn, CLE	18
M. Parnell, BOS	18

Saves

M. Harris, WAS	15
J. Page, NY	13
T. Ferrick, NY, STL	11
E. Kinder, BOS	9
L. Brissie, PHI	8

Strikeouts

B. Lemon, CLE	170
A. Reynolds, NY	160
V. Raschi, NY	155
E. Wynn, CLE	143
B. Feller, CLE	119

Complete Games

N. Garver, STL	22
B. Lemon, CLE	22
M. Parnell, BOS	21
A. Houtteman, DET	21
S. Hudson, WAS	17
V. Raschi, NY	17

Fewest Hits per 9 Innings

E. Wynn, CLE	6.99
B. Pierce, CHI	7.76
B. Cain, CHI	8.02

Shutouts

A. Houtteman, DET	4

Fewest Walks per 9 Innings

F. Hutchinson, DET	1.86
E. Lopat, NY	2.48
D. Trout, DET	3.12

Most Strikeouts per 9 Inn.

E. Wynn, CLE	6.02
A. Reynolds, NY	5.98
V. Raschi, NY	5.44

Innings

B. Lemon, CLE	288
A. Houtteman, DET	275
N. Garver, STL	260

Games Pitched

M. Harris, WAS	53
E. Kinder, BOS	48

	W	L	PCT	GB	R	OR	2B	3B	HR	BA	SA	SB	E	DP	FA	CG	BB	SO	ShO	SV	ERA
NY	98	56	.636		914	691	234	70	159	.282	.441	41	119	188	.980	66	708	712	12	31	4.15
DET	95	59	.617	3	837	713	285	50	114	.282	.417	23	120	194	.981	72	553	576	9	20	4.12
BOS	94	60	.610	4	1027	804	287	61	161	.302	.464	32	111	181	.981	66	748	630	6	28	4.88
CLE	92	62	.597	6	806	654	222	46	164	.269	.422	40	129	160	.978	69	647	674	11	16	4.66
WAS	67	87	.435	31	690	813	190	53	76	.260	.360	42	167	181	.972	59	648	486	7	18	4.41
CHI	60	94	.390	38	625	749	172	47	93	.260	.364	19	140	181	.977	62	734	448	7	9	4.41
STL	58	96	.377	40	684	916	235	43	106	.246	.370	39	196	155	.967	56	651	448	7	14	5.20
PHI	52	102	.338	46	670	913	204	53	100	.261	.378	42	155	208	.974	50	729	466	3	18	5.49
					6253	6253	1829	423	973	.271	.402	278	1137	1448	.976	500	5418	4558	62	154	4.58

National League 1951

	POS	Player	AB	BA	HR	RBI	PO	A	E	DP	TC/G	FA	Pitcher	G	IP	W	L	SV	ERA
N. Y.	1B	W. Lockman	614	.282	12	73	1045	89	16	113	9.7	.986	S. Maglie	42	298	23	6	4	2.93
W-98 L-59	2B	E. Stanky	515	.247	14	43	356	412	18	117	5.6	.977	L. Jansen	39	278	23	11	0	3.04
Leo Durocher	SS	A. Dark	646	.303	14	69	295	465	45	114	5.2	.944	J. Hearn	34	211	17	9	0	3.62
	3B	H. Thompson	264	.235	8	33	64	120	15	16	2.8	.925	D. Koslo	39	150	10	9	3	3.31
	RF	D. Mueller	469	.277	16	69	233	5	4	1	2.1	.983	G. Spencer	57	132	10	4	6	3.75
	CF	W. Mays	464	.274	20	68	353	12	9	2	3.1	.976	S. Jones	41	120	6	11	4	4.26
	LF	M. Irvin	558	.312	24	121	237	10	1	1	2.2	.996							
	C	W. Westrum	361	.219	20	70	554	62	8	9	5.1	.987							
	O3	B. Thomson	518	.293	32	101	258	139	20	14		.952							
	C	R. Noble	141	.234	5	26	144	8	4	3	3.8	.974							

	POS	Player	AB	BA	HR	RBI	PO	A	E	DP	TC/G	FA	Pitcher	G	IP	W	L	SV	ERA
Bkn. W-97 L-60 Chuck Dressen	1B	G. Hodges	582	.268	40	103	1365	**126**	12	**171**	9.5	.992	D. Newcombe	40	272	20	9	0	3.28
	2B	J. Robinson	548	.338	19	88	**390**	**435**	7	**137**	5.4	**.992**	P. Roe	34	258	22	3	0	3.04
	SS	P. Reese	616	.286	10	84	292	422	35	106	4.9	.953	R. Branca	42	204	13	12	3	3.26
	3B	B. Cox	455	.279	9	51	140	264	14	26	3.0	.967	C. Erskine	46	190	16	12	4	4.46
	RF	C. Furillo	**667**	.295	16	91	330	24	5	6	2.3	.986	C. King	48	121	14	7	6	4.15
	CF	D. Snider	606	.277	29	101	382	12	5	1	2.7	.987							
	LF	A. Pafko	277	.249	18	58	144	8	1	0	2.0	.993							
	C	R. Campanella	505	.325	33	108	**722**	72	**11**	12	**5.8**	.986							
St. L. W-81 L-73 Marty Marion	1B	N. Jones	300	.263	3	41	698	48	7	7	10.6	.991	G. Staley	42	227	19	13	3	3.81
	2B	Schoendienst	553	.289	6	54	339	386	7	113	5.9	.990	T. Poholsky	38	195	7	13	1	4.43
	SS	S. Hemus	420	.281	2	32	181	344	19	72	**5.2**	.965	M. Lanier	31	160	11	9	1	3.26
	3B	B. Johnson	442	.262	14	64	99	316	10	32	3.4	**.976**	A. Brazle	56	154	6	5	7	3.09
	RF	E. Slaughter	409	.281	4	64	198	10	1	3	2.0	.995	H. Brecheen	24	139	8	4	2	3.25
	CF	P. Lowrey	370	.303	5	40	220	6	4	3	2.7	.983	C. Chambers	21	129	11	6	0	3.83
	LF	S. Musial	578	**.355**	32	108	216	13	6	4	2.6	.974	G. Munger	23	95	4	6	0	5.32
	C	D. Rice	374	.251	9	47	447	66	8	**12**	4.3	.985	J. Presko	15	89	7	4	2	3.45
	OF	W. Westlake	267	.255	6	39	154	7	3	1	2.4	.982							
	OF	H. Rice	236	.254	4	38	116	6	6	0	2.0	.953							
	SS	S. Rojek	186	.274	0	14	95	131	6	36	4.5	.974							
Bos. W-76 L-78 Billy Southworth W-28 L-31 Tommy Holmes W-48 L-47	1B	E. Torgeson	581	.263	24	92	1330	107	**17**	137	9.4	.988	W. Spahn	39	311	22	14	0	2.98
	2B	R. Hartsfield	450	.271	6	31	336	293	20	87	5.7	.969	M. Surkont	37	237	12	16	1	3.99
	SS	B. Kerr	172	.186	1	18	110	173	9	34	4.6	.969	V. Bickford	25	165	11	9	0	3.12
	3B	B. Elliott	480	.285	15	70	138	242	**24**	31	3.2	.941	J. Sain	26	160	5	13	1	4.21
	RF	W. Marshall	469	.281	11	62	220	11	0	3	1.8	**1.000**	C. Nichols	33	156	11	8	2	**2.88**
	CF	S. Jethroe	572	.280	18	65	356	18	**10**	5	2.7	.974	J. Wilson	20	110	7	7	1	5.40
	LF	S. Gordon	550	.287	29	109	249	4	4	1	2.1	.984	B. Chipman	33	52	4	3	4	4.85
	C	W. Cooper	342	.313	18	59	367	57	8	9	4.8	.981							
	2S	S. Sisti	362	.279	2	38	220	227	18	47		.961							
	C	E. St. Claire	220	.282	1	25	267	29	7	5	4.9	.977							
	OF	B. Addis	199	.276	1	24	107	1	2	1	2.4	.982							
	SS	J. Logan	169	.219	0	16	98	155	11	31	4.6	.958							
Phi. W-73 L-81 Eddie Sawyer	1B	E. Waitkus	610	.257	1	46	1214	94	10	121	9.2	.992	R. Roberts	44	**315**	21	15	2	3.03
	2B	P. Caballero	161	.186	1	11	133	124	4	37	4.6	.985	B. Church	38	247	15	11	1	3.53
	SS	G. Hamner	589	.255	9	72	255	458	31	93	5.0	.958	R. Meyer	28	168	8	9	0	3.48
	3B	W. Jones	564	.285	22	81	190	286	17	**33**	3.4	.966	J. Thompson	29	119	4	8	1	3.85
	RF	D. Ennis	532	.267	15	73	268	14	9	3	2.0	.969	Heintzelman	35	118	6	12	2	4.18
	CF	R. Ashburn	643	.344	4	63	**538**	15	7	6	3.6	.988	J. Konstanty	58	116	4	11	9	4.05
	LF	D. Sisler	428	.287	8	52	233	8	8	3	2.2	.968	K. Johnson	20	106	5	8	0	4.57
	C	A. Seminick	291	.227	11	37	378	47	9	6	4.8	.979							
	C	D. Wilber	245	.278	8	34	326	26	8	5	4.9	.978							
	2B	E. Pellagrini	197	.234	5	30	80	110	2	19	3.6	.990							
	UT	T. Brown	196	.219	10	32	174	36	8	14		.963							
	OF	B. Nicholson	170	.241	8	30	75	1	1	0	1.9	.987							
Cin. W-68 L-86 Luke Sewell	1B	T. Kluszewski	607	.259	13	77	**1381**	88	5	**115**	9.6	**.997**	Raffensberger	42	249	16	**17**	5	3.44
	2B	C. Ryan	473	.237	16	53	332	344	21	73	5.8	.970	E. Blackwell	38	232	16	15	2	3.45
	SS	V. Stallcup	428	.241	8	49	190	333	17	61	4.6	.970	H. Fox	40	228	9	14	2	3.83
	3B	G. Hatton	331	.254	4	37	103	178	8	24	3.3	.972	W. Ramsdell	31	196	9	**17**	0	4.04
	RF	J. Wyrostek	537	.311	2	61	255	8	8	2	1.9	.970	H. Wehmeier	39	185	7	10	2	3.70
	CF	L. Merriman	359	.242	5	36	309	5	1	2	3.1	.997	H. Perkowski	35	102	3	6	1	2.82
	LF	J. Adcock	395	.243	10	47	221	8	4	2	2.2	.983	F. Smith	50	76	5	5	11	3.20
	C	D. Howell	207	.251	2	18	275	24	4	5	4.2	.987							
	32	B. Adams	403	.266	5	24	184	215	18	33		.957							
	OF	B. Usher	303	.208	5	25	218	9	6	4	2.4	.974							
	C	J. Pramesa	227	.229	6	22	241	27	9	4	4.4	.968							
	SS	R. McMillan	199	.211	1	8	78	132	8	23	4.0	.963							
	OF	H. Edwards	127	.315	3	20	64	0	1	0	1.9	.985							
Pit. W-64 L-90 Billy Meyer	1B	J. Phillips	156	.237	0	12	322	21	3	37	6.5	.991	M. Dickson	45	289	20	16	2	4.02
	2B	D. Murtaugh	151	.199	1	11	110	113	7	35	3.5	.970	M. Queen	39	168	7	9	0	4.44
	SS	G. Strickland	454	.216	9	47	222	386	37	89	5.2	.943	B. Werle	59	150	8	6	6	5.65
	3B	Castiglione	482	.261	7	42	103	228	15	25	3.5	.957	B. Friend	34	150	6	10	0	4.27
	RF	G. Bell	600	.278	16	89	267	18	4	4	2.0	.986	H. Pollet	21	129	6	10	0	5.04
	CF	C. Metkovich	423	.293	4	40	171	4	1	0	2.6	.994	V. Law	28	114	6	9	2	4.50
	LF	R. Kiner	531	.309	**42**	109	195	7	7	1	2.2	.977	T. Wilks	48*	83	3	5	12*	2.83
	C	McCullough	259	.297	8	39	364	52	5	10	4.9	.988							
	OF	B. Howerton	219	.274	11	37	93	3	5	1	1.9	.950							
	C	J. Garagiola	212	.255	9	35	255	30	4	4	4.7	.986							
	1B	R. Nelson	195	.267	1	14	275	24	3	32	9.4	.990							
	3B	W. Westlake	181	.282	16	45	32	87	12	12	3.9	.908							

	POS	Player	AB	BA	HR	RBI	PO	A	E	DP	TC/G	FA		Pitcher	G	IP	W	L	SV	ERA
Chi.	1B	C. Connors	201	.239	2	18	452	33	8	41	8.6	.984		B. Rush	37	211	11	12	2	3.83
W-62 L-92	2B	E. Miksis	421	.266	4	35	279	317	19	71	6.0*	.969		P. Minner	33	202	6	**17**	1	3.79
Frankie Frisch	SS	R. Smalley	238	.231	8	31	117	190	15	42	4.4	.953		C. McLish	30	146	4	10	0	4.45
W-35 L-45	3B	R. Jackson	557	.275	16	76	**198**	**323**	**24**	32	3.8	.956		F. Hiller	24	141	6	12	1	4.84
Phil Cavarretta	RF	H. Jeffcoat	278	.273	4	27	166	11	2	5	2.1	.989		T. Lown	31	127	4	9	0	5.46
W-27 L-47	CF	F. Baumholtz	560	.284	2	50	307	6	8	2	2.3	.975		J. Klippstein	35	124	6	6	2	4.29
	LF	H. Sauer	525	.263	30	89	286	19	6	2	2.4	.981		B. Kelly	35	124	7	4	0	4.66
	C	S. Burgess	219	.251	2	20	210	35	5	6	3.9	.980		D. Leonard	41	82	10	6	3	2.64
	OF	G. Hermanski	231	.281	3	20	134	9	5	1	2.0	.966								
	1B	P. Cavarretta	206	.311	6	28	444	42	3	51	9.2	.994								
	2B	Terwilliger	192	.214	0	10	136	142	9	37	5.9	.969								
	OF	A. Pafko	178	.264	12	35	119	6	1	3	2.6	.992								
	1B	D. Fondy	170	.271	3	20	387	27	10	40	9.6	.976								
	SS	J. Cusick	164	.177	2	16	78	147	11	25	4.2	.953								
	SS	B. Ramazzotti	158	.247	1	15	73	137	11	32	4.3	.950								

BATTING AND BASE RUNNING LEADERS

Batting Average
S. Musial, STL	.355
R. Ashburn, PHI	.344
J. Robinson, BKN	.338
R. Campanella, BKN	.325
M. Irvin, NY	.312

Slugging Average
R. Kiner, PIT	.627
S. Musial, STL	.614
R. Campanella, BKN	.590
B. Thomson, NY	.562
G. Hodges, BKN	.527

Home Runs
R. Kiner, PIT	42
G. Hodges, BKN	40
R. Campanella, BKN	33
B. Thomson, NY	32
S. Musial, STL	32

Total Bases
S. Musial, STL	355
R. Kiner, PIT	333
G. Hodges, BKN	307
R. Campanella, BKN	298
D. Snider, BKN	293
A. Dark, NY	293

Runs Batted In
M. Irvin, NY	121
R. Kiner, PIT	109
S. Gordon, BOS	109
R. Campanella, BKN	108
S. Musial, STL	108

Stolen Bases
S. Jethroe, BOS	35
R. Ashburn, PHI	29
J. Robinson, BKN	25
E. Torgeson, BOS	20
P. Reese, BKN	20

Hits
R. Ashburn, PHI	221
S. Musial, STL	205
C. Furillo, BKN	197

Base on Balls
R. Kiner, PIT	137
E. Stanky, NY	127
W. Westrum, NY	104

Home Run Percentage
R. Kiner, PIT	7.9
G. Hodges, BKN	6.9
A. Pafko, BKN, CHI	6.6

Runs Scored
R. Kiner, PIT	124
S. Musial, STL	124
G. Hodges, BKN	118

Doubles
A. Dark, NY	41
T. Kluszewski, CIN	35
R. Campanella, BKN	33
J. Robinson, BKN	33

Triples
S. Musial, STL	12
G. Bell, PIT	12
M. Irvin, NY	11

PITCHING LEADERS

Winning Percentage
P. Roe, BKN	.880
S. Maglie, NY	.793
D. Newcombe, BKN	.690
L. Jansen, NY	.676
J. Hearn, NY	.654

Earned Run Average
C. Nichols, BOS	2.88
S. Maglie, NY	2.93
W. Spahn, BOS	2.98
R. Roberts, PHI	3.03
P. Roe, BKN	3.04

Wins
S. Maglie, NY	23
L. Jansen, NY	23
P. Roe, BKN	22
W. Spahn, BOS	22
R. Roberts, PHI	21

Saves
T. Wilks, PIT, STL	13
F. Smith, CIN	11
J. Konstanty, PHI	9
A. Brazle, STL	7

Strikeouts
D. Newcombe, BKN	164
W. Spahn, BOS	164
S. Maglie, NY	146
L. Jansen, NY	145
B. Rush, CHI	129

Complete Games
W. Spahn, BOS	26
S. Maglie, NY	22
R. Roberts, PHI	22
P. Roe, BKN	19
M. Dickson, PIT	19

Fewest Hits per 9 Innings
S. Maglie, NY	7.67
D. Newcombe, BKN	7.78
E. Blackwell, CIN	7.90

Shutouts
R. Roberts, PHI	6
Raffensberger, CIN	5

Fewest Walks per 9 Innings
Raffensberger, CIN	1.38
L. Jansen, NY	1.81
R. Roberts, PHI	1.83

Most Strikeouts per 9 Inn.
M. Queen, PIT	6.58
B. Rush, CHI	5.49
D. Newcombe, BKN	5.43

Innings
R. Roberts, PHI	315
W. Spahn, BOS	311
S. Maglie, NY	298

Games Pitched
T. Wilks, PIT, STL	65
B. Werle, PIT	59
J. Konstanty, PHI	58

	W	L	PCT	GB	R	OR	Batting 2B	3B	HR	BA	SA	SB	Fielding E	DP	FA	Pitching CG	BB	SO	ShO	SV	ERA
NY *	98	59	.624		781	641	201	53	179	.260	.418	55	171	175	.972	64	**482**	625	9	18	**3.48**
BKN	97	60	.618	1	855	672	249	37	**184**	**.275**	**.434**	89	129	**192**	.979	64	549	**693**	10	13	3.88
STL	81	73	.526	15.5	683	671	230	**57**	95	.264	.382	30	**125**	187	**.980**	58	568	546	9	**23**	3.95
BOS	76	78	.494	20.5	723	662	234	37	130	.262	.394	78	145	157	.976	**73**	595	604	10	12	3.75
PHI	73	81	.474	23.5	648	644	199	47	108	.260	.375	64	138	146	.977	57	496	570	**19**	15	3.81
CIN	68	86	.442	28.5	559	667	215	33	88	.248	.351	44	140	141	.977	55	490	584	14	**23**	3.70
PIT	64	90	.416	32.5	689	845	218	56	137	.258	.397	26	170	178	.972	40	627	582	9	22	4.78
CHI	62	92	.403	34.5	614	750	200	47	103	.250	.364	63	181	161	.971	48	572	544	10	10	4.34
					5552	5552	1746	367	1024	.260	.390	449	1199	1337	.975	459	4379	4748	90	136	3.96

* Defeated Brooklyn in a playoff 2 games to 1.

POS	Player	AB	BA	HR	RBI	PO	A	E	DP	TC/G	FA	Pitcher	G	IP	W	L	SV	ERA
N. Y. W-98 L-56 Casey Stengel																		
1B	J. Collins	262	.286	9	48	556	56	8	65	5.4	.987	V. Raschi	35	258	21	10	0	3.27
2B	J. Coleman	362	.249	3	43	245	268	17	84	5.2	.968	E. Lopat	31	235	21	9	0	2.91
SS	P. Rizzuto	540	.274	2	43	317	407	24	113	5.2	.968	A. Reynolds	40	221	17	8	7	3.05
3B	B. Brown	313	.268	6	51	80	151	11	14	2.7	.955	T. Morgan	27	125	9	3	2	3.68
RF	H. Bauer	348	.296	10	54	188	7	2	1	1.8	.990	S. Shea	25	96	5	5	0	4.33
CF	J. DiMaggio	415	.263	12	71	288	11	3	3	2.7	.990	J. Ostrowski	34	95	6	4	5	3.49
LF	G. Woodling	420	.281	15	71	265	5	2	0	2.3	.993	B. Kuzava	23	82	8	4	5	2.40
C	Y. Berra	547	.294	27	88	693	82	13	25	5.6	.984							
32	G. McDougald	402	.306	14	63	174	249	14	46		.968							
OF	M. Mantle	341	.267	13	65	135	4	6	1	1.7	.959							
1B	J. Mize	332	.259	10	49	632	44	4	86	7.3	.994							
OF	J. Jensen	168	.298	8	25	106	6	3	1	2.4	.974							
Cle. W-93 L-61 Al Lopez																		
1B	L. Easter	486	.270	27	103	1043	68	14	108	9.0	.988	E. Wynn	37	**274**	20	13	1	3.02
2B	B. Avila	542	.304	10	58	349	417	14	87	5.7	.982	B. Lemon	42	263	17	14	2	3.52
SS	R. Boone	544	.233	12	51	311	425	**33**	108	5.1	.957	M. Garcia	47	254	20	13	6	3.15
3B	A. Rosen	573	.265	24	102	157	277	19	20	2.9	.958	B. Feller	33	250	**22**	8	0	3.50
RF	B. Kennedy	321	.246	7	29	174	9	6	2	1.8	.968	L. Brissie	54	112	4	3	9	3.20
CF	L. Doby	447	.295	20	69	321	12	8	3	2.6	.977	S. Gromek	27	107	7	4	1	2.77
LF	D. Mitchell	510	.290	11	62	253	3	2	0	2.1	.992							
C	J. Hegan	416	.238	6	43	597	66	6	8	5.2	**.991**							
O1	H. Simpson	332	.229	7	24	458	20	8	29		.984							
OF	S. Chapman	246	.228	6	36	132	2	2	1	1.6	.985							
Bos. W-87 L-67 Steve O'Neill																		
1B	W. Dropo	360	.239	11	57	878	63	12	91	10.2	.987	M. Parnell	36	221	18	11	2	3.26
2B	B. Doerr	402	.289	13	73	303	311	12	99	5.9	.981	Scarborough	42	184	12	9	0	5.09
SS	J. Pesky	480	.313	3	41	204	340	22	74	5.3	.961	M. McDermott	34	172	8	8	3	3.35
3B	V. Stephens	377	.300	17	78	105	207	7	19	3.6	.978	C. Stobbs	34	170	10	9	0	4.76
RF	C. Vollmer	386	.251	22	85	206	5	3	0	2.0	.986	E. Kinder	**63**	127	11	2	**14**	2.55
CF	D. DiMaggio	**639**	.296	12	72	376	15	11	1	2.8	.973	W. Nixon	33	125	7	4	1	4.90
LF	T. Williams	531	.318	30	126	315	12	4	**6**	2.3	.988	B. Wight	34	118	7	7	0	5.10
C	L. Moss	202	.198	3	26	284	28	5	4	4.6	.984	L. Kiely	17	113	7	7	0	3.34
UT	B. Goodman	546	.297	0	50	742	170	14	96		.985	H. Taylor	31	81	4	9	2	5.75
SS	L. Boudreau	273	.267	5	47	80	153	12	45	4.7	.951							
C	B. Rosar	170	.229	1	13	235	20	1	6	4.6	.996							
3B	F. Hatfield	163	.172	2	14	40	124	7	15	3.5	.959							
Chi. W-81 L-73 Paul Richards																		
1B	E. Robinson	564	.282	29	117	**1296**	91	**17**	**143**	9.6	.988	B. Pierce	37	240	15	**14**	2	3.03
2B	N. Fox	604	.313	4	55	413	449	17	112	**6.0**	.981	S. Rogovin	22	193	11	7	0	2.48*
SS	C. Carrasquel	538	.264	2	58	306	**477**	20	107	5.5	**.975**	K. Holcombe	28	159	11	12	0	3.78
3B	B. Dillinger	299	.301	0	20	70	116	14	10	2.9	.930	J. Dobson	28	147	7	6	3	3.62
RF	A. Zarilla	382	.257	10	60	164	7	3	2	1.5	.983	R. Gumpert	33	142	9	8	2	4.32
CF	J. Busby	477	.283	5	68	360	16	7	4	2.8	.982	L. Kretlow	26	137	6	9	0	4.20
LF	M. Minoso	516	.324	10	74	145	6	6	0	1.9	.961	H. Judson	27	122	5	6	1	3.77
C	P. Masi	225	.271	4	28	299	24	7	7	4.2	.979	H. Dorish	32	97	5	6	0	3.54
OF	B. Stewart	217	.276	6	40	111	4	2	0	1.9	.983							
OF	D. Lenhardt	199	.266	10	45	116	2	2	0	2.3	.983							
OF	R. Coleman	181	.276	3	21	141	3	3	1	2.9	.980							
C	G. Niarhos	168	.256	1	10	240	31	4	5	4.7	.985							
Det. W-73 L-81 Red Rolfe																		
1B	D. Kryhoski	421	.287	12	57	964	81	9	95	9.4	.991	T. Gray	34	197	7	**14**	1	4.06
2B	B. Priddy	584	.260	8	57	**437**	**463**	18	**118**	6.0	.980	D. Trout	42	192	9	**14**	5	4.04
SS	J. Lipon	487	.265	0	38	244	364	**33**	80	5.1	.949	F. Hutchinson	31	188	10	10	2	3.68
3B	G. Kell	598	.319	2	59	175	**310**	20	**34**	**3.4**	**.960**	V. Trucks	37	154	13	8	1	4.33
RF	V. Wertz	501	.285	27	94	254	7	3	1	2.0	.989	B. Cain	35	149	11	10	2	4.70
CF	J. Groth	428	.299	3	49	266	12	2	2	2.5	.993	M. Stuart	29	124	4	6	1	3.77
LF	H. Evers	393	.224	11	46	334	9	6	1	2.3	.976	G. Bearden	30	106	3	4	0	4.33
C	J. Ginsberg	304	.260	8	37	388	56	10	7	4.8	.978	H. Newhouser	15	96	6	6	0	3.92
OF	P. Mullin	295	.281	12	51	151	4	10	1	2.0	.939	H. White	38	76	3	4	4	4.74
1B	D. Kolloway	212	.255	1	17	452	49	4	53	8.6	.992							
OF	S. Souchock	188	.245	11	28	92	3	6	1	1.7	.941							
UT	N. Berry	157	.229	0	9	78	127	12	22		.945							
PH	C. Keller	62	.258	3	21													
Phi. W-70 L-84 Jimmy Dykes																		
1B	F. Fain	425	.344	6	57	931	**113**	11	124	**9.8**	.990	A. Kellner	33	210	11	**14**	2	4.46
2B	P. Suder	440	.245	1	42	274	313	8	93	5.8	**.987**	B. Shantz	32	205	18	10	0	3.94
SS	E. Joost	553	.289	19	78	**325**	422	20	**115**	5.5	.974	B. Hooper	38	189	12	10	5	4.38
3B	H. Majeski	323	.285	5	42	82	217	8	17	3.5	.974	C. Scheib	46	143	1	12	10	4.47
RF	E. Valo	444	.302	7	55	247	5	5	0	2.2	.981	M. Martin	35	138	11	4	0	3.78
CF	D. Philley	468	.263	7	59	299	15	7	4	2.7	.978	S. Zoldak	26	128	6	10	0	3.16
LF	G. Zernial	552	.274	33*	125*	321	17*	9	3	2.5	.974	D. Fowler	22	125	5	11	0	5.62
C	J. Tipton	213	.239	3	20	230	52	9	12	4.0	.969	J. Kucab	30	75	4	3	4	4.22
32	B. Hitchcock	222	.306	1	36	92	150	14	30		.945							
1B	L. Limmer	214	.159	5	30	450	40	6	54	8.6	.988							
C	J. Astroth	187	.246	2	19	228	18	2	2	4.4	.992							
OF	A. Clark	161	.248	4	22	60	2	1	1	2.0	.984							

POS	Player	AB	BA	HR	RBI	PO	A	E	DP	TC/G	FA	Pitcher	G	IP	W	L	SV	ERA
Was.												C. Marrero	25	187	11	9	0	3.90
1B	M. Vernon	546	.293	9	87	1157	87	8	121	9.1	.994	S. Consuegra	40	146	7	8	3	4.01
W-62 L-92	2B	C. Michaels	485	.258	4	45	258	391	24	86	5.3	.964	D. Johnson	21	144	7	11	0	3.95
Bucky Harris	SS	P. Runnels	273	.278	0	25	159	176	18	41	4.8	.949	S. Hudson	23	139	5	12	0	5.13
	3B	E. Yost	568	.283	12	65	203	234	21	22	3.0	.954	Porterfield	19	133	9	8	0	3.24
	RF	S. Mele	558	.274	5	94	263	8	2	1	2.2	.993	J. Moreno	31	133	5	11	2	4.88
	CF	I. Noren	509	.279	8	86	420	15	10	1	3.5	.978	M. Harris	41	87	6	8	4	3.81
	LF	G. Coan	538	.303	9	62	374	17	14	2	3.1	.965	A. Sima	18	77	3	7	0	4.79
	C	M. Guerra	214	.201	1	20	192	25	5	0	3.4	.977							
	SS	S. Dente	273	.238	0	29	128	173	12	43	4.8	.962							
	OF	M. McCormick	243	.288	1	23	134	7	5	0	2.4	.966							
	S2	G. Verble	177	.203	0	15	101	123	5	28		.978							
	C	M. Grasso	175	.206	1	14	182	26	7	6	4.4	.967							
	C	C. Kluttz	159	.308	1	22	162	15	6	2	4.2	.967							
St. L.												N. Garver	33	246	20	12	0	3.73
1B	H. Arft	345	.261	7	42	820	86	10	100	9.4	.989	D. Pillette	35	191	6	14	0	4.99
W-52 L-102	2B	B. Young	611	.260	1	31	361	462	17	118	5.7	.980	T. Byrne	19	123	4	10	0	3.82
Zack Taylor	SS	B. Jennings	195	.179	0	13	141	165	15	39	5.0	.953	A. Widmar	26	108	4	9	0	6.52
	3B	F. Marsh	445	.243	4	43	137	225	28	31	3.3	.928	J. McDonald	16	84	4	7	1	4.07
	RF	K. Wood	333	.237	15	44	179	7	8	0	1.9	.959	L. Sleater	20	81	1	9	1	5.11
	CF	J. Delsing	449	.249	8	45	340	15	6	5	2.9	.983	S. Paige	23	62	3	4	5	4.79
	LF	R. Coleman	341	.282	5	55	185	9	5	1	2.3	.975							
	C	S. Lollar	310	.252	8	44	361	48	2	8	4.8	.995							
	C	M. Batts	248	.302	5	31	259	30	12*	4	4.7	.960							
	OF	C. Mapes	201	.274	7	30	111	4	2	1	2.2	.983							
	SS	J. Bero	160	.213	5	17	91	137	11	30	4.3	.954							

BATTING AND BASE RUNNING LEADERS

Batting Average

F. Fain, PHI	.344
M. Minoso, CHI, CLE	.326
G. Kell, DET	.319
T. Williams, BOS	.318
N. Fox, CHI	.313

Slugging Average

T. Williams, BOS	.556
L. Doby, CLE	.512
G. Zernial, CHI, PHI	.511
V. Wertz, DET	.511
M. Minoso, CHI, CLE	.500

Home Runs

G. Zernial, CHI, PHI	33
T. Williams, BOS	30
E. Robinson, CHI	29
L. Easter, CLE	27
V. Wertz, DET	27
Y. Berra, NY	27

Total Bases

T. Williams, BOS	295
G. Zernial, CHI, PHI	292
E. Robinson, CHI	279
Y. Berra, NY	269
D. DiMaggio, BOS	267

Runs Batted In

G. Zernial, CHI, PHI	129
T. Williams, BOS	126
E. Robinson, CHI	117
L. Easter, CLE	103
A. Rosen, CLE	102

Stolen Bases

M. Minoso, CHI, CLE	31
J. Busby, CHI	26
P. Rizzuto, NY	18
G. McDougald, NY	14
C. Carrasquel, CHI	14
B. Avila, CLE	14

Hits

G. Kell, DET	191
N. Fox, CHI	189
D. DiMaggio, BOS	189

Base on Balls

T. Williams, BOS	143
E. Yost, WAS	126
E. Joost, PHI	106

Home Run Percentage

G. Zernial, CHI, PHI	5.8
T. Williams, BOS	5.6
L. Easter, CLE	5.6

Runs Scored

D. DiMaggio, BOS	113
M. Minoso, CHI, CLE	112
T. Williams, BOS	109
E. Yost, WAS	109

Doubles

S. Mele, WAS	36
E. Yost, WAS	36
G. Kell, DET	36

Triples

M. Minoso, CHI, CLE	14
R. Coleman, CHI, STL	12
N. Fox, CHI	12

PITCHING LEADERS

Winning Percentage

B. Feller, CLE	.733
E. Lopat, NY	.700
A. Reynolds, NY	.680
V. Raschi, NY	.677
B. Shantz, PHI	.643

Earned Run Average

S. Rogovin, CHI, DET	2.78
E. Lopat, NY	2.91
E. Wynn, CLE	3.02
B. Pierce, CHI	3.03
A. Reynolds, NY	3.05

Wins

B. Feller, CLE	22
E. Lopat, NY	21
V. Raschi, NY	21
N. Garver, STL	20
M. Garcia, CLE	20
E. Wynn, CLE	20

Saves

E. Kinder, BOS	14
C. Scheib, PHI	10
L. Brissie, CLE, PHI	9
A. Reynolds, NY	7
M. Garcia, CLE	6

Strikeouts

V. Raschi, NY	164
E. Wynn, CLE	133
B. Lemon, CLE	132
T. Gray, DET	131
M. McDermott, BOS	127

Complete Games

N. Garver, STL	24
E. Wynn, CLE	21
E. Lopat, NY	20
B. Pierce, CHI	18
S. Rogovin, CHI, DET	17
B. Lemon, CLE	17

Fewest Hits per 9 Innings

A. Reynolds, NY	6.96
M. McDermott, BOS	7.38
E. Wynn, CLE	7.45

Shutouts

A. Reynolds, NY	7
E. Lopat, NY	5

Fewest Walks per 9 Innings

F. Hutchinson, DET	1.29
E. Lopat, NY	2.72
B. Pierce, CHI	2.73

Most Strikeouts per 9 Inn.

M. McDermott, BOS	6.65
T. Gray, DET	5.97
V. Raschi, NY	5.71

Innings

E. Wynn, CLE	274
B. Lemon, CLE	263
V. Raschi, NY	258

Games Pitched

E. Kinder, BOS	63
L. Brissie, CLE, PHI	56
M. Garcia, CLE	47

	W	L	PCT	GB	R	OR	2B	3B	HR	BA	SA	SB	E	DP	FA	CG	BB	SO	ShO	SV	ERA
									Batting					**Fielding**				**Pitching**			
NY	98	56	.636		798	621	208	48	**140**	.269	**.408**	78	144	190	.975	66	562	**664**	24	22	3.56
CLE	93	61	.604	5	696	594	208	35	**140**	.256	.389	52	**134**	151	.978	76	577	642	10	19	**3.38**
BOS	87	67	.565	11	**804**	725	233	32	127	.266	.392	20	141	184	.977	46	599	658	7	**24**	4.14
CHI	81	73	.526	17	714	644	229	**64**	86	**.270**	.385	**99**	151	176	.975	74	**549**	572	11	14	3.50
DET	73	81	.474	25	685	741	231	35	104	.265	.380	37	163	166	.973	51	602	597	8	17	4.29
PHI	70	84	.455	28	736	745	**262**	43	102	.262	.386	48	136	**204**	.978	52	569	437	7	22	4.47
WAS	62	92	.403	36	672	764	242	45	54	.263	.355	45	160	148	.973	58	630	475	6	13	4.49
STL	52	102	.338	46	611	882	223	47	86	.247	.357	35	172	179	.971	56	801	550	5	9	5.17
					5716	5716	1836	349	839	.262	.381	414	1201	1398	.975	479	4889	4595	78	140	4.12

National League 1952

	POS	Player	AB	BA	HR	RBI	PO	A	E	DP	TC/G	FA	Pitcher	G	IP	W	L	SV	ERA
Bkn. W-96 L-57 Chuck Dressen	1B	G. Hodges	508	.254	32	102	1322	**116**	11	152	9.5	.992	C. Erskine	33	207	14	6	2	2.70
	2B	J. Robinson	510	.308	19	75	353	400	20	**113**	5.3	.974	B. Loes	39	187	13	8	1	2.69
	SS	P. Reese	559	.272	6	58	282	376	21	89	4.7	.969	B. Wade	37	180	11	9	3	3.60
	3B	B. Cox	455	.259	6	34	100	157	8	26	2.7	**.970**	P. Roe	27	159	11	2	0	3.12
	RF	C. Furillo	425	.247	8	59	225	12	3	2	1.8	.988	J. Black	56	142	15	4	15	2.15
	CF	D. Snider	534	.303	21	92	341	13	3	3	2.5	.992	C. Van Cuyk	23	98	5	6	1	5.16
	LF	A. Pafko	551	.287	19	85	229	18	3	2	1.8	.988	J. Rutherford	22	97	7	7	2	4.25
	C	R. Campanella	468	.269	22	97	662	55	4	7	5.9	**.994**	C. Labine	25	77	8	4	0	5.14
	OF	G. Shuba	256	.305	9	40	116	2	1	0	1.8	.992							
	3B	B. Morgan	191	.236	7	16	45	107	5	10	2.6	.968							
N. Y. W-92 L-62 Leo Durocher	1B	W. Lockman	606	.290	13	58	**1435**	111	13	**155**	10.1	.992	J. Hearn	37	224	14	7	1	3.78
	2B	D. Williams	540	.254	13	55	279	375	18	102	4.9	.973	S. Maglie	35	216	18	8	1	2.92
	SS	A. Dark	589	.301	14	73	**324**	423	27	**116**	5.2	.965	L. Jansen	34	167	11	11	2	4.09
	3B	B. Thomson	608	.270	24	108	82	184	17	13	3.1	.940	D. Koslo	41	166	10	7	5	3.19
	RF	D. Mueller	456	.281	12	49	221	8	3	4	1.9	.987	H. Wilhelm	71	159	15	3	11	**2.43**
	CF	H. Thompson	423	.260	17	67	182	5	4	1	2.7	.979	M. Lanier	37	137	7	12	5	3.94
	LF	B. Elliott	272	.228	10	35	83	6	2	0	1.4	.978	G. Spencer	35	60	3	5	3	5.55
	C	W. Westrum	322	.220	14	43	481	64	12	**11**	5.0	.978							
	OF	D. Rhodes	176	.250	10	36	97	3	9	0	1.9	.917							
	OF	W. Mays	127	.236	4	23	109	6	1	2	3.4	.991							
	OF	M. Irvin	126	.310	4	21	44	3	0	1	1.5	1.000							
St. L. W-88 L-66 Eddie Stanky	1B	D. Sisler	418	.261	13	60	1022	84	17*	116	9.9	.985	G. Staley	35	240	17	14	0	3.27
	2B	Schoendienst	620	.303	7	67	**399**	424	19	108	**5.9**	.977	V. Mizell	30	190	10	8	0	3.65
	SS	S. Hemus	570	.268	15	52	253	452	29	104	5.0	.960	J. Presko	28	147	7	10	0	4.05
	3B	B. Johnson	282	.252	2	34	56	177	12	10	2.8	.951	C. Boyer	23	110	6	6	0	4.24
	RF	E. Slaughter	510	.300	11	101	202	11	3	3	1.9	.989	A. Brazle	46	109	12	5	**16**	2.72
	CF	S. Musial	578	**.336**	21	91	298	6	4	2	2.3	.987	H. Brecheen	25	100	7	5	3	3.32
	LF	P. Lowrey	374	.286	1	48	174	3	4	1	1.7	.978	E. Yuhas	54	99	12	2	6	2.72
	C	D. Rice	495	.259	11	65	**677**	81	6	8	5.2	.992							
	OF	H. Rice	295	.288	7	45	132	5	4	0	1.7	.972							
	3B	T. Glaviano	162	.241	3	19	46	95	10	5	2.9	.934							
Phi. W-87 L-67 Eddie Sawyer W-28 L-35 Steve O'Neill W-59 L-32	1B	E. Waitkus	499	.289	2	49	1281	95	12	119	9.7	.991	R. Roberts	39	**330**	**28**	7	2	2.59
	2B	C. Ryan	577	.241	12	49	348	**462**	23	95	5.4	.972	R. Meyer	37	232	13	14	1	3.14
	SS	G. Hamner	596	.275	17	87	267	470	38	102	5.1	.951	K. Drews	33	229	14	15	0	2.72
	3B	W. Jones	541	.250	18	72	**216**	281	16	31	3.5	.969	C. Simmons	28	201	14	8	0	2.82
	RF	J. Wyrostek	321	.274	1	37	202	10	6	1	2.5	.972	J. Konstanty	42	80	5	3	6	3.94
	CF	R. Ashburn	613	.282	1	42	**428**	23	9	5	3.0	.980	A. Hansen	43	77	5	6	4	3.26
	LF	D. Ennis	592	.289	20	107	277	11	9	1	2.0	.970							
	C	S. Burgess	371	.296	6	56	439	47	11	6	4.8	.978							
	C	S. Lopata	179	.274	4	27	274	21	4	6	5.4	.987							
	OF	M. Clark	155	.335	1	15	81	5	0	1	2.3	1.000							
Chi. W-77 L-77 Phil Cavarretta	1B	D. Fondy	554	.300	10	67	1257	103	14	92	9.6	.990	B. Rush	34	250	17	13	0	2.70
	2B	E. Miksis	383	.232	2	19	126	140	14	22	5.2	.950	J. Klippstein	41	203	9	14	3	4.44
	SS	R. Smalley	261	.222	5	30	139	200	17	33	4.3	.952	W. Hacker	33	185	15	9	1	2.58
	3B	R. Jackson	379	.232	9	34	91	203	13	13	3.0	.958	P. Minner	28	181	14	9	0	3.74
	RF	F. Baumholtz	409	.325	4	35	248	10	7	3	2.6	.974	T. Lown	33	157	4	11	0	4.37
	CF	H. Jeffcoat	297	.219	4	30	218	16	1	2	2.5	.996	B. Kelly	31	125	4	9	0	3.59
	LF	H. Sauer	567	.270	**37**	**121**	327	17	6	3	2.3	.983	D. Leonard	45	67	2	2	11	2.16
	C	T. Atwell	362	.290	2	31	451	50	12	2	5.1	.977							
	32	B. Serena	390	.274	15	61	198	234	8	30		.982							
	OF	B. Addis	292	.295	1	20	160	8	2	2	2.2	.988							
	OF	G. Hermanski	275	.255	4	34	146	7	3	3	2.1	.981							
	SS	T. Brown	200	.320	3	24	58	85	14	17	4.0	.911							
	2B	B. Ramazzotti	183	.284	1	12	90	143	5	28	4.8	.979							

	POS	Player	AB	BA	HR	RBI	PO	A	E	DP	TC/G	FA	Pitcher	G	IP	W	L	SV	ERA
Cin.	1B	T. Kluszewski	497	.320	16	86	1121	66	8	116	9.0	**.993**	Raffensberger	38	247	17	13	1	2.81
W-69 L-85	2B	G. Hatton	433	.212	9	57	316	289	6	68	5.1	**.990**	H. Perkowski	33	194	12	10	0	3.80
Luke Sewell	SS	R. McMillan	540	.244	7	57	297	**495**	24	101	5.3	.971	H. Wehmeier	33	190	9	11	0	5.15
W-39 L-59	3B	B. Adams	637	.283	6	48	176	**328**	20	28	3.4	.962	B. Church	29	153	5	9	0	4.34
Earle Brucker	RF	W. Marshall	397	.267	8	46	188	13	3	2*	1.9	.985	F. Hiller	28	124	5	8	1	4.63
W-3 L-2	CF	B. Borkowski	377	.252	4	24	219	5	2	1	2.2	.991	F. Smith	53	122	12	11	7	3.75
Rogers Hornsby	LF	J. Adcock	378	.278	13	52	189	5	3	1	2.3	.985	E. Blackwell	23	102	3	12	0	5.38
W-27 L-24	C	A. Seminick	336	.256	14	50	416	47	13	7	4.8	.973	B. Podbielan	24	87	4	5	1	2.80
	OF	H. Edwards	184	.283	6	28	80	2	1	0	1.6	.988							
	OF	W. Westlake	183	.202	3	14	127	5	1	0	2.4	.992							
	OF	C. Abrams	158	.278	2	13	87	1	0	1	2.0	1.000							
	OF	J. Greengrass	68	.309	5	24	55	0	2	0	3.4	.965							
Bos.	1B	E. Torgeson	382	.230	5	34	931	73	11	86	9.7	.989	W. Spahn	40	290	14	19	3	2.98
W-64 L-89	2B	J. Dittmer	326	.193	7	41	228	267	9	60	5.6	.982	J. Wilson	33	234	12	14	0	4.23
Tommy Holmes	SS	J. Logan	456	.283	4	42	247	385	18	81	**5.6**	**.972**	M. Surkont	31	215	12	13	0	3.77
W-13 L-22	3B	E. Mathews	528	.242	25	58	160	259	19	21	3.1	.957	V. Bickford	26	161	7	12	0	3.74
Charlie Grimm	RF	B. Thorpe	292	.260	3	26	132	9	4	3	2.0	.972	L. Burdette	45	137	6	11	7	3.61
W-51 L-67	CF	S. Jethroe	608	.232	13	58	413	10	13	3	2.9	.970	E. Johnson	29	92	6	3	1	4.11
	LF	S. Gordon	522	.289	25	75	263	9	1	0	1.9	**.996**							
	C	W. Cooper	349	.235	10	55	417	55	8	8	5.4	.983							
	UT	S. Sisti	245	.212	4	24	142	129	16	22		.944							
	OF	J. Daniels	219	.187	2	14	119	6	3	2	1.5	.977							
	1B	G. Crowe	217	.258	4	20	476	42	8	40	9.6	.985							
	C	P. Burris	168	.220	2	21	208	16	0	3	4.5	1.000							
Pit.	1B	T. Bartirome	355	.220	0	16	909	72	11	91	8.4	.989	M. Dickson	43	278	14	**21**	2	3.57
W-42 L-112	2B	J. Merson	398	.246	5	38	190	214	9	59	5.1	.978	H. Pollet	31	214	7	16	0	4.12
Billy Meyer	SS	D. Groat	384	.284	1	29	229	272	25	61	5.6	.952	B. Friend	35	185	7	17	0	4.18
	3B	Castiglione	214	.266	4	18	67	129	10	7	3.6	.951	W. Main	48	153	2	12	2	4.46
	RF	G. Bell	468	.250	16	59	202	8	6	2	1.8	.972	T. Wilks	44	72	5	5	4	3.61
	CF	B. Del Greco	341	.217	1	20	246	11	6	3	2.8	.977							
	LF	R. Kiner	516	.244	**37**	87	250	9	8	0	1.8	.970							
	C	J. Garagiola	344	.273	8	54	418	63	11	9	4.7	.978							
	1O	C. Metkovich	373	.271	7	41	602	34	7	59		.989							
	UT	C. Koshorek	322	.261	0	15	149	232	18	47		.955							
	2S	G. Strickland	232	.177	5	22	142	217	19	54		.950							
	C	McCullough	172	.233	1	15	227	38	5	4	4.4	.981							

BATTING AND BASE RUNNING LEADERS

Batting Average

S. Musial, STL	.336
F. Baumholtz, CHI	.325
T. Kluszewski, CIN	.320
J. Robinson, BKN	.308
D. Snider, BKN	.303

Slugging Average

S. Musial, STL	.538
H. Sauer, CHI	.531
T. Kluszewski, CIN	.509
R. Kiner, PIT	.500
G. Hodges, BKN	.500

Home Runs

R. Kiner, PIT	37
H. Sauer, CHI	37
G. Hodges, BKN	32
S. Gordon, BOS	25
E. Mathews, BOS	25

Total Bases

S. Musial, STL	311
H. Sauer, CHI	301
B. Thomson, NY	293
D. Ennis, PHI	281
D. Snider, BKN	264

Runs Batted In

H. Sauer, CHI	121
B. Thomson, NY	108
D. Ennis, PHI	107
G. Hodges, BKN	102
E. Slaughter, STL	101

Stolen Bases

P. Reese, BKN	30
S. Jethroe, BOS	28
J. Robinson, BKN	24
R. Ashburn, PHI	16
D. Fondy, PHI	13
C. Ryan, PHI	13

Hits

S. Musial, STL	194
Schoendienst, STL	188
B. Adams, CIN	180

Base on Balls

R. Kiner, PIT	110
G. Hodges, BKN	107
J. Robinson, BKN	106

Home Run Percentage

R. Kiner, PIT	7.2
H. Sauer, CHI	6.5
G. Hodges, BKN	6.3

Runs Scored

S. Hemus, STL	105
S. Musial, STL	105
J. Robinson, BKN	104

Doubles

S. Musial, STL	42
Schoendienst, STL	40
R. McMillan, CIN	32

Triples

B. Thomson, NY	14
E. Slaughter, STL	12
T. Kluszewski, CIN	11

PITCHING LEADERS

Winning Percentage

S. Wilhelm, NY	.833
R. Roberts, PHI	.800
J. Black, BKN	.789
S. Maglie, NY	.692
W. Hacker, CHI	.625

Earned Run Average

H. Wilhelm, NY	2.43
W. Hacker, CHI	2.58
R. Roberts, PHI	2.59
B. Loes, BKN	2.69
B. Rush, CHI	2.70

Wins

R. Roberts, PHI	28
S. Maglie, NY	18
Raffensberger, CIN	17
B. Rush, CHI	17
G. Staley, STL	17

Saves

A. Brazle, STL	16
J. Black, BKN	15
H. Wilhelm, NY	11
D. Leonard, CHI	11
F. Smith, CIN	7
L. Burdette, BOS	7

Strikeouts

W. Spahn, BOS	183
B. Rush, CHI	157
R. Roberts, PHI	148
V. Mizell, STL	146
C. Simmons, PHI	141

Complete Games

R. Roberts, PHI	30
M. Dickson, PIT	21
W. Spahn, BOS	19
Raffensberger, CIN	18
B. Rush, CHI	17

Fewest Hits per 9 Innings

W. Hacker, CHI	7.01
H. Wilhelm, NY	7.17
C. Erskine, BKN	7.27

Shutouts

C. Simmons, PHI	6
Raffensberger, CIN	6

Fewest Walks per 9 Innings

R. Roberts, PHI	1.23
W. Hacker, CHI	1.51
Raffensberger, CIN	1.64

Most Strikeouts per 9 Inn.

V. Mizell, STL	6.92
C. Simmons, PHI	6.30
H. Wilhelm, NY	6.10

Innings

R. Roberts, PHI	330
W. Spahn, BOS	290
M. Dickson, PIT	278

Games Pitched

H. Wilhelm, NY	71
J. Black, BKN	56
E. Yuhas, STL	54

	W	L	PCT	GB	R	OR	2B	3B	Batting HR	BA	SA	SB	E	Fielding DP	FA	CG	BB	Pitching SO	ShO	SV	ERA
BKN	96	57	.627		775	603	199	32	153	.262	.399	90	106	169	.982	45	544	773	11	24	3.53
NY	92	62	.597	4.5	722	639	186	56	151	.256	.399	30	158	175	.974	49	538	655	11	31	3.59
STL	88	66	.571	8.5	677	630	247	54	97	.267	.391	33	141	159	.977	49	501	712	11	27	3.66
PHI	87	67	.565	9.5	657	552	237	45	93	.260	.376	60	150	145	.975	80	373	609	16	16	3.07
CHI	77	77	.500	19.5	628	631	223	45	107	.264	.383	50	146	123	.976	59	544	661	15	15	3.58
CIN	69	85	.448	27.5	615	659	212	45	104	.249	.366	32	107	145	.982	56	517	579	11	12	4.01
BOS	64	89	.418	32	569	651	187	31	110	.233	.343	58	154	143	.975	63	525	687	11	13	3.78
PIT	42	112	.273	54.5	515	793	181	30	92	.231	.331	43	182	167	.970	43	615	564	4	8	4.65
					5158	5158	1672	338	907	.253	.374	396	1144	1226	.976	444	4147	5240	90	146	3.73

American League 1952

	POS	Player	AB	BA	HR	RBI	PO	A	E	DP	TC/G	FA	Pitcher	G	IP	W	L	SV	ERA
N. Y. W-95 L-59 Casey Stengel	1B	J. Collins	428	.280	18	59	1047	73	11	123	9.5	.990	A. Reynolds	35	244	20	8	6	2.06
	2B	B. Martin	363	.267	3	33	244	323	9	92	5.4	.984	V. Raschi	31	223	16	6	0	2.78
	SS	P. Rizzuto	578	.254	2	43	308	458	19	116	5.2	.976	E. Lopat	20	149	10	5	0	2.53
	3B	G. McDougald	555	.263	11	78	124	273	13	38	3.5	.968	J. Sain	35	148	11	6	7	3.46
	RF	H. Bauer	553	.293	17	74	233	16	4	2	1.8	.984	B. Kuzava	28	133	8	8	3	3.45
	CF	M. Mantle	549	.311	23	87	347	15	12	5	2.7	.968	T. Morgan	16	94	5	4	2	3.07
	LF	G. Woodling	408	.309	12	63	241	12	1	4	2.2	.996	B. Miller	21	88	4	6	0	3.48
	C	Y. Berra	534	.273	30	98	700	73	6	10	5.6	.992	B. Hogue	27	47	3	5	4	5.32
	OF	I. Noren	272	.235	5	21	95	3	0	1	1.6	1.000							
	1B	J. Mize	137	.263	4	29	218	18	3	32	8.9	.987							
Cle. W-93 L-61 Al Lopez	1B	L. Easter	437	.263	31	97	940	90	18	87	8.9	.983	B. Lemon	42	310	22	11	4	2.50
	2B	B. Avila	597	.300	7	45	355	431	28	81	5.5	.966	M. Garcia	46	292	22	11	4	2.37
	SS	R. Boone	316	.263	7	45	177	251	27	55	4.7	.941	E. Wynn	42	286	23	12	3	2.90
	3B	A. Rosen	567	.302	28	105	159	256	18	25	2.9	.958	B. Feller	30	192	9	13	0	4.74
	RF	H. Simpson	545	.266	10	65	226	11	3	4	1.9	.988	S. Gromek	29	123	7	7	1	3.67
	CF	L. Doby	519	.276	32	104	398	11	6	3	3.1	.986							
	LF	D. Mitchell	511	.323	5	58	258	6	2	2	2.0	.992							
	C	J. Hegan	333	.225	4	41	498	53	7	7	5.2	.987							
	OF	J. Fridley	175	.251	4	16	87	3	2	0	1.7	.978							
	C	J. Tipton	105	.248	6	22	118	18	4	1	4.0	.971							
Chi. W-81 L-73 Paul Richards	1B	E. Robinson	594	.296	22	104	1329	89	14	145	9.2	.990	B. Pierce	33	255	15	12	1	2.57
	2B	N. Fox	648	.296	0	39	406	433	13	111	5.6	.985	S. Rogovin	33	232	14	9	1	3.85
	SS	C. Carrasquel	359	.248	1	42	176	248	16	50	4.4	.964	J. Dobson	29	201	14	10	1	2.51
	3B	H. Rodriguez	407	.265	1	40	145	232	16	26	3.5	.959	M. Grissom	28	166	12	10	0	3.74
	RF	S. Mele	423	.248	14	59	157	8	0	1	1.5	1.000	C. Stobbs	38	135	7	12	1	3.13
	CF	R. Coleman	195	.215	2	14	130	5	3	0	1.9	.978	H. Dorish	39	91	8	4	11	2.47
	LF	M. Minoso	569	.281	13	61	322	11	7	3	2.4	.979	L. Aloma	25	40	3	1	6	4.28
	C	S. Lollar	375	.240	13	50	590	53	7	4	5.4	.989							
	OF	B. Stewart	225	.267	5	30	108	1	2	0	1.9	.982							
	OF	J. Rivera	201	.249	3	18	157	2	2	1	3.0	.988							
	OF	T. Wright	132	.258	1	21	60	2	2	0	1.9	.969							
Phi. W-79 L-75 Jimmy Dykes	1B	F. Fain	538	.327	2	59	1245	150	22	124	9.8	.984	B. Shantz	33	280	24	7	0	2.48
	2B	B. Kell	213	.221	0	17	143	169	12	35	4.8	.963	A. Kellner	34	231	12	14	0	4.36
	SS	E. Joost	540	.244	20	75	278	431	28	81	5.0	.962	H. Byrd	37	228	15	15	2	3.31
	3B	H. Hitchcock	407	.246	1	56	105	222	20	26	3.3	.942	C. Scheib	30	158	11	7	2	4.39
	RF	E. Valo	388	.281	5	47	223	7	9	1	2.0	.962	B. Hooper	43	144	8	15	6	5.18
	CF	D. Philley	586	.263	7	71	442	13	4	3	3.1	.991							
	LF	G. Zernial	549	.262	29	100	302	6	9	0	2.2	.972							
	C	J. Astroth	337	.249	1	36	436	36	4	9	4.7	.992							
	UT	P. Suder	228	.241	1	20	136	179	4	40		.975							
	2B	C. Michaels	200	.250	1	18	151	133	2	30	5.2	.993							
	OF	A. Clark	186	.274	7	29	78	2	1	0	1.7	.988							
	3B	H. Majeski	117	.256	2	20	33	87	3	9	3.6	.976							
Was. W-78 L-76 Bucky Harris	1B	M. Vernon	569	.251	10	80	1291	115	10	139	9.3	.993	Porterfield	31	231	13	14	0	2.72
	2B	F. Baker	263	.262	0	33	151	176	2	36	4.8	.994	C. Marrero	22	184	11	8	0	2.88
	SS	P. Runnels	555	.285	1	64	314	406	25	97	5.1	.966	S. Shea	22	169	11	7	0	2.93
	3B	E. Yost	587	.233	12	49	212	249	18	26	3.1	.962	W. Masterson	24	161	9	8	2	3.70
	RF	J. Jensen	570	.286	10	80	283	17*	7	1	2.1	.977	J. Moreno	26	147	9	9	0	3.97
	CF	J. Busby	512	.244	2	47	430*	4	3	0	3.4*	.993	R. Gumpert	20	104	4	9	0	4.24
	LF	G. Coan	332	.205	5	20	185	4	3	1	2.2	.984	S. Consuegra	30	74	6	5	5	3.05
	C	M. Grasso	361	.216	0	27	485	64	17	4	5.0	.970							
	OF	K. Wood	210	.238	6	32	161	6	8	1	3.1	.954							
	2B	M. Hoderlein	208	.269	0	17	138	168	7	43	5.4	.978							

POS	Player	AB	BA	HR	RBI	PO	A	E	DP	TC/G	FA	Pitcher	G	IP	W	L	SV	ERA
Bos. W-76 L-78 Lou Boudreau																		
1B	D. Gernert	367	.243	19	67	877	67	12	104	9.7	.987	M. Parnell	33	214	12	12	2	3.62
2B	B. Goodman	513	.306	4	56	284	340	16	95	6.2	.975	M. McDermott	30	162	10	9	0	3.72
SS	J. Lipon	234	.205	0	18	118	218	6	53	5.0	.982*	S. Hudson	21	134	7	9	0	3.62
3B	G. Kell	276	.319	6	40	75	138	9	14	3.0	.959	D. Trout	26	134	9	8	1	3.64
RF	Throneberry	310	.258	5	23	141	9	7	5	1.8	.955	D. Brodowski	20	115	5	5	0	4.40
CF	D. DiMaggio	486	.294	6	33	303	12	8	4	2.6	.975	W. Nixon	23	104	5	4	0	4.86
LF	H. Evers	401	.262	14	59	219	8	6	3	2.2	.974	E. Kinder	23	98	5	6	4	2.58
C	S. White	381	.281	10	49	464	59	9	7	4.8	.983	I. Delock	39	95	4	9	5	4.26
S3	V. Stephens	295	.254	7	44	110	227	16	48		.955	Scarborough	28	77	1	5	4	4.81
23	T. Lepcio	274	.263	5	26	164	212	14	46		.964	A. Benton	24	38	4	3	6	2.39
OF	C. Vollmer	250	.264	11	50	143	3	0	1	2.1	1.000							
SO	J. Piersall	161	.267	1	16	79	78	9	13		.946							
C	D. Wilber	135	.267	3	23	160	22	1	5	4.7	.995							
1B	W. Dropo	132	.265	6	27	319	21	2	31	9.8	.994							
OF	D. Lenhardt	105	.295	7	24	52	0	1	0	2.0	.981							
St. L. W-64 L-90 Rogers Hornsby W-22 L-28 Marty Marion W-42 L-62																		
1B	D. Kryhoski	342	.243	11	42	680	49	8	80	8.6	.989	D. Pillette	30	205	10	13	0	3.59
2B	B. Young	575	.247	4	39	380	407	13	127	5.4	.984	T. Byrne	29	196	7	14	0	4.68
SS	J. DeMaestri	186	.226	1	18	105	156	17	29	3.6	.939	B. Cain	29	170	12	10	2	4.13
3B	J. Dyck	402	.269	15	64	79	152	9	14	3.2	.963	G. Bearden	34	151	7	8	0	4.30
RF	B. Nieman	478	.289	18	74	230	10	6	5	2.0	.976	N. Garver	21	149	7	10	0	3.69
CF	J. Rivera	336	.256	4	30	273	7	7	1	3.3	.976	S. Paige	46	138	12	10	10	3.07
LF	J. Delsing	298	.255	1	34	206	4	3	2	2.5	.986	E. Harrist	36	117	2	8	5	4.01
C	C. Courtney	413	.286	5	50	487	60	2	7	4.9	.996							
1B	G. Goldsberry	227	.229	3	17	524	40	10	56	8.0	.983							
UT	F. Marsh	247	.279	2	37	72	117	11	32		.945							
SS	M. Marion	186	.247	2	19	105	138	5	41	3.9	.980							
3B	C. Michaels	166	.265	3	25	43	88	12	12	3.4	.916							
Det. W-50 L-104 Red Rolfe W-23 L-49 Fred Hutchinson W-27 L-55																		
1B	W. Dropo	459	.279	23	70	1005	78	12	104	9.5	.989	T. Gray	35	224	12	17	0	4.14
2B	G. Priddy	279	.283	4	20	211	209	14	48	5.8	.968	A. Houtteman	35	221	8	20	1	4.36
SS	N. Berry	189	.228	0	13	90	158	9	26	3.9	.965	V. Trucks	35	197	5	19	1	3.97
3B	F. Hatfield	441	.236	2	25	114	253*	12	32	3.5	.968*	H. Newhouser	25	154	9	9	0	3.74
RF	V. Wertz	285	.246	17	51	134	8	2	3	1.8	.986	B. Wight	23	144	5	9	0	3.88
CF	J. Groth	524	.284	4	51	329	14	5	3	2.5	.986	B. Hoeft	34	125	2	7	4	4.32
LF	P. Mullin	255	.251	7	35	131	6	3	2	2.2	.979	H. White	41	63	1	8	5	3.69
C	J. Ginsberg	307	.221	6	36	442	41	8	7	4.9	.984							
OF	S. Souchock	265	.249	13	45	103	4	4	2	2.0	.964							
2B	A. Federoff	231	.242	0	14	136	184	8	42	4.7	.976							
OF	C. Mapes	193	.197	9	23	86	3	3	1	1.5	.967							
S2	J. Pesky	177	.254	1	9	105	137	11	37		.957							
1B	D. Kolloway	173	.243	2	21	252	28	6	15	8.9	.979							
C	M. Batts	173	.237	3	13	262	36	5	4	5.5	.983							

BATTING AND BASE RUNNING LEADERS

Batting Average

F. Fain, PHI	.327
D. Mitchell, CLE	.323
M. Mantle, NY	.311
G. Kell, BOS, DET	.311
G. Woodling, NY	.309

Slugging Average

L. Doby, CLE	.541
M. Mantle, NY	.530
A. Rosen, CLE	.524
L. Easter, CLE	.513
V. Wertz, DET, STL	.506

Home Runs

L. Doby, CLE	32
L. Easter, CLE	31
Y. Berra, NY	30
G. Zernial, PHI	29
W. Dropo, BOS, DET	29

Total Bases

A. Rosen, CLE	297
M. Mantle, NY	291
W. Dropo, BOS, DET	282
L. Doby, CLE	281
E. Robinson, CHI	277

Runs Batted In

A. Rosen, CLE	105
L. Doby, CLE	104
E. Robinson, CHI	104
G. Zernial, PHI	100
Y. Berra, NY	98

Stolen Bases

M. Minoso, CHI	22
J. Rivera, CHI, STL	21
J. Jensen, NY, WAS	18
P. Rizzuto, NY	17
Throneberry, BOS	16

Hits

N. Fox, CHI	192
B. Avila, CLE	179
F. Fain, PHI	176
E. Robinson, CHI	176

Base on Balls

E. Yost, WAS	129
E. Joost, PHI	122
F. Fain, PHI	105

Home Run Percentage

L. Easter, CLE	7.1
L. Doby, CLE	6.2
Y. Berra, NY	5.6

Runs Scored

L. Doby, CLE	104
B. Avila, CLE	102
A. Rosen, CLE	101

PITCHING LEADERS

Winning Percentage

B. Shantz, PHI	.774
V. Raschi, NY	.727
A. Reynolds, NY	.714
M. Garcia, CLE	.667
B. Lemon, CLE	.667

Earned Run Average

A. Reynolds, NY	2.06
M. Garcia, CLE	2.37
B. Shantz, PHI	2.48
B. Lemon, CLE	2.50
J. Dobson, CHI	2.51

Wins

B. Shantz, PHI	24
E. Wynn, CLE	23
M. Garcia, CLE	22
B. Lemon, CLE	22
A. Reynolds, NY	20

Saves

H. Dorish, CHI	11
S. Paige, STL	10
J. Sain, NY	7

Strikeouts

A. Reynolds, NY	160
E. Wynn, CLE	153
B. Shantz, PHI	152
B. Pierce, CHI	144
M. Garcia, CLE	143

Complete Games

B. Lemon, CLE	28
B. Shantz, PHI	27
A. Reynolds, NY	24
E. Wynn, CLE	19
M. Garcia, CLE	19

Fewest Hits per 9 Innings

B. Lemon, CLE	6.86
V. Raschi, NY	7.02
A. Reynolds, NY	7.15

Shutouts

A. Reynolds, NY	6
M. Garcia, CLE	6
B. Shantz, PHI	5
B. Lemon, CLE	5

Fewest Walks per 9 Innings

B. Shantz, PHI	2.03
D. Pillette, STL	2.41
C. Marrero, WAS	2.59

Most Strikeouts per 9 Inn.

M. McDermott, BOS	6.50
A. Reynolds, NY	5.89
V. Trucks, DET	5.89

BATTING AND BASE RUNNING LEADERS

Doubles		Triples		Innings		Games Pitched	
F. Fain, PHI	43	B. Avila, CLE	11	B. Lemon, CLE	310	B. Kennedy, CHI	47
M. Mantle, NY	37	H. Simpson, CLE	10	M. Garcia, CLE	292	M. Garcia, CLE	46
M. Vernon, WAS	33	P. Rizzuto, NY	10	E. Wynn, CLE	286	S. Paige, STL	46
E. Robinson, CHI	33	N. Fox, CHI	10			B. Hooper, PHI	43

PITCHING LEADERS

	W	L	PCT	GB	R	OR	2B	3B	Batting HR	BA	SA	SB	E	Fielding DP	FA	CG	BB	SO	Pitching ShO	SV	ERA
NY	95	59	.617		727	557	221	56	129	.267	.403	52	127	199	.979	72	581	666	17	27	3.14
CLE	93	61	.604	2	763	606	211	49	148	.262	.404	46	155	141	.975	80	556	671	16	18	3.32
CHI	81	73	.526	14	610	568	199	38	80	.252	.348	61	123	158	.980	53	578	774	13	28	3.25
PHI	79	75	.513	16	664	723	212	35	89	.253	.359	52	140	148	.977	73	526	562	11	16	4.15
WAS	78	76	.506	17	598	608	225	44	50	.239	.326	48	132	152	.978	75	577	574	10	15	3.37
BOS	76	78	.494	19	668	658	233	34	113	.255	.377	59	145	181	.976	53	623	624	7	24	3.80
STL	64	90	.416	31	604	733	225	46	82	.250	.356	30	155	176	.974	48	598	581	6	18	4.12
DET	50	104	.325	45	557	738	190	37	103	.243	.352	27	152	145	.975	51	591	702	10	14	4.25
					5191	5191	1716	339	794	.253	.365	375	1129	1300	.977	505	4630	5154	90	160	3.67

National League 1953

	POS	Player	AB	BA	HR	RBI	PO	A	E	DP	TC/G	FA	Pitcher	G	IP	W	L	SV	ERA
Bkn. W-105 L-49 Chuck Dressen	1B	G. Hodges	520	.302	31	122	1025	99	8	105	8.9	.993	C. Erskine	39	247	20	6	3	3.54
	2B	J. Gilliam	605	.278	6	63	332	426	19	102	5.2	.976	R. Meyer	34	191	15	5	0	4.56
	SS	P. Reese	524	.271	13	61	265	380	23	83	4.9	.966	B. Loes	32	163	14	8	0	4.54
	3B	B. Cox	327	.291	10	44	86	142	6	20	2.6	.974	P. Roe	25	157	11	3	0	4.36
	RF	C. Furillo	479	.344	21	92	232	11	3	3	1.9	.988	B. Milliken	37	118	8	4	2	3.37
	CF	D. Snider	590	.336	42	126	370	7	5	3	2.5	.987	J. Podres	33	115	9	4	0	4.23
	LF	J. Robinson	484	.329	12	95	145	9	3	0	2.1	.981	C. Labine	37	110	11	6	7	2.77
	C	R. Campanella	519	.312	41	142	807	57	10	9	6.2	.989	B. Wade	32	90	7	5	3	3.79
	3S	B. Morgan	196	.260	7	33	71	105	10	19		.946	J. Hughes	48	86	4	3	9	3.47
	OF	G. Shuba	169	.254	5	23	59	1	1	1	1.4	.984	J. Black	34	73	6	3	5	5.33
	1B	W. Belardi	163	.239	11	34	283	23	5	34	8.2	.984							
Mil. W-92 L-62 Charlie Grimm	1B	J. Adcock	590	.285	18	80	1389	96	13	146	9.5	.991	W. Spahn	35	266	23	7	3	2.10
	2B	J. Dittmer	504	.266	9	63	290	343	23	95	4.8	.965	L. Burdette	46	175	15	5	8	3.24
	SS	J. Logan	611	.273	11	73	295	481	20	104	5.3	.975	J. Antonelli	31	175	12	12	1	3.18
	3B	E. Mathews	579	.302	47	135	154	311	30	33	3.2	.939	M. Surkont	28	170	11	5	0	4.18
	RF	A. Pafko	516	.297	17	72	241	5	6	1	1.8	.976	B. Buhl	30	154	13	8	0	2.97
	CF	B. Bruton	613	.250	1	41	397	15	9	5	2.8	.979	D. Liddle	31	129	7	6	2	3.08
	LF	S. Gordon	464	.274	19	75	245	10	6	2	1.9	.977	J. Wilson	20	114	4	9	0	4.34
	C	D. Crandall	382	.272	15	51	566	62	9	13	5.9	.986							
	OF	J. Pendleton	251	.299	7	27	141	7	6	1	1.5	.961							
Phi. W-83 L-71 Steve O'Neill	1B	E. Torgeson	379	.274	11	64	916	65	13	83	9.5	.987	R. Roberts	44	347	23	16	2	2.75
	2B	G. Hamner	609	.276	21	92	194	290	15	65	5.4	.970	C. Simmons	32	238	16	13	0	3.21
	SS	T. Kazanski	360	.217	2	27	185	239	23	53	4.7	.949	K. Drews	47	185	9	10	3	4.52
	3B	W. Jones	481	.225	19	70	176	253	11	36	3.0	.975	J. Konstanty	48	171	14	10	5	4.43
	RF	J. Wyrostek	409	.271	6	47	192	11	8	2	1.9	.962	B. Miller	35	157	8	9	2	4.00
	CF	R. Ashburn	622	.330	2	57	496	18	5	4	3.3	.990	S. Ridzik	42	124	9	6	0	3.77
	LF	D. Ennis	578	.285	29	125	284	14	6	4	2.0	.980							
	C	S. Burgess	312	.292	4	36	395	23	3	8	4.4	.993							
	1B	E. Waitkus	247	.291	1	16	480	37	6	65	8.9	.989							
	2B	C. Ryan	247	.296	5	26	134	166	13	39	4.8	.958							
	C	S. Lopata	234	.239	8	31	344	27	5	2	4.7	.987							
	OF	M. Clark	198	.298	0	19	104	2	1	0	2.1	.991							
St. L. W-83 L-71 Eddie Stanky	1B	S. Bilko	570	.251	21	84	1446	124	15	145	10.3	.991	H. Haddix	36	253	20	9	1	3.06
	2B	Schoendienst	564	.342	15	79	365	430	14	109	5.8	.983	G. Staley	40	230	18	9	4	3.99
	SS	S. Hemus	585	.279	14	61	257	476	27	90	5.1	.964	V. Mizell	33	224	13	11	0	3.49
	3B	R. Jablonski	604	.268	21	112	94	278	27	27	2.5	.932	J. Presko	34	162	6	13	1	5.01
	RF	E. Slaughter	492	.291	6	89	235	2	1	0	1.7	.996	S. Miller	40	138	7	8	4	5.56
	CF	R. Repulski	567	.275	15	66	361	7	5	1	2.4	.987	A. Brazle	60	92	6	7	18	4.21
	LF	S. Musial	593	.337	30	113	294	9	5	1	2.0	.984	H. White	49	85	6	5	7	2.98
	C	D. Rice	419	.236	6	37	627	60	8	6	5.3	.988							
	OF	P. Lowrey	182	.269	5	27	42	1	0	0	1.1	1.000							

POS	Player	AB	BA	HR	RBI	PO	A	E	DP	TC/G	FA	Pitcher	G	IP	W	L	SV	ERA
N. Y. W-70 L-84 Leo Durocher																		
1B	W. Lockman	607	.295	9	61	1042	100	13	96	9.6	.989	R. Gomez	29	204	13	11	0	3.40
2B	D. Williams	340	.297	3	34	191	254	8	54	4.8	.982	J. Hearn	36	197	9	12	0	4.53
SS	A. Dark	647	.300	23	88	219	343	19	79	5.3	.967	L. Jansen	36	185	11	16	1	4.14
3B	H. Thompson	388	.302	24	74	90	194	13	18	2.9	.956	H. Wilhelm	68	145	7	8	15	3.04
RF	D. Mueller	480	.333	6	60	203	7	6	0	1.8	.972	S. Maglie	27	145	8	9	0	4.15
CF	B. Thomson	608	.288	26	106	391	16	7	0	2.7	.983	D. Koslo	37	112	6	12	2	4.76
LF	M. Irvin	444	.329	21	97	244	10	7	4	2.3	.973	A. Corwin	48	107	6	4	2	4.98
C	W. Westrum	290	.224	12	30	441	53	9	9	4.7	.982	Worthington	20	102	4	8	0	3.44
UT	D. Spencer	408	.208	20	56	179	269	32	52		.933							
32	B. Hofman	169	.266	12	34	55	83	7	18		.952							
OF	D. Rhodes	163	.233	11	30	76	6	3	4	1.8	.965							
1B	T. Gilbert	160	.169	3	16	381	26	2	34	9.3	.995							
Cin. W-68 L-86 Rogers Hornsby W-64 L-82 Buster Mills W-4 L-4																		
1B	T. Kluszewski	570	.316	40	108	1285	58	7	149	9.2	.995	H. Perkowski	33	193	12	11	2	4.52
2B	R. Bridges	432	.227	1	21	329	320	16	94	5.8	.976	B. Podbielan	36	186	6	16	1	4.73
SS	R. McMillan	557	.233	5	43	288	519	23	114	5.4	.972	Raffensberger	26	174	7	14	0	3.93
3B	B. Adams	607	.275	8	49	159	324	25	39	3.4	.951	J. Nuxhall	30	142	9	11	2	4.32
RF	W. Marshall	357	.266	17	62	187	11	1	1	2.1	.995	F. Baczewski	24	138	11	4	1	3.45
CF	G. Bell	610	.300	30	105	447	16	11	5	3.1	.977	J. Collum	30	125	7	11	3	3.75
LF	J. Greengrass	606	.285	20	100	341	11	6	0	2.3	.983	F. Smith	50	84	8	1	2	5.49
C	A. Seminick	387	.235	19	64	436	44	9	2	4.4	.982	C. King	35	76	3	6	2	5.21
OF	B. Borkowski	249	.269	7	29	104	3	2	0	1.6	.982							
2B	G. Hatton	159	.233	7	22	56	49	1	15	3.0	.991							
C	H. Landrith	154	.240	3	16	179	13	3	4	4.1	.985							
Chi. W-65 L-89 Phil Cavarretta																		
1B	D. Fondy	595	.309	18	78	1274	115	18	105	9.4	.987	W. Hacker	39	222	12	19	2	4.38
2B	E. Miksis	577	.251	8	39	210	262	23	65	5.4	.954	P. Minner	31	201	12	15	1	4.21
SS	R. Smalley	253	.249	6	25	153	191	25	39	4.8	.932	J. Klippstein	48	168	10	11	6	4.83
3B	R. Jackson	498	.285	19	66	141	265	22	24	3.2	.949	B. Rush	29	167	9	14	0	4.54
RF	H. Sauer	395	.263	19	60	221	5	7	1	2.2	.970	T. Lown	49	148	8	7	3	5.16
CF	F. Baumholtz	520	.306	3	25	290	6	6	0	2.3	.980	H. Pollet	25	111	5	6	1	4.12
LF	R. Kiner	414	.283	28	87	211	6	8	2	1.9	.964	B. Church	27	104	4	5	1	5.00
C	McCullough	229	.258	6	23	273	31	4	7	4.2	.987	D. Leonard	45	63	2	3	8	4.60
23	B. Serena	275	.251	10	52	135	160	7	31		.977							
C	J. Garagiola	228	.272	1	21	296	34	4	2	4.9	.988							
OF	H. Jeffcoat	183	.235	4	22	175	6	5	2	1.9	.973							
Pit. W-50 L-104 Fred Haney																		
1B	P. Ward	281	.210	8	27	693	64	7	65	9.8	.991	M. Dickson	45	201	10	19	4	4.53
2B	J. O'Brien	279	.247	2	22	172	210	7	48	5.1	.982	P. LaPalme	35	176	8	16	2	4.59
SS	E. O'Brien	261	.238	0	14	122	207	23	39	4.3	.935	J. Lindell	27	176	5	16	0	4.71
3B	D. O'Connell	588	.294	7	55	119	221	15	16	3.4	.958	B. Friend	32	171	8	11	0	4.90
RF	C. Abrams	448	.286	15	43	205	13	6	3	2.0	.973	B. Hall	37	152	3	12	1	5.39
CF	C. Bernier	310	.213	3	31	220	8	7	1	2.7	.970	R. Face	41	119	6	8	0	6.58
LF	F. Thomas	455	.255	30	102	306	17	8	1	2.8	.976	J. Hetki	54	118	3	6	3	3.95
C	M. Sandlock	186	.231	0	12	290	49	3	4	5.3	.991							
1B	P. Smith	389	.283	4	44	622	52	10	53	9.2	.985							
OF	H. Rice	286	.311	4	42	167	14	5	2	2.7	.973							
SS	D. Cole	235	.272	0	23	139	192	12	40	4.5	.965							
23	E. Pellagrini	174	.253	4	19	75	95	6	13		.966							
3B	Castiglione	159	.208	4	21	44	88	3	6	3.1	.978							
OF	R. Kiner	148	.270	7	29	71	5	0	1	1.9	1.000							

BATTING AND BASE RUNNING LEADERS

Batting Average

C. Furillo, BKN	.344
Schoendienst, STL	.342
S. Musial, STL	.337
D. Snider, BKN	.336
D. Mueller, NY	.333

Slugging Average

D. Snider, BKN	.627
E. Mathews, MIL	.627
R. Campanella, BKN	.611
S. Musial, STL	.609
C. Furillo, BKN	.580

Home Runs

E. Mathews, MIL	47
D. Snider, BKN	42
R. Campanella, BKN	41
T. Kluszewski, CIN	40
R. Kiner, CHI, PIT	35

Total Bases

D. Snider, BKN	370
E. Mathews, MIL	363
S. Musial, STL	361
T. Kluszewski, CIN	325
G. Bell, CIN	320

Runs Batted In

R. Campanella, BKN	142
E. Mathews, MIL	135
D. Snider, BKN	126
D. Ennis, PHI	125
G. Hodges, BKN	122

Stolen Bases

B. Bruton, MIL	26
P. Reese, BKN	22
J. Gilliam, BKN	21
J. Robinson, BKN	17
D. Snider, BKN	16

Hits

R. Ashburn, PHI	205
S. Musial, STL	200
D. Snider, BKN	198

Base on Balls

S. Musial, STL	105
R. Kiner, CHI, PIT	100
J. Gilliam, BKN	100

PITCHING LEADERS

Winning Percentage

C. Erskine, BKN	.769
W. Spahn, MIL	.767
L. Burdette, MIL	.750
R. Meyer, BKN	.750
H. Haddix, STL	.690

Earned Run Average

W. Spahn, MIL	2.10
R. Roberts, PHI	2.75
B. Buhl, MIL	2.97
H. Haddix, STL	3.06
J. Antonelli, MIL	3.18

Wins

W. Spahn, MIL	23
R. Roberts, PHI	23
C. Erskine, BKN	20
H. Haddix, STL	20
G. Staley, STL	18

Saves

A. Brazle, STL	18
H. Wilhelm, NY	15
J. Hughes, BKN	9
L. Burdette, MIL	8
D. Leonard, CHI	8

Strikeouts

R. Roberts, PHI	198
C. Erskine, BKN	187
V. Mizell, STL	173
H. Haddix, STL	163
W. Spahn, MIL	148

Complete Games

R. Roberts, PHI	33
W. Spahn, MIL	24
C. Simmons, PHI	19
H. Haddix, STL	19
C. Erskine, BKN	16

Fewest Hits per 9 Innings

W. Spahn, MIL	7.15
R. Gomez, NY	7.32
V. Mizell, STL	7.74

Shutouts

H. Haddix, STL	6
W. Spahn, MIL	5
R. Roberts, PHI	5

BATTING AND BASE RUNNING LEADERS

Home Run Percentage

E. Mathews, MIL	8.1
R. Campanella, BKN	7.9
D. Snider, BKN	7.1

Doubles

S. Musial, STL	53
A. Dark, NY	41
C. Furillo, BKN	38
D. Snider, BKN	38

Runs Scored

D. Snider, BKN	132
S. Musial, STL	127
A. Dark, NY	126
J. Gilliam, BKN	125

Triples

J. Gilliam, BKN	17
B. Bruton, MIL	14
S. Hemus, STL	11
D. Fondy, CHI	11

PITCHING LEADERS

Fewest Walks per 9 Innings

R. Roberts, PHI	1.58
Raffensberger, CIN	1.71
P. Minner, CHI	1.79

Innings

R. Roberts, PHI	347
W. Spahn, MIL	266
H. Haddix, STL	253

Most Strikeouts per 9 Inn.

V. Mizell, STL	6.94
C. Erskine, BKN	6.82
J. Antonelli, MIL	6.72

Games Pitched

H. Wilhelm, NY	68
A. Brazle, STL	60
J. Hetki, PIT	54

	W	L	PCT	GB	R	OR	2B	3B	Batting HR	BA	SA	SB	E	Fielding DP	FA	CG	BB	Pitching SO	ShO	SV	ERA
BKN	105	49	.682		955	689	274	59	208	.285	.474	90	118	161	.980	51	509	819	11	29	4.10
MIL	92	62	.597	13	738	589	227	52	156	.266	.415	46	143	169	.976	72	539	738	14	15	3.30
PHI	83	71	.539	22	716	666	228	62	115	.265	.396	42	147	161	.975	76	410	637	13	15	3.80
STL	83	71	.539	22	768	713	281	56	140	.273	.424	18	138	161	.977	51	533	732	11	36	4.23
NY	70	84	.455	35	768	747	195	45	176	.271	.422	31	151	151	.975	46	610	647	10	20	4.25
CIN	68	86	.442	37	714	788	190	34	166	.261	.403	25	129	176	.978	47	488	506	7	15	4.64
CHI	65	89	.422	40	633	835	204	57	137	.260	.399	49	193	141	.967	38	554	623	3	22	4.79
PIT	50	104	.325	55	622	887	178	49	99	.247	.356	41	163	139	.973	49	577	607	4	10	5.22
					5914	5914	1777	414	1197	.266	.411	342	1182	1259	.975	430	4220	5309	73	162	4.29

American League 1953

	POS	Player	AB	BA	HR	RBI	PO	A	E	DP	TC/G	FA	Pitcher	G	IP	W	L	SV	ERA
N. Y. W-99 L-52 Casey Stengel	1B	J. Collins	387	.269	17	44	826	65	10	100	8.0	.989	W. Ford	32	207	18	6	0	3.00
	2B	B. Martin	587	.257	15	75	376	390	12	121	5.3	.985	J. Sain	40	189	14	7	9	3.00
	SS	P. Rizzuto	413	.271	2	54	214	409	24	100	4.9	.963	V. Raschi	28	181	13	6	1	3.33
	3B	G. McDougald	541	.285	10	83	147	299	22	36	3.4	.953	E. Lopat	25	178	16	4	0	2.42
	RF	H. Bauer	437	.304	10	57	230	13	2	3	1.9	.992	A. Reynolds	41	145	13	7	13	3.41
	CF	M. Mantle	461	.295	21	92	322	10	6	2	2.8	.982	J. McDonald	27	130	9	7	0	3.82
	LF	G. Woodling	395	.306	10	58	240	6	1	2	2.1	.996	B. Kuzava	33	92	6	5	4	3.31
	C	Y. Berra	503	.296	27	108	566	64	9	9	4.8	.986	T. Gorman	40	77	4	5	6	3.39
	OF	I. Noren	345	.267	6	46	208	11	2	1	2.3	.991							
	1B	D. Bollweg	155	.297	6	24	323	15	6	37	8.0	.983							
	1B	J. Mize	104	.250	4	27	113	7	0	19	8.0	1.000							
Cle. W-92 L-62 Al Lopez	1B	B. Glynn	411	.243	3	30	1036	81	8	133	8.3	.993	B. Lemon	41	287	21	15	1	3.36
	2B	B. Avila	559	.286	8	55	346	445	11	114	5.7	.986	M. Garcia	38	272	18	9	0	3.25
	SS	G. Strickland	419	.284	5	47	238	400	17	103	5.4	.974	E. Wynn	36	252	17	12	0	3.93
	3B	A. Rosen	599	.336	43	145	174	338	19	38	3.4	.964	B. Feller	25	176	10	7	0	3.59
	RF	W. Westlake	218	.330	9	46	128	5	3	2	1.9	.963	D. Hoskins	26	113	9	3	1	3.99
	CF	L. Doby	513	.263	29	102	354	10	6	3	2.5	.984	A. Houtteman	22	109	7	7	3	3.80
	LF	D. Mitchell	500	.300	13	60	224	2	7	1	1.9	.970	B. Hooper	43	69	5	4	7	4.02
	C	J. Hegan	299	.217	9	37	399	42	11	3	4.3	.976							
	OF	H. Simpson	242	.227	7	22	118	4	4	0	1.8	.968							
	1B	L. Easter	211	.303	7	31	442	30	9	54	8.6	.981							
	OF	B. Kennedy	161	.236	3	22	91	2	0	0	1.0	1.000							
	SS	R. Boone	112	.241	4	21	64	94	8	24	5.4	.952							
Chi. W-89 L-65 Paul Richards	1B	F. Fain	446	.256	6	52	1108	106	13	98	9.7	.989	B. Pierce	40	271	18	12	3	2.72
	2B	N. Fox	624	.285	3	72	451	426	15	101	5.8	.983	V. Trucks	24	176	15	6	1	2.86
	SS	C. Carrasquel	552	.279	2	47	278	462	18	87	5.1	.976	M. Fornieles	39	153	8	7	3	3.59
	3B	B. Elliott	208	.260	4	32	54	104	6	9	2.8	.963	H. Dorish	55	146	10	6	18	3.40
	RF	S. Mele	481	.274	12	82	213	14	1	1	1.7	.996	S. Rogovin	22	131	7	12	1	5.22
	CF	J. Rivera	567	.259	11	78	385	15	10	10	2.6	.976	S. Consuegra	29	124	7	5	3	2.54
	LF	M. Minoso	556	.313	15	104	279	15	10	3	2.1	.967	J. Dobson	23	101	5	5	1	3.67
	C	S. Lollar	334	.287	8	54	470	51	3	2	4.9	.994	B. Keegan	22	99	7	5	1	2.74
	1O	B. Boyd	165	.297	3	23	301	16	1	25		.997							
	C	R. Wilson	164	.250	0	10	282	24	6	1	5.0	.981							
	OF	T. Wright	132	.250	2	25	44	1	1	0	1.4	.978							
Bos. W-84 L-69 Lou Boudreau	1B	D. Gernert	494	.253	21	71	1223	84	19	139	9.8	.986	M. Parnell	38	241	21	8	0	3.06
	2B	B. Goodman	514	.313	2	41	267	306	15	88	5.3	.974	M. McDermott	32	206	18	10	0	3.01
	SS	M. Bolling	323	.263	5	28	174	321	23	71	4.8	.956	H. Brown	30	166	11	6	0	4.65
	3B	G. Kell	460	.307	12	73	114	231	10	23	2.9	.972	S. Hudson	30	156	6	9	2	3.52
	RF	J. Piersall	585	.272	3	52	352	15	5	7	2.5	.987	W. Nixon	23	117	4	8	0	3.93
	CF	T. Umphlett	495	.283	3	59	382	12	7	1	2.9	.983	E. Kinder	69	107	10	6	27	1.85
	LF	H. Evers	300	.240	11	31	161	3	2	0	1.8	.988	B. Henry	21	86	5	5	1	3.26
	C	S. White	476	.273	13	64	588	68	9	9	5.1	.986							
	OF	G. Stephens	221	.204	3	18	113	2	4	0	1.7	.966							
	32	F. Baker	172	.273	0	24	67	93	4	18		.976							
	UT	T. Lepcio	161	.236	4	11	96	155	6	37		.977							
	C	D. Wilber	112	.241	7	29	90	7	2	0	3.5	.980							
	OF	T. Williams	91	.407	13	34	31	1	1	1	1.3	.970							

	POS	Player	AB	BA	HR	RBI	PO	A	E	DP	TC/G	FA	Pitcher	G	IP	W	L	SV	ERA
Was.	1B	M. Vernon	608	.337	15	115	1376	94	12	158	9.8	.992	Porterfield	34	255	22	10	0	3.35
W-76 L-76	2B	Terwilliger	464	.252	4	46	333	395	13	108	5.6	.982	W. Masterson	29	166	10	12	0	3.63
Bucky Harris	SS	P. Runnels	486	.257	2	50	195	324	23	87	4.5	.958	S. Shea	23	165	12	7	0	3.94
	3B	E. Yost	577	.272	9	45	190	300	18	31	3.3	.965	C. Stobbs	27	153	11	8	0	3.29
	RF	J. Jensen	552	.266	10	84	274	9	5	0	2.0	.983	C. Marrero	22	146	8	7	2	3.03
	CF	J. Busby	586	.312	6	82	482	15	6	4	3.4	.988	S. Dixon	43	120	5	8	3	3.75
	LF	C. Vollmer	408	.260	11	74	227	8	5	1	2.3	.979	J. Schmitz	24	108	2	7	4	3.68
	C	Fitz Gerald	288	.250	3	39	319	33	4	3	4.2	.989							
	C	M. Grasso	196	.209	2	22	219	24	4	4	4.2	.984							
	OF	G. Coan	168	.196	2	17	105	2	0	1	2.3	1.000							
Det.	1B	W. Dropo	606	.248	13	96	1260	127	14	121	9.3	.990	N. Garver	30	198	11	11	1	4.45
W-60 L-94	2B	J. Pesky	308	.292	2	24	166	183	3	49	4.8	.991	B. Hoeft	29	198	9	14	2	4.83
Fred Hutchinson	SS	H. Kuenn	679	.308	2	48	308	441	21	78	5.0	.973	T. Gray	30	176	10	15	0	4.60
	3B	R. Boone	385	.312	22	93	111	211	14	32	3.5	.958	S. Gromek	19	126	6	8	1	4.51
	RF	D. Lund	421	.257	9	47	275	12	6	0	2.4	.980	D. Marlowe	42	120	6	7	0	5.26
	CF	J. Delsing	479	.288	11	62	354	7	3	2	2.7	.992	R. Branca	17	102	4	7	1	4.15
	LF	B. Nieman	508	.281	15	69	271	10	6	1	2.1	.979	R. Herbert	43	88	4	6	6	5.24
	C	M. Batts	374	.278	6	42	463	44	7	7	5.0	.986							
	32	F. Hatfield	311	.254	3	19	120	208	9	34		.973							
	OF	S. Souchock	278	.302	11	46	144	7	6	3	2.0	.962							
	2B	G. Priddy	196	.235	1	24	111	106	5	28	4.9	.977							
	C	J. Bucha	158	.222	1	14	218	22	4	4	4.4	.984							
Phi.	1B	E. Robinson	615	.247	22	102	1366	71	17	135	9.4	.988	H. Byrd	40	237	11	20	0	5.51
W-59 L-95	2B	C. Michaels	411	.251	12	42	304	302	19	81	5.7	.970	M. Fricano	39	211	9	12	0	3.88
Jimmy Dykes	SS	J. DeMaestri	420	.255	6	35	191	297	18	53	4.7	.964	A. Kellner	25	202	11	12	0	3.93
	3B	L. Babe	343	.224	0	20	114	192	16	24	3.5	.950	C. Bishop	39	161	3	14	2	5.66
	RF	D. Philley	620	.303	9	59	296	18	6	0	2.0	.981	M. Martin	58	156	10	12	7	4.43
	CF	E. McGhee	358	.263	1	29	319	4	6	0	3.3	.982	B. Shantz	16	106	5	9	0	4.09
	LF	G. Zernial	556	.284	42	108	300	17	9	2	2.3	.972	C. Scheib	28	96	3	7	2	4.88
	C	J. Astroth	260	.296	3	24	341	47	5	13	5.0	.987							
	32	P. Suder	454	.286	4	35	178	279	10	42		.979							
	C	R. Murray	268	.284	6	41	330	45	4	8	4.9	.989							
	SS	E. Joost	177	.249	6	15	102	147	11	33	5.1	.958							
	OF	C. Mauro	165	.267	0	17	119	5	4	0	2.6	.969							
St. L.	1B	D. Kryhoski	338	.278	16	50	685	66	6	7	8.6	.992	D. Larsen	38	193	7	12	2	4.16
W-54 L-100	2B	B. Young	537	.255	4	25	397	363	18	120	5.3	.977	D. Pillette	31	167	7	13	0	4.48
Marty Marion	SS	B. Hunter	567	.219	1	37	284	512	25	99	5.4	.970	Littlefield	36	152	7	12	0	5.08
	3B	J. Dyck	334	.213	9	27	62	101	13	12	3.5	.926	S. Paige	57	117	3	9	11	3.53
	RF	V. Wertz	440	.268	19	70	243	15	7	4	2.2	.974	H. Brecheen	26	117	5	13	1	3.07
	CF	J. Groth	557	.253	10	57	425	18	4	5	3.2	.991	M. Stuart	60	114	8	2	7	3.94
	LF	D. Kokos	299	.241	13	38	152	5	6	1	2.0	.963	B. Cain	32	100	4	10	1	6.23
	C	C. Courtney	355	.251	4	19	436	47	10	7	4.8	.980	V. Trucks	16	88	5	4	2	3.07
	OF	D. Lenhardt	303	.317	10	35	148	8	5	1	2.1	.969	B. Holloman	22	65	3	7	0	5.23
	1B	R. Sievers	285	.270	8	35	604	31	5	64	8.4	.992							
	C	L. Moss	239	.276	2	28	296	21	7	4	4.6	.978							
	3B	V. Stephens	165	.321	4	17	54	91	7	9	3.3	.954							
	3B	B. Elliott	160	.250	5	29	51	93	7	12	3.4	.954							

BATTING AND BASE RUNNING LEADERS

Batting Average

M. Vernon, WAS	.337
A. Rosen, CLE	.336
B. Goodman, BOS	.313
M. Minoso, CHI	.313
J. Busby, WAS	.312

Slugging Average

A. Rosen, CLE	.613
G. Zernial, PHI	.559
Y. Berra, NY	.523
R. Boone, CLE, DET	.519
M. Vernon, WAS	.518

Home Runs

A. Rosen, CLE	43
G. Zernial, PHI	42
L. Doby, CLE	29
Y. Berra, NY	27
R. Boone, CLE, DET	26

Total Bases

A. Rosen, CLE	367
M. Vernon, WAS	315
G. Zernial, PHI	311
Y. Berra, NY	263
D. Philley, PHI	263

Runs Batted In

A. Rosen, CLE	145
M. Vernon, WAS	115
R. Boone, CLE, DET	114
Y. Berra, NY	108
G. Zernial, PHI	108

Stolen Bases

M. Minoso, CHI	25
J. Rivera, CHI	22
J. Jensen, WAS	18
J. Busby, WAS	13
D. Philley, PHI	13

Hits

H. Kuenn, DET	209
M. Vernon, WAS	205
A. Rosen, CLE	201

Base on Balls

E. Yost, WAS	123
F. Fain, CHI	108
L. Doby, CLE	96

PITCHING LEADERS

Winning Percentage

E. Lopat, NY	.800
W. Ford, NY	.750
M. Parnell, BOS	.724
Porterfield, WAS	.688
V. Trucks, CHI, STL	.667
M. Garcia, CLE	.667

Earned Run Average

E. Lopat, NY	2.42
B. Pierce, CHI	2.72
V. Trucks, CHI, STL	2.93
W. Ford, NY	3.00
J. Sain, NY	3.00

Wins

Porterfield, WAS	22
M. Parnell, BOS	21
B. Lemon, CLE	21
V. Trucks, CHI, STL	20

Saves

E. Kinder, BOS	27
H. Dorish, CHI	18
A. Reynolds, NY	13
S. Paige, STL	11
J. Sain, NY	9

Strikeouts

B. Pierce, CHI	186
V. Trucks, CHI, STL	149
E. Wynn, CLE	138
M. Parnell, BOS	136
M. Garcia, CLE	134

Complete Games

Porterfield, WAS	24
B. Lemon, CLE	23
M. Garcia, CLE	21
B. Pierce, CHI	19
V. Trucks, CHI, STL	17

Fewest Hits per 9 Innings

B. Pierce, CHI	7.16
M. McDermott, BOS	7.37
V. Raschi, NY	7.46

Shutouts

Porterfield, WAS	9
B. Pierce, CHI	7

BATTING AND BASE RUNNING LEADERS

Home Run Percentage

G. Zernial, PHI	7.6
A. Rosen, CLE	7.2
L. Doby, CLE	5.7

Runs Scored

A. Rosen, CLE	115
E. Yost, WAS	107
M. Mantle, NY	105

Doubles

M. Vernon, WAS	43
G. Kell, BOS	41
S. White, BOS	34

Triples

J. Rivera, CHI	16
M. Vernon, WAS	11
J. Piersall, BOS	9
D. Philley, PHI	9

PITCHING LEADERS

Fewest Walks per 9 Innings

E. Lopat, NY	1.61
J. Sain, NY	2.14
A. Kellner, PHI	2.28

Most Strikeouts per 9 Inn.

B. Pierce, CHI	6.17
T. Gray, DET	5.88
W. Masterson, WAS	5.14

Innings

B. Lemon, CLE	287
M. Garcia, CLE	272
B. Pierce, CHI	271

Games Pitched

E. Kinder, BOS	69
M. Stuart, STL	60
M. Martin, PHI	58

	W	L	PCT	GB	R	OR	Batting 2B	3B	HR	BA	SA	SB	Fielding E	DP	FA	CG	BB	Pitching SO	ShO	SV	ERA
NY	99	52	.656		801	547	226	52	139	.273	.417	34	126	182	.979	50	500	604	16	39	3.20
CLE	92	62	.597	8.5	770	627	201	29	160	.270	.410	33	127	197	.979	81	519	586	11	15	3.64
CHI	89	65	.578	11.5	716	592	226	53	74	.258	.364	73	125	144	.980	57	583	714	16	33	3.41
BOS	84	69	.549	16	656	632	255	37	101	.264	.384	33	148	173	.975	41	584	642	14	37	3.59
WAS	76	76	.500	23.5	687	614	230	53	69	.263	.368	65	120	173	.979	76	478	515	16	10	3.66
DET	60	94	.390	40.5	695	923	259	44	108	.266	.387	30	135	149	.978	50	585	645	2	16	5.25
PHI	59	95	.383	41.5	632	799	205	38	116	.256	.372	41	137	161	.977	51	594	566	6	11	4.67
STL	54	100	.351	46.5	555	778	214	25	112	.249	.363	17	152	165	.974	28	626	639	7	24	4.48
					5512	5512	1816	331	879	.262	.383	326	1070	1344	.978	434	4469	4911	88	185	4.00

National League 1954

	POS	Player	AB	BA	HR	RBI	PO	A	E	DP	TC/G	FA	Pitcher	G	IP	W	L	SV	ERA
N. Y. W-97 L-57 Leo Durocher	1B	W. Lockman	570	.251	16	60	1261	88	18	122	9.4	.987	J. Antonelli	39	259	21	7	2	2.30
	2B	D. Williams	544	.222	9	46	353	396	14	112	5.4	.982	R. Gomez	37	222	17	9	0	2.88
	SS	A. Dark	644	.293	20	70	289	487	36	105	5.3	.956	S. Maglie	34	218	14	6	2	3.26
	3B	H. Thompson	448	.263	26	86	125	267	23	27	3.2	.945	J. Hearn	29	130	8	8	1	4.15
	RF	D. Mueller	619	.342	4	71	263	14	6	5	1.8	.979	D. Liddle	28	127	9	4	0	3.06
	CF	W. Mays	565	.345	41	110	448	13	7	9	3.1	.985	M. Grissom	56	122	10	7	19	2.35
	LF	M. Irvin	432	.262	19	64	274	7	7	0	2.3	.976	H. Wilhelm	57	111	12	4	7	2.10
	C	W. Westrum	246	.187	8	27	419	45	7	8	4.8	.985							
	C	R. Katt	200	.255	9	33	265	23	8	4	3.6	.973							
	OF	D. Rhodes	164	.341	15	50	62	1	1	0	1.7	.984							
	UT	B. Hofman	125	.224	8	30	192	32	4	25		.982							
Bkn. W-92 L-62 Walter Alston	1B	G. Hodges	579	.304	42	130	1381	132	7	129	9.9	.995	C. Erskine	38	260	18	15	1	4.15
	2B	J. Gilliam	607	.282	13	52	340	388	17	99	5.2	.977	R. Meyer	36	180	11	6	0	3.99
	SS	P. Reese	554	.309	10	69	270	426	25	74	5.2	.965	J. Podres	29	152	11	7	0	4.27
	3B	D. Hoak	261	.245	7	26	71	139	11	12	2.9	.950	B. Loes	28	148	13	5	0	4.14
	RF	C. Furillo	547	.294	19	96	306	10	9	3	2.2	.972	D. Newcombe	29	144	9	8	0	4.55
	CF	D. Snider	584	.341	40	130	360	8	7	1	2.5	.981	C. Labine	47	108	7	6	5	4.15
	LF	S. Amoros	263	.274	9	34	149	6	2	1	2.2	.987	J. Hughes	60	87	8	4	24	3.22
	C	R. Campanella	397	.207	19	51	600	58	7	7	6.0	.989							
	O3	J. Robinson	386	.311	15	59	153	99	7	6		.973							
	3B	B. Cox	226	.235	2	17	57	90	6	7	2.6	.961							
	C	R. Walker	155	.181	5	23	259	19	1	4	5.9	.996							
Mil. W-89 L-65 Charlie Grimm	1B	J. Adcock	500	.308	23	87	1229	67	6	125	9.8	.995	W. Spahn	39	283	21	12	3	3.14
	2B	D. O'Connell	541	.279	2	37	244	314	12	83	5.5	.979	L. Burdette	38	238	15	14	0	2.76
	SS	J. Logan	560	.275	8	66	324	489	26	104	5.4	.969	G. Conley	28	194	14	9	0	2.96
	3B	E. Mathews	476	.290	40	103	112	254	13	28	3.0	.966	J. Wilson	27	128	8	2	0	3.52
	RF	A. Pafko	510	.286	14	69	245	9	8	3	1.9	.969	C. Nichols	35	122	9	11	1	4.41
	CF	B. Bruton	567	.284	4	30	350	14	7	3	2.6	.981	D. Jolly	47	111	11	6	10	2.43
	LF	H. Aaron	468	.280	13	69	223	5	7	0	2.0	.970	B. Buhl	31	110	2	7	3	4.00
	C	D. Crandall	463	.242	21	64	665	79	8	11	5.5	.989							
	2B	J. Dittmer	192	.245	6	20	119	141	6	31	4.8	.977							
	OF	J. Pendleton	173	.220	1	16	90	5	5	0	2.0	.950							
Phi. W-75 L-79 Steve O'Neill W-40 L-37 Terry Moore W-35 L-42	1B	E. Torgeson	490	.271	5	54	1146	74	12	103	9.3	.990	R. Roberts	45	337	23	15	4	2.97
	2B	G. Hamner	596	.299	13	89	361	412	17	97	5.2	.978	C. Simmons	34	253	14	15	1	2.81
	SS	B. Morgan	455	.262	14	50	237	361	29	71	4.9	.954	M. Dickson	40	226	10	20	3	3.78
	3B	W. Jones	535	.271	12	56	184	277	15	23	3.4	.968	B. Miller	30	150	7	9	0	4.56
	RF	M. Clark	233	.240	1	24	114	9	5	2	2.0	.961	H. Wehmeier	25	138	10	8	0	3.85
	CF	R. Ashburn	559	.313	1	41	483	12	8	2	3.3	.984							
	LF	D. Ennis	556	.261	25	119	303	9	14	1	2.3	.957							
	C	S. Burgess	345	.368	4	46	356	30	10	4	4.4	.975							
	OF	D. Schell	272	.283	7	33	143	4	4	0	2.2	.974							
	OF	J. Wyrostek	259	.239	3	28	90	5	1	1	1.7	.990							
	C	S. Lopata	259	.290	14	42	336	26	4	1	4.9	.989							

POS	Player	AB	BA	HR	RBI	PO	A	E	DP	TC/G	FA	Pitcher	G	IP	W	L	SV	ERA
Cin. W-74 L-80 Birdie Tebbetts																		
1B	T. Kluszewski	573	.326	49	141	1237	101	5	166	9.0	.996	A. Fowler	40	228	12	10	0	3.83
2B	J. Temple	505	.307	0	44	428	374	22	117	5.7	.973	C. Valentine	36	194	12	11	1	4.45
SS	R. McMillan	588	.250	4	42	341	464	34	129	5.4	.959	J. Nuxhall	35	167	12	5	0	3.89
3B	B. Adams	390	.269	3	23	127	186	16	24	3.5	.951	B. Podbielan	27	131	7	10	0	5.36
RF	W. Post	451	.255	18	83	231	13	11	2	2.2	.957	F. Baczewski	29	130	6	6	0	5.26
CF	G. Bell	619	.299	17	101	406	12	6	2	2.8	.986	H. Perkowski	28	96	2	8	0	6.11
LF	J. Greengrass	542	.280	27	95	298	9	10	0	2.3	.968	H. Judson	37	93	5	7	3	3.95
C	A. Seminick	247	.235	7	30	327	44	4	11	4.6	.989	F. Smith	50	81	5	8	20	2.67
3B	C. Harmon	286	.238	2	25	70	129	8	19	3.1	.961	J. Collum	36	79	7	3	0	3.74
C	E. Bailey	183	.197	9	20	194	20	6	2	3.6	.973							
OF	B. Borkowski	162	.265	1	19	69	3	0	0	2.0	1.000							
St. L. W-72 L-82 Eddie Stanky																		
1B	J. Cunningham	310	.284	11	50	814	68	10	96	10.5	.989	H. Haddix	43	260	18	13	4	3.57
2B	Schoendienst	610	.315	5	79	394	477	18	137	6.2	.980	V. Raschi	30	179	8	9	0	4.73
SS	A. Grammas	401	.264	2	29	252	432	24	100	5.0	.966	B. Lawrence	35	159	15	6	1	3.74
3B	R. Jablonski	611	.296	12	104	122	298	34	25	3.0	.925	G. Staley	48	156	7	13	2	5.26
RF	S. Musial	591	.330	35	126	271	13	3	4	1.9	.990	T. Poholsky	25	106	5	7	0	3.06
CF	W. Moon	635	.304	12	76	387	11	9	2	2.8	.978	A. Brazle	58	84	5	4	8	4.16
LF	R. Repulski	619	.283	19	79	302	4	8	0	2.1	.975	J. Presko	37	72	4	9	0	6.91
C	B. Sarni	380	.300	9	70	486	41	2	12	4.5	.996							
1B	T. Alston	244	.246	4	34	552	72	7	57	9.7	.989							
UT	S. Hemus	214	.304	2	27	85	151	10	29		.959							
Chi. W-64 L-90 Stan Hack																		
1B	D. Fondy	568	.285	9	49	1228	119	9	129	9.8	.993	B. Rush	33	236	13	15	0	3.77
2B	G. Baker	541	.275	13	61	355	385	25	102	5.7	.967	P. Minner	32	218	11	11	1	3.96
SS	E. Banks	593	.275	19	79	312	475	34	105	5.3	.959	W. Hacker	39	159	6	13	2	4.25
3B	R. Jackson	484	.273	19	67	118	266	18	21	3.2	.955	J. Klippstein	36	148	4	11	1	5.29
RF	H. Sauer	520	.288	41	103	282	8	11	2	2.1	.963	H. Pollet	20	128	8	10	0	3.58
CF	D. Talbot	403	.241	1	19	245	10	4	1	2.4	.985	J. Davis	46	128	11	7	4	3.52
LF	R. Kiner	557	.285	22	73	298	6	9	1	2.1	.971	H. Jeffcoat	43	104	5	6	1	5.19
C	J. Garagiola	153	.281	5	21	191	23	4	0	4.0	.982	D. Cole	18	84	3	8	0	5.36
OF	F. Baumholtz	303	.297	4	28	168	2	2	0	2.4	.988							
C	W. Cooper	158	.310	7	32	190	31	5	4	4.7	.978							
Pit. W-53 L-101 Fred Haney																		
1B	B. Skinner	470	.249	8	46	1026	84	16	87	9.5	.986	M. Surkont	33	208	9	18	0	4.41
2B	C. Roberts	496	.232	1	36	357	394	24	82	5.9	.969	B. Friend	35	170	7	12	2	5.07
SS	G. Allie	418	.199	3	30	192	260	23	59	5.0	.952	V. Law	39	162	9	13	3	5.51
3B	D. Cole	486	.270	1	40	48	112	10	7	3.1	.941	Littlefield	23	155	10	11	0	3.60
RF	S. Gordon	363	.306	12	49	121	9	3	1	1.8	.977	B. Purkey	36	131	3	8	0	5.07
CF	F. Thomas	577	.298	23	94	418	14	5	2	2.9	.989	J. Thies	33	130	3	9	0	3.87
LF	J. Lynch	284	.239	8	36	127	10	5	2	1.7	.965	P. LaPalme	33	121	4	10	0	5.52
C	T. Atwell	287	.289	3	26	360	39	4	4	4.6	.990	G. O'Donnell	21	87	3	9	1	4.53
UT	P. Ward	360	.269	7	48	419	69	15	34		.970	J. Hetki	58	83	4	4	9	4.99
OF	D. Hall	310	.239	2	27	235	5	11	1	2.5	.956							
C	J. Shepard	227	.304	3	22	257	46	7	5	4.6	.977							

BATTING AND BASE RUNNING LEADERS

Batting Average

W. Mays, NY	.345
D. Mueller, NY	.342
D. Snider, BKN	.341
S. Musial, STL	.330
T. Kluszewski, CIN	.326

Slugging Average

W. Mays, NY	.667
D. Snider, BKN	.647
T. Kluszewski, CIN	.642
S. Musial, STL	.607
E. Mathews, MIL	.603

Home Runs

T. Kluszewski, CIN	49
G. Hodges, BKN	42
H. Sauer, CHI	41
W. Mays, NY	41
E. Mathews, MIL	40
D. Snider, BKN	40

Total Bases

D. Snider, BKN	378
W. Mays, NY	377
T. Kluszewski, CIN	368
S. Musial, STL	359
G. Hodges, BKN	335

Runs Batted In

T. Kluszewski, CIN	141
G. Hodges, BKN	130
D. Snider, BKN	130
S. Musial, STL	126
D. Ennis, PHI	119

Stolen Bases

B. Bruton, MIL	34
J. Temple, CIN	21
D. Fondy, CHI	20
W. Moon, STL	18
R. Ashburn, PHI	11

Hits

D. Mueller, NY	212
D. Snider, BKN	199
W. Mays, NY	195
S. Musial, STL	195

Base on Balls

R. Ashburn, PHI	125
E. Mathews, MIL	113
S. Musial, STL	103

Home Run Percentage

T. Kluszewski, CIN	8.6
E. Mathews, MIL	8.4
H. Sauer, CHI	7.9

Runs Scored

D. Snider, BKN	120
S. Musial, STL	120
W. Mays, NY	119

PITCHING LEADERS

Winning Percentage

J. Antonelli, NY	.750
B. Lawrence, STL	.714
R. Gomez, NY	.654
W. Spahn, MIL	.636
R. Roberts, PHI	.605

Earned Run Average

J. Antonelli, NY	2.30
L. Burdette, MIL	2.76
C. Simmons, PHI	2.81
R. Gomez, NY	2.88
G. Conley, MIL	2.96

Wins

R. Roberts, PHI	23
J. Antonelli, NY	21
W. Spahn, MIL	21
H. Haddix, STL	18
C. Erskine, BKN	18

Saves

J. Hughes, BKN	24
F. Smith, CIN	20
M. Grissom, NY	19
D. Jolly, MIL	10
J. Hetki, PIT	9

Strikeouts

R. Roberts, PHI	185
H. Haddix, STL	184
C. Erskine, BKN	166
J. Antonelli, NY	152
W. Spahn, MIL	136

Complete Games

R. Roberts, PHI	29
W. Spahn, MIL	23
C. Simmons, PHI	21
J. Antonelli, NY	18
L. Burdette, MIL	13
H. Haddix, STL	13

Fewest Hits per 9 Innings

J. Antonelli, NY	7.27
R. Roberts, PHI	7.73
G. Conley, MIL	7.92

Shutouts

J. Antonelli, NY	6

Fewest Walks per 9 Innings

R. Roberts, PHI	1.50
P. Minner, CHI	2.06
W. Hacker, CHI	2.10

Most Strikeouts per 9 Inn.

H. Haddix, STL	6.38
C. Erskine, BKN	5.74
Littlefield, PIT	5.34

BATTING AND BASE RUNNING LEADERS

Doubles		Triples		Innings		Games Pitched	
S. Musial, STL	41	W. Mays, NY	13	R. Roberts, PHI	337	J. Hughes, BKN	60
D. Snider, BKN	39	G. Hamner, PHI	11	W. Spahn, MIL	283	A. Brazle, STL	58
G. Hamner, PHI	39	D. Snider, BKN	10	C. Erskine, BKN	260	J. Hetki, PIT	58
R. Repulski, STL	39						

PITCHING LEADERS

	W	L	PCT	GB	R	OR	Batting 2B	3B	HR	BA	SA	SB	Fielding E	DP	FA	Pitching CG	BB	SO	ShO	SV	ERA
NY	97	57	.630		732	550	194	42	186	.264	.424	30	154	172	.975	45	613	692	19	33	3.09
BKN	92	62	.597	5	778	740	246	56	186	.270	.444	46	129	138	.978	39	533	762	8	36	4.31
MIL	89	65	.578	8	670	556	217	41	139	.265	.401	54	116	171	.981	63	553	698	13	21	3.19
PHI	75	79	.487	22	659	614	243	58	102	.267	.395	30	145	133	.975	78	450	570	14	12	3.59
CIN	74	80	.481	23	729	763	221	46	147	.262	.406	47	137	194	.977	34	547	537	8	27	4.50
STL	72	82	.468	25	799	790	285	58	119	.281	.421	63	146	178	.976	40	535	680	11	18	4.50
CHI	64	90	.416	33	700	766	229	45	159	.263	.412	46	154	164	.974	41	619	622	6	19	4.51
PIT	53	101	.344	44	557	845	181	57	76	.248	.350	21	173	136	.971	37	564	525	4	15	4.92
					5624	5624	1816	403	1114	.265	.407	337	1154	1286	.976	377	4414	5086	83	181	4.07

American League 1954

	POS	Player	AB	BA	HR	RBI	PO	A	E	DP	TC/G	FA	Pitcher	G	IP	W	L	SV	ERA
Cle. W-111 L-43 Al Lopez	1B	B. Glynn	171	.251	5	18	424	35	6	38	4.8	.987	E. Wynn	40	271	23	11	2	2.73
	2B	B. Avila	555	.341	15	67	356	406	19	100	5.5	.976	B. Lemon	36	258	23	7	0	2.72
	SS	G. Strickland	361	.213	6	37	193	321	21	61	4.8	.961	M. Garcia	45	259	19	8	5	2.64
	3B	A. Rosen	466	.300	24	102	110	149	11	14	3.1	.959	A. Houtteman	32	188	15	7	0	3.35
	RF	D. Philley	452	.226	12	60	237	6	4	0	1.9	.984	B. Feller	19	140	13	3	0	3.09
	CF	L. Doby	577	.272	32	126	411	14	2	6	2.8	.995	D. Mossi	40	93	6	1	7	1.94
	LF	A. Smith	481	.281	11	50	241	8	4	1	2.3	.984	R. Narleski	42	89	3	3	13	2.22
	C	J. Hegan	423	.234	11	40	661	49	4	9	5.2	.994	H. Newhouser	26	47	7	2	7	2.51
	1B	V. Wertz	295	.275	14	48	557	52	7	57	7.4	.989							
	OF	W. Westlake	240	.263	11	42	131	1	5	0	2.0	.964							
	3B	R. Regalado	180	.250	2	24	62	84	5	7	3.0	.967							
	SS	S. Dente	169	.266	1	19	66	133	6	33	3.4	.971							
N. Y. W-103 L-51 Casey Stengel	1B	J. Collins	343	.271	12	46	759	60	7	105	7.1	.992	W. Ford	34	211	16	8	1	2.82
	2B	G. McDougald	394	.259	12	48	224	233	5	84	5.0	.989	B. Grim	37	199	20	6	0	3.26
	SS	P. Rizzuto	307	.195	2	15	184	294	16	84	3.9	.968	E. Lopat	26	170	12	4	0	3.55
	3B	A. Carey	411	.302	8	65	154	283	15	32	3.8	.967	A. Reynolds	36	157	13	4	7	3.32
	RF	H. Bauer	377	.294	12	54	179	6	2	1	1.7	.989	T. Morgan	32	143	11	5	1	3.34
	CF	M. Mantle	543	.300	27	102	327	20	9	5	2.5	.975	H. Byrd	25	132	9	7	0	2.99
	LF	I. Noren	426	.319	12	66	242	9	5	2	2.2	.980	J. Sain	45	77	6	6	22	3.16
	C	Y. Berra	584	.307	22	125	717	63	8	14	5.3	.990							
	OF	G. Woodling	304	.250	3	40	164	5	3	1	1.9	.983							
	2B	J. Coleman	300	.217	3	21	183	198	9	62	4.9	.977							
	1B	B. Skowron	215	.340	7	41	395	28	6	48	7.0	.986							
	1B	E. Robinson	142	.261	3	27	227	19	5	21	8.7	.980							
Chi. W-94 L-60 Paul Richards W-91 L-54 Marty Marion W-3 L-6	1B	F. Fain	235	.302	5	51	565	31	8	54	9.4	.987	V. Trucks	40	265	19	12	3	2.79
	2B	N. Fox	631	.319	2	47	400	392	9	103	5.2	.989	B. Keegan	31	210	16	9	2	3.09
	SS	C. Carrasquel	620	.255	12	62	280	492	20	102	5.1	.975	B. Pierce	36	189	9	10	3	3.48
	3B	C. Michaels	282	.262	7	44	95	180	12	10	3.2	.958	J. Harshman	35	177	14	8	1	2.95
	RF	J. Rivera	490	.286	13	61	255	5	11	0	1.9	.959	S. Consuegra	39	154	16	3	3	2.69
	CF	J. Groth	422	.275	7	60	314	7	4	3	2.6	.988	D. Johnson	46	144	8	7	7	3.13
	LF	M. Minoso	568	.320	19	116	340	14	8	3	2.5	.978	H. Dorish	37	109	6	4	6	2.72
	C	S. Lollar	316	.244	7	34	395	38	3	8	4.7	.993	M. Martin	35	70	5	4	5	2.06
	13	G. Kell	233	.283	5	48	272	56	4	31		.988							
	1B	P. Cavarretta	158	.316	3	24	261	17	2	29	6.4	.993							
	C	M. Batts	158	.228	3	19	225	19	2	3	5.9	.992							
Bos. W-69 L-85 Lou Boudreau	1B	H. Agganis	434	.251	11	57	1064	89	12	101	9.8	.990	F. Sullivan	36	206	15	12	1	3.14
	2B	T. Lepcio	398	.256	8	45	233	230	14	58	6.0	.971	W. Nixon	31	200	11	12	0	4.06
	SS	M. Bolling	370	.249	6	36	186	370	32	73	5.5	.946	T. Brewer	33	163	10	9	0	4.65
	3B	G. Hatton	302	.281	5	33	77	204	10	20	3.1	.966*	L. Kiely	28	131	5	8	0	3.50
	RF	J. Piersall	474	.285	8	38	249	10	4	2	2.1	.985	H. Brown	40	118	1	8	0	4.12
	CF	J. Jensen	580	.276	25	117	331	12	5	0	2.3	.986	E. Kinder	48	107	8	8	15	3.62
	LF	T. Williams	386	.345	29	89	213	5	4	0	1.9	.982	B. Henry	24	96	3	7	0	4.52
	C	S. White	493	.282	14	75	677	80	16	11	5.8	.979	M. Parnell	19	92	3	7	0	3.70
	UT	B. Goodman	489	.303	1	36	393	248	14	90		.979	S. Hudson	33	71	3	4	5	4.42
	UT	B. Consolo	242	.227	1	11	113	184	15	30		.952							
	OF	K. Olson	227	.260	1	20	122	10	6	1	1.8	.957							
	1O	S. Mele	132	.318	7	23	188	9	2	18		.990							

	POS	Player	AB	BA	HR	RBI	PO	A	E	DP	TC/G	FA	Pitcher	G	IP	W	L	SV	ERA
Det.	1B	W. Dropo	320	.281	4	44	681	54	3	60	7.8	.996	S. Gromek	36	253	18	16	1	2.74
W-68 L-86	2B	F. Bolling	368	.236	6	38	248	232	13	54	4.4	.974	N. Garver	35	246	14	11	1	2.81
Fred Hutchinson	SS	H. Kuenn	656	.306	5	48	294	496	28	85	5.3	.966	G. Zuverink	35	203	9	13	4	3.59
	3B	R. Boone	543	.295	20	85	170	332	19	22	3.5	.964	B. Hoeft	34	175	7	15	1	4.58
	RF	A. Kaline	504	.276	4	43	283	16	9	0	2.3	.971	A. Aber	32	125	5	11	3	3.97
	CF	B. Tuttle	530	.266	7	58	364	18	6	3	2.7	.985	D. Marlowe	38	84	5	4	2	4.18
	LF	J. Delsing	371	.248	6	38	221	5	1	0	2.1	.996							
	C	F. House	352	.250	9	38	434	56	4	7	4.6	.992							
	OF	B. Nieman	251	.263	8	35	119	2	2	0	2.0	.984							
	1B	W. Belardi	250	.232	11	24	636	51	8	54	8.8	.988							
	2B	F. Hatfield	218	.294	2	25	114	126	7	29	4.6	.972							
	C	R. Wilson	170	.282	2	22	245	25	1	7	5.1	.996							
Was.	1B	M. Vernon	597	.290	20	97	1365	76	11	144	9.8	.992	Porterfield	32	244	13	15	0	3.32
W-66 L-88	2B	Terwilliger	337	.208	3	24	213	243	13	72	5.2	.972	M. McDermott	30	196	7	15	1	3.44
Bucky Harris	SS	P. Runnels	488	.268	3	56	174	313	24	69	4.8	.953	J. Schmitz	29	185	11	8	1	2.91
	3B	E. Yost	539	.256	11	47	170	347	17	29	3.4	.968	C. Stobbs	31	182	11	11	0	4.10
	RF	T. Umphlett	342	.219	1	33	169	13	2	4	1.8	.989	D. Stone	31	179	12	10	0	3.22
	CF	J. Busby	628	.298	7	80	491	6	6	1	3.2	.988	C. Pascual	48	119	4	7	3	4.22
	LF	R. Sievers	514	.232	24	102	296	10	9	1	2.4	.971	S. Shea	23	71	2	9	0	6.18
	C	Fitz Gerald	360	.289	4	40	396	38	12	5	4.2	.973							
	OF	T. Wright	171	.246	1	17	84	0	0	0	2.0	1.000							
	2B	J. Pesky	158	.253	0	9	92	91	4	22	5.1	.979							
	C	J. Tipton	157	.223	1	10	220	30	2	6	4.8	.992							
	SS	J. Snyder	154	.234	0	17	81	145	5	31	4.8	.978							
Bal.	1B	E. Waitkus	311	.283	2	33	618	48	0	72	8.5	1.000	B. Turley	35	247	14	15	0	3.46
W-54 L-100	2B	B. Young	432	.245	4	24	299	310	15	76	4.9	.976	J. Coleman	33	221	13	17	0	3.50
Jimmy Dykes	SS	B. Hunter	411	.243	2	27	249	333	32	76	5.0	.948	D. Larsen	29	202	3	21	0	4.37
	3B	V. Stephens	365	.285	8	46	102	186	10	19	3.1	.966	D. Pillette	25	179	10	14	0	3.12
	RF	C. Abrams	423	.293	6	25	248	6	6	1	2.3	.977	L. Kretlow	32	167	6	11	0	4.37
	CF	C. Diering	418	.258	2	29	330	17	6	6	3.0	.983	B. Chakales	38	89	3	7	3	3.73
	LF	J. Fridley	240	.246	4	36	132	1	2	0	2.0	.985							
	C	C. Courtney	397	.270	4	37	539	53	6	8	5.4	.990							
	3B	B. Kennedy	323	.251	6	45	81	131	14	10	3.2	.938							
	1B	D. Kryhoski	300	.260	1	34	591	52	5	52	9.4	.992							
	OF	G. Coan	265	.279	2	20	148	1	5	0	2.3	.968							
	OF	S. Mele	230	.239	5	32	97	5	4	1	1.7	.962							
	SS	J. Brideweser	204	.265	0	12	67	103	10	22	3.8	.944							
Phi.	1B	L. Limmer	316	.231	14	32	597	56	8	63	8.4	.988	Portocarrero	34	248	9	18	0	4.06
W-51 L-103	2B	S. Jacobs	508	.258	0	26	347	300	17	98	5.1	.974	A. Kellner	27	174	6	17	0	5.39
Eddie Joost	SS	J. DeMaestri	539	.230	8	40	285	406	25	90	5.0	.965	M. Fricano	37	152	5	11	1	5.16
	3B	J. Finigan	487	.302	7	51	151	305	25	34	3.5	.968	B. Trice	19	119	7	8	0	5.60
	RF	B. Renna	422	.232	13	53	226	13	7	5	2.1	.972	S. Dixon	38*	107	5	7	4	4.86
	CF	B. Wilson	323	.238	15	33	270	7	3	4	3.1	.989	J. Gray	18	105	3	12	0	6.51
	LF	V. Power	462	.255	8	38	256	13	4	3	2.7	.985	C. Bishop	20	96	6	1	4	4.41
	C	J. Astroth	226	.221	1	23	300	39	4	5	4.8	.988	M. Burtschy	46	95	5	4	4	3.80
	OF	G. Zernial	336	.250	14	62	180	4	9	1	2.1	.953							
	1B	D. Bollweg	268	.224	5	24	530	51	13	55	8.4	.978							
	OF	E. Valo	224	.214	1	33	135	3	5	1	2.3	.965							
	23	P. Suder	205	.200	0	16	97	134	8	25	4.0	.967							
	C	B. Shantz	164	.256	1	17	170	28	5	1	4.0	.975							

BATTING AND BASE RUNNING LEADERS

Batting Average
B. Avila, CLE	.341
M. Minoso, CHI	.320
I. Noren, NY	.319
N. Fox, CHI	.319
Y. Berra, NY	.307

Slugging Average
T. Williams, BOS	.635
M. Minoso, CHI	.535
M. Mantle, NY	.525
A. Rosen, CLE	.506
M. Vernon, WAS	.492

Home Runs
L. Doby, CLE	32
T. Williams, BOS	29
M. Mantle, NY	27
J. Jensen, BOS	25
A. Rosen, CLE	24
R. Sievers, WAS	24

Total Bases
M. Minoso, CHI	304
M. Vernon, WAS	294
M. Mantle, NY	285
Y. Berra, NY	285
L. Doby, CLE	279

Runs Batted In
L. Doby, CLE	126
Y. Berra, NY	125
J. Jensen, BOS	117
M. Minoso, CHI	116

Stolen Bases
J. Jensen, BOS	22
J. Rivera, CHI	18
M. Minoso, CHI	18
S. Jacobs, PHI	17
J. Busby, WAS	17

Hits
N. Fox, CHI	201
H. Kuenn, DET	201
B. Avila, CLE	189

Base on Balls
T. Williams, BOS	136
E. Yost, WAS	131
M. Mantle, NY	102
A. Smith, CLE	88

PITCHING LEADERS

Winning Percentage
S. Consuegra, CHI	.842
B. Grim, NY	.769
B. Lemon, CLE	.767
M. Garcia, CLE	.704
A. Houtteman, CLE	.682

Earned Run Average
M. Garcia, CLE	2.64
S. Consuegra, CHI	2.69
B. Lemon, CLE	2.72
E. Wynn, CLE	2.73
S. Gromek, DET	2.74

Wins
B. Lemon, CLE	23
E. Wynn, CLE	23
B. Grim, NY	20
M. Garcia, CLE	19
V. Trucks, CHI	19

Saves
J. Sain, NY	22
E. Kinder, BOS	15
R. Narleski, CLE	13

Strikeouts
B. Turley, BAL	185
E. Wynn, CLE	155
V. Trucks, CHI	152
B. Pierce, CHI	148
J. Harshman, CHI	134

Complete Games
Porterfield, WAS	21
B. Lemon, CLE	21
E. Wynn, CLE	20
S. Gromek, DET	17

Fewest Hits per 9 Innings
B. Turley, BAL	6.48
W. Ford, NY	7.26
E. Wynn, CLE	7.48
J. Coleman, BAL	7.48

Shutouts
V. Trucks, CHI	5
M. Garcia, CLE	5

BATTING AND BASE RUNNING LEADERS

Home Run Percentage

L. Doby, CLE	5.5
A. Rosen, CLE	5.2
M. Mantle, NY	5.0
R. Sievers, WAS	4.7

Runs Scored

M. Mantle, NY	129
M. Minoso, CHI	119
B. Avila, CLE	112

Doubles

M. Vernon, WAS	33
A. Smith, CLE	29
M. Minoso, CHI	29

Triples

M. Minoso, CHI	18
P. Runnels, WAS	15
M. Vernon, WAS	14

PITCHING LEADERS

Fewest Walks per 9 Innings

E. Lopat, NY	1.75
S. Gromek, DET	2.03
S. Consuegra, CHI	2.05

Most Strikeouts per 9 Inn.

B. Pierce, CHI	7.06
J. Harshman, CHI	6.81
B. Turley, BAL	6.73

Innings

E. Wynn, CLE	271
V. Trucks, CHI	265
M. Garcia, CLE	259

Games Pitched

S. Dixon, PHI, WAS	54
M. Martin, CHI, PHI	48
C. Pascual, WAS	48
E. Kinder, BOS	48

	W	L	PCT	GB	R	OR	2B	3B	HR	BA	SA	SB	E	DP	FA	CG	BB	SO	ShO	SV	ERA
CLE	111	43	.721		746	504	188	39	156	.262	.403	30	128	148	.979	77	486	678	12	36	2.78
NY	103	51	.669	8	805	563	215	59	133	.268	.408	34	126	198	.979	51	552	655	15	37	3.26
CHI	94	60	.610	17	711	521	203	47	94	.267	.379	98	108	149	.982	60	517	701	21	33	3.05
BOS	69	85	.448	42	700	728	244	41	123	.266	.395	51	176	163	.972	41	612	707	9	22	4.01
DET	68	86	.442	43	584	664	215	41	90	.258	.367	48	129	131	.978	58	506	603	13	13	3.81
WAS	66	88	.429	45	632	680	188	69	81	.246	.355	37	137	172	.977	69	573	562	10	7	3.84
BAL	54	100	.351	57	483	668	195	49	52	.251	.338	30	147	152	.975	58	688	668	6	8	3.88
PHI	51	103	.331	60	542	875	191	41	94	.236	.342	30	169	163	.972	49	685	555	3	13	5.18
	5203	5203			1639		386	823	.257	.373		358	1120	1276	.977	463	4619	5129	89	169	3.72

National League 1955

	POS	Player	AB	BA	HR	RBI	PO	A	E	DP	TC/G	FA	Pitcher	G	IP	W	L	SV	ERA
Bkn. W-98 L-55 Walter Alston	1B	G. Hodges	546	.289	27	102	1274	105	12	126	10.0	.991	D. Newcombe	34	234	20	5	0	3.20
	2B	J. Gilliam	538	.249	7	40	213	269	16	64	5.0	.968	C. Erskine	31	195	11	8	1	3.79
	SS	P. Reese	553	.282	10	61	239	404	23	86	4.7	.965	J. Podres	27	159	9	10	0	3.95
	3B	J. Robinson	317	.256	8	36	74	180	9	18	3.1	.966	C. Labine	60	144	13	5	11	3.24
	RF	C. Furillo	523	.314	26	95	249	10	5	4	1.9	.981	B. Loes	22	128	10	4	0	3.59
	CF	D. Snider	538	.309	42	136	348	9	4	0	2.5	.989	K. Spooner	29	99	8	6	2	3.65
	LF	S. Amoros	388	.247	10	51	201	10	6	1	2.0	.972	R. Craig	21	91	5	3	2	2.78
	C	R. Campanella	446	.318	32	107	672	54	6	8	6.0	.992	E. Roebuck	47	84	5	6	12	4.71
	2S	D. Zimmer	280	.239	15	50	182	199	12	63		.969	D. Bessent	24	63	8	1	3	2.70
	3B	D. Hoak	279	.240	5	19	82	183	11	15	3.5	.960							
	P	D. Newcombe	117	.359	7	23	15	24	4	5	1.3	.907							
Mil. W-85 L-69 Charlie Grimm	1B	G. Crowe	303	.281	15	55	677	61	8	62	9.4	.989	W. Spahn	39	246	17	14	1	3.26
	2B	D. O'Connell	453	.225	6	40	309	357	13	76	6.0	.981	L. Burdette	42	230	13	8	0	4.03
	SS	J. Logan	595	.297	13	83	268	511	30	100	5.3	.963	B. Buhl	38	202	13	11	1	3.21
	3B	E. Mathews	499	.289	41	101	140	280	21	23	3.2	.952	G. Conley	22	158	11	7	0	4.16
	RF	H. Aaron	602	.314	27	106	254	9	9	2	2.2	.967	C. Nichols	34	144	9	8	1	4.00
	CF	B. Bruton	636	.275	9	47	412	17	14	6	3.0	.968	R. Crone	33	140	10	9	0	3.46
	LF	B. Thomson	343	.257	12	56	182	5	6	0	2.1	.969	E. Johnson	40	92	5	7	4	3.42
	C	D. Crandall	440	.236	26	62	611	67	10	8	5.3	.985							
	1B	J. Adcock	288	.264	15	45	725	44	8	68	10.0	.990							
	OF	A. Pafko	252	.266	5	34	96	1	2	0	1.7	.980							
	OF	C. Tanner	243	.247	6	27	101	4	2	0	1.7	.981							
N. Y. W-80 L-74 Leo Durocher	1B	G. Harris	263	.232	12	36	617	50	12	65	9.1	.982	J. Antonelli	38	235	14	16	1	3.33
	2B	J. Terwilliger	257	.257	1	18	212	240	7	70	5.9	.985	J. Hearn	39	227	14	16	0	3.73
	SS	A. Dark	475	.282	9	45	213	324	21	70	4.9	.962	R. Gomez	33	185	9	10	1	4.56
	3B	H. Thompson	432	.245	17	63	104	262	22	23	3.1	.943	S. Maglie	23	130	9	5	0	3.75
	RF	D. Mueller	605	.306	8	83	239	5	6	1	1.7	.976	D. Liddle	33	106	10	4	1	4.23
	CF	W. Mays	580	.319	51	127	407	23	8	8	2.9	.982	H. Wilhelm	59	103	4	1	0	3.93
	LF	W. Lockman	576	.273	15	49	167	4	3	1	2.1	.983	W. McCall	42	95	6	5	3	3.69
	C	R. Katt	326	.215	7	28	482	45	7	7	4.4	.987	R. Monzant	28	95	4	8	0	3.99
	2B	D. Williams	247	.251	4	15	139	162	10	39	4.4	.968	M. Grissom	55	89	5	4	8	2.92
	UT	B. Hofman	207	.266	10	28	259	59	1	30		.997							
	OF	D. Rhodes	187	.305	6	32	68	2	1	0	1.6	.986							
	SS	B. Gardner	187	.203	3	17	65	122	12	28	5.2	.940							
	3O	S. Gordon	144	.243	7	25	57	61	0	6		1.000							
Phi. W-77 L-77 Mayo Smith	1B	M. Blaylock	259	.208	3	24	528	44	5	35	7.5	.991	R. Roberts	41	305	23	14	3	3.28
	2B	B. Morgan	483	.232	10	49	192	204	8	46	4.6	.980	M. Dickson	36	216	12	11	0	3.50
	SS	R. Smalley	260	.196	7	39	136	205	9	32	4.0	.974	H. Wehmeier	31	194	10	12	0	4.41
	3B	W. Jones	516	.258	16	81	202	235	18	22	3.1	.960	C. Simmons	25	130	8	8	0	4.92
	RF	J. Greengrass	323	.272	12	37	159	10	2	0	2.1	.988	J. Meyer	50	110	6	11	16	3.43
	CF	R. Ashburn	533	.338	3	42	387	10	7	3	2.9	.983	B. Miller	40	90	8	4	1	2.41
	LF	D. Ennis	564	.296	29	120	298	9	4	2	2.1	.987							
	C	A. Seminick	289	.246	11	34	435	45	3	6	5.5	.994*							
	2B	G. Hamner	405	.257	5	43	152	183	14	39	4.3	.960							
	C	S. Lopata	303	.271	22	58	332	37	2	9	5.6	.995							
	OF	G. Gorbous	224	.237	4	23	113	10	2	2	2.2	.984							

	POS	Player	AB	BA	HR	RBI	PO	A	E	DP	TC/G	FA	Pitcher	G	IP	W	L	SV	ERA
Cin.	1B	T. Kluszewski	612	.314	47	113	**1388**	86	8	**153**	9.7	**.995**	J. Nuxhall	50	257	17	12	3	3.47
W-75 L-79	2B	J. Temple	588	.281	0	50	408	410	24	**119**	5.7	.971	A. Fowler	46	208	11	10	2	3.90
Birdie Tebbetts	SS	R. McMillan	470	.268	1	37	290	495	25	**111**	5.4	.969	J. Klippstein	39	138	9	10	0	3.39
	3B	R. Bridges	168	.286	1	18	48	88	5	7	2.4	.965	J. Collum	32	134	9	8	1	3.63
	RF	W. Post	601	.309	40	109	298	13	7	2	2.1	.978	G. Staley	30	120	5	8	0	4.66
	CF	G. Bell	610	.308	27	104	364	4	5	0	2.4	.987	R. Minarcin	41	116	5	9	1	4.90
	LF	S. Palys	222	.230	7	30	116	3	1	0	2.2	.992	J. Black	32	102	5	2	3	4.22
	C	S. Burgess	421	.306	20	77	457	35	7	6	4.7	.986	H. Freeman	52	92	7	4	11	2.16
	O3	R. Jablonski	221	.240	9	28	69	46	11	3		.913							
	3O	C. Harmon	198	.253	5	28	114	50	6	4		.965							
	OF	B. Thurman	152	.217	7	22	54	2	3	0	1.6	.949							
	3B	B. Adams	150	.273	2	20	35	88	4	11	3.0	.969							
Chi.	1B	D. Fondy	574	.265	17	65	1304	**107**	13	135	9.7	.991	S. Jones	36	242	14	**20**	0	4.10
W-72 L-81	2B	G. Baker	609	.268	11	52	**432**	**444**	30	114	5.9	.967	B. Rush	33	234	13	11	0	3.50
Stan Hack	SS	E. Banks	596	.295	44	117	290	482	22	102	5.2	**.972**	W. Hacker	35	213	11	15	3	4.27
	3B	R. Jackson	499	.265	21	70	125	247	20	**26**	2.9	.949	P. Minner	22	158	9	9	0	3.48
	RF	J. King	301	.256	11	45	184	10	2	2	2.1	.990	J. Davis	42	134	7	11	3	4.44
	CF	E. Miksis	481	.235	9	41	267	6	3	1	2.5	**.989**	H. Jeffcoat	50	101	8	6	6	2.95
	LF	H. Sauer	261	.211	12	28	122	4	2	1	1.9	.984	H. Pollet	24	61	4	3	5	5.61
	C	H. Chiti	338	.231	11	41	495	**69**	9	**10**	5.1	.984							
	OF	F. Baumholtz	280	.289	1	27	131	3	1	1	2.1	.993							
	OF	B. Speake	261	.218	12	43	90	4	4	1	1.8	.959							
	OF	J. Bolger	160	.206	0	7	125	1	6	0	2.6	.955							
St. L.	1B	S. Musial	562	.319	33	108	925	92	8	93	9.3	.992	H. Haddix	37	208	12	16	1	4.46
W-68 L-86	2B	Schoendienst	553	.268	11	51	296	381	10	96	4.8	**.985**	L. Jackson	37	177	9	14	2	4.31
Eddie Stanky	SS	A. Grammas	366	.240	3	25	235	340	19	76	4.7	.968	L. Arroyo	35	159	11	8	0	4.19
W-17 L-19	3B	K. Boyer	530	.264	18	62	124	253	19	24	2.8	.952	T. Poholsky	30	151	9	11	0	3.81
Harry Walker	RF	W. Moon	593	.295	19	76	188	5	5	1	2.0	.975	W. Schmidt	20	130	7	6	0	2.78
W-51 L-67	CF	B. Virdon	534	.281	17	68	339	7	12	1	2.5	.966	B. Lawrence	46	96	3	8	1	6.56
	LF	R. Repulski	512	.270	23	73	260	5	7	1	1.9	.974	P. LaPalme	56	92	4	3	3	2.75
	C	B. Sarni	325	.255	3	34	482	39	7	8	5.3	.987							
	32	S. Hemus	206	.243	5	21	56	90	5	10		.967							
	C	N. Burbrink	170	.276	0	15	261	24	6	4	5.3	.979							
Pit.	1B	D. Long	419	.291	16	79	968	97	13	114	9.1	.988	V. Law	43	201	10	10	1	3.81
W-60 L-94	2B	J. O'Brien	278	.299	1	25	185	220	13	53	5.4	.969	B. Friend	44	200	14	9	2	**2.83**
Fred Haney	SS	D. Groat	521	.267	4	51	**330**	450	**32**	107	5.4	.961	M. Surkont	35	166	7	14	2	5.57
	3B	G. Freese	455	.253	14	44	55	127	-11	16	3.0	.943	R. Kline	36	137	6	13	2	4.15
	RF	R. Clemente	474	.255	5	47	253	18	6	5	2.3	.978	Littlefield	35	130	5	12	0	5.12
	CF	E. O'Brien	236	.233	0	8	132	8	1	1	2.5	.993	R. Face	42	126	5	7	5	3.58
	LF	F. Thomas	510	.245	25	72	307	8	5	3	2.3	.984	L. Donoso	25	95	4	6	1	5.31
	C	J. Shepard	264	.239	2	23	288	34	6	6	4.3	.982	D. Hall	15	94	6	6	1	3.91
	OF	J. Lynch	282	.284	5	28	104	11	6	3	1.7	.950	B. Purkey	14	68	2	7	1	5.32
	UT	D. Cole	239	.226	0	21	103	158	10	25		.963							
	C	T. Atwell	207	.213	1	18	334	24	3	3	5.4	.992							
	1B	P. Ward	179	.212	5	25	384	35	1	41	8.8	.998							
	3B	G. Freese	179	.257	3	22	50	82	9	3	2.8	.936							
	OF	R. Mejias	167	.216	3	21	67	8	6	2	1.9	.926							

BATTING AND BASE RUNNING LEADERS

Batting Average

R. Ashburn, PHI	.338
W. Mays, NY	.319
S. Musial, STL	.319
R. Campanella, BKN	.318
H. Aaron, MIL	.314

Slugging Average

W. Mays, NY	.659
D. Snider, BKN	.628
E. Mathews, MIL	.601
E. Banks, CHI	.596
T. Kluszewski, CIN	.585

PITCHING LEADERS

Winning Percentage

D. Newcombe, BKN	.800
R. Roberts, PHI	.622
J. Nuxhall, CIN	.586
W. Spahn, MIL	.548

Earned Run Average

B. Friend, PIT	2.83
D. Newcombe, BKN	3.20
B. Buhl, MIL	3.21
W. Spahn, MIL	3.26
R. Roberts, PHI	3.28

Home Runs

W. Mays, NY	51
T. Kluszewski, CIN	47
E. Banks, CHI	44
D. Snider, BKN	42
E. Mathews, MIL	41

Total Bases

W. Mays, NY	382
T. Kluszewski, CIN	358
E. Banks, CHI	355
W. Post, CIN	345
D. Snider, BKN	338

Wins

R. Roberts, PHI	23
D. Newcombe, BKN	20
J. Nuxhall, CIN	17
W. Spahn, MIL	17

Saves

J. Meyer, NY	16
E. Roebuck, BKN	12
C. Labine, BKN	11
H. Freeman, CIN	11
M. Grissom, NY	8

Runs Batted In

D. Snider, BKN	136
W. Mays, NY	127
D. Ennis, PHI	120
E. Banks, CHI	117
T. Kluszewski, CIN	113

Stolen Bases

B. Bruton, MIL	25
W. Mays, NY	24
K. Boyer, STL	22
J. Temple, CIN	19
J. Gilliam, BKN	15

Strikeouts

S. Jones, CHI	198
R. Roberts, PHI	160
H. Haddix, STL	150
D. Newcombe, BKN	143
J. Antonelli, NY	143

Complete Games

R. Roberts, PHI	26
D. Newcombe, BKN	17
W. Spahn, MIL	16
J. Nuxhall, CIN	14
B. Rush, CHI	14
J. Antonelli, NY	14

Hits

T. Kluszewski, CIN	192
H. Aaron, MIL	189
G. Bell, CIN	188

Base on Balls

E. Mathews, MIL	109
R. Ashburn, PHI	105
D. Snider, BKN	104
H. Thompson, NY	84

Fewest Hits per 9 Innings

S. Jones, CHI	6.52
B. Buhl, MIL	7.50
B. Rush, CHI	7.85

Shutouts

J. Nuxhall, CIN	5
M. Dickson, PHI	4
S. Jones, CHI	4

BATTING AND BASE RUNNING LEADERS

Home Run Percentage			Runs Scored	
W. Mays, NY	8.8	D. Snider, BKN	126
E. Mathews, MIL	8.2	W. Mays, NY	123
D. Snider, BKN	7.8	W. Post, CIN	116
		T. Kluszewski, CIN	116

Doubles			Triples	
J. Logan, MIL	37	D. Long, PIT	13
H. Aaron, MIL	37	W. Mays, NY	13
D. Snider, BKN	34	B. Bruton, MIL	12
		R. Clemente, PIT	11

PITCHING LEADERS

Fewest Walks per 9 Innings			Most Strikeouts per 9 Inn.	
D. Newcombe, BKN	1.46	S. Jones, CHI	7.37
R. Roberts, PHI	1.56	H. Haddix, STL	6.49
W. Hacker, CHI	1.82	J. Podres, BKN	6.44

Innings			Games Pitched	
R. Roberts, PHI	305	C. Labine, BKN	60
J. Nuxhall, CIN	257	H. Wilhelm, NY	59
W. Spahn, MIL	246	P. LaPalme, STL	56

	W	L	PCT	GB	R	OR	2B	3B	Batting HR	BA	SA	SB	E	Fielding DP	FA	CG	BB	Pitching SO	ShO	SV	ERA
BKN	98	55	.641		857	650	230	44	201	.271	.448	79	133	156	.978	46	483	773	11	37	3.68
MIL	85	69	.552	13.5	743	668	219	55	182	.261	.427	42	152	155	.975	61	591	654	5	12	3.85
NY	80	74	.519	18.5	702	673	173	34	169	.260	.402	38	142	165	.976	52	560	721	6	14	3.77
PHI	77	77	.500	21.5	675	666	214	50	132	.255	.395	44	110	117	.981	58	477	657	11	21	3.93
CIN	75	79	.487	23.5	761	684	216	28	181	.270	.425	51	139	169	.977	38	443	576	12	22	3.95
CHI	72	81	.471	26	626	713	187	55	164	.247	.398	37	147	147	.975	47	601	686	10	23	4.17
STL	68	86	.442	30.5	654	757	228	36	143	.261	.400	64	146	152	.975	42	549	730	10	15	4.56
PIT	60	94	.390	38.5	560	767	210	60	91	.244	.361	22	166	175	.972	41	536	622	5	16	4.39
					5578	5578	1677	362	1263	.259	.407	377	1135	1236	.976	385	4240	5419	70	160	4.04

American League 1955

	POS	Player	AB	BA	HR	RBI	PO	A	E	DP	TC/G	FA	Pitcher	G	IP	W	L	SV	ERA
N. Y. W-96 L-58 Casey Stengel	1B	B. Skowron	288	.319	12	61	517	37	6	63	7.6	.989	W. Ford	39	254	**18**	7	2	2.63
	2B	G. McDougald	533	.285	13	53	352	348	11	**119**	5.6	**.985**	B. Turley	36	247	17	13	1	3.06
	SS	B. Hunter	255	.227	3	20	115	249	16	60	3.9	.958	T. Byrne	27	160	16	5	2	3.15
	3B	A. Carey	510	.257	7	47	**154**	**301**	22	**37**	**3.5**	.954	J. Kucks	29	127	8	7	0	3.41
	RF	H. Bauer	492	.278	20	53	248	13	5	3	2.0	.981	D. Larsen	19	97	9	2	2	3.06
	CF	M. Mantle	517	.306	**37**	99	372	11	2	2	2.7	.995	B. Grim	26	92	7	5	4	4.19
	LF	I. Noren	371	.253	8	59	238	9	5	0	2.0	.980	E. Lopat	16	87	4	8	0	3.74
	C	Y. Berra	541	.272	27	108	**721**	54	13	10	5.4	.984	J. Konstanty	45	74	7	2	**11**	2.32
													T. Morgan	40	72	7	3	**10**	3.25
	OF	E. Howard	279	.290	10	43	124	10	3	3	1.8	.978							
	1B	J. Collins	278	.234	13	45	395	42	1	63	6.0	.998							
	1B	E. Robinson	173	.208	16	42	390	20	2	35	9.0	.995							
	OF	B. Cerv	85	.341	3	22	25	1	0	0	1.3	1.000							
Cle. W-93 L-61 Al Lopez	1B	V. Wertz	257	.253	14	55	449	33	8	49	7.8	.984	E. Wynn	32	230	17	11	0	2.82
	2B	B. Avila	537	.272	13	61	348	342	13	108	5.0	.982	H. Score	33	227	16	10	0	2.85
	SS	G. Strickland	388	.209	2	34	221	360	14	84	4.6	**.976**	B. Lemon	35	211	**18**	10	2	3.88
	3B	A. Rosen	492	.244	21	81	119	195	12	17	3.1	.963	M. Garcia	38	211	11	13	3	4.02
	RF	A. Smith	607	.306	22	77	206	5	5	1	1.8	.977	A. Houtteman	35	124	10	6	0	3.98
	CF	L. Doby	491	.291	26	75	313	6	2	1	2.5	.994	R. Narleski	**60**	112	9	1	**19**	3.71
	LF	R. Kiner	321	.243	18	54	141	2	2	0	1.7	.986	D. Mossi	57	82	4	3	9	2.42
	C	J. Hegan	304	.220	9	40	583	34	2	12	5.6	.997							
	OF	G. Woodling	259	.278	5	35	129	4	1	0	1.9	.993*							
	OF	D. Pope	104	.298	6	22	62	0	3	0	2.1	.954							
Chi. W-91 L-63 Marty Marion	1B	W. Dropo	453	.280	19	79	1101	62	6	**104**	8.4	.995	B. Pierce	33	206	15	10	1	**1.97**
	2B	N. Fox	**636**	.311	6	59	**399**	**483**	24	110	**5.9**	.974	D. Donovan	29	187	15	9	0	3.32
	SS	C. Carrasquel	523	.256	11	52	222	424	18	81	4.6	.973	J. Harshman	32	179	11	7	0	3.36
	3B	G. Kell	429	.312	8	41	83	165	6	8	2.4	**.976**	V. Trucks	32	175	13	8	0	3.96
	RF	J. Rivera	454	.264	10	52	288	22	6	7	2.2	.981	S. Consuegra	44	126	6	5	7	2.64
	CF	J. Busby	337	.243	1	27	243	6	4	3	2.6	.984	C. Johnson	17	99	7	4	0	3.45
	LF	M. Minoso	517	.288	10	70	287	19	9	3	2.3	.971	H. Byrd	25	91	4	6	1	4.65
	C	S. Lollar	426	.261	16	61	664	62	4	12	5.4	.995	M. Fornieles	26	86	6	3	2	3.86
	OF	B. Nieman	272	.283	11	53	118	4	3	2	1.6	.976	D. Howell	35	74	8	3	9	2.93
	3B	B. Kennedy	214	.304	9	43	32	73	7	10	2.0	.938							
Bos. W-84 L-70 Pinky Higgins	1B	N. Zauchin	477	.239	27	93	1137	84	6	**106**	9.7	**.995**	F. Sullivan	35	**260**	**18**	13	0	2.91
	2B	B. Goodman	599	.294	0	52	348	373	23	93	5.2	.969	W. Nixon	31	208	12	10	0	4.07
	SS	B. Klaus	541	.283	7	60	207	391	28	55	5.0	.955	T. Brewer	31	193	11	10	0	4.20
	3B	G. Hatton	380	.245	4	49	97	225	8	22	3.0	.976	G. Susce	29	144	9	7	1	3.06
	RF	J. Jensen	574	.275	26	**116**	281	11	7	3	2.0	.977	I. Delock	29	144	9	7	3	3.76
	CF	J. Piersall	515	.283	13	62	425	7	3	2	3.0	.993	L. Kiely	33	90	3	3	6	2.80
	LF	T. Williams	320	.356	28	83	170	5	2	0	1.9	.989	T. Hurd	43	81	8	6	5	3.01
	C	S. White	544	.261	11	64	671	71	12	8	5.3	.984	E. Kinder	43	67	5	5	**18**	2.84
	OF	G. Stephens	157	.293	3	18	82	7	5	1	1.3	.947							
	OF	Throneberry	144	.257	6	27	69	3	3	0	2.2	.960							

	POS	Player	AB	BA	HR	RBI	PO	A	E	DP	TC/G	FA	Pitcher	G	IP	W	L	SV	ERA
Det. W-79 L-75 Bucky Harris	1B	E. Torgeson	300	.283	9	50	695	53	6	79	9.1	.992	F. Lary	36	235	14	15	1	3.10
	2B	F. Hatfield	413	.232	8	33	216	251	12	74	5.2	.975	N. Garver	33	231	12	16	0	3.98
	SS	H. Kuenn	620	.306	8	62	253	378	29	83	4.7	.956	B. Hoeft	32	220	16	7	0	2.99
	3B	R. Boone	500	.284	20	116	135	252	19	33	3.2	.953	S. Gromek	28	181	13	10	0	3.98
	RF	A. Kaline	588	.340	27	102	306	14	7	4	2.2	.979	D. Maas	18	87	5	6	0	4.88
	CF	B. Tuttle	603	.279	14	78	442	12	7	2	3.0	.985	B. Birrer	36	80	4	3	3	4.15
	LF	J. Delsing	356	.239	10	60	178	3	1	1	1.8	.995	A. Aber	39	80	6	3	3	3.38
	C	F. House	328	.259	15	53	423	35	6	5	5.0	.987							
	C	R. Wilson	241	.220	2	17	292	25	5	5	4.5	.984							
	2B	H. Malmberg	208	.216	0	19	155	181	5	42	5.2	.985							
	OF	B. Phillips	184	.234	3	23	128	2	1	0	2.0	.992							
	1B	F. Fain	140	.264	2	23	370	29	5	42	9.2	.988							
	1B	J. Phillips	117	.316	1	20	236	13	2	16	7.2	.992							
K. C. W-63 L-91 Lou Boudreau	1B	V. Power	596	.319	19	76	1281	130	10	140	9.9	.993	A. Ditmar	35	175	12	12	1	5.03
	2B	J. Finigan	545	.255	9	68	236	228	12	72	5.3	.975	A. Kellner	30	163	11	8	0	4.20
	SS	J. DeMaestri	457	.249	6	37	206	358	21	78	4.8	.964	B. Shantz	23	125	5	10	0	4.54
	3B	H. Lopez	483	.290	15	68	104	233	23	26	3.9	.936	A. Ceccarelli	31	124	4	7	0	5.31
	RF	E. Slaughter	267	.322	5	34	126	5	2	2	1.7	.985	Portocarrero	24	111	5	9	0	4.77
	CF	H. Simpson	396	.301	5	52	262	5	6	2	2.7	.978	T. Gorman	57	109	7	6	18	3.55
	LF	G. Zernial	413	.254	30	84	231	9	9	4	2.4	.964	V. Raschi	20	101	4	6	0	5.42
	C	J. Astroth	274	.252	5	23	420	50	5	9	4.8	.989	C. Boyer	30	98	5	5	0	6.22
	OF	E. Valo	283	.364	3	37	147	5	2	2	2.1	.987							
	OF	B. Wilson	273	.223	15	38	186	4	6	0	2.4	.969							
	OF	B. Renna	249	.213	7	28	118	5	1	2	1.6	.992							
	C	B. Shantz	217	.258	1	12	261	27	3	8	3.7	.990							
Bal. W-57 L-97 Paul Richards	1B	G. Triandos	481	.277	12	65	839	69	10	92	8.9	.989	J. Wilson	34	235	12	**18**	0	3.44
	2B	F. Marsh	303	.218	2	19	197	158	6	51	4.8	.983	E. Palica	33	170	5	11	2	4.14
	SS	W. Miranda	487	.255	1	38	300	481	34	101	5.3	.958	R. Moore	46	152	10	10	6	3.92
	3B	W. Causey	175	.194	1	9	25	79	10	10	2.1	.912	B. Wight	19	117	6	8	2	2.45
	RF	C. Abrams	309	.243	6	32	191	7	3	1	2.1	.985	G. Zuverink	28	86	4	3	4	2.19
	CF	C. Diering	371	.256	3	31	242	6	6	2	2.4	.976	H. Dorish	35	66	3	3	6	3.15
	LF	D. Philley	311	.299	6	41	154	6	5	2	2.0	.970							
	C	H. Smith	424	.271	4	52	497	58	8	9	4.5	.986							
	OF	D. Pope	222	.248	1	30	152	3	0	1	2.1	1.000							
	OF	J. Dyck	197	.279	2	22	86	4	1	1	2.0	.989							
	32	B. Cox	194	.211	3	14	53	95	3	9		.980							
	2B	B. Young	186	.199	1	8	121	146	4	42	4.7	.985							
	OF	H. Evers	185	.238	6	30	106	1	1	0	2.0	.991							
	1B	B. Hale	182	.357	0	29	300	33	9	25	7.8	.974							
Was. W-53 L-101 Chuck Dressen	1B	M. Vernon	538	.301	14	85	1258	69	8	137	9.3	.994	D. Stone	43	180	6	13	1	4.15
	2B	P. Runnels	503	.284	2	49	349	338	17	107	5.3	.976	Porterfield	30	178	10	17	0	4.45
	SS	Valdivielso	294	.221	2	28	160	317	22	69	5.3	.958	J. Schmitz	32	165	7	10	1	3.71
	3B	E. Yost	375	.243	7	48	100	217	19	22	3.1	.943	M. McDermott	31	156	10	10	1	3.75
	RF	C. Paula	351	.299	6	45	154	5	10	3	2.0	.941	C. Stobbs	41	140	4	14	3	5.00
	CF	T. Umphlett	323	.217	2	19	237	8	3	1	2.4	.988	P. Ramos	45	130	5	11	5	3.88
	LF	R. Sievers	509	.271	25	106	247	5	3	6	2.0	.988	C. Pascual	43	129	2	12	3	6.14
	C	Fitz Gerald	236	.237	4	19	304	30	6	5	4.7	.982	T. Abernathy	40	119	5	9	0	5.96
	OF	E. Oravetz	263	.270	0	25	117	1	4	0	2.1	.967							
	C	C. Courtney	238	.298	2	30	252	27	5	4	4.2	.982							
	OF	J. Busby	191	.230	6	14	132	1	1	0	2.9	.993							
	OF	J. Groth	183	.219	2	17	121	2	2	1	2.6	.984							

BATTING AND BASE RUNNING LEADERS

Batting Average
A. Kaline, DET	.340
V. Power, KC	.319
G. Kell, CHI	.312
N. Fox, CHI	.311
H. Kuenn, DET	.306

Slugging Average
M. Mantle, NY	.611
A. Kaline, DET	.546
G. Zernial, KC	.508
L. Doby, CLE	.505
V. Power, KC	.505

Home Runs
M. Mantle, NY	37
G. Zernial, KC	30
T. Williams, BOS	28
N. Zauchin, BOS	27
Y. Berra, NY	27
A. Kaline, DET	27

Total Bases
A. Kaline, DET	321
M. Mantle, NY	316
V. Power, KC	301
A. Smith, CLE	287
J. Jensen, BOS	275

Runs Batted In
R. Boone, DET	116
J. Jensen, BOS	116
Y. Berra, NY	108
R. Sievers, WAS	106
A. Kaline, DET	102

Stolen Bases
J. Rivera, CHI	25
M. Minoso, CHI	19
J. Jensen, BOS	16
J. Busby, CHI, WAS	12
A. Smith, CLE	11

Hits
A. Kaline, DET	200
N. Fox, CHI	198
V. Power, KC	190
H. Kuenn, DET	190

Base on Balls
M. Mantle, NY	113
B. Goodman, BOS	99
E. Yost, WAS	95

PITCHING LEADERS

Winning Percentage
T. Byrne, NY	.762
W. Ford, NY	.720
B. Hoeft, DET	.696
B. Lemon, CLE	.643
D. Donovan, CHI	.625

Earned Run Average
B. Pierce, CHI	1.97
W. Ford, NY	2.63
E. Wynn, CLE	2.82
H. Score, CLE	2.85
F. Sullivan, BOS	2.91

Wins
W. Ford, NY	18
B. Lemon, CLE	18
F. Sullivan, BOS	18
E. Wynn, CLE	17
B. Turley, NY	17

Saves
R. Narleski, CLE	19
T. Gorman, KC	18
E. Kinder, BOS	18
J. Konstanty, NY	11
T. Morgan, NY	10

Strikeouts
H. Score, CLE	245
B. Turley, NY	210
B. Pierce, CHI	157
W. Ford, NY	137
B. Hoeft, DET	133

Complete Games
W. Ford, NY	18
B. Hoeft, DET	17

Fewest Hits per 9 Innings
B. Turley, NY	6.13
H. Score, CLE	6.26
W. Ford, NY	6.67

Shutouts
B. Hoeft, DET	7
B. Pierce, CHI	6
E. Wynn, CLE	6
B. Turley, NY	6

BATTING AND BASE RUNNING LEADERS

Home Run Percentage

G. Zernial, KC	7.3
M. Mantle, NY	7.2
N. Zauchin, BOS	5.7

Runs Scored

A. Smith, CLE	123
M. Mantle, NY	121
A. Kaline, DET	121

Doubles

H. Kuenn, DET	38
V. Power, KC	34
B. Goodman, BOS	31

Triples

A. Carey, NY	11
M. Mantle, NY	11
V. Power, KC	10

PITCHING LEADERS

Fewest Walks per 9 Innings

S. Gromek, DET	1.84
D. Donovan, CHI	2.31
M. Garcia, CLE	2.39

Most Strikeouts per 9 Inn.

H. Score, CLE	9.70
B. Turley, NY	7.66
B. Pierce, CHI	6.87

Innings

F. Sullivan, BOS	260
W. Ford, NY	254
B. Turley, NY	247

Games Pitched

R. Narleski, CLE	60
T. Gorman, KC	57
D. Mossi, CLE	57

	W	L	PCT	GB	R	OR	2B	3B	Batting HR	BA	SA	SB	E	Fielding DP	FA	CG	BB	SO	Pitching ShO	SV	ERA
NY	96	58	.623		762	569	179	55	175	.260	.418	55	128	180	.978	52	689	731	18	33	3.23
CLE	93	61	.604	3	698	601	195	31	148	.257	.394	28	108	152	.981	45	558	877	13	36	3.39
CHI	91	63	.591	5	725	557	204	36	116	.268	.388	69	111	147	.981	55	499	720	17	23	3.37
BOS	84	70	.545	12	755	652	241	39	137	.264	.402	43	136	140	.977	44	582	674	9	34	3.72
DET	79	75	.513	17	775	658	211	38	130	.266	.394	41	139	159	.976	66	517	629	15	12	3.79
KC	63	91	.409	33	638	911	189	46	121	.261	.382	22	146	174	.976	29	707	572	7	23	5.35
BAL	57	97	.370	39	540	754	177	39	54	.240	.320	34	167	159	.972	35	625	595	9	22	4.21
WAS	53	101	.344	43	598	789	178	54	80	.248	.351	25	154	170	.974	37	637	607	9	16	4.62
					5491	5491	1574	338	961	.258	.381	317	1089	1281	.977	363	4814	5405	97	199	3.96

National League 1956

	POS	Player	AB	BA	HR	RBI	PO	A	E	DP	TC/G	FA	Pitcher	G	IP	W	L	SV	ERA
Bkn. W-93 L-61 Walter Alston	1B	G. Hodges	550	.265	32	87	1190	103	10	105	9.4	.992	D. Newcombe	38	268	27	7	0	3.06
	2B	J. Gilliam	594	.300	6	43	233	326	11	64	5.6	.981	R. Craig	35	199	12	11	1	3.71
	SS	P. Reese	572	.257	9	46	263	367	23	79	4.8	.965	S. Maglie	28	191	13	5	0	2.87
	3B	R. Jackson	307	.274	8	53	84	184	2	19	3.4	.993	C. Erskine	31	186	13	11	0	4.25
	RF	C. Furillo	523	.289	21	83	358	10	4	1	2.5	.984	C. Labine	62	116	10	6	19	3.35
	CF	D. Snider	542	.292	43	101	358	11	6	1	2.5	.984	D. Drysdale	25	99	5	5	0	2.64
	LF	S. Amoros	292	.260	16	58	123	3	6	0	1.5	.955	E. Roebuck	43	89	5	4	1	3.93
	C	R. Campanella	388	.219	20	73	659	49	11	3	5.9	.985	D. Bessent	38	79	4	3	9	2.50
	UT	J. Robinson	357	.275	10	43	169	230	9	37		.978							
	C	R. Walker	146	.212	3	20	184	20	3	4	4.8	.986							
Mil. W-92 L-62 Charlie Grimm W-24 L-22 Fred Haney W-68 L-40	1B	J. Adcock	454	.291	38	103	1086	75	6	109	9.0	.995	W. Spahn	39	281	20	11	3	2.78
	2B	D. O'Connell	498	.239	2	42	295	381	10	98	5.0	.985	L. Burdette	39	256	19	10	1	2.70
	SS	J. Logan	545	.281	15	46	266	467	24	94	5.1	.968	B. Buhl	38	217	18	8	0	3.32
	3B	E. Mathews	552	.272	37	95	133	287	25	22	3.0	.944	R. Crone	35	170	11	10	2	3.87
	RF	H. Aaron	609	.328	26	92	316	17	13	4	2.3	.962	G. Conley	31	158	8	9	3	3.13
	CF	B. Bruton	525	.272	8	56	391	10	13	1	2.9	.974	T. Phillips	23	88	5	3	2	2.26
	LF	B. Thomson	451	.235	20	74	257	7	7	0	2.0	.974	E. Johnson	36	51	4	3	6	3.71
	C	D. Crandall	311	.238	16	48	448	44	2	9	4.5	.996	D. Jolly	29	46	2	3	7	3.74
	C	D. Rice	188	.213	3	17	271	21	5	2	4.6	.983							
	1B	F. Torre	159	.258	0	16	390	42	3	34	4.9	.993							
Cin. W-91 L-63 Birdie Tebbetts	1B	T. Kluszewski	517	.302	35	102	1166	89	13	110	9.7	.990	B. Lawrence	49	219	19	10	0	3.99
	2B	J. Temple	632	.285	2	41	389	432	16	89	5.4	.981	J. Klippstein	37	211	12	11	1	4.09
	SS	R. McMillan	479	.263	3	62	319	511	21	105	5.7	.975	J. Nuxhall	44	201	13	11	1	3.72
	3B	R. Jablonski	407	.256	15	66	117	172	9	11	2.3	.970	A. Fowler	45	178	11	11	1	4.05
	RF	W. Post	539	.249	36	83	292	16	10	1	2.3	.969	H. Jeffcoat	38	171	8	2	2	3.84
	CF	G. Bell	603	.292	29	84	330	12	5	4	2.3	.986	H. Freeman	64	109	14	5	18	3.40
	LF	F. Robinson	572	.290	38	83	323	5	8	1	2.2	.976							
	C	E. Bailey	383	.300	28	75	511	52	9	10	5.4	.984							
	C	S. Burgess	229	.275	12	39	257	18	0	2	5.0	1.000							
	1B	G. Crowe	144	.250	10	23	225	25	3	15	7.9	.988							
	OF	B. Thurman	139	.295	8	22	39	2	2	1	1.5	.953							
St. L. W-76 L-78 Fred Hutchinson	1B	S. Musial	594	.310	27	109	870	90	7	96	9.4	.993	V. Mizell	33	209	14	14	0	3.62
	2B	D. Blasingame	587	.261	0	27	280	303	8	89	6.0	.986	T. Poholsky	33	203	9	14	0	3.59
	SS	A. Dark	413	.286	4	37	178	292	20	66	4.9	.959	M. Dickson	28	196	13	8	0	3.07
	3B	K. Boyer	595	.306	26	98	130	309	18	37	3.1	.961	H. Wehmeier	34	171	12	9	1	3.69
	RF	W. Moon	540	.298	16	68	159	8	2	2	1.7	.988	W. Schmidt	33	148	6	8	1	3.84
	CF	B. Del Greco	270	.215	5	18	217	3	3	0	2.3	.987	L. McDaniel	39	116	7	6	0	3.40
	LF	R. Repulski	376	.277	11	55	187	3	5	0	2.0	.974	L. Jackson	51	85	2	2	9	4.11
	C	H. Smith	227	.282	5	23	300	34	6	3	5.2	.982	J. Collum	38	60	6	2	7	4.20
	OF	W. Lockman	193	.249	0	10	103	2	5	0	1.9	.955							
	C	R. Katt	158	.259	6	20	231	16	4	0	5.3	.984							
	OF	H. Sauer	151	.298	5	24	55	2	0	1	1.5	1.000							
	C	B. Sarni	148	.291	5	22	219	25*	2	1*	6.0	.992							
	UT	B. Morgan	113	.195	3	20	42	56	6	6		.942							

	POS	Player	AB	BA	HR	RBI	PO	A	E	DP	TC/G	FA	Pitcher	G	IP	W	L	SV	ERA
Phi. W-71 L-83 Mayo Smith	1B	M. Blaylock	460	.254	10	50	949	72	8	86	8.3	.992	R. Roberts	43	297	19	**18**	3	4.45
	2B	T. Kazanski	379	.211	4	34	246	261	11	68	4.5	.979	H. Haddix	31	207	12	8	2	3.48
	SS	G. Hamner	401	.224	4	42	177	302	32	69	4.6	.937	C. Simmons	33	198	15	10	0	3.36
	3B	W. Jones	520	.277	17	78	202	264	13	23	3.2	.973	B. Miller	49	122	3	6	5	3.24
	RF	E. Valo	291	.289	5	37	167	4	6	0	2.0	.966	S. Rogovin	22	107	7	6	0	4.98
	CF	R. Ashburn	628	.303	3	50	503	11	9	3	3.4	.983	S. Miller	24	107	5	8	0	4.47
	LF	D. Ennis	630	.260	26	95	269	8	11	0	1.9	.962	J. Meyer	41	96	7	11	2	4.41
	C	S. Lopata	535	.267	32	95	573	24	11	10	6.0	.982							
	OF	J. Greengrass	215	.205	5	25	104	3	1	1	1.7	.991							
	2B	S. Hemus	187	.289	5	24	94	93	5	18	3.9	.974							
	SS	R. Smalley	168	.226	0	16	81	142	12	32	3.9	.949							
	C	A. Seminick	161	.199	7	23	266	23	7	2	5.5	.976							
N. Y. W-67 L-87 Billy Rigney	1B	B. White	508	.256	22	59	1256	111	15	106	10.0	.989	J. Antonelli	41	258	20	13	1	2.86
	2B	Schoendienst	334	.296	2	14	199	215	3	52	4.9	.993*	R. Gomez	40	196	7	17	0	4.58
	SS	D. Spencer	489	.221	14	42	113	169	6	33	4.4	.979	R. Worthington	28	166	7	14	0	3.97
	3B	F. Castleman	385	.226	14	45	90	213	17	10	3.0	.947	J. Hearn	30	129	5	11	1	3.97
	RF	D. Mueller	453	.269	5	41	180	4	2	2	1.6	.989	Littlefield	31	97	4	4	2	4.08
	CF	W. Mays	578	.296	36	84	415	14	9	6	2.9	.979	J. Margoneri	23	92	6	6	0	3.93
	LF	J. Brandt	351	.299	11	47	165	8	2	0	1.8	.989*	H. Wilhelm	64	89	4	9	8	3.83
	C	B. Sarni	238	.231	5	23	367	36*	3	9*	5.4	.993	W. McCall	46	77	3	4	7	3.61
	OF	D. Rhodes	244	.217	8	33	85	6	4	1	1.4	.958							
	SS	A. Dark	206	.252	2	17	89	132	9	27	4.8	.961							
	3B	H. Thompson	183	.235	8	29	25	94	12	7	3.0	.908							
	OF	W. Lockman	169	.272	1	10	69	3	3	1	1.9	.960							
	SS	E. Bressoud	163	.227	0	9	67	125	10	26	4.2	.950							
Pit. W-66 L-88 Bobby Bragan	1B	D. Long	517	.263	27	91	1201	99	**24**	92	9.6	.982	B. Friend	49	**314**	17	17	3	3.46
	2B	B. Mazeroski	255	.243	3	14	163	242	8	56	5.1	.981	R. Kline	44	264	14	**18**	2	3.38
	SS	D. Groat	520	.273	0	37	287	420	**34**	74	5.3	.954	V. Law	39	196	8	16	2	4.32
	3B	F. Thomas	588	.282	25	80	118	176	18	21	2.8	.942	R. Face	**68**	135	12	13	6	3.52
	RF	R. Clemente	543	.311	7	60	274	17	**13**	2	2.2	.957	G. Munger	35	107	3	4	2	4.04
	CF	B. Virdon	509	.334	8	37	334	10	4	2	2.7	.989	N. King	38	60	4	1	5	3.15
	LF	L. Walls	474	.274	11	54	284	10	10	1	2.3	.967							
	C	J. Shepard	256	.242	7	30	356	36	4	4	4.6	.990							
	O1	B. Skinner	233	.202	5	29	216	8	2	21		.991							
	C	H. Foiles	222	.212	7	25	291	30	4	8	4.5	.988							
	32	G. Freese	207	.208	3	14	69	115	4	9		.979							
Chi. W-60 L-94 Stan Hack	1B	D. Fondy	543	.269	9	46	1048	94	17	101	8.7	.985	B. Rush	32	240	13	10	0	3.19
	2B	G. Baker	546	.258	12	57	362	426	**25**	99	5.8	.969	S. Jones	33	189	9	14	0	3.91
	SS	E. Banks	538	.297	28	85	279	357	25	92	4.8	.962	W. Hacker	34	168	3	13	0	4.66
	3B	D. Hoak	424	.215	5	37	122	158	15	16	2.7	.947	D. Kaiser	27	150	4	9	0	3.59
	RF	W. Moryn	529	.285	23	67	268	**18**	5	2	2.1	.983	J. Davis	46	120	5	7	2	3.66
	CF	P. Whisenant	314	.239	11	46	242	6	2	0	2.7	.991	T. Lown	61	111	9	8	13	3.58
	LF	M. Irvin	339	.271	15	50	216	6	2	0	2.3	.991	Valentinetti	42	95	6	4	1	3.78
	C	H. Landrith	312	.221	4	32	483	55	14	9	5.6	.975	J. Brosnan	30	95	5	9	1	3.79
	UT	E. Miksis	356	.239	9	27	144	151	7	14		.977							
	OF	J. King	317	.249	15	54	187	10	2	2	2.4	.990							
	OF	S. Drake	215	.256	2	15	142	3	1	1	2.8	.993							
	C	H. Chiti	203	.212	4	18	327	35	7	2	5.5	.981							

BATTING AND BASE RUNNING LEADERS

Batting Average
H. Aaron, MIL	.328
B. Virdon, PIT, STL	.319
R. Clemente, PIT	.311
S. Musial, STL	.310
K. Boyer, STL	.306

Slugging Average
D. Snider, BKN	.598
J. Adcock, MIL	.597
H. Aaron, MIL	.558
F. Robinson, CIN	.558
W. Mays, NY	.557

Home Runs
D. Snider, BKN	43
J. Adcock, MIL	38
F. Robinson, CIN	38
E. Mathews, MIL	37
W. Post, CIN	36
W. Mays, NY	36

Total Bases
H. Aaron, MIL	340
D. Snider, BKN	324
W. Mays, NY	322
F. Robinson, CIN	319
S. Musial, STL	310

Runs Batted In
S. Musial, STL	109
J. Adcock, MIL	103
T. Kluszewski, CIN	102
D. Snider, BKN	101
K. Boyer, STL	98

Stolen Bases
W. Mays, NY	40
J. Gilliam, BKN	21
B. White, NY	15
J. Temple, CIN	14
P. Reese, BKN	13

Hits
H. Aaron, MIL	200
R. Ashburn, PHI	190
B. Virdon, PIT, STL	185

Base on Balls
D. Snider, BKN	99
J. Gilliam, BKN	95
W. Jones, PHI	92

PITCHING LEADERS

Winning Percentage
D. Newcombe, BKN	.794
B. Buhl, MIL	.692
L. Burdette, MIL	.655
B. Lawrence, CIN	.655
W. Spahn, MIL	.645

Earned Run Average
L. Burdette, MIL	2.70
W. Spahn, MIL	2.78
J. Antonelli, NY	2.86
S. Maglie, BKN	2.87
D. Newcombe, BKN	3.06

Wins
D. Newcombe, BKN	27
W. Spahn, MIL	20
J. Antonelli, NY	20
L. Burdette, MIL	19
B. Lawrence, CIN	19
R. Roberts, PHI	19

Saves
C. Labine, BKN	19
H. Freeman, CIN	18
T. Lown, CHI	13
D. Bessent, BKN	9
L. Jackson, STL	9

Strikeouts
S. Jones, CHI	176
H. Haddix, PHI, STL	170
B. Friend, PIT	166
R. Roberts, PHI	157
V. Mizell, STL	153

Complete Games
R. Roberts, PHI	22
W. Spahn, MIL	20
B. Friend, PIT	19
D. Newcombe, BKN	18
L. Burdette, MIL	16

Fewest Hits per 9 Innings
S. Maglie, BKN	7.26
D. Newcombe, BKN	7.35
S. Jones, CHI	7.39

Shutouts
J. Antonelli, NY	6
L. Burdette, MIL	6
D. Newcombe, BKN	5
B. Friend, PIT	4

BATTING AND BASE RUNNING LEADERS   PITCHING LEADERS

Home Run Percentage			Runs Scored			Fewest Walks per 9 Innings			Most Strikeouts per 9 Inn.	
J. Adcock, MIL	8.4		F. Robinson, CIN	122		R. Roberts, PHI	1.21		S. Jones, CHI	8.40
D. Snider, BKN	7.9		D. Snider, BKN	112		D. Newcombe, BKN	1.54		H. Haddix, PHI, STL	6.64
T. Kluszewski, CIN	6.8		H. Aaron, MIL	106		W. Spahn, MIL	1.66		V. Mizell, STL	6.60

Doubles			Triples			Innings			Games Pitched	
H. Aaron, MIL	34		B. Bruton, MIL	15		B. Friend, PIT	314		R. Face, PIT	68
S. Lopata, PHI	33		H. Aaron, MIL	14		R. Roberts, PHI	297		H. Freeman, CIN	64
D. Snider, BKN	33		L. Walls, PIT	11		W. Spahn, MIL	281		H. Wilhelm, NY	64
S. Musial, STL	33		W. Moon, STL	11						

	W	L	PCT	GB	R	OR	2B	3B	Batting HR	BA	SA	SB	E	Fielding DP	FA	CG	BB	Pitching SO	ShO	SV	ERA
BKN	93	61	.604		720	601	212	36	179	.258	.419	65	111	149	.981	46	441	772	12	30	3.57
MIL	92	62	.597	1	709	569	212	54	177	.259	.423	29	130	159	.979	64	467	639	12	27	3.11
CIN	91	63	.591	2	775	658	201	32	221	.266	.441	45	113	147	.981	47	458	653	4	29	3.85
STL	76	78	.494	17	678	698	234	49	124	.268	.399	41	134	172	.978	41	546	709	12	30	3.97
PHI	71	83	.461	22	668	738	207	49	121	.252	.381	45	144	140	.975	57	437	750	4	15	4.20
NY	67	87	.435	26	540	650	192	45	145	.244	.382	67	144	143	.976	31	551	765	9	28	3.78
PIT	66	88	.429	27	588	653	199	57	110	.257	.380	24	162	140	.973	37	469	662	8	24	3.74
CHI	60	94	.390	33	597	708	202	50	142	.244	.382	55	144	141	.976	37	613	744	6	17	3.96
					5275	5275	1659	372	1219	.256	.401	371	1082	1191	.977	360	3982	5694	67	200	3.77

American League 1956

	POS	Player	AB	BA	HR	RBI	PO	A	E	DP	TC/G	FA	Pitcher	G	IP	W	L	SV	ERA
N. Y. W-97 L-57 Casey Stengel	1B	B. Skowron	464	.308	23	90	968	80	7	138	8.8	.993	W. Ford	31	226	19	6	1	2.47
	2B	B. Martin	458	.264	9	49	241	260	10	84	4.9	.980	J. Kucks	34	224	18	9	0	3.85
	SS	G. McDougald	438	.311	13	56	177	273	14	77	5.0	.970	D. Larsen	38	180	11	5	1	3.26
	3B	A. Carey	422	.237	7	50	114	265	21	26	3.1	.948	T. Sturdivant	32	158	16	8	5	3.30
	RF	H. Bauer	539	.241	26	84	242	10	8	2	1.8	.969	B. Turley	27	132	8	4	1	5.05
	CF	M. Mantle	533	.353	52	130	370	10	4	3	2.7	.990	T. Byrne	37	110	7	3	6	3.36
	LF	E. Howard	290	.262	5	34	97	2	1	0	1.5	.990	R. Coleman	29	88	3	5	2	3.67
	C	Y. Berra	521	.298	30	105	732	55	11	15	5.9	.986	B. Grim	26	75	6	1	5	2.77
	O1	J. Collins	262	.225	7	43	346	32	1	37		.997	T. Morgan	41	71	6	7	11	4.16
	UT	J. Coleman	183	.257	0	18	138	152	9	46		.970							
	OF	N. Siebern	162	.204	4	21	100	1	3	0	2.0	.971							
	OF	B. Cerv	115	.304	3	25	59	4	1	2	1.5	.984							
Cle. W-88 L-66 Al Lopez	1B	V. Wertz	481	.264	32	106	971	77	9	99	7.9	.991	E. Wynn	38	278	20	9	2	2.72
	2B	B. Avila	513	.224	10	54	322	351	16	83	5.1	.977	B. Lemon	39	255	20	14	3	3.03
	SS	C. Carrasquel	474	.243	7	48	240	352	20	70	4.3	.967	H. Score	35	249	20	9	0	2.53
	3B	A. Rosen	416	.267	15	61	89	219	18	20	2.8	.945	M. Garcia	35	198	11	12	0	3.78
	RF	R. Colavito	322	.276	21	65	177	6	6	0	1.9	.968	D. Mossi	48	88	6	5	11	3.59
	CF	J. Busby	494	.235	12	50	344	3	4	0	2.6	.989							
	LF	A. Smith	526	.274	16	71	248	6	5	1	2.1	.981							
	C	J. Hegan	315	.222	6	34	648	28	10	2	5.8	.985							
	OF	G. Woodling	317	.262	8	38	154	3	3	0	1.9	.981							
	UT	G. Strickland	171	.211	3	17	118	145	5	34		.981							
	1B	P. Ward	150	.253	6	21	226	21	3	20	4.2	.988							
	OF	S. Mele	114	.254	4	20	29	2	1	0	1.6	.969							
Chi. W-85 L-69 Marty Marion	1B	W. Dropo	361	.266	8	52	855	50	6	95	7.8	.993	B. Pierce	35	276	20	9	1	3.32
	2B	N. Fox	649	.296	4	52	478	396	12	124	5.8	.986	D. Donovan	34	235	12	10	0	3.64
	SS	L. Aparicio	533	.266	3	56	250	474	35	91	5.0	.954	J. Harshman	34	227	15	11	0	3.10
	3B	F. Hatfield	321	.262	7	33	83	189	11	21	2.8	.961	J. Wilson	28	160	9	12	0	4.06
	RF	J. Rivera	491	.255	12	66	271	9	7	4	2.1	.976	B. Keegan	20	105	5	7	0	3.93
	CF	L. Doby	504	.268	24	102	371	4	5	2	2.8	.987	G. Staley	26	102	8	3	0	2.92
	LF	M. Minoso	545	.316	21	88	284	10	8	1	2.0	.974	D. Howell	34	64	5	6	4	4.62
	C	S. Lollar	450	.293	11	75	679	40	5	6	5.5	.993							
	1O	D. Philley	279	.265	4	47	349	19	7	31		.981							
	3B	S. Esposito	184	.228	3	25	41	109	6	17	2.6	.962							
	C	L. Moss	127	.244	10	22	149	10	1	1	3.3	.994							
	PH	R. Northey	48	.354	3	23													

POS	Player	AB	BA	HR	RBI	PO	A	E	DP	TC/G	FA	Pitcher	G	IP	W	L	SV	ERA
1B	M. Vernon	403	.310	15	84	930	58	11	96	9.3	.989	T. Brewer	32	244	19	9	0	3.50
2B	B. Goodman	399	.293	2	38	215	266	17	69	5.2	.966	F. Sullivan	34	242	14	7	0	3.42
SS	D. Buddin	377	.239	5	37	213	370	29	98	5.4	.953	W. Nixon	23	145	9	8	0	4.21
3B	B. Klaus	520	.271	7	59	120	242	21	18	3.6	.945	D. Sisler	39	142	9	8	0	4.62
RF	J. Jensen	578	.315	20	97	291	13	12	2	2.1	.962	M. Parnell	21	131	7	6	0	3.77
CF	J. Piersall	601	.293	14	87	455	10	4	1	3.0	.991	I. Delock	48	128	13	7	9	4.21
LF	T. Williams	400	.345	24	82	174	7	5	2	1.7	.973	Porterfield	25	126	3	12	0	5.14
C	S. White	392	.245	5	44	547	60	10	13	5.4	.984	T. Hurd	40	76	3	4	5	5.33
O1	D. Gernert	306	.291	16	68	367	41	4	38		.990							
2B	T. Lepcio	284	.261	15	51	143	166	11	47	5.6	.966							
C	P. Daley	187	.267	5	29	228	14	2	1	4.3	.992							

Bos.
W-84 L-70
Pinky Higgins

POS	Player	AB	BA	HR	RBI	PO	A	E	DP	TC/G	FA	Pitcher	G	IP	W	L	SV	ERA
1B	E. Torgeson	318	.264	12	42	623	32	5	62	8.0	.992	F. Lary	41	294	21	13	1	3.15
2B	F. Bolling	366	.281	7	45	223	260	11	72	4.8	.978	P. Foytack	43	256	15	13	1	3.59
SS	H. Kuenn	591	.332	12	88	219	388	20	86	4.4	.968	B. Hoeft	38	248	20	14	0	4.06
3B	R. Boone	481	.308	25	81	151	243	17	23	3.2	.959	S. Gromek	40	141	8	6	4	4.28
RF	A. Kaline	617	.314	27	128	343	18	6	4	2.4	.984	V. Trucks	22	120	6	5	1	3.83
CF	B. Tuttle	546	.253	9	65	348	13	9	2	2.7	.976	A. Aber	42	63	4	4	7	3.43
LF	C. Maxwell	500	.326	28	87	281	12	4	1	2.2	.987							
C	F. House	321	.240	10	44	450	33	7	8	5.6	.986							
C	R. Wilson	228	.289	7	38	393	34	4	7	5.5	.991							
1B	J. Phillips	224	.295	1	20	422	32	9	49	8.3	.981							
O3	B. Kennedy	177	.232	4	22	87	40	12	3		.914							
S2	J. Brideweser	156	.218	0	10	111	134	5	32		.980							
1B	W. Belardi	154	.279	6	15	240	17	3	21	8.4	.988							

Det.
W-82 L-72
Bucky Harris

POS	Player	AB	BA	HR	RBI	PO	A	E	DP	TC/G	FA	Pitcher	G	IP	W	L	SV	ERA
1B	B. Boyd	225	.311	2	11	469	24	5	46	8.3	.990	R. Moore	32	185	12	7	0	4.18
2B	B. Gardner	515	.231	11	50	274	331	16	76	4.7	.974	C. Johnson	26	184	9	10	0	3.43
SS	W. Miranda	461	.217	2	34	229	436	26	91	4.7	.962	B. Wight	35	175	9	12	0	4.02
3B	G. Kell	345	.261	8	37	97	165	7	19	2.8	.974*	H. Brown	35	152	9	7	2	4.04
RF	T. Francona	445	.258	9	57	240	10	6	1	2.1	.977	E. Palica	29	116	4	11	0	4.49
CF	D. Williams	353	.286	11	37	205	2	2	0	2.6	.990	M. Fornieles	30	111	4	7	1	3.97
LF	B. Nieman	388	.322	12	64	243	4	5	1	2.2	.980	D. Ferrarese	36	102	4	10	2	5.03
C	G. Triandos	452	.279	21	88	417	50	5	12	5.3	.989	G. Zuverink	62	97	7	6	16	4.16
C	H. Smith	229	.262	3	18	313	33	2	11	4.9	.994	B. Loes	21	57	2	7	3	4.76
1B	B. Hale	207	.237	1	24	366	29	10	33	7.9	.975							
OF	J. Pyburn	156	.173	2	11	114	5	3	3	1.6	.975							

Bal.
W-69 L-85
Paul Richards

POS	Player	AB	BA	HR	RBI	PO	A	E	DP	TC/G	FA	Pitcher	G	IP	W	L	SV	ERA
1B	R. Sievers	550	.253	29	95	638	51	7	75	9.2	.990	C. Stobbs	37	240	15	15	1	3.60
2B	P. Runnels	578	.310	8	76	179	177	10	56	5.3	.973	C. Pascual	39	189	6	18	2	5.87
SS	Valdivielso	246	.236	4	29	144	266	23	58	4.8	.947	P. Ramos	37	152	12	10	0	5.27
3B	E. Yost	515	.231	11	53	164	303	18	31	3.6	.963	D. Stone	41	132	5	7	3	6.27
RF	J. Lemon	538	.271	27	96	301	11	12	6	2.3	.963	B. Wiesler	37	123	3	12	0	6.44
CF	K. Olson	313	.246	4	22	192	4	2	0	2.0	.990	B. Stewart	33	105	5	7	2	5.57
LF	W. Herzog	421	.245	4	35	240	9	5	0	2.5	.980	B. Chakales	43	96	4	4	4	4.03
C	C. Courtney	283	.300	5	44	290	35	7	7	4.4	.979	C. Grob	37	79	4	5	1	7.83
2B	H. Plews	256	.270	1	25	137	166	17	38	4.8	.947	B. Byerly	25	52	2	4	4	2.96
C	L. Berberet	207	.261	4	27	266	28	1	6	5.0	.997							

Was.
W-59 L-95
Chuck Dressen

POS	Player	AB	BA	HR	RBI	PO	A	E	DP	TC/G	FA	Pitcher	G	IP	W	L	SV	ERA
1B	V. Power	530	.309	14	63	671	62	5	73	9.7	.993	A. Ditmar	44	254	12	22	1	4.42
2B	J. Finigan	250	.216	2	21	114	105	7	35	4.3	.969	T. Gorman	52	171	9	10	3	3.83
SS	J. DeMaestri	561	.273	6	39	210	407	23	95	4.8	.964	J. Crimian	54	129	4	8	3	5.51
3B	H. Lopez	561	.273	18	69	152	254	26	23	3.6	.940	W. Burnette	18	121	6	8	0	2.89
RF	H. Simpson	543	.293	21	105	188	3	7	2	1.8	.965	L. Kretlow	25	119	4	9	0	5.31
CF	J. Groth	244	.258	5	37	140	8	0	3	1.8	1.000	T. Herriage	31	103	1	13	0	6.64
LF	L. Skizas	297	.316	11	39	148	9	4	0	2.2	.975	B. Shantz	45	101	2	7	4	4.35
C	T. Thompson	268	.272	1	27	328	38	7	7	5.5	.981	A. Kellner	20	92	7	4	0	4.32
OF	G. Zernial	272	.224	16	44	111	9	2	1	1.8	.984							
OF	A. Pilarcik	239	.251	4	22	154	9	4	1	2.5	.976							
OF	E. Slaughter	223	.278	2	23	105	1	2	0	1.9	.981							
C	J. Ginsberg	195	.246	1	12	238	28	3	3	4.7	.989							
1B	E. Robinson	172	.198	2	12	360	19	9	43	8.3	.977							
C	H. Smith	142	.275	2	24	183	22	3	3	5.8	.986							

K. C.
W-52 L-102
Lou Boudreau

BATTING AND BASE RUNNING LEADERS

Batting Average

M. Mantle, NY	.353
T. Williams, BOS	.345
H. Kuenn, DET	.332
C. Maxwell, DET	.326
B. Nieman, BAL, CHI	.320

Slugging Average

M. Mantle, NY	.705
T. Williams, BOS	.605
C. Maxwell, DET	.534
Y. Berra, NY	.534
A. Kaline, DET	.530

Home Runs

M. Mantle, NY	52
V. Wertz, CLE	32
Y. Berra, NY	30
R. Sievers, WAS	29
C. Maxwell, DET	28

Total Bases

M. Mantle, NY	376
A. Kaline, DET	327
J. Jensen, BOS	287
M. Minoso, CHI	286
Y. Berra, NY	278
H. Kuenn, DET	278

PITCHING LEADERS

Winning Percentage

W. Ford, NY	.760
B. Pierce, CHI	.690
H. Score, CLE	.690
E. Wynn, CLE	.690
T. Brewer, BOS	.679

Earned Run Average

W. Ford, NY	2.47
H. Score, CLE	2.53
E. Wynn, CLE	2.72
B. Lemon, CLE	3.03
J. Harshman, CHI	3.10

Wins

F. Lary, DET	21
B. Pierce, CHI	20
H. Score, CLE	20
E. Wynn, CLE	20
B. Hoeft, DET	20
B. Lemon, CLE	20

Saves

G. Zuverink, BAL	16
T. Morgan, NY	11
D. Mossi, CLE	11
I. Delock, BOS	9
B. Shantz, KC	9

BATTING AND BASE RUNNING LEADERS

Runs Batted In
M. Mantle, NY 130
A. Kaline, DET 128
V. Wertz, CLE 106
Y. Berra, NY 105
H. Simpson, KC 105

Stolen Bases
L. Aparicio, CHI 21
J. Rivera, CHI 20
B. Avila, CLE 17
M. Minoso, CHI 12
T. Francona, BAL 11
J. Jensen, BOS 11

Hits
H. Kuenn, DET 196
A. Kaline, DET 194
N. Fox, CHI 192

Base on Balls
E. Yost, WAS 151
M. Mantle, NY 112
T. Williams, BOS 102
L. Doby, CHI 102

Home Run Percentage
M. Mantle, NY 9.8
V. Wertz, CLE 6.7
T. Williams, BOS 6.0

Runs Scored
M. Mantle, NY 132
N. Fox, CHI 109
M. Minoso, CHI 106

Doubles
J. Piersall, BOS 40
H. Kuenn, DET 32
A. Kaline, DET 32

Triples
J. Lemon, WAS 11
H. Simpson, KC 11
M. Minoso, CHI 11
J. Jensen, BOS 11

PITCHING LEADERS

Strikeouts
H. Score, CLE 263
B. Pierce, CHI 192
P. Foytack, DET 184
B. Hoeft, DET 172
F. Lary, DET 165

Complete Games
B. Pierce, CHI 21
B. Lemon, CLE 21
F. Lary, DET 20
W. Ford, NY 18
B. Hoeft, DET 18
E. Wynn, CLE 18

Fewest Hits per 9 Innings
H. Score, CLE 5.85
D. Larsen, NY 6.66
J. Harshman, CHI 7.27

Shutouts
H. Score, CLE 5

Fewest Walks per 9 Innings
C. Stobbs, WAS 2.03
D. Donovan, CHI 2.26
J. Kucks, NY 2.89

Most Strikeouts per 9 Inn.
H. Score, CLE 9.49
C. Pascual, WAS 7.73
P. Foytack, DET 6.47

Innings
F. Lary, DET 294
E. Wynn, CLE 278
B. Pierce, CHI 276

Games Pitched
G. Zuverink, BAL 62
J. Crimian, KC 54
T. Gorman, KC 52

	W	L	PCT	GB	R	OR	Batting					SB	E	Fielding		CG	BB	Pitching			
							2B	3B	HR	BA	SA			DP	FA			SO	ShO	SV	ERA
NY	97	57	.630		857	631	193	55	190	.270	.434	51	136	214	.977	50	652	732	9	35	3.63
CLE	88	66	.571	9	712	581	199	23	153	.244	.381	40	129	130	.978	67	564	845	17	24	3.32
CHI	85	69	.552	12	776	634	218	43	128	.267	.397	70	122	160	.979	65	524	722	11	13	3.73
BOS	84	70	.545	13	780	751	261	45	139	.275	.419	28	169	168	.972	50	668	712	8	20	4.17
DET	82	72	.532	15	789	699	209	50	150	.279	.420	43	140	151	.976	62	655	788	10	15	4.06
BAL	69	85	.448	28	571	705	198	34	91	.244	.350	39	137	142	.977	38	547	715	10	24	4.20
WAS	59	95	.383	38	652	924	198	62	112	.250	.377	37	171	173	.972	36	730	663	1	18	5.33
KC	52	102	.338	45	619	831	204	41	112	.252	.370	40	166	187	.973	30	679	636	3	18	4.86
					5756	5756	1680	353	1075	.260	.394	348	1170	1325	.975	398	5019	5813	69	167	4.16

National League 1957

	POS	Player	AB	BA	HR	RBI	PO	A	E	DP	TC/G	FA	Pitcher	G	IP	W	L	SV	ERA
Mil. W-95 L-59 Fred Haney	1B	F. Torre	364	.272	5	40	859	71	4	89	8.0	.996	W. Spahn	39	271	21	11	3	2.69
	2B	Schoendienst	394	.310	6	32	238	282	7	72	5.7	.987	L. Burdette	37	257	17	9	0	3.72
	SS	J. Logan	494	.273	10	49	263	440	29	94	5.7	.960	B. Buhl	34	217	18	7	0	2.74
	3B	E. Mathews	572	.292	32	94	131	299	16	27	3.0	.964	G. Conley	35	148	9	9	1	3.16
	RF	H. Aaron	615	.322	44	132	346	9	6	0	2.4	.983	B. Trowbridge	32	126	7	5	1	3.64
	CF	B. Bruton	306	.278	5	30	206	5	4	2	2.7	.981	J. Pizarro	24	99	5	6	0	4.62
	LF	W. Covington	328	.284	21	65	150	9	3	1	1.8	.981	E. Johnson	30	65	7	3	4	3.88
	C	D. Crandall	383	.253	15	46	414	59	6	11	4.7	.987	D. McMahon	32	47	2	3	9	1.54
	OF	A. Pafko	220	.277	8	27	108	1	2	1	1.6	.982							
	1B	J. Adcock	209	.287	12	38	477	30	2	60	9.1	.996							
	2B	D. O'Connell	183	.235	1	8	128	145	5	43	5.8	.982							
	UT	F. Mantilla	182	.236	4	21	87	136	12	28		.949							
	OF	B. Thomson	148	.236	4	23	78	2	1	0	2.1	.988							
	C	D. Rice	144	.229	9	20	235	14	2	3	5.2	.992							
	OF	B. Hazle	134	.403	7	27	57	1		6	0	1.6	.906							
St. L. W-87 L-67 Fred Hutchinson	1B	S. Musial	502	.351	29	102	1167	99	10	131	9.8	.992	L. Jackson	41	210	15	9	1	3.47
	2B	D. Blasingame	650	.271	8	58	372	512	14	128	5.8	.984	L. McDaniel	30	191	15	9	0	3.49
	SS	A. Dark	583	.290	4	64	276	419	25	105	5.2	.965	S. Jones	28	183	12	9	0	3.60
	3B	E. Kasko	479	.273	1	35	100	224	13	21	2.8	.961	H. Wehmeier	36	165	10	7	0	4.31
	RF	D. Ennis	490	.286	24	105	180	3	11	0	1.5	.943	V. Mizell	33	149	8	10	0	3.74
	CF	K. Boyer	544	.265	19	62	275	2	1	1	2.6	.996	W. Schmidt	40	117	10	3	0	4.78
	LF	W. Moon	516	.295	24	73	245	8	9	1	2.0	.966	V. McDaniel	17	87	7	5	0	3.22
	C	H. Smith	333	.279	2	37	468	42	5	8	5.3	.990	L. Merritt	44	65	1	2	7	3.31
	1O	J. Cunningham	261	.318	9	52	360	18	3	17		.992	H. Wilhelm	40	55	1	4	11	4.25
	C	H. Landrith	214	.243	3	26	339	29	5	3	5.6	.987	B. Muffett	23	44	3	2	8	2.25
	OF	B. Smith	185	.211	3	18	138	6	4	4	1.9	.973							

	POS	Player	AB	BA	HR	RBI	PO	A	E	DP	TC/G	FA	Pitcher	G	IP	W	L	SV	ERA
Bkn.	1B	G. Hodges	579	.299	27	98	1317	115	14	115	9.6	.990	D. Drysdale	34	221	17	9	0	2.69
W-84 L-70	2B	J. Gilliam	617	.250	2	37	407	390	11	90	5.5	.986	D. Newcombe	28	199	11	12	0	3.49
Walter Alston	SS	C. Neal	448	.270	12	62	151	298	24	60	4.7	.949	J. Podres	31	196	12	9	3	2.66
	3B	P. Reese	330	.224	1	29	51	166	13	5	3.1	.943	D. McDevitt	22	119	7	4	0	3.25
	RF	C. Furillo	395	.306	12	66	153	7	2	1	1.5	.988	R. Craig	32	111	6	9	0	4.61
	CF	D. Snider	508	.274	40	92	304	6	3	1	2.3	.990	C. Labine	58	105	5	7	17	3.44
	LF	G. Cimoli	532	.293	10	57	265	11	6	2	2.0	.979	S. Koufax	34	104	5	4	0	3.88
	C	R. Campanella	330	.242	13	62	618	51	5	5	6.7	.993	S. Maglie	19	101	6	6	1	2.93
	3S	D. Zimmer	269	.219	6	19	99	170	13	20		.954	E. Roebuck	44	96	8	2	8	2.71
	OF	S. Amoros	238	.277	7	26	122	2	2	0	1.9	.984							
	C	R. Walker	166	.181	2	23	230	20	2	3	5.0	.992							
	OF	E. Valo	161	.273	4	26	57	0	0	0	1.6	1.000							
Cin.	1B	G. Crowe	494	.271	31	92	932	86	11	86	8.6	.989	B. Lawrence	49	250	16	13	4	3.52
W-80 L-74	2B	J. Temple	557	.284	0	37	391	372	20	81	5.4	.974	H. Jeffcoat	37	207	12	13	0	4.52
Birdie Tebbetts	SS	R. McMillan	448	.272	1	55	253	418	16	86	4.5	.977	J. Nuxhall	39	174	10	10	1	4.75
	3B	D. Hoak	529	.293	19	89	193	269	14	29	3.2	.971	D. Gross	43	148	7	9	1	4.31
	RF	W. Post	467	.244	20	74	252	12	4	4	2.2	.985	J. Klippstein	46	146	8	11	3	5.05
	CF	G. Bell	510	.292	13	61	311	7	4	1	2.7	.988	T. Acker	49	109	10	5	4	4.97
	LF	F. Robinson	611	.322	29	75	336	11	4	3	2.6	.989	H. Freeman	52	84	7	2	8	4.52
	C	E. Bailey	391	.261	20	48	542	41	5	5	5.1	.991	R. Sanchez	38	62	3	2	5	4.76
	C	S. Burgess	205	.283	14	39	223	15	3	0	5.4	.988							
	OF	B. Thurman	190	.247	16	40	75	3	1	1	1.8	.987							
	1B	T. Kluszewski	127	.268	6	21	161	15	2	11	7.7	.989							
Phi.	1B	E. Bouchee	574	.293	17	76	1182	125	16	93	8.6	.988	R. Roberts	39	250	10	22	2	4.07
W-77 L-77	2B	G. Hamner	502	.227	10	62	260	282	21	54	4.5	.963	J. Sanford	33	237	19	8	0	3.08
Mayo Smith	SS	C. Fernandez	500	.262	5	51	241	377	26	69	4.3	.960	C. Simmons	32	212	12	11	0	3.44
	3B	W. Jones	440	.218	9	47	140	197	12	18	2.8	.966	H. Haddix	27	171	10	13	0	4.06
	RF	R. Repulski	516	.260	20	68	264	6	9	2	2.1	.968	D. Cardwell	30	128	4	8	1	4.91
	CF	R. Ashburn	626	.297	0	33	502	18	7	7	3.4	.967	D. Farrell	52	83	10	2	10	2.38
	LF	H. Anderson	400	.268	17	61	213	5	3	1	2.0	.986	B. Miller	32	60	2	5	6	2.69
	C	S. Lopata	388	.237	18	67	634	36	8	9	6.3	.988							
	OF	B. Bowman	237	.266	6	23	123	8	10	2	1.7	.929							
	32	T. Kazanski	185	.265	3	11	63	95	5	21		.969							
	C	J. Lonnett	160	.169	5	15	305	16	1	3	5.0	.997							
N. Y.	1B	W. Lockman	456	.248	7	30	981	71	10	94	10.4	.991	R. Gomez	38	238	15	13	0	3.78
W-69 L-85	2B	D. O'Connell	364	.266	7	28	156	194	7	50	5.3	.980	J. Antonelli	40	212	12	18	0	3.77
Billy Rigney	SS	D. Spencer	534	.249	11	50	213	342	29	95	5.3	.950	C. Barclay	37	183	9	9	0	3.44
	3B	R. Jablonski	305	.289	9	57	44	130	11	15	2.6	.941	Worthington	55	158	8	11	4	4.22
	RF	D. Mueller	450	.258	6	37	174	13	2	4	1.6	.989	S. Miller	38	124	7	9	1	3.63
	CF	W. Mays	585	.333	35	97	422	14	9	5	3.0	.980	R. Crone	25	121	4	8	1	4.33
	LF	H. Sauer	378	.259	26	76	125	4	1	0	1.3	.992	M. Grissom	55	83	4	4	14	2.61
	C	V. Thomas	241	.249	6	31	396	31	4	8	4.9	.991							
	2B	Schoendienst	254	.307	9	33	141	166	5	41	5.5	.984							
	3B	O. Virgil	226	.235	4	24	27	111	11	10	2.4	.926							
	1B	G. Harris	225	.240	9	31	502	37	8	53	9.0	.985							
	OF	B. Thomson	215	.242	8	38	124	2	1	0	1.8	.992							
	OF	D. Rhodes	190	.205	4	19	63	0	0	0	1.4	1.000							
	C	R. Katt	165	.230	2	17	238	25	5	4	3.9	.981							
Chi.	1B	D. Long	397	.305	21	62	908	72	5	81	9.5	.995	M. Drabowsky	36	240	13	15	0	3.53
W-62 L-92	2B	B. Morgan	425	.207	5	27	220	343	14	58	5.0	.976	D. Drott	38	229	15	11	0	3.58
Bob Scheffing	SS	E. Banks	594	.285	43	102	168	261	18	59	4.4	.975	B. Rush	31	205	6	16	0	4.38
	3B	B. Adams	187	.251	1	10	43	68	6	5	2.5	.949	D. Elston	39	144	6	7	8	3.56
	RF	W. Moryn	568	.289	19	88	276	13	12	3	2.0	.960	D. Hillman	32	103	6	11	1	4.35
	CF	C. Tanner	318	.286	7	42	156	5	2	2	2.0	.988	J. Brosnan	41	99	5	5	0	3.38
	LF	L. Walls	366	.240	6	33	174	6	3	0	1.9	.984	T. Lown	67	93	5	7	12	3.77
	C	C. Neeman	415	.258	10	39	703	56	8	13	6.5	.990							
	O1	B. Speake	418	.232	16	50	480	41	7	21		.987							
	OF	J. Bolger	273	.275	5	29	152	4	2	1	2.5	.987							
	UT	J. Kindall	181	.160	6	12	73	109	15	10		.924							
Pit.	1B	D. Fondy	323	.313	2	35	698	54	14	63	10.5	.982	B. Friend	40	277	14	18	0	3.38
W-62 L-92	2B	B. Mazeroski	526	.283	8	54	308	443	17	96	5.3	.978	R. Kline	40	205	9	16	0	4.04
Bobby Bragan	SS	D. Groat	501	.315	7	54	226	380	20	74	5.1	.968	B. Purkey	48	180	11	14	2	3.86
W-36 L-67	3B	G. Freese	346	.283	6	31	62	132	16	16	2.8	.924	V. Law	31	173	10	8	1	2.87
Danny Murtaugh	RF	R. Clemente	451	.253	4	30	272	9	6	1	2.6	.979	L. Arroyo	54	131	3	11	1	4.68
W-26 L-25	CF	B. Virdon	561	.251	8	50	403	13	6	2	3.0	.986	R. Face	59	94	4	6	10	3.07
	LF	B. Skinner	387	.305	13	45	172	9	7	2	2.0	.963							
	C	H. Foiles	281	.270	9	36	436	32	9	2	4.4	.981							
	UT	F. Thomas	594	.290	23	89	729	119	25	60		.971							
	UT	G. Baker	365	.266	2	36	129	219	20	35		.946							

BATTING AND BASE RUNNING LEADERS

Batting Average

S. Musial, STL	.351
W. Mays, NY	.333
F. Robinson, CIN	.322
H. Aaron, MIL	.322
D. Groat, PIT	.315

Slugging Average

W. Mays, NY	.626
S. Musial, STL	.612
H. Aaron, MIL	.600
D. Snider, BKN	.587
E. Banks, CHI	.579

PITCHING LEADERS

Winning Percentage

B. Buhl, MIL	.720
J. Sanford, PHI	.704
W. Spahn, MIL	.656
L. Burdette, MIL	.654
D. Drysdale, BKN	.654

Earned Run Average

J. Podres, BKN	2.66
D. Drysdale, BKN	2.69
W. Spahn, MIL	2.69
B. Buhl, MIL	2.74
V. Law, PIT	2.87

BATTING AND BASE RUNNING LEADERS

Home Runs

H. Aaron, MIL	44
E. Banks, CHI	43
D. Snider, BKN	40
W. Mays, NY	35
E. Mathews, MIL	32

Total Bases

H. Aaron, MIL	369
W. Mays, NY	366
E. Banks, CHI	344
F. Robinson, CIN	323
E. Mathews, MIL	309

Runs Batted In

H. Aaron, MIL	132
D. Ennis, STL	105
S. Musial, STL	102
E. Banks, CHI	102
G. Hodges, BKN	98

Stolen Bases

W. Mays, NY	38
J. Gilliam, BKN	26
D. Blasingame, STL	21
J. Temple, CIN	19
C. Fernandez, PHI	18

Hits

Schoendienst, MIL, NY	200
H. Aaron, MIL	198
F. Robinson, CIN	197

Base on Balls

J. Temple, CIN	94
R. Ashburn, PHI	94
E. Mathews, MIL	90

Home Run Percentage

D. Snider, BKN	7.9
E. Banks, CHI	7.2
H. Aaron, MIL	7.2

Runs Scored

H. Aaron, MIL	118
E. Banks, CHI	113
W. Mays, NY	112

Doubles

D. Hoak, CIN	39
S. Musial, STL	38
E. Bouchee, PHI	35

Triples

W. Mays, NY	20
B. Virdon, PIT	11
B. Bruton, MIL	9
E. Mathews, MIL	9

PITCHING LEADERS

Wins

W. Spahn, MIL	21
J. Sanford, PHI	19
B. Buhl, MIL	18
L. Burdette, MIL	17
D. Drysdale, BKN	17

Saves

C. Labine, BKN	17
M. Grissom, NY	14
T. Lown, CHI	12
H. Wilhelm, STL	11
D. Farrell, PHI	10
R. Face, PIT	10

Strikeouts

J. Sanford, PHI	188
D. Drott, CHI	170
M. Drabowsky, CHI	170
S. Jones, STL	154
D. Drysdale, BKN	148

Complete Games

W. Spahn, MIL	18
B. Friend, PIT	17
R. Gomez, NY	16
J. Sanford, PHI	15

Fewest Hits per 9 Innings

J. Sanford, PHI	7.38
J. Podres, BKN	7.71
D. Drott, CHI	7.86

Shutouts

J. Podres, BKN	6
D. Newcombe, BKN	4
D. Drysdale, BKN	4
W. Spahn, MIL	4

Fewest Walks per 9 Innings

D. Newcombe, BKN	1.49
R. Roberts, PHI	1.55
V. Law, PIT	1.67

Most Strikeouts per 9 Inn.

S. Jones, STL	7.59
H. Haddix, PHI	7.17
J. Sanford, PHI	7.15

Innings

B. Friend, PIT	277
W. Spahn, MIL	271
L. Burdette, MIL	257

Games Pitched

T. Lown, CHI	67
R. Face, PIT	59
C. Labine, BKN	58

	W	L	PCT	GB	R	OR	2B	3B	HR	BA	SA	SB	E	DP	FA	CG	BB	SO	ShO	SV	ERA
MIL	95	59	.617		772	613	221	62	199	.269	.442	35	120	173	.981	60	570	693	9	24	3.47
STL	87	67	.565	8	737	666	235	43	132	.274	.405	58	131	168	.979	46	506	778	11	29	3.78
BKN	84	70	.545	11	690	591	188	38	147	.253	.387	60	127	136	.979	44	456	891	18	29	3.35
CIN	80	74	.519	15	747	781	251	33	187	.269	.432	51	107	139	.982	40	429	707	5	29	4.62
PHI	77	77	.500	18	623	656	213	44	117	.250	.375	57	136	117	.976	54	412	858	9	23	3.80
NY	69	85	.448	26	643	701	171	54	157	.252	.393	64	161	180	.974	35	471	701	9	20	4.01
CHI	62	92	.403	33	628	722	223	31	147	.244	.380	28	149	140	.975	30	601	859	5	26	4.13
PIT	62	92	.403	33	586	696	231	60	92	.268	.384	46	170	143	.972	47	421	663	9	15	3.88
					5426	5426	1733	365	1178	.260	.400	399	1101	1196	.977	356	3866	6150	75	195	3.88

American League 1957

	POS	Player	AB	BA	HR	RBI	PO	A	E	DP	TC/G	FA	Pitcher	G	IP	W	L	SV	ERA
N. Y. W-98 L-56 Casey Stengel	1B	B. Skowron	457	.304	17	88	1026	86	9	116	9.7	.992	T. Sturdivant	28	202	16	6	0	2.54
	2B	B. Richardson	305	.256	0	19	206	223	9	60	4.7	.979	J. Kucks	37	179	8	10	2	3.56
	SS	G. McDougald	539	.289	13	62	247	391	16	104	5.4	.976	B. Turley	32	176	13	6	3	2.71
	3B	A. Carey	247	.255	6	33	66	147	5	9	2.7	.977	B. Shantz	30	173	11	5	5	2.45
	RF	H. Bauer	479	.259	18	65	200	7	3	1	1.6	.986	D. Larsen	27	140	10	4	0	3.74
	CF	M. Mantle	474	.365	34	94	324	6	7	1	2.4	.979	W. Ford	24	129	11	5	0	2.57
	LF	E. Slaughter	209	.254	5	34	97	2	0	0	1.5	1.000	A. Ditmar	46	127	8	3	6	3.25
	C	Y. Berra	482	.251	24	82	704	61	4	12	6.4	.995	T. Byrne	30	85	4	6	2	4.36
	UT	T. Kubek	431	.297	3	39	189	183	20	33		.949	B. Grim	46	72	12	8	19	2.63
	OC	E. Howard	356	.253	8	44	246	16	6	4		.978							
	O1	H. Simpson	224	.250	7	39	198	13	3	19		.986							
	23	J. Coleman	157	.268	2	12	89	115	7	33		.967							
Chi. W-90 L-64 Al Lopez	1B	E. Torgeson	251	.295	7	46	612	29	1	72	9.2	.998	B. Pierce	37	257	20	12	2	3.26
	2B	N. Fox	619	.317	6	61	453	453	13	141	5.9	.986	D. Donovan	28	221	16	6	0	2.77
	SS	L. Aparicio	575	.257	3	41	246	449	20	85	5.0	.972	J. Wilson	30	202	15	8	0	3.48
	3B	B. Phillips	393	.270	7	42	91	227	14	17	3.4	.985	J. Harshman	30	151	8	8	1	4.10
	RF	J. Landis	274	.212	2	16	192	8	3	4	2.3	.985	B. Keegan	30	143	10	8	2	3.53
	CF	L. Doby	416	.288	14	79	255	3	4	0	2.4	.985	B. Fischer	33	124	7	8	1	3.48
	LF	M. Minoso	568	.310	12	103	293	9	5	2	2.0	.984	G. Staley	47	105	5	1	7	2.06
	C	S. Lollar	351	.256	11	70	454	45	1	5	5.2	.998	D. Howell	37	68	6	5	6	3.29
	OF	J. Rivera	402	.256	14	52	141	6	4	0	1.8	.974	P. LaPalme	35	40	1	4	7	3.35
	1B	W. Dropo	223	.256	13	49	483	39	7	49	7.7	.987							
	3S	S. Esposito	176	.205	2	15	80	165	9	22		.965							

POS	Player	AB	BA	HR	RBI	PO	A	E	DP	TC/G	FA	Pitcher	G	IP	W	L	SV	ERA
Bos.																		
1B	D. Gernert	316	.237	14	58	681	50	8	82	10.4	.989	F. Sullivan	31	241	14	11	0	2.73
2B	T. Lepcio	232	.241	9	37	136	194	8	58	5.0	.976	T. Brewer	32	238	16	13	0	3.85
SS	B. Klaus	477	.252	10	42	204	417	25	93	5.5	.961	W. Nixon	29	191	12	13	0	3.68
3B	F. Malzone	634	.292	15	103	151	370	25	31	3.6	.954	M. Fornieles	25	125	8	7	2	3.52
RF	J. Jensen	544	.281	23	103	251	16	11	4	1.9	.960	D. Sisler	22	122	7	8	1	4.71
CF	J. Piersall	609	.261	19	63	397	12	4	0	2.7	.990	Porterfield	28	102	4	4	1	4.05
LF	T. Williams	420	**.388**	38	87	215	2	1	0	1.7	.995	I. Delock	49	94	9	8	11	3.83
C	S. White	340	.215	3	31	489	49	8	13	4.9	.985	G. Susce	29	88	7	3	1	4.28
W-82 L-72 Pinky Higgins																		
1B	M. Vernon	270	.241	7	38	662	51	6	47	10.3	.992							
2B	G. Mauch	222	.270	2	28	127	153	11	41	5.0	.962							
SS	B. Consolo	196	.270	4	19	61	149	15	30	5.4	.933							
C	P. Daley	191	.225	3	25	289	20	0	5	4.0	**1.000**							
OF	G. Stephens	173	.266	3	26	70	4	1	2	.8	.987							
Det.																		
1B	R. Boone	462	.273	12	65	972	45	10	103	8.8	.990	J. Bunning	45	**267**	**20**	8	1	2.69
2B	F. Bolling	576	.259	15	40	394	401	16	112	5.6	.980	F. Lary	40	238	11	16	3	3.98
SS	H. Kuenn	624	.277	9	44	225	354	27	86	4.5	.955	D. Maas	45	219	10	14	6	3.28
3B	R. Bertoia	295	.275	4	28	76	125	10	8	2.5	.953	P. Foytack	38	212	14	11	1	3.14
RF	A. Kaline	577	.295	23	90	319	13	5	2	2.3	.985	B. Hoeft	34	207	9	11	1	3.48
CF	B. Tuttle	451	.251	5	47	331	5	6	1	2.7	.982	H. Byrd	37	59	4	3	5	3.36
LF	C. Maxwell	492	.276	24	82	317	6	1	1	2.4	**.997**							
C	F. House	348	.259	7	36	535	54	2	5	6.1	.997							
W-78 L-76 Jack Tighe																		
C	R. Wilson	178	.242	3	13	277	29	0	5	5.2	1.000							
3B	J. Finigan	174	.270	0	17	58	108	8	9	2.9	.954							
1O	D. Philley	173	.283	2	16	219	25	2	19		.992							
Bal.																		
1B	B. Boyd	485	.318	4	34	**1073**	70	10	107	8.7	.991	C. Johnson	35	242	14	11	0	3.20
2B	B. Gardner	**644**	.262	6	55	393	424	11	96	5.6	**.987**	R. Moore	34	227	11	13	0	3.72
SS	W. Miranda	314	.194	0	20	166	324	17	59	4.4	.966	B. Loes	31	155	12	7	4	3.24
3B	G. Kell	310	.297	9	44	66	122	4	15	2.4	.979	H. Brown	25	150	7	8	1	3.90
RF	A. Pilarcik	407	.278	9	49	234	15	1	2	2.0	.996	B. O'Dell	35	140	4	10	4	2.69
CF	J. Busby	288	.250	3	19	233	8	4	1	2.9	.984	B. Wight	27	121	6	6	0	3.64
LF	B. Nieman	445	.276	13	70	237	6	5	0	2.1	.980	G. Zuverink	**56**	113	10	6	9	2.48
C	G. Triandos	418	.254	19	72	580	64	5	13	5.4	.992	K. Lehman	30	68	8	3	6	2.78
W-76 L-76 Paul Richards																		
OF	T. Francona	279	.233	7	38	119	0	1	0	1.6	.992							
UT	B. Goodman	263	.308	3	33	134	110	11	20		.957							
C	J. Ginsberg	175	.274	1	18	252	20	4	6	4.2	.986							
UT	D. Williams	167	.234	1	17	150	41	2	15		.990							
OF	J. Durham	157	.185	4	17	70	1	0	0	1.2	1.000							
Cle.																		
1B	V. Wertz	515	.282	28	105	1025	83	14	**122**	8.1	.988	E. Wynn	40	263	14	17	1	4.31
2B	B. Avila	463	.268	5	48	280	254	9	72	5.1	.983	M. Garcia	38	211	12	8	0	3.75
SS	C. Carrasquel	392	.276	8	57	212	357	24	75	4.9	.960	D. Mossi	36	159	11	10	2	4.13
3B	A. Smith	507	.247	11	49	95	156	24	16	3.3	.913	R. Narleski	46	154	11	5	16	3.09
RF	R. Colavito	461	.252	25	84	268	12	11	2	2.2	.962	C. McLish	42	144	9	7	1	2.74
CF	R. Maris	358	.235	14	51	266	10	7	2	2.5	.975	B. Lemon	21	117	6	11	0	4.60
LF	G. Woodling	430	.321	19	78	225	10	2	0	2.1	.992	B. Daley	34	87	2	8	2	4.43
C	J. Hegan	148	.216	4	15	287	14	0	4	5.2	1.000							
W-76 L-77 Kerby Farrell																		
UT	L. Raines	244	.262	2	16	84	109	13	15		.937							
O3	D. Williams	205	.283	6	17	94	31	6	5		.954							
UT	G. Strickland	201	.234	1	19	146	164	6	38		.981							
C	R. Nixon	185	.281	2	18	268	31	5	5	5.3	.984							
C	D. Brown	114	.263	4	22	190	18	3	4	6.4	.986							
K. C.																		
1B	V. Power	467	.259	14	42	968	**99**	2	95	9.5	**.998**	N. Garver	24	145	6	13	0	3.84
2B	B. Hunter	319	.191	8	29	111	152	7	40	4.2	.974	T. Morgan	46	144	9	7	7	4.64
SS	J. DeMaestri	461	.245	9	33	**248**	387	13	87	4.8	**.980**	A. Kellner	28	133	6	5	0	4.27
3B	H. Lopez	391	.294	11	35	117	227	23	20	3.3	.937	R. Terry	21	131	4	11	0	3.38
RF	B. Cerv	345	.272	11	44	157	6	6	1	1.9	.964	J. Urban	31	129	7	4	0	3.34
CF	W. Held	326	.239	20	50	266	12	1	2	3.0	.996	T. Gorman	38	125	5	9	3	3.83
LF	G. Zernial	437	.236	27	69	213	4	11	1	2.0	.952	V. Trucks	48	116	9	7	7	3.03
C	H. Smith	360	.303	13	41	463	55	9	8	5.1	.983	Portocarrero	33	115	4	9	0	3.92
W-59 L-94 Lou Boudreau W-36 L-67 Harry Craft W-23 L-27																		
OF	L. Skizas	376	.245	18	44	119	5	3	2	1.7	.976	W. Burnette	38	113	7	12	1	4.30
23	B. Martin	265	.257	9	27	150	135	5	32		.983							
C	T. Thompson	230	.204	7	19	272	29	2	7	4.9	.993							
1O	H. Simpson	179	.296	6	24	272	24	2	21		.993							
1B	I. Noren	160	.213	2	16	191	12	2	24	8.2	.990							
2B	M. Graff	155	.181	0	10	110	127	3	36	4.5	.988							
Was.																		
1B	P. Runnels	473	.230	2	35	616	44	3	59	9.2	.995	P. Ramos	43	231	12	16	0	4.79
2B	H. Plews	329	.271	1	26	199	175	8	42	4.8	.979	C. Stobbs	42	212	8	**20**	1	5.36
SS	R. Bridges	391	.228	3	47	226	382	18	77	5.8	.971	C. Pascual	29	176	8	17	0	4.10
3B	E. Yost	414	.251	9	38	109	207	16	18	3.1	.952	R. Kemmerer	39	172	7	11	0	4.96
RF	J. Lemon	518	.284	17	64	227	4	7	2	1.8	.971	T. Clevenger	52	140	7	6	8	4.19
CF	B. Usher	295	.261	5	27	228	7	5	2	2.5	.979	D. Hyde	52	109	4	3	1	4.12
LF	R. Sievers	572	.301	42	114	254	6	4	2	2.0	.985	B. Byerly	47	95	6	6	3	3.13
C	L. Berberet	264	.261	7	36	349	48	0	8	5.2	**1.000**	T. Abernathy	26	85	2	10	0	6.78
W-55 L-99 Chuck Dressen W-5 L-16 Cookie Lavagetto W-50 L-83																		
2S	M. Bolling	277	.227	4	19	168	232	11	53		.973							
1O	A. Schult	247	.263	4	35	366	15	6	35		.984							
C	C. Courtney	232	.267	6	27	288	35	2	6	5.5	.994							
OF	Throneberry	195	.185	2	12	116	2	0	0	2.1	.983							
1B	J. Becquer	186	.226	2	22	300	19	0	29	7.4	1.000							

BATTING AND BASE RUNNING LEADERS

Batting Average

T. Williams, BOS	.388
M. Mantle, NY	.365
G. Woodling, CLE	.321
B. Boyd, BAL	.318
N. Fox, CHI	.317

Slugging Average

T. Williams, BOS	.731
M. Mantle, NY	.665
R. Sievers, WAS	.579
G. Woodling, CLE	.521
V. Wertz, CLE	.485

Home Runs

R. Sievers, WAS	42
T. Williams, BOS	38
M. Mantle, NY	34
V. Wertz, CLE	28
G. Zernial, KC	27

Total Bases

R. Sievers, WAS	331
M. Mantle, NY	315
T. Williams, BOS	307
A. Kaline, DET	276
F. Malzone, BOS	271

Runs Batted In

R. Sievers, WAS	114
V. Wertz, CLE	105
J. Jensen, BOS	103
M. Minoso, CHI	103
F. Malzone, BOS	103

Stolen Bases

L. Aparicio, CHI	28
J. Rivera, CHI	18
M. Minoso, CHI	18
M. Mantle, NY	16

Hits

N. Fox, CHI	196
F. Malzone, BOS	185
M. Minoso, CHI	176

Base on Balls

M. Mantle, NY	146
T. Williams, BOS	119
A. Smith, CLE	79
M. Minoso, CHI	79

Home Run Percentage

T. Williams, BOS	9.0
R. Sievers, WAS	7.3
M. Mantle, NY	7.2

Runs Scored

M. Mantle, NY	121
N. Fox, CHI	110
J. Piersall, BOS	103

Doubles

M. Minoso, CHI	36
B. Gardner, BAL	36
F. Malzone, BOS	31

Triples

H. Simpson, KC, NY	9
H. Bauer, NY	9
G. McDougald, NY	9

PITCHING LEADERS

Winning Percentage

D. Donovan, CHI	.727
T. Sturdivant, NY	.727
J. Bunning, DET	.714
J. Wilson, CHI	.652
B. Pierce, CHI	.625

Earned Run Average

B. Shantz, NY	2.45
T. Sturdivant, NY	2.54
J. Bunning, DET	2.69
B. Turley, NY	2.71
F. Sullivan, BOS	2.73

Wins

J. Bunning, DET	20
B. Pierce, CHI	20
D. Donovan, CHI	16
T. Sturdivant, NY	16
T. Brewer, BOS	16

Saves

B. Grim, NY	19
R. Narleski, CLE	16
I. Delock, BOS	11
G. Zuverink, BAL	9
T. Clevenger, WAS	8

Strikeouts

E. Wynn, CLE	184
J. Bunning, DET	182
C. Johnson, BAL	177
B. Pierce, CHI	171
B. Turley, NY	152

Complete Games

D. Donovan, CHI	16
B. Pierce, CHI	16
T. Brewer, BOS	15
J. Bunning, DET	14
C. Johnson, BAL	14
F. Sullivan, BOS	14

Fewest Hits per 9 Innings

B. Turley, NY	6.12
J. Bunning, DET	7.20
P. Foytack, DET	7.43

Shutouts

J. Wilson, CHI	5
B. Turley, NY	4
B. Pierce, CHI	4

Fewest Walks per 9 Innings

F. Sullivan, BOS	1.79
D. Donovan, CHI	1.84
B. Shantz, NY	2.08

Most Strikeouts per 9 Inn.

B. Turley, NY	7.76
C. Johnson, BAL	6.58
E. Wynn, CLE	6.30

Innings

J. Bunning, DET	267
E. Wynn, CLE	263
B. Pierce, CHI	257

Games Pitched

G. Zuverink, BAL	56
T. Clevenger, WAS	52
D. Hyde, WAS	52

	W	L	PCT	GB	R	OR	Batting 2B	3B	HR	BA	SA	SB	E	Fielding DP	FA	CG	BB	Pitching SO	ShO	SV	ERA
NY	98	56	.636		723	534	200	54	145	**.268**	**.409**	49	123	183	.980	41	580	**810**	13	**42**	3.00
CHI	90	64	.584	8	707	566	208	41	106	.260	.375	**109**	107	169	**.982**	**59**	470	665	**16**	27	3.35
BOS	82	72	.532	16	721	668	231	32	153	.262	.405	29	149	179	.976	55	498	692	9	23	3.88
DET	78	76	.506	20	614	614	224	37	116	.257	.378	36	121	151	.980	52	505	756	9	21	3.56
BAL	76	76	.500	21	597	588	191	39	87	.252	.353	57	112	159	.981	44	493	767	13	23	3.46
CLE	76	77	.497	21.5	682	722	199	26	140	.252	.382	40	153	154	.974	46	618	807	7	23	4.05
KC	59	94	.386	38.5	563	710	195	40	**166**	.244	.394	35	125	162	.979	26	565	626	6	19	4.19
WAS	55	99	.357	43	603	808	215	38	111	.244	.363	13	128	159	.979	31	580	691	5	16	4.85
					5210	5210	1663	307	1024	.255	.382	368	1018	1316	.979	354	4309	5814	78	196	3.79

National League 1958

		POS	Player	AB	BA	HR	RBI	PO	A	E	DP	TC/G	FA	Pitcher	G	IP	W	L	SV	ERA
Mil.		1B	F. Torre	372	.309	6	55	960	80	6	85	8.6	**.994**	W. Spahn	38	**290**	**22**	11	1	3.07
W-92	L-62	2B	Schoendienst	427	.262	1	24	233	301	7	77	5.2	**.987**	L. Burdette	40	275	20	10	0	2.91
Fred Haney		SS	J. Logan	530	.226	11	53	273	481	32	99	5.5	.959	B. Rush	28	147	10	6	0	3.42
		3B	E. Mathews	546	.251	31	77	116	351	22	24	3.3	.955	C. Willey	23	140	9	7	0	2.70
		RF	H. Aaron	601	.326	30	95	305	12	5	0	2.1	.984	J. Pizarro	16	97	6	4	1	2.70
		CF	B. Bruton	325	.280	3	28	203	6	5	0	2.2	.977	J. Jay	18	97	7	5	0	2.14
		LF	W. Covington	294	.330	24	74	118	3	6	2	1.5	.953	D. McMahon	38	59	7	2	8	3.68
		C	D. Crandall	427	.272	18	63	659	64	7	6	5.9	**.990**							
		1B	J. Adcock	320	.275	19	54	525	36	6	55	8.0	.989							
		O2	F. Mantilla	226	.221	7	19	114	49	4	12		.976							
		OF	A. Pafko	164	.238	3	23	107	2	0	0	1.2	1.000							

Pit. W-84 L-70 Danny Murtaugh

POS	Player	AB	BA	HR	RBI	PO	A	E	DP	TC/G	FA
1B	T. Kluszewski	301	.292	4	37	591	36	4	62	8.8	.994
2B	B. Mazeroski	567	.275	19	68	344	496	17	118	5.6	.980
SS	D. Groat	584	.300	3	66	307	461	20	127	5.3	.975
3B	F. Thomas	562	.281	35	109	122	240	21	21	2.8	.926
RF	R. Clemente	519	.289	6	50	312	22	6	3	2.5	.982
CF	B. Virdon	604	.267	9	46	401	11	3	0	2.9	.993
LF	B. Skinner	529	.321	13	70	232	19	6	2	1.8	.977
C	H. Foiles	264	.205	8	30	456	41	6	5	4.9	.990
1B	D. Stuart	254	.268	16	48	529	49	16	69	9.3	.973
OF	R. Mejias	157	.268	5	19	104	3	3	0	1.9	.973

Pitcher	G	IP	W	L	SV	ERA
B. Friend	38	274	22	14	0	3.68
R. Kline	32	237	13	16	0	3.53
V. Law	35	202	14	12	3	3.96
C. Raydon	31	134	8	4	1	3.62
G. Witt	18	106	9	2	0	1.61
Porterfield	37	88	4	6	5	3.29
R. Face	57	84	5	2	20	2.89
D. Gross	40	75	5	7	3	3.98

S. F. W-80 L-74 Billy Rigney

POS	Player	AB	BA	HR	RBI	PO	A	E	DP	TC/G	FA
1B	O. Cepeda	603	.312	25	96	1322	97	16	131	9.8	.989
2B	D. O'Connell	306	.232	3	23	222	278	7	70	4.9	.986
SS	E. Spencer	539	.256	17	74	238	438	32	95	5.3	.955
3B	J. Davenport	434	.256	12	41	92	221	13	19	2.5	.960
RF	W. Kirkland	418	.258	14	56	187	12	8	4	1.8	.961
CF	W. Mays	600	.347	29	96	429	17	9	2	3.0	.980
LF	F. Alou	182	.253	4	16	126	2	2	1	1.9	.985
C	B. Schmidt	393	.244	14	54	616	54	12	10	5.5	.982
OF	H. Sauer	236	.250	12	46	93	3	5	1	1.5	.950
3B	R. Jablonski	230	.230	12	46	49	91	8	2	2.6	.946
OF	L. Wagner	221	.317	13	35	89	5	5	0	1.7	.949

Pitcher	G	IP	W	L	SV	ERA
J. Antonelli	41	242	16	13	3	3.28
R. Gomez	42	208	10	12	1	4.38
S. Miller	41	182	6	9	0	2.47
M. McCormick	42	178	11	8	1	4.59
Worthington	54	151	11	7	6	3.63
R. Monzant	43	151	8	11	1	4.72
M. Grissom	51	65	7	5	10	3.99

Cin. W-76 L-78 Birdie Tebbetts W-52 L-61 Jimmy Dykes W-24 L-17

POS	Player	AB	BA	HR	RBI	PO	A	E	DP	TC/G	FA
1B	G. Crowe	345	.275	7	61	713	53	6	65	8.3	.992
2B	J. Temple	542	.306	3	47	395	353	16	90	5.4	.979
SS	R. McMillan	393	.229	1	25	278	394	14	81	4.7	.980
3B	D. Hoak	417	.261	6	50	132	244	14	29	3.5	.964
RF	J. Lynch	420	.312	16	68	154	5	5	2	1.6	.970
CF	G. Bell	385	.252	10	46	235	7	1	2	2.3	.996
LF	F. Robinson	554	.269	31	83	310	12	3	1	2.4	.991
C	E. Bailey	360	.250	11	59	438	44	6	6	4.9	.988
C	S. Burgess	251	.283	6	31	297	21	4	2	5.6	.988
UT	A. Grammas	216	.218	0	12	126	174	6	32		.980
OF	P. Whisenant	203	.236	11	40	122	3	0	1	1.9	1.000
OF	B. Thurman	178	.230	4	20	80	2	2	1	2.0	.976
1B	W. Dropo	162	.290	7	31	300	27	0	31	7.6	1.000

Pitcher	G	IP	W	L	SV	ERA
B. Purkey	37	250	17	11	0	3.60
H. Haddix	29	184	8	7	0	3.52
B. Lawrence	46	181	8	13	5	4.13
J. Nuxhall	36	176	12	11	0	3.79
D. Newcombe	20	133	7	7	1	3.85
T. Acker	38	125	4	3	1	4.55
A. Kellner	18	82	7	3	0	2.30
H. Jeffcoat	49	75	6	8	9	3.72

Chi. W-72 L-82 Bob Scheffing

POS	Player	AB	BA	HR	RBI	PO	A	E	DP	TC/G	FA
1B	D. Long	480	.271	20	75	1173	84	10	130	9.2	.992
2B	T. Taylor	497	.235	6	27	311	374	23	103	5.2	.968
SS	E. Banks	617	.313	47	129	292	468	32	100	5.1	.960
3B	A. Dark	464	.295	3	43	107	225	18	24	3.2	.949
RF	L. Walls	513	.304	24	72	241	10	2	1	1.9	.992
CF	B. Thomson	547	.283	21	82	353	13	4	3	2.5	.989
LF	W. Moryn	512	.264	26	77	265	4	6	1	2.0	.978
C	S. Taylor	301	.259	6	36	460	23	6	4	5.6	.988
32	J. Goryl	219	.242	4	14	91	153	16	26		.938
C	C. Neeman	201	.259	12	29	340	25	3	6	5.2	.992

Pitcher	G	IP	W	L	SV	ERA
T. Phillips	39	170	7	10	1	4.76
G. Hobbie	55	168	10	6	2	3.74
D. Drott	39	167	7	11	0	5.43
D. Hillman	31	126	4	8	1	3.15
M. Drabowsky	22	126	9	11	0	4.51
D. Elston	69	97	9	8	10	2.88
J. Briggs	20	96	5	5	0	4.52
B. Henry	44	81	5	4	6	2.88

St. L. W-72 L-82 Fred Hutchinson W-69 L-75 Stan Hack W-3 L-7

POS	Player	AB	BA	HR	RBI	PO	A	E	DP	TC/G	FA
1B	S. Musial	472	.337	17	62	1019	100	13	127	9.1	.989
2B	D. Blasingame	547	.274	2	36	312	380	26	97	5.2	.964
SS	E. Kasko	259	.220	2	22	111	186	12	47	4.0	.961
3B	K. Boyer	570	.307	23	90	156	350	20	41	3.7	.962
RF	W. Moon	290	.238	7	38	122	5	2	0	1.6	.984
CF	C. Flood	422	.261	10	41	346	18	8	3	3.1	.978
LF	D. Ennis	329	.261	3	47	122	11	1	2	1.6	.993
C	H. Smith	220	.227	1	24	346	22	4	4	5.2	.989
OC	G. Green	442	.281	13	55	428	35	9	5		.981
1O	J. Cunningham	337	.312	12	57	418	26	3	21		.993
S2	G. Freese	191	.257	6	16	77	77	12	14		.928
OF	I. Noren	178	.264	4	22	75	1	2	0	1.0	.974

Pitcher	G	IP	W	L	SV	ERA
S. Jones	35	250	14	13	0	2.88
L. Jackson	49	198	13	13	8	3.68
V. Mizell	30	190	10	14	0	3.42
J. Brosnan	33	115	8	4	7	3.44
B. Mabe	31	112	3	9	0	4.51
L. McDaniel	26	109	5	7	0	5.80
B. Muffett	35	84	4	6	5	4.93

L. A. W-71 L-83 Walter Alston

POS	Player	AB	BA	HR	RBI	PO	A	E	DP	TC/G	FA
1B	G. Hodges	475	.259	22	64	907	69	8	134	8.1	.992
2B	C. Neal	473	.254	22	65	334	343	17	121	5.3	.976
SS	D. Zimmer	455	.262	17	60	265	372	23	100	5.8	.965
3B	D. Gray	197	.249	9	30	56	139	15	18	3.8	.929
RF	C. Furillo	411	.290	18	83	187	5	5	0	1.7	.975
CF	D. Snider	327	.312	15	58	151	4	2	0	1.7	.987
LF	G. Cimoli	325	.246	9	27	180	10	5	2	1.9	.974
C	J. Roseboro	384	.271	14	43	594	36	8	5	6.1	.987
UT	J. Gilliam	555	.261	2	43	245	176	12	37		.972
O1	N. Larker	253	.277	4	29	239	17	5	18		.981

Pitcher	G	IP	W	L	SV	ERA
D. Drysdale	44	212	12	13	0	4.17
J. Podres	39	210	13	15	1	3.72
S. Koufax	40	159	11	11	1	4.48
S. Williams	27	119	9	7	0	4.01
C. Labine	52	104	6	6	14	4.15
F. Kipp	40	102	6	6	0	5.01
J. Klippstein	45	90	3	5	9	3.80

Phi. W-69 L-85 Mayo Smith W-39 L-44 Eddie Sawyer W-30 L-41

POS	Player	AB	BA	HR	RBI	PO	A	E	DP	TC/G	FA
1B	E. Bouchee	334	.257	9	39	690	58	5	59	8.5	.993
2B	S. Hemus	334	.284	8	36	188	220	13	52	5.0	.969
SS	C. Fernandez	522	.230	6	51	296	415	18	88	4.9	.975
3B	W. Jones	398	.271	14	60	137	186	11	13	3.0	.967
RF	W. Post	379	.282	12	62	185	12	10	0	2.3	.952
CF	R. Ashburn	615	.350	2	33	495	8	8	2	3.4	.984
LF	H. Anderson	515	.301	23	97	155	4	1	1	1.9	.975
C	S. Lopata	258	.248	9	33	418	28	6	6	5.7	.987
UT	T. Kazanski	289	.228	3	35	140	175	8	41		.975
OF	R. Repulski	238	.244	13	40	90	3	5	0	1.8	.949
O1	D. Philley	207	.309	3	31	183	12	1	12		.995
OF	B. Bowman	184	.288	8	24	82	1	1	0	1.5	.988
C	C. Sawatski	183	.230	5	12	271	17	4	2	5.5	.986

Pitcher	G	IP	W	L	SV	ERA
R. Roberts	35	270	17	14	0	3.24
R. Semproch	36	204	13	11	0	3.92
J. Sanford	38	186	10	13	0	4.44
C. Simmons	29	168	7	14	1	4.38
D. Cardwell	16	108	3	6	0	4.51
D. Farrell	54	94	8	9	11	3.35
J. Meyer	37	90	3	6	2	3.59

BATTING AND BASE RUNNING LEADERS   PITCHING LEADERS

Batting Average

R. Ashburn, PHI	.350
W. Mays, SF	.347
S. Musial, STL	.337
H. Aaron, MIL	.326
B. Skinner, PIT	.321

Slugging Average

E. Banks, CHI	.614
W. Mays, SF	.583
H. Aaron, MIL	.546
F. Thomas, PIT	.528
S. Musial, STL	.528

Winning Percentage

W. Spahn, MIL	.667
L. Burdette, MIL	.667
B. Friend, PIT	.611
B. Purkey, CIN	.607
J. Antonelli, SF	.552

Earned Run Average

S. Miller, SF	2.47
S. Jones, STL	2.88
L. Burdette, MIL	2.91
W. Spahn, MIL	3.07
R. Roberts, PHI	3.24

Home Runs

E. Banks, CHI	47
F. Thomas, PIT	35
E. Mathews, MIL	31
F. Robinson, CIN	31
H. Aaron, MIL	30

Total Bases

E. Banks, CHI	379
W. Mays, SF	350
H. Aaron, MIL	328
O. Cepeda, SF	309
F. Thomas, PIT	297

Wins

W. Spahn, MIL	22
B. Friend, PIT	22
L. Burdette, MIL	20
B. Purkey, CIN	17
R. Roberts, PHI	17

Saves

R. Face, PIT	20
C. Labine, LA	14
D. Farrell, PHI	11
D. Elston, CHI	10
M. Grissom, SF	10
J. Klippstein, CIN, LA	10

Runs Batted In

E. Banks, CHI	129
F. Thomas, PIT	109
H. Anderson, PHI	97
W. Mays, SF	96
O. Cepeda, SF	96

Stolen Bases

W. Mays, SF	31
R. Ashburn, PHI	30
T. Taylor, CHI	21
D. Blasingame, STL	20
J. Gilliam, LA	18

Strikeouts

S. Jones, STL	225
W. Spahn, MIL	150
J. Podres, LA	143
J. Antonelli, SF	143
B. Friend, PIT	135

Complete Games

W. Spahn, MIL	23
R. Roberts, PHI	21
L. Burdette, MIL	19
B. Purkey, CIN	17
B. Friend, PIT	16

Hits

R. Ashburn, PHI	215
W. Mays, SF	208
H. Aaron, MIL	196

Base on Balls

R. Ashburn, PHI	97
J. Temple, CIN	91
E. Mathews, MIL	85

Fewest Hits per 9 Innings

S. Jones, STL	7.34
S. Koufax, LA	7.49
S. Miller, SF	7.91

Shutouts

C. Willey, MIL	4

Home Run Percentage

E. Banks, CHI	7.6
F. Thomas, PIT	6.2
E. Mathews, MIL	5.7

Runs Scored

W. Mays, SF	121
E. Banks, CHI	119
H. Aaron, MIL	109

Fewest Walks per 9 Innings

L. Burdette, MIL	1.63
R. Roberts, PHI	1.70
V. Law, PIT	1.73

Most Strikeouts per 9 Inn.

S. Jones, STL	8.10
S. Koufax, LA	7.43
D. Drott, CHI	6.83

Doubles

O. Cepeda, SF	38
D. Groat, PIT	36
S. Musial, STL	35

Triples

R. Ashburn, PHI	13
W. Mays, SF	11
B. Virdon, PIT	11
E. Banks, CHI	11

Innings

W. Spahn, MIL	290
L. Burdette, MIL	275
B. Friend, PIT	274

Games Pitched

D. Elston, CHI	69
J. Klippstein, CIN, LA	57
R. Face, PIT	57

	W	L	PCT	GB	R	OR	2B	3B	HR	BA	SA	SB	E	DP	FA	CG	BB	SO	ShO	SV	ERA
MIL	92	62	.597		675	541	221	21	167	.266	.412	26	120	152	.980	72	426	773	16	17	3.21
PIT	84	70	.545	8	662	607	229	68	134	.264	.410	30	133	173	.978	43	470	679	10	41	3.56
SF	80	74	.519	12	727	698	250	42	170	.263	.422	64	152	156	.975	38	512	775	7	25	3.98
CIN	76	78	.494	16	695	621	242	40	123	.258	.389	61	100	148	.983	50	419	705	7	20	3.73
CHI	72	82	.468	20	709	725	207	49	182	.265	.426	39	150	161	.975	27	619	805	5	24	4.22
STL	72	82	.468	20	619	704	216	39	111	.261	.380	44	153	163	.974	45	567	822	6	15	4.12
LA	71	83	.461	21	668	761	166	50	172	.251	.402	73	146	198	.975	30	606	855	7	31	4.47
PHI	69	85	.448	23	664	762	238	56	124	.266	.400	51	129	136	.978	51	446	778	6	15	4.32
					5419	5419	1769	365	1183	.262	.405	388	1083	1287	.977	356	4065	6192	64	198	3.95

American League 1958

	POS	Player	AB	BA	HR	RBI	PO	A	E	DP	TC/G	FA	Pitcher	G	IP	W	L	SV	ERA
N. Y.	1B	B. Skowron	465	.273	14	73	1040	71	8	112	9.5	.993	B. Turley	33	245	21	7	1	2.97
W-92 L-62	2B	G. McDougald	503	.250	14	65	265	298	13	97	5.0	.977	W. Ford	30	219	14	7	1	2.01
Casey Stengel	SS	T. Kubek	559	.265	2	48	242	453	28	98	5.4	.961	A. Ditmar	38	140	9	8	4	3.42
	3B	A. Carey	315	.286	12	45	99	195	12	22	3.1	.961	B. Shantz	33	126	7	6	0	3.36
	RF	H. Bauer	452	.268	12	50	186	7	4	0	1.6	.980	J. Kucks	34	126	8	8	4	3.93
	CF	M. Mantle	519	.304	42	97	331	5	8	2	2.3	.977	D. Larsen	19	114	9	6	0	3.07
	LF	N. Siebern	460	.300	14	55	259	8	5	2	2.0	.982	D. Maas	22	101	7	3	0	3.82
	C	Y. Berra	433	.266	22	90	509	41	0	8	6.5	1.000	R. Duren	44	76	6	4	20	2.02
	CO	E. Howard	376	.314	11	66	409	27	2	8		.995							
	3B	J. Lumpe	232	.254	3	32	57	126	11	13	3.0	.943							
	2B	B. Richardson	182	.247	0	14	104	110	6	35	4.3	.973							

POS	Player	AB	BA	HR	RBI	PO	A	E	DP	TC/G	FA	Pitcher	G	IP	W	L	SV	ERA
Chi.												D. Donovan	34	248	15	14	0	3.01
1B	E. Torgeson	188	.266	10	30	470	30	11	54	7.0	.978	B. Pierce	35	245	17	11	2	2.68
W-82 L-72	2B N. Fox	623	.300	0	49	**444**	399	13	**117**	5.5	.985	E. Wynn	40	240	14	16	2	4.13
Al Lopez	SS L. Aparicio	557	.266	2	40	**289**	463	21	90	5.3	.973	J. Wilson	28	156	9	9	1	4.10
	3B B. Goodman	425	.299	0	40	67	204	14	16	2.6	.951	R. Moore	32	137	9	7	2	3.82
	RF J. Rivera	276	.225	9	35	153	7	1	3	1.6	.994	G. Staley	50	85	4	5	8	3.16
	CF J. Landis	523	.277	15	64	331	9	5	1	2.4	.986	T. Lown	27	41	3	3	8	3.98
	LF A. Smith	480	.252	12	58	249	9	8	2	1.9	.970							
	C S. Lollar	421	.273	20	84	597	63	9	8	5.8	.987							
	3O B. Phillips	260	.273	5	30	122	87	8	13		.963							
	1B R. Boone	246	.244	7	41	511	34	8	45	8.8	.986							
	C E. Battey	168	.226	8	26	220	27	3	6	5.1	.988							
	OF D. Mueller	166	.253	0	16	57	3	2	1	1.4	.968							
	1B R. Jackson	146	.233	7	21	289	16	1	29	8.1	.997							
Bos.	1B D. Gernert	431	.237	20	69	**1101**	**93**	11	**118**	**10.6**	.991	T. Brewer	33	227	12	12	0	3.72
W-79 L-75	2B P. Runnels	568	.322	8	59	267	320	9	88	**5.6**	.985	F. Sullivan	32	199	13	9	3	3.57
Pinky Higgins	SS D. Buddin	497	.237	12	43	269	445	31	102	**5.5**	.958	I. Delock	31	160	14	8	2	3.38
	3B F. Malzone	**627**	.295	15	87	139	**378**	27	**36**	**3.5**	.950	D. Sisler	30	149	8	9	0	4.94
	RF J. Jensen	548	.286	35	**122**	293	14	6	3	2.0	.981	M. Wall	52	114	8	9	10	3.62
	CF J. Piersall	417	.237	8	48	314	8	5	2	2.6	.985	M. Fornieles	37	111	4	6	1	4.96
	LF T. Williams	411	**.328**	26	85	154	3	7	0	1.4	.957	L. Kiely	47	81	5	2	12	3.00
	C S. White	328	.259	6	35	450	38	6	8	4.8	.988							
	OF G. Stephens	270	.219	9	25	149	5	4	2	1.4	.975							
	C L. Berberet	167	.210	2	18	234	18	4	2	5.2	.984							
Cle.	1B M. Vernon	355	.293	8	55	774	50	11	90	8.7	.987	C. McLish	39	226	16	8	1	2.99
W-77 L-76	2B B. Avila	375	.253	5	30	175	177	5	62	4.4	.986	M. Grant	44	204	10	11	4	3.84
Bobby Bragan	SS B. Hunter	190	.195	0	9	124	165	16	46	4.1	.948	R. Narleski	44	183	13	10	1	4.07
W-31 L-36	3B B. Harrell	229	.218	7	19	21	50	1	7	1.6	.986	G. Bell	33	182	12	10	1	3.31
Joe Gordon	RF R. Colavito	489	.303	41	113	243	14	5	6	2.0	.981	D. Mossi	43	102	7	8	3	3.90
W-46 L-40	CF L. Doby	247	.283	13	45	141	5	0	0	2.1	1.000	H. Wilhelm	30	90	2	7	2	2.49
	LF M. Minoso	556	.302	24	80	301	13	8	1	2.2	.975	H. Woodeshick	14	72	6	6	0	3.64
	C R. Nixon	376	.301	9	46	499	31	5	4	5.3	.991							
	UT V. Power	385	.317	12	53	365	172	8	68		.985							
	2S B. Moran	257	.226	1	18	174	210	15	56		.962							
	OF G. Geiger	195	.231	1	6	133	3	2	2	2.6	.986							
	OF R. Maris	182	.225	9	27	109	6	4*	1	2.5	.966							
	C D. Brown	173	.237	7	20	278	23	4	6	4.9	.987							
	S3 C. Carrasquel	156	.256	2	21	54	84	8	17		.945							
	31 P. Ward	148	.338	4	21	162	40	2	12		.990							
Det.	1B G. Harris	451	.273	20	83	942	79	**15**	90	8.5	.986	F. Lary	39	**260**	16	15	1	2.90
W-77 L-77	2B F. Bolling	610	.269	14	75	342	**445**	12	109	5.2	.985	P. Foytack	39	230	15	13	1	3.44
Jack Tighe	SS B. Martin	498	.255	7	42	159	229	17	58	4.6	.958	J. Bunning	35	220	14	12	0	3.52
W-21 L-28	3B R. Bertoia	240	.233	6	27	70	139	11	13	3.2	.950	B. Hoeft	36	143	10	9	3	4.15
Bill Norman	RF A. Kaline	543	.313	16	85	316	**23**	2	4	2.4	.994	H. Moford	25	110	4	9	1	3.61
W-56 L-49	CF H. Kuenn	561	.319	8	54	**358**	9	6	1	**2.7**	.984	H. Aguirre	44	70	3	4	5	3.75
	LF C. Maxwell	397	.272	13	65	201	4	3	0	1.8	.986							
	C R. Wilson	298	.299	3	29	565	34	5	6	6.0	.992							
	SS C. Veal	207	.256	0	16	95	160	5	30	4.5	.981							
	3B O. Virgil	193	.244	3	19	55	101	3	7	3.2	.981							
	OF G. Zernial	124	.323	5	23	30	1	2	0	1.4	.939							
	1B R. Boone	114	.237	6	20	236	15	3	26	7.9	.988							
Bal.	1B B. Boyd	401	.309	7	36	757	53	5	85	8.2	.994	J. Harshman	34	236	12	15	4	2.89
W-74 L-79	2B B. Gardner	560	.225	3	33	349	350	11	103	4.7	.985	B. O'Dell	41	221	14	11	8	2.97
Paul Richards	SS W. Miranda	214	.201	1	8	137	216	14	53	3.6	.962	Portocarrero	32	205	15	11	3	3.25
	3B B. Robinson	463	.238	3	32	**151**	275	21	30	3.2	.953	M. Pappas	31	135	10	10	0	4.06
	RF A. Pilarcik	379	.243	1	24	213	5	3	0	1.9	.986	C. Johnson	26	118	6	9	1	3.88
	CF J. Busby	215	.237	3	19	196	1	1	0	1.9	**.995**	B. Loes	32	114	3	9	5	3.63
	LF G. Woodling	413	.276	15	65	181	7	5	1	1.7	.974	H. Brown	19	97	7	5	1	3.07
	C G. Triandos	474	.245	30	79	**698**	61	**10**	11	5.8	.987	G. Zuverink	45	69	2	2	7	3.39
	UT D. Williams	409	.276	4	32	359	61	8	27		.981							
	OF B. Nieman	366	.325	16	60	145	3	6	0	1.5	.961							
	SS F. Castleman	200	.170	3	14	102	165	10	37	3.0	.964							
	1B J. Marshall	191	.215	5	19	382	19	0	37	7.7	1.000							
K. C.	1B V. Power	205	.302	4	27	439	48	4	54	9.6	.992	R. Terry	40	217	11	13	2	4.24
W-73 L-81	2B H. Lopez	564	.261	17	73	251	282	**14**	78	5.7	.974	N. Garver	31	201	12	11	1	4.03
Harry Craft	SS J. DeMaestri	442	.219	6	38	226	417	13	95	4.8	**.980**	R. Herbert	42	175	8	8	3	3.50
	3B H. Smith	315	.273	5	46	44	87	7	9	3.2	.940	J. Urban	30	132	8	11	1	5.93
	RF R. Maris	401	.247	19	53	194	9	5*	3	2.1	.976	B. Grim	26	114	7	6	0	3.56
	CF B. Tuttle	511	.231	11	51	311	12	4	2	2.3	.988	M. Dickson	27	99	9	5	1	3.27
	LF B. Cerv	515	.305	38	104	311	13	5	3	2.4	.985	T. Gorman	50	90	4	4	8	3.51
	C H. Chiti	295	.268	9	44	425	41	6	9	5.7	.987	D. Tomanek	36	72	5	5	5	3.61
	13 P. Ward	268	.254	6	24	358	76	12	34		.973	D. Maas	10	55	4	5	1	3.90
	2B M. Baxes	231	.212	0	8	134	151	9	40	4.8	.969							
	OF B. Martyn	226	.261	2	23	112	4	4	2	1.9	.967							
	1B H. Simpson	212	.264	7	27	384	18	4	44	9.4	.990							
	C F. House	202	.252	4	24	236	22	2	4	4.7	.992							
	3S C. Carrasquel	160	.213	2	13	53	97	4	16		.974							

POS	Player	AB	BA	HR	RBI	PO	A	E	DP	TC/G	FA	Pitcher	G	IP	W	L	SV	ERA
1B	N. Zauchin	303	.228	15	37	749	56	4	74	8.9	.995	P. Ramos	43	259	14	18	3	4.23
2B	K. Aspromonte	253	.225	5	27	139	184	12	49	4.7	.964	R. Kemmerer	40	224	6	15	0	4.61
SS	R. Bridges	377	.263	5	28	191	331	13	73	4.8	.976	C. Pascual	31	177	8	12	0	3.15
3B	E. Yost	406	.224	8	37	109	186	11	20	2.7	.964	H. Griggs	32	137	3	11	0	5.52
RF	J. Lemon	501	.246	26	75	255	8	6	2	2.0	.978	T. Clevenger	55	124	9	9	6	4.35
CF	A. Pearson	530	.275	3	33	338	6	7	1	2.5	.980	D. Hyde	53	103	10	3	18	1.75
LF	R. Sievers	550	.295	39	108	216	5	2	0	2.0	.991	Valentinetti	23	96	4	6	0	5.08
C	C. Courtney	450	.251	8	62	682	64	7	17	5.9	.991							
23	H. Plews	380	.258	2	29	156	208	16	45		.958							
OF	N. Chrisley	233	.215	5	26	117	6	1	2	1.8	.992							
SS	O. Alvarez	196	.209	0	5	113	158	9	33	4.4	.968							
1B	J. Becquer	164	.238	0	12	319	34	2	26	8.5	.994							

Was.
W-61　L-93
Cookie Lavagetto

BATTING AND BASE RUNNING LEADERS

Batting Average
T. Williams, BOS	.328
P. Runnels, BOS	.322
H. Kuenn, DET	.319
A. Kaline, DET	.313
V. Power, CLE, KC	.312

Slugging Average
R. Colavito, CLE	.620
B. Cerv, KC	.592
M. Mantle, NY	.592
T. Williams, BOS	.584
R. Sievers, WAS	.544

Home Runs
M. Mantle, NY	42
R. Colavito, CLE	41
R. Sievers, WAS	39
B. Cerv, KC	38
J. Jensen, BOS	35

Total Bases
M. Mantle, NY	307
B. Cerv, KC	305
R. Colavito, CLE	303
R. Sievers, WAS	299
J. Jensen, BOS	293

Runs Batted In
J. Jensen, BOS	122
R. Colavito, CLE	113
R. Sievers, WAS	108
B. Cerv, KC	104
M. Mantle, NY	97

Stolen Bases
L. Aparicio, CHI	29
J. Rivera, CHI	21
J. Landis, CHI	19
M. Mantle, NY	18
M. Minoso, CLE	14

Hits
N. Fox, CHI	187
F. Malzone, BOS	185
V. Power, CLE, KC	184

Base on Balls
M. Mantle, NY	129
J. Jensen, BOS	99
T. Williams, BOS	98

Home Run Percentage
R. Colavito, CLE	8.4
M. Mantle, NY	8.1
B. Cerv, KC	7.4

Runs Scored
M. Mantle, NY	127
P. Runnels, BOS	103
V. Power, CLE, KC	98

Doubles
H. Kuenn, DET	39
V. Power, CLE, KC	37
A. Kaline, DET	34

Triples
V. Power, CLE, KC	10
J. Lemon, WAS	9
B. Tuttle, KC	9
L. Aparicio, CHI	9

PITCHING LEADERS

Winning Percentage
B. Turley, NY	.750
C. McLish, CLE	.667
B. Pierce, CHI	.607
Portocarrero, BAL	.577
P. Foytack, DET	.536

Earned Run Average
W. Ford, NY	2.01
B. Pierce, CHI	2.68
J. Harshman, BAL	2.89
F. Lary, DET	2.90
B. O'Dell, BAL	2.97

Wins
B. Turley, NY	21
B. Pierce, CHI	17
C. McLish, CLE	16
F. Lary, DET	16

Saves
R. Duren, NY	20
D. Hyde, WAS	18
L. Kiely, BOS	12
M. Wall, BOS	10

Strikeouts
E. Wynn, CHI	179
J. Bunning, DET	177
B. Turley, NY	168
J. Harshman, BAL	161
C. Pascual, WAS	146

Complete Games
B. Turley, NY	19
B. Pierce, CHI	19
F. Lary, DET	19
J. Harshman, BAL	17
P. Foytack, DET	16
D. Donovan, CHI	16

Fewest Hits per 9 Innings
B. Turley, NY	6.53
G. Bell, CLE	6.97
W. Ford, NY	7.14

Shutouts
W. Ford, NY	7
B. Turley, NY	6

Fewest Walks per 9 Innings
D. Donovan, CHI	1.92
B. O'Dell, BAL	2.07
F. Sullivan, BOS	2.21

Most Strikeouts per 9 Inn.
C. Pascual, WAS	7.41
J. Bunning, DET	7.25
E. Wynn, CHI	6.72

Innings
F. Lary, DET	260
P. Ramos, WAS	259
D. Donovan, CHI	248

Games Pitched
T. Clevenger, WAS	55
D. Tomanek, CLE, KC	54
D. Hyde, WAS	53

	W	L	PCT	GB	R	OR	2B	3B	HR	BA	SA	SB	E	DP	FA	CG	BB	SO	ShO	SV	ERA
NY	92	62	.597		759	577	212	39	164	.268	.416	48	128	182	.978	53	557	796	21	33	3.22
CHI	82	72	.532	10	634	615	191	42	101	.257	.367	101	114	160	.981	55	515	751	15	25	3.61
BOS	79	75	.513	13	697	691	229	30	155	.256	.400	29	145	172	.976	44	521	695	5	28	3.92
CLE	77	76	.503	14.5	694	635	210	31	161	.258	.403	50	152	171	.974	51	604	766	2	20	3.73
DET	77	77	.500	15	659	606	229	41	109	.266	.389	48	106	140	.982	59	437	797	8	19	3.59
BAL	74	79	.484	17.5	521	575	195	19	108	.241	.350	33	114	159	.980	55	403	749	15	28	3.40
KC	73	81	.474	19	642	713	196	50	138	.247	.381	22	125	166	.979	42	467	720	9	25	4.15
WAS	61	93	.396	31	553	747	161	38	121	.240	.357	22	118	163	.980	28	558	762	6	28	4.53
					5159	5159	1623	290	1057	.254	.383	353	1002	1313	.979	387	4062	6036	81	206	3.77

POS	Player	AB	BA	HR	RBI	PO	A	E	DP	TC/G	FA	Pitcher	G	IP	W	L	SV	ERA
L. A. W-88 L-68 Walter Alston																		
1B	G. Hodges	413	.276	25	80	891	66	8	77	8.5	.992	D. Drysdale	44	271	17	13	2	3.46
2B	C. Neal	616	.287	19	83	386	413	9	110	5.4	.989	J. Podres	34	195	14	9	0	4.11
SS	D. Zimmer	249	.165	4	28	115	226	10	43	4.0	.972	S. Koufax	35	153	8	6	2	4.05
3B	J. Gilliam	553	.282	3	34	121	245	16	18	2.9	.958	R. Craig	29	153	11	5	0	2.06
RF	D. Snider	370	.308	23	88	157	2	4	1	1.5	.975	D. McDevitt	39	145	10	8	4	3.97
CF	D. Demeter	371	.256	18	70	223	5	4	1	1.9	.983	S. Williams	35	125	5	5	0	3.97
LF	W. Moon	543	.302	19	74	224	13	4	2	1.7	.983	L. Sherry	23	94	7	2	3	2.19
C	J. Roseboro	397	.232	10	38	**848**	54	8	10	**7.8**	.991	C. Labine	56	85	5	10	9	3.93
1O	N. Larker	311	.289	8	49	491	48	5	53		.991							
OF	R. Fairly	244	.238	4	23	97	8	4	1	1.2	.963							
SS	M. Wills	242	.260	0	7	121	220	12	39	4.3	.966							
Mil. W-86 L-70 Fred Haney																		
1B	J. Adcock	404	.292	25	76	761	80	2	67	9.5	.998	W. Spahn	40	**292**	**21**	15	0	2.96
2B	F. Mantilla	251	.215	3	19	97	126	7	26	3.8	.970	L. Burdette	41	290	**21**	15	1	4.07
SS	J. Logan	470	.291	13	50	260	431	18	78	5.1	.975	B. Buhl	31	198	15	9	0	2.86
3B	E. Mathews	594	.306	**46**	114	144	305	18	21	3.2	.961	J. Jay	34	136	6	11	0	4.09
RF	H. Aaron	629	**.355**	39	123	261	12	5	3	1.8	.982	J. Pizarro	29	134	6	2	0	3.77
CF	B. Bruton	478	.289	6	41	309	6	3	2	2.4	.991	C. Willey	26	117	5	9	0	4.15
LF	W. Covington	373	.279	7	45	148	6	6	2	1.7	.963	B. Rush	31	101	5	6	0	2.40
C	D. Crandall	518	.257	21	72	783	**71**	5	**15**	5.9	**.994**	D. McMahon	60	81	5	3	**15**	2.57
1B	F. Torre	263	.228	1	33	622	46	4	43	7.7	.994							
2B	B. Avila	172	.238	3	19	103	131	8	21	4.7	.967							
S. F. W-83 L-71 Billy Rigney																		
1B	O. Cepeda	605	.317	27	105	929	70	16	74	8.3	.984	J. Antonelli	40	282	19	10	1	3.10
2B	D. Spencer	555	.265	12	62	350	413	24	82	5.2	.970	S. Jones	50	271	**21**	15	4	**2.83**
SS	E. Bressoud	315	.251	9	26	151	267	11	37	4.7	.974	M. McCormick	47	226	12	16	4	3.99
3B	J. Davenport	469	.258	6	38	91	221	7	15	2.6	**.978**	J. Sanford	36	222	15	12	1	3.16
RF	W. Kirkland	463	.272	22	68	212	8	7	0	1.9	.969	S. Miller	59	168	8	7	8	2.84
CF	W. Mays	575	.313	34	104	353	6	6	2	2.5	.984							
LF	J. Brandt	429	.270	12	57	176	10	3	2	1.6	.984							
C	H. Landrith	283	.251	3	29	576	45	5	5	5.7	.992							
OF	F. Alou	247	.275	10	33	111	2	3	0	1.7	.974							
SS	A. Rodgers	228	.250	6	24	110	197	22	35	5.0	.933							
1B	W. McCovey	192	.354	13	38	424	29	5	29	9.0	.989							
C	B. Schmidt	181	.243	5	20	307	30	0	1	4.8	1.000							
OF	L. Wagner	129	.225	5	22	48	0	3	0	1.8	.941							
Pit. W-78 L-76 Danny Murtaugh																		
1B	D. Stuart	397	.297	27	78	831	81	**22**	87	8.9	.976	V. Law	34	266	18	9	1	2.98
2B	B. Mazeroski	493	.241	7	59	303	373	13	100	5.2	.981	B. Friend	35	235	8	**19**	0	4.03
SS	D. Groat	593	.275	5	51	**301**	473	**29**	**97**	**5.5**	.964	H. Haddix	31	224	12	12	0	3.13
3B	D. Hoak	564	.294	8	65	**169**	**322**	20	31	**3.3**	.961	R. Kline	33	186	11	13	0	4.26
RF	R. Clemente	432	.296	4	50	229	10	**13**	1	2.4	.948	B. Daniels	34	101	7	9	1	5.45
CF	B. Virdon	519	.254	8	41	404	16	9	**5**	**3.0**	.979	R. Face	57	93	18	1	10	2.70
LF	B. Skinner	547	.280	13	61	285	9	11	1	2.1	.964							
C	S. Burgess	377	.297	11	59	441	39	8	4	4.8	.984							
OF	R. Mejias	276	.236	7	28	155	8	5	2	2.0	.970							
1B	R. Nelson	175	.291	6	32	337	18	2	45	6.4	.994							
C	D. Kravitz	162	.253	3	21	198	19	3	3	4.9	.986							
Chi. W-74 L-80 Bob Scheffing																		
1B	D. Long	296	.236	14	37	731	49	12	63	9.3	.985	B. Anderson	37	235	12	13	0	4.13
2B	T. Taylor	624	.280	8	38	352	**456**	**25**	105	**5.6**	.970	G. Hobbie	46	234	16	13	0	3.69
SS	E. Banks	589	.304	45	**143**	271	**519**	12	95	5.2	**.985**	D. Hillman	39	191	8	11	0	3.53
3B	A. Dark	477	.264	6	45	111	255	20	20	2.9	.948	M. Drabowsky	31	142	5	10	0	4.13
RF	L. Walls	354	.257	8	33	203	1	7	0	1.8	.967	B. Henry	65	134	9	8	12	2.68
CF	G. Altman	420	.245	12	47	278	7	3	2	2.4	.990	A. Ceccarelli	18	102	5	5	0	4.76
LF	B. Thomson	374	.259	11	52	223	9	3	4	2.0	.987	J. Buzhardt	31	101	4	5	0	4.97
C	S. Taylor	353	.269	13	43	497	37	**10**	1	5.0	.982	D. Elston	65	98	10	8	13	3.32
OF	W. Moryn	381	.234	14	48	175	9	2	1	1.8	.989							
1B	J. Marshall	294	.252	11	40	558	51	2	52	8.5	.997							
UT	E. Averill	186	.237	10	34	197	49	13	4		.950							
OF	I. Noren	156	.321	4	19	81	4	0	1	2.1	1.000							
Cin. W-74 L-80 Mayo Smith W-35 L-45 Fred Hutchinson W-39 L-35																		
1B	F. Robinson	540	.311	36	125	998	75	17	**111**	8.7	.984	D. Newcombe	30	222	13	8	1	3.16
2B	J. Temple	598	.311	8	67	322	390	19	96	4.9	.974	B. Purkey	38	218	13	18	1	4.25
SS	E. Kasko	329	.283	2	31	182	271	11	61	5.5	.976	O. Pena	46	136	5	9	5	4.76
3B	W. Jones	233	.249	7	31	92	105	7	9	3.0	.966	J. Nuxhall	28	132	9	9	1	4.24
RF	G. Bell	580	.293	19	115	269	15	1	1	2.0	**.996**	J. O'Toole	28	129	5	8	0	5.15
CF	V. Pinson	**648**	.316	20	84	**423**	11	7	4	2.9	.984	B. Lawrence	43	128	7	12	10	4.77
LF	J. Lynch	379	.269	17	58	180	5	4	3	1.9	.979	J. Brosnan	26	83	8	3	2	3.35
C	E. Bailey	379	.264	12	40	549	64	6	6	5.3	.990	J. Hook	17	79	5	5	0	5.13
UT	F. Thomas	374	.225	12	47	206	126	19	19		.946							
SS	R. McMillan	246	.264	9	24	163	205	10	50	5.2	.974							
C	D. Dotterer	161	.267	2	17	230	20	2	3	4.9	.992							
P	D. Newcombe	105	.305	3	21	14	31	1	4	1.5	.978							

POS	Player	AB	BA	HR	RBI	PO	A	E	DP	TC/G	FA	Pitcher	G	IP	W	L	SV	ERA
St. L. W-71 L-83 Solly Hemus																		
1B	S. Musial	341	.255	14	44	623	63	7	72	7.7	.990	L. Jackson	40	256	14	13	0	3.30
2B	D. Blasingame	615	.289	1	24	362	439	17	104	5.5	.979	V. Mizell	31	201	13	10	0	4.20
SS	A. Grammas	368	.269	3	30	216	373	22	80	4.7	.964	E. Broglio	35	181	7	12	0	4.72
3B	K. Boyer	563	.309	28	94	134	300	20	32	3.2	.956	L. McDaniel	62	132	14	12	15	3.82
RF	J. Cunningham	458	.345	7	60	201	5	6	1	1.8	.972	G. Blaylock	26	100	4	5	0	5.13
CF	G. Cimoli	519	.279	8	72	267	12	6	2	2.0	.979	M. Bridges	27	76	6	3	1	4.26
LF	B. White	517	.302	12	72	175	2	7	1	2.0	.962							
C	H. Smith	452	.270	13	50	758	60	9	13	5.9	.989							
OF	C. Flood	208	.255	7	26	147	1	5	1	1.4	.967							
OF	G. Oliver	172	.244	6	28	62	1	3	0	1.6	.955							
PH	G. Crowe	103	.301	8	29													
Phi. W-64 L-90 Eddie Sawyer																		
1B	E. Bouchee	499	.285	15	74	1127	95	17	96	9.2	.986	R. Roberts	35	257	15	17	0	4.27
2B	S. Anderson	477	.218	0	34	343	403	12	70	5.0	.984	J. Owens	31	221	12	12	1	3.21
SS	J. Koppe	422	.261	7	28	218	347	27	67	5.2	.954	G. Conley	25	180	12	7	1	3.00
3B	G. Freese	400	.268	23	70	83	156	22	15	2.4	.916	D. Cardwell	25	153	9	10	0	4.06
RF	W. Post	468	.254	22	94	226	12	2	3	2.0	.992	R. Semproch	30	112	3	10	3	5.40
CF	R. Ashburn	564	.266	1	20	359	4	11	1	2.5	.971	R. Gomez	20	72	3	8	1	6.10
LF	H. Anderson	508	.240	14	63	283	17	6	4	2.2	.980	D. Farrell	38	57	1	6	6	4.74
C	C. Sawatski	198	.293	9	43	306	23	7	4	4.9	.979							
O1	D. Philley	254	.291	7	37	238	15	4	18		.984							
3B	W. Jones	160	.269	7	24	40	76	3	5	2.6	.975							

BATTING AND BASE RUNNING LEADERS

Batting Average
H. Aaron, MIL	.355
J. Cunningham, STL	.345
O. Cepeda, SF	.317
V. Pinson, CIN	.316
W. Mays, SF	.313

Slugging Average
H. Aaron, MIL	.636
E. Banks, CHI	.596
E. Mathews, MIL	.593
F. Robinson, CIN	.583
W. Mays, SF	.583

Home Runs
E. Mathews, MIL	46
E. Banks, CHI	45
H. Aaron, MIL	39
F. Robinson, CIN	36
W. Mays, SF	34

Total Bases
H. Aaron, MIL	400
E. Mathews, MIL	352
E. Banks, CHI	351
W. Mays, SF	335
V. Pinson, CIN	330

Runs Batted In
E. Banks, CHI	143
F. Robinson, CIN	125
H. Aaron, MIL	123
G. Bell, CIN	115
E. Mathews, MIL	114

Stolen Bases
W. Mays, SF	27
J. Gilliam, LA	23
O. Cepeda, SF	23
T. Taylor, CHI	23
V. Pinson, CIN	21

Hits
H. Aaron, MIL	223
V. Pinson, CIN	205
O. Cepeda, SF	192

Base on Balls
J. Gilliam, LA	96
J. Cunningham, STL	88
W. Moon, LA	81

Home Run Percentage
E. Mathews, MIL	7.7
E. Banks, CHI	7.6
F. Robinson, CIN	6.7

Runs Scored
V. Pinson, CIN	131
W. Mays, SF	125
E. Mathews, MIL	118

Doubles
V. Pinson, CIN	47
H. Aaron, MIL	46
W. Mays, SF	43

Triples
W. Moon, LA	11
C. Neal, LA	11

PITCHING LEADERS

Winning Percentage
R. Face, PIT	.947
V. Law, PIT	.667
J. Antonelli, SF	.655
B. Buhl, MIL	.625

Earned Run Average
S. Jones, SF	2.83
S. Miller, SF	2.84
B. Buhl, MIL	2.86
W. Spahn, MIL	2.96
V. Law, PIT	2.98

Wins
L. Burdette, MIL	21
S. Jones, SF	21
W. Spahn, MIL	21
J. Antonelli, SF	19
R. Face, PIT	18
V. Law, PIT	18

Saves
L. McDaniel, STL	15
D. McMahon, MIL	15
D. Elston, CHI	13
B. Henry, CHI	12
R. Face, PIT	10
B. Lawrence, CIN	10

Strikeouts
D. Drysdale, LA	242
S. Jones, SF	209
S. Koufax, LA	173
J. Antonelli, SF	165
M. McCormick, SF	151

Complete Games
W. Spahn, MIL	21
V. Law, PIT	20
L. Burdette, MIL	20
R. Roberts, PHI	19
D. Newcombe, CIN	17
J. Antonelli, SF	17

Fewest Hits per 9 Innings
H. Haddix, PIT	7.58
S. Jones, SF	7.71
G. Hobbie, CHI	7.85

Shutouts
7 tied with	4

Fewest Walks per 9 Innings
D. Newcombe, CIN	1.09
L. Burdette, MIL	1.18
R. Roberts, PHI	1.22

Most Strikeouts per 9 Inn.
D. Drysdale, LA	8.05
S. Jones, SF	6.95
J. Podres, LA	6.69

Innings
W. Spahn, MIL	292
L. Burdette, MIL	290
J. Antonelli, SF	282

Games Pitched
B. Henry, CHI	65
D. Elston, CHI	65
L. McDaniel, STL	62

	W	L	PCT	GB	R	OR	Batting 2B	3B	HR	BA	SA	SB	Fielding E	DP	FA	CG	BB	Pitching SO	ShO	SV	ERA
LA *	88	68	.564		705	670	196	46	148	.257	.396	84	114	154	.981	43	614	1077	14	26	3.79
MIL	86	70	.551	2	724	623	216	36	177	.265	.417	41	127	138	.979	69	429	775	18	18	3.51
SF	83	71	.539	4	705	613	239	35	167	.261	.414	81	152	118	.974	52	500	873	12	23	3.47
PIT	78	76	.506	9	651	680	230	42	112	.263	.384	32	154	165	.975	48	418	730	7	17	3.90
CHI	74	80	.481	13	673	688	209	44	163	.249	.398	32	140	142	.977	30	519	765	11	25	4.01
CIN	74	80	.481	13	764	738	258	34	161	.274	.427	65	126	157	.978	44	456	690	7	26	4.31
STL	71	83	.461	16	641	725	244	49	118	.269	.400	65	146	158	.975	36	564	846	8	25	4.34
PHI	64	90	.416	23	599	725	196	38	113	.242	.362	39	154	132	.973	54	474	769	8	15	4.27
					5462	5462	1788	324	1159	.260	.400	439	1113	1164	.977	376	3974	6525	85	175	3.95

* Defeated Milwaukee in playoff 2 games to 0.

Chi.
W-94 L-60
Al Lopez

POS	Player	AB	BA	HR	RBI	PO	A	E	DP	TC/G	FA	Pitcher	G	IP	W	L	SV	ERA
1B	E. Torgeson	277	.220	9	45	717	37	13	58	7.4	.983	E. Wynn	37	**256**	**22**	10	0	3.17
2B	N. Fox	**624**	.306	2	70	**364**	**453**	10	93	5.3	**.988**	B. Shaw	47	231	18	6	3	2.69
SS	L. Aparicio	612	.257	6	51	**282**	**460**	23	87	5.0	.970	B. Pierce	34	224	14	15	0	3.62
3B	B. Phillips	379	.264	5	40	90	202	15	13	3.1	.951	D. Donovan	31	180	9	10	0	3.66
RF	J. McAnany	210	.276	0	27	106	6	4	4	1.7	.966	B. Latman	37	156	8	5	0	3.75
CF	J. Landis	515	.272	5	60	**420**	10	3	2	**2.9**	.993	G. Staley	**67**	116	8	5	14	2.24
LF	A. Smith	472	.237	17	55	303	8	6	2	2.5	.981	T. Lown	60	93	9	2	**15**	2.89
C	S. Lollar	505	.265	22	84	623	51	5	**14**	5.6	.993							
3B	B. Goodman	268	.250	1	28	57	135	10	10	2.7	.950							
OF	J. Rivera	177	.220	4	19	75	5	2	3	1.2	.976							
C	J. Romano	126	.294	5	25	169	16	4	5	5.0	.979							

Cle.
W-89 L-65
Joe Gordon

POS	Player	AB	BA	HR	RBI	PO	A	E	DP	TC/G	FA	Pitcher	G	IP	W	L	SV	ERA
1B	V. Power	595	.289	10	60	**1039**	110	6	**98**	**9.5**	.995	C. McLish	35	235	19	8	1	3.63
2B	B. Martin	242	.260	9	24	147	149	1	37	4.4	.997	G. Bell	44	234	16	11	5	4.04
SS	W. Held	525	.251	29	71	177	277	18	43	4.6	.962	M. Grant	38	165	10	7	3	4.14
3B	G. Strickland	441	.238	3	48	69	131	6	11	2.6	.971	H. Score	30	161	9	11	0	4.71
RF	R. Colavito	588	.257	**42**	111	319	7	5	1	2.1	.985	J. Perry	44	153	12	10	4	2.65
CF	J. Piersall	317	.246	4	30	216	3	4	2	2.5	.982	M. Garcia	29	72	3	6	1	4.00
LF	M. Minoso	570	.302	21	92	314	14	5	1	2.3	.985							
C	R. Nixon	258	.240	1	29	374	31	6	8	5.6	.985							
O1	T. Francona	399	.363	20	79	432	21	5	21		.989							
23	J. Baxes	247	.239	15	34	123	148	15	31		.948							

N. Y.
W-79 L-75
Casey Stengel

POS	Player	AB	BA	HR	RBI	PO	A	E	DP	TC/G	FA	Pitcher	G	IP	W	L	SV	ERA
1B	B. Skowron	282	.298	15	59	626	43	6	68	9.4	.991	W. Ford	35	204	16	10	1	3.04
2B	B. Richardson	469	.301	2	33	256	292	17	85	5.2	.970	A. Ditmar	38	202	13	9	1	2.90
SS	T. Kubek	512	.279	6	51	121	217	11	42	5.2	.968	B. Turley	33	154	8	11	0	4.32
3B	H. Lopez	406	.283	16	69	66	147	17	15	3.0	.926	D. Maas	38	138	14	8	4	4.43
RF	H. Bauer	341	.238	9	39	139	2	4	0	1.3	.972	R. Terry	24	127	3	7	0	3.39
CF	M. Mantle	541	.285	31	75	366	7	2	3	2.6	**.995**	D. Larsen	25	125	6	7	0	4.33
LF	N. Siebern	380	.271	11	53	175	1	2	0	1.9	.989	J. Coates	37	100	6	1	3	2.87
C	Y. Berra	472	.284	19	69	**698**	61	4	9	6.6	.997	B. Shantz	33	95	7	3	3	2.38
UT	E. Howard	443	.273	18	73	712	49	10	41		.987	R. Duren	41	77	3	6	14	1.88
UT	G. McDougald	434	.251	4	34	190	345	10	70		.982							
1B	Throneberry	192	.240	8	22	337	27	4	40	6.8	.989							
OF	E. Slaughter	99	.172	6	21	27	0	1	0	1.1	.964							

Det.
W-76 L-78
Bill Norman
W-2 L-15
Jimmy Dykes
W-74 L-63

POS	Player	AB	BA	HR	RBI	PO	A	E	DP	TC/G	FA	Pitcher	G	IP	W	L	SV	ERA
1B	G. Harris	349	.221	9	39	728	57	6	59	8.5	.992	J. Bunning	40	250	17	13	1	3.89
2B	F. Bolling	459	.266	13	55	281	340	8	81	5.0	.987	P. Foytack	39	240	14	14	1	4.64
SS	R. Bridges	381	.268	3	35	179	293	24	66	4.5	.952	D. Mossi	34	228	17	9	0	3.36
3B	E. Yost	521	.278	21	61	**168**	259	17	21	3.0	**.962**	F. Lary	32	223	17	10	0	3.55
RF	H. Kuenn	561	**.353**	9	71	247	6	3	0	1.9	.988	R. Narleski	42	104	4	12	5	5.78
CF	A. Kaline	511	.327	27	94	364	4	4	0	2.7	.989	T. Morgan	46	93	1	4	9	3.98
LF	C. Maxwell	518	.251	31	95	285	6	4	1	2.2	.986	D. Sisler	32	52	1	3	7	4.01
C	L. Berberet	338	.216	13	44	511	39	6	4	5.9	.989							
C	R. Wilson	228	.263	4	35	374	25	5	8	6.3	.988							
UT	T. Lepcio	215	.279	7	24	96	143	11	30		.956							
1B	B. Osborne	209	.191	3	21	377	27	7	36	7.3	.983							
1B	G. Zernial	132	.227	7	26	197	10	6	20	6.7	.972							

Bos.
W-75 L-79
Pinky Higgins
W-31 L-42
Rudy York
W-0 L-1
Bill Jurges
W-44 L-36

POS	Player	AB	BA	HR	RBI	PO	A	E	DP	TC/G	FA	Pitcher	G	IP	W	L	SV	ERA
1B	D. Gernert	298	.262	11	42	552	49	3	54	8.1	.995	T. Brewer	36	215	10	12	2	3.76
2B	P. Runnels	560	.314	6	57	273	272	10	82	5.5	.982	J. Casale	31	180	13	8	0	4.31
SS	D. Buddin	485	.241	10	53	235	412	**35**	**89**	4.5	.949	F. Sullivan	30	178	9	11	1	3.95
3B	F. Malzone	604	.280	19	92	134	**357**	24	**40**	3.3	.953	Monbouquette	34	152	7	7	0	4.15
RF	J. Jensen	535	.277	28	**112**	311	12	6	4	2.3	.982	I. Delock	28	134	11	6	0	2.95
CF	G. Geiger	335	.245	11	48	173	5	2	1	1.9	.989	F. Baumann	26	96	6	4	1	4.05
LF	T. Williams	272	.254	10	43	94	4	3	0	1.3	.970	M. Fornieles	46	82	5	3	11	3.07
C	S. White	377	.284	1	42	557	56	6	8	5.2	.990	L. Kiely	41	56	3	3	7	4.20
OF	G. Stephens	270	.278	3	39	141	11	3	0	1.8	.981							
OF	M. Keough	251	.243	7	27	147	5	1	1	2.2	.993							
1B	V. Wertz	247	.275	7	49	440	38	4	44	7.5	.992							
2B	P. Green	172	.233	1	10	109	132	7	38	5.5	.972							
C	P. Daley	169	.225	1	11	245	28	1	5	4.7	.996							

Bal.
W-74 L-80
Paul Richards

POS	Player	AB	BA	HR	RBI	PO	A	E	DP	TC/G	FA	Pitcher	G	IP	W	L	SV	ERA
1B	B. Boyd	415	.265	3	41	927	46	15	88	9.1	.985	H. Wilhelm	32	226	15	11	0	**2.19**
2B	B. Gardner	401	.217	6	27	333	392	18	104	5.3	.976	M. Pappas	33	209	15	9	3	3.27
SS	C. Carrasquel	346	.223	4	28	124	237	11	63	4.2	.970	B. O'Dell	38	199	10	12	1	2.93
3B	B. Robinson	313	.284	4	24	92	187	13	25	3.4	.955	J. Walker	30	182	11	10	4	2.92
RF	G. Woodling	440	.300	14	77	210	2	4	0	1.7	.981	H. Brown	31	164	11	9	3	3.79
CF	W. Tasby	505	.250	13	48	320	13	11	4	2.3	.968	B. Loes	37	64	4	7	14	4.06
LF	B. Nieman	360	.292	21	60	171	6	5	0	1.9	.973							
C	G. Triandos	393	.216	25	73	597	63	13	5	5.4	.981							
S3	B. Klaus	321	.249	3	25	120	231	13	28		.964							
OF	A. Pilarcik	273	.282	3	16	133	3	3	1	1.3	.978							
C	J. Ginsberg	166	.181	1	14	241	29	2	4	4.4	.993							
1B	W. Dropo	151	.278	6	21	386	18	4	42	7.6	.990							

	POS	Player	AB	BA	HR	RBI	PO	A	E	DP	TC/G	FA	Pitcher	G	IP	W	L	SV	ERA
K. C.	1B	K. Hadley	288	.253	10	39	656	42	8	66	7.4	.989	B. Daley	39	216	16	13	1	3.16
W-66 L-88	2B	Terwilliger	180	.267	2	18	144	166	9	42	5.1	.972	N. Garver	32	201	10	13	1	3.71
Harry Craft	SS	J. DeMaestri	352	.244	6	34	167	320	22	63	4.4	.957	R. Herbert	37	184	11	11	1	4.85
	3B	D. Williams	488	.266	16	75	83	164	11	10	3.2	.957	J. Kucks	33	151	8	11	1	3.87
	RF	R. Maris	433	.273	16	72	231	7	6	4	2.1	.975	B. Grim	40	125	6	10	4	4.09
	CF	B. Tuttle	463	.300	7	43	294	17	5	3	2.6	.984	R. Coleman	29	81	2	10	2	4.56
	LF	B. Cerv	463	.285	20	87	231	8	5	2	2.1	.980	T. Sturdivant	36	72	2	6	5	4.65
	C	F. House	347	.236	1	30	447	43	9	7	5.3	.982							
	2S	J. Lumpe	403	.243	3	28	218	306	12	80		.978							
	3B	H. Smith	292	.288	5	31	85	119	10	10	2.8	.953							
	OF	R. Snyder	243	.313	3	21	127	9	2	2	2.2	.986							
	C	H. Chiti	162	.272	5	25	228	25	3	5	5.4	.988							
	2B	H. Lopez	135	.281	6	24	81	71	11	15	4.9	.933							
Was.	1B	R. Sievers	385	.242	21	49	846	72	10	72	10.0	.989	C. Pascual	32	239	17	10	0	2.64
W-63 L-91	2B	R. Bertoia	308	.237	8	29	139	198	10	40	4.9	.971	P. Ramos	37	234	13	19	0	4.16
Cookie Lavagetto	SS	B. Consolo	202	.213	0	10	111	229	17	44	4.8	.952	R. Kemmerer	37	206	8	17	0	4.50
	3B	H. Killebrew	546	.242	**42**	105	129	325	**30**	18	3.2	.938	B. Fischer	34	187	9	11	0	4.28
	RF	Throneberry	327	.251	10	42	136	7	7	2	1.7	.953	T. Clevenger	50	117	8	5	8	3.91
	CF	B. Allison	570	.261	30	85	333	8	9	1	2.3	.974	H. Griggs	37	98	2	8	2	5.25
	LF	J. Lemon	531	.279	33	100	281	4	9	0	2.1	.969	C. Stobbs	41	91	1	8	7	2.98
	C	H. Naragon	195	.241	0	11	262	13	2	0	5.1	.993	D. Hyde	37	54	2	5	4	4.97
	SS	R. Samford	237	.224	5	22	92	177	15	33	4.4	.947							
	2B	K. Aspromonte	225	.244	2	14	101	137	10	25	4.8	.960							
	1B	J. Becquer	220	.268	1	26	454	32	5	38	9.3	.990							
	OF	L. Green	190	.242	2	15	89	4	2	0	1.6	.979							
	C	C. Courtney	189	.233	2	18	213	11	3	2	4.3	.987							

BATTING AND BASE RUNNING LEADERS

Batting Average
H. Kuenn, DET	.353
A. Kaline, DET	.327
P. Runnels, BOS	.314
N. Fox, CHI	.306
M. Minoso, CLE	.302

Slugging Average
A. Kaline, DET	.530
H. Killebrew, WAS	.516
M. Mantle, NY	.514
R. Colavito, CLE	.512
J. Lemon, WAS	.510

Home Runs
H. Killebrew, WAS	42
R. Colavito, CLE	42
J. Lemon, WAS	33
C. Maxwell, DET	31
M. Mantle, NY	31

Total Bases
R. Colavito, CLE	301
H. Killebrew, WAS	282
H. Kuenn, DET	281
M. Mantle, NY	278
B. Allison, WAS	275

Runs Batted In
J. Jensen, BOS	112
R. Colavito, CLE	111
H. Killebrew, WAS	105
J. Lemon, WAS	100
C. Maxwell, DET	95

Stolen Bases
L. Aparicio, CHI	56
M. Mantle, NY	21
J. Landis, CHI	20
J. Jensen, BOS	20
B. Allison, WAS	13

Hits
H. Kuenn, DET	198
N. Fox, CHI	191
P. Runnels, BOS	176

Base on Balls
E. Yost, DET	135
P. Runnels, BOS	95
M. Mantle, NY	94

Home Run Percentage
H. Killebrew, WAS	7.7
R. Colavito, CLE	7.1
J. Lemon, WAS	6.2

Runs Scored
E. Yost, DET	115
M. Mantle, NY	104
V. Power, CLE	102

Doubles
H. Kuenn, DET	42
F. Malzone, BOS	34
N. Fox, CHI	34

Triples
B. Allison, WAS	9
G. McDougald, NY	8

PITCHING LEADERS

Winning Percentage
B. Shaw, CHI	.750
C. McLish, CLE	.704
E. Wynn, CHI	.688
D. Mossi, DET	.654
F. Lary, DET	.630
C. Pascual, WAS	.630

Earned Run Average
H. Wilhelm, BAL	2.19
C. Pascual, WAS	2.64
B. Shaw, CHI	2.69
A. Ditmar, NY	2.90
J. Walker, BAL	2.92

Wins
E. Wynn, CHI	22
C. McLish, CLE	19
B. Shaw, CHI	18

Saves
T. Lown, CHI	15
G. Staley, CHI	14
B. Loes, BAL	14
R. Duren, NY	14
M. Fornieles, BOS	11

Strikeouts
J. Bunning, DET	201
C. Pascual, WAS	185
E. Wynn, CHI	179
H. Score, CLE	147
H. Wilhelm, BAL	139

Complete Games
C. Pascual, WAS	17
M. Pappas, BAL	15
D. Mossi, DET	15
J. Bunning, DET	14
E. Wynn, CHI	14

Fewest Hits per 9 Innings
H. Score, CLE	6.89
A. Ditmar, NY	6.95
H. Wilhelm, BAL	7.09

Shutouts
C. Pascual, WAS	6
E. Wynn, CHI	5
M. Pappas, BAL	4

Fewest Walks per 9 Innings
H. Brown, BAL	1.76
F. Lary, DET	1.86
N. Garver, KC	1.88

Most Strikeouts per 9 Inn.
H. Score, CLE	8.23
J. Bunning, DET	7.25
C. Pascual, WAS	6.98

Innings
E. Wynn, CHI	256
J. Bunning, DET	250
P. Foytack, DET	240

Games Pitched
G. Staley, CHI	67
T. Lown, CHI	60
T. Clevenger, WAS	50

	W	L	PCT	GB	R	OR	2B	3B	Batting HR	BA	SA	SB	E	Fielding DP	FA	CG	BB	Pitching SO	ShO	SV	ERA
CHI	94	60	.610		669	**588**	220	**46**	97	.250	.364	**113**	130	141	**.979**	44	525	761	13	**36**	3.29
CLE	89	65	.578	5	**745**	646	216	25	**167**	.263	**.408**	33	126	138	.978	**58**	635	799	7	23	3.75
NY	79	75	.513	15	687	647	224	40	153	.260	.402	45	131	160	.978	38	594	**836**	**15**	28	3.60
DET	76	78	.494	18	713	732	196	30	160	.258	.400	34	131	131	.978	53	**432**	829	9	24	4.20
BOS	75	79	.487	19	726	696	**248**	28	125	.256	.385	68	131	**167**	.978	38	589	724	9	25	4.17
BAL	74	80	.481	20	551	621	182	23	109	.238	.345	36	147	163	.976	45	476	735	**15**	30	3.56
KC	66	88	.429	28	681	760	231	43	117	.263	.390	34	159	156	.973	44	492	703	8	21	4.35
WAS	63	91	.409	31	619	701	173	32	163	.237	.379	51	162	140	.973	46	467	694	10	21	4.01
					5391	5391	1690	267	1091	.253	.384	414	1110	1196	.977	366	4210	6081	86	208	3.86

National League 1960

POS	Player	AB	BA	HR	RBI	PO	A	E	DP	TC/G	FA	Pitcher	G	IP	W	L	SV	ERA
Pit. W-95 L-59 Danny Murtaugh																		
1B	D. Stuart	438	.260	23	83	920	77	**14**	90	9.4	.986	B. Friend	38	276	18	12	1	3.00
2B	B. Mazeroski	538	.273	11	64	**413**	**449**	10	**127**	5.8	**.989**	V. Law	35	272	20	9	0	3.08
SS	D. Groat	573	**.325**	2	50	237	443	24	92	5.2	.966	H. Haddix	29	172	11	10	1	3.97
3B	D. Hoak	553	.282	16	79	132	**324**	25	34	3.1	.948	V. Mizell	23	156	13	5	0	3.12
RF	R. Clemente	570	.314	16	94	246	19	8	2	1.9	.971	R. Face	**68**	115	10	8	24	2.90
CF	B. Virdon	409	.264	8	40	272	10	5	0	2.6	.983	F. Green	45	70	8	4	3	3.21
LF	B. Skinner	571	.273	15	86	250	13	5	2	1.9	.981							
C	S. Burgess	337	.294	7	39	485	38	3	7	5.9	**.994**							
OF	G. Cimoli	307	.267	0	28	181	5	7	1	2.1	.964							
C	H. Smith	258	.295	11	45	356	30	6	5	5.5	.985							
1B	R. Nelson	200	.300	7	35	463	37	2	48	6.9	.996							
Mil. W-88 L-66 Chuck Dressen																		
1B	J. Adcock	514	.298	25	91	**1229**	104	9	105	9.9	**.993**	L. Burdette	45	276	19	13	4	3.36
2B	C. Cottier	229	.227	3	19	180	214	13	40	4.4	.968	W. Spahn	40	268	**21**	10	2	3.50
SS	J. Logan	482	.245	7	42	235	417	30	77	5.0	.956	B. Buhl	36	239	16	9	0	3.09
3B	E. Mathews	548	.277	39	124	141	280	22	23	2.9	.950	C. Willey	28	145	6	7	0	4.35
RF	H. Aaron	590	.292	40	**126**	320	13	6	**6**	2.2	.982	J. Jay	32	133	9	8	1	3.24
CF	B. Bruton	629	.286	12	54	351	10	5	3	2.5	.986	J. Pizarro	21	115	6	7	0	4.55
LF	W. Covington	281	.249	10	35	106	2	4	1	1.6	.964	D. McMahon	48	64	3	6	10	5.94
C	D. Crandall	537	.294	19	77	**764**	70	10	9	6.0	.988	R. Piche	37	48	3	5	3	3.56
2B	Schoendienst	226	.257	1	19	120	148	10	34	4.5	.964							
St. L. W-86 L-68 Solly Hemus																		
1B	B. White	554	.283	16	79	994	65	11	**109**	8.7	.990	L. Jackson	43	**282**	18	13	0	3.48
2B	J. Javier	451	.237	4	21	272	338	24	71	5.3	.962	E. Broglio	52	226	**21**	9	0	2.74
SS	D. Spencer	507	.258	16	58	215	323	31	66	4.1	.946	R. Sadecki	26	157	9	9	0	3.78
3B	K. Boyer	552	.304	32	97	140	300	19	**37**	3.1	.959	C. Simmons	23	152	7	4	0	2.66
RF	J. Cunningham	492	.280	6	39	184	6	10	1	1.7	.950	R. Kline	34	118	4	9	1	6.04
CF	C. Flood	396	.237	8	38	290	7	2	0	2.2	**.993**	L. McDaniel	65	116	12	4	**26**	2.09
LF	S. Musial	331	.275	17	63	97	2	1	0	1.7	.990							
C	H. Smith	337	.228	2	28	664	61	7	9	5.9	.990							
OF	W. Moryn	200	.245	11	35	100	4	1	0	1.7	.990							
UT	A. Grammas	196	.245	4	17	102	171	9	33		.968							
OF	B. Nieman	188	.287	4	31	63	0	4	0	1.2	.940							
C	C. Sawatski	179	.229	6	27	279	25	2	5	4.6	.993							
L. A. W-82 L-72 Walter Alston																		
1B	N. Larker	440	.323	5	78	914	80	7	81	8.4	.993	D. Drysdale	41	269	15	14	2	2.84
2B	C. Neal	477	.256	8	40	250	291	13	78	4.1	.977	J. Podres	34	228	14	12	0	3.08
SS	M. Wills	516	.295	0	27	260	431	**40**	78	5.0	.945	S. Williams	38	207	14	10	1	3.00
3B	J. Gilliam	557	.248	5	40	101	262	15	21	2.9	.960	S. Koufax	37	175	8	13	1	3.91
RF	F. Howard	448	.268	23	77	177	8	3	1	1.6	.984	L. Sherry	57	142	14	10	7	3.79
CF	T. Davis	352	.276	11	44	151	7	4	2	1.9	.975	E. Roebuck	58	117	8	3	8	2.78
LF	W. Moon	469	.299	13	69	194	15	3	3	1.9	.986	R. Craig	21	116	8	3	0	3.27
C	J. Roseboro	287	.213	8	42	640	48	5	10	8.0	.993							
OF	D. Snider	235	.243	14	36	108	3	4	1	1.5	.965							
1B	G. Hodges	197	.198	8	30	403	33	2	40	4.8	.995							
OF	D. Demeter	168	.274	9	29	92	2	1	1	1.5	.989							
S. F. W-79 L-75 Billy Rigney W-33 L-25 Tom Sheehan W-46 L-50																		
1B	W. McCovey	260	.238	13	51	557	39	9	42	8.5	.985	M. McCormick	40	253	15	12	3	**2.70**
2B	D. Blasingame	523	.235	2	31	318	329	14	66	5.0	.979	S. Jones	39	234	18	14	0	3.19
SS	E. Bressoud	386	.225	9	43	191	339	22	53	4.8	.960	J. Sanford	37	219	12	14	0	3.82
3B	J. Davenport	363	.251	6	38	77	171	10	12	2.5	**.961**	B. O'Dell	43	203	8	13	2	3.20
RF	W. Kirkland	515	.252	21	65	252	16	6	5	1.9	.978	J. Antonelli	41	112	6	7	11	3.77
CF	W. Mays	595	.319	29	103	392	12	8	2	2.7	.981	S. Miller	47	102	7	6	2	3.90
LF	O. Cepeda	569	.297	24	96	163	10	3	3	1.9	.983	B. Loes	37	46	3	2	5	4.93
C	B. Schmidt	344	.267	8	37	631	31	13	6	6.3	.981							
32	J. Amalfitano	328	.277	1	27	99	184	14	24		.953							
OF	F. Alou	322	.264	8	44	156	5	7	0	1.8	.958							
UT	A. Rodgers	217	.244	2	22	112	129	12	26		.953							
C	H. Landrith	190	.242	1	20	346	23	13	5	5.5	.966							

POS	Player	AB	BA	HR	RBI	PO	A	E	DP	TC/G	FA	Pitcher	G	IP	W	L	SV	ERA
1B	F. Robinson	464	.297	31	83	663	54	5	60	9.3	.993	B. Purkey	41	253	17	11	0	3.60
2B	B. Martin	317	.246	3	16	228	207	11	52	4.6	.975	J. Hook	36	222	11	18	0	4.50
SS	R. McMillan	399	.236	10	42	171	315	18	68	4.3	.964	J. O'Toole	34	196	12	12	1	3.80
3B	E. Kasko	479	.292	6	51	98	186	10	20	3.4	.966	C. McLish	37	151	4	14	0	4.16
RF	G. Bell	515	.262	12	62	239	13	3	1	1.9	.988	J. Nuxhall	38	112	1	8	0	4.42
CF	V. Pinson	652	.287	20	61	401	11	8	1	2.7	.981	J. Brosnan	57	99	7	2	12	2.36
LF	W. Post	249	.281	17	38	125	8	2	0	2.0	.985	D. Newcombe	16	83	4	6	0	4.57
C	E. Bailey	441	.261	13	67	621	52	7	8	5.3	.990	B. Henry	51	68	1	5	17	3.19
1B	G. Coleman	251	.271	6	32	559	63	1	69	9.4	.998							
OF	J. Lynch	159	.289	6	27	41	1	4	1	1.4	.913							
3B	W. Jones	149	.268	3	27	43	59	4	5	2.3	.962							

Cin.
W-67 L-87
Fred Hutchinson

POS	Player	AB	BA	HR	RBI	PO	A	E	DP	TC/G	FA	Pitcher	G	IP	W	L	SV	ERA
1B	E. Bouchee	299	.237	5	44	709	56	7	56	9.7	.991	G. Hobbie	46	259	16	20	1	3.97
2B	J. Kindall	246	.240	2	23	147	218	13	44	4.6	.966	B. Anderson	38	204	9	11	1	4.11
SS	E. Banks	597	.271	41	117	283	488	18	94	5.1	.977	D. Cardwell	31	177	8	14	0	4.37
3B	R. Santo	347	.251	9	44	78	144	13	6	2.5	.945	D. Ellsworth	31	177	7	13	0	3.72
RF	B. Will	475	.255	6	53	224	10	2	2	2.0	.992	D. Elston	60	127	8	9	11	3.40
CF	R. Ashburn	547	.291	0	40	317	11	8	2	2.3	.976	S. Morehead	45	123	2	9	4	3.94
LF	G. Altman	334	.266	13	51	144	2	1	0	1.9	.993							
C	M. Thacker	90	.156	0	6	170	23	4	2	3.9	.980							
UT	F. Thomas	479	.238	21	64	528	92	17	40		.973							
23	D. Zimmer	368	.258	6	35	208	266	16	30		.967							

Chi.
W-60 L-94
Charlie Grimm
W-6 L-11
Lou Boudreau
W-54 L-83

POS	Player	AB	BA	HR	RBI	PO	A	E	DP	TC/G	FA	Pitcher	G	IP	W	L	SV	ERA
1B	P. Herrera	512	.281	17	71	1017	109	14	88	8.5	.988	R. Roberts	35	237	12	16	1	4.02
2B	T. Taylor	505	.287	4	35	283	356	21	67	5.4	.968	J. Buzhardt	30	200	5	16	0	3.86
SS	R. Amaro	264	.231	0	16	153	230	14	47	4.3	.965	G. Conley	29	183	8	14	0	3.68
3B	A. Dark	198	.242	3	14	57	84	7	7	2.8	.953	J. Owens	31	150	4	14	0	5.04
RF	K. Walters	426	.239	8	37	220	17	3	4	2.0	.988	D. Green	23	109	3	6	0	4.06
CF	B. Del Greco	300	.237	10	26	247	10	8	1	3.0	.970	C. Short	42	107	6	9	3	3.94
LF	J. Callison	288	.260	9	30	176	7	2	4	2.2	.989	D. Farrell	59	103	10	6	11	2.70
C	J. Coker	252	.214	6	34	394	43	8	5	5.9	.982	A. Mahaffey	14	93	7	3	0	2.31
OF	T. Curry	245	.261	6	34	96	2	8	0	1.7	.925							
OF	T. Gonzalez	241	.299	6	33	146	6	3	0	2.3	.981							
OF	B. Smith	217	.286	4	27	125	4	0	1	1.8	1.000							
UT	L. Walls	181	.199	3	19	75	49	6	8		.954							
SS	J. Koppe	170	.171	1	13	107	133	11	23	4.6	.956							
C	C. Neeman	160	.181	4	13	252	31	6	2	5.6	.979							
C	C. Dalrymple	158	.272	4	21	172	25	7	3	4.3	.966							

Phi.
W-59 L-95
Eddie Sawyer
W-0 L-1
Andy Cohen
W-1 L-0
Gene Mauch
W-58 L-94

BATTING AND BASE RUNNING LEADERS

Batting Average

D. Groat, PIT	.325
W. Mays, SF	.319
R. Clemente, PIT	.314
K. Boyer, STL	.304
W. Moon, LA	.299

Slugging Average

F. Robinson, CIN	.595
H. Aaron, MIL	.566
K. Boyer, STL	.562
W. Mays, SF	.555
E. Banks, CHI	.554

Home Runs

E. Banks, CHI	41
H. Aaron, MIL	40
E. Mathews, MIL	39
K. Boyer, STL	32
F. Robinson, CIN	31

Total Bases

H. Aaron, MIL	334
E. Banks, CHI	331
W. Mays, SF	330
K. Boyer, STL	310
V. Pinson, CIN	308

Runs Batted In

H. Aaron, MIL	126
E. Mathews, MIL	124
E. Banks, CHI	117
W. Mays, SF	103
K. Boyer, STL	97

Stolen Bases

M. Wills, LA	50
V. Pinson, CIN	32
T. Taylor, CHI, PHI	26
W. Mays, SF	25
B. Bruton, MIL	22

Hits

W. Mays, SF	190
V. Pinson, CIN	187
D. Groat, PIT	186

Base on Balls

R. Ashburn, CHI	116
E. Mathews, MIL	111
J. Gilliam, LA	96

Home Run Percentage

E. Mathews, MIL	7.1
E. Banks, CHI	6.9
H. Aaron, MIL	6.8

Runs Scored

B. Bruton, MIL	112
E. Mathews, MIL	108
W. Mays, SF	107
V. Pinson, CIN	107

Doubles

V. Pinson, CIN	37
O. Cepeda, SF	36
F. Robinson, CIN	33
B. Skinner, PIT	33

Triples

B. Bruton, MIL	13
W. Mays, SF	12
V. Pinson, CIN	12
H. Aaron, MIL	11

PITCHING LEADERS

Winning Percentage

E. Broglio, STL	.700
V. Law, PIT	.690
W. Spahn, MIL	.677
B. Buhl, MIL	.640
B. Purkey, CIN	.607

Earned Run Average

M. McCormick, SF	2.70
E. Broglio, STL	2.74
D. Drysdale, LA	2.84
S. Williams, LA	3.00
B. Friend, PIT	3.00

Wins

E. Broglio, STL	21
W. Spahn, MIL	21
V. Law, PIT	20
L. Burdette, MIL	19

Saves

L. McDaniel, STL	26
R. Face, PIT	24
B. Henry, CIN	17
J. Brosnan, CIN	12

Strikeouts

D. Drysdale, LA	246
S. Koufax, LA	197
S. Jones, SF	190
E. Broglio, STL	188
B. Friend, PIT	183

Complete Games

L. Burdette, MIL	18
W. Spahn, MIL	18
V. Law, PIT	18
G. Hobbie, CHI	16
B. Friend, PIT	16

Fewest Hits per 9 Innings

E. Broglio, STL	6.84
S. Koufax, LA	6.84
S. Williams, LA	7.03

Shutouts

J. Sanford, SF	6
D. Drysdale, LA	5

Fewest Walks per 9 Innings

L. Burdette, MIL	1.14
R. Roberts, PHI	1.29
V. Law, PIT	1.33

Most Strikeouts per 9 Inn.

S. Koufax, LA	10.13
D. Drysdale, LA	8.23
S. Williams, LA	7.60

Innings

L. Jackson, STL	282
L. Burdette, MIL	276
B. Friend, PIT	276

Games Pitched

R. Face, PIT	68
L. McDaniel, STL	65
D. Elston, CHI	60

	W	L	PCT	GB	R	OR	2B	3B	Batting HR	BA	SA	SB	E	Fielding DP	FA	CG	BB	Pitching SO	ShO	SV	ERA
PIT	95	59	.617		**734**	593	**236**	56	120	**.276**	.407	34	128	**163**	.979	47	**386**	811	11	33	3.49
MIL	88	66	.571	7	724	658	198	48	**170**	.265	**.417**	69	141	137	.976	55	518	807	13	28	3.76
STL	86	68	.558	9	639	616	213	48	138	.254	.393	48	141	152	.976	37	511	906	11	30	3.64
LA	82	72	.532	13	662	593	216	38	126	.255	.383	95	**125**	142	**.979**	46	564	**1122**	13	20	**3.40**
SF	79	75	.513	16	671	631	220	**62**	130	.255	.393	86	166	117	.972	55	512	897	**16**	26	3.44
CIN	67	87	.435	28	640	692	230	40	140	.250	.388	73	**125**	155	.979	33	442	740	8	**35**	4.00
CHI	60	94	.390	35	634	658	213	48	119	.243	.369	51	143	133	.977	36	565	805	6	25	4.35
PHI	59	95	.383	36	546	691	196	44	99	.239	.351	45	155	129	.974	45	439	736	6	16	4.01
					5250	5250	1722	384	1042	.255	.388	501	1124	1128	.977	354	3937	6824	84	213	3.76

American League 1960

	POS	Player	AB	BA	HR	RBI	PO	A	E	DP	TC/G	FA	Pitcher	G	IP	W	L	SV	ERA
N. Y. W-97 L-57 Casey Stengel	1B	B. Skowron	538	.309	26	91	**1202**	115	**12**	130	9.4	.991	A. Ditmar	34	200	15	9	0	3.06
	2B	B. Richardson	460	.252	1	26	312	337	18	103	4.7	.973	W. Ford	33	193	12	9	0	3.08
	SS	T. Kubek	568	.273	14	62	228	443	22	84	5.1	.968	B. Turley	34	173	9	3	5	3.27
	3B	C. Boyer	393	.242	14	46	102	219	11	24	3.4	.967	R. Terry	35	167	10	8	1	3.40
	RF	R. Maris	499	.283	39	**112**	263	6	4	1	2.1	.985	J. Coates	35	149	13	3	1	4.28
	CF	M. Mantle	527	.275	**40**	94	326	9	3	1	2.3	.991	E. Grba	24	81	6	4	1	3.68
	LF	H. Lopez	408	.284	9	42	199	8	5	2	2.0	.976	D. Maas	35	70	5	1	4	4.09
	C	E. Howard	323	.245	6	39	410	40	6	9	5.0	.987	B. Shantz	42	68	5	4	11	2.79
	CO	Y. Berra	359	.276	15	62	312	24	5	6		.985	R. Duren	42	49	3	4	9	4.96
	32	G. McDougald	337	.258	8	34	127	236	13	31		.965	L. Arroyo	29	41	5	1	7	2.88
	OF	B. Cerv	216	.250	8	28	101	6	2	0	2.1	.982							
Bal. W-89 L-65 Paul Richards	1B	J. Gentile	384	.292	21	98	885	52	7	98	7.6	.993	C. Estrada	36	209	**18**	11	2	3.58
	2B	M. Breeding	551	.267	3	43	359	422	18	116	5.3	.977	M. Pappas	30	206	15	11	0	3.37
	SS	R. Hansen	530	.255	22	86	**325**	456	29	110	5.3	.964	J. Fisher	40	198	12	11	2	3.41
	3B	B. Robinson	595	.294	14	88	**171**	**328**	12	34	**3.4**	**.977**	S. Barber	30	182	10	7	2	3.22
	RF	G. Stephens	193	.238	5	11	124	5	1	0	1.7	.992	H. Brown	30	159	12	5	0	3.06
	CF	J. Brandt	511	.254	15	65	284	10	5	2	2.1	.983	H. Wilhelm	41	147	11	8	7	3.31
	LF	G. Woodling	435	.283	11	62	202	7	1	0	1.7	.995	J. Walker	29	118	3	4	5	3.74
	C	G. Triandos	364	.269	12	54	516	45	6	5	5.4	.989							
	OF	A. Pilarcik	194	.247	4	17	75	4	0	0	1.1	1.000							
	1B	W. Dropo	179	.268	4	21	397	27	3	50	6.4	.993							
	OF	J. Busby	159	.258	0	12	133	2	2	1	1.9	.985							
	C	C. Courtney	154	.227	1	12	246	23	7	2	4.8	.975							
Chi. W-87 L-67 Al Lopez	1B	R. Sievers	444	.295	28	93	1079	63	8	117	**10.1**	.993	E. Wynn	36	237	13	12	1	3.49
	2B	N. Fox	**605**	.289	2	59	412	**447**	13	**126**	5.9	.985	B. Pierce	32	196	14	7	0	3.62
	SS	L. Aparicio	600	.277	2	61	305	551	18	**117**	5.7	.979	B. Shaw	36	193	13	13	0	4.06
	3B	G. Freese	455	.273	17	79	88	263	20	29	3.0	.946	F. Baumann	44	185	13	6	3	**2.67**
	RF	A. Smith	536	.315	12	72	252	5	9	2	1.9	.966	R. Kemmerer	36	121	6	3	2	2.98
	CF	J. Landis	494	.253	10	49	372	10	6	3	2.6	.985	G. Staley	64	115	13	8	10	2.42
	LF	M. Minoso	591	.311	20	105	282	14	6	3	2.0	.980	H. Score	23	114	5	10	0	3.72
	C	S. Lollar	421	.252	7	46	555	54	3	**12**	5.0	**.995**	D. Donovan	33	79	6	1	3	5.38
	1B	T. Kluszewski	181	.293	5	39	325	19	1	38	8.8	.997	T. Lown	45	67	2	3	5	3.88
Cle. W-76 L-78 Joe Gordon W-49 L-46 Jo-Jo White W-1 L-0 Jimmy Dykes W-26 L-32	1B	V. Power	580	.288	10	84	1177	**145**	5	**145**	9.0	**.996**	J. Perry	41	261	**18**	10	1	3.62
	2B	K. Aspromonte	459	.290	10	48	192	215	10	63	5.2	.976	M. Grant	33	160	9	8	0	4.40
	SS	W. Held	376	.258	21	67	208	345	19	87	5.2	.967	G. Bell	28	155	9	10	1	4.13
	3B	B. Phillips	304	.207	4	33	87	135	11	18	2.7	.953	B. Latman	31	147	7	7	0	4.03
	RF	H. Kuenn	474	.308	9	54	222	7	8	3	2.0	.966	D. Stigman	41	134	5	11	9	4.51
	CF	J. Piersall	486	.282	18	66	355	5	3	0	2.7	.992	L. Locke	32	123	3	5	2	3.37
	LF	T. Francona	544	.292	17	79	278	4	3	0	2.1	.989	J. Klippstein	49	74	5	5	**14**	2.91
	C	J. Romano	316	.272	16	52	470	30	6	6	5.1	.988							
	2B	J. Temple	381	.268	2	19	169	164	9	55	4.4	.974							
	SS	de la Hoz	160	.256	6	23	58	94	8	13	4.2	.950							
Was. W-73 L-81 Cookie Lavagetto	1B	J. Becquer	298	.252	4	35	611	38	7	59	8.5	.989	P. Ramos	43	274	11	**18**	2	3.45
	2B	B. Gardner	592	.257	9	56	355	407	**21**	101	5.4	.973	D. Lee	44	165	8	7	3	3.44
	SS	Valdivielso	268	.213	2	19	178	294	23	68	4.3	.954	C. Pascual	26	152	12	8	2	3.03
	3B	R. Bertoia	460	.265	4	45	94	227	13	19	3.0	.961	J. Kralick	35	151	8	6	1	3.04
	RF	B. Allison	501	.251	15	69	290	10	11	3	2.2	.965	T. Clevenger	53	129	5	11	7	4.20
	CF	L. Green	330	.294	5	33	219	4	2	0	2.3	.991	C. Stobbs	40	119	12	7	2	3.32
	LF	J. Lemon	528	.269	38	100	251	11	11	1	1.9	.960	H. Woodeshick	41	115	4	5	4	4.70
	C	E. Battey	466	.270	15	60	749	65	15	10	6.1	.982	R. Moore	37	66	3	2	13	2.88
	13	H. Killebrew	442	.276	31	80	629	135	17	76		.978							
	OF	D. Dobbek	248	.218	10	30	141	5	4	1	1.9	.973							
	SS	B. Consolo	174	.207	3	15	83	158	16	36	3.1	.938							
	OF	Throneberry	157	.248	1	23	52	2	3	0	1.7	.947							

	POS	Player	AB	BA	HR	RBI	PO	A	E	DP	TC/G	FA	Pitcher	G	IP	W	L	SV	ERA
Det.	1B	N. Cash	353	.286	18	63	739	59	7	68	8.1	.991	F. Lary	38	**274**	15	15	1	3.51
W-71 L-83	2B	F. Bolling	536	.254	9	59	375	377	17	93	5.6	.978	J. Bunning	36	252	11	14	0	2.79
Jimmy Dykes	SS	C. Fernandez	435	.241	4	35	226	381	34	67	4.9	.947	D. Mossi	23	158	9	8	0	3.47
W-44 L-52	3B	E. Yost	497	.260	14	47	155	208	26	18	2.7	.933	B. Bruce	34	130	4	7	0	3.74
Billy Hitchcock	RF	R. Colavito	555	.249	35	87	271	11	7	5	2.0	.976	P. Burnside	31	114	7	7	2	4.28
W-1 L-0	CF	A. Kaline	551	.278	15	68	367	5	5	1	2.7	.987	P. Foytack	28	97	2	11	2	6.14
Joe Gordon	LF	C. Maxwell	482	.237	24	81	254	5	1	0	2.2	**.996**	H. Aguirre	37	95	5	3	10	2.85
W-26 L-31	C	L. Berberet	232	.194	5	23	396	36	3	4	5.4	.993	D. Sisler	41	80	7	5	6	2.48
	1B	S. Bilko	222	.207	9	25	501	36	5	47	8.7	.991							
	OF	N. Chrisley	220	.255	5	24	101	2	2	0	2.2	.981							
Bos.	1B	V. Wertz	443	.282	19	103	841	78	12	89	8.0	.987	Monbouquette	35	215	14	11	0	3.64
W-65 L-89	2B	P. Runnels	528	**.320**	2	35	274	360	9	99	5.0	**.986**	T. Brewer	34	187	10	15	1	4.82
Bill Jurges	SS	D. Buddin	428	.245	6	36	230	356	30	79	5.0	.951	F. Sullivan	40	154	6	16	1	5.10
W-34 L-47	3B	F. Malzone	595	.271	14	79	159	318	26	36	3.3	.948	I. Delock	24	129	9	10	0	4.73
Pinky Higgins	RF	L. Clinton	298	.228	6	37	165	4	6	2	2.0	.966	B. Muffett	23	125	6	4	0	3.24
W-31 L-42	CF	W. Tasby	385	.281	7	37	232	6	5	1	2.4	.979	M. Fornieles	70	109	10	5	**14**	2.64
	LF	T. Williams	310	.316	29	72	131	6	1	1	1.6	.993	T. Sturdivant	40	101	3	3	1	4.97
	C	R. Nixon	272	.298	5	33	354	26	5	3	5.2	.987	J. Casale	29	96	2	9	0	6.17
	2S	P. Green	260	.242	3	21	151	169	11	33		.967							
	OF	G. Geiger	245	.302	9	33	121	9	0	1	2.0	1.000							
	OF	B. Repulski	136	.243	3	20	56	0	0	0	1.7	1.000							
	OF	B. Thomson	114	.263	5	20	65	1	2	1	2.5	.971							
K. C.	1B	Throneberry	236	.250	11	41	508	40	5	56	7.8	.991	R. Herbert	37	253	14	15	1	3.28
W-58 L-96	2B	J. Lumpe	574	.272	8	53	355	364	13	99	5.5	.982	B. Daley	37	231	16	16	0	4.56
Bob Elliott	SS	K. Hamlin	428	.224	2	24	195	341	25	61	4.0	.955	D. Hall	29	182	8	13	0	4.05
	3B	A. Carey	343	.233	12	53	95	180	7	26	3.1	.975	N. Garver	28	122	4	9	0	3.83
	RF	R. Snyder	304	.260	4	26	135	4	2	2	1.5	.986	K. Johnson	42	120	5	10	3	4.26
	CF	B. Tuttle	559	.256	8	40	**381**	16	5	3	**2.7**	.988	J. Kucks	31	114	4	10	0	6.00
	LF	N. Siebern	520	.279	19	69	151	4	2	0	2.1	.987	D. Larsen	22	84	1	10	0	5.38
	C	P. Daley	228	.263	5	25	263	33	3	3	4.9	.990							
	UT	D. Williams	420	.288	12	65	376	131	11	28		.979							
	OF	H. Bauer	255	.275	3	31	85	4	2	1	1.4	.978							
	OF	W. Herzog	252	.266	8	38	128	4	2	1	1.9	.985							
	C	H. Chiti	190	.221	5	28	263	24	5	1	5.6	.983							
	C	D. Kravitz	175	.234	4	14	216	16	7	3	5.1	.971							

BATTING AND BASE RUNNING LEADERS

Batting Average

P. Runnels, BOS	.320
A. Smith, CHI	.315
M. Minoso, CHI	.311
B. Skowron, NY	.309
H. Kuenn, CLE	.308

Slugging Average

R. Maris, NY	.581
M. Mantle, NY	.558
H. Killebrew, WAS	.534
R. Sievers, CHI	.534
B. Skowron, NY	.528

Home Runs

M. Mantle, NY	40
R. Maris, NY	39
J. Lemon, WAS	38
R. Colavito, DET	35
H. Killebrew, WAS	31

Total Bases

M. Mantle, NY	294
R. Maris, NY	290
B. Skowron, NY	284
M. Minoso, CHI	284
J. Lemon, WAS	268

Runs Batted In

R. Maris, NY	112
M. Minoso, CHI	105
V. Wertz, BOS	103
J. Lemon, WAS	100
J. Gentile, BAL	98

Stolen Bases

L. Aparicio, CHI	51
J. Landis, CHI	23
L. Green, WAS	21
A. Kaline, DET	19
J. Piersall, CLE	18

Hits

M. Minoso, CHI	184
B. Robinson, BAL	175
N. Fox, CHI	175

Base on Balls

E. Yost, DET	125
M. Mantle, NY	111
B. Allison, WAS	92

Home Run Percentage

R. Maris, NY	7.8
M. Mantle, NY	7.6
J. Lemon, WAS	7.2

Runs Scored

M. Mantle, NY	119
R. Maris, NY	98
J. Landis, CHI	89
M. Minoso, CHI	89

Doubles

T. Francona, CLE	36
B. Skowron, NY	34
G. Freese, CHI	32
M. Minoso, CHI	32

Triples

N. Fox, CHI	10
B. Robinson, BAL	9

PITCHING LEADERS

Winning Percentage

J. Perry, CLE	.643
A. Ditmar, NY	.625
C. Estrada, BAL	.621
M. Pappas, BAL	.577

Earned Run Average

F. Baumann, CHI	2.67
J. Bunning, DET	2.79
H. Brown, BAL	3.06
A. Ditmar, NY	3.06
W. Ford, NY	3.08

Wins

J. Perry, CLE	18
C. Estrada, BAL	18
B. Daley, KC	16
A. Ditmar, NY	15
M. Pappas, BAL	15
F. Lary, DET	15

Saves

M. Fornieles, BOS	14
J. Klippstein, CLE	14
R. Moore, CHI, WAS	13
B. Shantz, NY	11
G. Staley, CHI	10
H. Aguirre, DET	10

Strikeouts

J. Bunning, DET	201
P. Ramos, WAS	160
E. Wynn, CHI	158
F. Lary, DET	149
C. Estrada, BAL	144

Complete Games

F. Lary, DET	15
R. Herbert, KC	14
P. Ramos, WAS	14
B. Daley, KC	13
E. Wynn, CHI	13

Fewest Hits per 9 Innings

C. Estrada, BAL	6.99
B. Turley, NY	7.17
S. Barber, BAL	7.33

Shutouts

W. Ford, NY	4
E. Wynn, CHI	4
J. Perry, CLE	4

Fewest Walks per 9 Innings

H. Brown, BAL	1.25
D. Mossi, DET	1.82
D. Hall, KC	1.88

Most Strikeouts per 9 Inn.

J. Bunning, DET	7.18
G. Bell, CLE	6.34
C. Estrada, BAL	6.21

Innings

F. Lary, DET	274
P. Ramos, WAS	274
J. Perry, CLE	261

Games Pitched

M. Fornieles, BOS	70
G. Staley, CHI	64
T. Clevenger, WAS	53

	W	L	PCT	GB	R	OR	2B	3B	Batting HR	BA	SA	SB	E	Fielding DP	FA	CG	BB	Pitching SO	ShO	SV	ERA
NY	97	57	.630		**746**	627	215	40	**193**	.260	**.426**	37	129	162	.979	38	609	712	**16**	**42**	**3.52**
BAL	89	65	.578	8	682	**606**	206	33	123	.253	.377	37	**108**	172	**.982**	**48**	552	785	11	22	3.52
CHI	87	67	.565	10	741	617	**242**	38	112	**.270**	.396	**122**	109	**175**	**.982**	42	533	695	11	26	3.60
CLE	76	78	.494	21	667	693	218	20	127	.267	.388	58	128	165	.978	32	636	771	10	30	3.95
WAS	73	81	.474	24	672	696	205	**43**	147	.244	.384	52	165	159	.973	34	538	775	10	35	3.77
DET	71	83	.461	26	633	644	188	34	150	.239	.375	66	138	138	.977	40	**474**	**824**	7	25	3.64
BOS	65	89	.422	32	658	775	234	32	124	.261	.389	34	141	156	.976	34	580	767	6	23	4.62
KC	58	96	.377	39	615	756	212	34	110	.249	.366	16	127	149	.979	44	525	664	4	14	4.38
					5414	5414	1720	274	1086	.255	.388	422	1045	1276	.978	312	4447	5993	75	217	3.87

National League 1961

	POS	Player	AB	BA	HR	RBI	PO	A	E	DP	TC/G	FA	Pitcher	G	IP	W	L	SV	ERA
Cin. W-93 L-61 Fred Hutchinson	1B	G. Coleman	520	.287	26	87	1162	**121**	11	93	8.6	.991	J. O'Toole	39	253	19	9	2	3.10
	2B	D. Blasingame	450	.222	1	21	277	304	17	53	5.2	.972	J. Jay	34	247	**21**	10	0	3.53
	SS	E. Kasko	469	.271	2	27	201	286	18	59	4.5	.964	B. Purkey	36	246	16	12	1	3.73
	3B	G. Freese	575	.277	26	87	123	254	20	23	2.6	.950	K. Hunt	29	136	9	10	0	3.96
	RF	F. Robinson	545	.323	37	124	284	15	3	3	2.0	.990	J. Maloney	27	95	6	7	2	4.37
	CF	V. Pinson	607	.343	16	87	391	19	10	4	**2.7**	.976	J. Brosnan	53	80	10	4	16	3.04
	LF	W. Post	282	.294	20	57	133	7	6	3	1.8	.959	B. Henry	47	53	2	1	16	2.19
	C	J. Zimmerman	204	.206	0	10	374	22	10	8	5.3	.975							
	OF	G. Bell	235	.255	3	33	112	1	1	0	1.5	.991							
	SS	L. Cardenas	198	.308	5	24	83	133	6	21	3.5	.973							
	OF	J. Lynch	181	.315	13	50	53	2	3	0	1.3	.948							
L. A. W-89 L-65 Walter Alston	1B	G. Hodges	215	.242	8	31	454	37	1	44	4.9	.998	S. Koufax	42	256	18	13	1	3.52
	2B	C. Neal	341	.235	10	48	211	246	11	63	4.5	.976	D. Drysdale	40	244	13	10	0	3.69
	SS	M. Wills	**613**	.282	1	31	253	428	29	104	4.8	.959	S. Williams	41	235	15	12	0	3.90
	3B	J. Gilliam	439	.244	4	32	48	104	7	9	2.1	.956	J. Podres	32	183	18	5	0	3.74
	RF	T. Davis	460	.278	15	58	143	3	4	2	1.7	.973	R. Craig	40	113	5	6	2	6.15
	CF	W. Davis	339	.254	12	45	224	4	4	1	2.0	.983	L. Sherry	53	95	4	4	15	3.90
	LF	W. Moon	463	.328	17	88	186	5	6	1	1.5	.970	R. Perranoski	53	92	7	5	6	2.65
	C	J. Roseboro	394	.251	18	59	**877**	56	13	**16**	7.6	.986	D. Farrell	50	89	6	6	10	5.06
	1B	N. Larker	282	.270	5	38	589	52	3	68	7.5	.995							
	OF	F. Howard	267	.296	15	45	79	6	6	0	1.4	.934							
	OF	R. Fairly	245	.322	10	48	85	7	1	1	1.3	.989							
	OF	D. Snider	233	.296	16	56	113	6	3	3	1.8	.975							
	3B	D. Spencer	189	.243	8	27	42	92	5	14	2.4	.964							
	C	N. Sherry	121	.256	5	21	253	16	2	3	6.0	.993							
S. F. W-85 L-69 Alvin Dark	1B	W. McCovey	328	.271	18	50	669	55	11	55	8.8	.985	M. McCormick	40	250	13	16	0	3.20
	2B	J. Amalfitano	384	.255	2	23	201	223	13	48	4.6	.970	J. Sanford	38	217	13	9	0	4.22
	SS	J. Pagan	434	.253	5	46	227	334	21	55	4.4	.964	J. Marichal	29	185	13	10	0	3.89
	3B	J. Davenport	436	.278	12	65	119	235	13	25	2.8	**.965**	B. O'Dell	46	130	7	5	2	3.59
	RF	F. Alou	415	.289	18	52	196	10	2	1	1.7	.990	S. Jones	37	128	8	8	1	4.49
	CF	W. Mays	572	.308	40	123	385	7	8	3	2.6	.980	S. Miller	63	122	14	5	**17**	2.66
	LF	H. Kuenn	471	.265	5	46	157	9	2	0	1.8	.988	B. Loes	26	115	6	5	0	4.24
	C	E. Bailey	340	.238	13	51	629	40	10	4	6.6	.985	D. LeMay	27	83	3	6	3	3.56
	1O	O. Cepeda	585	.311	**46**	**142**	774	51	5	50		.994							
	2B	C. Hiller	240	.238	2	12	133	158	8	34	4.5	.973							
	OF	M. Alou	200	.310	6	24	85	2	2	0	1.5	.978							
Mil. W-71 L-58 Chuck Dressen W-12 L-13 Birdie Tebbetts	1B	J. Adcock	562	.285	35	108	**1471**	102	11	**133**	**10.7**	**.993**	L. Burdette	40	**272**	18	11	0	4.00
	2B	F. Bolling	585	.262	15	56	326	489	10	112	5.6	**.988**	W. Spahn	38	263	**21**	13	0	**3.02**
	SS	R. McMillan	505	.220	7	48	**257**	**496**	19	110	5.0	.975	B. Buhl	32	188	9	10	0	4.11
	3B	E. Mathews	572	.306	32	91	168	281	18	30	3.1	.961	C. Willey	35	160	6	12	0	3.83
	RF	L. Maye	373	.271	14	41	169	6	5	0	1.9	.972	D. Nottebart	38	126	6	7	3	4.06
	CF	H. Aaron	603	.327	34	120	377	13	7	3	2.6	.982	B. Hendley	19	97	5	7	0	3.90
	LF	F. Thomas	423	.284	25	67	202	4	10	2	2.0	.954	D. McMahon	53	92	6	4	8	2.84
	C	J. Torre	406	.278	10	42	494	50	10	4	4.9	.982							
St. L. W-80 L-74 Solly Hemus W-33 L-41 Johnny Keane W-47 L-33	1B	B. White	591	.286	20	90	1373	104	17	125	9.9	.989	R. Sadecki	31	223	14	10	0	3.72
	2B	J. Javier	445	.279	2	41	239	332	20	82	5.2	.966	L. Jackson	33	211	14	11	0	3.75
	SS	A. Grammas	170	.212	0	21	81	136	9	29	3.5	.960	B. Gibson	35	211	13	12	1	3.24
	3B	K. Boyer	589	.329	24	95	117	**346**	24	23	3.2	.951	C. Simmons	30	196	9	10	0	3.13
	RF	C. James	349	.255	4	44	151	3	6	1	1.8	.963	E. Broglio	29	175	9	12	0	4.12
	CF	C. Flood	335	.322	2	21	241	13	4	4	2.2	.984	L. McDaniel	55	94	10	6	9	4.87
	LF	S. Musial	372	.288	15	70	149	9	1	0	1.5	**.994**							
	C	J. Schaffer	153	.255	1	16	244	23	1	6	3.9	.996							
	OF	J. Cunningham	322	.286	7	40	131	2	5	1	1.6	.964							
	SS	B. Lillis	230	.217	0	21	73	134	16	19	4.0	.928							
	OF	D. Taussig	188	.287	2	25	123	6	1	2	1.5	.992							
	C	C. Sawatski	174	.299	10	33	218	19	1	3	4.0	.996							
	SS	D. Spencer	130	.254	4	21	66	109	8	26	4.9	.956							

	POS	Player	AB	BA	HR	RBI	PO	A	E	DP	TC/G	FA	Pitcher	G	IP	W	L	SV	ERA
Pit. W-75 L-79 Danny Murtaugh	1B	D. Stuart	532	.301	35	117	1152	99	21	**141**	9.6	.983	B. Friend	41	236	14	**19**	1	3.85
	2B	B. Mazeroski	558	.265	13	59	410	505	23	**144**	**6.2**	.975	J. Gibbon	30	195	13	10	0	3.32
	SS	D. Groat	596	.275	6	55	235	473	32	**117**	5.1	.957	H. Haddix	29	156	10	6	0	4.10
	3B	D. Hoak	503	.298	12	61	137	267	20	29	3.0	.953	E. Francis	23	103	2	8	0	4.21
	RF	R. Clemente	572	**.351**	23	89	256	27	9	5	2.0	.969	V. Mizell	25	100	7	10	0	5.04
	CF	B. Virdon	599	.260	9	58	384	6	6	4	2.7	.985	C. Labine	56	93	4	1	8	3.69
	LF	B. Skinner	381	.268	3	42	175	5	5	1	1.9	.973	R. Face	62	92	6	12	17	3.82
	C	S. Burgess	323	.303	12	52	426	27	4	4	5.0	**.991**	B. Shantz	43	89	6	3	2	3.32
	C	H. Smith	193	.223	3	26	290	18	3	1	4.8	.990							
	OF	Christopher	186	.263	0	14	86	2	2	1	1.6	.978							
Chi. W-64 L-90 Vedie Himsl W-10 L-21 Harry Craft W-7 L-9 El Tappe W-42 L-53 Lou Klein W-5 L-7	1B	E. Bouchee	319	.248	12	38	852	76	16	97	8.8	.983	D. Cardwell	39	259	15	14	0	3.82
	2B	D. Zimmer	477	.252	13	40	282	323	17	99	5.4	.973	G. Hobbie	36	199	7	13	2	4.26
	SS	E. Banks	511	.278	29	80	173	358	19	68	**5.3**	.965	D. Ellsworth	37	187	10	11	0	3.86
	3B	R. Santo	578	.284	23	83	157	307	31	**41**	**3.2**	.937	J. Curtis	31	180	10	13	0	4.89
	RF	G. Altman	518	.303	27	96	258	11	6	2	2.1	.978	B. Anderson	57	152	7	10	8	4.26
	CF	A. Heist	321	.255	7	37	211	9	5	0	2.3	.978	J. Schultz	58	93	6	7	8	5.59
	LF	B. Williams	529	.278	25	86	220	9	11	3	1.8	.954	B. Schultz	41	67	7	6	7	2.70
	C	D. Bertell	267	.273	2	33	396	49	8	10	5.0	.982							
	2S	J. Kindall	310	.242	9	44	206	233	26	61		.944							
	OF	R. Ashburn	307	.257	0	19	131	4	3	0	1.8	.978							
	C	S. Taylor	235	.238	8	23	319	25	4	5	4.6	.989							
	1S	A. Rodgers	214	.266	6	23	404	83	9	44		.982							
Phi. W-47 L-107 Gene Mauch	1B	P. Herrera	400	.258	13	51	1003	96	8	104	9.6	.993	A. Mahaffey	36	219	11	**19**	0	4.10
	2B	T. Taylor	400	.250	2	26	231	270	10	74	5.6	.980	J. Buzhardt	41	202	6	18	0	4.49
	SS	R. Amaro	381	.257	1	32	243	379	19	91	4.9	.970	F. Sullivan	49	159	3	16	6	4.29
	3B	C. Smith	411	.248	9	47	75	194	22	19	3.1	.924	D. Ferrarese	42	139	5	12	1	3.76
	RF	D. Demeter	382	.257	20	68	173	9	1	2	2.3	.995	D. Green	42	128	2	4	1	4.85
	CF	T. Gonzalez	426	.277	12	58	246	7	4	4	2.2	.984	C. Short	39	127	6	12	1	5.94
	LF	J. Callison	455	.266	9	47	227	10	8	2	2.0	.967	R. Roberts	26	117	1	10	0	5.85
	C	C. Dalrymple	378	.220	5	42	551	**86**	**14**	10	5.3	.978	J. Owens	20	107	5	10	0	4.47
	UT	B. Malkmus	342	.231	7	31	210	299	12	67		.977	J. Baldschun	**65**	100	5	3	3	3.88
	UT	L. Walls	261	.280	8	30	247	59	8	33		.975							
	OF	K. Walters	180	.228	2	14	73	4	2	0	1.4	.975							
	OF	B. Smith	174	.253	2	18	91	8	3	1	2.2	.971							
	OF	W. Covington	165	.303	7	26	53	4	3	1	1.3	.950							

BATTING AND BASE RUNNING LEADERS

Batting Average

R. Clemente, PIT	.351
V. Pinson, CIN	.343
K. Boyer, STL	.329
W. Moon, LA	.328
H. Aaron, MIL	.327

Slugging Average

F. Robinson, CIN	.611
O. Cepeda, SF	.609
H. Aaron, MIL	.594
W. Mays, SF	.584
D. Stuart, PIT	.581

Home Runs

O. Cepeda, SF	46
W. Mays, SF	40
F. Robinson, CIN	37
D. Stuart, PIT	35
J. Adcock, MIL	35

Total Bases

H. Aaron, MIL	358
O. Cepeda, SF	356
W. Mays, SF	334
F. Robinson, CIN	333
R. Clemente, PIT	320

Runs Batted In

O. Cepeda, SF	142
F. Robinson, CIN	124
W. Mays, SF	123
H. Aaron, MIL	120
D. Stuart, PIT	117

Stolen Bases

M. Wills, LA	35
V. Pinson, CIN	23
F. Robinson, CIN	22
H. Aaron, MIL	21
W. Mays, SF	18

Hits

V. Pinson, CIN	208
R. Clemente, PIT	201
H. Aaron, MIL	197

Base on Balls

E. Mathews, MIL	93
W. Moon, LA	89
W. Mays, SF	81

Home Run Percentage

O. Cepeda, SF	7.9
W. Mays, SF	7.0
F. Robinson, CIN	6.8

Runs Scored

W. Mays, SF	129
F. Robinson, CIN	117
H. Aaron, MIL	115

Doubles

H. Aaron, MIL	39
V. Pinson, CIN	34

Triples

G. Altman, CHI	12
J. Callison, PHI	11
K. Boyer, STL	11
B. White, STL	11

PITCHING LEADERS

Winning Percentage

J. Podres, LA	.783
J. O'Toole, CIN	.679
J. Jay, CIN	.677
L. Burdette, MIL	.621
W. Spahn, MIL	.618

Earned Run Average

W. Spahn, MIL	3.02
J. O'Toole, CIN	3.10
C. Simmons, STL	3.13
M. McCormick, SF	3.20
B. Gibson, STL	3.24

Wins

J. Jay, CIN	21
W. Spahn, MIL	21
J. O'Toole, CIN	19
J. Podres, LA	18
L. Burdette, MIL	18
S. Koufax, LA	18

Saves

S. Miller, SF	17
R. Face, PIT	17
J. Brosnan, CIN	16
B. Henry, CIN	16
L. Sherry, LA	15

Strikeouts

S. Koufax, LA	269
S. Williams, LA	205
D. Drysdale, LA	182
J. O'Toole, CIN	178
B. Gibson, STL	166

Complete Games

W. Spahn, MIL	21
S. Koufax, LA	15
J. Jay, CIN	14
L. Burdette, MIL	14

Fewest Hits per 9 Innings

S. Koufax, LA	7.46
J. Jay, CIN	7.90
B. Gibson, STL	7.92

Shutouts

J. Jay, CIN	4
W. Spahn, MIL	4

Fewest Walks per 9 Innings

L. Burdette, MIL	1.09
B. Friend, PIT	1.72
B. Purkey, CIN	1.86

Most Strikeouts per 9 Inn.

S. Koufax, LA	9.47
S. Williams, LA	7.84
B. Gibson, STL	7.07

Innings

L. Burdette, MIL	272
W. Spahn, MIL	263
D. Cardwell, CHI	259

Games Pitched

J. Baldschun, PHI	65
S. Miller, SF	63
R. Face, PIT	62

	W	L	PCT	GB	R	OR	Batting						Fielding			Pitching					
							2B	3B	HR	BA	SA	SB	E	DP	FA	CG	BB	SO	ShO	SV	ERA
CIN	93	61	.604		710	**653**	**247**	35	158	.270	.421	70	134	124	.977	46	500	829	**12**	**40**	3.78
LA	89	65	.578	4	735	697	193	40	157	.262	.405	**86**	144	162	.975	40	544	**1105**	10	35	4.04
SF	85	69	.552	8	**773**	655	219	32	183	.264	**.423**	79	133	126	.977	39	502	924	9	30	3.77
MIL	83	71	.539	10	712	656	199	34	**188**	.258	.415	70	**111**	152	**.982**	**57**	493	652	8	16	3.89
STL	80	74	.519	13	703	668	236	51	103	.271	.393	46	166	165	.972	49	570	823	10	24	**3.74**
PIT	75	79	.487	18	694	675	232	**57**	128	**.273**	.410	26	150	**187**	.975	34	**400**	759	9	29	3.92
CHI	64	90	.416	29	689	800	238	51	176	.255	.418	35	183	175	.970	34	465	755	6	25	4.48
PHI	47	107	.305	46	584	796	185	50	103	.243	.357	56	146	179	.976	29	521	775	9	13	4.61
					5600	5600	1749	350	1196	.262	.405	468	1167	1270	.976	328	3995	6622	73	212	4.03

American League 1961

	POS	Player	AB	BA	HR	RBI	PO	A	E	DP	TC/G	FA	Pitcher	G	IP	W	L	SV	ERA
N. Y. W-109 L-53 Ralph Houk	1B	B. Skowron	561	.267	28	89	1228	102	10	**146**	9.0	.993	W. Ford	39	**283**	**25**	4	0	3.21
	2B	B. Richardson	662	.261	3	49	**413**	376	18	**136**	5.0	.978	B. Stafford	36	195	14	9	2	2.68
	SS	T. Kubek	617	.276	8	46	261	449	30	107	5.1	.959	R. Terry	31	188	16	3	0	3.15
	3B	C. Boyer	504	.224	11	55	151	**353**	17	36	3.7	.967	R. Sheldon	35	163	11	5	0	3.60
	RF	R. Maris	590	.269	**61**	**142**	266	9	9	1	1.8	.968	J. Coates	43	141	11	5	5	3.44
	CF	M. Mantle	514	.317	54	128	351	6	6	0	2.4	.983	B. Daley	23	130	8	9	0	3.96
	LF	Y. Berra	395	.271	22	61	161	7	2	2	2.0	.988	L. Arroyo	**65**	119	15	5	**29**	2.19
	C	E. Howard	446	.348	21	77	635	43	5	4	6.2	.993							
	OF	H. Lopez	243	.222	3	22	123	7	3	0	1.8	.977							
	C	J. Blanchard	243	.305	21	54	268	18	3	2	6.0	.990							
	OF	B. Cerv	118	.271	6	20	55	2	1	0	1.9	.983							
Det. W-101 L-61 Bob Scheffing	1B	N. Cash	535	**.361**	41	132	**1231**	127	11	121	8.7	.992	F. Lary	36	275	23	9	0	3.24
	2B	J. Wood	663	.258	11	69	380	396	**25**	83	4.9	.969	J. Bunning	38	268	17	11	1	3.19
	SS	C. Fernandez	435	.248	3	40	207	312	23	59	4.5	.958	D. Mossi	35	240	15	7	1	2.96
	3B	S. Boros	396	.270	5	62	115	192	15	15	2.8	.953	P. Foytack	32	170	11	10	0	3.93
	RF	A. Kaline	586	.324	19	82	378	9	4	3	2.7	.990	P. Regan	32	120	10	7	2	5.25
	CF	B. Bruton	596	.257	17	63	**410**	4	5	2	2.7	.988	T. Fox	39	57	5	2	12	1.41
	LF	R. Colavito	583	.290	45	140	329	**16**	9	4	2.2	.975	H. Aguirre	45	55	4	4	8	3.25
	C	D. Brown	308	.266	16	45	460	38	5	7	5.5	.990							
	SS	D. McAuliffe	285	.246	6	33	79	115	14	29	3.8	.933							
	C	M. Roarke	229	.223	2	22	383	22	5	5	4.8	.988							
Bal. W-95 L-67 Paul Richards W-78 L-57 Lum Harris W-17 L-10	1B	J. Gentile	486	.302	46	141	1209	100	14	129	9.2	.989	S. Barber	37	248	18	12	1	3.33
	2B	J. Adair	386	.264	9	37	233	237	6	57	4.4	.987	C. Estrada	33	212	15	9	0	3.69
	SS	R. Hansen	533	.248	12	51	256	437	30	**110**	4.9	.959	J. Fisher	36	196	10	13	1	3.90
	3B	B. Robinson	668	.287	7	61	151	331	14	34	3.0	**.972**	M. Pappas	26	178	13	9	1	3.04
	RF	W. Herzog	323	.291	5	35	143	2	0	0	1.5	**1.000**	H. Brown	27	167	10	6	1	3.19
	CF	J. Brandt	516	.297	16	72	293	6	8	2	2.3	.974	B. Hoeft	35	138	7	4	3	2.02
	LF	R. Snyder	312	.292	1	13	168	3	6	0	1.6	.966	D. Hall	29	122	7	5	4	3.09
	C	G. Triandos	397	.244	17	63	642	55	8	**9**	6.2	.989	H. Wilhelm	51	110	9	7	18	2.30
	OF	D. Williams	310	.206	8	24	86	4	3	1	1.2	.968							
	2B	M. Breeding	244	.209	1	16	179	179	11	53	4.6	.970							
	OF	E. Robinson	222	.266	8	30	136	6	4	3	1.8	.973							
	OF	D. Philley	144	.250	1	23	21	0	0	0	.8	1.000							
Chi. W-86 L-76 Al Lopez	1B	R. Sievers	492	.295	27	92	1096	94	8	93	9.1	.993	J. Pizarro	39	195	14	7	2	3.05
	2B	N. Fox	606	.251	2	51	**413**	407	15	97	5.3	.982	F. Baumann	53	188	10	13	3	5.61
	SS	L. Aparicio	625	.272	6	45	264	**487**	30	86	5.0	**.962**	B. Pierce	39	180	10	9	3	3.80
	3B	A. Smith	532	.278	28	93	58	161	12	12	2.9	.948	C. McLish	31	162	10	13	1	4.38
	RF	F. Robinson	432	.310	11	59	218	7	2	0	2.1	.991	R. Herbert	21	138	9	6	0	4.05
	CF	J. Landis	534	.283	22	85	389	9	5	3	**2.9**	.988	E. Wynn	17	110	8	2	0	3.51
	LF	M. Minoso	540	.280	14	82	273	10	13	2	2.0	.956	T. Lown	59	101	7	5	11	2.76
	C	S. Lollar	337	.282	7	41	464	48	1	6	4.8	**.998**	D. Larsen	25	74	7	2	2	4.12
	13	J. Martin	274	.230	5	32	353	118	10	38		.979	W. Hacker	42	57	3	3	8	3.77
	C	C. Carreon	229	.271	4	27	395	25	2	6	5.9	.995							
Cle. W-78 L-83 Jimmy Dykes W-78 L-82 Mel Harder W-0 L-1	1B	V. Power	563	.268	5	63	1154	**142**	8	101	9.2	.994	M. Grant	35	245	15	9	0	3.86
	2B	J. Temple	518	.276	3	30	239	317	18	79	4.4	.969	G. Bell	34	228	12	16	0	4.10
	SS	W. Held	509	.267	23	78	258	393	27	90	4.7	.960	J. Perry	35	224	10	17	0	4.71
	3B	B. Phillips	546	.264	18	72	**188**	246	19	23	3.2	.958	B. Latman	45	177	13	5	5	4.02
	RF	W. Kirkland	525	.259	27	95	290	12	8	**5**	2.2	.974	W. Hawkins	30	133	7	9	1	4.06
	CF	J. Piersall	484	.322	6	40	328	9	3	3	2.8	**.991**	A. Locke	37	95	4	4	2	4.53
	LF	T. Francona	592	.301	16	85	289	5	4	1	2.2	.987	F. Funk	56	92	11	11	1	3.31
	C	J. Romano	509	.299	21	80	752	58	9	8	5.8	.989							
	UT	de la Hoz	173	.260	3	23	77	116	9	10		.955							
	OF	C. Essegian	166	.289	12	35	85	5	3	1	1.9	.968							

	POS	Player	AB	BA	HR	RBI	PO	A	E	DP	TC/G	FA	Pitcher	G	IP	W	L	SV	ERA
Bos. W-76 L-86 Pinky Higgins	1B	P. Runnels	360	.317	3	38	701	50	4	92	6.7	**.995**	Monbouquette	32	236	14	14	0	3.39
	2B	C. Schilling	646	.259	5	62	397	**449**	8	121	5.4	.991	G. Conley	33	200	11	14	1	4.91
	SS	D. Buddin	339	.263	6	42	204	294	23	70	4.8	.956	D. Schwall	25	179	15	7	0	3.22
	3B	F. Malzone	590	.266	14	87	136	304	**23**	45	3.1	.950	I. Delock	28	156	6	9	0	4.90
	RF	J. Jensen	498	.263	13	66	274	14	4	2	2.2	.986	T. Stallard	43	133	2	7	2	4.88
	CF	G. Geiger	499	.232	18	64	324	12	4	1	2.5	.988	M. Fornieles	57	119	9	8	15	4.68
	LF	Yastrzemski	583	.266	11	80	248	12	10	1	1.8	.963	B. Muffett	38	113	3	11	5	5.67
	C	J. Pagliaroni	376	.242	16	58	586	39	**10**	5	5.9	.984	A. Earley	33	50	2	4	7	3.99
	1B	V. Wertz	317	.262	11	60	664	67	7	65	8.6	.991							
	OF	C. Hardy	281	.263	3	36	142	7	6	3	2.0	.961							
	C	R. Nixon	242	.289	1	19	330	24	9	2	5.5	.975							
	SS	P. Green	219	.260	6	27	84	166	16	35	4.7	.940							
Min. W-70 L-90 Cookie Lavagetto W-29 L-45 Sam Mele W-41 L-45	1B	H. Killebrew	541	.288	46	122	972	67	14	91	8.8	.987	P. Ramos	42	264	11	**20**	2	3.95
	2B	B. Martin	374	.246	6	36	217	224	17	61	4.4	.963	C. Pascual	35	252	15	16	0	3.46
	SS	Z. Versalles	510	.280	7	53	229	371	30	74	4.9	.952	J. Kralick	33	242	13	11	0	3.61
	3B	B. Tuttle	370	.246	5	38	66	165	14	15	2.9	.943	J. Kaat	36	201	9	17	0	3.90
	RF	B. Allison	556	.245	29	105	300	14	8	3	2.1	.975	D. Lee	37	115	3	6	3	3.52
	CF	L. Green	600	.285	9	50	356	3	8	0	2.4	.978	R. Moore	46	56	4	4	14	3.67
	LF	J. Lemon	423	.258	14	52	182	7	12	0	1.7	.940							
	C	E. Battey	460	.302	17	55	**812**	**60**	6	**9**	**6.7**	.993							
L. A. W-70 L-91 Billy Rigney	1B	S. Bilko	294	.279	20	59	577	61	7	56	7.5	.989	K. McBride	38	242	12	15	1	3.65
	2B	K. Aspromonte	238	.223	2	14	156	196	11	55	5.9	.970	E. Grba	40	212	11	13	2	4.25
	SS	J. Koppe	338	.251	5	40	127	250	21	51	4.5	.947	T. Bowsfield	41	157	11	8	0	3.73
	3B	E. Yost	213	.202	3	15	57	103	6	4	2.5	.964	R. Moeller	33	113	4	8	0	5.83
	RF	A. Pearson	427	.288	7	41	233	7	11	2	2.2	.954	R. Kline	26	105	3	6	1	4.90
	CF	K. Hunt	479	.255	25	84	261	6	**14**	1	2.1	.950	J. Donohue	38	100	4	6	5	4.31
	LF	L. Wagner	453	.280	28	79	187	12	6	2	1.8	.971	R. Duren	40	99	6	12	2	5.18
	C	E. Averill	323	.266	21	59	542	38	5	6	6.6	.991	T. Morgan	59	92	8	2	10	2.36
	OF	L. Thomas	450	.284	24	70	159	9	6	1	2.0	.966	A. Fowler	53	89	5	8	11	3.64
	O3	G. Thomas	282	.280	13	59	96	63	13	5		.924							
	1B	T. Kluszewski	263	.243	15	39	520	28	6	51	8.4	.989							
	2S	R. Bridges	229	.240	2	15	145	196	6	35		.983							
	3B	G. Leek	199	.226	5	20	54	127	8	11	3.9	.958							
	2B	B. Moran	173	.260	2	22	108	116	8	31	4.5	.966							
	C	E. Sadowski	164	.232	4	12	295	17	4	4	5.6	.987							
K. C. W-61 L-100 Joe Gordon W-26 L-43 Hank Bauer W-35 L-57	1B	N. Siebern	560	.296	18	98	907	76	11	88	9.1	.989	J. Archer	39	205	9	15	5	3.20
	2B	J. Lumpe	569	.293	3	54	403	426	18	105	**5.8**	.979	N. Bass	40	171	11	11	0	4.69
	SS	D. Howser	611	.280	3	45	**299**	427	**38**	85	4.9	.950	J. Walker	36	168	8	14	2	4.82
	3B	W. Causey	312	.276	8	49	102	193	14	20	3.5	.955	B. Shaw	26	150	9	10	0	4.31
	RF	D. Johnson	283	.216	8	42	104	6	6	0	2.0	.948	J. Nuxhall	37	128	5	8	1	5.34
	CF	B. Del Greco	239	.230	5	21	168	8	3	2	2.5	.983	E. Rakow	45	125	2	8	1	4.76
	LF	L. Posada	344	.253	7	53	205	8	6	0	2.1	.973	B. Kunkel	58	89	3	4	5	5.18
	C	H. Sullivan	331	.242	6	40	387	32	7	7	4.8	.984	B. Daley	16	64	4	8	1	4.95
	C	J. Pignatano	243	.243	4	22	379	35	9	7	5.1	.979							
	OF	G. Stephens	183	.208	4	26	114	6	4	4*	2.3	.968							
	OF	J. Hankins	173	.185	3	6	97	1	3	0	1.6	.970							
	1B	Throneberry	130	.238	6	24	241	25	1	31	8.9	.996							
Was. W-61 L-100 Mickey Vernon	1B	D. Long	377	.249	17	49	827	62	**15**	87	9.5	.983	J. McClain	33	212	8	18	1	3.86
	2B	C. Cottier	337	.234	2	34	233	316	10	73	5.6	.982	B. Daniels	32	212	12	11	0	3.44
	SS	C. Veal	218	.202	0	8	130	172	8	43	4.9	.974	D. Donovan	23	169	10	10	0	**2.40**
	3B	D. O'Connell	493	.260	1	37	75	173	16	14	3.6	.939	M. Kutyna	50	143	6	8	3	3.97
	RF	M. Keough	390	.249	9	34	213	7	5	2	2.3	.978	E. Hobaugh	26	126	7	9	0	4.42
	CF	W. Tasby	494	.251	17	63	332	5	5	0	2.5	.983	P. Burnside	33	113	4	9	2	4.53
	LF	C. Hinton	339	.260	6	34	175	6	7	4	2.0	.963	J. Gabler	29	93	3	8	4	4.86
	C	G. Green	364	.280	18	62	326	22	5	3	4.5	.986	D. Sisler	45	60	2	8	11	4.18
	OF	G. Woodling	342	.313	10	57	154	8	2	0	1.8	.988							
	OF	J. King	263	.270	11	46	138	7	3	2	1.6	.980							
	3B	B. Klaus	251	.227	7	30	40	107	6	3	3.0	.961							
	SS	B. Johnson	224	.295	6	28	110	172	13	31	5.2	.956							
	C	P. Daley	203	.192	2	17	285	35	4	6	4.5	.988							
	3B	H. Bright	183	.240	4	21	47	95	11	14	3.8	.928							
	1B	B. Zipfel	170	.200	4	18	429	25	8	40	10.5	.983							

BATTING AND BASE RUNNING LEADERS

Batting Average		Slugging Average	
N. Cash, DET	.361	M. Mantle, NY	.687
A. Kaline, DET	.324	N. Cash, DET	.662
J. Piersall, CLE	.322	J. Gentile, BAL	.646
M. Mantle, NY	.317	R. Maris, NY	.620
J. Gentile, BAL	.302	H. Killebrew, MIN	.606

Home Runs		Total Bases	
R. Maris, NY	61	R. Maris, NY	366
M. Mantle, NY	54	N. Cash, DET	354
J. Gentile, BAL	46	M. Mantle, NY	353
H. Killebrew, MIN	46	R. Colavito, DET	338
R. Colavito, DET	45	H. Killebrew, MIN	328

PITCHING LEADERS

Winning Percentage		Earned Run Average	
W. Ford, NY	.862	D. Donovan, WAS	2.40
R. Terry, NY	.842	B. Stafford, NY	2.68
L. Arroyo, NY	.750	D. Mossi, DET	2.96
F. Lary, DET	.719	M. Pappas, BAL	3.04
D. Mossi, DET	.682	J. Pizarro, CHI	3.05
D. Schwall, BOS	.682		

Wins		Saves	
W. Ford, NY	25	L. Arroyo, NY	29
F. Lary, DET	23	H. Wilhelm, BAL	18
S. Barber, BAL	18	M. Fornieles, BOS	15
J. Bunning, DET	17	R. Moore, MIN	14
R. Terry, NY	16	T. Fox, DET	12

BATTING AND BASE RUNNING LEADERS

Runs Batted In

R. Maris, NY	142
J. Gentile, BAL	141
R. Colavito, DET	140
N. Cash, DET	132
M. Mantle, NY	128

Hits

N. Cash, DET	193
B. Robinson, BAL	192
A. Kaline, DET	190

Home Run Percentage

M. Mantle, NY	10.5
R. Maris, NY	10.3
J. Gentile, BAL	9.5

Doubles

A. Kaline, DET	41
T. Kubek, NY	38
B. Robinson, BAL	38

Stolen Bases

L. Aparicio, CHI	53
D. Howser, KC	37
J. Wood, DET	30
C. Hinton, WAS	22
B. Bruton, DET	22

Base on Balls

M. Mantle, NY	126
N. Cash, DET	124
R. Colavito, DET	113

Runs Scored

M. Mantle, NY	132
R. Maris, NY	132
R. Colavito, DET	129

Triples

J. Wood, DET	14
M. Keough, WAS	9
J. Lumpe, KC	9

PITCHING LEADERS

Strikeouts

C. Pascual, MIN	221
W. Ford, NY	209
J. Bunning, DET	194
J. Pizarro, CHI	188
K. McBride, LA	180

Fewest Hits per 9 Innings

C. Estrada, BAL	6.75
M. Pappas, BAL	6.79
S. Barber, BAL	7.03

Fewest Walks per 9 Innings

D. Mossi, DET	1.76
H. Brown, BAL	1.78
D. Donovan, WAS	1.87

Innings

W. Ford, NY	283
F. Lary, DET	275
J. Bunning, DET	268

Complete Games

F. Lary, DET	22
C. Pascual, MIN	15
S. Barber, BAL	14

Shutouts

C. Pascual, MIN	8
S. Barber, BAL	8

Most Strikeouts per 9 Inn.

J. Pizarro, CHI	8.69
C. Pascual, MIN	7.88
C. Estrada, BAL	6.79

Games Pitched

L. Arroyo, NY	65
T. Lown, CHI	59
T. Morgan, LA	59

	W	L	PCT	GB	R	OR	2B	3B	HR	BA	SA	SB	E	DP	FA	CG	BB	SO	ShO	SV	ERA
NY	109	53	.673		827	612	194	40	**240**	.263	**.442**	28	**124**	180	**.980**	47	542	866	14	**39**	3.46
DET	101	61	.623	8	**841**	671	215	**53**	180	**.266**	.421	98	146	147	.976	**62**	**469**	836	12	30	3.55
BAL	95	67	.586	14	691	**588**	227	36	149	.254	.390	39	128	173	.980	54	617	926	21	33	**3.22**
CHI	86	76	.531	23	765	726	216	46	138	.265	.395	**100**	128	138	.980	39	498	814	3	33	4.06
CLE	78	83	.484	30.5	737	752	**257**	39	150	.266	.406	34	139	142	.977	35	599	801	12	23	4.15
BOS	76	86	.469	33	729	792	251	37	112	.254	.374	56	144	170	.977	35	679	831	6	30	4.29
MIN	70	90	.438	38	707	778	215	40	167	.250	.397	47	174	150	.971	49	570	914	14	23	4.28
LA	70	91	.435	38.5	744	784	218	22	189	.245	.398	37	192	154	.969	25	713	**973**	5	34	4.31
KC	61	100	.379	47.5	683	863	216	47	90	.247	.354	58	175	160	.972	32	629	703	5	23	4.74
WAS	61	100	.379	47.5	618	776	217	44	119	.244	.367	81	156	171	.975	39	586	666	8	21	4.23
					7342	7342	2226	404	1534	.256	.395	578	1506	1585	.976	417	5902	8330	100	289	4.02

National League 1962

	POS	Player	AB	BA	HR	RBI	PO	A	E	DP	TC/G	FA	Pitcher	G	IP	W	L	SV	ERA
S. F. W-103 L-62 Alvin Dark	1B	O. Cepeda	625	.306	35	114	1353	88	13	125	9.1	.991	B. O'Dell	43	281	19	14	0	3.53
	2B	C. Hiller	602	.276	3	48	367	417	**29**	105	5.0	.964	J. Sanford	39	265	24	7	0	3.43
	SS	J. Pagan	580	.259	7	57	286	461	21	84	4.7	**.973**	J. Marichal	37	263	18	11	1	3.36
	3B	J. Davenport	485	.297	14	58	125	256	19	28	2.8	.953	B. Pierce	30	162	16	6	1	3.49
	RF	F. Alou	561	.316	25	98	262	7	8	3	1.8	.971	S. Miller	59	107	5	8	19	4.12
	CF	W. Mays	621	.304	**49**	141	**429**	6	4	1	**2.7**	.991	M. McCormick	28	99	5	5	0	5.38
	LF	H. Kuenn	487	.304	10	68	160	3	5	1	1.6	.970	B. Bolin	41	92	7	3	5	3.62
	C	T. Haller	272	.261	18	55	472	38	4	6	5.6	.992	D. Larsen	49	86	5	4	11	4.38
	C	E. Bailey	254	.232	17	45	419	25	6	3	6.0	.987							
	OF	W. McCovey	229	.293	20	54	81	2	2	1	1.5	.976							
	OF	M. Alou	195	.292	3	14	80	3	2	0	1.5	.976							
L. A. W-102 L-63 Walter Alston	1B	R. Fairly	460	.278	14	71	968	43	11	76	8.5	.989	D. Drysdale	43	**314**	**25**	9	1	2.83
	2B	L. Burright	249	.205	4	30	176	206	15	35	3.6	.962	J. Podres	40	255	15	13	0	3.81
	SS	M. Wills	**695**	.299	6	48	295	493	36	86	5.0	.956	S. Williams	40	186	14	12	1	4.46
	3B	J. Gilliam	588	.270	4	43	51	126	11	12	2.1	.941	S. Koufax	28	184	14	7	1	**2.54**
	RF	F. Howard	493	.296	31	119	187	19	6	4	1.6	.972	E. Roebuck	64	119	10	2	9	3.09
	CF	W. Davis	600	.285	21	85	379	13	15	0	2.6	.963	R. Perranoski	**70**	107	6	6	20	2.85
	LF	T. Davis	665	**.346**	27	**153**	240	9	10	0	1.8	.961	L. Sherry	58	90	7	3	11	3.20
	C	J. Roseboro	389	.249	7	55	**842**	57	14	10	**7.1**	.985	J. Moeller	19	86	6	5	1	5.25
	O1	W. Moon	244	.242	4	31	300	20	7	29		.979							
	OF	D. Snider	158	.278	5	30	56	3	2	0	1.6	.967							
	C	D. Camilli	88	.284	4	22	162	8	3	1	4.4	.983							

	POS	Player	AB	BA	HR	RBI	PO	A	E	DP	TC/G	FA	Pitcher	G	IP	W	L	SV	ERA
Cin. W-98 L-64 Fred Hutchinson	1B	G. Coleman	476	.277	28	86	1021	83	12	100	8.7	.989	B. Purkey	37	288	23	5	0	2.81
	2B	D. Blasingame	494	.281	2	35	334	352	17	66	5.1	.976	J. Jay	39	273	21	14	0	3.76
	SS	L. Cardenas	589	.294	10	60	273	443	21	84	4.9	.972	J. O'Toole	36	252	16	13	0	3.50
	3B	E. Kasko	533	.278	4	41	101	204	19	18	2.8	.941	J. Maloney	22	115	9	7	1	3.51
	RF	F. Robinson	609	.342	39	136	315	10	2	2	2.0	.994	J. Klippstein	40	109	7	6	4	4.47
	CF	V. Pinson	619	.292	23	100	344	13	4	1	2.4	.989	J. Brosnan	48	65	4	4	13	3.34
	LF	W. Post	285	.263	17	62	110	5	8	0	1.4	.935	B. Henry	40	37	4	2	11	4.58
	C	J. Edwards	452	.254	8	50	807	92	12	11	7.0	.987							
	OF	J. Lynch	288	.281	12	57	89	7	3	1	1.4	.970							
	OF	M. Keough	230	.278	7	27	88	2	3	1	1.3	.968							
	3B	D. Zimmer	192	.250	2	16	45	66	6	6	2.7	.949							
	C	H. Foiles	131	.275	7	25	249	14	5	1	6.5	.981							
Pit. W-93 L-68 Danny Murtaugh	1B	D. Stuart	394	.228	16	64	868	78	17	98	9.5	.982	B. Friend	39	262	18	14	1	3.06
	2B	B. Mazeroski	572	.271	14	81	425	509	14	138	6.0	.985	A. McBean	33	190	15	10	0	3.70
	SS	D. Groat	678	.294	2	61	314	521	38	126	5.4	.956	E. Francis	36	176	9	8	0	3.07
	3B	D. Hoak	411	.241	5	48	93	220	10	19	2.8	.969	H. Haddix	28	141	9	6	0	4.20
	RF	R. Clemente	538	.312	10	74	269	19	8	1	2.1	.973	V. Law	23	139	10	7	0	3.94
	CF	B. Virdon	663	.247	6	47	360	11	9	0	2.4	.976	T. Sturdivant	49	125	9	5	2	3.73
	LF	B. Skinner	510	.302	20	75	210	6	9	0	1.6	.960	R. Face	63	91	8	7	28	1.88
	C	S. Burgess	360	.328	13	61	550	45	7	5	6.0	.988	D. Olivo	62	84	5	1	7	2.77
	1B	D. Clendenon	222	.302	7	28	382	24	4	44	7.9	.990							
Mil. W-86 L-76 Birdie Tebbetts	1B	J. Adcock	391	.248	29	78	907	57	3	72	8.6	.997	W. Spahn	34	269	18	14	0	3.04
	2B	F. Bolling	406	.271	9	43	252	298	6	70	4.7	.989	B. Shaw	38	225	15	9	2	2.80
	SS	R. McMillan	468	.246	12	41	243	424	19	85	5.1	.972	B. Hendley	35	200	11	13	1	3.60
	3B	E. Mathews	536	.265	29	90	141	283	16	22	3.1	.964	L. Burdette	37	144	10	9	2	4.89
	RF	M. Jones	333	.255	10	36	142	3	4	0	1.6	.973	T. Cloninger	24	111	8	3	0	4.30
	CF	H. Aaron	592	.323	45	128	340	11	7	1	2.3	.980	C. Raymond	26	43	5	5	10	2.74
	LF	L. Maye	349	.244	10	41	209	2	5	1	2.3	.977							
	C	D. Crandall	350	.297	8	45	460	54	3	7	5.7	.994							
	1B	T. Aaron	334	.231	8	38	507	45	6	55	5.1	.989							
	C	J. Torre	220	.282	5	26	325	39	5	4	5.9	.986							
	OF	G. Bell	214	.285	5	24	75	3	1	0	1.4	.987							
	S2	A. Samuel	209	.206	3	20	81	155	10	29		.959							
St. L. W-84 L-78 Johnny Keane	1B	B. White	614	.324	20	102	1221	94	9	114	9.1	.993	L. Jackson	36	252	16	11	0	3.75
	2B	J. Javier	598	.263	7	39	344	414	18	96	5.1	.977	B. Gibson	32	234	15	13	1	2.85
	SS	J. Gotay	369	.255	2	27	179	339	24	65	4.5	.956	E. Broglio	34	222	12	9	0	3.00
	3B	K. Boyer	611	.291	24	98	158	318	22	34	3.1	.956	R. Washburn	34	176	12	9	0	4.10
	RF	C. James	388	.276	8	59	156	7	2	1	1.4	.988	C. Simmons	31	154	10	10	0	3.51
	CF	C. Flood	635	.296	12	70	387	12	4	5	2.7	.990	L. McDaniel	55	107	3	10	14	4.12
	LF	S. Musial	433	.330	19	82	164	6	4	1	1.5	.977	R. Sadecki	22	102	6	8	1	5.54
	C	G. Oliver	345	.258	14	45	494	46	5	7	5.6	.991	B. Shantz	28	58	5	3	4	2.18
	C	C. Sawatski	222	.252	13	42	354	24	1	4	5.4	.997							
	SS	D. Maxvill	189	.222	1	18	111	169	11	41	3.8	.962							
	1B	F. Whitfield	158	.266	8	34	282	25	4	32	8.2	.987							
Phi. W-81 L-80 Gene Mauch	1B	R. Sievers	477	.262	21	80	975	93	10	102	8.3	.991	A. Mahaffey	41	274	19	14	0	3.94
	2B	T. Taylor	625	.259	7	43	372	385	22	101	5.2	.972	J. Hamilton	41	182	9	12	2	5.09
	SS	B. Wine	311	.244	4	25	140	237	8	51	4.3	.979	D. Bennett	31	175	9	9	3	3.81
	3B	D. Demeter	550	.307	29	107	91	177	18	18	2.7	.937	C. McLish	32	155	11	5	1	4.25
	RF	J. Callison	603	.300	23	83	327	24	7	7	2.4	.980	C. Short	47	142	11	9	3	3.42
	CF	T. Gonzalez	437	.302	20	63	268	8	0	2	2.4	**1.000**	D. Green	37	129	6	6	1	3.83
	LF	T. Savage	335	.266	7	39	185	4	5	1	1.8	.974	J. Baldschun	67	113	12	7	13	2.96
	C	C. Dalrymple	370	.276	11	54	635	61	9	11	5.9	.987							
	OF	W. Covington	304	.283	9	44	98	3	6	2	1.2	.944							
	UT	B. Klaus	248	.206	4	20	93	142	9	21		.963							
	SS	R. Amaro	226	.243	0	19	143	224	12	50	4.9	.968							
	1B	F. Torre	168	.310	0	20	347	37	8	40	5.2	.980							
Hou. W-64 L-96 Harry Craft	1B	N. Larker	506	.263	9	63	1148	103	11	103	9.3	.991	D. Farrell	43	242	10	20	4	3.02
	2B	J. Amalfitano	380	.237	1	27	230	268	13	72	4.7	.967	K. Johnson	33	197	7	16	0	3.84
	SS	B. Lillis	457	.249	1	30	169	290	13	54	4.8	.972	B. Bruce	32	175	10	9	0	4.06
	3B	B. Aspromonte	534	.266	11	59	150	233	13	21	2.8	.967	J. Golden	37	153	7	11	1	4.07
	RF	R. Mejias	566	.286	24	76	217	10	13	2	1.7	.946	H. Woodeshick	31	139	5	16	0	4.39
	CF	C. Warwick	477	.260	16	60	262	12	4	1	2.2	.986	D. McMahon	51	77	5	5	8	1.53
	LF	A. Spangler	418	.285	5	35	183	7	8	2	1.6	.960	R. Kemmerer	36	68	5	3	3	4.10
	C	H. Smith	345	.235	12	35	570	65	9	9	7.0	.986							
	OF	J. Pendleton	321	.246	8	36	126	4	5	0	1.5	.963							
	C	M. Ranew	218	.234	4	24	357	35	8	1	6.9	.980							
Chi. W-59 L-103 El Tappe W-4 L-16 Lou Klein W-12 L-18 Charlie Metro W-43 L-69	1B	E. Banks	610	.269	37	104	**1458**	106	11	134	10.6	.993	B. Buhl	34	212	12	13	0	3.69
	2B	K. Hubbs	661	.260	5	49	363	489	15	103	5.5	.983	D. Ellsworth	37	209	9	20	1	5.09
	SS	A. Rodgers	461	.278	5	44	239	433	28	91	5.3	.960	D. Cardwell	41	196	7	16	4	4.92
	3B	R. Santo	604	.227	17	83	161	332	23	33	3.3	.955	C. Koonce	35	191	10	10	4	3.97
	RF	G. Altman	534	.318	22	74	234	8	7	3	1.9	.973	G. Hobbie	42	162	5	14	0	5.22
	CF	L. Brock	434	.263	9	35	243	7	9	2	2.4	.965	B. Anderson	57	108	2	7	5	5.02
	LF	B. Williams	618	.298	12	91	273	18	10	4	1.9	.967	B. Schultz	51	78	5	5	5	3.82
	C	D. Bertell	215	.302	2	18	306	36	5	0	4.6	.986	D. Elston	57	66	4	8	8	2.44
	OF	D. Landrum	238	.282	1	15	122	3	4	3	2.2	.969							

POS	Player	AB	BA	HR	RBI	PO	A	E	DP	TC/G	FA	Pitcher	G	IP	W	L	SV	ERA
1B	Throneberry	357	.244	16	49	785	77	17	87	9.1	.981	R. Craig	42	233	10	24	3	4.51
2B	C. Neal	508	.260	11	58	187	240	13	54	5.2	.970	A. Jackson	36	231	8	20	0	4.40
SS	E. Chacon	368	.236	2	27	204	332	22	64	5.1	.961	J. Hook	37	214	8	19	0	4.84
3B	F. Mantilla	466	.275	11	59	76	179	14	22	2.8	.948	B. Miller	33	144	1	12	1	4.89
RF	R. Ashburn	389	.306	7	28	187	9	5	1	2.1	.975	C. Anderson	50	131	3	17	4	5.35
CF	J. Hickman	392	.245	13	46	265	7	8	0	2.3	.971	B. Moorhead	38	105	0	2	0	4.53
LF	F. Thomas	571	.266	34	94	216	14	9	0	1.9	.962	MacKenzie	42	80	5	4	1	4.95
C	C. Cannizzaro	133	.241	0	9	218	34	7	3	4.6	.973							
UT	R. Kanehl	351	.248	4	27	235	230	32	57		.936							
OF	Christopher	271	.244	6	32	133	5	4	4	1.5	.972							
OF	G. Woodling	190	.274	5	24	68	0	1	0	1.4	.986							
C	S. Taylor	158	.222	3	20	202	25	2	3	4.6	.991							

N. Y.
W-40 L-120
Casey Stengel

BATTING AND BASE RUNNING LEADERS

Batting Average
T. Davis, LA	.346
F. Robinson, CIN	.342
S. Musial, STL	.330
B. White, STL	.324
H. Aaron, MIL	.323

Slugging Average
F. Robinson, CIN	.624
H. Aaron, MIL	.618
W. Mays, SF	.615
F. Howard, LA	.560
T. Davis, LA	.535

Home Runs
W. Mays, SF	49
H. Aaron, MIL	45
F. Robinson, CIN	39
E. Banks, CHI	37
O. Cepeda, SF	35

Total Bases
W. Mays, SF	382
F. Robinson, CIN	380
H. Aaron, MIL	366
T. Davis, LA	356
O. Cepeda, SF	324

Runs Batted In
T. Davis, LA	153
W. Mays, SF	141
F. Robinson, CIN	136
H. Aaron, MIL	128
F. Howard, LA	119

Stolen Bases
M. Wills, LA	104
W. Davis, LA	32
J. Javier, STL	26
V. Pinson, CIN	26
T. Taylor, PHI	20

Hits
T. Davis, LA	230
F. Robinson, CIN	208
M. Wills, LA	208

Base on Balls
E. Mathews, MIL	101
J. Gilliam, LA	93
R. Ashburn, NY	81
W. Mays, SF	78

Home Run Percentage
W. Mays, SF	7.9
H. Aaron, MIL	7.6
F. Robinson, CIN	6.4

Runs Scored
F. Robinson, CIN	134
W. Mays, SF	130
M. Wills, LA	130

Doubles
F. Robinson, CIN	51
W. Mays, SF	36
D. Groat, PIT	34

Triples
W. Davis, LA	10
J. Callison, PHI	10
B. Virdon, PIT	10
M. Wills, LA	10

PITCHING LEADERS

Winning Percentage
B. Purkey, CIN	.821
J. Sanford, SF	.774
D. Drysdale, LA	.735
B. Pierce, SF	.727
B. Shaw, MIL	.625

Earned Run Average
S. Koufax, LA	2.54
B. Shaw, MIL	2.80
B. Purkey, CIN	2.81
D. Drysdale, LA	2.83
B. Gibson, STL	2.85

Wins
D. Drysdale, LA	25
J. Sanford, SF	24
B. Purkey, CIN	23
J. Jay, CIN	21
A. Mahaffey, PHI	19
B. O'Dell, SF	19

Saves
R. Face, PIT	28
R. Perranoski, LA	20
S. Miller, SF	19
L. McDaniel, STL	14
J. Baldschun, PHI	13
J. Brosnan, CIN	13

Strikeouts
D. Drysdale, LA	232
S. Koufax, LA	216
B. Gibson, STL	208
D. Farrell, HOU	203
B. O'Dell, SF	195

Complete Games
W. Spahn, MIL	22
A. Mahaffey, PHI	20
B. O'Dell, SF	20
D. Drysdale, LA	19
J. Marichal, SF	18
B. Purkey, CIN	18

Fewest Hits per 9 Innings
S. Koufax, LA	6.54
B. Gibson, STL	6.70
D. Bennett, PHI	7.42

Shutouts
| B. Gibson, STL | 5 |
| B. Friend, PIT | 5 |

Fewest Walks per 9 Innings
B. Shaw, MIL	1.76
B. Friend, PIT	1.82
W. Spahn, MIL	1.84

Most Strikeouts per 9 Inn.
S. Koufax, LA	10.55
K. Johnson, HOU	8.13
B. Gibson, STL	8.01

Innings
D. Drysdale, LA	314
B. Purkey, CIN	288
B. O'Dell, SF	281

Games Pitched
R. Perranoski, LA	70
J. Baldschun, PHI	67
E. Roebuck, LA	64

	W	L	PCT	GB	R	OR	Batting					SB	Fielding			CG	BB	Pitching			
							2B	3B	HR	BA	SA		E	DP	FA			SO	ShO	SV	ERA
SF *	103	62	.624	—	**878**	690	235	32	**204**	**.278**	**.441**	73	142	153	.977	**62**	503	886	10	39	3.79
LA	102	63	.618	1	842	697	192	**65**	140	.268	.400	**198**	193	144	.970	44	588	**1104**	8	**46**	3.62
CIN	98	64	.605	3.5	802	685	**252**	40	167	.270	.417	66	145	144	.977	51	567	964	13	35	3.75
PIT	93	68	.578	8	706	**626**	240	**65**	108	.268	.394	50	152	**177**	.976	40	466	897	13	41	**3.37**
MIL	86	76	.531	15.5	730	665	204	38	181	.252	.403	57	**124**	154	**.980**	59	**407**	802	10	24	3.68
STL	84	78	.519	17.5	774	664	221	31	137	.271	.394	86	132	170	.979	53	517	914	**17**	25	3.55
PHI	81	80	.503	20	705	759	199	39	142	.260	.390	79	138	167	.977	43	574	863	7	24	4.28
HOU	64	96	.400	36.5	592	717	170	47	105	.246	.351	42	173	149	.973	34	471	1047	9	19	3.83
CHI	59	103	.364	42.5	632	827	196	56	126	.253	.377	78	146	171	.977	29	601	783	4	26	4.54
NY	40	120	.250	60.5	617	948	166	40	139	.240	.361	59	210	167	.967	43	571	772	4	10	5.04
					7278	7278	2075	453	1449	.261	.393	788	1555	1596	.975	458	5265	9032	95	289	3.94

* Defeated Los Angeles in a playoff 2 games to 1.

	POS	Player	AB	BA	HR	RBI	PO	A	E	DP	TC/G	FA	Pitcher	G	IP	W	L	SV	ERA
N. Y. W-96 L-66 Ralph Houk	1B	B. Skowron	478	.270	23	80	1054	77	10	101	8.5	.991	R. Terry	43	299	23	12	2	3.19
	2B	B. Richardson	692	.302	8	59	378	452	15	116	5.2	.982	W. Ford	38	258	17	8	0	2.90
	SS	T. Tresh	622	.286	20	93	201	312	16	51	4.8	.970	B. Stafford	35	213	14	9	0	3.67
	3B	C. Boyer	566	.272	18	68	187	396	22	41	3.9	.964	J. Bouton	36	133	7	7	2	3.99
	RF	R. Maris	590	.256	33	100	316	4	3	0	2.1	.991	R. Sheldon	34	118	7	8	1	5.49
	CF	M. Mantle	377	.321	30	89	214	4	5	1	1.9	.978	J. Coates	50	118	7	6	6	4.44
	LF	H. Lopez	335	.275	6	48	176	3	3	0	2.2	.984	B. Daley	43	105	7	5	4	3.59
	C	E. Howard	494	.279	21	91	713	44	4	12	5.9	.995	M. Bridges	52	72	8	4	18	3.14
	OF	J. Blanchard	246	.232	13	39	76	2	1	0	1.7	.987	L. Arroyo	27	34	1	3	7	4.81
	CO	Y. Berra	232	.224	10	35	238	17	6	6		.977							
	SS	T. Kubek	169	.314	4	17	71	117	9	27	5.6	.954							
Min. W-91 L-71 Sam Mele	1B	V. Power	611	.290	16	63	1193	134	10	133	9.4	.993	J. Kaat	39	269	18	14	1	3.14
	2B	B. Allen	573	.269	12	64	357	394	13	109	4.8	.983	C. Pascual	34	258	20	11	0	3.32
	SS	Z. Versalles	568	.241	17	67	335	501	26	127	5.4	.970	J. Kralick	39	243	12	11	0	3.86
	3B	R. Rollins	624	.298	16	96	137	324	28	33	3.1	.943	D. Stigman	40	143	12	5	3	3.66
	RF	B. Allison	519	.266	29	102	287	10	7	1	2.1	.977	J. Bonikowski	30	100	5	7	2	3.88
	CF	J. Green	619	.271	14	63	361	8	2	2	2.4	.995	L. Stange	44	95	4	3	4	4.45
	LF	H. Killebrew	552	.243	48	126	227	5	8	0	1.6	.967	R. Moore	49	65	8	3	9	4.73
	C	E. Battey	522	.280	11	57	872	82	9	9	6.6	.991	B. Pleis	21	45	2	5	3	4.40
	1B	D. Mincher	121	.240	9	29	211	13	5	17	9.2	.978	F. Sullivan	21	33	4	1	5	3.24
L. A. W-86 L-76 Billy Rigney	1B	L. Thomas	583	.290	26	104	735	42	14	66	8.8	.982	D. Chance	50	207	14	10	8	2.96
	2B	B. Moran	659	.282	17	74	422	477	13	103	5.7	.986	B. Belinsky	33	187	10	11	1	3.56
	SS	J. Koppe	375	.227	4	40	197	356	25	63	4.9	.957	E. Grba	40	176	8	9	1	4.54
	3B	F. Torres	451	.259	11	74	110	250	24	20	3.1	.938	D. Lee	27	153	8	8	2	3.11
	RF	G. Thomas	181	.238	4	12	107	4	5	1	2.3	.957	K. McBride	24	149	11	5	0	3.50
	CF	A. Pearson	614	.261	5	42	366	8	4	0	2.4	.989	T. Bowsfield	34	139	9	8	1	4.40
	LF	L. Wagner	612	.268	37	107	269	7	8	1	1.8	.972	A. Fowler	48	77	4	3	5	2.81
	C	B. Rodgers	565	.258	6	61	826	73	10	14	6.1	.989	R. Duren	42	71	2	9	8	4.42
	OF	E. Averill	187	.219	4	22	70	2	0	0	1.5	1.000	J. Spring	57	65	4	2	6	4.02
	SS	J. Fregosi	175	.291	3	23	96	150	15	35	5.0	.943	T. Morgan	48	59	5	2	9	2.91
	1B	S. Bilko	164	.287	8	38	371	28	2	36	8.0	.995	D. Osinski	33	54	6	4	4	2.82
Det. W-85 L-76 Bob Scheffing	1B	N. Cash	507	.243	39	89	1081	116	10	94	8.3	.992	J. Bunning	41	258	19	10	6	3.59
	2B	J. Wood	367	.226	8	30	185	197	20	33	4.5	.950	H. Aguirre	42	216	16	8	3	2.21
	SS	C. Fernandez	503	.249	20	59	235	336	24	53	4.3	.960	D. Mossi	35	180	11	13	1	4.19
	3B	S. Boros	356	.228	16	47	105	151	19	15	2.6	.931	P. Regan	35	171	11	9	0	4.04
	RF	A. Kaline	398	.304	29	94	225	8	4	1	2.4	.983	P. Foytack	29	144	10	7	0	4.39
	CF	B. Bruton	561	.278	16	74	394	5	7	2	2.8	.983	R. Kline	36	77	3	6	2	4.31
	LF	R. Colavito	601	.273	37	112	359	10	3	1	2.3	.992	R. Nischwitz	48	65	4	5	4	3.90
	C	D. Brown	431	.241	12	40	742	42	5	8	6.0	.994	T. Fox	44	58	3	1	16	1.71
	UT	D. McAuliffe	471	.263	12	63	260	257	30	45		.945							
	OF	B. Morton	195	.262	4	17	110	4	1	1	1.9	.991							
Chi. W-85 L-77 Al Lopez	1B	J. Cunningham	526	.295	8	70	1282	90	8	118	9.7	.994	R. Herbert	35	237	20	9	0	3.27
	2B	N. Fox	621	.267	2	54	376	428	8	93	5.3	.990	J. Pizarro	36	203	12	14	1	3.81
	SS	L. Aparicio	581	.241	7	40	280	452	20	102	4.9	.973	E. Fisher	57	183	9	5	5	3.10
	3B	A. Smith	511	.292	16	82	76	185	18	8	2.7	.935	E. Wynn	27	168	7	15	0	4.46
	RF	Hershberger	427	.262	4	46	236	7	4	0	1.8	.984	J. Buzhardt	28	152	8	12	0	4.19
	CF	J. Landis	534	.228	15	61	360	2	2	1	2.5	.995	F. Baumann	40	120	7	6	4	3.38
	LF	F. Robinson	600	.312	11	109	278	13	8	2	1.9	.973	J. Horlen	20	109	7	6	0	4.89
	C	C. Carreon	313	.256	4	37	519	30	3	5	5.9	.995	D. Zanni	44	86	6	5	5	3.75
	C	S. Lollar	220	.268	2	26	298	23	3	0	4.9	.991	T. Lown	42	56	4	2	6	3.04
	OF	C. Maxwell	206	.296	9	43	100	2	1	1	1.8	.990							
	32	B. Sadowski	130	.231	6	24	33	62	2	9		.979							
Cle. W-80 L-82 Mel McGaha	1B	T. Francona	621	.272	14	70	1402	127	22	5	9.8	.986	D. Donovan	34	251	20	10	0	3.59
	2B	J. Kindall	530	.232	13	55	358	494	19	114	5.7	.978	P. Ramos	37	201	10	12	1	3.71
	SS	W. Held	466	.249	19	58	221	387	27	101	4.7	.956	J. Perry	35	194	12	12	0	4.14
	3B	B. Phillips	562	.258	10	54	175	243	10	16	3.0	.977	B. Latman	45	179	8	13	5	4.17
	RF	W. Kirkland	419	.200	21	72	233	11	7	0	2.0	.972	M. Grant	26	150	7	10	0	4.27
	CF	T. Cline	375	.248	2	28	238	3	2	1	2.3	.992	G. Bell	57	108	10	9	12	4.26
	LF	C. Essegian	336	.274	21	50	154	1	1	0	1.7	.994	S. McDowell	25	88	3	7	1	6.06
	C	J. Romano	459	.261	25	81	657	63	7	6	5.6	.990							
	OF	A. Luplow	318	.277	14	45	162	4	7	0		.960							
	OF	W. Tasby	199	.241	4	17	105	1	0	0	1.6	1.000							
	OF	D. Dillard	174	.230	5	14	54	1	2	0	1.1	.965							
	OF	G. Green	143	.280	11	28	51	2	2	1	1.7	.964							
Bal. W-77 L-85 Billy Hitchcock	1B	J. Gentile	545	.251	33	87	1214	121	16	121	9.0	.988	C. Estrada	34	223	9	17	0	3.83
	2B	M. Breeding	240	.246	2	18	146	196	8	47	4.8	.977	M. Pappas	35	205	12	10	0	4.03
	SS	J. Adair	538	.284	11	48	216	285	16	72	4.6	.969	R. Roberts	27	191	10	9	0	2.78
	3B	B. Robinson	634	.303	23	86	163	339	11	32	3.2	.979	J. Fisher	32	152	7	9	1	5.09
	RF	R. Snyder	416	.305	9	40	218	8	6	2	1.9	.974	S. Barber	28	140	9	6	0	3.46
	CF	J. Brandt	505	.255	19	75	310	9	8	2	2.4	.976	D. Hall	43	118	6	6	6	2.28
	LF	B. Powell	400	.243	15	53	184	1	6	0	1.7	.969	B. Hoeft	57	114	4	8	7	4.59
	C	G. Triandos	207	.159	6	23	355	28	6	2	6.2	.985	H. Wilhelm	52	93	7	10	15	1.94
	2B	J. Temple	270	.263	1	17	141	169	6	41	4.5	.981	H. Brown	22	86	6	4	1	4.10
	OF	W. Herzog	263	.266	7	35	132	4	3	0	2.0	.978							
	C	C. Lau	197	.294	6	37	269	15	1	1	5.1	.996							
	SS	R. Hansen	196	.173	3	17	114	159	10	37	4.4	.965							
	O1	D. Williams	178	.247	1	18	180	13	0	13		1.000							
	OF	D. Nicholson	173	.173	9	15	111	4	2	0	1.5	.983							
	C	H. Landrith	167	.222	4	17	289	34	6	5	5.5	.982							

POS	Player	AB	BA	HR	RBI	PO	A	E	DP	TC/G	FA	Pitcher	G	IP	W	L	SV	ERA
1B	P. Runnels	562	.326	10	60	1309	104	10	125	9.4	.993	G. Conley	34	242	15	14	1	3.95
2B	C. Schilling	413	.230	7	35	267	331	9	85	5.1	.985	Monbouquette	35	235	15	13	0	3.33
SS	E. Bressoud	599	.277	14	68	291	482	28	107	5.2	.965	E. Wilson	31	191	12	8	0	3.90
3B	F. Malzone	619	.283	21	95	154	313	16	32	3.1	.967	D. Schwall	33	182	9	15	0	4.94
RF	L. Clinton	398	.294	18	75	185	6	4	1	1.9	.979	D. Radatz	62	125	9	6	24	2.24
CF	G. Geiger	466	.249	16	54	287	8	4	1	2.3	.987	G. Cisco	23	83	4	7	0	6.72
LF	Yastrzemski	646	.296	19	94	329	15	11	3	2.2	.969	M. Fornieles	42	82	3	6	5	5.36
C	J. Pagliaroni	260	.258	11	37	411	33	6	4	6.2	.987	A. Earley	38	68	4	5	5	5.80
OF	C. Hardy	362	.215	8	36	205	7	2	1	2.0	.991							
C	B. Tillman	249	.229	14	38	389	19	7	1	6.3	.983							
2B	B. Gardner	199	.271	0	12	67	91	6	21	4.3	.963							

Bos.
W-76 L-84
Pinky Higgins

POS	Player	AB	BA	HR	RBI	PO	A	E	DP	TC/G	FA	Pitcher	G	IP	W	L	SV	ERA
1B	N. Siebern	600	.308	25	117	1405	127	10	122	9.5	.994	E. Rakow	42	235	14	17	1	4.25
2B	J. Lumpe	641	.301	10	83	343	435	11	97	5.1	.986	D. Pfister	41	196	4	14	1	4.54
SS	D. Howser	286	.238	6	34	138	191	13	37	4.8	.962	J. Walker	31	143	8	9	0	5.90
3B	E. Charles	535	.288	17	74	145	285	16	27	3.2	.964	B. Fischer	34	128	4	12	2	3.95
RF	G. Cimoli	550	.275	10	71	231	8	8	2	1.7	.968	J. Wyatt	59	125	10	7	11	4.46
CF	B. Del Greco	338	.254	9	38	245	9	4	0	2.1	.984	D. Segui	37	117	8	5	6	3.86
LF	M. Jimenez	479	.301	11	69	185	7	3	0	1.6	.985	D. Wickersham	30	110	11	4	1	4.17
C	H. Sullivan	274	.248	4	29	447	31	10	2	5.2	.980	O. Pena	13	90	6	4	0	3.01
OF	J. Tartabull	310	.277	0	22	185	6	5	0	2.3	.974	G. Jones	21	33	3	2	6	6.34
UT	W. Causey	305	.252	4	38	143	200	14	25		.961							
C	J. Azcue	223	.229	2	25	363	42	6	5	5.9	.985							
OF	G. Alusik	209	.273	11	35	87	3	3	0	1.9	.968							

K. C.
W-72 L-90
Hank Bauer

POS	Player	AB	BA	HR	RBI	PO	A	E	DP	TC/G	FA	Pitcher	G	IP	W	L	SV	ERA
1B	H. Bright	392	.273	17	67	800	70	10	83	8.9	.989	D. Stenhouse	34	197	11	12	0	3.65
2B	C. Cottier	443	.242	6	40	368	354	14	100	5.5	.981	D. Rudolph	37	176	8	10	0	3.62
SS	K. Hamlin	292	.253	3	22	126	210	13	47	4.0	.963	T. Cheney	37	173	7	9	1	3.17
3B	B. Johnson	466	.288	12	43	79	142	13	12	3.3	.944	B. Daniels	44	161	7	16	2	4.85
RF	J. King	333	.243	11	35	178	9	4	4	1.9	.979	C. Osteen	28	150	8	13	1	3.65
CF	J. Piersall	471	.244	4	31	308	5	1	0	2.4	.997	P. Burnside	40	150	5	11	2	4.45
LF	C. Hinton	542	.310	17	75	233	7	3	1	1.8	.988	S. Hamilton	41	107	3	8	2	3.77
C	K. Retzer	340	.285	8	37	488	44	8	5	5.5	.985	M. Kutyna	54	78	5	6	0	4.04
C	B. Schmidt	256	.242	10	31	342	40	1	3	4.4	.997	J. Hannan	42	68	2	4	4	3.31
32	D. O'Connell	236	.263	2	18	70	141	10	21		.955							
3B	J. Schaive	225	.253	6	29	42	105	5	7	3.1	.967							
OF	D. Lock	225	.253	12	37	144	2	4	0	2.2	.973							
1B	D. Long	191	.241	4	24	459	32	2	67	9.7	.996							
1O	B. Zipfel	184	.239	6	21	228	17	8	13		.968							
OF	J. Hicks	174	.224	6	14	74	1	3	1	1.9	.962							

Was.
W-60 L-101
Mickey Vernon

BATTING AND BASE RUNNING LEADERS

Batting Average

P. Runnels, BOS	.326
F. Robinson, CHI	.312
C. Hinton, WAS	.310
N. Siebern, KC	.308
B. Robinson, BAL	.303

Home Runs

H. Killebrew, MIN	48
N. Cash, DET	39
R. Colavito, DET	37
L. Wagner, LA	37
J. Gentile, BAL	33
R. Maris, NY	33

Runs Batted In

H. Killebrew, MIN	126
N. Siebern, KC	117
R. Colavito, DET	112
F. Robinson, CHI	109
L. Wagner, LA	107

Hits

B. Richardson, NY	209
J. Lumpe, KC	193
B. Robinson, BAL	192

Home Run Percentage

H. Killebrew, MIN	8.7
N. Cash, DET	7.7
R. Colavito, DET	6.2

Doubles

F. Robinson, CHI	45
Yastrzemski, BOS	43
E. Bressoud, BOS	40
B. Richardson, NY	38

Slugging Average

H. Killebrew, MIN	.545
R. Colavito, DET	.514
N. Cash, DET	.513
B. Allison, MIN	.511
L. Wagner, LA	.500

Total Bases

R. Colavito, DET	309
B. Robinson, BAL	308
L. Wagner, LA	306
Yastrzemski, BOS	303
H. Killebrew, MIN	301

Stolen Bases

L. Aparicio, CHI	31
C. Hinton, WAS	28
J. Wood, DET	24
E. Charles, KC	20

Base on Balls

M. Mantle, NY	122
N. Siebern, KC	110
H. Killebrew, MIN	106

Runs Scored

A. Pearson, LA	115
N. Siebern, KC	114
B. Allison, MIN	102

Triples

G. Cimoli, KC	15
L. Clinton, BOS	10
F. Robinson, CHI	10
J. Lumpe, KC	10

PITCHING LEADERS

Winning Percentage

R. Herbert, CHI	.690
W. Ford, NY	.680
D. Donovan, CLE	.667
H. Aguirre, DET	.667
R. Terry, NY	.657

Wins

R. Terry, NY	23
R. Herbert, CHI	20
D. Donovan, CLE	20
C. Pascual, MIN	20
J. Bunning, DET	19

Strikeouts

C. Pascual, MIN	206
J. Bunning, DET	184
R. Terry, NY	176
J. Pizarro, CHI	173
J. Kaat, MIN	173

Fewest Hits per 9 Innings

H. Aguirre, DET	6.75
T. Cheney, WAS	6.96
B. Belinsky, LA	7.16

Fewest Walks per 9 Innings

D. Donovan, CLE	1.69
R. Terry, NY	1.72
D. Mossi, DET	1.80

Innings

R. Terry, NY	299
J. Kaat, MIN	269
J. Bunning, DET	258

Earned Run Average

H. Aguirre, DET	2.21
R. Roberts, BAL	2.78
W. Ford, NY	2.90
D. Chance, LA	2.96
E. Fisher, CHI	3.10

Saves

D. Radatz, BOS	24
M. Bridges, NY	18
T. Fox, DET	16
H. Wilhelm, BAL	15
G. Bell, CLE	12

Complete Games

C. Pascual, MIN	18
D. Donovan, CLE	16
J. Kaat, MIN	16
R. Terry, NY	14
J. Bunning, DET	12
R. Herbert, CHI	12

Shutouts

C. Pascual, MIN	5
D. Donovan, CLE	5
J. Kaat, MIN	5

Most Strikeouts per 9 Inn.

J. Pizarro, CHI	7.66
T. Cheney, WAS	7.63
C. Pascual, MIN	7.20

Games Pitched

D. Radatz, BOS	62
J. Wyatt, KC	59

	W	L	PCT	GB	R	OR	2B	3B	HR	BA	SA	SB	E	DP	FA	CG	BB	SO	ShO	SV	ERA
NY	96	66	.593		817	680	240	29	199	.267	.426	42	131	151	.979	33	499	838	10	42	3.70
MIN	91	71	.562	5	798	713	215	39	185	.260	.412	33	129	173	.979	53	493	948	11	27	3.89
LA	86	76	.531	10	718	706	232	35	137	.250	.380	46	175	153	.972	23	616	858	15	47	3.70
DET	85	76	.528	10.5	758	692	191	36	209	.248	.411	69	156	114	.974	46	503	873	8	35	3.81
CHI	85	77	.525	11	707	658	250	56	92	.257	.372	76	110	153	.982	50	537	821	13	28	3.73
CLE	80	82	.494	16	682	745	202	22	180	.245	.388	35	139	168	.977	45	594	780	12	31	4.14
BAL	77	85	.475	19	652	680	225	34	156	.248	.387	45	122	152	.980	32	549	898	8	33	3.69
BOS	76	84	.475	19	707	756	257	53	146	.258	.403	39	131	152	.979	34	632	923	10	40	4.22
KC	72	90	.444	24	745	837	220	58	116	.263	.386	76	132	131	.979	32	655	825	4	33	4.79
WAS	60	101	.373	35.5	599	716	206	38	132	.250	.373	99	139	160	.978	38	593	771	11	13	4.04
					7183	7183	2238	400	1552	.255	.394	560	1364	1507	.978	386	5671	8535	102	329	3.97

National League 1963

	POS	Player	AB	BA	HR	RBI	PO	A	E	DP	TC/G	FA	Pitcher	G	IP	W	L	SV	ERA
L. A. W-99 L-63 Walter Alston	1B	R. Fairly	490	.271	12	77	884	45	5	74	7.8	.995	D. Drysdale	42	315	19	17	0	2.63
	2B	J. Gilliam	525	.282	6	49	242	277	8	61	4.4	.985	S. Koufax	40	311	25	5	0	1.88
	SS	M. Wills	527	.302	0	34	171	322	21	47	4.7	.959	J. Podres	37	198	14	12	1	3.54
	3B	K. McMullen	233	.236	5	28	47	133	13	8	2.7	.933	B. Miller	42	187	10	8	1	2.89
	RF	F. Howard	417	.273	28	64	190	4	8	0	1.8	.960	R. Perranoski	69	129	16	3	21	1.67
	CF	W. Davis	515	.245	9	60	337	16	8	3	2.4	.978	L. Sherry	36	80	2	6	3	3.73
	LF	T. Davis	556	.326	16	88	181	7	6	3	1.5	.969							
	C	J. Roseboro	470	.236	9	49	908	66	8	6	7.3	.992							
	OF	W. Moon	343	.262	8	48	125	2	5	0	1.4	.962							
	1B	B. Skowron	237	.203	4	19	518	34	5	44	8.4	.991							
	SS	D. Tracewski	217	.226	1	10	92	196	13	32	3.7	.957							
	2B	N. Oliver	163	.239	1	9	109	112	9	26	4.0	.961							
St. L. W-93 L-69 Johnny Keane	1B	B. White	658	.304	27	109	1389	105	13	126	9.3	.991	B. Gibson	36	255	18	9	0	3.39
	2B	J. Javier	609	.263	9	46	377	415	25	93	5.1	.969	E. Broglio	39	250	18	8	0	2.99
	SS	D. Groat	631	.319	6	73	257	448	26	91	4.6	.964	C. Simmons	32	233	15	9	0	2.48
	3B	K. Boyer	617	.285	24	111	129	293	34	23	2.9	.925	R. Sadecki	36	193	10	10	1	4.10
	RF	G. Altman	464	.274	9	47	220	8	5	1	1.9	.979	R. Taylor	54	133	9	7	11	2.84
	CF	C. Flood	662	.302	5	63	401	12	5	2	2.6	.988	L. Burdette	21	98	3	8	2	3.75
	LF	C. James	347	.268	10	45	169	4	1	1	1.7	.994	B. Shantz	55	79	6	4	11	2.61
	C	T. McCarver	405	.289	4	51	722	55	5	7	6.2	.994	E. Bauta	38	53	3	4	3	3.93
	OF	S. Musial	337	.255	12	58	121	1	4	0	1.3	.968							
	P	B. Gibson	87	.207	3	20	27	28	5	0	1.7	.917							
S. F. W-88 L-74 Alvin Dark	1B	O. Cepeda	579	.316	34	97	1262	83	21	91	9.1	.985	J. Marichal	41	321	25	8	0	2.41
	2B	C. Hiller	417	.223	6	33	224	277	19	48	4.8	.963	J. Sanford	42	284	16	13	0	3.51
	SS	J. Pagan	483	.234	6	39	262	375	20	69	4.6	.970	B. O'Dell	36	222	14	10	1	3.16
	3B	J. Davenport	460	.252	4	36	122	183	12	9	2.5	.962	B. Bolin	47	137	10	6	7	3.28
	RF	F. Alou	565	.281	20	82	279	9	4	2	1.9	.986	J. Fisher	36	116	6	10	1	4.58
	CF	W. Mays	596	.314	38	103	397	7	8	1	2.6	.984	B. Pierce	38	99	3	11	8	4.27
	LF	W. McCovey	564	.280	44	102	220	7	14	0	1.8	.942	D. Larsen	46	62	7	7	3	3.05
	C	E. Bailey	308	.263	21	68	560	44	8	3	7.0	.987							
	O3	H. Kuenn	417	.290	6	31	115	60	13	3		.931							
	C	T. Haller	298	.255	14	44	499	38	3	7	6.4	.994							
Phi. W-87 L-75 Gene Mauch	1B	R. Sievers	450	.240	19	82	981	77	12	93	8.5	.989	C. McLish	32	210	13	11	0	3.26
	2B	T. Taylor	640	.281	5	49	319	396	10	86	4.9	.986	R. Culp	34	203	14	11	0	2.97
	SS	B. Wine	418	.215	6	44	220	359	17	73	4.5	.971	C. Short	38	198	9	12	0	2.95
	3B	D. Hoak	377	.231	6	24	88	205	13	13	2.9	.958	A. Mahaffey	26	149	7	10	0	3.99
	RF	J. Callison	626	.284	26	78	298	26	2	4	2.1	.994	D. Green	40	120	7	5	2	3.23
	CF	T. Gonzalez	555	.306	4	66	263	11	4	2	1.8	.986	D. Bennett	23	119	9	5	1	2.64
	LF	W. Covington	353	.303	17	64	114	4	8	0	1.2	.937	J. Baldschun	65	114	11	7	16	2.30
	C	C. Dalrymple	452	.252	10	40	881	90	19	16	7.0	.981	J. Klippstein	49	112	5	6	8	1.93
	UT	D. Demeter	515	.258	22	83	375	86	14	15		.971	R. Duren	33	87	6	2	2	3.30
	S3	R. Amaro	217	.217	2	19	105	169	13	28		.955							
Cin. W-86 L-76 Fred Hutchinson	1B	G. Coleman	365	.247	14	59	752	65	11	66	7.7	.987	J. Maloney	33	250	23	7	0	2.77
	2B	P. Rose	623	.273	6	41	360	366	22	78	4.8	.991	J. O'Toole	33	234	17	14	0	2.88
	SS	L. Cardenas	565	.235	7	48	270	420	28	84	4.5	.972	J. Nuxhall	35	217	15	8	2	2.61
	3B	G. Freese	217	.244	6	26	44	103	11	8	2.5	.930	J. Tsitouris	30	191	12	8	0	3.16
	RF	T. Harper	408	.260	10	37	224	7	4	1	2.0	.983	J. Jay	30	170	7	18	1	4.29
	CF	V. Pinson	652	.313	22	106	357	9	8	0	2.3	.979	B. Purkey	21	137	6	10	0	3.55
	LF	F. Robinson	482	.259	21	91	237	13	4	1	1.8	.984	Worthington	50	81	4	4	10	2.99
	C	J. Edwards	495	.259	11	67	1008	87	6	16	7.4	.995	B. Henry	47	52	1	3	14	4.15
	3B	E. Kasko	199	.241	3	10	41	75	5	5	2.5	.959							
	OF	B. Skinner	194	.253	3	11	74	3	0	1	1.5	1.000							
	1B	D. Pavletich	183	.208	5	18	317	16	3	20	5.9	.991							
	1O	M. Keough	172	.227	6	21	250	24	2	25		.993							
	3B	D. Spencer	155	.239	1	23	45	92	3	9	2.9	.979							

POS	Player	AB	BA	HR	RBI	PO	A	E	DP	TC/G	FA	Pitcher	G	IP	W	L	SV	ERA
Mil. W-84 L-78 Bobby Bragan																		
1B	G. Oliver	296	.250	11	47	440	19	7	39	8.5	.985	W. Spahn	33	260	23	7	0	2.60
2B	F. Bolling	542	.244	5	43	326	379	14	107	5.1	.981	D. Lemaster	46	237	11	14	1	3.04
SS	R. McMillan	320	.250	4	29	143	283	9	60	4.6	.979	B. Hendley	41	169	9	9	3	3.93
3B	E. Mathews	547	.263	23	84	113	276	13	23	3.3	.968	B. Shaw	48	159	7	11	13	2.66
RF	H. Aaron	631	.319	44	130	267	10	6	1	1.8	.979	T. Cloninger	41	145	9	11	1	3.78
CF	M. Jones	228	.219	3	22	135	1	3	0	1.7	.978	B. Sadowski	19	117	5	7	0	2.62
LF	L. Maye	442	.271	11	34	231	4	4	1	2.2	.983	L. Burdette	15	84	6	5	0	3.63
C	J. Torre	501	.293	14	71	584	46	4	9	6.0	.994	C. Raymond	45	53	4	6	5	5.40
UT	D. Menke	518	.234	11	50	234	398	24	67		.963							
C	D. Crandall	259	.201	3	28	413	38	4	2	6.1	.991							
OF	T. Cline	174	.236	0	10	116	5	1	3	2.0	.992							
Chi. W-82 L-80 Bob Kennedy																		
1B	E. Banks	432	.227	18	64	1178	78	9	97	10.1	.993	D. Ellsworth	37	291	22	10	0	2.11
2B	K. Hubbs	566	.235	8	47	338	493	22	96	5.6	.974	L. Jackson	37	275	14	18	0	2.55
SS	A. Rodgers	516	.229	5	33	271	454	35	100	5.1	.954	B. Buhl	37	226	11	14	0	3.38
3B	R. Santo	630	.297	25	99	136	374	26	25	3.3	.951	G. Hobbie	36	165	7	10	0	3.92
RF	L. Brock	547	.258	9	37	269	17	8	7	2.1	.973	P. Toth	27	131	5	9	0	3.10
CF	E. Burton	322	.230	12	41	151	6	4	1	1.8	.975	L. McDaniel	57	88	13	7	22	2.86
LF	B. Williams	612	.286	25	95	298	13	4	2	2.0	.987							
C	D. Bertell	322	.233	2	14	549	84	8	15	6.5	.988							
OF	D. Landrum	227	.242	1	10	100	3	3	0	1.9	.972							
Pit. W-74 L-88 Danny Murtaugh																		
1B	D. Clendenon	563	.275	15	57	1450	118	15	154	10.5	.991	B. Friend	39	269	17	16	0	2.34
2B	B. Mazeroski	534	.245	8	52	340	506	14	131	6.2	.984	D. Cardwell	33	214	13	15	0	3.07
SS	D. Schofield	541	.246	3	32	232	366	21	95	5.3	.966	D. Schwall	33	168	6	12	0	3.33
3B	B. Bailey	570	.228	12	45	113	332	32	38	3.1	.933	J. Gibbon	37	147	5	12	1	3.30
RF	R. Clemente	600	.320	17	76	239	11	11	2	1.7	.958	A. McBean	55	122	13	3	11	2.57
CF	B. Virdon	554	.269	8	53	323	6	4	2	2.3	.988	T. Sisk	57	108	1	3	1	2.92
LF	W. Stargell	304	.243	11	47	78	3	4	0	1.3	.953	E. Francis	33	97	4	6	0	4.53
C	J. Pagliaroni	252	.230	11	26	435	56	6	4	5.8	.988	B. Veale	34	78	5	2	3	1.04
C	S. Burgess	264	.280	6	37	364	40	4	4	5.7	.990	R. Face	56	70	3	9	16	3.23
OF	J. Lynch	237	.266	10	36	70	2	3	0	1.2	.960							
SS	J. Logan	181	.232	0	9	74	122	17	28	4.8	.920							
Hou. W-66 L-96 Harry Craft																		
1B	R. Staub	513	.224	6	45	881	58	10	52	8.7	.989	K. Johnson	37	224	11	17	1	2.65
2B	E. Fazio	228	.184	2	5	132	145	8	18	3.4	.972	D. Farrell	34	202	14	13	1	3.02
SS	B. Lillis	469	.198	1	19	223	336	25	52	4.7	.957	D. Nottebart	31	193	11	8	0	3.17
3B	B. Aspromonte	468	.214	8	49	134	213	23	4	2.8	.938	B. Bruce	30	170	5	9	0	3.59
RF	C. Warwick	528	.254	7	47	240	7	3	2	1.8	.988	H. Brown	26	141	5	11	0	3.31
CF	H. Goss	411	.209	9	44	276	7	2	2	2.3	.993	H. Woodeshick	55	114	11	9	10	1.97
LF	A. Spangler	430	.281	4	27	215	5	3	1	2.0	.987	D. Drott	27	98	2	12	0	4.98
C	J. Bateman	404	.210	10	59	690	81	23	7	6.9	.971	D. McMahon	49	80	1	5	5	4.05
12	P. Runnels	388	.253	2	23	590	104	6	49		.991							
23	J. Temple	322	.264	1	17	146	188	16	19		.954							
OS	J. Wynn	250	.244	4	27	121	33	8	3		.951							
N. Y. W-51 L-111 Casey Stengel																		
1B	T. Harkness	375	.211	10	41	898	112	14	73	9.7	.986	R. Craig	46	236	5	22	2	3.78
2B	R. Hunt	533	.272	10	42	350	416	26	85	5.6	.967	A. Jackson	37	227	13	17	1	3.96
SS	A. Moran	331	.193	1	23	189	332	27	57	4.7	.951	C. Willey	30	183	9	14	0	3.10
3B	C. Neal	253	.225	3	18	61	135	8	10	3.1	.961	G. Cisco	51	156	7	15	0	4.34
RF	D. Snider	354	.243	14	45	139	5	2	0	1.4	.986	T. Stallard	39	155	6	17	1	4.71
CF	J. Hickman	494	.229	17	51	149	6	6	2	2.0	.963	J. Hook	41	153	4	14	1	5.48
LF	F. Thomas	420	.260	15	60	158	8	2	1	1.8	.988	L. Bearnarth	58	126	3	8	4	3.42
C	C. Coleman	247	.178	3	9	418	54	15	9	5.4	.969							
OF	E. Kranepool	273	.209	2	14	78	5	4	1	1.6	.954							
UT	R. Kanehl	191	.241	1	9	128	35	12	7		.931							
OF	J. Hicks	159	.226	5	22	83	1	3	0	2.1	.966							

BATTING AND BASE RUNNING LEADERS

Batting Average

T. Davis, LA	.326
R. Clemente, PIT	.320
H. Aaron, MIL	.319
D. Groat, STL	.319
O. Cepeda, SF	.316

Slugging Average

H. Aaron, MIL	.586
W. Mays, SF	.582
W. McCovey, SF	.566
O. Cepeda, SF	.563
V. Pinson, CIN	.514

Home Runs

W. McCovey, SF	44
H. Aaron, MIL	44
W. Mays, SF	38
O. Cepeda, SF	34
F. Howard, LA	28

Total Bases

H. Aaron, MIL	370
W. Mays, SF	347
V. Pinson, CIN	335
O. Cepeda, SF	326
B. White, STL	323

Runs Batted In

H. Aaron, MIL	130
K. Boyer, STL	111
B. White, STL	109
V. Pinson, CIN	106
W. Mays, SF	103

Stolen Bases

M. Wills, LA	40
H. Aaron, MIL	31
V. Pinson, CIN	27
F. Robinson, CIN	26
W. Davis, LA	25

PITCHING LEADERS

Winning Percentage

R. Perranoski, LA	.842
S. Koufax, LA	.833
J. Maloney, CIN	.767
W. Spahn, MIL	.767
J. Marichal, SF	.758

Earned Run Average

S. Koufax, LA	1.88
D. Ellsworth, CHI	2.11
B. Friend, PIT	2.34
J. Marichal, SF	2.41
C. Simmons, STL	2.48

Wins

S. Koufax, LA	25
J. Marichal, SF	25
J. Maloney, CIN	23
W. Spahn, MIL	23
D. Ellsworth, CHI	22

Saves

L. McDaniel, CHI	22
R. Perranoski, LA	21
J. Baldschun, PHI	16
R. Face, PIT	16
B. Henry, CIN	14

Strikeouts

S. Koufax, LA	306
J. Maloney, CIN	265
D. Drysdale, LA	251
J. Marichal, SF	248
B. Gibson, STL	204

Complete Games

W. Spahn, MIL	22
S. Koufax, LA	20
D. Ellsworth, CHI	19
J. Marichal, SF	18
D. Drysdale, LA	17

BATTING AND BASE RUNNING LEADERS

Hits
V. Pinson, CIN	204
H. Aaron, MIL	201
D. Groat, STL	201

Base on Balls
E. Mathews, MIL	124
F. Robinson, CIN	81
H. Aaron, MIL	78

Home Run Percentage
W. McCovey, SF	7.8
H. Aaron, MIL	7.0
W. Mays, SF	6.4

Runs Scored
H. Aaron, MIL	121
W. Mays, SF	115
C. Flood, STL	112

Doubles
D. Groat, STL	43
V. Pinson, CIN	37

Triples
V. Pinson, CIN	14
T. Gonzalez, PHI	12

PITCHING LEADERS

Fewest Hits per 9 Innings
S. Koufax, LA	6.19
R. Culp, PHI	6.55
J. Maloney, CIN	6.58

Shutouts
S. Koufax, LA	11
W. Spahn, MIL	7
C. Simmons, STL	6
J. Maloney, CIN	6

Fewest Walks per 9 Innings
B. Friend, PIT	1.47
D. Farrell, HOU	1.56
J. Nuxhall, CIN	1.61

Most Strikeouts per 9 Inn.
J. Maloney, CIN	9.53
S. Koufax, LA	8.86
R. Culp, PHI	7.79

Innings
J. Marichal, SF	321
D. Drysdale, LA	315
S. Koufax, LA	311

Games Pitched
R. Perranoski, LA	69
J. Baldschun, PHI	65
L. Bearnarth, NY	58

	W	L	PCT	GB	R	OR	Batting 2B	3B	HR	BA	SA	SB	Fielding E	DP	FA	CG	BB	Pitching SO	ShO	SV	ERA
LA	99	63	.611		640	550	178	34	110	.251	.357	124	159	129	.975	51	402	1095	24	29	2.85
STL	93	69	.574	6	747	628	231	66	128	.271	.403	77	147	136	.976	49	463	978	17	32	3.32
SF	88	74	.543	11	725	641	206	35	197	.258	.414	55	156	113	.975	46	464	954	9	30	3.35
PHI	87	75	.537	12	642	578	228	54	126	.252	.381	56	142	147	.978	45	553	1052	12	31	3.09
CIN	86	76	.531	13	648	594	225	44	122	.246	.371	92	135	127	.978	55	425	1048	22	36	3.29
MIL	84	78	.519	15	677	603	204	39	139	.244	.370	75	129	161	.980	56	489	924	18	25	3.26
CHI	82	80	.506	17	570	578	205	44	127	.238	.363	68	155	172	.976	45	400	851	15	28	3.08
PIT	74	88	.457	25	567	595	181	49	108	.250	.359	57	182	195	.972	34	457	900	16	33	3.10
HOU	66	96	.407	33	464	640	170	39	62	.220	.301	39	162	100	.974	36	378	937	16	20	3.44
NY	51	111	.315	48	501	774	156	35	96	.219	.315	41	210	151	.967	42	529	806	5	12	4.12
					6181	6181	1984	439	1215	.245	.364	684	1577	1431	.975	459	4560	9545	154	276	3.29

American League 1963

	POS	Player	AB	BA	HR	RBI	PO	A	E	DP	TC/G	FA	Pitcher	G	IP	W	L	SV	ERA
N. Y. W-104 L-57 Ralph Houk	1B	J. Pepitone	580	.271	27	89	1140	103	6	111	8.7	.995	W. Ford	38	269	24	7	1	2.74
	2B	B. Richardson	630	.265	3	48	335	424	12	105	5.1	.984	R. Terry	40	268	17	15	1	3.22
	SS	T. Kubek	557	.257	7	44	227	403	13	80	4.9	.980	J. Bouton	40	249	21	7	1	2.53
	3B	C. Boyer	557	.251	12	54	165	309	23	32	3.5	.954	A. Downing	24	176	13	5	0	2.56
	RF	R. Maris	312	.269	23	53	162	6	2	1	2.0	.988	S. Williams	29	146	9	8	0	3.20
	CF	T. Tresh	520	.269	25	71	305	6	6	1	2.2	.981	B. Stafford	28	90	4	8	3	6.02
	LF	H. Lopez	433	.249	14	52	187	11	9	2	1.7	.957	H. Reniff	48	89	4	3	18	2.62
	C	E. Howard	487	.287	28	85	786	51	5	8	6.4	.994	S. Hamilton	34	62	5	1	5	2.60
	OF	J. Blanchard	218	.225	16	45	76	2	1	0	1.2	.987							
	UT	P. Linz	186	.269	2	12	69	103	4	17		.977							
	OF	M. Mantle	172	.314	15	35	99	2	1	0	2.0	.990							
	1B	H. Bright	157	.236	7	23	263	8	4	32	7.9	.985							
	C	Y. Berra	147	.293	8	28	244	13	3	5	7.4	.988							
Chi. W-94 L-68 Al Lopez	1B	T. McCraw	280	.254	6	33	673	47	5	65	7.5	.993	G. Peters	41	243	19	8	1	**2.33**
	2B	N. Fox	539	.260	2	42	305	342	8	71	4.9	**.988**	R. Herbert	33	225	13	10	0	3.24
	SS	R. Hansen	482	.226	13	67	247	483	13	95	5.2	.983	J. Pizarro	32	215	16	8	1	2.39
	3B	P. Ward	600	.295	22	84	156	302	38	27	3.2	.923	H. Wilhelm	55	136	5	8	21	2.64
	RF	F. Robinson	527	.283	13	71	245	8	4	4	1.9	.984	J. Buzhardt	19	126	9	4	0	2.42
	CF	J. Landis	396	.225	13	45	264	6	2	0	2.2	.993	J. Horlen	33	124	11	7	0	3.27
	LF	D. Nicholson	449	.229	22	70	213	10	7	1	1.9	.970	E. Fisher	33	121	9	8	0	3.95
	C	J. Martin	259	.205	5	28	468	48	9	9	5.4	.983	J. Brosnan	45	73	3	8	14	2.84
	OF	Hershberger	476	.279	3	45	230	13	6	3	2.1	.976							
	C	C. Carreon	270	.274	2	35	429	36	6	7	5.1	.987							
	2S	A. Weis	210	.271	0	18	123	168	10	41		.967							
	1B	J. Cunningham	210	.286	1	31	535	24	6	39	9.7	.989							
Min. W-91 L-70 Sam Mele	1B	V. Power	541	.270	10	52	896	76	8	86	7.9	.992	C. Pascual	31	248	21	9	0	2.46
	2B	B. Allen	421	.240	9	43	236	256	12	65	3.9	.976	D. Stigman	33	241	15	15	0	3.25
	SS	Z. Versalles	621	.261	10	54	301	448	30	87	4.9	.961	J. Kaat	31	178	10	10	1	4.19
	3B	R. Rollins	531	.307	16	61	121	225	26	22	2.8	.930	J. Perry	35	168	9	9	1	3.74
	RF	B. Allison	527	.271	35	91	326	11	10	4	2.4	.971	L. Stange	32	165	12	5	0	2.62
	CF	J. Hall	497	.260	33	80	306	13	6	5	2.3	.982	B. Dailey	66	109	6	3	21	1.99
	LF	H. Killebrew	515	.258	45	96	219	7	3	0	1.7	.987	G. Roggenburk	36	50	2	4	4	2.16
	C	E. Battey	508	.285	26	84	861	66	6	11	6.4	.994							
	OF	L. Green	280	.239	4	27	165	1	2	0	1.4	.988							
	1B	D. Mincher	225	.258	17	42	446	27	8	34	8.0	.983							
	UT	J. Goryl	150	.287	9	24	75	92	7	18		.960							

	POS	Player	AB	BA	HR	RBI	PO	A	E	DP	TC/G	FA	Pitcher	G	IP	W	L	SV	ERA
Bal. W-86 L-76 Billy Hitchcock	1B	J. Gentile	496	.248	24	72	1185	110	6	122	9.1	.995	S. Barber	39	259	20	13	0	2.75
	2B	J. Adair	382	.228	6	30	242	268	8	67	5.0	.985	R. Roberts	35	251	14	13	0	3.33
	SS	L. Aparicio	601	.250	5	45	275	403	12	76	4.8	.983	M. Pappas	34	217	16	9	0	3.03
	3B	B. Robinson	589	.251	11	67	153	330	12	43	3.1	.976	M. McCormick	25	136	6	8	0	4.30
	RF	R. Snyder	429	.256	7	36	238	5	3	1	1.9	.988	D. McNally	29	126	7	8	1	4.58
	CF	J. Brandt	451	.248	15	61	272	9	4	1	2.1	.986	S. Miller	71	112	5	8	27	2.24
	LF	B. Powell	491	.265	25	82	181	6	6	1	1.6	.969	D. Hall	47	112	5	5	12	2.98
	C	J. Orsino	379	.272	19	56	636	37	7	8	6.2	.990							
	OF	A. Smith	368	.272	10	39	160	6	5	0	1.8	.971							
	2B	B. Johnson	254	.295	8	32	97	131	3	34	4.6	.987							
	C	D. Brown	171	.246	2	13	317	23	5	7	5.9	.986							
	UT	B. Saverine	167	.234	1	12	99	89	2	19		.989							
	OF	J. Gaines	126	.286	6	20	52	0	3	0	1.4	.945							
Cle. W-79 L-83 Birdie Tebbetts	1B	F. Whitfield	346	.251	21	54	690	51	10	64	8.2	.987	M. Grant	38	229	13	14	1	3.69
	2B	W. Held	416	.248	17	61	188	251	8	50	4.7	.982	D. Donovan	30	206	11	13	0	4.24
	SS	J. Kindall	234	.205	5	20	63	97	7	15	3.6	.958	J. Kralick	28	197	13	9	0	2.92
	3B	M. Alvis	602	.274	22	67	170	285	28	32	3.1	.942	P. Ramos	36	185	9	8	0	3.12
	RF	W. Kirkland	427	.230	15	47	234	11	4	2	2.2	.984	B. Latman	38	149	7	12	2	4.94
	CF	V. Davalillo	370	.292	7	36	247	10	3	0	2.9	.988	G. Bell	58	119	8	5	5	2.95
	LF	T. Francona	500	.228	10	41	215	2	3	0	1.8	.986	J. Walker	39	88	6	6	1	4.91
	C	J. Azcue	320	.284	14	46	564	42	5	13*	6.7	.992	T. Abernathy	43	59	7	2	12	2.88
	OF	A. Luplow	295	.234	7	27	157	7	1	1	1.9	.994							
	1B	J. Adcock	283	.251	13	49	608	36	3	46	8.3	.995							
	C	J. Romano	255	.216	10	34	408	28	3	5	6.2	.993							
	S2	L. Brown	247	.255	5	18	113	176	14	25		.954							
	SS	D. Howser	162	.247	1	10	80	90	9	15	4.1	.950							
	2B	de la Hoz	150	.267	5	25	63	89	6	20	4.6	.962							
Det. W-79 L-83 Bob Scheffing W-24 L-36 Chuck Dressen W-55 L-47	1B	N. Cash	493	.270	26	79	1161	99	7	93	8.9	.994	J. Bunning	39	248	12	13	1	3.88
	2B	J. Wood	351	.271	11	27	188	202	17	47	5.0	.958	H. Aguirre	38	226	14	15	0	3.67
	SS	D. McAuliffe	568	.262	13	61	220	356	22	68	4.5	.963	P. Regan	38	189	15	9	1	3.86
	3B	B. Phillips	464	.246	5	45	116	226	14	26	3.0	.961	M. Lolich	33	144	5	9	0	3.55
	RF	A. Kaline	551	.312	27	101	257	5	2	0	1.9	.992	D. Mossi	24	123	7	7	2	3.74
	CF	B. Bruton	524	.256	8	48	339	6	3	3	2.5	.991	F. Lary	16	107	4	9	0	3.27
	LF	R. Colavito	597	.271	22	91	319	10	4	0	2.1	.988	B. Faul	28	97	5	6	1	4.64
	C	G. Triandos	327	.239	14	41	535	29	1	4	6.3	.998	T. Fox	46	80	8	6	11	3.59
	C	B. Freehan	300	.243	9	36	407	22	2	5	5.9	.995							
	UT	D. Wert	251	.259	7	25	85	173	10	20		.963							
	2B	G. Smith	171	.216	0	17	120	157	5	28	5.4	.982							
Bos. W-76 L-85 Johnny Pesky	1B	D. Stuart	612	.261	42	118	1207	134	29	100	8.8	.979	Monbouquette	37	267	20	10	0	3.81
	2B	C. Schilling	576	.234	8	33	276	369	10	74	4.6	.985	E. Wilson	37	211	11	16	0	3.76
	SS	E. Bressoud	497	.260	20	60	260	351	24	76	4.6	.962	D. Morehead	29	175	10	13	0	3.81
	3B	F. Malzone	580	.291	15	71	151	283	16	18	3.0	.964	J. Lamabe	65	151	7	4	6	3.15
	RF	L. Clinton	560	.232	22	77	319	7	6	0	2.3	.982	D. Radatz	66	132	15	6	25	1.97
	CF	G. Geiger	399	.263	16	44	234	11	4	1	2.6	.984	B. Heffner	20	125	4	9	0	4.26
	LF	Yastrzemski	570	.321	14	68	283	18	6	3	2.0	.980	A. Earley	53	116	3	7	1	4.75
	C	B. Tillman	307	.225	8	32	621	26	5	5	6.9	.992							
	OF	R. Mejias	357	.227	11	39	177	6	5	1	2.2	.973							
	C	R. Nixon	287	.268	5	30	483	22	4	1	6.7	.992							
	UT	F. Mantilla	178	.315	6	15	83	74	4	19		.975							
K. C. W-73 L-89 Ed Lopat	1B	N. Siebern	556	.272	16	83	1193	102	12	95	10.0	.991	D. Wickersham	38	238	12	15	1	4.09
	2B	J. Lumpe	595	.271	5	59	341	452	10	92	5.2	.988	O. Pena	35	217	12	20	0	3.69
	SS	W. Causey	554	.280	8	44	266	402	15	81	5.1	.978	E. Rakow	34	174	9	10	0	3.92
	3B	E. Charles	603	.267	15	79	153	310	25	19	3.1	.949	M. Drabowsky	26	174	7	13	0	3.05
	RF	G. Cimoli	529	.263	4	48	256	14	4	3	2.0	.985	D. Segui	38	167	9	6	0	3.77
	CF	B. Del Greco	306	.212	8	29	207	5	4	0	2.0	.981	T. Bowsfield	41	111	5	7	3	4.45
	LF	J. Tartabull	242	.240	1	19	135	3	2	1	2.0	.986	B. Fischer	45	96	6	3	1	3.57
	C	D. Edwards	240	.250	6	35	341	30	5	4	6.0	.987	J. Wyatt	63	92	6	4	21	3.13
	OF	C. Essegian	231	.225	5	27	95	2	1	0	1.8	.990							
	1O	K. Harrelson	226	.230	6	23	326	17	7	24		.980							
	OF	G. Alusik	221	.267	9	37	98	5	0	1	1.6	1.000							
	C	C. Lau	187	.294	3	26	258	15	5	2	5.6	.982							
L. A. W-70 L-91 Billy Rigney	1B	L. Thomas	528	.220	9	55	961	84	4	88	10.1	.996	K. McBride	36	251	13	12	0	3.26
	2B	B. Moran	597	.275	7	65	352	455	22	98	5.5	.973	D. Chance	45	248	13	18	3	3.19
	SS	J. Fregosi	592	.287	9	50	271	446	27	90	4.9	.964	D. Osinski	47	159	8	8	0	3.28
	3B	F. Torres	463	.261	4	51	101	237	22	29	3.0	.939	Lee	40	154	8	11	1	3.68
	RF	B. Perry	166	.253	3	14	86	1	5	0	1.7	.946	J. Navarro	57	90	4	5	12	2.89
	CF	A. Pearson	578	.304	6	47	340	10	6	5	2.4	.983	A. Fowler	57	89	5	3	10	2.42
	LF	L. Wagner	550	.291	26	90	254	7	11	1	1.9	.960	B. Belinsky	13	77	2	9	0	5.75
	C	B. Rodgers	300	.233	4	23	416	48	10	5	5.6	.979	P. Foytack	25	70	5	5	0	3.71
	1B	C. Dees	202	.307	3	27	474	32	7	41	9.2	.986							
	C	E. Sadowski	174	.172	4	14	340	38	1	7	5.6	.997							
	OF	G. Thomas	167	.210	4	15	63	1	4	0	1.7	.941							
	OF	B. Sadowski	144	.250	1	22	41	0	0	0	1.6	1.000							

POS	Player	AB	BA	HR	RBI	PO	A	E	DP	TC/G	FA	Pitcher	G	IP	W	L	SV	ERA
1B	B. Osborne	358	.212	12	44	713	55	9	68	9.6	.988	C. Osteen	40	212	9	14	0	3.35
2B	C. Cottier	337	.205	5	21	200	221	16	49	5.1	.963	D. Rudolph	37	174	7	19	1	4.55
SS	E. Brinkman	514	.228	7	45	241	462	37	97	5.2	.950	B. Daniels	35	169	5	10	1	4.38
3B	D. Zimmer	298	.248	13	44	88	173	18	17	3.6	.935	T. Cheney	23	136	8	9	0	2.71
RF	J. King	459	.231	24	62	213	13	3	2	1.9	.987	J. Duckworth	37	121	4	12	0	6.04
CF	D. Lock	531	.252	27	82	**377**	14	8	6	2.7	.980	R. Kline	62	94	3	8	17	2.79
LF	C. Hinton	566	.269	15	55	274	8	3	1	2.3	.989	S. Ridzik	20	90	5	6	1	4.82
C	K. Retzer	265	.242	5	31	320	35	7	5	4.5	.981	D. Stenhouse	16	87	3	9	0	4.55
1B	D. Phillips	321	.237	10	32	655	59	4	73	10.6	.994							
OF	M. Minoso	315	.229	4	30	103	4	5	0	1.5	.955							
2B	D. Blasingame	254	.256	2	12	162	177	3	52	5.3	.991							
C	D. Leppert	211	.237	6	24	281	20	5	4	5.1	.984							
32	M. Breeding	197	.274	1	14	76	110	11	15		.944							

Was.
W-56 L-106
Mickey Vernon
W-14 L-26
Gil Hodges
W-42 L-80

BATTING AND BASE RUNNING LEADERS   PITCHING LEADERS

Batting Average
Yastrzemski, BOS	.321
A. Kaline, DET	.312
R. Rollins, MIN	.307
A. Pearson, LA	.304
P. Ward, CHI	.295

Slugging Average
H. Killebrew, MIN	.555
B. Allison, MIN	.533
E. Howard, NY	.528
D. Stuart, BOS	.521
J. Hall, MIN	.521

Winning Percentage
W. Ford, NY	.774
J. Bouton, NY	.750
D. Radatz, BOS	.714
G. Peters, CHI	.704
C. Pascual, MIN	.700

Earned Run Average
G. Peters, CHI	2.33
J. Pizarro, CHI	2.39
C. Pascual, MIN	2.46
J. Bouton, NY	2.53
A. Downing, NY	2.56

Home Runs
H. Killebrew, MIN	45
D. Stuart, BOS	42
B. Allison, MIN	35
J. Hall, MIN	33
E. Howard, NY	28

Total Bases
D. Stuart, BOS	319
P. Ward, CHI	289
H. Killebrew, MIN	286
A. Kaline, DET	283
B. Allison, MIN	281

Wins
W. Ford, NY	24
J. Bouton, NY	21
C. Pascual, MIN	21
Monbouquette, BOS	20
S. Barber, BAL	20

Saves
S. Miller, BAL	27
D. Radatz, BOS	25
B. Dailey, MIN	21
J. Wyatt, KC	21
H. Wilhelm, CHI	21

Runs Batted In
D. Stuart, BOS	118
A. Kaline, DET	101
H. Killebrew, MIN	96
B. Allison, MIN	91
R. Colavito, DET	91

Stolen Bases
L. Aparicio, BAL	40
C. Hinton, WAS	25
J. Wood, DET	18
R. Snyder, BAL	18
A. Pearson, LA	17

Strikeouts
C. Pascual, MIN	202
J. Bunning, DET	196
D. Stigman, MIN	193
G. Peters, CHI	189
W. Ford, NY	189

Complete Games
C. Pascual, MIN	18
R. Terry, NY	18
D. Stigman, MIN	15
H. Aguirre, DET	14
R. Herbert, CHI	14

Hits
Yastrzemski, BOS	183
P. Ward, CHI	177
A. Pearson, LA	176

Base on Balls
Yastrzemski, BOS	95
A. Pearson, LA	92
B. Allison, MIN	90

Fewest Hits per 9 Innings
A. Downing, NY	5.84
J. Bouton, NY	6.89
M. Drabowsky, KC	6.97

Shutouts
R. Herbert, CHI	7
J. Bouton, NY	6

Home Run Percentage
H. Killebrew, MIN	8.7
D. Stuart, BOS	6.9
B. Allison, MIN	6.6

Runs Scored
B. Allison, MIN	99
A. Pearson, LA	92

Fewest Walks per 9 Innings
D. Donovan, CLE	1.22
R. Terry, NY	1.31
R. Herbert, CHI	1.40

Most Strikeouts per 9 Inn.
A. Downing, NY	8.76
P. Ramos, CLE	8.24
C. Pascual, MIN	7.32

Doubles
Yastrzemski, BOS	40
P. Ward, CHI	34

Triples
Z. Versalles, MIN	13
C. Hinton, WAS	12
J. Fregosi, LA	12

Innings
W. Ford, NY	269
R. Terry, NY	268
Monbouquette, BOS	267

Games Pitched
S. Miller, BAL	71
D. Radatz, BOS	66
B. Dailey, MIN	66

	W	L	PCT	GB	R	OR	Batting 2B	3B	HR	BA	SA	SB	Fielding E	DP	FA	Pitching CG	BB	SO	ShO	SV	ERA
NY	104	57	.646		714	547	197	35	188	.252	.403	42	110	162	.982	**59**	476	965	17	31	3.07
CHI	94	68	.580	10.5	683	**544**	208	**40**	114	.250	.365	64	131	163	.979	49	**440**	932	**19**	39	**2.97**
MIN	91	70	.565	13	**767**	602	223	35	**225**	**.255**	**.430**	32	144	140	.976	58	459	941	12	30	3.28
BAL	86	76	.531	18.5	644	621	207	32	146	.249	.380	**97**	**99**	157	**.984**	35	507	913	8	**43**	3.45
CLE	79	83	.488	25.5	635	702	214	29	169	.239	.381	59	143	129	.977	40	478	**1018**	11	25	3.79
DET	79	83	.488	25.5	700	703	195	36	148	.252	.382	73	113	124	.981	42	477	930	6	28	3.90
BOS	76	85	.472	28	666	704	**247**	34	171	.252	.400	27	135	119	.978	29	539	1009	6	32	3.97
KC	73	89	.451	31.5	615	704	225	38	95	.247	.353	47	127	131	.980	35	540	887	9	29	3.92
LA	70	91	.435	34	597	660	208	38	95	.250	.354	43	163	155	.974	30	578	889	9	31	3.52
WAS	56	106	.346	48.5	578	812	190	35	138	.227	.351	68	182	**165**	.971	29	537	744	8	25	4.42
					6599	6599	2114	352	1489	.247	.380	552	1347	1445	.978	406	5031	9228	105	313	3.63

POS	Player	AB	BA	HR	RBI	PO	A	E	DP	TC/G	FA	Pitcher	G	IP	W	L	SV	ERA
St. L. W-93 L-69 Johnny Keane																		
1B	B. White	631	.303	21	102	1513	101	6	**125**	10.1	**.996**	B. Gibson	40	287	19	12	1	3.01
2B	J. Javier	535	.241	12	65	**360**	401	27	97	5.1	.966	C. Simmons	34	244	18	9	0	3.43
SS	D. Groat	636	.292	1	70	249	**499**	40	**91**	4.9	.949	R. Sadecki	37	220	20	11	1	3.68
3B	K. Boyer	628	.295	24	**119**	131	337	24	30	3.0	.951	R. Craig	39	166	7	9	5	3.25
RF	M. Shannon	253	.261	9	43	110	7	2	2	1.4	.983	R. Taylor	63	101	8	4	7	4.62
CF	C. Flood	**679**	.311	5	46	391	10	5	2	2.5	.988	M. Cuellar	32	72	5	5	4	4.50
LF	L. Brock	419	.348	12	44	180	7	10*	0	1.9	.949	B. Schultz	30	49	1	3	14	1.64
C	T. McCarver	465	.288	9	52	762	43	11	9	6.0	.987							
OF	C. James	233	.223	5	17	76	3	3	0	1.4	.963							
Cin. W-92 L-70 Fred Hutchinson W-60 L-49 Dick Sisler W-32 L-21																		
1B	D. Johnson	477	.273	21	79	940	81	10	82	7.9	.990	J. O'Toole	30	220	17	7	0	2.66
2B	P. Rose	516	.269	4	34	263	301	12	63	4.5	.979	J. Maloney	31	216	15	10	0	2.71
SS	L. Cardenas	597	.251	9	69	**336**	436	32	87	4.9	.960	B. Purkey	34	196	11	9	1	3.04
3B	S. Boros	370	.257	2	31	95	204	12	18	2.7	.961	J. Jay	34	183	11	11	2	3.39
RF	F. Robinson	568	.306	29	96	279	7	4	3	1.9	.986	J. Tsitouris	37	175	9	13	2	3.80
CF	V. Pinson	625	.266	23	84	299	14	9	1	2.1	.972	J. Nuxhall	32	155	9	8	2	4.07
LF	T. Harper	317	.243	4	22	149	4	1	2	1.7	.994	S. Ellis	52	122	10	3	14	2.57
C	J. Edwards	423	.281	7	55	**890**	73	8	**17**	8.1	.992	B. McCool	40	89	6	5	7	2.42
32	C. Ruiz	311	.244	2	16	95	149	11	28		.957	B. Henry	37	52	2	2	6	0.87
OF	M. Keough	276	.257	9	28	105	4	1	1	1.4	.991							
1B	G. Coleman	198	.242	5	27	352	35	4	28	8.0	.990							
Phi. W-92 L-70 Gene Mauch																		
1B	J. Herrnstein	303	.234	6	25	488	22	5	33	7.6	.990	J. Bunning	41	284	19	8	2	2.63
2B	T. Taylor	570	.251	4	46	325	358	16	94	4.7	.977	C. Short	42	221	17	9	2	2.20
SS	B. Wine	283	.212	4	34	153	257	15	55	3.9	.965	D. Bennett	41	208	12	14	1	3.68
3B	R. Allen	632	.318	29	91	154	325	**41**	30	3.2	.921	A. Mahaffey	34	157	12	9	0	4.52
RF	J. Callison	654	.274	31	104	319	**19**	4	3	2.1	.988	R. Culp	30	135	8	7	0	4.13
CF	T. Gonzalez	421	.278	4	40	243	5	1	2	2.1	**.996**	J. Baldschun	71	118	6	9	21	3.12
LF	W. Covington	339	.280	13	58	99	4	3	0	1.0	.972	E. Roebuck	60	77	5	3	12	2.21
C	C. Dalrymple	382	.238	6	46	737	61	7	11	6.5	.991							
UT	C. Rojas	340	.291	2	31	164	76	7	11		.972							
S1	R. Amaro	299	.264	4	34	295	200	10	55		.980							
C	G. Triandos	188	.250	8	33	371	24	6	4	6.3	.985							
1B	F. Thomas	143	.294	7	26	297	28	8	37	8.5	.976							
S. F. W-90 L-72 Alvin Dark																		
1B	O. Cepeda	529	.304	31	97	1211	80	**18**	89	9.4	.986	J. Marichal	33	269	21	8	0	2.48
2B	H. Lanier	383	.274	2	28	224	294	11	48	5.4	.979	G. Perry	44	206	12	11	5	2.75
SS	J. Pagan	367	.223	1	28	204	302	22	52	4.0	.958	B. Bolin	38	175	6	9	3	3.25
3B	J. Hart	566	.286	31	81	139	277	28	24	3.0	.937	B. Hendley	30	163	10	11	0	3.64
RF	F. Alou	376	.274	3	28	172	8	5	2	1.7	.973	R. Herbel	40	161	9	9	1	3.07
CF	W. Mays	578	.296	**47**	111	370	10	6	4	2.5	.984	J. Sanford	18	106	5	7	1	3.30
LF	W. McCovey	364	.220	18	54	96	5	7	1	1.3	.935	B. Shaw	61	93	7	6	11	3.76
C	T. Haller	388	.253	16	48	739	50	9	12	7.1	.989	B. O'Dell	36	85	8	7	2	5.40
OF	H. Kuenn	351	.262	4	22	97	2	5	0	1.2	.952							
UT	J. Davenport	297	.236	2	26	138	237	11	29		.972							
OF	M. Alou	250	.264	1	14	120	2	3	1	1.6	.976							
2B	C. Hiller	205	.180	1	17	111	143	6	29	4.3	.977							
C	D. Crandall	195	.231	3	11	402	30	3	7	6.7	.993							
OF	D. Snider	167	.210	4	17	44	2	1	0	1.1	.979							
Mil. W-88 L-74 Bobby Bragan																		
1B	G. Oliver	279	.276	13	49	622	34	12	50	8.8	.982	T. Cloninger	38	243	19	14	2	3.56
2B	F. Bolling	352	.199	5	34	212	255	7	68	4.1	**.985**	D. Lemaster	39	221	17	11	1	4.15
SS	D. Menke	505	.283	20	65	253	422	25	76	5.0	.964	W. Spahn	38	174	6	13	4	5.29
3B	E. Mathews	502	.233	23	74	130	247	15	19	3.1	.962	H. Fischer	37	168	11	10	2	4.01
RF	H. Aaron	570	.328	24	95	270	13	5	5	2.1	.983	B. Sadowski	51	167	9	10	5	4.10
CF	L. Maye	588	.304	10	74	264	7	11	1	2.1	.961	W. Blasingame	28	117	9	5	2	4.24
LF	R. Carty	455	.330	22	88	176	5	4	1	1.5	.978	B. Tiefenauer	46	73	4	6	13	3.21
C	J. Torre	601	.321	20	109	518	46	3	4	5.9	**.995**							
OF	F. Alou	415	.253	9	51	191	2	5	0	2.2	.975							
C	E. Bailey	271	.262	5	34	416	28	8	3	5.7	.982							
UT	de la Hoz	189	.291	4	12	65	109	10	17		.946							
L. A. W-80 L-82 Walter Alston																		
1B	R. Fairly	454	.256	10	74	1081	82	15	89	8.4	.987	D. Drysdale	40	**321**	18	16	0	2.18
2B	N. Oliver	321	.243	0	21	194	247	15	44	4.7	.967	S. Koufax	29	223	19	5	1	**1.74**
SS	M. Wills	630	.275	2	34	273	422	27	77	4.8	.963	P. Ortega	34	157	7	9	1	4.00
3B	J. Gilliam	334	.228	2	27	54	121	12	7	2.2	.936	J. Moeller	27	145	7	13	0	4.21
RF	F. Howard	433	.226	24	69	183	2	4	0	1.5	.979	B. Miller	**74**	138	7	7	9	2.62
CF	W. Davis	613	.294	12	77	**400**	16	7	2	**2.7**	.983	R. Perranoski	72	125	5	7	14	3.09
LF	T. Davis	592	.275	14	86	264	9	5	1	1.9	.982	L. Miller	16	80	4	8	0	4.18
C	J. Roseboro	414	.287	3	45	809	64	6	8	6.9	.993							
UT	D. Tracewski	304	.247	1	26	152	218	15	35		.961							
3O	D. Griffith	238	.290	4	23	57	56	23	3		.831							
O1	W. Parker	214	.257	3	10	326	26	6	18		.983							

	POS	Player	AB	BA	HR	RBI	PO	A	E	DP	TC/G	FA	Pitcher	G	IP	W	L	SV	ERA
Pit. W-80 L-82 Danny Murtaugh	1B	D. Clendenon	457	.282	12	64	1153	75	14	116	10.4	.989	B. Veale	40	280	18	12	0	2.74
	2B	B. Mazeroski	601	.268	10	64	346	543	23	122	5.6	.975	B. Friend	35	240	13	18	0	3.33
	SS	D. Schofield	398	.246	3	36	184	349	28	78	5.1	.950	V. Law	35	192	12	13	0	3.61
	3B	B. Bailey	530	.281	11	51	81	218	18	19	3.0	.943	J. Gibbon	28	147	10	7	0	3.68
	RF	R. Clemente	622	.339	12	87	289	13	10	2	2.0	.968	S. Blass	24	105	5	8	0	4.04
	CF	B. Virdon	473	.243	3	27	243	5	6	1	1.9	.976	A. McBean	58	90	8	3	22	1.91
	LF	M. Mota	271	.277	5	32	120	4	5	1	1.4	.961	R. Face	55	80	3	3	4	5.20
	C	J. Pagliaroni	302	.295	10	36	584	42	5	5	6.6	.992							
	O1	W. Stargell	421	.273	21	78	565	24	10	50		.983							
	OF	J. Lynch	297	.273	16	66	59	0	1	0	.8	.983							
	3B	G. Freese	289	.225	9	40	48	112	14	12	2.4	.920							
	SS	G. Alley	209	.211	6	13	100	211	11	43	5.3	.966							
	C	S. Burgess	171	.246	2	17	237	18	2	3	5.8	.992							
Chi. W-76 L-86 Bob Kennedy	1B	E. Banks	591	.264	23	95	1565	132	10	122	10.9	.994	L. Jackson	40	298	24	11	0	3.14
	2B	J. Amalfitano	324	.241	4	27	201	254	17	47	5.5	.964	D. Ellsworth	37	257	14	18	0	3.75
	SS	A. Rodgers	448	.239	12	46	232	428	24	68	5.4	.965	B. Buhl	36	228	15	14	0	3.83
	3B	R. Santo	592	.313	30	114	156	367	20	31	3.4	.963	L. Burdette	28	131	9	9	0	4.88
	RF	L. Gabrielson	272	.246	5	23	116	5	2	0	1.8	.984	E. Broglio	18	100	4	7	1	4.04
	CF	B. Cowan	497	.241	19	50	297	2	10	0	2.3	.968	L. McDaniel	63	95	1	7	15	3.88
	LF	B. Williams	645	.312	33	98	233	14	13	0	1.6	.950							
	C	D. Bertell	353	.238	4	35	531	52	11	3	5.4	.981							
	2S	J. Stewart	415	.253	3	33	214	307	12	64		.977							
	OF	L. Brock	215	.251	2	14	86	8	4*	1	1.9	.959							
Hou. W-66 L-96 Harry Craft W-61 L-88 Lum Harris W-5 L-8	1B	W. Bond	543	.254	20	85	685	40	8	46	9.6	.989	K. Johnson	35	218	11	16	0	3.63
	2B	N. Fox	442	.265	0	28	231	317	13	51	4.9	.977	B. Bruce	35	202	15	9	0	2.76
	SS	E. Kasko	448	.243	0	22	228	388	14	72	4.9	.978	D. Farrell	32	198	11	10	0	3.27
	3B	B. Aspromonte	553	.280	12	69	133	261	11	10	2.6	.973	D. Nottebart	28	157	6	11	0	3.90
	RF	J. Gaines	307	.254	7	34	130	4	6	1	1.7	.957	H. Brown	27	132	3	15	1	3.95
	CF	M. White	280	.271	0	27	127	4	3	1	1.9	.978	J. Owens	48	118	8	7	6	3.28
	LF	A. Spangler	449	.245	4	38	185	3	7	1	1.5	.964	D. Larsen	30	103	4	8	1	2.26
	C	J. Grote	298	.181	3	24	522	52	9	5	5.9	.985	C. Raymond	38	80	5	5	0	2.82
	UT	B. Lillis	332	.268	0	17	169	236	10	40		.976	H. Woodeshick	61	78	2	9	23	2.76
	1O	R. Staub	292	.216	8	35	512	30	9	34		.984							
	C	J. Bateman	221	.190	5	19	400	43	6	4	6.2	.987							
	OF	J. Wynn	219	.224	5	18	129	8	6	3	2.2	.958							
N. Y. W-53 L-109 Casey Stengel	1B	E. Kranepool	420	.257	10	45	975	80	10	78	10.2	.991	J. Fisher	40	228	10	17	0	4.23
	2B	R. Hunt	475	.303	6	42	244	317	12	73	5.3	.979	T. Stallard	36	226	10	20	0	3.79
	SS	R. McMillan	379	.211	1	25	217	353	14	64	5.3	.976	A. Jackson	40	213	11	16	1	4.26
	3B	C. Smith	443	.239	20	58	89	166	23	9	3.3	.917	G. Cisco	36	192	6	19	0	3.62
	RF	Christopher	543	.300	16	76	251	10	7	2	1.8	.974	B. Wakefield	62	120	3	5	2	3.61
	CF	J. Hickman	409	.257	11	57	237	8	6	1	2.2	.976	L. Bearnarth	44	78	5	5	3	4.15
	LF	G. Altman	422	.230	9	47	202	12	7	3	2.0	.968	W. Hunter	41	49	3	3	5	4.41
	C	J. Gonder	341	.270	7	35	397	70	10	7	4.9	.979							
	UT	R. Kanehl	254	.232	1	11	161	125	6	26		.979							
	C	H. Taylor	225	.240	4	23	182	28	4	5	4.8	.981							
	OF	L. Elliot	224	.228	9	22	130	2	2	1	2.1	.985							
	32	B. Klaus	209	.244	2	11	81	128	6	14		.972							
	O1	F. Thomas	197	.254	3	19	200	16	1	12		.995							
	C	C. Cannizzaro	164	.311	0	10	225	28	3	6	4.8	.988							

BATTING AND BASE RUNNING LEADERS

Batting Average

R. Clemente, PIT	.339
H. Aaron, MIL	.328
J. Torre, MIL	.321
R. Allen, PHI	.318
L. Brock, CHI, STL	.315

Slugging Average

W. Mays, SF	.607
R. Santo, CHI	.564
R. Allen, PHI	.557
F. Robinson, CIN	.548
O. Cepeda, SF	.539

Home Runs

W. Mays, SF	47
B. Williams, CHI	33
O. Cepeda, SF	31
J. Hart, SF	31
J. Callison, PHI	31

Total Bases

R. Allen, PHI	352
W. Mays, SF	351
B. Williams, CHI	343
R. Santo, CHI	334
J. Callison, PHI	322

Runs Batted In

K. Boyer, STL	119
R. Santo, CHI	114
W. Mays, SF	111
J. Torre, MIL	109
J. Callison, PHI	104

Stolen Bases

M. Wills, LA	53
L. Brock, CHI, STL	43
W. Davis, LA	42
T. Harper, CIN	24
F. Robinson, CIN	23

Hits

R. Clemente, PIT	211
C. Flood, STL	211
R. Allen, PHI	201
B. Williams, CHI	201

Base on Balls

R. Santo, CHI	86
E. Mathews, MIL	85
W. Mays, SF	82

PITCHING LEADERS

Winning Percentage

S. Koufax, LA	.792
J. Marichal, SF	.724
J. O'Toole, CIN	.708
J. Bunning, PHI	.704
L. Jackson, CHI	.686

Earned Run Average

S. Koufax, LA	1.74
D. Drysdale, LA	2.18
C. Short, PHI	2.20
J. Marichal, SF	2.48
J. Bunning, PHI	2.63

Wins

L. Jackson, CHI	24
J. Marichal, SF	21
R. Sadecki, STL	20

Saves

H. Woodeshick, HOU	23
A. McBean, PIT	22
J. Baldschun, PHI	21
L. McDaniel, CHI	15

Strikeouts

B. Veale, PIT	250
B. Gibson, STL	245
D. Drysdale, LA	237
S. Koufax, LA	223
J. Bunning, PHI	219

Complete Games

J. Marichal, SF	22
D. Drysdale, LA	21
L. Jackson, CHI	19
B. Gibson, STL	17
D. Ellsworth, CHI	16

Fewest Hits per 9 Innings

S. Koufax, LA	6.22
D. Drysdale, LA	6.78
C. Short, PHI	7.10

Shutouts

S. Koufax, LA	7

BATTING AND BASE RUNNING LEADERS

Home Run Percentage			Runs Scored	
W. Mays, SF	8.1		R. Allen, PHI	125
O. Cepeda, SF	5.9		W. Mays, SF	121
J. Hart, SF	5.5		L. Brock, CHI, STL	111

Doubles			Triples	
L. Maye, MIL	44		R. Santo, CHI	13
R. Clemente, PIT	40		R. Allen, PHI	13
B. Williams, CHI	39		V. Pinson, CIN	11
			L. Brock, CHI, STL	11

PITCHING LEADERS

Fewest Walks per 9 Innings			Most Strikeouts per 9 Inn.	
J. Bunning, PHI	1.46		S. Koufax, LA	9.00
B. Bruce, HOU	1.47		J. Maloney, CIN	8.92
V. Law, PIT	1.50		B. Veale, PIT	8.05

Innings			Games Pitched	
D. Drysdale, LA	321		B. Miller, LA	74
L. Jackson, CHI	298		R. Perranoski, LA	72
B. Gibson, STL	287		J. Baldschun, PHI	71

	W	L	PCT	GB	R	OR	2B	3B	HR	BA	SA	SB	E	DP	FA	CG	BB	SO	ShO	SV	ERA
STL	93	69	.574		715	652	240	53	109	.272	.392	73	172	147	.973	47	410	877	10	38	3.43
CIN	92	70	.568	1	660	566	220	38	130	.249	.372	90	130	137	.979	54	436	**1122**	14	35	3.07
PHI	92	70	.568	1	693	632	241	51	130	.258	.391	30	157	150	.975	37	440	1009	17	41	3.36
SF	90	72	.556	3	656	587	185	38	**165**	.246	.382	64	159	136	.975	48	480	1023	17	30	3.19
MIL	88	74	.543	5	**803**	744	**274**	32	159	**.272**	**.418**	53	143	139	.977	45	452	906	14	39	4.12
LA	80	82	.494	13	614	572	180	39	79	.250	.340	**141**	170	126	.973	47	458	1062	**19**	27	**2.95**
PIT	80	82	.494	13	663	636	225	**54**	121	.264	.389	39	177	**179**	.972	42	476	951	14	29	3.52
CHI	76	86	.469	17	649	724	239	50	145	.251	.390	70	162	147	.975	**58**	423	737	11	19	4.08
HOU	66	96	.407	27	495	628	162	41	70	.229	.315	40	149	124	.976	30	**353**	852	9	31	3.41
NY	53	109	.327	40	569	776	195	31	103	.246	.348	36	167	154	.974	40	466	717	10	15	4.25
					6517	6517	2161	427	1211	.254	.374	636	1586	1439	.975	448	4394	9256	135	304	3.54

American League 1964

	POS	Player	AB	BA	HR	RBI	PO	A	E	DP	TC/G	FA	Pitcher	G	IP	W	L	SV	ERA
N. Y. W-99 L-63 Yogi Berra	1B	J. Pepitone	613	.251	28	100	**1333**	121	18	**128**	9.5	.988	J. Bouton	38	271	18	13	0	3.02
	2B	B. Richardson	**679**	.267	4	50	**400**	410	15	108	5.3	.982	W. Ford	39	245	17	6	1	2.13
	SS	T. Kubek	415	.229	8	31	186	307	11	52	5.1	.978	A. Downing	37	244	13	8	2	3.47
	3B	C. Boyer	510	.218	8	52	118	278	13	28	**3.3**	.968	R. Terry	27	115	7	11	4	4.54
	RF	R. Maris	513	.281	26	71	250	6	1	0	1.9	.996	R. Sheldon	19	102	5	2	1	3.61
	CF	M. Mantle	465	.303	35	111	217	3	5	1	1.7	.978	Stottlemyre	13	96	9	3	0	2.06
	LF	T. Tresh	533	.246	16	73	259	7	1	0	1.8	**.996**	P. Mikkelsen	50	86	7	4	12	3.56
	C	E. Howard	550	.313	15	84	**939**	67	2	9	6.9	**.998**	H. Reniff	41	69	6	4	9	3.12
	S3	P. Linz	368	.250	5	25	121	275	20	42		.952	S. Hamilton	30	60	7	2	3	3.28
	OF	H. Lopez	285	.260	10	34	130	2	4	1	1.3	.971							
	CO	J. Blanchard	161	.255	7	28	139	8	2	1		.987							
Chi. W-98 L-64 Al Lopez	1B	T. McCraw	368	.261	6	36	601	37	5	57	7.7	.992	G. Peters	37	274	**20**	8	0	2.50
	2B	A. Weis	328	.247	2	23	199	255	16	64	4.1	.966	J. Pizarro	33	239	19	9	0	2.56
	SS	R. Hansen	575	.261	20	68	**292**	514	21	105	**5.2**	.975	J. Horlen	32	211	13	9	0	1.88
	3B	P. Ward	539	.282	23	94	126	309	19	24	3.3	.958	J. Buzhardt	31	160	10	8	0	2.98
	RF	Hershberger	452	.230	2	31	231	10	4	2	1.8	.984	H. Wilhelm	73	131	12	9	27	1.99
	CF	J. Landis	298	.208	1	18	183	7	1	2	1.9	.995	E. Fisher	59	125	6	3	9	3.02
	LF	F. Robinson	525	.301	11	59	225	5	3	0	1.7	.987	R. Herbert	20	112	6	7	0	3.47
	C	J. Martin	294	.197	4	22	530	43	8	6	4.8	.986	D. Mossi	34	40	3	1	7	2.93
	2B	D. Buford	442	.262	4	30	196	198	13	60	4.4	.968							
	OF	D. Nicholson	294	.204	13	39	136	4	4	0	1.6	.972							
	1B	B. Skowron	273	.293	4	38	621	40	1	53	9.5*	.998							
	C	J. McNertney	186	.215	3	23	360	30	5	5	5.7	.987							
Bal. W-97 L-65 Hank Bauer	1B	N. Siebern	478	.245	12	56	1171	101	6	**121**	8.6	.995	M. Pappas	37	252	16	7	0	2.97
	2B	J. Adair	569	.248	9	47	395	422	5	107	5.4	**.994**	W. Bunker	29	214	19	5	0	2.69
	SS	L. Aparicio	578	.266	10	37	260	437	15	98	4.9	**.979**	R. Roberts	31	204	13	7	0	2.91
	3B	B. Robinson	612	.317	28	118	153	**327**	14	**40**	3.0	.972	D. McNally	30	159	9	11	0	3.67
	RF	S. Bowens	501	.263	22	71	249	8	5	1	1.9	.981	S. Barber	36	157	9	13	1	3.84
	CF	J. Brandt	523	.243	13	47	345	14	7	2	**2.7**	.981	S. Miller	66	97	7	7	23	3.06
	LF	B. Powell	424	.290	39	99	178	13	5	1	1.6	.974	H. Haddix	49	90	5	5	10	2.31
	C	D. Brown	230	.257	8	32	380	29	5	4	4.9	.988	D. Hall	45	88	9	1	7	1.85
	C	J. Orsino	248	.222	8	23	384	31	10	3	6.4	.976							
	UT	B. Johnson	210	.248	3	29	164	77	5	27		.980							
	OF	W. Kirkland	150	.200	3	22	86	7	1	3	1.6	.989							

POS	Player	AB	BA	HR	RBI	PO	A	E	DP	TC/G	FA	Pitcher	G	IP	W	L	SV	ERA
Det. W-85 L-77 Chuck Dressen																		
1B	N. Cash	479	.257	23	83	1105	92	4	97	8.8	.997	D. Wickersham	40	254	19	12	1	3.44
2B	J. Lumpe	624	.256	6	46	339	394	13	95	4.7	.983	M. Lolich	44	232	18	9	2	3.26
SS	D. McAuliffe	557	.241	24	66	262	467	32	84	4.8	.958	H. Aguirre	32	162	5	10	1	3.79
3B	D. Wert	525	.257	9	55	126	283	15	30	3.0	.965	E. Rakow	42	152	8	9	3	3.72
RF	A. Kaline	525	.293	17	68	278	6	3	2	2.1	.990	P. Regan	32	147	5	10	1	5.03
CF	G. Thomas	308	.286	12	44	164	4	2	1	1.9	.988	D. McLain	19	100	4	5	0	4.05
LF	G. Brown	426	.272	15	54	205	4	4	0	2.0	.981	J. Sparma	21	84	5	6	0	3.00
C	B. Freehan	520	.300	18	80	923	61	7	7	7.0	.993	F. Gladding	42	67	7	4	7	3.07
OF	D. Demeter	441	.256	22	80	164	3	0	1	1.9	1.000	L. Sherry	38	66	7	5	11	3.66
OF	B. Bruton	296	.277	5	33	143	7	2	3	1.9	.987	T. Fox	32	61	4	3	5	3.39
L. A. W-82 L-80 Billy Rigney																		
1B	J. Adcock	366	.268	21	64	959	54	7	94	9.7	.993	D. Chance	46	**278**	**20**	9	4	**1.65**
2B	B. Knoop	486	.216	7	38	357	**522**	20	123	5.6	.978	F. Newman	32	190	13	10	0	2.75
SS	J. Fregosi	505	.277	18	72	225	421	23	89	4.9	.966	B. Latman	40	138	6	10	2	3.85
3B	F. Torres	277	.231	12	28	73	122	6	10	2.8	.970	B. Lee	64	137	6	5	19	1.51
RF	L. Clinton	306	.248	9	38	123	12	2	3	1.6	.985	B. Belinsky	23	135	9	8	0	2.86
CF	A. Pearson	265	.223	2	16	132	1	3	1	2.1	.978	K. McBride	29	116	4	13	1	5.26
LF	W. Smith	359	.301	11	51	128	2	3	0	1.5	.977	D. Lee	33	89	5	4	2	2.72
C	B. Rodgers	514	.243	4	54	884	87	13	14	6.7	.987	B. Duliba	58	73	6	4	9	3.59
UT	T. Satriano	255	.200	1	17	383	72	8	32		.983							
OF	J. Piersall	255	.314	2	13	164	2	0	2	1.6	1.000							
13	V. Power	221	.249	3	13	302	79	3	26		.992							
OF	B. Perry	221	.276	3	16	115	2	3	0	1.9	.975							
OF	Kirkpatrick	219	.242	2	22	90	3	3	0	1.5	.969							
3B	B. Moran	198	.268	0	11	47	86	10	5	3.0	.930							
OF	L. Thomas	172	.273	2	24	71	4	4	1	1.7	.949							
Cle. W-79 L-83 Birdie Tebbetts																		
1B	B. Chance	390	.279	14	75	567	24	7	47	7.4	.988	J. Kralick	30	191	12	7	0	3.21
2B	L. Brown	335	.230	12	40	185	270	9	56	4.5	.981	S. McDowell	31	173	11	6	1	2.70
SS	D. Howser	637	.256	3	52	291	463	20	100	4.8	.974	D. Donovan	30	158	7	9	1	4.55
3B	M. Alvis	381	.252	18	53	83	191	13	18	2.7	.955	S. Siebert	41	156	7	9	3	3.23
RF	T. Francona	270	.248	8	24	65	2	1	0	1.0	.985	P. Ramos	36	133	7	10	0	5.14
CF	V. Davalillo	577	.270	6	51	346	11	5	5	2.5	.986	L. Tiant	19	127	10	4	1	2.83
LF	L. Wagner	641	.253	31	100	254	5	11	0	1.7	.959	G. Bell	56	106	8	6	4	4.33
C	J. Romano	352	.241	19	47	714	38	7	3	7.9	.991	D. McMahon	70	101	6	4	16	2.41
UT	W. Held	364	.236	18	49	183	182	14	40		.963	T. John	25	94	2	9	0	3.91
1B	F. Whitfield	293	.270	10	29	596	36	5	63	8.1	.992	L. Stange	23	92	4	8	0	4.12
UT	C. Salmon	283	.307	4	25	191	67	2	14		.992	T. Abernathy	53	73	2	6	11	4.33
C	J. Azcue	271	.273	4	34	510	36	4	2	7.2	.993							
Min. W-79 L-83 Sam Mele																		
1B	B. Allison	492	.287	32	86	715	55	11	63	8.4	.986	C. Pascual	36	267	15	12	0	3.30
2B	B. Allen	243	.214	6	20	161	173	7	40	4.8	.979	J. Kaat	36	243	17	11	1	3.22
SS	Z. Versalles	659	.259	20	64	271	427	31	89	4.6	.957	D. Stigman	32	190	6	15	0	4.03
3B	R. Rollins	596	.270	12	68	134	297	24	17	3.1	.947	M. Grant	26	166	11	9	1	2.82
RF	T. Oliva	672	**.323**	32	94	313	5	6	0	2.0	.981	J. Arrigo	41	105	7	4	1	3.84
CF	J. Hall	510	.282	25	75	323	13	5	0	2.5	.985	J. Roland	30	94	2	6	3	4.10
LF	H. Killebrew	577	.270	**49**	111	232	1	7	0	1.5	.971	Worthington	41	72	5	6	14	1.37
C	E. Battey	405	.272	12	52	813	52	9	4	7.0	.990	J. Perry	42	65	6	3	2	3.44
1B	D. Mincher	287	.237	23	56	549	43	5	50	7.9	.992							
Bos. W-72 L-90 Johnny Pesky W-70 L-90 Billy Herman W-2 L-0																		
1B	D. Stuart	603	.279	33	114	1159	104	24	105	8.3	.981	Monbouquette	36	234	13	14	1	4.04
2B	D. Jones	374	.230	6	39	181	193	16	41	4.6	.959	E. Wilson	33	202	11	12	0	4.49
SS	E. Bressoud	566	.293	15	55	248	411	19	78	4.3	.972	J. Lamabe	39	177	9	13	1	5.89
3B	F. Malzone	537	.264	13	56	141	259	17	24	2.9	.959	D. Morehead	32	167	8	15	0	4.97
RF	L. Thomas	401	.257	13	42	176	6	1	1	1.7	.995	B. Heffner	55	159	7	9	6	4.08
CF	Yastrzemski	567	.289	15	67	372	19	11	3	2.7	.973	D. Radatz	79	157	16	9	29	2.29
LF	T. Conigliaro	404	.290	24	52	176	7	5	0	1.8	.973	E. Connolly	27	81	4	11	0	4.91
C	B. Tillman	425	.278	17	61	897	49	11	5	7.3	.989							
UT	F. Mantilla	425	.289	30	64	173	146	5	29		.985							
2B	C. Schilling	163	.196	0	7	89	101	5	20	4.6	.974							
C	R. Nixon	163	.233	1	20	273	11	3	3	6.4	.990							
Was. W-62 L-100 Gil Hodges																		
1B	B. Skowron	262	.271	13	41	591	40	4	41	9.6*	.994	C. Osteen	37	257	15	13	0	3.33
2B	D. Blasingame	506	.267	1	34	259	336	14	70	4.5	.977	B. Narum	38	199	9	15	0	4.30
SS	E. Brinkman	447	.224	8	34	234	364	19	75	4.9	.969	B. Daniels	33	163	8	10	0	3.70
3B	J. Kennedy	482	.230	7	35	97	190	16	14	2.9	.947	A. Koch	32	114	3	10	0	4.89
RF	J. King	415	.241	18	56	240	10	7	0	2.1	.973	S. Ridzik	49	112	5	5	2	2.89
CF	D. Lock	512	.248	28	80	354	19	5	3	2.5	.987	J. Hannan	49	106	4	7	3	4.16
LF	C. Hinton	514	.274	11	53	258	7	4	3	2.1	.985	D. Stenhouse	26	88	2	7	1	4.81
C	M. Brumley	426	.244	2	35	628	44	6	4	5.1	.991	R. Kline	61	81	10	7	14	2.32
3B	D. Zimmer	341	.246	12	38	68	143	10	6	2.5	.955	J. Duckworth	30	56	1	6	3	4.34
1B	D. Phillips	234	.231	2	23	473	39	3	50	8.4	.994							
OF	F. Valentine	212	.226	4	20	86	2	2	1	1.6	.978							

	POS	Player	AB	BA	HR	RBI	PO	A	E	DP	TC/G	FA	Pitcher	G	IP	W	L	SV	ERA
K. C.	1B	J. Gentile	439	.251	28	71	1018	84	13	92	8.7	.988	O. Pena	40	219	12	14	0	4.43
W-57 L-105	2B	D. Green	435	.264	11	37	262	361	6	69	5.2	.990	D. Segui	40	217	8	17	0	4.56
Ed Lopat	SS	W. Causey	604	.281	8	49	266	352	21	75	4.9	.967	J. O'Donoghue	39	174	10	14	0	4.92
W-17 L-35	3B	E. Charles	557	.241	16	63	138	259	19	25	2.8	.954	M. Drabowsky	53	168	5	13	1	5.29
Mel McGaha	RF	R. Colavito	588	.274	34	102	275	10	8	1	1.8	.973	J. Wyatt	81	128	9	8	20	3.59
W-40 L-70	CF	N. Mathews	573	.239	14	60	384	5	13	2	2.6	.968	T. Bowsfield	50	119	4	7	0	4.10
	LF	M. Jimenez	204	.225	12	38	59	3	4	1	1.3	.939	W. Stock	50	93	6	3	5	1.94
	C	D. Edwards	294	.224	5	28	469	31	7	5	6.4	.986							
	SO	B. Campaneris	269	.257	4	22	97	96	5	14		.975							
	C	B. Bryan	220	.241	13	36	317	22	3	5	5.3	.991							
	OF	G. Alusik	204	.240	3	19	61	1	1	1	1.4	.984							

BATTING AND BASE RUNNING LEADERS

Batting Average
T. Oliva, MIN	.323
B. Robinson, BAL	.317
E. Howard, NY	.313
M. Mantle, NY	.303
F. Robinson, CHI	.301

Slugging Average
B. Powell, BAL	.606
M. Mantle, NY	.591
T. Oliva, MIN	.557
B. Allison, MIN	.553
H. Killebrew, MIN	.548

Home Runs
H. Killebrew, MIN	49
B. Powell, BAL	39
M. Mantle, NY	35
R. Colavito, KC	34
D. Stuart, BOS	33

Total Bases
T. Oliva, MIN	374
B. Robinson, BAL	319
H. Killebrew, MIN	316
R. Colavito, KC	298
D. Stuart, BOS	296

Runs Batted In
B. Robinson, BAL	118
D. Stuart, BOS	114
M. Mantle, NY	111
H. Killebrew, MIN	111
R. Colavito, KC	102

Stolen Bases
L. Aparicio, BAL	57
A. Weis, CHI	22
V. Davalillo, CLE	21
D. Howser, CLE	20
C. Hinton, WAS	17

Hits
T. Oliva, MIN	217
B. Robinson, BAL	194
B. Richardson, NY	181

Base on Balls
N. Siebern, BAL	106
M. Mantle, NY	99
H. Killebrew, MIN	93

Home Run Percentage
H. Killebrew, MIN	8.5
M. Mantle, NY	7.5
B. Allison, MIN	6.5

Runs Scored
T. Oliva, MIN	109
D. Howser, CLE	101
H. Killebrew, MIN	95

Doubles
T. Oliva, MIN	43
E. Bressoud, BOS	41
B. Robinson, BAL	35
Z. Versalles, MIN	33

Triples
R. Rollins, MIN	10
Z. Versalles, MIN	10

PITCHING LEADERS

Winning Percentage
W. Bunker, BAL	.792
W. Ford, NY	.739
G. Peters, CHI	.714
M. Pappas, BAL	.696
D. Chance, LA	.690

Earned Run Average
D. Chance, LA	1.65
J. Horlen, CHI	1.88
W. Ford, NY	2.13
G. Peters, CHI	2.50
J. Pizarro, CHI	2.56

Wins
G. Peters, CHI	20
D. Chance, LA	20
W. Bunker, BAL	19
J. Pizarro, CHI	19
D. Wickersham, DET	19

Saves
D. Radatz, BOS	29
H. Wilhelm, CHI	27
S. Miller, BAL	23
J. Wyatt, KC	20
B. Lee, LA	19

Strikeouts
A. Downing, NY	217
C. Pascual, MIN	213
D. Chance, LA	207
G. Peters, CHI	205
M. Lolich, DET	192

Complete Games
D. Chance, LA	15
C. Pascual, MIN	14
J. Kaat, MIN	13
C. Osteen, WAS	13
M. Pappas, BAL	13

Fewest Hits per 9 Innings
J. Horlen, CHI	6.07
D. Chance, LA	6.27
W. Bunker, BAL	6.77

Shutouts
D. Chance, LA	11
W. Ford, NY	8
M. Pappas, BAL	7

Fewest Walks per 9 Innings
Monbouquette, BOS	1.54
M. Pappas, BAL	1.72
F. Newman, LA	1.85

Most Strikeouts per 9 Inn.
S. McDowell, CLE	9.19
A. Downing, NY	8.00
O. Pena, KC	7.55

Innings
D. Chance, LA	278
G. Peters, CHI	274
J. Bouton, NY	271

Games Pitched
J. Wyatt, KC	81
D. Radatz, BOS	79
H. Wilhelm, CHI	73

	W	L	PCT	GB	R	OR		Batting					SB		Fielding					Pitching			
							2B	3B	HR	BA	SA		E	DP	FA	CG	BB	SO	ShO	SV	ERA		
NY	99	63	.611		730	577	208	35	162	.253	.387	54	109	158	.983	46	504	989	18	**45**	3.15		
CHI	98	64	.605	1	642	501	184	40	106	.247	.353	75	122	164	.981	44	**401**	955	20	**45**	**2.72**		
BAL	97	65	.599	2	679	567	229	20	162	.248	.387	78	**95**	159	**.985**	44	456	939	17	41	3.16		
DET	85	77	.525	14	699	678	199	**57**	157	.253	.395	60	111	137	.982	35	536	993	11	35	3.84		
LA	82	80	.506	17	544	551	186	27	102	.242	.344	49	138	**168**	.978	30	530	965	**28**	41	2.91		
CLE	79	83	.488	20	689	693	208	22	164	.247	.380	**79**	118	149	.981	37	565	**1162**	16	37	3.75		
MIN	79	83	.488	20	**737**	678	227	46	**221**	.252	**.427**	46	145	131	.977	**47**	545	1099	4	29	3.57		
BOS	72	90	.444	27	688	793	**253**	29	186	**.258**	.416	18	138	123	.977	21	571	1094	9	38	4.50		
WAS	62	100	.383	37	578	733	199	28	125	.231	.348	47	127	145	.979	27	505	794	5	26	3.98		
KC	57	105	.352	42	621	836	216	29	166	.239	.379	34	158	152	.974	18	614	966	6	27	4.71		
					6607	6607	2109	333	1551	.247	.382	540	1261	1486	.980	349	5227	9956	134	364	3.63		

POS	Player	AB	BA	HR	RBI	PO	A	E	DP	TC/G	FA	Pitcher	G	IP	W	L	SV	ERA
L. A. W-97 L-65 Walter Alston																		
1B	W. Parker	542	.238	8	51	1434	95	5	112	10.0	.997	S. Koufax	43	336	26	8	2	2.04
2B	J. Lefebvre	544	.250	12	69	349	429	24	91	5.1	.970	D. Drysdale	44	308	23	12	1	2.77
SS	M. Wills	650	.286	0	33	267	535	25	89	5.3	.970	C. Osteen	40	287	15	15	0	2.79
3B	J. Gilliam	372	.280	4	39	55	135	8	13	2.5	.960	J. Podres	27	134	7	6	1	3.43
RF	R. Fairly	555	.274	9	70	262	7	5	1	1.9	.982	R. Perranoski	59	105	6	6	17	2.24
CF	W. Davis	558	.238	10	57	318	6	11	1	2.4	.967	B. Miller	61	103	6	7	9	2.97
LF	L. Johnson	468	.259	12	58	199	3	3	2	1.6	.985	H. Reed	38	78	7	5	1	3.12
C	J. Roseboro	437	.233	8	57	824	55	5	7	6.7	.994							
3B	J. Kennedy	105	.171	1	5	35	64	3	5	1.1	.971							
3B	D. Tracewski	186	.215	1	20	30	103	7	6	2.6	.950							
S. F. W-95 L-67 Herman Franks																		
1B	W. McCovey	540	.276	39	92	1310	87	13	93	9.0	.991	J. Marichal	39	295	22	13	1	2.13
2B	H. Lanier	522	.226	0	39	294	445	18	75	4.8	.976	B. Shaw	42	235	16	9	2	2.64
SS	D. Schofield	379	.203	2	19	145	274	7	52	4.6	.984*	G. Perry	47	196	8	12	1	4.19
3B	J. Hart	591	.299	23	96	134	231	32	16	2.8	.919	R. Herbel	47	171	12	9	1	3.85
RF	J. Alou	543	.298	9	52	238	7	5	0	1.8	.980	B. Bolin	45	163	14	6	2	2.76
CF	W. Mays	558	.317	52	112	337	13	6	4	2.4	.983	J. Sanford	23	91	4	5	2	3.96
LF	M. Alou	324	.231	2	18	139	6	2	1	1.4	.986	F. Linzy	57	82	9	3	21	1.43
C	T. Haller	422	.251	16	49	864	50	12	9	7.0	.987	M. Murakami	45	74	4	1	8	3.75
UT	J. Davenport	271	.251	4	31	97	147	14	21		.946							
OF	L. Gabrielson	269	.301	4	26	112	3	3	1	1.5	.975							
Pit. W-90 L-72 Harry Walker																		
1B	D. Clendenon	612	.301	14	96	1572	119	28	161	10.9	.984	B. Veale	39	266	17	12	0	2.84
2B	B. Mazeroski	494	.271	6	54	290	439	9	113	5.8	.988	D. Cardwell	37	240	13	10	0	3.18
SS	G. Alley	500	.252	5	47	163	376	18	79	5.1	.968	B. Friend	34	222	8	12	0	3.24
3B	B. Bailey	626	.256	11	49	96	243	22	25	2.5	.939	V. Law	29	217	17	9	0	2.15
RF	R. Clemente	589	.329	10	65	288	16	10	1	2.2	.968	A. McBean	62	114	6	6	18	2.29
CF	B. Virdon	481	.279	4	24	260	3	8	1	2.1	.970	T. Sisk	38	111	7	3	0	3.40
LF	W. Stargell	533	.272	27	107	208	12	8	3	1.7	.965	J. Gibbon	31	106	4	9	1	4.51
C	J. Pagliaroni	403	.268	17	65	669	42	4	14	5.5	.994	D. Schwall	43	77	9	6	4	2.92
OF	M. Mota	294	.279	4	29	127	5	2	1	1.4	.985							
UT	A. Rodgers	178	.287	2	25	88	110	8	27		.961							
Cin. W-89 L-73 Dick Sisler																		
1B	T. Perez	281	.260	12	47	525	40	6	55	6.1	.989	S. Ellis	44	264	22	10	2	3.79
2B	P. Rose	670	.312	11	81	382	403	20	93	5.0	.975	J. Maloney	33	255	20	9	0	2.54
SS	L. Cardenas	557	.287	11	57	292	440	19	92	4.8	.975	J. Jay	37	156	9	8	1	4.22
3B	D. Johnson	616	.287	32	130	132	266	22	26	2.6	.948	J. Nuxhall	32	149	11	4	2	3.45
RF	F. Robinson	582	.296	33	113	282	5	3	1	1.9	.990	J. Tsitouris	31	131	6	9	1	4.95
CF	V. Pinson	669	.305	22	94	354	9	3	1	2.3	.992	J. O'Toole	29	128	3	10	1	5.92
LF	T. Harper	646	.257	18	64	277	6	5	0	1.8	.983	B. McCool	62	105	9	10	21	4.27
C	J. Edwards	371	.267	17	51	761	61	8	9	7.5	.990							
1B	G. Coleman	325	.302	14	57	621	48	6	52	7.6	.991							
C	D. Pavletich	191	.319	8	32	335	16	5	5	6.6	.986							
Mil. W-86 L-76 Bobby Bragan																		
1B	G. Oliver	392	.270	21	58	374	37	7	30	8.0	.983	T. Cloninger	40	279	24	11	1	3.29
2B	F. Bolling	535	.264	7	50	310	393	17	90	4.9	.976	W. Blasingame	38	225	16	10	1	3.77
SS	W. Woodward	265	.208	0	11	146	243	9	61	3.7	.977	K. Johnson	29	180	13	8	2	3.21
3B	E. Mathews	546	.251	32	95	113	301	19	19	2.8	.956	D. Lemaster	32	146	7	13	0	4.43
RF	H. Aaron	570	.318	32	89	298	9	4	2	2.1	.987	B. Sadowski	34	123	5	9	3	4.32
CF	M. Jones	504	.262	31	75	239	2	5	2	1.8	.980	H. Fischer	31	123	8	9	0	3.89
LF	F. Alou	555	.297	23	78	148	2	3	0	1.7	.980	B. O'Dell	62	111	10	6	18	2.18
C	J. Torre	523	.291	27	80	589	43	6	4	6.4	.991	P. Niekro	41	75	2	3	6	2.89
OF	R. Carty	271	.310	10	35	112	3	5	1	1.6	.958							
OF	T. Cline	220	.191	0	10	119	5	4	1	1.5	.969							
SS	D. Menke	181	.243	4	18	65	140	7	22	3.9	.967							
UT	de la Hoz	176	.256	2	11	61	99	8	20		.952							
Phi. W-85 L-76 Gene Mauch																		
1B	D. Stuart	538	.234	28	95	1119	98	17	100	8.6	.986	C. Short	47	297	18	11	2	2.82
2B	T. Taylor	323	.229	3	27	169	220	17	51	4.7	.958	J. Bunning	39	291	19	9	0	2.60
SS	B. Wine	394	.228	5	33	221	387	21	84	4.7	.967	R. Culp	33	204	14	10	0	3.22
3B	R. Allen	619	.302	20	85	129	305	26	29	2.9	.943	R. Herbert	25	131	5	8	1	3.86
RF	J. Callison	619	.262	32	101	313	21	6	2	2.1	.982	B. Belinsky	30	110	4	9	1	4.84
CF	T. Gonzalez	370	.295	13	41	167	3	3	1	1.7	.983	G. Wagner	59	105	7	7	7	3.00
LF	A. Johnson	262	.294	8	28	109	3	4	0	1.4	.966	J. Baldschun	65	99	5	8	6	3.82
C	C. Dalrymple	301	.213	4	23	657	70	5	10	7.2	.993	E. Roebuck	44	50	5	3	3	3.40
2O	C. Rojas	521	.303	3	42	264	236	7	57		.986							
OF	W. Covington	235	.247	15	45	88	2	3	0	1.5	.968							
OF	J. Briggs	229	.236	4	23	110	2	2	0	1.7	.982							
S1	R. Amaro	184	.212	0	15	172	126	10	32		.968							
C	P. Corrales	174	.224	2	15	358	24	7	2	6.3	.982							
St. L. W-80 L-81 Red Schoendienst																		
1B	B. White	543	.289	24	73	1308	109	11	114	9.9	.992	B. Gibson	38	299	20	12	1	3.07
2B	J. Javier	229	.227	2	23	128	179	8	40	4.6	.975	C. Simmons	34	203	9	15	0	4.08
SS	D. Groat	587	.254	0	52	442	450	27	86	4.9	.962	T. Stallard	40	194	11	8	0	3.38
3B	K. Boyer	535	.260	13	75	113	250	12	18	2.6	.968	R. Sadecki	36	173	6	15	1	5.21
RF	M. Shannon	244	.221	3	25	170	5	1	1	1.7	.994	B. Purkey	32	124	10	9	2	5.79
CF	C. Flood	617	.310	11	83	349	7	5	3	2.4	.986	R. Washburn	28	119	9	11	2	3.62
LF	L. Brock	631	.288	16	69	272	11	12	1	1.9	.959	N. Briles	37	82	3	3	4	3.50
C	T. McCarver	409	.276	11	48	687	43	4	4	6.6	.995	H. Woodeshick	51	60	3	2	15	1.81
UT	P. Gagliano	363	.240	8	53	201	169	16	34		.959	D. Dennis	41	55	2	3	6	2.29
OF	T. Francona	174	.259	5	19	35	0	1	0	1.1	.972							
2S	J. Buchek	166	.247	3	21	92	154	5	38		.980							
OF	B. Skinner	152	.309	5	26	43	0	3	0	1.4	.935							

	POS	Player	AB	BA	HR	RBI	PO	A	E	DP	TC/G	FA	Pitcher	G	IP	W	L	SV	ERA
Chi.	1B	E. Banks	612	.265	28	106	**1682**	93	15	143	**11.0**	.992	L. Jackson	39	257	14	21	0	3.85
W-72 L-90	2B	G. Beckert	614	.239	3	30	326	**494**	23	101	5.5	.973	D. Ellsworth	36	222	14	15	1	3.81
Bob Kennedy	SS	D. Kessinger	309	.201	0	14	176	338	**28**	69	5.2	.948	B. Buhl	32	184	13	11	0	4.39
W-24 L-32	3B	R. Santo	608	.285	33	101	**155**	**373**	24	27	**3.4**	.957	C. Koonce	38	173	7	9	0	3.69
Lou Klein	RF	B. Williams	645	.315	34	108	296	10	10	2	1.9	.968	T. Abernathy	**84**	136	4	6	**31**	2.57
W-48 L-58	CF	D. Landrum	425	.226	6	34	241	3	3	0	2.1	.988	L. McDaniel	71	129	5	6	2	2.59
	LF	D. Clemens	340	.221	4	26	145	7	3	0	1.5	.981	B. Faul	17	97	6	6	0	3.54
	C	V. Roznovsky	172	.221	3	15	270	30	5	6	4.8	.984							
	OS	J. Stewart	282	.223	0	19	117	58	8	11		.956							
	OF	G. Altman	196	.235	4	23	66	0	4	0	1.6	.943							
	SS	R. Pena	170	.218	2	12	74	151	17	29	4.8	.930							
	C	C. Krug	169	.201	5	24	273	27	6	5	5.3	.980							
	C	E. Bailey	150	.253	5	23	237	23	5	3	4.9	.981							
Hou.	1B	W. Bond	407	.263	7	47	650	49	12	52	9.6	.983	B. Bruce	35	230	9	18	0	3.72
W-65 L-97	2B	J. Morgan	601	.271	14	40	348	492	**27**	82	5.5	.969	D. Farrell	33	208	11	11	1	3.50
Lum Harris	SS	B. Lillis	408	.221	0	20	188	273	15	49	4.6	.968	D. Nottebart	29	158	4	15	0	4.67
	3B	B. Aspromonte	578	.263	5	52	123	281	16	25	2.9	.962	L. Dierker	26	147	7	8	0	3.50
	RF	R. Staub	410	.256	14	63	202	12	11	1	2.0	.951	D. Giusti	38	131	8	7	3	4.32
	CF	J. Wynn	564	.275	22	73	**382**	13	9	1	**2.6**	.978	C. Raymond	33	96	7	4	5	2.90
	LF	L. Maye	415	.251	3	36	177	6	9	1	1.9	.953	J. Owens	50	71	6	5	8	3.28
	C	R. Brand	391	.235	2	37	585	54	8	8	6.3	.988	R. Taylor	32	58	1	5	4	6.40
	OF	J. Gaines	229	.227	6	31	83	1	8	0	1.4	.913	H. Woodeshick	27	32	3	4	3	3.06
	1B	J. Gentile	227	.242	7	31	544	43	4	41	8.2	.993							
	SS	E. Kasko	215	.247	1	10	96	152	6	27	4.3	.976							
N.Y.	1B	E. Kranepool	525	.253	10	53	1375	93	12	116	10.1	.992	J. Fisher	43	254	8	**24**	1	3.94
W-50 L-112	2B	C. Hiller	286	.238	5	21	145	182	14	39	4.3	.959	A. Jackson	37	205	8	20	1	4.34
Casey Stengel	SS	R. McMillan	528	.242	1	42	248	477	27	80	4.9	.964	W. Spahn	20	126	4	12	0	4.36
W-31 L-64	3B	C. Smith	499	.244	16	62	119	281	18	27	3.2	.957	G. Cisco	35	112	4	8	0	4.49
Wes Westrum	RF	J. Lewis	477	.245	15	45	257	14	7	3	2.0	.975	T. McGraw	37	98	2	7	1	3.32
W-19 L-48	CF	J. Hickman	369	.236	15	40	136	3	5	0	1.6	.965	T. Parsons	35	91	1	10	1	4.67
	LF	R. Swoboda	399	.228	19	50	188	9	11	2	1.9	.947	G. Kroll	32	87	6	6	1	4.45
	C	C. Cannizzaro	251	.183	0	7	435	69	**12**	8	4.6	.977							
	OF	Christopher	437	.249	5	40	180	3	2	0	1.7	.989							
	UT	B. Klaus	288	.191	2	12	179	254	11	54		.975							
	2B	R. Hunt	196	.240	1	10	106	128	5	17	5.2	.979							

BATTING AND BASE RUNNING LEADERS

Batting Average
R. Clemente, PIT	.329
H. Aaron, MIL	.318
W. Mays, SF	.317
B. Williams, CHI	.315
P. Rose, CIN	.312

Slugging Average
W. Mays, SF	.645
H. Aaron, MIL	.560
B. Williams, CHI	.552
F. Robinson, CIN	.540
W. McCovey, SF	.539

Home Runs
W. Mays, SF	52
W. McCovey, SF	39
B. Williams, CHI	34
F. Robinson, CIN	33
R. Santo, CHI	33

Total Bases
W. Mays, SF	360
B. Williams, CHI	356
V. Pinson, CIN	324
H. Aaron, MIL	319
D. Johnson, CIN	317

Runs Batted In
D. Johnson, CIN	130
F. Robinson, CIN	113
W. Mays, SF	112
B. Williams, CHI	108
W. Stargell, PIT	107

Stolen Bases
M. Wills, LA	94
L. Brock, STL	63
J. Wynn, HOU	43
T. Harper, CIN	35
W. Davis, LA	25

Hits
P. Rose, CIN	209
V. Pinson, CIN	204
B. Williams, CHI	203

Base on Balls
J. Morgan, HOU	97
W. McCovey, SF	88
R. Santo, CHI	88

Home Run Percentage
W. Mays, SF	9.3
W. McCovey, SF	7.2
M. Jones, MIL	6.2

Runs Scored
T. Harper, CIN	126
W. Mays, SF	118
P. Rose, CIN	117

Doubles
H. Aaron, MIL	40
B. Williams, CHI	39
L. Brock, STL	35
P. Rose, CIN	35

Triples
J. Callison, PHI	16
R. Clemente, PIT	14
D. Clendenon, PIT	14
R. Allen, PHI	14

PITCHING LEADERS

Winning Percentage
S. Koufax, LA	.765
J. Maloney, CIN	.690
S. Ellis, CIN	.688
T. Cloninger, MIL	.686
J. Bunning, PHI	.679

Earned Run Average
S. Koufax, LA	2.04
J. Marichal, SF	2.13
V. Law, PIT	2.15
J. Maloney, CIN	2.54
J. Bunning, PHI	2.60

Wins
S. Koufax, LA	26
T. Cloninger, MIL	24
D. Drysdale, LA	23
S. Ellis, CIN	22
J. Marichal, SF	22

Saves
T. Abernathy, CHI	31
F. Linzy, SF	21
B. McCool, CIN	21
B. O'Dell, MIL	18
H. Woodeshick, HOU, STL	18
A. McBean, PIT	18

Strikeouts
S. Koufax, LA	382
B. Veale, PIT	276
B. Gibson, STL	270
J. Bunning, PHI	268
J. Maloney, CIN	244

Complete Games
S. Koufax, LA	27
J. Marichal, SF	24
B. Gibson, STL	20
D. Drysdale, LA	20
T. Cloninger, MIL	16

Fewest Hits per 9 Innings
S. Koufax, LA	5.79
J. Maloney, CIN	6.66
J. Marichal, SF	6.83

Shutouts
J. Marichal, SF	10
S. Koufax, LA	8

Fewest Walks per 9 Innings
J. Marichal, SF	1.40
V. Law, PIT	1.45
B. Bruce, HOU	1.49

Most Strikeouts per 9 Inn.
S. Koufax, LA	10.24
B. Veale, PIT	9.34
J. Maloney, CIN	8.60

Innings
S. Koufax, LA	336
D. Drysdale, LA	308
B. Gibson, STL	299

Games Pitched
T. Abernathy, CHI	84
H. Woodeshick, HOU, STL	78
L. McDaniel, CHI	71
J. Baldschun, PHI	65

	W	L	PCT	GB	R	OR	2B	3B	Batting HR	BA	SA	SB	E	Fielding DP	FA	CG	BB	Pitching SO	ShO	SV	ERA
LA	97	65	.599		608	521	193	32	78	.245	.335	172	134	135	.979	58	425	1079	23	34	2.81
SF	95	67	.586	2	682	593	169	43	159	.252	.385	47	148	124	.976	42	408	1060	17	42	3.20
PIT	90	72	.556	7	675	580	217	57	111	.265	.382	51	152	189	.977	49	469	882	17	27	3.01
CIN	89	73	.549	8	825	704	268	61	183	.273	.439	82	117	142	.981	43	587	1113	9	34	3.88
MIL	86	76	.531	11	708	633	243	28	196	.256	.416	64	140	145	.978	43	541	966	4	38	3.52
PHI	85	76	.528	11.5	654	667	205	53	144	.250	.384	46	157	153	.975	50	466	1071	18	21	3.53
STL	80	81	.497	16.5	707	674	234	46	109	.254	.371	100	130	152	.979	40	467	916	11	35	3.77
CHI	72	90	.444	25	635	723	202	33	134	.238	.358	65	171	166	.974	33	481	855	9	35	3.78
HOU	65	97	.401	32	569	711	188	42	97	.237	.340	90	166	130	.974	29	388	931	7	26	3.84
NY	50	112	.309	47	495	752	203	27	107	.221	.327	28	171	153	.974	29	498	776	11	14	4.06
					6558	6558	2122	422	1318	.249	.374	745	1486	1489	.977	416	4730	9649	126	306	3.54

American League 1965

	POS	Player	AB	BA	HR	RBI	PO	A	E	DP	TC/G	FA	Pitcher	G	IP	W	L	SV	ERA
Min. W-102 L-60 Sam Mele	1B	D. Mincher	346	.251	22	65	818	45	7	64	8.8	.992	M. Grant	41	270	21	7	0	3.30
	2B	J. Kindall	342	.196	6	36	242	252	19	62	4.8	.963	J. Kaat	45	264	18	11	2	2.83
	SS	Z. Versalles	666	.273	19	77	248	487	39	105	4.8	.950	J. Perry	36	168	12	7	0	2.63
	3B	R. Rollins	469	.249	5	32	112	229	15	21	3.2	.958	C. Pascual	27	156	9	3	0	3.35
	RF	T. Oliva	576	.321	16	98	284	10	11	3	2.1	.964	D. Boswell	27	106	6	5	0	3.40
	CF	J. Hall	522	.285	20	86	282	7	7	2	2.1	.976	Worthington	62	80	10	7	21	2.13
	LF	B. Allison	438	.233	23	78	231	11	7	4	2.0	.972	J. Merritt	16	77	5	4	2	3.17
	C	E. Battey	394	.297	6	60	652	56	10	10	5.6	.986	J. Klippstein	56	76	9	3	5	2.24
	13	H. Killebrew	401	.269	25	75	743	113	12	67		.986	D. Stigman	33	70	4	2	4	4.37
	OF	S. Valdespino	245	.261	1	22	94	4	1	1	1.7	.990	B. Pleis	41	51	4	4	4	2.98
	OF	J. Nossek	170	.218	2	16	64	1	2	1	1.4	.970							
Chi. W-95 L-67 Al Lopez	1B	B. Skowron	559	.274	18	78	1297	74	8	116	9.5	.994	J. Horlen	34	219	13	13	0	2.88
	2B	D. Buford	586	.283	10	47	326	357	13	93	5.0	.981	J. Buzhardt	32	189	13	8	1	3.01
	SS	R. Hansen	587	.235	11	66	287	527	26	97	5.2	.969	T. John	39	184	14	7	3	3.09
	3B	P. Ward	507	.247	10	57	97	319	21	22	3.3	.952	G. Peters	33	176	10	12	0	3.62
	RF	F. Robinson	577	.265	14	66	254	6	4	0	1.7	.985	E. Fisher	82	165	15	7	24	2.40
	CF	K. Berry	472	.218	12	42	331	6	7	1	2.2	.980	B. Howard	30	148	9	8	0	3.47
	LF	D. Cater	514	.270	14	55	174	6	4	2	1.4	.978	H. Wilhelm	66	144	7	7	20	1.81
	C	J. Romano	356	.242	18	48	569	61	6	5	5.7	.992							
	1O	T. McCraw	273	.238	5	21	336	24	4	18		.989							
	C	J. Martin	230	.261	2	21	348	41	7	4	3.5	.982							
	PH	S. Burgess	77	.286	2	24													
Bal. W-94 L-68 Hank Bauer	1B	B. Powell	472	.248	17	72	538	52	5	50	7.6	.992	M. Pappas	34	221	13	9	0	2.60
	2B	J. Adair	582	.259	7	66	395	446	12	99	5.4	.986	S. Barber	37	221	15	10	0	2.69
	SS	L. Aparicio	564	.225	8	40	238	439	20	87	4.9	.971	D. McNally	35	199	11	6	0	2.85
	3B	B. Robinson	559	.297	18	80	144	296	15	36	3.2	.967	W. Bunker	34	189	10	8	2	3.38
	RF	R. Snyder	345	.270	1	29	188	4	0	0	1.8	1.000	S. Miller	67	119	14	7	24	1.89
	CF	P. Blair	364	.234	5	25	241	5	2	0	2.1	.992	R. Roberts	20	115	5	7	0	3.38
	LF	C. Blefary	462	.260	22	70	227	10	5	3	1.8	.979	J. Miller	16	93	6	4	0	3.18
	C	D. Brown	255	.231	5	30	466	40	9	6	5.6	.983	D. Hall	48	94	11	8	12	3.07
	1B	N. Siebern	297	.256	8	32	631	48	6	64	9.0	.991	J. Palmer	27	92	5	4	1	3.72
	UT	B. Johnson	273	.242	5	27	310	106	9	29		.979							
	OF	J. Brandt	243	.243	8	24	143	6	6	0	1.8	.961							
	C	J. Orsino	232	.233	9	28	342	25	5	3	6.0	.987							
	OF	S. Bowens	203	.163	7	20	108	3	2	1	1.7	.982							
Det. W-89 L-73 Chuck Dressen	1B	N. Cash	467	.266	30	82	1091	97	9	96	8.6	.992	M. Lolich	43	244	15	9	3	3.44
	2B	J. Lumpe	502	.257	4	39	281	308	9	69	4.3	.985	D. McLain	33	220	16	6	1	2.61
	SS	D. McAuliffe	404	.260	15	54	190	286	22	58	4.4	.956	H. Aguirre	32	208	14	10	0	3.59
	3B	D. Wert	609	.261	12	54	163	331	12	33	3.1	.976	D. Wickersham	34	195	9	14	0	3.78
	RF	A. Kaline	399	.281	18	72	193	2	3	0	1.8	.985	J. Sparma	30	167	13	8	0	3.18
	CF	D. Demeter	389	.278	16	58	158	1	2	1	2.0	.988	L. Sherry	39	78	3	6	5	3.10
	LF	W. Horton	512	.273	29	104	249	7	3	1	1.8	.988	T. Fox	42	78	6	4	10	2.78
	C	B. Freehan	431	.234	10	43	865	57	4	4	7.2	.996	F. Gladding	46	70	6	2	5	2.83
	OF	G. Brown	227	.256	10	43	108	1	3	0	2.0	.973	O. Pena	30	57	4	6	4	2.51
	OF	J. Northrup	219	.205	2	16	82	0	2	0	1.6	.976							
	SS	R. Oyler	194	.186	5	13	79	156	11	17	4.3	.955							
	OF	G. Thomas	169	.213	3	10	87	4	5	0	1.6	.948							
Cle. W-87 L-75 Birdie Tebbetts	1B	F. Whitfield	468	.293	26	90	932	80	7	79	8.4	.993	S. McDowell	42	273	17	11	4	2.18
	2B	P. Gonzalez	400	.253	5	39	265	287	11	59	5.0	.980	L. Tiant	41	196	11	11	1	3.53
	SS	L. Brown	438	.253	8	40	167	262	10	55	4.6	.977	S. Siebert	39	189	16	8	1	2.43
	3B	M. Alvis	604	.247	21	61	169	264	19	17	2.9	.958	R. Terry	30	166	11	6	0	3.69
	RF	R. Colavito	592	.287	26	108	265	9	0	1	1.7	1.000	L. Stange	41	132	8	4	0	3.34
	CF	V. Davalillo	505	.301	5	40	320	5	4	0	2.5	.988	G. Bell	60	104	6	5	17	3.04
	LF	L. Wagner	517	.294	28	79	175	3	8	0	1.4	.957	J. Kralick	30	86	5	11	0	4.92
	C	J. Azcue	335	.230	2	35	714	53	5	2	7.1	.994	D. McMahon	58	85	3	3	11	3.28
	UT	C. Hinton	431	.255	18	54	408	71	13	30		.974							
	SS	D. Howser	307	.235	1	6	119	173	7	33	4.1	.977							

POS	Player	AB	BA	HR	RBI	PO	A	E	DP	TC/G	FA	Pitcher	G	IP	W	L	SV	ERA
N. Y. W-77 L-85 Johnny Keane																		
1B	J. Pepitone	531	.247	18	62	1036	71	3	104	9.7	.997	Stottlemyre	37	291	20	9	0	2.63
2B	B. Richardson	664	.247	6	47	372	403	15	121	5.0	.981	W. Ford	37	244	16	13	1	3.24
SS	T. Kubek	339	.218	5	35	134	237	14	53	4.1	.964	A. Downing	35	212	12	14	0	3.40
3B	C. Boyer	514	.251	18	58	134	354	16	46	3.4	.968	J. Bouton	30	151	4	15	0	4.82
RF	H. Lopez	283	.261	7	39	94	3	6	0	1.4	.942	B. Stafford	22	111	3	8	0	3.56
CF	T. Tresh	602	.279	26	74	283	11	9	1	2.0	.970	P. Ramos	65	92	5	5	19	2.92
LF	M. Mantle	361	.255	19	46	165	3	6	0	1.6	.966	H. Reniff	51	85	3	4	3	3.80
C	E. Howard	391	.233	9	45	614	43	6	6	7.0	.991	P. Mikkelsen	41	82	4	9	1	3.28
SS	P. Linz	285	.207	2	16	126	205	16	29	4.9	.954							
OF	R. Repoz	218	.220	12	28	133	1	1	0	2.0	.993							
1B	R. Barker	205	.254	7	31	398	45	4	41	7.3	.991							
OF	R. Maris	155	.239	8	27	66	1	2	0	1.6	.971							
Cal. W-75 L-87 Billy Rigney																		
1B	J. Adcock	349	.241	14	47	789	45	3	68	8.6	.996	F. Newman	36	261	14	16	0	2.93
2B	B. Knoop	465	.269	7	43	331	402	22	89	5.3	.971	D. Chance	36	226	15	10	0	3.15
SS	J. Fregosi	602	.277	15	64	312	481	26	93	5.1	.968	M. Lopez	35	215	14	13	1	2.93
3B	P. Schaal	483	.224	9	45	101	321	13	20	2.8	.970	G. Brunet	41	197	9	11	2	2.56
RF	A. Pearson	360	.278	4	21	166	5	2	1	1.7	.988	B. Lee	69	131	9	7	23	1.92
CF	J. Cardenal	512	.250	11	57	286	12	11	2	2.4	.964	R. May	30	124	4	9	0	3.92
LF	W. Smith	459	.261	14	57	187	10	4	1	1.6	.980							
C	B. Rodgers	411	.209	1	32	682	52	7	5	5.8	.991							
OF	L. Clinton	222	.243	1	8	107	6	2	1	1.6	.983							
1B	V. Power	197	.259	1	20	419	41	2	35	4.3	.996							
Was. W-70 L-92 Gil Hodges																		
1B	D. Nen	246	.260	6	31	519	61	4	48	9.0	.993	P. Richert	34	194	15	12	0	2.60
2B	D. Blasingame	403	.223	1	18	235	248	8	60	4.5	.984	P. Ortega	35	180	12	15	0	5.11
SS	E. Brinkman	444	.185	5	35	292	369	25	76	4.6	.954	B. Narum	46	174	4	12	0	4.46
3B	K. McMullen	555	.263	18	54	155	299	22	29	3.4	.954	M. McCormick	44	158	8	8	1	3.36
RF	W. Held	332	.247	16	54	175	5	7	2	1.8	.963	B. Daniels	33	116	5	13	1	4.72
CF	D. Lock	418	.215	16	39	278	6	9	3	2.2	.969	S. Ridzik	63	110	6	4	8	4.02
LF	F. Howard	516	.289	21	84	204	5	4	0	1.5	.981	H. Koplitz	33	107	4	7	1	4.05
C	M. Brumley	216	.208	3	15	376	25	4	2	6.1	.990	R. Kline	74	99	7	6	29	2.63
2S	K. Hamlin	362	.273	4	22	185	210	12	45		.971							
OF	W. Kirkland	312	.231	14	54	151	3	2	0	1.7	.987							
OF	J. King	258	.213	14	49	127	7	1	1	1.5	.993							
UT	D. Zimmer	226	.199	2	17	181	81	12	7		.956							
1B	J. Cunningham	201	.229	3	20	393	24	6	44	7.2	.986							
1B	B. Chance	199	.256	4	14	391	25	5	39	8.8	.988							
C	D. Camilli	193	.192	3	18	319	23	7	2	5.9	.980							
Bos. W-62 L-100 Billy Herman																		
1B	L. Thomas	521	.271	22	75	1035	97	18	86	9.1	.984	E. Wilson	36	231	13	14	0	3.98
2B	F. Mantilla	534	.275	18	92	251	286	13	64	4.5	.976	Monbouquette	35	229	10	18	0	3.70
SS	R. Petrocelli	323	.232	13	33	151	278	19	45	4.8	.958	D. Morehead	34	193	10	18	0	4.06
3B	F. Malzone	364	.239	3	34	79	170	8	19	2.7	.969	J. Lonborg	32	185	9	17	0	4.47
RF	T. Conigliaro	521	.269	32	82	277	11	7	1	2.2	.976	D. Bennett	34	142	5	7	0	4.38
CF	L. Green	373	.276	7	24	198	2	4	1	2.1	.980	D. Radatz	63	124	9	11	22	3.91
LF	Yastrzemski	494	.312	20	72	222	11	3	2	1.8	.987							
C	B. Tillman	368	.215	6	35	676	45	9	6	6.9	.988							
3B	D. Jones	367	.270	5	37	63	163	17	14	3.0	.930							
OF	J. Gosger	324	.256	9	35	195	4	5	2	2.5	.975							
SS	E. Bressoud	296	.226	8	25	147	195	13	45	4.1	.963							
2B	C. Schilling	171	.240	3	9	90	116	5	22	5.1	.976							
1B	T. Horton	163	.294	7	23	311	24	7	30	7.8	.980							
K. C. W-59 L-103 Mel McGaha W-5 L-21 Haywood Sullivan W-54 L-82																		
1B	K. Harrelson	483	.238	23	66	1044	70	9	93	9.0	.992	F. Talbot	39	198	10	12	0	4.14
2B	D. Green	474	.232	15	55	252	341	12	73	4.8	.980	R. Sheldon	32	187	10	8	0	3.95
SS	B. Campaneris	578	.270	6	42	187	269	30	50	4.5	.938	J. O'Donoghue	34	178	9	18	0	3.95
3B	E. Charles	480	.269	8	56	150	251	12	28	3.2	.971	D. Segui	40	163	5	15	0	4.64
RF	Hershberger	491	.245	3	48	238	14	3	7	1.8	.968	C. Hunter	32	133	8	8	0	4.26
CF	J. Landis	364	.239	3	36	258	0	4	0	2.4	.985	J. Wyatt	65	89	2	6	18	3.25
LF	T. Reynolds	270	.237	1	22	154	8	3	2	2.0	.982	D. Mossi	51	55	5	8	7	3.74
C	B. Bryan	325	.252	14	45	527	44	9	6	6.1	.984	J. Aker	34	51	4	3	3	3.16
UT	W. Causey	513	.261	3	34	221	313	15	60		.973							
OF	J. Tartabull	218	.312	1	19	133	5	2	0	2.6	.986							
C	R. Lachemann	216	.227	9	29	361	27	8	3	5.3	.980							
OF	N. Mathews	184	.212	2	15	103	1	2	0	1.9	.981							
1B	J. Gentile	118	.246	10	22	239	17	5	24	7.5	.981							

BATTING AND BASE RUNNING LEADERS

Batting Average

T. Oliva, MIN	.321
Yastrzemski, BOS	.312
V. Davalillo, CLE	.301
B. Robinson, BAL	.297
L. Wagner, CLE	.294

Home Runs

T. Conigliaro, BOS	32
N. Cash, DET	30
W. Horton, DET	29
L. Wagner, CLE	28

Slugging Average

Yastrzemski, BOS	.536
T. Conigliaro, BOS	.512
N. Cash, DET	.512
L. Wagner, CLE	.495
T. Oliva, MIN	.491

Total Bases

Z. Versalles, MIN	308
T. Tresh, NY	287
T. Oliva, MIN	283
R. Colavito, CLE	277
T. Conigliaro, BOS	267

PITCHING LEADERS

Winning Percentage

M. Grant, MIN	.750
D. McLain, DET	.727
Stottlemyre, NY	.690
E. Fisher, CHI	.682
S. Siebert, CLE	.667

Wins

M. Grant, MIN	21
Stottlemyre, NY	20
J. Kaat, MIN	18
S. McDowell, CLE	17

Earned Run Average

S. McDowell, CLE	2.18
E. Fisher, CHI	2.40
S. Siebert, CLE	2.43
G. Brunet, CAL	2.56
P. Richert, WAS	2.60

Saves

R. Kline, WAS	29
E. Fisher, CHI	24
S. Miller, BAL	24
B. Lee, CAL	23
D. Radatz, BOS	22

BATTING AND BASE RUNNING LEADERS

Runs Batted In

R. Colavito, CLE	108
W. Horton, DET	104
T. Oliva, MIN	98
F. Mantilla, BOS	92
F. Whitfield, CLE	90

Stolen Bases

B. Campaneris, KC	51
J. Cardenal, CAL	37
Z. Versalles, MIN	27
V. Davalillo, CLE	26
L. Aparicio, BAL	26

Hits

T. Oliva, MIN	185
Z. Versalles, MIN	182
R. Colavito, CLE	170

Base on Balls

R. Colavito, CLE	93
C. Blefary, BAL	88
F. Mantilla, BOS	79

Home Run Percentage

N. Cash, DET	6.4
T. Conigliaro, BOS	6.1
W. Horton, DET	5.7

Runs Scored

Z. Versalles, MIN	126
T. Oliva, MIN	107
T. Tresh, NY	94

Doubles

Yastrzemski, BOS	45
Z. Versalles, MIN	45
T. Oliva, MIN	40

Triples

B. Campaneris, KC	12
Z. Versalles, MIN	12
L. Aparicio, BAL	10

PITCHING LEADERS

Strikeouts

S. McDowell, CLE	325
M. Lolich, DET	226
D. McLain, DET	192
S. Siebert, CLE	191
A. Downing, NY	179

Complete Games

Stottlemyre, NY	18
S. McDowell, CLE	14
M. Grant, MIN	14
D. McLain, DET	13

Fewest Hits per 9 Innings

S. McDowell, CLE	5.87
E. Fisher, CHI	6.42
S. Siebert, CLE	6.63

Shutouts

M. Grant, MIN	6

Fewest Walks per 9 Innings

R. Terry, CLE	1.25
Monbouquette, BOS	1.57
J. Horlen, CHI	1.60

Most Strikeouts per 9 Inn.

S. McDowell, CLE	10.71
S. Siebert, CLE	9.11
M. Lolich, DET	8.35

Innings

Stottlemyre, NY	291
S. McDowell, CLE	273
M. Grant, MIN	270

Games Pitched

E. Fisher, CHI	82
R. Kline, WAS	74
B. Lee, CAL	69

	W	L	PCT	GB	R	OR	2B	3B	HR	BA	SA	SB	E	DP	FA	CG	BB	SO	ShO	SV	ERA
MIN	102	60	.630		774	600	257	42	150	.254	.399	92	172	158	.973	32	503	934	12	45	3.14
CHI	95	67	.586	7	647	555	200	38	125	.246	.364	50	127	156	.980	21	460	946	14	53	2.99
BAL	94	68	.580	8	641	578	227	38	125	.238	.363	67	126	152	.980	32	510	939	15	41	2.98
DET	89	73	.549	13	680	602	190	27	162	.238	.374	57	116	126	.981	45	509	1069	14	31	3.35
CLE	87	75	.537	15	663	613	198	21	156	.250	.379	109	114	127	.981	41	500	1156	13	41	3.30
NY	77	85	.475	25	611	604	196	31	149	.235	.364	35	137	166	.978	41	511	1001	11	31	3.28
CAL	75	87	.463	27	527	569	200	36	92	.239	.341	107	123	149	.981	39	563	847	14	33	3.17
WAS	70	92	.432	32	591	721	179	33	136	.228	.350	30	143	148	.976	21	633	867	8	40	3.93
BOS	62	100	.383	40	669	791	244	40	165	.251	.400	47	162	129	.974	33	543	993	9	25	4.24
KC	59	103	.364	43	585	755	186	59	110	.240	.358	110	139	142	.977	18	574	882	7	32	4.24
					6388	6388	2077	365	1370	.242	.369	704	1359	1453	.978	323	5306	9634	117	372	3.46

National League 1966

	POS	Player	AB	BA	HR	RBI	PO	A	E	DP	TC/G	FA	Pitcher	G	IP	W	L	SV	ERA
L. A. W-95 L-67 Walter Alston	1B	W. Parker	475	.253	12	51	1118	70	9	74	8.6	.992	S. Koufax	41	323	27	9	0	1.73
	2B	J. Lefebvre	544	.274	24	74	246	332	12	59	5.0	.980	D. Drysdale	40	274	13	16	0	3.42
	SS	M. Wills	594	.273	1	39	227	453	23	79	5.1	.967	C. Osteen	39	240	17	14	0	2.85
	3B	J. Kennedy	274	.201	3	24	39	127	6	10	2.0	.965	D. Sutton	37	226	12	12	0	2.99
	RF	R. Fairly	351	.288	14	61	110	2	3	0	1.2	.974	P. Regan	65	117	14	1	21	1.62
	CF	W. Davis	624	.284	11	61	347	9	11	0	2.4	.970	B. Miller	46	84	4	2	5	2.77
	LF	L. Johnson	526	.272	17	73	249	8	4	2	1.8	.985	R. Perranoski	55	82	6	7	7	3.18
	C	J. Roseboro	445	.276	9	53	904	65	7	11	7.1	.993							
	OF	T. Davis	313	.313	3	27	98	5	3	1	1.3	.972							
	3B	J. Gilliam	235	.217	1	16	40	103	7	8	2.1	.953							
	OF	E. Ferrara	115	.270	5	23	43	0	2	0	1.4	.956							
S. F. W-93 L-68 Herman Franks	1B	W. McCovey	502	.295	36	96	1287	81	21	91	9.6	.984	J. Marichal	37	307	25	6	0	2.23
	2B	H. Lanier	459	.231	3	37	254	313	5	66	5.1	.991	G. Perry	36	256	21	8	0	2.99
	SS	T. Fuentes	541	.261	9	40	145	233	17	44	5.2	.957	B. Bolin	36	224	11	10	1	2.89
	3B	J. Hart	578	.285	33	93	100	282	24	24	2.9	.941	R. Herbel	32	130	4	5	1	4.16
	RF	O. Brown	348	.233	7	33	163	12	4	1	1.6	.978	L. McDaniel	64	122	10	5	6	2.66
	CF	W. Mays	552	.288	37	103	370	8	7	2	2.6	.982	R. Sadecki	26	105	3	7	0	5.40
	LF	J. Alou	370	.259	1	20	141	4	5	1	1.5	.967	F. Linzy	51	100	7	11	16	2.96
	C	T. Haller	471	.240	27	67	797	57	8	5	6.3	.991	B. Priddy	38	91	6	3	1	3.96
	UT	J. Davenport	305	.249	9	30	107	201	14	27		.957	J. Gibbon	37	81	4	6	1	3.67
	OF	L. Gabrielson	240	.217	4	16	72	1	4	0	1.1	.948							
	OF	C. Peterson	190	.237	2	19	62	2	0	1	1.3	1.000							

	POS	Player	AB	BA	HR	RBI	PO	A	E	DP	TC/G	FA	Pitcher	G	IP	W	L	SV	ERA
Pit.	1B	D. Clendenon	571	.299	28	98	**1452**	96	24	**182**	10.3	.985	B. Veale	38	268	16	12	0	3.02
W-92 L-70	2B	B. Mazeroski	621	.262	16	82	411	**538**	8	**161**	5.9	**.992**	W. Fryman	36	182	12	9	1	3.81
Harry Walker	SS	G. Alley	579	.299	7	43	235	472	15	**128**	5.0	.979	V. Law	31	178	12	8	0	4.05
	3B	B. Bailey	380	.279	13	46	57	201	12	20	2.8	.956	S. Blass	34	156	11	7	0	3.87
	RF	R. Clemente	638	.317	29	119	318	17	12	3	2.3	.965	T. Sisk	34	150	10	5	1	4.14
	CF	M. Alou	535	**.342**	2	27	264	11	8	3	2.1	.972	P. Mikkelsen	71	126	9	8	14	3.07
	LF	W. Stargell	485	.315	33	102	180	9	11	0	1.6	.945	D. Cardwell	32	102	6	6	1	4.60
	C	J. Pagliaroni	374	.235	11	49	613	37	2	6	5.5	.997	A. McBean	47	87	4	3	3	3.22
	3B	J. Pagan	368	.264	4	58	57	166	12	18	2.8	.949	R. Face	54	70	6	6	18	2.70
	OF	M. Mota	322	.332	5	46	150	3	1	0	1.6	.994							
Phi.	1B	B. White	577	.276	22	103	1422	**109**	9	**118**	9.7	**.994**	J. Bunning	43	314	19	14	1	2.41
W-87 L-75	2B	C. Rojas	626	.268	6	55	218	288	9	68	4.9	.983	C. Short	42	272	20	10	0	3.54
Gene Mauch	SS	D. Groat	584	.260	2	53	260	454	19	79	**5.3**	.974	L. Jackson	35	247	15	13	0	2.99
	3B	R. Allen	524	.317	40	110	81	180	9	15	3.0	.967	B. Buhl	32	132	6	8	1	4.77
	RF	J. Callison	612	.276	11	55	275	12	3	2	1.9	.990	R. Culp	34	111	7	4	1	5.04
	CF	J. Briggs	255	.282	10	23	126	3	3	0	1.9	.977	D. Knowles	69	100	6	5	13	3.05
	LF	T. Gonzalez	384	.286	6	40	206	7	3	1	1.8	.986	R. Wise	22	99	5	6	0	3.71
	C	C. Dalrymple	331	.245	4	39	615	48	5	5	6.1	.993							
	23	T. Taylor	434	.242	5	40	187	281	9	45		.981							
	C	B. Uecker	207	.208	7	30	368	33	6	7	5.4	.985							
	OF	J. Brandt	164	.250	1	15	78	3	1	0	1.2	.988							
Atl.	1B	F. Alou	**666**	.327	31	74	769	53	10	63	9.2	.988	T. Cloninger	39	258	14	11	1	4.12
W-85 L-77	2B	W. Woodward	455	.264	0	43	154	208	10	46	4.7	.973	K. Johnson	32	216	14	8	0	3.30
Bobby Bragan	SS	D. Menke	454	.251	15	60	165	282	21	50	4.4	.955	D. Lemaster	27	171	11	8	0	3.74
W-52 L-59	3B	E. Mathews	452	.250	16	53	114	237	20	31	2.9	.946	C. Carroll	**73**	144	8	7	11	2.37
Billy Hitchcock	RF	H. Aaron	603	.279	**44**	**127**	315	12	4	**5**	2.1	.988	D. Kelley	20	81	7	5	0	3.22
W-33 L-18	CF	M. Jones	417	.264	23	66	251	1	5	0	2.3	.981	W. Blasingame	16	68	3	7	0	5.32
	LF	R. Carty	521	.326	15	76	226	8	7	0	1.9	.971	C. Olivo	47	66	5	4	7	4.23
	C	J. Torre	546	.315	36	101	607	67	11	9	6.0	.984	T. Abernathy	38	65	4	4	4	3.86
	2B	F. Bolling	227	.211	1	18	134	150	5	35	4.3	.983	B. O'Dell	24	41	2	3	6	2.40
	C	G. Oliver	191	.194	8	24	286	22	3	3	6.5	.990							
	P	T. Cloninger	111	.234	5	23	14	43	8	1	1.7	.877							
St. L.	1B	O. Cepeda	452	.303	17	58	1109	62	13	111	9.9	.989	B. Gibson	35	280	21	12	0	2.44
W-83 L-79	2B	J. Javier	460	.228	7	31	306	364	13	89	4.7	.981	A. Jackson	36	233	13	15	0	2.51
Red Schoendienst	SS	D. Maxvill	394	.244	0	24	219	428	22	88	5.2	.967	R. Washburn	27	170	11	9	0	3.76
	3B	C. Smith	391	.266	10	43	84	213	11	26	2.9	.964	N. Briles	49	154	4	15	6	3.21
	RF	M. Shannon	459	.288	16	64	247	10	4	4	2.0	.985	L. Jaster	26	152	11	5	0	3.26
	CF	C. Flood	626	.267	10	78	**391**	5	0	1	2.5	**1.000**	J. Hoerner	57	76	5	1	13	1.54
	LF	L. Brock	643	.285	15	46	269	9	**19**	1	1.9	.936							
	C	T. McCarver	543	.274	12	68	841	62	7	7	6.1	.992							
	2S	J. Buchek	284	.236	4	25	148	220	18	52		.953							
	3B	P. Gagliano	213	.254	2	15	30	77	2	7	2.7	.982							
Cin.	1B	T. Perez	257	.265	4	39	530	23	6	46	7.5	.989	J. Maloney	32	225	16	8	0	2.80
W-76 L-84	2B	P. Rose	654	.313	16	70	385	344	14	79	5.3	.981	S. Ellis	41	221	12	19	0	5.29
Don Heffner	SS	L. Cardenas	568	.255	20	81	**279**	446	15	87	4.6	**.980**	M. Pappas	33	210	12	11	0	4.29
W-37 L-46	3B	T. Helms	542	.284	9	49	110	208	13	16	2.9	.961	J. O'Toole	25	142	5	7	0	3.55
Dave Bristol	RF	T. Harper	553	.278	5	31	257	5	1	2	1.8	.996	J. Nuxhall	35	130	6	8	0	4.50
W-39 L-38	CF	V. Pinson	618	.288	16	76	344	9	13	1	2.4	.964	D. Nottebart	59	111	5	4	11	3.07
	LF	D. Johnson	505	.257	24	81	141	4	3	1	1.4	.980	B. McCool	57	105	8	8	18	2.48
	C	J. Edwards	282	.191	6	39	617	40	5	3	6.8	.992	T. Davidson	54	85	5	4	4	3.90
	C	D. Pavletich	235	.294	12	38	323	30	9	2	6.6	.975							
	OF	A. Shamsky	234	.231	21	47	104	3	3	1	1.5	.973							
	1B	G. Coleman	227	.251	5	37	399	29	6	33	6.7	.986							
Hou.	1B	C. Harrison	434	.256	9	52	974	78	8	68	9.3	.992	M. Cuellar	38	227	12	10	2	2.22
W-72 L-90	2B	J. Morgan	425	.285	5	42	256	316	21	61	5.1	.965	D. Giusti	34	210	15	14	0	4.20
Grady Hatton	SS	S. Jackson	596	.292	3	25	270	449	**37**	73	5.0	.951	L. Dierker	29	187	10	8	0	3.18
	3B	B. Aspromonte	560	.252	8	52	149	261	16	18	2.9	**.962**	D. Farrell	32	153	6	10	2	4.60
	RF	R. Staub	554	.280	13	81	289	13	12	2	2.1	.962	B. Bruce	25	130	3	13	0	5.34
	CF	J. Wynn	418	.256	18	62	259	6	6	4	2.6	.978	B. Latman	31	103	2	7	1	2.71
	LF	L. Maye	358	.288	9	36	145	4	8	0	1.6	.949	C. Raymond	62	92	7	5	16	3.13
	C	J. Bateman	433	.279	17	70	731	63	**15**	14	6.7	.981	J. Owens	40	50	4	7	2	4.68
	OF	D. Nicholson	280	.246	10	31	139	11	5	0	1.7	.968							
	OF	R. Davis	194	.247	2	19	98	9	2	1	2.3	.982							
	UT	B. Lillis	164	.232	0	11	99	109	10	24		.954							
	UT	F. Mantilla	151	.219	6	22	124	46	4	11		.977							
N. Y.	1B	E. Kranepool	464	.254	16	57	1161	85	10	100	9.5	.992	J. Fisher	38	230	11	14	0	3.68
W-66 L-95	2B	R. Hunt	479	.288	3	33	295	384	21	81	5.7	.970	D. Ribant	39	188	11	9	3	3.20
Wes Westrum	SS	E. Bressoud	405	.225	10	49	135	252	16	52	4.3	.960	B. Shaw	26	168	11	10	0	3.92
	3B	K. Boyer	496	.266	14	61	113	292	21	33	3.3	.951	J. Hamilton	57	149	6	13	13	3.93
	RF	A. Luplow	334	.251	7	31	147	4	2	1	1.5	.987	R. Gardner	41	134	4	8	1	5.12
	CF	C. Jones	495	.275	8	57	275	10	6	2	2.3	.979	B. Friend	22	86	5	8	1	4.40
	LF	R. Swoboda	342	.222	8	50	145	7	2	0	1.6	.987	D. Selma	30	81	4	6	1	4.24
	C	J. Grote	317	.237	3	31	516	55	11	7	5.1	.981	T. McGraw	15	62	2	9	0	5.34
	UT	C. Hiller	254	.280	2	14	110	153	5	32		.981							
	SS	R. McMillan	220	.214	1	12	112	203	8	35	4.5	.975							
	OF	L. Elliot	199	.246	5	32	73	10	8	0	1.7	.912							
	OF	J. Lewis	166	.193	5	20	77	2	1	1	1.6	.988							

POS	Player	AB	BA	HR	RBI	PO	A	E	DP	TC/G	FA
1B	E. Banks	511	.272	15	75	1178	81	10	88	9.8	.992
2B	G. Beckert	656	.287	1	59	373	402	24	89	5.3	.970
SS	D. Kessinger	533	.274	1	43	202	474	35	68	4.8	.951
3B	R. Santo	561	.312	30	94	150	391	25	36	3.7	.956
RF	B. Williams	648	.276	29	91	319	9	8	3	2.1	.976
CF	A. Phillips	416	.262	16	36	258	14	6	2	2.5	.978
LF	B. Browne	419	.243	16	51	200	3	7	0	1.8	.967
C	R. Hundley	526	.236	19	63	871	85	14	8	6.5	.986
O1	J. Boccabella	206	.228	6	25	230	18	1	13		.996
OF	G. Altman	185	.222	5	17	42	4	2	0	1.1	.958

Chi. W-59 L-103   Leo Durocher

Pitcher	G	IP	W	L	SV	ERA
D. Ellsworth	38	269	8	22	0	3.98
K. Holtzman	34	221	11	16	0	3.79
F. Jenkins	60	182	6	8	5	3.31
B. Hands	41	159	8	13	2	4.58
C. Koonce	45	109	5	5	2	3.81
B. Hendley	43	90	4	5	7	3.91
C. Simmons	19	77	4	7	0	4.07

BATTING AND BASE RUNNING LEADERS

Batting Average
M. Alou, PIT	.342
F. Alou, ATL	.327
R. Carty, ATL	.326
R. Allen, PHI	.317
R. Clemente, PIT	.317

Slugging Average
R. Allen, PHI	.632
W. McCovey, SF	.586
W. Stargell, PIT	.581
J. Torre, ATL	.560
W. Mays, SF	.556

Home Runs
H. Aaron, ATL	44
R. Allen, PHI	40
W. Mays, SF	37
W. McCovey, SF	36
J. Torre, ATL	36

Total Bases
F. Alou, ATL	355
R. Clemente, PIT	342
R. Allen, PHI	331
H. Aaron, ATL	325
W. Mays, SF	307

Runs Batted In
H. Aaron, ATL	127
R. Clemente, PIT	119
R. Allen, PHI	110
W. Mays, SF	103
B. White, PHI	103

Stolen Bases
L. Brock, STL	74
S. Jackson, HOU	49
M. Wills, LA	38
A. Phillips, CHI, PHI	32
T. Harper, CIN	29

Hits
F. Alou, ATL	218
P. Rose, CIN	205
R. Clemente, PIT	202

Base on Balls
R. Santo, CHI	95
J. Morgan, HOU	89
W. McCovey, SF	76
H. Aaron, ATL	76

Home Run Percentage
R. Allen, PHI	7.6
H. Aaron, ATL	7.3
W. McCovey, SF	7.2

Runs Scored
F. Alou, ATL	122
H. Aaron, ATL	117
R. Allen, PHI	112

Doubles
J. Callison, PHI	40
P. Rose, CIN	38
V. Pinson, CIN	35

Triples
T. McCarver, STL	13
L. Brock, STL	12
R. Clemente, PIT	11

PITCHING LEADERS

Winning Percentage
J. Marichal, SF	.806
S. Koufax, LA	.750
G. Perry, SF	.724
C. Short, PHI	.667
J. Maloney, CIN	.667

Earned Run Average
S. Koufax, LA	1.73
M. Cuellar, HOU	2.22
J. Marichal, SF	2.23
J. Bunning, PHI	2.41
B. Gibson, STL	2.44

Wins
S. Koufax, LA	27
J. Marichal, SF	25
G. Perry, SF	21
B. Gibson, STL	21
C. Short, PHI	20

Saves
P. Regan, LA	21
B. McCool, CIN	18
R. Face, PIT	18
F. Linzy, SF	16
C. Raymond, HOU	16

Strikeouts
S. Koufax, LA	317
J. Bunning, PHI	252
B. Veale, PIT	229
B. Gibson, STL	225
J. Marichal, SF	222

Complete Games
S. Koufax, LA	27
J. Marichal, SF	25
B. Gibson, STL	20
C. Short, PHI	19
J. Bunning, PHI	16

Fewest Hits per 9 Innings
J. Marichal, SF	6.68
S. Koufax, LA	6.72
B. Gibson, STL	6.74

Shutouts
5 tied with	5

Fewest Walks per 9 Innings
J. Marichal, SF	1.05
V. Law, PIT	1.22
G. Perry, SF	1.41

Most Strikeouts per 9 Inn.
S. Koufax, LA	8.83
J. Maloney, CIN	8.65
D. Sutton, LA	8.34

Innings
S. Koufax, LA	323
J. Bunning, PHI	314
J. Marichal, SF	307

Games Pitched
C. Carroll, ATL	73
P. Mikkelsen, PIT	71
D. Knowles, PHI	69

	W	L	PCT	GB	R	OR	Batting 2B	3B	HR	BA	SA	SB	Fielding E	DP	FA	Pitching CG	BB	SO	ShO	SV	ERA
LA	95	67	.586		606	490	201	27	108	.256	.362	94	133	128	.979	52	356	1084	20	35	2.62
SF	93	68	.578	1.5	675	626	195	31	181	.248	.392	29	168	131	.974	52	359	973	14	27	3.24
PIT	92	70	.568	3	759	640	238	66	158	.279	.428	64	141	215	.978	35	463	898	12	43	3.52
PHI	87	75	.537	8	696	640	224	49	117	.258	.378	56	113	147	.982	52	412	928	15	23	3.57
ATL	85	77	.525	10	782	683	220	32	207	.263	.424	59	154	139	.976	37	485	884	10	36	3.68
STL	83	79	.512	12	571	577	196	61	108	.251	.368	144	145	166	.977	47	448	892	19	32	3.11
CIN	76	84	.475	18	692	702	232	33	149	.260	.395	70	122	133	.972	34	391	929	13	26	3.76
HOU	72	90	.444	23	612	695	203	35	112	.255	.365	90	174	126	.975	37	521	773	9	22	4.17
NY	66	95	.410	28.5	587	761	187	35	98	.239	.342	55	159	171	.975	28	479	908	6	24	4.33
CHI	59	103	.364	36	644	809	203	43	140	.254	.380	76	166	132	.974	28	490	1043	10	35	4.33
					6624	6624	2099	412	1378	.256	.384	737	1475	1488	.977	402	4404	9312	128	303	3.61

POS	Player	AB	BA	HR	RBI	PO	A	E	DP	TC/G	FA	Pitcher	G	IP	W	L	SV	ERA
Bal. W-97 L-63 Hank Bauer																		
1B	B. Powell	491	.287	34	109	1094	68	13	96	8.6	.989	D. McNally	34	213	13	6	0	3.17
2B	D. Johnson	501	.257	7	56	288	347	19	75	5.2	.971	J. Palmer	30	208	15	10	0	3.46
SS	L. Aparicio	659	.276	6	41	303	441	17	104	5.0	.978	E. Watt	43	146	9	7	4	3.83
3B	B. Robinson	620	.269	23	100	174	313	12	26	3.2	.976	W. Bunker	29	143	10	6	0	4.29
RF	F. Robinson	576	.316	49	122	254	4	4	0	1.7	.985	S. Barber	25	133	10	5	0	2.30
CF	P. Blair	303	.277	6	33	204	4	2	2	1.7	.990	J. Miller	23	101	4	8	0	4.74
LF	R. Snyder	373	.306	3	41	209	6	3	2	2.1	.986	M. Drabowsky	44	96	6	0	7	2.81
C	Etchebarren	412	.221	11	50	799	65	10	7	7.2	.989	S. Miller	51	92	9	4	18	2.25
OF	C. Blefary	419	.255	23	64	159	5	4	0	1.5	.976	E. Fisher	44*	72	5	3	13	2.64
OF	S. Bowens	243	.210	6	20	114	7	5	2	1.9	.960	D. Hall	32	66	6	2	7	3.95
Min. W-89 L-73 Sam Mele																		
1B	D. Mincher	431	.251	14	62	995	85	9	62	8.4	.992	J. Kaat	41	305	25	13	0	2.75
2B	B. Allen	319	.238	5	30	191	214	11	46	4.7	.974	M. Grant	35	249	13	13	0	3.25
SS	Z. Versalles	543	.249	7	36	195	377	35	69	4.5	.942	J. Perry	33	184	11	7	0	2.54
3B	H. Killebrew	569	.281	39	110	83	190	14	11	2.7	.951	D. Boswell	28	169	12	5	0	3.14
RF	T. Oliva	622	.307	25	87	335	9	10	3	2.2	.972	J. Merritt	31	144	7	14	3	3.38
CF	T. Uhlaender	367	.226	2	22	258	4	4	2	2.7	.985	C. Pascual	21	103	8	6	0	4.89
LF	J. Hall	356	.239	20	47	175	6	4	1	1.8	.978	Worthington	65	91	6	3	16	2.46
C	E. Battey	364	.255	4	34	705	45	4	9	6.7	.995	P. Cimino	35	65	2	5	4	2.92
UT	C. Tovar	465	.260	2	41	254	274	14	44		.974							
3B	R. Rollins	269	.245	10	40	54	107	8	13	2.6	.953							
OF	B. Allison	168	.220	8	19	86	3	3	0	1.6	.967							
Det. W-88 L-74 Chuck Dressen W-16 L-10 Bob Swift W-32 L-25 Frank Skaff W-40 L-39																		
1B	N. Cash	603	.279	32	93	1271	114	17	118	8.9	.988	D. McLain	38	264	20	14	0	3.92
2B	J. Lumpe	385	.231	1	26	202	223	4	51	4.5	.991	M. Lolich	40	204	14	14	3	4.77
SS	D. McAuliffe	430	.274	23	56	160	292	17	49	4.5	.964	E. Wilson	23	163	13	6	0	2.59
3B	D. Wert	559	.268	11	70	128	253	11	20	2.6	.972	D. Wickersham	38	141	8	3	1	3.20
RF	J. Northrup	419	.265	16	58	241	8	5	1	2.2	.980	O. Pena	54	108	4	2	7	3.08
CF	A. Kaline	479	.288	29	88	279	7	2	1	2.1	.993	J. Podres	36	108	4	5	4	3.43
LF	W. Horton	526	.262	27	100	233	4	5	1	1.8	.979	H. Aguirre	30	104	3	9	0	3.82
C	B. Freehan	492	.234	12	46	898	56	4	11	7.3	.996	Monbouquette	30	103	7	8	0	4.73
OF	M. Stanley	235	.289	3	19	163	6	0	1	2.1	1.000	L. Sherry	55	78	8	5	20	3.82
OF	J. Wood	230	.252	2	27	109	100	7	25	4.2	.968							
SS	R. Oyler	210	.171	1	9	107	194	11	42	4.5	.965							
OF	G. Brown	169	.266	7	27	46	4	1	1	1.2	.980							
Chi. W-83 L-79 Eddie Stanky																		
1B	T. McCraw	389	.229	5	48	843	67	9	56	7.6	.990	T. John	34	223	14	11	0	2.62
2B	A. Weis	187	.155	0	9	130	173	4	44	3.2	.987	J. Horlen	37	211	10	13	1	2.43
SS	L. Elia	195	.205	3	22	103	186	14	39	4.0	.954	G. Peters	30	205	12	10	0	1.98
3B	D. Buford	607	.244	8	52	98	301	26	24	3.2	.939	J. Buzhardt	33	150	6	11	1	3.83
RF	F. Robinson	342	.237	5	35	148	2	6	0	1.4	.962	B. Howard	27	149	9	5	0	2.30
CF	T. Agee	629	.273	22	86	376	12	7	7	2.5	.982	J. Lamabe	34	121	7	9	0	3.93
LF	K. Berry	443	.271	8	34	208	10	2	1	1.6	.991	B. Locker	56	95	9	8	12	2.46
C	J. Romano	329	.231	15	47	622	46	4	7	6.6	.994	J. Pizarro	34	89	8	6	3	3.76
S2	J. Adair	370	.243	4	36	198	328	12	54		.978	H. Wilhelm	46	81	5	2	6	1.66
1B	B. Skowron	337	.249	6	29	722	60	7	75	8.1	.991	E. Fisher	23*	35	1	3	6	2.29
OF	P. Ward	251	.219	3	28	83	3	1	1	1.5	.989							
2B	W. Causey	164	.244	0	13	86	110	4	15	3.3	.980							
C	J. Martin	157	.255	2	20	243	23	5	3	4.3	.982							
Cle. W-81 L-81 Birdie Tebbetts W-66 L-57 George Strickland W-15 L-24																		
1B	F. Whitfield	502	.241	27	78	1104	76	11	96	9.0	.991	G. Bell	40	254	14	15	0	3.22
2B	P. Gonzalez	352	.233	2	17	237	257	8	62	4.8	.984	S. Siebert	34	241	16	8	1	2.80
SS	L. Brown	340	.229	3	17	131	238	15	45	4.3	.961	S. McDowell	35	194	9	8	3	2.87
3B	M. Alvis	596	.245	17	55	180	280	20	24	3.1	.958	S. Hargan	38	192	13	10	0	2.48
RF	R. Colavito	533	.238	30	72	261	10	5	0	1.9	.982	L. Tiant	46	155	12	11	0	2.79
CF	V. Davalillo	344	.250	3	19	208	6	3	1	2.0	.986	J. O'Donoghue	32	108	6	8	0	3.83
LF	L. Wagner	549	.279	23	66	185	4	2	0	1.4	.990	T. Kelley	31	95	4	8	0	4.34
C	J. Azcue	302	.275	9	37	588	40	7	3	6.5	.989	D. Radatz	39	57	0	3	10	4.61
UT	C. Salmon	422	.256	7	40	315	225	19	53		.966							
OF	C. Hinton	348	.256	12	50	176	6	5	1	1.8	.973							
Cal. W-80 L-82 Billy Rigney																		
1B	N. Siebern	336	.247	5	41	1014	65	7	96	11.0	.994	D. Chance	41	260	12	17	1	3.08
2B	B. Knoop	590	.232	17	72	381	488	17	135	5.5	.981	G. Brunet	41	212	13	13	0	3.31
SS	J. Fregosi	611	.252	13	67	297	531	35	125	5.3	.959	M. Lopez	37	199	7	14	1	3.93
3B	P. Schaal	386	.244	6	24	97	249	19	21	2.8	.948	J. Sanford	50	108	13	7	5	3.83
RF	J. Kirkpatrick	312	.192	9	44	151	4	1	1	1.5	.994	F. Newman	21	103	4	7	0	4.73
CF	J. Cardenal	561	.276	16	48	351	10	3	4	2.5	.992	B. Lee	61	102	5	4	16	2.74
LF	R. Reichardt	319	.288	16	44	153	8	4	1	1.9	.976	C. Wright	20	91	4	7	0	3.74
C	B. Rodgers	454	.236	7	48	662	69	6	7	5.5	.992	M. Rojas	47	84	7	4	10	2.88
OF	J. Johnstone	254	.264	3	17	114	2	3	1	2.0	.975	L. Burdette	54	80	7	2	5	3.39
1B	J. Adcock	231	.273	18	48	565	39	2	60	8.5	.997							
UT	T. Satriano	226	.239	0	24	283	58	6	13		.983							
OF	W. Smith	195	.185	1	20	71	4	2	1	1.5	.974							

POS	Player	AB	BA	HR	RBI	PO	A	E	DP	TC/G	FA	Pitcher	G	IP	W	L	SV	ERA
	K. C. W-74 L-86 Alvin Dark																	
1B	K. Harrelson	210	.224	5	22	485	48	8	42	9.3	.985	L. Krausse	36	178	14	9	3	2.99
2B	D. Green	507	.250	9	62	300	389	15	86	5.1	.979	C. Hunter	30	177	9	11	0	4.02
SS	B. Campaneris	573	.267	5	42	283	350	19	80	4.7	.971	J. Nash	18	127	12	1	1	2.06
3B	E. Charles	385	.286	9	42	85	201	11	21	2.9	.963	P. Lindblad	38	121	5	10	1	4.17
RF	Hershberger	538	.253	2	57	285	14	7	3	2.1	.977	J. Aker	66	113	8	4	32	1.99
CF	J. Gosger	272	.224	5	27	158	3	1	0	2.1	.994	B. Odom	14	90	5	5	0	2.49
LF	L. Stahl	312	.250	5	34	142	6	3	1	1.6	.980	C. Dobson	14	84	4	6	0	4.09
C	P. Roof	369	.209	7	44	680	52	11	7	6.0	.985	R. Sheldon	14	69	4	7	0	3.13
UT	D. Cater	425	.292	7	52	545	104	9	55		.986							
O1	R. Repoz	319	.216	11	34	445	22	5	27		.989							
OF	J. Nossek	230	.261	1	27	161	8	3	1	2.2	.983							
UT	O. Chavarria	191	.241	2	10	105	86	7	23		.965							
	Was. W-71 L-88 Gil Hodges																	
1B	D. Nen	235	.213	6	30	566	38	6	44	8.0	.990	P. Richert	36	246	14	14	0	3.37
2B	B. Saverine	406	.251	5	24	149	169	9	35	4.7	.972	M. McCormick	41	216	11	14	0	3.46
SS	E. Brinkman	582	.229	7	48	263	501	28	83	5.0	.965	P. Ortega	33	197	12	12	0	3.92
3B	K. McMullen	524	.233	13	54	125	280	21	26	3.0	.951	J. Hannan	30	114	3	9	0	4.26
RF	F. Valentine	508	.276	16	59	290	6	6	2	2.2	.980	C. Cox	66	113	4	5	7	3.50
CF	D. Lock	386	.233	16	48	295	8	7	1	2.4	.977	B. Humphreys	58	112	7	3	3	2.82
LF	H. Howard	493	.278	18	71	216	5	4	1	1.7	.982	R. Kline	63	90	6	4	23	2.39
C	P. Casanova	429	.254	13	44	674	53	14	12	6.2	.981	D. Segui	21	72	3	7	0	5.00
OF	J. King	310	.248	10	30	147	4	2	0	1.8	.987							
1B	K. Harrelson	250	.248	7	28	641	38	6	53	9.8	.991							
2B	D. Blasingame	200	.215	1	11	119	132	4	32	4.4	.984							
OF	W. Kirkland	163	.190	6	17	56	3	1	0	.9	.983							
	Bos. W-64 L-90 Billy Herman W-64 L-82 Pete Runnels W-8 L-8																	
1B	G. Scott	601	.245	27	90	1362	112	14	130	9.4	.991	J. Lonborg	45	182	10	10	2	3.86
2B	G. Smith	403	.213	8	37	239	287	17	76	5.0	.969	J. Santiago	35	172	12	13	2	3.66
SS	R. Petrocelli	522	.238	18	59	206	381	28	69	4.8	.954	D. Brandon	40	158	8	8	2	3.31
3B	J. Foy	554	.262	15	63	150	279	21	28	3.2	.953	L. Stange	28	153	7	9	0	3.35
RF	T. Conigliaro	558	.265	28	93	244	8	7	1	1.8	.973	E. Wilson	15	101	5	5	0	3.84
CF	D. Demeter	226	.292	9	46	109	3	2	0	2.0	.982	D. McMahon	49	78	8	7	9	2.65
LF	Yastrzemski	594	.278	16	80	310	15	5	2	2.1	.985	J. Wyatt	42	72	3	4	8	3.14
C	M. Ryan	369	.214	2	32	685	50	6	7	6.5	.992	K. Sanders	24	47	3	6	2	3.80
2B	D. Jones	252	.234	4	23	129	121	10	26	3.7	.962							
C	B. Tillman	204	.230	3	24	372	24	4	5	5.6	.990							
OF	J. Tartabull	195	.277	0	11	90	1	1	0	2.0	.989							
OF	G. Thomas	173	.237	5	20	84	4	0	0	1.8	1.000							
	N. Y. W-70 L-89 Johnny Keane W-4 L-16 Ralph Houk W-66 L-73																	
1B	J. Pepitone	585	.255	31	83	1044	92	6	92	9.6	.995	Stottlemyre	37	251	12	20	1	3.80
2B	B. Richardson	610	.251	7	42	322	408	15	91	5.1	.980	F. Peterson	34	215	12	11	0	3.31
SS	H. Clarke	312	.266	6	28	102	154	8	37	4.2	.970	A. Downing	30	200	10	11	0	3.56
3B	C. Boyer	500	.240	14	57	87	226	11	12	3.8	.966	F. Talbot	23	124	7	7	0	4.15
RF	R. Maris	348	.233	13	43	133	3	1	0	1.4	.993	J. Bouton	24	120	3	8	1	2.69
CF	M. Mantle	333	.288	23	56	172	2	0	0	1.8	1.000	H. Reniff	56	95	3	7	9	3.21
LF	T. Tresh	537	.233	27	68	181	12	3	3	2.3	.985	S. Hamilton	44	90	8	3	3	3.00
C	E. Howard	410	.256	6	35	553	44	9	6	6.1	.985	P. Ramos	52	90	3	9	13	3.61
OF	R. White	316	.225	7	20	153	3	7	0	2.0	.957	D. Womack	42	75	7	3	4	2.64
C	J. Gibbs	182	.258	3	20	295	27	4	4	6.0	.988							
OF	L. Clinton	159	.220	5	21	80	2	2	0	1.3	.976							

BATTING AND BASE RUNNING LEADERS

Batting Average
F. Robinson, BAL	.316
T. Oliva, MIN	.307
A. Kaline, DET	.288
B. Powell, BAL	.287
H. Killebrew, MIN	.281

Slugging Average
F. Robinson, BAL	.637
H. Killebrew, MIN	.538
A. Kaline, DET	.534
B. Powell, BAL	.532
T. Oliva, MIN	.502

Home Runs
F. Robinson, BAL	49
H. Killebrew, MIN	39
B. Powell, BAL	34
N. Cash, DET	32
J. Pepitone, NY	31

Total Bases
F. Robinson, BAL	367
T. Oliva, MIN	312
H. Killebrew, MIN	306
N. Cash, DET	288
T. Agee, CHI	281

Runs Batted In
F. Robinson, BAL	122
H. Killebrew, MIN	110
B. Powell, BAL	109
W. Horton, DET	100
B. Robinson, BAL	100

Stolen Bases
B. Campaneris, KC	52
D. Buford, CHI	51
T. Agee, CHI	44
L. Aparicio, BAL	25
J. Cardenal, CAL	24

Hits
T. Oliva, MIN	191
F. Robinson, BAL	182
L. Aparicio, BAL	182

Base on Balls
H. Killebrew, MIN	103
J. Foy, BOS	91
F. Robinson, BAL	87

PITCHING LEADERS

Winning Percentage
S. Siebert, CLE	.667
J. Kaat, MIN	.658
E. Wilson, BOS, DET	.621
J. Palmer, BAL	.600
D. McLain, DET	.588

Earned Run Average
G. Peters, CHI	1.98
J. Horlen, CHI	2.43
S. Hargan, CLE	2.48
J. Perry, MIN	2.54
T. John, CHI	2.62

Wins
J. Kaat, MIN	25
D. McLain, DET	20
E. Wilson, BOS, DET	18
S. Siebert, CLE	16
J. Palmer, BAL	15

Saves
J. Aker, KC	32
R. Kline, WAS	23
L. Sherry, DET	20
E. Fisher, BAL, CHI	19
S. Miller, BAL	18

Strikeouts
S. McDowell, CLE	225
J. Kaat, MIN	205
E. Wilson, BOS, DET	200
P. Richert, WAS	195
G. Bell, CLE	194

Complete Games
J. Kaat, MIN	19
D. McLain, DET	14
E. Wilson, BOS, DET	13
G. Bell, CLE	12

Fewest Hits per 9 Innings
S. McDowell, CLE	6.02
D. Boswell, MIN	6.38
G. Peters, CHI	6.86

Shutouts
L. Tiant, CLE	5
S. McDowell, CLE	5
T. John, CHI	5

BATTING AND BASE RUNNING LEADERS

Home Run Percentage

F. Robinson, BAL	8.5
B. Powell, BAL	6.9
H. Killebrew, MIN	6.9

Runs Scored

F. Robinson, BAL	122
T. Oliva, MIN	99
N. Cash, DET	98
T. Agee, CHI	98

Doubles

Yastrzemski, BOS	39
B. Robinson, BAL	35
F. Robinson, BAL	34

Triples

B. Knoop, CAL	11
B. Campaneris, KC	10
E. Brinkman, WAS	9

PITCHING LEADERS

Fewest Walks per 9 Innings

J. Kaat, MIN	1.62
F. Peterson, NY	1.67
M. Grant, MIN	1.77

Most Strikeouts per 9 Inn.

S. McDowell, CLE	10.42
D. Boswell, MIN	9.19
M. Lolich, DET	7.64

Innings

J. Kaat, MIN	305
D. McLain, DET	264
E. Wilson, BOS, DET	264

Games Pitched

E. Fisher, BAL, CHI	67
J. Aker, KC	66
C. Cox, WAS	66

	W	L	PCT	GB	R	OR	2B	3B	HR	BA	SA	SB	E	DP	FA	CG	BB	SO	ShO	SV	ERA
BAL	97	63	.606		755	601	243	35	175	.258	.409	55	115	142	.981	23	514	1070	13	51	3.32
MIN	89	73	.549	9	663	581	219	33	144	.249	.382	67	139	118	.977	52	392	1015	11	28	3.13
DET	88	74	.543	10	719	698	224	45	179	.251	.406	41	120	142	.980	36	520	1026	11	38	3.85
CHI	83	79	.512	15	574	517	193	40	87	.231	.331	153	159	149	.976	38	403	896	22	34	2.68
CLE	81	81	.500	17	574	586	156	25	155	.237	.360	53	138	132	.977	49	489	1111	15	28	3.23
CAL	80	82	.494	18	604	643	179	54	122	.232	.354	80	136	186	.979	31	511	836	12	40	3.56
KC	74	86	.463	23	564	648	212	56	70	.236	.337	132	138	154	.977	19	630	854	11	47	3.55
WAS	71	88	.447	25.5	557	659	185	40	126	.234	.355	53	142	139	.977	25	448	866	6	35	3.70
BOS	72	90	.444	26	655	731	228	44	145	.240	.376	35	155	153	.975	32	577	977	10	31	3.92
NY	70	89	.440	26.5	611	612	182	36	162	.235	.374	49	142	142	.977	29	443	842	7	32	3.42
					6276	6276	2021	408	1365	.240	.369	718	1384	1457	.978	334	4927	9493	118	364	3.44

National League 1967

	POS	Player	AB	BA	HR	RBI	PO	A	E	DP	TC/G	FA	Pitcher	G	IP	W	L	SV	ERA
St. L. W-101 L-60 Red Schoendienst	1B	O. Cepeda	563	.325	25	111	1304	90	10	103	9.3	.993	D. Hughes	37	222	16	6	3	2.67
	2B	J. Javier	520	.281	14	64	311	352	24	72	5.0	.965	S. Carlton	30	193	14	9	1	2.98
	SS	D. Maxvill	476	.227	1	41	236	470	19	74	4.9	.974	R. Washburn	27	186	10	7	0	3.53
	3B	M. Shannon	482	.245	12	77	88	239	29	18	2.9	.919	B. Gibson	24	175	13	7	0	2.98
	RF	R. Maris	410	.261	9	55	224	5	2	1	2.0	.991	N. Briles	49	155	14	5	6	2.43
	CF	C. Flood	514	.335	5	50	314	4	4	1	2.6	.988	L. Jaster	34	152	9	7	3	3.01
	LF	L. Brock	689	.299	21	76	272	12	13	2	1.9	.956	A. Jackson	38	107	9	4	1	3.95
	C	T. McCarver	471	.295	14	69	819	67	3	10	6.8	.997	R. Willis	65	81	6	5	10	2.67
	OF	B. Tolan	265	.253	6	32	118	4	1	1	1.5	.992	J. Hoerner	57	66	4	4	15	2.59
	UT	P. Gagliano	217	.221	2	21	115	99	8	16		.964	J. Lamabe	23	48	3	4	4	2.83
	OF	A. Johnson	175	.223	1	12	91	7	3	2	1.8	.970							
S. F. W-91 L-71 Herman Franks	1B	W. McCovey	456	.276	31	91	1221	81	15	102	10.4	.989	G. Perry	39	293	15	17	1	2.61
	2B	T. Fuentes	344	.209	5	29	274	313	12	79	4.6	.980	M. McCormick	40	262	22	10	0	2.85
	SS	H. Lanier	525	.213	0	42	197	440	17	73	4.8	.974	J. Marichal	26	202	14	10	0	2.76
	3B	J. Hart	578	.289	29	99	60	177	16	10	2.8	.937	R. Sadecki	35	188	12	6	0	2.78
	RF	O. Brown	412	.267	13	53	190	5	3	0	1.7	.985	R. Herbel	42	126	4	5	1	3.08
	CF	W. Mays	486	.263	22	70	277	3	7	0	2.1	.976	B. Bolin	37	120	6	8	4	4.88
	LF	J. Alou	510	.292	5	30	195	5	11	2	1.7	.948	F. Linzy	57	96	7	7	17	1.51
	C	T. Haller	455	.251	14	49	797	64	3	5	6.4	.997	L. McDaniel	41	73	2	6	3	3.72
	UT	J. Davenport	295	.275	5	30	83	192	4	24		.986							
	OF	K. Henderson	179	.190	4	14	86	3	5	1	1.8	.947							
	1B	J. Hiatt	153	.275	6	26	288	17	3	25	8.6	.990							
Chi. W-87 L-74 Leo Durocher	1B	E. Banks	573	.276	23	95	1383	91	10	111	10.1	.993	F. Jenkins	38	289	20	13	0	2.80
	2B	G. Beckert	597	.280	5	40	327	422	25	89	5.4	.968	R. Nye	35	205	13	10	0	3.20
	SS	D. Kessinger	580	.231	0	42	215	457	19	77	4.9	.973	J. Niekro	36	170	10	7	0	3.34
	3B	R. Santo	586	.300	31	98	187	393	26	33	3.8	.957	R. Culp	30	153	8	11	0	3.89
	RF	T. Savage	225	.218	5	33	133	5	3	1	1.6	.979	B. Hands	49	150	7	8	6	2.46
	CF	A. Phillips	448	.268	17	70	340	13	7	0	2.6	.981	C. Simmons	17	82	3	7	0	4.94
	LF	B. Williams	634	.278	28	84	271	3	3	1	1.7	.989	Hartenstein	45	73	9	5	10	3.08
	C	R. Hundley	539	.267	14	60	865	59	4	7	6.1	.996	B. Stoneman	28	63	2	4	4	3.29
	OF	L. Thomas	191	.220	2	23	60	2	2	0	1.5	.969							
Cin. W-87 L-75 Dave Bristol	1B	L. May	438	.265	12	57	621	43	4	49	8.2	.994	G. Nolan	33	227	14	8	0	2.58
	2B	T. Helms	497	.274	2	35	185	224	9	50	4.8	.978	M. Pappas	34	218	16	13	0	3.35
	SS	L. Cardenas	379	.256	2	21	190	316	15	57	4.8	.971	J. Maloney	30	196	15	11	0	3.25
	3B	T. Perez	600	.290	26	102	113	221	13	13	2.5	.963	M. Queen	31	196	14	8	0	2.76
	RF	T. Harper	365	.225	7	22	208	6	1	0	2.2	.995	S. Ellis	32	176	8	11	0	3.84
	CF	V. Pinson	650	.288	18	66	341	4	5	1	2.2	.986	T. Abernathy	70	106	6	3	28	1.27
	LF	P. Rose	585	.301	12	76	211	5	4	0	1.8	.982	B. McCool	31	97	3	7	2	3.42
	C	J. Edwards	209	.206	2	20	454	30	5	4	6.7	.990	J. Arrigo	32	74	6	6	1	3.16
	1B	D. Johnson	361	.224	13	53	587	41	2	47	7.8	.997							
	UT	C. Ruiz	250	.220	0	13	131	168	10	33		.968							
	C	D. Pavletich	231	.238	6	34	383	31	6	5	6.4	.986							

	POS	Player	AB	BA	HR	RBI	PO	A	E	DP	TC/G	FA	Pitcher	G	IP	W	L	SV	ERA
Phi. W-82 L-80 Gene Mauch	1B	B. White	308	.250	8	33	775	52	6	85	8.8	.993	J. Bunning	40	302	17	15	0	2.29
	2B	C. Rojas	528	.259	4	45	282	360	15	92	4.8	.977	L. Jackson	40	262	13	15	0	3.10
	SS	B. Wine	363	.190	2	28	201	390	12	90	4.5	.980	C. Short	29	199	9	11	1	2.39
	3B	R. Allen	463	.307	23	77	95	249	35	23	3.1	.908	R. Wise	36	181	11	11	0	3.28
	RF	J. Callison	556	.261	14	64	286	12	7	1	2.1	.977	D. Ellsworth	32	125	6	7	0	4.38
	CF	J. Briggs	332	.232	9	30	182	2	4	0	2.0	.979	D. Farrell	50	92	9	6	12	2.05
	LF	T. Gonzalez	508	.339	9	59	260	10	2	1	1.9	.993	D. Hall	48	86	10	8	8	2.20
	C	C. Dalrymple	268	.172	3	21	558	59	4	7	6.4	.994	J. Boozer	28	75	5	4	1	4.10
	UT	T. Taylor	462	.238	2	34	524	182	9	73		.987							
	OF	D. Lock	313	.252	14	51	172	8	5	2	1.9	.973							
	C	G. Oliver	263	.224	7	34	425	30	6	3	5.8	.987							
	SS	G. Sutherland	231	.247	1	19	77	115	15	33	3.1	.928							
Pit. W-81 L-81 Harry Walker W-42 L-42 Danny Murtaugh W-39 L-39	1B	D. Clendenon	478	.249	13	56	1199	89	15	122	10.6	.988	T. Sisk	37	208	13	13	1	3.34
	2B	B. Mazeroski	639	.261	9	77	417	498	18	131	5.7	.981	B. Veale	33	203	16	8	0	3.64
	SS	G. Alley	550	.287	6	55	257	500	26	105	5.4	.967	D. Ribant	38	172	9	8	0	4.08
	3B	M. Wills	616	.302	3	45	98	343	24	31	3.2	.948	A. McBean	51	131	7	4	4	2.54
	RF	R. Clemente	585	.357	23	110	273	17	9	4	2.1	.970	S. Blass	32	127	6	8	0	3.55
	CF	M. Alou	550	.338	2	28	249	9	3	3	1.9	.989	W. Fryman	28	113	3	8	1	4.05
	LF	W. Stargell	462	.271	20	73	140	12	10	1	1.7	.938	J. Pizarro	50	107	8	10	9	3.95
	C	J. May	325	.271	3	22	550	52	4	9	5.5	.993	B. O'Dell	27	87	5	6	0	5.82
	OF	M. Mota	349	.321	4	56	153	9	2	2	1.7	.988	R. Face	61	74	7	5	17	2.42
	UT	J. Pagan	211	.289	1	19	73	109	7	14		.963							
Atl. W-77 L-85 Billy Hitchcock W-77 L-82 Ken Silvestri W-0 L-3	1B	F. Alou	574	.274	15	43	774	28	6	67	9.5	.993	D. Lemaster	31	215	9	9	0	3.34
	2B	W. Woodward	429	.226	0	25	270	339	11	81	5.2	.982	K. Johnson	29	210	13	9	0	2.74
	SS	D. Menke	418	.227	7	39	181	349	19	65	4.4	.965	P. Niekro	46	207	11	9	9	1.87
	3B	C. Boyer	572	.245	26	96	166	291	14	30	3.1	.970	P. Jarvis	32	194	15	10	0	3.66
	RF	H. Aaron	600	.307	39	109	321	12	7	3	2.2	.979	D. Kelley	39	98	2	9	2	3.77
	CF	M. Jones	454	.253	17	50	252	7	4	1	2.1	.985	C. Carroll	42	93	6	12	0	5.52
	LF	R. Carty	444	.255	15	64	203	7	9	3	2.0	.959	J. Ritchie	52	82	4	6	2	3.17
	C	J. Torre	477	.277	20	68	580	63	6	12	5.7	.991	T. Cloninger	16	77	4	7	0	5.17
	1B	T. Francona	254	.248	6	25	503	32	5	36	9.6	.991	C. Upshaw	30	45	2	3	8	2.58
L. A. W-73 L-89 Walter Alston	1B	W. Parker	413	.247	5	31	913	68	4	72	8.8	.996	C. Osteen	39	288	17	17	0	3.22
	2B	R. Hunt	388	.263	3	33	211	224	9	50	4.9	.980	D. Drysdale	38	282	13	16	0	2.74
	SS	G. Michael	223	.202	0	7	117	204	17	30	4.1	.950	D. Sutton	37	233	11	15	1	3.95
	3B	J. Lefebvre	494	.261	8	50	49	205	12	12	2.9	.955	B. Singer	32	204	12	8	0	2.64
	RF	R. Fairly	486	.220	10	55	129	8	2	1	1.4	.986	R. Perranoski	70	110	6	7	16	2.45
	CF	W. Davis	569	.257	6	41	300	6	9	2	2.3	.971	J. Brewer	30	101	5	4	1	2.68
	LF	L. Johnson	330	.270	11	41	153	7	4	0	1.8	.976	P. Regan	55	96	6	9	6	2.99
	C	J. Roseboro	334	.272	4	24	550	60	10	6	5.8	.984	B. Miller	52	86	2	9	0	4.31
	OF	A. Ferrara	347	.277	16	50	135	1	3	0	1.5	.978							
	3O	B. Bailey	322	.227	4	28	77	152	14	11		.942							
	OF	L. Gabrielson	238	.261	7	29	92	7	2	0	1.5	.980							
	SS	D. Schofield	232	.216	2	15	107	213	8	37	4.8	.976							
	2S	N. Oliver	232	.237	0	7	124	157	12	35		.959							
	C	J. Torborg	196	.214	2	12	413	30	5	3	6.0	.989							
Hou. W-69 L-93 Grady Hatton	1B	E. Mathews	328	.238	10	38	572	40	8	50	7.8	.987	M. Cuellar	36	246	16	11	1	3.03
	2B	J. Morgan	494	.275	6	42	297	344	14	67	5.0	.979	D. Giusti	37	222	11	15	1	4.18
	SS	S. Jackson	520	.237	0	25	204	379	35	63	4.8	.943	D. Wilson	31	184	10	9	0	2.79
	3B	B. Aspromonte	486	.294	6	58	130	237	14	17	2.9	.963	B. Belinsky	27	115	3	9	0	4.68
	RF	R. Staub	546	.333	10	74	269	10	11	2	2.0	.962	L. Dierker	15	99	6	5	0	3.36
	CF	J. Wynn	594	.249	37	107	364	4	12	1	2.4	.968	W. Blasingame	15	77	4	7	0	5.96
	LF	R. Davis	285	.256	7	38	114	7	3	2	1.6	.976	D. Eilers	35	59	6	4	1	3.94
	C	J. Bateman	252	.190	2	17	483	46	6	5	7.5	.989	C. Sembera	45	60	2	6	3	4.83
	2S	J. Gotay	234	.282	2	15	91	137	8	27		.966							
	C	R. Brand	215	.242	0	18	397	36	1	3	6.5	.998							
	OF	N. Miller	190	.205	1	14	84	3	3	1	1.7	.967							
	1B	C. Harrison	177	.243	2	26	438	27	6	24	8.0	.987							
	1B	D. Rader	162	.333	2	26	263	18	8	26	8.0	.972							
N. Y. W-61 L-101 Wes Westrum W-57 L-94 Salty Parker W-4 L-7	1B	E. Kranepool	469	.269	10	54	1137	87	10	103	8.9	.992	T. Seaver	35	251	16	13	0	2.76
	2B	J. Buchek	411	.236	14	41	203	255	11	54	4.9	.977	J. Fisher	39	220	9	18	0	4.70
	SS	B. Harrelson	540	.254	1	28	254	467	32	88	5.1	.958	D. Cardwell	26	118	5	9	0	3.57
	3B	E. Charles	323	.238	3	31	85	201	17	16	3.4	.944	B. Shaw	23	99	3	9	0	4.29
	RF	R. Swoboda	449	.281	13	53	190	8	9	0	1.9	.957	R. Taylor	50	73	4	6	8	2.34
	CF	C. Jones	411	.246	5	30	210	5	5	3	1.9	.977	D. Shaw	40	51	4	5	3	2.98
	LF	T. Davis	577	.302	16	73	231	5	6	0	1.6	.975	H. Reniff	29	43	3	3	4	3.35
	C	J. Grote	344	.195	4	23	609	62	7	8	5.7	.990							
	UT	B. Johnson	230	.348	5	27	222	105	7	37		.979							
	3B	K. Boyer	166	.235	3	13	27	84	6	7	2.7	.949							

BATTING AND BASE RUNNING LEADERS   PITCHING LEADERS

Batting Average		Slugging Average		Winning Percentage		Earned Run Average	
R. Clemente, PIT	.357	H. Aaron, ATL	.573	D. Hughes, STL	.727	P. Niekro, ATL	1.87
T. Gonzalez, PHI	.339	R. Allen, PHI	.566	M. McCormick, SF	.688	J. Bunning, PHI	2.29
M. Alou, PIT	.338	R. Clemente, PIT	.554	B. Veale, PIT	.667	C. Short, PHI	2.39
C. Flood, STL	.335	W. McCovey, SF	.535	F. Jenkins, CHI	.606	G. Nolan, CIN	2.58
R. Staub, HOU	.333	O. Cepeda, STL	.524	P. Jarvis, ATL	.600	G. Perry, SF	2.61

BATTING AND BASE RUNNING LEADERS

PITCHING LEADERS

Home Runs

H. Aaron, ATL	39
J. Wynn, HOU	37
W. McCovey, SF	31
R. Santo, CHI	31
J. Hart, SF	29

Total Bases

H. Aaron, ATL	344
L. Brock, STL	325
R. Clemente, PIT	324
B. Williams, CHI	305
R. Santo, CHI	300

Wins

M. McCormick, SF	22
F. Jenkins, CHI	20
J. Bunning, PHI	17
C. Osteen, LA	17

Saves

T. Abernathy, CIN	28
R. Face, PIT	17
F. Linzy, SF	17
R. Perranoski, LA	16
J. Hoerner, STL	15

Runs Batted In

O. Cepeda, STL	111
R. Clemente, PIT	110
H. Aaron, ATL	109
J. Wynn, HOU	107
T. Perez, CIN	102

Stolen Bases

L. Brock, STL	52
J. Morgan, HOU	29
M. Wills, PIT	29
V. Pinson, CIN	26
A. Phillips, CHI	24

Strikeouts

J. Bunning, PHI	253
F. Jenkins, CHI	236
G. Perry, SF	230
G. Nolan, CIN	206
M. Cuellar, HOU	203

Complete Games

F. Jenkins, CHI	20
J. Marichal, SF	18
T. Seaver, NY	18
G. Perry, SF	18
M. Cuellar, HOU	16
J. Bunning, PHI	16

Hits

R. Clemente, PIT	209
L. Brock, STL	206
V. Pinson, CIN	187

Base on Balls

R. Santo, CHI	96
J. Morgan, HOU	81
A. Phillips, CHI	80

Fewest Hits per 9 Innings

D. Hughes, STL	6.64
D. Wilson, HOU	6.90
G. Perry, SF	7.10

Shutouts

J. Bunning, PHI	6
G. Nolan, CIN	5
M. McCormick, SF	5
C. Osteen, LA	5

Home Run Percentage

W. McCovey, SF	6.8
H. Aaron, ATL	6.5
J. Wynn, HOU	6.2

Runs Scored

H. Aaron, ATL	113
L. Brock, STL	113
R. Santo, CHI	107

Fewest Walks per 9 Innings

M. Pappas, CIN	1.57
C. Osteen, LA	1.62
K. Johnson, ATL	1.63

Most Strikeouts per 9 Inn.

G. Nolan, CIN	8.18
B. Veale, PIT	7.94
S. Carlton, STL	7.83

Doubles

R. Staub, HOU	44
O. Cepeda, STL	37
H. Aaron, ATL	37

Triples

V. Pinson, CIN	13
B. Williams, CHI	12
L. Brock, STL	12

Innings

J. Bunning, PHI	302
G. Perry, SF	293
F. Jenkins, CHI	289

Games Pitched

R. Perranoski, LA	70
T. Abernathy, CIN	70
R. Willis, STL	65
R. Face, PIT	61

	W	L	PCT	GB	R	OR	2B	3B	Batting HR	BA	SA	SB	E	Fielding DP	FA	CG	BB	Pitching SO	ShO	SV	ERA
STL	101	60	.627		695	557	225	40	115	.263	.379	102	140	127	.978	44	431	956	17	45	3.05
SF	91	71	.562	10.5	652	551	201	39	140	.245	.372	22	134	149	.979	64	453	990	17	25	2.92
CHI	87	74	.540	14	702	624	211	49	128	.251	.378	63	121	143	.981	47	463	888	7	28	3.48
CIN	87	75	.537	14.5	604	563	251	54	109	.248	.372	92	121	124	.980	34	498	1065	18	39	3.05
PHI	82	80	.506	19.5	612	581	221	47	103	.242	.357	79	137	174	.978	46	403	967	17	23	3.10
PIT	81	81	.500	20.5	679	693	193	62	91	.277	.380	79	141	186	.978	35	561	820	5	35	3.74
ATL	77	85	.475	24.5	631	640	191	29	158	.240	.372	55	138	148	.978	35	449	862	5	32	3.47
LA	73	89	.451	28.5	519	595	203	38	82	.236	.332	56	160	144	.975	41	393	967	17	24	3.21
HOU	69	93	.426	32.5	626	742	259	46	93	.249	.364	88	159	120	.974	35	485	1060	8	21	4.03
NY	61	101	.377	40.5	498	672	178	23	83	.238	.325	58	157	147	.975	36	536	893	10	19	3.73
					6218	6218	2133	427	1102	.249	.363	694	1408	1462	.978	417	4672	9468	121	291	3.38

American League 1967

	POS	Player	AB	BA	HR	RBI	PO	A	E	DP	TC/G	FA	Pitcher	G	IP	W	L	SV	ERA
Bos. W-92 L-70 Dick Williams	1B	G. Scott	565	.303	19	82	1321	94	19	115	9.4	.987	J. Lonborg	39	273	22	9	0	3.16
	2B	M. Andrews	494	.263	8	40	303	345	16	63	4.8	.976	L. Stange	35	182	8	10	1	2.77
	SS	R. Petrocelli	491	.259	17	66	223	432	19	73	4.8	.972	G. Bell	29	165	12	8	3	3.16
	3B	J. Foy	446	.251	16	49	109	204	27	13	2.9	.921	D. Brandon	39	158	5	11	3	4.17
	RF	T. Conigliaro	349	.287	20	67	172	5	3	1	1.9	.983	J. Santiago	50	145	12	4	5	3.59
	CF	R. Smith	565	.246	15	61	335	10	6	3	2.4	.983	J. Wyatt	60	93	10	7	20	2.60
	LF	Yastrzemski	579	.326	44	121	297	13	7	1	2.0	.978							
	C	M. Ryan	226	.199	2	27	473	34	6	11	6.5	.988							
	UT	J. Adair	316	.291	3	26	105	175	8	30		.972							
	OF	J. Tartabull	247	.223	0	10	90	3	1	1	1.1	.989							
	32	D. Jones	159	.289	3	25	23	60	6	6		.933							
Det. W-91 L-71 Mayo Smith	1B	N. Cash	488	.242	22	72	1135	112	6	89	8.6	.995	E. Wilson	39	264	22	11	0	3.27
	2B	D. McAuliffe	557	.239	22	65	270	307	21	74	4.1	.965	D. McLain	37	235	17	16	0	3.79
	SS	R. Oyler	367	.207	1	29	185	374	21	61	4.0	.964	J. Sparma	37	218	16	9	0	3.76
	3B	D. Wert	534	.257	6	40	112	280	9	21	2.9	.978	M. Lolich	31	204	14	13	0	3.04
	RF	A. Kaline	458	.308	25	78	217	14	4	2	1.8	.983	D. Wickersham	36	85	4	5	4	2.74
	CF	J. Northrup	495	.271	10	61	271	3	8	1	2.0	.972	F. Gladding	42	77	6	4	12	1.99
	LF	W. Horton	401	.274	19	67	165	5	5	2	1.6	.971	J. Hiller	23	65	4	3	3	2.63
	C	B. Freehan	517	.282	20	74	950	63	8	9	6.9	.992	M. Marshall	37	59	1	3	10	1.98
	OF	M. Stanley	333	.210	7	24	216	3	4	2	1.7	.982	F. Lasher	17	30	2	1	9	3.90
	2B	J. Lumpe	177	.232	4	17	70	85	6	12	3.0	.963							

	POS	Player	AB	BA	HR	RBI	PO	A	E	DP	TC/G	FA	Pitcher	G	IP	W	L	SV	ERA
Min.	1B	H. Killebrew	547	.269	**44**	113	1283	86	11	100	8.6	.992	D. Chance	41	284	20	14	1	2.73
	2B	R. Carew	514	.292	8	51	289	314	15	60	4.6	.976	J. Kaat	42	263	16	13	0	3.04
W-91 L-71	SS	Z. Versalles	581	.200	6	50	229	454	**30**	81	4.5	.958	J. Merritt	37	228	13	7	0	2.53
Sam Mele	3B	R. Rollins	339	.245	6	39	83	153	9	13	2.5	.963	D. Boswell	37	223	14	12	0	3.27
W-25 L-25	RF	T. Oliva	557	.289	17	83	286	8	4	2	2.0	.987	J. Perry	37	131	8	7	0	3.03
Cal Ermer	CF	T. Uhlaender	415	.258	6	49	255	6	1	3	2.2	.996	M. Grant	27	95	5	6	0	4.72
W-66 L-46	LF	B. Allison	496	.258	24	75	220	6	5	0	1.6	.978	Worthington	59	92	8	9	16	2.84
	C	J. Zimmerman	234	.167	1	12	572	44	5	7	6.0	.992	R. Kline	54	72	7	1	5	3.77
	UT	C. Tovar	**649**	.267	6	47	307	184	17	23		.967							
	C	R. Nixon	170	.235	1	22	308	26	2	1	4.9	.994							
	1B	R. Reese	101	.248	4	20	93	3	1	5	2.7	.990							
Chi.	1B	T. McCraw	453	.236	11	45	1167	110	11	92	**10.5**	.991	G. Peters	38	260	16	11	0	2.28
	2B	W. Causey	292	.226	1	28	153	199	8	36	3.8	.978	J. Horlen	35	258	19	7	0	**2.06**
W-89 L-73	SS	R. Hansen	498	.233	8	51	243	**482**	27	91	4.4	.964	T. John	31	178	10	13	0	2.47
Eddie Stanky	3B	D. Buford	535	.241	4	32	95	250	19	16	3.0	.948	B. Locker	**77**	125	7	5	20	2.09
	RF	K. Berry	485	.241	7	41	233	9	2	1	1.7	.992	B. Howard	30	113	3	10	0	3.43
	CF	T. Agee	529	.234	14	52	337	6	**11**	2	2.3	.969	W. Wood	51	95	4	2	4	2.45
	LF	P. Ward	467	.233	18	62	107	3	1	0	1.2	.991	H. Wilhelm	49	89	8	3	12	1.31
	C	J. Martin	252	.234	4	22	478	39	7	3	5.5	.987	J. Buzhardt	28	89	3	9	0	3.96
	OF	W. Williams	275	.240	3	15	112	6	2	2	1.6	.983							
	OF	R. Colavito	190	.221	3	29	83	2	2	3	1.5	.977							
	C	D. Josephson	189	.238	1	9	292	24	0	3	5.4	1.000							
	31	K. Boyer	180	.261	4	21	154	79	5	16		.979							
Cal.	1B	D. Mincher	487	.273	25	76	1177	88	8	92	9.0	.994	G. Brunet	40	250	11	**19**	1	3.31
	2B	B. Knoop	511	.245	9	38	**376**	392	11	91	4.9	.986	McGlothlin	32	197	12	8	0	2.96
W-84 L-77	SS	J. Fregosi	590	.290	9	56	258	435	25	73	4.8	.965	R. Clark	32	174	12	11	0	2.59
Billy Rigney	3B	P. Schaal	272	.188	6	20	73	156	7	9	2.7	.970	M. Rojas	72	122	12	9	**27**	2.52
	RF	J. Hall	401	.249	16	55	197	6	2	1	1.7	.990	J. Hamilton	26	119	9	6	0	3.24
	CF	J. Cardenal	381	.236	6	27	195	10	3	0	2.1	.986	B. Kelso	69	112	5	3	11	2.97
	LF	R. Reichardt	498	.265	17	69	254	10	7	4	2.0	.974	C. Wright	20	77	5	5	0	3.26
	C	B. Rodgers	429	.219	6	41	728	**73**	7	11	6.0	.991							
	OF	J. Johnstone	230	.209	2	10	141	3	4	0	2.3	.973							
	UT	T. Satriano	201	.224	4	21	150	85	7	10		.971							
	OF	B. Morton	201	.313	0	32	83	1	0	0	1.4	1.000							
	OF	R. Repoz	176	.250	5	20	135	3	5	0	2.3	.965							
Bal.	1B	B. Powell	415	.234	13	55	903	64	14	82	8.6	.986	T. Phoebus	33	208	14	9	0	3.33
	2B	D. Johnson	510	.247	10	64	340	348	13	75	4.9	.981	P. Richert	26	132	7	10	2	2.99
W-76 L-85	SS	L. Aparicio	546	.233	4	31	221	333	25	67	4.4	.957	B. Dillman	32	124	5	9	3	4.35
Hank Bauer	3B	B. Robinson	610	.269	22	77	147	**405**	11	37	3.6	**.980**	D. McNally	24	119	7	7	0	4.54
	RF	F. Robinson	479	.311	30	94	191	7	2	2	1.6	.990	J. Hardin	19	111	8	3	0	2.27
	CF	P. Blair	552	.293	11	64	369	13	6	3	**2.7**	.985	E. Watt	49	104	3	5	8	2.26
	LF	C. Blefary	554	.242	22	81	170	13	6	5	1.8	.968	M. Drabowsky	43	95	7	5	12	1.60
	C	Etchebarren	330	.215	7	35	673	57	8	10	6.7	.989	G. Brabender	14	94	6	4	0	3.35
	OF	R. Snyder	275	.236	4	23	127	3	2	0	1.9	.985	W. Bunker	29	88	3	7	1	4.09
	S2	M. Belanger	184	.174	1	10	98	134	9	23		.963	S. Miller	42	81	3	10	8	2.55
	C	L. Haney	164	.268	3	20	311	31	3	3	6.1	.991	S. Barber	15	75	4	9	0	4.10
Was.	1B	M. Epstein	284	.229	9	29	718	54	10	72	9.8	.987	P. Ortega	34	220	10	10	0	3.03
	2B	B. Allen	254	.193	3	18	177	200	4	57	5.1	.990	C. Pascual	28	165	12	10	0	3.28
W-76 L-85	SS	E. Brinkman	320	.188	1	18	160	309	10	54	4.4	.979	B. Moore	27	144	7	11	0	3.76
Gil Hodges	3B	K. McMullen	563	.245	16	67	153	348	18	**38**	3.6	.965	J. Coleman	28	134	8	9	0	4.63
	RF	C. Peterson	405	.240	8	46	190	5	6	1	2.0	.970	D. Knowles	61	113	6	8	14	2.70
	CF	F. Valentine	457	.234	11	44	258	7	3	0	2.0	.989	B. Priddy	46	110	3	7	4	3.44
	LF	F. Howard	519	.256	36	89	210	5	3	1	1.5	.986	B. Humphreys	48	106	6	2	4	4.17
	C	P. Casanova	528	.248	9	53	827	70	15	19	6.7	.984	F. Bertaina	18	96	6	5	0	2.92
	UT	T. Cullen	402	.236	2	31	219	361	27	67		.956	D. Lines	54	86	2	5	4	3.36
	OF	H. Allen	292	.233	3	17	148	1	3	1	1.5	.980	C. Cox	54	73	7	4	1	2.96
	1B	D. Nen	238	.218	6	29	516	42	3	49	8.6	.995	D. Baldwin	58	69	2	4	12	1.70
	2B	B. Saverine	233	.236	0	8	80	98	8	22	3.9	.957							
	OF	E. Stroud	204	.201	1	10	117	1	2	0	1.5	.983							
Cle.	1B	T. Horton	363	.281	10	44	763	46	7	62	8.7	.991	S. McDowell	37	236	13	15	0	3.85
	2B	P. Gonzalez	189	.228	1	8	114	120	7	29	3.8	.971	S. Hargan	30	223	14	13	0	2.62
W-75 L-87	SS	L. Brown	485	.227	7	37	233	414	22	90	4.5	.967	L. Tiant	33	214	12	9	2	2.74
Joe Adcock	3B	M. Alvis	637	.256	21	70	**169**	304	17	20	3.0	.965	S. Siebert	34	185	10	12	4	2.38
	RF	C. Hinton	498	.245	10	37	239	5	6	0	1.8	.976	J. O'Donoghue	33	131	8	9	2	3.24
	CF	V. Davalillo	359	.287	2	22	202	5	3	1	1.7	.986	O. Pena	48	88	0	3	8	3.36
	LF	L. Wagner	433	.242	15	54	142	4	3	1	1.3	.980	S. Williams	16	79	6	4	1	2.62
	C	J. Azcue	295	.251	11	34	636	57	1	4	8.1	**.999**	G. Culver	53	75	7	3	3	3.96
	OF	L. Maye	297	.259	9	27	102	2	2	0	1.4	.981	B. Allen	47	54	0	5	5	2.98
	C	D. Sims	272	.202	12	37	561	56	7	7	7.3	.989							
	1B	F. Whitfield	257	.218	9	31	494	40	4	51	8.2	.993							
	2B	V. Fuller	206	.223	7	21	133	144	4	39	4.4	.986							
	UT	C. Salmon	203	.227	2	19	199	103	5	26		.984							
	OF	R. Colavito	191	.241	5	21	75	2	3	0	1.6	.963							

	POS	Player	AB	BA	HR	RBI	PO	A	E	DP	TC/G	FA	Pitcher	G	IP	W	L	SV	ERA
N. Y.	1B	M. Mantle	440	.245	22	55	1089	91	8	82	9.1	.993	Stottlemyre	36	255	15	15	0	2.96
	2B	H. Clarke	588	.272	3	29	348	410	8	79	5.5	.990	A. Downing	31	202	14	10	0	2.63
W-72 L-90	SS	R. Amaro	417	.223	1	17	212	374	16	73	4.9	.973	F. Peterson	36	181	8	14	0	3.47
Ralph Houk	3B	C. Smith	425	.224	9	38	92	283	21	22	3.4	.947	F. Talbot	29	139	6	8	0	4.22
	RF	S. Whitaker	441	.243	11	50	202	12	4	6	1.9	.982	Monbouquette	33	133	6	5	1	2.36
	CF	J. Pepitone	501	.251	13	64	277	7	7	1	2.4	.976	T. Tillotson	43	98	3	9	2	4.03
	LF	T. Tresh	448	.219	14	53	198	9	6	1	1.8	.972	D. Womack	65	97	5	6	18	2.41
	C	J. Gibbs	374	.233	4	25	582	55	16	7	6.6	.975	S. Barber	17	98	6	9	0	4.05
	OF	B. Robinson	342	.196	7	29	169	10	6	1	1.8	.968	S. Hamilton	44	62	2	4	4	3.48
	O3	R. White	214	.224	2	18	79	29	10	1		.915							
	C	E. Howard	199	.196	3	17	289	26	5	5	6.7	.984							
	S3	J. Kennedy	179	.196	1	17	74	151	16	21		.934							
K. C.	1B	R. Webster	360	.256	11	51	615	41	7	42	8.0	.989	C. Hunter	35	260	13	17	0	2.81
	2B	J. Donaldson	377	.276	0	28	210	230	8	40	4.4	.982	J. Nash	37	222	12	17	0	3.76
W-62 L-99	SS	B. Campaneris	601	.248	3	32	259	365	30	75	4.5	.954	C. Dobson	32	198	10	10	0	3.69
Alvin Dark	3B	D. Green	349	.198	5	37	54	86	8	5	2.5	.946	L. Krausse	48	160	7	17	6	4.28
W-52 L-69	RF	Hershberger	480	.254	1	49	206	17	4	2	1.7	.982	P. Lindblad	46	116	5	8	6	3.58
Luke Appling	CF	R. Monday	406	.251	14	58	260	14	8	6	2.5	.972	B. Odom	29	104	3	8	0	5.04
W-10 L-30	LF	J. Gosger	356	.242	5	36	201	6	4	1	1.9	.981	T. Pierce	49	98	3	4	7	3.04
	C	P. Roof	327	.205	6	24	677	55	7	6	6.5	.991	J. Aker	57	88	3	8	12	4.30
	UT	D. Cater	529	.270	4	46	424	109	13	35		.976							
	1B	K. Harrelson	174	.305	6	30	333	25	3	21	8.0	.992							
	OF	J. Nossek	166	.205	0	10	105	2	2	0	1.7	.982							

BATTING AND BASE RUNNING LEADERS

Batting Average			**Slugging Average**	
Yastrzemski, BOS	.326		Yastrzemski, BOS	.622
F. Robinson, BAL	.311		F. Robinson, BAL	.576
A. Kaline, DET	.308		H. Killebrew, MIN	.558
G. Scott, BOS	.303		A. Kaline, DET	.541
P. Blair, BAL	.293		F. Howard, WAS	.511

Home Runs			**Total Bases**	
H. Killebrew, MIN	44		Yastrzemski, BOS	360
Yastrzemski, BOS	44		H. Killebrew, MIN	305
F. Howard, WAS	36		F. Robinson, BAL	276
F. Robinson, BAL	30		F. Howard, WAS	265
A. Kaline, DET	25		B. Robinson, BAL	265
D. Mincher, CAL	25			

Runs Batted In			**Stolen Bases**	
Yastrzemski, BOS	121		B. Campaneris, KC	55
H. Killebrew, MIN	113		D. Buford, CHI	34
F. Robinson, BAL	94		T. Agee, CHI	28
F. Howard, WAS	89		T. McCraw, CHI	24
T. Oliva, MIN	83		H. Clarke, NY	21

Hits			**Base on Balls**	
Yastrzemski, BOS	189		H. Killebrew, MIN	131
C. Tovar, MIN	173		M. Mantle, NY	107
G. Scott, BOS	171		D. McAuliffe, DET	105
J. Fregosi, CAL	171			

Home Run Percentage			**Runs Scored**	
H. Killebrew, MIN	8.0		Yastrzemski, BOS	112
Yastrzemski, BOS	7.6		H. Killebrew, MIN	105
F. Howard, WAS	6.9		C. Tovar, MIN	98

Doubles			**Triples**	
T. Oliva, MIN	34		P. Blair, BAL	12
C. Tovar, MIN	32		D. Buford, CHI	9
Yastrzemski, BOS	31			

PITCHING LEADERS

Winning Percentage			**Earned Run Average**	
J. Horlen, CHI	.731		J. Horlen, CHI	2.06
J. Lonborg, BOS	.710		G. Peters, CHI	2.28
E. Wilson, DET	.667		S. Siebert, CLE	2.38
J. Sparma, DET	.640		T. John, CHI	2.47
G. Peters, CHI	.593		J. Merritt, MIN	2.53

Wins			**Saves**	
J. Lonborg, BOS	22		M. Rojas, CAL	27
E. Wilson, DET	22		J. Wyatt, BOS	20
D. Chance, MIN	20		B. Locker, CHI	20
J. Horlen, CHI	19		D. Womack, NY	18
D. McLain, DET	17		Worthington, MIN	16

Strikeouts			**Complete Games**	
J. Lonborg, BOS	246		D. Chance, MIN	18
S. McDowell, CLE	236		S. Hargan, CLE	15
D. Chance, MIN	220		J. Lonborg, BOS	15
L. Tiant, CLE	219		J. Horlen, CHI	13
G. Peters, CHI	215		C. Hunter, KC	13
			J. Kaat, MIN	13

Fewest Hits per 9 Innings			**Shutouts**	
G. Peters, CHI	6.47		S. Hargan, CLE	6
D. Boswell, MIN	6.55		T. John, CHI	6
J. Horlen, CHI	6.56		McGlothlin, CAL	6
			M. Lolich, DET	6

Fewest Walks per 9 Innings			**Most Strikeouts per 9 Inn.**	
J. Merritt, MIN	1.19		L. Tiant, CLE	9.22
J. Kaat, MIN	1.44		S. McDowell, CLE	8.99
L. Stange, BOS	1.59		D. Boswell, MIN	8.25

Innings			**Games Pitched**	
D. Chance, MIN	284		B. Locker, CHI	77
J. Lonborg, BOS	273		M. Rojas, CAL	72
E. Wilson, DET	264		B. Kelso, CAL	69

	W	L	PCT	GB	R	OR	2B	3B	HR	BA	SA	SB	E	DP	FA	CG	BB	SO	ShO	SV	ERA
								Batting					Fielding				Pitching				
BOS	92	70	.568		722	614	216	39	158	.255	.395	68	142	142	.977	41	477	1010	9	44	3.36
DET	91	71	.562	1	683	587	192	36	152	.243	.376	37	131	126	.979	46	472	1038	17	40	3.32
MIN	91	71	.562	1	671	590	216	48	131	.240	.369	55	132	123	.978	58	396	1089	18	24	3.14
CHI	89	73	.549	3	531	491	181	34	89	.225	.320	124	138	149	.979	36	465	927	24	39	2.45
CAL	84	77	.522	7.5	567	587	170	37	114	.238	.349	40	111	135	.982	19	525	892	14	46	3.19
BAL	76	85	.472	15.5	654	592	215	44	138	.240	.372	54	124	144	.980	29	566	1034	17	36	3.32
WAS	76	85	.472	15.5	550	637	168	25	115	.223	.326	53	144	167	.978	24	495	878	14	39	3.38
CLE	75	87	.463	17	559	613	213	35	131	.235	.359	53	117	138	.981	49	559	1189	14	27	3.25
NY	72	90	.444	20	522	621	166	17	100	.225	.317	63	154	144	.976	37	480	898	16	27	3.24
KC	62	99	.385	29.5	533	660	212	50	69	.233	.330	132	132	120	.978	26	558	990	10	34	3.68
					5992	5992	1949	365	1197	.236	.351	679	1325	1388	.979	365	4993	9945	153	356	3.23

National League 1968

	POS	Player	AB	BA	HR	RBI	PO	A	E	DP	TC/G	FA	Pitcher	G	IP	W	L	SV	ERA
St. L. W-97 L-65 Red Schoendienst	1B	O. Cepeda	600	.248	16	73	1362	90	17	109	9.5	.988	B. Gibson	34	305	22	9	0	1.12
	2B	J. Javier	519	.260	4	52	304	339	16	68	4.7	.976	N. Briles	33	244	19	11	0	2.81
	SS	D. Maxvill	459	.253	1	24	232	458	22	81	4.7	.969	S. Carlton	34	232	13	11	0	2.99
	3B	M. Shannon	576	.266	15	79	110	310	21	25	2.8	.952	R. Washburn	31	215	14	8	0	2.26
	RF	R. Maris	310	.255	5	45	169	4	3	1	2.1	.983	L. Jaster	31	154	9	13	0	3.51
	CF	C. Flood	618	.301	5	60	386	11	7	4	2.7	.983	J. Hoerner	47	49	8	2	17	1.47
	LF	L. Brock	660	.279	6	51	269	9	14	1	1.9	.952	W. Granger	34	44	4	2	4	2.25
	C	T. McCarver	434	.253	5	48	708	54	11	6	7.1	.986							
	OF	B. Tolan	278	.230	5	17	116	3	4	1	1.8	.967							
	C	J. Edwards	230	.239	3	29	350	25	3	2	7.0	.992							
S. F. W-88 L-74 Herman Franks	1B	W. McCovey	523	.293	36	105	1305	103	21	91	9.8	.985	J. Marichal	38	326	26	9	0	2.43
	2B	R. Hunt	529	.250	2	28	289	410	20	66	4.9	.972	G. Perry	39	291	16	15	1	2.45
	SS	H. Lanier	486	.206	0	27	282	496	17	72	5.3	.979	R. Sadecki	38	254	12	18	0	2.91
	3B	J. Davenport	272	.224	1	17	49	120	7	12	2.1	.960	M. McCormick	38	198	12	14	1	3.58
	RF	B. Bonds	307	.254	9	35	169	6	4	1	2.2	.978	B. Bolin	34	177	10	5	0	1.99
	CF	W. Mays	498	.289	23	79	301	7	7	2	2.2	.978	F. Linzy	57	95	9	8	12	2.08
	LF	J. Alou	419	.263	0	39	175	10	2	2	1.8	.989							
	C	D. Dietz	301	.272	6	38	497	37	13	10	6.1	.976							
	3O	J. Hart	480	.258	23	78	165	112	19	12		.936							
	OF	T. Cline	291	.223	1	28	93	6	3	1	1.5	.971							
	C	J. Hiatt	224	.232	4	34	328	31	2	4	6.2	.994							
	OF	D. Marshall	174	.264	1	16	58	3	5	3	1.3	.924							
	UT	F. Johnson	174	.190	1	7	61	83	9	6		.941							
Chi. W-84 L-78 Leo Durocher	1B	E. Banks	552	.246	32	83	1379	88	6	118	10.0	.996	F. Jenkins	40	308	20	15	0	2.63
	2B	G. Beckert	643	.294	4	37	356	461	19	107	5.4	.977	B. Hands	38	259	16	10	0	2.89
	SS	D. Kessinger	655	.240	1	32	263	573	33	97	5.5	.962	K. Holtzman	34	215	11	14	1	3.35
	3B	R. Santo	577	.246	26	98	130	378	15	33	3.2	.971	J. Niekro	34	177	14	10	2	4.31
	RF	J. Hickman	188	.223	5	23	115	4	3	0	1.8	.975	R. Nye	27	133	7	12	1	3.80
	CF	A. Phillips	439	.241	13	33	311	11	7	3	2.3	.979	P. Regan	68	127	10	5	25*	2.20
	LF	B. Williams	642	.288	30	98	261	4	9	0	1.7	.967							
	C	R. Hundley	553	.226	7	65	885	81	5	11	6.1	.995							
	OF	L. Johnson	205	.244	1	14	97	0	3	0	1.8	.970							
	OF	A. Spangler	177	.271	2	18	71	2	2	1	1.6	.973							
	OF	W. Smith	142	.275	5	25	42	1	0	0	1.1	1.000							
Cin. W-83 L-79 Dave Bristol	1B	L. May	559	.290	22	80	1040	70	5	86	9.1	.996	G. Culver	42	226	11	16	2	3.23
	2B	T. Helms	507	.288	2	47	322	370	15	82	5.6	.979	J. Maloney	33	207	16	10	0	3.61
	SS	L. Cardenas	452	.235	7	41	221	388	29	66	4.7	.955	J. Arrigo	36	205	12	10	0	3.33
	3B	T. Perez	625	.282	18	92	151	343	25	33	3.2	.952	G. Nolan	23	150	9	4	0	2.40
	RF	P. Rose	626	.335	10	49	268	20	3	4	2.0	.990	T. Abernathy	78	135	10	7	13	2.46
	CF	V. Pinson	499	.271	5	48	258	7	6	0	2.2	.978	C. Carroll	58	122	7	7	17	2.29
	LF	A. Johnson	603	.312	2	58	243	8	14	2	1.9	.947							
	C	J. Bench	564	.275	15	82	942	102	9	10	6.8	.991							
	OF	M. Jones	234	.252	10	34	82	1	1	0	1.4	.988							
	1B	F. Whitfield	171	.257	6	32	285	21	6	28	7.6	.981							
Atl. W-81 L-81 Lum Harris	1B	D. Johnson	342	.208	8	33	738	46	3	66	8.1	.996	P. Niekro	37	257	14	12	2	2.59
	2B	F. Millan	570	.289	1	33	330	438	16	91	5.4	.980	P. Jarvis	34	256	16	12	0	2.60
	SS	S. Jackson	358	.226	1	19	132	307	22	35	4.7	.952	R. Reed	35	202	11	10	0	3.35
	3B	C. Boyer	273	.227	4	17	74	135	4	17	3.1	.981	K. Johnson	31	135	5	8	0	3.47
	RF	H. Aaron	606	.287	29	86	330	13	3	2	2.3	.991	M. Pappas	22	121	10	8	0	2.37
	CF	F. Alou	662	.317	11	57	379	8	8	2	2.5	.980	C. Upshaw	52	117	8	7	13	2.47
	LF	M. Lum	232	.224	3	21	115	7	3	0	1.3	.976	J. Britton	34	90	4	6	3	3.09
	C	J. Torre	424	.271	10	55	492	37	2	7	5.8	.996	G. Stone	17	75	7	4	0	2.76
	UT	M. Martinez	356	.230	0	12	169	264	18	44		.960	C. Raymond	36	60	3	5	10	2.83
	O1	T. Francona	346	.286	2	47	382	12	4	18		.990							
	O1	T. Aaron	283	.244	1	25	287	20	5	13		.984							
	C	B. Tillman	236	.220	5	20	359	29	4	7	5.2	.990							
	3B	B. Johnson	187	.262	0	11	45	101	8	9	3.2	.948							

POS	Player	AB	BA	HR	RBI	PO	A	E	DP	TC/G	FA	Pitcher	G	IP	W	L	SV	ERA
Pit. W-80 L-82 Larry Shepard																		
1B	D. Clendenon	584	.257	17	87	**1587**	128	17	**134**	11.2	.990	B. Veale	36	245	13	14	0	2.05
2B	B. Mazeroski	506	.251	3	42	319	**467**	15	107	5.6	.981	S. Blass	33	220	18	6	0	2.12
SS	G. Alley	474	.245	4	39	162	394	15	86	5.2	.974	A. McBean	36	198	9	12	0	3.58
3B	M. Wills	627	.278	0	31	105	276	17	27	2.8	.957	B. Moose	38	171	8	12	3	2.74
RF	R. Clemente	502	.291	18	57	297	9	5	1	2.4	.984	J. Bunning	27	160	4	14	0	3.88
CF	M. Alou	558	.332	0	52	298	8	5	0	2.2	.984	R. Kline	56	113	12	5	7	1.68
LF	W. Stargell	435	.237	24	67	144	12	9	0	1.5	.945	D. Ellis	26	104	6	5	0	2.50
C	J. May	416	.219	1	33	752	70	10	10	6.2	.988	T. Sisk	33	96	5	5	1	3.28
OF	M. Mota	331	.281	1	33	149	5	3	1	1.7		R. Face	43	52	2	4	13	2.60
SS	F. Patek	208	.255	2	18	80	164	6	23	4.8	.976							
UT	J. Pagan	163	.221	4	21	40	65	7	7		.938							
L. A. W-76 L-86 Walter Alston																		
1B	W. Parker	468	.239	3	27	939	69	1	74	8.9	**.999**	B. Singer	37	256	13	17	0	2.88
2B	P. Popovich	418	.232	2	25	172	229	7	48	4.6	.983	C. Osteen	39	254	12	**18**	0	3.08
SS	Z. Versalles	403	.196	2	24	204	380	28	62	5.1	.954	D. Drysdale	31	239	14	12	0	2.15
3B	B. Bailey	322	.227	8	39	81	164	12	14	2.9	.953	D. Sutton	35	208	11	15	1	2.60
RF	R. Fairly	441	.234	4	43	159	13	2	7	1.7	.989	M. Kekich	25	115	2	10	0	3.91
CF	W. Davis	643	.250	7	31	345	9	10	2	2.3	.973	M. Grant	37	95	6	4	3	2.08
LF	L. Gabrielson	304	.270	10	35	114	6	3	1	1.4	.976	J. Brewer	54	76	8	3	14	2.49
C	T. Haller	474	.285	4	53	863	81	6	**23**	6.8	.994	J. Billingham	50	71	3	0	8	2.14
2B	J. Lefebvre	286	.241	5	31	126	137	6	29	4.3	.978							
31	K. Boyer	221	.271	6	41	275	64	10	29		.971							
OF	W. Crawford	175	.251	4	14	78	6	3	1	1.8	.966							
Phi. W-76 L-86 Gene Mauch W-26 L-27 George Myatt W-2 L-0 Bob Skinner W-48 L-59																		
1B	B. White	385	.239	9	40	982	77	6	94	9.6	.994	C. Short	42	270	19	13	1	2.94
2B	C. Rojas	621	.232	9	48	**365**	424	10	**110**	5.3	**.987**	L. Jackson	34	244	13	17	0	2.77
SS	R. Pena	500	.260	1	38	230	434	32	93	5.2	.954	W. Fryman	34	214	12	14	0	2.78
3B	T. Taylor	547	.250	3	38	112	315	15	25	3.2	.966	R. Wise	30	182	9	15	0	4.54
RF	J. Callison	398	.244	14	40	187	10	0	1	1.8	**1.000**	J. James	29	116	4	4	0	4.28
CF	T. Gonzalez	416	.264	3	38	227	4	5	1	2.0	.979	D. Farrell	54	83	4	6	12	3.48
LF	R. Allen	521	.263	33	90	208	5	6	0	1.6	.973	G. Wagner	44	78	4	4	8	3.00
C	M. Ryan	296	.179	1	15	501	62	5	7	5.9	.991							
O1	J. Briggs	338	.254	7	31	423	23	7	33		.985							
OF	D. Lock	248	.210	8	34	145	2	7	1	2.0	.955							
C	C. Dalrymple	241	.207	3	26	463	34	5	3	6.3	.990							
N. Y. W-73 L-89 Gil Hodges																		
1B	E. Kranepool	373	.231	3	20	921	75	6	76	8.9	.994	T. Seaver	36	278	16	12	1	2.20
2B	P. Linz	258	.209	0	17	136	162	10	36	4.3	.968	J. Koosman	35	264	19	12	0	2.08
SS	B. Harrelson	402	.219	0	14	199	317	15	58	5.0	.972	D. Cardwell	29	180	7	13	1	2.95
3B	E. Charles	369	.276	15	53	69	200	13	19	2.7	.954	D. Selma	33	170	9	10	0	2.75
RF	R. Swoboda	450	.242	11	59	217	14	6	4	1.9	.975	N. Ryan	21	134	6	9	0	3.09
CF	T. Agee	368	.217	5	17	216	6	5	2	1.8	.978	C. Koonce	55	97	6	4	11	2.42
LF	C. Jones	509	.297	14	55	226	7	9	0	1.7	.963	A. Jackson	25	93	3	7	3	3.69
C	J. Grote	404	.282	3	31	754	60	5	8	7.1	.994	J. McAndrew	12	79	4	7	0	2.28
OF	A. Shamsky	345	.238	12	48	128	6	1	2	1.6	.993	R. Taylor	58	77	1	5	13	2.70
2B	K. Boswell	284	.261	4	11	154	203	13	37	5.4	.965							
S2	A. Weis	274	.172	1	14	138	242	14	43		.964							
C	J. Martin	244	.225	3	31	334	24	2	4	6.8	.994							
UT	J. Buchek	192	.182	1	11	57	91	7	11		.955							
OF	L. Stahl	183	.235	3	10	110	5	2	1	2.5	.983							
Hou. W-72 L-90 Grady Hatton W-23 L-38 Harry Walker W-49 L-52																		
1B	R. Staub	591	.291	6	72	1313	93	11	100	9.6	.992	D. Giusti	37	251	11	14	1	3.19
2B	D. Menke	542	.249	6	56	269	285	10	47	4.7	.982	L. Dierker	32	234	12	15	0	3.31
SS	H. Torres	466	.223	1	24	159	391	24	55	4.5	.958	D. Lemaster	33	224	10	15	0	2.81
3B	D. Rader	333	.267	6	43	83	168	19	14	3.1	.930	D. Wilson	33	209	13	16	0	3.28
RF	N. Miller	257	.237	6	28	131	1	4	1	1.8	.971	M. Cuellar	28	171	8	11	1	2.74
CF	R. Davis	217	.212	1	12	131	4	4	0	2.7	.971	J. Buzhardt	39	84	4	4	5	3.12
LF	J. Wynn	542	.269	26	67	298	**20**	4	8	2.1	.988	S. Shea	30	35	4	4	6	3.38
C	J. Bateman	350	.249	3	36	690	49	11	6	6.9	.985							
3O	B. Aspromonte	409	.225	1	46	110	153	10	9		.963							
OF	L. Thomas	201	.194	1	11	67	5	2	0	1.5	.973							
OF	D. Simpson	177	.186	3	11	63	2	2	1	1.4	.970							
2B	J. Gotay	165	.248	1	11	116	103	4	28	4.6	.982							

BATTING AND BASE RUNNING LEADERS

Batting Average

P. Rose, CIN	.335
M. Alou, PIT	.332
F. Alou, ATL	.317
A. Johnson, CIN	.312
C. Flood, STL	.301

Slugging Average

W. McCovey, SF	.545
R. Allen, PHI	.520
B. Williams, CHI	.500
H. Aaron, ATL	.498
W. Mays, SF	.488

Home Runs

W. McCovey, SF	36
R. Allen, PHI	33
E. Banks, CHI	32
B. Williams, CHI	30
H. Aaron, ATL	29

Total Bases

B. Williams, CHI	321
H. Aaron, ATL	302
P. Rose, CIN	294
F. Alou, ATL	290
W. McCovey, SF	285

PITCHING LEADERS

Winning Percentage

S. Blass, PIT	.750
J. Marichal, SF	.743
B. Gibson, STL	.710
N. Briles, STL	.633
B. Hands, CHI	.615
J. Maloney, CIN	.615

Earned Run Average

B. Gibson, STL	1.12
B. Bolin, SF	1.99
B. Veale, PIT	2.05
J. Koosman, NY	2.08
S. Blass, PIT	2.12

Wins

J. Marichal, SF	26
B. Gibson, STL	22
F. Jenkins, CHI	20
N. Briles, STL	19
J. Koosman, NY	19
C. Short, PHI	19

Saves

P. Regan, CHI, LA	25
J. Hoerner, STL	17
C. Carroll, ATL, CIN	17
J. Brewer, LA	14

BATTING AND BASE RUNNING LEADERS

Runs Batted In
W. McCovey, SF	105
R. Santo, CHI	98
B. Williams, CHI	98
T. Perez, CIN	92
R. Allen, PHI	90

Stolen Bases
L. Brock, STL	62
M. Wills, PIT	52
W. Davis, LA	36
H. Aaron, ATL	28
C. Jones, NY	23

Hits
P. Rose, CIN	210
F. Alou, ATL	210
G. Beckert, CHI	189

Base on Balls
R. Santo, CHI	96
J. Wynn, HOU	90
R. Hunt, SF	78

Home Run Percentage
W. McCovey, SF	6.9
R. Allen, PHI	6.3
E. Banks, CHI	5.8

Runs Scored
G. Beckert, CHI	98
P. Rose, CIN	94
T. Perez, CIN	93

Doubles
L. Brock, STL	46
P. Rose, CIN	42
J. Bench, CIN	40

Triples
L. Brock, STL	14
R. Clemente, PIT	12
W. Davis, LA	10

PITCHING LEADERS

Strikeouts
B. Gibson, STL	268
F. Jenkins, CHI	260
B. Singer, LA	227
J. Marichal, SF	218
R. Sadecki, SF	206

Complete Games
J. Marichal, SF	30
B. Gibson, STL	28
F. Jenkins, CHI	20
G. Perry, SF	19
J. Koosman, NY	17

Fewest Hits per 9 Innings
B. Gibson, STL	5.85
B. Bolin, SF	6.52
B. Veale, PIT	6.86

Shutouts
B. Gibson, STL	13
D. Drysdale, LA	8
S. Blass, PIT	7
J. Koosman, NY	7

Fewest Walks per 9 Innings
B. Hands, CHI	1.25
J. Marichal, SF	1.27
T. Seaver, NY	1.55

Most Strikeouts per 9 Inn.
B. Singer, LA	7.97
B. Gibson, STL	7.92
J. Maloney, CIN	7.87

Innings
J. Marichal, SF	326
F. Jenkins, CHI	308
B. Gibson, STL	305

Games Pitched
T. Abernathy, CIN	78
P. Regan, CHI, LA	73
C. Carroll, ATL, CIN	68

	W	L	PCT	GB	R	OR	2B	3B	HR	BA	SA	SB	E	DP	FA	CG	BB	SO	ShO	SV	ERA
STL	97	65	.599		583	472	227	**48**	73	.249	.346	110	140	135	.978	63	375	971	**30**	32	**2.49**
SF	88	74	.543	9	599	529	162	33	108	.239	.341	50	162	125	.975	**77**	**344**	942	20	16	2.71
CHI	84	78	.519	13	612	611	203	43	**130**	.242	.366	41	**119**	149	**.981**	46	392	894	12	32	3.41
CIN	83	79	.512	14	**690**	673	**281**	36	106	**.273**	**.389**	59	144	144	.978	24	573	963	16	**38**	3.56
ATL	81	81	.500	16	514	549	179	31	80	.252	.339	83	125	139	.980	44	362	871	16	29	2.92
PIT	80	82	.494	17	583	532	180	44	80	.252	.343	**130**	139	162	.979	42	485	897	19	30	2.74
LA	76	86	.469	21	470	509	202	36	67	.230	.319	57	144	144	.977	38	414	994	23	31	2.69
PHI	76	86	.469	21	543	615	178	30	100	.233	.333	58	127	**163**	.980	42	421	935	12	27	3.36
NY	73	89	.451	24	473	499	178	30	81	.228	.315	72	133	142	.979	45	430	1014	25	32	2.72
HOU	72	90	.444	25	510	588	205	28	66	.231	.317	44	156	129	.975	50	479	**1021**	12	23	3.26
					5577	5577	1995	359	891	.243	.341	704	1389	1432	.978	471	4275	9502	185	290	2.99

American League 1968

	POS	Player	AB	BA	HR	RBI	PO	A	E	DP	TC/G	FA	Pitcher	G	IP	W	L	SV	ERA
Det. W-103 L-59 Mayo Smith	1B	N. Cash	411	.263	25	63	924	88	8	66	8.7	.992	D. McLain	41	**336**	**31**	6	0	1.96
	2B	D. McAuliffe	570	.249	16	56	288	348	9	79	4.4	.986	E. Wilson	34	224	13	12	0	2.85
	SS	R. Oyler	215	.135	1	12	139	207	8	31	3.2	.977	M. Lolich	39	220	17	9	1	3.19
	3B	D. Wert	536	.200	12	37	142	284	15	22	2.9	.966	J. Sparma	34	182	10	10	0	3.70
	RF	J. Northrup	580	.264	21	90	321	7	7	1	2.2	.979	J. Hiller	39	128	9	6	2	2.39
	CF	M. Stanley	583	.259	11	60	297	7	0	2	2.3	**1.000**	P. Dobson	47	125	5	8	7	2.66
	LF	W. Horton	512	.285	36	85	212	6	6	2	1.6	.973	D. Patterson	38	68	2	3	7	2.12
	C	B. Freehan	540	.263	25	84	**971**	73	6	**15**	7.6	.994	F. Lasher	34	49	5	1	5	3.33
	OF	A. Kaline	327	.287	10	53	131	1	3	3	1.8	.978							
	SS	T. Matchick	227	.203	3	14	53	118	9	20	3.1	.950							
	UT	D. Tracewski	212	.156	4	15	82	157	5	27		.980							
Bal. W-91 L-71 Hank Bauer W-43 L-37 Earl Weaver W-48 L-34	1B	B. Powell	550	.249	22	85	**1293**	79	14	**102**	9.3	.990	D. McNally	35	273	22	10	0	1.95
	2B	D. Johnson	504	.242	9	56	260	330	13	67	4.7	.978	J. Hardin	35	244	18	13	0	2.51
	SS	M. Belanger	472	.208	2	21	248	444	22	73	4.9	.969	T. Phoebus	36	241	15	15	0	2.62
	3B	B. Robinson	608	.253	17	75	168	**353**	16	31	3.3	**.970**	D. Leonhard	28	126	7	7	1	3.13
	RF	F. Robinson	421	.268	15	52	173	5	7	0	1.6	.962	G. Brabender	37	125	6	7	3	3.32
	CF	P. Blair	421	.211	7	38	271	10	2	2	2.1	.993	E. Watt	59	83	5	5	11	2.27
	LF	C. Blefary	451	.200	15	39	144	9	6	1	1.7	.962	P. Richert	36	62	6	3	6	3.47
	C	Etchebarren	189	.233	5	20	414	29	1	3	6.3	.998	M. Drabowsky	45	61	4	4	7	1.91
	O2	D. Buford	426	.282	15	46	239	111	8	22		.978							
	OF	C. Motton	217	.198	8	25	91	2	1	0	1.7	.989							
	C	E. Hendricks	183	.202	7	23	303	21	3	3	6.2	.991							

Cle. — W-86 L-75 — Alvin Dark

POS	Player	AB	BA	HR	RBI	PO	A	E	DP	TC/G	FA	Pitcher	G	IP	W	L	SV	ERA
1B	T. Horton	477	.249	14	59	972	63	8	80	8.1	.992	S. McDowell	38	269	15	14	0	1.81
2B	V. Fuller	244	.242	0	18	112	129	3	24	3.3	.988	L. Tiant	34	258	21	9	0	**1.60**
SS	L. Brown	495	.234	6	35	255	371	22	70	4.2	.966	S. Siebert	31	206	12	10	0	2.97
3B	M. Alvis	452	.223	8	37	114	202	13	18	2.6	.960	S. Williams	44	194	13	11	9	2.50
RF	T. Harper	235	.217	6	26	121	0	2	0	1.1	.984	J. Hargan	32	158	8	15	0	4.15
CF	J. Cardenal	583	.257	7	44	367	12	10	7	2.5	.974	E. Fisher	54	95	4	2	4	2.85
LF	L. Maye	299	.281	4	26	123	4	2	0	1.6	.984	M. Paul	36	92	5	8	3	3.93
C	J. Azcue	357	.280	4	42	699	50	3	11	7.8	**.996**	V. Romo	40	83	5	3	12	1.62
C	D. Sims	361	.249	11	44	523	41	**10**	7	6.8	.983							
UT	C. Salmon	276	.214	3	12	152	145	8	29		.974							
OF	R. Snyder	217	.281	2	23	106	4	1	3	2.1	.991							
OF	L. Johnson	202	.257	5	23	87	5	1	1	1.6	.989							
2B	D. Nelson	189	.233	0	19	115	114	3	26	3.9	.987							
OF	V. Davalillo	180	.239	2	13	84	4	3	1	1.9	.967							

Bos. — W-86 L-76 — Dick Williams

POS	Player	AB	BA	HR	RBI	PO	A	E	DP	TC/G	FA	Pitcher	G	IP	W	L	SV	ERA
1B	G. Scott	350	.171	3	25	807	55	11	68	7.8	.987	R. Culp	35	216	16	6	0	2.91
2B	M. Andrews	536	.271	7	45	330	375	17	93	5.2	.976	G. Bell	35	199	11	11	1	3.12
SS	R. Petrocelli	406	.234	12	46	169	360	12	66	4.6	.978	D. Ellsworth	31	196	16	7	0	3.03
3B	J. Foy	515	.225	10	60	116	313	**30**	36	3.1	.935	J. Santiago	18	124	9	4	0	2.25
RF	K. Harrelson	535	.275	35	**109**	241	8	0	1	1.9	**1.000**	J. Lonborg	23	113	6	10	0	4.29
CF	R. Smith	558	.265	15	69	**390**	8	6	1	2.6	.985	J. Pizarro	19	108	6	8	2	3.59
LF	Yastrzemski	539	**.301**	23	74	301	12	3	3	2.0	.991	G. Waslewski	34	105	4	7	2	3.67
C	R. Gibson	231	.225	3	20	428	36	8	7	6.4	.983	L. Stange	50	103	5	5	12	3.93
12	D. Jones	354	.234	5	29	481	65	3	55		.995	J. Stephenson	23	69	2	8	0	5.64
UT	J. Adair	208	.216	2	12	90	139	8	22		.966	S. Lyle	49	66	6	1	11	2.74
C	E. Howard	203	.241	5	18	377	30	2	3	6.0	.995							

N. Y. — W-83 L-79 — Ralph Houk

POS	Player	AB	BA	HR	RBI	PO	A	E	DP	TC/G	FA	Pitcher	G	IP	W	L	SV	ERA
1B	M. Mantle	435	.237	18	54	1195	76	15	91	9.8	.988	Stottlemyre	36	279	21	12	0	2.45
2B	H. Clarke	579	.230	2	26	**357**	**444**	13	80	5.9	.984	S. Bahnsen	37	267	17	12	0	2.05
SS	T. Tresh	507	.195	11	52	199	409	31	70	5.4	.951	F. Peterson	36	212	12	11	0	2.63
3B	B. Cox	437	.229	7	41	98	279	17	22	3.0	.957	S. Barber	20	128	6	5	0	3.23
RF	B. Robinson	342	.240	6	40	195	3	3	1	2.1	.985	F. Talbot	29	99	1	9	0	3.36
CF	J. Pepitone	380	.245	15	56	190	4	4	1	2.2	.980	J. Verbanic	40	97	6	7	4	3.15
LF	R. White	577	.267	17	62	283	14	1	4	1.9	.997	Monbouquette	17	89	5	7	0	4.43
C	J. Gibbs	423	.213	3	29	642	55	6	7	5.8	.991	D. Womack	45	62	3	7	2	3.21
OF	A. Kosco	466	.240	15	59	160	9	7	0	1.9	.960	L. McDaniel	24	51	4	1	10	1.75
C	F. Fernandez	135	.170	7	30	240	27	3	2	6.0	.989	S. Hamilton	40	51	2	2	11	2.13

Oak. — W-82 L-80 — Bob Kennedy

POS	Player	AB	BA	HR	RBI	PO	A	E	DP	TC/G	FA	Pitcher	G	IP	W	L	SV	ERA
1B	D. Cater	504	.290	6	62	985	68	5	89	8.7	**.995**	C. Hunter	36	234	13	13	1	3.35
2B	J. Donaldson	363	.220	2	27	169	263	13	48	4.5	.971	B. Odom	32	231	16	10	0	2.45
SS	B. Campaneris	**642**	.276	4	38	**279**	458	34	86	5.0	.956	J. Nash	34	229	13	13	0	2.28
3B	S. Bando	605	.251	9	67	**188**	272	17	27	2.9	.964	C. Dobson	35	225	12	14	0	3.00
RF	R. Jackson	553	.250	29	74	269	14	**12**	5	2.0	.959	L. Krausse	36	185	10	11	4	3.11
CF	R. Monday	482	.274	8	49	299	11	7	3	2.2	.978	D. Segui	52	83	6	5	6	2.39
LF	Hershberger	246	.272	5	32	128	5	3	0	1.5	.978	J. Aker	54	75	4	4	11	4.10
C	D. Duncan	246	.191	7	28	474	41	7	5	6.6	.987	E. Sprague	47	69	3	4	4	3.28
2B	D. Green	202	.233	6	18	124	170	8	35	5.0	.974							
C	J. Pagliaroni	199	.246	6	20	375	16	1	3	6.2	.997							
1B	R. Webster	196	.214	3	23	454	27	6	33	8.9	.988							
OF	J. Rudi	181	.177	1	12	77	1	1	0	1.4	.987							

Min. — W-79 L-83 — Cal Ermer

POS	Player	AB	BA	HR	RBI	PO	A	E	DP	TC/G	FA	Pitcher	G	IP	W	L	SV	ERA
1B	R. Reese	332	.259	4	28	620	38	6	36	7.6	.991	D. Chance	43	292	16	16	1	2.53
2B	R. Carew	461	.273	1	42	262	280	**18**	48	4.8	.968	J. Merritt	38	238	12	16	1	3.25
SS	J. Hernandez	199	.176	2	17	119	197	25	43	4.3	.927	J. Kaat	30	208	14	12	0	2.94
3B	C. Tovar	613	.272	6	47	48	147	14	8	2.8	.933	D. Boswell	34	190	10	13	0	3.32
RF	T. Oliva	470	.289	18	68	227	7	4	1	1.9	.983	J. Perry	32	139	8	6	1	2.27
CF	T. Uhlaender	488	.283	7	52	283	3	4	1	2.2	.986	R. Perranoski	66	87	8	7	6	3.10
LF	B. Allison	469	.247	22	52	166	4	6	0	1.5	.966	Worthington	54	76	4	5	18	2.71
C	J. Roseboro	380	.216	8	39	689	52	7	5	6.4	.991							
1B	H. Killebrew	295	.210	17	40	594	56	4	50	8.5	.994							
23	F. Quilici	229	.245	1	22	121	165	3	30		.990							
3S	R. Clark	227	.185	1	13	73	157	16	18		.935							
3B	R. Rollins	203	.241	6	30	28	93	9	4	2.3	.931							

Cal. — W-67 L-95 — Billy Rigney

POS	Player	AB	BA	HR	RBI	PO	A	E	DP	TC/G	FA	Pitcher	G	IP	W	L	SV	ERA
1B	D. Mincher	399	.236	13	48	949	59	9	90	9.0	.991	G. Brunet	39	245	13	**17**	0	2.86
2B	B. Knoop	494	.249	3	39	350	425	15	**94**	5.2	.981	McGlothlin	40	208	10	15	3	3.54
SS	J. Fregosi	614	.244	9	49	273	454	29	**92**	4.8	.962	S. Ellis	42	164	9	10	2	3.95
3B	A. Rodriguez	223	.242	1	16	61	113	15	18	2.7	.921	C. Wright	41	126	10	6	3	3.94
RF	R. Repoz	375	.240	13	54	226	4	3	1	2.0	.987	T. Murphy	15	99	5	6	0	2.17
CF	V. Davalillo	339	.298	1	18	212	4	1	2	2.5	.995	R. Clark	21	94	1	11	0	3.53
LF	R. Reichardt	534	.255	21	73	267	9	3	2	1.9	.989	M. Pattin	52	84	4	3	0	2.79
C	B. Rodgers	258	.190	1	14	407	50	7	11	5.3	.985	Messersmith	28	81	4	2	4	2.21
C	T. Satriano	297	.253	8	35	404	40	5	6	5.3	.989	T. Burgmeier	56	73	1	4	5	4.33
UT	C. Hinton	267	.195	7	40	390	60	7	32		.985	M. Rojas	38	55	4	3	6	4.25
3B	P. Schaal	219	.210	2	16	61	142	9	13	3.7	.958							
OF	B. Morton	163	.270	1	18	64	1	1	1	1.3	.985							

	POS	Player	AB	BA	HR	RBI	PO	A	E	DP	TC/G	FA	Pitcher	G	IP	W	L	SV	ERA
Chi.	1B	T. McCraw	477	.235	9	44	1285	93	20	103	10.4	.986	J. Horlen	35	224	12	14	0	2.37
W-67 L-95	2B	S. Alomar	363	.253	0	12	188	221	18	48	4.3	.958	J. Fisher	35	181	8	13	0	2.99
Eddie Stanky	SS	L. Aparicio	622	.264	4	36	269	535	19	92	5.3	.977	T. John	25	177	10	5	0	1.98
W-34 L-45	3B	P. Ward	399	.216	15	50	59	151	12	7	2.9	.946	G. Peters	31	163	4	13	1	3.76
Les Moss	RF	B. Bradford	281	.217	5	24	162	4	6	0	1.7	.965	W. Wood	88	159	13	12	16	1.87
W-0 L-2	CF	K. Berry	504	.252	7	32	352	11	7	2	2.5	.981	C. Carlos	29	122	4	14	0	3.90
Al Lopez	LF	T. Davis	456	.268	8	50	171	8	7	2	1.6	.962	B. Priddy	35	114	3	11	0	3.63
W-33 L-48	C	D. Josephson	434	.247	6	45	641	86	7	15	6.0	.990	H. Wilhelm	72	94	4	4	12	1.73
	C	J. McNertney	169	.219	3	18	299	39	5	8	5.4	.985	B. Locker	70	90	5	4	10	2.29
	OF	B. Voss	167	.156	2	15	73	5	3	3	1.5	.963							
	OF	L. Wagner	162	.284	1	18	48	0	3	0	1.1	.941							
Was.	1B	M. Epstein	385	.234	13	33	947	70	13	83	9.4	.987	J. Coleman	33	223	12	16	0	3.27
W-65 L-96	2B	B. Allen	373	.241	6	40	263	271	5	63	4.9	**.991**	C. Pascual	31	201	13	12	0	2.69
Jim Lemon	SS	R. Hansen	275	.185	8	28	137	256	15	45	5.0	.963	J. Hannan	25	140	10	6	0	3.01
	3B	K. McMullen	557	.248	20	62	185	296	19	26	3.4	.962	D. Bosman	46	139	2	9	1	3.69
	RF	E. Stroud	306	.239	4	23	139	2	3	1	1.7	.979	F. Bertaina	27	127	7	13	0	4.66
	CF	D. Unser	635	.230	1	30	388	22	5	10	2.7	.988	B. Moore	32	118	4	6	3	3.37
	LF	F. Howard	598	.274	44	106	160	11	8	1	1.7	.955	P. Ortega	31	116	5	12	0	4.98
	C	P. Casanova	322	.196	4	25	472	46	6	3	5.7	.989	D. Higgins	59	100	4	4	13	3.25
	OF	C. Peterson	226	.204	3	18	82	2	0	0	1.6	1.000	B. Humphreys	56	93	5	7	2	3.69
	SS	E. Brinkman	193	.187	0	6	97	197	10	28	4.1	.967							
	2B	F. Coggins	171	.175	0	7	122	122	12	33	4.9	.953							
	C	J. French	165	.194	1	10	268	42	5	2	5.9	.984							
	OF	B. Alyea	150	.267	6	23	76	0	0	0	1.9	1.000							

BATTING AND BASE RUNNING LEADERS

Batting Average
Yastrzemski, BOS	.301
D. Cater, OAK	.290
T. Oliva, MIN	.289
W. Horton, DET	.285
T. Uhlaender, MIN	.283

Home Runs
F. Howard, WAS	44
W. Horton, DET	36
K. Harrelson, BOS	35
R. Jackson, OAK	29
N. Cash, DET	25
B. Freehan, DET	25

Runs Batted In
K. Harrelson, BOS	109
F. Howard, WAS	106
J. Northrup, DET	90
W. Horton, DET	85
B. Powell, BAL	85

Hits
B. Campaneris, OAK	177
C. Tovar, MIN	167
F. Howard, WAS	164
L. Aparicio, CHI	164

Home Run Percentage
F. Howard, WAS	7.4
W. Horton, DET	7.0
K. Harrelson, BOS	6.5

Doubles
R. Smith, BOS	37
B. Robinson, BAL	36
Yastrzemski, BOS	32

Slugging Average
F. Howard, WAS	.552
W. Horton, DET	.543
K. Harrelson, BOS	.518
Yastrzemski, BOS	.495
T. Oliva, MIN	.477

Total Bases
F. Howard, WAS	330
W. Horton, DET	278
K. Harrelson, BOS	277
Yastrzemski, BOS	267
J. Northrup, DET	259

Stolen Bases
B. Campaneris, OAK	62
J. Cardenal, CLE	40
C. Tovar, MIN	35
D. Buford, BAL	27
J. Foy, BOS	26

Base on Balls
Yastrzemski, BOS	119
M. Mantle, NY	106
J. Foy, BOS	84

Runs Scored
D. McAuliffe, DET	95
Yastrzemski, BOS	90
R. White, NY	89
C. Tovar, MIN	89

Triples
J. Fregosi, CAL	13
T. McCraw, CHI	12
E. Stroud, WAS	10
D. McAuliffe, DET	10

PITCHING LEADERS

Winning Percentage
D. McLain, DET	.838
R. Culp, BOS	.727
L. Tiant, CLE	.700
D. Ellsworth, BOS	.696
D. McNally, BAL	.688

Wins
D. McLain, DET	31
D. McNally, BAL	22
L. Tiant, CLE	21
Stottlemyre, NY	21
J. Hardin, BAL	18

Strikeouts
S. McDowell, CLE	283
D. McLain, DET	280
L. Tiant, CLE	264
D. Chance, MIN	234
D. McNally, BAL	202

Fewest Hits per 9 Innings
L. Tiant, CLE	5.30
D. McNally, BAL	5.77
S. McDowell, CLE	6.06

Fewest Walks per 9 Innings
F. Peterson, NY	1.23
D. McLain, DET	1.69
D. Ellsworth, BOS	1.70

Innings
D. McLain, DET	336
D. Chance, MIN	292
Stottlemyre, NY	279

Earned Run Average
L. Tiant, CLE	1.60
S. McDowell, CLE	1.81
D. McNally, BAL	1.95
D. McLain, DET	1.96
T. John, CHI	1.98

Saves
Worthington, MIN	18
W. Wood, CHI	16
D. Higgins, WAS	13
L. Stange, BOS	12
V. Romo, CLE	12
H. Wilhelm, CHI	12

Complete Games
D. McLain, DET	28
L. Tiant, CLE	19
Stottlemyre, NY	19
D. McNally, BAL	18
J. Hardin, BAL	16

Shutouts
L. Tiant, CLE	9

Most Strikeouts per 9 Inn.
S. McDowell, CLE	9.47
L. Tiant, CLE	9.20
M. Lolich, DET	8.06

Games Pitched
W. Wood, CHI	88
H. Wilhelm, CHI	72
B. Locker, CHI	70

	W	L	PCT	GB	R	OR	2B	3B	Batting HR	BA	SA	SB	E	Fielding DP	FA	CG	BB	Pitching SO	ShO	SV	ERA
DET	103	59	.636		671	492	190	39	185	.235	.385	26	105	133	.983	59	486	1115	19	29	2.71
BAL	91	71	.562	12	579	497	215	28	133	.225	.352	78	120	131	.981	53	502	1044	16	31	2.66
CLE	86	75	.534	16.5	516	504	210	36	75	.234	.327	115	127	130	.979	48	540	1157	23	32	2.66
BOS	86	76	.531	17	614	611	207	17	125	.236	.352	76	128	147	.979	55	523	972	17	31	3.33
NY	83	79	.512	20	536	531	154	34	109	.214	.318	90	139	142	.979	45	424	831	14	27	3.33
OAK	82	80	.506	21	569	544	192	40	94	.240	.343	147	145	136	.976	45	505	997	18	29	2.79
MIN	79	83	.488	24	562	546	207	41	105	.237	.350	98	170	117	.973	45	414	996	14	29	2.94
CAL	67	95	.414	36	498	615	170	33	83	.227	.318	62	140	156	.977	46	519	869	11	31	2.89
CHI	67	95	.414	36	463	527	169	33	71	.228	.311	90	151	152	.977	20	451	834	11	40	3.43
WAS	65	96	.404	37.5	524	665	160	37	124	.224	.336	29	148	144	.976	26	517	826	11	28	3.64
					5532	5532	1874	338	1104	.230	.339	811	1373	1388	.978	426	4881	9641	154	307	2.98

National League 1969

	POS	Player	AB	BA	HR	RBI	PO	A	E	DP	TC/G	FA	Pitcher	G	IP	W	L	SV	ERA

East

N. Y. W-100 L-62   Gil Hodges

POS	Player	AB	BA	HR	RBI	PO	A	E	DP	TC/G	FA	Pitcher	G	IP	W	L	SV	ERA
1B	E. Kranepool	353	.238	11	49	809	64	6	76	8.3	.993	T. Seaver	36	273	25	7	0	2.21
2B	K. Boswell	362	.279	3	32	190	229	18	51	4.6	.959	J. Koosman	32	241	17	9	0	2.28
SS	B. Harrelson	395	.248	0	24	243	347	19	70	5.1	.969	G. Gentry	35	234	13	12	0	3.43
3B	W. Garrett	400	.218	1	39	40	115	8	10	2.3	.951	D. Cardwell	30	152	8	10	0	3.01
RF	R. Swoboda	327	.235	9	52	163	5	2	0	1.8	.988	J. McAndrew	27	135	6	7	0	3.47
CF	T. Agee	565	.271	26	76	334	7	5	0	2.4	.986	T. McGraw	42	100	9	3	12	2.24
LF	C. Jones	483	.340	12	75	223	4	2	0	1.9	.991	N. Ryan	25	89	6	3	1	3.53
C	J. Grote	365	.252	6	40	718	63	7	11	7.0	.991	C. Koonce	40	83	6	3	7	4.99
OF	A. Shamsky	303	.300	14	47	117	2	1	2	1.5	.992	R. Taylor	59	76	9	4	13	2.72
S2	A. Weis	247	.215	2	23	138	218	13	50	1.5	.965							
OF	R. Gaspar	215	.228	1	14	104	12	2	6	1.3	.983							
3B	B. Pfeil	211	.232	0	10	32	88	3	8	2.5	.976							
1B	D. Clendenon	202	.252	12	37	418	25	7	46	7.8	.984							
C	J. Martin	177	.209	4	21	275	9	1	2	5.9	.996							
3B	E. Charles	169	.207	3	18	37	86	7	9	2.5	.946							

Chi. W-92 L-70   Leo Durocher

POS	Player	AB	BA	HR	RBI	PO	A	E	DP	TC/G	FA	Pitcher	G	IP	W	L	SV	ERA
1B	E. Banks	565	.253	23	106	1419	87	4	116	9.9	.997	F. Jenkins	43	311	21	15	1	3.21
2B	G. Beckert	543	.291	1	37	262	401	24	71	5.3	.965	B. Hands	41	300	20	14	0	2.49
SS	D. Kessinger	664	.273	4	53	266	542	20	101	5.3	.976	K. Holtzman	39	261	17	13	0	3.59
3B	R. Santo	575	.289	29	123	144	334	27	23	3.2	.947	D. Selma	36	169	10	8	1	3.63
RF	J. Hickman	338	.237	21	54	153	6	3	0	1.3	.981	P. Regan	71	112	12	6	17	3.70
CF	D. Young	272	.239	6	27	191	4	5	0	2.0	.975	T. Abernathy	56	85	4	3	3	3.18
LF	B. Williams	642	.293	21	95	250	15	12	2	1.7	.957	R. Nye	34	69	3	5	3	5.09
C	R. Hundley	522	.255	18	64	978	79	8	17	7.1	.992							
OF	A. Spangler	213	.211	4	23	75	1	4	0	1.4	.950							
O1	W. Smith	195	.246	9	25	185	9	3	14		.985							

Pit. W-88 L-74   Larry Shepard W-84 L-73   Alex Grammas W-4 L-1

POS	Player	AB	BA	HR	RBI	PO	A	E	DP	TC/G	FA	Pitcher	G	IP	W	L	SV	ERA
1B	A. Oliver	463	.285	17	70	869	49	8	87	8.7	.991	B. Veale	34	226	13	14	0	3.23
2B	B. Mazeroski	227	.229	3	25	134	192	4	46	5.1	.988	D. Ellis	35	219	11	17	0	3.58
SS	F. Patek	460	.239	5	32	227	399	30	81	4.5	.954	S. Blass	38	210	16	10	2	4.46
3B	R. Hebner	459	.301	8	47	79	240	19	31	2.7	.944	B. Moose	44	170	14	3	4	2.91
RF	R. Clemente	507	.345	19	91	226	14	5	1	1.8	.980	J. Bunning	25	156	10	9	0	3.81
CF	M. Alou	698	.331	1	48	327	10	8	4	2.1	.977	L. Walker	31	119	4	6	0	3.63
LF	W. Stargell	522	.307	29	92	159	4	5	1	1.4	.970	Hartenstein	56	96	5	4	10	3.94
C	M. Sanguillen	459	.303	5	57	825	71	17	11	8.1	.981	Dal Canton	57	86	8	2	5	3.35
2S	G. Alley	285	.246	8	32	145	213	11	56		.970	J. Gibbon	35	51	5	1	9	1.93
3O	J. Pagan	274	.285	9	42	56	76	5	7		.964							
O1	C. Taylor	221	.348	4	33	267	16	8	26		.973							
C	J. May	190	.232	7	23	325	22	2	3	6.7	.994							
UT	J. Martinez	168	.268	1	16	86	132	6	31		.973							

St. L. W-87 L-75   Red Schoendienst

POS	Player	AB	BA	HR	RBI	PO	A	E	DP	TC/G	FA	Pitcher	G	IP	W	L	SV	ERA
1B	J. Torre	602	.289	18	101	1270	83	6	117	9.4	.996	B. Gibson	35	314	20	13	0	2.18
2B	J. Javier	493	.282	10	42	244	374	21	70	4.5	.967	S. Carlton	31	236	17	11	0	2.17
SS	D. Maxvill	372	.175	2	32	216	408	20	78	4.9	.969	N. Briles	36	228	15	13	0	3.51
3B	M. Shannon	551	.254	12	55	123	258	22	22	2.7	.945	R. Washburn	28	132	3	8	1	3.07
RF	V. Pinson	495	.255	10	70	218	6	1	2	1.8	.996	C. Taylor	27	127	7	5	0	2.55
CF	C. Flood	606	.285	4	57	362	14	4	2	2.5	.989	M. Torrez	24	108	10	4	0	3.58
LF	L. Brock	655	.298	12	47	255	7	14	2	1.8	.949	D. Giusti	22	100	3	7	0	3.60
C	T. McCarver	515	.260	7	51	925	66	14	10	7.4	.986	M. Grant	30	63	7	5	7	4.12

Phi.
W-63 L-99
Bob Skinner W-44 L-64
George Myatt W-19 L-35

POS	Player	AB	BA	HR	RBI	PO	A	E	DP	TC/G	FA
1B	R. Allen	438	.288	32	89	1024	54	16	100	9.4	.985
2B	C. Rojas	391	.228	4	30	259	229	10	68	5.2	.980
SS	D. Money	450	.229	6	42	212	443	21	82	5.4	.969
3B	T. Taylor	557	.262	3	30	57	150	7	8	3.0	.967
RF	J. Callison	495	.265	16	64	273	12	3	3	2.2	.990
CF	L. Hisle	482	.266	20	56	324	11	8	2	2.5	.977
LF	J. Briggs	361	.238	12	46	197	6	6	0	1.9	.971
C	M. Ryan	446	.204	12	44	769	79	8	13	6.5	.991
UT	D. Johnson	475	.255	17	80	250	99	11	12		.969
3B	R. Joseph	264	.273	6	37	49	103	7	11	2.7	.956
OF	R. Stone	222	.239	1	24	85	6	2	0	1.3	.978
S2	T. Harmon	201	.239	0	16	94	168	7	42		.974

Pitcher	G	IP	W	L	SV	ERA
G. Jackson	38	253	14	18	1	3.34
W. Fryman	36	228	12	15	0	4.42
R. Wise	33	220	15	13	0	3.23
J. Johnson	33	147	6	13	1	4.29
B. Champion	23	117	5	10	1	5.00
L. Palmer	26	90	2	8	0	5.20
D. Farrell	46	74	3	4	3	4.01
B. Wilson	37	62	2	5	6	3.34

Mon.
W-52 L-110
Gene Mauch

POS	Player	AB	BA	HR	RBI	PO	A	E	DP	TC/G	FA
1B	B. Bailey	358	.265	9	53	704	67	6	77	9.1	.992
2B	G. Sutherland	544	.239	3	53	318	381	21	110	5.2	.971
SS	B. Wine	370	.200	3	25	208	367	31	96	5.1	.949
3B	C. Laboy	562	.258	18	83	115	307	25	28	2.9	.944
RF	R. Staub	549	.302	29	79	265	16	10	2	1.9	.966
CF	A. Phillips	199	.216	4	7	99	3	2	0	2.0	.981
LF	M. Jones	455	.270	22	79	226	6	10	0	1.9	.959
C	R. Brand	287	.258	0	20	492	44	8	7	6.5	.985
1B	R. Fairly	253	.289	12	39	409	36	4	53	8.6	.991
C	J. Bateman	235	.209	8	19	433	26	7	5	7.1	.985
OF	T. Cline	209	.239	2	12	77	2	1	1	2.0	.988
SS	M. Wills	189	.222	0	8	72	139	11	31	4.8	.950

Pitcher	G	IP	W	L	SV	ERA
B. Stoneman	42	236	11	19	0	4.39
J. Robertson	38	180	5	16	1	3.96
M. Wegener	32	166	5	14	0	4.40
D. McGinn	74	132	7	10	6	3.94
G. Waslewski	30	109	3	7	1	3.29
H. Reed	31	106	6	7	1	4.84
S. Renko	18	103	6	7	0	4.02
R. Face	44	59	4	2	5	3.94

West

Atl.
W-93 L-69
Lum Harris

POS	Player	AB	BA	HR	RBI	PO	A	E	DP	TC/G	FA
1B	O. Cepeda	573	.257	22	88	1318	101	9	91	9.3	.994
2B	F. Millan	652	.267	6	57	373	444	17	72	5.1	.980
SS	S. Jackson	318	.239	1	27	161	254	17	48	4.5	.961
3B	C. Boyer	496	.250	14	57	139	275	15	18	3.0	.965
RF	H. Aaron	547	.300	44	97	267	11	5	3	2.0	.982
CF	F. Alou	476	.282	5	32	260	4	3	1	2.3	.989
LF	T. Gonzalez	320	.294	10	50	173	1	2	0	2.1	.989
C	B. Didier	352	.256	0	32	633	52	4	3	6.0	.994
OF	R. Carty	304	.342	16	58	118	0	6	0	1.6	.952
SS	G. Garrido	227	.220	0	10	99	192	8	32	3.7	.973
UT	B. Aspromonte	198	.253	3	24	74	46	8	2		.938
C	B. Tillman	190	.195	12	29	309	15	4	5	4.8	.988
OF	M. Lum	168	.268	1	22	119	2	1	1	1.4	.992
O1	T. Francona	88	.295	2	22	64	4	2	4		.971

Pitcher	G	IP	W	L	SV	ERA
P. Niekro	40	284	23	13	1	2.57
R. Reed	36	241	18	10	0	3.47
P. Jarvis	37	217	13	11	0	4.44
G. Stone	36	165	13	10	3	3.65
M. Pappas	26	144	6	10	0	3.63
C. Upshaw	62	105	6	4	27	2.91
J. Britton	24	88	7	5	1	3.78

S. F.
W-90 L-72
Clyde King

POS	Player	AB	BA	HR	RBI	PO	A	E	DP	TC/G	FA
1B	W. McCovey	491	.320	45	126	1392	79	12	116	10.0	.992
2B	R. Hunt	478	.262	3	41	254	356	13	67	5.0	.979
SS	H. Lanier	495	.228	0	35	252	530	25	98	5.4	.969
3B	J. Davenport	303	.241	2	42	77	158	8	15	2.3	.967
RF	B. Bonds	622	.259	32	90	339	9	8	2	2.3	.976
CF	W. Mays	403	.283	13	58	199	4	5	0	1.9	.976
LF	K. Henderson	374	.225	6	44	175	10	6	2	1.7	.969
C	D. Dietz	244	.230	11	35	432	31	13	5	6.5	.973
OF	D. Marshall	267	.232	2	33	106	3	5	0	1.3	.956
23	D. Mason	250	.228	0	13	132	174	18	36		.944
OF	J. Hart	236	.254	3	26	80	2	5	1	1.3	.943
C	J. Hiatt	194	.196	7	34	335	30	3	6	6.1	.992
3S	T. Fuentes	183	.295	1	14	50	117	13	18		.928
1B	B. Burda	161	.230	6	27	206	12	1	15	4.9	.995

Pitcher	G	IP	W	L	SV	ERA
G. Perry	40	325	19	14	0	2.49
J. Marichal	37	300	21	11	0	2.10
M. McCormick	32	197	11	9	0	3.34
B. Bolin	30	146	7	7	0	4.44
R. Sadecki	29	138	5	8	0	4.24
F. Linzy	58	116	14	9	11	3.65

Cin.
W-89 L-73
Dave Bristol

POS	Player	AB	BA	HR	RBI	PO	A	E	DP	TC/G	FA
1B	L. May	607	.278	38	110	1387	102	11	128	9.6	.993
2B	T. Helms	480	.269	1	40	320	344	17	87	5.4	.975
SS	W. Woodward	241	.261	0	15	147	248	14	36	4.4	.966
3B	T. Perez	629	.294	37	122	136	342	32	35	3.2	.937
RF	P. Rose	627	.348	16	82	316	10	4	3	2.1	.968
CF	B. Tolan	637	.305	21	93	362	6	10	3	2.5	.974
LF	A. Johnson	523	.315	17	80	222	5	18	1	1.9	.927
C	J. Bench	532	.293	26	90	793	76	7	10	6.0	.992
OF	J. Stewart	221	.253	4	24	68	4	2	0	1.1	.973
SS	D. Chaney	209	.191	0	15	115	191	17	44	3.5	.947
UT	C. Ruiz	196	.245	0	13	120	147	12	36		.957

Pitcher	G	IP	W	L	SV	ERA
J. Merritt	42	251	17	9	0	4.37
T. Cloninger	35	190	11	17	0	5.02
J. Maloney	30	179	12	5	0	2.77
C. Carroll	71	151	12	6	7	3.52
W. Granger	90	145	9	6	27	2.79
J. Fisher	34	113	4	4	1	5.50
G. Nolan	16	109	8	8	0	3.55
G. Culver	32	101	5	7	4	4.28
J. Arrigo	20	91	4	7	0	4.14

L. A.
W-85 L-77
Walter Alston

POS	Player	AB	BA	HR	RBI	PO	A	E	DP	TC/G	FA
1B	W. Parker	471	.278	13	68	1189	79	6	87	10.0	.995
2B	T. Sizemore	590	.271	4	46	283	331	13	76	5.3	.979
SS	M. Wills	434	.297	4	39	168	357	17	61	5.2	.969
3B	B. Sudakis	462	.234	14	53	98	272	21	26	3.2	.946
RF	A. Kosco	424	.248	19	74	153	6	3	2	1.5	.981
CF	W. Davis	498	.311	11	59	271	8	6	1	2.3	.979
LF	W. Crawford	389	.247	11	41	177	5	5	0	1.7	.973
C	T. Haller	445	.263	6	39	800	48	7	4	6.5	.992
OF	M. Mota	294	.323	3	30	118	8	4	2	1.6	.969
32	J. Lefebvre	275	.236	4	44	96	181	6	23		.979
OF	B. Russell	212	.226	5	15	132	4	3	1	1.6	.978
OF	L. Gabrielson	178	.270	1	18	50	1	1	0	1.1	.981

Pitcher	G	IP	W	L	SV	ERA
C. Osteen	41	321	20	15	0	2.66
B. Singer	41	316	20	12	1	2.34
D. Sutton	41	293	17	18	0	3.47
A. Foster	24	103	3	9	0	4.37
J. Brewer	59	88	7	6	20	2.56
P. Mikkelsen	48	81	7	5	4	2.78
A. McBean	31	48	2	6	4	3.91

POS	Player	AB	BA	HR	RBI	PO	A	E	DP	TC/G	FA	Pitcher	G	IP	W	L	SV	ERA
Hou. W-81 L-81 Harry Walker																		
1B	C. Blefary	542	.253	12	67	1235	103	17	117	8.9	.987	L. Dierker	39	305	20	13	0	2.33
2B	J. Morgan	535	.236	15	43	303	328	18	79	4.9	.972	D. Lemaster	38	245	13	17	1	3.16
SS	D. Menke	553	.269	10	90	161	356	24	63	4.1	.956	D. Wilson	34	225	16	12	0	4.00
3B	D. Rader	569	.246	11	83	126	307	25	34	3.0	.945	T. Griffin	31	188	11	10	0	3.54
RF	N. Miller	409	.264	4	50	172	7	3	3	1.6	.984	J. Ray	40	115	8	2	0	3.91
CF	J. Wynn	495	.269	33	87	318	9	5	3	2.2	.985	J. Billingham	52	83	6	7	2	4.23
LF	J. Alou	452	.248	5	34	173	8	14	1	1.7	.928	F. Gladding	57	73	4	8	29	4.19
C	J. Edwards	496	.232	6	50	1135	79	7	9	8.1	.994							
UT	M. Martinez	198	.308	0	15	77	66	11	8		.929							
S. D. W-52 L-110 Preston Gomez																		
1B	N. Colbert	483	.255	24	66	1217	87	13	96	9.8	.990	C. Kirby	35	216	7	20	0	3.79
2B	J. Arcia	302	.215	0	10	162	176	8	33	5.1	.977	J. Niekro	37	202	8	17	0	3.70
SS	T. Dean	273	.176	2	9	139	255	9	41	4.2	.978	A. Santorini	32	185	8	14	0	3.94
3B	E. Spiezio	355	.234	13	43	93	198	19	10	3.2	.939	T. Sisk	53	143	2	13	6	4.78
RF	O. Brown	568	.264	20	61	269	14	7	4	2.0	.976	D. Kelley	27	136	4	8	0	3.57
CF	C. Gaston	391	.230	2	28	243	12	11	4	2.4	.959	G. Ross	46	110	3	12	3	4.19
LF	A. Ferrara	366	.260	14	56	131	5	6	2	1.5	.958	J. Baldschun	61	77	7	2	1	4.79
C	C. Cannizzaro	418	.220	4	33	644	69	9	8	5.5	.988	J. Podres	17	65	5	6	0	4.29
UT	R. Pena	472	.250	4	30	289	285	13	54		.978	B. McCool	54	59	3	5	7	4.27
OF	I. Murrell	247	.255	3	25	137	3	6	0	2.0	.959							
2B	J. Sipin	229	.223	2	9	106	173	7	41	4.8	.976							
3B	V. Kelly	209	.244	3	15	42	91	4	10	2.8	.971							
OF	T. Gonzalez	182	.225	2	8	114	2	3	0	2.4	.975							
OF	L. Stahl	162	.198	3	10	48	3	1	0	1.4	.981							

BATTING AND BASE RUNNING LEADERS

Batting Average
P. Rose, CIN	.348
R. Clemente, PIT	.345
C. Jones, NY	.340
M. Alou, PIT	.331
W. McCovey, SF	.320

Slugging Average
W. McCovey, SF	.656
H. Aaron, ATL	.607
R. Allen, PHI	.573
W. Stargell, PIT	.556
R. Clemente, PIT	.544

Home Runs
W. McCovey, SF	45
H. Aaron, ATL	44
L. May, CIN	38
T. Perez, CIN	37
J. Wynn, HOU	33

Total Bases
H. Aaron, ATL	332
T. Perez, CIN	331
W. McCovey, SF	322
L. May, CIN	321
P. Rose, CIN	321

Runs Batted In
W. McCovey, SF	126
R. Santo, CHI	123
T. Perez, CIN	122
L. May, CIN	110
E. Banks, CHI	106

Stolen Bases
L. Brock, STL	53
J. Morgan, HOU	49
B. Bonds, SF	45
M. Wills, LA, MON	40
B. Tolan, CIN	26

Hits
M. Alou, PIT	231
P. Rose, CIN	218
L. Brock, STL	195

Base on Balls
J. Wynn, HOU	148
W. McCovey, SF	121
J. Morgan, HOU	110
R. Staub, MON	110

Home Run Percentage
W. McCovey, SF	9.2
H. Aaron, ATL	8.0
R. Allen, PHI	7.3

Runs Scored
B. Bonds, SF	120
P. Rose, CIN	120
J. Wynn, HOU	113

Doubles
M. Alou, PIT	41
D. Kessinger, CHI	38

Triples
R. Clemente, PIT	12
P. Rose, CIN	11

PITCHING LEADERS

Winning Percentage
T. Seaver, NY	.781
J. Marichal, SF	.656
J. Merritt, CIN	.654
J. Koosman, NY	.654
R. Reed, ATL	.643

Earned Run Average
J. Marichal, SF	2.10
S. Carlton, STL	2.17
B. Gibson, STL	2.18
T. Seaver, NY	2.21
J. Koosman, NY	2.28

Wins
T. Seaver, NY	25
P. Niekro, ATL	23
J. Marichal, SF	21
F. Jenkins, CHI	21

Saves
F. Gladding, HOU	29
W. Granger, CIN	27
C. Upshaw, ATL	27
J. Brewer, LA	20
P. Regan, CHI	17

Strikeouts
F. Jenkins, CHI	273
B. Gibson, STL	269
B. Singer, LA	247
D. Wilson, HOU	235
G. Perry, SF	233

Complete Games
B. Gibson, STL	28
J. Marichal, SF	27
G. Perry, SF	26
F. Jenkins, CHI	23
P. Niekro, ATL	21

Fewest Hits per 9 Innings
T. Seaver, NY	6.65
J. Maloney, CIN	6.79
B. Singer, LA	6.95

Shutouts
J. Marichal, SF	8
C. Osteen, LA	7
F. Jenkins, CHI	7

Fewest Walks per 9 Innings
J. Marichal, SF	1.62
P. Niekro, ATL	1.81
F. Jenkins, CHI	2.05

Most Strikeouts per 9 Inn.
D. Wilson, HOU	9.40
B. Moose, PIT	8.74
D. Selma, CHI, SD	8.54

Innings
G. Perry, SF	325
C. Osteen, LA	321
B. Singer, LA	316

Games Pitched
W. Granger, CIN	90
D. McGinn, MON	74
C. Carroll, CIN	71
P. Regan, CHI	71

	W	L	PCT	GB	R	OR	2B	3B	Batting HR	BA	SA	SB	E	Fielding DP	FA	CG	BB	Pitching SO	ShO	SV	ERA
EAST																					
NY	100	62	.617		632	541	184	41	109	.242	.351	66	122	146	.980	51	517	1012	**28**	35	2.99
CHI	92	70	.568	8	720	611	215	40	142	.253	.384	30	136	149	.979	58	475	1017	22	27	3.34
PIT	88	74	.543	12	725	652	220	**52**	119	**.277**	.398	74	155	169	.975	39	553	1124	9	33	3.61
STL	87	75	.537	13	595	**540**	**228**	44	90	.253	.359	87	138	144	.978	63	511	1004	12	26	**2.94**
PHI	63	99	.389	37	645	745	227	35	137	.241	.372	73	136	157	.978	47	570	921	14	21	4.17
MON	52	110	.321	48	582	791	202	33	125	.240	.359	52	184	**179**	.971	26	702	973	8	21	4.33
WEST																					
ATL	93	69	.574		691	631	195	22	141	.258	.380	59	**115**	114	**.981**	38	438	893	7	42	3.53
SF	90	72	.556	3	713	636	187	28	136	.242	.361	71	169	155	.974	**71**	461	906	15	17	3.25
CIN	89	73	.549	4	**798**	768	224	42	**171**	.277	**.422**	79	168	158	.973	23	611	818	11	**44**	4.13
LA	85	77	.525	8	645	561	185	**52**	97	.254	.359	80	126	130	.980	47	**420**	975	20	31	3.09
HOU	81	81	.500	12	676	668	208	40	104	.240	.352	**101**	153	136	.975	52	547	**1221**	11	34	3.60
SD	52	110	.321	41	468	746	180	42	99	.225	.329	45	156	140	.975	16	592	764	9	25	4.24
					7890	7890	2455	471	1470	.250	.369	817	1758	1777	.977	531	6397	11628	166	356	3.60

American League 1969

POS	Player	AB	BA	HR	RBI	PO	A	E	DP	TC/G	FA	Pitcher	G	IP	W	L	SV	ERA

East

Bal.
W-109 L-53
Earl Weaver

POS	Player	AB	BA	HR	RBI	PO	A	E	DP	TC/G	FA	Pitcher	G	IP	W	L	SV	ERA
1B	B. Powell	533	.304	37	121	1192	84	7	105	8.9	.995	M. Cuellar	39	291	23	11	0	2.38
2B	D. Johnson	511	.280	7	57	355	369	12	93	5.2	.984	D. McNally	41	269	20	7	0	3.22
SS	M. Belanger	530	.287	2	50	251	449	23	79	4.9	.968	T. Phoebus	35	202	14	7	0	3.52
3B	B. Robinson	598	.234	23	84	163	**370**	13	37	3.5	.976	J. Palmer	26	181	16	4	0	2.34
RF	F. Robinson	539	.308	32	100	226	9	3	2	1.8	.987	J. Hardin	30	138	6	7	1	3.60
CF	P. Blair	625	.285	26	76	**407**	14	5	5	**2.8**	.988	D. Leonhard	37	94	7	4	1	2.49
LF	D. Buford	554	.291	11	64	228	7	4	1	1.9	.983	E. Watt	56	71	5	2	16	1.65
C	E. Hendricks	295	.244	12	38	479	40	1	2	6.0	**.998**	D. Hall	39	66	5	2	6	1.92
C	Etchebarren	217	.249	3	26	380	27	4	1	5.7	.990	P. Richert	44	57	7	4	12	2.20
OF	M. Rettenmund	190	.247	4	25	105	3	1	0	1.4	.991							
OF	C. Motton	89	.303	6	21	26	0	0	0	1.3	1.000							

Det.
W-90 L-72
Mayo Smith

POS	Player	AB	BA	HR	RBI	PO	A	E	DP	TC/G	FA	Pitcher	G	IP	W	L	SV	ERA
1B	N. Cash	483	.280	22	74	1016	96	7	99	8.4	.994	D. McLain	42	**325**	**24**	9	0	2.80
2B	D. McAuliffe	271	.262	11	33	167	196	9	40	5.2	.976	M. Lolich	37	281	19	11	1	3.14
SS	M. Tresh	331	.224	13	37	118	187	11	38	4.1	.965	E. Wilson	35	215	12	10	0	3.31
3B	D. Wert	423	.225	14	50	114	259	13	20	3.0	.966	M. Kilkenny	39	128	8	6	2	3.37
RF	A. Kaline	456	.272	21	69	192	9	7	4	1.8	.966	P. Dobson	49	105	5	10	9	3.60
CF	J. Northrup	543	.295	25	66	323	8	5	2	2.3	.985	J. Hiller	40	99	4	4	4	3.99
LF	W. Horton	508	.262	28	91	272	8	8	0	2.1	.972	J. Sparma	23	93	6	8	0	4.76
C	B. Freehan	489	.262	16	49	**821**	49	7	7	**7.3**	.992	D. McMahon	34	37	3	5	11	3.89
OS	M. Stanley	592	.235	16	70	300	137	10	22		.978							
23	T. Matchick	298	.242	0	32	104	167	7	34		.975							
C	J. Price	192	.234	9	28	337	18	4	4	7.0	.989							
2B	I. Brown	170	.229	5	12	75	100	7	18	4.0	.962							

Bos.
W-87 L-75
Dick Williams
W-82 L-71
Eddie Popowski
W-5 L-4

POS	Player	AB	BA	HR	RBI	PO	A	E	DP	TC/G	FA	Pitcher	G	IP	W	L	SV	ERA
1B	D. Jones	336	.220	3	33	692	54	6	61	9.3	.992	R. Culp	32	227	17	8	0	3.81
2B	M. Andrews	464	.293	15	59	297	334	18	82	5.4	.972	M. Nagy	33	197	12	2	0	3.11
SS	R. Petrocelli	535	.297	40	97	269	466	14	103	4.9	**.981**	S. Siebert	43	163	14	10	5	3.80
3B	G. Scott	549	.253	16	52	106	203	15	29	3.0	.954	J. Lonborg	29	144	7	11	0	4.51
RF	T. Conigliaro	506	.255	20	82	207	4	4	2	1.6	.981	L. Stange	41	137	6	9	3	3.68
CF	R. Smith	543	.309	25	93	321	8	**14**	1	2.5	.959	V. Romo	52	127	7	9	11	3.18
LF	Yastrzemski	603	.255	40	111	246	17	4	2	1.9	.985	S. Lyle	71	103	8	3	17	2.54
C	R. Gibson	287	.251	3	27	466	41	11	2	6.2	.979	R. Jarvis	29	100	5	6	1	4.75
UT	S. O'Brien	263	.243	9	29	65	143	15	30		.933	B. Landis	45	82	5	5	1	5.25
UT	D. Schofield	226	.257	2	20	97	150	7	30		.972							
OF	J. Lahoud	218	.188	9	21	91	3	2	0	1.5	.979							

Was.
W-86 L-76
Ted Williams

POS	Player	AB	BA	HR	RBI	PO	A	E	DP	TC/G	FA	Pitcher	G	IP	W	L	SV	ERA
1B	M. Epstein	403	.278	30	85	1035	69	11	99	9.4	.990	J. Coleman	40	248	12	13	1	3.27
2B	B. Allen	365	.247	9	45	239	281	14	70	4.9	.974	D. Bosman	31	193	14	5	1	**2.19**
SS	E. Brinkman	576	.266	2	43	248	511	19	92	5.2	.976	C. Cox	52	172	12	7	0	2.78
3B	K. McMullen	562	.272	19	87	185	347	13	35	3.5	.976	J. Hannan	35	158	7	6	0	3.64
RF	H. Allen	271	.277	1	17	120	6	9	2	1.5	.933	B. Moore	31	134	9	8	0	4.30
CF	D. Unser	581	.286	7	57	339	8	10	3	2.4	.972	D. Higgins	55	85	10	9	16	3.48
LF	F. Howard	592	.296	48	111	147	3	4	0	1.4	.974	Shellenback	30	85	4	7	1	4.04
C	P. Casanova	379	.216	4	37	583	59	5	5	5.3	.992	D. Knowles	53	84	9	2	13	2.24
2B	T. Cullen	249	.209	1	15	166	188	7	44	3.4	.981	B. Humphreys	47	80	3	3	5	3.05
OF	L. Maye	238	.290	9	26	100	1	6	1	1.6	.944	D. Baldwin	43	67	2	4	4	4.05
OF	B. Alyea	237	.249	11	40	84	6	6	0	1.4	.938							
OF	E. Stroud	206	.252	4	29	109	1	2	0	1.3	.982							

POS	Player	AB	BA	HR	RBI	PO	A	E	DP	TC/G	FA	Pitcher	G	IP	W	L	SV	ERA
N. Y.																		
1B	J. Pepitone	513	.242	27	70	1254	74	7	118	10.1	.995	Stottlemyre	39	303	20	14	0	2.82
2B	H. Clarke	641	.285	4	48	373	429	15	112	5.2	.982	F. Peterson	37	272	17	16	0	2.55
SS	G. Michael	412	.272	2	31	205	365	19	64	5.0	.968	S. Bahnsen	40	221	9	16	1	3.83
3B	J. Kenney	447	.257	2	34	63	207	7	20	3.3	.975	B. Burbach	31	141	6	8	0	3.65
RF	B. Murcer	564	.259	26	82	212	4	8	0	1.9	.964	A. Downing	30	131	7	5	0	3.38
CF	B. Robinson	222	.171	3	21	99	5	4	0	1.7	.963	M. Kekich	28	105	4	6	1	4.54
LF	R. White	448	.290	7	74	267	9	3	1	2.2	.989	L. McDaniel	51	84	5	6	5	3.55
C	J. Gibbs	219	.224	0	18	364	31	4	6	6.0	.990	J. Aker	38	66	8	4	11	2.06
W-80 L-81																		
Ralph Houk																		
C	F. Fernandez	229	.223	12	29	321	29	2	2	5.4	.994							
OF	J. Hall	212	.236	3	26	78	1	3	0	1.6	.963							
3B	B. Cox	191	.215	2	17	37	122	11	14	3.0	.935							
OF	R. Woods	171	.175	1	7	129	2	0	0	2.0	1.000							
Cle.																		
1B	T. Horton	625	.278	27	93	1179	100	14	130	8.2	.989	S. McDowell	39	285	18	14	1	2.94
2B	V. Fuller	254	.236	4	22	217	192	9	53	4.1	.978	L. Tiant	38	250	9	20	0	3.71
SS	L. Brown	469	.239	4	24	172	276	19	59	4.6	.959	S. Williams	61	178	6	14	12	3.94
3B	M. Alvis	191	.225	1	15	49	96	4	10	2.6	.973	S. Hargan	32	144	5	14	0	5.70
RF	K. Harrelson	519	.222	27	84	257	7	4	2	1.9	.985	D. Ellsworth	34	135	6	9	0	4.13
CF	J. Cardenal	557	.257	11	45	327	9	6	2	2.4	.982	M. Paul	47	117	5	10	2	3.61
LF	R. Snyder	266	.248	2	24	144	2	6	1	1.8	.961	J. Pizarro	48	83	3	3	4	3.16
C	D. Sims	326	.236	18	45	634	51	6	8	6.8	.991							
W-62 L-99																		
Alvin Dark																		
3B	L. Klimchock	258	.287	6	26	46	82	9	7	2.4	.934							
23	Z. Versalles	217	.226	1	13	100	125	6	24		.974							
SS	E. Leon	213	.239	3	19	114	185	15	43	4.9	.952							
OF	R. Scheinblum	199	.186	1	13	71	4	2	1	1.5	.974							
OF	F. Baker	172	.256	3	15	71	5	4	0	1.7	.950							

West

POS	Player	AB	BA	HR	RBI	PO	A	E	DP	TC/G	FA	Pitcher	G	IP	W	L	SV	ERA
Min.																		
1B	R. Reese	419	.322	16	69	924	56	7	97	8.4	.993	J. Perry	46	262	20	6	0	2.82
2B	R. Carew	458	.332	8	56	244	302	17	80	4.8	.970	D. Boswell	39	256	20	12	0	3.23
SS	L. Cardenas	578	.280	10	70	310	570	32	126	5.7	.965	J. Kaat	40	242	14	13	1	3.49
3B	H. Killebrew	555	.276	49	140	75	185	20	12	2.7	.929	T. Hall	31	141	8	7	0	3.33
RF	T. Oliva	637	.309	24	101	311	14	6	3	2.2	.982	R. Perranoski	75	120	9	10	31	2.11
CF	C. Tovar	535	.288	11	52	225	9	4	3	2.1	.983	B. Miller	48	119	5	5	3	3.02
LF	T. Uhlaender	554	.273	8	62	278	8	1	1	1.9	.997	D. Woodson	44	110	7	5	1	3.67
C	J. Roseboro	361	.263	3	32	585	52	13	16	5.9	.980							
W-97 L-65																		
Billy Martin																		
OF	G. Nettles	225	.222	7	26	76	2	1	0	1.5	.987							
OF	B. Allison	189	.228	8	27	91	2	0	1	1.6	1.000							
C	G. Mitterwald	187	.257	5	13	340	33	5	6	6.0	.987							
OF	C. Manuel	164	.207	2	24	57	2	2	0	1.3	.967							
Oak.																		
1B	D. Cater	584	.262	10	76	1087	97	9	112	9.0	.992	C. Hunter	38	247	12	15	0	3.35
2B	D. Green	483	.275	12	64	302	379	10	93	5.3	.986	C. Dobson	35	235	15	13	0	3.86
SS	B. Campaneris	547	.260	2	25	220	391	21	72	5.1	.967	B. Odom	32	231	15	6	0	2.92
3B	S. Bando	609	.281	31	113	178	321	24	36	3.2	.954	L. Krausse	43	140	7	7	7	4.44
RF	R. Jackson	549	.275	47	118	278	14	11	2	2.0	.964	R. Fingers	60	119	6	7	12	3.71
CF	R. Monday	399	.271	12	54	262	3	10	0	2.3	.964	J. Nash	26	115	8	8	0	3.67
LF	T. Reynolds	315	.257	2	20	184	5	4	2	2.2	.979	P. Lindblad	60	78	9	6	9	4.14
C	P. Roof	247	.235	2	19	493	40	9	4	5.1	.983							
W-88 L-74																		
Hank Bauer																		
W-80 L-69																		
John McNamara																		
W-8 L-5																		
S2	T. Kubiak	305	.249	2	27	153	215	10	41		.974							
OF	J. Tartabull	266	.267	0	11	134	2	1	0	2.2	.993							
C	D. Duncan	127	.126	3	22	209	15	4	1	4.1	.982							
1B	T. Francona	85	.341	3	20	158	6	2	11	8.7	.988							
Cal.																		
1B	J. Spencer	386	.254	10	31	926	66	9	81	9.4	.991	Messersmith	40	250	16	11	2	2.52
2B	S. Alomar	559	.250	1	30	294	354	21*	94	5.0	.969	T. Murphy	36	216	10	16	0	4.21
SS	J. Fregosi	580	.260	12	47	255	465	21	88	4.6	.972	McGlothlin	37	201	8	16	0	3.18
3B	A. Rodriguez	561	.232	7	49	145	352	24	42	3.3	.954	R. May	43	180	10	13	2	3.44
RF	B. Voss	349	.261	2	40	175	11	1	3	1.7	.995	G. Brunet	23	101	6	7	0	3.84
CF	J. Johnstone	540	.270	10	59	331	12	6	4	2.4	.984	K. Tatum	45	86	7	2	22	1.36
LF	R. Reichardt	493	.254	13	68	244	13	5	4	1.9	.981	H. Wilhelm	44	66	5	7	10	2.47
C	J. Azcue	248	.218	1	19	437	52*	4	10	9.0	.992							
W-71 L-91																		
Billy Rigney																		
W-11 L-28																		
Lefty Phillips																		
W-60 L-63																		
O1	R. Repoz	219	.164	8	19	296	22	2	26		.994							
OF	B. Morton	172	.244	7	32	70	5	0	1	1.5	1.000							
K. C.																		
1B	M. Fiore	339	.274	12	35	696	94	10	54	8.8	.988	W. Bunker	35	223	12	11	2	3.23
2B	J. Adair	432	.250	5	48	223	261	8	41	4.5	.984	D. Drago	41	201	11	13	1	3.77
SS	J. Hernandez	504	.222	4	40	306	375	33	60	5.0	.954	B. Butler	34	194	9	10	0	3.90
3B	J. Foy	519	.262	11	71	117	209	12	20	3.0	.964	R. Nelson	29	193	7	13	0	3.31
RF	B. Oliver	394	.254	13	43	199	11	5	4	2.2	.977	J. Rooker	28	158	4	16	0	3.75
CF	P. Kelly	417	.264	8	32	237	12	5	3	2.4	.980	M. Hedlund	34	125	3	6	2	3.24
LF	L. Piniella	493	.282	11	68	278	13	7	1	2.3	.977	M. Drabowsky	52	98	11	9	11	2.94
C	E. Rodriguez	267	.236	2	20	433	39	5	2	5.3	.990	D. Wickersham	34	50	2	3	5	3.96
W-69 L-93																		
Joe Gordon																		
OF	Kirkpatrick	315	.257	14	49	180	8	1	1	2.3	.995							
1B	C. Harrison	213	.221	3	18	415	36	3	27	8.3	.993							
C	B. Martinez	205	.229	4	23	290	25	9	7	5.9	.972							
3B	P. Schaal	205	.263	1	13	27	77	12	3	2.4	.897							
2S	J. Rios	196	.224	1	5	101	105	9	23		.958							
OF	J. Keough	166	.187	0	7	82	2	0	1	1.7	1.000							
OF	H. Taylor	89	.270	3	21	19	1	2	1	1.2	.909							

	POS	Player	AB	BA	HR	RBI	PO	A	E	DP	TC/G	FA	Pitcher	G	IP	W	L	SV	ERA
Chi. W-68 L-94 Al Lopez W-8 L-9 Don Gutteridge W-60 L-85	1B	G. Hopkins	373	.265	8	46	903	51	6	81	9.5	.994	J. Horlen	36	236	13	16	0	3.78
	2B	B. Knoop	345	.229	6	41	271	320	9	76	5.8*	.985	T. John	33	232	9	11	0	3.25
	SS	L. Aparicio	599	.280	5	51	248	563	20	94	5.4	.976	G. Peters	36	219	10	15	0	4.53
	3B	B. Melton	556	.255	23	87	112	322	22	36	3.1	.952	B. Wynne	20	129	7	7	0	4.06
	RF	W. Williams	471	.304	3	32	183	13	3	4	1.8	.985	W. Wood	76	120	10	11	15	3.01
	CF	K. Berry	297	.232	4	18	215	7	0	1	1.9	1.000	D. Osinski	51	61	5	5	2	3.56
	LF	C. May	367	.281	18	62	154	10	3	0	1.7	.982							
	C	E. Herrmann	290	.231	8	31	420	41	8	7	5.1	.983							
	OF	B. Bradford	273	.256	11	27	141	5	6	1	1.7	.961							
	1O	T. McCraw	240	.258	2	25	302	15	3	21		.991							
	UT	P. Ward	199	.246	6	32	193	48	3	13		.988							
	C	D. Pavletich	188	.245	6	33	195	26	6	3	4.5	.974							
	UT	R. Hansen	185	.259	2	22	216	83	8	28		.974							
	C	D. Josephson	162	.241	1	20	227	27	4	1	5.5	.984							
Sea. W-64 L-98 Joe Schultz	1B	D. Mincher	427	.246	25	78	1033	93	6	98	9.3	.995	G. Brabender	40	202	13	14	0	4.36
	2B	J. Donaldson	338	.234	1	19	209	242	12	56	5.1	.974	M. Pattin	34	159	7	12	0	5.62
	SS	R. Oyler	255	.165	7	22	143	266	15	47	4.0	.965	D. Segui	66	142	12	6	0	3.35
	3B	T. Harper	537	.235	9	41	70	123	10	9	3.4	.951	F. Talbot	25	115	5	8	0	4.16
	RF	S. Hovley	329	.277	3	20	175	8	2	3	2.2	.989	J. Gelnar	39	109	3	10	3	3.31
	CF	W. Comer	481	.245	15	54	287	14	6	6	2.2	.980	M. Marshall	20	88	3	10	0	5.13
	LF	T. Davis	454	.271	6	80	174	3	6	0	1.6	.967	S. Barber	25	86	4	7	0	4.80
	C	J. McNertney	410	.241	8	55	697	67	9	13	6.3	.988	B. Locker	51	78	3	3	6	2.18
	OF	M. Hegan	267	.292	8	37	100	7	5	1	1.8	.955	J. O'Donoghue	55	70	2	2	6	2.96
	UT	G. Gil	221	.222	0	17	65	130	9	16		.956	G. Bell	13	61	2	6	2	4.70
	3B	R. Rollins	187	.225	4	20	42	103	8	6	3.3	.948							
	UT	R. Clark	163	.196	0	12	79	116	9	17		.956							
	1B	G. Goossen	139	.309	10	24	265	23	2	15	9.4	.993							

BATTING AND BASE RUNNING LEADERS

Batting Average

R. Carew, MIN	.332
R. Smith, BOS	.309
T. Oliva, MIN	.309
F. Robinson, BAL	.308
B. Powell, BAL	.304

Slugging Average

R. Jackson, OAK	.608
R. Petrocelli, BOS	.589
H. Killebrew, MIN	.584
F. Howard, WAS	.574
B. Powell, BAL	.559

Home Runs

H. Killebrew, MIN	49
F. Howard, WAS	48
R. Jackson, OAK	47
R. Petrocelli, BOS	40
Yastrzemski, BOS	40

Total Bases

F. Howard, WAS	340
R. Jackson, OAK	334
H. Killebrew, MIN	324
T. Oliva, MIN	316
R. Petrocelli, BOS	315

Runs Batted In

H. Killebrew, MIN	140
B. Powell, BAL	121
R. Jackson, OAK	118
S. Bando, OAK	113
F. Howard, WAS	111
Yastrzemski, BOS	111

Stolen Bases

T. Harper, SEA	73
B. Campaneris, OAK	62
C. Tovar, MIN	45
P. Kelly, KC	40
J. Foy, KC	37

Hits

T. Oliva, MIN	197
H. Clarke, NY	183
P. Blair, BAL	178

Base on Balls

H. Killebrew, MIN	145
R. Jackson, OAK	114
S. Bando, OAK	111

Home Run Percentage

H. Killebrew, MIN	8.8
R. Jackson, OAK	8.6
F. Howard, WAS	8.1

Runs Scored

R. Jackson, OAK	123
F. Robinson, BAL	111
F. Howard, WAS	111

Doubles

T. Oliva, MIN	39
R. Jackson, OAK	36
D. Johnson, BAL	34

Triples

D. Unser, WAS	8
R. Smith, BOS	7
H. Clarke, NY	7

PITCHING LEADERS

Winning Percentage

J. Palmer, BAL	.800
J. Perry, MIN	.769
D. McNally, BAL	.741
D. McLain, DET	.727
B. Odom, OAK	.714

Earned Run Average

D. Bosman, WAS	2.19
J. Palmer, BAL	2.34
M. Cuellar, BAL	2.38
Messersmith, CAL	2.52
F. Peterson, NY	2.55

Wins

D. McLain, DET	24
M. Cuellar, BAL	23
J. Perry, MIN	20
D. McNally, BAL	20
D. Boswell, MIN	20
Stottlemyre, NY	20

Saves

R. Perranoski, MIN	31
K. Tatum, CAL	22
S. Lyle, BOS	17
D. Higgins, WAS	16
E. Watt, BAL	16

Strikeouts

S. McDowell, CLE	279
M. Lolich, DET	271
Messersmith, CAL	211
D. Boswell, MIN	190
J. Coleman, WAS	182
M. Cuellar, BAL	182

Complete Games

Stottlemyre, NY	24
D. McLain, DET	23
S. McDowell, CLE	18
M. Cuellar, BAL	18
F. Peterson, NY	16

Fewest Hits per 9 Innings

Messersmith, CAL	6.08
J. Palmer, BAL	6.51
M. Cuellar, BAL	6.59

Shutouts

D. McLain, DET	9
J. Palmer, BAL	6
M. Cuellar, BAL	5

Fewest Walks per 9 Innings

F. Peterson, NY	1.42
D. Bosman, WAS	1.82
D. McLain, DET	1.86

Most Strikeouts per 9 Inn.

S. McDowell, CLE	8.81
M. Lolich, DET	8.68
Messersmith, CAL	7.60

Innings

D. McLain, DET	325
Stottlemyre, NY	303
M. Cuellar, BAL	291

Games Pitched

W. Wood, CHI	76
R. Perranoski, MIN	75
S. Lyle, BOS	71

	W	L	PCT	GB	R	OR	Batting 2B	3B	HR	BA	SA	SB	Fielding E	DP	FA	CG	BB	Pitching SO	ShO	SV	ERA
EAST																					
BAL	109	53	.673		779	517	234	29	175	.265	.414	82	**101**	145	**.984**	50	**498**	897	**20**	36	**2.83**
DET	90	72	.556	19	701	601	188	29	182	.242	.387	35	130	130	.979	**55**	586	**1032**	**20**	28	3.32
BOS	87	75	.537	22	743	736	234	37	**197**	.251	**.415**	41	157	**178**	.975	30	685	935	7	41	3.93
WAS	86	76	.531	23	694	644	171	40	148	.251	.378	52	140	159	.978	28	656	835	10	41	3.49
NY	80	81	.497	28.5	562	587	210	**44**	94	.235	.344	119	131	158	.979	53	522	801	13	20	3.23
CLE	62	99	.385	46.5	573	717	173	24	119	.237	.345	85	145	153	.976	35	681	1000	7	22	3.94
WEST																					
MIN	97	65	.599		**790**	618	**246**	32	163	**.268**	.408	115	150	177	.977	41	524	906	8	**43**	3.25
OAK	88	74	.543	9	740	678	210	28	148	.249	.376	100	137	162	.978	42	586	887	14	36	3.71
CAL	71	91	.438	26	528	652	151	29	88	.230	.319	54	136	164	.978	25	517	885	9	39	3.55
KC	69	93	.426	28	586	688	179	32	98	.240	.338	129	157	114	.975	42	560	894	10	25	3.72
CHI	68	94	.420	29	625	723	210	27	112	.247	.357	54	122	163	.981	29	564	810	10	25	4.21
SEA	64	98	.395	33	639	799	179	27	125	.234	.346	**167**	167	149	.974	21	653	963	6	33	4.35
					7960	7960	2385	378	1649	.246	.369	1033	1673	1852	.978	451	7032	10845	134	389	3.63

National League 1970

POS	Player	AB	BA	HR	RBI	PO	A	E	DP	TC/G	FA	Pitcher	G	IP	W	L	SV	ERA

East

Pit.
W-89 L-73
Danny Murtaugh

POS	Player	AB	BA	HR	RBI	PO	A	E	DP	TC/G	FA	Pitcher	G	IP	W	L	SV	ERA
1B	B. Robertson	390	.287	27	82	907	78	5	107	10.0	.995	D. Ellis	30	202	13	10	0	3.21
2B	B. Mazeroski	367	.229	7	39	227	325	7	87	5.5	.987	B. Veale	34	202	10	15	0	3.92
SS	G. Alley	426	.244	8	41	202	381	15	84	5.5	.975	S. Blass	31	197	10	12	0	3.52
3B	R. Hebner	420	.290	11	46	64	235	19	24	2.7	.940	B. Moose	28	190	11	10	0	3.98
RF	R. Clemente	412	.352	14	60	189	12	7	2	2.0	.966	L. Walker	42	163	15	6	3	3.04
CF	M. Alou	**677**	.297	1	47	297	15	8	1	2.1	.975	D. Giusti	66	103	9	3	26	3.06
LF	W. Stargell	474	.264	31	85	184	16	5	1	1.6	.976	Dal Canton	41	85	9	4	1	4.55
C	M. Sanguillen	486	.325	7	61	775	66	10	12	6.8	.988							
O1	A. Oliver	551	.270	12	83	718	52	9	69		.988							
SS	F. Patek	237	.245	1	19	122	212	10	42	5.3	.971							
3B	J. Pagan	230	.265	7	29	43	91	6	14	2.6	.957							
2B	D. Cash	210	.314	1	28	147	156	8	46	5.7	.974							

Chi.
W-84 L-78
Leo Durocher

POS	Player	AB	BA	HR	RBI	PO	A	E	DP	TC/G	FA	Pitcher	G	IP	W	L	SV	ERA
1B	J. Hickman	514	.315	32	115	563	60	6	46	8.5	.990	F. Jenkins	40	313	22	16	0	3.39
2B	G. Beckert	591	.288	3	36	302	412	**22**	88	5.3	.970	K. Holtzman	39	288	17	11	0	3.38
SS	D. Kessinger	631	.266	1	39	257	**501**	22	86	5.1	.972	B. Hands	39	265	18	15	1	3.70
3B	R. Santo	555	.267	26	114	143	320	27	36	3.2	.945	M. Pappas	21	145	10	8	0	2.68
RF	J. Callison	477	.264	19	68	244	8	7	3	1.8	.973	J. Decker	24	109	2	7	0	4.62
CF	C. James	176	.210	3	14	115	5	0	1	1.3	1.000	P. Regan	54	76	5	9	12	4.74
LF	B. Williams	636	.322	42	129	259	13	3	1	1.7	.989							
C	R. Hundley	250	.244	7	36	455	26	5	2	6.7	.990							
1B	E. Banks	222	.252	12	44	528	35	4	53	9.1	.993							
OF	J. Pepitone	213	.268	12	44	121	1	1	0	2.2	.992							
UT	P. Popovich	186	.253	4	20	75	97	4	26		.977							
C	J. Hiatt	178	.242	2	22	380	22	4	1	6.4	.990							
1B	W. Smith	167	.216	5	24	318	11	2	32	7.7	.994							

N. Y.
W-83 L-79
Gil Hodges

POS	Player	AB	BA	HR	RBI	PO	A	E	DP	TC/G	FA	Pitcher	G	IP	W	L	SV	ERA
1B	D. Clendenon	396	.288	22	97	722	62	7	72	7.9	.991	T. Seaver	37	291	18	12	0	**2.81**
2B	K. Boswell	351	.254	5	44	204	244	2	49	4.5	.996	J. Koosman	30	212	12	7	0	3.14
SS	B. Harrelson	564	.243	1	42	**305**	401	21	84	4.7	.971	G. Gentry	32	188	9	9	1	3.69
3B	J. Foy	322	.236	6	37	90	179	18	20	3.0	.937	J. McAndrew	32	184	10	14	2	3.57
RF	R. Swoboda	245	.233	9	40	117	3	2	1	1.2	.984	R. Sadecki	28	139	8	4	0	3.88
CF	T. Agee	636	.286	24	75	**374**	4	**13**	3	**2.6**	.967	N. Ryan	27	132	7	11	1	3.41
LF	C. Jones	506	.277	10	63	243	10	5	3	2.0	.981	T. McGraw	57	91	4	6	10	3.26
C	J. Grote	415	.255	2	34	855	46	8	12	7.3	.991	D. Frisella	30	66	8	3	1	3.00
O1	A. Shamsky	403	.293	11	49	482	37	2	30		.996	R. Taylor	57	66	5	4	13	3.95
32	W. Garrett	366	.254	12	45	151	205	12	34		.967							
OF	K. Singleton	198	.263	5	26	90	1	3	0	1.8	.968							
OF	D. Marshall	189	.243	6	29	71	2	2	0	1.7	.973							

St. L.
W-76 L-86
Red Schoendienst

POS	Player	AB	BA	HR	RBI	PO	A	E	DP	TC/G	FA	Pitcher	G	IP	W	L	SV	ERA
1B	J. Hague	451	.271	14	68	672	48	4	65	8.8	.994	B. Gibson	34	294	**23**	7	0	3.12
2B	J. Javier	513	.251	2	42	329	413	15	84	5.5	.980	S. Carlton	34	254	10	19	0	3.72
SS	D. Maxvill	399	.201	0	28	216	426	12	80	4.8	**.982**	M. Torrez	30	179	8	10	0	4.22
3B	J. Torre	624	.325	21	100	68	133	11	12	2.9	.948	J. Reuss	20	127	7	8	0	4.11
RF	L. Lee	264	.227	6	23	120	3	4	0	1.6	.969	C. Taylor	56	124	6	7	8	3.12
CF	J. Cardenal	552	.293	10	74	276	6	9	0	2.2	.969	N. Briles	30	107	6	7	0	6.22
LF	L. Brock	664	.304	13	57	247	9	10	2	1.8	.962	F. Linzy	47	61	3	5	2	3.67
C	T. Simmons	284	.243	3	24	466	37	5	2	6.4	.990							
13	R. Allen	459	.279	34	101	703	108	16	70		.981							
OF	C. Taylor	245	.249	6	45	66	3	1	1	1.5	.986							
OF	V. Davalillo	183	.311	1	33	67	3	2	1	1.3	.972							
3B	M. Shannon	174	.213	0	22	32	59	8	4	1.9	.919							

	POS	Player	AB	BA	HR	RBI	PO	A	E	DP	TC/G	FA	Pitcher	G	IP	W	L	SV	ERA
Phi. W-73 L-88 Frank Lucchesi	1B	D. Johnson	574	.256	27	93	1178	73	6	104	8.2	.995	R. Wise	35	220	13	14	0	4.17
	2B	D. Doyle	413	.208	2	16	251	228	11	55	4.8	.978	J. Bunning	34	219	10	15	0	4.11
	SS	L. Bowa	547	.250	0	34	202	418	13	69	4.4	.979	C. Short	36	199	9	16	1	4.30
	3B	D. Money	447	.295	14	66	131	236	15	27	3.2	.961	G. Jackson	32	150	5	15	0	5.28
	RF	R. Stone	321	.262	3	39	148	5	5	0	1.6	.968	B. Lersch	42	138	6	3	3	3.26
	CF	L. Hisle	405	.205	10	44	262	5	6	0	2.3	.978	D. Selma	73	134	8	9	22	2.75
	LF	J. Briggs	341	.270	9	47	188	7	4	1	2.1	.980	W. Fryman	27	128	8	6	0	4.08
	C	T. McCarver	164	.287	4	14	314	18	3	2	7.6	.991	L. Palmer	38	102	1	2	0	5.47
	UT	T. Taylor	439	.301	9	55	220	215	5	48		.989	J. Hoerner	44	58	9	5	9	2.64
	OF	O. Gamble	275	.262	1	19	148	4	7	0	2.1	.956							
	OF	B. Browne	270	.248	10	36	150	4	4	1	1.8	.975							
Mon. W-73 L-89 Gene Mauch	1B	R. Fairly	385	.288	15	61	944	90	5	112	8.8	.995	C. Morton	43	285	18	11	0	3.60
	2B	G. Sutherland	359	.206	3	26	178	254	11	72	4.6	.975	S. Renko	41	223	13	11	1	4.32
	SS	B. Wine	501	.232	3	51	284	481	19	137	4.9	.976	B. Stoneman	40	208	7	15	0	4.59
	3B	C. Laboy	432	.199	5	53	105	194	17	19	2.4	.946	D. McGinn	52	131	7	10	0	5.43
	RF	R. Staub	569	.274	30	94	308	14	5	4	2.0	.985	M. Wegener	25	104	3	6	0	5.28
	CF	A. Phillips	214	.238	6	21	130	1	2	0	1.8	.985	H. Reed	57	89	6	5	5	3.13
	LF	M. Jones	271	.240	14	32	118	3	4	1	1.4	.968	C. Raymond	59	83	6	7	23	4.45
	C	J. Bateman	520	.237	15	68	824	62	15	19	6.6	.983	M. Marshall	24	65	3	7	3	3.48
	UT	B. Bailey	352	.287	28	84	179	86	8	18		.971							
	2B	M. Staehle	321	.218	0	26	152	208	14	53	4.1	.963							
	OF	J. Gosger	274	.263	5	37	124	5	0	1	1.8	1.000							
	OF	J. Fairey	211	.242	3	25	86	1	2	0	1.5	.978							

West

	POS	Player	AB	BA	HR	RBI	PO	A	E	DP	TC/G	FA	Pitcher	G	IP	W	L	SV	ERA
Cin. W-102 L-60 Sparky Anderson	1B	L. May	605	.253	34	94	1362	109	10	143	9.7	.993	G. Nolan	37	251	18	7	0	3.26
	2B	T. Helms	575	.237	1	45	350	410	13	107	5.2	.983	J. Merritt	35	234	20	12	0	4.08
	SS	D. Concepcion	265	.260	1	19	137	244	22	51	4.3	.945	McGlothlin	35	211	14	10	0	3.58
	3B	T. Perez	587	.317	40	129	131	286	35	34	3.0	.923	W. Simpson	26	176	14	3	0	3.02
	RF	P. Rose	649	.316	15	52	309	8	1	2	2.0	.997	T. Cloninger	30	148	9	7	1	3.83
	CF	B. Tolan	589	.316	16	80	349	7	8	0	2.4	.978	C. Carroll	65	104	9	4	16	2.60
	LF	B. Carbo	365	.310	21	63	177	8	4	2	1.6	.979	W. Granger	67	85	6	5	35	2.65
	C	J. Bench	605	.293	45	148	759	73	12	12	6.0	.986	D. Gullett	44	78	5	2	6	2.42
	SS	W. Woodward	264	.223	1	14	101	226	9	48	4.4	.973							
	OF	H. McRae	165	.248	8	23	52	1	1	0	1.2	.981							
L. A. W-87 L-74 Walter Alston	1B	W. Parker	614	.319	10	111	1498	125	7	116	10.1	.996	D. Sutton	38	260	15	13	0	4.08
	2B	B. Sizemore	340	.306	1	34	194	232	7	47	5.0	.984	C. Osteen	37	259	16	14	0	3.82
	SS	M. Wills	522	.270	0	34	171	396	24	58	4.7	.959	A. Foster	33	199	10	13	0	4.25
	3B	Grabarkewitz	529	.289	17	84	88	190	12	19	3.0	.959	J. Moeller	31	135	7	9	4	3.93
	RF	M. Mota	417	.305	3	37	172	8	5	3	1.7	.973	S. Vance	20	115	7	7	0	3.13
	CF	W. Davis	593	.305	8	93	342	12	3	4	2.5	.992	B. Singer	16	106	8	5	0	3.14
	LF	W. Crawford	554	.234	8	40	160	9	7	1	1.9	.960	J. Brewer	58	89	7	6	24	3.13
	C	T. Haller	325	.286	10	47	524	26	4	7	5.2	.993	P. Mikkelsen	33	62	4	2	6	2.76
	2B	J. Lefebvre	314	.252	4	44	142	177	4	34	4.6	.988	J. Pena	29	57	4	3	4	4.42
	OF	B. Russell	278	.259	0	28	167	8	3	1	2.3	.983							
	C3	B. Sudakis	269	.264	14	44	188	99	14	9		.953							
	OF	A. Kosco	224	.228	8	27	101	2	2	0	1.8	.981							
S. F. W-86 L-76 Clyde King W-19 L-25 Charlie Fox W-67 L-51	1B	W. McCovey	495	.289	39	126	1217	134	15	117	9.4	.989	G. Perry	41	329	23	13	0	3.20
	2B	R. Hunt	367	.281	6	41	162	173	11	38	4.1	.968	J. Marichal	34	243	12	10	0	4.11
	SS	H. Lanier	438	.231	2	41	256	397	22	83	5.2	.967	R. Robertson	41	184	8	9	1	4.84
	3B	A. Gallagher	282	.266	4	28	70	128	6	12	2.2	.971	F. Reberger	45	152	7	8	2	5.57
	RF	B. Bonds	663	.302	26	78	326	14	11	7	2.2	.969	R. Bryant	34	96	5	8	0	4.78
	CF	W. Mays	478	.291	28	83	269	6	7	3	2.2	.975	D. McMahon	61	94	9	5	19	2.97
	LF	K. Henderson	554	.294	17	88	272	15	10	2	2.1	.966	S. Pitlock	18	87	5	5	0	4.66
	C	D. Dietz	493	.300	22	107	820	58	14	9	6.4	.984	J. Johnson	33	65	3	4	3	4.27
	UT	T. Fuentes	435	.267	2	32	202	324	19	57		.965							
	3B	J. Hart	255	.282	8	37	39	69	11	2	2.1	.908							
	O1	F. Johnson	161	.273	3	31	199	14	5	16		.977							
	S2	B. Heise	154	.234	1	22	78	124	13	24		.940							
Hou. W-79 L-83 Harry Walker	1B	B. Watson	327	.272	11	61	695	39	6	54	8.9	.992	L. Dierker	37	270	16	12	1	3.87
	2B	J. Morgan	548	.268	8	52	349	430	17	98	5.6	.979	J. Billingham	46	188	13	9	0	3.97
	SS	D. Menke	562	.304	13	92	192	394	28	66	4.6	.954	D. Wilson	29	184	11	6	0	3.91
	3B	D. Rader	576	.252	25	87	147	357	18	39	3.4	.966	D. Lemaster	39	162	7	12	3	4.56
	RF	J. Alou	458	.306	1	44	169	6	7	2	1.7	.962	T. Griffin	23	111	3	13	0	5.76
	CF	C. Cedeno	355	.310	7	42	211	1	7	0	2.4	.968	J. Ray	52	105	6	3	5	3.26
	LF	J. Wynn	554	.282	27	88	293	14	4	4	2.1	.968	R. Cook	41	82	4	4	2	3.73
	C	J. Edwards	458	.221	7	49	854	74	5	11	6.7	.995	J. Bouton	29	73	4	6	0	5.42
	1O	J. Pepitone	279	.251	14	35	428	30	3	45		.993	F. Gladding	63	71	7	4	18	4.06
	OF	N. Miller	226	.239	4	29	101	6	6	1	1.6	.947							
	OF	T. Davis	213	.282	3	30	71	4	4	1	1.5	.949							

	POS	Player	AB	BA	HR	RBI	PO	A	E	DP	TC/G	FA	Pitcher	G	IP	W	L	SV	ERA
Atl.	1B	O. Cepeda	567	.305	34	111	1288	112	12	100	9.5	.992	P. Jarvis	36	254	16	16	0	3.61
W-76 L-86	2B	F. Millan	590	.310	2	37	337	359	15	83	5.0	.979	P. Niekro	34	230	12	18	0	4.27
Lum Harris	SS	S. Jackson	328	.259	0	20	123	240	26	40	4.5	.933	J. Nash	34	212	13	9	0	4.08
	3B	C. Boyer	475	.246	16	62	107	268	18	21	3.1	.954	G. Stone	35	207	11	11	0	3.87
	RF	H. Aaron	516	.298	38	118	246	6	6	1	2.1	.977	R. Reed	21	135	7	10	0	4.40
	CF	T. Gonzalez	430	.265	7	55	235	1	3	0	2.0	.987	H. Wilhelm	50	78	6	4	13	3.10
	LF	R. Carty	478	.366	25	101	219	5	6	0	1.7	.974	B. Priddy	41	73	5	5	8	5.42
	C	B. Tillman	223	.238	11	30	404	22	5	0	6.2	.988							
	SS	G. Garrido	367	.264	1	19	119	233	9	36	4.5	.975							
	OF	M. Lum	291	.254	7	28	168	3	2	0	1.8	.988							
	C	H. King	204	.260	11	30	316	14	5	1	5.4	.985							
	C	B. Didier	168	.149	0	7	297	25	4	3	5.7	.988							
S. D.	1B	N. Colbert	572	.259	38	86	1406	90	14	126	9.9	.991	P. Dobson	40	251	14	15	1	3.76
W-63 L-99	2B	D. Campbell	581	.219	12	40	359	455	22	96	5.5	.974	C. Kirby	36	215	10	16	0	4.52
Preston Gomez	SS	J. Arcia	229	.223	0	17	89	146	11	32	3.7	.955	D. Coombs	35	188	10	14	0	3.30
	3B	E. Spiezio	316	.285	12	42	66	178	12	10	2.8	.953	D. Roberts	43	182	8	14	1	3.81
	RF	O. Brown	534	.292	23	89	258	12	10	3	2.0	.964	M. Corkins	24	111	5	6	0	4.62
	CF	C. Gaston	584	.318	29	93	310	7	8	0	2.3	.975	R. Herbel	64*	111	7	5	9	4.95
	LF	I. Murrell	347	.245	12	35	183	8	6	2	2.0	.970	A. Santorini	21	76	1	8	1	6.04
	C	C. Cannizzaro	341	.279	5	42	559	44	12	5	5.6	.980	T. Dukes	53	69	1	6	10	4.04
	OF	A. Ferrara	372	.277	13	51	119	2	4	0	1.3	.968							
	S3	S. Huntz	352	.219	11	37	118	257	20	39		.949							
	C	B. Barton	188	.218	4	16	347	28	2	5	6.4	.995							

BATTING AND BASE RUNNING LEADERS

Batting Average

R. Carty, ATL	.366
J. Torre, STL	.325
M. Sanguillen, PIT	.325
B. Williams, CHI	.322
W. Parker, LA	.319

Slugging Average

W. McCovey, SF	.612
T. Perez, CIN	.589
J. Bench, CIN	.587
B. Williams, CHI	.586
R. Carty, ATL	.584

Home Runs

J. Bench, CIN	45
B. Williams, CHI	42
T. Perez, CIN	40
W. McCovey, SF	39
H. Aaron, ATL	38
N. Colbert, SD	38

Total Bases

B. Williams, CHI	373
J. Bench, CIN	355
T. Perez, CIN	346
B. Bonds, SF	334
C. Gaston, SD	317

Runs Batted In

J. Bench, CIN	148
T. Perez, CIN	129
B. Williams, CHI	129
W. McCovey, SF	126
H. Aaron, ATL	118

Stolen Bases

B. Tolan, CIN	57
L. Brock, STL	51
B. Bonds, SF	48
J. Morgan, HOU	42
W. Davis, LA	38

Hits

B. Williams, CHI	205
P. Rose, CIN	205
J. Torre, STL	203

Base on Balls

W. McCovey, SF	137
R. Staub, MON	112
D. Dietz, SF	109

Home Run Percentage

W. McCovey, SF	7.9
J. Bench, CIN	7.4
R. Allen, STL	7.4

Runs Scored

B. Williams, CHI	137
B. Bonds, SF	134
P. Rose, CIN	120

Doubles

W. Parker, LA	47
W. McCovey, SF	39
P. Rose, CIN	37

Triples

W. Davis, LA	16
D. Kessinger, CHI	14
R. Clemente, PIT	10
B. Bonds, SF	10

PITCHING LEADERS

Winning Percentage

B. Gibson, STL	.767
G. Nolan, CIN	.720
L. Walker, PIT	.714
G. Perry, SF	.639
J. Merritt, CIN	.625

Earned Run Average

T. Seaver, NY	2.81
W. Simpson, CIN	3.02
L. Walker, PIT	3.04
B. Gibson, STL	3.12
J. Koosman, NY	3.14

Wins

B. Gibson, STL	23
G. Perry, SF	23
F. Jenkins, CHI	22
J. Merritt, CIN	20

Saves

W. Granger, CIN	35
D. Giusti, PIT	26
J. Brewer, LA	24
C. Raymond, MON	23
D. Selma, PHI	22

Strikeouts

T. Seaver, NY	283
B. Gibson, STL	274
F. Jenkins, CHI	274
G. Perry, SF	214
K. Holtzman, CHI	202

Complete Games

F. Jenkins, CHI	24
B. Gibson, STL	23
G. Perry, SF	23
T. Seaver, NY	19
L. Dierker, HOU	17

Fewest Hits per 9 Innings

W. Simpson, CIN	6.39
T. Seaver, NY	7.11
L. Walker, PIT	7.12

Shutouts

G. Perry, SF	5

Fewest Walks per 9 Innings

F. Jenkins, CHI	1.73
J. Marichal, SF	1.78
C. Osteen, LA	1.81

Most Strikeouts per 9 Inn.

T. Seaver, NY	8.75
B. Gibson, STL	8.39
B. Veale, PIT	7.93

Innings

G. Perry, SF	329
F. Jenkins, CHI	313
B. Gibson, STL	294

Games Pitched

R. Herbel, NY, SD	76
D. Selma, PHI	73
F. Linzy, SF, STL	67
W. Granger, CIN	67

	W	L	PCT	GB	R	OR	Batting 2B	3B	HR	BA	SA	SB	Fielding E	DP	FA	CG	BB	Pitching SO	ShO	SV	ERA
EAST																					
PIT	89	73	.549		729	664	235	70	130	.270	.406	66	137	195	.979	36	625	990	13	43	3.70
CHI	84	78	.519	5	806	679	228	44	179	.259	.415	39	137	146	.978	59	475	1000	9	25	3.76
NY	83	79	.512	6	695	630	211	42	120	.249	.370	118	124	136	.979	47	575	1064	10	32	3.46
STL	76	86	.469	13	744	747	218	51	113	.263	.379	117	150	159	.977	51	632	960	11	20	4.05
PHI	73	88	.453	15.5	594	730	224	58	101	.238	.356	72	114	134	.981	24	538	1047	8	36	4.17
MON	73	89	.451	16	687	807	211	35	136	.237	.365	65	141	193	.977	29	716	914	10	32	4.50
WEST																					
CIN	102	60	.630		775	681	253	45	191	.270	.436	115	151	173	.976	32	592	843	15	60	3.71
LA	87	74	.540	14.5	749	684	233	67	87	.270	.382	138	135	135	.978	37	496	880	17	42	3.82
SF	86	76	.531	16	831	826	257	35	165	.262	.409	83	170	153	.973	50	604	931	7	30	4.50
HOU	79	83	.488	23	744	763	250	47	129	.259	.391	114	140	144	.978	36	577	942	6	35	4.23
ATL	76	86	.469	26	736	772	215	24	160	.270	.404	58	141	118	.977	45	478	960	9	24	4.35
SD	63	99	.389	39	681	788	208	36	172	.246	.391	60	158	159	.975	24	611	886	9	32	4.38
					8771	8771	2743	554	1683	.258	.392	1045	1698	1845	.977	470	6919	11417	124	411	4.05

American League 1970

	POS	Player	AB	BA	HR	RBI	PO	A	E	DP	TC/G	FA	Pitcher	G	IP	W	L	SV	ERA

East

Bal.
W-108 L-54
Earl Weaver

POS	Player	AB	BA	HR	RBI	PO	A	E	DP	TC/G	FA	Pitcher	G	IP	W	L	SV	ERA
1B	B. Powell	526	.297	35	114	1209	89	10	107	9.0	.992	J. Palmer	39	305	20	10	0	2.71
2B	D. Johnson	530	.281	10	53	379	390	8	101	5.2	.990	M. Cuellar	40	298	24	8	0	3.47
SS	M. Belanger	459	.218	1	36	212	412	19	78	4.5	.970	D. McNally	40	296	24	9	0	3.22
3B	B. Robinson	608	.276	18	94	157	321	17	30	3.2	.966	J. Hardin	36	145	6	5	1	3.54
RF	F. Robinson	471	.306	25	78	221	9	3	3	1.9	.987	T. Phoebus	27	135	5	5	0	3.07
CF	P. Blair	480	.267	18	65	368	10	4	3	3.0	.990	D. Hall	32	61	10	5	3	3.10
LF	D. Buford	504	.272	17	66	221	13	3	3	1.8	.987	E. Watt	53	55	7	7	12	3.27
C	E. Hendricks	322	.242	12	41	509	35	8	6	5.8	.986	P. Richert	50	55	7	2	13	1.96
OF	M. Rettenmund	338	.322	18	58	201	6	5	1	2.3	.976							
C	Etchebarren	230	.243	4	28	392	29	7	3	5.6	.984							
UT	C. Salmon	172	.250	7	22	61	87	9	12		.943							
O1	T. Crowley	152	.257	5	20	138	6	2	9		.986							

N. Y.
W-93 L-69
Ralph Houk

POS	Player	AB	BA	HR	RBI	PO	A	E	DP	TC/G	FA	Pitcher	G	IP	W	L	SV	ERA
1B	D. Cater	582	.301	6	76	981	70	8	79	8.1	.992	Stottlemyre	37	271	15	13	0	3.09
2B	H. Clarke	686	.251	4	46	379	478	18	95	5.6	.979	F. Peterson	39	260	20	11	0	2.91
SS	G. Michael	435	.214	2	38	248	379	28	78	5.3	.957	S. Bahnsen	36	233	14	11	0	3.32
3B	J. Kenney	404	.193	4	35	111	300	17	18	3.2	.960	L. McDaniel	62	112	9	5	29	2.01
RF	C. Blefary	269	.212	9	37	103	1	3	0	1.4	.972	S. Kline	16	100	6	6	0	3.42
CF	B. Murcer	581	.251	23	78	375	15	3	3	2.5	.992	R. Klimkowski	45	98	6	7	1	2.66
LF	R. White	609	.296	22	94	315	6	2	0	2.0	.994	J. Aker	41	70	4	2	16	2.06
C	T. Munson	453	.302	6	53	631	80	8	11	5.8	.989	S. Hamilton	35	45	4	3	3	2.78
1B	J. Ellis	226	.248	7	29	449	37	4	35	9.2	.992							
OF	R. Woods	225	.227	8	27	108	6	3	1	1.5	.974							
C	J. Gibbs	153	.301	8	26	208	19	3	1	5.2	.987							

Bos.
W-87 L-75
Eddie Kasko

POS	Player	AB	BA	HR	RBI	PO	A	E	DP	TC/G	FA	Pitcher	G	IP	W	L	SV	ERA
1B	Yastrzemski	566	.329	40	102	696	61	8	62	8.1	.990	R. Culp	33	251	17	14	0	3.05
2B	M. Andrews	589	.253	17	65	342	350	19	74	4.8	.973	S. Siebert	33	223	15	8	0	3.43
SS	R. Petrocelli	583	.261	29	103	262	393	20	77	4.8	.970	G. Peters	34	222	16	11	0	4.05
3B	G. Scott	480	.296	16	63	71	113	13	13	2.9	.934	K. Brett	41	139	8	9	2	4.08
RF	T. Conigliaro	560	.266	36	116	252	7	6	1	1.8	.977	M. Nagy	23	129	6	5	0	4.47
CF	R. Smith	580	.303	22	74	361	15	9	1	2.7	.977	V. Romo	48	108	7	3	6	4.08
LF	B. Conigliaro	398	.271	18	58	201	8	7	0	2.0	.968	S. Lyle	63	67	1	7	20	3.90
C	G. Moses	315	.263	6	35	578	45	6	3	7.1	.990	G. Wagner	38	40	3	1	7	3.38
3S	L. Alvarado	183	.224	1	10	45	134	8	17		.957							
C	T. Satriano	165	.236	3	13	318	19	5	5	6.7	.985							

Det.
W-79 L-83
Mayo Smith

POS	Player	AB	BA	HR	RBI	PO	A	E	DP	TC/G	FA	Pitcher	G	IP	W	L	SV	ERA
1B	N. Cash	370	.259	15	53	868	70	10	76	8.3	.989	M. Lolich	40	273	14	19	0	3.79
2B	D. McAuliffe	530	.234	12	50	280	333	16	75	5.0	.975	J. Niekro	38	213	12	13	0	4.06
SS	C. Gutierrez	415	.243	0	22	183	326	23	60	3.9	.957	L. Cain	29	181	12	7	0	3.83
3B	D. Wert	363	.218	6	33	94	191	14	20	2.6	.953	M. Kilkenny	36	129	7	6	0	5.16
RF	A. Kaline	467	.278	16	71	156	3	2	1	1.8	.988	J. Hiller	47	104	6	6	3	3.03
CF	M. Stanley	568	.252	13	47	317	3	0	0	2.4	1.000	E. Wilson	18	96	4	6	0	4.41
LF	J. Northrup	504	.262	24	80	284	4	2	1	2.1	.993	T. Timmerman	61	85	6	7	27	4.13
C	B. Freehan	395	.241	16	52	742	42	2	6	6.9	.997	D. Patterson	43	78	7	1	2	4.85
OF	W. Horton	371	.305	17	69	154	10	3	1	1.7	.982							
UT	E. Maddox	258	.248	3	24	104	100	14	10		.936							
UT	D. Jones	191	.220	6	21	111	99	4	26		.981							
OF	G. Brown	124	.226	3	24	37	1	2	0	1.5	.950							

	POS	Player	AB	BA	HR	RBI	PO	A	E	DP	TC/G	FA	Pitcher	G	IP	W	L	SV	ERA
Cle. W-76 L-86 Alvin Dark	1B	T. Horton	413	.269	17	59	898	73	6	106	8.7	.994	S. McDowell	39	305	20	12	0	2.92
	2B	E. Leon	549	.248	10	56	342	378	13	102	5.2	.982	R. Hand	35	160	6	13	3	3.83
	SS	J. Heidemann	445	.211	6	37	216	354	23	79	4.5	.961	D. Chance	45	155	9	8	4	4.24
	3B	G. Nettles	549	.235	26	62	134	**358**	17	40	3.3	**.967**	S. Hargan	23	143	11	3	0	2.90
	RF	V. Pinson	574	.286	24	82	265	8	5	3	2.0	.982	S. Dunning	19	94	4	9	0	4.98
	CF	T. Uhlaender	473	.268	11	46	225	5	2	1	1.7	.991	D. Higgins	58	90	4	6	11	4.00
	LF	R. Foster	477	.268	23	60	188	6	7	0	1.5	.965	M. Paul	30	88	2	8	0	4.81
	C	R. Fosse	450	.307	18	61	**854**	70	10	7	**7.8**	.989	P. Hennigan	42	72	6	3	3	4.00
	UT	D. Sims	345	.264	23	56	505	34	8	18		.985	R. Austin	31	68	2	5	3	4.76
	UT	C. Hinton	195	.318	9	29	229	15	2	14		.992	F. Lasher	43	58	1	7	5	4.06
	OF	B. Bradford	163	.196	7	23	117	1	2	0	1.9	.983							
Was. W-70 L-92 Ted Williams	1B	M. Epstein	430	.256	20	56	1100	70	10	104	**9.7**	.992	D. Bosman	36	231	16	12	0	3.00
	2B	T. Cullen	262	.214	1	18	211	262	3	65	4.3	**.994**	J. Coleman	39	219	8	12	0	3.58
	SS	E. Brinkman	625	.262	1	40	**301**	**569**	23	103	5.7	.974	C. Cox	37	192	8	12	1	4.45
	3B	A. Rodriguez	547	.247	19	76	97	343	18	36*	3.4	.961	J. Hannan	42	128	9	11	0	4.01
	RF	E. Stroud	433	.266	5	32	271	8	2	3	2.4	.993	D. Knowles	71	119	2	14	27	2.04
	CF	D. Unser	322	.258	5	30	173	8	3	2	1.8	.984	G. Brunet	24	118	8	6	0	4.42
	LF	F. Howard	566	.283	**44**	**126**	172	6	5	4	1.5	.973	Shellenback	39	117	6	7	0	3.69
	C	P. Casanova	328	.229	6	30	461	48	6	**12**	5.2	.988	J. Grzenda	49	85	3	6	6	4.98
	OF	R. Reichardt	277	.253	15	46	134	0	2	0	1.7	.985	H. Pina	61	71	5	3	6	2.79
	2B	B. Allen	261	.234	8	29	169	175	11	47	4.4	.969							
	OF	L. Maye	255	.263	7	30	75	4	0	1	1.2	1.000							
	C	J. French	166	.211	1	13	267	23	8	4	4.8	.973							

West

	POS	Player	AB	BA	HR	RBI	PO	A	E	DP	TC/G	FA	Pitcher	G	IP	W	L	SV	ERA
Min. W-98 L-64 Billy Rigney	1B	R. Reese	501	.261	10	56	1118	82	10	94	8.3	.992	J. Perry	40	279	**24**	12	0	3.03
	2B	D. Thompson	302	.219	0	22	144	204	5	35	4.4	.986	J. Kaat	45	230	14	10	0	3.56
	SS	L. Cardenas	588	.247	11	65	280	487	17	91	4.9	.978	B. Blyleven	27	164	10	9	0	3.18
	3B	H. Killebrew	527	.271	41	113	108	203	17	14	2.4	.948	T. Hall	52	155	11	6	4	2.55
	RF	T. Oliva	628	.325	23	107	351	12	**12**	4	2.4	.968	B. Zepp	43	151	9	4	2	3.22
	CF	C. Tovar	650	.300	10	54	370	12	9	1	2.6	.977	S. Williams	68	113	10	1	15	1.99
	LF	J. Holt	319	.266	3	40	201	2	1	0	1.6	.995	R. Perranoski	67	111	7	8	**34**	2.43
	C	G. Mitterwald	369	.222	15	46	740	62	3	8	6.9	.996	L. Tiant	18	93	7	3	0	3.39
	OF	B. Alyea	258	.291	16	61	93	4	2	0	1.3	.980	D. Boswell	18	69	3	7	0	6.39
	2B	R. Carew	191	.366	4	28	73	122	8	26	4.5	.961							
	3O	R. Renick	179	.229	7	25	52	54	2	5		.981							
	C	P. Ratliff	149	.268	5	22	183	11	4	4	3.7	.980							
Oak. W-89 L-73 John McNamara	1B	D. Mincher	463	.246	27	74	1109	91	**12**	107	8.8	.990	C. Dobson	41	267	16	15	0	3.74
	2B	D. Green	384	.190	4	29	259	332	13	66	4.8	.978	C. Hunter	40	262	18	14	0	3.81
	SS	B. Campaneris	603	.279	22	64	267	414	19	92	4.9	.973	D. Segui	47	162	10	10	2	**2.56**
	3B	S. Bando	502	.263	20	75	158	258	20	22	2.9	.954	B. Odom	29	156	9	8	0	3.81
	RF	R. Jackson	426	.237	23	66	251	8	12	0	1.9	.956	R. Fingers	45	148	7	9	2	3.65
	CF	R. Monday	376	.290	10	37	257	3	5	2	2.4	.981	M. Grant	72	123	6	2	24	1.83
	LF	F. Alou	575	.271	8	55	287	11	7	3	2.1	.977	P. Lindblad	62	63	8	2	3	2.71
	C	F. Fernandez	252	.214	15	44	405	25	3	6	5.7	.993	B. Locker	38	56	3	3	4	2.88
	O1	J. Rudi	350	.309	11	42	302	18	4	17		.988							
	C	D. Duncan	232	.259	10	29	373	28	9	9	5.6	.978							
	OF	T. Davis	200	.290	1	27	51	1	2	0	1.2	.963							
	C	G. Tenace	105	.305	7	20	180	18	2	7	6.7	.990							
Cal. W-86 L-76 Lefty Phillips	1B	J. Spencer	511	.274	12	68	**1212**	85	7	**131**	9.2	**.995**	C. Wright	39	261	22	12	0	2.83
	2B	S. Alomar	672	.251	2	36	375	460	18	**119**	5.6	.979	T. Murphy	39	227	16	13	0	4.24
	SS	J. Fregosi	601	.278	22	82	264	468	20	99	5.0	.973	R. May	38	209	7	13	0	4.00
	3B	K. McMullen	422	.232	14	61	128	266	17	32	3.4*	.959	Messersmith	37	195	11	10	5	3.00
	RF	R. Repoz	407	.238	18	47	203	6	1	2	1.9	.995	E. Fisher	67	130	4	4	8	3.05
	CF	J. Johnstone	320	.238	11	39	200	7	4	3	2.1	.981	K. Tatum	32	89	7	4	17	2.93
	LF	A. Johnson	614	.329	14	86	269	11	**12**	0	1.9	.959	G. Garrett	32	75	5	6	0	2.64
	C	J. Azcue	351	.242	2	25	587	51	6	10	5.8	.991	M. Queen	34	60	3	6	9	4.20
	C	T. Egan	210	.238	4	20	367	31	5	4	5.1	.988							
	OF	J. Tatum	181	.238	0	6	108	2	2	0	1.9	.982							
	OF	B. Voss	181	.243	3	30	86	7	2	1	1.7	.979							
	O1	B. Cowan	134	.276	5	25	95	6	2	7		.981							
K. C. W-65 L-97 Charlie Metro W-19 L-35 Bob Lemon W-46 L-62	1B	B. Oliver	612	.260	27	99	1020	65	8	100	9.5	.993	D. Drago	35	240	9	15	0	3.75
	2B	C. Rojas	384	.260	2	28	217	283	9	69	5.2	.982	B. Johnson	40	214	8	13	4	3.07
	SS	J. Hernandez	238	.231	2	10	142	187	17	38	4.5	.951	J. Rooker	38	204	10	15	1	3.53
	3B	P. Schaal	380	.268	5	35	69	159	15	12	2.5	.938	B. Butler	25	141	4	12	0	3.77
	RF	P. Kelly	452	.235	6	38	254	8	10	2	2.3	.963	D. Morehead	28	122	3	5	1	3.61
	CF	A. Otis	620	.284	11	58	**388**	15	4	6	2.6	.990	W. Bunker	24	122	2	11	0	4.20
	LF	L. Piniella	542	.301	11	88	247	6	4	2	1.8	.984	A. Fitzmorris	43	118	8	5	1	4.42
	C	Kirkpatrick	424	.229	18	62	463	61	**12**	**12**	6.0	.978	T. Burgmeier	41	68	6	6	1	3.18
	S2	R. Severson	240	.250	1	22	127	202	12	45		.965	T. Abernathy	36	56	9	3	12	2.57
	C	E. Rodriguez	231	.225	1	15	451	32	6	5	6.5	.988							
	O1	J. Keough	183	.322	4	21	176	13	4	13		.979							

POS	Player	AB	BA	HR	RBI	PO	A	E	DP	TC/G	FA	Pitcher	G	IP	W	L	SV	ERA
Mil. W-65 L-97 Dave Bristol																		
1B	M. Hegan	476	.244	11	52	1097	113	7	104	8.8	.994	M. Pattin	37	233	14	12	0	3.40
2B	T. Kubiak	540	.252	4	41	233	238	5	63	5.2	.989	L. Krausse	37	216	13	18	0	4.75
SS	R. Pena	416	.238	3	42	149	272	8	58	4.3	.981*	S. Lockwood	27	174	5	12	0	4.29
3B	T. Harper	604	.296	31	82	123	275	24	23	3.3	.943	B. Bolin	32	132	5	11	1	4.91
RF	D. May	342	.240	7	31	255	6	3	0	2.7	.989	G. Brabender	29	129	6	15	1	6.00
CF	R. Snyder	276	.232	4	31	140	1	5	0	1.4	.966	A. Downing	17	94	2	10	0	3.34
LF	D. Walton	397	.257	17	66	162	4	6	0	1.5	.965	K. Sanders	50	92	5	2	13	1.76
C	P. Roof	321	.227	13	37	596	47	8	6	6.1	.988	J. Gelnar	53	92	4	3	4	4.21
C	J. McNertney	296	.243	6	22	387	46	7	3	4.7	.984							
OF	T. Savage	276	.279	12	50	119	3	6	0	1.6	.953							
OF	B. Burda	222	.248	4	20	71	3	1	1	1.2	.987							
Chi. W-56 L-106 Don Gutteridge W-49 L-87 Bill Adair W-4 L-6 Chuck Tanner W-3 L-13																		
1B	G. Hopkins	287	.286	6	29	629	42	9	67	8.8	.987	T. John	37	269	12	17	0	3.28
2B	B. Knoop	402	.229	5	36	276	403	11	102	5.5	.984	G. Janeski	35	206	10	17	0	4.76
SS	L. Aparicio	552	.313	5	43	251	483	18	99	5.2	.976	J. Horlen	28	172	6	16	0	4.87
3B	B. Melton	514	.263	33	96	47	179	18	19	3.5	.926	W. Wood	77	122	9	13	21	2.80
RF	W. Williams	315	.251	3	15	119	12	7	1	1.7	.949	J. Crider	32	91	4	7	4	4.45
CF	K. Berry	463	.276	7	50	331	9	4	2	2.5	.988	B. Johnson	18	90	4	7	0	4.80
LF	C. May	555	.285	12	68	203	12	2	2	1.5	.991	D. Murphy	51	81	2	3	5	5.67
C	E. Herrmann	297	.283	19	52	433	51	6	10	5.6	.988	B. Miller	15	70	4	6	0	5.01
32	S. O'Brien	441	.247	8	44	155	264	23	49		.948							
1O	T. McCraw	332	.220	6	31	427	35	9	34		.981							
C	D. Josephson	285	.316	4	41	353	38	6	7	4.7	.985							

BATTING AND BASE RUNNING LEADERS

Batting Average
A. Johnson, CAL	.329
Yastrzemski, BOS	.329
T. Oliva, MIN	.325
L. Aparicio, CHI	.313
F. Robinson, BAL	.306

Slugging Average
Yastrzemski, BOS	.592
B. Powell, BAL	.549
H. Killebrew, MIN	.546
F. Howard, WAS	.546
T. Harper, MIL	.522

Home Runs
F. Howard, WAS	44
H. Killebrew, MIN	41
Yastrzemski, BOS	40
T. Conigliaro, BOS	36
B. Powell, BAL	35

Total Bases
Yastrzemski, BOS	335
T. Oliva, MIN	323
T. Harper, MIL	315
F. Howard, WAS	309
B. Powell, BAL	289

Runs Batted In
F. Howard, WAS	126
T. Conigliaro, BOS	116
B. Powell, BAL	114
H. Killebrew, MIN	113
T. Oliva, MIN	107

Stolen Bases
B. Campaneris, OAK	42
T. Harper, MIL	38
S. Alomar, CAL	35
P. Kelly, KC	34
A. Otis, KC	33

Hits
T. Oliva, MIN	204
A. Johnson, CAL	202
C. Tovar, MIN	195

Base on Balls
F. Howard, WAS	132
H. Killebrew, MIN	128
Yastrzemski, BOS	128

Home Run Percentage
H. Killebrew, MIN	7.8
F. Howard, WAS	7.8
Yastrzemski, BOS	7.1

Runs Scored
Yastrzemski, BOS	125
C. Tovar, MIN	120
R. Smith, BOS	109
R. White, NY	109

Doubles
A. Otis, KC	36
T. Oliva, MIN	36
C. Tovar, MIN	36

Triples
C. Tovar, MIN	13
M. Stanley, DET	11
A. Otis, KC	9

PITCHING LEADERS

Winning Percentage
M. Cuellar, BAL	.750
D. McNally, BAL	.727
J. Perry, MIN	.667
J. Palmer, BAL	.667
S. Siebert, BOS	.652

Earned Run Average
D. Segui, OAK	2.56
J. Palmer, BAL	2.71
C. Wright, CAL	2.83
F. Peterson, NY	2.91
S. McDowell, CLE	2.92

Wins
M. Cuellar, BAL	24
D. McNally, BAL	24
J. Perry, MIN	24
C. Wright, CAL	22

Saves
R. Perranoski, MIN	34
L. McDaniel, NY	29
T. Timmerman, DET	27
D. Knowles, WAS	27
M. Grant, OAK	24

Strikeouts
S. McDowell, CLE	304
M. Lolich, DET	230
B. Johnson, KC	206
J. Palmer, BAL	199
R. Culp, BOS	197

Complete Games
M. Cuellar, BAL	21
S. McDowell, CLE	19
J. Palmer, BAL	17
D. McNally, BAL	16
R. Culp, BOS	15

Fewest Hits per 9 Innings
Messersmith, CAL	6.65
S. McDowell, CLE	6.96
D. Segui, OAK	7.22

Shutouts
J. Palmer, BAL	5
C. Dobson, OAK	5

Fewest Walks per 9 Innings
F. Peterson, NY	1.38
J. Perry, MIN	1.84
C. Cox, WAS	2.06

Most Strikeouts per 9 Inn.
S. McDowell, CLE	8.97
B. Johnson, KC	8.66
L. Cain, DET	7.76

Innings
S. McDowell, CLE	305
J. Palmer, BAL	305
M. Cuellar, BAL	298

Games Pitched
W. Wood, CHI	77
M. Grant, OAK	72
D. Knowles, WAS	71

	W	L	PCT	GB	R	OR	Batting 2B	3B	HR	BA	SA	SB	Fielding E	DP	FA	Pitching CG	BB	SO	ShO	SV	ERA
EAST																					
BAL	108	54	.667		792	574	213	25	179	.257	.401	84	117	148	.981	60	469	941	12	31	3.15
NY	93	69	.574	15	680	612	208	41	111	.251	.365	105	130	146	.980	36	451	777	6	49	3.25
BOS	87	75	.537	21	786	722	252	28	203	.262	.428	50	156	131	.974	38	594	1003	8	44	3.90
DET	79	83	.488	29	666	731	207	38	148	.238	.374	29	133	142	.978	33	623	1045	9	39	4.09
CLE	76	86	.469	32	649	675	197	23	183	.249	.394	25	133	168	.979	34	689	1076	8	35	3.91
WAS	70	92	.432	38	626	689	184	28	138	.238	.358	72	116	173	.982	20	611	823	11	40	3.80
WEST																					
MIN	98	64	.605		744	605	230	41	153	.262	.403	57	123	130	.980	26	486	940	12	58	3.23
OAK	89	73	.549	9	678	593	208	24	114	.249	.392	131	141	152	.977	33	542	858	15	40	3.30
CAL	86	76	.531	12	631	630	197	40	114	.251	.363	69	127	169	.980	21	559	922	10	49	3.48
KC	65	97	.401	33	611	705	202	41	97	.244	.348	97	152	162	.976	30	641	915	11	25	3.78
MIL	65	97	.401	33	613	751	202	24	126	.242	.358	91	136	142	.978	31	587	895	2	27	4.20
CHI	56	106	.346	42	633	822	192	20	123	.253	.362	54	165	187	.975	20	556	762	6	30	4.54
					8109	8109	2492	373	1746	.250	.379	864	1629	1850	.978	382	6808	10957	110	467	3.72

East

POS	Player	AB	BA	HR	RBI	PO	A	E	DP	TC/G	FA	Pitcher	G	IP	W	L	SV	ERA
Pit. W-97 L-65 Danny Murtaugh																		
1B	B. Robertson	469	.271	26	72	1089	128	9	107	9.7	.993	S. Blass	33	240	15	8	0	2.85
2B	D. Cash	478	.289	2	34	228	304	7	80	5.1	.987	D. Ellis	31	227	19	9	0	3.05
SS	G. Alley	348	.227	6	28	187	316	22	55	4.9	.958	B. Johnson	31	175	9	10	0	3.45
3B	R. Hebner	388	.271	17	67	89	172	14	21	2.5	.949	L. Walker	28	160	10	8	0	3.54
RF	R. Clemente	522	.341	13	86	267	11	2	4	2.3	.993	B. Moose	30	140	11	7	1	4.11
CF	A. Oliver	529	.282	14	64	305	4	6	2	2.7	.981	N. Briles	37	136	8	4	1	3.04
LF	W. Stargell	511	.295	48	125	237	8	4	4	1.8	.984	B. Kison	18	95	6	5	0	3.41
C	M. Sanguillen	533	.319	7	81	712	72	5	12	5.8	.994	D. Giusti	58	86	5	6	30	2.93
OF	V. Davalillo	295	.285	1	33	112	5	2	0	2.0	.983	M. Grant	42	75	5	3	7	3.60
OF	G. Clines	273	.308	1	24	146	8	3	2	2.1	.981							
SS	J. Hernandez	233	.206	3	26	105	235	18	42	4.8	.950							
2B	B. Mazeroski	193	.254	1	16	95	121	3	22	4.8	.986							
C	M. May	126	.278	6	25	168	12	0	3	5.8	1.000							
St. L. W-90 L-72 Red Schoendienst																		
1B	J. Hague	380	.226	16	54	618	50	3	63	7.4	.996	S. Carlton	37	273	20	9	0	3.56
2B	T. Sizemore	478	.264	3	42	206	237	11	55	4.9	.976	B. Gibson	31	246	16	13	0	3.04
SS	D. Maxvill	356	.225	0	24	188	413	13	71	4.4	.979	R. Cleveland	34	222	12	12	0	4.01
3B	J. Torre	634	.363	24	137	136	271	21	22	2.7	.951	J. Reuss	36	211	14	14	0	4.78
RF	M. Alou	609	.315	7	74	203	8	4	0	2.3	.981	C. Zachary	23	90	3	10	0	5.30
CF	J. Cruz	292	.274	9	27	197	2	5	1	2.5	.975	M. Drabowsky	51	60	6	1	8	3.45
LF	L. Brock	640	.313	7	61	262	7	14	3	1.8	.951	F. Linzy	50	59	4	3	6	2.14
C	T. Simmons	510	.304	7	77	747	52	9	11	6.2	.989	D. Shaw	45	51	7	2	2	2.65
OF	J. Cardenal	301	.243	7	48	181	9	6	1	2.4	.969							
2B	J. Javier	259	.259	3	28	163	186	8	45	4.5	.978							
OF	L. Melendez	173	.225	0	11	90	3	4	0	1.5	.959							
1B	J. Beauchamp	162	.235	2	16	311	19	6	27	7.6	.982							
C	J. McNertney	128	.289	4	22	192	7	3	1	5.6	.985							
Chi. W-83 L-79 Leo Durocher																		
1B	J. Pepitone	427	.307	16	61	872	64	9	75	9.9	.990	F. Jenkins	39	325	24	13	0	2.77
2B	G. Beckert	530	.342	2	42	275	382	9	76	5.2	.986	M. Pappas	35	261	17	14	0	3.52
SS	D. Kessinger	617	.258	2	38	263	512	27	97	5.2	.966	B. Hands	36	242	12	18	0	3.42
3B	R. Santo	555	.267	21	88	118	274	17	29	2.7	.958	K. Holtzman	30	195	9	15	0	4.48
RF	J. Callison	290	.210	8	38	158	3	3	0	1.8	.982	J. Pizarro	16	101	7	6	0	3.48
CF	B. Davis	301	.256	0	28	213	5	4	1	2.4	.982	P. Regan	48	73	5	5	6	3.95
LF	B. Williams	594	.301	28	93	284	8	7	3	1.9	.977							
C	C. Cannizzaro	197	.213	5	23	311	26	6	2	4.9	.983							
O1	J. Hickman	383	.256	19	60	470	34	3	28		.994							
2B	P. Popovich	226	.217	4	28	74	119	3	26	4.9	.985							
P	F. Jenkins	115	.243	6	20	31	48	7	1	2.2	.919							
N. Y. W-83 L-79 Gil Hodges																		
1B	E. Kranepool	421	.280	14	58	786	61	2	67	7.9	**.998**	T. Seaver	36	286	20	10	0	**1.76**
2B	K. Boswell	392	.273	5	40	191	234	12	56	4.0	.973	G. Gentry	32	203	12	11	0	3.24
SS	B. Harrelson	547	.252	0	32	257	441	16	86	5.1	.978	J. Koosman	26	166	6	11	0	3.04
3B	B. Aspromonte	342	.225	5	33	76	145	8	10	2.4	.965	R. Sadecki	34	163	7	7	0	2.93
RF	K. Singleton	298	.245	13	46	143	5	4	0	1.6	.974	N. Ryan	30	152	10	14	0	3.97
CF	T. Agee	425	.285	14	50	265	7	6	0	2.6	.978	T. McGraw	51	111	11	4	8	1.70
LF	C. Jones	505	.319	14	69	248	4	5	1	1.9	.981	D. Frisella	53	91	8	5	12	1.98
C	J. Grote	403	.270	2	35	892	41	9	4	7.7	.990	C. Williams	31	90	5	6	0	4.80
UT	T. Foli	288	.226	0	24	150	199	12	43		.967							
1B	D. Clendenon	263	.247	11	37	505	37	8	49	7.6	.985							
OF	D. Marshall	214	.238	3	21	92	2	1	0	1.5	.989							
3B	W. Garrett	202	.213	1	11	30	89	4	7	2.3	.967							
OF	D. Hahn	178	.236	1	11	140	2	4	1	1.8	.973							
C	D. Dyer	169	.231	2	18	336	21	3	3	6.8	.992							
Mon. W-71 L-90 Gene Mauch																		
1B	R. Fairly	447	.257	13	71	1108	104	10	110	9.1	.992	B. Stoneman	39	295	17	16	0	3.14
2B	R. Hunt	520	.279	5	38	270	370	14	72	4.9	.979	S. Renko	40	276	15	14	0	3.75
SS	B. Wine	340	.200	1	16	221	321	10	76	4.6	.982	C. Morton	36	214	10	18	1	4.79
3B	B. Bailey	545	.251	14	83	69	194	11	14	2.3	.960	E. McAnally	31	178	11	12	0	3.89
RF	R. Staub	599	.311	19	97	290	20	18	5	2.0	.945	J. Strohmayer	27	114	7	5	1	4.34
CF	B. Day	371	.283	4	33	262	10	5	1	2.3	.982	M. Marshall	66	111	5	8	23	4.30
LF	J. Fairey	200	.245	1	19	85	7	3	1	1.6	.968							
C	J. Bateman	492	.242	10	56	726	56	12	12	5.8	.985							
2S	G. Sutherland	304	.257	4	26	154	249	21	59		.950							
C1	J. Boccabella	177	.220	3	15	334	33	4	30		.989							
Phi. W-67 L-95 Frank Lucchesi																		
1B	D. Johnson	582	.265	34	95	1219	88	7	124	9.7	.995	R. Wise	38	272	17	14	0	2.88
2B	D. Doyle	342	.231	3	24	241	264	17	62	5.7	.967	B. Lersch	38	214	5	14	0	3.79
SS	L. Bowa	650	.249	0	25	272	560	11	97	5.4	**.987**	C. Short	31	173	7	14	1	3.85
3B	J. Vukovich	217	.166	0	14	58	137	9	8	2.8	.956	K. Reynolds	35	162	5	9	0	4.50
RF	H. Freed	348	.221	6	37	184	4	2	1	1.8	.989	W. Fryman	37	149	10	7	2	3.38
CF	W. Montanez	599	.255	30	99	364	11	11	3	2.4	.972	J. Bunning	29	110	5	12	1	5.48
LF	O. Gamble	280	.221	6	23	125	4	4	1	1.7	.970	B. Champion	37	109	3	5	0	4.38
C	T. McCarver	474	.278	8	46	673	51	11	8	5.9	.985	D. Brandon	52	83	6	6	4	3.90
UT	D. Money	439	.223	7	38	167	197	11	21		.971	J. Hoerner	49	73	4	5	9	1.97
2B	T. Harmon	221	.204	0	12	122	166	4	39	5.0	.986	B. Wilson	38	59	4	6	7	3.05
OF	R. Stone	185	.227	2	23	76	5	3	0	1.6	.964							

West

S. F.
W-90 L-72
Charlie Fox

POS	Player	AB	BA	HR	RBI	PO	A	E	DP	TC/G	FA	Pitcher	G	IP	W	L	SV	ERA
1B	W. McCovey	329	.277	18	70	828	63	15	80	9.5	.983	G. Perry	37	280	16	12	0	2.76
2B	T. Fuentes	630	.273	4	52	373	465	23	109	5.7	.973	J. Marichal	37	279	18	11	0	2.94
SS	C. Speier	601	.235	8	46	239	517	33	95	5.1	.958	J. Cumberland	45	185	9	6	2	2.92
3B	A. Gallagher	429	.277	5	57	88	204	15	18	2.4	.951	R. Bryant	27	140	7	10	0	3.79
RF	B. Bonds	619	.288	33	102	329	10	2	1	2.2	.994	S. Stone	24	111	5	9	0	4.14
CF	W. Mays	417	.271	18	61	192	2	6	1	2.4	.970	J. Johnson	67	109	12	9	18	2.97
LF	K. Henderson	504	.264	15	65	277	3	10	1	2.1	.966	D. McMahon	61	82	10	6	4	4.06
C	D. Dietz	453	.252	19	72	712	37	14	4	5.7	.982							
3B	H. Lanier	206	.233	1	13	33	79	5	6	1.4	.957							
OF	J. Rosario	192	.224	0	13	151	1	0	0	2.3	1.000							
1O	D. Kingman	115	.278	6	24	168	9	4	9		.978							

L. A.
W-89 L-73
Walter Alston

POS	Player	AB	BA	HR	RBI	PO	A	E	DP	TC/G	FA	Pitcher	G	IP	W	L	SV	ERA
1B	W. Parker	533	.274	6	62	1215	97	5	113	8.9	.996	D. Sutton	38	265	17	12	1	2.55
2B	J. Lefebvre	388	.245	12	68	244	260	6	69	5.0	.988	A. Downing	37	262	20	9	0	2.68
SS	M. Wills	601	.281	3	44	220	484	16	86	5.0	.978	C. Osteen	38	259	14	11	0	3.51
3B	S. Garvey	225	.227	7	26	53	161	14	11	2.9	.939	B. Singer	31	203	10	17	0	4.17
RF	B. Buckner	358	.277	5	41	165	5	1	0	2.0	.994	D. Alexander	17	92	6	6	0	3.82
CF	W. Davis	641	.309	10	74	404	7	8	0	2.7	.981	J. Brewer	55	81	6	5	22	1.89
LF	W. Crawford	342	.281	9	40	146	5	3	1	1.6	.981	P. Mikkelsen	41	74	8	5	5	3.65
C	D. Sims	230	.274	6	25	345	33	3	5	5.1	.992							
UT	R. Allen	549	.295	23	90	382	151	21	38		.962							
UT	B. Valentine	281	.249	1	25	123	176	16	31		.949							
OF	M. Mota	269	.312	0	34	108	3	4	1	1.4	.965							
2O	B. Russell	211	.227	2	15	130	109	7	21		.972							
C	T. Haller	202	.267	5	32	320	34	8	3	5.4	.978							

Atl.
W-82 L-80
Lum Harris

POS	Player	AB	BA	HR	RBI	PO	A	E	DP	TC/G	FA	Pitcher	G	IP	W	L	SV	ERA
1B	H. Aaron	495	.327	47	118	629	38	3	56	9.4	.996	P. Niekro	42	269	15	14	2	2.98
2B	F. Millan	577	.289	2	45	373	437	15	120	5.9	.982	R. Reed	32	222	13	14	0	3.73
SS	M. Perez	410	.227	4	32	195	382	27	91	4.8	.955	G. Stone	27	173	6	8	0	3.59
3B	D. Evans	260	.242	12	38	71	138	14	13	3.1	.937	P. Jarvis	35	162	6	14	1	4.11
RF	M. Lum	454	.269	13	55	286	10	3	2	2.4	.990	T. Kelley	28	143	9	5	0	2.96
CF	S. Jackson	547	.258	2	25	336	8	7	0	2.4	.980	J. Nash	32	133	9	7	2	4.94
LF	R. Garr	639	.343	9	44	315	15	11	3	2.2	.968	C. Upshaw	49	82	11	6	17	3.51
C	E. Williams	497	.260	33	87	375	35	8	4	5.8	.981	B. Priddy	40	64	4	9	4	4.22
1B	O. Cepeda	250	.276	14	44	586	49	5	60	10.2	.992							
C	H. King	198	.207	5	19	274	23	5	0	5.0	.983							
3S	Z. Versalles	194	.191	5	22	61	105	13	13		.927							

Cin.
W-79 L-83
Sparky Anderson

POS	Player	AB	BA	HR	RBI	PO	A	E	DP	TC/G	FA	Pitcher	G	IP	W	L	SV	ERA
1B	L. May	553	.278	39	98	1261	78	8	118	9.4	.994	G. Nolan	35	245	12	15	0	3.16
2B	T. Helms	547	.258	3	52	395	468	9	130	5.9	.990	D. Gullett	35	218	16	6	0	2.64
SS	D. Concepcion	327	.205	1	20	160	294	12	62	4.2	.974	McGlothlin	30	171	8	12	0	3.21
3B	T. Perez	609	.269	25	91	113	304	18	26	2.9	.959	R. Grimsley	26	161	10	7	0	3.58
RF	P. Rose	632	.304	13	44	306	13	2	1	2.0	.994	W. Simpson	22	117	4	7	0	4.77
CF	G. Foster	368	.234	10	50	267	8	4	3	2.7	.986	J. Merritt	28	107	1	11	0	4.37
LF	H. McRae	337	.264	9	34	167	6	6	1	2.0	.966	W. Granger	70	100	7	6	11	3.33
C	J. Bench	562	.238	27	61	687	59	9	9	5.4	.988	C. Carroll	61	94	10	4	15	2.49
OF	B. Carbo	310	.219	5	20	154	7	3	0	1.8	.982	J. Gibbon	50	64	5	6	11	2.95
S3	W. Woodward	273	.242	0	18	114	236	7	44		.980							

Hou.
W-79 L-83
Harry Walker

POS	Player	AB	BA	HR	RBI	PO	A	E	DP	TC/G	FA	Pitcher	G	IP	W	L	SV	ERA
1B	D. Menke	475	.246	1	43	845	59	3	77	9.0	.997	D. Wilson	35	268	16	10	0	2.45
2B	J. Morgan	583	.256	13	56	336	482	12	93	5.3	.986	J. Billingham	33	228	10	16	0	3.39
SS	R. Metzger	562	.235	0	26	275	459	17	91	5.1	.977	K. Forsch	33	188	8	8	0	2.54
3B	D. Rader	484	.244	12	56	93	275	21	28	2.9	.946	L. Dierker	24	159	12	6	0	2.72
RF	J. Wynn	404	.203	7	45	232	9	3	5	2.1	.988	W. Blasingame	30	158	9	11	0	4.61
CF	C. Cedeno	611	.264	10	81	345	6	4	0	2.3	.989	J. Ray	47	98	10	4	3	2.11
LF	B. Watson	468	.288	9	67	131	2	2	0	1.6	.985	G. Culver	59	95	5	8	7	2.65
C	J. Edwards	317	.233	1	23	555	48	3	7	5.8	.995	F. Gladding	48	51	4	5	12	2.12
OF	J. Alou	433	.279	2	40	229	7	4	3	2.2	.983							
C	J. Hiatt	174	.276	1	16	329	20	3	6	5.4	.991							

S. D.
W-61 L-100
Preston Gomez

POS	Player	AB	BA	HR	RBI	PO	A	E	DP	TC/G	FA	Pitcher	G	IP	W	L	SV	ERA
1B	N. Colbert	565	.264	27	84	1372	106	10	125	9.7	.993	D. Roberts	37	270	14	17	0	2.10
2B	D. Mason	344	.212	2	11	188	231	15	47	4.8	.965	C. Kirby	38	267	15	13	0	2.83
SS	E. Hernandez	549	.222	0	12	260	445	33	82	5.2	.955	S. Arlin	36	228	9	19	0	3.47
3B	E. Spiezio	308	.231	7	36	57	168	9	12	2.6	.962	T. Phoebus	29	133	3	11	0	4.47
RF	O. Brown	484	.273	9	55	263	9	5	2	2.1	.982	F. Norman	20	127	3	12	0	3.32
CF	C. Gaston	518	.228	17	61	271	8	5	1	2.1	.982	A. Severinsen	59	70	2	5	8	3.47
LF	L. Stahl	308	.253	8	36	141	11	2	4	2.1	.980	B. Miller	38	64	7	3	7	1.41
C	B. Barton	376	.250	5	23	698	67	15	10	6.6	.981							
23	D. Campbell	365	.227	7	29	169	254	17	48		.961							
OF	L. Lee	256	.273	4	21	86	6	8	1	1.5	.920							
OF	I. Murrell	255	.235	7	24	133	2	3	0	1.9	.978							
32	G. Jestadt	189	.291	0	13	63	141	12	11		.944							

BATTING AND BASE RUNNING LEADERS

PITCHING LEADERS

Batting Average		Slugging Average		Winning Percentage		Earned Run Average	
J. Torre, STL	.363	H. Aaron, ATL	.669	D. Gullett, CIN	.727	T. Seaver, NY	1.76
R. Garr, ATL	.343	W. Stargell, PIT	.628	S. Carlton, STL	.690	D. Roberts, HOU	2.10
G. Beckert, CHI	.342	J. Torre, STL	.555	A. Downing, LA	.690	D. Wilson, HOU	2.45
R. Clemente, PIT	.341	L. May, CIN	.532	D. Ellis, PIT	.679	K. Forsch, HOU	2.54
H. Aaron, ATL	.327	B. Bonds, SF	.512	T. Seaver, NY	.667	D. Sutton, LA	2.55

BATTING AND BASE RUNNING LEADERS

PITCHING LEADERS

Home Runs		Total Bases		Wins		Saves	
W. Stargell, PIT	48	J. Torre, STL	352	F. Jenkins, CHI	24	D. Giusti, PIT	30
H. Aaron, ATL	47	H. Aaron, ATL	331	S. Carlton, STL	20	M. Marshall, MON	23
L. May, CIN	39	W. Stargell, PIT	321	A. Downing, LA	20	J. Brewer, LA	22
D. Johnson, PHI	34	B. Bonds, SF	317	T. Seaver, NY	20	J. Johnson, SF	18
E. Williams, ATL	33	B. Williams, CHI	300	D. Ellis, PIT	19	C. Upshaw, ATL	17
B. Bonds, SF	33						

Runs Batted In		Stolen Bases		Strikeouts		Complete Games	
J. Torre, STL	137	L. Brock, STL	64	T. Seaver, NY	289	F. Jenkins, CHI	30
W. Stargell, PIT	125	J. Morgan, HOU	40	F. Jenkins, CHI	263	T. Seaver, NY	21
H. Aaron, ATL	118	R. Garr, ATL	30	B. Stoneman, MON	251	B. Gibson, STL	20
B. Bonds, SF	102	T. Agee, NY	28	C. Kirby, SD	231	B. Stoneman, MON	20
W. Montanez, PHI	99	B. Harrelson, NY	28	D. Sutton, LA	194		
		L. Bowa, PHI	28				

Hits		Base on Balls		Fewest Hits per 9 Innings		Shutouts	
J. Torre, STL	230	W. Mays, SF	112	D. Wilson, HOU	6.55	B. Gibson, STL	5
R. Garr, ATL	219	D. Dietz, SF	97	T. Seaver, NY	6.61	S. Blass, PIT	5
L. Brock, STL	200	B. Bailey, MON	97	C. Kirby, SD	7.18	M. Pappas, CHI	5
						A. Downing, LA	5

Home Run Percentage		Runs Scored		Fewest Walks per 9 Innings		Most Strikeouts per 9 Inn.	
H. Aaron, ATL	9.5	L. Brock, STL	126	F. Jenkins, CHI	1.02	T. Seaver, NY	9.09
W. Stargell, PIT	9.4	B. Bonds, SF	110	J. Marichal, SF	1.81	C. Kirby, SD	7.79
L. May, CIN	7.1	W. Stargell, PIT	104	G. Stone, ATL	1.82	B. Stoneman, MON	7.66

Doubles		Triples		Innings		Games Pitched	
C. Cedeno, HOU	40	R. Metzger, HOU	11	F. Jenkins, CHI	325	W. Granger, CIN	70
L. Brock, STL	37	J. Morgan, HOU	11	B. Stoneman, MON	295	J. Johnson, SF	67
R. Staub, MON	34	W. Davis, LA	10	T. Seaver, NY	286	M. Marshall, MON	66
J. Torre, STL	34	C. Gaston, SD	9				

	W	L	PCT	GB	R	OR	2B	3B	HR	BA	SA	SB	E	DP	FA	CG	BB	SO	ShO	SV	ERA
EAST																					
PIT	97	65	.599		**788**	599	223	**61**	**154**	.274	**.416**	65	133	164	.979	43	470	813	15	**48**	3.31
STL	90	72	.556	7	739	699	225	54	95	**.275**	.385	**124**	142	155	.978	56	576	911	14	22	3.87
CHI	83	79	.512	14	637	648	202	34	128	.258	.378	44	126	150	.980	**75**	411	900	17	13	3.61
NY	83	79	.512	14	588	**550**	203	29	98	.249	.351	89	114	135	.981	42	529	**1157**	13	22	**3.00**
MON	71	90	.441	25.5	622	729	197	29	88	.246	.343	51	150	164	.976	49	658	829	8	25	4.12
PHI	67	95	.414	30	558	688	209	35	123	.233	.350	63	122	158	.981	31	525	838	10	25	3.71
WEST																					
SF	90	72	.556		706	644	224	36	140	.247	.378	101	179	153	.972	45	471	831	14	30	3.33
LA	89	73	.549	1	663	587	213	38	95	.266	.370	76	131	159	.979	48	**399**	853	**18**	33	3.23
ATL	82	80	.506	8	643	699	192	30	153	.257	.385	57	146	**180**	.977	40	485	823	11	31	3.75
CIN	79	83	.488	11	586	581	203	28	138	.241	.366	59	**103**	174	**.984**	27	501	750	11	38	3.35
HOU	79	83	.488	11	585	540	**230**	52	71	.240	.340	101	106	152	.983	43	475	914	10	25	3.13
SD	61	100	.379	28.5	486	610	184	31	96	.233	.332	70	161	144	.974	47	559	923	10	17	3.23
					7601	7601	2505	457	1379	.252	.366	900	1613	1888	.979	546	6059	10542	151	329	3.47

American League 1971

	POS	Player	AB	BA	HR	RBI	PO	A	E	DP	TC/G	FA	Pitcher	G	IP	W	L	SV	ERA

East

	POS	Player	AB	BA	HR	RBI	PO	A	E	DP	TC/G	FA	Pitcher	G	IP	W	L	SV	ERA
Bal. W-101 L-57 Earl Weaver	1B	B. Powell	418	.256	22	92	1031	67	5	97	8.9	.995	M. Cuellar	38	292	20	9	0	3.08
	2B	D. Johnson	510	.282	18	72	361	367	12	**103**	5.3	.984	P. Dobson	38	282	20	8	1	2.90
	SS	M. Belanger	500	.266	0	35	280	443	16	77	5.0	.978	J. Palmer	37	282	20	9	0	2.68
	3B	B. Robinson	589	.272	20	92	131	354	16	35	3.2	.968	D. McNally	30	224	21	5	0	2.89
	RF	M. Rettenmund	491	.318	11	75	292	7	7	4	2.3	.977	D. Hall	27	43	6	6	1	5.02
	CF	P. Blair	516	.262	10	44	331	4	3	1	2.4	.991	E. Watt	35	40	3	1	11	1.80
	LF	D. Buford	449	.290	19	54	217	6	3	0	2.0	.987	T. Dukes	28	38	1	5	4	3.55
	C	E. Hendricks	316	.250	9	42	429	33	7	5	5.2	.985	P. Richert	35	36	3	5	4	3.50
	OF	F. Robinson	455	.281	28	99	177	3	5	0	2.0	.973							
	C	Etchebarren	222	.270	9	29	337	24	5	2	5.2	.986							

Det.
W-91 L-71 — Billy Martin

POS	Player	AB	BA	HR	RBI	PO	A	E	DP	TC/G	FA	Pitcher	G	IP	W	L	SV	ERA
1B	N. Cash	452	.283	32	91	1020	75	9	105	8.4	.992	M. Lolich	45	376	25	14	0	2.92
2B	D. McAuliffe	477	.208	18	57	322	308	8	86	5.2	.987	J. Coleman	39	286	20	9	0	3.15
SS	E. Brinkman	527	.228	1	37	235	513	15	91	4.8	.980	L. Cain	26	145	10	9	0	4.34
3B	A. Rodriguez	604	.253	15	39	127	341	23	33	3.2	.953	J. Niekro	31	122	6	7	1	4.50
RF	A. Kaline	405	.294	15	54	207	6	0	0	1.7	1.000	F. Scherman	69	113	11	6	20	2.71
CF	M. Stanley	401	.292	7	41	315	10	4	3	2.4	.988	D. Chance	31	90	4	6	0	3.50
LF	W. Horton	450	.289	22	72	176	8	7	1	1.6	.963	M. Kilkenny	30	86	4	5	1	5.02
C	B. Freehan	516	.277	21	71	912	50	4	6	6.7	.996	T. Timmerman	52	84	7	6	4	3.86
OF	J. Northrup	459	.270	16	71	205	4	4	0	2.0	.981							
OF	G. Brown	195	.338	11	29	68	2	1	0	1.3	.986							
2B	T. Taylor	181	.287	3	19	114	107	1	29	4.4	.995							

Bos.
W-85 L-77 — Eddie Kasko

POS	Player	AB	BA	HR	RBI	PO	A	E	DP	TC/G	FA	Pitcher	G	IP	W	L	SV	ERA
1B	G. Scott	537	.263	24	78	1256	75	11	122	9.4	.992	R. Culp	35	242	14	16	0	3.61
2B	D. Griffin	483	.244	3	27	311	344	9	90	5.4	.986	S. Siebert	32	235	16	10	0	2.91
SS	L. Aparicio	491	.232	4	45	194	338	16	56	4.5	.971	G. Peters	34	214	14	11	1	4.37
3B	R. Petrocelli	553	.251	28	89	118	334	11	37	3.0	.976	J. Lonborg	27	168	10	7	0	4.13
RF	R. Smith	618	.283	30	96	386	15	14	2	2.6	.966	B. Lee	47	102	9	2	2	2.74
CF	B. Conigliaro	351	.262	11	33	232	5	4	2	2.4	.983	B. Bolin	52	70	5	3	6	4.24
LF	C. Yastrzemski	508	.254	15	70	281	16	2	4	2.0	.993	K. Tatum	36	54	2	4	9	4.17
C	D. Josephson	306	.245	10	39	491	32	6	5	6.1	.989	S. Lyle	50	52	6	4	16	2.77
2S	J. Kennedy	272	.276	5	22	112	150	13	34		.953							
OF	J. Lahoud	256	.215	14	32	139	4	1	3	2.1	.993							
C	B. Montgomery	205	.239	2	24	361	15	4	3	5.8	.989							

N. Y.
W-82 L-80 — Ralph Houk

POS	Player	AB	BA	HR	RBI	PO	A	E	DP	TC/G	FA	Pitcher	G	IP	W	L	SV	ERA
1B	D. Cater	428	.276	4	50	564	62	3	54	8.1	.995	F. Peterson	37	274	15	13	1	3.05
2B	H. Clarke	625	.250	2	41	386	455	16	97	5.5	.981	Stottlemyre	35	270	16	12	0	2.87
SS	G. Michael	456	.224	3	35	243	474	20	88	5.4	.973	S. Bahnsen	36	242	14	12	0	3.35
3B	J. Kenney	325	.262	0	20	69	237	15	20	2.9	.953	S. Kline	31	222	12	13	0	2.96
RF	F. Alou	461	.289	8	69	129	3	2	0	1.7	.985	M. Kekich	37	170	10	9	0	4.08
CF	B. Murcer	529	.331	25	94	317	10	5	1	2.3	.985	L. McDaniel	44	70	5	10	4	5.01
LF	R. White	524	.292	19	84	306	8	0	1	2.2	1.000	J. Aker	41	56	4	4	4	2.57
C	T. Munson	451	.251	10	42	547	67	1	4	5.3	.998							
1B	J. Ellis	238	.244	3	34	625	35	7	66	10.3	.990							
C	J. Gibbs	206	.218	5	21	229	12	3	1	4.8	.988							
OF	R. Blomberg	199	.322	7	31	96	1	3	1	1.8	.970							
3B	R. Hansen	145	.207	2	20	16	51	6	9	2.4	.918							
OF	R. Swoboda	138	.261	2	20	80	2	3	0	1.8	.965							

Was.
W-63 L-96 — Ted Williams

POS	Player	AB	BA	HR	RBI	PO	A	E	DP	TC/G	FA	Pitcher	G	IP	W	L	SV	ERA
1B	D. Mincher	323	.291	10	45	705	59	8	80	8.8	.990	D. Bosman	35	237	12	16	0	3.72
2B	T. Cullen	403	.191	2	26	165	213	1	47	4.9	.997	D. McLain	33	217	10	22	0	4.27
SS	T. Harrah	383	.230	2	22	181	307	23	69	4.4	.955	P. Broberg	18	125	5	9	0	3.46
3B	D. Nelson	329	.280	5	33	63	149	14	15	2.7	.938	B. Gogolewski	27	124	6	5	0	2.76
RF	D. Unser	581	.255	9	41	394	10	8	2	2.7	.981	C. Cox	54	124	5	7	7	3.99
CF	E. Maddox	258	.217	1	18	197	7	2	1	2.0	.990	Shellenback	40	120	3	11	0	3.53
LF	F. Howard	549	.279	26	83	141	7	1	0	1.5	.993	P. Lindblad	43	84	6	4	8	2.58
C	P. Casanova	311	.203	5	26	416	40	7	4	5.6	.985	J. Grzenda	46	70	5	2	5	1.93
CO	D. Billings	349	.246	6	48	378	37	4	5		.990							
23	B. Allen	229	.266	4	22	85	126	10	16		.955							
2B	L. Randle	215	.219	2	13	178	178	12	50	5.6	.967							
O1	T. McCraw	207	.213	7	25	134	2	5	3		.965							
OF	J. Burroughs	181	.232	5	25	82	3	3	0	1.8	.966							
OF	L. Biittner	171	.257	0	16	72	6	5	0	2.0	.940							

Cle.
W-60 L-102 — Alvin Dark
W-42 L-61 — Johnny Lipon
W-18 L-41

POS	Player	AB	BA	HR	RBI	PO	A	E	DP	TC/G	FA	Pitcher	G	IP	W	L	SV	ERA
1B	C. Chambliss	415	.275	9	48	943	55	8	85	9.3	.992	S. McDowell	35	215	13	17	1	3.39
2B	E. Leon	429	.261	4	35	235	271	9	71	4.8	.983	S. Dunning	31	184	8	14	1	4.50
SS	J. Heidemann	240	.208	0	17	113	188	7	34	3.8	.977	A. Foster	36	182	8	12	0	4.15
3B	G. Nettles	598	.261	28	86	159	412	16	54	3.7	.973	R. Lamb	43	158	6	12	1	3.36
RF	V. Pinson	566	.263	11	35	305	11	7	2	2.3	.978	V. Colbert	50	143	7	6	2	3.97
CF	T. Uhlaender	500	.288	2	47	245	6	2	0	1.9	.992	S. Hargan	37	113	1	13	1	6.21
LF	R. Foster	396	.245	18	45	174	9	6	2	1.8	.968	P. Hennigan	57	82	4	3	14	4.94
C	R. Fosse	486	.276	12	62	748	73	10	16	6.6	.988	E. Farmer	43	79	5	4	4	4.33
OF	T. Ford	196	.194	2	14	107	4	0	0	2.0	1.000							
OF	F. Baker	181	.210	1	23	65	2	1	1	1.3	.985							

West

Oak.
W-101 L-60 — Dick Williams

POS	Player	AB	BA	HR	RBI	PO	A	E	DP	TC/G	FA	Pitcher	G	IP	W	L	SV	ERA
1B	M. Epstein	329	.234	18	51	714	52	4	93*	8.0	.995	V. Blue	39	312	24	8	0	1.82
2B	D. Green	475	.244	12	49	366	384	11	98	5.3	.986	C. Hunter	37	274	21	11	0	2.96
SS	B. Campaneris	569	.251	5	47	231	303	26	85	4.2	.954	C. Dobson	30	189	15	5	0	3.81
3B	S. Bando	538	.271	24	94	141	267	12	22	2.7	.971	D. Segui	26	146	10	8	0	3.14
RF	R. Jackson	567	.277	32	80	285	15	7	3	2.1	.977	B. Odom	25	141	10	12	0	4.28
CF	R. Monday	355	.245	18	56	238	6	4	1	2.1	.984	R. Fingers	48	129	4	6	17	3.00
LF	J. Rudi	513	.267	10	52	249	5	1	1	2.1	.996	B. Locker	47	72	7	2	6	2.88
C	D. Duncan	363	.253	15	40	678	41	12	3	7.2	.984	D. Knowles	43	53	5	2	7	3.59
OF	A. Mangual	287	.286	4	30	163	3	2	1	2.1	.988							
1O	T. Davis	219	.324	4	42	274	30	5	24		.984							
UT	L. Brown	189	.196	1	9	82	141	6	31		.974							
C	G. Tenace	179	.274	7	25	300	20	2	3	6.2	.994							

	POS	Player	AB	BA	HR	RBI	PO	A	E	DP	TC/G	FA	Pitcher	G	IP	W	L	SV	ERA
K. C. W-85 L-76 Bob Lemon	1B	G. Hopkins	295	.278	9	47	669	57	7	76	8.8	.990	D. Drago	35	241	17	11	0	2.99
	2B	C. Rojas	414	.300	6	59	252	293	5	76	5.0	.991	M. Hedlund	32	206	15	8	0	2.71
	SS	F. Patek	591	.267	6	36	301	459	25	107	5.3	.968	P. Splittorff	22	144	8	9	0	2.69
	3B	P. Schaal	548	.274	11	63	107	335	28	31	2.9	.940	Dal Canton	25	141	8	6	0	3.45
	RF	J. Keough	351	.248	3	30	164	4	3	1	1.7	.982	A. Fitzmorris	36	127	7	5	0	4.18
	CF	A. Otis	555	.301	15	79	404	10	4	4	2.9	.990	J. York	53	93	5	5	3	2.90
	LF	L. Piniella	448	.279	3	51	201	6	3	2	1.8	.986	T. Burgmeier	67	88	9	7	17	1.74
	C	J. May	218	.252	1	24	314	38	1	6	5.0	.997	T. Abernathy	63	81	4	6	23	2.56
	1O	B. Oliver	373	.244	8	52	564	34	8	52		.987	K. Wright	21	78	3	6	1	3.69
	OC	Kirkpatrick	365	.219	9	46	412	30	8	6		.982							
	1B	C. Harrison	143	.217	2	21	335	24	3	31	9.3	.992							
Chi. W-79 L-83 Chuck Tanner	1B	C. May	500	.294	7	70	1189	71	18	90	9.8	.986	W. Wood	44	334	22	13	1	1.91
	2B	M. Andrews	330	.282	12	47	177	191	17	51	5.1	.956	T. Bradley	45	286	15	15	2	2.96
	SS	L. Alvarado	264	.216	0	8	89	189	12	34	4.1	.959	T. John	38	229	13	16	0	3.62
	3B	B. Melton	543	.269	33	86	116	371	16	26	3.4	.968	B. Johnson	53	178	12	10	14	2.93
	RF	W. Williams	361	.294	8	35	157	4	0	2	1.8	1.000	J. Horlen	34	137	8	9	2	4.27
	CF	J. Johnstone	388	.260	16	40	232	9	8	1	2.1	.984	S. Kealey	54	77	2	2	6	3.86
	LF	R. Reichardt	496	.278	19	62	283	4	4	0	2.3	.986	V. Romo	45	72	1	7	5	3.38
	C	E. Herrmann	294	.214	11	35	556	56	3	5	6.3	.995							
	2O	R. McKinney	369	.271	8	46	192	160	10	34		.972							
	SS	L. Richard	260	.231	2	17	87	210	26	30	4.8	.920							
	C	T. Egan	251	.239	10	34	443	41	7	2	6.4	.986							
	OF	P. Kelly	213	.291	3	22	100	7	1	0	1.8	.991							
	SS	R. Morales	185	.243	2	14	66	138	5	14	3.7	.976							
	OF	Hershberger	177	.260	2	15	96	1	4	0	1.7	.960							
Cal. W-76 L-86 Lefty Phillips	1B	J. Spencer	510	.237	18	59	1296	93	5	117	9.6	.996	Messersmith	38	277	20	13	0	2.99
	2B	S. Alomar	689	.260	4	42	350	432	9	100	5.8	.989	C. Wright	37	277	16	17	0	2.99
	SS	J. Fregosi	347	.233	5	33	93	237	22	31	4.8	.938	T. Murphy	37	243	6	17	0	3.78
	3B	K. McMullen	593	.250	21	68	137	344	17	27	3.2	.966	R. May	32	208	11	12	0	3.03
	RF	R. Repoz	297	.199	13	42	172	6	0	2	1.8	1.000	E. Fisher	57	119	10	8	3	2.72
	CF	K. Berry	298	.221	3	22	237	5	3	0	2.4	.988	L. Allen	54	94	4	6	15	2.49
	LF	T. Gonzalez	343	.245	3	38	146	4	2	1	1.7	.987	D. LaRoche	56	72	5	1	9	2.50
	C	J. Stephenson	279	.219	3	25	434	33	4	3	5.4	.992							
	OF	M. Rivers	268	.265	1	12	159	5	4	2	2.2	.976							
	OF	T. Conigliaro	266	.222	4	15	155	6	1	1	2.3	.994							
	SS	S. O'Brien	251	.199	5	21	87	136	9	30	4.5	.961							
	OF	A. Johnson	242	.260	2	21	84	3	7	0	1.5	.926							
	C	G. Moses	181	.227	4	15	299	38	8	3	5.5	.977							
	OF	B. Cowan	174	.276	4	20	69	1	0	0	1.8	1.000							
Min. W-74 L-86 Billy Rigney	1B	R. Reese	329	.219	10	39	673	43	4	71	7.6	.994	B. Blyleven	38	278	16	15	0	2.82
	2B	R. Carew	577	.307	2	48	321	329	16	76	4.7	.976	J. Perry	40	270	17	17	1	4.23
	SS	L. Cardenas	554	.264	18	75	266	445	11	89	4.7	.985	J. Kaat	39	260	13	14	0	3.32
	3B	S. Braun	343	.254	5	35	48	106	11	7	2.3	.933	R. Corbin	52	140	8	11	3	4.11
	RF	T. Oliva	487	.337	22	81	216	6	7	3	1.9	.969	T. Hall	48	130	4	7	9	3.32
	CF	J. Holt	340	.259	1	29	209	4	3	2	2.0	.986	S. Williams	46	78	4	5	4	4.15
	LF	C. Tovar	657	.311	1	45	348	14	5	3	2.4	.986	R. Perranoski	36	43	1	4	5	6.75
	C	G. Mitterwald	388	.250	13	44	656	53	10	7	6.0	.986							
	13	H. Killebrew	500	.254	28	119	700	149	13	55		.985							
	OF	J. Nettles	168	.250	6	24	139	3	2	1	2.3	.986							
Mil. W-69 L-92 Dave Bristol	1B	J. Briggs	375	.264	21	59	458	40	5	53	8.4	.990	M. Pattin	36	265	14	14	0	3.12
	2B	R. Theobald	388	.276	1	23	233	311	15	81	5.0	.973	B. Parsons	36	245	13	17	0	3.20
	SS	R. Auerbach	236	.203	1	9	120	193	12	31	4.2	.963	S. Lockwood	33	208	10	15	0	3.33
	3B	T. Harper	585	.258	14	52	71	115	13	10	2.8	.935	L. Krausse	43	180	8	12	0	2.95
	RF	B. Voss	275	.251	10	30	151	1	2	1	1.9	.987	J. Slaton	26	148	10	8	0	3.77
	CF	D. May	501	.277	16	65	342	10	9	3	2.5	.975	K. Sanders	83	136	7	12	31	1.92
	LF	J. Cardenal	198	.258	3	32	133	6	3	0	2.7	.979							
	C	E. Rodriguez	319	.210	1	30	520	67	5	8	5.2	.992							
	UT	R. Pena	274	.237	3	28	290	112	4	38		.990							
	UT	A. Kosco	264	.227	10	39	264	25	3	23		.990							
	2S	T. Kubiak	260	.227	3	17	171	222	14	44		.966							
	SS	B. Heise	189	.254	0	7	85	138	9	36	4.5	.961							

BATTING AND BASE RUNNING LEADERS

Batting Average		Slugging Average	
T. Oliva, MIN	.337	T. Oliva, MIN	.546
B. Murcer, NY	.331	B. Murcer, NY	.543
M. Rettenmund, BAL	.318	N. Cash, DET	.531
C. Tovar, MIN	.311	F. Robinson, BAL	.510
R. Carew, MIN	.307	R. Jackson, OAK	.508

Home Runs		Total Bases	
B. Melton, CHI	33	R. Smith, BOS	302
N. Cash, DET	32	R. Jackson, OAK	288
R. Jackson, OAK	32	B. Murcer, NY	287
R. Smith, BOS	30	B. Melton, CHI	267
		T. Oliva, MIN	266

PITCHING LEADERS

Winning Percentage		Earned Run Average	
D. McNally, BAL	.808	V. Blue, OAK	1.82
V. Blue, OAK	.750	W. Wood, CHI	1.91
C. Dobson, OAK	.750	J. Palmer, BAL	2.68
P. Dobson, BAL	.714	M. Hedlund, KC	2.71
		B. Blyleven, MIN	2.82

Wins		Saves	
M. Lolich, DET	25	K. Sanders, MIL	31
V. Blue, OAK	24	T. Abernathy, KC	23
W. Wood, CHI	22	F. Scherman, DET	20
D. McNally, BAL	21	T. Burgmeier, KC	17
C. Hunter, OAK	21	R. Fingers, OAK	17

BATTING AND BASE RUNNING LEADERS

Runs Batted In			Stolen Bases	
H. Killebrew, MIN	119		A. Otis, KC	52
F. Robinson, BAL	99		F. Patek, KC	49
R. Smith, BOS	96		S. Alomar, CAL	39
B. Murcer, NY	94		B. Campaneris, OAK	34
S. Bando, OAK	94		V. Pinson, CLE	25
			T. Harper, MIL	25

Hits			Base on Balls	
C. Tovar, MIN	204		H. Killebrew, MIN	114
S. Alomar, CAL	179		Yastrzemski, BOS	106
R. Carew, MIN	177		P. Schaal, KC	103

Home Run Percentage			Runs Scored	
N. Cash, DET	7.1		D. Buford, BAL	99
F. Robinson, BAL	6.2		B. Murcer, NY	94
B. Melton, CHI	6.1		C. Tovar, MIN	94

Doubles			Triples	
R. Smith, BOS	33		F. Patek, KC	11
P. Schaal, KC	31		R. Carew, MIN	10
T. Oliva, MIN	30		P. Blair, BAL	8
A. Rodriguez, DET	30			

PITCHING LEADERS

Strikeouts			Complete Games	
M. Lolich, DET	308		M. Lolich, DET	29
V. Blue, OAK	301		V. Blue, OAK	24
J. Coleman, DET	236		W. Wood, CHI	22
B. Blyleven, MIN	224		M. Cuellar, BAL	21
W. Wood, CHI	210		J. Palmer, BAL	20

Fewest Hits per 9 Innings			Shutouts	
V. Blue, OAK	6.03		V. Blue, OAK	8
S. McDowell, CLE	6.70		Stottlemyre, NY	7
R. May, CAL	6.92		W. Wood, CHI	7

Fewest Walks per 9 Innings			Most Strikeouts per 9 Inn.	
F. Peterson, NY	1.38		V. Blue, OAK	8.68
S. Kline, NY	1.50		S. McDowell, CLE	8.04
J. Kaat, MIN	1.63		B. Johnson, CHI	7.74

Innings			Games Pitched	
M. Lolich, DET	376		K. Sanders, MIL	83
W. Wood, CHI	334		F. Scherman, DET	69
V. Blue, OAK	312		T. Burgmeier, KC	67
			T. Abernathy, KC	63

	W	L	PCT	GB	R	OR	2B	3B	Batting HR	BA	SA	SB	E	Fielding DP	FA	CG	BB	Pitching SO	ShO	SV	ERA
EAST																					
BAL	101	57	.639		742	530	207	25	158	.261	.398	66	112	148	.981	71	416	793	15	22	3.00
DET	91	71	.562	12	701	645	214	38	179	.254	.405	35	106	156	.983	53	609	1000	11	32	3.64
BOS	85	77	.525	18	691	667	246	28	161	.252	.397	51	116	149	.981	44	535	871	11	35	3.83
NY	82	80	.506	21	648	641	195	43	97	.254	.360	75	125	159	.981	67	423	707	15	12	3.45
WAS	63	96	.396	38.5	537	660	189	30	86	.230	.326	68	141	170	.977	30	554	762	10	26	3.70
CLE	60	102	.370	43	543	747	200	20	109	.238	.342	57	116	159	.981	21	770	937	7	32	4.28
WEST																					
OAK	101	60	.627		691	564	195	25	160	.252	.384	80	117	157	.981	57	501	999	18	36	3.06
KC	85	76	.528	16	603	566	225	40	80	.250	.353	130	134	178	.978	34	468	775	15	44	3.25
CHI	79	83	.488	22.5	617	597	185	30	138	.250	.373	83	160	128	.975	46	468	976	19	32	3.13
CAL	76	86	.469	25.5	511	576	213	18	96	.231	.329	72	131	159	.980	39	607	904	11	32	3.10
MIN	74	86	.463	26.5	654	670	197	31	116	.260	.372	66	118	134	.980	43	529	895	9	25	3.82
MIL	69	92	.429	32	534	609	160	23	104	.229	.329	82	138	152	.977	32	569	795	**23**	32	3.38
					7472	7472	2426	351	1484	.247	.364	865	1514	1849	.980	537	6477	10414	164	360	3.47

National League 1972

	POS	Player	AB	BA	HR	RBI	PO	A	E	DP	TC/G	FA	Pitcher	G	IP	W	L	SV	ERA

East

Pit.
W-96 L-59
Bill Virdon

POS	Player	AB	BA	HR	RBI	PO	A	E	DP	TC/G	FA	Pitcher	G	IP	W	L	SV	ERA
1B	W. Stargell	495	.293	33	112	881	40	15	96	9.3	.984	S. Blass	33	250	19	8	0	2.49
2B	D. Cash	425	.282	3	30	260	342	5	81	6.3	.992	B. Moose	31	226	13	10	1	2.91
SS	G. Alley	347	.248	3	36	181	339	16	88	4.7	.970	N. Briles	28	196	14	11	0	3.08
3B	R. Hebner	427	.300	19	72	76	210	9	17	2.4	.969	D. Ellis	25	163	15	7	0	2.70
RF	R. Clemente	378	.312	10	60	199	5	0	2	2.2	1.000	B. Kison	32	152	9	7	3	3.26
CF	A. Oliver	565	.312	12	89	332	4	5	1	2.5	.985	B. Johnson	31	116	4	4	3	2.96
LF	V. Davalillo	368	.318	4	28	181	4	4	0	1.9	.979	L. Walker	26	93	4	6	2	3.40
C	M. Sanguillen	520	.298	7	71	721	50	9	4	6.1	.988	D. Giusti	54	75	7	4	22	1.93
2O	R. Stennett	370	.286	3	30	192	164	9	43		.975	R. Hernandez	53	70	5	0	14	1.67
OF	G. Clines	311	.334	0	17	131	7	6	0	1.7	.958	B. Miller	36	54	5	2	3	2.65
1B	B. Robertson	306	.193	12	41	502	60	4	57	6.4	.993							
SS	J. Hernandez	176	.188	1	14	110	180	22	34	4.6	.929							

Chi.
W-85 L-70
Leo Durocher
W-46 L-44
Whitey Lockman
W-39 L-26

POS	Player	AB	BA	HR	RBI	PO	A	E	DP	TC/G	FA	Pitcher	G	IP	W	L	SV	ERA
1B	J. Hickman	368	.272	17	64	670	70	6	61	9.7	.992	F. Jenkins	36	289	20	12	0	3.21
2B	G. Beckert	474	.270	3	43	256	396	16	71	5.7	.976	B. Hooton	33	218	11	14	0	2.80
SS	D. Kessinger	577	.274	1	39	259	504	28	90	5.4	.965	M. Pappas	29	195	17	7	0	2.77
3B	R. Santo	464	.302	17	74	108	274	21	19	3.1	.948	B. Hands	32	189	11	8	0	2.99
RF	J. Cardenal	533	.291	17	70	223	11	7	1	1.8	.971	R. Reuschel	21	129	10	8	0	2.93
CF	R. Monday	434	.249	11	42	268	6	1	2	2.1	**.996**	T. Phoebus	37	83	3	3	6	3.78
LF	B. Williams	574	**.333**	37	122	233	9	4	0	1.7	.984	J. Aker	48	67	6	6	17	2.96
C	R. Hundley	357	.218	5	30	569	53	3	7	5.5	**.995**	J. Pizarro	16	59	4	5	1	3.97
UT	C. Fanzone	222	.225	8	42	243	115	9	21		.975							
1B	J. Pepitone	214	.262	8	21	552	31	2	51	8.9	.997							

	POS	Player	AB	BA	HR	RBI	PO	A	E	DP	TC/G	FA	Pitcher	G	IP	W	L	SV	ERA
N. Y. W-83 L-73 Yogi Berra	1B	E. Kranepool	327	.269	8	34	705	48	3	65	7.0	.996	T. Seaver	35	262	21	12	0	2.92
	2B	K. Boswell	355	.211	9	33	208	183	4	53	4.2	.990	J. Matlack	34	244	15	10	0	2.32
	SS	B. Harrelson	418	.215	1	24	191	334	16	51	4.7	.970	G. Gentry	32	164	7	10	0	4.01
	3B	J. Fregosi	340	.232	5	32	71	144	15	9	2.7	.935	J. Koosman	34	163	11	12	1	4.14
	RF	R. Staub	239	.293	9	38	108	4	2	2	1.8	.982	J. McAndrew	28	161	11	8	1	2.80
	CF	T. Agee	422	.227	13	47	273	6	11	1	2.7	.962	T. McGraw	54	106	8	6	27	1.70
	LF	C. Jones	375	.245	5	52	136	8	2	1	1.7	.986	D. Frisella	39	67	5	8	9	3.34
	C	D. Dyer	325	.231	8	36	690	61	5	**12**	**8.3**	.993							
	OF	J. Milner	362	.238	17	38	160	7	6	0	1.9	.965							
	UT	T. Martinez	330	.224	1	19	175	194	5	30		.987							
	3B	W. Garrett	298	.232	2	29	66	150	9	13	2.7	.960							
	C	J. Grote	205	.210	3	21	405	42	1	5	7.6	.998							
	OF	W. Mays	195	.267	8	19	109	3	3	1	2.3	.974							
St. L. W-75 L-81 Red Schoendienst	1B	M. Alou	404	.314	3	31	535	40	7	53	8.8	.988	B. Gibson	34	278	19	11	0	2.46
	2B	T. Sizemore	439	.264	2	38	222	342	14	68	5.2	.976	R. Wise	35	269	16	16	0	3.11
	SS	D. Maxvill	276	.221	1	23	145	243	8	56	4.2	.980	R. Cleveland	33	231	14	15	0	3.94
	3B	J. Torre	544	.289	11	81	102	182	11	17	2.5	.963	A. Santorini	30	134	8	11	0	4.11
	RF	L. Melendez	332	.238	5	28	206	5	9	0	2.1	.959	S. Spinks	16	118	5	5	0	2.67
	CF	J. Cruz	332	.235	2	23	220	9	5	**5**	2.3	.979	D. Segui	33	56	3	1	9	3.07
	LF	L. Brock	621	.311	3	42	253	6	**13**	1	1.8	.952							
	C	T. Simmons	594	.303	16	96	**842**	**78**	8	6	6.9	.991							
	OF	B. Carbo	302	.258	7	34	162	15*	6	3	2.0	.967							
	UT	E. Crosby	276	.217	0	19	130	197	10	42		.970							
Mon. W-70 L-86 Gene Mauch	1B	M. Jorgensen	372	.231	13	47	757	56	4	66	10.8	.995	B. Stoneman	36	251	12	14	0	2.98
	2B	R. Hunt	443	.253	0	18	257	353	11	61	5.1	.982	M. Torrez	34	243	16	12	0	3.33
	SS	T. Foli	540	.241	2	35	**281**	487	27	94	5.4	.966	C. Morton	27	172	7	13	0	3.92
	3B	B. Bailey	489	.233	16	57	83	250	22	21	2.6	.938	E. McAnally	29	170	6	15	0	3.81
	RF	K. Singleton	507	.274	14	50	236	9	7	3	1.8	.972	B. Moore	22	148	9	9	0	3.47
	CF	B. Day	386	.233	0	30	225	7	5	3	2.0	.979	M. Marshall	**65**	116	14	8	18	1.78
	LF	R. Fairly	446	.278	17	68	125	8	2	2	1.9	.985	S. Renko	30	97	1	10	0	5.20
	C	J. Boccabella	207	.227	1	10	316	33	6	6	4.9	.983							
	CO	T. McCarver	239	.251	5	20	312	24	4	2		.988							
	OF	R. Woods	221	.258	10	31	110	2	1	0	1.5	.991							
	C	T. Humphrey	215	.186	1	9	322	37	5	4	5.6	.986							
	2B	H. Torres	181	.155	2	7	86	132	8	28	3.8	.965							
	OF	C. Mashore	176	.227	3	23	80	3	1	0	1.1	.988							
Phi. W-59 L-97 Frank Lucchesi W-26 L-50 Paul Owens W-33 L-47	1B	T. Hutton	381	.260	4	38	555	36	5	46	6.9	.992	S. Carlton	41	**346**	**27**	10	0	**1.97**
	2B	D. Doyle	442	.249	1	26	265	288	10	66	4.7	.982	K. Reynolds	33	154	2	15	0	4.26
	SS	L. Bowa	579	.250	1	31	212	494	9	88	4.7	**.987**	W. Twitchell	49	140	5	9	1	4.06
	3B	D. Money	536	.222	15	52	**139**	316	10	**31**	3.1	**.978**	B. Champion	30	133	4	14	0	5.09
	RF	B. Robinson	188	.239	8	21	109	2	2	1	1.6	.982	W. Fryman	23	120	4	10	1	4.36
	CF	W. Montanez	531	.247	13	64	318	**15**	5	2	2.6	.985	D. Brandon	42	104	7	7	2	3.45
	LF	G. Luzinski	563	.281	18	68	255	9	11	2	1.9	.960	B. Lersch	36	101	4	6	0	3.04
	C	J. Bateman	252	.222	3	17	447	38	14*	6	6.2	.972	D. Selma	46	99	2	9	3	5.56
	1B	D. Johnson	230	.213	9	31	479	24	9	43	8.3	.982							
	2B	T. Harmon	218	.284	2	13	106	136	1	31	4.9	.996							

West

	POS	Player	AB	BA	HR	RBI	PO	A	E	DP	TC/G	FA	Pitcher	G	IP	W	L	SV	ERA
Cin. W-95 L-59 Sparky Anderson	1B	T. Perez	515	.283	21	90	1207	68	9	111	9.4	.993	J. Billingham	36	218	12	12	1	3.18
	2B	J. Morgan	552	.292	16	73	**370**	436	8	92	5.5	**.990**	R. Grimsley	30	198	14	8	1	3.05
	SS	D. Concepcion	378	.209	2	29	194	365	18	75	5.1	.969	G. Nolan	25	176	15	5	0	1.99
	3B	D. Menke	447	.233	9	50	85	258	16	20	2.8	.955	McGlothlin	31	145	9	8	0	3.91
	RF	C. Geronimo	255	.275	4	29	150	10	3	1	1.5	.982	D. Gullett	31	135	9	10	2	3.94
	CF	B. Tolan	604	.283	8	82	**401**	9	4	3	2.8	.990	W. Simpson	24	130	8	5	0	4.14
	LF	P. Rose	**645**	.307	6	57	330	15	2	2	2.3	.994	T. Hall	47	124	10	1	8	2.61
	C	J. Bench	538	.270	40	125	742	56	6	9	6.2	.993	P. Borbon	62	122	8	3	11	3.17
	SS	D. Chaney	196	.250	2	19	83	149	9	24	3.8	.963	C. Carroll	**65**	96	6	4	**37**	2.25
	1O	J. Hague	138	.246	4	20	196	9	0	13		1.000							
	O3	H. McRae	97	.278	5	26	16	14	6	1		.833							
Hou. W-84 L-69 Harry Walker W-67 L-54 Salty Parker W-1 L-0 Leo Durocher W-16 L-15	1B	L. May	592	.284	29	98	**1318**	76	6	**133**	9.6	.996	D. Wilson	33	228	15	10	0	2.68
	2B	T. Helms	518	.259	5	60	353	**441**	17	**115**	**5.8**	.979	L. Dierker	31	215	15	8	0	3.40
	SS	R. Metzger	641	.222	2	38	238	504	22	**101**	5.0	.971	J. Reuss	33	192	9	13	1	4.17
	3B	D. Rader	553	.237	22	90	119	**340**	20	31	3.2	.958	D. Roberts	35	192	12	7	2	4.50
	RF	J. Wynn	542	.273	24	90	284	8	5	2	2.1	.983	K. Forsch	30	156	6	8	0	3.91
	CF	C. Cedeno	559	.320	22	82	345	9	7	1	2.6	.981	G. Culver	45	97	6	2	3	3.05
	LF	B. Watson	548	.312	16	86	218	6	5	0	1.6	.978	T. Griffin	39	94	5	4	3	3.24
	C	J. Edwards	332	.268	5	40	645	41	8	8	6.6	.988	J. Ray	54	90	10	9	8	4.30

POS	Player	AB	BA	HR	RBI	PO	A	E	DP	TC/G	FA	Pitcher	G	IP	W	L	SV	ERA
L. A. W-85 L-70 Walter Alston																		
1B	W. Parker	427	.279	4	59	1074	68	4	91	9.6	.997	D. Sutton	33	273	19	9	0	2.08
2B	L. Lacy	243	.259	0	12	125	161	8	38	5.1	.973	C. Osteen	33	252	20	11	0	2.64
SS	B. Russell	434	.272	4	34	197	439	34	69	5.5	.949	A. Downing	31	203	9	9	0	2.98
3B	S. Garvey	294	.269	9	30	71	187	28	18	3.4	.902	T. John	29	187	11	5	0	2.89
RF	F. Robinson	342	.251	19	59	168	6	6	2	1.9	.967	B. Singer	26	169	6	16	0	3.67
CF	W. Davis	615	.289	19	79	373	10	5	1	2.7	.987	J. Brewer	51	78	8	7	17	1.26
LF	M. Mota	371	.323	5	48	141	3	1	1	1.5	.993	P. Mikkelsen	33	58	5	5	5	4.06
C	C. Cannizzaro	200	.240	2	18	312	26	6	4	4.8	.983	P. Richert	37	52	2	3	6	2.25
UT	B. Valentine	391	.274	3	32	178	245	23	38		.948							
O1	B. Buckner	383	.319	5	37	434	22	4	28		.991							
OF	W. Crawford	243	.251	8	27	111	2	2	0	1.6	.983							
2B	J. Lefebvre	169	.201	5	24	66	82	2	21	4.5	.987							
Atl. W-70 L-84 Lum Harris W-47 L-57 Eddie Mathews W-23 L-27																		
1B	H. Aaron	449	.265	34	77	968	66	14	75	9.6	.987	P. Niekro	38	282	16	12	0	3.06
2B	F. Millan	498	.257	1	38	273	339	8	67	5.2	.987	R. Reed	31	213	11	15	0	3.93
SS	M. Perez	479	.228	1	28	220	378	27	73	4.4	.957	R. Schueler	37	145	5	8	2	3.66
3B	D. Evans	418	.254	19	71	126	273	25	20	3.4	.941	T. Kelley	27	116	5	7	0	4.58
RF	M. Lum	369	.228	9	38	241	4	6	1	2.3	.976	G. Stone	31	111	6	11	1	5.51
CF	D. Baker	446	.321	17	76	344	8	4	1	2.9	.989	P. Jarvis	37	99	11	7	2	4.09
LF	R. Garr	554	.325	12	53	246	8	10	1	2.0	.962	C. Upshaw	42	54	3	5	13	3.67
C	E. Williams	565	.258	28	87	584	49	13	7	5.6	.980							
OF	R. Carty	271	.277	6	29	139	3	3	1	1.9	.979							
OF	O. Brown	164	.226	3	16	82	7	10	2	1.7	.899							
S. F. W-69 L-86 Charlie Fox																		
1B	W. McCovey	263	.213	14	35	617	32	9	52	8.9	.986	R. Bryant	35	214	14	7	0	2.90
2B	T. Fuentes	572	.264	7	53	361	417	29	89	5.3	.964	J. Barr	44	179	8	10	2	2.87
SS	C. Speier	562	.269	15	71	243	517	20	69	5.2	.974	J. Marichal	25	165	6	16	0	3.71
3B	A. Gallagher	233	.223	2	18	64	120	5	7	2.7	.974	S. McDowell	28	164	10	8	0	4.34
RF	B. Bonds	626	.259	26	80	345	8	8	3	2.4	.978	S. Stone	27	124	6	8	0	2.98
CF	G. Maddox	458	.266	12	58	279	7	6	3	2.4	.979	D. Carrithers	25	90	4	8	1	5.80
LF	K. Henderson	439	.257	18	51	247	14	7	3	2.2	.974	J. Willoughby	11	88	6	4	0	2.35
C	D. Rader	459	.259	6	41	661	45	11	7	5.6	.985	J. Johnson	48	73	8	6	8	4.44
UT	D. Kingman	472	.225	29	83	496	159	22	49		.968	R. Moffitt	40	71	1	5	4	3.68
1B	E. Goodson	150	.280	6	30	299	27	3	28	7.8	.991	D. McMahon	44	63	3	3	5	3.71
S. D. W-58 L-95 Preston Gomez W-4 L-7 Don Zimmer W-54 L-88																		
1B	N. Colbert	563	.250	38	111	1290	103	6	119	9.3	.996	S. Arlin	38	250	10	21	0	3.60
2B	D. Thomas	500	.230	5	36	197	239	15	52	5.4	.967	C. Kirby	34	239	12	14	0	3.13
SS	E. Hernandez	329	.195	1	15	169	319	19	59	4.7	.963	F. Norman	42	212	9	11	2	3.44
3B	D. Roberts	418	.244	5	33	62	166	17	20	2.9	.931	M. Caldwell	42	164	7	11	2	4.01
RF	C. Gaston	379	.269	7	44	158	10	4	3	1.8	.977	M. Corkins	47	140	6	9	6	3.54
CF	J. Morales	347	.239	4	18	214	8	3	2	2.3	.987	B. Greif	34	125	5	16	2	5.60
LF	L. Lee	370	.300	12	47	186	6	5	2	2.1	.975	G. Ross	60	92	4	3	3	2.45
C	F. Kendall	273	.216	6	18	504	41	3	11	6.7	.995							
OF	J. Jeter	326	.221	7	21	222	1	3	0	2.5	.987							
OF	L. Stahl	297	.226	7	20	139	4	2	1	1.9	.986							
23	G. Jestadt	256	.246	6	22	104	131	13	27		.948							

BATTING AND BASE RUNNING LEADERS

Batting Average
B. Williams, CHI	.333
R. Garr, ATL	.325
C. Cedeno, HOU	.320
B. Watson, HOU	.312
A. Oliver, PIT	.312

Slugging Average
B. Williams, CHI	.606
W. Stargell, PIT	.558
J. Bench, CIN	.541
C. Cedeno, HOU	.537
H. Aaron, ATL	.514

Home Runs
J. Bench, CIN	40
N. Colbert, SD	38
B. Williams, CHI	37
H. Aaron, ATL	34
W. Stargell, PIT	33

Total Bases
B. Williams, CHI	348
C. Cedeno, HOU	300
J. Bench, CIN	291
L. May, HOU	290
N. Colbert, SD	286

Runs Batted In
J. Bench, CIN	125
B. Williams, CHI	122
W. Stargell, PIT	112
N. Colbert, SD	111
L. May, HOU	98

Stolen Bases
L. Brock, STL	63
J. Morgan, CIN	58
C. Cedeno, HOU	55
B. Bonds, SF	44
B. Tolan, CIN	42

Hits
P. Rose, CIN	198
L. Brock, STL	193
B. Williams, CHI	191

Base on Balls
J. Morgan, CIN	115
J. Wynn, HOU	103
J. Bench, CIN	100

Home Run Percentage
H. Aaron, ATL	7.6
J. Bench, CIN	7.4
N. Colbert, SD	6.7

Runs Scored
J. Morgan, CIN	122
B. Bonds, SF	118
J. Wynn, HOU	117

PITCHING LEADERS

Winning Percentage
G. Nolan, CIN	.750
S. Carlton, PHI	.730
M. Pappas, CHI	.708
S. Blass, PIT	.704
D. Ellis, PIT	.682

Earned Run Average
S. Carlton, PHI	1.97
G. Nolan, CIN	1.99
D. Sutton, LA	2.08
J. Matlack, NY	2.32
B. Gibson, STL	2.46

Wins
S. Carlton, PHI	27
T. Seaver, NY	21
C. Osteen, LA	20
F. Jenkins, CHI	20

Saves
C. Carroll, CIN	37
T. McGraw, NY	27
D. Giusti, PIT	22
M. Marshall, MON	18
J. Brewer, LA	17
J. Aker, CHI	17

Strikeouts
S. Carlton, PHI	310
T. Seaver, NY	249
B. Gibson, STL	208
D. Sutton, LA	207
F. Jenkins, CHI	184

Complete Games
S. Carlton, PHI	30
B. Gibson, STL	23
F. Jenkins, CHI	23
R. Wise, STL	20
D. Sutton, LA	18

Fewest Hits per 9 Innings
D. Sutton, LA	6.14
S. Carlton, PHI	6.68
B. Gibson, STL	7.32

Shutouts
D. Sutton, LA	9
S. Carlton, PHI	8
F. Norman, SD	6

Fewest Walks per 9 Innings
M. Pappas, CHI	1.34
G. Nolan, CIN	1.53
P. Niekro, ATL	1.69

Most Strikeouts per 9 Inn.
T. Seaver, NY	8.55
J. Reuss, HOU	8.16
J. Koosman, NY	8.12

BATTING AND BASE RUNNING LEADERS   **PITCHING LEADERS**

Doubles		Triples		Innings		Games Pitched	
W. Montanez, PHI	39	L. Bowa, PHI	13	S. Carlton, PHI	346	M. Marshall, MON	65
C. Cedeno, HOU	39	P. Rose, CIN	11	F. Jenkins, CHI	289	C. Carroll, CIN	65
T. Simmons, STL	36			P. Niekro, ATL	282	P. Borbon, CIN	62
B. Williams, CHI	34					G. Ross, SD	60

	W	L	PCT	GB	R	OR	2B	3B	Batting HR	BA	SA	SB	E	Fielding DP	FA	CG	BB	Pitching SO	ShO	SV	ERA
EAST																					
PIT	96	59	.619		691	512	251	47	110	.274	.397	49	136	171	.978	39	433	838	15	48	2.81
CHI	85	70	.548	11	685	567	206	40	133	.257	.387	69	132	148	.979	54	421	824	19	32	3.22
NY	83	73	.532	13.5	528	578	175	31	105	.225	.332	41	116	122	.980	32	486	1059	12	41	3.27
STL	75	81	.481	21.5	568	600	214	42	70	.260	.355	104	141	146	.977	64	531	912	13	13	3.42
MON	70	86	.449	26.5	513	609	156	22	91	.234	.325	68	134	141	.978	39	579	888	11	23	3.60
PHI	59	97	.378	37.5	503	635	200	36	98	.236	.344	42	116	142	.981	43	536	927	13	15	3.67
WEST																					
CIN	95	59	.617		707	557	214	44	124	.251	.380	140	110	143	.982	25	435	806	15	60	3.21
HOU	84	69	.549	10.5	708	636	233	38	134	.258	.393	111	116	151	.980	38	498	971	14	31	3.77
LA	85	70	.548	10.5	584	527	178	39	98	.256	.360	82	162	145	.974	50	429	856	23	29	2.78
ATL	70	84	.455	25	628	730	186	17	144	.258	.382	47	156	130	.974	40	512	732	4	27	4.27
SF	69	86	.445	26.5	662	649	211	36	150	.244	.384	123	156	121	.974	44	507	771	8	23	3.70
SD	58	95	.379	36.5	488	665	168	38	102	.227	.332	78	144	146	.976	39	618	960	17	19	3.78
					7265	7265	2392	430	1359	.248	.365	954	1619	1706	.978	507	5985	10544	164	361	3.46

American League 1972

	POS	Player	AB	BA	HR	RBI	PO	A	E	DP	TC/G	FA	Pitcher	G	IP	W	L	SV	ERA

East

Det.
W-86 L-70
Billy Martin

	POS	Player	AB	BA	HR	RBI	PO	A	E	DP	TC/G	FA	Pitcher	G	IP	W	L	SV	ERA
	1B	N. Cash	440	.259	22	61	1060	70	8	102	8.5	.993	M. Lolich	41	327	22	14	0	2.50
	2B	D. McAuliffe	408	.240	8	30	266	249	13	63	4.6	.975	J. Coleman	40	280	19	14	0	2.80
	SS	E. Brinkman	516	.203	6	49	233	495	7	81	4.7	.990	T. Timmerman	34	150	8	10	0	2.88
	3B	A. Rodriguez	601	.236	13	56	150	348	16	33	3.4	.969	W. Fryman	16	114	10	3	0	2.05
	RF	J. Northrup	426	.261	8	42	215	8	5	2	1.8	.978	C. Seelbach	61	112	9	8	14	2.89
	CF	M. Stanley	435	.234	14	55	309	9	2	1	2.3	.994	F. Scherman	57	94	7	3	12	3.64
	LF	W. Horton	333	.231	11	36	131	6	0	0	1.4	1.000	B. Slayback	23	82	5	6	0	3.18
	C	B. Freehan	374	.262	10	56	648	57	8	9	6.8	.989							
	OF	A. Kaline	278	.313	10	32	111	5	1	0	1.4	.991							
	OF	G. Brown	252	.230	10	31	122	5	3	1	1.8	.977							
	2B	T. Taylor	228	.303	1	20	121	108	8	25	3.5	.966							

Bos.
W-85 L-70
Eddie Kasko

	POS	Player	AB	BA	HR	RBI	PO	A	E	DP	TC/G	FA	Pitcher	G	IP	W	L	SV	ERA
	1B	D. Cater	317	.237	8	39	656	61	5	65	8.0	.993	M. Pattin	38	253	17	13	0	3.24
	2B	D. Griffin	470	.260	2	35	321	331	15	81	5.2	.978	S. Siebert	32	196	12	12	0	3.81
	SS	L. Aparicio	436	.257	3	39	183	304	16	54	4.6	.968	L. Tiant	43	179	15	6	3	1.91
	3B	R. Petrocelli	521	.240	15	75	146	278	13	38	3.0	.970	J. Curtis	26	154	11	8	0	3.74
	RF	R. Smith	467	.270	21	74	247	8	5	2	2.0	.981	L. McGlothen	22	145	8	7	0	3.41
	CF	T. Harper	556	.254	14	49	321	4	5	4	2.3	.985	R. Culp	16	105	5	8	0	4.46
	LF	Yastrzemski	455	.264	12	68	141	10	4	1	1.9	.994	B. Lee	47	84	7	4	5	3.21
	C	C. Fisk	457	.293	22	61	846	72	15	10	7.1	.984	D. Newhauser	31	37	4	2	4	2.43
	OF	B. Oglivie	253	.241	8	30	98	5	2	2	1.6	.981							
	UT	J. Kennedy	212	.245	2	22	110	141	13	34		.951							

Bal.
W-80 L-74
Earl Weaver

	POS	Player	AB	BA	HR	RBI	PO	A	E	DP	TC/G	FA	Pitcher	G	IP	W	L	SV	ERA
	1B	B. Powell	465	.252	21	81	1116	70	15	111	9.0	.988	J. Palmer	36	274	21	10	0	2.07
	2B	D. Johnson	376	.221	5	32	286	307	6	81	5.2	.990	P. Dobson	38	268	16	18	0	2.65
	SS	M. Belanger	285	.186	2	16	180	285	12	53	4.5	.975	M. Cuellar	35	248	18	12	0	2.58
	3B	B. Robinson	556	.250	8	64	129	333	11	27	3.1	.977	D. McNally	36	241	13	17	0	2.95
	RF	M. Rettenmund	301	.233	6	21	174	6	2	2	1.9	.989	D. Alexander	35	106	6	8	2	2.46
	CF	P. Blair	477	.233	8	49	337	10	3	1	2.5	.991	R. Harrison	39	94	3	4	4	2.30
	LF	D. Buford	408	.206	5	22	173	6	2	1	1.7	.975	E. Watt	38	46	2	3	7	2.15
	C	J. Oates	253	.261	4	21	391	31	2	4	5.2	.995	G. Jackson	32	41	1	1	8	2.63
	UT	B. Grich	460	.278	12	50	299	338	20	81		.970							
	OF	D. Baylor	320	.253	11	38	152	2	4	0	1.9	.975							
	OF	T. Crowley	247	.231	11	29	95	2	1	1	1.4	.990							
	C	Etchebarren	188	.202	2	21	334	22	3	2	5.1	.992							

	POS	Player	AB	BA	HR	RBI	PO	A	E	DP	TC/G	FA	Pitcher	G	IP	W	L	SV	ERA
N. Y. W-79 L-76 Ralph Houk	1B	R. Blomberg	299	.268	14	49	813	32	13	88	9.0	.985	Stottlemyre	36	260	14	18	0	3.22
	2B	H. Clarke	547	.241	3	37	347	399	11	104	5.3	.985	F. Peterson	35	250	17	15	0	3.24
	SS	G. Michael	391	.233	1	32	218	437	21	89	5.6	.969	S. Kline	32	236	16	9	0	2.40
	3B	C. Sanchez	250	.248	0	22	47	167	14	13	3.4	.939	M. Kekich	29	175	10	13	0	3.70
	RF	J. Callison	275	.258	9	34	127	4	1	1	1.8	.992	S. Lyle	59	108	9	5	35	1.92
	CF	B. Murcer	585	.292	33	96	382	11	3	1	2.6	.992	R. Gardner	20	97	8	5	0	3.06
	LF	R. White	556	.270	10	54	323	8	2	1	2.1	.994							
	C	T. Munson	511	.280	7	46	575	71	15	11	5.0	.977							
	1B	F. Alou	324	.278	6	37	648	54	7	69	7.5	.990							
	32	B. Allen	220	.227	9	21	75	132	9	26		.958							
	OF	R. Torres	199	.211	3	13	86	4	2	0	1.5	.978							
	C	J. Ellis	136	.294	5	25	127	11	5	1	5.7	.965							
Cle. W-72 L-84 Ken Aspromonte	1B	C. Chambliss	466	.292	6	44	1109	56	8	109	9.9	.993	G. Perry	41	343	24	16	1	1.92
	2B	J. Brohamer	527	.233	5	35	285	393	16	87	5.3	.977	D. Tidrow	39	237	14	15	0	2.77
	SS	F. Duffy	385	.239	3	27	197	360	13	75	4.5	.977	M. Wilcox	32	156	7	14	0	3.40
	3B	G. Nettles	557	.253	17	70	114	358	21	27	3.3	.957	R. Lamb	34	108	5	6	0	3.08
	RF	B. Bell	466	.255	9	36	274	10	3	4	2.3	.990	S. Dunning	16	105	6	4	0	3.26
	CF	D. Unser	383	.238	1	17	248	10	3	1	2.2	.989	P. Hennigan	38	67	5	3	6	2.69
	LF	A. Johnson	356	.239	8	37	145	4	7	1	1.6	.955	E. Farmer	46	61	2	5	7	4.43
	C	R. Fosse	457	.241	10	41	713	70	12	9	6.4	.985	S. Mingori	41	57	0	6	10	3.95
	O1	T. McCraw	391	.258	7	33	504	28	3	29		.994							
	2S	E. Leon	225	.200	4	16	103	179	6	39		.979							
	OF	J. Lowenstein	151	.212	6	21	77	7	0	3	1.4	1.000							
Mil. W-65 L-91 Dave Bristol W-10 L-20 Roy McMillan W-1 L-1 Del Crandall W-54 L-70	1B	G. Scott	578	.266	20	88	1210	73	10	106	9.3	.992	J. Lonborg	33	223	14	12	1	2.83
	2B	R. Theobald	391	.220	1	19	193	299	6	68	4.4	.988	B. Parsons	33	214	13	13	0	3.91
	SS	R. Auerbach	554	.218	2	30	256	452	30	90	4.8	.959	S. Lockwood	29	170	8	15	0	3.60
	3B	M. Ferraro	381	.255	2	29	93	174	14	16	2.4	.950	J. Colborn	39	148	7	7	0	3.10
	RF	J. Lahoud	316	.237	12	34	189	2	5	0	2.0	.974	K. Brett	26	133	7	12	0	4.53
	CF	D. May	500	.238	9	45	376	9	6	3	2.8	.985	G. Ryerson	20	102	3	8	0	3.62
	LF	J. Briggs	418	.266	21	65	194	6	4	1	1.9	.980	K. Sanders	62	92	2	9	17	3.13
	C	E. Rodriguez	355	.285	2	35	542	54	10	6	5.3	.983	F. Linzy	47	77	2	2	12	3.04
	UT	B. Heise	271	.266	0	12	125	170	6	31		.980							
	OF	B. Conigliaro	191	.230	7	16	120	5	1	2	2.5	.992							
	OF	O. Brown	179	.279	3	25	116	8	1	3	2.2	.992							

West

	POS	Player	AB	BA	HR	RBI	PO	A	E	DP	TC/G	FA	Pitcher	G	IP	W	L	SV	ERA
Oak. W-93 L-62 Dick Williams	1B	M. Epstein	455	.270	26	70	1111	73	12	101	8.7	.990	C. Hunter	38	295	21	7	0	2.04
	2B	T. Cullen	142	.261	0	15	103	117	11	24	3.6	.952	K. Holtzman	39	265	19	11	0	2.51
	SS	B. Campaneris	625	.240	8	32	283	494	18	93	5.4	.977	B. Odom	31	194	15	6	0	2.51
	3B	S. Bando	535	.236	15	77	123	337	19	29	3.2	.960	V. Blue	25	151	6	10	0	2.80
	RF	R. Jackson	499	.265	25	75	301	5	9	5	2.3	.971	R. Fingers	65	111	11	9	21	2.51
	CF	A. Mangual	272	.246	5	32	166	4	5	2	2.4	.971	D. Hamilton	25	101	6	6	0	2.94
	LF	J. Rudi	593	.305	19	75	247	9	2	1	1.8	.994	B. Locker	56	78	6	1	10	2.65
	C	D. Duncan	403	.218	19	59	661	43	5	9	6.3	.993	D. Knowles	54	66	5	1	11	1.36
	C	G. Tenace	227	.225	5	32	266	18	6	1	5.9	.979							
Chi. W-87 L-67 Chuck Tanner	1B	R. Allen	506	.308	37	113	1234	67	7	94	9.1	.995	W. Wood	49	377	24	17	0	2.51
	2B	M. Andrews	505	.220	7	50	354	325	19	69	4.8	.973	T. Bradley	40	260	15	14	0	2.98
	SS	R. Morales	287	.206	2	20	120	213	11	32	4.0	.968	S. Bahnsen	43	252	21	16	0	3.60
	3B	E. Spiezio	277	.238	2	22	67	172	12	11	3.4	.952	T. Forster	62	100	6	5	29	2.25
	RF	P. Kelly	402	.261	5	24	173	8	6	3	1.7	.968	D. Lemonds	31	95	4	7	0	2.95
	CF	R. Reichardt	291	.251	8	43	157	2	3	1	1.8	.981	G. Gossage	36	80	7	1	2	4.28
	LF	C. May	523	.308	12	68	215	13	4	2	1.6	.983							
	C	E. Herrmann	354	.249	10	40	641	69	8	10	6.4	.989							
	OF	J. Johnstone	261	.188	4	17	154	5	2	1	1.7	.988							
	SS	L. Alvarado	254	.213	4	29	98	213	14	28	4.0	.957							
	OF	W. Williams	221	.249	2	11	93	6	1	2	1.8	.990							
	3B	B. Melton	208	.245	7	30	47	125	12	12	3.3	.935							
Min. W-77 L-77 Billy Rigney W-36 L-34 Frank Quilici W-41 L-43	1B	H. Killebrew	433	.231	26	74	995	99	9	82	8.5	.992	B. Blyleven	39	287	17	17	0	2.73
	2B	R. Carew	535	.318	0	51	331	378	16	85	5.2	.957	D. Woodson	36	252	14	14	0	2.71
	SS	D. Thompson	573	.276	4	48	247	468	32	76	5.2	.957	J. Perry	35	218	13	16	0	3.34
	3B	E. Soderholm	287	.188	13	39	66	163	14	17	3.1	.942	R. Corbin	31	162	8	9	0	2.61
	RF	C. Tovar	548	.265	2	31	287	10	5	2	2.2	.983	J. Kaat	15	113	10	2	0	2.07
	CF	B. Darwin	513	.267	22	80	289	8	6	1	2.1	.980	D. LaRoche	62	95	5	7	10	2.84
	LF	S. Brye	253	.241	0	12	170	9	1	1	1.9	.994	W. Granger	63	90	4	6	19	3.00
	C	G. Borgmann	175	.234	3	14	304	31	12	4	6.2	.965							
	UT	S. Braun	402	.289	2	50	110	207	13	26		.961							
	OF	J. Nettles	235	.204	4	15	156	5	3	1	2.1	.982							
	1B	R. Reese	197	.218	5	26	392	33	5	55	4.4	.988							
	C	G. Mitterwald	163	.184	1	8	272	33	5	4	5.1	.984							

		POS	Player	AB	BA	HR	RBI	PO	A	E	DP	TC/G	FA	Pitcher	G	IP	W	L	SV	ERA
K. C.		1B	J. Mayberry	503	.298	25	100	**1338**	82	7	**141**	9.8	.995	D. Drago	34	239	12	17	0	3.01
W-76 L-78		2B	C. Rojas	487	.261	3	53	265	360	9	82	4.8	.986	P. Splittorff	35	216	12	12	0	3.13
Bob Lemon		SS	F. Patek	518	.212	0	32	230	**510**	22	**113**	5.6	.971	R. Nelson	34	173	11	6	2	2.08
		3B	P. Schaal	435	.228	6	41	77	245	18	16	2.8	.947	Dal Canton	35	132	6	6	2	3.41
		RF	R. Scheinblum	450	.300	8	66	215	6	8	2	1.9	.965	M. Hedlund	29	113	5	7	0	4.78
		CF	A. Otis	540	.293	11	54	351	6	3	3	2.6	.992	A. Fitzmorris	38	101	2	5	3	3.74
		LF	L. Piniella	574	.312	11	72	275	8	7	2	1.9	.976	J. Rooker	18	72	5	6	0	4.38
		C	Kirkpatrick	364	.275	9	43	590	49	6	5	6.0	.991	T. Abernathy	45	58	3	4	5	1.71
		OF	S. Hovley	196	.270	3	24	103	6	2	0	1.6	.982	T. Burgmeier	51	55	6	2	9	4.25
Cal.		1B	B. Oliver	509	.269	19	70	1079	54	7	93	9.0	.994	N. Ryan	39	284	19	16	0	2.28
W-75 L-80		2B	S. Alomar	610	.239	1	25	350	388	17	92	4.9	.977	C. Wright	35	251	18	11	0	2.98
Del Rice		SS	L. Cardenas	551	.223	6	42	241	471	22	82	4.9	.970	R. May	35	205	12	11	1	2.94
		3B	K. McMullen	472	.269	9	34	89	267	11	26	2.7	.970	Messersmith	25	170	8	11	2	2.81
		RF	L. Stanton	402	.251	12	39	225	6	4	2	1.9	.983	R. Clark	26	110	4	9	1	4.50
		CF	K. Berry	409	.289	5	39	272	**13**	0	**5**	2.5	**1.000**	L. Allen	42	85	3	7	5	3.49
		LF	V. Pinson	484	.275	7	49	205	11	2	3	1.6	.991	E. Fisher	43	81	4	5	4	3.76
		C	A. Kusnyer	179	.207	2	13	362	33	10	3	6.4	.975	S. Barber	34	58	4	4	2	2.02
		1O	J. Spencer	212	.222	1	14	289	23	3	25		.990							
Tex.		1B	F. Howard	287	.244	9	31	441	27	9	39	7.2	.981	P. Broberg	39	176	5	12	1	4.30
W-54 L-100		2B	L. Randle	249	.193	2	21	151	166	16	38	5.1	.952	D. Bosman	29	173	8	10	0	3.64
Ted Williams		SS	T. Harrah	374	.259	1	31	166	308	20	64	4.7	.960	R. Hand	30	171	10	14	0	3.32
		3B	D. Nelson	499	.226	2	28	107	222	19	25	2.9	.945	M. Paul	49	162	8	9	1	2.17
		RF	T. Ford	429	.235	14	50	242	11	6	2	2.2	.977	B. Gogolewski	36	151	4	11	2	4.23
		CF	E. Maddox	294	.252	0	10	199	7	2	4	2.2	.990	D. Stanhouse	24	105	2	9	0	3.77
		LF	J. Lovitto	330	.224	1	19	233	7	6	2	2.4	.976	P. Lindblad	66	100	5	8	9	2.61
		C	D. Billings	469	.254	5	58	478	45	10	13	5.8	.981	J. Panther	58	94	5	9	0	4.12
		01	L. Biittner	382	.259	3	31	503	41	8	37		.986	H. Pina	60	76	2	7	15	3.20
		1B	D. Mincher	191	.236	6	39	467	44	3	45	8.7	.994	C. Cox	35	65	3	5	4	4.41
		2B	V. Harris	186	.140	0	10	110	132	10	29	4.3	.960							

BATTING AND BASE RUNNING LEADERS

Batting Average

R. Carew, MIN	.318
L. Piniella, KC	.312
R. Allen, CHI	.308
C. May, CHI	.308
J. Rudi, OAK	.305

Slugging Average

R. Allen, CHI	.603
C. Fisk, BOS	.538
B. Murcer, NY	.537
J. Mayberry, KC	.507
M. Epstein, OAK	.490

Home Runs

R. Allen, CHI	37
B. Murcer, NY	33
H. Killebrew, MIN	26
M. Epstein, OAK	26
R. Jackson, OAK	25
J. Mayberry, KC	25

Total Bases

B. Murcer, NY	314
R. Allen, CHI	305
J. Rudi, OAK	288
J. Mayberry, KC	255
L. Piniella, KC	253

Runs Batted In

R. Allen, CHI	113
J. Mayberry, KC	100
B. Murcer, NY	96
G. Scott, MIL	88
B. Powell, BAL	81

Stolen Bases

B. Campaneris, OAK	52
D. Nelson, TEX	51
F. Patek, KC	33
P. Kelly, CHI	32
A. Otis, KC	28

Hits

J. Rudi, OAK	181
L. Piniella, KC	179
B. Murcer, NY	171

Base on Balls

R. Allen, CHI	99
R. White, NY	99
H. Killebrew, MIN	94
C. May, CHI	79

Home Run Percentage

R. Allen, CHI	7.3
H. Killebrew, MIN	6.0
M. Epstein, OAK	5.7

Runs Scored

B. Murcer, NY	102
J. Rudi, OAK	94
T. Harper, BOS	92

Doubles

L. Piniella, KC	33
J. Rudi, OAK	32
B. Murcer, NY	30

Triples

C. Fisk, BOS	9
J. Rudi, OAK	9
P. Blair, BAL	8

PITCHING LEADERS

Winning Percentage

C. Hunter, OAK	.750
B. Odom, OAK	.714
L. Tiant, BOS	.714
J. Palmer, BAL	.677
S. Kline, NY	.640

Earned Run Average

L. Tiant, BOS	1.91
G. Perry, CLE	1.92
C. Hunter, OAK	2.04
J. Palmer, BAL	2.07
R. Nelson, KC	2.08

Wins

G. Perry, CLE	24
W. Wood, CHI	24
M. Lolich, DET	22
C. Hunter, OAK	21
J. Palmer, BAL	21
S. Bahnsen, CHI	21

Saves

S. Lyle, NY	35
T. Forster, CHI	29
R. Fingers, OAK	21
W. Granger, MIN	19
K. Sanders, MIL	17

Strikeouts

N. Ryan, CAL	329
M. Lolich, DET	250
G. Perry, CLE	234
B. Blyleven, MIN	228
J. Coleman, DET	222

Complete Games

G. Perry, CLE	29
M. Lolich, DET	23
N. Ryan, CAL	20
W. Wood, CHI	20
J. Palmer, BAL	18

Fewest Hits per 9 Innings

N. Ryan, CAL	5.26
C. Hunter, OAK	6.10
R. Nelson, KC	6.23

Shutouts

N. Ryan, CAL	9
W. Wood, CHI	8
Stottlemyre, NY	7

Fewest Walks per 9 Innings

F. Peterson, NY	1.58
R. Nelson, KC	1.61
S. Kline, NY	1.68

Most Strikeouts per 9 Inn.

N. Ryan, CAL	10.43
Messersmith, CAL	7.52
R. May, CAL	7.42

Innings

W. Wood, CHI	377
G. Perry, CLE	343
M. Lolich, DET	327

Games Pitched

P. Lindblad, TEX	66
R. Fingers, OAK	65
W. Granger, MIN	63

	W	L	PCT	GB	R	OR	2B	3B	Batting HR	BA	SA	SB	E	Fielding DP	FA	CG	BB	Pitching SO	ShO	SV	ERA
EAST																					
DET	86	70	.551		558	514	179	32	122	.237	.356	17	**96**	137	**.984**	46	465	952	11	33	2.96
BOS	85	70	.548	.5	**640**	620	**229**	**34**	124	.248	**.376**	66	130	141	.978	48	512	918	20	25	3.47
BAL	80	74	.519	5	519	**430**	193	29	100	.229	.339	78	100	150	.983	**62**	**395**	788	20	21	**2.54**
NY	79	76	.510	6.5	557	527	201	24	103	.249	.357	71	134	**179**	.978	35	419	625	19	39	3.05
CLE	72	84	.462	14	472	519	187	18	91	.234	.330	49	116	157	.981	47	534	846	13	25	2.97
MIL	65	91	.417	21	493	595	167	22	88	.235	.328	64	139	145	.977	37	486	740	14	32	3.45
WEST																					
OAK	93	62	.600		604	457	195	29	**134**	.240	.366	87	130	146	.979	42	418	862	**23**	**43**	2.58
CHI	87	67	.565	5.5	566	538	170	28	108	.238	.346	100	135	136	.977	36	431	936	14	42	3.12
MIN	77	77	.500	15.5	537	535	182	31	93	.244	.344	53	159	133	.974	37	444	838	17	34	2.86
KC	76	78	.494	16.5	580	545	220	26	78	**.255**	.353	85	120	164	.980	44	405	801	16	28	3.24
CAL	75	80	.484	18	454	533	171	26	78	.242	.330	57	114	135	.981	57	620	**1000**	18	16	3.06
TEX	54	100	.351	38.5	461	628	166	17	56	.217	.290	**126**	166	147	.972	11	613	868	8	34	3.53
					6441	6441	2260	316	1175	.239	.343	853	1539	1770	.979	502	5742	10174	193	372	3.07

National League 1973

POS	Player	AB	BA	HR	RBI	PO	A	E	DP	TC/G	FA	Pitcher	G	IP	W	L	SV	ERA

East

N. Y. — W-82 L-79 — Yogi Berra

POS	Player	AB	BA	HR	RBI	PO	A	E	DP	TC/G	FA	Pitcher	G	IP	W	L	SV	ERA
1B	J. Milner	451	.239	23	72	771	47	9	66	8.7	.989	T. Seaver	36	290	19	10	0	**2.08**
2B	F. Millan	638	.290	3	37	410	411	9	99	5.4	.989	J. Koosman	35	263	14	15	0	2.84
SS	B. Harrelson	356	.258	0	20	153	315	10	49	4.6	.979	J. Matlack	34	242	14	16	0	3.20
3B	W. Garrett	504	.256	16	58	80	280	22	36	2.9	.942	G. Stone	27	148	12	3	1	2.80
RF	R. Staub	585	.279	15	76	297	17	7	5	2.1	.978	T. McGraw	60	119	5	6	25	3.87
CF	D. Hahn	262	.229	2	21	176	2	2	0	2.1	.989	R. Sadecki	31	117	5	4	1	3.39
LF	C. Jones	339	.260	11	48	168	6	6	0	2.0	.967	H. Parker	38	97	8	4	5	3.35
C	J. Grote	285	.256	1	32	545	34	3	0	7.2	.995	J. McAndrew	23	80	3	8	1	5.38
1O	E. Kranepool	284	.239	1	35	448	28	2	39		.996	B. Capra	24	42	2	7	4	3.86
UT	T. Martinez	263	.255	1	14	119	139	12	15		.956							
OF	W. Mays	209	.211	6	25	103	2	1	0	2.4	.991							
C	D. Dyer	189	.185	1	9	308	26	2	7	5.6	.994							

St. L. — W-81 L-81 — Red Schoendienst

POS	Player	AB	BA	HR	RBI	PO	A	E	DP	TC/G	FA	Pitcher	G	IP	W	L	SV	ERA
1B	J. Torre	519	.287	13	69	833	60	6	80	7.9	.993	R. Wise	35	259	16	12	0	3.37
2B	T. Sizemore	521	.282	1	54	312	463	15	83	**5.7**	.981	R. Cleveland	32	224	14	10	0	3.01
SS	M. Tyson	469	.243	1	33	202	352	**33**	68	4.6	.944	A. Foster	35	204	13	9	0	3.14
3B	K. Reitz	426	.235	6	42	85	211	8	19	2.3	**.974**	B. Gibson	25	195	12	10	0	2.77
RF	L. Melendez	341	.267	2	35	196	8	2	4	2.2	.990	D. Segui	65	100	7	6	17	2.78
CF	J. Cruz	406	.227	10	57	276	2	6	1	2.4	.977	T. Murphy	19	89	3	7	0	3.76
LF	L. Brock	650	.297	7	63	310	3	12	1	2.0	.963	R. Folkers	34	82	4	4	3	3.61
C	T. Simmons	619	.310	13	91	**888**	74	13	13	6.4	.987	O. Pena	42	62	4	4	6	2.18
1B	T. McCarver	331	.266	3	49	545	30	8	47	7.6	.986	A. Hrabosky	44	56	2	4	5	2.09
OF	J. Carbo	308	.286	8	40	171	11	4	3	2.0	.978	W. Granger	33	47	2	4	5	4.24

Pit. — W-80 L-82 — Bill Virdon — Danny Murtaugh W-67 L-69 — W-13 L-13

POS	Player	AB	BA	HR	RBI	PO	A	E	DP	TC/G	FA	Pitcher	G	IP	W	L	SV	ERA
1B	B. Robertson	397	.239	14	40	957	79	5	91	9.7	**.995**	N. Briles	33	219	14	13	0	2.84
2B	D. Cash	436	.271	2	31	227	276	11	46	5.6	.979	B. Moose	33	201	12	13	0	3.53
SS	D. Maxvill	217	.189	0	17	105	234	10	46	4.7	.971	D. Ellis	28	192	12	14	0	3.05
3B	R. Hebner	509	.271	25	74	92	260	23	19	2.7	.939	J. Rooker	41	170	10	6	5	2.85
RF	R. Zisk	333	.324	10	54	139	12	2	4	1.8	.987	L. Walker	37	122	7	12	1	4.65
CF	A. Oliver	654	.292	20	99	238	5	9	0	2.3	.964	D. Giusti	67	99	9	2	20	2.37
LF	W. Stargell	522	.299	**44**	119	261	14	7	1	2.0	.975	B. Johnson	50	92	4	2	4	3.62
C	M. Sanguillen	589	.282	12	65	493	35	9	9	6.0	.983	R. Hernandez	59	90	4	5	11	2.41
2S	R. Stennett	466	.242	10	55	277	348	14	84		.978	S. Blass	23	89	3	9	0	9.85
OF	G. Clines	304	.263	1	23	145	6	5	0	2.0	.968							
C	M. May	283	.269	7	31	402	36	12	4	5.7	.973							

Mon. — W-79 L-83 — Gene Mauch

POS	Player	AB	BA	HR	RBI	PO	A	E	DP	TC/G	FA	Pitcher	G	IP	W	L	SV	ERA
1B	M. Jorgensen	413	.230	9	47	990	80	5	88	8.7	**.995**	S. Renko	36	250	15	11	1	2.81
2B	R. Hunt	401	.309	0	18	219	280	9	54	5.0	.982	M. Torrez	35	208	9	12	0	4.46
SS	T. Foli	458	.240	2	36	245	396	27	84	**5.4**	.960	M. Marshall	**92**	179	14	11	**31**	2.66
3B	B. Bailey	513	.273	26	86	93	275	17	25	2.6	.956	B. Moore	35	176	7	16	0	4.49
RF	K. Singleton	560	.302	23	103	278	20	5	3	1.9	.983	E. McAnally	27	147	7	9	0	4.04
CF	R. Woods	318	.230	3	31	208	7	5	1	1.9	.977	S. Rogers	17	134	10	5	0	1.54
LF	R. Fairly	413	.298	17	49	182	4	5	0	1.6	.974	B. Stoneman	29	97	4	8	1	6.80
C	J. Boccabella	403	.233	7	46	610	65	14	10	5.9	.980	T. Walker	54	92	7	5	4	3.63
1B	H. Breeden	258	.275	15	43	515	45	5	50	8.6	.991							
S2	P. Frias	225	.231	0	22	120	211	15	46		.957							
OF	B. Day	207	.275	4	28	86	2	0	0	1.7	1.000							

POS	Player	AB	BA	HR	RBI	PO	A	E	DP	TC/G	FA	Pitcher	G	IP	W	L	SV	ERA
Chi. W-77 L-84 Whitey Lockman																		
1B	J. Hickman	201	.244	3	20	398	31	5	37	8.5	.988	F. Jenkins	38	271	14	16	0	3.89
2B	G. Beckert	372	.255	0	29	163	262	7	50	4.9	.984	B. Hooton	42	240	14	17	0	3.68
SS	D. Kessinger	577	.262	0	43	274	526	30	109	5.3	.964	R. Reuschel	36	237	14	15	0	3.00
3B	R. Santo	536	.267	20	77	107	271	20	17	2.7	.950	M. Pappas	30	162	7	12	0	4.28
RF	J. Cardenal	522	.303	11	68	234	13	5	2	1.8	.980	B. Bonham	44	152	7	5	6	3.02
CF	R. Monday	554	.267	26	56	317	9	9	2	2.3	.973	B. Locker	63	106	10	6	18	2.55
LF	B. Williams	576	.288	20	86	253	14	4	1	2.0	.985	J. Aker	47	64	4	5	12	4.08
C	R. Hundley	368	.226	10	43	648	59	5	7	5.8	.993							
2B	P. Popovich	280	.236	2	24	171	247	8	53	5.1	.981							
C	K. Rudolph	170	.206	2	17	259	28	9	4	4.6	.970							
UT	C. Fanzone	150	.273	6	22	193	41	8	13		.967							
1B	P. Bourque	139	.209	7	20	327	35	5	32	9.7	.986							
Phi. W-71 L-91 Danny Ozark																		
1B	W. Montanez	552	.263	11	65	785	52	5	87	8.5	.994	S. Carlton	40	**293**	13	**20**	0	3.90
2B	D. Doyle	370	.273	3	26	231	296	14	71	4.7	.974	W. Twitchell	34	223	13	9	0	2.50
SS	L. Bowa	446	.211	0	23	191	361	12	87	4.6	.979	K. Brett	31	212	13	9	0	3.44
3B	M. Schmidt	367	.196	18	52	101	251	17	30	3.0	.954	J. Lonborg	38	199	13	16	0	4.88
RF	B. Robinson	452	.288	25	65	227	8	5	1	2.1	.979	D. Ruthven	25	128	6	9	1	4.21
CF	D. Unser	440	.289	11	52	329	14	4	4	2.6	.988	B. Lersch	42	98	3	6	1	4.39
LF	G. Luzinski	610	.285	29	97	262	7	2	1	1.7	**.993**	M. Scarce	52	71	1	8	12	2.42
C	B. Boone	521	.261	10	61	868	**89**	10	16	6.7	.990							
UT	C. Tovar	328	.268	1	21	113	113	12	32		.950							
1B	T. Hutton	247	.263	5	29	527	43	1	61	8.0	.998							
OF	M. Anderson	193	.254	9	28	99	4	2	1	1.6	.981							

West

POS	Player	AB	BA	HR	RBI	PO	A	E	DP	TC/G	FA	Pitcher	G	IP	W	L	SV	ERA
Cin. W-99 L-63 Sparky Anderson																		
1B	T. Perez	564	.314	27	101	**1318**	85	**13**	**131**	9.4	.991	J. Billingham	40	**293**	19	10	0	3.04
2B	J. Morgan	576	.290	26	82	417	440	9	**106**	5.6	.990	R. Grimsley	38	242	13	10	1	3.23
SS	D. Concepcion	328	.287	8	46	165	292	12	56	5.3	.974	D. Gullett	45	228	18	8	2	3.51
3B	D. Menke	241	.191	3	26	68	189	9	19	2.2	.966	F. Norman	24	166	12	6	0	3.30
RF	C. Geronimo	324	.210	4	33	243	9	2	2	2.0	.992	P. Borbon	80	121	11	4	14	2.15
CF	B. Tolan	457	.206	9	51	279	9	10	1	2.5	.966	T. Hall	54	104	8	5	8	3.47
LF	P. Rose	**680**	**.338**	5	64	343	15	3	0	2.3	.992	C. Carroll	53	93	8	8	14	3.69
C	J. Bench	557	.253	25	104	693	61	4	7	5.7	.995							
3B	D. Driessen	366	.301	4	47	62	150	12	19	2.6	.946							
SS	D. Chaney	227	.181	0	14	103	216	12	44	4.4	.964							
OF	A. Kosco	118	.280	9	21	50	1	0	0	1.4	1.000							
L. A. W-95 L-66 Walter Alston																		
1B	B. Buckner	575	.275	8	46	888	50	2	93	10.1	.998	D. Sutton	33	256	18	10	0	2.42
2B	D. Lopes	535	.275	6	37	319	379	11	90	5.3	.984	Messersmith	33	250	14	10	0	2.70
SS	B. Russell	615	.265	4	56	243	**560**	31	106	5.1	.963	C. Osteen	33	237	16	11	0	3.31
3B	R. Cey	507	.245	15	80	111	**328**	18	**39**	3.1	.961	T. John	36	218	16	7	0	3.10
RF	W. Crawford	457	.295	14	66	250	13	6	4	1.9	.978	A. Downing	30	193	9	9	0	3.31
CF	W. Davis	599	.285	16	77	344	6	7	0	2.4	.980	C. Hough	37	72	4	2	5	2.76
LF	M. Mota	293	.314	0	23	96	4	0	0	1.4	1.000	J. Brewer	56	72	6	8	20	3.01
C	J. Ferguson	487	.263	25	88	757	57	3	17	6.7	**.996**	P. Richert	39	51	3	3	7	3.18
1B	S. Garvey	349	.304	8	50	718	26	5	58	9.9	.993	G. Culver	28	42	4	4	2	3.00
OF	T. Paciorek	195	.262	5	18	92	2	2	0	1.2	.979							
S. F. W-88 L-74 Charlie Fox																		
1B	W. McCovey	383	.266	29	75	930	76	12	89	8.7	.988	R. Bryant	41	270	**24**	12	0	3.54
2B	T. Fuentes	656	.277	6	63	386	478	6	102	5.4	.963	J. Barr	41	231	11	17	2	3.82
SS	C. Speier	542	.249	11	71	255	470	33	92	5.1	.956	T. Bradley	35	224	13	12	0	3.90
3B	E. Goodson	384	.302	12	53	64	171	23	13	2.8	.911	J. Marichal	34	209	11	15	0	3.79
RF	B. Bonds	643	.283	39	96	346	12	11	5	2.3	.974	J. Willoughby	39	123	4	5	1	4.70
CF	G. Maddox	587	.319	11	76	370	4	**12**	0	2.8	.969	E. Sosa	71	107	10	4	18	3.28
LF	G. Matthews	540	.300	12	58	277	11	5	0	2.0	.983	R. Moffitt	60	100	4	4	14	2.43
C	D. Rader	462	.229	9	41	701	48	7	5	5.1	.991	D. McMahon	22	30	4	0	6	1.50
31	D. Kingman	305	.203	24	55	313	146	22	30		.954							
1O	G. Thomasson	235	.285	4	30	312	15	6	15		.982							
Hou. W-82 L-80 Leo Durocher																		
1B	L. May	545	.270	28	105	1220	78	9	112	9.1	.993	J. Reuss	41	279	16	13	0	3.74
2B	T. Helms	543	.287	4	61	325	438	9	104	5.3	.988	D. Roberts	39	249	17	11	0	2.85
SS	R. Metzger	580	.250	1	35	231	429	12	83	4.5	**.982**	D. Wilson	37	239	11	16	2	3.20
3B	D. Rader	574	.254	21	89	134	296	**25**	24	3.0	.945	K. Forsch	46	201	9	12	4	4.20
RF	J. Wynn	481	.220	20	55	270	9	4	1	2.1	.986	T. Griffin	25	100	4	6	0	4.15
CF	C. Cedeno	525	.320	25	70	357	10	7	2	2.8	.981	J. Crawford	48	70	2	4	6	4.50
LF	B. Watson	573	.312	16	94	271	8	9	0	2.0	.984	J. Ray	42	69	6	4	6	4.43
C	S. Jutze	278	.223	0	18	450	31	8	4	5.7	.984	J. York	41	53	3	4	6	4.42
C	J. Edwards	250	.244	5	27	435	22	5	3	6.1	.989							
OF	T. Agee	204	.235	8	15	114	2	2	2	1.8	.983							

	POS	Player	AB	BA	HR	RBI	PO	A	E	DP	TC/G	FA	Pitcher	G	IP	W	L	SV	ERA
Atl. W-76 L-85 Eddie Mathews	1B	M. Lum	513	.294	16	82	707	42	7	64	9.0	.991	C. Morton	38	256	15	10	0	3.41
	2B	D. Johnson	559	.270	43	99	383	464	30	106	5.7	.966	P. Niekro	42	245	13	10	4	3.31
	SS	M. Perez	501	.250	8	57	215	416	25	78	4.7	.962	R. Schueler	39	186	8	7	2	3.86
	3B	D. Evans	595	.281	41	104	124	325	22	33	3.2	.953	R. Harrison	38	177	11	8	5	4.16
	RF	H. Aaron	392	.301	40	96	206	5	5	0	2.1	.977	R. Reed	20	116	4	11	1	4.42
	CF	D. Baker	604	.288	21	99	390	10	7	1	2.6	.983	G. Gentry	16	87	4	6	1	3.41
	LF	R. Garr	668	.299	11	55	293	9	10	2	2.1	.968	T. House	52	67	4	2	4	4.70
	C	J. Oates	322	.248	4	27	409	57	9	6	5.5	.981	P. Dobson	12	58	3	7	0	4.97
	C	P. Casanova	236	.216	7	18	330	48	9	3	5.0	.977	D. Frisella	42	45	1	2	8	4.20
	OS	S. Jackson	206	.209	0	12	93	89	6	10		.968							
	1B	F. Tepedino	148	.304	4	29	331	28	3	30	6.2	.992							
	1C	D. Dietz	139	.295	3	24	325	29	6	19		.983							
S. D. W-60 L-102 Don Zimmer	1B	N. Colbert	529	.270	22	80	1300	98	11	124	9.8	.992	B. Greif	36	199	10	17	1	3.21
	2B	R. Morales	244	.164	0	16	176	239	5	45	5.3	.988	C. Kirby	34	192	8	18	0	4.79
	SS	D. Thomas	404	.238	0	16	115	227	32	39	5.1	.914	S. Arlin	34	180	11	14	0	5.10
	3B	D. Roberts	479	.286	21	64	77	245	20	25	3.1	.942	R. Troedson	50	152	7	9	1	4.25
	RF	C. Gaston	476	.250	16	57	198	16	12	4	1.9	.947	M. Caldwell	55	149	5	14	10	3.74
	CF	J. Grubb	389	.311	8	37	229	11	3	1	2.4	.988	R. Jones	20	140	7	6	0	3.16
	LF	J. Morales	388	.281	9	34	214	5	2	1	2.2	.991	M. Corkins	47	122	5	8	3	4.50
	C	F. Kendall	507	.282	10	59	749	64	13	7	6.0	.984	V. Romo	49	88	2	3	7	3.70
	OF	L. Lee	333	.237	3	30	154	7	5	0	2.0	.970							
	SS	E. Hernandez	247	.223	0	9	106	190	7	42	4.5	.977							
	32	D. Hilton	234	.197	5	16	79	141	6	19		.973							
	O1	I. Murrell	210	.229	9	21	249	16	5	14		.981							
	OF	G. Locklear	154	.240	3	25	77	2	4	0	2.2	.952							

BATTING AND BASE RUNNING LEADERS

Batting Average

P. Rose, CIN	.338
C. Cedeno, HOU	.320
G. Maddox, SF	.319
T. Perez, CIN	.314
B. Watson, HOU	.312

Slugging Average

W. Stargell, PIT	.646
D. Evans, ATL	.556
D. Johnson, ATL	.546
C. Cedeno, HOU	.537
B. Bonds, SF	.530

Home Runs

W. Stargell, PIT	44
D. Johnson, ATL	43
D. Evans, ATL	41
H. Aaron, ATL	40
B. Bonds, SF	39

Total Bases

B. Bonds, SF	341
W. Stargell, PIT	337
D. Evans, ATL	331
D. Johnson, ATL	305
A. Oliver, PIT	303

Runs Batted In

W. Stargell, PIT	119
L. May, HOU	105
J. Bench, CIN	104
D. Evans, ATL	104
K. Singleton, MON	103

Stolen Bases

L. Brock, STL	70
J. Morgan, CIN	67
C. Cedeno, HOU	56
B. Bonds, SF	43
D. Lopes, LA	36

Hits

P. Rose, CIN	230
R. Garr, ATL	200
L. Brock, STL	193

Base on Balls

D. Evans, ATL	124
K. Singleton, MON	123
J. Morgan, CIN	111

Home Run Percentage

W. Stargell, PIT	8.4
D. Johnson, ATL	7.7
D. Evans, ATL	6.9

Runs Scored

B. Bonds, SF	131
J. Morgan, CIN	116
P. Rose, CIN	115

Doubles

W. Stargell, PIT	43
A. Oliver, PIT	38

Triples

R. Metzger, HOU	14
G. Matthews, SF	10
G. Maddox, SF	10
W. Davis, LA	9

PITCHING LEADERS

Winning Percentage

T. John, LA	.696
D. Gullett, CIN	.692
R. Bryant, SF	.667
T. Seaver, NY	.655
J. Billingham, CIN	.655

Earned Run Average

T. Seaver, NY	2.08
D. Sutton, LA	2.42
W. Twitchell, PHI	2.50
M. Marshall, MON	2.66
Messersmith, LA	2.70

Wins

R. Bryant, SF	24
T. Seaver, NY	19
J. Billingham, CIN	19
D. Gullett, CIN	18
D. Sutton, LA	18

Saves

M. Marshall, MON	31
T. McGraw, NY	25
D. Giusti, PIT	20
J. Brewer, LA	20
B. Locker, CHI	18
E. Sosa, SF	18

Strikeouts

T. Seaver, NY	251
S. Carlton, PHI	223
J. Matlack, NY	205
D. Sutton, LA	200
Messersmith, LA	177
J. Reuss, HOU	177

Complete Games

T. Seaver, NY	18
S. Carlton, PHI	18
J. Billingham, CIN	16
D. Sutton, LA	14
R. Wise, STL	14
J. Matlack, NY	14

Fewest Hits per 9 Innings

T. Seaver, NY	6.80
D. Sutton, LA	6.88
W. Twitchell, PHI	6.93

Shutouts

J. Billingham, CIN	7
D. Roberts, HOU	6
W. Twitchell, PHI	5
R. Wise, STL	5

Fewest Walks per 9 Innings

J. Marichal, SF	1.59
F. Jenkins, CHI	1.89
J. Barr, SF	1.91

Most Strikeouts per 9 Inn.

T. Seaver, NY	7.79
B. Moore, MON	7.71
J. Matlack, NY	7.62

Innings

S. Carlton, PHI	293
J. Billingham, CIN	293
T. Seaver, NY	290

Games Pitched

M. Marshall, MON	92
P. Borbon, CIN	80
E. Sosa, SF	71

	W	L	PCT	GB	R	OR	Batting 2B	3B	HR	BA	SA	SB	Fielding E	DP	FA	CG	BB	Pitching SO	ShO	SV	ERA
EAST																					
NY	82	79	.509		608	588	198	24	85	.246	.338	27	126	140	.980	47	490	**1027**	15	40	3.27
STL	81	81	.500	1.5	643	603	240	35	75	.259	.357	100	159	149	.975	42	486	867	14	36	3.25
PIT	80	82	.494	2.5	704	693	**257**	44	154	.261	.405	23	151	156	.976	26	564	839	11	**44**	3.74
MON	79	83	.488	3.5	668	702	190	23	125	.251	.364	77	163	156	.974	26	681	866	6	38	3.73
CHI	77	84	.478	5	614	655	201	21	117	.247	.357	65	157	155	.975	27	**438**	885	13	40	3.66
PHI	71	91	.438	11.5	642	717	218	29	134	.249	.371	51	134	**179**	.979	**49**	632	919	11	22	4.00
WEST																					
CIN	99	63	.611		741	621	232	34	137	.254	.383	**148**	115	162	**.982**	39	518	801	**17**	43	3.43
LA	95	66	.590	3.5	675	**565**	219	29	110	.263	.371	109	125	166	.981	45	461	961	15	38	**3.00**
SF	88	74	.543	11	739	702	212	**52**	161	.262	.407	112	163	138	.974	33	485	787	8	**44**	3.79
HOU	82	80	.506	17	681	672	216	35	134	.251	.376	92	116	140	.981	45	575	907	14	26	3.78
ATL	76	85	.472	22.5	**799**	774	219	34	**206**	**.266**	**.427**	84	166	142	.974	34	575	803	9	35	4.25
SD	60	102	.370	39	548	770	198	26	112	.244	.351	88	170	152	.973	34	548	845	10	23	4.16
					8062	8062	2600	386	1550	.254	.376	976	1745	1835	.977	447	6453	10507	143	429	3.67

American League 1973

POS	Player	AB	BA	HR	RBI	PO	A	E	DP	TC/G	FA	Pitcher	G	IP	W	L	SV	ERA

East

Bal.
W-97 L-65
Earl Weaver

POS	Player	AB	BA	HR	RBI	PO	A	E	DP	TC/G	FA	Pitcher	G	IP	W	L	SV	ERA
1B	B. Powell	370	.265	11	54	988	77	12	95	9.7	.989	J. Palmer	38	296	22	9	1	**2.40**
2B	B. Grich	581	.251	12	50	**431**	**509**	5	**130**	**5.8**	**.995**	M. Cuellar	38	267	18	13	0	3.27
SS	M. Belanger	470	.226	0	27	241	**530**	23	100	5.2	.971	D. McNally	38	266	17	17	0	3.21
3B	B. Robinson	549	.257	9	72	129	354	15	25	3.2	.970	D. Alexander	29	175	12	8	0	3.86
RF	R. Coggins	389	.319	7	41	220	6	3	3	2.3	.987	B. Reynolds	42	111	7	5	9	1.95
CF	P. Blair	500	.280	10	64	369	14	4	4	2.7	.990	J. Jefferson	18	101	6	5	0	4.10
LF	D. Baylor	405	.286	11	51	204	5	4	0	1.9	.981	G. Jackson	45	80	8	0	9	1.90
C	E. Williams	459	.237	22	83	407	33	6	5	4.7	.987	E. Watt	30	71	3	4	5	3.30
DH	T. Davis	552	.306	7	89					.0								
OF	A. Bumbry	356	.337	7	34	134	2	3	0	1.6	.978							
OF	M. Rettenmund	321	.262	9	44	196	4	3	1	2.3	.985							
C	Etchebarren	152	.257	2	23	201	14	2	5	4.3	.991							

Bos.
W-89 L-73
Eddie Kasko

POS	Player	AB	BA	HR	RBI	PO	A	E	DP	TC/G	FA	Pitcher	G	IP	W	L	SV	ERA
1B	Yastrzemski	540	.296	19	95	912	56	6	85	9.1	.994	B. Lee	38	285	17	11	1	2.75
2B	D. Griffin	396	.255	1	33	294	284	6	77	5.2	.990	L. Tiant	35	272	20	13	0	3.34
SS	L. Aparicio	499	.271	0	49	190	404	21	68	4.7	.966	J. Curtis	35	221	13	13	0	3.58
3B	R. Petrocelli	356	.244	13	45	73	224	6	22	3.1	.980	M. Pattin	34	219	15	15	1	4.31
RF	R. Smith	423	.303	21	69	275	8	5	1	2.8	.983	R. Moret	30	156	13	2	3	3.17
CF	R. Miller	441	.261	6	43	301	4	7	1	2.3	.978	B. Bolin	39	53	3	4	15	2.70
LF	T. Harper	566	.281	17	71	251	13	4	2	1.9	.985	B. Veale	32	36	2	3	11	3.47
C	C. Fisk	508	.246	26	71	**739**	50	**14**	8	6.1	.983							
DH	O. Cepeda	550	.289	20	86					.0								
OF	D. Evans	282	.223	10	32	178	4	1	0	1.6	.995							
S2	M. Guerrero	219	.233	0	11	106	183	8	49		.973							
13	D. Cater	195	.313	1	24	303	56	6	45		.984							
C	B. Montgomery	128	.320	7	25	168	19	5	2	5.8	.974							

Det.
W-85 L-77
Billy Martin
W-76 L-67
Joe Schultz
W-9 L-10

POS	Player	AB	BA	HR	RBI	PO	A	E	DP	TC/G	FA	Pitcher	G	IP	W	L	SV	ERA
1B	N. Cash	363	.262	19	40	856	64	8	72	8.1	.991	M. Lolich	42	309	16	15	0	3.82
2B	D. McAuliffe	343	.274	12	47	217	265	7	62	4.8	.986	J. Coleman	40	288	23	15	0	3.53
SS	E. Brinkman	515	.237	7	40	249	480	24	89	4.6	.968	J. Perry	35	203	14	13	0	4.03
3B	A. Rodriguez	555	.222	9	58	135	335	14	30	3.0	.971	W. Fryman	34	170	6	13	0	5.36
RF	J. Northrup	404	.307	12	44	207	6	4	2	1.9	.982	J. Hiller	65	125	10	5	38	1.44
CF	M. Stanley	602	.244	17	57	420	10	3	3	2.8	.993							
LF	W. Horton	411	.316	17	53	160	2	10	0	1.6	.942							
C	B. Freehan	380	.234	6	29	584	50	3	3	6.5	**.995**							
DH	G. Brown	377	.236	12	50					.0								
O1	A. Kaline	310	.255	10	45	347	13	1	32		.997							
2B	T. Taylor	275	.229	5	24	134	165	4	37	4.2	.987							
C	D. Sims	252	.242	8	30	375	39	9	7	6.2	.979							
DH	F. Howard	227	.256	12	29					.0								
OF	D. Sharon	178	.242	7	16	124	5	4	1	1.5	.970							

N. Y.
W-80 L-82
Ralph Houk

POS	Player	AB	BA	HR	RBI	PO	A	E	DP	TC/G	FA	Pitcher	G	IP	W	L	SV	ERA
1B	F. Alou	280	.236	4	27	467	30	6	43	7.5	.988	Stottlemyre	38	273	16	16	0	3.07
2B	H. Clarke	590	.263	2	35	378	442	18	107	5.7	.979	D. Medich	34	235	14	9	0	2.95
SS	G. Michael	418	.225	3	47	208	433	23	84	5.1	.965	F. Peterson	31	184	8	15	0	3.95
3B	G. Nettles	552	.234	22	81	117	**410**	26	39	**3.5**	.953	L. McDaniel	47	160	12	6	10	2.86
RF	M. Alou	497	.296	2	28	146	6	4	2	1.8	.974	P. Dobson	22	142	9	8	0	4.17
CF	B. Murcer	616	.304	22	95	380	14	6	2	2.5	.985	S. McDowell	16	96	5	8	0	3.95
LF	R. White	**639**	.246	18	60	339	4	8	0	2.2	.977	S. Lyle	51	82	5	9	27	2.51
C	T. Munson	519	.301	20	74	673	**80**	12	**11**	5.4	.984	S. Kline	14	74	4	7	0	4.01
DH	J. Hart	339	.254	13	52					.0								
O1	M. Alou	497	.296	2	28	522	26	12	46		.979							
1B	R. Blomberg	301	.329	12	57	359	28	8	38		.980							

	POS	Player	AB	BA	HR	RBI	PO	A	E	DP	TC/G	FA	Pitcher	G	IP	W	L	SV	ERA
Mil. W-74 L-88 Del Crandall	1B	G. Scott	604	.306	24	107	1388	118	9	144	9.6	.994	J. Colborn	43	314	20	12	1	3.18
	2B	P. Garcia	580	.245	15	54	405	470	27	111	5.6	.970	J. Slaton	38	276	13	15	0	3.71
	SS	T. Johnson	465	.213	0	32	253	381	25	88	4.9	.962	J. Bell	31	184	9	9	1	3.97
	3B	D. Money	556	.284	11	61	112	224	10	24	2.8	.971	S. Lockwood	37	155	5	12	0	3.90
	RF	B. Coluccio	438	.224	15	58	236	12	2	3	2.3	.992	B. Champion	37	136	5	8	1	3.70
	CF	D. May	624	.303	25	93	401	9	9	3	2.8	.979	E. Rodriguez	30	76	9	7	5	3.30
	LF	J. Briggs	488	.246	18	57	294	9	10	1	2.3	.968	C. Short	42	72	3	5	2	5.13
	C	D. Porter	350	.254	16	67	372	47	10	9	4.8	.977	F. Linzy	42	63	2	6	13	3.57
	DH	O. Brown	296	.280	7	32					.0								
	C	E. Rodriguez	290	.269	0	30	324	40	5	5	4.9	.986							
	OF	J. Lahoud	225	.204	5	26	85	2	0	1		1.000							
	OF	B. Mitchell	130	.223	5	20	24	0	1	0		.960							
Cle. W-71 L-91 Ken Aspromonte	1B	C. Chambliss	572	.273	11	53	1437	114	14	153	10.2	.991	G. Perry	41	344	19	19	0	3.38
	2B	J. Brohamer	300	.220	4	29	215	279	15	67	5.2	.971	D. Tidrow	42	275	14	16	0	4.42
	SS	F. Duffy	361	.263	8	50	198	377	8	82	5.1	.986	M. Wilcox	26	134	8	10	0	5.83
	3B	B. Bell	631	.268	14	59	144	363	22	44	3.4	.958	T. Timmerman	29	124	8	7	2	4.92
	RF	R. Torres	312	.205	7	28	191	9	5	1	1.8	.976	B. Strom	27	123	2	10	0	4.61
	CF	G. Hendrick	440	.268	21	61	242	7	3	1	2.3	.988	T. Hilgendorf	48	95	5	3	6	3.14
	LF	C. Spikes	506	.237	23	73	202	13	8	0	2.0	.964	J. Johnson	39	60	5	6	5	6.18
	C	D. Duncan	344	.233	17	43	533	41	7	8	6.8	.988	K. Sanders	15	27	5	1	5	1.65
	DH	O. Gamble	390	.267	20	44	0	0	0	0	.0	.000							
	CC	J. Ellis	437	.270	14	68	370	27	8	5		.980							
	OF	W. Williams	350	.289	8	38	123	7	4	0	2.2	.970							
	UT	J. Lowenstein	305	.292	6	40	124	85	7	22		.968							
	SS	L. Cardenas	195	.215	0	12	87	154	9	33	3.7	.964							
	2B	T. Ragland	183	.257	0	12	136	166	5	43	4.7	.984							

West

	POS	Player	AB	BA	HR	RBI	PO	A	E	DP	TC/G	FA	Pitcher	G	IP	W	L	SV	ERA
Oak. W-94 L-68 Dick Williams	1B	G. Tenace	510	.259	24	84	1095	61	13	104	8.7	.989	K. Holtzman	40	297	21	13	0	2.97
	2B	D. Green	332	.262	3	42	264	297	7	86	4.3	.988	V. Blue	37	264	20	9	0	3.28
	SS	B. Campaneris	601	.250	4	46	228	496	23	87	5.0	.969	C. Hunter	36	256	21	5	0	3.34
	3B	S. Bando	592	.287	29	98	126	281	22	24	2.7	.949	B. Odom	30	150	5	12	0	4.49
	RF	R. Jackson	539	.293	32	117	302	4	9	0	2.2	.971	R. Fingers	62	127	7	8	22	1.92
	CF	B. North	554	.285	5	34	429	14	9	5	3.3	.980	D. Knowles	52	99	6	8	9	3.09
	LF	J. Rudi	437	.270	12	66	231	6	2	2	2.0	.992	H. Pina	47	88	6	3	8	2.76
	C	R. Fosse	492	.256	7	52	712	63	10	5	5.6	.987	D. Hamilton	16	70	6	4	0	4.39
	DH	D. Johnson	464	.246	19	81	0	0	0	0	.0	.000							
	OF	A. Mangual	192	.224	3	13	88	2	5	0	1.9	.947							
	2B	T. Kubiak	182	.220	3	17	89	129	6	28	2.7	.973							
K. C. W-88 L-74 Jack McKeon	1B	J. Mayberry	510	.278	26	100	1457	81	9	156	10.4	.994	P. Splittorff	38	262	20	11	0	3.98
	2B	C. Rojas	551	.276	6	69	302	424	13	114	5.4	.982	S. Busby	37	238	16	15	0	4.23
	SS	F. Patek	501	.234	5	45	242	503	26	115	5.7	.966	D. Drago	37	213	12	14	0	4.23
	3B	P. Schaal	396	.288	8	42	77	237	30	14	2.8	.913	G. Garber	48	153	9	9	11	4.24
	RF	Kirkpatrick	429	.263	6	45	198	3	2	0	1.9	.990	D. Bird	54	102	4	4	20	2.99
	CF	A. Otis	583	.300	26	93	330	10	5	4	2.6	.986	Dal Canton	32	97	4	3	3	4.82
	LF	L. Piniella	513	.250	9	69	196	9	3	3	1.6	.986	A. Fitzmorris	15	89	8	3	0	2.83
	C	F. Healy	279	.276	6	34	429	43	10	4	5.2	.979	K. Wright	25	81	6	5	0	4.91
	DH	H. McRae	338	.234	9	50					.0								
	UT	K. Bevacqua	276	.257	2	40	120	90	9	20		.959							
	OF	S. Hovley	232	.254	2	24	114	4	3	1	1.5	.975							
Min. W-81 L-81 Frank Quilici	1B	J. Lis	253	.245	9	25	626	48	9	59	7.1	.987	B. Blyleven	40	325	20	17	0	2.52
	2B	R. Carew	580	.350	6	62	383	413	13	96	5.5	.984	J. Kaat	29	182	11	12	0	4.41
	SS	D. Thompson	347	.225	1	36	131	326	24	50	5.1	.950	J. Decker	29	170	10	10	0	4.17
	3B	S. Braun	361	.283	6	42	79	175	16	21	2.6	.941	R. Corbin	51	148	8	5	14	3.03
	RF	J. Holt	441	.297	11	58	193	6	2	2	2.0	.990	B. Hands	39	142	7	10	2	3.49
	CF	B. Darwin	560	.252	18	90	233	13	5	1	1.8	.980	D. Woodson	23	141	10	8	0	3.95
	LF	L. Hisle	545	.272	15	64	337	11	9	0	2.5	.975	D. Goltz	32	106	6	4	1	5.25
	C	G. Mitterwald	432	.259	16	64	676	59	6	6	6.1	.992	B. Campbell	28	52	3	3	7	3.14
	DH	T. Oliva	571	.291	16	92					.0		K. Sanders	27	44	2	4	8	6.09
	UT	J. Terrell	438	.265	1	32	170	298	18	55		.963							
	OF	S. Brye	278	.263	6	33	209	4	3	1	2.5	.986							
	1B	H. Killebrew	248	.242	5	32	431	45	1	42	8.4	.998							
Cal. W-79 L-83 Bobby Winkles	1B	M. Epstein	312	.215	8	32	710	50	5	61	8.9	.993	N. Ryan	41	326	21	16	1	2.87
	2B	S. Alomar	470	.238	0	28	243	267	11	70	4.7	.979	B. Singer	40	316	20	14	0	3.22
	SS	R. Meoli	305	.223	2	23	122	252	27	52	4.2	.933	C. Wright	37	257	11	19	0	3.68
	3B	A. Gallagher	311	.273	0	26	59	185	10	13	2.6	.961	R. May	34	185	7	17	0	4.38
	RF	L. Stanton	306	.235	8	34	160	5	6	2	1.6	.965	D. Sells	51	68	7	2	10	3.71
	CF	K. Berry	415	.284	3	36	309	5	1	0	2.4	.997							
	LF	V. Pinson	466	.260	8	57	210	11	8	2	1.9	.965							
	C	J. Torborg	255	.220	1	18	611	37	6	2	6.4	.991							
	DH	F. Robinson	534	.266	30	97	0	0	0	0	.0	.000							
	UT	B. Oliver	544	.265	18	89	396	121	11	26		.979							
	UT	T. McCraw	264	.265	3	24	268	25	1	28		.997							
	OF	R. Scheinblum	229	.328	3	21	92	3	3	0	1.8	.969							
	UT	W. Llenas	130	.269	1	25	42	37	1	3		.988							

	POS	Player	AB	BA	HR	RBI	PO	A	E	DP	TC/G	FA	Pitcher	G	IP	W	L	SV	ERA
Chi.	1B	T. Muser	309	.285	4	30	680	38	6	70	8.1	.992	W. Wood	49	359	24	20	0	3.46
W-77 L-85	2B	J. Orta	425	.266	6	40	254	300	18	75	4.7	.969	S. Bahnsen	42	282	18	21	0	3.57
Chuck Tanner	SS	E. Leon	399	.228	3	30	198	382	17	78	4.9	.972	S. Stone	36	176	6	11	1	4.24
	3B	B. Melton	560	.277	20	87	115	347	23	31	3.2	.953	T. Forster	51	173	6	11	16	3.23
	RF	P. Kelly	550	.280	1	44	254	9	6	2	1.9	.978	E. Fisher	26	111	6	7	0	4.88
	CF	J. Jeter	300	.240	7	26	144	3	7	0	2.1	.955	C. Acosta	48	97	10	6	18	2.23
	LF	B. Sharp	196	.276	4	22	146	10	3	2	2.3	.981							
	C	E. Herrmann	379	.224	10	39	617	70	11	11	6.1	.984							
	DH	C. May	553	.268	20	96					.0								
	OF	K. Henderson	262	.260	6	32	102	1	3	0		.972							
	1B	R. Allen	250	.316	16	41	597	43	4	55	9.6	.994							
	UT	J. Hairston	210	.271	0	23	194	13	5	11		.976							
	UT	L. Alvarado	203	.232	0	20	120	158	9	31		.969							
	OF	B. Bradford	168	.238	8	15	114	9	1	2	2.4	.992							
Tex.	1B	J. Spencer	352	.267	4	43	790	67	1	110	8.7	.999*	J. Bibby	26	180	9	10	1	3.24
W-57 L-105	2B	D. Nelson	576	.286	7	48	327	364	11	98	5.0	.984	J. Merritt	35	160	5	13	1	4.05
Whitey Herzog	SS	J. Mason	238	.206	3	19	113	206	18	43	4.6	.947	B. Gogolewski	49	124	3	6	6	4.22
W-47 L-91	3B	T. Harrah	461	.260	10	50	39	79	8	4	2.4	.937	P. Broberg	22	119	5	9	0	5.61
Del Wilber	RF	J. Burroughs	526	.279	30	85	304	13	8	2	2.2	.975	S. Siebert	25	120	7	11	2	3.99
W-1 L-0	CF	V. Harris	555	.249	8	44	297	5	7	1	2.7	.977	D. Clyde	18	93	4	8	0	5.01
Billy Martin	LF	L. Biittner	258	.252	1	12	91	6	2	1	1.7	.980	M. Paul	36	87	5	4	2	4.95
W-9 L-14	C	K. Suarez	278	.248	1	27	501	44	6	4	6.1	.989	J. Brown	25	67	5	5	2	3.92
	DH	A. Johnson	624	.287	8	68	0	0	0	0	.0	.000	S. Foucault	32	56	2	4	8	3.88
	OF	R. Carty	306	.232	3	33	87	2	0	0		1.000							
	C	D. Billings	280	.179	3	32	356	32	10	3	5.5	.975							
	UT	B. Sudakis	235	.255	15	43	216	62	5	21		.982							
	OF	E. Maddox	172	.238	1	17	144	7	3	1	1.7	.981							
	OF	T. Grieve	123	.309	7	21	68	0	0	0	1.2	1.000							

BATTING AND BASE RUNNING LEADERS

Batting Average

R. Carew, MIN	.350
G. Scott, MIL	.306
T. Davis, BAL	.306
B. Murcer, NY	.304
D. May, MIL	.303

Slugging Average

R. Jackson, OAK	.531
S. Bando, OAK	.498
F. Robinson, CAL	.489
G. Scott, MIL	.488
T. Munson, NY	.487

Home Runs

R. Jackson, OAK	32
J. Burroughs, TEX	30
F. Robinson, CAL	30
S. Bando, OAK	29

Total Bases

G. Scott, MIL	295
D. May, MIL	295
S. Bando, OAK	294
R. Jackson, OAK	286
B. Murcer, NY	286

Runs Batted In

R. Jackson, OAK	117
G. Scott, MIL	107
J. Mayberry, KC	100
S. Bando, OAK	98
F. Robinson, CAL	97

Stolen Bases

T. Harper, BOS	54
B. North, OAK	53
D. Nelson, TEX	43
R. Carew, MIN	41
F. Patek, KC	36

Hits

R. Carew, MIN	203
D. May, MIL	189
B. Murcer, NY	187

Base on Balls

J. Mayberry, KC	122
B. Grich, BAL	107
Yastrzemski, BOS	105

Home Run Percentage

R. Jackson, OAK	5.9
J. Burroughs, TEX	5.7
F. Robinson, CAL	5.6

Runs Scored

R. Jackson, OAK	99
B. North, OAK	98
R. Carew, MIN	98
G. Scott, MIL	98

Doubles

P. Garcia, MIL	32
S. Bando, OAK	32

Triples

A. Bumbry, BAL	11
R. Carew, MIN	11
J. Orta, CHI	10

PITCHING LEADERS

Winning Percentage

C. Hunter, OAK	.808
J. Palmer, BAL	.710
V. Blue, OAK	.690
P. Splittorff, KC	.645
J. Colborn, MIL	.625

Earned Run Average

J. Palmer, BAL	2.40
B. Blyleven, MIN	2.52
B. Lee, BOS	2.74
N. Ryan, CAL	2.87
D. Medich, NY	2.95

Wins

W. Wood, CHI	24
J. Coleman, DET	23
J. Palmer, BAL	22
C. Hunter, OAK	21
K. Holtzman, OAK	21
N. Ryan, CAL	21

Saves

J. Hiller, DET	38
S. Lyle, NY	27
R. Fingers, OAK	22
D. Bird, KC	20
C. Acosta, CHI	18

Strikeouts

N. Ryan, CAL	383
B. Blyleven, MIN	258
B. Singer, CAL	241
G. Perry, CLE	238
M. Lolich, DET	214

Complete Games

G. Perry, CLE	29
N. Ryan, CAL	26
B. Blyleven, MIN	25
L. Tiant, BOS	23
J. Colborn, MIL	22

Fewest Hits per 9 Innings

J. Bibby, TEX	6.05
N. Ryan, CAL	6.57
J. Palmer, BAL	6.84

Shutouts

B. Blyleven, MIN	9
G. Perry, CLE	7
J. Palmer, BAL	6

Fewest Walks per 9 Innings

J. Kaat, CHI, MIN	1.73
B. Blyleven, MIN	1.86
K. Holtzman, OAK	2.00

Most Strikeouts per 9 Inn.

N. Ryan, CAL	10.57
J. Bibby, TEX	7.75
B. Blyleven, MIN	7.14

Innings

W. Wood, CHI	359
G. Perry, CLE	344
N. Ryan, CAL	326

Games Pitched

J. Hiller, DET	65
R. Fingers, OAK	62
D. Bird, KC	54
D. Knowles, OAK	52

(cont'd) American League 1973

	W	L	PCT	GB	R	OR	2B	3B	HR	BA	SA	SB	E	DP	FA	CG	BB	SO	ShO	SV	ERA
							Batting						Fielding					Pitching			
EAST																					
BAL	97	65	.599		754	**561**	229	**48**	119	.266	.389	**146**	119	184	.981	67	475	715	14	26	**3.07**
BOS	89	73	.549	8	738	647	235	30	147	.267	**.401**	114	127	162	.979	67	499	808	10	33	3.65
DET	85	77	.525	12	642	674	213	32	157	.254	.390	28	**112**	144	**.982**	39	493	911	11	**46**	3.90
NY	80	82	.494	17	641	610	212	17	131	.261	.378	47	156	172	.976	47	**457**	708	16	39	3.34
MIL	74	88	.457	23	708	731	229	40	145	.253	.388	110	145	167	.977	50	623	671	11	28	3.98
CLE	71	91	.438	26	680	826	205	29	**158**	.256	.387	60	139	174	.978	55	602	883	9	21	4.58
WEST																					
OAK	94	68	.580		**758**	615	216	28	147	.260	.389	4	137	170	.978	46	494	797	16	41	3.29
KC	88	74	.543	6	755	752	239	40	114	.261	.381	105	167	**192**	.974	40	617	790	7	41	4.21
MIN	81	81	.500	13	738	692	**240**	44	120	**.270**	.393	87	139	147	.978	48	519	880	**18**	34	3.77
CAL	79	83	.488	15	629	657	183	29	93	.253	.348	59	156	153	.975	**72**	614	**1010**	13	19	3.57
CHI	77	85	.475	17	652	705	228	38	111	.256	.372	83	144	165	.977	48	574	848	15	35	3.86
TEX	57	105	.352	37	619	844	195	29	110	.255	.361	91	161	164	.974	35	680	831	10	27	4.64
					8314	8314	2624	404	1552	.259	.381	934	1702	1994	.977	614	6647	9852	150	390	3.82

National League 1974

	POS	Player	AB	BA	HR	RBI	PO	A	E	DP	TC/G	FA	Pitcher	G	IP	W	L	SV	ERA

East

Pit.
W-88 L-74
Danny Murtaugh

POS	Player	AB	BA	HR	RBI	PO	A	E	DP	TC/G	FA	Pitcher	G	IP	W	L	SV	ERA
1B	B. Robertson	236	.229	16	48	494	37	5	44	8.5	.991	J. Rooker	33	263	15	11	0	2.77
2B	R. Stennett	673	.291	7	56	441	475	19	115	6.1	.980	J. Reuss	35	260	16	11	0	3.50
SS	F. Taveras	333	.246	0	26	170	321	31	60	4.2	.941	K. Brett	27	191	13	9	0	3.30
3B	R. Hebner	550	.291	18	68	115	304	**28**	34	3.2	.937	D. Ellis	26	177	12	9	0	3.15
RF	R. Zisk	536	.313	17	100	312	9	5	3	2.3	.985	B. Kison	40	129	9	8	2	3.49
CF	A. Oliver	617	.321	11	85	284	3	4	1	3.0	.986	D. Giusti	64	106	7	5	12	3.31
LF	W. Stargell	508	.301	25	96	253	8	9	1	2.0	.967	L. Demery	19	95	6	6	0	4.26
C	M. Sanguillen	596	.287	7	68	713	76	12	8	5.3	.985							
OF	G. Clines	276	.225	0	14	177	6	2	1	2.4	.989							
1B	Kirkpatrick	271	.247	6	38	512	31	4	55	9.3	.993							
OF	D. Parker	220	.282	4	29	101	5	4	1	2.2	.964							
SS	M. Mendoza	163	.221	0	15	77	187	10	21	3.1	.964							

St. L.
W-86 L-75
Red Schoendienst

POS	Player	AB	BA	HR	RBI	PO	A	E	DP	TC/G	FA	Pitcher	G	IP	W	L	SV	ERA
1B	J. Torre	529	.282	11	70	1165	**102**	10	**144**	9.2	.992	B. Gibson	33	240	11	13	0	3.83
2B	T. Sizemore	504	.250	2	47	335	412	15	109	6.0	.980	L. McGlothen	31	237	16	12	0	2.70
SS	M. Tyson	422	.223	1	37	231	410	30	108	4.7	.955	J. Curtis	33	195	10	14	1	3.78
3B	K. Reitz	579	.271	7	54	131	278	11	29	2.8	**.974**	A. Foster	31	162	7	10	0	3.89
RF	R. Smith	517	.309	23	100	275	9	7	3	2.2	.976	S. Siebert	28	134	8	8	0	3.83
CF	B. McBride	559	.309	6	56	395	9	4	1	2.8	.990	B. Forsch	19	100	7	4	0	2.97
LF	L. Brock	635	.306	3	48	283	8	10	2	2.0	.967	R. Folkers	55	90	6	2	2	3.00
C	T. Simmons	599	.272	20	103	717	82	11	13	5.7	.986	A. Hrabosky	65	88	8	1	9	2.97
OF	J. Cruz	161	.261	5	20	76	2	2	1	1.5	.975	M. Garman	64	82	7	2	6	2.63

Phi.
W-80 L-82
Danny Ozark

POS	Player	AB	BA	HR	RBI	PO	A	E	DP	TC/G	FA	Pitcher	G	IP	W	L	SV	ERA
1B	W. Montanez	527	.304	7	79	1216	79	10	126	9.5	.992	S. Carlton	39	291	16	13	0	3.22
2B	D. Cash	**687**	.300	2	58	396	**519**	22	141	5.8	.977	J. Lonborg	39	283	17	13	0	3.21
SS	L. Bowa	669	.275	1	36	256	462	12	104	4.5	**.984**	D. Ruthven	35	213	9	13	0	4.01
3B	M. Schmidt	568	.282	**36**	116	134	**404**	26	40	3.5	.954	R. Schueler	44	203	11	16	1	3.72
RF	M. Anderson	395	.251	5	34	238	12	5	3	1.9	.980	W. Twitchell	25	112	6	9	0	5.22
CF	D. Unser	454	.264	11	61	300	13	6	0	2.4	.981	M. Scarce	58	70	3	8	5	5.01
LF	G. Luzinski	302	.272	7	48	146	10	3	0	1.9	.981							
C	B. Boone	488	.242	3	52	825	77	**22**	7	6.3	.976							
OF	B. Robinson	280	.236	5	29	162	8	5	0	2.0	.971							
1O	T. Hutton	208	.240	4	33	285	15	2	25		.993							
OF	J. Johnstone	200	.295	6	30	88	4	3	1	1.6	.968							

Mon.
W-79 L-82
Gene Mauch

POS	Player	AB	BA	HR	RBI	PO	A	E	DP	TC/G	FA	Pitcher	G	IP	W	L	SV	ERA
1B	M. Jorgensen	287	.310	11	59	606	51	1	47	7.2	.998	S. Rogers	38	254	15	**22**	0	4.46
2B	J. Cox	236	.220	2	26	148	220	12	45	5.3	.968	S. Renko	37	228	12	16	0	4.03
SS	T. Foli	441	.254	0	39	220	412	19	85	5.4	.971	M. Torrez	32	186	15	8	0	3.58
3B	R. Hunt	403	.268	0	26	37	140	11	14	2.5	.941	D. Blair	22	146	11	7	0	3.27
RF	K. Singleton	511	.276	9	74	224	7	11	0	1.7	.955	E. McAnally	25	129	6	13	0	4.47
CF	W. Davis	611	.295	12	89	369	8	**12**	1	2.6	.969	C. Taylor	61	108	6	2	11	2.17
LF	B. Bailey	507	.280	20	73	105	8	3	3	1.5	.974	T. Walker	33	92	4	5	2	3.82
C	B. Foote	420	.262	11	60	640	**83**	12	12	6.0	.984	J. Montague	46	83	3	4	3	3.14
2S	L. Lintz	319	.238	0	20	168	250	18	48		.959	D. Murray	32	70	1	1	10	1.03
1B	R. Fairly	282	.245	12	43	572	42	7	41	9.3	.989							
1B	H. Breeden	190	.247	2	20	422	31	6	43	8.2	.987							

POS	Player	AB	BA	HR	RBI	PO	A	E	DP	TC/G	FA	Pitcher	G	IP	W	L	SV	ERA
N. Y. W-71 L-91 Yogi Berra																		
1B	J. Milner	507	.252	20	63	1147	77	7	103	9.3	.994	J. Matlack	34	265	13	15	0	2.41
2B	F. Millan	518	.268	1	33	374	315	15	81	5.3	.979	J. Koosman	35	265	15	11	0	3.36
SS	B. Harrelson	331	.227	1	13	196	325	17	65	5.5	.968	T. Seaver	32	236	11	11	0	3.20
3B	W. Garrett	522	.224	13	53	111	318	20	31	3.1	.955	H. Parker	40	131	4	12	4	3.92
RF	R. Staub	561	.258	19	78	262	19	5	5	1.9	.983	B. Apodaca	35	103	6	6	3	3.50
CF	D. Hahn	323	.251	4	28	217	8	3	0	2.2	.987	R. Sadecki	34	100	8	8	0	3.48
LF	C. Jones	461	.282	13	60	220	8	7	0	2.0	.970	T. McGraw	41	89	6	11	3	4.15
C	J. Grote	319	.257	5	36	549	36	7	1	6.3	.988							
UT	T. Martinez	334	.219	2	43	164	257	20	38		.955							
OF	D. Schneck	254	.205	5	25	179	7	5	2	2.3	.974							
UT	K. Boswell	222	.216	2	15	94	113	6	18		.972							
O1	E. Kranepool	217	.300	4	24	207	9	5	18		.977							
Chi. W-66 L-96 Whitey Lockman W-41 L-52 Jim Marshall W-25 L-44																		
1B	A. Thornton	303	.261	10	46	760	70	7	61	9.3	.992	B. Bonham	44	243	11	22	1	3.85
2B	V. Harris	200	.195	0	11	122	144	16	20	5.0	.943	R. Reuschel	41	241	13	12	0	4.29
SS	D. Kessinger	599	.259	1	42	259	476	32	87	5.1	.958	B. Hooton	48	176	7	11	1	4.81
3B	B. Madlock	453	.313	9	54	84	229	18	14	2.7	.946	S. Stone	38	170	8	6	0	4.13
RF	J. Cardenal	542	.293	13	72	262	15	10	4	2.1	.965	K. Frailing	55	125	6	9	1	3.89
CF	R. Monday	538	.294	20	58	302	10	5	5	2.3	.984	D. LaRoche	49	92	5	6	5	4.79
LF	J. Morales	534	.273	15	82	266	5	7	2	1.9	.975	O. Zamora	56	84	3	9	10	3.11
C	S. Swisher	280	.214	5	27	493	50	7	8	6.1	.987	H. Pina	34	47	3	4	4	4.02
1O	B. Williams	404	.280	16	68	635	53	11	50		.984							
C	G. Mitterwald	215	.251	7	28	335	40	10	4	5.7	.974							
UT	C. Fanzone	158	.190	4	22	87	82	15	14		.918							

West

POS	Player	AB	BA	HR	RBI	PO	A	E	DP	TC/G	FA	Pitcher	G	IP	W	L	SV	ERA
L. A. W-102 L-60 Walter Alston																		
1B	S. Garvey	642	.312	21	111	**1536**	62	8	108	**10.3**	.995	Messersmith	39	292	**20**	6	0	2.59
2B	D. Lopes	530	.266	10	35	309	360	24	71	4.8	.965	D. Sutton	40	276	19	9	0	3.23
SS	B. Russell	553	.269	5	58	194	491	39	68	4.5	.946	M. Marshall	106	208	15	12	21	2.42
3B	R. Cey	577	.262	18	97	155	365	22	25	3.4	.959	D. Rau	36	198	13	11	0	3.73
RF	W. Crawford	468	.295	11	61	225	3	8	1	1.8	.966	T. John	22	153	13	3	0	2.59
CF	J. Wynn	535	.271	32	108	365	10	3	3	2.6	.992	A. Downing	21	98	5	6	0	3.67
LF	B. Buckner	580	.314	7	58	235	4	6	0	1.8	.976	C. Hough	49	96	9	4	1	3.75
C	S. Yeager	316	.266	12	41	552	58	5	4	6.6	.992							
C	J. Ferguson	349	.252	16	57	436	40	6	2	5.9	.988							
OF	T. Paciorek	175	.240	1	24	83	1	5	1	1.2	.944							
Cin. W-98 L-64 Sparky Anderson																		
1B	T. Perez	596	.265	28	101	1292	75	6	111	8.7	**.996**	D. Gullett	36	243	17	11	0	3.04
2B	J. Morgan	512	.293	22	67	344	385	13	92	5.2	.982	C. Kirby	36	231	12	9	0	3.27
SS	D. Concepcion	594	.281	14	82	239	536	30	99	5.0	.963	J. Billingham	36	212	19	11	0	3.95
3B	D. Driessen	470	.281	7	56	67	192	24	19	2.2	.915	F. Norman	35	186	13	12	0	3.15
RF	C. Geronimo	474	.281	7	54	355	13	5	2	2.6	.987	P. Borbon	73	139	10	7	14	3.24
CF	G. Foster	276	.264	7	41	172	2	2	1	1.8	.989	C. Carroll	57	101	12	5	6	2.14
LF	P. Rose	652	.284	3	51	346	11	1	3	2.2	**.997**							
C	J. Bench	621	.280	33	**129**	757	68	6	**16**	6.1	.993							
OF	K. Griffey	227	.251	2	19	115	5	0	1	1.7	1.000							
OF	M. Rettenmund	208	.216	6	28	103	3	0	0	1.5	1.000							
OF	T. Crowley	125	.240	1	20	29	1	0	0	1.4	1.000							
Atl. W-88 L-74 Eddie Mathews W-50 L-49 Clyde King W-38 L-25																		
1B	D. Johnson	454	.251	15	62	641	54	5	57	9.6	.993	P. Niekro	41	**302**	**20**	13	1	2.38
2B	M. Perez	447	.260	2	34	225	311	8	64	5.3	.985	C. Morton	38	275	16	12	0	3.14
SS	C. Robinson	452	.230	0	29	238	395	29	73	4.7	.956	B. Capra	39	217	16	8	1	**2.28**
3B	D. Evans	571	.240	25	79	**185**	367	26	**45**	**3.6**	.955	R. Reed	28	186	10	11	0	3.39
RF	D. Baker	574	.256	20	69	359	10	7	2	2.5	.981	R. Harrison	20	126	6	11	0	4.71
CF	R. Office	248	.246	3	31	171	0	1	0	1.4	.994	T. House	56	103	6	2	11	1.92
LF	R. Garr	606	**.353**	11	54	255	8	9	2	2.0	.967	M. Leon	34	75	4	7	3	2.64
C	J. Oates	291	.223	1	21	434	55	4	5	5.4	.992	D. Frisella	36	42	3	4	6	5.14
1O	M. Lum	361	.233	11	50	554	26	4	44		.993							
OF	H. Aaron	340	.268	20	69	142	3	2	0	1.7	.986							
C	V. Correll	202	.238	4	29	282	40	4	4	5.5	.988							
1B	F. Tepedino	169	.231	0	16	307	26	4	35	7.3	.988							
Hou. W-81 L-81 Preston Gomez																		
1B	L. May	556	.268	24	85	1253	88	8	116	9.3	.994	L. Dierker	33	224	11	10	0	2.89
2B	T. Helms	452	.279	5	50	308	360	10	99	5.1	**.985**	T. Griffin	34	211	14	10	0	3.54
SS	R. Metzger	572	.253	0	30	238	451	17	85	4.9	.976	D. Wilson	33	205	11	13	0	3.07
3B	D. Rader	533	.257	17	78	128	347	17	28	3.2	.965	D. Roberts	34	204	10	12	1	3.40
RF	G. Gross	589	.314	0	36	296	15	2	4	2.1	.994	C. Osteen	23	138	9	9	0	3.71
CF	C. Cedeno	610	.269	26	102	**446**	11	3	4	2.9	.993	K. Forsch	70	103	8	7	10	2.80
LF	B. Watson	524	.298	11	67	202	7	4	2	1.5	.981	M. Cosgrove	45	90	7	3	2	3.49
C	M. May	405	.289	7	54	525	63	4	10	5.1	**.993**	F. Scherman	53	61	2	5	4	4.13
C1	C. Johnson	171	.228	10	29	270	18	4	17		.986							

POS	Player	AB	BA	HR	RBI	PO	A	E	DP	TC/G	FA	Pitcher	G	IP	W	L	SV	ERA
S. F. 1B	D. Kingman	350	.223	18	55	680	60	13	66	8.3	.983	J. Barr	44	240	13	9	2	2.74
W-72 L-90 2B	T. Fuentes	390	.249	0	22	238	287	11	70	5.2	.979	J. D'Acquisto	38	215	12	14	0	3.77
Charlie Fox SS	C. Speier	501	.250	9	53	210	445	21	82	5.0	.969	M. Caldwell	31	189	14	5	0	2.95
W-34 L-42 3B	S. Ontiveros	343	.265	4	33	64	144	16	16	3.0	.929	T. Bradley	30	134	8	11	0	5.17
Wes Westrum RF	B. Bonds	567	.256	21	71	305	11	11	3	2.2	.966	R. Bryant	41	127	3	15	0	5.60
CF	G. Maddox	538	.284	8	50	345	3	5	0	2.7	.986	R. Moffitt	61	102	5	7	15	4.50
W-38 L-48 LF	G. Matthews	561	.287	16	82	281	9	9	2	2.0	.970	E. Sosa	68	101	9	7	6	3.48
C	D. Rader	323	.291	1	26	461	38	8	4	4.7	.984	C. Williams	39	100	1	3	0	2.79
OF	G. Thomasson	315	.244	2	29	149	4	3	1	2.1	.981							
1B	E. Goodson	298	.272	6	48	593	30	2	52	8.6	.997							
UT	M. Phillips	283	.219	2	20	125	195	19	33		.944							
UT	B. Miller	198	.278	0	16	55	161	12	11		.947							
2B	C. Arnold	174	.241	1	26	64	86	4	16	5.0	.974							
S. D. 1B	W. McCovey	344	.253	22	63	815	47	11	59	8.4	.987	B. Greif	43	226	9	19	1	4.66
W-60 L-102 2B	D. Thomas	523	.247	3	41	232	294	13	45	5.2	.976	D. Freisleben	33	212	9	14	0	3.65
John McNamara SS	E. Hernandez	512	.232	0	34	229	449	24	64	4.8	.966	R. Jones	40	208	8	22	2	4.46
3B	D. Roberts	318	.167	5	18	83	170	12	15	2.6	.955	D. Spillner	30	148	9	11	0	4.01
RF	D. Winfield	498	.265	20	75	276	11	12	2	2.3	.960	L. Hardy	76	102	9	4	2	4.68
CF	J. Grubb	444	.286	8	42	321	8	8	1	2.8	.976	V. Romo	54	71	5	5	9	4.56
LF	B. Tolan	357	.266	8	40	161	5	5	0	1.9	.971							
C	F. Kendall	424	.231	8	45	631	64	12	12	5.3	.983							
1O	N. Colbert	368	.207	14	54	605	52	9	43		.986							
OF	C. Gaston	267	.213	6	33	119	7	1	1	2.0	.992							
3B	D. Hilton	217	.240	1	12	51	94	8	13	2.8	.948							
2B	G. Beckert	172	.256	0	7	70	80	10	16	4.4	.938							

BATTING AND BASE RUNNING LEADERS

Batting Average
R. Garr, ATL	.353
A. Oliver, PIT	.321
G. Gross, HOU	.314
B. Buckner, LA	.314
R. Zisk, PIT	.313

Slugging Average
M. Schmidt, PHI	.546
W. Stargell, PIT	.537
R. Smith, STL	.528
J. Bench, CIN	.507
R. Garr, ATL	.503

Home Runs
M. Schmidt, PHI	36
J. Bench, CIN	33
J. Wynn, LA	32
T. Perez, CIN	28
C. Cedeno, HOU	26

Total Bases
J. Bench, CIN	315
M. Schmidt, PHI	310
R. Garr, ATL	305
S. Garvey, LA	301
A. Oliver, PIT	293

Runs Batted In
J. Bench, CIN	129
M. Schmidt, PHI	116
S. Garvey, LA	111
J. Wynn, LA	108
T. Simmons, STL	103

Stolen Bases
L. Brock, STL	118
D. Lopes, LA	59
J. Morgan, CIN	58
C. Cedeno, HOU	57
L. Lintz, MON	50

Hits
R. Garr, ATL	214
D. Cash, PHI	206
S. Garvey, LA	200

Base on Balls
D. Evans, ATL	126
J. Morgan, CIN	120
J. Wynn, LA	108

Home Run Percentage
M. Schmidt, PHI	6.3
J. Wynn, LA	6.0
J. Bench, CIN	5.3

Runs Scored
P. Rose, CIN	110
M. Schmidt, PHI	108
J. Bench, CIN	108

Doubles
P. Rose, CIN	45
A. Oliver, PIT	38
J. Bench, CIN	38

Triples
R. Garr, ATL	17
A. Oliver, PIT	12
D. Cash, PHI	11

PITCHING LEADERS

Winning Percentage
Messersmith, LA	.769
D. Sutton, LA	.679
B. Capra, ATL	.667
M. Torrez, MON	.652
J. Billingham, CIN	.633

Earned Run Average
B. Capra, ATL	2.28
P. Niekro, ATL	2.38
J. Matlack, NY	2.41
M. Marshall, LA	2.42
Messersmith, LA	2.59

Wins
Messersmith, LA	20
P. Niekro, ATL	20
D. Sutton, LA	19
J. Billingham, CIN	19
D. Gullett, CIN	17
J. Lonborg, PHI	17

Saves
M. Marshall, LA	21
R. Moffitt, SF	15
P. Borbon, CIN	14
D. Giusti, PIT	12
C. Taylor, MON	11
T. House, ATL	11

Strikeouts
S. Carlton, PHI	240
Messersmith, LA	221
T. Seaver, NY	201
J. Matlack, NY	195
P. Niekro, ATL	195

Complete Games
P. Niekro, ATL	18
S. Carlton, PHI	17
J. Lonborg, PHI	16
J. Rooker, PIT	15
J. Matlack, NY	14
J. Reuss, PIT	14

Fewest Hits per 9 Innings
B. Capra, ATL	6.76
Messersmith, LA	7.00
P. Niekro, ATL	7.42

Shutouts
J. Matlack, NY	7
P. Niekro, ATL	6

Fewest Walks per 9 Innings
J. Barr, SF	1.76
R. Reed, ATL	1.98
D. Ellis, PIT	2.08

Most Strikeouts per 9 Inn.
T. Seaver, NY	7.67
S. Carlton, PHI	7.42
B. Bonham, CHI	7.07

Innings
P. Niekro, ATL	302
Messersmith, LA	292
S. Carlton, PHI	291

Games Pitched
M. Marshall, LA	106
L. Hardy, SD	76
P. Borbon, CIN	73

	W	L	PCT	GB	R	OR	Batting					SB	Fielding			Pitching					
							2B	3B	HR	BA	SA		E	DP	FA	CG	BB	SO	ShO	SV	ERA
EAST																					
PIT	88	74	.543		751	657	238	46	114	.274	.391	55	162	154	.975	51	543	721	9	17	3.49
STL	86	75	.534	1.5	677	643	216	46	83	.265	.365	172	147	192	.977	37	616	794	13	20	3.48
PHI	80	82	.494	8	676	701	233	50	95	.261	.373	115	148	168	.976	46	682	892	4	19	3.92
MON	79	82	.491	8.5	662	657	201	29	86	.254	.350	124	153	157	.976	35	544	822	8	27	3.60
NY	71	91	.438	17	572	646	183	22	96	.235	.329	43	158	150	.975	46	504	908	15	14	3.42
CHI	66	96	.407	22	669	826	221	42	110	.251	.365	78	199	141	.969	23	576	895	6	26	4.28
WEST																					
LA	102	60	.630		798	561	231	34	139	.272	.401	149	157	122	.975	33	464	943	19	23	2.97
CIN	98	64	.605	4	776	631	271	35	135	.260	.394	146	134	151	.979	34	536	875	11	27	3.42
ATL	88	74	.543	14	661	563	202	37	120	.249	.363	72	132	161	.979	46	488	772	21	22	3.05
HOU	81	81	.500	21	653	632	222	41	110	.263	.378	108	113	161	.982	36	601	738	18	18	3.48
SF	72	90	.444	30	634	723	228	38	93	.252	.358	107	175	153	.972	27	559	756	11	25	3.80
SD	60	102	.370	42	541	830	196	27	99	.229	.330	85	170	126	.973	25	715	855	7	19	4.61
					8070	8070	2642	447	1280	.255	.367	1254	1848	1836	.976	439	6828	9971	142	257	3.62

American League 1974

POS	Player	AB	BA	HR	RBI	PO	A	E	DP	TC/G	FA	Pitcher	G	IP	W	L	SV	ERA

East

Bal.
W-91 L-71
Earl Weaver

POS	Player	AB	BA	HR	RBI	PO	A	E	DP	TC/G	FA	Pitcher	G	IP	W	L	SV	ERA
1B	B. Powell	344	.265	12	45	866	61	4	102	9.1	.996	R. Grimsley	40	296	18	13	1	3.07
2B	B. Grich	582	.263	19	82	484	453	20	132	6.0	.977	M. Cuellar	38	269	22	10	0	3.11
SS	M. Belanger	493	.225	5	36	243	552	13	100	5.2	.984	D. McNally	39	259	16	10	1	3.58
3B	B. Robinson	553	.288	7	59	115	410	18	44	3.5	.967	J. Palmer	26	179	7	12	0	3.27
RF	R. Coggins	411	.243	4	32	238	3	4	1	2.3	.984	D. Alexander	30	114	6	9	0	4.03
CF	P. Blair	552	.261	17	62	447	7	7	2	3.1	.985	W. Garland	20	91	5	5	1	2.97
LF	D. Baylor	489	.272	10	59	218	1	5	0	1.7	.978	B. Reynolds	54	69	7	5	7	2.74
C	E. Williams	413	.254	14	52	308	33	6	5	4.6	.983	G. Jackson	49	67	6	4	12	2.55
DH	T. Davis	626	.289	11	84					.0								
OF	A. Bumbry	270	.233	1	19	115	7	6	0	1.9	.953							
OF	J. Fuller	189	.222	7	28	116	3	5	1	2.1	.960							
C	Etchebarren	180	.222	2	15	269	19	7	3	4.9	.976							
UT	E. Cabell	174	.241	3	17	223	45	4	18		.985							

N. Y.
W-89 L-73
Bill Virdon

POS	Player	AB	BA	HR	RBI	PO	A	E	DP	TC/G	FA	Pitcher	G	IP	W	L	SV	ERA
1B	C. Chambliss	400	.243	6	43	873	78	8	93	9.0	.992	P. Dobson	39	281	19	15	0	3.07
2B	S. Alomar	279	.269	1	27	140	136	9	37	3.8	.968	D. Medich	38	280	19	15	0	3.60
SS	J. Mason	440	.250	5	37	241	430	25	87	4.6	.964	D. Tidrow	33	191	11	9	1	3.86
3B	G. Nettles	566	.246	22	75	147	377	21	29	3.5	.961	S. Lyle	66	114	9	3	15	1.66
RF	B. Murcer	606	.274	10	88	297	21	7	2	2.1	.978	R. May	17	114	8	4	0	2.29
CF	E. Maddox	466	.303	3	45	334	18	5	4	2.6	.986	Stottlemyre	16	113	6	7	0	3.58
LF	L. Piniella	518	.305	9	70	265	16	3	0	2.2	.989	C. Upshaw	36	60	1	5	6	3.00
C	T. Munson	517	.261	13	60	743	75	22	10	6.1	.974							
DH	R. White	473	.275	7	43					.0								
DH	R. Blomberg	264	.311	10	48					.0								
1B	B. Sudakis	259	.232	7	39	277	3	3	31		.990							
2S	G. Michael	177	.260	0	13	121	169	9	40		.970							

Bos.
W-84 L-78
Darrell Johnson

POS	Player	AB	BA	HR	RBI	PO	A	E	DP	TC/G	FA	Pitcher	G	IP	W	L	SV	ERA
1B	Yastrzemski	515	.301	15	79	707	44	2	67	9.0	.997	L. Tiant	38	311	22	13	0	2.92
2B	D. Griffin	312	.266	0	33	178	242	9	53	4.7	.979	B. Lee	38	282	17	15	0	3.51
SS	M. Guerrero	284	.246	0	23	136	266	13	50	4.5	.969	R. Cleveland	41	221	12	14	0	4.32
3B	R. Petrocelli	454	.267	15	76	83	219	12	23	2.7	.962	D. Drago	33	176	7	10	3	3.48
RF	D. Evans	463	.281	10	70	294	8	3	2	2.5	.990	R. Moret	31	173	9	10	2	3.75
CF	R. Miller	280	.261	5	22	253	7	3	3	2.5	.989	D. Segui	58	108	6	8	10	4.00
LF	J. Beniquez	389	.267	5	33	264	4	6	2	2.8	.978							
C	B. Montgomery	254	.252	4	38	318	28	8	3	4.5	.977							
DH	T. Harper	443	.237	5	24					.0								
1B	C. Cooper	414	.275	8	43	637	40	12	66		.983							
SS	R. Burleson	384	.284	4	44	142	249	18	41	4.6	.956							
OF	B. Carbo	338	.249	12	61	164	5	1	1	2.0	.994							
23	D. McAuliffe	272	.210	5	24	150	177	11	37		.967							
C	C. Fisk	187	.299	11	26	267	26	6	2	6.0	.980							
1B	D. Cater	126	.246	5	20	126	10	0	9		1.000							

Cle.
W-77 L-85
Ken Aspromonte

POS	Player	AB	BA	HR	RBI	PO	A	E	DP	TC/G	FA	Pitcher	G	IP	W	L	SV	ERA
1B	J. Ellis	477	.285	10	64	667	37	6	57	10.3	.992	G. Perry	37	322	21	13	0	2.52
2B	J. Brohamer	315	.270	2	30	203	269	6	67	4.8	.987	J. Perry	36	252	17	12	0	2.96
SS	F. Duffy	549	.233	8	48	242	491	15	83	4.7	.980	F. Peterson	29	153	9	14	0	4.35
3B	B. Bell	423	.262	7	46	112	274	15	31	3.5	.963	D. Bosman	25	127	7	5	0	4.11
RF	C. Spikes	568	.271	22	80	284	16	10	3	2.0	.968	T. Buskey	51	93	2	6	17	3.19
CF	G. Hendrick	495	.279	19	67	355	9	4	2	2.8	.989	F. Beene	32	73	4	4	2	4.93
LF	J. Lowenstein	508	.242	8	48	200	6	3	1	2.1	.986	S. Kline	16	71	3	8	0	5.07
C	D. Duncan	425	.200	16	46	557	47	15	7	4.6	.976	T. Hilgendorf	35	48	4	3	3	4.88
DH	O. Gamble	454	.291	19	59					.0								
OF	L. Lee	232	.233	5	25	131	5	6	1	2.3	.958							

	POS	Player	AB	BA	HR	RBI	PO	A	E	DP	TC/G	FA	Pitcher	G	IP	W	L	SV	ERA
Mil. W-76 L-86 Del Crandall	1B	G. Scott	604	.281	17	82	1345	114	12	137	9.9	.992	J. Slaton	40	250	13	16	0	3.92
	2B	P. Garcia	452	.199	12	54	382	365	23	102	5.5	.970	C. Wright	38	232	9	20	0	4.42
	SS	R. Yount	344	.250	3	26	148	327	19	55	4.6	.962	J. Colborn	33	224	10	13	0	4.06
	3B	D. Money	629	.283	15	65	131	336	5	42	3.0	.989	K. Kobel	34	169	6	14	0	3.99
	RF	B. Coluccio	394	.223	6	31	346	10	4	2	2.7	.989	B. Champion	31	162	11	4	0	3.61
	CF	D. May	477	.226	10	42	249	10	3	2	2.2	.989	T. Murphy	70	123	10	10	20	1.90
	LF	J. Briggs	554	.253	17	73	309	10	9	2	2.2	.973	E. Rodriguez	43	112	7	4	4	3.62
	C	D. Porter	432	.241	12	56	484	60	12	8	4.8	.978							
	DH	B. Mitchell	173	.243	5	20						.0							
	OF	K. Berry	267	.240	1	24	187	8	1	1	2.4	.995							
	S2	T. Johnson	245	.245	0	25	138	230	9	51		.976							
	C	C. Moore	204	.245	0	19	229	28	4	5	4.3	.985							
	UT	M. Hegan	190	.237	7	32	136	5	1	12		.993							
Det. W-72 L-90 Ralph Houk	1B	B. Freehan	445	.297	18	60	590	36	4	49	9.7	.994	M. Lolich	41	308	16	21	0	4.15
	2B	G. Sutherland	619	.254	5	49	337	360	17	101	4.9	.976	J. Coleman	41	286	14	12	0	4.31
	SS	E. Brinkman	502	.221	14	54	237	493	21	88	5.0	.972	L. LaGrow	37	216	8	19	0	4.67
	3B	A. Rodriguez	571	.222	5	49	132	389	21	40	3.4	.961	J. Hiller	59	150	17	14	13	2.64
	RF	J. Northrup	376	.237	11	42	209	5	6	0	2.3	.973	W. Fryman	27	142	6	9	0	4.31
	CF	M. Stanley	394	.221	8	34	252	4	2	2	2.8	.992	L. Walker	28	92	5	5	0	4.99
	LF	W. Horton	238	.298	15	47	106	2	6	0	1.8	.947							
	C	G. Moses	198	.237	4	19	377	26	6	6	5.5	.985							
	DH	A. Kaline	558	.262	13	64						.0							
	OF	R. LeFlore	254	.260	2	13	151	8	11	3	2.9	.935							
	OF	B. Oglivie	252	.270	4	29	87	3	5	0	1.5	.947							

West

	POS	Player	AB	BA	HR	RBI	PO	A	E	DP	TC/G	FA	Pitcher	G	IP	W	L	SV	ERA
Oak. W-90 L-72 Alvin Dark	1B	G. Tenace	484	.211	26	73	816	41	4	80	8.1	.995	C. Hunter	41	318	**25**	12	0	**2.49**
	2B	D. Green	287	.213	2	22	233	243	8	67	4.8	.983	V. Blue	40	282	17	15	0	3.26
	SS	B. Campaneris	527	.290	2	41	207	423	22	76	4.9	.966	K. Holtzman	39	255	19	17	0	3.07
	3B	S. Bando	498	.243	22	103	113	287	23	28	3.0	.946	R. Fingers	**76**	119	9	5	18	2.65
	RF	R. Jackson	506	.289	29	93	296	8	10	2	2.5	.968	D. Hamilton	29	117	7	4	0	3.15
	CF	B. North	543	.260	4	33	437	9	4	2	**3.3**	.991	P. Lindblad	45	101	4	4	6	2.05
	LF	J. Rudi	593	.293	22	99	234	7	4	0	1.8	.984	G. Abbott	19	96	5	7	0	3.00
	C	R. Fosse	204	.196	4	23	299	28	9	6	4.9	.973							
	DH	J. Alou	220	.268	2	15	0	0	0	0	.0	.000							
	OF	A. Mangual	365	.233	9	43	142	5	6	0		.961							
	OF	C. Washington	221	.285	0	19	63	2	1	0		.985							
	UT	T. Kubiak	220	.209	0	18	129	175	6	38		.981							
	1B	D. Johnson	174	.195	7	23	211	9	2	15		.991							
Tex. W-84 L-76 Billy Martin	1B	M. Hargrove	415	.323	4	66	631	72	9	57	7.8	.987	F. Jenkins	41	328	**25**	12	0	2.83
	2B	D. Nelson	474	.236	3	42	295	337	20	74	5.4	.969	J. Bibby	41	264	19	19	0	4.74
	SS	T. Harrah	573	.260	21	74	281	466	**29**	98	4.9	.963	S. Brown	35	217	13	12	0	3.57
	3B	L. Randle	520	.302	1	49	92	167	18	23	3.1	.935	S. Hargan	37	187	12	9	0	3.95
	RF	J. Burroughs	554	.301	25	**118**	231	10	7	5	1.7	.972	S. Foucault	69	144	8	9	12	2.25
	CF	J. Lovitto	283	.223	2	26	201	7	6	1	2.0	.980	D. Clyde	28	117	3	9	0	4.38
	LF	C. Tovar	562	.292	4	58	331	13	7	3	2.6	.980							
	C	J. Sundberg	368	.247	3	36	722	69	8	15	6.1	.990							
	DH	J. Spencer	352	.278	7	44						.0							
	OF	A. Johnson	453	.291	4	41	168	6	8	2	2.2	.956							
	OF	T. Grieve	259	.255	9	32	62	5	0	1		1.000							
	13	J. Fregosi	230	.261	12	34	331	73	5	35		.988							
Min. W-82 L-80 Frank Quilici	1B	C. Kusick	201	.239	8	26	479	42	2	45	7.0	.996	B. Blyleven	37	281	17	17	0	2.66
	2B	R. Carew	599	**.364**	3	55	375	416	**33**	114	5.6	.960	J. Decker	37	249	16	14	0	3.29
	SS	D. Thompson	264	.250	4	25	127	183	12	39	3.7	.963	D. Goltz	28	174	10	10	1	3.26
	3B	E. Soderholm	464	.276	10	51	100	273	17	19	3.0	.956	V. Albury	32	164	8	9	0	4.12
	RF	S. Brye	488	.283	2	41	301	10	1	2	2.4	.997	B. Campbell	63	120	8	7	19	2.63
	CF	B. Darwin	575	.264	25	94	254	8	8	1	1.9	.970	B. Hands	35	115	4	5	3	4.46
	LF	L. Hisle	510	.286	19	79	279	4	6	1	2.1	.979	R. Corbin	29	112	7	6	0	5.30
	C	G. Borgmann	345	.252	3	45	652	52	2	4	5.5	.997	B. Butler	26	99	4	6	1	4.09
	DH	T. Oliva	459	.285	13	57						.0	T. Burgmeier	50	92	5	3	4	4.50
	OF	S. Braun	453	.280	8	40	180	10	7	2	1.8	.964							
	1B	H. Killebrew	333	.222	13	54	218	21	2	21		.992							
	UT	J. Terrell	229	.245	0	19	114	179	9	35		.970							
	1B	J. Holt	197	.254	0	16	449	43	2	57	7.4	.996							
	SS	L. Gomez	168	.208	0	3	97	190	12	37	4.0	.960							
Chi. W-80 L-80 Chuck Tanner	1B	R. Allen	462	.301	**32**	88	998	49	**15**	112	8.5	.986	W. Wood	42	320	20	19	0	3.60
	2B	J. Orta	525	.316	10	67	297	313	18	93	5.1	.971	J. Kaat	42	277	21	13	0	2.92
	SS	B. Dent	496	.274	5	45	251	499	22	**108**	5.0	.972	S. Bahnsen	38	216	12	15	0	4.71
	3B	B. Melton	495	.242	21	63	100	272	**24**	29	3.2	.939	T. Forster	59	134	7	8	**24**	3.63
	RF	B. Sharp	320	.253	4	24	210	3	3	0	2.2	.986	B. Johnson	18	122	10	4	0	2.73
	CF	K. Henderson	602	.292	20	95	**462**	7	6	3	2.9	.987	S. Pitlock	40	106	3	3	1	4.42
	LF	C. May	551	.249	8	58	246	11	3	1	2.0	.988	G. Gossage	39	89	4	6	1	4.15
	C	E. Herrmann	367	.259	10	39	561	55	8	8	5.8	.987							
	DH	P. Kelly	424	.281	4	21						.0							
	UT	R. Santo	375	.221	5	41	135	148	8	49		.973							
	CO	B. Downing	293	.225	10	39	337	30	2	5		.995							
	1B	T. Muser	206	.291	1	18	419	13	1	46	5.4	.998							

	POS	Player	AB	BA	HR	RBI	PO	A	E	DP	TC/G	FA	Pitcher	G	IP	W	L	SV	ERA
K. C.	1B	J. Mayberry	427	.234	22	69	963	61	10	101	9.8	.990	S. Busby	38	292	22	14	0	3.39
W-77 L-85	2B	C. Rojas	542	.271	6	60	292	368	9	94	4.7	.987	P. Splittorff	36	226	13	19	0	4.10
Jack McKeon	SS	F. Patek	537	.225	3	38	250	493	25	108	5.2	.967	A. Fitzmorris	34	190	13	6	1	2.79
	3B	G. Brett	457	.282	2	47	102	279	21	16	3.0	.948	Dal Canton	31	175	8	10	0	3.14
	RF	J. Wohlford	501	.271	2	44	273	7	5	4	2.1	.982	M. Pattin	25	117	3	7	0	4.00
	CF	A. Otis	552	.284	12	73	425	8	6	3	3.1	.986	L. McDaniel	38	107	1	4	1	3.45
	LF	V. Pinson	406	.276	6	41	188	9	4	2	1.8	.980	N. Briles	18	103	5	7	0	4.02
	C	F. Healy	445	.252	9	53	620	64	16	4	5.1	.977	D. Bird	55	92	7	6	10	2.74
	DH	H. McRae	539	.310	15	88					.0								
	OF	A. Cowens	269	.242	1	25	151	13	2	2	1.6	.988							
	1B	T. Solaita	239	.268	7	30	508	40	5	36	8.5	.991							
	UT	F. White	204	.221	1	18	119	189	12	40		.963							
Cal.	1B	J. Doherty	223	.256	3	15	538	30	5	55	8.2	.991	N. Ryan	42	333	22	16	0	2.89
W-68 L-94	2B	D. Doyle	511	.260	1	34	311	404	12	99	5.0	.983	F. Tanana	39	269	14	19	0	3.11
Bobby Winkles	SS	D. Chalk	465	.252	5	31	168	269	29	55	4.7	.938	A. Hassler	23	162	7	11	1	2.61
W-32 L-46	3B	P. Schaal	165	.248	2	20	24	78	11	9	2.2	.903	D. Lange	21	114	3	8	0	3.79
Dick Williams	RF	L. Stanton	415	.267	11	62	226	11	6	0	2.1	.975	B. Singer	14	109	7	4	0	2.97
W-36 L-48	CF	M. Rivers	466	.285	3	31	309	9	2	3	2.8	.994	E. Figueroa	25	105	2	8	0	3.69
	LF	J. Lahoud	325	.271	13	44	156	6	4	2	1.6	.976							
	C	E. Rodriguez	395	.253	7	36	782	75	7	7	6.3	.992							
	DH	F. Robinson	427	.251	20	63					.0								
	UT	B. Valentine	371	.261	3	39	160	116	17	10		.942							
	13	B. Oliver	359	.248	8	55	400	83	12	46		.976							
	O1	B. Bochte	196	.270	5	26	248	9	5	16		.981							
	OF	M. Nettles	175	.274	0	8	99	0	1	0	1.9	.990							

BATTING AND BASE RUNNING LEADERS

Batting Average

R. Carew, MIN	.364
J. Orta, CHI	.316
H. McRae, KC	.310
L. Piniella, NY	.305
E. Maddox, NY	.303

Home Runs

R. Allen, CHI	32
R. Jackson, OAK	29
G. Tenace, OAK	26
J. Burroughs, TEX	25
B. Darwin, MIN	25

Runs Batted In

J. Burroughs, TEX	118
S. Bando, OAK	103
J. Rudi, OAK	99
K. Henderson, CHI	95
B. Darwin, MIN	94

Hits

R. Carew, MIN	218
T. Davis, BAL	181
D. Money, MIL	178

Home Run Percentage

R. Allen, CHI	6.9
R. Jackson, OAK	5.7
G. Tenace, OAK	5.4

Doubles

J. Rudi, OAK	39
H. McRae, KC	36
G. Scott, MIL	36

Slugging Average

R. Allen, CHI	.563
R. Jackson, OAK	.514
J. Burroughs, TEX	.504
J. Rudi, OAK	.484
H. McRae, KC	.475

Total Bases

J. Rudi, OAK	287
K. Henderson, CHI	281
J. Burroughs, TEX	279
R. Carew, MIN	267
G. Scott, MIL	261
D. Money, MIL	261

Stolen Bases

B. North, OAK	54
R. Carew, MIN	38
J. Lowenstein, CLE	36
B. Campaneris, OAK	34
F. Patek, KC	33

Base on Balls

G. Tenace, OAK	110
Yastrzemski, BOS	104
J. Burroughs, TEX	91

Runs Scored

Yastrzemski, BOS	93
B. Grich, BAL	92
R. Jackson, OAK	90

Triples

M. Rivers, CAL	11
A. Otis, KC	9

PITCHING LEADERS

Winning Percentage

M. Cuellar, BAL	.688
C. Hunter, OAK	.676
F. Jenkins, TEX	.676
L. Tiant, BOS	.629
J. Kaat, CHI	.618
G. Perry, CLE	.618

Wins

C. Hunter, OAK	25
F. Jenkins, TEX	25
M. Cuellar, BAL	22
L. Tiant, BOS	22
S. Busby, KC	22
N. Ryan, CAL	22

Strikeouts

N. Ryan, CAL	367
B. Blyleven, MIN	249
F. Jenkins, TEX	225
G. Perry, CLE	216
M. Lolich, DET	202

Fewest Hits per 9 Innings

N. Ryan, CAL	5.97
G. Perry, CLE	6.43
Dal Canton, KC	6.94

Fewest Walks per 9 Innings

F. Jenkins, TEX	1.23
C. Hunter, OAK	1.30
K. Holtzman, OAK	1.80

Innings

N. Ryan, CAL	333
F. Jenkins, TEX	328
G. Perry, CLE	322

Earned Run Average

C. Hunter, OAK	2.49
G. Perry, CLE	2.52
A. Hassler, CAL	2.61
B. Blyleven, MIN	2.66
A. Fitzmorris, KC	2.79

Saves

T. Forster, CHI	24
T. Murphy, MIL	20
B. Campbell, MIN	19
R. Fingers, OAK	18
T. Buskey, CLE, NY	18

Complete Games

F. Jenkins, TEX	29
G. Perry, CLE	28
M. Lolich, DET	27
N. Ryan, CAL	26
L. Tiant, BOS	25

Shutouts

L. Tiant, BOS	7
C. Hunter, OAK	6
F. Jenkins, TEX	6

Most Strikeouts per 9 Inn.

N. Ryan, CAL	9.92
B. Blyleven, MIN	7.98
F. Jenkins, TEX	6.17

Games Pitched

R. Fingers, OAK	76
T. Murphy, MIL	70
S. Foucault, TEX	69

	W	L	PCT	GB	R	OR	2B	3B	Batting HR	BA	SA	SB	E	Fielding DP	FA	CG	BB	Pitching SO	ShO	SV	ERA
EAST																					
BAL	91	71	.562		659	612	226	27	116	.256	.370	145	128	174	.980	57	480	701	16	25	3.27
NY	89	73	.549	2	671	623	220	30	101	.263	.368	53	142	158	.977	53	528	829	13	24	3.31
BOS	84	78	.519	7	696	661	236	31	109	.264	.377	104	145	156	.977	71	463	751	12	18	3.72
CLE	77	85	.475	14	662	694	201	19	131	.255	.370	79	146	157	.977	45	479	650	8	27	3.80
MIL	76	86	.469	15	647	660	228	49	120	.244	.369	106	127	168	.980	43	493	621	11	24	3.77
DET	72	90	.444	19	620	768	200	35	131	.247	.366	67	158	155	.975	54	621	869	7	15	4.17
WEST																					
OAK	90	72	.556		689	551	205	37	132	.247	.373	164	141	154	.977	49	430	755	12	28	2.95
TEX	84	76	.525	5	690	698	198	39	99	.272	.377	113	163	164	.974	62	449	871	16	12	3.82
MIN	82	80	.506	8	673	669	190	37	111	.272	.378	74	151	164	.976	43	513	934	11	29	3.64
CHI	80	80	.500	9	684	721	225	23	135	.268	.389	64	147	188	.977	55	548	826	11	29	3.94
KC	77	85	.475	13	667	662	232	42	89	.259	.364	146	152	166	.976	54	482	731	14	17	3.51
CAL	68	94	.420	22	618	657	203	31	95	.254	.356	119	147	150	.977	64	649	986	13	12	3.52
					7976	7976	2564	400	1369	.258	.371	1234	1747	1954	.977	650	6135	9524	144	260	3.62

National League 1975

	POS	Player	AB	BA	HR	RBI	PO	A	E	DP	TC/G	FA	Pitcher	G	IP	W	L	SV	ERA

East

Pit.
W-92 L-69
Danny Murtaugh

POS	Player	AB	BA	HR	RBI	PO	A	E	DP	TC/G	FA	Pitcher	G	IP	W	L	SV	ERA
1B	W. Stargell	461	.295	22	90	1121	54	10	112	9.7	.992	J. Reuss	32	237	18	11	0	2.54
2B	R. Stennett	616	.286	7	62	379	463	18	98	6.0	.979	J. Rooker	28	197	13	11	0	2.97
SS	F. Taveras	378	.212	0	23	200	369	28	74	4.5	.953	B. Kison	33	192	12	11	0	3.23
3B	R. Hebner	472	.246	15	57	86	244	19	17	2.8	.946	D. Ellis	27	140	8	9	0	3.79
RF	D. Parker	558	.308	25	101	311	7	9	2	2.3	.972	J. Candelaria	18	121	8	6	0	2.75
CF	A. Oliver	628	.280	18	84	380	5	5	3	2.5	.987	K. Brett	23	118	9	5	0	3.36
LF	R. Zisk	504	.290	20	75	264	7	7	1	2.0	.975	L. Demery	45	115	7	5	4	2.90
C	M. Sanguillen	481	.328	9	58	650	53	9	4	5.4	.987	D. Giusti	61	92	5	4	17	2.93
OF	B. Robinson	200	.280	6	33	107	3	1	1	1.9	.991	R. Hernandez	46	64	7	2	5	2.95

Phi.
W-86 L-76
Danny Ozark

POS	Player	AB	BA	HR	RBI	PO	A	E	DP	TC/G	FA	Pitcher	G	IP	W	L	SV	ERA
1B	R. Allen	416	.233	12	62	900	70	18	79	8.7	.982	S. Carlton	37	255	15	14	0	3.56
2B	D. Cash	699	.305	4	57	400	481	17	126	5.5	.981	T. Underwood	35	219	14	13	0	4.15
SS	L. Bowa	583	.305	2	38	227	403	25	82	4.9	.962	Christenson	29	172	11	6	1	3.66
3B	M. Schmidt	562	.249	38	95	132	368	24	30	3.5	.954	J. Lonborg	27	159	8	6	0	4.13
RF	M. Anderson	247	.259	4	28	161	6	4	0	1.6	.977	W. Twitchell	36	134	5	10	0	4.43
CF	G. Maddox	374	.291	4	46	288	10	5	4	3.1*	.983	G. Garber	71	110	10	12	14	3.60
LF	G. Luzinski	596	.300	34	120	248	10	9	0	1.7	.966	T. McGraw	56	103	9	6	14	2.97
C	B. Boone	289	.246	2	20	456	44	5	7	5.5	.990	T. Hilgendorf	53	97	7	3	0	2.13
OF	J. Johnstone	350	.329	7	54	152	10	4	3	1.6	.976							
C	J. Oates	269	.286	1	25	429	44	5	10*	5.8	.990							
1B	T. Hutton	165	.248	3	24	307	32	2	37	4.8	.994							
OF	O. Brown	145	.303	6	26	67	0	0	0	1.8	1.000							

N. Y.
W-82 L-80
Yogi Berra
W-56 L-53
Roy McMillan
W-26 L-27

POS	Player	AB	BA	HR	RBI	PO	A	E	DP	TC/G	FA	Pitcher	G	IP	W	L	SV	ERA
1B	E. Kranepool	325	.323	4	43	666	46	2	51	8.7	.997	T. Seaver	36	280	22	9	0	2.38
2B	F. Millan	676	.283	1	56	379	420	23	95	5.1	.972	J. Koosman	36	240	14	13	2	3.41
SS	M. Phillips	383	.256	1	28	185	334	31*	52	4.8	.944	J. Matlack	33	229	16	12	0	3.38
3B	W. Garrett	274	.266	6	34	64	160	8	24	2.5	.966	R. Tate	26	138	5	13	0	4.43
RF	R. Staub	574	.282	19	105	267	15	4	3	1.9	.986	H. Webb	29	115	7	6	0	4.07
CF	D. Unser	531	.294	10	53	362	13	5	2	2.6	.987	B. Baldwin	54	97	3	5	6	3.34
LF	D. Kingman	502	.231	36	88	134	3	6	0	2.0	.958	B. Apodaca	46	85	3	4	13	1.48
C	J. Grote	386	.295	2	39	706	55	4	8	6.9	.995							
3B	J. Torre	361	.247	6	35	61	148	11	14	2.7	.950							
O1	J. Milner	220	.191	7	29	267	27	3	21		.990							
OF	G. Clines	203	.227	0	10	98	9	2	2	1.8	.982							
C	J. Stearns	169	.189	3	10	297	40	2	9	6.3	.994							
OF	M. Vail	162	.302	3	17	92	9	3	1	2.9	.971							

St. L.
W-82 L-80
Red Schoendienst

POS	Player	AB	BA	HR	RBI	PO	A	E	DP	TC/G	FA	Pitcher	G	IP	W	L	SV	ERA
1B	R. Smith	477	.302	19	76	524	33	10	51	8.6	.982	L. McGlothen	35	239	15	13	0	3.92
2B	T. Sizemore	562	.240	3	49	329	405	21	82	4.9	.972	B. Forsch	34	230	15	10	0	2.86
SS	M. Tyson	368	.266	2	37	154	246	12	44	4.3	.971	R. Reed	24	176	9	8	0	3.23
3B	K. Reitz	592	.269	5	63	124	279	23	21	2.7	.946	J. Curtis	39	147	8	9	1	3.43
RF	B. McBride	413	.300	5	36	289	4	3	1	2.8	.990	J. Denny	25	136	10	7	0	3.97
CF	W. Davis	350	.291	6	50	187	5	6	2	2.2	.970	B. Gibson	22	109	3	10	2	5.04
LF	L. Brock	528	.309	3	47	247	5	9	0	2.0	.966	A. Hrabosky	65	97	13	3	22	1.67
C	T. Simmons	581	.332	18	100	803	62	15	5	5.7	.983	E. Rasmussen	14	81	5	5	0	3.78
OF	L. Melendez	291	.265	2	27	169	3	3	1	2.0	.983	M. Garman	66	79	3	8	10	2.39
1B	R. Fairly	229	.301	7	37	351	33	8	33	7.0	.980							
1B	K. Hernandez	188	.250	3	20	469	36	2	34	9.1	.996							
SS	M. Guerrero	184	.239	0	11	76	198	13	29	4.5	.955							

POS	Player	AB	BA	HR	RBI	PO	A	E	DP	TC/G	FA	Pitcher	G	IP	W	L	SV	ERA
Chi. W-75 L-87 Jim Marshall																		
1B	A. Thornton	372	.293	18	60	982	77	13	88	9.5	.988	R. Burris	36	238	15	10	0	4.12
2B	M. Trillo	545	.248	7	70	350	509	29	103	5.8	.967	R. Reuschel	38	234	11	17	1	3.73
SS	D. Kessinger	601	.243	0	46	205	436	22	100	4.7	.967	B. Bonham	38	229	13	15	0	4.72
3B	B. Madlock	514	.354	7	64	79	250	20	14	2.7	.943	S. Stone	33	214	12	8	0	3.95
RF	J. Cardenal	574	.317	9	68	313	14	8	3	2.2	.976	D. Knowles	58	88	6	9	15	5.83
CF	R. Monday	491	.267	17	60	315	6	9	0	2.5	.973	O. Zamora	52	71	5	2	10	5.07
LF	J. Morales	578	.270	12	91	273	11	6	1	1.9	.979	G. Zahn	16	63	2	7	1	4.45
C	S. Swisher	254	.213	1	22	426	36	10	5	5.1	.979							
1O	P. LaCock	249	.229	6	30	479	45	6	39		.989							
C	G. Mitterwald	200	.220	5	26	247	32	7	4	4.8	.976							
C	T. Hosley	141	.255	6	20	254	16	9	3	5.3	.968							
Mon. W-75 L-87 Gene Mauch																		
1B	M. Jorgensen	445	.261	18	67	1150	91	7	123	9.4	.994	S. Rogers	35	252	11	12	0	3.29
2B	P. Mackanin	448	.225	12	44	300	410	25	100	5.8	.966	S. Renko	31	170	6	12	1	4.08
SS	T. Foli	572	.238	1	29	**260**	**497**	21	**104**	5.2	.973	D. Warthen	40	168	8	6	3	3.11
3B	L. Parrish	532	.274	10	65	105	291	35	33	3.0	.919	D. Blair	30	163	8	15	0	3.81
RF	L. Biittner	346	.315	3	28	166	8	5	0	1.9	.972	W. Fryman	38	157	9	12	3	3.32
CF	P. Mangual	514	.245	9	45	308	8	9	2	2.4	.972	D. Murray	63	111	15	8	9	3.97
LF	G. Carter	503	.270	17	68	150	1	4	1	1.7	.974	D. Carrithers	19	101	5	3	0	3.30
C	B. Foote	387	.194	7	30	590	50	10	**10**	5.7	.985	D. De Mola	60	98	4	7	1	4.13
OF	B. Bailey	227	.273	5	30	88	4	2	1	1.5	.979	C. Taylor	54	74	2	2	6	3.53
OF	J. Dwyer	175	.286	3	20	86	8	4	1	1.9	.959							
1B	J. Morales	163	.301	2	24	201	26	4	19	8.6	.983							

West

POS	Player	AB	BA	HR	RBI	PO	A	E	DP	TC/G	FA	Pitcher	G	IP	W	L	SV	ERA
Cin. W-108 L-54 Sparky Anderson																		
1B	T. Perez	511	.282	20	109	1192	72	9	113	9.6	.993	G. Nolan	32	211	15	9	0	3.16
2B	J. Morgan	498	.327	17	94	356	425	11	96	5.6	**.986**	J. Billingham	33	208	15	10	0	4.11
SS	D. Concepcion	507	.274	5	49	238	445	16	102	**5.4**	.977	F. Norman	34	188	12	4	0	3.73
3B	P. Rose	662	.317	7	74	106	230	13	21	2.5	.963	D. Gullett	22	160	15	4	0	2.42
RF	K. Griffey	463	.305	4	46	202	6	7	0	1.8	.967	P. Darcy	27	131	11	5	1	3.57
CF	C. Geronimo	501	.257	6	53	**408**	12	3	5	2.9	.993	P. Borbon	67	125	9	5	5	2.95
LF	G. Foster	463	.300	23	78	299	11	3	3	2.5	.990	C. Kirby	26	111	10	6	0	4.70
C	J. Bench	530	.283	28	110	568	51	7	9	5.2	.989	C. Carroll	56	96	7	5	7	2.63
1O	D. Driessen	210	.281	7	38	309	20	5	34		.985	W. McEnaney	70	91	5	2	15	2.47
OF	M. Rettenmund	188	.239	2	19	99	1	0	1	1.6	1.000	R. Eastwick	58	90	5	3	**22**	2.60
UT	D. Chaney	160	.219	2	26	77	164	7	27		.972							
UT	D. Flynn	127	.268	1	20	57	118	2	20		.989							
L. A. W-88 L-74 Walter Alston																		
1B	S. Garvey	659	.319	18	95	**1500**	77	8	96	**9.9**	**.995**	Messersmith	42	**322**	19	14	1	2.29
2B	D. Lopes	618	.262	8	41	307	377	15	58	5.1	.979	D. Rau	38	258	15	9	0	3.10
SS	B. Russell	252	.206	0	14	94	230	11	27	4.0	.967	D. Sutton	35	254	16	13	0	2.87
3B	R. Cey	566	.283	25	101	144	309	19	23	3.0	.960	B. Hooton	31	224	18	7	0	2.82
RF	W. Crawford	373	.263	9	46	201	2	2	0	1.8	.990	M. Marshall	57	109	9	14	13	3.30
CF	J. Wynn	412	.248	18	58	282	6	5	2	2.4	.983	C. Hough	38	61	3	7	4	2.95
LF	B. Buckner	288	.243	6	31	138	4	2	0	2.0	.986							
C	S. Yeager	452	.228	12	54	**806**	62	7	4	6.5	.992							
O2	L. Lacy	306	.314	7	40	151	75	13	11		.946							
OF	J. Hale	204	.211	6	22	128	2	3	0	2.0	.977							
CO	J. Ferguson	202	.208	5	23	215	20	2	4		.992							
SS	R. Auerbach	170	.224	0	12	77	137	9	17	2.8	.960							
S. F. W-80 L-81 Wes Westrum																		
1B	W. Montanez	518	.305	8	85	1150	81*	8	114*	9.2	.994	J. Montefusco	35	244	15	9	0	2.88
2B	D. Thomas	540	.276	6	48	348	372	19	100	5.2	.974	J. Barr	35	244	13	14	0	3.06
SS	C. Speier	487	.271	10	69	247	420	12	81	5.0	**.982**	P. Falcone	34	190	12	11	0	4.17
3B	S. Ontiveros	325	.289	3	31	64	188	21	14	3.1	.923	M. Caldwell	38	163	7	13	1	4.80
RF	B. Murcer	526	.298	11	91	201	10	4	3	1.5	.981	E. Halicki	24	160	9	13	0	3.49
CF	V. Joshua	507	.318	7	43	279	10	2	3	2.5	**.993**	C. Williams	55	98	5	3	3	3.49
LF	G. Matthews	425	.280	12	58	225	11	8	2	2.2	.967	G. Lavelle	65	82	6	3	8	2.96
C	D. Rader	292	.291	5	31	457	37	8	7	5.3	.984	R. Moffitt	55	74	4	5	11	3.89
OF	G. Thomasson	326	.227	7	32	172	9	4	2	2.5	.994							
3B	B. Miller	309	.239	1	31	66	120	10	11	2.9	.949							
C	M. Hill	182	.214	5	23	282	27	2	7	5.2	.994							
S. D. W-71 L-91 John McNamara																		
1B	W. McCovey	413	.252	23	68	979	73	15	94	9.3	.986	R. Jones	37	285	20	12	0	**2.24**
2B	T. Fuentes	565	.280	4	43	389	448	26	105	**6.1**	.970	J. McIntosh	37	183	8	15	0	3.69
SS	E. Hernandez	344	.218	0	19	168	327	18	70	4.6	.965	D. Freisleben	36	181	5	14	0	4.28
3B	T. Kubiak	196	.224	0	14	36	110	7	9	2.4	.954	D. Spillner	37	167	5	13	1	4.26
RF	D. Winfield	509	.267	15	76	302	9	9	1	2.3	.972	R. Folkers	45	142	6	11	0	4.18
CF	J. Grubb	553	.269	4	38	334	3	3	0	2.4	.991	B. Strom	18	120	8	8	0	2.55
LF	B. Tolan	506	.255	5	43	230	5	7	1	2.0	.971	D. Frisella	65	98	1	6	9	3.12
C	F. Kendall	286	.199	0	24	337	38	9	6	4.5	.977	B. Greif	59	72	4	6	9	3.88
13	M. Ivie	377	.249	8	46	539	138	23	54		.967							
UT	H. Torres	352	.259	5	40	128	338	13	55		.973							
OF	G. Locklear	237	.321	5	27	92	4	3	1	1.9	.970							
C	R. Hundley	180	.206	2	14	237	20	8	3	5.2	.970							
OF	D. Sharon	160	.194	4	20	91	1	5	0	1.7	.948							

	POS	Player	AB	BA	HR	RBI	PO	A	E	DP	TC/G	FA	Pitcher	G	IP	W	L	SV	ERA
Atl. W-67 L-94 Clyde King W-59 L-76 Connie Ryan W-8 L-18	1B	E. Williams	383	.240	11	50	844	50	10	77	10.0	.989	C. Morton	39	278	17	16	0	3.50
	2B	M. Perez	461	.275	2	34	259	341	9	74	5.3	.985	P. Niekro	39	276	15	15	1	3.20
	SS	L. Blanks	471	.234	3	38	183	414	25	68	4.8	.960	T. House	58	79	7	7	11	3.19
	3B	D. Evans	567	.243	22	73	161	381	36	41	3.7	.938	B. Capra	12	78	4	7	0	4.27
	RF	D. Baker	494	.261	19	72	287	10	3	0	2.2	.990	J. Easterly	21	69	2	9	0	4.96
	CF	R. Office	355	.290	3	30	229	6	8	0	2.3	.967	Dal Canton	26	67	2	7	3	3.36
	LF	R. Garr	625	.278	6	31	298	12	11	2	2.2	.966							
	C	V. Correll	325	.215	11	39	413	63	13	2	5.0	.973							
	1O	M. Lum	364	.228	8	36	657	34	5	41		.993							
	OF	D. May	203	.276	12	40	103	3	4	2	2.1	.964							
	2B	R. Gilbreath	202	.243	2	16	121	125	5	29	4.8	.980							
	C	B. Pocoroba	188	.255	1	22	237	25	8	2	4.4	.970							
Hou. W-64 L-97 Preston Gomez W-47 L-80 Bill Virdon W-17 L-17	1B	B. Watson	485	.324	18	85	1077	69	8	106	9.8	.993	L. Dierker	34	232	14	16	0	4.00
	2B	R. Andrews	277	.238	0	19	191	237	8	65	4.6	.982	J. Richard	33	203	12	10	0	4.39
	SS	R. Metzger	450	.227	2	26	186	441	15	83	5.1	.977	D. Roberts	32	198	8	14	1	4.27
	3B	D. Rader	448	.223	12	48	111	257	11	24	3.1	.971	D. Konieczny	32	171	6	13	0	4.47
	RF	J. Cruz	315	.257	9	49	187	6	4	0	2.1	.980	K. Forsch	34	109	4	8	2	3.22
	CF	C. Cedeno	500	.288	13	63	322	8	6	2	2.6	.982	J. Niekro	40	88	6	4	4	3.07
	LF	G. Gross	483	.294	0	41	216	14	10	2	2.0	.958	J. Crawford	44	87	3	5	4	3.62
	C	M. May	386	.241	4	52	568	70	9	8	6.3	.986	T. Griffin	17	79	3	8	0	5.35
	OF	W. Howard	392	.283	0	21	194	7	1	0	2.1	.995	W. Granger	55	74	2	5	5	3.65
	UT	E. Cabell	348	.264	2	43	197	58	6	17		.977							
	1C	C. Johnson	340	.276	20	65	602	37	12	37		.982							
	23	K. Boswell	178	.242	0	21	54	103	6	13		.963							

BATTING AND BASE RUNNING LEADERS

Batting Average
B. Madlock, CHI	.354
T. Simmons, STL	.332
M. Sanguillen, PIT	.328
J. Morgan, CIN	.327
B. Watson, HOU	.324

Slugging Average
D. Parker, PIT	.541
G. Luzinski, PHI	.540
M. Schmidt, PHI	.523
J. Bench, CIN	.519
G. Foster, CIN	.518

Home Runs
M. Schmidt, PHI	38
D. Kingman, NY	36
G. Luzinski, PHI	34
J. Bench, CIN	28
D. Parker, PIT	25
R. Cey, LA	25

Total Bases
G. Luzinski, PHI	322
S. Garvey, LA	314
D. Parker, PIT	302
M. Schmidt, PHI	294
P. Rose, CIN	286

Runs Batted In
G. Luzinski, PHI	120
J. Bench, CIN	110
T. Perez, CIN	109
R. Staub, NY	105

Stolen Bases
D. Lopes, LA	77
J. Morgan, CIN	67
L. Brock, STL	56
C. Cedeno, HOU	50
J. Cardenal, CHI	34

Hits
D. Cash, PHI	213
S. Garvey, LA	210
P. Rose, CIN	210

Base on Balls
J. Morgan, CIN	132
J. Wynn, LA	110
D. Evans, ATL	105

Home Run Percentage
D. Kingman, NY	7.2
M. Schmidt, PHI	6.8
G. Luzinski, PHI	5.7

Runs Scored
P. Rose, CIN	112
D. Cash, PHI	111
D. Lopes, LA	108

Doubles
P. Rose, CIN	47
D. Cash, PHI	40
J. Bench, CIN	39
A. Oliver, PIT	39

Triples
R. Garr, ATL	11

PITCHING LEADERS

Winning Percentage
T. Seaver, NY	.710
B. Hooton, CHI, LA	.667
R. Jones, SD	.625
G. Nolan, CIN	.625
J. Montefusco, SF	.625
D. Rau, LA	.625

Earned Run Average
R. Jones, SD	2.24
Messersmith, LA	2.29
T. Seaver, NY	2.38
J. Reuss, PIT	2.54
B. Forsch, STL	2.86

Wins
T. Seaver, NY	22
R. Jones, SD	20
Messersmith, LA	19
B. Hooton, CHI, LA	18
J. Reuss, PIT	18

Saves
A. Hrabosky, STL	22
R. Eastwick, CIN	22
D. Giusti, PIT	17
D. Knowles, CHI	15
W. McEnaney, CIN	15

Strikeouts
T. Seaver, NY	243
J. Montefusco, SF	215
Messersmith, LA	213
S. Carlton, PHI	192
J. Richard, HOU	176

Complete Games
Messersmith, LA	19
R. Jones, SD	18
J. Reuss, PIT	15
T. Seaver, NY	15
L. Dierker, HOU	14
S. Carlton, PHI	14

Fewest Hits per 9 Innings
Messersmith, LA	6.82
D. Warthen, MON	6.96
T. Seaver, NY	6.98

Shutouts
Messersmith, LA	7
J. Reuss, PIT	6
R. Jones, SD	6
T. Seaver, NY	5

Fewest Walks per 9 Innings
G. Nolan, CIN	1.24
R. Jones, SD	1.77
R. Reed, ATL, STL	1.90

Most Strikeouts per 9 Inn.
J. Montefusco, SF	7.93
T. Seaver, NY	7.81
D. Warthen, MON	6.86

Innings
Messersmith, LA	322
R. Jones, SD	285
T. Seaver, NY	280

Games Pitched
G. Garber, PHI	71
W. McEnaney, CIN	70
P. Borbon, CIN	67
D. Tomlin, SD	67

	W	L	PCT	GB	R	OR	Batting							Fielding			Pitching				
							2B	3B	HR	BA	SA	SB	E	DP	FA	CG	BB	SO ShO	SV	ERA

EAST

	W	L	PCT	GB	R	OR	2B	3B	HR	BA	SA	SB	E	DP	FA	CG	BB	SO	ShO	SV	ERA
PIT	92	69	.571		712	565	255	47	**138**	.263	**.402**	49	151	147	.976	43	551	768	14	31	3.02
PHI	86	76	.531	6.5	735	694	**283**	42	125	.269	.402	126	152	156	.976	33	546	897	11	30	3.82
NY	82	80	.506	10.5	646	625	217	34	101	.256	.361	32	151	144	.976	40	580	**989**	14	31	3.39
STL	82	80	.506	10.5	662	689	239	46	81	**.273**	.375	116	171	140	.973	33	571	824	13	36	3.58
CHI	75	87	.463	17.5	712	827	229	41	95	.259	.368	67	179	152	.972	27	551	850	8	33	4.57
MON	75	87	.463	17.5	601	690	216	31	98	.244	.348	108	180	**179**	.973	30	665	831	12	25	3.73

WEST

	W	L	PCT	GB	R	OR	2B	3B	HR	BA	SA	SB	E	DP	FA	CG	BB	SO	ShO	SV	ERA
CIN	108	54	.667		**840**	586	278	37	124	.271	.401	**168**	**102**	173	**.984**	22	487	663	8	**50**	3.37
LA	88	74	.543	20	648	**534**	217	31	118	.248	.365	138	127	106	.979	**51**	**448**	894	**18**	21	**2.92**
SF	80	81	.497	27.5	659	671	235	45	84	.259	.365	99	146	164	.976	37	612	856	9	24	3.74
SD	71	91	.438	37	552	683	215	22	78	.244	.335	85	188	163	.971	40	521	713	12	20	3.51
ATL	67	94	.416	40.5	583	739	179	28	107	.244	.346	55	175	147	.972	32	519	669	4	25	3.93
HOU	64	97	.398	43.5	664	711	218	**54**	84	.254	.359	133	137	166	.979	39	679	839	6	25	4.05
					8014	8014	2781	458	1233	.257	.369	1176	1859	1837	.976	427	6730	9793	129	351	3.63

American League 1975

East

	POS	Player	AB	BA	HR	RBI	PO	A	E	DP	TC/G	FA	Pitcher	G	IP	W	L	SV	ERA
Bos. W-95 L-65 Darrell Johnson	1B	Yastrzemski	543	.269	14	60	1202	87	5	103	9.2	.996	B. Lee	41	260	17	9	0	3.95
	2B	D. Griffin	287	.240	1	29	195	215	14	45	4.3	.967	L. Tiant	35	260	18	14	0	4.02
	SS	R. Burleson	580	.252	6	62	266	495	29	102	5.0	.963	R. Wise	35	255	19	12	0	3.95
	3B	R. Petrocelli	402	.239	7	59	84	228	13	13	2.9	.960	R. Cleveland	31	171	13	9	0	4.42
	RF	D. Evans	412	.274	13	56	281	15	4	8	2.6	.987	R. Moret	36	145	14	3	1	3.60
	CF	F. Lynn	528	.331	21	105	404	11	7	1	2.9	.983	D. Pole	18	90	4	6	0	4.40
	LF	J. Rice	564	.309	22	102	162	6	0	0	1.9	1.000	D. Drago	40	73	2	2	15	3.82
	C	C. Fisk	263	.331	10	52	347	30	8	2	5.4	.978	D. Segui	33	71	2	5	6	4.82
	DH	C. Cooper	305	.311	14	44							J. Willoughby	24	48	5	2	8	3.56
	OF	B. Carbo	319	.257	15	50	157	7	4	1	2.0	.976							
	2B	D. Doyle	310	.310	4	36	141	193	9	35	4.1	.974							
	UT	J. Beniquez	254	.291	2	17	110	17	1	2		.992							
	C	B. Montgomery	195	.226	2	26	210	23	3	6	4.5	.987							
	3B	B. Heise	126	.214	0	21	36	90	8	7	3.0	.940							
Bal. W-90 L-69 Earl Weaver	1B	L. May	580	.262	20	99	**1312**	106	10	**138**	9.9	.993	J. Palmer	39	323	**23**	11	1	**2.09**
	2B	B. Grich	524	.260	13	57	**423**	**484**	21	**122**	6.2	.977	M. Torrez	36	271	20	9	0	3.06
	SS	M. Belanger	442	.226	3	27	259	508	17	**105**	5.2	.978	M. Cuellar	36	256	14	12	0	3.66
	3B	B. Robinson	482	.201	6	53	96	326	9	30	3.0	**.979**	R. Grimsley	35	197	10	13	0	4.07
	RF	K. Singleton	586	.300	15	55	283	9	3	2	1.9	.990	D. Alexander	32	133	8	8	1	3.05
	CF	P. Blair	440	.218	5	31	327	8	3	1	2.4	.991	W. Garland	29	87	2	5	4	3.72
	LF	D. Baylor	524	.282	25	76	268	8	5	0	2.1	.982	G. Jackson	41	48	4	3	7	3.38
	C	D. Duncan	307	.205	12	41	397	41	8	5	4.7	.982	D. Miller	30	46	6	3	8	2.74
	DH	T. Davis	460	.283	6	57					.0								
	OF	A. Bumbry	349	.269	2	32	70	2	0	1		1.000							
	C	E. Hendricks	223	.215	8	38	332	36	2	3	4.5	**.995**							
	UT	D. DeCinces	167	.251	4	23	92	115	7	20		.967							
N. Y. W-83 L-77 Bill Virdon W-53 L-51 Billy Martin W-30 L-26	1B	C. Chambliss	562	.304	9	72	1222	106	12	113	9.1	.991	C. Hunter	39	**328**	**23**	14	0	2.58
	2B	S. Alomar	489	.239	2	39	340	368	11	93	4.8	**.985**	D. Medich	38	272	16	16	0	3.50
	SS	J. Mason	223	.152	2	16	134	209	16	45	3.9	.955	R. May	32	212	14	12	0	3.06
	3B	G. Nettles	581	.267	21	91	135	**379**	19	31	3.4	.964	P. Dobson	33	208	11	14	0	4.07
	RF	B. Bonds	529	.270	32	85	287	12	4	6	2.3	.987	L. Gura	26	151	7	8	0	3.51
	CF	E. Maddox	218	.307	1	23	157	5	0	3	2.9	1.000	S. Lyle	49	89	5	7	6	3.12
	LF	R. White	556	.290	12	59	303	11	5	0	2.4	.984	D. Tidrow	37	69	6	3	5	3.13
	C	T. Munson	597	.318	12	102	700	95	23	**14**	6.3	.972	T. Martinez	23	37	1	2	8	2.68
	DH	E. Herrmann	200	.255	6	30					.0								
	SS	F. Stanley	252	.222	0	15	105	189	7	36	3.6	.977							
	OF	L. Piniella	199	.196	0	22	65	5	1	0	1.5	.986							
	UT	W. Williams	185	.281	5	16	57	4	1	0		.984							
Cle. W-79 L-80 Frank Robinson	1B	B. Powell	435	.297	27	86	997	69	3	92	8.8	**.997**	D. Eckersley	34	187	13	7	2	2.60
	2B	D. Kuiper	346	.292	0	25	192	230	12	65	5.0	.972	F. Peterson	25	146	14	8	0	3.94
	SS	F. Duffy	482	.243	1	47	225	464	25	85	4.9	.977	D. Hood	29	135	6	10	0	4.39
	3B	B. Bell	553	.271	10	59	**146**	330	25	29	3.3	.950	R. Harrison	19	126	7	7	0	4.79
	RF	G. Hendrick	561	.258	24	86	338	4	6	1	2.4	.983	G. Perry	15	122	6	9	0	3.55
	CF	R. Manning	480	.285	3	35	331	12	9	2	3.0	.974	J. Bibby	24	113	5	9	1	3.20
	LF	C. Spikes	345	.229	11	33	176	13	5	5	1.9	.974	E. Raich	18	93	7	8	0	5.54
	C	A. Ashby	254	.226	5	32	441	43	5	6	5.6	.990	D. LaRoche	61	82	5	3	17	2.19
	DH	R. Carty	383	.308	18	64					.0		T. Buskey	50	77	5	3	7	2.57
	C	J. Ellis	296	.230	7	32	396	44	11	3	5.4	.976							
	UT	J. Lowenstein	265	.242	12	33	61	16	2	1		.975							
	2B	J. Brohamer	217	.244	6	16	166	162	8	52	5.1	.976							
	DH	F. Robinson	118	.237	9	24					.0								

Mil.
W-68 L-94
Del Crandall
W-67 L-94
Harvey Kuenn
W-1 L-0

POS	Player	AB	BA	HR	RBI	PO	A	E	DP	TC/G	FA
1B	G. Scott	617	.285	36	109	1202	109	14	118	9.2	.989
2B	P. Garcia	302	.225	6	38	230	293	8	67	5.6	.985
SS	R. Yount	558	.267	8	52	273	402	44	80	5.0	.939
3B	D. Money	405	.277	15	43	95	179	14	22	2.9	.951
RF	G. Thomas	240	.179	10	28	215	5	9	1	2.0	.961
CF	S. Lezcano	429	.247	11	43	240	10	6	1	2.0	.977
LF	B. Sharp	373	.255	1	34	294	12	2	4	2.5	.994
C	D. Porter	409	.232	18	60	532	82	13	10	5.1	.979
DH	H. Aaron	465	.234	12	60					.0	
32	K. Bevacqua	258	.229	2	24	145	159	12	32		.962
CO	C. Moore	241	.290	1	29	234	23	10	2		.963
OF	B. Mitchell	229	.249	9	41	128	2	1	1	1.8	.992
O1	M. Hegan	203	.251	5	22	241	21	2	19		.992
OF	B. Darwin	186	.247	8	23	82	5	2	1	2.1	.978
2B	B. Sheldon	181	.287	0	14	87	122	5	33	4.9	.977

Pitcher	G	IP	W	L	SV	ERA
P. Broberg	38	220	14	16	0	4.13
J. Slaton	37	217	11	18	0	4.52
J. Colborn	36	206	11	13	2	4.27
B. Travers	28	136	6	11	1	4.29
T. Hausman	29	112	3	6	0	4.10
B. Champion	27	110	6	6	0	5.89
E. Rodriguez	43	88	7	0	7	3.49
T. Murphy	52	72	1	9	20	4.48

Det.
W-57 L-102
Ralph Houk

POS	Player	AB	BA	HR	RBI	PO	A	E	DP	TC/G	FA
1B	D. Meyer	470	.236	8	47	441	37	5	39	10.5	.990
2B	G. Sutherland	503	.258	6	39	278	365	21	83	5.2	.968
SS	T. Veryzer	404	.252	5	48	215	358	24	62	4.7	.960
3B	A. Rodriguez	507	.245	13	60	136	375	25	33	3.5	.953
RF	L. Roberts	447	.257	10	38	268	10	5	2	2.2	.982
CF	R. LeFlore	550	.258	8	37	317	13	9	3	2.5	.973
LF	B. Oglivie	332	.286	9	36	192	4	5	1	2.3	.975
C	B. Freehan	427	.246	14	47	582	64	6	8	5.8	.991
DH	W. Horton	615	.275	25	92					.0	
1B	J. Pierce	170	.235	8	22	407	26	13	38	9.1	.971
UT	M. Stanley	164	.256	3	19	183	22	2	9		.990

Pitcher	G	IP	W	L	SV	ERA
M. Lolich	32	241	12	18	0	3.78
J. Coleman	31	201	10	18	0	5.55
V. Ruhle	32	190	11	12	0	4.03
L. LaGrow	32	164	7	14	0	4.38
R. Bare	29	151	8	13	0	4.48
T. Walker	36	115	3	8	0	4.45
D. Lemanczyk	26	109	2	7	0	4.46
J. Hiller	36	71	2	3	14	2.17

West

Oak.
W-98 L-64
Alvin Dark

POS	Player	AB	BA	HR	RBI	PO	A	E	DP	TC/G	FA
1B	J. Rudi	468	.278	21	75	732	36	7	64	8.5	.991
2B	P. Garner	488	.246	6	54	354	426	26	93	5.0	.968
SS	B. Campaneris	509	.265	4	46	199	378	23	58	4.4	.962
3B	S. Bando	562	.230	15	78	122	314	15	36	2.8	.967
RF	R. Jackson	593	.253	36	104	315	13	12	5	2.3	.965
CF	B. North	524	.273	1	43	420	10	11	1	3.2	.975
LF	C. Washington	590	.308	10	77	305	8	7	1	2.2	.978
C	G. Tenace	498	.255	29	87	541	63	10	10	4.9	.984
DH	B. Williams	520	.244	23	81					.0	

Pitcher	G	IP	W	L	SV	ERA
V. Blue	39	278	22	11	1	3.01
K. Holtzman	39	266	18	14	0	3.14
R. Fingers	75	127	10	6	24	2.98
J. Todd	58	122	8	3	12	2.29
P. Lindblad	68	122	9	1	7	2.72
D. Bosman	22	123	11	4	0	3.52
G. Abbott	30	114	5	5	0	4.25
S. Bahnsen	21	100	6	7	0	3.24

K. C.
W-91 L-71
Jack McKeon
W-50 L-46
Whitey Herzog
W-41 L-25

POS	Player	AB	BA	HR	RBI	PO	A	E	DP	TC/G	FA
1B	J. Mayberry	554	.291	34	106	1199	100	16	105	10.0	.988
2B	C. Rojas	406	.254	2	37	233	303	11	65	4.7	.980
SS	F. Patek	483	.228	5	45	231	405	27	78	4.9	.959
3B	G. Brett	634	.308	11	89	131	355	26	27	3.2	.949
RF	A. Cowens	328	.277	4	42	214	4	5	2	2.0	.978
CF	A. Otis	470	.247	9	46	310	9	4	3	2.5	.988
LF	H. McRae	480	.306	5	71	207	7	3	2	1.9	.986
C	B. Martinez	226	.226	3	23	361	39	8	4	5.2	.980
DH	H. Killebrew	312	.199	14	44					.0	
OF	J. Wohlford	353	.255	0	30	175	9	9	1	1.9	.953
OF	V. Pinson	319	.223	4	22	144	6	1	0	1.8	.993
2S	F. White	304	.250	7	36	179	265	11	55		.976
1B	T. Solaita	231	.260	16	44	282	28	2	24		.994
C	F. Healy	188	.255	2	18	258	17	5	2	5.5	.982

Pitcher	G	IP	W	L	SV	ERA
S. Busby	34	260	18	12	0	3.08
A. Fitzmorris	35	242	16	12	0	3.57
D. Leonard	32	212	15	7	0	3.77
M. Pattin	44	177	10	10	5	3.24
P. Splittorff	35	159	9	10	1	3.17
N. Briles	24	112	6	6	2	4.26
D. Bird	51	105	9	6	11	3.25

Tex.
W-79 L-83
Billy Martin
W-44 L-51
Frank Lucchesi
W-35 L-32

POS	Player	AB	BA	HR	RBI	PO	A	E	DP	TC/G	FA
1B	J. Spencer	403	.266	11	47	844	70	5	92	9.3	.995
2B	L. Randle	601	.276	4	57	205	232	12	61	5.7	.973
SS	T. Harrah	522	.293	20	93	198	375	22	68	5.0	.963
3B	B. Howell	383	.251	10	51	80	214	21	32	2.7	.933
RF	J. Burroughs	585	.226	29	94	249	10	9	2	1.8	.966
CF	W. Davis	169	.249	5	17	100	1	1	1	2.4	.990
LF	M. Hargrove	519	.303	11	62	187	2	7	0	2.0	.964
C	J. Sundberg	472	.199	6	36	791	101	17	11	5.9	.981
DH	C. Tovar	427	.258	3	28					.0	
OF	T. Grieve	369	.276	14	61	93	3	1	0		.990
SS	R. Smalley	250	.228	3	33	80	175	16	30	4.6	.941
1B	J. Fregosi	191	.262	7	33	355	34	6	31	7.3	.985
OF	D. Moates	175	.274	3	14	114	6	2	1	2.4	.984
2B	M. Cubbage	143	.224	4	21	67	111	7	24	5.0	.962

Pitcher	G	IP	W	L	SV	ERA
F. Jenkins	37	270	17	18	0	3.93
S. Hargan	33	189	9	10	0	3.80
G. Perry	22	184	12	8	0	3.03
J. Umbarger	56	131	8	7	2	4.12
B. Hands	18	110	6	7	0	4.02
S. Foucault	59	107	8	4	10	4.12
C. Wright	25	93	4	6	0	4.44
S. Thomas	46	81	4	4	3	3.10
J. Brown	17	70	5	5	0	4.22

Min.
W-76 L-83
Frank Quilici

POS	Player	AB	BA	HR	RBI	PO	A	E	DP	TC/G	FA
1B	C. Kusick	156	.237	6	27	372	31	4	45	8.0	.990
2B	R. Carew	535	.359	14	80	285	369	18	79	5.5	.973
SS	D. Thompson	355	.270	5	37	138	245	24	40	4.1	.941
3B	B. Soderholm	419	.286	11	58	94	277	12	14	3.4	.969
RF	L. Bostock	369	.282	0	29	188	3	3	0	2.1	.985
CF	D. Ford	440	.280	15	59	246	3	3	2	2.1	.988
LF	S. Braun	453	.302	11	45	195	6	6	1	2.0	.971
C	G. Borgmann	352	.207	2	33	618	81	8	6	5.7	.989
DH	T. Oliva	455	.270	13	58					.0	
UT	J. Terrell	385	.286	1	36	267	232	14	60		.973
1O	J. Briggs	264	.231	7	39	483	55	8	38		.985
OF	L. Hisle	255	.314	11	51	118	2	3	0	2.1	.976
OF	S. Brye	246	.252	9	34	112	7	2	0	1.7	.983
OF	B. Darwin	169	.219	5	18	28	3	1	0		.969
C	P. Roof	126	.302	7	21	245	30	3	4	4.4	.989

Pitcher	G	IP	W	L	SV	ERA
B. Blyleven	35	276	15	10	0	3.00
J. Hughes	37	250	16	14	0	3.82
D. Goltz	32	243	14	14	0	3.67
V. Albury	32	135	6	7	1	4.53
B. Campbell	47	121	4	6	5	3.79
R. Corbin	18	90	5	7	0	5.12
T. Burgmeier	46	76	5	8	11	3.09

	POS	Player	AB	BA	HR	RBI	PO	A	E	DP	TC/G	FA	Pitcher	G	IP	W	L	SV	ERA
Chi.	1B	C. May	454	.271	8	53	508	46	6	54	8.9	.989	J. Kaat	43	304	20	14	0	3.11
	2B	J. Orta	542	.304	11	83	354	354	16	95	5.4	.978	W. Wood	43	291	16	20	0	4.11
W-75 L-86	SS	B. Dent	602	.264	3	58	279	543	16	105	5.3	.981	C. Osteen	37	204	7	16	0	4.32
Chuck Tanner	3B	B. Melton	512	.240	15	70	131	313	26	23	3.4	.945	G. Gossage	62	142	9	8	26	1.84
	RF	P. Kelly	471	.274	9	45	222	4	2	1	2.0	.991	J. Jefferson	22	108	5	9	0	5.10
	CF	N. Nyman	327	.226	2	28	177	6	8	0	2.0	.958	D. Hamilton	30	70	6	5	6	2.84
	LF	K. Henderson	513	.251	9	53	394	7	4	0	3.0	.990	S. Bahnsen	12	67	4	6	0	6.01
	C	B. Downing	420	.240	7	41	730	84	8	5	6.0	.990	T. Forster	17	37	3	3	4	2.19
	DH	D. Johnson	555	.232	18	72					.0								
	UT	B. Stein	226	.270	3	21	87	118	9	21		.958							
	OF	J. Hairston	219	.283	0	23	111	6	6	1	2.1	.951							
Cal.	1B	B. Bochte	375	.285	3	48	850	51	12	90	8.7	.987	F. Tanana	34	257	16	9	0	2.62
	2B	J. Remy	569	.258	1	46	336	427	14	111	5.3	.982	E. Figueroa	33	245	16	13	0	2.91
W-72 L-89	SS	M. Miley	224	.174	4	26	107	186	19	53	4.5	.939	N. Ryan	28	198	14	12	0	3.45
Dick Williams	3B	D. Chalk	513	.273	3	56	108	333	11	30	3.0	.976	B. Singer	29	179	7	15	1	4.98
	RF	L. Stanton	440	.261	14	82	230	16	10	2	2.0	.961	A. Hassler	30	133	3	12	0	5.94
	CF	M. Rivers	616	.284	1	53	371	13	9	3	2.6	.977	D. Lange	30	102	4	6	1	5.21
	LF	D. Collins	319	.266	3	29	159	3	2	2	2.2	.988	D. Kirkwood	44	84	6	5	7	3.11
	C	E. Rodriguez	226	.235	3	27	492	33	5	2	5.9	.991							
	DH	T. Harper	285	.239	3	31					.0								
	OF	J. Lahoud	192	.214	6	33	41	1	0	0		1.000							

BATTING AND BASE RUNNING LEADERS

Batting Average
R. Carew, MIN	.359
F. Lynn, BOS	.331
T. Munson, NY	.318
J. Rice, BOS	.309
C. Washington, OAK	.308

Slugging Average
F. Lynn, BOS	.566
J. Mayberry, KC	.547
G. Scott, MIL	.515
B. Bonds, NY	.512
R. Jackson, OAK	.511

Home Runs
R. Jackson, OAK	36
G. Scott, MIL	36
J. Mayberry, KC	34
B. Bonds, NY	32
G. Tenace, OAK	29
J. Burroughs, TEX	29

Total Bases
G. Scott, MIL	318
J. Mayberry, KC	303
R. Jackson, OAK	303
F. Lynn, BOS	299
G. Brett, KC	289

Runs Batted In
G. Scott, MIL	109
J. Mayberry, KC	106
F. Lynn, BOS	105
R. Jackson, OAK	104
J. Rice, BOS	102
T. Munson, NY	102

Stolen Bases
M. Rivers, CAL	70
C. Washington, OAK	40
A. Otis, KC	39
R. Carew, MIN	35
J. Remy, CAL	34

Hits
G. Brett, KC	195
R. Carew, MIN	192
T. Munson, NY	190

Base on Balls
J. Mayberry, KC	119
K. Singleton, BAL	118
B. Grich, BAL	107

Home Run Percentage
J. Mayberry, KC	6.1
R. Jackson, OAK	6.1
B. Bonds, NY	6.0

Runs Scored
F. Lynn, BOS	103
J. Mayberry, KC	95
B. Bonds, NY	93

Doubles
F. Lynn, BOS	47
R. Jackson, OAK	39

Triples
M. Rivers, CAL	13
G. Brett, KC	13
J. Orta, CHI	10
A. Cowens, KC	8

PITCHING LEADERS

Winning Percentage
M. Torrez, BAL	.690
D. Leonard, KC	.682
J. Palmer, BAL	.676
V. Blue, OAK	.667
B. Lee, BOS	.654

Earned Run Average
J. Palmer, BAL	2.09
C. Hunter, NY	2.58
D. Eckersley, CLE	2.60
F. Tanana, CAL	2.62
E. Figueroa, CAL	2.91

Wins
J. Palmer, BAL	23
C. Hunter, NY	23
V. Blue, OAK	22
M. Torrez, BAL	20
J. Kaat, CHI	20

Saves
G. Gossage, CHI	26
R. Fingers, OAK	24
T. Murphy, MIL	20
D. LaRoche, CLE	17
D. Drago, BOS	15

Strikeouts
F. Tanana, CAL	269
B. Blyleven, MIN	233
G. Perry, CLE, TEX	233
J. Palmer, BAL	193
V. Blue, OAK	189

Complete Games
C. Hunter, NY	30
G. Perry, CLE, TEX	25
J. Palmer, BAL	25
F. Jenkins, TEX	22
B. Blyleven, MIN	20

Fewest Hits per 9 Innings
C. Hunter, NY	6.80
N. Ryan, CAL	6.91
J. Palmer, BAL	7.05

Shutouts
J. Palmer, BAL	10
C. Hunter, NY	7

Fewest Walks per 9 Innings
F. Jenkins, TEX	1.87
G. Perry, CLE, TEX	2.06
R. Grimsley, BAL	2.15

Most Strikeouts per 9 Inn.
F. Tanana, CAL	9.41
N. Ryan, CAL	8.45
B. Blyleven, MIN	7.61

Innings
C. Hunter, NY	328
J. Palmer, BAL	323
G. Perry, CLE, TEX	306

Games Pitched
R. Fingers, OAK	75
P. Lindblad, OAK	68
G. Gossage, CHI	62

	W	L	PCT	GB	R	OR	Batting 2B	3B	HR	BA	SA	SB	Fielding E	DP	FA	Pitching CG	BB	SO	ShO	SV	ERA
EAST																					
BOS	95	65	.594		796	709	284	44	134	.275	.417	66	139	142	.977	62	490	720	11	31	3.99
BAL	90	69	.566	4.5	682	553	224	33	124	.252	.373	104	107	175	.983	70	500	717	19	21	3.17
NY	83	77	.519	12	681	588	230	39	110	.264	.382	102	135	148	.978	70	502	809	11	20	3.29
CLE	79	80	.497	15.5	688	703	201	25	153	.261	.392	106	134	156	.978	37	599	800	6	32	3.84
MIL	68	94	.420	28	675	792	242	34	146	.250	.389	65	180	162	.971	36	624	643	10	34	4.34
DET	57	102	.358	37.5	570	786	171	39	125	.249	.366	63	173	141	.972	52	533	787	10	17	4.29
WEST																					
OAK	98	64	.605		758	606	220	33	151	.254	.391	183	143	140	.977	36	523	784	10	44	3.29
KC	91	71	.562	7	710	649	263	58	118	.261	.394	155	154	151	.976	52	498	815	11	25	3.49
TEX	79	83	.488	19	714	733	208	17	134	.256	.371	102	191	173	.971	60	518	792	16	17	3.90
MIN	76	83	.478	20.5	724	736	215	28	121	.271	.386	81	170	147	.973	57	617	846	7	22	4.05
CHI	75	86	.466	22.5	655	703	209	38	94	.255	.358	101	140	155	.978	34	657	802	7	39	3.94
CAL	72	89	.447	25.5	628	723	195	41	55	.246	.328	220	184	164	.971	59	613	975	19	16	3.89
					8281	8281	2662	429	1465	.258	.379	1348	1850	1854	.975	625	6674	9490	137	318	3.79

POS	Player	AB	BA	HR	RBI	PO	A	E	DP	TC/G	FA	Pitcher	G	IP	W	L	SV	ERA

East

Phi.
W-101 L-61
Danny Ozark

POS	Player	AB	BA	HR	RBI	PO	A	E	DP	TC/G	FA	Pitcher	G	IP	W	L	SV	ERA
1B	R. Allen	298	.268	15	49	671	44	8	71	8.5	.989	S. Carlton	35	253	20	7	0	3.13
2B	D. Cash	666	.284	1	56	407	424	10	118	5.3	.988	J. Kaat	38	228	12	14	0	3.48
SS	L. Bowa	624	.248	0	49	180	492	17	90	4.4	.975	J. Lonborg	33	222	18	10	1	3.08
3B	M. Schmidt	584	.262	38	107	139	377	21	29	3.4	.961	Christenson	32	169	13	8	0	3.68
RF	J. Johnstone	440	.318	5	53	266	8	5	1	2.3	.982	T. Underwood	33	156	10	5	2	3.53
CF	G. Maddox	531	.330	6	68	441	10	5	0	3.2	.989	R. Reed	59	128	8	7	14	2.46
LF	G. Luzinski	533	.304	21	95	204	8	8	0	1.5	.964	T. McGraw	58	97	7	6	11	2.50
C	B. Boone	361	.271	4	54	557	36	4	5	5.5	.993	G. Garber	59	93	9	3	11	2.82
1O	B. Tolan	272	.261	5	35	395	14	5	36		.988							
OF	O. Brown	209	.254	5	30	105	7	6	2	1.6	.949							
C	T. McCarver	155	.277	3	29	254	9	0	1	6.4	1.000							

Pit.
W-92 L-70
Danny Murtaugh

POS	Player	AB	BA	HR	RBI	PO	A	E	DP	TC/G	FA	Pitcher	G	IP	W	L	SV	ERA
1B	W. Stargell	428	.257	20	65	1037	53	13	76	9.9	.988	J. Candelaria	32	220	16	7	1	3.15
2B	R. Stennett	654	.257	2	60	430	502	18	111	6.1	.981	J. Reuss	31	209	14	9	2	3.53
SS	F. Taveras	519	.258	0	24	210	481	35	74	5.1	.952	J. Rooker	30	199	15	8	1	3.35
3B	R. Hebner	434	.249	8	51	87	236	16	16	2.7	.953	B. Kison	31	193	14	9	1	3.08
RF	D. Parker	537	.313	13	90	294	12	14	0	2.4	.956	D. Medich	29	179	8	11	0	3.51
CF	A. Oliver	443	.323	12	61	301	4	5	0	2.9	.984	L. Demery	36	145	10	7	2	3.17
LF	R. Zisk	581	.289	21	89	300	11	4	2	2.1	.987	K. Tekulve	64	103	5	3	9	2.45
C	M. Sanguillen	389	.290	2	36	518	52	13	7	5.3	.978	B. Moose	53	88	3	9	10	3.70
03	B. Robinson	393	.303	21	64	164	53	8	7		.964	D. Giusti	40	58	5	4	6	4.32
C	D. Dyer	184	.223	3	9	279	37	2	4	5.5	.994							
1B	B. Robertson	129	.217	2	25	257	17	1	28	9.5	.996							

N.Y.
W-86 L-76
Joe Frazier

POS	Player	AB	BA	HR	RBI	PO	A	E	DP	TC/G	FA	Pitcher	G	IP	W	L	SV	ERA
1B	E. Kranepool	415	.292	10	49	675	33	3	48	8.3	.996	T. Seaver	35	271	14	11	0	2.59
2B	F. Millan	531	.282	1	35	311	315	15	68	4.7	.977	J. Matlack	35	262	17	10	0	2.95
SS	B. Harrelson	359	.234	1	26	183	330	20	44	4.6	.962	J. Koosman	34	247	21	10	0	2.70
3B	R. Staiger	304	.220	2	26	55	209	9	18	2.9	.967	M. Lolich	31	193	8	13	0	3.22
RF	J. Milner	443	.271	15	78	195	7	3	2	1.8	.985	C. Swan	23	132	6	9	0	3.55
CF	D. Unser	276	.228	5	25	180	5	1	0	2.4	.995	S. Lockwood	56	94	10	7	19	2.67
LF	D. Kingman	474	.238	37	86	202	10	9	0	2.0	.959	B. Apodaca	43	90	3	7	5	2.80
C	J. Grote	323	.272	4	28	617	49	5	6	7.1	.993							
1B	J. Torre	310	.306	5	31	590	49	7	40	8.3	.989							
OF	B. Boisclair	286	.287	2	13	156	3	3	1	1.9	.981							
UT	M. Phillips	262	.256	4	29	115	191	11	26		.965							
3B	W. Garrett	251	.223	4	26	47	137	10	12	3.0	.948							
C	R. Hodges	155	.226	4	24	262	18	7	0	5.5	.976							

Chi.
W-75 L-87
Jim Marshall

POS	Player	AB	BA	HR	RBI	PO	A	E	DP	TC/G	FA	Pitcher	G	IP	W	L	SV	ERA
1B	P. LaCock	244	.221	8	28	435	30	12	47	8.8	.975	R. Reuschel	38	260	14	12	1	3.46
2B	M. Trillo	582	.239	4	59	349	527	19	103	5.7	.981	R. Burris	37	249	15	13	0	3.11
SS	M. Kelleher	337	.228	0	22	147	289	9	52	4.4	.980	B. Bonham	32	196	9	13	0	4.27
3B	B. Madlock	514	.339	15	84	107	234	14	21	2.6	.961	S. Renko	28	163	8	11	0	3.86
RF	J. Morales	537	.274	16	67	273	12	5	6	2.1	.983	B. Sutter	52	83	6	3	10	2.71
CF	R. Monday	534	.272	32	77	278	4	2	0	2.8	.993	J. Coleman	39	79	2	8	4	4.10
LF	J. Cardenal	521	.299	8	47	246	10	5	1	2.0	.981	D. Knowles	58	72	5	7	9	2.88
C	S. Swisher	377	.236	5	42	574	49	11	6	5.9	.983	O. Zamora	40	55	5	3	3	5.24
OF	J. Wallis	338	.254	5	21	193	11	5	3	2.3	.976							
C	G. Mitterwald	303	.215	5	28	320	40	7	2	5.7	.981							
SS	D. Rosello	227	.242	1	11	128	217	12	45	4.2	.966							
1O	L. Biittner	192	.245	0	17	266	34	4	20		.987							

St. L.
W-72 L-90
Red Schoendienst

POS	Player	AB	BA	HR	RBI	PO	A	E	DP	TC/G	FA	Pitcher	G	IP	W	L	SV	ERA
1B	K. Hernandez	374	.289	7	46	862	107	10	87	8.9	.990	P. Falcone	32	212	12	16	0	3.23
2B	M. Tyson	245	.286	3	28	158	237	12	54	5.5	.971	J. Denny	30	207	11	9	0	2.52
SS	D. Kessinger	502	.239	1	40	212	350	18	84	5.1	.969	L. McGlothen	33	205	13	15	0	3.91
3B	H. Cruz	526	.228	13	71	100	270	26	19	2.7	.934	B. Forsch	33	194	8	10	0	3.94
RF	W. Crawford	392	.304	9	50	209	6	4	1	2.0	.982	E. Rasmussen	43	150	6	12	0	3.53
CF	J. Mumphrey	384	.258	1	26	261	6	2	1	2.9	.993	J. Curtis	37	134	6	11	1	4.50
LF	L. Brock	498	.301	4	67	221	6	4	0	1.9	.983	A. Hrabosky	68	95	8	6	13	3.30
C	T. Simmons	546	.291	5	75	493	66	4	4	5.0	.993	B. Greif	47	55	1	5	6	4.12
OF	B. McBride	272	.335	3	24	201	5	4	0	3.2	.981							
UT	V. Harris	259	.228	1	19	173	103	14	21		.952							
SS	G. Templeton	213	.291	1	17	111	172	24	41	5.8	.922							
OF	M. Anderson	199	.291	1	12	106	5	2	1	1.9	.982							
C	J. Ferguson	189	.201	4	21	238	32	6	6	5.8	.978							
UT	R. Smith	170	.218	8	23	184	44	2	18		.991							
1B	R. Fairly	110	.264	0	21	174	21	1	19	7.3	.995							

Mon.
W-55 L-107
Karl Kuehl
W-43 L-85
Charlie Fox
W-12 L-22

POS	Player	AB	BA	HR	RBI	PO	A	E	DP	TC/G	FA	Pitcher	G	IP	W	L	SV	ERA
1B	M. Jorgensen	343	.254	6	23	599	57	7	59	8.2	.989	S. Rogers	33	230	7	17	1	3.21
2B	P. Mackanin	380	.224	8	33	201	289	18	60	5.1	.965	W. Fryman	34	216	13	13	2	3.37
SS	T. Foli	546	.264	6	54	247	469	18	102	5.0	.975	D. Stanhouse	34	184	9	12	1	3.77
3B	L. Parrish	543	.232	11	61	122	310	25	35	3.0	.945	D. Carrithers	34	140	6	12	0	4.43
RF	E. Valentine	305	.279	7	39	162	12	5	4	2.0	.972	D. Murray	81	113	4	9	13	3.26
CF	P. Mangual	215	.260	3	16	146	3	5	1	2.5	.968	D. Warthen	23	90	2	10	0	5.30
LF	J. White	278	.245	2	21	157	4	3	0	1.8	.982							
C	B. Foote	350	.234	7	27	476	59	6	13	5.6	.989							
CO	G. Carter	311	.219	6	38	364	42	2	8		.995							
OF	D. Unser	220	.227	7	15	108	5	2	2	1.8	.983							
1B	E. Williams	190	.237	8	29	377	41	8	37	9.1	.981							
OF	B. Rivera	185	.276	2	19	89	7	5	3	1.8	.950							
1B	A. Thornton	183	.191	9	24	326	26	2	43	8.2	.994							
2B	W. Garrett	177	.243	2	11	121	157	5	32	5.2	.982							
1C	J. Morales	158	.316	4	37	137	21	3	9		.981							

West

Cin.
W-102 L-60
Sparky Anderson

POS	Player	AB	BA	HR	RBI	PO	A	E	DP	TC/G	FA	Pitcher	G	IP	W	L	SV	ERA
1B	T. Perez	527	.260	19	91	1158	73	5	110	9.1	.996	G. Nolan	34	239	15	9	0	3.46
2B	J. Morgan	472	.320	27	111	342	335	13	85	5.2	.981	P. Zachry	38	204	14	7	0	2.74
SS	D. Concepcion	576	.281	9	69	304	506	27	93	5.6	.968	F. Norman	33	180	12	7	0	3.10
3B	P. Rose	665	.323	10	63	115	293	13	25	2.6	.969	J. Billingham	34	177	12	10	1	4.32
RF	K. Griffey	562	.336	6	74	270	10	6	2	2.0	.979	S. Alcala	30	132	11	4	0	4.70
CF	C. Geronimo	486	.307	2	49	386	4	6	2	2.7	.985	D. Gullett	23	126	11	3	1	3.00
LF	G. Foster	562	.306	29	121	322	9	2	3	2.3	.994	P. Borbon	69	121	4	3	8	3.35
C	J. Bench	465	.234	16	74	651	60	2	11	5.6	.997	R. Eastwick	71	108	11	5	26	2.08
1O	D. Driessen	219	.247	7	44	314	23	2	33		.994	W. McEnaney	55	72	2	6	7	4.88
UT	D. Flynn	219	.283	1	20	107	152	4	33		.985							
OF	M. Lum	136	.228	3	20	48	0	0	0	1.3	1.000							
OF	B. Bailey	124	.298	6	23	35	2	1	1	1.2	.974							

L. A.
W-92 L-70
Walter Alston
W-90 L-68
Tom Lasorda
W-2 L-2

POS	Player	AB	BA	HR	RBI	PO	A	E	DP	TC/G	FA	Pitcher	G	IP	W	L	SV	ERA
1B	S. Garvey	631	.317	13	80	1583	67	3	138	10.2	.998	D. Sutton	35	268	21	10	0	3.06
2B	D. Lopes	427	.241	4	20	218	266	18	56	5.0	.964	D. Rau	34	231	16	12	0	2.57
SS	B. Russell	554	.274	5	65	251	476	28	90	5.1	.963	B. Hooton	33	227	11	15	0	3.26
3B	R. Cey	502	.277	23	80	111	334	16	22	3.2	.965	T. John	31	207	10	10	0	3.09
RF	R. Smith	225	.280	10	26	130	3	2	2	2.3	.985	R. Rhoden	27	181	12	3	0	2.98
CF	D. Baker	384	.242	4	39	254	3	1	1	2.4	.996	C. Hough	77	143	12	8	18	2.21
LF	B. Buckner	642	.301	7	60	315	7	5	0	2.1	.985	M. Marshall	30	63	4	3	8	4.45
C	S. Yeager	359	.214	11	35	522	77	9	9	5.3	.985							
2B	T. Sizemore	266	.241	0	18	168	191	5	51	5.1	.986							
OC	J. Ferguson	185	.222	6	18	156	12	6	2		.966							

Hou.
W-80 L-82
Bill Virdon

POS	Player	AB	BA	HR	RBI	PO	A	E	DP	TC/G	FA	Pitcher	G	IP	W	L	SV	ERA
1B	B. Watson	585	.313	16	102	1395	96	15	126	9.7	.990	J. Richard	39	291	20	15	0	2.75
2B	R. Andrews	410	.256	0	23	228	354	14	66	5.6	.977	L. Dierker	28	188	13	14	0	3.69
SS	R. Metzger	481	.210	0	29	253	462	10	93	4.8	.986	J. Andujar	28	172	9	10	0	3.61
3B	E. Cabell	586	.273	2	43	128	263	17	24	2.9	.958	J. Niekro	36	118	4	8	0	3.36
RF	J. Cruz	439	.303	4	61	265	10	8	4	2.3	.972	D. Larson	13	92	5	8	0	3.03
CF	C. Cedeno	575	.297	18	83	377	11	8	5	2.7	.980	K. Forsch	52	92	4	3	19	2.15
LF	G. Gross	426	.286	0	27	208	13	5	4	2.0	.978	McLaughlin	17	79	4	5	1	2.85
C	E. Herrmann	265	.204	3	25	412	37	6	5	5.8	.987	G. Pentz	40	64	3	3	5	2.95
UT	C. Johnson	318	.226	10	49	468	35	9	10		.982							
OF	L. Roberts	235	.289	7	33	99	1	2	0	1.7	.980							
OF	W. Howard	191	.220	1	18	96	2	4	1	1.6	.961							
UT	J. DaVanon	107	.290	1	20	53	94	7	16		.955							

S. F.
W-74 L-88
Billy Rigney

POS	Player	AB	BA	HR	RBI	PO	A	E	DP	TC/G	FA	Pitcher	G	IP	W	L	SV	ERA
1B	D. Evans	257	.222	10	36	681	68	7	53	9.1	.991	J. Montefusco	37	253	16	14	0	2.84
2B	M. Perez	332	.259	2	26	189	273	10	51	5.3	.979	J. Barr	37	252	15	12	0	2.89
SS	C. Speier	495	.226	3	40	225	441	18	81	5.1	.974	E. Halicki	32	186	12	14	0	3.62
3B	K. Reitz	577	.267	5	66	140	303	19	32	3.0	.959	G. Lavelle	65	110	10	6	12	2.69
RF	B. Murcer	533	.259	23	90	282	11	12	2	2.1	.961	R. Dressler	25	108	3	10	0	4.43
CF	L. Herndon	337	.288	2	23	226	8	8	4	2.2	.967	M. Caldwell	50	107	1	7	2	4.86
LF	G. Matthews	587	.279	20	84	265	8	7	0	1.8	.975	J. D'Acquisto	28	106	3	8	0	5.35
C	D. Rader	255	.263	1	22	349	32	6	4	4.8	.984	R. Moffitt	58	103	6	6	14	2.27
1O	G. Thomasson	328	.259	8	38	436	20	12	28		.974							
2B	D. Thomas	272	.232	2	19	160	212	14	52	5.6	.964							
1B	W. Montanez	230	.309	2	22	583	51*	7*	54*	11.1*	.989							

S. D.
W-73 L-89
John McNamara

POS	Player	AB	BA	HR	RBI	PO	A	E	DP	TC/G	FA	Pitcher	G	IP	W	L	SV	ERA
1B	M. Ivie	405	.291	7	70	1020	70	5	89	8.1	.995	R. Jones	40	315	22	14	0	2.74
2B	T. Fuentes	520	.263	2	36	339	387	22	91	5.9	.971	B. Strom	36	211	12	16	0	3.29
SS	E. Hernandez	340	.256	1	24	132	344	18	64	4.9	.964	D. Freisleben	34	172	10	13	1	3.51
3B	D. Rader	471	.257	9	55	109	318	20	22	3.3	.955	B. Metzger	77	123	11	4	16	2.92
RF	J. Grubb	384	.284	5	27	183	3	5	0	1.9	.974	D. Spillner	32	107	2	11	0	5.06
CF	W. Davis	493	.268	5	46	349	6	3	2	2.8	.992							
LF	D. Winfield	492	.283	13	69	304	15	6	4	2.4	.982							
C	F. Kendall	456	.246	2	39	582	54	4	6	4.4	.994							
OF	J. Turner	281	.267	5	37	115	6	5	0	1.7	.960							
SS	H. Torres	215	.195	4	15	64	160	12	29	3.7	.949							
UT	T. Kubiak	212	.236	0	26	77	110	4	21		.979							
1B	W. McCovey	202	.203	7	36	420	44	4	39	9.2	.991							

Atl.
W-70 L-92
Dave Bristol

POS	Player	AB	BA	HR	RBI	PO	A	E	DP	TC/G	FA	Pitcher	G	IP	W	L	SV	ERA
1B	W. Montanez	420	.321	9	64	986	56*	15*	87*	10.3*	.986	P. Niekro	38	271	17	11	0	3.29
2B	R. Gilbreath	383	.251	1	32	239	311	14	76	5.4	.975	D. Ruthven	36	240	14	17	0	4.20
SS	D. Chaney	496	.252	1	50	243	466	37	88	4.9	.950	Messersmith	29	207	11	11	1	3.04
3B	J. Royster	533	.248	5	45	156	306	18	35	3.2	.963	C. Morton	26	140	4	9	0	4.18
RF	R. Office	435	.262	13	61	219	3	3	0	1.8	.987	F. LaCorte	19	105	3	12	0	4.71
CF	R. Office	359	.281	4	34	204	3	3	2	2.3	.986	A. Devine	48	73	5	6	9	3.21
LF	J. Wynn	449	.207	17	66	287	17	9	2	2.3	.971	E. Sosa	21	35	4	4	3	5.35
C	V. Correll	200	.225	5	16	319	36	7	1	5.6	.981							
OF	T. Paciorek	324	.290	4	36	115	3	2	0	1.4	.983							
OF	D. May	214	.215	3	23	98	5	3	1	1.8	.972							
C1	E. Williams	184	.212	9	26	298	18	1	9		.997							
2B	L. Lacy	180	.272	3	20	88	101	6	25	4.4	.969							
C	B. Pocoroba	174	.241	0	14	273	39	7	5	5.9	.978							
OF	C. Gaston	134	.291	4	25	42	1	1	0	1.6	.977							

BATTING AND BASE RUNNING LEADERS

Batting Average		Slugging Average	
B. Madlock, CHI	.339	J. Morgan, CIN	.576
K. Griffey, CIN	.336	G. Foster, CIN	.530
G. Maddox, PHI	.330	M. Schmidt, PHI	.524
P. Rose, CIN	.323	R. Monday, CHI	.507
J. Morgan, CIN	.320	B. Madlock, CHI	.500

Home Runs		Total Bases	
M. Schmidt, PHI	38	M. Schmidt, PHI	306
D. Kingman, NY	37	P. Rose, CIN	299
R. Monday, CHI	32	G. Foster, CIN	298
G. Foster, CIN	29	S. Garvey, LA	284
J. Morgan, CIN	27	J. Morgan, CIN	272
		W. Montanez, ATL, SF	272

Runs Batted In		Stolen Bases	
G. Foster, CIN	121	D. Lopes, LA	63
J. Morgan, CIN	111	J. Morgan, CIN	60
M. Schmidt, PHI	107	F. Taveras, PIT	58
B. Watson, HOU	102	C. Cedeno, HOU	58
G. Luzinski, PHI	95	L. Brock, STL	56

Hits		Base on Balls	
P. Rose, CIN	215	J. Wynn, ATL	127
W. Montanez, ATL, SF	206	J. Morgan, CIN	114
S. Garvey, LA	200	M. Schmidt, PHI	100

Home Run Percentage		Runs Scored	
M. Schmidt, PHI	6.5	P. Rose, CIN	130
R. Monday, CHI	6.0	J. Morgan, CIN	113
J. Morgan, CIN	5.7	M. Schmidt, PHI	112

Doubles		Triples	
P. Rose, CIN	42	D. Cash, PHI	12
J. Johnstone, PHI	38	C. Geronimo, CIN	11
G. Maddox, PHI	37	W. Davis, SD	10
S. Garvey, LA	37	D. Parker, PIT	10

PITCHING LEADERS

Winning Percentage		Earned Run Average	
S. Carlton, PHI	.741	J. Denny, STL	2.52
J. Candelaria, PIT	.696	D. Rau, LA	2.57
D. Sutton, LA	.677	T. Seaver, NY	2.59
J. Koosman, NY	.677	J. Koosman, NY	2.70
J. Rooker, PIT	.652	P. Zachry, CIN	2.74

Wins		Saves	
R. Jones, SD	22	R. Eastwick, CIN	26
D. Sutton, LA	21	S. Lockwood, NY	19
J. Koosman, NY	21	K. Forsch, HOU	19
S. Carlton, PHI	20	C. Hough, LA	18
J. Richard, HOU	20	B. Metzger, SD	16

Strikeouts		Complete Games	
T. Seaver, NY	235	R. Jones, SD	25
J. Richard, HOU	214	J. Koosman, NY	17
J. Koosman, NY	200	J. Matlack, NY	16
S. Carlton, PHI	195	D. Sutton, LA	15
P. Niekro, ATL	173	J. Richard, HOU	14

Fewest Hits per 9 Innings		Shutouts	
J. Richard, HOU	6.84	J. Matlack, NY	6
T. Seaver, NY	7.01	J. Montefusco, SF	6
J. Candelaria, PIT	7.08	T. Seaver, NY	5
		R. Jones, SD	5

Fewest Walks per 9 Innings		Most Strikeouts per 9 Inn.	
G. Nolan, CIN	1.02	T. Seaver, NY	7.80
J. Kaat, PHI	1.26	J. Koosman, NY	7.29
R. Jones, SD	1.43	S. Carlton, PHI	6.95

Innings		Games Pitched	
R. Jones, SD	315	D. Murray, MON	81
J. Richard, HOU	291	C. Hough, LA	77
P. Niekro, ATL	271	B. Metzger, SD	77
T. Seaver, NY	271		

	W	L	PCT	GB	R	OR	Batting					SB	Fielding			CG	BB	Pitching			
							2B	3B	HR	BA	SA		E	DP	FA			SO	ShO	SV	ERA
EAST																					
PHI	101	61	.623		770	557	259	45	110	.272	.395	127	115	148	.981	34	397	918	9	44	3.10
PIT	92	70	.568	9	708	630	249	56	110	.267	.391	130	163	142	.975	45	460	762	12	35	3.37
NY	86	76	.531	15	615	538	198	34	102	.246	.352	66	131	116	.979	53	419	1025	18	25	2.94
CHI	75	87	.463	26	611	728	216	24	105	.251	.356	74	140	145	.978	27	490	850	12	33	3.93
STL	72	90	.444	29	629	671	243	57	63	.260	.359	123	174	163	.973	35	581	731	15	26	3.61
MON	55	107	.340	46	531	734	224	32	94	.235	.340	86	155	179	.976	26	659	783	10	21	3.99
WEST																					
CIN	102	60	.630		857	633	271	63	141	.280	.424	210	102	157	.984	33	491	790	12	45	3.51
LA	92	70	.568	10	608	543	200	34	91	.251	.349	144	128	154	.980	47	479	747	17	28	3.02
HOU	80	82	.494	22	625	657	195	50	66	.256	.347	150	140	155	.978	42	662	780	17	29	3.55
SF	74	88	.457	28	595	686	211	37	85	.246	.345	88	186	153	.971	27	518	746	18	31	3.53
SD	73	89	.451	29	570	662	216	37	64	.247	.337	92	141	148	.978	47	543	652	11	18	3.65
ATL	70	92	.432	32	620	700	170	30	82	.245	.334	74	167	151	.973	33	564	818	13	27	3.87
					7739	7739	2652	499	1113	.255	.361	1364	1742	1811	.977	449	6263	9602	164	362	3.50

POS	Player	AB	BA	HR	RBI	PO	A	E	DP	TC/G	FA	Pitcher	G	IP	W	L	SV	ERA

East

N. Y.
W-97 L-62
Billy Martin

POS	Player	AB	BA	HR	RBI	PO	A	E	DP	TC/G	FA	Pitcher	G	IP	W	L	SV	ERA
1B	C. Chambliss	641	.293	17	96	1440	109	9	123	10.1	.994	C. Hunter	36	299	17	15	0	3.53
2B	W. Randolph	430	.267	1	40	307	415	19	87	6.0	.974	E. Figueroa	34	257	19	10	0	3.02
SS	F. Stanley	260	.238	1	20	145	251	7	36	3.7	.983	D. Ellis	32	212	17	8	0	3.19
3B	G. Nettles	583	.254	32	93	137	383	19	30	3.4	.965	K. Holtzman	21	149	9	7	0	4.17
RF	O. Gamble	340	.232	17	57	199	10	4	3	2.0	.981	D. Alexander	19	137	10	5	0	3.29
CF	M. Rivers	590	.312	8	67	407	6	6	0	3.1	.986	S. Lyle	64	104	7	8	23	2.26
LF	R. White	626	.286	14	65	380	9	5	1	2.5	.987	D. Tidrow	47	92	4	5	10	2.63
C	T. Munson	616	.302	17	105	537	78	12	8	5.2	.981							
DH	C. May	288	.278	3	40						.0							
OF	L. Piniella	327	.281	3	38	106	4	2	0		.982							
SS	J. Mason	217	.180	1	14	128	245	13	47	4.2	.966							
UT	S. Alomar	163	.239	1	10	95	114	7	18		.968							

Bal.
W-88 L-74
Earl Weaver

POS	Player	AB	BA	HR	RBI	PO	A	E	DP	TC/G	FA	Pitcher	G	IP	W	L	SV	ERA
1B	T. Muser	326	.227	1	30	683	62	7	65	6.9	.991	J. Palmer	40	315	22	13	0	2.51
2B	B. Grich	518	.266	13	54	389	400	12	91	5.7	.985	W. Garland	38	232	20	7	1	2.68
SS	M. Belanger	522	.270	1	40	239	545	14	97	5.2	.982	R. May	24	152	11	7	0	3.78
3B	D. DeCinces	440	.234	11	42	96	208	19	9	3.0	.941	R. Grimsley	28	137	8	7	0	3.94
RF	R. Jackson	498	.277	27	91	284	8	11	3	2.5	.964	M. Cuellar	26	107	4	13	1	4.96
CF	P. Blair	375	.197	3	16	327	6	7	1	2.4	.979	D. Miller	49	89	2	4	7	2.93
LF	K. Singleton	544	.278	13	70	278	9	5	2	2.2	.983	T. Martinez	28	42	3	1	8	2.59
C	D. Duncan	284	.204	4	17	371	35	6	9	4.4	.985							
DH	L. May	530	.258	25	109						.0							
OF	A. Bumbry	450	.251	9	36	251	9	3	2	2.3	.989							
OF	A. Mora	220	.218	6	25	55	3	3	0		.951							
3B	B. Robinson	218	.211	3	11	59	126	6	11	2.7	.969							
C	R. Dempsey	174	.213	0	10	263	34	4	8	5.2	.987							

Bos.
W-83 L-79
Darrell Johnson
W-41 L-45
Don Zimmer
W-42 L-34

POS	Player	AB	BA	HR	RBI	PO	A	E	DP	TC/G	FA	Pitcher	G	IP	W	L	SV	ERA
1B	Yastrzemski	546	.267	21	102	829	52	2	78	9.4	.998	L. Tiant	38	279	21	12	0	3.06
2B	D. Doyle	432	.250	0	26	209	311	12	67	4.7	.977	R. Wise	34	224	14	11	0	3.54
SS	R. Burleson	540	.291	7	42	274	478	34	88	5.2	.957	F. Jenkins	30	209	12	11	0	3.27
3B	B. Hobson	269	.234	8	34	60	146	14	11	2.9	.936	R. Cleveland	41	170	10	9	2	3.07
RF	D. Evans	501	.242	17	62	324	15	2	4	2.4	.994	D. Pole	31	121	6	5	0	4.31
CF	F. Lynn	507	.314	10	65	367	13	6	4	3.0	.984	R. Jones	24	104	5	3	0	3.36
LF	J. Rice	581	.282	25	85	199	8	7	0	2.2	.967	J. Willoughby	54	99	3	12	10	2.82
C	C. Fisk	487	.255	17	58	649	73	12	9	5.5	.984	B. Lee	24	96	5	7	3	5.63
DH	C. Cooper	451	.282	15	78						.0	T. Murphy	37	81	4	5	8	3.44
OF	R. Miller	269	.283	0	27	220	4	2	1	2.8	.991							
3B	R. Petrocelli	240	.213	3	24	57	120	6	11	2.5	.967							
UT	S. Dillard	167	.275	1	15	58	102	11	21		.936							

Cle.
W-81 L-78
Frank Robinson

POS	Player	AB	BA	HR	RBI	PO	A	E	DP	TC/G	FA	Pitcher	G	IP	W	L	SV	ERA
1B	B. Powell	293	.215	9	33	698	61	10	76	8.6	.987	P. Dobson	35	217	16	12	0	3.48
2B	D. Kuiper	506	.263	0	37	300	365	9	92	5.3	.987	D. Eckersley	36	199	13	12	1	3.44
SS	F. Duffy	392	.212	2	30	222	344	10	83	4.4	.983	J. Brown	32	180	9	11	0	4.25
3B	B. Bell	604	.281	7	60	104	330	20	23	2.9	.956	J. Bibby	34	163	13	7	1	3.20
RF	R. Manning	552	.292	6	43	359	8	5	1	2.7	.987	R. Waits	26	124	7	9	0	3.99
CF	G. Hendrick	551	.265	25	81	288	13	4	6	2.1	.987	J. Kern	50	118	10	7	15	2.36
LF	C. Spikes	334	.237	3	31	185	7	3	0	2.0	.985	S. Thomas	37	106	4	4	6	2.29
C	A. Ashby	247	.239	4	32	475	51	7	7	6.2	.987	D. LaRoche	61	96	1	4	21	2.25
DH	R. Carty	552	.310	13	83						.0	T. Buskey	39	94	5	4	1	3.64
S2	L. Blanks	328	.280	5	41	152	213	11	53		.971							
C	R. Fosse	276	.301	2	30	483	42	7	9	6.3	.987							
OF	J. Lowenstein	229	.205	2	14	97	7	3	1	1.8	.972							
OF	T. Smith	164	.256	2	12	90	4	2	0	1.9	.979							

Det.
W-74 L-87
Ralph Houk

POS	Player	AB	BA	HR	RBI	PO	A	E	DP	TC/G	FA	Pitcher	G	IP	W	L	SV	ERA
1B	J. Thompson	412	.218	17	54	1157	88	8	104	10.7	.994	D. Roberts	36	252	16	17	0	4.00
2B	P. Garcia	227	.198	3	20	168	219	17	53	5.2	.958	M. Fidrych	31	250	19	9	0	2.34
SS	T. Veryzer	354	.234	1	25	164	313	17	53	5.1	.966	V. Ruhle	32	200	9	12	0	3.92
3B	A. Rodriguez	480	.240	8	50	120	280	9	21	3.2	.978	R. Bare	30	134	7	8	0	4.63
RF	R. Staub	589	.299	15	96	218	8	7	3	1.8	.970	J. Hiller	56	121	12	8	13	2.38
CF	R. LeFlore	544	.316	4	39	381	14	11	1	3.1	.973	J. Crawford	32	109	1	8	2	4.53
LF	A. Johnson	429	.268	6	45	159	7	8	1	1.9	.954	D. Lemanczyk	20	81	4	6	0	5.11
C	B. Freehan	237	.270	5	27	312	28	6	2	5.7	.983							
DH	W. Horton	401	.262	14	56						.0							
OF	B. Oglivie	305	.285	15	47	136	7	2	0	2.3	.986							
OF	D. Meyer	294	.252	2	16	76	4	1	1	1.7	.988							
2S	C. Scrivener	222	.221	2	16	134	221	11	46		.970							
UT	M. Stanley	214	.257	4	29	187	47	5	14		.979							

Mil.
W-66 L-95
Alex Grammas

POS	Player	AB	BA	HR	RBI	PO	A	E	DP	TC/G	FA	Pitcher	G	IP	W	L	SV	ERA
1B	G. Scott	606	.274	18	77	1393	107	13	133	9.8	.991	J. Slaton	38	293	14	15	0	3.44
2B	T. Johnson	273	.275	0	14	161	222	8	42	3.9	.980	B. Travers	34	240	15	16	0	2.81
SS	R. Yount	638	.252	2	54	290	510	31	104	5.2	.963	J. Colborn	32	226	9	15	0	3.71
3B	D. Money	439	.267	12	62	96	202	13	21	3.0	.958	J. Augustine	39	172	9	12	0	3.30
RF	S. Lezcano	513	.285	7	56	345	10	10	3	2.6	.973	E. Rodriguez	45	136	5	13	8	3.64
CF	V. Joshua	423	.267	5	28	268	10	5	4	2.7	.982	B. Castro	39	70	4	6	8	3.45
LF	G. Thomas	227	.198	8	36	210	4	3	0	2.3	.986	D. Frisella	32	49	5	2	9	2.74
C	D. Porter	389	.208	5	32	491	52	14	7	5.0	.975							
DH	H. Aaron	271	.229	10	35						.0							
CO	C. Moore	241	.191	3	16	249	44	9	1		.970							
UT	M. Hegan	218	.248	5	31	88	6	2	8		.979							
OF	B. Carbo	183	.235	3	15	71	5	0	1		1.000							
OF	B. Sharp	180	.244	0	11	108	7	3	2	2.1	.975							

	POS	Player	AB	BA	HR	RBI	PO	A	E	DP	TC/G	FA	Pitcher	G	IP	W	L	SV	ERA

West

K. C.
W-90 L-72
Whitey Herzog

	POS	Player	AB	BA	HR	RBI	PO	A	E	DP	TC/G	FA	Pitcher	G	IP	W	L	SV	ERA
	1B	J. Mayberry	594	.232	13	95	1484	105	7	132	10.0	.996	D. Leonard	35	259	17	10	0	3.51
	2B	F. White	446	.229	2	46	255	387	18	75	5.1	.973	A. Fitzmorris	35	220	15	11	0	3.07
	SS	F. Patek	432	.241	1	43	233	426	26	87	4.8	.962	D. Bird	39	198	12	10	2	3.36
	3B	G. Brett	645	.333	7	67	140	335	26	22	3.2	.948	P. Splittorff	26	159	11	8	0	3.96
	RF	A. Cowens	581	.265	3	59	329	13	5	3	2.3	.986	M. Pattin	44	141	8	14	5	2.49
	CF	A. Otis	592	.279	18	86	373	5	3	1	2.5	.992	M. Littell	60	104	8	4	16	2.08
	LF	T. Poquette	344	.302	2	34	188	1	4	0	2.0	.979	A. Hassler	19	100	5	6	0	2.89
	C	B. Martinez	267	.228	5	34	420	40	4	4	4.9	.991	S. Mingori	55	85	5	5	10	2.33
	DH	H. McRae	527	.332	8	73						.0							
	OF	J. Wohlford	293	.249	1	24	189	6	5	0	2.2	.975							
	C	B. Stinson	209	.263	2	25	304	30	7	4	4.3	.979							

Oak.
W-87 L-74
Chuck Tanner

	POS	Player	AB	BA	HR	RBI	PO	A	E	DP	TC/G	FA	Pitcher	G	IP	W	L	SV	ERA
	1B	D. Baylor	595	.247	15	68	629	44	9	40	9.9	.987	V. Blue	37	298	18	13	0	2.36
	2B	P. Garner	555	.261	8	74	378	465	22	91	5.4	.975	M. Torrez	39	266	16	12	0	2.50
	SS	B. Campaneris	536	.256	1	52	231	490	23	66	5.0	.969	S. Bahnsen	35	143	8	7	0	3.34
	3B	S. Bando	550	.240	27	84	125	304	17	26	2.9	.962	P. Mitchell	26	142	9	7	0	4.25
	RF	C. Washington	490	.257	5	53	276	10	11	2	2.4	.963	R. Fingers	70	135	13	11	20	2.47
	CF	B. North	590	.276	2	31	397	8	9	1	2.9	.978	P. Lindblad	65	115	6	5	5	3.05
	LF	J. Rudi	500	.270	13	94	258	6	3	2	2.1	.989	D. Bosman	27	112	4	2	0	4.10
	C	L. Haney	177	.226	0	10	290	45	9	2	4.0	.974	J. Todd	49	83	7	8	4	3.80
	DH	B. Williams	351	.211	11	41	0	0	0	0	.0	.000							
	1C	G. Tenace	417	.249	22	66	840	56	8	50		.991							
	UT	K. McMullen	186	.220	5	23	222	39	2	20		.992							

Min.
W-85 L-77
Gene Mauch

	POS	Player	AB	BA	HR	RBI	PO	A	E	DP	TC/G	FA	Pitcher	G	IP	W	L	SV	ERA
	1B	R. Carew	605	.331	9	90	1394	108	16	149	10.0	.989	D. Goltz	36	249	14	14	0	3.36
	2B	B. Randall	475	.267	1	34	327	423	24	124	5.1	.969	J. Hughes	37	177	9	14	0	4.98
	SS	R. Smalley	384	.271	2	36	189	338	18	70	5.3	.967	B. Singer	26	172	9	9	0	3.77
	3B	M. Cubbage	342	.260	3	49	71	209	18	22	3.0	.940	B. Campbell	78	168	17	5	20	3.00
	RF	D. Ford	514	.267	20	86	267	6	9	1	2.0	.968	S. Luebber	38	119	4	5	2	4.01
	CF	L. Bostock	474	.323	4	60	320	10	4	2	2.7	.988	P. Redfern	23	118	8	8	0	3.51
	LF	L. Hisle	581	.272	14	96	361	16	6	1	2.5	.984	T. Burgmeier	57	115	8	1	1	2.50
	C	B. Wynegar	534	.260	10	69	650	78	16	6	5.4	.978	E. Bane	17	79	4	7	0	5.13
	DH	C. Kusick	266	.259	11	36						.0							
	UT	S. Braun	417	.288	3	61	71	32	6	3		.945							
	OF	S. Brye	258	.264	2	23	147	1	2	0	1.9	.987							
	UT	J. Terrell	171	.246	0	8	82	122	8	27		.962							

Cal.
W-76 L-86
Dick Williams
W-39 L-57
Norm Sherry
W-37 L-29

	POS	Player	AB	BA	HR	RBI	PO	A	E	DP	TC/G	FA	Pitcher	G	IP	W	L	SV	ERA
	1B	B. Bochte	466	.258	2	49	489	39	5	37	9.0	.991	F. Tanana	34	288	19	10	0	2.44
	2B	J. Remy	502	.263	0	28	279	406	16	77	5.3	.977	N. Ryan	39	284	17	18	0	3.36
	SS	D. Chalk	438	.217	0	33	141	293	13	45	4.4	.971	G. Ross	34	225	8	16	0	3.00
	3B	R. Jackson	410	.227	8	40	85	222	16	19	2.8	.950	P. Hartzell	37	166	7	4	2	2.77
	RF	R. Torres	264	.205	6	27	195	5	2	0	1.9	.990	D. Kirkwood	28	158	6	12	0	4.61
	CF	B. Bonds	378	.265	10	54	199	9	5	3	2.2	.977	S. Monge	32	118	6	7	0	3.36
	LF	D. Collins	365	.263	4	28	160	3	1	0	2.3	.994	D. Drago	43	79	7	8	6	2.70
	C	Etchebarren	247	.227	0	21	539	46	12	7	5.9	.980							
	DH	B. Melton	341	.208	6	42						.0							
	S2	M. Guerrero	268	.284	1	18	129	172	14	32		.956							
	1O	D. Briggs	248	.214	1	14	358	26	5	33		.987							
	OF	L. Stanton	231	.190	2	25	128	1	2	0	1.7	.985							
	DH	T. Davis	219	.265	3	26													
	1B	T. Solaita	215	.270	9	33	451	54	1	32	9.4	.998							
	C	T. Humphrey	196	.245	1	19	397	42	9	4	6.3	.980							
	OF	B. Jones	166	.211	6	17	98	6	1	0	1.7	.990							

Tex.
W-76 L-86
Frank Lucchesi

	POS	Player	AB	BA	HR	RBI	PO	A	E	DP	TC/G	FA	Pitcher	G	IP	W	L	SV	ERA
	1B	M. Hargrove	541	.287	7	58	1222	110	21	103	9.6	.984	G. Perry	32	250	15	14	0	3.24
	2B	L. Randle	539	.224	1	51	291	319	18	63	5.6	.971	N. Briles	32	210	11	9	1	3.26
	SS	T. Harrah	584	.260	15	67	290	473	36	81	5.5	.955	B. Blyleven	24	202	9	11	0	2.76
	3B	R. Howell	491	.253	8	53	103	245	28	20	2.9	.926	J. Umbarger	30	197	10	12	0	3.15
	RF	J. Burroughs	604	.237	18	86	289	12	4	3	2.0	.987	S. Hargan	35	124	8	8	1	3.63
	CF	J. Beniquez	478	.255	0	33	410	18	6	3	3.1	.986	S. Foucault	46	76	8	8	5	3.32
	LF	G. Clines	446	.276	0	38	215	9	3	1	2.2	.987	J. Hoerner	41	35	0	4	8	5.14
	C	J. Sundberg	448	.228	3	34	719	96	7	11	5.9	.991							
	DH	T. Grieve	546	.255	20	81						.0							
	UT	D. Thompson	196	.214	1	13	60	117	4	12		.978							

Chi.
W-64 L-97
Paul Richards

	POS	Player	AB	BA	HR	RBI	PO	A	E	DP	TC/G	FA	Pitcher	G	IP	W	L	SV	ERA
	1B	J. Spencer	518	.253	14	70	1206	112	2	116	9.2	.998	G. Gossage	31	224	9	17	1	3.94
	2B	J. Brohamer	354	.251	7	40	263	334	10	74	5.2	.984	B. Johnson	32	211	9	16	0	4.73
	SS	B. Dent	562	.246	2	52	279	468	18	96	4.8	.976	K. Brett	27	201	10	12	1	3.32
	3B	K. Bell	230	.248	5	20	70	124	6	10	3.0	.970	F. Barrios	35	142	5	9	3	4.31
	RF	J. Orta	636	.274	14	72	156	9	5	1	2.2	.971	T. Forster	29	111	2	12	1	4.38
	CF	C. Lemon	451	.246	4	38	353	12	3	1	2.8	.992	P. Vuckovich	33	110	7	4	0	4.66
	LF	R. Garr	527	.300	4	36	254	7	6	2	2.1	.978	D. Hamilton	45	90	6	6	10	3.60
	C	B. Downing	317	.256	3	30	450	38	6	4	5.3	.988	C. Carroll	29	77	4	4	6	2.57
	DH	P. Kelly	311	.254	5	34						.0							
	32	B. Stein	392	.268	4	36	153	241	19	39		.954							
	1B	L. Johnson	222	.320	4	33	210	18	4	20		.983							
	C	J. Essian	199	.246	0	21	319	53	10	10	5.0	.974							

BATTING AND BASE RUNNING LEADERS

Batting Average
G. Brett, KC	.333
H. McRae, KC	.332
R. Carew, MIN	.331
L. Bostock, MIN	.323
R. LeFlore, DET	.316

Slugging Average
R. Jackson, BAL	.502
J. Rice, BOS	.482
G. Nettles, NY	.475
F. Lynn, BOS	.467
R. Carew, MIN	.463

Home Runs
G. Nettles, NY	32
R. Jackson, BAL	27
S. Bando, OAK	27
L. May, BAL	25
G. Hendrick, CLE	25
J. Rice, BOS	25

Total Bases
G. Brett, KC	298
C. Chambliss, NY	283
J. Rice, BOS	280
R. Carew, MIN	280
G. Nettles, NY	277

Runs Batted In
L. May, BAL	109
T. Munson, NY	105
Yastrzemski, BOS	102
L. Hisle, MIN	96
R. Staub, DET	96
C. Chambliss, NY	96

Stolen Bases
B. North, OAK	75
R. LeFlore, DET	58
B. Campaneris, OAK	54
D. Baylor, OAK	52
F. Patek, KC	51

Hits
G. Brett, KC	215
R. Carew, MIN	200
C. Chambliss, NY	188

Base on Balls
M. Hargrove, TEX	97
T. Harrah, TEX	91
B. Grich, BAL	86

Home Run Percentage
G. Nettles, NY	5.5
R. Jackson, BAL	5.4
S. Bando, OAK	4.9

Runs Scored
R. White, NY	104
R. Carew, MIN	97
M. Rivers, NY	95
G. Brett, KC	94

Doubles
A. Otis, KC	40

Triples
G. Brett, KC	14
P. Garner, OAK	12
R. Carew, MIN	12

PITCHING LEADERS

Winning Percentage
B. Campbell, MIN	.773
W. Garland, BAL	.741
D. Ellis, NY	.680
M. Fidrych, DET	.679
E. Figueroa, NY	.655
F. Tanana, CAL	.655

Earned Run Average
M. Fidrych, DET	2.34
V. Blue, OAK	2.36
F. Tanana, CAL	2.44
M. Torrez, OAK	2.50
J. Palmer, BAL	2.51

Wins
J. Palmer, BAL	22
L. Tiant, BOS	21
W. Garland, BAL	20
M. Fidrych, DET	19
E. Figueroa, NY	19
F. Tanana, CAL	19

Saves
S. Lyle, NY	23
D. LaRoche, CLE	21
B. Campbell, MIN	20
R. Fingers, OAK	20
M. Littell, KC	16

Strikeouts
N. Ryan, CAL	327
F. Tanana, CAL	261
B. Blyleven, MIN, TEX	219
D. Eckersley, CLE	200
C. Hunter, NY	173

Complete Games
M. Fidrych, DET	24
F. Tanana, CAL	23
J. Palmer, BAL	23
G. Perry, TEX	21
C. Hunter, NY	21
N. Ryan, CAL	21

Fewest Hits per 9 Innings
N. Ryan, CAL	6.12
F. Tanana, CAL	6.62
D. Eckersley, CLE	7.01

Shutouts
N. Ryan, CAL	7
B. Blyleven, MIN, TEX	6
V. Blue, OAK	6
J. Palmer, BAL	6

Fewest Walks per 9 Innings
D. Bird, KC	1.41
F. Jenkins, BOS	1.85
G. Perry, TEX	1.87

Most Strikeouts per 9 Inn.
N. Ryan, CAL	10.36
D. Eckersley, CLE	9.05
F. Tanana, CAL	8.16

Innings
J. Palmer, BAL	315
C. Hunter, NY	299
V. Blue, OAK	298

Games Pitched
B. Campbell, MIN	78
R. Fingers, OAK	70
P. Lindblad, OAK	65

	W	L	PCT	GB	R	OR	2B	3B	HR	BA	SA	SB	E	DP	FA	CG	BB	SO	ShO	SV	ERA
EAST																					
NY	97	62	.610		730	**575**	231	36	120	.269	.389	163	126	141	.980	62	448	674	15	37	**3.19**
BAL	88	74	.543	10.5	619	598	213	28	119	.243	.358	150	**118**	157	**.982**	59	489	678	16	23	3.31
BOS	83	79	.512	15.5	716	660	257	53	134	.263	**.402**	95	141	148	.978	49	**409**	673	13	27	3.52
CLE	81	78	.509	16	615	615	189	38	85	.263	.359	75	121	159	.980	30	533	928	**17**	**46**	3.48
DET	74	87	.460	24	609	709	207	38	101	.257	.365	107	168	161	.974	55	550	738	12	20	3.87
MIL	66	95	.410	32	570	655	170	38	88	.246	.340	62	152	160	.975	45	567	677	10	27	3.64
WEST																					
KC	90	72	.556		713	611	**259**	**57**	65	.269	.371	218	139	147	.978	41	493	735	12	35	3.21
OAK	87	74	.540	2.5	686	598	208	33	113	.246	.361	**341**	144	130	.977	39	415	711	15	29	3.26
MIN	85	77	.525	5	**743**	704	222	51	81	**.274**	.375	146	172	**182**	.973	29	610	762	11	23	3.72
CAL	76	86	.469	14	550	631	210	23	63	.235	.318	126	150	139	.977	**64**	553	**992**	15	17	3.36
TEX	76	86	.469	14	616	652	213	26	80	.250	.341	87	156	142	.976	63	461	773	15	15	3.47
CHI	64	97	.398	25.5	586	745	209	46	73	.255	.349	120	130	155	.979	54	600	802	10	22	4.25
					7753	7753	2588	467	1122	.256	.361	1690	1717	1821	.977	590	6128	9143	161	321	3.52

East

POS	Player	AB	BA	HR	RBI	PO	A	E	DP	TC/G	FA	Pitcher	G	IP	W	L	SV	ERA
Phi. W-101 L-61 Danny Ozark																		
1B	R. Hebner	397	.285	18	62	927	65	9	91	9.7	.991	S. Carlton	36	283	**23**	10	0	2.64
2B	T. Sizemore	519	.281	4	47	348	427	11	**104**	5.2	.986	Christenson	34	219	19	6	0	4.07
SS	L. Bowa	624	.280	4	41	222	518	13	94	4.9	.983	R. Lerch	32	169	10	6	0	5.06
3B	M. Schmidt	544	.274	38	101	106	**396**	19	33	**3.5**	.964	J. Kaat	35	160	6	11	0	5.40
RF	B. McBride	280	.339	11	41	140	6	2	1	2.0	.986	J. Lonborg	25	158	11	4	0	4.10
CF	G. Maddox	571	.292	14	74	383	7	9	2	**2.9**	.977	R. Reed	60	124	7	5	15	2.76
LF	G. Luzinski	554	.309	39	130	205	11	8	2	1.5	.964	G. Garber	64	103	8	6	19	2.36
C	B. Boone	440	.284	11	66	653	80	8	9	5.7	.989	T. McGraw	45	79	7	3	9	2.62
OF	J. Johnstone	363	.284	15	59	163	9	0	1	1.9	1.000	W. Brusstar	46	71	7	2	3	2.66
OF	J. Martin	215	.260	6	28	117	4	2	1	1.2	.984							
C	T. McCarver	169	.320	6	30	233	14	3	3	6.0	.988							
1B	D. Johnson	156	.321	8	36	291	14	0	26	7.1	1.000							
Pit. W-96 L-66 Chuck Tanner																		
1B	B. Robinson	507	.304	26	104	695	34	6	62	8.5	.992	J. Candelaria	33	231	20	5	0	**2.34**
2B	R. Stennett	453	.336	5	51	269	315	11	70	5.3	.982	J. Reuss	33	208	10	13	0	4.11
SS	F. Taveras	544	.252	1	29	178	449	25	62	4.5	.962	J. Rooker	30	204	14	9	0	3.09
3B	P. Garner	585	.260	17	77	98	240	10	28	3.3	.971	B. Kison	33	193	9	10	0	4.90
RF	D. Parker	637	.338	21	88	389	26	15	0	2.7	.965	G. Gossage	72	133	11	9	26	1.62
CF	O. Moreno	492	.240	7	34	366	10	9	4	2.6	.977	O. Jones	34	108	3	7	0	5.08
LF	A. Oliver	568	.308	19	82	305	6	6	1	2.1	.981	K. Tekulve	72	103	10	1	7	3.06
C	D. Dyer	270	.241	3	19	502	41	2	10	5.9	**.996**	G. Jackson	49	91	5	3	4	3.86
C	E. Ott	311	.264	7	38	455	49	9	6	5.7	.982	L. Demery	39	90	6	5	1	5.10
1B	W. Stargell	186	.274	13	35	449	27	7	26	8.8	.986	T. Forster	33	87	6	4	1	4.45
UT	F. Gonzalez	181	.276	4	27	43	66	2	6		.982							
St. L. W-83 L-79 Vern Rapp																		
1B	K. Hernandez	560	.291	15	91	1453	106	12	**146**	9.9	.992	E. Rasmussen	34	233	11	17	0	3.48
2B	M. Tyson	418	.246	7	57	267	423	15	99	5.2	.979	B. Forsch	35	217	20	7	0	3.48
SS	G. Templeton	621	.322	8	79	285	453	32	98	5.1	.958	J. Denny	26	150	8	8	0	4.50
3B	K. Reitz	587	.261	17	79	121	320	9	35	2.9	**.980**	J. Urrea	41	140	7	6	4	3.15
RF	H. Cruz	339	.236	6	42	154	9	6	1	1.6	.964	P. Falcone	27	124	4	8	1	5.44
CF	J. Mumphrey	463	.287	2	38	291	8	9	1	2.3	.971	T. Underwood	19	100	6	9	0	4.95
LF	L. Brock	489	.272	2	46	184	2	9	1	1.5	.954	B. Metzger	58	93	4	2	7	3.11
C	T. Simmons	516	.318	21	95	683	75	10	5	5.3	.987	C. Carroll	51	90	4	2	4	2.50
OF	T. Scott	292	.291	3	41	223	5	1	0	2.6	.996	A. Hrabosky	65	86	6	5	10	4.40
OF	B. McBride	122	.262	4	20	48	2	0	1	1.5	1.000	R. Eastwick	41	54	3	7	4	4.70
1B	R. Freed	83	.398	5	21	102	7	0	13	6.1	1.000							
Chi. W-81 L-81 Herman Franks																		
1B	B. Buckner	426	.284	11	60	966	58	10	75	10.4	.990	R. Reuschel	39	252	20	10	1	2.79
2B	M. Trillo	504	.280	7	57	330	**467**	25	81	**5.5**	.970	R. Burris	39	221	14	16	0	4.72
SS	I. DeJesus	624	.266	3	40	234	**595**	33	94	5.6	.962	B. Bonham	34	215	10	13	0	4.35
3B	S. Ontiveros	546	.299	10	68	100	324	20	24	2.9	.955	M. Krukow	34	172	8	14	0	4.40
RF	B. Murcer	554	.265	27	89	237	11	5	5	1.7	.980	W. Hernandez	67	110	8	7	4	3.03
CF	J. Morales	490	.290	11	69	247	8	4	3	2.0	.985	B. Sutter	62	107	7	3	31	1.35
LF	G. Gross	239	.322	5	32	109	3	1	0	1.6	.991	P. Reuschel	39	107	5	6	4	4.37
C	G. Mitterwald	349	.238	9	43	621	78	8	13	6.5	.989							
1O	L. Biittner	493	.298	12	62	792	65	11	51		.987							
OF	G. Clines	239	.293	3	41	68	3	1	0	1.1	.986							
OF	J. Cardenal	226	.239	3	18	85	1	1	0	1.4	.989							
C	S. Swisher	205	.190	5	15	327	38	9	3	5.2	.976							
Mon. W-75 L-87 Dick Williams																		
1B	T. Perez	559	.283	19	91	1312	110	11	88	9.7	.992	S. Rogers	40	302	17	16	0	3.10
2B	D. Cash	650	.289	0	43	343	443	11	73	5.2	.986	J. Brown	42	186	9	12	0	4.50
SS	C. Speier	531	.235	5	38	236	435	21	75	5.0	.970	D. Stanhouse	47	158	10	10	10	3.42
3B	L. Parrish	402	.246	11	46	81	225	21	11	2.8	.936	W. Twitchell	22	139	6	5	0	4.21
RF	E. Valentine	508	.293	25	76	232	9	7	1	2.0	.972	S. Bahnsen	23	127	8	9	0	4.82
CF	A. Dawson	525	.282	19	65	352	9	4	1	2.7	.989	S. Alcala	31	102	2	6	2	4.69
LF	W. Cromartie	620	.282	5	50	319	10	8	1	2.2	.976	J. Kerrigan	66	89	3	5	11	3.24
C	G. Carter	522	.284	31	84	811	101	9	14	6.3	.990	W. McEnaney	69	87	3	5	3	3.93
OF	D. Unser	289	.273	12	40	120	2	3	0	1.7	.976	B. Atkinson	55	83	7	2	7	3.36
3B	W. Garrett	159	.270	2	22	34	101	0	2	2.8	1.000							
N. Y. W-64 L-98 Joe Frazier W-15 L-30 Joe Torre W-49 L-68																		
1B	J. Milner	388	.255	12	57	672	48	4	64	8.3	.994	J. Koosman	32	227	8	**20**	0	3.49
2B	F. Millan	314	.248	2	21	197	188	9	43	4.4	.977	N. Espinosa	32	200	10	13	0	3.42
SS	B. Harrelson	269	.178	1	12	141	239	6	41	3.9	.984	J. Matlack	26	169	7	15	0	4.21
3B	L. Randle	513	.304	5	27	98	221	13	25	3.0	.961	C. Swan	26	147	9	10	0	4.22
RF	M. Vail	279	.262	8	35	159	5	6	2	2.0	.965	P. Zachry	19	120	7	6	0	3.76
CF	L. Mazzilli	537	.250	6	46	386	9	3	1	2.6	.992	S. Lockwood	63	104	4	8	20	3.38
LF	S. Henderson	350	.297	12	65	189	4	4	1	2.0	.980	T. Seaver	13	96	7	3	0	3.00
C	J. Stearns	431	.251	12	55	742	76	15	12	6.6	.982	B. Apodaca	59	84	4	8	5	3.43
OF	B. Boisclair	307	.293	4	44	140	1	6	0	1.6	.959							
S2	D. Flynn	282	.191	0	14	155	203	13	38		.965							
O1	E. Kranepool	281	.281	10	40	347	30	4	21		.990							
OF	D. Kingman	211	.209	9	28	76	0	2	0	1.7	.974							
UT	J. Youngblood	182	.253	0	11	99	88	7	21		.964							

POS	Player	AB	BA	HR	RBI	PO	A	E	DP	TC/G	FA	Pitcher	G	IP	W	L	SV	ERA

West

L. A.
W-98 L-64
Tom Lasorda

POS	Player	AB	BA	HR	RBI	PO	A	E	DP	TC/G	FA	Pitcher	G	IP	W	L	SV	ERA
1B	S. Garvey	646	.297	33	115	1606	55	8	137	10.4	.995	D. Sutton	33	240	14	8	0	3.19
2B	D. Lopes	502	.283	11	53	287	380	14	74	5.2	.979	B. Hooton	32	223	12	7	1	2.62
SS	B. Russell	634	.278	4	51	234	523	29	102	5.1	.963	T. John	31	220	20	7	0	2.78
3B	R. Cey	564	.241	30	110	138	346	18	29	3.3	.964	R. Rhoden	31	216	16	10	0	3.75
RF	R. Smith	488	.307	32	87	240	7	5	0	1.8	.980	D. Rau	32	212	14	8	0	3.44
CF	R. Monday	392	.230	15	48	208	3	2	0	1.9	.991	C. Hough	70	127	6	12	22	3.33
LF	D. Baker	533	.291	30	86	227	8	3	2	1.6	.987	M. Garman	49	63	4	4	12	2.71
C	S. Yeager	387	.256	16	55	690	89	18	12	6.5	.977							
UT	L. Lacy	169	.266	6	21	56	69	4	11		.969							
OF	G. Burke	169	.254	1	13	98	1	3	0	1.4	.971							

Cin.
W-88 L-74
Sparky Anderson

POS	Player	AB	BA	HR	RBI	PO	A	E	DP	TC/G	FA	Pitcher	G	IP	W	L	SV	ERA
1B	D. Driessen	536	.300	17	91	1182	75	7	116	8.5	.994	F. Norman	35	221	14	13	0	3.38
2B	J. Morgan	521	.288	22	78	351	359	5	100	4.7	.993	T. Seaver	20	165	14	3	0	2.34
SS	D. Concepcion	572	.271	8	64	280	490	11	101	5.0	.986	J. Billingham	36	162	10	10	0	5.22
3B	P. Rose	655	.311	9	64	98	268	16	18	2.4	.958	P. Borbon	73	127	10	5	18	3.19
RF	K. Griffey	585	.318	12	57	298	10	3	3	2.1	.990	P. Moskau	20	108	6	6	0	4.00
CF	C. Geronimo	492	.266	10	52	375	9	3	2	2.6	.992	D. Capilla	22	106	7	8	0	4.23
LF	G. Foster	615	.320	52	149	352	12	3	1	2.3	.992	D. Murray	61	102	7	2	4	4.94
C	J. Bench	494	.275	31	109	705	66	10	10	5.8	.987	P. Zachry	12	75	3	7	0	5.04

Hou.
W-81 L-81
Bill Virdon

POS	Player	AB	BA	HR	RBI	PO	A	E	DP	TC/G	FA	Pitcher	G	IP	W	L	SV	ERA
1B	B. Watson	554	.289	22	110	1331	118	9	100	10.0	.994	J. Richard	36	267	18	12	0	2.97
2B	A. Howe	413	.264	8	58	192	279	7	49	5.0	.985	M. Lemongello	34	215	9	14	0	3.47
SS	R. Metzger	269	.186	0	16	130	260	11	45	4.2	.973	J. Niekro	44	181	13	8	5	3.03
3B	E. Cabell	625	.282	16	68	140	280	23	17	3.1	.948	J. Andujar	26	159	11	8	0	3.68
RF	J. Cruz	579	.299	17	87	311	11	9	1	2.1	.973	F. Bannister	24	143	8	9	0	4.03
CF	C. Cedeno	530	.279	14	71	335	14	1	2	2.6	.997	J. Sambito	54	89	5	5	7	2.33
LF	T. Puhl	229	.301	0	10	119	3	1	0	2.1	.992	K. Forsch	42	86	5	8	8	2.72
C	J. Ferguson	421	.257	16	61	634	80	11	10	5.9	.985	McLaughlin	46	85	4	7	5	4.24
S2	J. Gonzalez	383	.245	1	27	154	293	27	56		.943							
OF	W. Howard	187	.257	2	13	100	2	1	1	1.7	.990							
OF	C. Johnson	144	.299	10	23	49	4	3	0	1.6	.946							

S. F.
W-75 L-87
Joe Altobelli

POS	Player	AB	BA	HR	RBI	PO	A	E	DP	TC/G	FA	Pitcher	G	IP	W	L	SV	ERA
1B	W. McCovey	478	.280	28	86	1072	60	13	93	8.4	.989	E. Halicki	37	258	16	12	0	3.31
2B	R. Andrews	436	.264	0	25	225	314	20	66	4.9	.964	J. Barr	38	234	12	16	0	4.77
SS	T. Foli	368	.228	4	27	184	302	13	72	4.9	.974	B. Knepper	27	166	11	9	0	3.36
3B	B. Madlock	533	.302	12	46	96	220	17	16	2.6	.949	J. Montefusco	26	157	7	12	0	3.50
RF	J. Clark	413	.252	13	51	226	11	6	2	2.1	.975	C. Williams	55	119	6	5	0	4.01
CF	T. Whitfield	326	.285	7	36	167	4	5	0	2.1	.972	G. Lavelle	73	118	7	7	20	2.06
LF	G. Thomasson	446	.256	17	71	255	2	11	1	2.4	.959	R. Moffitt	64	88	4	9	11	3.58
C	M. Hill	320	.250	9	50	505	57	6	4	5.6	.989	L. McGlothen	21	80	2	9	0	5.63
UT	D. Thomas	506	.267	8	44	307	158	14	24		.971							
UT	D. Evans	461	.254	17	72	324	83	13	15		.969							
OF	R. Elliott	167	.240	7	26	68	5	2	1	1.6	.973							
UT	V. Harris	165	.261	2	14	69	96	8	21		.954							
C	G. Alexander	119	.303	5	20	174	8	6	0	5.7	.968							

S. D.
W-69 L-93
John McNamara
W-20 L-28
Bob Skinner
W-1 L-0
Alvin Dark
W-48 L-65

POS	Player	AB	BA	HR	RBI	PO	A	E	DP	TC/G	FA	Pitcher	G	IP	W	L	SV	ERA
1B	M. Ivie	489	.272	9	66	863	56	7	76	8.8	.992	B. Shirley	39	214	12	18	0	3.70
2B	M. Champion	507	.229	1	43	301	348	17	82	4.5	.974	B. Owchinko	30	170	9	12	0	4.45
SS	B. Almon	613	.261	2	43	303	538	41	87	5.7	.954	T. Griffin	38	151	6	9	0	4.47
3B	T. Ashford	249	.217	3	24	32	145	12	14	2.6	.937	R. Jones	27	147	6	12	0	4.59
RF	G. Richards	525	.290	5	32	193	13	8	0	2.0	.963	D. Freisleben	33	139	7	9	0	4.60
CF	G. Hendrick	541	.311	23	81	386	11	7	2	2.8	.983	R. Fingers	78	132	8	9	35	3.00
LF	D. Winfield	615	.275	25	92	368	15	11	3	2.5	.972	D. Spillner	76	123	7	6	6	3.73
C	G. Tenace	437	.233	15	61	523	61	12	9	6.0	.980	R. Sawyer	56	111	7	6	1	5.84
OF	J. Turner	289	.246	10	48	114	10	7	2	1.9	.947	D. Tomlin	76	102	4	4	3	3.00
C	D. Roberts	186	.220	1	23	254	24	5	2	4.5	.982							
3B	D. Rader	170	.271	5	27	43	104	6	9	3.0	.961							
O1	D. Kingman	168	.238	11	39	142	14	3	5		.981							

Atl.
W-61 L-101
Dave Bristol
W-8 L-21
Ted Turner
W-0 L-1
Dave Bristol
W-53 L-79

POS	Player	AB	BA	HR	RBI	PO	A	E	DP	TC/G	FA	Pitcher	G	IP	W	L	SV	ERA
1B	W. Montanez	544	.287	20	68	1129	70	10	88	9.0	.992	P. Niekro	44	330	16	20	0	4.04
2B	R. Gilbreath	407	.243	8	43	277	305	13	61	4.9	.978	D. Ruthven	25	151	7	13	0	4.23
SS	P. Rockett	264	.254	1	24	152	209	23	38	4.6	.940	B. Capra	45	139	6	11	0	5.37
3B	J. Moore	361	.260	5	34	86	189	17	10	2.8	.942	Messersmith	16	102	5	4	0	4.41
RF	G. Matthews	555	.283	17	64	262	11	10	1	2.0	.965	E. Solomon	18	89	6	6	0	4.55
CF	G. Office	428	.241	5	39	249	8	3	3	2.5	.988	D. Campbell	65	89	6	6	13	3.03
LF	J. Burroughs	579	.271	41	114	249	9	7	3	1.7	.974	R. Camp	54	79	6	3	10	3.99
C	B. Pocoroba	321	.290	8	44	542	78	7	8	6.3	.989	D. Collins	40	71	3	9	2	5.07
UT	J. Royster	445	.216	6	28	182	267	28	40		.941							
OF	B. Bonnell	360	.300	1	45	181	3	4	2	1	.989							
S2	D. Chaney	209	.201	3	15	113	182	8	30	2.5	.974							
PH	C. Gaston	85	.271	3	21													

BATTING AND BASE RUNNING LEADERS

Batting Average

D. Parker, PIT	.338
G. Templeton, STL	.322
G. Foster, CIN	.320
K. Griffey, CIN	.318
T. Simmons, STL	.318

Slugging Average

G. Foster, CIN	.631
G. Luzinski, PHI	.594
R. Smith, LA	.576
M. Schmidt, PHI	.574
J. Bench, CIN	.540

PITCHING LEADERS

Winning Percentage

J. Candelaria, PIT	.800
T. Seaver, CIN, NY	.778
Christenson, PHI	.760
T. John, LA	.741
B. Forsch, STL	.741

Earned Run Average

J. Candelaria, PIT	2.34
T. Seaver, CIN, NY	2.58
B. Hooton, LA	2.62
S. Carlton, PHI	2.64
T. John, LA	2.78

BATTING AND BASE RUNNING LEADERS

Home Runs

G. Foster, CIN	52
J. Burroughs, ATL	41
G. Luzinski, PHI	39
M. Schmidt, PHI	38
S. Garvey, LA	33

Runs Batted In

G. Foster, CIN	149
G. Luzinski, PHI	130
S. Garvey, LA	115
J. Burroughs, ATL	114
B. Watson, HOU	110
R. Cey, LA	110

Hits

D. Parker, PIT	215
P. Rose, CIN	204
G. Templeton, STL	200

Home Run Percentage

G. Foster, CIN	8.5
J. Burroughs, ATL	7.1
G. Luzinski, PHI	7.0

Doubles

D. Parker, PIT	44
D. Cash, MON	42
K. Hernandez, STL	41
W. Cromartie, MON	41

Total Bases

G. Foster, CIN	388
D. Parker, PIT	338
G. Luzinski, PHI	329
S. Garvey, LA	322
M. Schmidt, PHI	312

Stolen Bases

F. Taveras, PIT	70
C. Cedeno, HOU	61
G. Richards, SD	56
O. Moreno, PIT	53
J. Morgan, CIN	49

Base on Balls

G. Tenace, SD	125
J. Morgan, CIN	117
R. Smith, LA	104
M. Schmidt, PHI	104

Runs Scored

G. Foster, CIN	124
K. Griffey, CIN	117
M. Schmidt, PHI	114

Triples

G. Templeton, STL	18
G. Richards, SD	11
M. Schmidt, PHI	11
B. Almon, SD	11

PITCHING LEADERS

Wins

S. Carlton, PHI	23
T. Seaver, CIN, NY	21
J. Candelaria, PIT	20
T. John, LA	20
B. Forsch, STL	20
R. Reuschel, CHI	20

Strikeouts

P. Niekro, ATL	262
J. Richard, HOU	214
S. Rogers, MON	206
S. Carlton, PHI	198
T. Seaver, CIN, NY	196

Fewest Hits per 9 Innings

T. Seaver, CIN, NY	6.85
J. Richard, HOU	7.15
S. Carlton, PHI	7.28

Fewest Walks per 9 Innings

J. Candelaria, PIT	1.95
T. John, LA	2.05
D. Rau, LA	2.08

Innings

P. Niekro, ATL	330
S. Rogers, MON	302
S. Carlton, PHI	283

Saves

R. Fingers, SD	35
B. Sutter, CHI	31
G. Gossage, PIT	26
C. Hough, LA	22
G. Lavelle, SF	20
S. Lockwood, NY	20

Complete Games

P. Niekro, ATL	20
T. Seaver, CIN, NY	19
S. Carlton, PHI	17
S. Rogers, MON	17
J. Richard, HOU	13

Shutouts

T. Seaver, CIN, NY	7
R. Reuschel, CHI	4
S. Rogers, MON	4

Most Strikeouts per 9 Inn.

J. Koosman, NY	7.61
J. Richard, HOU	7.21
P. Niekro, ATL	7.15

Games Pitched

R. Fingers, SD	78
D. Spillner, SD	76
D. Tomlin, SD	76

	W	L	PCT	GB	R	OR	2B	3B	HR	BA	SA	SB	E	DP	FA	CG	BB	SO	ShO	SV	ERA
EAST																					
PHI	101	61	.623		847	668	266	56	186	.279	.448	135	120	168	.981	31	482	856	4	47	3.71
PIT	96	66	.593	5	734	665	278	57	133	.274	.413	260	145	137	.977	25	485	890	15	39	3.61
STL	83	79	.512	18	737	688	252	56	96	.270	.388	134	139	174	.978	26	532	768	10	31	3.81
CHI	81	81	.500	20	692	739	271	37	111	.266	.387	64	153	147	.977	16	489	942	10	44	4.01
MON	75	87	.463	26	665	736	294	50	138	.260	.402	88	129	128	.980	31	579	856	11	33	4.01
NY	64	98	.395	37	587	663	227	30	88	.244	.346	98	134	132	.978	27	490	911	12	28	3.77
WEST																					
LA	98	64	.605		769	582	223	28	191	.266	.418	114	124	160	.981	34	438	930	13	39	3.22
CIN	88	74	.543	10	802	725	269	42	181	.274	.436	170	95	154	.984	33	544	868	12	32	4.22
HOU	81	81	.500	17	680	650	263	60	114	.254	.385	187	142	136	.978	37	529	871	11	28	3.54
SF	75	87	.463	23	673	711	227	41	134	.253	.383	90	179	136	.972	27	529	854	10	33	3.75
SD	69	93	.426	29	692	834	245	49	120	.249	.375	133	189	142	.971	6	673	827	5	44	4.43
ATL	61	101	.377	37	678	895	218	20	139	.254	.376	82	175	127	.972	28	701	915	5	31	4.85
					8556	8556	3033	526	1631	.262	.396	1555	1724	1741	.977	321	6487	10488	118	429	3.91

American League 1977

		POS	Player	AB	BA	HR	RBI	PO	A	E	DP	TC/G	FA	Pitcher	G	IP	W	L	SV	ERA

East

		POS	Player	AB	BA	HR	RBI	PO	A	E	DP	TC/G	FA	Pitcher	G	IP	W	L	SV	ERA
N. Y.		1B	C. Chambliss	600	.287	17	90	1368	98	16	129	9.4	.989	E. Figueroa	32	239	16	11	0	3.58
W-100 L-62		2B	W. Randolph	551	.274	4	40	350	454	16	108	5.6	.980	M. Torrez	31	217	14	12	0	3.86
Billy Martin		SS	B. Dent	477	.247	8	49	250	434	18	90	4.5	.974	R. Guidry	31	211	16	7	1	2.82
		3B	G. Nettles	589	.255	37	107	132	321	12	31	3.0	.974	D. Gullett	22	158	14	4	0	3.59
		RF	R. Jackson	525	.286	32	110	236	7	13	0	2.0	.949	D. Tidrow	49	151	11	4	5	3.16
		CF	M. Rivers	565	.326	12	69	380	11	7	1	2.9	.982	C. Hunter	22	143	9	9	0	4.72
		LF	R. White	519	.268	14	52	301	7	6	4	2.3	.981	S. Lyle	72	137	13	5	26	2.17
		C	T. Munson	595	.308	18	100	657	73	12	4	5.5	.984							
		DH	L. Piniella	339	.330	12	45					.0								
		DH	C. May	181	.227	2	16					.0								
		OF	P. Blair	164	.262	4	25	125	1	4	0	1.6	.969							
		UT	C. Johnson	142	.296	12	31	145	14	1	13		.994							

POS	Player	AB	BA	HR	RBI	PO	A	E	DP	TC/G	FA	Pitcher	G	IP	W	L	SV	ERA
Bal. W-97 L-64 Earl Weaver																		
1B	L. May	585	.253	27	99	907	56	5	101	8.8	.995	J. Palmer	39	**319**	**20**	11	0	2.91
2B	B. Smith	367	.215	5	29	260	272	5	78	5.2	.991	R. May	37	252	18	14	0	3.61
SS	M. Belanger	402	.206	2	30	244	417	10	82	4.7	**.985**	M. Flanagan	36	235	15	10	1	3.64
3B	D. DeCinces	522	.259	19	69	124	**330**	20	**34**	3.2	.958	R. Grimsley	34	218	14	10	0	3.96
RF	K. Singleton	536	.328	24	99	278	8	4	2	1.9	.986	D. Martinez	42	167	14	7	4	4.10
CF	A. Bumbry	518	.317	4	41	329	7	3	0	2.6	.991	S. McGregor	29	114	3	5	4	4.42
LF	P. Kelly	360	.256	10	49	181	2	3	1	1.7	.984	T. Martinez	41	50	5	1	9	2.70
C	R. Dempsey	270	.226	3	34	416	52	11	10	5.3	.977	D. Drago	36	40	6	3	3	3.63
DH	E. Murray	611	.283	27	88					.0								
2B	R. Dauer	304	.243	5	25	179	213	7	55	4.8	.982							
OF	A. Mora	233	.245	13	44	66	2	0	0	1.2	1.000							
C	D. Skaggs	216	.287	1	24	344	34	2	4	4.8	.995							
Bos. W-97 L-64 Don Zimmer																		
1B	G. Scott	584	.269	33	95	1446	115	**24**	150	10.1	.985	F. Jenkins	28	193	10	10	0	3.68
2B	D. Doyle	455	.240	2	49	230	412	14	90	4.8	.979	R. Cleveland	36	190	11	8	2	4.26
SS	R. Burleson	**663**	.293	3	52	**285**	482	24	111	5.1	.970	L. Tiant	32	189	12	8	0	4.53
3B	B. Hobson	593	.265	30	112	128	272	23	27	2.7	.946	B. Stanley	41	151	8	7	3	3.99
RF	D. Evans	230	.287	14	36	126	2	1	0	2.0	.992	B. Campbell	69	140	13	9	**31**	2.96
CF	F. Lynn	497	.260	18	76	333	7	2	1	2.7	.994	B. Lee	27	128	9	5	1	4.77
LF	Yastrzemski	558	.296	28	102	287	**16**	0	1	2.2	**1.000**	R. Wise	26	128	11	5	0	4.78
C	C. Fisk	536	.315	26	102	779	69	11	7	5.7	.987	M. Paxton	29	108	10	5	0	3.83
DH	J. Rice	644	.320	**39**	114					.0		J. Willoughby	31	55	6	2	2	4.94
OF	B. Carbo	228	.289	15	34	131	5	7	1	2.1	.951							
OF	R. Miller	189	.254	0	24	118	5	1	3	1.6	.992							
Det. W-74 L-88 Ralph Houk																		
1B	J. Thompson	585	.270	31	105	**1599**	97	16	135	**10.8**	.991	D. Rozema	28	218	15	7	0	3.10
2B	T. Fuentes	615	.309	5	51	**379**	459	**26**	115	5.7	.970	F. Arroyo	38	209	8	18	0	4.18
SS	T. Veryzer	350	.197	2	28	185	377	18	62	4.7	.969	B. Sykes	32	133	5	7	0	4.40
3B	A. Rodriguez	306	.219	10	32	60	222	8	19	3.1	.972	D. Roberts	22	129	4	10	0	5.16
RF	B. Oglivie	450	.262	21	61	236	10	6	3	2.1	.976	J. Crawford	37	126	7	8	1	4.79
CF	R. LeFlore	652	.325	16	57	365	12	11	0	2.5	.972	J. Hiller	45	124	8	14	7	3.56
LF	S. Kemp	552	.257	18	88	252	10	5	1	1.8	.981	M. Wilcox	20	106	6	2	0	3.65
C	M. May	397	.249	12	46	551	78	9	**12**	5.7	.986	M. Fidrych	11	81	6	4	0	2.89
DH	R. Staub	623	.278	22	101					.0		S. Foucault	44	74	7	7	13	3.16
3B	P. Mankowski	286	.276	3	27	73	196	10	15	3.3	.964							
OF	M. Stanley	222	.230	8	23	101	2	3	0	1.9	.972							
C	J. Wockenfuss	164	.274	9	25	175	20	3	2	5.4	.985							
Cle. W-71 L-90 Frank Robinson W-26 L-31 Jeff Torborg W-45 L-59																		
1B	A. Thornton	433	.263	28	70	1026	71	6	97	9.4	.995	W. Garland	38	283	13	**19**	0	3.59
2B	D. Kuiper	610	.277	1	50	334	449	12	104	5.4	.985	D. Eckersley	33	247	14	13	0	3.53
SS	F. Duffy	334	.201	4	31	145	301	15	62	3.8	.967	J. Bibby	37	207	12	13	2	3.57
3B	B. Bell	479	.292	11	64	111	253	15	23	3.2	.960	R. Waits	37	135	9	7	2	4.00
RF	J. Norris	440	.270	2	37	320	9	6	1	2.7	.982	A. Fitzmorris	29	133	6	10	0	5.41
CF	R. Manning	252	.226	5	18	191	2	2	0	2.9	.990	P. Dobson	33	133	3	12	1	6.16
LF	P. Dade	461	.291	3	45	167	10	2	2	1.8	.989	D. Hood	41	105	2	1	0	3.00
C	F. Kendall	317	.249	3	39	506	35	5	5	5.4	.991	J. Kern	60	92	8	10	18	3.42
DH	R. Carty	461	.280	15	80					.0								
O1	B. Bochte	392	.304	5	43	438	28	9	18		.981							
UT	L. Blanks	322	.286	6	38	100	181	11	27		.962							
C	R. Fosse	238	.265	6	27	427	48	8	4	6.3	.983							
OF	R. Pruitt	219	.288	2	32	104	2	3	0	1.6	.972							
Mil. W-67 L-95 Alex Grammas																		
1B	C. Cooper	643	.300	20	78	1386	118	12	134	10.2	.992	J. Slaton	32	221	10	14	0	3.58
2B	D. Money	570	.279	25	83	256	357	12	82	5.4	.981	J. Augustine	32	209	12	18	0	4.48
SS	R. Yount	605	.288	4	49	256	449	26	94	4.8	.964	M. Haas	32	198	10	12	0	4.32
3B	S. Bando	580	.250	17	82	96	277	13	31	2.9	.966	E. Rodriguez	42	143	5	6	4	4.34
RF	S. Lezcano	400	.273	21	49	238	11	3	2	2.3	.988	L. Sorensen	23	142	7	10	0	4.37
CF	V. Joshua	536	.261	9	49	311	8	10	0	2.4	.970	B. Travers	19	122	4	12	0	5.24
LF	J. Wohlford	391	.248	2	36	246	6	5	1	2.1	.981	M. Caldwell	21	94	5	8	0	4.60
C	C. Moore	375	.248	5	45	566	78	**13**	10	4.8	.980	B. Castro	51	69	8	6	13	4.17
DH	J. Quirk	221	.217	3	13					.0								
OF	S. Brye	241	.249	7	28	166	8	0	1	2.1	1.000							
Tor. W-54 L-107 Roy Hartsfield																		
1B	D. Ault	445	.245	11	64	1113	103	16	91	10.1	.987	D. Lemanczyk	34	252	13	16	0	4.25
2B	S. Staggs	291	.258	2	28	169	194	13	35	5.2	.965	J. Garvin	34	245	10	18	0	4.19
SS	H. Torres	266	.241	5	26	82	165	5	29	3.7	.980	J. Jefferson	33	217	9	17	0	4.31
3B	R. Howell	364	.316	10	44	81	165	12	12	3.0	.953	P. Vuckovich	53	148	7	7	8	3.47
RF	B. Bailor	496	.310	5	32	156	10	2	2	2.7	.988	M. Willis	43	107	2	6	5	3.95
CF	G. Woods	227	.216	0	17	154	4	0	0	2.6	1.000	J. Byrd	17	87	2	13	0	6.21
LF	A. Woods	440	.284	6	35	215	6	7	1	2.0	.969	J. Johnson	43	86	2	4	5	4.60
C	A. Ashby	396	.210	2	29	619	71	11	11	5.7	.984	J. Clancy	13	77	4	9	0	5.03
DH	R. Fairly	458	.279	19	64					.0		B. Singer	13	60	2	8	0	6.75
OF	O. Velez	360	.256	16	62	140	5	4	1	1.9	.973							
3B	D. Rader	313	.240	13	40	38	103	5	2		.966							
UT	D. McKay	274	.197	3	22	141	205	14	36		.961							
OF	S. Ewing	244	.287	4	34	65	1	3	0		.957							
OF	J. Scott	233	.240	2	15	127	3	5	2	2.0	.963							
OF	S. Bowling	194	.206	1	13	139	14	2	0	1.8	.987							

West

	POS	Player	AB	BA	HR	RBI	PO	A	E	DP	TC/G	FA	Pitcher	G	IP	W	L	SV	ERA
K. C. W-102 L-60 Whitey Herzog	1B	J. Mayberry	543	.230	23	82	1296	81	7	118	9.5	.995	D. Leonard	38	293	20	12	1	3.04
	2B	F. White	474	.245	5	50	310	434	8	86	4.9	.989	J. Colborn	36	239	18	14	0	3.62
	SS	F. Patek	497	.262	5	60	252	413	29	70	4.5	.958	P. Splittorff	37	229	16	6	0	3.69
	3B	G. Brett	564	.312	22	88	115	325	20	33	3.4	.957	A. Hassler	29	156	9	6	0	4.21
	RF	A. Cowens	606	.312	23	112	307	14	6	1	2.1	.982	M. Pattin	31	128	10	3	0	3.59
	CF	A. Otis	478	.251	17	78	326	10	3	0	2.4	.991	D. Bird	53	118	11	4	14	3.89
	LF	T. Poquette	342	.292	2	33	177	4	0	1	1.9	1.000	L. Gura	52	106	8	5	10	3.14
	C	D. Porter	425	.275	16	60	663	61	13	4	5.9	.982	M. Littell	48	105	8	4	12	3.60
	DH	H. McRae	641	.298	21	92					.0		S. Mingori	43	64	2	4	4	3.09
	UT	P. LaCock	218	.303	3	29	203	19	2	16		.991							
	OF	J. Zdeb	195	.297	2	23	93	4	3	0	1.1	.970							
	C	J. Wathan	119	.328	2	21	130	9	1	0	4.0	.993							
Tex. W-94 L-68 Frank Lucchesi Eddie Stanky W-1 L-0 Connie Ryan W-2 L-4	1B	M. Hargrove	525	.305	18	69	1393	100	11	134	9.9	.993	G. Perry	34	238	15	12	0	3.37
	2B	B. Wills	541	.287	9	62	321	492	15	89	5.5	.982	D. Alexander	34	237	17	11	0	3.65
	SS	B. Campaneris	552	.254	5	46	269	483	25	91	5.2	.968	B. Blyleven	30	235	14	12	0	2.72
	3B	T. Harrah	539	.263	27	87	108	278	15	20	2.5	.963	D. Ellis	23	167	10	6	1	2.90
	RF	C. Washington	521	.284	12	68	255	11	6	3	2.1	.978	N. Briles	30	108	6	4	1	4.07
	CF	J. Beniquez	424	.269	10	50	311	10	4	1	2.6	.988	A. Devine	56	106	11	6	15	3.57
	LF	D. May	340	.241	7	42	181	8	6	2	1.8	.969	P. Lindblad	42	99	4	5	4	4.18
	C	J. Sundberg	453	.291	6	65	801	103	5	12	6.1	.994	R. Moret	18	72	3	3	4	3.75
	DH	W. Horton	519	.289	15	75					.0		D. Knowles	42	50	5	2	4	3.24
Billy Hunter W-60 L-33	OF	K. Henderson	244	.258	5	23	113	0	2	0	1.8	.983							
	OF	T. Grieve	236	.225	7	30	77	5	2	1	1.4	.976							
	UT	K. Bevacqua	96	.333	5	28	42	31	1	4		.986							
Chi. W-90 L-72 Bob Lemon	1B	J. Spencer	470	.247	18	69	977	90	10	76	8.6	.991	F. Barrios	33	231	14	7	0	4.13
	2B	J. Orta	564	.282	11	84	287	335	19	64	4.6	.970	S. Stone	31	207	15	12	0	4.52
	SS	A. Bannister	560	.275	3	57	259	325	40	51	4.7	.936	K. Kravec	26	167	11	8	0	4.10
	3B	E. Soderholm	460	.280	25	67	99	249	8	18	2.8	.978	C. Knapp	27	146	12	7	0	4.81
	RF	R. Garr	543	.300	10	54	225	10	3	2	1.9	.987	W. Wood	24	123	7	8	0	4.98
	CF	C. Lemon	553	.273	19	67	512	12	12	2	3.6	.978	L. LaGrow	66	99	7	3	25	2.45
	LF	R. Zisk	531	.290	30	101	210	9	4	3	2.0	.982	B. Johnson	29	92	4	5	2	4.01
	C	J. Essian	322	.273	10	44	592	62	9	8	6.0	.986	K. Brett	13	83	6	4	0	5.01
	DH	O. Gamble	408	.297	31	83					.0		D. Hamilton	55	67	4	5	9	3.63
	1B	L. Johnson	374	.302	18	65	346	32	4	31		.990							
	C	B. Downing	169	.284	4	25	320	28	6	5	5.8	.983							
	32	J. Brohamer	152	.257	2	20	54	100	8	15		.951							
	OF	W. Nordhagen	124	.315	4	22	50	1	3	0	1.2	.944							
Min. W-84 L-77 Gene Mauch	1B	R. Carew	616	.388	14	100	1459	121	10	161	10.5	.994	D. Goltz	39	303	20	11	0	3.36
	2B	B. Randall	306	.239	0	22	222	297	8	74	5.2	.985	Thormodsgard	37	218	11	15	0	4.52
	SS	R. Smalley	584	.231	6	56	255	504	33	116	5.3	.958	G. Zahn	34	198	12	14	0	4.68
	3B	M. Cubbage	417	.264	9	55	90	266	18	29	3.0	.952	T. Johnson	71	147	16	7	15	3.12
	RF	D. Ford	453	.267	11	60	205	9	8	2	1.6	.964	P. Redfern	30	137	6	9	0	5.19
	CF	L. Hisle	546	.302	28	119	287	11	8	2	2.3	.974	R. Schueler	52	135	8	7	3	4.40
	LF	L. Bostock	593	.336	14	90	349	10	4	0	2.4	.989	T. Burgmeier	61	97	6	4	7	5.10
	C	B. Wynegar	532	.261	10	79	676	84	5	8	5.4	.993							
	DH	C. Kusick	268	.254	12	45					.0								
	OF	G. Adams	269	.338	6	49	60	3	2	1	1.5	.969							
	DH	R. Chiles	261	.264	3	36					.0								
	UT	J. Terrell	214	.224	1	20	58	129	6	20		.969							
	2B	R. Wilfong	171	.246	1	13	114	164	12	40	4.4	.959							
	OF	B. Gorinski	118	.195	3	22	44	0	3	0	1.3	.936							
Cal. W-74 L-88 Norm Sherry W-39 L-42 Dave Garcia W-35 L-46	1B	T. Solaita	324	.241	14	53	641	57	7	50	7.7	.990	N. Ryan	37	299	19	16	0	2.77
	2B	J. Remy	575	.252	4	44	307	420	19	90	4.9	.975	F. Tanana	31	241	15	9	0	2.54
	SS	R. Mulliniks	271	.269	3	21	112	229	13	37	4.6	.963	P. Hartzell	41	189	8	12	4	3.57
	3B	D. Chalk	519	.277	3	45	114	266	21	21	2.8	.948	K. Brett	21	142	7	10	0	4.25
	RF	B. Bonds	592	.264	37	115	272	5	4	0	2.0	.986	W. Simpson	27	122	6	12	0	5.83
	CF	G. Flores	342	.278	1	26	177	5	4	2	2.2	.978	D. Miller	41	92	4	4	4	3.02
	LF	J. Rudi	242	.264	13	53	131	3	0	0	2.2	1.000	D. LaRoche	46	81	6	5	13	3.10
	C	T. Humphrey	304	.227	2	34	661	63	8	10	6.0	.989							
	DH	D. Baylor	561	.251	25	75					.0								
	UT	R. Jackson	292	.243	8	28	314	75	6	33		.985							
	UT	M. Guerrero	244	.283	1	28	61	105	2	18		.988							
	OF	T. Bosley	212	.297	0	19	130	1	5	0	2.5	.963							
	SS	B. Grich	181	.243	7	23	88	141	4	23	4.5	.983							
Sea. W-64 L-98 Darrell Johnson	1B	D. Meyer	582	.273	22	90	1407	109	12	134	9.6	.992	G. Abbott	36	204	12	13	0	4.46
	2B	J. Baez	305	.259	1	17	151	250	11	54	5.4	.973	J. Montague	47	182	8	12	4	4.50
	SS	C. Reynolds	420	.248	4	28	197	397	28	86	4.6	.955	D. Pole	25	122	7	12	0	5.16
	3B	B. Stein	556	.259	13	67	146	255	15	20	2.8	.964	E. Romo	58	114	8	10	16	2.84
	RF	C. Lopez	297	.283	8	34	160	11	5	5	2.0	.972	D. Segui	40	111	0	7	2	5.68
	CF	R. Jones	597	.263	24	76	465	11	9	3	3.1	.981	M. Kekich	41	90	5	4	3	5.60
	LF	S. Braun	451	.235	5	31	186	11	5	3	2.0	.975	T. House	26	89	4	5	1	3.93
	C	B. Stinson	297	.269	8	32	494	43	9	11	5.5	.984	G. Wheelock	17	88	6	9	0	4.91
	DH	D. Collins	402	.239	5	28					.0								
	OF	L. Stanton	454	.275	27	90	175	9	9	2	2.1	.953							
	3B	J. Bernhardt	305	.243	7	30	18	37	1	1		.982							
	2S	L. Milbourne	242	.219	2	21	120	209	11	46		.968							
	2B	J. Cruz	199	.256	1	7	114	171	5	29	5.4	.983							

POS	Player	AB	BA	HR	RBI	PO	A	E	DP	TC/G	FA	Pitcher	G	IP	W	L	SV	ERA
1B	R. Allen	171	.240	5	31	389	37	7	36	8.7	.984	V. Blue	38	280	14	19	0	3.83
2B	M. Perez	373	.231	2	23	192	287	13	48	4.7	.974	R. Langford	37	208	8	19	0	4.02
SS	R. Picciolo	419	.200	2	22	213	381	21	70	4.2	.966	D. Medich	26	148	10	6	0	4.69
3B	W. Gross	485	.233	22	63	126	242	27	26	2.7	.932	J. Coleman	43	128	4	4	2	2.95
RF	J. Tyrone	294	.245	5	26	167	5	9	0	2.2	.950	B. Lacey	64	122	6	8	7	3.02
CF	T. Armas	363	.240	13	53	294	9	6	4	2.8	.981	P. Torrealba	41	117	4	6	2	2.62
LF	M. Page	501	.307	21	75	279	11	14	0	2.3	.954	D. Bair	45	83	4	6	8	3.47
C	J. Newman	162	.222	4	15	251	36	9	5	3.1	.970	D. Giusti	40	60	3	3	6	3.00
DH	M. Sanguillen	571	.275	6	58					.0								
2S	R. Scott	364	.261	0	20	198	270	21	49		.957							
UT	E. Williams	348	.241	13	38	305	26	3	14		.991							
1O	M. Jorgensen	203	.246	8	32	365	32	4	26		.990							
UT	R. McKinney	198	.177	6	21	213	27	9	22		.964							
OF	B. North	184	.261	1	9	112	1	2	0	2.2	.983							
OF	L. Murray	162	.179	1	9	114	3	1	3	1.5	.992							

Oak.
W-63 L-98
Jack McKeon
W-26 L-27
Bobby Winkles
W-37 L-71

BATTING AND BASE RUNNING LEADERS

Batting Average
R. Carew, MIN	.388
L. Bostock, MIN	.336
K. Singleton, BAL	.328
M. Rivers, NY	.326
R. LeFlore, DET	.325

Slugging Average
J. Rice, BOS	.593
R. Carew, MIN	.570
R. Jackson, NY	.550
L. Hisle, MIN	.533
G. Brett, KC	.532

Home Runs
J. Rice, BOS	39
G. Nettles, NY	37
B. Bonds, CAL	37
G. Scott, BOS	33
R. Jackson, NY	32

Total Bases
J. Rice, BOS	382
R. Carew, MIN	351
H. McRae, KC	330
A. Cowens, KC	318
R. LeFlore, DET	310

Runs Batted In
L. Hisle, MIN	119
B. Bonds, CAL	115
J. Rice, BOS	114
B. Hobson, BOS	112
A. Cowens, KC	112

Stolen Bases
F. Patek, KC	53
M. Page, OAK	42
J. Remy, CAL	41
B. Bonds, CAL	41
R. LeFlore, DET	39

Hits
R. Carew, MIN	239
R. LeFlore, DET	212
J. Rice, BOS	206

Base on Balls
T. Harrah, TEX	109
K. Singleton, BAL	107
M. Hargrove, TEX	103

Home Run Percentage
A. Thornton, CLE	6.5
G. Nettles, NY	6.3
B. Bonds, CAL	6.3

Runs Scored
R. Carew, MIN	128
C. Fisk, BOS	106
G. Brett, KC	105

Doubles
H. McRae, KC	54
R. Jackson, NY	39
C. Lemon, CHI	38
R. Carew, MIN	38

Triples
R. Carew, MIN	16
J. Rice, BOS	15
A. Cowens, KC	14

PITCHING LEADERS

Winning Percentage
P. Splittorff, KC	.727
R. Guidry, NY	.696
D. Rozema, DET	.682
J. Palmer, BAL	.645
D. Goltz, MIN	.645

Earned Run Average
F. Tanana, CAL	2.54
B. Blyleven, TEX	2.72
N. Ryan, CAL	2.77
R. Guidry, NY	2.82
J. Palmer, BAL	2.91

Wins
J. Palmer, BAL	20
D. Goltz, MIN	20
D. Leonard, KC	20
N. Ryan, CAL	19
R. May, BAL	18
J. Colborn, KC	18

Saves
B. Campbell, BOS	31
S. Lyle, NY	26
L. LaGrow, CHI	25
J. Kern, CLE	18
D. LaRoche, CAL, CLE	17

Strikeouts
N. Ryan, CAL	341
D. Leonard, KC	244
F. Tanana, CAL	205
J. Palmer, BAL	193
D. Eckersley, CLE	191

Complete Games
N. Ryan, CAL	22
J. Palmer, BAL	22
D. Leonard, KC	21
W. Garland, CLE	21
F. Tanana, CAL	20

Fewest Hits per 9 Innings
N. Ryan, CAL	5.96
B. Blyleven, TEX	6.93
J. Palmer, BAL	7.42

Shutouts
F. Tanana, CAL	7
R. Guidry, NY	5
B. Blyleven, TEX	5
D. Leonard, KC	5

Fewest Walks per 9 Innings
D. Rozema, DET	1.40
F. Jenkins, BOS	1.68
P. Hartzell, CAL	1.81

Most Strikeouts per 9 Inn.
N. Ryan, CAL	10.26
F. Tanana, CAL	7.64
R. Guidry, NY	7.51

Innings
J. Palmer, BAL	319
D. Goltz, MIN	303
N. Ryan, CAL	299

Games Pitched
S. Lyle, NY	72
T. Johnson, MIN	71
B. Campbell, BOS	69

	W	L	PCT	GB	R	OR	2B	3B	HR	BA	SA	SB	E	DP	FA	CG	BB	SO	ShO	SV	ERA
EAST																					
NY	100	62	.617		831	651	267	47	184	.281	.444	93	132	151	.979	52	486	758	16	34	3.61
BAL	97	64	.602	2.5	719	653	231	25	148	.261	.393	90	**106**	**189**	**.983**	**65**	494	737	11	23	3.74
BOS	97	64	.602	2.5	859	712	258	56	**213**	.281	.465	66	133	162	.978	65	**378**	758	13	40	4.16
DET	74	88	.457	26	714	751	228	45	166	.264	.410	60	142	153	.978	44	470	784	3	23	4.13
CLE	71	90	.441	28.5	676	739	221	46	100	.269	.380	87	130	145	.979	45	550	876	8	30	4.10
MIL	67	95	.414	33	639	765	255	46	125	.258	.389	85	139	165	.978	38	566	719	6	25	4.32
TOR	54	107	.335	45.5	605	822	230	41	100	.252	.365	65	164	133	.974	40	623	771	3	20	4.57
WEST																					
KC	102	60	.630		822	651	**299**	**77**	146	.277	.436	170	137	145	.978	41	499	850	15	**42**	3.52
TEX	94	68	.580	8	767	657	265	39	135	.270	.405	154	117	156	.982	49	471	864	**17**	31	3.56
CHI	90	72	.556	12	844	771	254	52	192	.278	.444	42	159	125	.974	34	516	842	3	40	4.25
MIN	84	77	.522	17.5	**867**	776	273	60	123	**.282**	.417	105	143	184	.978	35	507	737	4	25	4.38
CAL	74	88	.457	28	675	695	233	40	131	.255	.386	159	147	137	.976	53	572	**965**	13	26	3.76
SEA	64	98	.395	38	624	855	218	33	133	.256	.381	110	147	162	.976	18	578	785	1	31	4.83
OAK	63	98	.391	38.5	605	749	176	37	117	.240	.352	**176**	190	136	.970	32	560	788	4	26	4.05
					10247	10247	3408	644	2013	.266	.405	1462	1986	2143	.977	586	7270	11234	117	416	4.07

POS	Player	AB	BA	HR	RBI	PO	A	E	DP	TC/G	FA	Pitcher	G	IP	W	L	SV	ERA

East

Phi.
W-90 L-72
Danny Ozark

POS	Player	AB	BA	HR	RBI	PO	A	E	DP	TC/G	FA	Pitcher	G	IP	W	L	SV	ERA
1B	R. Hebner	435	.283	17	71	987	49	6	86	8.9	.994	S. Carlton	34	247	16	13	0	2.84
2B	T. Sizemore	351	.219	0	25	232	302	12	61	5.1	.978	Christenson	33	228	13	14	0	3.24
SS	L. Bowa	654	.294	3	43	224	502	10	87	4.7	.986	R. Lerch	33	184	11	8	0	3.96
3B	M. Schmidt	513	.251	21	78	98	324	16	34	3.1	.963	D. Ruthven	20	151	13	5	0	2.99
RF	B. McBride	472	.269	10	49	234	8	1	3	2.0	.996	J. Kaat	26	140	8	5	0	4.11
CF	G. Maddox	598	.288	11	68	444	7	8	1	3.0	.983	J. Lonborg	22	114	8	10	0	5.21
LF	G. Luzinski	540	.265	35	101	232	7	4	2	1.6	.984	R. Reed	66	109	3	4	17	2.23
C	B. Boone	435	.283	12	62	619	55	6	6	5.3	.991	T. McGraw	55	90	8	7	9	3.20
OF	J. Martin	266	.271	9	36	148	8	2	1	1.4	.987							
1B	J. Cardenal	201	.249	4	33	360	17	4	39	7.6	.990							

Pit.
W-88 L-73
Chuck Tanner

POS	Player	AB	BA	HR	RBI	PO	A	E	DP	TC/G	FA	Pitcher	G	IP	W	L	SV	ERA
1B	W. Stargell	390	.295	28	97	875	57	6	76	8.4	.994	B. Blyleven	34	244	14	10	0	3.02
2B	R. Stennett	333	.243	3	35	164	208	11	40	4.8	.971	D. Robinson	35	228	14	6	1	3.47
SS	F. Taveras	654	.278	0	38	216	448	38	80	4.5	.946	J. Candelaria	30	189	12	11	1	3.24
3B	P. Garner	528	.261	10	66	67	172	18	12	3.2	.930	J. Rooker	28	163	9	11	0	4.25
RF	D. Parker	581	.334	30	117	302	12	13	3	2.2	.960	K. Tekulve	91	135	8	7	31	2.33
CF	O. Moreno	515	.235	2	33	409	9	7	2	2.8	.984	J. Bibby	34	107	8	7	1	3.53
LF	B. Robinson	499	.246	14	80	235	8	3	2	1.9	.988	B. Kison	28	96	6	6	0	3.19
C	E. Ott	379	.269	9	38	537	42	15	7	6.1	.975	G. Jackson	60	77	7	5	5	3.27
OF	J. Milner	295	.271	6	38	118	1	0	0	1.7	1.000	E. Whitson	43	74	5	6	4	3.28
1C	M. Sanguillen	220	.264	3	16	438	20	0	26		1.000							
C	D. Dyer	175	.211	0	13	326	22	3	2	6.4	.991							

Chi.
W-79 L-83
Herman Franks

POS	Player	AB	BA	HR	RBI	PO	A	E	DP	TC/G	FA	Pitcher	G	IP	W	L	SV	ERA
1B	B. Buckner	446	.323	5	74	1075	83	6	85	11.1	.995	R. Reuschel	35	243	14	15	0	3.41
2B	M. Trillo	552	.261	4	55	354	505	19	99	5.9	.978	D. Lamp	37	224	7	15	0	3.29
SS	I. DeJesus	619	.278	3	35	232	558	27	96	5.1	.967	R. Burris	40	199	7	13	1	4.75
3B	S. Ontiveros	276	.243	1	22	57	194	9	16	3.4	.965	D. Roberts	35	142	6	8	1	5.26
RF	B. Murcer	499	.281	9	64	225	8	5	0	1.7	.979	M. Krukow	27	138	9	3	0	3.91
CF	G. Gross	347	.265	1	39	182	6	4	1	1.7	.979	D. Moore	71	103	9	7	4	4.11
LF	D. Kingman	395	.266	28	79	170	8	4	2	1.8	.978	B. Sutter	64	99	8	10	27	3.18
C	D. Rader	305	.203	3	36	412	51	11	7	4.2	.977	W. Hernandez	54	60	8	2	3	3.75
1O	L. Biittner	343	.257	4	50	601	53	9	53		.986							
OF	G. Clines	229	.258	0	17	84	6	2	0	1.4	.978							
3B	R. Scott	227	.282	0	15	43	101	11	15	2.6	.929							
OF	M. Vail	180	.333	4	33	50	1	1	0	1.2	.981							

Mon.
W-76 L-86
Dick Williams

POS	Player	AB	BA	HR	RBI	PO	A	E	DP	TC/G	FA	Pitcher	G	IP	W	L	SV	ERA
1B	T. Perez	544	.290	14	78	1181	82	11	116	8.8	.991	R. Grimsley	36	263	20	11	0	3.05
2B	D. Cash	658	.252	3	43	362	400	11	91	4.9	.986	S. Rogers	30	219	13	10	1	2.47
SS	C. Speier	501	.251	5	51	245	467	18	93	4.9	.975	D. Schatzeder	29	144	7	7	0	3.06
3B	L. Parrish	520	.277	15	70	122	288	23	20	3.1	.947	R. May	27	144	8	10	0	3.88
RF	E. Valentine	570	.289	25	76	296	24	10	3	2.3	.970	W. Twitchell	33	112	4	12	0	5.38
CF	A. Dawson	609	.253	25	72	411	17	5	2	2.8	.988	H. Dues	25	99	5	6	1	2.36
LF	W. Cromartie	607	.297	10	56	340	24	8	5	2.4	.978	W. Fryman	19	95	5	7	1	3.61
C	G. Carter	533	.255	20	72	781	83	10	9	5.8	.989	S. Bahnsen	44	75	1	5	7	3.84
1O	D. Unser	179	.196	2	15	232	12	2	16		.992	D. Knowles	60	72	3	3	6	2.38

St. L.
W-69 L-93
Vern Rapp
W-5 L-10
Jack Krol
W-2 L-1
Ken Boyer
W-62 L-82

POS	Player	AB	BA	HR	RBI	PO	A	E	DP	TC/G	FA	Pitcher	G	IP	W	L	SV	ERA
1B	K. Hernandez	542	.255	11	64	1436	96	10	124	9.8	.994	B. Forsch	34	234	11	17	0	3.69
2B	M. Tyson	377	.233	3	26	246	306	13	78	4.6	.977	J. Denny	33	234	14	11	0	2.96
SS	G. Templeton	647	.280	2	47	285	523	40	108	5.5	.953	P. Vuckovich	45	198	12	12	1	2.55
3B	K. Reitz	540	.246	10	75	111	314	12	18	2.9	.973	S. Martinez	22	138	9	8	0	3.65
RF	J. Morales	457	.239	4	46	254	5	6	0	2.1	.977	M. Littell	72	106	4	8	11	2.80
CF	G. Hendrick	382	.288	17	67	241	5	1	0	2.4	.996	J. Urrea	27	99	4	9	0	5.36
LF	J. Mumphrey	367	.262	2	37	178	10	1	1	1.6	.995	B. Schultz	62	83	2	4	6	3.80
C	T. Simmons	516	.287	22	80	670	88	9	6	5.7	.988							
OF	L. Brock	298	.221	0	12	114	2	3	0	1.5	.975							
OF	T. Scott	219	.228	1	14	100	6	6	0	1.5	.946							
2B	M. Phillips	164	.268	1	28	93	110	6	24	3.8	.971							
1B	R. Freed	92	.239	2	20	110	10	1	13	8.1	.992							

N. Y.
W-66 L-96
Joe Torre

POS	Player	AB	BA	HR	RBI	PO	A	E	DP	TC/G	FA	Pitcher	G	IP	W	L	SV	ERA
1B	W. Montanez	609	.256	17	96	1350	104	8	138	9.3	.995	J. Koosman	38	235	3	15	2	3.75
2B	D. Flynn	532	.237	0	36	249	299	8	70	4.3	.986	C. Swan	29	207	9	6	0	2.43
SS	T. Foli	413	.257	1	27	190	314	18	78	4.7	.966	N. Espinosa	32	204	11	15	0	4.72
3B	L. Randle	437	.233	2	35	108	215	11	21	2.7	.967	P. Zachry	21	138	10	6	0	3.33
RF	E. Maddox	389	.257	2	39	155	8	2	3	2.1	.988	M. Bruhert	27	134	4	11	0	4.77
CF	L. Mazzilli	542	.273	16	61	386	8	5	3	2.8	.987	K. Kobel	32	108	5	6	0	2.92
LF	S. Henderson	587	.266	10	65	315	18	11	3	2.2	.968	S. Lockwood	57	91	7	13	15	3.56
C	J. Stearns	477	.264	15	73	711	84	12	7	5.7	.985	D. Murray	53	86	8	5	5	3.65
UT	J. Youngblood	266	.252	7	30	160	96	6	21		.977							
OF	B. Boisclair	214	.224	4	15	114	3	2	0	1.7	.983							

West

POS	Player	AB	BA	HR	RBI	PO	A	E	DP	TC/G	FA	Pitcher	G	IP	W	L	SV	ERA
L. A. W-95 L-67 Tom Lasorda																		
1B	S. Garvey	639	.316	21	113	**1546**	74	9	121	**10.1**	.994	D. Sutton	34	238	15	11	0	3.55
2B	D. Lopes	587	.278	17	58	337	424	**20**	88	5.3	.974	B. Hooton	32	236	19	10	0	2.71
SS	B. Russell	625	.286	3	46	245	533	31	91	5.2	.962	T. John	33	213	17	10	1	3.30
3B	R. Cey	555	.270	23	84	116	336	16	26	3.0	.966	D. Rau	30	199	15	9	0	3.26
RF	R. Smith	447	.295	29	93	220	8	12	4	1.9	.950	R. Rhoden	30	165	10	8	0	3.65
CF	R. Monday	342	.254	19	57	209	3	1	0	2.1	.995	B. Welch	23	111	7	4	3	2.03
LF	D. Baker	522	.262	11	66	250	13	4	1	1.8	.985	C. Hough	55	93	5	5	7	3.29
C	S. Yeager	228	.193	4	23	373	55	5	3	4.8		T. Forster	47	65	5	4	22	1.94
OF	B. North	304	.234	0	10	232	2	6	1	2.3	.975							
UT	L. Lacy	245	.261	13	40	114	64	9	7		.952							
C	J. Ferguson	198	.237	7	28	284	23	5	2	5.0	.984							
Cin. W-92 L-69 Sparky Anderson																		
1B	D. Driessen	524	.250	16	70	1264	93	6	92	9.0	**.996**	T. Seaver	36	260	16	14	0	2.87
2B	J. Morgan	441	.236	13	75	252	290	11	49	4.5	.980	F. Norman	36	177	11	9	1	3.71
SS	D. Concepcion	565	.301	6	67	255	459	23	72	4.8	.969	T. Hume	42	174	8	11	1	4.14
3B	P. Rose	655	.302	7	52	117	256	15	23	2.5	.961	P. Moskau	26	145	6	4	1	3.97
RF	K. Griffey	614	.288	10	63	296	13	10	2	2.1	.969	B. Bonham	23	140	11	5	0	3.54
CF	C. Geronimo	296	.226	5	27	259	4	5	1	2.3	.981	M. Sarmiento	63	127	9	7	5	4.39
LF	G. Foster	604	.281	**40**	**120**	319	10	10	1	2.2	.971	D. Bair	70	100	7	6	28	1.98
C	J. Bench	393	.260	23	73	605	48	7	6	**6.2**	.989	P. Borbon	62	99	8	2	4	5.00
OF	M. Lum	146	.267	6	23	69	6	1	2	1.8	.987	M. LaCoss	16	96	4	8	0	4.50
S. F. W-89 L-73 Joe Altobelli																		
1B	W. McCovey	351	.228	12	64	721	44	10	49	8.0	.987	B. Knepper	36	260	17	11	0	2.63
2B	B. Madlock	447	.309	15	44	223	299	14	48	4.7	.974	V. Blue	35	258	18	10	0	2.79
SS	J. LeMaster	272	.235	1	14	135	260	14	40	4.3	.966	J. Montefusco	36	239	11	9	0	3.80
3B	D. Evans	547	.243	20	78	**147**	348	**25**	25	3.4	.952	E. Halicki	29	199	9	10	1	2.85
RF	J. Clark	592	.306	25	98	320	16	6	**5**	2.3	.982	J. Barr	32	163	8	11	1	3.53
CF	L. Herndon	471	.259	1	32	369	3	10	0	2.6	.974	G. Lavelle	67	98	13	10	14	3.31
LF	T. Whitfield	488	.289	10	32	249	7	3	2	1.8	.988	R. Moffitt	70	82	8	4	12	3.29
C	M. Hill	358	.243	3	36	586	56	9	3	5.6	.986							
1B	M. Ivie	318	.308	11	55	550	18	3	33	7.5	.995							
SS	R. Metzger	235	.260	0	17	112	184	8	30	4.1	.974							
OF	H. Cruz	197	.223	6	24	82	5	2	3	1.7	.978							
2B	R. Andrews	177	.220	1	11	120	131	6	23	4.1	.977							
O1	J. Dwyer	173	.225	5	22	197	14	2	14		.991							
S. D. W-84 L-78 Roger Craig																		
1B	G. Tenace	401	.224	16	61	668	37	5	61	8.9	.993	G. Perry	37	261	**21**	6	0	2.72
2B	F. Gonzalez	320	.250	2	29	190	256	8	68	4.8	.982	R. Jones	37	253	13	14	0	2.88
SS	O. Smith	590	.258	1	46	264	548	25	98	5.3	.970	B. Owchinko	36	202	10	13	0	3.56
3B	B. Almon	405	.252	0	21	72	221	21	20	2.8	.933	B. Shirley	50	166	8	11	5	3.69
RF	O. Gamble	375	.275	7	47	172	12	4	3	1.8	.979	E. Rasmussen	27	146	12	10	0	4.06
CF	G. Richards	555	.308	4	45	210	8	8	0	1.8	.965	R. Fingers	67	107	6	13	**37**	2.52
LF	D. Winfield	587	.308	24	97	321	7	7	1	2.2	.979	J. D'Acquisto	45	93	4	3	10	2.13
C	R. Sweet	226	.221	1	11	337	33	6	3	4.9	.984							
UT	D. Thomas	352	.227	3	26	328	168	12	39		.976							
OF	J. Turner	225	.280	8	37	91	5	3	0	1.7	.970							
1B	B. Perkins	217	.240	2	33	538	41	4	56	9.9	.983							
UT	T. Ashford	155	.245	3	26	108	53	6	22		.964							
Hou. W-74 L-88 Bill Virdon																		
1B	B. Watson	461	.289	14	79	974	95	9	63	8.4	.992	J. Richard	36	275	18	11	0	3.11
2B	A. Howe	420	.293	7	55	224	289	12	51	4.9	.977	M. Lemongello	33	210	9	14	1	3.94
SS	R. Landestoy	218	.266	0	9	65	132	4	18	4.0	.980	J. Niekro	35	203	14	14	0	3.86
3B	E. Cabell	**660**	.295	7	71	136	274	18	15	2.8	.958	T. Dixon	30	140	7	11	1	3.99
RF	J. Cruz	565	.315	10	83	311	4	8	0	2.1	.975	K. Forsch	52	133	10	6	7	2.71
CF	C. Cedeno	192	.281	7	23	149	2	2	1	3.1	.981	J. Andujar	35	111	5	7	1	3.41
LF	T. Puhl	585	.289	3	35	386	6	3	2	2.7	.992	F. Bannister	28	110	3	9	0	4.83
C	L. Pujols	153	.131	1	11	271	33	6	2	5.6	.981	J. Sambito	62	88	4	9	11	3.07
OF	D. Walling	247	.251	3	36	140	4	3	2	1.9	.980							
2B	J. Gonzalez	223	.233	1	16	62	112	3	21	3.3	.983							
1O	D. Bergman	186	.231	0	12	328	16	4	26		.990							
C	J. Ferguson	150	.207	7	22	288	29	2	0	6.3	.994							
Atl. W-69 L-93 Bobby Cox																		
1B	D. Murphy	530	.226	23	79	1137	92	**20**	84	9.7	.984	P. Niekro	44	**334**	19	**18**	1	2.88
2B	J. Royster	529	.259	2	35	186	193	10	39	5.2	.974	P. Hanna	29	140	7	13	0	5.14
SS	D. Chaney	245	.224	3	20	97	189	7	30	3.8	.976	M. Mahler	34	135	4	11	0	4.67
3B	B. Horner	323	.266	23	63	81	199	13	17	3.3	.956	E. Solomon	37	106	4	6	2	4.08
RF	G. Matthews	474	.285	18	62	238	10	8	0	2.0	.969	McWilliams	15	99	9	3	0	2.82
CF	R. Office	404	.250	9	40	291	4	3	2	2.2	.990	J. Easterly	37	78	3	6	1	5.65
LF	J. Burroughs	488	.301	23	77	224	13	6	2	1.7	.975	G. Garber	43	78	4	4	22	2.53
C	B. Pocoroba	289	.242	6	34	454	43	5	1	6.4	.990	A. Devine	31	65	5	4	3	5.95
32	R. Gilbreath	326	.245	3	31	108	204	9	22		.972	T. Boggs	16	59	2	8	0	6.71
OF	B. Bonnell	304	.240	1	16	172	7	3	1	1.7	.984							
C	J. Nolan	213	.230	4	22	295	24	7	3	5.3	.979							
1B	B. Beall	185	.243	1	16	275	24	4	23	7.6	.987							
2B	G. Hubbard	163	.258	2	13	102	130	5	30	5.4	.979							

BATTING AND BASE RUNNING LEADERS

Batting Average

D. Parker, PIT	.334
S. Garvey, LA	.316
J. Cruz, HOU	.315
D. Winfield, SD	.308
G. Richards, SD	.308

Slugging Average

D. Parker, PIT	.585
R. Smith, LA	.559
G. Foster, CIN	.546
J. Clark, SF	.537
J. Burroughs, ATL	.529

PITCHING LEADERS

Winning Percentage

G. Perry, SD	.778
D. Robinson, PIT	.700
B. Hooton, LA	.655
R. Grimsley, MON	.645
V. Blue, SF	.643

Earned Run Average

C. Swan, NY	2.43
S. Rogers, MON	2.47
P. Vuckovich, STL	2.55
B. Knepper, SF	2.63
B. Hooton, LA	2.71

Home Runs

G. Foster, CIN	40
G. Luzinski, PHI	35
D. Parker, PIT	30
R. Smith, LA	29
W. Stargell, PIT	28
D. Kingman, CHI	28

Total Bases

D. Parker, PIT	340
G. Foster, CIN	330
S. Garvey, LA	319
J. Clark, SF	318
D. Winfield, SD	293

Wins

G. Perry, SD	21
R. Grimsley, MON	20
B. Hooton, LA	19
P. Niekro, ATL	19
V. Blue, SF	18
J. Richard, HOU	18

Saves

R. Fingers, SD	37
K. Tekulve, PIT	31
D. Bair, CIN	28
B. Sutter, CHI	27
G. Garber, ATL, PHI	25

Runs Batted In

G. Foster, CIN	120
D. Parker, PIT	117
S. Garvey, LA	113
G. Luzinski, PHI	101
J. Clark, SF	98

Stolen Bases

O. Moreno, PIT	71
F. Taveras, PIT	46
D. Lopes, LA	45
I. DeJesus, CHI	41
O. Smith, SD	40

Strikeouts

J. Richard, HOU	303
P. Niekro, ATL	248
T. Seaver, CIN	226
B. Blyleven, PIT	182
J. Montefusco, SF	177

Complete Games

P. Niekro, ATL	22
R. Grimsley, MON	19
B. Knepper, SF	16
J. Richard, HOU	16
S. Carlton, PHI	12
D. Sutton, LA	12

Hits

S. Garvey, LA	202
P. Rose, CIN	198
E. Cabell, HOU	195

Base on Balls

J. Burroughs, ATL	117
D. Evans, SF	105
G. Tenace, SD	101

Fewest Hits per 9 Innings

J. Richard, HOU	6.28
C. Swan, NY	7.13
B. Hooton, LA	7.47

Shutouts

B. Knepper, SF	6

Home Run Percentage

G. Foster, CIN	6.6
R. Smith, LA	6.5
G. Luzinski, PHI	6.5

Runs Scored

I. DeJesus, CHI	104
P. Rose, CIN	103
D. Parker, PIT	102

Fewest Walks per 9 Innings

Christenson, PHI	1.86
J. Barr, SF	1.93
R. Reuschel, CHI	2.00

Most Strikeouts per 9 Inn.

J. Richard, HOU	9.92
T. Seaver, CIN	7.82
P. Vuckovich, STL	6.77

Doubles

P. Rose, CIN	51
J. Clark, SF	46
T. Simmons, STL	40

Triples

G. Templeton, STL	13
G. Richards, SD	12
D. Parker, PIT	12

Innings

P. Niekro, ATL	334
J. Richard, HOU	275
R. Grimsley, MON	263

Games Pitched

K. Tekulve, PIT	91
M. Littell, STL	72
D. Moore, CHI	71

	W	L	PCT	GB	R	OR	Batting 2B	3B	HR	BA	SA	SB	Fielding E	DP	FA	CG	BB	Pitching SO	ShO	SV	ERA
EAST																					
PHI	90	72	.556		708	586	248	32	133	.258	.388	152	**104**	155	**.983**	38	**393**	813	9	29	3.33
PIT	88	73	.547	1.5	684	637	239	54	115	.257	.385	**213**	167	133	.973	30	499	880	13	44	3.41
CHI	79	83	.488	11	664	724	224	48	72	**.264**	.361	110	144	154	.978	24	539	768	7	38	4.05
MON	76	86	.469	14	633	611	269	31	121	.254	.379	80	134	150	.979	42	572	740	13	32	3.42
STL	69	93	.426	21	600	657	263	44	79	.249	.358	97	136	155	.978	32	600	859	13	22	3.58
NY	66	96	.407	24	607	690	227	47	86	.245	.352	100	132	159	.979	21	531	775	7	26	3.87
WEST																					
LA	95	67	.586		**727**	**573**	251	27	**149**	.264	**.402**	137	140	138	.978	46	440	800	16	38	**3.12**
CIN	92	69	.571	2.5	710	688	**270**	32	136	.256	.393	137	134	120	.978	16	567	908	10	46	3.81
SF	89	73	.549	6	613	594	240	41	117	.248	.374	87	146	118	.977	42	453	840	17	29	3.30
SD	84	78	.519	11	591	598	208	42	75	.252	.348	152	160	**171**	.975	21	483	744	10	**55**	3.28
HOU	74	88	.457	21	605	634	231	45	70	.258	.355	178	133	109	.978	**48**	578	**930**	17	23	3.63
ATL	69	93	.426	26	600	750	191	39	123	.244	.363	90	153	126	.975	29	624	848	12	32	4.08
					7742	7742	2861	482	1276	.254	.372	1533	1683	1688	.978	389	6279	9905	144	414	3.58

POS	Player	AB	BA	HR	RBI	PO	A	E	DP	TC/G	FA	Pitcher	G	IP	W	L	SV	ERA

East

N. Y.
W-100 L-63
Billy Martin
W-52 L-42
Dick Howser
W-0 L-1
Bob Lemon
W-48 L-20

POS	Player	AB	BA	HR	RBI	PO	A	E	DP	TC/G	FA	Pitcher	G	IP	W	L	SV	ERA
1B	C. Chambliss	625	.274	12	90	1366	111	4	119	9.6	.997	R. Guidry	35	274	**25**	3	0	**1.74**
2B	W. Randolph	499	.279	3	42	296	400	16	80	5.3	.978	E. Figueroa	35	253	20	9	0	2.99
SS	B. Dent	379	.243	5	40	178	341	10	56	4.3	.981	D. Tidrow	31	185	7	11	0	3.84
3B	G. Nettles	587	.276	27	93	109	326	11	**30**	2.8	.975	G. Gossage	63	134	10	11	27	2.01
RF	R. Jackson	511	.274	27	97	212	6	3	1	2.1	.986	J. Beattie	25	128	6	9	0	3.73
CF	M. Rivers	559	.265	11	48	384	8	8	2	2.9	.980	C. Hunter	21	118	12	6	0	3.58
LF	L. Piniella	472	.314	6	69	213	4	7	0	2.2	.969	S. Lyle	59	112	9	3	9	3.47
C	T. Munson	617	.297	6	71	666	61	10	4	5.9	.986							
DH	C. Johnson	174	.184	6	19					.0								
OF	R. White	346	.269	8	43	128	1	1	0	1.8	.992							
DH	J. Spencer	150	.227	7	24					.0								
OF	G. Thomasson	116	.276	3	20	101	4	3	1	2.2	.972							

Bos.
W-99 L-64
Don Zimmer

POS	Player	AB	BA	HR	RBI	PO	A	E	DP	TC/G	FA	Pitcher	G	IP	W	L	SV	ERA
1B	G. Scott	412	.233	12	54	1052	55	10	99	9.9	.991	D. Eckersley	35	268	20	8	0	2.99
2B	J. Remy	583	.278	2	44	327	444	13	**114**	5.6	.983	M. Torrez	36	250	16	13	0	3.96
SS	R. Burleson	626	.248	5	49	285	482	15	100	5.4	.981	L. Tiant	32	212	13	8	0	3.31
3B	B. Hobson	512	.250	17	80	122	261	**43**	25	3.2	.899	B. Lee	28	177	10	10	0	3.46
RF	D. Evans	497	.247	24	63	305	14	6	2	2.3	.982	B. Stanley	52	142	15	2	10	2.60
CF	F. Lynn	541	.298	22	82	408	11	7	2	2.9	.984	J. Wright	24	116	8	4	0	3.57
LF	J. Rice	677	.315	**46**	**139**	245	13	3	1	2.3	.989	D. Drago	37	77	4	4	7	3.03
C	C. Fisk	571	.284	20	88	733	90	**17**	13	5.5	.980	B. Campbell	29	51	7	5	4	3.91
DH	Yastrzemski	523	.277	17	81					.0								
UT	J. Brohamer	244	.234	1	25	64	103	5	18		.971							

Mil.
W-93 L-69
George Bamberger

POS	Player	AB	BA	HR	RBI	PO	A	E	DP	TC/G	FA	Pitcher	G	IP	W	L	SV	ERA
1B	C. Cooper	407	.312	13	54	842	66	11	71	10.9	.988	M. Caldwell	37	293	22	9	1	2.36
2B	P. Molitor	521	.273	6	45	197	283	12	57	5.4	.976	L. Sorensen	37	281	18	12	1	3.21
SS	R. Yount	502	.293	9	71	246	453	30	78	5.8	.959	J. Augustine	35	188	13	12	0	4.54
3B	S. Bando	540	.285	17	78	89	329	14	25	3.2	.968	B. Travers	28	176	12	11	0	4.41
RF	S. Lezcano	442	.292	15	61	262	**18**	6	5	2.3	.979	A. Replogle	32	149	9	5	0	3.93
CF	G. Thomas	452	.246	32	86	345	5	6	0	2.6	.983	E. Rodriguez	32	105	5	5	2	3.93
LF	L. Hisle	520	.290	34	115	172	6	4	2	2.1	.978	B. McClure	44	65	2	6	9	3.74
C	C. Moore	268	.269	5	31	314	41	6	3	3.8	.983	B. Castro	42	50	5	4	8	1.81
DH	D. Davis	218	.248	5	26					.0								
UT	D. Money	518	.293	14	54	705	216	9	88		.990							
OF	B. Oglivie	469	.303	18	72	187	5	4	0	2.2	.980							
C	B. Martinez	256	.219	1	20	327	32	8	7	4.1	.978							

Bal.
W-90 L-71
Earl Weaver

POS	Player	AB	BA	HR	RBI	PO	A	E	DP	TC/G	FA	Pitcher	G	IP	W	L	SV	ERA
1B	E. Murray	610	.285	27	95	**1504**	106	5	143	10.3	.997	J. Palmer	38	**296**	21	12	0	2.46
2B	R. Dauer	459	.264	6	46	193	239	1	60	5.0	.998	M. Flanagan	40	281	19	15	0	4.03
SS	M. Belanger	348	.213	0	16	184	409	9	76	4.5	.985	D. Martinez	40	276	16	11	0	3.52
3B	D. DeCinces	511	.286	28	80	111	280	10	27	3.1	.975	S. McGregor	35	233	15	13	1	3.32
RF	K. Singleton	502	.293	20	81	244	1	6	0	1.8	.976	D. Stanhouse	56	75	6	9	24	2.89
CF	L. Harlow	460	.243	8	26	313	7	7	2	2.4	.979	T. Martinez	42	69	3	3	5	4.83
LF	C. Lopez	193	.238	4	20	151	7	2	2	1.4	.988							
C	R. Dempsey	441	.259	6	32	636	79	11	14	5.4	.985							
DH	L. May	556	.246	25	80					.0								
OF	P. Kelly	274	.274	11	40	123	3	4	1	1.6	.969							
2B	B. Smith	250	.260	5	30	146	208	5	43	4.3	.986							
OF	A. Mora	229	.214	8	14	129	4	3	0	2.0	.978							
SS	K. Garcia	186	.263	0	13	86	173	15	35	3.7	.945							

Det.
W-86 L-76
Ralph Houk

POS	Player	AB	BA	HR	RBI	PO	A	E	DP	TC/G	FA	Pitcher	G	IP	W	L	SV	ERA
1B	J. Thompson	589	.287	26	96	1503	92	11	**153**	10.6	.993	J. Slaton	35	234	17	11	0	4.12
2B	L. Whitaker	484	.285	3	58	301	458	17	95	5.7	.978	M. Wilcox	29	215	13	12	0	3.76
SS	A. Trammell	448	.268	2	34	239	421	14	95	4.8	.979	D. Rozema	28	209	9	12	0	3.14
3B	A. Rodriguez	385	.265	7	43	79	228	4	20	2.4	**.987**	J. Billingham	30	202	15	8	0	3.88
RF	T. Corcoran	324	.265	1	27	186	6	3	4	1.8	.985	J. Morris	28	106	3	5	0	4.33
CF	R. LeFlore	666	.297	12	62	**440**	9	11	4	3.0	.976	K. Young	14	106	6	7	0	2.81
LF	S. Kemp	582	.277	15	79	325	11	8	2	2.2	.977	B. Sykes	22	94	6	6	2	3.94
C	M. May	352	.250	10	37	406	58	10	5	5.0	.979	J. Hiller	51	92	9	4	15	2.34
DH	R. Staub	642	.273	24	121					.0		S. Foucault	24	37	2	4	4	3.16
C	L. Parrish	288	.219	14	41	353	39	5	5	5.0	.987							
3B	P. Mankowski	222	.275	4	20	42	129	5	17	2.2	.972							
OF	J. Wockenfuss	187	.283	7	22	89	2	2	0	1.6	.978							

Cle.
W-69 L-90
Jeff Torborg

POS	Player	AB	BA	HR	RBI	PO	A	E	DP	TC/G	FA	Pitcher	G	IP	W	L	SV	ERA
1B	A. Thornton	508	.262	33	105	1327	106	7	106	9.9	.995	R. Waits	34	230	13	15	0	3.20
2B	D. Kuiper	547	.283	0	43	341	408	16	91	5.1	.979	R. Wise	33	213	9	**19**	0	4.32
SS	T. Veryzer	421	.271	1	32	177	375	21	58	4.4	.963	M. Paxton	33	191	12	11	1	3.86
3B	B. Bell	556	.282	6	62	125	**355**	15	**30**	3.6	.970	D. Hood	36	155	5	6	0	4.47
RF	J. Grubb	378	.265	14	61	199	14	6	4	2.0	.973	D. Clyde	28	153	8	11	0	4.28
CF	R. Manning	566	.263	3	50	377	7	2	1	2.7	.995	J. Kern	58	99	10	10	13	3.08
LF	J. Norris	315	.283	2	27	153	6	2	2	2.1	.988	S. Monge	48	85	4	3	6	2.76
C	G. Alexander	324	.235	17	62	305	34	6	3	5.2	.983							
DH	B. Carbo	174	.287	4	16					.0								
OF	P. Dade	307	.254	3	20	171	6	7	2	2.3	.962							
UT	T. Cox	227	.233	1	19	100	42	4	6		.973							
S2	L. Blanks	193	.254	2	20	81	138	13	25		.944							
CO	R. Pruitt	187	.235	6	17	199	15	4	4		.982							
DH	W. Horton	169	.249	5	22					.0								

Tor.
W-59 L-102
Roy Hartsfield

POS	Player	AB	BA	HR	RBI	PO	A	E	DP	TC/G	FA	Pitcher	G	IP	W	L	SV	ERA
1B	J. Mayberry	515	.250	22	70	1143	52	8	120	8.7	.993	J. Jefferson	31	212	7	16	0	4.38
2B	D. McKay	504	.238	7	45	310	408	12	96	5.2	.984	T. Underwood	31	198	6	14	0	4.10
SS	L. Gomez	413	.223	0	32	247	400	16	97	4.3	.976	J. Clancy	31	194	10	12	0	4.09
3B	R. Howell	551	.270	8	61	109	306	22	27	3.3	.950	B. Moore	37	144	6	9	0	4.68
RF	B. Bailor	621	.264	1	52	303	15	12	7	2.6	.964	J. Garvin	26	145	4	12	0	5.52
CF	R. Bosetti	568	.259	5	42	417	17	6	1	3.3	.986	D. Lemanczyk	29	137	4	14	0	6.26
LF	O. Velez	248	.266	9	38	150	10	3	4	2.2	.982	M. Willis	44	101	3	7	7	4.56
C	R. Cerone	282	.223	3	20	426	44	4	7	5.6	.992	T. Murphy	50	94	6	9	7	3.93
DH	R. Carty	387	.284	20	68							V. Cruz	32	47	7	3	9	1.71
C	A. Ashby	264	.261	9	29	399	38	6	6	5.5	.986							
UT	W. Upshaw	224	.237	1	17	131	4	7	5		.951							
OF	A. Woods	220	.241	3	25	131	2	3	0	2.3	.978							
OF	T. Hutton	173	.254	2	9	85	2	0	0	1.6	1.000							

West

K. C.
W-92 L-70
Whitey Herzog

POS	Player	AB	BA	HR	RBI	PO	A	E	DP	TC/G	FA	Pitcher	G	IP	W	L	SV	ERA
1B	P. LaCock	322	.295	5	48	700	39	5	67	7.0	.993	D. Leonard	40	295	21	17	0	3.33
2B	F. White	461	.275	7	50	325	385	16	96	5.2	.978	P. Splittorff	39	262	19	13	0	3.40
SS	F. Patek	440	.248	2	46	240	350	32	84	4.5	.949	L. Gura	35	222	16	4	0	2.72
3B	G. Brett	510	.294	9	62	104	289	16	25	3.2	.961	R. Gale	31	192	14	8	0	3.09
RF	A. Cowens	485	.274	5	63	275	10	3	5	2.3	.990	D. Bird	40	99	6	6	1	5.29
CF	A. Otis	486	.298	22	96	382	9	2	1	2.9	.995	M. Pattin	32	79	3	3	4	3.32
LF	T. Poquette	204	.216	4	30	144	5	7	0	2.5	.955	A. Hrabosky	58	75	8	7	20	2.88
C	D. Porter	520	.265	18	78	608	62	8	10	4.7	.988	S. Mingori	45	69	1	4	7	2.74
DH	H. McRae	623	.273	16	72						.0							
O1	C. Hurdle	417	.264	7	56	544	30	12	48		.980							
OF	W. Wilson	198	.217	0	16	171	6	4	2	1.6	.978							
1C	J. Wathan	190	.300	2	28	385	28	2	20		.995							

Cal.
W-87 L-75
Dave Garcia
W-25 L-20
Jim Fregosi
W-62 L-55

POS	Player	AB	BA	HR	RBI	PO	A	E	DP	TC/G	FA	Pitcher	G	IP	W	L	SV	ERA
1B	R. Fairly	235	.217	10	40	482	31	1	47	6.6	.998	F. Tanana	33	239	18	12	0	3.65
2B	B. Grich	487	.251	6	42	325	419	13	77	5.3	.983	N. Ryan	31	235	10	13	0	3.72
SS	D. Chalk	470	.253	1	34	168	237	19	46	4.4	.955	C. Knapp	30	188	14	8	0	4.21
3B	C. Lansford	453	.294	8	52	93	182	17	18	2.5	.942	D. Aase	29	179	11	8	0	4.03
RF	R. Miller	475	.263	1	37	353	9	4	5	2.8	.989	P. Hartzell	54	157	6	10	6	3.44
CF	L. Bostock	568	.296	5	71	366	7	4	2	2.6	.989	K. Brett	31	100	3	5	1	4.95
LF	J. Rudi	497	.256	17	79	231	4	2	1	2.1	.992	D. LaRoche	59	96	10	9	25	2.81
C	B. Downing	412	.255	7	46	681	82	5	6	6.0	.993							
DH	D. Baylor	591	.255	34	99						.0							
13	R. Jackson	387	.297	6	57	605	88	7	56		.990							
OF	K. Landreaux	260	.223	5	23	138	6	2	0	1.8	.986							

Tex.
W-87 L-75
Billy Hunter

POS	Player	AB	BA	HR	RBI	PO	A	E	DP	TC/G	FA	Pitcher	G	IP	W	L	SV	ERA
1B	M. Hargrove	494	.251	7	40	1221	116	17	90	9.7	.987	J. Matlack	35	270	15	13	1	2.27
2B	B. Wills	539	.250	9	57	350	526	17	84	5.7	.981	F. Jenkins	34	249	18	8	0	3.04
SS	B. Campaneris	269	.186	1	17	151	263	20	44	4.9	.954	D. Alexander	31	191	9	10	0	3.86
3B	T. Harrah	450	.229	12	59	54	167	8	15	2.5	.965	D. Medich	28	171	9	8	2	3.74
RF	B. Bonds	475	.265	29	82	213	13	7	5	2.1	.970	D. Ellis	22	141	9	7	0	4.20
CF	J. Beniquez	473	.260	11	50	309	8	9	1	2.6	.972	S. Comer	30	117	11	5	1	2.30
LF	A. Oliver	525	.324	14	89	219	8	3	1	2.1	.987	J. Umbarger	32	98	5	8	1	4.88
C	J. Sundberg	518	.278	6	58	769	91	3	14	5.8	.997	R. Cleveland	53	76	5	7	12	3.09
DH	R. Zisk	511	.262	22	85						.0	L. Barker	29	52	1	5	4	4.82
UT	K. Bevacqua	248	.222	6	30	62	116	18	12		.908							
UT	J. Lowenstein	176	.222	5	21	34	42	6	2		.927							

Min.
W-73 L-89
Gene Mauch

POS	Player	AB	BA	HR	RBI	PO	A	E	DP	TC/G	FA	Pitcher	G	IP	W	L	SV	ERA
1B	R. Carew	564	.333	5	70	1362	105	16	134	10.0	.989	R. Erickson	37	266	14	13	0	3.96
2B	B. Randall	330	.270	0	21	231	345	10	81	5.1	.983	G. Zahn	35	252	14	14	0	3.03
SS	R. Smalley	586	.273	19	77	287	527	25	121	5.3	.970	D. Goltz	39	220	15	10	0	2.49
3B	M. Cubbage	394	.282	7	57	65	233	9	24	2.7	.971	G. Serum	34	184	9	9	1	4.10
RF	D. Ford	592	.274	11	82	376	6	9	2	2.6	.977	M. Marshall	54	99	10	12	21	2.36
CF	H. Powell	381	.247	3	31	219	9	4	2	2.0	.983	D. Jackson	19	92	4	6	0	4.48
LF	W. Norwood	428	.255	8	46	227	7	14	1	1.9	.944	Perzanowski	13	57	2	7	1	5.24
C	B. Wynegar	454	.229	4	45	582	70	8	12	5.0	.988							
DH	G. Adams	310	.258	7	35						.0							
OF	B. Rivera	251	.271	3	23	162	5	3	0	1.8	.982							
DH	J. Morales	242	.314	2	38						.0							
3B	L. Wolfe	235	.234	3	25	60	143	10	9	2.6	.953							
2B	R. Wilfong	199	.266	1	11	152	196	5	37	4.4	.986							
OF	R. Chiles	198	.268	1	22	108	3	4	0	1.9	.965							
UT	C. Kusick	191	.173	4	20	228	22	4	14		.984							

Chi.
W-71 L-90
Bob Lemon
W-34 L-40
Larry Doby
W-37 L-50

POS	Player	AB	BA	HR	RBI	PO	A	E	DP	TC/G	FA	Pitcher	G	IP	W	L	SV	ERA
1B	L. Johnson	498	.273	8	72	887	71	8	74	8.9	.992	S. Stone	30	212	12	12	0	4.37
2B	J. Orta	420	.274	13	53	275	290	9	62	5.0	.984	K. Kravec	30	203	11	16	0	4.08
SS	D. Kessinger	431	.255	1	31	171	321	13	60	4.1	.974	F. Barrios	33	196	9	15	0	4.05
3B	E. Soderholm	457	.258	20	67	128	245	14	17	3.0	.964	W. Wood	28	168	10	10	0	5.20
RF	C. Washington	314	.264	6	31	159	6	7	0	2.1	.959	J. Willoughby	59	93	1	6	13	3.86
CF	C. Lemon	357	.300	13	55	284	8	5	2	3.1	.983	L. LaGrow	52	88	6	5	16	4.40
LF	R. Garr	443	.275	3	29	205	5	9	2	2.0	.959							
C	B. Nahorodny	347	.236	8	35	486	53	11	6	5.3	.980							
DH	B. Molinaro	286	.262	6	27						.0							
UT	G. Pryor	222	.261	2	15	100	202	11	31		.965							
OF	T. Bosley	219	.269	2	13	155	3	4	0	2.5	.975							
UT	W. Nordhagen	206	.301	5	35	87	12	6	2		.943							
DH	R. Blomberg	156	.231	5	22						.0							
C	M. Colbern	141	.270	2	20	203	19	7	1	4.9	.969							

POS	Player	AB	BA	HR	RBI	PO	A	E	DP	TC/G	FA	Pitcher	G	IP	W	L	SV	ERA
Oak.																		
1B	D. Revering	521	.271	16	46	1013	110	13	98	8.2	.989	M. Keough	32	197	8	15	0	3.24
2B	M. Edwards	414	.273	1	23	228	309	20	71	4.2	.964	J. Johnson	33	186	11	10	0	3.39
SS	M. Guerrero	505	.275	3	38	258	330	26	67	4.3	.958	R. Langford	37	176	7	13	0	3.43
3B	W. Gross	285	.200	7	23	72	150	20	22	2.3	.917	P. Broberg	35	166	10	12	0	4.62
RF	T. Armas	239	.213	2	13	214	3	2	0	2.6	.991	S. Renko	27	151	6	12	0	4.29
CF	M. Dilone	258	.229	1	14	195	3	3	1	2.0	.985	D. Heaverlo	69	130	3	6	10	3.25
LF	M. Page	516	.285	17	70	211	4	6	0	1.9	.973	B. Lacey	74	120	8	9	5	3.01
C	J. Essian	278	.223	3	26	431	78	10	12	4.4	.981	E. Sosa	68	109	8	2	14	2.64
DH	G. Alexander	174	.207	10	22	0	0	0	0	.0	.000	A. Wirth	16	81	5	6	0	3.43
3B	T. Duncan	319	.257	2	37	63	119	9	4	2.3	.953							
OF	J. Wallis	279	.237	6	26	187	7	4	5	2.5	.980							
C1	J. Newman	268	.239	9	32	399	41	12	20		.973							
OF	G. Burke	200	.235	1	14	152	1	2	0	2.3	.987							
OF	D. Alston	173	.208	1	10	86	0	4	0	1.8	.956							
DH	R. Carty	141	.277	11	31					.0								
Sea.																		
1B	D. Meyer	444	.227	8	56	1104	79	13	119	9.9	.989	P. Mitchell	29	168	8	14	0	4.18
2B	J. Cruz	550	.235	1	25	286	472	10	101	5.4	.987	G. Abbott	29	155	7	15	0	5.27
SS	C. Reynolds	548	.292	5	44	243	461	29	102	5.0	.960	R. Honeycutt	26	134	5	11	0	4.89
3B	B. Stein	403	.261	4	37	72	244	24	21	3.1	.929	T. House	34	116	5	4	0	4.66
RF	B. Bochte	486	.263	11	51	172	7	3	2	2.0	.984	J. Colborn	20	114	3	10	0	5.37
CF	R. Jones	472	.235	6	46	393	10	6	2	3.2	.985	S. Rawley	52	111	4	9	4	4.12
LF	L. Roberts	472	.301	22	92	296	10	8	4	2.5	.975	E. Romo	56	107	11	7	10	3.69
C	B. Stinson	364	.258	11	55	472	60	7	7	4.4	.987	McLaughlin	20	107	4	8	0	4.37
DH	L. Stanton	302	.182	3	24					.0		J. Todd	49	107	3	4	3	3.88
OF	T. Paciorek	251	.299	4	30	95	3	2	0	1.9	.980	D. Pole	21	99	4	11	0	6.48
UT	L. Milbourne	234	.226	2	20	92	169	9	27		.967							
OF	J. Hale	211	.171	4	22	160	1	2	0	1.7	.988							
1B	B. Robertson	174	.230	8	28	141	8	0	16		1.000							
13	J. Bernhardt	165	.230	2	12	263	63	6	21		.982							

Oak.
W-69 L-93
Bobby Winkles
W-24 L-15
Jack McKeon
W-45 L-78

Sea.
W-56 L-104
Darrell Johnson

BATTING AND BASE RUNNING LEADERS

Batting Average

R. Carew, MIN	.333
A. Oliver, TEX	.324
J. Rice, BOS	.315
L. Piniella, NY	.314
B. Oglivie, MIL	.303

Home Runs

J. Rice, BOS	46
L. Hisle, MIL	34
D. Baylor, CAL	34
A. Thornton, CLE	33
G. Thomas, MIL	32

Runs Batted In

J. Rice, BOS	139
R. Staub, DET	121
L. Hisle, MIL	115
A. Thornton, CLE	105
R. Carty, OAK, TOR	99
D. Baylor, CAL	99

Hits

J. Rice, BOS	213
R. LeFlore, DET	198
R. Carew, MIN	188

Home Run Percentage

G. Thomas, MIL	7.1
J. Rice, BOS	6.8
L. Hisle, MIL	6.5

Doubles

G. Brett, KC	45
C. Fisk, BOS	39
H. McRae, KC	39

Slugging Average

J. Rice, BOS	.600
L. Hisle, MIL	.533
D. DeCinces, BAL	.526
A. Otis, KC	.525
A. Thornton, CLE	.516

Total Bases

J. Rice, BOS	406
E. Murray, BAL	293
D. Baylor, CAL	279
R. Staub, DET	279
J. Thompson, DET	278

Stolen Bases

R. LeFlore, DET	68
J. Cruz, SEA	59
B. Wills, TEX	52
M. Dilone, OAK	50
W. Wilson, KC	46

Base on Balls

M. Hargrove, TEX	107
K. Singleton, BAL	98
S. Kemp, DET	97

Runs Scored

R. LeFlore, DET	126
J. Rice, BOS	121
D. Baylor, CAL	103

Triples

J. Rice, BOS	15
R. Carew, MIN	10
D. Ford, MIN	10

PITCHING LEADERS

Winning Percentage

R. Guidry, NY	.893
B. Stanley, BOS	.882
L. Gura, KC	.800
D. Eckersley, BOS	.714
M. Caldwell, MIL	.710

Wins

R. Guidry, NY	25
M. Caldwell, MIL	22
J. Palmer, BAL	21
D. Leonard, KC	21
D. Eckersley, BOS	20
E. Figueroa, NY	20

Strikeouts

N. Ryan, CAL	260
R. Guidry, NY	248
D. Leonard, KC	183
M. Flanagan, BAL	167
D. Eckersley, BOS	162

Fewest Hits per 9 Innings

R. Guidry, NY	6.15
N. Ryan, CAL	7.01
L. Gura, KC	7.43

Fewest Walks per 9 Innings

F. Jenkins, TEX	1.48
L. Sorensen, MIL	1.60
M. Caldwell, MIL	1.66

Innings

J. Palmer, BAL	296
D. Leonard, KC	295
M. Caldwell, MIL	293

Earned Run Average

R. Guidry, NY	1.74
J. Matlack, TEX	2.27
M. Caldwell, MIL	2.36
J. Palmer, BAL	2.46
D. Goltz, MIN	2.49

Saves

G. Gossage, NY	27
D. LaRoche, CAL	25
D. Stanhouse, BAL	24
M. Marshall, MIN	21
A. Hrabosky, KC	20

Complete Games

M. Caldwell, MIL	23
D. Leonard, KC	20
J. Palmer, BAL	19
J. Matlack, TEX	18
L. Sorensen, MIL	17
M. Flanagan, BAL	17

Shutouts

R. Guidry, NY	9
M. Caldwell, MIL	6
J. Palmer, BAL	6
L. Tiant, BOS	5

Most Strikeouts per 9 Inn.

N. Ryan, CAL	9.96
R. Guidry, NY	8.16
K. Kravec, CHI	6.83

Games Pitched

B. Lacey, OAK	74
D. Heaverlo, OAK	69
E. Sosa, OAK	68
G. Gossage, NY	63

	W	L	PCT	GB	R	OR	Batting					SB	Fielding			CG	BB	Pitching			
							2B	3B	HR	BA	SA		E	DP	FA			SO	ShO	SV	ERA
EAST																					
NY *	100	63	.613	-	735	582	228	38	125	.267	.388	98	113	136	.982	39	478	817	16	**36**	**3.18**
BOS	99	64	.607	1	796	657	270	46	172	.267	.424	74	146	172	.977	57	464	706	15	26	3.54
MIL	93	69	.574	6.5	**804**	650	265	38	**173**	**.276**	**.432**	95	150	144	.977	62	**398**	577	**19**	24	3.65
BAL	90	71	.559	9	659	633	248	19	154	.258	.396	75	**110**	166	**.982**	**65**	509	754	16	33	3.56
DET	86	76	.531	13.5	714	653	218	34	129	.271	.392	90	118	**177**	.981	60	503	684	12	21	3.64
CLE	69	90	.434	29	639	694	223	45	106	.261	.379	64	123	142	.980	36	568	739	6	28	3.97
TOR	59	102	.366	40	590	775	217	39	98	.250	.359	28	131	163	.979	35	614	758	5	23	4.55
WEST																					
KC	92	70	.568	-	743	634	**305**	**59**	98	.268	.399	**216**	150	152	.976	53	478	657	14	33	3.44
CAL	87	75	.537	5	691	666	226	28	108	.259	.370	86	136	136	.978	44	599	**892**	13	33	3.65
TEX	87	75	.537	5	692	632	216	36	132	.253	.381	196	153	140	.976	54	421	776	12	25	3.42
MIN	73	89	.451	19	666	678	259	47	82	.267	.375	99	146	171	.977	48	520	703	9	26	3.69
CHI	71	90	.441	20.5	634	731	221	41	106	.264	.379	83	139	130	.977	38	586	710	9	33	4.22
OAK	69	93	.426	23	532	690	200	31	100	.245	.351	144	179	142	.971	26	582	750	11	29	3.62
SEA	56	104	.350	35	614	834	229	37	97	.248	.359	123	141	172	.978	28	567	630	4	20	4.72
					9509	9509	3325	538	1680	.261	.385	1471	1935	2143	.978	645	7287	10153	161	390	3.77

* Defeated Boston in a 1 game playoff.

National League 1979

	POS	Player	AB	BA	HR	RBI	PO	A	E	DP	TC/G	FA	Pitcher	G	IP	W	L	SV	ERA

East

Pit.
W-98 L-64
Chuck Tanner

	POS	Player	AB	BA	HR	RBI	PO	A	E	DP	TC/G	FA	Pitcher	G	IP	W	L	SV	ERA
	1B	W. Stargell	424	.281	32	82	949	47	3	102	8.8	**.997**	B. Blyleven	37	237	12	5	0	3.61
	2B	P. Garner	549	.293	11	59	175	234	8	58	5.0	.981	J. Candelaria	33	207	14	9	0	3.22
	SS	T. Foli	525	.291	1	65	255	404	15	97	5.1	.978	B. Kison	33	172	13	7	0	3.19
	3B	B. Madlock	311	.328	7	44	63	153	7	12	2.6	.969	D. Robinson	29	161	8	8	0	3.86
	RF	D. Parker	622	.310	25	94	341	15	15	1	2.3	.960	J. Bibby	34	138	12	4	0	2.80
	CF	O. Moreno	695	.282	8	69	**490**	11	13	3	3.2	.975	K. Tekulve	**94**	134	10	8	31	2.75
	LF	B. Robinson	421	.264	24	75	161	6	3	0	1.4	.982	E. Romo	84	129	10	5	5	3.00
	C	E. Ott	403	.273	7	51	612	53	4	5	5.8	.994	J. Rooker	19	104	4	7	0	4.59
	O1	J. Milner	326	.276	16	60	367	20	8	28		.980	G. Jackson	72	82	8	5	14	2.96
	2B	R. Stennett	319	.238	0	24	172	282	12	63	4.6	.974							
	C	S. Nicosia	191	.288	4	13	320	25	3	4	5.4	.991							
	OF	L. Lacy	182	.247	5	15	70	3	2	0	1.8	.973							

Mon.
W-95 L-65
Dick Williams

	POS	Player	AB	BA	HR	RBI	PO	A	E	DP	TC/G	FA	Pitcher	G	IP	W	L	SV	ERA
	1B	T. Perez	489	.270	13	73	1114	65	11	81	9.2	.991	S. Rogers	37	249	13	12	0	3.00
	2B	R. Scott	562	.238	3	42	301	324	13	71	**5.6**	.980	B. Lee	33	222	16	10	0	3.04
	SS	C. Speier	344	.227	7	26	194	355	17	52	5.1	.970	S. Sanderson	34	168	9	8	1	3.43
	3B	L. Parrish	544	.307	30	82	119	290	23	25	2.8	.947	D. Schatzeder	32	162	10	5	1	2.83
	RF	E. Valentine	548	.276	21	82	281	10	5	2	2.1	.983	R. Grimsley	32	151	10	9	0	5.36
	CF	A. Dawson	639	.275	25	92	394	7	5	1	2.7	.988	D. Palmer	36	123	10	2	2	2.63
	LF	W. Cromartie	659	.275	8	46	343	16	9	4	2.3	.976	E. Sosa	62	97	8	7	18	1.95
	C	G. Carter	505	.283	22	75	**751**	88	9	**12**	6.1	.989	R. May	33	94	10	3	0	2.30
	2B	D. Cash	187	.321	2	19	88	110	6	18	4.3	.971	W. Fryman	44	58	3	6	10	2.79

St. L.
W-86 L-76
Ken Boyer

	POS	Player	AB	BA	HR	RBI	PO	A	E	DP	TC/G	FA	Pitcher	G	IP	W	L	SV	ERA
	1B	K. Hernandez	610	**.344**	11	105	**1489**	**146**	8	**145**	10.3	.995	P. Vuckovich	34	233	15	10	0	3.59
	2B	K. Oberkfell	369	.301	1	35	213	323	8	65	4.6	**.985**	B. Forsch	33	219	11	11	0	3.82
	SS	G. Templeton	672	.314	9	62	292	525	34	**102**	5.7	.960	S. Martinez	32	207	15	8	0	3.26
	3B	K. Reitz	605	.268	8	73	124	290	12	26	2.7	.972	J. Denny	31	206	8	11	0	4.85
	RF	G. Hendrick	493	.300	16	75	254	**20**	2	**7**	2.0	.993	M. Littell	63	82	9	4	13	2.20
	CF	T. Scott	587	.259	6	68	427	14	7	5	3.0	.984	D. Knowles	48	49	2	5	6	4.04
	LF	L. Brock	405	.304	5	38	152	7	7	7	1.7	.985	B. Schultz	31	42	4	3	3	4.50
	C	T. Simmons	448	.283	26	87	606	69	10	10	5.6	.985							
	OF	J. Mumphrey	339	.295	3	32	180	3	3	0	1.6	.984							
	2B	M. Tyson	190	.221	5	20	125	184	8	42	4.5	.975							
	OF	D. Iorg	179	.291	1	21	51	2	2	0	1.4	.964							

Phi.
W-84 L-78
Danny Ozark
W-65 L-67
Dallas Green
W-19 L-11

	POS	Player	AB	BA	HR	RBI	PO	A	E	DP	TC/G	FA	Pitcher	G	IP	W	L	SV	ERA
	1B	P. Rose	628	.331	4	59	1424	87	8	124	9.6	.995	S. Carlton	35	251	18	11	0	3.62
	2B	M. Trillo	431	.260	6	42	270	368	10	84	5.5	.985	R. Lerch	37	214	10	13	0	3.74
	SS	L. Bowa	539	.241	0	31	229	448	6	80	4.7	**.991**	N. Espinosa	33	212	14	12	0	3.65
	3B	M. Schmidt	541	.253	45	114	114	361	23	**36**	3.2	.954	D. Ruthven	20	122	7	5	0	4.28
	RF	B. McBride	582	.280	12	60	341	12	4	2	2.4	.989	Christenson	19	106	5	10	0	4.50
	CF	G. Maddox	548	.281	13	61	433	13	2	2	**3.2**	.996	R. Reed	61	102	13	8	5	4.15
	LF	G. Luzinski	452	.252	18	81	156	3	9	1	1.3	.946	T. McGraw	65	84	4	3	16	5.14
	C	B. Boone	398	.286	9	58	527	65	7	8	5.1	.988	R. Eastwick	51	83	3	6	6	4.88
	OF	G. Gross	174	.333	0	15	82	5	2	2	1.2	.978							
	O1	D. Unser	141	.298	6	29	118	5	3	6		.976							

POS	Player	AB	BA	HR	RBI	PO	A	E	DP	TC/G	FA	Pitcher	G	IP	W	L	SV	ERA

Chi.
W-80 L-82
Herman Franks
W-78 L-77
Joey Amalfitano
W-2 L-5

POS	Player	AB	BA	HR	RBI	PO	A	E	DP	TC/G	FA	Pitcher	G	IP	W	L	SV	ERA
1B	B. Buckner	591	.284	14	66	1258	124	7	118	9.9	.995	R. Reuschel	36	239	18	12	0	3.62
2B	T. Sizemore	330	.248	2	24	230	312	15	68	5.8	.973	L. McGlothen	42	212	13	14	2	4.12
SS	I. DeJesus	636	.283	5	52	235	507	32	97	4.8	.959	D. Lamp	38	200	11	10	0	3.51
3B	S. Ontiveros	519	.285	4	57	98	268	23	27	2.7	.941	M. Krukow	28	165	9	9	0	4.20
RF	S. Thompson	346	.289	2	29	161	7	5	3	1.7	.971	K. Holtzman	23	118	6	9	0	4.58
CF	J. Martin	534	.272	19	73	297	11	6	4	2.2	.981	D. Tidrow	63	103	11	5	4	2.71
LF	D. Kingman	532	.288	48	115	240	11	12	3	1.9	.954	B. Sutter	62	101	6	6	37	2.23
C	B. Foote	429	.254	16	56	713	63	17	9	6.1	.979							
O1	L. Biittner	272	.290	3	50	282	23	6	24		.981							
OF	B. Murcer	190	.258	7	22	110	4	0	0	2.1	1.000							
OF	M. Vail	179	.335	7	35	51	3	2	0	1.4	.964							
2B	S. Dillard	166	.283	5	24	111	132	3	31	4.1	.988							

N. Y.
W-63 L-99
Joe Torre

POS	Player	AB	BA	HR	RBI	PO	A	E	DP	TC/G	FA	Pitcher	G	IP	W	L	SV	ERA
1B	W. Montanez	410	.234	5	47	905	76	11	95	9.2	.989	C. Swan	35	251	14	13	0	3.30
2B	D. Flynn	555	.243	4	61	369	380	13	98	5.1	.983	P. Falcone	33	184	6	14	0	4.16
SS	F. Taveras	635	.263	1	33	270	438	25	88	4.8	.966	K. Kobel	30	162	6	8	0	3.50
3B	R. Hebner	473	.268	10	79	99	246	22	26	2.7	.940	N. Allen	50	99	6	10	8	3.55
RF	J. Youngblood	590	.275	16	60	308	18	5	3	2.3	.985	D. Murray	58	97	4	8	4	4.82
CF	L. Mazzilli	597	.303	15	79	358	12	4	1	2.6	.989	D. Ellis	17	85	3	7	0	6.04
LF	S. Henderson	350	.306	5	39	201	6	2	3	2.2	.990	A. Hassler	29	80	4	5	4	3.71
C	J. Stearns	538	.243	9	66	628	85	12	11	6.0	.983	T. Hausman	19	79	2	6	2	2.73
OF	E. Maddox	224	.268	1	12	129	5	2	1	2.1	.985	E. Glynn	46	60	1	4	7	3.00
UT	A. Trevino	207	.271	0	20	229	71	9	14		.971	S. Lockwood	27	42	2	5	9	1.50

West

Cin.
W-90 L-71
John McNamara

POS	Player	AB	BA	HR	RBI	PO	A	E	DP	TC/G	FA	Pitcher	G	IP	W	L	SV	ERA
1B	D. Driessen	515	.250	18	75	1289	79	9	112	9.6	.993	T. Seaver	32	215	16	6	0	3.14
2B	J. Morgan	436	.250	9	32	259	329	12	74	5.0	.980	M. LaCoss	35	206	14	8	0	3.50
SS	D. Concepcion	590	.281	16	84	284	495	27	102	5.4	.967	F. Norman	34	195	11	13	0	3.65
3B	R. Knight	551	.318	10	79	120	262	15	26	2.7	.962	B. Bonham	29	176	9	7	0	3.78
RF	K. Griffey	380	.316	8	32	175	8	3	1	2.0	.984	T. Hume	57	163	10	9	17	2.76
CF	C. Geronimo	356	.239	4	38	291	11	2	2	2.6	.993	P. Moskau	21	106	9	3	0	3.91
LF	G. Foster	440	.302	30	98	214	7	4	1	1.9	.982	F. Pastore	30	95	6	7	4	4.26
C	J. Bench	464	.276	22	80	619	68	10	11	5.5	.986	D. Bair	65	94	11	7	16	4.31
OF	D. Collins	396	.318	3	35	159	2	4	2	1.8	.976							
2B	J. Kennedy	220	.273	1	17	95	144	5	28	4.1	.980							
OF	H. Cruz	182	.242	4	27	119	8	2	4	1.9	.984							

Hou.
W-89 L-73
Bill Virdon

POS	Player	AB	BA	HR	RBI	PO	A	E	DP	TC/G	FA	Pitcher	G	IP	W	L	SV	ERA
1B	C. Cedeno	470	.262	6	54	832	33	17	79	9.7	.981	J. Richard	38	292	18	13	0	2.71
2B	R. Landestoy	282	.270	0	30	166	234	12	53	3.6	.971	J. Niekro	38	264	21	11	0	3.00
SS	C. Reynolds	555	.265	0	39	208	428	23	88	4.6	.965	J. Andujar	46	194	12	12	4	3.43
3B	E. Cabell	603	.272	6	67	109	178	13	11	2.3	.957	K. Forsch	26	178	11	6	0	3.03
RF	J. Leonard	411	.290	0	47	227	6	10	1	2.0	.959	R. Williams	31	121	4	7	0	3.27
CF	T. Puhl	600	.287	8	49	352	7	0	3	2.4	1.000	J. Sambito	63	91	8	7	22	1.78
LF	J. Cruz	558	.289	9	72	320	7	14	0	2.2	.959							
C	A. Ashby	336	.202	2	35	548	57	8	5	5.8	.987							
23	A. Howe	355	.248	6	33	173	258	7	39		.984							
UT	J. Gonzalez	181	.249	0	10	92	146	5	27		.979							
1B	B. Watson	163	.239	3	18	371	33	3	23	9.3	.993							
OF	D. Walling	147	.327	3	31	65	2	1	0	1.6	.985							

L. A.
W-79 L-83
Tom Lasorda

POS	Player	AB	BA	HR	RBI	PO	A	E	DP	TC/G	FA	Pitcher	G	IP	W	L	SV	ERA
1B	S. Garvey	648	.315	28	110	1402	93	7	101	9.3	.995	R. Sutcliffe	39	242	17	10	0	3.46
2B	D. Lopes	582	.265	28	73	341	384	14	82	4.9	.981	D. Sutton	33	226	12	15	1	3.82
SS	B. Russell	627	.271	7	56	218	452	30	70	4.7	.957	B. Hooton	29	212	11	10	0	2.97
3B	R. Cey	487	.281	28	81	123	265	9	25	2.6	.977	J. Reuss	39	160	7	14	3	3.54
RF	G. Thomasson	315	.248	14	45	194	4	4	1	2.0	.980	C. Hough	42	151	7	5	0	4.77
CF	D. Thomas	406	.256	5	44	269	10	1	4	2.4	.996	B. Welch	25	81	5	6	5	4.00
LF	D. Baker	554	.274	23	88	289	14	3	4	2.0	.990	D. Patterson	36	53	4	1	6	5.26
C	S. Yeager	310	.216	13	41	513	56	9	7	5.6	.984	L. LaGrow	31	37	5	1	4	3.41
CO	J. Ferguson	363	.262	20	69	414	37	9	8		.980							
OF	R. Smith	234	.274	10	32	159	5	2	0	2.7	.988							

S. F.
W-71 L-91
Joe Altobelli
W-61 L-79
Dave Bristol
W-10 L-12

POS	Player	AB	BA	HR	RBI	PO	A	E	DP	TC/G	FA	Pitcher	G	IP	W	L	SV	ERA
1B	M. Ivie	402	.286	27	89	724	40	4	51	7.8	.995	V. Blue	34	237	14	14	0	5.01
2B	J. Strain	257	.241	1	12	147	188	6	32	5.1	.982	B. Knepper	34	207	9	12	0	4.65
SS	J. LeMaster	343	.254	3	29	160	303	20	32	4.6	.959	J. Montefusco	22	137	3	8	0	3.94
3B	D. Evans	562	.253	17	70	129	369	30	28	3.3	.943	E. Halicki	33	126	5	8	0	4.57
RF	J. Clark	527	.273	26	86	261	13	5	7	2.0	.982	J. Curtis	27	121	10	9	0	4.17
CF	B. North	460	.259	5	30	300	8	4	2	2.4	.987	P. Nastu	25	100	3	4	0	4.32
LF	L. Herndon	354	.257	7	36	196	10	8	2	1.8	.963	E. Whitson	18	100	5	8	0	3.95
C	D. Littlejohn	193	.197	1	13	366	43	6	7	6.6	.986	G. Lavelle	70	97	7	9	20	2.51
OF	T. Whitfield	394	.287	5	44	167	10	8	3	1.7	.957	T. Griffin	59	94	5	6	2	3.93
1B	W. McCovey	353	.249	15	57	740	48	10	60	9.0	.987	G. Minton	46	80	4	3	4	1.80
SS	R. Metzger	259	.251	0	31	108	219	15	34	4.4	.956	P. Borbon	30	46	4	3	3	4.89
2B	B. Madlock	249	.261	7	41	137	144	7	32	4.6	.976							
C	M. Hill	169	.207	3	15	283	31	3	4	5.5	.991							

POS	Player	AB	BA	HR	RBI	PO	A	E	DP	TC/G	FA	Pitcher	G	IP	W	L	SV	ERA
1B	D. Briggs	227	.207	8	30	326	28	5	20	7.2	.986	R. Jones	39	263	11	12	0	3.63
2B	F. Gonzalez	323	.217	9	34	217	225	11	52	4.4	.976	G. Perry	32	233	12	11	0	3.05
SS	O. Smith	587	.211	0	27	256	555	20	86	5.4	.976	B. Shirley	49	205	8	16	0	3.38
3B	P. Dade	283	.276	1	19	44	162	11	12	3.1	.949	E. Rasmussen	45	157	6	9	3	3.27
RF	J. Turner	448	.248	9	61	197	7	9	2	1.9	.958	B. Owchinko	42	149	6	12	0	3.74
CF	G. Richards	545	.279	4	41	320	7	9	2	2.5	.973	J. D'Acquisto	51	134	9	13	2	4.90
LF	D. Winfield	597	.308	34	**118**	344	14	5	3	2.3	.986	R. Fingers	54	84	9	9	13	4.50
C	G. Tenace	463	.263	20	67	413	51	1	10	4.9	**.998**	S. Mura	38	73	4	4	2	3.08
UT	K. Bevacqua	297	.253	1	34	115	156	11	21		.961	M. Lee	46	65	2	4	5	4.29
C	B. Fahey	209	.287	3	19	277	33	2	5	4.6	.994							
O1	J. Johnstone	201	.294	0	32	185	18	4	10		.981							
2B	B. Almon	198	.227	1	8	116	150	4	37	4.4	.985							
3B	B. Evans	162	.216	1	14	30	108	7	12	2.7	.952							

S. D.
W-68 L-93
Roger Craig

POS	Player	AB	BA	HR	RBI	PO	A	E	DP	TC/G	FA	Pitcher	G	IP	W	L	SV	ERA
1B	D. Murphy	384	.276	21	57	685	42	15	61	9.8	.980	P. Niekro	44	**342**	**21**	**20**	0	3.39
2B	G. Hubbard	325	.231	3	29	193	268	**15**	57	5.2	.968	E. Solomon	31	186	7	14	0	4.21
SS	P. Frias	475	.259	1	44	229	432	32	79	5.1	.954	R. Matula	28	171	8	10	0	4.16
3B	B. Horner	487	.314	33	98	56	143	15	11	2.6	.930	T. Brizzolara	20	107	6	9	0	5.30
RF	J. Burroughs	397	.224	11	47	175	8	7	1	1.7	.963	G. Garber	68	106	6	16	25	4.33
CF	B. Bonnell	375	.259	12	45	220	8	4	2	1.9	.983	M. Mahler	26	100	5	11	0	5.85
LF	G. Matthews	631	.304	27	90	292	12	8	4	2.0	.974	McLaughlin	37	69	5	3	5	2.48
C	B. Benedict	204	.225	0	15	344	35	6	3	5.1	.984							
32	J. Royster	601	.273	3	51	261	405	22	62		.968							
OF	R. Office	277	.249	2	37	164	4	2	0	1.8	.988							
C	J. Nolan	230	.248	4	21	328	27	6	2	4.9	.983							
1B	M. Lum	217	.249	6	27	414	30	1	36	8.7	.998							
OF	C. Spikes	93	.280	3	21	16	0	3	0	1.3	.842							

Atl.
W-66 L-94
Bobby Cox

BATTING AND BASE RUNNING LEADERS

Batting Average

K. Hernandez, STL	.344
P. Rose, PHI	.331
R. Knight, CIN	.318
S. Garvey, LA	.315
B. Horner, ATL	.314

Slugging Average

D. Kingman, CHI	.613
M. Schmidt, PHI	.564
D. Winfield, SD	.558
B. Horner, ATL	.552
L. Parrish, MON	.551

Home Runs

D. Kingman, CHI	48
M. Schmidt, PHI	45
D. Winfield, SD	34
B. Horner, ATL	33
W. Stargell, PIT	32

Total Bases

D. Winfield, SD	333
D. Parker, PIT	327
D. Kingman, CHI	326
S. Garvey, LA	322
G. Matthews, ATL	317

Runs Batted In

D. Winfield, SD	118
D. Kingman, CHI	115
M. Schmidt, PHI	114
S. Garvey, LA	110
K. Hernandez, STL	105

Stolen Bases

O. Moreno, PIT	77
B. North, SF	58
D. Lopes, LA	44
F. Taveras, NY, PIT	44
R. Scott, MON	39

Hits

G. Templeton, STL	211
K. Hernandez, STL	210
P. Rose, PHI	208

Base on Balls

M. Schmidt, PHI	120
G. Tenace, SD	105
D. Lopes, LA	97

Home Run Percentage

D. Kingman, CHI	9.0
M. Schmidt, PHI	8.3
B. Horner, ATL	6.8

Runs Scored

K. Hernandez, STL	116
O. Moreno, PIT	110

Doubles

K. Hernandez, STL	48
W. Cromartie, MON	46
D. Parker, PIT	45

Triples

G. Templeton, STL	19
B. McBride, PHI	12
A. Dawson, MON	12
O. Moreno, PIT	12

PITCHING LEADERS

Winning Percentage

T. Seaver, CIN	.727
J. Niekro, HOU	.656
S. Martinez, STL	.652
R. Sutcliffe, LA	.630
S. Carlton, PHI	.621

Earned Run Average

J. Richard, HOU	2.71
T. Hume, CIN	2.76
D. Schatzeder, MON	2.83
B. Hooton, LA	2.97
J. Niekro, HOU	3.00
S. Rogers, MON	3.00

Wins

J. Niekro, HOU	21
P. Niekro, ATL	21
S. Carlton, PHI	18
R. Reuschel, CHI	18
J. Richard, HOU	18

Saves

B. Sutter, CHI	37
K. Tekulve, PIT	31
G. Garber, ATL	25
J. Sambito, HOU	22
G. Lavelle, SF	20

Strikeouts

J. Richard, HOU	313
S. Carlton, PHI	213
P. Niekro, ATL	208
B. Blyleven, PIT	172
L. McGlothen, CHI	147

Complete Games

P. Niekro, ATL	23
J. Richard, HOU	19
S. Carlton, PHI	13
S. Rogers, MON	13
B. Hooton, LA	12

Fewest Hits per 9 Innings

J. Richard, HOU	6.78
S. Carlton, PHI	7.24
J. Niekro, HOU	7.53

Shutouts

T. Seaver, CIN	5
S. Rogers, MON	5
J. Niekro, HOU	5

Fewest Walks per 9 Innings

K. Forsch, HOU	1.77
J. Candelaria, PIT	1.78
T. Hume, CIN	1.82

Most Strikeouts per 9 Inn.

J. Richard, HOU	9.65
S. Carlton, PHI	7.64
S. Sanderson, MON	7.39

Innings

P. Niekro, ATL	342
J. Richard, HOU	292
J. Niekro, HOU	264

Games Pitched

K. Tekulve, PIT	94
E. Romo, PIT	84
G. Jackson, PIT	72

	W	L	PCT	GB	R	OR	Batting 2B	3B	HR	BA	SA	SB	Fielding E	DP	FA	Pitching CG	BB	SO	ShO	SV	ERA
EAST																					
PIT	98	64	.605		**775**	643	264	52	148	.272	**.416**	180	134	163	.979	24	504	904	7	**52**	3.41
MON	95	65	.594	2	701	**581**	273	42	143	.264	.408	121	131	123	.979	33	**450**	813	18	39	**3.14**
STL	86	76	.531	12	731	693	**279**	63	100	**.278**	.401	116	132	166	.980	38	501	788	10	25	3.72
PHI	84	78	.519	14	683	718	250	53	119	.266	.396	128	**106**	148	**.983**	33	477	787	14	29	4.16
CHI	80	82	.494	18	706	707	250	43	135	.269	.403	73	159	163	.975	20	521	**933**	11	44	3.88
NY	63	99	.389	35	593	706	255	41	74	.250	.350	135	140	**168**	.978	16	607	819	10	36	3.84
WEST																					
CIN	90	71	.559		731	644	266	31	132	.264	.396	99	124	152	.980	27	485	773	10	40	3.58
HOU	89	73	.549	1.5	583	582	224	52	49	.256	.344	**190**	138	146	.978	**55**	504	854	**19**	31	3.19
LA	79	83	.488	11.5	739	717	220	24	**183**	.263	.412	106	118	123	.981	30	555	811	6	34	3.83
SF	71	91	.438	19.5	672	751	192	36	125	.246	.365	140	163	138	.974	25	577	880	6	34	4.16
SD	68	93	.422	22	603	681	193	53	93	.242	.348	100	141	154	.978	29	513	779	7	25	3.69
ATL	66	94	.413	23.5	669	763	220	28	126	.256	.377	98	183	139	.970	32	494	779	3	34	4.18
					8186	8186	2886	518	1427	.261	.385	1486	1669	1783	.978	362	6188	9920	121	423	3.73

American League 1979

POS	Player	AB	BA	HR	RBI	PO	A	E	DP	TC/G	FA	Pitcher	G	IP	W	L	SV	ERA

East

Bal. W-102 L-57 Earl Weaver

POS	Player	AB	BA	HR	RBI	PO	A	E	DP	TC/G	FA	Pitcher	G	IP	W	L	SV	ERA
1B	E. Murray	606	.295	25	99	**1456**	107	10	135	10.0	.994	D. Martinez	40	**292**	15	16	0	3.67
2B	R. Dauer	479	.257	9	61	213	260	10	68	4.7	.979	M. Flanagan	39	266	**23**	9	0	3.08
SS	K. Garcia	417	.247	5	24	173	271	21	66	4.1	.955	S. Stone	32	186	11	7	0	3.77
3B	D. DeCinces	422	.230	16	61	99	247	13	21	3.0	.964	S. McGregor	38	251	13	6	0	3.34
RF	K. Singleton	570	.295	35	111	247	8	5	2	1.8	.981	J. Palmer	23	156	10	6	0	3.29
CF	A. Bumbry	569	.285	7	49	367	7	7	1	2.6	.982	S. Stewart	31	118	8	5	1	3.51
LF	G. Roenicke	376	.261	25	64	246	10	5	1	2.0	.981	T. Martinez	39	78	10	3	3	2.88
C	R. Dempsey	368	.239	6	41	615	**81**	7	13	**5.7**	.990	D. Stanhouse	52	73	7	3	21	2.84
DH	L. May	456	.254	19	69	0	0	0	0	.0	.000							
SS	M. Belanger	198	.167	0	9	110	195	3	38	3.1	.990							
OF	J. Lowenstein	197	.254	11	34	120	4	1	2	1.7	.992							
2B	B. Smith	189	.249	6	33	107	142	5	33	4.0	.980							
OF	P. Kelly	153	.288	9	25	36	0	0	0		1.000							

Mil. W-95 L-66 George Bamberger

POS	Player	AB	BA	HR	RBI	PO	A	E	DP	TC/G	FA	Pitcher	G	IP	W	L	SV	ERA
1B	C. Cooper	590	.308	24	106	1323	78	10	119	10.5	.993	L. Sorensen	34	235	15	14	0	3.98
2B	P. Molitor	584	.322	9	62	289	413	15	81	**5.9**	.979	M. Caldwell	30	235	16	6	0	3.29
SS	R. Yount	577	.267	8	51	267	517	25	97	5.4	.969	J. Slaton	32	213	15	9	0	3.63
3B	S. Bando	476	.246	9	43	87	222	12	16	2.9	.963	B. Travers	30	187	14	8	0	3.90
RF	S. Lezcano	473	.321	28	101	281	10	4	4	2.2	.986	M. Haas	29	185	11	11	0	4.77
CF	G. Thomas	557	.244	**45**	123	435	4	4	2	2.9	.991	J. Augustine	43	86	9	6	5	3.45
LF	B. Oglivie	514	.282	29	81	252	7	4	0	2.2	.985	R. Cleveland	29	55	1	5	4	6.71
C	C. Moore	337	.300	5	38	414	58	10	7	4.5	.979	B. McClure	36	51	5	2	5	3.88
DH	D. Davis	335	.266	12	41	0	0	0	0	.0	.000	B. Castro	39	44	3	1	6	2.05
UT	D. Money	350	.237	6	38	240	117	2	33		.994							
32	J. Gantner	208	.284	3	22	78	147	7	24		.970							
C	B. Martinez	196	.270	4	26	198	39	8	2	3.6	.967							
OF	J. Wohlford	175	.263	1	17	126	0	4	0	2.4	.969							

Bos. W-91 L-69 Don Zimmer

POS	Player	AB	BA	HR	RBI	PO	A	E	DP	TC/G	FA	Pitcher	G	IP	W	L	SV	ERA
1B	B. Watson	312	.337	13	53	525	47	7	58	10.0	.988	M. Torrez	36	252	16	13	0	4.50
2B	J. Remy	306	.297	0	29	147	205	11	43	4.8	.970	D. Eckersley	33	247	17	10	0	2.99
SS	R. Burleson	627	.278	5	60	272	523	16	109	5.3	**.980**	B. Stanley	40	217	16	12	1	3.98
3B	B. Hobson	528	.261	28	93	110	251	25	17	2.7	.935	S. Renko	27	171	11	9	0	4.11
RF	D. Evans	489	.274	21	58	307	15	4	5	2.2	.988	C. Rainey	20	104	8	5	1	3.81
CF	F. Lynn	531	**.333**	39	122	381	10	5	4	2.8	.987	D. Drago	53	89	10	6	13	3.03
LF	J. Rice	619	.325	39	130	241	8	4	1	2.0	.984	B. Campbell	41	55	3	4	9	4.25
C	G. Allenson	241	.203	3	22	407	40	9	3	4.4	.980							
DH	Yastrzemski	518	.270	21	87	0	0	0	0	.0	.000							
CC	C. Fisk	320	.272	10	42	155	8	3	1		.982							
23	J. Brohamer	192	.266	1	11	74	140	5	27		.977							
1B	G. Scott	156	.224	4	23	400	25	6	40	10.5	.986							
OF	T. Poquette	154	.331	2	23	73	2	4	1	1.8	.949							

N. Y. W-89 L-71 Bob Lemon W-34 L-30 Billy Martin W-55 L-41

POS	Player	AB	BA	HR	RBI	PO	A	E	DP	TC/G	FA	Pitcher	G	IP	W	L	SV	ERA
1B	C. Chambliss	554	.280	18	63	1299	95	7	135	**10.5**	.995	T. John	37	276	21	9	0	2.97
2B	W. Randolph	574	.270	5	61	**355**	**478**	13	**128**	5.5	.985	R. Guidry	33	236	18	8	2	**2.78**
SS	B. Dent	431	.230	2	32	219	512	17	107	5.3	.977	L. Tiant	30	196	13	8	0	3.90
3B	G. Nettles	521	.253	20	73	110	339	16	30	3.2	.966	E. Figueroa	16	105	4	6	0	4.11
RF	R. Jackson	465	.297	29	89	274	7	4	2	2.3	.986	C. Hunter	19	105	2	9	0	5.31
CF	M. Rivers	286	.287	3	25	147	4	4	0	2.2	.974	R. Davis	44	85	14	2	9	2.86
LF	L. Piniella	461	.297	11	69	204	13	4	1	2.0	.982	K. Clay	32	78	1	7	2	5.42
C	T. Munson	382	.288	3	39	405	44	10	5	5.2	.978	G. Gossage	36	58	5	3	18	2.64
DH	J. Spencer	295	.288	23	53	0	0	0	0	.0	.000							
OF	B. Murcer	264	.273	8	33	169	4	3	0	2.5	.983							
OF	R. White	205	.215	3	27	45	3	0	0		1.000							
OF	O. Gamble	113	.389	11	32	47	3	3	2		.943							

Det. (W-85 L-76)
Les Moss W-27 L-26 · Dick Tracewski W-2 L-1 · Sparky Anderson W-56 L-49

POS	Player	AB	BA	HR	RBI	PO	A	E	DP	TC/G	FA	Pitcher	G	IP	W	L	SV	ERA
1B	J. Thompson	492	.246	20	79	1176	91	8	135	9.1	.994	J. Morris	27	198	17	7	0	3.27
2B	L. Whitaker	423	.286	3	42	280	369	9	103	5.2	.986	M. Wilcox	33	196	12	10	0	4.36
SS	A. Trammell	460	.276	6	50	245	388	26	99	4.6	.961	J. Billingham	35	158	10	7	3	3.30
3B	A. Rodriguez	343	.254	5	36	72	211	13	23	2.8	.956	A. Lopez	61	127	10	5	21	2.41
RF	J. Morales	440	.211	14	56	206	6	3	2	1.8	.986	P. Underwood	27	122	6	4	0	4.57
CF	R. LeFlore	600	.300	9	57	293	6	3	3	2.7	.990	D. Petry	15	98	6	5	0	3.95
LF	S. Kemp	490	.318	26	105	229	12	6	2	2.1	.976	J. Hiller	43	79	4	7	9	5.24
C	L. Parrish	493	.276	19	65	707	79	9	10	5.6	.989	D. Tobik	37	69	3	5	3	4.30
DH	R. Staub	246	.236	9	40	0	0	0	0	.0	.000							
OF	C. Summers	246	.313	20	51	87	3	1	0	1.3	.989							
UT	J. Wockenfuss	231	.264	15	46	318	26	3	22		.991							
OF	L. Jones	213	.296	4	26	142	3	3	1	1.8	.980							
32	T. Brookens	190	.263	4	21	76	141	11	21		.952							

Cle. (W-81 L-80)
Jeff Torborg W-43 L-52 · Dave Garcia W-38 L-28

POS	Player	AB	BA	HR	RBI	PO	A	E	DP	TC/G	FA	Pitcher	G	IP	W	L	SV	ERA
1B	A. Thornton	515	.233	26	93	1089	82	7	100	9.1	.994	R. Wise	34	232	15	10	0	3.72
2B	D. Kuiper	479	.255	0	39	345	380	9	89	5.2	.988	R. Waits	34	231	16	13	0	4.44
SS	T. Veryzer	449	.220	0	34	238	446	18	90	4.7	.974	M. Paxton	33	160	8	8	0	5.91
3B	T. Harrah	527	.279	20	77	91	160	16	19	2.1	.940	D. Spillner	49	158	9	5	1	4.61
RF	B. Bonds	538	.275	25	85	267	9	6	1	2.4	.979	L. Barker	29	137	6	6	0	4.93
CF	R. Manning	560	.259	3	51	417	9	6	2	3.1	.986	S. Monge	76	131	12	10	19	2.40
LF	J. Norris	353	.246	3	30	214	2	4	0	2.4	.982	W. Garland	18	95	4	10	0	5.21
C	G. Alexander	358	.229	15	54	404	40	18	5	5.1	.961	V. Cruz	61	79	3	9	10	4.22
DH	C. Johnson	240	.271	18	61	0	0	0	0	.0	.000							
O1	M. Hargrove	338	.325	10	56	356	16	2	23		.995							
C	R. Hassey	223	.287	4	32	345	29	3	4	5.5	.992							
3B	T. Cox	189	.212	4	22	29	78	4	11	2.1	.964							
OF	P. Dade	170	.282	3	18	73	4	3	1	2.2	.963							
UT	R. Pruitt	166	.283	2	21	66	5	2	1		.973							

Tor. (W-53 L-109)
Roy Hartsfield

POS	Player	AB	BA	HR	RBI	PO	A	E	DP	TC/G	FA	Pitcher	G	IP	W	L	SV	ERA
1B	J. Mayberry	464	.274	21	74	1192	74	6	129	9.4	.995	T. Underwood	33	227	9	16	0	3.69
2B	D. Ainge	308	.237	2	19	198	261	11	67	5.5	.977	P. Huffman	31	173	6	18	0	5.77
SS	A. Griffin	624	.287	2	31	272	501	36	124	5.3	.956	D. Lemanczyk	22	143	8	10	0	3.71
3B	R. Howell	511	.247	15	72	108	290	20	28	3.1	.952	B. Moore	34	139	5	7	0	4.86
RF	B. Bailor	414	.229	1	38	210	16	3	2	1.9	.987	D. Stieb	18	129	8	8	0	4.33
CF	R. Bosetti	619	.260	8	65	466	18	13	4	3.1	.974	J. Jefferson	34	116	2	10	1	5.51
LF	A. Woods	436	.278	5	36	251	10	9	2	2.1	.967	M. Lemongello	18	83	1	9	0	6.29
C	R. Cerone	469	.239	7	61	560	68	13	10	4.7	.980	T. Buskey	44	79	6	10	7	3.42
DH	R. Carty	461	.256	12	55	0	0	0	0	.0	.000							
OF	O. Velez	274	.288	15	48	130	3	4	1	1.9	.971							
UT	L. Gomez	163	.239	0	11	70	116	3	25		.984							

West

Cal. (W-88 L-74)
Jim Fregosi

POS	Player	AB	BA	HR	RBI	PO	A	E	DP	TC/G	FA	Pitcher	G	IP	W	L	SV	ERA
1B	R. Carew	409	.318	3	44	804	55	10	101	8.4	.988	D. Frost	36	239	16	10	1	3.58
2B	B. Grich	534	.294	30	101	340	438	13	111	5.2	.984	N. Ryan	34	223	16	14	0	3.59
SS	B. Anderson	234	.248	3	23	126	189	17	42	4.0	.949	J. Barr	36	197	10	12	0	4.20
3B	C. Lansford	654	.287	19	79	135	263	7	29	2.6	.983	D. Aase	37	185	9	10	2	4.82
RF	D. Ford	569	.290	21	101	332	10	8	2	2.5	.977	M. Clear	52	109	11	5	14	3.63
CF	R. Miller	427	.293	2	28	349	3	4	1	3.0	.989	C. Knapp	20	98	5	5	0	5.51
LF	D. Baylor	628	.296	36	139	198	3	5	0	2.1	.976	F. Tanana	18	90	7	5	0	3.90
C	B. Downing	509	.326	12	75	669	55	11	5	5.5	.985	D. LaRoche	53	86	7	11	10	5.55
DH	W. Aikens	379	.280	21	81	0	0	0	0	.0	.000							
OF	J. Rudi	330	.242	11	61	174	5	2	2	2.3	.989							
SS	B. Campaneris	239	.234	0	15	136	220	16	69	4.5	.957							

K. C. (W-85 L-77)
Whitey Herzog

POS	Player	AB	BA	HR	RBI	PO	A	E	DP	TC/G	FA	Pitcher	G	IP	W	L	SV	ERA
1B	P. LaCock	408	.277	3	56	829	68	3	79	8.3	.997	P. Splittorff	36	240	15	17	0	4.24
2B	F. White	467	.266	10	48	317	332	12	78	5.3	.982	D. Leonard	32	236	14	12	0	4.08
SS	F. Patek	306	.252	1	37	153	249	19	54	4.0	.955	L. Gura	39	234	13	12	0	4.46
3B	G. Brett	645	.329	23	107	129	373	30	28	3.6	.944	R. Gale	34	182	9	10	0	5.64
RF	A. Cowens	516	.295	9	73	288	3	4	0	2.2	.986	S. Busby	22	94	6	6	0	3.64
CF	A. Otis	577	.295	18	90	385	11	3	5	2.7	.992	M. Pattin	31	94	5	2	3	4.60
LF	W. Wilson	588	.315	6	49	384	13	6	0	2.7	.985	A. Hrabosky	58	65	9	4	11	3.74
C	D. Porter	533	.291	20	112	628	68	13	15	5.0	.982	Quisenberry	32	40	3	2	5	3.15
DH	H. McRae	393	.288	10	74	0	0	0	0	.0	.000							
S2	U. Washington	268	.254	2	25	174	242	18	68		.959							
UT	J. Wathan	199	.206	2	28	336	24	3	30		.992							
OF	C. Hurdle	171	.240	3	30	88	2	3	0	1.9	.968							
1B	G. Scott	146	.267	1	20	335	21	4	27	8.8	.989							

Tex. (W-83 L-79)
Pat Corrales

POS	Player	AB	BA	HR	RBI	PO	A	E	DP	TC/G	FA	Pitcher	G	IP	W	L	SV	ERA
1B	P. Putnam	426	.277	18	64	832	62	5	65	9.4	.994	F. Jenkins	37	259	16	14	0	4.07
2B	B. Wills	543	.273	5	46	337	468	20	95	5.7	.976	S. Comer	36	242	17	12	0	3.68
SS	N. Norman	343	.222	0	21	177	302	24	64	3.5	.952	D. Medich	29	149	10	7	0	4.17
3B	B. Bell	670	.299	18	101	112	364	15	22	3.3	.969	J. Kern	71	143	13	5	29	1.57
RF	R. Zisk	503	.262	18	64	234	10	7	6	1.9	.972	D. Alexander	23	113	5	7	0	4.46
CF	A. Oliver	492	.323	12	76	260	9	7	2	2.3	.975	S. Lyle	67	95	5	8	13	3.13
LF	B. Sample	325	.292	5	35	173	7	0	1	1.7	1.000							
C	J. Sundberg	495	.275	5	64	754	75	4	13	5.6	.995							
DH	J. Ellis	316	.285	12	61	0	0	0	0	.0	.000							
OF	J. Grubb	289	.273	10	37	135	8	2	4	1.8	.986							
OF	M. Rivers	247	.300	6	25	153	4	3	1	2.8	.981							
OF	O. Gamble	161	.335	8	32	41	2	0	2		1.000							
1B	W. Montanez	144	.319	8	24	191	16	1	14		.995							

POS	Player	AB	BA	HR	RBI	PO	A	E	DP	TC/G	FA	Pitcher	G	IP	W	L	SV	ERA
Min. W-82 L-80 Gene Mauch																		
1B	R. Jackson	583	.271	14	68	1447	**137**	9	**175**	10.1	.994	J. Koosman	37	264	20	13	0	3.38
2B	R. Wilfong	419	.313	9	59	287	379	14	92	5.1	.979	D. Goltz	36	251	14	13	0	4.16
SS	R. Smalley	621	.271	24	95	**296**	**572**	29	**144**	**5.6**	.968	G. Zahn	26	169	13	7	0	3.57
3B	J. Castino	393	.285	5	52	85	277	14	**31**	2.6	.963	P. Hartzell	28	163	6	10	0	5.36
RF	B. Rivera	263	.281	2	31	169	12	2	0	1.7	.989	M. Marshall	**90**	143	10	15	**32**	2.64
CF	K. Landreaux	564	.305	15	83	292	10	6	1	2.1	.981	R. Erickson	24	123	3	10	0	5.63
LF	H. Powell	338	.293	2	36	165	6	4	3	1.9	.977	P. Redfern	40	108	7	3	1	3.50
C	B. Wynegar	504	.270	7	57	653	65	6	10	5.0	.992							
DH	J. Morales	191	.267	2	27	0	0	0	0	.0	.000							
OF	G. Adams	326	.301	8	50	66	2	3	0		.958							
OF	W. Norwood	270	.248	6	30	147	4	4	0	2.2	.974							
3B	M. Cubbage	243	.276	2	23	34	94	10	9	2.2	.928							
OF	D. Edwards	229	.249	8	35	165	7	3	0	2.0	.983							
2B	B. Randall	199	.246	0	14	130	166	5	48	4.2	.983							
DH	D. Goodwin	159	.289	5	27	0	0	0	0	.0	.000							
Chi. W-73 L-87 Don Kessinger W-46 L-60 Tony LaRussa W-27 L-27																		
1B	L. Johnson	479	.309	12	74	748	63	11	62	8.7	.987	K. Kravec	36	250	15	13	1	3.74
2B	A. Bannister	506	.285	2	55	150	160	12	32	5.0	.963	R. Wortham	34	204	14	14	0	4.90
SS	G. Pryor	476	.275	3	34	161	362	21	54	4.6	.961	R. Baumgarten	28	191	13	8	0	3.53
3B	K. Bell	200	.245	4	22	51	153	17	11	3.3	.923	S. Trout	34	155	11	8	4	3.89
RF	C. Washington	471	.280	13	66	256	7	7	3	2.2	.974	R. Scarbery	45	101	2	8	4	4.63
CF	C. Lemon	556	.318	17	86	411	10	10	2	2.9	.977	F. Barrios	15	95	8	3	0	3.60
LF	R. Torres	170	.253	8	24	117	4	3	0	1.5	.976	M. Proly	38	88	3	8	9	3.89
C	M. May	202	.252	7	28	277	27	6	1	4.8	.981	E. Farmer	42	81	3	7	14	2.44
DH	J. Orta	325	.262	11	46	0	0	0	0	.0	.000							
OF	R. Garr	307	.280	9	39	94	3	5	1	1.5	.951							
1B	M. Squires	295	.264	2	22	741	60	4	62	7.3	.995							
23	J. Morrison	240	.275	14	35	121	185	9	38		.971							
3B	E. Soderholm	210	.252	6	34	55	154	3	12	3.8	.986							
OF	J. Moore	201	.264	1	23	83	3	3	0	1.5	.966							
DH	W. Nordhagen	193	.280	7	25	0	0	0	0	.0	.000							
C	B. Nahorodny	179	.257	6	29	223	25	7	3	4.3	.973							
Sea. W-67 L-95 Darrell Johnson																		
1B	B. Bochte	554	.316	16	100	1361	114	**14**	140	10.1	.991	M. Parrott	38	229	14	12	0	3.77
2B	J. Cruz	414	.271	1	29	258	361	13	87	5.9	.979	R. Honeycutt	33	194	11	12	0	4.04
SS	M. Mendoza	373	.198	1	29	177	422	20	91	4.2	.968	F. Bannister	30	182	10	15	0	4.05
3B	D. Meyer	525	.278	20	74	76	201	19	22	2.9	.936	McLaughlin	47	124	7	7	14	4.21
RF	J. Simpson	265	.283	2	27	162	10	6	4	1.7	.966	O. Jones	25	119	3	11	0	6.05
CF	R. Jones	622	.267	21	78	453	13	5	4	2.9	.989	G. Abbott	23	117	4	10	0	5.15
LF	L. Roberts	450	.271	15	54	286	6	5	2	2.2	.983	J. Montague	41	116	6	4	1	5.59
C	L. Cox	293	.215	4	36	408	49	9	6	4.7	.981	R. Dressler	21	104	3	2	0	4.93
DH	W. Horton	646	.279	29	106	0	0	0	0	.0	.000	S. Rawley	48	84	5	9	11	3.86
S2	L. Milbourne	356	.278	2	26	136	250	11	57		.972							
OF	T. Paciorek	310	.287	6	42	137	2	0	0	1.9	1.000							
3B	B. Stein	250	.248	7	27	45	120	7	13	2.6	.959							
C	B. Stinson	247	.243	6	28	376	29	9	2	4.5	.978							
Oak. W-54 L-108 Jim Marshall																		
1B	D. Revering	472	.288	19	77	828	80	13	77	8.9	.986	R. Langford	34	219	12	16	0	4.27
2B	M. Edwards	400	.233	1	23	244	314	**22**	54	5.1	.962	S. McCatty	31	186	11	12	0	4.21
SS	R. Picciolo	348	.253	2	27	191	265	17	51	4.5	.964	M. Keough	30	177	2	17	0	5.03
3B	W. Gross	442	.224	14	50	120	211	20	19	2.9	.943	M. Norris	29	146	5	8	0	4.81
RF	L. Murray	226	.186	2	20	173	7	7	2	2.1	.963	C. Minetto	36	118	1	5	0	5.57
CF	D. Murphy	388	.255	11	40	322	10	4	0	2.8	.988	B. Kingman	18	113	8	7	0	4.30
LF	R. Henderson	351	.274	1	26	215	5	6	0	2.6	.973	D. Heaverlo	62	86	4	11	9	4.19
C	J. Newman	516	.231	22	71	378	53	10	7	5.4	.977	J. Johnson	14	85	2	8	0	4.34
DH	M. Page	478	.247	9	42	0	0	0	0	.0	.000	D. Hamilton	40	83	3	4	5	3.69
C	J. Essian	313	.243	8	40	348	57	8	5	5.9	.981	M. Morgan	13	77	2	10	0	5.96
OF	T. Armas	278	.248	11	34	194	7	5	2	2.6	.976	B. Lacey	42	48	1	5	4	5.81
UT	M. Heath	258	.256	3	27	167	32	5	2		.975							
UT	D. Chalk	212	.222	2	13	122	151	11	31		.961							
SS	M. Guerrero	166	.229	0	18	68	129	10	33	4.8	.952							

BATTING AND BASE RUNNING LEADERS

Batting Average
F. Lynn, BOS	.333
G. Brett, KC	.329
B. Downing, CAL	.326
J. Rice, BOS	.325
A. Oliver, TEX	.323

Slugging Average
F. Lynn, BOS	.637
J. Rice, BOS	.596
S. Lezcano, MIL	.573
G. Brett, KC	.563
R. Jackson, NY	.544

Home Runs
G. Thomas, MIL	45
F. Lynn, BOS	39
J. Rice, BOS	39
D. Baylor, CAL	36
K. Singleton, BAL	35

Total Bases
J. Rice, BOS	369
G. Brett, KC	363
F. Lynn, BOS	338
D. Baylor, CAL	333
K. Singleton, BAL	304

Runs Batted In
D. Baylor, CAL	139
J. Rice, BOS	130
G. Thomas, MIL	123
F. Lynn, BOS	122
D. Porter, KC	112

Stolen Bases
W. Wilson, KC	83
R. LeFlore, DET	78
J. Cruz, SEA	49
A. Bumbry, BAL	37
B. Wills, TEX	35

PITCHING LEADERS

Winning Percentage
M. Caldwell, MIL	.727
M. Flanagan, BAL	.719
J. Morris, DET	.708
T. John, NY	.700
R. Guidry, NY	.692

Earned Run Average
R. Guidry, NY	2.78
T. John, NY	2.97
D. Eckersley, BOS	2.99
M. Flanagan, BAL	3.08
J. Morris, DET	3.27

Wins
M. Flanagan, BAL	23
T. John, NY	21
J. Koosman, MIN	20
R. Guidry, NY	18

Saves
M. Marshall, MIN	32
J. Kern, TEX	29
A. Lopez, DET	21
D. Stanhouse, BAL	21
S. Monge, CLE	19

Strikeouts
N. Ryan, CAL	223
R. Guidry, NY	201
M. Flanagan, BAL	190
F. Jenkins, TEX	164
J. Koosman, MIN	157

Complete Games
D. Martinez, BAL	18
D. Eckersley, BOS	17
N. Ryan, CAL	17
T. John, NY	17

BATTING AND BASE RUNNING LEADERS

Hits
G. Brett, KC	212
J. Rice, BOS	201
B. Bell, TEX	200

Base on Balls
D. Porter, KC	121
K. Singleton, BAL	109
G. Thomas, MIL	98

Home Run Percentage
G. Thomas, MIL	8.1
F. Lynn, BOS	7.3
J. Rice, BOS	6.3

Runs Scored
D. Baylor, CAL	120
G. Brett, KC	119
J. Rice, BOS	117

Doubles
C. Lemon, CHI	44
C. Cooper, MIL	44

Triples
G. Brett, KC	20
P. Molitor, MIL	16
W. Randolph, NY	13
W. Wilson, KC	13

PITCHING LEADERS

Fewest Hits per 9 Innings
N. Ryan, CAL	6.82
K. Kravec, CHI	7.49
R. Guidry, NY	7.74

Shutouts
D. Leonard, KC	5
N. Ryan, CAL	5
M. Flanagan, BAL	5

Fewest Walks per 9 Innings
S. McGregor, BAL	1.18
M. Caldwell, MIL	1.49
L. Sorensen, MIL	1.61

Most Strikeouts per 9 Inn.
N. Ryan, CAL	9.00
R. Guidry, NY	7.67
M. Flanagan, BAL	6.43

Innings
D. Martinez, BAL	292
T. John, NY	276
M. Flanagan, BAL	266

Games Pitched
M. Marshall, MIN	90
S. Monge, CLE	76
J. Kern, TEX	71

	W	L	PCT	GB	R	OR	2B	3B	HR	BA	SA	SB	E	DP	FA	CG	BB	SO	ShO	SV	ERA
EAST																					
BAL	102	57	.642		757	**582**	258	24	181	.261	.419	99	125	161	.980	52	467	786	**12**	30	**3.26**
MIL	95	66	.590	8	807	722	291	41	185	.280	.448	100	127	153	.980	**61**	381	580	**12**	23	4.03
BOS	91	69	.569	11.5	841	711	310	34	**194**	.283	.456	60	142	166	.977	47	463	731	11	29	4.03
NY	89	71	.556	13.5	734	672	226	40	150	.266	.406	65	122	183	.981	43	455	731	10	37	3.83
DET	85	76	.528	18	770	738	221	35	164	.269	.415	176	**120**	184	.981	25	547	802	5	37	4.28
CLE	81	80	.503	22	760	805	206	29	138	.258	.384	143	134	149	.978	28	570	781	7	32	4.57
TOR	53	109	.327	50.5	613	862	253	34	95	.251	.363	75	159	187	.975	44	594	613	7	11	4.82
WEST																					
CAL	88	74	.543		**866**	768	242	43	164	.282	.429	100	135	172	.978	46	573	**820**	9	33	4.34
KC	85	77	.525	3	851	816	286	**79**	116	.282	.422	**207**	146	160	.977	42	536	640	7	27	4.45
TEX	83	79	.512	5	750	698	252	26	140	.278	.409	79	130	151	.979	26	532	773	10	**42**	3.86
MIN	82	80	.506	6	764	725	256	46	112	.278	.402	66	134	**203**	.979	31	452	721	6	33	4.13
CHI	73	87	.456	14	730	748	290	33	127	.275	.410	97	173	142	.972	28	618	675	9	37	4.10
SEA	67	95	.414	21	711	820	250	52	132	.269	.404	126	141	170	.978	37	571	736	7	26	4.58
OAK	54	108	.333	34	573	860	188	32	108	.239	.346	104	174	137	.972	41	654	726	4	20	4.75
					10527	10527	3529	548	2006	.270	.408	1497	1962	2318	.978	551	7413	10115	116	417	4.22

National League 1980

East

POS	Player	AB	BA	HR	RBI	PO	A	E	DP	TC/G	FA	Pitcher	G	IP	W	L	SV	ERA
Phi. W-91 L-71 Dallas Green																		
1B	P. Rose	655	.282	1	64	1427	123	5	113	9.6	.997	S. Carlton	38	304	24	9	0	2.34
2B	M. Trillo	531	.292	7	43	360	467	11	91	6.0	.987	D. Ruthven	33	223	17	10	0	3.55
SS	L. Bowa	540	.267	2	39	225	449	17	70	4.7	.975	B. Walk	27	152	11	7	0	4.56
3B	M. Schmidt	548	.286	48	121	98	372	27	31	3.3	.946	R. Lerch	30	150	4	14	0	5.16
RF	B. McBride	554	.309	9	87	282	6	3	1	2.2	.990	T. McGraw	57	92	5	4	20	1.47
CF	G. Maddox	549	.259	11	73	405	7	10	0	3.0	.976	R. Reed	55	91	7	5	9	4.05
LF	G. Luzinski	368	.228	19	56	137	2	1	0	1.3	.993	D. Noles	48	81	1	4	6	3.89
C	B. Boone	480	.229	9	55	741	88	**18**	7	6.1	.979	K. Saucier	40	50	7	3	0	3.42
OF	L. Smith	298	.339	3	20	121	2	4	0	1.5	.969							
C	K. Moreland	159	.314	4	29	183	21	7	7	5.4	.967							
Mon. W-90 L-72 Dick Williams																		
1B	W. Cromartie	597	.288	14	70	1457	93	**14**	104	9.9	.991	S. Rogers	37	281	16	11	0	2.98
2B	R. Scott	567	.224	0	46	287	380	12	73	5.3	.982	S. Sanderson	33	211	16	11	0	3.11
SS	C. Speier	388	.265	1	32	187	396	21	62	4.8	.965	B. Gullickson	24	141	10	5	0	3.00
3B	L. Parrish	452	.254	15	72	106	231	18	15	2.9	.949	D. Palmer	24	130	8	6	0	2.98
RF	E. Valentine	311	.315	13	67	154	6	5	1	2.0	.970	B. Lee	24	118	4	6	0	4.96
CF	A. Dawson	577	.308	17	87	410	14	6	3	2.9	.986	C. Lea	21	104	7	5	0	3.72
LF	R. LeFlore	521	.257	4	39	233	14	**11**	1	2.0	.957	F. Norman	48	98	4	4	4	4.05
C	G. Carter	549	.264	29	101	**822**	108	7	8	6.3	**.993**	E. Sosa	67	94	9	6	9	3.06
OF	R. Office	292	.267	6	30	150	2	2	1	1.6	.987	S. Bahnsen	57	91	7	6	4	3.07
OF	J. White	214	.262	7	23	101	5	6	1	1.3	.946	W. Fryman	61	80	7	4	17	2.25
2S	T. Bernazard	183	.224	5	18	82	151	9	25		.963							

	POS	Player	AB	BA	HR	RBI	PO	A	E	DP	TC/G	FA	Pitcher	G	IP	W	L	SV	ERA
Pit.	1B	J. Milner	238	.244	8	34	502	32	5	48	7.7	.991	J. Bibby	35	238	19	6	0	3.33
W-83 L-79	2B	P. Garner	548	.259	5	58	349	499	21	116	5.8	.976	J. Candelaria	35	233	11	14	1	4.02
Chuck Tanner	SS	T. Foli	495	.265	3	38	212	402	12	87	5.0	.981	B. Blyleven	34	217	8	13	0	3.82
	3B	B. Madlock	494	.277	10	53	86	214	14	18	2.5	.955	D. Robinson	29	160	7	10	1	3.99
	RF	D. Parker	518	.295	17	79	235	14	9	0	2.0	.965	R. Rhoden	20	127	7	5	0	3.83
	CF	O. Moreno	676	.249	5	36	479	15	5	2	3.1	.990	E. Romo	74	124	5	5	11	3.27
	LF	M. Easler	393	.338	21	74	201	6	3	1	1.8	.986	E. Solomon	26	100	7	3	0	2.70
	C	E. Ott	392	.260	8	41	569	73	11	5	5.6	.983	K. Tekulve	78	93	8	12	21	3.39
	OF	L. Lacy	278	.335	7	33	173	7	3	1	2.1	.984	G. Jackson	61	71	8	4	9	2.92
	1O	B. Robinson	272	.287	12	36	427	22	7	30		.985							
	3S	D. Berra	245	.220	6	31	82	167	11	23		.958							
	1B	W. Stargell	202	.262	11	38	460	33	4	54	9.2	.992							
	C	S. Nicosia	176	.216	1	22	284	25	5	4	5.4	.984							
St. L.	1B	K. Hernandez	595	.321	16	99	1572	115	9	146	10.8	.995	P. Vuckovich	32	222	12	9	1	3.41
W-74 L-88	2B	K. Oberkfell	422	.303	3	46	223	310	6	62	5.3	.989	B. Forsch	31	215	11	10	0	3.77
Ken Boyer	SS	G. Templeton	504	.319	4	43	223	451	29	85	6.1	.959	J. Kaat	49	130	8	7	4	3.81
W-18 L-33	3B	K. Reitz	523	.270	8	58	86	293	8	25	2.6	.979	B. Sykes	27	126	6	10	0	4.64
Jack Krol	RF	G. Hendrick	572	.302	25	109	322	10	2	2	2.2	.994	S. Martinez	25	120	5	10	0	4.80
W-0 L-1	CF	T. Scott	415	.251	0	28	324	5	1	2	2.5	.997	J. Fulgham	15	85	4	6	0	3.39
Whitey Herzog	LF	L. Durham	303	.271	8	42	136	14	2	1	1.9	.987	D. Hood	33	82	4	6	0	3.40
W-38 L-35	C	T. Simmons	495	.303	21	98	520	71	9	12	4.7	.985	Littlefield	52	66	5	5	9	3.14
Red Schoendienst																			
W-18 L-19	OF	D. Iorg	251	.303	3	36	108	2	1	0	1.8	.991							
	CO	T. Kennedy	248	.254	4	34	231	22	7	3		.973							
	OF	B. Bonds	231	.203	5	24	114	5	4	2	1.8	.967							
	2B	T. Herr	222	.248	0	15	107	136	4	37	4.3	.984							
N. Y.	1B	L. Mazzilli	578	.280	16	76	708	49	13	67	8.4	.983	R. Burris	29	170	7	13	0	4.02
W-67 L-95	2B	D. Flynn	443	.255	0	24	283	370	6	70	5.1	.991	P. Zachry	28	165	6	10	0	3.00
Joe Torre	SS	F. Taveras	562	.279	0	25	237	347	25	63	4.4	.959	M. Bomback	36	163	10	8	0	4.09
	3B	E. Maddox	411	.246	4	34	96	209	14	18	2.8	.956	P. Falcone	37	157	7	10	1	4.53
	RF	C. Washington	284	.275	10	42	123	12	3	1	2.0	.978	C. Swan	21	128	5	9	0	3.59
	CF	J. Youngblood	514	.276	8	69	292	18	5	6	2.6	.984	T. Hausman	55	122	6	5	1	3.98
	LF	S. Henderson	513	.290	8	58	299	7	6	1	2.3	.981	J. Reardon	61	110	8	7	6	2.62
	C	A. Trevino	355	.256	0	37	443	63	12	5	6.0	.977	N. Allen	59	97	7	10	22	3.71
	1O	M. Jorgensen	321	.255	7	43	562	37	4	33		.993							
	C	J. Stearns	319	.285	0	45	432	41	7	6	6.5	.985							
	OF	J. Morales	193	.254	3	30	107	3	3	1	1.8	.973							
Chi.	1B	B. Buckner	578	**.324**	10	68	826	73	6	67	9.6	.993	R. Reuschel	38	257	11	13	0	3.40
W-64 L-98	2B	M. Tyson	341	.238	3	23	222	329	18	69	4.9	.968	M. Krukow	34	205	10	15	0	4.39
Preston Gomez	SS	I. DeJesus	618	.259	3	33	229	529	24	99	5.0	.969	D. Lamp	41	203	10	14	0	5.19
W-38 L-52	3B	L. Randle	489	.276	5	39	76	225	23	7	2.9	.929	L. McGlothen	39	182	12	14	0	4.80
Joey Amalfitano	RF	S. Thompson	226	.212	2	13	100	4	4	2	1.6	.963	B. Caudill	72	128	4	6	1	2.18
W-26 L-46	CF	J. Martin	494	.227	23	73	262	8	6	0	2.1	.978	D. Tidrow	84	116	6	5	6	2.79
	LF	D. Kingman	255	.278	18	57	103	8	7	0	1.9	.941	W. Hernandez	53	108	1	9	0	4.42
	C	T. Blackwell	320	.272	5	30	572	93	12	16	6.6	.982	B. Sutter	60	102	5	8	28	2.65
	OF	M. Vail	312	.298	6	47	126	5	5	1	1.8	.963	D. Capilla	39	90	2	8	0	4.10
	1O	L. Biittner	273	.249	1	34	305	23	2	16		.994							
	32	S. Dillard	244	.225	4	27	89	169	14	19		.949							
	C	B. Foote	202	.238	6	28	317	36	3	5	6.5	.992							
	OF	J. Figueroa	198	.253	1	11	89	6	2	2	1.7	.979							
	1B	C. Johnson	196	.235	10	34	468	16	4	34	10.6	.992							

West

	POS	Player	AB	BA	HR	RBI	PO	A	E	DP	TC/G	FA	Pitcher	G	IP	W	L	SV	ERA
Hou.	1B	A. Howe	321	.283	10	46	580	49	9	47	8.3	.986	J. Niekro	37	256	20	12	0	3.55
W-93 L-70	2B	J. Morgan	461	.243	11	49	244	348	7	68	4.6	.988	N. Ryan	35	234	11	10	0	3.35
Bill Virdon	SS	C. Reynolds	381	.226	3	28	162	362	17	59	4.0	.969	K. Forsch	32	222	12	13	0	3.20
	3B	E. Cabell	604	.276	2	55	118	250	29	15	2.6	.927	V. Ruhle	28	159	12	4	0	2.38
	RF	T. Puhl	535	.282	13	55	311	14	3	3	2.4	.991	J. Andujar	35	122	3	8	2	3.91
	CF	C. Cedeno	499	.309	10	73	338	9	8	3	2.6	.977	J. Richard	17	114	10	4	0	1.89
	LF	J. Cruz	612	.302	11	91	323	16	11	6	2.2	.969	D. Smith	57	103	7	5	10	1.92
	C	A. Ashby	352	.256	3	48	608	60	6	10	5.9	.991	J. Sambito	64	90	8	4	17	2.20
	2S	R. Landestoy	393	.247	1	27	184	291	9	67		.981	F. LaCorte	55	83	8	5	11	2.82
	1B	D. Walling	284	.299	3	29	505	31	6	46	8.6	.989							
	C	L. Pujols	221	.199	0	20	348	35	4	5	5.2	.990							
	OF	J. Leonard	216	.213	3	20	87	6	2	0	1.7	.979							
L. A.	1B	S. Garvey	658	.304	26	106	1502	112	6	122	10.0	.996	J. Reuss	37	229	18	6	3	2.52
W-92 L-71	2B	D. Lopes	553	.251	10	49	304	416	15	85	5.3	.980	B. Welch	32	214	14	9	0	3.28
Tom Lasorda	SS	B. Russell	466	.264	3	34	179	387	19	57	4.5	.968	D. Sutton	32	212	13	5	1	**2.21**
	3B	R. Cey	551	.254	28	77	127	317	13	24	2.9	.972	B. Hooton	34	207	14	8	1	3.65
	RF	R. Smith	311	.322	15	55	153	15	1	5	2.0	.994	D. Goltz	35	171	7	11	1	4.32
	CF	R. Law	388	.260	1	23	233	6	3	3	2.3	.994	R. Sutcliffe	42	110	3	9	5	5.56
	LF	D. Baker	579	.294	29	97	308	5	3	3	2.1	.991	B. Castillo	61	98	8	6	5	2.76
	C	S. Yeager	227	.211	2	20	382	36	7	4	4.5	.984	S. Howe	59	85	7	9	17	2.65
	UT	D. Thomas	297	.266	1	22	203	175	14	39		.964	D. Stanhouse	21	25	2	2	7	5.04
	OF	J. Johnstone	251	.307	2	20	100	9	4	0	1.9	.965							
	OF	R. Monday	194	.268	10	25	92	1	3	0	1.9	.969							
	OF	P. Guerrero	183	.322	7	31	74	1	1	0	1.9	.987							
	C	J. Ferguson	172	.238	9	29	297	23	6	4	4.9	.982							

POS	Player	AB	BA	HR	RBI	PO	A	E	DP	TC/G	FA	Pitcher	G	IP	W	L	SV	ERA
Cin. W-89 L-73 John McNamara																		
1B	D. Driessen	524	.265	14	74	1349	85	7	115	9.5	.995	M. Soto	53	190	10	8	4	3.08
2B	J. Kennedy	337	.261	1	34	200	303	6	53	4.9	.988	F. Pastore	27	185	13	7	0	3.26
SS	D. Concepcion	622	.260	5	77	265	451	16	98	4.7	.978	C. Leibrandt	36	174	10	9	0	4.24
3B	R. Knight	618	.264	14	78	120	291	13	19	2.6	.969	M. LaCoss	34	169	10	12	0	4.63
RF	K. Griffey	544	.294	13	85	266	5	6	3	2.0	.978	T. Seaver	26	168	10	8	0	3.64
CF	D. Collins	551	.303	3	35	337	5	5	1	2.5	.986	P. Moskau	33	153	9	7	2	4.00
LF	G. Foster	528	.273	25	93	295	6	1	1	2.1	.997	T. Hume	78	137	9	10	25	2.56
C	J. Bench	360	.250	24	68	505	39	5	7	5.2	.991	J. Price	24	111	7	3	0	3.57
2B	R. Oester	303	.277	2	20	144	194	7	42	4.4	.980	D. Bair	61	85	3	6	6	4.24
C	J. Nolan	154	.312	3	24	251	23	5	6	5.5	.982							
Atl. W-81 L-80 Bobby Cox																		
1B	C. Chambliss	602	.282	18	72	1626	101	12	140	11.0	.993	P. Niekro	40	275	15	18	1	3.63
2B	G. Hubbard	431	.248	9	43	268	405	15	91	5.9	.978	D. Alexander	35	232	14	11	0	4.19
SS	L. Gomez	278	.191	0	24	135	319	15	55	3.9	.968	T. Boggs	32	192	12	9	0	3.42
3B	B. Horner	463	.268	35	89	78	251	23	20	2.9	.935	R. Matula	33	177	11	13	0	4.58
RF	J. Burroughs	278	.263	13	51	129	0	3	0	1.8	.977	McWilliams	30	164	9	14	0	4.94
CF	D. Murphy	569	.281	33	89	374	14	6	4	2.6	.985	R. Camp	77	108	6	4	22	1.92
LF	G. Matthews	571	.278	19	75	258	8	11	0	1.9	.960	G. Garber	68	82	5	5	7	3.84
C	B. Benedict	359	.253	2	34	502	76	7	6	4.9	.988	L. Bradford	56	55	3	4	4	2.45
UT	J. Royster	392	.242	1	20	195	166	18	32		.953							
S3	L. Blanks	221	.204	2	12	64	189	17	31		.937							
OF	B. Asselstine	218	.284	3	25	102	0	4	0	1.7	.962							
SS	R. Ramirez	165	.267	2	11	63	140	11	25	4.7	.949							
S. F. W-75 L-86 Dave Bristol																		
1B	M. Ivie	286	.241	4	25	669	32	5	46	9.8	.993	V. Blue	31	224	14	10	0	2.97
2B	R. Stennett	397	.244	2	37	244	293	15	53	5.0	.973	B. Knepper	35	215	9	16	0	4.10
SS	J. LeMaster	405	.215	3	31	200	372	26	54	4.5	.957	E. Whitson	34	212	11	13	0	3.10
3B	D. Evans	556	.264	20	78	113	328	25	26	3.3	.946	A. Ripley	23	113	9	10	0	4.14
RF	J. Clark	437	.284	22	82	229	7	8	1	2.0	.967	J. Montefusco	22	113	4	8	0	4.38
CF	B. North	415	.251	1	19	313	6	6	1	2.8	.982	T. Griffin	42	108	5	1	0	2.75
LF	L. Herndon	493	.258	8	49	247	8	11	1	2.2	.959	G. Lavelle	62	100	6	8	9	3.42
C	M. May	358	.260	6	50	500	59	8	12	5.5	.986	G. Minton	68	91	4	6	19	2.47
OF	T. Whitfield	321	.296	4	26	140	11	2	1	1.6	.987	A. Holland	54	82	5	3	7	1.76
1B	R. Murray	194	.216	4	24	508	35	7	32	10.4	.987	Hargesheimer	15	75	4	6	0	4.32
OF	J. Wohlford	193	.280	1	24	89	2	1	0	1.9	.989							
UT	J. Pettini	190	.232	1	9	66	147	8	24		.964							
2B	J. Strain	189	.286	0	16	85	102	2	15	4.5	.989							
S. D. W-73 L-89 Jerry Coleman																		
1B	W. Montanez	481	.274	6	63	1185	84	8	105	10.3	.994	J. Curtis	30	187	10	8	0	3.51
2B	D. Cash	397	.227	1	23	290	326	8	72	5.1	.987	S. Mura	37	169	8	7	2	3.67
SS	O. Smith	609	.230	0	35	288	621	24	113	5.9	.974	R. Jones	24	154	5	13	0	3.92
3B	A. Rodriguez	175	.200	2	13	38	128	6	12	2.0	.965	R. Wise	27	154	6	8	0	3.68
RF	D. Winfield	558	.276	20	87	273	20	4	4	1.9	.987	G. Lucas	46	150	5	8	3	3.24
CF	J. Mumphrey	564	.298	4	59	398	10	11	1	2.7	.974	B. Shirley	59	137	11	12	7	3.55
LF	G. Richards	642	.301	4	41	307	21	4	7	2.1	.979	E. Rasmussen	40	111	4	11	1	4.38
C	G. Tenace	316	.222	17	50	415	46	10	7	4.5	.979	R. Fingers	66	103	11	9	23	2.80
23	T. Flannery	292	.240	2	25	145	204	8	34		.977	D. Kinney	50	83	4	6	1	4.23
C	B. Fahey	241	.257	1	22	309	34	8	6	4.1	.977							
3B	L. Salazar	169	.337	1	25	29	88	7	7	3.0	.944							

BATTING AND BASE RUNNING LEADERS

Batting Average

B. Buckner, CHI	.324
K. Hernandez, STL	.321
G. Templeton, STL	.319
B. McBride, PHI	.309
C. Cedeno, HOU	.309

Home Runs

M. Schmidt, PHI	48
B. Horner, ATL	35
D. Murphy, ATL	33
G. Carter, MON	29
D. Baker, LA	29

Runs Batted In

M. Schmidt, PHI	121
G. Hendrick, STL	109
S. Garvey, LA	106
G. Carter, MON	101
K. Hernandez, STL	99

Hits

S. Garvey, LA	200
G. Richards, SD	193
K. Hernandez, STL	191

Slugging Average

M. Schmidt, PHI	.624
J. Clark, SF	.517
D. Murphy, ATL	.510
T. Simmons, STL	.505
D. Baker, LA	.503

Total Bases

M. Schmidt, PHI	342
S. Garvey, LA	307
K. Hernandez, STL	294
D. Baker, LA	291
D. Murphy, ATL	290

Stolen Bases

R. LeFlore, MON	97
O. Moreno, PIT	96
D. Collins, CIN	79
R. Scott, MON	63
G. Richards, SD	61

Base on Balls

J. Morgan, HOU	93
D. Driessen, CIN	93
G. Tenace, SD	92

PITCHING LEADERS

Winning Percentage

J. Bibby, PIT	.760
J. Reuss, LA	.750
S. Carlton, PHI	.727
D. Ruthven, PHI	.630
J. Niekro, HOU	.625

Wins

S. Carlton, PHI	24
J. Niekro, HOU	20
J. Bibby, PIT	19
J. Reuss, LA	18
D. Ruthven, PHI	17

Strikeouts

S. Carlton, PHI	286
N. Ryan, HOU	200
M. Soto, CIN	182
P. Niekro, ATL	176
B. Blyleven, PIT	168

Fewest Hits per 9 Innings

M. Soto, CIN	5.97
D. Sutton, LA	6.92
S. Carlton, PHI	7.19

Earned Run Average

D. Sutton, LA	2.21
S. Carlton, PHI	2.34
J. Reuss, LA	2.52
V. Blue, SF	2.97
S. Rogers, MON	2.98

Saves

B. Sutter, CHI	28
T. Hume, CIN	25
R. Fingers, SD	23
N. Allen, NY	22
R. Camp, ATL	22

Complete Games

S. Rogers, MON	14
S. Carlton, PHI	13
J. Niekro, HOU	11
P. Niekro, ATL	11
J. Reuss, LA	10
V. Blue, SF	10

Shutouts

J. Reuss, LA	6
J. Richard, HOU	4
S. Rogers, MON	4

BATTING AND BASE RUNNING LEADERS

PITCHING LEADERS

Home Run Percentage

M. Schmidt, PHI	8.8
D. Murphy, ATL	5.8
G. Carter, MON	5.3

Runs Scored

K. Hernandez, STL	111
M. Schmidt, PHI	104
D. Murphy, ATL	98

Fewest Walks per 9 Innings

B. Forsch, STL	1.38
J. Reuss, LA	1.57
K. Forsch, HOU	1.66

Most Strikeouts per 9 Inn.

M. Soto, CIN	8.62
S. Carlton, PHI	8.47
N. Ryan, HOU	7.69

Doubles

P. Rose, PHI	42
A. Dawson, MON	41
B. Buckner, CHI	41

Triples

R. Scott, MON	13
O. Moreno, PIT	13
L. Herndon, SF	11
R. LeFlore, MON	11

Innings

S. Carlton, PHI	304
S. Rogers, MON	281
P. Niekro, ATL	275

Games Pitched

D. Tidrow, CHI	84
T. Hume, CIN	78
K. Tekulve, PIT	78

	W	L	PCT	GB	R	OR	2B	3B	HR	BA	SA	SB	E	DP	FA	CG	BB	SO	ShO	SV	ERA
EAST																					
PHI	91	71	.562		728	639	272	54	117	.270	.400	140	136	136	.979	25	530	889	8	40	3.43
MON	90	72	.556	1	694	629	250	61	114	.257	.388	237	144	126	.977	33	460	823	15	36	3.48
PIT	83	79	.512	8	666	646	249	38	116	.266	.388	209	137	154	.978	25	451	832	8	43	3.58
STL	74	88	.457	17	738	710	300	49	101	.275	.400	117	122	174	.981	34	495	664	9	27	3.93
NY	67	95	.414	24	611	702	218	41	61	.257	.345	158	154	132	.975	17	510	886	9	33	3.85
CHI	64	98	.395	27	614	728	251	35	107	.251	.365	93	174	149	.974	13	589	923	6	35	3.89
WEST																					
HOU*	93	70	.571		637	589	231	67	75	.261	.367	194	140	145	.978	31	466	929	18	41	3.10
LA	92	71	.564	1	663	591	209	24	148	.263	.388	123	123	149	.981	24	480	835	19	42	3.24
CIN	89	73	.549	3.5	707	670	256	45	113	.262	.386	156	106	144	.983	30	506	833	12	37	3.85
ATL	81	80	.503	11	630	660	226	22	144	.250	.380	73	162	156	.975	29	454	696	9	37	3.77
SF	75	86	.466	17	573	634	199	44	80	.244	.342	100	159	124	.975	27	492	811	10	35	3.46
SD	73	89	.451	19.5	591	654	195	43	67	.255	.342	239	132	157	.980	19	536	728	9	39	3.65
					7852	7852	2856	523	1243	.259	.374	1839	1689	1746	.978	307	5969	9849	132	445	3.60

* Defeated Los Angeles in a 1 game playoff.

American League 1980

	POS	Player	AB	BA	HR	RBI	PO	A	E	DP	TC/G	FA	Pitcher	G	IP	W	L	SV	ERA

East

N. Y.
W-103 L-59
Dick Howser

POS	Player	AB	BA	HR	RBI	PO	A	E	DP	TC/G	FA	Pitcher	G	IP	W	L	SV	ERA
1B	B. Watson	469	.307	13	68	851	63	9	87	8.9	.990	T. John	36	265	22	9	0	3.43
2B	W. Randolph	513	.294	7	46	361	401	19	97	5.7	.976	R. Guidry	37	220	17	10	1	3.56
SS	B. Dent	489	.262	5	52	224	489	13	77	5.1	.982	T. Underwood	38	187	13	9	2	0.00
3B	G. Nettles	324	.244	16	45	58	182	10	18	2.8	.960	R. May	41	175	15	5	3	2.47
RF	R. Jackson	514	.300	41	111	174	3	7	0	2.0	.962	L. Tiant	25	136	8	9	0	4.90
CF	B. Brown	412	.260	14	47	303	7	9	0	2.4	.972	R. Davis	53	131	9	3	7	2.95
LF	L. Piniella	321	.287	2	27	157	8	5	1	1.6	.971	G. Gossage	64	99	6	2	33	2.27
C	R. Cerone	519	.277	14	85	800	73	9	9	6.0	.990							
DH	E. Soderholm	275	.287	11	35	0	0	0	0	.0	.000							
OF	R. Jones	328	.223	9	42	246	4	3	1	3.1	.988							
OF	B. Murcer	297	.269	13	57	82	2	4	0		.955							
1B	J. Spencer	259	.236	13	43	567	41	6	51	8.2	.990							
OF	O. Gamble	194	.278	14	50	65	2	0	1	1.4	1.000							
3B	A. Rodriguez	164	.220	3	14	26	77	5	5	2.2	.954							
OF	J. Lefebvre	150	.227	8	21	75	3	2	1	1.1	.975							

Bal.
W-100 L-62
Earl Weaver

POS	Player	AB	BA	HR	RBI	PO	A	E	DP	TC/G	FA	Pitcher	G	IP	W	L	SV	ERA
1B	E. Murray	621	.300	32	116	1369	77	9	158	9.4	.994	S. McGregor	36	252	20	8	0	3.32
2B	R. Dauer	557	.284	2	63	320	368	6	110	5.1	.991	S. Stone	37	251	25	7	0	3.23
SS	K. Garcia	311	.199	1	27	135	240	10	52	4.0	.974	M. Flanagan	37	251	16	13	0	4.12
3B	D. DeCinces	489	.249	16	64	120	340	19	41	3.4	.960	J. Palmer	34	224	16	10	0	3.98
RF	K. Singleton	583	.304	24	104	248	3	4	1	1.7	.984	S. Stewart	33	119	7	7	3	3.55
CF	A. Bumbry	645	.318	9	53	488	7	5	1	3.1	.990	D. Martinez	25	100	6	4	1	3.96
LF	G. Roenicke	297	.239	10	28	197	8	0	1	1.8	1.000	T. Stoddard	64	86	5	3	26	2.51
C	R. Dempsey	362	.262	9	40	531	54	8	8	5.3	.987	T. Martinez	53	81	4	4	10	3.00
DH	T. Crowley	233	.288	12	50	0	0	0	0	.0	.000							
SS	M. Belanger	268	.228	0	22	133	258	10	49	3.7	.975							
C	D. Graham	266	.278	15	54	328	35	7	3	5.1	.981							
DH	L. May	222	.243	7	31	0	0	0	0	.0	.000							
OF	P. Kelly	200	.260	3	26	48	4	0	0		1.000							
OF	J. Lowenstein	196	.311	4	33	128	3	1	0	1.5	.992							
OF	B. Ayala	170	.265	10	33	20	2	0	1		1.000							

POS	Player	AB	BA	HR	RBI	PO	A	E	DP	TC/G	FA	Pitcher	G	IP	W	L	SV	ERA
Mil.																		
1B	C. Cooper	622	.352	25	**122**	1336	**106**	5	**160**	10.2	**.997**	M. Haas	33	252	16	15	0	3.11
2B	P. Molitor	450	.304	9	37	240	294	16	80	6.0	.971	M. Caldwell	34	225	13	11	1	4.04
SS	R. Yount	611	.293	23	87	239	455	28	89	5.4	.961	L. Sorensen	35	196	12	10	1	3.67
3B	J. Gantner	415	.282	4	40	41	126	11	15	2.6	.938	B. Travers	29	154	12	6	0	3.92
RF	S. Lezcano	411	.229	18	55	228	8	4	4	2.2	.983	R. Cleveland	45	154	11	9	4	3.74
CF	G. Thomas	628	.239	38	105	455	6	7	1	2.9	.985	B. McClure	52	91	5	8	10	3.07
LF	B. Oglivie	592	.304	**41**	118	384	18	9	3	2.7	.978	P. Mitchell	17	89	5	5	1	3.54
C	C. Moore	320	.291	2	30	319	28	4	3	3.3	.989	B. Castro	56	84	2	4	8	2.79
DH	D. Davis	365	.271	4	30	0	0	0	0	.0	.000							
UT	D. Money	289	.256	17	46	176	129	12	35		.962							
3B	S. Bando	254	.197	5	31	46	110	11	12	2.9	.934							
C	B. Martinez	219	.224	3	17	293	33	5	0	4.4	.985							

W-86 L-76
Buck Rodgers
W-26 L-21
George Bamberger
W-47 L-45
Buck Rodgers
W-13 L-10

POS	Player	AB	BA	HR	RBI	PO	A	E	DP	TC/G	FA	Pitcher	G	IP	W	L	SV	ERA
Bos.																		
1B	T. Perez	585	.275	25	105	1301	87	10	150	10.2	.993	M. Torrez	36	207	9	16	0	5.09
2B	D. Stapleton	449	.321	7	45	178	327	11	90	5.5	.979	D. Eckersley	30	198	12	14	0	4.27
SS	R. Burleson	644	.278	8	51	**301**	**528**	22	**147**	5.5	.974	B. Stanley	52	175	10	8	14	3.39
3B	G. Hoffman	312	.285	4	42	72	193	15	17	2.5	.946	S. Renko	32	165	9	9	0	4.20
RF	D. Evans	463	.266	18	60	268	11	5	7	2.0	.982	D. Drago	43	133	7	7	3	4.13
CF	F. Lynn	415	.301	12	61	302	11	2	4	2.9	.994	T. Burgmeier	62	99	5	4	24	2.00
LF	J. Rice	504	.294	24	86	233	10	3	2	2.3	.988	J. Tudor	16	92	8	5	0	3.03
C	C. Fisk	478	.289	18	62	522	56	**10**	8	5.1	.983	C. Rainey	16	87	8	3	0	4.86
DH	Yastrzemski	364	.275	15	50	0	0	0	0	.0	.000							
3B	B. Hobson	324	.228	11	39	52	109	16	5		.910							
OF	J. Dwyer	260	.285	9	38	111	7	3	2	1.9	.975							
2B	J. Remy	230	.313	0	9	109	189	7	30	5.1	.977							

W-83 L-77
Don Zimmer
W-82 L-74
Johnny Pesky
W-1 L-3

POS	Player	AB	BA	HR	RBI	PO	A	E	DP	TC/G	FA	Pitcher	G	IP	W	L	SV	ERA
Det.																		
1B	R. Hebner	341	.290	12	82	466	35	1	35	8.2	.998	J. Morris	36	250	16	15	0	4.18
2B	L. Whitaker	477	.233	1	45	340	428	12	93	5.5	.985	M. Wilcox	32	199	13	11	0	4.48
SS	A. Trammell	560	.300	9	65	225	412	13	89	4.5	.980	D. Schatzeder	32	193	11	13	0	4.01
3B	T. Brookens	509	.275	10	66	112	279	**29**	27	3.0	.931	D. Petry	27	165	10	9	0	3.93
RF	A. Cowens	403	.280	5	42	199	8	3	2	2.0	.986	D. Rozema	42	145	6	9	4	3.91
CF	R. Peters	477	.291	2	42	296	1	7	1	2.8	.977	A. Lopez	67	124	13	6	21	3.77
LF	S. Kemp	508	.293	21	101	197	4	1	3	2.4	.995	P. Underwood	49	113	3	6	5	3.58
C	L. Parrish	553	.286	24	82	557	66	6	8	5.2	.990							
DH	C. Summers	347	.297	17	60	0	0	0	0	.0	.000							
UT	J. Wockenfuss	372	.274	16	65	575	47	11	44		.983							
OF	K. Gibson	175	.263	9	16	122	1	1	0	2.5	.992							
1B	J. Thompson	126	.214	4	20	328	30	0	33	9.9	1.000							

W-84 L-78
Sparky Anderson

POS	Player	AB	BA	HR	RBI	PO	A	E	DP	TC/G	FA	Pitcher	G	IP	W	L	SV	ERA
Cle.																		
1B	M. Hargrove	589	.304	11	85	**1391**	88	10	128	9.3	.993	L. Barker	36	246	19	12	0	4.17
2B	A. Bannister	262	.328	1	32	77	106	6	20	4.6	.968	R. Waits	33	224	13	14	0	4.46
SS	T. Veryzer	358	.271	2	28	169	331	15	59	4.8	.971	D. Spillner	34	194	16	11	0	5.29
3B	T. Harrah	561	.267	11	72	120	317	13	27	2.9	.971	W. Garland	25	150	6	9	0	4.62
RF	J. Orta	481	.291	10	64	269	10	5	1	2.4	.982	B. Owchinko	29	114	2	9	0	5.29
CF	R. Manning	471	.234	3	52	379	7	4	1	2.8	.990	J. Denny	16	109	8	6	0	4.38
LF	M. Dilone	528	.341	0	40	249	7	7	2	2.2	.973	S. Monge	67	94	3	5	14	3.64
C	R. Hassey	390	.318	8	65	549	52	4	8	5.4	.993	V. Cruz	55	86	6	7	12	3.45
DH	J. Charboneau	453	.289	23	87	0	0	0	0	.0	.000							
S2	J. Dybzinski	248	.230	1	23	142	261	13	45		.969							
C	B. Diaz	207	.227	3	32	317	35	4	4	4.7	.989							
DH	G. Alexander	178	.225	5	31					.0								
DH	C. Johnson	174	.230	6	28	0	0	0	0	.0	.000							

W-79 L-81
Dave Garcia

POS	Player	AB	BA	HR	RBI	PO	A	E	DP	TC/G	FA	Pitcher	G	IP	W	L	SV	ERA
Tor.																		
1B	J. Mayberry	501	.248	30	82	1243	79	8	138	9.8	.994	J. Clancy	34	251	13	16	0	3.30
2B	D. Garcia	543	.278	4	46	316	471	16	112	**5.8**	.980	D. Stieb	34	243	12	15	0	3.70
SS	A. Griffin	653	.254	2	41	295	489	**37**	126	5.3	.955	McLaughlin	36	136	6	9	4	4.50
3B	R. Howell	528	.269	10	57	105	257	16	24	2.7	.958	P. Mirabella	33	131	5	12	0	4.33
RF	L. Moseby	389	.229	9	46	208	12	4	1	2.2	.982	J. Jefferson	29	122	4	13	0	5.46
CF	B. Bonnell	463	.268	13	56	271	15	8	3	2.4	.973	J. Garvin	61	83	4	7	8	2.28
LF	A. Woods	373	.300	15	47	205	5	2	1	2.4	.991	J. Kucek	23	68	3	8	1	6.75
C	E. Whitt	295	.237	6	34	436	56	7	11	4.8	.986							
DH	O. Velez	357	.269	20	62	0	0	0	0	.0	.000							
OF	B. Bailor	347	.236	1	16	205	16	2	5	2.3	.991							
UT	G. Iorg	222	.248	2	14	122	155	3	45		.989							
C	B. Davis	218	.216	4	19	317	28	6	6	3.9	.983							
OF	R. Bosetti	188	.213	4	18	124	4	2	0	2.5	.985							

W-67 L-95
Bobby Mattick

West

POS	Player	AB	BA	HR	RBI	PO	A	E	DP	TC/G	FA	Pitcher	G	IP	W	L	SV	ERA
K. C.																		
1B	W. Aikens	543	.278	20	98	1081	65	**12**	95	8.4	.990	L. Gura	36	283	18	10	0	2.96
2B	F. White	560	.264	7	60	395	448	10	103	5.6	.988	D. Leonard	38	280	20	11	0	3.79
SS	U. Washington	549	.273	6	53	237	467	32	86	4.8	.957	P. Splittorff	34	204	14	11	0	4.15
3B	G. Brett	449	**.390**	24	118	103	256	17	28	3.4	.955	R. Gale	32	191	13	9	1	3.91
RF	C. Hurdle	395	.294	10	60	233	8	10	1	2.0	.960	R. Martin	32	137	10	10	2	4.40
CF	A. Otis	394	.251	10	53	310	6	4	1	3.0	.988	Quisenberry	75	128	12	7	**33**	3.09
LF	W. Wilson	**705**	.326	3	49	482	9	6	1	3.1	.988							
C	D. Porter	418	.249	7	51	322	37	8	6	4.5	.978							
DH	H. McRae	489	.297	14	83	0	0	0	0	.0	.000							
CO	J. Wathan	453	.305	6	58	360	26	7	5		.982							
UT	D. Chalk	167	.251	1	20	57	88	6	10		.960							
UT	J. Quirk	163	.276	5	21	78	66	8	3		.947							

W-97 L-65
Jim Frey

POS	Player	AB	BA	HR	RBI	PO	A	E	DP	TC/G	FA	Pitcher	G	IP	W	L	SV	ERA
Oak. W-83 L-79 Billy Martin																		
1B	D. Revering	376	.290	15	62	724	67	9	56	8.4	.989	R. Langford	35	290	19	12	0	3.26
2B	D. McKay	295	.244	1	29	99	151	6	24	4.1	.977	M. Norris	33	284	22	9	0	2.54
SS	M. Guerrero	381	.239	2	23	184	276	18	50	4.1	.962	M. Keough	34	250	16	13	0	2.92
3B	W. Gross	366	.281	14	61	69	130	11	13	2.1	.948	S. McCatty	33	222	14	14	0	3.85
RF	T. Armas	628	.279	35	109	374	17	10	2	2.5	.975	B. Kingman	32	211	8	**20**	0	3.84
CF	D. Murphy	573	.274	13	68	**507**	13	5	0	**3.3**	.990	B. Lacey	47	80	3	2	6	2.93
LF	R. Henderson	591	.303	9	53	407	15	7	1	2.7	.984							
C	J. Essian	285	.232	5	29	333	46	5	5	5.6	.987							
DH	M. Page	348	.244	17	51	0	0	0	0	.0	.000							
1C	J. Newman	438	.233	15	56	675	54	15	28		.980							
C	M. Heath	305	.243	1	33	268	19	4	5		.986							
S2	R. Picciolo	271	.240	5	18	163	208	6	39		.984							
3B	M. Klutts	197	.269	4	21	46	80	7	3	2.1	.947							
2B	J. Cox	169	.213	0	9	107	167	6	28	4.8	.979							
Min. W-77 L-84 Gene Mauch W-54 L-71 John Goryl W-23 L-13																		
1B	R. Jackson	396	.265	5	42	983	74	10	105	9.0	.991	J. Koosman	38	243	16	13	2	4.04
2B	R. Wilfong	416	.248	8	45	238	337	3	85	4.8	**.995**	G. Zahn	38	233	14	18	0	4.40
SS	R. Smalley	486	.278	12	63	210	446	17	100	5.4	.975	R. Erickson	32	191	7	13	0	3.25
3B	J. Castino	546	.302	13	64	105	**340**	18	34	3.4	.961	D. Jackson	32	172	9	9	1	3.87
RF	H. Powell	485	.262	6	35	265	11	9	1	2.2	.968	D. Corbett	73	136	8	6	23	1.99
CF	K. Landreaux	484	.281	7	62	231	8	6	0	2.0	.976	P. Redfern	23	105	7	7	2	4.54
LF	R. Sofield	417	.247	9	49	267	7	6	0	2.2	.979	J. Verhoeven	44	100	3	4	0	3.96
C	B. Wynegar	486	.255	5	57	670	72	9	13	5.3	.988	F. Arroyo	21	92	6	6	0	4.70
DH	J. Morales	241	.303	8	36	0	0	0	0	.0	.000							
2S	P. Mackanin	319	.266	4	35	156	279	17	74		.962							
13	M. Cubbage	285	.246	8	42	541	98	4	62		.994							
DH	G. Adams	262	.286	6	38	0	0	0	0	.0	.000							
OF	D. Edwards	200	.250	2	20	144	7	11	1	2.3	.932							
Tex. W-76 L-85 Pat Corrales																		
1B	P. Putnam	410	.263	13	55	979	80	9	107	7.8	.992	J. Matlack	35	235	10	10	1	3.68
2B	B. Wills	578	.263	5	58	340	473	13	112	5.7	.984	D. Medich	34	204	14	11	0	3.93
SS	P. Frias	227	.242	0	10	117	167	16	38	2.8	.947	F. Jenkins	29	198	12	12	0	3.77
3B	B. Bell	490	.329	17	83	125	282	8	26	3.4	**.981**	G. Perry	24	155	6	9	0	3.43
RF	J. Grubb	274	.277	9	32	112	6	6	1	1.6	.952	D. Darwin	53	110	13	4	8	2.62
CF	M. Rivers	630	.333	7	60	342	**19**	8	4	2.6	.978	S. Lyle	49	81	3	2	8	4.67
LF	A. Oliver	656	.319	19	117	314	9	9	2	2.1	.973	J. Kern	38	63	3	11	2	4.86
C	J. Sundberg	505	.273	10	63	853	76	7	7	6.2	.993							
DH	R. Zisk	448	.290	19	77	0	0	0	0	.0	.000							
UT	R. Staub	340	.300	9	55	262	14	6	28		.979							
UT	D. Roberts	235	.238	10	30	138	100	11	11		.956							
OF	B. Sample	204	.260	4	19	105	2	3	0	1.5	.973							
1B	J. Ellis	182	.236	1	23	240	12	2	22		.992							
SS	B. Harrelson	180	.272	1	9	118	220	17	57	4.1	.952							
OF	J. Norris	174	.247	0	16	73	3	0	0	.9	1.000							
Chi. W-70 L-90 Tony LaRussa																		
1B	M. Squires	343	.283	2	33	904	68	5	79	8.6	.995	B. Burns	34	238	15	13	0	2.84
2B	J. Morrison	604	.283	15	57	**422**	481	29	117	5.8	.969	S. Trout	32	200	9	16	0	3.69
SS	T. Cruz	293	.232	2	18	138	298	20	62	5.1	.956	R. Dotson	33	198	12	10	0	4.27
3B	K. Bell	191	.178	1	11	35	151	15	12	2.4	.925	M. Proly	62	147	5	10	8	3.06
RF	H. Baines	491	.255	13	49	229	6	9	1	1.8	.963	R. Baumgarten	24	136	2	12	0	3.44
CF	C. Lemon	514	.292	11	51	347	11	7	2	2.6	.981	L. Hoyt	24	112	9	3	0	4.58
LF	W. Nordhagen	415	.277	15	59	120	6	4	1	1.8	.969	E. Farmer	64	100	7	9	30	3.33
C	B. Kimm	251	.243	0	19	375	26	6	4	4.2	.985	R. Wortham	41	92	4	7	1	5.97
DH	L. Johnson	541	.277	13	81	0	0	0	0	.0	.000							
OF	B. Molinaro	344	.291	5	36	85	3	4	0		.957							
S3	G. Pryor	338	.240	1	29	125	333	16	53		.966							
Cal. W-65 L-95 Jim Fregosi																		
1B	R. Carew	540	.331	3	59	897	57	6	82	9.3	.994	F. Tanana	32	204	11	12	0	4.15
2B	B. Grich	498	.271	14	62	326	463	9	101	5.5	.989	D. Aase	40	175	8	13	2	4.06
SS	F. Patek	273	.264	5	34	129	199	16	42	4.2	.953	F. Martinez	30	149	7	9	0	4.53
3B	C. Lansford	602	.261	15	80	151	250	19	29	2.8	.955	D. LaRoche	52	128	3	5	4	4.08
RF	L. Harlow	301	.276	4	27	234	11	6	5	2.7	.955	C. Knapp	32	117	2	11	1	6.15
CF	R. Miller	412	.274	2	38	299	11	5	3	2.7	.984	M. Clear	58	106	11	11	9	3.31
LF	J. Rudi	372	.237	16	53	220	5	2	1	2.5	.991	A. Hassler	41	83	5	1	10	2.49
C	T. Donohue	218	.188	2	14	330	29	5	5	4.3	.986	D. Frost	15	78	4	8	0	5.31
DH	J. Thompson	312	.317	17	70	0	0	0	0	.0	.000							
OF	D. Baylor	340	.250	5	51	119	4	4	0		.969							
UT	D. Thon	267	.255	0	15	70	128	10	28		.952							
OF	B. Clark	261	.230	5	23	213	6	4	2	2.9	.982							
OF	D. Ford	226	.279	7	26	75	3	5	0	1.8	.940							
SS	B. Campaneris	210	.252	2	18	108	157	12	41	4.3	.957							
C	B. Downing	93	.290	2	25	69	6	0	0		1.000							
Sea. W-59 L-103 Darrell Johnson W-39 L-65 Maury Wills W-20 L-38																		
1B	B. Bochte	520	.300	13	78	1273	98	6	143	**10.4**	.996	F. Bannister	32	218	9	13	0	3.47
2B	J. Cruz	422	.209	2	16	269	355	11	85	5.5	.983	G. Abbott	31	215	12	12	0	4.10
SS	M. Mendoza	277	.245	2	14	149	290	19	68	4.0	.959	R. Honeycutt	30	203	10	17	0	3.95
3B	T. Cox	247	.243	2	18	47	142	11	20	2.5	.945	J. Beattie	33	187	5	15	0	4.86
RF	L. Roberts	374	.251	10	33	238	6	4	1	2.4	.984	R. Dressler	30	149	4	10	0	3.99
CF	J. Simpson	365	.249	3	34	205	10	5	1	1.8	.977	S. Rawley	59	114	7	13	13	3.32
LF	D. Meyer	531	.276	11	71	189	10	8	2	1.7	.961	M. Parrott	27	94	1	16	3	7.28
C	L. Cox	243	.202	4	20	412	45	3	5	4.4	**.993**	McLaughlin	45	91	3	6	2	6.82
DH	W. Horton	335	.221	8	36	0	0	0	0	.0	.000	D. Heaverlo	60	79	6	3	4	3.87
UT	T. Paciorek	418	.282	15	59	360	22	5	25		.987							
S3	J. Anderson	317	.227	8	30	118	253	22	45		.944							
UT	L. Milbourne	258	.264	0	26	103	195	8	50		.974							
OF	R. Craig	240	.283	3	20	155	2	2	1	2.5	.987							
OF	J. Beniquez	237	.228	6	21	176	3	8	0	2.9	.957							
UT	B. Stein	198	.268	5	27	119	115	4	21		.983							

BATTING AND BASE RUNNING LEADERS

Batting Average
G. Brett, KC	.390
C. Cooper, MIL	.352
M. Dilone, CLE	.341
M. Rivers, TEX	.333
R. Carew, CAL	.331

Slugging Average
G. Brett, KC	.664
R. Jackson, NY	.597
B. Oglivie, MIL	.563
C. Cooper, MIL	.539
R. Yount, MIL	.519

Home Runs
R. Jackson, NY	41
B. Oglivie, MIL	41
G. Thomas, MIL	38
T. Armas, OAK	35
E. Murray, BAL	32

Total Bases
C. Cooper, MIL	335
B. Oglivie, MIL	333
E. Murray, BAL	322
R. Yount, MIL	317
A. Oliver, TEX	315

Runs Batted In
C. Cooper, MIL	122
G. Brett, KC	118
B. Oglivie, MIL	118
A. Oliver, TEX	117
E. Murray, BAL	116

Stolen Bases
R. Henderson, OAK	100
W. Wilson, KC	79
M. Dilone, CLE	61
J. Cruz, SEA	45
A. Bumbry, BAL	44

Hits
W. Wilson, KC	230
C. Cooper, MIL	219
M. Rivers, TEX	210

Base on Balls
W. Randolph, NY	119
R. Henderson, OAK	117
M. Hargrove, CLE	111

Home Run Percentage
R. Jackson, NY	8.0
B. Oglivie, MIL	6.9
G. Thomas, MIL	6.1

Runs Scored
W. Wilson, KC	133
R. Yount, MIL	121
A. Bumbry, BAL	118

Doubles
R. Yount, MIL	49
A. Oliver, TEX	43
J. Morrison, CHI	40

Triples
A. Griffin, TOR	15
W. Wilson, KC	15
K. Landreaux, MIN	11
U. Washington, KC	11

PITCHING LEADERS

Winning Percentage
S. Stone, BAL	.781
R. May, NY	.750
S. McGregor, BAL	.714
T. John, NY	.710
M. Norris, OAK	.710

Earned Run Average
R. May, NY	2.47
M. Norris, OAK	2.54
B. Burns, CHI	2.84
M. Keough, OAK	2.92
L. Gura, KC	2.96

Wins
S. Stone, BAL	25
T. John, NY	22
M. Norris, OAK	22
S. McGregor, BAL	20
D. Leonard, KC	20

Saves
Quisenberry, KC	33
G. Gossage, NY	33
E. Farmer, CHI	30
T. Stoddard, BAL	26
T. Burgmeier, BOS	24

Strikeouts
L. Barker, CLE	187
M. Norris, OAK	180
R. Guidry, NY	166
F. Bannister, SEA	155
D. Leonard, KC	155

Complete Games
R. Langford, OAK	28
M. Norris, OAK	24
M. Keough, OAK	20
T. John, NY	16
L. Gura, KC	16

Fewest Hits per 9 Innings
M. Norris, OAK	6.81
R. May, NY	7.41
J. Clancy, TOR	7.78

Shutouts
T. John, NY	6
G. Zahn, MIN	5

Fewest Walks per 9 Innings
J. Matlack, TEX	1.84
P. Splittorff, KC	1.90
T. John, NY	1.90

Most Strikeouts per 9 Inn.
L. Barker, CLE	6.84
R. May, NY	6.84
R. Guidry, NY	6.79

Innings
R. Langford, OAK	290
M. Norris, OAK	284
L. Gura, KC	283

Games Pitched
Quisenberry, KC	75
D. Corbett, MIN	73
A. Lopez, DET	67
S. Monge, CLE	67

	W	L	PCT	GB	R	OR	Batting 2B	3B	HR	BA	SA	SB	Fielding E	DP	FA	Pitching CG	BB	SO	ShO	SV	ERA
EAST																					
NY	103	59	.636		820	662	239	34	189	.267	.425	86	138	160	.978	29	463	845	**15**	**50**	3.58
BAL	100	62	.617	3	805	**640**	258	29	156	.273	.413	111	**95**	178	**.985**	42	507	789	10	41	3.64
MIL	86	76	.531	17	811	682	**298**	36	203	.275	**.448**	131	147	189	.977	48	**420**	575	14	30	3.71
BOS	83	77	.519	19	757	767	297	36	162	.283	.436	79	149	**206**	.977	30	481	696	8	43	4.38
DET	84	78	.519	19	**830**	757	232	53	143	.273	.409	75	133	165	.979	40	558	741	9	30	4.25
CLE	79	81	.494	23	738	807	221	40	89	.277	.381	118	105	143	.983	35	552	842	8	32	4.68
TOR	67	95	.414	36	624	762	249	53	126	.251	.383	67	133	**206**	.979	39	635	705	9	23	4.19
WEST																					
KC	97	65	.599		809	694	266	**59**	115	**.286**	.413	**185**	141	150	.978	37	465	614	10	42	3.83
OAK	83	79	.512	14	686	642	212	35	137	.259	.385	175	130	115	.979	94	521	769	9	13	**3.46**
MIN	77	84	.478	19.5	670	724	252	46	99	.265	.381	62	148	192	.977	35	468	744	9	30	3.93
TEX	76	85	.472	20.5	756	752	263	27	124	.284	.405	91	147	169	.977	35	519	**890**	6	25	4.02
CHI	70	90	.438	26	587	722	255	38	91	.259	.370	68	171	162	.973	32	563	724	12	42	3.92
CAL	65	95	.406	31	698	797	236	32	106	.265	.378	91	134	144	.978	22	529	725	6	30	4.52
SEA	59	103	.364	38	610	793	211	35	104	.248	.356	116	149	189	.977	31	540	703	7	26	4.38
					10201	10201	3489	553	1844	.269	.399	1455	1920	2368	.978	549	7221	10362	132	457	4.03

East

POS	Player	AB	BA	HR	RBI	PO	A	E	DP	TC/G	FA	Pitcher	G	IP	W	L	SV	ERA
St. L.																		
W-59 L-43																		
Whitey Herzog																		
1B	K. Hernandez	376	.306	8	48	**1054**	86	3	**99**	11.7	.997	L. Sorensen	23	140	7	7	0	3.28
2B	T. Herr	411	.268	0	46	211	**374**	5	74	5.7	.992	B. Forsch	20	124	10	5	0	3.19
SS	G. Templeton	333	.288	1	33	160	272	18	54	5.9	.960	J. Martin	17	103	8	5	0	3.41
3B	K. Oberkfell	376	.293	2	45	77	246	15	23	3.3	.956	B. Sutter	48	82	3	5	25	2.63
RF	S. Lezcano	214	.266	5	28	103	5	3	1	1.7	.973	B. Shirley	28	79	6	4	1	4.10
CF	G. Hendrick	394	.284	18	61	227	6	4	0	2.3	.983	J. Kaat	41	53	6	6	4	3.40
LF	D. Iorg	217	.327	2	39	78	0	3	0	1.4	.963							
C	D. Porter	174	.224	6	31	206	31	5	2	4.7	.979							
OF	T. Scott	176	.227	2	17	120	2	0	0	2.8	1.000							
C	G. Tenace	129	.233	5	22	126	18	3	1	3.9	.980							
SS	M. Ramsey	124	.258	0	9	52	118	6	20	5.0	.966							
OF	T. Landrum	119	.261	0	10	72	6	0	1	1.2	1.000							
Mon.																		
W-60 L-48																		
Dick Williams																		
W-44 L-37																		
Jim Fanning																		
W-16 L-11																		
1B	W. Cromartie	358	.304	6	42	488	32	4	38	8.5	.992	S. Rogers	22	161	12	8	0	3.41
2B	R. Scott	336	.205	0	26	187	278	8	41	5.1	.983	B. Gullickson	22	157	7	9	0	2.81
SS	C. Speier	307	.225	2	25	175	280	17	57	4.9	.964	S. Sanderson	22	137	9	7	0	2.96
3B	L. Parrish	349	.244	8	44	**91**	141	16	7	2.6	.935	R. Burris	22	136	9	7	0	3.04
RF	J. White	119	.218	3	11	58	2	3	1	1.6	.952	B. Lee	31	89	5	6	6	2.93
CF	A. Dawson	394	.302	24	64	**327**	10	7	1	3.3	.980	W. Fryman	35	43	5	3	7	1.88
LF	T. Raines	313	.304	5	37	160	6	4	0	2.1	.976							
C	G. Carter	374	.251	16	68	**509**	58	4	11	5.7	.993							
UT	T. Wallach	212	.236	4	13	207	31	1	9		.996							
Phi.																		
W-59 L-48																		
Dallas Green																		
1B	P. Rose	431	.325	0	33	929	91	4	69	9.6	.996	S. Carlton	24	190	13	4	0	2.42
2B	M. Trillo	349	.287	6	36	**245**	286	7	61	5.7	.987	D. Ruthven	23	147	12	7	0	5.14
SS	L. Bowa	360	.283	0	31	117	309	11	50	4.3	.975	Christenson	20	107	4	7	1	3.53
3B	M. Schmidt	354	.316	31	91	74	**249**	15	20	3.3	.956	S. Lyle	48	75	9	6	2	4.44
RF	B. McBride	221	.271	2	21	76	2	1	1	1.4	.987	R. Reed	39	61	5	3	8	3.10
CF	G. Maddox	323	.263	5	40	251	8	6	4	2.8	.977	T. McGraw	34	44	2	4	10	2.66
LF	G. Matthews	359	.301	9	67	170	11	7	1	1.9	.963							
C	B. Boone	227	.211	4	24	365	32	6	1	5.4	.985							
C	K. Moreland	196	.255	6	37	256	20	5	2	5.6	.982							
OF	L. Smith	176	.324	2	11	89	10	3	2	2.0	.971							
OF	G. Gross	102	.225	0	7	48	7	1	2	1.0	.982							
Pit.																		
W-46 L-56																		
Chuck Tanner																		
1B	J. Thompson	223	.242	15	42	590	46	7	65	8.2	.989	R. Rhoden	21	136	9	4	0	3.90
2B	P. Garner	181	.254	1	20	121	148	9	31	5.6	.968	E. Solomon	22	127	8	6	1	3.12
SS	T. Foli	316	.247	0	20	140	247	14	52	5.0	.965	R. Scurry	27	74	4	5	3	3.77
3B	B. Madlock	279	**.341**	6	45	50	147	9	17	2.6	.956	K. Tekulve	45	65	5	5	3	2.49
RF	D. Parker	240	.258	9	48	110	1	7	0	2.0	.941	E. Romo	33	42	1	3	9	4.50
CF	O. Moreno	434	.276	1	35	302	6	1	1	3.0	.997							
LF	M. Easler	339	.286	7	42	188	13	4	2	2.3	.980							
C	T. Pena	210	.300	2	17	286	41	5	10	5.2	.985							
UT	D. Berra	232	.241	2	27	89	167	8	27		.970							
OF	L. Lacy	213	.268	2	10	121	7	3	1	2.1	.977							
C	S. Nicosia	169	.231	2	18	257	23	5	2	5.5	.982							
2B	J. Ray	102	.245	0	6	52	96	2	22	4.8	.987							
N. Y.																		
W-41 L-62																		
Joe Torre																		
1B	D. Kingman	353	.221	22	59	462	31	13	39	9.0	.974	P. Zachry	24	139	7	**14**	0	4.14
2B	D. Flynn	325	.222	1	20	220	301	7	58	5.3	.987	M. Scott	23	136	5	10	0	3.90
SS	F. Taveras	283	.230	0	11	120	202	24	44	4.4	.931	N. Allen	43	67	7	6	18	2.96
3B	H. Brooks	358	.307	4	38	65	192	**21**	14	3.0	.924							
RF	E. Valentine	169	.207	5	21	83	6	4	0	2.0	.957							
CF	M. Wilson	328	.271	3	14	226	3	4	2	2.9	.983							
LF	L. Mazzilli	324	.228	6	34	192	5	6	1	2.3	.970							
C	J. Stearns	273	.271	1	24	302	38	6	7	5.2	.983							
1B	R. Staub	161	.317	5	21	339	20	4	26	8.9	.989							
C	A. Trevino	149	.262	0	10	211	22	9	1	5.4	.963							
OF	J. Youngblood	143	.350	4	25	70	6	3	0	1.9	.962							
1O	M. Jorgensen	122	.205	3	15	143	9	1	8		.993							
Chi.																		
W-38 L-65																		
Joey Amalfitano																		
1B	B. Buckner	421	.311	10	75	996	81	**17**	92	10.4	.984	M. Krukow	25	144	9	9	0	3.69
2B	P. Tabler	101	.188	1	5	70	93	3	14	4.7	.982	R. Martz	33	108	5	7	6	3.67
SS	I. DeJesus	403	.194	0	13	**221**	343	24	81	5.5	.959	R. Reuschel	13	86	4	7	0	3.45
3B	K. Reitz	260	.215	2	28	57	157	5	11	2.7	**.977**	D. Tidrow	51	75	3	10	9	5.04
RF	L. Durham	328	.290	10	35	159	4	5	1	2.0	.970	L. Smith	40	67	3	6	1	3.49
CF	S. Henderson	287	.293	5	35	152	4	8	2	2.1	.951							
LF	J. Morales	245	.286	1	25	142	2	2	1	2.0	.986							
C	J. Davis	180	.256	4	21	274	44	9	4	5.8	.972							
OF	B. Bonds	163	.215	6	19	108	2	2	0	2.5	.982							
C	T. Blackwell	158	.234	1	11	268	28	2	1	5.3	.993							
2B	S. Dillard	119	.218	2	11	54	96	4	21	4.8	.974							
OF	S. Thompson	115	.165	0	8	49	1	1	0	1.7	.980							
3O	H. Cruz	109	.229	7	15	33	26	3	0		.952							

West

	POS	Player	AB	BA	HR	RBI	PO	A	E	DP	TC/G	FA	Pitcher	G	IP	W	L	SV	ERA
Cin. W-66 L-42 John McNamara	1B	D. Driessen	233	.236	7	33	558	30	3	54	8.0	.995	M. Soto	25	175	12	9	0	3.29
	2B	R. Oester	354	.271	5	42	202	328	11	61	5.3	.980	T. Seaver	23	166	14	2	0	2.55
	SS	D. Concepcion	421	.306	5	67	208	322	22	71	5.2	.960	F. Pastore	22	132	4	9	0	4.02
	3B	R. Knight	386	.259	6	34	69	176	11	18	2.4	.957	B. Berenyi	21	126	9	6	0	3.50
	RF	D. Collins	360	.272	3	23	167	4	4	2	1.9	.977	M. LaCoss	20	78	4	7	1	6.12
	CF	K. Griffey	396	.311	2	34	268	8	3	1	2.8	.989	T. Hume	51	68	9	4	13	3.44
	LF	G. Foster	414	.295	22	90	224	8	2	1	2.2	.991	J. Price	41	54	6	1	4	2.50
	C	J. Nolan	236	.309	1	26	393	18	2	2	5.1	.995							
	1B	J. Bench	178	.309	8	25	334	23	6	35	9.6	.983							
	C	M. O'Berry	111	.180	1	5	208	22	4	2	4.3	.983							
L. A. W-63 L-47 Tom Lasorda	1B	S. Garvey	431	.283	10	64	1019	55	1	84	9.8	.999	F. Valenzuela	25	192	13	7	0	2.48
	2B	D. Lopes	214	.206	5	17	129	161	2	30	5.3	.993	J. Reuss	22	153	10	4	0	2.29
	SS	B. Russell	262	.233	0	22	128	261	14	49	5.0	.965	B. Hooton	23	142	11	6	0	2.28
	3B	R. Cey	312	.288	13	50	71	184	16	15	3.2	.941	B. Welch	23	141	9	5	0	3.45
	RF	P. Guerrero	347	.300	12	48	145	4	4	0	2.0	.974	D. Goltz	26	77	2	7	1	4.09
	CF	K. Landreaux	390	.251	7	41	210	4	0	0	2.3	1.000	S. Howe	41	54	5	3	8	2.50
	LF	D. Baker	400	.320	9	49	181	8	2	1	1.9	.990	B. Castillo	34	51	2	4	5	5.29
	C	M. Scioscia	290	.276	2	29	493	48	7	4	6.0	.987	D. Stewart	32	43	4	3	6	2.51
	UT	D. Thomas	218	.248	4	24	133	144	14	30		.952							
	OF	R. Monday	130	.315	11	25	50	1	2	0	1.3	.962							
	2B	S. Sax	119	.277	2	9	64	93	4	22	5.6	.975							
Hou. W-61 L-49 Bill Virdon	1B	C. Cedeno	306	.271	5	34	428	27	4	27	10.0	.991	J. Niekro	24	166	9	9	0	2.82
	2B	J. Pittman	135	.281	0	7	56	89	3	14	4.2	.980	D. Sutton	23	159	11	9	0	2.60
	SS	C. Reynolds	323	.260	4	31	139	261	11	36	4.8	.973	B. Knepper	22	157	9	5	0	2.18
	3B	A. Howe	361	.296	3	36	52	206	9	16	2.7	.966	N. Ryan	21	149	11	5	0	1.69
	RF	T. Puhl	350	.251	3	28	185	5	0	1	2.2	1.000	V. Ruhle	20	102	4	6	1	2.91
	CF	T. Scott	225	.293	2	22	127	5	2	0	2.4	.985	D. Smith	42	75	5	3	8	2.76
	LF	J. Cruz	409	.267	13	55	237	5	4	2	2.3	.984	J. Sambito	49	64	5	5	10	1.83
	C	A. Ashby	255	.271	4	33	434	58	9	6	6.2	.982	F. LaCorte	37	42	4	2	5	3.64
	O1	D. Walling	158	.234	5	23	226	9	2	18		.992							
	UT	K. Garcia	136	.272	0	15	58	119	11	14		.941							
	C	L. Pujols	117	.239	1	14	192	14	1	1	5.3	.995							
	2B	P. Garner	113	.239	0	6	62	102	3	17	5.4	.982							
	OF	G. Woods	110	.209	0	12	61	1	1	0	1.6	.984							
S. F. W-56 L-55 Frank Robinson	1B	E. Cabell	396	.255	2	36	620	63	9	56	10.0	.987	D. Alexander	24	152	11	7	0	2.90
	2B	J. Morgan	308	.240	8	31	177	258	4	61	5.0	.991	T. Griffin	22	129	8	8	0	3.77
	SS	J. LeMaster	324	.253	0	28	166	294	17	57	4.6	.964	V. Blue	18	125	8	6	0	2.45
	3B	D. Evans	357	.258	12	48	74	187	13	10	3.1	.953	E. Whitson	22	123	6	9	0	4.02
	RF	J. Clark	385	.268	17	53	193	14	4	4	2.2	.981	A. Holland	47	101	7	5	7	2.41
	CF	J. Martin	241	.241	4	25	138	4	1	1	2.2	.993	G. Minton	55	84	4	5	21	2.89
	LF	L. Herndon	364	.288	5	41	207	8	5	1	2.4	.977	G. Lavelle	34	66	2	6	4	3.82
	C	M. May	316	.310	2	33	468	48	6	4	5.6	.989							
	1O	D. Bergman	145	.255	3	13	252	24	3	21		.989							
	OF	B. North	131	.221	1	12	84	1	3	1	2.4	.966							
	1B	J. Leonard	127	.307	4	26	79	2	0	0	2.9	1.000							
Atl. W-50 L-56 Bobby Cox	1B	C. Chambliss	404	.272	8	51	1046	94	4	83	10.7	.997	G. Perry	23	151	8	9	0	3.93
	2B	G. Hubbard	361	.235	6	33	188	344	5	50	5.5	.991	T. Boggs	25	143	3	13	0	4.09
	SS	R. Ramirez	307	.218	2	20	181	306	30	55	5.4	.942	P. Niekro	22	139	7	7	0	3.11
	3B	B. Horner	300	.277	15	42	51	129	12	6	2.4	.938	R. Mahler	34	112	8	6	2	2.81
	RF	C. Washington	320	.291	5	37	145	5	1	0	1.9	.993	R. Camp	48	76	9	3	17	1.78
	CF	D. Murphy	369	.247	13	50	254	11	5	4	2.6	.981	G. Garber	35	59	4	6	2	2.59
	LF	R. Linares	253	.265	5	25	124	6	5	1	2.3	.963							
	C	B. Benedict	295	.264	5	35	404	73	7	7	5.4	.986							
	OF	E. Miller	134	.231	0	7	65	2	1	0	1.9	.985							
	OF	B. Butler	126	.254	0	4	76	2	1	0	2.1	.987							
	3B	B. Pocoroba	122	.180	0	8	15	30	3	4	2.3	.938							
S. D. W-41 L-69 Frank Howard	1B	B. Perkins	254	.280	2	40	598	38	2	56	8.0	.997	Eichelberger	25	141	8	8	0	3.51
	2B	J. Bonilla	369	.290	1	25	229	290	13	72	5.5	.976	S. Mura	23	139	5	14	0	4.27
	SS	O. Smith	450	.222	0	21	220	422	16	72	6.0	.976	C. Welsh	22	124	6	7	0	3.77
	3B	L. Salazar	400	.303	3	38	63	189	12	16	2.8	.955	R. Wise	18	98	4	8	0	3.77
	RF	G. Richards	393	.288	3	42	178	14	5	1	1.9	.975	G. Lucas	57	90	7	7	13	2.00
	CF	R. Jones	397	.249	4	39	295	9	2	3	2.9	.993	T. Lollar	24	77	2	8	1	6.08
	LF	J. Lefebvre	246	.256	8	31	167	6	1	2	2.1	.994							
	C	T. Kennedy	382	.301	2	41	465	63	20	12	5.5	.964							
	1B	R. Bass	176	.210	4	20	390	35	3	38	8.6	.993							
	OF	D. Edwards	112	.214	2	13	59	6	2	2	1.4	.970							

BATTING AND BASE RUNNING LEADERS

Batting Average		Slugging Average	
B. Madlock, PIT	.341	M. Schmidt, PHI	.644
P. Rose, PHI	.325	A. Dawson, MON	.553
D. Baker, LA	.320	G. Foster, CIN	.519
M. Schmidt, PHI	.316	B. Madlock, PIT	.495
B. Buckner, CHI	.311	G. Hendrick, STL	.485

PITCHING LEADERS

Winning Percentage		Earned Run Average	
T. Seaver, CIN	.875	N. Ryan, HOU	1.69
S. Carlton, PHI	.765	B. Knepper, HOU	2.18
J. Reuss, LA	.714	B. Hooton, LA	2.28
N. Ryan, HOU	.688	J. Reuss, LA	2.29
B. Forsch, STL	.667	S. Carlton, PHI	2.42

BATTING AND BASE RUNNING LEADERS

Home Runs			Total Bases	
M. Schmidt, PHI	31		M. Schmidt, PHI	228
A. Dawson, MON	24		A. Dawson, MON	218
D. Kingman, NY	22		G. Foster, CIN	215
G. Foster, CIN	22		B. Buckner, CHI	202
G. Hendrick, STL	18		G. Hendrick, STL	191

Runs Batted In			Stolen Bases	
M. Schmidt, PHI	91		T. Raines, MON	71
G. Foster, CIN	90		O. Moreno, PIT	39
B. Buckner, CHI	75		R. Scott, MON	30
G. Carter, MON	68		B. North, SF	26
G. Matthews, PHI	67		D. Collins, CIN	26
D. Concepcion, CIN	67		A. Dawson, MON	26

Hits			Base on Balls	
P. Rose, PHI	140		M. Schmidt, PHI	73
B. Buckner, CHI	131		J. Morgan, SF	66
D. Concepcion, CIN	129		K. Hernandez, STL	61

Home Run Percentage			Runs Scored	
M. Schmidt, PHI	8.8		M. Schmidt, PHI	78
D. Kingman, NY	6.2		P. Rose, PHI	73
A. Dawson, MON	6.1		A. Dawson, MON	71

Doubles			Triples	
B. Buckner, CHI	35		C. Reynolds, HOU	12
R. Jones, SD	34		G. Richards, SD	12
D. Concepcion, CIN	28		T. Herr, STL	9

PITCHING LEADERS

Wins			Saves	
T. Seaver, CIN	14		B. Sutter, STL	25
S. Carlton, PHI	13		G. Minton, SF	21
F. Valenzuela, LA	13		N. Allen, NY	18
D. Ruthven, PHI	12		R. Camp, ATL	17
S. Rogers, MON	12		T. Hume, CIN	13
M. Soto, CIN	12		G. Lucas, SD	13

Strikeouts			Complete Games	
F. Valenzuela, LA	180		F. Valenzuela, LA	11
S. Carlton, PHI	179		S. Carlton, PHI	10
M. Soto, CIN	151		M. Soto, CIN	10
N. Ryan, HOU	140		J. Reuss, LA	8
B. Gullickson, MON	115		S. Rogers, MON	7

Fewest Hits per 9 Innings			Shutouts	
N. Ryan, HOU	5.98		F. Valenzuela, LA	8
T. Seaver, CIN	6.51		B. Knepper, HOU	5
F. Valenzuela, LA	6.56		B. Hooton, LA	4

Fewest Walks per 9 Innings			Most Strikeouts per 9 Inn.	
G. Perry, ATL	1.43		S. Carlton, PHI	8.48
J. Reuss, LA	1.59		N. Ryan, HOU	8.46
D. Sutton, HOU	1.64		F. Valenzuela, LA	8.44

Innings			Games Pitched	
F. Valenzuela, LA	192		G. Lucas, SD	57
S. Carlton, PHI	190		G. Minton, SF	55
M. Soto, CIN	175		D. Tidrow, CHI	51
			T. Hume, CIN	51

	W	L	PCT	GB	R	OR	2B	3B	HR	BA	SA	SB	E	DP	FA	CG	BB	SO	ShO	SV	ERA
EAST																					
STL	59	43	.578		464	417	158	45	50	.265	.377	88	82	108	.981	11	290	388	5	33	3.63
MON	60	48	.556	2	443	394	146	28	81	.246	.370	138	81	88	.980	20	268	520	12	23	3.30
PHI	59	48	.551	2.5	491	472	165	25	69	.273	.389	103	86	90	.980	19	347	580	5	23	4.05
PIT	46	56	.451	13	407	425	176	30	55	.257	.369	122	86	106	.979	11	346	492	5	29	3.56
NY	41	62	.398	18.5	348	432	136	35	57	.248	.356	103	130	89	.968	7	336	490	3	24	3.55
CHI	38	65	.369	21.5	370	483	138	29	57	.236	.340	72	113	103	.974	6	388	532	2	20	4.01
WEST																					
CIN	66	42	.611		464	440	190	24	64	.267	.385	58	80	99	.981	25	393	593	14	20	3.73
LA	63	47	.573	4	450	356	133	20	82	.262	.374	73	87	101	.980	26	302	603	19	24	3.01
HOU	61	49	.555	6	394	331	160	35	45	.257	.356	81	87	81	.980	23	300	610	19	25	2.66
SF	56	55	.505	11.5	427	414	161	26	63	.250	.357	89	102	102	.977	8	393	561	9	33	3.28
ATL	50	56	.472	15	395	416	148	22	64	.243	.349	98	102	93	.976	11	330	471	4	24	3.45
SD	41	69	.373	26	382	455	170	35	32	.256	.346	83	102	117	.977	9	414	492	6	23	3.72
					5035	5035	1881	354	719	.255	.364	1108	1138	1177	.978	176	4107	6332	103	301	3.49

First Half

	W	L	PCT	GB
EAST				
PHI	34	21	.618	
STL	30	20	.600	1.5
MON	30	25	.545	4
PIT	25	23	.521	5.5
NY	17	34	.333	15
CHI	15	37	.288	17.5

*Defeated Philadelphia in playoff 3 games to 2.

	W	L	PCT	GB
WEST				
LA*	36	21	.632	
CIN	35	21	.625	.5
HOU	28	29	.491	8
ATL	25	29	.463	9.5
SF	27	32	.458	10
SD	23	33	.411	12.5

*Defeated Houston in playoff 3 games to 2.

Second Half

	W	L	PCT	GB
EAST				
MON*	30	23	.566	
STL	29	23	.558	.5
PHI	25	27	.481	4.5
NY	24	28	.462	5.5
CHI	23	28	.451	6
PIT	21	33	.389	9.5

	W	L	PCT	GB
WEST				
HOU	33	20	.623	
CIN	31	21	.596	1.5
SF	29	23	.558	3.5
LA	27	26	.509	6
ATL	25	27	.481	7.5
SD	18	36	.333	15.5

POS	Player	AB	BA	HR	RBI	PO	A	E	DP	TC/G	FA	Pitcher	G	IP	W	L	SV	ERA

East

Mil.
W-62 L-47
Buck Rodgers

POS	Player	AB	BA	HR	RBI	PO	A	E	DP	TC/G	FA	Pitcher	G	IP	W	L	SV	ERA
1B	C. Cooper	416	.320	12	60	987	72	9	111	10.6	.992	P. Vuckovich	24	150	14	4	0	3.54
2B	J. Gantner	352	.267	2	33	251	352	10	95	5.7	.984	M. Caldwell	24	144	11	9	0	3.94
SS	R. Yount	377	.273	10	49	161	370	8	83	5.8	.985	M. Haas	24	137	11	7	0	4.47
3B	R. Howell	244	.238	6	33	38	98	6	9	2.7	.958	J. Slaton	24	117	5	7	0	4.38
RF	M. Brouhard	186	.274	2	20	92	7	1	2	2.0	.990	R. Lerch	23	111	7	9	0	4.30
CF	G. Thomas	363	.259	21	65	221	8	5	3	2.4	.979	R. Fingers	47	78	6	3	28	1.04
LF	B. Oglivie	400	.243	14	72	211	3	4	1	2.2	.982	J. Easterly	44	62	3	3	4	3.19
C	T. Simmons	380	.216	14	61	300	37	7	3	4.6	.980							
DH	P. Molitor	251	.267	2	19	0	0	0	0	.0	.000							
3B	D. Money	185	.216	2	14	27	100	3	8	2.3	.977							
C	C. Moore	156	.301	1	9	147	16	5	0	4.9	.970							
OF	T. Bosley	105	.229	0	3	55	1	2	0	1.6	.966							

Bal.
W-59 L-46
Earl Weaver

POS	Player	AB	BA	HR	RBI	PO	A	E	DP	TC/G	FA	Pitcher	G	IP	W	L	SV	ERA
1B	E. Murray	378	.294	22	78	899	91	1	98	10.0	.999	D. Martinez	25	179	14	5	0	3.32
2B	R. Dauer	369	.263	4	38	201	253	5	71	4.9	.989	S. McGregor	24	160	13	5	0	3.26
SS	M. Belanger	139	.165	1	10	86	162	7	21	4.0	.973	J. Palmer	22	127	7	8	0	3.76
3B	D. DeCinces	346	.263	13	55	86	191	17	31	2.9	.942	M. Flanagan	20	116	9	6	0	4.19
RF	K. Singleton	363	.278	13	49	125	2	0	2	1.8	1.000	S. Stewart	29	112	4	8	4	2.33
CF	A. Bumbry	392	.273	1	27	255	6	2	2	2.6	.992	S. Stone	15	63	4	7	0	4.57
LF	G. Roenicke	219	.269	3	20	175	2	3	1	2.2	.983	T. Martinez	37	59	3	3	11	2.90
C	R. Dempsey	251	.215	6	15	384	35	1	6	4.7	.998	T. Stoddard	31	37	4	2	7	3.89
DH	T. Crowley	134	.246	4	25	0	0	0	0	.0	.000							
OF	J. Lowenstein	189	.249	6	20	100	3	1	0	1.4	.990							
S2	L. Sakata	150	.227	5	15	82	148	7	33		.970							
C	D. Graham	142	.176	2	11	138	20	4	1	4.1	.975							
OF	J. Dwyer	134	.224	3	10	84	2	2	0	1.5	.977							

N. Y.
W-59 L-48
Gene Michael
W-46 L-33
Bob Lemon
W-13 L-15

POS	Player	AB	BA	HR	RBI	PO	A	E	DP	TC/G	FA	Pitcher	G	IP	W	L	SV	ERA
1B	B. Watson	156	.212	6	12	367	25	1	42	7.9	.997	R. May	27	148	6	11	1	4.14
2B	W. Randolph	357	.232	2	24	205	268	11	74	5.2	.977	T. John	20	140	9	8	0	2.64
SS	B. Dent	227	.238	7	27	104	217	10	49	4.5	.970	R. Guidry	23	127	11	5	0	2.76
3B	G. Nettles	349	.244	15	46	63	214	8	14	2.9	.972	D. Righetti	15	105	8	4	0	2.06
RF	R. Jackson	334	.237	15	54	111	3	3	0	1.9	.974	R. Davis	43	73	4	5	6	2.71
CF	J. Mumphrey	319	.307	6	32	219	5	8	0	2.9	.966	G. Gossage	32	47	3	2	20	0.77
LF	D. Winfield	388	.294	13	68	196	1	3	0	2.0	.985							
C	R. Cerone	234	.244	2	21	353	26	3	1	5.5	.992							
DH	B. Murcer	117	.265	6	24	0	0	0	0	.0	.000							
OF	O. Gamble	189	.238	10	27	77	0	0	0		1.000							
UT	L. Milbourne	163	.313	1	12	74	121	8	26		.961							
OF	L. Piniella	159	.277	5	18	69	2	1	1		.986							
C	B. Foote	125	.208	6	10	227	14	1	3	7.1	.996							
1B	D. Revering	119	.235	2	7	276	30	2	24	7.0	.994							

Det.
W-60 L-49
Sparky Anderson

POS	Player	AB	BA	HR	RBI	PO	A	E	DP	TC/G	FA	Pitcher	G	IP	W	L	SV	ERA
1B	R. Hebner	226	.226	5	28	531	29	3	36	9.2	.995	J. Morris	25	198	14	7	0	3.05
2B	L. Whitaker	335	.263	5	36	227	354	9	77	5.5	.985	M. Wilcox	24	166	12	9	0	3.04
SS	A. Trammell	392	.258	2	31	181	347	9	65	5.1	.983	D. Petry	23	141	10	9	0	3.00
3B	T. Brookens	239	.243	4	25	58	139	10	13	2.9	.952	D. Rozema	28	104	5	5	3	3.63
RF	K. Gibson	290	.328	9	40	142	1	4	0	2.2	.973	A. Lopez	29	82	5	2	3	3.62
CF	A. Cowens	253	.261	1	18	166	3	1	0	2.0	.994	D. Schatzeder	17	71	6	8	0	6.08
LF	S. Kemp	372	.277	9	49	207	4	3	0	2.3	.986	K. Saucier	38	49	4	2	13	1.65
C	L. Parrish	348	.244	10	46	407	40	3	6	5.0	.993							
DH	C. Summers	165	.255	3	21	0	0	0	0	.0	.000							
OF	R. Peters	207	.256	0	15	103	3	1	1		.991							
OF	L. Jones	174	.259	2	19	85	5	1	2	1.5	.989							
1B	J. Wockenfuss	172	.215	9	25	179	5	3	27		.984							

Bos.
W-59 L-49
Ralph Houk

POS	Player	AB	BA	HR	RBI	PO	A	E	DP	TC/G	FA	Pitcher	G	IP	W	L	SV	ERA
1B	T. Perez	306	.252	9	39	519	37	4	63	10.0	.993	D. Eckersley	23	154	9	8	0	4.27
2B	J. Remy	358	.307	0	31	162	272	7	58	5.1	.984	F. Tanana	24	141	4	10	0	4.02
SS	G. Hoffman	242	.231	1	20	131	233	15	62	4.9	.960	M. Torrez	22	127	10	3	0	3.69
3B	C. Lansford	399	.336	4	52	70	180	13	17	3.1	.951	B. Stanley	35	99	10	8	0	3.82
RF	D. Evans	412	.296	22	71	259	9	2	1	2.5	.993	M. Clear	34	77	8	3	9	4.09
CF	R. Miller	316	.291	2	33	219	5	3	0	2.4	.987	T. Burgmeier	32	60	4	5	6	2.85
LF	J. Rice	451	.284	17	62	237	9	3	0	2.3	.988							
C	R. Gedman	205	.288	5	26	275	30	3	1	5.2	.990							
DH	Yastrzemski	338	.246	7	53	0	0	0	0	.0	.000							
UT	D. Stapleton	355	.285	10	42	260	204	17	50		.965							
C	G. Allenson	139	.223	5	25	235	18	8	3	5.6	.969							
DH	J. Rudi	122	.180	6	24	0	0	0	0	.0	.000							

Cle.
W-52 L-51
Dave Garcia

POS	Player	AB	BA	HR	RBI	PO	A	E	DP	TC/G	FA	Pitcher	G	IP	W	L	SV	ERA
1B	M. Hargrove	322	.317	2	49	766	76	9	67	9.7	.989	B. Blyleven	20	159	11	7	0	2.89
2B	D. Kuiper	206	.257	0	14	118	174	5	24	4.1	.983	L. Barker	22	154	8	7	0	3.92
SS	T. Veryzer	221	.244	0	14	121	207	10	48	4.5	.970	J. Denny	19	146	10	6	0	3.14
3B	T. Harrah	361	.291	5	44	63	179	13	12	2.5	.949	R. Waits	22	126	8	10	0	4.93
RF	J. Orta	338	.272	5	34	150	11	1	2	1.9	.994	D. Spillner	32	97	4	4	7	3.15
CF	R. Manning	360	.244	4	33	305	6	4	3	3.1	.987	S. Monge	31	58	3	5	4	4.34
LF	M. Dilone	269	.290	0	19	126	7	4	1	2.4	.971	W. Garland	12	56	3	7	0	5.79
C	R. Hassey	190	.232	1	25	296	38	3	6	6.0	.991							
DH	A. Thornton	226	.239	6	30	0	0	0	0	.0	.000							
O2	A. Bannister	232	.263	1	17	121	76	2	14		.990							
C	B. Diaz	182	.313	7	38	247	27	7	0	5.5	.975							
OF	J. Charboneau	138	.210	4	18	51	1	2	0		.963							
UT	V. Hayes	109	.257	1	17	30	4	3	1		.919							

Tor.
W-37 L-69
Bobby Mattick

POS	Player	AB	BA	HR	RBI	PO	A	E	DP	TC/G	FA	Pitcher	G	IP	W	L	SV	ERA
1B	J. Mayberry	290	.248	17	43	647	36	5	65	8.6	.993	D. Stieb	25	184	11	10	0	3.18
2B	D. Garcia	250	.252	1	13	132	181	9	32	5.2	.972	L. Leal	29	130	7	13	1	3.67
SS	A. Griffin	388	.209	0	21	186	275	31	64	5.1	.937	J. Clancy	22	125	6	12	0	4.90
3B	D. Ainge	246	.187	0	14	73	133	11	19	2.8	.949	M. Bomback	20	90	5	5	0	3.90
RF	B. Bonnell	227	.220	4	28	148	5	4	1	2.4	.975	J. Berenguer	12	71	2	9*	0	4.31
CF	L. Moseby	378	.233	9	43	259	4	3	0	2.7	.989	R. Jackson	39	62	1	2	7	2.61
LF	A. Woods	288	.247	1	21	179	4	5	0	2.4	.973	McLaughlin	40	60	1	5	10	2.85
C	E. Whitt	195	.236	1	16	297	46	3	5	4.8	.991							
DH	O. Velez	240	.213	11	28	0	0	0	0	.0	.000							
23	G. Iorg	215	.242	0	10	94	178	12	32		.958							
OF	G. Bell	163	.233	5	12	92	3	3	2	2.2	.969							
C	B. Martinez	128	.227	4	21	192	22	2	3	4.8	.991							
UT	W. Upshaw	111	.171	4	10	72	6	0	8		1.000							

West

Oak.
W-64 L-45
Billy Martin

POS	Player	AB	BA	HR	RBI	PO	A	E	DP	TC/G	FA	Pitcher	G	IP	W	L	SV	ERA
1B	J. Spencer	171	.205	2	9	344	36	1	30	7.9	.997	R. Langford	24	195	12	10	0	3.00
2B	S. Babitt	156	.256	0	14	84	125	6	12	4.1	.972	S. McCatty	22	186	14	7	0	**2.32**
SS	R. Picciolo	179	.268	4	13	99	157	5	30	3.2	.981	M. Norris	23	173	12	9	0	3.75
3B	W. Gross	243	.206	10	31	65	127	11	7	2.8	.946	M. Keough	19	140	10	6	0	3.41
RF	T. Armas	440	.261	22	76	259	8	2	2	2.5	.993	B. Kingman	18	100	3	6	0	3.96
CF	D. Murphy	390	.251	15	60	326	6	5	0	3.2	.985							
LF	R. Henderson	423	.319	6	35	**327**	7	7	0	**3.2**	.979							
C	M. Heath	301	.236	8	30	391	45	**10**	6	5.7	.978							
DH	C. Johnson	273	.260	17	59	0	0	0	0	.0	.000							
32	D. McKay	224	.263	4	21	112	167	13	26		.955							
C1	J. Newman	216	.231	3	15	367	28	2	14		.995							
SS	F. Stanley	145	.193	0	7	94	118	3	25	3.5	.986							

Tex.
W-57 L-48
Don Zimmer

POS	Player	AB	BA	HR	RBI	PO	A	E	DP	TC/G	FA	Pitcher	G	IP	W	L	SV	ERA
1B	P. Putnam	297	.266	8	35	769	64	6	65	8.9	.993	D. Darwin	22	146	9	9	0	3.64
2B	B. Wills	410	.251	2	41	**268**	326	10	70	**6.0**	.983	D. Medich	20	143	10	6	0	3.08
SS	M. Mendoza	229	.231	0	22	114	270	12	47	4.5	.970	R. Honeycutt	20	128	11	6	0	3.30
3B	B. Bell	360	.294	10	64	66	**281**	14	18	**3.8**	.961	F. Jenkins	19	106	5	8	0	4.50
RF	J. Grubb	199	.231	3	26	95	2	1	0	1.7	.990	J. Matlack	17	104	4	7	0	4.15
CF	M. Rivers	399	.286	3	26	225	12	1	3	2.5	.996	S. Comer	36	77	8	2	6	2.57
LF	B. Sample	230	.283	3	25	132	4	1	1	2.1	.993							
C	J. Sundberg	339	.277	3	28	464	**52**	2	9	5.3	.996							
DH	A. Oliver	421	.309	4	55	0	0	0	0	.0	.000							
OF	L. Roberts	233	.279	4	31	130	2	1	0	1.9	.992							
UT	B. Stein	115	.330	2	22	166	26	2	10		.990							

Chi.
W-54 L-52
Tony LaRussa

POS	Player	AB	BA	HR	RBI	PO	A	E	DP	TC/G	FA	Pitcher	G	IP	W	L	SV	ERA
1B	M. Squires	294	.265	0	25	729	58	6	68	9.0	.992	B. Burns	24	157	10	6	0	2.64
2B	T. Bernazard	384	.276	6	34	228	320	7	66	5.3	.987	R. Dotson	24	141	9	8	0	3.77
SS	B. Almon	349	.301	4	41	190	340	17	78	5.3	.969	D. Lamp	27	127	7	6	0	2.41
3B	J. Morrison	290	.234	10	44	64	199	12	14	3.2	.956	S. Trout	20	125	8	7	0	3.46
RF	H. Baines	280	.286	10	41	120	10	2	1	1.7	.985	R. Baumgarten	19	102	5	9	0	4.06
CF	C. Lemon	328	.302	9	50	240	2	4	1	2.6	.984	L. Hoyt	43	99	9	3	10	3.56
LF	R. LeFlore	337	.246	0	24	162	6	7	2	2.1	.960	E. Farmer	42	53	3	3	10	4.58
C	C. Fisk	338	.263	7	45	**470**	44	5	**10**	5.5	.990							
DH	G. Luzinski	378	.265	21	62	0	0	0	0	.0	.000							
OF	W. Nordhagen	208	.308	6	33	85	4	5	1	1.6	.947							
1B	L. Johnson	134	.276	1	15	264	15	3	31	7.8	.989							

K. C.
W-50 L-53
Jim Frey
W-30 L-40
Dick Howser
W-20 L-13

POS	Player	AB	BA	HR	RBI	PO	A	E	DP	TC/G	FA	Pitcher	G	IP	W	L	SV	ERA
1B	W. Aikens	349	.266	17	53	844	56	7	79	9.2	.992	D. Leonard	26	**202**	13	11	0	2.99
2B	F. White	364	.250	9	38	226	263	6	70	5.3	.988	L. Gura	23	172	11	8	0	2.72
SS	U. Washington	339	.227	2	29	135	297	12	58	4.5	.973	R. Gale	19	102	6	6	0	5.38
3B	G. Brett	347	.314	6	43	74	170	14	7	2.9	.946	P. Splittorff	21	99	5	5	0	4.34
RF	D. Motley	125	.232	2	8	88	3	3	1	2.4	.968	Quisenberry	40	62	1	4	18	1.74
CF	A. Otis	372	.269	9	57	294	6	2	1	3.1	.993	R. Martin	29	62	4	5	4	2.76
LF	W. Wilson	439	.303	1	32	299	**14**	4	3	3.1	.987							
C	J. Wathan	301	.252	1	19	300	26	7	1	4.6	.979							
DH	H. McRae	389	.272	7	36	0	0	0	0	.0	.000							
OF	C. Geronimo	118	.246	2	13	96	1	2	0	1.7	.980							

Cal.
W-51 L-59
Jim Fregosi

POS	Player	AB	BA	HR	RBI	PO	A	E	DP	TC/G	FA	Pitcher	G	IP	W	L	SV	ERA
1B	R. Carew	364	.305	2	21	877	60	5	90	10.5	.995	G. Zahn	25	161	10	11	0	4.42
2B	B. Grich	352	.304	**22**	61	230	349	10	85	5.9	.983	K. Forsch	20	153	11	7	0	2.88
SS	R. Burleson	430	.293	5	33	**208**	**394**	13	**88**	5.6	.979	M. Witt	22	129	8	9	0	3.28
3B	B. Hobson	268	.235	4	36	85	139	**17**	13	2.9	.929	S. Renko	22	102	8	4	1	3.44
RF	D. Ford	375	.277	15	48	188	3	**8**	0	2.1	.960	A. Hassler	42	76	4	3	5	3.20
CF	F. Lynn	256	.219	5	31	176	4	4	1	2.7	.978	D. Aase	39	65	4	4	11	2.35
LF	B. Downing	317	.249	9	41	97	1	1	0	1.8	.990							
C	E. Ott	258	.217	2	22	287	36	7	1	4.6	.979							
DH	D. Baylor	377	.239	17	66	0	0	0	0	.0	.000							
OF	J. Beniquez	166	.181	3	13	117	0	5	0	2.2	.959							

	POS	Player	AB	BA	HR	RBI	PO	A	E	DP	TC/G	FA	Pitcher	G	IP	W	L	SV	ERA
Sea. W-44 L-65 Maury Wills W-6 L-18 Rene Lachemann W-38 L-47	1B	B. Bochte	335	.260	6	30	745	49	4	70	9.7	.995	G. Abbott	22	130	4	9	0	3.95
	2B	J. Cruz	352	.256	2	24	239	294	10	72	5.9	.982	F. Bannister	21	121	9	9	0	4.46
	SS	J. Anderson	162	.204	2	19	88	181	15	44	4.2	.947	K. Clay	22	101	2	7	0	4.63
	3B	L. Randle	273	.231	4	25	38	105	2	8	2.5	.986	J. Gleaton	20	85	4	7	0	4.76
	RF	T. Paciorek	405	.326	14	66	253	10	7	1	2.6	.974	M. Parrott	24	85	3	6	1	5.08
	CF	J. Simpson	288	.222	2	30	219	5	5	1	2.6	.978	S. Rawley	46	68	4	6	8	3.97
	LF	J. Burroughs	319	.254	10	41	127	4	2	1	1.5	.985	L. Andersen	41	68	3	3	5	2.65
	C	J. Narron	203	.222	3	17	248	11	1	3	4.0	.996	D. Drago	39	54	4	6	5	5.50
	DH	R. Zisk	357	.311	16	43	0	0	0	0	.0	.000							
	3B	D. Meyer	252	.262	3	22	36	87	5	12	2.6	.961							
	1B	G. Gray	208	.245	13	31	275	16	2	34		.993							
	C	T. Bulling	154	.247	2	15	239	21	6	3	4.3	.977							
	OF	D. Henderson	126	.167	6	13	105	4	0	1	1.9	1.000							
Min. W-41 L-68 Johnny Goryl W-11 L-25 Billy Gardner W-30 L-43	1B	D. Goodwin	151	.225	2	17	341	20	3	27	9.1	.992	A. Williams	23	150	6	10	0	4.08
	2B	R. Wilfong	305	.246	3	19	183	268	9	52	4.9	.980	P. Redfern	24	142	9	8	0	4.06
	SS	R. Smalley	167	.263	7	22	52	89	8	14	4.0	.946	F. Arroyo	23	128	7	10	0	3.94
	3B	J. Castino	381	.268	6	36	86	224	8	24	3.2	.975	J. Koosman	19	94	3	9*	5	4.21
	CF	M. Hatcher	377	.255	3	37	239	3	2	0	2.7	.992	R. Erickson	14	91	3	8	0	3.86
	LF	G. Ward	295	.264	3	29	185	8	5	4	2.5	.975	D. Corbett	54	88	6	17	2.56
	C	S. Butera	167	.240	0	18	254	41	9	0	5.2	.970							
	DH	G. Adams	220	.209	2	24	0	0	0	0	.0	.000							
	OF	H. Powell	264	.239	2	25	122	6	4	1	2.1	.970							
	UT	P. Mackanin	225	.231	4	18	171	149	12	40		.964							
	UT	R. Jackson	175	.263	4	28	329	30	5	26		.986							
	C	B. Wynegar	150	.247	0	10	162	24	1	4	5.1	.995							
	OF	R. Sofield	102	.176	0	5	54	5	1	0	1.8	.983							

BATTING AND BASE RUNNING LEADERS

Batting Average
C. Lansford, BOS	.336
T. Paciorek, SEA	.326
C. Cooper, MIL	.320
R. Henderson, OAK	.319
M. Hargrove, CLE	.317

Slugging Average
B. Grich, CAL	.543
E. Murray, BAL	.534
D. Evans, BOS	.522
T. Paciorek, SEA	.509
C. Cooper, MIL	.495

Home Runs
B. Grich, CAL	22
E. Murray, BAL	22
D. Evans, BOS	22
T. Armas, OAK	22
G. Thomas, MIL	21
G. Luzinski, CHI	21

Total Bases
D. Evans, BOS	215
T. Armas, OAK	211
T. Paciorek, SEA	206
C. Cooper, MIL	206
E. Murray, BAL	202

Runs Batted In
E. Murray, BAL	78
T. Armas, OAK	76
B. Oglivie, MIL	72
D. Evans, BOS	71
D. Winfield, NY	68

Stolen Bases
R. Henderson, OAK	56
J. Cruz, SEA	43
R. LeFlore, CHI	36
W. Wilson, KC	34
M. Dilone, CLE	29

Hits
R. Henderson, OAK	135
C. Lansford, BOS	134
C. Cooper, MIL	133
W. Wilson, KC	133

Base on Balls
D. Evans, BOS	85
D. Murphy, OAK	73
S. Kemp, DET	70

Home Run Percentage
B. Grich, CAL	6.3
J. Mayberry, TOR	5.9
E. Murray, BAL	5.8

Runs Scored
R. Henderson, OAK	89
D. Evans, BOS	84
C. Cooper, MIL	70

Doubles
C. Cooper, MIL	35
A. Oliver, TEX	29
T. Paciorek, SEA	28

Triples
J. Castino, MIN	9

PITCHING LEADERS

Winning Percentage
P. Vuckovich, MIL	.778
M. Torrez, BOS	.769
D. Martinez, BAL	.737
S. McGregor, BAL	.722
R. Guidry, NY	.688

Earned Run Average
S. McCatty, OAK	2.32
S. Stewart, BAL	2.33
D. Lamp, CHI	2.41
T. John, NY	2.64
B. Burns, CHI	2.64

Wins
P. Vuckovich, MIL	14
D. Martinez, BAL	14
S. McCatty, OAK	14
J. Morris, DET	14
S. McGregor, BAL	13
D. Leonard, KC	13

Saves
R. Fingers, MIL	28
G. Gossage, NY	20
Quisenberry, KC	18
D. Corbett, MIN	17
K. Saucier, DET	13

Strikeouts
L. Barker, CLE	127
B. Burns, CHI	108
B. Blyleven, CLE	107
D. Leonard, KC	107
R. Guidry, NY	104

Complete Games
R. Langford, OAK	18
S. McCatty, OAK	16
J. Morris, DET	15
M. Norris, OAK	12
L. Gura, KC	12

Fewest Hits per 9 Innings
S. McCatty, OAK	6.77
J. Morris, DET	6.95
R. Guidry, NY	7.09

Shutouts
K. Forsch, CAL	4
D. Medich, TEX	4
S. McCatty, OAK	4
R. Dotson, CHI	4

Fewest Walks per 9 Innings
R. Honeycutt, TEX	1.20
K. Forsch, CAL	1.59
D. Leonard, KC	1.83

Most Strikeouts per 9 Inn.
L. Barker, CLE	7.42
R. Guidry, NY	7.37
F. Bannister, SEA	6.32

Innings
D. Leonard, KC	202
J. Morris, DET	198
R. Langford, OAK	195

Games Pitched
D. Corbett, MIN	54
R. Fingers, MIL	47
S. Rawley, SEA	46

	W	L	PCT	GB	R	OR	Batting 2B	3B	HR	BA	SA	SB	Fielding E	DP	FA	Pitching CG	BB	SO	ShO	SV	ERA
EAST																					
MIL	62	47	.569		493	459	173	20	96	.257	.391	39	79	135	.982	11	352	448	4	35	3.91
BAL	59	46	.562	1	429	437	165	11	88	.251	.379	41	68	114	.983	25	347	489	10	23	3.70
NY	59	48	.551	2	421	343	148	22	100	.252	.391	46	72	100	.982	16	287	606	13	30	2.90
DET	60	49	.550	2	427	404	148	29	65	.256	.368	61	67	109	.984	33	373	472	13	22	3.53
BOS	59	49	.546	2.5	519	481	168	17	90	.275	.399	32	91	108	.979	19	354	536	4	24	3.81
CLE	52	51	.505	7	431	442	150	21	39	.263	.351	119	87	91	.978	33	311	569	10	13	3.88
TOR	37	69	.349	23.5	329	466	137	23	61	.226	.330	66	105	102	.975	20	377	451	4	18	3.82
WEST																					
OAK	64	45	.587		458	403	119	26	104	.247	.379	98	81	74	.980	60	370	505	11	10	3.30
TEX	57	48	.543	5	452	389	178	15	49	.270	.369	46	69	102	.984	23	322	488	13	18	3.40
CHI	54	52	.509	8.5	476	423	135	27	76	.272	.387	86	87	113	.979	20	336	529	8	23	3.47
KC	50	53	.485	11	397	405	169	29	61	.267	.383	100	72	94	.982	24	273	404	8	24	3.56
CAL	51	59	.464	13.5	476	453	134	16	97	.256	.380	44	101	120	.977	27	323	426	8	19	3.70
SEA	44	65	.404	20	426	521	148	13	89	.251	.368	100	91	122	.979	10	360	478	5	23	4.23
MIN	41	68	.376	23	378	486	147	36	47	.240	.338	34	96	103	.978	13	376	500	6	22	3.98
					6112	6112	2119	305	1062	.256	.373	912	1166	1487	.980	334	4761	6905	117	304	3.66

First Half

	W	L	PCT	GB
EAST				
NY*	34	22	.607	
BAL	31	23	.574	2
MIL	31	25	.554	3
DET	31	26	.544	3.5
BOS	30	26	.536	4
CLE	26	24	.520	5
TOR	16	42	.276	19

*Defeated Milwaukee in playoff 3 games to 2.

	W	L	PCT	GB
WEST				
OAK*	37	23	.617	
TEX	33	22	.600	1.5
CHI	31	22	.585	2.5
CAL	31	29	.517	6
KC	20	30	.400	12
SEA	21	36	.368	14.5
MIN	17	39	.304	18

*Defeated Kansas City in playoff 3 games to 0.

Second Half

	W	L	PCT	GB
EAST				
MIL	31	22	.585	
BOS	29	23	.558	1.5
DET	29	23	.558	1.5
BAL	28	23	.549	2
CLE	26	27	.491	5
NY	25	26	.490	5
TOR	21	27	.438	7.5
WEST				
KC	30	23	.566	
OAK	27	22	.551	1
TEX	24	26	.480	4.5
MIN	24	29	.453	6
SEA	23	29	.442	6.5
CHI	23	30	.434	7
CAL	20	30	.400	8.5

National League 1982

East

POS	Player	AB	BA	HR	RBI	PO	A	E	DP	TC/G	FA	Pitcher	G	IP	W	L	SV	ERA
1B	K. Hernandez	579	.299	7	94	1586	135	11	140	11.0	.994	J. Andujar	38	266	15	10	0	2.47
2B	T. Herr	493	.266	0	36	263	427	9	97	5.5	.987	B. Forsch	36	233	15	9	1	3.48
SS	O. Smith	488	.248	2	43	279	535	13	101	5.9	.984	S. Mura	35	184	12	11	0	4.05
3B	K. Oberkfell	470	.289	2	34	78	304	11	23	2.9	.972	D. LaPoint	42	153	9	3	0	3.42
RF	G. Hendrick	515	.282	19	104	238	6	5	1	1.9	.980	J. Stuper	23	137	9	7	0	3.36
CF	W. McGee	422	.296	4	56	245	3	11	0	2.2	.958	B. Sutter	70	102	9	8	36	2.90
LF	L. Smith	592	.307	8	69	303	16	10	3	2.2	.970	D. Bair	63	92	5	3	8	2.55
C	D. Porter	373	.231	12	48	469	64	9	8	4.9	.983	J. Kaat	62	75	5	3	2	4.08
UT	M. Ramsey	256	.230	1	21	135	219	10	42		.973							
OF	D. Iorg	238	.294	0	34	99	2	3	0	1.7	.971							
OF	D. Green	166	.283	2	23	111	4	1	1	1.7	.991							

St. L.
W-92 L-70
Whitey Herzog

POS	Player	AB	BA	HR	RBI	PO	A	E	DP	TC/G	FA	Pitcher	G	IP	W	L	SV	ERA
1B	P. Rose	634	.271	3	54	1428	123	8	114	9.6	.995	S. Carlton	38	296	23	11	0	3.10
2B	M. Trillo	549	.271	0	39	343	441	5	101	5.3	.994	Christenson	33	223	9	10	0	3.47
SS	I. DeJesus	536	.239	3	59	216	469	19	80	4.6	.973	M. Krukow	33	208	13	11	0	3.12
3B	M. Schmidt	514	.280	35	87	110	324	23	28	3.1	.950	D. Ruthven	33	204	11	11	0	3.79
RF	G. Vukovich	335	.272	6	42	168	4	4	3	1.7	.977	R. Reed	57	98	5	5	14	2.66
CF	G. Maddox	412	.284	8	61	253	8	2	4	2.4	.992	M. Bystrom	19	89	5	6	0	4.85
LF	G. Matthews	616	.281	19	83	268	14	10	2	1.8	.966	E. Farmer	47	76	2	6	6	4.86
C	B. Diaz	525	.288	18	85	850	80	10	7	6.5	.989	S. Monge	47	72	7	1	2	3.75
OF	B. Dernier	370	.249	4	21	255	5	5	0	2.2	.981	T. McGraw	34	40	3	3	5	4.31

Phi.
W-89 L-73
Pat Corrales

	POS	Player	AB	BA	HR	RBI	PO	A	E	DP	TC/G	FA	Pitcher	G	IP	W	L	SV	ERA
Mon. W-86 L-76 Jim Fanning	1B	A. Oliver	617	.331	22	109	1286	92	19	96	8.8	.986	S. Rogers	35	277	19	8	0	2.40
	2B	D. Flynn	193	.244	0	20	135	157	5	40	5.1	.983	B. Gullickson	34	237	12	14	0	3.57
	SS	C. Speier	530	.257	7	60	291	405	13	76	4.6	.982	S. Sanderson	32	224	12	12	0	3.46
	3B	T. Wallach	596	.268	28	97	132	287	23	23	2.8	.948	C. Lea	27	178	12	10	0	3.24
	RF	W. Cromartie	497	.254	14	62	275	10	6	1	2.1	.979	R. Burris	37	124	4	14	2	4.73
	CF	A. Dawson	608	.301	23	83	419	8	8	2	3.0	.982	J. Reardon	75	109	7	4	26	2.06
	LF	T. Raines	647	.277	4	43	232	7	2	1	2.0	.992	D. Palmer	13	74	6	4	0	3.18
	C	G. Carter	557	.293	29	97	954	104	10	6	7.0	.991	W. Fryman	60	70	9	4	12	3.75
Pit. W-84 L-78 Chuck Tanner	1B	J. Thompson	550	.284	31	101	1395	105	10	114	9.7	.993	R. Rhoden	35	230	11	14	0	4.14
	2B	J. Ray	647	.281	7	63	381	512	21	89	5.6	.977	D. Robinson	38	227	15	13	0	4.28
	SS	D. Berra	529	.263	10	61	238	498	30	77	5.0	.961	J. Candelaria	31	175	12	7	1	2.94
	3B	B. Madlock	568	.319	19	95	92	266	18	23	2.6	.952	M. Sarmiento	35	165	9	4	1	3.39
	RF	L. Lacy	359	.312	5	31	186	7	7	1	1.8	.965	K. Tekulve	85	129	12	8	20	2.87
	CF	O. Moreno	645	.245	3	44	396	10	7	3	2.6	.983	McWilliams	19	122	6	5	1	3.11
	LF	M. Easler	475	.276	15	58	243	8	7	2	1.9	.973	R. Scurry	76	104	4	5	14	1.74
	C	T. Pena	497	.296	11	63	763	89	16	6	6.3	.982	E. Romo	45	87	9	3	1	4.36
	OF	D. Parker	244	.270	6	29	108	2	5	1	1.8	.957							
Chi. W-73 L-89 Lee Elia	1B	B. Buckner	657	.306	15	105	1547	159	12	89	10.7	.993	F. Jenkins	34	217	14	15	0	3.15
	2B	B. Wills	419	.272	6	38	199	297	19	45	5.0	.963	D. Bird	35	191	9	14	0	5.14
	SS	L. Bowa	499	.246	0	29	210	396	17	64	4.5	.973	D. Noles	31	171	10	13	0	4.42
	3B	R. Sandberg	635	.271	7	54	79	278	11	19	2.8	.970	R. Martz	28	148	11	10	1	4.21
	RF	J. Johnstone	269	.249	10	43	154	8	3	0	1.9	.982	A. Ripley	28	123	5	7	0	4.26
	CF	L. Durham	539	.312	22	90	301	11	12	1	2.3	.963	L. Smith	72	117	2	5	17	2.69
	LF	K. Moreland	476	.261	15	68	169	9	2	0	2.1	.989	D. Tidrow	65	104	8	3	6	3.39
	C	J. Davis	418	.261	12	52	598	89	11	11	5.4	.984	B. Campbell	62	100	3	6	8	3.69
	OF	S. Henderson	257	.233	2	29	126	5	6	0	2.0	.956	W. Hernandez	75	75	4	6	10	3.00
	OF	G. Woods	245	.269	4	30	161	6	0	1	1.6	1.000							
	2S	J. Kennedy	242	.219	2	25	137	220	12	35		.967							
	OF	J. Morales	116	.284	4	30	72	5	0	1	1.9	1.000							
N.Y. W-65 L-97 George Bamberger	1B	D. Kingman	535	.204	37	99	1232	69	18	88	9.2	.986	C. Puleo	36	171	9	9	1	4.47
	2B	W. Backman	261	.272	3	22	169	202	14	30	4.4	.964	P. Falcone	40	171	8	10	2	3.84
	SS	R. Gardenhire	384	.240	3	33	234	398	29	68	4.9	.956	C. Swan	37	166	11	7	1	3.35
	3B	H. Brooks	457	.249	2	40	89	237	24	17	2.8	.931	M. Scott	37	147	7	13	3	5.14
	RF	E. Valentine	337	.288	8	48	159	10	3	4	1.8	.983	E. Lynch	43	139	4	8	2	3.55
	CF	M. Wilson	639	.279	5	55	415	12	5	4	2.8	.988	P. Zachry	36	138	6	9	1	4.05
	LF	G. Foster	550	.247	13	70	289	12	8	4	2.2	.974	J. Orosco	54	109	4	10	4	2.72
	C	J. Stearns	352	.293	4	28	379	61	6	9	5.5	.987	R. Jones	28	108	7	10	0	4.60
	UT	B. Bailor	376	.277	0	31	166	272	11	42		.976	N. Allen	50	65	3	7	19	3.06
	C	R. Hodges	228	.246	5	27	362	35	8	4	5.5	.980							
	O1	R. Staub	219	.242	3	27	172	19	2	12		.990							
	OF	J. Youngblood	202	.257	3	21	88	5	3	1	1.5	.969							
	OF	G. Rajsich	162	.259	2	12	60	0	0	0	1.7	1.000							

West

	POS	Player	AB	BA	HR	RBI	PO	A	E	DP	TC/G	FA	Pitcher	G	IP	W	L	SV	ERA
Atl. W-89 L-73 Joe Torre	1B	C. Chambliss	534	.270	20	86	1352	138	10	144	9.9	.993	P. Niekro	35	234	17	4	0	3.61
	2B	G. Hubbard	532	.248	9	59	312	505	14	111	5.8	.983	R. Mahler	39	205	9	10	0	4.21
	SS	R. Ramirez	609	.278	10	52	300	528	38	130	5.5	.956	R. Camp	51	177	11	13	5	3.65
	3B	B. Horner	499	.261	32	97	102	217	10	20	2.4	.970	B. Walk	32	164	11	9	0	4.87
	RF	C. Washington	563	.266	16	80	221	9	12	3	1.7	.950	S. Bedrosian	64	138	8	6	11	2.42
	CF	D. Murphy	598	.281	36	109	407	6	9	2	2.6	.979	G. Garber	69	119	8	10	30	2.34
	LF	B. Butler	240	.217	0	7	129	2	0	0	1.000		K. Dayley	20	71	5	6	0	4.54
	C	B. Benedict	386	.246	3	44	602	73	5	9	5.8	.993							
	UT	J. Royster	261	.295	2	25	105	112	11	20		.952							
	OF	R. Linares	191	.298	2	17	92	4	0	1	1.8	1.000							
	C	B. Pocoroba	120	.275	2	22	143	16	2	4	2.5	.988							
	1B	B. Watson	114	.246	5	22	206	8	0	18	7.9	1.000							
L.A. W-88 L-74 Tom Lasorda	1B	R. Garvey	625	.282	16	86	1539	111	8	132	10.5	.995	F. Valenzuela	37	285	19	13	0	2.87
	2B	S. Sax	638	.282	4	47	347	452	19	83	5.5	.977	J. Reuss	39	255	18	11	0	3.11
	SS	B. Russell	497	.274	3	46	216	502	29	64	5.0	.961	B. Welch	36	236	16	11	0	3.36
	3B	R. Cey	556	.254	24	79	93	320	16	23	2.9	.963	D. Stewart	45	146	9	8	1	3.81
	RF	P. Guerrero	575	.304	32	100	269	11	7	6	2.1	.976	B. Hooton	21	121	4	7	0	4.03
	CF	K. Landreaux	487	.284	7	50	281	3	4	1	2.5	.986	S. Howe	66	99	7	5	13	2.08
	LF	D. Baker	570	.300	23	88	226	7	6	1	1.7	.975	T. Forster	56	83	5	6	3	3.04
	C	M. Scioscia	365	.219	5	38	631	57	10	10	5.7	.986	T. Niedenfuer	55	70	3	4	9	2.71
	OF	R. Monday	210	.257	11	42	62	4	4	0	1.2	.943							
	C	S. Yeager	196	.245	2	18	338	42	4	8	5.1	.990							
S.F. W-87 L-75 Frank Robinson	1B	R. Smith	349	.284	18	56	792	78	16	61	8.9	.982	B. Laskey	32	189	13	12	0	3.14
	2B	J. Morgan	463	.289	14	61	254	364	7	69	5.2	.989	A. Hammaker	29	175	12	8	0	4.11
	SS	J. LeMaster	436	.216	2	30	223	382	23	63	4.8	.963	R. Gale	33	170	7	14	0	4.23
	3B	D. Evans	465	.256	16	61	59	150	15	12	2.7	.933	F. Breining	54	143	11	6	0	3.08
	RF	J. Clark	563	.274	27	103	281	10	6	2	1.9	.980	R. Martin	29	141	7	10	0	4.66
	CF	C. Davis	641	.261	19	76	404	16	12	4	2.8	.972	A. Holland	58	130	7	3	5	3.33
	LF	J. Leonard	278	.259	9	49	135	2	6	0	1.9	.958	J. Barr	53	129	4	3	2	3.29
	C	M. May	395	.263	9	39	552	61	8	5	5.6	.987	G. Minton	78	123	10	4	30	1.83
	3B	T. O'Malley	291	.275	2	27	59	160	8	9	2.7	.965	G. Lavelle	68	105	10	7	8	2.67
	OF	J. Wohlford	250	.256	2	25	122	4	1	0	1.8	.992							
	2B	D. Kuiper	218	.280	0	17	101	124	5	24	4.5	.978							
	C	B. Brenly	180	.283	4	15	265	32	12	2	5.1	.961							

	POS	Player	AB	BA	HR	RBI	PO	A	E	DP	TC/G	FA	Pitcher	G	IP	W	L	SV	ERA
S. D.	1B	B. Perkins	347	.271	2	34	817	64	5	61	9.0	.994	T. Lollar	34	233	16	9	0	3.13
W-81 L-81	2B	T. Flannery	379	.264	0	30	221	260	13	46	4.8	.974	J. Montefusco	32	184	10	11	0	4.00
Dick Williams	SS	G. Templeton	563	.247	6	64	220	422	26	70	4.9	.961	Eichelberger	31	178	7	14	0	4.20
	3B	L. Salazar	524	.242	8	62	104	291	26	28	3.3	.938	E. Show	47	150	10	6	3	2.64
	RF	S. Lezcano	470	.289	16	84	275	16	3	8	2.2	.990	C. Welsh	28	139	8	8	0	4.91
	CF	R. Jones	424	.283	12	61	314	3	5	1	2.8	.984	J. Curtis	26	116	8	6	0	4.10
	LF	G. Richards	521	.286	3	28	200	8	5	1	2.1	.977	D. Dravecky	31	105	5	3	2	2.57
	C	T. Kennedy	562	.295	21	97	666	56	7	11	5.2	.990	L. DeLeon	61	102	9	5	15	2.03
	OF	A. Wiggins	254	.256	1	15	140	8	5	2	2.3	.967	G. Lucas	65	97	1	10	16	3.24
	3O	J. Lefebvre	239	.238	4	21	70	74	3	6		.980	F. Chiffer	51	79	4	3	4	2.95
	OF	T. Gwynn	190	.289	1	17	110	1	1	0	2.2	.991							
	2B	J. Bonilla	182	.280	0	8	99	134	6	26	5.3	.975							
	1B	K. Bevacqua	123	.252	0	24	253	16	3	13	9.1	.989							
Hou.	1B	R. Knight	609	.294	6	70	945	55	10	76	10.5	.990	J. Niekro	35	270	17	12	0	2.47
W-77 L-85	2B	P. Garner	588	.274	13	83	273	429	14	90	5.3	.980	N. Ryan	35	250	16	12	0	3.16
Bill Virdon	SS	D. Thon	496	.276	3	36	177	399	15	80	5.0	.975	D. Sutton	27	195	13	8	0	3.00
W-49 L-62	3B	A. Howe	365	.238	5	38	53	153	6	13	2.9	.972	B. Knepper	33	180	5	15	1	4.45
Bob Lillis	RF	T. Puhl	507	.262	8	50	257	4	3	3	1.9	.989	V. Ruhle	31	149	9	13	1	3.93
W-28 L-23	CF	T. Scott	460	.239	1	29	262	7	5	0	2.1	.982	M. LaCoss	41	115	6	6	0	2.90
	LF	J. Cruz	570	.275	9	68	340	9	13	3	2.3	.964	F. LaCorte	55	76	1	5	7	4.48
	C	A. Ashby	339	.257	12	49	530	55	14	5	6.3	.977	D. Smith	49	63	5	4	11	3.84
	OF	D. Heep	198	.237	4	22	62	2	0	1	1.6	1.000							
	C	L. Pujols	176	.199	4	15	295	39	3	3	5.3	.991							
Cin.	1B	D. Driessen	516	.269	17	57	1239	78	3	123	9.2	.998	M. Soto	35	258	14	13	0	2.79
W-61 L-101	2B	R. Oester	549	.260	9	47	258	325	17	72	5.1	.972	B. Berenyi	34	222	9	18	0	3.36
John McNamara	SS	D. Concepcion	572	.287	5	53	262	459	17	94	5.1	.977	F. Pastore	31	188	8	13	0	3.97
W-34 L-58	3B	J. Bench	399	.258	13	38	54	155	19	10	2.1	.917	B. Shirley	41	153	8	13	0	3.60
Russ Nixon	RF	H. Householder	417	.211	9	34	220	14	2	4	1.8	.992	T. Seaver	21	111	5	13	0	5.50
W-27 L-43	CF	C. Cedeno	492	.289	8	57	301	4	3	2	2.4	.990	C. Leibrandt	36	108	5	7	2	5.10
	LF	E. Milner	407	.268	4	31	215	8	3	1	2.1	.987	J. Kern	50	76	3	5	2	2.84
	C	A. Trevino	355	.251	1	33	725	61	17	7	6.9	.979	J. Price	59	73	3	4	3	2.85
	OF	D. Walker	239	.218	5	22	110	7	1	1	1.7	.992	T. Hume	46	64	2	6	17	3.11
	OF	M. Vail	189	.254	4	29	72	7	1	0	1.5	.988							
	3B	W. Krenchicki	187	.283	2	21	35	93	6	7	1.9	.955							
	O1	L. Biittner	184	.310	2	24	170	14	2	13		.989							
	2B	T. Lawless	165	.212	0	4	87	136	5	35	4.9	.978							

BATTING AND BASE RUNNING LEADERS

Batting Average
A. Oliver, MON	.331
B. Madlock, PIT	.319
L. Durham, CHI	.312
L. Smith, STL	.307
B. Buckner, CHI	.306

Slugging Average
M. Schmidt, PHI	.547
P. Guerrero, LA	.536
L. Durham, CHI	.521
A. Oliver, MON	.514
J. Thompson, PIT	.511

Home Runs
D. Kingman, NY	37
D. Murphy, ATL	36
M. Schmidt, PHI	35
B. Horner, ATL	32
P. Guerrero, LA	32

Total Bases
A. Oliver, MON	317
P. Guerrero, LA	308
D. Murphy, ATL	303
A. Dawson, MON	303
B. Buckner, CHI	290

Runs Batted In
D. Murphy, ATL	109
A. Oliver, MON	109
B. Buckner, CHI	105
G. Hendrick, STL	104
J. Clark, SF	103

Stolen Bases
T. Raines, MON	78
L. Smith, STL	68
O. Moreno, PIT	60
M. Wilson, NY	58
S. Sax, LA	49

Hits
A. Oliver, MON	204
B. Buckner, CHI	201
A. Dawson, MON	183

Base on Balls
M. Schmidt, PHI	107
J. Thompson, PIT	101
K. Hernandez, STL	100

Home Run Percentage
D. Kingman, NY	6.9
M. Schmidt, PHI	6.8
B. Horner, ATL	6.4

Runs Scored
L. Smith, STL	120
D. Murphy, ATL	113
M. Schmidt, PHI	108

Doubles
A. Oliver, MON	43
T. Kennedy, SD	42
A. Dawson, MON	37
R. Knight, HOU	36

Triples
D. Thon, HOU	10
T. Puhl, HOU	9
M. Wilson, NY	9
O. Moreno, PIT	9

PITCHING LEADERS

Winning Percentage
P. Niekro, ATL	.810
S. Rogers, MON	.704
M. Sarmiento, PIT	.692
S. Carlton, PHI	.676
T. Lollar, SD	.640

Earned Run Average
S. Rogers, MON	2.40
J. Niekro, HOU	2.47
J. Andujar, STL	2.47
M. Soto, CIN	2.79
F. Valenzuela, LA	2.87

Wins
S. Carlton, PHI	23
S. Rogers, MON	19
F. Valenzuela, LA	19
J. Reuss, LA	18
P. Niekro, ATL	17
J. Niekro, HOU	17

Saves
B. Sutter, STL	36
G. Minton, SF	30
G. Garber, ATL	30
J. Reardon, MON	26
K. Tekulve, PIT	20

Strikeouts
S. Carlton, PHI	286
M. Soto, CIN	274
N. Ryan, HOU	245
F. Valenzuela, LA	199
S. Rogers, MON	179

Complete Games
S. Carlton, PHI	19
F. Valenzuela, LA	18
J. Niekro, HOU	16
S. Rogers, MON	14
M. Soto, CIN	13

Fewest Hits per 9 Innings
N. Ryan, HOU	7.05
M. Soto, CIN	7.06
C. Lea, MON	7.35

Shutouts
S. Carlton, PHI	6
J. Niekro, HOU	5
J. Andujar, STL	5

Fewest Walks per 9 Innings
D. Bird, CHI	1.41
A. Hammaker, SF	1.44
J. Andujar, STL	1.69

Most Strikeouts per 9 Inn.
M. Soto, CIN	9.57
N. Ryan, HOU	8.81
S. Carlton, PHI	8.71

Innings
S. Carlton, PHI	296
F. Valenzuela, LA	285
S. Rogers, MON	277

Games Pitched
K. Tekulve, PIT	85
G. Minton, SF	78
R. Scurry, PIT	76

	W	L	PCT	GB	R	OR	2B	3B	Batting HR	BA	SA	SB	E	Fielding DP	FA	CG	BB	Pitching SO	ShO	SV	ERA
EAST																					
STL	92	70	.568		685	609	239	52	67	.264	.364	200	124	169	.981	25	502	689	10	47	3.37
PHI	89	73	.549	3	664	654	245	25	112	.260	.376	128	121	138	.981	38	472	1002	13	33	3.61
MON	86	76	.531	6	697	616	270	38	133	.262	.396	156	122	117	.980	34	448	936	10	43	3.31
PIT	84	78	.519	8	724	696	272	40	134	.273	.408	161	145	133	.977	19	521	933	7	39	3.81
CHI	73	89	.451	19	676	709	239	46	102	.260	.375	132	132	110	.979	9	452	764	7	43	3.92
NY	65	97	.401	27	609	723	227	26	97	.247	.350	137	175	134	.972	15	582	759	5	37	3.88
WEST																					
ATL	89	73	.549		739	702	215	22	146	.256	.383	151	137	186	.979	15	502	813	11	51	3.82
LA	88	74	.543	1	691	612	222	32	138	.264	.388	151	139	131	.979	37	468	932	16	28	3.26
SF	87	75	.537	2	673	687	213	30	133	.253	.376	130	173	125	.973	18	466	810	4	45	3.64
SD	81	81	.500	8	675	658	217	52	81	.257	.359	165	152	142	.976	20	502	765	11	41	3.52
HOU	77	85	.475	12	569	620	236	48	74	.247	.349	140	136	154	.978	37	479	899	16	31	3.41
CIN	61	101	.377	28	545	661	228	34	82	.251	.350	131	128	158	.980	22	570	998	7	31	3.66
					7947	7947	2823	445	1299	.258	.373	1782	1684	1697	.978	289	5964	10300	117	469	3.60

American League 1982

East

	POS	Player	AB	BA	HR	RBI	PO	A	E	DP	TC/G	FA	Pitcher	G	IP	W	L	SV	ERA
Mil. W-95 L-67 Buck Rodgers W-23 L-24 Harvey Kuenn W-72 L-43	1B	C. Cooper	654	.313	32	121	1428	98	5	156	9.9	.997	M. Caldwell	35	258	17	13	0	3.91
	2B	J. Gantner	447	.295	4	43	307	398	13	104	5.5	.982	P. Vuckovich	30	224	18	6	0	3.34
	SS	R. Yount	635	.331	29	114	253	489	24	95	5.0	.969	M. Haas	32	193	11	8	1	4.47
	3B	P. Molitor	666	.302	19	71	128	340	29	48	3.3	.942	M. McClure	34	173	12	7	0	4.22
	RF	C. Moore	456	.254	6	45	231	13	3	6	2.1	.988	J. Slaton	39	118	10	6	6	3.29
	CF	G. Thomas	567	.245	39	112	427	11	4	4	2.8	.991	R. Lerch	21	109	8	7	0	4.97
	LF	B. Oglivie	602	.244	34	102	359	15	7	3	2.4	.982	D. Bernard	47	79	3	1	6	3.76
	C	T. Simmons	539	.269	23	97	570	62	3	8	5.2	.995	R. Fingers	50	80	5	6	29	2.60
	DH	R. Howell	300	.260	4	38	0	0	0	0	.0	.000							
	DH	D. Money	275	.284	16	55	0	0	0	0	.0	.000							
	OF	M. Edwards	178	.247	2	14	119	2	2	1	2.3	.984							
Bal. W-94 L-68 Earl Weaver	1B	E. Murray	550	.316	32	110	1269	97	4	106	9.2	.997	D. Martinez	40	252	16	12	0	4.21
	2B	R. Dauer	558	.280	8	57	261	268	7	67	4.4	.987	M. Flanagan	36	236	15	11	0	3.97
	SS	C. Ripken	598	.264	28	93	155	289	13	47	4.9	.972	J. Palmer	36	227	15	5	1	3.13
	3B	G. Gulliver	145	.200	1	5	34	97	4	6	2.7	.970	S. McGregor	37	226	14	12	0	4.61
	RF	D. Ford	421	.235	10	43	263	6	7	2	2.3	.975	S. Stewart	38	139	10	9	5	4.14
	CF	A. Bumbry	562	.262	5	40	404	9	6	1	2.9	.986	S. Davis	29	101	8	4	0	3.49
	LF	J. Lowenstein	322	.320	24	66	202	2	0	0	1.8	1.000	T. Martinez	76	95	8	8	16	3.41
	C	R. Dempsey	344	.256	5	36	491	46	5	8	4.4	.991	T. Stoddard	50	56	3	4	12	4.02
	DH	K. Singleton	561	.251	14	77	0	0	0	0	.0	.000							
	OF	G. Roenicke	393	.270	21	74	288	7	3	0	2.4	.990							
	2S	L. Sakata	343	.259	6	31	182	299	16	61		.968							
	C	J. Nolan	219	.233	6	35	292	22	7	2	4.5	.978							
	OF	B. Ayala	128	.305	6	24	35	0	1	0		.972							
Bos. W-89 L-73 Ralph Houk	1B	D. Stapleton	538	.264	14	65	964	77	9	98	9.9	.991	D. Eckersley	33	224	13	13	0	3.73
	2B	J. Remy	636	.280	0	47	290	432	13	104	4.8	.982	J. Tudor	32	196	13	10	0	3.63
	SS	G. Hoffman	469	.209	7	49	246	439	20	93	4.7	.972	M. Torrez	31	176	9	9	0	5.23
	3B	C. Lansford	482	.301	11	63	83	216	10	19	2.7	.968	B. Stanley	48	168	12	7	14	3.10
	RF	D. Evans	609	.292	32	98	346	9	10	3	2.3	.973	C. Rainey	27	125	7	5	0	5.02
	CF	R. Miller	409	.254	4	38	277	6	5	2	2.3	.983	B. Hurst	28	117	3	7	0	5.77
	LF	J. Rice	573	.309	24	97	273	10	9	3	2.0	.969	M. Clear	55	105	14	9	14	3.00
	C	G. Allenson	264	.205	6	33	454	39	4	8	5.5	.992	T. Burgmeier	40	102	7	0	2	2.29
	DH	Yastrzemski	459	.275	16	72	0	0	0	0	.0	.000	B. Ojeda	22	78	4	6	0	5.63
	13	W. Boggs	338	.349	5	44	488	168	8	51		.988							
	C	R. Gedman	289	.249	4	26	397	29	10	5	5.1	.977							
	OF	R. Nichols	245	.302	7	33	169	9	2	4	2.2	.989							
	DH	T. Perez	196	.260	6	31	0	0	0	0	.0	.000							
Det. W-83 L-79 Sparky Anderson	1B	E. Cabell	464	.261	2	37	548	52	5	62	7.3	.992	J. Morris	37	266	17	16	0	4.06
	2B	L. Whitaker	560	.286	15	65	331	470	10	120	5.4	.988	D. Petry	35	246	15	9	0	3.22
	SS	A. Trammell	489	.258	9	57	259	459	16	97	4.7	.978	M. Wilcox	29	194	12	10	0	3.62
	3B	T. Brookens	398	.231	9	58	72	206	18	20	2.6	.939	J. Ujdur	25	178	10	10	0	3.69
	RF	C. Lemon	436	.266	19	52	242	11	4	2	2.1	.984	P. Underwood	33	99	4	8	3	4.73
	CF	G. Wilson	322	.292	12	34	215	8	3	1	2.8	.987	D. Tobik	51	99	4	9	9	3.56
	LF	L. Herndon	614	.292	23	88	328	11	6	3	2.2	.983	D. Rucker	27	64	5	6	0	3.38
	C	L. Parrish	486	.284	32	87	627	76	8	8	5.4	.989	E. Sosa	38	61	3	3	4	4.43
	DH	M. Ivie	259	.232	14	38	0	0	0	0	.0	.000							
	OF	K. Gibson	266	.278	8	35	167	4	1	3	2.7	.994							
	1B	R. Leach	218	.239	3	12	410	28	2	36	7.9	.995							
	DH	J. Turner	210	.248	8	27	0	0	0	0	.0	.000							
	UT	J. Wockenfuss	193	.301	8	32	228	14	2	9		.992							
	1B	R. Hebner	179	.274	8	18	286	25	3	15		.990							

N. Y.
W-79 L-83
Bob Lemon
W-6 L-8
Gene Michael
W-44 L-42
Clyde King
W-29 L-33

POS	Player	AB	BA	HR	RBI	PO	A	E	DP	TC/G	FA	Pitcher	G	IP	W	L	SV	ERA
1B	J. Mayberry	215	.209	8	27	455	25	2	49	7.7	.996	R. Guidry	34	222	14	8	0	3.81
2B	W. Randolph	553	.280	3	36	352	380	14	100	5.3	.981	T. John	30	187	10	10	0	3.66
SS	R. Smalley	486	.257	20	67	109	238	8	42	4.0	.977	D. Righetti	33	183	11	10	1	3.79
3B	G. Nettles	405	.232	18	55	73	255	23	23	3.1	.934	S. Rawley	47	164	11	10	3	4.06
RF	K. Griffey	484	.277	12	54	282	8	5	2	2.4	.983	M. Morgan	30	150	7	11	0	4.37
CF	J. Mumphrey	477	.300	9	68	336	5	5	2	2.8	.986	G. Frazier	63	112	4	4	1	3.47
LF	D. Winfield	539	.280	37	106	279	17	8	2	2.3	.974	R. May	41	106	6	6	3	2.89
C	R. Cerone	300	.227	5	28	509	25	6	5	6.1	.989	G. Gossage	56	93	4	5	30	2.23
DH	O. Gamble	316	.272	18	57	0	0	0	0	.0	.000	R. Erickson	16	71	4	5	1	4.46
O1	D. Collins	348	.253	3	25	498	28	7	30		.987							
OF	L. Piniella	261	.307	6	37	68	2	0	1		1.000							
C	B. Wynegar	191	.293	3	20	395	17	3	6	6.7*	.993							
DH	B. Murcer	141	.227	7	30	0	0	0	0	.0	.000							

Cle.
W-78 L-84
Dave Garcia

POS	Player	AB	BA	HR	RBI	PO	A	E	DP	TC/G	FA	Pitcher	G	IP	W	L	SV	ERA
1B	M. Hargrove	591	.271	4	65	1293	123	5	110	9.3	.996	L. Barker	33	245	15	11	0	3.90
2B	J. Perconte	219	.237	0	15	131	199	8	23	4.1	.976	R. Sutcliffe	34	216	14	8	1	2.96
SS	M. Fischlin	276	.268	0	21	136	253	12	42	4.0	.970	L. Sorensen	32	189	10	15	0	5.61
3B	T. Harrah	602	.304	25	78	126	279	12	25	2.6	.971	J. Denny	21	138	6	11	0	5.01
RF	V. Hayes	527	.250	14	82	306	9	6	4	2.3	.981	D. Spillner	65	134	12	10	21	2.49
CF	R. Manning	562	.270	8	44	387	10	9	1	2.7	.978	R. Waits	25	115	2	13	0	5.40
LF	M. Dilone	379	.235	3	25	187	3	7	1	2.0	.964	E. Whitson	40	108	4	2	2	3.26
C	R. Hassey	323	.251	5	34	562	38	4	6	5.8	.993	E. Glynn	47	50	5	2	4	4.17
DH	A. Thornton	589	.273	32	116	0	0	0	0	.0	.000							
O2	A. Bannister	348	.267	4	41	206	124	10	22		.971							
UT	L. Milbourne	291	.275	2	25	149	224	14	41		.964							
SS	J. Dybzinski	212	.231	0	22	118	239	16	39	4.8	.957							
C	C. Bando	184	.212	3	16	268	23	3	1	4.7	.990							

Tor.
W-78 L-84
Bobby Cox

POS	Player	AB	BA	HR	RBI	PO	A	E	DP	TC/G	FA	Pitcher	G	IP	W	L	SV	ERA
1B	W. Upshaw	580	.267	21	75	1438	101	17	123	10.0	.989	D. Stieb	38	288	17	14	0	3.25
2B	D. Garcia	597	.310	5	42	273	461	15	94	5.3	.980	J. Clancy	40	267	16	14	0	3.71
SS	A. Griffin	539	.241	1	48	319	479	26	92	5.1	.968	L. Leal	38	250	12	15	0	3.93
3B	R. Mulliniks	311	.244	4	35	60	137	13	13	2.1	.938	J. Gott	30	136	5	10	0	4.43
RF	J. Barfield	394	.246	18	58	217	15	9	4	1.8	.963	D. Murray	56	111	8	7	11	3.16
CF	L. Moseby	487	.236	9	52	361	4	3	0	2.5	.992	R. Jackson	48	97	8	8	6	3.06
LF	B. Bonnell	437	.293	6	49	232	3	5	0	1.9	.979	McLaughlin	44	70	8	6	8	3.21
C	E. Whitt	284	.261	11	42	406	30	8	0	4.5	.982							
DH	W. Nordhagen	185	.270	1	20	0	0	0	0	.0	.000							
3B	G. Iorg	417	.285	1	36	57	155	12	13	2.2	.946							
OF	H. Powell	265	.275	3	26	111	2	3	0	1.5	.974							
C	B. Martinez	260	.242	10	37	382	35	5	8	4.5	.988							
OF	A. Woods	201	.234	3	24	96	2	3	1	1.6	.970							

West

Cal.
W-93 L-69
Gene Mauch

POS	Player	AB	BA	HR	RBI	PO	A	E	DP	TC/G	FA	Pitcher	G	IP	W	L	SV	ERA
1B	R. Carew	523	.319	3	44	1339	94	12	115	10.8	.992	G. Zahn	34	229	18	8	0	3.73
2B	B. Grich	506	.261	19	65	338	450	11	112	5.6	.980	K. Forsch	37	228	13	11	0	3.87
SS	T. Foli	480	.252	3	56	235	432	10	87	4.9	.985	M. Witt	33	180	8	6	0	3.51
3B	D. DeCinces	575	.301	30	97	112	399	21	41	3.5	.961	S. Renko	31	156	11	6	0	4.44
RF	R. Jackson	530	.275	39	101	200	6	6	1	1.5	.972	B. Kison	33	142	10	5	1	3.17
CF	F. Lynn	472	.299	21	86	317	6	3	3	2.5	.991	L. Sanchez	46	93	7	4	5	3.21
LF	B. Downing	623	.281	28	84	321	9	0	0	2.1	1.000	D. Goltz	28	86	8	5	3	4.08
C	B. Boone	472	.256	7	58	650	87	8	8	5.2	.989	D. Corbett	33	57	1	7	8	5.05
DH	D. Baylor	608	.263	24	93	0	0	0	0	.0	.000	D. Aase	24	52	3	3	4	3.46
OF	J. Beniquez	196	.265	3	24	113	4	2	1	1.1	.983	A. Moreno	13	49	3	7	1	4.74

K. C.
W-90 L-72
Dick Howser

POS	Player	AB	BA	HR	RBI	PO	A	E	DP	TC/G	FA	Pitcher	G	IP	W	L	SV	ERA
1B	W. Aikens	466	.281	17	74	1048	75	7	95	8.8	.992	L. Gura	37	248	18	12	0	4.03
2B	F. White	524	.298	11	56	361	389	17	99	5.3	.978	V. Blue	31	181	13	12	0	3.78
SS	U. Washington	437	.286	10	60	173	371	22	63	4.8	.961	P. Splittorff	29	162	10	10	0	4.28
3B	G. Brett	552	.301	21	82	107	294	17	22	3.1	.969	Quisenberry	72	137	9	7	35	2.57
RF	J. Martin	519	.266	15	65	333	4	7	2	2.4	.980	D. Leonard	21	131	10	6	0	5.10
CF	A. Otis	475	.286	11	88	308	5	1	1	2.5	.997	M. Armstrong	52	113	5	5	6	3.20
LF	W. Wilson	585	.332	3	46	376	4	5	0	2.9	.987	B. Black	22	88	4	6	0	4.58
C	J. Wathan	448	.270	3	51	463	38	10	3	4.3	.980	D. Frost	21	82	6	6	0	5.51
DH	H. McRae	613	.308	27	133	0	0	0	0	.0	.000							
S2	O. Concepcion	205	.234	0	15	92	168	11	28		.959							
OF	C. Geronimo	119	.269	4	23	93	3	0	0	2.2	1.000							

Chi.
W-87 L-75
Tony LaRussa

POS	Player	AB	BA	HR	RBI	PO	A	E	DP	TC/G	FA	Pitcher	G	IP	W	L	SV	ERA
1B	M. Squires	195	.267	1	21	512	48	3	59	5.2	.995	L. Hoyt	39	240	19	15	0	3.53
2B	T. Bernazard	540	.256	11	56	353	443	12	116	5.9	.985	R. Dotson	34	197	11	15	0	3.84
SS	B. Almon	308	.256	4	26	164	317	26	72	4.7	.949	D. Lamp	44	190	11	8	5	3.99
3B	A. Rodriguez	257	.241	3	31	78	204	9	19	2.6	.969	J. Koosman	42	173	11	7	3	3.84
RF	H. Baines	608	.271	25	105	326	10	7	4	2.1	.980	B. Burns	28	169	13	5	0	4.04
CF	R. Law	336	.318	3	32	215	2	6	0	2.4	.973	S. Trout	25	120	6	9	0	4.26
LF	S. Kemp	580	.286	19	98	280	6	7	1	1.9	.976	S. Barojas	61	107	6	6	21	3.54
C	C. Fisk	476	.267	14	65	639	62	4	7	5.3	.994	K. Hickey	60	78	4	4	6	3.00
DH	G. Luzinski	583	.292	18	102	0	0	0	0	.0	.000							
1B	T. Paciorek	382	.312	11	55	833	66	6	85	8.9	.993							
S3	V. Law	359	.281	5	54	145	294	23	47		.950							
OF	R. LeFlore	334	.287	4	25	179	7	12	1	2.4	.939							
3B	J. Morrison	166	.223	7	19	19	87	10	10	2.3	.914							

	POS	Player	AB	BA	HR	RBI	PO	A	E	DP	TC/G	FA	Pitcher	G	IP	W	L	SV	ERA
Sea.	1B	G. Gray	269	.257	7	29	476	31	8	36	8.6	.984	F. Bannister	35	247	12	13	0	3.43
W-76 L-86	2B	J. Cruz	549	.242	8	49	320	434	10	98	5.1	.987	G. Perry	32	217	10	12	0	4.40
Rene Lachemann	SS	T. Cruz	492	.230	16	57	215	439	25	98	5.0	.963	J. Beattie	28	172	8	12	0	3.34
	3B	M. Castillo	506	.257	3	49	96	209	20	18	2.5	.938	M. Moore	28	144	7	14	0	5.36
	RF	A. Cowens	560	.270	20	78	280	14	4	1	2.1	.987	G. Nelson	22	123	6	9	0	4.62
	CF	J. Simpson	296	.257	2	23	177	7	3	0	1.9	.984	B. Clark	37	115	5	2	0	2.75
	LF	B. Bochte	509	.297	12	70	161	5	2	1	1.7	.988	B. Caudill	70	96	12	9	26	2.35
	C	R. Sweet	258	.256	4	24	431	26	3	6	5.5	.993	E. Vande Berg	78	76	9	4	5	2.37
	DH	R. Zisk	503	.292	21	62	0	0	0	0	.0	.000	M. Stanton	56	71	2	4	7	4.16
	OF	D. Henderson	324	.253	14	48	249	11	4	4	2.6	.985							
	OF	B. Brown	245	.241	4	17	148	5	5	1	2.3	.968							
	1B	J. Maler	221	.226	4	26	529	41	5	45	10.1	.991							
	UT	P. Serna	169	.225	3	8	63	126	9	23		.955							
	C	J. Essian	153	.275	3	20	282	26	2	1	6.5	.994							
Oak.	1B	D. Meyer	383	.240	8	59	373	31	4	38	7.0	.990	R. Langford	32	237	11	16	0	4.21
W-68 L-94	2B	D. Lopes	450	.242	11	42	289	338	15	82	5.1	.977	M. Keough	34	209	11	18	0	5.72
Billy Martin	SS	F. Stanley	228	.193	2	17	112	223	13	42	3.6	.963	M. Norris	28	166	7	11	0	4.76
	3B	W. Gross	386	.251	9	41	113	182	9	25	2.8	.970	T. Underwood	56	153	10	6	7	3.29
	RF	T. Armas	536	.233	28	89	333	9	6	1	2.6	.983	S. McCatty	21	129	6	3	0	3.99
	CF	D. Murphy	543	.238	27	94	452	14	8	3	3.2	.983	B. Kingman	23	123	4	12	1	4.48
	LF	R. Henderson	536	.267	10	51	379	2	9	0	2.7	.977	B. Owchinko	54	102	2	4	3	5.21
	C	M. Heath	318	.242	3	39	350	50	11	8	4.6	.973	D. Beard	54	92	10	9	11	3.44
	DH	J. Burroughs	285	.277	16	48	0	0	0	0	.0	.000							
	C	J. Newman	251	.199	6	30	320	27	4	5	5.2	.989							
	DH	C. Johnson	214	.238	7	31	0	0	0	0	.0	.000							
	2B	D. McKay	212	.198	4	17	99	116	7	22	3.8	.968							
	1B	J. Rudi	193	.212	5	18	398	20	4	37	8.6	.991							
Tex.	1B	D. Hostetler	418	.232	22	67	1099	48	12	102	10.6	.990	C. Hough	34	228	16	13	0	3.95
W-64 L-98	2B	M. Richardt	402	.241	3	43	234	278	6	68	5.3	.988	F. Tanana	30	194	7	18	0	4.21
Don Zimmer	SS	M. Wagner	179	.240	0	8	77	197	13	32	4.8	.955	R. Honeycutt	30	164	5	17	0	5.27
W-38 L-58	3B	B. Bell	537	.296	13	67	131	396	13	35	3.7	.976	J. Matlack	33	148	7	7	1	3.53
Darrell Johnson	RF	L. Parrish	440	.264	17	62	190	12	8	4	1.7	.962	D. Medich	21	123	7	11	0	5.06
W-26 L-40	CF	G. Wright	557	.264	11	50	398	14	8	3	2.8	.981	D. Schmidt	33	110	4	6	6	3.20
	LF	B. Sample	360	.261	10	29	196	6	4	1	2.3	.981	S. Comer	37	97	1	6	6	5.10
	C	J. Sundberg	470	.251	10	47	607	69	6	15	5.2	.991	D. Darwin	56	89	10	8	7	3.44
	DH	L. Johnson	324	.259	7	38	0	0	0	0	.0	.000							
	OF	J. Grubb	308	.279	3	26	135	4	5	1	1.9	.965							
	2S	D. Flynn	270	.211	0	19	161	254	9	48		.979							
	OF	L. Mazzilli	195	.241	4	17	51	1	3	1		.945							
	UT	B. Stein	184	.239	1	16	72	122	6	28		.970							
Min.	1B	K. Hrbek	532	.301	23	92	1174	88	9	125	9.2	.993	B. Castillo	40	219	13	11	0	3.66
W-60 L-102	2B	J. Castino	410	.241	6	37	193	228	2	63	4.4	.995	B. Havens	33	209	10	14	0	4.31
Billy Gardner	SS	R. Washington	451	.271	5	39	127	186	9	38	3.5	.972	A. Williams	26	154	9	7	0	4.22
	3B	G. Gaetti	508	.230	25	84	106	286	15	35	2.9	.963	F. Viola	22	126	4	10	0	5.21
	RF	T. Brunansky	463	.272	20	46	343	8	5	0	2.8	.986	J. O'Connor	23	126	8	9	0	4.29
	CF	B. Mitchell	454	.249	2	28	350	8	1	3	3.0	.997	T. Felton	48	117	0	13	3	4.99
	LF	G. Ward	570	.289	28	91	343	13	4	3	2.4	.989	R. Davis	63	106	3	9	22	4.42
	C	T. Laudner	306	.255	7	33	454	41	12	5	5.5	.976	P. Redfern	27	94	5	11	0	6.58
	DH	R. Johnson	234	.248	10	33	0	0	0	0	.0	.000							
	OF	M. Hatcher	277	.249	3	26	78	7	1	0		.988							
	SS	L. Faedo	255	.243	3	22	129	218	12	52	4.1	.967							
	1B	J. Vega	199	.266	5	29	106	8	3	9		.974							
	OF	D. Engle	186	.226	4	16	63	3	1	1		.985							

BATTING AND BASE RUNNING LEADERS

Batting Average		Slugging Average	
W. Wilson, KC	.332	R. Yount, MIL	.578
R. Yount, MIL	.331	D. Winfield, NY	.560
R. Carew, CAL	.319	E. Murray, BAL	.549
E. Murray, BAL	.316	D. DeCinces, CAL	.548
C. Cooper, MIL	.313	H. McRae, KC	.542

Home Runs		Total Bases	
R. Jackson, CAL	39	R. Yount, MIL	367
G. Thomas, MIL	39	C. Cooper, MIL	345
D. Winfield, NY	37	H. McRae, KC	332
B. Oglivie, MIL	34	D. Evans, BOS	325
		D. DeCinces, CAL	315

Runs Batted In		Stolen Bases	
H. McRae, KC	133	R. Henderson, OAK	130
C. Cooper, MIL	121	D. Garcia, TOR	54
A. Thornton, CLE	116	J. Cruz, SEA	46
R. Yount, MIL	114	P. Molitor, MIL	41
G. Thomas, MIL	112	W. Wilson, KC	37

PITCHING LEADERS

Winning Percentage		Earned Run Average	
P. Vuckovich, MIL	.750	R. Sutcliffe, CLE	2.96
J. Palmer, BAL	.750	B. Stanley, BOS	3.10
B. Burns, CHI	.722	J. Palmer, BAL	3.13
G. Zahn, CAL	.692	D. Petry, DET	3.22
R. Guidry, NY	.636	D. Stieb, TOR	3.25
R. Sutcliffe, CLE	.636		

Wins		Saves	
L. Hoyt, CHI	19	Quisenberry, KC	35
P. Vuckovich, MIL	18	G. Gossage, NY	30
G. Zahn, CAL	18	R. Fingers, MIL	29
L. Gura, KC	18	B. Caudill, SEA	26
		R. Davis, MIN	22

Strikeouts		Complete Games	
F. Bannister, SEA	209	D. Stieb, TOR	19
L. Barker, CLE	187	J. Morris, DET	17
D. Righetti, NY	163	R. Langford, OAK	15
R. Guidry, NY	162	L. Hoyt, CHI	14
J. Tudor, BOS	146		

BATTING AND BASE RUNNING LEADERS   PITCHING LEADERS

Hits			Base on Balls	
R. Yount, MIL	210		R. Henderson, OAK	116
C. Cooper, MIL	205		D. Evans, BOS	112
P. Molitor, MIL	201		A. Thornton, CLE	109

Fewest Hits per 9 Innings			Shutouts	
R. Sutcliffe, CLE	7.25		D. Stieb, TOR	5
J. Ujdur, DET	7.58		G. Zahn, CAL	4
D. Righetti, NY	7.62		K. Forsch, CAL	4

Home Run Percentage			Runs Scored	
R. Jackson, CAL	7.4		P. Molitor, MIL	136
G. Thomas, MIL	6.9		R. Yount, MIL	129
D. Winfield, NY	6.9		D. Evans, BOS	122

Fewest Walks per 9 Innings			Most Strikeouts per 9 Inn.	
T. John, CAL, NY	1.58		D. Righetti, NY	8.02
D. Eckersley, BOS	1.73		F. Bannister, SEA	7.62
L. Hoyt, CHI	1.80		J. Beattie, SEA	7.31

Doubles			Triples	
H. McRae, KC	46		W. Wilson, KC	15
R. Yount, MIL	46		L. Herndon, DET	13
F. White, KC	45		R. Yount, MIL	12
			J. Mumphrey, NY	10

Innings			Games Pitched	
D. Stieb, TOR	288		E. Vande Berg, SEA	78
J. Clancy, TOR	267		T. Martinez, BAL	76
J. Morris, DET	266		Quisenberry, KC	72

	W	L	PCT	GB	R	OR	2B	3B	Batting HR	BA	SA	SB	E	Fielding DP	FA	CG	BB	Pitching SO	ShO	SV	ERA
EAST																					
MIL	95	67	.586		891	717	277	41	216	.279	.455	84	125	184	.980	34	511	717	6	47	3.98
BAL	94	68	.580	1	774	687	259	27	179	.266	.419	49	101	140	.984	38	488	719	8	34	3.99
BOS	89	73	.549	6	753	713	271	31	136	.274	.407	42	121	172	.981	23	478	816	11	33	4.03
DET	83	79	.512	12	729	685	237	40	177	.266	.418	93	117	164	.981	45	554	740	5	27	3.80
NY	79	83	.488	16	709	716	225	37	161	.256	.398	69	128	157	.979	24	491	939	8	39	3.99
CLE	78	84	.481	17	683	748	225	32	109	.262	.373	151	123	127	.980	31	589	882	9	30	4.11
TOR	78	84	.481	17	651	701	262	45	106	.262	.383	118	136	146	.978	41	493	776	13	25	3.95
WEST																					
CAL	93	69	.574		814	670	268	26	186	.274	.433	55	108	171	.983	40	482	728	10	27	3.82
KC	90	72	.556	3	784	717	295	58	132	.285	.428	133	127	140	.979	16	471	650	12	45	4.08
CHI	87	75	.537	6	786	710	266	52	136	.273	.413	136	154	173	.976	30	460	753	10	41	3.87
SEA	76	86	.469	17	651	712	259	33	130	.254	.381	131	139	157	.978	23	547	1002	11	39	3.88
OAK	68	94	.420	25	691	819	211	27	149	.236	.367	232	160	135	.974	42	648	697	6	22	4.54
TEX	64	98	.395	29	590	749	204	26	115	.249	.359	63	121	168	.981	32	483	690	5	24	4.28
MIN	60	102	.370	33	657	819	234	44	148	.257	.396	38	108	162	.982	26	643	812	7	30	4.72
					10163	10163	3493	519	2080	.264	.402	1394	1768	2196	.980	445	7338	10921	121	463	4.07

National League 1983

	POS	Player	AB	BA	HR	RBI	PO	A	E	DP	TC/G	FA	Pitcher	G	IP	W	L	SV	ERA

East

Phi.
W-90 L-72
Pat Corrales
W-43 L-42
Paul Owens
W-47 L-30

	POS	Player	AB	BA	HR	RBI	PO	A	E	DP	TC/G	FA	Pitcher	G	IP	W	L	SV	ERA
	1B	P. Rose	493	.245	0	45	786	74	9	57	7.8	.990	S. Carlton	37	284	15	16	0	3.11
	2B	J. Morgan	404	.230	16	59	231	331	17	63	4.9	.971	J. Denny	36	243	19	6	0	2.37
	SS	I. DeJesus	497	.254	4	45	214	438	23	64	4.3	.966	C. Hudson	26	169	8	8	0	3.35
	3B	M. Schmidt	534	.255	40	109	107	332	19	29	3.0	.959	M. Bystrom	24	119	6	9	0	4.60
	RF	V. Hayes	351	.265	6	32	165	7	5	0	1.7	.972	K. Gross	17	96	4	6	0	3.56
	CF	G. Maddox	324	.275	4	32	216	1	5	0	2.3	.977	W. Hernandez	63	96	8	4	7	3.29
	LF	G. Matthews	446	.258	10	50	174	11	5	2	1.6	.974	R. Reed	61	96	9	1	8	3.48
	C	B. Diaz	471	.236	15	64	903	97	14	7	7.6	.986	A. Holland	68	92	8	4	25	2.26
	OF	J. Lefebvre	258	.310	8	38	92	4	1	0	1.3	.990							
	1B	T. Perez	253	.241	6	43	514	40	1	36	8.0	.998							
	OF	G. Gross	245	.302	0	29	104	1	1	0	1.0	.991							
	OF	B. Dernier	221	.231	1	15	164	3	2	1	1.0	.988							
	C	O. Virgil	140	.214	6	23	228	24	9	2	5.1	.966							

Pit.
W-84 L-78
Chuck Tanner

	POS	Player	AB	BA	HR	RBI	PO	A	E	DP	TC/G	FA	Pitcher	G	IP	W	L	SV	ERA
	1B	J. Thompson	517	.259	18	76	1266	89	9	131	9.0	.993	R. Rhoden	36	244	13	13	1	3.09
	2B	J. Ray	576	.283	5	53	319	452	13	102	5.2	.983	McWilliams	35	238	15	8	0	3.25
	SS	D. Berra	537	.251	10	52	286	505	30	103	5.1	.963	J. Candelaria	33	198	15	8	0	3.23
	3B	B. Madlock	473	.323	12	68	59	193	11	20	2.1	.958	L. Tunnell	35	178	11	6	0	3.65
	RF	D. Parker	552	.279	12	69	282	3	8	2	2.1	.973	J. DeLeon	15	108	7	3	0	3.63
	CF	M. Wynne	366	.243	7	26	223	3	4	2	2.3	.983	C. Guante	49	100	2	6	9	3.32
	LF	M. Easler	381	.307	10	54	158	6	6	1	1.6	.965	K. Tekulve	76	99	7	5	18	1.64
	C	T. Pena	542	.301	15	70	976	90	9	9	7.2	.992	M. Sarmiento	52	84	3	5	4	2.99
	OF	L. Lacy	288	.302	4	13	167	2	0	0	1.7	1.000	J. Bibby	29	78	5	12	2	6.69
	OF	L. Mazzilli	246	.240	5	24	130	3	2	1	2.4	.985	R. Scurry	61	68	4	9	7	5.56
	3B	R. Hebner	162	.265	5	26	16	43	2	1	1.5	.967							
	UT	J. Morrison	158	.304	6	25	55	99	7	21	.957							
	OF	B. Harper	131	.221	7	20	40	0	0	0	1.1	1.000							

POS	Player	AB	BA	HR	RBI	PO	A	E	DP	TC/G	FA	Pitcher	G	IP	W	L	SV	ERA
Mon. W-82 L-80 Bill Virdon																		
1B	A. Oliver	614	.300	8	84	1207	118	13	93	8.7	.990	S. Rogers	36	273	17	12	0	3.23
2B	D. Flynn	452	.237	0	26	205	290	7	57	4.7	.986	B. Gullickson	34	242	17	12	0	3.75
SS	C. Speier	261	.257	2	22	107	196	12	31	4.3	.962	C. Lea	33	222	16	11	0	3.12
3B	T. Wallach	581	.269	19	70	151	265	19	25	2.8	.956	B. Smith	49	155	6	11	3	2.49
RF	W. Cromartie	360	.278	3	43	208	12	6	2	2.2	.973	R. Burris	40	154	4	7	0	3.68
CF	A. Dawson	633	.299	32	113	435	6	9	2	2.9	.980	J. Reardon	66	92	7	9	21	3.03
LF	T. Raines	615	.298	11	71	307	21	4	3	2.2	.988	S. Sanderson	18	81	6	7	1	4.65
C	G. Carter	541	.270	17	79	847	107	5	14	6.7	.995							
S2	B. Little	350	.260	1	36	181	248	9	44		.979							
O1	T. Francona	230	.257	3	22	172	10	3	10		.984							
St. L. W-79 L-83 Whitey Herzog																		
1B	G. Hendrick	529	.318	18	97	819	77	7	72	9.8	.992	J. Andujar	39	225	6	16	1	4.16
2B	T. Herr	313	.323	2	31	178	245	6	60	5.0	.986	J. Stuper	40	198	12	11	1	3.68
SS	O. Smith	552	.243	3	50	304	519	21	100	5.3	.975	D. LaPoint	37	191	12	9	0	3.95
3B	K. Oberkfell	488	.293	3	38	79	231	13	27	2.5	.960	B. Forsch	34	187	10	12	0	4.28
RF	D. Green	422	.284	8	69	214	10	7	2	1.7	.970	N. Allen	25	122	10	6	0	3.70
CF	W. McGee	601	.286	5	75	385	7	5	1	2.7	.987	B. Sutter	60	89	9	10	21	4.23
LF	L. Smith	492	.321	8	45	225	14	15	4	2.0	.941							
C	D. Porter	443	.262	15	66	578	70	7	8	4.9	.989							
O3	A. Van Slyke	309	.262	8	38	132	54	4	3		.979							
1B	K. Hernandez	218	.284	3	26	581*	51	6*	62*	11.8*	.991							
2S	M. Ramsey	175	.263	1	16	91	140	8	31		.967							
Chi. W-71 L-91 Lee Elia W-54 L-69 Charlie Fox W-17 L-22																		
1B	B. Buckner	626	.280	16	66	1366	161	13	132	10.7	.992	C. Rainey	34	191	14	13	0	4.48
2B	R. Sandberg	633	.261	8	48	330	571	13	126	5.8	.986	S. Trout	34	180	10	14	0	4.65
SS	L. Bowa	499	.267	2	43	230	464	11	102	4.9	.984	F. Jenkins	33	167	6	9	0	4.30
3B	R. Cey	581	.275	24	90	90	270	17	12	2.4	.955	D. Ruthven	25	149	12	9	0	4.10
RF	K. Moreland	533	.302	16	70	236	7	6	1	1.6	.976	B. Campbell	82	122	6	8	8	4.49
CF	M. Hall	410	.283	17	56	239	8	3	2	2.2	.988	N. Noles	24	116	5	10	0	4.72
LF	L. Durham	337	.258	12	55	168	2	6	0	1.9	.966	L. Smith	66	103	4	10	29	1.65
C	J. Davis	510	.271	24	84	730	75	13	7	5.5	.984							
OF	G. Woods	190	.242	4	22	97	4	3	0	1.4	.971							
OF	J. Johnstone	140	.257	6	22	55	3	4	1	1.4	.935							
N. Y. W-68 L-94 George Bamberger W-16 L-30 Frank Howard W-52 L-64																		
1B	K. Hernandez	320	.306	9	37	837*	96	7*	85*	10.4*	.993	T. Seaver	34	231	9	14	0	3.55
2B	B. Giles	400	.245	2	27	299	380	14	87	5.0	.980	M. Torrez	39	222	10	17	0	4.37
SS	J. Oquendo	328	.213	1	17	182	326	21	65	4.6	.960	E. Lynch	30	175	10	10	0	4.28
3B	H. Brooks	586	.251	5	58	107	289	21	25	2.9	.950	W. Terrell	21	134	8	8	0	3.57
RF	D. Strawberry	420	.257	26	74	232	8	4	0	2.1	.984	J. Orosco	62	110	13	7	17	1.47
CF	M. Wilson	638	.276	7	51	422	5	7	1	2.9	.984	D. Sisk	67	104	5	4	11	2.24
LF	G. Foster	601	.241	28	90	314	12	4	3	2.2	.988	S. Holman	35	101	1	7	0	3.74
C	R. Hodges	250	.260	0	21	360	45	12	4	4.3	.971	C. Swan	27	96	2	8	1	5.51
S2	B. Bailor	340	.250	1	30	157	282	16	60		.965	N. Allen	21	54	2	7	2	4.50
OF	D. Heep	253	.253	8	21	90	4	0	1	1.5	1.000							
1B	D. Kingman	248	.198	13	29	443	28	3	43	9.5	.994							
C	J. Ortiz	185	.254	0	12	273	31	11	2	4.7	.965							
PH	R. Staub	115	.296	3	28													

West

POS	Player	AB	BA	HR	RBI	PO	A	E	DP	TC/G	FA	Pitcher	G	IP	W	L	SV	ERA
L. A. W-91 L-71 Tom Lasorda																		
1B	G. Brock	455	.224	20	66	1162	106	12	94	9.1	.991	F. Valenzuela	35	257	15	10	0	3.75
2B	S. Sax	623	.281	5	41	331	399	30	74	5.0	.961	J. Reuss	32	223	12	11	0	2.94
SS	B. Russell	451	.246	1	30	192	392	22	61	4.8	.964	B. Welch	31	204	15	12	0	2.65
3B	P. Guerrero	584	.298	32	103	123	305	30	22	2.9	.934	A. Pena	34	177	12	9	1	2.75
RF	M. Marshall	465	.284	17	65	160	3	4	1	1.5	.976	B. Hooton	33	160	9	8	0	4.22
CF	K. Landreaux	481	.281	17	66	299	4	3	1	2.2	.990	T. Niedenfuer	66	95	8	3	11	1.90
LF	D. Baker	531	.260	15	73	249	4	5	2	1.8	.981	D. Stewart	46	76	5	2	8	2.96
C	S. Yeager	335	.203	15	41	579	63	10	10	5.8	.985	S. Howe	46	69	4	7	18	1.44
OF	D. Thomas	192	.250	2	8	97	3	1	0	1.2	.990							
OF	R. Monday	178	.247	6	20	62	1	2	0	1.5	.969							
C	J. Fimple	148	.250	2	22	336	32	4	2	6.9	.989							
Atl. W-88 L-74 Joe Torre																		
1B	C. Chambliss	447	.280	20	78	1092	89	5	117	9.4	.996	C. McMurtry	36	225	15	9	0	3.08
2B	G. Hubbard	517	.263	12	70	313	484	12	103	5.5	.985	P. Perez	33	215	15	8	0	3.43
SS	R. Ramirez	622	.297	7	58	232	490	39	116	5.0	.949	P. Niekro	34	202	11	10	0	3.97
3B	B. Horner	386	.303	20	68	76	153	10	18	2.3	.958	R. Camp	40	140	10	9	0	3.79
RF	C. Washington	496	.278	9	44	218	8	6	3	1.8	.974	S. Bedrosian	70	120	9	10	19	3.60
CF	D. Murphy	589	.302	36	121	373	10	6	0	2.4	.985	P. Falcone	33	107	9	4	0	3.63
LF	B. Butler	549	.281	5	37	284	13	4	4	2.1	.987	K. Dayley	24	105	5	8	0	4.30
C	B. Benedict	423	.298	2	43	738	91	7	12	6.2	.992	T. Forster	56	79	3	2	13	2.16
UT	J. Royster	268	.235	3	30	112	156	10	29		.996	D. Moore	43	69	2	3	6	3.67
OF	T. Harper	201	.264	3	26	95	5	5	0	1.8	.952	G. Garber	43	61	4	5	9	4.60
1B	B. Watson	149	.309	6	37	280	19	5	23	8.9	.984							

POS	Player	AB	BA	HR	RBI	PO	A	E	DP	TC/G	FA	Pitcher	G	IP	W	L	SV	ERA
Hou. W-85 L-77 Bob Lillis																		
1B	R. Knight	507	.304	9	70	1285	73	9	131	9.6	.993	J. Niekro	38	264	15	14	0	3.48
2B	B. Doran	535	.271	8	39	347	461	17	109	5.4	.979	B. Knepper	35	203	6	13	0	3.19
SS	D. Thon	619	.286	20	79	258	533	28	114	5.3	.966	N. Ryan	29	196	14	9	0	2.98
3B	P. Garner	567	.238	14	79	100	311	24	22	2.8	.945	M. Scott	24	145	10	6	0	3.72
RF	T. Puhl	465	.292	8	44	220	4	2	1	1.8	.991	M. LaCoss	38	138	5	7	1	4.43
CF	O. Moreno	405	.242	0	25	251	8	6	3	2.7	.977	V. Ruhle	41	115	8	5	3	3.69
LF	J. Cruz	594	.318	14	92	322	9	7	1	2.1	.979	M. Madden	28	95	9	5	0	3.14
C	A. Ashby	275	.229	8	34	435	56	13	2	5.9	.974	B. Dawley	48	80	6	6	14	2.82
OF	K. Bass	195	.236	2	18	68	1	4	1	1.4	.945	D. Smith	42	73	3	1	6	3.10
OF	T. Scott	186	.226	2	17	89	2	0	1	1.5	1.000	F. DiPino	53	71	3	4	20	2.65
S. D. W-81 L-81 Dick Williams																		
1B	S. Garvey	388	.294	14	59	888	49	6	69	9.4	.994	E. Show	35	201	15	12	0	4.17
2B	J. Bonilla	556	.237	4	45	335	414	11	90	5.1	.986	D. Dravecky	28	184	14	10	0	3.58
SS	G. Templeton	460	.263	3	40	219	355	24	66	4.9	.960	T. Lollar	30	176	7	12	0	4.61
3B	L. Salazar	481	.258	14	45	102	250	19	17	3.1	.949	E. Whitson	31	144	5	7	1	4.30
RF	S. Lezcano	317	.233	8	49	171	6	6	1	2.0	.968	A. Hawkins	21	120	5	7	0	2.93
CF	R. Jones	335	.233	12	49	249	3	5	2	2.3	.981	M. Thurmond	21	115	7	3	0	2.65
LF	A. Wiggins	503	.276	0	22	242	6	2	1	2.4	.992	L. DeLeon	63	111	6	6	13	2.68
C	T. Kennedy	549	.284	17	98	782	79	12	8	6.1	.986	J. Montefusco	31	95	9	4	4	3.30
OF	T. Gwynn	304	.309	1	37	163	9	1	1	2.1	.994	G. Lucas	62	91	5	8	17	2.87
OF	G. Richards	233	.275	3	22	96	2	2	0	1.9	.980	S. Monge	47	69	7	3	7	3.15
OF	B. Brown	225	.267	5	22	103	1	4	0	2.0	.963							
32	T. Flannery	214	.234	3	19	58	148	4	19		.981							
UT	K. Bevacqua	156	.244	2	24	207	28	2	16		.992							
S. F. W-79 L-83 Frank Robinson																		
1B	D. Evans	523	.277	30	82	979	88	7	60	9.5	.993	F. Breining	32	203	11	12	0	3.82
2B	B. Wellman	182	.214	1	16	91	160	9	26	3.5	.965	M. Krukow	31	184	11	11	0	3.95
SS	J. LeMaster	534	.240	6	30	215	402	23	58	4.6	.964	A. Hammaker	23	172	10	9	0	2.25
3B	T. O'Malley	410	.259	5	45	70	213	18	12	2.6	.940	B. Laskey	25	148	13	10	0	4.19
RF	J. Clark	492	.268	20	66	249	17	9	3	2.1	.967	McGaffigan	43	134	3	9	2	4.29
CF	C. Davis	486	.233	11	59	357	7	9	1	2.8	.976	M. Davis	20	111	6	4	0	3.49
LF	J. Leonard	516	.279	21	87	253	17	7	2	2.0	.975	G. Minton	73	107	7	11	22	3.54
C	B. Brenly	281	.224	7	34	403	70	8	9	5.3	.983	J. Barr	53	93	5	3	2	3.98
UT	J. Youngblood	373	.292	17	53	147	182	19	28		.945	G. Lavelle	56	87	7	4	20	2.59
OF	M. Venable	228	.219	6	27	141	5	1	0	2.2	.993							
C	M. May	186	.247	6	20	285	32	6	5	5.8	.981							
2B	D. Kuiper	176	.250	0	14	107	140	3	17	3.9	.988							
1B	D. Bergman	140	.286	6	24	291	27	2	20	6.4	.994							
Cin. W-74 L-88 Russ Nixon																		
1B	D. Driessen	386	.277	12	57	917	71	4	73	8.9	**.996**	M. Soto	34	274	17	13	0	2.70
2B	R. Oester	549	.264	11	58	315	413	17	80	4.8	.977	B. Berenyi	32	186	9	14	0	3.86
SS	D. Concepcion	528	.233	1	47	225	376	13	67	4.4	.979	F. Pastore	36	184	9	12	0	4.88
3B	N. Esasky	302	.265	12	46	53	133	13	11	2.4	.935	J. Price	21	144	10	6	0	2.88
RF	Householder	380	.255	6	43	221	5	2	0	2.0	**.991**	C. Puleo	27	144	6	12	0	4.89
CF	E. Milner	502	.261	9	33	392	9	4	0	2.9	.990	T. Power	49	111	5	6	2	4.54
LF	G. Redus	453	.247	17	51	235	11	7	0	2.1	.972	B. Scherrer	73	92	2	3	10	2.74
C	D. Bilardello	298	.238	9	38	494	72	5	4	5.4	.991	R. Gale	33	90	4	6	1	5.82
OF	C. Cedeno	332	.232	9	39	138	5	1	1	2.0	.993	B. Hayes	60	69	4	6	7	6.49
31	J. Bench	310	.255	12	54	275	72	9	26		.975	T. Hume	48	66	3	5	9	4.77
OF	D. Walker	225	.236	2	29	104	4	5	0	1.9	.956							
C	A. Trevino	167	.216	1	13	359	28	5	2	6.2	.987							

BATTING AND BASE RUNNING LEADERS

Batting Average

B. Madlock, PIT	.323
L. Smith, STL	.321
J. Cruz, HOU	.318
G. Hendrick, STL	.318
R. Knight, HOU	.304

Slugging Average

D. Murphy, ATL	.540
A. Dawson, MON	.539
P. Guerrero, LA	.531
M. Schmidt, PHI	.524
D. Evans, SF	.516

Home Runs

M. Schmidt, PHI	40
D. Murphy, ATL	36
P. Guerrero, LA	32
A. Dawson, MON	32
D. Evans, SF	30

Total Bases

A. Dawson, MON	341
D. Murphy, ATL	318
P. Guerrero, LA	310
D. Thon, HOU	283
M. Schmidt, PHI	280

Runs Batted In

D. Murphy, ATL	121
A. Dawson, MON	113
M. Schmidt, PHI	109
P. Guerrero, LA	103
T. Kennedy, SD	98

Stolen Bases

T. Raines, MON	90
A. Wiggins, SD	66
S. Sax, LA	56
M. Wilson, NY	54
L. Smith, STL	43

Hits

J. Cruz, HOU	189
A. Dawson, MON	189
R. Ramirez, ATL	185

Base on Balls

M. Schmidt, PHI	128
J. Thompson, PIT	99
T. Raines, MON	97

PITCHING LEADERS

Winning Percentage

J. Denny, PHI	.760
J. Candelaria, PIT	.652
McWilliams, PIT	.652
P. Perez, ATL	.652
L. Tunnell, PIT	.647

Earned Run Average

A. Hammaker, SF	2.25
J. Denny, PHI	2.37
B. Welch, LA	2.65
M. Soto, CIN	2.70
A. Pena, LA	2.75

Wins

J. Denny, PHI	19
B. Gullickson, MON	17
S. Rogers, MON	17
M. Soto, CIN	17
C. Lea, MON	16

Saves

L. Smith, CHI	29
A. Holland, PHI	25
G. Minton, SF	22
B. Sutter, STL	21
J. Reardon, MON	21

Strikeouts

S. Carlton, PHI	275
M. Soto, CIN	242
McWilliams, PIT	199
F. Valenzuela, LA	189
N. Ryan, HOU	183

Complete Games

M. Soto, CIN	18
S. Rogers, MON	13
B. Gullickson, MON	10
D. Dravecky, SD	9
F. Valenzuela, LA	9
J. Niekro, HOU	9

Fewest Hits per 9 Innings

N. Ryan, HOU	6.14
M. Soto, CIN	6.81
B. Welch, LA	7.24

Shutouts

S. Rogers, MON	5
C. Lea, MON	4
McWilliams, PIT	4
F. Valenzuela, LA	4

BATTING AND BASE RUNNING LEADERS

PITCHING LEADERS

Home Run Percentage
M. Schmidt, PHI	7.5
D. Murphy, ATL	6.1
D. Evans, SF	5.7

Runs Scored
T. Raines, MON	133
D. Murphy, ATL	131
M. Schmidt, PHI	104
A. Dawson, MON	104

Fewest Walks per 9 Innings
A. Hammaker, SF	1.67
D. Ruthven, CHI, PHI	1.87
J. Denny, PHI	1.97

Most Strikeouts per 9 Inn.
S. Carlton, PHI	8.72
N. Ryan, HOU	8.39
M. Soto, CIN	7.96

Doubles
J. Ray, PIT	38
A. Oliver, MON	38
B. Buckner, CHI	38

Triples
B. Butler, ATL	13
O. Moreno, HOU	11
D. Green, STL	10
A. Dawson, MON	10

Innings
S. Carlton, PHI	284
M. Soto, CIN	274
S. Rogers, MON	273

Games Pitched
B. Campbell, CHI	82
K. Tekulve, PIT	76
W. Hernandez, CHI, PHI	74

	W	L	PCT	GB	R	OR	2B	3B	HR	BA	SA	SB	E	DP	FA	CG	BB	SO	ShO	SV	ERA
EAST																					
PHI	90	72	.556		696	635	209	45	125	.249	.373	143	152	117	.976	20	464	1092	10	41	3.34
PIT	84	78	.519	6	659	648	238	29	121	.264	.383	124	115	165	.982	25	563	1061	14	41	3.55
MON	82	80	.506	8	677	646	297	41	102	.264	.386	138	116	130	.981	38	479	899	15	34	3.58
STL	79	83	.488	11	679	710	262	63	83	.270	.384	207	152	173	.976	22	525	709	10	27	3.79
CHI	71	91	.438	19	701	719	272	42	140	.261	.401	84	115	164	.982	9	498	807	10	42	4.07
NY	68	94	.420	22	575	680	172	26	112	.241	.344	141	151	171	.976	18	615	717	7	33	3.68
WEST																					
LA	91	71	.562		654	609	197	34	146	.250	.379	166	168	132	.974	27	495	1000	12	40	3.10
ATL	88	74	.543	3	746	640	218	45	130	.272	.400	146	137	176	.978	18	540	895	4	48	3.67
HOU	85	77	.525	6	643	646	239	60	97	.257	.375	164	147	165	.977	22	570	904	14	48	3.45
SD	81	81	.500	10	653	653	207	34	93	.250	.351	179	129	135	.979	23	528	850	5	44	3.62
SF	79	83	.488	12	687	697	206	30	142	.247	.375	140	171	109	.973	20	520	881	9	47	3.70
CIN	74	88	.457	17	623	710	236	35	107	.239	.356	154	114	121	.981	34	627	934	5	29	3.98
					7993	7993	2753	484	1398	.255	.376	1786	1667	1758	.978	276	6424	10749	115	474	3.63

American League 1983

POS	Player	AB	BA	HR	RBI	PO	A	E	DP	TC/G	FA	Pitcher	G	IP	W	L	SV	ERA

East

Bal. W-98 L-64 Joe Altobelli

POS	Player	AB	BA	HR	RBI	PO	A	E	DP	TC/G	FA	Pitcher	G	IP	W	L	SV	ERA
1B	E. Murray	582	.306	33	111	1393	114	10	136	9.9	.993	S. McGregor	36	260	18	7	0	3.18
2B	R. Dauer	459	.235	5	41	273	322	7	78	4.6	.988	S. Davis	34	200	13	7	0	3.59
SS	C. Ripken	663	.318	27	102	272	534	25	113	5.1	.970	M. Boddicker	27	179	16	8	0	2.77
3B	T. Cruz	221	.208	3	27	49	162	13	19	2.8	.942	D. Martinez	32	153	7	16	0	5.53
RF	D. Ford	407	.280	9	55	218	2	3	0	2.2	.987	S. Stewart	58	144	9	4	7	3.62
CF	J. Shelby	325	.258	5	27	200	9	4	3	1.9	.981	M. Flanagan	20	125	12	4	0	3.30
LF	J. Lowenstein	310	.281	15	60	155	8	3	1	1.6	.982	T. Martinez	65	103	9	3	21	2.35
C	R. Dempsey	347	.231	4	32	591	65	2	7	5.1	.997	T. Stoddard	47	58	4	3	9	6.09
DH	K. Singleton	507	.276	18	84						.0							
OF	A. Bumbry	378	.275	3	31	235	3	3	1	2.3	.988							
OF	G. Roenicke	323	.260	19	64	159	7	3	0	1.7	.982							
3B	L. Hernandez	203	.246	6	26	44	109	13	3	2.6	.922							
OF	J. Dwyer	196	.286	8	38	85	1	3	1	1.6	.966							
C	J. Nolan	184	.277	5	24	223	16	5	2	3.8	.980							

Det. W-92 L-70 Sparky Anderson

POS	Player	AB	BA	HR	RBI	PO	A	E	DP	TC/G	FA	Pitcher	G	IP	W	L	SV	ERA
1B	E. Cabell	392	.311	5	46	830	79	3	76	8.6	.997	J. Morris	37	294	20	13	0	3.34
2B	L. Whitaker	643	.320	12	72	299	447	13	92	4.7	.983	D. Petry	38	266	19	11	0	3.92
SS	A. Trammell	505	.319	14	66	236	367	13	71	4.4	.970	M. Wilcox	26	186	11	10	0	3.97
3B	T. Brookens	332	.214	6	32	54	164	17	21	2.3	.928	J. Berenguer	37	158	9	5	1	3.14
RF	G. Wilson	503	.268	11	65	225	12	3	2	1.7	.988	A. Lopez	57	115	9	8	18	2.81
CF	C. Lemon	491	.255	24	69	406	6	5	3	2.9	.988	D. Rozema	29	105	8	3	2	3.43
LF	L. Herndon	603	.302	20	92	283	6	15	1	2.3	.951	H. Bailey	33	72	5	5	0	4.88
C	L. Parrish	605	.269	27	114	695	73	4	8	5.9	.995	D. Bair	27	56	7	3	4	3.88
DH	K. Gibson	401	.227	15	51						.0							
UT	J. Wockenfuss	245	.269	9	44	225	21	2	10		.992							
1B	R. Leach	242	.248	3	26	447	45	3	37	6.8	.994							
OF	J. Grubb	134	.254	4	22	34	1	0	0		1.000							

N. Y. W-91 L-71 Billy Martin

POS	Player	AB	BA	HR	RBI	PO	A	E	DP	TC/G	FA	Pitcher	G	IP	W	L	SV	ERA
1B	K. Griffey	458	.306	11	46	830	57	7	82	8.9	.992	R. Guidry	31	250	21	9	0	3.42
2B	W. Randolph	420	.279	2	38	265	298	12	77	5.5	.979	S. Rawley	34	238	14	14	1	3.78
SS	R. Smalley	451	.275	18	62	125	230	15	40	4.1	.959	D. Righetti	31	217	14	8	0	3.44
3B	G. Nettles	462	.266	20	75	78	273	16	18	2.9	.956	G. Frazier	61	115	4	4	8	3.43
RF	S. Kemp	373	.241	12	49	215	5	3	3	2.2	.987	B. Shirley	25	108	5	8	0	5.08
CF	J. Mumphrey	267	.262	7	36	227	7	4	1	2.9	.983	R. Fontenot	15	97	8	2	0	3.33
LF	D. Winfield	598	.283	32	116	313	5	7	2	2.2	.978	G. Gossage	57	87	13	5	22	2.27
C	B. Wynegar	301	.296	6	42	480	29	8	4	5.6	.985							
DH	D. Baylor	534	.303	21	85						.0							
SS	A. Robertson	322	.248	1	22	91	242	14	49	4.4	.960							
O1	D. Mattingly	279	.283	4	32	350	15	3	31		.992							
C	R. Cerone	246	.220	2	22	412	18	4	2	5.6	.991							
OF	O. Gamble	180	.261	7	26	64	1	4	1		.942							

POS	Player	AB	BA	HR	RBI	PO	A	E	DP	TC/G	FA	Pitcher	G	IP	W	L	SV	ERA
Tor. W-89 L-73 Bobby Cox																		
1B	W. Upshaw	579	.306	27	104	1294	117	21	131	9.0	.985	D. Stieb	36	278	17	12	0	3.04
2B	D. Garcia	525	.307	3	38	266	360	12	75	4.9	.981	J. Clancy	34	223	15	11	0	3.91
SS	A. Griffin	528	.250	4	47	280	413	25	84	4.6	.965	L. Leal	35	217	13	12	0	4.31
3B	R. Mulliniks	364	.275	10	49	70	161	7	12	2.1	.971	J. Gott	34	177	9	14	0	4.74
RF	J. Barfield	388	.253	27	68	213	16	8	4	2.0	.966	D. Alexander	17	117	7	6	0	3.93
CF	L. Moseby	539	.315	18	81	399	10	7	1	2.8	.983	R. Jackson	49	92	8	3	7	4.50
LF	D. Collins	402	.271	1	34	251	8	3	1	2.3	.989	McLaughlin	50	65	7	4	9	4.45
C	E. Whitt	344	.256	17	56	554	50	5	5	5.1	.992	R. Moffitt	45	57	6	2	10	3.77
DH	C. Johnson	407	.265	22	76					.0								
OF	B. Bonnell	377	.318	10	54	212	7	3	0	1.9	.986							
32	G. Iorg	375	.275	2	39	105	223	9	31		.973							
DH	J. Orta	245	.237	10	38					.0								
C	B. Martinez	221	.253	10	33	331	25	4	3	4.2	.989							
Mil. W-87 L-75 Harvey Kuenn																		
1B	C. Cooper	661	.307	30	**126**	1452	87	11	**144**	9.8	.993	M. Caldwell	32	228	12	11	0	4.53
2B	J. Gantner	603	.282	11	74	374	**512**	14	**128**	5.7	.984	D. Sutton	31	220	8	13	0	4.08
SS	R. Yount	578	.308	17	80	256	420	19	86	5.0	.973	M. Haas	25	179	13	3	0	3.27
3B	P. Molitor	608	.270	15	47	105	343	16	37	3.2	.966	B. McClure	24	142	9	9	0	4.50
RF	C. Moore	529	.284	2	49	301	9	7	1	2.1	.978	C. Porter	25	134	7	9	0	4.50
CF	R. Manning	375	.229	3	33	325*	1	3	0	3.0		J. Slaton	46	112	14	6	5	4.33
LF	B. Oglivie	411	.280	13	66	259	8	4	1	2.4	.985	T. Tellmann	44	100	6	3		2.80
C	T. Simmons	600	.308	13	108	395	41	11	4	5.2	.975	P. Ladd	44	49	3	4	25	2.55
DH	R. Howell	194	.278	4	25					.0								
C	N. Yost	196	.224	6	28	252	16	8	2	4.5	.971							
OF	M. Brouhard	185	.276	7	23	112	1	1	0	2.7	.991							
OF	G. Thomas	164	.183	5	18	126	0	1	0	2.8	.992							
Bos. W-78 L-84 Ralph Houk																		
1B	D. Stapleton	542	.247	10	66	1242	95	9	129	9.3	.993	J. Tudor	34	242	13	12	0	4.09
2B	J. Remy	592	.275	0	43	295	376	7	104	4.7	.990	B. Hurst	33	211	12	12	0	4.09
SS	G. Hoffman	473	.260	4	41	240	417	26	82	4.8	.962	D. Eckersley	28	176	9	13	0	5.61
3B	W. Boggs	582	.361	5	74	118	368	27	40	3.4	.947	B. Ojeda	29	174	12	7	0	4.04
RF	D. Evans	470	.238	22	58	222	6	3	1	2.3	.987	B. Stanley	64	145	8	10	33	2.85
CF	T. Armas	574	.218	36	107	326	5	5	0	2.9	.985	M. Brown	19	104	6	6	0	4.67
LF	J. Rice	626	.305	39	126	339	21	6	5	2.4	.984	O. Boyd	15	99	4	8	0	3.28
C	G. Allenson	230	.230	3	30	393	29	7	6	5.1	.984	M. Clear	48	96	4	5	4	6.28
DH	Yastrzemski	380	.266	10	56					.0		L. Aponte	34	62	5	4	3	3.63
OF	R. Nichols	274	.285	6	22	168	4	1	1	2.4	.994							
OF	R. Miller	262	.286	2	21	141	4	1	1	2.2	.993							
C	R. Gedman	204	.294	2	18	274	26	6	5	4.4	.980							
Cle. W-70 L-92 Mike Ferraro W-40 L-60 Pat Corrales W-30 L-32																		
1B	M. Hargrove	469	.286	3	57	1098	115	7	131	9.3	.994	R. Sutcliffe	36	243	17	11	0	4.29
2B	M. Trillo	320	.272	1	29	172	269	5	58	5.1	.989	L. Sorensen	36	223	12	11	0	4.24
SS	J. Franco	560	.273	8	80	247	438	28	92	4.8	.961	B. Blyleven	24	156	7	10	0	3.91
3B	T. Harrah	526	.266	9	53	101	273	11	32	2.8	**.971**	N. Heaton	39	149	11	7	7	4.16
RF	G. Vukovich	312	.247	3	44	203	3	3	0	1.7	.986	L. Barker	24	150	8	13	0	5.11
CF	G. Thomas	371	.221	17	51	313	7	6	2	3.1	.982	Eichelberger	28	134	4	11	0	4.90
LF	A. Bannister	377	.265	5	45	148	7	5	2	1.8	.969	D. Spillner	60	92	2	9	8	5.07
C	R. Hassey	341	.270	6	42	514	43	3	4	5.0	.995	B. Anderson	39	68	1	6	7	4.08
DH	A. Thornton	508	.281	17	77					.0								
OF	P. Tabler	430	.291	6	65	180	4	10	0	2.4	.948							
OF	B. McBride	230	.291	1	18	81	4	2	1	1.9	.977							
2B	M. Fischlin	225	.209	2	23	151	179	12	46	4.8	.965							
OF	R. Manning	194	.278	1	10	146*	1	2	0	3.0								
UT	B. Perkins	184	.272	0	24	148	6	2	12		.987							

West

POS	Player	AB	BA	HR	RBI	PO	A	E	DP	TC/G	FA	Pitcher	G	IP	W	L	SV	ERA
Chi. W-99 L-63 Tony LaRussa																		
1B	M. Squires	153	.222	1	11	515	40	2	55	4.5	**.996**	L. Hoyt	36	261	**24**	10	0	3.66
2B	J. Cruz	525	.251	1	40	213	298	9	71	5.4	.983	R. Dotson	35	240	22	7	0	3.23
SS	J. Dybzinski	256	.230	1	32	140	252	14	47	3.4	.966	F. Bannister	34	217	16	10	0	3.35
3B	V. Law	408	.243	4	42	91	309	14	28	3.0	.966	B. Burns	29	174	10	11	0	3.58
RF	H. Baines	596	.280	20	99	312	10	9	3	2.1	.973	J. Koosman	37	170	11	7	2	4.77
CF	R. Law	501	.283	3	34	302	5	2	2	2.3	**.994**	D. Lamp	49	116	7	7	15	3.71
LF	R. Kittle	520	.254	35	100	234	7	9	0	1.8	.964	D. Tidrow	50	92	4	4	7	4.22
C	C. Fisk	488	.289	26	86	709	46	7	5	5.7	.991	S. Barojas	52	87	3	3	12	2.47
DH	G. Luzinski	502	.255	32	95					.0		J. Agosto	39	42	2	2	7	4.10
1O	T. Paciorek	420	.307	9	63	629	38	1	42		.999							
1B	G. Walker	307	.270	10	55	426	19	7	40	7.7	.985							
SS	S. Fletcher	262	.237	3	31	107	275	14	52	4.0	.965							
2B	T. Bernazard	233	.262	2	26	96	189	7	38	4.9	.976							
OF	J. Hairston	126	.294	5	22	29	1		0	1.0	.968							
K. C. W-79 L-83 Dick Howser																		
1B	W. Aikens	410	.302	23	72	884	64	11	101	8.6	.989	L. Gura	34	200	11	**18**	0	4.90
2B	F. White	549	.260	11	77	390	442	8	123	5.8	**.990**	B. Black	24	161	10	7	0	3.79
SS	U. Washington	547	.236	5	41	201	448	36	91	4.9	.947	P. Splittorff	27	156	13	8	0	3.63
3B	G. Brett	464	.310	25	93	85	188	24	25	2.9	.919	Quisenberry	69	139	5	3	45	1.94
RF	A. Otis	356	.261	4	41	233	6	1	1	2.5	.996	S. Renko	25	121	6	11	1	4.30
CF	W. Wilson	576	.276	2	33	354	9	9	0	2.7	.975	M. Armstrong	58	103	10	7	3	3.86
LF	P. Sheridan	333	.270	7	36	237	6	3	2	2.5	.988							
C	J. Wathan	437	.245	2	32	360	32	6	5	4.3	.985							
DH	H. McRae	589	.311	12	82					.0								
C	D. Slaught	276	.312	0	28	299	18	12	7	4.2	.964							
UT	O. Concepcion	219	.242	0	20	92	175	15	35		.947							
OF	L. Roberts	213	.258	8	24	139	3	3	0	1.9	.979							

	POS	Player	AB	BA	HR	RBI	PO	A	E	DP	TC/G	FA	Pitcher	G	IP	W	L	SV	ERA
Tex. W-77 L-85 Doug Rader	1B	P. O'Brien	524	.237	8	53	1144	**120**	9	104	9.6	.993	C. Hough	34	252	15	13	0	3.18
	2B	W. Tolleson	470	.260	3	20	246	315	16	69	5.2	.972	M. Smithson	33	223	10	14	0	3.91
	SS	B. Dent	417	.237	2	34	150	369	11	71	4.1	**.979**	D. Darwin	28	183	8	13	0	3.49
	3B	B. Bell	618	.277	14	66	123	**383**	17	29	**3.4**	.967	R. Honeycutt	25	175	14	8	0	**2.42**
	RF	L. Parrish	555	.272	26	88	215	11	9	1	1.8	.962	F. Tanana	29	159	7	9	0	3.16
	CF	G. Wright	634	.276	18	80	460	6	7	1	2.9	.985	J. Butcher	36	123	6	6	5	3.51
	LF	B. Sample	554	.274	12	57	329	8	4	0	2.3	.988	O. Jones	42	67	3	6	10	3.09
	C	J. Sundberg	378	.201	2	28	618	56	5	2	5.2	.993	D. Tobik	27	44	2	1	9	3.68
	DH	D. Hostetler	304	.220	11	46						.0							
	OF	M. Rivers	309	.285	1	20	48	1	1	1	0	.980							
	UT	B. Stein	232	.310	2	33	222	103	5	40		.985							
	C	B. Johnson	175	.211	5	16	252	15	0	4	4.3	1.000							
Oak. W-74 L-88 Steve Boros	1B	W. Gross	339	.233	12	44	426	21	2	41	6.1	.996	C. Codiroli	37	206	12	12	1	4.46
	2B	D. Lopes	494	.277	17	67	254	278	9	81	4.4	.983	S. McCatty	38	167	6	9	5	3.99
	SS	T. Phillips	412	.248	4	35	112	257	23	59	3.9	.941	T. Conroy	39	162	7	10	0	3.94
	3B	C. Lansford	299	.308	10	45	60	163	10	19	3.0	.957	T. Underwood	51	145	9	7	4	4.04
	RF	M. Davis	443	.275	8	62	278	16	8	4	2.5	.974	B. Krueger	17	110	7	6	0	3.61
	CF	D. Murphy	471	.227	17	75	365	7	8	0	3.1	.979	T. Burgmeier	49	96	6	7	4	2.81
	LF	R. Henderson	513	.292	9	48	349	9	3	1	2.5	.992	K. Atherton	29	68	2	5	4	2.77
	C	B. Kearney	298	.255	8	32	437	41	9	5	4.8	.982	D. Beard	43	61	5	5	10	5.61
	DH	J. Burroughs	401	.269	10	56						.0	S. Baker	35	54	3	3	5	4.33
	UT	B. Almon	451	.266	4	63	327	176	20	33		.962							
	C	M. Heath	345	.281	6	33	316	47	10	6	4.7	.973							
	O1	G. Hancock	256	.273	8	30	249	10	4	17		.985							
	OF	R. Peters	178	.287	0	20	141	3	2	1	3.1	.986							
	UT	D. Meyer	169	.189	1	13	305	16	4	28		.988							
Cal. W-70 L-92 John McNamara	1B	R. Carew	472	.339	2	44	890	42	6	94	10.5	.994	T. John	34	235	11	13	0	4.33
	2B	B. Grich	387	.292	16	62	270	415	**22**	94	**6.0**	.969	K. Forsch	31	219	11	12	0	4.06
	SS	T. Foli	330	.252	2	29	115	274	10	51	5.4	.975	G. Zahn	29	203	9	11	0	3.33
	3B	D. DeCinces	370	.281	18	65	79	216	14	26	3.7	.955	M. Witt	43	154	7	14	5	4.91
	RF	E. Valentine	271	.240	13	43	152	5	6	1	1.9	.963	B. Kison	26	127	11	5	2	4.05
	CF	F. Lynn	437	.272	22	74	274	8	2	4	2.5	.993	L. Sanchez	56	98	10	8	7	3.66
	LF	B. Downing	403	.246	19	53	160	9	1	0	2.0	.994							
	C	B. Boone	468	.256	9	52	606	**83**	14	12	5.0	.980							
	DH	R. Jackson	397	.194	14	49						.0							
	UT	R. Jackson	348	.230	8	39	402	114	13	43		.975							
	OF	J. Beniquez	315	.305	3	34	174	8	6	1	2.2	.968							
	1B	D. Sconiers	314	.274	8	46	473	23	7	46		.986							
	OF	B. Clark	212	.231	5	21	122	0	0	0	1.7	1.000							
	UT	R. Wilfong	177	.254	2	17	107	144	2	33		.992							
Min. W-70 L-92 Billy Gardner	1B	K. Hrbek	515	.297	16	84	1151	89	13	125	9.1	.990	F. Viola	35	210	7	15	0	5.49
	2B	J. Castino	563	.277	11	57	301	406	7	94	5.4	.990	K. Schrom	33	196	15	8	0	3.71
	SS	R. Washington	317	.246	4	26	121	204	13	49	4.2	.962	A. Williams	36	193	11	14	1	4.14
	3B	G. Gaetti	584	.245	21	78	**131**	360	17	**46**	3.3	.967	B. Castillo	27	158	6	12	0	4.77
	RF	T. Brunansky	542	.227	28	82	375	16	6	**8**	2.7	.985	R. Lysander	61	125	5	12	3	3.38
	CF	D. Brown	309	.272	0	22	188	2	1	0	2.4	.995	R. Davis	66	89	5	8	30	3.34
	LF	G. Ward	623	.278	19	88	374	**24**	9	6	2.7	.978	B. Havens	16	80	5	8	0	8.18
	C	D. Engle	374	.305	8	43	299	26	9	3	4.6	.973	L. Whitehouse	60	74	7	1	2	4.15
	DH	R. Bush	373	.249	11	56						.0							
	OF	M. Hatcher	375	.317	9	47	137	4	3	1		.979							
	SS	L. Faedo	173	.277	1	18	53	133	9	22	3.8	.954							
	C	T. Laudner	168	.185	6	18	259	22	4	5	5.0	.986							
Sea. W-60 L-102 Rene Lachemann W-26 L-47 Del Crandall W-34 L-55	1B	P. Putnam	469	.269	19	67	1067	85	7	105	9.3	.994	M. Young	33	204	11	15	0	3.27
	2B	T. Bernazard	300	.267	6	30	166	233	12	51	5.2	.971	J. Beattie	30	197	10	15	0	3.84
	SS	S. Owen	306	.196	2	21	122	233	11	45	4.6	.970	B. Stoddard	35	176	9	17	0	4.41
	3B	J. Allen	273	.223	4	21	55	155	9	16	2.7	.959	B. Clark	41	162	7	10	0	3.94
	RF	R. Nelson	291	.254	5	36	122	10	4	1	1.5	.971	M. Moore	22	128	6	8	0	4.71
	CF	D. Henderson	484	.269	17	55	304	17	6	4	2.5	.982	G. Perry	16	102	3	10	0	4.94
	LF	S. Henderson	436	.294	10	54	182	15	6	2	1.8	.970	B. Caudill	63	73	2	8	26	4.71
	C	R. Sweet	249	.221	1	22	413	34	6	6	5.3	.987	M. Stanton	50	65	2	3	7	3.32
	DH	R. Zisk	285	.242	12	36						.0	E. Vande Berg	68	64	2	4	5	3.36
	OF	A. Cowens	356	.205	7	37	124	7	2	1		.985							
	SS	T. Cruz	216	.190	7	21	97	224	12	42	5.3	.964							
	3B	M. Castillo	203	.207	0	24	35	101	4	9	2.5	.971							
	OF	R. Roenicke	198	.253	4	23	124	12	1	3	2.5	.993							
	2B	J. Cruz	181	.254	2	12	131	173	5	41	5.2	.984							
	C	O. Mercado	178	.197	1	16	342	27	2	2	5.7	.995							

BATTING AND BASE RUNNING LEADERS

Batting Average

W. Boggs, BOS	.361
R. Carew, CAL	.339
L. Whitaker, DET	.320
A. Trammell, DET	.319
C. Ripken, BAL	.318

Slugging Average

G. Brett, KC	.563
J. Rice, BOS	.550
E. Murray, BAL	.538
C. Fisk, CHI	.518
C. Ripken, BAL	.517

PITCHING LEADERS

Winning Percentage

M. Haas, MIL	.813
R. Dotson, CHI	.759
S. McGregor, BAL	.720
L. Hoyt, CHI	.706
R. Guidry, NY	.700

Earned Run Average

R. Honeycutt, TEX	2.42
M. Boddicker, BAL	2.77
D. Stieb, TOR	3.04
C. Hough, TEX	3.18
S. McGregor, BAL	3.18

BATTING AND BASE RUNNING LEADERS
PITCHING LEADERS

Home Runs
J. Rice, BOS	39
T. Armas, BOS	36
R. Kittle, CHI	35
E. Murray, BAL	33
G. Luzinski, CHI	32
D. Winfield, NY	32

Total Bases
J. Rice, BOS	344
C. Ripken, BAL	343
C. Cooper, MIL	336
E. Murray, BAL	313
D. Winfield, NY	307

Wins
L. Hoyt, CHI	24
R. Dotson, CHI	22
R. Guidry, NY	21
J. Morris, DET	20
D. Petry, DET	19

Saves
Quisenberry, KC	45
B. Stanley, BOS	33
R. Davis, MIN	30
B. Caudill, SEA	26
P. Ladd, MIL	25

Runs Batted In
J. Rice, BOS	126
C. Cooper, MIL	126
D. Winfield, NY	116
L. Parrish, DET	114
E. Murray, BAL	111

Stolen Bases
R. Henderson, OAK	108
R. Law, CHI	77
W. Wilson, KC	59
J. Cruz, CHI, SEA	57
B. Sample, TEX	44

Strikeouts
J. Morris, DET	232
F. Bannister, CHI	193
D. Stieb, TOR	187
D. Righetti, NY	169
R. Sutcliffe, CLE	160

Complete Games
R. Guidry, NY	21
J. Morris, DET	20
D. Stieb, TOR	14
S. Rawley, NY	13
S. McGregor, BAL	12

Hits
C. Ripken, BAL	211
W. Boggs, BOS	210
L. Whitaker, DET	206

Base on Balls
R. Henderson, OAK	103
K. Singleton, BAL	99
W. Boggs, BOS	92

Fewest Hits per 9 Innings
M. Boddicker, BAL	7.09
D. Stieb, TOR	7.22
T. Conroy, OAK	7.82

Shutouts
M. Boddicker, BAL	5
B. Burns, CHI	4
D. Stieb, TOR	4

Home Run Percentage
R. Kittle, CHI	6.7
G. Luzinski, CHI	6.4
T. Armas, BOS	6.3

Runs Scored
C. Ripken, BAL	121
E. Murray, BAL	115
C. Cooper, MIL	106

Fewest Walks per 9 Innings
L. Hoyt, CHI	1.07
S. McGregor, BAL	1.56
T. John, CAL	1.88

Most Strikeouts per 9 Inn.
F. Bannister, CHI	7.99
J. Morris, DET	7.11
D. Righetti, NY	7.01

Doubles
C. Ripken, BAL	47
W. Boggs, BOS	44
R. Yount, MIL	42
L. Parrish, DET	42

Triples
R. Yount, MIL	10
K. Gibson, DET	9
A. Griffin, TOR	9
L. Herndon, DET	9

Innings
J. Morris, DET	294
D. Stieb, TOR	278
D. Petry, DET	266

Games Pitched
Quisenberry, KC	69
E. Vande Berg, SEA	68
R. Davis, MIN	66

	W	L	PCT	GB	R	OR	2B	3B	HR	BA	SA	SB	E	DP	FA	CG	BB	SO	ShO	SV	ERA
EAST																					
BAL	98	64	.605		799	652	283	27	**168**	.269	.421	61	121	159	.981	36	452	774	**15**	38	3.63
DET	92	70	.568	6	789	679	283	53	156	.274	.427	93	125	142	.980	42	522	875	9	28	3.80
NY	91	71	.562	7	770	703	269	40	153	.273	.416	84	139	157	.978	47	492	892	12	32	3.85
TOR	89	73	.549	9	795	726	268	**58**	167	**.277**	**.436**	131	115	148	.981	43	517	835	8	32	4.12
MIL	87	75	.537	11	764	708	281	57	132	.277	.418	101	**113**	162	.982	35	491	689	10	43	4.02
BOS	78	84	.481	20	724	775	**287**	32	142	.270	.401	30	130	168	.979	29	493	767	7	42	4.34
CLE	70	92	.432	28	704	785	249	31	86	.265	.369	109	122	174	.980	34	529	794	8	25	4.43
WEST																					
CHI	99	63	.611		**800**	650	270	42	157	.262	.413	165	120	158	.981	35	**447**	877	12	48	3.67
KC	79	83	.488	20	696	767	273	54	109	.271	.397	182	165	178	.974	19	471	593	8	**49**	4.25
TEX	77	85	.475	22	639	**609**	242	33	106	.255	.366	119	113	150	**.982**	43	471	826	11	32	**3.31**
OAK	74	88	.457	25	708	782	237	28	121	.262	.381	**235**	157	157	.974	22	626	719	12	33	4.35
CAL	70	92	.432	29	722	779	241	22	154	.260	.393	41	154	**190**	.977	39	496	668	7	23	4.31
MIN	70	92	.432	29	709	822	280	41	141	.261	.401	44	121	170	.980	20	580	748	5	39	4.67
SEA	60	102	.370	39	558	740	247	31	111	.240	.360	144	136	159	.978	25	544	**910**	9	39	4.12
					10177	10177	3710	549	1903	.266	.401	1539	1831	2272	.979	469	7094	10967	133	503	4.06

National League 1984

	POS	Player	AB	BA	HR	RBI	PO	A	E	DP	TC/G	FA	Pitcher	G	IP	W	L	SV	ERA

East

Chi.
W-96 L-65
Jim Frey

	POS	Player	AB	BA	HR	RBI	PO	A	E	DP	TC/G	FA	Pitcher	G	IP	W	L	SV	ERA
	1B	L. Durham	473	.279	23	96	1162	96	7	96	9.7	.994	S. Trout	32	190	13	7	0	3.41
	2B	R. Sandberg	636	.314	19	84	314	550	6	102	5.6	**.993**	D. Eckersley	24	160	10	8	0	3.03
	SS	L. Bowa	391	.223	0	17	217	378	16	64	4.6	.974	R. Sutcliffe	20	150	16	1	0	2.69
	3B	R. Cey	505	.240	25	97	97	230	11	22	2.3	.967	S. Sanderson	24	141	8	5	0	3.14
	RF	K. Moreland	495	.279	16	80	154	6	4	0	1.6	.976	D. Ruthven	23	127	6	10	0	5.04
	CF	B. Dernier	536	.278	3	32	355	5	5	1	2.6	.986	L. Smith	69	101	9	7	33	3.65
	LF	G. Matthews	491	.291	14	82	224	7	11	0	1.7	.955	R. Reuschel	19	92	5	5	0	5.17
	C	J. Davis	523	.256	19	94	811	89	15	9	6.3	.984	T. Stoddard	58	92	10	6	7	3.82
	OF	M. Hall	150	.280	4	22	69	5	3	2	1.7	.961	C. Rainey	17	88	5	7	0	4.28

POS	Player	AB	BA	HR	RBI	PO	A	E	DP	TC/G	FA	Pitcher	G	IP	W	L	SV	ERA
N. Y. W-90 L-72 Davy Johnson																		
1B	K. Hernandez	550	.311	15	94	1214	142	8	127	8.9	.994	D. Gooden	31	218	17	9	0	2.60
2B	W. Backman	436	.280	1	26	218	295	10	72	4.5	.981	W. Terrell	33	215	11	12	0	3.52
SS	J. Oquendo	189	.222	0	10	95	152	7	33	3.8	.972	R. Darling	33	206	12	9	0	3.81
3B	H. Brooks	561	.283	16	73	79	211	22	22	2.4	.929	E. Lynch	40	124	9	8	2	4.50
RF	D. Strawberry	522	.251	26	97	276	11	6	3	2.0	.980	B. Berenyi	19	115	9	6	0	3.76
CF	M. Wilson	587	.276	10	54	396	8	4	6	2.8	.990	S. Fernandez	15	90	6	6	0	3.50
LF	G. Foster	553	.269	24	86	278	6	7	1	2.1	.976	J. Orosco	60	87	10	6	31	2.59
C	M. Fitzgerald	360	.242	2	33	715	47	4	6	7.2	.995	D. Sisk	50	78	1	3	15	2.09
S2	R. Gardenhire	207	.246	1	10	96	143	10	20		.960							
OF	D. Heep	199	.231	1	12	86	1	3	1	1.9	.967							
2B	K. Chapman	197	.289	3	23	104	130	5	32	4.3	.979							
St. L. W-84 L-78 Whitey Herzog																		
1B	D. Green	452	.268	15	65	1088	69	10	98	10.0	.991	J. Andujar	36	261	20	14	0	3.34
2B	T. Herr	558	.276	4	49	328	452	6	106	5.5	.992	D. LaPoint	33	193	12	10	0	3.96
SS	O. Smith	412	.257	1	44	233	437	12	94	5.5	.982	D. Cox	29	156	9	11	0	4.03
3B	T. Pendleton	262	.324	1	33	59	155	13	10	3.4	.943	R. Horton	37	126	9	4	1	3.44
RF	G. Hendrick	441	.277	9	69	188	9	2	1	1.7	.990	B. Sutter	71	123	5	7	45	1.54
CF	W. McGee	571	.291	6	50	374	10	6	4	2.8	.985	N. Allen	57	119	9	6	3	3.55
LF	L. Smith	504	.250	6	49	184	18	11	0	1.5	.948	K. Kepshire	17	109	6	5	0	3.30
C	D. Porter	422	.232	11	68	620	58	11	6	5.6	.984							
UT	A. Van Slyke	361	.244	7	50	357	82	8	40		.982							
OF	T. Landrum	173	.272	3	26	93	1	2	0	1.1	.979							
Phi. W-81 L-81 Paul Owens																		
1B	L. Matuszek	262	.248	12	43	643	55	7	40	8.7	.990	S. Carlton	33	229	13	7	0	3.58
2B	J. Samuel	701	.272	15	69	388	438	33	77	5.4	.962	J. Koosman	36	224	14	15	0	3.25
SS	I. DeJesus	435	.257	0	35	166	400	29	57	4.2	.951	C. Hudson	30	174	9	11	0	4.04
3B	M. Schmidt	528	.277	36	106	85	329	26	19	3.0	.941	J. Denny	22	154	7	7	0	2.45
RF	S. Lezcano	256	.277	14	40	151	3	3	0	1.8	.981	K. Gross	44	129	8	5	1	4.12
CF	V. Hayes	561	.292	16	67	341	2	4	1	2.3	.988	S. Rawley	18	120	10	6	0	3.81
LF	G. Wilson	341	.240	6	31	147	4	5	0	1.4	.968	A. Holland	68	98	5	10	29	3.39
C	O. Virgil	456	.261	18	68	722	58	6	6	5.7	.992	L. Andersen	64	91	3	7	4	2.38
OF	G. Maddox	241	.282	5	19	160	3	0	1	2.4	1.000	B. Campbell	57	81	6	5	1	3.43
1B	T. Corcoran	208	.341	5	36	318	21	1	20	6.7	.997							
O1	G. Gross	202	.322	0	16	195	13	2	9		.990							
OF	J. Stone	185	.362	1	15	75	1	7	0	1.8	.916							
1C	J. Wockenfuss	180	.289	6	24	323	20	7	21		.980							
Mon. W-78 L-83 Bill Virdon W-64 L-67 Jim Fanning W-14 L-16																		
1B	T. Francona	214	.346	1	18	427	49	3	43	9.6	.994	B. Gullickson	32	227	12	9	0	3.61
2B	D. Flynn	366	.243	0	17	148	223	8	47	4.3	.979	C. Lea	30	224	15	10	0	2.89
SS	A. Salazar	174	.155	0	12	88	155	10	35	3.2	.960	B. Smith	28	179	12	13	0	3.32
3B	T. Wallach	582	.246	18	72	162	332	21	29	3.2	.959	S. Rogers	31	169	6	15	0	4.31
RF	A. Dawson	533	.248	17	86	297	11	8	2	2.4	.975	D. Schatzeder	36	136	7	7	1	2.71
CF	T. Raines	622	.309	8	60	420	8	5	1	2.7	.988	D. Palmer	20	105	7	3	0	3.84
LF	J. Wohlford	213	.300	5	29	85	3	1	1	1.5	.989	B. James	62	96	6	6	10	3.66
C	G. Carter	596	.294	27	106	772	65	6	6	5.9	.993	J. Reardon	68	87	7	7	23	2.90
1O	P. Rose	278	.259	0	23	349	44	6	22		.985	G. Lucas	55	53	0	3	8	2.72
2B	B. Little	266	.244	0	9	137	197	6	44	4.4	.982							
UT	D. Thomas	243	.255	0	20	118	135	10	33		.962							
OF	M. Stenhouse	175	.183	4	16	67	4	1	2	1.5	.986							
1B	D. Driessen	169	.254	9	32	363	23	2	38	8.6	.995							
OF	M. Dilone	169	.278	1	10	76	1	1	0	1.9	.987							
Pit. W-75 L-87 Chuck Tanner																		
1B	J. Thompson	543	.254	17	74	1337	74	14	111	9.4	.990	R. Rhoden	33	238	14	9	0	2.72
2B	J. Ray	555	.312	6	67	331	400	12	90	5.0	.984	McWilliams	34	227	12	11	1	2.93
SS	D. Berra	450	.222	9	52	186	449	30	65	4.9	.955	J. Tudor	32	212	12	11	0	3.27
3B	B. Madlock	403	.253	4	44	66	176	15	17	2.6	.942	J. DeLeon	30	192	7	13	0	3.74
RF	L. Lacy	474	.321	12	70	268	15	1	4	2.2	.996	J. Candelaria	33	185	12	11	2	2.72
CF	M. Wynne	653	.266	0	39	373	8	4	1	2.5	.990	D. Robinson	51	122	5	6	10	3.02
LF	L. Mazzilli	266	.237	4	21	92	2	1	0	1.3	.989	K. Tekulve	72	88	3	9	13	2.66
C	T. Pena	546	.286	15	78	895	95	9	15	6.8	.991	R. Scurry	43	46	5	6	4	2.53
32	J. Morrison	304	.286	11	45	81	163	10	21		.961							
OF	D. Frobel	276	.203	12	28	188	9	9	3	1.8	.956							

West

POS	Player	AB	BA	HR	RBI	PO	A	E	DP	TC/G	FA	Pitcher	G	IP	W	L	SV	ERA
S. D. W-92 L-70 Dick Williams																		
1B	S. Garvey	617	.284	8	86	1232	87	0	117	8.2	1.000	E. Show	32	207	15	9	0	3.40
2B	A. Wiggins	596	.258	3	34	391	410	32	95	5.3	.962	T. Lollar	31	196	11	13	0	3.91
SS	G. Templeton	493	.258	2	35	225	407	26	79	4.5	.960	E. Whitson	31	189	14	8	0	3.24
3B	G. Nettles	395	.228	20	65	93	201	20	14	2.6	.936	M. Thurmond	32	179	14	8	0	2.97
RF	T. Gwynn	606	.351	5	71	345	11	4	4	2.3	.989	D. Dravecky	50	157	9	8	8	2.93
CF	McReynolds	525	.278	20	75	422	10	4	1	3.0	.991	A. Hawkins	36	146	8	9	0	4.68
LF	C. Martinez	488	.250	13	66	312	15	8	4	2.4	.976	C. Lefferts	62	106	3	4	10	2.13
C	T. Kennedy	530	.240	14	57	708	54	14	6	5.3	.982	G. Gossage	62	102	10	6	25	2.90
3O	L. Salazar	228	.241	3	17	84	92	6	5		.967							
OF	B. Brown	171	.251	3	29	100	2	3	0	2.0	.971							

	POS	Player	AB	BA	HR	RBI	PO	A	E	DP	TC/G	FA	Pitcher	G	IP	W	L	SV	ERA
Atl.	1B	C. Chambliss	389	.257	9	44	996	70	8	84	9.9	.993	R. Mahler	38	222	13	10	0	3.12
W-80 L-82	2B	G. Hubbard	397	.234	9	43	237	405	8	78	5.6	.988	P. Perez	30	212	14	8	0	3.74
Joe Torre	SS	R. Ramirez	591	.266	2	48	251	443	30	94	5.0	.959	C. McMurtry	37	183	9	17	0	4.32
	3B	R. Johnson	294	.279	5	30	44	171	14	14	2.8	.939	R. Camp	31	149	8	6	0	3.27
	RF	C. Washington	416	.286	17	61	170	4	6	0	1.7	.967	L. Barker	21	126	7	8	0	3.85
	CF	D. Murphy	607	.290	36	100	369	10	5	1	2.4	.987	P. Falcone	35	120	5	7	2	4.13
	LF	G. Perry	347	.265	7	47	74	2	6	0	1.5	.927	G. Garber	62	106	3	6	11	3.06
	C	B. Benedict	300	.223	4	25	504	37	5	2	5.7	.991	S. Bedrosian	40	84	9	6	11	2.37
	OF	B. Komminsk	301	.203	8	36	135	2	1	0	1.7	.993	J. Dedmon	54	81	4	3	4	3.78
	C	A. Trevino	266	.244	3	28	399	60	5	5	5.9	.989	D. Moore	47	64	4	5	16	2.94
	UT	J. Royster	227	.207	1	21	99	162	9	23		.967							
	3B	K. Oberkfell	172	.233	1	10	31	77	4	8	2.5	.964							
Hou.	1B	E. Cabell	436	.310	8	44	971	66	7	97	9.3	.993	J. Niekro	38	248	16	12	0	3.04
W-80 L-82	2B	B. Doran	548	.261	4	41	261	419	10	83	5.0	.986	B. Knepper	35	234	15	10	0	3.20
Bob Lillis	SS	C. Reynolds	527	.260	6	60	212	472	25	91	5.0	.965	N. Ryan	30	184	12	11	0	3.04
	3B	P. Garner	374	.278	4	45	71	163	5	16	2.9	.979	M. Scott	31	154	5	11	0	4.68
	RF	T. Puhl	449	.301	9	55	213	6	3	4	1.8	.986	M. LaCoss	39	132	7	5	3	4.02
	CF	J. Mumphrey	524	.290	9	83	317	5	4	2	2.4	.988	B. Dawley	60	98	11	4	5	1.93
	LF	J. Cruz	600	.312	12	95	310	11	8	1	2.1	.976	V. Ruhle	40	90	1	9	2	4.58
	C	M. Bailey	344	.212	9	34	629	56	12	4	6.5	.983	D. Smith	53	77	5	4	5	2.21
	OF	K. Bass	331	.260	2	29	149	4	4	2	1.9	.975	F. DiPino	57	75	4	9	14	3.35
	31	R. Knight	278	.223	2	29	236	95	7	22		.979							
	3B	D. Walling	249	.281	3	31	30	100	6	14	2.6	.956							
	C	A. Ashby	191	.262	4	27	303	42	5	3	5.6	.986							
L. A.	1B	G. Brock	271	.225	14	34	703	65	4	61	9.3	.995	F. Valenzuela	34	261	12	17	0	3.03
W-79 L-83	2B	S. Sax	569	.243	1	35	318	450	21	99	5.6	.973	A. Pena	28	199	12	6	0	**2.48**
Tom Lasorda	SS	D. Anderson	374	.251	3	34	169	334	18	63	4.7	.965	O. Hershiser	45	190	11	8	2	2.66
	3B	P. Guerrero	535	.303	16	72	36	141	16	12	2.5	.917	R. Honeycutt	29	184	10	9	0	2.84
	RF	C. Maldonado	254	.268	5	28	124	4	6	0	1.3	.955	B. Welch	31	179	13	13	0	3.78
	CF	K. Landreaux	438	.251	11	47	212	3	3	2	1.7	.986	B. Hooton	54	110	3	6	4	3.44
	LF	M. Marshall	495	.257	21	65	200	9	4	1	1.8	.981	J. Reuss	30	99	5	7	1	3.82
	C	M. Scioscia	341	.273	5	38	701	64	12	8	6.9	.985	P. Zachry	58	83	5	6	2	3.81
	SS	B. Russell	262	.267	0	19	81	165	9	29	3.9	.965	K. Howell	32	51	5	5	6	3.33
	OF	R. Reynolds	240	.258	2	24	104	4	3	1	1.8	.973	T. Niedenfuer	33	47	2	5	11	2.47
	3B	G. Rivera	227	.260	2	17	55	167	15	12	2.6	.937							
	1B	F. Stubbs	217	.194	8	17	395	37	3	31	8.5	.993							
	C	S. Yeager	197	.228	4	29	317	30	2	1	5.4	.994							
	OF	T. Whitfield	180	.244	4	18	76	4	1	0	1.4	.988							
Cin.	1B	D. Driessen	218	.280	7	28	507	29	5	31	7.7	.991	M. Soto	33	237	18	7	0	3.53
W-70 L-92	2B	R. Oester	553	.242	3	38	357	388	15	75	5.2	.980	J. Russell	33	182	6	18	0	4.26
Vern Rapp	SS	D. Concepcion	531	.245	4	58	156	247	9	41	4.0	.978	J. Price	30	172	7	13	0	4.19
W-51 L-69	3B	N. Esasky	322	.193	10	45	51	130	18	8	2.4	.910	T. Hume	54	113	4	13	3	5.64
Pete Rose	RF	D. Parker	607	.285	16	94	296	6	8	1	2.1	.974	T. Power	78	109	9	7	11	2.82
W-19 L-23	CF	E. Milner	336	.232	7	29	285	8	5	4	2.8	.983	J. Tibbs	14	101	6	2	0	2.86
	LF	G. Redus	394	.254	7	22	200	6	7	3	1.9	.967	F. Pastore	24	98	3	6	0	6.50
	C	B. Gulden	292	.226	4	33	485	53	14	8	5.5	.975	B. Owchinko	49	94	3	5	2	4.12
	O1	C. Cedeno	380	.276	10	47	355	21	7	16		.982	J. Franco	54	79	6	2	4	2.61
	SS	T. Foley	277	.253	5	27	104	197	11	31	3.8	.965	B. Berenyi	13	51	3	7	0	6.00
	OF	D. Walker	195	.292	10	28	110	3	6	0	1.8	.950							
	C	D. Bilardello	182	.209	2	10	323	34	3	3	5.3	.992							
	3B	W. Krenchicki	181	.298	6	22	25	91	4	5	1.9	.967							
	OF	E. Davis	174	.224	10	30	125	4	1	2	2.5	.992							
S. F.	1B	S. Thompson	245	.306	1	31	555	36	1	48	6.8	.998	B. Laskey	35	208	9	14	0	4.33
W-66 L-96	2B	M. Trillo	401	.254	4	36	215	287	6	67	5.3	.988	M. Krukow	35	199	11	12	1	4.56
Frank Robinson	SS	J. LeMaster	451	.217	4	32	222	391	23	70	4.9	.964	M. Davis	46	175	5	17	0	5.36
W-42 L-64	3B	J. Youngblood	469	.254	10	51	87	195	36	11	2.7	.887	J. Robinson	34	172	7	15	0	4.56
Danny Ozark	RF	C. Davis	499	.315	21	81	292	9	9	2	2.5	.971	G. Minton	74	124	4	9	19	3.76
W-24 L-32	CF	D. Gladden	342	.351	4	31	232	8	3	1	2.9	.988	F. Williams	61	106	9	4	3	3.55
	LF	J. Leonard	514	.302	21	86	247	14	8	4	2.1	.970	G. Lavelle	77	101	5	4	12	2.76
	C	B. Brenly	506	.291	20	80	635	69	10	4	5.6	.986	R. Lerch	37	72	5	3	2	4.23
	1B	A. Oliver	339	.298	0	34	665	55	11	50	8.9	.985							
	UT	B. Wellman	265	.226	2	25	151	258	11	37		.974							
	OF	D. Baker	243	.292	3	32	112	1	3	0	1.9	.974							
	OF	J. Clark	203	.320	11	44	94	3	1	0	1.8	.990							

BATTING AND BASE RUNNING LEADERS

Batting Average
T. Gwynn, SD .351
L. Lacy, PIT .321
C. Davis, SF .315
R. Sandberg, CHI .314
J. Ray, PIT .312

Slugging Average
D. Murphy, ATL .547
M. Schmidt, PHI .536
R. Sandberg, CHI .520
C. Davis, SF .507
L. Durham, CHI .505

Home Runs
M. Schmidt, PHI 36
D. Murphy, ATL 36
G. Carter, MON 27
D. Strawberry, NY 26
R. Cey, CHI 25

Total Bases
D. Murphy, ATL 332
R. Sandberg, CHI 331
J. Samuel, PHI 310
G. Carter, MON 290
M. Schmidt, PHI 283

PITCHING LEADERS

Winning Percentage
M. Soto, CIN .720
A. Pena, LA .667
D. Gooden, NY .654
S. Carlton, PHI .650
S. Trout, CHI .650

Earned Run Average
A. Pena, LA 2.48
D. Gooden, NY 2.60
O. Hershiser, LA 2.66
R. Rhoden, PIT 2.72
J. Candelaria, PIT 2.72

Wins
J. Andujar, STL 20
M. Soto, CIN 18
D. Gooden, NY 17
R. Sutcliffe, CHI 16
J. Niekro, HOU 16

Saves
B. Sutter, STL 45
L. Smith, CHI 33
J. Orosco, NY 31
A. Holland, PHI 29
G. Gossage, SD 25

BATTING AND BASE RUNNING LEADERS

Runs Batted In
M. Schmidt, PHI	106
G. Carter, MON	106
D. Murphy, ATL	100
R. Cey, CHI	97
D. Strawberry, NY	97

Stolen Bases
T. Raines, MON	75
J. Samuel, PHI	72
A. Wiggins, SD	70
L. Smith, STL	50
G. Redus, CIN	48
V. Hayes, PHI	48

Hits
T. Gwynn, SD	213
R. Sandberg, CHI	200
T. Raines, MON	192

Base on Balls
G. Matthews, CHI	103
K. Hernandez, NY	97
M. Schmidt, PHI	92

Home Run Percentage
M. Schmidt, PHI	6.8
D. Murphy, ATL	5.9
D. Strawberry, NY	5.0

Runs Scored
R. Sandberg, CHI	114
A. Wiggins, SD	106
T. Raines, MON	106

Doubles
J. Ray, PIT	38
T. Raines, MON	38
R. Sandberg, CHI	36
J. Samuel, PHI	36

Triples
R. Sandberg, CHI	19
J. Samuel, PHI	19
J. Cruz, HOU	13

PITCHING LEADERS

Strikeouts
D. Gooden, NY	276
F. Valenzuela, LA	240
N. Ryan, HOU	197
M. Soto, CIN	185
S. Carlton, PHI	163

Complete Games
M. Soto, CIN	13
F. Valenzuela, LA	12
J. Andujar, STL	12
B. Knepper, HOU	11
R. Mahler, ATL	9

Fewest Hits per 9 Innings
D. Gooden, NY	6.65
M. Soto, CIN	6.86
J. DeLeon, PIT	6.88

Shutouts
O. Hershiser, LA	4
A. Pena, LA	4
J. Andujar, STL	4

Fewest Walks per 9 Innings
B. Gullickson, MON	1.47
J. Candelaria, PIT	1.65
E. Whitson, SD	2.00

Most Strikeouts per 9 Inn.
D. Gooden, NY	11.39
N. Ryan, HOU	9.65
F. Valenzuela, LA	8.28

Innings
J. Andujar, STL	261
F. Valenzuela, LA	261
J. Niekro, HOU	248

Games Pitched
T. Power, CIN	78
G. Lavelle, SF	77
G. Minton, SF	74

	W	L	PCT	GB	R	OR	2B	3B	Batting HR	BA	SA	SB	E	Fielding DP	FA	CG	BB	Pitching SO	ShO	SV	ERA
EAST																					
CHI	96	65	.596		762	658	239	47	136	.260	.397	154	121	137	.981	19	442	879	8	50	3.75
NY	90	72	.556	6.5	652	676	235	25	107	.257	.369	149	129	154	.979	12	573	1028	15	50	3.60
STL	84	78	.519	12.5	652	645	225	44	75	.252	.351	220	118	184	.982	19	494	808	12	51	3.58
PHI	81	81	.500	15.5	720	690	248	51	147	.266	.407	186	161	112	.975	11	448	904	6	35	3.62
MON	78	83	.484	18	593	585	242	36	96	.251	.362	131	132	147	.978	19	474	861	10	48	3.31
PIT	75	87	.463	21.5	615	567	237	33	98	.255	.363	96	128	142	.980	27	502	995	13	34	**3.11**
WEST																					
SD	92	70	.568		686	634	207	42	109	.259	.371	152	138	144	.978	13	563	812	17	44	3.48
ATL	80	82	.494	12	632	655	234	27	111	.247	.361	140	139	153	.978	17	525	859	7	49	3.57
HOU	80	82	.494	12	693	630	222	67	79	.264	.371	105	133	160	.979	24	502	950	13	29	3.32
LA	79	83	.488	13	580	600	213	23	102	.244	.348	109	163	146	.975	39	499	1033	16	27	3.17
CIN	70	92	.432	22	627	747	238	30	106	.244	.356	160	139	116	.977	25	578	946	6	25	4.16
SF	66	96	.407	26	682	807	229	26	112	.265	.375	126	173	134	.973	9	549	854	7	38	4.39
					7894	7894	2769	451	1278	.255	.369	1728	1674	1729	.978	234	6149	10929	130	480	3.59

American League 1984

	POS	Player	AB	BA	HR	RBI	PO	A	E	DP	TC/G	FA	Pitcher	G	IP	W	L	SV	ERA

East

Det.
W-104 L-58
Sparky Anderson

	POS	Player	AB	BA	HR	RBI	PO	A	E	DP	TC/G	FA	Pitcher	G	IP	W	L	SV	ERA
	1B	D. Bergman	271	.273	7	44	657	75	8	63	6.5	.989	J. Morris	35	241	19	11	0	3.65
	2B	L. Whitaker	558	.289	13	56	290	405	15	83	5.0	.979	D. Petry	35	233	18	8	0	3.24
	SS	A. Trammell	555	.314	14	69	180	314	10	71	4.4	.980	M. Wilcox	33	194	17	8	0	4.00
	3B	H. Johnson	355	.248	12	50	58	140	12	16	2.0	.944	J. Berenguer	31	168	11	10	0	3.48
	RF	K. Gibson	531	.282	27	91	245	4	12	2	1.9	.954	W. Hernandez	80	140	9	3	32	1.92
	CF	C. Lemon	509	.287	20	76	427	6	2	1	3.1	.995	A. Lopez	71	138	10	1	14	2.94
	LF	L. Herndon	407	.280	7	43	199	7	3	0	1.8	.986	D. Rozema	29	101	7	6	0	3.74
	C	L. Parrish	578	.237	33	98	720	67	7	11	6.3	.991	D. Bair	47	94	5	3	4	3.75
	DH	D. Evans	401	.232	16	63	0	0	0	0	.0	.000							
	UT	B. Garbey	327	.287	5	52	411	58	12	53		.975							
	UT	T. Brookens	224	.246	5	26	98	187	12	35		.960							
	OF	R. Jones	215	.284	12	37	150	4	0	1	2.1	1.000							
	OF	J. Grubb	176	.267	8	17	47	0	0	0		1.000							
	OF	R. Kuntz	140	.286	2	22	74	2	1	1	1.1	.987							

Tor.
W-89 L-73
Bobby Cox

	POS	Player	AB	BA	HR	RBI	PO	A	E	DP	TC/G	FA	Pitcher	G	IP	W	L	SV	ERA
	1B	W. Upshaw	569	.278	19	84	1246	103	14	133	9.0	.990	D. Stieb	35	**267**	16	8	0	2.83
	2B	D. Garcia	633	.284	5	46	267	427	14	95	4.8	.980	D. Alexander	36	262	17	6	0	3.13
	SS	A. Griffin	419	.241	4	30	189	269	18	65	4.1	.962	L. Leal	35	222	13	8	0	3.89
	3B	R. Mulliniks	343	.324	3	42	65	148	7	8	1.8	**.968**	J. Clancy	36	220	13	15	0	5.12
	RF	G. Bell	606	.292	26	87	289	11	9	1	2.1	.971	J. Gott	35	110	7	6	2	4.02
	CF	L. Moseby	592	.280	18	92	473	8	5	2	3.1	.990	R. Jackson	54	86	7	8	10	3.56
	LF	D. Collins	441	.308	2	44	203	8	2	3	2.0	.991	D. Lamp	56	85	8	8	9	4.55
	C	E. Whitt	315	.238	15	46	583	40	4	8	5.3	.994	J. Key	63	62	4	5	10	4.65
	DH	C. Johnson	359	.304	16	61	0	0	0	0	.0	.000							
	OF	J. Barfield	320	.284	14	49	190	9	10	5	2.4	.952							
	3B	G. Iorg	247	.227	1	25	62	110	10	15	1.6	.945							
	DH	W. Aikens	234	.205	11	26	0	0	0	0	.0	.000							
	SS	T. Fernandez	233	.270	3	19	116	178	8	40	4.1	.974							
	C	B. Martinez	232	.220	5	37	360	34	2	5	4.0	.995							

POS	Player	AB	BA	HR	RBI	PO	A	E	DP	TC/G	FA	Pitcher	G	IP	W	L	SV	ERA
N. Y. W-87 L-75 Yogi Berra																		
1B	D. Mattingly	603	.343	23	110	1107	124	5	135	9.3	.996	P. Niekro	32	216	16	8	0	3.09
2B	W. Randolph	564	.287	2	31	334	419	13	112	5.4	.983	R. Guidry	29	196	10	11	0	4.51
SS	B. Meacham	360	.253	2	25	136	269	19	52	4.4	.955	R. Fontenot	33	169	8	9	0	3.61
3B	T. Harrah	253	.217	1	27	51	128	6	17	2.5	.968	D. Rasmussen	24	148	9	6	0	4.57
RF	D. Winfield	567	.340	19	100	306	3	2	1	2.2	.994	B. Shirley	41	114	3	3	0	3.38
CF	O. Moreno	355	.259	4	38	262	9	4	2	2.5	.985	J. Howell	61	104	9	4	7	2.69
LF	S. Kemp	313	.291	7	41	138	2	4	0	1.9	.972	D. Righetti	64	96	5	6	31	2.34
C	B. Wynegar	442	.267	6	45	757	59	6	9	6.5	.993	J. Cowley	16	83	9	2	0	3.56
DH	D. Baylor	493	.262	27	89	0	0	0	0	.0	.000	J. Rijo	24	62	2	8	2	4.76
OF	K. Griffey	399	.273	7	56	181	6	5	0	2.3	.974							
UT	R. Smalley	209	.239	7	26	66	99	12	17		.932							
3B	M. Pagliarulo	201	.239	7	34	44	106	7	16	2.3	.955							
UT	T. Foli	163	.252	0	16	88	122	6	32		.972							
OF	B. Dayett	127	.244	4	23	80	3	1	0	1.4	.988							
OF	O. Gamble	125	.184	10	27	15	1	0	0		1.000							
Bos. W-86 L-76 Ralph Houk																		
1B	B. Buckner	439	.278	11	67	974	96	15	75	9.6	.986	B. Hurst	33	218	12	12	0	3.92
2B	M. Barrett	475	.303	3	45	245	417	9	67	4.9	.987	B. Ojeda	33	217	12	12	0	3.99
SS	J. Gutierrez	449	.263	2	29	228	347	31	60	4.0	.949	O. Boyd	29	198	12	12	0	4.37
3B	W. Boggs	625	.325	6	55	141	330	20	30	3.2	.959	A. Nipper	29	183	11	6	0	3.89
RF	D. Evans	630	.295	32	104	311	7	2	2	2.0	.994	R. Clemens	21	133	9	4	0	4.32
CF	T. Armas	639	.268	43	123	329	4	9	2	2.7	.974	B. Stanley	57	107	9	10	22	3.54
LF	J. Rice	657	.280	28	122	336	12	4	3	2.2	.989	M. Clear	47	67	8	3	8	4.03
C	R. Gedman	449	.269	24	72	693	58	18	5	6.2	.977							
DH	M. Easler	601	.313	27	91	0	0	0	0	.0	.000							
Bal. W-85 L-77 Joe Altobelli																		
1B	E. Murray	588	.306	29	110	**1538**	143	13	**152**	**10.7**	.992	M. Boddicker	34	261	**20**	11	0	**2.79**
2B	R. Dauer	397	.254	2	24	225	325	11	76	4.6	.980	M. Flanagan	34	227	13	13	0	3.53
SS	C. Ripken	641	.304	27	86	**297**	**583**	26	**122**	**5.6**	.971	S. Davis	35	225	14	9	1	3.12
3B	W. Gross	342	.216	22	64	64	205	18	13	2.5	.937	S. McGregor	30	196	15	12	0	3.94
RF	M. Young	401	.252	17	52	216	4	4	0	1.9	.982	D. Martinez	34	142	6	9	0	5.02
CF	J. Shelby	383	.209	6	30	261	9	2	1	2.2	.993	S. Stewart	60	93	7	4	13	3.29
LF	G. Roenicke	326	.224	10	44	197	6	1	0	1.7	.995	T. Martinez	55	90	4	9	17	3.91
C	R. Dempsey	330	.230	11	34	453	43	4	5	4.6	.992							
DH	K. Singleton	363	.215	6	36	0	0	0	0	.0	.000							
OF	A. Bumbry	344	.270	3	24	230	7	3	1	2.4	.988							
OF	J. Lowenstein	270	.237	8	28	94	5	3	0	1.5	.971							
C	F. Rayford	250	.256	4	27	287	35	3	2	4.9	.991							
OF	J. Dwyer	161	.255	2	21	83	3	3	1	1.7	.966							
DH	B. Ayala	118	.212	4	24	0	0	0	0	.0	.000							
Cle. W-75 L-87 Pat Corrales																		
1B	M. Hargrove	352	.267	2	44	790	83	8	86	7.1	.991	B. Blyleven	33	245	19	7	0	2.87
2B	T. Bernazard	439	.221	2	38	264	397	20	85	5.0	.971	N. Heaton	38	199	12	15	0	5.21
SS	J. Franco	658	.286	3	79	280	481	36	116	5.0	.955	S. Comer	22	117	4	8	0	5.68
3B	B. Jacoby	439	.264	7	40	86	187	14	17	2.3	.951	S. Farr	31	116	3	11	1	4.58
RF	G. Vukovich	437	.304	9	60	316	13	2	5	2.5	.994	E. Camacho	69	100	5	9	23	2.43
CF	B. Butler	602	.269	3	49	448	13	4	3	3.0	.991	T. Waddell	58	97	7	4	6	3.06
LF	M. Hall	257	.257	7	30	143	3	1	0	2.1	.993	R. Smith	22	86	5	5	0	4.59
C	J. Willard	246	.224	10	37	335	35	7	7	5.0	.981							
DH	A. Thornton	587	.271	33	99	0	0	0	0	.0	.000							
UT	P. Tabler	473	.290	10	68	532	89	7	54		.989							
OF	J. Carter	244	.275	13	41	122	9	6	0	2.3	.956							
C	C. Bando	220	.291	12	41	305	30	6	4	5.4	.982							
OF	C. Castillo	211	.261	10	36	123	2	9	0	1.9	.933							
Mil. W-67 L-94 Rene Lachemann																		
1B	C. Cooper	603	.275	11	67	1061	98	10	106	9.6	.991	D. Sutton	33	213	14	12	0	3.77
2B	J. Gantner	613	.282	3	56	**362**	469	13	111	5.5	.985	M. Haas	31	189	9	11	0	3.99
SS	R. Yount	624	.298	16	80	199	402	18	80	5.2	.971	J. Cocanower	33	175	8	16	0	4.02
3B	E. Romero	357	.252	1	31	38	111	9	13	2.7	.943	B. McClure	39	140	4	8	1	4.38
RF	D. James	387	.295	1	30	252	7	3	1	2.2	.989	M. Caldwell	26	126	6	13	0	4.64
CF	R. Manning	341	.249	7	31	231	2	3	2	2.1	.987	P. Ladd	54	91	4	9	3	5.24
LF	B. Oglivie	461	.262	12	60	256	6	8	1	2.2	.970	C. Porter	17	81	6	4	0	3.87
C	J. Sundberg	348	.261	7	43	556	55	3	6	5.6	.995	T. Tellmann	50	81	6	3	4	2.78
DH	T. Simmons	497	.221	4	52	0	0	0	0	.0	.000	R. Fingers	33	46	1	2	23	1.96
C	B. Schroeder	210	.257	14	25	274	24	4	2	5.2	.987							
OF	M. Brouhard	197	.239	6	22	107	6	2	2	2.2	.983							
OF	C. Moore	188	.234	2	17	119	2	2	0	2.0	.984							
OF	B. Clark	169	.260	2	16	106	0	2	0	1.9	.981							
3B	R. Howell	164	.232	4	17	21	67	9	7	2.1	.907							
3B	W. Lozado	107	.271	1	20	23	51	6	7	2.2	.925							

West

K. C.
W-84 L-78
Dick Howser

POS	Player	AB	BA	HR	RBI	PO	A	E	DP	TC/G	FA	Pitcher	G	IP	W	L	SV	ERA
1B	S. Balboni	438	.244	28	77	1102	79	15	102	9.6	.987	B. Black	35	257	17	12	0	3.12
2B	F. White	479	.271	17	56	299	425	11	97	5.7	.985	M. Gubicza	29	189	10	14	0	4.05
SS	O. Concepcion	287	.282	1	23	105	280	11	53	4.7	.972	L. Gura	31	169	12	9	0	5.18
3B	G. Brett	377	.284	13	69	59	201	14	18	2.7	.949	B. Saberhagen	38	158	10	11	1	3.48
RF	P. Sheridan	481	.283	8	53	273	8	4	1	2.1	.986	C. Leibrandt	23	144	11	7	0	3.63
CF	W. Wilson	541	.301	2	44	383	6	4	2	3.1	.990	Quisenberry	72	129	6	3	44	2.64
LF	D. Motley	522	.284	15	70	301	7	5	2	2.3	.984	J. Beckwith	49	101	8	4	2	3.40
C	D. Slaught	409	.264	4	42	547	44	11	8	4.9	.982							
DH	H. McRae	317	.303	3	42	0	0	0	0	.0	.000							
DH	J. Orta	403	.298	9	50	0	0	0	0	.0	.000							
3B	G. Pryor	270	.263	4	25	59	138	6	13	1.9	.970							
1O	D. Iorg	235	.255	5	30	399	22	3	33		.993							
C1	J. Wathan	171	.181	2	10	304	31	6	10		.982							
SS	U. Washington	170	.224	1	10	81	166	10	40	4.2	.961							

Cal.
W-81 L-81
John McNamara

POS	Player	AB	BA	HR	RBI	PO	A	E	DP	TC/G	FA	Pitcher	G	IP	W	L	SV	ERA
1B	R. Carew	329	.295	3	31	724	59	15	73	9.6	.981	M. Witt	34	247	15	11	0	3.47
2B	R. Wilfong	307	.248	6	33	161	266	11	48	4.5	.975	R. Romanick	33	230	12	12	0	3.76
SS	D. Schofield	400	.193	4	21	218	420	12	95	4.6	.982	G. Zahn	28	199	13	10	0	3.12
3B	D. DeCinces	547	.269	20	82	107	266	14	22	2.8	.964	T. John	32	181	7	13	0	4.52
RF	F. Lynn	517	.271	23	79	321	12	6	5	2.4	.982	J. Slaton	32	163	7	10	0	4.97
CF	G. Pettis	397	.227	2	29	337	11	6	4	2.6	.983	D. Corbett	45	85	5	1	4	2.12
LF	B. Downing	539	.275	23	91	272	5	0	0	2.1	1.000	L. Sanchez	49	84	9	7	11	3.33
C	B. Boone	450	.202	3	32	660	71	12	10	5.4	.984	B. Kison	20	65	4	5	2	5.37
DH	R. Jackson	525	.223	25	81	0	0	0	0	.0	.000	D. Aase	23	39	4	1	8	1.62
UT	B. Grich	363	.256	18	58	311	282	12	84		.980							
OF	J. Beniquez	354	.336	8	39	197	5	6	1	2.1	.971							
OF	M. Brown	148	.284	7	22	57	4	2	0	1.4	.968							

Min.
W-81 L-81
Billy Gardner

POS	Player	AB	BA	HR	RBI	PO	A	E	DP	TC/G	FA	Pitcher	G	IP	W	L	SV	ERA
1B	K. Hrbek	559	.311	27	107	1320	99	14	113	9.7	.990	F. Viola	35	258	18	12	0	3.21
2B	T. Teufel	568	.262	14	61	315	485	13	81	5.2	.984	M. Smithson	36	252	15	13	0	3.68
SS	H. Jimenez	298	.201	0	19	145	273	18	59	4.1	.959	J. Butcher	34	225	13	11	0	3.44
3B	G. Gaetti	588	.262	5	65	142	334	20	26	3.2	.960	K. Schrom	25	137	5	11	0	4.47
RF	T. Brunansky	567	.252	32	85	304	13	5	6	2.1	.984	P. Filson	55	119	6	5	1	4.10
CF	K. Puckett	557	.296	0	31	438	16	3	4	3.6	.993	E. Hodge	25	100	4	3	0	4.77
LF	M. Hatcher	576	.302	5	69	249	11	7	1	2.7	.974	R. Davis	64	83	7	11	29	4.55
C	D. Engle	391	.266	4	38	376	34	8	3	4.9	.981	R. Lysander	36	57	4	3	5	3.65
DH	R. Bush	311	.225	11	43	0	0	0	0	.0	.000							
C	T. Laudner	262	.206	10	35	362	38	9	2	5.0	.978							
OF	D. Brown	260	.273	1	19	144	4	1	0	2.7	.993							
SS	R. Washington	197	.294	3	23	60	114	4	19	2.5	.978							

Oak.
W-77 L-85
Steve Boros
W-20 L-24
Jackie Moore
W-57 L-61

POS	Player	AB	BA	HR	RBI	PO	A	E	DP	TC/G	FA	Pitcher	G	IP	W	L	SV	ERA
1B	B. Bochte	469	.264	5	52	1048	66	8	119	7.8	.993	R. Burris	34	212	13	10	0	3.15
2B	J. Morgan	369	.244	6	44	201	229	10	62	4.4	.977	L. Sorensen	46	183	6	13	1	4.91
SS	T. Phillips	451	.266	4	37	133	235	23	54	4.3	.941	S. McCatty	33	180	8	14	0	4.76
3B	C. Lansford	597	.300	14	74	137	268	18	27	2.8	.957	B. Krueger	26	142	10	10	0	4.75
RF	M. Davis	382	.230	9	46	287	6	12	4	2.4	.961	C. Young	20	109	9	4	0	4.06
CF	D. Murphy	559	.256	33	88	474	14	6	2	3.2	.988	K. Atherton	57	104	7	6	2	4.33
LF	R. Henderson	502	.293	16	58	341	7	11	1	2.6	.969	B. Caudill	68	96	9	7	36	2.71
C	M. Heath	472	.250	13	64	423	54	7	7	4.5	.986	C. Codiroli	28	89	6	4	1	5.84
DH	D. Kingman	549	.268	35	118	0	0	0	0	.0	.000							
UT	D. Lopes	230	.257	9	36	99	47	6	10		.961							
UT	B. Almon	212	.217	7	16	255	15	2	19		.993							
SS	D. Hill	174	.230	2	16	99	125	12	28	3.6	.949							

Chi.
W-74 L-88
Tony LaRussa

POS	Player	AB	BA	HR	RBI	PO	A	E	DP	TC/G	FA	Pitcher	G	IP	W	L	SV	ERA
1B	G. Walker	442	.294	24	75	791	51	4	66	8.4	.995	R. Dotson	32	246	14	15	0	3.59
2B	J. Cruz	415	.222	5	43	273	452	18	92	5.3	.976	T. Seaver	34	237	15	11	0	3.95
SS	S. Fletcher	456	.250	3	35	193	381	16	75	4.4	.973	L. Hoyt	34	236	13	18	0	4.47
3B	V. Law	481	.252	17	59	79	199	13	24	2.1	.955	F. Bannister	34	218	14	11	0	4.83
RF	H. Baines	569	.304	29	94	307	8	6	1	2.2	.981	B. Burns	34	117	4	12	3	5.00
CF	R. Law	487	.251	6	37	322	5	5	2	2.6	.985	R. Reed	51	73	0	6	12	3.08
LF	R. Kittle	466	.215	32	74	226	14	7	2	2.0	.972	J. Agosto	49	55	2	1	7	3.09
C	C. Fisk	359	.231	21	43	421	38	6	4	5.2	.987							
DH	G. Luzinski	412	.238	13	58	0	0	0	0	.0	.000							
1O	T. Paciorek	363	.256	4	29	596	25	6	50		.990							
OF	J. Hairston	227	.260	5	19	57	2	2	0		.967							
C	M. Hill	193	.233	5	20	308	17	3	4	4.6	.991							

Sea.
W-74 L-88
Del Crandall
W-59 L-76
Chuck Cottier
W-15 L-12

POS	Player	AB	BA	HR	RBI	PO	A	E	DP	TC/G	FA	Pitcher	G	IP	W	L	SV	ERA
1B	A. Davis	567	.284	27	116	1271	94	11	108	9.4	.992	M. Langston	35	225	17	10	0	3.40
2B	J. Perconte	612	.294	0	31	303	438	14	90	5.0	.981	M. Moore	34	212	7	17	0	4.97
SS	S. Owen	530	.245	3	43	245	463	17	86	4.8	.977	J. Beattie	32	211	12	16	0	3.41
3B	J. Presley	251	.227	10	36	48	113	7	12	2.4	.958	E. Vande Berg	50	130	8	12	7	4.76
RF	A. Cowens	524	.277	15	78	228	8	3	0	1.8	.987	M. Young	22	113	6	8	0	5.72
CF	D. Henderson	350	.280	14	43	242	11	3	5	2.6	.988	S. Barojas	19	95	6	5	1	3.98
LF	S. Henderson	325	.262	10	35	84	4	6	0	1.8	.936	D. Beard	43	76	3	2	5	5.80
C	B. Kearney	431	.225	7	43	823	63	11	9	6.7	.985	E. Nunez	37	68	2	2	7	3.18
DH	K. Phelps	290	.241	24	51	0	0	0	0	.0	.000	P. Mirabella	52	68	2	5	3	4.37
OF	B. Bonnell	363	.264	8	48	153	8	1	0	1.7	.994	M. Stanton	54	61	4	4	8	3.54
OF	P. Bradley	322	.301	0	24	235	3	2	1	2.1	.992							
UT	L. Milbourne	211	.265	1	22	53	86	12	14		.921							

	POS	Player	AB	BA	HR	RBI	PO	A	E	DP	TC/G	FA	Pitcher	G	IP	W	L	SV	ERA
Tex.	1B	P. O'Brien	520	.287	18	80	1270	105	11	103	9.8	.992	C. Hough	36	266	16	14	0	3.76
W-69 L-92	2B	W. Tolleson	338	.213	0	9	191	276	10	61	4.4	.979	F. Tanana	35	246	15	15	0	3.25
Doug Rader	SS	C. Wilkerson	484	.248	1	26	151	285	26	50	4.0	.944	D. Darwin	35	224	8	12	0	3.94
	3B	B. Bell	553	.315	11	83	129	323	20	28	3.2	.958	D. Stewart	32	192	7	14	0	4.73
	RF	G. Ward	602	.284	21	79	376	11	5	1	2.6	.987	M. Mason	36	184	9	13	0	3.61
	CF	G. Wright	383	.243	9	48	175	3	3	0	2.3	.983	D. Schmidt	43	70	6	6	12	2.56
	LF	B. Sample	489	.247	5	33	285	3	4	2	2.4	.986	D. Tobik	24	42	1	6	5	3.61
	C	D. Scott	235	.221	3	20	400	41	12	9	5.7	.974							
	DH	L. Parrish	613	.285	22	101						.0							
	OF	M. Rivers	313	.300	4	33	49	3	0	2		1.000							
	C	N. Yost	242	.182	6	25	368	20	2	1	5.0	.995							
	O1	B. Jones	143	.259	4	22	139	7	1	8		.993							

BATTING AND BASE RUNNING LEADERS

Batting Average

D. Mattingly, NY	.343
D. Winfield, NY	.340
W. Boggs, BOS	.325
B. Bell, TEX	.315
A. Trammell, DET	.314

Slugging Average

H. Baines, CHI	.541
D. Mattingly, NY	.537
D. Evans, BOS	.532
T. Armas, BOS	.531
K. Hrbek, MIN	.522

PITCHING LEADERS

Winning Percentage

D. Alexander, TOR	.739
B. Blyleven, CLE	.731
D. Petry, DET	.692
M. Wilcox, DET	.680
P. Niekro, NY	.667
D. Stieb, TOR	.667

Earned Run Average

M. Boddicker, BAL	2.79
D. Stieb, TOR	2.83
B. Blyleven, CLE	2.87
P. Niekro, NY	3.09
G. Zahn, CAL	3.12

Home Runs

T. Armas, BOS	43
D. Kingman, OAK	35
D. Murphy, OAK	33
L. Parrish, DET	33
A. Thornton, CLE	33

Total Bases

T. Armas, BOS	339
D. Evans, BOS	335
C. Ripken, BAL	327
D. Mattingly, NY	324
M. Easler, BOS	310

Wins

M. Boddicker, BAL	20
B. Blyleven, CLE	19
J. Morris, DET	19
D. Petry, DET	18
F. Viola, MIN	18

Saves

Quisenberry, KC	44
B. Caudill, OAK	36
W. Hernandez, DET	32
D. Righetti, NY	31
R. Davis, MIN	29

Runs Batted In

T. Armas, BOS	123
J. Rice, BOS	122
D. Kingman, OAK	118
A. Davis, SEA	116
E. Murray, BAL	110
D. Mattingly, NY	110

Stolen Bases

R. Henderson, OAK	66
D. Collins, TOR	60
B. Butler, CLE	52
G. Pettis, CAL	48
W. Wilson, KC	47

Strikeouts

M. Langston, SEA	204
D. Stieb, TOR	198
M. Witt, CAL	196
B. Blyleven, CLE	170
C. Hough, TEX	165

Complete Games

C. Hough, TEX	17
M. Boddicker, BAL	16
R. Dotson, CHI	14
B. Blyleven, CLE	12
J. Beattie, SEA	12

Hits

D. Mattingly, NY	207
W. Boggs, BOS	203
C. Ripken, BAL	195

Base on Balls

E. Murray, BAL	107
A. Davis, SEA	97
D. Evans, BOS	96

Fewest Hits per 9 Innings

D. Stieb, TOR	7.25
B. Blyleven, CLE	7.49
M. Boddicker, BAL	7.51

Shutouts

G. Zahn, CAL	5
B. Ojeda, BOS	5

Home Run Percentage

R. Kittle, CHI	6.9
T. Armas, BOS	6.7
D. Kingman, OAK	6.4

Runs Scored

D. Evans, BOS	121
R. Henderson, OAK	113
W. Boggs, BOS	109

Fewest Walks per 9 Innings

L. Hoyt, CHI	1.64
M. Smithson, MIN	1.93
R. Guidry, NY	2.02

Most Strikeouts per 9 Inn.

M. Langston, SEA	8.16
M. Witt, CAL	7.15
M. Moore, SEA	6.71

Doubles

D. Mattingly, NY	44
L. Parrish, TEX	42
G. Bell, TOR	39

Triples

D. Collins, TOR	15
L. Moseby, TOR	15
K. Gibson, DET	10
H. Baines, CHI	10

Innings

D. Stieb, TOR	267
C. Hough, TEX	266
D. Alexander, TOR	262

Games Pitched

W. Hernandez, DET	80
Quisenberry, KC	72
A. Lopez, DET	71

	W	L	PCT	GB	R	OR	2B	3B	Batting HR	BA	SA	SB	E	Fielding DP	FA	CG	BB	Pitching SO	ShO	SV	ERA
EAST																					
DET	104	58	.642		829	643	254	46	187	.271	.432	106	127	162	.979	19	489	914	8	51	3.49
TOR	89	73	.549	15	750	696	275	68	143	.273	.421	193	123	166	.980	34	528	875	10	33	3.86
NY	87	75	.537	17	758	679	276	32	130	.276	.405	62	142	177	.977	15	518	992	12	43	3.78
BOS	86	76	.531	18	810	764	259	45	181	.283	.441	37	143	127	.977	40	517	927	12	32	4.18
BAL	85	77	.525	19	681	667	234	23	160	.252	.391	51	123	166	.981	48	512	713	13	32	3.72
CLE	75	87	.463	29	761	766	222	39	123	.265	.384	126	146	163	.977	21	545	803	7	35	4.25
MIL	67	94	.416	36.5	641	734	232	36	96	.262	.370	52	136	156	.978	13	480	785	7	41	4.06
WEST																					
KC	84	78	.519		673	686	268	52	117	.268	.399	106	131	157	.979	18	433	724	9	50	3.91
CAL	81	81	.500	3	696	697	211	30	150	.249	.381	79	128	170	.980	36	474	754	12	26	3.96
MIN	81	81	.500	3	673	675	259	33	114	.265	.385	39	120	133	.980	32	463	713	9	38	3.86
OAK	77	85	.475	7	738	796	257	29	158	.259	.404	145	146	159	.975	15	592	695	6	44	4.49
CHI	74	88	.457	10	679	736	225	38	172	.247	.395	109	122	160	.978	43	483	840	9	32	4.13
SEA	74	88	.457	10	682	774	244	34	129	.258	.384	116	128	141	.979	26	619	972	4	35	4.31
TEX	69	92	.429	14.5	656	714	227	29	120	.261	.377	80	138	137	.977	38	518	864	6	21	3.91
					10027	10027	3443	534	1980	.264	.398	1301	1853	2174	.979	398	7171	11571	124	513	3.99

PART SIX

Home/Road Performance

YEAR-BY-YEAR BREAKDOWNS OF TEAM PERFORMANCE

AT HOME AND ON THE ROAD FOR WINS AND LOSSES,

RUNS SCORED AND ALLOWED, AND HOME RUNS

HIT AND ALLOWED

Home/Road Performance

The Home/Road Performance section is a chronological listing of team performance at home and on the road for every team since 1900. Categories listed for each team are wins and losses at home and on the road; runs scored and allowed at home and on the road; and home runs hit and allowed at home and on the road.

In the sixteen years since the publication of the first edition of The Baseball Encyclopedia, a wide range of new methods of analyzing player performance have emerged. Perhaps the most significant of these are the methods examining players in light of the characteristics of the parks in which they play the majority of their games. Baseball fans have known for years that some ball parks are good hitters' parks or good pitchers' parks. Few could have known, until recent research, just how large an effect the park can have on performance. In 1978, to take one example, the Atlanta Braves scored 364 runs in 81 games at home and 236 runs in 81 games on the road: a 54.2% increase in runs scored in their home games. That same year, the Houston Astros allowed 254 runs in 81 games at home, and 380 runs in 81 games on the road: a 33.1% difference. In evaluating the statistics for players on these two teams, it is important to note the advantages given to a hitter in Atlanta, and the disadvantages faced by one in Houston.

Historical research has indicated that a normal home-field advantage will be 5% for both hitters and pitchers; in a theoretically neutral home park with no unusual configuration or visibility problems, a team should score 5% more runs in home games and allow 5% fewer. The task facing each team seeking to construct a team for its peculiar park is to improve on these theoretical advantages, or to ensure that their club is better able to take advantage of its park's oddities. In examining the statistics that follow, then, it is important to note those parks which have distinct pro-hitter or pro-pitcher tendencies, like Wrigley Field, Fenway Park, Yankee Stadium, or the Houston Astrodome, but also to note those teams which adapt particularly well to their parks, as reflected in a substantial increase in runs and decrease in runs allowed at home.

Finally, the separation of home and road statistics allows for the possibility of examining team performance in a neutral setting: performance in road games, with an appropriate fraction of home performance factored in. It is tempting for the statistician to proclaim this a "truer" measure of a club than its overall performance. It is also misleading; teams that have done especially well in adapting themselves to the place where they play half their games will inevitably suffer in such a comparison. Let's just say it is a less biased measure, while acknowledging that the bias it eliminates is, in fact, an integral part of the rules of the game.

We are deeply indebted to Pete Palmer for supplying us with this material.

TEAM	Home Games			Road Games			Home Games						Road Games					
	W	L	Pct.	W	L	Pct.	HR	OHR	R	OR	RF	ORF	HR	OHR	R	OR	RF	ORF
National League 1968																		
STL	47	34	.580	50	31	.617	31	35	267	218	-15.5	-14.1	42	47	316	254	12.7	11.1
SF	42	39	.519	46	35	.568	60	32	299	242	0.8	-14.6	48	54	300	287	8.6	-0.2
CHI	47	34	.580	37	44	.457	83	83	363	332	44.0	17.5	47	55	249	279	-5.6	-0.8
CIN	40	41	.494	43	38	.531	55	66	377	400	18.9	44.7	51	48	313	273	15.7	-1.3
ATL	41	40	.506	40	41	.494	42	43	241	241	-10.6	-20.7	38	44	273	308	-2.2	-6.9
PIT	40	41	.494	40	41	.494	33	30	289	268	-0.4	2.7	47	43	294	264	6.3	6.1
LA	41	40	.506	35	46	.432	25	24	212	215	-17.8	-26.8	42	41	258	294	-8.1	-1.5
PHI	38	43	.469	38	43	.469	52	46	274	297	1.8	-6.6	48	45	269	318	-2.3	-12.1
NY	32	49	.395	41	40	.506	49	50	224	270	-11.1	16.4	32	37	249	229	-10.6	17.2
HOU	42	39	.519	30	51	.370	22	30	279	269	20.7	-15.6	44	38	231	319	-14.5	-11.4

TEAM INFORMATION EXPLANATION

The abbreviations for the teams appear as listed below:

ATL	Atlanta	MIN	Minnesota
BAL	Baltimore	MON	Montreal
BOS	Boston	NWK	Newark
BKN	Brooklyn	NY	New York
BUF	Buffalo	OAK	Oakland
CAL	California	PHI	Philadelphia
CHI	Chicago	PIT	Pittsburgh
CIN	Cincinnati	SD	San Diego
CLE	Cleveland	SEA	Seattle
DET	Detroit	SF	San Francisco
HOU	Houston	STL	St. Louis
IND	Indianapolis	TEX	Texas
KC	Kansas City	TOR	Toronto
LA	Los Angeles	WAS	Washington
MIL	Milwaukee		

Within each league (or division) teams are listed in their order of standings for the year. For further details on a club's performance in that season, see The Teams and Their Players.

COLUMN HEADINGS INFORMATION

W	Wins
L	Losses
Pct.	Winning Percentage
HR	Home Runs
OHR	Opposition Home Runs
R	Runs Scored
OR	Opposition Runs Scored
RF	Run Factor
ORF	Opposition Run Factor

The above categories are listed for both home games and road games. The statistics should be familiar, with the exception of Run Factor and Opposition Run Factor, which are explained below, both briefly and in depth.

Run Factor and Opposition Run Factor (Home Games). Home game Run Factors show how much better or worse a team hit or pitched at home. The higher the home RF or ORF, the better the hitters' park. The lower the RF or ORF, the better the pitchers' park. (A complete explanation is given below.)

Run Factor and Opposition Run Factor (Road Games). Road game Run Factors and Opposition Run Factors use road games as a neutral setting to compare all teams under similar conditions, away from the peculiarities of their home park. The league average in every year would be 0.0; an above-zero RF means the team's offense was better than average; below zero is worse than average. The same is true of the ORF: positive numbers mean better-than-average pitching; negative numbers mean worse-than-average pitching.

A more detailed explanation of the methods used to determine these factors follows.

RF and ORF (Home Games). The Run Factors and Opposition Run Factors listed for home games are an attempt to measure the influence of the home park on a team's ability to score and prevent runs. Each is expressed as a percentage showing the increase or decrease in a team's runs scored and allowed in home games when compared to its road games. The formula for (home) RF is Runs Per Game at home divided by Runs Per Game on the road, all minus one. A home RF of 10.0 means that the team scored ten percent more runs per game at home than on the road; an RF of −10.0 means the club scored ten percent fewer runs per game at home. The same applies to a team's ORF, which is calculated by taking Opposition Runs Per Game at home and dividing by Opposition Runs Per Game on the road (and subtracting one).

Run Factor and Opposition Run Factor (Road Games). Unlike the RF and ORF for home games, the factors for road games compare a team not to its own performance, but to the league's as as a whole. They are an effort to devise an absolute rating of the hitting and pitching talents of a team in a given year. (It should be noted that the formulas for home and road RFs and ORFs are the Encyclopedia's own; Pete Palmer's own methods of analyzing these statistics take more outside factors into account, and are therefore more precise. The methods chosen here were selected to balance accuracy with simplicity.)

The formula for road RF is a bit more complex than those for the home factors. A team's road runs scored total is added to a portion of its home runs scored, representing one season series' worth of games. (In an eight-team league, one-seventh of home runs scored is; in a ten-team league, one-ninth; in a twelve-team league, one-eleventh; in a fourteen-team league, one-thirteenth.) This total, representing a theoretically equal number of games played in every park for every team, is divided by the average in these categories for the league as a whole. The entire figure minus one gives a percentage over or under the league average for a club's offense.

A team's road ORF is calculated the same way: total road opposition runs plus a portion of home opposition runs divided by a league average in those categories. That percentage is then subtracted from one to give a percentage over or under the league average for the club's pitching and defense. Since the final figure is compared to the average, the higher the ORF, the better the pitching staff.

Road Run and Opposition Run Factors are useful measures of a team within a league and year. Since they are dependent upon league performance, however, they are not very helpful in comparing teams from one year against those from another, except as a measure of dominance. For what it's worth, the highest road RF belongs to the 1930 Yankees (42.7); the lowest belongs to the 1903 Washington Senators (-33.6); the highest road ORF was turned in by the 1906 Chicago Cubs (36.4); the lowest by the 1911 Boston Braves (-41.2).

League leaders. For each year, the leaders in a league are indicated, as in The Teams and Their Players, by listing that statistic in boldface type. Leaders are listed in the following categories:

Home Games:	*Road Games:*
Highest Winning Percentage	Highest Winning Pecentage
Most Home Runs	Most Home Runs
Fewest Home Runs	Fewest Opposition Home Runs
Most Opposition Home Runs	Most Runs
Fewest Opposition Home Runs	Fewest Opposition Runs
Most Runs	Highest Run Factor
Fewest Runs	Highest Opposition Run Factor
Most Opposition Runs	
Fewest Opposition Runs	
Highest Run Factor	
Lowest Run Factor	
Highest Opposition Run Factor	
Lowest Opposition Run Factor	

It might seem curious to "credit" the team scoring the fewest runs at home, or allowing the most. Bear in mind, though, that the home game statistics are primarily intended to measure the effects of the home park; highest and lowest may simply mean "best for hitters" or "best for pitchers." This is particularly true of homers and run factors; the benefit of the doubt should be given to the team. No such presumption applies to road statistics; only the best performances are listed in bold.

TEAM	Home Games W	L	Pct.	Road Games W	L	Pct.	Home Games HR	OHR	R	OR	RF	ORF	Road Games HR	OHR	R	OR	RF	ORF
National League 1900																		
BKN	43	26	.623	39	28	**.582**	15	15	452	394	17.3	13.5	10	**15**	364	328	5.2	12.6
PIT	42	28	.600	37	32	.536	14	7	359	315	-4.0	6.0	12	17	374	**297**	4.4	**22.2**
PHI	45	23	**.662**	30	40	.429	13	7	434	353	17.0	-18.2	15	22	376	438	7.5	-10.9
BOS	42	29	.592	24	43	.358	**40**	**43**	507	420	76.8	24.4	8	16	271	319	-15.6	13.8
CHI	45	30	.600	20	45	.308	**12**	**5**	337	329	1.3	**-30.1**	**21**	16	298	422	-14.9	-6.5
STL	40	31	.563	25	44	.362	23	13	382	316	2.8	-28.7	13	19	361	431	2.0	-8.1
CIN	27	34	.443	35	43	.449	12	9	255	309	-26.6	-8.8	18	19	**447**	436	18.7	-9.1
NY	38	31	.551	22	47	.319	13	8	393	375	21.0	-17.4	10	18	320	448	-7.6	-13.9
National League 1901																		
PIT	45	24	.652	45	25	**.643**	15	8	372	255	-5.2	-5.9	13	**12**	404	279	**24.6**	15.9
PHI	46	23	**.667**	37	34	.521	11	**6**	349	**247**	12.5	-14.1	13	13	319	296	0.5	11.7
BKN	43	25	.632	36	32	.529	13	**6**	**400**	303	17.9	3.5	**19**	**12**	344	297	9.3	9.3
STL	40	31	.563	36	33	.522	21	19	392	338	-4.7	-6.3	18	19	400	351	24.3	-6.3
BOS	41	29	.586	28	40	.412	18	17	297	298	**26.9**	15.5	10	**12**	234	**258**	-24.6	**19.9**
CHI	30	39	.435	23	47	.329	**7**	10	293	357	2.8	4.3	11	17	285	342	-10.8	-4.7
NY	30	38	.441	22	47	.319	8	11	**255**	350	-13.0	-14.8	11	13	289	405	-11.2	-21.2
CIN	27	43	.386	25	44	.362	**23**	**33**	279	**409**	-3.8	-2.7	15	18	282	409	-12.2	-24.5
American League 1901																		
CHI	49	21	.700	34	32	**.515**	14	11	**441**	285	8.4	-23.4	17	16	378	346	23.4	0.1
BOS	49	20	**.710**	30	37	.448	**20**	16	383	**252**	1.8	**-29.2**	16	16	376	356	20.7	-1.3
DET	42	27	.609	32	34	.485	15	10	438	369	36.2	7.0	14	12	303	**325**	1.9	**2.9**
PHI	42	24	.636	32	38	.457	15	**9**	410	352	11.6	-7.4	**20**	11	**395**	409	**27.1**	-18.4
BAL	40	25	.615	28	40	.412	11	11	430	367	36.2	0.1	13	**9**	330	383	9.3	-12.1
WAS	31	35	.470	30	38	.441	17	**36**	333	375	-2.0	-2.9	17	15	345	392	10.1	-14.8
CLE	29	39	.426	26	43	.377	**0**	13	317	399	-7.0	-5.4	12	**9**	346	428	9.8	-25.0
MIL	32	37	.464	16	52	.235	15	14	342	373	12.7	-19.2	11	19	299	455	-2.6	-31.2
National League 1902																		
PIT	56	15	**.789**	47	21	**.691**	9	**2**	410	207	12.3	-11.1	10	**2**	**365**	233	34.8	19.3
BKN	45	23	.662	30	40	.429	8	**2**	277	210	0.7	**-29.0**	**11**	8	287	309	3.9	-4.1
BOS	42	27	.609	31	37	.456	**13**	**11**	283	230	-4.8	-21.8	1	4	289	286	4.9	2.0
CIN	35	35	.500	35	35	.500	11	8	353	305	**27.8**	18.5	7	8	280	261	5.2	6.4
CHI	31	38	.449	37	31	.544	**1**	3	228	249	**-23.4**	0.2	5	7	302	252	6.5	11.6
STL	28	38	.424	28	40	.412	3	7	262	336	2.7	-6.4	7	9	255	359	-6.8	-25.0
PHI	29	39	.426	27	42	.391	**1**	6	264	**351**	19.9	17.7	4	6	220	298	-17.9	-6.9
NY	24	44	.353	24	44	.353	7	7	**214**	297	9.6	-2.9	1	9	187	293	-30.7	-3.0
American League 1902																		
PHI	56	17	**.767**	27	36	.429	19	12	**477**	330	40.3	**-5.4**	19	21	298	**306**	3.7	**15.8**
STL	49	21	.700	29	37	.439	16	14	350	289	19.4	-16.5	13	22	269	318	-9.6	14.3
BOS	43	27	.614	34	33	**.507**	24	15	348	284	**3.9**	-15.1	18	**12**	316	316	3.5	14.9
CHI	48	19	.716	26	41	.388	**5**	**2**	371	**238**	15.1	**-38.3**	9	28	304	364	1.1	5.1
CLE	40	25	.615	29	42	.408	15	7	357	257	20.1	-30.5	18	19	**329**	410	**7.6**	-6.5
WAS	40	28	.588	21	47	.309	**35**	**38**	407	341	39.6	-21.8	12	18	300	449	1.4	-18.6
DET	35	33	.515	17	50	.254	13	8	**312**	286	24.6	-21.7	9	**12**	254	371	-15.4	1.8
BAL	32	31	.508	18	57	.240	17	18	391	**369**	45.1	-7.3	16	**12**	324	479	7.5	-26.7
National League 1903																		
PIT	46	24	**.657**	45	25	**.643**	17	**5**	393	327	-0.3	15.9	17	**3**	**400**	286	**19.7**	13.2
NY	41	27	.603	43	28	.606	9	10	368	296	4.8	12.3	11	10	361	271	8.5	**18.2**
CHI	45	28	.616	37	28	.569	**2**	7	345	**285**	-10.8	**-17.9**	7	6	350	314	4.8	7.4
CIN	41	35	.539	33	30	.524	12	7	**440**	389	15.7	24.6	16	8	325	**267**	1.8	15.8
BKN	40	33	.548	30	33	.476	8	9	359	361	5.3	1.6	7	9	308	321	-5.6	2.8
BOS	31	35	.470	27	45	.375	11	**19**	283	314	1.5	-13.6	14	11	295	385	-11.9	-12.1
PHI	25	33	.431	24	53	.312	9	6	250	298	**-12.9**	-13.4	3	15	367	440	5.7	-25.8
STL	22	45	.328	21	49	.300	7	13	**248**	**393**	-2.1	-0.8	1	13	257	402	-23.2	-19.5
American League 1903																		
BOS	49	20	**.710**	42	27	**.609**	**35**	12	**395**	266	28.0	**13.3**	13	11	**313**	238	21.8	**20.2**
PHI	44	21	.677	31	39	.443	16	8	323	238	23.1	-11.5	15	12	274	281	5.6	8.9
CLE	49	25	.662	28	38	.424	11	5	364	256	18.0	-29.3	**20**	11	275	323	7.8	-3.9
NY	41	26	.612	31	36	.463	10	6	301	269	11.5	-8.8	8	13	278	304	5.8	1.0
DET	37	28	.569	28	43	.394	**5**	7	279	**222**	7.3	-22.4	7	12	288	317	8.1	-0.8
STL	38	32	.543	27	42	.391	7	15	250	228	-1.4	-24.3	5	**10**	250	297	-5.7	4.7
CHI	41	28	.594	19	49	.279	**5**	**2**	284	244	18.9	**-35.7**	9	21	232	369	-10.0	-16.7
WAS	29	40	.420	14	54	.206	15	**24**	275	**349**	64.9	-0.8	2	14	162	342	-33.6	-13.2

TEAM	W	L	Pct.	W	L	Pct.	HR	OHR	R	OR	RF	ORF	HR	OHR	R	OR	RF	ORF
	Home Games			**Road Games**			**Home Games**						**Road Games**					
National League 1904																		
NY	56	26	.683	50	21	.704	23	30	397	258	0.7	4.2	8	6	347	218	18.8	28.5
CHI	49	27	.645	44	33	.571	6	10	303	240	2.3	-13.3	16	6	296	277	0.0	12.7
CIN	49	27	.645	39	38	.506	12	7	409	295	41.1	15.5	9	7	286	252	1.4	17.5
PIT	48	30	.615	39	36	.520	5	2	338	286	0.2	-6.5	10	11	337	306	13.4	2.7
STL	39	36	.520	36	43	.456	14	15	298	280	1.8	-7.6	10	8	304	315	2.0	0.4
BKN	31	44	.413	25	53	.321	3	11	234	287	-8.6	-9.9	12	16	263	327	-12.7	-3.1
BOS	34	45	.430	21	53	.284	13	10	269	363	16.5	-9.5	11	14	222	386	-23.3	-22.7
PHI	28	43	.394	24	57	.296	7	7	269	348	0.0	-10.3	16	15	302	436	0.2	-36.1
American League 1904																		
BOS	49	30	.620	46	29	.613	18	18	325	240	7.7	-0.3	8	13	283	226	5.9	19.2
NY	46	29	.613	46	30	.605	22	25	321	288	23.6	29.0	5	4	277	238	3.8	13.3
CHI	50	27	.649	39	38	.506	0	2	297	226	-1.9	-11.7	14	11	303	256	11.0	10.5
CLE	44	31	.587	42	34	.553	14	2	329	242	0.8	-1.7	13	8	318	240	17.3	14.8
PHI	47	31	.603	34	39	.466	19	8	308	235	18.9	-15.6	12	5	249	268	-5.8	6.4
STL	32	43	.427	33	44	.429	2	14	231	288	-7.6	-8.8	8	11	250	316	-9.0	-10.8
DET	34	40	.459	28	50	.359	3	4	237	295	-7.0	-6.6	8	12	268	332	-2.9	-16.0
WAS	23	52	.307	15	61	.197	3	2	221	350	3.6	-9.8	7	17	216	393	-20.4	-37.4
National League 1905																		
NY	54	21	.720	51	27	.654	33	19	377	234	-2.2	-10.2	6	6	401	271	29.0	18.7
PIT	49	28	.636	47	29	.618	4	1	362	287	8.2	0.1	18	11	330	283	8.2	13.4
CHI	54	25	.684	38	36	.514	7	5	365	212	10.4	-15.8	5	10	302	230	0.4	30.5
PHI	39	36	.520	44	33	.571	8	9	353	314	3.3	13.3	8	12	355	288	15.0	11.1
CIN	50	28	.641	29	46	.387	12	2	438	330	41.8	-13.7	15	20	297	368	2.0	-10.8
STL	32	45	.416	26	51	.338	13	10	245	342	-15.5	-12.7	8	18	290	392	-7.8	-17.7
BOS	29	46	.387	22	57	.278	14	14	234	344	5.2	-6.4	3	22	234	387	-24.1	-16.4
BKN	29	47	.382	19	57	.250	16	16	273	379	18.6	-10.3	13	8	233	428	-22.8	-28.7
American League 1905																		
PHI	50	23	.685	42	33	.560	12	12	337	247	24.2	6.2	12	9	286	245	5.2	15.7
CHI	50	29	.633	42	31	.575	5	2	300	207	-10.8	-21.3	6	9	312	244	11.8	17.7
DET	45	30	.600	34	44	.436	5	5	267	275	11.8	-13.6	8	6	245	327	-10.7	-10.1
BOS	44	32	.579	34	42	.447	21	20	296	281	3.2	-2.0	8	13	283	283	2.4	2.8
CLE	40	37	.519	36	41	.468	5	13	290	284	6.0	-5.0	13	10	277	303	0.3	-3.3
NY	40	35	.533	31	43	.419	15	15	316	303	20.1	-2.4	8	11	270	319	-0.7	-8.9
WAS	33	42	.440	31	45	.408	10	4	289	340	7.0	20.1	12	8	270	283	-1.9	0.2
STL	34	42	.447	20	57	.260	5	7	250	267	-6.6	-23.6	11	12	261	341	-6.5	-14.0
National League 1906																		
CHI	56	21	.727	60	15	.800	7	6	345	214	-7.8	23.2	13	6	360	167	29.5	36.4
NY	51	24	.680	45	32	.584	9	8	309	239	1.6	-8.2	6	5	316	271	14.0	1.8
PIT	49	27	.645	44	33	.571	4	8	325	232	9.0	-2.5	8	5	298	238	9.0	12.8
PHI	37	40	.481	34	42	.447	2	5	226	270	-25.1	-8.1	10	13	302	294	5.8	-6.9
BKN	31	44	.413	35	42	.455	9	5	191	287	-36.5	-13.9	16	10	305	338	5.1	-21.8
CIN	36	40	.474	28	47	.373	10	10	316	333	43.7	32.0	6	4	217	249	-17.0	4.6
STL	28	48	.368	24	50	.324	6	10	241	313	5.2	6.4	4	7	229	294	-16.6	-8.9
BOS	28	47	.373	21	55	.276	11	16	218	329	14.7	2.8	5	8	190	320	-30.0	-18.0
American League 1906																		
CHI	54	23	.701	39	35	.527	2	1	275	180	-11.5	-38.9	5	10	295	280	9.2	8.9
NY	53	23	.697	37	38	.493	14	8	398	294	68.1	22.7	3	13	246	249	-1.0	13.3
CLE	47	30	.610	42	34	.553	4	8	351	229	11.0	-10.6	8	8	312	253	18.3	14.9
PHI	48	23	.676	30	44	.405	21	4	285	211	7.5	-33.6	11	5	276	331	3.4	-7.5
STL	40	34	.541	36	39	.480	12	10	272	225	-2.4	-15.4	8	4	286	273	6.1	9.1
DET	42	34	.553	29	44	.397	4	5	315	317	45.2	5.2	6	9	203	282	-18.9	2.5
WAS	33	41	.446	22	54	.289	7	5	260	288	2.1	-22.3	19	10	258	376	-3.5	-24.1
BOS	22	54	.289	27	51	.346	10	22	230	364	0.4	7.8	3	15	232	342	-13.4	-17.3
National League 1907																		
CHI	54	19	.740	53	26	.671	2	5	282	198	1.0	7.1	11	6	290	192	14.0	28.5
PIT	47	29	.618	44	34	.564	7	3	330	258	12.7	6.3	12	9	304	252	21.2	6.3
PHI	45	30	.600	38	34	.528	2	4	265	247	5.8	6.4	10	9	247	229	-1.6	14.2
NY	45	30	.600	37	41	.474	19	19	317	250	24.9	-2.6	4	6	257	260	4.3	4.0
BKN	37	38	.493	28	45	.384	9	10	223	232	-1.3	-21.0	9	6	223	290	-11.9	-4.8
CIN	43	36	.544	23	51	.311	3	5	287	227	11.1	-28.0	12	11	239	292	-3.3	-5.2
BOS	31	42	.425	27	48	.360	14	20	253	304	7.0	-7.9	8	8	249	348	-1.5	-26.9
STL	31	47	.397	21	54	.280	9	10	223	289	9.4	-12.3	10	10	196	317	-21.3	-16.2

TEAM	Home Games W	L	Pct.	Road Games W	L	Pct.	Home Games HR	OHR	R	OR	RF	ORF	Road Games HR	OHR	R	OR	RF	ORF
American League 1907																		
DET	50	27	.649	42	31	**.575**	3	5	**373**	265	8.8	-7.0	8	4	**321**	267	**19.8**	8.2
PHI	50	20	**.714**	38	37	.507	**14**	6	324	235	**32.4**	-10.2	8	6	258	276	-2.5	6.8
CHI	48	29	.623	39	35	.527	0	5	316	**222**	14.7	-13.0	5	8	272	**252**	1.5	**14.6**
CLE	46	31	.597	39	36	.520	7	3	267	226	-5.9	**-29.9**	4	3	263	299	-3.5	0.2
NY	33	40	.452	37	38	.493	10	7	331	**372**	24.0	**30.3**	5	7	274	293	2.9	-4.1
STL	36	40	.474	33	43	.434	5	**11**	261	262	-3.4	-7.0	4	6	281	293	1.9	0.5
BOS	34	41	.453	25	49	.338	12	**11**	249	270	14.3	-7.4	6	**11**	215	288	-19.7	1.7
WAS	27	47	.365	22	55	.286	1	3	**228**	310	**-13.6**	-14.3	**11**	7	278	381	-0.5	-28.0
National League 1908																		
CHI	47	30	.610	52	25	.675	9	15	294	264	-8.6	**37.4**	10	5	330	**197**	24.2	**19.5**
NY	52	25	**.675**	46	31	.597	10	11	**343**	235	6.8	2.3	10	15	309	221	19.5	12.7
PIT	42	35	.545	56	21	**.727**	12	4	227	255	**-35.7**	20.7	13	12	**358**	214	30.3	14.1
PHI	43	34	.558	40	37	.519	0	3	251	**213**	-2.0	-9.3	11	5	253	232	-3.5	10.0
CIN	40	37	.519	33	44	.429	8	7	260	272	15.0	1.2	6	12	229	272	-11.1	-6.5
BOS	35	42	.455	28	49	.364	13	20	295	**328**	21.9	11.5	4	9	242	294	-5.1	-16.7
BKN	27	50	.351	26	51	.338	16	3	179	243	-9.6	**-10.9**	12	14	198	273	-25.3	-5.4
STL	28	49	.364	21	56	.273	9	11	185	295	-0.5	-10.8	8	**5**	186	331	-29.0	-27.8
American League 1908																		
DET	44	33	.571	46	30	**.605**	6	6	315	300	**-7.5**	18.3	13	6	332	247	**27.2**	8.2
CLE	51	26	.662	39	38	.506	8	6	305	223	17.4	-3.4	10	9	263	**234**	3.4	**15.8**
CHI	51	25	**.671**	37	39	.487	1	4	271	**184**	1.8	**-35.6**	2	7	266	286	2.8	1.1
STL	46	31	.597	37	38	.493	11	2	292	234	14.3	-7.2	9	5	252	249	-0.8	10.5
BOS	37	40	.481	38	39	.494	9	9	273	249	-4.9	-4.4	5	9	291	264	11.3	5.1
PHI	46	30	.605	22	55	.286	11	5	294	272	**55.0**	-5.0	10	6	192	290	-21.0	-4.1
WAS	43	32	.573	24	53	.312	2	8	249	237	6.8	-22.5	6	7	230	302	-10.3	-6.3
NY	30	47	.390	21	56	.273	11	16	**234**	352	5.3	-1.2	1	10	225	361	-12.7	-30.2
National League 1909																		
PIT	56	21	**.727**	54	21	.720	10	6	354	237	-1.3	8.5	15	6	345	210	**19.5**	23.2
CHI	47	29	.618	57	20	**.740**	8	0	281	**199**	**-19.6**	5.5	12	6	**354**	191	19.0	**30.9**
NY	44	33	.571	48	28	.632	19	23	298	294	-3.5	22.7	7	6	325	252	11.0	7.4
CIN	39	38	.506	38	38	.500	5	2	282	299	-17.3	-5.3	17	3	324	300	10.0	-7.8
PHI	40	37	.519	34	42	.447	6	10	266	279	6.4	16.7	6	13	250	239	-12.9	12.2
BKN	34	45	.430	21	53	.284	12	9	238	311	**11.1**	**-5.3**	4	22	206	316	-27.4	-13.4
STL	26	48	.351	28	50	.359	9	12	271	**387**	-10.8	15.4	6	10	312	344	5.9	-25.6
BOS	27	47	.365	18	61	.228	11	9	**219**	326	5.3	-5.0	4	14	216	357	-25.2	-27.0
American League 1909																		
DET	57	19	**.750**	41	35	.539	13	12	377	246	**33.7**	2.1	6	7	289	247	19.3	12.3
PHI	49	27	.645	46	31	**.597**	8	4	293	**200**	**-4.8**	-2.5	**12**	5	312	**208**	23.2	26.5
BOS	47	28	.627	41	35	.539	18	12	329	**295**	26.0	**18.7**	3	**4**	268	255	9.6	7.7
CHI	42	34	.553	36	40	.474	1	8	256	201	4.4	-26.1	3	5	236	262	-5.1	9.7
NY	41	35	.539	33	42	.440	11	6	338	263	32.3	-19.8	5	12	252	324	4.5	-12.3
CLE	39	37	.513	32	45	.416	2	0	262	259	14.8	-3.9	8	10	231	273	-6.5	3.7
STL	40	37	.519	21	52	.288	5	5	242	235	15.4	**-34.3**	5	10	199	340	-18.6	-16.0
WAS	27	48	.360	15	62	.195	5	3	**197**	271	10.4	-27.7	4	10	183	385	-26.4	-31.6
National League 1910																		
CHI	58	19	**.753**	46	31	**.597**	18	9	354	**231**	-1.1	-13.8	16	**9**	358	**268**	17.0	**17.8**
NY	52	26	.667	39	37	.513	20	17	352	255	**-6.7**	**-21.3**	11	13	**363**	312	**18.3**	4.8
PIT	46	30	.605	40	37	.519	17	8	**365**	308	29.1	17.9	16	12	290	**268**	-2.0	14.8
PHI	40	36	.526	38	39	.494	12	18	333	290	-1.1	-15.8	10	18	341	349	11.2	-6.6
CIN	39	37	.513	36	42	.462	6	8	320	341	9.4	1.9	17	19	300	343	-0.9	-6.9
BKN	39	39	.500	25	51	.329	9	**5**	255	287	0.1	-18.8	16	12	242	336	-20.2	-2.9
STL	35	41	.461	28	49	.364	3	14	312	316	-3.3	-20.3	12	16	327	402	6.4	-22.1
BOS	29	48	.377	24	52	.316	25	25	292	**396**	45.6	31.5	6	11	203	305	-29.9	1.2
American League 1910																		
PHI	57	19	**.750**	45	29	**.608**	9	0	339	211	**0.1**	-9.4	10	8	**334**	230	**20.4**	22.5
NY	49	25	.662	39	38	.506	13	4	343	284	24.3	6.7	7	10	283	273	4.5	6.6
DET	46	31	.597	40	37	.519	17	23	346	306	2.5	9.4	9	13	333	276	**20.4**	4.7
BOS	51	28	.646	30	44	.405	32	21	338	262	9.8	-15.4	11	8	300	302	9.6	-1.1
CLE	39	36	.520	32	45	.416	4	2	278	330	4.2	2.1	5	7	270	327	-2.4	-11.4
CHI	41	37	.526	27	48	.360	2	2	233	198	1.3	**-31.3**	5	14	224	281	-18.9	7.8
WAS	38	35	.521	28	50	.359	3	7	265	252	16.6	-12.1	6	12	236	298	-13.7	0.5
STL	26	51	.338	21	56	.273	4	2	**229**	359	3.1	-6.5	8	12	222	384	-19.8	-29.6

TEAM	Home Games			Road Games			Home Games						Road Games					
	W	L	Pct.	W	L	Pct.	HR	OHR	R	OR	RF	ORF	HR	OHR	R	OR	RF	ORF
National League 1911																		
NY	49	25	**.662**	50	29	**.633**	24	15	357	267	-5.7	2.2	16	20	**399**	**275**	**15.7**	**21.2**
CHI	49	32	.605	43	30	.589	26	14	380	306	-12.4	-11.6	**29**	**13**	377	301	10.9	13.3
PIT	48	29	.623	37	40	.481	27	6	**393**	**246**	10.5	-21.9	21	29	351	311	4.6	12.9
PHI	42	34	.553	37	39	.487	**48**	26	352	357	16.5	15.9	12	17	306	312	-8.3	8.7
STL	36	38	.486	39	36	.520	11	12	343	380	4.5	4.1	16	27	328	365	-3.0	-5.4
CIN	38	42	.475	32	41	.438	5	6	331	317	-11.4	**-23.4**	16	30	351	389	2.4	-9.2
BKN	31	42	.425	33	44	.429	10	11	**247**	303	-8.5	-7.9	18	15	292	356	-15.8	-0.4
BOS	19	54	.260	25	53	.321	28	**47**	391	**536**	**37.1**	19.3	9	28	308	485	-6.4	-41.2
American League 1911																		
PHI	54	20	**.730**	47	30	**.610**	11	24	384	253	-17.3	-25.3	5	12	**477**	348	**33.1**	6.0
DET	51	25	.671	38	40	.487	**21**	9	**468**	403	**32.3**	10.8	15	13	363	373	7.6	-5.3
CLE	46	30	.605	34	43	.442	**7**	13	368	344	16.8	-4.1	4	13	323	368	-5.9	-2.0
BOS	39	37	.513	39	38	.506	20	15	328	312	-5.6	-4.5	16	6	352	331	-0.1	8.1
CHI	40	37	.519	37	37	.500	8	12	341	299	-12.1	-10.3	13	9	378	325	6.8	10.0
NY	36	40	.474	40	36	.526	14	11	365	**422**	12.9	**37.9**	14	11	319	**302**	-7.0	**11.4**
WAS	39	38	.506	25	52	.325	10	6	323	356	6.9	-13.1	**21**	18	302	410	-12.8	-12.7
STL	25	53	.321	20	54	.270	9	8	**296**	396	3.6	-9.6	10	18	271	416	-21.5	-15.5
National League 1912																		
NY	49	25	**.662**	54	23	**.701**	**31**	21	387	302	-8.9	15.2	16	15	**436**	**269**	**21.2**	**22.5**
PIT	45	31	.592	48	27	.640	15	10	347	**275**	**-14.1**	-5.1	**24**	18	404	290	11.8	18.3
CHI	46	29	.613	45	30	.600	22	18	394	347	6.0	5.2	21	**15**	362	321	3.1	8.0
CIN	45	32	.584	30	46	.395	**7**	**2**	309	311	-9.8	**-23.3**	14	26	347	411	-3.5	-12.9
PHI	34	41	.453	39	38	.506	25	26	318	352	-7.2	7.5	18	17	352	336	-1.9	4.1
STL	37	40	.481	26	50	.342	14	9	354	414	14.5	-1.7	13	22	305	416	-12.2	-17.8
BKN	33	43	.434	25	52	.325	17	20	**303**	368	-11.7	-3.4	15	25	348	386	-3.4	-8.8
BOS	31	47	.397	21	54	.280	22	**28**	**407**	471	36.9	16.1	13	15	286	390	-15.1	-13.4
American League 1912																		
BOS	57	20	**.740**	48	27	**.640**	10	10	**417**	286	6.3	8.0	**19**	8	382	258	12.1	**23.5**
WAS	45	33	.577	46	28	.622	13	12	336	295	-11.8	-2.0	7	11	362	286	4.0	16.0
PHI	45	32	.584	45	30	.600	11	6	381	342	-7.9	4.0	11	6	**398**	316	**14.8**	6.6
CHI	34	43	.442	44	33	.571	11	11	**276**	340	-21.8	13.9	6	14	362	306	1.9	9.2
CLE	39	35	.527	36	43	.456	**3**	6	338	326	6.6	-1.7	7	9	338	354	-1.9	-2.5
DET	37	39	.487	32	45	.416	8	6	344	370	-6.1	**-6.7**	11	10	376	407	7.9	-17.7
STL	27	50	.351	26	51	.338	6	11	287	379	6.9	-2.8	13	6	265	385	-22.3	-12.4
NY	31	44	.413	19	58	.247	**14**	**16**	352	**423**	**28.2**	2.2	4	12	278	419	-16.6	-22.7
National League 1913																		
NY	54	23	**.701**	47	28	**.627**	23	22	367	**250**	7.1	-12.6	8	**16**	317	**265**	0.5	**17.9**
PHI	43	33	.566	45	30	.600	**51**	**23**	361	366	12.9	**40.7**	**22**	17	332	270	4.4	12.0
CHI	51	25	.671	37	40	.481	37	19	**372**	273	11.1	**-19.3**	**22**	19	348	352	**9.2**	-6.7
PIT	41	35	.539	37	36	.507	13	6	324	277	-10.7	-13.4	**22**	20	**349**	308	7.6	5.1
BOS	34	40	.459	35	42	.455	14	12	298	337	**-13.1**	-4.5	18	26	343	353	4.9	-9.4
BKN	29	47	.382	36	37	.493	20	14	296	343	-3.5	23.7	19	19	299	270	-7.0	12.9
CIN	32	44	.421	32	45	.416	15	13	307	**380**	2.3	12.7	12	27	300	337	-6.3	-6.7
STL	25	48	.342	26	51	.338	**8**	20	**239**	346	-10.1	-9.6	6	37	284	409	-13.3	-25.1
American League 1913																		
PHI	50	26	**.658**	46	31	.597	**19**	14	**388**	271	-3.1	**-14.4**	14	10	**406**	321	**33.0**	-5.1
WAS	43	35	.551	47	29	**.618**	10	**29**	297	318	-4.4	25.8	10	6	299	**243**	-1.5	15.6
CLE	45	31	.592	41	35	.539	4	9	336	284	8.8	8.4	12	11	297	252	-0.5	14.4
BOS	41	34	.547	38	37	.507	**3**	**0**	342	306	9.6	6.0	14	6	303	298	0.8	-0.1
CHI	40	37	.519	38	37	.507	6	4	**216**	**233**	-21.6	-13.2	17	6	272	265	-12.7	12.8
DET	34	42	.447	32	45	.416	9	4	312	**368**	1.3	7.1	15	8	312	348	2.7	-17.0
NY	27	47	.365	30	47	.390	5	20	265	339	4.3	7.1	4	12	264	329	-12.9	-10.3
STL	31	46	.403	26	50	.342	13	11	247	309	-10.9	-6.0	5	10	281	333	-8.8	-10.2
National League 1914																		
BOS	51	25	**.671**	43	34	**.558**	17	16	339	279	6.6	3.7	18	22	318	269	10.4	12.6
NY	43	36	.544	41	34	.547	17	**24**	316	288	**-15.6**	-5.0	14	23	**356**	288	**20.9**	6.9
STL	42	34	.553	39	38	.506	20	14	285	280	3.0	**6.3**	13	12	273	**260**	-5.4	**15.1**
CHI	46	30	.605	32	46	.410	22	20	318	281	16.6	-17.1	**20**	17	287	357	0.1	-12.2
BKN	45	34	.570	30	45	.400	17	17	342	306	15.9	-6.8	14	19	280	312	-0.8	-0.5
PHI	48	30	.615	26	50	.342	**50**	16	**377**	321	**34.0**	-14.5	12	**11**	274	366	-1.1	-16.4
PIT	39	36	.520	30	49	.380	**3**	6	**234**	**214**	-8.5	**-30.9**	15	21	269	326	-8.8	-0.8
CIN	34	42	.447	26	52	.333	4	5	290	**328**	25.5	5.5	12	25	240	323	-15.1	-4.5

	Home Games			Road Games			Home Games						Road Games					
TEAM	W	L	Pct.	W	L	Pct.	HR	OHR	R	OR	RF	ORF	HR	OHR	R	OR	RF	ORF
American League 1914																		
PHI	51	24	.680	48	29	.623	17	13	354	247	-8.0	-10.1	12	5	395	282	36.4	4.4
BOS	44	31	.587	47	31	.603	3	5	270	247	-14.0	-5.2	15	13	318	264	9.1	9.8
WAS	40	33	.548	41	40	.506	8	7	282	246	2.2	-5.2	10	13	290	273	1.1	7.1
DET	42	35	.545	38	38	.500	11	9	315	318	6.3	7.3	14	8	300	300	5.6	-4.0
STL	42	36	.538	29	46	.387	11	14	271	298	3.5	-9.1	6	6	252	316	-11.0	-8.0
CHI	43	37	.538	27	47	.365	7	4	271	285	17.7	-2.7	12	11	216	275	-22.0	4.9
NY	36	40	.474	34	44	.436	8	24	278	259	8.2	-9.8	4	6	260	291	-8.2	1.2
CLE	32	47	.405	19	55	.257	4	3	289	380	14.5	14.0	6	7	249	329	-11.1	-15.4
Federal League 1914																		
IND	53	23	.697	35	42	.455	14	8	439	339	30.8	15.2	19	21	323	283	8.5	12.0
CHI	41	34	.547	46	33	.582	30	19	248	208	-27.3	-26.4	22	23	373	309	14.9	10.1
BAL	53	26	.671	31	44	.413	25	15	350	298	10.0	-16.2	7	19	295	330	-2.8	1.1
BUF	47	29	.618	33	42	.440	21	18	345	300	20.6	-4.4	17	27	275	302	-8.7	8.4
BKN	47	32	.595	30	45	.400	27	13	358	335	13.3	-5.7	15	18	304	342	0.0	-3.4
KC	38	37	.507	29	47	.382	28	21	322	306	2.6	-16.7	11	16	322	377	3.6	-11.6
PIT	37	37	.500	27	49	.355	11	10	297	307	1.5	-17.3	23	29	308	391	-1.3	-15.3
STL	31	44	.413	31	45	.408	12	23	304	368	19.5	14.7	13	15	261	329	-14.2	-1.2
National League 1915																		
PHI	49	27	.645	41	35	.539	46	18	313	235	14.8	4.4	12	8	276	228	1.8	21.0
BOS	49	27	.645	34	42	.447	3	5	280	263	-6.1	-5.5	14	18	302	282	8.6	3.5
BKN	51	26	.662	29	46	.387	9	14	299	263	22.9	-13.7	5	15	237	297	-11.1	-1.0
CHI	42	34	.553	31	46	.403	31	16	296	314	10.8	5.2	22	12	274	306	0.4	-5.9
PIT	40	37	.519	33	44	.429	8	6	290	241	5.8	-15.8	16	15	267	279	-2.0	5.3
STL	42	36	.538	30	45	.400	11	10	320	303	11.2	-4.6	9	20	270	298	0.3	-3.0
CIN	39	37	.513	32	46	.410	6	7	265	295	8.2	4.2	9	21	251	290	-8.2	-0.2
NY	37	38	.493	32	45	.416	15	20	275	270	-6.8	-21.6	9	20	307	358	10.0	-19.7
American League 1915																		
BOS	55	20	.733	46	30	.605	5	4	323	221	-2.6	-17.3	9	14	345	278	11.6	12.2
DET	50	26	.658	50	28	.641	11	7	410	314	17.2	16.7	12	7	368	283	21.7	7.0
CHI	54	24	.692	39	37	.513	9	4	353	236	-6.7	-16.8	16	10	364	273	18.3	13.0
WAS	48	28	.632	37	40	.481	2	2	277	235	-3.9	-7.0	10	10	292	256	-5.3	17.9
NY	37	44	.457	32	39	.451	28	32	310	309	-3.2	-5.2	3	9	274	279	-9.1	8.3
STL	35	38	.479	28	53	.346	6	7	237	315	-8.8	-5.5	13	14	284	364	-9.2	-15.9
CLE	27	50	.351	30	45	.400	7	9	277	362	5.7	17.5	13	10	262	308	-13.9	-1.9
PHI	20	55	.267	23	54	.299	9	18	285	457	9.6	6.0	7	3	260	431	-14.1	-40.6
Federal League 1915																		
CHI	44	32	.579	42	34	.553	21	10	310	252	-7.2	-13.0	29	23	330	286	6.8	8.7
STL	43	34	.558	44	33	.571	12	15	334	280	4.5	6.4	11	7	300	247	-0.7	18.6
PIT	45	31	.592	41	36	.532	4	10	292	269	-0.1	8.2	16	27	300	255	-2.4	16.8
KC	46	31	.597	35	41	.461	15	19	274	249	-0.9	-18.6	13	10	273	302	-10.8	4.3
IND	40	39	.506	40	33	.548	4	2	267	271	-19.2	-10.4	13	13	318	291	1.6	6.5
BUF	37	40	.481	37	38	.493	21	21	290	324	0.7	3.1	19	14	284	310	-7.1	-1.0
BKN	34	40	.459	36	42	.462	20	11	315	324	1.2	-0.9	16	16	332	349	7.6	-12.0
BAL	24	51	.320	23	56	.291	29	36	299	419	25.4	29.4	7	16	251	341	-16.1	-13.6
National League 1916																		
BKN	50	27	.649	44	33	.571	19	9	300	233	5.2	-2.1	9	15	285	238	7.7	12.1
PHI	50	29	.633	41	33	.554	29	17	281	233	-11.0	-13.6	13	11	300	256	11.8	6.2
BOS	41	31	.569	48	32	.600	6	4	224	207	-27.7	-13.7	16	20	318	246	15.0	10.7
NY	47	30	.610	39	36	.520	21	23	291	229	-6.1	-17.8	21	9	306	275	14.2	0.3
CHI	37	41	.474	30	45	.400	34	22	309	317	42.7	37.9	12	10	211	224	-16.1	12.7
PIT	37	40	.481	28	49	.364	9	5	268	298	25.6	4.8	11	19	216	288	-16.4	-7.0
CIN	32	44	.421	28	49	.364	4	10	242	312	-4.3	6.3	10	25	263	305	-2.1	-13.2
STL	36	40	.474	24	53	.312	12	15	251	295	13.0	-10.5	13	16	225	334	-14.2	-21.8
American League 1916																		
BOS	49	28	.636	42	35	.545	1	1	252	205	-15.4	-25.4	13	9	298	275	4.1	9.5
CHI	49	28	.636	40	37	.519	9	5	326	254	20.0	5.8	8	9	275	243	0.2	16.9
DET	49	28	.636	38	39	.494	7	8	350	313	10.7	12.4	10	4	320	282	15.3	2.8
NY	46	31	.597	34	43	.442	22	22	306	277	10.0	-4.9	13	15	271	284	-1.8	3.7
STL	45	32	.584	34	43	.442	7	10	290	238	-2.6	-22.4	7	5	298	307	5.8	-1.4
CLE	44	33	.571	33	44	.429	4	9	323	293	6.5	-3.9	12	7	307	309	10.1	-4.3
WAS	49	28	.636	27	49	.355	6	1	294	248	16.9	-19.0	6	13	242	295	-11.4	1.7
PHI	23	53	.303	13	64	.169	15	17	231	399	9.7	8.6	4	9	216	377	-22.3	-29.0

TEAM	Home Games W	L	Pct.	Road Games W	L	Pct.	HR	OHR	R	OR	RF	ORF	HR	OHR	R	OR	RF	ORF
National League 1917																		
NY	50	28	.641	48	28	.632	21	17	294	220	-15.9	-9.5	18	12	341	237	19.4	13.1
PHI	46	29	.613	41	36	.532	26	20	297	270	8.4	20.4	12	5	281	230	0.9	13.1
STL	38	38	.500	44	32	.579	15	15	266	302	-2.2	11.0	11	14	265	265	-5.4	0.3
CIN	39	38	.506	39	38	.506	10	3	279	296	-16.6	-9.5	16	17	322	315	12.8	-15.5
CHI	35	42	.455	39	38	.506	11	14	273	305	1.6	20.9	6	20	279	262	-0.8	1.1
BOS	35	42	.455	37	39	.487	13	3	240	269	-15.7	-1.2	9	16	296	283	3.0	-3.9
BKN	36	38	.486	34	43	.442	14	14	270	288	12.0	6.2	11	18	241	271	-12.7	-0.9
PIT	25	53	.321	26	50	.342	2	4	232	307	-1.2	5.2	7	10	232	288	-17.2	-7.3
American League 1917																		
CHI	56	21	.727	44	33	.571	7	3	327	204	-3.1	-23.5	11	7	329	260	15.8	10.8
BOS	45	33	.577	45	29	.608	3	4	293	245	7.6	12.8	11	8	262	209	-6.2	24.7
CLE	43	34	.558	45	32	.584	5	8	317	314	21.8	40.6	8	9	267	229	-3.6	15.5
DET	34	41	.453	44	34	.564	5	5	285	303	-17.3	13.4	20	7	354	274	21.7	2.2
WAS	42	36	.538	32	43	.427	1	3	264	255	-11.2	-23.0	3	9	279	311	-2.3	-7.0
NY	35	40	.467	36	42	.462	19	24	269	292	12.5	17.0	8	4	255	266	-9.4	5.1
STL	31	46	.403	26	51	.338	7	11	252	337	-3.5	-4.9	8	8	258	350	-9.3	-22.7
PHI	29	47	.382	26	51	.338	11	17	264	319	2.2	-12.0	6	6	265	372	-6.6	-28.7
National League 1918																		
CHI	50	26	.658	34	19	.642	9	5	300	235	-8.7	7.6	12	8	238	158	8.0	27.9
NY	35	21	.625	36	32	.529	9	13	204	181	-10.2	-6.0	4	7	276	234	17.3	2.3
CIN	46	24	.657	22	36	.379	9	5	298	256	4.9	-12.8	6	14	232	240	5.6	-3.9
PIT	41	27	.603	24	33	.421	9	4	270	232	13.7	6.4	6	9	196	180	-9.7	19.8
BKN	33	21	.611	24	48	.333	4	12	173	185	23.3	-11.2	6	10	187	278	-18.5	-14.4
PHI	27	29	.482	28	39	.418	19	13	220	261	24.9	26.5	6	9	210	246	-7.1	-6.4
BOS	23	29	.442	30	42	.417	5	2	163	183	-13.5	-11.4	8	12	261	286	9.3	-17.3
STL	32	40	.444	19	38	.333	14	7	241	280	-10.1	-9.9	13	9	213	247	-4.8	-7.8
American League 1918																		
BOS	49	21	.700	26	30	.464	2	3	272	165	7.7	-38.6	13	6	202	215	-5.7	12.7
CLE	38	22	.633	35	32	.522	1	4	274	219	28.7	3.7	8	6	230	228	5.3	5.2
WAS	41	32	.562	31	24	.564	2	6	268	238	5.0	3.5	3	4	193	174	-9.4	23.9
NY	37	29	.561	23	34	.404	10	22	251	237	-8.6	-12.3	10	3	242	238	8.7	0.6
STL	23	30	.434	35	34	.507	1	7	178	195	-5.2	1.7	4	4	248	253	7.0	-2.6
CHI	30	26	.536	27	41	.397	4	4	216	194	8.8	-6.5	5	5	241	252	6.4	-2.2
DET	28	29	.491	27	42	.391	2	7	221	246	4.5	-4.5	11	4	255	311	12.1	-26.5
PHI	35	32	.522	17	44	.279	15	8	256	273	49.6	-6.0	7	5	156	265	-24.6	-11.1
National League 1919																		
CIN	52	19	.732	44	25	.638	10	5	315	189	16.8	-13.3	10	16	262	212	10.2	21.1
NY	46	23	.667	41	30	.577	28	17	310	209	8.1	-17.6	12	17	295	261	21.8	4.0
CHI	40	31	.563	35	34	.507	11	7	232	190	1.5	-14.9	10	7	222	217	-8.3	19.4
PIT	40	30	.571	31	38	.449	8	7	273	218	35.2	-13.3	9	16	199	248	-14.5	7.9
BKN	36	33	.522	33	38	.465	12	10	243	227	-10.0	-17.1	13	11	282	286	13.7	-5.0
BOS	29	38	.433	28	44	.389	11	9	231	265	4.5	-5.8	13	20	234	298	-4.1	-10.7
STL	34	35	.493	20	48	.294	9	10	240	244	7.6	-20.7	9	15	223	308	-7.5	-13.0
PHI	26	44	.371	21	46	.313	29	24	307	378	42.7	11.1	13	16	203	321	-11.3	-23.6
American League 1919																		
CHI	48	22	.686	40	30	.571	5	11	344	279	6.5	9.4	20	14	323	255	16.1	11.9
CLE	44	25	.638	40	30	.571	12	4	340	276	16.5	7.2	13	15	296	261	7.5	10.2
NY	46	25	.648	34	34	.500	33	30	326	255	20.5	-5.3	12	17	252	251	-6.7	14.1
DET	46	24	.657	34	36	.486	10	14	307	243	-1.2	-27.4	13	21	311	335	10.7	-10.4
BOS	35	30	.538	31	41	.431	10	3	233	241	-23.2	-15.4	23	13	331	311	13.7	-3.1
STL	40	30	.571	27	42	.391	19	23	280	249	10.6	-21.7	12	12	253	318	-8.5	-5.5
WAS	32	40	.444	24	44	.353	2	5	265	282	-3.8	-4.8	22	15	268	288	-4.5	1.9
PHI	21	49	.300	15	55	.214	29	31	266	400	39.2	16.9	6	13	191	342	-28.5	-19.1
National League 1920																		
BKN	49	29	.628	44	32	.579	17	14	360	291	18.4	21.2	11	11	300	237	2.6	21.8
NY	45	35	.563	41	33	.554	31	33	334	282	-10.0	1.2	15	11	348	261	15.5	15.5
CIN	42	34	.553	40	37	.519	5	1	281	238	-21.5	-28.1	13	25	358	331	16.2	-2.3
PIT	42	35	.545	37	40	.481	6	4	276	263	7.2	-10.1	10	21	254	289	-14.3	8.4
CHI	43	34	.558	32	45	.416	19	15	322	302	8.4	-9.3	15	22	297	333	0.1	-5.4
STL	38	38	.500	37	41	.474	10	10	330	332	-0.5	-1.4	22	20	345	350	14.5	-11.4
BOS	36	37	.493	26	53	.329	5	11	271	292	14.8	-17.5	18	28	252	378	-15.1	-17.6
PHI	32	45	.416	30	46	.395	50	30	339	380	48.0	12.2	14	5	226	334	-19.8	-8.8

TEAM	Home Games W	L	Pct.	Road Games W	L	Pct.	HR	OHR	R	OR	RF	ORF	HR	OHR	R	OR	RF	ORF
American League 1920																		
CLE	51	27	.654	47	29	.618	20	10	441	330	3.2	3.0	15	21	416	312	15.5	15.3
CHI	52	25	.675	44	33	.571	18	10	381	298	-7.7	-18.8	19	35	413	367	12.7	3.4
NY	49	28	.636	46	31	.597	71	36	424	308	2.4	-4.0	44	12	414	321	14.5	13.9
STL	40	38	.513	36	39	.480	31	33	473	415	42.2	15.2	19	20	324	351	-5.5	3.2
BOS	41	35	.539	31	46	.403	3	14	327	300	3.9	-22.6	19	25	323	398	-10.8	-3.9
WAS	37	38	.493	31	46	.403	5	7	343	386	-8.5	-5.9	31	44	380	416	3.5	-11.1
DET	32	46	.410	29	47	.382	12	24	336	452	4.9	17.1	18	22	316	381	-12.1	-5.0
PHI	25	50	.333	23	56	.291	35	40	254	401	-14.2	-4.9	9	16	304	433	-17.9	-15.6
National League 1921																		
NY	53	26	.671	41	33	.554	47	46	407	321	-11.9	-4.8	28	33	433	316	22.5	10.4
PIT	45	31	.592	45	32	.584	13	10	343	295	0.8	0.9	24	27	349	300	-0.6	15.3
STL	48	29	.623	39	37	.513	43	25	397	307	-6.1	-20.0	40	36	412	374	16.9	-3.4
BOS	42	32	.568	37	42	.468	20	18	332	292	-8.8	-23.0	41	36	389	405	8.9	-10.6
BKN	41	37	.526	36	38	.486	32	23	360	361	11.2	7.0	27	23	307	320	-10.5	8.0
CIN	40	36	.526	30	47	.390	5	2	321	306	9.5	-9.6	15	35	297	343	-14.4	4.2
CHI	32	44	.421	32	45	.416	23	37	345	434	8.2	29.7	14	30	323	339	-7.0	0.7
PHI	29	47	.382	22	56	.282	67	49	326	485	14.9	14.6	21	30	291	434	-15.7	-24.6
American League 1921																		
NY	53	25	.679	45	30	.600	83	34	500	355	7.3	-3.3	51	17	448	353	17.9	12.2
CLE	51	26	.662	43	34	.558	15	10	467	330	1.9	-13.6	27	33	458	382	19.1	6.7
STL	43	34	.558	38	39	.494	42	43	423	434	2.6	5.5	25	28	412	411	7.2	-2.7
WAS	46	30	.605	34	43	.442	14	13	358	332	6.1	-16.0	28	38	346	406	-9.8	1.4
BOS	41	36	.532	34	43	.442	3	16	332	333	-1.2	-8.2	14	37	336	363	-12.9	10.7
DET	37	40	.481	34	42	.447	19	28	433	412	-3.7	-6.3	39	43	450	440	16.2	-8.4
CHI	37	40	.481	25	52	.325	13	20	378	399	23.9	-13.0	22	32	305	459	-18.4	-12.1
PHI	28	47	.373	25	53	.321	65	59	353	464	17.6	9.3	17	26	304	430	-19.5	-7.8
National League 1922																		
NY	51	27	.654	42	34	.553	48	38	439	333	3.6	-0.1	32	33	413	325	9.2	17.1
CIN	48	29	.623	38	39	.494	8	13	378	297	-5.0	-23.8	37	36	388	380	1.5	6.0
PIT	45	33	.577	40	36	.526	22	16	439	390	1.7	11.2	30	35	426	346	12.2	10.6
STL	42	35	.545	43	34	.558	59	31	446	414	6.9	2.2	48	30	417	405	10.3	-3.2
CHI	39	37	.513	41	37	.526	22	37	344	382	-15.2	-5.6	20	40	427	426	9.3	-6.9
BKN	44	34	.564	32	44	.421	25	35	380	326	3.3	-24.8	31	39	363	428	-4.1	-5.6
PHI	35	41	.461	22	55	.286	94	60	449	517	55.3	28.2	21	29	289	403	-18.9	-6.1
BOS	32	43	.427	21	57	.269	6	15	287	373	-4.6	-14.7	26	42	309	449	-19.6	-11.7
American League 1922																		
NY	50	27	.649	44	33	.571	53	48	387	291	4.3	-11.0	42	25	371	327	5.0	14.7
STL	54	23	.701	39	38	.506	70	41	471	314	18.9	-4.5	28	30	396	329	14.1	13.4
DET	43	34	.558	36	41	.468	15	32	426	370	7.3	-10.9	39	30	402	421	14.0	-9.6
CLE	44	35	.557	34	41	.453	12	20	423	424	14.9	1.1	20	38	345	393	-0.1	-4.9
CHI	43	34	.558	34	43	.442	10	21	351	335	4.5	-4.6	35	36	340	356	-3.8	6.5
WAS	40	39	.506	29	46	.387	15	3	329	295	-2.7	-31.8	30	46	321	411	-9.3	-4.8
PHI	38	39	.494	27	50	.351	80	82	388	437	20.8	9.7	31	25	317	393	-8.2	-5.4
BOS	31	42	.425	30	51	.370	6	17	280	344	-2.3	-10.1	39	31	318	425	-11.7	-9.7
National League 1923																		
NY	47	30	.610	48	28	.632	41	53	408	362	-9.7	12.7	44	29	446	317	15.7	12.1
CIN	46	32	.590	45	31	.592	6	4	337	300	-11.5	-11.1	39	24	371	329	-3.7	11.4
PIT	47	30	.610	40	37	.519	16	9	381	322	-5.9	-13.9	33	44	405	374	5.4	0.0
CHI	46	31	.597	37	40	.481	63	57	402	354	13.5	1.1	27	29	354	350	-5.5	4.5
STL	42	35	.545	37	39	.487	22	27	335	320	-20.5	-24.3	41	43	411	412	5.3	-9.0
BKN	37	40	.481	39	38	.506	26	27	348	383	-15.1	5.6	36	28	405	358	4.4	1.6
BOS	22	55	.286	32	45	.416	7	27	291	429	-14.5	17.7	25	37	345	369	-11.2	-2.5
PHI	20	55	.267	30	49	.380	76	77	418	597	35.1	54.9	36	23	330	411	-10.5	-18.2
American League 1923																		
NY	46	30	.605	52	24	.684	62	50	407	329	-2.1	12.2	43	18	416	293	14.4	20.3
DET	45	32	.584	38	39	.494	21	31	400	351	-5.9	-8.8	20	27	431	390	17.8	-3.1
CLE	42	36	.538	40	35	.533	22	16	455	393	1.0	7.0	37	20	433	353	20.1	4.1
WAS	43	34	.558	32	44	.421	7	16	363	339	-2.1	-20.0	19	40	357	408	-1.3	-6.9
STL	40	36	.526	34	42	.447	50	43	377	364	18.1	-0.3	32	15	311	356	-11.9	4.3
PHI	34	41	.453	35	42	.455	28	32	345	360	13.5	-6.6	24	36	316	401	-11.8	-6.0
CHI	30	45	.400	39	40	.494	13	24	327	348	-3.2	-4.3	29	25	365	393	-0.6	-3.7
BOS	37	40	.481	24	51	.320	11	15	327	402	23.9	-3.7	23	33	257	407	-26.7	-8.8

TEAM	Home Games			Road Games			Home Games						Road Games					
	W	L	Pct.	W	L	Pct.	HR	OHR	R	OR	RF	ORF	HR	OHR	R	OR	RF	ORF
National League 1924																		
NY	51	26	**.662**	42	34	.553	51	40	385	**272**	-18.4	-26.2	44	37	**472**	369	**34.1**	-0.8
BKN	46	31	.597	46	31	**.597**	26	30	342	338	-8.8	0.2	**46**	28	375	337	7.9	4.7
PIT	49	28	.636	41	35	.539	19	17	393	293	17.1	-1.9	24	25	331	**295**	-1.4	16.7
CIN	43	33	.566	40	37	.519	3	3	311	283	-6.7	-3.1	33	27	338	296	-2.6	**16.8**
CHI	46	31	.597	35	41	.461	33	**68**	373	341	11.8	-7.2	33	21	325	358	-3.6	-0.5
STL	40	37	.519	25	52	.325	32	37	**419**	359	**30.5**	-8.1	35	32	321	391	-3.0	-9.3
PHI	26	49	.347	29	47	.382	**58**	64	369	**483**	20.1	**31.9**	36	**20**	307	366	-8.4	-7.5
BOS	28	48	.368	25	52	.325	9	8	**254**	366	-2.0	-13.4	16	41	266	434	-23.0	-20.1
American League 1924																		
WAS	47	30	**.610**	45	32	.584	1	7	371	**280**	-5.8	-18.0	21	27	384	**333**	1.0	**16.1**
NY	45	32	.584	44	31	**.587**	**57**	46	397	324	-4.8	-9.1	**41**	13	401	343	5.8	12.4
DET	45	33	.577	41	35	.539	17	28	**427**	393	1.1	-2.4	18	27	**422**	403	**11.6**	-3.2
STL	41	36	.532	33	42	.440	44	49	426	**445**	19.4	**17.5**	23	19	343	364	-6.6	3.8
PHI	36	39	.480	35	42	.455	32	24	**328**	391	-5.6	3.7	31	19	357	387	-6.6	0.4
CLE	37	38	.493	30	48	.385	13	18	374	375	2.0	-11.1	28	25	381	439	0.4	-10.7
BOS	41	36	.532	26	51	.338	8	17	402	391	**24.6**	-2.1	22	26	335	415	-9.2	-5.8
CHI	37	39	.487	29	48	.377	13	23	403	414	3.3	-6.7	28	29	390	444	3.4	-13.1
National League 1925																		
PIT	52	25	**.675**	43	33	**.566**	27	31	481	342	10.1	-9.5	51	50	**431**	373	**15.2**	6.5
NY	47	29	.618	39	37	.513	55	39	362	334	-3.2	-9.2	**59**	34	374	368	-1.8	7.8
CIN	44	32	.579	36	41	.468	10	5	334	**285**	-4.9	-19.3	34	**30**	356	**358**	-6.9	**11.6**
STL	48	28	.632	29	48	.377	66	41	449	359	20.0	-10.2	43	45	379	405	2.1	-1.1
BOS	37	39	.487	33	44	.429	15	14	**315**	383	-18.8	-7.3	26	53	393	419	0.9	-4.9
BKN	40	37	.519	28	48	.368	25	41	383	407	-6.2	-12.4	39	34	403	459	5.5	-14.6
PHI	38	39	.494	30	46	.395	73	74	488	**547**	48.6	**40.9**	27	43	324	383	-9.2	-2.1
CHI	37	40	.481	31	46	.403	57	63	367	359	3.0	-13.2	29	39	356	414	-5.8	-3.1
American League 1925																		
WAS	53	22	**.707**	43	33	**.566**	13	**13**	408	**298**	-3.0	-19.9	43	36	421	372	5.9	10.3
PHI	51	26	.662	37	38	.493	35	37	435	351	8.4	-4.3	41	23	396	**362**	1.3	**10.8**
STL	45	32	.584	37	39	.487	**73**	**73**	**503**	501	23.4	20.5	37	26	397	405	3.6	-3.1
DET	43	34	.558	38	39	.494	18	36	451	399	2.3	-4.8	32	34	**452**	430	**14.1**	-5.3
CHI	44	33	.571	35	42	.455	13	32	366	378	-17.7	-3.5	25	37	445	392	9.9	3.5
CLE	37	39	.487	33	45	.423	23	19	421	430	18.1	12.5	29	**22**	361	387	-6.8	2.9
NY	42	36	.538	27	49	.355	54	56	354	356	-1.9	-16.9	**56**	**22**	352	418	-10.9	-1.4
BOS	28	47	.373	19	58	.247	**10**	28	**309**	441	-3.8	-5.8	31	39	330	481	-17.2	-17.6
National League 1926																		
STL	47	30	.610	42	35	**.545**	54	42	411	359	-1.3	9.6	**36**	34	**406**	319	**20.2**	10.8
CIN	53	23	**.697**	34	44	.436	8	8	372	**259**	3.0	-31.3	27	32	375	392	10.8	-3.2
PIT	49	28	.636	35	41	.461	17	16	**446**	374	**36.3**	**17.2**	27	35	323	315	0.0	11.3
CHI	49	28	.636	33	44	.429	38	17	377	295	22.0	-5.1	28	21	305	**307**	-7.1	**15.9**
NY	43	33	.566	31	44	.413	45	**43**	333	317	-0.4	-10.8	28	27	330	351	-2.2	4.5
BKN	38	38	.500	33	44	.429	23	26	314	331	5.6	-8.0	17	24	309	374	-8.4	-1.4
BOS	43	34	.558	23	52	.307	4	5	296	266	**-10.9**	**-42.0**	12	41	328	453	-4.1	-18.2
PHI	33	42	.440	25	51	.329	51	42	392	**470**	32.8	9.3	24	26	295	430	-9.1	-19.6
American League 1926																		
NY	50	25	**.667**	41	38	.519	**58**	33	**417**	326	3.4	-10.1	**63**	23	**430**	387	**17.2**	-4.3
CLE	49	31	.613	39	35	.527	11	19	376	301	-3.9	-10.4	16	30	362	311	-0.4	14.8
PHI	44	27	.620	39	40	.494	34	27	365	314	**30.1**	**36.4**	27	**11**	312	**256**	-12.7	**27.5**
WAS	42	30	.583	39	39	.500	4	15	373	378	-8.3	4.0	39	30	429	383	15.5	-5.1
CHI	47	31	.603	34	41	.453	8	19	332	**294**	-19.7	**-23.7**	24	28	398	371	6.6	0.6
DET	39	41	.488	40	34	**.541**	16	38	380	**445**	-13.6	8.4	20	20	413	385	11.9	-7.9
STL	40	39	.506	22	53	.293	53	**64**	375	429	17.5	-0.8	19	22	307	416	-13.6	-14.8
BOS	25	51	.329	21	56	.273	9	16	**288**	438	5.1	10.3	23	29	274	397	-24.5	-10.6
National League 1927																		
PIT	48	31	.608	46	29	**.613**	25	23	406	345	-3.7	**7.0**	29	35	411	314	18.8	12.0
STL	55	25	**.688**	37	36	.507	55	**51**	433	354	**23.0**	3.8	29	**21**	321	**311**	-2.9	**12.4**
NY	49	25	.662	43	37	.538	**62**	49	389	342	-0.5	-0.9	**47**	28	**428**	378	**22.5**	-3.4
CHI	50	28	.641	35	40	.467	37	19	398	315	8.7	-12.4	37	31	352	346	3.6	5.2
CIN	45	35	.563	30	43	.411	3	11	348	320	7.6	-12.3	26	25	295	333	-12.6	8.2
BKN	34	39	.466	31	49	.388	20	35	**266**	**296**	4.5	-0.9	19	28	275	323	-20.6	11.5
BOS	32	41	.438	28	53	.346	5	10	296	339	**-8.7**	**-14.1**	32	33	355	432	0.7	-16.3
PHI	34	43	.442	17	60	.221	32	46	375	**429**	22.1	-10.6	25	38	303	474	-9.6	-29.6

TEAM	Home Games			Road Games			Home Games						Road Games					
	W	L	Pct.	W	L	Pct.	HR	OHR	R	OR	RF	ORF	HR	OHR	R	OR	RF	ORF
American League 1927																		
NY	57	19	**.750**	53	25	**.679**	83	30	**479**	**267**	-2.1	-18.5	75	12	**496**	**332**	34.1	17.7
PHI	50	27	.649	41	36	.532	26	36	412	327	-2.7	-16.9	30	29	429	399	15.9	0.9
WAS	51	28	.646	34	41	.453	10	19	416	308	12.2	-27.9	19	34	366	422	1.1	-3.5
DET	44	32	.579	38	39	.494	25	28	467	433	23.5	16.3	26	24	378	372	5.7	3.5
CHI	38	37	.507	32	46	.410	6	22	337	343	7.8	-2.2	30	33	325	365	-11.3	7.9
CLE	35	42	.455	31	45	.408	10	11	333	367	-1.8	-9.2	16	26	335	399	-9.0	-0.3
STL	38	38	.500	21	56	.273	42	57	440	**457**	52.9	0.9	13	22	284	447	-17.5	-13.8
BOS	29	49	.372	22	54	.289	5	29	**299**	409	-2.2	-10.8	23	27	298	447	-19.0	-12.3
National League 1928																		
STL	42	35	.545	53	24	**.688**	62	51	367	336	**-16.6**	11.9	51	35	**440**	**300**	20.4	16.2
NY	51	26	.662	42	35	.545	80	46	411	315	5.1	-5.6	38	31	396	338	11.2	7.7
CHI	52	25	**.675**	39	38	.506	40	18	335	**264**	-11.6	-24.7	52	38	379	351	4.4	6.4
PIT	47	30	.610	38	37	.507	16	**14**	479	356	30.3	-0.3	36	51	358	348	4.3	3.9
CIN	44	33	.571	34	41	.453	3	17	324	318	-3.8	-16.9	29	41	324	368	-9.4	0.4
BKN	41	35	.539	36	41	.468	31	25	330	296	-0.2	-12.8	35	34	335	344	-6.5	7.0
BOS	25	51	.329	25	52	.325	24	62	**309**	448	-2.7	5.5	28	38	322	430	-10.4	-18.9
PHI	26	49	.347	17	60	.221	54	**67**	360	**521**	23.2	**22.6**	31	42	300	436	-14.0	-22.8
American League 1928																		
NY	52	25	**.675**	49	28	**.636**	69	36	400	301	**-19.0**	**-21.6**	64	23	**494**	384	31.3	-1.7
PHI	52	25	**.675**	46	30	.605	54	33	**430**	**295**	6.3	-9.0	35	33	399	320	9.7	13.7
STL	44	33	.571	38	39	.494	51	**64**	398	389	6.4	10.1	12	29	374	353	2.6	2.6
WAS	37	43	.463	38	36	.514	16	**12**	363	378	-4.1	8.3	24	28	355	327	-3.0	9.2
CHI	37	40	.481	35	42	.455	11	28	316	369	-8.2	2.3	13	38	340	356	-8.2	-9.6
DET	36	41	.468	32	45	.416	33	26	382	400	5.5	-0.9	29	32	362	404	-0.7	-9.8
CLE	29	48	.377	33	44	.429	**10**	**15**	366	**443**	20.3	15.9	24	37	308	387	-14.1	-7.2
BOS	26	47	.356	31	49	.388	**10**	**15**	**283**	363	0.0	-3.5	28	34	306	407	-17.4	-9.3
National League 1929																		
CHI	52	25	**.675**	46	29	**.613**	76	41	490	374	-0.4	-2.6	63	**36**	**492**	384	20.0	8.1
PIT	45	31	.592	43	34	.558	28	37	471	382	11.6	-1.5	32	58	433	398	6.8	4.9
NY	39	37	.513	45	30	.600	79	59	418	374	**-15.0**	8.7	57	43	479	**335**	15.0	**18.4**
STL	43	32	.573	35	42	.455	48	50	414	386	-0.7	-8.1	52	51	417	420	1.7	0.1
PHI	39	37	.513	32	45	.416	86	**74**	503	**580**	31.0	31.6	67	49	394	452	-0.5	-12.3
BKN	42	35	.545	28	48	.368	53	48	371	413	-4.6	-14.1	46	44	384	475	-6.6	-12.1
CIN	38	39	.494	28	49	.364	7	18	356	**356**	6.4	-13.0	27	43	330	404	-18.6	4.4
BOS	34	43	.442	22	55	.286	11	39	**318**	403	-6.2	**-14.8**	22	64	339	473	-17.8	-11.4
American League 1929																		
PHI	57	16	**.781**	47	30	**.610**	72	47	**484**	**302**	20.7	0.3	50	**26**	417	**313**	13.4	**20.5**
NY	49	28	.636	39	38	.506	69	55	463	362	6.1	-12.3	**73**	28	436	413	17.1	-3.6
CLE	44	32	.579	37	39	.487	27	21	359	363	0.2	-2.6	35	35	358	373	-4.4	5.2
STL	41	36	.532	38	37	.507	22	**58**	370	341	1.9	-8.3	24	42	363	372	-2.9	6.1
WAS	37	40	.481	34	41	.453	**10**	**17**	376	390	2.1	-2.8	38	31	354	386	-4.8	1.4
DET	38	39	.494	32	45	.416	57	33	476	**453**	7.1	-3.4	53	40	**450**	475	20.8	-20.3
CHI	35	41	.461	24	52	.316	19	41	**306**	366	**-4.6**	**-14.0**	18	43	321	426	-14.8	-6.6
BOS	32	45	.416	26	51	.338	11	36	328	399	16.8	-2.5	17	42	277	404	-24.4	-2.8
National League 1930																		
STL	53	24	**.688**	39	38	.506	52	50	541	383	16.8	-4.4	52	**37**	463	**401**	9.4	10.6
CHI	51	26	.662	39	38	.506	**93**	62	538	454	13.9	6.3	**78**	49	460	416	8.7	5.7
NY	47	31	.603	40	36	**.526**	91	63	468	395	-7.1	-8.1	52	54	491	419	**13.0**	6.8
BKN	49	27	.645	37	41	.474	73	66	438	**336**	3.8	-14.2	49	49	433	402	0.4	**11.7**
PIT	42	35	.545	38	39	.494	26	51	433	454	-5.4	-4.2	60	77	458	474	5.3	-5.6
BOS	39	38	.506	31	46	.403	29	51	329	401	-9.6	-7.6	37	66	364	434	-16.7	3.6
CIN	37	40	.481	22	55	.286	**20**	**21**	**300**	368	**-17.8**	**-24.7**	54	54	365	489	-17.3	-6.1
PHI	35	42	.455	17	60	.221	72	**72**	543	**644**	38.9	19.0	54	70	401	555	-3.0	-26.8
American League 1930																		
PHI	58	18	**.763**	44	34	**.564**	76	49	485	329	6.8	-19.9	49	**35**	466	422	16.0	4.6
WAS	56	21	.727	38	39	.494	17	**15**	474	**300**	13.3	**-22.8**	40	37	418	**389**	5.3	12.1
NY	47	29	.618	39	39	.500	69	54	471	390	**-18.2**	-21.2	**83**	39	**591**	508	42.7	-14.6
CLE	44	33	.571	37	40	.481	34	46	**494**	469	24.7	5.1	38	39	396	446	1.1	-4.3
DET	45	33	.577	30	46	.395	45	48	441	419	25.6	-1.3	37	38	342	414	-12.1	3.6
STL	38	40	.487	26	50	.342	35	**72**	432	**475**	31.9	12.6	40	52	319	411	-17.4	2.6
CHI	34	44	.436	28	48	.368	25	42	393	457	13.9	4.2	38	32	336	427	-14.9	-0.1
BOS	30	46	.395	22	56	.282	**15**	31	**287**	354	-9.3	-21.0	32	44	325	460	-20.6	-3.8

	Home Games			Road Games			Home Games						Road Games					
TEAM	W	L	Pct.	W	L	Pct.	HR	OHR	R	OR	RF	ORF	HR	OHR	R	OR	RF	ORF
National League 1931																		
STL	54	24	.692	47	29	.618	31	29	439	320	13.7	6.0	29	36	376	294	15.6	17.4
NY	50	27	.649	37	38	.493	80	47	379	274	-6.3	-18.9	21	24	389	325	16.8	11.5
CHI	50	27	.649	34	43	.442	40	22	414	311	2.5	-20.0	44	32	414	399	24.7	-7.7
BKN	46	29	.613	33	44	.429	46	22	363	317	15.6	-9.7	25	34	318	356	-2.5	2.5
PIT	44	33	.571	31	46	.403	25	16	343	327	15.5	-11.3	16	39	293	364	-9.8	0.2
PHI	40	36	.526	26	52	.333	53	33	391	423	38.7	8.5	28	42	293	405	-8.0	-13.0
BOS	36	41	.468	28	49	.364	16	24	278	318	9.0	-12.1	18	42	255	362	-22.3	1.0
CIN	38	39	.494	20	57	.260	6	3	312	328	11.4	-20.7	15	48	280	414	-14.4	-11.9
American League 1931																		
PHI	60	15	.800	47	30	.610	61	37	446	289	12.5	-10.8	57	36	412	337	9.9	20.4
NY	51	25	.671	43	34	.558	84	39	545	337	5.7	-19.3	71	28	522	423	38.6	0.8
WAS	55	22	.714	37	40	.481	13	24	453	308	13.2	-21.6	36	49	390	383	5.0	10.1
CLE	45	31	.592	33	45	.423	38	32	503	405	36.8	-1.6	33	32	382	428	4.8	-2.2
STL	39	38	.506	24	53	.312	42	48	407	425	29.2	-4.5	34	36	315	445	-13.7	-6.4
BOS	39	40	.494	23	50	.315	11	29	332	362	3.3	-24.5	26	25	293	438	-21.3	-3.0
DET	36	41	.468	25	52	.325	19	43	349	432	15.5	6.9	24	36	302	404	-18.6	2.0
CHI	31	45	.408	25	52	.325	11	45	341	421	-3.6	-16.6	16	37	363	518	-4.8	-21.6
National League 1932																		
CHI	53	24	.688	37	40	.481	32	33	390	303	18.1	-8.1	37	35	330	330	-3.0	9.7
PIT	45	31	.592	41	37	.526	22	25	352	338	3.5	-7.0	26	61	349	373	0.3	-1.8
BKN	44	34	.564	37	39	.487	59	31	378	353	-1.5	-12.7	51	41	374	394	7.5	-7.4
PHI	45	32	.584	33	44	.429	86	71	507	429	50.4	16.8	36	36	337	367	2.8	-3.5
BOS	44	33	.571	33	44	.429	27	20	299	285	-13.4	-21.9	36	41	350	370	-1.3	0.6
NY	37	40	.481	35	42	.455	78	71	362	359	-7.8	3.4	38	41	393	347	11.7	3.6
STL	42	35	.545	30	47	.390	36	38	354	357	4.5	-3.3	40	38	330	360	-4.3	0.5
CIN	33	44	.429	27	50	.351	11	11	270	344	-10.3	-6.0	36	58	305	371	-13.6	-1.6
American League 1932																		
NY	62	15	.805	45	32	.584	81	44	482	300	-4.9	-27.4	79	49	520	424	32.0	1.4
PHI	51	26	.662	43	34	.558	109	80	572	406	39.8	17.3	63	32	409	346	10.0	14.7
WAS	51	26	.662	42	35	.545	21	26	431	325	5.3	-16.8	40	47	409	391	5.5	7.6
CLE	43	33	.566	44	32	.579	36	33	460	401	17.9	14.3	42	37	385	346	1.1	14.8
DET	42	34	.553	34	41	.453	29	50	423	399	8.1	-1.1	51	39	376	388	-2.1	6.0
STL	33	42	.440	30	49	.380	47	56	385	428	15.5	-4.0	20	47	351	470	-8.9	-12.1
CHI	28	49	.364	21	53	.284	10	36	300	390	-20.3	-25.0	26	52	367	507	-8.0	-18.8
BOS	27	50	.351	16	61	.208	18	31	295	439	8.8	-7.7	35	48	271	476	-29.7	-13.7
National League 1933																		
NY	48	27	.640	43	34	.558	55	44	298	241	-9.5	-9.7	27	17	338	274	10.1	13.2
PIT	50	27	.649	37	40	.481	12	13	332	272	-0.9	-21.6	27	41	335	347	10.6	-8.5
CHI	55	24	.696	31	44	.413	40	32	334	239	1.6	-23.6	32	19	312	297	4.1	6.8
BOS	45	31	.592	38	40	.487	27	26	265	230	-5.2	-21.6	27	28	287	301	-5.9	6.1
STL	46	31	.597	36	40	.474	18	25	347	315	2.0	7.1	39	30	340	294	12.7	4.6
BKN	36	41	.468	29	47	.382	33	29	306	352	-5.3	-1.2	29	22	311	343	2.6	-10.5
PHI	32	40	.444	28	52	.350	45	46	355	437	56.5	50.3	15	41	252	323	-12.4	-8.3
CIN	37	42	.468	21	52	.288	5	10	264	321	6.5	-6.6	29	37	232	322	-21.9	-3.4
American League 1933																		
WAS	46	30	.605	53	23	.697	14	16	358	338	-26.2	4.7	46	48	492	327	24.6	13.2
NY	51	23	.689	40	36	.526	79	26	421	324	-14.5	-25.0	65	40	506	444	29.8	-13.3
PHI	46	29	.613	33	43	.434	82	50	414	387	-10.2	-16.9	57	27	461	466	19.3	-20.4
CLE	45	32	.584	30	44	.405	22	24	353	341	12.7	0.0	28	36	301	328	-19.3	12.9
DET	43	35	.551	32	44	.421	27	36	394	382	18.5	7.4	30	48	328	351	-11.8	6.2
CHI	35	41	.461	32	42	.432	20	42	355	426	4.0	5.5	23	43	328	388	-13.1	-3.7
BOS	32	40	.444	31	46	.403	23	35	341	377	1.5	5.8	27	40	359	381	-6.4	-0.5
STL	30	46	.395	25	50	.333	43	68	389	480	37.1	39.3	21	28	280	340	-23.0	5.5
National League 1934																		
STL	48	29	.623	47	29	.618	56	43	451	363	29.5	23.8	48	34	348	293	4.6	17.8
NY	49	26	.653	44	34	.564	75	43	363	254	-4.9	-19.7	51	32	397	329	13.9	12.9
CHI	47	30	.610	39	35	.527	53	44	347	301	-5.6	-13.2	48	36	358	338	3.4	9.2
BOS	40	35	.533	38	38	.500	36	27	280	280	-28.6	-33.7	47	51	403	434	12.4	-12.9
PIT	45	32	.584	29	44	.397	22	38	421	369	25.4	0.3	30	40	314	344	-5.0	5.4
BKN	43	33	.566	28	48	.368	40	38	390	355	7.5	-20.3	39	43	358	440	5.0	-16.9
PHI	35	36	.493	21	57	.269	28	72	384	400	44.9	11.5	28	54	291	394	-12.2	-7.5
CIN	30	47	.390	22	52	.297	17	24	331	406	21.2	-2.4	38	37	259	395	-22.2	-7.9

TEAM	Home Games W	L	Pct.	Road Games W	L	Pct.	Home Games HR	OHR	R	OR	RF	ORF	Road Games HR	OHR	R	OR	RF	ORF
American League 1934
DET	54	26	.675	47	27	**.635**	28	32	**479**	345	**-7.5**	-12.0	46	54	**479**	**363**	**24.1**	**10.3**
NY	53	24	**.688**	41	36	.532	75	34	416	**275**	-2.3	**-30.2**	60	37	426	394	10.1	5.8
CLE	47	31	.603	38	38	.500	45	34	435	362	11.8	-12.0	55	36	379	401	0.0	1.5
BOS	42	35	.545	34	41	.453	23	**24**	447	405	**18.2**	**8.0**	28	46	373	370	-0.8	6.9
PHI	34	40	.459	34	42	.447	**81**	48	371	410	-4.3	-2.9	**63**	36	393	428	1.1	-5.7
STL	36	39	.480	31	46	.403	35	60	**356**	405	14.8	5.2	27	**34**	318	395	-16.3	1.5
WAS	34	40	.459	32	46	.410	**14**	26	368	397	5.9	0.8	37	48	361	409	-6.1	-1.2
CHI	29	46	.387	24	53	.312	47	**82**	370	**464**	15.2	0.1	24	57	334	482	-12.2	-19.2
National League 1935
CHI	56	21	**.727**	44	33	**.571**	43	40	426	**264**	1.1	-20.7	45	45	**421**	333	**20.9**	14.0
STL	53	24	.688	43	34	.558	39	27	**441**	298	13.6	-8.8	47	41	388	327	13.2	14.2
NY	50	27	.649	41	35	.539	**84**	66	386	302	-2.0	-21.0	39	40	384	373	10.2	3.4
PIT	46	31	.597	40	36	.526	32	25	398	340	13.8	9.3	34	**38**	345	**307**	0.8	**17.5**
BKN	38	38	.500	32	45	.416	32	43	349	346	**-3.6**	-17.8	27	45	362	421	3.3	-9.1
CIN	41	35	.539	27	50	.351	18	18	331	320	7.8	**-27.3**	**55**	47	315	452	-9.0	-15.4
PHI	35	43	.449	29	46	.387	52	68	416	**499**	**50.7**	**30.7**	40	**38**	269	372	-17.5	-2.8
BOS	25	50	.333	13	65	.167	34	41	**309**	381	20.8	-15.8	41	40	266	471	-22.1	-21.8
American League 1935
DET	53	25	**.679**	40	33	.548	45	38	**467**	304	-4.5	**-22.1**	**61**	40	452	361	17.6	9.6
NY	41	33	.554	48	27	**.640**	60	51	**341**	**294**	**-27.5**	-11.8	44	40	**477**	338	**19.2**	**15.1**
CLE	48	29	.623	34	42	.447	53	30	391	340	4.1	-12.5	40	38	385	399	0.0	0.0
BOS	41	37	.526	37	38	.493	26	29	393	404	14.7	16.9	43	38	**325**	**328**	-13.5	13.8
CHI	42	34	.553	32	44	.421	50	**61**	418	396	**28.9**	10.4	24	44	320	354	-13.9	8.2
WAS	37	39	.487	30	47	.390	5	**28**	388	414	-10.8	-15.3	27	**61**	435	489	11.2	-22.4
STL	31	44	.413	34	43	.442	36	49	374	**513**	13.0	**27.8**	37	43	344	417	-9.8	-9.5
PHI	30	42	.417	28	49	.364	**63**	39	369	414	15.7	-2.7	49	**34**	341	455	-10.7	-14.8
National League 1936
NY	52	26	**.667**	40	36	.526	68	54	378	296	1.1	-11.2	29	**21**	364	325	0.7	12.3
CHI	50	27	.649	37	40	.481	34	41	404	**290**	15.0	-7.3	42	35	351	**313**	-1.4	**15.4**
STL	43	33	.566	44	34	**.564**	38	43	363	386	-14.8	-4.1	50	46	**432**	408	**16.6**	-10.5
PIT	46	30	.605	38	40	.487	23	25	375	342	-7.9	-4.2	37	49	429	376	16.3	-1.3
CIN	42	34	.553	32	46	.410	24	**21**	358	350	0.9	**-12.3**	**58**	30	364	410	0.0	-9.7
BOS	35	43	.449	36	40	.474	26	23	**292**	339	**-14.9**	-10.9	41	46	339	376	-8.2	-1.2
BKN	37	40	.481	30	47	.390	15	46	360	397	16.1	9.0	18	39	302	355	-14.8	1.7
PHI	30	48	.385	24	52	.316	**69**	**56**	**408**	**499**	**25.0**	**29.6**	34	31	318	375	-9.3	-6.5
American League 1936
NY	56	21	**.727**	46	30	**.605**	**82**	41	492	**311**	**-13.0**	**-25.0**	**100**	43	**573**	420	**31.8**	9.5
DET	44	33	.571	39	38	.506	51	58	448	399	-5.2	-15.4	43	42	473	472	10.0	-3.0
CHI	43	32	.573	38	38	.500	23	55	453	419	0.8	-4.0	37	49	467	454	8.9	0.0
WAS	42	35	.545	40	36	.526	16	**27**	433	380	-6.2	-10.4	46	46	456	419	6.1	7.8
CLE	49	30	.620	31	44	.413	73	33	**535**	433	30.0	-5.3	50	**40**	386	429	-5.2	4.4
BOS	47	29	.618	27	51	.346	38	31	437	360	**30.9**	-9.7	48	47	338	**404**	-17.9	**11.3**
STL	31	43	.419	26	52	.333	47	63	443	**552**	24.3	**9.2**	32	52	361	512	-13.0	-15.0
PHI	31	46	.403	22	54	.289	43	**77**	**383**	531	15.7	3.3	29	54	331	514	-20.9	-14.8
National League 1937
NY	50	25	**.667**	45	32	.584	**76**	57	353	288	-4.3	-5.8	35	28	379	**314**	7.4	**10.2**
CHI	46	32	.590	47	29	**.618**	47	48	**412**	361	0.6	9.5	49	43	**399**	321	**14.6**	5.8
PIT	46	32	.590	40	36	.526	13	28	360	332	1.9	3.0	34	43	344	**314**	-1.0	8.6
STL	45	33	.577	36	40	.474	52	51	406	379	2.0	3.0	42	44	383	354	10.3	-3.1
BOS	43	33	.566	36	40	.474	26	15	**252**	**224**	-22.9	**-32.5**	37	45	327	332	-9.1	8.0
BKN	36	39	.480	26	52	.333	20	30	336	389	**24.7**	5.5	17	38	280	383	-17.9	-10.8
PHI	29	45	.392	32	47	.405	65	**69**	379	**481**	20.2	**35.6**	38	47	345	388	-0.1	-15.3
CIN	28	51	.354	28	47	.373	13	**14**	268	347	**-26.9**	-9.6	**60**	**24**	344	360	-4.3	-3.4
American League 1937
NY	57	20	**.740**	45	32	**.584**	**94**	41	520	**298**	11.8	-21.1	**80**	51	**459**	373	**18.3**	**13.1**
DET	49	28	.636	40	37	.519	91	58	**521**	448	**27.4**	**15.4**	59	44	414	393	8.4	4.4
CHI	47	30	.610	39	38	.506	39	62	397	365	3.6	0.0	28	53	383	**365**	-2.4	12.8
CLE	50	28	.641	33	43	.434	48	**22**	430	329	11.1	**-25.0**	55	**39**	387	439	-0.4	-1.5
BOS	44	29	.603	36	43	.456	53	43	420	368	13.2	-2.2	47	49	401	407	2.3	3.9
WAS	43	35	.551	30	45	.400	**14**	30	376	381	-3.7	-19.2	33	**66**	381	460	-3.5	-7.5
PHI	27	50	.351	27	47	.365	51	47	**333**	**419**	**-13.6**	-8.5	43	58	366	435	-8.2	-3.4
STL	25	51	.329	21	57	.269	39	**74**	385	**513**	16.6	0.5	32	69	330	510	-14.5	-21.9

TEAM	Home Games			Road Games			Home Games						Road Games					
	W	L	Pct.	W	L	Pct.	HR	OHR	R	OR	RF	ORF	HR	OHR	R	OR	RF	ORF
National League 1938																		
CHI	44	33	.571	45	30	**.600**	24	41	349	326	-4.1	19.8	41	30	364	**272**	6.4	**16.3**
PIT	44	33	.571	42	31	.575	22	22	348	330	-8.0	4.3	43	49	359	300	5.1	8.8
NY	43	30	.589	40	37	.519	**89**	**58**	365	297	16.1	-5.4	36	**29**	340	340	0.8	-0.3
CIN	43	34	.558	39	34	.534	50	31	344	323	-12.7	-0.1	**60**	44	379	311	10.1	6.2
BOS	45	30	**.600**	32	45	.416	12	19	233	241	**-26.1**	**-33.5**	42	47	328	377	-7.0	-7.9
STL	36	41	.468	35	39	.473	58	45	**414**	425	23.2	32.9	33	32	311	296	-4.7	6.3
BKN	31	41	.431	38	39	.494	38	44	319	349	-13.7	0.5	23	44	**385**	361	**10.7**	-7.8
PHI	26	48	.351	19	57	.250	18	40	286	**439**	9.7	10.9	22	36	264	401	-21.5	-21.7
American League 1938																		
NY	55	22	**.714**	44	31	**.587**	112	43	**524**	**342**	17.0	-8.2	62	42	**442**	368	12.1	13.0
BOS	52	23	.693	36	38	.486	67	52	481	356	14.2	-9.8	31	50	421	395	6.2	7.0
CLE	46	30	.605	40	36	.526	54	35	425	363	2.0	-12.2	59	65	422	419	4.7	1.8
DET	48	31	.608	36	39	.480	83	60	447	392	3.6	-6.4	54	50	415	403	3.9	4.2
WAS	44	33	.571	31	43	.419	33	**27**	412	413	-2.7	**-14.8**	52	65	402	460	0.0	-8.2
CHI	33	39	.458	32	44	.421	**24**	**41**	326	364	**-11.3**	-2.3	43	60	383	388	-6.7	8.2
STL	31	43	.419	24	54	.308	52	62	385	**487**	6.7	5.1	40	70	370	475	-7.7	-13.5
PHI	28	47	.373	25	52	.325	55	**64**	378	486	11.4	**6.1**	43	78	348	470	-12.7	-12.5
National League 1939																		
CIN	55	25	**.688**	42	32	**.568**	48	39	404	307	3.0	-1.3	**50**	42	363	288	10.7	17.4
STL	51	27	.654	41	34	.547	63	42	**431**	317	19.1	-3.5	35	34	348	316	7.8	10.1
BKN	51	27	.654	33	42	.440	41	49	385	329	20.7	5.4	37	44	323	316	-0.4	9.7
CHI	44	34	.564	40	36	.526	44	35	379	343	4.3	-2.7	47	39	345	335	5.1	4.4
NY	41	33	.554	36	41	.468	**84**	**58**	360	315	9.2	-11.4	32	**28**	343	370	3.8	-3.2
PIT	35	42	.455	33	43	.434	22	29	339	365	2.3	1.1	41	41	327	356	-1.1	-1.5
BOS	37	35	.514	26	53	.329	13	14	**254**	**272**	**-13.5**	**-23.9**	43	49	318	387	-6.7	-5.9
PHI	29	44	.397	16	62	.205	19	49	288	**384**	14.5	-14.2	30	57	265	472	-19.3	-31.0
American League 1939																		
NY	52	25	**.675**	54	20	**.730**	**84**	48	382	**261**	**-36.4**	-13.8	**82**	**37**	**585**	295	**37.5**	**26.1**
BOS	42	32	.568	47	30	.610	57	39	458	445	8.8	30.5	67	38	432	350	6.9	8.0
CLE	44	33	.571	43	34	.558	30	33	363	347	-16.3	-1.7	55	42	434	353	4.4	10.4
CHI	50	27	.649	35	42	.455	38	51	414	366	**22.9**	0.0	26	48	341	371	-13.9	5.8
DET	42	35	.545	39	38	.506	66	65	**461**	434	17.2	**30.6**	58	39	388	328	-2.4	13.2
WAS	37	39	.487	28	48	.368	11	**19**	326	337	-14.4	**-27.7**	33	56	376	460	-9.1	-12.9
PHI	28	48	.368	27	49	.355	45	**83**	354	523	0.4	6.1	53	65	357	499	-12.3	-27.5
STL	18	59	.234	25	52	.325	47	80	372	**561**	3.0	18.3	44	53	361	474	-10.9	-23.2
National League 1940																		
CIN	55	21	**.724**	45	32	.584	47	36	352	**240**	0.4	**-15.5**	42	37	355	288	4.2	16.4
BKN	41	37	.526	47	28	**.627**	40	55	369	358	4.1	26.0	**53**	46	328	**263**	-2.1	18.5
STL	41	36	.532	43	33	.566	**69**	47	368	364	-0.3	11.4	50	36	379	335	10.9	-0.3
PIT	40	34	.541	38	42	.475	26	**22**	390	354	0.5	-10.8	50	50	419	429	**22.0**	-24.3
CHI	40	37	.519	35	42	.455	40	32	333	316	-4.3	-1.2	46	42	348	320	1.7	5.3
NY	33	43	.434	39	37	.513	61	75	323	339	-5.0	5.9	30	**35**	340	320	-0.7	4.4
BOS	35	40	.467	30	47	.390	**25**	30	328	352	14.1	-8.0	34	53	295	393	-12.1	-14.9
PHI	24	55	.304	26	48	.351	33	50	**232**	**403**	**-17.0**	8.7	42	42	262	347	-24.1	-4.9
American League 1940																		
DET	50	29	.633	40	35	**.533**	82	64	**512**	389	**31.0**	14.0	52	**38**	376	328	4.8	14.7
CLE	51	30	.630	38	35	.521	37	**27**	350	**281**	**-13.4**	**-29.7**	64	59	360	356	-4.3	11.9
NY	52	24	**.684**	36	42	.462	83	60	414	284	6.7	-23.7	**72**	56	403	387	7.8	4.9
BOS	45	34	.570	37	38	.493	73	64	468	421	9.9	-1.0	**72**	60	**404**	404	9.8	-3.2
CHI	41	36	.532	41	36	.532	36	65	357	363	-6.7	**15.9**	37	46	378	**309**	0.1	**19.7**
STL	37	39	.487	30	48	.385	68	**68**	419	**460**	27.1	11.8	50	45	338	422	-7.1	-8.4
WAS	36	41	.468	28	49	.364	**19**	28	**316**	368	-9.4	-16.9	33	65	349	443	-8.0	-10.2
PHI	29	42	.408	25	58	.301	44	62	336	409	7.0	-8.5	61	73	367	523	-3.1	-29.3
National League 1941																		
BKN	52	25	.675	48	29	**.623**	55	40	**421**	282	9.6	-6.8	46	41	**379**	299	**18.4**	11.0
STL	53	24	**.688**	44	32	.579	37	53	405	324	**18.4**	17.6	33	32	329	**265**	4.3	**18.3**
CIN	45	34	.570	43	32	.573	27	27	308	**273**	-5.0	-10.9	37	34	308	291	-5.1	13.4
PIT	45	32	.584	36	41	.468	20	28	346	336	0.5	9.4	36	38	344	307	6.0	6.9
NY	38	39	.494	36	40	.474	**68**	**69**	360	358	17.2	2.8	27	**21**	307	348	-3.3	-4.6
CHI	38	39	.494	32	45	.416	37	**20**	311	306	**-11.2**	**-14.8**	**62**	40	355	364	7.6	-6.9
BOS	32	44	.421	30	48	.385	17	28	276	321	-8.0	**-15.3**	31	47	316	399	-4.1	-16.6
PHI	23	52	.307	20	59	.253	34	37	**255**	**384**	7.7	-2.4	30	42	246	409	-23.8	-21.6

TEAM	Home Games W	L	Pct.	Road Games W	L	Pct.	Home Games HR	OHR	R	OR	RF	ORF	Road Games HR	OHR	R	OR	RF	ORF
American League 1941																		
NY	51	26	**.662**	50	27	**.649**	**76**	44	396	**295**	-8.7	-12.2	**75**	37	**434 336**		**18.2**	**11.7**
BOS	47	30	.610	37	40	.481	70	51	**461**	371	15.5	-0.8	54	37	404	379	13.2	-0.8
CHI	38	39	.494	39	38	.506	17	40	**288**	297	-19.8	-17.7	30	49	350	352	-5.7	7.9
CLE	42	35	.545	33	44	.429	45	35	340	322	2.1	-5.7	58	**36**	337	346	-7.0	8.4
DET	43	34	.558	32	45	.416	51	43	381	377	**26.5**	4.3	30	37	305	366	-13.3	1.9
STL	40	37	.519	30	47	.390	49	63	407	408	12.2	-2.9	42	57	358	415	0.2	-10.5
WAS	40	37	.519	30	47	.390	**13**	**19**	367	387	1.6	-5.8	39	50	361	411	-0.3	-8.8
PHI	36	41	.468	28	49	.364	43	**75**	373	**432**	9.7	**5.8**	42	61	340	408	-5.2	-9.6
National League 1942																		
STL	60	17	**.779**	46	31	.597	31	24	**419 229**		**24.7**	-9.4	29	25	336	**253**	20.0	**19.2**
BKN	57	22	.722	47	28	**.627**	30	35	381	250	1.5	-7.5	32	38	**361**	260	**25.9**	16.3
NY	47	31	.603	38	36	.514	**80**	**67**	376	296	20.9	-6.3	29	27	299	304	6.9	2.0
CIN	38	39	.494	38	37	.507	30	23	264	276	-2.2	**0.0**	36	**24**	263	269	-8.8	12.7
PIT	41	34	.547	25	47	.347	**15**	**21**	333	301	23.5	-14.7	**39**	41	252	330	-9.1	-5.4
CHI	36	41	.468	32	45	.416	36	27	298	318	0.4	-9.5	**39**	43	293	347	1.7	-10.9
BOS	33	36	.478	26	53	.329	36	34	250	271	9.1	**-16.1**	32	48	265	374	-8.8	-16.7
PHI	23	51	.311	19	58	.247	18	31	**182 340**		**-10.6**	-3.3	26	30	212	366	-27.8	-17.2
American League 1942																		
NY	58	19	**.753**	45	32	**.584**	62	39	394	**226**	-3.2	**-19.5**	46	32	**407 281**		25.2	16.3
BOS	53	24	.688	40	35	.533	54	33	**403**	299	9.6	-1.2	**49**	32	358	295	12.3	9.8
STL	40	37	.519	42	32	.568	55	37	376	350	2.0	**17.2**	43	26	354	287	10.2	10.0
CLE	39	39	.500	36	40	.474	20	24	266	308	**-22.0**	-16.6	30	37	324	351	-0.1	-5.4
DET	43	34	.558	30	47	.390	50	40	344	302	**44.0**	8.7	26	**20**	245	285	-20.4	12.3
CHI	35	35	.500	31	47	.397	**6**	31	256	275	1.1	-8.2	19	43	282	334	-13.8	0.3
WAS	35	42	.455	27	47	.365	13	**11**	339	409	3.7	-3.6	27	39	314	408	-2.0	-24.5
PHI	25	51	.329	30	48	.385	16	**42**	**249 415**		-14.8	10.3	17	47	300	386	-9.2	-18.8
National League 1943																		
STL	58	21	**.734**	47	28	**.627**	33	17	355	**243**	2.8	-1.7	**37**	**16**	324	**232**	8.4	**24.6**
CIN	48	29	.623	39	38	.506	**17**	**15**	282	280	**-14.6**	5.1	26	23	326	263	5.9	14.4
BKN	46	31	.597	35	41	.461	21	30	**389**	323	17.4	-9.1	18	29	327	351	**10.7**	-12.1
PIT	47	30	.610	33	44	.429	20	**15**	364	296	**20.8**	-2.9	22	29	305	309	3.3	0.8
CHI	36	38	.486	38	41	.481	24	19	292	300	-9.5	5.3	28	34	**340**	300	10.4	3.1
BOS	38	39	.494	30	46	.395	25	34	**247 327**		11.8	**13.2**	14	32	218	285	-26.7	6.3
PHI	33	43	.434	31	47	.397	29	18	269	314	-9.7	-12.1	**37**	41	302	362	-1.5	-14.8
NY	34	43	.442	21	55	.276	**63**	**52**	291	326	11.8	**-13.5**	18	28	267	387	-10.7	-22.4
American League 1943																		
NY	54	23	**.701**	44	33	**.571**	**60**	33	321	**241**	-6.5	-18.9	**40**	27	**348**	301	**15.6**	2.6
WAS	44	32	.579	40	37	.519	**9**	**14**	**345**	307	8.8	7.9	38	34	321	288	8.7	3.7
CLE	44	33	.571	38	38	.500	16	21	269	**247**	**-19.7**	**-26.1**	39	31	331	330	8.4	-5.9
CHI	40	36	.526	42	36	.538	20	25	264	311	-11.2	**14.2**	13	29	309	283	1.8	4.9
DET	45	32	.584	33	44	.429	45	26	**345**	284	18.6	1.5	32	25	287	**276**	-1.2	**8.1**
STL	44	33	.571	28	47	.373	49	**51**	319	290	13.6	-8.8	29	**23**	277	314	-5.2	-3.1
BOS	39	36	.520	29	48	.377	29	25	293	312	9.9	7.1	28	36	270	295	-8.4	1.4
PHI	27	51	.346	22	54	.289	14	36	**261 387**		6.3	12.8	12	37	236	330	-19.7	-11.8
National League 1944																		
STL	54	22	**.711**	51	27	**.654**	39	**14**	360	**230**	-9.2	-8.1	**61**	41	**412 260**		**23.1**	**22.9**
PIT	49	28	.636	41	35	.539	23	31	**399**	357	9.9	**11.2**	47	34	345	305	6.8	6.3
CIN	45	33	.577	44	32	.579	**14**	23	**253**	252	-21.9	-12.7	37	37	320	285	-5.3	15.5
CHI	35	42	.455	40	37	.519	33	40	346	342	-1.5	5.9	38	35	356	327	7.7	1.1
NY	39	36	.520	28	51	.354	**75**	**86**	372	382	**28.0**	4.2	18	30	310	391	-3.4	-17.1
BOS	38	40	.487	27	49	.355	51	44	293	307	-3.5	**-17.4**	28	36	300	367	-9.1	-8.0
BKN	37	39	.487	26	52	.333	27	34	372	**413**	18.4	-0.1	29	41	318	419	-1.3	-25.7
PHI	29	49	.372	32	43	.427	20	21	271	346	-4.0	5.2	35	**28**	268	312	-18.4	4.9
American League 1944																		
STL	54	23	**.701**	35	42	.455	45	24	368	272	16.4	-13.6	27	34	316	315	6.7	6.2
DET	43	34	.558	45	32	**.584**	38	21	325	318	-2.4	**20.9**	22	**18**	333	**263**	9.9	**18.2**
NY	47	31	.603	36	40	.474	**58**	**45**	388	307	**32.1**	-3.5	38	37	286	310	-1.0	6.2
BOS	47	30	.610	30	47	.390	48	34	**389**	311	11.1	-14.8	21	32	**350**	365	17.5	-8.4
CLE	39	38	.506	33	44	.429	27	16	345	**328**	14.2	-7.2	**43**	24	298	349	0.6	-4.8
PHI	39	37	.513	33	45	.423	18	28	**277**	270	16.1	-13.3	18	30	248	324	-16.6	3.9
CHI	41	36	.532	30	47	.390	11	24	302	304	25.3	-15.0	12	44	241	358	-17.6	-6.3
WAS	40	37	.519	24	53	.312	**9**	**13**	286	**268**	**-6.5**	**-32.3**	24	35	306	396	0.5	-15.0

TEAM	Home Games			Road Games			Home Games						Road Games					
	W	L	Pct.	W	L	Pct.	HR	OHR	R	OR	RF	ORF	HR	OHR	R	OR	RF	ORF
National League 1945																		
CHI	49	26	.653	49	30	.620	24	17	330	253	-15.3	-5.7	33	40	405	279	16.1	20.8
STL	48	29	.623	47	30	.610	28	29	368	286	-6.3	-4.9	36	41	388	297	13.1	15.1
BKN	48	30	.615	39	37	.513	29	34	387	347	-6.3	-9.1	28	40	408	377	18.9	-7.1
PIT	45	34	.570	37	38	.493	31	25	407	352	13.1	1.3	41	36	346	334	3.8	3.4
NY	47	30	.610	31	44	.413	83	47	366	325	18.0	-15.5	31	38	302	375	-9.0	-5.8
BOS	36	38	.486	31	47	.397	68	63	411	395	39.6	24.9	33	36	310	333	-5.3	2.1
CIN	36	41	.468	25	52	.325	25	23	267	307	-0.7	-20.6	31	47	269	387	-21.1	-8.2
PHI	22	55	.286	24	53	.312	23	28	261	450	-9.0	8.4	33	33	287	415	-16.7	-20.3
American League 1945																		
DET	50	26	.658	38	39	.494	43	28	333	285	15.3	5.8	34	20	300	280	6.6	9.9
WAS	46	31	.597	41	36	.532	1	6	278	255	-19.1	-16.9	26	36	344	307	17.7	3.5
STL	47	27	.635	34	43	.442	32	33	353	291	48.4	16.2	31	26	244	257	-9.6	16.1
NY	48	28	.632	33	43	.434	65	51	395	297	40.5	-3.8	28	15	281	309	3.5	1.2
CLE	44	33	.571	29	39	.426	27	15	292	273	0.1	-9.7	38	24	265	275	-5.9	11.8
CHI	44	29	.603	27	49	.355	8	34	305	277	7.6	-20.0	14	29	291	356	2.6	-11.1
BOS	42	35	.545	29	48	.377	22	28	306	299	5.7	-19.2	28	30	293	375	3.2	-17.3
PHI	39	35	.527	13	63	.171	16	21	265	270	14.2	-27.5	17	34	229	368	-18.1	-14.2
National League 1946																		
STL	49	29	.628	49	29	.628	39	36	370	288	8.1	12.0	42	27	342	257	14.7	16.8
BKN	56	22	.718	40	38	.513	20	22	374	273	12.9	-9.2	35	36	327	297	10.5	6.2
CHI	44	33	.571	38	38	.500	24	30	291	260	-12.0	-17.9	32	28	335	321	9.4	0.0
BOS	45	31	.592	36	41	.468	14	31	300	268	-9.1	-17.2	30	45	330	324	8.3	-1.1
PHI	41	36	.532	28	49	.364	38	34	280	335	-1.2	-10.6	42	39	280	370	-6.9	-16.6
CIN	35	42	.455	32	45	.416	37	39	267	289	7.0	5.5	28	31	256	281	-14.4	10.0
PIT	37	40	.481	26	51	.338	24	23	303	342	20.1	3.5	36	27	249	326	-15.0	-4.6
NY	38	39	.494	23	54	.299	76	75	340	336	25.0	-3.7	45	39	272	349	-6.8	-10.7
American League 1946																		
BOS	61	16	.792	43	34	.558	65	44	469	315	45.2	12.9	44	45	323	279	10.0	11.2
DET	48	30	.615	44	32	.579	75	68	391	300	20.1	8.0	33	29	313	267	4.0	15.1
NY	47	30	.610	40	37	.519	68	34	342	262	0.0	-8.0	68	32	342	285	10.2	11.6
WAS	38	38	.500	38	40	.487	16	25	253	343	-25.9	-1.7	44	56	355	363	10.3	-12.8
CHI	40	38	.513	34	42	.447	17	46	272	290	-9.7	-8.5	20	34	290	305	-7.2	5.1
CLE	36	41	.468	32	45	.416	25	36	231	264	-22.5	-27.5	54	48	306	374	-4.3	-12.7
STL	35	41	.461	31	47	.397	46	29	313	344	4.2	-3.5	38	44	308	366	-0.5	-13.7
PHI	31	46	.403	18	59	.234	21	38	297	351	26.3	5.3	19	45	232	329	-22.5	-3.8
National League 1947																		
BKN	52	25	.675	42	35	.545	37	57	409	343	10.6	4.1	46	47	365	325	5.0	7.9
STL	46	31	.597	43	34	.558	45	49	400	331	7.9	12.0	70	57	380	303	8.4	13.8
BOS	50	27	.649	36	41	.468	29	39	332	289	-10.0	-13.2	56	54	369	333	3.3	7.9
NY	45	31	.592	36	42	.462	131	75	417	380	4.9	3.6	90	47	413	381	17.2	-7.0
CIN	42	35	.545	31	46	.403	48	47	318	330	-12.4	-22.3	47	55	363	425	1.3	-16.1
CHI	36	43	.456	33	42	.440	29	51	280	384	-6.1	9.2	42	55	287	338	-18.8	3.3
PHI	38	38	.500	24	54	.308	24	43	309	323	11.7	-10.1	36	55	280	364	-19.5	-0.9
PIT	32	45	.416	30	47	.390	95	87	384	437	3.9	12.0	61	68	360	380	2.9	-8.8
American League 1947																		
NY	55	22	.714	42	35	.545	54	49	392	242	-1.2	-24.8	61	46	402	326	23.7	1.8
DET	46	31	.597	39	38	.506	62	47	370	345	4.8	13.2	41	32	344	297	7.2	5.7
BOS	49	30	.620	34	41	.453	61	39	421	355	32.1	6.0	42	45	299	314	-2.9	0.6
CLE	38	39	.494	42	35	.545	52	51	314	279	-14.7	-8.5	60	43	373	309	12.9	5.0
PHI	39	38	.506	39	38	.506	33	41	296	324	-12.1	11.7	28	44	337	290	2.4	8.4
CHI	32	43	.427	38	41	.481	20	31	244	322	-15.7	1.3	33	45	309	339	-7.0	-4.8
WAS	36	41	.468	28	49	.364	10	20	244	326	-3.1	-6.6	32	43	252	349	-22.4	-7.7
STL	29	48	.377	30	47	.390	52	57	286	401	2.8	16.9	38	46	278	343	-13.8	-9.0
National League 1948																		
BOS	45	31	.592	46	31	.597	32	40	349	297	-8.1	6.2	63	53	390	287	10.3	14.4
STL	44	33	.571	41	36	.532	47	43	359	327	-5.0	3.8	58	60	383	319	8.9	5.0
BKN	36	41	.468	48	29	.623	43	68	352	386	-11.3	35.6	48	51	392	281	10.9	12.7
PIT	47	31	.603	36	40	.474	69	64	384	370	13.2	6.8	39	56	322	329	-5.4	0.8
NY	37	40	.481	41	36	.532	89	82	366	374	-10.4	14.8	75	40	414	330	16.9	0.4
PHI	32	44	.421	34	44	.436	32	44	276	332	-8.9	-13.0	59	51	315	397	-11.1	-15.3
CIN	32	45	.416	32	44	.421	68	52	312	398	11.5	10.9	36	52	276	354	-19.6	-6.6
CHI	35	42	.455	29	48	.377	38	34	282	323	-11.6	-16.7	49	55	315	383	-10.9	-11.4

	Home Games			Road Games			Home Games					Road Games				
TEAM	W	L	Pct.	W	L	Pct.	HR	OHR	R	OR	RF	ORF	HR	OHR	R	OR	RF	ORF

American League 1948

TEAM	W	L	Pct.	W	L	Pct.	HR	OHR	R	OR	RF	ORF	HR	OHR	R	OR	RF	ORF
CLE	48	30	.615	49	28	.636	77	41	398	272	-12.2	-10.4	78	41	442	296	19.5	19.7
BOS	55	23	.705	41	36	.532	60	43	481	336	11.4	-13.6	61	40	426	384	18.5	-3.5
NY	50	27	.649	44	33	.571	70	54	413	315	-6.9	-0.9	69	40	444	318	20.5	12.9
PHI	36	41	.468	48	29	.623	33	47	347	396	-9.1	16.8	35	39	382	339	3.4	5.1
DET	39	38	.506	39	38	.506	39	61	327	355	-12.3	-4.3	39	31	373	371	0.5	-1.1
STL	34	42	.447	25	52	.325	29	64	363	451	22.5	17.7	34	39	308	398	-13.7	-10.8
WAS	29	48	.377	27	49	.355	11	24	312	419	14.2	8.2	20	57	266	377	-25.6	-4.7
CHI	27	48	.360	24	53	.312	21	36	278	378	1.5	-11.0	34	53	281	436	-23.1	-17.4

National League 1949

TEAM	W	L	Pct.	W	L	Pct.	HR	OHR	R	OR	RF	ORF	HR	OHR	R	OR	RF	ORF
BKN	48	29	.623	49	28	.636	86	73	431	335	-3.8	6.0	66	59	448	316	28.6	11.4
STL	51	26	.662	45	32	.584	48	33	427	325	24.3	10.2	54	54	339	291	0.9	17.9
PHI	40	37	.519	41	36	.532	61	35	336	326	3.0	-4.6	61	69	326	342	-5.6	5.4
BOS	43	34	.558	32	45	.416	40	40	344	328	-1.2	-12.8	63	70	362	391	3.7	-6.5
NY	43	34	.558	30	47	.390	94	78	404	331	18.6	-10.8	53	54	332	362	-1.6	0.4
PIT	36	41	.468	35	42	.455	77	75	341	397	0.2	9.3	49	67	340	363	-1.8	-2.1
CIN	35	42	.455	27	50	.351	50	54	326	349	8.3	-17.1	36	70	301	421	-12.2	-14.5
CHI	33	44	.429	28	49	.364	53	38	285	365	-7.4	-10.5	44	66	308	408	-11.9	-11.9

American League 1949

TEAM	W	L	Pct.	W	L	Pct.	HR	OHR	R	OR	RF	ORF	HR	OHR	R	OR	RF	ORF
NY	54	23	.701	43	34	.558	72	53	419	304	0.8	-9.8	43	45	410	333	17.8	11.7
BOS	61	16	.792	35	42	.455	71	43	514	310	36.3	-12.0	60	39	382	357	14.2	5.9
CLE	49	28	.636	40	37	.519	61	42	319	263	-10.4	-15.4	51	40	356	311	0.7	18.2
DET	50	27	.649	37	40	.481	57	60	402	350	13.7	13.2	31	42	349	305	1.9	16.7
PHI	52	25	.675	29	48	.377	42	42	389	326	15.4	-18.3	40	63	337	399	-1.5	-4.4
CHI	32	45	.416	31	46	.403	15	52	327	353	1.8	-8.0	28	56	321	384	-7.7	-1.8
STL	36	41	.468	17	60	.221	69	56	394	426	46.1	-11.3	48	57	273	487	-17.4	-28.4
WAS	26	51	.338	24	53	.312	20	14	254	426	-23.0	-3.6	61	65	330	442	-8.1	-17.9

National League 1950

TEAM	W	L	Pct.	W	L	Pct.	HR	OHR	R	OR	RF	ORF	HR	OHR	R	OR	RF	ORF
PHI	47	30	.610	44	33	.571	58	53	348	279	-5.7	-18.1	67	69	374	345	5.6	8.7
BKN	48	30	.615	41	35	.539	110	96	458	386	16.2	12.7	84	67	389	338	13.3	6.8
NY	44	32	.579	42	36	.538	84	67	362	290	-0.4	-15.6	49	73	373	353	5.9	6.5
BOS	46	31	.597	37	40	.481	59	45	343	294	-24.3	-35.1	89	84	442	442	22.4	-14.7
STL	47	29	.618	31	46	.403	50	43	389	303	29.6	-16.3	52	76	304	367	-10.3	2.7
CIN	38	38	.500	28	49	.364	52	81	355	373	20.2	4.6	47	64	299	361	-12.8	1.7
CHI	35	42	.455	29	47	.382	79	63	352	411	17.8	10.9	82	67	291	361	-14.9	0.5
PIT	33	44	.429	24	52	.316	81	79	370	447	18.9	9.0	57	73	311	410	-9.2	-12.3

American League 1950

TEAM	W	L	Pct.	W	L	Pct.	HR	OHR	R	OR	RF	ORF	HR	OHR	R	OR	RF	ORF
NY	53	24	.688	45	32	.584	78	51	440	333	-5.9	-5.7	81	67	474	358	22.3	10.8
DET	50	30	.625	45	29	.608	60	72	405	346	-12.0	-11.5	54	69	432	367	11.6	8.4
BOS	55	22	.714	39	38	.506	100	67	625	427	55.4	13.2	61	54	402	377	11.9	3.6
CLE	49	28	.636	43	34	.558	102	57	386	297	-6.9	-15.7	62	63	420	357	8.3	12.1
WAS	35	42	.455	32	45	.416	18	28	347	407	-0.1	-1.0	58	71	343	406	-10.5	-2.0
CHI	35	42	.455	25	52	.325	52	55	316	352	-0.3	-13.5	41	52	309	397	-19.2	1.6
STL	27	47	.365	31	49	.388	52	69	368	484	25.8	21.1	54	60	316	432	-15.9	-10.2
PHI	29	48	.377	23	54	.299	45	67	314	406	-11.8	-19.9	55	71	356	507	-8.6	-24.2

National League 1951

TEAM	W	L	Pct.	W	L	Pct.	HR	OHR	R	OR	RF	ORF	HR	OHR	R	OR	RF	ORF
NY	50	28	.641	48	31	.608	115	89	399	308	5.7	-6.3	64	59	382	333	12.6	6.5
BKN	49	29	.628	48	31	.608	100	81	412	316	-4.6	-8.9	84	69	443	356	28.8	0.6
STL	44	34	.564	37	39	.487	44	56	370	323	13.7	-10.7	51	63	313	348	-6.1	2.3
BOS	42	35	.545	34	43	.442	59	37	367	310	1.7	-13.0	71	59	356	352	4.8	1.8
PHI	38	39	.494	35	42	.455	43	50	312	305	-7.1	-10.0	65	60	336	339	-2.3	5.2
CIN	35	42	.455	33	44	.429	44	46	289	320	8.4	-6.5	44	73	270	347	-20.1	2.6
PIT	32	45	.416	32	45	.416	72	84	388	465	27.2	20.8	65	73	301	380	-8.5	-10.6
CHI	32	45	.416	30	47	.390	45	59	304	364	-0.6	-4.4	58	66	310	386	-9.2	-8.5

American League 1951

TEAM	W	L	Pct.	W	L	Pct.	HR	OHR	R	OR	RF	ORF	HR	OHR	R	OR	RF	ORF
NY	56	22	.718	42	34	.553	72	43	366	258	-17.4	-30.7	68	49	432	363	19.7	2.9
CLE	53	24	.688	40	37	.519	76	42	324	249	-11.7	-26.8	64	44	372	345	3.4	7.6
BOS	50	25	.667	37	42	.468	80	65	460	348	40.8	-2.7	47	35	344	377	1.3	-3.5
CHI	39	38	.506	42	35	.545	28	47	334	310	-13.2	-8.3	58	62	380	334	5.7	8.2
DET	36	41	.468	37	40	.481	58	60	358	402	9.4	18.5	46	42	327	339	-6.5	3.8
PHI	38	41	.481	32	43	.427	54	59	406	407	16.8	14.3	48	50	330	338	-4.0	3.8
WAS	32	44	.421	30	48	.385	13	35	319	362	-7.2	-7.5	41	75	353	402	-1.4	-10.0
STL	24	53	.312	28	49	.364	41	66	327	486	15.1	22.7	45	65	284	396	-18.2	-12.9

TEAM	Home Games			Road Games			Home Games						Road Games					
	W	L	Pct.	W	L	Pct.	HR	OHR	R	OR	RF	ORF	HR	OHR	R	OR	RF	ORF
National League 1952																		
BKN	45	33	.577	51	24	**.680**	76	78	**389**	324	-5.5	8.8	**77**	43	386	279	20.0	11.8
NY	50	27	**.649**	42	35	.545	103	74	369	327	4.5	4.8	48	47	353	312	10.2	2.7
STL	48	29	.623	40	37	.519	46	59	343	291	2.6	-14.1	51	60	334	339	4.1	-3.1
PHI	47	29	.618	40	38	.513	42	43	318	269	-3.7	-2.4	51	52	339	283	4.4	12.8
CHI	42	35	.545	35	42	.455	51	40	329	316	11.4	1.6	56	61	299	315	-5.9	2.3
CIN	38	39	.494	31	46	.403	43	43	318	319	7.0	-6.1	61	68	297	340	-6.9	-4.5
BOS	31	45	.408	33	44	.429	48	44	257	314	-16.5	-5.6	62	62	312	337	-5.2	-3.4
PIT	23	54	.299	19	58	.247	45	72	261	**414**	4.0	10.6	47	61	254	379	-20.8	-18.7
American League 1952																		
NY	49	28	.636	46	31	**.597**	64	48	345	264	-9.6	-9.9	65	**46**	382	293	19.0	**12.8**
CLE	49	28	.636	44	33	.571	72	43	333	260	-21.5	-23.8	76	51	**430**	346	31.8	-1.0
CHI	44	33	.571	37	40	.481	42	39	305	276	-2.5	-7.8	38	47	305	292	-3.7	12.6
PHI	45	32	.584	34	43	.442	55	60	382	**403**	33.7	24.3	34	53	282	320	-7.1	0.4
WAS	42	35	.545	36	41	.468	13	18	299	292	1.2	-6.4	37	60	299	316	-5.6	5.7
BOS	50	27	**.649**	26	51	.338	68	49	**406**	309	54.9	-11.4	45	58	262	349	-11.6	-3.6
STL	42	35	.545	22	55	.286	47	52	321	346	11.9	-11.7	35	59	283	387	-9.2	-15.0
DET	32	45	.416	18	59	.234	65	59	**284**	366	6.7	0.9	38	52	273	372	-13.4	-11.8
National League 1953																		
BKN	60	17	**.779**	45	32	.584	110	82	**517**	333	16.5	-7.6	98	87	**438**	356	25.1	7.4
MIL	45	31	.592	47	31	**.603**	51	44	332	260	-19.2	-21.9	105	63	406	**329**	10.8	16.0
PHI	48	29	.623	35	42	.455	63	65	363	304	2.8	-16.0	52	73	353	362	-1.0	7.0
STL	48	30	.615	35	41	.461	65	58	420	321	22.2	-17.0	75	81	348	392	-0.2	-0.4
NY	38	39	.494	32	45	.416	109	81	395	345	7.2	-13.0	67	65	373	402	5.0	-3.5
CIN	38	39	.494	30	47	.390	89	96	367	391	4.4	-2.7	77	83	347	397	-2.3	-3.8
CHI	43	34	.558	22	55	.286	74	69	351	417	26.0	1.0	63	82	282	418	-18.7	-9.5
PIT	26	51	.338	24	53	.312	53	88	338	**460**	19.0	**7.7**	46	80	284	427	-18.7	-13.0
American League 1953																		
NY	50	27	.649	49	25	**.662**	64	39	347	**255**	-26.5	-16.0	75	55	**454**	292	**24.7**	14.4
CLE	53	24	**.688**	39	38	.506	90	46	**379**	272	-4.3	-24.3	70	46	391	355	10.3	-2.6
CHI	41	36	.532	48	29	.623	30	56	349	328	-4.9	24.2	44	57	367	264	3.2	19.0
BOS	38	38	.500	46	31	.597	57	59	335	354	5.7	29.0	44	**33**	321	278	-8.6	14.4
WAS	39	36	.520	37	40	.481	10	31	305	283	-18.0	-12.2	59	81	382	331	5.4	3.2
DET	30	47	.390	30	47	.390	55	97	369	**462**	13.1	0.2	53	57	326	461	-6.1	-37.2
PHI	27	50	.351	32	45	.416	49	74	299	447	-9.0	28.6	67	47	333	352	-6.9	-8.3
STL	23	54	.299	31	46	.403	58	64	**281**	447	2.5	35.0	54	37	274	331	-22.1	-2.8
National League 1954																		
NY	53	23	**.697**	44	34	.564	120	67	387	254	15.1	-11.9	66	**46**	345	296	-1.3	16.4
BKN	45	32	.584	47	30	**.610**	101	92	380	393	-4.5	13.2	85	72	398	347	11.5	-1.3
MIL	43	34	.558	46	31	.597	43	**29**	285	251	-25.9	**-17.7**	96	77	385	305	4.9	14.3
PHI	39	39	.500	36	40	.474	47	60	315	305	-10.7	-3.8	55	73	344	309	-4.0	11.3
CIN	41	36	.532	33	44	.429	94	105	380	407	8.8	14.3	53	64	349	356	-0.5	-4.0
STL	33	44	.429	39	38	.506	57	90	386	**431**	-6.5	20.0	62	80	**413**	359	15.4	-5.7
CHI	40	37	.519	24	53	.312	86	59	366	385	9.5	1.0	73	72	334	381	-4.7	-9.5
PIT	31	46	.403	22	55	.286	**22**	42	**277**	422	-1.0	-0.2	54	86	280	423	-21.2	-21.4
American League 1954																		
CLE	59	18	**.766**	52	25	**.675**	78	57	376	**252**	4.2	2.5	78	**32**	370	252	12.2	21.3
NY	54	23	.701	49	28	.636	68	42	**388**	274	-8.1	-6.4	65	44	**417**	289	25.1	10.3
CHI	45	32	.584	49	28	.636	39	51	327	294	-15.9	27.8	55	43	384	**227**	14.1	**26.4**
BOS	38	39	.494	31	46	.403	69	70	357	384	1.4	8.8	54	48	343	344	4.4	-9.0
DET	35	42	.455	33	44	.429	44	80	285	336	-3.4	3.7	46	58	299	328	-9.9	-2.7
WAS	37	41	.474	29	47	.382	27	27	320	335	1.2	-4.1	54	52	312	345	-5.2	-7.3
BAL	32	45	.416	22	55	.286	19	23	**235**	313	-5.2	**-11.8**	33	55	248	355	-25.3	-9.2
PHI	29	47	.382	22	56	.282	44	85	260	**467**	-5.4	17.4	50	56	282	408	-15.4	-29.7
National League 1955																		
BKN	56	21	**.727**	42	34	**.553**	119	85	**461**	318	16.4	-4.2	82	83	396	332	21.6	9.5
MIL	46	31	.597	39	38	.506	75	51	342	**297**	-14.7	-19.9	107	87	**401**	371	18.5	0.9
NY	44	35	.557	36	39	.480	95	91	362	327	1.0	-10.2	74	**64**	340	346	3.1	5.8
PHI	46	31	.597	31	46	.403	76	78	371	309	22.0	-13.4	56	83	304	357	-5.9	3.8
CIN	46	31	.597	29	48	.377	102	91	425	341	26.4	-0.5	79	70	336	343	4.5	6.1
CHI	43	33	.566	29	48	.377	80	62	348	322	25.1	-17.6	84	91	278	391	-13.6	-4.7
STL	41	36	.532	27	50	.351	84	92	358	**362**	20.9	-8.3	59	93	296	395	-8.5	-7.0
PIT	36	39	.480	24	55	.304	**34**	48	298	337	19.8	-17.4	57	94	262	430	-19.7	-14.5

TEAM	Home Games W	L	Pct.	Road Games W	L	Pct.	Home Games HR	OHR	R	OR	RF	ORF	Road Games HR	OHR	R	OR	RF	ORF
American League 1955																		
NY	52	25	.675	44	33	.571	89	44	378	248	-1.5	-22.7	86	64	384	321	13.2	10.4
CLE	49	28	.636	44	33	.571	84	58	343	318	-3.3	12.3	64	53	355	283	4.5	17.4
CHI	49	28	.636	42	35	.545	54	47	357	262	-1.7	-10.0	62	64	368	295	8.3	16.4
BOS	47	31	.603	37	39	.487	84	79	470	395	60.6	49.7	53	49	285	257	-8.9	21.2
DET	46	31	.597	33	44	.429	81	59	386	301	-0.7	-15.6	49	67	389	357	14.8	-0.5
KC	33	43	.434	30	48	.385	70	110	333	477	13.4	14.2	51	65	305	434	-8.8	-26.2
BAL	30	47	.390	27	50	.351	15	42	249	335	-16.6	-22.0	39	61	291	419	-15.5	-17.3
WAS	28	49	.364	25	52	.325	20	25	282	357	-10.7	-17.3	60	74	316	432	-7.8	-21.4
National League 1956																		
BKN	52	25	.675	41	36	.532	102	89	369	300	5.1	-0.3	77	82	351	301	10.3	11.3
MIL	47	29	.618	45	33	.577	77	53	344	265	-4.5	-11.7	100	80	365	304	13.1	11.8
CIN	51	26	.662	40	37	.519	128	75	426	346	23.6	12.3	93	66	349	312	12.0	6.7
STL	43	34	.558	33	44	.429	58	73	358	328	11.8	-11.3	66	82	320	370	1.4	-7.5
PHI	40	37	.519	31	46	.403	61	74	337	335	1.8	-16.8	60	98	331	403	3.6	-16.2
NY	37	40	.481	30	47	.390	94	86	269	306	-0.7	-11.0	51	58	271	344	-15.4	0.0
PIT	35	43	.449	31	45	.408	49	45	301	328	6.2	2.2	61	97	287	325	-9.8	4.0
CHI	39	38	.506	21	56	.273	78	77	335	328	23.0	-16.9	64	84	262	380	-15.3	-10.1
American League 1956																		
NY	49	28	.623	48	29	.623	88	48	412	303	-7.4	-7.6	102	66	445	328	21.8	9.1
CLE	46	31	.597	42	35	.545	71	61	340	287	-7.4	-1.1	82	55	372	294	1.7	18.0
CHI	46	31	.597	39	38	.506	69	47	403	320	8.0	1.9	59	71	373	314	4.1	12.0
BOS	43	34	.558	41	36	.532	68	64	408	388	8.2	5.5	71	66	372	363	4.0	-2.3
DET	37	40	.481	45	32	.584	75	77	359	357	-17.5	3.0	75	63	430	342	16.3	3.8
BAL	41	36	.532	28	49	.364	35	39	275	315	-7.1	-19.2	56	60	296	390	-18.9	-6.4
WAS	32	45	.416	27	50	.351	63	95	354	481	20.3	9.9	49	76	298	443	-15.7	-25.1
KC	22	55	.286	30	47	.390	62	113	305	449	-2.8	17.5	50	74	314	382	-13.5	-9.1
National League 1957																		
MIL	45	32	.584	50	27	.649	75	51	312	289	-33.0	-11.9	124	73	460	324	29.5	5.2
STL	42	35	.545	45	32	.584	64	70	356	348	-6.5	9.4	82	70	381	318	10.8	4.6
BKN	43	34	.558	41	36	.532	84	88	383	348	24.7	43.2	63	56	307	243	-7.1	24.0
CIN	45	32	.584	35	42	.455	118	101	417	410	26.3	10.5	69	78	330	371	0.0	-11.4
PHI	38	39	.494	39	38	.506	60	60	299	322	-7.7	-3.6	57	79	324	334	-5.8	1.4
NY	37	40	.481	32	45	.416	99	86	353	341	21.7	-5.2	58	64	290	360	-12.6	-6.0
CHI	31	46	.403	31	46	.403	81	68	301	353	-7.9	-4.3	66	76	327	369	-5.0	-8.7
PIT	36	41	.468	26	51	.338	20	53	273	321	-11.6	-13.2	72	105	313	375	-9.6	-9.1
American League 1957																		
NY	48	29	.623	50	27	.649	60	51	316	241	-22.3	-17.7	85	59	407	293	23.1	13.1
CHI	45	32	.584	45	32	.584	40	59	347	263	-2.3	-12.0	66	65	360	303	11.5	9.6
BOS	44	33	.571	38	39	.494	72	67	408	360	30.3	16.8	81	49	313	308	1.1	4.6
DET	45	32	.584	33	44	.429	71	86	351	304	33.4	-1.9	45	61	263	310	-14.7	6.2
BAL	42	33	.560	34	43	.442	36	30	283	248	-9.8	-27.0	51	65	314	340	-3.4	0.4
CLE	40	37	.519	36	40	.474	71	74	348	384	2.8	12.1	69	56	334	338	4.4	-4.1
KC	37	40	.481	22	54	.289	91	77	294	344	9.2	-6.0	75	76	269	366	-15.3	-10.0
WAS	28	49	.364	27	50	.351	60	79	304	415	1.6	5.5	51	70	299	393	-6.7	-19.9
National League 1958																		
MIL	48	29	.623	44	33	.571	72	48	291	207	-24.2	-38.0	95	77	384	334	9.5	5.7
PIT	49	28	.636	35	42	.455	41	40	323	260	-4.7	-25.0	93	83	339	347	-0.8	0.4
SF	44	33	.571	36	41	.468	85	88	363	354	-0.2	2.9	85	78	364	344	7.0	-2.2
CIN	40	37	.519	36	41	.468	71	86	364	337	9.9	18.6	52	62	331	284	-1.4	13.9
CHI	35	42	.455	37	40	.481	101	72	350	381	-2.5	10.7	81	70	359	344	5.3	-3.2
STL	39	38	.506	33	44	.429	62	88	329	381	13.4	17.9	49	70	290	323	-13.2	2.1
LA	39	38	.506	32	45	.416	92	101	359	405	16.1	13.7	80	72	309	356	-7.2	-7.2
PHI	35	42	.455	34	43	.442	59	77	318	397	-8.1	8.7	65	71	346	365	0.7	-9.3
American League 1958																		
NY	44	33	.571	48	29	.623	78	62	362	318	-9.9	21.2	86	54	397	259	23.1	18.3
CHI	47	30	.610	35	42	.455	47	68	318	282	1.9	-14.2	54	84	316	333	-0.8	-0.1
BOS	49	28	.636	30	47	.390	73	65	384	350	24.2	3.9	82	56	313	341	0.9	-4.9
CLE	42	34	.553	35	42	.455	72	59	324	293	-11.2	-13.2	89	64	370	342	14.2	-3.0
DET	43	34	.558	34	43	.442	59	79	348	306	11.8	1.9	50	54	311	300	-1.0	7.7
BAL	46	31	.597	28	48	.368	46	36	248	256	-11.4	-21.8	62	70	273	319	-15.3	4.5
KC	43	34	.558	30	47	.390	88	96	365	363	31.7	3.7	50	54	277	350	-9.6	-7.8
WAS	33	44	.429	28	49	.364	49	80	269	373	-5.2	-0.2	72	76	284	374	-11.5	-14.6

TEAM	W	L	Pct.	W	L	Pct.	HR	OHR	R	OR	RF	ORF	HR	OHR	R	OR	RF	ORF
	Home Games			**Road Games**			**Home Games**						**Road Games**					
National League 1959																		
LA	46	32	.590	42	36	**.538**	82	**90**	363	333	6.1	-1.1	66	67	342	**337**	4.0	4.3
MIL	49	29	**.628**	37	41	.474	83	64	350	274	**-7.6**	**-22.4**	**94**	64	374	349	**12.0**	3.4
SF	42	35	.545	41	36	.532	80	63	339	**271**	-7.3	-20.7	87	76	366	342	9.5	**5.2**
PIT	47	30	.610	31	46	.403	**47**	**53**	348	334	16.3	-2.2	65	81	303	346	-6.7	2.0
CHI	38	39	.494	36	41	.468	87	76	336	329	0.9	-7.1	76	76	337	359	1.7	-1.0
CIN	43	34	.558	31	46	.403	**101**	84	**423**	**367**	24.0	**-1.0**	60	78	341	371	6.0	-5.3
STL	42	35	.545	29	48	.377	64	64	366	359	**33.0**	-1.9	54	73	275	366	-13.5	-3.8
PHI	37	40	.481	27	50	.351	55	66	**316**	354	10.2	-5.8	58	84	283	371	-13.2	-4.8
American League 1959																		
CHI	47	30	**.610**	47	30	**.610**	44	61	313	**272**	-12.0	**-13.9**	53	68	356	**316**	3.7	**7.6**
CLE	43	34	.558	46	31	.597	84	74	346	316	-13.2	-4.2	83	74	**399**	330	**16.1**	2.3
NY	40	37	.519	39	38	.506	63	45	293	305	**-24.6**	-9.6	**90**	75	394	342	12.8	-0.3
DET	41	36	.532	35	42	.455	**95**	**105**	401	**411**	28.5	28.0	65	72	312	321	-4.3	1.1
BOS	43	34	.558	32	45	.416	62	66	**404**	356	25.4	4.7	63	69	322	340	-1.6	-1.7
BAL	38	39	.494	36	41	.468	53	50	**260**	299	-11.8	-8.3	56	61	291	322	-15.0	5.0
KC	37	40	.481	29	48	.377	58	80	362	386	13.4	3.2	59	68	319	374	-3.9	-11.7
WAS	34	43	.442	29	48	.377	83	68	307	360	-1.6	5.5	80	**55**	312	341	-7.8	-2.1
National League 1960																		
PIT	52	25	**.675**	43	34	**.558**	51	36	362	287	-3.9	-7.4	69	69	372	306	14.9	9.0
MIL	51	26	.662	37	40	.481	**90**	56	342	270	-10.4	**-30.4**	80	74	**382**	388	**16.8**	-11.8
STL	51	26	.662	35	42	.455	78	64	361	308	31.5	1.2	60	63	278	308	-10.5	7.7
LA	42	35	.545	40	37	.519	89	**97**	**379**	334	33.9	28.9	37	**57**	283	**259**	-8.5	**19.5**
SF	45	32	.584	34	43	.442	**46**	**34**	**296**	**256**	**-19.0**	-29.9	**84**	73	375	375	13.2	-7.9
CIN	37	40	.481	30	47	.390	75	68	314	347	-3.6	0.5	65	66	326	345	0.6	-3.4
CHI	33	44	.429	27	50	.351	52	78	331	**390**	6.4	-1.5	67	74	303	386	-4.9	-15.8
PHI	31	46	.403	28	49	.364	54	74	300	373	21.9	17.2	45	59	246	318	-21.6	2.6
American League 1960																		
NY	55	22	**.714**	42	35	.545	**92**	**52**	350	**273**	-10.4	**-21.8**	**101**	71	**396**	354	**15.3**	-1.5
BAL	44	33	.571	45	32	**.584**	50	**52**	332	313	-5.1	6.8	73	65	350	**293**	2.7	**12.7**
CHI	51	26	.662	36	41	.468	57	54	**379**	298	4.6	-6.5	55	73	362	319	7.6	6.5
CLE	39	38	.506	37	40	.481	62	84	315	351	**-10.5**	2.6	65	77	352	342	2.6	-1.3
WAS	32	45	.416	41	36	.532	75	74	336	360	0.0	10.9	72	**56**	336	330	-0.6	1.1
DET	40	37	.519	31	46	.403	78	85	322	323	3.5	0.6	72	**56**	311	321	-7.6	5.0
BOS	36	41	.468	29	48	.377	65	69	347	**413**	11.5	**14.0**	59	58	311	362	-6.7	-8.8
KC	34	43	.442	24	53	.312	58	79	327	369	**12.0**	-5.8	52	81	288	387	-13.4	-13.6
National League 1961																		
CIN	47	30	.610	46	31	**.597**	70	75	345	355	-5.4	**19.1**	88	72	365	**298**	3.3	**12.6**
LA	45	32	.584	44	33	.571	83	**109**	373	358	3.0	5.6	74	**58**	362	339	3.5	2.2
SF	45	32	.584	40	37	.519	97	77	371	316	-6.5	-5.5	86	75	**402**	339	**13.5**	3.7
MIL	45	32	.584	38	39	.494	84	72	324	**280**	-15.4	**-24.5**	**104**	81	388	376	8.3	-4.2
STL	48	29	**.623**	32	45	.416	54	69	**413**	362	**40.5**	16.7	49	67	290	306	-12.9	10.3
PIT	38	39	.494	37	40	.481	49	**54**	338	338	-5.0	0.2	79	67	356	337	0.8	3.4
CHI	40	37	.519	24	53	.312	**102**	81	372	391	17.3	-4.4	74	84	317	409	-7.6	-16.4
PHI	22	55	.286	25	52	.325	**43**	77	**256**	**408**	**-22.9**	3.8	60	78	328	388	-9.0	-11.8
American League 1961																		
NY	65	16	**.802**	44	37	.543	112	59	411	**251**	0.0	**-29.6**	128	78	416	361	15.2	6.3
DET	50	31	.617	51	30	**.630**	90	95	389	324	**-14.9**	-7.7	90	75	**452**	347	**23.6**	7.7
BAL	48	33	.593	47	34	.580	61	**46**	320	283	-14.8	-8.3	88	63	371	**305**	1.5	**18.9**
CHI	53	28	.654	33	48	.407	80	55	411	320	17.5	-20.2	58	103	354	406	-0.2	-6.3
CLE	40	41	.494	38	42	.475	74	98	342	380	-14.4	0.8	76	80	395	372	8.1	0.2
BOS	50	31	.617	26	55	.321	63	91	401	386	20.7	-6.0	49	76	328	406	-6.9	-8.0
MIN	36	44	.450	34	46	.425	92	89	380	423	14.7	**17.6**	75	74	327	355	-7.8	3.2
LA	46	36	.561	24	55	.304	122	**126**	447	421	**46.8**	13.1	67	**54**	297	363	-13.4	1.3
KC	33	47	.413	28	53	.346	**33**	61	365	**434**	17.6	3.6	57	80	318	429	-10.4	-14.9
WAS	33	46	.418	28	54	.341	34	53	**288**	366	-9.4	-7.3	85	78	330	410	-9.6	-8.5
National League 1962																		
SF	61	21	**.744**	42	41	.506	**109**	**74**	**479**	299	21.5	-22.6	95	74	399	391	14.8	-2.2
LA	54	29	.651	48	34	**.585**	47	**39**	409	**289**	-6.6	**-30.0**	93	76	**433**	408	**21.5**	-6.0
CIN	58	23	.716	40	41	.494	95	68	456	294	**31.7**	-24.8	72	81	346	391	0.7	-2.0
PIT	51	30	.630	42	38	.525	48	56	358	315	1.6	0.0	60	**62**	348	311	-1.4	16.6
MIL	49	32	.605	37	44	.457	93	74	374	307	5.0	-14.2	88	77	356	358	1.0	5.5
STL	44	37	.543	40	41	.494	64	83	407	362	12.2	21.3	73	66	367	**302**	4.7	**17.5**
PHI	46	34	.575	35	46	.432	70	66	341	346	-1.5	-15.1	72	89	364	413	2.1	-8.7
HOU	32	48	.400	32	48	.400	**44**	41	**268**	340	**-19.3**	-12.0	61	72	324	377	-10.1	0.0
CHI	32	49	.395	27	54	.333	71	94	333	456	11.3	**22.9**	55	65	299	371	-14.6	-1.5
NY	22	58	.275	18	62	.225	93	**120**	335	**510**	20.2	17.8	46	72	282	438	-18.9	-19.1

TEAM	Home Games W	L	Pct.	Road Games W	L	Pct.	Home Games HR	OHR	R	OR	RF	ORF	Road Games HR	OHR	R	OR	RF	ORF
American League 1962																		
NY	50	30	**.625**	46	36	.561	92	67	369	306	-15.5	-16.1	107	79	**448**	374	**23.6**	-1.3
MIN	45	36	.556	46	35	**.568**	97	97	417	378	8.1	**11.4**	88	69	381	335	8.0	6.3
LA	40	41	.494	46	35	**.568**	50	**50**	357	368	-1.1	8.8	87	68	361	338	1.2	5.8
DET	49	33	.598	36	43	.456	117	91	**448**	368	**39.2**	9.4	92	78	310	**324**	-9.0	**9.3**
CHI	43	38	.531	42	39	.519	36	58	315	319	-19.6	-5.9	56	**65**	392	339	7.9	6.9
CLE	43	38	.531	37	44	.457	103	89	348	350	4.1	-11.4	77	85	334	395	-5.7	-7.7
BAL	44	38	**.537**	33	47	.413	66	65	328	**299**	-1.2	**-23.4**	90	82	324	381	-8.8	-2.8
BOS	39	40	.494	37	44	.457	72	76	369	377	11.9	1.9	74	83	338	379	-4.1	-4.5
KC	39	42	.481	33	48	.407	64	**118**	387	**423**	8.1	2.1	52	81	358	414	1.3	-14.5
WAS	27	53	.338	33	48	.407	65	79	**293**	364	-1.8	5.9	67	72	306	352	-14.4	2.5
National League 1963																		
LA	53	28	**.654**	46	35	**.568**	42	43	296	**248**	**-12.9**	-16.8	68	68	344	302	12.8	6.6
STL	53	28	**.654**	40	41	.494	79	70	**429**	311	**34.9**	-1.9	49	54	318	317	9.5	0.4
SF	50	31	.617	38	43	.469	101	64	363	289	0.2	-17.9	96	62	**362**	352	**20.5**	-8.8
PHI	45	36	.556	42	39	.519	61	60	340	282	12.5	-4.7	65	53	302	296	1.7	7.2
CIN	46	35	.568	40	41	.494	65	46	344	300	13.1	2.0	57	71	304	294	2.5	7.2
MIL	45	36	.556	39	42	.481	68	81	341	307	0.2	2.4	71	68	336	296	11.9	6.4
CHI	43	38	.531	39	42	.481	63	70	298	302	9.5	**9.4**	64	49	272	**276**	-8.6	**12.3**
PIT	42	39	.519	32	49	.395	47	42	275	295	-5.8	-1.6	61	57	292	300	-3.3	5.7
HOU	44	37	.543	22	59	.272	25	**34**	**236**	268	3.5	**-27.9**	37	61	228	372	-23.8	-13.8
NY	34	47	.420	17	64	.210	61	**93**	276	**381**	22.6	-3.0	35	69	225	393	-23.4	-23.3
American League 1963																		
NY	58	22	**.725**	46	35	**.568**	88	55	367	**246**	7.0	-17.2	100	60	347	301	7.8	12.1
CHI	49	33	.598	45	35	.563	63	46	362	272	10.0	-2.4	51	**54**	321	**272**	0.4	**19.1**
MIN	48	33	.593	43	37	.538	112	99	377	306	-4.5	2.1	113	63	390	296	**20.1**	11.6
BAL	48	33	.593	38	43	.469	72	56	311	268	-6.6	**-24.0**	74	81	333	353	2.2	-2.4
CLE	41	40	.506	38	43	.469	88	87	308	341	-5.8	-5.5	81	89	327	361	0.4	-6.7
DET	47	34	.580	32	49	.395	94	109	**395**	339	29.5	-6.8	54	86	305	364	-2.9	-7.4
BOS	44	36	.550	32	49	.395	95	73	383	346	37.0	-2.1	76	79	283	358	-9.4	-6.0
KC	36	45	.444	37	44	.457	52	87	326	390	12.8	**24.2**	43	69	289	314	-9.5	4.3
LA	39	42	.481	31	49	.388	24	**44**	264	306	**-21.7**	-14.6	71	76	333	354	0.7	-3.8
WAS	31	49	.388	25	57	.305	63	82	286	**406**	0.3	2.5	75	94	292	406	-9.9	-20.7
National League 1964																		
STL	48	33	**.593**	45	36	.556	59	81	386	378	17.3	**37.9**	50	52	329	274	2.9	12.9
CIN	47	34	.580	45	36	.556	62	59	331	294	-0.6	6.7	68	53	329	**272**	1.2	**16.0**
PHI	46	35	.568	46	35	**.568**	59	61	352	298	3.2	-10.7	71	68	341	334	5.2	-1.1
SF	44	37	.543	46	35	**.568**	86	63	314	299	-8.1	3.8	**79**	55	342	288	4.3	11.4
MIL	45	36	.556	43	38	.531	**89**	78	405	356	1.7	-8.2	70	82	**398**	398	**22.6**	-17.8
LA	41	40	.506	39	42	.481	26	38	259	**259**	**-25.2**	-15.2	53	**50**	355	313	6.2	5.8
PIT	42	39	.519	38	43	.469	55	**31**	340	315	5.2	-1.8	66	61	323	321	-0.1	1.9
CHI	40	41	.494	36	45	.444	85	**87**	337	**397**	8.0	21.4	60	57	312	327	-3.2	-2.2
HOU	41	40	.506	25	56	.309	29	44	**246**	290	-1.2	-14.2	41	61	249	338	-23.5	-2.0
NY	33	48	.407	20	61	.247	58	61	298	363	8.6	-13.1	45	69	271	413	-15.8	-24.9
American League 1964																		
NY	50	31	.617	49	32	**.605**	69	56	363	290	1.3	3.5	93	73	**367**	287	**12.4**	14.1
CHI	52	29	**.642**	46	35	.568	43	42	306	**213**	-8.9	-26.0	63	82	336	288	2.1	16.2
BAL	49	32	.605	48	33	.593	79	64	351	296	5.7	7.8	83	**65**	328	**271**	1.3	**18.2**
DET	46	35	.568	39	42	.481	85	89	340	320	-6.4	-11.7	72	75	359	358	9.5	-5.8
LA	45	36	.556	37	44	.457	32	**31**	230	226	**-26.7**	**-30.4**	70	69	314	325	-6.2	5.8
CLE	41	40	.506	38	43	.469	84	82	365	351	12.6	2.6	80	72	324	342	0.6	-2.4
MIN	40	41	.494	39	42	.481	115	88	386	336	8.6	-2.9	106	93	351	342	8.7	-1.9
BOS	45	36	.556	27	54	.333	100	87	**393**	382	**33.2**	-7.0	86	91	295	411	-6.5	-21.9
WAS	31	50	.383	31	50	.383	71	95	294	380	3.5	7.6	54	77	284	353	-12.5	-6.2
KC	26	55	.321	31	50	.383	107	**132**	330	**455**	14.8	**20.8**	59	88	291	381	-9.5	-16.0
National League 1965																		
LA	50	31	.617	47	34	**.580**	26	41	268	**218**	-21.1	**-28.0**	52	86	340	303	2.3	10.9
SF	51	30	**.630**	44	37	.543	81	81	365	327	16.5	**24.4**	78	56	317	**266**	-1.0	**17.6**
PIT	49	32	.605	41	40	.506	37	38	334	284	-3.2	-5.2	74	51	341	296	4.6	10.8
CIN	49	32	.605	40	41	.494	108	69	**450**	352	19.9	0.0	75	67	**375**	352	**17.5**	-6.4
MIL	44	37	.543	42	39	.519	98	75	366	331	7.0	9.6	**98**	48	342	302	5.8	7.7
PHI	45	35	.563	40	41	.494	77	55	312	300	-6.5	-16.2	67	61	342	367	4.2	-9.0
STL	42	39	.519	38	43	.475	68	**103**	379	361	15.5	15.3	61	63	328	313	2.4	3.8
CHI	40	41	.494	32	49	.395	79	94	330	**380**	5.5	8.1	55	60	305	343	-5.4	-4.8
HOU	36	45	.444	29	52	.358	25	**32**	250	313	-21.6	-21.3	72	91	319	398	-4.0	-17.8
NY	29	52	.358	21	60	.259	50	81	258	**380**	8.8	2.1	57	66	237	372	-26.4	-12.7

| | Home Games | | | Road Games | | | Home Games | | | | | | Road Games | | | | | |
TEAM	W	L	Pct.	W	L	Pct.	HR	OHR	R	OR	RF	ORF	HR	OHR	R	OR	RF	ORF
American League 1965																		
MIN	51	30	.630	51	30	**.630**	67	89	**379**	308	-4.0	5.4	**83**	77	**395**	**292**	24.4	9.0
CHI	48	33	.593	47	34	.580	45	51	288	**241**	-19.7	-23.2	80	71	359	314	11.3	4.9
BAL	46	33	.582	48	35	.578	62	71	302	282	-6.4	0.0	63	49	339	296	6.0	8.7
DET	47	34	.580	42	39	.519	96	85	362	310	13.8	6.1	66	52	318	**292**	2.0	8.9
CLE	52	30	**.634**	35	45	.438	90	58	342	287	3.9	-14.1	66	71	321	326	2.2	0.2
NY	40	43	.482	37	42	.468	77	63	320	306	4.6	-2.2	72	63	291	298	-7.0	7.4
CAL	46	34	.575	29	53	.354	36	35	**265**	254	3.6	-17.3	56	56	262	315	-17.0	4.3
WAS	36	45	.444	34	47	.420	62	86	302	366	4.4	3.0	74	74	289	355	-8.1	-10.3
BOS	34	47	.420	28	53	.346	94	88	375	**433**	27.5	20.9	71	70	294	358	-4.4	-13.2
KC	33	48	.407	26	55	.321	47	68	301	365	5.9	-6.4	63	93	284	390	-9.6	-20.0
National League 1966																		
LA	53	28	**.654**	42	39	.519	**43**	36	286	**220**	-10.6	**-18.5**	65	48	320	**270**	-3.2	20.9
SF	47	34	.580	46	34	**.575**	91	77	317	312	**-12.5**	-1.8	90	63	358	314	8.1	6.3
PIT	46	35	.568	46	35	.568	48	48	384	317	2.3	-2.1	110	77	375	324	14.8	3.5
PHI	48	33	.593	39	42	.481	52	65	354	319	3.5	-0.6	65	72	342	321	4.8	4.3
ATL	43	38	.531	42	39	.519	119	82	394	335	0.3	-4.9	88	47	388	348	18.7	-3.4
STL	43	38	.531	40	41	.494	48	64	274	288	-7.7	-0.3	60	66	297	289	-9.9	13.8
CIN	46	33	.582	30	51	.370	91	93	417	372	55.4	15.5	58	60	275	330	-11.6	0.3
HOU	45	36	.556	27	54	.333	48	48	318	317	9.4	-15.1	64	82	294	378	-9.4	-10.9
NY	32	49	.395	34	46	.425	51	94	276	372	-12.3	-5.5	47	72	311	389	-6.0	-15.5
CHI	32	49	.395	27	54	.333	80	**100**	342	**410**	13.2	2.7	60	84	302	399	-6.4	-19.3
American League 1966																		
BAL	48	31	**.608**	49	32	**.605**	85	65	**375**	296	1.1	-0.5	**90**	62	**380**	305	22.9	4.6
MIN	49	32	.605	40	41	.494	94	83	**375**	311	30.2	15.1	50	**56**	288	**270**	-3.8	14.0
DET	42	39	.519	46	35	.568	97	101	360	374	0.2	15.4	82	84	359	324	16.3	-3.1
CHI	45	36	.556	38	43	.469	31	36	**273**	217	-8.1	-26.7	56	65	301	300	-3.4	8.5
CLE	41	40	.506	40	41	.494	82	65	283	300	-2.7	4.8	73	64	291	286	-5.9	9.8
CAL	42	39	.519	38	43	.469	54	67	303	315	0.6	-3.9	68	69	301	328	-2.4	-2.4
KC	42	39	.519	32	47	.405	18	**27**	284	292	-1.0	-20.0	52	79	280	356	-9.1	-9.6
WAS	42	36	.538	29	52	.358	62	84	**273**	292	-0.1	-17.3	64	70	284	367	-8.3	-12.7
BOS	40	41	.494	32	49	.395	80	97	374	**397**	33.0	18.8	65	67	281	334	-5.9	-6.7
NY	35	46	.432	35	43	.449	74	63	302	280	-7.0	-19.7	88	61	309	332	-0.1	-2.4
National League 1967																		
STL	49	32	.605	52	28	**.650**	53	54	326	301	-12.7	**16.1**	62	43	**369**	**256**	21.5	19.0
SF	51	31	**.622**	40	40	.500	65	59	333	271	1.8	-5.5	**75**	54	319	280	6.8	13.2
CHI	49	34	.590	38	40	.487	70	90	366	332	1.1	5.5	58	52	336	292	13.0	8.7
CIN	49	32	.605	38	43	.469	57	66	343	287	31.4	3.9	52	**35**	261	276	-10.2	13.9
PHI	45	35	.563	37	45	.451	48	44	320	292	12.3	3.5	55	42	292	289	-1.7	10.1
PIT	49	32	.605	32	49	.395	43	49	370	321	21.2	-12.6	48	59	309	372	5.0	-13.9
ATL	48	33	.593	29	52	.358	91	74	352	316	26.1	-2.4	67	44	279	324	-4.5	-0.4
LA	42	39	.519	31	50	.383	36	35	241	230	-13.3	-36.9	46	58	278	365	-8.5	-9.2
HOU	46	35	.568	23	58	.284	31	32	337	315	16.6	-26.2	62	88	289	427	-2.0	-29.1
NY	36	42	.462	25	59	.298	44	61	258	307	15.7	-9.4	39	63	240	365	-19.3	-11.6
American League 1967																		
BOS	49	32	.605	43	38	**.531**	90	88	**408**	355	29.9	37.0	68	54	314	**259**	9.8	11.8
DET	52	29	**.642**	39	42	.481	83	79	360	272	10.0	-14.7	69	72	323	315	10.9	-1.9
MIN	52	29	**.642**	39	42	.481	70	63	372	292	27.4	0.4	61	52	299	298	4.0	2.4
CHI	49	33	.598	40	40	.500	38	38	**243**	222	-17.6	-19.4	51	**49**	288	269	-3.7	13.2
CAL	53	30	.639	31	47	.397	56	59	288	276	-3.0	-16.6	58	59	279	311	-4.9	-0.8
BAL	35	42	.455	41	43	.488	64	49	283	275	-16.7	-5.3	74	67	**371**	317	23.0	-2.6
WAS	40	40	.500	36	45	.444	57	54	277	332	2.7	10.2	58	59	273	305	-7.1	-0.9
CLE	36	45	.444	39	42	.481	76	69	274	316	-3.8	6.3	55	51	285	297	-3.5	1.9
NY	43	38	.531	29	52	.358	60	47	268	271	4.2	**-23.5**	40	63	254	350	-13.2	-12.2
KC	37	44	.457	25	55	.313	19	**38**	288	320	16.0	-7.0	50	87	245	340	-15.3	-10.8
National League 1968																		
STL	47	34	**.580**	50	31	**.617**	31	35	267	218	-15.5	-14.1	42	47	**316**	254	12.7	11.1
SF	42	39	.519	46	35	.568	60	32	299	242	0.8	-14.6	48	54	300	287	8.6	-0.2
CHI	47	34	**.580**	37	44	.457	83	83	363	332	44.0	17.5	47	55	249	279	-5.6	-0.8
CIN	40	41	.494	43	38	.531	55	66	377	**400**	18.9	44.7	51	48	313	273	15.7	-1.3
ATL	41	40	.506	40	41	.494	42	43	241	241	-10.6	-20.7	38	44	273	308	-2.2	-6.9
PIT	40	41	.494	40	41	.494	33	30	289	268	-0.4	2.7	47	43	294	264	6.3	6.1
LA	41	40	.506	35	46	.432	25	**24**	212	215	-17.8	-26.8	42	41	258	294	-8.1	-1.5
PHI	38	43	.469	38	43	.469	52	46	274	297	1.8	-6.6	48	45	269	318	-2.3	-12.1
NY	32	49	.395	41	40	.506	49	50	224	270	-11.1	16.4	32	**37**	249	**229**	-10.6	17.2
HOU	42	39	.519	30	51	.370	**22**	30	279	269	20.7	-15.6	44	38	231	319	-14.5	-11.4

TEAM	Home Games W	L	Pct.	Road Games W	L	Pct.	Home Games HR	OHR	R	OR	RF	ORF	Road Games HR	OHR	R	OR	RF	ORF
American League 1968																		
DET	56	25	**.691**	47	34	**.580**	107	**75**	348	254	10.3	9.3	78	54	**323**	238	**18.1**	**13.7**
BAL	47	33	.588	44	38	.537	57	54	288	**248**	1.4	2.0	76	47	291	249	5.5	10.4
CLE	43	37	.538	43	38	.531	36	56	246	262	-8.8	8.2	39	42	270	242	-2.8	12.1
BOS	46	35	.568	40	41	.494	58	61	325	299	12.4	-4.1	67	54	289	312	6.2	-11.8
NY	39	42	.481	44	37	.543	56	50	268	268	0.0	1.8	53	49	268	263	-2.6	5.1
OAK	44	38	.537	38	42	.475	38	58	296	258	4.5	-13.0	56	66	273	286	0.0	-1.9
MIN	41	40	.506	38	43	.469	50	51	299	290	13.6	13.2	55	**41**	263	256	-3.2	6.6
CAL	32	49	.395	35	46	.432	49	66	229	299	**-14.8**	-5.3	34	65	269	316	-3.7	-13.1
CHI	36	45	.444	31	50	.383	**29**	**47**	**225**	273	-5.4	7.4	42	50	238	254	-14.0	7.8
WAS	34	47	.420	31	49	.388	53	53	257	**300**	-4.9	**-18.8**	71	65	267	365	-3.4	-29.0
National League 1969																		
EAST																		
NY	52	30	.634	48	32	**.600**	56	59	312	270	-4.8	-2.8	53	60	320	271	-2.4	17.9
CHI	49	32	.605	43	38	.531	84	64	387	321	14.7	9.3	58	**54**	333	290	3.0	11.3
PIT	47	34	.580	41	40	.506	**41**	**33**	324	322	**-19.2**	-2.4	**78**	63	**401**	330	**20.5**	0.2
STL	42	38	.525	45	37	.549	41	43	273	273	-13.1	4.8	49	56	322	**267**	-2.8	**18.9**
PHI	30	51	.370	33	48	.407	75	64	317	378	-3.3	2.9	62	70	328	367	0.0	-11.4
MON	24	57	.296	28	53	.346	73	**87**	288	**421**	-2.0	13.7	52	58	294	370	-10.3	-13.3
WEST																		
ATL	50	31	.617	43	38	.531	77	84	360	321	8.7	3.5	64	60	331	310	1.8	5.8
SF	52	29	**.642**	38	43	.469	77	61	362	317	3.1	-0.6	59	59	351	319	7.5	3.4
CIN	50	31	.617	39	42	.481	**97**	74	**407**	373	5.3	-4.4	74	75	391	395	19.8	-19.0
LA	50	31	.617	35	46	.432	41	55	325	**258**	1.5	**-14.8**	56	67	320	303	-2.1	9.3
HOU	52	29	**.642**	29	52	.358	47	43	371	313	21.6	-11.8	57	68	305	355	-5.1	-6.4
SD	28	53	.346	24	57	.296	47	47	**239**	358	4.3	-7.7	52	66	229	388	-29.8	-16.7
American League 1969																		
EAST																		
BAL	60	21	**.741**	49	32	**.605**	82	**51**	402	251	6.6	-5.6	**93**	66	377	**266**	16.5	**21.6**
DET	46	35	.568	44	37	.543	104	72	361	305	6.1	3.0	78	56	340	296	5.0	12.2
BOS	46	35	.568	41	40	.506	**105**	78	392	391	11.6	13.3	92	77	351	345	8.9	-3.2
WAS	47	34	.580	39	42	.481	77	62	353	290	3.5	-18.0	71	73	341	354	5.1	-3.1
NY	48	32	.600	32	49	.395	44	51	284	**245**	4.7	**-26.5**	50	67	278	342	-14.4	1.2
CLE	33	48	.407	29	51	.363	56	60	**276**	341	-8.2	-10.4	63	74	297	376	-9.2	-10.3
WEST																		
MIN	57	24	.704	40	41	.494	79	61	**414**	298	10.1	-6.8	84	58	376	320	16.5	5.8
OAK	49	32	.605	39	42	.481	73	70	330	315	**-19.5**	-13.2	75	93	**410**	363	**23.9**	-6.2
CAL	43	38	.531	28	53	.346	49	65	277	305	11.7	-11.0	39	61	251	347	-22.1	-1.6
KC	36	45	.444	33	48	.407	**39**	63	301	362	4.3	9.6	59	73	273	336	-14.0	-0.6
CHI	41	40	.506	27	54	.333	61	80	352	387	**28.9**	**15.1**	51	66	273	336	-14.0	-0.6
SEA	34	47	.420	30	51	.370	74	**93**	329	**399**	4.8	-1.4	51	79	310	400	-4.2	-18.3
National League 1970																		
EAST																		
PIT	50	32	.610	39	41	.488	43	**41**	356	315	-6.8	-11.9	87	65	373	349	2.5	6.0
CHI	46	34	.575	38	44	.463	109	92	471	394	**44.1**	**41.7**	70	**51**	335	**285**	-4.4	20.2
NY	44	38	.537	39	41	.488	63	75	374	**314**	13.6	-3.0	57	60	321	316	-10.2	14.3
STL	34	47	.420	42	39	.519	51	44	377	**418**	2.7	27.0	62	58	367	329	1.5	8.7
PHI	40	40	.500	33	48	.407	48	63	**293**	337	-1.4	-13.1	53	69	301	393	-17.1	-5.3
MON	39	41	.488	34	48	.415	77	91	363	385	14.8	-6.4	59	71	324	422	-9.7	-13.6
WEST																		
CIN	57	24	**.704**	45	36	**.556**	100	58	416	334	15.8	-3.7	91	60	359	347	0.3	6.1
LA	39	42	.481	48	32	**.600**	**35**	82	310	316	**-30.2**	**-15.2**	52	82	**439**	368	**18.1**	1.3
SF	48	33	.593	38	43	.469	84	77	413	386	-1.2	-12.2	78	79	418	440	15.2	-18.1
HOU	44	37	.543	35	46	.432	51	64	350	351	-11.1	-14.8	78	67	394	412	7.7	-10.4
ATL	42	39	.519	34	47	.420	92	**119**	395	398	15.8	6.4	68	66	341	374	-4.6	-2.0
SD	31	50	.383	32	49	.395	68	56	312	393	-15.4	-0.5	**104**	93	369	395	0.5	-7.1
American League 1970																		
EAST																		
BAL	59	22	**.728**	49	32	**.605**	88	58	386	**256**	-4.9	-19.5	**91**	81	**406**	318	**22.0**	9.1
NY	53	28	**.654**	40	41	.494	60	**40**	317	257	-11.6	**-26.7**	51	90	363	355	8.4	-0.6
BOS	52	29	.642	35	46	.432	117	75	**455**	382	37.4	12.3	86	81	331	340	3.0	0.2
DET	42	39	.519	37	44	.457	86	86	348	379	9.4	7.6	62	67	318	352	-3.2	-2.8
CLE	43	38	.531	33	48	.407	**133**	**103**	386	370	**46.7**	21.3	50	**60**	263	**305**	-17.5	**9.8**
WAS	40	41	.494	30	51	.370	72	61	303	330	-6.2	-8.0	66	78	323	359	-3.0	-3.5
WEST																		
MIN	51	30	.630	47	34	.580	66	53	366	285	-3.1	-10.9	87	77	378	320	13.7	7.9
OAK	49	32	.605	40	41	.494	83	56	337	265	-1.1	-19.2	88	78	341	328	2.8	6.3
CAL	43	38	.531	43	38	.531	**41**	59	**287**	274	-16.5	-23.0	73	95	344	356	2.3	-1.3
KC	35	44	.443	30	53	.361	46	48	305	331	4.7	-7.0	51	90	306	374	-7.6	-7.5
MIL	38	42	.475	27	55	.329	68	72	313	362	5.6	-5.8	58	74	300	389	-9.1	-12.2
CHI	31	53	.369	25	53	.321	78	97	346	**469**	11.9	**23.3**	45	67	287	353	-11.9	-5.2

TEAM	Home Games W	L	Pct.	Road Games W	L	Pct.	Home Games HR	OHR	R	OR	RF	ORF	Road Games HR	OHR	R	OR	RF	ORF
National League 1971																		
EAST																		
PIT	52	28	**.650**	45	37	.549	66	49	**393**	279	1.9	-10.6	**88**	59	**395**	320	**26.5**	1.4
STL	45	36	.556	45	36	.556	38	49	376	358	2.3	3.7	57	55	363	341	16.6	-6.5
CHI	44	37	.543	39	42	.481	74	70	363	342	**32.4**	11.7	54	62	274	306	-9.8	3.8
NY	44	37	.543	39	42	.481	48	50	281	256	-8.4	-12.9	50	50	307	**294**	-2.3	**9.5**
MON	36	44	.450	35	46	.432	50	68	304	366	-2.0	3.3	38	65	318	363	1.5	-13.0
PHI	34	47	.420	33	48	.407	73	80	296	353	12.9	5.3	50	52	262	335	-15.1	-4.7
WEST																		
SF	51	30	.630	39	42	.481	71	58	372	300	11.3	-12.8	69	70	334	344	8.0	-5.9
LA	42	39	.519	47	34	**.580**	43	56	324	286	-4.4	-4.9	52	54	339	301	8.2	6.7
ATL	43	39	.524	39	41	.488	**96**	90	366	**384**	28.9	**18.9**	57	62	277	315	-8.8	0.1
CIN	46	35	.568	33	48	.407	69	51	303	**251**	7.0	**-23.9**	69	61	283	330	-8.7	-0.6
HOU	39	42	.481	40	41	.494	**18**	**27**	256	263	**-22.2**	-13.4	53	**48**	329	304	3.4	6.4
SD	33	48	.407	28	52	.350	42	43	**233**	296	-9.0	-6.9	54	50	253	314	-19.4	2.7
American League 1971																		
EAST																		
BAL	53	24	**.688**	48	33	.593	78	67	374	**254**	6.9	-3.2	80	58	**368**	276	**18.4**	12.0
DET	54	27	.667	37	44	.457	**90**	70	352	289	0.8	-18.8	**89**	56	349	356	12.2	-12.4
BOS	47	33	.588	38	44	.463	88	75	**375**	338	21.6	5.3	73	61	316	329	3.1	-5.8
NY	44	37	.543	38	43	.469	39	61	327	297	1.8	-13.6	58	65	321	344	3.3	-9.1
WAS	35	46	.432	28	50	.359	34	59	268	296	-4.0	**-21.7**	52	73	269	364	-13.5	-15.0
CLE	29	52	.358	31	50	.383	62	**99**	297	**400**	20.7	15.2	47	55	246	347	-19.5	-12.8
WEST																		
OAK	46	35	.568	55	25	**.688**	84	74	325	300	-12.3	12.2	76	57	366	**264**	16.5	**14.3**
KC	44	37	.543	41	39	.513	**23**	**36**	296	277	-4.7	-5.3	57	48	307	289	-1.6	7.5
CHI	39	42	.481	40	41	.494	60	53	278	310	**-18.0**	8.0	78	47	339	287	7.3	7.2
CAL	35	46	.432	41	40	.506	39	55	**233**	297	-16.1	6.4	57	**46**	278	279	-11.8	9.9
MIN	37	42	.468	37	44	.457	57	71	332	356	5.7	**16.2**	59	68	322	314	3.7	-1.9
MIL	34	48	.415	35	44	.443	46	64	282	319	7.8	5.9	58	66	252	290	-18.2	6.1
National League 1972																		
EAST																		
PIT	49	29	**.628**	47	30	.610	53	**34**	351	259	1.9	1.0	57	56	340	**253**	12.2	**16.0**
CHI	46	31	.597	39	39	.500	83	63	**392**	305	**37.2**	19.4	50	49	293	262	-0.7	12.0
NY	41	37	.526	42	36	.538	45	56	254	264	-7.3	-15.9	60	62	274	314	-10.3	-2.6
STL	40	37	.519	35	44	.443	31	38	298	308	13.2	8.2	39	49	270	292	-10.3	2.8
MON	35	43	.449	35	43	.449	50	56	252	324	-3.4	13.6	41	47	261	285	-14.3	4.4
PHI	28	51	.354	31	46	.403	49	57	246	316	-6.7	-3.4	49	60	257	319	-15.6	-5.6
WEST																		
CIN	42	34	.553	53	25	**.679**	58	59	300	266	-24.3	-6.1	66	70	**407**	291	**31.1**	4.2
HOU	41	36	.532	43	33	.566	58	56	367	355	6.2	**24.6**	76	58	341	281	13.0	4.8
LA	41	34	.547	44	36	.550	46	37	267	**221**	-10.1	**-22.9**	52	**46**	317	306	3.0	0.9
ATL	36	41	.468	34	43	.442	**86**	**88**	339	**392**	15.7	14.4	58	67	289	338	-3.4	-13.4
SF	34	43	.442	35	43	.449	**86**	65	336	321	4.4	-0.8	64	65	326	328	7.6	-8.4
SD	26	54	.325	32	41	.438	41	64	**217**	315	**-26.9**	-17.8	61	57	271	350	-12.2	-15.0
American League 1972																		
EAST																		
DET	44	34	.564	42	36	.538	68	67	312	288	26.8	**27.4**	54	**34**	246	226	-1.9	17.5
BOS	52	26	.667	33	44	.429	71	49	**373**	303	37.9	-5.6	53	52	267	317	7.5	-12.6
BAL	38	39	.494	42	35	.545	44	40	240	211	**-13.9**	-3.6	56	45	279	229	7.5	**22.1**
NY	46	31	.597	33	45	.423	53	37	270	219	-4.7	-27.9	50	50	287	308	11.3	-7.2
CLE	43	34	.558	29	50	.367	59	**79**	263	261	29.1	3.7	32	44	209	258	-16.7	7.8
MIL	37	42	.468	28	49	.364	36	45	243	286	-5.2	-9.7	52	71	250	309	-2.7	-9.5
WEST																		
OAK	48	29	.623	45	33	**.577**	68	52	287	**210**	-8.2	-13.8	**66**	44	**317**	247	**22.6**	13.0
CHI	55	23	**.705**	32	44	.421	65	44	341	252	**47.6**	-14.1	43	50	225	286	-8.4	-1.0
MIN	42	32	.568	35	45	.438	52	54	299	255	35.8	-1.5	41	51	238	280	-5.2	0.8
KC	44	33	.571	32	45	.416	**29**	**28**	309	257	14.0	-10.7	49	57	271	288	6.9	-1.8
CAL	44	36	.550	31	44	.413	30	31	**221**	218	-11.0	**-35.1**	48	59	233	315	-9.5	-9.4
TEX	31	46	.403	23	54	.299	33	41	235	288	3.9	-15.3	23	51	226	340	-11.5	-19.7

	Home Games			Road Games			Home Games						Road Games					
TEAM	W	L	Pct.	W	L	Pct.	HR	OHR	R	OR	RF	ORF	HR	OHR	R	OR	RF	ORF
National League 1973																		
EAST																		
NY	43	38	.531	39	41	.488	39	61	314	283	5.4	-8.3	46	66	294	305	-10.7	10.9
STL	43	38	.531	38	43	.469	27	30	290	255	-17.8	-26.7	48	75	353	348	4.9	0.1
PIT	41	40	.506	39	42	.481	72	42	334	301	-9.7	-23.2	82	68	370	392	10.7	-12.8
MON	43	38	.531	36	45	.444	63	70	364	353	19.7	1.1	62	58	304	349	-6.7	-2.5
CHI	41	39	.513	36	45	.444	66	72	327	356	15.3	20.5	51	56	287	299	-12.3	10.8
PHI	38	43	.469	33	48	.407	78	80	358	381	26.0	13.3	56	51	284	336	-12.4	0.2
WEST																		
CIN	50	31	.617	49	32	.605	47	67	330	287	-19.7	-14.0	90	68	411	334	22.0	3.0
LA	50	31	.617	45	35	.563	63	62	338	271	0.2	-7.8	47	67	337	294	1.7	14.2
SF	47	34	.580	41	40	.506	85	79	395	363	14.8	7.0	76	66	344	339	5.1	-0.1
HOU	41	40	.506	41	40	.506	58	53	315	322	-13.9	-8.0	76	58	366	350	9.2	-2.0
ATL	40	40	.500	36	45	.444	118	87	460	437	35.6	29.6	88	57	339	337	5.3	-1.3
SD	31	50	.383	29	52	.358	51	80	273	355	-0.7	-14.4	61	77	275	415	-17.0	-20.3
American League 1973																		
EAST																		
BAL	50	31	.617	47	34	.580	63	60	408	284	17.9	2.5	56	64	346	277	2.5	20.7
BOS	48	33	.593	41	40	.506	83	83	390	339	12.0	10.0	64	75	348	308	2.6	11.3
DET	47	34	.580	38	43	.469	86	71	329	332	5.1	-2.9	71	83	313	342	-8.2	2.6
NY	50	31	.617	30	51	.370	74	42	359	263	27.3	-24.2	57	67	282	347	-15.8	2.9
MIL	40	41	.494	34	47	.420	73	52	349	343	-2.7	-11.6	72	67	359	388	4.5	-9.6
CLE	34	47	.420	37	44	.457	92	100	320	427	-11.1	7.0	66	72	360	399	4.1	-14.5
WEST																		
OAK	50	31	.617	44	37	.543	70	70	313	253	-29.6	-30.1	77	73	445	362	26.7	-0.7
KC	48	33	.593	40	41	.494	54	61	422	404	26.7	16.0	60	53	333	348	-0.6	-0.6
MIN	37	44	.457	44	37	.543	56	60	357	386	-6.3	26.1	64	55	381	306	10.6	10.7
CAL	43	38	.531	36	45	.444	41	49	316	294	0.9	-19.0	52	55	313	363	-8.5	-1.9
CHI	40	41	.494	37	44	.457	56	58	329	368	1.8	9.2	55	52	323	337	-5.5	3.0
TEX	35	46	.432	22	59	.272	47	51	321	408	7.7	-6.4	63	79	298	436	-12.4	-23.7
National League 1974																		
EAST																		
PIT	52	29	.642	36	45	.444	47	32	380	303	2.4	-14.4	67	61	371	354	12.4	-2.3
STL	44	37	.543	42	38	.525	45	46	356	329	9.5	3.4	38	51	321	314	-2.0	7.7
PHI	46	35	.568	34	47	.420	55	56	378	337	26.8	-7.4	40	55	298	364	-7.8	-5.8
MON	42	38	.525	37	44	.457	50	49	356	329	17.7	1.5	36	50	306	328	-6.1	4.0
NY	36	45	.444	35	46	.432	43	49	279	325	-4.7	1.2	53	50	293	321	-11.7	6.0
CHI	32	49	.395	34	47	.420	67	72	344	424	5.8	5.4	43	50	325	402	-1.2	-18.1
WEST																		
LA	52	29	.642	50	31	.617	68	51	355	250	-19.8	-19.6	71	61	443	311	31.7	10.5
CIN	50	31	.617	48	33	.593	74	62	389	295	-0.7	-13.2	61	64	387	336	17.1	2.7
ATL	46	35	.568	42	39	.519	65	44	337	290	5.2	7.5	55	53	324	273	-1.6	19.7
HOU	46	35	.568	35	46	.432	58	35	330	293	2.1	-13.5	52	49	323	339	-2.1	1.9
SF	37	44	.457	35	46	.432	50	61	340	398	15.6	22.4	43	55	294	325	-9.9	3.1
SD	36	45	.444	24	57	.296	47	54	272	381	1.1	-15.1	52	70	269	449	-18.5	-29.6
American League 1974																		
EAST																		
BAL	46	35	.568	45	36	.556	48	46	281	293	-25.6	-8.1	68	55	378	319	12.1	5.3
NY	47	34	.580	42	39	.519	42	50	315	295	-11.5	-10.0	59	54	356	328	6.8	2.8
BOS	46	35	.568	38	43	.469	58	66	375	348	16.8	11.1	51	60	321	313	-1.3	5.6
CLE	40	41	.494	37	44	.457	72	92	338	349	4.3	1.1	59	46	324	345	-1.4	-3.1
MIL	40	41	.494	36	45	.444	58	69	342	329	12.1	-0.6	62	57	305	331	-6.6	1.1
DET	36	45	.444	36	45	.444	74	84	335	412	17.5	15.7	57	64	285	356	-12.3	-7.7
WEST																		
OAK	49	32	.605	41	40	.506	69	43	345	265	0.2	-7.3	63	47	344	286	4.2	15.1
TEX	42	38	.525	42	38	.525	43	57	321	340	-11.9	-3.8	56	69	369	358	10.6	-6.4
MIN	48	33	.593	34	47	.420	60	56	365	317	17.0	-11.0	51	59	308	352	-5.2	-4.2
CHI	46	34	.575	34	46	.425	66	43	360	365	9.7	1.2	69	60	324	356	-0.8	-6.5
KC	40	41	.494	37	44	.457	38	42	355	353	13.7	14.2	51	49	312	309	-4.3	6.6
CAL	36	45	.444	32	49	.395	46	47	291	287	-9.9	-21.4	49	54	327	370	-1.8	-8.4

TEAM	Home Games W	L	Pct.	Road Games W	L	Pct.	Home Games HR	OHR	R	OR	RF	ORF	Road Games HR	OHR	R	OR	RF	ORF
National League 1975																		
EAST																		
PIT	52	28	.650	40	41	.494	67	41	348	270	-3.2	-7.3	71	38	364	295	10.8	14.0
PHI	51	30	.630	35	46	.432	72	47	401	326	20.0	-11.4	53	64	334	368	3.8	-6.9
NY	42	39	.519	40	41	.494	52	48	294	301	-16.4	-7.1	49	51	352	324	6.1	5.5
STL	45	36	.556	37	44	.457	46	39	351	352	11.4	3.1	35	59	311	337	-3.8	0.7
CHI	42	39	.519	33	48	.407	54	71	392	427	22.5	6.7	41	59	320	400	-0.3	-18.0
MON	39	42	.481	36	45	.444	53	57	326	375	18.5	19.0	45	45	275	315	-14.6	6.1
WEST																		
CIN	64	17	**.790**	44	37	**.543**	70	52	**457**	275	19.3	-11.5	54	60	**383**	311	**18.9**	9.6
LA	49	32	.605	39	42	.481	64	52	319	**221**	-3.0	-29.4	54	52	329	313	0.3	10.4
SF	46	35	.568	34	46	.425	36	**37**	346	335	9.1	-1.5	48	55	313	336	-3.4	1.4
SD	38	43	.469	33	48	.407	**33**	38	**279**	338	2.1	-2.0	45	61	273	345	-16.3	-1.0
ATL	37	43	.463	30	51	.370	58	63	280	350	-6.4	-8.9	49	**38**	303	389	-7.9	-13.1
HOU	37	44	.457	27	53	.338	40	43	313	338	-10.8	-9.3	44	63	351	373	6.3	-8.5
American League 1975																		
EAST																		
BOS	47	34	.580	48	31	**.608**	74	83	**427**	399	12.8	**25.5**	60	62	369	**310**	8.5	8.1
BAL	44	33	.571	46	36	.561	46	45	**282**	**231**	-24.9	-23.6	78	65	**400**	322	**13.2**	9.0
NY	43	35	.551	40	42	.488	50	56	323	276	-5.1	-7.0	60	**48**	358	312	3.0	**10.6**
CLE	41	39	.513	38	41	.481	79	85	331	367	-8.4	7.8	74	51	357	336	3.0	2.0
MIL	36	45	.444	32	49	.395	72	63	348	398	6.4	1.0	74	70	327	394	-4.5	-14.0
DET	31	49	.388	26	53	.329	63	83	301	**421**	10.4	13.9	62	54	269	365	-21.1	-6.9
WEST																		
OAK	54	27	**.667**	44	37	.543	75	**43**	366	247	-6.6	**-31.2**	76	59	392	359	13.1	-1.1
KC	51	30	.630	40	41	.494	46	45	377	309	13.2	-9.1	72	63	333	340	-2.2	2.3
TEX	39	41	.488	40	42	.488	52	70	349	366	-2.0	2.2	**82**	53	365	367	5.5	-6.1
MIN	39	43	.476	37	40	.481	75	**88**	401	410	16.5	18.1	46	49	323	326	-4.3	3.6
CHI	42	39	.519	33	47	.413	42	54	350	359	13.3	3.0	52	53	305	344	-10.3	0.1
CAL	35	46	.432	37	43	.463	**24**	52	294	349	-13.0	-7.8	31	71	334	374	-4.0	-7.6
National League 1976																		
EAST																		
PHI	53	28	**.654**	48	33	.593	63	49	424	277	22.5	-1.0	47	49	346	280	10.5	14.1
PIT	47	34	.580	45	36	.556	54	44	366	302	7.0	-7.9	56	51	342	328	7.8	0.0
NY	45	37	.549	41	39	.513	43	43	269	245	-24.1	-18.4	59	54	346	293	6.4	11.3
CHI	42	39	.519	33	48	.407	71	**84**	355	385	**38.6**	12.2	34	39	256	343	-17.1	-6.2
STL	37	44	.457	35	46	.432	**27**	40	335	346	13.9	6.4	36	51	294	325	-6.7	-0.2
MON	27	53	.338	28	54	.341	45	41	266	374	2.8	6.4	49	48	265	360	-16.9	-10.7
WEST																		
CIN	49	32	.605	53	28	**.654**	**73**	46	**426**	337	-1.1	13.8	**68**	54	**431**	296	**34.9**	8.1
LA	49	32	.605	43	38	.531	42	48	296	265	-5.1	-4.6	49	49	312	**278**	-2.6	**15.0**
HOU	46	36	.561	34	46	.425	30	**27**	277	264	-22.3	**-34.4**	36	55	348	393	7.2	-17.2
SF	40	41	.494	34	47	.420	44	32	314	352	11.7	5.3	41	36	281	334	-11.0	-2.9
SD	42	38	.525	31	51	.378	30	38	**254**	271	-17.6	-28.9	34	49	316	391	-2.5	-16.8
ATL	34	47	.420	36	45	.444	43	56	338	**401**	19.8	**34.1**	39	**30**	282	299	-10.1	5.6
American League 1976																		
EAST																		
NY	45	35	.563	52	27	**.658**	67	51	349	294	-9.5	3.3	53	46	**381**	**281**	**17.7**	**13.1**
BAL	42	39	.519	46	35	.568	58	38	280	306	**-17.4**	4.7	61	42	339	292	3.9	9.7
BOS	46	35	.568	37	44	.457	71	61	**408**	352	**32.4**	14.2	**63**	48	308	308	-1.5	4.0
CLE	44	35	.557	37	43	.463	40	43	311	295	3.5	-6.6	45	**37**	304	320	-5.2	2.1
DET	36	44	.450	38	43	.469	51	**62**	305	**381**	1.5	**17.6**	50	39	304	328	-5.3	-2.3
MIL	36	45	.444	30	50	.375	45	43	292	321	3.7	-5.0	43	56	278	334	-13.1	-2.4
WEST																		
KC	49	32	.605	41	40	.506	37	35	368	287	6.6	-11.4	28	48	345	324	7.9	1.2
OAK	51	30	**.630**	36	44	.450	56	57	353	**284**	4.6	-10.6	57	39	333	314	4.1	4.1
MIN	44	37	.543	41	40	.506	34	52	368	348	-1.8	-2.2	47	**37**	375	356	16.5	-9.3
CAL	38	43	.469	38	43	.469	**24**	35	249	284	-17.2	**-18.1**	39	60	301	347	-7.6	-5.2
TEX	39	42	.481	37	44	.457	40	57	319	330	7.4	2.4	40	49	297	322	-6.9	0.6
CHI	35	45	.438	29	52	.358	31	**34**	300	369	6.2	-0.6	42	53	286	376	-10.6	-15.5

TEAM	Home Games W	L	Pct.	Road Games W	L	Pct.	Home Games HR	OHR	R	OR	RF	ORF	Road Games HR	OHR	R	OR	RF	ORF

National League 1977

EAST

TEAM	W	L	Pct.	W	L	Pct.	HR	OHR	R	OR	RF	ORF	HR	OHR	R	OR	RF	ORF
PHI	60	21	.741	41	40	.506	101	63	453	299	14.9	-18.9	85	71	394	369	15.1	0.9
PIT	58	23	.716	38	43	.469	64	76	396	315	17.1	-10.0	69	73	338	350	-1.0	5.2
STL	52	31	.627	31	48	.392	41	53	379	314	0.7	-20.0	55	86	358	374	3.8	-0.6
CHI	46	35	.568	35	46	.432	69	82	411	402	46.2	19.2	42	46	281	337	-15.8	6.5
MON	38	43	.469	37	44	.457	66	65	329	362	-2.0	-3.2	72	70	336	374	-3.2	-1.7
NY	35	44	.443	29	54	.349	46	56	282	297	-2.8	-14.7	42	62	305	366	-12.5	1.6

WEST

TEAM	W	L	Pct.	W	L	Pct.	HR	OHR	R	OR	RF	ORF	HR	OHR	R	OR	RF	ORF
LA	51	30	.630	47	34	.580	96	65	386	273	0.7	-11.6	95	54	383	309	10.5	16.5
CIN	48	33	.593	40	41	.494	83	83	408	355	3.5	-4.0	98	73	394	370	14.0	-0.6
HOU	46	35	.568	35	46	.432	40	33	309	291	-16.7	-18.9	74	77	371	359	5.5	3.5
SF	38	43	.469	37	44	.457	62	56	353	371	10.3	9.1	72	58	320	340	-6.8	6.5
SD	35	46	.432	34	47	.420	53	70	299	368	-23.9	-21.0	67	90	393	466	11.1	-24.9
ATL	40	41	.494	21	60	.259	97	111	416	488	58.7	19.9	42	58	262	407	-20.7	-12.9

American League 1977

EAST

TEAM	W	L	Pct.	W	L	Pct.	HR	OHR	R	OR	RF	ORF	HR	OHR	R	OR	RF	ORF
NY	55	26	.679	45	36	.556	84	63	412	305	-1.6	-11.8	100	76	419	346	15.4	7.1
BAL	54	27	.667	43	37	.538	74	62	356	269	-3.1	-30.8	74	62	363	384	0.0	-1.7
BOS	51	29	.638	46	35	.568	124	95	495	407	37.6	35.1	89	63	364	305	2.9	15.4
DET	39	42	.481	35	46	.432	81	100	369	401	6.9	14.5	85	62	345	350	-4.3	4.2
CLE	37	44	.457	34	46	.425	54	66	339	357	-0.6	-7.7	46	70	337	382	-7.0	-2.9
MIL	37	44	.457	30	51	.370	49	54	305	365	-8.6	-8.7	76	82	334	400	-8.4	-7.6
TOR	25	55	.313	29	52	.358	45	94	297	444	-2.3	18.9	55	58	308	378	-15.2	-3.6

WEST

TEAM	W	L	Pct.	W	L	Pct.	HR	OHR	R	OR	RF	ORF	HR	OHR	R	OR	RF	ORF
KC	55	26	.679	47	34	.580	56	50	408	320	-1.4	-3.3	90	60	414	331	14.0	10.5
TEX	44	37	.543	50	31	.617	62	78	369	368	-7.2	27.3	73	56	398	289	9.1	20.2
CHI	48	33	.593	42	39	.519	85	58	434	370	5.8	-7.7	107	78	410	401	13.5	-7.9
MIN	48	32	.600	36	45	.444	61	79	469	376	19.3	-4.8	62	72	398	400	11.1	-7.8
CAL	39	42	.481	35	46	.432	69	65	320	321	-9.8	-14.1	62	71	355	374	-2.8	-0.2
SEA	29	52	.358	35	46	.432	75	103	303	419	-5.6	-3.9	58	91	321	436	-11.8	-17.7
OAK	35	46	.432	28	52	.350	58	69	302	347	-1.5	-14.7	59	76	303	402	-16.4	-7.7

National League 1978

EAST

TEAM	W	L	Pct.	W	L	Pct.	HR	OHR	R	OR	RF	ORF	HR	OHR	R	OR	RF	ORF
PHI	54	28	.659	36	44	.450	80	70	405	279	30.4	-11.3	53	48	303	307	1.1	9.6
PIT	55	26	.679	33	47	.413	57	61	389	310	30.2	-6.3	58	42	295	327	-1.6	3.4
CHI	44	38	.537	35	45	.438	41	76	393	387	41.4	12.0	31	49	271	337	-8.6	-1.1
MON	41	39	.513	35	47	.427	46	49	299	283	-8.2	-11.5	75	68	334	328	7.5	3.8
STL	37	44	.457	32	49	.395	29	32	289	307	-7.0	-12.2	50	62	311	350	0.4	-2.7
NY	33	47	.413	33	49	.402	37	60	295	340	-3.0	-0.4	49	54	312	350	0.8	-3.5

WEST

TEAM	W	L	Pct.	W	L	Pct.	HR	OHR	R	OR	RF	ORF	HR	OHR	R	OR	RF	ORF
LA	54	27	.667	41	40	.506	78	59	361	272	-1.3	-9.6	71	48	366	301	18.7	11.4
CIN	49	31	.613	43	38	.531	74	61	379	338	15.9	-2.2	62	61	331	350	8.8	-3.4
SF	50	31	.617	39	42	.481	47	30	291	244	-9.6	-30.2	70	54	322	350	3.7	-1.1
SD	50	31	.617	34	47	.420	31	23	291	245	-3.0	-30.6	44	51	300	353	-2.8	-1.9
HOU	50	31	.617	24	57	.296	30	29	327	254	17.6	-33.1	40	57	278	380	-8.3	-9.5
ATL	39	42	.481	30	51	.370	87	89	364	400	54.2	14.2	36	43	236	350	-19.8	-4.9

American League 1978

EAST

TEAM	W	L	Pct.	W	L	Pct.	HR	OHR	R	OR	RF	ORF	HR	OHR	R	OR	RF	ORF
NY	55	26	.679	45	37	.549	68	59	358	275	-3.8	-9.3	57	52	377	307	16.9	14.8
BOS	59	23	.720	40	41	.494	94	72	445	334	25.2	2.1	78	65	351	323	11.3	9.5
MIL	54	27	.667	39	42	.481	94	50	446	318	24.5	-4.2	79	59	358	332	13.3	7.5
BAL	51	30	.630	39	41	.488	74	42	316	258	-9.0	-32.0	80	65	343	375	6.1	-2.4
DET	47	34	.580	39	42	.481	74	78	395	338	23.8	7.3	55	57	319	315	0.9	11.5
CLE	42	36	.538	27	54	.333	50	37	319	287	3.5	-26.7	56	63	320	407	-0.4	-11.3
TOR	37	44	.457	22	58	.275	50	75	334	366	28.8	-11.6	48	74	256	409	-18.5	-13.4

WEST

TEAM	W	L	Pct.	W	L	Pct.	HR	OHR	R	OR	RF	ORF	HR	OHR	R	OR	RF	ORF
KC	56	25	.691	36	45	.444	43	44	434	264	40.4	-28.6	55	64	309	370	-1.0	-1.2
CAL	50	31	.617	37	44	.457	56	58	371	316	15.9	-9.7	52	67	320	350	0.7	2.9
TEX	52	30	.634	35	45	.438	62	49	348	289	-1.3	-17.8	70	59	344	343	7.1	5.2
MIN	38	43	.469	35	46	.432	44	39	322	308	-6.4	-16.7	38	63	344	370	6.5	-2.1
CHI	38	42	.475	33	48	.407	56	58	342	349	18.5	-7.5	50	70	292	382	-8.0	-6.0
OAK	38	42	.475	31	51	.378	52	51	281	330	14.7	-6.0	48	55	251	360	-21.2	0.0
SEA	32	49	.395	24	55	.304	58	93	343	423	23.4	0.3	39	62	271	411	-14.0	-15.0

TEAM	Home Games W	L	Pct.	Road Games W	L	Pct.	Home Games HR	OHR	R	OR	RF	ORF	Road Games HR	OHR	R	OR	RF	ORF
National League 1979																		
EAST																		
PIT	48	33	.593	50	31	**.617**	74	77	399	339	7.4	12.8	74	48	**376**	**304**	**11.8**	10.8
MON	56	25	**.691**	39	40	.494	68	51	378	275	14.1	-12.3	75	65	323	306	-3.0	**11.8**
STL	42	39	.519	44	37	.543	48	65	379	372	6.3	14.4	52	62	352	321	4.8	5.5
PHI	43	38	.531	41	40	.506	52	72	332	342	-4.2	-7.9	67	63	351	376	3.4	-8.3
CHI	45	36	.556	35	46	.432	79	72	**423**	370	49.4	9.7	56	55	283	337	-12.7	1.3
NY	28	53	.346	35	46	.432	30	58	**267**	354	-19.1	-0.6	44	62	326	352	-4.9	-2.2
WEST																		
CIN	48	32	.600	42	39	.519	71	53	360	298	-1.7	-12.8	61	50	371	346	9.5	0.6
HOU	52	29	.642	37	44	.457	**15**	**31**	269	**234**	-14.3	**-32.7**	34	59	314	348	-8.1	1.7
LA	46	35	.568	33	48	.407	**106**	55	389	341	11.1	-9.3	**77**	46	350	376	4.5	-8.3
SF	38	43	.469	33	48	.407	53	61	298	361	**-20.3**	-7.4	72	82	374	390	8.8	-12.5
SD	39	42	.481	29	51	.363	36	47	287	335	-10.3	-4.3	57	61	316	346	-7.1	-0.2
ATL	34	45	.430	32	49	.395	73	**80**	359	**425**	18.7	**28.9**	53	52	310	338	-7.0	-0.2
American League 1979																		
EAST																		
BAL	55	24	**.696**	47	33	**.588**	74	57	369	**259**	-3.7	-18.8	**107**	76	388	**323**	5.4	**17.3**
MIL	52	29	.642	43	37	.538	91	81	401	362	-2.4	-0.6	94	81	406	360	10.6	6.5
BOS	51	29	.638	40	40	.500	**121**	59	**470**	357	26.6	0.8	73	74	371	354	3.1	8.0
NY	51	30	.630	38	41	.481	77	59	360	308	-6.1	-17.4	73	64	374	364	1.7	6.5
DET	46	34	.575	39	42	.481	101	74	394	323	6.0	-21.2	63	93	376	415	2.9	-6.0
CLE	47	34	.580	34	46	.425	87	72	428	409	27.3	2.0	51	66	332	396	-7.5	-3.0
TOR	32	49	.395	21	60	.259	50	74	345	**432**	28.7	0.4	45	91	268	430	-25.4	-11.6
WEST																		
CAL	49	32	.605	39	42	.481	71	**55**	408	339	-10.9	-20.9	93	76	**458**	429	**23.9**	-9.6
KC	46	35	.568	39	42	.481	53	81	462	421	18.7	6.5	63	84	389	395	7.5	-2.9
TEX	44	37	.543	39	42	.481	69	63	382	335	3.8	-7.7	71	72	368	363	0.6	6.3
MIN	39	42	.481	43	38	.531	67	61	415	390	18.9	16.4	45	67	349	335	-3.5	12.0
CHI	33	46	.418	40	41	.494	56	60	349	401	-6.0	18.4	71	54	381	347	3.2	8.9
SEA	36	45	.444	31	50	.383	88	**94**	371	404	9.1	-2.8	44	71	340	416	-6.6	-7.7
OAK	31	50	.383	23	58	.284	**46**	65	**262**	371	**-15.7**	**-24.1**	62	82	311	489	-16.1	-24.7
National League 1980																		
EAST																		
PHI	49	32	.605	42	39	.519	64	44	**398**	334	20.6	9.5	53	**43**	330	**305**	6.3	**9.2**
MON	51	29	.638	39	43	.476	51	40	357	286	8.5	-14.5	63	60	337	343	7.2	0.1
PIT	47	34	.580	36	45	.444	63	53	355	322	14.1	-0.6	53	57	311	324	-0.3	4.3
STL	41	40	.506	33	48	.407	41	42	396	357	15.7	1.1	60	48	342	353	9.7	-4.3
NY	38	44	.463	29	51	.363	35	**80**	306	336	-2.1	-10.4	26	60	305	366	-3.3	-7.3
CHI	37	44	.457	27	54	.333	54	62	338	**385**	22.4	**12.2**	53	47	276	343	-10.9	-2.3
WEST																		
HOU	55	26	**.679**	38	44	.463	26	**22**	329	**255**	8.1	-22.7	49	47	308	334	-1.8	3.3
LA	55	27	**.671**	37	44	.457	82	58	327	272	**-3.8**	-15.7	**66**	47	336	319	6.2	6.9
CIN	44	37	.543	45	36	**.556**	66	70	356	349	0.1	7.3	47	**43**	351	321	**11.3**	4.5
ATL	50	30	.625	31	50	.383	**84**	79	352	297	28.2	-17.1	60	52	278	363	-9.9	-5.5
SF	44	37	.543	31	49	.388	**24**	41	**283**	293	-3.6	-15.1	56	51	290	341	-8.3	0.5
SD	45	36	.556	28	53	.346	29	33	295	274	0.8	**-27.0**	38	64	296	380	-6.2	-9.5
American League 1980																		
EAST																		
NY	53	28	**.654**	50	31	**.617**	**91**	47	409	315	-0.4	-9.2	98	55	411	347	13.7	6.2
BAL	50	31	.617	50	31	**.617**	75	81	397	319	-2.7	-0.6	81	**53**	408	**321**	12.7	**12.6**
MIL	40	42	.488	46	34	.575	90	65	443	346	**-18.9**	-5.2	**113**	72	**443**	346	**21.1**	6.0
BOS	36	45	.444	47	32	.595	79	74	370	**420**	-6.7	**18.0**	83	55	387	347	6.8	4.1
DET	43	38	.531	41	40	.506	77	95	**440**	404	11.4	13.0	66	57	390	353	8.9	2.9
CLE	44	35	.557	35	46	.432	55	66	400	389	21.3	-4.5	34	71	338	418	-5.1	-13.1
TOR	35	46	.432	32	49	.395	56	75	311	386	-0.6	2.6	70	60	313	376	-13.3	-2.5
WEST																		
KC	49	32	.605	48	33	.593	47	51	397	335	-3.6	-6.6	68	78	412	359	13.7	2.7
OAK	46	35	.568	37	44	.457	58	57	337	**277**	-3.4	**-24.1**	79	85	349	365	-3.6	2.3
MIN	44	36	.550	33	48	.407	51	63	392	361	**42.7**	0.6	48	57	278	363	-20.7	1.2
TEX	39	41	.488	37	44	.457	58	57	380	365	4.8	-2.1	66	62	376	387	4.1	-4.8
CHI	37	42	.468	33	48	.407	**41**	**37**	281	350	-8.1	-5.9	50	71	306	372	-15.7	-0.8
CAL	30	51	.370	35	44	.443	49	76	330	403	-12.5	-0.2	57	65	368	394	1.1	-7.3
SEA	36	45	.444	23	58	.284	74	**99**	340	389	27.4	-2.5	30	60	270	404	-23.8	-9.6

TEAM	Home Games W	L	Pct.	Road Games W	L	Pct.	Home Games HR	OHR	R	OR	RF	ORF	Road Games HR	OHR	R	OR	RF	ORF
National League 1981																		
EAST																		
STL	32	21	.604	27	22	.551	22	26	244	218	4.6	3.3	28	26	220	199	8.3	6.6
MON	38	18	**.679**	22	30	.423	39	23	255	170	25.9	-29.5	42	35	188	224	-5.4	-2.2
PHI	36	19	.655	23	29	.442	**41**	39	**295**	**261**	42.3	**16.9**	28	33	196	211	-0.2	-0.1
PIT	22	28	.440	24	28	.462	29	29	189	207	-11.6	-3.1	26	31	218	218	5.2	-1.0
NY	24	27	.471	17	35	.327	30	38	186	207	17.0	-6.2	27	36	162	225	-19.9	-4.0
CHI	27	30	.474	11	35	.239	**41**	38	239	254	50.9	-8.2	16	21	131	229	-31.6	-7.6
WEST																		
CIN	32	22	.593	34	20	**.630**	26	**41**	226	230	-5.0	9.5	38	26	**238**	210	**15.7**	1.4
LA	33	23	.589	30	24	.556	37	34	221	171	-6.9	-10.8	**45**	**20**	229	**185**	11.4	**14.4**
HOU	31	20	.608	30	29	.508	16	9	**166**	**106**	-15.7	**-45.5**	29	31	228	225	8.7	-0.1
SF	29	24	.547	27	31	.466	28	19	218	204	14.1	6.3	35	38	209	210	2.4	2.4
ATL	22	27	.449	28	29	.491	37	**41**	182	195	-2.6	0.5	27	21	213	221	2.7	-1.8
SD	20	35	.364	21	34	.382	**9**	27	168	223	**-21.5**	-3.8	23	37	214	232	2.6	-7.6
American League 1981																		
EAST																		
MIL	28	21	.571	34	26	**.567**	33	29	203	203	-14.2	-2.9	**63**	43	**290**	256	**30.3**	-15.2
BAL	33	22	.600	26	24	.520	49	47	231	217	6.0	-10.3	39	36	198	220	-7.9	-0.4
NY	32	19	**.627**	27	29	.482	47	**24**	203	154	2.2	-10.5	53	40	218	**189**	-0.3	**14.7**
DET	32	23	.582	28	26	.519	43	44	241	196	**27.2**	-7.4	22	39	186	208	-12.7	5.3
BOS	30	23	.566	29	26	.527	52	47	**278**	247	19.7	9.5	38	43	241	234	11.9	-7.3
CLE	25	29	.463	27	22	.551	19	33	210	216	-13.7	-13.2	20	34	221	226	1.1	-2.9
TOR	17	36	.321	20	33	.377	34	41	172	272	9.5	**40.2**	27	31	157	194	-27.4	8.8
WEST																		
OAK	35	21	.625	29	24	.547	**57**	46	234	183	-1.1	-21.2	47	34	224	220	3.2	0.6
TEX	32	24	.571	25	24	.510	21	**24**	232	168	-7.7	**-33.4**	28	43	220	221	1.4	0.7
CHI	25	24	.510	29	28	.509	31	33	215	198	-4.1	2.3	45	40	261	225	18.3	-1.9
KC	19	28	.404	31	25	.554	**17**	27	**163**	197	**-17.0**	12.8	44	48	234	208	5.1	5.3
CAL	26	28	.481	25	31	.446	48	39	244	233	9.0	9.8	49	42	232	220	6.9	-0.9
SEA	20	37	.351	24	28	.462	52	**53**	226	271	5.0	0.7	37	**23**	200	250	-7.3	-14.9
MIN	24	36	.400	17	32	.347	25	47	213	**292**	3.6	20.9	22	32	165	194	-22.6	8.1
National League 1982																		
EAST																		
STL	46	35	.568	46	35	.568	**27**	48	338	325	-2.6	14.4	40	46	347	284	4.1	12.8
PHI	51	30	**.630**	38	43	.469	57	46	301	307	**-17.0**	-11.5	55	**40**	363	347	7.6	-4.2
MON	40	41	.494	46	35	.568	59	65	335	352	-7.4	**33.3**	74	45	362	**264**	8.2	**17.7**
PIT	42	39	.519	42	39	.519	77	65	**391**	**394**	17.4	30.4	57	53	333	302	1.6	6.1
CHI	38	43	.469	35	46	.432	53	62	352	371	8.6	9.7	49	63	324	338	-1.8	-3.3
NY	33	48	.407	32	49	.395	48	60	307	357	1.6	-2.4	49	59	302	366	-9.0	-10.7
WEST																		
ATL	42	39	.519	47	34	**.580**	**95**	**86**	388	387	10.5	22.8	51	**40**	351	315	6.4	2.6
LA	43	38	.531	45	36	.556	57	35	321	**283**	-13.2	-13.9	**81**	46	**370**	329	**10.0**	1.4
SF	45	36	.556	42	39	.519	55	54	319	312	-9.8	-16.8	78	55	354	375	5.5	-12.1
SD	43	38	.531	38	43	.469	33	76	316	286	-11.9	**-23.1**	48	63	359	372	6.9	-10.6
HOU	43	38	.531	34	47	.420	31	**26**	**290**	294	3.9	-9.8	43	61	279	326	-15.8	1.9
CIN	33	48	.407	28	53	.346	37	47	296	325	18.8	-3.2	45	58	249	336	-23.9	-1.6
American League 1982																		
EAST																		
MIL	48	34	.585	47	33	**.588**	89	64	431	319	-7.4	**-20.8**	**127**	88	**460**	398	**29.4**	-5.4
BAL	53	28	.654	41	40	.506	87	87	397	330	4.0	-8.7	92	60	377	357	6.9	4.5
BOS	49	32	.605	40	41	.494	67	82	**434**	370	**36.0**	7.8	69	73	319	343	-7.5	7.3
DET	47	34	.580	36	45	.444	**108**	100	378	328	7.6	-8.1	69	72	351	357	-0.2	4.6
NY	42	39	.519	37	44	.457	73	55	346	338	-4.6	-10.5	88	58	363	378	2.2	-0.8
CLE	41	40	.506	37	44	.457	49	64	342	377	0.2	1.6	60	58	341	371	-3.6	0.1
TOR	44	37	.543	34	47	.420	62	70	353	379	18.4	17.7	44	77	298	**322**	-14.6	**12.3**
WEST																		
CAL	52	29	.642	41	40	.506	99	69	414	322	3.5	-7.4	87	**55**	400	348	13.3	6.9
KC	56	25	**.691**	34	47	.420	61	64	431	**318**	22.0	-20.3	71	99	353	399	1.3	-5.6
CHI	49	31	.613	38	44	.463	51	**43**	383	332	-2.5	-9.9	85	56	403	378	13.4	-0.7
SEA	42	39	.519	34	47	.420	78	104	356	388	20.6	**19.7**	52	69	295	324	-15.4	11.6
OAK	36	45	.444	32	49	.395	71	83	328	398	**-9.6**	-5.4	78	94	363	421	1.8	-12.7
TEX	38	43	.469	26	55	.321	**43**	66	**286**	333	-5.9	-19.9	72	62	304	416	-14.4	-10.2
MIN	37	44	.457	23	58	.284	81	**110**	351	**401**	14.7	-4.0	67	98	306	418	-12.6	-12.0

TEAM	Home Games			Road Games			Home Games						Road Games					
	W	L	Pct.	W	L	Pct.	HR	OHR	R	OR	RF	ORF	HR	OHR	R	OR	RF	ORF
National League 1983																		
EAST																		
PHI	50	31	**.617**	40	41	.494	61	61	361	310	6.4	-5.7	64	50	335	325	3.1	4.5
PIT	41	40	.506	43	38	**.531**	60	63	335	336	3.3	**7.6**	61	46	324	**312**	-0.5	7.4
MON	46	35	.568	36	45	.444	40	56	341	325	2.7	2.4	62	64	336	321	2.9	5.2
STL	44	37	.543	35	46	.432	38	58	334	350	-3.1	-2.7	45	57	345	360	5.2	-5.8
CHI	43	38	.531	28	53	.346	71	69	384	341	21.1	-9.7	69	48	317	378	-1.3	-10.5
NY	41	41	.500	27	53	.338	63	53	300	329	6.4	-8.5	49	**44**	275	351	-15.2	-2.9
WEST																		
LA	48	32	.600	43	39	.524	**74**	49	316	296	-3.0	-1.8	**72**	48	338	313	2.8	**8.1**
ATL	46	34	.575	42	40	.512	66	71	**394**	327	14.7	7.0	64	61	**352**	313	**8.7**	7.4
HOU	46	36	.561	39	41	.488	26	28	294	278	-17.8	-26.3	71	66	349	368	5.3	-6.2
SD	47	34	.580	34	47	.420	53	82	350	299	14.1	-16.5	40	62	303	354	-6.0	-2.9
SF	43	38	.531	36	45	.444	73	67	346	356	1.4	4.3	69	60	341	341	4.4	-0.8
CIN	36	45	.444	38	43	.469	52	64	331	**360**	13.3	2.8	55	71	292	350	-9.6	-3.4
American League 1983																		
EAST																		
BAL	50	31	.617	48	33	**.593**	79	66	389	328	-5.1	1.2	**89**	64	410	324	14.9	12.7
DET	48	33	.593	44	37	.543	83	87	377	314	-8.5	-13.9	73	83	**412**	365	**15.2**	2.7
NY	51	30	.630	40	41	.494	67	55	398	323	6.9	-15.0	86	61	372	380	5.2	-1.1
TOR	48	33	.593	41	40	.506	101	84	**437**	385	22.0	12.9	66	61	358	341	2.3	7.4
MIL	52	29	.642	35	46	.432	64	57	356	305	-12.7	-24.3	68	76	408	403	13.7	-6.5
BOS	38	43	.469	40	41	.494	65	76	373	390	6.2	1.3	77	82	351	385	-0.7	-3.6
CLE	36	45	.444	34	47	.420	48	71	367	424	8.9	17.4	38	**49**	337	361	-4.5	1.6
WEST																		
CHI	55	26	**.679**	44	37	.543	84	64	432	306	17.3	-11.0	73	64	368	344	4.8	8.1
KC	45	36	.556	34	47	.420	50	66	381	369	19.4	-8.4	59	67	315	398	-10.0	-6.5
TEX	44	37	.543	33	48	.407	**45**	**33**	326	**294**	5.4	-5.5	61	64	313	**315**	-11.6	**15.6**
OAK	42	39	.519	32	49	.395	60	54	348	367	-3.3	-11.5	61	81	360	415	1.0	-10.7
CAL	35	46	.432	35	46	.432	86	67	368	354	3.9	-16.7	68	63	354	425	0.0	-12.9
MIN	37	44	.457	33	48	.407	56	**91**	389	**427**	21.5	8.1	85	72	320	395	-8.5	-6.9
SEA	30	51	.370	30	51	.370	64	80	**281**	369	1.4	-0.5	47	65	277	371	-21.9	0.2
National League 1984																		
EAST																		
CHI	51	29	**.638**	45	36	**.556**	**86**	70	**414**	360	20.4	22.3	50	**29**	348	298	7.3	7.7
NY	48	33	.593	42	39	.519	56	47	336	327	6.3	-6.3	51	57	316	349	-3.5	-5.6
STL	44	37	.543	40	41	.494	29	42	327	310	0.6	-7.4	46	52	325	335	-1.2	-1.3
PHI	39	42	.481	42	39	.519	79	45	353	369	-3.8	14.9	**68**	56	367	321	11.1	1.0
MON	39	42	.481	39	41	.488	45	56	**266**	**260**	-19.6	-20.9	51	58	327	325	-2.2	2.7
PIT	41	40	.506	34	47	.420	48	44	282	263	-15.3	-13.4	50	58	333	304	-0.1	8.5
WEST																		
SD	48	33	.593	44	37	.543	60	61	344	300	0.5	-10.1	49	61	342	334	3.9	-0.7
ATL	38	43	.469	42	39	.519	53	72	328	376	7.8	**34.7**	58	50	304	**279**	-7.0	12.6
HOU	43	38	.531	37	44	.457	18	29	309	292	-19.5	-13.6	61	62	**384**	338	**14.7**	-1.7
LA	40	41	.494	39	42	.481	49	40	287	321	-2.0	15.0	53	36	293	**279**	-11.1	**14.0**
CIN	39	42	.481	31	50	.383	58	**73**	356	381	31.3	4.0	48	55	271	366	-15.5	-11.7
SF	35	46	.432	31	50	.383	55	63	340	**393**	-0.5	-5.0	57	62	342	414	3.8	-25.4
American League 1984																		
EAST																		
DET	53	29	**.646**	51	29	**.638**	85	69	406	295	-6.3	-17.3	**102**	61	**423**	348	**20.1**	5.7
TOR	49	32	.605	40	41	.494	59	78	387	339	7.9	-3.8	84	62	363	357	3.8	2.5
NY	51	30	.630	36	45	.444	62	**49**	372	**292**	-3.6	-24.5	68	71	386	387	9.6	-4.1
BOS	41	40	.506	45	36	.556	100	76	**456**	413	28.8	17.6	81	65	354	351	2.9	2.6
BAL	44	37	.543	41	40	.506	82	59	319	306	-11.8	-15.2	78	78	362	361	2.2	2.2
CLE	41	39	.513	34	48	.415	65	73	411	399	18.8	10.0	58	68	350	367	0.9	-1.1
MIL	38	43	.469	29	51	.363	42	68	**286**	344	-20.4	-12.8	54	69	355	390	-0.3	-5.9
WEST																		
KC	44	37	.543	40	41	.494	48	59	344	326	4.5	-9.4	69	77	329	360	-6.0	2.0
CAL	37	44	.457	44	37	.543	79	**83**	341	364	-3.9	9.3	71	60	355	**333**	0.8	**8.2**
MIN	47	34	.580	34	47	.420	63	77	372	337	23.5	-0.3	51	82	301	338	-12.8	7.4
OAK	44	37	.543	33	48	.407	77	72	356	344	-6.8	-23.9	81	83	382	452	8.2	-21.6
CHI	43	38	.531	31	50	.383	103	77	394	389	38.2	12.1	69	78	285	347	-16.6	4.1
SEA	42	39	.519	32	49	.395	68	82	357	394	9.8	3.6	61	**56**	325	380	-6.7	-4.3
TEX	34	46	.425	35	46	.432	55	70	327	357	0.6	1.2	65	78	329	357	-6.3	2.2

PART SEVEN

Manager Register

ALPHABETICAL LIST OF EVERY MAN WHO EVER

MANAGED IN THE MAJOR LEAGUES

AND HIS COMPLETE MANAGERIAL RECORD

Manager Register

The Manager Register is an alphabetical listing of every man who has managed a major league team from 1876 through today. Included are facts about the managers and their year-by-year managerial records for both the regular season and lifetime totals for Championship Series and World Series. All managers who played in the major leagues can also be found in the Player Register.

Managers included here are defined as men who were in charge of a team while the team was on the field. This definition includes interim managers (those who served between outgoing and incoming managers), but not "acting managers," men who took over a team while the regular manager was temporarily absent because of illness, injury, or suspension. All information and abbreviations that may appear unfamiliar are explained in the sample format presented below. The man, John Doe, used in the sample is fictitious and serves only to illustrate the information:

		G	W	L	PCT	Standing		

John Doe

DOE, JOHN LEE (Slim)
Born John Lee Doughnut.
Brother of Bill Doe.
B. Jan. 1, 1850, New York, N. Y.
D. July 1, 1955, New York, N.Y.
Hall of Fame 1946.

Year	Team	Lg	G	W	L	PCT	Standing		
1908	BOS	N	100	70	.30	.700	4	1	
1909	NY	N	155	90	64	.584	3		
1910			154	96	58	.623	1		
1911			105	60	45	.571	5	6	
1912	CHI	A	154	101	53	.656	1		
1913	STL	N	154	90	64	.584	2		
1914	CHI	F	25	8	17	.320	4	6	5
1915	NY	A	54	20	34	.370	6	4	
1915	CLE	A	100	65	35	.650	5	2	
8 yrs.			1001	600	400	.600			
						3rd			

LEAGUE CHAMPIONSHIP SERIES

Year	Team	Lg	G	W	L	PCT
1974	OAK	A	4	3	1	.750
1975			3	0	3	.000
2 yrs.			7	3	4	.429

WORLD SERIES

Year	Team	Lg	G	W	L	PCT
1962	SF	N	7	3	4	.429
1974	OAK	A	5	4	1	.800
2 yrs.			12	7	5	.583

MANAGER INFORMATION

John Doe — This shortened version of the manager's full name is the name most familiar to the fans. All managers in this section are alphabetically arranged by the last name part of this name.

DOE, JOHN LEE — Manager's full name. The arrangement is last name first, then first and middle name(s).

(Slim) — Nickname. Any name or names appearing in parentheses indicates a nickname.

The name the manager was given at birth. A name shown in this form means that the man never used this name while he was a major league manager.

Born John Lee Doughnut

The manager's brother. (Relatives indicated here are fathers, sons, brothers, grandfathers, and grandsons who played or managed in the major leagues and the National Association.)

Brother of Bill Doe

Date and place of birth.

B. Jan. 1, 1850, New York, N.Y.

Date and place of death. (For those managers who are listed simply as "deceased," it means that, although no certification of death or other information is presently available, it is reasonably certain they are dead.)

D. July 1, 1955, New York, N.Y.

Doe was elected into the Hall of Fame in 1946.

Hall of Fame 1946

COLUMN HEADINGS

G	W	L	PCT	Standing

G	Games Managed (includes tie games)
W	Wins
L	Losses
PCT	Winning Percentage
STANDING	(explained under Statistical Information)

LEAGUE AND TEAM INFORMATION

Year	Team	League
1908	BOS	N
1909	NY	N
1910		
1911		
1912	CHI	A
1913	STL	N
1914	CHI	F
1915	NY	A
1915	CLE	A
8 yrs.		

Although Doe's record does not include managing in each of the six different major leagues that will appear in this section, the symbols for all the leagues are listed below:

N	National League (1876 to date)
A	American League (1901 to date)
F	Federal League (1914–15)
AA	American Association (1882–91)
P	Players' League (1890)
U	Union Association (1884)

BOS The abbreviation of the city in which the team played. Doe, for example, managed Boston in 1908. All teams in this section are listed by an abbreviation of the city in which the team played. The abbreviations follow:

ALT	Altoona	NWK	Newark
ATL	Atlanta	NY	New York
BAL	Baltimore	OAK	Oakland
BKN	Brooklyn	PHI	Philadelphia
BOS	Boston	PIT	Pittsburgh
BUF	Buffalo	PRO	Providence
CAL	California	RIC	Richmond
CHI	Chicago	ROC	Rochester
CIN	Cincinnati	SD	San Diego
CLE	Cleveland	SEA	Seattle
COL	Columbus	SF	San Francisco
DET	Detroit	STL	St. Louis
HAR	Hartford	STP	St. Paul
HOU	Houston	SYR	Syracuse
IND	Indianapolis	TEX	Texas
KC	Kansas City	TOL	Toledo
LA	Los Angeles	TOR	Toronto
LOU	Louisville	TRO	Troy
MIL	Milwaukee	WAS	Washington
MIN	Minnesota	WIL	Wilmington
MON	Montreal	WOR	Worcester

Three franchises in the history of major league baseball changed their location during the season. These teams are designated by the first letter of the two cities they represented. They are:

B-B   Brooklyn-Baltimore (American Association, 1890)

C-M   Cincinnati-Milwaukee (American Association, 1891)

C-P   Chicago-Pittsburgh (Union Association, 1884)

Blank space appearing beneath a team and league indicates that the team and league are the same. Doe, for example, managed New York in the National League from 1909 through 1911.

Separate Managerial Records. Whenever a manager served with more than one team in the same year, the information is shown on separate lines. Doe, for example, managed two teams in 1915.

Total Playing Years. This information, which appears directly beneath the last team, indicates the total number of years in which the man managed for at least one game. Doe, for example, managed in at least one game for eight years.

	G	W	L	PCT	Standing

John Doe

DOE, JOHN LEE (Slim)
Born John Lee Doughnut.
Brother of Bill Doe.
B. Jan. 1, 1850, New York, N. Y.
D. July 1, 1955, New York, N.Y.
Hall of Fame 1946.

Year	Team	Lg	G	W	L	PCT	St1	St2	St3
1908	**BOS**	N	100	70	.30	.700	4	1	
1909	**NY**	N	155	90	64	.584	3		
1910			154	96	58	.623	1		
1911			105	60	45	.571	5	6	
1912	**CHI**	A	154	101	53	.656	1		
1913	**STL**	N	154	90	64	.584	2		
1914	**CHI**	F	25	8	17	.320	4	6	5
1915	**NY**	A	54	20	34	.370	6	4	
1915	**CLE**	A	100	65	35	.650	5	2	
8 yrs.			1001	600	400	.600			
						3rd			

LEAGUE CHAMPIONSHIP SERIES RECORD

	G	W	L	PCT
3 yrs.	13	8	5	.615

WORLD SERIES RECORD

	G	W	L	PCT
2 yrs.	12	4	8	.333

Standing. The figures in this column indicate the standing of the team at the end of the season and when there was a managerial change. The four possible cases are as follows:

Only Manager for the Team That Year. Indicated by a single bold faced figure that appears in the extreme left-hand column and shows the final standing of the team. See Doe in 1909, 1910, 1912, and 1913.

Manager Started Season, but Did Not Finish. Indicated by two figures: the first is bold faced and shows the standing of the team when this manager left; the second shows the final standing of the team. See Doe in 1911 and 1915, New York.

Manager Finished Season, but Did Not Start. Indicated by two figures: the first shows the standing of the team when this manager started; the second is bold faced and shows the final standing of the team. See Doe in 1908 and 1915, Cleveland.

Manager Did Not Start or Finish Season. Indicated by three figures: the first shows the standing of the team when this manager started; the second is bold faced and shows the standing of the team when this manager left; the third shows the final standing of the team. See Doe in 1914.

Split Season Indicator. The 1981 season was divided into two halves as a result of the players' strike. Each half-season is listed separately in the Manager Register. A figure in parentheses to the right of the Standing column indicates whether the record is for the first or second half-season.

Lifetime Leaders. The top ten men are shown for Games, Wins, Losses, and Winning Percentage. Doe has a "3rd" shown below his lifetime winning percentage total. This means that, lifetime, Doe ranks third among major league managers for the highest winning percentage based on a minimum of 1000 games. Managers who tied for a position receive the same ranking.

	G	W	L	PCT	Standing			G	W	L	PCT	Standing

Bill Adair
ADAIR, MARION DANNE
B. Feb. 10, 1916, Mobile, Ala.

		G	W	L	PCT			
1970	CHI A	10	4	6	.400	6	**6**	6

Joe Adcock
ADCOCK, JOSEPH WILBUR
B. Oct. 30, 1927, Coushatta, La.

1967	CLE A	162	75	87	.463	8

Bob Addy
ADDY, ROBERT EDWARD (The Magnet)
B. 1838, Rochester, N. Y.
D. Apr. 10, 1910, Pocatello, Ida.

1877	CIN N	44	12	31	.279	6	**6**

Bob Allen
ALLEN, ROBERT GILMAN
B. July 10, 1867, Marion, Ohio
D. May 14, 1943, Little Rock, Ark.

1900	CIN N	144	62	77	.446	7

Walter Alston
ALSTON, WALTER EMMONS (Smokey)
B. Dec. 1, 1911, Venice, Ohio
D. Oct. 1, 1984, Oxford, Ohio
Hall of Fame 1983.

		G	W	L	PCT	Standing	
1954	BKN N	154	92	62	.597	2	
1955		154	98	55	.641	1	
1956		154	93	61	.604	1	
1957		154	84	70	.545	3	
1958	LA N	154	71	83	.461	7	
1959		156	88	68	.564	1	
1960		154	82	72	.532	4	
1961		154	89	65	.578	2	
1962		165	102	63	.618	2	
1963		163	99	63	.611	1	
1964		164	80	82	.494	6	
1965		162	97	65	.599	1	
1966		162	95	67	.586	1	
1967		162	73	89	.451	8	
1968		162	76	86	.469	7	
1969		162	85	77	.525	4	
1970		161	87	74	.540	2	
1971		162	89	73	.549	2	
1972		155	85	70	.548	3	
1973		161	95	66	.590	2	
1974		162	102	60	.630	1	
1975		162	88	74	.543	2	
1976		158	90	68	.570	2	2
23 yrs.		3657	2040	1613	.558		
			6th	**5th**	**8th**		

LEAGUE CHAMPIONSHIP SERIES

1974	LA N	4	3	1	.750

WORLD SERIES

		G	W	L	PCT	
1955	BKN N	7	4	3	.571	
1956		7	3	4	.429	
1959	LA N	6	4	2	.667	
1963		4	4	0	1.000	
1965		7	4	3	.571	
1966		4	0	4	.000	
1974		5	1	4	.200	
7 yrs.		40	20	20	.500	
		5th	**5th**	**3rd**	**8th**	

Joe Altobelli
ALTOBELLI, JOSEPH SALVATORE
B. May 26, 1932, Detroit, Mich.

		G	W	L	PCT	Standing	
1977	SF N	162	75	87	.463	4	
1978		162	89	73	.549	3	
1979		140	61	79	.436	4	4
1983	BAL A	162	98	64	.605	1	
1984		162	85	77	.525	5	
5 yrs.		788	408	380	.518		

Joe Altobelli   continued

LEAGUE CHAMPIONSHIP SERIES

1983	BAL A	4	3	1	.750

WORLD SERIES

1983	BAL A	5	4	1	.800

Joey Amalfitano
AMALFITANO, JOHN JOSEPH
B. Jan. 23, 1934, San Pedro, Calif.

		G	W	L	PCT	Standing		
1979	CHI N	7	2	5	.286	5	5	
1980		72	26	46	.361	6	6	
1981		54	15	37	.288	6		(1st)
1981		52	23	28	.451	5		(2nd)
3 yrs.		185	66	116	.363			

Sparky Anderson
ANDERSON, GEORGE LEE
B. Feb. 22, 1934, Bridgewater, S. D.

		G	W	L	PCT	Standing		
1970	CIN N	162	102	60	.630	1		
1971		162	79	83	.488	4		
1972		154	95	59	.617	1		
1973		162	99	63	.611	1		
1974		162	98	64	.605	2		
1975		162	108	54	.667	1		
1976		162	102	60	.630	1		
1977		162	88	74	.543	2		
1978		161	92	69	.571	2		
1979	DET A	105	56	49	.533	5	5	
1980		163	84	78	.519	4		
1981		57	31	26	.544	4		(1st)
1981		52	29	23	.558	2		(2nd)
1982		162	83	79	.512	4		
1983		162	92	70	.568	2		
1984		162	104	58	.642	1		
15 yrs.		2312	1342	969	.581			
					10th			

LEAGUE CHAMPIONSHIP SERIES

		G	W	L	PCT			
1970	CIN N	3	3	0	1.000			
1972		5	3	2	.600			
1973		5	2	3	.400			
1975		3	3	0	1.000			
1976		3	3	0	1.000			
1984	DET A	3	3	0	1.000			
6 yrs.		22	17	5	.773			
		1st	**1st**	**9th**	**1st**			

WORLD SERIES

		G	W	L	PCT			
1970	CIN N	5	1	4	.200			
1972		7	3	4	.429			
1975		7	4	3	.571			
1976		4	4	0	1.000			
1984	DET A	5	4	1	.800			
5 yrs.		28	16	12	.571			
		7th	**7th**	**10th**	**3rd**			

Cap Anson
ANSON, ADRIAN CONSTANTINE (Pop)
B. Apr. 17, 1852, Marshalltown, Iowa
D. Apr. 14, 1922, Chicago, Ill.
Hall of Fame 1939.

		G	W	L	PCT	Standing
1879	CHI N	83	46	33	.582	4
1880		86	67	17	.798	1
1881		84	56	28	.667	1
1882		84	55	29	.655	1
1883		98	59	39	.602	2
1884		113	62	50	.554	4
1885		113	87	25	.777	1
1886		126	90	34	.726	1
1887		127	71	50	.587	3
1888		135	77	58	.570	2
1889		136	67	65	.508	3
1890		139	84	53	.613	2
1891		137	82	53	.607	2
1892		147	70	76	.479	7
1893		128	56	71	.441	9
1894		135	57	75	.432	8

	G	W	L	PCT	Standing				G	W	L	PCT	Standing

Cap Anson continued

		G	W	L	PCT	Standing	
1895		133	72	58	.554	4	
1896		132	71	57	.555	5	
1897		138	59	73	.447	9	
1898	**NY N**	22	9	13	.409	6	7 7
20 yrs.		2296	1297	957	.575		

Luke Appling

APPLING, LUCIUS BENJAMIN (Old Aches and Pains)
B. Apr. 2, 1907, High Point, N. C.
Hall of Fame 1964.

		G	W	L	PCT	Standing	
1967	**KC A**	40	10	30	.250	10	10

Bill Armour

ARMOUR, WILLIAM R.
B. Sept. 3, 1869, Homestead, Pa.
D. Dec. 2, 1922, Minneapolis, Minn.

		G	W	L	PCT	Standing
1902	**CLE A**	137	69	67	.507	5
1903		140	77	63	.550	3
1904		154	86	65	.570	4
1905	**DET A**	153	79	74	.516	3
1906		151	71	78	.477	6
5 yrs.		735	382	347	.524	

Ken Aspromonte

ASPROMONTE, KENNETH JOSEPH
Brother of Bob Aspromonte.
B. Sept. 22, 1931, Brooklyn, N. Y.

		G	W	L	PCT	Standing
1972	**CLE A**	156	72	84	.462	5
1973		162	71	91	.438	6
1974		162	77	85	.475	4
3 yrs.		480	220	260	.458	

Jimmy Austin

AUSTIN, JAMES PHILIP (Pepper)
B. Dec. 8, 1879, Swansea, Wales
D. Apr. 6, 1965, Laguna Beach, Calif.

		G	W	L	PCT	Standing	
1913	**STL A**	8	2	6	.250	7	8 8
1918		14	6	8	.429	1	6 5
1923		53	23	29	.442	3	5
3 yrs.		75	31	43	.419		

Del Baker

BAKER, DELMAR DAVID
B. May 3, 1892, Sherwood, Ore.
D. Sept. 11, 1973, San Antonio, Tex.

		G	W	L	PCT	Standing	
1933	**DET A**	2	2	0	1.000	5	5
1938		58	37	20	.649	4	4
1939		155	81	73	.526	5	
1940		155	90	64	.584	1	
1941		155	75	79	.487	4	
1942		156	73	81	.474	5	
6 yrs.		681	358	317	.530		

WORLD SERIES

		G	W	L	PCT
1940	**DET A**	7	3	4	.429

George Bamberger

BAMBERGER, GEORGE IRVIN
B. Aug. 1, 1925, Staten Island, N. Y.

		G	W	L	PCT	Standing	
1978	**MIL A**	162	93	69	.574	3	
1979		161	95	66	.590	2	
1980		92	47	45	.511	2	4 3
1982	**NY N**	162	65	97	.401	6	
1983		46	16	30	.348	6	6
5 yrs.		623	316	307	.507		

Dave Bancroft

BANCROFT, DAVID JAMES (Beauty)
B. Apr. 20, 1891, Sioux City, Iowa
D. Oct. 9, 1972, Superior, Wis.
Hall of Fame 1971.

		G	W	L	PCT	Standing
1924	**BOS N**	154	53	100	.346	8
1925		153	70	83	.458	5
1926		153	66	86	.434	7
1927		155	60	94	.390	7
4 yrs.		615	249	363	.407	

Frank Bancroft

BANCROFT, FRANK CARTER
B. May 9, 1846, Lancaster, Mass.
D. Mar. 31, 1921, Cincinnati, Ohio

		G	W	L	PCT	Standing	
1880	**WOR N**	85	40	43	.482	5	
1881	**DET N**	84	41	43	.488	4	
1882		86	42	41	.506	6	
1883	**CLE N**	100	55	42	.567	4	
1884	**PRO N**	114	84	28	.750	1	
1885		110	53	57	.482	4	
1887	**PHI AA**	47	22	25	.468	5	5
1889	**IND N**	67	25	42	.373	7	7
1902	**CIN N**	17	10	7	.588	7	5 4
9 yrs.		710	372	328	.531		

Sam Barkley

BARKLEY, SAMUEL E
B. May 24, 1858, Wheeling, W. Va.
D. Apr. 20, 1912, Wheeling, W. Va.

		G	W	L	PCT	Standing	
1888	**KC AA**	69	26	43	.377	8	8 8

Billy Barnie

BARNIE, WILLIAM HARRISON (Bald Billy)
B. Jan. 26, 1853, New York, N. Y.
D. July 15, 1900, Hartford, Conn.

		G	W	L	PCT	Standing	
1883	**BAL AA**	96	28	68	.292	8	
1884		108	63	43	.594	6	
1885		110	41	68	.376	8	
1886		139	48	83	.366	8	
1887		141	77	58	.570	3	
1888		137	57	80	.416	5	
1889		139	70	65	.519	5	
1890	**B-B AA**	34	15	19	.441	8	8
1891	**BAL AA**	133	68	61	.527	3	3
1891	**PHI AA**	8	4	3	.571	4	4
1892	**WAS N**	34	13	21	.382	9	10
1893	**LOU N**	126	50	75	.400	11	
1894		130	36	94	.277	12	
1897	**BKN N**	136	61	71	.462	6	
1898		35	15	20	.429	9	10
14 yrs.		1506	646	829	.438		

Ed Barrow

BARROW, EDWARD GRANT (Cousin Ed)
B. May 10, 1868, Springfield, Ill.
D. Dec. 15, 1953, Port Chester, N. Y.
Hall of Fame 1953.

		G	W	L	PCT	Standing	
1903	**DET A**	137	65	71	.478	5	
1904		84	32	46	.410	7	7
1918	**BOS A**	126	75	51	.595	1	
1919		138	66	71	.482	6	
1920		154	72	81	.471	5	
5 yrs.		639	310	320	.492		

WORLD SERIES

		G	W	L	PCT
1918	**BOS A**	6	4	2	.667

Jack Barry

BARRY, JOHN JOSEPH
B. Apr. 26, 1887, Meriden, Conn.
D. Apr. 23, 1961, Shrewsbury, Mass.

		G	W	L	PCT	Standing
1917	**BOS A**	157	90	62	.592	2

	G	W	L	PCT	Standing					G	W	L	PCT	Standing		

Joe Battin

BATTIN, JOSEPH V.
B. Nov. 11, 1851, Philadelphia, Pa.
D. Oct. 11, 1937, Akron, Ohio

		G	W	L	PCT	Standing		
1883	**PIT AA**	13	2	11	.154	7	**7**	
1884		4	1	3	.250	11	11	
1884	**C-P U**	6	1	5	.167	6	**7**	6
2 yrs.		23	4	19	.174			

Hank Bauer

BAUER, HENRY ALBERT
B. July 31, 1922, East St. Louis, Ill.

		G	W	L	PCT	Standing	
1961	**KC A**	92	35	57	.380	8	**9**
1962		162	72	90	.444	9	
1964	**BAL A**	163	97	65	.599	3	
1965		162	94	68	.580	3	
1966		160	97	63	.606	1	
1967		161	76	85	.472	6	
1968		80	43	37	.538	3	2
1969	**OAK A**	149	80	69	.537	2	2
8 yrs.		1129	594	534	.527		

WORLD SERIES
1966	**BAL A**	4	4	0	1.000		

Yogi Berra

BERRA, LAWRENCE PETER
Father of Dale Berra.
B. May 12, 1925, St. Louis, Mo.
Hall of Fame 1971.

		G	W	L	PCT	Standing	
1964	**NY A**	164	99	63	.611	1	
1972	**NY N**	156	83	73	.532	3	
1973		161	82	79	.509	1	
1974		162	71	91	.438	5	
1975		109	56	53	.514	3	3
1984	**NY A**	162	87	75	.537	3	
6 yrs.		914	478	434	.524		

LEAGUE CHAMPIONSHIP SERIES
1973	**NY N**	5	3	2	.600		

WORLD SERIES
1964	**NY N**	7	3	4	.429		
1973	**NY N**	7	3	4	.429		
2 yrs.		14	6	8	.429		

Hugo Bezdek

BEZDEK, HUGO FRANCIS
B. Apr. 1, 1883, Prague, Czechoslovakia
D. Sept. 19, 1952, Atlantic City, N. J.

		G	W	L	PCT	Standing	
1917	**PIT N**	91	30	59	.337	8	**8**
1918		126	65	60	.520	4	
1919		139	71	68	.511	4	
3 yrs.		356	166	187	.470		

Joe Birmingham

BIRMINGHAM, JOSEPH LEE (Dode)
B. Aug. 6, 1884, Elmira, N. Y.
D. Apr. 24, 1946, Tampico, Mexico

		G	W	L	PCT	Standing	
1912	**CLE A**	28	21	7	.750	6	5
1913		155	86	66	.566	3	
1914		157	51	102	.333	8	
1915		28	12	16	.429	6	7
4 yrs.		368	170	191	.471		

Del Bissonette

BISSONETTE, ADELPHIA LOUIS
B. Sept. 6, 1899, Winthrop, Me.
D. June 9, 1972, Augusta, Me.

		G	W	L	PCT	Standing	
1945	**BOS N**	61	25	36	.410	7	**6**

Lena Blackburne

BLACKBURNE, RUSSELL AUBREY (Slats)
B. Oct. 23, 1886, Clifton Heights, Pa.
D. Feb. 29, 1968, Riverside, N. J.

		G	W	L	PCT	Standing	
1928	**CHI A**	80	40	40	.500	6	5
1929		152	59	93	.388	7	
2 yrs.		232	99	133	.427		

Ray Blades

BLADES, FRANCIS RAYMOND
B. Aug. 6, 1896, Mt. Vernon, Ill.
D. May 18, 1979, Lincoln, Ill.

		G	W	L	PCT	Standing	
1939	**STL N**	155	92	61	.601	2	
1940		40	15	24	.385	7	3
2 yrs.		195	107	85	.557		

Walter Blair

BLAIR, WALTER ALLAN (Heavy)
B. Oct. 13, 1883, Arnot, Pa.
D. Aug. 20, 1948, Lewisburg, Pa.

		G	W	L	PCT	Standing		
1915	**BUF F**	2	1	1	.500	8	**8**	6

Ossie Bluege

BLUEGE, OSWALD LOUIS
Brother of Otto Bluege.
B. Oct. 24, 1900, Chicago, Ill.

		G	W	L	PCT	Standing	
1943	**WAS A**	153	84	69	.549	2	
1944		154	64	90	.416	8	
1945		156	87	67	.565	2	
1946		155	76	78	.494	4	
1947		154	64	90	.416	7	
5 yrs.		772	375	394	.488		

Tommy Bond

BOND, THOMAS HENRY
B. Apr. 2, 1856, Granard, Ireland
D. Jan. 24, 1941, Boston, Mass.

		G	W	L	PCT	Standing		
1882	**WOR N**	27	5	22	.185	8	**8**	8

Steve Boros

BOROS, STEPHEN
B. Sept. 3, 1936, Flint, Mich.

		G	W	L	PCT	Standing	
1983	**OAK A**	162	74	88	.457	4	
1984		44	20	24	.455	4	4
2 yrs.		206	94	112	.456		

Jim Bottomley

BOTTOMLEY, JAMES LeROY (Sunny Jim)
B. Apr. 23, 1900, Oglesby, Ill.
D. Dec. 11, 1959, St. Louis, Mo.
Hall of Fame 1974.

		G	W	L	PCT	Standing	
1937	**STL A**	80	21	58	.266	8	**8**

Lou Boudreau

BOUDREAU, LOUIS
B. July 17, 1917, Harvey, Ill.
Hall of Fame 1970.

		G	W	L	PCT	Standing	
1942	**CLE A**	156	75	79	.487	4	
1943		153	82	71	.536	3	
1944		155	72	82	.468	5	
1945		147	73	72	.503	5	
1946		156	68	86	.442	6	
1947		157	80	74	.519	4	
1948		156	97	58	.626	1	
1949		154	89	65	.578	3	
1950		155	92	62	.597	4	
1952	**BOS A**	154	76	78	.494	6	
1953		153	84	69	.549	4	
1954		156	69	85	.448	4	

	G	W	L	PCT	Standing			G	W	L	PCT	Standing

Lou Boudreau continued

		G	W	L	PCT		
1955	KC A	155	63	91	.409	6	
1956		154	52	102	.338	8	
1957		104	36	67	.350	8	7
1960	CHI N	139	54	83	.394	8	7
16 yrs.		2404	1162	1224	.487		

WORLD SERIES
| 1948 | CLE A | 6 | 4 | 2 | .667 | | |

Frank Bowerman

BOWERMAN, FRANK EUGENE (Mike)
B. Dec. 5, 1868, Romeo, Mich.
D. Nov. 30, 1948, Romeo, Mich.

		G	W	L	PCT		
1909	BOS N	79	23	55	.295	8	8

Ken Boyer

BOYER, KENTON LLOYD
Brother of Cloyd Boyer.
Brother of Clete Boyer.
B. May 20, 1931, Liberty, Mo.
D. Sept. 7, 1982, St. Louis, Mo.

		G	W	L	PCT		
1978	STL N	144	62	82	.431	5	5
1979		162	86	76	.531	3	
1980		51	18	33	.353	6	4
3 yrs.		357	166	191	.465		

Bill Bradley

BRADLEY, WILLIAM JOSEPH
B. Feb. 13, 1878, Cleveland, Ohio
D. Mar. 11, 1954, Cleveland, Ohio

		G	W	L	PCT		
1914	BKN F	157	77	77	.500	5	

Bobby Bragan

BRAGAN, ROBERT RANDALL
B. Oct. 30, 1917, Birmingham, Ala.

		G	W	L	PCT		
1956	PIT N	157	66	88	.429	7	
1957		104	36	67	.350	8	7
1958	CLE A	67	31	36	.463	5	4
1963	MIL N	163	84	78	.519	6	
1964		162	88	74	.543	5	
1965		162	86	76	.531	5	
1966	ATL N	112	52	59	.468	5	5
7 yrs.		927	443	478	.481		

Roger Bresnahan

BRESNAHAN, ROGER PHILIP (The Duke of Tralee)
B. June 11, 1879, Toledo, Ohio
D. Dec. 4, 1944, Toledo, Ohio
Hall of Fame 1945.

		G	W	L	PCT		
1909	STL N	154	54	98	.355	7	
1910		153	63	90	.412	7	
1911		158	75	74	.503	5	
1912		153	63	90	.412	6	
1915	CHI N	156	73	80	.477	4	
5 yrs.		774	328	432	.432		

Dave Bristol

BRISTOL, JAMES DAVID
B. June 23, 1933, Macon, Ga.

		G	W	L	PCT		
1966	CIN N	77	39	38	.506	8	7
1967		162	87	75	.537	4	
1968		163	83	79	.512	4	
1969		163	89	73	.549	3	
1970	MIL A	162	65	97	.401	5	
1971		161	69	92	.429	6	
1972		30	10	20	.333	6	6
1976	ATL N	162	70	92	.432	6	
1977		29	8	21	.276	6	6
1977		132	53	79	.402	6	6
1979	SF N	22	10	12	.455	4	4
1980		161	75	86	.466	5	
11 yrs.		1424	658	764	.463		

Ed Brown

BROWN, EDWARD P.
B. Chicago, Ill.
Deceased.

		G	W	L	PCT		
1882	STL AA	21	10	11	.476	5	5

Freeman Brown

BROWN, FREEMAN
B. Jan. 31, 1845, Hubbardstown, Mass.
D. Dec. 27, 1916, Worcester, Mass.

		G	W	L	PCT		
1881	WOR N	83	32	50	.390	8	
1882		23	4	19	.174	8	8
2 yrs.		106	36	69	.343		

Three Finger Brown

BROWN, MORDECAI PETER CENTENNIAL (Miner)
B. Oct. 19, 1876, Nyesville, Ind.
D. Feb. 14, 1948, Terre Haute, Ind.
Hall of Fame 1949.

		G	W	L	PCT		
1914	STL F	114	50	63	.442	7	8

Tom Brown

BROWN, THOMAS T.
B. Sept. 21, 1860, Liverpool, England
D. Oct. 27, 1927, Washington, D. C.

		G	W	L	PCT		
1897	WAS N	99	52	46	.531	11	6
1898		16	3	13	.188	12	11
2 yrs.		115	55	59	.482		

Earle Brucker

BRUCKER, EARLE FRANCIS
Father of Earle Brucker.
B. May 6, 1901, Albany, N. Y.
D. May 8, 1981, San Diego, Calif.

		G	W	L	PCT		
1952	CIN N	5	3	2	.600	7	7	6

Al Buckenberger

BUCKENBERGER, ALBERT C.
B. Jan. 31, 1861, Detroit, Mich.
D. July 1, 1917, Syracuse, N. Y.

		G	W	L	PCT		
1889	COL AA	140	60	78	.435	6	
1890		84	42	42	.500	5	2
1892	PIT N	99	55	43	.561	9	6
1893		131	81	48	.628	2	
1894		109	53	55	.491	7	7
1895	STL N	49	16	32	.333	11	11
1902	BOS N	142	73	64	.533	3	
1903		140	58	80	.420	6	
1904		155	55	98	.359	7	
9 yrs.		1049	493	540	.477		

Charlie Buffinton

BUFFINTON, CHARLES G.
B. June 14, 1861, Fall River, Mass.
D. Sept. 23, 1907, Fall River, Mass.

		G	W	L	PCT		
1890	PHI P	47	21	25	.457	4	5

Jim Bullock

BULLOCK, JAMES LEONARD
B. Jan. 13, 1845, Bristol, R. I.
D. Aug. 12, 1914

		G	W	L	PCT		
1880	PRO N	87	52	32	.619	2	
1881		34	17	17	.500	3	2
2 yrs.		121	69	49	.585		

	G	W	L	PCT	Standing		

Jack Burdock

BURDOCK, JOHN JOSEPH (Black Jack)
B. 1851, Brooklyn, N. Y.
D. Nov. 28, 1931, Brooklyn, N. Y.

		G	W	L	PCT	Standing	
1883	BOS N	57	31	26	.544	2	1

Jimmy Burke

BURKE, JAMES TIMOTHY (Sunset Jimmy)
B. Oct. 12, 1874, St. Louis, Mo.
D. Mar. 26, 1942, St. Louis, Mo.

		G	W	L	PCT	Standing		
1905	STL N	49	17	32	.347	6	6	6
1918	STL A	62	29	32	.475	6	5	
1919		140	67	72	.482	5		
1920		154	76	77	.497	4		
4 yrs.		405	189	213	.470			

Watch Burnham

BURNHAM, GEORGE WALTER
B. May 20, 1860, Albion, Mich.
D. Nov. 18, 1902, Detroit, Mich.

		G	W	L	PCT	Standing	
1887	IND N	28	6	22	.214	8	8

Tom Burns

BURNS, THOMAS EVERETT
B. Mar. 30, 1857, Honesdale, Pa.
D. Mar. 19, 1902, Jersey City, N. J.

		G	W	L	PCT	Standing	
1892	PIT N	56	25	30	.455	9	6
1898	CHI N	152	85	65	.567	4	
1899		152	75	73	.507	8	
3 yrs.		360	185	168	.524		

Bill Burwell

BURWELL, WILLIAM EDWIN
B. Mar. 27, 1895, Jarbalo, Kans.
D. June 11, 1973, Ormond Beach, Fla.

		G	W	L	PCT	Standing	
1947	PIT N	1	1	0	1.000	8	7

Donie Bush

BUSH, OWEN JOSEPH
B. Oct. 8, 1887, Indianapolis, Ind.
D. Mar. 28, 1972, Indianapolis, Ind.

		G	W	L	PCT	Standing	
1923	WAS A	155	75	78	.490	4	
1927	PIT N	156	94	60	.610	1	
1928		152	85	67	.559	4	
1929		119	67	51	.568	2	2
1930	CHI A	154	62	92	.403	7	
1931		156	56	97	.366	8	
1933	CIN N	153	58	94	.382	8	
7 yrs.		1045	497	539	.480		

WORLD SERIES							
1927	PIT N	4	0	4	.000		

Ormond Butler

BUTLER, ORMOND HOOK
B. Nov. 18, 1854, West Virginia
D. Sept. 12, 1915, Baltimore, Md.

		G	W	L	PCT	Standing		
1883	PIT AA	53	17	36	.321	6	7	7

Charlie Byrne

BYRNE, CHARLES H.
B. Sept., 1843, New York, N. Y.
D. Jan. 4, 1898, New York, N. Y.

		G	W	L	PCT	Standing	
1885	BKN AA	39	25	14	.641	7	5
1886		141	76	61	.555	3	
1887		138	60	74	.448	6	
3 yrs.		318	161	149	.519		

Nixey Callahan

CALLAHAN, JAMES JOSEPH
B. Mar. 18, 1874, Fitchburg, Mass.
D. Oct. 4, 1934, Boston, Mass.

		G	W	L	PCT	Standing	
1903	CHI A	138	60	77	.438	7	
1904		41	22	18	.550	4	3
1912		158	78	76	.506	4	
1913		153	78	74	.513	5	
1914		157	70	84	.455	6	
1916	PIT N	157	65	89	.422	6	
1917		61	20	40	.333	8	8
7 yrs.		865	393	458	.462		

Bill Cammeyer

CAMMEYER, WILLIAM HENRY
B. Mar. 20, 1821, New York, N. Y.
D. Sept. 4, 1898, New York, N. Y.

		G	W	L	PCT	Standing	
1876	NY N	57	21	35	.375	6	

Count Campau

CAMPAU, CHARLES COLUMBUS
B. Oct. 17, 1863, Detroit, Mich.
D. Apr. 3, 1938, New Orleans, La.

		G	W	L	PCT	Standing	
1890	STL AA	62	33	26	.559	2	3

Joe Cantillon

CANTILLON, JOSEPH D. (Pongo)
B. Aug. 19, 1861, Janesville, Wis.
D. Jan. 31, 1930, Hickman, Ky.

		G	W	L	PCT	Standing	
1907	WAS A	154	49	102	.325	8	
1908		155	67	85	.441	7	
1909		156	42	110	.276	8	
3 yrs.		465	158	297	.347		

Max Carey

CAREY, MAX GEORGE (Scoops)
Also known as Maximilian Carnarius.
B. Jan. 11, 1890, Terre Haute, Ind.
D. May 30, 1976, Miami, Fla.
Hall of Fame 1961.

		G	W	L	PCT	Standing	
1932	BKN N	154	81	73	.526	3	
1933		157	65	88	.425	6	
2 yrs.		311	146	161	.476		

Bill Carrigan

CARRIGAN, WILLIAM FRANCIS (Rough)
B. Oct. 22, 1883, Lewiston, Me.
D. July 8, 1969, Lewiston, Me.

		G	W	L	PCT	Standing	
1913	BOS A	70	40	30	.571	5	4
1914		160	91	62	.595	2	
1915		155	101	50	.669	1	
1916		156	91	63	.591	1	
1927		154	51	103	.331	8	
1928		154	57	96	.373	8	
1929		155	58	96	.377	8	
7 yrs.		1004	489	500	.494		

WORLD SERIES							
1915	BOS A	5	4	1	.800		
1916		5	4	1	.800		
2 yrs.		10	8	2	.800		

Phil Cavarretta

CAVARRETTA, PHILIP JOSEPH
B. July 19, 1916, Chicago, Ill.

		G	W	L	PCT	Standing	
1951	CHI N	74	27	47	.365	7	8
1952		155	77	77	.500	5	
1953		155	65	89	.422	7	
3 yrs.		384	169	213	.442		

	G	W	L	PCT	Standing			G	W	L	PCT	Standing

O. P. Caylor

CAYLOR, OLIVER PERRY
B. Dec. 14, 1849, Dayton, Ohio
D. Oct. 19, 1897, Winona, Minn.

		G	W	L	PCT	Standing
1885	CIN AA	112	63	49	.563	2
1886		141	65	73	.471	5
1887	NY AA	42	10	29	.256	7	7
3 yrs.		295	138	151	.478	

Frank Chance

CHANCE, FRANK LEROY (Husk, The Peerless Leader)
B. Sept. 9, 1877, Fresno, Calif.
D. Sept. 14, 1924, Los Angeles, Calif.
Hall of Fame 1946.

		G	W	L	PCT	Standing
1905	CHI N	65	40	23	.635	4	3
1906		154	116	36	.763	1
1907		155	107	45	.704	1
1908		158	99	55	.643	1
1909		155	104	49	.680	2
1910		154	104	50	.675	1
1911		157	92	62	.597	2
1912		152	91	59	.607	3
1913	NY A	153	57	94	.377	7
1914		140	61	76	.445	7	6
1923	BOS A	154	61	91	.401	8
11 yrs.		1597	932	640	.593	
						7th

WORLD SERIES

		G	W	L	PCT
1906	CHI N	6	2	4	.333
1907		5	4	0	1.000
1908		5	4	1	.800
1910		5	1	4	.200
4 yrs.		21	11	9	.550
			9th		5th

Ben Chapman

CHAPMAN, WILLIAM BENJAMIN
B. Dec. 25, 1908, Nashville, Tenn.

		G	W	L	PCT	Standing
1945	PHI N	87	29	58	.333	8	8
1946		155	69	85	.448	5
1947		155	62	92	.403	7
1948		79	37	42	.468	7	6
4 yrs.		476	197	277	.416	

Jack Chapman

CHAPMAN, JOHN CURTIS
B. May 8, 1843, Brooklyn, N. Y.
D. June 10, 1916, Brooklyn, N. Y.

		G	W	L	PCT	Standing
1877	LOU N	61	35	25	.583	2
1878	MIL N	61	15	45	.250	6
1882	WOR N	34	9	25	.265	8	8
1883	DET N	101	40	58	.408	7
1884		114	28	84	.250	8
1885	BUF N	31	12	19	.387	6	7
1889	LOU AA	10	1	9	.100	8	8
1890		136	88	44	.667	1
1891		141	55	84	.396	7
1892	LOU N	58	23	35	.397	11	9
10 yrs.		747	306	428	.417	

Hal Chase

CHASE, HAROLD HOMER (Prince Hal)
B. Feb. 13, 1883, Los Gatos, Calif.
D. May 18, 1947, Colusa, Calif.

		G	W	L	PCT	Standing
1910	NY A	11	9	2	.818	2	2
1911		153	76	76	.500	6
2 yrs.		164	85	78	.521	

John Clapp

CLAPP, JOHN EDGAR
Brother of Aaron Clapp.
B. July 17, 1851, Ithaca, N. Y.
D. Dec. 17, 1904, Ithaca, N. Y.

		G	W	L	PCT	Standing
1878	IND N	63	24	36	.400	5

John Clapp continued

		G	W	L	PCT	Standing
1879	BUF N	79	46	32	.590	3
1880	CIN N	83	21	59	.263	8
1883	NY N	98	46	50	.479	6
4 yrs.		323	137	177	.436	

Fred Clarke

CLARKE, FRED CLIFFORD (Cap)
Brother of Josh Clarke.
B. Oct. 3, 1872, Winterset, Iowa
D. Aug. 14, 1960, Winfield, Kans.
Hall of Fame 1945.

		G	W	L	PCT	Standing
1897	LOU N	89	35	52	.402	9	11
1898		154	70	81	.464	9
1899		155	75	77	.493	9
1900	PIT N	140	79	60	.568	2
1901		140	90	49	.647	1
1902		142	103	36	.741	1
1903		141	91	49	.650	1
1904		156	87	66	.569	4
1905		155	96	57	.627	2
1906		154	93	60	.608	3
1907		157	91	63	.591	2
1908		155	98	56	.636	2
1909		154	110	42	.724	1
1910		154	86	67	.562	3
1911		155	85	69	.552	3
1912		152	93	58	.616	2
1913		155	78	71	.523	4
1914		158	69	85	.448	7
1915		156	73	81	.474	5
19 yrs.		2822	1602	1179	.576	

WORLD SERIES

		G	W	L	PCT
1903	PIT N	8	3	5	.375
1909		7	4	3	.571
2 yrs.		15	7	8	.467

Ty Cobb

COBB, TYRUS RAYMOND (The Georgia Peach)
B. Dec. 18, 1886, Narrows, Ga.
D. July 17, 1961, Atlanta, Ga.
Hall of Fame 1936.

		G	W	L	PCT	Standing
1921	DET A	154	71	82	.464	6
1922		155	79	75	.513	3
1923		155	83	71	.539	2
1924		156	86	68	.558	3
1925		156	81	73	.526	4
1926		157	79	75	.513	6
6 yrs.		933	479	444	.519	

Mickey Cochrane

COCHRANE, GORDON STANLEY (Black Mike)
B. Apr. 6, 1903, Bridgewater, Mass.
D. June 28, 1962, Lake Forest, Ill.
Hall of Fame 1947.

		G	W	L	PCT	Standing
1934	DET A	154	101	53	.656	1
1935		152	93	58	.616	1
1936		154	83	71	.539	2
1937		155	89	65	.578	2
1938		97	47	50	.485	4	4
5 yrs.		712	413	297	.582	

WORLD SERIES

		G	W	L	PCT
1934	DET A	7	3	4	.429
1935		6	4	2	.667
2 yrs.		13	7	6	.538

Andy Cohen

COHEN, ANDREW HOWARD
Brother of Sid Cohen.
B. Oct. 25, 1904, Baltimore, Md.

		G	W	L	PCT	Standing
1960	PHI N	1	1	0	1.000	8	4	8

	G	W	L	PCT	Standing			G	W	L	PCT	Standing

Bob Coleman
COLEMAN, ROBERT HUNTER
B. Sept. 26, 1890, Huntingburg, Ind.
D. July 16, 1959, Boston, Mass.

		G	W	L	PCT	Standing
1944	BOS N	155	65	89	.422	6
1945		93	42	49	.462	7 6
2 yrs.		248	107	138	.437	

Jerry Coleman
COLEMAN, GERALD FRANCIS
B. Sept. 14, 1924, San Jose, Calif.

		G	W	L	PCT	Standing
1980	SD N	163	73	89	.451	6

Eddie Collins
COLLINS, EDWARD TROWBRIDGE, SR. (Cocky)
Played as Eddie Sullivan 1906.
Father of Eddie Collins.
B. May 2, 1887, Millerton, N. Y.
D. Mar. 25, 1951, Boston, Mass.
Hall of Fame 1939.

		G	W	L	PCT	Standing
1925	CHI A	154	79	75	.513	5
1926		155	81	72	.529	5
2 yrs.		309	160	147	.521	

Jimmy Collins
COLLINS, JAMES JOSEPH
B. Jan. 16, 1870, Buffalo, N. Y.
D. Mar. 6, 1943, Buffalo, N. Y.
Hall of Fame 1945.

		G	W	L	PCT	Standing
1901	BOS A	138	79	57	.581	2
1902		138	77	60	.562	3
1903		141	91	47	.659	1
1904		157	95	59	.617	1
1905		153	78	74	.513	4
1906		137	44	92	.324	8 8
6 yrs.		864	464	389	.544	

WORLD SERIES

		G	W	L	PCT	Standing
1903	BOS A	8	5	3	.625	

Shano Collins
COLLINS, JOHN FRANCIS
B. Dec. 4, 1885, Charlestown, Mass.
D. Sept. 10, 1955, Newton, Mass.

		G	W	L	PCT	Standing
1931	BOS A	153	62	90	.408	6
1932		57	11	46	.193	8 8
2 yrs.		210	73	136	.349	

Charlie Comiskey
COMISKEY, CHARLES ALBERT (Commy, The Old Roman)
B. Aug. 15, 1859, Chicago, Ill.
D. Oct. 26, 1931, Eagle River, Wis.
Hall of Fame 1939.

		G	W	L	PCT	Standing
1883	STL AA	18	12	6	.667	2 2
1885		112	79	33	.705	1
1886		139	93	46	.669	1
1887		138	95	40	.704	1
1888		137	92	43	.681	1
1889		141	90	45	.667	2
1890	CHI P	138	75	62	.547	4
1891	STL AA	141	86	52	.623	2
1892	CIN N	155	82	68	.547	5
1893		131	65	63	.508	6
1894		132	55	75	.423	10
11 yrs.		1382	824	533	.607	
						3rd

Roger Connor
CONNOR, ROGER
Brother of Joe Connor.
B. July 1, 1857, Waterbury, Conn.
D. Jan. 4, 1931, Waterbury, Conn.
Hall of Fame 1976.

		G	W	L	PCT	Standing
1896	STL N	46	9	37	.196	11 11 11

Dusty Cooke
COOKE, ALLEN LINDSEY
B. June 23, 1907, Swepsonville, N. C.

		G	W	L	PCT	Standing
1948	PHI N	12	6	5	.545	7 6 6

Jack Coombs
COOMBS, JOHN WESLEY (Colby Jack)
B. Nov. 18, 1882, LeGrand, Iowa
D. Apr. 15, 1957, LeGrand, Iowa

		G	W	L	PCT	Standing
1919	PHI N	62	18	44	.290	8 8

Pat Corrales
CORRALES, PATRICK
B. Mar. 20, 1941, Los Angeles, Calif.

		G	W	L	PCT	Standing
1979	TEX A	162	83	79	.512	3
1980		163	76	85	.472	4
1982	PHI N	162	89	73	.549	2
1983		86	43	42	.506	1 1
1983	CLE A	62	30	32	.484	7 7
1984		163	75	87	.463	6
5 yrs.		798	396	398	.499	

Red Corriden
CORRIDEN, JOHN MICHAEL, SR.
Father of John Corriden.
B. Sept. 4, 1887, Logansport, Ind.
D. Sept. 28, 1959, Indianapolis, Ind.

		G	W	L	PCT	Standing
1950	CHI A	126	52	72	.419	8 6

Chuck Cottier
COTTIER, CHARLES KEITH
B. Jan. 8, 1936, Delta, Colo.

		G	W	L	PCT	Standing
1984	SEA A	27	15	12	.556	7 6

Bobby Cox
COX, ROBERT JOE
B. May 21, 1941, Tulsa, Okla.

		G	W	L	PCT	Standing	
1978	ATL N	162	69	93	.426	6	
1979		160	66	94	.413	6	
1980		161	81	80	.503	4	
1981		55	25	29	.463	4	(1st)
1981		52	25	27	.481	5	(2nd)
1982	TOR A	162	78	84	.481	6	
1983		162	89	73	.549	4	
1984		163	89	73	.549	2	
7 yrs.		1077	522	553	.486		

Harry Craft
CRAFT, HARRY FRANCIS
B. Apr. 19, 1915, Ellisville, Miss.

		G	W	L	PCT	Standing
1957	KC A	50	23	27	.460	8 7
1958		156	73	81	.474	7
1959		154	66	88	.429	7
1961	CHI N	16	7	9	.438	7 7 7
1962	HOU N	162	64	96	.400	8
1963		162	66	96	.407	9
1964		149	61	88	.409	9 9
7 yrs.		849	360	485	.426	

Roger Craig
CRAIG, ROGER LEE
B. Feb. 17, 1931, Durham, N. C.

		G	W	L	PCT	Standing
1978	SD N	162	84	78	.519	4
1979		161	68	93	.422	5
2 yrs.		323	152	171	.471	

	G	W	L	PCT	Standing			G	W	L	PCT	Standing

Del Crandall

CRANDALL, DELMAR WESLEY
B. Mar. 5, 1930, Ontario, Calif.

		G	W	L	PCT	Standing	
1972	MIL A	124	54	70	.435	6	6
1973		162	74	88	.457	5	
1974		162	76	86	.469	5	
1975		161	67	94	.416	5	5
1983	SEA A	89	34	55	.382	7	7
1984		135	59	76	.437	7	6
6 yrs.		833	364	469	.437		

Sam Crane

CRANE, SAMUEL NEWHALL
B. Jan. 2, 1854, Springfield, Mass.
D. June 26, 1925, New York, N. Y.

		G	W	L	PCT	Standing	
1880	BUF N	68	20	45	.308	8	7
1884	CIN U	43	36	7	.837	3	3
2 yrs.		111	56	52	.519		

Gavvy Cravath

CRAVATH, CLIFFORD CARLTON (Cactus)
B. Mar. 23, 1881, Escondido, Calif.
D. May 23, 1963, Laguna Beach, Calif.

		G	W	L	PCT	Standing	
1919	PHI N	76	29	46	.387	8	8
1920		153	62	91	.405	8	
2 yrs.		229	91	137	.399		

George Creamer

CREAMER, GEORGE W.
Born George W. Triebel.
B. 1855, Philadelphia, Pa.
D. June 27, 1886, Philadelphia, Pa.

		G	W	L	PCT	Standing	
1884	PIT AA	9	2	7	.222	11	12	11

Joe Cronin

CRONIN, JOSEPH EDWARD
B. Oct. 12, 1906, San Francisco, Calif.
D. Sept. 7, 1984, Osterville, Mass.
Hall of Fame 1956.

		G	W	L	PCT	Standing
1933	WAS A	153	99	53	.651	1
1934		155	66	86	.434	7
1935	BOS A	154	78	75	.510	4
1936		155	74	80	.481	6
1937		154	80	72	.526	5
1938		150	88	61	.591	2
1939		152	89	62	.589	2
1940		154	82	72	.532	4
1941		155	84	70	.545	2
1942		152	93	59	.612	2
1943		155	68	84	.447	7
1944		156	77	77	.500	4
1945		157	71	83	.461	7
1946		156	104	50	.675	1
1947		157	83	71	.539	3
15 yrs.		2315	1236	1055	.540	

WORLD SERIES		G	W	L	PCT	
1933	WAS A	5	1	4	.200	
1946	BOS A	7	3	4	.429	
2 yrs.		12	4	8	.333	

Lave Cross

CROSS, LAFAYETTE NAPOLEON
Brother of Frank Cross.
Brother of Amos Cross.
B. May 11, 1867, Milwaukee, Wis.
D. Sept. 4, 1927, Toledo, Ohio

		G	W	L	PCT	Standing	
1899	CLE N	38	8	30	.211	12	12

Ed Curtis

CURTIS, EDWIN R.
Deceased.

		G	W	L	PCT	Standing
1884	ALT U	25	6	19	.240	10

Charlie Cushman

CUSHMAN, CHARLES H.
B. May 25, 1850, New York, N. Y.
D. June 29, 1909, Milwaukee, Wis.

		G	W	L	PCT	Standing	
1891	C-M AA	36	21	15	.583	7	5

Ned Cuthbert

CUTHBERT, EDGAR EDWARD
B. June 20, 1845, Philadelphia, Pa.
D. Feb. 6, 1905, St. Louis, Mo.

		G	W	L	PCT	Standing	
1882	STL AA	59	27	32	.458	5	5

Bill Dahlen

DAHLEN, WILLIAM FREDERICK (Bad Bill)
B. Jan. 5, 1870, Nelliston, N. Y.
D. Dec. 5, 1950, Brooklyn, N. Y.

		G	W	L	PCT	Standing
1910	BKN N	156	64	90	.416	6
1911		154	64	86	.427	7
1912		153	58	95	.379	7
1913		152	65	84	.436	6
4 yrs.		615	251	355	.414	

Alvin Dark

DARK, ALVIN RALPH (Blackie)
B. Jan. 7, 1922, Comanche, Okla.

		G	W	L	PCT	Standing	
1961	SF N	155	85	69	.552	3	
1962		165	103	62	.624	1	
1963		162	88	74	.543	3	
1964		162	90	72	.556	4	
1966	KC A	160	74	86	.463	7	
1967		121	52	69	.430	10	10
1968	CLE A	161	86	75	.534	3	
1969		161	62	99	.385	6	
1970		162	76	86	.469	5	
1971		103	42	61	.408	6	6
1974	OAK A	162	90	72	.556	1	
1975		162	98	64	.605	1	
1977	SD N	113	48	65	.425	5	5
13 yrs.		1949	994	954	.510		

LEAGUE CHAMPIONSHIP SERIES		G	W	L	PCT	
1974	OAK A	4	3	1	.750	
1975		3	0	3	.000	
2 yrs.		7	3	4	.429	

WORLD SERIES		G	W	L	PCT	
1962	SF N	7	3	4	.429	
1974	OAK A	5	4	1	.800	
2 yrs.		12	7	5	.583	

Mordecai Davidson

DAVIDSON, MORDECAI H.
B. Nov. 30, 1846, Port Washington, Ohio
D. Sept. 6, 1940, Louisville, Ky.

		G	W	L	PCT	Standing	
1888	LOU AA	96	37	55	.402	8	7

George Davis

DAVIS, GEORGE STACEY
B. Aug. 23, 1870, Cohoes, N. Y.
D. Oct. 17, 1940, Philadelphia, Pa.

		G	W	L	PCT	Standing	
1895	NY N	34	17	17	.500	8	9
1900		77	39	37	.513	8	8
1901		141	52	85	.380	7	
3 yrs.		252	108	139	.437		

Harry Davis

DAVIS, HARRY H (Jasper)
B. July 10, 1873, Philadelphia, Pa.
D. Aug. 11, 1947, Philadelphia, Pa.

		G	W	L	PCT	Standing	
1912	CLE A	127	54	71	.432	6	5

	G	W	L	PCT	Standing			G	W	L	PCT	Standing

Spud Davis

DAVIS, VIRGIL LAWRENCE
B. Dec. 20, 1904, Birmingham, Ala.
D. Aug. 14, 1984, Birmingham, Ala.

		G	W	L	PCT	Standing	
1946	PIT N	3	1	2	.333	7	7

John Day

DAY, JOHN B.
B. Sept. 23, 1847, Colchester, Mass.
D. Jan. 25, 1925, Cliffside, N. J.

		G	W	L	PCT	Standing	
1899	NY N	71	30	40	.429	9	10

Herman Dehlman

DEHLMAN, HERMAN J.
B. 1850, Catasauqua, Pa.
D. Mar. 13, 1885, Wilkes-Barre, Pa.

		G	W	L	PCT	Standing
1876	STL N	64	45	19	.703	2

Bill Dickey

DICKEY, WILLIAM MALCOLM
Brother of George Dickey.
B. June 6, 1907, Bastrop, La.
Hall of Fame 1954.

		G	W	L	PCT	Standing		
1946	NY A	105	57	48	.543	2	3	3

Harry Diddlebock

DIDDLEBOCK, HENRY H.
B. June 27, 1854, Philadelphia, Pa.
D. Feb. 5, 1900, Philadelphia, Pa.

		G	W	L	PCT	Standing	
1896	STL N	18	7	11	.389	10	11

Larry Doby

DOBY, LAWRENCE EUGENE
B. Dec. 13, 1923, Camden, S. C.

		G	W	L	PCT	Standing	
1978	CHI A	87	37	50	.425	5	5

Patsy Donovan

DONOVAN, PATRICK JOSEPH
B. Mar. 16, 1865, County Cork, Ireland
D. Dec. 25, 1953, Lawrence, Mass.

		G	W	L	PCT	Standing	
1897	PIT N	135	60	71	.458	8	
1899		129	68	57	.544	10	7
1901	STL N	142	76	64	.543	4	
1902		140	56	78	.418	6	
1903		139	43	94	.314	8	
1904	WAS A	139	37	97	.276	8	8
1906	BKN N	153	66	86	.434	5	
1907		153	65	83	.439	5	
1908		154	53	101	.344	7	
1910	BOS A	158	81	72	.529	4	
1911		153	78	75	.510	5	
11 yrs.		1595	683	878	.438		

Wild Bill Donovan

DONOVAN, WILLIAM EDWARD
B. Oct. 13, 1876, Lawrence, Mass.
D. Dec. 9, 1923, Forsyth, N. Y.

		G	W	L	PCT	Standing	
1915	NY A	154	69	83	.454	5	
1916		156	80	74	.519	4	
1917		155	71	82	.464	6	
1921	PHI N	102	31	71	.304	8	8
4 yrs.		567	251	310	.447		

Red Dooin

DOOIN, CHARLES SEBASTIAN
B. June 12, 1879, Cincinnati, Ohio
D. May 14, 1952, Rochester, N. Y.

		G	W	L	PCT	Standing
1910	PHI N	157	78	75	.510	4
1911		153	79	73	.520	4
1912		152	73	79	.480	5
1913		159	88	63	.583	2
1914		154	74	80	.481	6
5 yrs.		775	392	370	.514	

Mike Dorgan

DORGAN, MICHAEL CORNELIUS
Brother of Jerry Dorgan.
B. Oct. 2, 1853, Middletown, Conn.
D. Apr. 26, 1909, Hartford, Conn.

		G	W	L	PCT	Standing
1879	SYR N	71	22	48	.314	7

Tommy Dowd

DOWD, THOMAS JEFFERSON (Buttermilk Tommy)
B. Apr. 20, 1869, Holyoke, Mass.
D. July 2, 1933, Holyoke, Mass.

		G	W	L	PCT	Standing	
1896	STL N	62	24	38	.387	11	11
1897		32	6	25	.194	12	12
2 yrs.		94	30	63	.323		

Jack Doyle

DOYLE, JOHN JOSEPH (Dirty Jack)
B. Oct. 25, 1869, Killorgin, Ireland
D. Dec. 31, 1958, Holyoke, Mass.

		G	W	L	PCT	Standing		
1895	NY N	63	31	31	.500	8	9	9
1898	WAS N	44	20	24	.455	12	10	11
2 yrs.		107	51	55	.481			

Joe Doyle

DOYLE, JOSEPH J.
B. Apr. 9, 1838, New York, N. Y.
D. Jan. 7, 1906, White Plains, N. Y.

		G	W	L	PCT	Standing	
1885	BKN AA	33	13	20	.394	7	5

Chuck Dressen

DRESSEN, CHARLES WALTER
B. Sept. 20, 1898, Decatur, Ill.
D. Aug. 10, 1966, Detroit, Mich.

		G	W	L	PCT	Standing	
1934	CIN N	66	25	41	.379	8	8
1935		154	68	85	.444	6	
1936		154	74	80	.481	5	
1937		130	51	78	.395	8	8
1951	BKN N	158	97	60	.618	2	
1952		155	96	57	.627	1	
1953		155	105	49	.682	1	
1955	WAS A	154	53	101	.344	8	
1956		155	59	95	.383	7	
1957		21	5	16	.238	8	8
1960	MIL N	154	88	66	.571	2	
1961		130	71	58	.550	3	4
1963	DET A	102	55	47	.539	9	5
1964		163	85	77	.525	4	
1965		162	89	73	.549	4	
1966		26	16	10	.615	3	3
16 yrs.		2039	1037	993	.511		

WORLD SERIES						
1952	BKN N	7	3	4	.429	
1953		6	2	4	.333	
2 yrs.		13	5	8	.385	

	G	W	L	PCT	Standing			G	W	L	PCT	Standing

Hugh Duffy

DUFFY, HUGH
B. Nov. 26, 1866, Cranston, R. I.
D. Oct. 19, 1954, Boston, Mass.
Hall of Fame 1945.

		G	W	L	PCT	Standing
1901	MIL A	139	48	89	.350	8
1904	PHI N	155	52	100	.342	8
1905		155	83	69	.546	4
1906		154	71	82	.464	4
1910	CHI A	156	68	85	.444	6
1911		154	77	74	.510	4
1921	BOS A	154	75	79	.487	5
1922		154	61	93	.396	8
8 yrs.		1221	535	671	.444	

Fred Dunlap

DUNLAP, FREDERICK C. (Sure Shot)
B. May 21, 1859, Philadelphia, Pa.
D. Dec. 1, 1902, Philadelphia, Pa.

		G	W	L	PCT	Standing		
1889	PIT N	16	7	9	.438	7	7	5

Leo Durocher

DUROCHER, LEO ERNEST (The Lip)
B. July 27, 1905, W. Springfield, Mass.

		G	W	L	PCT	Standing	
1939	BKN N	157	84	69	.549	3	
1940		156	88	65	.575	2	
1941		157	100	54	.649	1	
1942		155	104	50	.675	2	
1943		153	81	72	.529	3	
1944		155	63	91	.409	7	
1945		155	87	67	.565	3	
1946		157	96	60	.615	2	
1948		75	37	38	.493	5	3
1948	NY N	79	41	38	.519	4	5
1949		156	73	81	.474	5	
1950		154	86	68	.558	3	
1951		157	98	59	.624	1	
1952		154	92	62	.597	2	
1953		155	70	84	.455	5	
1954		154	97	57	.630	1	
1955		154	80	74	.519	3	
1966	CHI N	162	59	103	.364	10	
1967		162	87	74	.540	3	
1968		163	84	78	.519	3	
1969		163	92	70	.568	2	
1970		162	84	78	.519	2	
1971		162	83	79	.512	3	
1972		90	46	44	.511	4	2
1972	HOU N	31	16	15	.516	2	2
1973		162	82	80	.506	4	
24 yrs.		3740	2010	1710	.540		
			5th	6th	7th		

WORLD SERIES		G	W	L	PCT	
1941	BKN N	5	1	4	.200	
1951	NY N	6	2	4	.333	
1954		4	4	0	1.000	
3 yrs.		15	7	8	.467	

Frank Dwyer

DWYER, JOHN FRANCIS
B. Mar. 25, 1868, Lee, Mass.
D. Feb. 4, 1943, Pittsfield, Mass.

		G	W	L	PCT	Standing
1902	DET A	137	52	83	.385	7

Eddie Dyer

DYER, EDWIN HAWLEY
B. Oct. 11, 1900, Morgan City, La.
D. Apr. 20, 1964, Houston, Tex.

		G	W	L	PCT	Standing
1946	STL N	156	98	58	.628	1
1947		156	89	65	.578	2
1948		155	85	69	.552	2
1949		157	96	58	.623	2
1950		153	78	75	.510	5
5 yrs.		777	446	325	.578	

WORLD SERIES		G	W	L	PCT
1946	STL N	7	4	3	.571

Jimmy Dykes

DYKES, JAMES JOSEPH
B. Nov. 10, 1896, Philadelphia, Pa.
D. June 15, 1976, Philadelphia, Pa.

		G	W	L	PCT	Standing	
1934	CHI A	136	49	86	.363	8	8
1935		153	74	78	.487	5	
1936		153	81	70	.536	3	
1937		154	86	68	.558	3	
1938		149	65	83	.439	6	
1939		155	85	69	.552	4	
1940		155	82	72	.532	4	
1941		156	77	77	.500	3	
1942		148	66	82	.446	6	
1943		155	82	72	.532	4	
1944		154	71	83	.461	7	
1945		150	71	78	.477	6	
1946		30	10	20	.333	7	5
1951	PHI A	154	70	84	.455	6	
1952		155	79	75	.513	4	
1953		157	59	95	.383	7	
1954	BAL A	154	54	100	.351	7	
1958	CIN N	41	24	17	.585	7	4
1959	DET A	137	74	63	.540	8	4
1960		96	44	52	.458	6	6
1960	CLE A	58	26	32	.448	4	4
1961		160	78	82	.488	5	5
21 yrs.		2960	1407	1538	.478		
					9th		

John Dyler

DYLER, JOHN F.
B. June, 1852, Louisville, Ky.
Deceased.

		G	W	L	PCT	Standing		
1882	LOU AA	13	6	7	.462	4	3	

Charlie Ebbets

EBBETS, CHARLES HERCULES
B. Oct. 29, 1859, New York, N. Y.
D. Apr. 18, 1925, New York, N. Y.

		G	W	L	PCT	Standing		
1898	BKN N	110	38	68	.358	9	10	

Kid Elberfeld

ELBERFELD, NORMAN ARTHUR (The Tabasco Kid)
B. Apr. 13, 1875, Pomeroy, Ohio
D. Jan. 13, 1944, Chattanooga, Tenn.

		G	W	L	PCT	Standing		
1908	NY A	98	27	71	.276	6	8	

Lee Elia

ELIA, LEE CONSTANTINE
B. July 16, 1937, Philadelphia, Pa.

		G	W	L	PCT	Standing	
1982	CHI N	162	73	89	.451	5	
1983		123	54	69	.439	5	5
2 yrs.		285	127	158	.446		

Joe Ellick

ELLICK, JOSEPH J.
B. Apr. 3, 1854, Cincinnati, Ohio
D. Apr. 21, 1923, Kansas City, Mo.

		G	W	L	PCT	Standing		
1884	C-P U	13	6	6	.500	7	6	

Bob Elliott

ELLIOTT, ROBERT IRVING
B. Nov. 26, 1916, San Francisco, Calif.
D. May 4, 1966, San Diego, Calif.

		G	W	L	PCT	Standing
1960	KC A	155	58	96	.377	8

| | G | W | L | PCT | Standing | | | | G | W | L | PCT | Standing | |

Jewel Ens

ENS, JEWEL WILLOUGHBY
Brother of Mutz Ens.
B. Aug. 24, 1889, St. Louis, Mo.
D. Jan. 17, 1950, Syracuse, N. Y.

		G	W	L	PCT	Standing	
1929	PIT N	35	21	14	.600	2	2
1930		154	80	74	.519	5	
1931		155	75	79	.487	5	
3 yrs.		344	176	167	.513		

Cal Ermer

ERMER, CALVIN COOLIDGE
B. Nov. 10, 1923, Baltimore, Md.

		G	W	L	PCT	Standing	
1967	MIN A	114	66	46	.589	6	2
1968		162	79	83	.488	7	
2 yrs.		276	145	129	.529		

Dude Esterbrook

ESTERBROOK, THOMAS JEFFERSON
B. June 20, 1860, Staten Island, N. Y.
D. Apr. 30, 1901, Middletown, N. Y.

		G	W	L	PCT	Standing	
1889	LOU AA	10	2	8	.200	8	8

Ford Evans

EVANS, J. FORD
D. Oct. 14, 1884, Akron, Ohio

		G	W	L	PCT	Standing	
1882	CLE N	84	42	40	.512	5	

Johnny Evers

EVERS, JOHN JOSEPH (The Trojan, The Crab)
Brother of Joe Evers.
B. July 21, 1881, Troy, N. Y.
D. Mar. 28, 1947, Albany, N. Y.
Hall of Fame 1946.

		G	W	L	PCT	Standing	
1913	CHI N	154	88	65	.575	3	
1921		98	42	56	.429	7	7
1924	CHI A	154	66	87	.431	8	
3 yrs.		406	196	208	.485		

Buck Ewing

EWING, WILLIAM
Brother of John Ewing.
B. Oct. 17, 1859, Hoaglands, Ohio
D. Oct. 20, 1906, Cincinnati, Ohio
Hall of Fame 1939.

		G	W	L	PCT	Standing	
1890	NY P	132	74	57	.565	3	
1895	CIN N	132	66	64	.508	8	
1896		128	77	50	.606	3	
1897		134	76	56	.576	4	
1898		157	92	60	.605	3	
1899		156	83	67	.553	6	
1900	NY N	64	21	41	.339	8	8
7 yrs.		903	489	395	.553		

Jay Faatz

FAATZ, JAYSON S.
B. Oct. 24, 1860, Weedsport, N. Y.
D. Apr. 10, 1923, Syracuse, N. Y.

		G	W	L	PCT	Standing	
1890	CLE P	35	10	25	.286	7	7

Jim Fanning

FANNING, WILLIAM JAMES
B. Sept. 14, 1927, Chicago, Ill.

		G	W	L	PCT	Standing		
1981	MON N	27	16	11	.593	2	1	(2nd)
1982		162	86	76	.531	3		
1984		30	14	16	.467	5	5	
3 yrs.		219	116	103	.530			

DIVISIONAL PLAYOFF SERIES
		G	W	L	PCT		
1981	MON N	5	3	2	.600		

LEAGUE CHAMPIONSHIP SERIES
		G	W	L	PCT		
1981	MON N	5	2	3	.400		

Kerby Farrell

FARRELL, MAJOR KERBY
B. Sept. 3, 1913, Leapwood, Tenn.
D. Dec. 17, 1975, Nashville, Tenn.

		G	W	L	PCT	Standing	
1957	CLE A	153	76	77	.497	6	

Bob Ferguson

FERGUSON, ROBERT V. (Death to Flying Things)
B. Jan. 31, 1845, Brooklyn, N. Y.
D. May 3, 1894, Brooklyn, N. Y.

		G	W	L	PCT	Standing		
1876	HAR N	69	47	21	.691	3		
1877		60	31	27	.534	3		
1878	CHI N	61	30	30	.500	4		
1879	TRO N	18	7	10	.412	8	8	
1880		83	41	42	.494	4		
1881		85	39	45	.464	5		
1882		85	35	48	.422	7		
1883	PHI N	17	4	13	.235	8	8	
1884	PIT AA	26	5	21	.192	12	12	11
1886	NY AA	119	47	70	.402	8	7	
1887		30	6	24	.200	8	7	
11 yrs.		653	292	351	.454			

Mike Ferraro

FERRARO, MICHAEL DENNIS
B. Aug. 14, 1944, Kingston, N. Y.

		G	W	L	PCT	Standing	
1983	CLE A	100	40	60	.400	7	7

Freddie Fitzsimmons

FITZSIMMONS, FREDERICK LANDIS (Fat Freddie)
B. July 28, 1901, Mishawaka, Ind.
D. Nov. 18, 1979, Yucca Valley, Calif.

		G	W	L	PCT	Standing	
1943	PHI N	62	24	37	.393	5	7
1944		154	61	92	.399	8	
1945		67	17	50	.254	8	8
3 yrs.		283	102	179	.363		

Art Fletcher

FLETCHER, ARTHUR
B. Jan. 5, 1885, Collinsville, Ill.
D. Feb. 6, 1950, Los Angeles, Calif.

		G	W	L	PCT	Standing	
1923	PHI N	155	50	104	.325	8	
1924		152	55	96	.364	7	
1925		153	68	85	.444	6	
1926		152	58	93	.384	8	
1929	NY A	11	6	5	.545	2	2
5 yrs.		623	237	383	.382		

Jim Fogarty

FOGARTY, JAMES G.
Brother of Joe Fogarty.
B. Feb. 12, 1864, San Francisco, Calif.
D. May 20, 1891, Philadelphia, Pa.

		G	W	L	PCT	Standing		
1890	PHI P	49	30	19	.612	5	4	5

Horace Fogel

FOGEL, HORACE S.
B. Mar. 2, 1861, Macungie, Pa.
D. Nov. 15, 1928, Philadelphia, Pa.

		G	W	L	PCT	Standing	
1887	IND N	70	20	49	.290	8	8
1902	NY N	42	18	23	.439	4	8
2 yrs.		112	38	72	.345		

	G	W	L	PCT	Standing			G	W	L	PCT	Standing

Lee Fohl

FOHL, LEO ALEXANDER
B. Nov. 28, 1876, Lowell, Ohio
D. Oct. 30, 1965, Cleveland, Ohio

		G	W	L	PCT	Standing	
1915	CLE A	126	45	79	.363	6	7
1916		157	77	77	.500	6	
1917		156	88	66	.571	3	
1918		129	73	54	.575	2	
1919		79	45	34	.570	3	2
1921	STL A	154	81	73	.526	3	
1922		154	93	61	.604	2	
1923		101	51	49	.510	3	5
1924	BOS A	156	67	87	.435	7	
1925		152	47	105	.309	8	
1926		154	46	107	.301	8	
11 yrs.		1518	713	792	.474		

Lew Fonseca

FONSECA, LEWIS ALBERT
B. Jan. 21, 1899, Oakland, Calif.

		G	W	L	PCT	Standing	
1932	CHI A	152	49	102	.325	7	
1933		151	67	83	.447	6	
1934		17	4	13	.235	8	8
3 yrs.		320	120	198	.377		

Dave Foutz

FOUTZ, DAVID LUTHER (Scissors)
B. Sept. 7, 1856, Carroll County, Md.
D. Mar. 5, 1897, Waverly, Md.

		G	W	L	PCT	Standing
1893	BKN N	130	65	63	.508	6
1894		134	70	61	.534	5
1895		133	71	60	.542	5
1896		133	58	73	.443	9
4 yrs.		530	264	257	.507	

Charlie Fox

FOX, CHARLES FRANCIS (Irish)
B. Oct. 7, 1921, New York, N. Y.

		G	W	L	PCT	Standing	
1970	SF N	118	67	51	.568	5	3
1971		162	90	72	.556	1	
1972		155	69	86	.445	5	
1973		162	88	74	.543	3	
1974		76	34	42	.447	5	5
1976	MON N	34	12	22	.353	6	6
1983	CHI N	39	17	22	.436	5	5
7 yrs.		746	377	369	.505		

LEAGUE CHAMPIONSHIP SERIES

		G	W	L	PCT	Standing
1971	SF N	4	1	3	.250	

Herman Franks

FRANKS, HERMAN LOUIS
B. Jan. 4, 1914, Price, Utah

		G	W	L	PCT	Standing	
1965	SF N	163	95	67	.586	2	
1966		161	93	68	.578	2	
1967		162	91	71	.562	2	
1968		163	88	74	.543	2	
1977	CHI N	162	81	81	.500	4	
1978		162	79	83	.488	3	
1979		155	78	77	.503	5	5
7 yrs.		1128	605	521	.537		

George Frazer

FRAZER, GEORGE KASSON
B. Jan. 7, 1861, Syracuse, N. Y.
D. Feb. 5, 1913, Philadelphia, Pa.

		G	W	L	PCT	Standing
1890	SYR AA	128	55	72	.433	6

Joe Frazier

FRAZIER, JOSEPH FILMORE (Cobra Joe)
B. Oct. 6, 1922, Liberty, N. C.

		G	W	L	PCT	Standing	
1976	NY N	162	86	76	.531	3	
1977		45	15	30	.333	6	6
2 yrs.		207	101	106	.488		

Jim Fregosi

FREGOSI, JAMES LOUIS
B. Apr. 4, 1942, San Francisco, Calif.

		G	W	L	PCT	Standing		
1978	CAL A	117	62	55	.530	3	2	
1979		162	88	74	.543	1		
1980		160	65	95	.406	6		
1981		47	22	25	.468	4	4	(1st)
4 yrs.		486	237	249	.488			

LEAGUE CHAMPIONSHIP SERIES

		G	W	L	PCT	Standing
1979	CAL A	4	1	3	.250	

Jim Frey

FREY, JAMES GOTTFRIED
B. May 26, 1931, Cleveland, Ohio

		G	W	L	PCT	Standing		
1980	KC A	162	97	65	.599	1		
1981		50	20	30	.400	5		(1st)
1981		20	10	10	.500	2	1	(2nd)
1984	CHI N	161	96	65	.596	1		
3 yrs.		393	223	170	.567			

LEAGUE CHAMPIONSHIP SERIES

		G	W	L	PCT	Standing
1980	KC A	3	3	0	1.000	
1984	CHI N	5	2	3	.400	
2 yrs.		8	5	3	.625	

WORLD SERIES

		G	W	L	PCT	Standing
1980	KC A	6	2	4	.333	

Frankie Frisch

FRISCH, FRANK FRANCIS (The Fordham Flash)
B. Sept. 9, 1898, Queens, N. Y.
D. Mar. 12, 1973, Wilmington, Del.
Hall of Fame 1947.

		G	W	L	PCT	Standing	
1933	STL N	63	36	26	.581	5	5
1934		154	95	58	.621	1	
1935		154	96	58	.623	2	
1936		155	87	67	.565	2	
1937		157	81	73	.526	4	
1938		138	62	72	.463	6	6
1940	PIT N	156	78	76	.506	4	
1941		156	81	73	.526	4	
1942		151	66	81	.449	5	
1943		157	80	74	.519	4	
1944		158	90	63	.588	2	
1945		155	82	72	.532	4	
1946		152	62	89	.411	7	7
1949	CHI N	104	42	62	.404	8	8
1950		154	64	89	.418	7	
1951		81	35	45	.438	7	8
16 yrs.		2245	1137	1078	.513		

WORLD SERIES

		G	W	L	PCT	Standing
1934	STL N	7	4	3	.571	

Judge Fuchs

FUCHS, EMIL EDWIN
B. Apr. 17, 1878, New York, N. Y.
D. Dec. 5, 1961, Boston, Mass.

		G	W	L	PCT	Standing
1929	BOS N	154	56	98	.364	8

Chick Fulmer

FULMER, CHARLES JOHN
B. Feb. 12, 1851, Philadelphia, Pa.
D. Feb. 15, 1940, Philadelphia, Pa.

		G	W	L	PCT	Standing
1876	LOU N	69	30	36	.455	5

Tom Furniss

FURNISS, THOMAS
B. Conn.
Deceased.

		G	W	L	PCT	Standing		
1884	BOS U	10	4	6	.400	5	5	5

	G	W	L	PCT	Standing			G	W	L	PCT	Standing

John Gaffney

GAFFNEY, JOHN H. (Honest John, King of the Umpires)
B. June 29, 1855, Roxbury, Mass.
D. Aug. 8, 1913, New York, N. Y.

	G	W	L	PCT	Standing	
1886 WAS N	43	15	26	.366	8	8
1887	126	46	76	.377	7	
2 yrs.	169	61	102	.374		

Pud Galvin

GALVIN, JAMES FRANCIS (Gentle Jeems, The Little Steam Engine)
Brother of Lou Galvin.
B. Dec. 25, 1855, St. Louis, Mo.
D. Mar. 7, 1902, Pittsburgh, Pa.
Hall of Fame 1965.

	G	W	L	PCT	Standing	
1885 BUF N	30	8	22	.267	7	7

John Ganzel

GANZEL, JOHN HENRY
Brother of Charlie Ganzel.
B. Apr. 7, 1874, Kalamazoo, Mich.
D. Jan. 14, 1959, Orlando, Fla.

	G	W	L	PCT	Standing	
1908 CIN N	155	73	81	.474	5	
1915 BKN F	35	17	18	.486	7	7
2 yrs.	190	90	99	.476		

Dave Garcia

GARCIA, DAVID
B. Sept. 15, 1920, East St. Louis, Mo.

	G	W	L	PCT	Standing		
1977 CAL A	81	35	46	.432	5	5	
1978	45	25	20	.556	3	2	
1979 CLE A	66	38	28	.576	6	6	
1980	160	79	81	.494	6		
1981	50	26	24	.520	6		(1st)
1981	53	26	27	.491	5		(2nd)
1982	162	78	84	.481	6		
6 yrs.	617	307	310	.498			

Billy Gardner

GARDNER, WILLIAM FREDERICK (Shotgun)
B. July 19, 1927, Waterford, Conn.

	G	W	L	PCT	Standing		
1981 MIN A	20	6	14	.300	5	7	(1st)
1981	53	24	29	.453	4		(2nd)
1982	162	60	102	.370	7		
1983	162	70	92	.432	5		
1984	162	81	81	.500	2		
4 yrs.	559	241	318	.431			

Joe Gerhardt

GERHARDT, JOHN JOSEPH (Move Up Joe)
B. Feb. 14, 1855, Washington, D. C.
D. Mar. 11, 1922, Middletown, N. Y.

	G	W	L	PCT	Standing	
1883 LOU AA	36	16	19	.457	4	5
1884	58	39	18	.684	3	3
2 yrs.	94	55	37	.598		

Doc Gessler

GESSLER, HARRY HOMER
B. Dec. 23, 1880, Indiana, Pa.
D. Dec. 26, 1924, Indiana, Pa.

	G	W	L	PCT	Standing	
1914 PIT F	18	6	12	.333	8	7

George Gibson

GIBSON, GEORGE (Moon)
B. July 22, 1880, London, Ont., Canada
D. Jan. 25, 1967, London, Ont., Canada

	G	W	L	PCT	Standing
1920 PIT N	155	79	75	.513	4
1921	154	90	63	.588	2

George Gibson continued

	G	W	L	PCT	Standing	
1922	65	32	33	.492	5	3
1925 CHI N	26	12	14	.462	8	8
1932 PIT N	154	86	68	.558	2	
1933	154	87	67	.565	2	
1934	52	27	24	.529	4	5
7 yrs.	760	413	344	.546		

Jim Gifford

GIFFORD, JAMES H.
B. Oct. 18, 1845, Warren, N. Y.
D. Dec. 19, 1901, Columbus, Ohio

	G	W	L	PCT	Standing	
1884 IND AA	86	25	59	.298	11	12
1885 NY AA	108	44	64	.407	7	
1886	18	6	12	.333	8	7
3 yrs.	212	75	135	.357		

Jack Glasscock

GLASSCOCK, JOHN WESLEY (Pebbly Jack)
B. July 22, 1859, Wheeling, W. Va.
D. Feb. 24, 1947, Wheeling, W. Va.

	G	W	L	PCT	Standing	
1889 IND N	68	34	33	.507	7	7

Kid Gleason

GLEASON, WILLIAM J.
Brother of Harry Gleason.
B. Oct. 26, 1866, Camden, N. J.
D. Jan. 2, 1933, Philadelphia, Pa.

	G	W	L	PCT	Standing
1919 CHI A	140	88	52	.629	1
1920	154	96	58	.623	2
1921	154	62	92	.403	7
1922	155	77	77	.500	5
1923	156	69	85	.448	7
5 yrs.	759	392	364	.519	

WORLD SERIES					
1919 CHI A	8	3	5	.375	

Preston Gomez

GOMEZ, PEDRO MARTINEZ
B. Apr. 20, 1923, Central Preston, Cuba

	G	W	L	PCT	Standing	
1969 SD N	162	52	110	.321	6	
1970	162	63	99	.389	6	
1971	161	61	100	.379	6	
1972	11	4	7	.364	4	6
1974 HOU N	162	81	81	.500	4	
1975	128	47	80	.370	6	6
1980 CHI N	90	38	52	.422	6	6
7 yrs.	876	346	529	.395		

Mike Gonzalez

GONZALEZ, MIGUEL ANGEL
B. Sept. 24, 1890, Havana, Cuba
D. Feb. 19, 1977, Havana, Cuba

	G	W	L	PCT	Standing		
1938 STL N	18	9	8	.529	6	6	
1940	5	0	5	.000	7	6	3
2 yrs.	23	9	13	.409			

Joe Gordon

GORDON, JOSEPH LOWELL (Flash)
B. Feb. 18, 1915, Los Angeles, Calif.
D. Apr. 14, 1978, Sacramento, Calif.

	G	W	L	PCT	Standing	
1958 CLE A	86	46	40	.535	5	4
1959	154	89	65	.578	2	
1960	95	49	46	.516	4	4
1960 DET A	57	26	31	.456	6	6
1961 KC A	70	26	43	.377	8	9
1969	163	69	93	.426	4	
5 yrs.	625	305	318	.490		

	G	W	L	PCT	Standing			G	W	L	PCT	Standing

John Goryl

GORYL, JOHN ALBERT
B. Oct. 21, 1933, Cumberland, R. I.

		G	W	L	PCT		
1980	MIN A	36	23	13	.639	6	3
1981		37	11	25	.306	5	7	(1st)
2 yrs.		73	34	38	.472		

Charlie Gould

GOULD, CHARLES HARVEY
B. Aug. 21, 1847, Cincinnati, Ohio
D. Apr. 10, 1917, Flushing, N. Y.

		G	W	L	PCT	
1876	CIN N	65	9	56	.138	8

Alex Grammas

GRAMMAS, ALEXANDER PETER
B. Apr. 3, 1926, Birmingham, Ala.

		G	W	L	PCT	
1969	PIT N	5	4	1	.800	3	3
1976	MIL A	161	66	95	.410	6
1977		162	67	95	.414	6
3 yrs.		328	137	191	.418	

Dallas Green

GREEN, GEORGE DALLAS
B. Aug. 4, 1934, Newport, Del.

		G	W	L	PCT	
1979	PHI N	30	19	11	.633	5	4
1980		162	91	71	.562	1
1981		56	34	21	.618	1	(1st)
1981		53	25	27	.481	3	(2nd)
3 yrs.		301	169	130	.565	

DIVISIONAL PLAYOFF SERIES
1981	PHI N	5	2	3	.400	

LEAGUE CHAMPIONSHIP SERIES
1980	PHI N	5	3	2	.600	

WORLD SERIES
1980	PHI N	6	4	2	.667	

Mike Griffin

GRIFFIN, MICHAEL JOSEPH
B. Mar. 20, 1865, Utica, N. Y.
D. Apr. 10, 1908, Utica, N. Y.

		G	W	L	PCT		
1898	BKN N	4	1	3	.250	9	9	10

Sandy Griffin

GRIFFIN, TOBIAS CHARLES
B. July 19, 1858, Fayetteville, N. Y.
D. June 5, 1926, Fayetteville, N. Y.

		G	W	L	PCT		
1891	WAS AA	17	4	13	.235	8	8

Clark Griffith

GRIFFITH, CLARK CALVIN (The Old Fox)
B. Nov. 20, 1869, Stringtown, Mo.
D. Oct. 27, 1955, Washington, D. C.
Hall of Fame 1946.

		G	W	L	PCT		
1901	CHI A	137	83	53	.610	1
1902		138	74	60	.552	4
1903	NY A	136	72	62	.537	4
1904		155	92	59	.609	2
1905		152	71	78	.477	6
1906		155	90	61	.596	2
1907		152	70	78	.473	5
1908		57	24	32	.429	6	8
1909	CIN N	157	77	76	.503	4
1910		156	75	79	.487	5
1911		159	70	83	.458	6
1912	WAS A	154	91	61	.599	2
1913		155	90	64	.584	2
1914		157	81	73	.526	3
1915		155	85	68	.556	4
1916		159	76	77	.497	7
1917		157	74	79	.484	5
1918		130	72	56	.563	3

Clark Griffith continued

		G	W	L	PCT	
1919		142	56	84	.400	7
1920		153	68	84	.447	6
20 yrs.		2916	1491	1367	.522	

Burleigh Grimes

GRIMES, BURLEIGH ARLAND (Ol' Stubblebeard)
B. Aug. 18, 1893, Clear Lake, Wis.
Hall of Fame 1964.

		G	W	L	PCT	
1937	BKN N	155	62	91	.405	6
1938		150	68	80	.459	7
2 yrs.		305	130	171	.432	

Charlie Grimm

GRIMM, CHARLES JOHN (Jolly Cholly)
B. Aug. 28, 1898, St. Louis, Mo.
D. Nov. 15, 1983, Scottsdale, Ariz.

		G	W	L	PCT		
1932	CHI N	57	37	20	.649	2	1
1933		154	86	68	.558	3
1934		152	86	65	.570	3
1935		154	100	54	.649	1
1936		154	87	67	.565	2
1937		154	93	61	.604	2
1938		81	45	36	.556	3	1
1944		146	74	69	.517	8	4
1945		155	98	56	.636	1
1946		155	82	71	.536	3
1947		155	69	85	.448	6
1948		155	64	90	.416	8
1949		50	19	31	.380	8	8
1952	BOS N	120	51	67	.432	6	7
1953	MIL N	157	92	62	.597	2
1954		154	89	65	.578	3
1955		154	85	69	.552	2
1956		46	24	22	.522	5	2
1960	CHI N	17	6	11	.353	8	7
19 yrs.		2370	1287	1069	.546	

WORLD SERIES
		G	W	L	PCT	
1932	CHI N	4	0	4	.000	
1935		6	2	4	.333	
1945		7	3	4	.429	
3 yrs.		17	5	12	.294	
					10th	

Heinie Groh

GROH, HENRY KNIGHT
Brother of Lew Groh.
B. Sept. 18, 1889, Rochester, N. Y.
D. Aug. 22, 1968, Cincinnati, Ohio

		G	W	L	PCT		
1918	CIN N	10	7	3	.700	4	3

Don Gutteridge

GUTTERIDGE, DONALD JOSEPH
B. June 19, 1912, Pittsburg, Kans.

		G	W	L	PCT		
1969	CHI A	145	60	85	.414	4	5
1970		136	49	87	.360	6	6
2 yrs.		281	109	172	.388	

Stan Hack

HACK, STANLEY CAMFIELD (Smiling Stan)
B. Dec. 6, 1909, Sacramento, Calif.
D. Dec. 15, 1979, Dickson, Ill.

		G	W	L	PCT		
1954	CHI N	154	64	90	.416	7
1955		154	72	81	.471	6
1956		157	60	94	.390	8
1958	STL N	10	3	7	.300	5	5
4 yrs.		475	199	272	.423	

	G	W	L	PCT	Standing				G	W	L	PCT	Standing	

Charlie Hackett

HACKETT, CHARLES M.
B. Holyoke, Mass.
D. Aug. 1, 1898, Holyoke, Mass.

	G	W	L	PCT	Standing	
1884 **CLE N**	113	35	77	.313	7	
1885 **BKN AA**	40	15	25	.375	7	7	5
2 yrs.	153	50	102	.329		

Bill Hallman

HALLMAN, WILLIAM WILSON
B. Mar. 30, 1867, Pittsburgh, Pa.
D. Sept. 11, 1920, Philadelphia, Pa.

	G	W	L	PCT	Standing		
1897 **STL N**	59	13	46	.220	12	12	12

Fred Haney

HANEY, FRED GIRARD (Pudge)
B. Apr. 25, 1898, Albuquerque, N. M.
D. Nov. 9, 1977, Beverly Hills, Calif.

	G	W	L	PCT	Standing	
1939 **STL A**	156	43	111	.279	8	
1940	156	67	87	.435	6	
1941	44	15	29	.341	7	6
1953 **PIT N**	154	50	104	.325	8	
1954	154	53	101	.344	8	
1955	154	60	94	.390	8	
1956 **MIL N**	109	68	40	.630	5	2
1957	155	95	59	.617	1	
1958	154	92	62	.597	1	
1959	157	86	70	.551	2	
10 yrs.	1393	629	757	.454		

WORLD SERIES

	G	W	L	PCT	
1957 **MIL N**	7	4	3	.571	
1958	7	3	4	.429	
2 yrs.	14	7	7	.500	

Ned Hanlon

HANLON, EDWARD HUGH
B. Aug. 22, 1857, Montville, Conn.
D. Apr. 14, 1937, Baltimore, Md.

	G	W	L	PCT	Standing	
1889 **PIT N**	47	26	19	.578	7	5
1890 **PIT P**	128	60	68	.469	6	
1891 **PIT N**	78	31	47	.397	8	8
1892 **BAL N**	135	45	85	.346	12	12
1893	130	60	70	.462	8	
1894	129	89	39	.695	1	
1895	132	87	43	.669	1	
1896	132	90	39	.698	1	
1897	136	90	40	.692	2	
1898	154	96	53	.644	2	
1899 **BKN N**	150	101	47	.682	1	
1900	142	82	54	.603	1	
1901	137	79	57	.581	3	
1902	141	75	63	.543	2	
1903	139	70	66	.515	5	
1904	154	56	97	.366	6	
1905	155	48	104	.316	8	
1906 **CIN N**	155	64	87	.424	6	
1907	156	66	87	.431	6	
19 yrs.	2530	1315	1165	.530		

Mel Harder

HARDER, MELVIN LeROY (Chief, Wimpy)
B. Oct. 15, 1909, Beemer, Neb.

	G	W	L	PCT	Standing	
1961 **CLE A**	1	0	1	.000	5	5

Bucky Harris

HARRIS, STANLEY RAYMOND
B. Nov. 8, 1896, Port Jervis, N. Y.
D. Nov. 8, 1977, Bethesda, Md.
Hall of Fame 1975.

	G	W	L	PCT	Standing	
1924 **WAS A**	156	92	62	.597	1	
1925	152	96	55	.636	1	
1926	152	81	69	.540	4	
1927	157	85	69	.552	3	

Bucky Harris continued

	G	W	L	PCT	Standing	
1928	155	75	79	.487	4	
1929 **DET A**	155	70	84	.455	6	
1930	154	75	79	.487	5	
1931	154	61	93	.396	7	
1932	152	76	75	.503	5	
1933	153	73	79	.480	5	5
1934 **BOS A**	153	76	76	.500	4	
1935 **WAS A**	154	67	86	.438	6	
1936	153	82	71	.536	4	
1937	158	73	80	.477	6	
1938	152	75	76	.497	5	
1939	153	65	87	.428	6	
1940	154	64	90	.416	7	
1941	156	70	84	.455	6	
1942	151	62	89	.411	7	
1943 **PHI N**	95	40	53	.430	5	7
1947 **NY A**	155	97	57	.630	1	
1948	154	94	60	.610	3	
1950 **WAS A**	155	67	87	.435	5	
1951	154	62	92	.403	7	
1952	157	78	76	.506	5	
1953	152	76	76	.500	5	
1954	155	66	88	.429	6	
1955 **DET A**	154	79	75	.513	5	
1956	155	82	72	.532	5	
29 yrs.	4410	2159	2219	.493		
		3rd	**3rd**	**2nd**		

WORLD SERIES

	G	W	L	PCT	
1924 **WAS A**	7	4	3	.571	
1925	7	3	4	.429	
1947 **NY A**	7	4	3	.571	
3 yrs.	21	11	10	.524	
		9th		**7th**	

Lum Harris

HARRIS, CHALMER LUMAN
B. Jan. 17, 1915, New Castle, Ala.

	G	W	L	PCT	Standing	
1961 **BAL A**	27	17	10	.630	3	3
1964 **HOU N**	13	5	8	.385	9	9
1965	162	65	97	.401	9	
1968 **ATL N**	163	81	81	.500	5	
1969	162	93	69	.574	1	
1970	162	76	86	.469	5	
1971	162	82	80	.506	3	
1972	104	47	57	.452	5	4
8 yrs.	955	466	488	.488		

LEAGUE CHAMPIONSHIP SERIES

	G	W	L	PCT	
1969 **ATL N**	3	0	3	.000	

Jim Hart

HART, JAMES ARISTOTLE
B. July 10, 1855, Fairview, Pa.
D. July 18, 1919, Chicago, Ill.

	G	W	L	PCT	Standing	
1885 **LOU AA**	112	53	59	.473	5	
1886	138	66	70	.485	4	
1889 **BOS N**	133	83	45	.648	2	
3 yrs.	383	202	174	.537		

Gabby Hartnett

HARTNETT, CHARLES LEO
B. Dec. 20, 1900, Woonsocket, R. I.
D. Dec. 20, 1972, Park Ridge, Ill.
Hall of Fame 1955.

	G	W	L	PCT	Standing	
1938 **CHI N**	73	44	27	.620	3	1
1939	156	84	70	.545	4	
1940	154	75	79	.487	5	
3 yrs.	383	203	176	.536		

WORLD SERIES

	G	W	L	PCT	
1938 **CHI N**	4	0	4	.000	

| | G | W | L | PCT | Standing | | | | G | W | L | PCT | Standing | |

Roy Hartsfield

HARTSFIELD, ROY THOMAS
B. Oct. 25, 1925, Chattahoochee, Ga.

		G	W	L	PCT	Standing
1977	TOR A	161	54	107	.335	7
1978		161	59	102	.366	7
1979		162	53	109	.327	7
3 yrs.		484	166	318	.343	

Grady Hatton

HATTON, GRADY EDGEBERT
B. Oct. 7, 1922, Beaumont, Tex.

		G	W	L	PCT	Standing	
1966	HOU N	163	72	90	.444	8	
1967		162	69	93	.426	9	
1968		61	23	38	.377	10	10
3 yrs.		386	164	221	.426		

Guy Hecker

HECKER, GUY JACKSON (Blond Guy)
B. Apr. 3, 1856, Youngville, Pa.
D. Dec. 3, 1938, Wooster, Ohio

		G	W	L	PCT	Standing
1890	PIT N	138	23	113	.169	8

Don Heffner

HEFFNER, DONALD HENRY (Jeep)
B. Feb. 8, 1911, Rouzerville, Pa.

		G	W	L	PCT	Standing	
1966	CIN N	83	37	46	.446	8	7

Louie Heilbroner

HEILBRONER, LOUIS WILBUR
B. July 4, 1861, Ft. Wayne, Ind.
D. Dec. 21, 1933, Ft. Wayne, Ind.

		G	W	L	PCT	Standing	
1900	STL N	38	17	20	.459	7	5

Solly Hemus

HEMUS, SOLOMON JOSEPH
B. Apr. 17, 1923, Phoenix, Ariz.

		G	W	L	PCT	Standing	
1959	STL N	154	71	83	.461	7	
1960		155	86	68	.558	3	
1961		75	33	41	.446	6	5
3 yrs.		384	190	192	.497		

Bill Henderson

HENDERSON, WILLIAM C.
D. Oct. 6, 1966

		G	W	L	PCT	Standing	
1884	BAL U	17	5	12	.294	4	4

Jack Hendricks

HENDRICKS, JOHN CHARLES
B. Apr. 9, 1875, Joliet, Ill.
D. May 13, 1943, Chicago, Ill.

		G	W	L	PCT	Standing
1918	STL N	131	51	78	.395	8
1924	CIN N	153	83	70	.542	4
1925		153	80	· 73	.523	3
1926		157	87	67	.565	2
1927		153	75	78	.490	5
1928		153	78	74	.513	5
1929		155	66	88	.429	7
7 yrs.		1055	520	528	.496	

Ed Hengle

HENGLE, EDWARD S.
B. Chicago, Ill.
Deceased.

		G	W	L	PCT	Standing	
1884	C-P U	74	34	39	.466	6	6

Billy Herman

HERMAN, WILLIAM JENNINGS (Bryan)
B. July 7, 1909, New Albany, Ind.
Hall of Fame 1975.

		G	W	L	PCT	Standing	
1947	PIT N	155	61	92	.399	8	7
1964	BOS A	2	2	0	1.000	8	8
1965		162	62	100	.383	9	
1966		146	64	82	.438	10	9
4 yrs.		465	189	274	.408		

Buck Herzog

HERZOG, CHARLES LINCOLN
B. July 9, 1885, Baltimore, Md.
D. Sept. 4, 1953, Baltimore, Md.

		G	W	L	PCT	Standing	
1914	CIN N	157	60	94	.390	8	
1915		160	71	83	.461	7	
1916		83	34	49	.410	8	7
3 yrs.		400	165	226	.422		

Whitey Herzog

HERZOG, DORREL NORMAN ELVERT
B. Nov. 9, 1931, New Athens, Ill.

		G	W	L	PCT	Standing		
1973	TEX A	138	47	91	.341	6	6	
1975	KC A	66	41	25	.621	2	2	
1976		162	90	72	.556	1		
1977		162	102	60	.630	1		
1978		162	92	70	.568	1		
1979		162	85	77	.525	2		
1980	STL N	73	38	35	.521	6	5	4
1981		51	30	20	.600	2		(1st)
1981		52	29	23	.558	2		(2nd)
1982		162	92	70	.568	1		
1983		162	79	83	.488	4		
1984		162	84	78	.519	3		
11 yrs.		1514	809	704	.535			

LEAGUE CHAMPIONSHIP SERIES							
1976	KC A	5	2	3	.400		
1977		5	2	3	.400		
1978		4	1	3	.250		
1982	STL N	3	3	0	1.000		
4 yrs.		17	8	9	.471		
		5th	5th	3rd	5th		

WORLD SERIES						
1982	STL N	7	4	3	.571	

Walter Hewett

HEWETT, WALTER F.
B. 1861, Washington, D. C.
D. Oct. 7, 1944, Washington, D. C.

		G	W	L	PCT	Standing	
1888	WAS N	42	12	29	.293	8	8

Pinky Higgins

HIGGINS, MICHAEL FRANKLIN
B. May 27, 1909, Red Oak, Tex.
D. Mar. 21, 1969, Dallas, Tex.

		G	W	L	PCT	Standing	
1955	BOS A	154	84	70	.545	4	
1956		155	84	70	.545	4	
1957		154	82	72	.532	3	
1958		155	79	75	.513	3	
1959		73	31	42	.425	8	5
1960		73	31	42	.425	8	7
1961		163	76	86	.469	6	
1962		160	76	84	.475	8	
8 yrs.		1087	543	541	.501		

Ben Hilt

HILT, BENJAMIN FRANKLIN
B. Philadelphia, Pa.
Deceased.

		G	W	L	PCT	Standing	
1890	PHI P	36	17	19	.472	5	5

	G	W	L	PCT	Standing				G	W	L	PCT	Standing

Vedie Himsl

HIMSL, AVITUS BERNARD
B. Apr. 2, 1917, Plevna, Mont.

		G	W	L	PCT	Standing	
1961	CHI N	32	10	21	.323	7	7

Billy Hitchcock

HITCHCOCK, WILLIAM CLYDE
Brother of Jim Hitchcock.
B. July 31, 1916, Inverness, Ala.

		G	W	L	PCT	Standing		
1960	DET A	1	1	0	1.000	6	6	6
1962	BAL A	162	77	85	.475	7		
1963		162	86	76	.531	4		
1966	ATL N	51	33	18	.647	5	5	
1967		159	77	82	.484	7	7	
5 yrs.		535	274	261	.512			

Gil Hodges

HODGES, GILBERT RAYMOND
B. Apr. 4, 1924, Princeton, Ind.
D. Apr. 2, 1972, West Palm Beach, Fla.

		G	W	L	PCT	Standing	
1963	WAS A	122	42	80	.344	10	10
1964		162	62	100	.383	9	
1965		162	70	92	.432	8	
1966		159	71	88	.447	8	
1967		161	76	85	.472	6	
1968	NY N	163	73	89	.451	9	
1969		162	100	62	.617	1	
1970		162	83	79	.512	3	
1971		162	83	79	.512	3	
9 yrs.		1415	660	754	.467		

LEAGUE CHAMPIONSHIP SERIES

		G	W	L	PCT	
1969	NY N	3	3	0	1.000	

WORLD SERIES

		G	W	L	PCT	
1969	NY N	5	4	1	.800	

Fred Hoey

HOEY, FREDERICK C.
B. New York, N. Y.
D. Dec. 7, 1933, Paris, France

		G	W	L	PCT	Standing	
1899	NY N	81	30	50	.375	9	10

Holly Hollingshead

HOLLINGSHEAD, JOHN SAMUEL
B. Jan. 17, 1853, Washington, D. C.
D. Oct. 6, 1926, Washington, D. C.

		G	W	L	PCT	Standing
1884	WAS AA	63	12	51	.190	13

Tommy Holmes

HOLMES, THOMAS FRANCIS (Kelly)
B. Mar. 29, 1917, Brooklyn, N. Y.

		G	W	L	PCT	Standing	
1951	BOS N	95	48	47	.505	5	4
1952		35	13	22	.371	6	7
2 yrs.		130	61	69	.469		

Rogers Hornsby

HORNSBY, ROGERS (Rajah)
B. Apr. 27, 1896, Winters, Tex.
D. Jan. 5, 1963, Chicago, Ill.
Hall of Fame 1942.

		G	W	L	PCT	Standing	
1925	STL N	115	64	51	.557	8	4
1926		156	89	65	.578	1	
1928	BOS N	122	39	83	.320	7	7
1930	CHI N	4	4	0	1.000	2	2
1931		156	84	70	.545	3	
1932		97	53	44	.546	2	1
1933	STL A	56	20	34	.370	8	8
1934		154	67	85	.441	6	
1935		155	65	87	.428	7	
1936		155	57	95	.375	7	
1937		76	25	50	.333	8	8
1952		50	22	28	.440	7	7

Rogers Hornsby continued

		G	W	L	PCT	Standing	
1952	CIN N	51	27	24	.529	7	6
1953		147	64	82	.438	6	6
13 yrs.		1494	680	798	.460		

WORLD SERIES

		G	W	L	PCT	
1926	STL N	7	4	3	.571	

Ralph Houk

HOUK, RALPH GEORGE (Major)
B. Aug. 9, 1919, Lawrence, Kans.

		G	W	L	PCT	Standing	
1961	NY A	163	109	53	.673	1	
1962		162	96	66	.593	1	
1963		161	104	57	.646	1	
1966		140	66	73	.475	10	10
1967		163	72	90	.444	9	
1968		164	83	79	.512	5	
1969		162	80	81	.497	5	
1970		162	93	69	.574	2	
1971		162	82	80	.506	4	
1972		155	79	76	.510	4	
1973		162	80	82	.494	4	
1974	DET A	162	72	90	.444	6	
1975		159	57	102	.358	6	
1976		161	74	87	.460	5	
1977		162	74	88	.457	4	
1978		162	86	76	.531	5	
1981	BOS A	56	30	26	.536	5	(1st)
1981		52	29	23	.558	2	(2nd)
1982		162	89	73	.549	3	
1983		162	78	84	.481	6	
1984		162	86	76	.531	4	
20 yrs.		3156	1619	1531	.514		
		10th	10th	10th			

WORLD SERIES

		G	W	L	PCT	Standing	
1961	NY A	5	4	1	.800		
1962		7	4	3	.571		
1963		4	0	4	.000		
3 yrs.		16	8	8	.500		
						8th	

Frank Howard

HOWARD, FRANK OLIVER (The Capital Punisher, Hondo)
B. Aug. 8, 1936, Columbus, Ohio

		G	W	L	PCT	Standing	
1981	SD N	56	23	33	.411	6	(1st)
1981		54	18	36	.333	6	(2nd)
1983	NY N	116	52	64	.448	6	6
2 yrs.		226	93	133	.412		

Dan Howley

HOWLEY, DANIEL PHILIP (Dapper Dan)
B. Oct. 16, 1885, E. Weymouth, Mass.
D. Mar. 10, 1944, E. Weymouth, Mass.

		G	W	L	PCT	Standing
1927	STL A	155	59	94	.386	7
1928		154	82	72	.532	3
1929		154	79	73	.520	4
1930	CIN N	154	59	95	.383	7
1931		154	58	96	.377	8
1932		155	60	94	.390	8
6 yrs.		926	397	524	.431	

Dick Howser

HOWSER, RICHARD DALTON
B. May 14, 1937, Miami, Fla.

		G	W	L	PCT	Standing		
1978	NY A	1	0	1	.000	3	3	1
1980		162	103	59	.636	1		
1981	KC A	33	20	13	.606	2	1	(2nd)
1982		162	90	72	.556	2		
1983		163	79	83	.488	2		
1984		162	84	78	.519	1		
6 yrs.		683	376	306	.551			

DIVISIONAL PLAYOFF SERIES

		G	W	L	PCT	
1981	KC A	3	0	3	.000	

LEAGUE CHAMPIONSHIP SERIES

		G	W	L	PCT	
1980	NY A	3	0	3	.000	

	G	W	L	PCT	Standing		

Dick Howser continued

		G	W	L	PCT	Standing
1984 KC	A	3	0	3	.000	
2 yrs.		6	0	6	.000	

George Huff

HUFF, GEORGE A.
B. June 11, 1872, Champaign, Ill.
D. Oct. 1, 1936, Champaign, Ill.

		G	W	L	PCT	Standing		
1907 BOS	A	8	3	5	.375	5	6	7

Miller Huggins

HUGGINS, MILLER JAMES (Hug, The Mighty Mite)
B. Mar. 27, 1879, Cincinnati, Ohio
D. Sept. 25, 1929, New York, N. Y.
Hall of Fame 1964.

		G	W	L	PCT	Standing	
1913 STL	N	152	51	99	.340	8	
1914		157	81	72	.529	3	
1915		157	72	81	.471	6	
1916		153	60	93	.392	7	
1917		154	82	70	.539	3	
1918 NY	A	126	60	63	.488	4	
1919		141	80	59	.576	3	
1920		154	95	59	.617	3	
1921		153	98	55	.641	1	
1922		154	94	60	.610	1	
1923		152	98	54	.645	1	
1924		153	89	63	.586	2	
1925		156	69	85	.448	7	
1926		155	91	63	.591	1	
1927		155	110	44	.714	1	
1928		154	101	53	.656	1	
1929		143	82	61	.573	2	2
17 yrs.		2569	1413	1134	.555		

WORLD SERIES

		G	W	L	PCT
1921 NY	A	8	3	5	.375
1922		5	0	4	.000
1923		6	4	2	.667
1926		7	3	4	.429
1927		4	4	0	1.000
1928		4	4	0	1.000
6 yrs.		34	18	15	.545
		6th	6th	5th	6th

George Hughson

HUGHSON, GEORGE H.
B. Aug. 1, 1834, Erie County, N. Y.
D. Apr. 22, 1912

		G	W	L	PCT	Standing		
1885 BUF	N	51	18	33	.353	6	7	7

Billy Hunter

HUNTER, GORDON WILLIAM
B. June 4, 1928, Punxsutawney, Pa.

		G	W	L	PCT	Standing	
1977 TEX	A	93	60	33	.645	4	2
1978		162	87	75	.537	2	
2 yrs.		255	147	108	.576		

Tim Hurst

HURST, TIMOTHY CARROLL
B. June 30, 1865, Ashland, Pa.
D. June 4, 1915, Pottsville, Pa.

		G	W	L	PCT	Standing
1898 STL	N	154	39	111	.260	12

Fred Hutchinson

HUTCHINSON, FREDERICK CHARLES
B. Aug. 12, 1919, Seattle, Wash.
D. Nov. 12, 1964, Bradenton, Fla.

		G	W	L	PCT	Standing	
1952 DET	A	83	27	55	.329	8	8
1953		158	60	94	.390	6	
1954		155	68	86	.442	5	
1956 STL	N	156	76	78	.494	4	

Fred Hutchinson continued

		G	W	L	PCT	Standing	
1957		154	87	67	.565	2	
1958		144	69	75	.479	5	5
1959 CIN	N	74	39	35	.527	7	5
1960		154	67	87	.435	6	
1961		154	93	61	.604	1	
1962		162	98	64	.605	3	
1963		162	86	76	.531	5	
1964		110	60	49	.550	3	2
12 yrs.		1666	830	827	.501		

WORLD SERIES

		G	W	L	PCT
1961 CIN	N	5	1	4	.200

Arthur Irwin

IRWIN, ARTHUR ALBERT
Brother of John Irwin.
B. Feb. 14, 1858, Toronto, Ont., Canada
D. July 16, 1921, Atlantic Ocean

		G	W	L	PCT	Standing		
1889 WAS	N	73	28	44	.389	8	8	
1891 BOS	AA	139	93	42	.689	1		
1892 WAS	N	82	34	46	.425	9	12	10
1894 PHI	N	129	71	57	.555	4		
1895		133	78	53	.595	3		
1896 NY	N	93	38	53	.418	9	7	
1898 WAS	N	25	9	15	.375	11	11	
1899		155	54	98	.355	11		
8 yrs.		829	405	408	.498			

Hughie Jennings

JENNINGS, HUGH AMBROSE (Ee-Yah)
B. Apr. 2, 1869, Pittston, Pa.
D. Feb. 1, 1928, Scranton, Pa.
Hall of Fame 1945.

		G	W	L	PCT	Standing
1907 DET	A	153	92	58	.613	1
1908		153	90	63	.588	1
1909		158	98	54	.645	1
1910		155	86	68	.558	3
1911		154	89	65	.578	2
1912		154	69	84	.451	6
1913		153	66	87	.431	6
1914		157	80	73	.523	4
1915		156	100	54	.649	2
1916		155	87	67	.565	3
1917		154	78	75	.510	4
1918		128	55	71	.437	7
1919		140	80	60	.571	4
1920		155	61	93	.396	7
14 yrs.		2125	1131	972	.538	

WORLD SERIES

		G	W	L	PCT
1907 DET	A	4	0	4	.000
1908		5	1	4	.200
1909		7	3	4	.429
3 yrs.		16	4	12	.250
				10th	

Darrell Johnson

JOHNSON, DARRELL DEAN
B. Aug. 25, 1928, Horace, Neb.

		G	W	L	PCT	Standing	
1974 BOS	A	162	84	78	.519	3	
1975		160	95	65	.594	1	
1976		86	41	45	.477	3	3
1977 SEA	A	162	64	98	.395	6	
1978		160	56	104	.350	7	
1979		162	67	95	.414	6	
1980		105	39	65	.375	7	7
1982 TEX	A	66	26	40	.394	6	6
8 yrs.		1063	472	590	.444		

LEAGUE CHAMPIONSHIP SERIES

		G	W	L	PCT
1975 BOS	A	3	3	0	1.000

WORLD SERIES

		G	W	L	PCT
1975 BOS	A	7	3	4	.429

	G	W	L	PCT	Standing			G	W	L	PCT	Standing

Davy Johnson

JOHNSON, DAVID ALLEN
B. Jan. 30, 1943, Orlando, Fla.

	G	W	L	PCT	Standing
1984 NY N	162	90	72	.556	2

Roy Johnson

JOHNSON, ROY CLEVELAND
Brother of Bob Johnson.
B. Feb. 23, 1903, Pryor, Okla.
D. Sept. 11, 1973, Tacoma, Wash.

	G	W	L	PCT	Standing	
1944 CHI N	1	0	1	.000	8	8	4

Walter Johnson

JOHNSON, WALTER PERRY (The Big Train, Barney)
B. Nov. 6, 1887, Humboldt, Kans.
D. Dec. 10, 1946, Washington, D. C.
Hall of Fame 1936.

	G	W	L	PCT	Standing	
1929 WAS A	153	71	81	.467	5	
1930	154	94	60	.610	2	
1931	156	92	62	.597	3	
1932	154	93	61	.604	3	
1933 CLE A	100	49	51	.490	5	4
1934	154	85	69	.552	3	
1935	96	46	48	.489	5	3
7 yrs.	967	530	432	.551		

Fielder Jones

JONES, FIELDER ALLISON
B. Aug. 13, 1871, Shinglehouse, Pa.
D. Mar. 13, 1934, Portland, Ore.

	G	W	L	PCT	Standing	
1904 CHI A	115	67	47	.588	4	3
1905	157	92	60	.605	2	
1906	154	93	58	.616	1	
1907	157	87	64	.576	3	
1908	156	88	64	.579	3	
1914 STL F	40	12	26	.316	7	8
1915	159	87	67	.565	2	
1916 STL A	158	79	75	.513	5	
1917	155	57	97	.370	7	
1918	47	23	24	.489	5	5
10 yrs.	1298	685	582	.541		

WORLD SERIES

	G	W	L	PCT
1906 CHI A	6	4	2	.667

Eddie Joost

JOOST, EDWIN DAVID
B. June 5, 1916, San Francisco, Calif.

	G	W	L	PCT	Standing
1954 PHI A	156	51	103	.331	8

Bill Joyce

JOYCE, WILLIAM MICHAEL (Scrappy Bill)
B. Sept. 21, 1865, St. Louis, Mo.
D. May 8, 1941, St. Louis, Mo.

	G	W	L	PCT	Standing	
1896 NY N	40	26	14	.650	9	7
1897	137	83	48	.634	3	
1898	45	23	21	.523	6	7
1898	90	45	39	.536	7	7
3 yrs.	312	177	122	.592		

Bill Jurges

JURGES, WILLIAM FREDERICK
B. May 9, 1908, Bronx, N. Y.

	G	W	L	PCT	Standing	
1959 BOS A	80	44	36	.550	8	5
1960	81	34	47	.420	8	7
2 yrs.	161	78	83	.484		

Eddie Kasko

KASKO, EDWARD MICHAEL
B. June 27, 1932, Linden, N. J.

	G	W	L	PCT	Standing
1970 BOS A	162	87	75	.537	3
1971	162	85	77	.525	3
1972	155	85	70	.548	2
1973	162	89	73	.549	2
4 yrs.	641	346	295	.540	

Johnny Keane

KEANE, JOHN JOSEPH
B. Nov. 3, 1911, St. Louis, Mo.
D. Jan. 6, 1967, Houston, Tex.

	G	W	L	PCT	Standing	
1961 STL N	80	47	33	.588	6	5
1962	163	84	78	.519	6	
1963	162	93	69	.574	2	
1964	162	93	69	.574	1	
1965 NY A	162	77	85	.475	6	
1966	20	4	16	.200	10	10
6 yrs.	749	398	350	.532		

WORLD SERIES

	G	W	L	PCT
1964 STL N	7	4	3	.571

Joe Kelley

KELLEY, JOSEPH JAMES
B. Dec. 9, 1871, Cambridge, Mass.
D. Aug. 14, 1943, Baltimore, Md.
Hall of Fame 1971.

	G	W	L	PCT	Standing	
1902 CIN N	59	33	26	.559	5	4
1903	141	74	65	.532	4	
1904	157	88	65	.575	3	
1905	155	79	74	.516	5	
1908 BOS N	156	63	91	.409	6	
5 yrs.	668	337	321	.512		

John Kelly

KELLY, JOHN O. (Honest John)
B. 1856, New York, N. Y.
D. Mar. 27, 1926, Malba, N. Y.

	G	W	L	PCT	Standing
1887 LOU AA	139	76	60	.559	4

King Kelly

KELLY, MICHAEL JOSEPH
B. Dec. 31, 1857, Troy, N. Y.
D. Nov. 8, 1894, Boston, Mass.
Hall of Fame 1945.

	G	W	L	PCT	Standing	
1890 BOS P	130	81	48	.628	1	
1891 C-M AA	102	43	57	.430	7	5
2 yrs.	232	124	105	.541		

Bob Kennedy

KENNEDY, ROBERT DANIEL
Father of Terry Kennedy.
B. Aug. 18, 1920, Chicago, Ill.

	G	W	L	PCT	Standing	
1963 CHI N	162	82	80	.506	7	
1964	162	76	86	.469	8	
1965	58	24	32	.429	9	8
1968 OAK A	163	82	80	.506	6	
4 yrs.	545	264	278	.487		

Jim Kennedy

KENNEDY, JAMES C.
B. 1867, New York, N. Y.
D. Apr. 20, 1904, Brighton Beach, N. Y.

	G	W	L	PCT	Standing	
1890 B-B AA	100	26	73	.263	8	8

G	W	L	PCT	Standing		G	W	L	PCT	Standing

John Kerins

KERINS, JOHN NELSON
B. Dec. 22, 1858, Indianapolis, Ind.
D. Sept. 15, 1919, Louisville, Ky.

		G	W	L	PCT	Standing	
1888	LOU AA	43	11	32	.256	8	7

Don Kessinger

KESSINGER, DONALD EULON
B. July 17, 1942, Forrest City, Ark.

		G	W	L	PCT	Standing	
1979	CHI A	106	46	60	.434	5	5

Bill Killefer

KILLEFER, WILLIAM LAVIER (Reindeer Bill)
Brother of Red Killefer.
B. Oct. 10, 1887, Bloomingdale, Mich.
D. July 2, 1960, Elsmere, Del.

		G	W	L	PCT	Standing	
1921	CHI N	55	22	33	.400	7	7
1922		156	80	74	.519	5	
1923		154	83	71	.539	4	
1924		154	81	72	.529	5	
1925		75	33	42	.440	7	8
1930	STL A	154	64	90	.416	6	
1931		154	63	91	.409	5	
1932		154	63	91	.409	6	
1933		93	34	59	.366	8	8
9 yrs.		1149	523	623	.456		

Clyde King

KING, CLYDE EDWARD
B. May 23, 1925, Goldsboro, N. C.

		G	W	L	PCT	Standing	
1969	SF N	162	90	72	.556	2	
1970		44	19	25	.432	5	3
1974	ATL N	63	38	25	.603	4	3
1975		135	59	76	.437	5	5
1982	NY A	62	29	33	.468	5	5
5 yrs.		466	235	231	.504		

Malachi Kittredge

KITTREDGE, MALACHI J.
B. Oct. 12, 1869, Clinton, Mass.
D. June 23, 1928, Gary, Ind.

		G	W	L	PCT	Standing	
1904	WAS A	18	1	16	.059	8	8

Lou Klein

KLEIN, LOUIS FRANK
B. Oct. 22, 1918, New Orleans, La.
D. June 20, 1976, Metairie, La.

		G	W	L	PCT	Standing		
1961	CHI N	12	5	7	.417	7	7	
1962		30	12	18	.400	9	9	9
1965		106	48	58	.453	9	8	
3 yrs.		148	65	83	.439			

Johnny Kling

KLING, JOHN (Noisy)
Brother of Bill Kling.
B. Feb. 25, 1875, Kansas City, Mo.
D. Jan. 31, 1947, Kansas City, Mo.

		G	W	L	PCT	Standing
1912	BOS N	153	52	101	.340	8

Otto Knabe

KNABE, FRANZ OTTO (Dutch)
B. June 12, 1884, Carrick, Pa.
D. May 17, 1961, Philadelphia, Pa.

		G	W	L	PCT	Standing
1914	BAL F	160	84	70	.545	3
1915		154	47	107	.305	8
2 yrs.		314	131	177	.425	

Lon Knight

KNIGHT, ALONZO P.
B. June 16, 1853, Philadelphia, Pa.
D. Apr. 23, 1932, Philadelphia, Pa.

		G	W	L	PCT	Standing	
1885	PHI AA	35	16	19	.457	3	4

Jack Krol

KROL, JOHN THOMAS
B. July 5, 1936, Chicago, Ill.

		G	W	L	PCT	Standing		
1978	STL N	3	2	1	.667	6	5	5
1980		1	0	1	.000	6	6	4
2 yrs.		4	2	2	.500			

Karl Kuehl

KUEHL, KARL OTTO
B. Sept. 5, 1937, Monterey Park, Calif.

		G	W	L	PCT	Standing	
1976	MON N	128	43	85	.336	6	6

Harvey Kuenn

KUENN, HARVEY EDWARD
B. Dec. 4, 1930, Milwaukee, Wis.

		G	W	L	PCT	Standing		
1975	MIL A	1	1	0	1.000	5	5	
1982		115	72	43	.626	5	1	
1983		162	87	75	.537	5		
3 yrs.		278	160	118	.576			

LEAGUE CHAMPIONSHIP SERIES

		G	W	L	PCT
1982	MIL A	5	3	2	.600

WORLD SERIES

		G	W	L	PCT
1982	MIL A	7	3	4	.429

Joe Kuhel

KUHEL, JOSEPH ANTHONY
B. June 25, 1906, Kansas City, Kans.
D. Feb. 26, 1984, Kansas City, Mo.

		G	W	L	PCT	Standing
1948	WAS A	154	56	97	.366	7
1949		154	50	104	.325	8
2 yrs.		308	106	201	.345	

Rene Lachemann

LACHEMANN, RENE GEORGE
Brother of Marcel Lachemann.
B. May 4, 1945, Los Angeles, Calif.

		G	W	L	PCT	Standing		
1981	SEA A	33	15	18	.455	7	6	(1st)
1981		52	23	29	.442	5		(2nd)
1982		162	76	86	.469	4		
1983		73	26	47	.356	7	7	
1984	MIL A	161	67	94	.416	7		
4 yrs.		481	207	274	.430			

Nap Lajoie

LAJOIE, NAPOLEON (Larry)
B. Sept. 5, 1875, Woonsocket, R. I.
D. Feb. 7, 1959, Daytona Beach, Fla.
Hall of Fame 1937.

		G	W	L	PCT	Standing	
1905	CLE A	154	76	78	.494	5	
1906		157	89	64	.582	3	
1907		158	85	67	.559	4	
1908		157	90	64	.584	2	
1909		114	57	57	.500	6	6
5 yrs.		740	397	330	.546		

Fred Lake

LAKE, FREDERICK LOVETT
B. Oct. 16, 1866, Nova Scotia, Canada
D. Nov. 24, 1931, Boston, Mass.

		G	W	L	PCT	Standing	
1908	BOS A	40	22	17	.564	6	5
1909		152	88	63	.583	3	
1910	BOS N	157	53	100	.346	8	
3 yrs.		349	163	180	.475		

	G	W	L	PCT	Standing					G	W	L	PCT	Standing	

Henry Larkin

LARKIN, HENRY E. (Ted)
B. Jan. 12, 1860, Reading, Pa.
D. Jan. 31, 1942, Reading, Pa.

		G	W	L	PCT			
1890	CLE P	60	27	33	.450	7	**7**	7

Tony LaRussa

LaRUSSA, ANTHONY
B. Oct. 4, 1944, Tampa, Fla.

		G	W	L	PCT			
1979	CHI A	54	27	27	.500	5	**5**	
1980		162	70	90	.438	5		
1981		53	31	22	.585	3		(1st)
1981		53	23	30	.434	6		(2nd)
1982		162	87	75	.537	3		
1983		162	99	63	.611	1		
1984		162	74	88	.457	5		
6 yrs.		808	411	395	.510			

LEAGUE CHAMPIONSHIP SERIES

		G	W	L	PCT
1983	CHI A	4	1	3	.250

Tom Lasorda

LASORDA, THOMAS CHARLES
B. Sept. 22, 1927, Norristown, Pa.

		G	W	L	PCT			
1976	LA N	4	2	2	.500	2	**2**	
1977		162	98	64	.605	1		
1978		162	95	67	.586	1		
1979		162	79	83	.488	3		
1980		163	92	71	.564	2		
1981		57	36	21	.632	1		(1st)
1981		53	27	26	.509	4		(2nd)
1982		162	88	74	.543	2		
1983		162	91	71	.562	1		
1984		162	79	83	.488	4		
9 yrs.		1249	687	562	.550			

DIVISIONAL PLAYOFF SERIES

		G	W	L	PCT
1981	LA N	5	3	2	.600

LEAGUE CHAMPIONSHIP SERIES

		G	W	L	PCT
1977	LA N	4	3	1	.750
1978		4	3	1	.750
1981		5	3	2	.600
1983		4	1	3	.250
4 yrs.		17	10	7	.588
		5th	**3rd**	**6th**	**3rd**

WORLD SERIES

		G	W	L	PCT
1977	LA N	6	2	4	.333
1978		6	2	4	.333
1981		6	4	2	.667
3 yrs.		18	8	10	.444

Arlie Latham

LATHAM, WALTER ARLINGTON (The Freshest Man on Earth)
B. Mar. 15, 1859, W. Lebanon, N. H.
D. Nov. 29, 1952, Garden City, N. Y.

		G	W	L	PCT			
1896	STL N	2	0	2	.000	10	**10**	11

Cookie Lavagetto

LAVAGETTO, HARRY ARTHUR
B. Dec. 1, 1912, Oakland, Calif.

		G	W	L	PCT			
1957	WAS A	133	50	83	.376	8	**8**	
1958		156	61	93	.396	8		
1959		154	63	91	.409	8		
1960		154	73	81	.474	5		
1961	MIN A	74	29	45	.392	9		7
5 yrs.		671	276	393	.413			

Bob Leadley

LEADLEY, ROBERT H.
B. 1851, Detroit, Mich.
Deceased.

		G	W	L	PCT			
1888	DET N	38	19	18	.514	3	**5**	
1890	CLE N	58	23	33	.411	7		7
1891		65	31	34	.477	6		5
3 yrs.		161	73	85	.462			

Bob Lemon

LEMON, ROBERT GRANVILLE
B. Sept. 22, 1920, San Bernardino, Calif.
Hall of Fame 1976.

		G	W	L	PCT			
1970	KC A	108	46	62	.426	6	**4**	
1971		161	85	76	.528	2		
1972		154	76	78	.494	4		
1977	CHI A	162	90	72	.556	3		
1978		74	34	40	.459	5		5
1978	NY A	68	48	20	.706	3		1
1979		64	34	30	.531	4		4
1981		28	13	15	.464	5		6	(2nd)
1982		14	6	8	.429	4		5
8 yrs.		833	432	401	.519			

DIVISIONAL PLAYOFF SERIES

		G	W	L	PCT
1981	NY A	5	3	2	.600

LEAGUE CHAMPIONSHIP SERIES

		G	W	L	PCT
1978	NY A	4	3	1	.750
1981		3	3	0	1.000
2 yrs.		7	6	1	.857

WORLD SERIES

		G	W	L	PCT
1978	NY A	6	4	2	.667
1981		6	2	4	.333
2 yrs.		12	6	6	.500

Jim Lemon

LEMON, JAMES ROBERT
B. Mar. 23, 1928, Covington, Va.

		G	W	L	PCT		
1968	WAS A	161	65	96	.404	10	

Charlie Levis

LEVIS, CHARLES H.
B. June 21, 1860, St. Louis, Mo.
D. Oct. 16, 1926, St. Louis, Mo.

		G	W	L	PCT			
1884	BAL U	89	53	35	.602	4	**4**	

Bob Lillis

LILLIS, ROBERT PERRY (Flea)
B. June 2, 1930, Altadena, Calif.

		G	W	L	PCT			
1982	HOU N	51	28	23	.549	5	**5**	
1983		162	85	77	.525	3		
1984		162	80	82	.494	2		
3 yrs.		375	193	182	.515			

Johnny Lipon

LIPON, JOHN JOSEPH (Skids)
B. Nov. 10, 1922, Martin's Ferry, Ohio

		G	W	L	PCT			
1971	CLE A	59	18	41	.305	6	**6**	

Hans Lobert

LOBERT, JOHN BERNARD (Honus)
Brother of Frank Lobert.
B. Oct. 18, 1881, Wilmington, Del.
D. Sept. 14, 1968, Philadelphia, Pa.

		G	W	L	PCT			
1938	PHI N	2	0	2	.000	8	**8**	
1942		151	42	109	.278	8		
2 yrs.		153	42	111	.275			

Whitey Lockman

LOCKMAN, CARROLL WALTER
B. July 25, 1926, Lowell, N. C.

		G	W	L	PCT			
1972	CHI N	65	39	26	.600	4	**2**	
1973		161	77	84	.478	5		
1974		93	41	52	.441	5		6
3 yrs.		319	157	162	.492			

	G	W	L	PCT	Standing			G	W	L	PCT	Standing

Tom Loftus

LOFTUS, THOMAS JOSEPH
B. Nov. 15, 1856, Jefferson City, Mo.
D. Apr. 16, 1910, Concord, Mass.

		G	W	L	PCT	Standing	
1884	MIL U	12	8	4	.667	2	
1888	CLE AA	74	31	41	.431	7	6
1889	CLE N	136	61	72	.459	6	
1890	CIN N	134	77	55	.583	4	
1891		138	56	81	.409	7	
1900	CHI N	146	65	75	.464	5	
1901		140	53	86	.381	6	
1902	WAS A	138	61	75	.449	6	
1903		140	43	94	.314	8	
9 yrs.		1058	455	583	.438		

Ed Lopat

LOPAT, EDMUND WALTER (Steady Eddie)
Born Edmund Walter Lopatynski.
B. June 21, 1918, New York, N. Y.

		G	W	L	PCT	Standing	
1963	KC A	162	73	89	.451	8	
1964		52	17	35	.327	10	10
2 yrs.		214	90	124	.421		

Al Lopez

LOPEZ, ALFONSO RAYMOND
B. Aug. 20, 1908, Tampa, Fla.
Hall of Fame 1977.

		G	W	L	PCT	Standing	
1951	CLE A	155	93	61	.604	2	
1952		155	93	61	.604	2	
1953		155	92	62	.597	2	
1954		156	111	43	.721	1	
1955		154	93	61	.604	2	
1956		155	88	66	.571	2	
1957	CHI A	155	90	64	.584	2	
1958		155	82	72	.532	2	
1959		156	94	60	.610	1	
1960		154	87	67	.565	3	
1961		163	86	76	.531	4	
1962		162	85	77	.525	5	
1963		162	94	68	.580	2	
1964		162	98	64	.605	2	
1965		162	95	67	.586	2	
1968		81	33	48	.407	9	9
1969		17	8	9	.471	4	5
17 yrs.		2459	1422	1026	.581		
						9th	

		G	W	L	PCT	Standing	
WORLD SERIES							
1954	CLE A	4	0	4	.000		
1959	CHI A	6	2	4	.333		
2 yrs.		10	2	8	.200		

Harry Lord

LORD, HARRY DONALD
B. Mar. 8, 1882, Porter, Me.
D. Aug. 9, 1948, Westbrook, Me.

		G	W	L	PCT	Standing	
1915	BUF F	108	59	48	.551	8	6

Bobby Lowe

LOWE, ROBERT LINCOLN (Link)
B. July 10, 1868, Pittsburgh, Pa.
D. Dec. 8, 1951, Detroit, Mich.

		G	W	L	PCT	Standing	
1904	DET A	78	30	44	.405	7	7

Henry Lucas

LUCAS, HENRY V.
B. Sept. 5, 1857, St. Louis, Mo.
D. Nov. 15, 1910, St. Louis, Mo.

		G	W	L	PCT	Standing	
1884	STL U	114	94	19	.832	1	
1885	STL N	111	36	72	.333	8	
2 yrs.		225	130	91	.588		

John Lucas

LUCAS, JOHN R. C.
Deceased.

		G	W	L	PCT	Standing	
1877	STL N	26	14	12	.538	3	4

Frank Lucchesi

LUCCHESI, FRANK JOSEPH
B. Apr. 24, 1926, San Francisco, Calif.

		G	W	L	PCT	Standing	
1970	PHI N	161	73	88	.453	5	
1971		162	67	95	.414	6	
1972		76	26	50	.342	6	6
1975	TEX A	67	35	32	.522	4	3
1976		162	76	86	.469	5	
1977		62	31	31	.500	4	2
6 yrs.		690	308	382	.446		

Harry Lumley

LUMLEY, HARRY G
B. Sept. 29, 1880, Forest City, Pa.
D. May 22, 1938, Binghamton, N. Y.

		G	W	L	PCT	Standing	
1909	BKN N	155	55	98	.359	6	

Ted Lyons

LYONS, THEODORE AMAR
B. Dec. 28, 1900, Lake Charles, La.
Hall of Fame 1955.

		G	W	L	PCT	Standing	
1946	CHI A	125	64	60	.516	7	5
1947		155	70	84	.455	6	
1948		154	51	101	.336	8	
3 yrs.		434	185	245	.430		

Connie Mack

MACK, CORNELIUS (The Tall Tactician)
Born Cornelius McGillicuddy.
Father of Earle Mack.
B. Dec. 22, 1862, E. Brookfield, Mass.
D. Feb. 8, 1956, Philadelphia, Pa.
Hall of Fame 1937.

		G	W	L	PCT	Standing	
1894	PIT N	23	12	10	.545	7	7
1895		134	71	61	.538	7	
1896		131	66	63	.512	6	
1901	PHI A	137	74	62	.544	4	
1902		137	83	53	.610	1	
1903		137	75	60	.556	2	
1904		155	81	70	.536	5	
1905		152	92	56	.622	1	
1906		149	78	67	.538	4	
1907		150	88	57	.607	2	
1908		157	68	85	.444	6	
1909		153	95	58	.621	2	
1910		155	102	48	.680	1	
1911		152	101	50	.669	1	
1912		153	90	62	.592	3	
1913		153	96	57	.627	1	
1914		157	99	53	.651	1	
1915		154	43	109	.283	8	
1916		154	36	117	.235	8	
1917		154	55	98	.359	8	
1918		130	52	76	.406	8	
1919		140	36	104	.257	8	
1920		156	48	106	.312	8	
1921		155	53	100	.346	8	
1922		155	65	89	.422	7	
1923		153	69	83	.454	6	
1924		152	71	81	.467	5	
1925		153	88	64	.579	2	
1926		150	83	67	.553	3	
1927		155	91	63	.591	2	
1928		153	98	55	.641	2	
1929		151	104	46	.693	1	
1930		154	102	52	.662	1	
1931		153	107	45	.704	1	
1932		154	94	60	.610	2	

	G	W	L	PCT	Standing				G	W	L	PCT	Standing	

Connie Mack continued

Year		G	W	L	PCT	Standing
1933		152	79	72	.523	3
1934		153	68	82	.453	5
1935		149	58	91	.389	8
1936		154	53	100	.346	8
1937		154	54	97	.358	7
1938		154	53	99	.349	8
1939		153	55	97	.362	7
1940		154	54	100	.351	8
1941		154	64	90	.416	8
1942		154	55	99	.357	8
1943		155	49	105	.318	8
1944		155	72	82	.468	5
1945		153	52	98	.347	8
1946		155	49	105	.318	8
1947		156	78	76	.506	5
1948		154	84	70	.545	4
1949		154	81	73	.526	5
1950		154	52	102	.338	8
53 yrs.		7878	3776	4025	.484	
		1st	**1st**	**1st**		

WORLD SERIES

Year		G	W	L	PCT
1905	PHI A	5	1	4	.200
1910		5	4	1	.800
1911		6	4	2	.667
1913		5	4	1	.800
1914		4	0	4	.000
1929		5	4	1	.800
1930		6	4	2	.667
1931		7	3	4	.429
8 yrs.		43	24	19	.558
		3rd	**4th**	**4th**	**4th**

Lee Magee

MAGEE, LEO CHRISTOPHER
Born Leopold Christopher Hoernschemeyer.
B. June 4, 1889, Cincinnati, Ohio
D. Mar. 14, 1966, Columbus, Ohio

Year		G	W	L	PCT	Standing	
1915	BKN F	118	53	64	.453	7	7

Fergy Malone

MALONE, FERGUSON G.
B. 1842, Ireland
D. Jan. 18, 1905, Seattle, Wash.

Year		G	W	L	PCT	Standing	
1884	PHI U	41	11	30	.268	6	8

Jimmy Manning

MANNING, JAMES H.
B. Jan. 31, 1862, Fall River, Mass.
D. Oct. 22, 1929, Edinburg, Tex.

Year		G	W	L	PCT	Standing
1901	WAS A	138	61	73	.455	6

Rabbit Maranville

MARANVILLE, WALTER JAMES VINCENT
B. Nov. 11, 1891, Springfield, Mass.
D. Jan. 5, 1954, New York, N. Y.
Hall of Fame 1954.

Year		G	W	L	PCT	Standing		
1925	CHI N	53	23	30	.434	7	8	8

Marty Marion

MARION, MARTIN WHITFORD (Slats, The Octopus)
Brother of Red Marion.
B. Dec. 1, 1917, Richburg, S. C.

Year		G	W	L	PCT	Standing	
1951	STL N	156	81	73	.526	3	
1952	STL A	105	42	62	.404	7	7
1953		154	54	100	.351	8	
1954	CHI A	9	3	6	.333	3	3
1955		155	91	63	.591	3	
1956		154	85	69	.552	3	
6 yrs.		733	356	373	.488		

Jim Marshall

MARSHALL, RUFUS JAMES
B. May 25, 1932, Danville, Ill.

Year		G	W	L	PCT	Standing	
1974	CHI N	69	25	44	.362	5	6
1975		162	75	87	.463	5	
1976		162	75	87	.463	4	
1979	OAK A	162	54	108	.333	7	
4 yrs.		555	229	326	.413		

Billy Martin

MARTIN, ALFRED MANUEL
B. May 16, 1928, Berkeley, Calif.

Year		G	W	L	PCT	Standing		
1969	MIN A	162	97	65	.599	1		
1971	DET A	162	91	71	.562	2		
1972		156	86	70	.551	1		
1973		143	76	67	.531	3	3	
1973	TEX A	23	9	14	.391	6	6	6
1974		160	84	76	.525	2		
1975		95	44	51	.463	4	3	
1975	NY A	56	30	26	.536	3	3	
1976		159	97	62	.610	1		
1977		162	100	62	.617	1		
1978		94	52	42	.553	3	1	
1979		96	55	41	.573	4	4	
1980	OAK A	162	83	79	.512	2		
1981		60	37	23	.617	1		(1st)
1981		49	27	22	.551	2		(2nd)
1982		162	68	94	.420	5		
1983	NY A	162	91	71	.562	3		
14 yrs.		2063	1127	936	.546			

DIVISIONAL PLAYOFF SERIES

Year		G	W	L	PCT
1981	OAK A	3	3	0	1.000

LEAGUE CHAMPIONSHIP SERIES

Year		G	W	L	PCT	Standing		
1969	MIN A	3	0	3	.000			
1972	DET A	5	2	3	.400			
1976	NY A	5	3	2	.600			
1977		5	3	2	.600			
1981	OAK A	3	0	3	.000			
5 yrs.		21	8	13	.381			
		3rd	**5th**	**1st**	**7th**			

WORLD SERIES

Year		G	W	L	PCT
1976	NY A	4	0	4	.000
1977		6	4	2	.667
2 yrs.		10	4	6	.400

Leech Maskrey

MASKREY, SAMUEL LEECH
Brother of Harry Maskrey.
B. Feb. 16, 1856, Mercer, Pa.
D. Apr. 1, 1922, Mercer, Pa.

Year		G	W	L	PCT	Standing		
1882	LOU AA	25	12	13	.480	2	3	
1883		40	24	16	.600	5	4	5
2 yrs.		65	36	29	.554			

Charlie Mason

MASON, CHARLES E.
B. June 25, 1853, New Orleans, La.
D. Oct. 21, 1936, Philadelphia, Pa.

Year		G	W	L	PCT	Standing		
1882	PHI AA	36	21	15	.583	3	3	
1884		51	28	23	.549	7	7	
1885		39	17	21	.447	3	4	4
3 yrs.		126	66	59	.528			

Eddie Mathews

MATHEWS, EDWIN LEE
B. Oct. 13, 1931, Texarkana, Tex.
Hall of Fame 1978.

Year		G	W	L	PCT	Standing	
1972	ATL N	50	23	27	.460	5	4
1973		161	76	85	.472	5	
1974		99	50	49	.505	4	3
3 yrs.		310	149	161	.481		

	G	W	L	PCT	Standing				G	W	L	PCT	Standing

Christy Mathewson

MATHEWSON, CHRISTOPHER (Big Six)
Brother of Henry Mathewson.
B. Aug. 12, 1880, Factoryville, Pa.
D. Oct. 7, 1925, Saranac Lake, N. Y.
Hall of Fame 1936.

		G	W	L	PCT	Standing	
1916	CIN N	70	25	43	.368	8	7
1917		157	78	76	.506	4	
1918		119	61	57	.517	4	3
3 yrs.		346	164	176	.482		

Bobby Mattick

MATTICK, ROBERT JAMES
Son of Wally Mattick.
B. Dec. 5, 1915, Sioux City, Iowa

		G	W	L	PCT	Standing	
1980	TOR A	162	67	95	.414	7	
1981		58	16	42	.276	7	(1st)
1981		48	21	27	.438	7	(2nd)
2 yrs.		268	104	164	.388		

Gene Mauch

MAUCH, GENE WILLIAM (Skip)
B. Nov. 18, 1925, Salina, Kans.

		G	W	L	PCT	Standing	
1960	PHI N	152	58	94	.382	4	8
1961		155	47	107	.305	8	
1962		161	81	80	.503	7	
1963		162	87	75	.537	4	
1964		162	92	70	.568	2	
1965		162	85	76	.528	6	
1966		162	87	75	.537	4	
1967		162	82	80	.506	5	
1968		53	26	27	.491	4	8
1969	MON N	162	52	110	.321	6	
1970		162	73	89	.451	6	
1971		162	71	90	.441	5	
1972		156	70	86	.449	5	
1973		162	79	83	.488	4	
1974		161	79	82	.491	4	
1975		162	75	87	.463	5	
1976	MIN A	162	85	77	.525	3	
1977		161	84	77	.522	4	
1978		162	73	89	.451	4	
1979		162	82	80	.506	4	
1980		125	54	71	.432	6	3
1981	CAL A	13	9	4	.692	4	4	(1st)
1981		50	20	30	.400	7		(2nd)
1982		162	93	69	.574	1	
23 yrs.		3455	1644	1808	.476		
			9th	9th	5th		

LEAGUE CHAMPIONSHIP SERIES

		G	W	L	PCT		
1982	CAL A	5	2	3	.400		

Jimmy McAleer

McALEER, JAMES ROBERT
B. July 10, 1864, Youngstown, Ohio
D. Apr. 29, 1931, Youngstown, Ohio

		G	W	L	PCT	Standing
1901	CLE A	138	55	82	.401	7
1902	STL A	140	78	58	.574	2
1903		139	65	74	.468	6
1904		156	65	87	.428	6
1905		156	54	99	.353	8
1906		154	76	73	.510	5
1907		155	69	83	.454	6
1908		155	83	69	.546	4
1909		154	61	89	.407	7
1910	WAS A	157	66	85	.437	7
1911		154	64	90	.416	7
11 yrs.		1658	736	889	.453	

George McBride

McBRIDE, GEORGE FLORIAN
B. Nov. 20, 1880, Milwaukee, Wis.
D. July 2, 1973, Milwaukee, Wis.

		G	W	L	PCT	Standing
1921	WAS A	154	80	73	.523	4

Jack McCallister

McCALLISTER, JACK
B. Jan. 19, 1879, Marietta, Ohio
D. Oct. 18, 1946

		G	W	L	PCT	Standing
1927	CLE A	153	66	87	.431	6

Joe McCarthy

McCARTHY, JOSEPH VINCENT (Marse Joe)
B. Apr. 21, 1887, Philadelphia, Pa.
D. Jan. 3, 1978, Buffalo, N. Y.
Hall of Fame 1957.

		G	W	L	PCT	Standing	
1926	CHI N	155	82	72	.532	4	
1927		153	85	68	.556	4	
1928		154	91	63	.591	3	
1929		156	98	54	.645	1	
1930		152	86	64	.573	2	2
1931	NY A	155	94	59	.614	2	
1932		155	107	47	.695	1	
1933		152	91	59	.607	2	
1934		154	94	60	.610	2	
1935		149	89	60	.597	2	
1936		155	102	51	.667	1	
1937		157	102	52	.662	1	
1938		157	99	53	.651	1	
1939		152	106	45	.702	1	
1940		155	88	66	.571	3	
1941		156	101	53	.656	1	
1942		154	103	51	.669	1	
1943		155	98	56	.636	1	
1944		154	83	71	.539	3	
1945		152	81	71	.533	4	
1946		35	22	13	.629	2	3
1948	BOS A	155	96	59	.619	2	
1949		155	96	58	.623	2	
1950		62	32	30	.516	4	3
24 yrs.		3489	2126	1335	.614		
			8th	4th		1st	

WORLD SERIES		G	W	L	PCT	Standing	
1929	CHI N	5	1	4	.200		
1932	NY A	4	4	0	1.000		
1936		6	4	2	.667		
1937		5	4	1	.800		
1938		4	4	0	1.000		
1939		4	4	0	1.000		
1941		5	4	1	.800		
1942		5	1	4	.200		
1943		5	4	1	.800		
9 yrs.		43	30	13	.698		
			3rd	2nd	8th	1st	

Tommy McCarthy

McCARTHY, THOMAS FRANCIS MICHAEL
B. July 24, 1864, Boston, Mass.
D. Aug. 5, 1922, Boston, Mass.
Hall of Fame 1946.

		G	W	L	PCT	Standing	
1890	STL AA	26	13	13	.500	4	3

John McCloskey

McCLOSKEY, JOHN JAMES (Honest John)
B. Apr. 4, 1862, Louisville, Ky.
D. Nov. 17, 1940, Louisville, Ky.

		G	W	L	PCT	Standing	
1895	LOU N	133	35	96	.267	12	
1896		44	9	34	.209	12	12
1906	STL N	154	52	98	.347	7	
1907		155	52	101	.340	8	
1908		154	49	105	.318	8	
5 yrs.		640	197	434	.312		

Jim McCormick

McCORMICK, JAMES
B. 1856, Glasgow, Scotland
D. Mar. 10, 1918, Paterson, N. J.

		G	W	L	PCT	Standing
1879	CLE N	82	27	55	.329	6
1880		85	47	37	.560	3
2 yrs.		167	74	92	.446	

	G	W	L	PCT	Standing			G	W	L	PCT	Standing

Mel McGaha

McGAHA, FRED MELVIN
B. Sept. 26, 1926, Bastrop, La.

		G	W	L	PCT	Standing	
1962	CLE A	162	80	82	.494	6	
1964	KC A	111	40	70	.364	10	10
1965		26	5	21	.192	10	10
3 yrs.		299	125	173	.419		

Mike McGeary

McGEARY, MICHAEL HENRY
B. 1851, Philadelphia, Pa.
Deceased.

		G	W	L	PCT	Standing
1881	CLE N	85	36	48	.429	7

John McGraw

McGRAW, JOHN JOSEPH (Little Napoleon)
B. Apr. 7, 1873, Truxton, N. Y.
D. Feb. 25, 1934, New Rochelle, N. Y.
Hall of Fame 1937.

		G	W	L	PCT	Standing	
1899	BAL N	152	86	62	.581	4	
1901	BAL A	135	68	65	.511	5	
1902		63	28	34	.452	7	8
1902	NY N	65	25	38	.397	8	8
1903		142	84	55	.604	2	
1904		157	106	47	.693	1	
1905		155	105	48	.686	1	
1906		152	96	56	.632	2	
1907		155	82	71	.536	4	
1908		157	98	56	.636	2	
1909		156	92	61	.601	3	
1910		155	91	63	.591	2	
1911		154	99	54	.647	1	
1912		154	103	48	.682	1	
1913		156	101	51	.664	1	
1914		156	84	70	.545	2	
1915		155	69	83	.454	8	
1916		155	86	66	.566	4	
1917		158	98	56	.636	1	
1918		124	71	53	.573	2	
1919		140	87	53	.621	2	
1920		155	86	68	.558	2	
1921		153	94	59	.614	1	
1922		156	93	61	.604	1	
1923		153	95	58	.621	1	
1924		154	93	60	.608	1	
1925		152	86	66	.566	2	
1926		151	74	77	.490	5	
1927		155	92	62	.597	3	
1928		155	93	61	.604	2	
1929		152	84	67	.556	3	
1930		154	87	67	.565	3	
1931		153	87	65	.572	2	
1932		40	17	23	.425	8	6
33 yrs.		4879	2840	1984	.589		
			2nd	**2nd**	**3rd**	**8th**	

WORLD SERIES

		G	W	L	PCT		
1905	NY N	5	4	1	.800		
1911		6	2	4	.333		
1912		7	3	4	.429		
1913		5	1	4	.200		
1917		6	2	4	.333		
1921		8	5	3	.625		
1922		5	4	0	1.000		
1923		6	2	4	.333		
1924		7	3	4	.429		
9 yrs.		55	26	28	.481		
			2nd	**3rd**	**1st**		

Deacon McGuire

McGUIRE, JAMES THOMAS
B. Nov. 2, 1865, Youngstown, Ohio
D. Oct. 31, 1936, Albion, Mich.

		G	W	L	PCT	Standing		
1898	WAS N	70	19	49	.279	10	11	11
1907	BOS A	111	45	61	.425	8	7	
1908		115	53	62	.461	6	5	
1909	CLE A	41	14	25	.359	6	6	
1910		161	71	81	.467	5		
1911		17	6	11	.353	5	3	
6 yrs.		515	208	289	.419			

Bill McGunnigle

McGUNNIGLE, WILLIAM HENRY (Gunner)
B. Jan. 1, 1855, E. Stoughton, Mass.
D. Mar. 9, 1899, Brockton, Mass.

		G	W	L	PCT	Standing	
1880	BUF N	17	4	13	.235	8	7
1888	BKN AA	143	88	52	.629	2	
1889		140	93	44	.679	1	
1890	BKN N	129	86	43	.667	1	
1891	PIT N	59	24	33	.421	8	8
1896	LOU N	89	29	59	.330	12	12
6 yrs.		577	324	244	.570		

Stuffy McInnis

McINNIS, JOHN PHALEN
B. Sept. 19, 1890, Gloucester, Mass.
D. Feb. 16, 1960, Ipswich, Mass.

		G	W	L	PCT	Standing
1927	PHI N	155	51	103	.331	8

Bill McKechnie

McKECHNIE, WILLIAM BOYD (Deacon)
B. Aug. 7, 1886, Wilkinsburg, Pa.
D. Oct. 29, 1965, Bradenton, Fla.
Hall of Fame 1962.

		G	W	L	PCT	Standing	
1915	NWK F	102	54	45	.545	6	5
1922	PIT N	90	53	36	.596	5	3
1923		154	87	67	.565	3	
1924		153	90	63	.588	3	
1925		153	95	58	.621	1	
1926		157	84	69	.549	3	
1928	STL N	154	95	59	.617	1	
1929		62	33	29	.532	4	4
1930	BOS N	154	70	84	.455	6	
1931		156	64	90	.416	7	
1932		155	77	77	.500	5	
1933		156	83	71	.539	4	
1934		152	78	73	.517	4	
1935		153	38	115	.248	8	
1936		157	71	83	.461	6	
1937		152	79	73	.520	5	
1938	CIN N	151	82	68	.547	4	
1939		156	97	57	.630	1	
1940		155	100	53	.654	1	
1941		154	88	66	.571	3	
1942		154	76	76	.500	4	
1943		155	87	67	.565	2	
1944		155	89	65	.578	3	
1945		154	61	93	.396	7	
1946		156	67	87	.435	6	
25 yrs.		3650	1898	1724	.524		
			7th	**8th**	**6th**		

WORLD SERIES

		G	W	L	PCT	
1925	PIT N	7	4	3	.571	
1928	STL N	4	0	4	.000	
1939	CIN N	4	0	4	.000	
1940		7	4	3	.571	
4 yrs.		22	8	14	.364	
			10th		**6th**	

Jack McKeon

McKEON, JOHN ALOYSIUS
B. Nov. 23, 1930, South Amboy, N. J.

		G	W	L	PCT	Standing	
1973	KC A	162	88	74	.543	2	
1974		162	77	85	.475	5	
1975		96	50	46	.521	2	2
1977	OAK A	53	26	27	.491	7	7
1978		123	45	78	.366	6	6
5 yrs.		596	286	310	.480		

Denny McKnight

McKNIGHT, HENRY DENNIS
B. 1847, Pittsburgh, Pa.
D. May 5, 1900, Pittsburgh, Pa.

		G	W	L	PCT	Standing		
1884	PIT AA	30	12	17	.414	12	12	11

	G	W	L	PCT	Standing

George McManus

McMANUS, GEORGE
B. Oct., 1846
D. Oct. 2, 1918, New York, N. Y.

		G	W	L	PCT		Standing
1877	STL N	34	14	20	.412	3	4

Marty McManus

McMANUS, MARTIN JOSEPH
B. Mar. 14, 1900, Chicago, Ill.
D. Feb. 18, 1966, St. Louis, Mo.

		G	W	L	PCT		Standing
1932	BOS A	97	32	65	.330	8	8
1933		149	63	86	.423	7	
2 yrs.		246	95	151	.386		

Roy McMillan

McMILLAN, ROY DAVID
B. July 17, 1930, Bonham, Tex.

		G	W	L	PCT		Standing	
1972	MIL A	2	1	1	.500	6	6	6
1975	NY N	53	26	27	.491	3	3	
2 yrs.		55	27	28	.491			

John McNamara

McNAMARA, JOHN FRANCIS
B. June 4, 1932, Sacramento, Calif.

		G	W	L	PCT		Standing	
1969	OAK A	13	8	5	.615	2	2	
1970		162	89	73	.549	2		
1974	SD N	162	60	102	.370	6		
1975		162	71	91	.438	4		
1976		162	73	89	.451	5		
1977		48	20	28	.417	5	5	
1979	CIN N	161	90	71	.559	1		
1980		163	89	73	.549	3		
1981		56	35	21	.625	2		(1st)
1981		52	31	21	.596	2		(2nd)
1982		92	34	58	.370	6	6	
1983	CAL A	162	70	92	.432	5		
1984		162	81	81	.500	2		
12 yrs.		1557	751	805	.483			

LEAGUE CHAMPIONSHIP SERIES

		G	W	L	PCT	
1979	CIN N	3	0	3	.000	

Bid McPhee

McPHEE, JOHN ALEXANDER
B. Nov. 1, 1859, Massena, N. Y.
D. Jan. 3, 1943, San Diego, Calif.

		G	W	L	PCT		Standing
1901	CIN N	142	52	87	.374	8	
1902		65	27	37	.422	7	4
2 yrs.		207	79	124	.389		

Cal McVey

McVEY, CALVIN ALEXANDER
B. Aug. 30, 1850, Montrose Lee County, Iowa
D. Aug. 20, 1926, San Francisco, Calif.

		G	W	L	PCT		Standing
1878	CIN N	61	37	23	.617	2	
1879		64	35	29	.547	5	5
2 yrs.		125	72	52	.581		

Sam Mele

MELE, SABATH ANTHONY
B. Jan. 21, 1923, Astoria, N. Y.

		G	W	L	PCT		Standing
1961	MIN A	87	41	45	.477	9	7
1962		163	91	71	.562	2	
1963		161	91	70	.565	3	
1964		163	79	83	.488	6	
1965		162	102	60	.630	1	
1966		162	89	73	.549	2	
1967		50	25	25	.500	6	2
7 yrs.		948	518	427	.548		

WORLD SERIES

		G	W	L	PCT
1965	MIN A	7	3	4	.429

Charlie Metro

METRO, CHARLES
Born Charles Moreskonich.
B. Apr. 28, 1919, Nanty-Glo, Pa.

		G	W	L	PCT		Standing
1962	CHI N	112	43	69	.384	9	9
1970	KC A	54	19	35	.352	6	4
2 yrs.		166	62	104	.373		

Billy Meyer

MEYER, WILLIAM ADAM
B. Jan. 14, 1892, Knoxville, Tenn.
D. Mar. 31, 1957, Knoxville, Tenn.

		G	W	L	PCT		Standing
1948	PIT N	156	83	71	.539	4	
1949		154	71	83	.461	6	
1950		154	57	96	.373	8	
1951		155	64	90	.416	7	
1952		155	42	112	.273	8	
5 yrs.		774	317	452	.412		

Gene Michael

MICHAEL, GENE RICHARD (Stick)
B. June 2, 1938, Kent, Ohio

		G	W	L	PCT			Standing	
1981	NY A	56	34	22	.607	1			(1st)
1981		23	12	11	.522	5	6		(2nd)
1982		86	44	42	.512	4	5	5	
2 yrs.		165	90	75	.545				

Clyde Milan

MILAN, JESSE CLYDE (Deerfoot)
Brother of Horace Milan.
B. Mar. 25, 1887, Linden, Tenn.
D. Mar. 3, 1953, Orlando, Fla.

		G	W	L	PCT		Standing
1922	WAS A	154	69	85	.448	6	

George Miller

MILLER, GEORGE C.
B. Feb. 19, 1853, Newport, Ky.
D. July 25, 1929, Cincinnati, Ohio

		G	W	L	PCT		Standing
1894	STL N	132	56	76	.424	9	

Buster Mills

MILLS, COLONEL BUSTER
B. Sept. 16, 1908, Ranger, Tex.

		G	W	L	PCT		Standing
1953	CIN N	8	4	4	.500	6	6

Fred Mitchell

MITCHELL, FREDERICK FRANCIS
Born Frederick Francis Yapp.
B. June 5, 1878, Cambridge, Mass.
D. Oct. 13, 1970, Newton, Mass.

		G	W	L	PCT		Standing
1917	CHI N	157	74	80	.481	5	
1918		131	84	45	.651	1	
1919		140	75	65	.536	3	
1920		154	75	79	.487	5	
1921	BOS N	153	79	74	.516	4	
1922		154	53	100	.346	8	
1923		155	54	100	.351	7	
7 yrs.		1044	494	543	.476		

WORLD SERIES

		G	W	L	PCT
1918	CHI N	6	2	4	.333

Jackie Moore

MOORE, JACKIE SPENCER
B. Feb. 19, 1939, Jay, Fla.

		G	W	L	PCT		Standing
1984	OAK A	118	57	61	.483	4	4

	G	W	L	PCT	Standing				G	W	L	PCT	Standing

Terry Moore

MOORE, TERRY BLUFORD
B. May 27, 1912, Vernon, Ala.

		G	W	L	PCT	Standing
1954	PHI N	77	35	42	.455	3 4

Pat Moran

MORAN, PATRICK JOSEPH
B. Feb. 7, 1876, Fitchburg, Mass.
D. Mar. 7, 1924, Orlando, Fla.

		G	W	L	PCT	Standing
1915	PHI N	153	90	62	.592	1
1916		154	91	62	.595	2
1917		154	87	65	.572	2
1918		125	55	68	.447	6
1919	CIN N	140	96	44	.686	1
1920		153	82	71	.536	3
1921		153	70	83	.458	6
1922		156	86	68	.558	2
1923		154	91	63	.591	2
9 yrs.		1342	748	586	.561	

WORLD SERIES
		G	W	L	PCT	
1915	PHI N	5	1	4	.200	
1919	CIN N	8	5	3	.625	
2 yrs.		13	6	7	.462	

George Moriarty

MORIARTY, GEORGE JOSEPH
Brother of Bill Moriarty.
B. July 7, 1884, Chicago, Ill.
D. Apr. 8, 1964, Miami, Fla.

		G	W	L	PCT	Standing
1927	DET A	156	82	71	.536	4
1928		154	68	86	.442	6
2 yrs.		310	150	157	.489	

John Morrill

MORRILL, JOHN FRANCIS (Honest John)
B. Feb. 19, 1855, Boston, Mass.
D. Apr. 2, 1932, Boston, Mass.

		G	W	L	PCT	Standing
1882	BOS N	85	45	39	.536	3
1883		41	32	9	.780	2 1
1884		116	73	38	.658	2
1885		113	46	66	.411	5
1886		118	56	61	.479	5
1887		127	61	60	.504	5
1888		137	70	64	.522	4
1889	WAS N	54	13	39	.250	8 8
8 yrs.		791	396	376	.513	

Bob Morrow

MORROW, ROBERT
B. Sept. 27, 1838, England
D. Feb. 6, 1898

		G	W	L	PCT	Standing
1881	PRO N	51	30	20	.600	3 2

Jake Morse

MORSE, JACOB CHARLES
B. June 7, 1860, Concord, N. H.
D. Apr. 12, 1937, Brookine, Mass.

		G	W	L	PCT	Standing
1884	BOS U	75	46	28	.622	5 5

Charlie Morton

MORTON, CHARLES HAZEN
B. Oct. 12, 1854, Kingsville, Ohio
D. Dec. 13, 1921, Akron, Ohio

		G	W	L	PCT	Standing
1884	TOL AA	110	46	58	.442	8
1885	DET N	57	18	39	.316	7 6
1890	TOL AA	134	68	64	.515	4
3 yrs.		301	132	161	.451	

Felix Moses

MOSES, FELIX I.
B. Richmond, Va.
Deceased.

		G	W	L	PCT	Standing
1884	RIC AA	46	12	30	.286	10

Les Moss

MOSS, JOHN LESTER
B. May 14, 1925, Tulsa, Okla.

		G	W	L	PCT	Standing
1968	CHI A	2	0	2	.000	9 9 9
1979	DET A	53	27	26	.509	5 5
2 yrs.		55	27	28	.491	

Tim Murnane

MURNANE, TIMOTHY HAYES
B. June 4, 1852, Naugatuck, Conn.
D. Feb. 13, 1917, Boston, Mass.

		G	W	L	PCT	Standing
1884	BOS U	26	8	17	.320	5 5

Billy Murray

MURRAY, WILLIAM JEREMIAH
B. Apr. 13, 1864, Peabody, Mass.
D. Mar. 25, 1937, Youngstown, Ohio

		G	W	L	PCT	Standing
1907	PHI N	149	83	64	.565	3
1908		155	83	71	.539	4
1909		153	74	79	.484	5
3 yrs.		457	240	214	.529	

Danny Murtaugh

MURTAUGH, DANIEL EDWARD
B. Oct. 8, 1917, Chester, Pa.
D. Dec. 2, 1976, Chester, Pa.

		G	W	L	PCT	Standing
1957	PIT N	51	26	25	.510	8 7
1958		154	84	70	.545	2
1959		155	78	76	.506	4
1960		155	95	59	.617	1
1961		154	75	79	.487	6
1962		161	93	68	.578	4
1963		162	74	88	.457	8
1964		162	80	82	.494	6
1967		79	39	39	.500	6 6
1970		162	89	73	.549	1
1971		162	97	65	.599	1
1973		26	13	13	.500	2 3
1974		162	88	74	.543	1
1975		161	92	69	.571	1
1976		162	92	70	.568	2
15 yrs.		2068	1115	950	.540	

LEAGUE CHAMPIONSHIP SERIES
		G	W	L	PCT	Standing
1970	PIT N	3	0	3	.000	
1971		4	3	1	.750	
1974		4	1	3	.250	
1975		3	0	3	.000	
4 yrs.		14	4	10	.286	
		7th	7th	2nd	8th	

WORLD SERIES
		G	W	L	PCT	
1960	PIT N	7	4	3	.571	
1971		7	4	3	.571	
2 yrs.		14	8	6	.571	

Jim Mutrie

MUTRIE, JAMES J. (Truthful Jim)
B. June 13, 1851, Chelsea, Mass.
D. Jan. 24, 1938, New York, N. Y.

		G	W	L	PCT	Standing
1883	NY AA	97	54	42	.563	4
1884		112	75	32	.701	1
1885	NY N	112	85	27	.759	2
1886		124	75	44	.630	2
1887		129	68	55	.553	4
1888		137	84	47	.641	1
1889		131	83	43	.659	1
1890		135	63	68	.481	6
1891		136	71	61	.538	3
9 yrs.		1113	658	419	.611	
						2nd

	G	W	L	PCT	Standing				G	W	L	PCT	Standing

George Myatt

MYATT, GEORGE EDWARD (Mercury, Stud, Foghorn)
B. June 14, 1914, Denver, Colo.

		G	W	L	PCT	Standing	
1968	PHI N	2	2	0	1.000	4 5	8
1969		54	19	35	.352	5 5	
2 yrs.		56	21	35	.375		

Henry Myers

MYERS, HENRY C.
B. May, 1858, Philadelphia, Pa.
D. Apr. 18, 1895, Philadelphia, Pa.

		G	W	L	PCT	Standing
1882	BAL AA	74	19	54	.260	6

Billy Nash

NASH, WILLIAM MITCHELL
B. June 24, 1865, Richmond, Va.
D. Nov. 16, 1929, East Orange, N. J.

		G	W	L	PCT	Standing
1896	PHI N	131	62	68	.477	8

Johnny Neun

NEUN, JOHN HENRY
B. Oct. 28, 1900, Baltimore, Md.

		G	W	L	PCT	Standing
1946	NY A	14	8	6	.571	3 3
1947	CIN N	154	73	81	.474	5
1948		100	44	56	.440	7 7
3 yrs.		268	125	143	.466	

Kid Nichols

NICHOLS, CHARLES AUGUSTUS
B. Sept. 14, 1869, Madison, Wis.
D. Apr. 11, 1953, Kansas City, Mo.
Hall of Fame 1949.

		G	W	L	PCT	Standing
1904	STL N	155	75	79	.487	5
1905		48	19	29	.396	6 6
2 yrs.		203	94	108	.465	

Hugh Nicol

NICOL, HUGH N.
B. Jan. 1, 1858, Campsie, Scotland
D. June 27, 1921, Lafayette, Ind.

		G	W	L	PCT	Standing	
1897	STL N	38	9	29	.237	12 12	12

Russ Nixon

NIXON, RUSSELL EUGENE
B. Feb. 19, 1935, Cleveland, Ohio

		G	W	L	PCT	Standing
1982	CIN N	70	27	43	.386	6 6
1983		162	74	88	.457	6
2 yrs.		232	101	131	.435	

Bill Norman

NORMAN, HENRY WILLIS PATRICK
B. July 16, 1910, St. Louis, Mo.
D. Apr. 21, 1962, Milwaukee, Wis.

		G	W	L	PCT	Standing
1958	DET A	105	56	49	.533	5 5
1959		17	2	15	.118	8 4
2 yrs.		122	58	64	.475	

Rebel Oakes

OAKES, ENNIS TELFLAIR
B. Dec. 17, 1886, Homer, La.
D. Feb. 29, 1948, Shreveport, La.

		G	W	L	PCT	Standing
1914	PIT F	136	58	74	.439	8 7
1915		156	86	67	.562	3
2 yrs.		292	144	141	.505	

Jack O'Connor

O'CONNOR, JOHN JOSEPH (Peach Pie)
B. Mar. 3, 1867, St. Louis, Mo.
D. Nov. 14, 1937, St. Louis, Mo.

		G	W	L	PCT	Standing
1910	STL A	157	47	107	.305	8

Hank O'Day

O'DAY, HENRY FRANCIS
B. July 8, 1863, Chicago, Ill.
D. July 2, 1935, Chicago, Ill.

		G	W	L	PCT	Standing
1912	CIN N	155	75	78	.490	4
1914	CHI N	156	78	76	.506	4
2 yrs.		311	153	154	.498	

Bob O'Farrell

O'FARRELL, ROBERT ARTHUR
B. Oct. 19, 1896, Waukegan, Ill.

		G	W	L	PCT	Standing	
1927	STL N	153	92	61	.601	2	
1934	CIN N	85	26	58	.310	8	8
2 yrs.		238	118	119	.498		

Dan O'Leary

O'LEARY, DANIEL (Hustling Dan)
B. Oct. 22, 1856, Detroit, Mich.
D. June 24, 1922, Chicago, Ill.

		G	W	L	PCT	Standing
1884	CIN U	62	33	29	.532	3 3

Steve O'Neill

O'NEILL, STEPHEN FRANCIS
Brother of Jim O'Neill.
Brother of Jack O'Neill.
Brother of Mike O'Neill.
B. July 6, 1891, Minooka, Pa.
D. Jan. 26, 1962, Cleveland, Ohio

		G	W	L	PCT	Standing	
1935	CLE A	60	36	23	.610	5	3
1936		157	80	74	.519	5	
1937		156	83	71	.539	4	
1943	DET A	155	78	76	.506	5	
1944		156	88	66	.571	2	
1945		155	88	65	.575	1	
1946		155	92	62	.597	2	
1947		158	85	69	.552	2	
1948		154	78	76	.506	5	
1950	BOS A	92	62	30	.674	4	3
1951		154	87	67	.565	3	
1952	PHI N	91	59	32	.648	6	4
1953		156	83	71	.539	3	
1954		77	40	37	.519	3	4
14 yrs.		1876	1039	819	.559		

WORLD SERIES		G	W	L	PCT	
1945	DET A	7	4	3	.571	

Jack Onslow

ONSLOW, JOHN JAMES
Brother of Eddie Onslow.
B. Oct. 13, 1888, Scottdale, Pa.
D. Dec. 22, 1960, Concord, Mass.

		G	W	L	PCT	Standing	
1949	CHI A	154	63	91	.409	6	
1950		30	8	22	.267	8	6
2 yrs.		184	71	113	.386		

Jim O'Rourke

O'ROURKE, JAMES HENRY (Orator Jim)
Father of Queenie O'Rourke.
B. Aug. 24, 1852, Bridgeport, Conn.
D. Jan. 8, 1919, Bridgeport, Conn.
Hall of Fame 1945.

		G	W	L	PCT	Standing
1881	BUF N	83	45	38	.542	3
1882		84	45	39	.536	3
1883		98	52	45	.536	5
1884		114	64	47	.577	3

	G	W	L	PCT	Standing		

Jim O'Rourke continued

		G	W	L	PCT	Standing	
1893	WAS N	130	40	89	.310	12	
5 yrs.		509	246	258	.488		

Dave Orr

ORR, DAVID L.
B. Sept. 29, 1859, New York, N. Y.
D. June 3, 1915, Brooklyn, N. Y.

		G	W	L	PCT	Standing		
1887	NY AA	66	28	36	.438	8	7	7

Mel Ott

OTT, MELVIN THOMAS (Master Melvin)
B. Mar. 2, 1909, Gretna, La.
D. Nov. 21, 1958, New Orleans, La.
Hall of Fame 1951.

		G	W	L	PCT	Standing	
1942	NY N	154	85	67	.559	3	
1943		156	55	98	.359	8	
1944		155	67	87	.435	5	
1945		154	78	74	.513	5	
1946		154	61	93	.396	8	
1947		155	81	73	.526	4	
1948		76	37	38	.493	4	5
7 yrs.		1004	464	530	.467		

Paul Owens

OWENS, PAUL FRANCIS (The Pope)
B. Feb. 7, 1924, Salamanca, N. Y.

		G	W	L	PCT	Standing	
1972	PHI N	80	33	47	.413	6	6
1983		77	47	30	.610	1	1
1984		162	81	81	.500	4	
3 yrs.		319	161	158	.505		

LEAGUE CHAMPIONSHIP SERIES

		G	W	L	PCT	
1983	PHI N	4	3	1	.750	

WORLD SERIES

		G	W	L	PCT	
1983	PHI N	5	1	4	.200	

Danny Ozark

OZARK, DANIEL LEONARD (Ozark Ike)
B. Nov. 24, 1923, Buffalo, N. Y.

		G	W	L	PCT	Standing	
1973	PHI N	162	71	91	.438	6	
1974		162	80	82	.494	3	
1975		162	86	76	.531	2	
1976		162	101	61	.623	1	
1977		162	101	61	.623	1	
1978		162	90	72	.556	1	
1979		132	65	67	.492	5	4
1984	SF N	56	24	32	.429	6	6
8 yrs.		1160	618	542	.533		

LEAGUE CHAMPIONSHIP SERIES

		G	W	L	PCT	
1976	PHI N	3	0	3	.000	
1977		4	1	3	.250	
1978		4	1	3	.250	
3 yrs.		11	2	9	.182	
		8th	9th	3rd	9th	

Salty Parker

PARKER, FRANCIS JAMES
B. July 8, 1913, East St. Louis, Ill.

		G	W	L	PCT	Standing		
1967	NY N	11	4	7	.364	10	10	
1972	HOU N	1	1	0	1.000	3	2	2
2 yrs.		12	5	7	.417			

Roger Peckinpaugh

PECKINPAUGH, ROGER THORPE
B. Feb. 5, 1891, Wooster, Ohio
D. Nov. 17, 1977, Cleveland, Ohio

		G	W	L	PCT	Standing	
1914	NY A	17	9	8	.529	7	6
1928	CLE A	155	62	92	.403	7	
1929		152	81	71	.533	3	
1930		154	81	73	.526	4	
1931		155	78	76	.506	4	

Roger Peckinpaugh continued

	G	W	L	PCT	Standing	
1932	153	87	65	.572	4	
1933	51	26	25	.510	5	4
1941	155	75	79	.487	4	
8 yrs.	992	499	489	.505		

Johnny Pesky

PESKY, JOHN MICHAEL
Born John Michael Paveskovich.
B. Sept. 27, 1919, Portland, Ore.

		G	W	L	PCT	Standing	
1963	BOS A	161	76	85	.472	7	
1964		160	70	90	.438	8	8
1980		4	1	3	.250	4	4
3 yrs.		325	147	178	.452		

Fred Pfeffer

PFEFFER, NATHANIEL FREDERICK (Dandelion)
B. Mar. 17, 1860, Louisville, Ky.
D. Apr. 10, 1932, Chicago, Ill.

		G	W	L	PCT	Standing	
1892	LOU N	96	40	54	.426	11	9

Lew Phelan

PHELAN, LEWIS G.
Deceased.

		G	W	L	PCT	Standing		
1895	STL N	31	8	21	.276	11	11	11

Bill Phillips

PHILLIPS, WILLIAM CORCORAN (Whoa Bill,
Silver Bill)
B. Nov. 9, 1868, Allenport, Pa.
D. Oct. 25, 1941, Charleroi, Pa.

		G	W	L	PCT	Standing	
1914	IND F	157	88	65	.575	1	
1915	NWK F	53	26	27	.491	6	5
2 yrs.		210	114	92	.553		

Horace Phillips

PHILLIPS, HORACE B. (Hustling Horace)
B. May 14, 1853, Salem, Ohio
Deceased.

		G	W	L	PCT	Standing		
1879	TRO N	59	12	46	.207	8	8	
1883	COL AA	97	32	65	.330	6		
1884	PIT AA	41	10	30	.250	12	11	
1885		111	56	55	.505	3		
1886		140	80	57	.584	2		
1887	PIT N	125	55	69	.444	6		
1888		138	66	68	.493	6		
1889		71	28	43	.394	7	5	
8 yrs.		782	339	433	.439			

Lefty Phillips

PHILLIPS, HAROLD ROSS
B. May 16, 1919, Los Angeles, Calif.
D. June 10, 1972, Fullerton, Calif.

		G	W	L	PCT	Standing	
1969	CAL A	124	60	63	.488	6	3
1970		162	86	76	.531	3	
1971		162	76	86	.469	4	
3 yrs.		448	222	225	.497		

Lip Pike

PIKE, LIPMAN EMANUEL
Brother of Jay Pike.
B. May 25, 1845, New York, N. Y.
D. Oct. 10, 1893, Brooklyn, N. Y.

		G	W	L	PCT	Standing		
1877	CIN N	14	3	11	.214	6	6	

	G	W	L	PCT	Standing				G	W	L	PCT	Standing

Eddie Popowski
POPOWSKI, EDWARD JOSEPH (Pop)
B. Aug. 20, 1913, Sayreville, N. J.

	G	W	L	PCT	Standing
1969 BOS A	9	5	4	.556	3 3

Pat Powers
POWERS, PATRICK THOMAS
B. June 27, 1860, Trenton, N. J.
D. Aug. 29, 1925, Belmar, N. J.

	G	W	L	PCT	Standing
1890 ROC AA	133	63	63	.500	5
1892 NY N	153	71	80	.470	8
2 yrs.	286	134	143	.484	

Al Pratt
PRATT, ALBERT G. (Uncle Al)
B. Nov. 19, 1847, Pittsburgh, Pa.
D. Nov. 21, 1937, Pittsburgh, Pa.

	G	W	L	PCT	Standing
1882 PIT AA	79	39	39	.500	4
1883	32	12	20	.375	6 7
2 yrs.	111	51	59	.464	

Tom Pratt
PRATT, THOMAS J.
B. 1844, Worcester, Mass.
D. Sept. 28, 1908, Philadelphia, Pa.

	G	W	L	PCT	Standing
1884 PHI U	26	10	16	.385	6 8

James Price
PRICE, JAMES L.
Deceased.

	G	W	L	PCT	Standing
1884 NY N	100	56	42	.571	4 4

Doc Prothro
PROTHRO, JAMES THOMPSON
B. July 16, 1893, Memphis, Tenn.
D. Oct. 14, 1971, Memphis, Tenn.

	G	W	L	PCT	Standing
1939 PHI N	152	45	106	.298	8
1940	153	50	103	.327	8
1941	155	43	111	.279	8
3 yrs.	460	138	320	.301	

Blondie Purcell
PURCELL, WILLIAM ALOYSIUS
B. Mar. 16, 1854, Paterson, N. J.
Deceased.

	G	W	L	PCT	Standing
1883 PHI N	82	13	68	.160	8 8

Frank Quilici
QUILICI, FRANK RALPH (Guido)
B. May 11, 1939, Chicago, Ill.

	G	W	L	PCT	Standing
1972 MIN A	84	41	43	.488	3 3
1973	162	81	81	.500	3
1974	162	82	80	.506	3
1975	159	76	83	.478	4
4 yrs.	567	280	287	.494	

Joe Quinn
QUINN, JOSEPH J.
B. Dec. 25, 1864, Sydney, Australia
D. Nov. 12, 1940, St. Louis, Mo.

	G	W	L	PCT	Standing
1895 STL N	41	13	27	.325	11 11 11
1899 CLE N	116	12	104	.103	12 12
2 yrs.	157	25	131	.160	

Doug Rader
RADER, DOUGLAS LEE (Rojo, The Red Rooster)
B. July 30, 1944, Chicago, Ill.

	G	W	L	PCT	Standing
1983 TEX A	163	77	85	.475	3
1984	161	69	92	.429	7
2 yrs.	324	146	177	.452	

Vern Rapp
RAPP, VERNON FRED
B. May 11, 1928, St. Louis, Mo.

	G	W	L	PCT	Standing
1977 STL N	162	83	79	.512	3
1978	15	5	10	.333	6 5
1984 CIN N	120	51	69	.425	5 5
3 yrs.	297	139	158	.468	

Bill Reccius
RECCIUS, J. WILLIAM
Brother of John Reccius.
Brother of Phil Reccius.
B. 1847, Frankfurt-on-Main, Germany
D. Jan. 25, 1911, Louisville, Ky.

	G	W	L	PCT	Standing
1882 LOU AA	42	24	18	.571	4 2 3
1883	22	12	10	.545	5 5
2 yrs.	64	36	28	.563	

Del Rice
RICE, DELBERT W.
B. Oct. 27, 1922, Portsmouth, Ohio
D. Jan. 26, 1983, Buena Park, Calif.

	G	W	L	PCT	Standing
1972 CAL A	155	75	80	.484	5

Paul Richards
RICHARDS, PAUL RAPIER
B. Nov. 21, 1908, Waxahachie, Tex.

	G	W	L	PCT	Standing
1951 CHI A	155	81	73	.526	4
1952	156	81	73	.526	3
1953	156	89	65	.578	3
1954	146	91	54	.628	3 3
1955 BAL A	156	57	97	.370	7
1956	154	69	85	.448	6
1957	154	76	76	.500	5
1958	154	74	79	.484	6
1959	155	74	80	.481	6
1960	154	89	65	.578	2
1961	135	78	57	.578	3 3
1976 CHI A	161	64	97	.398	6
12 yrs.	1836	923	901	.506	

Danny Richardson
RICHARDSON, DANIEL
B. Jan. 25, 1863, Elmira, N. Y.
D. Sept. 12, 1926, New York, N. Y.

	G	W	L	PCT	Standing
1892 WAS N	37	11	26	.297	12 10

Branch Rickey
RICKEY, WESLEY BRANCH (The Mahatma)
B. Dec. 20, 1881, Stockdale, Ohio
D. Dec. 9, 1965, Columbia, Mo.
Hall of Fame 1967.

	G	W	L	PCT	Standing
1913 STL A	12	5	6	.455	8 8
1914	159	71	82	.464	5
1915	159	63	91	.409	6
1919 STL N	138	54	83	.394	7
1920	155	75	79	.487	5
1921	154	87	66	.569	3
1922	154	85	69	.552	3
1923	154	79	74	.516	5
1924	154	65	89	.422	6
1925	38	13	25	.342	8 4
10 yrs.	1277	597	664	.473	

		G	W	L	PCT	Standing				G	W	L	PCT	Standing

Billy Rigney

RIGNEY, WILLIAM JOSEPH (Specs, The Cricket)
B. Jan. 29, 1918, Alameda, Calif.

		G	W	L	PCT	Standing
1956	NY N	154	67	87	.435	6
1957		154	69	85	.448	6
1958	SF N	154	80	74	.519	3
1959		154	83	71	.539	3
1960		58	33	25	.569	2 5
1961	LA A	162	70	91	.435	8
1962		162	86	76	.531	3
1963		161	70	91	.435	9
1964		162	82	80	.506	5
1965	CAL A	162	75	87	.463	7
1966		162	80	82	.494	6
1967		161	84	77	.522	5
1968		162	67	95	.414	8
1969		39	11	28	.282	6 3
1970	MIN A	162	98	64	.605	1
1971		160	74	86	.463	5
1972		70	36	34	.514	3 3
1976	SF N	162	74	88	.457	4
18 yrs.		2561	1239	1321	.484	

LEAGUE CHAMPIONSHIP SERIES

1970	MIN A	3	0	3	.000	

Frank Robinson

ROBINSON, FRANK
B. Aug. 31, 1935, Beaumont, Tex.
Hall of Fame 1982.

		G	W	L	PCT	Standing	
1975	CLE A	159	79	80	.497	4	
1976		159	81	78	.509	4	
1977		57	26	31	.456	6 5	
1981	SF N	59	27	32	.458	5	(1st)
1981		52	29	23	.558	3	(2nd)
1982		162	87	75	.537	3	
1983		162	79	83	.488	5	
1984		106	42	64	.396	6 6	
7 yrs.		916	450	466	.491		

Wilbert Robinson

ROBINSON, WILBERT (Uncle Robbie)
Brother of Fred Robinson.
B. June 2, 1863, Bolton, Mass.
D. Aug. 8, 1934, Atlanta, Ga.
Hall of Fame 1945.

		G	W	L	PCT	Standing	
1902	BAL A	78	22	54	.289	7 8	
1914	BKN N	154	75	79	.487	5	
1915		154	80	72	.526	3	
1916		156	94	60	.610	1	
1917		156	70	81	.464	7	
1918		126	57	69	.452	5	
1919		141	69	71	.493	5	
1920		155	93	61	.604	1	
1921		152	77	75	.507	5	
1922		155	76	78	.494	6	
1923		155	76	78	.494	6	
1924		154	92	62	.597	2	
1925		153	68	85	.444	6	
1926		155	71	82	.464	6	
1927		154	65	88	.425	6	
1928		155	77	76	.503	6	
1929		153	70	83	.458	6	
1930		154	86	68	.558	4	
1931		153	79	73	.520	4	
19 yrs.		2813	1397	1395	.500		

WORLD SERIES

1916	BKN N	5	1	4	.200	
1920		7	2	5	.286	
2 yrs.		12	3	9	.250	

Matt Robison

ROBISON, MATTHEW STANLEY
B. Mar. 30, 1859, Pittsburgh, Pa.
D. Mar. 24, 1911, St. Louis, Mo.

		G	W	L	PCT	Standing	
1905	STL N	57	22	35	.386	6 6	

Buck Rodgers

RODGERS, ROBERT LEROY
B. Aug. 16, 1938, Delaware, Ohio

		G	W	L	PCT	Standing	
1980	MIL A	47	26	21	.553	2 3	
1980		23	13	10	.565	4 3	
1981		56	31	25	.554	3	(1st)
1981		53	31	22	.585	1	(2nd)
1982		47	23	24	.489	5 1	
3 yrs.		226	124	102	.549		

DIVISIONAL PLAYOFF SERIES

1981	MIL A	5	2	3	.400	

Jim Rogers

ROGERS, JAMES F.
B. Apr. 9, 1872, Hartford, Conn.
D. Jan. 21, 1900, Bridgeport, Conn.

		G	W	L	PCT	Standing	
1897	LOU N	45	17	26	.395	9 11	

Red Rolfe

ROLFE, ROBERT ABIAL
B. Oct. 17, 1908, Penacook, N. H.
D. July 8, 1969, Gilford, N. H.

		G	W	L	PCT	Standing	
1949	DET A	155	87	67	.565	4	
1950		157	95	59	.617	2	
1951		154	73	81	.474	5	
1952		73	23	49	.319	8 8	
4 yrs.		539	278	256	.521		

Pete Rose

ROSE, PETER EDWARD (Charlie Hustle)
B. Apr. 14, 1941, Cincinnati, Ohio

		G	W	L	PCT	Standing	
1984	CIN N	42	19	23	.452	5 5	

Chief Roseman

ROSEMAN, JAMES JOHN
B. 1856, New York, N. Y.
D. July 4, 1938, Brooklyn, N. Y.

		G	W	L	PCT	Standing	
1890	STL AA	51	32	19	.627	4 2 3	

Dave Rowe

ROWE, DAVID ELI
Brother of Jack Rowe.
B. Feb., 1856, Jacksonville, Ill.
D. Oct. 12, 1918.

		G	W	L	PCT	Standing	
1886	KC N	123	30	91	.248	7	
1888	KC AA	49	14	35	.286	8 8	
2 yrs.		172	44	126	.259		

Jack Rowe

ROWE, JOHN CHARLES
Brother of Dave Rowe.
B. Dec. 18, 1856, Harrisburg, Pa.
D. Apr. 25, 1911, St. Louis, Mo.

		G	W	L	PCT	Standing	
1890	BUF P	134	36	96	.273	8	

Pants Rowland

ROWLAND, CLARENCE HENRY
B. Feb. 12, 1879, Platteville, Wis.
D. May 17, 1969, Chicago, Ill.

		G	W	L	PCT	Standing	
1915	CHI A	155	93	61	.604	3	
1916		155	89	65	.578	2	
1917		156	100	54	.649	1	
1918		124	57	67	.460	6	
4 yrs.		590	339	247	.578		

WORLD SERIES

1917	CHI A	6	4	2	.667	

	G	W	L	PCT	Standing		

Muddy Ruel

RUEL, HEROLD DOMINIC
B. Feb. 20, 1896, St. Louis, Mo.
D. Nov. 13, 1963, Palo Alto, Calif.

		G	W	L	PCT	Standing	
1947	STL A	154	59	95	.383	8	

Pete Runnels

RUNNELS, JAMES EDWARD
B. Jan. 28, 1928, Lufkin, Tex.

		G	W	L	PCT	Standing	
1966	BOS A	16	8	8	.500	10	9

Connie Ryan

RYAN, CORNELIUS JOSEPH
B. Feb. 27, 1920, New Orleans, La.

		G	W	L	PCT	Standing	
1975	ATL N	26	8	18	.308	5	5
1977	TEX A	6	2	4	.333	2	4	2
2 yrs.		32	10	22	.313		

Eddie Sawyer

SAWYER, EDWIN MILBY
B. Sept. 10, 1910, Westerly, R. I.

		G	W	L	PCT	Standing	
1948	PHI N	64	23	41	.359	6	6
1949		154	81	73	.526	3	
1950		157	91	63	.591	1	
1951		154	73	81	.474	5	
1952		63	28	35	.444	6	4
1958		71	30	41	.423	7	8
1959		155	64	90	.416	8	
1960		1	0	1	.000	8	8
8 yrs.		819	390	425	.479		

WORLD SERIES

		G	W	L	PCT		
1950	PHI N	4	0	4	.000		

Mike Scanlon

SCANLON, MICHAEL B.
B. 1847, Cork, Ireland
D. Jan. 18, 1929, Washington, D. C.

		G	W	L	PCT	Standing	
1884	WAS U	115	47	66	.416	7	
1886	WAS N	79	13	66	.165	8	8
2 yrs.		194	60	132	.313		

Ray Schalk

SCHALK, RAYMOND WILLIAM (Cracker)
B. Aug. 12, 1892, Harvel, Ill.
D. May 19, 1970, Chicago, Ill.
Hall of Fame 1955.

		G	W	L	PCT	Standing	
1927	CHI A	153	70	83	.458	5	
1928		75	32	42	.432	6	5
2 yrs.		228	102	125	.449		

Bob Scheffing

SCHEFFING, ROBERT BODEN
B. Aug. 11, 1915, Overland, Mo.

		G	W	L	PCT	Standing	
1957	CHI N	156	62	92	.403	7	
1958		154	72	82	.468	5	
1959		155	74	80	.481	5	
1961	DET A	163	101	61	.623	2	
1962		161	85	76	.528	4	
1963		60	24	36	.400	9	5
6 yrs.		849	418	427	.495		

Larry Schlafly

SCHLAFLY, HARRY LAWRENCE
B. Sept. 20, 1878, Port Washington, Ohio
D. June 27, 1919, Beach City, Ohio

		G	W	L	PCT	Standing	
1914	BUF F	155	80	71	.530	4	
1915		43	14	29	.326	8	6
2 yrs.		198	94	100	.485		

Gus Schmelz

SCHMELZ, GUSTAVUS HEINRICH
B. Sept. 26, 1850, Columbus, Ohio
D. Oct. 14, 1925, Columbus, Ohio

		G	W	L	PCT	Standing	
1884	COL AA	110	69	39	.639	2	
1886	STL N	126	43	79	.352	6	
1887	CIN AA	136	81	54	.600	2	
1888		137	80	54	.597	4	
1889		141	76	63	.547	4	
1890	CLE N	78	21	55	.276	7	7
1890	COL AA	56	37	13	.740	5	2
1891		138	61	76	.445	6	
1894	WAS N	132	45	87	.341	11	
1895		132	43	85	.336	10	
1896		133	58	73	.443	9	
1897		36	9	25	.265	11	6
11 yrs.		1355	623	703	.470		

Red Schoendienst

SCHOENDIENST, ALBERT FRED
B. Feb. 2, 1923, Germantown, Ill.

		G	W	L	PCT	Standing	
1965	STL N	162	80	81	.497	7	
1966		162	83	79	.512	6	
1967		161	101	60	.627	1	
1968		162	97	65	.599	1	
1969		162	87	75	.537	4	
1970		162	76	86	.469	4	
1971		163	90	72	.556	2	
1972		156	75	81	.481	4	
1973		162	81	81	.500	2	
1974		161	86	75	.534	2	
1975		163	82	80	.506	3	
1976		162	72	90	.444	5	
1980		37	18	19	.486	5	4
13 yrs.		1975	1028	944	.521		

WORLD SERIES

		G	W	L	PCT		
1967	STL N	7	4	3	.571		
1968		7	3	4	.429		
2 yrs.		14	7	7	.500		

Joe Schultz

SCHULTZ, JOSEPH CHARLES, JR. (Dode)
Son of Joe Schultz.
B. Aug. 29, 1918, Chicago, Ill.

		G	W	L	PCT	Standing	
1969	SEA A	163	64	98	.395	6	
1973	DET A	19	9	10	.474	3	3
2 yrs.		182	73	108	.403		

Frank Selee

SELEE, FRANK GIBSON
B. Oct. 26, 1859, Amherst, N. H.
D. July 5, 1909, Denver, Colo.

		G	W	L	PCT	Standing	
1890	BOS N	134	76	57	.571	5	
1891		140	87	51	.630	1	
1892		152	102	48	.680	1	
1893		131	86	43	.667	1	
1894		133	83	49	.629	3	
1895		132	71	60	.542	5	
1896		132	74	57	.565	4	
1897		135	93	39	.705	1	
1898		152	102	47	.685	1	
1899		153	95	57	.625	2	
1900		142	66	72	.478	4	
1901		140	69	69	.500	5	
1902	CHI N	141	68	69	.496	5	
1903		139	82	56	.594	3	
1904		156	93	60	.608	2	
1905		90	52	38	.578	4	3
16 yrs.		2202	1299	872	.598		
						4th	

	G	W	L	PCT	Standing				G	W	L	PCT	Standing

Luke Sewell

SEWELL, JAMES LUTHER
Brother of Tommy Sewell.
Brother of Joe Sewell.
B. Jan. 5, 1901, Titus, Ala.

		G	W	L	PCT	Standing	
1941	**STL A**	113	55	55	.500	7	6
1942		151	82	69	.543	3	
1943		153	72	80	.474	6	
1944		154	89	65	.578	1	
1945		154	81	70	.536	3	
1946		126	53	71	.427	7	7
1949	**CIN N**	3	1	2	.333	7	7
1950		153	66	87	.431	6	
1951		155	68	86	.442	6	
1952		98	39	59	.398	7	6
10 yrs.		1260	606	644	.485		

WORLD SERIES
1944	**STL A**	6	2	4	.333		

Dan Shannon

SHANNON, DANIEL W.
B. Mar. 23, 1865, Bridgeport, Conn.
D. Oct. 25, 1913, Bridgeport, Conn.

		G	W	L	PCT	Standing		
1889	**LOU AA**	54	9	43	.173	8	8	8
1891	**WAS AA**	39	12	25	.324	7	8	8
2 yrs.		93	21	68	.236			

Bill Sharsig

SHARSIG, WILLIAM A.
B. 1855, Philadelphia, Pa.
D. Feb. 1, 1902, Philadelphia, Pa.

		G	W	L	PCT	Standing	
1884	**PHI AA**	57	33	23	.589	7	7
1885		39	22	17	.564	4	4
1886		41	22	17	.564	6	6
1887		90	42	44	.488	5	5
1888		136	81	52	.609	3	
1889		138	75	58	.564	3	
1890		136	54	78	.409	7	
1891		34	15	17	.469	4	4
8 yrs.		671	344	306	.529		

Bob Shawkey

SHAWKEY, JAMES ROBERT
B. Dec. 4, 1890, Brookville, Pa.
D. Dec. 31, 1980, Syracuse, N. Y.

		G	W	L	PCT	Standing
1930	**NY A**	154	86	68	.558	3

Tom Sheehan

SHEEHAN, THOMAS CLANCY
B. Mar. 31, 1894, Grand Ridge, Ill.
D. Dec., 1982, Chillicote, Ohio

		G	W	L	PCT	Standing	
1960	**SF N**	98	46	50	.479	2	5

Larry Shepard

SHEPARD, LAWRENCE WILLIAM
B. Apr. 3, 1919, Lakewood, Ohio

		G	W	L	PCT	Standing	
1968	**PIT N**	163	80	82	.494	6	
1969		157	84	73	.535	3	3
2 yrs.		320	164	155	.514		

Norm Sherry

SHERRY, NORMAN BURT
Brother of Larry Sherry.
B. July 16, 1931, New York, N. Y.

		G	W	L	PCT	Standing	
1976	**CAL A**	66	37	29	.561	4	4
1977		81	39	42	.481	5	5
2 yrs.		147	76	71	.517		

Bill Shettsline

SHETTSLINE, WILLIAM JOSEPH
B. Oct. 25, 1863, Philadelphia, Pa.
D. Feb. 22, 1933, Philadelphia, Pa.

		G	W	L	PCT	Standing	
1898	**PHI N**	104	59	44	.573	8	6
1899		154	94	58	.618	3	
1900		141	75	63	.543	3	
1901		140	83	57	.593	2	
1902		138	56	81	.409	7	
5 yrs.		677	367	303	.548		

Burt Shotton

SHOTTON, BURTON EDWIN (Barney)
B. Oct. 18, 1884, Brownhelm, Ohio
D. July 29, 1962, Lake Wales, Fla.

		G	W	L	PCT	Standing		
1928	**PHI N**	152	43	109	.283	8		
1929		154	71	82	.464	5		
1930		156	52	102	.338	8		
1931		155	66	88	.429	6		
1932		154	78	76	.506	4		
1933		152	60	92	.395	7		
1934	**CIN N**	1	1	0	1.000	8	8	8
1947	**BKN N**	154	93	60	.608	1	1	
1948		79	47	32	.595	5	3	
1949		156	97	57	.630	1		
1950		155	89	65	.578	2		
11 yrs.		1468	697	763	.477			

WORLD SERIES
		G	W	L	PCT	Standing
1947	**BKN N**	7	3	4	.429	
1949		5	1	4	.200	
2 yrs.		12	4	8	.333	

Ken Silvestri

SILVESTRI, KENNETH JOSEPH (Hawk)
B. May 3, 1916, Chicago, Ill.

		G	W	L	PCT	Standing	
1967	**ATL N**	3	0	3	.000	7	7

Joe Simmons

SIMMONS, JOSEPH S.
B. June 13, 1845, New York, N. Y.
Deceased.

		G	W	L	PCT	Standing	
1884	**WIL U**	18	2	16	.111	12	

Lew Simmons

SIMMONS, LEWIS
B. Aug. 27, 1838, New Castle, Pa.
D. Sept. 2, 1911, Jamestown, Pa.

		G	W	L	PCT	Standing	
1882	**PHI AA**	39	20	19	.513	3	3
1883		98	66	32	.673	1	
1886		98	41	55	.427	6	6
3 yrs.		235	127	106	.545		

Dick Sisler

SISLER, RICHARD ALLAN
Son of George Sisler.
Brother of Dave Sisler.
B. Nov. 2, 1920, St. Louis, Mo.

		G	W	L	PCT	Standing	
1964	**CIN N**	53	32	21	.604	3	2
1965		162	89	73	.549	4	
2 yrs.		215	121	94	.563		

George Sisler

SISLER, GEORGE HAROLD (Gorgeous George)
Father of Dick Sisler.
Father of Dave Sisler.
B. Mar. 24, 1893, Manchester, Ohio
D. Mar. 26, 1973, St. Louis, Mo.
Hall of Fame 1939.

		G	W	L	PCT	Standing	
1924	**STL A**	152	74	78	.487	4	
1925		154	82	71	.536	3	
1926		155	62	92	.403	7	
3 yrs.		461	218	241	.475		

| | G | W | L | PCT | Standing | | | | G | W | L | PCT | Standing | |

Frank Skaff

SKAFF, FRANCIS MICHAEL
B. Sept. 30, 1913, LaCrosse, Wis.

		G	W	L	PCT	Standing	
1966	DET A	79	40	39	.506	3	3

Bob Skinner

SKINNER, ROBERT RALPH
Father of Joel Skinner.
B. Oct. 3, 1931, La Jolla, Calif.

		G	W	L	PCT	Standing		
1968	PHI N	107	48	59	.449	5	8	
1969		108	44	64	.407	5	5	
1977	SD N	1	1	0	1.000	5	5	5
3 yrs.		216	93	123	.431			

Jack Slattery

SLATTERY, JOHN TERRENCE
B. Jan. 6, 1877, Boston, Mass.
D. July 17, 1949, Boston, Mass.

		G	W	L	PCT	Standing	
1928	BOS N	31	11	20	.355	7	7

Harry Smith

SMITH, HARRY W.
B. Feb. 5, 1856, N. Vernon, Ind.
D. June 4, 1898, N. Vernon, Ind.

		G	W	L	PCT	Standing	
1909	BOS N	76	22	53	.293	8	8

Heinie Smith

SMITH, GEORGE HENRY
B. Oct. 24, 1871, Pittsburgh, Pa.
D. June 25, 1939, Buffalo, N. Y.

		G	W	L	PCT	Standing		
1902	NY N	32	5	27	.156	4	8	8

Mayo Smith

SMITH, EDWARD MAYO
B. Jan. 17, 1915, New London, Mo.
D. Nov. 24, 1977, Boynton Beach, Fla.

		G	W	L	PCT	Standing	
1955	PHI N	154	77	77	.500	4	
1956		154	71	83	.461	5	
1957		156	77	77	.500	5	
1958		83	39	44	.470	7	8
1959	CIN N	80	35	45	.438	7	5
1967	DET A	163	91	71	.562	2	
1968		164	103	59	.636	1	
1969		162	90	72	.556	2	
1970		162	79	83	.488	4	
9 yrs.		1278	662	611	.520		

WORLD SERIES						
1968	DET A	7	4	3	.571	

Pop Snyder

SNYDER, CHARLES N.
B. Oct. 6, 1854, Washington, D. C.
D. Oct. 29, 1924, Washington, D. C.

		G	W	L	PCT	Standing		
1882	CIN AA	80	55	25	.688	1		
1883		98	61	37	.622	3		
1884		41	25	16	.610	4	5	
1891	WAS AA	70	23	46	.333	6	7	8
4 yrs.		289	164	124	.569			

Allen Sothoron

SOTHORON, ALLEN SUTTON
B. Apr. 29, 1893, Laura, Ohio
D. June 17, 1939, St. Louis, Mo.

		G	W	L	PCT	Standing		
1933	STL A	4	1	3	.250	8	8	8

Billy Southworth

SOUTHWORTH, WILLIAM HARRISON
B. Mar. 9, 1893, Harvard, Neb.
D. Nov. 15, 1969, Columbus, Ohio

		G	W	L	PCT	Standing	
1929	STL N	89	43	45	.489	4	4
1940		111	69	40	.633	6	3
1941		155	97	56	.634	2	
1942		156	106	48	.688	1	
1943		157	105	49	.682	1	
1944		157	105	49	.682	1	
1945		155	95	59	.617	2	
1946	BOS N	154	81	72	.529	4	
1947		154	86	68	.558	3	
1948		154	91	62	.595	1	
1949		157	75	79	.487	4	
1950		156	83	71	.539	4	
1951		60	28	31	.475	5	4
13 yrs.		1815	1064	729	.593		
						6th	

WORLD SERIES						
1942	STL N	5	4	1	.800	
1943		5	1	4	.200	
1944		6	4	2	.667	
1948	BOS N	6	2	4	.333	
4 yrs.		22	11	11	.500	
		10th	9th			8th

Al Spalding

SPALDING, ALBERT GOODWILL
B. Sept. 2, 1850, Byron, Ill.
D. Sept. 9, 1915, Point Loma, Calif.
Hall of Fame 1939.

		G	W	L	PCT	Standing	
1876	CHI N	66	52	14	.788	1	
1877		60	26	33	.441	5	
2 yrs.		126	78	47	.624		

Tris Speaker

SPEAKER, TRISTRAM E (The Grey Eagle, Spoke)
B. Apr. 4, 1888, Hubbard, Tex.
D. Dec. 8, 1958, Lake Whitney, Tex.
Hall of Fame 1937.

		G	W	L	PCT	Standing	
1919	CLE A	60	39	21	.650	3	2
1920		154	98	56	.636	1	
1921		154	94	60	.610	2	
1922		155	78	76	.506	4	
1923		153	82	71	.536	3	
1924		153	67	86	.438	6	
1925		155	70	84	.455	6	
1926		154	88	66	.571	2	
8 yrs.		1138	616	520	.542		

WORLD SERIES						
1920	CLE A	7	5	2	.714	

Harry Spence

SPENCE, HARRISON L.
B. 1858, Virginia
D. May 17, 1908, Chicago, Ill.

		G	W	L	PCT	Standing	
1888	IND N	136	50	85	.370	7	

Chick Stahl

STAHL, CHARLES SYLVESTER
Brother of Jake Stahl.
B. Jan. 10, 1873, Fort Wayne, Ind.
D. Mar. 28, 1907, West Baden, Ind.

		G	W	L	PCT	Standing	
1906	BOS A	18	5	13	.278	8	8

	G	W	L	PCT	Standing				G	W	L	PCT	Standing

Jake Stahl

STAHL, GARLAND
Brother of Chick Stahl.
B. Apr. 13, 1879, Elkhart, Ind.
D. Sept. 18, 1922, Los Angeles, Calif.

		G	W	L	PCT	Standing	
1905	**WAS A**	156	64	87	.424	7	
1906		151	55	95	.367	7	
1912	**BOS A**	154	105	47	.691	1	
1913		81	39	41	.488	5	4
4 yrs.		542	263	270	.493		

WORLD SERIES

		G	W	L	PCT		
1912	**BOS A**	8	4	3	.571		

George Stallings

STALLINGS, GEORGE TWEEDY (The Miracle Man)
B. Nov. 17, 1867, Augusta, Ga.
D. May 13, 1929, Haddock, Ga.

		G	W	L	PCT	Standing	
1897	**PHI N**	134	55	77	.417	10	
1898		46	19	27	.413	8	6
1901	**DET A**	136	74	61	.548	3	
1909	**NY A**	153	74	77	.490	5	
1910		145	79	61	.564	2	2
1913	**BOS N**	154	69	82	.457	5	
1914		158	94	59	.614	1	
1915		157	83	69	.546	2	
1916		158	89	63	.586	3	
1917		157	72	81	.471	6	
1918		124	53	71	.427	7	
1919		140	57	82	.410	6	
1920		153	62	90	.408	7	
13 yrs.		1815	880	900	.494		

WORLD SERIES

		G	W	L	PCT		
1914	**BOS N**	4	4	0	1.000		

Eddie Stanky

STANKY, EDWARD RAYMOND (The Brat, Muggsy)
B. Sept. 3, 1916, Philadelphia, Pa.

		G	W	L	PCT	Standing	
1952	**STL N**	154	88	66	.571	3	
1953		157	83	71	.539	3	
1954		154	72	82	.468	6	
1955		36	17	19	.472	5	7
1966	**CHI A**	163	83	79	.512	4	
1967		162	89	73	.549	4	
1968		79	34	45	.430	9	9
1977	**TEX A**	1	1	0	1.000	4	2	2
8 yrs.		906	467	435	.518		

Casey Stengel

STENGEL, CHARLES DILLON (The Old Professor)
B. July 30, 1890, Kansas City, Mo.
D. Sept. 29, 1975, Glendale, Calif.
Hall of Fame 1966.

		G	W	L	PCT	Standing	
1934	**BKN N**	153	71	81	.467	6	
1935		154	70	83	.458	5	
1936		156	67	87	.435	7	
1938	**BOS N**	153	77	75	.507	5	
1939		152	63	88	.417	7	
1940		152	65	87	.428	7	
1941		156	62	92	.403	7	
1942		150	59	89	.399	7	
1943		153	68	85	.444	6	
1949	**NY A**	155	97	57	.630	1	
1950		155	98	56	.636	1	
1951		154	98	56	.636	1	
1952		154	95	59	.617	1	
1953		151	99	52	.656	1	
1954		155	103	51	.669	2	
1955		154	96	58	.623	1	
1956		154	97	57	.630	1	
1957		154	98	56	.636	1	
1958		155	92	62	.597	1	
1959		155	79	75	.513	3	
1960		155	97	57	.630	1	
1962	**NY N**	161	40	120	.250	10	
1963		162	51	111	.315	10	
1964		163	53	109	.327	10	
1965		96	31	64	.326	10	10
25 yrs.		3812	1926	1867	.508		
			4th	**7th**		**4th**	

Casey Stengel continued

WORLD SERIES

		G	W	L	PCT		
1949	**NY A**	5	4	1	.800		
1950		4	4	0	1.000		
1951		6	4	2	.667		
1952		7	4	3	.571		
1953		6	4	2	.667		
1955		7	3	4	.429		
1956		7	4	3	.571		
1957		7	3	4	.429		
1958		7	4	3	.571		
1960		7	3	4	.429		
10 yrs.		63	37	26	.587		
			1st	**1st**	**2nd**	**2nd**	

George Stovall

STOVALL, GEORGE THOMAS (Firebrand)
Brother of Jesse Stovall.
B. Nov. 23, 1878, Independence, Mo.
D. Nov. 5, 1951, Burlington, Iowa

		G	W	L	PCT	Standing	
1911	**CLE A**	139	74	62	.544	5	3
1912	**STL A**	117	41	74	.357	8	7
1913		135	50	84	.373	7	8
1914	**KC F**	154	67	84	.444	6	
1915		153	81	72	.529	4	
5 yrs.		698	313	376	.454		

Gabby Street

STREET, CHARLES EVARD (Old Sarge)
B. Sept. 30, 1882, Huntsville, Ala.
D. Feb. 6, 1951, Joplin, Mo.

		G	W	L	PCT	Standing	
1929	**STL N**	2	2	0	1.000	4	4	4
1930		154	92	62	.597	1	
1931		154	101	53	.656	1	
1932		156	72	82	.468	6	
1933		91	46	45	.505	5	5
1938	**STL N**	156	55	97	.362	7	
6 yrs.		713	368	339	.521		

WORLD SERIES

		G	W	L	PCT		
1930	**STL N**	6	2	4	.333		
1931		7	4	3	.571		
2 yrs.		13	6	7	.462		

George Strickland

STRICKLAND, GEORGE BEVAN (Bo)
B. Jan. 10, 1926, New Orleans, La.

		G	W	L	PCT	Standing	
1966	**CLE A**	39	15	24	.385	5	5

Clyde Sukeforth

SUKEFORTH, CLYDE LeROY (Sukey)
B. Nov. 30, 1901, Washington, Me.

		G	W	L	PCT	Standing	
1947	**BKN N**	1	1	0	1.000	1	1

Billy Sullivan

SULLIVAN, WILLIAM JOSEPH, SR.
Father of Billy Sullivan.
B. Feb. 1, 1875, Oakland, Wis.
D. Jan. 28, 1965, Newberg, Ore.

		G	W	L	PCT	Standing	
1909	**CHI A**	159	78	74	.513	4	

Haywood Sullivan

SULLIVAN, HAYWOOD COOPER
Father of Marc Sullivan.
B. Dec. 15, 1930, Donalsonville, Ga.

		G	W	L	PCT	Standing	
1965	**KC A**	136	54	82	.397	10	10

Ted Sullivan

SULLIVAN, THEODORE PAUL
B. 1852, County Clare, Ireland
D. July 5, 1929, Washington, D. C.

	G	W	L	PCT	Standing	
1883 STL AA	80	53	27	.663	2	2
1884 KC U	82	16	63	.203	11	
1888 WAS N	94	36	57	.387	8	8
3 yrs.	256	105	147	.417		

Bob Swift

SWIFT, ROBERT VIRGIL
B. Mar. 6, 1915, Salina, Kans.
D. Oct. 17, 1966, Detroit, Mich.

	G	W	L	PCT	Standing	
1966 DET A	57	32	25	.561	3	3

Chuck Tanner

TANNER, CHARLES WILLIAM
B. July 4, 1929, New Castle, Pa.

	G	W	L	PCT	Standing		
1970 CHI A	16	3	13	.188	6	6	
1971	162	79	83	.488	3		
1972	154	87	67	.565	2		
1973	162	77	85	.475	5		
1974	160	80	80	.500	4		
1975	161	75	86	.466	5		
1976 OAK A	161	87	74	.540	2		
1977 PIT N	162	96	66	.593	2		
1978	161	88	73	.547	2		
1979	162	98	64	.605	1		
1980	162	83	79	.512	3		
1981	49	25	23	.521	4		(1st)
1981	54	21	33	.389	6		(2nd)
1982	162	84	78	.519	4		
1983	162	84	78	.519	2		
1984	162	75	87	.463	6		
15 yrs.	2212	1142	1069	.517			

LEAGUE CHAMPIONSHIP SERIES
	G	W	L	PCT		
1979 PIT N	3	3	0	1.000		

WORLD SERIES
	G	W	L	PCT		
1979 PIT N	7	4	3	.571		

El Tappe

TAPPE, ELVIN WALTER
B. May 21, 1927, Quincy, Ill.

	G	W	L	PCT	Standing		
1961 CHI N	96	42	53	.442	7	7	7
1962	20	4	16	.200	9	9	
2 yrs.	116	46	69	.400			

George Taylor

TAYLOR, GEORGE J.
B. Nov. 22, 1853, New York, N. Y.
Deceased.

	G	W	L	PCT	Standing
1884 BKN AA	109	40	64	.385	9

Zack Taylor

TAYLOR, JAMES WREN
B. July 27, 1898, Yulee, Fla.
D. July 6, 1974, Orlando, Fla.

	G	W	L	PCT	Standing	
1946 STL A	30	13	17	.433	7	7
1948	155	59	94	.386	6	
1949	155	53	101	.344	7	
1950	154	58	96	.377	7	
1951	154	52	102	.338	8	
5 yrs.	648	235	410	.364		

Birdie Tebbetts

TEBBETTS, GEORGE ROBERT
B. Nov. 10, 1912, Burlington, Vt.

	G	W	L	PCT	Standing
1954 CIN N	154	74	80	.481	5
1955	154	75	79	.487	5
1956	155	91	63	.591	3

Birdie Tebbetts continued

	G	W	L	PCT	Standing	
1957	154	80	74	.519	4	
1958	113	52	61	.460	7	4
1961 MIL N	25	12	13	.480	3	4
1962	162	86	76	.531	5	
1963 CLE A	162	79	83	.488	5	
1964	164	79	83	.488	6	
1965	162	87	75	.537	5	
1966	123	66	57	.537	5	5
11 yrs.	1528	781	744	.512		

Patsy Tebeau

TEBEAU, OLIVER WENDELL
Brother of White Wings Tebeau.
B. Dec. 5, 1864, St. Louis, Mo.
D. May 15, 1918, St. Louis, Mo.

	G	W	L	PCT	Standing	
1890 CLE P	36	18	17	.514	7	7
1891 CLE N	76	34	40	.459	6	5
1892	153	93	56	.624	2	
1893	129	73	55	.570	3	
1894	130	68	61	.527	6	
1895	131	84	46	.646	2	
1896	135	80	48	.625	2	
1897	132	69	62	.527	5	
1898	156	81	68	.544	5	
1899 STL N	155	84	67	.556	5	
1900	104	48	55	.466	7	5
11 yrs.	1337	732	575	.560		

Fred Tenney

TENNEY, FREDERICK CLAY
B. June 9, 1859, Georgetown, Mass.
D. July 3, 1952, Boston, Mass.

	G	W	L	PCT	Standing
1905 BOS N	156	51	103	.331	7
1906	152	49	102	.325	8
1907	152	58	90	.392	7
1911	156	44	107	.291	8
4 yrs.	616	202	402	.334	

Bill Terry

TERRY, WILLIAM HAROLD (Memphis Bill)
B. Oct. 30, 1898, Atlanta, Ga.
Hall of Fame 1954.

	G	W	L	PCT	Standing	
1932 NY N	114	55	59	.482	8	6
1933	156	91	61	.599	1	
1934	153	93	60	.608	2	
1935	156	91	62	.595	3	
1936	154	92	62	.597	1	
1937	152	95	57	.625	1	
1938	152	83	67	.553	3	
1939	151	77	74	.510	5	
1940	152	72	80	.474	6	
1941	156	74	79	.484	5	
10 yrs.	1496	823	661	.555		

WORLD SERIES
	G	W	L	PCT	
1933 NY N	5	4	1	.800	
1936	6	2	4	.333	
1937	5	1	4	.200	
3 yrs.	16	7	9	.438	

Fred Thomas

THOMAS, FREDERICK L.
B. Ind.
Deceased.

	G	W	L	PCT	Standing		
1887 IND N	29	11	18	.379	8	8	8

A. M. Thompson

THOMPSON, A. M.
B. St. Paul, Minn.
Deceased.

	G	W	L	PCT	Standing
1884 STP U	9	2	6	.250	9

	G	W	L	PCT	Standing				G	W	L	PCT	Standing	

Jack Tighe
TIGHE, JOHN THOMAS
B. Aug. 9, 1913, Kearny, N. J.

	G	W	L	PCT	Standing
1957 **DET A**	154	78	76	.506	4
1958	49	21	28	.429	5 5
2 yrs.	203	99	104	.488	

Joe Tinker
TINKER, JOSEPH BERT
B. July 27, 1880, Muscotah, Kans.
D. July 27, 1948, Orlando, Fla.
Hall of Fame 1946.

	G	W	L	PCT	Standing
1913 **CIN N**	156	64	89	.418	7
1914 **CHI F**	157	87	67	.565	2
1915	155	86	66	.566	1
1916 **CHI N**	156	67	86	.438	5
4 yrs.	624	304	308	.497	

Jeff Torborg
TORBORG, JEFFREY ALLEN
B. Nov. 26, 1941, Plainfield, N. J.

	G	W	L	PCT	Standing
1977 **CLE A**	104	45	59	.433	6 5
1978	159	69	90	.434	6
1979	95	43	52	.453	6 6
3 yrs.	358	157	201	.439	

Joe Torre
TORRE, JOSEPH PAUL
Brother of Frank Torre.
B. July 18, 1940, Brooklyn, N. Y.

	G	W	L	PCT	Standing	
1977 **NY N**	117	49	68	.419	6 6	
1978	162	66	96	.407	6	
1979	162	63	99	.389	6	
1980	162	67	95	.414	5	
1981	52	17	34	.333	5	(1st)
1981	53	24	28	.462	4	(2nd)
1982 **ATL N**	162	89	73	.549	1	
1983	162	88	74	.543	2	
1984	162	80	82	.494	2	
8 yrs.	1194	543	649	.456		

LEAGUE CHAMPIONSHIP SERIES

	G	W	L	PCT
1982 **ATL N**	3	0	3	.000

Dick Tracewski
TRACEWSKI, RICHARD JOSEPH
B. Feb. 3, 1935, Eynon, Pa.

	G	W	L	PCT	Standing
1979 **DET A**	3	2	1	.667	5 5 5

Pie Traynor
TRAYNOR, HAROLD JOSEPH
B. Nov. 11, 1899, Framingham, Mass.
D. Mar. 16, 1972, Pittsburgh, Pa.
Hall of Fame 1948.

	G	W	L	PCT	Standing
1934 **PIT N**	99	47	52	.475	4 5
1935	153	86	67	.562	4
1936	156	84	70	.545	4
1937	154	86	68	.558	3
1938	152	86	64	.573	2
1939	153	68	85	.444	6
6 yrs.	867	457	406	.530	

Sam Trott
TROTT, SAMUEL W.
B. 1858, Washington, D. C.
D. June 5, 1925, Cantonsville, Md.

	G	W	L	PCT	Standing
1891 **WAS AA**	13	4	8	.333	6 8

Ted Turner
TURNER, ROBERT EDWARDS
B. Nov. 19, 1938, Cincinnati, Ohio

	G	W	L	PCT	Standing
1977 **ATL N**	1	0	1	.000	6 6 6

Bob Unglaub
UNGLAUB, ROBERT ALEXANDER
B. July 31, 1881, Baltimore, Md.
D. Nov. 29, 1916, Baltimore, Md.

	G	W	L	PCT	Standing
1907 **BOS A**	29	8	20	.286	6 8 7

George Van Haltren
VAN HALTREN, GEORGE EDWARD MARTIN
B. Mar. 30, 1866, St. Louis, Mo.
D. Sept. 29, 1945, Oakland, Calif.

	G	W	L	PCT	Standing
1891 **BAL AA**	6	4	2	.667	3 3
1892 **BAL N**	15	1	14	.067	12 12
2 yrs.	21	5	16	.238	

Mickey Vernon
VERNON, JAMES BARTON
B. Apr. 22, 1918, Marcus Hook, Pa.

	G	W	L	PCT	Standing
1961 **WAS A**	161	61	100	.379	9
1962	162	60	101	.373	10
1963	40	14	26	.350	10 10
3 yrs.	363	135	227	.373	

Bill Virdon
VIRDON, WILLIAM CHARLES
B. June 9, 1931, Hazel Park, Mich.

	G	W	L	PCT	Standing	
1972 **PIT N**	155	96	59	.619	1	
1973	136	67	69	.493	2 3	
1974 **NY A**	162	89	73	.549	2	
1975	104	53	51	.510	3 3	
1975 **HOU N**	34	17	17	.500	6 6	
1976	162	80	82	.494	3	
1977	162	81	81	.500	3	
1978	162	74	88	.457	5	
1979	162	89	73	.549	2	
1980	163	93	70	.571	1	
1981	57	28	29	.491	3	(1st)
1981	53	33	20	.623	1	(2nd)
1982	111	49	62	.441	5 5	
1983 **MON N**	163	82	80	.506	3	
1984	131	64	67	.489	5 5	
13 yrs.	1917	995	921	.519		

DIVISIONAL PLAYOFF SERIES

	G	W	L	PCT
1981 **HOU N**	5	2	3	.400

LEAGUE CHAMPIONSHIP SERIES

	G	W	L	PCT	
1972 **PIT N**	5	2	3	.400	
1980 **HOU N**	5	2	3	.400	
2 yrs.	10	4	6	.400	9th 7th 8th 6th

Ossie Vitt
VITT, OSCAR JOSEPH
B. Jan. 4, 1890, San Francisco, Calif.
D. Jan. 31, 1963, Oakland, Calif.

	G	W	L	PCT	Standing
1938 **CLE A**	153	86	66	.566	3
1939	154	87	67	.565	3
1940	155	89	65	.578	2
3 yrs.	462	262	198	.570	

Chris Von Der Ahe
VON DER AHE, CHRISTIAN FREDERICK WILHELM
B. Nov. 7, 1851, Hille, Germany
D. June 7, 1913, St. Louis, Mo.

	G	W	L	PCT	Standing
1892 **STL N**	155	56	94	.373	11
1895	14	2	12	.143	11 11
1896	3	0	2	.000	10 11 11
1897	3	1	2	.333	12 12
4 yrs.	175	59	110	.349	

	G	W	L	PCT	Standing			G	W	L	PCT	Standing

Heinie Wagner

WAGNER, CHARLES F.
B. Sept. 23, 1881, New York, N. Y.
D. Mar. 20, 1943, New Rochelle, N. Y.

		G	W	L	PCT	Standing
1930	BOS A	154	52	102	.338	8

Honus Wagner

WAGNER, JOHN PETER (The Flying Dutchman)
Brother of Butts Wagner.
B. Feb. 24, 1874, Carnegie, Pa.
D. Dec. 6, 1955, Carnegie, Pa.
Hall of Fame 1936.

		G	W	L	PCT	Standing		
1917	PIT N	5	1	4	.200	8	8	8

Harry Walker

WALKER, HARRY WILLIAM (The Hat)
Son of Dixie Walker.
Brother of Dixie Walker.
B. Oct. 22, 1918, Pascagoula, Miss.

		G	W	L	PCT	Standing	
1955	STL N	118	51	67	.432	5	7
1965	PIT N	163	90	72	.556	3	
1966		162	92	70	.568	3	
1967		84	42	42	.500	6	6
1968	HOU N	101	49	52	.485	10	10
1969		162	81	81	.500	5	
1970		162	79	83	.488	4	
1971		162	79	83	.488	4	
1972		121	67	54	.554	3	2
9 yrs.		1235	630	604	.511		

Bobby Wallace

WALLACE, RODERICK JOHN (Rhody)
B. Nov. 4, 1873, Pittsburgh, Pa.
D. Nov. 3, 1960, Torrance, Calif.
Hall of Fame 1953.

		G	W	L	PCT	Standing	
1911	STL A	152	45	107	.296	8	
1912		40	12	27	.308	8	7
1937	CIN N	25	5	20	.200	8	8
3 yrs.		217	62	154	.287		

Mike Walsh

WALSH, MICHAEL JOHN
B. Aug. 6, 1852, Baltimore, Md.
D. Mar. 17, 1924, Springfield, Mo.

		G	W	L	PCT	Standing	
1884	LOU AA	52	29	22	.569	3	3

Bucky Walters

WALTERS, WILLIAM HENRY
B. Apr. 19, 1909, Philadelphia, Pa.

		G	W	L	PCT	Standing	
1948	CIN N	53	20	33	.377	7	7
1949		153	61	90	.404	7	7
2 yrs.		206	81	123	.397		

John Waltz

WALTZ, JOHN J.
Deceased.

		G	W	L	PCT	Standing		
1892	BAL N	2	0	2	.000	12	12	12

Monte Ward

WARD, JOHN MONTGOMERY
B. Mar. 3, 1860, Bellefonte, Pa.
D. Mar. 4, 1925, Augusta, Ga.
Hall of Fame 1964.

		G	W	L	PCT	Standing	
1884	NY N	16	6	8	.429	4	4
1890	BKN P	133	76	56	.576	2	
1891	BKN N	137	61	76	.445	6	
1892		158	95	59	.617	3	
1893	NY N	136	68	64	.515	5	
1894		137	88	44	.667	2	
6 yrs.		717	394	307	.562		

George Ware

WARE, GEORGE
Deceased.

		G	W	L	PCT	Standing
1878	PRO N	62	33	27	.550	3

Bill Watkins

WATKINS, WILLIAM HENRY
B. May 5, 1859, Brantford, Ont., Canada
D. June 9, 1937, Port Huron, Mich.

		G	W	L	PCT	Standing	
1884	IND AA	24	4	19	.174	11	12
1885	DET N	51	23	28	.451	7	6
1886		126	87	36	.707	2	
1887		127	79	45	.637	1	
1888		96	49	45	.521	3	5
1888	KC AA	14	3	11	.214	8	8
1889		139	55	82	.401	7	
1893	STL N	135	57	75	.432	10	
1898	PIT N	152	72	76	.486	8	
1899		25	8	16	.333	10	7
9 yrs.		889	437	433	.502		

Harvey Watkins

WATKINS, HARVEY L.
Deceased.

		G	W	L	PCT	Standing	
1895	NY N	35	18	17	.514	9	9

Earl Weaver

WEAVER, EARL SIDNEY
B. Aug. 14, 1930, St. Louis, Mo.

		G	W	L	PCT	Standing		
1968	BAL A	82	48	34	.585	3	2	
1969		162	109	53	.673	1		
1970		162	108	54	.667	1		
1971		158	101	57	.639	1		
1972		154	80	74	.519	3		
1973		162	97	65	.599	1		
1974		162	91	71	.562	1		
1975		159	90	69	.566	2		
1976		162	88	74	.543	2		
1977		161	97	64	.602	2		
1978		161	90	71	.559	4		
1979		159	102	57	.642	1		
1980		162	100	62	.617	2		
1981		54	31	23	.574	2		(1st)
1981		51	28	23	.549	4		(2nd)
1982		162	94	68	.580	2		
15 yrs.		2273	1354	919	.596			
					5th			

LEAGUE CHAMPIONSHIP SERIES

		G	W	L	PCT	
1969	BAL A	3	3	0	1.000	
1970		3	3	0	1.000	
1971		3	3	0	1.000	
1973		5	2	3	.400	
1974		4	1	3	.250	
1979		4	3	1	.750	
6 yrs.		22	15	7	.682	
		1st	**2nd**	**6th**	**2nd**	

WORLD SERIES

		G	W	L	PCT
1969	BAL A	5	1	4	.200
1970		5	4	1	.800
1971		7	3	4	.429
1979		7	3	4	.429
4 yrs.		24	11	13	.458
		9th	**9th**	**8th**	

Wes Westrum

WESTRUM, WESLEY NOREEN
B. Nov. 28, 1922, Clearbrook, Minn.

		G	W	L	PCT	Standing	
1965	NY N	68	19	48	.284	10	10
1966		161	66	95	.410	9	
1967		151	57	94	.377	10	10
1974	SF N	86	38	48	.442	5	5
1975		161	80	81	.497	3	
5 yrs.		627	260	366	.415		

	G	W	L	PCT	Standing				G	W	L	PCT	Standing	

Deacon White
WHITE, JAMES LAURIE
Brother of Will White.
B. Dec. 7, 1847, Caton, N. Y.
D. July 7, 1939, Aurora, Ill.

1879 CIN N	17	8	8	.500	5	5

Jo-Jo White
WHITE, JOYNER CLIFFORD
Father of Mike White.
B. June 1, 1909, Red Oak, Ga.

1960 CLE A	1	1	0	1.000	4	4	4

Will White
WHITE, WILLIAM HENRY (Whoop-La)
Brother of Deacon White.
B. Oct. 11, 1854, Caton, N. Y.
D. Aug. 31, 1911, Port Carling, Ont., Canada

1884 CIN AA	71	43	25	.632	4	5

Del Wilber
WILBER, DELBERT QUENTIN (Babe)
B. Feb. 24, 1919, Lincoln Park, Mich.

1973 TEX A	1	1	0	1.000	6	6

Kaiser Wilhelm
WILHELM, IRVIN KEY
B. Jan. 26, 1874, Wooster Ohio
D. May 21, 1936, Rochester, N. Y.

1921 PHI N	52	20	32	.385	8	8
1922	154	57	96	.373	7	
2 yrs.	206	77	128	.376		

Dick Williams
WILLIAMS, RICHARD HIRSHFIELD
B. May 7, 1928, St. Louis, Mo.

1967 BOS A	162	92	70	.568	1		
1968	162	86	76	.531	4		
1969	153	82	71	.536	3	3	
1971 OAK A	161	101	60	.627	1		
1972	155	93	62	.600	1		
1973	162	94	68	.580	1		
1974 CAL A	84	36	48	.429	6	6	
1975	161	72	89	.447	6		
1976	96	39	57	.406	4	4	
1977 MON N	162	75	87	.463	5		
1978	162	76	86	.469	4		
1979	160	95	65	.594	2		
1980	162	90	72	.556	2		
1981	55	30	25	.545	3		(1st)
1981	26	14	12	.538	2	1	(2nd)
1982 SD N	162	81	81	.500	4		
1983	162	81	81	.500	4		
1984	162	92	70	.568	1		
17 yrs.	2509	1329	1180	.530			

LEAGUE CHAMPIONSHIP SERIES

1971 OAK A	3	0	3	.000
1972	5	3	2	.600
1973	5	3	2	.600
1984 SD N	5	3	2	.600
4 yrs.	18	9	9	.500
	4th	4th	3rd	4th

WORLD SERIES

1967 BOS A	7	3	4	.429
1972 OAK A	7	4	3	.571
1973	7	4	3	.571
1984 SD N	5	1	4	.200
4 yrs.	26	12	14	.462
	8th	8th	6th	

Jimmy Williams
WILLIAMS, JAMES ANDREWS
B. Jan. 3, 1848, Columbus, Ohio
D. Oct. 24, 1918, North Hempstead, N. Y.

1884 STL AA	110	67	40	.626	4	
1887 CLE AA	133	39	92	.298	8	
1888	61	19	41	.317	7	6
3 yrs.	304	125	173	.419		

Ted Williams
WILLIAMS, THEODORE SAMUEL (The Splendid Splinter, The Thumper)
B. Aug. 30, 1918, San Diego, Calif.
Hall of Fame 1966.

1969 WAS A	162	86	76	.531	4
1970	162	70	92	.432	6
1971	159	63	96	.396	5
1972 TEX A	154	54	100	.351	6
4 yrs.	637	273	364	.429	

Maury Wills
WILLS, MAURICE MORNING
Father of Bump Wills.
B. Oct. 2, 1932, Washington, D. C.

1980 SEA A	58	20	38	.345	7	7	
1981	25	6	18	.250	7	6	(1st)
2 yrs.	83	26	56	.317			

Jimmie Wilson
WILSON, JAMES (Ace)
B. July 23, 1900, Philadelphia, Pa.
D. May 31, 1947, Bradenton, Fla.

1934 PHI N	149	56	93	.376	7	
1935	156	64	89	.418	7	
1936	154	54	100	.351	8	
1937	155	61	92	.399	7	
1938	149	45	103	.304	8	8
1941 CHI N	155	70	84	.455	6	
1942	155	68	86	.442	6	
1943	154	74	79	.484	5	
1944	10	1	9	.100	8	4
9 yrs.	1237	493	735	.401		

Ivy Wingo
WINGO, IVEY BROWN
Brother of Al Wingo.
B. July 8, 1890, Gainesville, Ga.
D. Mar. 1, 1941, Norcross, Ga.

1916 CIN N	2	1	1	.500	8	8	7

Bobby Winkles
WINKLES, BOBBY BROOKS (Winks)
B. Mar. 11, 1932, Swifton, Ark.

1973 CAL A	162	79	83	.488	4	
1974	78	32	46	.410	6	6
1977 OAK A	108	37	71	.343	7	7
1978	39	24	15	.615	6	6
4 yrs.	387	172	215	.444		

Chicken Wolf
WOLF, WILLIAM VAN WINKLE
B. May 12, 1862, Louisville, Ky.
D. May 16, 1903, Louisville, Ky.

1889 LOU AA	66	15	51	.227	8	8	8

	G	W	L	PCT	Standing			G	W	L	PCT	Standing

Harry Wolverton
WOLVERTON, HARRY STERLING
B. Dec. 6, 1873, Mt. Vernon, Ohio
D. Feb. 4, 1937, Oakland, Calif.

		G	W	L	PCT	Standing
1912	NY A	153	50	102	.329	8

George Wood
WOOD, GEORGE A. (Dandy)
B. Nov. 9, 1858, Boston, Mass.
D. Apr. 4, 1924, Harrisburg, Pa.

		G	W	L	PCT	Standing		
1891	PHI AA	101	54	46	.540	4	4	4

Al Wright
WRIGHT, ALFRED HECTOR
B. Mar. 30, 1842, Cedar Grove, N. J.
D. Apr. 20, 1905

		G	W	L	PCT	Standing
1876	PHI N	60	14	45	.237	7

George Wright
WRIGHT, GEORGE
Brother of Harry Wright.
Brother of Sam Wright.
B. Jan. 28, 1847, Yonkers, N. Y.
D. Aug. 21, 1937, Boston, Mass.
Hall of Fame 1937.

		G	W	L	PCT	Standing
1879	PRO N	85	59	25	.702	1

Harry Wright
WRIGHT, WILLIAM HENRY
Brother of Sam Wright.
Brother of George Wright.
B. Jan. 10, 1835, Sheffield, England
D. Oct. 3, 1895, Atlantic City, N. J.
Hall of Fame 1953.

		G	W	L	PCT	Standing
1876	BOS N	70	39	31	.557	4
1877		61	42	18	.700	1
1878		60	41	19	.683	1
1879		84	54	30	.643	2
1880		86	40	44	.476	6
1881		83	38	45	.458	6
1882	PRO N	84	52	32	.619	2
1883		98	58	40	.592	3
1884	PHI N	113	39	73	.348	6
1885		111	56	54	.509	3
1886		119	71	43	.623	4
1887		128	75	48	.610	2
1888		131	69	61	.531	3
1889		130	63	64	.496	4
1890		133	78	54	.591	3
1891		138	68	69	.496	4
1892		155	87	66	.569	4
1893		133	72	57	.558	4
18 yrs.		1917	1042	848	.551	

Rudy York
YORK, RUDOLPH PRESTON
B. Aug. 17, 1913, Ragland, Ala.
D. Feb. 2, 1970, Rome, Ga.

		G	W	L	PCT	Standing		
1959	BOS A	1	0	1	.000	8	8	5

Cy Young
YOUNG, DENTON TRUE
B. Mar. 29, 1867, Gilmore, Ohio
D. Nov. 4, 1955, Peoli, Ohio
Hall of Fame 1937.

		G	W	L	PCT	Standing	
1907	BOS A	7	3	4	.429	5	7

Chief Zimmer
ZIMMER, CHARLES LOUIS
B. Nov. 23, 1860, Marietta, Ohio
D. Aug. 22, 1949, Cleveland, Ohio

		G	W	L	PCT	Standing
1903	PHI N	139	49	86	.363	7

Don Zimmer
ZIMMER, DONALD WILLIAM
B. Jan. 17, 1931, Cincinnati, Ohio

		G	W	L	PCT	Standing		
1972	SD N	142	54	88	.380	4	6	
1973		162	60	102	.370	6		
1976	BOS A	76	42	34	.553	3	3	
1977		161	97	64	.602	2		
1978		163	99	64	.607	2		
1979		160	91	69	.569	3		
1980		156	82	74	.526	4	4	
1981	TEX A	55	33	22	.600	2		(1st)
1981		50	24	26	.480	3		(2nd)
1982		96	38	58	.396	6	6	
9 yrs.		1221	620	601	.508			

PART EIGHT

Player Register

ALPHABETICAL LIST OF EVERY MAN

(EXCEPT CERTAIN PITCHERS)

WHO EVER PLAYED IN THE MAJOR LEAGUES

AND HIS BATTING RECORD

Player Register

The Player Register is an alphabetical listing of every man who has played in the major leagues from 1876 through today, except those players who were primarily pitchers. However, pitchers who pinch hit and played in other positions for a total of 25 games or more are listed in this Player Register. Included are facts about the players and their year-by-year batting records and their lifetime totals of league Championship Series and World Series.

Much of this information has never been compiled, especially for the period 1876 through 1919. For certain other years some statistics are still missing or incomplete. Research in this area is still in progress, and the years that lack complete information are indicated. In fact, all information and abbreviations that may appear unfamiliar are explained in the sample format presented below. John Doe, the player used in the sample, is fictitious and serves only to illustrate the information.

	G	AB	H	2B	3B	HR	HR %	R	RBI	BB	SO	SB	BA	SA	Pinch Hit AB	Pinch Hit H	G by POS

John Doe

DOE, JOHN LEE (Slim)
Played as John Cherry part of 1900.
Born John Lee Doughnut.   Brother of Bill Doe.
B. Jan. 1,1850, New York, N. Y.   D. July 1, 1955, New York, N. Y.
Manager 1908-15.
Hall of Fame 1946.

BR TR 6'2"   165 lbs.
BB 1884   BL 1906

Year	Team	Lg	G	AB	H	2B	3B	HR	HR %	R	RBI	BB	SO	SB	BA	SA	PH AB	PH H	G by POS
1884	STL	U	125	435	121	18	1	3	0.7	44		37	42	7	.278	.345	9	2	SS-99, P-26
1885	LOU	AA	155	547	138	22	3	3	0.6	50	58	42	48	8	.252	.320	8	4	SS-115, P-40
1886	CLE	N	147	485	134	38	5	0	0.0	66	54	48	50	8	.276	.375	7	1	SS-107, P-40
1887	BOS	N	129	418	117	15	3	1	0.2	38	52	32	37	1	.280	.337	1	0	SS-102, P-27
1888	NY	N	144	506	135	26	2	6	1.2	50	63	43	50	1	.267	.362	10	8	SS-105, P-39
1889	3 teams		DET	N	(10G –	.300)		PIT	N	(32G –	.241)		PHI	N	(41G –	.364)		
"	total		83	237	75	31	16	7	3.0	90	42	25	35	3	.316	.671	6	3	SS-61, P-22
1890	NY	P	123	430	119	27	5	1	0.2	63	59	39	39	2	.277	.370	12	10	SS-85, P-38
1900	CHI	N	146	498	116	29	4	3	0.6	51	46	59	53	1	.233	.325	13	8	SS-114, P-35
1901	NY	N	149	540	147	19	6	4	0.7	57	74	49	58	3	.272	.352	23	15	SS-113, P-31
1906	BOS	N	144	567	143	26	4	4	0.7	70	43	37	54	1	.252	.333	7	1	SS-97, P-37
1907			134	515	140	31	2	5	1.0	61	70	37	42	0	.272	.369	13	8	SS-105, P-1
1908			106	372	92	10	2	4	1.1	36	40	4	55	1	.247	.317	1	0	P-6
1914	CHI	F	6	6	0	0	0	0	0.0	0	0	0	1	0	.000	.000	0	0	SS-1
1915	NY	A	1	0	0	0	0	0	–	0	0	0	0	0	–	–	0	0	SS-
14 yrs.			1592	5556	1927	292 4th	53	41	0.7	676	601	452	564	36	.266	.360	110	60	SS-1215, P-377

LEAGUE CHAMPIONSHIP SERIES																	
1 yr.	3	14	5	2	0	3	21.4	3	7	0	1	0	.357	1.143	0	0	OF-3

WORLD SERIES																	
2 yrs.	14	55	20	2	1	3	5.5	8	9	5	12	0	.364	.600	0	0	OF-14

John Doe — This shortened version of the player's full name is the name most familiar to the fans. All players in this section are alphabetically arranged by the last name part of this name.

DOE, JOHN LEE — Player's full name. The arrangement is last name first, then first and middle name(s).

(Slim) — Player's nickname. Any name or names appearing in parentheses indicates a nickname.

The player's main batting and throwing style. Doe, for instance, batted and threw right handed. The information listed directly below the main batting information indicates that at various times in a player's career he changed his batting style. The "BB" for Doe in 1884 means he was a switch hitter that year, and the "BL" means he batted left handed in 1906. For the years that are not shown it can be assumed that Doe batted right, as his main batting information indicates.

BR TR
BB 1884
BL 1906

Player's height.

6'2"

Player's average playing weight.

165 lbs

The player at one time in his major league career played under another name and can be found only in box scores or newspaper stories under that name.

Played as
John Cherry
part of 1900

The name the player was given at birth. (For the most part, the player never used this name while playing in the major leagues, but, if he did, it would be listed as "played as," which is explained above under the heading "Played as John Cherry part of 1900.")

Born John Lee
Doughnut

The player's brother. (Relatives indicated here are fathers, sons, brothers, grandfathers, and grandsons who played or managed in the major leagues and the National Association.)

Brother of
Bill Doe

Date and place of birth.

B. Jan. 1, 1850,
New York, N.Y.

Date and place of death. (For those players who are listed simply as "deceased," it means that, although no certification of death or other information is presently available, it is reasonably certain they are dead.)

D. July 1, 1955,
New York, N.Y.

Doe also served as a major league manager. All men who were managers can be found also in the Manager Register, where their complete managerial record is shown.

Manager
1908–15

Doe was elected to the Baseball Hall of Fame in 1946.

Hall of Fame
1946

COLUMN HEADINGS INFORMATION

G	AB	H	2B	3B	HR	HR %	R	RBI	BB	SO	SB	BA	SA	Pinch Hit AB	H	G by POS

G	Games
AB	At Bats
H	Hits
2B	Doubles
3B	Triples
HR	Home Runs
HR %	Home Run Percentage (the number of home runs per 100 times at bat)
R	Runs Scored
RBI	Runs Batted In
BB	Bases on Balls
SO	Strikeouts
SB	Stolen Bases
BA	Batting Average
SA	Slugging Average

Pinch Hit

AB	Pinch Hit At Bats
H	Pinch Hits

G by POS Games by Position. (All fielding positions a man played within the given year are shown. The position where the most games were played is listed first. Any man who pitched, as Doe did, is listed also in the alphabetically arranged Pitcher Register, where his complete pitching record can be found.) If no fielding positions are shown in a particular year, it means the player only pinch-hit, pinch-ran, or was a "designated hitter." In the case of a designated hitter, the number of games he has played as a designated hitter will be shown alongside the letters DH.

```
1884 STL  U    125 |
1885 LOU  AA   155 |
1886 CLE  N    147 |
1887 BOS  N    129 |
1888 NY   N    144 |
1889 3 teams   DET N (10G - .300)   PIT N (32G - .241)   PHI N (41G - .364)
"    total  83 | 237  75 | 31'  16  7  3.0 | 90  42 | 25  35 | 3 | .316  .671 | 6  3 |SS-61, P-22
1890 NY   P
1900 CHI  N
1901 NY   N
1906 BOS  N

1907
1908
1914 CHI  F
1915 NY   A
 14 yrs.
```

Doe's record has been exaggerated so that his playing career spans all the years of the six different major leagues. Directly alongside the year and team information is the symbol for the league:

N	National League (1876 to date)
A	American League (1901 to date)
F	Federal League (1914–15)
AA	American Association (1882–91)
P	Players' League (1890)
U	Union Association (1884)

STL—The abbreviation of the city in which the team played. Doe, for example, played for St. Louis in 1884. All teams in this section are listed by an abbreviation of the city in which the team played. The abbreviations follow:

ALT	Altoona	NWK	Newark
ATL	Atlanta	NY	New York
BAL	Baltimore	OAK	Oakland
BOS	Boston	PHI	Philadelphia
BKN	Brooklyn	PIT	Pittsburgh
BUF	Buffalo	PRO	Providence
CAL	California	RIC	Richmond
CHI	Chicago	ROC	Rochester
CIN	Cincinnati	SD	San Diego
CLE	Cleveland	SEA	Seattle
COL	Columbus	SF	San Francisco
DET	Detroit	STL	St. Louis
HAR	Hartford	STP	St. Paul
HOU	Houston	SYR	Syracuse
IND	Indianapolis	TEX	Texas
KC	Kansas City	TOL	Toledo
LA	Los Angeles	TOR	Toronto
LOU	Louisville	TRO	Troy
MIL	Milwaukee	WAS	Washington
MIN	Minnesota	WIL	Wilmington
MON	Montreal	WOR	Worcester

Three franchises in the history of major league baseball changed their location during the season. These teams are designated by the first letter of the two cities they represented. They are:

B-B   Brooklyn-Baltimore (American Association, 1890)
C-M   Cincinnati-Milwaukee (American Association, 1891)
C-P   Chicago-Pittsburgh (Union Association, 1884)

Blank space appearing beneath a team and league indicates that the team and league are the same. Doe, for example, played for Boston in the National League from 1906 through 1908.

3 Teams Total. Indicates a player played for more than one team in the same year. Doe played for three teams in 1889. The number of games he played and his batting average for each team are also shown. Directly beneath this line, following the word "total," is Doe's combined record for all three teams for 1889.

Total Playing Years. This information, which appears as the first item on the player's lifetime total line, indicates the total number of years in which he played at least one game. Doe, for example, played in at least one game for 14 years.

STATISTICAL INFORMATION

	G	AB	H	2B	3B	HR	HR %	R	RBI	BB	SO	SB	BA	SA	Pinch Hit AB	Pinch Hit H	G by POS

John Doe

DOE, JOHN LEE (Slim)
Played as John Cherry part of 1900.
Born John Lee Doughnut.   Brother of Bill Doe.
B. Jan. 1,1850, New York, N. Y.   D. July 1, 1955, New York, N. Y.
Manager 1908-15.
Hall of Fame 1946.

BR TR 6'2"   165 lbs.
BB 1884 BL 1906

	G	AB	H	2B	3B	HR	HR %	R	RBI	BB	SO	SB	BA	SA	PH AB	PH H	G by POS
1884 STL U	125	435	121	18	1	3	0.7	44		37	42	7	.278	.345	9	2	SS-99, P-26
1885 LOU AA	155	547	138	22	3	3	0.6	50	58	42	48	8	.252	.320	8	4	SS-115, P-40
1886 CLE N	147	485	134	38	5	0	0.0	66	54	48	50	8	.276	.375	7	1	SS-107, P-40
1887 BOS N	129	418	117	15	3	1	0.2	38	52	32	37	1	.280	.337	1	0	SS-102, P-27
1888 NY N	144	506	135	26	2	6	1.2	50	63	43	50	1	.267	.362	10	8	SS-105, P-39
1889 3 teams	DET	N	(10G	–	.300)	PIT	N	(32G	–	.241)	PHI	N	(41G	–	.364)		
" total	83	237	75	31	16	7	3.0	90	42	25	35	3	.316	.671	6	3	SS-61, P-22
1890 NY P	123	430	119	27	5	1	0.2	63	59	39	39	2	.277	.370	12	10	SS-85, P-38
1900 CHI N	146	498	116	29	4	3	0.6	51	46	59	53	1	.233	.325	13	8	SS-114, P-35
1901 NY N	149	540	147	19	6	4	0.7	57	74	49	58	3	.272	.352	23	15	SS-113, P-31
1906 BOS N	144	567	143	26	4	4	0.7	70	43	37	54	1	.252	.333	7	1	SS-97, P-37
1907	134	515	140	31	2	5	1.0	61	70	37	42	0	.272	.369	13	8	SS-105, P-1
1908	106	372	92	10	2	4	1.1	36	40	4	55	1	.247	.317	0	0	P-6
1914 CHI F	6	6	0	0	0	0	0.0	0	0	0	0	0	.000	.000	0	0	SS-1
1915 NY A	1	0	0	0	0	0	–	0	0	0	0	0	–	.360	0	0	SS-1
14 yrs.	1592	5556	1927	292	53 4th	41	0.7	676	601	452	564	36	.266	.360	110	60	SS-1215, P-377

League Leaders. Statistics that appear in bold faced print indicate the player led his league that year in a particular statistical category. Doe, for example, led the National League in doubles in 1889. When there is a tie for league lead, the figures for all the men who tied are shown in bold face.

All-Time Single Season Leaders. Indicated by the small number that appears next to the statistic. Doe, for example, is shown by a small number "1" next to his doubles total in 1889. This means he is first on the all-time major league list for hitting the most doubles in a single season. All players who tied for first are also shown by the same number.

Lifetime Leaders. Indicated by the figure that appears beneath the line showing the player's lifetime totals. Doe has a "4th" shown below his lifetime triples total. This means that, lifetime, Doe ranks fourth among major league players for hitting the most triples. Once again, only the top ten are indicated, and players who are tied receive the same number.

Unavailable Information. Any time a blank space is shown in a particular statistical column, such as in Doe's 1884 RBI total, it indicates the information was unavailable or incomplete.

Meaningless Averages. Indicated by use of a dash (—). In the case of Doe, a dash is shown for his 1915 batting average. This means that, although he played one game, he had no official at bats. A batting average of .000 would mean he had at least one at bat with no hits.

League Leaders Qualifications. Throughout baseball there have been different rules used to determine the minimum appearances necessary to qualify for league leader in categories concerning averages (Batting Average, Earned Run Average, etc.). For the rules and the years they were in effect, see Appendix C.

WORLD SERIES AND CHAMPIONSHIP PLAYOFFS

	G	AB	H	2B	3B	HR	HR %	R	RBI	BB	SO	SB	BA	SA	Pinch Hit AB	H	G by POS
DIVISIONAL PLAYOFF SERIES																	
1 yr.	3	14	5	2	0	3	21.4	3	7	0	1	0	.357	1.143	0	0	OF-3
LEAGUE CHAMPIONSHIP SERIES																	
1 yr.	3	14	5	2	0	3	21.4	3	7	0	1	0	.357	1.143	0	0	OF-3
WORLD SERIES																	
2 yrs.	14	55	20	2	1	3	5.5	8	9	5	12	0	.364	.600	0	0	OF-14
					5th				9th								

World Series Lifetime Leaders. Indicated by the figure that appears beneath the player's lifetime totals. Doe has a "5th" shown below his lifetime home run total. This means that, lifetime, Doe ranks fifth among major league players for hitting the most home runs in total World Series play. Players who tied for a position in the top ten are shown by the same number, so that, if two men tied for fourth and fifth place, the appropriate information for both men would be followed by the small number "4," and the next man would be considered sixth in the ranking.

	G	AB	H	2B	3B	HR	HR%	R	RBI	BB	SO	SB	BA	SA	Pinch Hit AB	Pinch Hit H	G by POS

Hank Aaron

AARON, HENRY LOUIS
Brother of Tommie Aaron.
B. Feb. 5, 1934, Mobile, Ala.
Hall of Fame 1982.

BR TR 6' 180 lbs.

Year/Team	G	AB	H	2B	3B	HR	HR%	R	RBI	BB	SO	SB	BA	SA	PH AB	PH H	G by POS
1954 MIL N	122	468	131	27	6	13	2.8	58	69	28	39	2	.280	.447	6	1	OF-116
1955	153	602	189	37	9	27	4.5	105	106	49	61	3	.314	.540	2	1	OF-126, 2B-27
1956	153	609	200	34	14	26	4.3	106	92	37	54	2	.328	.558	1	0	OF-152
1957	151	615	198	27	6	44	7.2	118	132	57	58	1	.322	.600	1	0	OF-150
1958	153	601	196	34	4	30	5.0	109	95	59	49	4	.326	.546	0	0	OF-153
1959	154	629	223	46	7	39	6.2	116	123	51	54	8	.355	.636	0	0	OF-152, 3B-5
1960	153	590	172	20	11	40	6.8	102	126	60	63	16	.292	.566	0	0	OF-153, 3B-5
1961	155	603	197	39	10	34	5.6	115	120	56	64	21	.327	.594	0	0	OF-153, 3B-2
1962	156	592	191	28	6	45	7.6	127	128	66	73	15	.323	.618	1	0	OF-154, 3B-2
1963	161	631	201	29	4	44	7.0	121	130	78	94	31	.319	.586	2	1	OF-153, 1B-1
1964	145	570	187	30	2	24	4.2	103	95	62	46	22	.328	.514	0	0	OF-161
1965	150	570	181	40	1	32	5.6	109	89	60	81	24	.318	.560	1	0	OF-139, 2B-11
1966 ATL N	158	603	168	23	1	44	7.3	117	127	76	96	21	.279	.539	2	1	OF-148
1967	155	600	184	37	3	39	6.5	113	109	63	97	17	.307	.573	1	1	OF-158, 2B-2
1968	160	606	174	33	4	29	4.8	84	86	64	62	28	.287	.498	3	0	OF-152, 2B-1
1969	147	547	164	30	3	44	8.0	100	97	87	47	9	.300	.607	2	0	OF-151, 1B-14
1970	150	516	154	26	1	38	7.4	103	118	74	63	9	.298	.574	0	0	OF-144, 1B-4
1971	139	495	162	22	3	47	9.5	95	118	71	58	1	.327	.669	9	1	OF-125, 1B-11
1972	129	449	119	10	0	34	7.6	75	77	92	55	4	.265	.514	8	2	1B-71, OF-60
1973	120	392	118	12	1	40	10.2	84	96	68	51	1	.301	.643	5	2	1B-109, OF-15
1974	112	340	91	16	0	20	5.9	47	69	39	29	1	.268	.491	11	3	OF-105
1975 MIL A	137	465	109	16	2	12	2.6	45	60	70	51	0	.234	.355	17	1	OF-89
1976	85	271	62	8	0	10	3.7	22	35	35	38	0	.229	.369	5	1	DH-128, OF-3
23 yrs.	3298	12364	3771	624	98	755	6.1	2174	2297	1402	1383	240	.305	.555	10	2	DH-74, OF-1
	3rd	2nd	3rd	8th		1st		2nd	1st						86	17	OF-2760, 1B-210,
																	DH-202, 2B-43, 3B-7

LEAGUE CHAMPIONSHIP SERIES

1969 ATL N	3	14	5	2	0	3	21.4	3	7	0	1	0	.357	1.143	0	0	OF-3

WORLD SERIES

1957 MIL N	7	28	11	0	1	3	10.7	5	7	1	6	0	.393	.786	0	0	OF-7
1958	7	27	9	2	0	0	0.0	3	2	4	6	0	.333	.407	0	0	OF-7
2 yrs.	14	55	20	2	1	3	5.5	8	9	5	12	0	.364	.600	0	0	OF-14
													4th	10th			

Tommie Aaron

AARON, TOMMIE LEE
Brother of Hank Aaron.
B. Aug. 5, 1939, Mobile, Ala. D. Aug. 16, 1984, Atlanta, Ga.

BR TR 5'11" 195 lbs.

Year/Team	G	AB	H	2B	3B	HR	HR%	R	RBI	BB	SO	SB	BA	SA	PH AB	PH H	G by POS
1962 MIL N	141	334	77	20	2	8	2.4	54	38	41	58	6	.231	.374	11	3	1B-110, OF-42, 3B-1, 2B-1
1963	72	135	27	6	1	1	0.7	6	15	11	27	0	.200	.281	16	2	1B-45, OF-14, 2B-6, 3B-1
1965	8	16	3	0	0	0	0.0	1	1	1	2	0	.188	.188	2	1	1B-6
1968 ATL N	98	283	69	10	3	1	0.4	21	25	21	37	3	.244	.311	18	3	OF-62, 1B-28, 3B-1
1969	49	60	15	2	0	1	1.7	13	5	6	6	0	.250	.333	23	4	1B-16, OF-8
1970	44	63	13	2	0	2	3.2	3	7	3	10	0	.206	.333	16	2	1B-16, OF-12
1971	25	53	12	2	0	0	0.0	4	3	3	5	0	.226	.264	6	2	1B-11, 3B-7
7 yrs.	437	944	216	42	6	13	1.4	102	94	86	145	9	.229	.327	92	17	1B-232, OF-138, 3B-10, 2B-7

LEAGUE CHAMPIONSHIP SERIES

1969 ATL N	1	1	0	0	0	0	0.0	0	0	0	0	0	.000	.000	1	0	

Ed Abbaticchio

ABBATICCHIO, EDWARD JAMES
B. Apr. 15, 1877, Latrobe, Pa. D. Jan. 6, 1957, Fort Lauderdale, Fla.

BR TR 5'11" 170 lbs.

Year/Team	G	AB	H	2B	3B	HR	HR%	R	RBI	BB	SO	SB	BA	SA	PH AB	PH H	G by POS
1897 PHI N	3	10	3	0	0	0	0.0	0			1			.300	.300	0	0	2B-3
1898	25	92	21	4	0	0	0.0	9		14	7		0	.228	.272	0	0	3B-20, 2B-4, OF-1
1903 BOS N	136	489	111	18	5	1	0.2	61	46	52		4	23	.227	.290	3	1	2B-116, SS-17
1904	154	579	148	18	10	3	0.5	76	54	40		24	.256	.337	0	0	SS-154
1905	153	610	170	25	12	3	0.5	70	41	35		30	.279	.374	0	0	SS-152, OF-1
1907 PIT N	147	496	130	14	7	2	0.4	63	82	65		35	.262	.331	0	0	2B-147
1908	146	500	125	16	7	1	0.2	43	61	58		22	.250	.316	2	0	2B-144
1909	36	87	20	0	0	1	1.1	13	16	19		2	.230	.264	11	2	SS-18, 2B-4, OF-1
1910 2 teams	PIT N (3G – .000)			BOS N (52G – .247)													
" total	55	181	44	4	2	0	0.0	20	10	12	16	2	.243	.287	7	0	SS-47, 2B-1
9 yrs.	855	3044	772	99	43	11	0.4	355	324	289	16	142	.254	.325	23	3	2B-419, SS-388, 3B-20, OF-3

WORLD SERIES

1909 PIT N	1	1	0	0	0	0	0.0	0	0	0	1	0	.000	.000	1	0	

Charlie Abbey

ABBEY, CHARLES S.
B. Oct., 1868, Falls City, Neb. Deceased.

BL 5'8½" 169 lbs.

Year/Team	G	AB	H	2B	3B	HR	HR%	R	RBI	BB	SO	SB	BA	SA	PH AB	PH H	G by POS
1893 WAS N	31	116	30	1	4	0	0.0	11	12	6		9	.259	.336	0	0	OF-31
1894	129	523	164	26	18	7	1.3	95	101	58	38	31	.314	.472	0	0	OF-129
1895	132	511	141	14	10	8	1.6	102	84	43	41	28	.276	.389	0	0	OF-132
1896	79	301	79	12	6	1	0.3	47	49	27	20	16	.262	.352	2	1	OF-78, P-1
1897	80	300	78	14	8	3	1.0	52	34	27		9	.260	.390	0	0	OF-80
5 yrs.	451	1751	492	67	46	19	1.1	307	280	167	105	93	.281	.404	2	1	OF-450, P-1

Fred Abbott

ABBOTT, FREDERICK HARRY
Born Harry Frederick Winbigler.
B. Oct. 22, 1874, Versailles, Ohio D. June 11, 1935, Los Angeles, Calif.

BR TR

Year/Team	G	AB	H	2B	3B	HR	HR%	R	RBI	BB	SO	SB	BA	SA	PH AB	PH H	G by POS
1903 CLE A	77	255	60	11	3	1	0.4	25	25	7		8	.235	.314	3	0	C-71, 1B-3
1904	41	130	22	4	2	0	0.0	14	12	6		1	.169	.231	1	0	C-33, 1B-7
1905 PHI N	42	128	25	6	1	0	0.0	9	12	6		4	.195	.258	2	0	C-34, 1B-5
3 yrs.	160	513	107	21	6	1	0.2	48	49	19	14		.209	.279	6	0	C-138, 1B-15

	G	AB	H	2B	3B	HR	HR %	R	RBI	BB	SO	SB	BA	SA	Pinch Hit AB	Pinch Hit H	G by POS

Ody Abbott

ABBOTT, ODY CLEON (Toby)
B. Sept. 5, 1886, New Eagle, Pa.   D. Apr. 13, 1933, Washington, D. C.
BR TR 6'2"   180 lbs.

	G	AB	H	2B	3B	HR	HR %	R	RBI	BB	SO	SB	BA	SA	PH AB	PH H	G by POS
1910 STL N	22	70	13	2	1	0	0.0	2	6	6	20	3	.186	.243	1	0	OF-21

Cliff Aberson

ABERSON, CLIFFORD ALEXANDER
B. Aug. 28, 1921, Chicago, Ill.   D. June 23, 1973, Vallejo, Calif.
BR TR 6'   200 lbs.

	G	AB	H	2B	3B	HR	HR %	R	RBI	BB	SO	SB	BA	SA	PH AB	PH H	G by POS
1947 CHI N	47	140	39	6	3	4	2.9	24	20	20	32	0	.279	.450	6	2	OF-40
1948	12	32	6	0	1	1	3.1	1	6	5	10	0	.188	.313	3	1	OF-8
1949	4	7	0	0	0	0	0.0	0	0	0	2	0	.000	.000	3	0	OF-1
3 yrs.	63	179	45	7	3	5	2.8	25	26	25	44	0	.251	.408	12	3	OF-49

Cal Abrams

ABRAMS, CALVIN ROSS
B. Mar. 2, 1924, Philadelphia, Pa.
BL TL 5'11½"   195 lbs.

	G	AB	H	2B	3B	HR	HR %	R	RBI	BB	SO	SB	BA	SA	PH AB	PH H	G by POS
1949 BKN N	8	24	2	1	0	0	0.0	6	0	7	6	1	.083	.125	1	0	OF-7
1950	38	44	9	1	0	0	0.0	5	4	9	13	0	.205	.227	20	4	OF-15
1951	67	150	42	8	0	3	2.0	27	19	36	26	3	.280	.393	22	5	OF-34
1952 2 teams		BKN	N (10G – .200)					CIN	N	(71G – .278)							
" total	81	168	46	9	2	2	1.2	24	13	21	29	1	.274	.387	35	6	OF-46
1953 PIT N	119	448	128	10	6	15	3.3	66	43	58	70	4	.286	.435	7	2	OF-112
1954 2 teams		PIT	N (17G – .143)					BAL	A	(115G – .293)							
" total	132	465	130	23	8	6	1.3	73	27	82	76	1	.280	.402	5	1	OF-128
1955 BAL A	118	309	75	12	3	6	1.9	56	32	89	69	2	.243	.359	16	2	OF-96, 1B-4
1956 CHI A	4	3	1	0	0	0	0.0	0	0	2	1	0	.333	.333	2	1	OF-2
8 yrs.	567	1611	433	64	19	32	2.0	257	138	304	290	12	.269	.392	108	21	OF-440, 1B-4

Joe Abreu

ABREU, JOSEPH LAWRENCE (The Magician)
B. May 24, 1916, Oakland, Calif.
BR TR 5'8"   160 lbs.

	G	AB	H	2B	3B	HR	HR %	R	RBI	BB	SO	SB	BA	SA	PH AB	PH H	G by POS
1942 CIN N	9	28	6	1	0	1	3.6	4	3	4	4	0	.214	.357	1	0	3B-6, 2B-2

Bill Abstein

ABSTEIN, WILLIAM HENRY (Big Bill)
B. Feb. 2, 1885, St. Louis, Mo.   D. Apr. 8, 1940, St. Louis, Mo.
BR TR 6'   185 lbs.

	G	AB	H	2B	3B	HR	HR %	R	RBI	BB	SO	SB	BA	SA	PH AB	PH H	G by POS
1906 PIT N	8	20	4	0	0	0	0.0	2	3	0		2	.200	.200	3	0	2B-3, OF-2
1909	137	512	133	20	10	1	0.2	51	70	27		16	.260	.344	2	0	1B-135
1910 STL A	25	87	13	2	0	0	0.0	1	3	2		3	.149	.172	2	0	1B-23
3 yrs.	170	619	150	22	10	1	0.2	54	76	29		21	.242	.315	7	0	1B-158, 2B-3, OF-2

WORLD SERIES
| 1909 PIT N | 7 | 26 | 6 | 2 | 0 | 0 | 0.0 | 3 | 2 | 3 | 10 | 1 | .231 | .308 | 0 | 0 | 1B-7 |

Merito Acosta

ACOSTA, BALMADERO PEDRO
Brother of Jose Acosta.
B. June 2, 1896, Havana, Cuba   D. Nov. 16, 1963, Miami, Fla.
BL TL 5'7"   140 lbs.

	G	AB	H	2B	3B	HR	HR %	R	RBI	BB	SO	SB	BA	SA	PH AB	PH H	G by POS
1913 WAS A	9	20	6	0	1	0	0.0	3	1	4	2	2	.300	.400	2	1	OF-7
1914	38	74	19	2	2	0	0.0	10	4	11	18	3	.257	.338	12	2	OF-24
1915	72	163	34	4	1	0	0.0	20	8	28	15	8	.209	.245	15	4	OF-53
1916	4	7	1	0	0	0	0.0	0	0	2	0	0	.143	.143	0	0	OF-4
1918 2 teams		WAS	A (3G – .000)					PHI	A	(49G – .302)							
" total	52	171	51	3	3	0	0.0	23	14	18	11	4	.298	.351	6	1	OF-45
5 yrs.	175	435	111	9	7	0	0.0	56	37	63	46	17	.255	.308	35	8	OF-133

Jerry Adair

ADAIR, KENNETH JERRY
B. Dec. 17, 1936, Sand Springs, Okla.
BR TR 6'   175 lbs.

	G	AB	H	2B	3B	HR	HR %	R	RBI	BB	SO	SB	BA	SA	PH AB	PH H	G by POS
1958 BAL A	11	19	2	0	0	0	0.0	1	0	1	7	0	.105	.105	0	0	SS-10, 2B-1
1959	12	35	11	0	1	0	0.0	3	2	1	5	0	.314	.371	0	0	2B-11, SS-1
1960	3	5	1	0	0	1	20.0	1	1	0	0	0	.200	.800	0	0	2B-3
1961	133	386	102	21	6	9	2.3	41	37	35	51	5	.264	.394	0	0	2B-107, SS-27, 3B-2
1962	139	538	153	29	4	11	2.0	67	48	27	77	7	.284	.414	4	0	SS-113, 2B-34, 3B-1
1963	109	382	87	21	3	6	1.6	34	30	9	51	3	.228	.346	5	2	2B-103
1964	155	569	141	20	9	9	1.6	56	47	28	72	3	.248	.341	2	1	2B-153
1965	157	582	151	26	3	7	1.2	51	66	35	65	6	.259	.351	0	0	2B-157
1966 2 teams		BAL	A (17G – .288)					CHI	A	(105G – .243)							
" total	122	422	105	19	2	4	0.9	30	39	21	52	3	.249	.332	4	1	SS-75, 2B-63
1967 2 teams		CHI	A (28G – .204)					BOS	A	(89G – .291)							
" total	117	414	112	17	1	3	0.7	47	35	17	52	1	.271	.338	8	2	2B-50, 3B-35, SS-30
1968 BOS A	74	208	45	1	0	2	1.0	18	12	9	28	0	.216	.250	13	3	SS-46, 2B-12, 3B-7, 1B-1
1969 KC A	126	432	108	9	1	5	1.2	29	48	20	36	1	.250	.310	6	1	2B-109, SS-8, 3B-1
1970	7	27	4	0	0	0	0.0	1	1	5	3	0	.148	.148	0	0	2B-7
13 yrs.	1165	4019	1022	163	19	57	1.4	378	366	208	499	29	.254	.347	42	10	2B-810, SS-310, 3B-46, 1B-1

WORLD SERIES
| 1967 BOS A | 5 | 16 | 2 | 0 | 0 | 0 | 0.0 | 0 | 1 | 0 | 3 | 1 | .125 | .125 | 0 | 0 | 2B-4 |

Jimmy Adair

ADAIR, JAMES AUBREY (Choppy)
B. Jan. 25, 1907, Waxahachie, Tex.   D. Dec. 9, 1982, Dallas, Tex.
BR TR 5'10½"   154 lbs.

	G	AB	H	2B	3B	HR	HR %	R	RBI	BB	SO	SB	BA	SA	PH AB	PH H	G by POS
1931 CHI N	18	76	21	3	1	0	0.0	9	3	1	8	1	.276	.342	0	0	SS-18

Bert Adams

ADAMS, JOHN BERTRAM
B. June 21, 1891, Wharton, Tex.   D. June 24, 1940, Los Angeles, Calif.
BR TR 6'1"   185 lbs.

	G	AB	H	2B	3B	HR	HR %	R	RBI	BB	SO	SB	BA	SA	PH AB	PH H	G by POS
1910 CLE A	5	13	3	0	0	0	0.0	0	1	1		0	.231	.231	0	0	C-5
1911	2	5	1	0	0	0	0.0	0	0	0		0	.200	.200	0	0	C-2
1912	20	54	11	2	1	0	0.0	5	6	4		0	.204	.278	0	0	C-20
1915 PHI N	24	27	3	0	0	0	0.0	1	2	2	3	0	.111	.111	0	1	C-23, 1B-1
1916	11	13	3	0	0	0	0.0	2	1	0		0	.231	.231	1	0	C-11
1917	43	107	22	4	1	1	0.9	4	7	0	20	0	.206	.290	4	1	C-38, 1B-1
1918	84	227	40	4	0	0	0.0	10	12	10	26	5	.176	.194	8	3	C-76
1919	78	232	54	7	2	1	0.4	14	17	6	27	4	.233	.293	4	0	C-73
8 yrs.	267	678	137	17	4	3	0.3	37	45	23	79	9	.202	.248	17	4	C-248, 1B-2

	G	AB	H	2B	3B	HR	HR %	R	RBI	BB	SO	SB	BA	SA	Pinch Hit AB	Pinch Hit H	G by POS

Bob Adams

ADAMS, ROBERT MELVIN
B. Jan. 6, 1952, Pittsburgh, Pa.
BR TR 6'2" 200 lbs.

	G	AB	H	2B	3B	HR	HR %	R	RBI	BB	SO	SB	BA	SA	PH AB	PH H	G by POS
1977 DET A	15	24	6	1	0	2	8.3	2	2	0	5	0	.250	.542	12	4	1B-2, C-1

Bobby Adams

ADAMS, ROBERT HENRY
Brother of Dick Adams. Father of Mike Adams.
B. Dec. 14, 1921, Tuolumburgh, Calif.
BR TR 5'10½" 160 lbs.

	G	AB	H	2B	3B	HR	HR %	R	RBI	BB	SO	SB	BA	SA	PH AB	PH H	G by POS
1946 CIN N	94	311	76	13	3	4	1.3	35	24	18	32	16	.244	.344	13	4	2B-74, OF-2, 3B-1
1947	81	217	59	11	2	4	1.8	39	20	25	23	9	.272	.396	1	1	2B-69
1948	87	262	78	20	3	1	0.4	33	21	25	23	6	.298	.408	14	5	2B-64, 3B-7
1949	107	277	70	16	2	0	0.0	32	25	25	36	4	.253	.325	23	6	2B-63, 3B-14
1950	115	348	98	21	8	3	0.9	57	25	26	36	4	.282	.414	9	1	2B-53, 3B-42
1951	125	403	107	12	5	5	1.2	57	24	43	40	30	.266	.357	30	10	3B-60, 2B-42, OF-1
1952	154	637	180	25	4	6	0.9	85	48	49	67	11	.283	.363	0	0	3B-154
1953	150	607	167	14	6	8	1.3	99	49	58	67	3	.275	.357	0	0	3B-150
1954	110	390	105	25	4	3	0.8	69	23	55	46	2	.269	.387	11	4	3B-93, 2B-2
1955 2 teams		CIN	N (64G –	.273)		CHI	A	(28G –	.095)								
" total	92	171	43	11	3	2	1.2	31	23	24	25	2	.251	.386	20	5	3B-51, 2B-6
1956 BAL A	41	111	25	6	1	0	0.0	19	7	25	15	1	.225	.297	0	0	3B-24, 2B-18
1957 CHI N	60	187	47	10	2	1	0.5	21	10	17	28	0	.251	.342	8	1	3B-47, 2B-1
1958	62	96	27	4	0	0	0.0	14	4	6	15	2	.281	.406	35	9	1B-11, 3B-9, 2B-7
1959	3	2	0	0	0	0	0.0	0	0	0	1	0	.000	.000	2	0	1B-1
14 yrs.	1281	4019	1082	188	49	37	0.9	591	303	414	447	67	.269	.368	166	46	3B-652, 2B-399, 1B-12, OF-3

Buster Adams

ADAMS, ELVIN CLARK
B. June 24, 1915, Trinidad, Colo.
BR TR 6' 180 lbs.

	G	AB	H	2B	3B	HR	HR %	R	RBI	BB	SO	SB	BA	SA	PH AB	PH H	G by POS
1939 STL N	2	1	0	0	0	0	0.0	1	0	0	0	0	.000	.000	1	0	
1943 2 teams		STL	N (8G –	.091)		PHI	N	(111G –	.256)								
" total	119	429	108	15	7	4	0.9	49	39	43	71	2	.252	.347	2	1	OF-113
1944 PHI N	151	584	165	35	3	17	2.9	86	64	74	74	2	.283	.440	0	0	OF-151
1945 2 teams		PHI	N (14G –	.232)		STL	N	(140G –	.292)								
" total	154	634	182	29	6	22	3.5	104	109	62	80	3	.287	.440	0	0	OF-153
1946 STL N	81	173	32	6	0	5	2.9	21	22	29	27	3	.185	.306	21	6	OF-58
1947 PHI N	69	182	45	11	1	2	1.1	21	15	26	29	2	.247	.352	15	6	OF-51
6 yrs.	576	2003	532	96	12	50	2.5	282	249	234	281	12	.266	.400	39	13	OF-526

Dick Adams

ADAMS, RICHARD LEROY
Brother of Bobby Adams.
B. Apr. 8, 1920, Tuolumne, Calif.
BR TL 6' 185 lbs.

	G	AB	H	2B	3B	HR	HR %	R	RBI	BB	SO	SB	BA	SA	PH AB	PH H	G by POS
1947 PHI A	37	89	18	2	3	2	2.2	9	11	2	18	0	.202	.360	10	1	1B-24, OF-3

Doug Adams

ADAMS, HAROLD DOUGLAS
B. Jan. 27, 1943, Blue River, Wis.
BL TR 6'3" 185 lbs.

	G	AB	H	2B	3B	HR	HR %	R	RBI	BB	SO	SB	BA	SA	PH AB	PH H	G by POS
1969 CHI A	8	14	3	0	0	0	0.0	1	1	1	3	0	.214	.214	5	2	C-4

George Adams

ADAMS, GEORGE (Partridge)
B. Grafton, Mass. Deceased.

	G	AB	H	2B	3B	HR	HR %	R	RBI	BB	SO	SB	BA	SA	PH AB	PH H	G by POS
1879 SYR N	4	13	3	0	0	0	0.0	0	0	1	1		.231	.231	0	0	OF-2, 1B-2

Glenn Adams

ADAMS, GLENN CHARLES
B. Oct. 4, 1947, Northbridge, Mass.
BL TR 6'1" 180 lbs.

	G	AB	H	2B	3B	HR	HR %	R	RBI	BB	SO	SB	BA	SA	PH AB	PH H	G by POS
1975 SF N	61	90	27	2	1	4	4.4	10	15	11	25	1	.300	.478	33	12	OF-25
1976	69	74	18	4	0	0	0.0	2	3	1	12	1	.243	.297	59	13	OF-6
1977 MIN A	95	269	91	17	0	6	2.2	32	49	18	30	0	.338	.468	11	6	OF-44
1978	116	310	80	18	1	7	2.3	27	35	17	32	0	.258	.390	23	8	DH-101, OF-5
1979	119	326	98	13	1	8	2.5	34	50	25	27	2	.301	.420	21	2	DH-55, OF-53
1980	99	262	75	11	2	6	2.3	32	38	15	26	2	.286	.412	16	2	DH-81, OF-12
1981	72	220	46	10	0	2	0.9	13	24	20	26	0	.209	.282	13	6	DH-62
1982 TOR A	30	66	17	4	0	1	1.5	2	11	4	5	0	.258	.364	9	2	DH-27
8 yrs.	661	1617	452	79	5	34	2.1	152	225	111	183	6	.280	.398	185	51	DH-326, OF-145

Herb Adams

ADAMS, HERBERT LOREN
B. Apr. 14, 1928, Hollywood, Calif.
BL TL 5'9" 160 lbs.

	G	AB	H	2B	3B	HR	HR %	R	RBI	BB	SO	SB	BA	SA	PH AB	PH H	G by POS
1948 CHI A	5	11	3	1	0	0	0.0	1	0	1	1	0	.273	.364	0	0	OF-4
1949	56	208	61	5	3	0	0.0	26	16	9	16	1	.293	.346	0	0	OF-48
1950	34	118	24	2	3	0	0.0	12	2	12	7	3	.203	.271	1	0	OF-33
3 yrs.	95	337	88	8	6	0	0.0	39	18	22	24	4	.261	.320	1	0	OF-85

Jim Adams

ADAMS, JAMES J.
B. 1868, East St. Louis, Ill. Deceased.

	G	AB	H	2B	3B	HR	HR %	R	RBI	BB	SO	SB	BA	SA	PH AB	PH H	G by POS
1890 STL AA	1	4	1	0	0	0	0.0	1	0	0		0	.250	.250	0	0	C-1

Mike Adams

ADAMS, ROBERT MICHAEL
Son of Bobby Adams.
B. July 22, 1948, Cincinnati, Ohio
BR TR 5'9" 180 lbs.

	G	AB	H	2B	3B	HR	HR %	R	RBI	BB	SO	SB	BA	SA	PH AB	PH H	G by POS
1972 MIN A	3	6	2	0	0	0	0.0	0	0	0	1	0	.333	.333	1	0	OF-1
1973	55	66	14	2	0	3	4.5	21	6	17	18	2	.212	.379	1	0	OF-24, DH-2
1976 CHI N	25	29	4	2	0	0	0.0	1	2	8	7	0	.138	.207	16	2	OF-4, 3B-3, 2B-1
1977	2	2	0	0	0	0	0.0	0	0	0	1	0	.000	.000	1	0	OF-2
1978 OAK A	15	15	3	1	0	0	0.0	5	1	7	2	0	.200	.267	5	0	2B-6, DH-3, 3B-3
5 yrs.	100	118	23	5	0	3	2.5	27	9	32	29	2	.195	.314	24	1	OF-31, 2B-7, 3B-6, DH-5

Ricky Adams

ADAMS, RICKY LEE
B. Jan. 21, 1959, Upland, Calif.
BR TR 6'2" 180 lbs.

	G	AB	H	2B	3B	HR	HR %	R	RBI	BB	SO	SB	BA	SA	PH AB	PH H	G by POS
1982 CAL A	8	14	2	0	0	0	0.0	1	0	0	2	1	.143	.143	1	1	SS-8

	G	AB	H	2B	3B	HR	HR %	R	RBI	BB	SO	SB	BA	SA	Pinch Hit AB	Pinch Hit H	G by POS

Ricky Adams continued

	G	AB	H	2B	3B	HR	HR %	R	RBI	BB	SO	SB	BA	SA	AB	H	G by POS
1983	58	112	28	2	0	2	1.8	22	6	5	12	1	.250	.321	0	0	SS-38, 3B-16, 2B-4
2 yrs.	66	126	30	2	0	2	1.6	23	6	5	14	2	.238	.302	1	1	SS-46, 3B-16, 2B-4

Sparky Adams

ADAMS, EARL JOHN
B. Aug. 26, 1894, Newtown, Pa.   BR TR 5'5½" 151 lbs.

		G	AB	H	2B	3B	HR	HR %	R	RBI	BB	SO	SB	BA	SA	AB	H	G by POS
1922	CHI N	11	44	11	0	1	0	0.0	5	3	4	3	1	.250	.295	0	0	2B-11
1923		95	311	90	12	4	4	1.3	40	35	26	10	20	.289	.367	10	4	SS-79, OF-1
1924		117	418	117	11	5	1	0.2	66	27	40	20	15	.280	.337	7	2	SS-88, 2B-19
1925		149	627	180	29	8	2	0.3	95	48	44	15	26	.287	.368	0	0	2B-144, SS-5
1926		154	624	193	35	3	0	0.0	95	39	52	27	27	.309	.375	2	0	2B-136, 3B-19, SS-2
1927		146	647	189	17	7	0	0.0	100	49	42	26	26	.292	.340	0	0	2B-60, 3B-53, SS-40
1928	PIT N	135	539	149	14	6	0	0.0	91	38	64	18	8	.276	.325	1	0	2B-107, SS-27, OF-1
1929		74	196	51	8	1	0	0.0	37	11	15	5	3	.260	.311	4	2	SS-30, 2B-20, 3B-15, OF-2
1930	STL N	137	570	179	36	9	0	0.0	98	55	45	27	7	.314	.409	2	1	3B-104, 2B-25, SS-7
1931		143	608	178	46	5	1	0.2	97	40	42	24	16	.293	.390	1	0	3B-138, SS-6
1932		31	127	35	3	1	0	0.0	22	13	14	5	0	.276	.315	0	0	3B-30
1933	2 teams	STL	N (8G – .167)			CIN	N (137G – .262)											
"	total	145	568	146	22	1	1	0.2	60	22	45	33	3	.257	.305	0	0	3B-135, SS-13
1934	CIN N	87	278	70	16	1	0	0.0	38	14	20	10	2	.252	.317	12	4	3B-38, 2B-29
13 yrs.		1424	5557	1588	249	48	9	0.2	844	394	453	223	154	.286	.353	39	13	2B-551, 3B-532, SS-297, OF-4

WORLD SERIES																		
1930	STL N	6	21	3	0	0	0	0.0	0	1	0	4	0	.143	.143	0	0	3B-6
1931		2	4	1	0	0	0	0.0	0	0	0	1	0	.250	.250	0	0	3B-2
2 yrs.		8	25	4	0	0	0	0.0	0	1	0	5	0	.160	.160	0	0	3B-8

Spencer Adams

ADAMS, SPENCER DEWEY
B. June 21, 1897, Layton, Utah   D. Nov. 25, 1970, Salt Lake City, Utah   BL TR 5'9" 158 lbs.

		G	AB	H	2B	3B	HR	HR %	R	RBI	BB	SO	SB	BA	SA	AB	H	G by POS
1923	PIT N	25	56	14	0	1	0	0.0	11	4	6	6	2	.250	.286	1	1	2B-11, SS-6
1925	WAS A	39	55	15	4	1	0	0.0	11	4	5	4	1	.273	.382	1	0	2B-15, SS-8, 3B-3
1926	NY A	28	25	3	1	0	0	0.0	7	1	3	7	1	.120	.160	10	0	2B-4, 3B-1
1927	STL A	88	259	69	11	3	0	0.0	32	29	24	33	1	.266	.332	5	0	2B-54, 3B-28
4 yrs.		180	395	101	16	5	0	0.0	61	38	38	50	5	.256	.322	17	1	2B-84, 3B-32, SS-14

WORLD SERIES																		
1925	WAS A	2	1	0	0	0	0	0.0	0	0	0	0	0	.000	.000	1	0	2B-1
1926	NY A	2	0	0	0	0	0	–	0	0	0	0	0	–	–	0	0	
2 yrs.		4	1	0	0	0	0	0.0	0	0	0	0	0	.000	.000	1	0	2B-1

Joe Adcock

ADCOCK, JOSEPH WILBUR
B. Oct. 30, 1927, Coushatta, La.   BR TR 6'4" 210 lbs.
Manager 1967.

		G	AB	H	2B	3B	HR	HR %	R	RBI	BB	SO	SB	BA	SA	AB	H	G by POS
1950	CIN N	102	372	109	16	1	8	2.2	46	55	24	24	2	.293	.406	4	0	OF-75, 1B-24
1951		113	395	96	16	4	10	2.5	40	47	24	29	1	.243	.380	5	2	OF-107
1952		117	378	105	22	4	13	3.4	43	52	23	38	1	.278	.460	14	4	OF-85, 1B-17
1953	MIL N	157	590	168	33	6	18	3.1	71	80	42	82	3	.285	.453	0	0	1B-157
1954		133	500	154	27	4	23	4.6	73	87	44	58	1	.308	.520	1	1	1B-133
1955		84	288	76	14	0	15	5.2	40	45	31	44	0	.264	.469	5	1	1B-78
1956		137	454	132	23	1	38	8.4	76	103	32	86	1	.291	.597	8	2	1B-129
1957		65	209	60	13	2	12	5.7	31	38	20	51	0	.287	.541	6	1	1B-56
1958		105	320	88	15	1	19	5.9	40	54	21	63	0	.275	.506	14	3	1B-71, OF-22
1959		115	404	118	19	2	25	6.2	53	76	32	77	0	.292	.535	10	3	1B-89, OF-21
1960		138	514	153	21	4	25	4.9	55	91	46	86	2	.298	.500	2	1	1B-136
1961		152	562	160	20	0	35	6.2	77	108	59	94	2	.285	.507	4	1	1B-148
1962		121	391	97	12	1	29	7.4	48	78	50	91	2	.248	.506	8	3	1B-112
1963	CLE A	97	283	71	7	1	13	4.6	28	49	30	53	1	.251	.420	22	5	1B-78
1964	LA A	118	366	98	13	0	21	5.7	39	64	48	61	0	.268	.475	11	4	1B-105
1965	CAL A	122	349	84	14	0	14	4.0	30	47	37	74	2	.241	.401	23	4	1B-97
1966		83	231	63	10	3	18	7.8	33	48	31	48	2	.273	.576	16	4	1B-71
17 yrs.		1959	6606	1832	295	35	336	5.1	823	1122	594	1059	20	.277	.485	153	39	1B-1501, OF-310

WORLD SERIES																		
1957	MIL N	5	15	3	0	0	0	0.0	1	2	0	2	0	.200	.200	1	0	1B-5
1958		4	13	4	0	0	0	0.0	1	0	1	3	0	.308	.308	1	1	1B-4
2 yrs.		9	28	7	0	0	0	0.0	2	2	1	5	0	.250	.250	2	1	1B-9

Bob Addis

ADDIS, ROBERT GORDON
B. Nov. 6, 1925, Mineral, Ohio   BL TR 6' 175 lbs.

		G	AB	H	2B	3B	HR	HR %	R	RBI	BB	SO	SB	BA	SA	AB	H	G by POS
1950	BOS N	16	28	7	1	0	0	0.0	7	2	3	5	1	.250	.286	10	1	OF-7
1951		85	199	55	7	0	1	0.5	23	24	9	10	3	.276	.327	36	12	OF-46
1952	CHI N	93	292	86	13	2	1	0.3	38	20	23	30	4	.295	.363	15	4	OF-76
1953	2 teams	CHI	N (10G – .167)			PIT	N (4G – .000)											
"	total	14	15	2	1	0	0	0.0	1	2	2	2	0	.133	.200	8	1	OF-3
4 yrs.		208	534	150	22	2	2	0.4	70	47	37	47	8	.281	.341	69	18	OF-132

Jim Adduci

ADDUCI, JAMES DAVID
B. Aug. 9, 1959, Chicago, Ill.   BL TL 6'4" 200 lbs.

		G	AB	H	2B	3B	HR	HR %	R	RBI	BB	SO	SB	BA	SA	AB	H	G by POS
1983	STL N	10	20	1	0	0	0	0.0	0	0	1	6	0	.050	.050	3	0	1B-6, OF-1

Bob Addy

ADDY, ROBERT EDWARD (The Magnet)
B. 1838, Rochester, N. Y.   D. Apr. 10, 1910, Pocatello, Ida.   BL TL 5'8" 160 lbs.
Manager 1877.

		G	AB	H	2B	3B	HR	HR %	R	RBI	BB	SO	SB	BA	SA	AB	H	G by POS
1876	CHI N	32	142	40	4	1	0	0.0	36	16	5	0		.282	.324	0	0	OF-32
1877	CIN N	57	245	68	2	3	0	0.0	27	31	6	5		.278	.310	0	0	OF-57
2 yrs.		89	387	108	6	4	0	0.0	63	47	11	5		.279	.315	0	0	OF-89

	G	AB	H	2B	3B	HR	HR %	R	RBI	BB	SO	SB	BA	SA	Pinch Hit AB	Pinch Hit H	G by POS

Morrie Aderholt

ADERHOLT, MORRIS WOODROW
B. Sept. 13, 1915, Mt. Olive, N. C.   D. Mar. 18, 1955, Sarasota, Fla.   BL TR 6'1"   188 lbs.

	G	AB	H	2B	3B	HR	HR %	R	RBI	BB	SO	SB	BA	SA	AB	H	G by POS
1939 WAS A	7	25	5	0	0	1	4.0	5	4	2	6	0	.200	.320	1	0	2B-7
1940	1	2	0	0	0	0	0.0	0	0	0	0	0	.000	.000	0	0	2B-1
1941	11	14	2	0	0	0	0.0	0	0	0	0	0	.143	.143	0	0	2B-1
1944 BKN N	17	59	16	2	3	0	0.0	3	1	1	3	0	.271	.143	5	1	2B-2, 3B-1
1945 2 teams					BKN N (39G – .217)			BOS N (31G – .333)									OF-13
" total	70	162	47	5	0	2	1.2	19	17	4	4	0	.290	.407	3	0	OF-32, 2B-1
5 yrs.	106	262	70	7	3	3	1.1	36	32	12	16	3	.267	.358	36	8	OF-45, 2B-11, 3B-1

Dick Adkins

ADKINS, RICHARD EARL
B. Mar. 3, 1920, Electra, Tex.   D. Sept. 12, 1955, Electra, Tex.   BR TR 5'10"   165 lbs.

	G	AB	H	2B	3B	HR	HR %	R	RBI	BB	SO	SB	BA	SA	AB	H	G by POS
1942 PHI A	3	7	1	0	0	0	0.0	2	0	0	2	0	.143	.143	0	0	SS-3

Henry Adkinson

ADKINSON, HENRY MAGEE
B. Sept. 1, 1874, Chicago, Ill.   D. May 1, 1923, Salt Lake City, Utah

	G	AB	H	2B	3B	HR	HR %	R	RBI	BB	SO	SB	BA	SA	AB	H	G by POS
1895 STL N	1	5	2	0	0	0	0.0	0		0	2	0	.400	.400	0	0	OF-1

Dave Adlesh

ADLESH, DAVID GEORGE
B. July 15, 1943, Long Beach, Calif.   BR TR 6'   187 lbs.

	G	AB	H	2B	3B	HR	HR %	R	RBI	BB	SO	SB	BA	SA	AB	H	G by POS
1963 HOU N	6	8	0	0	0	0	0.0	0	0	0	4	0	.000	.000	2	0	C-6
1964	3	10	2	0	0	0	0.0	0	0	0	5	0	.200	.200	2	0	C-3
1965	15	34	5	1	0	0	0.0	2	3	2	12	0	.147	.176	2	1	C-13
1966	3	6	0	0	0	0	0.0	0	0	0	4	0	.000	.000	3	0	C-1
1967	39	94	17	1	0	1	1.1	4	4	11	28	0	.181	.223	8	2	C-31
1968	40	104	19	1	1	0	0.0	3	4	5	27	0	.183	.212	4	2	C-36
6 yrs.	106	256	43	3	1	1	0.4	9	11	18	80	0	.168	.199	19	5	C-90

Tommie Agee

AGEE, TOMMIE LEE
B. Aug. 9, 1942, Magnolia, Ala.   BR TR 5'11"   195 lbs.

	G	AB	H	2B	3B	HR	HR %	R	RBI	BB	SO	SB	BA	SA	AB	H	G by POS
1962 CLE A	5	14	3	0	0	0	0.0	0	0	0	4	0	.214	.214	2	0	OF-3
1963	13	27	4	1	0	1	3.7	3	3	2	9	0	.148	.296	2	0	OF-13
1964	13	12	2	0	0	0	0.0	0	0	0	3	0	.167	.167	0	0	OF-12
1965 CHI A	10	19	3	1	0	0	0.0	2	3	2	6	0	.158	.211	1	0	OF-9
1966	160	629	172	27	8	22	3.5	98	86	41	127	44	.273	.447	0	0	OF-159
1967	158	529	124	26	2	14	2.6	73	52	44	129	28	.234	.371	2	1	OF-152
1968 NY N	132	368	80	12	3	5	1.4	30	17	15	103	13	.217	.307	3	0	OF-127
1969	149	565	153	23	4	26	4.6	97	76	59	137	12	.271	.464	3	1	OF-146
1970	153	636	182	30	7	24	3.8	107	75	55	156	31	.286	.469	3	1	OF-150
1971	113	425	121	19	0	14	3.3	58	50	50	84	28	.285	.428	6	3	OF-107
1972	114	422	96	23	2	13	3.1	52	47	53	92	8	.227	.374	4	0	OF-109
1973 2 teams					HOU N (83G – .235)			STL N (26G – .177)									
" total	109	266	59	8	3	11	4.1	38	22	21	68	3	.222	.398	19	4	OF-86
12 yrs.	1129	3912	999	170	27	130	3.3	558	433	342	918	167	.255	.412	43	11	OF-1073
LEAGUE CHAMPIONSHIP SERIES																	
1969 NY N	3	14	5	1	0	2	14.3	4	4	1	5	2	.357	.857	0	0	OF-3
WORLD SERIES																	
1969 NY N	5	18	3	0	0	1	5.6	1	1	2	5	1	.167	.333	0	0	OF-5

Harry Agganis

AGGANIS, HARRY (The Golden Greek)
B. Apr. 20, 1930, Lynn, Mass.   D. June 27, 1955, Cambridge, Mass.   BL TL 6'2"   200 lbs.

	G	AB	H	2B	3B	HR	HR %	R	RBI	BB	SO	SB	BA	SA	AB	H	G by POS
1954 BOS A	132	434	109	13	8	11	2.5	54	57	47	57	6	.251	.394	11	3	1B-119
1955	25	83	26	10	1	0	0.0	11	10	10	10	2	.313	.458	3	0	1B-20
2 yrs.	157	517	135	23	9	11	2.1	65	67	57	67	8	.261	.404	14	3	1B-139

Joe Agler

AGLER, JOSEPH ABRAM
B. June 12, 1889, Coshocton, Ohio   D. Apr. 26, 1971, Massillon, Ohio   BL TL 5'11"   165 lbs.

	G	AB	H	2B	3B	HR	HR %	R	RBI	BB	SO	SB	BA	SA	AB	H	G by POS
1912 WAS A	1	1	0	0	0	0	0.0	0	0	0		0	.000	.000	1	0	
1914 BUF F	135	463	126	17	6	0	0.0	82	20	77		21	.272	.335	3	1	1B-76, OF-54
1915 2 teams					BUF F (25G – .178)			BAL F (72G – .215)									
" total	97	287	59	5	4	0	0.0	39	16	54		17	.206	.251	7	0	1B-59, OF-24, 2B-3
3 yrs.	233	751	185	22	10	0	0.0	121	36	131		38	.246	.302	11	1	1B-135, OF-78, 2B-3

Sam Agnew

AGNEW, SAMUEL LESTER
B. Apr. 12, 1887, Farmington, Mo.   D. July 19, 1951, Sonoma, Calif.   BR TR 5'11"   185 lbs.

	G	AB	H	2B	3B	HR	HR %	R	RBI	BB	SO	SB	BA	SA	AB	H	G by POS
1913 STL A	104	307	64	9	5	2	0.7	27	24	20	49	11	.208	.290	0	0	C-103
1914	113	311	66	5	4	0	0.0	22	16	24	63	10	.212	.254	0	0	C-113
1915 BOS A	104	295	60	4	2	0	0.0	18	19	12	36	5	.203	.231	0	0	C-102
1916 BOS A	40	67	14	2	1	0	0.0	4	7	6	4	0	.209	.269	2	0	C-38
1917	85	260	54	6	2	0	0.0	17	16	19	30	2	.208	.246	0	0	C-85
1918	72	199	33	8	0	0	0.0	11	6	11	26	0	.166	.206	0	0	C-72
1919 WAS A	42	98	23	7	0	0	0.0	6	10	10	8	1	.235	.306	5	1	C-36
7 yrs.	560	1537	314	41	14	2	0.1	105	98	102	216	29	.204	.253	8	1	C-549
WORLD SERIES																	
1918 BOS A	4	9	0	0	0	0	0.0	0	0	0	0	0	.000	.000	0	0	C-4

Luis Aguayo

AGUAYO, LUIS
Also known as Luis Muriel.
B. Mar. 13, 1959, Vega Baja, Puerto Rico   BR TR 5'9"   173 lbs.

	G	AB	H	2B	3B	HR	HR %	R	RBI	BB	SO	SB	BA	SA	AB	H	G by POS
1980 PHI N	20	47	13	1	2	1	2.1	7	8	2	3	1	.277	.447	1	0	2B-14, SS-5
1981	45	84	18	4	0	1	1.2	11	7	6	15	1	.214	.298	3	1	SS-21, 2B-21, 3B-3
1982	50	56	15	1	2	3	5.4	11	7	5	7	1	.268	.518	6	1	2B-21, SS-15, 3B-5
1983	2	4	1	0	0	0	0.0	1	0	1	2	0	.250	.250	0	0	SS-2
1984	58	72	20	4	0	3	4.2	15	11	8	16	0	.278	.458	16	3	3B-14, 2B-12, SS-10
5 yrs.	175	263	67	10	4	8	3.0	45	33	22	43	3	.255	.414	25	5	2B-68, SS-53, 3B-22
DIVISIONAL PLAYOFF SERIES																	
1981 PHI N	2	0	0	0	0	0	–	1	0	0	0	0	–	–	0	0	

	G	AB	H	2B	3B	HR	HR %	R	RBI	BB	SO	SB	BA	SA	Pinch Hit AB	Pinch Hit H	G by POS

Charlie Ahearn

AHEARN, CHARLES
B. Troy, N. Y. Deceased.

	G	AB	H	2B	3B	HR	HR%	R	RBI	BB	SO	SB	BA	SA	PH AB	PH H	G by POS
1880 TRO N	1	4	1	0	0	0	0.0	1		0	0		.250	.250	0	0	C-1

BL TR 6'3" 220 lbs.

Willie Aikens

AIKENS, WILLIE MAYS
B. Oct. 14, 1954, Seneca, S. C.

	G	AB	H	2B	3B	HR	HR%	R	RBI	BB	SO	SB	BA	SA	PH AB	PH H	G by POS
1977 CAL A	42	91	18	4	0	0	0.0	5	6	10	23	1	.198	.242	15	1	DH-13, 1B-13
1979	116	379	106	18	0	21	5.5	59	81	61	79	1	.280	.493	11	3	1B-55, DH-51
1980 KC A	151	543	151	24	0	20	3.7	70	98	64	88	1	.278	.433	0	0	1B-138, DH-13
1981	101	349	93	16	0	17	4.9	45	53	62	47	0	.266	.458	2	0	1B-99
1982	134	466	131	29	1	17	3.6	50	74	45	70	0	.281	.457	10	4	1B-128
1983	125	410	124	26	1	23	5.6	49	72	45	75	0	.302	.539	8	2	1B-112, DH-6
1984 TOR A	93	234	48	7	0	11	4.7	21	26	29	56	0	.205	.376	15	3	1B-81, 1B-2
7 yrs.	762	2472	671	124	2	109	4.4	299	410	316	438	3	.271	.456	61	13	1B-547, DH-164
DIVISIONAL PLAYOFF SERIES																	
1981 KC A	3	9	3	0	0	0	0.0	0	0	3	2	0	.333	.333	0	0	1B-3
LEAGUE CHAMPIONSHIP SERIES																	
1980 KC A	3	11	4	0	0	0	0.0	0	2	0	1	0	.364	.364	0	0	1B-3
WORLD SERIES																	
1980 KC A	6	20	8	0	1	4	20.0	5	8	6	8	0	.400	1.100	0	0	1B-6

BR TR 6'4" 175 lbs.

Danny Ainge

AINGE, DANIEL RAE
B. Mar. 17, 1959, Eugene, Ore.

	G	AB	H	2B	3B	HR	HR%	R	RBI	BB	SO	SB	BA	SA	PH AB	PH H	G by POS
1979 TOR A	87	308	73	7	1	2	0.6	26	19	12	58	1	.237	.286	0	0	2B-86, DH-1
1980	38	111	27	6	1	0	0.0	11	4	2	29	3	.243	.315	3	0	OF-29, 3B-3, DH-2, 2B-1
1981	86	246	46	6	2	0	0.0	20	14	23	41	8	.187	.228	0	0	3B-77, SS-6, OF-4, 2B-2
3 yrs.	211	665	146	19	4	2	0.3	57	37	37	128	12	.220	.269	3	0	2B-89, 3B-80, OF-33, SS-6, DH-3

BR TR 5'11" 180 lbs.

Eddie Ainsmith

AINSMITH, EDWARD WILBUR
B. Feb. 4, 1890, Cambridge, Mass. D. Sept. 6, 1981, Fort Lauderdale, Fla.

	G	AB	H	2B	3B	HR	HR%	R	RBI	BB	SO	SB	BA	SA	PH AB	PH H	G by POS
1910 WAS A	33	104	20	2	0	0	0.0	4	9	6		0	.192	.240	0	0	C-30
1911	61	149	33	2	3	0	0.0	12	14	10		5	.221	.275	7	1	C-49
1912	60	186	42	7	2	0	0.0	22	22	14		4	.226	.285	2	0	C-58
1913	79	229	49	4	4	0	0.0	26	20	12	41	17	.214	.293	0	0	C-79, P-1
1914	58	151	34	7	0	0	0.0	11	13	9	28	8	.225	.272	3	2	C-51
1915	47	120	24	4	2	0	0.0	13	6	10	18	7	.200	.267	3	0	C-42
1916	51	100	17	4	0	0	0.0	11	8	8	14	3	.170	.210	1	0	C-46
1917	125	350	67	17	4	0	0.0	38	42	40	48	16	.191	.263	5	0	C-119
1918	96	292	62	10	9	0	0.0	22	20	29	44	6	.212	.308	4	1	C-89
1919 DET A	114	364	99	17	12	3	0.8	42	32	45	30	9	.272	.409	0	0	C-106
1920	69	186	43	5	3	1	0.5	19	19	14	19	4	.231	.306	7	2	C-61
1921 2 teams	DET A (35G – .276)				STL N (27G – .290)												
" total	62	160	45	5	3	0	0.0	11	17	16	11	1	.281	.350	4	0	C-57, 1B-1
1922 STL N	119	379	111	14	4	13	3.4	46	59	28	43	2	.293	.454	2	1	C-116
1923 2 teams	STL N (82G – .213)				BKN N (2G – .200)												
" total	84	273	58	11	6	3	1.1	22	36	22	19	4	.212	.330	2	1	C-82
1924 NY N	10	5	3	0	0	0	0.0	0	0	0	0	0	.600	.600	1	1	C-9
15 yrs.	1068	3048	707	108	54	22	0.7	299	317	263	315	86	.232	.324	49	10	C-994, 1B-1, P-1

BR TR 6'1" 180 lbs.

John Ake

AKE, JOHN LECKIE
B. Aug. 29, 1861, Altoona, Pa. D. May 11, 1887, La Crosse, Wis.

	G	AB	H	2B	3B	HR	HR%	R	RBI	BB	SO	SB	BA	SA	PH AB	PH H	G by POS
1884 BAL AA	13	52	10	0	1	0	0.0	1		0			.192	.231	0	0	3B-9, OF-3, SS-1

BR TR 5'11" 178 lbs.

Bill Akers

AKERS, THOMAS ERNEST
B. Dec. 25, 1904, Chattanooga, Tenn. D. Apr. 13, 1962, Chattanooga, Tenn.

	G	AB	H	2B	3B	HR	HR%	R	RBI	BB	SO	SB	BA	SA	PH AB	PH H	G by POS
1929 DET A	24	83	22	4	1	1	1.2	15	9	10	9	2	.265	.373	0	0	SS-24
1930	85	233	65	8	5	9	3.9	36	40	36	34	5	.279	.472	5	2	SS-49, 3B-26
1931	29	66	13	2	0	0	0.0	5	3	7	6	0	.197	.288	5	1	SS-21, 2B-2
1932 BOS N	36	93	24	3	1	1	1.1	8	17	10	15	0	.258	.344	6	1	3B-20, SS-5, 2B-5
4 yrs.	174	475	124	17	9	11	2.3	64	69	63	64	7	.261	.404	16	5	SS-99, 3B-46, 2B-7

BR TR 6'2" 205 lbs.

Butch Alberts

ALBERTS, FRANCIS BURT
B. May 4, 1950, Williamsport, Pa.

	G	AB	H	2B	3B	HR	HR%	R	RBI	BB	SO	SB	BA	SA	PH AB	PH H	G by POS
1978 TOR A	6	18	5	1	0	0	0.0	1	0	0	2	0	.278	.333	2	0	DH-4

BR TR 5'6½" 180 lbs.

Gus Alberts

ALBERTS, AUGUST P.
B. 1861, Reading, Pa. D. May 8, 1912, Idaho Springs, Colo.

	G	AB	H	2B	3B	HR	HR%	R	RBI	BB	SO	SB	BA	SA	PH AB	PH H	G by POS
1884 2 teams	PIT AA (2G – .200)				WAS U (4G – .250)												
" total	6	21	5	0	0	0	0.0	5		4			.238	.238	0	0	SS-6
1888 CLE AA	102	364	75	10	6	1	0.3	51	48	41	26		.206	.275	0	0	SS-53, 3B-49
1891 C-M AA	12	41	4	0	0	0	0.0	6	2	7	5	1	.098	.098	0	0	3B-12
3 yrs.	120	426	84	10	6	1	0.2	62	49	52	5	27	.197	.256	0	0	3B-61, SS-59

BR TR 5'9" 175 lbs.

Jack Albright

ALBRIGHT, HAROLD JOHN
B. June 30, 1921, St. Petersburg, Fla.

	G	AB	H	2B	3B	HR	HR%	R	RBI	BB	SO	SB	BA	SA	PH AB	PH H	G by POS
1947 PHI N	41	99	23	4	0	2	2.0	5	10	11	1		.232	.333	2	0	SS-33

BR TR 5'9" 165 lbs.

Luis Alcaraz

ALCARAZ, ANGEL LUIS
B. June 20, 1941, Humacao, Puerto Rico

	G	AB	H	2B	3B	HR	HR%	R	RBI	BB	SO	SB	BA	SA	PH AB	PH H	G by POS
1967 LA N	17	60	14	1	0	0	0.0	1	3	1	13	1	.233	.250	0	0	2B-17
1968	41	106	16	1	0	2	1.9	4	5	9	23	1	.151	.217	5	1	2B-20, 3B-13, SS-1
1969 KC A	22	79	20	2	1	1	1.3	15	7	7	9	0	.253	.342	1	0	2B-19, 3B-2, SS-1
1970	35	120	20	5	1	1	0.8	10	14	4	13	0	.167	.242	3	1	2B-31
4 yrs.	115	365	70	9	2	4	1.1	30	29	21	58	2	.192	.260	9	2	2B-87, 3B-15, SS-2

	G	AB	H	2B	3B	HR	HR %	R	RBI	BB	SO	SB	BA	SA	Pinch Hit AB	Pinch Hit H	G by POS

Scotty Alcock

ALCOCK, JOHN FORBES
B. Nov. 29, 1885, Wooster, Ohio   D. Jan. 30, 1973, Wooster, Ohio
BR TR 5'9½" 160 lbs.

	G	AB	H	2B	3B	HR	HR%	R	RBI	BB	SO	SB	BA	SA	AB	H	G by POS
1914 CHI A	54	156	27	4	2	0	0.0	12	7	7	14	4	.173	.224	3	0	3B-48, 2B-1

Chuck Aleno

ALENO, CHARLES
B. Feb. 19, 1917, St. Louis, Mo.
BR TR 6'1½" 215 lbs.

	G	AB	H	2B	3B	HR	HR%	R	RBI	BB	SO	SB	BA	SA	AB	H	G by POS
1941 CIN N	54	169	41	7	3	1	0.6	23	18	11	16	3	.243	.337	11	2	3B-40, 1B-2
1942	7	14	2	1	0	0	0.0	1	0	3	3	0	.143	.214	3	0	3B-2, 2B-1
1943	7	10	3	0	0	0	0.0	0	1	2	1	0	.300	.300	4	2	OF-2
1944	50	127	21	3	0	1	0.8	10	15	15	15	0	.165	.213	2	0	3B-42, SS-3, 1B-3
4 yrs.	118	320	67	11	3	2	0.6	34	34	31	35	3	.209	.281	20	4	3B-84, 1B-5, SS-3, OF-2, 2B-1

Dale Alexander

ALEXANDER, DAVID DALE (Moose)
B. Apr. 26, 1903, Greenville, Tenn.   D. Mar. 2, 1979, Greenville, Tenn.
BR TR 6'3" 210 lbs.

	G	AB	H	2B	3B	HR	HR%	R	RBI	BB	SO	SB	BA	SA	AB	H	G by POS
1929 DET A	155	626	215	43	15	25	4.0	110	137	56	63	5	.343	.580	0	0	1B-155
1930	154	602	196	33	8	20	3.3	86	135	42	56	6	.326	.507	0	0	1B-154
1931	135	517	168	47	3	3	0.6	75	87	64	35	7	.325	.445	6	0	1B-126, OF-4
1932 2 teams			DET A (23G – .250)					BOS A (101G – .372)									
" total	124	392	144	27	3	8	2.0	58	60	61	21	4	.367	.513	15	4	1B-103
1933 BOS A	94	313	88	14	1	5	1.6	40	40	25	22	0	.281	.380	15	4	1B-79
5 yrs.	662	2450	811	164	30	61	2.5	369	459	248	197	20	.331	.497	36	8	1B-617, OF-4

Gary Alexander

ALEXANDER, GARY WAYNE
B. Mar. 27, 1953, Los Angeles, Calif.
BR TR 6'2" 195 lbs.

	G	AB	H	2B	3B	HR	HR%	R	RBI	BB	SO	SB	BA	SA	AB	H	G by POS
1975 SF N	3	3	0	0	0	0	0.0	1	0	1	2	0	.000	.000	3	0	C-2
1976	23	73	13	1	1	2	2.7	12	7	10	16	1	.178	.301	0	0	C-23
1977	51	119	36	4	2	5	4.2	17	20	20	33	3	.303	.496	17	7	C-33, OF-1
1978 2 teams			OAK A (58G – .207)					CLE A (90G – .235)									
" total	148	498	112	20	4	27	5.4	57	84	57	166	0	.225	.444	10	1	DH-71, C-66, OF-6, 1B-1
1979 CLE A	110	358	82	9	2	15	4.2	54	54	46	100	4	.229	.391	6	2	C-91, DH-13, OF-2
1980	76	178	40	7	1	5	2.8	22	31	17	52	0	.225	.360	23	7	DH-40, C-13, OF-2
1981 PIT N	21	47	10	4	1	1	2.1	6	6	3	12	0	.213	.404	5	0	1B-9, OF-8
7 yrs.	432	1276	293	45	11	55	4.3	169	202	154	381	8	.230	.411	64	17	C-228, DH-124, OF-19, 1B-10

Hugh Alexander

ALEXANDER, HUGH
B. July 10, 1917, Buffalo, Mo.
BR TR 6' 190 lbs.

	G	AB	H	2B	3B	HR	HR%	R	RBI	BB	SO	SB	BA	SA	AB	H	G by POS
1937 CLE A	7	11	1	0	0	0	0.0	0	0	0	5	1	.091	.091	3	0	OF-3

Matt Alexander

ALEXANDER, MATTHEW
B. Jan. 30, 1947, Shreveport, La.
BB TR 5'11" 168 lbs.

	G	AB	H	2B	3B	HR	HR%	R	RBI	BB	SO	SB	BA	SA	AB	H	G by POS
1973 CHI N	12	5	1	0	0	0	0.0	4	1	1	2	2	.200	.200	1	0	OF-3
1974	45	54	11	2	1	0	0.0	15	0	12	12	8	.204	.278	11	3	3B-19, OF-4, 2B-2
1975 OAK A	63	10	1	0	0	0	0.0	16	0	1	1	17	.100	.100	2	0	DH-17, OF-11, 2B-3, 3B-2
1976	61	30	1	0	0	0	0.0	16	0	0	5	20	.033	.033	1	0	OF-23, DH-19
1977	90	42	10	1	0	0	0.0	24	3	4	6	26	.238	.262	0	0	OF-31, DH-12, SS-12, 2B-4, 3B-1
1978 PIT N	7	0	0	0	0	0	–	2	0	0	0	4	–	–	0	0	OF-3
1979	44	13	7	0	1	0	0.0	16	1	0	0	13	.538	.692	1	0	OF-11, SS-1
1980	37	3	1	1	0	0	0.0	13	0	0	0	10	.333	.667	0	0	OF-4, 2B-1
1981	15	11	4	0	0	0	0.0	5	0	0	1	3	.364	.364	0	0	OF-6
9 yrs.	374	168	36	4	2	0	0.0	111	4	18	26	103	.214	.262	20	3	OF-93, DH-48, 3B-22, SS-13, 2B-10

LEAGUE CHAMPIONSHIP SERIES

	G	AB	H	2B	3B	HR	HR%	R	RBI	BB	SO	SB	BA	SA	AB	H	G by POS
1979 PIT N	1	0	0	0	0	0	–	1	0	0	0	0	–	–	0	0	

WORLD SERIES

	G	AB	H	2B	3B	HR	HR%	R	RBI	BB	SO	SB	BA	SA	AB	H	G by POS
1979 PIT N	1	0	0	0	0	0	–	0	0	0	0	0	–	–	0	0	OF-1

Nin Alexander

ALEXANDER, WILLIAM HENRY
B. Nov. 24, 1858, Pana, Ill.   D. Dec. 22, 1933, Pana, Ill.
BR TR 5'2" 135 lbs.

	G	AB	H	2B	3B	HR	HR%	R	RBI	BB	SO	SB	BA	SA	AB	H	G by POS
1884 2 teams			KC U (19G – .138)					STL AA (1G – .000)									
" total	20	69	9	0	0	0	0.0	2		1			.130	.130	0	0	C-18, OF-3, SS-2

Walt Alexander

ALEXANDER, WALTER ERNEST
B. Mar. 5, 1891, Atlanta, Ga.   D. Dec. 29, 1978, Ft. Worth, Tex.
BR TR 5'10½" 165 lbs.

	G	AB	H	2B	3B	HR	HR%	R	RBI	BB	SO	SB	BA	SA	AB	H	G by POS
1912 STL A	37	97	17	4	0	0	0.0	5	5	8		1	.175	.216	0	0	C-37
1913	43	110	15	2	1	0	0.0	5	7	4	36	1	.136	.173	0	0	C-43
1915 2 teams			STL A (1G – .000)					NY A (25G – .250)									
" total	26	69	17	4	0	1	1.4	7	5	13	16	2	.246	.348	0	0	C-25
1916 NY A	36	78	20	6	1	0	0.0	8	3	13	20	0	.256	.359	8	2	C-27
1917	20	51	7	2	1	0	0.0	1	4	4	11	1	.137	.216	0	0	C-20
5 yrs.	162	405	76	18	3	1	0.2	26	24	42	83	5	.188	.254	8	2	C-152

Bernie Allen

ALLEN, BERNARD KEITH
B. Apr. 16, 1939, East Liverpool, Ohio
BL TR 6' 175 lbs.

	G	AB	H	2B	3B	HR	HR%	R	RBI	BB	SO	SB	BA	SA	AB	H	G by POS
1962 MIN A	159	573	154	27	7	12	2.1	79	64	62	82	0	.269	.403	1	1	2B-158
1963	139	421	101	20	1	9	2.1	52	43	38	52	0	.240	.356	5	2	2B-128
1964	74	243	52	8	1	6	2.5	28	20	33	30	1	.214	.329	3	0	2B-71
1965	19	39	9	2	0	0	0.0	2	6	6	8	0	.231	.282	3	0	2B-10, 3B-1
1966	101	319	76	18	1	5	1.6	34	30	26	40	2	.238	.348	6	0	2B-89, 3B-2
1967 WAS A	87	254	49	5	1	3	1.2	13	18	18	43	1	.193	.256	12	1	2B-75
1968	120	373	90	12	4	6	1.6	31	40	28	35	2	.241	.343	15	3	2B-110, 3B-2
1969	122	365	90	17	4	9	2.5	33	45	50	35	5	.247	.389	13	5	2B-110, 3B-6
1970	104	261	61	7	1	8	3.1	31	29	43	21	0	.234	.360	23	5	2B-80, 3B-12
1971	97	229	61	11	1	4	1.7	18	22	33	27	2	.266	.376	32	7	2B-41, 3B-34
1972 NY A	84	220	50	9	0	9	4.1	26	21	23	42	0	.227	.391	20	0	3B-44, 2B-20

	G	AB	H	2B	3B	HR	HR %	R	RBI	BB	SO	SB	BA	SA	Pinch Hit AB	H	G by POS

Bernie Allen continued

1973 2 teams	NY	A	(17G – .228)			MON	N	(16G – .180)									
1973 2 teams	NY A	(17G – .228)						10	13	10	9	0	.206	.299	3	0	2B-22, 3B-8, DH-4
" total	33	107	22	4	0	2	1.9	10	13	10	9	0	.206	.299	3	0	2B-22, 3B-8, DH-4
12 yrs.	1139	3404	815	140	21	73	2.1	357	351	370	424	13	.239	.357	141	25	2B-914, 3B-109, DH-4

ALLEN, ROBERT
B. 1896

BR TR 5'10" 180 lbs.

Bob Allen

1919 PHI A	9	22	3	1	0	0	0.0	3	0	3	7	0	.136	.182	2	1	OF-6

ALLEN, ROBERT GILMAN
B. July 10, 1867, Marion, Ohio   D. May 14, 1943, Little Rock, Ark.
Manager 1900.

BR TR 5'11" 175 lbs.

Bob Allen

1890 PHI N	133	456	103	15	11	2	0.4	69	57	87	54	13	.226	.320	0	0	SS-133
1891	118	438	97	7	4	1	0.2	46	51	43	44	12	.221	.263	0	0	SS-118
1892	152	563	128	20	14	2	0.4	77	64	61	60	15	.227	.323	0	0	SS-152
1893	124	471	126	19	12	8	1.7	86	90	71	40	8	.268	.410	0	0	SS-124
1894	40	149	38	10	3	0	0.0	26	19	17	11	4	.255	.362	0	0	SS-40
1897 BOS N	34	119	38	5	0	1	0.8	33	24	18		1	.319	.387	0	0	SS-32, OF-1, 2B-1
1900 CIN N	5	15	2	1	0	0	0.0	0	1	0		0	.133	.200	0	0	SS-5
7 yrs.	606	2211	532	77	44	14	0.6	337	306	297	209	53	.241	.334	0	0	SS-604, OF-1, 2B-1

ALLEN, ETHAN NATHAN
B. Jan. 1, 1904, Cincinnati, Ohio

BR TR 6'1" 180 lbs.

Ethan Allen

1926 CIN N	18	13	4	1	0	0	0.0	3	0	0	3	0	.308	.385	2	0	OF-9
1927	111	359	106	26	4	2	0.6	54	20	14	23	12	.295	.407	2	1	OF-98
1928	129	485	148	30	7	1	0.2	55	62	27	29	6	.305	.402	0	0	OF-129
1929	143	538	157	27	11	6	1.1	69	64	20	21	21	.292	.416	2	0	OF-137
1930 2 teams	CIN	N	(21G – .217)			NY	N	(76G – .307)									
" total	97	284	83	10	2	10	3.5	58	38	17	25	6	.292	.447	18	5	OF-77
1931 NY N	94	298	98	18	2	5	1.7	58	43	15	15	6	.329	.453	14	8	OF-77
1932	54	103	18	6	2	1	1.0	13	7	1	12	0	.175	.301	22	1	OF-24
1933 STL N	91	261	63	7	3	0	0.0	25	36	13	22	3	.241	.291	21	3	OF-67
1934 PHI N	145	581	192	42	4	10	1.7	87	85	33	47	6	.330	.468	0	0	OF-145
1935	156	645	198	46	1	8	1.2	90	63	43	54	5	.307	.419	0	0	OF-156
1936 2 teams	PHI	N	(30G – .296)			CHI	N	(91G – .295)									
" total	121	498	147	21	7	4	0.8	68	48	17	38	16	.295	.390	0	0	OF-119
1937 STL A	103	320	101	18	1	0	0.0	39	31	21	17	3	.316	.378	23	8	OF-78
1938	19	33	10	3	1	0	0.0	4	4	2	4	0	.303	.455	12	3	OF-7
13 yrs.	1281	4418	1325	255	45	47	1.1	623	501	223	310	84	.300	.410	116	29	OF-1123

ALLEN, HAROLD ANDREW
Brother of Richie Allen.   Brother of Ron Allen.
B. July 23, 1940, Wampum, Pa.

BR TR 6' 190 lbs.

Hank Allen

1966 WAS A	9	31	12	0	0	1	3.2	6	3	6	6	0	.387	.484	0	0	OF-9
1967	116	292	68	8	4	3	1.0	34	17	13	53	3	.233	.318	21	7	OF-99
1968	68	128	28	2	1	1	0.8	16	9	7	16	0	.219	.289	22	5	OF-25, 3B-16, 2B-11
1969	109	271	75	9	4	1	0.4	42	17	13	28	12	.277	.343	23	5	OF-91, 3B-6, 2B-3
1970 2 teams	WAS	A	(22G – .211)			MIL	A	(28G – .230)									
" total	50	99	22	6	0	0	0.0	7	8	12	14	0	.222	.283	14	2	OF-31, 2B-5, 1B-4
1972 CHI A	9	21	3	0	0	0	0.0	1	0	0	2	0	.143	.143	0	0	3B-6
1973	28	39	4	2	0	0	0.0	2	0	1	9	0	.103	.154	5	0	3B-9, 1B-8, OF-5, 2B-1, C-1
7 yrs.	389	881	212	27	9	6	0.7	104	57	49	128	15	.241	.312	85	19	OF-260, 3B-37, 2B-20, 1B-12, C-1

ALLEN, HEZEKIAH
B. Feb. 25, 1863, Westport, Conn.   D. Sept. 21, 1916, Westport, Conn.

5'11" 160 lbs.

Hezekiah Allen

1884 PHI N	1	3	2	0	0	0	0.0	0		0		0	.667	.667	0	0	C-1

ALLEN, HORACE TANNER (Pug)
B. June 11, 1899, DeLand, Fla.   D. July 5, 1981, Canton, N. C.

BB TR 6' 187 lbs.

Horace Allen

1919 BKN N	4	7	0	0	0	0	0.0	0	0	0	2	0	.000	.000	1	0	OF-2

ALLEN, CYRUS ALBAN
B. Oct. 2, 1855, Woodstock, Ill.   D. Apr. 21, 1915, Girard, Pa.

Jack Allen

1879 2 teams	SYR	N	(11G – .188)			CLE	N	(16G – .117)									
" total	27	108	16	3	2	0	0.0	14	7	2	14		.148	.213	0	0	3B-22, OF-5

ALLEN, JAMES BRADLEY
B. May 29, 1958, Yakima, Wash.

BR TR 5'11" 210 lbs.

Jamie Allen

1983 SEA A	86	273	61	10	0	4	1.5	23	21	33	52	6	.223	.304	3	2	3B-82, DH-2

ALLEN, KIM BRYANT
B. Apr. 5, 1953, Fontana, Calif.

BR TR 5'11" 175 lbs.

Kim Allen

1980 SEA A	23	51	12	3	0	0	0.0	9	3	8	3	10	.235	.294	0	0	2B-15, OF-4, SS-1
1981	19	3	0	0	0	0	0.0	1	0	0	2	2	.000	.000	2	0	DH-2, OF-2, 2B-2
2 yrs.	42	54	12	3	0	0	0.0	10	3	8	5	12	.222	.278	2	0	2B-17, OF-6, DH-2, SS-1

ALLEN, MYRON SMITH
B. Mar. 22, 1854, Kingston, N. Y.   D. Mar. 8, 1924, Kingston, N. Y.

BR TR 5'8" 150 lbs.

Myron Allen

1883 NY N	1	4	0	0	0	0	0.0	0		0	2		.000	.000	0	0	P-1
1886 BOS N	1	3	0	0	0	0	0.0	0		0	1		.000	.000	0	0	2B-1
1887 CLE AA	117	463	128	22	10	4	0.9	66		36		26	.276	.393	0	0	OF-115, 3B-3, SS-2, P-2
1888 KC AA	37	136	29	6	4	0	0.0	23	10	9		4	.213	.316	0	0	OF-35, P-2
4 yrs.	156	606	157	28	14	4	0.7	89	9	45	3	30	.259	.371	0	0	OF-150, P-5, 3B-3, SS-2, 2B-1

	G	AB	H	2B	3B	HR	HR %	R	RBI	BB	SO	SB	BA	SA	Pinch Hit AB	Pinch Hit H	G by POS

Nick Allen

ALLEN, ARTEMUS WARD
B. Sept. 14, 1888, Udall, Kans.   D. Oct. 16, 1939, Hines, Ill.   BR TR 6'   180 lbs.

	G	AB	H	2B	3B	HR	HR %	R	RBI	BB	SO	SB	BA	SA	PH AB	PH H	G by POS
1914 BUF F	32	63	15	1	0	0	0.0	3	4	3		4	.238	.254	5	2	C-26
1915	84	215	44	7	1	0	0.0	14	17	18		4	.205	.247	4	1	C-80
1916 CHI N	5	16	1	0	0	0	0.0	1	1	0	3	0	.063	.063	1	0	C-4
1918 CIN N	37	96	25	2	2	0	0.0	6	5	4	7	0	.260	.323	4	3	C-31
1919	15	25	8	0	1	0	0.0	7	5	2	6	0	.320	.400	2	0	C-12
1920	43	85	23	3	1	0	0.0	10	4	6	11	0	.271	.329	6	2	C-36
6 yrs.	216	500	116	13	5	0	0.0	41	36	33	27	8	.232	.278	22	8	C-189

Pete Allen

ALLEN, JESSE HALL
B. May 1, 1868, Columbiana, Ohio   D. Apr. 16, 1946, Philadelphia, Pa.   BR TR 5'8½" 185 lbs.

	G	AB	H	2B	3B	HR	HR %	R	RBI	BB	SO	SB	BA	SA	PH AB	PH H	G by POS
1893 CLE N	1	4	0	0	0	0	0.0	0	0	0	0	0	.000	.000	0	0	C-1

Richie Allen

ALLEN, RICHARD ANTHONY
Brother of Hank Allen.   Brother of Ron Allen.   BR TR 5'11" 187 lbs.
B. Mar. 8, 1942, Wampum, Pa.

	G	AB	H	2B	3B	HR	HR %	R	RBI	BB	SO	SB	BA	SA	PH AB	PH H	G by POS
1963 PHI N	10	24	7	2	1	0	0.0	6	2	0	5	0	.292	.458	2	0	OF-7, 3B-1
1964	162	632	201	38	13	29	4.6	125	91	67	138	3	.318	.557	0	0	3B-162
1965	161	619	187	31	14	20	3.2	93	85	74	150	15	.302	.494	0	0	3B-160, SS-2
1966	141	524	166	25	10	40	7.6	112	110	68	136	10	.317	.632	4	1	3B-91, OF-47
1967	122	463	142	31	10	23	5.0	89	77	75	117	20	.307	.566	1	0	3B-121, SS-1, 2B-1
1968	152	521	137	17	9	33	6.3	87	90	74	161	7	.263	.520	8	0	OF-139, 3B-10
1969	118	438	126	23	3	32	7.3	79	89	64	144	9	.288	.573	1	1	1B-119
1970 STL N	122	459	128	17	5	34	7.4	88	101	71	118	5	.279	.560	3	1	1B-79, 3B-38, OF-3
1971 LA N	155	549	162	24	1	23	4.2	82	90	93	113	8	.295	.468	3	0	3B-67, OF-60, 1B-28
1972 CHI A	148	506	156	28	5	37	7.3	90	113	99	126	19	.308	.603	7	1	3B-143, DH-2
1973	72	250	79	20	3	16	6.4	39	41	33	51	7	.316	.612	3	0	1B-67, 2B-2, DH-1
1974	128	462	139	23	1	32	6.9	84	88	57	89	7	.301	.563	4	0	1B-125, DH-1, 2B-1
1975 PHI N	119	416	97	21	3	12	2.9	54	62	58	109	11	.233	.385	5	0	1B-113
1976	85	298	80	16	1	15	5.0	52	49	37	63	11	.268	.480	2	1	1B-85
1977 OAK A	54	171	41	4	0	5	2.9	19	31	24	36	1	.240	.351	2	0	1B-50, DH-1
15 yrs.	1749	6332	1848	320	79	351	5.5	1099	1119	894	1556 10th	133	.292	.534	46	5	1B-807, 3B-652, OF-256, 2B-4, DH-3, SS-3

LEAGUE CHAMPIONSHIP SERIES

	G	AB	H	2B	3B	HR	HR %	R	RBI	BB	SO	SB	BA	SA	PH AB	PH H	G by POS
1976 PHI N	3	9	2	0	0	0	0.0	1	0	3	2	0	.222	.222	0	0	1B-3

Rod Allen

ALLEN, RODERICK BERNET
B. Oct. 5, 1959, Los Angeles, Calif.   BR TR 6'1" 185 lbs.

	G	AB	H	2B	3B	HR	HR %	R	RBI	BB	SO	SB	BA	SA	PH AB	PH H	G by POS
1983 SEA A	11	12	2	0	0	0	0.0	1	0	0	1	0	.167	.167	4	1	DH-3, OF-2
1984 DET A	15	27	8	1	0	0	0.0	6	3	2	8	1	.296	.333	3	1	DH-11, OF-2
2 yrs.	26	39	10	1	0	0	0.0	7	3	2	9	1	.256	.282	7	2	DH-14, OF-4

Ron Allen

ALLEN, RONALD FREDERICK
Brother of Hank Allen.   Brother of Richie Allen.   BB TR 6'3" 205 lbs.
B. Dec. 23, 1943, Ellwood City, Pa.

	G	AB	H	2B	3B	HR	HR %	R	RBI	BB	SO	SB	BA	SA	PH AB	PH H	G by POS
1972 STL N	7	11	1	0	0	1	9.1	2	1	3	5	0	.091	.364	0	0	1B-5

Sled Allen

ALLEN, FLETCHER MANSON
B. Aug. 23, 1886, West Plains, Mo.   D. Oct. 16, 1959, Lubbock, Tex.   BR TR 6'1" 180 lbs.

	G	AB	H	2B	3B	HR	HR %	R	RBI	BB	SO	SB	BA	SA	PH AB	PH H	G by POS
1910 STL A	14	23	3	1	0	0	0.0	3	1	1		0	.130	.174	1	0	C-12, 1B-1

Gary Allenson

ALLENSON, GARY MARTIN (Hardrock)
B. Feb. 4, 1955, Culver City, Calif.   BR TR 5'11" 185 lbs.

	G	AB	H	2B	3B	HR	HR %	R	RBI	BB	SO	SB	BA	SA	PH AB	PH H	G by POS
1979 BOS A	108	241	49	10	2	3	1.2	27	22	20	42	1	.203	.299	0	0	C-104, 3B-3
1980	36	70	25	6	0	0	0.0	9	10	13	11	2	.357	.443	1	0	C-24, DH-6, 3B-5
1981	47	139	31	8	0	5	3.6	23	25	23	33	0	.223	.388	0	0	C-47
1982	92	264	54	11	0	6	2.3	25	33	38	39	0	.205	.314	1	0	C-91
1983	84	230	53	11	0	3	1.3	19	30	27	43	0	.230	.317	1	0	C-84
1984	35	83	19	2	0	2	2.4	9	8	9	14	0	.229	.325	0	0	C-35
6 yrs.	402	1027	231	48	2	19	1.9	112	128	130	182	3	.225	.331	3	0	C-385, 3B-8, DH-6

Gene Alley

ALLEY, LEONARD EUGENE
B. July 10, 1940, Richmond, Va.   BR TR 5'10" 160 lbs.

	G	AB	H	2B	3B	HR	HR %	R	RBI	BB	SO	SB	BA	SA	PH AB	PH H	G by POS
1963 PIT N	17	51	11	1	0	0	0.0	3	0	2	12	0	.216	.235	1	0	3B-7, SS-4, 2B-4
1964	81	209	44	3	1	6	2.9	30	13	21	56	0	.211	.321	9	1	SS-61, 3B-3, 2B-1
1965	153	500	126	21	6	5	1.0	47	47	32	82	7	.252	.348	2	0	SS-110, 2B-40, 3B-1
1966	147	579	173	28	10	7	1.2	88	43	27	83	8	.299	.418	1	0	SS-143
1967	152	550	158	25	7	6	1.1	59	55	36	70	10	.287	.391	4	0	SS-146
1968	133	474	116	20	2	4	0.8	48	39	39	78	13	.245	.321	4	0	SS-109, 2B-24
1969	82	285	70	3	2	8	2.8	28	32	19	48	4	.246	.354	1	0	2B-53, SS-25, 3B-5
1970	121	426	104	16	5	8	1.9	46	41	31	70	7	.244	.362	5	0	SS-108, 2B-8, 3B-2
1971	114	348	79	8	7	6	1.7	38	28	35	43	9	.227	.342	4	2	SS-108, 3B-1
1972	119	347	86	12	2	3	0.9	30	36	38	52	4	.248	.320	5	3	SS-114, 3B-4
1973	76	158	32	3	2	2	1.3	25	8	20	28	1	.203	.285	12	0	SS-49, 3B-8
11 yrs.	1195	3927	999	140	44	55	1.4	442	342	300	622	63	.254	.354	48	6	SS-977, 2B-130, 3B-31

LEAGUE CHAMPIONSHIP SERIES

	G	AB	H	2B	3B	HR	HR %	R	RBI	BB	SO	SB	BA	SA	PH AB	PH H	G by POS
1970 PIT N	2	7	0	0	0	0	0.0	0	0	1	2	0	.000	.000	0	0	SS-2
1971	1	2	1	0	0	0	0.0	1	0	0	0	0	.500	.500	0	0	SS-1
1972	5	16	0	0	0	0	0.0	1	0	0	3	0	.000	.000	0	0	SS-5
3 yrs.	8	25	1	0	0	0	0.0	2	0	1	5	0	.040	.040	0	0	SS-8

WORLD SERIES

	G	AB	H	2B	3B	HR	HR %	R	RBI	BB	SO	SB	BA	SA	PH AB	PH H	G by POS
1971 PIT N	2	2	0	0	0	0	0.0	0	0	1	0	0	.000	.000	0	0	SS-2

	G	AB	H	2B	3B	HR	HR %	R	RBI	BB	SO	SB	BA	SA	Pinch Hit AB	Pinch Hit H	G by POS

Gair Allie

ALLIE, GAIR ROOSEVELT
B. Oct. 29, 1931, Statesville, N. C.
BR TR 6'1" 190 lbs.

	G	AB	H	2B	3B	HR	HR %	R	RBI	BB	SO	SB	BA	SA	PH AB	PH H	G by POS
1954 PIT N	121	418	83	8	6	3	0.7	38	30	56	84	1	.199	.268	4	0	SS-95, 3B-19

Bob Allietta

ALLIETTA, ROBERT GEORGE
B. May 1, 1952, New Bedford, Md.
BR TR 6' 190 lbs.

	G	AB	H	2B	3B	HR	HR %	R	RBI	BB	SO	SB	BA	SA	PH AB	PH H	G by POS
1975 CAL A	21	45	8	1	0	1	2.2	4	2	1	6	0	.178	.267	0	0	C-21

Art Allison

ALLISON, ARTHUR ALGERNON
Brother of Doug Allison.
B. Jan. 29, 1849, Philadelphia, Pa.   D. Feb. 25, 1916, Washington, D. C.
5'8" 150 lbs.

	G	AB	H	2B	3B	HR	HR %	R	RBI	BB	SO	SB	BA	SA	PH AB	PH H	G by POS
1876 LOU N	31	130	27	2	1	0	0.0	9	10	2	6		.208	.238	0	0	OF-23, 1B-8

Bob Allison

ALLISON, WILLIAM ROBERT
B. July 11, 1934, Raytown, Mo.
BR TR 6'3" 205 lbs.

	G	AB	H	2B	3B	HR	HR %	R	RBI	BB	SO	SB	BA	SA	PH AB	PH H	G by POS
1958 WAS A	11	35	7	1	0	0	0.0	1	0	2	5	0	.200	.229	0	0	OF-11
1959	150	570	149	18	9	30	5.3	83	85	60	92	13	.261	.482	1	0	OF-149
1960	144	501	126	30	3	15	3.0	79	69	92	94	11	.251	.413	4	0	OF-140, 1B-4
1961 MIN A	159	556	136	21	3	29	5.2	83	105	103	100	2	.245	.450	0	0	OF-150, 1B-18
1962	149	519	138	24	8	29	5.6	102	102	84	115	0	.266	.511	0	0	OF-147
1963	148	527	143	25	4	35	6.6	99	91	90	109	6	.271	.533	1	0	OF-147
1964	149	492	141	27	4	32	6.5	90	86	92	99	10	.287	.553	8	1	1B-93, OF-61
1965	135	438	102	14	5	23	5.3	71	78	73	114	10	.233	.445	14	2	OF-72, 1B-3
1966	70	168	37	6	1	8	4.8	34	19	30	34	6	.220	.411	11	5	OF-56
1967	153	496	128	21	6	24	4.8	73	75	74	114	6	.258	.470	6	4	OF-145
1968	145	469	116	16	8	22	4.7	63	52	52	98	9	.247	.456	13	2	OF-117, 1B-17
1969	81	189	43	8	2	8	4.2	18	27	29	39	2	.228	.418	20	4	OF-58, 1B-3
1970	47	72	15	5	0	1	1.4	15	7	14	20	1	.208	.319	20	7	OF-17, 1B-7
13 yrs.	1541	5032	1281	216	53	256	5.1	811	796	795	1033	84	.255	.471	98	25	OF-1320, 1B-145
LEAGUE CHAMPIONSHIP SERIES																	
1969 MIN A	2	8	0	0	0	0	0.0	0	1	0	0	0	.000	.000	0	0	OF-2
1970	3	2	0	0	0	0	0.0	0	0	1	1	0	.000	.000	2	0	
2 yrs.	5	10	0	0	0	0	0.0	0	1	1	1	0	.000	.000	2	0	OF-2
WORLD SERIES																	
1965 MIN A	5	16	2	1	0	1	6.3	3	2	2	9	1	.125	.375	0	0	OF-5

Doug Allison

ALLISON, DOUGLAS L.
Brother of Art Allison.
B. 1846, Philadelphia, Pa.   D. Dec. 19, 1916, Washington, D. C.
BR TR 5'10½" 160 lbs.

	G	AB	H	2B	3B	HR	HR %	R	RBI	BB	SO	SB	BA	SA	PH AB	PH H	G by POS
1876 HAR N	44	163	43	4	0	0	0.0	19	15	3	9		.264	.288	0	0	C-40, OF-6
1877	29	115	17	2	0	0	0.0	14	6	3	7		.148	.165	0	0	C-29
1878 PRO N	19	76	22	2	0	0	0.0	9	7	1	8		.289	.316	0	0	C-19, P-1
1879	1	5	0	0	0	0	0.0	0	0	0	1		.000	.000	0	0	C-1
1883 BAL AA	1	3	2	0	0	0	0.0	2			0		.667	.667	0	0	OF-1, C-1
5 yrs.	94	362	84	8	0	0	0.0	44	28	7	25		.232	.254	0	0	C-90, OF-7, P-1

Milo Allison

ALLISON, MILO HENRY (Pete)
B. Oct. 16, 1890, Elk Rapids, Mich.   D. June 18, 1957, Kenosha, Wis.
BL TR 6' 163 lbs.

	G	AB	H	2B	3B	HR	HR %	R	RBI	BB	SO	SB	BA	SA	PH AB	PH H	G by POS
1913 CHI N	2	6	2	0	0	0	0.0	1	0	0	1	1	.333	.333	0	0	OF-1
1914	1	1	1	0	0	0	0.0	0	0	0	0	0	1.000	1.000	1	1	
1916 CLE A	14	18	5	0	0	0	0.0	10	0	9	6	3	.278	.278	1	0	OF-5
1917	32	35	5	0	0	0	0.0	4	0	7	1	3	.143	.143	14	0	OF-11
4 yrs.	49	60	13	0	0	0	0.0	15	0	15	9	4	.217	.217	16	1	OF-17

Mel Almada

ALMADA, BALDOMERO MELO
B. Feb. 7, 1913, Hwatabampo, Mexico
BL TL 6' 170 lbs.

	G	AB	H	2B	3B	HR	HR %	R	RBI	BB	SO	SB	BA	SA	PH AB	PH H	G by POS
1933 BOS A	14	44	15	0	0	1	2.3	11	3	11	3	3	.341	.409	1	0	OF-13
1934	23	90	21	2	0	0	0.0	7	10	6	8	3	.233	.278	0	0	OF-23
1935	151	607	176	27	9	3	0.5	85	59	55	34	20	.290	.379	0	0	OF-149, 1B-3
1936	96	320	81	16	4	1	0.3	40	21	24	15	2	.253	.338	13	5	OF-81
1937 2 teams	BOS A (32G – .236)					STL A (100G – .309)											
" total	132	543	160	27	6	5	0.9	91	42	53	27	12	.295	.394	0	0	OF-127, 1B-4
1938 2 teams	WAS A (47G – .244)					STL A (102G – .342)											
" total	149	633	197	29	6	4	0.6	101	52	46	38	13	.311	.395	1	0	OF-148
1939 2 teams	STL A (42G – .239)					BKN N (39G – .214)											
" total	81	246	56	6	1	1	0.4	28	10	19	25	3	.228	.272	8	3	OF-66
7 yrs.	646	2483	706	107	27	15	0.6	363	197	214	150	56	.284	.367	23	8	OF-607, 1B-7

Rafael Almeida

ALMEIDA, RAFAEL D.
B. July 30, 1887, Havana, Cuba   D. Mar., 1968, Havana, Cuba
BR TR 5'9" 164 lbs.

	G	AB	H	2B	3B	HR	HR %	R	RBI	BB	SO	SB	BA	SA	PH AB	PH H	G by POS
1911 CIN N	36	96	30	5	1	0	0.0	9	15	9	16	3	.313	.385	4	1	3B-27, SS-1, 2B-1
1912	16	59	13	4	3	0	0.0	9	10	5	8	0	.220	.390	1	0	3B-16
1913	50	130	34	4	2	3	2.3	14	21	11	16	4	.262	.392	7	1	3B-37, OF-3, SS-2, 2B-1
3 yrs.	102	285	77	13	6	3	1.1	32	46	25	40	7	.270	.389	12	2	3B-80, OF-3, SS-3, 2B-2

Bill Almon

ALMON, WILLIAM FRANCIS
B. Nov. 21, 1952, Providence, R. I.
BR TR 6'3" 180 lbs.

	G	AB	H	2B	3B	HR	HR %	R	RBI	BB	SO	SB	BA	SA	PH AB	PH H	G by POS
1974 SD N	16	38	12	1	0	0	0.0	4	3	2	9	1	.316	.342	0	0	SS-14
1975	6	10	4	0	0	0	0.0	0	0	0	1	0	.400	.400	1	0	SS-2
1976	14	57	14	3	0	1	1.8	6	6	2	9	3	.246	.351	0	0	SS-14
1977	155	613	160	18	11	2	0.3	75	43	37	114	20	.261	.336	4	1	3B-114, SS-15, 2B-7
1978	138	405	102	19	2	0	0.0	39	21	33	74	17	.252	.309	4	0	2B-61, SS-25, OF-1
1979	100	198	45	3	0	1	0.5	20	8	21	48	6	.227	.258	3	0	SS-34, 2B-19, 3B-9
1980 2 teams	MON N (18G – .263)					NY N (48G – .170)											
" total	66	150	29	4	3	0	0.0	15	7	9	32	2	.193	.260	4	0	SS-103
1981 CHI A	103	349	105	10	2	4	1.1	46	41	21	60	16	.301	.375	0	0	

	G	AB	H	2B	3B	HR	HR %	R	RBI	BB	SO	SB	BA	SA	Pinch Hit AB	Pinch Hit H	G by POS

Bill Almon continued

	G	AB	H	2B	3B	HR	HR %	R	RBI	BB	SO	SB	BA	SA	PH AB	PH H	G by POS
1982	111	308	79	10	4	4	1.3	40	26	25	49	10	.256	.354	1	0	SS-108, DH-1
1983 OAK A	143	451	120	29	1	4	0.9	45	63	26	67	26	.266	.361	14	3	SS-52, 3B-40, 1B-38, OF-23, 2B-5, DH-4
1984	106	212	46	11	0	7	3.3	24	16	10	42	5	.217	.368	15	3	OF-48, 1B-44, DH-12, 3B-4, SS-1, C-1
11 yrs.	958	2791	716	108	23	23	0.8	314	234	186	505	106	.257	.336	42	7	SS-523, 3B-167, 2B-92, 1B-82, OF-72, DH-17, C-1

Sandy Alomar

ALOMAR, CONDE SANTOS
B. Oct. 19, 1943, Salinas, Puerto Rico

BB TR 5'9" 140 lbs.
BR 1964-66

	G	AB	H	2B	3B	HR	HR %	R	RBI	BB	SO	SB	BA	SA	PH AB	PH H	G by POS
1964 MIL N	19	53	13	1	0	0	0.0	3	6	0	11	1	.245	.264	0	0	SS-19
1965	67	108	26	1	1	0	0.0	16	8	4	12	12	.241	.269	0	0	SS-39, 2B-19
1966 ATL N	31	44	4	1	0	0	0.0	4	2	1	10	0	.091	.114	1	0	2B-21, SS-5
1967 2 teams	NY	N	(15G –	.000)		CHI	A	(12G –	.200)								
" total	27	37	3	0	0	0	0.0	5	0	2	6	2	.081	.081	1	0	SS-18, 2B-4, 3B-3
1968 CHI A	133	363	92	8	2	0	0.0	41	12	20	42	21	.253	.287	4	2	2B-99, 3B-27, SS-9, OF-1
1969 2 teams	CHI	A	(22G –	.224)		CAL	A	(134G –	.250)								
" total	156	617	153	12	2	1	0.2	68	34	40	54	20	.248	.279	0	0	2B-156
1970 CAL A	162	672	169	18	2	2	0.3	82	36	49	65	35	.251	.293	0	0	2B-153, SS-10, 3B-1
1971	162	689	179	24	3	4	0.6	77	42	41	60	39	.260	.321	0	0	2B-137, SS-28
1972	155	610	146	20	3	1	0.2	65	25	47	55	20	.239	.287	0	0	2B-154, SS-4
1973	136	470	112	7	1	0	0.0	45	28	34	44	25	.238	.257	0	0	2B-110, SS-31
1974 2 teams	CAL	A	(46G –	.222)		NY	A	(76G –	.269)								
" total	122	333	87	8	1	1	0.3	47	28	15	33	8	.261	.300	3	1	2B-91, SS-19, 3B-5, DH-1, OF-1
1975 NY A	151	489	117	18	4	2	0.4	61	39	26	58	28	.239	.305	0	0	2B-150, SS-1
1976	67	163	39	4	0	1	0.6	20	10	13	12	12	.239	.282	2	0	2B-38, DH-9, SS-6, 3B-3, OF-1, 1B-1
1977 TEX A	69	83	22	3	0	1	1.2	21	11	8	13	4	.265	.337	7	2	DH-26, 2B-18, SS-6, OF-5, 1B-4, 3B-1
1978	24	29	6	1	0	0	0.0	3	1	1	7	0	.207	.241	0	0	1B-9, 2B-6, DH-3, 3B-3, SS-2
15 yrs.	1481	4760	1168	126	19	13	0.3	558	282	301	482	227	.245	.288	18	5	2B-1156, SS-197, 3B-43, DH-39, 1B-14, OF-8

LEAGUE CHAMPIONSHIP SERIES

	G	AB	H	2B	3B	HR	HR %	R	RBI	BB	SO	SB	BA	SA	PH AB	PH H	G by POS
1976 NY A	2	1	0	0	0	0	0.0	0	0	0	0	0	.000	.000	1	0	DH-1

Felipe Alou

ALOU, FELIPE ROJAS
Brother of Jesus Alou. Brother of Matty Alou.
B. May 12, 1935, Santo Domingo, Dominican Republic

BR TR 6' 195 lbs.

	G	AB	H	2B	3B	HR	HR %	R	RBI	BB	SO	SB	BA	SA	PH AB	PH H	G by POS
1958 SF N	75	182	46	9	2	4	2.2	21	16	19	34	4	.253	.390	5	1	OF-70
1959	95	247	68	13	2	10	4.0	38	33	17	38	5	.275	.466	21	5	OF-69
1960	106	322	85	17	3	8	2.5	48	44	16	42	10	.264	.410	9	0	OF-95
1961	132	415	120	19	0	18	4.3	59	52	26	41	11	.289	.465	11	2	OF-122
1962	154	561	177	30	3	25	4.5	96	98	33	66	10	.316	.513	4	0	OF-150
1963	157	565	159	31	9	20	3.5	75	82	27	87	11	.281	.474	8	4	OF-153
1964 MIL N	121	415	105	26	3	9	2.2	60	51	30	41	5	.253	.395	18	5	OF-92, 1B-18
1965	143	555	165	29	2	23	4.1	80	78	31	63	8	.297	.481	9	3	OF-91, 1B-69, 3B-2, SS-1
1966 ATL N	154	666	218	32	6	31	4.7	122	74	24	51	5	.327	.533	0	0	1B-90, OF-79, 3B-3, SS-1
1967	140	574	157	26	3	15	2.6	76	43	32	50	6	.274	.408	3	1	1B-85, OF-56
1968	160	662	210	37	5	11	1.7	72	57	48	56	12	.317	.438	3	0	OF-158
1969	123	476	134	13	1	5	1.1	54	32	23	23	4	.282	.345	2	2	OF-116
1970 OAK A	154	575	156	25	3	8	1.4	70	55	32	31	10	.271	.367	9	1	OF-145, 1B-1
1971 2 teams	OAK	A	(2G –	.250)		NY	A	(131G –	.289)								
" total	133	469	135	21	6	8	1.7	52	69	32	25	5	.288	.409	19	7	OF-82, 1B-42
1972 NY A	120	324	90	18	1	6	1.9	33	37	22	27	1	.278	.395	29	10	1B-95, OF-15
1973 2 teams	NY	A	(93G –	.236)		MON	N	(19G –	.208)								
" total	112	328	76	13	0	5	1.5	29	31	11	29	0	.232	.317	21	6	1B-68, OF-37
1974 MIL N	3	3	0	0	0	0	0.0	0	0	0	2	0	.000	.000	3	0	OF-1
17 yrs.	2082	7339	2101	359	49	206	2.8	985	852	423	706	107	.286	.433	174	46	OF-1531, 1B-468, 3B-5, SS-2

LEAGUE CHAMPIONSHIP SERIES

	G	AB	H	2B	3B	HR	HR %	R	RBI	BB	SO	SB	BA	SA	PH AB	PH H	G by POS
1969 ATL N	1	1	0	0	0	0	0.0	0	0	0	0	0	.000	.000	1	0	

WORLD SERIES

	G	AB	H	2B	3B	HR	HR %	R	RBI	BB	SO	SB	BA	SA	PH AB	PH H	G by POS
1962 SF N	7	26	7	1	0	0	0.0	2	1	1	4	0	.269	.385	0	0	OF-7

Jesus Alou

ALOU, JESUS MARIA ROJAS (Jay)
Brother of Matty Alou. Brother of Felipe Alou.
B. Mar. 24, 1942, Haina, Dominican Republic

BR TR 6'2" 190 lbs.

	G	AB	H	2B	3B	HR	HR %	R	RBI	BB	SO	SB	BA	SA	PH AB	PH H	G by POS
1963 SF N	16	24	6	1	0	0	0.0	3	5	0	3	0	.250	.292	4	0	OF-12
1964	115	376	103	11	0	3	0.8	42	28	13	35	6	.274	.327	13	4	OF-108
1965	143	543	162	19	4	9	1.7	76	52	13	40	8	.298	.398	8	4	OF-136
1966	110	370	96	13	1	1	0.3	41	20	9	22	5	.259	.308	13	3	OF-100
1967	129	510	149	15	4	5	1.0	55	30	14	39	1	.292	.367	6	2	OF-123
1968	120	419	110	15	0	0	0.0	26	39	9	23	0	.263	.317	18	6	OF-105
1969 HOU N	115	452	112	19	4	5	1.1	49	34	15	30	4	.248	.341	0	0	OF-112
1970	117	458	140	27	3	1	0.2	59	44	21	15	3	.306	.384	11	2	OF-108
1971	122	433	121	21	4	2	0.5	41	40	13	17	3	.279	.360	17	5	OF-109
1972	52	93	29	4	1	0	0.0	8	11	7	5	0	.312	.376	31	8	OF-23
1973 2 teams	HOU	N	(28G –	.236)		OAK	A	(36G –	.306)								
" total	64	163	46	5	0	2	1.2	17	19	3	12	0	.282	.344	22	5	OF-35, DH-6
1974 OAK A	96	220	59	8	0	2	0.9	13	15	5	9	0	.268	.332	41	7	DH-41, OF-25
1975 NY N	62	102	27	3	0	0	0.0	8	11	4	5	0	.265	.294	39	14	OF-20
1978 HOU N	77	139	45	5	1	2	1.4	7	19	6	5	0	.324	.417	44	16	OF-28
1979	42	43	11	4	0	0	0.0	3	10	6	7	0	.256	.349	34	6	OF-6, 1B-1
15 yrs.	1380	4345	1216	170	26	32	0.7	448	377	138	267	31	.280	.353	301	82	OF-1050, DH-47, 1B-1

	G	AB	H	2B	3B	HR	HR %	R	RBI	BB	SO	SB	BA	SA	Pinch Hit AB	Pinch Hit H	G by POS

Jesus Alou continued

LEAGUE CHAMPIONSHIP SERIES

	G	AB	H	2B	3B	HR	HR%	R	RBI	BB	SO	SB	BA	SA	AB	H	G by POS
1973 OAK A	4	6	2	0	0	0	0.0	0	1	0	1	0	.333	.333	3	1	DH-1
1974	1	1	1	0	0	0	0.0	0	0	0	0	0	1.000	1.000	1	1	
2 yrs.	5	7	3	0	0	0	0.0	0	1	0	1	0	.429	.429	4	2	DH-1

WORLD SERIES

	G	AB	H	2B	3B	HR	HR%	R	RBI	BB	SO	SB	BA	SA	AB	H	G by POS
1973 OAK A	7	19	3	1	0	0	0.0	0	3	0	0	0	.158	.211	1	0	OF-6
1974	1	1	0	0	0	0	0.0	0	0	0	1	0	.000	.000	1	0	
2 yrs.	8	20	3	1	0	0	0.0	0	3	0	1	0	.150	.200	2	0	OF-6

Matty Alou

ALOU, MATEO ROJAS   BL TL 5'9"   160 lbs.
Brother of Jesus Alou.   Brother of Felipe Alou.
B. Dec. 22, 1938, Haina, Dominican Republic

	G	AB	H	2B	3B	HR	HR%	R	RBI	BB	SO	SB	BA	SA	AB	H	G by POS
1960 SF N	4	3	1	0	0	0	0.0	0	0	0	0	0	.333	.333	3	1	OF-1
1961	81	200	62	7	2	6	3.0	38	24	15	18	3	.310	.455	22	5	OF-58
1962	78	195	57	8	1	3	1.5	28	14	14	17	3	.292	.390	24	9	OF-57
1963	63	76	11	0	0	0	0.0	4	2	2	13	0	.145	.158	45	8	OF-20
1964	110	250	66	4	2	1	0.4	28	14	11	25	5	.264	.308	30	4	OF-80
1965	117	324	75	12	2	2	0.6	37	18	17	28	10	.231	.299	19	1	OF-103, P-1
1966 PIT N	141	535	183	18	9	2	0.4	86	27	24	44	23	.342	.421	7	4	OF-136
1967	139	550	186	21	7	2	0.4	87	28	24	42	16	.338	.413	10	2	OF-134, 1B-1
1968	146	558	185	28	4	0	0.0	59	52	27	26	18	.332	.396	2	1	OF-144
1969	162	698	231	41	6	1	0.1	105	48	42	35	22	.331	.411	0	0	OF-162
1970	155	677	201	21	8	1	0.1	97	47	30	18	19	.297	.356	2	0	OF-153
1971 STL N	149	609	192	28	6	7	1.1	85	74	34	27	19	.315	.415	6	2	OF-94, 1B-57
1972 2 teams		STL	N	(108G –	.314)		OAK	A	(32G –	.281)							
" total	140	525	161	22	2	4	0.8	57	47	35	35	13	.307	.379	9	1	OF-71, 1B-67
1973 2 teams		NY	A	(123G –	.296)		STL	N	(11G –	.273)							
" total	134	508	150	22	1	2	0.4	60	29	31	43	5	.295	.354	10	3	OF-86, 1B-41, DH-1
1974 SD N	48	81	16	3	0	0	0.0	8	3	5	6	0	.198	.235	30	5	OF-13, 1B-2
15 yrs.	1667	5789	1777	236	50	31	0.5	780	427	311	377	156	.307	.381	219	46	OF-1312, 1B-168, DH-1, P-1

LEAGUE CHAMPIONSHIP SERIES

	G	AB	H	2B	3B	HR	HR%	R	RBI	BB	SO	SB	BA	SA	AB	H	G by POS
1970 PIT N	3	12	3	1	0	0	0.0	1	0	2	1	0	.250	.333	0	0	OF-3
1972 OAK A	5	21	8	4	0	0	0.0	2	2	0	2	1	.381	.571	0	0	OF-5
2 yrs.	8	33	11	5	0	0	0.0	3	2	2	3	1	.333	.485	0	0	OF-8

WORLD SERIES

	G	AB	H	2B	3B	HR	HR%	R	RBI	BB	SO	SB	BA	SA	AB	H	G by POS
1962 SF N	6	12	4	1	0	0	0.0	2	1	0	1	0	.333	.417	3	2	OF-4
1972 OAK A	7	24	1	0	0	0	0.0	0	0	3	0	1	.042	.042	0	0	OF-7
2 yrs.	13	36	5	1	0	0	0.0	2	1	3	1	1	.139	.167	3	2	OF-11

Whitey Alperman

ALPERMAN, CHARLES AUGUSTUS   BR TR 5'10"   180 lbs.
B. Nov. 11, 1879, Etna, Pa.   D. Dec. 25, 1942, Pittsburgh, Pa.

	G	AB	H	2B	3B	HR	HR%	R	RBI	BB	SO	SB	BA	SA	AB	H	G by POS
1906 BKN N	128	441	111	15	7	3	0.7	38	46	6		13	.252	.338	1	0	2B-104, SS-24, 3B-1
1907	141	558	130	23	16	2	0.4	44	39	13		5	.233	.342	3	1	2B-115, 3B-14, SS-12
1908	70	213	42	3	1	1	0.5	17	15	9		2	.197	.235	11	1	2B-42, 3B-9, OF-5, SS-2
1909	111	420	104	19	12	1	0.2	35	41	2		7	.248	.357	3	0	2B-108
4 yrs.	450	1632	387	60	36	7	0.4	134	141	30		27	.237	.331	18	2	2B-369, SS-38, 3B-24, OF-5

Del Alston

ALSTON, WENDELL   BL TR 6'   180 lbs.
B. Sept. 22, 1952, White Plains, N. Y.

	G	AB	H	2B	3B	HR	HR%	R	RBI	BB	SO	SB	BA	SA	AB	H	G by POS
1977 NY A	22	40	13	4	0	1	2.5	10	4	3	4	3	.325	.500	8	3	DH-10, OF-2
1978 2 teams		NY	A	(3G –	.000)		OAK	A	(58G –	.208)							
" total	61	176	36	2	0	1	0.6	17	10	10	23	11	.205	.233	7	1	OF-50, 1B-9, DH-3
1979 CLE A	54	62	18	0	2	1	1.6	10	12	10	10	4	.290	.403	11	1	OF-30, DH-7
1980	52	54	12	1	2	0	0.0	11	9	5	7	2	.222	.315	7	1	OF-26, DH-6
4 yrs.	189	332	79	7	4	3	0.9	48	35	28	44	20	.238	.310	33	6	OF-108, DH-26, 1B-9

Tom Alston

ALSTON, THOMAS EDISON   BL TR 6'5"   210 lbs.
B. Jan. 31, 1931, Greensboro, N. C.

	G	AB	H	2B	3B	HR	HR%	R	RBI	BB	SO	SB	BA	SA	AB	H	G by POS
1954 STL N	66	244	60	14	2	4	1.6	28	34	24	41	3	.246	.369	2	1	1B-65
1955	13	8	1	0	0	0	0.0	0	0	0	0	0	.125	.125	6	1	1B-7
1956	3	2	0	0	0	0	0.0	0	0	0	0	0	.000	.000	0	0	1B-3
1957	9	17	5	1	0	0	0.0	2	2	1	5	0	.294	.353	3	2	1B-6
4 yrs.	91	271	66	15	2	4	1.5	30	36	25	46	3	.244	.358	11	4	1B-81

Walter Alston

ALSTON, WALTER EMMONS (Smokey)   BR TR 6'2"   195 lbs.
B. Dec. 1, 1911, Venice, Ohio   D. Oct. 1, 1984, Oxford, Ohio
Manager 1954-76.
Hall of Fame 1983.

	G	AB	H	2B	3B	HR	HR%	R	RBI	BB	SO	SB	BA	SA	AB	H	G by POS
1936 STL N	1	1	0	0	0	0	0.0	0	0	0	1	0	.000	.000	0	0	1B-1

Jesse Altenburg

ALTENBURG, JESSE HOWARD   BL TR 5'8"   158 lbs.
B. Jan. 2, 1893, Ashley, Mich.   D. Mar. 12, 1973, Lansing, Mich.

	G	AB	H	2B	3B	HR	HR%	R	RBI	BB	SO	SB	BA	SA	AB	H	G by POS
1916 PIT N	8	14	6	1	1	0	0.0	2	0	1	1	0	.429	.643	1	0	OF-8
1917	11	17	3	0	0	0	0.0	1	3	2	4	0	.176	.176	6	0	OF-4
2 yrs.	19	31	9	1	1	0	0.0	3	3	3	5	0	.290	.387	7	0	OF-12

Dave Altizer

ALTIZER, DAVID TILDON (Filipino)   BL TR 5'10½"   160 lbs.
B. Nov. 6, 1876, Pearl, Ill.   D. May 14, 1964, Pleasant Hill, Ill.

	G	AB	H	2B	3B	HR	HR%	R	RBI	BB	SO	SB	BA	SA	AB	H	G by POS
1906 WAS A	115	433	111	9	5	1	0.2	56	27	35		37	.256	.307	0	0	SS-113, OF-2
1907	147	540	145	15	5	1	0.2	60	42	34		38	.269	.320	0	0	SS-71, 1B-50, OF-26
1908 2 teams		WAS	A	(67G –	.224)		CLE	A	(29G –	.213)							
" total	96	294	65	2	3	0	0.0	30	23	20		15	.221	.248	7	1	2B-38, OF-24, 3B-16, SS-4, 1B-4

	G	AB	H	2B	3B	HR	HR %	R	RBI	BB	SO	SB	BA	SA	Pinch Hit AB	Pinch Hit H	G by POS

Dave Altizer continued

	G	AB	H	2B	3B	HR	HR %	R	RBI	BB	SO	SB	BA	SA	AB	H	G by POS
1909 CHI A	116	382	89	6	7	1	0.3	47	20	39		27	.233	.293	7	1	OF-62, 1B-45
1910 CIN N	3	10	6	0	0	0	0.0	3	0	3	0	0	.600	.600	0	0	SS-3
1911	37	75	17	4	1	0	0.0	8	4	9	5	2	.227	.307	4	1	SS-23, OF-1, 2B-1, 1B-1
6 yrs.	514	1734	433	36	21	3	0.2	204	116	140	5	119	.250	.300	18	3	SS-214, OF-115, 1B-100, 2B-39, 3B-16

George Altman

ALTMAN, GEORGE LEE
B. Mar. 20, 1933, Goldsboro, N. C.
BL TR 6'4" 200 lbs.

	G	AB	H	2B	3B	HR	HR %	R	RBI	BB	SO	SB	BA	SA	AB	H	G by POS
1959 CHI N	135	420	103	14	4	12	2.9	54	47	34	80	1	.245	.383	15	4	OF-121
1960	119	334	89	16	4	13	3.9	50	51	32	67	4	.266	.455	20	8	OF-79, 1B-21
1961	138	518	157	28	12	27	5.2	77	96	40	92	6	.303	.560	6	0	OF-130, 1B-3
1962	147	534	170	27	5	22	4.1	74	74	62	89	19	.318	.511	6	1	OF-129, 1B-16
1963 STL N	135	464	127	18	7	9	1.9	62	47	47	93	13	.274	.401	12	3	OF-124
1964 NY N	124	422	97	14	1	9	2.1	48	47	18	70	4	.230	.332	18	6	OF-109
1965 CHI N	90	196	46	7	1	4	2.0	24	23	19	36	3	.235	.342	43	6	OF-45, 1B-2
1966	88	185	41	6	0	5	2.7	19	17	14	37	2	.222	.335	44	9	OF-42, 1B-4
1967	15	18	2	2	0	0	0.0	1	1	2	8	0	.111	.222	9	2	OF-4, 1B-1
9 yrs.	991	3091	832	132	34	101	3.3	409	403	268	572	52	.269	.432	173	39	OF-783, 1B-47

Joe Altobelli

ALTOBELLI, JOSEPH SALVATORE
B. May 26, 1932, Detroit, Mich.
Manager 1977-79, 1983-84.
BL TL 6' 185 lbs.

	G	AB	H	2B	3B	HR	HR %	R	RBI	BB	SO	SB	BA	SA	AB	H	G by POS
1955 CLE A	42	75	15	3	0	2	2.7	8	5	5	14	0	.200	.320	1	0	1B-40
1957	83	87	18	3	2	0	0.0	9	9	5	14	3	.207	.287	22	4	1B-56, OF-7
1961 MIN A	41	95	21	2	1	3	3.2	10	14	13	14	0	.221	.358	12	4	OF-25, 1B-2
3 yrs.	166	257	54	8	3	5	1.9	27	28	23	42	3	.210	.323	35	8	1B-98, OF-32

George Alton

ALTON, GEORGE WILSON (Bill)
B. Dec. 29, 1890, Kingman, Kans.   D. Aug. 16, 1976, Van Nuys, Calif.
BB TR 5'11½" 175 lbs.

	G	AB	H	2B	3B	HR	HR %	R	RBI	BB	SO	SB	BA	SA	AB	H	G by POS
1912 STL A	8	17	4	0	0	0	0.0	1	1	4		0	.235	.235	1	0	OF-6

George Alusik

ALUSIK, GEORGE JOSEPH (Turk, Glider)
B. Feb. 11, 1935, Ashley, Pa.
BR TR 6'3½" 175 lbs.

	G	AB	H	2B	3B	HR	HR %	R	RBI	BB	SO	SB	BA	SA	AB	H	G by POS
1958 DET A	2	2	0	0	0	0	0.0	0	0	0	1	0	.000	.000	1	0	OF-1
1961	15	14	2	0	0	0	0.0	0	2	1	4	0	.143	.143	12	2	OF-1
1962 2 teams			DET	A	(2G –	.000)		KC	A	(90G –	.273)						
" total	92	211	57	10	1	11	5.2	29	35	16	29	1	.270	.483	38	11	OF-50, 1B-1
1963 KC A	87	221	59	11	0	9	4.1	28	37	26	33	0	.267	.439	19	9	OF-63
1964	102	204	49	10	1	3	1.5	18	19	30	36	0	.240	.343	40	6	OF-44, 1B-12
5 yrs.	298	652	167	31	2	23	3.5	75	93	73	103	1	.256	.416	110	28	OF-159, 1B-13

Luis Alvarado

ALVARADO, LUIS CESAR (Pimba)
B. Jan. 15, 1949, La Jas, Puerto Rico
BR TR 5'9" 162 lbs.

	G	AB	H	2B	3B	HR	HR %	R	RBI	BB	SO	SB	BA	SA	AB	H	G by POS
1968 BOS A	11	46	6	2	0	0	0.0	3	1	1	11	0	.130	.174	0	0	SS-11
1969	6	5	0	0	0	0	0.0	0	0	0	2	0	.000	.000	1	0	SS-5
1970	59	183	41	11	0	1	0.5	19	10	9	30	1	.224	.301	1	0	3B-29, SS-27
1971 CHI A	99	264	57	14	1	0	0.0	22	8	11	34	1	.216	.277	9	0	SS-71, 2B-16
1972	103	254	54	4	1	4	1.6	30	29	13	36	2	.213	.283	7	2	SS-81, 2B-16, 3B-2
1973	80	203	47	7	2	0	0.0	21	20	4	20	6	.232	.286	7	4	2B-45, SS-18, 3B-10
1974 3 teams			CHI	A	(8G –	.100)		CLE	A	(61G –	.219)		STL	N	(17G –	.139)	
" total	86	160	31	4	0	0	0.0	16	13	8	21	1	.194	.219	5	1	2B-47, SS-28, DH-3, 3B-1
1976 STL N	16	42	12	1	0	0	0.0	5	3	3	6	0	.286	.310	0	0	2B-16
1977 2 teams			DET	A	(2G –	.000)		NY	N	(1G –	.000)						
" total	3	3	0	0	0	0	0.0	0	0	0	0	0	.000	.000	0	0	3B-2, 2B-1
9 yrs.	463	1160	248	43	4	5	0.4	116	84	49	160	11	.214	.271	30	7	SS-241, 2B-141, 3B-44, DH-3

Jesus Alvarez

ALVAREZ, JESUS ORLANDO
B. Feb. 28, 1953, Cinega Baja, Puerto Rico
BR TR 6' 165 lbs.

	G	AB	H	2B	3B	HR	HR %	R	RBI	BB	SO	SB	BA	SA	AB	H	G by POS
1973 LA N	4	4	1	1	0	0	0.0	0	0	0	0	0	.250	.500	4	1	
1974	2	1	0	0	0	0	0.0	0	0	0	0	0	.000	.000	1	0	OF-1
1975	4	4	0	0	0	0	0.0	0	0	0	0	0	.000	.000	4	0	
1976 CAL A	15	42	7	1	0	2	4.8	4	8	0	3	0	.167	.333	5	0	OF-11, DH-2
4 yrs.	25	51	8	2	0	2	3.9	4	8	0	3	0	.157	.314	14	1	OF-12, DH-2

Ossie Alvarez

ALVAREZ, OSWALDO GONZALEZ
B. Oct. 19, 1933, Matanzas, Cuba
BR TR 5'10" 165 lbs.

	G	AB	H	2B	3B	HR	HR %	R	RBI	BB	SO	SB	BA	SA	AB	H	G by POS
1958 WAS A	87	196	41	3	0	0	0.0	20	5	16	26	1	.209	.224	3	0	SS-64, 2B-14, 3B-3
1959 DET A	8	2	1	0	0	0	0.0	0	0	0	1	0	.500	.500	2	1	
2 yrs.	95	198	42	3	0	0	0.0	20	5	16	27	1	.212	.227	5	1	SS-64, 2B-14, 3B-3

Rogelio Alvarez

ALVAREZ, ROGELIO HERNANDEZ (Gorrego)
B. Apr. 18, 1938, Pinar Del Rio, Cuba
BR TR 5'11" 183 lbs.

	G	AB	H	2B	3B	HR	HR %	R	RBI	BB	SO	SB	BA	SA	AB	H	G by POS
1960 CIN N	3	9	1	0	0	0	0.0	1	0	0	3	0	.111	.111	1	0	1B-2
1962	14	28	6	0	0	0	0.0	1	2	1	10	0	.214	.214	2	0	1B-13
2 yrs.	17	37	7	0	0	0	0.0	2	2	1	13	0	.189	.189	3	0	1B-15

Max Alvis

ALVIS, ROY MAXWELL
B. Feb. 2, 1938, Jasper, Tex.
BR TR 5'11" 185 lbs.

	G	AB	H	2B	3B	HR	HR %	R	RBI	BB	SO	SB	BA	SA	AB	H	G by POS
1962 CLE A	12	51	11	2	0	0	0.0	1	3	2	13	3	.216	.255	0	0	3B-12
1963	158	602	165	32	7	22	3.7	81	67	36	109	9	.274	.460	0	0	3B-158
1964	107	381	96	14	3	18	4.7	51	53	29	77	5	.252	.446	1	1	3B-105
1965	159	604	149	24	2	21	3.5	88	61	47	121	12	.247	.397	2	1	3B-156
1966	157	596	146	22	3	17	2.9	67	55	50	98	4	.245	.378	0	0	3B-157
1967	161	637	163	23	4	21	3.3	66	70	38	107	3	.256	.403	0	0	3B-161

	G	AB	H	2B	3B	HR	HR %	R	RBI	BB	SO	SB	BA	SA	Pinch Hit AB	Pinch Hit H	G by POS

Max Alvis continued

	G	AB	H	2B	3B	HR	HR%	R	RBI	BB	SO	SB	BA	SA	PH AB	PH H	G by POS
1968	131	452	101	17	3	8	1.8	38	37	41	91	5	.223	.327	6	1	3B-128
1969	66	191	43	6	0	1	0.5	13	15	14	26	1	.225	.272	9	0	3B-58, SS-1
1970 MIL A	62	115	21	2	0	3	2.6	16	12	5	20	1	.183	.278	15	3	3B-36
9 yrs.	1013	3629	895	142	22	111	3.1	421	373	262	662	43	.247	.390	33	6	3B-971, SS-1

Billy Alvord

ALVORD, WILLIAM C. (Uncle Bill)
B. St. Louis, Mo.   Deceased.   5'10"   187 lbs.

	G	AB	H	2B	3B	HR	HR%	R	RBI	BB	SO	SB	BA	SA	PH AB	PH H	G by POS
1885 STL N	2	5	0	0	0	0	0.0	0	0	1	2		.000	.000	0	0	3B-2
1889 KC AA	50	186	43	8	9	0	0.0	23	18	10	35	3	.231	.371	0	0	3B-34, SS-8, 2B-8
1890 TOL AA	116	495	135	13	16	2	0.4	69		22		21	.273	.376	0	0	3B-116
1891 2 teams	CLE	N (13G –	.288)		WAS	AA (81G –	.234)										
" total	94	371	90	10	5	1	0.3	35	37	11	45	3	.243	.305	0	0	3B-94
1893 CLE N	3	12	2	0	0	0	0.0	2	2	0	1	0	.167	.167	0	0	3B-3
5 yrs.	265	1069	270	31	30	3	0.3	129	57	44	83	27	.253	.346	0	0	3B-249, SS-8, 2B-8

Brant Alyea

ALYEA, GARRABRANT RYERSON
B. Dec. 8, 1940, Passaic, N. J.   BR TR 6'3"   215 lbs.

	G	AB	H	2B	3B	HR	HR%	R	RBI	BB	SO	SB	BA	SA	PH AB	PH H	G by POS
1965 WAS A	8	13	3	0	0	2	15.4	3	6	1	4	0	.231	.692	5	1	1B-3, OF-1
1968	53	150	40	11	1	6	4.0	18	23	10	39	0	.267	.473	18	3	OF-39
1969	104	237	59	4	0	11	4.6	29	40	34	67	1	.249	.405	41	8	OF-69, 1B-3
1970 MIN A	94	258	75	12	1	16	6.2	34	61	28	51	3	.291	.531	18	7	OF-75
1971	79	158	28	4	0	2	1.3	13	15	24	38	1	.177	.241	25	4	OF-48
1972 2 teams	OAK	A (20G –	.194)		STL	N (13G –	.158)										
" total	33	50	9	2	0	1	2.0	3	3	3	11	0	.180	.280	20	3	OF-11
6 yrs.	371	866	214	33	2	38	4.4	100	148	100	210	5	.247	.421	127	26	OF-243, 1B-6

LEAGUE CHAMPIONSHIP SERIES

	G	AB	H	2B	3B	HR	HR%	R	RBI	BB	SO	SB	BA	SA	PH AB	PH H	G by POS
1970 MIN A	3	7	0	0	0	0	0.0	1	0	1	3	0	.000	.000	1	0	OF-2

Joey Amalfitano

AMALFITANO, JOHN JOSEPH
B. Jan. 23, 1934, San Pedro, Calif.
Manager 1979-81.   BR TR 5'11"   175 lbs.

	G	AB	H	2B	3B	HR	HR%	R	RBI	BB	SO	SB	BA	SA	PH AB	PH H	G by POS
1954 NY N	9	5	0	0	0	0	0.0	2	0	0	4	0	.000	.000	0	0	3B-4, 2B-1
1955	36	22	5	1	1	0	0.0	8	1	2	2	0	.227	.364	4	0	SS-5, 3B-2
1960 SF N	106	328	91	15	3	1	0.3	47	27	26	31	2	.277	.351	13	5	2B-63, 2B-33, SS-3, OF-1
1961	109	384	98	11	4	2	0.5	64	23	44	59	7	.255	.320	12	4	2B-95, 3B-6
1962 HOU N	117	380	90	12	5	1	0.3	44	27	45	43	4	.237	.303	2	1	2B-110, 3B-5
1963 SF N	54	137	24	3	0	1	0.7	11	7	12	18	2	.175	.219	18	1	2B-37, 3B-7
1964 CHI N	100	324	78	19	6	4	1.2	51	27	40	42	2	.241	.373	10	3	2B-86, SS-1, 1B-1
1965	67	96	26	4	0	0	0.0	13	8	12	14	2	.271	.313	37	8	2B-24, SS-4
1966	41	38	6	2	0	0	0.0	8	3	4	10	0	.158	.211	9	2	2B-12, 3B-3, SS-2
1967	4	1	0	0	0	0	0.0	0	0	0	1	0	.000	.000	1	0	
10 yrs.	643	1715	418	67	19	9	0.5	248	123	185	224	19	.244	.321	106	24	2B-398, 3B-90, SS-15, OF-1, 1B-1

Ruben Amaro

AMARO, RUBEN MORA
B. Jan. 6, 1936, Vera Cruz, Mexico   BR TR 5'11"   170 lbs.

	G	AB	H	2B	3B	HR	HR%	R	RBI	BB	SO	SB	BA	SA	PH AB	PH H	G by POS
1958 STL N	40	76	17	2	1	0	0.0	8	0	5	8	0	.224	.276	1	0	SS-36, 2B-1
1960 PHI N	92	264	61	9	1	0	0.0	25	16	21	32	0	.231	.273	0	0	SS-92
1961	135	381	98	14	9	1	0.3	34	32	53	59	1	.257	.349	0	0	SS-132, 1B-3, 2B-1
1962	79	226	55	10	0	0	0.0	24	19	30	28	5	.243	.288	0	0	SS-63, 3B-45, 1B-5
1963	115	217	47	9	2	2	0.9	25	19	19	31	0	.217	.304	7	0	SS-78, 1B-1
1964	129	299	79	11	0	4	1.3	31	34	16	37	1	.264	.341	9	1	SS-71, 1B-58, 3B-3, 2B-3, OF-1
1965	118	184	39	7	0	0	0.0	26	15	27	22	1	.212	.250	7	0	SS-60, 1B-60, 2B-6
1966 NY A	14	23	5	0	0	0	0.0	0	3	0	2	0	.217	.217	0	0	SS-14
1967	130	417	93	10	0	1	0.2	31	17	43	49	3	.223	.259	2	0	SS-123, 3B-3, 1B-2
1968	47	41	5	1	0	0	0.0	3	0	9	6	0	.122	.146	1	0	SS-23, 1B-22
1969 CAL A	41	27	6	0	0	0	0.0	4	1	4	6	0	.222	.222	5	1	1B-18, 2B-9, SS-5, 3B-2
11 yrs.	940	2155	505	75	13	8	0.4	211	156	227	280	11	.234	.292	32	2	SS-705, 1B-169, 3B-53, 2B-20, OF-1

Wayne Ambler

AMBLER, WAYNE HARPER
B. Nov. 8, 1915, Abington, Pa.   BR TR 5'8½"   165 lbs.

	G	AB	H	2B	3B	HR	HR%	R	RBI	BB	SO	SB	BA	SA	PH AB	PH H	G by POS
1937 PHI A	56	162	35	5	0	0	0.0	3	11	13	8	1	.216	.247	0	0	2B-56
1938	120	393	92	21	2	0	0.0	42	38	48	31	2	.234	.298	0	0	SS-116, 2B-4
1939	95	227	48	13	0	0	0.0	15	24	22	25	1	.211	.269	0	0	SS-77, 2B-19
3 yrs.	271	782	175	39	2	0	0.0	60	73	83	64	4	.224	.279	0	0	SS-193, 2B-79

Ed Amelung

AMELUNG, EDWARD
B. Apr. 13, 1959, Stanton, Calif.   BL TL 6'   185 lbs.

	G	AB	H	2B	3B	HR	HR%	R	RBI	BB	SO	SB	BA	SA	PH AB	PH H	G by POS
1984 LA N	34	46	10	0	0	0	0.0	7	4	2	4	3	.217	.217	11	1	OF-23

Sandy Amoros

AMOROS, EDMUNDO ISASI
B. Jan. 30, 1930, Havana, Cuba   BL TL 5'7½"   170 lbs.

	G	AB	H	2B	3B	HR	HR%	R	RBI	BB	SO	SB	BA	SA	PH AB	PH H	G by POS
1952 BKN N	20	44	11	3	1	0	0.0	10	3	5	14	1	.250	.364	11	0	OF-10
1954	79	263	72	18	6	9	3.4	44	34	31	24	1	.274	.490	8	2	OF-70
1955	119	388	96	16	7	10	2.6	59	51	55	45	10	.247	.402	9	3	OF-109
1956	114	292	76	11	8	16	5.5	53	58	59	51	3	.260	.517	22	3	OF-86
1957	106	238	66	7	1	7	2.9	40	26	46	42	3	.277	.403	28	4	OF-66
1959 LA N	5	5	1	0	0	0	0.0	1	1	0	1	0	.200	.200	5	1	
1960 2 teams	LA	N (9G –	.143)		DET	A (65G –	.149)										
" total	74	81	12	0	0	1	1.2	8	7	15	12	0	.148	.185	48	8	OF-13
7 yrs.	517	1311	334	55	23	43	3.3	215	180	211	189	18	.255	.430	131	21	OF-354

WORLD SERIES

	G	AB	H	2B	3B	HR	HR%	R	RBI	BB	SO	SB	BA	SA	PH AB	PH H	G by POS
1952 BKN N	1	0	0	0	0	0	–	0	0	0	0	0	–	–	0	0	

	G	AB	H	2B	3B	HR	HR %	R	RBI	BB	SO	SB	BA	SA	Pinch Hit AB	Pinch Hit H	G by POS

Sandy Amoros *continued*

	G	AB	H	2B	3B	HR	HR %	R	RBI	BB	SO	SB	BA	SA	AB	H	G by POS
1955	5	12	4	0	0	1	8.3	3	3	4	4	0	.333	.583	0	0	OF-5
1956	6	19	1	0	0	0	0.0	1	1	2	4	0	.053	.053	0	0	OF-6
3 yrs.	12	31	5	0	0	1	3.2	4	4	6	8	0	.161	.258	0	0	OF-11

Alf Anderson

ANDERSON, ALFRED WALTON
B. Jan. 28, 1914, Gainesville, Ga.   BR TR 5'11"   165 lbs.

	G	AB	H	2B	3B	HR	HR %	R	RBI	BB	SO	SB	BA	SA	AB	H	G by POS
1941 PIT N	70	223	48	7	2	1	0.4	32	10	14	30	2	.215	.278	5	1	SS-58
1942	54	166	45	4	1	0	0.0	24	7	18	19	4	.271	.307	4	1	SS-48
1946	2	1	0	0	0	0	0.0	0	0	1	0	0	.000	.000	1	0	
3 yrs.	126	390	93	11	3	1	0.3	56	17	33	49	6	.238	.290	10	2	SS-106

Andy Anderson

ANDERSON, ANDY HOLM
B. Nov. 13, 1922, Bremerton, Wash. D. July 18, 1982, Seattle, Wash.   BR TR 5'11"   178 lbs.

	G	AB	H	2B	3B	HR	HR %	R	RBI	BB	SO	SB	BA	SA	AB	H	G by POS
1948 STL A	51	87	24	5	1	1	1.1	13	12	8	15	0	.276	.391	21	5	2B-21, SS-10, 1B-2
1949	71	136	17	3	0	1	0.7	10	5	14	21	0	.125	.169	12	1	SS-44, 3B-8, 2B-8
2 yrs.	122	223	41	8	1	2	0.9	23	17	22	36	0	.184	.256	33	6	SS-54, 2B-29, 3B-8, 1B-2

Dave Anderson

ANDERSON, DAVID CARTER
B. Aug. 1, 1960, Louisville, Ky.   BR TR 6'2"   185 lbs.

	G	AB	H	2B	3B	HR	HR %	R	RBI	BB	SO	SB	BA	SA	AB	H	G by POS
1983 LA N	61	115	19	4	2	1	0.9	12	2	12	15	6	.165	.261	2	1	SS-53, 3B-1
1984	121	374	94	16	2	3	0.8	51	34	45	55	15	.251	.329	5	0	SS-111, 3B-11
2 yrs.	182	489	113	20	4	4	0.8	63	36	57	70	21	.231	.313	7	1	SS-164, 3B-12

Dwain Anderson

ANDERSON, DWAIN CLEAVEN
B. Nov. 23, 1947, Berkeley, Calif.   BR TR 5'11"   165 lbs.

	G	AB	H	2B	3B	HR	HR %	R	RBI	BB	SO	SB	BA	SA	AB	H	G by POS
1971 OAK A	16	37	10	2	1	0	0.0	3	3	5	9	0	.270	.378	0	0	SS-10, 2B-5, 3B-1
1972 2 teams	OAK A	(3G –	.000)		STL N	(57G –	.267)										
" total	60	142	36	4	1	1	0.7	14	8	9	27	0	.254	.317	1	0	SS-44, 3B-14, 2B-1
1973 2 teams	STL N	(18G –	.118)		SD N	(53G –	.121)										
" total	71	124	15	0	0	0	0.0	16	3	18	33	2	.121	.121	15	1	SS-42, 3B-6, OF-2
1974 CLE A	2	3	1	0	0	0	0.0	0	0	0	1	0	.333	.333	0	0	2B-1
4 yrs.	149	306	62	6	2	1	0.3	33	14	32	70	2	.203	.245	16	1	SS-96, 3B-21, 2B-7, OF-2

Ferrell Anderson

ANDERSON, FERRELL JACK
B. Jan. 9, 1918, Maple City, Kans.   D. Mar. 12, 1978, Joplin, Mo.   BR TR 6'1"   200 lbs.

	G	AB	H	2B	3B	HR	HR %	R	RBI	BB	SO	SB	BA	SA	AB	H	G by POS
1946 BKN N	70	199	51	10	0	2	1.0	19	14	18	21	1	.256	.337	8	2	C-70
1953 STL N	18	35	10	2	0	0	0.0	1	1	0	4	0	.286	.343	7	0	C-12
2 yrs.	88	234	61	12	0	2	0.9	20	15	18	25	1	.261	.338	15	2	C-82

George Anderson

ANDERSON, GEORGE ANDREW JENDRUS
B. Sept. 26, 1889, Cleveland, Ohio   D. May 28, 1962, Warrensville Hts., Ohio   BL TR 5'8½"   160 lbs.

	G	AB	H	2B	3B	HR	HR %	R	RBI	BB	SO	SB	BA	SA	AB	H	G by POS
1914 BKN F	98	364	115	13	3	3	0.8	58	24	31		16	.316	.393	5	0	OF-92
1915	136	511	135	23	9	2	0.4	70	39	52		20	.264	.356	1	0	OF-134
1918 STL N	35	132	39	4	5	0	0.0	20	6	15	7	0	.295	.402	0	0	OF-35
3 yrs.	269	1007	289	40	17	5	0.5	148	69	98	7	36	.287	.375	6	0	OF-261

Goat Anderson

ANDERSON, EDWARD JOHN
B. Jan. 13, 1880, Cleveland, Ohio   D. Mar. 15, 1923, South Bend, Ind.   TR

	G	AB	H	2B	3B	HR	HR %	R	RBI	BB	SO	SB	BA	SA	AB	H	G by POS
1907 PIT N	127	413	85	3	1	1	0.2	73	12	80		27	.206	.225	5	1	OF-117, 2B-5

Hal Anderson

ANDERSON, HAROLD
B. Feb. 10, 1904, St. Louis, Mo.   D. May 1, 1974, St. Louis, Mo.   BR TR 5'11"   160 lbs.

	G	AB	H	2B	3B	HR	HR %	R	RBI	BB	SO	SB	BA	SA	AB	H	G by POS
1932 CHI A	9	32	8	0	0	0	0.0	4	2	0	1	0	.250	.250	0	0	OF-9

Harry Anderson

ANDERSON, HARRY WALTER
B. Sept. 10, 1931, North East, Md.   BL TR 6'3"   205 lbs.

	G	AB	H	2B	3B	HR	HR %	R	RBI	BB	SO	SB	BA	SA	AB	H	G by POS
1957 PHI N	118	400	107	15	4	17	4.3	53	61	36	61	2	.268	.453	11	3	OF-109
1958	140	515	155	34	6	23	4.5	80	97	59	95	0	.301	.524	10	1	OF-87, 1B-49
1959	142	508	122	28	6	14	2.8	50	63	43	95	1	.240	.402	6	1	OF-137
1960 2 teams	PHI N	(38G –	.247)		CIN N	(42G –	.167)										
" total	80	159	34	5	0	6	3.8	16	21	21	39	0	.214	.358	29	1	1B-27, OF-20
1961 CIN N	4	4	1	0	0	0	0.0	0	0	0	1	0	.250	.250	4	1	
5 yrs.	484	1586	419	82	16	60	3.8	199	242	159	291	3	.264	.450	60	7	OF-353, 1B-76

Jim Anderson

ANDERSON, JAMES LEA
B. Feb. 23, 1957, Los Angeles, Calif.   BR TR 6'   170 lbs.

	G	AB	H	2B	3B	HR	HR %	R	RBI	BB	SO	SB	BA	SA	AB	H	G by POS
1978 CAL A	48	108	21	7	0	0	0.0	6	7	11	16	0	.194	.259	0	0	SS-47, 2B-1
1979	96	234	58	13	1	3	1.3	33	23	17	31	3	.248	.350	0	0	SS-82, 3B-10, 2B-6, C-3
1980 SEA A	116	317	72	7	0	8	2.5	46	30	27	39	2	.227	.325	8	2	SS-65, 3B-33, DH-5, 2B-2, C-1
1981	70	162	33	7	0	2	1.2	12	19	17	29	3	.204	.284	0	0	SS-68, 3B-2
1983 TEX A	50	102	22	1	1	0	0.0	8	6	5	8	1	.216	.245	0	0	SS-27, 2B-17, OF-3, 3B-3, DH-2, C-1
1984	39	47	5	0	0	0	0.0	2	1	4	7	0	.106	.106	0	0	SS-31, 3B-6, 2B-1
6 yrs.	419	970	211	35	2	13	1.3	107	86	81	130	9	.218	.298	8	2	SS-320, 3B-54, 2B-27, DH-7, C-5, OF-3

LEAGUE CHAMPIONSHIP SERIES

	G	AB	H	2B	3B	HR	HR %	R	RBI	BB	SO	SB	BA	SA	AB	H	G by POS
1979 CAL A	4	11	1	0	0	0	0.0	0	0	0	1	0	.091	.091	0	0	SS-4

John Anderson

ANDERSON, JOHN JOSEPH (Honest John)
B. Dec. 14, 1873, Sasbourg, Norway   D. July 23, 1949, Worcester, Mass.   BB TR 6'2"   180 lbs.

	G	AB	H	2B	3B	HR	HR %	R	RBI	BB	SO	SB	BA	SA	AB	H	G by POS
1894 BKN N	17	63	19	1	3	1	1.6	14	19	3		7	.302	.460	0	0	OF-16, 3B-1
1895	102	419	120	11	14	9	2.1	76	87	12	29	24	.286	.444	0	0	OF-101
1896	108	430	135	23	17	1	0.2	70	55	18	23	37	.314	.453	1	0	OF-68, 1B-42
1897	117	492	160	28	12	4	0.8	93	85	17		29	.325	.455	0	0	OF-115, 1B-3

	G	AB	H	2B	3B	HR	HR %	R	RBI	BB	SO	SB	BA	SA	Pinch Hit AB	H	G by POS

John Anderson continued

1898 2 teams	BKN N (25G – .244)				WAS N (110G – .305)												
" total	135	520	153	33	22	9	1.7	82	81	29		20	.294	.494	1	0	OF-115, 1B-19
1899 BKN N	117	439	118	18	7	3	0.7	65	92	27		25	.269	.362	3	0	OF-76, 1B-41
1901 MIL A	138	576	190	46	7	8	1.4	90	99	24		35	.330	.476	0	0	1B-125, OF-13
1902 STL A	126	524	149	29	6	4	0.8	60	85	21		15	.284	.385	0	0	1B-126, OF-3
1903	138	550	156	34	8	2	0.4	65	78	23		16	.284	.385	0	0	1B-133, OF-7
1904 NY A	143	558	155	27	12	3	0.5	62	82	23		20	.278	.385	1	1	OF-111, 1B-33
1905 2 teams	NY A (32G – .232)				WAS N (93G – .290)												
" total	125	499	139	24	7	1	0.2	62	52	30		31	.279	.361	7	1	OF-111, 1B-7
1906 WAS A	151	583	158	25	4	3	0.5	62	70	19		39	.271	.343	0	0	OF-151
1907	87	333	96	12	4	0	0.0	33	44	34		19	.288	.348	0	0	1B-61, OF-26
1908 CHI A	123	355	93	17	1	0	0.0	36	47	30		21	.262	.315	25	5	OF-90, 1B-9
14 yrs.	1627	6341	1841	328	124	48	0.8	870	976	310	55	338	.290	.404	38	7	OF-1003, 1B-599, 3B-1

Mike Anderson

ANDERSON, MICHAEL ALLEN
B. June 22, 1951, Florence, S. C.

BR TR 6'2" 200 lbs.

1971 PHI N	26	89	22	5	1	2	2.2	11	5	13	28	0	.247	.393	0	0	OF-26
1972	36	103	20	5	1	2	1.9	8	5	19	36	1	.194	.320	0	0	OF-35
1973	87	193	49	9	1	9	4.7	32	28	19	53	0	.254	.451	26	4	OF-67
1974	145	395	99	22	2	5	1.3	35	34	37	75	2	.251	.354	19	5	OF-133, 1B-1
1975	115	247	64	10	3	4	1.6	24	28	17	66	1	.259	.372	16	5	OF-105, 1B-3
1976 STL N	86	199	58	8	1	1	0.5	17	12	26	30	1	.291	.357	21	7	OF-58, 1B-5
1977	94	154	34	4	1	4	2.6	18	17	14	31	2	.221	.338	20	5	OF-47
1978 BAL A	53	32	3	0	1	0	0.0	2	3	3	10	0	.094	.156	6	0	OF-70, P-1
1979 PHI N	79	78	18	4	0	1	1.3	12	2	13	14	1	.231	.321	11	0	OF-70, P-1
9 yrs.	721	1490	367	67	11	28	1.9	159	134	161	343	8	.246	.362	119	26	OF-618, 1B-9, P-1

Sparky Anderson

ANDERSON, GEORGE LEE
B. Feb. 22, 1934, Bridgewater, S. D.
Manager 1970-84.

BR TR 5'9" 170 lbs.

1959 PHI N	152	477	104	9	3	0	0.0	42	34	42	53	6	.218	.249	0	0	2B-152

Ernie Andres

ANDRES, ERNEST HENRY (Junie)
B. Jan. 11, 1918, Jeffersonville, Ind.

BR TR 6'1" 200 lbs.

1946 BOS A	15	41	4	2	0	0	0.0	0	1	3	5	0	.098	.146	0	0	3B-15

Kim Andrew

ANDREW, KIM DARRELL
B. Nov. 14, 1953, Glendale, Calif.

BR TR 5'10" 160 lbs.

1975 BOS A	2	2	1	0	0	0	0.0	0	0	0	0	0	.500	.500	0	0	2B-2

Ed Andrews

ANDREWS, GEORGE EDWARD
B. Apr. 5, 1859, Painesville, Ohio D. Aug. 12, 1934, West Palm Beach, Fla.

BR TR 5'8" 160 lbs.

1884 PHI N	109	420	93	21	2	0	0.0	74		9	42		.221	.281	0	0	OF-109
1885	103	421	112	15	3	0	0.0	77		32	25		.266	.316	0	0	OF-99, 2B-5
1886	107	437	109	15	4	2	0.5	93	28	31	35		.249	.316	0	0	OF-104, 2B-3
1887	104	464	151	19	7	4	0.9	110	67	21	21	57	.325	.422	0	0	OF-99, 2B-7, 1B-1
1888	124	528	126	14	4	3	0.6	75	44	21	41	35	.239	.297	0	0	OF-124
1889 2 teams	PHI N (10G – .282)				IND N (40G – .306)												
" total	50	212	64	12	0	0	0.0	42	29	7	14	14	.302	.358	0	0	OF-49, 2B-2
1890 BKN P	94	395	100	14	2	3	0.8	84	38	40	32	21	.253	.322	0	0	OF-94
1891 C-M AA	83	356	75	7	4	0	0.0	47	26	33	35	22	.211	.253	0	0	OF-83
8 yrs.	774	3233	830	117	26	12	0.4	602	231	194	245	149	.257	.320	0	0	OF-652, 2B-126, 1B-1

Fred Andrews

ANDREWS, FRED
B. May 4, 1952, Lafayette, La.

BR TR 5'8" 163 lbs.

1976 PHI N	4	6	4	0	0	0	0.0	1	0	2	0	1	.667	.667	0	0	2B-4
1977	12	23	4	0	1	0	0.0	3	2	1	5	1	.174	.261	5	2	2B-7
2 yrs.	16	29	8	0	1	0	0.0	4	2	3	5	2	.276	.345	5	2	2B-11

Jim Andrews

ANDREWS, JAMES PRATT
B. June 5, 1865, Shelburne Falls, Mass. D. Dec. 27, 1907, Chicago, Ill.

1890 CHI N	53	202	38	4	2	3	1.5	32	17	23	41	11	.188	.272	0	0	OF-53

Mike Andrews

ANDREWS, MICHAEL JAY
Brother of Rob Andrews.
B. July 9, 1943, Los Angeles, Calif.

BR TR 6'3" 195 lbs.

1966 BOS A	5	18	3	0	0	0	0.0	1	0	0	2	0	.167	.167	0	0	2B-5
1967	142	494	130	20	0	8	1.6	79	40	62	72	7	.263	.352	2	0	2B-139, SS-6
1968	147	536	145	22	1	7	1.3	77	45	81	57	3	.271	.354	5	1	2B-139, SS-4, 3B-1
1969	121	464	136	26	2	15	3.2	79	59	71	53	1	.293	.455	1	0	2B-120
1970	151	589	149	28	1	17	2.9	91	65	81	63	2	.253	.390	3	0	2B-148
1971 CHI A	109	330	93	16	0	12	3.6	45	47	67	36	3	.282	.439	12	4	2B-76, 1B-25
1972	148	505	111	18	0	7	1.4	58	50	70	78	2	.220	.297	1	1	2B-145, 1B-5
1973 2 teams	CHI A (52G – .201)				OAK A (18G – .190)												
" total	70	180	36	10	0	1	0.0	11	10	26	29	0	.200	.256	15	1	DH-32, 2B-15, 1B-9, 3B-5
8 yrs.	893	3116	803	140	4	66	2.1	441	316	458	390	18	.258	.369	39	7	2B-787, 1B-39, DH-32, SS-10, 3B-6

LEAGUE CHAMPIONSHIP SERIES																	
1973 OAK A	2	1	0	0	0	0	0.0	0	0	0	0	0	.000	.000	0	0	1B-1

WORLD SERIES																	
1967 BOS A	5	13	4	0	0	0	0.0	2	1	0	1	0	.308	.308	2	1	2B-3
1973 OAK A	2	3	0	0	0	0	0.0	0	0	1	1	0	.000	.000	2	0	2B-1
2 yrs.	7	16	4	0	0	0	0.0	2	1	1	2	0	.250	.250	4	1	2B-4

	G	AB	H	2B	3B	HR	HR %	R	RBI	BB	SO	SB	BA	SA	Pinch Hit AB	Pinch Hit H	G by POS

Rob Andrews

ANDREWS, ROBERT PATRICK
Brother of Mike Andrews.
B. Dec. 11, 1952, Santa Monica, Calif.
BR TR 6' 185 lbs.

	G	AB	H	2B	3B	HR	HR %	R	RBI	BB	SO	SB	BA	SA	PH AB	PH H	G by POS
1975 HOU N	103	277	66	5	4	0	0.0	29	19	31	34	12	.238	.285	1	0	2B-94, SS-6
1976	109	410	105	8	5	0	0.0	42	23	33	27	7	.256	.300	0	0	2B-107, SS-3
1977 SF N	127	436	115	11	3	0	0.0	60	25	56	33	5	.264	.303	9	1	2B-115
1978	79	177	39	3	3	1	0.6	21	11	20	18	5	.220	.288	12	2	2B-62, SS-1
1979	75	154	40	3	0	2	1.3	22	13	8	9	4	.260	.318	22	5	2B-53, 3B-3
5 yrs.	493	1454	365	30	15	3	0.2	174	91	148	121	33	.251	.298	44	8	2B-431, SS-10, 3B-3

Stan Andrews

ANDREWS, STANLEY JOSEPH (Polo)
Born Stanley Joseph Andruskewicz.
B. Apr. 17, 1917, Lynn, Mass.
BR TR 5'11" 178 lbs.

	G	AB	H	2B	3B	HR	HR %	R	RBI	BB	SO	SB	BA	SA	PH AB	PH H	G by POS
1939 BOS N	13	26	6	0	0	0	0.0	1	1	1	2	0	.231	.231	3	1	C-10
1940	19	33	6	0	0	0	0.0	1	2	0	3	1	.182	.182	5	1	C-14
1944 BKN N	4	8	1	0	0	0	0.0	1	1	1	2	0	.125	.125	0	0	C-4
1945 2 teams		BKN N	(21G –	.163)		PHI N	(13G –	.333)									
" total	34	82	19	2	1	1	1.2	8	8	6	9	1	.232	.317	1	0	C-33
4 yrs.	70	149	32	2	1	1	0.7	11	12	8	16	2	.215	.262	9	2	C-61

Wally Andrews

ANDREWS, WILLIAM WALTER
B. Sept. 18, 1859, Philadelphia, Pa.   D. Jan. 20, 1940, Indianapolis, Ind.
BR TR 6'3" 170 lbs.

	G	AB	H	2B	3B	HR	HR %	R	RBI	BB	SO	SB	BA	SA	PH AB	PH H	G by POS
1884 LOU AA	14	49	10	5	0	0	0.0	10		4			.204	.347	0	0	1B-9, 3B-3, OF-1, SS-1
1885 PRO N	1	4	0	0	0	0	0.0	0	0	0	1		.000	.000	0	0	3B-1
1888 LOU AA	26	93	18	6	3	0	0.0	12	6	13		5	.194	.323	0	0	1B-26
3 yrs.	41	146	28	11	4	0	0.0	22	5	17	1	5	.192	.322	0	0	1B-35, 3B-4, OF-1, SS-1

Bill Andrus

ANDRUS, WILLIAM MORGAN
B. July 25, 1907, Beaumont, Tex.   D. Mar. 12, 1982, Washington, D. C.
BR TR 6' 185 lbs.

	G	AB	H	2B	3B	HR	HR %	R	RBI	BB	SO	SB	BA	SA	PH AB	PH H	G by POS
1931 WAS A	3	7	0	0	0	0	0.0	0	1	0	1	0	.000	.000	1	0	3B-2
1937 PHI N	3	2	0	0	0	0	0.0	0	0	0	2	0	.000	.000	2	0	3B-1
2 yrs.	6	9	0	0	0	0	0.0	0	1	0	3	0	.000	.000	3	0	3B-3

Fred Andrus

ANDRUS, FREDERICK HOTHAM
B. Aug. 23, 1850, Washington, Mich.   D. Nov. 10, 1937, Detroit, Mich.
BR TR 6'2" 185 lbs.

	G	AB	H	2B	3B	HR	HR %	R	RBI	BB	SO	SB	BA	SA	PH AB	PH H	G by POS
1876 CHI N	8	36	11	3	0	0	0.0	6	2	0	5		.306	.389	0	0	OF-8
1884	1	5	1	0	0	0	0.0	3		1	0		.200	.200	0	0	P-1
2 yrs.	9	41	12	3	0	0	0.0	9	2	1	5		.293	.366	0	0	OF-8, P-1

Tom Angley

ANGLEY, THOMAS SAMUEL
B. Oct. 2, 1904, Baltimore, Md.   D. Oct. 26, 1952, Wichita, Kans.
BL TR 5'8" 190 lbs.

	G	AB	H	2B	3B	HR	HR %	R	RBI	BB	SO	SB	BA	SA	PH AB	PH H	G by POS
1929 CHI N	5	16	4	1	0	0	0.0	1	6	2	2	0	.250	.313	0	0	C-5

Pat Ankenman

ANKENMAN, FRED NORMAN
B. Dec. 23, 1912, Houston, Tex.
BR TR 5'4" 125 lbs.

	G	AB	H	2B	3B	HR	HR %	R	RBI	BB	SO	SB	BA	SA	PH AB	PH H	G by POS
1936 STL N	1	3	0	0	0	0	0.0	0	0	0	3	0	.000	.000	0	0	SS-1
1943 BKN N	1	2	1	0	0	0	0.0	1	0	0	0	0	.500	.500	0	0	SS-1
1944	13	24	6	1	0	0	0.0	1	3	0	2	0	.250	.292	1	0	2B-11, SS-2
3 yrs.	15	29	7	1	0	0	0.0	2	3	0	5	0	.241	.276	1	0	2B-11, SS-4

Bill Annis

ANNIS, WILLIAM PERLEY
B. Mar. 8, 1857, Stoneham, Mass.   D. June 10, 1923, Kennebunkport, Me.
5'7" 150 lbs.

	G	AB	H	2B	3B	HR	HR %	R	RBI	BB	SO	SB	BA	SA	PH AB	PH H	G by POS
1884 BOS N	27	96	17	2	0	0	0.0	17		0	8		.177	.198	0	0	OF-27

Cap Anson

ANSON, ADRIAN CONSTANTINE (Pop)
B. Apr. 17, 1852, Marshalltown, Iowa   D. Apr. 14, 1922, Chicago, Ill.
Manager 1879-98.
Hall of Fame 1939.
BR TR 6' 202 lbs.

	G	AB	H	2B	3B	HR	HR %	R	RBI	BB	SO	SB	BA	SA	PH AB	PH H	G by POS
1876 CHI N	66	309	110	13	7	1	0.3	63	59	12	8		.356	.453	0	0	3B-66, C-2
1877	59	255	86	19	1	0	0.0	52	32	9	3		.337	.420	0	0	3B-40, C-31
1878	60	261	89	12	2	0	0.0	55	40	13	1		.341	.402	0	0	OF-48, 2B-9, 3B-3, C-3
1879	51	227	90	20	1	0	0.0	40	34	2	2		.396	.493	0	0	1B-51
1880	86	356	120	24	1	1	0.3	54	74	14	12		.337	.419	0	0	1B-81, 3B-9, SS-1, 2B-1
1881	84	343	137	21	7	1	0.3	67	82	26	4		.399	.510	0	0	1B-84, C-2, SS-1
1882	82	348	126	29	8	1	0.3	69	83	20	7		.362	.500	0	0	1B-82, C-1
1883	98	413	127	36	5	0	0.0	70		18	9		.308	.419	0	0	1B-98, P-2, OF-1, C-1
1884	112	475	159	30	3	21	4.4	108		29	13		.335	.543	0	0	1B-112, C-3, SS-1, P-1
1885	112	464	144	35	7	7	1.5	100	114	34	13		.310	.461	0	0	1B-112, C-1
1886	125	504	187	35	11	10	2.0	117	147	55	19	29	.371	.544	0	0	1B-125, C-12
1887	122	472	164	33	13	7	1.5	107	102	60	18	27	.347	.517	0	0	1B-122, C-1
1888	134	515	177	20	12	12	2.3	101	84	47	24	28	.344	.499	0	0	1B-134
1889	134	518	177	32	7	7	1.4	100	117	86	19	27	.342	.471	0	0	1B-134
1890	139	504	157	14	5	7	1.4	95	107	113	23	29	.312	.401	0	0	1B-135, C-3, 2B-2
1891	136	540	157	24	8	8	1.5	81	120	75	17	17	.291	.409	0	0	1B-136, C-2
1892	146	559	152	25	9	1	0.2	62	74	67	30	13	.272	.354	0	0	1B-146
1893	103	398	125	24	2	0	0.0	70	91	68	12	13	.314	.384	1	1	1B-101
1894	83	347	137	28	4	5	1.4	82	99	40	15	17	.395	.542	0	0	1B-82, 2B-1
1895	122	474	159	23	6	2	0.4	87	91	55	23	12	.335	.422	0	0	1B-122
1896	108	402	133	18	2	2	0.5	72	90	49	10	24	.331	.400	1	0	1B-98, C-10
1897	114	424	128	17	3	3	0.7	67	75	60		11	.302	.377	0	0	1B-103, C-11
22 yrs.	2276	9108	3041	532	124	96	1.1	1719	1715	952	294	247	.334	.451	2	1	1B-2058, 3B-118, C-83, OF-49, 2B-13, SS-3, P-3

	G	AB	H	2B	3B	HR	HR %	R	RBI	BB	SO	SB	BA	SA	Pinch Hit AB	H	G by POS

Joe Antolick

ANTOLICK, JOSEPH
B. Apr. 11, 1916, Hokendauqua, Pa.

BR TR 6'　　185 lbs.

	G	AB	H	2B	3B	HR	HR %	R	RBI	BB	SO	SB	BA	SA	AB	H	G by POS
1944 PHI N	4	6	2	0	0	0	0.0	1	0	1	0	0	.333	.333	1	0	C-3

John Antonelli

ANTONELLI, JOHN LAWRENCE
B. July 15, 1915, Memphis, Tenn.

BR TR 5'10½" 165 lbs.

	G	AB	H	2B	3B	HR	HR %	R	RBI	BB	SO	SB	BA	SA	AB	H	G by POS
1944 STL N	8	21	4	1	0	0	0.0	0	1	0	4	0	.190	.238	0	0	3B-3, 1B-3, 2B-2
1945 2 teams	STL	N	(2G –	.000)		PHI	N	(125G –	.256)								
" total	127	507	129	27	2	1	0.2	50	28	24	25	1	.254	.321	2	0	3B-109, 2B-23, SS-1, 1B-1
2 yrs.	135	528	133	28	2	1	0.2	50	29	24	29	1	.252	.318	2	0	3B-112, 2B-25, 1B-4, SS-1

Bill Antonello

ANTONELLO, WILLIAM JAMES
B. May 19, 1927, Brooklyn, N. Y.

BR TR 5'11"　　185 lbs.

	G	AB	H	2B	3B	HR	HR %	R	RBI	BB	SO	SB	BA	SA	AB	H	G by POS
1953 BKN N	40	43	7	1	1	1	2.3	9	4	2	11	0	.163	.302	8	0	OF-25

Luis Aparicio

APARICIO, LUIS ERNESTO (Little Looie)
B. Apr. 29, 1934, Maracaibo, Venezuela
Hall of Fame 1984.

BR TR 5'9"　　160 lbs.

	G	AB	H	2B	3B	HR	HR %	R	RBI	BB	SO	SB	BA	SA	AB	H	G by POS
1956 CHI A	152	533	142	19	6	3	0.6	69	56	34	63	21	.266	.341	0	0	SS-152
1957	143	575	148	22	6	3	0.5	82	41	52	55	28	.257	.332	1	0	SS-145
1958	145	557	148	20	9	2	0.4	76	40	35	38	29	.266	.345	0	0	SS-145
1959	152	612	157	18	5	6	1.0	98	51	53	40	56	.257	.332	0	0	SS-152
1960	153	600	166	20	7	2	0.3	86	61	43	39	51	.277	.343	0	0	SS-153
1961	156	625	170	24	4	6	1.0	90	45	38	33	53	.272	.352	0	0	SS-156
1962	153	581	140	23	5	7	1.2	72	40	32	36	31	.241	.334	1	0	SS-152
1963 BAL A	146	601	150	18	8	5	0.8	73	45	36	40	40	.250	.331	0	0	SS-145
1964	146	578	154	20	3	10	1.7	93	37	49	51	57	.266	.363	1	0	SS-141
1965	144	564	127	20	10	8	1.4	67	40	46	56	26	.225	.339	1	0	SS-151
1966	151	659	182	25	8	6	0.9	97	41	33	42	25	.276	.366	2	0	SS-131
1967	134	546	127	22	5	4	0.7	55	31	29	44	18	.233	.313	2	0	SS-154
1968 CHI A	155	622	164	24	4	4	0.6	55	36	33	43	17	.264	.334	2	0	SS-154
1969	156	599	168	24	5	5	0.8	77	51	66	29	24	.280	.362	1	0	SS-146
1970	146	552	173	29	3	5	0.9	86	43	53	34	8	.313	.404	3	2	SS-121
1971 BOS A	125	491	114	23	0	4	0.8	56	45	35	43	6	.232	.303	2	1	SS-109
1972	110	436	112	26	3	3	0.7	47	39	26	28	3	.257	.351	1	0	SS-132
1973	132	499	135	17	1	0	0.0	56	49	43	33	13	.271	.309	0	0	SS-2581
18 yrs.	2599	10230	2677	394	92	83	0.8	1335	791	736	742	506	.262	.343	15	3	SS-2581
	10th											10th					

WORLD SERIES																	
1959 CHI A	6	26	8	1	0	0	0.0	1	0	2	3	1	.308	.346	0	1	SS-6
1966 BAL A	4	16	4	1	0	0	0.0	0	2	0	0	0	.250	.313	0	0	SS-4
2 yrs.	10	42	12	2	0	0	0.0	1	2	2	3	1	.286	.333	0	1	SS-10

Luke Appling

APPLING, LUCIUS BENJAMIN (Old Aches and Pains)
B. Apr. 2, 1907, High Point, N. C.
Manager 1967.
Hall of Fame 1964.

BR TR 5'10"　　183 lbs.

	G	AB	H	2B	3B	HR	HR %	R	RBI	BB	SO	SB	BA	SA	AB	H	G by POS
1930 CHI A	6	26	8	2	0	0	0.0	2	2	0	0	2	.308	.385	0	0	SS-6
1931	96	297	69	13	4	1	0.3	36	28	29	27	9	.232	.313	12	3	SS-76, 2B-1
1932	139	489	134	20	10	3	0.6	66	63	40	36	9	.274	.374	7	3	SS-85, 2B-30, 3B-14
1933	151	612	197	36	10	6	1.0	90	85	56	29	6	.322	.443	0	0	SS-151
1934	118	452	137	28	6	2	0.4	75	61	59	27	3	.303	.405	0	0	SS-110, 2B-8
1935	153	525	161	28	6	1	0.2	94	71	122	40	12	.307	.389	0	0	SS-153
1936	138	526	204	31	7	6	1.1	111	128	85	25	10	.388	.508	1	0	SS-137
1937	154	574	182	42	8	4	0.7	98	77	86	28	18	.317	.439	0	0	SS-154
1938	81	294	89	14	0	0	0.0	41	44	42	17	1	.303	.350	2	1	SS-78
1939	148	516	162	16	6	0	0.0	82	56	105	37	16	.314	.368	0	0	SS-148
1940	150	566	197	27	13	0	0.0	96	79	69	35	3	.348	.442	0	0	SS-150
1941	154	592	186	26	8	1	0.2	93	57	82	32	12	.314	.390	0	0	SS-154
1942	142	543	142	26	4	3	0.6	78	53	63	23	17	.262	.341	0	0	SS-155
1943	155	585	192	33	2	3	0.5	63	80	90	29	27	.328	.407	0	0	SS-17
1945	18	58	21	2	2	1	1.7	12	10	12	7	1	.362	.517	1	0	SS-149
1946	149	582	180	27	5	1	0.2	59	55	71	41	6	.309	.378	0	0	SS-149
1947	139	503	154	29	0	8	1.6	67	49	64	28	8	.306	.412	7	0	SS-129, 3B-2
1948	139	497	156	16	2	0	0.0	63	47	94	35	10	.314	.354	3	1	3B-72, SS-64
1949	142	492	148	21	5	5	1.0	82	58	121	24	7	.301	.394	1	0	SS-20, 1B-13, 2B-1
1950	50	128	30	3	4	0	0.0	11	13	12	8	2	.234	.320	15	1	SS-2218, 3B-88, 2B-40, 1B-13
20 yrs.	2422	8857	2749	440	102	45	0.5	1319	1116	1302	528	179	.310	.398	49	9	SS-2218, 3B-88, 2B-40, 1B-13

Angel Aragon

ARAGON, ANGEL VALDEZ SR. (Pete, Bing)
Father of Jack Aragon.
B. Aug. 2, 1893, Havana, Cuba　　D. Jan. 24, 1952, New York, N. Y.

BR TR 5'5"　　150 lbs.

	G	AB	H	2B	3B	HR	HR %	R	RBI	BB	SO	SB	BA	SA	AB	H	G by POS
1914 NY A	6	7	1	0	0	0	0.0	1	0	1	2	0	.143	.143	5	1	OF-1
1916	13	27	5	0	0	0	0.0	3	3	2	2	2	.185	.185	1	0	3B-8, OF-3
1917	14	45	3	1	0	0	0.0	2	2	2	2	0	.067	.089	2	0	OF-6, 3B-4, SS-2
3 yrs.	33	79	9	1	0	0	0.0	6	5	5	6	2	.114	.127	8	1	3B-12, OF-10, SS-2

Jack Aragon

ARAGON, ANGEL VALDEZ JR.
Son of Angel Aragon.
B. Nov. 20, 1915, Havana, Cuba

BR TR 5'10"　　176 lbs.

	G	AB	H	2B	3B	HR	HR %	R	RBI	BB	SO	SB	BA	SA	AB	H	G by POS
1941 NY N	1	0	0	0	0	0	–	0	0	0	0	–	–	0	0		

	G	AB	H	2B	3B	HR	HR%	R	RBI	BB	SO	SB	BA	SA	Pinch Hit AB	Pinch Hit H	G by POS

Maurice Archdeacon

ARCHDEACON, MAURICE JOHN (Flash, Comet)
B. Dec. 14, 1898, St. Louis, Mo.   D. Sept. 5, 1954, St. Louis, Mo.   BL TL 5'8"   153 lbs.

	G	AB	H	2B	3B	HR	HR%	R	RBI	BB	SO	SB	BA	SA	AB	H	G by POS
1923 CHI A	22	87	35	5	1	0	0.0	23	4	6	8	2	.402	.483	1	0	OF-20
1924	95	288	92	9	3	0	0.0	59	25	40	30	11	.319	.372	14	5	OF-77
1925	10	9	1	0	0	0	0.0	2	0	2	1	0	.111	.111	8	1	OF-1
3 yrs.	127	384	128	14	4	0	0.0	84	29	48	39	13	.333	.391	23	6	OF-98

Jimmy Archer

ARCHER, JAMES PETER
B. May 13, 1883, Dublin, Ireland   D. Mar. 29, 1958, Milwaukee, Wis.   BR TR 5'10"   168 lbs.

	G	AB	H	2B	3B	HR	HR%	R	RBI	BB	SO	SB	BA	SA	AB	H	G by POS
1904 PIT N	7	20	3	0	0	0	0.0		1	1		0	.150	.150	0	0	C-7, OF-1
1907 DET A	18	42	5	0	0	0	0.0	1	0	4		0	.119	.119	0	0	C-17, 2B-1
1909 CHI N	80	261	60	9	2	1	0.4	31	30	12		5	.230	.291	0	0	C-80
1910	98	313	81	17	6	2	0.6	36	41	14	49	6	.259	.371	8	3	C-49, 1B-40
1911	116	387	98	18	5	4	1.0	41	41	18	43	5	.253	.357	3	0	C-102, 1B-10, 2B-1
1912	120	385	109	20	2	5	1.3	35	58	22	36	7	.283	.384	1	0	C-118
1913	110	367	98	14	7	2	0.5	38	44	19	27	4	.267	.360	3	1	C-103, 1B-8
1914	79	248	64	9	2	0	0.0	17	19	9	9	1	.258	.310	3	1	C-76
1915	97	309	75	11	5	1	0.3	21	27	11	38	5	.243	.320	5	2	C-88
1916	77	205	45	6	2	1	0.5	11	30	12	24	3	.220	.283	16	2	C-65, 3B-1
1917	2	2	0	0	0	0	0.0		0		1	0	.000	.000	2	0	
1918 3 teams																	
" PIT N (24G – .155)					BKN N (9G – .273)				CIN N (9G – .269)								
" total	42	106	22	3	0	0	0.0	10	5	3	14	0	.208	.283	5	1	C-35, 1B-2
12 yrs.	846	2645	660	106	34	16	0.6	247	296	124	241	36	.250	.333	46	10	C-740, 1B-60, 2B-2, OF-1, 3B-1

WORLD SERIES

	G	AB	H	2B	3B	HR	HR%	R	RBI	BB	SO	SB	BA	SA	AB	H	G by POS
1907 DET A	1	3	0	0	0	0	0.0	0	0	0		0	.000	.000	0	0	C-1
1910 CHI N	3	11	2	1	0	0	0.0	1	0	0	4	0	.182	.273	0	0	1B-1
2 yrs.	4	14	2	1	0	0	0.0	1	0	0	5	0	.143	.214	0	0	1B-1, C-1

George Archie

ARCHIE, GEORGE ALBERT
B. Apr. 27, 1914, Nashville, Tenn.   BR TR 6'   170 lbs.

	G	AB	H	2B	3B	HR	HR%	R	RBI	BB	SO	SB	BA	SA	AB	H	G by POS
1938 DET A	3	2	0	0	0	0	0.0	0	0	1		0	.000	.000	2	0	
1941 2 teams			WAS A (105G – .269)			STL A (9G – .379)											
" total	114	408	113	23	4	3	0.7	48	53	37	45	10	.277	.375	9	1	3B-73, 1B-31
1946 STL A	4	11	2	1	0	0	0.0	1	0	0	1	0	.182	.273	0	0	1B-3
3 yrs.	121	421	115	24	4	3	0.7	49	53	37	47	10	.273	.371	11	1	3B-73, 1B-34

Jose Arcia

ARCIA, JOSE RAIMUNDO ORTA (Flaco)
B. Aug. 22, 1943, Havana, Cuba   BR TR 6'3"   170 lbs.

	G	AB	H	2B	3B	HR	HR%	R	RBI	BB	SO	SB	BA	SA	AB	H	G by POS
1968 CHI N	59	84	16	4	0	1	1.2	15	8	3	24	0	.190	.274	5	1	OF-17, 2B-10, SS-7, 3B-1
1969 SD N	120	302	65	11	3	0	0.0	35	10	14	47	14	.215	.272	0	0	2B-68, SS-37, 3B-8, OF-4, 1B-1
1970	114	229	51	9	3	0	0.0	28	17	12	36	3	.223	.288	1	0	SS-67, 2B-20, 3B-9, OF-7
3 yrs.	293	615	132	24	6	1	0.2	78	35	29	107	17	.215	.278	6	1	SS-111, 2B-98, OF-28, 3B-18, 1B-1

Dan Ardell

ARDELL, DANIEL MIERS
B. May 27, 1941, Seattle, Wash.   BL TL 6'2"   190 lbs.

	G	AB	H	2B	3B	HR	HR%	R	RBI	BB	SO	SB	BA	SA	AB	H	G by POS
1961 LA A	7	4	1	0	0	0	0.0	1	0	1	2	0	.250	.250	2	1	1B-1

Joe Ardner

ARDNER, JOSEPH A. (Old Hoss)
B. Feb. 27, 1858, Mt. Vernon, Ohio   D. Sept. 15, 1935, Cleveland, Ohio   BR

	G	AB	H	2B	3B	HR	HR%	R	RBI	BB	SO	SB	BA	SA	AB	H	G by POS
1884 CLE N	26	92	16	1	1	0	0.0	6	4	1	24		.174	.207	0	0	2B-25, 3B-1
1890	84	323	72	13	1	0	0.0	28	35	17	40	9	.223	.269	0	0	2B-84
2 yrs.	110	415	88	14	2	0	0.0	34	39	18	64	9	.212	.255	0	0	2B-109, 3B-1

Hank Arft

ARFT, HENRY IRVEN (Bow Wow)
B. Jan. 28, 1922, Manchester, Mo.   BL TL 5'10½"   190 lbs.

	G	AB	H	2B	3B	HR	HR%	R	RBI	BB	SO	SB	BA	SA	AB	H	G by POS
1948 STL A	69	248	59	10	3	5	2.0	25	38	45	43	1	.238	.363	1	0	1B-69
1949	6	5	1	1	0	0	0.0	1	2	0	1	0	.200	.400	5	1	
1950	98	280	75	16	4	5	1.0	45	32	46	48	3	.268	.364	13	3	1B-84
1951	112	345	90	16	5	7	2.0	44	42	41	34	4	.261	.397	15	5	1B-97
1952	15	28	4	3	1	0	0.0	1	4	5	7	0	.143	.321	5	0	1B-10
5 yrs.	300	906	229	46	13	13	1.4	116	118	137	133	8	.253	.375	38	9	1B-260

Buzz Arlett

ARLETT, RUSSELL LORIS
B. Jan. 3, 1899, Elmhurst, Calif.   D. May 16, 1964, Minneapolis, Minn.   BB TR 6'3½"   225 lbs.

	G	AB	H	2B	3B	HR	HR%	R	RBI	BB	SO	SB	BA	SA	AB	H	G by POS
1931 PHI N	121	418	131	26	7	18	4.3	65	72	45	39	3	.313	.538	14	4	OF-94, 1B-13

Tony Armas

ARMAS, ANTONIO RAFAEL
Also known as Antonio Rafael Machado.
B. July 12, 1953, Anzoateque, Venezuela   BR TR 5'11"   182 lbs.

	G	AB	H	2B	3B	HR	HR%	R	RBI	BB	SO	SB	BA	SA	AB	H	G by POS
1976 PIT N	4	6	2	0	0	0	0.0	0	1	0	2	0	.333	.333	2	0	OF-2
1977 OAK A	118	363	87	8	2	13	3.6	26	53	20	99	1	.240	.380	7	0	OF-112, SS-1
1978	91	239	51	6	1	2	0.8	17	13	10	62	1	.213	.272	4	0	OF-85, DH-3
1979	80	278	69	9	3	11	4.0	29	34	16	67	1	.248	.421	0	0	OF-80
1980	158	628	175	18	8	35	5.6	87	109	29	128	5	.279	.500	0	0	OF-158
1981	109	440	115	24	3	22	5.0	51	76	19	115	5	.261	.480	0	0	OF-109
1982	138	536	125	19	2	28	5.2	58	89	33	128	2	.233	.433	0	0	OF-135, DH-1
1983 BOS A	145	574	125	23	2	36	6.3	77	107	29	131	0	.218	.453	2	0	OF-116, DH-27
1984	157	639	171	29	5	43	6.7	107	123	32	156	1	.268	.531	0	0	OF-126, DH-31
9 yrs.	1000	3703	920	136	26	190	5.1	452	605	188	888	16	.248	.453	17	0	OF-923, DH-62, SS-1

DIVISIONAL PLAYOFF SERIES

	G	AB	H	2B	3B	HR	HR%	R	RBI	BB	SO	SB	BA	SA	AB	H	G by POS
1981 OAK A	3	11	6	2	0	0	0.0	1	3	1	1	0	.545	.727	0	0	OF-3

LEAGUE CHAMPIONSHIP SERIES

	G	AB	H	2B	3B	HR	HR%	R	RBI	BB	SO	SB	BA	SA	AB	H	G by POS
1981 OAK A	3	12	2	0	0	0	0.0	0	0	0	5	0	.167	.167	0	0	OF-3

	G	AB	H	2B	3B	HR	HR%	R	RBI	BB	SO	SB	BA	SA	Pinch Hit AB	Pinch Hit H	G by POS

Ed Armbrister

ARMBRISTER, EDISON ROSANDA
B. July 4, 1948, Nassau, Bahamas
BR TR 5'11" 160 lbs.

	G	AB	H	2B	3B	HR	HR%	R	RBI	BB	SO	SB	BA	SA	PH AB	PH H	G by POS
1973 CIN N	18	37	8	3	1	1	2.7	5	5	2	8	0	.216	.432	5	1	OF-14
1974	9	7	2	0	0	0	0.0	0	0	1	1	0	.286	.286	5	2	OF-4
1975	59	65	12	1	0	0	0.0	9	2	5	19	3	.185	.200	28	7	OF-19
1976	73	78	23	3	2	2	2.6	20	7	6	22	7	.295	.462	27	7	OF-32
1977	65	78	20	4	3	1	1.3	12	5	10	21	5	.256	.423	24	5	OF-27
5 yrs.	224	265	65	11	6	4	1.5	46	19	24	71	15	.245	.377	89	22	OF-96

LEAGUE CHAMPIONSHIP SERIES

	G	AB	H	2B	3B	HR	HR%	R	RBI	BB	SO	SB	BA	SA	PH AB	PH H	G by POS
1973 CIN N	3	6	1	0	0	0	0.0	0	0	0	5	0	.167	.167	2	0	OF-1
1975	1	0	0	0	0	0	–	0	1	0	0	0	–	–	0	0	
1976	1	0	0	0	0	0	–	0	0	0	0	0	–	–	0	0	
3 yrs.	5	6	1	0	0	0	0.0	0	1	0	5	0	.167	.167	2	0	OF-1

WORLD SERIES

	G	AB	H	2B	3B	HR	HR%	R	RBI	BB	SO	SB	BA	SA	PH AB	PH H	G by POS
1975 CIN N	5	1	0	0	0	0	0.0	1	0	2	0	0	.000	.000	1	0	

Charlie Armbruster

ARMBRUSTER, CHARLES A.
B. Aug. 30, 1880, Cincinnati, Ohio   D. Oct. 7, 1964, Grants Pass, Ore.
BR TR 5'9" 180 lbs.

	G	AB	H	2B	3B	HR	HR%	R	RBI	BB	SO	SB	BA	SA	PH AB	PH H	G by POS
1905 BOS A	35	91	18	4	0	0	0.0	13	6	18		3	.198	.242	0	0	C-35
1906	72	201	29	6	1	0	0.0	9	6	25		2	.144	.184	4	0	C-66, 1B-1
1907 2 teams	BOS A (23G – .100)				CHI A (1G – .000)												
" total	24	63	6	1	0	0	0.0	2	0	9		1	.095	.111	1	0	C-22
3 yrs.	131	355	53	11	1	0	0.0	24	12	52		6	.149	.186	5	0	C-123, 1B-1

Herman Armbruster

ARMBRUSTER, HERMAN (Buster)
B. Mar. 20, 1882, Cincinnati, Ohio   D. Dec. 10, 1953, Cincinnati, Ohio
BL TL

	G	AB	H	2B	3B	HR	HR%	R	RBI	BB	SO	SB	BA	SA	PH AB	PH H	G by POS
1906 PHI A	91	265	63	6	3	2	0.8	40	24	43		13	.238	.306	12	3	OF-74

George Armstrong

ARMSTRONG, GEORGE NOBLE (Dodo)
B. June 3, 1924, Orange, N. J.
BR TR 5'10" 190 lbs.

	G	AB	H	2B	3B	HR	HR%	R	RBI	BB	SO	SB	BA	SA	PH AB	PH H	G by POS
1946 PHI A	8	6	1	1	0	0	0.0	0	0	1		0	.167	.333	4	1	C-4

Harry Arndt

ARNDT, HARRY J.
B. Feb. 12, 1879, South Bend, Ind.   D. Mar. 24, 1921, South Bend, Ind.
TR

	G	AB	H	2B	3B	HR	HR%	R	RBI	BB	SO	SB	BA	SA	PH AB	PH H	G by POS
1902 2 teams	DET A (10G – .147)				BAL A (68G – .254)												
" total	78	282	68	7	5	2	0.7	45	35	41		9	.241	.323	0	0	OF-72, 2B-4, 3B-2, SS-1, 1B-1
1905 STL N	113	415	101	11	6	2	0.5	40	36	24		13	.243	.313	2	1	2B-90, OF-9, 3B-7, SS-5
1906	69	256	69	7	9	2	0.8	30	26	19		5	.270	.391	1	0	3B-65, OF-1, 1B-1
1907	11	32	6	1	0	0	0.0	3	2	1		0	.188	.219	4	1	1B-4, 3B-3
4 yrs.	271	985	244	26	20	6	0.6	118	99	85		27	.248	.333	7	2	2B-94, OF-82, 3B-77, SS-6, 1B-6

Chris Arnold

ARNOLD, CHRISTOPHER PAUL
B. Nov. 6, 1947, Long Beach, Calif.
BR TR 5'10" 160 lbs.

	G	AB	H	2B	3B	HR	HR%	R	RBI	BB	SO	SB	BA	SA	PH AB	PH H	G by POS
1971 SF N	6	13	3	0	0	1	7.7	2	3	1	2	0	.231	.462	4	1	2B-3
1972	51	84	19	3	1	1	1.2	8	4	8	12	0	.226	.321	21	4	3B-17, 2B-7, SS-4
1973	49	54	16	2	0	1	1.9	7	13	8	11	0	.296	.389	36	12	C-9, 3B-1, 2B-1
1974	78	174	42	7	3	1	0.6	22	26	15	27	1	.241	.333	38	9	2B-31, 3B-7, SS-1
1975	29	41	8	0	0	0	0.0	4	0	4	8	0	.195	.195	17	3	OF-4, 2B-4
1976	60	69	15	0	1	0	0.0	4	5	6	16	0	.217	.246	45	12	2B-8, 3B-4, SS-1, 1B-1
6 yrs.	273	435	103	12	5	4	0.9	47	51	42	76	1	.237	.315	161	41	2B-54, 3B-29, C-9, SS-6, OF-4, 1B-1

Morrie Arnovich

ARNOVICH, MORRIS (Snooker)
B. Nov. 20, 1910, Superior, Wis.   D. July 20, 1959, Superior, Wis.
BR TR 5'10" 168 lbs.

	G	AB	H	2B	3B	HR	HR%	R	RBI	BB	SO	SB	BA	SA	PH AB	PH H	G by POS
1936 PHI N	13	48	15	3	0	1	2.1	4	7	1	3	0	.313	.438	0	0	OF-13
1937	117	410	119	27	4	10	2.4	60	60	34	32	5	.290	.449	9	2	OF-107
1938	139	502	138	29	4	4	0.8	47	72	42	37	2	.275	.357	6	0	OF-133
1939	134	491	159	25	2	5	1.0	68	67	58	28	7	.324	.413	2	1	OF-132
1940 2 teams	PHI N (39G – .199)				CIN N (62G – .284)												
" total	101	352	88	12	3	0	0.0	30	33	27	25	1	.250	.301	4	1	OF-97
1941 NY N	85	207	58	8	3	2	1.0	25	22	23	14	2	.280	.377	20	5	OF-61
1946	1	3	0	0	0	0	0.0	0	0	0	0	0	.000	.000	0	0	OF-1
7 yrs.	590	2013	577	104	12	22	1.1	234	261	185	139	17	.287	.383	41	9	OF-544

WORLD SERIES

	G	AB	H	2B	3B	HR	HR%	R	RBI	BB	SO	SB	BA	SA	PH AB	PH H	G by POS
1940 CIN N	1	1	0	0	0	0	0.0	0	0	0	0	0	.000	.000	1	0	OF-1

Tug Arundel

ARUNDEL, JOHN THOMAS
Brother of Harry Arundel.
B. 1863, Auburn, N. Y.   D. Sept. 5, 1912, Auburn, N. Y.

	G	AB	H	2B	3B	HR	HR%	R	RBI	BB	SO	SB	BA	SA	PH AB	PH H	G by POS
1882 PHI AA	1	5	0	0	0	0	0.0	0		0			.000	.000	0	0	C-1
1884 TOL AA	15	47	4	0	0	0	0.0	6		3			.085	.085	0	0	C-15
1887 IND N	43	157	31	4	0	0	0.0	13	13	8	12	8	.197	.223	0	0	C-42, OF-2, 1B-1
1888 WAS N	17	51	10	0	1	0	0.0	2	2	5	10	1	.196	.235	0	0	C-17
4 yrs.	76	260	45	4	1	0	0.0	21	15	16	22	9	.173	.196	0	0	C-75, OF-2, 1B-1

Jim Asbell

ASBELL, JAMES MARION
B. June 22, 1914, Dallas, Tex.   D. July 6, 1967, San Mateo, Calif.
BR TR 6' 210 lbs.

	G	AB	H	2B	3B	HR	HR%	R	RBI	BB	SO	SB	BA	SA	PH AB	PH H	G by POS
1938 CHI N	17	33	6	2	0	0	0.0	6	3	3	9	0	.182	.242	6	3	OF-17

Asby Asbjornson

ASBJORNSON, ROBERT ANTHONY
B. June 19, 1909, Concord, Mass.   D. Jan. 21, 1970, Williamsport, Pa.
BR TR 6'1" 196 lbs.

	G	AB	H	2B	3B	HR	HR%	R	RBI	BB	SO	SB	BA	SA	PH AB	PH H	G by POS
1928 BOS A	6	16	3	1	0	0	0.0	0	1	1	1	0	.188	.250	0	0	C-6
1929	17	29	3	0	0	0	0.0	1	0	1	6	0	.103	.103	1	0	C-15
1931 CIN N	45	118	36	7	1	0	0.0	13	22	7	23	0	.305	.381	14	3	C-31

	G	AB	H	2B	3B	HR	HR%	R	RBI	BB	SO	SB	BA	SA	Pinch Hit AB	Pinch Hit H	G by POS

Asby Asbjornson continued

	G	AB	H	2B	3B	HR	HR%	R	RBI	BB	SO	SB	BA	SA	AB	H	G by POS
1932	29	58	10	2	0	1	1.7	5	4	0	15	0	.172	.259	13	0	C-16
4 yrs.	97	221	52	10	1	1	0.5	19	27	9	45	0	.235	.303	28	3	C-68

Richie Ashburn

ASHBURN, DON RICHARD (Whitey)
B. Mar. 19, 1927, Tilden, Neb.

BL TR 5'10" 170 lbs.

	G	AB	H	2B	3B	HR	HR%	R	RBI	BB	SO	SB	BA	SA	AB	H	G by POS
1948 PHI N	117	463	154	17	4	2	0.4	78	40	60	22	32	.333	.400	1	0	OF-116
1949	154	662	188	18	11	1	0.2	84	37	58	38	9	.284	.349	0	0	OF-154
1950	151	594	180	25	14	2	0.3	84	41	63	32	14	.303	.402	2	0	OF-147
1951	154	643	221	31	5	4	0.6	92	63	50	37	29	.344	.426	0	0	OF-154
1952	154	613	173	31	6	1	0.2	93	42	75	30	16	.282	.357	1	1	OF-154
1953	156	622	205	25	9	2	0.3	110	57	61	35	14	.330	.408	0	0	OF-156
1954	153	559	175	16	8	1	0.2	111	41	125	46	11	.313	.376	0	0	OF-153
1955	140	533	180	32	9	3	0.6	91	42	105	36	12	.338	.448	1	1	OF-140
1956	154	628	190	26	8	3	0.5	94	50	79	45	10	.303	.384	0	0	OF-154
1957	156	626	186	26	8	0	0.0	93	33	94	44	13	.297	.364	0	0	OF-156
1958	152	615	215	24	13	2	0.3	98	33	97	48	30	.350	.441	0	0	OF-152
1959	153	564	150	16	2	1	0.2	86	20	79	42	9	.266	.307	4	1	OF-149
1960 CHI N	151	547	159	16	5	0	0.0	99	40	116	50	16	.291	.338	6	1	OF-146
1961	109	307	79	7	4	0	0.0	49	19	55	27	7	.257	.306	34	10	OF-76
1962 NY N	135	389	119	7	3	7	1.8	60	28	81	39	12	.306	.393	31	13	OF-97, 2B-2
15 yrs.	2189	8365	2574	317	109	29	0.3	1322	586	1198	571	234	.308	.382	80	27	OF-2104, 2B-2

WORLD SERIES

	G	AB	H	2B	3B	HR	HR%	R	RBI	BB	SO	SB	BA	SA	AB	H	G by POS
1950 PHI N	4	17	3	1	0	0	0.0	0	1	0	4	0	.176	.235	0	0	OF-4

Alan Ashby

ASHBY, ALAN DEAN
B. July 8, 1951, Long Beach, Calif.

BB TR 6'2" 185 lbs.

	G	AB	H	2B	3B	HR	HR%	R	RBI	BB	SO	SB	BA	SA	AB	H	G by POS
1973 CLE A	11	29	5	1	0	1	3.4	4	3	2	11	0	.172	.310	1	0	C-11
1974	10	7	1	0	0	0	0.0	1	0	1	2	0	.143	.143	1	1	C-9
1975	90	254	57	10	1	5	2.0	32	32	30	42	3	.224	.331	1	0	C-87, 1B-2, DH-1, 3B-1
1976	89	247	59	5	1	4	1.6	26	32	27	49	0	.239	.316	5	0	C-86, 1B-2, 3B-1
1977 TOR A	124	396	83	16	3	2	0.5	25	29	50	50	0	.210	.280	0	0	C-124
1978	81	264	69	15	0	9	3.4	27	29	28	32	1	.261	.420	0	0	C-81
1979 HOU N	108	336	68	15	2	2	0.6	25	35	26	70	0	.202	.277	3	1	C-105
1980	116	352	90	19	2	3	0.9	30	48	35	40	0	.256	.347	5	1	C-114
1981	83	255	69	13	0	4	1.6	20	33	35	33	0	.271	.369	4	2	C-81
1982	100	339	87	14	2	12	3.5	40	49	27	53	2	.257	.416	6	3	C-95
1983	87	275	63	18	1	8	2.9	31	34	31	38	0	.229	.389	5	2	C-85
1984	66	191	50	7	0	4	2.1	16	27	20	22	0	.262	.361	4	2	C-63
12 yrs.	965	2945	701	133	12	54	1.8	277	351	312	442	6	.238	.346	35	12	C-941, 1B-4, 3B-2, DH-1

DIVISIONAL PLAYOFF SERIES

	G	AB	H	2B	3B	HR	HR%	R	RBI	BB	SO	SB	BA	SA	AB	H	G by POS
1981 HOU N	3	9	1	0	0	1	11.1	1	2	2	0	0	.111	.444	0	0	C-3

LEAGUE CHAMPIONSHIP SERIES

	G	AB	H	2B	3B	HR	HR%	R	RBI	BB	SO	SB	BA	SA	AB	H	G by POS
1980 HOU N	2	8	1	0	0	0	0.0	0	1	0	0	0	.125	.125	1	1	C-2

Tucker Ashford

ASHFORD, THOMAS STEVEN
B. Dec. 4, 1954, Memphis, Tenn.

BR TR 6'1" 195 lbs.

	G	AB	H	2B	3B	HR	HR%	R	RBI	BB	SO	SB	BA	SA	AB	H	G by POS
1976 SD N	4	5	3	1	0	0	0.0	0	0	1	0	2	.600	.800	2	1	3B-1
1977	81	249	54	18	0	3	1.2	25	24	21	35	2	.217	.325	1	0	3B-74, SS-10, 2B-4
1978	75	155	38	11	0	3	1.9	11	26	14	31	1	.245	.374	18	7	3B-32, 2B-18, 1B-14
1980 TEX A	15	32	4	0	0	0	0.0	2	3	3	3	0	.125	.125	0	0	3B-12, SS-2
1981 NY A	3	0	0	0	0	0	–	0	0	0	0	0	–	–	0	0	2B-2
1983 NY A	35	56	10	0	1	0	0.0	3	2	7	4	0	.179	.214	10	1	3B-15, 2B-13, C-1
1984 KC A	9	13	2	1	0	0	0.0	1	0	1	2	0	.154	.231	0	0	3B-9
7 yrs.	222	510	111	31	1	6	1.2	42	55	47	75	5	.218	.318	31	9	3B-143, 2B-37, 1B-14, SS-12, C-1

Tom Asmussen

ASMUSSEN, THOMAS WILLIAM
B. Sept. 26, 1876, Chicago, Ill.   D. Aug. 21, 1963, Arlington Heights, Ill.

TR

	G	AB	H	2B	3B	HR	HR%	R	RBI	BB	SO	SB	BA	SA	AB	H	G by POS
1907 BOS N	2	5	0	0	0	0	0.0	0	0	0		0	.000	.000	0	0	C-2

Bob Aspromonte

ASPROMONTE, ROBERT THOMAS
Brother of Ken Aspromonte.
B. June 19, 1938, Brooklyn, N. Y.

BR TR 6'2" 170 lbs.

	G	AB	H	2B	3B	HR	HR%	R	RBI	BB	SO	SB	BA	SA	AB	H	G by POS
1956 BKN N	1	1	0	0	0	0	0.0	0	0	0	1	0	.000	.000	1	0	
1960 LA N	21	55	10	1	0	1	1.8	1	6	0	6	1	.182	.255	5	1	SS-15, 3B-4
1961	47	58	14	3	0	0	0.0	7	2	4	12	0	.241	.293	31	9	3B-9, SS-4, 2B-2
1962 HOU N	149	534	142	18	4	11	2.1	59	59	46	54	4	.266	.376	1	0	3B-142, SS-11, 2B-1
1963	136	468	100	9	5	8	1.7	42	49	40	57	3	.214	.306	5	0	3B-131, 1B-1
1964	157	553	155	20	3	12	2.2	51	69	35	54	6	.280	.392	2	0	3B-155
1965	152	578	152	15	2	5	0.9	53	52	38	54	2	.263	.322	1	1	3B-146, 1B-6, SS-4
1966	152	560	141	16	3	8	1.4	55	52	35	63	0	.252	.334	3	0	3B-149, SS-2, 1B-2
1967	137	486	143	24	5	6	1.2	51	58	45	44	2	.294	.401	4	2	3B-133
1968	124	409	92	9	2	1	0.2	25	46	35	57	1	.225	.264	12	5	3B-75, OF-36, SS-1, 1B-1
1969 ATL N	82	198	50	8	1	3	1.5	16	24	13	19	0	.253	.348	26	5	OF-24, 3B-23, SS-18, 2B-2
1970	62	127	27	3	0	0	0.0	5	7	13	13	0	.213	.236	27	5	3B-30, SS-4, OF-1, 1B-1
1971 NY N	104	342	77	9	1	5	1.5	21	33	29	25	0	.225	.301	7	1	3B-97
13 yrs.	1324	4369	1103	135	26	60	1.4	386	457	333	459	19	.252	.336	125	27	3B-1094, OF-61, SS-59, 1B-11, 2B-5

LEAGUE CHAMPIONSHIP SERIES

	G	AB	H	2B	3B	HR	HR%	R	RBI	BB	SO	SB	BA	SA	AB	H	G by POS
1969 ATL N	3	3	0	0	0	0	0.0	0	0	0	0	0	.000	.000	3	0	

	G	AB	H	2B	3B	HR	HR%	R	RBI	BB	SO	SB	BA	SA	Pinch Hit AB	Pinch Hit H	G by POS

Ken Aspromonte

ASPROMONTE, KENNETH JOSEPH
Brother of Bob Aspromonte.
B. Sept. 22, 1931, Brooklyn, N. Y.
Manager 1972-74.

BR TR 6' 180 lbs.

	G	AB	H	2B	3B	HR	HR%	R	RBI	BB	SO	SB	BA	SA	PH AB	PH H	G by POS
1957 BOS A	24	78	21	5	0	0	0.0	9	4	17	10	0	.269	.333	0	0	2B-24
1958 2 teams	BOS	A (6G – .125)			WAS	A	(92G – .225)										
" total	98	269	59	9	4	5	1.9	15	27	28	29	1	.219	.316	9	2	2B-78, 3B-11, SS-1
1959 WAS A	70	225	55	12	0	2	0.9	31	14	26	39	2	.244	.324	5	0	2B-52, SS-12, OF-1, 1B-1
1960 2 teams	CLE	A (4G – .000)			CLE	A	(117G – .290)										
" total	121	462	133	20	1	10	2.2	65	48	53	34	4	.288	.400	6	0	2B-80, 3B-36
1961 2 teams	LA	A (66G – .223)			CLE	A	(22G – .229)										
" total	88	308	69	16	1	2	0.6	34	19	39	24	0	.224	.302	3	1	2B-83
1962 2 teams	CLE	A (20G – .143)			MIL	N	(34G – .291)										
" total	54	107	27	4	0	0	0.0	15	8	12	10	0	.252	.290	21	5	2B-18, 3B-9
1963 CHI N	20	34	5	3	0	0	0.0	2	4	4	4	0	.147	.235	8	0	2B-7, 1B-2
7 yrs.	475	1483	369	69	3	19	1.3	171	124	179	150	7	.249	.338	52	8	2B-342, 3B-56, SS-13, 1B-3, OF-1

Brian Asselstine

ASSELSTINE, BRIAN HANLY
B. Sept. 23, 1953, Santa Barbara, Calif.

BL TR 6'1" 175 lbs.

	G	AB	H	2B	3B	HR	HR%	R	RBI	BB	SO	SB	BA	SA	PH AB	PH H	G by POS
1976 ATL N	11	33	7	0	0	1	3.0	2	3	1	2	0	.212	.303	2	0	OF-9
1977	83	124	26	6	0	4	3.2	12	17	9	10	1	.210	.355	47	10	OF-35
1978	39	103	28	3	3	2	1.9	11	13	11	16	2	.272	.417	6	1	OF-35
1979	8	10	1	0	0	0	0.0	1	0	1	2	0	.100	.100	0	0	OF-1
1980	87	218	62	13	1	3	1.4	18	25	11	37	1	.284	.394	22	3	OF-61
1981	56	86	22	5	0	2	2.3	8	10	5	7	1	.256	.384	36	9	OF-16
6 yrs.	284	574	146	27	4	12	2.1	52	68	38	74	5	.254	.378	119	23	OF-157

Joe Astroth

ASTROTH, JOSEPH HENRY
B. Sept. 1, 1922, East Alton, Ill.

BR TR 5'9" 187 lbs.

	G	AB	H	2B	3B	HR	HR%	R	RBI	BB	SO	SB	BA	SA	PH AB	PH H	G by POS
1945 PHI A	10	17	1	0	0	0	0.0	1	1	0	1	0	.059	.059	2	0	C-8
1946	4	7	1	0	0	0	0.0	0	0	0	2	0	.143	.143	0	0	C-4
1949	55	148	36	4	1	0	0.0	18	12	21	13	1	.243	.284	8	2	C-44
1950	39	110	36	3	1	1	0.9	11	18	18	3	0	.327	.400	0	0	C-38
1951	64	187	46	10	2	2	1.1	30	19	18	13	0	.246	.353	6	1	C-57
1952	104	337	84	7	2	1	0.3	24	36	25	27	2	.249	.291	1	0	C-102
1953	82	260	77	15	2	3	1.2	28	24	27	12	1	.296	.404	3	0	C-79
1954	77	226	50	8	1	1	0.4	22	23	21	19	0	.221	.279	6	2	C-71
1955 KC A	101	274	69	4	1	5	1.8	29	23	47	33	2	.252	.328	2	1	C-100
1956	8	13	1	0	0	0	0.0	0	0	0	1	0	.077	.077	0	0	C-8
10 yrs.	544	1579	401	51	10	13	0.8	163	156	177	124	6	.254	.324	28	6	C-511

Charlie Atherton

ATHERTON, CHARLES MORGAN HERBERT (Prexy)
B. Oct. 19, 1873, New Brunswick N. J. D. Dec. 19, 1934, Vienna, Austria

BR TR 5'10" 160 lbs.

	G	AB	H	2B	3B	HR	HR%	R	RBI	BB	SO	SB	BA	SA	PH AB	PH H	G by POS
1899 WAS N	65	242	60	5	6	0	0.0	28	23	21		2	.248	.318	1	1	3B-63, OF-1

Lefty Atkinson

ATKINSON, HUBERT BURLEY
B. June 4, 1904, Chicago, Ill. D. Feb. 12, 1961, Chicago, Ill.

BL TL 5'6½" 149 lbs.

	G	AB	H	2B	3B	HR	HR%	R	RBI	BB	SO	SB	BA	SA	PH AB	PH H	G by POS
1927 WAS A	1	1	0	0	0	0	0.0	1	0	0	0	0	.000	.000	0	0	

Dick Attreau

ATTREAU, RICHARD GILBERT
B. Apr. 8, 1897, Chicago, Ill. D. July 5, 1964, Chicago, Ill.

BL TL 6' 160 lbs.

	G	AB	H	2B	3B	HR	HR%	R	RBI	BB	SO	SB	BA	SA	PH AB	PH H	G by POS
1926 PHI N	17	61	14	1	0	0	0.0	9	5	6	5	1	.230	.279	0	0	1B-17
1927	44	83	17	1	1	1	1.2	17	11	14	18	1	.205	.277	10	0	1B-26
2 yrs.	61	144	31	2	2	1	0.7	26	16	20	23	1	.215	.278	10	0	1B-43

Toby Atwell

ATWELL, MAURICE DAILEY
B. Mar. 8, 1924, Leesburg, Va.

BL TR 5'9½" 185 lbs.

	G	AB	H	2B	3B	HR	HR%	R	RBI	BB	SO	SB	BA	SA	PH AB	PH H	G by POS
1952 CHI N	107	362	105	16	3	2	0.6	36	31	40	22	2	.290	.367	5	0	C-101
1953 2 teams	CHI	N (24G – .230)			PIT	N	(53G – .245)										
" total	77	213	51	8	0	1	0.5	21	25	33	19	0	.239	.291	11	2	C-68
1954 PIT N	96	287	83	8	4	3	1.0	36	26	43	21	2	.289	.376	8	4	C-88
1955	71	207	44	8	0	1	0.5	21	18	40	16	0	.213	.266	6	0	C-67
1956 2 teams	PIT	N (12G – .111)			MIL	N	(15G – .167)										
" total	27	48	7	1	0	2	4.2	2	10	5	6	0	.146	.292	7	0	C-19
5 yrs.	378	1117	290	41	7	9	0.8	116	110	161	84	4	.260	.333	37	6	C-343

Bill Atwood

ATWOOD, WILLIAM FRANKLIN
B. Sept. 25, 1911, Rome, Ga.

BR TR 5'11½" 190 lbs.

	G	AB	H	2B	3B	HR	HR%	R	RBI	BB	SO	SB	BA	SA	PH AB	PH H	G by POS
1936 PHI N	71	192	58	9	2	2	1.0	21	29	11	15	0	.302	.401	15	4	C-53
1937	87	279	68	15	1	2	0.7	27	32	30	27	3	.244	.326	6	1	C-80
1938	102	281	55	8	1	3	1.1	27	28	25	26	0	.196	.263	5	2	C-94
1939	4	6	0	0	0	0	0.0	0	1	2	3	1	.000	.000	0	0	C-2
1940	78	203	39	9	0	0	0.0	7	22	25	18	0	.192	.236	6	1	C-69
5 yrs.	342	961	220	41	4	7	0.7	82	112	93	89	4	.229	.302	32	8	C-298

Jake Atz

ATZ, JACOB HENRY
B. July 1, 1879, Washington, D. C. D. May 22, 1945, New Orleans, La.

BR TR 5'9½" 160 lbs.

	G	AB	H	2B	3B	HR	HR%	R	RBI	BB	SO	SB	BA	SA	PH AB	PH H	G by POS
1902 WAS A	3	10	1	0	0	0	0.0	1	0	0		0	.100	.100	0	0	2B-3
1907 CHI A	3	7	1	0	0	0	0.0	0	0	0		0	.143	.143	0	0	3B-2
1908	83	206	40	3	0	0	0.0	24	27	31		9	.194	.209	17	4	2B-46, SS-18, 3B-1
1909	119	381	90	18	3	0	0.0	39	22	38		14	.236	.299	1	0	2B-118, OF-3, SS-1
4 yrs.	208	604	132	21	3	0	0.0	64	49	69		23	.219	.263	19	4	2B-167, SS-19, OF-3, 3B-3

	G	AB	H	2B	3B	HR	HR %	R	RBI	BB	SO	SB	BA	SA	Pinch Hit AB	H	G by POS

Harvey Aubrey

AUBREY, HARVEY HERBERT
B. July 5, 1880, St. Joseph, Mo. D. Sept. 18, 1953, Baltimore, Md. TR

	G	AB	H	2B	3B	HR	HR %	R	RBI	BB	SO	SB	BA	SA	PH AB	PH H	G by POS
1903 BOS N	96	325	69	8	2	0	0.0	26	27	18		7	.212	.249	0	0	SS-94, OF-1, 2B-1

Rick Auerbach

AUERBACH, FREDERICK STEVEN
B. Feb. 15, 1950, Glendale, Calif. BR TR 6' 165 lbs.

	G	AB	H	2B	3B	HR	HR %	R	RBI	BB	SO	SB	BA	SA	PH AB	PH H	G by POS
1971 MIL A	79	236	48	10	0	1	0.4	22	9	20	40	3	.203	.258	0	0	SS-78
1972	153	554	121	16	3	2	0.4	50	30	43	62	24	.218	.269	1	0	SS-153
1973	6	10	1	1	0	0	0.0	2	0	0	1	0	.100	.200	1	0	SS-2
1974 LA N	45	73	25	0	0	1	1.4	12	4	8	9	4	.342	.384	4	1	SS-19, 2B-16, 3B-3
1975	85	170	38	9	0	0	0.0	18	12	18	22	3	.224	.276	0	0	SS-81, 3B-1, 1B-1
1976	36	47	6	0	0	0	0.0	7	1	6	6	0	.128	.128	2	0	SS-12, 3B-8, 2B-7
1977 CIN N	33	45	7	2	0	0	0.0	5	3	4	7	0	.156	.200	2	0	2B-19, SS-12
1978	63	55	18	6	0	2	3.6	17	5	7	12	1	.327	.545	13	7	SS-26, 2B-10, 3B-3
1979	62	100	21	8	1	1	1.0	17	12	14	19	0	.210	.340	23	5	3B-18, SS-16, 2B-3
1980	24	33	11	1	1	1	3.0	5	4	3	5	0	.333	.515	17	3	SS-3, 3B-3, 2B-1
1981 SEA A	38	84	13	3	0	1	1.2	12	6	4	15	1	.155	.226	0	0	SS-38
11 yrs.	624	1407	309	56	5	9	0.6	167	86	127	198	36	.220	.286	63	16	SS-440, 2B-56, 3B-36, 1B-1

LEAGUE CHAMPIONSHIP SERIES

	G	AB	H	2B	3B	HR	HR %	R	RBI	BB	SO	SB	BA	SA	PH AB	PH H	G by POS
1974 LA N	1	1	1	1	0	0	0.0	0	0	0	0	0	1.000	2.000	1	1	
1979 CIN N	2	2	0	0	0	0	0.0	0	0	0	1	0	.000	.000	1	0	
2 yrs.	3	3	1	1	0	0	0.0	0	0	0	1	0	.333	.667	2	1	

WORLD SERIES

	G	AB	H	2B	3B	HR	HR %	R	RBI	BB	SO	SB	BA	SA	PH AB	PH H	G by POS
1974 LA N	1	0	0	0	0	0	–	0	0	0	0	0	–	–	0	0	

Dave Augustine

AUGUSTINE, DAVID RALPH
B. Nov. 28, 1949, Follansbee, W. Va. BB TR 6'2" 174 lbs.

	G	AB	H	2B	3B	HR	HR %	R	RBI	BB	SO	SB	BA	SA	PH AB	PH H	G by POS
1973 PIT N	11	7	2	1	0	0	0.0	1	0	0	1	0	.286	.429	0	0	OF-9
1974	18	22	4	0	0	0	0.0	3	0	0	5	0	.182	.182	0	0	OF-11
2 yrs.	29	29	6	1	0	0	0.0	4	0	0	6	0	.207	.241	0	0	OF-20

Doyle Aulds

AULDS, LEYCESTER DOYLE (Tex)
B. Dec. 28, 1920, Farmerville, La. BR TR 6'2" 185 lbs.

	G	AB	H	2B	3B	HR	HR %	R	RBI	BB	SO	SB	BA	SA	PH AB	PH H	G by POS
1947 BOS A	3	4	1	0	0	0	0.0	0	1	0	1	0	.250	.250	0	0	C-3

Doug Ault

AULT, DOUGLAS REAGAN
B. Mar. 9, 1950, Beaumont, Tex. BR TL 6'3" 200 lbs.

	G	AB	H	2B	3B	HR	HR %	R	RBI	BB	SO	SB	BA	SA	PH AB	PH H	G by POS
1976 TEX A	9	20	6	1	0	0	0.0	0	0	1	3	0	.300	.350	3	1	1B-4, DH-3
1977 TOR A	129	445	109	22	3	11	2.5	44	64	39	68	4	.245	.382	8	4	1B-122, DH-4
1978	54	104	25	1	1	3	2.9	10	7	17	14	0	.240	.356	20	5	1B-25, OF-7, DH-5
1980	64	144	28	5	1	3	2.1	12	15	14	23	0	.194	.306	14	5	1B-32, DH-21, OF-1
4 yrs.	256	713	168	29	5	17	2.4	66	86	71	108	4	.236	.362	45	15	1B-183, DH-33, OF-8

Jimmy Austin

AUSTIN, JAMES PHILIP (Pepper)
B. Dec. 8, 1879, Swansea, Wales D. Apr. 6, 1965, Laguna Beach, Calif. BB TR 5'7½" 155 lbs.
Manager 1913, 1918, 1923.

	G	AB	H	2B	3B	HR	HR %	R	RBI	BB	SO	SB	BA	SA	PH AB	PH H	G by POS
1909 NY A	136	437	101	11	5	1	0.2	37	39	32		30	.231	.286	1	1	3B-111, SS-23, 2B-1
1910	133	432	94	11	4	2	0.5	46	36	47		22	.218	.275	0	0	3B-133
1911 STL A	148	541	141	25	11	2	0.4	84	45	69		26	.261	.359	0	0	3B-148
1912	149	536	135	14	8	2	0.4	57	44	38		28	.252	.319	0	0	3B-149
1913	142	489	130	18	6	2	0.4	56	42	45	51	37	.266	.339	0	0	3B-142
1914	130	466	111	16	4	0	0.0	55	30	40	59	20	.238	.290	2	0	3B-127
1915	141	477	127	6	6	1	0.2	61	30	64	60	18	.266	.310	0	0	3B-141
1916	129	411	85	15	6	1	0.2	55	28	74	59	19	.207	.280	3	0	3B-124
1917	127	455	109	18	8	0	0.0	61	19	50	46	13	.240	.314	0	0	3B-121, SS-6
1918	110	367	97	14	4	0	0.0	42	20	53	32	18	.264	.324	4	2	SS-57, 3B-48
1919	106	396	94	9	9	1	0.3	54	21	42	31	8	.237	.313	6	2	3B-98
1920	83	280	76	11	3	1	0.4	38	32	31	15	2	.271	.343	7	1	3B-75
1921	27	66	18	2	1	0	0.0	8	2	4	7	2	.273	.333	2	1	SS-14, 2B-6, 3B-2
1922	15	31	9	3	1	0	0.0	6	1	3	2	0	.290	.452	4	0	3B-11, 2B-2
1923	1	0	0	0	0	0	–	0	0	0	0	0	–	–	0	0	C-1
1925	1	1	0	0	0	0	0.0	0	0	0	0	0	.000	.000	0	0	3B-1
1926	1	2	1	1	0	0	0.0	1	1	0	0	0	.500	1.000	0	0	3B-1
1929	1	1	0	0	0	0	0.0	0	0	0	0	1	.000	.000	0	0	3B-1
18 yrs.	1580	5388	1328	174	76	13	0.2	661	390	592	363	244	.246	.314	29	7	3B-1433, SS-100, 2B-9, C-1

Chick Autry

AUTRY, WILLIAM ASKEW
B. Jan. 2, 1885, Humboldt, Tenn. D. Jan. 16, 1976, Santa Rosa, Calif. BL TL 5'11" 168 lbs.

	G	AB	H	2B	3B	HR	HR %	R	RBI	BB	SO	SB	BA	SA	PH AB	PH H	G by POS
1907 CIN N	7	25	5	0	0	0	0.0	3	0	1		0	.200	.200	0	0	OF-7
1909 2 teams		CIN N (9G – .182)						BOS N (65G – .196)									
" total	74	232	45	6	0	0	0.0	19	17	23		6	.194	.220	0	0	1B-70, OF-4
2 yrs.	81	257	50	6	0	0	0.0	22	17	24		6	.195	.218	0	0	1B-70, OF-11

Martin Autry

AUTRY, MARTIN GORDON (Chick)
B. Mar. 5, 1903, Martindale, Tex. D. Jan. 26, 1950, Savannah, Ga. BR TR 6' 180 lbs.

	G	AB	H	2B	3B	HR	HR %	R	RBI	BB	SO	SB	BA	SA	PH AB	PH H	G by POS
1924 NY A	2	0	0	0	0	0	–	1	0	0	0	0	–	–	0	0	C-2
1926 CLE A	3	7	1	0	0	0	0.0	1	0	1	0	0	.143	.143	0	0	C-3
1927	16	43	11	4	1	0	0.0	5	7	0	6	0	.256	.395	1	0	C-14
1928	22	60	18	6	1	1	1.7	6	11	9	7	0	.300	.483	4	0	C-18
1929 CHI A	43	96	20	6	0	1	1.0	7	12	1	8	0	.208	.302	11	3	C-30
1930	34	71	18	1	1	0	0.0	1	5	4	1	0	.254	.296	5	1	C-29
6 yrs.	120	277	68	17	3	2	0.7	21	25	15	29	0	.245	.350	21	4	C-96

	G	AB	H	2B	3B	HR	HR %	R	RBI	BB	SO	SB	BA	SA	Pinch Hit AB	Pinch Hit H	G by POS

Earl Averill

AVERILL, EARL DOUGLAS
Son of Earl Averill.
B. Sept. 9, 1931, Cleveland, Ohio

BR TR 5'10" 185 lbs.

	G	AB	H	2B	3B	HR	HR %	R	RBI	BB	SO	SB	BA	SA	PH AB	PH H	G by POS
1956 CLE A	42	93	22	6	0	3	3.2	12	14	14	25	0	.237	.398	8	2	C-34
1958	17	55	10	1	0	2	3.6	2	7	4	7	1	.182	.309	0	0	3B-17
1959 CHI N	74	186	44	10	0	10	5.4	22	34	15	39	0	.237	.452	25	10	C-32, 3B-13, OF-5, 2B-2
1960 2 teams	CHI	N (52G –	.235)		CHI	A	(10G –	.214)									
" total	62	116	27	4	0	1	0.9	16	15	15	18	1	.233	.293	30	6	C-39, OF-1, 3B-1
1961 LA N	115	323	86	9	0	21	6.5	56	59	62	70	1	.266	.489	21	7	C-88, OF-9, 2B-1
1962	92	187	41	9	0	4	2.1	21	22	43	47	0	.219	.332	34	7	OF-49, C-6
1963 PHI N	47	71	19	2	0	3	4.2	8	8	9	14	0	.268	.423	24	4	C-20, OF-8, 3B-1, 1B-1
7 yrs.	449	1031	249	41	0	44	4.3	137	159	162	220	3	.242	.409	142	36	C-219, OF-72, 3B-32, 2B-3, 1B-1

Earl Averill

AVERILL, HOWARD EARL
Father of Earl Averill.
B. May 21, 1902, Snohomish, Wash.   D. Aug. 16, 1983, Everett, Wash.
Hall of Fame 1975.

BL TR 5'9½" 172 lbs.

	G	AB	H	2B	3B	HR	HR %	R	RBI	BB	SO	SB	BA	SA	PH AB	PH H	G by POS
1929 CLE A	152	602	199	43	13	18	3.0	110	97	64	53	13	.331	.535	0	0	OF-152
1930	139	534	181	33	8	19	3.6	102	119	56	48	10	.339	.537	5	2	OF-134
1931	155	627	209	36	10	32	5.1	140	143	68	38	9	.333	.576	0	0	OF-153
1932	153	631	198	37	14	32	5.1	116	124	75	40	5	.314	.569	0	0	OF-149
1933	151	599	180	39	16	11	1.8	83	92	54	29	3	.301	.474	2	1	OF-149
1934	154	598	187	48	6	31	5.2	128	113	99	44	4	.313	.569	0	0	OF-154
1935	140	563	162	34	13	19	3.4	109	79	70	58	8	.288	.496	1	0	OF-139
1936	152	614	232	39	15	28	4.6	136	126	65	35	3	.378	.627	2	1	OF-150
1937	156	609	182	33	11	21	3.4	121	92	88	65	5	.299	.493	0	0	OF-156
1938	134	482	159	27	15	14	2.9	101	93	81	48	5	.330	.535	3	0	OF-131
1939 2 teams	CLE	A (24G –	.273)		DET	A	(87G –	.262)									
" total	111	364	96	28	6	11	3.0	66	65	49	42	4	.264	.464	19	6	OF-91
1940 DET A	64	118	33	4	1	2	1.7	10	20	5	14	0	.280	.381	38	12	OF-22
1941 BOS N	8	17	2	0	0	0	0.0	2	2	1	4	0	.118	.118	3	0	OF-4
13 yrs.	1669	6358	2020	401	128	238	3.7	1224	1165	775	518	69	.318	.533	73	22	OF-1590

WORLD SERIES

	G	AB	H	2B	3B	HR	HR %	R	RBI	BB	SO	SB	BA	SA	PH AB	PH H	G by POS
1940 DET A	3	3	0	0	0	0	0.0	0	0	0	0	0	.000	.000	3	0	

Bobby Avila

AVILA, ROBERTO GONZALEZ (Beto)
B. Apr. 2, 1924, Vera Cruz, Mexico

BR TR 5'10" 175 lbs.

	G	AB	H	2B	3B	HR	HR %	R	RBI	BB	SO	SB	BA	SA	PH AB	PH H	G by POS
1949 CLE A	31	14	3	0	0	0	0.0	3	3	1	3	0	.214	.214	9	2	2B-5
1950	80	201	60	10	2	1	0.5	39	21	29	17	5	.299	.383	6	2	2B-62, SS-2
1951	141	542	165	21	3	10	1.8	76	58	60	31	14	.304	.410	4	1	2B-136
1952	150	597	179	26	11	7	1.2	102	45	67	36	12	.300	.415	1	0	2B-149
1953	141	559	160	22	3	8	1.4	85	55	58	27	10	.286	.379	2	0	2B-140
1954	143	555	189	27	2	15	2.7	112	67	59	31	9	.341	.477	1	0	2B-141, SS-7
1955	141	537	146	22	4	13	2.4	83	61	82	47	1	.272	.400	1	1	2B-141
1956	138	513	115	14	2	10	1.9	74	54	70	68	17	.224	.318	5	1	2B-135
1957	129	463	124	19	3	5	1.1	60	48	46	47	2	.268	.354	8	1	2B-107, 3B-16
1958	113	375	95	21	3	5	1.3	54	30	56	45	5	.253	.365	15	5	2B-82, 3B-33
1959 3 teams	BAL	A (20G –	.170)		BOS	N	(22G –	.244)		MIL	N	(51G –	.238)				
" total	93	264	60	3	2	6	2.3	37	23	34	47	3	.227	.322	14	2	2B-70, OF-10, 3B-1
11 yrs.	1300	4620	1296	185	35	80	1.7	725	465	562	399	78	.281	.388	66	15	2B-1168, 3B-50, OF-10, SS-9

WORLD SERIES

	G	AB	H	2B	3B	HR	HR %	R	RBI	BB	SO	SB	BA	SA	PH AB	PH H	G by POS
1954 CLE A	4	15	2	0	0	0	0.0	1	0	2	1	0	.133	.133	0	0	2B-4

Ramon Aviles

AVILES, RAMON ANTONIO
Also known as Ramon Antonio Miranda.
B. Jan. 22, 1952, Manati, Puerto Rico

BR TR 5'9" 155 lbs.

	G	AB	H	2B	3B	HR	HR %	R	RBI	BB	SO	SB	BA	SA	PH AB	PH H	G by POS
1977 BOS A	1	0	0	0	0	0	–	0	0	0	0	0	–	–	0	0	2B-1
1979 PHI N	27	61	17	2	0	0	0.0	7	12	8	8	0	.279	.311	3	1	2B-27
1980	51	101	28	6	0	2	2.0	12	9	10	9	0	.277	.396	6	2	SS-29, 2B-15
1981	38	28	6	1	0	0	0.0	2	3	3	5	0	.214	.250	4	0	2B-20, 3B-13, SS-5
4 yrs.	117	190	51	9	0	2	1.1	21	24	21	22	0	.268	.347	13	3	2B-63, SS-34, 3B-13

DIVISIONAL PLAYOFF SERIES

	G	AB	H	2B	3B	HR	HR %	R	RBI	BB	SO	SB	BA	SA	PH AB	PH H	G by POS
1981 PHI N	1	1	0	0	0	0	0.0	0	0	1	0	0	–	–	0	0	

LEAGUE CHAMPIONSHIP SERIES

	G	AB	H	2B	3B	HR	HR %	R	RBI	BB	SO	SB	BA	SA	PH AB	PH H	G by POS
1980 PHI N	1	1	0	0	0	0	–	1	0	0	0	0	–	–	0	0	

Benny Ayala

AYALA, BENIGNO FELIX
B. Feb. 7, 1951, Yavco, Puerto Rico

BR TR 6'1" 185 lbs.

	G	AB	H	2B	3B	HR	HR %	R	RBI	BB	SO	SB	BA	SA	PH AB	PH H	G by POS
1974 NY N	23	68	16	1	0	2	2.9	9	8	7	17	0	.235	.338	4	0	OF-20
1976	22	26	3	0	0	1	3.8	2	2	2	6	0	.115	.231	15	2	OF-7
1977 STL N	1	3	1	0	0	0	0.0	0	0	0	1	0	.333	.333	0	0	OF-1
1979 BAL A	42	86	22	5	0	6	7.0	15	13	6	9	0	.256	.523	13	3	OF-24, DH-10
1980	76	170	45	8	1	10	5.9	28	33	19	21	0	.265	.500	28	5	DH-41, OF-19
1981	44	86	24	2	0	3	3.5	12	13	11	9	0	.279	.407	16	5	DH-27, OF-4
1982	64	128	39	6	0	6	4.7	17	24	5	14	1	.305	.492	14	9	OF-25, DH-17, 1B-3
1983	47	104	23	7	0	4	3.8	12	13	9	18	0	.221	.404	14	4	OF-24, DH-11
1984	60	118	25	6	0	4	3.4	9	24	8	24	1	.212	.364	29	9	DH-34, OF-13
9 yrs.	379	789	198	35	1	36	4.6	104	130	67	119	2	.251	.435	143	37	DH-140, OF-137, 1B-3

LEAGUE CHAMPIONSHIP SERIES

	G	AB	H	2B	3B	HR	HR %	R	RBI	BB	SO	SB	BA	SA	PH AB	PH H	G by POS
1983 BAL A	1	1	0	0	0	0	–	0	1	0	0	0	–	–	0	0	DH-1

WORLD SERIES

	G	AB	H	2B	3B	HR	HR %	R	RBI	BB	SO	SB	BA	SA	PH AB	PH H	G by POS
1979 BAL A	4	6	2	0	0	1	16.7	1	2	1	0	0	.333	.833	0	0	OF-3
1983	1	1	1	0	0	0	0.0	1	1	0	0	0	1.000	1.000	1	1	
2 yrs.	5	7	3	0	0	1	14.3	2	3	1	0	0	.429	.857	1	1	OF-3

	G	AB	H	2B	3B	HR	HR %	R	RBI	BB	SO	SB	BA	SA	Pinch Hit AB	Pinch Hit H	G by POS

Dick Aylward

AYLWARD, RICHARD JOHN   BR TR 6'   190 lbs.
B. June 4, 1925, Baltimore, Md.   D. June 11, 1983, Spring Valley, Calif.

	G	AB	H	2B	3B	HR	HR%	R	RBI	BB	SO	SB	BA	SA	PH AB	PH H	G by POS
1953 CLE A	4	3	0	0	0	0	0.0	0	0	0	1	0	.000	.000	0	0	C-4

Joe Azcue

AZCUE, JOSE JOAQUIN (The Immortal Azcue)   BR TR 6'   190 lbs.
B. Aug. 18, 1939, Cienfuegos, Cuba

	G	AB	H	2B	3B	HR	HR%	R	RBI	BB	SO	SB	BA	SA	PH AB	PH H	G by POS
1960 CIN N	14	31	3	0	0	0	0.0	1	3	2	6	0	.097	.097	2	0	C-14
1962 KC A	72	223	51	9	1	2	0.9	18	25	17	27	1	.229	.305	2	2	C-70
1963 2 teams	KC	A (2G – .000)			CLE	A	(94G – .284)										
" total	96	324	91	16	0	14	4.3	26	46	15	47	1	.281	.460	8	2	C-92
1964 CLE A	83	271	74	9	1	4	1.5	20	34	16	38	0	.273	.358	7	1	C-76
1965	111	335	77	7	0	2	0.6	16	35	27	54	2	.230	.269	10	3	C-108
1966	98	302	83	10	1	9	3.0	22	37	20	22	0	.275	.404	3	1	C-97
1967	86	295	74	12	5	11	3.7	33	34	22	35	0	.251	.437	2	1	C-86
1968	115	357	100	10	0	4	1.1	23	42	28	33	1	.280	.342	17	4	C-97
1969 3 teams	CLE	A (7G – .292)		BOS	A	(19G – .216)		CAL	A	(80G – .218)						
" total	106	323	72	8	0	2	0.6	23	23	35	36	0	.223	.266	4	0	C-80
1970 CAL A	114	351	85	13	1	2	0.6	19	25	24	40	0	.242	.302	4	1	C-112
1972 2 teams	CAL	A (3G – .000)		MIL	A	(11G – .143)										
" total	14	16	2	0	0	0	0.0	0	0	1	6	0	.125	.125	3	1	C-11
11 yrs.	909	2828	712	94	9	50	1.8	201	304	207	344	5	.252	.344	62	16	C-843

Charlie Babb

BABB, CHARLES AMOS   BB TR 5'10½" 165 lbs.
B. Feb. 20, 1873, Milwaukie, Ore.   D. Mar. 20, 1954, Portland, Ore.

	G	AB	H	2B	3B	HR	HR%	R	RBI	BB	SO	SB	BA	SA	PH AB	PH H	G by POS
1903 NY N	121	424	105	15	8	0	0.0	68	46	45		22	.248	.321	0	0	SS-113, 3B-8
1904 BKN N	151	521	138	18	3	0	0.0	49	53	53		34	.265	.311	0	0	SS-151
1905	75	235	44	8	2	0	0.0	27	17	27		10	.187	.238	1	0	SS-36, 1B-31, 3B-5, 2B-2
3 yrs.	347	1180	287	41	13	0	0.0	144	116	125		66	.243	.300	1	0	SS-300, 1B-31, 3B-13, 2B-2

Loren Babe

BABE, LOREN ROLLAND (Bee Bee)   BL TR 5'10" 180 lbs.
B. Jan. 11, 1928, Pisgah, Iowa   D. Feb. 14, 1984, Omaha, Neb.

	G	AB	H	2B	3B	HR	HR%	R	RBI	BB	SO	SB	BA	SA	PH AB	PH H	G by POS
1952 NY A	12	21	2	1	0	0	0.0	1	0	4	4	1	.095	.143	2	0	3B-9
1953 2 teams	NY	A (5G – .333)		PHI	A	(103G – .224)										
" total	108	361	83	17	2	2	0.6	36	26	35	22	0	.230	.305	12	3	3B-98, SS-1
2 yrs.	120	382	85	18	2	2	0.5	37	26	39	26	1	.223	.296	14	3	3B-107, SS-1

Charlie Babington

BABINGTON, CHARLES PERCY   BR TR 6'   170 lbs.
B. May 4, 1895, Cranston, R. I.   D. Mar. 22, 1957, Providence, R. I.

	G	AB	H	2B	3B	HR	HR%	R	RBI	BB	SO	SB	BA	SA	PH AB	PH H	G by POS
1915 NY N	28	33	8	3	1	0	0.0	5	2	0	4	1	.242	.394	10	2	OF-12, 1B-1

Shooty Babitt

BABITT, MACK NEAL II   BR TR 5'8" 174 lbs.
B. Mar. 9, 1959, Oakland, Calif.

	G	AB	H	2B	3B	HR	HR%	R	RBI	BB	SO	SB	BA	SA	PH AB	PH H	G by POS
1981 OAK A	54	156	40	1	3	0	0.0	10	14	13	13	5	.256	.301	2	0	2B-52

Wally Backman

BACKMAN, WALTER WAYNE   BB TR 5'9" 160 lbs.
B. Sept. 22, 1959, Hillsboro, Ore.

	G	AB	H	2B	3B	HR	HR%	R	RBI	BB	SO	SB	BA	SA	PH AB	PH H	G by POS
1980 NY N	27	93	30	1	1	0	0.0	12	9	11	14	2	.323	.355	0	0	2B-20, SS-8
1981	26	36	10	2	0	0	0.0	5	0	4	7	1	.278	.333	15	3	2B-11, 3B-1
1982	96	261	71	13	2	3	1.1	37	22	49	47	8	.272	.372	5	0	2B-88, 3B-6, SS-1
1983	26	42	7	0	1	0	0.0	6	3	2	8	0	.167	.214	16	3	2B-14, 3B-2
1984	128	436	122	19	2	1	0.2	68	26	56	63	32	.280	.339	11	3	2B-115, SS-7
5 yrs.	303	868	240	35	6	4	0.5	128	60	122	139	43	.276	.344	47	9	2B-248, SS-16, 3B-9

Eddie Bacon

BACON, EDGAR SUTER   BR TR 5'10" 170 lbs.
B. Apr. 8, 1895, Frankfort, Ky.   D. Oct. 2, 1963, Frankfort, Ky.

	G	AB	H	2B	3B	HR	HR%	R	RBI	BB	SO	SB	BA	SA	PH AB	PH H	G by POS
1917 PHI A	4	6	3	1	0	0	0.0	1	2	0	0	0	.500	.667	3	1	P-1

Art Bader

BADER, ARTHUR HERMAN   BR TR 5'10" 170 lbs.
B. Sept. 21, 1886, St. Louis, Mo.   D. Apr. 5, 1957, St. Louis, Mo.

	G	AB	H	2B	3B	HR	HR%	R	RBI	BB	SO	SB	BA	SA	PH AB	PH H	G by POS
1904 STL A	2	3	0	0	0	0	0.0	0	0	1		0	.000	.000	1	0	OF-1

Red Badgro

BADGRO, MORRIS HIRAM   BL TR 6'   190 lbs.
B. Dec. 1, 1902, Orilla, Wash.

	G	AB	H	2B	3B	HR	HR%	R	RBI	BB	SO	SB	BA	SA	PH AB	PH H	G by POS
1929 STL A	54	148	42	12	0	1	0.7	27	18	11	15	1	.284	.385	15	4	OF-37
1930	89	234	56	18	3	1	0.4	30	27	13	27	3	.239	.355	24	9	OF-61
2 yrs.	143	382	98	30	3	2	0.5	57	45	24	42	4	.257	.366	39	13	OF-98

Jose Baez

BAEZ, JOSE ANTONIO   BR TR 5'8" 160 lbs.
B. Dec. 31, 1953, San Cristobal, Dominican Republic

	G	AB	H	2B	3B	HR	HR%	R	RBI	BB	SO	SB	BA	SA	PH AB	PH H	G by POS
1977 SEA A	91	305	79	14	1	1	0.3	39	17	19	20	6	.259	.321	7	1	2B-77, DH-3, 3B-1
1978	23	50	8	0	1	0	0.0	8	2	6	7	1	.160	.200	3	0	2B-14, 3B-3, DH-1
2 yrs.	114	355	87	14	2	1	0.3	47	19	25	27	7	.245	.304	10	1	2B-91, DH-4, 3B-4

Gene Bagley

BAGLEY, EUGENE T.
B. June, 1861, Brooklyn, N. Y.   Deceased.

	G	AB	H	2B	3B	HR	HR%	R	RBI	BB	SO	SB	BA	SA	PH AB	PH H	G by POS
1886 NY N	5	16	2	0	0	0	0.0	1	1	1	3		.125	.125	0	0	C-3, OF-2

Bill Bagwell

BAGWELL, WILLIAM MALLORY (Big Bill)   BL TL 6'1" 175 lbs.
B. Feb. 24, 1896, Choudrant, La.   D. Oct. 5, 1976, Choudrant, La.

	G	AB	H	2B	3B	HR	HR%	R	RBI	BB	SO	SB	BA	SA	PH AB	PH H	G by POS
1923 BOS A	56	93	27	4	2	2	2.2	8	10	6	12	0	.290	.441	32	6	OF-22
1925 PHI A	36	50	15	2	1	0	0.0	4	10	2	2	0	.300	.380	31	7	OF-4
2 yrs.	92	143	42	6	3	2	1.4	12	20	8	14	0	.294	.420	63	13	OF-26

	G	AB	H	2B	3B	HR	HR %	R	RBI	BB	SO	SB	BA	SA	Pinch Hit AB	Pinch Hit H	G by POS

Frank Bahret

BAHRET, FRANK J.
Deceased.

1884 2 teams	BAL	U	(2G –	.000)	IND	AA	(5G –	.077)									
" total	7	21	1	1	0	0	0.0	1	1		1		.048	.095	0	0	C-4, OF-3

Bill Bailey

BAILEY, HARRY LEWIS
B. Nov. 19, 1881, Shawnee, Ohio   D. Oct. 27, 1967, Seattle, Wash.

1911 NY A	5	9	1	0	0	0	0.0	1	0	0		0	.111	.111	2	0	OF-2, 3B-1

Bob Bailey

BR TR 6'1"   180 lbs.

BAILEY, ROBERT SHERWOOD
B. Oct. 13, 1942, Long Beach, Calif.

1962 PIT N	14	42	7	2	1	0	0.0	6	6	6	10	1	.167	.262	2	0	3B-12
1963	154	570	130	15	3	12	2.1	60	45	58	98	10	.228	.328	1	1	3B-153, SS-3
1964	143	530	149	26	3	11	2.1	73	51	44	78	10	.281	.404	13	3	3B-105, OF-35, SS-2
1965	159	626	160	28	3	11	1.8	87	49	70	93	10	.256	.363	2	0	3B-142, OF-28
1966	126	380	106	19	3	13	3.4	51	46	47	65	5	.279	.447	11	4	OF-96, OF-22
1967 LA N	116	322	73	8	2	4	1.2	21	28	40	50	1	.227	.301	19	3	3B-65, OF-27, 1B-4, SS-1
1968	105	322	73	9	3	8	2.5	24	39	38	69	1	.227	.348	16	2	3B-90, OF-1, SS-1
1969 MON N	111	358	95	16	6	9	2.5	46	53	40	76	3	.265	.419	15	4	1B-85, OF-12, 3B-1
1970	131	352	101	19	3	28	8.0	77	84	72	70	5	.287	.597	36	12	3B-48, OF-44, 1B-18
1971	157	545	137	21	4	14	2.6	65	83	97	105	13	.251	.382	0	0	3B-120, OF-51, 1B-9
1972	143	489	114	10	4	16	3.3	55	57	59	112	6	.233	.368	7	3	3B-134, OF-5, 1B-3
1973	151	513	140	25	4	26	5.1	77	86	88	99	5	.273	.489	5	0	3B-146, OF-2
1974	152	507	142	20	2	20	3.9	69	73	100	107	4	.280	.446	8	2	OF-78, 3B-68
1975	106	227	62	5	0	5	2.2	23	30	46	38	4	.273	.361	40	11	OF-61, 3B-3
1976 CIN N	69	124	37	6	1	6	4.8	17	23	16	26	0	.298	.508	27	10	OF-31, 3B-10
1977 2 teams	CIN	N	(49G –	.253)	BOS	A	(2G –	.000)								
" total	51	81	20	2	1	2	2.5	9	11	12	11	1	.247	.370	27	6	1B-19, OF-3
1978 BOS A	43	94	18	3	0	4	4.3	12	9	19	19	2	.191	.351	13	1	DH-34, OF-1, 3B-1
17 yrs.	1931	6082	1564	234	43	189	3.1	772	773	852	1126	85	.257	.403	242	62	3B-1194, OF-401, 1B-138, DH-34, SS-7

Ed Bailey

BL TR 6'2"   205 lbs.

BAILEY, LONAS EDGAR
Brother of Jim Bailey.
B. Apr. 15, 1931, Strawberry Plains, Tenn.

1953 CIN N	2	8	3	1	0	0	0.0	1	1	1	3	0	.375	.500	0	0	C-2
1954	73	183	36	2	3	9	4.9	21	20	35	34	1	.197	.388	12	0	C-61
1955	21	39	8	1	1	1	2.6	3	4	4	10	0	.205	.359	9	3	C-106
1956	118	383	115	8	2	28	7.3	59	75	52	50	2	.300	.551	13	8	C-115
1957	122	391	102	15	2	20	5.1	54	48	73	69	5	.261	.463	6	2	C-115
1958	112	360	90	23	1	11	3.1	39	59	47	61	2	.250	.411	11	1	C-99
1959	121	379	100	13	0	12	3.2	43	40	62	53	2	.264	.393	8	2	C-117
1960	133	441	115	19	3	13	2.9	52	67	59	70	1	.261	.406	9	2	C-129
1961 2 teams	CIN	N	(12G –	.302)	SF	N	(107G –	.238)								
" total	119	383	94	13	1	13	3.4	43	53	45	46	1	.245	.386	9	5	C-115, OF-1
1962 SF N	96	254	59	9	1	17	6.7	32	45	42	42	0	.232	.476	18	6	C-75
1963	105	308	81	8	0	21	6.8	41	68	50	64	0	.263	.494	16	3	C-88
1964 MIL N	95	271	71	10	1	5	1.8	30	34	34	39	2	.262	.362	14	3	C-80
1965 2 teams	SF	N	(24G –	.107)	CHI	N	(66G –	.253)								
" total	90	178	41	6	0	5	2.8	14	26	40	35	0	.230	.348	22	2	C-66, 1B-5
1966 CAL A	5	3	0	0	0	0	0.0	0	0	1	1	0	.000	.000	3	0	
14 yrs.	1212	3581	915	128	15	155	4.3	432	540	545	577	17	.256	.429	150	37	C-1064, 1B-5, OF-1
WORLD SERIES																	
1962 SF N	6	14	1	0	0	1	7.1	1	2	0	3	0	.071	.286	2	0	C-3

Fred Bailey

BL TL 5'11"   150 lbs.

BAILEY, FRED MIDDLETON (Penny)
B. Aug. 16, 1895, Mt. Hope, W. Va.   D. Aug. 16, 1972, Huntington, W. Va.

1916 BOS N	6	10	1	0	0	0	0.0	0	1	0	3	0	.100	.100	5	1	OF-2
1917	50	110	21	2	1	1	0.9	9	5	9	25	3	.191	.255	18	4	OF-31
1918	4	4	1	0	0	0	0.0	1	0	0	1	0	.250	.250	4	1	
3 yrs.	60	124	23	2	1	1	0.8	10	6	9	29	3	.185	.242	27	6	OF-33

Gene Bailey

BR TR 5'8"   160 lbs.

BAILEY, ARTHUR EUGENE
B. Nov. 25, 1893, Pearsall, Tex.   D. Nov. 14, 1973, Houston, Tex.

1917 PHI A	5	12	1	0	0	0	0.0	1	0	1	0	0	.083	.083	0	0	OF-4
1919 BOS N	4	6	2	0	0	0	0.0	1	0	0	2	1	.333	.333	1	1	OF-3
1920 2 teams	BOS	N	(13G –	.083)	BOS	A	(46G –	.230)								
" total	59	159	33	2	0	0	0.0	16	5	12	18	2	.208	.220	3	0	OF-48
1923 BKN N	127	411	109	11	7	1	0.2	71	42	43	34	9	.265	.333	12	3	OF-100, 1B-5
1924	18	46	11	3	0	1	2.2	7	4	7	6	1	.239	.370	0	0	OF-17
5 yrs.	213	634	156	16	7	2	0.3	95	52	63	61	13	.246	.303	16	4	OF-172, 1B-5

Mark Bailey

BR TR 6'4"   185 lbs.

BAILEY, JOHN MARK
B. Apr. 21, 1963, Escondido, Calif.

1984 HOU N	108	344	73	16	1	9	2.6	38	34	53	71	0	.212	.343	0	0	C-108

Bob Bailor

BR TR 5'11"   170 lbs.

BAILOR, ROBERT MICHAEL
B. July 10, 1951, Connellsville, Pa.

1975 BAL A	5	7	1	0	0	0	0.0	1	0	1	0	0	.143	.143	0	0	SS-2, 2B-1
1976	9	6	2	0	1	0	0.0	2	0	0	0	0	.333	.667	1	0	DH-1, SS-1
1977 TOR A	122	496	154	21	5	5	1.0	62	32	17	26	15	.310	.403	3	2	OF-63, SS-53, DH-7
1978	154	621	164	29	5	1	0.2	74	52	38	21	5	.264	.338	3	1	OF-125, 3B-28, SS-4
1979	130	414	95	11	5	1	0.2	50	38	36	27	14	.229	.287	4	1	OF-118, 2B-9, DH-1
1980	117	347	82	14	2	1	0.3	44	16	36	33	12	.236	.297	1	0	OF-98, SS-12, 3B-11, P-3, DH-1, 2B-1
1981 NY N	51	81	23	3	1	0	0.0	11	8	8	11	2	.284	.346	3	0	SS-22, OF-13, 2B-13, 3B-1

	G	AB	H	2B	3B	HR	HR %	R	RBI	BB	SO	SB	BA	SA	Pinch Hit AB	Pinch Hit H	G by POS

Bob Bailor continued

	G	AB	H	2B	3B	HR	HR%	R	RBI	BB	SO	SB	BA	SA	AB	H	G by POS
1982	110	376	104	14	1	0	0.0	44	31	20	17	20	.277	.319	13	6	SS-60, 2B-56, 3B-21, OF-4
1983	118	340	85	8	0	1	0.3	33	30	20	23	18	.250	.282	9	1	SS-75, 2B-50, 3B-11, OF-3
1984 LA N	65	131	36	4	0	0	0.0	11	8	8	1	3	.275	.305	7	2	2B-23, 3B-17, SS-16
10 yrs.	881	2819	746	104	22	9	0.3	331	215	184	159	89	.265	.327	44	14	OF-424, SS-245, 2B-153, 3B-89, DH-10, P-3

Harold Baines

BAINES, HAROLD DOUGLASS
B. Mar. 15, 1959, St. Michaels, Md.

BL TL 6'2"   175 lbs.

	G	AB	H	2B	3B	HR	HR%	R	RBI	BB	SO	SB	BA	SA	AB	H	G by POS
1980 CHI A	141	491	125	23	6	13	2.6	55	49	19	65	2	.255	.405	9	1	OF-137, DH-1
1981	82	280	80	11	7	10	3.6	42	41	12	41	6	.286	.482	5	1	OF-80, DH-1
1982	161	608	165	29	8	25	4.1	89	105	49	95	10	.271	.469	1	0	OF-161
1983	156	596	167	33	2	20	3.4	76	99	49	85	7	.280	.443	1	1	OF-155
1984	147	569	173	28	10	29	5.1	72	94	54	75	1	.304	.541	1	0	OF-147
5 yrs.	687	2544	710	124	33	97	3.8	334	388	183	361	26	.279	.468	17	3	OF-680, DH-2
LEAGUE CHAMPIONSHIP SERIES																	
1983 CHI A	4	16	2	0	0	0	0.0	0	0	1	3	0	.125	.125	0	0	OF-4

Al Baird

BAIRD, ALBERT WELLS
B. June 2, 1895, Cleburne, Tex.   D. Nov. 27, 1976, Shreveport, La.

BR TR 5'9"   160 lbs.

	G	AB	H	2B	3B	HR	HR%	R	RBI	BB	SO	SB	BA	SA	AB	H	G by POS
1917 NY N	10	24	7	0	0	0	0.0	1	4	2	2	2	.292	.292	0	0	2B-7, SS-3
1919	38	83	20	1	0	0	0.0	8	5	5	9	3	.241	.253	0	0	2B-24, SS-9, 3B-5
2 yrs.	48	107	27	1	0	0	0.0	9	9	7	11	5	.252	.262	0	0	2B-31, SS-12, 3B-5

Doug Baird

BAIRD, HOWARD DOUGLASS
B. Sept. 27, 1891, St. Charles, Mo.   D. June 13, 1967, Thomasville, Ga.

BR TR 5'9½" 148 lbs.

	G	AB	H	2B	3B	HR	HR%	R	RBI	BB	SO	SB	BA	SA	AB	H	G by POS
1915 PIT N	145	512	112	26	12	1	0.2	49	53	37	88	29	.219	.322	2	0	3B-131, OF-20, 2B-3
1916	128	430	93	10	7	1	0.2	41	28	24	49	20	.216	.279	3	0	3B-80, 2B-29, OF-16
1917 2 teams	147	PIT N (43G – .259)			STL	N	(104G – .253)										
" total	147	499	127	25	13	0	0.0	55	42	43	71	26	.255	.357	0	0	3B-144, OF-2, 2B-2
1918 STL N	82	316	78	12	8	2	0.6	41	25	42	25	22	.247	.354	0	0	3B-81, OF-1, SS-1
1919 3 teams	102	PHI N (66G – .252)			STL	N	(16G – .212)			BKN	N	(20G – .183)					
" total	102	335	79	13	5	2	0.6	43	42	25	41	18	.236	.322	5	1	3B-91, OF-1, 2B-1
1920 2 teams	13	BKN N (6G – .333)			NY	N	(7G – .125)										
" total	13	14	3	0	0	0	0.0	1	1	3	4	0	.214	.214	3	1	3B-6
6 yrs.	617	2106	492	86	45	6	0.3	230	191	157	295	118	.234	.326	13	2	3B-533, OF-40, 2B-35, SS-1

Bill Baker

BAKER, WILLIAM PRESLEY
B. Feb. 22, 1911, Paw Creek, N. C.

BR TR 6'   200 lbs.

	G	AB	H	2B	3B	HR	HR%	R	RBI	BB	SO	SB	BA	SA	AB	H	G by POS
1940 CIN N	27	69	15	1	1	0	0.0	5	7	4	8	2	.217	.261	3	0	C-24
1941 2 teams	37	CIN N (2G – .000)			PIT	N	(35G – .224)										
" total	37	68	15	3	0	0	0.0	5	6	12	1	0	.221	.265	3	0	C-34
1942 PIT N	18	17	2	0	0	0	0.0	1	2	1	0	0	.118	.118	7	0	C-11
1943	63	172	47	6	3	1	0.6	12	26	22	6	3	.273	.360	7	1	C-56
1946	53	113	27	4	0	1	0.9	7	8	12	6	0	.239	.301	9	2	C-41, 1B-1
1948 STL N	45	119	35	10	1	0	0.0	13	15	15	7	1	.294	.395	7	2	C-36
1949	20	30	4	1	0	0	0.0	2	4	2	2	0	.133	.167	10	1	C-10
7 yrs.	263	588	145	25	5	2	0.3	45	68	68	30	6	.247	.316	46	7	C-212, 1B-1
WORLD SERIES																	
1940 CIN N	3	4	1	0	0	0	0.0	1	0	0	1	0	.250	.250	1	0	C-3

Charlie Baker

BAKER, CHARLES
B. Hudson, Mass.   Deceased.

	G	AB	H	2B	3B	HR	HR%	R	RBI	BB	SO	SB	BA	SA	AB	H	G by POS
1884 C-P U	15	57	8	2	0	1	1.8	5		0				.140	.228	0	0	OF-11, SS-3, 2B-1

Chuck Baker

BAKER, CHARLES JOSEPH
B. Dec. 6, 1952, Seattle, Wash.

BR TR 5'11"   180 lbs.

	G	AB	H	2B	3B	HR	HR%	R	RBI	BB	SO	SB	BA	SA	AB	H	G by POS
1978 SD N	44	58	12	1	1	0	0.0	8	3	2	15	0	.207	.224	6	1	2B-24, SS-12
1980	9	22	3	1	0	0	0.0	0	0	0	4	0	.136	.182	1	0	SS-8
1981 MIN A	40	66	12	0	3	0	0.0	6	6	1	8	0	.182	.273	5	2	SS-31, 2B-3, DH-1, 3B-1
3 yrs.	93	146	27	2	3	0	0.0	14	9	3	27	0	.185	.240	12	3	SS-51, 2B-27, DH-1, 3B-1

Dave Baker

BAKER, DAVID GLEN
B. Nov. 8, 1956, Des Moines, Iowa

BL TR 6'1"   180 lbs.

	G	AB	H	2B	3B	HR	HR%	R	RBI	BB	SO	SB	BA	SA	AB	H	G by POS
1982 TOR A	9	20	5	1	0	0	0.0	3	2	3	3	0	.250	.300	0	0	3B-8

Del Baker

BAKER, DELMAR DAVID
B. May 3, 1892, Sherwood, Ore.   D. Sept. 11, 1973, San Antonio, Tex.
Manager 1933, 1938-42.

BR TR 5'11½" 176 lbs.

	G	AB	H	2B	3B	HR	HR%	R	RBI	BB	SO	SB	BA	SA	AB	H	G by POS
1914 DET A	43	70	15	2	1	0	0.0	4	1	6	9	0	.214	.271	3	0	C-38
1915	68	134	33	3	3	0	0.0	16	15	15	15	3	.246	.313	3	0	C-61
1916	61	98	15	4	0	0	0.0	7	6	11	8	2	.153	.194	1	0	C-59
3 yrs.	172	302	63	9	4	0	0.0	27	22	32	32	5	.209	.265	7	0	C-158

Doug Baker

BAKER, DOUGLAS
B. Apr. 13, 1961, Fullerton, Calif.

BB TR 5'9"   160 lbs.

	G	AB	H	2B	3B	HR	HR%	R	RBI	BB	SO	SB	BA	SA	AB	H	G by POS
1984 DET A	43	108	20	4	1	0	0.0	15	11	7	22	3	.185	.241	1	1	SS-39, 2B-5
LEAGUE CHAMPIONSHIP SERIES																	
1984 DET A	1	0	0	0	0	0	–	0	0	0	0	0	–	–	0	0	SS-1

	G	AB	H	2B	3B	HR	HR %	R	RBI	BB	SO	SB	BA	SA	Pinch Hit AB	Pinch Hit H	G by POS

Dusty Baker

BAKER, JOHNNIE B
B. June 15, 1949, Riverside, Calif.
BR TR 6'2" 183 lbs.

	G	AB	H	2B	3B	HR	HR %	R	RBI	BB	SO	SB	BA	SA	PH AB	PH H	G by POS
1968 ATL N	6	5	2	0	0	0	0.0	0	0	0	1	0	.400	.400	3	1	OF-3
1969	3	7	0	0	0	0	0.0	0	0	0	3	0	.000	.000	0	0	OF-3
1970	13	24	7	0	0	0	0.0	3	4	2	4	0	.292	.292	1	0	OF-11
1971	29	62	14	2	0	0	0.0	2	4	1	14	0	.226	.258	13	2	OF-18
1972	127	446	143	27	2	17	3.8	62	76	45	68	4	.321	.504	4	1	OF-123
1973	159	604	174	29	4	21	3.5	101	99	67	72	24	.288	.454	4	1	OF-156
1974	149	574	147	35	0	20	3.5	80	69	71	87	18	.256	.422	1	0	OF-148
1975	142	494	129	18	2	19	3.8	63	72	67	57	12	.261	.421	6	2	OF-136
1976 LA N	112	384	93	13	0	4	1.0	36	39	31	54	2	.242	.307	8	4	OF-106
1977	153	533	155	26	1	30	5.6	86	86	58	89	2	.291	.512	2	0	OF-152
1978	149	522	137	24	1	11	2.1	62	66	47	66	12	.262	.375	5	0	OF-145
1979	151	554	152	29	1	23	4.2	86	88	56	70	11	.274	.455	2	0	OF-150
1980	153	579	170	26	4	29	5.0	80	97	43	66	12	.294	.503	3	0	OF-151
1981	103	400	128	17	3	9	2.3	48	49	29	43	10	.320	.445	1	1	OF-101
1982	147	570	171	19	1	23	4.0	80	88	56	62	17	.300	.458	4	1	OF-144
1983	149	531	138	25	1	15	2.8	71	73	72	59	7	.260	.395	6	1	OF-143
1984 SF N	100	243	71	7	2	3	1.2	31	32	40	27	4	.292	.374	30	7	OF-62
17 yrs.	1845	6532	1831	297	22	224	3.4	891	942	685	842	135	.280	.435	93	21	OF-1752

DIVISIONAL PLAYOFF SERIES

	G	AB	H	2B	3B	HR	HR %	R	RBI	BB	SO	SB	BA	SA	PH AB	PH H	G by POS
1981 LA N	5	18	3	1	0	0	0.0	2	1	2	0	0	.167	.222	0	0	OF-5

LEAGUE CHAMPIONSHIP SERIES

	G	AB	H	2B	3B	HR	HR %	R	RBI	BB	SO	SB	BA	SA	PH AB	PH H	G by POS
1977 LA N	4	14	5	1	0	2	14.3	4	8	2	3	0	.357	.857	0	0	OF-4
1978	4	15	7	2	0	0	0.0	1	1	3	0	0	.467	.600	0	0	OF-4
1981	5	19	6	1	0	0	0.0	3	3	1	0	0	.316	.368	0	0	OF-5
1983	4	14	5	1	0	1	7.1	4	1	2	0	0	.357	.643	0	0	OF-4
4 yrs.	17	62	23	5	0	3	4.8	12	13	8	3	0	.371	.597	0	0	OF-17

WORLD SERIES

	G	AB	H	2B	3B	HR	HR %	R	RBI	BB	SO	SB	BA	SA	PH AB	PH H	G by POS
1977 LA N	6	24	7	0	0	1	4.2	4	5	0	2	0	.292	.417	0	0	OF-6
1978	6	21	5	0	0	1	4.8	4	1	1	3	0	.238	.381	0	0	OF-6
1981	6	24	4	0	0	0	0.0	3	1	1	6	0	.167	.167	0	0	OF-6
3 yrs.	18	69	16	0	0	2	2.9	9	7	2	11	0	.232	.319	0	0	OF-18

Floyd Baker

BAKER, FLOYD WILSON
B. Oct. 10, 1916, Luray, Va.
BL TR 5'9" 160 lbs.

	G	AB	H	2B	3B	HR	HR %	R	RBI	BB	SO	SB	BA	SA	PH AB	PH H	G by POS
1943 STL A	22	46	8	2	0	0	0.0	5	4	6	4	0	.174	.217	11	2	SS-10, 3B-1
1944	44	97	17	3	0	0	0.0	10	5	11	5	2	.175	.206	11	4	2B-17, SS-16
1945 CHI A	82	208	52	8	0	0	0.0	22	19	23	12	3	.250	.288	16	1	3B-58, 2B-11
1946	9	24	6	1	0	0	0.0	2	3	2	3	0	.250	.292	3	0	3B-6
1947	105	371	98	12	3	0	0.0	61	22	66	28	9	.264	.313	0	0	3B-101, SS-1, 2B-1
1948	104	335	72	8	3	0	0.0	47	18	73	26	4	.215	.257	11	4	3B-71, 2B-18, SS-1
1949	125	388	101	15	4	1	0.3	38	40	84	32	3	.260	.327	0	0	3B-122, SS-3, 2B-1
1950	83	186	59	7	0	0	0.0	26	11	32	10	1	.317	.355	24	9	3B-53, 2B-3, OF-2
1951	82	133	35	6	1	0	0.0	24	14	25	12	0	.263	.323	33	9	3B-44, 2B-5, SS-3
1952 WAS A	79	263	69	8	0	0	0.0	27	33	30	17	1	.262	.293	4	0	2B-68, SS-7, 3B-1
1953 2 teams	WAS A (9G – .000)			BOS A (81G – .273)													
" total	90	179	47	4	2	0	0.0	22	24	25	10	0	.263	.307	31	3	3B-38, SS-1
1954 2 teams	BOS A (21G – .200)			PHI N (23G – .227)													
" total	44	42	9	2	0	0	0.0	1	3	5	5	0	.214	.262	25	7	3B-14, 2B-3
1955 PHI N	5	8	0	0	0	0	0.0	0	0	0	1	0	.000	.000	4	0	3B-1
13 yrs.	874	2280	573	76	13	1	0.0	285	196	382	165	23	.251	.297	173	36	3B-510, 2B-143, SS-41, OF-2

WORLD SERIES

	G	AB	H	2B	3B	HR	HR %	R	RBI	BB	SO	SB	BA	SA	PH AB	PH H	G by POS
1944 STL A	2	2	0	0	0	0	0.0	0	0	0	2	0	.000	.000	2	0	2B-2

Frank Baker

BAKER, FRANK
B. Jan. 11, 1944, Fort Meade, Fla.
BL TR 5'10" 180 lbs.

	G	AB	H	2B	3B	HR	HR %	R	RBI	BB	SO	SB	BA	SA	PH AB	PH H	G by POS
1969 CLE A	52	172	44	5	3	3	1.7	21	15	14	34	2	.256	.372	7	1	OF-46
1971	73	181	38	12	1	1	0.6	18	23	12	34	1	.210	.304	23	3	OF-51
2 yrs.	125	353	82	17	4	4	1.1	39	38	26	68	3	.232	.337	30	4	OF-97

Frank Baker

BAKER, FRANK WATTS
B. Oct. 29, 1946, Meridian, Miss.
BL TR 6'2" 178 lbs.

	G	AB	H	2B	3B	HR	HR %	R	RBI	BB	SO	SB	BA	SA	PH AB	PH H	G by POS
1970 NY A	35	117	27	4	1	0	0.0	6	11	14	26	1	.231	.282	0	0	SS-35
1971	43	79	11	2	0	0	0.0	9	2	16	22	3	.139	.165	1	0	SS-38
1973 BAL A	44	63	12	1	2	1	1.6	10	11	7	7	0	.190	.317	2	1	SS-32, 2B-7, 3B-1, 1B-1
1974	24	29	5	1	0	0	0.0	3	0	3	5	0	.172	.207	0	0	SS-17, 2B-3, 3B-1
4 yrs.	146	288	55	8	3	1	0.3	28	24	40	60	4	.191	.250	3	1	SS-122, 2B-10, 3B-2, 1B-1

LEAGUE CHAMPIONSHIP SERIES

	G	AB	H	2B	3B	HR	HR %	R	RBI	BB	SO	SB	BA	SA	PH AB	PH H	G by POS
1973 BAL A	2	0	0	0	0	0	–	0	0	0	0	0	–	–	0	0	SS-2
1974	2	0	0	0	0	0	–	0	0	0	0	0	–	–	0	0	SS-4
2 yrs.	4	0	0	0	0	0	–	0	0	0	0	0	–	–	0	0	SS-6

Frank Baker

BAKER, JOHN FRANKLIN (Home Run)
B. Mar. 13, 1886, Trappe, Md. D. June 28, 1963, Trappe, Md.
Hall of Fame 1955.
BL TR 5'11" 173 lbs.

	G	AB	H	2B	3B	HR	HR %	R	RBI	BB	SO	SB	BA	SA	PH AB	PH H	G by POS
1908 PHI A	9	31	9	3	0	0	0.0	5	2	0			.290	.387	0	0	3B-9
1909	148	541	165	27	19	4	0.7	73	85	26		20	.305	.447	2	0	3B-146
1910	146	561	159	25	15	2	0.4	83	74	34		21	.283	.392	0	0	3B-146
1911	148	592	198	40	14	11	1.9	96	115	40		38	.334	.505	0	0	3B-148
1912	149	577	200	40	21	10	1.7	116	133	50		40	.347	.541	0	0	3B-149
1913	149	565	190	34	9	12	2.1	116	126	63	31	34	.336	.492	1	0	3B-149
1914	150	570	182	23	10	9	1.6	84	97	53	37	19	.319	.442	3	0	3B-149
1916 NY A	100	360	97	23	2	10	2.8	46	52	36	30	15	.269	.428	0	0	3B-96
1917	146	553	156	24	2	6	1.1	57	71	48	27	18	.282	.365	0	0	3B-146

	G	AB	H	2B	3B	HR	HR %	R	RBI	BB	SO	SB	BA	SA	Pinch Hit AB	Pinch Hit H	G by POS

Frank Baker continued

	G	AB	H	2B	3B	HR	HR%	R	RBI	BB	SO	SB	BA	SA	PH AB	PH H	G by POS
1918	126	504	154	24	5	6	1.2	65	68	38	13	8	.306	.409	0	0	3B-126
1919	141	567	166	22	1	10	1.8	70	83	44	18	13	.293	.388	0	0	3B-141
1921	94	330	97	16	2	9	2.7	46	71	26	12	8	.294	.436	0	0	3B-83
1922	69	234	65	12	3	7	3.0	30	36	15	14	1	.278	.444	9	0	3B-60
13 yrs.	1575	5985	1838	313	103	96	1.6	887	1013	473	182	235	.307	.442	8	1	3B-1548
WORLD SERIES																	
1910 PHI A	5	22	9	3	0	0	0.0	6	4	2	1	0	.409	.545	0	0	3B-5
1911	6	24	9	2	0	2	8.3	7	5	1	5	0	.375	.708	0	0	3B-6
1913	5	20	9	0	0	1	5.0	2	7	0	2	1	.450	.600	0	0	3B-5
1914 NY A	4	16	4	2	0	0	0.0	0	2	1	3	0	.250	.375	0	0	3B-4
1921	4	8	2	0	0	0	0.0	0	0	1	0	0	.250	.250	2	0	3B-2
1922	1	1	0	0	0	0	0.0	0	0	0	0	0	.000	.000	1	0	
6 yrs.	25	91	33	7	0	3	3.3	15	18	5	11	1	.363	.538	3	0	3B-22
				8th									5th				

Gene Baker

BAKER, EUGENE WALTER
B. June 15, 1925, Davenport, Iowa   BR TR 6'1"   170 lbs.

	G	AB	H	2B	3B	HR	HR%	R	RBI	BB	SO	SB	BA	SA	PH AB	PH H	G by POS
1953 CHI N	7	22	5	1	0	0	0.0	1	0	1	4	1	.227	.273	1	0	2B-6
1954	135	541	149	32	5	13	2.4	68	61	47	55	4	.275	.425	0	0	2B-134
1955	154	609	163	29	7	11	1.8	82	52	49	57	9	.268	.392	0	0	2B-154
1956	140	546	141	23	3	12	2.2	65	57	39	54	4	.258	.377	0	0	2B-140
1957 2 teams	123	CHI N (12G – .250)			PIT N (111G – .266)												
" total	123	409	108	22	5	3	0.7	40	46	35	32	3	.264	.364	16	3	3B-72, SS-28, 2B-13
1958 PIT N	29	56	14	2	1	0	0.0	3	7	8	6	0	.250	.321	14	6	3B-11, 2B-3
1960	33	37	9	0	0	0	0.0	5	4	2	9	0	.243	.243	18	4	3B-7, 2B-1
1961	9	10	1	0	0	0	0.0	1	0	3	2	0	.100	.100	3	0	3B-3
8 yrs.	630	2230	590	109	21	39	1.7	265	227	184	219	21	.265	.385	52	13	2B-451, 3B-93, SS-28
WORLD SERIES																	
1960 PIT N	3	3	0	0	0	0	0.0	0	0	0	1	0	.000	.000	3	0	

George Baker

BAKER, GEORGE F.
B. 1859, St. Louis, Mo.   Deceased.

	G	AB	H	2B	3B	HR	HR%	R	RBI	BB	SO	SB	BA	SA	PH AB	PH H	G by POS
1883 BAL AA	7	22	5	0	0	0	0.0	0		0			.227	.227	0	0	SS-4, C-3, OF-1
1884 STL U	80	317	52	6	0	0	0.0	39		5			.164	.183	0	0	C-68, OF-5, 2B-4, 3B-3, SS-2
1885 STL N	38	131	16	0	0	0	0.0	5	5	9	28		.122	.122	0	0	C-32, 3B-3, OF-2, 2B-1
1886 KC N	1	4	1	0	0	0	0.0	1	0	0	1		.250	.250	0	0	C-1
4 yrs.	126	474	74	6	0	0	0.0	45	4	14	29		.156	.169	0	0	C-104, OF-8, SS-6, 3B-6, 2B-5

Howard Baker

BAKER, HOWARD FRANCIS
B. Mar. 1, 1888, Bridgeport, Conn.   D. Jan. 16, 1964, Bridgeport, Conn.   BR TR 5'11"   175 lbs.

	G	AB	H	2B	3B	HR	HR%	R	RBI	BB	SO	SB	BA	SA	PH AB	PH H	G by POS
1912 CLE A	11	30	5	0	0	0	0.0	1	2	5		0	.167	.167	1	0	3B-10
1914 CHI A	15	47	13	1	1	0	0.0	4	5	3	8	2	.277	.340	0	0	3B-15
1915 2 teams	3	CHI A (2G – .000)			NY N (1G – .000)												
" total	3	5	0	0	0	0	0.0	0	0	0	2	0	.000	.000	2	0	3B-1
3 yrs.	29	82	18	1	1	0	0.0	5	7	8	10	2	.220	.256	3	0	3B-26

Jack Baker

BAKER, JACK EDWARD
B. May 4, 1950, Birmingham, Ala.   BR TR 6'5"   225 lbs.

	G	AB	H	2B	3B	HR	HR%	R	RBI	BB	SO	SB	BA	SA	PH AB	PH H	G by POS
1976 BOS A	12	23	3	0	0	1	4.3	1	2	1	5	0	.130	.261	4	0	1B-8, DH-1
1977	2	3	0	0	0	0	0.0	0	0	0	1	0	.000	.000	1	0	1B-1
2 yrs.	14	26	3	0	0	1	3.8	1	2	1	6	0	.115	.231	5	0	1B-9, DH-1

Jesse Baker

BAKER, JESSE EUGENE
B. Feb. 9, 1897, New York   D. July 25, 1960, Pomona, Calif.   BR TR 5'4"   140 lbs.

	G	AB	H	2B	3B	HR	HR%	R	RBI	BB	SO	SB	BA	SA	PH AB	PH H	G by POS
1919 WAS A	1	0	0	0	0	0	–	0	1	0	0	0	–	–	0	0	SS-1

Phil Baker

BAKER, PHILIP
B. Sept. 19, 1856, Philadelphia, Pa.   D. June 4, 1940, Washington, D. C.   BL TL 5'8"   152 lbs.

	G	AB	H	2B	3B	HR	HR%	R	RBI	BB	SO	SB	BA	SA	PH AB	PH H	G by POS
1883 BAL AA	28	121	33	2	1	1	0.8	22		8			.273	.331	0	0	C-19, OF-14, SS-1
1884 WAS U	86	371	107	12	5	1	0.3	75		11			.288	.356	0	0	1B-39, OF-32, C-27
1886 WAS N	81	325	72	6	5	1	0.3	37	34	20	32		.222	.280	0	0	1B-56, OF-21, C-16
3 yrs.	195	817	212	20	11	3	0.4	134	33	39	32		.259	.322	0	0	1B-95, OF-67, C-62, SS-1

Tracy Baker

BAKER, TRACY LEE
B. Nov. 7, 1891, Pendleton, Ore.   D. Mar. 14, 1975, Placerville, Calif.   BR TR 6'1"   180 lbs.

	G	AB	H	2B	3B	HR	HR%	R	RBI	BB	SO	SB	BA	SA	PH AB	PH H	G by POS
1911 BOS A	1	0	0	0	0	0	–	0	0	0		0	–	–	0	0	1B-1

John Balaz

BALAZ, JOHN LAWRENCE
B. Nov. 24, 1950, Toronto, Ontario, Canada   BR TR 6'3"   180 lbs.

	G	AB	H	2B	3B	HR	HR%	R	RBI	BB	SO	SB	BA	SA	PH AB	PH H	G by POS
1974 CAL A	14	42	10	0	0	1	2.4	4	5	2	10	0	.238	.310	1	1	OF-12
1975	45	120	29	8	1	1	0.8	10	10	5	25	0	.242	.350	7	2	OF-27, DH-11
2 yrs.	59	162	39	8	1	2	1.2	14	15	7	35	0	.241	.340	8	3	OF-39, DH-11

Steve Balboni

BALBONI, STEPHEN CHARLES (Bye-Bye)
B. Jan. 16, 1957, Brockton, Mass.   BR TR 6'3"   225 lbs.

	G	AB	H	2B	3B	HR	HR%	R	RBI	BB	SO	SB	BA	SA	PH AB	PH H	G by POS
1981 NY A	4	7	2	1	1	0	0.0	2	2	1	4	0	.286	.714	1	0	1B-3, DH-1
1982	33	107	20	2	1	2	1.9	8	4	6	34	0	.187	.280	5	1	1B-26, DH-5
1983	32	86	20	2	0	5	5.8	8	17	8	23	0	.233	.430	3	1	1B-23, DH-4
1984 KC A	126	438	107	23	2	28	6.4	58	77	45	139	0	.244	.498	1	0	1B-125, DH-1
4 yrs.	195	638	149	28	4	35	5.5	76	100	60	200	0	.234	.455	10	2	1B-177, DH-11
LEAGUE CHAMPIONSHIP SERIES																	
1984 KC A	3	10	1	0	0	0	0.0	0	0	1	4	0	.100	.100	0	0	1B-3

	G	AB	H	2B	3B	HR	HR %	R	RBI	BB	SO	SB	BA	SA	Pinch Hit AB	Pinch Hit H	G by POS

Bobby Balcena

BALCENA, ROBERT RUDOLPH
B. Aug. 1, 1928, San Pedro, Calif.

BR TL 5'7" 160 lbs.

	G	AB	H	2B	3B	HR	HR%	R	RBI	BB	SO	SB	BA	SA	PH AB	PH H	G by POS
1956 CIN N	7	2	0	0	0	0	0.0	2	0	0	1	0	.000	.000	2	0	OF-2

Bobby Baldwin

BALDWIN, ROBERT HARVEY
B. June 9, 1951, Tazewell, Va.

BL TL 6' 175 lbs.

	G	AB	H	2B	3B	HR	HR%	R	RBI	BB	SO	SB	BA	SA	PH AB	PH H	G by POS
1975 DET A	30	95	21	3	0	4	4.2	8	8	5	14	2	.221	.379	0	0	OF-25, DH-1
1976 NY N	9	22	6	1	1	1	4.5	4	5	1	2	0	.273	.545	3	1	OF-5
2 yrs.	39	117	27	4	1	5	4.3	12	13	6	16	2	.231	.410	3	1	OF-30, DH-1

Frank Baldwin

BALDWIN, FRANK DeWITT
B. Dec. 25, 1928, High Bridge, N. J.

BR TR 5'11" 195 lbs.

	G	AB	H	2B	3B	HR	HR%	R	RBI	BB	SO	SB	BA	SA	PH AB	PH H	G by POS
1953 CIN N	16	20	2	0	0	0	0.0	0	0	1	9	0	.100	.100	11	1	C-6

Henry Baldwin

BALDWIN, HENRY CLAY (Ted)
B. June 13, 1894, Chadds Ford, Pa. D. Feb. 24, 1964, West Chester, Pa.

BR TR 5'11" 180 lbs.

	G	AB	H	2B	3B	HR	HR%	R	RBI	BB	SO	SB	BA	SA	PH AB	PH H	G by POS
1927 PHI N	6	16	5	0	0	0	0.0	1	1	1	2	0	.313	.313	1	1	SS-3, 3B-2

Kid Baldwin

BALDWIN, CLARENCE GEOGHAN
B. Nov. 1, 1864, Newport, Ky. D. July 10, 1897, Cincinnati, Ohio

BR TR 5'6" 147 lbs.

	G	AB	H	2B	3B	HR	HR%	R	RBI	BB	SO	SB	BA	SA	PH AB	PH H	G by POS
1884 2 teams	KC	U	(50G –	.194)	C-P	U	(1G –	1.000)									
" total	51	192	38	5	3	1	0.5	19		4			.198	.271	0	0	C-45, OF-10, 3B-1, 2B-1
1885 CIN AA	34	126	17	1	0	1	0.8	9		3			.135	.167	0	0	C-25, OF-6, 2B-2, P-2, 3B-1
1886	87	315	72	8	7	3	1.0	41		8		13	.229	.327	0	0	C-71, 3B-13, OF-6
1887	96	388	98	15	10	1	0.3	46		6		13	.253	.351	0	0	C-96, OF-2
1888	67	271	59	11	3	1	0.4	27	25	3		4	.218	.292	0	0	C-65, OF-2, 1B-1
1889	60	223	55	14	2	1	0.4	34	34	5	32	7	.247	.341	0	0	C-55, OF-4, 3B-1, 1B-1
1890 2 teams	CIN	N	(22G –	.153)	PHI	AA	(24G –	.233)									
" total	46	162	32	1	2	0	0.0	10	10	7	6	4	.198	.228	0	0	C-39, 3B-5, OF-2
7 yrs.	441	1677	371	55	27	8	0.5	186	68	36	38	28	.221	.301	0	0	C-396, OF-32, 3B-21, 2B-3, 1B-2, P-2

Reggie Baldwin

BALDWIN, REGINALD CONRAD
B. Aug. 19, 1954, River Rouge, Mich.

BR TR 6'1" 195 lbs.

	G	AB	H	2B	3B	HR	HR%	R	RBI	BB	SO	SB	BA	SA	PH AB	PH H	G by POS
1978 HOU N	38	67	17	5	0	1	1.5	5	11	3	3	0	.254	.373	18	5	C-17
1979	14	20	4	1	0	0	0.0	0	1	0	1	0	.200	.250	12	3	C-3, 1B-1
2 yrs.	52	87	21	6	0	1	1.1	5	12	3	4	0	.241	.345	30	8	C-20, 1B-1

Mike Balenti

BALENTI, MICHAEL RICHARD
B. July 3, 1889, Calumet, Okla. D. Aug. 4, 1955, Altus, Okla.

BR TR 5'11" 175 lbs.

	G	AB	H	2B	3B	HR	HR%	R	RBI	BB	SO	SB	BA	SA	PH AB	PH H	G by POS
1911 CIN N	8	8	2	0	0	0	0.0	2	0	0	1	3	.250	.250	0	0	SS-2, OF-1
1913 STL A	70	211	38	2	4	0	0.0	17	11	6	32	3	.180	.227	4	1	SS-56, OF-8
2 yrs.	78	219	40	2	4	0	0.0	19	11	6	33	6	.183	.228	4	1	SS-58, OF-9

Lee Bales

BALES, WESLEY OWEN
B. Dec. 4, 1944, Los Angeles, Calif.

BB TR 5'10½" 165 lbs.

	G	AB	H	2B	3B	HR	HR%	R	RBI	BB	SO	SB	BA	SA	PH AB	PH H	G by POS
1966 ATL N	12	16	1	0	0	0	0.0	4	0	0	5	0	.063	.063	0	0	2B-7, 3B-3
1967 HOU N	19	27	3	0	0	0	0.0	4	2	8	7	1	.111	.111	6	0	2B-6, SS-1
2 yrs.	31	43	4	0	0	0	0.0	8	2	8	12	1	.093	.093	6	0	2B-13, 3B-3, SS-1

Art Ball

BALL, ARTHUR
B. Chicago, Ill. D. Dec. 26, 1915, Chicago, Ill.

TR

	G	AB	H	2B	3B	HR	HR%	R	RBI	BB	SO	SB	BA	SA	PH AB	PH H	G by POS
1894 STL N	1	3	1	0	0	0	0.0	0	0	0		1	.333	.333	0	0	2B-1
1898 BAL N	32	81	15	2	0	0	0.0	7	8	7		2	.185	.210	0	0	3B-15, SS-14, 2B-2, OF-1
2 yrs.	33	84	16	2	0	0	0.0	7	8	7	1	2	.190	.214	0	0	3B-15, SS-14, 2B-3, OF-1

Jim Ball

BALL, JAMES CHANDLER
B. Feb. 22, 1884, Hartford, Md. D. Apr. 7, 1963, Glendale, Calif.

BR TR 5'11" 175 lbs.

	G	AB	H	2B	3B	HR	HR%	R	RBI	BB	SO	SB	BA	SA	PH AB	PH H	G by POS
1907 BOS N	10	36	6	2	0	0	0.0	3	3	2		0	.167	.222	0	0	C-10
1908	6	15	1	0	0	0	0.0	1	0	1		0	.067	.067	0	0	C-6
2 yrs.	16	51	7	2	0	0	0.0	4	3	3		0	.137	.176	0	0	C-16

Neal Ball

BALL, CORNELIUS
B. Apr. 22, 1881, Grand Haven, Mich. D. Oct. 15, 1957, Bridgeport, Conn.

BR TR 5'7" 145 lbs.

	G	AB	H	2B	3B	HR	HR%	R	RBI	BB	SO	SB	BA	SA	PH AB	PH H	G by POS
1907 NY A	15	44	9	1	1	0	0.0	5	4	1		1	.205	.273	0	0	SS-11, 2B-5
1908	132	446	110	16	2	0	0.0	34	38	21		32	.247	.291	1	1	SS-130, 2B-1
1909 2 teams	NY	A	(8G –	.207)	CLE	A	(96G –	.256)									
" total	104	353	89	14	3	1	0.3	34	28	20		19	.252	.317	3	0	SS-95, 2B-8
1910 CLE A	53	119	25	3	1	0	0.0	12	12	9		4	.210	.252	3	0	SS-27, OF-6, 2B-6, 3B-3
1911	116	412	122	14	9	3	0.7	45	45	27		21	.296	.396	2	0	2B-95, 3B-17, SS-1
1912 2 teams	CLE	A	(37G –	.227)	BOS	A	(18G –	.200)									
" total	55	177	39	6	1	0	0.0	22	20	12		12	.220	.266	1	1	2B-54
1913 BOS A	21	58	10	2	0	0	0.0	9	4	9	13	3	.172	.207	2	0	2B-10, SS-8, 3B-1
7 yrs.	496	1609	404	56	17	4	0.2	161	151	99	13	92	.251	.314	8	2	SS-272, 2B-179, 3B-21, OF-6

WORLD SERIES

	G	AB	H	2B	3B	HR	HR%	R	RBI	BB	SO	SB	BA	SA	PH AB	PH H	G by POS
1912 BOS A	1	1	0	0	0	0	0.0	0	0	0	1	0	.000	.000	1	0	

Pelham Ballenger

BALLENGER, PELHAM ASHBY
B. Feb. 6, 1894, Gilreath Mill, S. C. D. Dec. 8, 1948, West Gantt Twp., S. C.

BR TR 5'11" 160 lbs.

	G	AB	H	2B	3B	HR	HR%	R	RBI	BB	SO	SB	BA	SA	PH AB	PH H	G by POS
1928 WAS A	3	9	1	0	0	0	0.0	0	0	0	1	0	.111	.111	0	0	3B-3

	G	AB	H	2B	3B	HR	HR %	R	RBI	BB	SO	SB	BA	SA	Pinch Hit AB	Pinch Hit H	G by POS

Hal Bamberger

BAMBERGER, HAROLD EARL (Dutch)
B. Oct. 29, 1924, Lebanon, Pa.
BL TR 6' 173 lbs.

	G	AB	H	2B	3B	HR	HR %	R	RBI	BB	SO	SB	BA	SA	PH AB	PH H	G by POS
1948 NY N	7	12	1	0	0	0	0.0	0	0	1	2	0	.083	.083	3	0	OF-3

Dave Bancroft

BANCROFT, DAVID JAMES (Beauty)
B. Apr. 20, 1891, Sioux City, Iowa   D. Oct. 9, 1972, Superior, Wis.
Manager 1924-27.
Hall of Fame 1971.
BB TR 5'9½" 160 lbs.

	G	AB	H	2B	3B	HR	HR %	R	RBI	BB	SO	SB	BA	SA	PH AB	PH H	G by POS
1915 PHI N	153	563	143	18	2	7	1.2	85	30	77	62	15	.254	.330	0	0	SS-153
1916	142	477	101	10	0	3	0.6	53	33	74	57	15	.212	.252	0	0	SS-142
1917	127	478	116	22	5	4	0.8	56	43	44	42	14	.243	.335	1	0	SS-120, 2B-3, OF-2
1918	125	499	132	19	4	0	0.0	69	26	54	36	11	.265	.319	0	0	SS-125
1919	92	335	91	13	7	0	0.0	45	25	31	30	8	.272	.352	4	1	SS-88
1920 2 teams		PHI	N	(42G –	.298)		NY	N	(108G –	.299)							
" total	150	613	183	36	9	0	0.0	102	36	42	44	8	.299	.387	0	0	SS-150
1921 NY N	153	606	193	26	15	6	1.0	121	67	66	23	17	.318	.441	0	0	SS-153
1922	156	651	209	41	5	4	0.6	117	60	79	27	16	.321	.418	0	0	SS-156
1923	107	444	135	33	3	1	0.2	80	31	62	23	8	.304	.399	0	0	SS-96, 2B-11
1924 BOS N	79	319	89	11	1	2	0.6	49	21	37	24	4	.279	.339	0	0	SS-79
1925	128	479	153	29	8	2	0.4	75	49	64	22	7	.319	.426	3	1	SS-125
1926	127	453	141	18	6	1	0.2	70	44	64	29	3	.311	.384	1	0	SS-123, 3B-2
1927	111	375	91	13	4	1	0.3	44	31	43	36	5	.243	.307	5	1	SS-104, 3B-1
1928 BKN N	149	515	127	19	5	0	0.0	47	51	59	20	7	.247	.303	0	0	SS-149
1929	104	358	99	11	3	1	0.3	35	44	29	11	7	.277	.332	2	0	SS-102
1930 NY N	10	17	1	1	0	0	0.0	0	0	2	1	0	.059	.118	1	0	SS-8
16 yrs.	1913	7182	2004	320	77	32	0.4	1048	591	827	487	145	.279	.358	17	3	SS-1873, 2B-14, 3B-3, OF-2

WORLD SERIES																	
1915 PHI N	5	17	5	0	0	0	0.0	2	1	2	2	0	.294	.294	0	0	SS-5
1921 NY N	8	33	5	1	0	0	0.0	3	3	1	5	0	.152	.182	0	0	SS-8
1922	5	19	4	0	0	0	0.0	4	2	2	1	0	.211	.211	0	0	SS-5
1923	6	24	2	0	0	0	0.0	1	1	1	2	1	.083	.083	0	0	SS-6
4 yrs.	24	93	16	1	0	0	0.0	10	7	6	10	1	.172	.183	0	0	SS-24

Chris Bando

BANDO, CHRISTOPHER MICHAEL
Brother of Sal Bando.
B. Feb. 4, 1956, Cleveland, Ohio
BB TR 6' 195 lbs.

	G	AB	H	2B	3B	HR	HR %	R	RBI	BB	SO	SB	BA	SA	PH AB	PH H	G by POS
1981 CLE A	21	47	10	3	0	0	0.0	3	6	2	2	0	.213	.277	9	2	C-15, DH-2
1982	66	184	39	6	1	3	1.6	13	16	24	30	0	.212	.304	12	4	C-63, 3B-2
1983	48	121	31	3	0	4	3.3	15	15	15	19	0	.256	.380	9	2	C-43
1984	75	220	64	11	0	12	5.5	38	41	33	35	1	.291	.505	11	2	C-63, DH-1, 3B-1, 1B-1
4 yrs.	210	572	144	23	1	19	3.3	69	78	74	86	1	.252	.395	41	8	C-184, DH-3, 3B-3, 1B-1

Sal Bando

BANDO, SALVATORE LEONARD
Brother of Chris Bando.
B. Feb. 13, 1944, Cleveland, Ohio
BR TR 6' 195 lbs.

	G	AB	H	2B	3B	HR	HR %	R	RBI	BB	SO	SB	BA	SA	PH AB	PH H	G by POS
1966 KC A	11	24	7	1	1	0	0.0	1	1	1	3	0	.292	.417	4	2	3B-7
1967	47	130	25	3	2	0	0.0	11	6	16	24	1	.192	.246	4	0	3B-44
1968 OAK A	162	605	152	25	5	9	1.5	67	67	51	78	13	.251	.354	0	0	3B-162, OF-1
1969	162	609	171	25	3	31	5.1	106	113	111	82	1	.281	.484	0	0	3B-162
1970	155	502	132	20	2	20	4.0	93	75	118	88	6	.263	.430	1	0	3B-152
1971	153	538	146	23	1	24	4.5	75	94	86	55	3	.271	.452	0	0	3B-153
1972	152	535	126	20	3	15	2.8	64	77	78	55	3	.236	.368	1	0	3B-151, 2B-1
1973	162	592	170	32	3	29	4.9	97	98	82	84	4	.287	.498	0	0	3B-159, DH-3
1974	146	498	121	21	2	22	4.4	84	103	86	79	2	.243	.426	4	2	3B-141, DH-3
1975	160	562	129	24	1	15	2.7	64	78	87	80	7	.230	.356	1	0	3B-160
1976	158	550	132	18	2	27	4.9	75	84	76	74	20	.240	.427	0	0	3B-155, SS-5, DH-2
1977 MIL A	159	580	145	27	3	17	2.9	65	82	75	89	4	.250	.395	0	0	3B-135, SS-1, 2B-1
1978	152	540	154	20	6	17	3.1	85	78	72	52	3	.285	.439	4	0	3B-134, DH-12, 1B-5
1979	130	476	117	14	3	9	1.9	57	43	57	42	2	.246	.345	1	1	3B-109, DH-19, 1B-4, 2B-1, P-1
1980	78	254	50	12	1	5	2.0	28	31	29	35	5	.197	.311	6	0	3B-57, DH-15, 1B-7
1981	32	65	13	4	0	2	3.1	10	9	6	3	1	.200	.354	6	1	3B-15, 1B-9, DH-2
16 yrs.	2019	7060	1790	289	38	242	3.4	982	40	1031	923	75	.254	.408	32	6	3B-1896, DH-56, 1B-25, SS-6, 2B-3, OF-1, P-1

DIVISIONAL PLAYOFF SERIES																	
1981 MIL A	5	17	5	3	0	0	0.0	1	1	2	3	0	.294	.471	0	0	3B-5

LEAGUE CHAMPIONSHIP SERIES																	
1971 OAK A	3	11	4	2	0	1	9.1	3	1	1	0	0	.364	.818	0	0	3B-3
1972	5	20	4	0	0	0	0.0	0	0	0	3	0	.200	.200	0	0	3B-5
1973	5	18	3	0	0	2	11.1	2	3	3	6	0	.167	.500	0	0	3B-5
1974	4	13	3	0	0	2	15.4	4	2	4	0	0	.231	.692	0	0	3B-4
1975	3	12	6	2	0	0	0.0	1	2	0	3	0	.500	.667	0	0	3B-3
5 yrs.	20	74	20	4	0	5	6.8	10	8	8	12	0	.270	.527	0	0	3B-20

WORLD SERIES																	
1972 OAK A	7	26	7	1	0	0	0.0	2	1	2	5	0	.269	.308	0	0	3B-7
1973	7	26	6	1	1	0	0.0	5	1	4	7	0	.231	.346	0	0	3B-7
1974	5	16	1	0	0	0	0.0	3	2	2	5	0	.063	.063	0	0	3B-5
3 yrs.	19	68	14	2	1	0	0.0	10	4	8	17	0	.206	.265	0	0	3B-19

Ernie Banks

BANKS, ERNEST
B. Jan. 31, 1931, Dallas, Tex.
Hall of Fame 1977.
BR TR 6'1" 180 lbs.

	G	AB	H	2B	3B	HR	HR %	R	RBI	BB	SO	SB	BA	SA	PH AB	PH H	G by POS
1953 CHI N	10	35	11	1	1	2	5.7	3	6	4	5	0	.314	.571	0	0	SS-10
1954	154	593	163	19	7	19	3.2	70	79	40	50	6	.275	.427	0	0	SS-154
1955	154	596	176	29	9	44	7.4	98	117	45	72	9	.295	.596	0	0	SS-154
1956	139	538	160	25	8	28	5.2	82	85	52	62	6	.297	.530	0	0	SS-139

	G	AB	H	2B	3B	HR	HR %	R	RBI	BB	SO	SB	BA	SA	Pinch Hit AB	Pinch Hit H	G by POS

Ernie Banks   continued

	G	AB	H	2B	3B	HR	HR %	R	RBI	BB	SO	SB	BA	SA	PH AB	PH H	G by POS
1957	156	594	169	34	6	43	7.2	113	102	70	85	8	.285	.579	0	0	SS-100, 3B-58
1958	154	617	193	23	11	47	7.6	119	129	52	87	4	.313	.614	0	0	SS-154
1959	155	589	179	25	6	45	7.6	97	143	64	72	2	.304	.596	1	0	SS-154
1960	156	597	162	32	7	41	6.9	94	117	71	69	1	.271	.554	0	0	SS-156
1961	138	511	142	22	4	29	5.7	75	80	54	75	1	.278	.507	4	1	SS-104, OF-23, 1B-7
1962	154	610	164	20	6	37	6.1	87	104	30	71	5	.269	.503	4	2	1B-149, 3B-3
1963	130	432	98	20	1	18	4.2	41	64	39	73	0	.227	.403	5	1	1B-125
1964	157	591	156	29	6	23	3.9	67	95	36	84	1	.264	.450	1	0	1B-157
1965	163	612	162	25	3	28	4.6	79	106	55	64	3	.265	.453	2	1	1B-162
1966	141	511	139	23	7	15	2.9	52	75	29	59	0	.272	.432	8	1	1B-130, 3B-8
1967	151	573	158	26	4	23	4.0	68	95	27	93	2	.276	.455	5	1	1B-147
1968	150	552	136	27	0	32	5.8	71	83	27	67	2	.246	.469	4	1	1B-147
1969	155	565	143	19	2	23	4.1	60	106	42	101	0	.253	.416	2	2	1B-153
1970	72	222	56	6	2	12	5.4	25	44	20	33	0	.252	.459	9	2	1B-62
1971	39	83	16	2	0	3	3.6	4	6	6	14	0	.193	.325	18	2	1B-20
19 yrs.	2528	9421	2583	407	90	512	5.4	1305	1636	763	1236	50	.274	.500	62	14	1B-1259, SS-1125, 3B-69, OF-23
							10th										

George Banks

BANKS, GEORGE EDWARD   BR TR 5'11"   185 lbs.
B. Sept. 24, 1938, Pacolet Mills, S. C.

	G	AB	H	2B	3B	HR	HR %	R	RBI	BB	SO	SB	BA	SA	PH AB	PH H	G by POS
1962 MIN A	63	103	26	0	2	4	3.9	22	15	21	27	0	.252	.408	28	5	OF-17, 3B-6
1963	25	71	11	4	0	3	4.2	5	8	9	21	0	.155	.338	3	0	3B-21
1964 2 teams		MIN	A (1G – .000)			CLE	A (9G – .294)										
" total	10	18	5	1	0	2	11.1	6	3	6	7	0	.278	.667	5	1	OF-3, 3B-1, 2B-1
1965 CLE A	4	5	1	0	0	0	0.0	0	0	1	3	0	.200	.400	3	0	3B-1
1966	4	4	1	0	0	0	0.0	0	1	0	1	0	.250	.250	4	1	
5 yrs.	106	201	44	6	2	9	4.5	33	27	37	59	0	.219	.403	43	7	3B-29, OF-20, 2B-1

Bill Bankston

BANKSTON, WILBORN EVERETT   BL TR 5'11"   180 lbs.
B. May 25, 1893, Barnesville, Ga.   D. Feb. 26, 1970, Griffin, Ga.

	G	AB	H	2B	3B	HR	HR %	R	RBI	BB	SO	SB	BA	SA	PH AB	PH H	G by POS
1915 PHI A	11	36	5	1	1	1	2.8	6	2	2	5	1	.139	.306	2	1	OF-8

Jim Banning

BANNING, JAMES M.   BL TR
B. 1866, New York, N. Y.   D. Glen Rock, N. J.

	G	AB	H	2B	3B	HR	HR %	R	RBI	BB	SO	SB	BA	SA	PH AB	PH H	G by POS
1888 WAS N	1	0	0	0	0	0	–	0	0	0	0	0	–	–	0	0	C-1
1889	2	1	0	0	0	0	0.0	0	0	0	0	0	.000	.000	0	0	C-2
2 yrs.	3	1	0	0	0	0	0.0	0	0	0	0	0	.000	.000	0	0	C-3

Alan Bannister

BANNISTER, ALAN   BR TR 5'11"   170 lbs.
B. Sept. 3, 1951, Montebello, Calif.

	G	AB	H	2B	3B	HR	HR %	R	RBI	BB	SO	SB	BA	SA	PH AB	PH H	G by POS
1974 PHI N	26	25	3	0	0	0	0.0	4	1	3	7	0	.120	.120	7	0	OF-8, SS-2
1975	24	61	16	3	1	0	0.0	10	0	1	9	2	.262	.344	1	0	OF-18, SS-1, 2B-1
1976 CHI A	73	145	36	6	2	0	0.0	19	8	14	21	12	.248	.317	2	0	OF-43, SS-14, DH-4, 2B-4, 3B-1
1977	139	560	154	20	3	3	0.5	87	57	54	49	4	.275	.338	1	0	SS-133, OF-3, 2B-3
1978	49	107	24	3	2	0	0.0	16	8	11	12	3	.224	.290	10	0	DH-19, OF-15, SS-8, 2B-2
1979	136	506	144	28	8	2	0.4	71	55	43	40	22	.285	.383	0	0	2B-65, OF-47, 3B-12, DH-9, 1B-1
1980 2 teams		CHI	A (45G – .192)			CLE	A (81G – .328)										
" total	126	392	111	23	4	1	0.3	57	41	40	19	14	.283	.370	12	0	OF-63, 2B-41, 3B-20, SS-2
1981 CLE A	68	232	61	11	1	4	1.7	36	17	16	19	16	.263	.332	11	4	OF-35, 2B-30, 1B-2, SS-1
1982	101	348	93	16	1	4	1.1	40	41	42	41	18	.267	.353	6	1	OF-55, 2B-48, SS-2, DH-1, 3B-1
1983	117	377	100	25	4	5	1.3	51	45	31	43	6	.265	.393	10	5	OF-91, 2B-27, DH-3, 1B-3
1984 2 teams		HOU	N (9G – .200)			TEX	A (47G – .300)										
" total	56	130	37	4	1	2	1.5	22	9	23	19	2	.285	.377	17	4	2B-25, DH-9, OF-4, SS-4, 3B-1, 1B-1
11 yrs.	915	2883	779	139	27	18	0.6	413	282	278	301	99	.270	.356	77	14	OF-382, 2B-246, SS-167, DH-45, 3B-35, 1B-7

Jimmy Bannon

BANNON, JAMES HENRY (Foxy Grandpa)   BR TR 5'5"   160 lbs.
Brother of Tom Bannon.
B. May 5, 1871, Amesbury, Mass.   D. Mar. 24, 1948, Glen Rock, N. J.

	G	AB	H	2B	3B	HR	HR %	R	RBI	BB	SO	SB	BA	SA	PH AB	PH H	G by POS
1893 STL N	26	107	36	3	4	0	0.0	9	15	4	5	8	.336	.439	0	0	OF-24, SS-1, P-1
1894 BOS N	128	494	166	29	10	13	2.6	130	114	62	42	47	.336	.514	0	0	OF-128, P-1
1895	123	489	171	35	5	6	1.2	101	74	54	31	28	.350	.479	1	0	OF-122, P-1
1896	89	343	86	9	5	0	0.0	52	50	32	23	16	.251	.306	1	0	OF-76, 2B-6, SS-5, 3B-3
4 yrs.	366	1433	459	76	24	19	1.3	292	253	152	101	99	.320	.447	2	0	OF-350, SS-7, 2B-6, 3B-3, P-3

Tom Bannon

BANNON, THOMAS EDWARD (Uncle Tom)   BR TR 5'8"   175 lbs.
Brother of Jimmy Bannon.
B. May 8, 1869, S. Groveland, Mass.   D. Jan. 26, 1950, Lynn, Mass.

	G	AB	H	2B	3B	HR	HR %	R	RBI	BB	SO	SB	BA	SA	PH AB	PH H	G by POS
1895 NY N	37	159	43	6	2	0	0.0	33	8	7	8	20	.270	.333	0	0	OF-21, 1B-16
1896	2	7	1	1	0	0	0.0	1	0	1	1	0	.143	.286	0	0	OF-2
2 yrs.	39	166	44	7	2	0	0.0	34	8	8	9	20	.265	.331	0	0	OF-23, 1B-16

Walter Barbare

BARBARE, WALTER LAWRENCE (Dinty)   BR TR 6'   162 lbs.
B. Aug. 11, 1891, Greenville, S. C.   D. Oct. 28, 1965, Greenville, S. C.

	G	AB	H	2B	3B	HR	HR %	R	RBI	BB	SO	SB	BA	SA	PH AB	PH H	G by POS
1914 CLE A	15	52	16	2	2	0	0.0	6	5	2	5	1	.308	.423	0	0	3B-14, SS-1
1915	77	246	47	3	1	0	0.0	15	11	10	27	6	.191	.211	5	1	3B-68, 1B-1
1916	13	48	11	1	0	0	0.0	3	3	4	9	0	.229	.250	1	0	3B-12
1918 BOS A	13	29	5	3	0	0	0.0	2	2	0	1	1	.172	.276	1	0	3B-11, SS-1
1919 PIT N	85	293	80	11	5	1	0.3	34	34	18	18	11	.273	.355	3	1	3B-80, 2B-1
1920	57	186	51	5	2	0	0.0	9	12	9	11	5	.274	.323	7	2	SS-34, 2B-12, 3B-5

	G	AB	H	2B	3B	HR	HR %	R	RBI	BB	SO	SB	BA	SA	Pinch Hit AB	Pinch Hit H	G by POS

Walter Barbare continued

	G	AB	H	2B	3B	HR	HR%	R	RBI	BB	SO	SB	BA	SA	PH AB	PH H	G by POS
1921 BOS N	134	550	166	22	7	0	0.0	66	49	24	28	11	.302	.367	2	2	SS-121, 2B-8, 3B-2
1922	106	373	86	5	4	0	0.0	38	40	21	22	2	.231	.265	11	3	2B-45, 3B-38, 1B-14
8 yrs.	500	1777	462	52	21	1	0.1	173	156	88	121	37	.260	.315	30	9	3B-230, SS-157, 2B-66, 1B-15

Red Barbary

BARBARY, DONALD ODELL
B. June 20, 1920, Simpsonville, S. C.   BR TR 6'3"   190 lbs.

	G	AB	H	2B	3B	HR	HR%	R	RBI	BB	SO	SB	BA	SA	PH AB	PH H	G by POS
1943 WAS A	1	1	0	0	0	0	0.0	0	0	0	0	0	.000	.000	1	0	

Jap Barbeau

BARBEAU, WILLIAM JOSEPH
B. June 10, 1882, New York, N. Y.   D. Sept. 10, 1969, Milwaukee, Wis.   BR TR 5'5"   140 lbs.

	G	AB	H	2B	3B	HR	HR%	R	RBI	BB	SO	SB	BA	SA	PH AB	PH H	G by POS
1905 CLE A	11	37	10	1	1	0	0.0	1	2	1		1	.270	.351	0	0	2B-11
1906	42	129	25	5	3	0	0.0	8	12	9		5	.194	.279	3	0	3B-32, SS-6
1909 2 teams	PIT	N	(91G –	.220)		STL	N	(47G –	.251)								
" total	138	525	121	19	3	0	0.0	83	30	65		33	.230	.278	7	0	3B-131
1910 STL N	7	21	4	0	1	0	0.0	4	2	3	3	0	.190	.286	0	0	3B-6, 2B-1
4 yrs.	198	712	160	25	8	0	0.0	96	46	78	3	39	.225	.282	10	0	3B-169, 2B-12, SS-6

Dave Barbee

BARBEE, DAVID MONROE
B. May 7, 1905, Greensboro, N. C.   D. July 1, 1968, Albemarle, N. C.   BR TR 5'11½" 178 lbs.

	G	AB	H	2B	3B	HR	HR%	R	RBI	BB	SO	SB	BA	SA	PH AB	PH H	G by POS
1926 PHI A	19	47	8	1	1	1	2.1	7	5	2	4	0	.170	.298	8	0	OF-10
1932 PIT N	97	327	84	22	6	5	1.5	37	55	18	38	1	.257	.407	19	8	OF-78
2 yrs.	116	374	92	23	7	6	1.6	44	60	20	42	1	.246	.393	27	8	OF-88

Charlie Barber

BARBER, CHARLES D.
B. 1854, Martinsburg, Pa.   D. Nov. 23, 1910, Philadelphia, Pa.   BR TR

	G	AB	H	2B	3B	HR	HR%	R	RBI	BB	SO	SB	BA	SA	PH AB	PH H	G by POS
1884 CIN U	55	204	41	1	4	0	0.0	38		11			.201	.245	0	0	3B-55

Turner Barber

BARBER, TYRUS TURNER
B. July 9, 1893, Lavinia, Tenn.   D. Oct. 20, 1968, Milan, Tenn.   BL TR 5'11"   170 lbs.

	G	AB	H	2B	3B	HR	HR%	R	RBI	BB	SO	SB	BA	SA	PH AB	PH H	G by POS
1915 WAS A	20	53	16	1	1	0	0.0	9	6	6	7	0	.302	.358	1	0	OF-19
1916	15	33	7	0	1	1	3.0	3	5	2	3	0	.212	.364	3	1	OF-9
1917 CHI N	7	28	6	1	0	0	0.0	2	2	2	8	1	.214	.250	0	0	OF-7
1918	55	123	29	3	2	0	0.0	11	10	9	16	3	.236	.293	20	4	OF-27, 1B-4
1919	76	230	72	9	4	0	0.0	26	21	14	17	7	.313	.387	6	1	OF-68
1920	94	340	90	10	5	0	0.0	27	50	9	26	5	.265	.324	5	2	1B-69, OF-17, 2B-2
1921	127	452	142	14	4	1	0.2	73	54	41	24	5	.314	.369	2	1	OF-123
1922	84	226	70	7	4	0	0.0	35	29	30	9	7	.310	.376	19	2	OF-47, 1B-16
1923 BKN N	13	46	10	2	0	0	0.0	3	8	2	2	0	.217	.261	1	1	OF-12
9 yrs.	491	1531	442	47	21	2	0.1	189	185	115	112	28	.289	.351	57	12	OF-329, 1B-89, 2B-2
WORLD SERIES																	
1918 CHI N	3	2	0	0	0	0	0.0	0	0	0	0	0	.000	.000	2	0	

Jim Barbieri

BARBIERI, JAMES PATRICK
B. Sept. 15, 1941, Schenectady, N. Y.   BL TR 5'7"   155 lbs.

	G	AB	H	2B	3B	HR	HR%	R	RBI	BB	SO	SB	BA	SA	PH AB	PH H	G by POS
1966 LA N	39	82	23	5	0	0	0.0	9	3	9	7	2	.280	.341	17	4	OF-20
WORLD SERIES																	
1966 LA N	1	1	0	0	0	0	0.0	0	0	0	1	0	.000	.000	1	0	

George Barclay

BARCLAY, GEORGE OLIVER (Deerfoot)
B. May 16, 1876, Millville, Pa.   D. Apr. 3, 1909, Philadelphia, Pa.   5'10"   162 lbs.

	G	AB	H	2B	3B	HR	HR%	R	RBI	BB	SO	SB	BA	SA	PH AB	PH H	G by POS
1902 STL N	137	543	163	14	2	3	0.6	79	53	31		30	.300	.350	0	0	OF-137
1903	108	419	104	10	8	0	0.0	37	42	15		12	.248	.310	0	0	OF-107
1904 2 teams	STL	N	(103G –	.200)		BOS	N	(24G –	.226)								
" total	127	468	96	10	5	1	0.2	46	38	14		17	.205	.254	0	0	OF-127
1905 BOS N	29	108	19	1	0	0	0.0	5	7	2		2	.176	.185	1	0	OF-28
4 yrs.	401	1538	382	35	15	4	0.3	167	140	62		61	.248	.298	1	0	OF-399

Jesse Barfield

BARFIELD, JESSE LEE
B. Oct. 29, 1959, Joliet, Ill.   BR TR 6'1"   170 lbs.

	G	AB	H	2B	3B	HR	HR%	R	RBI	BB	SO	SB	BA	SA	PH AB	PH H	G by POS
1981 TOR A	25	95	22	3	2	2	2.1	7	9	4	19	4	.232	.368	0	0	OF-25
1982	139	394	97	13	2	18	4.6	54	58	42	79	1	.246	.426	21	6	OF-137, DH-1
1983	128	388	98	13	3	27	7.0	58	68	22	110	2	.253	.510	16	6	OF-120, DH-5
1984	110	320	91	14	1	14	4.4	51	49	35	81	8	.284	.466	20	8	OF-88, DH-9
4 yrs.	402	1197	308	43	8	61	5.1	170	184	103	289	15	.257	.459	57	20	OF-370, DH-15

Cy Barger

BARGER, EROS BOLIVAR
B. May 18, 1885, Jamestown, Ky.   D. Sept. 23, 1964, Columbia, Ky.   BL TR 6'   160 lbs.

	G	AB	H	2B	3B	HR	HR%	R	RBI	BB	SO	SB	BA	SA	PH AB	PH H	G by POS
1906 NY A	2	3	1	0	0	0	0.0	0	0	0		0	.333	.333	0	0	P-2
1907	1	2	0	0	0	0	0.0	0	0	0		0	.000	.000	0	0	P-1
1910 BKN N	35	104	24	3	2	0	0.0	7	7	5	14	0	.231	.298	6	3	P-35
1911	57	145	33	1	1	0	0.0	16	9	5	20	2	.228	.248	10	2	P-30, OF-11, 1B-1
1912	17	37	7	1	0	0	0.0	3	3	3	7	1	.189	.216	1	0	P-16
1914 PIT F	38	83	17	1	2	0	0.0	4	9	2		0	.205	.265	0	0	P-33, SS-1
1915	36	54	15	2	0	0	0.0	3	3	1		0	.278	.315	0	0	P-34
7 yrs.	186	428	97	8	5	0	0.0	33	31	16	41	3	.227	.269	17	5	P-151, OF-11, SS-1, 1B-1

Ray Barker

BARKER, RAYMOND HERRELL (Buddy)
B. Mar. 12, 1936, Martinsburg, W. Va.   BL TR 6'   192 lbs.

	G	AB	H	2B	3B	HR	HR%	R	RBI	BB	SO	SB	BA	SA	PH AB	PH H	G by POS
1960 BAL A	5	6	0	0	0	0	0.0	0	0	0	3	0	.000	.000	5	0	OF-1
1965 2 teams	CLE	A	(11G –	.000)		NY	A	(98G –	.254)								
" total	109	211	52	11	0	7	3.3	21	31	22	48	1	.246	.398	44	11	1B-64, 3B-3
1966 NY A	61	75	14	5	0	3	4.0	11	13	4	20	0	.187	.373	11	0	1B-47

	G	AB	H	2B	3B	HR	HR%	R	RBI	BB	SO	SB	BA	SA	Pinch Hit AB	Pinch Hit H	G by POS

Ray Barker continued

	G	AB	H	2B	3B	HR	HR%	R	RBI	BB	SO	SB	BA	SA	PH AB	PH H	G by POS
1967	17	26	2	0	0	0	0.0	2	0	3	5	0	.077	.077	4	0	1B-13
4 yrs.	192	318	68	16	0	10	3.1	34	44	29	76	1	.214	.358	64	11	1B-124, 3B-3, OF-1

Red Barkley

BARKLEY, JOHN DUNCAN
B. Sept. 19, 1913, Childress, Tex. BR TR 5'11" 160 lbs.

	G	AB	H	2B	3B	HR	HR%	R	RBI	BB	SO	SB	BA	SA	PH AB	PH H	G by POS
1937 STL A	31	101	27	6	0	0	0.0	9	14	14	17	1	.267	.327	0	0	2B-31
1939 BOS N	12	11	0	0	0	0	0.0	1	0	1	2	0	.000	.000	1	0	SS-7, 3B-4
1943 BKN N	20	51	16	3	0	0	0.0	6	7	4	7	1	.314	.373	0	0	SS-18
3 yrs.	63	163	43	9	0	0	0.0	16	21	19	26	2	.264	.319	1	0	2B-31, SS-25, 3B-4

Sam Barkley

BARKLEY, SAMUEL E
B. May 24, 1858, Wheeling, W. Va. D. Apr. 20, 1912, Wheeling, W. Va. TR 5'11½"
Manager 1888.

	G	AB	H	2B	3B	HR	HR%	R	RBI	BB	SO	SB	BA	SA	PH AB	PH H	G by POS
1884 TOL AA	104	435	133	39	9	1	0.2	71		22			.306	.444	0	0	2B-103, C-2
1885 STL AA	106	418	112	18	10	2	0.5	67		25			.268	.373	0	0	2B-96, 1B-11
1886 PIT AA	122	478	127	32	8	0	0.0	77		58			.266	.366	0	0	2B-112, OF-8, 1B-2
1887 PIT N	89	340	76	10	4	1	0.3	44	35	30	24	6	.224	.285	0	0	1B-53, 2B-36
1888 KC AA	116	482	104	21	6	3	0.6	67	51	26		15	.216	.303	0	0	2B-116
1889	45	176	50	6	2	0	0.0	36	22	15	20	8	.284	.341	0	0	2B-41, 1B-4
6 yrs.	582	2329	602	126	39	7	0.3	362	108	176	44	29	.258	.355	0	0	2B-504, 1B-70, OF-8, C-2

Bruce Barmes

BARMES, BRUCE RAYMOND (Squeaky)
B. Oct. 23, 1929, Vincennes, Ind. BL TR 5'8" 165 lbs.

	G	AB	H	2B	3B	HR	HR%	R	RBI	BB	SO	SB	BA	SA	PH AB	PH H	G by POS
1953 WAS A	5	5	1	0	0	0	0.0	1	0	0	0	0	.200	.200	4	1	OF-1

Babe Barna

BARNA, HERBERT PAUL
B. Mar. 2, 1915, Clarksburg, W. Va. D. May 18, 1972, Charleston, W. Va. BL TR 6'2" 210 lbs.

	G	AB	H	2B	3B	HR	HR%	R	RBI	BB	SO	SB	BA	SA	PH AB	PH H	G by POS
1937 PHI A	14	36	14	2	0	2	5.6	10	9	2	6	1	.389	.611	3	1	OF-9, 1B-1
1938	9	30	4	0	0	0	0.0	4	2	3	5	0	.133	.133	2	0	OF-7
1941 NY N	10	42	9	3	0	1	2.4	5	5	2	6	0	.214	.357	0	0	OF-10
1942	104	331	85	8	7	6	1.8	39	58	38	48	3	.257	.378	13	5	OF-89
1943 2 teams	NY N (40G – .204)					BOS A (30G – .170)											
" total	70	225	42	9	3	3	1.3	30	22	31	33	5	.187	.284	9	2	OF-60
5 yrs.	207	664	154	22	9	12	1.8	88	76	76	98	9	.232	.346	27	8	OF-175, 1B-1

Bill Barnes

BARNES, WILLIAM H.
B. Indianapolis, Ind. Deceased.

	G	AB	H	2B	3B	HR	HR%	R	RBI	BB	SO	SB	BA	SA	PH AB	PH H	G by POS
1884 STP U	8	30	6	1	0	0	0.0	2		0			.200	.233	0	0	OF-8

Eppie Barnes

BARNES, EVERETT DUANE
B. Dec. 1, 1900, Ossining, N. Y. D. Nov. 11, 1980, Hamilton, N. Y. BL TR 5'9" 175 lbs.

	G	AB	H	2B	3B	HR	HR%	R	RBI	BB	SO	SB	BA	SA	PH AB	PH H	G by POS
1923 PIT N	2	2	1	0	0	0	0.0	0	0	0	1	0	.500	.500	0	0	1B-1
1924	2	5	0	0	0	0	0.0	0	0	0	1	0	.000	.000	1	0	1B-1
2 yrs.	4	7	1	0	0	0	0.0	0	0	0	2	0	.143	.143	1	0	1B-2

Honey Barnes

BARNES, JOHN FRANCIS
B. Jan. 29, 1900, Fulton, N. Y. D. June 18, 1981, Lockport, N. Y. BL TR 5'10" 175 lbs.

	G	AB	H	2B	3B	HR	HR%	R	RBI	BB	SO	SB	BA	SA	PH AB	PH H	G by POS
1926 NY A	1	0	0	0	0	0	–	0	0	1	0	0	–	–	0	0	C-1

Lute Barnes

BARNES, LUTHER OWEN
B. Apr. 28, 1947, Forest City, Iowa BR TR 5'10" 160 lbs.

	G	AB	H	2B	3B	HR	HR%	R	RBI	BB	SO	SB	BA	SA	PH AB	PH H	G by POS
1972 NY N	24	72	17	2	2	0	0.0	5	6	6	4	0	.236	.319	3	0	2B-14, SS-6
1973	3	2	1	0	0	0	0.0	2	1	0	1	0	.500	.500	2	1	
2 yrs.	27	74	18	2	2	0	0.0	7	6	5	5	0	.243	.324	5	1	2B-14, SS-6

Red Barnes

BARNES, EMILE DEERING
B. Dec. 25, 1903, Suggsville, Ala. D. July 3, 1959, Mobile, Ala. BL TR 5'10½" 158 lbs.

	G	AB	H	2B	3B	HR	HR%	R	RBI	BB	SO	SB	BA	SA	PH AB	PH H	G by POS
1927 WAS A	3	11	4	1	0	0	0.0	5	0	1	3	0	.364	.455	0	0	OF-3
1928	114	417	126	22	15	6	1.4	82	51	55	38	7	.302	.470	7	2	OF-104
1929	72	130	26	5	2	1	0.8	16	15	13	12	1	.200	.292	36	8	OF-30
1930 2 teams	WAS A (12G – .167)					CHI A (85G – .248)											
" total	97	278	68	13	7	1	0.4	49	31	26	23	4	.245	.353	22	3	OF-72
4 yrs.	286	836	224	41	24	8	1.0	152	97	95	76	12	.268	.403	65	13	OF-209

Ross Barnes

BARNES, ROSCOE CHARLES
B. May 8, 1850, Mt. Morris, N. Y. D. Feb. 5, 1915, Chicago, Ill. BR TR 5'8½" 145 lbs.

	G	AB	H	2B	3B	HR	HR%	R	RBI	BB	SO	SB	BA	SA	PH AB	PH H	G by POS
1876 CHI N	66	322	138	21	14	1	0.3	126	59	20	8		.429	.590	0	0	2B-66, P-1
1877	22	92	25	1	0	0	0.0	16	5	7	4		.272	.283	0	0	2B-22
1879 CIN N	77	323	86	9	2	1	0.3	55	30	16	25		.266	.316	0	0	SS-61, 2B-16
1881 BOS N	69	295	80	14	1	0	0.0	42	17	16	16		.271	.325	0	0	SS-63, 2B-7
4 yrs.	234	1032	329	45	17	2	0.2	239	111	59	53		.319	.401	0	0	SS-124, 2B-111, P-1

Sam Barnes

BARNES, SAMUEL THOMAS
B. Dec. 18, 1899, Suggsville, Ala. D. Feb. 19, 1981, Montgomery, Ala. BL TR 5'8" 150 lbs.

	G	AB	H	2B	3B	HR	HR%	R	RBI	BB	SO	SB	BA	SA	PH AB	PH H	G by POS
1921 DET A	7	11	2	1	0	0	0.0	2	0	2	1	0	.182	.273	2	0	2B-2

Skeeter Barnes

BARNES, WILLIAM HENRY
B. Mar. 3, 1957, Cincinnati, Ohio BR TR 5'11" 170 lbs.

	G	AB	H	2B	3B	HR	HR%	R	RBI	BB	SO	SB	BA	SA	PH AB	PH H	G by POS
1983 CIN N	15	34	7	0	0	1	2.9	5	4	7	3	2	.206	.294	2	0	3B-7, 1B-7
1984	32	42	5	0	0	1	2.4	5	3	4	6	0	.119	.190	16	1	3B-11, OF-3
2 yrs.	47	76	12	0	0	2	2.6	10	7	11	9	2	.158	.237	18	1	3B-18, 1B-7, OF-3

	G	AB	H	2B	3B	HR	HR %	R	RBI	BB	SO	SB	BA	SA	Pinch Hit AB	Pinch Hit H	G by POS

Ed Barney

BARNEY, EDMUND J. BL TR 5'10½" 178 lbs.
B. Jan. 23, 1890, Amery, Wis.   D. Oct. 4, 1967, Rice Lake, Wis.

	G	AB	H	2B	3B	HR	HR %	R	RBI	BB	SO	SB	BA	SA	PH AB	PH H	G by POS
1915 **2 teams**	**NY**	**A** (11G –	.194)		**PIT**	**N**	(32G –	.273)									
" total	43	135	34	1	2	0	0.0	17	13	14	18	9	.252	.289	6	2	OF-36
1916 **PIT N**	45	137	27	4	0	0	0.0	16	9	23	15	8	.197	.226	4	1	OF-40
2 yrs.	88	272	61	5	2	0	0.0	33	22	37	33	17	.224	.257	10	3	OF-76

Clyde Barnhart

BARNHART, CLYDE LEE (Pooch) BR TR 5'10" 155 lbs.
Father of Vic Barnhart.
B. Dec. 29, 1895, Buck Valley, Pa.   D. Jan. 21, 1980, Hagerstown, Md.

	G	AB	H	2B	3B	HR	HR %	R	RBI	BB	SO	SB	BA	SA	PH AB	PH H	G by POS
1920 **PIT N**	12	46	15	4	2	0	0.0	5	5	1	2	1	.326	.500	0	0	3B-12
1921	124	449	116	15	13	3	0.7	66	62	32	36	3	.258	.370	6	1	3B-118
1922	75	209	69	7	5	1	0.5	30	38	25	7	3	.330	.426	16	4	3B-30, OF-26
1923	114	327	106	25	13	9	2.8	60	72	47	21	5	.324	.563	17	4	OF-92
1924	102	344	95	6	11	3	0.9	49	51	30	17	8	.276	.384	12	2	OF-88
1925	142	539	175	32	11	4	0.7	85	114	59	25	9	.325	.447	3	1	OF-138
1926	76	203	39	3	0	0	0.0	26	10	23	13	1	.192	.207	15	2	OF-61
1927	108	360	115	25	5	3	0.8	66	54	37	19	2	.319	.442	11	1	OF-94
1928	61	196	58	6	2	4	2.0	18	30	11	9	3	.296	.408	10	2	OF-48, 3B-1
9 yrs.	814	2673	788	123	62	27	1.0	405	436	265	149	35	.295	.418	90	17	OF-547, 3B-161
WORLD SERIES																	
1925 **PIT N**	7	28	7	1	0	0	0.0	1	5	3	5	1	.250	.286	0	0	OF-7
1927	4	16	5	1	0	0	0.0	0	4	0	0	0	.313	.375	0	0	OF-4
2 yrs.	11	44	12	2	0	0	0.0	1	9	3	5	1	.273	.318	0	0	OF-11

Vic Barnhart

BARNHART, VICTOR DEE BR TR 6' 188 lbs.
Son of Clyde Barnhart.
B. Sept. 1, 1922, Hagerstown, Md.

	G	AB	H	2B	3B	HR	HR %	R	RBI	BB	SO	SB	BA	SA	PH AB	PH H	G by POS
1944 **PIT N**	1	2	1	0	0	0	0.0	0	1	1	1	0	.500	.500	0	0	SS-1
1945	71	201	54	7	0	0	0.0	21	19	9	11	2	.269	.303	2	2	SS-60, 3B-4
1946	2	1	0	0	0	0	0.0	0	0	0	0	0	.000	.000	1	0	
3 yrs.	74	204	55	7	0	0	0.0	21	19	10	12	2	.270	.304	3	2	SS-61, 3B-4

Billy Barnie

BARNIE, WILLIAM HARRISON (Bald Billy) 5'7" 157 lbs.
B. Jan. 26, 1853, New York, N. Y.   D. July 15, 1900, Hartford, Conn.
Manager 1883-89, 1892-94, 1897-98.

	G	AB	H	2B	3B	HR	HR %	R	RBI	BB	SO	SB	BA	SA	PH AB	PH H	G by POS
1883 **BAL AA**	17	55	11	0	0	0	0.0	7		2			.200	.200	0	0	C-13, OF-6, SS-1
1886	2	6	0	0	0	0	0.0	0		1			.000	.000	0	0	OF-1, C-1
2 yrs.	19	61	11	0	0	0	0.0	7		3			.180	.180	0	0	C-14, OF-7, SS-1

Dick Barone

BARONE, RICHARD ANTHONY BR TR 5'9" 165 lbs.
B. Oct. 13, 1932, San Jose, Calif.

	G	AB	H	2B	3B	HR	HR %	R	RBI	BB	SO	SB	BA	SA	PH AB	PH H	G by POS
1960 **PIT N**	3	6	0	0	0	0	0.0	0	0	0	1	0	.000	.000	0	0	SS-2

Bob Barr

BARR, ROBERT McCLELLAND 192 lbs.
B. 1856, Washington, D. C.   D. Mar. 11, 1930, Washington, D. C.

	G	AB	H	2B	3B	HR	HR %	R	RBI	BB	SO	SB	BA	SA	PH AB	PH H	G by POS
1883 **PIT AA**	37	142	35	4	3	0	0.0	12		5			.246	.317	0	0	P-26, OF-14, 1B-4, 3B-1
1884 **2 teams**	**WAS**	**AA** (39G –	.148)		**IND**	**AA**	(18G –	.185)									
" total	57	200	32	6	3	2	1.0	21		8			.160	.250	0	0	P-48, OF-7, 1B-2
1886 **WAS N**	22	79	13	2	0	0	0.0	6	2	4	23		.165	.190	0	0	P-22
1890 **ROC AA**	57	201	36	2	0	2	1.0	22		13		1	.179	.219	0	0	P-57
1891 **NY N**	5	11	1	0	0	0	0.0	0	0	2	3	0	.091	.091	0	0	P-5
5 yrs.	178	633	117	14	6	4	0.6	61		32	26	1	.185	.245	0	0	P-158, OF-21, 1B-6, 3B-1

Scotty Barr

BARR, HYDER EDWARD BR TR 6' 175 lbs.
B. Oct. 6, 1886, Bristol, Tenn.   D. Dec. 2, 1934, Fort Smith, Ark.

	G	AB	H	2B	3B	HR	HR %	R	RBI	BB	SO	SB	BA	SA	PH AB	PH H	G by POS
1908 **PHI A**	19	56	8	2	0	0	0.0	4	1	3		0	.143	.179	1	0	2B-11, 3B-4, 1B-2
1909	22	51	4	1	0	0	0.0	5	1	11		2	.078	.098	0	0	OF-15, 1B-7
2 yrs.	41	107	12	3	0	0	0.0	9	2	14		2	.112	.140	1	0	OF-15, 2B-11, 1B-9, 3B-4

Cuno Barragan

BARRAGAN, FACUNDO ANTHONY BR TR 5'11" 180 lbs.
B. June 20, 1932, Sacramento, Calif.

	G	AB	H	2B	3B	HR	HR %	R	RBI	BB	SO	SB	BA	SA	PH AB	PH H	G by POS
1961 **CHI N**	10	28	6	0	0	1	3.6	3	2	2	7	0	.214	.321	0	0	C-10
1962	58	134	27	6	1	0	0.0	11	12	21	28	0	.201	.261	7	0	C-55
1963	1	1	0	0	0	0	0.0	0	0	0	1	0	.000	.000	0	0	C-1
3 yrs.	69	163	33	6	1	1	0.6	14	14	23	36	0	.202	.270	7	0	C-66

German Barranca

BARRANCA, GERMAN BL TR 6' 160 lbs.
Also known as German Costales.
B. Oct. 19, 1956, Veracruz, Mexico

	G	AB	H	2B	3B	HR	HR %	R	RBI	BB	SO	SB	BA	SA	PH AB	PH H	G by POS
1979 **KC A**	5	5	3	1	0	0	0.0	3	0	0	0	3	.600	.800	0	0	DH-1, 3B-1, 2B-1
1980	7	0	0	0	0	0	–	3	0	0	0	0			0	0	
1981 **CIN N**	9	6	2	0	0	0	0.0	2	1	0	0	0	.333	.333	6	2	
1982	46	51	13	1	3	0	0.0	11	2	2	9	2	.255	.392	39	9	2B-6
4 yrs.	67	62	18	2	3	0	0.0	19	3	2	9	5	.290	.419	45	11	2B-7, DH-1, 3B-1

Bill Barrett

BARRETT, WILLIAM JOSEPH (Whispering Bill) BR TR 6' 175 lbs.
B. May 28, 1900, Cambridge, Mass.   D. Jan. 26, 1951, Cambridge, Mass.

	G	AB	H	2B	3B	HR	HR %	R	RBI	BB	SO	SB	BA	SA	PH AB	PH H	G by POS
1921 **PHI A**	14	30	7	2	1	0	0.0	3	3	0	5	0	.233	.367	0	0	SS-7, P-4, 3B-2, 1B-1
1923 **CHI A**	42	162	44	7	2	2	1.2	17	23	9	24	12	.272	.377	1	0	OF-40, 3B-1
1924	119	406	110	18	5	2	0.5	52	56	30	38	15	.271	.355	7	3	SS-77, OF-27, 3B-8
1925	81	245	89	23	3	3	1.2	44	40	24	27	5	.363	.518	7	1	2B-41, OF-27, SS-4, 3B-4
1926	111	368	113	31	4	6	1.6	46	61	25	26	9	.307	.462	6	3	OF-102, 1B-2
1927	147	556	159	35	9	4	0.7	62	83	52	46	20	.286	.403	0	0	OF-147
1928	76	235	65	11	2	3	1.3	34	26	14	30	8	.277	.379	9	2	OF-37, 2B-26

	G	AB	H	2B	3B	HR	HR %	R	RBI	BB	SO	SB	BA	SA	Pinch Hit AB	Pinch Hit H	G by POS

Bill Barrett continued

	G	AB	H	2B	3B	HR	HR%	R	RBI	BB	SO	SB	BA	SA	AB	H	G by POS
1929 2 teams	CHI	A (3G – .000)			BOS	A (111G – .270)											
" total	114	371	100	23	4	3	0.8	57	35	55	38	11	.270	.377	1	0	OF-109, 3B-1
1930 2 teams	BOS	A (6G – .167)			WAS	A (6G – .000)											
" total	12	22	3	1	0	0	0.0	3	1	2	5	0	.136	.182	5	0	OF-6
9 yrs.	716	2395	690	151	30	23	1.0	318	328	211	239	80	.288	.405	36	8	OF-495, SS-88, 2B-67, 3B-16, P-4, 1B-3

Bob Barrett

BARRETT, ROBERT SCHLEY (Jumbo)   BR TR 5'11" 175 lbs.
B. Jan. 27, 1899, Atlanta, Ga.   D. Jan. 18, 1982, Atlanta, Ga.

	G	AB	H	2B	3B	HR	HR%	R	RBI	BB	SO	SB	BA	SA	AB	H	G by POS
1923 CHI N	3	3	1	0	0	0	0.0	0	0	0	0	0	.333	.333	3	1	
1924	54	133	32	2	3	5	3.8	12	21	7	29	1	.241	.414	10	2	2B-25, 1B-10, 3B-8
1925 2 teams	CHI	N (14G – .313)			BKN	N (1G – .000)											
" total	15	33	10	1	0	0	0.0	1	8	1	4	1	.303	.333	5	2	3B-6, 2B-4
1927 BKN N	99	355	92	10	2	5	1.4	29	38	14	22	1	.259	.341	3	0	3B-96
1929 BOS A	68	126	34	10	0	0	0.0	15	19	10	6	3	.270	.349	23	7	3B-34, 1B-4, 2B-2, OF-1
5 yrs.	239	650	169	23	5	10	1.5	57	86	32	61	6	.260	.357	44	12	3B-144, 2B-31, 1B-14, OF-1

Jimmy Barrett

BARRETT, JAMES ERIGENA   BL TL 5'9" 170 lbs.
B. Mar. 28, 1875, Athol, Mass.   D. Oct. 24, 1921, Detroit, Mich.

	G	AB	H	2B	3B	HR	HR%	R	RBI	BB	SO	SB	BA	SA	AB	H	G by POS
1899 CIN N	26	92	34	2	4	0	0.0	30	10	18		4	.370	.478	0	0	OF-26
1900	137	545	172	11	7	5	0.9	114	42	72		44	.316	.389	0	0	OF-137
1901 DET A	135	542	159	16	9	4	0.7	110	65	76		26	.293	.378	0	0	OF-135
1902	136	509	154	19	6	4	0.8	93	44	74		24	.303	.387	0	0	OF-136
1903	136	517	163	13	10	2	0.4	95	31	74		27	.315	.391	0	0	OF-136
1904	162	624	167	10	5	0	0.0	83	31	79		15	.268	.300	0	0	OF-162
1905	20	67	17	1	0	0	0.0	2	3	6		0	.254	.269	2	0	OF-18
1906 CIN N	5	12	0	0	0	0	0.0	1	0	2			.000	.000	1	0	OF-4
1907 BOS A	106	390	95	11	6	1	0.3	52	28	38		3	.244	.310	7	3	OF-99
1908	2	8	1	0	0	0	0.0	0	1	1		0	.125	.125	0	0	OF-2
10 yrs.	865	3306	962	83	47	16	0.5	580	255	440		143	.291	.359	10	3	OF-855

Johnny Barrett

BARRETT, JOHN JOSEPH   BL TL 5'10½" 170 lbs.
B. Dec. 18, 1915, Lowell, Mass.   D. Aug. 17, 1974, Seabrook Beach, N. H.

	G	AB	H	2B	3B	HR	HR%	R	RBI	BB	SO	SB	BA	SA	AB	H	G by POS
1942 PIT N	111	332	82	11	6	0	0.0	56	26	48	42	10	.247	.316	13	4	OF-94
1943	130	290	67	12	3	1	0.3	41	32	32	23	5	.231	.303	27	11	OF-99
1944	149	568	153	24	19	7	1.2	99	83	86	56	28	.269	.415	2	1	OF-147
1945	142	507	130	29	4	15	3.0	97	67	79	68	25	.256	.418	6	3	OF-132
1946 2 teams	PIT	N (32G – .169)			BOS	N (24G – .233)											
" total	56	114	22	6	0	0	0.0	10	12	20	12	1	.193	.246	16	4	OF-38
5 yrs.	588	1811	454	82	32	23	1.3	303	220	265	201	69	.251	.369	64	23	OF-510

Marty Barrett

BARRETT, MARTIN F.   5'9" 170 lbs.
B. Nov., 1860, Port Huron, N. Y.   D. Jan. 29, 1910, Holyoke, Mass.

	G	AB	H	2B	3B	HR	HR%	R	RBI	BB	SO	SB	BA	SA	AB	H	G by POS
1884 BOS N	3	6	0	0	0	0	0.0	0		0	4		.000	.000	0	0	C-3

Marty Barrett

BARRETT, MARTIN GLENN   BR TR 5'9" 160 lbs.
B. June 23, 1958, Arcadia, Calif.

	G	AB	H	2B	3B	HR	HR%	R	RBI	BB	SO	SB	BA	SA	AB	H	G by POS
1982 BOS A	8	18	1	0	0	0	0.0	0	0	0	1	0	.056	.056	0	0	2B-7
1983	33	44	10	1	1	0	0.0	7	2	3	1	0	.227	.295	0	0	2B-23, DH-5
1984	139	475	144	23	3	3	0.6	56	45	42	25	4	.303	.383	0	0	2B-136
3 yrs.	180	537	155	24	4	3	0.6	63	47	45	27	4	.289	.365	1	0	2B-166, DH-5

Jose Barrios

BARRIOS, JOSE MANUEL   BR TR 6'4" 195 lbs.
B. June 26, 1957, New York, N. Y.

	G	AB	H	2B	3B	HR	HR%	R	RBI	BB	SO	SB	BA	SA	AB	H	G by POS
1982 SF N	19	19	3	0	0	0	0.0	2	0	1	4	0	.158	.158	3	0	1B-7

Red Barron

BARRON, DAVID IRENUS   BR TR 5'11½" 185 lbs.
B. June 21, 1900, Clarksville, Ga.   D. Oct. 4, 1982, Atlanta, Ga.

	G	AB	H	2B	3B	HR	HR%	R	RBI	BB	SO	SB	BA	SA	AB	H	G by POS
1929 BOS N	10	21	4	1	0	0	0.0	3	1	1	4	2	.190	.238	1	0	OF-6

Cuke Barrows

BARROWS, ROLAND   BR TL 5'8" 158 lbs.
B. Oct. 20, 1883, Gray, Me.   D. Feb. 10, 1955, Gorham, Me.

	G	AB	H	2B	3B	HR	HR%	R	RBI	BB	SO	SB	BA	SA	AB	H	G by POS
1909 CHI A	5	20	3	0	0	0	0.0	1	2	0		0	.150	.150	0	0	OF-5
1910	6	20	4	0	0	0	0.0	0	1	3		0	.200	.200	0	0	OF-6
1911	13	46	9	2	0	0	0.0	5	4	7		2	.196	.239	0	0	OF-13
1912	8	13	3	0	0	0	0.0	0	2	2		1	.231	.231	4	1	OF-3
4 yrs.	32	99	19	2	0	0	0.0	6	9	12		3	.192	.212	4	1	OF-27

Jack Barry

BARRY, JOHN JOSEPH   BR TR 5'9" 158 lbs.
B. Apr. 26, 1887, Meriden, Conn.   D. Apr. 23, 1961, Shrewsbury, Mass.
Manager 1917.

	G	AB	H	2B	3B	HR	HR%	R	RBI	BB	SO	SB	BA	SA	AB	H	G by POS
1908 PHI A	40	135	30	4	3	0	0.0	13	8	10		5	.222	.296	3	1	2B-20, SS-14, 3B-3
1909	124	409	88	11	2	1	0.2	56	23	44		17	.215	.259	0	0	SS-124
1910	145	487	126	19	5	3	0.6	64	60	52		14	.259	.337	0	0	SS-145
1911	127	442	117	18	7	1	0.2	73	63	38		30	.265	.344	0	0	SS-127
1912	139	483	126	19	9	0	0.0	76	55	47		22	.261	.337	0	0	SS-139
1913	134	455	125	20	6	3	0.7	62	85	44	32	15	.275	.365	0	0	SS-134
1914	140	467	113	12	0	0	0.0	57	42	53	34	2	.242	.268	0	0	SS-140
1915 2 teams	PHI	A (54G – .222)			BOS	A (78G – .262)											
" total	132	442	108	19	4	0	0.0	46	41	39	20	6	.244	.305	0	0	2B-78, SS-54
1916 BOS A	94	330	67	6	1	0	0.0	28	20	17	24	8	.203	.227	0	0	2B-94
1917	116	388	83	9	0	2	0.5	45	30	47	27	12	.214	.253	0	0	2B-116
1919	31	108	26	5	1	0	0.0	13	2	5	5	2	.241	.306	0	0	2B-31
11 yrs.	1222	4146	1009	142	38	10	0.2	533	429	396	142	153	.243	.303	3	1	SS-877, 2B-339, 3B-3

	G	AB	H	2B	3B	HR	HR %	R	RBI	BB	SO	SB	BA	SA	Pinch Hit AB	Pinch Hit H	G by POS

Jack Barry continued

WORLD SERIES

	G	AB	H	2B	3B	HR	HR %	R	RBI	BB	SO	SB	BA	SA	PH AB	PH H	G by POS
1910 PHI A	5	17	4	2	0	0	0.0	3	3	1	3	0	.235	.353	0	0	SS-5
1911	6	19	7	4	0	0	0.0	2	2	0	1	2	.368	.579	0	0	SS-6
1913	5	20	6	3	0	0	0.0	3	2	0	0	0	.300	.450	0	0	SS-5
1914	4	14	1	0	0	0	0.0	1	0	1	3	1	.071	.071	0	0	SS-4
1915 BOS A	5	17	3	0	0	0	0.0	1	1	1	2	0	.176	.176	0	0	2B-5
5 yrs.	25	87	21	9 3rd	0	0	0.0	10	8	3	9	3	.241	.345	0	0	SS-20, 2B-5

Rich Barry

BARRY, RICHARD DONOVAN
B. Sept. 12, 1940, Berkeley, Calif.　　　BR TR 6'4" 205 lbs.

	G	AB	H	2B	3B	HR	HR %	R	RBI	BB	SO	SB	BA	SA	PH AB	PH H	G by POS
1969 PHI N	20	32	6	1	0	0	0.0	4	0	5	6	0	.188	.219	11	2	OF-9

Shad Barry

BARRY, JOHN C.
B. Sept. 28, 1878, Newburgh, N. Y.　　D. Nov. 27, 1936, Los Angeles, Calif.　　BR TR

	G	AB	H	2B	3B	HR	HR %	R	RBI	BB	SO	SB	BA	SA	PH AB	PH H	G by POS
1899 WAS N	78	247	71	7	5	1	0.4	31	33	12		11	.287	.368	3	0	OF-23, 1B-22, SS-13, 3B-13, 2B-7
1900 BOS N	81	254	66	10	7	1	0.4	40	37	13		9	.260	.366	14	3	OF-24, SS-18, 2B-16, 1B-10, 3B-1
1901 2 teams		BOS	N (11G – .175)		PHI	N	(67G – .246)										
" total	78	292	69	12	0	1	0.3	38	28	17		14	.236	.288	4	0	2B-35, OF-24, 3B-16, SS-1
1902 PHI N	138	543	156	20	6	3	0.6	65	57	44		14	.287	.363	0	0	OF-137, 1B-1
1903	138	550	152	24	5	1	0.2	75	60	30		26	.276	.344	0	0	OF-107, 1B-30, 3B-1
1904 2 teams		PHI	N (35G – .205)		CHI	N	(73G – .262)										
" total	108	385	94	9	2	1	0.3	44	29	28		14	.244	.286	3	0	OF-62, 1B-18, 3B-17, SS-8, 2B-2
1905 2 teams		CHI	N (27G – .212)		CIN	N	(125G – .324)										
" total	152	598	182	13	12	1	0.2	100	66	38		21	.304	.371	1	0	1B-149, OF-2
1906 2 teams		CIN	N (73G – .287)		STL	N	(62G – .249)										
" total	135	516	139	19	6	1	0.2	64	45	41		17	.269	.335	0	0	OF-65, 1B-64, 3B-6
1907 STL N	80	292	72	5	2	0	0.0	30	19	28		4	.247	.277	0	0	OF-81
1908 2 teams		STL	N (74G – .228)		NY	N	(37G – .149)										
" total	111	335	71	9	2	0	0.0	29	16	28		10	.212	.251	7	1	OF-100, SS-2
10 yrs.	1099	4012	1072	128	47	10	0.2	516	390	279		140	.267	.330	32	4	OF-625, 1B-294, 2B-60, 3B-54, SS-42

Dick Bartell

BARTELL, RICHARD WILLIAM (Rowdy Richard)
B. Nov. 22, 1907, Chicago, Ill.　　　BR TR 5'9" 160 lbs.

	G	AB	H	2B	3B	HR	HR %	R	RBI	BB	SO	SB	BA	SA	PH AB	PH H	G by POS
1927 PIT N	1	2	0	0	0	0	0.0	0	0	2	0	0	.000	.000	0	0	SS-1
1928	72	233	71	8	4	1	0.4	27	36	21	18	4	.305	.386	2	0	2B-39, SS-27, 3B-1
1929	143	610	184	40	13	2	0.3	101	57	40	29	11	.302	.420	0	0	SS-97, 2B-70
1930	129	475	152	32	13	4	0.8	69	75	39	34	8	.320	.467	3	0	SS-126
1931 PHI N	135	554	160	43	7	0	0.0	88	34	27	38	6	.289	.392	0	0	SS-133, 2B-3
1932	154	614	189	48	7	1	0.2	118	53	64	47	8	.308	.414	0	0	SS-154
1933	152	587	159	25	5	1	0.2	78	37	56	46	6	.271	.336	0	0	SS-152
1934	146	604	187	30	4	0	0.0	102	37	64	59	13	.310	.373	0	0	SS-146
1935 NY N	137	539	141	28	4	14	2.6	60	53	37	52	5	.262	.406	0	0	SS-137
1936	145	510	152	31	3	8	1.6	71	42	40	36	6	.298	.418	0	0	SS-144
1937	128	516	158	38	2	14	2.7	91	62	40	38	5	.306	.469	0	0	SS-128
1938	127	481	126	26	1	9	1.9	67	49	55	60	4	.262	.376	0	0	SS-127
1939 CHI N	105	336	80	24	2	3	0.9	37	34	42	25	6	.238	.348	3	1	SS-101, 3B-1
1940 DET A	139	528	123	24	3	7	1.3	76	53	76	53	12	.233	.330	0	0	SS-139
1941 2 teams		DET	A (5G – .167)		NY	N	(104G – .303)										
" total	109	385	115	21	0	5	1.3	44	36	54	31	6	.299	.392	3	0	3B-84, SS-26
1942 NY N	90	316	77	10	3	5	1.6	53	24	44	34	4	.244	.342	8	1	3B-52, SS-31
1943	99	337	91	14	0	5	1.5	48	28	47	27	5	.270	.356	10	1	3B-54, SS-33
1946	5	2	0	0	0	0	0.0	0	0	0	0	0	.000	.000	0	0	3B-4, 2B-2
18 yrs.	2016	7629	2165	442	71	79	1.0	1130	710	748	627	109	.284	.391	29	3	SS-1702, 3B-196, 2B-114

WORLD SERIES

	G	AB	H	2B	3B	HR	HR %	R	RBI	BB	SO	SB	BA	SA	PH AB	PH H	G by POS
1936 NY N	6	21	8	3	0	1	4.8	5	3	4	4	0	.381	.667	0	0	SS-6
1937	5	21	5	1	0	0	0.0	3	1	0	3	0	.238	.286	0	0	SS-5
1940 DET A	7	26	7	2	0	0	0.0	2	3	3	3	0	.269	.346	0	0	SS-7
3 yrs.	18	68	20	6	0	1	1.5	10	7	7	10	0	.294	.426	0	0	SS-18

Tony Bartirome

BARTIROME, ANTHONY JOSEPH
B. May 9, 1932, Pittsburgh, Pa.　　　BL TL 5'10" 155 lbs.

	G	AB	H	2B	3B	HR	HR %	R	RBI	BB	SO	SB	BA	SA	PH AB	PH H	G by POS
1952 PIT N	124	355	78	10	3	0	0.0	32	16	26	37	3	.220	.265	1	0	1B-118

Boyd Bartley

BARTLEY, BOYD OWEN
B. Feb. 11, 1920, Chicago, Ill.　　　BR TR 5'8½" 165 lbs.

	G	AB	H	2B	3B	HR	HR %	R	RBI	BB	SO	SB	BA	SA	PH AB	PH H	G by POS
1943 BKN N	9	21	1	0	0	0	0.0	1	0	1	3	0	.048	.048	0	0	SS-9

Irv Bartling

BARTLING, IRVING HENRY
B. June 27, 1914, Bay City, Mich.　　D. June 12, 1973, Westland, Mich.　　BR TR 6' 175 lbs.

	G	AB	H	2B	3B	HR	HR %	R	RBI	BB	SO	SB	BA	SA	PH AB	PH H	G by POS
1938 PHI A	14	46	8	1	1	0	0.0	5	5	3	7	0	.174	.239	0	0	SS-13, 3B-1

Bob Barton

BARTON, ROBERT WILBUR
B. July 30, 1941, Norwood, Ohio　　　BR TR 6' 175 lbs.

	G	AB	H	2B	3B	HR	HR %	R	RBI	BB	SO	SB	BA	SA	PH AB	PH H	G by POS
1965 SF N	4	7	4	0	0	0	0.0	1	1	0	0	0	.571	.571	2	1	C-2
1966	43	91	16	2	1	0	0.0	1	3	5	5	0	.176	.220	4	0	C-39
1967	7	19	4	0	0	0	0.0	0	1	0	2	0	.211	.211	0	0	C-7
1968	46	92	24	0	0	0	0.0	4	5	7	18	0	.261	.283	2	0	C-45
1969	49	106	18	2	0	0	0.0	5	1	9	19	0	.170	.189	0	0	C-49
1970 SD N	61	188	41	6	0	4	2.1	15	16	15	37	1	.218	.314	2	0	C-59

	G	AB	H	2B	3B	HR	HR%	R	RBI	BB	SO	SB	BA	SA	Pinch Hit AB	Pinch Hit H	G by POS

Bob Barton continued

	G	AB	H	2B	3B	HR	HR%	R	RBI	BB	SO	SB	BA	SA	PH AB	PH H	G by POS
1971	121	376	94	17	2	5	1.3	23	23	35	49	0	.250	.346	3	1	C-119
1972	29	88	17	1	0	0	0.0	1	9	2	19	2	.193	.205	0	0	C-29
1973 CIN N	3	1	0	0	0	0	0.0	0	0	1	0	0	.000	.000	1	0	C-2
1974 SD N	30	81	19	1	0	0	0.0	4	7	13	19	0	.235	.247	1	1	C-29
10 yrs.	393	1049	237	31	3	9	0.9	54	66	87	168	3	.226	.287	15	3	C-380

Harry Barton

BARTON, HARRY LAMB
B. Jan. 20, 1875, Chester, Pa.   D. Jan. 25, 1955, Upland, Pa.
BB TR 5'6½" 155 lbs.

	G	AB	H	2B	3B	HR	HR%	R	RBI	BB	SO	SB	BA	SA	PH AB	PH H	G by POS
1905 PHI A	29	60	10	2	1	0	0.0	5	3	3		2	.167	.233	10	1	C-13, 3B-2, 1B-2, OF-1

Vince Barton

BARTON, VINCENT DAVID
B. Feb. 1, 1908, Edmonton, Alta., Canada   D. Sept. 13, 1972, Toronto, Ont., Canada
BL TR 6' 180 lbs.

	G	AB	H	2B	3B	HR	HR%	R	RBI	BB	SO	SB	BA	SA	PH AB	PH H	G by POS
1931 CHI N	66	239	57	10	1	13	5.4	45	50	21	40	1	.238	.452	4	1	OF-61
1932	36	134	30	2	3	3	2.2	19	15	8	22	0	.224	.351	2	0	OF-34
2 yrs.	102	373	87	12	4	16	4.3	64	65	29	62	1	.233	.416	6	1	OF-95

Dave Bartosch

BARTOSCH, DAVID ROBERT
B. Mar. 24, 1917, St. Louis, Mo.
BR TR 6'1" 190 lbs.

	G	AB	H	2B	3B	HR	HR%	R	RBI	BB	SO	SB	BA	SA	PH AB	PH H	G by POS
1945 STL N	24	47	12	1	0	0	0.0	9	1	6	3	0	.255	.277	13	5	OF-11

Monty Basgall

BASGALL, ROMANUS
B. Feb. 8, 1922, Pfeifer, Kans.
BR TR 5'10½" 175 lbs.

	G	AB	H	2B	3B	HR	HR%	R	RBI	BB	SO	SB	BA	SA	PH AB	PH H	G by POS
1948 PIT N	38	51	11	1	0	2	3.9	12	6	3	5	0	.216	.353	5	1	2B-22
1949	107	308	67	9	1	2	0.6	25	26	31	32	1	.218	.273	4	1	2B-98, 3B-3
1951	55	153	32	5	2	0	0.0	15	9	12	14	0	.209	.268	0	0	2B-55
3 yrs.	200	512	110	15	3	4	0.8	52	41	46	51	1	.215	.279	9	2	2B-175, 3B-3

Al Bashang

BASHANG, ALBERT C.
B. Aug. 22, 1888, Cincinnati, Ohio   D. June 23, 1967, Cincinnati, Ohio
BB TR 5'8" 150 lbs.

	G	AB	H	2B	3B	HR	HR%	R	RBI	BB	SO	SB	BA	SA	PH AB	PH H	G by POS
1912 DET A	5	12	1	0	0	0	0.0	3	0	3		0	.083	.083	0	0	OF-5
1918 BKN N	2	5	1	0	0	0	0.0	0	0	0		0	.200	.200	1	0	OF-1
2 yrs.	7	17	2	0	0	0	0.0	3	0	3	0	0	.118	.118	1	0	OF-6

Walt Bashore

BASHORE, WALTER FRANKLIN
B. Oct. 6, 1909, Harrisburg, Pa.
BR TR 6' 170 lbs.

	G	AB	H	2B	3B	HR	HR%	R	RBI	BB	SO	SB	BA	SA	PH AB	PH H	G by POS
1936 PHI N	10	10	2	0	0	0	0.0	1	0	1	3	0	.200	.200	2	0	OF-6, 3B-1

Eddie Basinski

BASINSKI, EDWIN FRANK (Fiddler)
B. Nov. 4, 1922, Buffalo, N. Y.
BR TR 6'1" 172 lbs.

	G	AB	H	2B	3B	HR	HR%	R	RBI	BB	SO	SB	BA	SA	PH AB	PH H	G by POS
1944 BKN N	39	105	27	4	1	0	0.0	13	9	6	10	1	.257	.314	1	0	2B-37, SS-3
1945	108	336	88	9	4	0	0.0	30	33	11	33	0	.262	.313	2	0	SS-101, 2B-6
1947 PIT N	56	161	32	6	2	4	2.5	15	17	18	27	0	.199	.335	0	0	2B-56
3 yrs.	203	602	147	19	7	4	0.7	58	59	35	70	1	.244	.319	3	0	SS-104, 2B-99

Doc Bass

BASS, WILLIAM CAPERS
B. Dec. 4, 1899, Macon, Ga.   D. Jan. 12, 1970, Macon, Ga.
5'10" 165 lbs.

	G	AB	H	2B	3B	HR	HR%	R	RBI	BB	SO	SB	BA	SA	PH AB	PH H	G by POS
1918 BOS N	1	1	1	0	0	0	0.0	1	0	0	0	0	1.000	1.000	1	1	

John Bass

BASS, JOHN E.
B. 1850, Baltimore, Md.   Deceased.
5'6" 150 lbs.

	G	AB	H	2B	3B	HR	HR%	R	RBI	BB	SO	SB	BA	SA	PH AB	PH H	G by POS
1877 HAR N	1	4	1	0	0	0	0.0	1	0	0	0		.250	.250	0	0	OF-1

Kevin Bass

BASS, KEVIN
B. May 12, 1959, Menlo Park, Calif.
BB TR 6' 180 lbs.

	G	AB	H	2B	3B	HR	HR%	R	RBI	BB	SO	SB	BA	SA	PH AB	PH H	G by POS
1982 2 teams	MIL A (18G – .000)				HOU N (12G – .042)												
" total	30	33	1	0	0	0	0.0	6	1	1	9	0	.030	.030	1	0	OF-21, DH-2
1983 HOU N	88	195	46	7	3	2	1.0	25	18	6	27	2	.236	.333	43	11	OF-52
1984	121	331	86	17	5	2	0.6	33	29	6	57	5	.260	.360	44	13	OF-81
3 yrs.	239	559	133	24	8	4	0.7	64	48	13	93	7	.238	.331	88	24	OF-154, DH-2

Randy Bass

BASS, RANDY WILLIAM
B. Mar. 13, 1954, Lawton, Okla.
BL TR 6'1" 210 lbs.

	G	AB	H	2B	3B	HR	HR%	R	RBI	BB	SO	SB	BA	SA	PH AB	PH H	G by POS
1977 MIN A	9	19	2	0	0	0	0.0	0	0	0	5	0	.105	.105	4	0	DH-6
1978 KC A	2	2	0	0	0	0	0.0	0	0	0	0	0	.000	.000	2	0	
1979 MON N	2	1	0	0	0	0	0.0	0	0	0	0	0	.000	.000	1	0	1B-1
1980 SD N	19	49	14	0	1	3	6.1	5	8	7	7	0	.286	.510	3	0	1B-15
1981	69	176	37	4	1	4	2.3	13	20	20	28	0	.210	.313	19	5	1B-50
1982 2 teams	SD N (13G – .200)				TEX A (16G – .208)												
" total	29	78	16	2	0	2	2.6	6	14	3	11	0	.205	.308	5	1	1B-15, DH-7
6 yrs.	130	325	69	6	2	9	2.8	24	42	30	51	0	.212	.326	34	6	1B-81, DH-13

Charley Bassett

BASSETT, CHARLES EDWIN
B. Feb. 9, 1863, Central Falls, R. I.   D. May 28, 1942, Pawtucket, R. I.
BR TR 5'10" 150 lbs.

	G	AB	H	2B	3B	HR	HR%	R	RBI	BB	SO	SB	BA	SA	PH AB	PH H	G by POS
1884 PRO N	27	79	11	2	1	0	0.0	10		4	15		.139	.190	0	0	3B-13, SS-7, OF-2, 2B-1
1885	82	285	41	8	2	0	0.0	21	16	19	60		.144	.186	0	0	2B-39, SS-23, 3B-20, C-1
1886 KC N	90	342	89	19	8	2	0.6	41	32	36	43		.260	.380	0	0	SS-82, 3B-8
1887 IND N	119	452	104	14	6	1	0.2	41	47	25	31	25	.230	.294	0	0	2B-119
1888	128	481	116	20	3	2	0.4	58	60	32	41	24	.241	.308	0	0	2B-128
1889	127	477	117	12	5	4	0.8	64	68	37	38	15	.245	.317	0	0	2B-127
1890 NY N	100	410	98	13	8	0	0.0	52	54	29	25	14	.239	.310	0	0	2B-100
1891	130	524	136	19	8	0	0.0	60	68	36	29	16	.260	.349	0	0	3B-121, 2B-9
1892 2 teams	NY N (35G – .208)				LOU N (79G – .214)												
" total	114	443	94	7	8	2	0.5	45	51	21	29	16	.212	.278	0	0	3B-78, 2B-36
9 yrs.	917	3493	806	114	49	15	0.4	392	395	239	311	110	.231	.304	0	0	2B-559, 3B-240, SS-112, OF-2, C-1

	G	AB	H	2B	3B	HR	HR %	R	RBI	BB	SO	SB	BA	SA	Pinch Hit AB	Pinch Hit H	G by POS

Johnny Bassler

BASSLER, JOHN LANDIS
B. June 3, 1895, Mechanics Grove, Pa.   D. June 29, 1979, Santa Monica, Calif.
BL TR 5'9"   170 lbs.

	G	AB	H	2B	3B	HR	HR%	R	RBI	BB	SO	SB	BA	SA	PH AB	PH H	G by POS
1913 CLE A	1	2	0	0	0	0	0.0	0	0	0	0	0	.000	.000	0	0	C-1
1914	43	77	14	1	1	0	0.0	5	6	15	8	3	.182	.221	10	1	C-25, OF-1, 3B-1
1921 DET A	119	388	119	18	5	0	0.0	37	56	58	16	2	.307	.379	3	1	C-115
1922	121	372	120	14	0	0	0.0	41	41	62	12	2	.323	.360	2	0	C-118
1923	135	383	114	12	3	0	0.0	45	49	76	13	2	.298	.345	5	2	C-128
1924	124	379	131	20	3	1	0.3	43	68	62	11	2	.346	.422	3	1	C-122
1925	121	344	96	19	3	0	0.0	40	52	74	6	1	.279	.352	3	0	C-118
1926	66	174	53	8	1	0	0.0	20	22	45	6	0	.305	.362	2	0	C-63
1927	81	200	57	7	0	0	0.0	19	24	45	9	1	.285	.320	12	2	C-67
9 yrs.	811	2319	704	99	16	1	0.0	250	318	437	81	13	.304	.361	40	7	C-757, OF-1, 3B-1

Charlie Bastian

BASTIAN, CHARLES J.
B. July 4, 1860, Philadelphia, Pa.   D. Jan. 18, 1932, Pennsauken, N. J.
BR TR 5'6½"   145 lbs.

	G	AB	H	2B	3B	HR	HR%	R	RBI	BB	SO	SB	BA	SA	PH AB	PH H	G by POS
1884 2 teams	WIL U (17G – .200)			KC U (11G – .196)													
" total	28	106	21	4	3	3	2.8	12		7			.198	.377	0	0	2B-27, SS-1, P-1
1885 PHI N	103	389	65	11	5	4	1.0	63		35	82		.167	.252	0	0	SS-103
1886	105	373	81	9	11	2	0.5	46	38	33	73		.217	.316	0	0	2B-87, SS-10, 3B-8
1887	60	221	47	11	1	1	0.5	33	21	19	29	11	.213	.285	0	0	2B-39, SS-18, 3B-4
1888	80	275	53	4	1	1	0.4	30	17	27	41	12	.193	.225	0	0	2B-65, 3B-14, SS-1
1889 CHI N	46	155	21	0	0	0	0.0	19	10	25	46	1	.135	.135	0	0	SS-45, 2B-1
1890 CHI P	80	283	54	10	5	0	0.0	38	29	33	37	4	.191	.261	0	0	SS-64, 2B-12, 3B-4
1891 2 teams	C-M AA (1G – .000)			PHI N (1G – .000)													
" total	2	4	0	0	0	0	0.0	0	0	0	0	0	.000	.000	0	0	SS-1, 2B-1
8 yrs.	504	1806	342	49	26	11	0.6	241	114	179	308	28	.189	.264	0	0	SS-243, 2B-232, 3B-30, P-1

Emil Batch

BATCH, EMIL HENRY (Heinie)
B. Jan. 21, 1880, Brooklyn, N. Y.   D. Aug. 23, 1926, Brooklyn, N. Y.
BR TR

	G	AB	H	2B	3B	HR	HR%	R	RBI	BB	SO	SB	BA	SA	PH AB	PH H	G by POS
1904 BKN N	28	94	24	1	2	2	2.1	9	7	1		6	.255	.372	0	0	3B-28
1905	145	568	143	20	11	5	0.9	64	49	26		21	.252	.352	0	0	3B-145
1906	59	203	52	7	6	0	0.0	23	11	15		3	.256	.350	6	1	OF-50, 3B-2
1907	116	388	96	10	3	0	0.0	38	31	23		7	.247	.289	8	1	OF-102, 3B-2, SS-1, 2B-1
4 yrs.	348	1253	315	38	22	7	0.6	134	98	65		37	.251	.334	14	2	3B-177, OF-152, SS-1, 2B-1

John Bateman

BATEMAN, JOHN ALVIN
B. July 21, 1942, Killeen, Tex.
BR TR 6'3"   210 lbs.

	G	AB	H	2B	3B	HR	HR%	R	RBI	BB	SO	SB	BA	SA	PH AB	PH H	G by POS
1963 HOU N	128	404	85	8	6	10	2.5	23	59	13	103	0	.210	.334	13	2	C-115
1964	74	221	42	8	0	5	2.3	18	19	17	48	0	.190	.294	2	0	C-72
1965	45	142	28	3	1	7	4.9	15	14	12	37	0	.197	.380	5	0	C-39
1966	131	433	121	24	3	17	3.9	39	70	20	74	0	.279	.467	11	2	C-121
1967	76	252	48	9	0	2	0.8	16	17	17	53	0	.190	.250	4	1	C-71
1968	111	350	87	19	0	4	1.1	28	33	23	46	1	.249	.337	2	0	C-108
1969 MON N	74	235	49	4	0	8	3.4	16	19	12	44	0	.209	.328	7	2	C-66
1970	139	520	123	21	5	15	2.9	51	68	28	75	8	.237	.383	2	0	C-137
1971	139	492	119	17	3	10	2.0	34	56	19	87	1	.242	.350	4	1	C-137
1972 2 teams	MON N (18G – .241)			PHI N (82G – .222)													
" total	100	281	63	10	0	3	1.1	10	20	11	47	0	.224	.292	14	2	C-87
10 yrs.	1017	3330	765	123	18	81	2.4	250	375	172	614	10	.230	.350	64	11	C-953

Bud Bates

BATES, HUBERT EDGAR
B. Mar. 16, 1912, Los Angeles, Calif.
BR TR 6'   165 lbs.

	G	AB	H	2B	3B	HR	HR%	R	RBI	BB	SO	SB	BA	SA	PH AB	PH H	G by POS
1939 PHI N	15	58	15	2	0	1	1.7	8	2	2	8	1	.259	.345	0	0	OF-14

Charlie Bates

BATES, CHARLES WILLIAM
B. Sept. 17, 1905, Philadelphia, Pa.
BR TR 5'10"   165 lbs.

	G	AB	H	2B	3B	HR	HR%	R	RBI	BB	SO	SB	BA	SA	PH AB	PH H	G by POS
1927 PHI A	9	38	9	2	2	0	0.0	5	2	3	5	3	.237	.395	0	0	OF-9

Del Bates

BATES, DELBERT OAKLEY JR.
B. June 12, 1941, Seattle, Wash.
BL TR 6'2"   195 lbs.

	G	AB	H	2B	3B	HR	HR%	R	RBI	BB	SO	SB	BA	SA	PH AB	PH H	G by POS
1970 PHI N	22	60	8	2	0	0	0.0	1	1	6	15	0	.133	.167	5	0	C-20

Johnny Bates

BATES, JOHN WILLIAM
B. Jan. 10, 1882, Steubenville, Ohio   D. Feb. 10, 1949, Steubenville, Ohio
BL TL 5'7"   168 lbs.

	G	AB	H	2B	3B	HR	HR%	R	RBI	BB	SO	SB	BA	SA	PH AB	PH H	G by POS
1906 BOS N	140	504	127	21	5	6	1.2	52	54	36		9	.252	.349	0	0	OF-140
1907	126	447	116	18	12	2	0.4	52	49	39		11	.260	.367	5	1	OF-120
1908	127	445	115	14	6	1	0.2	48	29	35		25	.258	.324	10	0	OF-117
1909 2 teams	BOS N (63G – .288)			PHI N (77G – .293)													
" total	140	502	146	26	4	2	0.4	70	38	48		37	.291	.371	5	1	OF-133
1910 PHI N	135	498	152	26	11	3	0.6	91	61	61	49	31	.305	.420	4	0	OF-131
1911 CIN N	148	518	151	24	13	1	0.2	89	61	103	59	33	.292	.394	1	0	OF-147
1912	81	239	69	12	7	1	0.4	45	29	47	16	10	.289	.410	12	3	OF-65
1913	131	407	113	13	7	6	1.5	63	51	67	30	21	.278	.388	17	5	OF-112
1914 3 teams	CIN N (67G – .245)			CHI N (9G – .125)			BAL F (59G – .305)										
" total	135	361	99	13	8	3	0.8	62	45	68	19	10	.274	.380	8	1	OF-119
9 yrs.	1163	3921	1088	167	73	25	0.6	572	417	504	173	187	.277	.376	62	12	OF-1084

Ray Bates

BATES, RAYMOND
B. Feb. 8, 1890, Paterson, N. J.   D. Aug. 15, 1970, Tuscon, Ariz.
BR TR 6'2"   165 lbs.

	G	AB	H	2B	3B	HR	HR%	R	RBI	BB	SO	SB	BA	SA	PH AB	PH H	G by POS
1913 CLE A	20	30	5	0	2	0	0.0	4	4	3	9	0	.167	.300	1	0	3B-12, OF-2
1917 PHI A	127	485	115	20	7	2	0.4	47	66	21	39	12	.237	.320	3	0	3B-124
2 yrs.	147	515	120	20	9	2	0.4	51	70	24	48	15	.233	.318	4	0	3B-136, OF-2

	G	AB	H	2B	3B	HR	HR %	R	RBI	BB	SO	SB	BA	SA	Pinch Hit AB	Pinch Hit H	G by POS

Rafael Batista

BATISTA, RAFAEL   BL TL 6'1"   195 lbs.
B. Nov. 21, 1945, San Pedro de Macoris, Dominican Republic

	G	AB	H	2B	3B	HR	HR%	R	RBI	BB	SO	SB	BA	SA	AB	H	G by POS
1973 HOU N	12	15	4	0	0	0	0.0	2	2	1	6	0	.267	.267	6	0	1B-8
1975	10	10	3	1	0	0	0.0	0	0	0	4	0	.300	.400	10	3	
2 yrs.	22	25	7	1	0	0	0.0	2	2	1	10	0	.280	.320	16	3	1B-8

Bill Batsch

BATSCH, WILLIAM McKINLEY   BR TR 5'10½" 168 lbs.
B. May 18, 1892, Mingo Junction, Ohio   D. Dec. 31, 1963, Canton, Ohio

	G	AB	H	2B	3B	HR	HR%	R	RBI	BB	SO	SB	BA	SA	AB	H	G by POS
1916 PIT N	1	0	0	0	0	0	–	0	1	0	0	0	–	–	0	0	

Larry Battam

BATTAM, LAWRENCE   5'11"
B. May 1, 1878, Brooklyn, N. Y.   D. Jan. 27, 1938, Brooklyn, N. Y.

	G	AB	H	2B	3B	HR	HR%	R	RBI	BB	SO	SB	BA	SA	AB	H	G by POS
1895 NY N	2	4	1	0	0	0	0.0	0	0	2	1	0	.250	.250	0	0	3B-2

George Batten

BATTEN, GEORGE BURNETT   BR TR 5'11"   165 lbs.
B. Oct. 7, 1891, Haddonfield, N. J.   D. Aug. 4, 1972, New Port Ritchey, Fla.

	G	AB	H	2B	3B	HR	HR%	R	RBI	BB	SO	SB	BA	SA	AB	H	G by POS
1912 NY A	1	3	0	0	0	0	0.0	0	0	0		0	.000	.000	0	0	2B-1

Earl Battey

BATTEY, EARL JESSE   BR TR 6'1"   205 lbs.
B. Jan. 5, 1935, Los Angeles, Calif.

	G	AB	H	2B	3B	HR	HR%	R	RBI	BB	SO	SB	BA	SA	AB	H	G by POS
1955 CHI A	5	7	2	0	0	0	0.0	1	1	1	1	0	.286	.286	1	0	C-5
1956	4	4	1	0	0	0	0.0	1	0	1	1	0	.250	.250	0	0	C-3
1957	48	115	20	2	3	3	2.6	12	6	11	38	0	.174	.322	4	3	C-43
1958	68	168	38	8	0	8	4.8	24	26	24	34	1	.226	.417	17	1	C-49
1959	26	64	14	1	2	2	3.1	9	7	8	13	0	.219	.391	5	0	C-20
1960 WAS A	137	466	126	24	2	15	3.2	49	60	48	68	4	.270	.427	4	2	C-136
1961 MIN A	133	460	139	24	1	17	3.7	70	55	53	66	3	.302	.470	2	0	C-131
1962	148	522	146	20	3	11	2.1	58	57	57	48	0	.280	.393	1	0	C-147
1963	147	508	145	17	1	26	5.1	64	84	61	75	0	.285	.476	2	0	C-146
1964	131	405	110	17	1	12	3.0	33	52	51	49	1	.272	.407	8	2	C-125
1965	131	394	117	22	2	6	1.5	36	60	50	23	0	.297	.409	5	0	C-128
1966	115	364	93	12	1	4	1.1	30	34	43	30	4	.255	.327	2	1	C-113
1967	48	109	18	3	1	0	0.0	6	8	13	24	0	.165	.211	9	3	C-41
13 yrs.	1141	3586	969	150	17	104	2.9	393	449	421	470	13	.270	.409	60	12	C-1087

WORLD SERIES

	G	AB	H	2B	3B	HR	HR%	R	RBI	BB	SO	SB	BA	SA	AB	H	G by POS
1965 MIN A	7	25	3	0	1	0	0.0	1	2	0	5	0	.120	.200	0	0	C-7

Joe Battin

BATTIN, JOSEPH V.   BR TR
B. Nov. 11, 1851, Philadelphia, Pa.   D. Oct. 11, 1937, Akron, Ohio
Manager 1883-84.

	G	AB	H	2B	3B	HR	HR%	R	RBI	BB	SO	SB	BA	SA	AB	H	G by POS
1876 STL N	64	283	85	11	4	0	0.0	34	46	6	6		.300	.367	0	0	3B-63, 2B-1
1877	57	226	45	3	7	1	0.4	28	22	6	17		.199	.288	0	0	3B-32, 2B-21, OF-5, P-1
1882 PIT AA	34	133	28	5	1	1	0.8	13		3			.211	.286	0	0	3B-34
1883	98	388	83	9	6	1	0.3	42		11			.214	.276	0	0	3B-98, P-2
1884 3 teams			PIT	AA (43G – .177)		C-P	U	(18G – .188)		BAL	U	(17G – .102)					
" total	78	286	47	4	2	0	0.0	21		3			.164	.192	0	0	3B-78
1890 SYR AA	29	119	25	2	1	0	0.0	15		8		8	.210	.244	0	0	3B-29
6 yrs.	360	1435	313	34	21	3	0.2	153	68	37	23	8	.218	.277	0	0	3B-334, 2B-22, OF-5, P-3

Jim Battle

BATTLE, JAMES MILTON   BR TR 6'1"   170 lbs.
B. Mar. 26, 1901, Bailer, Tex.   D. Sept. 30, 1965, Chico, Calif.

	G	AB	H	2B	3B	HR	HR%	R	RBI	BB	SO	SB	BA	SA	AB	H	G by POS
1927 CHI A	6	8	3	0	1	0	0.0	1	0	0	1	0	.375	.625	0	0	3B-4, SS-2

Matt Batts

BATTS, MATTHEW DANIEL   BR TR 5'11"   200 lbs.
B. Oct. 16, 1921, San Antonio, Tex.

	G	AB	H	2B	3B	HR	HR%	R	RBI	BB	SO	SB	BA	SA	AB	H	G by POS
1947 BOS A	7	16	8	1	0	1	6.3	3	5	1	1	0	.500	.750	1	0	C-6
1948	46	118	37	12	0	1	0.8	13	24	15	9	0	.314	.441	6	1	C-41
1949	60	157	38	9	1	3	1.9	23	31	25	22	1	.242	.369	11	1	C-50
1950	75	238	65	15	3	4	1.7	27	34	18	19	0	.273	.412	2	1	C-73
1951 2 teams			BOS	A (11G – .138)		STL	A	(79G – .302)									
" total	90	277	79	18	1	5	1.8	27	33	22	23	2	.285	.412	11	1	C-75
1952 DET A	56	173	41	4	1	3	1.7	11	13	14	22	1	.237	.324	2	0	C-55
1953	116	374	104	24	3	6	1.6	38	42	24	36	2	.278	.406	12	4	C-103
1954 2 teams			DET	A (12G – .286)		CHI	A	(55G – .228)									
" total	67	179	42	8	1	3	1.7	17	24	19	19	0	.235	.341	17	4	C-50
1955 CIN N	26	71	18	4	1	0	0.0	4	13	4	11	0	.254	.338	5	1	C-21
1956	3	2	0	0	0	0	0.0	0	0	1	1	0	.000	.000	2	0	
10 yrs.	546	1605	432	95	11	26	1.6	163	219	143	163	6	.269	.391	69	13	C-474

Hank Bauer

BAUER, HENRY ALBERT   BR TR 6'   192 lbs.
B. July 31, 1922, East St. Louis, Ill.
Manager 1961-62, 1964-69.

	G	AB	H	2B	3B	HR	HR%	R	RBI	BB	SO	SB	BA	SA	AB	H	G by POS
1948 NY A	19	50	9	1	1	1	2.0	6	9	6	13	1	.180	.300	2	0	OF-14
1949	103	301	82	6	6	10	3.3	56	45	37	42	2	.272	.432	5	2	OF-95
1950	113	415	133	16	2	13	3.1	72	70	33	41	2	.320	.463	2	1	OF-110
1951	118	348	103	19	3	10	2.9	53	54	42	39	5	.296	.454	13	5	OF-107
1952	141	553	162	31	6	17	3.1	86	74	50	61	6	.293	.463	2	1	OF-139
1953	133	437	133	20	6	10	2.3	77	57	59	45	2	.304	.446	16	3	OF-126
1954	114	377	111	16	5	12	3.2	73	54	40	42	4	.294	.459	9	4	OF-108
1955	139	492	137	20	5	20	4.1	97	53	56	65	8	.278	.461	6	1	OF-133, C-1
1956	147	539	130	18	7	26	4.8	96	84	59	72	4	.241	.445	7	4	OF-146
1957	137	479	124	22	9	18	3.8	70	65	42	64	7	.259	.455	4	1	OF-135
1958	128	452	121	22	6	12	2.7	62	50	32	56	3	.268	.423	6	2	OF-109
1959	114	341	81	20	0	9	2.6	44	39	33	54	4	.238	.375	7	1	OF-111
1960 KC A	95	255	70	15	0	3	1.2	30	31	21	36	1	.275	.369	33	10	OF-67

	G	AB	H	2B	3B	HR	HR %	R	RBI	BB	SO	SB	BA	SA	Pinch Hit AB	Pinch Hit H	G by POS

Hank Bauer continued

	G	AB	H	2B	3B	HR	HR%	R	RBI	BB	SO	SB	BA	SA	AB	H	G by POS
1961	43	106	28	3	1	3	2.8	11	18	9	8	1	.264	.396	9	1	OF-35
14 yrs.	1544	5145	1424	229	57	164	3.2	833	703	519	638	50	.277	.439	121	36	OF-1449, C-1
WORLD SERIES																	
1949 NY A	3	6	1	0	0	0	0.0	0	0	0	0	0	.167	.167	1	0	OF-3
1950	4	15	2	0	0	0	0.0	0	1	0	0	0	.133	.133	0	0	OF-4
1951	6	18	3	0	1	0	0.0	0	3	1	1	0	.167	.278	0	0	OF-6
1952	7	18	1	0	0	0	0.0	2	1	4	3	0	.056	.056	1	0	OF-7
1953	6	23	6	0	1	0	0.0	6	1	2	4	0	.261	.348	0	0	OF-6
1955	6	14	6	0	0	0	0.0	1	1	0	1	0	.429	.429	1	0	OF-5
1956	7	32	9	0	0	1	3.1	3	3	0	5	1	.281	.375	0	0	OF-7
1957	7	31	8	2	1	2	6.5	3	6	1	6	0	.258	.581	0	0	OF-7
1958	7	31	10	0	0	4	12.9	6	8	0	5	0	.323	.710	0	0	OF-7
9 yrs.	53	188	46	2	3	7	3.7	21	24	8	25	1	.245	.399	3	0	OF-52
	4th	6th	5th		4th	10th			10th	8th		7th					

Paddy Baumann

BAUMANN, CHARLES JOHN
B. Dec. 20, 1885, Indianapolis, Ind.   D. Nov. 20, 1969, Indianapolis, Ind.
BR TR 5'9"   160 lbs.

	G	AB	H	2B	3B	HR	HR%	R	RBI	BB	SO	SB	BA	SA	AB	H	G by POS
1911 DET A	26	94	24	2	4	0	0.0	8	11	6		1	.255	.362	0	0	2B-23, OF-3
1912	13	42	11	1	0	0	0.0	3	7	6		4	.262	.286	1	0	3B-6, 2B-5, OF-1
1913	49	191	57	7	4	1	0.5	31	22	16	18	4	.298	.393	0	0	2B-49
1914	3	11	0	0	0	0	0.0	1	0	2	1	0	.000	.000	0	0	2B-3
1915 NY A	76	219	64	13	1	2	0.9	30	28	28	32	9	.292	.388	10	2	2B-43, 3B-19
1916	79	237	68	5	3	1	0.4	35	25	19	16	10	.287	.346	14	5	OF-28, 3B-26, 2B-9
1917	49	110	24	2	1	0	0.0	10	8	4	9	2	.218	.255	21	6	2B-18, OF-7, 3B-1
7 yrs.	295	904	248	30	13	4	0.4	118	101	81	76	30	.274	.350	46	13	2B-150, 3B-52, OF-39

Jim Baumer

BAUMER, JAMES SLOAN
B. Jan. 29, 1931, Tulsa, Okla.
BR TR 6'2"   185 lbs.

	G	AB	H	2B	3B	HR	HR%	R	RBI	BB	SO	SB	BA	SA	AB	H	G by POS
1949 CHI A	8	10	4	1	1	0	0.0	2	2	2	1	0	.400	.700	0	0	SS-7
1961 CIN N	10	24	3	0	0	0	0.0	0	0	0	9	0	.125	.125	0	0	2B-9
2 yrs.	18	34	7	1	1	0	0.0	2	2	2	10	0	.206	.294	0	0	2B-9, SS-7

John Baumgartner

BAUMGARTNER, JOHN EDWARD
B. May 29, 1931, Birmingham, Ala.
BR TR 6'1"   190 lbs.

	G	AB	H	2B	3B	HR	HR%	R	RBI	BB	SO	SB	BA	SA	AB	H	G by POS
1953 DET A	7	27	5	0	0	0	0.0	3	2	0	5	0	.185	.185	0	0	3B-7

Frankie Baumholtz

BAUMHOLTZ, FRANK CONRAD
B. Oct. 7, 1918, Midvale, Ohio
BL TL 5'10½"   175 lbs.

	G	AB	H	2B	3B	HR	HR%	R	RBI	BB	SO	SB	BA	SA	AB	H	G by POS
1947 CIN N	151	643	182	32	9	5	0.8	96	45	56	53	6	.283	.384	1	1	OF-150
1948	128	415	123	19	5	4	1.0	57	30	27	32	8	.296	.395	15	7	OF-110
1949 2 teams		CIN	N (27G –	.235)		CHI	N (58G –	.226)									
" total	85	245	56	9	5	2	0.8	27	23	15	29	2	.229	.331	20	6	OF-63
1951 CHI N	146	560	159	28	10	2	0.4	62	50	49	36	5	.284	.380	4	2	OF-140
1952	103	409	133	17	4	4	1.0	59	35	27	27	5	.325	.416	2	0	OF-101
1953	133	520	159	36	7	3	0.6	75	25	42	36	3	.306	.419	3	0	OF-130
1954	90	303	90	12	6	4	1.3	38	28	20	15	1	.297	.416	17	2	OF-71
1955	105	280	81	12	5	1	0.4	23	27	16	24	0	.289	.379	37	15	OF-63
1956 PHI N	76	100	27	0	0	0	0.0	13	9	6	6	0	.270	.270	52	14	OF-15
1957	2	2	0	0	0	0	0.0	0	0	0	0	0	.000	.000	2	0	
10 yrs.	1019	3477	1010	165	51	25	0.7	450	272	258	258	30	.290	.389	153	47	OF-843

Jim Baxes

BAXES, DIMITRIOS SPEROS
Brother of Mike Baxes.
B. July 5, 1928, San Francisco, Calif.
BR TR 6'1"   190 lbs.

	G	AB	H	2B	3B	HR	HR%	R	RBI	BB	SO	SB	BA	SA	AB	H	G by POS
1959 2 teams		LA	N (11G –	.303)		CLE	A (77G –	.239)									
" total	88	280	69	12	0	17	6.1	39	39	25	54	1	.246	.471	12	3	2B-48, 3B-32

Mike Baxes

BAXES, MICHAEL
Brother of Jim Baxes.
B. Dec. 18, 1930, San Francisco, Calif.
BR TR 5'10"   175 lbs.

	G	AB	H	2B	3B	HR	HR%	R	RBI	BB	SO	SB	BA	SA	AB	H	G by POS
1956 KC A	73	106	24	3	1	1	0.9	9	5	18	15	0	.226	.302	9	1	SS-62, 2B-1
1958	73	231	49	10	1	0	0.0	31	8	21	24	1	.212	.264	4	0	2B-61, SS-4
2 yrs.	146	337	73	13	2	1	0.3	40	13	39	39	1	.217	.276	13	1	SS-66, 2B-62

John Baxter

BAXTER, JOHN
B. Spokane, Wash.

	G	AB	H	2B	3B	HR	HR%	R	RBI	BB	SO	SB	BA	SA	AB	H	G by POS
1907 STL N	6	21	4	0	0	0	0.0	0		0		0	.190	.190	0	0	1B-6

Harry Bay

BAY, HARRY ELBERT (Deerfoot)
B. Jan. 17, 1878, Pontiac, Ill.   D. Mar. 20, 1952, Peoria, Ill.
BL TL 5'8"   138 lbs.

	G	AB	H	2B	3B	HR	HR%	R	RBI	BB	SO	SB	BA	SA	AB	H	G by POS
1901 CIN N	41	157	33	1	2	1	0.6	25	3	13		4	.210	.261	1	1	OF-40
1902 2 teams		CIN	N (6G –	.375)		CLE	A (108G –	.290)									
" total	114	471	138	10	5	0	0.0	74	24	38		22	.293	.335	4	0	OF-110
1903 CLE A	140	579	169	15	12	1	0.2	94	35	29		45	.292	.364	0	0	OF-140
1904	132	506	132	12	9	3	0.6	69	36	43		38	.261	.338	0	0	OF-132
1905	143	550	164	18	10	0	0.0	90	22	36		36	.298	.367	0	0	OF-143
1906	68	280	77	8	3	0	0.0	47	14	26		17	.275	.325	0	0	OF-68
1907	34	95	17	1	1	0	0.0	14	7	10		7	.179	.211	3	1	OF-31
1908	1	0	0	0	0	0	–	0	0	0		0	–	–	0	0	
8 yrs.	673	2638	730	65	42	5	0.2	413	141	195		169	.277	.339	8	2	OF-664

	G	AB	H	2B	3B	HR	HR %	R	RBI	BB	SO	SB	BA	SA	Pinch Hit AB	Pinch Hit H	G by POS

Burley Bayer

BAYER, CHRISTOPHER A.
B. Dec. 19, 1875, Louisville, Ky.   D. May 30, 1933, Louisville, Ky.   175 lbs.

	G	AB	H	2B	3B	HR	HR %	R	RBI	BB	SO	SB	BA	SA	PH AB	PH H	G by POS
1899 LOU N	1	3	0	0	0	0	0.0	0	0	0		0	.000	.000	0	0	SS-1

Dick Bayless

BAYLESS, HARRY OWEN   BL TR 5'9"   178 lbs.
B. Sept. 6, 1883, Joplin, Mo.   D. Dec. 16, 1920, Santa Rita, N. M.

	G	AB	H	2B	3B	HR	HR %	R	RBI	BB	SO	SB	BA	SA	PH AB	PH H	G by POS
1908 CIN N	19	71	16	1	0	1	1.4	7	3	6		0	.225	.282	0	0	OF-19

Don Baylor

BAYLOR, DON EDWARD   BR TR 6'1"   190 lbs.
B. June 28, 1949, Austin, Tex.

	G	AB	H	2B	3B	HR	HR %	R	RBI	BB	SO	SB	BA	SA	PH AB	PH H	G by POS
1970 BAL A	8	17	4	0	0	0	0.0	4	4	2	3	1	.235	.235	0	0	OF-6
1971	1	2	0	0	0	0	0.0	0	1	2	1	0	.000	.000	0	0	OF-1
1972	102	320	81	13	3	11	3.4	33	38	29	50	24	.253	.416	16	5	OF-84, 1B-9
1973	118	405	116	20	4	11	2.7	64	51	35	48	32	.286	.437	12	2	OF-110, 1B-6, DH-1
1974	137	489	133	22	1	10	2.0	66	59	43	56	29	.272	.382	5	3	OF-129, 1B-8, DH-1
1975	145	524	148	21	6	25	4.8	79	76	53	64	32	.282	.489	1	1	OF-135, DH-7, 1B-2
1976 OAK A	157	595	147	25	1	15	2.5	85	68	58	72	52	.247	.368	2	0	OF-76, 1B-69, DH-23
1977 CAL A	154	561	141	27	0	25	4.5	87	75	62	76	26	.251	.433	1	0	OF-77, DH-61, 1B-18
1978	158	591	151	26	0	34	5.8	103	99	56	71	22	.255	.472	0	0	DH-100, OF-39, 1B-17
1979	162	628	186	33	3	36	5.7	120	139	71	51	22	.296	.530	0	0	OF-97, DH-65, 1B-1
1980	90	340	85	12	2	5	1.5	39	51	24	32	6	.250	.341	0	0	OF-54, DH-36
1981	103	377	90	18	1	17	4.5	52	66	42	51	3	.239	.427	1	1	DH-97, 1B-4, OF-1
1982	157	608	160	24	1	24	3.9	80	93	57	69	10	.263	.424	0	0	DH-155
1983 NY A	144	534	162	33	3	21	3.9	82	85	40	53	17	.303	.494	9	2	DH-136, OF-5, 1B-1
1984	134	493	129	29	1	27	5.5	84	89	39	67	1	.262	.489	10	2	DH-127, 1B-5
15 yrs.	1770	6484	1733	303	26	261	4.0	978	994	613	764	277	.267	.443	57	16	OF-814, DH-809, 1B-140
LEAGUE CHAMPIONSHIP SERIES																	
1973 BAL A	4	11	3	0	0	0	0.0	3	1	3	5	0	.273	.273	0	0	OF-3
1974	4	15	4	0	0	0	0.0	0	0	0	2	0	.267	.267	0	0	OF-4
1979 CAL A	4	16	3	0	0	1	6.3	2	2	1	2	0	.188	.375	0	0	OF-1
1982	5	17	5	1	1	1	5.9	2	10	2	0	0	.294	.647	0	0	DH-5
4 yrs.	17	59	15	1	1	2	3.4	7	13	6	9	0	.254	.407	0	0	OF-8, DH-5

Jack Beach

BEACH, JACKSON STONEWALL
B. Alexandria, Va.   D. July 23, 1896, Alexandria, Va.

	G	AB	H	2B	3B	HR	HR %	R	RBI	BB	SO	SB	BA	SA	PH AB	PH H	G by POS
1884 WAS AA	8	31	3	2	0	0	0.0	3		0			.097	.161	0	0	OF-8

Bob Beall

BEALL, ROBERT BROOKS   BB TL 5'11"   180 lbs.
B. Apr. 24, 1948, Portland, Ore.

	G	AB	H	2B	3B	HR	HR %	R	RBI	BB	SO	SB	BA	SA	PH AB	PH H	G by POS
1975 ATL N	20	31	7	2	0	0	0.0	2	1	6	9	0	.226	.290	9	0	1B-8
1978	108	185	45	8	0	1	0.5	29	16	36	27	4	.243	.303	50	10	1B-40, OF-8
1979	17	15	2	2	0	0	0.0	1	1	3	4	0	.133	.267	9	1	1B-3
1980 PIT N	3	3	0	0	0	0	0.0	0	0	0	1	0	.000	.000	3	0	
4 yrs.	148	234	54	12	0	1	0.4	32	18	45	41	4	.231	.295	71	11	1B-51, OF-8

Johnny Beall

BEALL, JOHN WOOLF   BL TR 6'   180 lbs.
B. Mar. 12, 1882, Beltsville, Md.   D. June 13, 1926, Beltsville, Md.

	G	AB	H	2B	3B	HR	HR %	R	RBI	BB	SO	SB	BA	SA	PH AB	PH H	G by POS
1913 2 teams			CLE	A	(6G –	.167)		CHI	A	(17G –	.267)						
" total	23	66	17	0	1	3	4.5	10	4	0	2	1	.258	.379	6	1	OF-17
1915 CIN N	10	34	8	1	0	0	0.0	3	3	5	10	0	.235	.265	0	0	OF-10
1916	6	21	7	2	0	1	4.8	3	4	3	7	1	.333	.571	1	0	OF-6
1918 STL N	19	49	11	1	0	0	0.0	2	6	3	6	0	.224	.245	5	2	OF-18
4 yrs.	58	170	43	4	1	3	1.8	18	17	11	25	2	.253	.341	12	3	OF-51

Tommy Beals

BEALS, THOMAS L.   5'5"   144 lbs.
B. Hartford, Conn.   D. Oct. 2, 1915, San Francisco, Calif.

	G	AB	H	2B	3B	HR	HR %	R	RBI	BB	SO	SB	BA	SA	PH AB	PH H	G by POS
1880 CHI N	13	46	7	0	0	0	0.0	4	3	1	6		.152	.152	0	0	OF-10, 2B-3

Charlie Beamon

BEAMON, CHARLES ALONZO   BL TL 6'1"   183 lbs.
Son of Charlie Beamon.
B. Dec. 4, 1953, Oakland, Calif.

	G	AB	H	2B	3B	HR	HR %	R	RBI	BB	SO	SB	BA	SA	PH AB	PH H	G by POS
1978 SEA A	10	11	2	0	0	0	0.0	2	0	1	1	0	.182	.182	1	0	DH-6, 1B-2
1979	27	25	5	1	0	0	0.0	5	0	0	5	1	.200	.240	14	3	1B-7, DH-5, OF-2
1981 TOR A	8	15	3	1	0	0	0.0	1	0	2	2	0	.200	.267	3	0	DH-4, 1B-1
3 yrs.	45	51	10	2	0	0	0.0	8	0	3	8	1	.196	.235	18	3	DH-15, 1B-10, OF-2

Joe Bean

BEAN, JOSEPH WILLIAM   BR TR 5'8"   138 lbs.
B. Mar. 18, 1874, Boston, Mass.   D. Feb. 15, 1961, Atlanta, Ga.

	G	AB	H	2B	3B	HR	HR %	R	RBI	BB	SO	SB	BA	SA	PH AB	PH H	G by POS
1902 NY N	48	176	39	2	1	0	0.0	13	5	5		9	.222	.244	0	0	SS-48

Billy Beane

BEANE, WILLIAM LAMAR   BR TR 6'4"   195 lbs.
B. Mar. 29, 1962, Orlando, Fla.

	G	AB	H	2B	3B	HR	HR %	R	RBI	BB	SO	SB	BA	SA	PH AB	PH H	G by POS
1984 NY N	5	10	1	0	0	0	0.0	0	0	0	2	0	.100	.100	2	0	OF-5

Ollie Beard

BEARD, OLIVER PERRY   BR TR 5'11"   180 lbs.
B. May 2, 1862, Lexington, Ky.   D. May 28, 1929, Cincinnati, Ohio

	G	AB	H	2B	3B	HR	HR %	R	RBI	BB	SO	SB	BA	SA	PH AB	PH H	G by POS
1889 CIN AA	141	558	159	13	14	1	0.2	96	77	35	39	36	.285	.364	0	0	SS-141
1890 CIN N	122	492	132	17	15	3	0.6	64	72	44	13	30	.268	.382	0	0	SS-113, 3B-9
1891 LOU AA	68	257	62	4	5	0	0.0	35	24	33	9	7	.241	.296	0	0	3B-61, SS-7
3 yrs.	331	1307	353	34	34	4	0.3	195	173	112	61	73	.270	.357	0	0	SS-261, 3B-70

Ted Beard

BEARD, CRAMER THEODORE   BL TL 5'8"   165 lbs.
B. Jan. 7, 1921, Woodsboro, Md.

	G	AB	H	2B	3B	HR	HR %	R	RBI	BB	SO	SB	BA	SA	PH AB	PH H	G by POS
1948 PIT N	25	81	16	1	3	0	0.0	15	7	12	18	5	.198	.284	2	1	OF-22
1949	14	24	2	0	0	0	0.0	1	1	2	2	0	.083	.083	3	0	OF-10
1950	61	177	41	6	2	4	2.3	32	12	27	45	3	.232	.356	12	3	OF-49

	G	AB	H	2B	3B	HR	HR %	R	RBI	BB	SO	SB	BA	SA	Pinch Hit AB	H	G by POS

Ted Beard continued

	G	AB	H	2B	3B	HR	HR %	R	RBI	BB	SO	SB	BA	SA	AB	H	G by POS
1951	22	48	9	1	0	1	2.1	7	3	6	14	0	.188	.271	6	2	OF-22
1952	15	44	8	2	1	0	0.0	5	3	7	9	2	.182	.273	1	0	OF-13
1957 CHI A	38	78	16	1	0	0	0.0	15	7	18	14	3	.205	.218	3	1	OF-28
1958	19	22	2	0	0	1	4.5	5	2	6	5	3	.091	.227	3	0	OF-15
7 yrs.	194	474	94	11	6	6	1.3	80	35	78	107	16	.198	.285	30	7	OF-159

Lew Beasley

BEASLEY, LEWIS PAIGE   BL TR 5'10" 172 lbs.
B. Aug. 27, 1949, Sparta, Va.

	G	AB	H	2B	3B	HR	HR %	R	RBI	BB	SO	SB	BA	SA	AB	H	G by POS
1977 TEX A	25	32	7	1	0	0	0.0	5	3	2	2	1	.219	.250	2	0	OF-18, DH-1, SS-1

Dave Beatle

BEATLE, DAVID   6'2" 200 lbs.
B. 1861, New York, N. Y. Deceased.

	G	AB	H	2B	3B	HR	HR %	R	RBI	BB	SO	SB	BA	SA	AB	H	G by POS
1884 DET N	1	3	0	0	0	0	0.0	0		0	2		.000	.000	0	0	OF-1, C-1

Des Beatty

BEATTY, ALOYSIUS DESMOND (Desperate)   BR TR 5'8½" 158 lbs.
B. Apr. 7, 1893, Baltimore, Md.   D. Oct. 6, 1969, Norway, Me.

	G	AB	H	2B	3B	HR	HR %	R	RBI	BB	SO	SB	BA	SA	AB	H	G by POS
1914 NY N	2	3	0	0	0	0	0.0	0	1	0	0	0	.000	.000	0	0	SS-1, 3B-1

Jim Beauchamp

BEAUCHAMP, JAMES EDWARD   BR TR 6'2" 190 lbs.
B. Aug. 21, 1939, Vinita, Okla.

	G	AB	H	2B	3B	HR	HR %	R	RBI	BB	SO	SB	BA	SA	AB	H	G by POS
1963 STL N	4	3	0	0	0	0	0.0	0	0	0	2	0	.000	.000	3	0	
1964 HOU N	23	55	9	2	0	2	3.6	6	4	5	16	0	.164	.309	6	1	OF-15, 1B-2
1965 2 teams	HOU N (24G – .189)				MIL N (4G – .000)												
" total	28	56	10	1	0	0	0.0	5	4	6	12	0	.179	.196	13	2	OF-9, 1B-5
1967 ATL N	4	3	0	0	0	0	0.0	0	1	0	0	0	.000	.000	3	0	
1968 CIN N	31	57	15	2	0	2	3.5	10	14	4	19	0	.263	.404	17	4	OF-13, 1B-1
1969	43	60	15	1	0	1	1.7	8	8	5	13	0	.250	.317	32	7	OF-9, 1B-3
1970 2 teams	HOU N (31G – .192)				STL N (44G – .259)												
" total	75	84	20	2	0	2	2.4	11	10	11	18	2	.238	.333	37	9	OF-26, 1B-5
1971 STL N	77	162	38	8	3	2	1.2	24	16	9	26	3	.235	.358	32	8	1B-44, OF-1
1972 NY N	58	120	29	1	0	5	4.2	10	19	7	33	0	.242	.375	21	6	1B-35, OF-3
1973	50	61	17	1	1	0	0.0	5	14	7	11	1	.279	.328	34	9	1B-11
10 yrs.	393	661	153	18	4	14	2.1	79	90	54	150	6	.231	.334	198	46	1B-106, OF-76

WORLD SERIES

	G	AB	H	2B	3B	HR	HR %	R	RBI	BB	SO	SB	BA	SA	AB	H	G by POS
1973 NY N	4	4	0	0	0	0	0.0	0	0	0	1	0	.000	.000	4	0	

Ginger Beaumont

BEAUMONT, CLARENCE HOWETH   BL TR 5'8" 190 lbs.
B. July 23, 1876, Rochester, Wis.   D. Apr. 10, 1956, Burlington, Wis.

	G	AB	H	2B	3B	HR	HR %	R	RBI	BB	SO	SB	BA	SA	AB	H	G by POS
1899 PIT N	111	437	154	15	8	3	0.7	90	38	41		31	.352	.444	6	3	OF-102, 1B-2
1900	138	567	158	14	9	4	0.7	105	50	40		27	.279	.356	0	0	OF-138
1901	133	558	185	14	6	8	1.4	120	72	44		36	.332	.421	0	0	OF-133
1902	131	544	194	21	6	0	0.0	101	67	39		33	.357	.417	0	0	OF-130
1903	141	613	209	30	6	7	1.1	137	68	44		23	.341	.444	0	0	OF-141
1904	153	615	185	12	12	3	0.5	97	54	34		28	.301	.374	0	0	OF-153
1905	103	384	126	12	8	3	0.8	60	40	22		21	.328	.424	4	1	OF-97
1906	80	310	82	9	3	2	0.6	48	32	19		1	.265	.332	1	0	OF-78
1907 BOS N	150	580	187	19	14	4	0.7	67	62	37		25	.322	.424	1	1	OF-149
1908	125	476	127	20	6	2	0.4	66	52	42		13	.267	.347	4	1	OF-121
1909	123	407	107	11	4	0	0.0	35	60	35		12	.263	.310	14	5	OF-111
1910 CHI N	56	172	46	5	1	2	1.2	30	22	28	14	4	.267	.343	13	3	OF-56
12 yrs.	1444	5663	1760	182	83	38	0.7	956	617	425	14	254	.311	.392	43	14	OF-1409, 1B-2

WORLD SERIES

	G	AB	H	2B	3B	HR	HR %	R	RBI	BB	SO	SB	BA	SA	AB	H	G by POS
1903 PIT N	8	34	9	0	1	0	0.0	6	0	2	4	2	.265	.324	0	0	OF-8
1910 CHI N	3	2	0	0	0	0	0.0	1	0	1	1	0	.000	.000	2	0	
2 yrs.	11	36	9	0	1	0	0.0	7	0	3	5	2	.250	.306	2	0	OF-8

George Bechtel

BECHTEL, GEORGE A.   5'11" 165 lbs.
B. 1848, Philadelphia, Pa. Deceased.

	G	AB	H	2B	3B	HR	HR %	R	RBI	BB	SO	SB	BA	SA	AB	H	G by POS
1876 2 teams	LOU N (14G – .182)				NY N (2G – .300)												
" total	16	65	13	1	0	0	0.0	4	2	0	1		.200	.215	0	0	OF-16

Clyde Beck

BECK, CLYDE EUGENE   BR TR 5'10" 150 lbs.
B. Jan. 6, 1902, Bassett, Calif.

	G	AB	H	2B	3B	HR	HR %	R	RBI	BB	SO	SB	BA	SA	AB	H	G by POS
1926 CHI N	30	81	16	0	0	1	1.2	10	4	7	15	0	.198	.235	0	0	2B-27
1927	117	391	101	20	5	2	0.5	44	44	43	37	0	.258	.350	0	0	2B-99, 3B-17, SS-1
1928	131	483	124	18	4	3	0.6	72	52	58	58	3	.257	.329	1	1	3B-87, SS-47, 2B-1
1929	54	190	40	7	0	0	0.0	28	9	19	24	3	.211	.247	5	1	3B-33, SS-14
1930	83	244	52	7	0	6	2.5	32	34	36	32	2	.213	.316	0	0	SS-57, 2B-24, 3B-2
1931 CIN N	53	136	21	4	2	0	0.0	17	19	21	14	1	.154	.213	8	2	3B-38, SS-6
6 yrs.	468	1525	354	56	11	12	0.8	203	162	184	180	9	.232	.307	14	4	3B-177, 2B-151, SS-125

Erve Beck

BECK, ERVIN THOMAS (Dutch)   BR TR 5'10" 168 lbs.
B. July 19, 1878, Toledo, Ohio   D. Dec. 23, 1916, Toledo, Ohio

	G	AB	H	2B	3B	HR	HR %	R	RBI	BB	SO	SB	BA	SA	AB	H	G by POS
1899 BKN N	8	24	4	2	0	0	0.0	2	2	0		0	.167	.250	2	0	2B-6, SS-2
1901 CLE A	135	539	156	26	8	6	1.1	78	79	23		7	.289	.401	3	1	2B-132
1902 2 teams	CIN N (48G – .305)				DET A (41G – .296)												
" total	89	349	105	14	3	3	0.9	42	42	7		5	.301	.384	4	1	1B-42, 2B-32, OF-11
3 yrs.	232	912	265	42	11	9	1.0	122	123	30		12	.291	.390	7	2	2B-170, 1B-42, OF-11, SS-2

Fred Beck

BECK, FREDERICK THOMAS   BL TL 6'1" 180 lbs.
B. Nov. 17, 1886, Havana, Ill.   D. Mar. 12, 1962, Havana, Ill.

	G	AB	H	2B	3B	HR	HR %	R	RBI	BB	SO	SB	BA	SA	AB	H	G by POS
1909 BOS N	96	334	66	4	6	3	0.9	20	27	17		5	.198	.272	8	0	OF-57, 1B-33
1910	154	571	157	32	9	10	1.8	52	64	19	55	8	.275	.415	1	0	OF-134, 1B-19

	G	AB	H	2B	3B	HR	HR %	R	RBI	BB	SO	SB	BA	SA	Pinch Hit AB	Pinch Hit H	G by POS

Fred Beck continued

		G	AB	H	2B	3B	HR	HR%	R	RBI	BB	SO	SB	BA	SA	AB	H	G by POS
1911 2 teams	CIN N (41G – .184)	PHI N (66G – .281)															
" total		107	297	75	9	5	5	1.7	33	45	18	34	5	.253	.367	21	4	OF-77, 1B-6
1914 CHI F		157	555	155	23	4	11	2.0	51	77	44		9	.279	.395	0	0	1B-157
1915		121	373	83	9	3	5	1.3	35	38	24		4	.223	.303	4	0	1B-117
5 yrs.		635	2130	536	77	27	34	1.6	191	251	122	89	31	.252	.361	34	4	1B-332, OF-268

Zinn Beck

BECK, ZINN BERTRAM
B. Sept. 30, 1885, Steubenville, Ohio   D. Mar. 19, 1981, West Palm Beach, Fla.
BR TR 5'10½" 160 lbs.

	G	AB	H	2B	3B	HR	HR%	R	RBI	BB	SO	SB	BA	SA	AB	H	G by POS
1913 STL N	10	30	5	1	0	0	0.0	4	2	4	10	1	.167	.200	0	0	SS-5, 3B-5
1914	137	457	106	15	11	3	0.7	42	45	28	32	14	.232	.333	0	0	3B-122, SS-16
1915	70	223	52	9	4	0	0.0	21	15	12	31	3	.233	.309	2	0	3B-60, SS-4, 2B-2
1916	62	184	41	7	1	0	0.0	8	10	14	21	3	.223	.272	9	2	3B-52, 2B-1, 1B-1
1918 NY A	11	8	0	0	0	0	0.0	0	1	0	1	0	.000	.000	4	0	1B-5
5 yrs.	290	902	204	32	16	3	0.3	75	73	58	95	21	.226	.307	15	2	3B-239, SS-25, 1B-6, 2B-3

Heinie Beckendorf

BECKENDORF, HENRY WARD
B. June 15, 1884, New York, N. Y.   D. Sept. 15, 1949, Jackson Heights, N. Y.
BR TR 5'9"   174 lbs.

		G	AB	H	2B	3B	HR	HR%	R	RBI	BB	SO	SB	BA	SA	AB	H	G by POS
1909 DET A		15	27	7	1	0	0	0.0	1	1	2		0	.259	.296	0	0	C-15
1910 2 teams	DET A (3G – .231)	WAS A (37G – .155)															
" total		40	110	18	1	0	0	0.0	8	12	6		0	.164	.173	2	1	C-38
2 yrs.		55	137	25	2	0	0	0.0	9	13	8		0	.182	.197	2	1	C-53

Beals Becker

BECKER, BEALS
B. July 5, 1886, El Dorado, Kans.   D. Aug. 16, 1943, Huntington Park, Calif.
BL TL 5'9"   170 lbs.

		G	AB	H	2B	3B	HR	HR%	R	RBI	BB	SO	SB	BA	SA	AB	H	G by POS
1908 2 teams	PIT N (20G – .154)	BOS N (43G – .275)															
" total		63	236	57	3	2	0	0.0	17	7	9		9	.242	.271	3	0	OF-60
1909 BOS N		152	562	138	15	6	6	1.1	60	24	47		21	.246	.326	0	0	OF-152
1910 NY N		80	126	36	2	4	3	2.4	18	24	14	25	11	.286	.437	30	5	OF-45, 1B-1
1911		88	172	45	11	1	1	0.6	28	20	26	22	19	.262	.355	26	3	OF-55
1912		125	402	106	18	8	6	1.5	66	58	54	35	30	.264	.393	5	1	OF-117
1913 2 teams	CIN N (30G – .296)	PHI N (88G – .324)															
" total		118	414	131	24	13	9	2.2	64	58	28	42	11	.316	.502	11	4	OF-105, 1B-1
1914 PHI N		138	514	167	25	5	9	1.8	76	66	37	59	16	.325	.446	12	3	OF-126
1915		112	338	83	16	4	11	3.3	38	35	26	48	12	.246	.414	13	2	OF-95
8 yrs.		876	2764	763	114	43	45	1.6	367	292	241	231	129	.276	.397	100	18	OF-755, 1B-2

WORLD SERIES

	G	AB	H	2B	3B	HR	HR%	R	RBI	BB	SO	SB	BA	SA	AB	H	G by POS
1911 NY N	3	3	0	0	0	0	0.0	0	0	0	0	0	.000	.000	3	0	OF-1
1912	2	4	0	0	0	0	0.0	1	0	2	0	0	.000	.000	0	0	OF-2
1915 PHI N	2	0	0	0	0	0	–	0	0	0	0	0	–	–	0	0	OF-2
3 yrs.	7	7	0	0	0	0	0.0	2	0	2	0	0	.000	.000	3	0	OF-3

Heinz Becker

BECKER, HEINZ REINHARD (Dutch)
B. Aug. 26, 1915, Berlin, Germany
BB TR 6'2"   200 lbs.
BL 1947

		G	AB	H	2B	3B	HR	HR%	R	RBI	BB	SO	SB	BA	SA	AB	H	G by POS
1943 CHI N		24	69	10	0	0	0	0.0	5	2	9	6	0	.145	.145	3	0	1B-18
1945		67	133	38	8	2	2	1.5	25	27	17	16	0	.286	.421	36	5	1B-28
1946 2 teams	CHI N (9G – .286)	CLE A (50G – .299)															
" total		59	154	46	10	1	0	0.0	15	18	24	19	1	.299	.377	11	3	1B-44
1947 CLE A		2	2	0	0	0	0	0.0	0	0	0	1	0	.000	.000	2	0	
4 yrs.		152	358	94	18	3	2	0.6	45	47	50	42	1	.263	.346	52	8	1B-90

WORLD SERIES

	G	AB	H	2B	3B	HR	HR%	R	RBI	BB	SO	SB	BA	SA	AB	H	G by POS
1945 CHI N	3	2	1	0	0	0	0.0	0	0	1	1	0	.500	.500	2	1	

Joe Becker

BECKER, JOSEPH EDWARD
B. June 25, 1909, St. Louis, Mo.
BR TR 6'1"   180 lbs.

	G	AB	H	2B	3B	HR	HR%	R	RBI	BB	SO	SB	BA	SA	AB	H	G by POS
1936 CLE A	22	50	9	3	1	1	2.0	5	11	5	4	0	.180	.340	7	0	C-15
1937	18	33	11	2	1	0	0.0	3	2	3	4	0	.333	.455	6	2	C-12
2 yrs.	40	83	20	5	2	1	1.2	8	13	8	8	0	.241	.386	13	2	C-27

Marty Becker

BECKER, MARTIN HENRY
B. Dec. 25, 1893, Tiffin, Ohio   D. Sept. 25, 1957, Cincinnati, Ohio
BB TR 5'7"   168 lbs.

	G	AB	H	2B	3B	HR	HR%	R	RBI	BB	SO	SB	BA	SA	AB	H	G by POS
1915 NY N	17	52	13	2	0	0	0.0	5	3	2	9	3	.250	.288	1	0	OF-16

Glenn Beckert

BECKERT, GLENN ALFRED
B. Oct. 12, 1940, Pittsburgh, Pa.
BR TR 6'1"   190 lbs.

	G	AB	H	2B	3B	HR	HR%	R	RBI	BB	SO	SB	BA	SA	AB	H	G by POS
1965 CHI N	154	614	147	21	3	3	0.5	73	30	28	52	6	.239	.298	2	2	2B-153
1966	153	656	188	23	7	1	0.2	73	59	26	36	10	.287	.348	1	0	2B-152, SS-1
1967	146	597	167	32	3	5	0.8	91	40	30	25	10	.280	.369	1	0	2B-144
1968	155	643	189	28	4	4	0.6	98	37	31	20	8	.294	.369	0	0	2B-155
1969	131	543	158	22	1	1	0.2	69	37	24	24	6	.291	.341	1	0	2B-129
1970	143	591	170	15	6	3	0.5	99	36	32	22	4	.288	.349	3	0	2B-138, OF-1
1971	131	530	181	18	5	2	0.4	80	42	24	24	3	.342	.406	2	1	2B-129
1972	120	474	128	22	2	3	0.6	51	43	23	17	2	.270	.344	2	1	2B-118
1973	114	372	95	13	0	0	0.0	38	29	30	15	0	.255	.290	25	6	2B-88
1974 SD N	64	172	44	1	0	0	0.0	11	7	11	8	0	.256	.262	26	4	2B-36, 3B-1
1975	9	16	6	1	0	0	0.0	2	0	1	0	0	.375	.438	5	1	3B-4
11 yrs.	1320	5208	1473	196	31	22	0.4	685	360	260	243	49	.283	.345	68	15	2B-1242, 3B-5, OF-1, SS-1

Jake Beckley

BECKLEY, JACOB PETER (Eagle Eye)
B. Aug. 4, 1867, Hannibal, Mo.   D. June 25, 1918, Kansas City, Mo.
Hall of Fame 1971.
BL TL 5'10"   200 lbs.

	G	AB	H	2B	3B	HR	HR%	R	RBI	BB	SO	SB	BA	SA	AB	H	G by POS
1888 PIT N	71	283	97	15	3	0	0.0	35	27	7	22	20	.343	.417	0	0	1B-71
1889	123	522	157	24	10	9	1.7	91	97	29	29	11	.301	.437	0	0	1B-122, OF-1
1890 PIT P	121	516	167	38	22	10	1.9	109	120	42	32	18	.324	.541	0	0	1B-121
1891 PIT N	133	554	162	20	20	4	0.7	94	73	44	46	13	.292	.422	0	0	1B-133

	G	AB	H	2B	3B	HR	HR %	R	RBI	BB	SO	SB	BA	SA	Pinch Hit AB	Pinch Hit H	G by POS

Jake Beckley continued

	G	AB	H	2B	3B	HR	HR %	R	RBI	BB	SO	SB	BA	SA	PH AB	PH H	G by POS
1892	151	614	145	21	19	10	1.6	102	96	31	44	30	.236	.381	0	0	1B-151
1893	131	542	164	32	19	5	0.9	108	106	54	26	15	.303	.459	0	0	1B-131
1894	131	533	183	36	17	8	1.5	121	120	43	16	21	.343	.520	0	0	1B-131
1895	129	530	174	30	20	5	0.9	104	110	24	20	20	.328	.489	0	0	1B-129
1896 2 teams	PIT	N (59G –	.253)		NY	N	(46G –	.302)									
" total	105	399	110	15	9	8	2.0	81	70	31	35	19	.276	.419	0	0	1B-101, OF-5, 2B-1
1897 2 teams	NY	N (17G –	.250)		CIN	N	(97G –	.345)									
" total	114	433	143	19	12	8	1.8	84	87	20		25	.330	.485	0	0	1B-114
1898 CIN N	118	459	135	20	12	4	0.9	86	72	28		6	.294	.416	0	0	1B-118
1899	134	513	171	27	16	3	0.6	87	99	40		20	.333	.466	0	0	1B-134
1900	141	558	190	26	10	2	0.4	98	94	40		23	.341	.434	1	0	1B-140
1901	140	580	178	39	13	3	0.5	78	79	28		4	.307	.434	0	0	1B-140
1902	129	532	176	23	7	5	0.9	82	69	34		15	.331	.429	0	0	1B-129, P-1
1903	120	459	150	29	10	2	0.4	85	81	42		23	.327	.447	1	1	1B-119
1904 STL N	142	551	179	22	9	1	0.2	72	67	35		17	.325	.403	0	0	1B-142
1905	134	514	147	20	10	1	0.2	48	57	30		12	.286	.370	0	0	1B-134
1906	87	320	79	16	6	0	0.0	29	44	13		3	.247	.334	2	1	1B-85
1907	32	115	24	3	0	0	0.0	6	7	1		0	.209	.235	0	0	1B-32
20 yrs.	2386	9527	2931	475	244	88	0.9	1600	1575	616	270	315	.308	.436	4	2	1B-2377, OF-6, 2B-1, P-1
								4th									

Julio Becquer

BECQUER, JULIO VILLEGAS
B. Dec. 20, 1931, Havana, Cuba

BL TL 5'11½" 178 lbs.

	G	AB	H	2B	3B	HR	HR %	R	RBI	BB	SO	SB	BA	SA	PH AB	PH H	G by POS
1955 WAS A	10	14	3	0	0	0	0.0	1	1	0	1	0	.214	.214	8	3	1B-2
1957	105	186	42	6	2	2	1.1	14	22	10	29	3	.226	.312	65	18	1B-43
1958	86	164	39	3	0	0	0.0	10	12	8	21	1	.238	.256	41	11	1B-42, OF-1
1959	108	220	59	12	5	1	0.5	20	26	8	17	3	.268	.382	56	12	1B-53
1960	110	298	75	15	7	4	1.3	41	35	12	35	1	.252	.389	39	8	1B-77, P-1
1961 2 teams	LA	A (11G –	.000)		MIN	A	(57G –	.238)									
" total	68	92	20	1	2	5	5.4	13	18	3	17	0	.217	.435	47	11	1B-23, OF-5, P-1
1963 MIN A	1	0	0	0	0	0	–	1	0	0	0	0	–	–	0	0	
7 yrs.	488	974	238	37	16	12	1.2	100	114	41	120	8	.244	.352	256	63	1B-240, OF-6, P-2

Howie Bedell

BEDELL, HOWARD WILLIAMS
B. Sept. 29, 1935, Clearfield, Pa.

BL TR 6'1" 185 lbs.

	G	AB	H	2B	3B	HR	HR %	R	RBI	BB	SO	SB	BA	SA	PH AB	PH H	G by POS
1962 MIL N	58	138	27	1	2	0	0.0	15	2	11	22	1	.196	.232	11	1	OF-45
1968 PHI N	9	7	1	0	0	0	0.0	0	1	1	0	0	.143	.143	7	1	
2 yrs.	67	145	28	1	2	0	0.0	15	3	12	22	1	.193	.228	18	2	OF-45

Jim Bedford

BEDFORD, JAMES ELDRED
B. May 25, 1904, Hudson, N. Y.   D. June 27, 1962, Poughkeepsie, N. Y.

BR TR 5'8" 155 lbs.

	G	AB	H	2B	3B	HR	HR %	R	RBI	BB	SO	SB	BA	SA	PH AB	PH H	G by POS
1925 CLE A	2	3	0	0	0	0	0.0	1	0	1	0	1	.000	.000	0	0	2B-2

Ed Beecher

BEECHER, EDWARD (Scrap Iron)
B. Aug. 27, 1873   Deceased.

	G	AB	H	2B	3B	HR	HR %	R	RBI	BB	SO	SB	BA	SA	PH AB	PH H	G by POS
1897 STL N	3	12	4	0	0	0	0.0	1	1	0		1	.333	.333	0	0	OF-3
1898 CLE N	8	25	5	2	0	0	0.0	1	0	0		0	.200	.280	0	0	OF-8
2 yrs.	11	37	9	2	0	0	0.0	2	1	0		1	.243	.297	0	0	OF-11

Ed Beecher

BEECHER, EDWARD H.
B. July 2, 1859, Guilford, Conn.   D. Sept. 12, 1935, Hartford, Conn.

5'10" 185 lbs.

	G	AB	H	2B	3B	HR	HR %	R	RBI	BB	SO	SB	BA	SA	PH AB	PH H	G by POS
1887 PIT N	41	169	41	8	0	2	1.2	15	22	7	8	8	.243	.325	0	0	OF-41
1889 WAS N	42	179	53	9	0	0	0.0	20	30	5	4	3	.296	.346	0	0	OF-39, 1B-3
1890 BUF P	126	536	159	22	10	3	0.6	69	90	29	23	14	.297	.392	0	0	OF-126, P-1
1891 2 teams	WAS	AA (58G –	.243)		PHI	AA	(16G –	.211)									
" total	74	306	72	13	7	2	0.7	44	35	30	13	24	.235	.343	0	0	OF-74
4 yrs.	283	1190	325	52	17	7	0.6	148	177	71	48	49	.273	.363	0	0	OF-280, 1B-3, P-1

Jodie Beeler

BEELER, JOSEPH SAM
B. Nov. 26, 1921, Dallas, Tex.

BR TR 6' 170 lbs.

	G	AB	H	2B	3B	HR	HR %	R	RBI	BB	SO	SB	BA	SA	PH AB	PH H	G by POS
1944 CIN N	3	3	0	0	0	0	0.0	0	0	0	2	0	.000	.000	0	0	3B-1, 2B-1

Jim Begley

BEGLEY, JAMES LAWRENCE (Imp)
B. Sept. 19, 1903, San Francisco, Calif.   D. Feb. 20, 1957, San Francisco, Calif.

BR TR 5'5½" 140 lbs.

	G	AB	H	2B	3B	HR	HR %	R	RBI	BB	SO	SB	BA	SA	PH AB	PH H	G by POS
1924 CIN N	2	5	1	0	0	0	0.0	1	0	2	0	0	.200	.200	0	0	2B-2

Steve Behel

BEHEL, STEVEN ARNOLD DOUGLAS
B. Nov. 6, 1860, Earlville, Ill.   D. Feb. 15, 1945, Los Angeles, Calif.

	G	AB	H	2B	3B	HR	HR %	R	RBI	BB	SO	SB	BA	SA	PH AB	PH H	G by POS
1884 MIL U	9	33	8	1	0	0	0.0	5		3			.242	.273	0	0	OF-9
1886 NY AA	59	224	46	5	2	0	0.0	32		22			.205	.246	0	0	OF-59
2 yrs.	68	257	54	6	2	0	0.0	37		25			.210	.249	0	0	OF-68

Ollie Bejma

BEJMA, ALOYSIUS FRANK
B. Sept. 12, 1907, South Bend, Ind.

BR TR 5'10" 115 lbs.

	G	AB	H	2B	3B	HR	HR %	R	RBI	BB	SO	SB	BA	SA	PH AB	PH H	G by POS
1934 STL A	95	262	71	16	3	2	0.8	39	29	40	36	3	.271	.378	22	6	SS-32, 2B-14, 3B-13, OF-9
1935	64	198	38	8	2	2	1.0	18	26	27	21	1	.192	.283	7	2	2B-47, SS-8, 3B-2
1936	67	139	36	2	3	2	1.4	19	18	27	21	0	.259	.360	21	6	2B-32, 3B-7, SS-1
1939 CHI A	90	307	77	9	3	8	2.6	52	44	36	27	1	.251	.378	6	1	2B-81, SS-1, 3B-1
4 yrs.	316	906	222	35	11	14	1.5	128	117	130	105	5	.245	.354	56	15	2B-174, SS-42, 3B-23, OF-9

	G	AB	H	2B	3B	HR	HR %	R	RBI	BB	SO	SB	BA	SA	Pinch Hit AB	Pinch Hit H	G by POS

Mark Belanger

BELANGER, MARK HENRY   BR TR 6'1"   170 lbs.
B. June 8, 1944, Pittsfield, Mass.

	G	AB	H	2B	3B	HR	HR %	R	RBI	BB	SO	SB	BA	SA	AB	H	G by POS
1965 BAL A	11	3	1	0	0	0	0.0	1	0	0	0	0	.333	.333	0	0	SS-4
1966	8	19	3	1	0	0	0.0	2	0	0	3	0	.158	.211	0	0	SS-6
1967	69	184	32	5	0	1	0.5	19	10	12	46	6	.174	.217	2	0	SS-38, 2B-26, 3B-2
1968	145	472	98	13	0	2	0.4	40	21	40	114	10	.208	.248	0	0	SS-145
1969	150	530	152	17	4	2	0.4	76	50	53	54	14	.287	.345	3	1	SS-148
1970	145	459	100	6	5	1	0.2	53	36	52	65	13	.218	.259	3	0	SS-143
1971	150	500	133	19	4	0	0.0	67	35	73	48	10	.266	.320	1	0	SS-149
1972	113	285	53	9	1	2	0.7	36	16	18	53	6	.186	.246	1	0	SS-105
1973	154	470	106	15	1	0	0.0	60	27	49	54	13	.226	.262	0	0	SS-154
1974	155	493	111	14	4	5	1.0	54	36	51	69	17	.225	.300	0	0	SS-155
1975	152	442	100	11	1	3	0.7	44	27	36	53	16	.226	.276	0	0	SS-152
1976	153	522	141	22	2	1	0.2	66	40	51	64	27	.270	.326	0	0	SS-153
1977	144	402	83	13	4	2	0.5	39	30	43	68	15	.206	.274	0	0	SS-142
1978	135	348	74	13	0	0	0.0	39	16	40	55	6	.213	.250	1	0	SS-134
1979	101	198	33	6	2	0	0.0	28	9	29	33	5	.167	.217	1	1	SS-98
1980	113	268	61	7	3	0	0.0	37	22	36	53	6	.228	.276	2	0	SS-109
1981	64	139	23	3	2	1	0.7	9	10	12	25	2	.165	.237	1	0	SS-63
1982 LA N	54	50	12	1	0	0	0.0	6	4	5	10	1	.240	.260	4	1	SS-44, 2B-1
18 yrs.	2016	5784	1316	175	33	20	0.3	676	389	576	839	167	.228	.280	19	3	SS-1942, 2B-27, 3B-2

LEAGUE CHAMPIONSHIP SERIES

	G	AB	H	2B	3B	HR	HR %	R	RBI	BB	SO	SB	BA	SA	AB	H	G by POS
1969 BAL A	3	15	4	0	1	1	6.7	4	1	0	0	0	.267	.600	0	0	SS-3
1970	3	12	4	0	0	0	0.0	5	1	1	0	0	.333	.333	0	0	SS-3
1971	3	8	2	0	0	0	0.0	1	1	3	2	0	.250	.250	0	0	SS-3
1973	5	16	2	0	0	0	0.0	0	1	1	1	0	.125	.125	0	0	SS-5
1974	4	9	0	0	0	0	0.0	0	0	1	3	0	.000	.000	0	0	SS-4
1979	3	5	1	0	0	0	0.0	0	1	0	2	0	.200	.200	0	0	SS-3
6 yrs.	21	65	13	0	1	1	1.5	10	5	6	8	0	.200	.277	0	0	SS-21

WORLD SERIES

	G	AB	H	2B	3B	HR	HR %	R	RBI	BB	SO	SB	BA	SA	AB	H	G by POS
1969 BAL A	5	15	3	0	0	0	0.0	2	1	2	1	0	.200	.200	0	0	SS-5
1970	5	19	2	0	0	0	0.0	0	1	1	2	0	.105	.105	0	0	SS-5
1971	7	21	5	0	1	0	0.0	4	0	5	2	1	.238	.333	0	0	SS-7
1979	5	6	0	0	0	0	0.0	1	0	1	1	0	.000	.000	0	0	SS-4
4 yrs.	22	61	10	0	1	0	0.0	7	2	9	6	1	.164	.197	0	0	SS-21

Wayne Belardi

BELARDI, CARROLL WAYNE (Footsie)   BL TL 6'1"   185 lbs.
B. Sept. 5, 1930, Calistoga, Calif.

	G	AB	H	2B	3B	HR	HR %	R	RBI	BB	SO	SB	BA	SA	AB	H	G by POS
1950 BKN N	10	10	0	0	0	0	0.0	0	0	0	4	0	.000	.000	9	0	1B-1
1951	3	3	1	0	0	0	0.0	1	0	0	2	0	.333	1.000	3	1	
1953	69	163	39	3	2	11	6.7	19	34	16	40	0	.239	.485	28	9	1B-38
1954 2 teams				BKN N (11G – .222)				DET A (88G – .232)									
" total	99	259	60	7	1	11	4.2	27	25	35	37	1	.232	.394	21	4	1B-79
1955 DET A	3	3	0	0	0	0	0.0	0	0	0	1	0	.000	.000	3	0	
1956	79	154	43	3	1	6	3.9	24	15	15	13	0	.279	.429	37	8	1B-31, OF-2
6 yrs.	263	592	143	13	5	28	4.7	71	74	66	97	1	.242	.422	101	22	1B-149, OF-2

WORLD SERIES

	G	AB	H	2B	3B	HR	HR %	R	RBI	BB	SO	SB	BA	SA	AB	H	G by POS
1953 BKN N	2	2	0	0	0	0	0.0	0	0	0	1	0	.000	.000	2	0	

Ira Belden

BELDEN, IRA ALLISON   BL TR 5'11"   175 lbs.
B. Apr. 16, 1874, Cleveland, Ohio   D. July 15, 1916, Lakewood, Ohio

	G	AB	H	2B	3B	HR	HR %	R	RBI	BB	SO	SB	BA	SA	AB	H	G by POS
1897 CLE N	8	30	8	0	2	0	0.0	5	4	2		0	.267	.400	0	0	OF-8

Beau Bell

BELL, ROY CHESTER   BR TR 6'2"   185 lbs.
B. Aug. 20, 1907, Bellville, Tex.   D. Sept. 14, 1977, College Station, Tex.

	G	AB	H	2B	3B	HR	HR %	R	RBI	BB	SO	SB	BA	SA	AB	H	G by POS
1935 STL A	76	220	55	8	2	3	1.4	20	17	16	16	1	.250	.345	24	4	OF-37, 1B-15, 3B-3
1936	155	616	212	40	12	11	1.8	100	123	60	55	4	.344	.502	0	0	OF-142, 1B-17
1937	156	642	218	51	8	14	2.2	82	117	53	54	2	.340	.509	0	0	OF-131, 1B-26, 3B-2
1938	147	526	138	35	3	13	2.5	91	84	71	46	1	.262	.414	8	3	OF-132, 1B-4
1939 2 teams				STL A (54G – .219)				DET A (11G – .239)									
" total	65	166	39	5	2	1	0.6	18	29	28	19	0	.235	.307	17	3	OF-46
1940 CLE A	120	444	124	22	2	4	0.9	55	58	34	41	2	.279	.365	9	0	OF-97, 1B-14
1941	48	104	20	4	3	0	0.0	12	9	10	8	1	.192	.288	23	3	OF-14, 1B-10
7 yrs.	767	2718	806	165	32	46	1.7	378	437	272	239	11	.297	.432	81	13	OF-599, 1B-86, 3B-5

Buddy Bell

BELL, DAVID GUS   BR TR 6'1"   180 lbs.
Son of Gus Bell.
B. Aug. 27, 1951, Pittsburgh, Pa.

	G	AB	H	2B	3B	HR	HR %	R	RBI	BB	SO	SB	BA	SA	AB	H	G by POS
1972 CLE A	132	466	119	21	1	9	1.9	49	36	34	29	5	.255	.363	3	1	OF-123, 3B-6
1973	156	631	169	23	7	14	2.2	86	59	49	47	7	.268	.393	1	0	3B-154, OF-2
1974	116	423	111	15	1	7	1.7	51	46	35	29	1	.262	.352	0	0	3B-115, DH-1
1975	153	553	150	20	4	10	1.8	66	59	51	72	6	.271	.376	0	0	3B-153
1976	159	604	170	26	2	7	1.2	75	60	44	49	3	.281	.366	1	1	3B-158, 1B-2
1977	129	479	140	23	4	11	2.3	64	64	45	63	1	.292	.426	3	1	3B-118, OF-11
1978	142	556	157	27	8	6	1.1	71	62	39	43	1	.282	.392	3	0	3B-139, DH-1
1979 TEX A	162	670	200	42	3	18	2.7	89	101	30	45	5	.299	.451	0	0	3B-147, SS-33
1980	129	490	161	24	4	17	3.5	76	83	40	39	3	.329	.498	9	2	3B-123, SS-3
1981	97	360	106	16	1	10	2.8	44	64	42	30	3	.294	.428	1	0	3B-96, SS-1
1982	148	537	159	27	2	13	2.4	62	67	70	56	5	.296	.426	1	0	3B-145, SS-4
1983	156	618	171	35	3	14	2.3	75	66	50	48	3	.277	.411	2	0	3B-154
1984	148	553	174	36	5	11	2.0	87	83	63	54	2	.315	.458	0	0	3B-147
13 yrs.	1827	6940	1987	335	45	147	2.1	895	850	592	598	45	.286	.411	24	6	3B-1655, OF-136, SS-41, DH-2, 1B-2

	G	AB	H	2B	3B	HR	HR %	R	RBI	BB	SO	SB	BA	SA	Pinch Hit AB	Pinch Hit H	G by POS

Fern Bell

BELL, FERN LEE (Danny)
B. Jan. 21, 1913, Ada, Okla.　　　　BR TR 6'　　180 lbs.

	G	AB	H	2B	3B	HR	HR %	R	RBI	BB	SO	SB	BA	SA	PH AB	PH H	G by POS
1939 PIT N	83	262	75	5	8	2	0.8	44	34	42	18	2	.286	.389	8	1	OF-67, 3B-1
1940	6	3	0	0	0	0	0.0	0	1	1	1	0	.000	.000	3	0	
2 yrs.	89	265	75	5	8	2	0.8	44	35	43	19	2	.283	.385	11	1	OF-67, 3B-1

Frank Bell

BELL, FRANK GUSTAV
Brother of Charlie Bell.
B. 1863, Cincinnati, Ohio　　D. Apr. 14, 1891, Cincinnati, Ohio

	G	AB	H	2B	3B	HR	HR %	R	RBI	BB	SO	SB	BA	SA	PH AB	PH H	G by POS
1885 BKN AA	10	29	5	0	1	0	0.0	5		0			.172	.241	0	0	C-5, OF-4, 3B-2

George Bell

BELL, JORGE ANTONIO
B. Oct. 21, 1959, San Pedro, Dominican Republic　　BR TR 6'1"　　190 lbs.

	G	AB	H	2B	3B	HR	HR %	R	RBI	BB	SO	SB	BA	SA	PH AB	PH H	G by POS
1981 TOR A	60	163	38	2	1	5	3.1	19	12	5	27	3	.233	.350	5	3	OF-44, DH-8
1983	39	112	30	5	4	2	1.8	5	17	4	17	1	.268	.438	3	1	OF-34, DH-2
1984	159	606	177	39	4	26	4.3	85	87	24	86	11	.292	.498	8	3	OF-147, DH-7, 3B-3
3 yrs.	258	881	245	46	9	33	3.7	109	116	33	130	15	.278	.463	16	7	OF-225, DH-17, 3B-3

Gus Bell

BELL, DAVID RUSSELL
Father of Buddy Bell.
B. Nov. 15, 1928, Louisville, Ky.　　BL TR 6'1½"　190 lbs.

	G	AB	H	2B	3B	HR	HR %	R	RBI	BB	SO	SB	BA	SA	PH AB	PH H	G by POS
1950 PIT N	111	422	119	22	11	8	1.9	62	53	28	46	4	.282	.443	6	1	OF-104
1951	149	600	167	27	12	16	2.7	80	89	42	41	1	.278	.443	2	1	OF-145
1952	131	468	117	21	5	16	3.4	53	59	36	72	1	.250	.419	8	0	OF-123
1953 CIN N	151	610	183	37	5	30	4.9	102	105	48	72	0	.300	.525	1	1	OF-151
1954	153	619	185	38	7	17	2.7	104	101	48	58	5	.299	.465	1	0	OF-153
1955	154	610	188	30	6	27	4.4	88	104	54	57	4	.308	.510	0	0	OF-154
1956	150	603	176	31	4	29	4.8	82	84	50	66	6	.292	.501	1	0	OF-149
1957	121	510	149	20	3	13	2.5	65	61	30	54	0	.292	.420	0	0	OF-121
1958	112	385	97	16	2	10	2.6	42	46	36	40	2	.252	.382	7	1	OF-107
1959	148	580	170	27	2	19	3.3	59	115	29	44	2	.293	.445	5	2	OF-145
1960	143	515	135	19	5	12	2.3	65	62	29	40	1	.262	.388	13	3	OF-131
1961	103	235	60	10	1	3	1.3	27	33	18	21	1	.255	.345	36	11	OF-75
1962 2 teams	NY	N	(30G –	.149)		MIL	N	(79G –	.285)								
" total	109	315	76	13	3	6	1.9	36	30	22	24	0	.241	.359	26	4	OF-84
1963 MIL N	3	3	1	0	0	0	0.0	0	0	0	0	0	.333	.333	3	1	
1964	3	3	0	0	0	0	0.0	0	0	0	1	0	.000	.000	3	0	
15 yrs.	1741	6478	1823	311	66	206	3.2	865	942	470	636	30	.281	.445	112	25	OF-1642
WORLD SERIES																	
1961 CIN N	3	3	0	0	0	0	0.0	0	0	0	0	0	.000	.000	3	0	

Kevin Bell

BELL, KEVIN ROBERT
B. July 13, 1955, Los Angeles, Calif.　　BR TR 6'　195 lbs.

	G	AB	H	2B	3B	HR	HR %	R	RBI	BB	SO	SB	BA	SA	PH AB	PH H	G by POS
1976 CHI A	68	230	57	7	6	5	2.2	24	20	18	56	2	.248	.396	1	0	3B-67, DH-1
1977	9	28	5	1	0	1	3.6	4	6	3	8	0	.179	.321	0	0	SS-5, 3B-4, OF-1
1978	54	68	13	0	0	2	2.9	9	5	5	19	1	.191	.279	2	0	3B-52, DH-1
1979	70	200	49	8	1	4	2.0	20	22	15	43	2	.245	.355	2	0	3B-68, SS-2
1980	92	191	34	5	2	1	0.5	16	11	29	37	0	.178	.241	3	2	3B-83, DH-3, SS-3
1982 OAK A	4	9	3	1	0	0	0.0	1	0	0	2	0	.333	.444	0	0	3B-3, DH-1
6 yrs.	297	726	161	22	9	13	1.8	74	64	70	165	5	.222	.331	8	2	3B-277, SS-10, DH-6, OF-1

Les Bell

BELL, LESTER ROWLAND
B. Dec. 14, 1901, Harrisburg, Pa.　　BR TR 5'11"　165 lbs.

	G	AB	H	2B	3B	HR	HR %	R	RBI	BB	SO	SB	BA	SA	PH AB	PH H	G by POS
1923 STL N	15	51	19	2	1	0	0.0	5	9	9	7	1	.373	.451	0	0	SS-15
1924	17	57	14	3	2	1	1.8	5	5	3	7	0	.246	.421	0	0	SS-17
1925	153	586	167	29	9	11	1.9	80	88	43	47	4	.285	.422	0	0	3B-153, SS-1
1926	155	581	189	33	14	17	2.9	85	100	54	62	9	.325	.518	0	0	3B-155
1927	115	390	101	26	6	9	2.3	48	65	34	63	5	.259	.426	1	0	3B-100, SS-10
1928 BOS N	153	591	164	36	7	10	1.7	58	91	40	45	1	.277	.413	0	0	3B-153
1929	139	483	144	23	5	9	1.9	58	72	50	42	4	.298	.422	9	2	3B-127, SS-1, 2B-1
1930 CHI N	74	248	69	15	4	5	2.0	35	47	24	27	1	.278	.431	2	0	3B-70, 1B-2
1931	75	252	71	17	1	4	1.6	30	32	19	22	0	.282	.405	5	1	3B-70
9 yrs.	896	3239	938	184	49	66	2.0	404	509	276	322	25	.290	.438	21	3	3B-828, SS-44, 1B-2, 2B-1
WORLD SERIES																	
1926 STL N	7	27	7	1	0	1	3.7	4	6	2	5	0	.259	.407	0	0	3B-7

Rudy Bell

BELL, RUDOLPH FRED
Born John Baerwald.
B. Jan. 1, 1881, Wausau, Wis.　　D. July 28, 1955, Albuquerque, N. M.　　BR TR 5'8½"　158 lbs.

	G	AB	H	2B	3B	HR	HR %	R	RBI	BB	SO	SB	BA	SA	PH AB	PH H	G by POS
1907 NY A	17	52	11	2	1	0	0.0	4	3	3		4	.212	.288	0	0	OF-17

Zeke Bella

BELLA, JOHN
B. Aug. 23, 1930, Greenwich, Conn.　　BR TL 5'11"　185 lbs.

	G	AB	H	2B	3B	HR	HR %	R	RBI	BB	SO	SB	BA	SA	PH AB	PH H	G by POS
1957 NY A	5	10	1	0	0	0	0.0	0	0	1	2	0	.100	.100	1	0	OF-4
1959 KC A	47	82	17	2	1	1	1.2	10	9	9	14	0	.207	.293	22	5	OF-25, 1B-1
2 yrs.	52	92	18	2	1	1	1.1	10	9	10	16	0	.196	.272	23	5	OF-29, 1B-1

Rafael Belliard

BELLIARD, RAFAEL
B. Oct. 24, 1961, Pueblo Nuevo, Dominican Republic　　BR TR 5'8½"　139 lbs.

	G	AB	H	2B	3B	HR	HR %	R	RBI	BB	SO	SB	BA	SA	PH AB	PH H	G by POS
1982 PIT N	9	2	1	0	0	0	0.0	3	0	0	0	1	.500	.500	1	1	SS-4
1983	4	1	0	0	0	0	0.0	1	0	0	1	0	.000	.000	0	0	SS-3
1984	20	22	5	0	0	0	0.0	3	0	0	1	4	.227	.227	0	0	SS-12, 2B-1
3 yrs.	33	25	6	0	0	0	0.0	7	0	0	2	5	.240	.240	1	1	SS-19, 2B-1

	G	AB	H	2B	3B	HR	HR %	R	RBI	BB	SO	SB	BA	SA	Pinch Hit AB	Pinch Hit H	G by POS

John Bellman

BELLMAN, JOHN HUTCHINS
B. Mar. 4, 1864, Taylorsville, Ky.   D. Dec. 8, 1931, Louisville, Ky.

	G	AB	H	2B	3B	HR	HR%	R	RBI	BB	SO	SB	BA	SA	PH AB	PH H	G by POS
1889 STL AA	1	2	1	0	0	0	0.0	1	0	1	0	0	.500	.500	0	0	C-1

Bob Belloir

BELLOIR, ROBERT ELWOOD
B. July 13, 1948, Heidelberg, Germany
BR TR 5'10" 155 lbs.

	G	AB	H	2B	3B	HR	HR%	R	RBI	BB	SO	SB	BA	SA	PH AB	PH H	G by POS
1975 ATL N	43	105	23	2	1	0	0.0	11	9	7	8	0	.219	.257	2	0	SS-38, 2B-1
1976	30	60	12	2	0	0	0.0	5	4	5	7	0	.200	.233	3	0	SS-12, 3B-10, 2B-5
1977	6	1	0	0	0	0	0.0	2	0	0	0	0	.000	.000	1	0	SS-3
1978	2	1	1	1	0	0	0.0	0	0	0	0	0	1.000	2.000	1	1	SS-1, 3B-1
4 yrs.	81	167	36	5	1	0	0.0	18	13	12	15	0	.216	.257	7	1	SS-54, 3B-11, 2B-6

Harry Bemis

BEMIS, HARRY PARKER
B. Feb. 1, 1874, Farmington, N. H.   D. May 23, 1947, Cleveland, Ohio
BL TR 5'6½" 155 lbs.

	G	AB	H	2B	3B	HR	HR%	R	RBI	BB	SO	SB	BA	SA	PH AB	PH H	G by POS
1902 CLE A	93	317	99	12	7	1	0.3	42	29	19		3	.312	.404	3	1	C-87, OF-2, 2B-1
1903	92	314	82	20	3	1	0.3	31	41	8		5	.261	.354	8	3	C-74, 1B-10, 2B-1
1904	97	336	76	11	6	0	0.0	35	25	8		6	.226	.295	4	1	C-79, 1B-13, 2B-1
1905	69	226	66	13	3	0	0.0	27	28	13		3	.292	.376	4	1	C-58, 2B-4, 3B-2, 1B-1
1906	93	297	82	13	5	2	0.7	28	30	12		8	.276	.374	12	2	C-81
1907	65	172	43	7	0	0	0.0	12	19	7		5	.250	.291	12	4	C-51, 1B-2
1908	91	277	62	9	1	0	0.0	23	33	7		14	.224	.264	12	1	C-76, 1B-2
1909	42	123	23	2	3	0	0.0	4	13	0		2	.187	.252	5	2	C-36
1910	61	167	36	5	1	1	0.6	11	16	5		3	.216	.275	12	3	C-46
9 yrs.	703	2229	569	92	29	5	0.2	213	234	79		49	.255	.329	72	18	C-588, 1B-28, 2B-7, OF-2, 3B-2

Johnny Bench

BENCH, JOHNNY LEE
B. Dec. 7, 1947, Oklahoma City, Okla.
BR TR 6'1" 197 lbs.

	G	AB	H	2B	3B	HR	HR%	R	RBI	BB	SO	SB	BA	SA	PH AB	PH H	G by POS
1967 CIN N	26	86	14	3	1	1	1.2	7	6	5	19	0	.163	.256	0	0	C-26
1968	154	564	155	40	2	15	2.7	67	82	31	96	1	.275	.433	2	0	C-154
1969	148	532	156	23	1	26	4.9	83	90	49	86	6	.293	.487	10	2	C-147
1970	158	605	177	35	4	45	7.4	97	148	54	102	5	.293	.587	4	1	C-140, OF-23, 1B-12, 3B-1
1971	149	562	134	19	2	27	4.8	80	61	49	83	2	.238	.423	2	0	C-141, OF-12, 1B-12, 3B-3
1972	147	538	145	22	2	40	7.4	87	125	100	84	6	.270	.541	0	0	C-130, OF-17, 1B-6, 3B-4
1973	152	557	141	17	3	25	4.5	83	104	83	83	4	.253	.429	1	0	C-134, OF-23, 1B-4, 3B-1
1974	160	621	174	38	2	33	5.3	108	129	80	90	5	.280	.507	1	0	C-137, 3B-36, 1B-5
1975	142	530	150	39	1	28	5.3	83	110	65	108	11	.283	.519	5	1	C-121, OF-19, 1B-9
1976	135	465	109	24	1	16	3.4	62	74	81	95	13	.234	.394	8	1	C-128, OF-5, 1B-1
1977	142	494	136	34	2	31	6.3	67	109	58	95	2	.275	.540	2	0	C-135, OF-8, 1B-4, 3B-1
1978	120	393	102	17	1	23	5.9	52	73	50	83	4	.260	.483	11	2	C-107, 1B-11, OF-2
1979	130	464	128	19	0	22	4.7	73	80	67	73	4	.276	.459	4	0	C-126, 1B-2
1980	114	360	90	12	0	24	6.7	52	68	41	64	4	.250	.483	13	2	C-105
1981	52	178	55	8	0	8	4.5	14	25	17	21	0	.309	.489	8	3	1B-38, C-7
1982	119	399	103	16	0	13	3.3	44	38	37	58	1	.258	.396	9	1	3B-107, 1B-8, C-1
1983	110	310	79	15	2	12	3.9	32	54	24	38	0	.255	.432	34	9	3B-42, 1B-32, C-5, OF-1
17 yrs.	2158	7658	2048	381	24	389	5.1	1091	1376	891	1278	68	.267	.476	114	22	C-1744, 3B-195, 1B-144, OF-110

LEAGUE CHAMPIONSHIP SERIES

	G	AB	H	2B	3B	HR	HR%	R	RBI	BB	SO	SB	BA	SA	PH AB	PH H	G by POS
1970 CIN N	3	9	2	0	0	1	11.1	2	1	3	1	0	.222	.556	0	0	C-3
1972	5	18	6	1	1	1	5.6	3	2	1	3	2	.333	.667	0	0	C-5
1973	5	19	5	2	0	1	5.3	1	1	2	2	0	.263	.526	0	0	C-5
1975	3	13	1	0	0	0	0.0	1	0	1	6	1	.077	.077	0	0	C-3
1976	3	12	4	1	0	1	8.3	3	1	1	2	1	.333	.667	0	0	C-3
1979	3	12	3	0	1	1	8.3	1	1	2	2	0	.250	.667	0	0	C-3
6 yrs.	22	83	21	4	2	5	6.0	11	6	10	16	4	.253	.530	0	0	C-22

WORLD SERIES

	G	AB	H	2B	3B	HR	HR%	R	RBI	BB	SO	SB	BA	SA	PH AB	PH H	G by POS
1970 CIN N	5	19	4	0	0	1	5.3	3	3	1	2	0	.211	.368	0	0	C-5
1972	7	23	6	1	0	1	4.3	4	1	5	5	2	.261	.435	0	0	C-7
1975	7	29	6	2	0	1	3.4	5	4	2	4	0	.207	.379	0	0	C-7
1976	4	15	8	1	1	2	13.3	4	6	0	1	0	.533	1.133	0	0	C-4
4 yrs.	23	86	24	4	1	5	5.8	16	14	8	12	2	.279	.523	0	0	C-23

Chief Bender

BENDER, CHARLES ALBERT
B. May 5, 1883, Brainerd, Minn.   D. May 22, 1954, Philadelphia, Pa.
Hall of Fame 1953.
BR TR 6'2" 185 lbs.

	G	AB	H	2B	3B	HR	HR%	R	RBI	BB	SO	SB	BA	SA	PH AB	PH H	G by POS
1903 PHI A	43	120	22	4	1	0	0.0	10	8	3		3	.183	.233	3	2	P-36, 1B-3, OF-1
1904	31	79	18	3	2	0	0.0	8	5	5		3	.228	.316	1	0	P-29
1905	38	92	20	3	2	0	0.0	11	14	3		3	.217	.293	3	0	P-35
1906	44	99	25	4	0	3	3.0	9	13	9		2	.253	.384	2	0	P-36, OF-4
1907	45	100	23	6	1	0	0.0	10	8	5		2	.230	.310	7	1	P-33, 1B-2, OF-1, 2B-1
1908	20	50	11	1	0	0	0.0	5	2	10		1	.220	.240	1	0	P-18, 1B-1
1909	40	93	20	5	0	0	0.0	6	9	5		1	.215	.269	5	1	P-34
1910	36	93	25	3	2	0	0.0	6	16	6		0	.269	.344	6	1	P-30
1911	32	79	13	0	0	0	0.0	9	8	2		0	.165	.165	1	0	P-31
1912	27	60	9	1	1	0	0.0	5	4	6		2	.150	.200	0	0	P-27
1913	48	78	12	3	1	0	0.0	7	10	6	17	1	.154	.218	0	0	P-48
1914	28	62	9	1	0	1	1.6	4	8	4	13	0	.145	.210	0	0	P-28
1915 BAL F	26	60	16	2	0	1	1.7	7	2	6		0	.267	.350	0	0	P-26
1916 PHI N	28	43	12	4	0	0	0.0	2	5	3	9	0	.279	.372	0	0	P-27, 3B-1
1917	20	39	8	0	0	1	2.6	3	4	2	3	0	.205	.282	0	0	P-20
1925 CHI A	1	0	0	0	0	0	–	0	0	0	0	0	–	–	0	0	P-1
16 yrs.	507	1147	243	40	10	6	0.5	102	116	75	42	20	.212	.280	29	5	P-459, OF-6, 1B-6, 3B-1, 2B-1

WORLD SERIES

	G	AB	H	2B	3B	HR	HR%	R	RBI	BB	SO	SB	BA	SA	PH AB	PH H	G by POS
1905 PHI A	2	5	0	0	0	0	0.0	0	0	1	0	0	.000	.000	0	0	P-2

	G	AB	H	2B	3B	HR	HR %	R	RBI	BB	SO	SB	BA	SA	Pinch Hit AB	Pinch Hit H	G by POS

Chief Bender continued

	G	AB	H	2B	3B	HR	HR%	R	RBI	BB	SO	SB	BA	SA	AB	H	G by POS
1910	2	6	2	0	0	0	0.0	1	1	1	1	0	.333	.333	0	0	P-2
1911	3	11	1	0	0	0	0.0	0	0	0	1	0	.091	.091	0	0	P-3
1913	2	8	0	0	0	0	0.0	0	1	0	1	0	.000	.000	0	0	P-2
1914	1	2	0	0	0	0	0.0	0	0	0	0	0	.000	.000	0	0	P-1
5 yrs.	10	32	3	0	0	0	0.0	1	2	1	4	0	.094	.094	0	0	P-10

Art Benedict

BENEDICT, ARTHUR M.
B. Mar. 31, 1862, Cornwall, Ill.   D. Jan. 20, 1948, Blue Rapids, Kans.

	G	AB	H	2B	3B	HR	HR%	R	RBI	BB	SO	SB	BA	SA	AB	H	G by POS
1883 PHI N	3	15	4	1	0	0	0.0	3		0	4		.267	.333	0	0	2B-3

Bruce Benedict

BENEDICT, BRUCE EDWIN   BR TR 6'1"   175 lbs.
B. Aug. 18, 1955, Birmingham, Ala.

	G	AB	H	2B	3B	HR	HR%	R	RBI	BB	SO	SB	BA	SA	AB	H	G by POS
1978 ATL N	22	52	13	2	0	0	0.0	3	1	6	6	0	.250	.288	0	0	C-22
1979	76	204	46	11	0	0	0.0	14	15	33	18	1	.225	.279	1	0	C-76
1980	120	359	91	14	1	2	0.6	18	34	28	36	3	.253	.315	0	0	C-120
1981	90	295	78	12	1	5	1.7	26	35	33	21	1	.264	.363	0	0	C-90
1982	118	386	95	11	1	3	0.8	34	44	37	41	4	.246	.303	1	0	C-118
1983	134	423	126	13	1	2	0.5	43	43	61	24	1	.298	.348	0	0	C-134
1984	95	300	67	8	1	4	1.3	26	25	34	25	1	.223	.297	0	0	C-95
7 yrs.	655	2019	516	71	5	16	0.8	164	197	232	171	11	.256	.319	2	0	C-655

LEAGUE CHAMPIONSHIP SERIES

	G	AB	H	2B	3B	HR	HR%	R	RBI	BB	SO	SB	BA	SA	AB	H	G by POS
1982 ATL N	3	8	2	1	0	0	0.0	1	0	2	1	0	.250	.375	0	0	C-3

Joe Benes

BENES, JOSEPH ANTHONY (Bananas)   BR TR 5'8½"   158 lbs.
B. Jan. 8, 1901, Long Island City, N. Y.   D. Mar. 7, 1975, Elmhurst, N. Y.

	G	AB	H	2B	3B	HR	HR%	R	RBI	BB	SO	SB	BA	SA	AB	H	G by POS
1931 STL N	10	12	2	0	0	0	0.0	1	0	2	1	0	.167	.167	0	0	SS-6, 2B-2, 3B-1

Benny Bengough

BENGOUGH, BERNARD OLIVER   BR TR 5'7½"   168 lbs.
B. July 27, 1898, Niagara Falls, N. Y.   D. Dec. 22, 1968, Philadelphia, Pa.

	G	AB	H	2B	3B	HR	HR%	R	RBI	BB	SO	SB	BA	SA	AB	H	G by POS
1923 NY A	19	53	7	2	0	0	0.0	1	3	4	2	0	.132	.170	0	0	C-19
1924	11	16	5	1	1	0	0.0	4	3	2	0	0	.313	.500	0	0	C-11
1925	95	283	73	14	2	0	0.0	17	23	19	9	0	.258	.322	1	0	C-94
1926	36	84	32	6	0	0	0.0	9	14	7	4	1	.381	.452	1	0	C-35
1927	31	85	21	3	3	0	0.0	6	10	4	4	0	.247	.353	1	0	C-30
1928	58	161	43	3	1	0	0.0	12	9	7	8	0	.267	.298	0	0	C-58
1929	23	62	12	2	1	0	0.0	5	7	0	2	0	.194	.258	0	0	C-23
1930	44	102	24	4	2	0	0.0	10	12	3	8	1	.235	.314	0	0	C-44
1931 STL A	40	140	35	4	1	0	0.0	6	12	4	4	0	.250	.293	3	0	C-37
1932	54	139	35	7	1	0	0.0	13	15	12	4	0	.252	.317	5	1	C-47
10 yrs.	411	1125	287	46	12	0	0.0	83	108	62	45	2	.255	.317	11	1	C-398

WORLD SERIES

	G	AB	H	2B	3B	HR	HR%	R	RBI	BB	SO	SB	BA	SA	AB	H	G by POS
1927 NY A	2	4	0	0	0	0	0.0	1	0	1	0	0	.000	.000	0	0	C-2
1928	4	13	3	0	0	0	0.0	1	1	1	1	0	.231	.231	0	0	C-4
2 yrs.	6	17	3	0	0	0	0.0	2	1	2	1	0	.176	.176	0	0	C-6

Juan Beniquez

BENIQUEZ, JUAN JOSE   BR TR 5'11"   150 lbs.
B. May 13, 1950, San Sebastian, Puerto Rico

	G	AB	H	2B	3B	HR	HR%	R	RBI	BB	SO	SB	BA	SA	AB	H	G by POS
1971 BOS A	16	57	17	2	0	0	0.0	8	4	3	4	3	.298	.333	0	0	SS-15
1972	33	99	24	4	1	1	1.0	10	8	7	11	2	.242	.333	3	1	SS-27
1974	106	389	104	14	3	5	1.3	60	33	25	61	19	.267	.357	8	0	OF-97, DH-4
1975	78	254	74	14	4	2	0.8	43	17	25	26	7	.291	.402	8	5	OF-44, DH-20, 3B-14
1976 TEX A	145	478	122	14	4	0	0.0	49	33	39	56	17	.255	.301	4	1	OF-141, 2B-1
1977	123	424	114	19	6	10	2.4	56	50	43	43	26	.269	.413	0	0	OF-123
1978	127	473	123	17	3	11	2.3	61	50	20	59	10	.260	.378	2	0	OF-126
1979 NY A	62	142	36	6	1	4	2.8	19	17	9	17	3	.254	.394	1	0	OF-60, 3B-3
1980 SEA A	70	237	54	10	0	6	2.5	26	21	17	25	2	.228	.346	5	0	OF-65, DH-1
1981 CAL A	58	166	30	5	0	3	1.8	18	13	15	16	2	.181	.265	2	0	OF-55, DH-1
1982	112	196	52	11	2	3	1.5	25	24	15	21	3	.265	.388	3	1	OF-107
1983	92	315	96	15	0	3	1.0	44	34	15	29	4	.305	.381	3	1	OF-84, DH-6
1984	110	354	119	17	0	8	2.3	60	39	18	43	0	.336	.452	10	3	OF-98
13 yrs.	1132	3584	965	148	24	56	1.6	479	343	251	411	98	.269	.371	49	12	OF-1000, SS-42, DH-32, 3B-17, 2B-1

LEAGUE CHAMPIONSHIP SERIES

	G	AB	H	2B	3B	HR	HR%	R	RBI	BB	SO	SB	BA	SA	AB	H	G by POS
1975 BOS A	3	12	3	0	0	0	0.0	2	1	0	1	2	.250	.250	0	0	DH-3
1982 CAL A	2	0	0	0	0	0	–	0	0	0	0	0	–	–	0	0	OF-2
2 yrs.	5	12	3	0	0	0	0.0	2	1	0	1	2	.250	.250	0	0	DH-3, OF-2

WORLD SERIES

	G	AB	H	2B	3B	HR	HR%	R	RBI	BB	SO	SB	BA	SA	AB	H	G by POS
1975 BOS A	3	8	1	0	0	0	0.0	0	1	1	1	0	.125	.125	1	0	OF-2

Stan Benjamin

BENJAMIN, ALFRED STANLEY   BR TR 6'2"   194 lbs.
B. May 20, 1914, Framingham, Mass.

	G	AB	H	2B	3B	HR	HR%	R	RBI	BB	SO	SB	BA	SA	AB	H	G by POS
1939 PHI N	13	50	7	2	1	0	0.0	4	2	1	6	1	.140	.220	0	0	OF-7, 3B-5
1940	8	9	2	0	0	0	0.0	1	1	1	1	0	.222	.222	4	1	OF-2
1941	129	480	113	20	7	3	0.6	47	27	20	81	17	.235	.325	9	1	OF-110, 1B-8, 2B-2, 3B-1
1942	78	210	47	8	3	2	1.0	24	8	10	27	5	.224	.319	15	4	OF-45, 1B-15
1945 CLE A	14	21	7	2	0	0	0.0	1	3	0	0	0	.333	.429	10	3	OF-4
5 yrs.	242	770	176	32	11	5	0.6	77	41	32	115	23	.229	.318	38	9	OF-168, 1B-23, 3B-6, 2B-2

Ike Benners

BENNERS, ISAAC (Windy)
B. Philadelphia, Pa.   Deceased.

	G	AB	H	2B	3B	HR	HR%	R	RBI	BB	SO	SB	BA	SA	AB	H	G by POS
1884 2 teams	BKN	AA	(49G –	.201)		WIL	U	(6G –	.045)								
" total	55	211	39	11	5	1	0.5	25		8			.185	.299	0	0	OF-54, 1B-1

	G	AB	H	2B	3B	HR	HR %	R	RBI	BB	SO	SB	BA	SA	Pinch Hit AB	Pinch Hit H	G by POS

Charlie Bennett

BENNETT, CHARLES WESLEY   BR TR 5'11"   180 lbs.
B. Nov. 21, 1854, New Castle, Pa.   D. Feb. 24, 1927, Detroit, Mich.

	G	AB	H	2B	3B	HR	HR %	R	RBI	BB	SO	SB	BA	SA	AB	H	G by POS
1878 MIL N	49	184	45	9	0	1	0.5	16	12	10	26		.245	.310	0	0	C-35, OF-20
1880 WOR N	51	193	44	9	3	0	0.0	20		10	30		.228	.306	0	0	C-46, OF-6
1881 DET N	76	299	90	18	7	7	2.3	44	64	18	37		.301	.478	0	0	C-70, 3B-5, OF-3
1882	84	342	103	16	10	5	1.5	43	51	20	33		.301	.450	0	0	C-65, 3B-11, 2B-7, SS-1, 1B-1
1883	92	371	113	34	7	5	1.3	56		26	59		.305	.474	0	0	C-72, 2B-15, OF-12
1884	90	341	90	18	6	3	0.9	37		36	40		.264	.378	0	0	C-80, OF-5, SS-4, 3B-1, 2B-1, 1B-1
1885	91	349	94	24	13	5	1.4	49	60	47	37		.269	.456	0	0	C-62, OF-19, 3B-10
1886	72	235	57	13	4	5	2.1	37	34	48	29		.243	.396	0	0	C-69, OF-4, SS-1
1887	46	160	39	6	5	3	1.9	26	20	30	22	7	.244	.400	0	0	C-45, OF-1, 1B-1
1888	74	258	68	12	4	5	1.9	32	29	31	40	4	.264	.399	0	0	C-73, 1B-1
1889 BOS N	82	247	57	8	2	4	1.6	42	28	21	43	7	.231	.328	0	0	C-82
1890	85	281	60	17	2	3	1.1	59	40	72	56	6	.214	.320	0	0	C-85
1891	75	256	55	9	3	5	2.0	35	39	42	61	3	.215	.332	0	0	C-75
1892	35	114	23	4	0	1	0.9	19	16	27	23	6	.202	.263	0	0	C-35
1893	60	191	40	6	0	4	2.1	34	27	40	36	5	.209	.304	0	0	C-60
15 yrs.	1062	3821	978	203	66	56	1.5	549	420	478	572	38	.256	.388	0	0	C-954, OF-70, 3B-27, 2B-23, SS-6, 1B-4

Fred Bennett

BENNETT, JAMES FRED (Red)   BR TR 5'9"   185 lbs.
B. Mar. 15, 1902, Atkins, Ark.   D. May 12, 1957, Atkins, Ark.

	G	AB	H	2B	3B	HR	HR %	R	RBI	BB	SO	SB	BA	SA	AB	H	G by POS
1928 STL A	7	8	2	1	0	0	0.0	0	0	0	2	0	.250	.375	6	1	OF-1
1931 PIT N	32	89	25	5	0	1	1.1	6	7	7	4	0	.281	.371	9	2	OF-21
2 yrs.	39	97	27	6	0	1	1.0	6	7	7	6	0	.278	.371	15	3	OF-22

Herschel Bennett

BENNETT, HERSCHEL EMMETT   BL TR 5'9½"   160 lbs.
B. Sept. 21, 1896, Elwood, Mo.   D. Sept. 9, 1964, Springfield, Mo.

	G	AB	H	2B	3B	HR	HR %	R	RBI	BB	SO	SB	BA	SA	AB	H	G by POS
1923 STL A	5	4	0	0	0	0	0.0	0	0	1	1	0	.000	.000	3	0	OF-1
1924	41	94	31	4	3	1	1.1	16	11	3	6	1	.330	.468	18	6	OF-21
1925	98	298	83	11	6	2	0.7	46	37	18	16	4	.279	.376	16	9	OF-73
1926	80	225	60	14	2	1	0.4	33	26	22	21	2	.267	.360	28	12	OF-50
1927	93	256	68	12	2	3	1.2	40	30	14	21	6	.266	.363	30	5	OF-55
5 yrs.	317	877	242	41	13	7	0.8	135	104	58	65	13	.276	.376	95	32	OF-200

Joe Bennett

BENNETT, JOSEPH ROSENBLUM   BR TR 5'9"   168 lbs.
B. July 2, 1900, New York, N. Y.

	G	AB	H	2B	3B	HR	HR %	R	RBI	BB	SO	SB	BA	SA	AB	H	G by POS
1923 PHI N	1	0	0	0	0	0	–	0	0	0	0	0	–	–	0	0	3B-1

Pug Bennett

BENNETT, JUSTIN TITUS   TR
B. Feb. 20, 1874, Ponca, Neb.   D. Sept. 12, 1935, Kirkland, Wash.

	G	AB	H	2B	3B	HR	HR %	R	RBI	BB	SO	SB	BA	SA	AB	H	G by POS
1906 STL N	153	595	156	16	7	1	0.2	66	34	56		20	.262	.318	0	0	2B-153
1907	87	324	72	8	2	0	0.0	20	21	21		7	.222	.259	1	0	2B-83, 3B-3
2 yrs.	240	919	228	24	9	1	0.1	86	55	77		27	.248	.297	1	0	2B-236, 3B-3

Vern Benson

BENSON, VERNON ADAIR   BL TR 5'10"   160 lbs.
B. Sept. 19, 1924, Granite Quarry, N. C.

	G	AB	H	2B	3B	HR	HR %	R	RBI	BB	SO	SB	BA	SA	AB	H	G by POS
1943 PHI A	2	2	0	0	0	0	0.0	0	0	0	0	0	.000	.000	2	0	
1946	7	5	0	0	0	0	0.0	1	0	1	3	0	.000	.000	0	0	OF-2
1951 STL N	13	46	12	3	1	1	2.2	8	7	6	8	0	.261	.435	0	0	3B-9, OF-4
1952	20	47	9	2	0	2	4.3	6	5	5	9	0	.191	.362	5	2	3B-15
1953	13	4	0	0	0	0	0.0	2	0	1	2	0	.000	.000	4	0	
5 yrs.	55	104	21	5	1	3	2.9	17	12	13	22	0	.202	.356	11	2	3B-24, OF-6

Jack Bentley

BENTLEY, JOHN NEEDLES   BL TL 5'11½"   200 lbs.
B. Mar. 8, 1895, Sandy Spring, Md.   D. Oct. 24, 1969, Downey, Md.

	G	AB	H	2B	3B	HR	HR %	R	RBI	BB	SO	SB	BA	SA	AB	H	G by POS
1913 WAS A	3	3	0	0	0	0	0.0	0	0	0	0	0	.000	.000	0	0	P-3
1914	30	40	11	2	0	0	0.0	7	4	0	5	0	.275	.325	0	0	P-30
1915	4	2	0	0	0	0	0.0	0	0	0	1	0	.000	.000	0	0	P-4
1916	2	0	0	0	0	0	–	0	0	0	0	0	–	–	0	0	P-2
1923 NY N	52	89	38	6	2	1	1.1	9	14	3	4	0	.427	.573	20	10	P-31
1924	46	98	26	5	1	0	0.0	12	6	3	13	0	.265	.337	18	4	P-28
1925	64	99	30	5	2	3	3.0	10	18	9	11	0	.303	.485	28	9	P-28, OF-3, 1B-1
1926 2 teams	PHI	N (75G –	.258)		NY	N (3G –	.250)										
" total	78	244	63	12	3	2	0.8	19	27	5	4	0	.258	.357	16	2	1B-56, P-8
1927 NY N	8	9	2	0	0	1	11.1	1	2	1	1	0	.222	.556	1	0	P-4, 1B-2
9 yrs.	287	584	170	30	8	7	1.2	58	71	21	39	0	.291	.406	83	25	P-138, 1B-59, OF-3

WORLD SERIES																	
1923 NY N	5	5	3	1	0	0	0.0	0	0	0	0	0	.600	.800	3	2	P-2
1924	5	7	2	0	0	1	14.3	1	2	1	1	0	.286	.714	1	0	P-3
2 yrs.	10	12	5	1	0	1	8.3	1	2	1	1	0	.417	.750	4	2	P-5

Butch Benton

BENTON, ALFRED LEE   BR TR 6'1"   190 lbs.
B. Aug. 24, 1957, Tampa, Fla.

	G	AB	H	2B	3B	HR	HR %	R	RBI	BB	SO	SB	BA	SA	AB	H	G by POS
1978 NY N	4	4	2	0	0	0	0.0	1	0	0	0	0	.500	.500	1	0	C-1
1980	12	21	1	0	0	0	0.0	0	0	2	4	0	.048	.048	4	0	C-8
1982 CHI N	4	7	1	0	0	0	0.0	0	1	0	1	0	.143	.143	0	0	C-4
3 yrs.	20	32	4	0	0	0	0.0	1	3	2	5	0	.125	.125	5	0	C-13

Stan Benton

BENTON, STANLEY (Rabbit)   BL TR 5'7½"   160 lbs.
B. Sept. 29, 1901, Cannel City, Ky.

	G	AB	H	2B	3B	HR	HR %	R	RBI	BB	SO	SB	BA	SA	AB	H	G by POS
1922 PHI N	6	19	4	1	0	0	0.0	1	3	2	1	0	.211	.263	1	0	2B-5

	G	AB	H	2B	3B	HR	HR %	R	RBI	BB	SO	SB	BA	SA	Pinch Hit AB	Pinch Hit H	G by POS

Johnny Berardino

BERARDINO, JOHN
B. May 1, 1917, Los Angeles, Calif.
BR TR 5'11½" 175 lbs.

	G	AB	H	2B	3B	HR	HR%	R	RBI	BB	SO	SB	BA	SA	AB	H	G by POS
1939 STL A	126	468	120	24	5	5	1.1	42	58	37	36	6	.256	.361	2	1	2B-114, 3B-8, SS-2
1940	142	523	135	31	4	16	3.1	71	85	32	46	6	.258	.424	8	2	SS-112, 2B-13, 3B-9
1941	128	469	127	30	4	5	1.1	48	89	41	27	3	.271	.384	4	0	SS-123, 3B-1
1942	29	74	21	6	0	1	1.4	11	10	4	2	3	.284	.405	8	1	SS-6, 3B-6, 1B-5, 2B-4
1946	144	582	154	29	5	5	0.9	70	68	34	58	2	.265	.357	1	0	2B-143
1947	90	306	80	22	1	1	0.3	29	20	44	26	6	.261	.350	2	0	2B-86
1948 CLE A	66	147	28	5	1	2	1.4	19	10	27	16	0	.190	.279	11	2	2B-20, 1B-18, SS-12, 3B-3
1949	50	116	23	6	1	0	0.0	11	13	14	14	0	.198	.267	14	2	3B-25, 2B-8, SS-3
1950 2 teams	CLE	A	(4G –	.400)		PIT	N	(40G –	.206)								
" total	44	136	29	3	1	1	0.7	13	15	20	11	0	.213	.272	3	2	2B-37, 3B-4
1951 STL A	39	119	27	7	1	0	0.0	13	13	17	18	1	.227	.303	3	0	3B-31, 2B-2, OF-1, 1B-1
1952 2 teams	CLE	A	(35G –	.094)		PIT	N	(19G –	.143)								
" total	54	88	11	4	0	0	0.0	7	6	14	14	0	.125	.170	8	0	2B-26, SS-8, 3B-4, 1B-2
11 yrs.	912	3028	755	167	23	36	1.2	334	387	284	268	27	.249	.355	64	10	2B-453, SS-266, 3B-91, 1B-26, OF-1

Lou Berberet

BERBERET, LOUIS JOSEPH
B. Nov. 20, 1929, Long Beach, Calif.
BL TR 5'11" 200 lbs.

	G	AB	H	2B	3B	HR	HR%	R	RBI	BB	SO	SB	BA	SA	AB	H	G by POS
1954 NY A	5	5	2	0	0	0	0.0	1	3	1	1	0	.400	.400	2	1	C-3
1955	5	5	2	0	0	0	0.0	1	2	1	0	0	.400	.400	1	1	C-1
1956 WAS A	95	207	54	6	3	4	1.9	25	27	46	33	0	.261	.377	33	6	C-59
1957	99	264	69	11	2	7	2.7	24	36	41	38	0	.261	.398	16	3	C-77
1958 2 teams	WAS	A	(5G –	.167)		BOS	A	(57G –	.210)								
" total	62	173	36	5	3	2	1.2	11	18	35	33	0	.208	.306	8	0	C-51
1959 DET A	100	338	73	8	2	13	3.8	38	44	35	59	0	.216	.367	3	0	C-95
1960	85	232	45	4	0	5	2.2	18	23	41	31	2	.194	.276	4	1	C-81
7 yrs.	448	1224	281	34	10	31	2.5	118	153	200	195	2	.230	.350	67	12	C-367

Moe Berg

BERG, MORRIS
B. Mar. 2, 1902, New York, N. Y.   D. May 29, 1972, Belleville, N. J.
BR TR 6'1" 185 lbs.

	G	AB	H	2B	3B	HR	HR%	R	RBI	BB	SO	SB	BA	SA	AB	H	G by POS
1923 BKN N	49	129	24	3	2	0	0.0	9	6	2	5	1	.186	.240	0	0	SS-47, 2B-1
1926 CHI A	41	113	25	6	0	0	0.0	4	7	6	9	0	.221	.274	6	1	SS-31, 2B-2, 3B-1
1927	35	69	17	4	0	0	0.0	4	4	4	10	0	.246	.304	6	1	2B-10, C-10, SS-6, 3B-3
1928	76	224	55	16	0	0	0.0	25	29	14	25	2	.246	.317	3	1	C-73
1929	106	351	101	7	0	0	0.0	32	47	17	16	5	.288	.308	0	0	C-106
1930	20	61	7	3	0	0	0.0	4	7	1	5	0	.115	.164	0	0	C-20
1931 CLE A	10	13	1	1	0	0	0.0	1	0	1	1	0	.077	.154	1	0	C-8
1932 WAS A	75	195	46	8	1	1	0.5	16	26	8	13	1	.236	.303	0	0	C-75
1933	40	65	12	3	0	2	3.1	8	9	4	5	0	.185	.323	4	0	C-35
1934 2 teams	WAS	A	(33G –	.244)		CLE	A	(29G –	.258)								
" total	62	183	46	7	1	0	0.0	9	15	7	11	2	.251	.301	3	0	C-62
1935 BOS A	38	98	28	5	0	2	2.0	13	12	5	3	0	.286	.398	1	0	C-37
1936	39	125	30	4	1	0	0.0	9	19	2	6	0	.240	.288	0	0	C-39
1937	47	141	36	3	1	0	0.0	13	20	5	4	0	.255	.291	0	0	C-47
1938	10	12	4	0	0	0	0.0	0	0	0	1	0	.333	.333	3	2	C-7, 1B-1
1939	14	33	9	1	0	1	3.0	3	5	2	3	0	.273	.394	1	0	C-13
15 yrs.	662	1812	441	71	6	6	0.3	150	206	78	117	11	.243	.299	28	5	C-532, SS-84, 2B-13, 3B-4, 1B-1

Augie Bergamo

BERGAMO, AUGUST SAMUEL
B. Feb. 14, 1918, Detroit, Mich.   D. Aug. 19, 1974, Grosse Point City, Mich.
BL TL 5'9" 165 lbs.

	G	AB	H	2B	3B	HR	HR%	R	RBI	BB	SO	SB	BA	SA	AB	H	G by POS
1944 STL N	80	192	55	6	3	2	1.0	35	19	35	23	0	.286	.380	26	4	OF-50, 1B-2
1945	94	304	96	17	2	3	1.0	51	44	43	21	0	.316	.414	15	4	OF-77, 1B-2
2 yrs.	174	496	151	23	5	5	1.0	86	63	78	44	0	.304	.401	41	8	OF-127, 1B-4

WORLD SERIES

	G	AB	H	2B	3B	HR	HR%	R	RBI	BB	SO	SB	BA	SA	AB	H	G by POS
1944 STL N	3	6	0	0	0	0	0.0	0	1	2	3	0	.000	.000	0	0	OF-2

Bill Bergen

BERGEN, WILLIAM ALOYSIUS
Brother of Marty Bergen.
B. June 13, 1873, N. Brookfield, Mass.   D. Dec. 19, 1943, Worcester, Mass.
BR TR 6' 184 lbs.

	G	AB	H	2B	3B	HR	HR%	R	RBI	BB	SO	SB	BA	SA	AB	H	G by POS
1901 CIN N	87	308	55	6	4	1	0.3	15	17	8		2	.179	.234	0	0	C-87
1902	89	322	58	8	3	0	0.0	19	36	14		2	.180	.224	0	0	C-89
1903	58	207	47	4	2	0	0.0	21	19	7		2	.227	.266	0	0	C-58
1904 BKN N	96	329	60	4	2	0	0.0	17	12	9		3	.182	.207	0	0	C-93, 1B-1
1905	79	247	47	3	2	0	0.0	12	22	7		4	.190	.219	3	0	C-76
1906	103	353	56	3	3	0	0.0	19	19	7		2	.159	.184	0	0	C-103
1907	51	138	22	3	0	0	0.0	2	14	1		1	.159	.181	0	0	C-51
1908	99	302	53	8	2	0	0.0	8	15	5		1	.175	.215	0	0	C-99
1909	112	346	48	1	1	1	0.3	16	15	10		4	.139	.156	0	0	C-112
1910	89	249	40	2	1	0	0.0	11	14	6	39	0	.161	.177	0	0	C-89
1911	84	227	30	3	1	0	0.0	8	10	14	42	2	.132	.154	0	0	C-84
11 yrs.	947	3028	516	45	21	2	0.1	138	193	88	81	23	.170	.201	3	0	C-941, 1B-1

Marty Bergen

BERGEN, MARTIN
Brother of Bill Bergen.
B. Oct. 25, 1871, N. Brookfield, Mass.   D. Jan. 19, 1900, N. Brookfield, Mass.
TR 5'10" 170 lbs.

	G	AB	H	2B	3B	HR	HR%	R	RBI	BB	SO	SB	BA	SA	AB	H	G by POS
1896 BOS N	65	245	66	6	4	4	1.6	39	37	11	22	6	.269	.376	1	0	C-63, 1B-1
1897	87	327	81	11	3	2	0.6	47	45	18		5	.248	.318	0	0	C-85, 1B-1
1898	120	446	125	16	5	3	0.7	62	60	13		9	.280	.359	1	1	C-117, 1B-2
1899	72	260	67	11	3	1	0.4	32	34	10		4	.258	.335	0	0	C-72
4 yrs.	344	1278	339	44	15	10	0.8	180	176	52	22	24	.265	.347	2	1	C-337, 1B-3, OF-1

Boze Berger

BERGER, LOUIS WILLIAM
B. May 13, 1910, Baltimore, Md.
BR TR 6'2" 180 lbs.

	G	AB	H	2B	3B	HR	HR%	R	RBI	BB	SO	SB	BA	SA	AB	H	G by POS
1932 CLE A	1	1	0	0	0	0	0.0	0	0	0	1	0	.000	.000	0	0	SS-1
1935	124	461	119	27	5	5	1.1	62	43	34	97	7	.258	.371	0	0	2B-120, SS-3, 1B-2, 3B-1

	G	AB	H	2B	3B	HR	HR %	R	RBI	BB	SO	SB	BA	SA	Pinch Hit AB	H	G by POS

Boze Berger continued

	G	AB	H	2B	3B	HR	HR %	R	RBI	BB	SO	SB	BA	SA	PH AB	PH H	G by POS
1936	28	52	9	2	0	0	0.0	1	3	1	14	0	.173	.212	1	0	2B-8, 1B-8, 3B-7, SS-2
1937 CHI A	52	130	31	5	0	5	3.8	19	13	15	24	1	.238	.392	6	2	3B-40, SS-1, 2B-1
1938	118	470	102	15	3	3	0.6	60	36	43	80	4	.217	.281	0	0	SS-67, 2B-42, 3B-9
1939 BOS A	20	30	9	2	0	0	0.0	4	2	1	10	0	.300	.367	3	1	SS-10, 3B-5, 2B-2
6 yrs.	343	1144	270	51	8	13	1.1	146	97	94	226	12	.236	.329	10	3	2B-173, SS-84, 3B-62, 1B-10

Clarence Berger

BERGER, CLARENCE EDWARD BL TR 6' 185 lbs.
B. Nov. 1, 1894, Cleveland, Ohio   D. June 30, 1959, Washington, D. C.

	G	AB	H	2B	3B	HR	HR %	R	RBI	BB	SO	SB	BA	SA	PH AB	PH H	G by POS
1914 PIT N	6	13	1	0	0	0	0.0	2	0	1	4	0	.077	.077	1	0	OF-5

Joe Berger

BERGER, JOSEPH AUGUST (Fats) BR TR 5'10½" 170 lbs.
B. Dec. 20, 1886, St. Louis, Mo.   D. Mar. 5, 1956, Rock Island, Ill.

	G	AB	H	2B	3B	HR	HR %	R	RBI	BB	SO	SB	BA	SA	PH AB	PH H	G by POS
1913 CHI A	77	223	48	6	2	2	0.9	27	20	36	28	5	.215	.287	2	0	2B-69, SS-4, 3B-1
1914	47	148	23	3	1	0	0.0	11	3	13	9	2	.155	.189	1	0	SS-27, 2B-12, 3B-7
2 yrs.	124	371	71	9	3	2	0.5	38	23	49	37	7	.191	.248	3	0	2B-81, SS-31, 3B-8

Johnny Berger

BERGER, JOHN HENNE BR TR 5'9" 165 lbs.
B. Aug. 27, 1901, Philadelphia, Pa.   D. May 7, 1979, Lake Charles, La.

	G	AB	H	2B	3B	HR	HR %	R	RBI	BB	SO	SB	BA	SA	PH AB	PH H	G by POS
1922 PHI A	2	1	1	0	0	0	0.0	0	0	0	0	1	1.000	1.000	0	0	C-2
1927 WAS A	9	15	4	0	0	0	0.0	1	1	2	3	0	.267	.267	0	0	C-9
2 yrs.	11	16	5	0	0	0	0.0	1	1	2	3	1	.313	.313	0	0	C-11

Tun Berger

BERGER, JOHN HENRY
B. Dec. 6, 1867, Pittsburgh, Pa.   D. June 11, 1907, Pittsburgh, Pa.

	G	AB	H	2B	3B	HR	HR %	R	RBI	BB	SO	SB	BA	SA	PH AB	PH H	G by POS
1890 PIT N	104	391	104	18	4	0	0.0	64	40	35	23	11	.266	.332	0	0	OF-41, SS-33, C-21, 2B-6, 3B-1
1891	43	134	32	2	1	1	0.7	15	14	12	10	4	.239	.291	0	0	C-18, 2B-17, SS-6, OF-2
1892 WAS N	26	97	14	2	1	0	0.0	9	3	7	9	3	.144	.186	0	0	SS-18, C-9
3 yrs.	173	622	150	22	6	1	0.2	88	57	54	42	18	.241	.301	0	0	SS-57, C-48, OF-43, 2B-23, 3B-1

Wally Berger

BERGER, WALTER ANTON BR TR 6'2" 198 lbs.
B. Oct. 10, 1905, Chicago, Ill.

	G	AB	H	2B	3B	HR	HR %	R	RBI	BB	SO	SB	BA	SA	PH AB	PH H	G by POS
1930 BOS N	151	555	172	27	14	38	6.8	98	119	54	69	3	.310	.614	6	1	OF-145
1931	156	617	199	44	8	19	3.1	94	84	55	70	13	.323	.512	0	0	OF-156, 1B-1
1932	145	602	185	34	6	17	2.8	90	73	33	66	5	.307	.468	1	0	OF-134, 1B-11
1933	137	528	165	37	8	27	5.1	84	106	41	77	2	.313	.566	1	1	OF-136
1934	150	615	183	35	8	34	5.5	92	121	49	65	2	.298	.546	0	0	OF-150
1935	150	589	174	39	4	34	5.8	91	130	50	80	3	.295	.548	1	0	OF-149
1936	138	534	154	23	3	25	4.7	88	91	53	84	1	.288	.483	5	1	OF-133
1937 2 teams	89	BOS N (30G – .274)						NY N (59G – .291)									
" total	89	312	89	20	3	17	5.4	54	65	29	63	3	.285	.532	9	1	OF-80
1938 2 teams		NY N (16G – .188)						CIN N (99G – .307)									
" total	115	439	131	23	4	16	3.6	76	60	31	48	2	.298	.478	5	2	OF-107
1939 CIN N	97	329	85	15	1	14	4.3	36	44	36	63	1	.258	.438	2	0	OF-95
1940 2 teams		CIN N (2G – .000)						PHI N (20G – .317)									
" total	22	43	13	2	0	1	2.3	3	5	4	9	1	.302	.419	9	0	OF-11, 1B-1
11 yrs.	1350	5163	1550	299	59	242	4.7	806	898	435	694	36	.300	.522	39	6	OF-1296, 1B-13

WORLD SERIES

	G	AB	H	2B	3B	HR	HR %	R	RBI	BB	SO	SB	BA	SA	PH AB	PH H	G by POS
1937 NY N	3	3	0	0	0	0	0.0	0	0	0	1	0	.000	.000	3	0	OF-4
1939 CIN N	4	15	0	0	0	0	0.0	0	1	0	4	0	.000	.000	0	0	OF-4
2 yrs.	7	18	0	0	0	0	0.0	0	1	0	5	0	.000	.000	3	0	OF-4

John Bergh

BERGH, JOHN BAPTIST
B. Oct. 8, 1857, Boston, Mass.   D. Apr. 16, 1883, Boston, Mass.

	G	AB	H	2B	3B	HR	HR %	R	RBI	BB	SO	SB	BA	SA	PH AB	PH H	G by POS
1876 PHI N	1	4	0	0	0	0	0.0	0	0	0	2	0	.000	.000	0	0	OF-1, C-1
1880 BOS N	11	40	8	3	0	0	0.0	2	0	2	5	0	.200	.275	0	0	C-11
2 yrs.	12	44	8	3	0	0	0.0	2	0	2	7	0	.182	.250	0	0	C-12, OF-1

Marty Berghammer

BERGHAMMER, MARTIN ANDREW BL TR 5'9" 172 lbs.
B. Jan. 18, 1886, Pittsburgh, Pa.   D. Dec. 21, 1957, Pittsburgh, Pa.

	G	AB	H	2B	3B	HR	HR %	R	RBI	BB	SO	SB	BA	SA	PH AB	PH H	G by POS
1911 CHI A	2	5	0	0	0	0	0.0	0	0	0	0	0	.000	.000	0	0	2B-2
1913 CIN N	74	188	41	4	1	1	0.5	25	13	10	29	16	.218	.266	0	0	SS-53, 2B-13
1914	77	112	25	2	0	0	0.0	15	6	10	18	4	.223	.241	13	2	SS-33, 2B-13
1915 PIT F	132	469	114	10	6	0	0.0	96	33	83		26	.243	.290	0	0	SS-132
4 yrs.	285	774	180	16	7	1	0.1	136	52	103	47	46	.233	.275	13	2	SS-218, 2B-28

Al Bergman

BERGMAN, ALFRED HENRY (Dutch) BR TR 5'7" 155 lbs.
B. Sept. 27, 1890, Peru, Ind.   D. June 20, 1961, Fort Wayne, Ind.

	G	AB	H	2B	3B	HR	HR %	R	RBI	BB	SO	SB	BA	SA	PH AB	PH H	G by POS
1916 CLE A	8	14	3	0	1	0	0.0	2	0	2	4	0	.214	.357	3	0	2B-3

Dave Bergman

BERGMAN, DAVID BRUCE BL TL 6'1½" 185 lbs.
B. June 6, 1953, Park Ridge, Ill.

	G	AB	H	2B	3B	HR	HR %	R	RBI	BB	SO	SB	BA	SA	PH AB	PH H	G by POS
1975 NY A	7	17	0	0	0	0	0.0	0	0	2	4	0	.000	.000	0	0	OF-6
1977	5	4	1	0	0	0	0.0	1	1	0	0	0	.250	.250	0	0	OF-3, 1B-2
1978 HOU N	104	186	43	5	1	0	0.0	15	12	39	32	2	.231	.269	16	2	1B-66, OF-29
1979	13	15	6	0	0	1	6.7	4	2	0	3	0	.400	.600	10	5	1B-4
1980	90	78	20	6	1	0	0.0	12	3	10	10	1	.256	.359	24	4	1B-59, OF-5
1981 2 teams		HOU N (6G – .167)						SF N (63G – .255)									
" total	69	151	38	9	0	4	2.6	17	14	19	18	2	.252	.391	23	4	1B-34, OF-15
1982 SF N	100	121	33	3	1	4	3.3	22	14	18	11	3	.273	.413	21	5	1B-69, OF-6
1983	90	140	40	4	1	6	4.3	16	24	24	21	2	.286	.457	31	11	1B-50, OF-6
1984 DET A	120	271	74	8	5	7	2.6	42	44	33	40	3	.273	.417	21	6	1B-114, OF-2
9 yrs.	598	983	255	35	9	22	2.2	129	114	145	139	13	.259	.380	146	37	1B-398, OF-72

	G	AB	H	2B	3B	HR	HR %	R	RBI	BB	SO	SB	BA	SA	Pinch Hit AB	Pinch Hit H	G by POS

Dave Bergman continued

LEAGUE CHAMPIONSHIP SERIES

	G	AB	H	2B	3B	HR	HR%	R	RBI	BB	SO	SB	BA	SA	PH AB	PH H	G by POS
1980 HOU N	4	3	1	0	1	0	0.0	0	2	0	0	0	.333	1.000	0	0	1B-4
1984 DET A	2	1	1	0	0	0	0.0	1	0	0	0	1	1.000	1.000	0	0	1B-1
2 yrs.	6	4	2	0	1	0	0.0	1	2	0	0	1	.500	1.000	0	0	1B-5

WORLD SERIES

	G	AB	H	2B	3B	HR	HR%	R	RBI	BB	SO	SB	BA	SA	PH AB	PH H	G by POS
1984 DET A	5	5	0	0	0	0	0.0	0	0	0	1	0	.000	.000	0	0	1B-5

Frank Berkelbach

BERKELBACH, FRANCIS P.
B. Philadelphia, Pa. Deceased.   6'   182 lbs.

	G	AB	H	2B	3B	HR	HR%	R	RBI	BB	SO	SB	BA	SA	PH AB	PH H	G by POS
1884 CIN AA	6	25	6	0	1	0	0.0	3		0			.240	.320	0	0	OF-6

Bob Berman

BERMAN, ROBERT LEON
B. Jan. 24, 1899, New York, N. Y.   BR TR 5'7½" 155 lbs.

	G	AB	H	2B	3B	HR	HR%	R	RBI	BB	SO	SB	BA	SA	PH AB	PH H	G by POS
1918 WAS A	2	0	0	0	0	0	—	0	0	0	0	0	—	—	0	0	C-1

Curt Bernard

BERNARD, CURTIS HENRY
B. Feb. 18, 1878, Parkersburg, W. Va.   D. Apr. 10, 1955, Culver City, Calif.   BL TR 5'10½" 150 lbs.

	G	AB	H	2B	3B	HR	HR%	R	RBI	BB	SO	SB	BA	SA	PH AB	PH H	G by POS
1900 NY N	20	71	18	2	0	0	0.0	9	8	6			.254	.282	0	0	OF-19, SS-1
1901	23	76	17	0	2	0	0.0	11	6	7		2	.224	.276	1	0	OF-15, 2B-4, SS-2, 3B-1
2 yrs.	43	147	35	2	2	0	0.0	20	14	13		3	.238	.279	1	0	OF-34, 2B-4, SS-3, 3B-1

Tony Bernazard

BERNAZARD, ANTONIO
Also known as Antonio Garcia.
B. Aug. 24, 1956, Caguas, Puerto Rico   BB TR 5'9" 150 lbs.

	G	AB	H	2B	3B	HR	HR%	R	RBI	BB	SO	SB	BA	SA	PH AB	PH H	G by POS
1979 MON N	22	40	12	2	0	1	2.5	11	8	15	12	1	.300	.425	2	0	2B-14
1980	82	183	41	7	1	5	2.7	26	18	17	41	9	.224	.355	22	4	2B-39, SS-22
1981 CHI A	106	384	106	14	4	6	1.6	53	34	54	66	4	.276	.380	2	0	2B-104, SS-1
1982	137	540	138	25	9	11	2.0	90	56	67	88	11	.256	.396	0	0	2B-137
1983 2 teams	CHI A (59G – .262)					SEA A (80G – .267)											
" total	139	533	141	34	3	8	1.5	65	56	55	97	23	.265	.385	2	0	2B-138
1984 CLE A	140	439	97	15	4	2	0.5	44	38	43	70	20	.221	.287	3	0	2B-136, DH-1
6 yrs.	626	2119	535	97	21	33	1.6	289	210	251	374	68	.252	.365	31	4	2B-568, SS-23, DH-1

Juan Bernhardt

BERNHARDT, JUAN RAMON
Also known as Juan Ramon Coraoin.
B. Aug. 31, 1953, San Pedro, Dominican Republic   BR TR 5'11" 160 lbs.

	G	AB	H	2B	3B	HR	HR%	R	RBI	BB	SO	SB	BA	SA	PH AB	PH H	G by POS
1976 NY A	10	21	4	1	0	0	0.0	1	1	0	4	0	.190	.238	5	0	OF-4, DH-2, 3B-1
1977 SEA A	89	305	74	9	2	7	2.3	32	30	5	26	2	.243	.354	12	2	DH-54, 3B-21, 1B-8
1978	54	165	38	9	0	2	1.2	13	12	9	10	1	.230	.321	5	1	1B-25, 3B-22, DH-2
1979	1	1	1	0	0	0	0.0	0	0	0	0	0	1.000	1.000	1	1	
4 yrs.	154	492	117	19	2	9	1.8	46	43	14	40	3	.238	.339	23	4	DH-58, 3B-44, 1B-33, OF-4

Carlos Bernier

BERNIER, CARLOS RODRIGUEZ
B. Jan. 28, 1929, Juan Diaz, Puerto Rico   BR TR 5'9" 180 lbs.

	G	AB	H	2B	3B	HR	HR%	R	RBI	BB	SO	SB	BA	SA	PH AB	PH H	G by POS
1953 PIT N	105	310	66	7	8	3	1.0	48	31	51	53	15	.213	.316	16	3	OF-87

Johnny Bero

BERO, JOHN GEORGE
B. Dec. 22, 1922, Gary, W. Va.   BL TR 6' 170 lbs.

	G	AB	H	2B	3B	HR	HR%	R	RBI	BB	SO	SB	BA	SA	PH AB	PH H	G by POS
1948 DET A	4	9	0	0	0	0	0.0	2	0	1	1	0	.000	.000	1	0	2B-2
1951 STL A	61	160	34	5	0	5	3.1	24	17	26	30	1	.213	.338	7	2	SS-55, 2B-1
2 yrs.	65	169	34	5	0	5	3.0	26	17	27	31	1	.201	.320	8	2	SS-55, 2B-3

Dale Berra

BERRA, DALE ANTHONY
Son of Yogi Berra.
B. Dec. 13, 1956, Ridgewood, N. J.   BR TR 6' 180 lbs.

	G	AB	H	2B	3B	HR	HR%	R	RBI	BB	SO	SB	BA	SA	PH AB	PH H	G by POS
1977 PIT N	17	40	7	1	0	0	0.0	0	3	1	8	0	.175	.200	2	0	3B-14
1978	56	135	28	2	0	6	4.4	16	14	13	20	3	.207	.356	0	0	3B-55, SS-2
1979	44	123	26	5	0	3	2.4	11	15	11	17	0	.211	.325	0	0	SS-22, 3B-22
1980	93	245	54	8	2	6	2.4	21	31	16	52	2	.220	.343	4	1	3B-48, SS-45, 2B-4
1981	81	232	56	12	0	2	0.9	21	27	17	34	11	.241	.319	3	0	3B-42, SS-30, 2B-18
1982	156	529	139	25	5	10	1.9	64	61	33	83	6	.263	.386	0	0	SS-153, 3B-6
1983	161	537	135	25	1	10	1.9	51	52	61	84	8	.251	.358	0	0	SS-161
1984	136	450	100	16	0	9	2.0	31	52	34	78	1	.222	.318	1	1	SS-135, 3B-1
8 yrs.	744	2291	545	94	8	46	2.0	215	255	186	376	31	.238	.346	10	2	SS-548, 3B-188, 2B-22

Yogi Berra

BERRA, LAWRENCE PETER
Father of Dale Berra.
B. May 12, 1925, St. Louis, Mo.
Manager 1964, 1972-75, 1984.
Hall of Fame 1971.   BL TR 5'7½" 185 lbs.

	G	AB	H	2B	3B	HR	HR%	R	RBI	BB	SO	SB	BA	SA	PH AB	PH H	G by POS
1946 NY A	7	22	8	1	0	2	9.1	3	4	1	1	0	.364	.682	1	0	C-6
1947	83	293	82	15	3	11	3.8	41	54	13	12	0	.280	.464	8	2	C-51, OF-24
1948	125	469	143	24	10	14	3.0	70	98	25	24	3	.305	.488	10	5	C-71, OF-50
1949	116	415	115	20	2	20	4.8	59	91	22	25	2	.277	.480	7	3	C-109
1950	151	597	192	30	6	28	4.7	116	124	55	12	4	.322	.533	3	1	C-148
1951	141	547	161	19	4	27	4.9	92	88	44	20	5	.294	.492	0	0	C-141
1952	142	534	146	17	1	30	5.6	97	98	66	24	2	.273	.478	3	0	C-140
1953	137	503	149	23	5	27	5.4	80	108	50	32	0	.296	.523	10	4	C-133
1954	151	584	179	28	6	22	3.8	88	125	56	29	0	.307	.488	1	0	C-149, 3B-1
1955	147	541	147	20	3	27	5.0	84	108	60	20	1	.272	.470	4	1	C-145
1956	140	521	155	29	2	30	5.8	93	105	65	29	3	.298	.534	4	0	C-135, OF-1
1957	134	482	121	14	2	24	5.0	74	82	57	25	1	.251	.438	10	1	C-121, OF-6
1958	122	433	115	17	3	22	5.1	60	90	35	35	3	.266	.471	10	3	C-85, OF-21, 1B-2

	G	AB	H	2B	3B	HR	HR %	R	RBI	BB	SO	SB	BA	SA	Pinch Hit AB	H	G by POS

Yogi Berra continued

	G	AB	H	2B	3B	HR	HR %	R	RBI	BB	SO	SB	BA	SA	AB	H	G by POS
1959	131	472	134	25	1	19	4.0	64	69	43	38	1	.284	.462	11	3	C-116, OF-7
1960	120	359	99	14	1	15	4.2	46	62	38	23	2	.276	.446	24	5	C-63, OF-36
1961	119	395	107	11	0	22	5.6	62	61	35	28	2	.271	.466	19	5	OF-87, C-15
1962	86	232	52	8	0	10	4.3	25	35	24	18	0	.224	.388	23	6	C-31, OF-28
1963	64	147	43	6	0	8	5.4	20	28	15	17	1	.293	.497	28	5	C-35
1965 NY N	4	9	2	0	0	0	0.0	1	0	0	3	0	.222	.222	2	0	C-2
19 yrs.	2120	7555	2150	321	49	358	4.7	1175	1430	704	415	30	.285	.482	178	44	C-1696, OF-260, 1B-2, 3B-1

WORLD SERIES

	G	AB	H	2B	3B	HR	HR %	R	RBI	BB	SO	SB	BA	SA	AB	H	G by POS
1947 NY A	6	19	3	0	0	1	5.3	2	2	1	2	0	.158	.316	1	1	C-4
1949	4	16	1	0	0	0	0.0	2	1	1	3	0	.063	.063	0	0	C-4
1950	4	15	3	0	0	1	6.7	2	2	2	1	0	.200	.400	0	0	C-4
1951	6	23	6	1	0	0	0.0	4	0	2	1	0	.261	.304	0	0	C-6
1952	7	28	6	1	0	2	7.1	2	3	2	4	0	.214	.464	0	0	C-7
1953	6	21	9	1	0	1	4.8	3	4	3	3	0	.429	.619	0	0	C-6
1955	7	24	10	1	0	1	4.2	5	2	3	1	0	.417	.583	0	0	C-7
1956	7	25	9	2	0	3	12.0	5	10	4	1	0	.360	.800	0	0	C-7
1957	7	25	8	1	0	1	4.0	5	2	4	0	0	.320	.480	0	0	C-7
1958	7	27	6	3	0	0	0.0	3	2	1	0	0	.222	.333	0	0	C-7
1960	7	22	7	0	0	1	4.5	6	8	2	0	0	.318	.455	1	0	C-3
1961	4	11	3	0	0	1	9.1	2	3	5	1	0	.273	.545	0	0	OF-4
1962	2	2	0	0	0	0	0.0	0	0	2	0	0	.000	.000	0	0	C-1
1963	1	1	0	0	0	0	0.0	0	0	0	0	0	.000	.000	1	0	
14 yrs.	75	259	71	10	0	12	4.6	41	39	32	17	0	.274	.452	3	1	C-63, OF-4
	1st	1st	1st	1st		3rd		2nd	2nd	3rd							

Joe Berran

BERRAN, DENNIS MARTIN　　　　　　　　　BR TL
B. 1887, Merrimac, Mass.　D. Apr. 28, 1943, Boston, Mass.

	G	AB	H	2B	3B	HR	HR %	R	RBI	BB	SO	SB	BA	SA	AB	H	G by POS
1912 CHI A	2	4	1	0	0	0	0.0	1	0	0		0	.250	.250	0	0	OF-2

Ray Berres

BERRES, RAYMOND FREDERICK　　　　　　BR TR 5'9"　170 lbs.
B. Aug. 21, 1908, Kenosha, Wis.

	G	AB	H	2B	3B	HR	HR %	R	RBI	BB	SO	SB	BA	SA	AB	H	G by POS
1934 BKN N	39	79	17	4	0	0	0.0	7	3	1	16	0	.215	.266	1	0	C-37
1936	105	267	64	10	1	1	0.4	16	13	14	35	1	.240	.296	0	0	C-105
1937 PIT N	2	6	1	0	0	0	0.0	0	0	0	0	0	.167	.167	0	0	C-2
1938	40	100	23	2	0	0	0.0	7	6	8	10	0	.230	.250	0	0	C-40
1939	81	231	53	6	1	0	0.0	22	16	11	25	1	.229	.264	1	1	C-80
1940 2 teams		PIT	N (21G –	.188)		BOS	N (85G –	.192)									
" total	106	261	50	4	1	0	0.0	14	16	19	20	0	.192	.215	0	0	C-106
1941 BOS N	120	279	56	10	0	1	0.4	21	19	17	20	2	.201	.247	0	0	C-120
1942 NY N	12	32	6	0	0	0	0.0	1	0	1	3	0	.188	.188	0	0	C-12
1943	20	28	4	1	0	0	0.0	1	0	1	2	0	.143	.179	3	1	C-17
1944	16	17	8	0	0	1	5.9	4	2	1	0	0	.471	.647	0	0	C-12
1945	20	30	5	0	0	0	0.0	4	2	2	3	0	.167	.167	0	0	C-20
11 yrs.	561	1330	287	37	3	3	0.2	96	78	76	134	4	.216	.255	5	2	C-551

Charlie Berry

BERRY, CHARLES FRANCIS　　　　　　　　BR TR 6'　185 lbs.
Son of Charlie Berry.
B. Oct. 18, 1902, Phillipsburg, N. J.　D. Sept. 6, 1972, Evanston, Ill.

	G	AB	H	2B	3B	HR	HR %	R	RBI	BB	SO	SB	BA	SA	AB	H	G by POS
1925 PHI A	10	14	3	1	0	0	0.0	1	3	0	2	0	.214	.286	6	1	C-4
1928 BOS A	80	177	46	7	3	1	0.6	18	19	21	19	1	.260	.350	14	4	C-63
1929	77	207	50	11	4	1	0.5	19	21	15	29	2	.242	.348	4	3	C-72
1930	88	256	74	9	6	6	2.3	31	35	16	22	2	.289	.441	3	2	C-85
1931	111	357	101	16	2	6	1.7	41	49	29	38	4	.283	.389	9	2	C-102
1932 2 teams		BOS	A (10G –	.188)		CHI	A (72G –	.305)									
" total	82	258	75	18	6	4	1.6	33	37	24	25	3	.291	.453	2	0	C-80
1933 CHI A	86	271	69	8	3	2	0.7	25	28	17	16	0	.255	.328	3	0	C-83
1934 PHI A	99	269	72	10	2	0	0.0	14	34	22	23	1	.268	.320	0	0	C-99
1935	62	190	48	7	3	3	1.6	14	29	10	20	0	.253	.368	6	1	C-56
1936	13	17	1	1	0	0	0.0	0	1	6	2	0	.059	.118	1	0	C-12
1938	1	2	0	0	0	0	0.0	0	0	0	0	0	.000	.000	0	0	C-1
11 yrs.	709	2018	539	88	29	23	1.1	196	256	160	196	13	.267	.374	48	13	C-657

Charlie Berry

BERRY, CHARLES JOSEPH　　　　　　　　BR TR 5'11"　175 lbs.
Father of Charlie Berry.
B. Sept. 6, 1860, Elizabeth, N. J.　D. Jan. 22, 1940, Phillipsburg, N. J.

	G	AB	H	2B	3B	HR	HR %	R	RBI	BB	SO	SB	BA	SA	AB	H	G by POS
1884 3 teams		ALT	U (7G –	.240)		KC	U (29G –	.246)		C-P	U (7G –	.111)					
" total	43	170	38	8	1	1	0.6	21		1		1	.224	.300	0	0	2B-36, OF-8, 3B-1

Claude Berry

BERRY, CLAUDE ELZY (Admiral)　　　　　BR TR 5'7"　165 lbs.
B. Feb. 4, 1880, Losantville, Ind.　D. Feb. 1, 1974, Richmond, Ind.

	G	AB	H	2B	3B	HR	HR %	R	RBI	BB	SO	SB	BA	SA	AB	H	G by POS
1904 CHI A	3	1	0	0	0	0	0.0	1	0	1		0	.000	.000	0	0	C-3
1906 PHI A	10	30	7	0	0	0	0.0	2	2	2		1	.233	.233	0	0	C-10
1907	8	19	4	2	0	0	0.0	2	1	2		0	.211	.316	0	0	C-8
1914 PIT F	124	411	98	18	9	2	0.5	35	36	26		6	.238	.341	1	0	C-122
1915	100	292	56	11	1	1	0.3	32	26	29		7	.192	.247	0	0	C-99
5 yrs.	245	753	165	31	10	3	0.4	72	65	60		14	.219	.299	1	0	C-242

Joe Berry

BERRY, JOSEPH HOWARD (Hodge)　　　　BB TR 5'9"　172 lbs.
Father of Joe Berry.
B. Sept. 10, 1872, Wheeling, W. Va.　D. Mar. 13, 1961, Philadelphia, Pa.

	G	AB	H	2B	3B	HR	HR %	R	RBI	BB	SO	SB	BA	SA	AB	H	G by POS
1902 PHI N	1	4	1	0	0	0	0.0	0	1	1		1	.250	.250	0	0	C-1

	G	AB	H	2B	3B	HR	HR %	R	RBI	BB	SO	SB	BA	SA	Pinch Hit AB	H	G by POS

Joe Berry

BERRY, JOSEPH HOWARD JR. (Nig)
Son of Joe Berry.
B. Dec. 31, 1894, Philadelphia, Pa.   D. Apr. 29, 1976

BR TR 5'10½" 159 lbs.
BB 1922

	G	AB	H	2B	3B	HR	HR %	R	RBI	BB	SO	SB	BA	SA	AB	H	G by POS
1921 NY N	9	6	2	0	1	0	0.0	0	2	1	1	0	.333	.667	0	0	2B-7
1922	6	0	0	0	0	0	–	0	0	0	0	0	–	–	0	0	2B-6
2 yrs.	15	6	2	0	1	0	0.0	0	2	1	1	0	.333	.667	0	0	2B-13

Ken Berry

BERRY, ALLEN KENNETH
B. May 10, 1941, Kansas City, Mo.

BR TR 6' 175 lbs.

	G	AB	H	2B	3B	HR	HR %	R	RBI	BB	SO	SB	BA	SA	AB	H	G by POS
1962 CHI A	3	6	2	0	0	0	0.0	2	0	0	0	0	.333	.333	1	1	OF-2
1963	4	5	1	0	0	0	0.0	2	0	1	1	0	.200	.200	0	0	OF-2, 2B-1
1964	12	32	12	1	0	1	3.1	4	4	5	3	0	.375	.500	0	0	OF-12
1965	157	472	103	17	4	12	2.5	51	42	28	96	4	.218	.347	1	0	OF-156
1966	147	443	120	20	2	8	1.8	50	34	28	63	7	.271	.379	3	0	OF-141
1967	147	485	117	14	4	7	1.4	49	41	46	68	9	.241	.330	4	0	OF-143
1968	153	504	127	21	4	7	1.4	49	32	25	64	6	.252	.343	2	1	OF-151
1969	130	297	69	12	2	4	1.3	25	18	24	50	1	.232	.327	2	0	OF-120
1970	141	463	128	12	2	7	1.5	45	50	43	61	6	.276	.356	2	1	OF-138
1971 CAL A	111	298	66	17	0	3	1.0	29	22	18	33	3	.221	.309	10	5	OF-101
1972	119	409	118	15	3	5	1.2	41	39	35	47	5	.289	.377	4	1	OF-116
1973	136	415	118	11	2	3	0.7	48	36	26	50	1	.284	.342	3	0	OF-129
1974 MIL A	98	267	64	9	2	1	0.4	21	24	18	26	3	.240	.300	9	1	OF-82, DH-13
1975 CLE A	25	40	8	1	0	0	0.0	6	1	1	7	0	.200	.225	1	0	OF-18, DH-5
14 yrs.	1383	4136	1053	150	23	58	1.4	422	343	298	569	45	.255	.344	42	10	OF-1311, DH-18, 2B-1

Neil Berry

BERRY, CORNELIUS JOHN
B. Jan. 11, 1922, Kalamazoo, Mich.

BR TR 5'10" 168 lbs.

	G	AB	H	2B	3B	HR	HR %	R	RBI	BB	SO	SB	BA	SA	AB	H	G by POS
1948 DET A	87	256	68	8	1	0	0.0	46	16	37	23	1	.266	.305	5	1	SS-41, 2B-26
1949	109	329	78	9	1	0	0.0	38	18	27	24	4	.237	.271	4	0	2B-95, SS-4
1950	38	39	10	1	0	0	0.0	9	7	6	11	0	.256	.282	4	0	SS-11, 2B-2, 3B-1
1951	67	157	36	5	2	0	0.0	17	9	10	15	4	.229	.287	4	1	SS-38, 2B-10, 3B-7
1952	73	189	43	4	3	0	0.0	22	13	22	19	1	.228	.280	1	1	SS-66, 3B-2
1953 2 teams	STL	A	(57G –	.283)		CHI	A	(5G –	.125)								
" total	62	107	29	1	2	0	0.0	15	11	10	11	1	.271	.318	6	1	3B-18, 2B-18, SS-6
1954 BAL A	5	9	1	0	0	0	0.0	1	0	1	2	0	.111	.111	0	0	SS-5
7 yrs.	441	1086	265	28	9	0	0.0	148	74	113	105	11	.244	.286	24	3	SS-171, 2B-151, 3B-28

Harry Berte

BERTE, HARRY THOMAS
B. May 10, 1872, Covington, Ky.   D. May 6, 1952, Los Angeles, Calif.

TR

	G	AB	H	2B	3B	HR	HR %	R	RBI	BB	SO	SB	BA	SA	AB	H	G by POS
1903 STL N	4	15	5	0	0	0	0.0	1	1	1		0	.333	.333	0	0	2B-3, SS-1

Dick Bertell

BERTELL, RICHARD GEORGE
B. Nov. 21, 1935, Oak Park, Ill.

BR TR 6'½" 200 lbs.

	G	AB	H	2B	3B	HR	HR %	R	RBI	BB	SO	SB	BA	SA	AB	H	G by POS
1960 CHI N	5	15	2	0	0	0	0.0	0	2	3	1	0	.133	.133	0	0	C-5
1961	92	267	73	7	1	2	0.7	20	33	15	33	0	.273	.330	6	2	C-90
1962	77	215	65	6	2	2	0.9	19	18	13	30	0	.302	.377	5	1	C-76
1963	100	322	75	7	2	2	0.6	15	14	24	41	0	.233	.286	1	0	C-99
1964	112	353	84	11	3	4	1.1	29	35	33	67	2	.238	.320	3	0	C-110
1965 2 teams	CHI	N	(34G –	.214)		SF	N	(22G –	.188)								
" total	56	132	27	3	0	0	0.0	7	10	18	15	0	.205	.227	4	0	C-56
1967 CHI N	2	6	1	0	1	0	0.0	1	0	0	1	0	.167	.500	0	0	C-2
7 yrs.	444	1310	327	34	9	10	0.8	91	112	106	188	2	.250	.312	15	3	C-438

Reno Bertoia

BERTOIA, RENO PETER
B. Jan. 8, 1935, St. Vito Udine, Italy

BR TR 5'11½" 185 lbs.

	G	AB	H	2B	3B	HR	HR %	R	RBI	BB	SO	SB	BA	SA	AB	H	G by POS
1953 DET A	1	1	0	0	0	0	0.0	0	0	0	1	0	.000	.000	0	0	2B-1
1954	54	37	6	2	0	1	2.7	13	2	5	9	1	.162	.297	2	0	2B-15, 3B-8, SS-3
1955	38	68	14	2	1	1	1.5	13	10	5	11	0	.206	.309	6	0	3B-14, 2B-6, SS-5
1956	22	66	12	2	0	1	1.5	7	5	6	12	0	.182	.258	0	0	2B-18, 3B-2
1957	97	295	81	16	2	4	1.4	28	28	19	43	2	.275	.383	9	0	3B-83, SS-7, 2B-2
1958	86	240	56	6	0	6	2.5	28	27	20	35	5	.233	.333	4	0	3B-68, SS-5, OF-1
1959 WAS A	90	308	73	10	0	8	2.6	33	29	29	48	2	.237	.347	14	3	2B-71, 3B-5, SS-1
1960	121	460	122	17	7	4	0.9	44	45	26	58	3	.265	.359	5	3	3B-112, 2B-21
1961 3 teams	MIN	A	(35G –	.212)		KC	A	(39G –	.242)		DET	A	(24G –	.217)			
" total	98	270	61	5	0	2	0.7	35	25	32	35	3	.226	.267	6	2	3B-74, 2B-13, SS-1
1962 DET A	5	0	0	0	0	0	–	3	0	0	0	0	–	–	0	0	SS-1, 3B-1, 2B-1
10 yrs.	612	1745	425	60	10	27	1.5	204	171	142	252	16	.244	.336	47	8	3B-367, 2B-148, SS-23, OF-1

Bob Bescher

BESCHER, ROBERT HENRY
B. Feb. 25, 1884, London, Ohio   D. Nov. 29, 1942, London, Ohio

BB TL 6'1" 200 lbs.

	G	AB	H	2B	3B	HR	HR %	R	RBI	BB	SO	SB	BA	SA	AB	H	G by POS
1908 CIN N	32	114	31	5	5	0	0.0	16	17	9		10	.272	.404	0	0	OF-32
1909	124	446	107	17	6	1	0.2	73	34	56		54	.240	.312	6	1	OF-117
1910	150	589	147	20	10	4	0.7	95	48	81	75	70	.250	.338	0	0	OF-150
1911	153	599	165	32	10	1	0.2	106	45	102	78	81	.275	.367	0	0	OF-153
1912	145	548	154	29	11	4	0.7	120	38	83	61	67	.281	.396	2	1	OF-143
1913	141	511	132	22	11	1	0.2	86	37	94	68	38	.258	.350	2	0	OF-138
1914 NY N	135	512	138	23	4	6	1.2	82	35	45	48	36	.270	.365	8	3	OF-126
1915 STL N	130	486	128	15	7	4	0.8	71	34	52	53	27	.263	.348	0	0	OF-130
1916	151	561	132	24	8	6	1.1	78	43	60	50	39	.235	.339	0	0	OF-151
1917	42	110	17	1	1	1	0.9	10	8	20	13	3	.155	.209	8	0	OF-32
1918 CLE A	25	60	20	2	1	0	0.0	12	6	17	5	3	.333	.400	4	3	OF-17
11 yrs.	1228	4536	1171	190	74	28	0.6	749	345	619	451	428	.258	.351	30	8	OF-1189

	G	AB	H	2B	3B	HR	HR %	R	RBI	BB	SO	SB	BA	SA	Pinch Hit AB	H	G by POS

Jim Beswick

BESWICK, JAMES WILLIAM
B. Feb. 12, 1958, Wilkensburg, Pa.
BB TR 6'1" 180 lbs.

	G	AB	H	2B	3B	HR	HR %	R	RBI	BB	SO	SB	BA	SA	PH AB	PH H	G by POS
1978 SD N	17	20	1	0	0	0	0.0	2	0	1	7	0	.050	.050	7	1	OF-6

Frank Betcher

BETCHER, FRANK LYLE
Also known as Frank Lyle Bettger.
B. Feb. 15, 1888, Philadelphia, Pa.   D. Nov. 27, 1981, Wynnewood, Pa.
BB TR 5'11" 173 lbs.

1910 STL N	35	89	18	2	0	0	0.0	7	6	7	14	1	.202	.225	8	2	SS-12, 3B-7, 2B-6, OF-2

Bill Bethea

BETHEA, WILLIAM LAMAR (Spot)
B. Jan. 1, 1942, Houston, Tex.
BR TR 6' 175 lbs.

1964 MIN A	10	30	5	1	0	0	0.0	4	2	4	4	0	.167	.200	0	0	2B-7, SS-3

Larry Bettencourt

BETTENCOURT, LAWRENCE JOSEPH
B. Sept. 22, 1905, Newark, Calif.   D. Sept. 15, 1978, New Orleans, La.
BR TR 5'11" 195 lbs.

	G	AB	H	2B	3B	HR	HR %	R	RBI	BB	SO	SB	BA	SA	PH AB	PH H	G by POS
1928 STL A	67	159	45	9	4	4	2.5	30	24	22	19	2	.283	.465	17	2	3B-41, OF-2, C-1
1931	74	206	53	9	2	3	1.5	27	26	31	35	4	.257	.364	14	2	OF-58
1932	27	30	4	1	0	1	3.3	4	3	7	6	1	.133	.267	17	2	OF-4, 3B-2
3 yrs.	168	395	102	19	6	8	2.0	61	53	60	60	7	.258	.397	48	6	OF-64, 3B-43, C-1

Bruno Betzel

BETZEL, CHRISTIAN FREDERICK ALBERT JOHN HENRY DAVID
B. Dec. 6, 1894, Chattanooga, Ohio   D. Feb. 7, 1965, West Hollywood, Fla.
BR TR 5'9" 158 lbs.

	G	AB	H	2B	3B	HR	HR %	R	RBI	BB	SO	SB	BA	SA	PH AB	PH H	G by POS
1914 STL N	7	9	0	0	0	0	0.0	2	0	1	1	0	.000	.000	2	0	2B-4, 3B-1
1915	117	367	92	12	4	0	0.0	42	27	18	48	10	.251	.305	3	1	3B-105, 2B-3, SS-2
1916	142	510	119	15	11	1	0.2	49	37	39	77	22	.233	.312	0	0	2B-113, 3B-33, OF-7
1917	106	328	71	4	3	1	0.3	24	17	20	47	9	.216	.256	3	2	2B-75, OF-23, 3B-4
1918	76	230	51	6	7	0	0.0	18	13	12	16	8	.222	.309	6	2	3B-34, OF-21, 2B-10
5 yrs.	448	1444	333	37	25	2	0.1	135	94	90	189	49	.231	.295	14	5	2B-205, 3B-177, OF-51, SS-2

Kurt Bevacqua

BEVACQUA, KURT ANTHONY
B. Jan. 23, 1947, Miami Beach, Fla.
BR TR 6' 180 lbs.

	G	AB	H	2B	3B	HR	HR %	R	RBI	BB	SO	SB	BA	SA	PH AB	PH H	G by POS
1971 CLE A	55	137	28	3	1	3	2.2	9	13	4	28	0	.204	.307	15	3	2B-36, OF-5, 3B-3, SS-2
1972	19	35	4	0	0	1	2.9	2	1	3	10	0	.114	.200	6	1	OF-11, 3B-1
1973 KC A	99	276	71	8	3	2	0.7	39	40	25	42	2	.257	.330	14	6	3B-40, 2B-16, OF-10, 1B-9
1974 2 teams					PIT N (18G – .114)			KC A (39G – .211)									
" total	57	125	23	1	0	0	0.0	11	3	11	30	1	.184	.192	15	2	3B-21, 1B-14, 2B-7, DH-3, SS-2, OF-1
1975 MIL A	104	258	59	14	0	2	0.8	30	24	26	45	3	.229	.306	5	1	3B-60, 2B-32, SS-5, 1B-3, DH-1
1976	12	7	1	0	0	0	0.0	3	0	0	0	0	.143	.143	2	0	2B-2
1977 TEX A	39	96	32	7	2	5	5.2	13	28	6	13	0	.333	.604	14	5	OF-14, 3B-11, 2B-5, 1B-5
1978	90	248	55	12	0	6	2.4	21	30	18	31	1	.222	.343	16	1	3B-49, DH-16, 2B-13, 1B-1
1979 SD N	114	297	75	12	4	1	0.3	23	34	38	25	2	.253	.330	29	6	3B-64, 2B-16, OF-8, 1B-8
1980 2 teams	SD N (62G – .268)					PIT N (22G – .163)											
" total	84	114	26	7	1	0	0.0	5	16	12	8	1	.228	.307	56	17	3B-22, OF-4, 1B-3, 2B-2
1981 PIT N	29	27	7	1	0	1	3.7	2	4	4	6	0	.259	.407	19	5	2B-4, 3B-2
1982 SD N	64	123	31	9	0	0	0.0	15	24	17	22	2	.252	.327	25	6	1B-30, OF-13, 3B-12
1983	74	156	38	7	0	2	1.3	17	24	18	33	0	.244	.327	34	14	1B-27, OF-12, 3B-12
1984	59	80	16	3	0	1	1.3	7	9	14	19	0	.200	.275	30	7	1B-20, 3B-10, OF-3
14 yrs.	899	1979	466	84	11	24	1.2	197	250	196	312	12	.235	.325	281	77	3B-296, 2B-133, 1B-120, OF-71, DH-20, SS-9

LEAGUE CHAMPIONSHIP SERIES

1984 SD N	2	2	0	0	0	0	0.0	0	0	0	0	0	.000	.000	2	0	

WORLD SERIES

1984 SD N	5	17	7	2	0	2	11.8	4	4	1	2	0	.412	.882	0	0	DH-5

Hal Bevan

BEVAN, HAROLD JOSEPH
B. Nov. 15, 1930, New Orleans, La.   D. Oct. 5, 1968, New Orleans, La.
BR TR 6'2" 198 lbs.

	G	AB	H	2B	3B	HR	HR %	R	RBI	BB	SO	SB	BA	SA	PH AB	PH H	G by POS
1952 2 teams	BOS A (1G – .000)					PHI A (8G – .353)											
" total	9	18	6	0	0	0	0.0	1	4	0	1	2	.333	.333	0	0	3B-7
1955 KC A	3	3	0	0	0	0	0.0	0	0	0	0	0	.000	.000	2	0	3B-1
1961 CIN N	3	3	1	0	0	1	33.3	1	1	0	2	0	.333	1.333	3	1	
3 yrs.	15	24	7	0	0	1	4.2	2	5	0	3	2	.292	.417	5	1	3B-8

Monte Beville

BEVILLE, HENRY MONTE
B. Feb. 24, 1875, Dublin, Ind.   D. Jan. 24, 1955, Grand Rapids, Mich.
BL TR 5'11" 180 lbs.

	G	AB	H	2B	3B	HR	HR %	R	RBI	BB	SO	SB	BA	SA	PH AB	PH H	G by POS
1903 NY A	82	258	50	14	1	0	0.0	23	29	16		4	.194	.256	4	1	C-75, 1B-3
1904 2 teams	NY A (9G – .273)					DET A (54G – .207)											
" total	63	196	42	7	1	0	0.0	16	15	10		2	.214	.260	4	0	C-33, 1B-28
2 yrs.	145	454	92	21	2	0	0.0	39	44	26		6	.203	.258	8	1	C-108, 1B-31

Buddy Biancalana

BIANCALANA, ROLAND AMERICO
B. Feb. 2, 1960, Larkspur, Calif.
BB TR 5'11" 155 lbs.

	G	AB	H	2B	3B	HR	HR %	R	RBI	BB	SO	SB	BA	SA	PH AB	PH H	G by POS
1982 KC A	3	2	1	0	0	0	0.0	0	0	1	0	0	.500	1.500	0	0	SS-3
1983	6	15	3	0	0	0	0.0	2	0	0	7	1	.200	.200	0	0	SS-6
1984	66	134	26	6	1	2	1.5	18	9	6	44	1	.194	.299	2	1	SS-33, 2B-29, DH-1
3 yrs.	75	151	30	6	2	2	1.3	20	9	7	51	2	.199	.305	2	1	SS-42, 2B-29, DH-1

LEAGUE CHAMPIONSHIP SERIES

1984 KC A	2	1	0	0	0	0	0.0	0	0	0	1	0	.000	.000	0	0	SS-2

Tommy Bianco

BIANCO, THOMAS ANTHONY
B. Dec. 16, 1952, Elmont, N. Y.
BB TR 5'11" 190 lbs.

1975 MIL A	18	34	6	1	0	0	0.0	6	3	7	0	.176	.206	5	0	3B-7, 1B-5, DH-2

	G	AB	H	2B	3B	HR	HR %	R	RBI	BB	SO	SB	BA	SA	Pinch Hit AB	Pinch Hit H	G by POS

Hank Biasetti

BIASETTI, HENRY ARCADO
B. Jan. 14, 1922, Beano, Italy
BL TL 5'11" 175 lbs.

	G	AB	H	2B	3B	HR	HR%	R	RBI	BB	SO	SB	BA	SA	AB	H	G by POS
1949 PHI A	21	24	2	2	0	0	0.0	6	2	8	5	0	.083	.167	9	0	1B-8

Oscar Bielaski

BIELASKI, OSCAR
B. Mar. 21, 1847, Washington, D. C.   D. Nov. 8, 1911, Washington, D. C.
BR TR

	G	AB	H	2B	3B	HR	HR%	R	RBI	BB	SO	SB	BA	SA	AB	H	G by POS
1876 CHI N	32	139	29	3	0	0	0.0	24	10	2	3		.209	.230	0	0	OF-32

Lou Bierbauer

BIERBAUER, LOUIS W.
Also appeared in box score as Bauer
B. Sept. 28, 1865, Erie, Pa.   D. Jan. 31, 1926, Erie, Pa.
BR TR 5'8" 140 lbs.

	G	AB	H	2B	3B	HR	HR%	R	RBI	BB	SO	SB	BA	SA	AB	H	G by POS
1886 PHI AA	137	522	118	17	5	2	0.4	56		21			.226	.289	0	0	2B-133, C-4, SS-2, P-2
1887	126	530	144	19	7	1	0.2	74		13		40	.272	.340	0	0	2B-126, P-1
1888	134	535	143	20	9	0	0.0	83	80	25		34	.267	.338	0	0	2B-121, 3B-13, P-1
1889	130	549	167	27	7	7	1.3	80	105	29	30	17	.304	.417	0	0	2B-130, C-1
1890 BKN P	133	589	180	31	11	7	1.2	128	99	40	15	16	.306	.431	0	0	2B-133
1891 PIT N	121	500	103	13	6	1	0.2	60	47	28	19	12	.206	.262	0	0	2B-121
1892	152	649	153	20	9	8	1.2	81	65	25	29	11	.236	.331	0	0	2B-152
1893	128	528	150	19	11	4	0.8	84	94	36	12	11	.284	.384	0	0	2B-128
1894	130	525	159	19	13	3	0.6	86	107	26	9	19	.303	.406	0	0	2B-130
1895	117	466	120	13	11	0	0.0	53	69	19	8	18	.258	.333	0	0	2B-117
1896	59	258	74	10	6	0	0.0	33	39	5	7	7	.287	.372	0	0	2B-59
1897 STL N	12	46	10	0	0	0	0.0	1	1	0		2	.217	.217	0	0	2B-12
1898	4	9	0	0	0	0	0.0	0	0	1		0	.000	.000	0	0	2B-2, SS-1, 3B-1
13 yrs.	1383	5706	1521	208	95	33	0.6	819	705	268	129	187	.267	.354	0	0	2B-1364, 3B-14, C-5, P-4, SS-3

Carson Bigbee

BIGBEE, CARSON LEE (Skeeter)
Brother of Lyle Bigbee.
B. Mar. 31, 1895, Waterloo, Ore.   D. Oct. 17, 1964, Portland, Ore.
BL TR 5'9" 157 lbs.

	G	AB	H	2B	3B	HR	HR%	R	RBI	BB	SO	SB	BA	SA	AB	H	G by POS
1916 PIT N	43	164	41	3	6	0	0.0	17	3	7	14	8	.250	.341	0	0	2B-23, OF-19, 3B-1
1917	133	469	112	11	6	0	0.0	46	21	37	16	19	.239	.288	5	2	OF-107, 2B-16, SS-2
1918	92	310	79	11	3	1	0.3	47	19	42	10	19	.255	.319	4	2	OF-92
1919	125	478	132	11	4	2	0.4	61	27	37	26	31	.276	.328	1	0	OF-124
1920	137	550	154	19	15	4	0.7	78	32	45	28	31	.280	.391	0	0	OF-133
1921	147	632	204	23	17	3	0.5	100	42	41	19	21	.323	.427	1	0	OF-146
1922	150	614	215	29	15	5	0.8	113	99	56	13	24	.350	.471	0	0	OF-150
1923	123	499	149	18	7	0	0.0	79	54	43	15	10	.299	.363	1	1	OF-122
1924	89	282	74	4	1	0	0.0	42	15	26	12	15	.262	.284	8	4	OF-75
1925	66	126	30	7	0	0	0.0	31	8	7	8	2	.238	.294	13	3	OF-42
1926	42	68	15	3	1	2	2.9	15	4	3	0	2	.221	.382	10	3	OF-21
11 yrs.	1147	4192	1205	139	75	17	0.4	629	324	344	161	182	.287	.369	43	15	OF-1031, 2B-39, SS-2, 3B-1

WORLD SERIES

	G	AB	H	2B	3B	HR	HR%	R	RBI	BB	SO	SB	BA	SA	AB	H	G by POS
1925 PIT N	4	3	1	1	0	0	0.0	1	1	0	0	1	.333	.667	3	1	OF-1

Lyle Bigbee

BIGBEE, LYLE RANDOLPH (Al)
Brother of Carson Bigbee.
B. Aug. 22, 1893, Sweet Home, Ore.   D. Aug. 5, 1942, Portland, Ore.
BL TR 6' 180 lbs.

	G	AB	H	2B	3B	HR	HR%	R	RBI	BB	SO	SB	BA	SA	AB	H	G by POS
1920 PHI A	37	70	13	1	0	1	1.4	4	8	8	10	1	.186	.243	10	3	OF-13, P-12
1921 PIT N	5	2	0	0	0	0	0.0	0	0	0	1	0	.000	.000	0	0	P-5
2 yrs.	42	72	13	1	0	1	1.4	4	8	8	11	1	.181	.236	10	3	P-17, OF-13

Elliott Bigelow

BIGELOW, ELLIOTT ALLARDICE (Gilly)
B. Oct. 13, 1898, Tarpon Springs, Fla.   D. Aug. 10, 1933, Tampa, Fla.
BL TL 5'11" 185 lbs.

	G	AB	H	2B	3B	HR	HR%	R	RBI	BB	SO	SB	BA	SA	AB	H	G by POS
1929 BOS A	100	211	60	16	0	1	0.5	23	26	23	18	1	.284	.374	35	6	OF-58

George Bignal

BIGNAL, GEORGE WILLIAM
B. July 18, 1858, Taunton, Mass.   D. Jan. 16, 1925, Providence, R. I.

	G	AB	H	2B	3B	HR	HR%	R	RBI	BB	SO	SB	BA	SA	AB	H	G by POS
1884 MIL U	4	9	2	0	0	0	0.0	4		1			.222	.222	0	0	C-4

Larry Biittner

BIITTNER, LARRY DAVID
B. July 27, 1946, Pocahontas, Iowa
BL TL 6'2" 205 lbs.

	G	AB	H	2B	3B	HR	HR%	R	RBI	BB	SO	SB	BA	SA	AB	H	G by POS
1970 WAS A	2	2	0	0	0	0	0.0	0	0	0	0	0	.000	.000	2	0	
1971	66	171	44	4	1	0	0.0	12	16	16	20	1	.257	.292	19	7	OF-41, 1B-3
1972 TEX A	137	382	99	18	1	3	0.8	34	31	29	37	1	.259	.335	17	4	OF-65, 1B-65
1973	83	258	65	8	2	1	0.4	19	12	20	21	1	.252	.310	7	1	OF-57, 1B-20, DH-3
1974 MON N	18	26	7	1	0	0	0.0	2	3	0	2	0	.269	.308	15	4	1B-4
1975	121	346	109	13	5	3	0.9	34	28	34	33	2	.315	.408	27	8	OF-93
1976 2 teams		MON N	(11G –	.188)		CHI N	(78G –	.245)									
" total	89	224	53	14	1	0	0.0	23	18	10	9	0	.237	.308	32	6	1B-33, OF-31
1977 CHI N	138	493	147	28	1	12	2.4	74	62	35	36	2	.298	.432	15	5	1B-80, OF-52, P-1
1978	120	343	88	15	1	4	1.2	32	50	23	37	0	.257	.341	33	11	1B-62, OF-29
1979	111	272	79	13	3	3	1.1	35	50	21	23	1	.290	.393	42	13	OF-44, 1B-32
1980	127	273	68	12	2	1	0.4	21	34	18	33	1	.249	.319	52	11	1B-41, OF-38
1981 CIN N	42	61	13	4	0	0	0.0	1	8	4	4	0	.213	.279	29	7	1B-8, OF-3
1982	97	184	57	9	2	2	1.1	18	24	17	16	1	.310	.413	49	10	OF-31, 1B-15
1983 TEX A	66	116	32	5	1	0	0.0	5	18	9	16	0	.276	.336	31	8	1B-22, DH-9, OF-2
14 yrs.	1217	3151	861	144	20	29	0.9	310	354	236	287	10	.273	.359	370	95	OF-486, 1B-385, DH-12, P-1
																10th	P-1

Dann Bilardello

BILARDELLO, DANN JAMES
B. May 26, 1959, Santa Cruz, Calif.
BR TR 6' 185 lbs.

	G	AB	H	2B	3B	HR	HR%	R	RBI	BB	SO	SB	BA	SA	AB	H	G by POS
1983 CIN N	109	298	71	18	0	9	3.0	27	38	15	49	2	.238	.389	5	0	C-105
1984	68	182	38	7	0	2	1.1	16	10	19	34	0	.209	.280	5	2	C-68
2 yrs.	177	480	109	25	0	11	2.3	43	48	34	83	2	.227	.348	10	2	C-173

	G	AB	H	2B	3B	HR	HR %	R	RBI	BB	SO	SB	BA	SA	Pinch Hit AB	Pinch Hit H	G by POS

Steve Bilko

BILKO, STEVEN THOMAS   BR TR 6'1"   230 lbs.
B. Nov. 13, 1928, Nanticoke, Pa.   D. Mar. 7, 1978, Wilkes Barre, Pa.

	G	AB	H	2B	3B	HR	HR %	R	RBI	BB	SO	SB	BA	SA	PH AB	PH H	G by POS
1949 STL N	6	17	5	2	0	0	0.0	3	2	5	6	0	.294	.412	1	0	1B-5
1950	10	33	6	1	0	0	0.0	1	2	4	10	0	.182	.212	1	1	1B-9
1951	21	72	16	4	0	2	2.8	5	12	9	10	0	.222	.361	2	1	1B-19
1952	20	72	19	6	1	1	1.4	7	6	4	15	0	.264	.417	0	0	1B-20
1953	154	570	143	23	3	21	3.7	72	84	70	125	0	.251	.412	0	0	1B-154
1954 2 teams	STL	N (8G –	.143)		CHI	N (47G –	.239)										
" total	55	106	24	8	1	4	3.8	12	13	14	25	0	.226	.434	24	6	1B-28
1958 2 teams	CIN	N (31G –	.264)		LA	N (47G –	.208)										
" total	78	188	44	5	4	11	5.9	25	35	18	57	0	.234	.479	27	5	1B-46
1960 DET A	78	222	46	11	2	9	4.1	20	25	27	31	0	.207	.396	17	1	1B-62
1961 LA A	114	294	82	16	1	20	6.8	49	59	58	81	1	.279	.544	24	8	1B-86, OF-3
1962	64	164	47	9	1	8	4.9	26	38	25	35	1	.287	.500	14	3	1B-50
10 yrs.	600	1738	432	85	13	76	4.4	220	276	234	395	2	.249	.444	110	25	1B-479, OF-3

Dick Billings

BILLINGS, RICHARD ARLIN   BR TR 6'1"   195 lbs.
B. Dec. 4, 1942, Detroit, Mich.

	G	AB	H	2B	3B	HR	HR %	R	RBI	BB	SO	SB	BA	SA	PH AB	PH H	G by POS
1968 WAS A	12	33	6	1	0	1	3.0	3	3	5	13	0	.182	.303	3	1	OF-8, 3B-4
1969	27	37	5	0	0	0	0.0	3	0	6	8	0	.135	.135	15	1	OF-6, 3B-1
1970	11	24	6	2	0	1	4.2	3	1	2	3	0	.250	.458	3	0	C-8
1971	116	349	86	14	0	6	1.7	32	48	21	54	2	.246	.338	24	8	C-62, OF-32, 3B-2
1972 TEX A	133	469	119	15	1	5	1.1	41	58	29	77	1	.254	.322	10	1	C-92, OF-41, 3B-5, 1B-1
1973	81	280	50	11	0	3	1.1	17	32	20	43	1	.179	.250	5	1	C-72, OF-4, 1B-3, DH-2
1974 2 teams	TEX	A (16G –	.226)		STL	N (1G –	.200)										
" total	17	36	8	1	0	0	0.0	2	0	4	7	2	.222	.250	1	0	C-14, DH-1, OF-1
1975 STL N	3	3	0	0	0	0	0.0	0	0	0	2	0	.000	.000	3	0	
8 yrs.	400	1231	280	44	1	16	1.3	101	142	87	207	6	.227	.304	64	12	C-248, OF-92, 3B-12, 1B-4, DH-3

Josh Billings

BILLINGS, JOHN AUGUSTUS   BR TR 5'11"   165 lbs.
B. Nov. 30, 1891, Grantville, Kans.   D. Dec. 30, 1981, Santa Monica, Calif.

	G	AB	H	2B	3B	HR	HR %	R	RBI	BB	SO	SB	BA	SA	PH AB	PH H	G by POS
1913 CLE A	1	3	0	0	0	0	0.0	0	0	0	3	0	.000	.000	0	0	C-1
1914	8	8	2	1	0	0	0.0	2	0	1	1	1	.250	.375	2	0	C-3
1915	8	21	4	1	0	0	0.0	2	0	0	6	1	.190	.238	0	0	C-7, OF-1
1916	22	31	5	0	0	0	0.0	2	1	2	11	0	.161	.161	9	1	C-12
1917	66	129	23	3	2	0	0.0	8	9	8	21	2	.178	.233	17	4	C-48
1918	2	3	1	0	0	0	0.0	0	0	0	0	0	.333	.333	1	0	C-1
1919 STL A	38	76	15	1	1	0	0.0	9	3	1	12	0	.197	.237	7	1	C-27, 1B-1
1920	66	155	43	5	2	0	0.0	19	11	11	10	1	.277	.335	22	9	C-40
1921	20	46	10	0	0	0	0.0	2	4	0	7	0	.217	.217	7	0	C-12
1922	5	7	3	1	0	0	0.0	0	1	0	0	0	.429	.571	1	0	C-3
1923	4	9	0	0	0	0	0.0	0	0	0	2	0	.000	.000	0	0	C-4
11 yrs.	240	488	106	12	5	0	0.0	44	29	23	73	5	.217	.262	66	15	C-158, OF-1, 1B-1

George Binks

BINKS, GEORGE EUGENE (Bingo)   BL TL 6'   175 lbs.
Born George Eugene Binkowski.
B. July 11, 1914, Chicago, Ill.

	G	AB	H	2B	3B	HR	HR %	R	RBI	BB	SO	SB	BA	SA	PH AB	PH H	G by POS
1944 WAS A	5	12	3	0	0	0	0.0	0	0	0	1	0	.250	.250	1	0	OF-3
1945	145	550	153	32	6	6	1.1	62	81	34	52	11	.278	.391	1	1	OF-128, 1B-20
1946	65	134	26	3	0	0	0.0	13	12	6	16	1	.194	.216	35	7	OF-28
1947 PHI A	104	333	86	19	4	2	0.6	33	34	23	36	8	.258	.357	15	4	OF-75, 1B-13
1948 2 teams	PHI	A (17G –	.098)		STL	A (15G –	.217)										
" total	32	64	9	1	0	0	0.0	4	3	4	3	1	.141	.156	9	1	OF-19, 1B-4
5 yrs.	351	1093	277	55	10	8	0.7	112	130	67	108	21	.253	.344	61	13	OF-253, 1B-37

Steve Biras

BIRAS, STEPHEN ALEXANDER   BR TR 5'11"   185 lbs.
B. Feb. 26, 1922, East St. Louis, Ill.   D. Apr. 21, 1965, St. Louis, Mo.

	G	AB	H	2B	3B	HR	HR %	R	RBI	BB	SO	SB	BA	SA	PH AB	PH H	G by POS
1944 CLE A	2	2	2	0	0	0	0.0	0	2	0	0	0	1.000	1.000	1	1	2B-1

Jud Birchall

BIRCHALL, A. JUDSON
B. 1858, Philadelphia, Pa.   D. Dec. 22, 1887, Philadelphia, Pa.

	G	AB	H	2B	3B	HR	HR %	R	RBI	BB	SO	SB	BA	SA	PH AB	PH H	G by POS
1882 PHI AA	75	338	89	12	1	0	0.0	65		8				.263	.305	0	0	OF-74, 2B-1
1883	96	449	108	10	1	1	0.2	95		19				.241	.274	0	0	OF-96
1884	54	221	57	2	2	0	0.0	36		4				.258	.285	0	0	OF-52, 3B-2
3 yrs.	225	1008	254	24	4	1	0.1	196		31				.252	.287	0	0	OF-222, 3B-2, 2B-1

Frank Bird

BIRD, FRANK ZEPHERIN (Dodo)   BR TR 5'10"   195 lbs.
B. Mar. 10, 1869, Spencer, Mass.   D. May 20, 1958, Worcester, Mass.

	G	AB	H	2B	3B	HR	HR %	R	RBI	BB	SO	SB	BA	SA	PH AB	PH H	G by POS
1892 STL N	17	50	10	3	1	1	2.0	9	1	6	11	2	.200	.360	0	0	C-17

Joe Birmingham

BIRMINGHAM, JOSEPH LEE (Dode)   BR TR 5'10"   185 lbs.
B. Aug. 6, 1884, Elmira, N. Y.   D. Apr. 24, 1946, Tampico, Mexico
Manager 1912-15.

	G	AB	H	2B	3B	HR	HR %	R	RBI	BB	SO	SB	BA	SA	PH AB	PH H	G by POS
1906 CLE A	10	37	11	3	1	0	0.0	4	6	1		2	.297	.432	0	0	OF-10
1907	138	476	112	10	9	1	0.2	55	33	16		23	.235	.300	1	0	OF-134, SS-3
1908	122	413	88	10	1	2	0.5	32	38	19		15	.213	.257	0	0	OF-121, SS-1
1909	100	343	99	10	5	1	0.3	29	38	19		12	.289	.356	2	0	OF-98
1910	104	364	84	11	2	0	0.0	41	35	23		18	.231	.272	0	0	OF-103, 3B-1
1911	125	447	136	18	5	2	0.4	55	51	15		16	.304	.380	6	1	OF-101, 3B-16
1912	107	369	94	19	3	0	0.0	49	45	26		15	.255	.322	2	0	OF-96, 1B-9
1913	47	131	37	9	1	0	0.0	16	15	8	22	7	.282	.366	10	0	OF-37
1914	19	47	6	0	0	0	0.0	2	4	2	5	0	.128	.128	4	0	OF-14
9 yrs.	772	2627	667	90	27	6	0.2	283	265	129	27	108	.254	.316	25	2	OF-714, 3B-17, 1B-9, SS-4

	G	AB	H	2B	3B	HR	HR %	R	RBI	BB	SO	SB	BA	SA	Pinch Hit AB	Pinch Hit H	G by POS

John Bischoff

BISCHOFF, JOHN GEORGE (Smiley)   BR TR 5'7"   165 lbs.
B. Oct. 28, 1894, Granite City, Ill.   D. Dec. 28, 1981, Granite City, Ill.

	G	AB	H	2B	3B	HR	HR %	R	RBI	BB	SO	SB	BA	SA	AB	H	G by POS
1925 **2 teams**		CHI	**A** (7G – .091)			BOS	**A** (41G – .278)										
" total	48	144	38	9	1	1	0.7	14	16	7	16	1	.264	.361	3	0	C-44
1926 **BOS A**	59	127	33	11	2	0	0.0	6	19	15	16	1	.260	.378	12	2	C-46
2 yrs.	107	271	71	20	3	1	0.4	20	35	22	32	2	.262	.369	15	2	C-90

Frank Bishop

BISHOP, FRANK H
B. Sept. 21, 1860, Belvidere, Ill.   D. June 18, 1929, Chicago, Ill.

	G	AB	H	2B	3B	HR	HR %	R	RBI	BB	SO	SB	BA	SA	AB	H	G by POS
1884 **C-P U**	4	16	3	1	0	0	0.0	1		0			.188	.250	0	0	3B-3, SS-1

Max Bishop

BISHOP, MAX FREDERICK (Tilly, Camera Eye)   BL TR 5'8½"   165 lbs.
B. Sept. 5, 1899, Waynesboro, Pa.   D. Feb. 24, 1962, Waynesboro, Pa.

	G	AB	H	2B	3B	HR	HR %	R	RBI	BB	SO	SB	BA	SA	AB	H	G by POS
1924 **PHI A**	91	294	75	13	2	2	0.7	52	21	54	30	4	.255	.333	5	1	2B-80
1925	105	368	103	18	4	4	1.1	66	27	87	37	5	.280	.383	1	0	2B-104
1926	122	400	106	20	2	0	0.0	77	33	116	41	4	.265	.325	2	0	2B-119
1927	117	372	103	15	1	0	0.0	80	22	105	28	8	.277	.323	7	1	2B-106
1928	126	472	149	27	5	6	1.3	104	50	97	36	9	.316	.432	0	0	2B-125
1929	129	475	110	19	6	3	0.6	102	36	**128**	44	1	.232	.316	0	0	2B-129
1930	130	441	111	27	6	10	2.3	117	38	128	60	3	.252	.408	3	2	2B-127
1931	130	497	146	30	4	5	1.0	115	37	112	51	3	.294	.400	0	0	2B-130
1932	114	409	104	24	2	5	1.2	89	37	110	43	2	.254	.359	6	0	2B-106
1933	117	391	115	27	1	4	1.0	80	42	106	46	1	.294	.399	2	0	2B-113
1934 **BOS A**	97	253	66	13	1	1	0.4	65	22	82	22	3	.261	.332	20	2	2B-57, 1B-15
1935	60	122	28	3	1	1	0.8	19	14	28	14	0	.230	.295	8	1	2B-34, 1B-11, SS-2
12 yrs.	1338	4494	1216	236	35	41	0.9	966	379	1153	452	43	.271	.366	54	7	2B-1230, 1B-26, SS-2

WORLD SERIES

	G	AB	H	2B	3B	HR	HR %	R	RBI	BB	SO	SB	BA	SA	AB	H	G by POS
1929 **PHI A**	5	21	4	0	0	0	0.0	2	1	2	3	0	.190	.190	0	0	2B-5
1930	6	18	4	0	0	0	0.0	5	0	7	3	0	.222	.222	0	0	2B-6
1931	7	27	4	0	0	0	0.0	4	0	3	5	0	.148	.148	0	0	2B-7
3 yrs.	18	66	12	0	0	0	0.0	11	1	12	11	0	.182	.182	0	0	2B-18

Mike Bishop

BISHOP, MICHAEL D.   BR TR 6'2"   185 lbs.
B. Nov. 5, 1958, Santa Maria, Calif.

	G	AB	H	2B	3B	HR	HR %	R	RBI	BB	SO	SB	BA	SA	AB	H	G by POS
1983 **NY N**	3	8	1	1	0	0	0.0	2	0	3	4	0	.125	.250	0	0	C-3

Rivington Bisland

BISLAND, RIVINGTON MARTIN   BR TR 5'9"   155 lbs.
B. Feb. 17, 1890, New York, N. Y.   D. Jan. 11, 1973, Salzburg, Austria

	G	AB	H	2B	3B	HR	HR %	R	RBI	BB	SO	SB	BA	SA	AB	H	G by POS
1912 **PIT N**	1	1	0	0	0	0	0.0	0	0	0	0	0	.000	.000	1	0	
1913 **STL A**	12	44	6	0	0	0	0.0	3	3	2	5	0	.136	.136	0	0	SS-12
1914 **CLE A**	18	57	6	1	0	0	0.0	9	2	6	2	2	.105	.123	1	0	SS-15, 3B-1
3 yrs.	31	102	12	1	0	0	0.0	12	5	8	7	2	.118	.127	2	0	SS-27, 3B-1

Del Bissonette

BISSONETTE, ADELPHIA LOUIS   BL TL 5'11"   180 lbs.
B. Sept. 6, 1899, Winthrop, Me.   D. June 9, 1972, Augusta, Me.
Manager 1945.

	G	AB	H	2B	3B	HR	HR %	R	RBI	BB	SO	SB	BA	SA	AB	H	G by POS
1928 **BKN N**	155	587	188	30	13	25	4.3	90	106	70	75	5	.320	.543	0	0	1B-155
1929	116	431	121	28	10	12	2.8	68	75	46	58	2	.281	.476	3	0	1B-113
1930	146	572	192	33	13	16	2.8	102	113	56	66	4	.336	.523	0	0	1B-146
1931	152	587	170	19	14	12	2.0	90	87	59	53	4	.290	.431	0	0	1B-152
1933	35	114	28	7	0	0	0.0	9	10	2	17	2	.246	.307	3	1	1B-32
5 yrs.	604	2291	699	117	50	65	2.8	359	391	233	269	17	.305	.485	6	1	1B-598

Red Bittmann

BITTMANN, HENRY
B. July 22, 1862, Cincinnati, Ohio   D. Nov. 8, 1929, Cincinnati, Ohio

	G	AB	H	2B	3B	HR	HR %	R	RBI	BB	SO	SB	BA	SA	AB	H	G by POS
1889 **KC AA**	4	14	4	0	0	0	0.0	2	2	1	1	1	.286	.286	0	0	2B-4

George Bjorkman

BJORKMAN, GEORGE ANTON   BR TR 6'2"   190 lbs.
B. Aug. 26, 1956, Ontario, Calif.

	G	AB	H	2B	3B	HR	HR %	R	RBI	BB	SO	SB	BA	SA	AB	H	G by POS
1983 **HOU N**	29	75	17	4	0	2	2.7	8	14	16	29	0	.227	.360	0	0	C-29

Bill Black

BLACK, JOHN WILLIAM (Jigger)   BL TR 5'11"   168 lbs.
B. Aug. 12, 1899, Philadelphia, Pa.   D. Jan. 14, 1968, Philadelphia, Pa.

	G	AB	H	2B	3B	HR	HR %	R	RBI	BB	SO	SB	BA	SA	AB	H	G by POS
1924 **CHI A**	6	5	1	0	0	0	0.0	0	0	0	0	0	.200	.200	0	0	2B-1

Bob Black

BLACK, ROBERT BENJAMIM
B. Dec. 10, 1864, Cincinnati, Ohio   D. Mar. 21, 1933, Sioux City, Iowa

	G	AB	H	2B	3B	HR	HR %	R	RBI	BB	SO	SB	BA	SA	AB	H	G by POS
1884 **KC U**	38	146	36	14	2	1	0.7	25		10			.247	.390	0	0	OF-19, P-16, 2B-6, SS-1

Jack Black

BLACK, JOHN FALCONER   BR TR 6'2"   175 lbs.
Born John Falconer Haddow.
B. Feb. 23, 1890, Covington, Ky.   D. Mar. 20, 1962, Rutherford, N. J.

	G	AB	H	2B	3B	HR	HR %	R	RBI	BB	SO	SB	BA	SA	AB	H	G by POS
1911 **STL A**	54	186	28	4	0	0	0.0	13	7	10		4	.151	.172	0	0	1B-54

Ethan Blackaby

BLACKABY, ETHAN ALLAN   BL TL 5'11"   190 lbs.
B. July 24, 1940, Cincinnati, Ohio

	G	AB	H	2B	3B	HR	HR %	R	RBI	BB	SO	SB	BA	SA	AB	H	G by POS
1962 **MIL N**	6	13	2	1	0	0	0.0	0	1	1	8	0	.154	.231	3	1	OF-3
1964	9	12	1	0	0	0	0.0	0	1	1	2	0	.083	.083	4	0	OF-5
2 yrs.	15	25	3	1	0	0	0.0	0	2	2	10	0	.120	.160	7	1	OF-8

Earl Blackburn

BLACKBURN, EARL STUART   BR TR 5'11"   180 lbs.
B. Nov. 1, 1892, Leesville, Ohio   D. Aug. 3, 1966, Mansfield, Ohio

	G	AB	H	2B	3B	HR	HR %	R	RBI	BB	SO	SB	BA	SA	AB	H	G by POS
1912 **2 teams**		PIT	**N** (1G – .000)			CIN	**N** (1G – .000)										
" total	2	0	0	0	0	0	–	0	0	1	0	0	–	–	0	0	C-2
1913 **CIN N**	17	27	7	0	0	0	0.0	1	3	2	5	2	.259	.259	5	1	C-12

	G	AB	H	2B	3B	HR	HR %	R	RBI	BB	SO	SB	BA	SA	Pinch Hit AB	Pinch Hit H	G by POS

Earl Blackburn continued

	G	AB	H	2B	3B	HR	HR%	R	RBI	BB	SO	SB	BA	SA	AB	H	G by POS
1915 BOS N	3	6	1	0	0	0	0.0	0	0	2	1	0	.167	.167	0	0	C-3
1916	47	110	30	4	4	0	0.0	12	7	9	21	2	.273	.382	3	1	C-44
1917 CHI N	2	2	0	0	0	0	0.0	0	0	0	0	0	.000	.000	2	0	
5 yrs.	71	145	38	4	4	0	0.0	13	10	14	27	4	.262	.345	10	2	C-61

Lena Blackburne

BLACKBURNE, RUSSELL AUBREY (Slats)   BR TR 5'11" 160 lbs.
B. Oct. 23, 1886, Clifton Heights, Pa.   D. Feb. 29, 1968, Riverside, N. J.
Manager 1928-29.

	G	AB	H	2B	3B	HR	HR%	R	RBI	BB	SO	SB	BA	SA	AB	H	G by POS
1910 CHI A	75	242	42	3	1	0	0.0	16	10	19		4	.174	.194	0	0	SS-74
1912	3	0	0	0	0	0	0.0	0	0	1		1	.000	.000	0	0	SS-2, 3B-1
1914	144	474	105	10	5	1	0.2	52	35	66	58	25	.222	.270	1	0	2B-143
1915	96	283	61	5	1	0	0.0	33	25	35	34	13	.216	.240	2	1	3B-81, SS-9
1918 CIN N	125	435	99	8	10	1	0.2	35	45	25	30	6	.228	.299	0	0	SS-125
1919 2 teams					BOS	N (31G –	.263)		PHI	N (72G –	.199)						
" total	103	371	79	13	6	2	0.5	37	23	16	29	5	.213	.296	4	1	3B-96, SS-2, 2B-2, 1B-2
1927 CHI A	1	1	1	0	0	0	0.0	0	1	0	0	0	1.000	1.000	1	1	
1929	1	0	0	0	0	0	–	0	0	0	0	0	–	–	0	0	P-1
8 yrs.	548	1807	387	39	23	4	0.2	174	139	162	151	54	.214	.268	8	3	SS-212, 3B-180, 2B-145, 1B-2, P-1

George Blackerby

BLACKERBY, GEORGE FRANKLIN   BR TR 6'1" 176 lbs.
B. Nov. 10, 1903, Gluther, Okla.

	G	AB	H	2B	3B	HR	HR%	R	RBI	BB	SO	SB	BA	SA	AB	H	G by POS
1928 CHI A	30	83	21	0	0	0	0.0	8	12	4	10	2	.253	.253	10	4	OF-20

Fred Blackwell

BLACKWELL, FREDERICK WILLIAM   BL TR 5'10½" 160 lbs.
B. Sept. 7, 1895, Bowling Green, Ky.   D. Dec. 8, 1975, Morgantown, Ky.

	G	AB	H	2B	3B	HR	HR%	R	RBI	BB	SO	SB	BA	SA	AB	H	G by POS
1917 PIT N	3	10	2	0	0	0	0.0	1	2	0	3	0	.200	.200	0	0	C-3
1918	8	13	2	0	0	0	0.0	1	4	3	4	0	.154	.154	0	0	C-8
1919	24	65	14	3	0	0	0.0	3	4	3	9	0	.215	.262	2	1	C-22
3 yrs.	35	88	18	3	0	0	0.0	5	10	6	16	0	.205	.239	2	1	C-33

Tim Blackwell

BLACKWELL, TIMOTHY P.   BB TR 5'11" 170 lbs.
B. Aug. 19, 1952, San Diego, Calif.

	G	AB	H	2B	3B	HR	HR%	R	RBI	BB	SO	SB	BA	SA	AB	H	G by POS
1974 BOS A	44	122	30	1	1	0	0.0	9	8	10	21	1	.246	.270	0	0	C-44
1975	59	132	26	3	2	0	0.0	15	6	19	13	0	.197	.250	0	0	C-57, DH-2
1976 PHI N	4	8	2	0	0	0	0.0	0	1	0	1	0	.250	.250	2	1	C-4
1977 2 teams					PHI	N (1G –	.000)		MON	N (16G –	.091)						
" total	17	22	2	1	0	0	0.0	4	0	2	7	0	.091	.136	2	0	C-15
1978 CHI N	49	103	23	3	0	0	0.0	8	7	23	17	0	.223	.252	0	0	C-49
1979	63	122	20	3	1	0	0.0	8	12	32	25	0	.164	.205	1	0	C-63
1980	103	320	87	16	4	5	1.6	24	30	41	62	0	.272	.394	0	0	C-103
1981	58	158	37	10	2	1	0.6	21	11	23	23	2	.234	.342	2	0	C-56
1982 MON N	23	42	8	2	1	0	0.0	2	3	3	11	0	.190	.286	6	1	C-18
1983	6	15	3	0	0	0	0.0	0	2	1	3	0	.200	.267	1	0	C-5
10 yrs.	426	1044	238	40	11	6	0.6	91	80	154	183	3	.228	.305	14	2	C-414, DH-2

Ray Blades

BLADES, FRANCIS RAYMOND   BR TR 5'7½" 163 lbs.
B. Aug. 6, 1896, Mt. Vernon, Ill.   D. May 18, 1979, Lincoln, Ill.
Manager 1939-40.

	G	AB	H	2B	3B	HR	HR%	R	RBI	BB	SO	SB	BA	SA	AB	H	G by POS
1922 STL N	37	130	39	2	4	3	2.3	27	21	25	21	3	.300	.446	0	0	OF-29, SS-4, 3B-1
1923	98	317	78	21	5	5	1.6	48	44	37	46	4	.246	.391	4	1	OF-83, 3B-4
1924	131	456	142	21	13	11	2.4	86	68	35	38	7	.311	.487	2	1	OF-109, 3B-7, 2B-7
1925	122	462	158	37	8	12	2.6	112	57	59	47	6	.342	.535	4	2	OF-114, 3B-1
1926	107	416	127	17	12	8	1.9	81	43	62	57	6	.305	.462	1	0	OF-105
1927	61	180	57	8	5	2	1.1	33	29	28	22	3	.317	.450	9	4	OF-50
1928	51	85	20	7	1	1	1.2	9	19	20	26	0	.235	.376	24	4	OF-19
1930	45	101	40	6	2	4	4.0	26	25	21	15	1	.396	.614	7	2	OF-32
1931	35	67	19	4	0	1	1.5	10	5	10	7	1	.284	.388	14	4	OF-20
1932	80	201	46	10	1	3	1.5	35	29	34	31	2	.229	.333	16	2	OF-62, 3B-1
10 yrs.	767	2415	726	133	51	50	2.1	467	340	331	310	33	.301	.460	81	20	OF-623, 3B-14, 2B-7, SS-4

WORLD SERIES	G	AB	H	2B	3B	HR	HR%	R	RBI	BB	SO	SB	BA	SA	AB	H	G by POS
1928 STL N	1	1	0	0	0	0	0.0	0	0	0	1	0	.000	.000	1	0	
1930	5	9	1	0	0	0	0.0	2	0	2	2	0	.111	.111	1	0	OF-3
1931	2	2	0	0	0	0	0.0	0	0	0	2	0	.000	.000	2	0	
3 yrs.	8	12	1	0	0	0	0.0	2	0	2	5	0	.083	.083	4	0	OF-3

Rick Bladt

BLADT, RICHARD ALAN   BR TR 6'1" 160 lbs.
B. Dec. 9, 1946, Santa Cruz, Calif.

	G	AB	H	2B	3B	HR	HR%	R	RBI	BB	SO	SB	BA	SA	AB	H	G by POS
1969 CHI N	10	13	2	0	0	0	0.0	1	1	0	5	0	.154	.154	1	0	1B-7
1975 NY A	52	117	26	3	1	1	0.9	13	11	11	8	6	.222	.291	1	1	OF-51
2 yrs.	62	130	28	3	1	1	0.8	14	12	11	13	6	.215	.277	2	1	OF-51, 1B-7

Rae Blaemire

BLAEMIRE, RAE BERTRAM   BR TR 6' 178 lbs.
B. Feb. 8, 1911, Gary, Ind.

	G	AB	H	2B	3B	HR	HR%	R	RBI	BB	SO	SB	BA	SA	AB	H	G by POS
1941 NY N	2	5	2	0	0	0	0.0	0	0	0	0	0	.400	.400	0	0	C-2

Buddy Blair

BLAIR, LOUIS NATHAN   BL TR 6' 186 lbs.
B. Sept. 10, 1910, Columbia, Miss.

	G	AB	H	2B	3B	HR	HR%	R	RBI	BB	SO	SB	BA	SA	AB	H	G by POS
1942 PHI A	137	484	135	26	8	5	1.0	48	66	30	30	1	.279	.397	12	2	3B-126

Footsie Blair

BLAIR, CLARENCE VICK   BL TR 6'1" 180 lbs.
B. July 13, 1900, Interprise, Okla.   D. July 1, 1982, Texarkana, Tex.

	G	AB	H	2B	3B	HR	HR%	R	RBI	BB	SO	SB	BA	SA	AB	H	G by POS
1929 CHI N	26	72	23	5	0	1	1.4	10	8	3	4	1	.319	.431	3	2	3B-8, 1B-7, 2B-2
1930	134	578	158	24	12	6	1.0	97	59	20	58	9	.273	.388	6	1	2B-115, 3B-13

	G	AB	H	2B	3B	HR	HR %	R	RBI	BB	SO	SB	BA	SA	Pinch Hit AB	H	G by POS

Footsie Blair continued

	G	AB	H	2B	3B	HR	HR %	R	RBI	BB	SO	SB	BA	SA	AB	H	G by POS
1931	86	240	62	19	5	2	0.8	31	29	14	26	1	.258	.404	16	2	2B-44, 1B-23, 3B-1
3 yrs.	246	890	243	48	17	9	1.0	138	96	37	88	11	.273	.396	25	5	2B-161, 1B-30, 3B-22

WORLD SERIES

	G	AB	H	2B	3B	HR	HR %	R	RBI	BB	SO	SB	BA	SA	AB	H	G by POS
1929 CHI N	1	1	0	0	0	0	0.0	0	0	0	0	0	.000	.000	1	0	

Paul Blair

BLAIR, PAUL L. D. (Motormouth)
B. Feb. 1, 1944, Cushing, Okla.   BR TR 6'   168 lbs.

	G	AB	H	2B	3B	HR	HR %	R	RBI	BB	SO	SB	BA	SA	AB	H	G by POS
1964 BAL A	8	1	0	0	0	0	0.0	0	0	0	1	0	.000	.000	0	0	OF-6
1965	119	364	85	19	2	5	1.4	49	25	32	52	8	.234	.338	0	0	OF-116
1966	133	303	84	20	2	6	2.0	35	33	15	36	5	.277	.416	5	1	OF-127
1967	151	552	162	27	12	11	2.0	72	64	50	68	8	.293	.446	5	1	OF-146
1968	141	421	89	22	1	7	1.7	48	38	37	60	4	.211	.318	11	2	OF-132, 3B-1
1969	150	625	178	32	5	26	4.2	102	76	40	72	20	.285	.477	1	0	OF-150
1970	133	480	128	24	2	18	3.8	79	65	56	93	24	.267	.438	6	0	OF-128, 3B-1
1971	141	516	135	24	8	10	1.9	75	44	32	94	14	.262	.397	4	1	OF-138
1972	142	477	111	20	8	8	1.7	47	49	25	78	7	.233	.358	11	3	OF-139
1973	146	500	140	25	3	10	2.0	73	64	43	72	18	.280	.402	8	0	OF-144, DH-1
1974	151	552	144	27	4	17	3.1	77	62	43	59	27	.261	.417	4	0	OF-151
1975	140	440	96	13	4	5	1.1	51	31	25	82	17	.218	.300	5	2	OF-138, DH-1, 1B-1
1976	145	375	74	16	0	3	0.8	29	16	22	49	15	.197	.264	11	2	OF-139, DH-1
1977 NY A	83	164	43	4	3	4	2.4	20	25	9	16	3	.262	.396	3	1	OF-79, DH-1
1978	75	125	22	5	0	2	1.6	10	13	9	17	1	.176	.264	16	5	OF-64, 2B-5, SS-4, 3B-3
1979 2 teams		NY	A (2G –	.200)		CIN	N	(75G –	.150)								
" total	77	145	22	4	1	2	1.4	7	15	11	28	0	.152	.234	8	0	OF-69
1980 NY A	12	2	0	0	0	0	0.0	2	0	0	0	0	.000	.000	0	0	OF-12
17 yrs.	1947	6042	1513	282	55	134	2.2	776	620	449	877	171	.250	.382	98	18	OF-1878, 3B-5, 2B-5, DH-4, SS-4, 1B-1

LEAGUE CHAMPIONSHIP SERIES

	G	AB	H	2B	3B	HR	HR %	R	RBI	BB	SO	SB	BA	SA	AB	H	G by POS
1969 BAL A	3	15	6	2	0	1	6.7	1	6	2	2	0	.400	.733	0	0	OF-3
1970	3	13	1	0	0	0	0.0	0	0	1	4	0	.077	.077	0	0	OF-3
1971	3	9	3	1	0	0	0.0	1	2	0	3	0	.333	.444	0	0	OF-3
1973	5	18	3	0	0	0	0.0	1	0	1	5	0	.167	.167	0	0	OF-5
1974	4	14	4	0	0	1	7.1	3	2	2	2	0	.286	.500	0	0	OF-4
1977 NY A	3	5	2	0	0	0	0.0	1	0	0	0	0	.400	.400	2	0	OF-3
1978	4	6	0	0	0	0	0.0	1	0	0	1	0	.000	.000	2	0	OF-4
7 yrs.	25	80	19	3	0	2	2.5	9	10	6	17	0	.238	.350	2	0	OF-24

WORLD SERIES

	G	AB	H	2B	3B	HR	HR %	R	RBI	BB	SO	SB	BA	SA	AB	H	G by POS
1966 BAL A	4	6	1	0	0	1	16.7	2	1	1	0	0	.167	.667	0	0	OF-4
1969	5	20	2	0	0	0	0.0	1	0	2	5	1	.100	.100	0	0	OF-5
1970	5	19	9	1	0	0	0.0	5	3	2	4	0	.474	.526	0	0	OF-5
1971	4	9	3	1	0	0	0.0	2	0	0	1	0	.333	.444	0	0	OF-3
1977 NY A	4	4	1	0	0	0	0.0	0	1	0	0	0	.250	.250	1	0	OF-3
1978	6	8	3	1	0	0	0.0	2	0	1	4	0	.375	.500	1	1	OF-6
6 yrs.	28	66	19	3	0	1	1.5	12	5	6	14	1	.288	.379	2	1	OF-26

Walter Blair

BLAIR, WALTER ALLAN (Heavy)
B. Oct. 13, 1883, Arnot, Pa.   D. Aug. 20, 1948, Lewisburg, Pa.   BR TR 6'   185 lbs.
Manager 1915.

	G	AB	H	2B	3B	HR	HR %	R	RBI	BB	SO	SB	BA	SA	AB	H	G by POS
1907 NY A	7	22	4	0	0	0	0.0	1	1	2		0	.182	.182	0	0	C-7
1908	76	211	40	5	1	1	0.5	9	13	11		4	.190	.237	3	1	C-60, OF-9, 1B-3
1909	42	110	23	2	2	0	0.0	5	11	7		2	.209	.264	0	0	C-42
1910	6	22	5	0	1	0	0.0	2	2	0		0	.227	.318	0	0	C-6
1911	85	222	43	9	2	0	0.0	18	26	16		2	.194	.252	0	0	C-84, 1B-1
1914 BUF F	128	378	92	11	2	0	0.0	22	33	32		6	.243	.283	0	0	C-128
1915	98	290	65	15	3	2	0.7	23	20	18		4	.224	.317	1	0	C-97
7 yrs.	442	1255	272	42	11	3	0.2	80	106	86		18	.217	.275	4	1	C-424, OF-9, 1B-4

Harry Blake

BLAKE, HARRY COOPER (Dude)
B. June 16, 1874, Portsmouth, Ohio   D. Oct. 14, 1919, Chicago, Ill.   BR TR 5'7"   165 lbs.

	G	AB	H	2B	3B	HR	HR %	R	RBI	BB	SO	SB	BA	SA	AB	H	G by POS
1894 CLE N	73	296	78	15	4	1	0.3	51	51	30	22	1	.264	.351	0	0	OF-73
1895	84	315	87	10	1	3	1.0	50	45	30	33	11	.276	.343	1	0	OF-83
1896	104	383	92	12	5	1	0.3	66	43	46	30	10	.240	.305	0	0	OF-103, SS-1
1897	32	117	30	3	1	1	0.9	17	15	12		5	.256	.325	0	0	OF-32
1898	136	474	116	18	7	0	0.0	65	58	69		12	.245	.312	0	0	OF-136, 1B-2
1899 STL N	97	292	70	9	4	2	0.7	50	41	43		16	.240	.318	4	2	OF-87, 2B-4, SS-1, 1B-1, C-1
6 yrs.	526	1877	473	67	22	8	0.4	299	253	230	85	55	.252	.324	5	2	OF-514, 2B-4, 1B-3, SS-2, C-1

Link Blakely

BLAKELY, LINCOLN HOWARD
B. Feb. 12, 1912, Oakland, Calif.   D. Sept. 28, 1976, Oakland, Ky.   BL TR 6'   180 lbs.

	G	AB	H	2B	3B	HR	HR %	R	RBI	BB	SO	SB	BA	SA	AB	H	G by POS
1934 CIN N	34	102	23	1	1	0	0.0	11	10	5	14	1	.225	.255	1	0	OF-28

Bob Blakiston

BLAKISTON, ROBERT J.
Born Robert J. Blackstone.
B. Oct. 2, 1855, San Francisco, Calif.   D. Dec. 25, 1918, San Francisco, Calif.

	G	AB	H	2B	3B	HR	HR %	R	RBI	BB	SO	SB	BA	SA	AB	H	G by POS
1882 PHI AA	72	281	64	4	1	0	0.0	40		9			.228	.249	0	0	OF-38, 3B-34, 2B-1
1883	44	167	41	3	3	0	0.0	26		9			.246	.299	0	0	OF-37, 1B-6, 3B-5
1884 2 teams		PHI	AA	(32G –	.258)		IND	AA	(6G –	.222)							
" total	38	146	37	7	0	0	0.0	21		12			.253	.301	0	0	OF-29, 1B-6, 3B-2, SS-1, 2B-1
3 yrs.	154	594	142	14	4	0	0.0	87		30			.239	.276	0	0	OF-104, 3B-41, 1B-12, 2B-2, SS-1

	G	AB	H	2B	3B	HR	HR %	R	RBI	BB	SO	SB	BA	SA	Pinch Hit AB	Pinch Hit H	G by POS

Johnny Blanchard

BLANCHARD, JOHN EDWIN   BL TR 6'1"   193 lbs.
B. Feb. 26, 1933, Minneapolis, Minn.

	G	AB	H	2B	3B	HR	HR %	R	RBI	BB	SO	SB	BA	SA	AB	H	G by POS
1955 NY A	1	3	0	0	0	0	0.0	0	0	1	0	0	.000	.000	0	0	C-1
1959	49	59	10	1	0	2	3.4	6	4	7	12	0	.169	.288	28	2	C-12, OF-8, 1B-1
1960	53	99	24	3	1	4	4.0	8	14	6	17	0	.242	.414	23	4	C-28
1961	93	243	74	10	1	21	8.6	38	54	27	28	1	.305	.613	26	7	C-48, OF-15
1962	93	246	57	7	0	13	5.3	33	39	28	32	0	.232	.419	25	3	OF-47, C-15, 1B-2
1963	76	218	49	4	0	16	7.3	22	45	26	30	0	.225	.463	14	1	OF-64
1964	77	161	41	8	0	7	4.3	18	28	24	24	1	.255	.435	31	8	C-25, OF-14, 1B-3
1965 3 teams	NY	A (12G – .147)		KC	A	(52G – .200)		MIL	N	(10G – .100)							
" total	74	164	30	3	0	4	2.4	12	16	17	20	0	.183	.274	30	4	C-26, OF-21
8 yrs.	516	1193	285	36	2	67	5.6	137	200	136	163	2	.239	.441	177	29	OF-169, C-155, 1B-6

WORLD SERIES

	G	AB	H	2B	3B	HR	HR %	R	RBI	BB	SO	SB	BA	SA	AB	H	G by POS
1960 NY A	5	11	5	2	0	0	0.0	2	2	0	0	0	.455	.636	3	1	C-2
1961	4	10	4	1	0	2	20.0	4	3	2	0	0	.400	1.100	2	1	OF-2
1962	1	1	0	0	0	0	0.0	0	0	0	1	0	.000	.000	1	0	
1963	1	3	0	0	0	0	0.0	0	0	0	0	0	.000	.000	0	0	OF-1
1964	4	4	1	1	0	0	0.0	0	0	0	1	0	.250	.500	4	1	
5 yrs.	15	29	10	4	0	2	6.9	6	5	2	2	0	.345	.690	10 (1st)	3 (1st)	OF-3, C-2

Damasco Blanco

BLANCO, DAMASCO   BR TR 5'10"   165 lbs.
B. Dec. 11, 1941, Curiepe, Venezuela

	G	AB	H	2B	3B	HR	HR %	R	RBI	BB	SO	SB	BA	SA	AB	H	G by POS
1972 SF N	39	20	7	1	0	0	0.0	5	2	4	3	2	.350	.400	0	0	3B-19, SS-8, 2B-3
1973	28	12	0	0	0	0	0.0	4	0	1	2	0	.000	.000	6	0	3B-7, SS-5, 2B-3
1974	5	1	0	0	0	0	0.0	0	0	0	1	1	.000	.000	1	0	
3 yrs.	72	33	7	1	0	0	0.0	9	2	5	6	3	.212	.242	7	0	3B-26, SS-13, 2B-6

Ossie Blanco

BLANCO, OSWALDO C.   BR TR 6'   185 lbs.
B. Sept. 8, 1945, Caracas, Venezuela

	G	AB	H	2B	3B	HR	HR %	R	RBI	BB	SO	SB	BA	SA	AB	H	G by POS
1970 CHI A	34	66	13	0	0	0	0.0	4	8	3	14	0	.197	.197	16	3	1B-22, OF-1
1974 CLE A	18	36	7	0	0	0	0.0	1	2	7	4	0	.194	.194	0	0	1B-16, DH-1
2 yrs.	52	102	20	0	0	0	0.0	5	10	10	18	0	.196	.196	16	3	1B-38, DH-1, OF-1

Coonie Blank

BLANK, FRANK IGNATZ   BR TR 5'11"   165 lbs.
B. Oct. 18, 1892, St. Louis, Mo.   D. Dec. 8, 1961, St. Louis, Mo.

	G	AB	H	2B	3B	HR	HR %	R	RBI	BB	SO	SB	BA	SA	AB	H	G by POS
1909 STL N	1	2	0	0	0	0	0.0	0	0	0	0	0	.000	.000	0	0	C-1

Cliff Blankenship

BLANKENSHIP, CLIFFORD DOUGLAS   BR TR 5'10½"   165 lbs.
B. Apr. 10, 1880, Columbus, Ga.   D. Apr. 26, 1956, Oakland, Calif.

	G	AB	H	2B	3B	HR	HR %	R	RBI	BB	SO	SB	BA	SA	AB	H	G by POS
1905 CIN N	19	56	11	1	1	0	0.0	8	7	4		1	.196	.250	3	0	1B-15
1907 WAS A	37	102	23	2	0	0	0.0	4	6	3		3	.225	.245	5	2	C-22, 1B-9
1909	39	60	15	0	0	0	0.0	4	9	0		2	.250	.250	16	3	C-17, OF-4
3 yrs.	95	218	49	3	1	0	0.0	16	22	7		6	.225	.248	24	5	C-39, 1B-24, OF-4

Larvell Blanks

BLANKS, LARVELL (Sugar Bear)   BR TR 5'8"   167 lbs.
B. Jan. 28, 1950, Del Rio, Tex.

	G	AB	H	2B	3B	HR	HR %	R	RBI	BB	SO	SB	BA	SA	AB	H	G by POS
1972 ATL N	33	85	28	5	0	1	1.2	10	7	7	12	0	.329	.424	7	3	2B-18, SS-4, 3B-2
1973	17	18	4	0	0	0	0.0	1	0	1	3	0	.222	.222	10	3	3B-3, SS-2, 2B-2
1974	3	8	2	0	0	0	0.0	0	1	0	0	0	.250	.250	1	1	SS-2
1975	141	471	110	13	3	3	0.6	49	38	38	43	4	.234	.293	2	0	SS-129, 2B-12
1976 CLE A	104	328	92	8	7	5	1.5	45	41	30	31	1	.280	.393	14	4	SS-56, 2B-46, 3B-2
1977	105	322	92	10	4	6	1.9	43	38	19	37	3	.286	.398	24	6	SS-66, 3B-18, 2B-12
1978	70	193	49	10	0	2	1.0	19	20	10	16	0	.254	.337	12	2	SS-43, 2B-17, 3B-3, DH-1
1979 TEX A	68	120	24	5	0	1	0.8	13	15	11	9	0	.200	.267	12	2	SS-49, 2B-16, DH-1
1980 ATL N	88	221	45	6	0	2	0.9	23	12	16	27	1	.204	.258	10	1	SS-56, 3B-43, 2B-1
9 yrs.	629	1766	446	57	14	20	1.1	203	172	132	178	9	.253	.335	92	22	SS-407, 2B-124, 3B-71, DH-2

Don Blasingame

BLASINGAME, DONALD LEE (The Blazer)   BL TR 5'10"   160 lbs.
B. Mar. 16, 1932, Corinth, Miss.

	G	AB	H	2B	3B	HR	HR %	R	RBI	BB	SO	SB	BA	SA	AB	H	G by POS
1955 STL N	5	16	6	1	0	0	0.0	4	0	6	0	1	.375	.438	0	0	2B-3, SS-2
1956	150	587	153	22	7	0	0.0	94	27	72	52	8	.261	.322	2	0	2B-98, SS-49, 3B-2
1957	154	650	176	25	7	8	1.2	108	58	71	49	21	.271	.368	0	0	2B-154
1958	143	547	150	19	10	2	0.4	71	36	57	47	20	.274	.356	4	0	2B-137
1959	150	615	178	26	7	1	0.2	90	24	67	42	15	.289	.359	1	0	2B-150
1960 SF N	136	523	123	12	8	2	0.4	72	31	49	53	14	.235	.300	3	0	2B-133
1961 2 teams	SF	N (3G – .000)		CIN	N	(123G – .222)											
" total	126	451	100	18	4	1	0.2	60	21	41	39	4	.222	.286	8	2	2B-116
1962 CIN N	141	494	139	9	7	2	0.4	77	35	63	44	4	.281	.340	6	2	2B-137
1963 2 teams	CIN	N (18G – .161)		WAS	A	(69G – .256)											
" total	87	285	70	12	2	2	0.7	33	12	31	23	3	.246	.323	9	2	2B-75, 3B-2
1964 WAS A	143	506	135	17	2	1	0.2	56	34	40	44	8	.267	.314	17	0	2B-135
1965	129	403	90	8	8	1	0.2	47	18	35	45	5	.223	.290	13	2	2B-110
1966 2 teams	WAS	A (68G – .215)		KC	A	(12G – .158)											
" total	80	219	46	9	0	1	0.5	19	12	20	24	2	.210	.265	10	1	2B-62, SS-1
12 yrs.	1444	5296	1366	178	62	21	0.4	731	308	552	462	105	.258	.327	73	9	2B-1310, SS-52, 3B-4

WORLD SERIES

	G	AB	H	2B	3B	HR	HR %	R	RBI	BB	SO	SB	BA	SA	AB	H	G by POS
1961 CIN N	3	7	1	0	0	0	0.0	1	0	1	0	0	.143	.143	0	0	2B-3

Johnny Blatnik

BLATNIK, JOHN LOUIS (Chief)   BR TR 6'   195 lbs.
B. Mar. 10, 1921, Bridgeport, Ohio   D. Nov. 5, 1974

	G	AB	H	2B	3B	HR	HR %	R	RBI	BB	SO	SB	BA	SA	AB	H	G by POS
1948 PHI N	121	415	108	27	8	6	1.4	56	45	31	77	3	.260	.407	15	4	OF-105
1949	6	8	1	0	0	0	0.0	3	0	4	1	0	.125	.125	3	1	OF-2
1950 2 teams	PHI	N (4G – .250)		STL	N	(7G – .150)											
" total	11	24	4	0	0	0	0.0	0	1	5	5	0	.167	.167	4	1	OF-8
3 yrs.	138	447	113	27	8	6	1.3	59	46	40	83	3	.253	.389	22	6	OF-115

	G	AB	H	2B	3B	HR	HR %	R	RBI	BB	SO	SB	BA	SA	Pinch Hit AB	Pinch Hit H	G by POS

Buddy Blattner

BLATTNER, ROBERT GARNETT
B. Feb. 8, 1920, St. Louis, Mo.
BR TR 6'½" 180 lbs.

	G	AB	H	2B	3B	HR	HR %	R	RBI	BB	SO	SB	BA	SA	AB	H	G by POS
1942 STL N	19	23	1	0	0	0	0.0	3	1	3	6	0	.043	.043	2	0	SS-13, 2B-3
1946 NY N	126	420	107	18	6	11	2.6	63	49	56	52	12	.255	.405	2	0	2B-114, 1B-1
1947	55	153	40	9	2	0	0.0	28	13	21	19	4	.261	.346	2	0	2B-34, 3B-4
1948	8	20	4	1	0	0	0.0	3	0	3	2	2	.200	.250	0	0	2B-7
1949 PHI N	64	97	24	6	0	5	5.2	15	21	19	17	0	.247	.464	29	7	3B-62, 2B-15, SS-7
5 yrs.	272	713	176	34	8	16	2.2	112	84	102	96	18	.247	.384	35	7	2B-173, 3B-66, SS-20, 1B-1

Marv Blaylock

BLAYLOCK, MARVIN EDWARD
B. Sept. 30, 1929, Fort Smith, Ark.
BL TL 6'1½" 175 lbs.

	G	AB	H	2B	3B	HR	HR %	R	RBI	BB	SO	SB	BA	SA	AB	H	G by POS
1950 NY N	1	1	0	0	0	0	0.0	0	0	0	0	0	.000	.000	1	0	
1955 PHI N	113	259	54	7	7	3	1.2	30	24	31	43	6	.208	.324	27	5	1B-77, OF-6
1956	136	460	117	14	8	10	2.2	61	50	50	86	5	.254	.385	8	0	1B-124, OF-1
1957	37	26	4	0	0	2	7.7	5	4	3	8	0	.154	.385	19	4	1B-12, OF-1
4 yrs.	287	746	175	21	15	15	2.0	96	78	84	137	11	.235	.363	55	9	1B-213, OF-8

Curt Blefary

BLEFARY, CURTIS LeROY
B. July 5, 1943, Brooklyn, N. Y.
BL TR 6'2" 195 lbs.

	G	AB	H	2B	3B	HR	HR %	R	RBI	BB	SO	SB	BA	SA	AB	H	G by POS
1965 BAL A	144	462	120	23	4	22	4.8	72	70	88	73	4	.260	.470	9	1	OF-136
1966	131	419	107	14	3	23	5.5	73	64	73	56	1	.255	.468	13	3	OF-109, 1B-20
1967	155	554	134	19	5	22	4.0	69	81	73	94	4	.242	.413	6	1	OF-103, 1B-52
1968	137	451	90	8	1	15	3.3	50	39	65	66	6	.200	.322	6	2	OF-92, C-40, 1B-12
1969 HOU N	155	542	137	26	7	12	2.2	66	67	77	79	8	.253	.393	2	0	1B-152, OF-1
1970 NY A	99	269	57	6	0	9	3.3	34	37	43	37	1	.212	.335	12	3	OF-79, 1B-6
1971 2 teams			NY	A (21G – .194)		OAK	A (50G – .218)										
" total	71	137	29	3	0	6	4.4	19	14	18	20	0	.212	.365	27	4	OF-20, C-14, 3B-5, 1B-4, 2B-2
1972 2 teams			OAK	A (8G – .455)		SD	N (74G – .196)										
" total	82	113	25	5	0	3	2.7	11	10	19	19	0	.221	.345	56	11	C-12, 1B-7, OF-4, 3B-3, 2B-1
8 yrs.	974	2947	699	104	20	112	3.8	394	382	456	444	24	.237	.400	131	25	OF-544, 1B-253, C-66, 3B-8, 2B-3

LEAGUE CHAMPIONSHIP SERIES

	G	AB	H	2B	3B	HR	HR %	R	RBI	BB	SO	SB	BA	SA	AB	H	G by POS
1971 OAK A	1	1	0	0	0	0	0.0	0	0	0	1	0	.000	.000	1	0	

WORLD SERIES

	G	AB	H	2B	3B	HR	HR %	R	RBI	BB	SO	SB	BA	SA	AB	H	G by POS
1966 BAL A	4	13	1	0	0	0	0.0	0	0	2	3	0	.077	.077	0	0	OF-4

Ike Blessitt

BLESSITT, ISIAH
B. Sept. 30, 1949, Detroit, Mich.
BR TR 5'11" 185 lbs.

	G	AB	H	2B	3B	HR	HR %	R	RBI	BB	SO	SB	BA	SA	AB	H	G by POS
1972 DET A	4	5	0	0	0	0	0.0	0	0	0	2	0	.000	.000	3	0	OF-1

Ned Bligh

BLIGH, EDWIN FORREST
B. June 30, 1864, Brooklyn, N. Y.   D. Apr. 18, 1892, Brooklyn, N. Y.
BR TR 5'11" 172 lbs.

	G	AB	H	2B	3B	HR	HR %	R	RBI	BB	SO	SB	BA	SA	AB	H	G by POS
1886 BAL AA	3	9	0	0	0	0	0.0	0		1			.000	.000	0	0	C-3
1888 CIN AA	3	5	0	0	0	0	0.0	0	0	0		0	.000	.000	0	0	C-2, OF-1
1889 COL AA	28	93	13	1	0	0	0.0	6	5	4	14	2	.140	.172	0	0	C-28
1890 2 teams			COL	AA (8G – .207)		LOU	AA (24G – .205)										
" total	32	102	21	2	0	1	1.0	11		11		1	.206	.255	0	0	C-32
4 yrs.	66	209	34	3	1	1	0.5	17	4	16	14	3	.163	.201	0	0	C-65, OF-1

Elmer Bliss

BLISS, ELMER WARD
B. Mar. 9, 1875, Penfield, Pa.   D. Mar. 18, 1962, Bradford, Pa.
BL TR 6' 180 lbs.

	G	AB	H	2B	3B	HR	HR %	R	RBI	BB	SO	SB	BA	SA	AB	H	G by POS
1903 NY A	1	3	0	0	0	0	0.0	0	0	0		0	.000	.000	0	0	P-1
1904	1	1	0	0	0	0	0.0	0	0	0		0	.000	.000	0	0	OF-1
2 yrs.	2	4	0	0	0	0	0.0	0	0	0		0	.000	.000	0	0	OF-1, P-1

Frank Bliss

BLISS, HOWARD FRANK
B. Feb. 15, 1844, Mount Carmel, Ill.   D. July 25, 1919, Janesville, Wis.

	G	AB	H	2B	3B	HR	HR %	R	RBI	BB	SO	SB	BA	SA	AB	H	G by POS
1878 MIL N	2	8	1	0	0	0	0.0	1	0	0		0	.125	.125	0	0	3B-1, C-1

John Bliss

BLISS, JOHN JOSEPH ALFRED
B. Jan. 9, 1882, Vancouver, Wash.   D. Oct. 23, 1968, Temple City, Calif.
BR TR 5'9" 185 lbs.

	G	AB	H	2B	3B	HR	HR %	R	RBI	BB	SO	SB	BA	SA	AB	H	G by POS
1908 STL N	44	136	29	4	0	1	0.7	9	5	8		3	.213	.265	2	1	C-43
1909	35	113	25	2	1	1	0.9	12	8	12		2	.221	.283	9	1	C-32
1910	16	33	2	0	0	0	0.0	2	3	4	8	0	.061	.061	3	0	C-13
1911	97	258	59	6	4	1	0.4	36	27	42	25	5	.229	.295	8	1	C-84, SS-1
1912	49	114	28	3	1	0	0.0	11	18	19	14	3	.246	.289	6	3	C-41
5 yrs.	241	654	143	15	6	3	0.5	70	61	85	47	13	.219	.274	28	6	C-213, SS-1

Bruno Block

BLOCK, JAMES JOHN
Born James John Blochowitz.
B. Mar. 14, 1885, Wisconsin Rapids, Wis.   D. Aug. 6, 1937, S. Milwaukee, Wis.
BR TR 5'9" 185 lbs.

	G	AB	H	2B	3B	HR	HR %	R	RBI	BB	SO	SB	BA	SA	AB	H	G by POS
1907 WAS A	24	57	8	2	1	0	0.0	3	2	2		0	.140	.211	3	0	C-21
1910 CHI A	55	152	32	1	1	0	0.0	12	9	13		3	.211	.230	6	0	C-47
1911	39	115	35	6	1	1	0.9	11	18	6		0	.304	.400	2	0	C-38
1912	46	136	35	5	6	0	0.0	8	26	7		1	.257	.382	0	0	C-46
1914 CHI F	43	100	19	4	1	0	0.0	8	13	11		1	.190	.250	10	2	C-33
5 yrs.	207	560	129	18	10	1	0.2	42	68	39		5	.230	.304	20	2	C-185

Cy Block

BLOCK, SEYMOUR
B. May 4, 1919, Brooklyn, N. Y.
BR TR 6' 180 lbs.

	G	AB	H	2B	3B	HR	HR %	R	RBI	BB	SO	SB	BA	SA	AB	H	G by POS
1942 CHI N	9	33	12	1	1	0	0.0	6	4	3	2	2	.364	.455	0	0	3B-8, 2B-1
1945	2	7	1	0	0	0	0.0	1	1	0	0	0	.143	.143	0	0	3B-1, 2B-1
1946	6	13	3	0	0	0	0.0	2	0	4	0	0	.231	.231	1	0	3B-4
3 yrs.	17	53	16	1	1	0	0.0	9	5	7	3	2	.302	.358	1	0	3B-13, 2B-2

	G	AB	H	2B	3B	HR	HR %	R	RBI	BB	SO	SB	BA	SA	Pinch Hit AB	Pinch Hit H	G by POS

Cy Block continued

	G	AB	H	2B	3B	HR	HR%	R	RBI	BB	SO	SB	BA	SA	PH AB	PH H	G by POS
WORLD SERIES																	
1945 CHI N	1	0	0	0	0	0	–	0	0	0	0	0	–	–	0	0	

Ron Blomberg

BLOMBERG, RONALD MARK
B. Aug. 23, 1948, Atlanta, Ga.   BL TR 6'1½" 195 lbs.

	G	AB	H	2B	3B	HR	HR%	R	RBI	BB	SO	SB	BA	SA	PH AB	PH H	G by POS
1969 NY A	4	6	3	0	0	0	0.0	0	0	1	0	0	.500	.500	1	1	OF-2
1971	64	199	64	6	2	7	3.5	30	31	14	23	2	.322	.477	11	2	OF-57
1972	107	299	80	22	1	14	4.7	36	49	38	26	0	.268	.488	15	5	1B-95
1973	100	301	99	13	1	12	4.0	45	57	34	25	2	.329	.498	6	2	DH-55, 1B-41
1974	90	264	82	11	2	10	3.8	39	48	29	33	2	.311	.481	10	5	DH-58, OF-19
1975	34	106	27	8	2	4	3.8	18	17	13	10	0	.255	.481	5	2	DH-27, OF-1
1976	1	2	0	0	0	0	0.0	0	0	0	0	0	.000	.000	1	0	DH-1
1978 CHI A	61	156	36	7	0	5	3.2	16	22	11	17	0	.231	.372	16	1	DH-36, 1B-7
8 yrs.	461	1333	391	67	8	52	3.9	184	224	140	134	6	.293	.473	65	19	DH-177, 1B-143, OF-79

Joe Blong

BLONG, JOSEPH MYLES
B. Sept. 17, 1853, St. Louis, Mo.   D. Sept. 22, 1892, St. Louis, Mo.   BR TR

	G	AB	H	2B	3B	HR	HR%	R	RBI	BB	SO	SB	BA	SA	PH AB	PH H	G by POS
1876 STL N	62	264	62	7	4	0	0.0	30	30	2	9		.235	.292	0	0	OF-62, P-1
1877	58	218	47	8	3	0	0.0	17	13	4	22		.216	.280	0	0	OF-40, P-25
2 yrs.	120	482	109	15	7	0	0.0	47	43	6	31		.226	.286	0	0	OF-102, P-26

Wes Blong

BLONG, WESLEY C.
B. Norfolk, Va.   D. Mar. 10, 1897

	G	AB	H	2B	3B	HR	HR%	R	RBI	BB	SO	SB	BA	SA	PH AB	PH H	G by POS
1883 PIT AA	9	34	5	0	0	0	0.0	0	0	0	0		.147	.147	0	0	C-6, OF-3

Jimmy Bloodworth

BLOODWORTH, JAMES HENRY
B. July 26, 1917, Tallahassee, Fla.   BR TR 5'11" 180 lbs.

	G	AB	H	2B	3B	HR	HR%	R	RBI	BB	SO	SB	BA	SA	PH AB	PH H	G by POS
1937 WAS A	15	50	11	2	1	0	0.0	3	8	5	8	0	.220	.300	1	0	2B-14
1939	83	318	92	24	1	4	1.3	34	40	10	26	3	.289	.409	5	2	2B-73, OF-5
1940	119	469	115	17	8	11	2.3	47	70	16	71	3	.245	.386	0	0	2B-96, 1B-17, 3B-6
1941	142	506	124	24	3	7	1.4	59	66	41	58	1	.245	.346	4	0	2B-132, 3B-6, SS-1
1942 DET A	137	533	129	23	1	13	2.4	62	57	35	63	2	.242	.362	1	0	2B-134, SS-2
1943	129	474	114	23	4	6	1.3	41	52	29	59	4	.241	.344	0	0	2B-129
1946	76	249	61	8	1	5	2.0	25	36	12	26	3	.245	.345	4	0	2B-71
1947 PIT N	88	316	79	9	0	7	2.2	27	48	16	39	1	.250	.345	1	0	2B-87
1949 CIN N	134	452	118	27	1	9	2.0	40	59	27	36	1	.261	.385	14	8	2B-92, 1B-23, 3B-8
1950 2 teams	CIN N (4G – .214)			PHI N (54G – .229)													
" total	58	110	25	3	0	0	0.0	7	14	8	12	0	.227	.255	16	4	2B-31, 1B-7, 3B-2
1951 PHI N	21	42	6	0	0	0	0.0	2	3	1	9	1	.143	.143	7	3	2B-8, 1B-6
11 yrs.	1002	3519	874	160	20	62	1.8	347	453	200	407	19	.248	.358	53	17	2B-867, 1B-53, 3B-22, OF-5, SS-3

	G	AB	H	2B	3B	HR	HR%	R	RBI	BB	SO	SB	BA	SA	PH AB	PH H	G by POS
WORLD SERIES																	
1950 PHI N	1	0	0	0	0	0	–	0	0	0	0	0	–	–	0	0	2B-1

Clyde Bloomfield

BLOOMFIELD, CLYDE STALCUP (Bud)
B. Jan. 5, 1937, Oklahoma City, Okla.   BR TR 5'11½" 175 lbs.

	G	AB	H	2B	3B	HR	HR%	R	RBI	BB	SO	SB	BA	SA	PH AB	PH H	G by POS
1963 STL N	1	0	0	0	0	0	0.0	0	0	0	0	0	–	–	0	0	3B-1
1964 MIN A	7	7	1	0	0	0	0.0	1	0	0	0	0	.143	.143	0	0	2B-3, SS-2
2 yrs.	8	7	1	0	0	0	0.0	1	0	0	0	0	.143	.143	0	0	2B-3, SS-2, 3B-1

Jack Blott

BLOTT, JACK LEONARD
B. Aug. 24, 1902, Girard, Ohio   D. June 11, 1964, Ann Arbor, Mich.   BR TR 6' 210 lbs.

	G	AB	H	2B	3B	HR	HR%	R	RBI	BB	SO	SB	BA	SA	PH AB	PH H	G by POS
1924 CIN N	2	1	0	0	0	0	0.0	0	0	0	0	0	.000	.000	1	0	C-1

Bert Blue

BLUE, BIRD WAYNE
B. Dec. 14, 1876, Bettsville, Ohio   D. Dec. 14, 1928, Detroit, Mich.   BR TR 6'3" 200 lbs.

	G	AB	H	2B	3B	HR	HR%	R	RBI	BB	SO	SB	BA	SA	PH AB	PH H	G by POS
1908 2 teams	STL A (11G – .360)			PHI N (6G – .158)													
" total	17	44	12	1	2	1	2.3	4	2	3		0	.273	.455	3	0	C-14

Lu Blue

BLUE, LUZERNE ATWELL
B. Mar. 5, 1897, Washington, D.C.   D. July 28, 1958, Alexandria, Va.   BB TL 5'10" 165 lbs.

	G	AB	H	2B	3B	HR	HR%	R	RBI	BB	SO	SB	BA	SA	PH AB	PH H	G by POS
1921 DET A	153	585	180	33	11	5	0.9	103	75	103	47	13	.308	.427	1	0	1B-152
1922	145	584	175	31	9	6	1.0	131	45	82	48	8	.300	.414	1	1	1B-144
1923	129	504	143	27	7	1	0.2	100	46	96	40	9	.284	.371	0	0	1B-129
1924	108	395	123	26	7	2	0.5	81	50	64	26	9	.311	.428	0	0	1B-108
1925	150	532	163	18	9	3	0.6	91	94	83	29	19	.306	.391	2	0	1B-148
1926	128	429	123	24	14	1	0.2	92	52	90	18	13	.287	.415	12	5	1B-109, OF-1
1927	112	365	95	17	9	1	0.3	71	42	71	28	13	.260	.364	5	2	1B-104
1928 STL A	154	549	154	32	11	14	2.6	116	80	105	43	12	.281	.455	0	0	1B-154
1929	151	573	168	40	10	6	1.0	111	61	126	32	12	.293	.429	0	0	1B-151
1930	117	425	100	27	5	4	0.9	85	42	81	44	12	.235	.351	4	1	1B-111
1931 CHI A	155	589	179	23	15	1	0.2	119	62	127	60	13	.304	.399	0	0	1B-155
1932	112	373	93	21	2	0	0.0	51	43	64	21	17	.249	.316	6	1	1B-105
1933 BKN N	1	1	0	0	0	0	0.0	0	0	0	0	0	.000	.000	0	0	1B-1
13 yrs.	1615	5904	1696	319	109	44	0.7	1151	692	1092	436	150	.287	.401	31	10	1B-1571, OF-1

Ossie Bluege

BLUEGE, OSWALD LOUIS
Brother of Otto Bluege.
B. Oct. 24, 1900, Chicago, Ill.
Manager 1943-47.   BR TR 5'11" 162 lbs.

	G	AB	H	2B	3B	HR	HR%	R	RBI	BB	SO	SB	BA	SA	PH AB	PH H	G by POS
1922 WAS A	19	61	12	1	0	0	0.0	5	2	7	7	1	.197	.213	1	0	3B-17, SS-2
1923	109	379	93	15	7	2	0.5	48	42	48	53	5	.245	.338	0	0	3B-107, 2B-2
1924	117	402	113	15	4	2	0.5	59	49	39	36	7	.281	.353	1	1	3B-102, 2B-10, SS-4
1925	145	522	150	27	4	4	0.8	77	79	59	59	16	.287	.377	0	0	3B-144, SS-4

	G	AB	H	2B	3B	HR	HR %	R	RBI	BB	SO	SB	BA	SA	Pinch Hit AB	Pinch Hit H	G by POS

Ossie Bluege continued

	G	AB	H	2B	3B	HR	HR%	R	RBI	BB	SO	SB	BA	SA	AB	H	G by POS
1926	139	487	132	19	8	3	0.6	69	65	70	46	12	.271	.361	0	0	3B-134, SS-8
1927	146	503	138	21	10	1	0.2	71	66	57	47	15	.274	.362	0	0	3B-146
1928	146	518	154	33	7	2	0.4	78	75	46	27	18	.297	.400	1	1	3B-144
1929	64	220	65	6	1	5	2.3	35	31	19	15	6	.295	.400	4	0	3B-34, 2B-14, SS-10
1930	134	476	138	27	7	3	0.6	64	69	51	40	15	.290	.395	0	0	3B-134
1931	152	570	155	25	7	8	1.4	82	98	50	39	16	.272	.382	0	0	3B-152, SS-1
1932	149	507	131	22	4	5	1.0	64	64	84	41	9	.258	.347	0	0	3B-149
1933	140	501	131	14	0	6	1.2	63	71	55	34	6	.261	.325	2	1	3B-138
1934	99	285	70	9	2	0	0.0	39	11	23	15	2	.246	.291	13	4	3B-41, SS-30, OF-5, 2B-5
1935	100	320	84	14	3	0	0.0	44	34	37	21	2	.263	.325	7	2	SS-58, 3B-25, 2B-4
1936	90	319	92	12	1	1	0.3	43	55	38	16	5	.288	.342	0	0	2B-52, SS-23, 3B-15
1937	42	127	36	4	2	1	0.8	12	13	13	19	1	.283	.370	7	2	SS-28, 3B-2, 1B-2
1938	58	184	48	12	1	0	0.0	25	21	21	11	3	.261	.337	8	1	2B-38, SS-10, 3B-1, 1B-1
1939	18	59	9	0	0	0	0.0	5	3	7	2	1	.153	.153	1	0	1B-11, SS-2, 3B-2, 2B-2
18 yrs.	1867	6440	1751	276	68	43	0.7	883	848	724	525	140	.272	.356	45	12	3B-1487, SS-180, 2B-127, 1B-14, OF-5

WORLD SERIES

	G	AB	H	2B	3B	HR	HR%	R	RBI	BB	SO	SB	BA	SA	AB	H	G by POS
1924 WAS A	7	26	5	0	0	0	0.0	2	3	3	4	1	.192	.192	0	0	3B-4
1925	5	18	5	1	0	0	0.0	2	2	1	4	0	.278	.333	0	0	3B-5
1933	5	16	2	1	0	0	0.0	1	0	1	6	0	.125	.188	0	0	3B-5
3 yrs.	17	60	12	2	0	0	0.0	5	5	5	14	1	.200	.233	0	0	3B-14

Otto Bluege

BLUEGE, OTTO ADAM (Squeaky)
Brother of Ossie Bluege.
B. July 20, 1909, Chicago, Ill.   D. June 28, 1977, Chicago, Ill.   BR TR 5'10"   154 lbs.

	G	AB	H	2B	3B	HR	HR%	R	RBI	BB	SO	SB	BA	SA	AB	H	G by POS
1932 CIN N	1	0	0	0	0	0	–	1	0	0	0	0	–	–	0	0	
1933	108	291	62	6	2	0	0.0	17	18	26	29	0	.213	.247	0	0	SS-95, 2B-10, 3B-1
2 yrs.	109	291	62	6	2	0	0.0	18	18	26	29	0	.213	.247	0	0	SS-95, 2B-10, 3B-1

Red Bluhm

BLUHM, HARVEY FRED
B. June 27, 1894, Cleveland, Ohio   D. May 7, 1952, Flint, Mich.   BR TR 5'11"   165 lbs.

	G	AB	H	2B	3B	HR	HR%	R	RBI	BB	SO	SB	BA	SA	AB	H	G by POS
1918 BOS A	1	1	0	0	0	0	0.0	0	0	0	0	0	.000	.000	1	0	

Chet Boak

BOAK, CHESTER ROBERT
B. June 19, 1935, New Castle, Pa.   D. Nov. 28, 1983, Emporium, Pa.   BR TR 6'   180 lbs.

	G	AB	H	2B	3B	HR	HR%	R	RBI	BB	SO	SB	BA	SA	AB	H	G by POS
1960 KC A	5	13	2	0	0	0	0.0	1	1	0	2	0	.154	.154	0	0	2B-5
1961 WAS A	5	7	0	0	0	0	0.0	0	0	1	1	1	.000	.000	4	0	2B-1
2 yrs.	10	20	2	0	0	0	0.0	1	1	1	3	1	.100	.100	4	0	2B-6

Randy Bobb

BOBB, MARK RANDALL
B. Jan. 1, 1948, Los Angeles, Calif.   BR TR 6'1"   195 lbs.

	G	AB	H	2B	3B	HR	HR%	R	RBI	BB	SO	SB	BA	SA	AB	H	G by POS
1968 CHI N	7	8	1	0	0	0	0.0	0	0	1	2	0	.125	.125	0	0	C-7
1969	3	2	0	0	0	0	0.0	0	0	0	1	0	.000	.000	0	0	C-2
2 yrs.	10	10	1	0	0	0	0.0	0	0	1	3	0	.100	.100	0	0	C-9

John Boccabella

BOCCABELLA, JOHN DOMINIC
B. June 29, 1941, San Francisco, Calif.   BR TR 6'1"   195 lbs.

	G	AB	H	2B	3B	HR	HR%	R	RBI	BB	SO	SB	BA	SA	AB	H	G by POS
1963 CHI N	24	74	14	4	1	1	1.4	7	5	6	21	0	.189	.311	1	0	1B-24
1964	9	23	9	2	1	0	0.0	4	6	0	3	0	.391	.565	3	1	1B-5, OF-2
1965	6	12	4	0	0	2	16.7	2	4	1	2	0	.333	.833	2	1	1B-2, OF-1
1966	75	206	47	9	0	6	2.9	22	25	14	39	0	.228	.359	16	2	OF-33, 1B-30, C-5
1967	25	35	6	1	1	0	0.0	0	8	3	7	0	.171	.257	11	2	OF-9, 1B-3, C-1
1968	7	14	1	0	0	0	0.0	0	1	2	2	0	.071	.071	2	0	C-4, OF-1
1969 MON N	40	86	9	2	0	1	1.2	4	6	4	30	1	.105	.163	7	1	C-32
1970	61	145	39	3	1	5	3.4	18	17	11	24	0	.269	.407	8	2	1B-33, C-24, 3B-1
1971	74	177	39	11	0	3	1.7	15	15	14	26	0	.220	.333	5	0	1B-37, C-37, 3B-2
1972	83	207	47	8	1	1	0.5	14	10	9	29	1	.227	.290	3	0	C-73, 1B-7, 3B-1
1973	118	403	94	13	0	7	1.7	25	46	26	57	1	.233	.318	1	0	C-117, 1B-1
1974 SF N	29	80	11	3	0	0	0.0	6	5	4	6	0	.138	.175	4	0	C-26
12 yrs.	551	1462	320	56	5	26	1.8	117	148	96	246	3	.219	.317	63	9	C-319, 1B-142, OF-46, 3B-4

Milt Bocek

BOCEK, MILTON FRANK
B. July 16, 1912, Chicago, Ill.   BR TR 6'1"   185 lbs.

	G	AB	H	2B	3B	HR	HR%	R	RBI	BB	SO	SB	BA	SA	AB	H	G by POS
1933 CHI A	11	22	8	1	0	1	4.5	3	3	4	6	0	.364	.545	5	1	OF-6
1934	19	38	8	1	0	0	0.0	3	3	5	5	0	.211	.237	6	0	OF-10
2 yrs.	30	60	16	2	0	1	1.7	6	6	9	11	0	.267	.350	11	1	OF-16

Bruce Bochte

BOCHTE, BRUCE ANTON
B. Nov. 12, 1950, Pasadena, Calif.   BL TL 6'3"   195 lbs.

	G	AB	H	2B	3B	HR	HR%	R	RBI	BB	SO	SB	BA	SA	AB	H	G by POS
1974 CAL A	57	196	53	4	1	5	2.6	24	26	18	23	6	.270	.378	1	0	OF-39, 1B-24
1975	107	375	107	19	3	3	0.8	41	48	45	43	3	.285	.376	3	1	1B-105, DH-1
1976	146	466	120	17	1	2	0.4	53	49	64	53	4	.258	.311	8	3	OF-86, 1B-59, DH-1
1977 2 teams							CAL A (25G – .290)			CLE A (112G – .304)							
" total	137	492	148	23	1	7	1.4	64	51	47	42	6	.301	.394	1	0	OF-100, 1B-36, DH-2
1978 SEA A	140	486	128	25	3	11	2.3	58	51	60	47	3	.263	.395	5	3	OF-91, DH-43, 1B-1
1979	150	554	175	38	6	16	2.9	81	100	67	64	2	.316	.493	4	2	1B-147
1980	148	520	156	34	4	13	2.5	62	78	72	81	2	.300	.456	6	1	1B-133, DH-11
1981	99	335	87	16	0	6	1.8	39	30	47	53	1	.260	.361	2	0	1B-82, OF-14, DH-1
1982	144	509	151	21	0	12	2.4	58	70	67	71	8	.297	.409	4	2	OF-99, 1B-34, DH-12
1984 OAK A	148	469	120	23	0	5	1.1	58	52	52	59	2	.264	.345	11	4	1B-144, DH-2
10 yrs.	1276	4402	1249	220	19	80	1.8	538	555	539	536	37	.284	.397	51	18	1B-765, OF-429, DH-73

	G	AB	H	2B	3B	HR	HR %	R	RBI	BB	SO	SB	BA	SA	Pinch Hit AB	Pinch Hit H	G by POS

Bruce Bochy

BOCHY, BRUCE DOUGLAS
B. Apr. 16, 1955, Landes De Bussac, France
BR TR 6'3" 205 lbs.

	G	AB	H	2B	3B	HR	HR%	R	RBI	BB	SO	SB	BA	SA	PH AB	PH H	G by POS
1978 HOU N	54	154	41	8	0	3	1.9	8	15	11	35	0	.266	.377	3	0	C-53
1979	56	129	28	4	0	1	0.8	11	6	13	25	0	.217	.271	3	0	C-55
1980	22	22	4	1	0	0	0.0	0	0	5	7	0	.182	.227	9	1	C-10, 1B-1
1982 NY N	17	49	15	4	0	2	4.1	4	8	4	6	0	.306	.510	0	0	C-16, 1B-1
1983 SD N	23	42	9	1	1	0	0.0	2	3	0	9	0	.214	.286	12	4	C-11
1984	37	92	21	5	1	4	4.3	10	15	3	21	0	.228	.435	1	0	C-36
6 yrs.	209	488	118	23	2	10	2.0	35	47	36	103	0	.242	.359	28	5	C-181, 1B-2

LEAGUE CHAMPIONSHIP SERIES

| 1980 HOU N | 1 | 1 | 0 | 0 | 0 | 0 | 0.0 | 0 | 0 | 0 | 0 | 0 | .000 | .000 | 0 | 0 | C-1 |

WORLD SERIES

| 1984 SD N | 1 | 1 | 1 | 0 | 0 | 0 | 0.0 | 0 | 0 | 0 | 0 | 0 | 1.000 | 1.000 | 1 | 1 | |

Eddie Bockman

BOCKMAN, JOSEPH EDWARD
B. July 26, 1920, Santa Ana, Calif.
BR TR 5'9" 175 lbs.

	G	AB	H	2B	3B	HR	HR%	R	RBI	BB	SO	SB	BA	SA	PH AB	PH H	G by POS
1946 NY A	4	12	1	1	0	0	0.0	2	0	1	4	0	.083	.167	0	0	3B-4
1947 CLE A	96	66	17	2	2	1	1.5	8	14	5	17	0	.258	.394	20	5	3B-12, 2B-4, OF-1, SS-1
1948 PIT N	70	176	42	7	1	4	2.3	23	23	17	35	2	.239	.358	11	2	3B-51, 2B-1
1949	79	220	49	6	1	6	2.7	21	19	23	31	3	.223	.341	5	2	3B-68, 2B-5
4 yrs.	249	474	109	16	4	11	2.3	54	56	46	87	5	.230	.350	36	9	3B-135, 2B-10, OF-1, SS-1

Ping Bodie

BODIE, FRANK STEPHAN
Born Francesco Stephano Pezzolo.
B. Oct. 8, 1887, San Francisco, Calif.   D. Dec. 17, 1961, San Francisco, Calif.
BR TR 5'8" 195 lbs.

	G	AB	H	2B	3B	HR	HR%	R	RBI	BB	SO	SB	BA	SA	PH AB	PH H	G by POS
1911 CHI A	145	551	159	27	13	4	0.7	75	97	49		14	.289	.407	1	0	OF-128, 2B-16
1912	137	472	139	24	7	5	1.1	58	72	43		12	.294	.407	7	3	OF-130
1913	127	406	107	14	8	8	2.0	43	48	35	57	5	.264	.397	6	0	OF-119
1914	107	327	75	9	5	3	0.9	21	29	21	35	12	.229	.315	10	2	OF-95
1917 PHI A	148	557	162	28	11	7	1.3	51	74	53	40	13	.291	.418	2	0	OF-145, 1B-1
1918 NY A	91	324	83	12	6	3	0.9	36	46	27	24	6	.256	.358	1	0	OF-90
1919	134	475	132	27	8	6	1.3	45	59	36	46	15	.278	.406	0	0	OF-134
1920	129	471	139	26	12	7	1.5	63	79	40	30	6	.295	.446	0	0	OF-129
1921	31	87	15	2	2	0	0.0	5	12	8	8	0	.172	.241	6	0	OF-25
9 yrs.	1049	3670	1011	169	72	43	1.2	397	516	312	240	83	.275	.396	33	5	OF-995, 2B-16, 1B-1

Tony Boeckel

BOECKEL, NORMAN DOXIE (Elmer)
B. Aug. 25, 1892, Los Angeles, Calif.   D. Feb. 16, 1924, Torrey Pines, Calif.
BR TR 5'10½" 175 lbs.

	G	AB	H	2B	3B	HR	HR%	R	RBI	BB	SO	SB	BA	SA	PH AB	PH H	G by POS
1917 PIT N	64	219	58	11	1	0	0.0	16	23	8	31	6	.265	.324	2	0	3B-62
1919 2 teams		PIT	N (45G – .250)					BOS	N (95G – .249)								
" total	140	517	129	20	7	1	0.2	60	42	53	33	21	.250	.321	2	1	3B-138
1920 BOS N	153	582	156	28	5	3	0.5	70	62	38	50	18	.268	.349	0	0	3B-151, SS-3, 2B-1
1921	153	592	185	20	13	10	1.7	93	84	52	41	20	.313	.441	0	0	3B-153
1922	119	402	116	19	6	6	1.5	61	47	35	32	14	.289	.410	13	4	3B-106
1923	148	568	169	32	4	7	1.2	72	79	51	31	11	.298	.405	0	0	3B-147, SS-1
6 yrs.	777	2880	813	130	36	27	0.9	372	337	237	218	90	.282	.381	17	5	3B-757, SS-4, 2B-1

Len Boehmer

BOEHMER, LEONARD JOSEPH
B. June 28, 1941, Flint Hill, Mo.
BR TR 6'1" 192 lbs.

	G	AB	H	2B	3B	HR	HR%	R	RBI	BB	SO	SB	BA	SA	PH AB	PH H	G by POS
1967 CIN N	2	3	0	0	0	0	0.0	0	0	0	0	0	.000	.000	0	0	2B-1
1969 NY A	45	108	19	4	0	0	0.0	5	7	8	10	0	.176	.213	15	1	1B-21, 3B-8, SS-1, 2B-1
1971	3	5	0	0	0	0	0.0	0	0	0	0	0	.000	.000	2	0	3B-1
3 yrs.	50	116	19	4	0	0	0.0	5	7	8	10	0	.164	.198	17	1	1B-21, 3B-9, 2B-2, SS-1

Terry Bogener

BOGENER, TERRENCE WAYNE
B. Sept. 28, 1955, Hannibal, Mo.
BL TL 6' 193 lbs.

	G	AB	H	2B	3B	HR	HR%	R	RBI	BB	SO	SB	BA	SA	PH AB	PH H	G by POS
1982 TEX A	24	60	13	2	1	1	1.7	6	4	8	2	.217	.333	3	0	OF-16, DH-4

Wade Boggs

BOGGS, WADE ANTHONY
B. June 15, 1958, Omaha, Neb.
BR TL 6'2" 185 lbs.

	G	AB	H	2B	3B	HR	HR%	R	RBI	BB	SO	SB	BA	SA	PH AB	PH H	G by POS
1982 BOS A	104	338	118	14	1	5	1.5	51	44	35	21	1	.349	.441	13	4	1B-49, 3B-44, DH-3, OF-1
1983	153	582	210	44	7	5	0.9	100	74	92	36	3	.361	.486	0	0	3B-155, DH-2
1984	158	625	203	31	4	6	1.0	109	55	89	44	3	.325	.416	1	0	3B-155, DH-2
3 yrs.	415	1545	531	89	12	16	1.0	260	173	216	101	7	.344	.448	14	4	3B-352, 1B-49, DH-5, OF-1

Charlie Bohn

BOHN, CHARLES
B. 1857, Cleveland, Ohio   D. Aug. 1, 1903, Cleveland, Ohio

	G	AB	H	2B	3B	HR	HR%	R	RBI	BB	SO	SB	BA	SA	PH AB	PH H	G by POS
1882 LOU AA	4	13	2	0	0	0	0.0	0		0			.154	.154	0	0	OF-2, P-2

Sammy Bohne

BOHNE, SAMMY ARTHUR
Born Sammy Arthur Cohen.
B. Oct. 22, 1896, San Francisco, Calif.   D. May 23, 1977, Menlo Park, Calif.
BR TR 5'7½" 170 lbs.

	G	AB	H	2B	3B	HR	HR%	R	RBI	BB	SO	SB	BA	SA	PH AB	PH H	G by POS
1916 STL N	14	38	9	0	0	0	0.0	3	0	4	6	3	.237	.237	0	0	SS-14
1921 CIN N	153	613	175	28	16	3	0.5	98	44	54	38	26	.285	.398	0	0	2B-102, 3B-53
1922	112	383	105	14	5	3	0.8	53	51	39	18	13	.274	.360	2	0	2B-85, SS-22
1923	139	539	136	18	10	3	0.6	77	47	48	37	16	.252	.340	0	0	2B-96, 3B-35, SS-9, 1B-1
1924	100	349	89	15	9	4	1.1	42	46	18	24	9	.255	.384	0	0	2B-48, 3B-40, 3B-12
1925	73	214	55	9	1	2	0.9	24	24	14	14	6	.257	.336	3	1	SS-49, 2B-10, OF-4, 3B-2, 1B-2
1926 2 teams		CIN	N (25G – .204)					BKN	N (47G – .200)								
" total	72	179	36	3	4	1	0.6	12	16	16	17	2	.201	.279	0	0	2B-31, SS-20, 3B-15
7 yrs.	663	2315	605	87	45	16	0.7	309	228	193	154	75	.261	.359	5	4	2B-372, SS-154, 3B-117, OF-4, 1B-3

	G	AB	H	2B	3B	HR	HR %	R	RBI	BB	SO	SB	BA	SA	Pinch Hit AB	Pinch Hit H	G by POS

Bruce Boisclair

BOISCLAIR, BRUCE ARMAND
B. Dec. 9, 1952, Putnam, Conn. BL TL 6'2" 185 lbs.

	G	AB	H	2B	3B	HR	HR %	R	RBI	BB	SO	SB	BA	SA	AB	H	G by POS
1974 NY N	7	12	3	1	0	0	0.0	0	1	1	4	0	.250	.333	0	0	OF-5
1976	110	286	82	13	3	2	0.7	42	13	28	55	9	.287	.374	21	12	OF-87
1977	127	307	90	21	1	4	1.3	41	44	31	57	6	.293	.407	30	9	OF-91, 1B-9
1978	107	214	48	7	1	4	1.9	24	15	23	43	3	.224	.322	47	12	OF-69, 1B-1
1979	59	98	18	5	1	0	0.0	7	4	3	24	0	.184	.255	35	5	OF-24, 1B-1
5 yrs.	410	917	241	47	6	10	1.1	114	77	86	183	18	.263	.360	133	38	OF-276, 1B-11

Bob Boken

BOKEN, ROBERT ANTHONY
B. Feb. 23, 1908, Maryville, Ill. BR TR 6'2" 165 lbs.

	G	AB	H	2B	3B	HR	HR %	R	RBI	BB	SO	SB	BA	SA	AB	H	G by POS
1933 WAS A	55	133	37	5	2	3	2.3	19	26	9	16	0	.278	.414	7	2	2B-31, 3B-19, SS-10
1934 2 teams			WAS A	(11G –	.222)			CHI A	(81G –	.236)							
" total	92	324	76	10	2	3	0.9	35	46	18	33	4	.235	.306	5	2	2B-58, SS-22, 3B-6
2 yrs.	147	457	113	15	4	6	1.3	54	72	27	49	4	.247	.337	12	4	2B-89, SS-32, 3B-25

Ed Boland

BOLAND, EDWARD JOHN
B. Apr. 18, 1908, Long Island City, N. Y. BL TL 5'10" 165 lbs.

	G	AB	H	2B	3B	HR	HR %	R	RBI	BB	SO	SB	BA	SA	AB	H	G by POS
1934 PHI N	8	30	9	1	0	0	0.0	2	5	0	2	1	.300	.400	1	0	OF-7
1935	30	47	10	0	0	0	0.0	5	4	4	6	1	.213	.213	17	2	OF-10
1944 WAS A	19	59	16	4	0	0	0.0	4	14	0	6	0	.271	.339	5	1	OF-14
3 yrs.	57	136	35	5	0	0	0.0	11	23	4	14	2	.257	.309	23	3	OF-31

Charlie Bold

BOLD, CHARLES DICKENS (Dutch)
B. Oct. 27, 1894, Karlskrong, Sweden   D. Jan. 29, 1978, Chelsea, Mass. BR TR 6'2" 185 lbs.

	G	AB	H	2B	3B	HR	HR %	R	RBI	BB	SO	SB	BA	SA	AB	H	G by POS
1914 STL A	2	1	0	0	0	0	0.0	0	0	0	1	0	.000	.000	0	0	1B-1

Carl Boles

BOLES, CARL THEODORE
B. Oct. 31, 1934, Center Point, Ark. BR TR 5'11" 185 lbs.

	G	AB	H	2B	3B	HR	HR %	R	RBI	BB	SO	SB	BA	SA	AB	H	G by POS
1962 SF N	19	24	9	0	0	0	0.0	4	1	0	6	0	.375	.375	11	4	OF-7

Joe Boley

BOLEY, JOHN PETER
Born John Peter Bolinsky.
B. July 19, 1896, Mahoney City, Pa.   D. Dec. 30, 1962, Mahoney City, Pa. BR TR 5'11" 170 lbs.

	G	AB	H	2B	3B	HR	HR %	R	RBI	BB	SO	SB	BA	SA	AB	H	G by POS
1927 PHI A	116	370	115	18	8	1	0.3	49	52	26	14	8	.311	.411	0	0	SS-114
1928	132	425	112	20	3	0	0.0	49	49	32	11	5	.264	.325	0	0	SS-132
1929	91	303	76	17	6	2	0.7	36	47	24	16	1	.251	.366	0	0	SS-88, 3B-1
1930	121	420	116	22	2	4	1.0	41	55	32	26	0	.276	.367	1	0	SS-120
1931	67	224	51	9	3	0	0.0	26	20	15	13	1	.228	.295	4	1	SS-62, 2B-1
1932 2 teams			PHI A	(10G –	.206)			CLE A	(1G –	.250)							
" total	11	38	8	2	0	0	0.0	2	4	1	4	0	.211	.263	0	0	SS-11
6 yrs.	538	1780	478	88	22	7	0.4	203	227	130	84	15	.269	.354	6	1	SS-527, 3B-1, 2B-1
WORLD SERIES																	
1929 PHI A	5	17	4	0	0	0	0.0	1	1	0	3	0	.235	.235	0	0	SS-5
1930	6	21	2	0	0	0	0.0	1	1	0	1	0	.095	.095	0	0	SS-6
1931	1	1	0	0	0	0	0.0	0	0	0	1	0	.000	.000	1	0	
3 yrs.	12	39	6	0	0	0	0.0	2	2	0	5	0	.154	.154	1	0	SS-11

Jim Bolger

BOLGER, JAMES CYRIL (Dutch)
B. Feb. 23, 1932, Cincinnati, Ohio BR TR 6'2" 180 lbs.

	G	AB	H	2B	3B	HR	HR %	R	RBI	BB	SO	SB	BA	SA	AB	H	G by POS
1950 CIN N	2	1	0	0	0	0	0.0	0	0	0	0	0	.000	.000	0	0	OF-2
1951	2	0	0	0	0	0	–	1	0	0	0	1	–	–	0	0	
1954	5	3	1	0	0	0	0.0	1	0	0	1	0	.333	.333	2	0	OF-2
1955 CHI N	64	160	33	5	4	0	0.0	19	7	9	17	2	.206	.288	1	1	OF-51
1957	112	273	75	4	1	5	1.8	28	29	10	36	0	.275	.352	48	17	OF-63, 3B-3
1958	84	120	27	4	1	1	0.8	15	11	9	20	0	.225	.300	51	10	OF-37
1959 2 teams			CLE A	(8G –	.000)			PHI N	(35G –	.083)							
" total	43	55	4	1	0	0	0.0	1	1	4	9	0	.073	.091	32	4	OF-9
7 yrs.	312	612	140	14	6	6	1.0	65	48	32	83	3	.229	.301	134	32	OF-164, 3B-3

Frank Bolling

BOLLING, FRANK ELMORE
Brother of Milt Bolling.
B. Nov. 16, 1931, Mobile, Ala. BR TR 6'1" 175 lbs.

	G	AB	H	2B	3B	HR	HR %	R	RBI	BB	SO	SB	BA	SA	AB	H	G by POS
1954 DET A	117	368	87	15	2	6	1.6	46	38	36	51	3	.236	.337	3	0	2B-113
1956	102	366	103	21	7	7	1.9	53	45	42	51	6	.281	.434	0	0	2B-102
1957	146	576	149	27	6	15	2.6	72	40	57	64	4	.259	.405	0	0	2B-146
1958	154	610	164	25	4	14	2.3	91	75	54	54	6	.269	.392	0	0	2B-154
1959	127	459	122	18	3	13	2.8	56	55	45	37	2	.266	.403	1	0	2B-126
1960	139	536	136	20	4	9	1.7	64	59	40	48	7	.254	.356	1	0	2B-138
1961 MIL N	148	585	153	16	4	15	2.6	86	56	57	62	7	.262	.379	0	0	2B-148
1962	122	406	110	17	4	9	2.2	45	43	35	45	2	.271	.399	5	1	2B-119
1963	142	542	132	18	2	5	0.9	73	43	41	47	2	.244	.312	0	0	2B-141
1964	120	352	70	11	1	5	1.4	35	34	21	44	0	.199	.278	7	0	2B-117
1965	148	535	141	26	3	7	1.3	55	50	24	41	0	.264	.363	1	0	2B-147
1966 ATL N	75	227	48	7	0	1	0.4	16	18	10	14	1	.211	.256	11	1	2B-67
12 yrs.	1540	5562	1415	221	40	106	1.9	692	556	462	558	40	.254	.366	29	2	2B-1518

John Bolling

BOLLING, JOHN EDWARD
B. Feb. 20, 1917, Mobile, Ala. BL TL 5'11" 168 lbs.

	G	AB	H	2B	3B	HR	HR %	R	RBI	BB	SO	SB	BA	SA	AB	H	G by POS
1939 PHI N	69	211	61	11	0	3	1.4	27	13	11	10	6	.289	.384	17	4	1B-48
1944 BKN N	56	131	46	14	1	1	0.8	21	25	14	4	0	.351	.496	24	6	1B-27
2 yrs.	125	342	107	25	1	4	1.2	48	38	25	14	6	.313	.427	41	10	1B-75

	G	AB	H	2B	3B	HR	HR%	R	RBI	BB	SO	SB	BA	SA	Pinch Hit AB	Pinch Hit H	G by POS

Milt Bolling

BOLLING, MILTON JOSEPH
Brother of Frank Bolling.
B. Aug. 9, 1930, Mississippi City, Miss.   BR TR 6'1"   177 lbs.

	G	AB	H	2B	3B	HR	HR%	R	RBI	BB	SO	SB	BA	SA	AB	H	G by POS
1952 BOS A	11	36	8	1	0	1	2.8	4	3	3	5	0	.222	.333	0	0	SS-11
1953	109	323	85	12	1	5	1.5	30	28	24	41	1	.263	.353	1	0	SS-109
1954	113	370	92	20	3	6	1.6	42	36	47	55	2	.249	.368	1	0	SS-107, 3B-5
1955	6	5	1	0	0	0	0.0	0	0	0	1	0	.200	.200	2	0	SS-2
1956	45	118	25	3	2	3	2.5	19	8	18	20	0	.212	.347	5	2	SS-26, 3B-11, 2B-1
1957 2 teams		BOS	A (1G – .000)				WAS	A	(91G – .227)								
" total	92	278	63	12	1	4	1.4	29	19	18	59	2	.227	.320	4	0	2B-53, SS-37, 3B-1
1958 DET A	24	31	6	2	0	0	0.0	3	0	5	7	0	.194	.258	4	0	SS-13, 3B-1, 2B-1
7 yrs.	400	1161	280	50	7	19	1.6	127	94	115	188	5	.241	.345	17	2	SS-305, 2B-55, 3B-18

Don Bollweg

BOLLWEG, DONALD RAYMOND
B. Feb. 12, 1921, Wheaton, Ill.   BL TL 6'1"   190 lbs.

	G	AB	H	2B	3B	HR	HR%	R	RBI	BB	SO	SB	BA	SA	AB	H	G by POS
1950 STL N	4	11	2	0	0	0	0.0	1	1	1	1	0	.182	.182	0	0	1B-4
1951	6	9	1	1	0	0	0.0	1	2	0	1	0	.111	.222	4	1	1B-2
1953 NY A	70	155	46	6	4	6	3.9	24	24	21	31	1	.297	.503	21	5	1B-43
1954 PHI A	103	268	60	15	3	5	1.9	35	24	35	33	1	.224	.358	29	6	1B-71
1955 KC A	12	9	1	0	0	0	0.0	1	2	3	2	0	.111	.111	9	1	1B-3
5 yrs.	195	452	110	22	7	11	2.4	62	53	60	68	2	.243	.396	63	13	1B-123
WORLD SERIES																	
1953 NY A	3	2	0	0	0	0	0.0	0	0	0	2	0	.000	.000	2	0	1B-1

Cecil Bolton

BOLTON, CECIL GLENFORD (Lefty)
B. Feb. 13, 1904, Boonville, Miss.   BL TL 6'4"   195 lbs.

	G	AB	H	2B	3B	HR	HR%	R	RBI	BB	SO	SB	BA	SA	AB	H	G by POS
1928 CLE A	4	13	2	0	2	0	0.0	1	0	2	2	0	.154	.462	0	0	1B-4

Cliff Bolton

BOLTON, WILLIAM CLIFTON
B. Apr. 10, 1907, High Point, N. C.   D. Apr. 21, 1979, Lexington, Ky.   BL TR 5'9"   160 lbs.

	G	AB	H	2B	3B	HR	HR%	R	RBI	BB	SO	SB	BA	SA	AB	H	G by POS
1931 WAS A	23	43	11	1	1	0	0.0	3	6	1	5	0	.256	.326	10	6	C-13
1933	33	39	16	1	1	0	0.0	4	6	6	3	0	.410	.487	22	9	C-9, OF-1
1934	42	148	40	9	1	1	0.7	12	17	11	9	2	.270	.365	3	2	C-39
1935	110	375	114	18	11	2	0.5	47	55	56	13	0	.304	.427	3	0	C-106
1936	86	289	84	18	4	2	0.7	41	51	25	12	1	.291	.401	5	1	C-83
1937 DET A	27	57	15	2	0	1	1.8	6	7	8	6	0	.263	.351	13	3	C-13
1941 WAS A	14	11	0	0	0	0	0.0	0	1	1	2	0	.000	.000	10	0	C-3
7 yrs.	335	962	280	49	18	6	0.6	113	143	108	50	3	.291	.398	66	21	C-266, OF-1
WORLD SERIES																	
1933 WAS A	2	2	0	0	0	0	0.0	0	0	0	0	0	.000	.000	2	0	

Tommy Bond

BOND, THOMAS HENRY
B. Apr. 2, 1856, Granard, Ireland   D. Jan. 24, 1941, Boston, Mass.
Manager 1882.   BR TR 5'7½"   160 lbs.

	G	AB	H	2B	3B	HR	HR%	R	RBI	BB	SO	SB	BA	SA	AB	H	G by POS
1876 HAR N	45	182	50	8	0	0	0.0	18	21	0	4		.275	.319	0	0	P-45
1877 BOS N	61	259	59	4	3	0	0.0	32	30	1	15		.228	.266	0	0	P-58, OF-3
1878	59	236	50	4	1	0	0.0	22	23	0	9		.212	.237	0	0	P-59, OF-2
1879	65	257	62	3	1	0	0.0	35	21	6	8		.241	.261	0	0	P-64, OF-5, 1B-1
1880	76	282	62	4	1	0	0.0	27	24	8	14		.220	.241	0	0	P-63, OF-26, 3B-1, 1B-1
1881	3	10	2	0	0	0	0.0	0	0	0	0		.200	.200	0	0	P-3
1882 WOR N	8	30	4	0	0	0	0.0	1	2	2	3		.133	.133	0	0	OF-8, P-2
1884 2 teams		BOS	U (37G – .296)				IND	AA	(7G – .130)								
" total	44	185	51	9	1	0	0.0	21		4			.276	.335	0	0	P-28, OF-19, 3B-1
8 yrs.	361	1441	340	32	7	0	0.0	156	121	21	53		.236	.268	0	0	P-322, OF-63, 3B-2, 1B-2

Walt Bond

BOND, WALTER FRANKLIN
B. Oct. 19, 1937, Denmark, Tenn.   D. Sept. 14, 1967, Houston, Tex.   BL TR 6'7"   228 lbs.

	G	AB	H	2B	3B	HR	HR%	R	RBI	BB	SO	SB	BA	SA	AB	H	G by POS
1960 CLE A	40	131	29	2	1	5	3.8	19	18	13	14	4	.221	.366	5	0	OF-36
1961	38	52	9	1	1	2	3.8	7	7	6	10	1	.173	.346	23	2	OF-12
1962	12	50	19	3	0	6	12.0	10	17	4	9	1	.380	.800	0	0	OF-12
1964 HOU N	148	543	138	16	7	20	3.7	63	85	38	90	2	.254	.420	2	0	1B-76, OF-71
1965	117	407	107	17	2	7	1.7	46	47	42	51	2	.263	.366	7	1	1B-74, OF-38
1967 MIN A	10	16	5	1	0	1	6.3	4	5	3	1	0	.313	.563	5	2	OF-3
6 yrs.	365	1199	307	40	11	41	3.4	149	179	106	175	10	.256	.410	42	5	OF-172, 1B-150

Bobby Bonds

BONDS, BOBBY LEE
B. Mar. 15, 1946, Riverside, Calif.   BR TR 6'1"   190 lbs.

	G	AB	H	2B	3B	HR	HR%	R	RBI	BB	SO	SB	BA	SA	AB	H	G by POS
1968 SF N	81	307	78	10	5	9	2.9	55	35	38	84	16	.254	.407	0	0	OF-80
1969	158	622	161	25	6	32	5.1	120	90	81	187	45	.259	.473	1	0	OF-155
1970	157	663	200	36	10	26	3.9	134	78	77	189	48	.302	.504	2	0	OF-157
1971	155	619	178	32	4	33	5.3	110	102	62	137	26	.288	.512	3	1	OF-154
1972	153	626	162	29	5	26	4.2	118	80	60	137	44	.259	.446	0	0	OF-153
1973	160	643	182	34	4	39	6.1	131	96	87	148	43	.283	.530	2	1	OF-158
1974	150	567	145	22	8	21	3.7	97	71	95	134	41	.256	.434	3	1	OF-148
1975 NY A	145	529	143	26	3	32	6.0	93	85	89	137	30	.270	.512	4	1	OF-129, DH-12
1976 CAL A	99	378	100	10	3	10	2.6	48	54	41	90	30	.265	.386	1	0	OF-98, DH-1
1977	158	592	156	23	9	37	6.3	103	115	74	141	41	.264	.520	1	0	OF-140, DH-18
1978 2 teams		CHI	A (26G – .278)				TEX	A	(130G – .265)								
" total	156	565	151	19	4	31	5.5	93	90	79	120	43	.267	.480	2	1	OF-133, DH-21
1979 CLE A	146	538	148	24	1	25	4.6	93	85	74	135	34	.275	.463	1	0	OF-116, DH-29
1980 STL N	86	231	47	5	3	5	2.2	37	24	33	74	15	.203	.316	15	2	OF-70
1981 CHI N	45	163	35	7	1	6	3.7	26	19	24	44	5	.215	.380	0	0	OF-44
14 yrs.	1849	7043	1886	302	66	332	4.7	1258	1024	914	1757 **4th**	461	.268	.471	35	7	OF-1736, DH-81
LEAGUE CHAMPIONSHIP SERIES																	
1971 SF N	3	8	2	0	0	0	0.0	0	0	2	4	0	.250	.250	0	0	OF-3

	G	AB	H	2B	3B	HR	HR%	R	RBI	BB	SO	SB	BA	SA	Pinch Hit AB	Pinch Hit H	G by POS

George Bone
BONE, GEORGE DRUMMOND
B. Aug. 28, 1876, New Haven, Conn.   D. May 26, 1918, West Haven, Conn.
TR 5'7"   152 lbs.

	G	AB	H	2B	3B	HR	HR%	R	RBI	BB	SO	SB	BA	SA	PH AB	PH H	G by POS
1901 MIL A	12	43	13	2	0	0	0.0	6	6	4			.302	.349	0	0	SS-12

Nino Bongiovanni
BONGIOVANNI, ANTHONY THOMAS
B. Dec. 21, 1911, Pike's Peak, La.
BL TL 5'10"   175 lbs.

	G	AB	H	2B	3B	HR	HR%	R	RBI	BB	SO	SB	BA	SA	PH AB	PH H	G by POS
1938 CIN N	2	7	2	1	0	0	0.0	0	0	0	0	0	.286	.429	0	0	OF-2
1939	66	159	41	6	0	0	0.0	17	16	9	8	0	.258	.296	27	7	OF-39
2 yrs.	68	166	43	7	0	0	0.0	17	16	9	8	0	.259	.301	27	7	OF-41

WORLD SERIES

	G	AB	H	2B	3B	HR	HR%	R	RBI	BB	SO	SB	BA	SA	PH AB	PH H	G by POS
1939 CIN N	1	1	0	0	0	0	0.0	0	0	0	0	0	.000	.000	1	0	

Juan Bonilla
BONILLA, JUAN GUILLERMO
B. Feb. 12, 1955, Santurce, Puerto Rico
BR TR 5'9"   170 lbs.

	G	AB	H	2B	3B	HR	HR%	R	RBI	BB	SO	SB	BA	SA	PH AB	PH H	G by POS
1981 SD N	99	369	107	13	2	1	0.3	30	25	25	23	4	.290	.344	0	0	2B-97
1982	45	182	51	6	2	0	0.0	21	8	11	15	0	.280	.335	0	0	2B-45
1983	152	556	132	17	4	4	0.7	55	45	50	40	3	.237	.304	4	1	2B-149
3 yrs.	296	1107	290	36	8	5	0.5	106	78	86	78	7	.262	.322	4	1	2B-291

Luther Bonin
BONIN, ERNEST LUTHER
B. Jan. 13, 1888, Green Hill, Ind.   D. Jan. 3, 1966, Sycamore, Ohio
BL TR 5'9½"   178 lbs.

	G	AB	H	2B	3B	HR	HR%	R	RBI	BB	SO	SB	BA	SA	PH AB	PH H	G by POS
1913 STL A	1	1	0	0	0	0	0.0	0	0	0	0	0	.000	.000	1	0	
1914 BUF F	20	76	14	4	1	0	0.0	6	4	7		3	.184	.263	0	0	OF-20
2 yrs.	21	77	14	4	1	0	0.0	6	4	7		3	.182	.260	1	0	OF-20

Barry Bonnell
BONNELL, ROBERT BARRY
B. Oct. 27, 1953, Cincinnati, Ohio
BR TR 6'3"   190 lbs.

	G	AB	H	2B	3B	HR	HR%	R	RBI	BB	SO	SB	BA	SA	PH AB	PH H	G by POS
1977 ATL N	100	360	108	11	0	1	0.3	41	45	37	32	7	.300	.339	7	1	OF-75, 3B-32
1978	117	304	73	11	3	1	0.3	36	16	20	30	12	.240	.306	1	0	OF-105, 3B-15
1979	127	375	97	20	3	12	3.2	47	45	26	55	8	.259	.424	4	1	OF-124, 3B-1
1980 TOR A	130	463	124	22	4	13	2.8	55	56	37	59	3	.268	.417	5	1	OF-122, DH-3
1981	66	227	50	7	4	4	1.8	21	28	12	25	4	.220	.339	2	0	OF-66
1982	140	437	128	26	3	6	1.4	59	49	32	51	14	.293	.407	22	4	OF-125, 3B-9, DH-6
1983	121	377	120	21	3	10	2.7	49	54	33	52	9	.318	.469	7	2	OF-117, 3B-4, DH-1
1984 SEA A	110	363	96	15	4	8	2.2	42	48	25	51	5	.264	.394	8	1	OF-94, 3B-10, 1B-5
8 yrs.	911	2906	796	133	24	55	1.9	350	341	222	355	62	.274	.393	56	10	OF-828, 3B-71, DH-10, 1B-5

Bob Bonner
BONNER, ROBERT AVERILL
B. Aug. 12, 1956, Uvalde, Tex.
BR TR 6'   185 lbs.

	G	AB	H	2B	3B	HR	HR%	R	RBI	BB	SO	SB	BA	SA	PH AB	PH H	G by POS
1980 BAL A	4	4	0	0	0	0	0.0	1	1	0	0	0	.000	.000	0	0	SS-3
1981	10	27	8	2	0	0	0.0	6	2	1	4	1	.296	.370	0	0	2B-9
1982	41	77	13	3	1	0	0.0	8	5	3	12	0	.169	.234	0	0	SS-38, 2B-3
1983	6	0	0	0	0	0	—	0	0	0	0	0	—	—	0	0	2B-5, DH-1
4 yrs.	61	108	21	5	1	0	0.0	15	8	4	16	1	.194	.259	0	0	SS-41, 2B-17, DH-1

Frank Bonner
BONNER, FRANK J (The Human Flea)
B. Aug. 20, 1869, Lowell, Mass.   D. Dec. 31, 1905, Kansas City, Mo.
TR 5'7½"   169 lbs.

	G	AB	H	2B	3B	HR	HR%	R	RBI	BB	SO	SB	BA	SA	PH AB	PH H	G by POS
1894 BAL N	33	118	38	10	2	0	0.0	27	24	17	5	12	.322	.441	1	0	2B-27, OF-4, 3B-2, SS-1
1895 2 teams	BAL N (11G – .333)							STL N (15G – .136)									
" total	26	101	22	1	2	1	1.0	12	15	6	9	6	.218	.297	0	0	3B-21, OF-5, C-1
1896 BKN N	9	34	6	2	0	0	0.0	8	5	2	8	1	.176	.235	0	0	2B-9
1899 WAS N	85	347	95	20	4	2	0.6	41	44	18		6	.274	.372	0	0	2B-85
1902 2 teams	CLE A (34G – .280)							PHI A (11G – .182)									
" total	45	176	45	6	0	0	0.0	16	17	5		1	.256	.290	0	0	2B-45
1903 BOS N	48	173	38	5	0	1	0.6	11	10	7		2	.220	.266	2	1	2B-24, SS-22
6 yrs.	246	949	244	44	8	4	0.4	115	115	55	22	28	.257	.333	3	1	2B-190, SS-23, 3B-23, OF-9, C-1

Zeke Bonura
BONURA, HENRY JOHN
B. Sept. 20, 1908, New Orleans, La.
BR TR 6'   210 lbs.

	G	AB	H	2B	3B	HR	HR%	R	RBI	BB	SO	SB	BA	SA	PH AB	PH H	G by POS
1934 CHI A	127	510	154	35	4	27	5.3	86	110	64	31	0	.302	.545	0	0	1B-127
1935	138	550	162	34	4	21	3.8	107	92	57	28	4	.295	.485	0	0	1B-138
1936	148	587	194	39	7	12	2.0	120	138	94	29	4	.330	.482	1	0	1B-146
1937	116	447	154	41	2	19	4.3	79	100	49	24	5	.345	.573	1	0	1B-115
1938 WAS A	137	540	156	27	3	22	4.1	72	114	44	29	2	.289	.472	8	2	1B-129
1939 NY N	123	455	146	26	6	11	2.4	75	85	46	22	1	.321	.477	0	0	1B-122
1940 2 teams	WAS A (79G – .273)							CHI N (49G – .264)									
" total	128	493	133	30	3	7	1.4	61	65	50	17	3	.270	.385	5	1	1B-123
7 yrs.	917	3582	1099	232	29	119	3.3	600	704	404	180	19	.307	.487	15	3	1B-900

Everett Booe
BOOE, EVERETT LITTLE
B. Sept. 28, 1890, Mocksville, N. C.   D. May 21, 1969, Kenedy, Tex.
BL TR 5'8½"   165 lbs.

	G	AB	H	2B	3B	HR	HR%	R	RBI	BB	SO	SB	BA	SA	PH AB	PH H	G by POS
1913 PIT N	29	80	16	0	2	0	0.0	9	2	6	9	2	.200	.250	6	1	OF-22
1914 2 teams	IND F (20G – .226)							BUF F (76G – .224)									
" total	96	272	61	10	2	0	0.0	34	20	28		12	.224	.276	14	3	OF-63, SS-11, 3B-2, 2B-1
2 yrs.	125	352	77	10	4	0	0.0	43	22	34	9	14	.219	.270	20	4	OF-85, SS-11, 3B-2, 2B-1

Buddy Booker
BOOKER, RICHARD LEE
B. May 28, 1942, Lynchburg, Va.
BL TR 5'10"   170 lbs.

	G	AB	H	2B	3B	HR	HR%	R	RBI	BB	SO	SB	BA	SA	PH AB	PH H	G by POS
1966 CLE A	18	28	6	1	0	2	7.1	6	5	2	6	0	.214	.464	8	0	C-12
1968 CHI A	5	5	0	0	0	0	0.0	0	0	1	2	0	.000	.000	4	0	C-3
2 yrs.	23	33	6	1	0	2	6.1	6	5	3	8	0	.182	.394	12	0	C-15

	G	AB	H	2B	3B	HR	HR %	R	RBI	BB	SO	SB	BA	SA	Pinch Hit AB	Pinch Hit H	G by POS

Al Bool

BOOL, ALBERT
B. Aug. 24, 1897, Lincoln, Neb.   D. Sept. 27, 1981, Lincoln, Neb.
BR TR 5'11"   180 lbs.

	G	AB	H	2B	3B	HR	HR %	R	RBI	BB	SO	SB	BA	SA	PH AB	PH H	G by POS
1928 WAS A	2	7	1	0	0	0	0.0	0	1	0	0	0	.143	.143	0	0	C-2
1930 PIT N	78	216	56	12	4	7	3.2	30	46	25	29	0	.259	.449	11	3	C-65
1931 BOS N	49	85	16	1	0	0	0.0	5	6	9	13	0	.188	.200	11	1	C-37
3 yrs.	129	308	73	13	4	7	2.3	35	53	34	42	0	.237	.373	22	4	C-104

Bob Boone

BOONE, ROBERT RAYMOND
Son of Ray Boone.
B. Nov. 19, 1947, San Diego, Calif.
BR TR 6'2½"   195 lbs.

	G	AB	H	2B	3B	HR	HR %	R	RBI	BB	SO	SB	BA	SA	PH AB	PH H	G by POS
1972 PHI N	16	51	14	1	0	1	2.0	4	4	5	7	1	.275	.353	3	0	C-14
1973	145	521	136	20	2	10	1.9	42	61	41	36	3	.261	.365	0	0	C-145
1974	146	488	118	24	3	3	0.6	41	52	35	29	3	.242	.322	0	0	C-146
1975	97	289	71	14	2	2	0.7	28	20	32	14	1	.246	.329	6	1	C-92, 3B-3
1976	121	361	98	18	2	4	1.1	40	54	45	44	2	.271	.366	12	4	C-108, 1B-4
1977	132	440	125	26	4	11	2.5	55	66	42	54	5	.284	.436	1	0	C-131, 3B-2
1978	132	435	123	18	4	12	2.8	48	62	46	37	2	.283	.425	5	1	C-129, 1B-3, OF-1
1979	119	398	114	21	3	9	2.3	38	58	49	33	1	.286	.422	1	0	C-117, 3B-2
1980	141	480	110	23	1	9	1.9	34	55	48	41	3	.229	.338	4	1	C-138
1981	76	227	48	7	0	4	1.8	19	24	22	16	2	.211	.295	4	0	C-75
1982 CAL A	143	472	121	17	0	7	1.5	42	58	39	34	0	.256	.337	0	0	C-143
1983	142	468	120	18	0	9	1.9	46	52	24	42	4	.256	.353	0	0	C-142
1984	139	450	91	16	1	3	0.7	33	32	25	45	3	.202	.262	2	2	C-137
13 yrs.	1549	5080	1289	223	22	84	1.7	470	598	453	432	30	.254	.356	39	10	C-1517, 3B-7, 1B-7, OF-1

DIVISIONAL PLAYOFF SERIES

	G	AB	H	2B	3B	HR	HR %	R	RBI	BB	SO	SB	BA	SA	PH AB	PH H	G by POS
1981 PHI N	3	5	0	0	0	0	0.0	0	0	0	0	0	.000	.000	0	0	C-3

LEAGUE CHAMPIONSHIP SERIES

	G	AB	H	2B	3B	HR	HR %	R	RBI	BB	SO	SB	BA	SA	PH AB	PH H	G by POS
1976 PHI N	3	7	2	0	0	0	0.0	1	1	0	0	0	.286	.286	0	0	C-3
1977	4	10	4	0	0	0	0.0	1	0	0	1	0	.400	.400	0	0	C-4
1978	3	11	2	0	0	0	0.0	0	0	0	0	0	.182	.182	0	0	C-3
1980	5	18	4	0	0	0	0.0	1	2	1	2	0	.222	.222	0	0	C-5
1982 CAL A	5	16	4	0	0	1	6.3	3	4	0	2	0	.250	.438	0	0	C-5
5 yrs.	20	62	16	0	0	1	1.6	5	7	2	5	0	.258	.306	0	0	C-20

WORLD SERIES

	G	AB	H	2B	3B	HR	HR %	R	RBI	BB	SO	SB	BA	SA	PH AB	PH H	G by POS
1980 PHI N	6	17	7	2	0	0	0.0	3	4	4	0	0	.412	.529	0	0	C-6

Ike Boone

BOONE, ISAAC MORGAN
Brother of Danny Boone.
B. Feb. 17, 1897, Samantha, Ala.   D. Aug. 1, 1958, Northport, Ala.
BL TR 6'   195 lbs.

	G	AB	H	2B	3B	HR	HR %	R	RBI	BB	SO	SB	BA	SA	PH AB	PH H	G by POS
1922 NY N	2	2	1	0	0	0	0.0	0	0	0	1	0	.500	.500	2	1	
1923 BOS A	5	15	4	0	1	0	0.0	1	2	1	0	0	.267	.400	1	0	OF-4
1924	128	486	162	29	3	13	2.7	71	96	55	32	2	.333	.486	4	1	OF-123
1925	133	476	157	34	5	9	1.9	79	68	60	19	1	.330	.479	11	3	OF-118
1927 CHI A	29	53	12	4	0	1	1.9	10	11	3	4	0	.226	.358	16	3	OF-11
1930 BKN N	40	101	30	1	1	3	3.0	13	13	14	8	0	.297	.495	9	3	OF-27
1931	6	5	1	0	0	0	0.0	0	0	2	2	0	.200	.200	5	1	
1932	13	21	3	1	0	0	0.0	2	2	5	2	0	.143	.190	5	0	OF-8
8 yrs.	356	1159	370	77	10	26	2.2	176	192	140	68	3	.319	.470	53	12	OF-291

Luke Boone

BOONE, LUTE JOSEPH (Danny)
B. May 6, 1890, Pittsburgh, Pa.   D. Aug. 21, 1982, Pittsburgh, Pa.
BR TR 5'9"   160 lbs.

	G	AB	H	2B	3B	HR	HR %	R	RBI	BB	SO	SB	BA	SA	PH AB	PH H	G by POS
1913 NY A	5	12	4	0	0	0	0.0	3	1	3	1	0	.333	.333	1	0	SS-4
1914	106	370	82	8	2	0	0.0	34	21	31	41	10	.222	.254	5	0	2B-90, 3B-9
1915	130	431	88	12	2	5	1.2	44	43	41	53	14	.204	.276	0	0	2B-115, SS-12, 3B-3
1916	46	124	23	4	0	1	0.8	14	8	8	10	7	.185	.242	0	0	3B-25, SS-12, 2B-7
1918 PIT N	27	91	18	3	0	0	0.0	7	3	8	6	1	.198	.231	0	0	SS-26, 2B-1
5 yrs.	314	1028	215	27	4	6	0.6	102	76	91	111	32	.209	.261	6	0	2B-213, SS-54, 3B-37

Ray Boone

BOONE, RAYMOND OTIS (Ike)
Father of Bob Boone.
B. July 27, 1923, San Diego, Calif.
BR TR 6'   172 lbs.

	G	AB	H	2B	3B	HR	HR %	R	RBI	BB	SO	SB	BA	SA	PH AB	PH H	G by POS
1948 CLE A	6	5	2	1	0	0	0.0	0	1	0	1	0	.400	.600	1	0	SS-4
1949	86	258	65	4	4	4	1.6	39	26	38	17	0	.252	.345	7	1	SS-76
1950	109	365	110	14	6	7	1.9	53	58	56	27	4	.301	.430	6	0	SS-102
1951	151	544	127	14	1	12	2.2	65	51	48	36	5	.233	.329	0	0	SS-96, 3B-2, 2B-1
1952	103	316	83	8	2	7	2.2	57	45	53	33	0	.263	.367	4	0	SS-102
1953 2 teams		CLE	A	(34G –	.241)			DET	A	(101G –	.312)						
" total	135	497	147	17	8	26	5.2	94	114	72	68	3	.296	.519	4	1	3B-97, SS-34
1954 DET A	148	543	160	19	7	20	3.7	76	85	71	53	4	.295	.466	0	0	3B-148, SS-1
1955	135	500	142	22	7	20	4.0	61	116	50	49	1	.284	.476	8	2	3B-126
1956	131	481	148	14	6	25	5.2	77	81	77	46	0	.308	.518	0	0	3B-130
1957	129	462	126	25	3	12	2.6	48	65	57	47	1	.273	.418	5	1	1B-117, 3B-4
1958 2 teams		DET	A	(39G –	.237)			CHI	A	(77G –	.244)						
" total	116	360	87	16	2	13	3.6	41	61	32	46	1	.242	.406	21	2	1B-95
1959 3 teams		CHI	A	(9G –	.238)			KC	A	(61G –	.273)	MIL	N	(13G –	.200)			
" total	83	168	44	6	0	4	2.4	25	19	38	24	2	.262	.369	37	11	1B-47, 3B-3
1960 2 teams		MIL	N	(7G –	.250)			BOS	A	(34G –	.205)						
" total	41	90	19	2	0	1	1.1	9	15	16	16	0	.211	.267	15	3	1B-26
13 yrs.	1373	4589	1260	162	46	151	3.3	645	737	608	463	21	.275	.429	108	21	3B-510, SS-464, 1B-285, 2B-1

WORLD SERIES

	G	AB	H	2B	3B	HR	HR %	R	RBI	BB	SO	SB	BA	SA	PH AB	PH H	G by POS
1948 CLE A	1	1	0	0	0	0	0.0	0	0	0	1	0	.000	.000	1	0	

Amos Booth

BOOTH, AMOS SMITH (The Darling)
B. Sept. 14, 1853, Cincinnati, Ohio   D. July 1, 1921, Miamisburg, Ohio
BR TR

	G	AB	H	2B	3B	HR	HR %	R	RBI	BB	SO	SB	BA	SA	PH AB	PH H	G by POS
1876 CIN N	63	272	71	3	0	0	0.0	31	14	9	11		.261	.272	0	0	3B-24, C-24, SS-22, OF-3, P-3

	G	AB	H	2B	3B	HR	HR %	R	RBI	BB	SO	SB	BA	SA	Pinch Hit AB	Pinch Hit H	G by POS

Amos Booth continued

	G	AB	H	2B	3B	HR	HR%	R	RBI	BB	SO	SB	BA	SA	PH AB	PH H	G by POS
1877	44	157	27	2	1	0	0.0	16	13	12	10		.172	.197	0	0	SS-13, C-12, P-12, 2B-10, 3B-3, OF-1
1880	1	2	0	0	0	0	0.0	0	0	0	0		.000	.000	0	0	3B-1
1882 2 teams	BAL	AA	(1G – .000)			LOU	AA	(1G – .000)									
" total	2	7	0	0	0	0	0.0	0		0			.000	.000	0	0	3B-1, 2B-1
4 yrs.	110	438	98	5	1	0	0.0	47	27	21	21		.224	.240	0	0	C-36, SS-35, 3B-29, P-15, 2B-11, OF-4

Eddie Booth

BOOTH, EDWARD H.
B. Brooklyn, N. Y.   Deceased.

	G	AB	H	2B	3B	HR	HR%	R	RBI	BB	SO	SB	BA	SA	PH AB	PH H	G by POS
1876 NY N	57	228	49	2	1	0	0.0	17	7	2	4		.215	.232	0	0	OF-53, 2B-5, P-1

Frenchy Bordagaray

BORDAGARAY, STANLEY GEORGE
B. Jan. 3, 1910, Coalinga, Calif.   BR TR 5'7½" 175 lbs.

	G	AB	H	2B	3B	HR	HR%	R	RBI	BB	SO	SB	BA	SA	PH AB	PH H	G by POS
1934 CHI A	29	87	28	3	1	0	0.0	12	2	3	8	1	.322	.379	12	8	OF-17
1935 BKN N	120	422	119	19	6	1	0.2	69	39	17	29	18	.282	.363	9	2	OF-105
1936	125	372	117	21	3	4	1.1	63	31	17	42	12	.315	.419	6	1	OF-92, 2B-11
1937 STL N	96	300	88	11	4	1	0.3	43	37	15	25	11	.293	.367	16	1	3B-50, OF-28
1938	81	156	44	5	1	0	0.0	19	21	8	9	2	.282	.327	43	20	OF-29, 3B-4
1939 CIN N	63	122	24	5	1	0	0.0	19	12	9	10	3	.197	.254	11	4	OF-43, 2B-2
1941 NY A	36	73	19	1	0	0	0.0	10	4	6	8	1	.260	.274	13	4	OF-19
1942 BKN N	48	58	14	2	0	0	0.0	11	5	3	3	2	.241	.276	15	4	OF-17
1943	89	268	81	18	2	0	0.0	47	19	30	15	6	.302	.384	6	2	OF-53, 3B-25
1944	130	501	141	26	4	6	1.2	85	51	36	22	2	.281	.385	10	3	3B-98, OF-25
1945	113	273	70	9	6	2	0.7	32	49	29	15	7	.256	.355	32	7	3B-57, OF-22
11 yrs.	930	2632	745	120	28	14	0.5	410	270	173	186	65	.283	.366	173	54	OF-450, 3B-234, 2B-13
WORLD SERIES																	
1939 CIN N	2	0	0	0	0	0	–	0	0	0	0	0	–	–	0	0	
1941 NY A	1	0	0	0	0	0	–	0	0	0	0	0	–	–	0	0	
2 yrs.	3	0	0	0	0	0	–	0	0	0	0	0	–	–	0	0	

Glenn Borgmann

BORGMANN, GLENN DENNIS
B. May 25, 1950, Paterson, N. J.   BR TR 6'4" 210 lbs.

	G	AB	H	2B	3B	HR	HR%	R	RBI	BB	SO	SB	BA	SA	PH AB	PH H	G by POS
1972 MIN A	56	175	41	4	0	3	1.7	11	14	25	25	0	.234	.309	0	0	C-56
1973	12	34	9	2	0	0	0.0	7	9	6	10	0	.265	.324	0	0	C-12
1974	128	345	87	8	1	3	0.9	33	45	39	44	2	.252	.307	1	0	C-128
1975	125	352	73	15	2	2	0.6	34	33	47	59	0	.207	.278	2	0	C-125
1976	24	65	16	3	0	1	1.5	10	6	19	7	1	.246	.338	1	1	C-24
1977	17	43	11	1	0	2	4.7	12	7	11	9	0	.256	.419	0	0	C-17
1978	49	123	26	4	1	3	2.4	16	15	18	17	0	.211	.333	3	1	C-46, DH-1
1979	31	70	14	3	0	0	0.0	4	8	12	11	1	.200	.243	0	0	C-31
1980 CHI A	32	87	19	2	0	2	2.3	10	14	14	9	0	.218	.310	1	0	C-32
9 yrs.	474	1294	296	42	4	16	1.2	137	151	191	191	4	.229	.304	11	2	C-471, DH-1

Bob Borkowski

BORKOWSKI, ROBERT VILARIAN (Bush)
B. Jan. 27, 1926, Dayton, Ohio   BR TR 6' 182 lbs.

	G	AB	H	2B	3B	HR	HR%	R	RBI	BB	SO	SB	BA	SA	PH AB	PH H	G by POS
1950 CHI N	85	256	70	7	4	4	1.6	27	27	16	30	1	.273	.379	14	2	OF-65, 1B-1
1951	58	89	14	1	0	0	0.0	9	10	3	16	0	.157	.169	23	3	OF-25
1952 CIN N	126	377	95	11	4	4	1.1	42	24	26	53	1	.252	.334	18	3	OF-103, 1B-5
1953	94	249	67	11	1	7	2.8	32	29	21	41	0	.269	.446	27	9	OF-67, 1B-3
1954	73	162	43	12	1	1	0.6	13	19	8	18	0	.265	.370	33	8	OF-36, 1B-3
1955 2 teams	CIN	N	(25G – .167)			BKN	N	(9G – .105)									
" total	34	37	5	1	0	0	0.0	3	1	2	8	0	.135	.162	9	2	OF-20, 1B-1
6 yrs.	470	1170	294	43	10	16	1.4	126	112	76	166	2	.251	.346	124	27	OF-316, 1B-12

Red Borom

BOROM, EDWARD JONES
B. Oct. 30, 1915, Spartanburg, S. C.   BL TR 5'11" 180 lbs.

	G	AB	H	2B	3B	HR	HR%	R	RBI	BB	SO	SB	BA	SA	PH AB	PH H	G by POS
1944 DET A	7	14	1	0	0	0	0.0	1	1	2	2	0	.071	.071	2	0	2B-4, SS-1
1945	55	130	35	4	0	0	0.0	19	9	7	8	4	.269	.300	12	2	2B-28, 3B-4, SS-2
2 yrs.	62	144	36	4	0	0	0.0	20	10	9	10	4	.250	.278	14	2	2B-32, 3B-4, SS-3
WORLD SERIES																	
1945 DET A	2	1	0	0	0	0	0.0	0	0	0	0	0	.000	.000	1	0	

Steve Boros

BOROS, STEPHEN
B. Sept. 3, 1936, Flint, Mich.
Manager 1983-84.   BR TR 6' 185 lbs.

	G	AB	H	2B	3B	HR	HR%	R	RBI	BB	SO	SB	BA	SA	PH AB	PH H	G by POS
1957 DET A	24	41	6	1	0	0	0.0	4	2	1	8	0	.146	.171	4	0	3B-9, SS-5
1958	6	2	0	0	0	0	0.0	0	0	0	0	0	.000	.000	0	0	2B-1
1961	116	396	107	18	2	5	1.3	51	62	68	42	0	.270	.364	0	0	3B-116
1962	116	356	81	14	1	16	4.5	46	47	53	62	3	.228	.407	0	0	3B-105, 2B-6
1963 CHI N	41	90	19	5	1	3	3.3	9	7	12	19	0	.211	.389	17	2	1B-14, OF-11
1964 CIN N	117	370	95	12	3	2	0.5	31	31	47	43	4	.257	.322	1	0	3B-114
1965	2	0	0	0	0	0	–	0	0	0	0	0	–	–	0	0	3B-2
7 yrs.	422	1255	308	50	7	26	2.1	141	149	181	174	11	.245	.359	30	2	3B-346, 1B-14, OF-11, 2B-7, SS-5

Babe Borton

BORTON, WILLIAM BAKER
B. Aug. 14, 1888, Marion, Ill.   D. July 29, 1954, Berkeley, Calif.   BL TL 6' 178 lbs.

	G	AB	H	2B	3B	HR	HR%	R	RBI	BB	SO	SB	BA	SA	PH AB	PH H	G by POS
1912 CHI A	31	105	39	3	1	0	0.0	15	17	8			.371	.419	1	1	1B-30
1913 2 teams	CHI	A	(28G – .275)			NY	A	(33G – .130)									
" total	61	188	36	6	0	1	0.5	17	24	41	24	2	.191	.239	2	0	1B-59
1915 STL F	159	549	157	20	14	3	0.5	97	83	92		17	.286	.390	0	0	1B-159
1916 STL A	66	98	22	1	2	1	1.0	10	12	19	13	1	.224	.306	35	6	1B-22
4 yrs.	317	940	254	30	17	5	0.5	139	136	160	37	21	.270	.354	38	7	1B-270

	G	AB	H	2B	3B	HR	HR%	R	RBI	BB	SO	SB	BA	SA	Pinch Hit AB	Pinch Hit H	G by POS

Don Bosch

BOSCH, DONALD JOHN   BB TR 5'10" 160 lbs.
B. July 15, 1942, San Francisco, Calif.

	G	AB	H	2B	3B	HR	HR%	R	RBI	BB	SO	SB	BA	SA	PH AB	PH H	G by POS
1966 PIT N	3	2	0	0	0	0	0.0	0	0	0	0	0	.000	.000	1	0	OF-1
1967 NY N	44	93	13	0	1	0	0.0	7	2	5	24	3	.140	.161	3	0	OF-39
1968	50	111	19	1	0	3	2.7	14	7	9	33	0	.171	.261	9	1	OF-33
1969 MON N	49	112	20	5	0	1	0.9	13	4	8	20	1	.179	.250	15	2	OF-32
4 yrs.	146	318	52	6	1	4	1.3	34	13	22	77	4	.164	.226	28	3	OF-105

Rick Bosetti

BOSETTI, RICHARD ALAN   BR TR 5'11" 185 lbs.
B. Aug. 5, 1953, Redding, Calif.

	G	AB	H	2B	3B	HR	HR%	R	RBI	BB	SO	SB	BA	SA	PH AB	PH H	G by POS
1976 PHI N	13	18	5	1	0	0	0.0	6	0	1	3	3	.278	.333	1	0	OF-6
1977 STL N	41	69	16	0	0	0	0.0	12	3	6	11	4	.232	.232	2	0	OF-35
1978 TOR A	136	568	147	25	5	5	0.9	61	42	30	65	6	.259	.347	0	0	OF-135
1979	162	619	161	35	2	8	1.3	59	65	22	70	13	.260	.362	0	0	OF-162
1980	53	188	40	7	1	4	2.1	24	18	15	29	1	.213	.324	1	0	OF-51
1981 2 teams	TOR A (25G – .234)				OAK A (9G – .105)												
" total	34	66	13	2	0	0	0.0	9	5	5	9	0	.197	.227	3	1	OF-24, DH-3
1982 OAK A	6	15	3	0	0	0	0.0	1	0	0	1	0	.200	.200	0	0	OF-6
7 yrs.	445	1543	385	70	8	17	1.1	172	133	79	188	30	.250	.338	7	1	OF-419, DH-3

DIVISIONAL PLAYOFF SERIES

	G	AB	H	2B	3B	HR	HR%	R	RBI	BB	SO	SB	BA	SA	PH AB	PH H	G by POS
1981 OAK A	1	0	0	0	0	0	–	0	0	0	0	0	–	–	0	0	OF-1

LEAGUE CHAMPIONSHIP SERIES

	G	AB	H	2B	3B	HR	HR%	R	RBI	BB	SO	SB	BA	SA	PH AB	PH H	G by POS
1981 OAK A	2	4	1	1	0	0	0.0	1	0	0	1	0	.250	.500	1	0	OF-1

Thad Bosley

BOSLEY, THADDIS   BL TL 6'3" 175 lbs.
B. Sept. 17, 1956, Oceanside, Calif.

	G	AB	H	2B	3B	HR	HR%	R	RBI	BB	SO	SB	BA	SA	PH AB	PH H	G by POS
1977 CAL A	58	212	63	10	2	0	0.0	19	19	16	32	5	.297	.363	4	2	OF-55
1978 CHI A	66	219	59	5	1	2	0.9	25	13	13	32	12	.269	.329	1	0	OF-64
1979	36	77	24	1	1	1	1.3	13	8	9	14	4	.312	.390	7	1	OF-28, DH-1
1980	70	147	33	2	0	2	1.4	12	14	10	27	3	.224	.279	25	8	OF-52
1981 MIL A	42	105	24	2	0	0	0.0	11	3	6	13	2	.229	.248	4	0	OF-37, DH-1
1982 SEA A	22	46	8	1	0	0	0.0	3	2	4	8	3	.174	.196	3	0	OF-19
1983 CHI N	43	72	21	4	1	2	2.8	12	12	10	12	1	.292	.458	18	4	OF-20
1984	55	98	29	2	2	2	2.0	17	14	13	22	5	.296	.418	23	6	OF-33
8 yrs.	392	976	261	27	7	9	0.9	112	85	81	160	35	.267	.337	85	21	OF-308, DH-2

DIVISIONAL PLAYOFF SERIES

	G	AB	H	2B	3B	HR	HR%	R	RBI	BB	SO	SB	BA	SA	PH AB	PH H	G by POS
1981 MIL A	1	0	0	0	0	0	–	0	0	0	0	0	–	–	0	0	DH-1

LEAGUE CHAMPIONSHIP SERIES

	G	AB	H	2B	3B	HR	HR%	R	RBI	BB	SO	SB	BA	SA	PH AB	PH H	G by POS
1984 CHI N	2	2	0	0	0	0	0.0	0	0	0	2	0	.000	.000	2	0	

Harley Boss

BOSS, ELMER HARLEY (Lefty)   BL TL 5'11½" 185 lbs.
B. Nov. 19, 1908, Hodge, La.   D. May 15, 1964, Nashville, Tenn.

	G	AB	H	2B	3B	HR	HR%	R	RBI	BB	SO	SB	BA	SA	PH AB	PH H	G by POS
1928 WAS A	12	12	3	0	0	0	0.0	1	2	3	1	0	.250	.250	4	0	1B-5
1929	28	66	18	2	1	0	0.0	9	6	2	6	0	.273	.333	9	1	1B-18
1930	3	3	0	0	0	0	0.0	0	0	0	0	0	.000	.000	2	0	1B-1
1933 CLE A	112	438	118	17	7	1	0.2	54	53	25	27	2	.269	.347	3	0	1B-110
4 yrs.	155	519	139	19	8	1	0.2	64	61	30	34	2	.268	.341	18	1	1B-134

Henry Bostick

BOSTICK, HENRY LANDERS   BR TR
Born Henry Lipschitz.
B. Jan. 11, 1895, Boston, Mass.   D. Sept. 16, 1968, Denver, Colo.

	G	AB	H	2B	3B	HR	HR%	R	RBI	BB	SO	SB	BA	SA	PH AB	PH H	G by POS
1915 PHI A	2	7	0	0	0	0	0.0	0	2	1	1	0	.000	.000	0	0	3B-2

Lyman Bostock

BOSTOCK, LYMAN WESLEY   BL TR 6'1" 180 lbs.
B. Nov. 22, 1950, Birmingham, Ala.   D. Sept. 23, 1978, Gary, Ind.

	G	AB	H	2B	3B	HR	HR%	R	RBI	BB	SO	SB	BA	SA	PH AB	PH H	G by POS
1975 MIN A	98	369	104	21	5	0	0.0	52	29	28	42	2	.282	.366	2	0	OF-92, DH-1
1976	128	474	153	21	9	4	0.8	75	60	33	37	12	.323	.430	9	4	OF-124
1977	153	593	199	36	12	14	2.4	104	90	51	59	16	.336	.508	10	1	OF-149
1978 CAL A	147	568	168	24	4	5	0.9	74	71	59	36	15	.296	.379	1	0	OF-146, DH-1
4 yrs.	526	2004	624	102	30	23	1.1	305	250	171	174	45	.311	.427	22	5	OF-511, DH-2

Daryl Boston

BOSTON, DARYL LAMONT   BL TL 6'3" 185 lbs.
B. Jan. 4, 1963, Cincinnati, Ohio

	G	AB	H	2B	3B	HR	HR%	R	RBI	BB	SO	SB	BA	SA	PH AB	PH H	G by POS
1984 CHI A	35	83	14	3	1	0	0.0	8	3	4	20	6	.169	.229	2	1	OF-34, DH-1

Ken Boswell

BOSWELL, KENNETH GEORGE   BL TR 6' 170 lbs.
B. Feb. 23, 1946, Austin, Tex.

	G	AB	H	2B	3B	HR	HR%	R	RBI	BB	SO	SB	BA	SA	PH AB	PH H	G by POS
1967 NY N	11	40	9	3	0	1	2.5	2	4	1	5	0	.225	.375	1	0	2B-6, 3B-4
1968	75	284	74	7	2	4	1.4	37	11	16	27	7	.261	.342	6	1	2B-69
1969	102	362	101	14	7	3	0.8	48	32	36	47	7	.279	.381	10	1	2B-96
1970	105	351	89	13	2	5	1.4	32	44	41	32	5	.254	.345	7	2	2B-101
1971	116	392	107	20	1	5	1.3	46	40	36	31	5	.273	.367	7	0	2B-109
1972	100	355	75	9	1	9	2.5	35	33	32	35	2	.211	.318	7	1	2B-94
1973	76	110	25	2	1	2	1.8	12	14	12	11	0	.227	.318	51	12	3B-17, 2B-3
1974	96	222	48	6	1	2	0.9	19	15	18	19	0	.216	.279	42	9	2B-28, 3B-20, OF-7
1975 HOU N	86	178	43	8	2	0	0.0	16	21	30	12	0	.242	.309	35	6	2B-31, 3B-23
1976	91	126	33	8	1	0	0.0	12	18	8	8	1	.262	.341	65	20	3B-16, 2B-3, OF-1
1977	72	97	21	1	1	0	0.0	7	12	10	12	0	.216	.247	53	14	2B-26, 3B-2
11 yrs.	930	2517	625	91	19	31	1.2	266	244	240	239	27	.248	.337	284	66	2B-566, 3B-82, OF-8

LEAGUE CHAMPIONSHIP SERIES

	G	AB	H	2B	3B	HR	HR%	R	RBI	BB	SO	SB	BA	SA	PH AB	PH H	G by POS
1969 NY N	3	12	4	0	0	2	16.7	4	5	1	2	0	.333	.833	0	0	2B-3
1973	1	1	0	0	0	0	0.0	0	0	0	0	0	.000	.000	1	0	
2 yrs.	4	13	4	0	0	2	15.4	4	5	1	2	0	.308	.769	1	0	2B-3

WORLD SERIES

	G	AB	H	2B	3B	HR	HR%	R	RBI	BB	SO	SB	BA	SA	PH AB	PH H	G by POS
1969 NY N	1	3	1	0	0	0	0.0	1	0	0	0	0	.333	.333	0	0	2B-1

	G	AB	H	2B	3B	HR	HR %	R	RBI	BB	SO	SB	BA	SA	Pinch Hit AB	Pinch Hit H	G by POS

Ken Boswell continued

	G	AB	H	2B	3B	HR	HR %	R	RBI	BB	SO	SB	BA	SA	PH AB	PH H	G by POS
1973	3	3	3	0	0	0	0.0	1	0	0	0	0	1.000	1.000	3	3	
2 yrs.	4	6	4	0	0	0	0.0	2	0	0	0	0	.667	.667	3	3	2B-1
																1st	

John Bottarini

BOTTARINI, JOHN CHARLES   BR TR 6'   190 lbs.
B. Sept. 14, 1908, Crockett, Calif.   D. Oct. 8, 1976, Jemez Springs, N. M.

	G	AB	H	2B	3B	HR	HR %	R	RBI	BB	SO	SB	BA	SA	PH AB	PH H	G by POS
1937 CHI N	26	40	11	3	0	1	2.5	3	7	5	10	0	.275	.425	7	2	C-18, OF-1

Jim Bottomley

BOTTOMLEY, JAMES LeROY (Sunny Jim)   BL TL 6'   180 lbs.
B. Apr. 23, 1900, Oglesby, Ill.   D. Dec. 11, 1959, St. Louis, Mo.
Manager 1937.
Hall of Fame 1974.

	G	AB	H	2B	3B	HR	HR %	R	RBI	BB	SO	SB	BA	SA	PH AB	PH H	G by POS
1922 STL N	37	151	49	8	5	5	3.3	29	35	6	13	3	.325	.543	3	1	1B-34
1923	134	523	194	34	14	8	1.5	79	94	45	44	4	.371	.535	4	1	1B-130
1924	137	528	167	31	12	14	2.7	87	111	35	35	5	.316	.500	3	1	1B-133, 2B-1
1925	153	619	227	44	12	21	3.4	92	128	47	36	3	.367	.578	0	0	1B-153
1926	154	603	180	40	14	19	3.2	98	120	58	52	4	.299	.506	0	0	1B-154
1927	152	574	174	31	15	19	3.3	95	124	74	49	8	.303	.509	0	0	1B-152
1928	149	576	187	42	20	31	5.4	123	136	71	54	10	.325	.628	0	0	1B-148
1929	146	560	176	31	12	29	5.2	108	137	70	54	4	.314	.568	1	0	1B-145
1930	131	487	148	33	7	15	3.1	92	97	44	36	5	.304	.493	7	2	1B-124
1931	108	382	133	34	5	9	2.4	73	75	34	24	3	.348	.534	14	3	1B-93
1932	91	311	92	16	3	11	3.5	45	48	25	32	2	.296	.473	16	7	1B-74
1933 CIN N	145	549	137	23	9	13	2.4	57	83	42	28	3	.250	.395	0	0	1B-145
1934	142	556	158	31	11	11	2.0	72	78	33	40	1	.284	.439	3	0	1B-139
1935	107	399	103	21	1	1	0.3	44	49	18	24	3	.258	.323	10	5	1B-97
1936 STL A	140	544	162	39	11	12	2.2	72	95	44	55	0	.298	.476	0	0	1B-140
1937	65	109	26	7	0	1	0.9	11	12	18	15	1	.239	.330	38	7	1B-24
16 yrs.	1991	7471	2313	465	151	219	2.9	1177	1422	664	591	58	.310	.500	99	27	1B-1885, 2B-1

WORLD SERIES

	G	AB	H	2B	3B	HR	HR %	R	RBI	BB	SO	SB	BA	SA	PH AB	PH H	G by POS
1926 STL N	7	29	10	3	0	0	0.0	4	5	1	2	0	.345	.448	0	0	1B-7
1928	4	14	3	0	1	1	7.1	1	3	2	6	0	.214	.571	0	0	1B-4
1930	6	22	1	1	0	0	0.0	1	0	2	9	0	.045	.091	0	0	1B-6
1931	7	25	4	1	0	0	0.0	2	2	2	5	0	.160	.200	0	0	1B-7
4 yrs.	24	90	18	5	1	1	1.1	8	10	7	22	0	.200	.311	0	0	1B-24

Ed Bouchee

BOUCHEE, EDWARD FRANCIS   BL TL 6'   200 lbs.
B. Mar. 7, 1933, Livingston, Mont.

	G	AB	H	2B	3B	HR	HR %	R	RBI	BB	SO	SB	BA	SA	PH AB	PH H	G by POS
1956 PHI N	9	22	6	2	0	0	0.0	0	1	5	6	0	.273	.364	2	0	1B-6
1957	154	574	168	35	8	17	3.0	78	76	84	91	1	.293	.470	0	0	1B-154
1958	89	334	86	19	5	9	2.7	55	39	51	74	1	.257	.425	0	0	1B-89
1959	136	499	142	29	4	15	3.0	75	74	70	74	0	.285	.449	2	1	1B-134
1960 2 teams		PHI	N (22G –	.262)		CHI	N (98G –	.237)									
" total	120	364	88	15	1	5	1.4	34	52	54	62	2	.242	.330	17	1	1B-102
1961 CHI N	112	319	79	12	3	12	3.8	49	38	58	77	1	.248	.417	12	1	1B-107
1962 NY N	50	87	14	2	0	3	3.4	7	10	18	17	0	.161	.287	28	5	1B-19
7 yrs.	670	2199	583	114	21	61	2.8	298	290	340	401	5	.265	.419	61	8	1B-611

Al Boucher

BOUCHER, ALEXANDER FRANCIS (Bo)   BR TR 5'8½" 156 lbs.
B. Nov. 13, 1881, Franklin, Mass.   D. June 23, 1974, Torrance, Calif.

	G	AB	H	2B	3B	HR	HR %	R	RBI	BB	SO	SB	BA	SA	PH AB	PH H	G by POS
1914 STL F	147	516	119	26	4	2	0.4	62	49	52		13	.231	.308	0	0	3B-147

Medric Boucher

BOUCHER, MEDRIC CHARLES FRANCIS   BR TR 5'10½" 165 lbs.
B. Mar. 12, 1886, St. Louis, Mo.   D. Mar. 12, 1974, Martinez, Calif.

	G	AB	H	2B	3B	HR	HR %	R	RBI	BB	SO	SB	BA	SA	PH AB	PH H	G by POS
1914 2 teams		BAL	F (16G –	.313)		PIT	F (1G –	.000)									
" total	17	17	5	1	1	0	0.0	2	2	1		0	.294	.471	6	2	C-7, OF-1, 1B-1

Lou Boudreau

BOUDREAU, LOUIS   BR TR 5'11"   185 lbs.
B. July 17, 1917, Harvey, Ill.
Manager 1942-50, 1952-57, 1960.
Hall of Fame 1970.

	G	AB	H	2B	3B	HR	HR %	R	RBI	BB	SO	SB	BA	SA	PH AB	PH H	G by POS
1938 CLE A	1	1	0	0	0	0	0.0	0	0	1	0	0	.000	.000	0	0	3B-1
1939	53	225	58	15	4	0	0.0	42	19	28	24	2	.258	.360	0	0	SS-53
1940	155	627	185	46	10	9	1.4	97	101	73	39	6	.295	.443	0	0	SS-155
1941	148	579	149	45	8	10	1.7	95	56	85	57	9	.257	.415	0	0	SS-147
1942	147	506	143	18	10	2	0.4	57	58	75	39	7	.283	.370	1	0	SS-146
1943	152	539	154	32	7	3	0.6	69	67	90	31	4	.286	.388	1	0	SS-152, C-1
1944	150	584	191	45	5	3	0.5	91	67	73	39	11	.327	.437	1	0	SS-149, C-1
1945	97	346	106	24	1	3	0.9	50	48	35	20	0	.306	.408	0	0	SS-97
1946	140	515	151	30	6	6	1.2	51	62	40	14	6	.293	.410	1	0	SS-139
1947	150	538	165	45	3	4	0.7	79	67	67	10	1	.307	.424	1	1	SS-148
1948	152	560	199	34	6	18	3.2	116	106	98	9	3	.355	.534	1	1	SS-151, C-1
1949	134	475	135	20	3	4	0.8	53	60	70	10	0	.284	.364	4	1	SS-88, 3B-38, 1B-6, 2B-1
1950	81	260	70	13	2	1	0.4	23	29	31	5	1	.269	.346	9	2	SS-61, 1B-8, 3B-2, 2B-2
1951 BOS A	82	273	73	18	1	5	1.8	37	47	30	12	1	.267	.396	11	1	SS-52, 3B-15, 1B-2
1952	4	2	0	0	0	0	0.0	1	2	0	0	0	.000	.000	2	0	SS-1, 3B-1
15 yrs.	1646	6030	1779	385	66	68	1.1	861	789	796	309	51	.295	.415	32	6	SS-1539, 3B-57, 1B-16, 2B-3, C-3

WORLD SERIES

	G	AB	H	2B	3B	HR	HR %	R	RBI	BB	SO	SB	BA	SA	PH AB	PH H	G by POS
1948 CLE A	6	22	6	4	0	0	0.0	1	3	1	1	0	.273	.455	0	0	SS-6

	G	AB	H	2B	3B	HR	HR %	R	RBI	BB	SO	SB	BA	SA	Pinch Hit AB	H	G by POS

Chris Bourjos

BOURJOS, CHRISTOPHER   BR TR 6'   185 lbs.
B. Oct. 16, 1955, Chicago, Ill.

	G	AB	H	2B	3B	HR	HR %	R	RBI	BB	SO	SB	BA	SA	PH AB	H	G by POS
1980 SF N	13	22	5	1	0	1	4.5	4	2	2	7	0	.227	.409	7	2	OF-6

Pat Bourque

BOURQUE, PATRICK DANIEL   BL TL 6'   210 lbs.
B. Mar. 23, 1947, Worcester, Mass.

	G	AB	H	2B	3B	HR	HR %	R	RBI	BB	SO	SB	BA	SA	PH AB	H	G by POS
1971 CHI N	14	37	7	0	1	1	2.7	3	3	3	9	0	.189	.324	3	1	1B-11
1972	11	27	7	1	0	0	0.0	3	5	2	2	0	.259	.296	4	0	1B-7
1973 2 teams	CHI	N (57G –	.209)		OAK	A	(23G –	.190)									
" total	80	181	37	10	1	9	5.0	19	29	31	31	1	.204	.420	20	4	1B-43, DH-15
1974 2 teams	OAK	A (73G –	.229)		MIN	A	(23G –	.219)									
" total	96	160	36	6	0	2	1.3	11	24	22	31	0	.225	.300	35	7	1B-60, DH-8
4 yrs.	201	405	87	17	2	12	3.0	36	61	58	73	1	.215	.356	62	12	1B-121, DH-23

LEAGUE CHAMPIONSHIP SERIES
| 1973 OAK A | 2 | 1 | 0 | 0 | 0 | 0 | 0.0 | 0 | 0 | 1 | 1 | 0 | .000 | .000 | 0 | 0 | DH-2 |

WORLD SERIES
| 1973 OAK A | 2 | 2 | 1 | 0 | 0 | 0 | 0.0 | 0 | 0 | 0 | 0 | 0 | .500 | .500 | 1 | 0 | 1B-2 |

Larry Bowa

BOWA, LAWRENCE ROBERT   BB TR 5'10"   155 lbs.
B. Dec. 6, 1945, Sacramento, Calif.

	G	AB	H	2B	3B	HR	HR %	R	RBI	BB	SO	SB	BA	SA	PH AB	H	G by POS
1970 PHI N	145	547	137	17	6	0	0.0	50	34	21	48	24	.250	.303	0	0	SS-143, 2B-1
1971	159	650	162	18	5	0	0.0	74	25	36	61	28	.249	.292	0	0	SS-157
1972	152	579	145	11	13	1	0.2	67	31	32	51	17	.250	.320	0	0	SS-150
1973	122	446	94	11	3	0	0.0	42	23	24	31	10	.211	.249	0	0	SS-122
1974	162	669	184	19	10	1	0.1	97	36	23	52	39	.275	.338	0	0	SS-162
1975	136	583	178	18	9	2	0.3	79	38	24	32	24	.305	.377	0	0	SS-135
1976	156	624	155	15	9	0	0.0	71	49	32	31	30	.248	.301	0	0	SS-156
1977	154	624	175	19	3	4	0.6	93	41	32	32	32	.280	.340	0	0	SS-154
1978	156	654	192	31	5	3	0.5	78	43	24	40	27	.294	.370	0	0	SS-156
1979	147	539	130	17	11	0	0.0	74	31	61	32	20	.241	.314	0	0	SS-146
1980	147	540	144	16	4	2	0.4	57	39	24	28	21	.267	.322	0	0	SS-147
1981	103	360	102	14	3	0	0.0	34	31	26	17	16	.283	.339	1	0	SS-102
1982 CHI N	142	499	123	15	7	0	0.0	50	29	39	38	8	.246	.305	2	1	SS-140
1983	147	499	133	20	5	2	0.4	73	43	35	30	7	.267	.339	4	1	SS-145
1984	133	391	87	14	2	0	0.0	33	17	28	24	10	.223	.269	2	1	SS-132
15 yrs.	2161	8204	2141	255	95	15	0.2	972	510	461	547	313	.261	.321	9	3	SS-2147, 2B-1

DIVISIONAL PLAYOFF SERIES
| 1981 PHI N | 5 | 17 | 3 | 1 | 0 | 0 | 0.0 | 0 | 1 | 0 | 0 | 0 | .176 | .235 | 0 | 0 | SS-5 |

LEAGUE CHAMPIONSHIP SERIES
1976 PHI N	3	8	1	1	0	0	0.0	1	1	3	0	0	.125	.250	0	0	SS-3
1977	4	17	2	0	0	0	0.0	2	1	1	0	0	.118	.118	0	0	SS-4
1978	4	18	6	0	0	0	0.0	2	0	1	2	0	.333	.333	0	0	SS-4
1980	5	19	6	0	0	0	0.0	2	0	3	3	1	.316	.316	0	0	SS-5
1984 CHI N	5	15	3	1	0	0	0.0	1	1	1	0	0	.200	.267	0	0	SS-5
5 yrs.	21	77	18	2	0	0	0.0	8	3	9	5	1	.234	.260	0	0	SS-21

WORLD SERIES
| 1980 PHI N | 6 | 24 | 9 | 1 | 0 | 0 | 0.0 | 3 | 2 | 0 | 0 | 3 | .375 | .417 | 0 | 0 | SS-6 |

Benny Bowcock

BOWCOCK, BENJAMIN JAMES   BR TR 5'7"   150 lbs.
B. Oct. 28, 1879, Fall River, Mass.   D. June 16, 1961, New Bedford, Mass.

	G	AB	H	2B	3B	HR	HR %	R	RBI	BB	SO	SB	BA	SA	PH AB	H	G by POS
1903 STL A	14	50	16	3	1	1	2.0	7	10	3		1	.320	.480	0	0	2B-14

Tim Bowden

BOWDEN, DAVID TIMON   BL TR 5'10"   175 lbs.
B. Aug. 15, 1891, McDonough, Ga.   D. Oct. 25, 1949, Emory University, Ga.

	G	AB	H	2B	3B	HR	HR %	R	RBI	BB	SO	SB	BA	SA	PH AB	H	G by POS
1914 STL A	7	9	2	0	0	0	0.0	0	0	1	6	0	.222	.222	3	1	OF-4

Chick Bowen

BOWEN, EMMONS JOSEPH   BR TR 5'7"   165 lbs.
B. July 26, 1897, New Haven, Conn.   D. Aug. 9, 1948, New Haven, Conn.

	G	AB	H	2B	3B	HR	HR %	R	RBI	BB	SO	SB	BA	SA	PH AB	H	G by POS
1919 NY N	3	5	1	0	0	0	0.0	0	1	1	2	0	.200	.200	0	0	OF-2

Sam Bowen

BOWEN, SAMUEL THOMAS   BR TR 5'9"   170 lbs.
B. Sept. 18, 1952, Brunswick, Ga.

	G	AB	H	2B	3B	HR	HR %	R	RBI	BB	SO	SB	BA	SA	PH AB	H	G by POS
1977 BOS A	3	2	0	0	0	0	0.0	0	0	0	2	0	.000	.000	0	0	OF-3
1978	6	7	1	0	0	1	14.3	3	1	1	2	0	.143	.571	0	0	OF-4
1980	7	13	2	0	0	0	0.0	0	0	2	3	1	.154	.154	0	0	OF-6
3 yrs.	16	22	3	0	0	1	4.5	3	1	3	7	1	.136	.273	0	0	OF-13

Sam Bowens

BOWENS, SAMUEL EDWARD   BR TR 6'1½"   188 lbs.
B. Mar. 23, 1939, Wilmington, N. C.

	G	AB	H	2B	3B	HR	HR %	R	RBI	BB	SO	SB	BA	SA	PH AB	H	G by POS
1963 BAL A	15	48	16	3	1	1	2.1	8	9	4	5	1	.333	.500	2	0	OF-13
1964	139	501	132	25	2	22	4.4	58	71	42	99	4	.263	.453	5	0	OF-135
1965	84	203	33	4	1	7	3.4	16	20	10	41	7	.163	.296	13	2	OF-68
1966	89	243	51	9	1	6	2.5	26	20	17	52	9	.210	.329	22	6	OF-68
1967	62	120	22	2	1	5	4.2	13	12	11	43	3	.183	.342	26	6	OF-32
1968 WAS A	57	115	22	4	0	4	3.5	14	7	11	39	0	.191	.330	29	6	OF-27
1969	33	57	11	1	0	0	0.0	6	4	5	14	1	.193	.211	3	0	OF-30
7 yrs.	479	1287	287	48	6	45	3.5	141	143	100	293	25	.223	.375	100	20	OF-373

Frank Bowerman

BOWERMAN, FRANK EUGENE (Mike)   BR TR 5'11"   185 lbs.
B. Dec. 5, 1868, Romeo, Mich.   D. Nov. 30, 1948, Romeo, Mich.
Manager 1909.

	G	AB	H	2B	3B	HR	HR %	R	RBI	BB	SO	SB	BA	SA	PH AB	H	G by POS
1895 BAL N	1	1	0	0	0	0	0.0	0	0	0	0	0	.000	.000	0	0	C-1
1896	4	16	2	0	0	0	0.0	0	4	1	1	0	.125	.125	0	0	C-3, 1B-1
1897	38	130	41	5	0	1	0.8	16	21	1		3	.315	.377	2	0	C-36

	G	AB	H	2B	3B	HR	HR %	R	RBI	BB	SO	SB	BA	SA	Pinch Hit AB	Pinch Hit H	G by POS

Frank Bowerman continued

		G	AB	H	2B	3B	HR	HR%	R	RBI	BB	SO	SB	BA	SA	AB	H	G by POS
1898	2 teams	BAL	N (5G –	.438)		PIT	N	(69G –	.274)									
"	total	74	257	73	7	3	0	0.0	22	30	9		5	.284	.335	2	0	C-63, 1B-9
1899	PIT N	109	424	110	16	10	3	0.7	49	53	11		10	.259	.366	2	4	C-79, 1B-28
1900	NY N	80	270	65	5	3	1	0.4	25	42	6		10	.241	.293	2	0	C-75, SS-2
1901		59	191	38	5	3	0	0.0	20	14	7		3	.199	.257	4	1	C-46, SS-3, 3B-3, 2B-3, 1B-1
1902		107	367	93	13	6	0	0.0	38	26	13		12	.253	.322	5	0	C-98, 1B-3
1903		64	210	58	6	2	1	0.5	22	31	6		5	.276	.338	4	3	C-55, 1B-4, OF-1
1904		93	289	67	11	4	2	0.7	38	27	16		7	.232	.318	3	0	C-79, 1B-9, 2B-2, P-1
1905		98	297	80	8	1	3	1.0	37	41	12		6	.269	.333	7	3	C-72, 1B-17, 2B-1
1906		103	285	65	7	3	1	0.4	23	42	15		5	.228	.284	5	2	C-67, 1B-8
1907		96	311	81	8	2	0	0.0	31	32	17		11	.260	.299	5	1	C-62, 1B-29
1908	BOS N	86	254	58	8	1	0	0.0	16	25	13		4	.228	.280	12	4	C-63, 1B-11
1909		33	99	21	2	0	0	0.0	6	4	2		0	.212	.232	6	0	C-27
15 yrs.		1045	3401	852	101	38	13	0.4	343	392	129		81	.251	.314	59	14	C-826, 1B-132, 2B-6, SS-5, 3B-3, OF-1, P-1

Billy Bowers

BOWERS, GROVER BILL
B. Mar. 25, 1923, Parkin, Ark.

BL TR 5'9½" 176 lbs.

	G	AB	H	2B	3B	HR	HR%	R	RBI	BB	SO	SB	BA	SA	AB	H	G by POS
1949 CHI A	26	78	15	2	1	0	0.0	5	6	4	5	1	.192	.244	6	0	OF-20

Frank Bowes

BOWES, FRANK M.
B. 1865, Bath, N.Y.   D. Jan. 25, 1895, New York, N.Y.

TR

	G	AB	H	2B	3B	HR	HR%	R	RBI	BB	SO	SB	BA	SA	AB	H	G by POS
1890 B-B AA	61	232	51	5	2	0	0.0	28		7		11	.220	.259	0	0	C-25, OF-19, 3B-13, 1B-3, SS-2

Hoss Bowlin

BOWLIN, LOIS WELDON
B. Dec. 10, 1940, Paragould, Ark.

BR TR 5'9" 155 lbs.

	G	AB	H	2B	3B	HR	HR%	R	RBI	BB	SO	SB	BA	SA	AB	H	G by POS
1967 KC A	2	5	1	0	0	0	0.0	0	0	0	0	0	.200	.200	0	0	3B-2

Steve Bowling

BOWLING, STEPHEN SHADDON
B. June 26, 1952, Tulsa, Okla.

BR TR 6' 185 lbs.

	G	AB	H	2B	3B	HR	HR%	R	RBI	BB	SO	SB	BA	SA	AB	H	G by POS
1976 MIL N	14	42	7	2	0	0	0.0	4	2	2	5	0	.167	.214	1	0	OF-13, DH-1
1977 TOR A	89	194	40	8	1	1	0.5	19	13	37	42	2	.206	.273	2	0	OF-87
2 yrs.	103	236	47	10	1	1	0.4	23	15	39	47	2	.199	.263	3	0	OF-100, DH-1

Bill Bowman

BOWMAN, WILLIAM G.
B. 1869, Chicago, Ill.   Deceased.

5'11" 180 lbs.

	G	AB	H	2B	3B	HR	HR%	R	RBI	BB	SO	SB	BA	SA	AB	H	G by POS
1891 CHI N	15	45	4	1	0	0	0.0	5	5	5	9	0	.089	.111	0	0	C-15

Bob Bowman

BOWMAN, ROBERT LEROY
B. May 10, 1931, Laytonville, Calif.

BR TR 6'1" 195 lbs.

	G	AB	H	2B	3B	HR	HR%	R	RBI	BB	SO	SB	BA	SA	AB	H	G by POS
1955 PHI N	3	3	0	0	0	0	0.0	0	0	0	0	0	.000	.000	0	0	OF-2
1956	6	16	3	0	1	1	6.3	2	2	0	6	0	.188	.500	1	0	OF-5
1957	99	237	63	8	2	6	2.5	31	23	27	50	0	.266	.392	15	1	OF-81
1958	91	184	53	11	2	8	4.3	31	24	16	30	0	.288	.500	31	13	OF-57
1959	57	79	10	0	0	2	2.5	7	5	5	23	0	.127	.203	32	7	OF-20, P-5
5 yrs.	256	519	129	19	5	17	3.3	71	54	48	109	0	.249	.403	79	21	OF-165, P-5

Elmer Bowman

BOWMAN, ELMER WILLIAM (Big Bow)
Also known as Elmari Wilhelm.
B. Mar. 19, 1897, Proctor, Vt.

BR TR 6'½" 193 lbs.

	G	AB	H	2B	3B	HR	HR%	R	RBI	BB	SO	SB	BA	SA	AB	H	G by POS
1920 WAS A	2	1	0	0	0	0	0.0	1	0	0	0	0	.000	.000	1	0	

Ernie Bowman

BOWMAN, ERNEST FERRELL
B. July 28, 1937, Johnson City, Tenn.

BR TR 5'10" 160 lbs.

	G	AB	H	2B	3B	HR	HR%	R	RBI	BB	SO	SB	BA	SA	AB	H	G by POS
1961 SF N	38	38	8	0	2	0	0.0	10	2	1	8	2	.211	.316	3	1	2B-13, SS-12, 3B-7
1962	46	42	8	1	0	1	2.4	9	4	1	10	0	.190	.286	3	0	2B-17, 3B-11, SS-10
1963	81	125	23	3	0	0	0.0	10	4	0	15	1	.184	.208	1	0	SS-40, 2B-26, 3B-12
3 yrs.	165	205	39	4	2	1	0.5	29	10	2	33	3	.190	.244	7	1	SS-62, 2B-56, 3B-30
WORLD SERIES																	
1962 SF N	2	1	0	0	0	0	0.0	1	0	0	0	0	.000	.000	0	0	SS-1

Joe Bowman

BOWMAN, JOSEPH EMIL
B. June 17, 1910, Argentine, Kans.

BL TR 6'2" 190 lbs.

		G	AB	H	2B	3B	HR	HR%	R	RBI	BB	SO	SB	BA	SA	AB	H	G by POS
1932 PHI A		7	1	1	0	0	0	0.0	0	0	0	0	0	1.000	1.000	0	0	P-7
1934 NY N		31	29	5	0	0	0	0.0	4	4	2	3	0	.172	.241	0	0	P-30
1935 PHI N		49	67	13	1	1	1	1.5	6	7	4	7	1	.194	.284	13	2	P-33, OF-1
1936		44	77	15	1	0	0	0.0	9	6	6	14	0	.195	.208	4	2	P-40
1937 PIT N		35	47	10	1	0	0	0.0	3	4	5	9	0	.213	.234	2	0	P-30
1938		18	21	7	0	1	0	0.0	5	1	1	3	0	.333	.429	0	0	P-17
1939		70	96	33	8	1	0	0.0	9	18	5	9	0	.344	.448	29	6	P-37
1940		57	90	22	5	1	1	1.1	11	14	14	14	0	.244	.356	17	4	P-32
1941		22	31	8	1	0	0	0.0	4	1	1	2	0	.258	.290	4	1	P-18
1944 BOS N		59	100	20	5	2	0	0.0	7	16	5	19	1	.200	.290	31	7	P-26
1945	2 teams	BOS	A (9G –	.222)		CIN	N	(29G –	.070)									
"	total	38	80	7	2	0	0	0.0	4	4	3	10	1	.088	.138	9	1	P-28
11 yrs.		430	639	141	24	8	2	0.3	62	75	46	90	3	.221	.293	109	24	P-298, OF-1

Red Bowser

BOWSER, JAMES H.
B. 1886, Greensburg, Pa.

	G	AB	H	2B	3B	HR	HR%	R	RBI	BB	SO	SB	BA	SA	AB	H	G by POS
1910 CHI A	1	2	0	0	0	0	0.0	0	0	0		0	.000	.000	0	0	OF-1

	G	AB	H	2B	3B	HR	HR %	R	RBI	BB	SO	SB	BA	SA	Pinch Hit AB	H	G by POS

Bob Boyd

BOYD, ROBERT RICHARD (The Rope)
B. Oct. 1, 1926, Potts Camp, Miss.

BL TL 5'10" 170 lbs.

	G	AB	H	2B	3B	HR	HR%	R	RBI	BB	SO	SB	BA	SA	PH AB	H	G by POS
1951 CHI A	12	18	3	0	1	0	0.0	3	4	3	3	0	.167	.278	5	1	1B-6
1953	55	165	49	6	2	3	1.8	20	23	13	11	1	.297	.412	8	4	1B-29, OF-16
1954	29	56	10	3	0	0	0.0	10	5	4	3	2	.179	.232	2	0	OF-13, 1B-12
1956 BAL A	70	225	70	8	3	2	0.9	28	11	30	14	0	.311	.400	10	3	1B-60, OF-8
1957	141	485	154	16	8	4	0.8	73	34	55	31	2	.318	.408	15	6	1B-132, OF-1
1958	125	401	124	21	5	7	1.7	58	36	25	24	1	.309	.439	32	4	1B-99
1959	128	415	110	20	2	3	0.7	42	41	29	14	3	.265	.345	20	4	1B-109
1960	71	82	26	5	2	0	0.0	9	9	6	5	0	.317	.427	56	17	1B-17
1961 2 teams		KC	A (26G –	.229)		MIL	N	(36G –	.244)								
" total	62	89	21	2	0	0	0.0	10	12	2	9	0	.236	.258	49	9	1B-11
9 yrs.	693	1936	567	81	23	19	1.0	253	175	167	114	9	.293	.388	197	48	1B-475, OF-38

Frank Boyd

BOYD, FRANK JOHN
B. Apr. 2, 1868, West Middletown, Pa.   D. Dec. 17, 1937, Oil City, Pa.

	G	AB	H	2B	3B	HR	HR%	R	RBI	BB	SO	SB	BA	SA	PH AB	H	G by POS
1893 CLE N	2	5	1	1	0	0	0.0	3	3	1	0	0	.200	.400	0	0	C-2

Jake Boyd

BOYD, JACOB HENRY
B. Jan. 19, 1874, Martinsburgh, W. Va.   D. Aug. 12, 1932, Gettysburg, Pa.

TL

	G	AB	H	2B	3B	HR	HR%	R	RBI	BB	SO	SB	BA	SA	PH AB	H	G by POS
1894 WAS N	6	21	3	0	0	0	0.0	1	1	1	4	2	.143	.143	0	0	OF-3, P-3
1895	51	157	42	5	1	1	0.6	29	16	20	28	2	.268	.331	0	0	OF-21, P-14, 2B-10, SS-8, 3B-1
1896	4	13	1	0	0	0	0.0	1	1	1	1	0	.077	.077	0	0	P-4
3 yrs.	61	191	46	5	1	1	0.5	31	18	22	33	4	.241	.293	0	0	OF-24, P-21, 2B-10, SS-8, 3B-1

Clete Boyer

BOYER, CLETIS LEROY
Brother of Ken Boyer.   Brother of Cloyd Boyer.
B. Feb. 8, 1937, Cassville, Mo.

BR TR 6' 165 lbs.

	G	AB	H	2B	3B	HR	HR%	R	RBI	BB	SO	SB	BA	SA	PH AB	H	G by POS
1955 KC A	47	79	19	1	0	0	0.0	3	6	3	17	0	.241	.253	9	0	SS-12, 3B-11, 2B-10
1956	67	129	28	3	1	1	0.8	15	4	11	24	1	.217	.279	5	1	2B-51, 3B-7
1957	10	0	0	0	0	0	–	0	0	0	0	0	–	–	0	0	3B-1, 2B-1
1959 NY A	47	114	20	2	0	0	0.0	4	3	6	23	1	.175	.193	6	0	SS-26, 3B-16
1960	124	393	95	20	1	14	3.6	54	46	23	85	2	.242	.405	2	0	3B-99, SS-33
1961	148	504	113	19	5	11	2.2	61	55	63	83	1	.224	.347	0	0	3B-141, SS-12, OF-1
1962	158	566	154	24	1	18	3.2	85	68	51	106	3	.272	.413	0	0	3B-157
1963	152	557	140	20	3	12	2.2	59	54	33	91	4	.251	.363	0	0	3B-141, SS-9, 2B-1
1964	147	510	111	10	5	8	1.6	43	52	36	93	6	.218	.304	3	0	3B-123, SS-21
1965	148	514	129	23	6	18	3.5	69	58	39	79	4	.251	.424	1	0	3B-147, SS-2
1966	144	500	120	22	4	14	2.8	59	57	46	48	6	.240	.384	2	0	3B-150, SS-59
1967 ATL N	154	572	140	18	3	26	4.5	63	96	39	81	6	.245	.423	2	0	3B-150, SS-6
1968	71	273	62	7	2	4	1.5	19	17	16	32	2	.227	.311	3	0	3B-69
1969	144	496	124	16	1	14	2.8	57	57	55	87	3	.250	.371	0	0	3B-141
1970	134	475	117	14	1	16	3.4	44	62	41	71	2	.246	.381	2	1	3B-126, SS-5
1971	30	98	24	1	0	6	6.1	10	19	8	11	0	.245	.439	3	1	3B-25, SS-1
16 yrs.	1725	5780	1396	200	33	162	2.8	645	654	470	931	41	.242	.372	38	3	3B-1439, SS-186, 2B-63, OF-1

LEAGUE CHAMPIONSHIP SERIES

	G	AB	H	2B	3B	HR	HR%	R	RBI	BB	SO	SB	BA	SA	PH AB	H	G by POS
1969 ATL N	3	9	1	0	0	0	0.0	0	3	2	3	0	.111	.111	0	0	3B-3

WORLD SERIES

	G	AB	H	2B	3B	HR	HR%	R	RBI	BB	SO	SB	BA	SA	PH AB	H	G by POS
1960 NY A	4	12	3	2	1	0	0.0	1	1	0	1	0	.250	.583	0	0	3B-4
1961	5	15	4	2	0	0	0.0	3	3	4	0	0	.267	.400	0	0	3B-5
1962	7	22	7	1	0	1	4.5	2	4	1	3	0	.318	.500	0	0	3B-7
1963	4	13	1	0	0	0	0.0	0	0	1	6	0	.077	.077	0	0	3B-4
1964	7	24	5	1	0	1	4.2	2	3	1	5	1	.208	.375	0	0	3B-7
5 yrs.	27	86	20	6	1	2	2.3	5	11	7	15	1	.233	.395	0	0	3B-27

Ken Boyer

BOYER, KENTON LLOYD
Brother of Cloyd Boyer.   Brother of Clete Boyer.
B. May 20, 1931, Liberty, Mo.   D. Sept. 7, 1982, St. Louis, Mo.
Manager 1978-80.

BR TR 6'1½" 190 lbs.

	G	AB	H	2B	3B	HR	HR%	R	RBI	BB	SO	SB	BA	SA	PH AB	H	G by POS
1955 STL N	147	530	140	27	2	18	3.4	78	62	37	67	22	.264	.425	1	0	3B-139, SS-18
1956	150	595	182	30	2	26	4.4	91	98	38	65	8	.306	.494	1	0	3B-149
1957	142	544	144	18	3	19	3.5	79	62	44	77	12	.265	.414	6	0	OF-105, 3B-41
1958	150	570	175	21	9	23	4.0	101	90	49	53	11	.307	.496	1	0	3B-144, OF-6, SS-1
1959	149	563	174	18	5	28	5.0	86	94	67	77	12	.309	.508	0	0	3B-143, SS-12
1960	151	552	168	26	10	32	5.8	95	97	56	77	8	.304	.562	5	1	3B-146
1961	153	589	194	26	11	24	4.1	109	95	68	91	6	.329	.533	0	0	3B-153
1962	160	611	178	27	5	24	3.9	92	98	75	104	12	.291	.470	0	0	3B-159
1963	159	617	176	28	2	24	3.9	86	111	70	90	1	.285	.454	0	0	3B-162
1964	162	628	185	30	10	24	3.8	100	119	70	85	3	.295	.489	0	0	3B-162
1965	144	535	139	18	2	13	2.4	71	75	57	73	2	.260	.374	3	0	3B-143
1966 NY N	136	496	132	28	2	14	2.8	62	61	30	64	4	.266	.415	7	3	3B-130, 1B-2
1967 2 teams		NY	N	(56G –	.235)		CHI	A	(57G –	.261)							
" total	113	346	86	12	3	7	2.0	34	34	33	47	2	.249	.361	15	4	3B-77, 1B-26
1968 2 teams		CHI	A (10G –	.125)		LA	N	(83G –	.271)								
" total	93	245	63	7	2	6	2.4	20	41	17	40	2	.257	.376	29	6	3B-39, 1B-33
1969 LA N	25	34	7	2	0	0	0.0	0	4	2	7	0	.206	.265	19	4	1B-4
15 yrs.	2034	7455	2143	318	68	282	3.8	1104	1141	713	1017	105	.287	.462	83	18	3B-1785, OF-111, 1B-65, SS-31

WORLD SERIES

	G	AB	H	2B	3B	HR	HR%	R	RBI	BB	SO	SB	BA	SA	PH AB	H	G by POS
1964 STL N	7	27	6	1	0	2	7.4	5	6	1	5	0	.222	.481	0	0	3B-7

	G	AB	H	2B	3B	HR	HR %	R	RBI	BB	SO	SB	BA	SA	Pinch Hit AB	Pinch Hit H	G by POS

Dorian Boyland

BOYLAND, DORIAN SCOTT
Also known as Dorian Scott Costales.
B. Jan. 6, 1955, Chicago, Ill.

BL TL 6'4" 200 lbs.

	G	AB	H	2B	3B	HR	HR%	R	RBI	BB	SO	SB	BA	SA	AB	H	G by POS
1978 PIT N	6	8	2	0	0	0	0.0	1	1	0	1	0	.250	.250	5	1	1B-1
1979	4	3	0	0	0	0	0.0	0	0	0	2	0	.000	.000	3	0	
1981	11	8	0	0	0	0	0.0	0	0	1	3	0	.000	.000	8	0	
3 yrs.	21	19	2	0	0	0	0.0	1	1	1	6	0	.105	.105	16	1	1B-1

Buzz Boyle

BOYLE, RALPH FRANCIS
Brother of Jim Boyle.
B. Feb. 9, 1908, Cincinnati, Ohio   D. Nov. 12, 1978, Cincinnati, Ohio

BL TL 5'11½" 170 lbs.

	G	AB	H	2B	3B	HR	HR%	R	RBI	BB	SO	SB	BA	SA	AB	H	G by POS
1929 BOS N	17	57	15	2	1	1	1.8	8	2	6	11	2	.263	.386	0	0	OF-17
1930	1	1	0	0	0	0	0.0	0	0	1	0	0	.000	.000	0	0	OF-1
1933 BKN N	93	338	101	13	4	0	0.0	38	31	16	24	7	.299	.361	3	1	OF-90
1934	128	472	144	26	10	7	1.5	88	48	51	44	8	.305	.447	6	2	OF-121
1935	127	475	129	17	9	4	0.8	51	44	43	45	7	.272	.371	2	0	OF-124
5 yrs.	366	1343	389	58	24	12	0.9	185	125	116	125	24	.290	.395	11	3	OF-353

Eddie Boyle

BOYLE, EDWARD J.
Brother of Jack Boyle.
B. May 8, 1874, Cincinnati, Ohio   D. Feb. 9, 1941, Cincinnati, Ohio

BR TR 6'3" 200 lbs.

	G	AB	H	2B	3B	HR	HR%	R	RBI	BB	SO	SB	BA	SA	AB	H	G by POS
1896 2 teams		LOU	N	(3G –	.000)		PIT	N	(2G –	.000)							
" total	5	14	0	0	0	0	0.0	0		2	3	0	.000	.000	0	0	C-5

Henry Boyle

BOYLE, HENRY J. (Handsome Henry)
B. Sept. 20, 1860, Philadelphia, Pa.   D. May 25, 1932, Philadelphia, Pa.

TR

	G	AB	H	2B	3B	HR	HR%	R	RBI	BB	SO	SB	BA	SA	AB	H	G by POS
1884 STL U	65	262	68	10	3	4	1.5	41			9		.260	.366	0	0	OF-43, P-19, 3B-4, SS-1, 2B-1, 1B-1
1885 STL N	72	258	52	9	1	1	0.4	24	21	13	38		.202	.256	0	0	P-42, OF-31, 2B-2
1886	30	108	27	2	2	1	0.9	8	13	5	19		.250	.333	0	0	P-25, OF-6
1887 IND N	41	141	27	9	1	2	1.4	17	13	9	18	2	.191	.312	0	0	P-38, OF-4
1888	37	125	18	2	0	1	0.8	13	6	6	31	1	.144	.184	0	0	P-37, 1B-1
1889	46	155	38	10	0	1	0.6	17	17	9	23	4	.245	.329	0	0	P-46, 3B-1
6 yrs.	291	1049	230	42	7	10	1.0	120	69	51	129	7	.219	.301	0	0	P-207, OF-84, 3B-5, 2B-3, 1B-2, SS-1

Jack Boyle

BOYLE, JOHN ANTHONY (Honest Jack)
Brother of Eddie Boyle.
B. Mar. 22, 1866, Cincinnati, Ohio   D. Jan. 7, 1913, Cincinnati, Ohio

BR TR 6'4" 190 lbs.

	G	AB	H	2B	3B	HR	HR%	R	RBI	BB	SO	SB	BA	SA	AB	H	G by POS
1886 CIN AA	1	5	1	0	0	0	0.0	0		0			.200	.200	0	0	C-1
1887 STL AA	88	350	66	3	1	2	0.6	48		20		7	.189	.220	0	0	C-86, OF-2, 1B-2, 3B-1
1888	71	257	62	8	1	1	0.4	33	23	13		11	.241	.292	0	0	C-70, OF-1
1889	99	347	85	11	4	4	1.2	54	42	21	42	5	.245	.334	0	0	C-80, 3B-12, OF-5, 1B-4, 2B-1
1890 CHI P	100	369	96	9	5	1	0.3	56	49	44	29	11	.260	.320	0	0	C-50, 3B-30, SS-16, 1B-7, OF-2
1891 STL AA	123	439	123	18	8	5	1.1	78	79	47	36	19	.280	.392	0	0	C-91, SS-26, 3B-8, OF-3, 2B-3, 1B-3
1892 NY N	120	436	80	8	8	0	0.0	52	32	36	40	10	.183	.239	0	0	C-79, 1B-40, OF-2, SS-2
1893 PHI N	116	504	144	29	9	4	0.8	105	81	41	30	22	.286	.403	0	0	1B-112, C-6, 2B-1
1894	114	495	149	21	10	4	0.8	98	88	45	26	21	.301	.408	0	0	1B-114, 3B-1, 2B-1
1895	133	565	143	17	4	0	0.0	90	67	35	23	13	.253	.297	0	0	1B-133
1896	40	145	43	4	1	1	0.7	17	28	6	7	3	.297	.359	0	0	C-28, 1B-12
1897	75	288	73	9	1	2	0.7	37	36	19		3	.253	.313	2	1	C-50, 1B-24
1898	6	22	2	0	1	0	0.0	0	3	1		0	.091	.182	0	0	1B-4, C-3
13 yrs.	1086	4222	1067	137	53	24	0.6	668	527	328	233	125	.253	.327	2	1	C-544, 1B-455, 3B-52, SS-44, OF-15, 2B-7

Jack Boyle

BOYLE, JOHN BELLEW
B. July 9, 1889, Morris, Ill.   D. Apr. 3, 1971, Ft. Lauderdale, Fla.

BL TR 5'11½" 165 lbs.

	G	AB	H	2B	3B	HR	HR%	R	RBI	BB	SO	SB	BA	SA	AB	H	G by POS
1912 PHI N	15	25	7	1	0	0	0.0	4	2	1	5	0	.280	.320	5	2	3B-6, SS-2

Jim Boyle

BOYLE, JAMES JOHN
Brother of Buzz Boyle.
B. Jan. 19, 1904, Cincinnati, Ohio   D. Dec. 24, 1958, Cincinnati, Ohio

BR TR 6' 180 lbs.

	G	AB	H	2B	3B	HR	HR%	R	RBI	BB	SO	SB	BA	SA	AB	H	G by POS
1926 NY N	1	0	0	0	0	0	0.0	0	0	0	0	0	–	–	0	0	C-1

Gib Brack

BRACK, GILBERT HERMAN (Gibby)
B. Mar. 29, 1908, Chicago, Ill.   D. Jan. 20, 1960, Greenville, Tex.

BR TR 5'9" 170 lbs.

	G	AB	H	2B	3B	HR	HR%	R	RBI	BB	SO	SB	BA	SA	AB	H	G by POS
1937 BKN N	112	372	102	27	9	5	1.3	60	38	44	93	9	.274	.435	6	1	OF-101
1938 2 teams		BKN	N	(40G –	.214)		PHI	N	(72G –	.287)							
" total	112	338	93	22	5	5	1.5	50	34	22	44	3	.275	.414	14	6	OF-81
1939 PHI N	91	270	78	21	4	6	2.2	40	41	26	49	1	.289	.463	19	5	OF-48, 1B-19
3 yrs.	315	980	273	70	18	16	1.6	150	113	92	186	13	.279	.436	39	12	OF-230, 1B-19

Buddy Bradford

BRADFORD, CHARLES WILLIAM
B. July 25, 1944, Mobile, Ala.

BR TR 5'11" 170 lbs.

	G	AB	H	2B	3B	HR	HR%	R	RBI	BB	SO	SB	BA	SA	AB	H	G by POS
1966 CHI A	14	28	4	0	0	0	0.0	3	0	2	6	0	.143	.143	0	0	OF-9
1967	24	20	2	1	0	0	0.0	6	1	1	7	1	.100	.150	3	1	OF-14
1968	103	281	61	11	0	5	1.8	32	24	23	67	8	.217	.310	6	1	OF-99
1969	93	273	70	8	2	11	4.0	36	27	34	75	5	.256	.421	5	0	OF-88
1970 2 teams		CHI	A	(32G –	.187)		CLE	A	(75G –	.196)							
" total	107	254	49	9	1	9	3.5	33	31	31	73	1	.193	.343	18	3	OF-91, 3B-1
1971 2 teams		CLE	A	(20G –	.158)		CIN	N	(79G –	.200)							
" total	99	138	26	5	1	2	1.4	21	15	20	33	4	.188	.283	14	2	OF-84
1972 CHI A	35	48	13	2	0	2	4.2	13	8	4	13	3	.271	.438	10	4	OF-28
1973	53	168	40	3	1	8	4.8	24	15	17	43	4	.238	.411	5	0	OF-51
1974	39	96	32	2	0	5	5.2	16	10	13	11	1	.333	.510	7	2	OF-32, DH-1

	G	AB	H	2B	3B	HR	HR %	R	RBI	BB	SO	SB	BA	SA	Pinch Hit AB	Pinch Hit H	G by POS

Buddy Bradford continued

	G	AB	H	2B	3B	HR	HR %	R	RBI	BB	SO	SB	BA	SA	AB	H	G by POS
1975 2 teams	CHI A (25G – .155)			STL N (50G – .272)													
" total	75	139	31	4	1	6	4.3	20	30	20	46	3	.223	.396	27	6	OF-43, DH-4
1976 CHI A	55	160	35	5	2	4	2.5	20	14	19	37	6	.219	.350	9	0	OF-48, DH-3
11 yrs.	697	1605	363	50	8	52	3.2	224	175	184	411	36	.226	.364	104	19	OF-587, DH-8, 3B-1

Vic Bradford

BRADFORD, HENRY VICTOR   BR TR 6'2"   190 lbs.
B. Mar. 5, 1915, Brownsville, Tenn.

	G	AB	H	2B	3B	HR	HR %	R	RBI	BB	SO	SB	BA	SA	AB	H	G by POS
1943 NY N	6	5	1	0	0	0	0.0	1	1	1	1	0	.200	.200	1	0	OF-1

Bill Bradley

BRADLEY, WILLIAM JOSEPH   BR TR 6'   185 lbs.
B. Feb. 13, 1878, Cleveland, Ohio   D. Mar. 11, 1954, Cleveland, Ohio
Manager 1914.

	G	AB	H	2B	3B	HR	HR %	R	RBI	BB	SO	SB	BA	SA	AB	H	G by POS
1899 CHI N	35	129	40	6	1	2	1.6	26	18	12		4	.310	.419	0	0	3B-30, SS-5
1900	122	444	125	21	8	5	1.1	63	49	27		14	.282	.399	1	1	3B-106, 1B-15
1901 CLE A	133	516	151	28	13	1	0.2	95	55	26		15	.293	.403	0	0	3B-133, P-1
1902	137	550	187	39	12	11	2.0	104	77	27		11	.340	.515	0	0	3B-137
1903	137	543	171	36	22	6	1.1	103	68	25		21	.315	.495	0	0	3B-137
1904	154	607	182	31	8	5	0.8	94	83	26		27	.300	.402	0	0	3B-154
1905	145	537	144	34	6	0	0.0	63	51	27		22	.268	.354	0	0	3B-145
1906	82	302	83	15	2	2	0.7	32	25	18		13	.275	.358	0	0	3B-82
1907	139	498	111	20	1	0	0.0	48	34	35		20	.223	.267	0	0	3B-139
1908	148	548	133	24	7	1	0.2	70	46	29		18	.243	.318	0	0	3B-116, SS-32
1909	95	334	62	6	3	0	0.0	30	22	19		8	.186	.222	2	1	3B-87, 2B-3, 1B-3
1910	61	214	42	3	0	0	0.0	12	12	10		6	.196	.210	0	0	3B-61
1914 BKN F	7	6	3	1	0	0	0.0	1	3	0		0	.500	.667	6	3	
1915 KC F	66	203	38	9	1	0	0.0	15	9	9		6	.187	.241	5	0	3B-61
14 yrs.	1461	5431	1472	273	84	33	0.6	756	552	290		185	.271	.370	14	5	3B-1388, SS-37, 1B-18, 2B-3, P-1

George Bradley

BRADLEY, GEORGE WASHINGTON (Grin)   BR TR 5'10½" 175 lbs.
B. July 13, 1852, Reading, Pa.   D. Oct. 2, 1931, Philadelphia, Pa.

	G	AB	H	2B	3B	HR	HR %	R	RBI	BB	SO	SB	BA	SA	AB	H	G by POS
1876 STL N	64	265	66	7	6	0	0.0	29	28	3	12		.249	.321	0	0	P-64
1877 CHI N	55	214	52	7	3	0	0.0	31	12	6	19		.243	.304	0	0	P-50, 3B-16, 1B-3, OF-1
1879 TRO N	63	251	62	9	5	0	0.0	36	23	1	20		.247	.323	0	0	P-54, 3B-5, 1B-3, OF-1, SS-1
1880 PRO N	82	309	70	7	6	0	0.0	32	23	5	38		.227	.288	0	0	3B-57, P-28, OF-7, 1B-2
1881 2 teams	DET N (1G – .000)			CLE N (60G – .249)													
" total	61	245	60	10	1	2	0.8	21	18	4	25		.245	.318	0	0	3B-48, SS-7, P-6, OF-1
1882 CLE N	30	115	21	5	0	0	0.0	16	6	4	16		.183	.226	0	0	P-18, OF-9, 1B-6
1883 2 teams	CLE N (4G – .313)			PHI AA (76G – .234)													
" total	80	328	78	8	6	1	0.3	47		8	1		.238	.308	0	0	3B-44, P-26, OF-11, SS-4, 1B-2
1884 CIN U	58	226	43	4	7	0	0.0	31		7			.190	.270	0	0	P-41, OF-16, SS-5, 1B-2
1886 PHI AA	13	48	4	0	1	0	0.0	1		1			.083	.125	0	0	SS-13
1888 BAL AA	1	3	0	0	0	0	0.0	0	0	0		0	.000	.000	0	0	SS-1
10 yrs.	507	2004	456	57	35	3	0.1	244	110	39	131		.228	.295	0	0	P-287, 3B-170, OF-46, SS-31, 1B-18

George Bradley

BRADLEY, GEORGE WASHINGTON   BR TR 6'1½" 185 lbs.
B. Apr. 1, 1914, Greenwood, Ark.

	G	AB	H	2B	3B	HR	HR %	R	RBI	BB	SO	SB	BA	SA	AB	H	G by POS
1946 STL A	4	12	2	1	0	0	0.0	2	3	0	1	0	.167	.250	0	0	OF-3

Hugh Bradley

BRADLEY, HUGH FREDERICK (Corns)   BR TR 5'10"   175 lbs.
B. May 23, 1885, Grafton, Mass.   D. Jan. 26, 1949, Worcester, Mass.

	G	AB	H	2B	3B	HR	HR %	R	RBI	BB	SO	SB	BA	SA	AB	H	G by POS
1910 BOS A	32	83	14	6	2	0	0.0	8	7	5		2	.169	.289	7	2	1B-21, C-3, OF-1
1911	12	41	13	2	0	1	2.4	9	4	2		1	.317	.439	0	0	1B-12
1912	40	137	26	11	1	1	0.7	16	19	15		3	.190	.307	0	0	1B-40
1914 PIT F	118	427	131	20	6	0	0.0	41	61	27		7	.307	.382	0	0	1B-118
1915 3 teams	PIT F (26G – .273)			BKN F (37G – .246)			NWK F (12G – .152)										
" total	75	225	54	7	3	0	0.0	10	26	10		10	.240	.298	18	3	1B-34, OF-22, C-1
5 yrs.	277	913	238	46	12	2	0.2	84	117	59		23	.261	.344	25	5	1B-225, OF-23, C-4

Jack Bradley

BRADLEY, JOHN THOMAS   BR TR 5'11"   175 lbs.
B. Sept. 20, 1893, Denver, Colo.   D. Mar. 18, 1969, Tulsa, Okla.

	G	AB	H	2B	3B	HR	HR %	R	RBI	BB	SO	SB	BA	SA	AB	H	G by POS
1916 CLE A	2	3	0	0	0	0	0.0	0	0	0	1	0	.000	.000	1	0	C-1

Mark Bradley

BRADLEY, MARK ALLEN   BR TR 6'1"   180 lbs.
B. Dec. 3, 1956, Elizabethtown, Ky.

	G	AB	H	2B	3B	HR	HR %	R	RBI	BB	SO	SB	BA	SA	AB	H	G by POS
1981 LA N	9	6	1	1	0	0	0.0	2	0	0	1	0	.167	.333	2	0	OF-6
1982	8	3	1	0	0	0	0.0	1	0	0	0	0	.333	.333	1	0	OF-3
1983 NY N	73	104	21	4	0	3	2.9	10	5	11	35	4	.202	.327	34	6	OF-35
3 yrs.	90	113	23	5	0	3	2.7	13	5	11	36	4	.204	.327	37	6	OF-44

Nick Bradley

BRADLEY, J. NICHOLS   5'10"   185 lbs.
B. Altoona, Pa.   D. Jan. 16, 1889

	G	AB	H	2B	3B	HR	HR %	R	RBI	BB	SO	SB	BA	SA	AB	H	G by POS
1884 WAS U	1	3	0	0	0	0	0.0	0		2			.000	.000	0	0	OF-1

Phil Bradley

BRADLEY, PHILIP POOLE   BR TR 6'2"   180 lbs.
B. Mar. 11, 1959, Bloomington, Ind.

	G	AB	H	2B	3B	HR	HR %	R	RBI	BB	SO	SB	BA	SA	AB	H	G by POS
1983 SEA A	23	67	18	2	0	0	0.0	8	5	8	5	3	.269	.299	3	0	OF-21, DH-1
1984	124	322	97	12	4	0	0.0	49	24	34	61	21	.301	.363	3	0	OF-117, DH-3
2 yrs.	147	389	115	14	4	0	0.0	57	29	42	66	24	.296	.352	6	0	OF-138, DH-4

	G	AB	H	2B	3B	HR	HR %	R	RBI	BB	SO	SB	BA	SA	Pinch Hit AB	Pinch Hit H	G by POS

Scott Bradley

BRADLEY, SCOTT WILLIAM
B. Mar. 22, 1960, Essex Fells, N. J.   BL TR 5'11"   175 lbs.

	G	AB	H	2B	3B	HR	HR%	R	RBI	BB	SO	SB	BA	SA	PH AB	PH H	G by POS
1984 NY A	9	21	6	1	0	0	0.0	3	2	1	1	0	.286	.333	1	0	OF-5, C-3

Dallas Bradshaw

BRADSHAW, DALLAS CARL (Rabbit)
B. Nov. 23, 1895, Herrin, Ill. D. Dec. 11, 1939, Herrin, Ill.   BL TR 5'7"   145 lbs.

	G	AB	H	2B	3B	HR	HR%	R	RBI	BB	SO	SB	BA	SA	PH AB	PH H	G by POS
1917 PHI A	2	4	0	0	0	0	0.0	0	0	0	1	0	.000	.000	1	0	2B-1

George Bradshaw

BRADSHAW, GEORGE THOMAS
B. Sept. 12, 1924, Salisbury, N. C.   BR TR 6'2"   185 lbs.

	G	AB	H	2B	3B	HR	HR%	R	RBI	BB	SO	SB	BA	SA	PH AB	PH H	G by POS
1952 WAS A	10	23	5	2	0	0	0.0	3	6	1	2	0	.217	.304	1	0	C-9

Bob Brady

BRADY, ROBERT JAY
B. Nov. 8, 1922, Lewistown, Pa.   BL TR 6'1"   175 lbs.

	G	AB	H	2B	3B	HR	HR%	R	RBI	BB	SO	SB	BA	SA	PH AB	PH H	G by POS
1946 BOS N	3	5	1	0	0	0	0.0	0	0	1	1	0	.200	.200	2	1	C-1
1947	1	1	0	0	0	0	0.0	0	0	0	0	0	.000	.000	1	0	
2 yrs.	4	6	1	0	0	0	0.0	0	0	1	1	0	.167	.167	3	1	C-1

Cliff Brady

BRADY, CLIFFORD FRANCIS
B. Mar. 6, 1897, St. Louis, Mo.   D. Sept. 25, 1974, Belleville, Ill.   BR TR 5'5½" 140 lbs.

	G	AB	H	2B	3B	HR	HR%	R	RBI	BB	SO	SB	BA	SA	PH AB	PH H	G by POS
1920 BOS A	53	180	41	5	1	0	0.0	16	12	13	12	0	.228	.267	0	0	2B-53

Fred Brady

Playing record listed under Larry Kopf

Steve Brady

BRADY, STEPHEN A.
Brother of Tom Brady.
B. July 14, 1851, Worcester, Mass.   D. Nov. 2, 1917, Hartford, Conn.

	G	AB	H	2B	3B	HR	HR%	R	RBI	BB	SO	SB	BA	SA	PH AB	PH H	G by POS
1883 NY AA	97	432	117	12	6	0	0.0	69		11			.271	.326	0	0	1B-81, OF-16
1884	112	485	122	11	3	0	0.0	102		21			.252	.287	0	0	OF-110, 1B-5, 2B-1
1885	108	434	128	14	5	3	0.7	60		25			.295	.371	0	0	OF-105, 1B-4, 2B-2, 3B-1
1886	124	466	112	8	5	0	0.0	56		35			.240	.279	0	0	OF-123, 1B-1
4 yrs.	441	1817	479	45	19	3	0.2	287		92			.264	.314	0	0	OF-354, 1B-91, 2B-3, 3B-1

Bobby Bragan

BRAGAN, ROBERT RANDALL
B. Oct. 30, 1917, Birmingham, Ala.   BR TR 5'10½" 175 lbs.
Manager 1956-58, 1963-66.

	G	AB	H	2B	3B	HR	HR%	R	RBI	BB	SO	SB	BA	SA	PH AB	PH H	G by POS
1940 PHI N	132	474	105	14	1	7	1.5	36	44	28	34	2	.222	.300	0	0	SS-132, 3B-2
1941	154	557	140	19	3	4	0.7	37	69	26	29	7	.251	.318	0	0	SS-154, 2B-2, 3B-1
1942	109	335	73	12	2	2	0.6	17	15	20	21	0	.218	.284	2	0	SS-78, C-22, 2B-4, 3B-3
1943 BKN N	74	220	58	7	2	2	0.9	17	24	15	16	0	.264	.341	1	0	C-57, 3B-12, SS-5
1944	94	266	71	8	4	0	0.0	26	17	13	14	2	.267	.327	3	1	SS-51, C-35, 2B-1
1947	25	36	7	2	0	0	0.0	3	3	7	3	1	.194	.250	4	0	C-24
1948	9	12	2	0	0	0	0.0	0	0	1	0	0	.167	.167	4	0	C-5
7 yrs.	597	1900	456	62	12	15	0.8	136	172	110	117	12	.240	.309	14	2	SS-420, C-143, 3B-18, 2B-7

WORLD SERIES

	G	AB	H	2B	3B	HR	HR%	R	RBI	BB	SO	SB	BA	SA	PH AB	PH H	G by POS
1947 BKN N	1	1	1	1	0	0	0.0	0	1	0	0	0	1.000	2.000	1	1	

Dave Brain

BRAIN, DAVID LEONARD
B. Jan. 24, 1879, Hereford, England   D. May 25, 1959, Los Angeles, Calif.   BR TR 5'10" 170 lbs.

	G	AB	H	2B	3B	HR	HR%	R	RBI	BB	SO	SB	BA	SA	PH AB	PH H	G by POS
1901 CHI A	5	20	7	1	0	0	0.0	2	5	1		0	.350	.400	0	0	2B-5
1903 STL N	119	464	107	8	15	1	0.2	44	60	25		21	.231	.319	0	0	SS-72, 3B-46
1904	127	488	130	24	12	7	1.4	57	72	17		18	.266	.408	2	0	SS-59, 3B-30, OF-19, 2B-13, 1B-4
1905 2 teams	STL N (44G – .228)				PIT N (85G – .257)												
" total	129	465	115	21	11	4	0.9	42	63	23		12	.247	.366	3	1	3B-84, SS-33, OF-6
1906 BOS N	139	525	131	19	5	5	1.0	43	45	29		10	.250	.333	0	0	3B-139
1907	133	509	142	24	9	10	2.0	60	56	29		11	.279	.420	0	0	3B-130, OF-3
1908 2 teams	CIN N (16G – .109)				NY N (11G – .176)												
" total	27	72	9	0	0	0	0.0	6	2	10		1	.125	.125	2	0	OF-19, 2B-3, 3B-2, SS-1
7 yrs.	679	2543	641	97	52	27	1.1	254	303	134		73	.252	.363	7	1	3B-431, SS-165, OF-47, 2B-21, 1B-4

Fred Brainerd

BRAINERD, FREDERICK F.
B. Jan. 17, 1892, Champaign, Ill.   D. Apr. 17, 1959, Galveston, Tex.   BR TR 6'   176 lbs.

	G	AB	H	2B	3B	HR	HR%	R	RBI	BB	SO	SB	BA	SA	PH AB	PH H	G by POS
1914 NY N	2	5	1	0	0	0	0.0	1		1	0	0	.200	.200	0	0	2B-2
1915	91	249	50	7	2	1	0.4	31	21	21	44	6	.201	.257	20	3	1B-45, 3B-16, SS-9, OF-1, 2B-1
1916	2	7	0	0	0	0	0.0	0	0	0	0	0	.000	.000	0	0	3B-2
3 yrs.	95	261	51	7	2	1	0.4	32	21	22	44	6	.195	.249	20	3	1B-45, 3B-18, SS-9, 2B-3, OF-1

Erv Brame

BRAME, ERVIN BECKHAM
B. Oct. 12, 1901, Big Rock, Tenn.   D. Nov. 22, 1949, Hopkinsville, Ky.   BL TR 6'2"   190 lbs.

	G	AB	H	2B	3B	HR	HR%	R	RBI	BB	SO	SB	BA	SA	PH AB	PH H	G by POS
1928 PIT N	35	49	13	4	0	1	2.0	6	11	4	3	0	.265	.408	9	1	P-24
1929	59	116	36	8	1	4	3.4	9	25	2	7	0	.310	.500	21	10	P-37
1930	50	116	41	5	0	3	2.6	20	22	0	2	0	.353	.474	16	6	P-32
1931	48	95	26	4	1	0	0.0	6	15	4	16	0	.274	.337	21	7	P-26
1932	26	20	5	0	0	0	0.0	2	2	0	4	0	.250	.250	3	1	P-23
5 yrs.	218	396	121	21	2	8	2.0	43	75	10	32	0	.306	.429	70	25	P-142

Art Bramhall

BRAMHALL, ARTHUR WASHINGTON
B. Feb. 22, 1909, Chicago, Ill.   BR TR 5'11" 170 lbs.

	G	AB	H	2B	3B	HR	HR%	R	RBI	BB	SO	SB	BA	SA	PH AB	PH H	G by POS
1935 PHI N	2	1	0	0	0	0	0.0	0	0	0	0	0	.000	.000	0	0	SS-1, 3B-1

Al Brancato

BRANCATO, ALBERT
B. May 29, 1919, Philadelphia, Pa.
BR TR 5'9½" 188 lbs.

	G	AB	H	2B	3B	HR	HR%	R	RBI	BB	SO	SB	BA	SA	PH AB	PH H	G by POS
1939 PHI A	21	68	14	5	0	1	1.5	12	8	8	4	1	.206	.324	0	0	3B-20, SS-1
1940	107	298	57	11	2	1	0.3	42	23	28	36	3	.191	.252	2	0	SS-80, 3B-25
1941	144	530	124	20	9	2	0.4	60	49	59	49	0	.234	.317	1	0	SS-139, 3B-7
1945	10	34	4	1	0	0	0.0	3	0	1	3	0	.118	.147	0	0	SS-10
4 yrs.	282	930	199	37	11	4	0.4	117	80	96	92	5	.214	.290	3	0	SS-230, 3B-52

Ron Brand

BRAND, RONALD GEORGE
B. Jan. 13, 1940, Los Angeles, Calif.
BR TR 5'7½" 167 lbs.

	G	AB	H	2B	3B	HR	HR%	R	RBI	BB	SO	SB	BA	SA	PH AB	PH H	G by POS
1963 PIT N	46	66	19	2	0	1	1.5	8	7	10	11	0	.288	.364	5	0	C-33, 3B-2, 2B-2
1965 HOU N	117	391	92	6	3	2	0.5	27	37	19	34	10	.235	.281	6	0	C-102, 3B-6, OF-5
1966	56	123	30	2	0	0	0.0	12	10	9	13	0	.244	.260	20	3	C-25, 2B-9, OF-3, 3B-1
1967	84	215	52	8	1	0	0.0	22	18	23	17	4	.242	.288	14	2	C-67, OF-1, 2B-1
1968	43	81	13	2	0	0	0.0	7	4	9	11	1	.160	.185	7	1	C-29, OF-1, 3B-1
1969 MON N	103	287	74	12	0	0	0.0	19	20	30	19	2	.258	.300	13	3	C-84, OF-2
1970	72	126	30	2	3	0	0.0	10	9	9	16	2	.238	.302	35	7	SS-19, 3B-12, C-9, OF-5, 2B-3
1971	47	56	12	0	0	0	0.0	3	1	3	5	1	.214	.214	15	3	SS-22, OF-4, 3B-4, 2B-1, C-1
8 yrs.	568	1345	322	34	7	3	0.2	108	106	112	126	20	.239	.282	115	19	C-350, SS-41, 3B-26, OF-21, 2B-16

Jackie Brandt

BRANDT, JOHN GEORGE
B. Apr. 28, 1934, Omaha, Neb.
BR TR 5'11" 165 lbs.

	G	AB	H	2B	3B	HR	HR%	R	RBI	BB	SO	SB	BA	SA	PH AB	PH H	G by POS
1956 2 teams	STL N (27G – .286)				NY N (98G – .299)												
" total	125	393	117	19	8	12	3.1	54	50	21	36	3	.298	.478	4	2	OF-122
1958 SF N	18	52	13	1	0	0	0.0	7	3	6	5	1	.250	.269	5	1	OF-14
1959	137	429	116	16	5	12	2.8	63	57	35	69	11	.270	.415	16	4	OF-116, 3B-18, 1B-3, 2B-1
1960 BAL A	145	511	130	24	6	15	2.9	73	65	47	69	5	.254	.413	4	0	OF-142, 3B-2, 2B-1
1961	139	516	153	18	5	16	3.1	93	72	62	51	10	.297	.444	0	0	OF-136, 3B-1
1962	143	505	129	29	5	19	3.8	76	75	55	64	9	.255	.446	6	1	OF-138, 3B-2
1963	142	451	112	15	5	15	3.3	49	61	34	85	4	.248	.404	8	1	OF-134, 3B-1
1964	137	523	127	25	1	13	2.5	66	47	45	104	1	.243	.369	4	0	OF-134
1965	96	243	59	17	0	8	3.3	35	24	21	40	1	.243	.412	14	2	OF-84
1966 PHI N	82	164	41	6	1	1	0.6	16	15	17	36	0	.250	.317	15	4	OF-71
1967 2 teams	PHI N (16G – .105)				HOU N (41G – .236)												
" total	57	108	23	5	1	1	0.9	8	16	8	15	0	.213	.306	33	9	1B-14, OF-9, 3B-1
11 yrs.	1221	3895	1020	175	37	112	2.9	540	485	351	574	45	.262	.412	109	24	OF-1100, 3B-25, 1B-18, 2B-1

Otis Brannan

BRANNAN, OTIS OWEN
B. Mar. 13, 1899, Greenbrier, Ark.   D. June 6, 1967, Little Rock, Ark.
BL TR 5'9" 160 lbs.

	G	AB	H	2B	3B	HR	HR%	R	RBI	BB	SO	SB	BA	SA	PH AB	PH H	G by POS
1928 STL A	135	483	118	18	3	10	2.1	68	66	60	19	3	.244	.356	0	0	2B-135
1929	23	51	14	1	0	1	2.0	4	8	4	4	0	.275	.353	4	1	2B-19
2 yrs.	158	534	132	19	3	11	2.1	72	74	64	23	3	.247	.356	4	1	2B-154

Dudley Branom

BRANOM, EDGAR DUDLEY
B. Nov. 30, 1897, Sulphur Springs, Tex.   D. Feb. 4, 1980, Sun City, Ariz.
BL TL 6'1" 190 lbs.

	G	AB	H	2B	3B	HR	HR%	R	RBI	BB	SO	SB	BA	SA	PH AB	PH H	G by POS
1927 PHI A	30	94	22	1	0	0	0.0	8	13	2	5	2	.234	.245	4	2	1B-26

Kitty Bransfield

BRANSFIELD, WILLIAM EDWARD
B. Jan. 7, 1875, Worcester, Mass.   D. May 1, 1947, Worcester, Mass.
BR TR 5'11" 207 lbs.

	G	AB	H	2B	3B	HR	HR%	R	RBI	BB	SO	SB	BA	SA	PH AB	PH H	G by POS
1898 BOS N	5	9	2	0	1	0	0.0	2	1	0		0	.222	.444	0	0	C-4, 1B-1
1901 PIT N	139	566	167	26	17	0	0.0	92	91	29		23	.295	.401	0	0	1B-139
1902	102	417	127	21	7	1	0.2	50	69	17		23	.305	.396	1	0	1B-101
1903	127	505	134	23	7	2	0.4	69	57	33		13	.265	.350	0	0	1B-127
1904	139	520	116	17	9	0	0.0	47	60	22		11	.223	.290	0	0	1B-139
1905 PHI N	151	580	150	23	9	0	0.5	55	76	27		27	.259	.345	0	0	1B-151
1906	140	524	144	28	5	1	0.2	47	60	16		12	.275	.353	1	0	1B-139
1907	94	348	81	15	2	0	0.0	25	38	14		8	.233	.287	2	0	1B-92
1908	144	527	160	25	7	3	0.6	53	71	23		30	.304	.395	1	1	1B-143
1909	140	527	154	27	6	1	0.2	47	59	18		17	.292	.372	2	0	1B-138
1910	123	427	102	17	4	3	0.7	39	52	20	34	10	.239	.319	12	2	1B-138
1911 2 teams	PHI N (23G – .256)				CHI N (3G – .400)												
" total	26	53	15	3	1	0	0.0	4	3	2	7	1	.283	.377	15	1	1B-11
12 yrs.	1330	5003	1352	225	75	14	0.3	530	637	221	41	175	.270	.354	34	4	1B-1291, C-4

WORLD SERIES	G	AB	H	2B	3B	HR	HR%	R	RBI	BB	SO	SB	BA	SA	PH AB	PH H	G by POS
1903 PIT N	8	30	6	0	2	0	0.0	3	1	1	6	1	.200	.333	0	0	1B-8

Marshall Brant

BRANT, MARSHALL LEE
B. Sept. 17, 1955, Garberville, Calif.
BR TR 6'5" 185 lbs.

	G	AB	H	2B	3B	HR	HR%	R	RBI	BB	SO	SB	BA	SA	PH AB	PH H	G by POS
1980 NY A	3	6	0	0	0	0	0.0	0	0	0	3	0	.000	.000	1	0	1B-2, DH-1
1983 OAK A	5	14	2	0	0	0	0.0	2	2	0	3	0	.143	.143	2	0	1B-3, DH-1
2 yrs.	8	20	2	0	0	0	0.0	2	2	0	6	0	.100	.100	3	0	1B-5, DH-2

Kitty Brashear

BRASHEAR, ROBERT NORMAN C.
Brother of Roy Brashear.
B. Aug. 27, 1877, Mansfield, Ohio   D. Dec. 22, 1934, Los Angeles, Calif.

	G	AB	H	2B	3B	HR	HR%	R	RBI	BB	SO	SB	BA	SA	PH AB	PH H	G by POS
1902 STL N	110	388	107	8	2	1	0.3	36	40	32		9	.276	.314	3	1	1B-67, 2B-21, OF-16, SS-3

Roy Brashear

BRASHEAR, ROY PARKS
Brother of Kitty Brashear.
B. Jan. 3, 1874, Ashtabula, Ohio   D. Apr. 20, 1951, Los Angeles, Calif.
BR TR

	G	AB	H	2B	3B	HR	HR%	R	RBI	BB	SO	SB	BA	SA	PH AB	PH H	G by POS
1899 LOU N	3	2	1	0	0	0	0.0	0	0	0		0	.500	.500	0	0	P-3

	G	AB	H	2B	3B	HR	HR %	R	RBI	BB	SO	SB	BA	SA	Pinch Hit AB	Pinch Hit H	G by POS

Roy Brashear continued

	G	AB	H	2B	3B	HR	HR%	R	RBI	BB	SO	SB	BA	SA	PH AB	PH H	G by POS
1903 PHI N	20	75	17	3	0	0	0.0	9	4	6		2	.227	.267	0	0	2B-18, 1B-2
2 yrs.	23	77	18	3	0	0	0.0	9	4	6		2	.234	.273	0	0	2B-18, P-3, 1B-2

Joe Bratcher

BRATCHER, JOSEPH WARLICK (Goobers)
B. July 22, 1898, Grand Saline, Tex.   BL TR 5'8½" 140 lbs.

	G	AB	H	2B	3B	HR	HR%	R	RBI	BB	SO	SB	BA	SA	PH AB	PH H	G by POS
1924 STL N	4	1	0	0	0	0	0.0	1	0	0	0	0	.000	.000	1	0	OF-1

Fred Bratchi

BRATCHI, FREDERICK OSCAR (Fritz)
B. Jan. 16, 1892, Alliance, Ohio   D. Jan. 10, 1962, Massillon, Ohio   BR TR 5'10" 170 lbs.

	G	AB	H	2B	3B	HR	HR%	R	RBI	BB	SO	SB	BA	SA	PH AB	PH H	G by POS
1921 CHI A	16	28	8	1	0	0	0.0	3	3	0	2	0	.286	.321	10	3	OF-5
1926 BOS A	72	167	46	10	1	0	0.0	12	19	14	15	0	.275	.347	30	7	OF-37
1927	1	1	0	0	0	0	0.0	0	0	0	0	0	.000	.000	1	0	
3 yrs.	89	196	54	11	1	0	0.0	12	22	14	17	0	.276	.342	41	10	OF-42

Steve Braun

BRAUN, STEPHEN RUSSELL
B. May 8, 1948, Trenton, N. J.   BL TR 5'10" 180 lbs.

	G	AB	H	2B	3B	HR	HR%	R	RBI	BB	SO	SB	BA	SA	PH AB	PH H	G by POS
1971 MIN A	128	343	87	12	2	5	1.5	51	35	48	50	8	.254	.344	26	7	3B-73, 2B-28, SS-10, OF-2
1972	121	402	116	21	0	2	0.5	40	50	45	38	4	.289	.356	14	4	3B-74, 2B-20, SS-11, OF-9
1973	115	361	102	28	5	6	1.7	46	42	74	48	4	.283	.438	5	1	3B-102, OF-6
1974	129	453	127	12	1	8	1.8	53	40	56	51	4	.280	.364	6	1	OF-108, 3B-17
1975	136	453	137	18	3	11	2.4	70	45	66	55	0	.302	.428	11	6	OF-106, DH-9, 1B-9, 3B-2, 2B-1
1976	122	417	120	12	3	3	0.7	73	61	67	43	12	.288	.353	9	5	DH-71, OF-32, 3B-16
1977 SEA A	139	451	106	19	1	5	1.1	51	31	80	59	8	.235	.315	11	0	OF-100, DH-32, 3B-1
1978 2 teams	SEA A (32G – .230)				KC	A	(64G – .263)										
" total	96	211	53	14	1	3	1.4	27	29	37	21	4	.251	.370	38	11	OF-37, DH-14, 3B-11
1979 KC A	58	116	31	2	0	4	3.4	15	10	22	11	0	.267	.388	28	8	OF-18, DH-11, 3B-2
1980 2 teams	KC A (14G – .043)				TOR	A	(37G – .273)										
" total	51	78	16	2	0	1	1.3	4	10	10	7	0	.205	.269	35	10	DH-14, OF-5, 3B-1
1981 STL N	44	46	9	2	1	0	0.0	9	2	15	7	1	.196	.283	25	5	OF-12, 3B-1
1982	58	62	17	4	0	0	0.0	6	4	11	10	0	.274	.339	41	12	OF-8, 3B-5
1983	78	92	25	2	1	3	3.3	8	7	21	7	0	.272	.413	48	15	OF-22, 3B-4
1984	86	98	27	3	1	0	0.0	6	16	17	17	0	.276	.327	60	17	OF-19, 3B-1
14 yrs.	1361	3583	973	151	19	51	1.4	459	382	569	424	45	.272	.367	357	102	OF-484, 3B-310, DH-151, 2B-49, SS-21, 1B-9
																9th	

LEAGUE CHAMPIONSHIP SERIES

	G	AB	H	2B	3B	HR	HR%	R	RBI	BB	SO	SB	BA	SA	PH AB	PH H	G by POS
1978 KC A	2	5	0	0	0	0	0.0	0	0	1	1	0	.000	.000	1	0	OF-1
1982 STL N	1	1	0	0	0	0	0.0	0	0	0	0	0	.000	.000	1	0	
2 yrs.	3	6	0	0	0	0	0.0	0	0	1	1	0	.000	.000	2	0	OF-1

WORLD SERIES

	G	AB	H	2B	3B	HR	HR%	R	RBI	BB	SO	SB	BA	SA	PH AB	PH H	G by POS
1982 STL N	2	2	1	0	0	0	0.0	0	2	1	0	0	.500	.500	1	0	DH-2

Angel Bravo

BRAVO, ANGEL ALFONSO
B. Aug. 4, 1942, Maracaibo, Venezuela   BL TL 5'8" 150 lbs.

	G	AB	H	2B	3B	HR	HR%	R	RBI	BB	SO	SB	BA	SA	PH AB	PH H	G by POS
1969 CHI A	27	90	26	4	2	1	1.1	10	3	3	5	2	.289	.411	2	0	OF-25
1970 CIN N	65	65	18	1	1	0	0.0	10	3	9	13	0	.277	.323	42	13	OF-22
1971 2 teams	CIN N (5G – .200)				SD	N	(52G – .155)										
" total	57	63	10	2	0	0	0.0	6	6	8	13	0	.159	.190	40	7	OF-9
3 yrs.	149	218	54	7	3	1	0.5	26	12	20	31	2	.248	.321	84	20	OF-56

LEAGUE CHAMPIONSHIP SERIES

	G	AB	H	2B	3B	HR	HR%	R	RBI	BB	SO	SB	BA	SA	PH AB	PH H	G by POS
1970 CIN N	1	1	0	0	0	0	0.0	0	0	0	0	0	.000	.000	1	0	

WORLD SERIES

	G	AB	H	2B	3B	HR	HR%	R	RBI	BB	SO	SB	BA	SA	PH AB	PH H	G by POS
1970 CIN N	4	2	0	0	0	0	0.0	0	0	1	1	0	.000	.000	2	0	

Buster Bray

BRAY, CLARENCE WILBUR
B. Apr. 1, 1913, Birmingham, Ala.   D. Sept. 4, 1982, Evansville, Ind.   BL TL 6' 170 lbs.

	G	AB	H	2B	3B	HR	HR%	R	RBI	BB	SO	SB	BA	SA	PH AB	PH H	G by POS
1941 BOS N	4	11	1	1	0	0	0.0	2	1	1	2	0	.091	.182	0	0	OF-3

Frank Brazill

BRAZILL, FRANK LEO
B. Aug. 11, 1899, Spangler, Pa.   D. Nov. 3, 1976, Oakland, Calif.   BL TR 5'11½" 175 lbs.

	G	AB	H	2B	3B	HR	HR%	R	RBI	BB	SO	SB	BA	SA	PH AB	PH H	G by POS
1921 PHI A	66	177	48	3	1	0	0.0	17	19	23	21	2	.271	.299	19	5	1B-36, 3B-9
1922	6	13	1	0	0	0	0.0	0	1	0	1	0	.077	.077	4	0	3B-2
2 yrs.	72	190	49	3	1	0	0.0	17	20	23	22	2	.258	.284	23	5	1B-36, 3B-11

Sid Bream

BREAM, SIDNEY EUGENE
B. Aug. 3, 1960, Carlisle, Pa.   BL TL 6'4" 215 lbs.

	G	AB	H	2B	3B	HR	HR%	R	RBI	BB	SO	SB	BA	SA	PH AB	PH H	G by POS
1983 LA N	15	11	2	0	0	0	0.0	2	2	2	2	0	.182	.182	10	2	1B-4
1984	27	49	9	3	0	0	0.0	2	6	6	9	1	.184	.245	11	1	1B-14
2 yrs.	42	60	11	3	0	0	0.0	2	8	8	11	1	.183	.233	21	3	1B-18

Jim Breazeale

BREAZEALE, JAMES LEO
B. Oct. 3, 1949, Houston, Tex.   BL TR 6'2" 210 lbs.

	G	AB	H	2B	3B	HR	HR%	R	RBI	BB	SO	SB	BA	SA	PH AB	PH H	G by POS
1969 ATL N	2	1	0	0	0	0	0.0	0	0	2	0	0	.000	.000	0	0	1B-1
1971	10	21	4	0	0	1	4.8	1	3	0	3	0	.190	.333	5	3	1B-4
1972	52	85	21	2	0	5	5.9	10	17	6	12	0	.247	.447	33	10	1B-16, 3B-1
1978 CHI A	25	72	15	3	0	3	4.2	8	13	8	10	0	.208	.375	2	1	1B-19, DH-4
4 yrs.	89	179	40	5	0	9	5.0	20	33	16	25	0	.223	.402	40	14	1B-40, DH-4, 3B-1

Danny Breeden

BREEDEN, DANIEL RICHARD
Brother of Hal Breeden.
B. June 27, 1942, Albany, Ga.   BR TR 5'11½" 185 lbs.

	G	AB	H	2B	3B	HR	HR%	R	RBI	BB	SO	SB	BA	SA	PH AB	PH H	G by POS
1969 CIN N	3	8	1	0	0	0	0.0	0	1	0	3	0	.125	.125	0	0	C-3

	G	AB	H	2B	3B	HR	HR %	R	RBI	BB	SO	SB	BA	SA	Pinch Hit AB	Pinch Hit H	G by POS

Danny Breeden continued

	G	AB	H	2B	3B	HR	HR%	R	RBI	BB	SO	SB	BA	SA	AB	H	G by POS
1971 CHI N	25	65	10	1	0	0	0.0	3	4	9	18	0	.154	.169	0	0	C-25
2 yrs.	28	73	11	1	0	0	0.0	3	5	9	21	0	.151	.164	0	0	C-28

Hal Breeden

BR TL 6'2"   200 lbs.

BREEDEN, HAROLD NOEL
Brother of Danny Breeden.
B. June 28, 1944, Albany, Ga.

	G	AB	H	2B	3B	HR	HR%	R	RBI	BB	SO	SB	BA	SA	AB	H	G by POS
1971 CHI N	23	36	5	1	0	1	2.8	1	2	2	7	0	.139	.250	14	0	1B-8
1972 MON N	42	87	20	2	0	3	3.4	6	10	7	15	0	.230	.356	17	5	1B-26, OF-10
1973	105	258	71	10	6	15	5.8	36	43	29	45	0	.275	.535	43	12	1B-66
1974	79	190	47	13	0	2	1.1	14	20	24	35	0	.247	.347	25	6	1B-56
1975	24	37	5	2	0	0	0.0	4	1	7	5	0	.135	.189	12	3	1B-12
5 yrs.	273	608	148	28	6	21	3.5	61	76	69	107	0	.243	.413	111	26	1B-168, OF-10

Marv Breeding

BR TR 6'   175 lbs.

BREEDING, MARVIN EUGENE
B. Mar. 8, 1934, Decatur, Ala.

	G	AB	H	2B	3B	HR	HR%	R	RBI	BB	SO	SB	BA	SA	AB	H	G by POS
1960 BAL A	152	551	147	25	2	3	0.5	69	43	35	80	10	.267	.336	0	0	2B-152
1961	90	244	51	8	0	1	0.4	32	16	14	33	5	.209	.254	3	0	2B-80
1962	95	240	59	10	1	2	0.8	27	18	8	41	2	.246	.321	10	1	2B-73, SS-1, 3B-1
1963 2 teams			WAS A	(58G –	.274)		LA N	(20G –	.167)								
" total	78	233	60	7	2	1	0.4	26	15	9	26	2	.258	.318	10	4	2B-39, 3B-30, SS-3
4 yrs.	415	1268	317	50	5	7	0.6	154	92	66	180	19	.250	.314	23	5	2B-344, 3B-31, SS-4

Ted Breitenstein

BL TL 5'9"   167 lbs.

BREITENSTEIN, THEODORE P.
B. June 1, 1869, St. Louis, Mo.   D. May 3, 1935, St. Louis, Mo.

	G	AB	H	2B	3B	HR	HR%	R	RBI	BB	SO	SB	BA	SA	AB	H	G by POS
1891 STL AA	6	12	0	0	0	0	0.0	0		2	0	1	.000	.000	0	0	P-6, OF-1
1892 STL N	47	131	16	1	1	0	0.0	16	6	16	20	4	.122	.145	0	0	P-39, OF-10
1893	49	160	29	1	1	1	0.6	20	14	18	15	3	.181	.219	0	0	P-48, OF-2
1894	63	182	40	7	2	0	0.0	27	13	31	19	3	.220	.280	0	0	P-56, OF-7
1895	72	218	42	2	0	0	0.0	25	18	29	22	5	.193	.202	1	1	P-54, OF-16
1896	51	162	42	5	2	0	0.0	21	12	13	26	8	.259	.315	1	1	P-44, OF-8
1897 CIN N	41	124	33	4	6	0	0.0	16	23	6		5	.266	.395	1	0	P-40
1898	41	121	26	2	1	0	0.0	16	17	16		0	.215	.248	0	0	P-39, OF-2
1899	33	105	37	4	1	1	1.0	18	11	10		1	.352	.438	0	0	P-26, OF-7
1900	41	126	24	1	1	2	1.6	12	12	9		0	.190	.262	5	1	P-24, OF-12
1901 STL N	3	6	2	0	0	0	0.0	1	0	0		0	.333	.333	0	0	P-3
11 yrs.	447	1347	291	27	15	4	0.3	174	126	150	102	30	.216	.267	8	3	P-379, OF-65

Herb Bremer

BR TR 6'   195 lbs.

BREMER, HERBERT FREDERICK
B. Oct. 25, 1913, Chicago, Ill.   D. Nov. 28, 1979, Columbus, Ga.

	G	AB	H	2B	3B	HR	HR%	R	RBI	BB	SO	SB	BA	SA	AB	H	G by POS
1937 STL N	11	33	7	1	0	0	0.0	2	3	2	4	0	.212	.242	0	0	C-10
1938	50	151	33	5	1	2	1.3	14	14	9	36	1	.219	.305	0	0	C-50
1939	9	9	1	0	0	0	0.0	0	1	0	2	0	.111	.111	1	0	C-8
3 yrs.	70	193	41	6	1	2	1.0	16	18	11	42	1	.212	.285	1	0	C-68

Sam Brenegan

BL TR 6'2"   185 lbs.

BRENEGAN, OLAF SELMER
B. Sept. 1, 1890, Galesville, Wis.   D. Apr. 20, 1956, Galesville, Wis.

	G	AB	H	2B	3B	HR	HR%	R	RBI	BB	SO	SB	BA	SA	AB	H	G by POS
1914 PIT N	1	0	0	0	0	0	–	0	0	0	0	0	–	–	0	0	C-1

Bob Brenly

BR TR 6'2"   210 lbs.

BRENLY, ROBERT EARL
B. Feb. 25, 1954, Coshocton, Ohio

	G	AB	H	2B	3B	HR	HR%	R	RBI	BB	SO	SB	BA	SA	AB	H	G by POS
1981 SF N	19	45	15	2	1	1	2.2	5	4	6	4	0	.333	.489	1	0	C-14, 3B-3, OF-1
1982	65	180	51	4	1	4	2.2	26	15	18	26	6	.283	.383	9	3	C-61, 3B-1
1983	104	281	63	12	2	7	2.5	36	34	37	48	10	.224	.356	13	2	C-90, 1B-10, OF-2
1984	145	506	147	28	4	20	4.0	74	80	48	52	6	.291	.464	6	1	C-127, 1B-22, OF-3
4 yrs.	333	1012	276	46	4	32	3.2	141	133	109	130	22	.273	.421	29	6	C-292, 1B-32, OF-6, 3B-4

Jim Brennan

BRENNAN, JAMES AUGUSTUS (Old Sport)
B. 1862, St. Louis, Mo.   D. Oct. 18, 1904, Philadelphia, Pa.

	G	AB	H	2B	3B	HR	HR%	R	RBI	BB	SO	SB	BA	SA	AB	H	G by POS
1884 STL U	56	231	50	6	1	0	0.0	38		12				.216	.251	0	0	C-33, OF-16, 3B-7, SS-1
1885 STL N	3	10	1	0	0	0	0.0	0		1		1		.100	.100	0	0	OF-2, 3B-1
1888 KC AA	34	118	20	2	0	0	0.0	5	6	3		3	.169	.186	0	0	C-25, OF-5, 3B-5
1889 PHI AA	31	113	25	4	0	0	0.0	12	15	10	15	1	.221	.257	0	0	C-13, OF-28, 2B-7, 3B-4
1890 CLE P	59	233	59	3	7	0	0.0	32	26	13	29	8	.253	.326	0	0	C-42, 3B-14, OF-6
5 yrs.	183	705	155	15	8	0	0.0	87	47	39	45	12	.220	.264	0	0	C-113, OF-36, 3B-31, 2B-7, SS-1

Bill Brenzel

BR TR 5'10"   173 lbs.

BRENZEL, WILLIAM RICHARD
B. Mar. 3, 1910, Oakland, Calif.   D. June 12, 1979, Oakland, Calif.

	G	AB	H	2B	3B	HR	HR%	R	RBI	BB	SO	SB	BA	SA	AB	H	G by POS
1932 PIT N	9	24	1	1	0	0	0.0	0	2	0	4	0	.042	.083	0	0	C-9
1934 CLE A	15	51	11	3	0	0	0.0	4	3	2	1	0	.216	.275	0	0	C-15
1935	52	142	31	5	1	0	0.0	12	14	6	10	2	.218	.268	0	0	C-51
3 yrs.	76	217	43	9	1	0	0.0	16	19	8	15	2	.198	.249	0	0	C-75

Roger Bresnahan

BR TR 5'9"   200 lbs.

BRESNAHAN, ROGER PHILIP (The Duke of Tralee)
B. June 11, 1879, Toledo, Ohio   D. Dec. 4, 1944, Toledo, Ohio
Manager 1909-12, 1915.
Hall of Fame 1945.

	G	AB	H	2B	3B	HR	HR%	R	RBI	BB	SO	SB	BA	SA	AB	H	G by POS
1897 WAS N	6	16	6	0	0	0	0.0	1	3	1		0	.375	.375	0	0	P-6, OF-1
1900 CHI N	2	2	0	0	0	0	0.0	0	0	0		0	.000	.000	0	0	C-1
1901 BAL A	86	293	77	9	9	1	0.3	40	32	23		10	.263	.365	1	0	C-69, OF-8, 3B-4, 2B-2, P-2
1902 2 teams			BAL A	(65G –	.272)		NY N	(51G –	.292)								
" total	116	413	116	22	9	5	1.2	47	56	37		18	.281	.414	2	2	OF-42, C-38, 3B-31, SS-4, 1B-4
1903 NY N	113	406	142	30	8	4	1.0	87	55	61		34	.350	.493	1	1	OF-84, 1B-13, C-11, 3B-4
1904	109	402	114	22	7	5	1.2	81	33	58		13	.284	.410	3	1	OF-93, 1B-10, SS-4, 3B-1, 2B-1

	G	AB	H	2B	3B	HR	HR %	R	RBI	BB	SO	SB	BA	SA	Pinch Hit AB	H	G by POS

Roger Bresnahan continued

	G	AB	H	2B	3B	HR	HR%	R	RBI	BB	SO	SB	BA	SA	PH AB	PH H	G by POS
1905	104	331	100	18	3	0	0.0	58	46	50		11	.302	.375	6	0	C-87, OF-8
1906	124	405	114	22	4	0	0.0	69	43	81		25	.281	.356	0	0	C-82, OF-40
1907	110	328	83	9	7	4	1.2	57	38	61		15	.253	.360	6	2	C-95, 1B-6, OF-2, 3B-1
1908	140	449	127	25	3	1	0.2	70	54	83		14	.283	.359	1	1	C-139
1909 STL N	72	234	57	4	1	0	0.0	27	23	46		11	.244	.269	2	0	C-59, 2B-9, 3B-1
1910	88	234	65	15	3	0	0.0	35	27	55	17	13	.278	.368	5	0	C-77, OF-2, P-1
1911	81	227	63	17	8	3	1.3	22	41	45	19	4	.278	.463	3	1	C-77, 2B-2
1912	48	108	36	7	2	1	0.9	8	15	14	9	4	.333	.463	14	7	C-28
1913 CHI N	68	161	37	5	2	1	0.6	20	21	21	11	7	.230	.304	9	4	C-58
1914	86	248	69	10	4	0	0.0	42	24	49	20	14	.278	.351	4	1	C-85, 2B-14, OF-1
1915	77	221	45	8	1	1	0.5	19	19	29	23	19	.204	.262	6	0	C-68
17 yrs.	1430	4478	1251	223	71	26	0.6	683	530	714	99	212	.279	.378	63	20	C-974, OF-281, 3B-42, 1B-33, 2B-28, P-9, SS-8

WORLD SERIES

	G	AB	H	2B	3B	HR	HR%	R	RBI	BB	SO	SB	BA	SA	PH AB	PH H	G by POS
1905 NY N	5	16	5	2	0	0	0.0	3	1	4	0	1	.313	.438	0	0	C-5

Rube Bressler

BRESSLER, RAYMOND BLOOM
B. Oct. 23, 1894, Coder, Pa.   D. Nov. 7, 1966, Cincinnati, Ohio   BR TL 6'   187 lbs.

	G	AB	H	2B	3B	HR	HR%	R	RBI	BB	SO	SB	BA	SA	PH AB	PH H	G by POS
1914 PHI A	29	51	11	1	1	0	0.0	6	4	6	7	0	.216	.275	0	0	P-29
1915	33	55	8	0	1	1	1.8	9	4	9	13	0	.145	.236	1	0	P-32
1916	4	5	1	0	1	0	0.0	1	1	0	0	0	.200	.400	0	0	P-4
1917 CIN N	3	5	1	0	0	0	0.0	0	0	0	2	0	.200	.200	1	0	P-2
1918	23	62	17	5	0	0	0.0	10	6	5	4	0	.274	.355	1	0	P-17, OF-3
1919	61	165	34	3	4	2	1.2	22	17	23	15	2	.206	.309	1	0	OF-48, P-13
1920	21	30	8	1	0	0	0.0	4	3	1	4	1	.267	.300	6	0	P-10, OF-3, 1B-2
1921	109	323	99	18	6	1	0.3	41	54	39	20	5	.307	.409	12	4	OF-85, 1B-6
1922	52	53	14	0	2	0	0.0	7	8	4	4	1	.264	.340	43	13	1B-3, OF-2
1923	54	119	33	3	1	0	0.0	25	18	20	4	3	.277	.319	24	9	1B-22, OF-6
1924	115	383	133	14	13	4	1.0	41	49	22	20	9	.347	.483	16	3	1B-50, OF-49
1925	97	319	111	17	6	4	1.3	43	61	40	16	9	.348	.476	4	0	1B-52, OF-38
1926	86	297	106	15	9	1	0.3	58	51	37	20	3	.357	.478	4	0	OF-80, 1B-4
1927	124	467	136	14	8	3	0.6	43	77	32	22	4	.291	.375	3	0	OF-120
1928 BKN N	145	501	148	29	13	4	0.8	78	70	80	33	2	.295	.429	7	3	OF-137
1929	136	456	145	22	8	9	2.0	72	77	67	27	4	.318	.461	12	3	OF-122
1930	109	335	100	12	8	3	0.9	53	52	51	19	4	.299	.409	8	0	OF-90, 1B-7
1931	67	153	43	4	5	0	0.0	22	26	11	10	0	.281	.373	29	2	OF-35, 1B-1
1932 2 teams		PHI	N (27G – .229)		STL	N	(10G –	.158)									
" total	37	102	22	6	1	0	0.0	9	8	2	6	0	.216	.294	14	5	OF-22
19 yrs.	1305	3881	1170	164	87	32	0.8	544	586	449	246	47	.301	.413	188	45	OF-840, 1B-147, P-107

Ed Bressoud

BRESSOUD, EDWARD FRANCIS
B. May 2, 1932, Los Angeles, Calif.   BR TR 6'1"   175 lbs.

	G	AB	H	2B	3B	HR	HR%	R	RBI	BB	SO	SB	BA	SA	PH AB	PH H	G by POS
1956 NY N	49	163	37	4	2	0	0.0	15	9	12	20	1	.227	.276	1	0	SS-48
1957	49	127	34	2	2	5	3.9	11	10	4	19	0	.268	.433	2	0	SS-33, 3B-12
1958 SF N	66	137	36	5	3	0	0.0	19	8	14	22	0	.263	.343	0	0	2B-57, 3B-6, SS-4
1959	104	315	79	17	2	9	2.9	36	26	28	55	0	.251	.403	5	0	SS-92, 3B-1, 2B-1, 1B-1
1960	116	386	87	19	6	9	2.3	37	43	35	72	1	.225	.376	1	0	SS-115
1961	59	114	24	6	0	3	2.6	14	11	11	23	1	.211	.342	20	4	SS-34, 3B-3, 2B-1
1962 BOS A	153	599	166	40	9	14	2.3	79	68	46	118	2	.277	.444	0	0	SS-153
1963	140	497	129	23	6	20	4.0	61	60	52	93	1	.260	.451	2	0	SS-137
1964	158	566	166	41	3	15	2.7	86	55	72	99	1	.293	.456	0	0	SS-158
1965	107	296	67	11	1	8	2.7	29	25	29	77	0	.226	.351	21	7	SS-86, 3B-2, OF-1
1966 NY N	133	405	91	15	5	10	2.5	48	49	47	107	2	.225	.360	12	2	SS-94, 3B-32, 1B-9, 2B-7
1967 STL N	52	67	9	1	1	1	1.5	8	1	9	18	0	.134	.224	3	1	SS-48, 3B-1
12 yrs.	1186	3672	925	184	40	94	2.6	443	365	359	723	9	.252	.401	67	14	SS-1002, 3B-66, 3B-57, 1B-10, OF-1

WORLD SERIES

	G	AB	H	2B	3B	HR	HR%	R	RBI	BB	SO	SB	BA	SA	PH AB	PH H	G by POS
1967 STL N	2	0	0	0	0	0	–	0	0	0	0	0	–	–	0	0	SS-2

Jim Breton

BRETON, JOHN FREDERICK
B. July 15, 1891, Chicago, Ill.   D. May 30, 1973, Beloit, Wis.   BR TR 5'10½" 178 lbs.

	G	AB	H	2B	3B	HR	HR%	R	RBI	BB	SO	SB	BA	SA	PH AB	PH H	G by POS
1913 CHI A	10	30	5	1	1	0	0.0	1	2	1	5	0	.167	.267	0	0	SS-7, 3B-3
1914	81	231	49	7	2	0	0.0	21	24	24	42	9	.212	.260	0	0	3B-79
1915	16	36	5	1	0	0	0.0	3	1	5	9	2	.139	.167	0	0	3B-14, SS-1, 2B-1
3 yrs.	107	297	59	9	3	0	0.0	25	27	30	56	11	.199	.249	0	0	3B-96, SS-8, 2B-1

George Brett

BRETT, GEORGE HOWARD
Brother of Ken Brett
B. May 15, 1953, Moundsville, W. Va.   BL TR 6'   185 lbs.

	G	AB	H	2B	3B	HR	HR%	R	RBI	BB	SO	SB	BA	SA	PH AB	PH H	G by POS
1973 KC A	13	40	5	2	0	0	0.0	2	0	0	5	0	.125	.175	1	0	3B-13
1974	133	457	129	21	5	2	0.4	49	47	21	38	8	.282	.363	2	0	3B-132, SS-1
1975	159	634	195	35	13	11	1.7	84	89	46	49	13	.308	.456	0	0	3B-159, SS-1
1976	159	645	215	34	14	7	1.1	94	67	49	36	21	.333	.462	0	0	3B-157, SS-4
1977	139	564	176	32	13	22	3.9	105	88	55	24	14	.312	.532	3	1	3B-135, DH-3, SS-1
1978	128	510	150	45	8	9	1.8	79	62	39	35	23	.294	.467	0	0	3B-128, SS-1
1979	154	645	212	42	20	23	3.6	119	107	51	36	17	.329	.563	0	0	3B-149, 1B-8, DH-1
1980	117	449	175	33	9	24	5.3	87	118	58	22	15	.390	.664	3	1	3B-112, 1B-1
1981	89	347	109	27	7	6	1.7	42	43	27	23	14	.314	.484	0	0	3B-88
1982	144	552	166	32	9	21	3.8	101	82	71	51	6	.301	.505	0	0	3B-134, OF-12
1983	123	464	144	38	2	25	5.4	90	93	57	39	0	.310	.563	1	1	3B-102, 1B-14, OF-13, DH-1
1984	104	377	107	21	3	13	3.4	42	69	38	37	0	.284	.459	3	1	3B-101
12 yrs.	1462	5684	1783	362	103	163	2.9	894	865	512	395	131	.314	.500	13	4	3B-1410, OF-25, 1B-23, SS-8, DH-5

	G	AB	H	2B	3B	HR	HR %	R	RBI	BB	SO	SB	BA	SA	Pinch Hit AB	Pinch Hit H	G by POS

George Brett continued

DIVISIONAL PLAYOFF SERIES

	G	AB	H	2B	3B	HR	HR %	R	RBI	BB	SO	SB	BA	SA	AB	H	G by POS
1981 KC A	3	12	2	0	0	0	0.0	0	0	0	0	0	.167	.167	0	0	3B-3

LEAGUE CHAMPIONSHIP SERIES

	G	AB	H	2B	3B	HR	HR %	R	RBI	BB	SO	SB	BA	SA	AB	H	G by POS
1976 KC A	5	18	8	1	1	1	5.6	4	5	2	1	0	.444	.778	0	0	3B-5
1977	5	20	6	0	2	0	0.0	2	2	1	0	0	.300	.500	0	0	3B-5
1978	4	18	7	1	1	3	16.7	7	3	0	1	0	.389	1.056	0	0	3B-4
1980	3	11	3	1	0	2	18.2	3	4	1	0	0	.273	.909	0	0	3B-3
1984	3	13	3	0	0	0	0.0	0	0	0	2	0	.231	.231	0	0	3B-3
5 yrs.	20	80	27	3	4	6	7.5	16	14	4	4	0	.338	.700	0	0	3B-20

WORLD SERIES

	G	AB	H	2B	3B	HR	HR %	R	RBI	BB	SO	SB	BA	SA	AB	H	G by POS
1980 KC A	6	24	9	2	1	1	4.2	3	3	2	4	1	.375	.667	0	0	3B-6

BL TL 6'   190 lbs.

Ken Brett

BRETT, KENNETH ALVIN
Brother of George Brett.
B. Sept. 18, 1948, Brooklyn, N. Y.

	G	AB	H	2B	3B	HR	HR %	R	RBI	BB	SO	SB	BA	SA	AB	H	G by POS
1967 BOS A	1	0	0	0	0	0	–	0	0	0	0	0	–	–	0	0	P-1
1969	8	10	3	1	0	1	10.0	1	3	1	1	0	.300	.700	0	0	P-8
1970	41	41	13	3	0	2	4.9	8	3	2	7	0	.317	.537	0	0	P-41
1971	29	10	2	0	0	0	0.0	0	0	2	2	0	.200	.200	0	0	P-29
1972 MIL N	31	44	10	1	0	0	0.0	6	1	2	10	0	.227	.250	1	0	P-26
1973 PHI N	37	80	20	5	0	4	5.0	6	16	4	17	0	.250	.463	2	0	P-31
1974 PIT N	43	87	27	4	1	2	2.3	13	15	4	20	0	.310	.448	15	3	P-27
1975	26	52	12	4	0	1	1.9	5	4	1	7	0	.231	.365	3	0	P-23
1976 2 teams				NY	A (2G –	.000)		CHI	A (33G –	.083)							
" total	35	12	1	0	0	0	0.0	0	0	0	1	0	.083	.083	6	1	P-29
1977 2 teams				CHI	A (13G –	.000)		CAL	A (21G –	.000)							
" total	34	0	0	0	0	0	–	0	0	0	0	0	–	–	0	0	P-34
1978 CAL A	31	0	0	0	0	0	–	0	0	0	0	0	–	–	0	0	P-31
1979 2 teams				MIN	A (9G –	.000)		LA	N (30G –	.273)							
" total	39	11	3	0	0	0	0.0	0	2	0	2	0	.273	.273	0	0	P-39
1980 KC A	8	0	0	0	0	0	–	0	0	0	0	0	–	–	0	0	P-8
1981	22	0	0	0	0	0	–	0	0	0	0	0	–	–	0	0	P-22
14 yrs.	385	347	91	18	1	10	2.9	39	44	14	67	0	.262	.406	27	4	P-349

LEAGUE CHAMPIONSHIP SERIES

	G	AB	H	2B	3B	HR	HR %	R	RBI	BB	SO	SB	BA	SA	AB	H	G by POS
1974 PIT N	1	1	0	0	0	0	0.0	0	0	0	1	0	.000	.000	0	0	P-1
1975	2	0	0	0	0	0	–	0	0	0	0	0	–	–	0	0	P-2
2 yrs.	3	1	0	0	0	0	0.0	0	0	0	1	0	.000	.000	0	0	P-3

WORLD SERIES

	G	AB	H	2B	3B	HR	HR %	R	RBI	BB	SO	SB	BA	SA	AB	H	G by POS
1967 BOS A	2	0	0	0	0	0	–	0	0	0	0	0	–	–	0	0	P-2

BR TR 5'11"   175 lbs.

Tony Brewer

BREWER, ANTHONY BRUCE
B. Nov. 25, 1957, Shreveport, La.

	G	AB	H	2B	3B	HR	HR %	R	RBI	BB	SO	SB	BA	SA	AB	H	G by POS
1984 LA N	24	37	4	1	0	1	2.7	3	4	4	9	1	.108	.216	14	1	OF-10

BR TR 5'8½"   175 lbs.

Charlie Brewster

BREWSTER, CHARLES LAWRENCE
B. Dec. 27, 1916, Marthaville, La.

	G	AB	H	2B	3B	HR	HR %	R	RBI	BB	SO	SB	BA	SA	AB	H	G by POS
1943 2 teams				CIN	N (7G –	.125)		PHI	N (49G –	.220)							
" total	56	167	36	2	0	0	0.0	13	12	10	20	1	.216	.228	2	0	SS-46, 2B-2
1944 CHI N	10	44	11	2	0	0	0.0	4	2	5	7	0	.250	.295	0	0	SS-10
1946 CLE A	3	2	0	0	0	0	0.0	0	0	1	1	0	.000	.000	1	0	SS-1
3 yrs.	69	213	47	4	0	0	0.0	17	14	16	28	1	.221	.239	3	0	SS-57, 2B-2

BL TR 5'7"   160 lbs.

Fred Brickell

BRICKELL, GEORGE FREDERICK
Father of Fritzie Brickell.
B. Nov. 9, 1906, Saffordville, Kans.   D. Apr. 8, 1961, Wichita, Kans.

	G	AB	H	2B	3B	HR	HR %	R	RBI	BB	SO	SB	BA	SA	AB	H	G by POS
1926 PIT N	24	55	19	3	1	0	0.0	11	3	6	0	0	.345	.436	4	2	OF-14
1927	32	21	6	1	0	1	4.8	6	4	1	0	0	.286	.476	15	4	OF-3
1928	81	202	65	4	4	3	1.5	34	41	20	18	5	.322	.426	24	7	OF-50
1929	60	118	37	4	2	0	0.0	13	17	7	12	3	.314	.381	29	6	OF-27
1930 2 teams				PIT	N (68G –	.297)		PHI	N (53G –	.246)							
" total	121	459	124	21	9	1	0.2	69	31	28	41	4	.270	.362	5	2	OF-114
1931 PHI N	130	514	130	14	5	1	0.2	77	31	42	39	5	.253	.305	5	2	OF-122
1932	45	66	22	6	1	0	0.0	9	2	4	5	2	.333	.455	20	5	OF-12
1933	8	13	4	1	1	0	0.0	2	1	1	0	0	.308	.538	2	0	OF-4
8 yrs.	501	1448	407	54	23	6	0.4	221	131	106	121	19	.281	.363	104	28	OF-346

WORLD SERIES

	G	AB	H	2B	3B	HR	HR %	R	RBI	BB	SO	SB	BA	SA	AB	H	G by POS
1927 PIT N	2	2	0	0	0	0	0.0	1	0	0	0	0	.000	.000	2	0	

BR TR 5'5½"   157 lbs.

Fritzie Brickell

BRICKELL, FRITZ DARRELL
Son of Fred Brickell.
B. Mar. 19, 1935, Wichita, Kans.   D. Oct. 15, 1965, Wichita, Kans.

	G	AB	H	2B	3B	HR	HR %	R	RBI	BB	SO	SB	BA	SA	AB	H	G by POS
1958 NY A	2	0	0	0	0	0	–	0	0	0	0	0	–	–	0	0	2B-2
1959	18	39	10	1	0	1	2.6	4	4	1	10	0	.256	.359	0	0	SS-15, 2B-3
1961 LA A	21	49	6	0	0	0	0.0	3	3	6	9	0	.122	.122	3	0	SS-17
3 yrs.	41	88	16	1	0	1	1.1	7	7	7	19	0	.182	.227	3	0	SS-32, 2B-5

BR TR 5'9"   180 lbs.

George Brickley

BRICKLEY, GEORGE VINCENT
B. July 19, 1894, Everett, Mass.   D. Feb. 23, 1947, Everett, Mass.

	G	AB	H	2B	3B	HR	HR %	R	RBI	BB	SO	SB	BA	SA	AB	H	G by POS
1913 PHI A	5	12	2	0	1	0	0.0	0	0	0	4	0	.167	.333	1	0	OF-4

BR TR 6'   165 lbs.

Jim Brideweser

BRIDEWESER, JAMES EHRENFELD
B. Feb. 13, 1927, Lancaster, Ohio

	G	AB	H	2B	3B	HR	HR %	R	RBI	BB	SO	SB	BA	SA	AB	H	G by POS
1951 NY A	2	8	3	0	0	0	0.0	1	0	0	0	0	.375	.375	0	0	SS-2
1952	42	38	10	0	0	0	0.0	12	2	3	5	0	.263	.263	9	1	SS-22, 2B-4, 3B-1

	G	AB	H	2B	3B	HR	HR%	R	RBI	BB	SO	SB	BA	SA	Pinch Hit AB	Pinch Hit H	G by POS

Jim Brideweser continued

	G	AB	H	2B	3B	HR	HR%	R	RBI	BB	SO	SB	BA	SA	PH AB	PH H	G by POS
1953	7	3	3	0	1	0	0.0	3	3	1	0	0	1.000	1.667	2	2	SS-3
1954 BAL A	73	204	54	7	2	0	0.0	18	12	15	27	1	.265	.319	11	2	SS-48, 2B-19
1955 CHI A	34	58	12	3	2	0	0.0	6	4	3	7	0	.207	.328	1	0	SS-26, 3B-3, 2B-2
1956 2 teams	CHI	A (10G –	.182)	DET	A	(70G –	.218)										
" total	80	167	36	5	0	0		23	11	20	22	3	.216	.246	1	1	SS-42, 2B-31, 3B-4
1957 BAL A	91	142	38	6	1	0	0.7	16	18	21	16	2	.268	.345	5	1	SS-74, 3B-3, 2B-1
7 yrs.	329	620	156	21	6	1	0.2	79	50	63	78	6	.252	.310	29	7	SS-217, 2B-57, 3B-11

Rocky Bridges

BRIDGES, EVERETT LAMAR B. Aug. 7, 1927, Refugio, Tex.   BR TR 5'8" 170 lbs.

	G	AB	H	2B	3B	HR	HR%	R	RBI	BB	SO	SB	BA	SA	PH AB	PH H	G by POS
1951 BKN N	63	134	34	7	0	1	0.7	13	15	10	10	0	.254	.328	2	0	3B-40, 2B-10, SS-9
1952	51	56	11	3	0	0	0.0	9	2	7	9	0	.196	.250	3	1	2B-24, SS-13, 3B-6
1953 CIN N	122	432	98	13	2	1	0.2	52	21	37	42	6	.227	.273	4	0	2B-115, SS-6, 3B-3
1954	53	52	12	1	0	0	0.0	4	2	7	7	0	.231	.250	1	0	SS-20, 2B-19, 3B-13
1955	95	168	48	4	0	1	0.6	20	18	15	19	1	.286	.327	0	0	3B-59, SS-26, 2B-9
1956	71	19	4	0	0	0	0.0	9	1	4	3	1	.211	.211	2	0	3B-51, 2B-8, SS-7, OF-1
1957 2 teams	CIN	N (5G –	.000)	WAS	A	(120G –	.228)										
" total	125	392	89	17	2	3	0.8	41	47	41	33	0	.227	.304	0	0	SS-109, 2B-16, 3B-2
1958 WAS A	116	377	99	14	3	5	1.3	38	28	27	32	0	.263	.355	4	0	SS-112, 3B-3, 2B-3
1959 DET A	116	381	102	16	3	3	0.8	38	35	30	35	1	.268	.349	2	0	SS-110, 2B-5
1960 3 teams	DET	A (10G –	.200)	CLE	A (10G –	.333)	STL	N (3G –	.000)								
" total	23	32	10	0	0	0	0.0	1	3	1	2	0	.313	.313	0	0	SS-10, 3B-10, 2B-3
1961 LA A	84	229	55	5	1	2	0.9	20	15	26	37	1	.240	.297	1	0	2B-58, SS-25, 3B-4
11 yrs.	919	2272	562	80	11	16	0.7	245	187	205	229	10	.247	.313	19	1	SS-447, 2B-270, 3B-191, OF-1

Al Bridwell

BRIDWELL, ALBERT HENRY B. Jan. 4, 1884, Friendship, Ohio   D. Jan. 23, 1969, Portsmouth, Ohio   BL TR 5'9" 150 lbs.

	G	AB	H	2B	3B	HR	HR%	R	RBI	BB	SO	SB	BA	SA	PH AB	PH H	G by POS
1905 CIN N	82	254	64	3	1	0	0.0	17	17	19		8	.252	.272	7	3	3B-43, OF-18, 2B-7, SS-5, 1B-1
1906 BOS N	120	459	104	9	1	0	0.0	41	22	44		6	.227	.251	0	0	SS-119, OF-1
1907	140	509	111	8	2	0	0.0	49	26	61		17	.218	.242	0	0	SS-140
1908 NY N	147	467	133	14	1	0	0.0	53	46	52		20	.285	.319	0	0	SS-147
1909	145	476	140	11	5	0	0.0	59	55	67		32	.294	.338	0	0	SS-144
1910	142	492	136	15	7	0	0.0	74	48	73	23	14	.276	.335	1	0	SS-141
1911 2 teams	NY	N (76G –	.270)	BOS	N	(51G –	.291)										
" total	127	445	124	15	1	0	0.0	57	41	66	18	10	.279	.317	0	0	SS-127
1912 BOS N	31	106	25	5	1	0	0.0	6	14	7	6	2	.236	.302	0	0	SS-31
1913 CHI N	135	405	97	6	1	0	0.2	35	37	74	28	12	.240	.291	0	0	SS-135
1914 STL F	117	381	90	6	5	1	0.3	46	33	71		9	.236	.286	3	0	SS-103, 2B-11
1915	65	175	40	3	2	0	0.0	20	9	25		6	.229	.269	6	2	2B-42, 3B-15, 1B-1
11 yrs.	1251	4169	1064	95	32	2	0.0	457	348	559	75	136	.255	.295	17	5	SS-1092, 2B-60, 3B-58, OF-19, 1B-2

Bunny Brief

BRIEF, ANTHONY VINCENT Born Antonio Bordetzki. B. July 3, 1892, Remus, Mich.   D. Feb. 10, 1963, Milwaukee, Wis.   BR TR 6' 185 lbs.

	G	AB	H	2B	3B	HR	HR%	R	RBI	BB	SO	SB	BA	SA	PH AB	PH H	G by POS
1912 STL A	15	42	13	3	0	0	0.0	9	5	6		2	.310	.381	2	0	OF-9, 1B-4
1913	84	258	56	11	6	1	0.4	24	26	21	46	3	.217	.318	14	1	1B-62, OF-8
1915 CHI A	48	154	33	6	2	2	1.3	13	17	16	28	8	.214	.318	2	0	1B-46
1917 PIT N	36	115	25	5	1	2	1.7	15	11	15	21	4	.217	.330	2	2	1B-34
4 yrs.	183	569	127	25	9	5	0.9	61	59	58	95	17	.223	.325	20	3	1B-146, OF-17

Charlie Briggs

BRIGGS, CHARLES R. D. Nov. 15, 1917, Chicago, Ill.

	G	AB	H	2B	3B	HR	HR%	R	RBI	BB	SO	SB	BA	SA	PH AB	PH H	G by POS
1884 C-P U	49	182	31	8	2	1	0.5	29		11			.170	.253	0	0	OF-37, 2B-12, SS-2

Dan Briggs

BRIGGS, DANIEL LEE B. Nov. 18, 1952, Scotia, Calif.   BL TL 6' 180 lbs.

	G	AB	H	2B	3B	HR	HR%	R	RBI	BB	SO	SB	BA	SA	PH AB	PH H	G by POS
1975 CAL A	13	31	7	1	0	1	3.2	3	3	2	6	0	.226	.355	1	0	1B-6, OF-5, DH-2
1976	77	248	53	13	2	1	0.4	19	14	13	47	0	.214	.294	4	2	1B-44, OF-40, DH-1
1977	59	74	12	2	0	1	1.4	6	4	8	14	0	.162	.230	3	0	1B-45, OF-13
1978 CLE A	15	49	8	0	1	1	2.0	4	1	4	9	0	.163	.265	0	0	OF-15
1979 SD N	104	227	47	4	3	8	3.5	34	30	18	45	2	.207	.357	29	3	1B-50, OF-44
1981 MON N	9	11	1	0	0	0	0.0	0	0	0	3	0	.091	.091	3	0	OF-3, 1B-3
1982 CHI N	48	48	6	0	0	0	0.0	1	1	0	9	0	.125	.125	37	4	OF-10, 1B-4
7 yrs.	325	688	134	20	6	12	1.7	67	53	45	133	2	.195	.294	77	9	1B-152, OF-130, DH-3

Grant Briggs

BRIGGS, GRANT B. Mar. 16, 1865, Pittsburgh, Pa.   D. May 31, 1928, Pittsburgh, Pa.

	G	AB	H	2B	3B	HR	HR%	R	RBI	BB	SO	SB	BA	SA	PH AB	PH H	G by POS
1890 SYR AA	86	316	57	6	5	0	0.0	44		16		7	.180	.231	0	0	C-46, OF-33, 3B-5, SS-4
1891 LOU AA	1	4	1	0	0	0	0.0	0	0	0	0	0	.250	.250	0	0	C-1
1892 STL N	23	57	4	1	0	0	0.0	2	1	6	16	3	.070	.088	0	0	C-15, OF-9
1895 LOU N	1	3	0	0	0	0	0.0	0	0	0	1	0	.000	.000	0	0	C-1
4 yrs.	111	380	62	7	5	0	0.0	46		22	17	10	.163	.208	0	0	C-63, OF-42, 3B-5, SS-4

John Briggs

BRIGGS, JOHN EDWARD B. Mar. 10, 1944, Paterson, N. J.   BL TL 6'1" 190 lbs.

	G	AB	H	2B	3B	HR	HR%	R	RBI	BB	SO	SB	BA	SA	PH AB	PH H	G by POS
1964 PHI N	61	66	17	2	0	1	1.5	16	6	9	12	1	.258	.333	29	7	OF-19, 1B-1
1965	93	229	54	9	4	4	1.7	47	23	42	44	3	.236	.362	32	7	OF-66
1966	81	255	72	13	5	10	3.9	43	23	41	55	3	.282	.490	17	2	OF-69
1967	106	332	77	12	4	9	2.7	47	30	41	72	3	.232	.373	13	2	OF-94
1968	110	338	86	13	1	7	2.1	36	31	58	72	8	.254	.361	14	7	OF-65, 1B-36
1969	124	361	86	20	3	12	3.3	51	46	64	78	9	.238	.410	16	3	OF-108, 1B-2
1970	110	341	92	15	7	9	2.6	43	47	39	65	5	.270	.434	15	6	OF-95

	G	AB	H	2B	3B	HR	HR %	R	RBI	BB	SO	SB	BA	SA	Pinch Hit AB	Pinch Hit H	G by POS

John Briggs continued

		G	AB	H	2B	3B	HR	HR%	R	RBI	BB	SO	SB	BA	SA	PH AB	PH H	G by POS
1971 2 teams	PHI N (10G – .182)					MIL A (125G – .264)												
" total		135	397	103	12	1	21	5.3	54	62	77	81	1	.259	.453	10	1	OF-73, 1B-60
1972 MIL A		135	418	111	14	1	21	5.0	58	65	54	67	1	.266	.455	10	4	OF-106, 1B-28
1973		142	488	120	20	7	18	3.7	78	57	87	83	15	.246	.426	2	0	OF-137, DH-1
1974		154	554	140	30	8	17	3.1	72	73	71	102	9	.253	.428	4	1	OF-149, DH-2
1975 2 teams	MIL A (28G – .297)					MIN A (87G – .231)												
" total		115	338	83	10	2	10	3.0	56	44	80	54	6	.246	.376	8	1	OF-56, 1B-49, DH-3
12 yrs.		1366	4117	1041	170	43	139	3.4	601	507	663	785	64	.253	.416	170	41	OF-1037, 1B-176, DH-6

Harry Bright

BRIGHT, HARRY JAMES
B. Sept. 22, 1929, Kansas City, Mo.   BR TR 6'   190 lbs.

		G	AB	H	2B	3B	HR	HR%	R	RBI	BB	SO	SB	BA	SA	PH AB	PH H	G by POS
1958 PIT N		15	24	6	1	0	1	4.2	4	3	1	6	0	.250	.417	4	1	3B-7
1959		40	48	12	1	0	3	6.3	4	8	5	10	0	.250	.458	31	7	OF-4, 3B-3, 2B-1
1960		4	4	0	0	0	0	0.0	0	0	0	2	0	.000	.000	4	0	
1961 WAS A		72	183	44	6	0	4	2.2	20	21	19	23	0	.240	.339	23	3	3B-40, C-8, 2B-1
1962		113	392	107	15	4	17	4.3	55	67	26	51	2	.273	.462	15	4	1B-99, C-3, 3B-1
1963 2 teams	CIN N (1G – .000)					NY A (60G – .236)												
" total		61	158	37	7	0	7	4.4	15	23	13	32	0	.234	.411	12	2	1B-36, 3B-12
1964 NY A		4	5	1	0	0	0	0.0	0	0	1	1	0	.200	.200	1	0	1B-2
1965 CHI N		27	25	7	1	0	0	0.0	1	4	0	8	0	.280	.320	25	7	
8 yrs.		336	839	214	31	4	32	3.8	99	126	65	133	2	.255	.416	115	24	1B-137, 3B-63, C-11, OF-4, 2B-2

WORLD SERIES

		G	AB	H	2B	3B	HR	HR%	R	RBI	BB	SO	SB	BA	SA	PH AB	PH H	G by POS
1963 NY A		2	2	0	0	0	0	0.0	0	0	0	2	0	.000	.000	2	0	

Bill Brinker

BRINKER, WILLIAM HUTCHINSON (Dode)
B. Aug. 30, 1883, Warrensburg, Mo.   D. Feb. 5, 1965, Arcadia, Calif.   BB TR 6'1"   190 lbs.

		G	AB	H	2B	3B	HR	HR%	R	RBI	BB	SO	SB	BA	SA	PH AB	PH H	G by POS
1912 PHI N		9	18	4	1	0	0	0.0	1	2	2	3	0	.222	.278	3	0	OF-2, 3B-2

Chuck Brinkman

BRINKMAN, CHARLES ERNEST
Brother of Ed Brinkman.
B. Sept. 16, 1944, Cincinnati, Ohio   BR TR 6'1"   185 lbs.

		G	AB	H	2B	3B	HR	HR%	R	RBI	BB	SO	SB	BA	SA	PH AB	PH H	G by POS
1969 CHI A		14	15	1	0	0	0	0.0	2	0	1	5	0	.067	.067	1	0	C-14
1970		9	20	5	1	0	0	0.0	4	0	3	3	0	.250	.300	0	0	C-9
1971		15	20	4	0	0	0	0.0	0	1	3	5	0	.200	.200	1	0	C-14
1972		35	52	7	0	0	0	0.0	1	0	4	7	0	.135	.135	3	1	C-33
1973		63	139	26	6	0	1	0.7	13	10	11	37	0	.187	.252	0	0	C-63
1974 2 teams	CHI A (8G – .143)					PIT N (4G – .143)												
" total		12	21	3	0	0	0	0.0	2	1	1	3	0	.143	.143	0	0	C-12
6 yrs.		148	267	46	7	0	1	0.4	22	12	23	60	0	.172	.210	5	1	C-145

Ed Brinkman

BRINKMAN, EDWIN ALBERT
Brother of Chuck Brinkman.
B. Dec. 8, 1941, Cincinnati, Ohio   BR TR 6'   170 lbs.

		G	AB	H	2B	3B	HR	HR%	R	RBI	BB	SO	SB	BA	SA	PH AB	PH H	G by POS
1961 WAS A		4	11	1	0	0	0	0.0	0	0	1	1	0	.091	.091	1	0	3B-3
1962		54	133	22	7	1	0	0.0	8	4	11	28	1	.165	.233	0	0	SS-38, 3B-10
1963		145	514	117	20	3	7	1.4	44	45	31	86	5	.228	.319	2	1	SS-143
1964		132	447	100	20	3	8	1.8	54	34	26	99	2	.224	.336	7	1	SS-125
1965		154	444	82	13	2	5	1.1	35	35	38	82	1	.185	.257	3	0	SS-150
1966		158	582	133	18	9	7	1.2	42	48	29	105	7	.229	.326	0	0	SS-158
1967		109	320	60	9	2	1	0.3	21	18	24	58	1	.188	.238	0	0	SS-109
1968		77	193	36	3	0	0	0.0	12	6	19	31	0	.187	.202	2	0	SS-74, 2B-2, OF-1
1969		151	576	153	18	5	2	0.3	71	43	50	42	2	.266	.325	1	1	SS-150
1970		158	625	164	17	2	1	0.2	63	40	60	41	8	.262	.301	2	1	SS-157
1971 DET A		159	527	120	18	2	1	0.2	40	37	44	54	1	.228	.275	0	0	SS-159
1972		156	516	105	19	1	6	1.2	42	49	38	51	0	.203	.279	0	0	SS-156
1973		162	515	122	16	4	7	1.4	55	40	34	79	0	.237	.324	0	0	SS-162
1974		153	502	111	15	3	14	2.8	55	54	29	71	2	.221	.347	0	0	SS-151, 3B-2
1975 3 teams	STL N (1G – .000)					TEX A (44G – .175)				NY A (44G – .175)								
" total		73	140	29	1	1	1	0.7	8	8	10	17	0	.207	.300	4	1	SS-63, 3B-4, 2B-3
15 yrs.		1845	6045	1355	201	38	60	1.0	550	461	444	845	30	.224	.300	22	5	SS-1795, 3B-19, 2B-5, OF-1

LEAGUE CHAMPIONSHIP SERIES

		G	AB	H	2B	3B	HR	HR%	R	RBI	BB	SO	SB	BA	SA	PH AB	PH H	G by POS
1972 DET A		1	4	1	1	0	0	0.0	0	0	0	0	0	.250	.500	0	0	SS-1

Leon Brinkopf

BRINKOPF, LEON CLARENCE
B. Oct. 20, 1926, Cape Girardeau, Mo.   BR TR 5'11½" 185 lbs.

		G	AB	H	2B	3B	HR	HR%	R	RBI	BB	SO	SB	BA	SA	PH AB	PH H	G by POS
1952 CHI N		9	22	4	0	0	0	0.0	1	2	4	5	0	.182	.182	2	1	SS-6

Fatty Briody

BRIODY, CHARLES F. (Alderman)
B. Sept. 13, 1858, Lansingburg, N. Y.   D. June 22, 1903, Chicago, Ill.   5'8½"   190 lbs.

		G	AB	H	2B	3B	HR	HR%	R	RBI	BB	SO	SB	BA	SA	PH AB	PH H	G by POS
1880 TRO N		1	4	0	0	0	0	0.0	0		0	0		.000	.000	0	0	C-1
1882 CLE N		53	194	50	13	0	0	0.0	30	13	9	13		.258	.325	0	0	C-53
1883		40	145	34	5	1	0	0.0	23		3	13		.234	.283	0	0	C-33, 2B-4, 1B-2, 3B-1
1884 2 teams	CLE N (43G – .169)					CIN U (22G – .337)												
" total		65	237	55	8	2	1	0.4	28	12	7	19		.232	.295	0	0	C-64, OF-1
1885 STL N		62	215	42	9	0	1	0.5	14	17	12	23		.195	.251	0	0	C-60, OF-1, 3B-1, 2B-1
1886 KC N		56	215	51	10	3	0	0.0	14	29	3	35		.237	.312	0	0	C-54, OF-2, 1B-1
1887 DET N		33	128	29	6	1	2	1.6	24	26	9	10	6	.227	.336	0	0	C-33
1888 KC AA		13	48	10	1	0	0	0.0	1	8	1		0	.208	.229	0	0	C-13
8 yrs.		323	1186	271	52	7	4	0.3	134	104	44	113	6	.228	.294	0	0	C-311, 2B-5, OF-4, 1B-3, 3B-2

	G	AB	H	2B	3B	HR	HR %	R	RBI	BB	SO	SB	BA	SA	Pinch Hit AB	Pinch Hit H	G by POS

George Bristow

BRISTOW, GEORGE
B. Pawpaw, Ill.   Deceased.

	G	AB	H	2B	3B	HR	HR%	R	RBI	BB	SO	SB	BA	SA	AB	H	G by POS
1899 CLE N	3	8	1	1	0	0	0.0	0	0	0		0	.125	.250	0	0	OF-3

Gus Brittain

BRITTAIN, AUGUST SCHUSTER   BR TR 5'10"   192 lbs.
B. Nov. 29, 1909, Wilmington, N. C.   D. Feb. 16, 1974, Wilmington, N. C.

	G	AB	H	2B	3B	HR	HR%	R	RBI	BB	SO	SB	BA	SA	AB	H	G by POS
1937 CIN N	3	6	1	0	0	0	0.0	0	0	0	3	0	.167	.167	2	0	C-1

Gil Britton

BRITTON, STEPHEN GILBERT   BR TR 5'10"   160 lbs.
B. Sept. 21, 1891, Parsons, Kans.   D. June 27, 1983, Parsons, Kans.

	G	AB	H	2B	3B	HR	HR%	R	RBI	BB	SO	SB	BA	SA	AB	H	G by POS
1913 PIT N	3	12	0	0	0	0	0.0	0	0	0	2	0	.000	.000	0	0	SS-3

Greg Brock

BROCK, GREGORY ALLEN   BL TR 6'3"   200 lbs.
B. June 14, 1957, McMinnville, Ore.

	G	AB	H	2B	3B	HR	HR%	R	RBI	BB	SO	SB	BA	SA	AB	H	G by POS
1982 LA N	18	17	2	0	0	0	0.0	1	1	1	5	0	.118	.176	13	2	1B-3
1983	146	455	102	14	2	20	4.4	64	66	83	81	5	.224	.396	6	1	1B-140
1984	88	271	61	6	0	14	5.2	33	34	39	37	8	.225	.402	8	0	1B-83
3 yrs.	252	743	165	21	2	34	4.6	98	101	123	123	13	.222	.393	27	3	1B-226
LEAGUE CHAMPIONSHIP SERIES																	
1983 LA N	3	9	0	0	0	0	0.0	1	0	0	3	0	.000	.000	0	0	1B-3

John Brock

BROCK, JOHN ROY   BR TR 5'8"   160 lbs.
B. Oct. 16, 1896, Hamilton, Ill.   D. Oct. 27, 1951, Clayton, Mo.

	G	AB	H	2B	3B	HR	HR%	R	RBI	BB	SO	SB	BA	SA	AB	H	G by POS
1917 STL N	7	15	6	1	0	0	0.0	4	2	0	2	2	.400	.467	3	1	C-4
1918	27	52	11	2	0	0	0.0	9	4	3	10	5	.212	.250	7	2	C-18, OF-1
2 yrs.	34	67	17	3	0	0	0.0	13	6	3	12	7	.254	.299	10	3	C-22, OF-1

Lou Brock

BROCK, LOUIS CLARK   BL TL 5'11½"   170 lbs.
B. June 18, 1939, El Dorado, Ark.
Hall of Fame 1985.

	G	AB	H	2B	3B	HR	HR%	R	RBI	BB	SO	SB	BA	SA	AB	H	G by POS
1961 CHI N	4	11	1	0	0	0	0.0	1	0	1	3	0	.091	.091	0	0	OF-3
1962	123	434	114	24	7	9	2.1	73	35	35	96	16	.263	.412	15	2	OF-106
1963	148	547	141	19	11	9	1.6	79	37	31	122	24	.258	.382	10	2	OF-140
1964 2 teams		CHI N (52G – .251)				STL N (103G – .348)											
" total	155	634	200	30	11	14	2.2	111	58	40	127	43	.315	.464	1	0	OF-154
1965 STL N	155	631	182	35	8	16	2.5	107	69	45	116	63	.288	.445	1	0	OF-153
1966	156	643	183	24	12	15	2.3	94	46	31	134	74	.285	.429	1	0	OF-154
1967	159	689	206	32	12	21	3.0	113	76	24	109	52	.299	.472	4	0	OF-157
1968	159	660	184	46	14	6	0.9	92	51	46	124	62	.279	.418	3	1	OF-156
1969	157	655	195	33	10	12	1.8	97	47	50	115	53	.298	.434	2	1	OF-157
1970	155	664	202	29	5	13	2.0	114	57	60	99	51	.304	.422	3	2	OF-152
1971	157	640	200	37	7	7	1.1	126	61	76	107	64	.313	.425	2	1	OF-157
1972	153	621	193	26	8	3	0.5	81	42	47	93	63	.311	.393	4	1	OF-149
1973	160	650	193	29	8	7	1.1	110	63	71	112	70	.297	.398	1	0	OF-159
1974	153	635	194	25	7	3	0.5	105	48	61	88	118	.306	.381	3	1	OF-152
1975	136	528	163	27	6	3	0.6	78	47	38	64	56	.309	.400	8	3	OF-128
1976	133	498	150	24	5	4	0.8	73	67	35	75	56	.301	.394	12	3	OF-123
1977	141	489	133	22	6	2	0.4	69	46	30	74	35	.272	.354	18	7	OF-130
1978	92	298	66	9	0	0	0.0	31	12	17	29	17	.221	.252	15	4	OF-79
1979	120	405	123	15	4	5	1.2	56	38	23	43	21	.304	.398	22	5	OF-98
19 yrs.	2616	10332	3023	486	141	149	1.4	1610	900	761	1730	938	.293	.410	125	33	OF-2507
			9th									1st					
WORLD SERIES																	
1964 STL N	7	30	9	2	0	1	3.3	2	5	0	3	0	.300	.467	0	0	OF-7
1967	7	29	12	2	1	1	3.4	8	3	2	3	7	.414	.655	0	0	OF-7
1968	7	28	13	3	1	2	7.1	6	5	3	4	7	.464	.857	0	0	OF-7
3 yrs.	21	87	34	7	2	4	4.6	16	13	5	10	14	.391	.655	0	0	OF-21
			8th									1st	2nd	5th			

Matt Broderick

BRODERICK, MATTHEW THOMAS   TR 5'6½"   135 lbs.
B. Dec. 1, 1877, Lattimer Mines, Pa.   D. Feb. 26, 1940, Freeland, Pa.

	G	AB	H	2B	3B	HR	HR%	R	RBI	BB	SO	SB	BA	SA	AB	H	G by POS
1903 BKN N	2	2	0	0	0	0	0.0	0	0	0		0	.000	.000	1	0	2B-1

Steve Brodie

BRODIE, WALTER SCOTT   BL TR 5'9½"   176 lbs.
B. Sept. 11, 1868, Warrenton, Va.   D. Oct. 30, 1935, Baltimore, Md.

	G	AB	H	2B	3B	HR	HR%	R	RBI	BB	SO	SB	BA	SA	AB	H	G by POS
1890 BOS N	132	514	152	19	9	0	0.0	77	67	66	20	29	.296	.368	0	0	OF-132
1891	133	523	136	13	6	2	0.4	84	78	63	39	25	.260	.319	0	0	OF-133
1892 STL N	154	602	152	10	9	4	0.7	85	60	52	31	28	.252	.319	0	0	OF-137, 2B-16, 3B-2
1893 2 teams		STL N (107G – .318)				BAL N (25G – .361)											
" total	132	566	184	23	10	2	0.4	89	98	45	18	49	.325	.412	0	0	OF-132
1894 BAL N	129	573	210	25	11	3	0.5	134	113	18	8	42	.366	.464	0	0	OF-129
1895	131	528	184	27	10	2	0.4	85	134	26	15	35	.348	.449	0	0	OF-131
1896	132	516	153	19	11	2	0.4	98	87	36	17	25	.297	.388	0	0	OF-132
1897 PIT N	100	370	108	7	12	2	0.5	47	53	25		11	.292	.392	0	0	OF-100
1898 2 teams		PIT N (42G – .263)				BAL N (23G – .306)											
" total	65	254	71	8	2	0	0.0	27	40	11		6	.280	.327	0	0	OF-65
1899 BAL N	137	531	164	26	1	3	0.6	82	87	31		19	.309	.379	0	0	OF-137
1901 BAL A	84	309	96	6	6	2	0.6	41	41	25		9	.311	.388	0	0	OF-83
1902 NY N	109	416	117	8	2	3	0.7	37	42	22		11	.281	.332	0	0	OF-109
12 yrs.	1438	5702	1727	191	89	25	0.4	886	900	420	148	289	.303	.381	0	0	OF-1420, 2B-16, 3B-2

Jack Brohamer

BROHAMER, JOHN ANTHONY   BL TR 5'10"   165 lbs.
B. Feb. 26, 1950, Maywood, Calif.

	G	AB	H	2B	3B	HR	HR%	R	RBI	BB	SO	SB	BA	SA	AB	H	G by POS
1972 CLE A	136	527	123	13	2	5	0.9	49	35	27	46	3	.233	.294	6	1	2B-132, 3B-1
1973	102	300	66	12	1	4	1.3	29	29	32	23	0	.220	.307	10	3	2B-97
1974	101	315	85	11	1	2	0.6	33	30	26	22	2	.270	.330	9	4	2B-99
1975	69	217	53	5	0	6	2.8	15	16	14	14	2	.244	.350	3	1	2B-66

	G	AB	H	2B	3B	HR	HR %	R	RBI	BB	SO	SB	BA	SA	Pinch Hit AB	Pinch Hit H	G by POS

Jack Brohamer continued

	G	AB	H	2B	3B	HR	HR %	R	RBI	BB	SO	SB	BA	SA	AB	H	G by POS
1976 CHI A	119	354	89	12	2	7	2.0	33	40	44	28	1	.251	.356	1	0	2B-117, 3B-1
1977	59	152	39	10	3	2	1.3	26	20	21	8	0	.257	.401	2	0	3B-38, 2B-18, DH-1
1978 BOS A	81	244	57	14	1	1	0.4	34	25	25	13	1	.234	.311	11	3	3B-30, DH-25, 2B-23
1979	64	192	51	7	1	1	0.5	25	11	15	15	0	.266	.328	8	1	2B-36, 3B-22
1980 2 teams	BOS A (21G – .316)					CLE A (53G – .225)											
" total	74	199	50	7	1	2	1.0	18	21	18	9	0	.251	.327	15	3	2B-51, 3B-13, DH-4
9 yrs.	805	2500	613	91	12	30	1.2	262	227	222	178	9	.245	.327	65	16	2B-639, 3B-105, DH-30

Herman Bronkie

BRONKIE, HERMAN CHARLES (Dutch)   BR TR 5'9"   165 lbs.
B. Mar. 30, 1885, S. Manchester, Conn.   D. May 27, 1968, Somers, Conn.

	G	AB	H	2B	3B	HR	HR %	R	RBI	BB	SO	SB	BA	SA	AB	H	G by POS
1910 CLE A	4	9	2	0	0	0	0.0	1	0	1		1	.222	.222	0	0	3B-3, SS-1
1911	2	6	1	0	0	0	0.0	0	0	0		0	.167	.167	0	0	3B-2
1912	6	16	0	0	0	0	0.0	1	0	1		0	.000	.000	0	0	3B-6
1914 CHI N	1	1	1	1	0	0	0.0	1	1	0	0	0	1.000	2.000	0	0	3B-1
1918 STL N	18	68	15	3	0	1	1.5	7	7	2	4	0	.221	.309	0	0	3B-18
1919 STL A	67	196	50	6	4	0	0.0	23	14	23	23	2	.255	.327	12	3	3B-34, 2B-16, 1B-2
1922	23	64	18	4	1	0	0.0	7	2	6	7	0	.281	.375	4	1	3B-18
7 yrs.	121	360	87	14	5	1	0.3	40	24	33	34	3	.242	.317	16	4	3B-82, 2B-16, 1B-2, SS-1

Tom Brookens

BROOKENS, THOMAS DALE   BR TR 5'10"   165 lbs.
B. Aug. 10, 1953, Chambersburg, Pa.

	G	AB	H	2B	3B	HR	HR %	R	RBI	BB	SO	SB	BA	SA	AB	H	G by POS
1979 DET A	60	190	50	5	2	4	2.1	23	21	11	40	10	.263	.374	0	0	3B-42, 2B-19, DH-1
1980	151	509	140	25	9	10	2.0	64	66	32	71	13	.275	.418	4	1	3B-138, 2B-9, DH-1, SS-1
1981	71	239	58	10	1	4	1.7	19	25	14	43	5	.243	.343	1	0	3B-71
1982	140	398	92	15	3	9	2.3	40	58	27	63	5	.231	.352	6	2	3B-113, 2B-26, SS-9, OF-1
1983	138	332	71	13	3	6	1.8	50	32	29	46	10	.214	.325	10	0	3B-103, SS-30, 2B-10, DH-1
1984	113	224	55	11	4	5	2.2	32	26	19	33	6	.246	.397	3	2	3B-68, SS-28, 2B-26, DH-1
6 yrs.	673	1892	466	79	22	38	2.0	228	228	132	296	49	.246	.372	24	6	3B-535, 2B-90, SS-68, DH-4, OF-1

LEAGUE CHAMPIONSHIP SERIES

	G	AB	H	2B	3B	HR	HR %	R	RBI	BB	SO	SB	BA	SA	AB	H	G by POS
1984 DET A	2	2	0	0	0	0	0.0	0	0	0	1	0	.000	.000	0	0	3B-2

WORLD SERIES

	G	AB	H	2B	3B	HR	HR %	R	RBI	BB	SO	SB	BA	SA	AB	H	G by POS
1984 DET A	3	3	0	0	0	0	0.0	0	0	0	1	0	.000	.000	2	0	3B-3

Bobby Brooks

BROOKS, ROBERT   BR TR 5'8½"   165 lbs.
B. Nov. 1, 1945, Los Angeles, Calif.

	G	AB	H	2B	3B	HR	HR %	R	RBI	BB	SO	SB	BA	SA	AB	H	G by POS
1969 OAK A	29	79	19	5	0	3	3.8	13	10	20	24	0	.241	.418	4	1	OF-21
1970	7	18	6	1	0	2	11.1	2	5	1	7	0	.333	.722	3	0	OF-5
1972	15	39	7	0	0	0	0.0	4	5	8	8	0	.179	.179	4	1	OF-11
1973 CAL A	4	7	1	0	0	0	0.0	0	0	0	3	0	.143	.143	3	0	OF-1
4 yrs.	55	143	33	6	0	5	3.5	19	20	29	42	0	.231	.378	14	2	OF-38

Hubie Brooks

BROOKS, HUBERT JR.   BR TR 6'   178 lbs.
B. Sept. 24, 1956, Los Angeles, Calif.

	G	AB	H	2B	3B	HR	HR %	R	RBI	BB	SO	SB	BA	SA	AB	H	G by POS
1980 NY N	24	81	25	2	1	1	1.2	8	10	5	9	1	.309	.395	1	0	3B-23
1981	98	358	110	21	2	4	1.1	34	38	23	65	9	.307	.411	2	0	3B-93, OF-3, SS-1
1982	126	457	114	21	2	2	0.4	40	40	28	76	6	.249	.317	1	0	3B-126
1983	150	586	147	18	4	5	0.9	53	58	24	96	6	.251	.321	2	1	3B-145, 2B-7
1984	153	561	159	23	2	16	2.9	61	73	48	79	6	.283	.417	0	0	3B-129, SS-26
5 yrs.	551	2043	555	85	11	28	1.4	196	219	128	325	28	.272	.365	6	1	3B-516, SS-27, 2B-7, OF-3

Mandy Brooks

BROOKS, JONATHAN JOSEPH   BR TR 5'9"   165 lbs.
Born Jonathan Joseph Brozek.
B. Aug. 18, 1898, Milwaukee, Wis.   D. June 17, 1962, Kirkwood, Mo.

	G	AB	H	2B	3B	HR	HR %	R	RBI	BB	SO	SB	BA	SA	AB	H	G by POS
1925 CHI N	90	349	98	25	7	13	3.7	55	72	19	28	10	.281	.504	1	0	OF-89
1926	26	48	9	1	0	1	2.1	7	6	5	5	0	.188	.271	6	1	OF-18
2 yrs.	116	397	107	26	7	14	3.5	62	78	24	33	10	.270	.476	7	1	OF-107

Siggy Broskie

BROSKIE, SIGMUND THEODORE (Chops)   BR TR 5'11½" 200 lbs.
B. Mar. 23, 1911, Iselin, Pa.   D. May 17, 1975, Canton, Ohio

	G	AB	H	2B	3B	HR	HR %	R	RBI	BB	SO	SB	BA	SA	AB	H	G by POS
1940 BOS N	11	22	6	1	0	0	0.0	1	4	1	2	0	.273	.318	0	0	C-11

Tony Brottem

BROTTEM, ANTON CHRISTIAN   BR TR 6'½"   176 lbs.
B. Apr. 30, 1892, Halstead, Minn.   D. Aug. 5, 1929, Chicago, Ill.

	G	AB	H	2B	3B	HR	HR %	R	RBI	BB	SO	SB	BA	SA	AB	H	G by POS
1916 STL N	26	33	6	1	0	0	0.0	3	4	3	10	1	.182	.212	7	4	C-15, OF-2
1918	2	4	0	0	0	0	0.0	0	0	1	0	0	.000	.000	1	0	1B-2
1921 2 teams	WAS A (4G – .143)					PIT N (30G – .242)											
" total	34	98	23	2	0	0	0.0	7	9	5	12	0	.235	.255	1	0	C-33
3 yrs.	62	135	29	3	0	0	0.0	10	13	9	22	1	.215	.237	9	4	C-48, OF-2, 1B-2

Cal Broughton

BROUGHTON, CECIL CALVERT   TL
B. Dec. 28, 1860, Magnolia, Wis.   D. Mar. 15, 1939, Evansville, Wis.

	G	AB	H	2B	3B	HR	HR %	R	RBI	BB	SO	SB	BA	SA	AB	H	G by POS
1883 2 teams	CLE N (4G – .200)					BAL AA (9G – .188)											
" total	13	42	8	0	0	0	0.0	3		3	2		.190	.190	0	0	C-12, OF-1
1884 MIL U	11	39	12	5	0	0	0.0	5		0			.308	.436	0	0	C-7, OF-5
1885 2 teams	STL AA (4G – .059)					NY AA (11G – .146)											
" total	15	58	7	1	0	0	0.0	2		1			.121	.138	0	0	C-15
1888 DET N	1	4	0	0	0	0	0.0	0		0		0	.000	.000	0	0	C-1
4 yrs.	40	143	27	6	0	0	0.0	10		4	2	0	.189	.231	0	0	C-35, OF-6

	G	AB	H	2B	3B	HR	HR %	R	RBI	BB	SO	SB	BA	SA	Pinch Hit AB	Pinch Hit H	G by POS

Mark Brouhard

BROUHARD, MARK STEVEN
B. May 22, 1956, Burbank, Calif.   BR TR 6'1" 210 lbs.

Year	Tm	G	AB	H	2B	3B	HR	HR%	R	RBI	BB	SO	SB	BA	SA	PH AB	PH H	G by POS
1980	MIL A	45	125	29	6	0	5	4.0	17	16	7	24	1	.232	.400	8	0	DH-21, OF-12, 1B-10
1981		60	186	51	6	3	2	1.1	19	20	7	41	1	.274	.371	4	1	OF-51, DH-7
1982		40	108	29	4	1	4	3.7	16	10	9	17	0	.269	.435	7	0	OF-30, DH-7
1983		56	185	51	10	1	7	3.8	25	23	9	39	0	.276	.454	6	2	OF-42, DH-11
1984		66	197	47	7	0	6	3.0	20	22	16	37	0	.239	.365	7	0	OF-52, DH-8
5 yrs.		267	801	207	33	5	24	3.0	97	91	48	158	2	.258	.402	32	3	OF-187, DH-54, 1B-10

LEAGUE CHAMPIONSHIP SERIES

| 1982 | MIL A | 1 | 4 | 3 | 1 | 0 | 1 | 25.0 | 4 | 3 | 0 | 0 | 0 | .750 | 1.750 | 0 | 0 | OF-1 |

Art Brouthers

BROUTHERS, ARTHUR H.
B. Nov. 25, 1882, Montgomery, Ala.   D. Sept. 28, 1959, Charleston, S. C.   TR 6'1"

| 1906 | PHI A | 36 | 144 | 30 | 5 | 1 | 0 | 0.0 | 18 | 14 | 5 | | 4 | .208 | .257 | 1 | 0 | 3B-33 |

Dan Brouthers

BROUTHERS, DENNIS JOSEPH (Big Dan)   BL TL 6'2" 207 lbs.
B. May 8, 1858, Sylvan Lake, N. Y.   D. Aug. 2, 1932, East Orange, N. J.
Hall of Fame 1945.

Year	Tm	G	AB	H	2B	3B	HR	HR%	R	RBI	BB	SO	SB	BA	SA	PH AB	PH H	G by POS
1879	TRO N	39	168	46	13	1	4	2.4	17	17	1	18		.274	.435	0	0	1B-37, P-3
1880		3	13	2	0	0	0	0.0	0		1	0		.154	.154	0	0	1B-3
1881	BUF N	65	270	86	18	9	8	3.0	60	45	18	22		.319	.541	0	0	OF-35, 1B-30
1882		84	351	129	23	11	6	1.7	71		21	7		.368	.547	0	0	1B-84
1883		98	425	159	41	17	3	0.7	85		16	17		.374	.572	0	0	1B-97, 3B-1, P-1
1884		94	398	130	22	16	14	3.5	82		33	20		.327	.568	0	0	1B-93, 3B-1
1885		98	407	146	32	11	7	1.7	87	60	34	10		.359	.543	0	0	1B-98
1886	DET N	121	489	181	40	15	11	2.2	139	72	66	16		.370	.581	0	0	1B-121
1887		123	500	169	36	20	12	2.4	153	101	71	9	34	.338	.562	0	0	1B-123
1888		129	522	160	33	11	9	1.7	118	66	68	13	34	.307	.464	0	0	1B-129
1889	BOS N	126	485	181	26	9	7	1.4	105	118	66	6	22	.373	.507	0	0	1B-126
1890	BOS P	123	464	160	36	9	1	0.2	117	97	99	17	28	.345	.468	0	0	1B-123
1891	BOS AA	130	486	170	26	19	5	1.0	117	108	87	20	31	.350	.512	0	0	1B-130
1892	BKN N	152	588	197	30	20	5	0.9	121	124	84	30	31	.335	.480	0	0	1B-152
1893		77	282	95	21	11	2	0.7	57	59	52	10	9	.337	.511	0	0	1B-77
1894	BAL N	123	525	182	39	23	9	1.7	137	128	67	9	38	.347	.560	0	0	1B-123
1895	2 teams		BAL	N (5G – .261)			LOU	N	(24G – .309)									
"	total	29	120	36	12	1	2	1.7	15	20	12	3	1	.300	.467	0	0	1B-29
1896	PHI N	57	218	75	13	3	1	0.5	42	41	44	11	7	.344	.445	0	0	1B-57
1904	NY N	2	5	0	0	0	0	0.0	0	0	0		0	.000	.000	1	0	1B-1
19 yrs.		1673	6716	2304	461	206	106	1.6	1523	1056	840	238	235	.343	.520	1	0	1B-1633, OF-35, P-4, 3B-2
					8th										9th			

Joe Brovia

BROVIA, JOSEPH JOHN (Ox)
B. Feb. 18, 1922, Davenport, Calif.   BL TR 6'3" 195 lbs.

| 1955 | CIN N | 21 | 18 | 2 | 0 | 0 | 0 | 0.0 | 0 | 4 | 1 | 6 | 0 | .111 | .111 | 18 | 2 | |

Frank Brower

BROWER, FRANCIS WILLARD (Turkeyfoot)   BL TR 6'2" 180 lbs.
B. Mar. 26, 1893, Gainesville, Va.   D. Nov. 20, 1960, Baltimore, Md.

Year	Tm	G	AB	H	2B	3B	HR	HR%	R	RBI	BB	SO	SB	BA	SA	PH AB	PH H	G by POS
1920	WAS A	36	119	37	7	2	1	0.8	21	13	9	11	1	.311	.429	5	2	OF-20, 1B-9, 3B-1
1921		83	203	53	12	3	1	0.5	31	35	18	7	1	.261	.365	27	6	OF-46, 1B-4
1922		139	471	138	20	6	9	1.9	61	71	52	25	8	.293	.418	9	1	OF-121, 1B-7
1923	CLE A	126	397	113	25	8	16	4.0	77	66	62	32	6	.285	.509	6	2	1B-112, OF-3
1924		66	107	30	10	1	3	2.8	16	20	27	9	1	.280	.477	24	5	1B-26, P-4, OF-3
5 yrs.		450	1297	371	74	20	30	2.3	206	205	168	84	17	.286	.443	71	16	OF-192, 1B-158, P-4, 3B-1

Lou Brower

BROWER, LOUIS LESTER
B. July 1, 1900, Cleveland, Ohio   BR TR 5'10" 155 lbs.

| 1931 | DET A | 21 | 62 | 10 | 1 | 0 | 0 | 0.0 | 3 | 6 | 8 | 5 | 1 | .161 | .177 | 0 | 0 | SS-20, 2B-2 |

Bill Brown

BROWN, WILLIAM VERNA
B. July 8, 1893, Coleman, Tex.   D. May 13, 1965, Lubbock, Tex.   BL TR

| 1912 | STL A | 9 | 20 | 4 | 0 | 0 | 0 | 0.0 | 0 | 1 | 0 | | 0 | .200 | .200 | 2 | 1 | OF-7 |

Bobby Brown

BROWN, ROBERT WILLIAM
B. Oct. 25, 1924, Seattle, Wash.   BL TR 6'1" 180 lbs.

Year	Tm	G	AB	H	2B	3B	HR	HR%	R	RBI	BB	SO	SB	BA	SA	PH AB	PH H	G by POS
1946	NY A	7	24	8	1	0	0	0.0	1	1	4	0	0	.333	.375	0	0	SS-5, 3B-2
1947		69	150	45	6	1	1	0.7	21	18	21	9	0	.300	.373	27	9	3B-27, SS-11, OF-3
1948		113	363	109	19	5	3	0.8	62	48	48	16	0	.300	.405	22	4	3B-41, SS-26, 2B-17, OF-4
1949		104	343	97	14	4	6	1.7	61	61	38	18	4	.283	.399	16	5	3B-86, OF-3
1950		95	277	74	4	2	4	1.4	33	37	39	18	3	.267	.339	14	3	3B-82
1951		103	313	84	15	2	6	1.9	44	51	47	18	1	.268	.387	10	1	3B-90
1952		29	89	22	2	0	1	1.1	6	14	9	6	1	.247	.303	4	0	3B-24
1954		28	60	13	1	0	1	1.7	5	7	8	3	0	.217	.283	9	3	3B-17
8 yrs.		548	1619	452	62	14	22	1.4	233	237	214	88	9	.279	.376	102	25	3B-369, SS-42, 2B-17, OF-10

WORLD SERIES

Year	Tm	G	AB	H	2B	3B	HR	HR%	R	RBI	BB	SO	SB	BA	SA	PH AB	PH H	G by POS
1947	NY A	4	3	3	2	0	0	0.0	2	3	1	0	0	1.000	1.667	3	3	
1949		4	12	6	1	2	0	0.0	4	5	2	2	0	.500	.917	0	0	3B-3
1950		4	12	4	1	1	0	0.0	2	1	0	0	0	.333	.583	1	0	3B-4
1951		5	14	5	1	0	0	0.0	1	0	2	1	0	.357	.429	1	0	3B-4
4 yrs.		17	41	18	5	3	0	0.0	9	9	5	3	0	.439	.707	6	3	3B-11
					4th										1st			

	G	AB	H	2B	3B	HR	HR %	R	RBI	BB	SO	SB	BA	SA	Pinch Hit AB	H	G by POS

Bobby Brown

BROWN, ROGERS LEE
B. May 25, 1954, Turbeville, Va.
BB TR 6'2" 190 lbs.

	G	AB	H	2B	3B	HR	HR %	R	RBI	BB	SO	SB	BA	SA	PH AB	PH H	G by POS
1979 2 teams	TOR A (4G – .000)				NY A (30G – .250)												
" total	34	78	17	3	1	0	0.0	8	3	4	18	2	.218	.282	2	0	OF-31, DH-1
1980 NY A	137	412	107	12	5	14	3.4	65	47	29	82	27	.260	.415	5	0	OF-131, DH-1
1981	31	62	14	1	0	0	0.0	5	6	5	15	4	.226	.242	1	0	OF-29, DH-2
1982 SEA A	79	245	59	7	1	4	1.6	29	17	17	32	28	.241	.327	7	2	OF-68, DH-3
1983 SD N	57	225	60	5	3	5	2.2	40	22	23	38	27	.267	.382	2	1	OF-54
1984	85	171	43	7	2	3	1.8	28	29	11	33	16	.251	.368	24	9	OF-53
6 yrs.	423	1193	300	35	12	26	2.2	175	124	89	218	104	.251	.366	41	12	OF-366, DH-7
DIVISIONAL PLAYOFF SERIES																	
1981 NY A	1	0	0	0	0	0	–	0	0	0	0	0	–	–	0	0	
LEAGUE CHAMPIONSHIP SERIES																	
1980 NY A	3	10	0	0	0	0	0.0	1	0	1	2	0	.000	.000	0	0	OF-3
1981	3	1	1	0	0	0	0.0	2	0	0	0	0	1.000	1.000	0	0	OF-2
1984 SD N	3	4	0	0	0	0	0.0	1	0	1	2	1	.000	.000	1	0	OF-3
3 yrs.	9	15	1	0	0	0	0.0	4	0	2	4	1	.067	.067	1	0	OF-8
WORLD SERIES																	
1981 NY A	4	1	0	0	0	0	0.0	1	0	0	1	0	.000	.000	1	0	OF-2
1984 SD N	5	15	1	0	0	0	0.0	1	2	0	4	0	.067	.067	0	0	OF-5
2 yrs.	9	16	1	0	0	0	0.0	2	2	0	5	0	.063	.063	1	0	OF-7

Chris Brown

BROWN, JOHN CHRISTOPHER
B. Aug. 15, 1961, Jackson, Miss.
BR TR 6' 185 lbs.

	G	AB	H	2B	3B	HR	HR %	R	RBI	BB	SO	SB	BA	SA	PH AB	PH H	G by POS
1984 SF N	23	84	24	7	0	1	1.2	6	11	9	19	2	.286	.405	0	0	3B-23

Curt Brown

BROWN, CURTIS JR.
B. Sept. 14, 1945, Sacramento, Calif.
BR TR 5'11" 180 lbs.

	G	AB	H	2B	3B	HR	HR %	R	RBI	BB	SO	SB	BA	SA	PH AB	PH H	G by POS
1973 MON N	1	4	0	0	0	0	0.0	0	0	0	0	0	.000	.000	0	0	OF-1

Darrell Brown

BROWN, DARRELL WAYNE
B. Oct. 29, 1955, Oklahoma City, Okla.
BB TR 6' 180 lbs.

	G	AB	H	2B	3B	HR	HR %	R	RBI	BB	SO	SB	BA	SA	PH AB	PH H	G by POS
1981 DET A	16	4	1	0	0	0	0.0	4	0	0	1	1	.250	.250	2	1	OF-6, DH-4
1982 OAK A	8	18	6	1	0	0	0.0	2	3	1	2	1	.333	.444	0	0	OF-7, DH-1
1983 MIN A	91	309	84	6	2	0	0.0	40	22	10	28	3	.272	.304	6	0	OF-81, DH-3
1984	95	260	71	9	3	1	0.4	36	19	14	16	4	.273	.342	35	10	OF-55, DH-13
4 yrs.	210	591	162	15	6	1	0.2	82	44	25	47	9	.274	.325	43	11	OF-149, DH-21

Delos Brown

BROWN, DELOS HIGHT
B. Oct. 4, 1892, Anna, Ill. D. Dec. 21, 1964, Carbondale, Ill.
BR TR 5'9" 160 lbs.

	G	AB	H	2B	3B	HR	HR %	R	RBI	BB	SO	SB	BA	SA	PH AB	PH H	G by POS
1914 CHI A	1	1	0	0	0	0	0.0	0	0	0	1	0	.000	.000	1	0	

Dick Brown

BROWN, RICHARD ERNEST
Brother of Larry Brown.
B. Jan. 17, 1935, Shinnston, W. Va. D. Apr. 12, 1970, Baltimore, Md.
BR TR 6'2" 176 lbs.

	G	AB	H	2B	3B	HR	HR %	R	RBI	BB	SO	SB	BA	SA	PH AB	PH H	G by POS
1957 CLE A	34	114	30	4	0	4	3.5	10	22	4	23	1	.263	.404	1	0	C-33
1958	68	173	41	5	0	7	4.0	20	20	12	27	1	.237	.387	6	0	C-62
1959	48	141	31	7	0	5	3.5	15	16	11	39	0	.220	.376	2	0	C-48
1960 CHI A	16	43	7	0	0	3	7.0	4	5	3	11	0	.163	.372	2	1	C-14
1961 DET A	98	308	82	12	2	16	5.2	32	45	22	57	0	.266	.474	3	2	C-91
1962	134	431	104	12	0	12	2.8	40	40	21	66	0	.241	.353	3	1	C-132
1963 BAL A	59	171	42	7	0	2	1.2	13	13	15	35	1	.246	.322	1	1	C-58
1964	88	230	59	6	0	8	3.5	24	32	12	45	2	.257	.387	7	0	C-84
1965	96	255	59	9	1	5	2.0	17	30	17	53	2	.231	.333	7	1	C-92
9 yrs.	641	1866	455	62	3	62	3.3	175	223	117	356	7	.244	.380	32	6	C-614

Don Brown

BROWN, JAMES DONALDSON (Moose)
B. Mar. 31, 1897, Laurel, Ind.
BR TR 6' 178 lbs.

	G	AB	H	2B	3B	HR	HR %	R	RBI	BB	SO	SB	BA	SA	PH AB	PH H	G by POS
1915 STL N	1	2	1	0	0	0	0.0	0	0	2	1	0	.500	.500	0	0	OF-1
1916 PHI A	14	42	10	2	1	1	2.4	6	5	4	9	0	.238	.405	2	0	OF-12
2 yrs.	15	44	11	2	1	1	2.3	6	5	6	10	0	.250	.409	2	0	OF-13

Drummond Brown

BROWN, DRUMMOND NICOL
B. Jan. 31, 1885, Los Angeles, Calif. D. Jan. 27, 1927, Platte County, Mo.
BR TR 6' 180 lbs.

	G	AB	H	2B	3B	HR	HR %	R	RBI	BB	SO	SB	BA	SA	PH AB	PH H	G by POS
1913 BOS N	15	34	11	1	0	1	2.9	3	2	2	9	0	.324	.441	3	0	C-12
1914 KC F	31	58	11	3	0	0	0.0	4	5	7		1	.190	.241	4	0	C-23, 1B-2
1915	77	227	55	10	1	1	0.4	13	26	12		3	.242	.308	11	2	C-65, 1B-1
3 yrs.	123	319	77	14	1	2	0.6	20	33	21	9	4	.241	.310	18	2	C-100, 1B-3

Ed Brown

BROWN, EDWARD P.
B. Chicago, Ill. Deceased.
Manager 1882.
TR

	G	AB	H	2B	3B	HR	HR %	R	RBI	BB	SO	SB	BA	SA	PH AB	PH H	G by POS
1882 STL AA	17	60	11	0	0	0	0.0	4			4		.183	.183	0	0	OF-15, 2B-2, P-1
1884 TOL AA	42	153	27	3	0	0	0.0	13			2		.176	.196	0	0	3B-39, OF-2, 2B-1, C-1, P-1
2 yrs.	59	213	38	3	0	0	0.0	17			6		.178	.192	0	0	3B-39, OF-17, 2B-3, P-2, C-1

Eddie Brown

BROWN, EDWARD WILLIAM (Glass Arm Eddie)
B. July 17, 1891, Milligan, Neb. D. Sept. 10, 1956, Vallejo, Calif.
BR TR 6'3" 190 lbs.

	G	AB	H	2B	3B	HR	HR %	R	RBI	BB	SO	SB	BA	SA	PH AB	PH H	G by POS
1920 NY N	3	8	1	1	0	0	0.0	1	0	0	3	0	.125	.250	1	0	OF-2
1921	70	128	36	6	2	0	0.0	16	12	4	11	1	.281	.359	37	11	OF-30
1924 BKN N	114	455	140	30	4	5	1.1	56	78	26	15	3	.308	.424	0	0	OF-114
1925	153	618	189	39	11	6	0.8	88	99	22	18	3	.306	.429	0	0	OF-153
1926 BOS N	153	612	201	31	8	2	0.3	71	84	23	20	5	.328	.415	0	0	OF-153
1927	155	558	171	35	6	2	0.4	64	75	28	20	11	.306	.401	4	2	OF-150, 1B-1

	G	AB	H	2B	3B	HR	HR %	R	RBI	BB	SO	SB	BA	SA	Pinch Hit AB	Pinch Hit H	G by POS

Eddie Brown continued

	G	AB	H	2B	3B	HR	HR %	R	RBI	BB	SO	SB	BA	SA	AB	H	G by POS
1928	142	523	140	28	2	2	0.4	45	59	24	22	6	.268	.340	10	4	OF-129, 1B-1
7 yrs.	790	2902	878	170	33	16	0.6	341	407	127	109	29	.303	.400	52	17	OF-731, 1B-2

Fred Brown

BROWN, FRED HERBERT
B. Apr. 12, 1879, Ossipee, N. H.   D. Feb. 3, 1955, Somersworth, N. H.
BR TR 5'10½" 180 lbs.

	G	AB	H	2B	3B	HR	HR %	R	RBI	BB	SO	SB	BA	SA	AB	H	G by POS
1901 BOS N	7	14	2	0	0	0	0.0	1	2	0		0	.143	.143	2	1	OF-5
1902	2	6	2	1	0	0	0.0	1	0	0		0	.333	.500	0	0	OF-2
2 yrs.	9	20	4	1	0	0	0.0	2	2	0		0	.200	.250	2	1	OF-7

Gates Brown

BROWN, WILLIAM JAMES
B. May 2, 1939, Crestline, Ohio
BL TR 5'11" 220 lbs.

	G	AB	H	2B	3B	HR	HR %	R	RBI	BB	SO	SB	BA	SA	AB	H	G by POS
1963 DET A	55	82	22	3	1	2	2.4	16	14	8	13	2	.268	.402	30	6	OF-16
1964	123	426	116	22	6	15	3.5	65	54	31	53	11	.272	.458	19	4	OF-106
1965	96	227	58	14	2	10	4.4	33	43	17	33	6	.256	.467	34	9	OF-56
1966	88	169	45	5	1	7	4.1	27	27	18	19	3	.266	.432	40	13	OF-43
1967	51	91	17	1	1	2	2.2	17	9	13	15	0	.187	.286	26	4	OF-20
1968	67	92	34	7	2	6	6.5	15	15	12	4	0	.370	.685	39	18	OF-17, 1B-1
1969	60	93	19	1	2	1	1.1	13	6	5	17	0	.204	.290	39	8	OF-14
1970	81	124	28	3	0	3	2.4	18	24	20	14	0	.226	.323	41	10	OF-26
1971	82	195	66	2	3	11	5.6	37	29	21	17	4	.338	.549	26	9	OF-56
1972	103	252	58	5	0	10	4.0	33	31	26	28	3	.230	.369	28	4	OF-72
1973	125	377	89	11	1	12	3.2	48	50	52	41	1	.236	.366	4	0	DH-119, OF-2
1974	73	99	24	2	0	4	4.0	7	17	10	15	0	.242	.384	53	16	DH-13
1975	47	35	6	2	0	1	2.9	1	3	9	6	0	.171	.314	35	6	
13 yrs.	1051	2262	582	78	19	84	3.7	330	322	242	275	30	.257	.420	414	107	OF-428, DH-132, 1B-1
															8th	7th	

LEAGUE CHAMPIONSHIP SERIES

	G	AB	H	2B	3B	HR	HR %	R	RBI	BB	SO	SB	BA	SA	AB	H	G by POS
1972 DET A	3	2	0	0	0	0	0.0	1	0	1	0	0	.000	.000	2	0	

WORLD SERIES

	G	AB	H	2B	3B	HR	HR %	R	RBI	BB	SO	SB	BA	SA	AB	H	G by POS
1968 DET A	1	1	0	0	0	0	0.0	0	0	0	0	0	.000	.000	1	0	

Ike Brown

BROWN, ISAAC
B. Apr. 13, 1942, Memphis, Tenn.
BR TR 6' 190 lbs.

	G	AB	H	2B	3B	HR	HR %	R	RBI	BB	SO	SB	BA	SA	AB	H	G by POS
1969 DET A	70	170	39	4	3	5	2.9	24	12	26	43	2	.229	.376	12	0	2B-45, 3B-12, OF-3, SS-1
1970	56	94	27	5	0	4	4.3	17	15	13	26	0	.287	.468	21	7	2B-23, OF-4, 3B-1
1971	59	110	28	1	0	8	7.3	20	19	19	25	0	.255	.482	19	6	1B-17, OF-9, 2B-8, 3B-4, SS-1
1972	51	84	21	3	0	2	2.4	12	10	17	23	1	.250	.357	12	1	OF-22, 1B-13, 2B-3, SS-1, 3B-1
1973	42	76	22	2	1	1	1.3	12	9	15	13	0	.289	.382	7	1	1B-21, OF-12, DH-2, 3B-2
1974	2	2	0	0	0	0	0.0	0	0	0	0	0	.000	.000	0	0	3B-2
6 yrs.	280	536	137	15	4	20	3.7	85	65	90	130	3	.256	.410	71	15	2B-79, 1B-51, OF-50, 3B-22, SS-3, DH-2

LEAGUE CHAMPIONSHIP SERIES

	G	AB	H	2B	3B	HR	HR %	R	RBI	BB	SO	SB	BA	SA	AB	H	G by POS
1972 DET A	1	2	1	0	0	0	0.0	0	2	0	1	0	.500	.500	0	0	1B-1

Jake Brown

BROWN, JERALD RAY
B. Mar. 22, 1946, Sumrall, Miss.
BR TR 6'2" 200 lbs.

	G	AB	H	2B	3B	HR	HR %	R	RBI	BB	SO	SB	BA	SA	AB	H	G by POS
1975 SF N	41	43	9	3	0	0	0.0	6	4	5	13	0	.209	.279	22	4	OF-14

Jimmy Brown

BROWN, JAMES ROBERSON
B. Apr. 25, 1910, Jamesville, N. C.   D. Dec. 29, 1977, Bath, N. C.
BB TR 5'8½" 165 lbs.

	G	AB	H	2B	3B	HR	HR %	R	RBI	BB	SO	SB	BA	SA	AB	H	G by POS
1937 STL N	138	525	145	20	9	2	0.4	86	53	27	29	10	.276	.360	6	1	2B-112, SS-25, 3B-1
1938	108	382	115	12	6	0	0.0	50	38	27	9	7	.301	.364	9	3	2B-49, SS-30, 3B-24
1939	147	645	192	31	8	3	0.5	88	51	32	18	4	.298	.384	1	0	SS-104, 2B-50
1940	107	454	127	17	4	0	0.0	56	30	24	15	9	.280	.335	1	0	2B-48, 3B-41, SS-28
1941	132	549	168	28	9	3	0.5	81	56	45	22	2	.306	.404	1	1	3B-123, 2B-11
1942	145	606	155	28	4	1	0.2	75	71	52	11	4	.256	.320	0	0	2B-82, 3B-66, SS-12
1943	34	110	20	4	2	0	0.0	6	8	6	1	0	.182	.255	1	0	2B-19, 3B-9, SS-6
1946 PIT N	79	241	58	6	0	0	0.0	23	12	18	5	3	.241	.266	20	7	SS-30, 2B-21, 3B-9
8 yrs.	890	3512	980	146	42	9	0.3	465	319	231	110	39	.279	.352	39	12	2B-392, 3B-273, SS-235

WORLD SERIES

	G	AB	H	2B	3B	HR	HR %	R	RBI	BB	SO	SB	BA	SA	AB	H	G by POS
1942 STL N	5	20	6	0	0	0	0.0	2	1	3	0	0	.300	.300	0	0	2B-5

Larry Brown

BROWN, LARRY LESLEY
Brother of Dick Brown.
B. Mar. 1, 1940, Shinnston, W. Va.
BR TR 5'10" 160 lbs.

	G	AB	H	2B	3B	HR	HR %	R	RBI	BB	SO	SB	BA	SA	AB	H	G by POS
1963 CLE A	74	247	63	6	0	5	2.0	28	18	22	27	4	.255	.340	5	1	SS-46, 2B-27
1964	115	335	77	12	1	12	3.6	33	40	24	55	1	.230	.379	12	1	2B-103, SS-4
1965	124	438	111	22	2	8	1.8	52	40	38	62	5	.253	.368	5	1	SS-95, 2B-26
1966	105	340	78	12	0	3	0.9	29	17	36	58	0	.229	.291	6	2	SS-90, 2B-10
1967	152	485	110	16	2	7	1.4	38	37	53	62	4	.227	.311	1	0	SS-150
1968	154	495	116	18	3	6	1.2	43	35	43	46	1	.234	.319	1	0	SS-154
1969	132	469	112	10	2	4	0.9	48	24	44	43	5	.239	.294	6	2	SS-101, 3B-29, 2B-5
1970	72	155	40	5	2	0	0.0	17	15	20	14	1	.258	.316	22	5	SS-27, 3B-17, 2B-16
1971 2 teams	CLE	A (13G – .220)				OAK	A (70G – .196)										
" total	83	239	48	3	1	4	1.7	18	14	10	22	1	.201	.234	8	0	SS-44, 2B-23, 3B-10
1972 OAK A	47	142	26	2	0	0	0.0	11	4	13	8	0	.183	.197	0	0	2B-46, 3B-1
1973 BAL A	17	28	7	0	0	1	3.6	4	5	5	4	0	.250	.357	3	0	3B-15, 2B-1
1974 TEX A	54	76	15	2	0	0	0.0	10	5	9	13	0	.197	.224	2	1	3B-47, 2B-8, SS-1
12 yrs.	1129	3449	803	108	13	47	1.4	331	254	317	414	22	.233	.313	71	13	SS-712, 2B-265, 3B-119

LEAGUE CHAMPIONSHIP SERIES

	G	AB	H	2B	3B	HR	HR %	R	RBI	BB	SO	SB	BA	SA	AB	H	G by POS
1973 BAL A	1	0	0	0	0	0	–	0	0	0	0	0	–	–	0	0	3B-1

	G	AB	H	2B	3B	HR	HR%	R	RBI	BB	SO	SB	BA	SA	Pinch Hit AB	Pinch Hit H	G by POS

Leon Brown

BROWN, LEON (Brownie)
B. Nov. 16, 1948, Sacramento, Calif.
BB TR 6' 185 lbs.

	G	AB	H	2B	3B	HR	HR%	R	RBI	BB	SO	SB	BA	SA	PH AB	PH H	G by POS
1976 NY N	64	70	15	3	0	0	0.0	11	2	4	4	2	.214	.257	7	1	OF-43

Lew Brown

BROWN, LEWIS J. (Blower)
B. Feb. 1, 1858, Leominster, Mass. D. Jan. 16, 1889, Boston, Mass.
BR TR 5'10½" 185 lbs.

	G	AB	H	2B	3B	HR	HR%	R	RBI	BB	SO	SB	BA	SA	PH AB	PH H	G by POS
1876 BOS N	45	195	41	6	6	2	1.0	23	21	3	22		.210	.333	0	0	C-45, OF-1
1877	58	221	56	12	8	1	0.5	27	31	6	33		.253	.394	0	0	C-55, 1B-4
1878 PRO N	58	243	74	21	6	1	0.4	44	43	7	37		.305	.453	0	0	C-45, 1B-15, OF-1, P-1
1879 2 teams	PRO N (53G – .258)				CHI N (6G – .286)												
" total	59	250	65	14	4	2	0.8	25	41	5	28		.260	.372	0	0	C-48, OF-6, 1B-6
1881 2 teams	DET N (27G – .241)				PRO N (18G – .240)												
" total	45	183	44	6	2	3	1.6	25	24	7	29		.240	.344	0	0	1B-32, OF-13
1883 2 teams	BOS N (14G – .241)				LOU AA (14G – .183)												
" total	28	114	24	6	2	0	0.0	11	9		4	6	.211	.298	0	0	1B-28, C-1
1884 BOS U	85	325	75	18	3	1	0.3	50			13		.231	.314	0	0	C-54, 1B-33, OF-2, P-1
7 yrs.	378	1531	379	83	31	10	0.7	205	169	45	155		.248	.362	0	0	C-248, 1B-118, OF-23, P-2

Lindsay Brown

BROWN, JOHN LINDSAY (Red)
B. July 22, 1911, Mason, Tex. D. Jan. 1, 1967, San Antonio, Tex.
BR TR 5'10" 160 lbs.

	G	AB	H	2B	3B	HR	HR%	R	RBI	BB	SO	SB	BA	SA	PH AB	PH H	G by POS
1937 BKN N	48	115	31	3	1	0	0.0	16	6	3	17	1	.270	.313	0	0	SS-45

Mike Brown

BROWN, MICHAEL CHARLES
B. Dec. 29, 1959, San Francisco, Calif.
BR TR 6'2" 190 lbs.

	G	AB	H	2B	3B	HR	HR%	R	RBI	BB	SO	SB	BA	SA	PH AB	PH H	G by POS
1983 CAL A	31	104	24	5	1	3	2.9	12	9	7	20	1	.231	.385	0	0	OF-31
1984	62	148	42	8	3	7	4.7	19	22	13	23	0	.284	.520	14	3	OF-44, DH-3
2 yrs.	93	252	66	13	4	10	4.0	31	31	20	43	1	.262	.464	14	3	OF-75, DH-3

Ollie Brown

BROWN, OLLIE LEE (Downtown)
Brother of Oscar Brown.
B. Feb. 11, 1944, Tuscaloosa, Ala.
BR TR 6'2" 178 lbs.

	G	AB	H	2B	3B	HR	HR%	R	RBI	BB	SO	SB	BA	SA	PH AB	PH H	G by POS
1965 SF N	6	10	2	1	0	0	0.0	0	0	0	2	0	.200	.300	1	0	OF-4
1966	115	348	81	7	1	7	2.0	32	33	33	66	2	.233	.319	3	0	OF-114
1967	120	412	110	12	1	13	3.2	44	53	25	65	0	.267	.396	4	1	OF-115
1968	40	95	22	4	0	0	0.0	7	11	3	23	1	.232	.274	6	1	OF-35
1969 SD N	151	568	150	18	3	20	3.5	76	61	44	97	10	.264	.412	1	0	OF-148
1970	139	534	156	34	1	23	4.3	79	89	34	78	5	.292	.489	3	0	OF-137
1971	145	484	132	16	4	9	1.9	36	55	52	74	3	.273	.362	11	3	OF-134
1972 3 teams	SD N (23G – .171)			OAK A (20G – .241)			MIL A (66G – .279)										
" total	109	303	75	11	0	4	1.3	29	32	28	47	1	.248	.323	24	1	OF-89, 3B-1
1973 MIL A	97	296	83	10	1	7	2.4	28	32	33	53	4	.280	.392	9	0	DH-82, OF-4
1974 2 teams	HOU N (27G – .217)			PHI N (43G – .242)													
" total	70	168	39	6	2	7	4.2	19	19	10	35	0	.232	.417	29	11	OF-53
1975 PHI N	84	145	44	12	0	6	4.1	19	26	15	29	1	.303	.510	30	8	OF-38
1976	92	209	53	10	1	5	2.4	30	30	33	33	2	.254	.383	26	9	OF-75
1977	50	70	17	3	1	1	1.4	5	13	4	14	1	.243	.357	31	7	OF-21
13 yrs.	1218	3642	964	144	11	102	2.8	404	454	314	616	30	.265	.394	178	42	OF-967, DH-82, 3B-1

LEAGUE CHAMPIONSHIP SERIES

	G	AB	H	2B	3B	HR	HR%	R	RBI	BB	SO	SB	BA	SA	PH AB	PH H	G by POS
1976 PHI N	1	2	0	0	0	0	0.0	0	0	1	1	0	.000	.000	0	0	OF-1
1977	2	2	0	0	0	0	0.0	0	0	0	1	0	.000	.000	2	0	
2 yrs.	3	4	0	0	0	0	0.0	0	0	1	2	0	.000	.000	2	0	OF-1

Oscar Brown

BROWN, OSCAR LEE
Brother of Ollie Brown.
B. Feb. 8, 1946, Long Beach, Calif.
BR TR 6' 175 lbs.

	G	AB	H	2B	3B	HR	HR%	R	RBI	BB	SO	SB	BA	SA	PH AB	PH H	G by POS
1969 ATL N	7	4	1	0	0	0	0.0	2	0	0	1	0	.250	.250	1	0	OF-3
1970	28	47	18	4	0	1	2.1	6	7	7	7	0	.383	.532	3	2	OF-25
1971	27	43	9	4	0	0	0.0	4	5	3	8	0	.209	.302	10	1	OF-15
1972	76	164	37	5	1	3	1.8	19	16	4	29	0	.226	.323	15	1	OF-59
1973	22	58	12	1	0	0	0.0	3	0	3	10	0	.207	.259	9	1	OF-13
5 yrs.	160	316	77	14	2	4	1.3	34	28	17	55	0	.244	.339	38	5	OF-115

Randy Brown

BROWN, EDWIN RANDOLPH
B. Aug. 29, 1944, Leesburg, Fla.
BL TR 5'7" 170 lbs.

	G	AB	H	2B	3B	HR	HR%	R	RBI	BB	SO	SB	BA	SA	PH AB	PH H	G by POS
1969 CAL A	13	25	4	1	0	0	0.0	3	0	6	1	0	.160	.200	3	0	C-10, OF-1
1970	5	4	0	0	0	0	0.0	0	0	0	0	0	.000	.000	0	0	C-5
2 yrs.	18	29	4	1	0	0	0.0	3	0	6	1	0	.138	.172	3	0	C-15, OF-1

Sam Brown

BROWN, SAMUEL WAKEFIELD
B. May 21, 1878, Webster, Pa. D. Nov. 8, 1931, Mount Pleasant, Pa.
BR TR

	G	AB	H	2B	3B	HR	HR%	R	RBI	BB	SO	SB	BA	SA	PH AB	PH H	G by POS
1906 BOS N	71	231	48	6	1	0	0.0	12	20	13			4	.208	.242	5	1	C-35, OF-13, 3B-12, 1B-3, 2B-2
1907	70	208	40	6	0	0	0.0	17	14	12			0	.192	.221	4	1	C-63, 1B-2
2 yrs.	141	439	88	12	1	0	0.0	29	34	25			4	.200	.232	9	2	C-98, OF-13, 3B-12, 1B-5, 2B-2

Tom Brown

BROWN, THOMAS T.
B. Sept. 21, 1860, Liverpool, England D. Oct. 27, 1927, Washington, D. C.
Manager 1897-98.
BL TR 5'10" 168 lbs.

	G	AB	H	2B	3B	HR	HR%	R	RBI	BB	SO	SB	BA	SA	PH AB	PH H	G by POS
1882 BAL AA	45	181	55	5	2	1	0.6	30			6			.304	.370	0	0	OF-45, P-2
1883 COL AA	97	420	115	12	7	5	1.2	69		20				.274	.371	0	0	OF-96, P-3
1884	107	451	123	9	11	5	1.1	93		24				.273	.375	0	0	OF-107, P-4
1885 PIT AA	108	437	134	16	12	4	0.9	81		34				.307	.426	0	0	OF-108, P-2
1886	115	460	131	11	11	1	0.2	106		56				.285	.363	0	0	OF-115, P-1
1887 2 teams	PIT N (47G – .245)			IND N (36G – .179)													
" total	83	332	72	6	4	2	0.6	50	15	19	65	25	.217	.277	0	0	OF-83
1888 BOS N	107	420	104	10	7	9	2.1	62	49	30	68	46	.248	.369	0	0	OF-107

	G	AB	H	2B	3B	HR	HR %	R	RBI	BB	SO	SB	BA	SA	Pinch Hit AB	Pinch Hit H	G by POS

Tom Brown continued

	G	AB	H	2B	3B	HR	HR%	R	RBI	BB	SO	SB	BA	SA	AB	H	G by POS
1889	90	362	84	10	5	2	0.6	93	24	59	56	63	.232	.304	0	0	OF-90
1890 BOS P	128	543	150	23	14	4	0.7	146	61	86	84	79	.276	.392	0	0	OF-128
1891 BOS AA	137	589	189	30	21	5	0.8	177	71	70	96	106	.321	.469	0	0	OF-137
1892 LOU N	153	660	150	16	8	2	0.3	105	45	47	94	78	.227	.285	0	0	OF-153
1893	122	529	127	15	7	5	0.9	104	54	56	63	66	.240	.323	0	0	OF-122
1894	129	536	136	22	14	9	1.7	122	57	60	73	66	.254	.397	0	0	OF-129
1895 2 teams	STL	N (83G –	.217)		WAS	N	(34G –	.239)									
" total	117	484	108	19	7	3	0.6	97	47	66	60	42	.223	.310	0	0	OF-117
1896 WAS N	116	435	128	17	6	2	0.5	87	59	58	49	28	.294	.375	0	0	OF-116
1897	116	469	137	17	2	5	1.1	91	45	52		25	.292	.369	0	0	OF-115
1898	16	55	9	1	0	0	0.0	8	2	5		3	.164	.182	0	0	OF-15
17 yrs.	1786	7363	1952	239	138	64	0.9	1521	528	748	708	627	.265	.361	0	0	OF-1783, P-12

Tom Brown

BROWN, THOMAS WILLIAM   BB TL 6'1"   190 lbs.
B. Dec. 12, 1940, Laureldale, Pa.

	G	AB	H	2B	3B	HR	HR%	R	RBI	BB	SO	SB	BA	SA	AB	H	G by POS
1963 WAS A	61	116	17	4	0	1	0.9	8	4	11	45	2	.147	.207	22	4	OF-16, 1B-14

Tommy Brown

BROWN, THOMAS MICHAEL (Buckshot)   BR TR 6'1"   170 lbs.
B. Dec. 6, 1927, Brooklyn, N. Y.

	G	AB	H	2B	3B	HR	HR%	R	RBI	BB	SO	SB	BA	SA	AB	H	G by POS
1944 BKN N	46	146	24	4	0	0	0.0	17	8	8	17	0	.164	.192	0	0	SS-46
1945	57	196	48	3	4	2	1.0	19	19	6	16	3	.245	.332	1	0	SS-55, OF-1
1947	15	34	8	1	0	0	0.0	3	2	1	6	0	.235	.265	4	1	3B-6, OF-3, SS-1
1948	54	145	35	4	0	2	1.4	18	20	7	17	1	.241	.310	9	1	3B-43, 1B-1
1949	41	89	27	2	0	3	3.4	14	18	6	8	0	.303	.427	13	4	OF-27
1950	48	86	25	2	1	8	9.3	15	20	11	9	0	.291	.616	29	7	OF-16
1951 2 teams	BKN	N (11G –	.160)		PHI	N	(78G –	.219)									
" total	89	221	47	4	1	10	4.5	26	33	17	25	1	.213	.376	26	4	OF-37, 2B-14, 1B-12, 3B-1
1952 2 teams	PHI	N (18G –	.160)		CHI	N	(61G –	.320)									
" total	79	225	68	12	0	4	1.8	26	26	16	27	1	.302	.409	15	3	SS-39, 2B-10, 1B-8, OF-3
1953 CHI N	65	138	27	7	1	2	1.4	19	13	13	17	1	.196	.304	30	5	SS-25, OF-6
9 yrs.	494	1280	309	39	7	31	2.4	151	159	85	142	7	.241	.355	127	25	SS-166, OF-93, 3B-50, 2B-24, 1B-21

WORLD SERIES
	G	AB	H	2B	3B	HR	HR%	R	RBI	BB	SO	SB	BA	SA	AB	H	G by POS
1949 BKN N	2	2	0	0	0	0	0.0	0	0	0	1	0	.000	.000	2	0	

Willard Brown

BROWN, WILLARD (Big Bill, California Brown)   BR TR 6'2"   190 lbs.
B. 1866, San Francisco, Calif.   D. Dec. 20, 1897, San Francisco, Calif.

	G	AB	H	2B	3B	HR	HR%	R	RBI	BB	SO	SB	BA	SA	AB	H	G by POS
1887 NY N	49	170	37	3	2	0	0.0	17	25	10	15	10	.218	.259	0	0	C-46, 3B-3, OF-2
1888	20	59	16	1	0	0	0.0	4	6	1	8	1	.271	.288	0	0	C-20
1889	40	139	36	10	0	1	0.7	16	29	9	9	6	.259	.353	0	0	C-37, OF-3
1890 NY P	60	230	64	8	4	4	1.7	47	43	13	13	5	.278	.400	0	0	C-34, OF-13, 1B-9, 3B-3, 2B-2
1891 PHI N	115	441	107	20	4	0	0.0	62	50	34	35	7	.243	.306	0	0	1B-97, C-19, OF-2
1893 2 teams	BAL	N (7G –	.125)		LOU	N	(111G –	.304)									
" total	118	493	144	26	7	1	0.2	85	90	51	35	9	.292	.379	0	0	1B-118, C-1
1894 2 teams	LOU	N (13G –	.208)		STL	N	(3G –	.111)									
" total	16	57	11	2	0	0	0.0	5	9	5	9	1	.193	.228	0	0	1B-16
7 yrs.	418	1589	415	70	17	6	0.4	236	252	123	124	39	.261	.338	0	0	1B-240, C-157, OF-20, 3B-6, 2B-2

Willard Brown

BROWN, WILLARD JESSIE   BR TR 5'11½" 200 lbs.
B. June 26, 1921, Shreveport, La.

	G	AB	H	2B	3B	HR	HR%	R	RBI	BB	SO	SB	BA	SA	AB	H	G by POS
1947 STL A	21	67	12	3	0	1	1.5	4	6	0	7	2	.179	.269	3	1	OF-18

Byron Browne

BROWNE, BYRON ELLIS   BR TR 6'2"   190 lbs.
B. Dec. 27, 1942, St. Joseph, Mo.

	G	AB	H	2B	3B	HR	HR%	R	RBI	BB	SO	SB	BA	SA	AB	H	G by POS
1965 CHI N	4	6	0	0	0	0	0.0	0	0	0	2	0	.000	.000	1	0	OF-4
1966	120	419	102	15	7	16	3.8	46	51	40	143	3	.243	.427	5	0	OF-114
1967	10	19	3	2	0	0	0.0	3	2	4	5	1	.158	.263	2	0	OF-8
1968 HOU N	10	13	3	0	0	0	0.0	0	1	4	6	0	.231	.231	6	1	OF-2
1969 STL N	22	53	12	0	1	1	1.9	9	7	11	14	0	.226	.321	7	0	OF-16
1970 PHI N	104	270	67	17	2	10	3.7	29	36	33	72	1	.248	.437	18	4	OF-88
1971	58	68	14	3	0	3	4.4	5	5	8	23	0	.206	.382	27	7	OF-30
1972	21	21	4	0	0	0	0.0	2	0	1	8	0	.190	.190	14	3	OF-9
8 yrs.	349	869	205	37	10	30	3.5	94	102	101	273	5	.236	.405	80	15	OF-271

Earl Browne

BROWNE, EARL JAMES (Snitz)   BL TL 6'   175 lbs.
B. Mar. 5, 1911, Louisville, Ky.

	G	AB	H	2B	3B	HR	HR%	R	RBI	BB	SO	SB	BA	SA	AB	H	G by POS
1935 PIT N	9	32	8	2	0	0	0.0	6	6	2	8	0	.250	.313	0	0	1B-9
1936	8	23	7	1	2	0	0.0	7	3	1	4	0	.304	.522	3	1	OF-4, 1B-1
1937 PHI N	105	332	97	19	3	6	1.8	42	52	21	41	4	.292	.422	26	7	OF-54, 1B-23
1938	21	74	19	4	0	0	0.0	4	8	5	11	0	.257	.311	3	1	1B-16, OF-2
4 yrs.	143	461	131	26	5	6	1.3	59	69	29	64	4	.284	.401	32	9	OF-60, 1B-49

George Browne

BROWNE, GEORGE EDWARD   BL TR 5'10½" 160 lbs.
B. Jan. 12, 1876, Richmond, Va.   D. Dec. 9, 1920, Hyde Park, N. Y.

	G	AB	H	2B	3B	HR	HR%	R	RBI	BB	SO	SB	BA	SA	AB	H	G by POS
1901 PHI N	8	26	5	1	0	0	0.0	2	4	1		2	.192	.231	0	0	OF-8
1902 2 teams	PHI	N (70G –	.260)		NY	N	(53G –	.319)									
" total	123	497	142	16	6	0	0.0	71	40	25		24	.286	.342	0	0	OF-123
1903 NY N	141	591	185	20	3	5	0.5	105	45	43		27	.313	.372	0	0	OF-141
1904	150	596	169	16	5	4	0.7	99	39	39		24	.284	.347	1	0	OF-149
1905	127	536	157	16	14	4	0.7	95	43	20		26	.293	.397	0	0	OF-127
1906	122	477	126	10	4	0	0.0	61	38	27		32	.264	.302	1	0	OF-121
1907	127	458	119	11	10	5	1.1	54	37	31		15	.260	.360	4	0	OF-121
1908 BOS N	138	536	122	10	6	1	0.2	61	34	36		17	.228	.274	3	1	OF-138

	G	AB	H	2B	3B	HR	HR %	R	RBI	BB	SO	SB	BA	SA	Pinch Hit AB	Pinch Hit H	G by POS

George Browne continued

	G	AB	H	2B	3B	HR	HR %	R	RBI	BB	SO	SB	BA	SA	AB	H	G by POS
1909 2 teams	CHI N (12G – .205)			WAS A (103G – .272)													
" total	115	432	115	15	6	1	0.2	47	17	22		16	.266	.336	2	0	OF-113
1910 2 teams	WAS A (7G – .182)			CHI A (30G – .241)													
" total	37	134	31	4	1	0	0.0	18	4	13		5	.231	.276	3	0	OF-34
1911 BKN N	8	12	4	0	0	0	0.0	1	2	1	1	2	.333	.333	4	0	OF-2
1912 PHI N	6	5	1	0	0	0	0.0	0	1	1		0	.200	.200	4	1	3B-1
12 yrs.	1102	4300	1176	119	55	18	0.4	614	303	259	1	190	.273	.339	22	2	OF-1077, 3B-1

WORLD SERIES

	G	AB	H	2B	3B	HR	HR %	R	RBI	BB	SO	SB	BA	SA	AB	H	G by POS
1905 NY N	5	22	4	0	0	0	0.0	2	1	0	2	2	.182	.182	0	0	OF-5

Pidge Browne

BROWNE, PRENTICE ALMONT   BL TL 6'1"   190 lbs.
B. Mar. 21, 1929, Peekskill, N. Y.

	G	AB	H	2B	3B	HR	HR %	R	RBI	BB	SO	SB	BA	SA	AB	H	G by POS
1962 HOU N	65	100	21	4	2	1	1.0	8	10	13	9	0	.210	.320	36	8	1B-26

Pete Browning

BROWNING, LOUIS ROGERS (The Gladiator)   BR TR 6'   180 lbs.
B. June 17, 1861, Louisville, Ky.   D. Sept. 10, 1905, Louisville, Ky.

	G	AB	H	2B	3B	HR	HR %	R	RBI	BB	SO	SB	BA	SA	AB	H	G by POS
1882 LOU AA	69	288	110	19	3	5	1.7	67		26			.382	.521	0	0	2B-42, SS-18, 3B-13
1883	84	360	121	14	11	4	1.1	95		23			.336	.469	0	0	OF-48, SS-26, 3B-10, 2B-3, 1B-1
1884	105	454	150	34	8	4	0.9	101		13			.330	.467	0	0	3B-52, OF-24, 1B-23, 2B-4, P-1
1885	112	481	174	34	10	9	1.9	98		25			.362	.530	0	0	OF-112
1886	112	467	159	29	6	3	0.6	86		30			.340	.448	0	0	OF-112
1887	134	547	220	36	18	4	0.7	137		55		103	.402	.556	0	0	OF-134
1888	99	383	120	23	8	3	0.8	58	72	37		36	.313	.439	0	0	OF-99
1889	83	324	83	19	5	2	0.6	39	32	34	30	21	.256	.364	0	0	OF-83
1890 CLE P	118	493	191	40	8	5	1.0	114	93	75	36	35	.387	.531	0	0	OF-118
1891 2 teams	PIT N (50G – .291)			CIN N (55G – .343)													
" total	105	419	133	24	4	4	1.0	64	61	51	54	16	.317	.422	0	0	OF-105
1892 2 teams	LOU N (21G – .247)			CIN N (83G – .303)													
" total	104	384	112	16	5	3	0.8	57	56	52	32	13	.292	.383	0	0	OF-103, 1B-2
1893 LOU N	57	220	78	11	3	1	0.5	38	37	44	15	8	.355	.445	0	0	OF-57
1894 2 teams	STL N (2G – .143)			BKN N (1G – 1.000)													
" total	3	9	3	0	0	0	0.0	2	1	0	1	0	.333	.333	0	0	OF-3
13 yrs.	1185	4829	1654	299	89	47	1.0	956	352	466	167	232	.343 10th	.470	0	0	OF-998, 3B-75, 2B-49, SS-44, 1B-26, P-1

Bill Brubaker

BRUBAKER, WILBUR LEE   BR TR 6'2"   185 lbs.
B. Nov. 7, 1910, Cleveland, Ohio   D. Apr. 2, 1978, Laguna Hills, Calif.

	G	AB	H	2B	3B	HR	HR %	R	RBI	BB	SO	SB	BA	SA	AB	H	G by POS
1932 PIT N	7	24	10	3	0	0	0.0	3	4	3	4	1	.417	.542	0	0	3B-7
1933	2	2	0	0	0	0	0.0	0	0	0	0	0	.000	.000	1	0	3B-1
1934	3	6	2	1	0	0	0.0	0	1	1	0	0	.333	.500	0	0	3B-3
1935	6	11	0	0	0	0	0.0	1	0	2	5	0	.000	.000	1	0	3B-5
1936	145	554	160	27	4	6	1.1	77	102	50	96	5	.289	.384	0	0	3B-145
1937	120	413	105	20	4	6	1.5	57	48	47	51	2	.254	.366	0	0	3B-115, SS-3, 1B-1
1938	45	112	33	5	0	3	2.7	18	19	9	14	2	.295	.420	9	3	3B-18, 1B-9, SS-3, OF-1
1939	100	345	80	23	1	7	2.0	41	43	29	51	3	.232	.365	5	1	2B-65, 3B-32, SS-1
1940	38	78	15	3	1	0	0.0	8	7	8	16	0	.192	.256	4	1	3B-19, SS-8, 1B-4
1943 BOS N	13	19	8	3	0	0	0.0	3	1	2	2	0	.421	.579	3	2	3B-5, 1B-3
10 yrs.	479	1564	413	85	10	22	1.4	208	225	151	239	13	.264	.373	23	7	3B-350, 2B-65, 1B-17, SS-15, OF-1

Lou Bruce

BRUCE, LOUIS   BL TR 5'5"   145 lbs.
B. Jan. 16, 1877, St. Regis, N. Y.   D. Feb. 9, 1968, Ilion, N. Y.

	G	AB	H	2B	3B	HR	HR %	R	RBI	BB	SO	SB	BA	SA	AB	H	G by POS
1904 PHI A	30	101	27	3	0	0	0.0	9	8	5		2	.267	.297	3	1	OF-25, P-2, 3B-1, 2B-1

Earle Brucker

BRUCKER, EARLE FRANCIS   BR TR 5'11"   175 lbs.
Father of Earle Brucker.
B. May 6, 1901, Albany, N. Y.   D. May 8, 1981, San Diego, Calif.
Manager 1952.

	G	AB	H	2B	3B	HR	HR %	R	RBI	BB	SO	SB	BA	SA	AB	H	G by POS
1937 PHI A	102	317	82	16	5	6	1.9	40	37	48	30	1	.259	.397	9	0	C-92
1938	53	171	64	21	1	3	1.8	26	35	19	16	1	.374	.561	7	2	C-44, 1B-1
1939	62	172	50	15	1	3	1.7	18	31	24	16	0	.291	.442	13	4	C-47
1940	23	46	9	1	1	0	0.0	3	2	6	3	0	.196	.261	9	2	C-13
1943	1	1	0	0	0	0	0.0	0	0	0	0	0	.000	.000	1	0	
5 yrs.	241	707	205	53	8	12	1.7	87	105	97	65	2	.290	.438	39	8	C-196, 1B-1

Earle Brucker

BRUCKER, EARLE FRANCIS, JR.   BL TR 6'2"   210 lbs.
Son of Earle Brucker.
B. Aug. 29, 1925, Los Angeles, Calif.

	G	AB	H	2B	3B	HR	HR %	R	RBI	BB	SO	SB	BA	SA	AB	H	G by POS
1948 PHI A	2	6	1	1	0	0	0.0	0	0	1	1	0	.167	.333	0	0	C-2

Frank Bruggy

BRUGGY, FRANK LEO   BR TR 5'11"   195 lbs.
B. May 4, 1891, Elizabeth, N. J.   D. Apr. 5, 1959, Elizabeth, N. J.

	G	AB	H	2B	3B	HR	HR %	R	RBI	BB	SO	SB	BA	SA	AB	H	G by POS
1921 PHI N	86	277	86	11	2	5	1.8	28	28	23	37	6	.310	.419	12	4	C-86, 1B-2
1922 PHI A	53	111	31	7	0	0	0.0	10	9	6	11	1	.279	.342	21	4	C-31
1923	54	105	22	3	0	1	1.0	4	6	4	9	1	.210	.267	13	1	C-34, 1B-5
1924	50	113	30	6	0	0	0.0	9	8	8	15	4	.265	.319	7	0	C-44
1925 CIN N	6	14	3	0	0	0	0.0	2	1	2	0	0	.214	.214	0	0	C-6
5 yrs.	249	620	172	27	2	6	1.0	53	52	43	72	12	.277	.356	53	9	C-201, 1B-7

Mike Brumley

BRUMLEY, TONY MIKE   BL TR 5'10"   195 lbs.
B. July 10, 1938, Granite, Okla.

	G	AB	H	2B	3B	HR	HR %	R	RBI	BB	SO	SB	BA	SA	AB	H	G by POS
1964 WAS A	136	426	104	19	2	2	0.5	36	35	40	54	1	.244	.312	14	3	C-132
1965	79	216	45	4	0	3	1.4	15	15	20	33	1	.208	.269	15	3	C-66

	G	AB	H	2B	3B	HR	HR %	R	RBI	BB	SO	SB	BA	SA	Pinch Hit AB	Pinch Hit H	G by POS

Mike Brumley continued

	G	AB	H	2B	3B	HR	HR %	R	RBI	BB	SO	SB	BA	SA	AB	H	G by POS
1966	9	18	2	1	0	0	0.0	1	0	0	2	0	.111	.167	2	0	C-7
3 yrs.	224	660	151	24	2	5	0.8	52	50	60	89	2	.229	.294	31	6	C-205

Glenn Brummer

BRUMMER, GLENN EDWARD
B. Nov. 23, 1954, Olney, Ill.
BR TR 6' 185 lbs.

	G	AB	H	2B	3B	HR	HR %	R	RBI	BB	SO	SB	BA	SA	AB	H	G by POS
1981 STL N	21	30	6	1	0	0	0.0	2	2	1	2	0	.200	.233	2	0	C-19
1982	35	64	15	4	0	0	0.0	4	8	0	12	2	.234	.297	1	1	C-32
1983	45	87	24	7	0	0	0.0	7	9	10	11	1	.276	.356	5	0	C-41
1984	28	58	12	0	0	1	1.7	3	3	3	7	0	.207	.259	2	0	C-26
4 yrs.	129	239	57	12	0	1	0.4	16	22	14	32	3	.238	.301	10	1	C-118

WORLD SERIES

	G	AB	H	2B	3B	HR	HR %	R	RBI	BB	SO	SB	BA	SA	AB	H	G by POS
1982 STL N	1	0	0	0	0	0	–	0	0	0	0	0	–	–	0	0	C-1

Tom Brunansky

BRUNANSKY, THOMAS ANDREW
B. Aug. 20, 1960, West Covina, Calif.
BR TR 6'4" 205 lbs.

	G	AB	H	2B	3B	HR	HR %	R	RBI	BB	SO	SB	BA	SA	AB	H	G by POS
1981 CAL A	11	33	5	0	0	3	9.1	7	6	8	10	1	.152	.424	0	0	OF-11
1982 MIN A	127	463	126	30	1	20	4.3	77	46	71	101	1	.272	.471	0	0	OF-127
1983	151	542	123	24	5	28	5.2	70	82	61	95	2	.227	.445	2	0	OF-146, DH-4
1984	155	567	143	21	0	32	5.6	75	85	57	94	4	.252	.459	2	0	OF-153, DH-1
4 yrs.	444	1605	397	75	6	83	5.2	229	219	197	300	8	.247	.457	4	0	OF-437, DH-5

Arlo Brunsberg

BRUNSBERG, ARLO ADOLPH
B. Aug. 15, 1940, Fertile, Minn.
BL TR 6' 195 lbs.

	G	AB	H	2B	3B	HR	HR %	R	RBI	BB	SO	SB	BA	SA	AB	H	G by POS
1966 DET A	2	3	1	1	0	0	0.0	1	0	0	0	0	.333	.667	0	0	C-2

Bob Brush

BRUSH, ROBERT
B. Mar. 8, 1875, Osage, Iowa   D. Apr. 2, 1944, San Berardino, Calif.

	G	AB	H	2B	3B	HR	HR %	R	RBI	BB	SO	SB	BA	SA	AB	H	G by POS
1907 BOS N	2	2	0	0	0	0	0.0	0	0	0		0	.000	.000	1	0	1B-1

Bill Bruton

BRUTON, WILLIAM HARON
B. Dec. 22, 1929, Panola, Ala.
BL TR 6'½" 169 lbs.

	G	AB	H	2B	3B	HR	HR %	R	RBI	BB	SO	SB	BA	SA	AB	H	G by POS
1953 MIL N	151	613	153	18	14	1	0.2	82	41	44	100	26	.250	.330	1	0	OF-150
1954	142	567	161	20	7	4	0.7	89	30	40	78	34	.284	.365	3	2	OF-141
1955	149	636	175	30	12	9	1.4	106	47	43	72	25	.275	.403	2	0	OF-149
1956	147	525	143	23	15	8	1.5	73	56	26	63	8	.272	.419	4	0	OF-145
1957	79	306	85	16	9	5	1.6	41	30	19	35	11	.278	.438	1	0	OF-79
1958	100	325	91	11	3	3	0.9	47	28	27	37	4	.280	.360	5	0	OF-96
1959	133	478	138	22	6	6	1.3	72	41	35	54	13	.289	.397	6	2	OF-133
1960	151	629	180	27	13	12	1.9	112	54	41	97	22	.286	.428	3	0	OF-149
1961 DET A	160	596	153	15	5	17	2.9	99	63	61	66	22	.257	.384	6	1	OF-155
1962	147	561	156	27	5	16	2.9	90	74	55	67	14	.278	.430	5	1	OF-145
1963	145	524	134	21	8	8	1.5	84	48	59	70	14	.256	.372	11	6	OF-138
1964	106	296	82	11	5	5	1.7	42	33	32	54	14	.277	.399	26	6	OF-81
12 yrs.	1610	6056	1651	241	102	94	1.6	937	545	482	793	207	.273	.393	73	18	OF-1561

WORLD SERIES

	G	AB	H	2B	3B	HR	HR %	R	RBI	BB	SO	SB	BA	SA	AB	H	G by POS
1958 MIL N	7	17	7	0	0	1	5.9	2	2	5	5	0	.412	.588	1	0	OF-7

Ed Bruyette

BRUYETTE, EDWARD T.
B. Aug. 31, 1874, Wanawa, Wis.   D. Aug. 5, 1940, Peshastin, Wash.
TR 5'10" 170 lbs.

	G	AB	H	2B	3B	HR	HR %	R	RBI	BB	SO	SB	BA	SA	AB	H	G by POS
1901 MIL A	26	82	15	3	0	0	0.0	7	4	12		1	.183	.220	0	0	OF-21, 2B-3, SS-1, 3B-1

Billy Bryan

BRYAN, WILLIAM RONALD
B. Dec. 4, 1938, Morgan, Ga.
BL TR 6'4" 200 lbs.

	G	AB	H	2B	3B	HR	HR %	R	RBI	BB	SO	SB	BA	SA	AB	H	G by POS
1961 KC A	9	19	3	0	0	1	5.3	2	2	2	7	0	.158	.316	5	1	C-4
1962	25	74	11	2	1	2	2.7	5	7	5	32	0	.149	.284	3	0	C-22
1963	24	65	11	1	1	3	4.6	11	7	9	22	0	.169	.354	0	0	C-24
1964	93	220	53	9	2	13	5.9	19	36	16	69	0	.241	.477	36	11	C-65
1965	108	325	82	11	5	14	4.3	36	51	29	87	0	.252	.446	14	1	C-95
1966 2 teams	59	KC A (32G – .132)		NY A (27G – .217)													
" total	59	145	25	6	0	4	2.8	5	12	11	36	0	.172	.297	22	3	C-35, 1B-6
1967 NY A	16	12	2	0	0	1	8.3	1	2	5	3	0	.167	.417	10	1	C-1
1968 WAS A	40	108	22	3	0	3	2.8	7	8	14	27	0	.204	.315	12	1	C-28
8 yrs.	374	968	209	32	9	41	4.2	86	125	91	283	0	.216	.395	102	18	C-274, 1B-6

Derek Bryant

BRYANT, DEREK ROSZELL
B. Oct. 9, 1951, Lexington, Ky.
BR TR 5'11" 185 lbs.

	G	AB	H	2B	3B	HR	HR %	R	RBI	BB	SO	SB	BA	SA	AB	H	G by POS
1979 OAK A	39	106	19	2	1	0	0.0	8	13	10	10	0	.179	.217	2	0	OF-33, DH-2

Don Bryant

BRYANT, DONALD RAY
B. July 13, 1941, Jasper, Fla.
BR TR 6'5" 200 lbs.

	G	AB	H	2B	3B	HR	HR %	R	RBI	BB	SO	SB	BA	SA	AB	H	G by POS
1966 CHI N	13	26	8	2	0	0	0.0	2	4	1	4	1	.308	.385	3	0	C-10
1969 HOU N	31	59	11	1	0	1	1.7	2	6	4	13	0	.186	.254	2	1	C-28
1970	15	24	5	0	0	0	0.0	2	3	1	8	0	.208	.208	3	0	C-13
3 yrs.	59	109	24	3	0	1	0.9	6	13	6	25	1	.220	.275	8	1	C-51

George Bryant

BRYANT, G.
D. Mar. 14, 1898, Martinsville, Ind.

	G	AB	H	2B	3B	HR	HR %	R	RBI	BB	SO	SB	BA	SA	AB	H	G by POS
1885 DET N	1	4	0	0	0	0	0.0	0	1	0	2		.000	.000	0	0	2B-1

Steve Brye

BRYE, STEPHEN ROBERT
B. Feb. 4, 1949, Alameda, Calif.
BR TR 6' 190 lbs.

	G	AB	H	2B	3B	HR	HR %	R	RBI	BB	SO	SB	BA	SA	AB	H	G by POS
1970 MIN A	9	11	2	1	0	0	0.0	1	2	2	4	0	.182	.273	1	0	OF-6
1971	28	107	24	1	0	3	2.8	10	11	7	15	3	.224	.318	0	0	OF-28

	G	AB	H	2B	3B	HR	HR %	R	RBI	BB	SO	SB	BA	SA	Pinch Hit AB	Pinch Hit H	G by POS

Steve Brye continued

	G	AB	H	2B	3B	HR	HR %	R	RBI	BB	SO	SB	BA	SA	PH AB	PH H	G by POS
1972	100	253	61	9	3	0	0.0	18	12	17	38	3	.241	.300	10	5	OF-93
1973	92	278	73	9	5	6	2.2	39	33	35	43	3	.263	.396	2	0	OF-87, DH-1
1974	135	488	138	32	1	2	0.4	52	41	22	59	1	.283	.365	5	1	OF-129
1975	86	246	62	13	1	9	3.7	41	34	21	37	2	.252	.423	10	5	OF-72, DH-6
1976	87	258	68	11	0	2	0.8	33	23	13	31	1	.264	.329	12	2	OF-78, DH-3
1977 MIL A	94	241	60	14	3	7	2.9	27	28	16	39	1	.249	.419	14	1	OF-83
1978 PIT N	66	115	27	7	0	1	0.9	16	9	11	10	2	.235	.322	21	3	OF-47
9 yrs.	697	1997	515	97	13	30	1.5	237	193	144	276	16	.258	.365	75	17	OF-623, DH-10

Hal Bubser

BUBSER, HAROLD FRED   BR TR 5'11"   170 lbs.
B. Sept. 28, 1895, Chicago, Ill.   D. June 22, 1959, Melrose Park, Ill.

	G	AB	H	2B	3B	HR	HR %	R	RBI	BB	SO	SB	BA	SA	PH AB	PH H	G by POS
1922 CHI A	3	3	0	0	0	0	0.0	0	0	0	2	0	.000	.000	3	0	

Johnny Bucha

BUCHA, JOHN GEORGE   BR TR 5'11"   190 lbs.
B. Jan. 22, 1925, Allentown, Pa.

	G	AB	H	2B	3B	HR	HR %	R	RBI	BB	SO	SB	BA	SA	PH AB	PH H	G by POS
1948 STL N	2	1	0	0	0	0	0.0	0	0	1	0	0	.000	.000	1	0	C-1
1950	22	36	5	1	0	0	0.0	1	1	4	7	0	.139	.167	5	2	C-17
1953 DET A	60	158	35	9	0	1	0.6	17	14	20	14	1	.222	.297	2	0	C-56
3 yrs.	84	195	40	10	0	1	0.5	18	15	25	21	1	.205	.272	8	2	C-74

Jerry Buchek

BUCHEK, GERALD PETER   BR TR 5'11"   185 lbs.
B. May 9, 1942, St. Louis, Mo.

	G	AB	H	2B	3B	HR	HR %	R	RBI	BB	SO	SB	BA	SA	PH AB	PH H	G by POS
1961 STL N	31	90	12	2	0	0	0.0	6	9	0	28	0	.133	.156	0	0	SS-31
1963	3	4	1	0	0	0	0.0	0	0	0	2	0	.250	.250	2	0	SS-1
1964	35	30	6	0	2	0	0.0	7	1	3	11	0	.200	.333	2	0	SS-20, 2B-9, 3B-1
1965	55	166	41	8	3	3	1.8	17	21	13	46	1	.247	.386	5	0	2B-33, SS-18, 3B-1
1966	100	284	67	10	4	4	1.4	23	25	23	71	0	.236	.342	9	1	2B-49, SS-48, 3B-4
1967 NY N	124	411	97	11	2	14	3.4	35	41	26	101	3	.236	.375	9	2	2B-95, 3B-17, SS-9
1968	73	192	35	4	0	1	0.5	8	11	10	53	1	.182	.219	18	3	3B-37, 2B-12, OF-9
7 yrs.	421	1177	259	35	11	22	1.9	96	108	75	312	5	.220	.325	45	6	2B-198, SS-127, 3B-60, OF-9

WORLD SERIES
	G	AB	H	2B	3B	HR	HR %	R	RBI	BB	SO	SB	BA	SA	PH AB	PH H	G by POS
1964 STL N	4	1	1	0	0	0	0.0	1	0	0	0	0	1.000	1.000	0	0	2B-4

Jim Bucher

BUCHER, JAMES QUINTER   BL TR 5'11"   170 lbs.
B. Mar. 11, 1911, Manassas, Va.

	G	AB	H	2B	3B	HR	HR %	R	RBI	BB	SO	SB	BA	SA	PH AB	PH H	G by POS
1934 BKN N	47	84	19	5	2	0	0.0	12	8	4	7	1	.226	.333	18	8	2B-20, 3B-6
1935	123	473	143	22	1	7	1.5	72	58	10	33	4	.302	.397	12	0	2B-41, 3B-39, OF-37
1936	110	370	93	12	8	2	0.5	49	41	29	27	5	.251	.343	10	3	3B-39, 2B-32, OF-30
1937	125	380	96	11	2	4	1.1	44	37	20	18	5	.253	.324	23	3	2B-49, 3B-43, OF-6
1938 STL N	17	57	13	3	1	0	0.0	7	7	2	2	0	.228	.316	2	1	2B-14, 3B-1
1944 BOS A	80	277	76	9	2	4	1.4	39	31	19	13	3	.274	.365	15	5	3B-44, 2B-21
1945	52	151	34	4	3	0	0.0	19	11	7	13	1	.225	.291	17	2	3B-32, 2B-2
7 yrs.	554	1792	474	66	19	17	0.9	242	193	91	113	19	.265	.351	97	22	3B-204, 2B-179, OF-73

Dick Buckley

BUCKLEY, RICHARD D.   TR 5'10"
B. Sept. 21, 1858, Troy, N. Y.   D. Dec. 12, 1929, Pittsburgh, Pa.

	G	AB	H	2B	3B	HR	HR %	R	RBI	BB	SO	SB	BA	SA	PH AB	PH H	G by POS
1888 IND N	71	260	71	9	3	5	1.9	28	22	6	24	4	.273	.388	0	0	C-51, 3B-22, OF-1, 1B-1
1889	68	260	67	11	0	8	3.1	35	41	15	32	5	.258	.392	0	0	C-55, 3B-12, OF-1, 1B-1
1890 NY N	70	266	68	11	0	2	0.8	39	26	23	35	3	.256	.320	0	0	C-62, 3B-8
1891	75	253	55	9	1	4	1.6	23	31	11	30	3	.217	.308	0	0	C-74, 3B-1
1892 STL N	121	410	93	17	4	5	1.2	43	52	22	34	7	.227	.324	0	0	C-119, 1B-2
1893	9	23	4	1	0	0	0.0	2	1	0	0	0	.174	.217	0	0	C-9
1894 2 teams	STL	N (29G – .180)			PHI	N	(43G – .294)										
" total	72	249	63	8	5	2	0.8	23	29	12	16	1	.253	.349	1	0	C-69, 1B-2
1895 PHI N	38	112	28	6	1	0	0.0	20	14	9	17	2	.250	.321	0	0	C-38
8 yrs.	524	1833	449	72	14	26	1.4	213	216	98	188	25	.245	.342	1	0	C-477, 3B-43, 1B-6, OF-2

Kevin Buckley

BUCKLEY, KEVIN JOHN   BR TR 6'1"   195 lbs.
B. Jan. 16, 1959, Quincy, Mass.

	G	AB	H	2B	3B	HR	HR %	R	RBI	BB	SO	SB	BA	SA	PH AB	PH H	G by POS
1984 TEX A	5	7	2	1	0	0	0.0	1	0	2	4	0	.286	.429	2	0	DH-3

Bill Buckner

BUCKNER, WILLIAM JOSEPH   BL TL 6'   185 lbs.
B. Dec. 14, 1949, Vallejo, Calif.

	G	AB	H	2B	3B	HR	HR %	R	RBI	BB	SO	SB	BA	SA	PH AB	PH H	G by POS
1969 LA N	1	1	0	0	0	0	0.0	0	0	0	0	0	.000	.000	1	0	
1970	28	68	13	3	1	0	0.0	6	4	3	7	0	.191	.265	8	2	OF-20, 1B-1
1971	108	358	99	15	1	5	1.4	37	41	11	18	4	.277	.366	17	3	OF-86, 1B-11
1972	105	383	122	14	3	5	1.3	47	37	17	13	10	.319	.410	11	3	OF-61, 1B-35
1973	140	575	158	20	0	8	1.4	68	46	17	34	12	.275	.351	9	2	1B-93, OF-48
1974	145	580	182	30	3	7	1.2	83	58	30	24	31	.314	.412	9	1	OF-137, 1B-6
1975	92	288	70	11	2	6	2.1	30	31	17	15	8	.243	.358	19	3	OF-72
1976	154	642	193	28	4	7	1.1	76	60	26	26	28	.301	.389	1	1	OF-153, 1B-1
1977 CHI N	122	426	121	27	0	11	2.6	40	60	21	23	7	.284	.425	22	7	1B-99
1978	117	446	144	26	1	5	1.1	47	74	18	17	7	.323	.419	12	2	1B-105
1979	149	591	168	34	7	14	2.4	72	66	30	28	9	.284	.437	8	3	1B-140
1980	145	578	187	41	3	10	1.7	69	68	30	18	1	.324	.457	6	0	1B-94, OF-50
1981	106	421	131	35	3	10	2.4	45	75	26	16	5	.311	.480	2	1	1B-105
1982	161	657	201	34	5	15	2.3	93	105	36	26	15	.306	.441	0	0	1B-161
1983	153	626	175	38	6	16	2.6	79	66	25	30	12	.280	.436	2	1	1B-144, OF-15
1984 2 teams	CHI	N (21G – .209)			BOS	A	(114G – .278)										
" total	135	482	131	21	2	11	2.3	54	69	25	39	2	.272	.392	12	3	1B-120, OF-2
16 yrs.	1861	7122	2095	377	41	130	1.8	846	860	332	334	151	.294	.413	139	32	1B-1115, OF-644

LEAGUE CHAMPIONSHIP SERIES
	G	AB	H	2B	3B	HR	HR %	R	RBI	BB	SO	SB	BA	SA	PH AB	PH H	G by POS
1974 LA N	4	18	3	1	0	0	0.0	0	0	0	2	0	.167	.222	0	0	OF-4

	G	AB	H	2B	3B	HR	HR %	R	RBI	BB	SO	SB	BA	SA	Pinch Hit AB	Pinch Hit H	G by POS

Bill Buckner continued

WORLD SERIES

	G	AB	H	2B	3B	HR	HR %	R	RBI	BB	SO	SB	BA	SA	PH AB	PH H	G by POS
1974 LA N	5	20	5	1	0	1	5.0	1	1	0	1	0	.250	.450	0	0	OF-5

Mark Budaska

BUDASKA, MARK DAVID
B. Dec. 27, 1952, Sharon, Pa.
BB TL 6'   180 lbs.

	G	AB	H	2B	3B	HR	HR %	R	RBI	BB	SO	SB	BA	SA	PH AB	PH H	G by POS
1978 OAK A	4	4	1	1	0	0	0.0	0	0	1	2	0	.250	.500	2	1	OF-2
1981	9	32	5	1	0	0	0.0	3	2	4	10	0	.156	.188	0	0	DH-9
2 yrs.	13	36	6	2	0	0	0.0	3	2	5	12	0	.167	.222	2	1	DH-9, OF-2

Budd

BUDD,
Deceased.

	G	AB	H	2B	3B	HR	HR %	R	RBI	BB	SO	SB	BA	SA	PH AB	PH H	G by POS
1890 CLE P	1	4	0	0	0	0	0.0	0	0	0	3	0	.000	.000	0	0	OF-1

Don Buddin

BUDDIN, DONALD THOMAS
B. May 5, 1934, Turbeville, S. C.
BR TR 5'11"   178 lbs.

	G	AB	H	2B	3B	HR	HR %	R	RBI	BB	SO	SB	BA	SA	PH AB	PH H	G by POS
1956 BOS A	114	377	90	24	0	5	1.3	49	37	65	62	2	.239	.342	1	0	SS-113
1958	136	497	118	25	2	12	2.4	74	43	82	106	0	.237	.368	0	0	SS-136
1959	151	485	117	24	1	10	2.1	75	53	92	99	6	.241	.357	0	0	SS-150
1960	124	428	105	21	5	6	1.4	60	36	62	59	4	.245	.360	0	0	SS-124
1961	115	339	89	22	3	6	1.8	58	42	72	45	2	.263	.398	4	1	SS-109
1962 2 teams		HOU N	(40G –	.163)		DET A	(31G –	.229)									
" total	71	163	32	7	1	2	1.2	24	14	37	33	1	.196	.288	12	3	SS-46, 3B-11, 2B-5
6 yrs.	711	2289	551	123	12	41	1.8	342	225	410	404	15	.241	.359	17	4	SS-678, 3B-11, 2B-5

Charlie Buelow

BUELOW, CHARLES JOHN
B. Jan. 12, 1877, Dubuque, Iowa   D. May 4, 1951, Dubuque, Iowa
BR TR

	G	AB	H	2B	3B	HR	HR %	R	RBI	BB	SO	SB	BA	SA	PH AB	PH H	G by POS
1901 NY N	22	72	8	4	0	0	0.0	3	4	2		0	.111	.167	3	0	3B-17, 2B-2

Fritz Buelow

BUELOW, FREDERICK WILLIAM
B. Feb. 13, 1876, Berlin, Germany   D. Dec. 27, 1933, Detroit, Mich.
BR TR 5'9½"

	G	AB	H	2B	3B	HR	HR %	R	RBI	BB	SO	SB	BA	SA	PH AB	PH H	G by POS
1899 STL N	7	15	7	0	2	0	0.0	4	2	2		0	.467	.733	1	0	C-4, OF-2
1900	6	17	4	0	0	0	0.0	2	3	0		0	.235	.235	1	1	C-4, OF-1
1901 DET A	70	231	52	5	5	2	0.9	28	29	11		2	.225	.316	1	0	C-69
1902	66	224	50	5	2	2	0.9	23	29	9		3	.223	.290	0	0	C-63, 1B-2
1903	63	192	41	3	6	1	0.5	24	13	6		4	.214	.307	0	0	C-60, 1B-2
1904 2 teams		DET	A (42G –	.110)		CLE	A (42G –	.176)									
" total	84	255	36	5	2	0	0.0	17	10	19		4	.141	.176	0	0	C-84
1905 CLE A	74	236	41	4	1	1	0.4	11	18	6		7	.174	.212	2	1	C-59, OF-8, 1B-3, 3B-2
1906	34	86	14	2	0	0	0.0	7	7	9		0	.163	.186	0	0	C-33, 1B-1
1907 STL A	26	75	11	1	0	0	0.0	9	1	7		0	.147	.160	1	0	C-25
9 yrs.	430	1331	256	25	18	6	0.5	125	112	69		20	.192	.252	6	2	C-401, OF-11, 1B-8, 3B-2

Art Bues

BUES, ARTHUR FREDERICK
B. Mar. 3, 1888, Milwaukee, Wis.   D. Nov. 7, 1954, Whitefish Bay, Wis.
BR TR 5'11"   184 lbs.

	G	AB	H	2B	3B	HR	HR %	R	RBI	BB	SO	SB	BA	SA	PH AB	PH H	G by POS
1913 BOS N	2	1	0	0	0	0	0.0	0	0	0	1	0	.000	.000	0	0	3B-1, 2B-1
1914 CHI N	14	45	10	1	1	0	0.0	3	4	5	6	1	.222	.289	2	0	3B-12
2 yrs.	16	46	10	1	1	0	0.0	3	4	5	7	1	.217	.283	2	0	3B-13, 2B-1

Charlie Buffinton

BUFFINTON, CHARLES G.
B. June 14, 1861, Fall River, Mass.   D. Sept. 23, 1907, Fall River, Mass.
Manager 1890.
BR TR 6'1"   180 lbs.

	G	AB	H	2B	3B	HR	HR %	R	RBI	BB	SO	SB	BA	SA	PH AB	PH H	G by POS
1882 BOS N	15	50	13	1	0	0	0.0	5	4	2	3		.260	.280	0	0	OF-7, P-6, 1B-4
1883	86	341	81	8	3	1	0.3	28	26	6	24		.238	.287	0	0	OF-51, P-43, 1B-2
1884	87	352	94	18	3	1	0.3	48		16	12		.267	.344	0	0	P-67, OF-13, 1B-11
1885	82	338	81	12	3	1	0.3	26	33	3	26		.240	.302	0	0	P-51, OF-18, 1B-15
1886	44	176	51	4	1	1	0.6	27	30	6	12		.290	.341	0	0	1B-19, P-18
1887 PHI N	66	269	72	12	1	1	0.4	34	46	11	3	8	.268	.331	0	0	P-40, OF-22, 1B-10
1888	46	160	29	4	1	0	0.0	14	12	7	5	1	.181	.219	0	0	P-46, OF-1
1889	47	154	32	2	0	0	0.0	16	21	9	5	0	.208	.221	0	0	P-47, OF-1
1890 PHI P	42	150	41	3	2	1	0.7	24	24	9	3	1	.273	.340	0	0	P-36, OF-5, 1B-3
1891 BOS AA	58	181	34	2	1	1	0.6	16	16	19	15	0	.188	.227	0	0	P-48, OF-10, 1B-4
1892 BAL N	13	43	15	1	1	0	0.0	7	4	3	6	1	.349	.419	0	0	P-13
11 yrs.	586	2214	543	67	16	7	0.3	245	216	91	114	11	.245	.299	0	0	P-415, OF-128, 1B-68

Don Buford

BUFORD, DONALD ALVIN
B. Feb. 2, 1937, Linden, Tex.
BB TR 5'7"   160 lbs.

	G	AB	H	2B	3B	HR	HR %	R	RBI	BB	SO	SB	BA	SA	PH AB	PH H	G by POS
1963 CHI A	12	42	12	1	2	0	0.0	9	5	5	7	1	.286	.405	1	0	3B-9, 2B-2
1964	135	442	116	14	6	4	0.9	62	30	46	62	11	.262	.348	10	1	2B-92, 3B-37
1965	155	586	166	22	5	10	1.7	93	47	67	76	17	.283	.389	8	2	2B-139, 3B-41
1966	163	607	148	26	7	8	1.3	85	52	69	71	51	.244	.349	1	0	3B-133, 2B-37, OF-11
1967	156	535	129	10	9	4	0.7	61	32	65	51	34	.241	.316	3	1	3B-121, 2B-51, OF-1
1968 BAL A	130	426	120	13	4	15	3.5	65	46	57	46	27	.282	.437	20	6	OF-65, 2B-58, 3B-2
1969	144	554	161	31	3	11	2.0	99	64	96	62	19	.291	.417	5	1	OF-128, 2B-10, 3B-6
1970	144	504	137	15	2	17	3.4	99	66	109	55	16	.272	.411	10	2	OF-130, 3B-3, 2B-3
1971	122	449	130	19	4	19	4.2	99	54	89	62	15	.290	.477	8	2	OF-115
1972	125	408	84	6	2	5	1.2	46	22	69	83	8	.206	.267	19	2	OF-105
10 yrs.	1286	4553	1203	157	44	93	2.0	718	418	672	575	200	.264	.379	85	17	OF-555, 2B-392, 3B-352

LEAGUE CHAMPIONSHIP SERIES

	G	AB	H	2B	3B	HR	HR %	R	RBI	BB	SO	SB	BA	SA	PH AB	PH H	G by POS
1969 BAL A	3	14	4	1	0	0	0.0	3	1	3	0	0	.286	.357	0	0	OF-3
1970	2	7	3	1	0	1	14.3	2	3	2	0	0	.429	1.000	0	0	OF-2
1971	2	7	3	0	1	0	0.0	1	0	2	1	0	.429	.714	0	0	OF-2
3 yrs.	7	28	10	2	1	1	3.6	6	4	7	1	0	.357	.607	0	0	OF-7

WORLD SERIES

	G	AB	H	2B	3B	HR	HR %	R	RBI	BB	SO	SB	BA	SA	PH AB	PH H	G by POS
1969 BAL A	5	20	2	1	0	1	5.0	1	2	2	4	0	.100	.300	0	0	OF-5
1970	4	15	4	0	0	1	6.7	3	1	3	2	0	.267	.467	0	0	OF-4

	G	AB	H	2B	3B	HR	HR %	R	RBI	BB	SO	SB	BA	SA	Pinch Hit AB	Pinch Hit H	G by POS

Don Buford continued

	G	AB	H	2B	3B	HR	HR%	R	RBI	BB	SO	SB	BA	SA	PH AB	PH H	G by POS
1971	6	23	6	1	0	2	8.7	3	4	3	3	0	.261	.565	0	0	OF-6
3 yrs.	15	58	12	2	0	4	6.9	7	7	8	9	0	.207	.448	0	0	OF-15

Harry Buker

BUKER, HENRY L. (Happy)
B. 1859, Chicago, Ill.   D. Sept. 10, 1899, Chicago, Ill.

	G	AB	H	2B	3B	HR	HR%	R	RBI	BB	SO	SB	BA	SA	PH AB	PH H	G by POS
1884 DET N	30	111	15	1	0	0	0.0	5		4	15		.135	.144	0	0	SS-19, OF-11

George Bullard

BULLARD, GEORGE DONALD (Curly)
B. Oct. 24, 1928, Lynn, Mass.   BR TR 5'9" 155 lbs.

	G	AB	H	2B	3B	HR	HR%	R	RBI	BB	SO	SB	BA	SA	PH AB	PH H	G by POS
1954 DET A	4	1	0	0	0	0	0.0	0	0	0	0	0	.000	.000	0	0	SS-1

Sim Bullas

BULLAS, SIMEON EDWARD (Derby)
B. Apr. 10, 1861, Cleveland, Ohio   D. Jan. 14, 1908, Cleveland, Ohio   BR TR 5'7½" 150 lbs.

	G	AB	H	2B	3B	HR	HR%	R	RBI	BB	SO	SB	BA	SA	PH AB	PH H	G by POS
1884 TOL AA	13	45	4	0	1	0	0.0	4		1			.089	.133	0	0	C-12, OF-2

Terry Bulling

BULLING, TERRY CHARLES
B. Dec. 15, 1952, Lynwood, Calif.   BR TR 6'1" 200 lbs.

	G	AB	H	2B	3B	HR	HR%	R	RBI	BB	SO	SB	BA	SA	PH AB	PH H	G by POS
1977 MIN A	15	32	5	1	0	0	0.0	2	5	5	5	0	.156	.188	1	0	C-10, DH-3
1981 SEA A	62	154	38	3	0	2	1.3	15	15	21	20	0	.247	.305	4	0	C-62
1982	56	154	34	7	0	1	0.6	17	8	19	16	2	.221	.286	1	0	C-56
1983	5	5	0	0	0	0	0.0	0	0	0	0	0	.000	.000	0	0	C-5
4 yrs.	138	345	77	11	0	3	0.9	34	28	45	41	2	.223	.281	6	0	C-133, DH-3

Al Bumbry

BUMBRY, ALONZA BENJAMIN
B. Apr. 21, 1947, Fredericksburg, Va.   BL TR 5'8" 170 lbs.

	G	AB	H	2B	3B	HR	HR%	R	RBI	BB	SO	SB	BA	SA	PH AB	PH H	G by POS
1972 BAL A	9	11	4	0	1	0	0.0	5	0	0	0	1	.364	.545	3	0	OF-2
1973	110	356	120	15	11	7	2.0	73	34	34	49	23	.337	.500	8	5	OF-86, DH-7
1974	94	270	63	10	3	1	0.4	35	19	21	46	12	.233	.304	7	1	OF-67, DH-7
1975	114	349	94	19	4	2	0.6	47	32	32	81	16	.269	.364	20	4	DH-48, OF-39, 3B-1
1976	133	450	113	15	7	9	2.0	71	36	43	76	42	.251	.376	7	1	OF-116, DH-10
1977	133	518	164	31	4	4	0.8	74	41	45	88	19	.317	.411	2	2	OF-130
1978	33	114	27	5	2	2	1.8	21	6	17	15	5	.237	.368	5	1	OF-28
1979	148	569	162	29	1	7	1.2	80	49	43	74	37	.285	.376	8	3	OF-146
1980	160	645	205	29	9	9	1.4	118	53	78	75	44	.318	.433	1	0	OF-160
1981	101	392	107	18	2	1	0.3	61	27	51	51	22	.273	.337	2	0	OF-100
1982	150	562	147	20	4	5	0.9	77	40	44	77	10	.262	.338	7	0	OF-147, DH-1
1983	124	378	104	14	4	3	0.8	63	31	31	33	12	.275	.357	12	3	OF-104, DH-11
1984	119	344	93	12	1	3	0.9	47	24	25	35	9	.270	.337	12	2	OF-99, DH-9
13 yrs.	1428	4958	1403	217	52	53	1.1	772	392	464	700	252	.283	.380	94	22	OF-1224, DH-93, 3B-1

LEAGUE CHAMPIONSHIP SERIES

	G	AB	H	2B	3B	HR	HR%	R	RBI	BB	SO	SB	BA	SA	PH AB	PH H	G by POS
1973 BAL A	2	7	0	0	0	0	0.0	1	0	2	2	0	.000	.000	0	0	OF-2
1974	2	1	0	0	0	0	0.0	0	0	0	1	0	.000	.000	1	0	
1979	4	16	4	0	1	0	0.0	5	0	4	3	2	.250	.375	0	0	OF-4
1983	3	8	1	1	0	0	0.0	0	1	0	2	0	.125	.250	0	0	OF-3
4 yrs.	11	32	5	1	1	0	0.0	6	1	6	8	2	.156	.250	1	0	OF-9

WORLD SERIES

	G	AB	H	2B	3B	HR	HR%	R	RBI	BB	SO	SB	BA	SA	PH AB	PH H	G by POS
1979 BAL A	7	21	3	0	0	0	0.0	3	1	2	1	0	.143	.143	2	0	OF-7
1983	4	11	1	1	0	0	0.0	0	1	0	1	0	.091	.182	0	0	OF-4
2 yrs.	11	32	4	1	0	0	0.0	3	2	2	2	0	.125	.156	2	0	OF-11

Josh Bunce

BUNCE, JOSHUA
B. May 10, 1847, Brooklyn, N. Y.   D. Apr. 28, 1912, Brooklyn, N. Y.

	G	AB	H	2B	3B	HR	HR%	R	RBI	BB	SO	SB	BA	SA	PH AB	PH H	G by POS
1877 HAR N	1	4	0	0	0	0	0.0	0	0	0	0		.000	.000	0	0	OF-1

Nels Burbrink

BURBRINK, NELSON EDWARD
B. Dec. 28, 1921, Cincinnati, Ohio   BR TR 5'10" 195 lbs.

	G	AB	H	2B	3B	HR	HR%	R	RBI	BB	SO	SB	BA	SA	PH AB	PH H	G by POS
1955 STL N	58	170	47	8	1	0	0.0	11	15	14	13	1	.276	.335	3	2	C-55

Al Burch

BURCH, ALBERT WILLIAM
B. Oct. 7, 1883, Albany, N. Y.   D. Oct. 5, 1926, Brooklyn, N. Y.   BL TR 5'8½" 160 lbs.

	G	AB	H	2B	3B	HR	HR%	R	RBI	BB	SO	SB	BA	SA	PH AB	PH H	G by POS
1906 STL N	91	335	89	5	1	0	0.0	40	11	37		15	.266	.287	0	0	OF-91
1907 2 teams		STL	N (48G – .227)		BKN	N	(40G – .292)										
" total	88	274	70	5	3	0	0.0	30	17	28		12	.255	.296	3	0	OF-84, 2B-1
1908 BKN N	123	456	111	8	4	2	0.4	45	18	33		15	.243	.292	6	1	OF-116
1909	152	601	163	20	6	1	0.2	80	30	51		38	.271	.329	0	0	OF-151, 1B-1
1910	103	352	83	8	3	1	0.3	41	20	22	30	13	.236	.284	18	7	OF-70, 1B-13
1911	54	167	38	2	3	0	0.0	18	7	15	22	3	.228	.275	6	0	OF-43, 2B-3
6 yrs.	611	2185	554	48	20	4	0.2	254	103	186	52	96	.254	.299	33	8	OF-555, 1B-14, 2B-4

Ernie Burch

BURCH, EDWARD A.
B. 1858, DeKalb County, Ill.   D. Nov. 8, 1933, Evanston, Ill.   BL

	G	AB	H	2B	3B	HR	HR%	R	RBI	BB	SO	SB	BA	SA	PH AB	PH H	G by POS
1884 CLE N	32	124	26	4	0	0	0.0	9	7	5	24		.210	.242	0	0	OF-32
1886 BKN AA	113	456	119	22	6	2	0.4	78		39			.261	.349	0	0	OF-113
1887	49	188	55	4	4	2	1.1	47		29		15	.293	.388	0	0	OF-49
3 yrs.	194	768	200	30	10	4	0.5	134	7	73	24	15	.260	.341	0	0	OF-194

Bob Burda

BURDA, EDWARD ROBERT
B. July 16, 1938, St. Louis, Mo.   BL TL 5'11" 174 lbs.

	G	AB	H	2B	3B	HR	HR%	R	RBI	BB	SO	SB	BA	SA	PH AB	PH H	G by POS
1962 STL N	7	14	1	0	0	0	0.0	0	1	0	3	1	1	.071	.071	1	0	OF-6
1965 SF N	31	27	3	0	0	0	0.0	0	5	5	6	0	.111	.111	12	1	1B-11, OF-1
1966	37	43	7	3	0	0	0.0	3	2	2	5	0	.163	.233	25	4	1B-7, OF-4
1969	97	161	37	8	0	6	3.7	20	27	21	12	0	.230	.391	35	8	1B-45, OF-19

	G	AB	H	2B	3B	HR	HR %	R	RBI	BB	SO	SB	BA	SA	Pinch Hit AB	Pinch Hit H	G by POS

Bob Burda continued

		G	AB	H	2B	3B	HR	HR%	R	RBI	BB	SO	SB	BA	SA	PH AB	PH H	G by POS
1970	2 teams	SF	N	(28G –	.261)		MIL	A	(78G –	.248)								
"	total	106	245	61	9	0	4	1.6	20	23	21	19	1	.249	.335	27	8	OF-65, 1B-15
1971	STL N	65	71	21	0	0	1	1.4	6	12	10	11	0	.296	.338	48	14	1B-13, OF-1
1972	BOS A	45	73	12	1	0	2	2.7	4	9	8	11	0	.164	.260	27	2	1B-15, OF-1
7 yrs.		388	634	142	21	0	13	2.1	53	78	70	65	2	.224	.319	175	37	1B-106, OF-97

Jack Burdock

BURDOCK, JOHN JOSEPH (Black Jack)
B. 1851, Brooklyn, N. Y. D. Nov. 28, 1931, Brooklyn, N. Y.
Manager 1883.

BR TR 5'9½" 158 lbs.

	G	AB	H	2B	3B	HR	HR%	R	RBI	BB	SO	SB	BA	SA	PH AB	PH H	G by POS
1876 HAR N	69	309	80	9	1	0	0.0	66	23	13	16		.259	.294	0	0	2B-69, 3B-1
1877	58	277	72	6	0	0	0.0	35	9	2	16		.260	.282	0	0	2B-55, 3B-3
1878 BOS N	60	246	64	12	6	0	0.0	37	25	3	17		.260	.358	0	0	2B-60
1879	84	359	86	10	3	0	0.0	64	36	9	28		.240	.284	0	0	2B-84
1880	86	356	90	17	4	2	0.6	58	35	8	26		.253	.340	0	0	2B-86
1881	73	282	67	12	4	1	0.4	36	24	7	18		.238	.319	0	0	2B-72, SS-1
1882	83	319	76	6	7	0	0.0	36	27	9	24		.238	.301	0	0	2B-83
1883	96	400	132	27	8	5	1.3	80	88	14	35		.330	.475	0	0	2B-96
1884	87	361	97	14	4	6	1.7	65		15	52		.269	.380	0	0	2B-87, 3B-1
1885	45	169	24	5	0	0	0.0	18	7	8	18		.142	.172	0	0	2B-45
1886	59	221	48	6	1	0	0.0	26	25	11	27		.217	.253	0	0	2B-59
1887	65	237	61	6	0	0	0.0	36	29	18	22	19	.257	.283	0	0	2B-65
1888 2 teams	BOS	N	(22G –	.203)		BKN	AA	(70G –	.122)								
" total	92	325	46	1	2	1	0.3	20	12	10	5	10	.142	.166	0	0	2B-92
1891 BKN N	3	12	1	0	0	0	0.0	1	1	1	1	0	.083	.083	0	0	2B-3
14 yrs.	960	3873	944	131	40	15	0.4	578	341	128	305	29	.244	.310	0	0	2B-956, 3B-5, SS-1

Pete Burg

BURG, JOSEPH PETER
B. June 4, 1882, Chicago, Ill. D. Apr. 28, 1969, Joliet, Ill.

BR TR 5'10" 165 lbs.

	G	AB	H	2B	3B	HR	HR%	R	RBI	BB	SO	SB	BA	SA	PH AB	PH H	G by POS
1910 BOS N	13	46	15	0	1	0	0.0	7	10	7	12	5	.326	.370	0	0	3B-12, SS-1

Smoky Burgess

BURGESS, FORREST HARRILL
B. Feb. 6, 1927, Caroleen, N. C.

BL TR 5'8½" 185 lbs.

	G	AB	H	2B	3B	HR	HR%	R	RBI	BB	SO	SB	BA	SA	PH AB	PH H	G by POS
1949 CHI N	46	56	15	0	0	1	1.8	4	12	4	4	0	.268	.321	37	12	C-8
1951	94	219	55	4	2	2	0.9	21	20	21	12	2	.251	.315	30	5	C-64
1952 PHI N	110	371	110	27	2	6	1.6	49	56	49	21	3	.296	.429	6	3	C-104
1953	102	312	91	17	5	4	1.3	31	36	37	17	3	.292	.417	9	3	C-95
1954	108	345	127	27	5	4	1.2	41	46	42	11	1	.368	.510	17	6	C-91
1955 2 teams	PHI	N	(7G –	.190)		CIN	N	(116G –	.306)								
" total	123	442	133	17	3	21	4.8	71	78	50	36	1	.301	.495	9	3	C-113
1956 CIN N	90	229	63	10	0	12	5.2	28	39	26	18	0	.275	.476	29	7	C-55
1957	90	205	58	14	1	14	6.8	29	39	24	16	0	.283	.566	39	11	C-45
1958	99	251	71	12	1	6	2.4	28	31	22	20	0	.283	.410	40	11	C-58
1959 PIT N	114	377	112	28	5	11	2.9	41	59	31	16	0	.297	.485	17	7	C-101
1960	110	337	99	15	2	7	2.1	33	39	35	13	0	.294	.412	20	9	C-89
1961	100	323	98	17	3	12	3.7	37	52	30	16	1	.303	.486	14	4	C-92
1962	130	360	118	19	2	13	3.6	38	61	31	19	0	.328	.500	5	1	C-101
1963	91	264	74	10	1	6	2.3	20	37	24	14	0	.280	.394	18	6	C-72
1964 2 teams	PIT	N	(68G –	.246)		CHI	A	(7G –	.200)								
" total	75	176	43	3	1	3	1.7	10	18	15	14	2	.244	.324	26	8	C-44
1965 CHI A	80	77	22	4	0	2	2.6	2	24	11	7	0	.286	.416	65	20	C-5
1966	79	67	21	5	0	0	0.0	0	15	11	8	0	.313	.388	66	21	C-2
1967	77	60	8	1	0	2	3.3	2	11	14	8	0	.133	.250	60	8	
18 yrs.	1718	4471	1318	230	33	126	2.8	485	673	477	270	13	.295	.446	507 1st	145 2nd	C-1139

WORLD SERIES

	G	AB	H	2B	3B	HR	HR%	R	RBI	BB	SO	SB	BA	SA	PH AB	PH H	G by POS
1960 PIT N	5	18	6	1	0	0	0.0	2	0	2	1	0	.333	.389	0	0	C-5

Tom Burgess

BURGESS, THOMAS ROLAND (Tim)
B. Sept. 1, 1927, London Ont., Canada

BL TL 6' 180 lbs.

	G	AB	H	2B	3B	HR	HR%	R	RBI	BB	SO	SB	BA	SA	PH AB	PH H	G by POS
1954 STL N	17	21	1	1	0	0	0.0	2	3	9	0	.048	.095	11	0	OF-4
1962 LA A	87	143	28	7	1	2	1.4	17	13	36	20	2	.196	.301	43	7	1B-35, OF-2
2 yrs.	104	164	29	8	1	2	1.2	19	14	39	29	2	.177	.274	54	7	1B-35, OF-6

Bill Burgo

BURGO, WILLIAM ROSS
B. Nov. 15, 1919, Johnstown, Pa.

BR TR 5'8" 185 lbs.

	G	AB	H	2B	3B	HR	HR%	R	RBI	BB	SO	SB	BA	SA	PH AB	PH H	G by POS
1943 PHI A	17	70	26	4	2	1	1.4	12	9	4	1	0	.371	.529	0	0	OF-17
1944	27	88	21	2	0	1	1.1	6	3	7	3	1	.239	.295	3	0	OF-22
2 yrs.	44	158	47	6	2	2	1.3	18	12	11	4	1	.297	.399	3	0	OF-39

Bill Burich

BURICH, WILLIAM MAX
B. May 29, 1918, Calumet, Mich.

BR TR 6' 180 lbs.

	G	AB	H	2B	3B	HR	HR%	R	RBI	BB	SO	SB	BA	SA	PH AB	PH H	G by POS
1942 PHI N	25	80	23	1	0	0	0.0	3	7	6	13	2	.288	.300	3	0	SS-19, 3B-3
1946	2	1	0	0	0	0	0.0	1	0	0	0	0	.000	.000	0	0	3B-1
2 yrs.	27	81	23	1	0	0	0.0	4	7	6	13	2	.284	.296	3	0	SS-19, 3B-4

Mack Burk

BURK, MACK EDWIN
B. Apr. 21, 1935, Nacogdoches, Tex.

BR TR 6'4" 180 lbs.

	G	AB	H	2B	3B	HR	HR%	R	RBI	BB	SO	SB	BA	SA	PH AB	PH H	G by POS
1956 PHI N	15	1	1	0	0	0	0.0	3	0	0	0	0	1.000	1.000	1	1	C-1
1958	1	1	0	0	0	0	0.0	0	0	0	1	0	.000	.000	1	0	
2 yrs.	16	2	1	0	0	0	0.0	3	0	0	1	0	.500	.500	2	1	C-1

Bob Burkam

BURKAM, ROBERT (Chris, Chauncey DePew)
B. Oct. 13, 1892, Benton Harbor, Mich. D. May 9, 1964, Kalamazoo, Mich.

BL TR

	G	AB	H	2B	3B	HR	HR%	R	RBI	BB	SO	SB	BA	SA	PH AB	PH H	G by POS
1915 STL A	1	1	0	0	0	0	0.0	0	0	0	1	0	.000	.000	1	0	

	G	AB	H	2B	3B	HR	HR %	R	RBI	BB	SO	SB	BA	SA	Pinch Hit AB	Pinch Hit H	G by POS

Dan Burke

BURKE, DANIEL L.   BR TR 5'10" 190 lbs.
B. Mar., 1869, Whitman, Mass.   D. Mar. 20, 1933, Taunton, Mass.

	G	AB	H	2B	3B	HR	HR %	R	RBI	BB	SO	SB	BA	SA	PH AB	PH H	G by POS
1890 2 teams	ROC	AA (32G –	.216)			SYR	AA (9G –	.000)									
" total	41	122	22	1	0	0	0.0	15		22		2	.180	.189	0	0	OF-29, C-13, 1B-2
1892 BOS N	1	4	0	0	0	0	0.0	0	0	0	2	0	.000	.000	0	0	C-1
2 yrs.	42	126	22	1	0	0	0.0	15		22	2	2	.175	.183	0	0	OF-29, C-14, 1B-2

Eddie Burke

BURKE, EDWARD D.   BR TR 5'6" 161 lbs.
B. Oct. 6, 1866, Northumberland, Pa.   D. Nov. 26, 1907, Utica, N. Y.

	G	AB	H	2B	3B	HR	HR %	R	RBI	BB	SO	SB	BA	SA	PH AB	PH H	G by POS
1890 2 teams	PHI	N (100G –	.263)			PIT	N (31G –	.210)									
" total	131	554	139	21	13	5	0.9	102	57	63	49	44	.251	.363	0	0	OF-127, 2B-4
1891 C-M AA	35	144	34	9	0	1	0.7	31	21	12	19	7	.236	.319	0	0	OF-35
1892 2 teams	CIN	N (15G –	.146)			NY	N (89G –	.259)									
" total	104	404	100	11	5	6	1.5	87	45	55	41	44	.248	.344	0	0	2B-59, OF-44, 3B-1
1893 NY N	135	537	150	23	10	9	1.7	122	80	51	32	54	.279	.410	0	0	OF-135
1894	136	566	172	23	11	5	0.9	121	77	37	35	34	.304	.410	0	0	OF-136
1895 2 teams	NY	N (40G –	.257)			CIN	N (56G –	.268)									
" total	96	395	104	14	8	2	0.5	90	40	29	23	33	.263	.354	0	0	OF-95
1896 CIN N	122	521	177	24	9	1	0.2	120	52	41	29	53	.340	.426	0	0	OF-122
1897	95	387	103	17	1	1	0.3	71	41	29		22	.266	.323	0	0	OF-95
8 yrs.	854	3508	979	142	57	30	0.9	744	413	317	228	291	.279	.378	0	0	OF-789, 2B-63, 3B-1

Frank Burke

BURKE, FRANK ALOYSIUS   TR
B. Feb. 16, 1880, Carbon County, Pa.   D. Sept. 17, 1946, Los Angeles, Calif.

	G	AB	H	2B	3B	HR	HR %	R	RBI	BB	SO	SB	BA	SA	PH AB	PH H	G by POS
1906 NY N	8	9	3	1	1	0	0.0	2	1	1		1	.333	.667	3	1	OF-4
1907 BOS N	43	129	23	0	1	0	0.0	6	8	11		3	.178	.194	6	1	OF-36
2 yrs.	51	138	26	1	2	0	0.0	8	9	12		4	.188	.225	9	2	OF-40

Glenn Burke

BURKE, GLENN LAWRENCE   BR TR 6' 195 lbs.
B. Nov. 16, 1952, Oakland, Calif.

	G	AB	H	2B	3B	HR	HR %	R	RBI	BB	SO	SB	BA	SA	PH AB	PH H	G by POS
1976 LA N	25	46	11	2	0	0	0.0	9	5	3	8	3	.239	.283	1	0	OF-20
1977	83	169	43	8	0	1	0.6	16	13	5	22	13	.254	.320	9	0	OF-74
1978 2 teams	LA	N (16G –	.211)			OAK	A (78G –	.235)									
" total	94	219	51	6	1	1	0.5	21	16	10	30	16	.233	.283	2	0	OF-82, DH-2, 1B-1
1979 OAK A	23	89	19	2	1	0	0.0	4	4	4	10	3	.213	.258	0	0	OF-23
4 yrs.	225	523	124	18	2	2	0.4	50	38	22	70	35	.237	.291	12	0	OF-199, DH-2, 1B-1

LEAGUE CHAMPIONSHIP SERIES

	G	AB	H	2B	3B	HR	HR %	R	RBI	BB	SO	SB	BA	SA	PH AB	PH H	G by POS
1977 LA N	4	7	0	0	0	0	0.0	0	0	0	3	0	.000	.000	0	0	OF-4

WORLD SERIES

	G	AB	H	2B	3B	HR	HR %	R	RBI	BB	SO	SB	BA	SA	PH AB	PH H	G by POS
1977 LA N	3	5	1	0	0	0	0.0	0	0	0	1	0	.200	.200	0	0	OF-3

Jimmy Burke

BURKE, JAMES TIMOTHY (Sunset Jimmy)   BR TR
B. Oct. 12, 1874, St. Louis, Mo.   D. Mar. 26, 1942, St. Louis, Mo.
Manager 1905, 1918-20.

	G	AB	H	2B	3B	HR	HR %	R	RBI	BB	SO	SB	BA	SA	PH AB	PH H	G by POS
1898 CLE N	13	38	4	1	0	0	0.0	1	1	2		1	.105	.132	0	0	3B-13
1901 3 teams	MIL	A (64G –	.206)			CHI	A (42G –	.264)			PIT	N (14G –	.196)				
" total	120	432	92	13	0	0	0.0	48	51	33		17	.225	.255	0	0	3B-89, SS-31
1902 PIT N	60	203	60	12	2	0	0.0	24	26	17		9	.296	.374	2	0	2B-27, OF-18, 3B-9, SS-4
1903 STL N	115	431	123	13	3	0	0.0	55	42	23		28	.285	.329	1	0	3B-93, 2B-15, OF-5
1904	118	406	92	10	3	0	0.0	37	37	15		17	.227	.266	0	0	3B-118
1905	122	431	97	9	5	1	0.2	34	30	21		15	.225	.276	0	0	3B-122
6 yrs.	548	1941	473	58	13	1	0.1	199	187	111		87	.244	.289	3	0	3B-444, 2B-42, SS-35, OF-23

Joe Burke

BURKE, JOSEPH M.   5'7" 160 lbs.
B. Cincinnati, Ohio   D. Dec. 29, 1896

	G	AB	H	2B	3B	HR	HR %	R	RBI	BB	SO	SB	BA	SA	PH AB	PH H	G by POS
1890 STL AA	2	6	4	0	0	0	0.0	3		1		0	.667	.667	0	0	3B-2
1891 C-M AA	1	4	1	0	0	0	0.0	0	1	0	2	0	.250	.250	0	0	2B-1
2 yrs.	3	10	5	0	0	0	0.0	3	1	1	2	0	.500	.500	0	0	3B-2, 2B-1

John Burke

BURKE, JOHN PATRICK
B. Jan. 27, 1877, Hazleton, Pa.   D. Aug. 4, 1950, Jersey City, N. J.

	G	AB	H	2B	3B	HR	HR %	R	RBI	BB	SO	SB	BA	SA	PH AB	PH H	G by POS
1899 STL N	2	6	2	0	0	0	0.0	1	0	1		0	.333	.333	0	0	2B-2
1902 NY N	4	13	2	0	0	0	0.0	0	0	0		0	.154	.154	0	0	OF-2, 2B-2, P-2
2 yrs.	6	19	4	0	0	0	0.0	1	0	1		0	.211	.211	0	0	OF-2, 2B-2, P-2

Leo Burke

BURKE, LEO PATRICK   BR TR 5'11" 185 lbs.
B. May 6, 1934, Hagerstown, Md.

	G	AB	H	2B	3B	HR	HR %	R	RBI	BB	SO	SB	BA	SA	PH AB	PH H	G by POS
1958 BAL A	7	11	5	1	0	1	9.1	4	4	1	2	0	.455	.818	3	1	OF-3, 3B-1
1959	5	10	2	0	0	0	0.0	0	1	0	5	0	.200	.200	2	0	3B-2, 2B-2
1961 LA A	6	5	0	0	0	0	0.0	0	0	0	1	0	.000	.000	5	0	OF-1
1962	19	64	17	1	0	4	6.3	8	14	5	11	0	.266	.469	2	0	OF-12, 3B-4, SS-1
1963 2 teams	STL	N (30G –	.204)			CHI	N (27G –	.184)									
" total	57	98	19	2	1	3	3.1	10	12	8	25	0	.194	.327	28	8	OF-11, 2B-10, 3B-5, 1B-4
1964 CHI N	59	103	27	3	1	1	1.0	11	14	7	31	0	.262	.340	34	10	OF-18, 2B-5, 3B-4, 1B-2, C-1
1965	12	10	2	0	0	0	0.0	0	0	0	4	0	.200	.200	9	1	C-2, OF-1
7 yrs.	165	301	72	7	2	9	3.0	33	45	21	79	0	.239	.365	83	20	OF-45, 2B-17, 3B-16, 1B-6, C-3, SS-1

Les Burke

BURKE, LESLIE KINGSTON (Buck)   BL TR 5'9" 168 lbs.
B. Dec. 18, 1902, Lynn, Mass.   D. May 6, 1975, Danvers, Mass.

	G	AB	H	2B	3B	HR	HR %	R	RBI	BB	SO	SB	BA	SA	PH AB	PH H	G by POS
1923 DET A	7	10	1	0	0	0	0.0	0	0	1		0	.100	.100	1	0	3B-2, 2B-1, C-1
1924	72	241	61	10	4	0	0.0	30	17	22	20	2	.253	.328	7	4	2B-58, SS-6
1925	77	180	52	6	3	0	0.0	32	24	17	8	4	.289	.356	22	4	2B-52
1926	38	75	17	1	0	0	0.0	9	4	7	3	1	.227	.240	13	1	2B-15, 3B-7, SS-1
4 yrs.	194	506	131	17	7	0	0.0	73	47	46	32	7	.259	.320	43	9	2B-126, 3B-9, SS-7, C-1

	G	AB	H	2B	3B	HR	HR %	R	RBI	BB	SO	SB	BA	SA	Pinch Hit AB	Pinch Hit H	G by POS

Mike Burke

BURKE, MICHAEL E.   BR TR 6'   190 lbs.
B. 1855, Cincinnati, Ohio   D. June 4, 1889, Albany, N. Y.

	G	AB	H	2B	3B	HR	HR %	R	RBI	BB	SO	SB	BA	SA	AB	H	G by POS
1879 CIN N	28	117	26	3	0	0	0.0	13	8	2	5		.222	.248	0	0	SS-19, OF-5, 3B-5

Pat Burke

BURKE, PATRICK EDWARD   BR TR 5'10½" 170 lbs.
B. May 13, 1901, St. Louis, Mo.   D. July 7, 1965, St. Louis, Mo.

	G	AB	H	2B	3B	HR	HR %	R	RBI	BB	SO	SB	BA	SA	AB	H	G by POS
1924 STL A	1	3	0	0	0	0	0.0	1	0	0	0		.000	.000	0	0	3B-1

Jesse Burkett

BURKETT, JESSE CAIL (The Crab)   BL TL 5'8"   155 lbs.
B. Dec. 4, 1868, Wheeling, W. Va.   D. May 27, 1953, Worcester, Mass.
Hall of Fame 1946.

	G	AB	H	2B	3B	HR	HR %	R	RBI	BB	SO	SB	BA	SA	AB	H	G by POS
1890 NY N	101	401	124	23	13	4	1.0	67	60	33	52	14	.309	.461	0	0	OF-90, P-21
1891 CLE N	42	167	45	7	4	0	0.0	29	13	23	19	1	.269	.359	0	0	OF-42
1892	145	608	167	15	14	6	1.0	119	66	67	59	36	.275	.375	0	0	OF-145
1893	125	511	178	25	15	6	1.2	145	82	98	23	39	.348	.491	0	0	OF-125
1894	125	523	187	27	14	8	1.5	138	94	84	27	28	.358	.509	0	0	OF-125, P-1
1895	132	555	**235**	21	15	5	0.9	149	83	74	31	47	**.423**	.542	0	0	OF-132
1896	133	**586**	**240**	27	16	6	1.0	**160**	72	49	19	34	**.410**	.541	0	0	OF-133
1897	128	519	199	28	8	2	0.4	128	60	76		28	.383	.480	0	0	OF-127
1898	150	624	**215**	18	9	0	0.0	115	42	69		19	.345	.402	0	0	OF-150
1899 STL N	141	567	228	17	10	7	1.2	115	71	67		22	.402	.504	0	0	OF-140, 2B-1
1900	142	560	203	14	12	7	1.3	88	68	62		32	.363	.468	0	0	OF-141
1901	142	**597**	**228**	21	17	10	1.7	**139**	75	59		27	**.382**	.524	0	0	OF-142
1902 STL A	137	549	168	29	9	5	0.9	97	52	71		23	.306	.419	0	0	OF-137, SS-1, 3B-1, P-1
1903	133	514	152	20	7	3	0.6	74	40	52		17	.296	.379	0	0	OF-132
1904	147	576	157	15	9	2	0.3	72	27	78		12	.273	.340	0	0	OF-147
1905 BOS A	149	573	147	13	13	4	0.7	78	47	67		13	.257	.346	0	0	OF-149
16 yrs.	2072	8430	2873	320	185	75	0.9	1713	952	1029	230	392	.341	.449	0	0	OF-2057, P-23, SS-1, 3B-1, 2B-1

Rick Burleson

BURLESON, RICHARD PAUL (Rooster)   BR TR 5'10"   165 lbs.
B. Apr. 29, 1951, Lynwood, Calif.

	G	AB	H	2B	3B	HR	HR %	R	RBI	BB	SO	SB	BA	SA	AB	H	G by POS
1974 BOS A	114	384	109	22	0	4	1.0	36	44	21	34	3	.284	.372	1	0	SS-88, 2B-31, 3B-2
1975	158	580	146	25	1	6	1.0	66	62	45	44	8	.252	.329	0	0	SS-157
1976	152	540	157	27	1	7	1.3	75	42	60	37	14	.291	.383	0	0	SS-152
1977	154	**663**	194	36	7	3	0.5	80	52	47	69	13	.293	.382	0	0	SS-154
1978	145	626	155	32	5	5	0.8	75	49	40	71	8	.248	.339	0	0	SS-144
1979	153	627	174	32	5	5	0.8	93	60	35	54	9	.278	.368	1	0	SS-153
1980	155	644	179	29	2	8	1.2	89	51	62	51	12	.278	.366	0	0	SS-155
1981 CAL A	109	430	126	17	1	5	1.2	53	33	42	38	4	.293	.372	0	0	SS-109
1982	11	45	7	1	0	0	0.0	4	2	6	3	0	.156	.178	0	0	SS-11
1983	33	119	34	7	0	0	0.0	22	11	12	12	0	.286	.345	2	1	SS-31
1984	7	4	0	0	0	0	0.0	2	0	0	2	0	.000	.000	4	0	
11 yrs.	1191	4662	1281	228	22	43	0.9	595	406	370	415	71	.275	.361	8	1	SS-1154, 2B-31, 3B-2
LEAGUE CHAMPIONSHIP SERIES																	
1975 BOS A	3	9	4	2	0	0	0.0	2	1	1	0	0	.444	.667	0	0	SS-3
WORLD SERIES																	
1975 BOS A	7	24	7	1	0	0	0.0	1	2	4	2	0	.292	.333	0	0	SS-7

Hercules Burnett

BURNETT, HERCULES H.
B. Aug. 13, 1865, Louisville, Ky.   D. Oct. 4, 1936, Louisville, Ky.

	G	AB	H	2B	3B	HR	HR %	R	RBI	BB	SO	SB	BA	SA	AB	H	G by POS
1888 LOU AA	1	4	0	0	0	0	0.0	0	0	1		1	.000	.000	0	0	OF-1
1895 LOU N	5	17	7	0	1	2	11.8	6	3	2	2	2	.412	.882	0	0	OF-4, 1B-1
2 yrs.	6	21	7	0	1	2	9.5	7	3	3	2	3	.333	.714	0	0	OF-5, 1B-1

John Burnett

BURNETT, JOHN P.
B. Unknown.

	G	AB	H	2B	3B	HR	HR %	R	RBI	BB	SO	SB	BA	SA	AB	H	G by POS
1907 STL N	59	206	49	8	4	0	0.0	18	12	15		5	.238	.316	0	0	OF-59

Johnny Burnett

BURNETT, JOHN HENDERSON   BL TR 5'11"   175 lbs.
B. Nov. 1, 1904, Bartow, Fla.   D. Aug. 13, 1959, Tampa, Fla.

	G	AB	H	2B	3B	HR	HR %	R	RBI	BB	SO	SB	BA	SA	AB	H	G by POS
1927 CLE A	17	8	0	0	0	0	0.0	5	0	0	3	1	.000	.000	6	0	2B-2
1928	3	10	5	0	0	0	0.0	3	1	0	1	0	.500	.500	1	1	SS-2
1929	19	33	5	1	0	0	0.0	2	2	1	2	0	.152	.182	1	0	SS-10, 2B-4
1930	54	170	53	13	0	0	0.0	28	20	17	8	2	.312	.388	8	3	3B-27, SS-19
1931	111	427	128	25	5	1	0.2	85	52	39	25	5	.300	.389	2	1	SS-63, 2B-35, 3B-21, OF-1
1932	129	512	152	23	5	4	0.8	81	53	46	27	2	.297	.385	1	1	SS-103, 2B-26
1933	83	261	71	11	2	1	0.4	39	29	23	14	3	.272	.341	12	1	SS-41, 3B-17, 3B-12
1934	72	208	61	11	2	3	1.4	28	30	18	11	1	.293	.409	14	3	3B-42, SS-9, 2B-3, OF-2
1935 STL A	70	206	46	10	1	0	0.0	17	26	19	16	1	.223	.282	16	4	3B-31, SS-18, 2B-12
9 yrs.	558	1835	521	94	15	9	0.5	288	213	163	107	15	.284	.366	61	14	SS-265, 3B-133, 2B-99, OF-3

Bill Burns

BURNS, CHARLES BIRMINGHAM (C. B.)
B. May 15, 1879, Bay View, Md.   D. June 6, 1968, Havre de Grace, Md.

	G	AB	H	2B	3B	HR	HR %	R	RBI	BB	SO	SB	BA	SA	AB	H	G by POS
1902 BAL A	1	1	1	0	0	0	0.0	0	0	0		0	1.000	1.000	1	1	

Dick Burns

BURNS, RICHARD SIMON   TL   140 lbs.
B. Dec. 26, 1863, Holyoke, Mass.   D. Nov. 18, 1937, Holyoke, Mass.

	G	AB	H	2B	3B	HR	HR %	R	RBI	BB	SO	SB	BA	SA	AB	H	G by POS
1883 DET N	37	140	26	7	1	0	0.0	11		2	22		.186	.250	0	0	OF-24, P-17
1884 CIN U	79	350	107	17	12	4	1.1	84		5			.306	.457	0	0	OF-44, P-40, SS-2
1885 STL N	14	54	12	2	1	0	0.0	2	4	3	8		.222	.296	0	0	OF-14, P-1
3 yrs.	130	544	145	26	14	4	0.7	97	3	10	30		.267	.388	0	0	OF-82, P-58, SS-2

	G	AB	H	2B	3B	HR	HR %	R	RBI	BB	SO	SB	BA	SA	Pinch Hit AB	Pinch Hit H	G by POS

Ed Burns

BURNS, EDWARD JAMES
B. Oct. 31, 1887, San Francisco, Calif.   D. June 1, 1942, Monterey, Calif.   BR TR 5'6"   165 lbs.

	G	AB	H	2B	3B	HR	HR %	R	RBI	BB	SO	SB	BA	SA	AB	H	G by POS
1912 STL N	1	1	0	0	0	0	0.0	0	1	0	0	0	.000	.000	0	0	C-1
1913 PHI N	17	30	6	3	0	0	0.0	3	3	6	3	2	.200	.300	1	0	C-15
1914	70	139	36	3	4	0	0.0	8	16	20	12	5	.259	.338	14	3	C-55
1915	67	174	42	5	0	0	0.0	11	16	20	12	1	.241	.270	5	2	C-67
1916	78	219	51	8	1	0	0.0	14	14	16	18	3	.233	.279	2	0	C-75, OF-1, SS-1
1917	20	49	10	1	0	0	0.0	2	6	1	5	2	.204	.224	5	0	C-15
1918	68	184	38	1	0	0	0.0	10	9	20	9	1	.207	.223	0	0	C-68
7 yrs.	321	796	183	21	6	0	0.0	48	65	83	59	14	.230	.271	27	5	C-296, OF-1, SS-1
WORLD SERIES																	
1915 PHI N	5	16	3	0	0	0	0.0	1	0	1	2	0	.188	.188	0	0	C-5

George Burns

BURNS, GEORGE HENRY (Tioga George)
B. Jan. 31, 1893, Niles, Ohio   D. Jan. 7, 1978, Kirkland, Wash.   BR TR 6'1½"   180 lbs.

	G	AB	H	2B	3B	HR	HR %	R	RBI	BB	SO	SB	BA	SA	AB	H	G by POS
1914 DET A	137	478	139	22	5	5	1.0	55	57	32	56	23	.291	.389	0	0	1B-137
1915	105	392	99	18	3	5	1.3	49	50	22	51	9	.253	.352	1	0	1B-104
1916	135	479	137	22	6	4	0.8	60	73	22	30	12	.286	.382	11	3	1B-124
1917	119	407	92	14	10	1	0.2	42	40	15	33	3	.226	.317	15	2	1B-104
1918 PHI A	130	505	**178**	22	9	6	1.2	61	70	23	25	8	.352	.467	0	0	1B-128, OF-2
1919	126	470	139	29	9	8	1.7	63	57	19	18	15	.296	.447	5	0	1B-86, OF-34
1920 2 teams			PHI	A	(22G –	.233)		CLE	A	(44G –	.268)						
" total	66	116	29	7	1	1	0.9	8	20	10	10	5	.250	.353	39	11	OF-13, 1B-12
1921 CLE A	84	244	88	21	4	0	0.0	52	48	13	19	2	.361	.480	10	2	1B-73
1922 BOS A	147	558	171	32	5	12	2.2	71	73	20	28	8	.306	.446	6	2	1B-140
1923	146	551	181	47	5	7	1.3	91	82	45	33	9	.328	.470	0	0	1B-146
1924 CLE A	129	462	143	37	5	4	0.9	64	66	29	27	14	.310	.437	2	0	1B-127
1925	127	488	164	41	4	6	1.2	69	79	24	24	16	.336	.473	1	1	1B-126
1926	151	603	**216**	**64**	3	4	0.7	97	114	28	33	13	.358	.494	0	0	1B-151
1927	140	549	175	51	2	3	0.5	84	78	42	27	13	.319	.435	1	0	1B-139
1928 2 teams			CLE	A	(82G –	.249)		NY	A	(4G –	.500)						
" total	86	213	54	12	1	5	2.3	30	30	17	12	2	.254	.390	30	6	1B-55
1929 2 teams			NY	A	(9G –	.000)		PHI	A	(29G –	.265)						
" total	38	58	13	5	0	1	1.7	5	11	2	7	1	.224	.362	17	0	1B-19
16 yrs.	1866	6573	2018	444	72	72	1.1	901	948	363	433	153	.307	.429	138	27	1B-1671, OF-49
WORLD SERIES																	
1920 CLE A	5	10	3	1	0	0	0.0	1	3	3	3	0	.300	.400	1	1	1B-4
1929 PHI A	1	2	0	0	0	0	0.0	0	0	0	1	0	.000	.000	2	0	
2 yrs.	6	12	3	1	0	0	0.0	1	3	3	4	0	.250	.333	3	1	1B-4

George Burns

BURNS, GEORGE JOSEPH
B. Nov. 24, 1889, Utica, N. Y.   D. Aug. 15, 1966, Gloversville, N. Y.   BR TR 5'7"   160 lbs.

	G	AB	H	2B	3B	HR	HR %	R	RBI	BB	SO	SB	BA	SA	AB	H	G by POS
1911 NY N	6	17	1	0	0	0	0.0	2	0	1	0	1	.059	.059	0	0	OF-6
1912	29	51	15	4	0	0	0.0	11	3	8	8	7	.294	.373	2	1	OF-23
1913	150	605	173	37	4	2	0.3	81	54	58	74	40	.286	.370	0	0	OF-150
1914	154	561	170	35	10	3	0.5	100	60	89	53	62	.303	.417	0	0	OF-154
1915	155	**622**	169	27	14	3	0.5	83	51	56	57	27	.272	.375	0	0	OF-155
1916	155	**623**	174	24	8	5	0.8	105	41	63	47	37	.279	.368	0	0	OF-155
1917	152	597	180	25	13	5	0.8	103	45	75	55	40	.302	.412	0	0	OF-152
1918	119	465	135	22	6	4	0.9	80	51	43	37	40	.290	.389	0	0	OF-119
1919	139	534	162	30	9	2	0.4	86	46	82	37	40	.303	.404	0	0	OF-139
1920	154	631	181	35	9	6	1.0	115	46	76	48	22	.287	.399	0	0	OF-154
1921	149	605	181	28	9	4	0.7	111	61	80	24	19	.299	.395	0	0	OF-149, 3B-1
1922 CIN N	156	631	180	20	10	1	0.2	104	53	78	38	30	.285	.353	0	0	OF-156
1923	154	614	168	27	13	3	0.5	99	45	101	46	12	.274	.375	0	0	OF-154
1924	93	336	86	19	2	2	0.6	43	33	29	21	3	.256	.342	3	2	OF-90
1925 PHI N	88	349	102	29	1	1	0.3	65	22	33	20	4	.292	.390	0	0	OF-88
15 yrs.	1853	7241	2077	362	108	41	0.6	1188	611	872	565	383	.287	.384	5	3	OF-1844, 3B-1
WORLD SERIES																	
1913 NY N	5	19	3	2	0	0	0.0	2	1	1	5	1	.158	.263	0	0	OF-5
1917	6	22	5	0	0	0	0.0	3	2	3	6	1	.227	.227	0	0	OF-6
1921	8	33	11	4	1	0	0.0	2	2	3	5	1	.333	.515	0	0	OF-8
3 yrs.	19	74	19	6	1	0	0.0	7	5	7	16	3	.257	.365	0	0	OF-19

Jack Burns

BURNS, JOHN IRVING (Slug)
B. Aug. 31, 1907, Cambridge, Mass.   D. Apr. 18, 1975, Boston, Mass.   BR TR 5'10½" 175 lbs.

	G	AB	H	2B	3B	HR	HR %	R	RBI	BB	SO	SB	BA	SA	AB	H	G by POS
1930 STL A	8	30	9	3	0	0	0.0	5	2	5	5	0	.300	.400	0	0	1B-8
1931	144	570	148	27	7	4	0.7	75	70	42	58	19	.260	.353	0	0	1B-143
1932	150	617	188	33	8	11	1.8	111	70	61	43	17	.305	.438	0	0	1B-150
1933	144	556	160	43	4	7	1.3	89	71	56	51	11	.288	.417	1	0	1B-143
1934	154	612	157	28	8	13	2.1	86	73	62	47	9	.257	.392	0	0	1B-154
1935	143	549	157	28	1	5	0.9	77	67	68	49	3	.286	.368	0	0	1B-141
1936 2 teams			STL	A	(9G –	.214)		DET	A	(138G –	.283)						
" total	147	572	161	37	4	4	0.7	98	64	82	46	4	.281	.378	6	3	1B-140
7 yrs.	890	3506	980	199	31	44	1.3	541	417	376	299	63	.280	.392	8	3	1B-879

Jim Burns

BURNS, JAMES M.
B. Quincy, Ill.   Deceased.   5'7"   168 lbs.

	G	AB	H	2B	3B	HR	HR %	R	RBI	BB	SO	SB	BA	SA	AB	H	G by POS
1888 KC AA	15	66	20	0	0	0	0.0	13	4	1		6	.303	.303	0	0	OF-15
1889	134	579	176	23	11	5	0.9	103	97	20	68	56	.304	.408	0	0	OF-134, 3B-1
1891 WAS AA	20	82	26	6	0	0	0.0	15	10	6	10	2	.317	.390	0	0	OF-21, SS-1
3 yrs.	169	727	222	29	11	5	0.7	131	111	27	78	64	.305	.396	0	0	OF-170, SS-1, 3B-1

	G	AB	H	2B	3B	HR	HR%	R	RBI	BB	SO	SB	BA	SA	Pinch Hit AB	Pinch Hit H	G by POS

Joe Burns

BURNS, JOSEPH FRANCIS   BL TL 5'11"   170 lbs.
B. Mar. 26, 1889, Ipswich, Mass.

	G	AB	H	2B	3B	HR	HR%	R	RBI	BB	SO	SB	BA	SA	P.H. AB	P.H. H	G by POS
1910 CIN N	1	1	1	0	0	0	0.0	0	0	0	0	1	1.000	1.000	1	1	
1913 DET A	4	13	5	0	0	0	0.0	0	1	2	4	0	.385	.385	0	0	OF-4
2 yrs.	5	14	6	0	0	0	0.0	0	1	2	4	1	.429	.429	1	1	OF-4

Joe Burns

BURNS, JOSEPH FRANCIS   BR TR 6'   175 lbs.
B. Feb. 25, 1900, Trenton, N. J.

	G	AB	H	2B	3B	HR	HR%	R	RBI	BB	SO	SB	BA	SA	P.H. AB	P.H. H	G by POS
1924 CHI A	8	19	2	0	0	0	0.0	1	0	0	2	0	.105	.105	2	0	C-6

Joe Burns

BURNS, JOSEPH JAMES   BR TR 5'10½" 175 lbs.
B. June 17, 1916, Bryn Mawr, Pa.   D. June 24, 1974, Bryn Mawr, Pa.

	G	AB	H	2B	3B	HR	HR%	R	RBI	BB	SO	SB	BA	SA	P.H. AB	P.H. H	G by POS
1943 BOS N	52	135	28	3	0	1	0.7	12	5	8	25	2	.207	.252	10	1	3B-34, OF-4
1944 PHI A	28	75	18	2	0	1	1.3	5	8	4	8	0	.240	.307	2	1	3B-17, 2B-9
1945	31	90	23	1	1	0	0.0	7	3	4	17	0	.256	.289	6	2	OF-19, 3B-5, 1B-1
3 yrs.	111	300	69	6	1	2	0.7	24	16	16	50	2	.230	.277	18	4	3B-56, OF-23, 2B-9, 1B-1

John Burns

BURNS, JOHN JOSEPH   BR TR 5'10"   160 lbs.
B. May 13, 1877, Moosic, Pa.   D. June 24, 1957, Pleasure Beach, Conn.

	G	AB	H	2B	3B	HR	HR%	R	RBI	BB	SO	SB	BA	SA	P.H. AB	P.H. H	G by POS
1903 DET A	11	37	10	0	0	0	0.0	2	3	1		0	.270	.270	0	0	2B-11
1904	4	16	2	0	0	0	0.0	3	1	1		1	.125	.125	0	0	2B-4
2 yrs.	15	53	12	0	0	0	0.0	5	4	2		1	.226	.226	0	0	2B-15

Oyster Burns

BURNS, THOMAS P.   BR TR 5'8"   183 lbs.
B. Sept. 6, 1864, Philadelphia, Pa.   D. Nov. 11, 1928, Brooklyn, N. Y.

	G	AB	H	2B	3B	HR	HR%	R	RBI	BB	SO	SB	BA	SA	P.H. AB	P.H. H	G by POS
1884 2 teams		WIL	U (2G – .143)		BAL	AA (35G – .298)											
" total	37	138	40	2	7	6	4.3	34		8			.290	.536	0	0	OF-24, 2B-10, SS-2, P-2, 3B-1
1885 BAL AA	78	321	74	11	6	5	1.6	47		16			.231	.349	0	0	OF-45, P-15, SS-10, 3B-6, 2B-6, 1B-1
1887	140	551	188	33	19	10	1.8	122		63		58	.341	.525	0	0	SS-98, 3B-42, P-3, 2B-1
1888 2 teams		BAL	AA (79G – .308)		BKN	AA (52G – .286)											
" total	131	528	158	27	15	6	1.1	95	67	38		44	.299	.441	0	0	OF-70, SS-59, P-5, 2B-4, 3B-2
1889 BKN AA	131	504	153	19	13	5	1.0	105	100	68	26	32	.304	.423	0	0	OF-113, SS-19
1890 BKN N	119	472	134	22	13	13	2.8	102	128	51	42	21	.284	.468	0	0	OF-116, 3B-3
1891	123	470	134	24	13	4	0.9	75	83	53	30	21	.285	.417	0	0	OF-113, SS-6, 3B-5
1892	141	542	171	27	18	4	0.7	91	96	65	42	33	.315	.454	0	0	OF-129, 3B-7, SS-5
1893	109	415	112	22	8	7	1.7	68	60	36	16	14	.270	.412	0	0	OF-108, SS-1
1894	126	513	185	32	14	5	1.0	107	109	44	18	30	.361	.507	0	0	OF-125
1895 2 teams		BKN	N (20G – .184)		NY	N (33G – .307)											
" total	53	190	49	5	8	1	0.5	28	32	22	8	10	.258	.384	1	0	OF-32, 1B-1
11 yrs.	1188	4644	1398	224	134	66	1.4	874	674	464	182	263	.301	.450	1	0	OF-875, SS-200, 3B-66, P-25, 2B-21, 1B-2

Pat Burns

BURNS, PATRICK
Deceased.

	G	AB	H	2B	3B	HR	HR%	R	RBI	BB	SO	SB	BA	SA	P.H. AB	P.H. H	G by POS
1884 2 teams		BAL	AA (6G – .200)		BAL	U (1G – .500)											
" total	7	29	7	2	1	0	0.0	3		3			.241	.379	0	0	1B-7

Tom Burns

BURNS, THOMAS EVERETT   BL TR 5'9"   165 lbs.
B. Mar. 30, 1857, Honesdale, Pa.   D. Mar. 19, 1902, Jersey City, N. J.
Manager 1892, 1898-99.

	G	AB	H	2B	3B	HR	HR%	R	RBI	BB	SO	SB	BA	SA	P.H. AB	P.H. H	G by POS
1880 CHI N	85	333	103	17	3	0	0.0	47	43	12	23		.309	.378	0	0	SS-79, 3B-9, C-2
1881	84	342	95	20	3	4	1.2	41	42	14	22		.278	.389	0	0	SS-80, 3B-3, 2B-3
1882	84	355	88	23	6	0	0.0	55	48	15	28		.248	.346	0	0	2B-43, SS-41
1883	97	405	119	37	7	2	0.5	69		13	31		.294	.435	0	0	SS-79, 2B-19, OF-1
1884	83	343	84	14	2	7	2.0	54		13	50		.245	.359	0	0	SS-80, 3B-3
1885	111	445	121	23	9	7	1.6	82	70	16	48		.272	.411	0	0	SS-111, 2B-1
1886	112	445	123	18	10	3	0.7	64	65	14	40		.276	.382	0	0	3B-112
1887	115	424	112	20	10	3	0.7	57	60	34	32	32	.264	.380	0	0	3B-107, OF-8
1888	134	483	115	12	6	3	0.6	60	70	26	49	34	.238	.306	0	0	3B-134
1889	136	525	127	27	6	4	0.8	64	66	32	57	18	.242	.339	0	0	3B-136
1890	139	538	149	16	6	6	1.1	86	86	57	45	44	.277	.362	0	0	3B-139
1891	59	243	55	8	1	1	0.4	36	17	21	21	18	.226	.280	0	0	3B-53, SS-4, OF-2
1892 PIT N	12	39	8	0	0	0	0.0	7	4	3	8	1	.205	.205	1	0	3B-8, OF-3
13 yrs.	1251	4920	1299	235	69	40	0.8	722	571	270	454	147	.264	.364	1	0	3B-704, SS-474, 2B-66, OF-14, C-2

Alex Burr

BURR, ALEXANDER THOMSON   BR TR 6'3½" 190 lbs.
B. Nov. 1, 1893, Chicago, Ill.   D. Nov. 1, 1918, France

	G	AB	H	2B	3B	HR	HR%	R	RBI	BB	SO	SB	BA	SA	P.H. AB	P.H. H	G by POS
1914 NY A	1	0	0	0	0	0	0.0	0	0	0	0	0	–	–	0	0	OF-1

Buster Burrell

BURRELL, FRANK ANDREW   BR TR 5'10"   165 lbs.
B. Dec. 8, 1866, E. Weymouth, Mass.   D. May 8, 1962, S. Weymouth, Mass.

	G	AB	H	2B	3B	HR	HR%	R	RBI	BB	SO	SB	BA	SA	P.H. AB	P.H. H	G by POS
1891 NY N	15	53	5	0	0	0	0.0	1	1	3	12	2	.094	.094	0	0	C-15, OF-1
1895 BKN N	12	28	4	0	0	1	3.6	7	5	4	3	0	.143	.250	0	0	C-12
1896	62	206	62	11	3	0	0.0	19	23	15	13	1	.301	.383	2	0	C-60
1897	33	103	25	2	0	2	1.9	15	18	10		1	.243	.320	2	1	C-27, 1B-4
4 yrs.	122	390	96	13	3	3	0.8	42	47	32	28	4	.246	.318	4	1	C-114, 1B-4, OF-1

Larry Burright

BURRIGHT, LARRY ALLEN (Possum)   BR TR 5'11"   170 lbs.
B. July 10, 1937, Roseville, Ill.

	G	AB	H	2B	3B	HR	HR%	R	RBI	BB	SO	SB	BA	SA	P.H. AB	P.H. H	G by POS
1962 LA N	115	249	51	6	5	4	1.6	35	30	21	67	4	.205	.317	1	0	2B-109, SS-1
1963 NY N	41	100	22	2	1	0	0.0	9	3	8	25	1	.220	.260	2	0	SS-19, 2B-15, 3B-1
1964	3	7	0	0	0	0	0.0	0	0	0	0	0	.000	.000	0	0	2B-3
3 yrs.	159	356	73	8	6	4	1.1	44	33	29	92	5	.205	.295	3	0	2B-127, SS-20, 3B-1

	G	AB	H	2B	3B	HR	HR %	R	RBI	BB	SO	SB	BA	SA	Pinch Hit AB	Pinch Hit H	G by POS

Paul Burris

BURRIS, PAUL ROBERT
B. July 21, 1923, Hickory, N. C.

BR TR 6'   190 lbs.

	G	AB	H	2B	3B	HR	HR %	R	RBI	BB	SO	SB	BA	SA	AB	H	G by POS
1948 BOS N	2	4	2	0	0	0	0.0	0	0	0	0	0	.500	.500	0	0	C-2
1950	10	23	4	1	0	0	0.0	1	3	1	2	0	.174	.217	2	1	C-8
1952	55	168	37	4	0	2	1.2	14	21	7	19	0	.220	.280	5	1	C-50
1953 MIL N	2	1	0	0	0	0	0.0	0	0	0	0	0	.000	.000	0	0	C-2
4 yrs.	69	196	43	5	0	2	1.0	15	24	8	21	0	.219	.276	7	2	C-62

Jeff Burroughs

BURROUGHS, JEFFREY ALLEN
B. Mar. 7, 1951, Long Beach, Calif.

BR TR 6'1"   200 lbs.

	G	AB	H	2B	3B	HR	HR %	R	RBI	BB	SO	SB	BA	SA	AB	H	G by POS
1970 WAS A	6	12	2	0	0	0	0.0	1	1	2	5	0	.167	.167	4	1	OF-3
1971	59	181	42	9	0	5	2.8	20	25	22	55	1	.232	.365	8	2	OF-50
1972 TEX A	22	65	12	1	0	1	1.5	4	3	5	22	0	.185	.246	5	1	OF-19, 1B-1
1973	151	526	147	17	1	30	5.7	71	85	67	88	0	.279	.487	5	0	OF-148, 1B-3, DH-1
1974	152	554	167	33	2	25	4.5	84	118	91	104	2	.301	.504	0	0	OF-150, 1B-2, DH-1
1975	152	585	132	20	0	29	5.0	81	94	79	155	4	.226	.409	2	1	OF-148, DH-3
1976	158	604	143	22	2	18	3.0	71	86	69	93	0	.237	.369	0	0	OF-155, DH-3
1977 ATL N	154	579	157	19	1	41	7.1	91	114	86	126	4	.271	.520	0	0	OF-154
1978	153	488	147	30	6	23	4.7	72	77	117	92	1	.301	.529	3	1	OF-147
1979	116	397	89	14	1	11	2.8	49	47	73	75	2	.224	.348	5	1	OF-110
1980	99	278	73	14	0	13	4.7	35	51	35	57	1	.263	.453	24	9	OF-73
1981 SEA A	89	319	81	13	1	10	3.1	32	41	41	64	0	.254	.395	1	0	OF-87, DH-1
1982 OAK A	113	285	79	13	2	16	5.6	42	48	45	61	1	.277	.505	33	11	DH-48, OF-34
1983	121	401	108	15	1	10	2.5	43	56	47	79	0	.269	.387	13	5	DH-114
1984	58	71	15	1	0	2	2.8	5	8	18	23	0	.211	.310	33	4	DH-23, OF-4
15 yrs.	1603	5345	1394	221	17	234	4.4	701	854	797	1099	16	.261	.440	136	36	OF-1282, DH-194, 1B-6

Dick Burrus

BURRUS, MAURICE LENNON
B. Jan. 29, 1898, Hatteras, N. C.   D. Dec. 2, 1972, Elizabeth City, N. C.

BL TL 5'11"   175 lbs.

	G	AB	H	2B	3B	HR	HR %	R	RBI	BB	SO	SB	BA	SA	AB	H	G by POS
1919 PHI A	70	194	50	3	4	0	0.0	17	8	9	25	2	.258	.314	21	4	1B-38, OF-10
1920	71	135	25	8	0	0	0.0	11	10	5	7	0	.185	.244	37	7	1B-31, OF-2
1925 BOS N	152	588	200	41	4	5	0.9	82	87	51	29	8	.340	.449	1	0	1B-151
1926	131	486	131	21	1	3	0.6	59	61	37	16	4	.270	.335	3	0	1B-130
1927	72	220	70	8	3	0	0.0	22	32	17	10	3	.318	.382	10	4	1B-61
1928	64	137	37	6	0	3	2.2	15	13	19	8	1	.270	.380	23	7	1B-32
6 yrs.	560	1760	513	87	12	11	0.6	206	211	138	95	18	.291	.373	95	22	1B-443, OF-12

Frank Burt

BURT, FRANK J.
B. Camden, N. J.   Deceased.

	G	AB	H	2B	3B	HR	HR %	R	RBI	BB	SO	SB	BA	SA	AB	H	G by POS
1882 BAL AA	10	36	4	2	1	0	0.0	2		1			.111	.222	0	0	OF-10

Ellis Burton

BURTON, ELLIS NARRINGTON
B. Aug. 12, 1936, Los Angeles, Calif.

BB TR 5'11"   160 lbs.

	G	AB	H	2B	3B	HR	HR %	R	RBI	BB	SO	SB	BA	SA	AB	H	G by POS
1958 STL N	8	30	7	0	1	2	6.7	5	4	3	8	0	.233	.500	1	0	OF-7
1960	29	28	6	1	0	0	0.0	5	2	4	14	0	.214	.250	5	2	OF-23
1963 2 teams					CLE	A	(26G –	.194)		CHI	N	(93G –	.230)				
" total	119	353	80	19	1	13	3.7	51	42	40	63	6	.227	.397	9	2	OF-106
1964 CHI N	42	105	20	3	2	2	1.9	12	7	17	22	4	.190	.314	12	2	OF-29
1965	17	40	7	1	0	0	0.0	6	4	1	10	1	.175	.200	8	2	OF-12
5 yrs.	215	556	120	24	4	17	3.1	79	59	65	117	11	.216	.365	35	8	OF-177

Jim Busby

BUSBY, JAMES FRANKLIN
B. Jan. 8, 1927, Kenedy, Tex.

BR TR 6'1"   175 lbs.

	G	AB	H	2B	3B	HR	HR %	R	RBI	BB	SO	SB	BA	SA	AB	H	G by POS
1950 CHI A	18	48	10	0	0	0	0.0	5	4	1	5	0	.208	.208	0	0	OF-12
1951	143	477	135	15	2	5	1.0	59	68	40	46	26	.283	.354	3	0	OF-139
1952 2 teams					CHI	A	(16G –	.128)		WAS	A	(129G –	.244)				
" total	145	551	130	24	4	2	0.4	63	47	24	55	5	.236	.305	1	0	OF-144
1953 WAS A	150	586	183	28	7	6	1.0	68	82	38	45	13	.312	.415	0	0	OF-150
1954	155	628	187	22	7	7	1.1	83	80	43	56	17	.298	.389	0	0	OF-155
1955 2 teams					WAS	A	(47G –	.230)		CHI	N	(99G –	.243)				
" total	146	528	126	19	6	7	1.3	61	41	38	59	12	.239	.337	0	0	OF-146
1956 CLE A	135	494	116	17	3	6	1.2	72	50	43	47	8	.235	.354	5	1	OF-133
1957 2 teams					CLE	A	(30G –	.189)		BAL	A	(86G –	.250)				
" total	116	362	86	12	2	5	1.4	40	23	24	44	6	.238	.323	8	2	OF-111
1958 BAL A	113	215	51	7	2	3	1.4	32	19	24	37	6	.237	.330	6	1	OF-103, 3B-1
1959 BOS A	61	102	23	8	0	1	1.0	16	5	5	18	0	.225	.333	18	1	OF-34
1960 2 teams					BOS	A	(1G –	.000)		BAL	A	(79G –	.258)				
" total	80	159	41	7	1	0	0.0	25	12	20	14	2	.258	.314	3	1	OF-72
1961 BAL A	75	89	23	3	1	0	0.0	15	6	8	10	2	.258	.315	4	1	OF-71
1962 HOU N	15	11	2	0	0	0	0.0	2	1	2	3	0	.182	.182	3	1	OF-10, C-1
13 yrs.	1352	4250	1113	162	35	48	1.1	541	438	310	439	97	.262	.350	51	8	OF-1280, 3B-1, C-1

Paul Busby

BUSBY, PAUL MILLER (Red)
B. Aug. 25, 1918, Waynesboro, Miss.

BL TR 6'1"   175 lbs.

	G	AB	H	2B	3B	HR	HR %	R	RBI	BB	SO	SB	BA	SA	AB	H	G by POS
1941 PHI N	10	16	5	0	0	0	0.0	3	2	1	1	0	.313	.313	6	1	OF-3
1943	26	40	10	1	0	0	0.0	13	5	1	1	2	.250	.275	11	3	OF-10
2 yrs.	36	56	15	1	0	0	0.0	16	7	2	2	2	.268	.286	17	4	OF-13

Ed Busch

BUSCH, EDGAR JOHN
B. Nov. 16, 1917, Lebanon, Ill.

BR TR 5'10"   175 lbs.

	G	AB	H	2B	3B	HR	HR %	R	RBI	BB	SO	SB	BA	SA	AB	H	G by POS
1943 PHI A	4	17	5	0	0	0	0.0	2	0	1	2	0	.294	.294	0	0	SS-4
1944	140	484	131	11	3	0	0.0	41	40	29	17	5	.271	.306	1	0	SS-111, 2B-27, 3B-4
1945	126	416	104	10	3	0	0.0	37	35	32	9	2	.250	.288	2	0	SS-116, 3B-5, 2B-2, 1B-1
3 yrs.	270	917	240	21	6	0	0.0	80	75	62	28	7	.262	.298	3	0	SS-231, 2B-29, 3B-9, 1B-1

	G	AB	H	2B	3B	HR	HR %	R	RBI	BB	SO	SB	BA	SA	Pinch Hit AB	H	G by POS

Donie Bush

BUSH, OWEN JOSEPH
B. Oct. 8, 1887, Indianapolis, Ind.   D. Mar. 28, 1972, Indianapolis, Ind.
Manager 1923, 1927-31, 1933.   BB TR 5'6"   140 lbs.

	G	AB	H	2B	3B	HR	HR %	R	RBI	BB	SO	SB	BA	SA	AB	H	G by POS
1908 DET A	20	68	20	1	1	0	0.0	13	4	7		2	.294	.338	0	0	SS-20
1909	157	532	145	18	2	0	0.0	114	33	88		53	.273	.314	0	0	SS-157
1910	142	496	130	13	4	3	0.6	90	34	78		49	.262	.323	0	0	SS-141, 3B-1
1911	150	561	130	18	5	1	0.2	126	36	98		40	.232	.287	0	0	SS-150
1912	144	511	118	14	8	2	0.4	107	38	117		35	.231	.301	0	0	SS-144
1913	153	593	149	19	10	1	0.2	98	40	80	32	44	.251	.322	0	0	SS-153
1914	157	596	150	18	4	0	0.0	97	32	112	54	35	.252	.295	0	0	SS-157
1915	155	561	128	12	8	1	0.2	99	44	118	44	35	.228	.283	0	0	SS-155
1916	145	550	124	5	9	0	0.0	73	34	75	42	19	.225	.267	0	0	SS-144
1917	147	581	163	18	3	0	0.0	112	24	80	40	34	.281	.322	0	0	SS-147
1918	128	500	117	10	3	0	0.0	74	22	79	31	9	.234	.266	0	0	SS-128
1919	129	509	124	11	6	0	0.0	82	26	75	36	22	.244	.289	0	0	SS-129
1920	141	506	133	18	5	1	0.2	85	33	73	32	15	.263	.324	1	1	SS-140
1921 2 teams	DET	A	(104G	–	.281)		WAS	A	(23G	–	.214)						
" total	127	486	131	7	5	0	0.0	87	29	57	27	10	.270	.305	2	1	SS-102, 2B-23
1922 WAS A	41	134	32	4	1	0	0.0	17	7	21	7	1	.239	.284	1	0	3B-37, 2B-1
1923	10	22	9	0	0	0	0.0	6	0	0	1	0	.409	.409	1	0	3B-6, 2B-1
16 yrs.	1946	7206	1803	186	74	9	0.1	1280	436	1158	346	403	.250	.300	7	2	SS-1867, 3B-44, 2B-25
WORLD SERIES																	
1909 DET A	7	23	6	1	0	0	0.0	5	2	5	3	1	.261	.304	0	0	SS-7

Joe Bush

BUSH, LESLIE AMBROSE (Bullet Joe)
B. Nov. 27, 1892, Brainerd, Minn.   D. Nov. 1, 1974, Ft. Lauderdale, Fla.   BR TR 5'9"   173 lbs.

	G	AB	H	2B	3B	HR	HR %	R	RBI	BB	SO	SB	BA	SA	AB	H	G by POS
1912 PHI A	1	4	2	0	1	0	0.0	1	3	0		0	.500	1.000	0	0	P-1
1913	39	70	11	3	1	0	0.0	8	1	2	21	0	.157	.229	0	0	P-39
1914	38	74	14	4	0	1	1.4	6	8	2	25	0	.189	.284	0	0	P-38
1915	25	49	7	0	0	0	0.0	2	0	1	22	0	.143	.143	0	0	P-25
1916	41	100	14	4	0	0	0.0	4	6	0	23	0	.140	.180	0	0	P-40
1917	37	80	16	2	1	0	0.0	9	4	5	12	0	.200	.250	0	0	P-37
1918 BOS A	36	98	27	3	2	0	0.0	8	14	6	11	0	.276	.347	0	0	P-36
1919	6	5	2	0	0	0	0.0	1	2	0	1	0	.400	.400	1	0	P-3
1920	45	102	25	2	0	0	0.0	14	7	9	15	0	.245	.265	5	1	P-35, OF-2
1921	51	120	39	5	4	0	0.0	19	14	3	14	2	.325	.433	8	2	P-37, OF-4
1922 NY A	39	95	31	6	2	0	0.0	15	12	3	11	0	.326	.432	0	0	P-39
1923	38	113	31	5	3	2	1.8	12	19	3	8	0	.274	.425	1	0	P-37
1924	60	124	42	9	3	1	0.8	13	14	7	6	0	.339	.484	16	8	P-39
1925 STL A	57	102	26	12	0	2	2.0	10	18	6	8	2	.255	.431	21	2	P-33, OF-1
1926 2 teams	WAS	A	(17G	–	.233)		PIT	N	(28G	–	.265)						
" total	45	79	20	4	0	1	1.3	6	10	4	12	0	.253	.342	10	1	P-31, OF-1
1927 2 teams	PIT	N	(7G	–	.600)		NY	N	(3G	–	.500)						
" total	10	9	5	0	0	0	0.0	0	2	1	1	0	.556	.556	1	1	P-8
1928 PHI A	15	15	1	0	0	0	0.0	0	0	1	2	0	.067	.067	1	0	P-11, OF-1
17 yrs.	583	1239	313	59	17	7	0.6	128	134	53	192	4	.253	.345	64	15	P-489, OF-9
WORLD SERIES																	
1913 PHI A	1	4	1	0	0	0	0.0	0	0	0	1	0	.250	.250	0	0	P-1
1914	1	5	0	0	0	0	0.0	0	0	0	2	0	.000	.000	0	0	P-1
1918 BOS A	2	2	0	0	0	0	0.0	0	0	1	0	0	.000	.000	0	0	P-2
1922 NY A	2	6	1	0	0	0	0.0	0	1	0	0	0	.167	.167	0	0	P-2
1923	4	7	3	1	0	0	0.0	2	1	1	1	0	.429	.571	0	0	P-3
5 yrs.	10	24	5	1	0	0	0.0	2	2	2	4	0	.208	.250	0	0	P-9

Randy Bush

BUSH, ROBERT RANDALL
B. Oct. 5, 1958, Dover, Del.   BL TL 6'1"   190 lbs.

	G	AB	H	2B	3B	HR	HR %	R	RBI	BB	SO	SB	BA	SA	AB	H	G by POS
1982 MIN A	55	119	29	6	1	4	3.4	13	13	8	28	0	.244	.412	25	3	DH-26, OF-6
1983	124	373	93	24	3	11	2.9	43	56	34	51	0	.249	.418	19	4	DH-103, 1B-3
1984	113	311	70	17	1	11	3.5	46	43	31	60	1	.225	.392	20	8	DH-89, 1B-2
3 yrs.	292	803	192	47	5	26	3.2	102	112	73	139	1	.239	.407	64	15	DH-218, OF-6, 1B-5

Doc Bushong

BUSHONG, ALBERT JOHN
B. Jan. 10, 1856, Philadelphia, Pa.   D. Aug. 19, 1908, Brooklyn, N. Y.   BR TR 5'11"   165 lbs.

	G	AB	H	2B	3B	HR	HR %	R	RBI	BB	SO	SB	BA	SA	AB	H	G by POS
1876 PHI N	5	21	1	0	0	0	0.0	4	1	0	0		.048	.048	0	0	C-5
1880 WOR N	41	146	25	3	0	0	0.0	13		1	16		.171	.192	0	0	C-40, OF-1, 3B-1
1881	76	275	64	7	4	0	0.0	35	21	21	23		.233	.287	0	0	C-76
1882	69	253	40	4	1	1	0.4	20	15	5	17		.158	.194	0	0	C-69
1883 CLE N	63	215	37	5	0	0	0.0	15		7	19		.172	.195	0	0	C-63
1884	62	203	48	6	1	0	0.0	24	10	17	11		.236	.276	0	0	C-62, OF-1
1885 STL AA	85	300	80	13	5	0	0.0	42		11			.267	.343	0	0	C-85, 3B-1
1886	107	386	86	8	0	1	0.3	56		31			.223	.251	0	0	C-106, 1B-1
1887	53	201	51	4	0	0	0.0	35		11		14	.254	.274	0	0	C-52, OF-2, 3B-2
1888 BKN AA	69	253	53	5	1	0	0.0	23	16	5		9	.209	.237	0	0	C-69
1889	25	84	13	1	0	0	0.0	15	8	9	7	2	.155	.167	0	0	C-25
1890 BKN N	16	55	13	2	0	0	0.0	5	7	6	4	2	.236	.273	0	0	C-15, OF-1
12 yrs.	671	2392	511	58	12	2	0.1	287	78	124	97	27	.214	.250	0	0	C-667, OF-5, 3B-4, 1B-1

Joe Buskey

BUSKEY, JOSEPH HENRY (Jazzbow)
B. Dec. 18, 1902, Cumberland, Md.   D. Apr. 11, 1949, Cumberland, Md.   BR TR 5'10"   175 lbs.

	G	AB	H	2B	3B	HR	HR %	R	RBI	BB	SO	SB	BA	SA	AB	H	G by POS
1926 PHI N	5	8	0	0	0	0	0.0	1	0	1	1	0	.000	.000	0	0	SS-5

Mike Buskey

BUSKEY, MICHAEL THOMAS
B. Jan. 13, 1950, San Francisco, Calif.   BR TR 5'11"   160 lbs.

	G	AB	H	2B	3B	HR	HR %	R	RBI	BB	SO	SB	BA	SA	AB	H	G by POS
1977 PHI N	6	7	2	0	1	0	0.0	1	1	0	1	0	.286	.571	0	0	SS-6

	G	AB	H	2B	3B	HR	HR %	R	RBI	BB	SO	SB	BA	SA	Pinch Hit AB	Pinch Hit H	G by POS

Ray Busse

BUSSE, RAYMOND EDWARD
B. Sept. 25, 1948, Daytona Beach, Fla.
BR TR 6'4" 175 lbs.

	G	AB	H	2B	3B	HR	HR %	R	RBI	BB	SO	SB	BA	SA	PH AB	PH H	G by POS
1971 HOU N	10	34	5	3	0	0	0.0	2	4	2	9	0	.147	.235	2	0	SS-5, 3B-3
1973 2 teams	STL N (24G – .143)						HOU N (15G – .059)										
" total	39	87	11	4	2	2	2.3	7	5	6	33	0	.126	.287	6	0	SS-28, 3B-3
1974 HOU N	19	34	7	1	0	0	0.0	3	0	3	12	0	.206	.235	11	1	3B-8
3 yrs.	68	155	23	8	2	2	1.3	12	9	11	54	0	.148	.265	19	1	SS-33, 3B-14

Hank Butcher

BUTCHER, HENRY JOSEPH
B. July 12, 1886, Chicago, Ill.   D. Dec. 28, 1979, Hazel Crest, Ill.
BR TR 5'10" 180 lbs.

	G	AB	H	2B	3B	HR	HR %	R	RBI	BB	SO	SB	BA	SA	PH AB	PH H	G by POS
1911 CLE A	38	133	32	7	3	1	0.8	21	11	11		9	.241	.361	4	1	OF-34
1912	24	82	16	4	1	1	1.2	9	10	6		1	.195	.305	4	0	OF-20
2 yrs.	62	215	48	11	4	2	0.9	30	21	17		10	.223	.340	8	1	OF-54

Sal Butera

BUTERA, SALVATORE PHILIP
B. Sept. 25, 1952, Richmond Hill, N. Y.
BR TR 6' 190 lbs.

	G	AB	H	2B	3B	HR	HR %	R	RBI	BB	SO	SB	BA	SA	PH AB	PH H	G by POS
1980 MIN A	34	85	23	1	0	0	0.0	4	2	3	6	0	.271	.282	2	0	C-32, DH-2
1981	62	167	40	7	1	0	0.0	13	18	22	14	0	.240	.293	1	0	C-59, DH-1, 1B-1
1982	54	126	32	2	0	0	0.0	9	8	17	12	0	.254	.270	1	0	C-53
1983 DET A	4	5	1	0	0	0	0.0	1	0	0	0	0	.200	.200	0	0	C-4
1984 MON N	3	3	0	0	0	0	0.0	0	0	1	0	0	.000	.000	0	0	C-2
5 yrs.	157	386	96	10	1	0	0.0	27	28	43	32	0	.249	.280	4	0	C-150, DH-3, 1B-1

Ed Butka

BUTKA, EDWARD LUKE (Babe)
B. Jan. 7, 1916, Canonsburg, Pa.
BR TR 6'3" 193 lbs.

	G	AB	H	2B	3B	HR	HR %	R	RBI	BB	SO	SB	BA	SA	PH AB	PH H	G by POS
1943 WAS A	3	9	3	1	0	0	0.0	1		0	3	0	.333	.444	1	1	1B-3
1944	15	41	8	1	0	0	0.0	1	1	2	11	0	.195	.220	1	0	1B-14
2 yrs.	18	50	11	2	0	0	0.0	2	1	2	14	0	.220	.260	2	1	1B-17

Art Butler

BUTLER, ARTHUR EDWARD
Born Arthur Edward Bouthillier.
B. Dec. 19, 1887, Fall River, Mass.   D. Oct. 7, 1984, Fall River, Mass.
BR TR 5'9" 160 lbs.

	G	AB	H	2B	3B	HR	HR %	R	RBI	BB	SO	SB	BA	SA	PH AB	PH H	G by POS
1911 BOS N	27	68	12	2	0	0	0.0	11	2	6	6	0	.176	.206	7	1	3B-14, 2B-4, SS-1
1912 PIT N	43	154	42	4	2	1	0.6	19	17	15	11	2	.273	.344	0	0	2B-43
1913	82	214	60	9	3	0	0.0	40	20	32	14	9	.280	.350	18	6	2B-27, SS-24, OF-2, 3B-2
1914 STL N	86	274	55	12	3	1	0.4	29	24	39	23	14	.201	.277	2	0	SS-84, OF-1
1915	130	469	119	12	5	1	0.2	73	31	47	34	26	.254	.307	2	0	SS-130
1916	86	110	23	5	0	0	0.0	9	7	7	12	3	.209	.255	54	13	OF-15, 2B-8, SS-1, 3B-1
6 yrs.	454	1289	311	44	13	3	0.2	181	101	146	100	54	.241	.303	83	20	SS-240, 2B-82, OF-18, 3B-17

Bill Butler

BUTLER, W. J.
B. 1861, New Orleans, La.   Deceased.

	G	AB	H	2B	3B	HR	HR %	R	RBI	BB	SO	SB	BA	SA	PH AB	PH H	G by POS
1884 IND AA	9	31	7	3	2	0	0.0	7		1			.226	.452	0	0	OF-9

Brett Butler

BUTLER, BRETT MORGAN
B. June 15, 1959, Los Angeles, Calif.
BL TL 5'10" 160 lbs.

	G	AB	H	2B	3B	HR	HR %	R	RBI	BB	SO	SB	BA	SA	PH AB	PH H	G by POS
1981 ATL N	40	126	32	2	3	0	0.0	17	4	19	17	9	.254	.317	2	1	OF-37
1982	89	240	52	2	0	0	0.0	35	7	25	35	21	.217	.225	6	1	OF-77
1983	151	549	154	21	13	5	0.9	84	37	54	56	39	.281	.393	6	0	OF-143
1984 CLE A	159	602	162	25	9	3	0.5	108	49	86	62	52	.269	.355	3	0	OF-156
4 yrs.	439	1517	400	50	25	8	0.5	244	97	184	170	121	.264	.345	17	3	OF-413

LEAGUE CHAMPIONSHIP SERIES

	G	AB	H	2B	3B	HR	HR %	R	RBI	BB	SO	SB	BA	SA	PH AB	PH H	G by POS
1982 ATL N	2	1	0	0	0	0	0.0	0	0	0	0	0	.000	.000	1	0	OF-1

Dick Butler

BUTLER, RICHARD H.
B. Brooklyn, N. Y.   Deceased.

	G	AB	H	2B	3B	HR	HR %	R	RBI	BB	SO	SB	BA	SA	PH AB	PH H	G by POS
1897 LOU N	10	38	7	0	0	0	0.0	3	2	0		1	.184	.184	0	0	C-10
1899 WAS N	12	36	10	0	1	0	0.0	4	1	2		1	.278	.333	1	0	C-11
2 yrs.	22	74	17	0	1	0	0.0	7	3	2		2	.230	.257	1	0	C-21

Frank Butler

BUTLER, FRANK DEAN (Stuffy)
B. July 18, 1860, Savannah, Ga.   D. July 10, 1945, Jacksonville, Fla.
BL TL

	G	AB	H	2B	3B	HR	HR %	R	RBI	BB	SO	SB	BA	SA	PH AB	PH H	G by POS
1895 NY N	5	22	6	1	0	0	0.0	5	2	1	1	0	.273	.318	0	0	OF-5

Frank Butler

BUTLER, FRANK E. (Kid)
B. 1862, Boston, Mass.   D. Apr. 9, 1921, South Boston, Mass.

	G	AB	H	2B	3B	HR	HR %	R	RBI	BB	SO	SB	BA	SA	PH AB	PH H	G by POS
1884 BOS U	71	255	43	15	0	0	0.0	36		12			.169	.227	0	0	OF-53, 2B-12, SS-6, 3B-2

John Butler

BUTLER, JOHN ALBERT
Born John Albert Butler.   Played as Fred King, 1901
B. July 26, 1879, Boston, Mass.   D. Feb. 2, 1950, Boston, Mass.
BR TR 5'7" 170 lbs.

	G	AB	H	2B	3B	HR	HR %	R	RBI	BB	SO	SB	BA	SA	PH AB	PH H	G by POS
1901 MIL A	1	3	0	0	0	0	0.0	0	0	0		0	.000	.000	0	0	C-1
1904 STL N	12	37	6	1	0	0	0.0	0	1	4		0	.162	.189	0	0	C-12
1906 BKN N	1	0	0	0	0	0	–	0	0	0		0	–	–	0	0	C-1
1907	30	79	10	1	0	0	0.0	6	2	9		0	.127	.139	1	0	C-28, OF-1
4 yrs.	44	119	16	2	0	0	0.0	6	3	13		0	.134	.151	1	0	C-42, OF-1

Johnny Butler

BUTLER, JOHN STEPHEN (Trolley Line)
B. Mar. 20, 1894, Eureka, Kans.   D. Apr. 29, 1967, Long Beach, Calif.
BR TR 6' 175 lbs.

	G	AB	H	2B	3B	HR	HR %	R	RBI	BB	SO	SB	BA	SA	PH AB	PH H	G by POS
1926 BKN N	147	501	135	27	5	1	0.2	54	68	54	44	6	.269	.349	0	0	SS-102, 3B-42, 2B-8
1927	149	521	124	13	6	2	0.4	39	57	34	33	9	.238	.298	1	0	SS-90, 3B-60
1928 CHI N	62	174	47	7	0	0	0.0	17	16	19	7	2	.270	.310	1	0	3B-59, SS-2
1929 STL N	17	55	9	1	1	0	0.0	5	5	4	5	0	.164	.218	0	0	3B-9, SS-8
4 yrs.	375	1251	315	48	12	3	0.2	115	146	111	89	17	.252	.317	2	0	SS-202, 3B-170, 2B-8

	G	AB	H	2B	3B	HR	HR%	R	RBI	BB	SO	SB	BA	SA	Pinch Hit AB	Pinch Hit H	G by POS

Kid Butler

BUTLER, WILLIS EVERETT BR TR 5'11" 155 lbs.
B. Aug. 9, 1887, Franklin, Pa.   D. Feb. 22, 1964, Richmond, Calif.

	G	AB	H	2B	3B	HR	HR%	R	RBI	BB	SO	SB	BA	SA	PH AB	PH H	G by POS
1907 STL A	20	59	13	2	0	0	0.0	4	6	2		1	.220	.254	3	0	2B-11, 3B-5, SS-1

Joe Buzas

BUZAS, JOSEPH JOHN BR TR 6'1" 180 lbs.
B. Oct. 2, 1919, Alpha, N. J.

	G	AB	H	2B	3B	HR	HR%	R	RBI	BB	SO	SB	BA	SA	PH AB	PH H	G by POS
1945 NY A	30	65	17	2	1	0	0.0	8	6	2	5	2	.262	.323	16	3	SS-12

Bill Byers

BYERS, JAMES WILLIAM (Big Bill) TR
B. Oct. 3, 1877, Bridgetown, Ind.   D. Sept. 8, 1948, Baltimore, Md.

	G	AB	H	2B	3B	HR	HR%	R	RBI	BB	SO	SB	BA	SA	PH AB	PH H	G by POS
1904 STL N	19	60	13	0	0	0	0.0	3	4	1		0	.217	.217	2	1	C-16, 1B-1

Sammy Byrd

BYRD, SAMUEL DEWEY (Babe Ruth's Legs) BR TR 5'10½" 175 lbs.
B. Oct. 15, 1906, Bremen, Ga.   D. May 11, 1981, Mesa, Ariz.

	G	AB	H	2B	3B	HR	HR%	R	RBI	BB	SO	SB	BA	SA	PH AB	PH H	G by POS
1929 NY A	62	170	53	12	0	5	2.9	32	28	28	18	1	.312	.471	8	0	OF-54
1930	92	218	62	12	2	6	2.8	46	31	30	18	5	.284	.440	4	2	OF-85
1931	115	248	67	18	2	3	1.2	51	32	29	26	5	.270	.395	25	5	OF-88
1932	104	209	62	12	1	8	3.8	49	30	30	20	1	.297	.478	9	4	OF-90
1933	85	107	30	6	1	2	1.9	26	11	15	12	0	.280	.411	9	2	OF-71
1934	106	191	47	8	0	3	1.6	32	23	18	22	1	.246	.335	1	0	OF-104
1935 CIN N	121	416	109	25	4	9	2.2	51	52	37	51	4	.262	.406	6	4	OF-115
1936	59	141	35	8	0	2	1.4	17	13	11	11	0	.248	.348	19	4	OF-37
8 yrs.	744	1700	465	101	10	38	2.2	304	220	198	178	17	.274	.412	81	21	OF-644
WORLD SERIES																	
1932 NY A	1	0	0	0	0	0	–	0	0	0	0	0	–	–	0	0	OF-1

Bobby Byrne

BYRNE, ROBERT MATTHEW BR TR 5'7½" 145 lbs.
B. Dec. 31, 1884, St. Louis, Mo.   D. Dec. 31, 1964, Wayne, Pa.

	G	AB	H	2B	3B	HR	HR%	R	RBI	BB	SO	SB	BA	SA	PH AB	PH H	G by POS
1907 STL N	148	558	143	11	5	0	0.0	55	29	35		21	.256	.294	0	0	3B-148, SS-1
1908	127	439	84	7	1	0	0.0	27	14	23		16	.191	.212	1	0	3B-122, SS-4
1909 2 teams	151		STL	N	(105G –	.214)		PIT	N	(46G –	.256)						
" total	151	589	133	19	8	1	0.2	92	40	78		29	.226	.290	0	0	3B-151
1910 PIT N	148	602	178	43	12	2	0.3	101	52	66	27	36	.296	.417	0	0	3B-148
1911	153	598	155	24	17	2	0.3	96	52	67	41	23	.259	.366	1	0	3B-152
1912	130	528	152	31	11	3	0.6	99	35	54	40	20	.288	.405	0	0	3B-130
1913 2 teams	132		PIT	N	(113G –	.270)		PHI	N	(19G –	.224)						
" total	132	506	134	23	0	2	0.4	63	51	34	31	12	.265	.322	5	1	3B-125
1914 PHI N	126	467	127	12	1	0	0.0	61	26	45	44	9	.272	.302	4	2	2B-101, 3B-22
1915	105	387	81	6	4	0	0.0	50	21	39	28	4	.209	.245	0	0	3B-105
1916	48	141	33	10	1	0	0.0	22	9	14	7	6	.234	.319	6	1	3B-40
1917 2 teams	14		PHI	N	(13G –	.357)		CHI	A	(1G –	.000)						
" total	14	15	5	0	0	0	0.0	1	0	1	2	0	.333	.333	9	2	3B-4, 2B-1
11 yrs.	1282	4830	1225	186	60	10	0.2	667	329	456	220	176	.254	.323	26	6	3B-1147, 2B-102, SS-5
WORLD SERIES																	
1909 PIT N	7	24	6	1	0	0	0.0	5	0	1	4	1	.250	.292	0	0	3B-7
1915 PHI N	1	1	0	0	0	0	0.0	0	0	0	0	0	.000	.000	1	0	
2 yrs.	8	25	6	1	0	0	0.0	5	0	1	4	1	.240	.280	1	0	3B-7

Tommy Byrne

BYRNE, THOMAS JOSEPH BL TL 6'1" 182 lbs.
B. Dec. 31, 1919, Baltimore, Md.

	G	AB	H	2B	3B	HR	HR%	R	RBI	BB	SO	SB	BA	SA	PH AB	PH H	G by POS
1943 NY A	13	11	1	0	0	0	0.0	0	0	2	3	0	.091	.091	1	0	P-11
1946	14	9	2	0	0	0	0.0	2	0	1	0	0	.222	.222	6	1	P-4
1947	4	0	0	0	0	0	–	0	0	1	0	0	–	–	0	0	P-4
1948	31	46	15	3	1	1	2.2	8	7	1	7	0	.326	.500	0	0	P-31
1949	35	83	16	4	2	0	0.0	8	13	2	20	0	.193	.289	1	0	P-32
1950	34	81	22	3	1	2	2.5	14	16	4	15	1	.272	.407	1	0	P-31
1951 2 teams	43		NY	A	(9G –	.222)		STL	A	(34G –	.281)						
" total	43	66	18	3	0	2	3.0	9	15	4	10	0	.273	.409	13	2	P-28
1952 STL A	40	84	21	5	1	1	1.2	9	12	5	18	0	.250	.369	9	0	P-29
1953 2 teams	32		CHI	A	(18G –	.167)		WAS	A	(14G –	.059)						
" total	32	35	4	0	1	1	2.9	5	5	5	13	0	.114	.200	18	1	P-12
1954 NY A	7	19	7	4	1	0	0.0	2	6	0	3	0	.368	.684	2	0	P-5
1955	45	78	16	1	1	1	1.3	6	6	8	15	0	.205	.282	14	0	P-27
1956	44	52	14	1	1	3	5.8	8	10	2	11	0	.269	.500	8	0	P-37
1957	35	37	7	2	0	3	8.1	5	8	3	11	0	.189	.486	7	2	P-30
13 yrs.	377	601	143	26	8	14	2.3	73	98	38	126	1	.238	.378	80	6	P-281
WORLD SERIES																	
1949 NY A	1	1	1	0	0	0	0.0	0	0	0	0	0	1.000	1.000	0	0	P-1
1955	3	6	1	0	0	0	0.0	0	2	0	2	0	.167	.167	1	0	P-2
1956	2	1	0	0	0	0	0.0	0	0	0	0	0	.000	.000	1	0	P-1
1957	2	2	1	0	0	0	0.0	0	0	0	1	0	.500	.500	0	0	P-2
4 yrs.	8	10	3	0	0	0	0.0	0	2	0	3	0	.300	.300	2	0	P-6

Jim Byrnes

BYRNES, JAMES JOSEPH BR TR
B. Jan. 5, 1880, San Francisco, Calif.   D. July 31, 1941, San Francisco, Calif.

	G	AB	H	2B	3B	HR	HR%	R	RBI	BB	SO	SB	BA	SA	PH AB	PH H	G by POS
1906 PHI A	9	23	4	0	0	0	0.0	2	0	0		0	.174	.261	1	0	C-8

Milt Byrnes

BYRNES, MILTON JOHN (Skippy) BL TL 5'10½" 170 lbs.
B. Nov. 15, 1916, St. Louis, Mo.   D. Feb. 1, 1979, St. Louis, Mo.

	G	AB	H	2B	3B	HR	HR%	R	RBI	BB	SO	SB	BA	SA	PH AB	PH H	G by POS
1943 STL A	129	429	120	28	7	4	0.9	58	50	54	49	1	.280	.406	14	1	OF-114
1944	128	407	120	20	4	4	1.0	63	45	68	50	1	.295	.393	5	3	OF-122
1945	133	442	110	29	4	8	1.8	53	59	78	84	1	.249	.387	7	2	OF-125, 1B-2
3 yrs.	390	1278	350	77	15	16	1.3	174	154	200	183	3	.274	.395	26	6	OF-361, 1B-2
WORLD SERIES																	
1944 STL A	3	2	0	0	0	0	0.0	0	0	1	2	0	.000	.000	2	0	

	G	AB	H	2B	3B	HR	HR %	R	RBI	BB	SO	SB	BA	SA	Pinch Hit AB	Pinch Hit H	G by POS

Putsy Caballero
CABALLERO, RALPH JOSEPH
B. Nov. 5, 1927, New Orleans, La.
BR TR 5'10" 170 lbs.

	G	AB	H	2B	3B	HR	HR %	R	RBI	BB	SO	SB	BA	SA	AB	H	G by POS
1944 PHI N	4	4	0	0	0	0	0.0	0	0	0	1	0	.000	.000	0	0	3B-2
1945	9	1	0	0	0	0	0.0	1	1	0	0	0	.000	.000	0	0	3B-5
1947	2	7	1	0	0	0	0.0	2	0	1	0	0	.143	.143	0	0	2B-2, 3B-1
1948	113	351	86	12	1	0	0.0	33	19	24	18	7	.245	.285	11	3	3B-79, 2B-23
1949	29	68	19	3	0	0	0.0	8	3	0	3	0	.279	.324	4	1	2B-21, SS-1
1950	46	24	4	0	0	0	0.0	12	0	2	2	1	.167	.167	5	2	2B-5, 3B-4, SS-2
1951	84	161	30	3	2	1	0.6	15	11	12	7	1	.186	.248	3	0	2B-57, SS-3, 3B-3
1952	35	42	10	3	0	0	0.0	10	6	2	3	1	.238	.310	1	1	SS-8, 3B-7, 2B-7
8 yrs.	322	658	150	21	3	1	0.2	81	40	41	34	10	.228	.274	24	7	2B-115, 3B-101, SS-14
WORLD SERIES																	
1950 PHI N	3	1	0	0	0	0	0.0	0	0	0	1	0	.000	.000	1	0	

Enos Cabell
CABELL, ENOS MILTON
B. Oct. 8, 1949, Fort Riley, Kans.
BR TR 6'4" 170 lbs.

	G	AB	H	2B	3B	HR	HR %	R	RBI	BB	SO	SB	BA	SA	AB	H	G by POS
1972 BAL A	3	5	0	0	0	0	0.0	0	1	0	0	0	.000	.000	1	0	1B-1
1973	32	47	10	2	0	1	2.1	12	3	3	7	1	.213	.319	4	1	1B-23, 3B-1
1974	80	174	42	4	2	3	1.7	24	17	7	20	5	.241	.339	4	0	1B-28, OF-22, 3B-19, 2B-1
1975 HOU N	117	348	92	17	6	2	0.6	43	43	18	53	12	.264	.365	17	7	OF-67, 1B-25, 3B-22
1976	144	586	160	13	7	2	0.3	85	43	29	79	35	.273	.329	1	0	3B-143, 1B-3
1977	150	625	176	36	7	16	2.6	101	68	27	55	42	.282	.438	3	0	3B-144, 1B-8, SS-1
1978	162	660	195	31	8	7	1.1	92	71	22	80	33	.295	.398	0	0	3B-153, 1B-14, SS-1
1979	155	603	164	30	5	6	1.0	60	67	21	68	37	.272	.368	0	0	3B-132, 1B-51
1980	152	604	167	23	8	2	0.3	69	55	26	84	21	.276	.351	1	1	3B-150, 1B-1
1981 SF N	96	396	101	20	1	2	0.5	41	36	10	47	6	.255	.326	6	1	1B-69, 3B-22
1982 DET A	125	464	121	17	3	2	0.4	45	37	15	48	15	.261	.323	10	2	1B-83, 3B-59, OF-3
1983	121	392	122	23	5	5	1.3	62	46	16	41	4	.311	.434	11	4	1B-106, DH-8, 3B-4, SS-1
1984 HOU N	127	436	135	17	3	8	1.8	52	44	21	47	8	.310	.417	17	5	1B-112
13 yrs.	1464	5340	1485	233	55	56	1.0	686	531	215	629	219	.278	.374	75	21	3B-849, 1B-524, OF-92, DH-8, SS-3, 2B-1
LEAGUE CHAMPIONSHIP SERIES																	
1974 BAL A	3	4	1	0	0	0	0.0	0	0	0	2	0	.250	.250	1	0	OF-1
1980 HOU N	5	21	5	1	0	0	0.0	1	0	1	3	0	.238	.286	0	0	3B-5
2 yrs.	8	25	6	1	0	0	0.0	1	0	1	5	0	.240	.280	1	0	3B-5, OF-1

Al Cabrera
CABRERA, ALFREDO A.
B. 1883, Canary Islands   D. Havana, Cuba
TR

	G	AB	H	2B	3B	HR	HR %	R	RBI	BB	SO	SB	BA	SA	AB	H	G by POS
1913 STL N	1	2	0	0	0	0	0.0	0	0	0	0	0	.000	.000	0	0	SS-1

Craig Cacek
CACEK, CRAIG THOMAS
B. Aug. 10, 1954, Hollywood, Calif.
BR TR 6'1" 200 lbs.

	G	AB	H	2B	3B	HR	HR %	R	RBI	BB	SO	SB	BA	SA	AB	H	G by POS
1977 HOU N	7	20	1	0	0	0	0.0	0	1	1	3	0	.050	.050	2	0	1B-6

Charlie Cady
CADY, CHARLES B.
B. Dec., 1865, Chicago, Ill.   D. June 9, 1909, Kankakee, Ill.

	G	AB	H	2B	3B	HR	HR %	R	RBI	BB	SO	SB	BA	SA	AB	H	G by POS
1883 CLE N	3	11	0	0	0	0	0.0	0		1	5		.000	.000	0	0	OF-2, P-1
1884 2 teams	C-P	U (6G – .100)			KC	U (2G – .000)											
" total	8	23	2	1	1	0	0.0	4		1			.087	.217	0	0	P-4, OF-2, 2B-1, C-1
2 yrs.	11	34	2	1	1	0	0.0	4		2	5		.059	.147	0	0	P-5, OF-4, 2B-1, C-1

Hick Cady
CADY, FORREST LeROY
B. Jan. 26, 1886, Bishop Hill, Ill.   D. Mar. 3, 1946, Cedar Rapids, Iowa
BR TR 6'2" 179 lbs.

	G	AB	H	2B	3B	HR	HR %	R	RBI	BB	SO	SB	BA	SA	AB	H	G by POS
1912 BOS A	47	135	35	13	2	0	0.0	19	9	10		0	.259	.385	0	0	C-43, 1B-4
1913	39	96	24	5	2	0	0.0	10	6	5	14	1	.250	.344	1	0	C-38
1914	61	159	41	6	1	0	0.0	14	8	12	22	2	.258	.308	3	0	C-58
1915	78	205	57	10	2	0	0.0	25	17	19	25	0	.278	.346	1	0	C-77
1916	78	162	31	6	3	0	0.0	5	13	15	16	0	.191	.265	12	4	C-63, 1B-3
1917	17	46	7	1	1	0	0.0	4	2	1	6	0	.152	.217	3	1	C-14
1918 CLE A	1	0	0	0	0	0	–	0	–	1	0	0	–	–	0	0	
1919 PHI N	34	98	21	6	0	1	1.0	6	19	4	8	1	.214	.306	5	2	C-29
8 yrs.	355	901	216	47	11	1	0.1	83	74	67	91	4	.240	.320	25	7	C-322, 1B-7
WORLD SERIES																	
1912 BOS A	7	22	3	0	0	0	0.0	1	1	0	3	0	.136	.136	0	0	C-7
1915	4	6	2	0	0	0	0.0	0	0	1	2	0	.333	.333	0	0	C-4
1916	2	4	1	0	0	0	0.0	1	0	3	0	0	.250	.250	0	0	C-2
3 yrs.	13	32	6	0	0	0	0.0	2	1	4	5	0	.188	.188	0	0	C-13

Tom Cafego
CAFEGO, THOMAS
B. Aug. 21, 1911, Whipple, W. Va.   D. Oct. 29, 1961, Detroit, Mich.
BL TR 5'10" 160 lbs.

	G	AB	H	2B	3B	HR	HR %	R	RBI	BB	SO	SB	BA	SA	AB	H	G by POS
1937 STL A	4	4	0	0	0	0	0.0	1	0	0	1	0	.000	.000	1	0	OF-1

Joe Caffie
CAFFIE, JOSEPH CLIFFORD (Rabbit)
B. Feb. 14, 1931, Ramer, Ala.
BL TR 5'10½" 180 lbs.

	G	AB	H	2B	3B	HR	HR %	R	RBI	BB	SO	SB	BA	SA	AB	H	G by POS
1956 CLE A	12	38	13	0	0	0	0.0	7	1	4	8	3	.342	.342	1	1	OF-10
1957	32	89	24	2	1	3	3.4	14	10	4	11	0	.270	.416	9	0	OF-19
2 yrs.	44	127	37	2	1	3	2.4	21	11	8	19	3	.291	.394	10	1	OF-29

Ben Caffyn
CAFFYN, BENJAMIN THOMAS
B. Feb. 10, 1880, Peoria, Ill.   D. Nov. 22, 1942, Peoria, Ill.

	G	AB	H	2B	3B	HR	HR %	R	RBI	BB	SO	SB	BA	SA	AB	H	G by POS
1906 CLE A	30	103	20	4	0	0	0.0	16	3	12		2	.194	.233	1	0	OF-29

	G	AB	H	2B	3B	HR	HR %	R	RBI	BB	SO	SB	BA	SA	Pinch Hit AB	Pinch Hit H	G by POS

Wayne Cage

CAGE, WAYNE LEVELL   BL TL 6'4"   205 lbs.
B. Nov. 23, 1951, Jonesboro, La.

	G	AB	H	2B	3B	HR	HR %	R	RBI	BB	SO	SB	BA	SA	PH AB	PH H	G by POS
1978 CLE A	36	98	24	6	1	4	4.1	11	13	9	28	1	.245	.449	6	0	DH-20, 1B-11
1979	29	56	13	2	0	1	1.8	6	6	5	16	0	.232	.321	12	1	DH-9, 1B-7
2 yrs.	65	154	37	8	1	5	3.2	17	19	14	44	1	.240	.403	18	1	DH-29, 1B-18

John Cahill

CAHILL, JOHN FRANCIS PATRICK (Patsy)   BR
B. Philadelphia, Pa.   D. Nov. 1, 1901, Pleasanton, Calif.

	G	AB	H	2B	3B	HR	HR %	R	RBI	BB	SO	SB	BA	SA	PH AB	PH H	G by POS
1884 COL AA	59	210	46	3	3	0	0.0	28		6				.219	.262	0	0	OF-56, SS-5
1886 STL N	125	463	92	17	6	1	0.2	43	32	9	79			.199	.268	0	0	OF-124, P-2, SS-1, 3B-1
1887 IND N	68	263	54	4	3	0	0.0	22	26	9	5	34	.205	.243	0	0	OF-56, 3B-9, P-6, SS-1
3 yrs.	252	936	192	24	12	1	0.1	93	57	24	84	34	.205	.260	0	0	OF-236, 3B-10, P-8, SS-7

Tom Cahill

CAHILL, THOMAS H.
B. Oct., 1868, Fall River, Mass.   D. Dec. 25, 1894, Scranton, Pa.

	G	AB	H	2B	3B	HR	HR %	R	RBI	BB	SO	SB	BA	SA	PH AB	PH H	G by POS
1891 LOU AA	120	433	111	18	7	3	0.7	70	47	41	51	39	.256	.351	0	0	C-56, SS-49, OF-12, 2B-6, 3B-2

George Caithamer

CAITHAMER, GEORGE THEODORE   BR TR 5'7½"   160 lbs.
B. July 22, 1910, Chicago, Ill.   D. June 1, 1954, Chicago, Ill.

	G	AB	H	2B	3B	HR	HR %	R	RBI	BB	SO	SB	BA	SA	PH AB	PH H	G by POS
1934 CHI A	5	19	6	1	0	0	0.0	1	3	1	5	0	.316	.368	0	0	C-5

Ivan Calderon

CALDERON, IVAN   BR TR 5'11"   160 lbs.
B. Mar. 19, 1962, Fajardo Puerto Rico

	G	AB	H	2B	3B	HR	HR %	R	RBI	BB	SO	SB	BA	SA	PH AB	PH H	G by POS
1984 SEA A	11	24	5	1	0	1	4.2	2	1	2	5	1	.208	.375	0	0	OF-11

Sammy Calderone

CALDERONE, SAMUEL FRANCIS   BR TR 5'10½"   185 lbs.
B. Feb. 6, 1926, Beverly, N. J.

	G	AB	H	2B	3B	HR	HR %	R	RBI	BB	SO	SB	BA	SA	PH AB	PH H	G by POS
1950 NY N	34	67	20	1	0	1	1.5	9	12	5	2	0	.299	.358	1	0	C-33
1953	35	45	10	2	0	0	0.0	4	8	1	4	0	.222	.267	6	0	C-31
1954 MIL N	22	29	11	2	0	0	0.0	3	5	4	4	0	.379	.448	7	2	C-16
3 yrs.	91	141	41	5	0	1	0.7	16	25	7	13	0	.291	.348	14	2	C-80

Bruce Caldwell

CALDWELL, BRUCE   BR TR 6'   195 lbs.
B. Feb. 8, 1906, Ashton, R. I.   D. Feb. 15, 1959, New Haven, Conn.

	G	AB	H	2B	3B	HR	HR %	R	RBI	BB	SO	SB	BA	SA	PH AB	PH H	G by POS
1928 CLE A	18	27	6	1	1	0	0.0	2	3	2	2	1	.222	.333	7	0	OF-10, 1B-1
1932 BKN N	7	11	1	0	0	0	0.0	2	2	2	2	0	.091	.091	1	1	1B-6
2 yrs.	25	38	7	1	1	0	0.0	4	5	4	4	1	.184	.263	8	1	OF-10, 1B-7

Ray Caldwell

CALDWELL, RAYMOND BENJAMIN (Slim)   BL TR 6'2"   190 lbs.
B. Apr. 26, 1888, Corydon, Pa.   D. Aug. 17, 1967, Salamanca, N. Y.

	G	AB	H	2B	3B	HR	HR %	R	RBI	BB	SO	SB	BA	SA	PH AB	PH H	G by POS
1910 NY A	6	6	0	0	0	0	0.0	0	0	0		0	.000	.000	0	0	P-6
1911	58	147	40	4	1	0	0.0	14	17	11	0	5	.272	.313	4	1	P-41, OF-11
1912	41	76	18	1	2	0	0.0	18	6	5		4	.237	.303	7	2	P-30
1913	55	97	28	3	2	0	0.0	10	11	3	15	3	.289	.361	19	4	P-27, OF-3
1914	59	113	22	4	0	0	0.0	9	10	7	24	2	.195	.230	21	4	P-31, 1B-6
1915	72	144	35	4	1	4	2.8	27	20	9	32	4	.243	.368	33	9	P-36
1916	45	93	19	2	0	0	0.0	6	4	2	17	1	.204	.226	19	3	P-21, OF-3
1917	63	124	32	6	1	2	1.6	12	12	16	16	2	.258	.371	15	5	P-32, OF-8
1918	65	151	44	10	0	1	0.7	14	18	13	23	2	.291	.377	19	6	P-24, OF-19
1919 2 teams		BOS	A (33G – .271)		CLE	A (6G – .348)											
" total	39	71	21	5	1	0	0.0	9	6	0	13	0	.296	.394	12	2	P-24, OF-2
1920 CLE A	41	89	19	3	0	0	0.0	17	7	10	13	0	.213	.247	4	0	P-34
1921	38	53	11	4	0	1	1.9	2	3	2	5	0	.208	.340	1	0	P-37
12 yrs.	582	1164	289	46	8	8	0.7	138	114	78	158	23	.248	.322	154	36	P-343, OF-46, 1B-6

WORLD SERIES

	G	AB	H	2B	3B	HR	HR %	R	RBI	BB	SO	SB	BA	SA	PH AB	PH H	G by POS
1920 CLE A	1	0	0	0	0	0	–	0	0	0	0	0	–	–	0	0	P-1

Bill Calhoun

CALHOUN, WILLIAM DAVITTE (Mary)   BL TL 6'   180 lbs.
B. June 23, 1890, Rockmart, Ga.   D. Feb. 11, 1955, Sandersville, Ga.

	G	AB	H	2B	3B	HR	HR %	R	RBI	BB	SO	SB	BA	SA	PH AB	PH H	G by POS
1913 BOS N	6	13	1	0	0	0	0.0	0	0		3	0	.077	.077	3	1	1B-3

John Calhoun

CALHOUN, JOHN CHARLES (Red)   BR TR 6'   185 lbs.
B. Dec. 14, 1879, Pittsburgh, Pa.   D. Feb. 27, 1947, Cincinnati, Ohio

	G	AB	H	2B	3B	HR	HR %	R	RBI	BB	SO	SB	BA	SA	PH AB	PH H	G by POS
1902 STL N	20	64	10	2	1	0	0.0	8	8	1		1	.156	.219	2	0	3B-12, 1B-5, OF-1

Marty Callaghan

CALLAGHAN, MARTIN FRANCIS   BL TL 5'10"   157 lbs.
B. June 9, 1900, Norwood, Mass.   D. June 23, 1975, Norwood, Kans.

	G	AB	H	2B	3B	HR	HR %	R	RBI	BB	SO	SB	BA	SA	PH AB	PH H	G by POS
1922 CHI N	74	175	45	7	4	0	0.0	31	20	17	17	2	.257	.343	17	3	OF-53
1923	61	129	29	1	3	0	0.0	18	14	8	18	2	.225	.279	16	3	OF-38
1928 CIN N	81	238	69	11	4	0	0.0	29	24	27	10	5	.290	.370	7	1	OF-69
1930	79	225	62	9	2	0	0.0	28	16	19	25	1	.276	.333	23	3	OF-54
4 yrs.	295	767	205	28	13	0	0.0	106	74	71	70	10	.267	.338	63	10	OF-214

Dave Callahan

CALLAHAN, DAVID JOSEPH   BL TR 5'10"   165 lbs.
B. July 20, 1888, Seneca, Ill.   D. Oct. 28, 1969, Ottawa, Ill.

	G	AB	H	2B	3B	HR	HR %	R	RBI	BB	SO	SB	BA	SA	PH AB	PH H	G by POS
1910 CLE A	13	44	8	1	0	0	0.0	6	2	4		5	.182	.205	1	0	OF-12
1911	5	12	4	0	1	0	0.0	1	0	1		0	.333	.500	2	1	OF-3
2 yrs.	18	56	12	1	1	0	0.0	7	2	5		5	.214	.268	3	1	OF-15

Ed Callahan

CALLAHAN, EDWARD J.
B. Boston, Mass.   Deceased.

	G	AB	H	2B	3B	HR	HR %	R	RBI	BB	SO	SB	BA	SA	PH AB	PH H	G by POS
1884 3 teams		STL	U (1G – .000)		KC	U (3G – .364)			BOS	U (4G – .385)							
" total	8	27	9	0	0	0	0.0	2		1			.333	.333	0	0	OF-5, SS-3

	G	AB	H	2B	3B	HR	HR %	R	RBI	BB	SO	SB	BA	SA	Pinch Hit AB	Pinch Hit H	G by POS

Jim Callahan

CALLAHAN, JAMES J.
B. Marlboro, Mass.

	G	AB	H	2B	3B	HR	HR%	R	RBI	BB	SO	SB	BA	SA	AB	H	G by POS
1902 NY N	1	4	0	0	0	0	0.0	0	0		1	0	.000	.000	0	0	OF-1

Leo Callahan

CALLAHAN, LEO DAVID   BL TL 5'8" 142 lbs.
B. Aug. 9, 1890, Jamaica Plain, Mass.   D. May 2, 1982, Erie, Pa.

	G	AB	H	2B	3B	HR	HR%	R	RBI	BB	SO	SB	BA	SA	AB	H	G by POS
1913 BKN N	33	41	7	3	1	0	0.0	6	3	4	5	0	.171	.293	24	5	OF-8
1919 PHI N	81	235	54	14	4	1	0.4	26	9	29	19	5	.230	.336	21	3	OF-58
2 yrs.	114	276	61	17	5	1	0.4	32	12	33	24	5	.221	.330	45	8	OF-66

Nixey Callahan

CALLAHAN, JAMES JOSEPH   BR TR 5'10½" 180 lbs.
B. Mar. 18, 1874, Fitchburg, Mass.   D. Oct. 4, 1934, Boston, Mass.
Manager 1903-04, 1912-14, 1916-17.

	G	AB	H	2B	3B	HR	HR%	R	RBI	BB	SO	SB	BA	SA	AB	H	G by POS
1894 PHI N	9	21	5	0	0	0	0.0	4	0	0	7	0	.238	.238	0	0	P-9
1897 CHI N	94	360	105	18	6	3	0.8	60	47	10		12	.292	.400	2	0	2B-30, P-23, OF-21, SS-18, 3B-2
1898	43	164	43	7	5	0	0.0	27	22	4		3	.262	.366	0	0	P-31, OF-9, SS-1, 2B-1, 1B-1
1899	47	150	39	4	3	0	0.0	21	18	8		9	.260	.327	1	0	P-35, OF-9, SS-2, 2B-1
1900	32	115	27	3	2	0	0.0	16	9	6		5	.235	.296	0	0	P-32
1901 CHI A	45	118	39	7	3	1	0.8	15	19	10		10	.331	.466	10	3	P-27, 3B-6, 2B-2
1902	70	218	51	7	2	0	0.0	27	13	6		4	.234	.284	12	2	P-35, OF-23, SS-1
1903	118	439	128	26	5	2	0.5	47	56	20		24	.292	.387	5	3	3B-102, OF-8, P-3
1904	132	482	126	23	2	0	0.0	66	54	39		29	.261	.317	1	0	OF-104, 2B-28
1905	96	345	94	18	6	1	0.3	50	43	29		26	.272	.368	3	1	OF-93
1911	120	466	131	13	5	3	0.6	64	60	15		45	.281	.350	5	1	OF-114
1912	111	408	111	9	7	1	0.2	45	52	12		19	.272	.336	4	1	OF-107
1913	6	9	2	0	0	0	0.0	0	1	0	2	0	.222	.222	5	1	OF-1
13 yrs.	923	3295	901	135	46	11	0.3	442	394	159	9	186	.273	.352	48	12	OF-489, P-195, 3B-110, 2B-62, SS-22, 1B-1

Pat Callahan

CALLAHAN, PATRICK HENRY
B. Oct. 15, 1866, Cleveland, Ohio   D. Feb. 4, 1940, Louisville, Ky.

	G	AB	H	2B	3B	HR	HR%	R	RBI	BB	SO	SB	BA	SA	AB	H	G by POS
1884 IND AA	61	258	67	8	5	2	0.8	38		8			.260	.353	0	0	3B-61

Wes Callahan

CALLAHAN, WESLEY LeROY   BR TR 5'7½" 155 lbs.
B. July 3, 1888, Lyons, Ind.   D. Sept. 13, 1953, Dayton, Ohio

	G	AB	H	2B	3B	HR	HR%	R	RBI	BB	SO	SB	BA	SA	AB	H	G by POS
1913 STL N	7	14	4	0	0	0	0.0	0	1	2	2	1	.286	.286	1	0	SS-6

Frank Callaway

CALLAWAY, FRANK BURNETT   BR TR 6' 170 lbs.
B. Feb. 26, 1898, Knoxville, Tenn.

	G	AB	H	2B	3B	HR	HR%	R	RBI	BB	SO	SB	BA	SA	AB	H	G by POS
1921 PHI A	14	50	12	1	1	0	0.0	7	2	2	11	1	.240	.300	0	0	SS-14
1922	29	48	13	0	2	0	0.0	5	4	0	13	0	.271	.354	4	1	2B-11, 3B-5, SS-4
2 yrs.	43	98	25	1	3	0	0.0	12	6	2	24	1	.255	.327	4	0	SS-18, 2B-11, 3B-5

Johnny Callison

CALLISON, JOHN WESLEY   BL TR 5'10" 175 lbs.
B. Mar. 12, 1939, Qualls, Okla.

	G	AB	H	2B	3B	HR	HR%	R	RBI	BB	SO	SB	BA	SA	AB	H	G by POS
1958 CHI A	18	64	19	4	2	1	1.6	10	12	6	14	1	.297	.469	0	0	OF-18
1959	49	104	18	3	0	3	2.9	12	12	13	20	0	.173	.288	4	0	OF-41
1960 PHI N	99	288	75	11	5	9	3.1	36	30	45	70	0	.260	.427	15	3	OF-86
1961	138	455	121	20	11	9	2.0	74	47	69	76	10	.266	.418	14	3	OF-124
1962	157	603	181	26	10	23	3.8	107	83	54	96	10	.300	.491	9	4	OF-152
1963	157	626	178	36	11	26	4.2	96	78	50	111	8	.284	.502	2	0	OF-157
1964	162	654	179	30	10	31	4.7	101	104	36	95	6	.274	.492	2	1	OF-162
1965	160	619	162	25	16	32	5.2	93	101	57	117	6	.262	.509	6	0	OF-159
1966	155	612	169	40	7	11	1.8	93	55	56	83	8	.276	.418	3	1	OF-154
1967	149	556	145	30	5	14	2.5	62	64	55	63	6	.261	.408	3	0	OF-147
1968	121	398	97	18	4	14	3.5	46	40	42	70	4	.244	.415	11	3	OF-109
1969	134	495	131	29	5	16	3.2	66	64	49	73	2	.265	.440	4	2	OF-129
1970 CHI N	147	477	126	23	2	19	4.0	65	68	60	63	7	.264	.440	3	1	OF-144
1971	103	290	61	12	1	8	2.8	27	38	36	55	2	.210	.341	14	1	OF-89
1972 NY A	92	275	71	10	0	9	3.3	28	34	18	34	3	.258	.393	19	4	OF-74
1973	45	136	24	4	0	1	0.7	10	10	4	21	1	.176	.228	5	2	OF-32, DH-10
16 yrs.	1886	6652	1757	321	89	226	3.4	926	840	650	1064	74	.264	.441	116	24	OF-1777, DH-10

Jack Calvo

CALVO, JACINTO   BL TL 5'10" 156 lbs.
B. June 11, 1894, Havana, Cuba   D. June 15, 1965, Miami, Fla.

	G	AB	H	2B	3B	HR	HR%	R	RBI	BB	SO	SB	BA	SA	AB	H	G by POS
1913 WAS A	16	33	8	0	0	1	3.0	5	2	1	4	0	.242	.333	2	0	OF-12
1920	17	23	1	0	1	0	0.0	5	2	2	2	0	.043	.130	7	1	OF-10
2 yrs.	33	56	9	0	1	1	1.8	10	4	3	6	0	.161	.250	9	1	OF-22

Hank Camelli

CAMELLI, HENRY RICHARD   BR TR 5'11" 190 lbs.
B. Dec. 9, 1914, Gloucester, Mass.

	G	AB	H	2B	3B	HR	HR%	R	RBI	BB	SO	SB	BA	SA	AB	H	G by POS
1943 PIT N	1	3	0	0	0	0	0.0	1	0	1	0	0	.000	.000	0	0	C-1
1944	63	125	37	5	1	1	0.8	14	10	18	12	0	.296	.376	1	1	C-61
1945	1	2	0	0	0	0	0.0	0	0	1	0	0	.000	.000	0	0	C-1
1946	42	96	20	2	2	0	0.0	8	5	8	9	0	.208	.271	2	0	C-34
1947 BOS N	52	150	29	8	1	1	0.7	10	11	18	18	0	.193	.280	1	1	C-51
5 yrs.	159	376	86	15	4	2	0.5	33	26	46	39	0	.229	.306	4	2	C-148

John Cameron

CAMERON, JOHN S. (Happy Jack)
B. Aug. 1, 1879, Truro, Nova Scotia, Canada   D. June 15, 1964, West Roxbury, Mass.

	G	AB	H	2B	3B	HR	HR%	R	RBI	BB	SO	SB	BA	SA	AB	H	G by POS
1906 BOS N	18	61	11	0	0	0	0.0	3	4	2		0	.180	.180	0	0	OF-16, P-2

	G	AB	H	2B	3B	HR	HR%	R	RBI	BB	SO	SB	BA	SA	Pinch Hit AB	Pinch Hit H	G by POS

Dolf Camilli

CAMILLI, ADOLF LOUIS
Father of Doug Camilli.
B. Apr. 23, 1907, San Francisco, Calif.
BL TL 5'10" 185 lbs.

	G	AB	H	2B	3B	HR	HR%	R	RBI	BB	SO	SB	BA	SA	PH AB	PH H	G by POS
1933 CHI N	16	58	13	2	1	2	3.4	8	7	4	11	3	.224	.397	0	0	1B-16
1934 2 teams	CHI N (32G – .275)					PHI N (102G – .265)											
" total	134	498	133	28	3	16	3.2	69	87	53	94	4	.267	.432	0	0	1B-134
1935 PHI N	156	602	157	23	5	25	4.2	88	83	65	113	9	.261	.440	0	0	1B-156
1936	151	530	167	29	13	28	5.3	106	102	116	84	5	.315	.577	1	1	1B-150
1937	131	475	161	23	7	27	5.7	101	80	90	82	6	.339	.587	0	0	1B-131
1938 BKN N	146	509	128	25	11	24	4.7	106	100	119	101	6	.251	.485	0	0	1B-145
1939	157	565	164	30	12	26	4.6	105	104	110	107	1	.290	.524	0	0	1B-157
1940	142	512	147	29	13	23	4.5	92	96	89	83	9	.287	.529	1	0	1B-140
1941	149	529	151	29	4	34	6.4	92	120	104	115	3	.285	.556	1	0	1B-148
1942	150	524	132	23	7	26	5.0	89	109	97	85	10	.252	.471	0	0	1B-150
1943	95	353	87	15	6	6	1.7	56	43	65	48	2	.246	.374	0	0	1B-95
1945 BOS A	63	198	42	5	2	2	1.0	24	19	35	38	2	.212	.288	8	1	1B-54
12 yrs.	1490	5353	1482	261	86	239	4.5	936	950	947	961	60	.277	.492	11	2	1B-1476

WORLD SERIES

	G	AB	H	2B	3B	HR	HR%	R	RBI	BB	SO	SB	BA	SA	PH AB	PH H	G by POS
1941 BKN N	5	18	3	1	0	0	0.0	1	1	1	6	0	.167	.222	0	0	1B-5

Doug Camilli

CAMILLI, DOUGLASS JOSEPH
Son of Dolf Camilli.
B. Sept. 22, 1936, Philadelphia, Pa.
BR TR 5'11" 195 lbs.

	G	AB	H	2B	3B	HR	HR%	R	RBI	BB	SO	SB	BA	SA	PH AB	PH H	G by POS
1960 LA N	6	24	8	2	0	1	4.2	4	3	1	4	0	.333	.542	1	0	C-6
1961	13	30	4	0	0	3	10.0	3	4	1	9	0	.133	.433	4	0	C-12
1962	45	88	25	5	2	4	4.5	16	22	12	21	0	.284	.523	6	3	C-39
1963	49	117	19	1	1	3	2.6	9	10	11	22	0	.162	.265	3	1	C-47
1964	50	123	22	3	0	0	0.0	1	10	8	19	0	.179	.203	3	0	C-46
1965 WAS A	75	193	37	6	1	3	1.6	13	18	16	34	0	.192	.280	14	2	C-59
1966	44	107	22	4	0	2	1.9	5	8	3	19	0	.206	.299	3	1	C-39
1967	30	82	15	1	0	2	2.4	5	5	4	16	0	.183	.268	6	2	C-24
1969	1	3	1	0	0	0	0.0	0	0	0	2	0	.333	.333	0	0	C-1
9 yrs.	313	767	153	22	4	18	2.3	56	80	56	146	0	.199	.309	40	9	C-273

Lou Camilli

CAMILLI, LOUIS STEVEN
B. Sept. 24, 1946, El Paso, Tex.
BB TR 5'10" 170 lbs.

	G	AB	H	2B	3B	HR	HR%	R	RBI	BB	SO	SB	BA	SA	PH AB	PH H	G by POS
1969 CLE A	13	14	0	0	0	0	0.0	0	0	0	3	0	.000	.000	0	0	3B-13
1970	16	15	0	0	0	0	0.0	0	0	2	2	0	.000	.000	12	0	SS-3, 2B-1, 3B-1
1971	39	81	16	2	0	0	0.0	5	0	8	10	0	.198	.222	4	0	SS-23, 2B-16
1972	39	41	6	2	0	0	0.0	2	3	3	8	0	.146	.195	29	5	SS-8, 2B-2
4 yrs.	107	151	22	4	0	0	0.0	7	3	13	23	0	.146	.172	45	5	SS-34, 2B-20, 3B-14

Howie Camp

CAMP, HOWARD LEE (Red)
B. July 1, 1893, Munford, Ala.   D. May 8, 1960, Eastaboga, Ala.
BL TR 5'9" 169 lbs.

	G	AB	H	2B	3B	HR	HR%	R	RBI	BB	SO	SB	BA	SA	PH AB	PH H	G by POS
1917 NY A	5	21	6	1	0	0	0.0	3	0	1	2	0	.286	.333	0	0	OF-5

Llewellan Camp

CAMP, LLEWELLAN ROBERT
Brother of Kid Camp.
B. Feb. 22, 1868, Columbus, Ohio   D. Oct. 1, 1948, Omaha, Neb.
TR 6'1½" 165 lbs.

	G	AB	H	2B	3B	HR	HR%	R	RBI	BB	SO	SB	BA	SA	PH AB	PH H	G by POS
1892 STL N	42	145	30	3	1	2	1.4	19	13	17	27	12	.207	.283	0	0	3B-39, OF-3
1893 CHI N	38	156	41	7	7	2	1.3	37	17	19	19	30	.263	.436	0	0	3B-16, OF-11, 2B-9, SS-3
1894	8	33	6	2	0	0	0.0	1	1	1	6	0	.182	.242	0	0	2B-8
3 yrs.	88	334	77	12	8	4	1.2	57	31	37	52	42	.231	.350	0	0	3B-55, 2B-17, OF-14, SS-3

Roy Campanella

CAMPANELLA, ROY
B. Nov. 19, 1921, Philadelphia, Pa.
Hall of Fame 1969.
BR TR 5'9½" 190 lbs.

	G	AB	H	2B	3B	HR	HR%	R	RBI	BB	SO	SB	BA	SA	PH AB	PH H	G by POS
1948 BKN N	83	279	72	11	3	9	3.2	32	45	36	45	3	.258	.416	4	1	C-78
1949	130	436	125	22	2	22	5.0	65	82	67	36	3	.287	.498	3	1	C-127
1950	126	437	123	19	3	31	7.1	70	89	55	51	1	.281	.551	3	2	C-123
1951	143	505	164	33	1	33	6.5	90	108	53	51	1	.325	.590	5	2	C-140
1952	128	468	126	18	1	22	4.7	73	97	57	59	8	.269	.453	6	1	C-122
1953	144	519	162	26	3	41	7.9	103	142	67	58	4	.312	.611	9	5	C-140
1954	111	397	82	14	3	19	4.8	43	51	42	49	1	.207	.401	1	0	C-111
1955	123	446	142	20	1	32	7.2	81	107	56	41	2	.318	.583	3	2	C-121
1956	124	388	85	6	1	20	5.2	39	73	66	61	1	.219	.394	7	0	C-121
1957	103	330	80	9	0	13	3.9	31	62	34	50	1	.242	.388	4	1	C-100
10 yrs.	1215	4205	1161	178	18	242	5.8	627	856	533	501	25	.276	.500	45	15	C-1183

WORLD SERIES

	G	AB	H	2B	3B	HR	HR%	R	RBI	BB	SO	SB	BA	SA	PH AB	PH H	G by POS
1949 BKN N	5	15	4	1	0	1	6.7	2	2	3	1	0	.267	.533	0	0	C-5
1952	7	28	6	0	0	0	0.0	0	1	1	6	0	.214	.214	0	0	C-7
1953	6	22	6	0	0	1	4.5	6	2	2	3	0	.273	.409	0	0	C-6
1955	7	27	7	3	0	2	7.4	4	4	3	3	0	.259	.593	0	0	C-7
1956	7	22	4	1	0	0	0.0	2	3	3	7	0	.182	.227	0	0	C-7
5 yrs.	32	114	27	5	0	4	3.5	14	12	12	20	0	.237	.386	0	0	C-32

Bert Campaneris

CAMPANERIS, BLANCO DAGOBERTO
Born Blanco Dagoberto Campaneria.
B. Mar. 9, 1942, Pueblo Nuevo, Cuba.
BR TR 5'10" 160 lbs.

	G	AB	H	2B	3B	HR	HR%	R	RBI	BB	SO	SB	BA	SA	PH AB	PH H	G by POS
1964 KC A	67	269	69	14	3	4	1.5	27	22	15	41	10	.257	.375	1	0	SS-38, OF-27, 3B-6
1965	144	578	156	23	12	6	1.0	67	42	41	71	51	.270	.382	2	1	SS-109, OF-39, 3B-1, 2B-1, 1B-1, C-1, P-1
1966	142	573	153	29	10	5	0.9	82	42	25	72	52	.267	.379	2	0	SS-138
1967	147	601	149	29	6	3	0.5	85	32	36	82	55	.248	.331	1	0	SS-145
1968 OAK A	159	642	177	25	9	4	0.6	87	38	50	69	62	.276	.361	1	0	SS-155, OF-3
1969	135	547	142	15	2	2	0.4	71	25	30	62	62	.260	.305	4	1	SS-125

	G	AB	H	2B	3B	HR	HR%	R	RBI	BB	SO	SB	BA	SA	Pinch Hit AB	Pinch Hit H	G by POS

Bert Campaneris continued

	G	AB	H	2B	3B	HR	HR%	R	RBI	BB	SO	SB	BA	SA	PH AB	PH H	G by POS
1970	147	603	168	28	4	22	3.6	97	64	36	73	**42**	.279	.448	5	2	SS-143
1971	134	569	143	18	4	5	0.9	80	47	29	64	34	.251	.323	1	1	SS-133
1972	149	**625**	150	25	2	8	1.3	85	32	32	88	**52**	.240	.325	0	0	SS-148
1973	151	601	150	17	6	4	0.7	89	46	50	79	34	.250	.318	0	0	SS-149
1974	134	527	153	18	8	2	0.4	77	41	47	81	34	.290	.366	0	0	SS-133, DH-1
1975	137	509	135	15	3	4	0.8	69	46	50	71	24	.265	.330	0	0	SS-137
1976	149	536	137	14	1	1	0.2	67	52	63	80	54	.256	.291	0	0	SS-149
1977 TEX A	150	552	140	19	7	5	0.9	77	46	47	86	27	.254	.341	1	0	SS-149
1978	98	269	50	5	3	1	0.4	30	17	20	36	22	.186	.238	1	0	SS-89, DH-4
1979 2 teams	TEX	A (8G − .111)		CAL	A	(85G −	.234)										
" total	93	248	57	4	4	0	0.0	29	15	20	35	13	.230	.278	0	0	SS-90, DH-1
1980 CAL A	77	210	53	8	1	2	1.0	32	18	14	33	10	.252	.329	3	0	SS-64, DH-2, 2B-1
1981	55	82	21	2	1	1	1.2	11	10	5	10	5	.256	.341	1	1	3B-45, SS-3, 2B-2
1983 NY A	60	143	46	5	0	0	0.0	19	11	8	9	6	.322	.357	2	2	2B-32, 3B-24
19 yrs.	2328	8684	2249	313	86	79	0.9	1181	646	618	1142	649	.259	.342	25	6	SS-2097, 3B-76, OF-69, 2B-36, DH-8, 1B-1, C-1, P-1
												7th					

LEAGUE CHAMPIONSHIP SERIES

	G	AB	H	2B	3B	HR	HR%	R	RBI	BB	SO	SB	BA	SA	PH AB	PH H	G by POS
1971 OAK A	3	12	2	1	0	0	0.0	0	0	0	1	0	.167	.250	0	0	SS-3
1972	2	7	3	0	0	0	0.0	3	0	1	0	2	.429	.429	0	0	SS-2
1973	5	21	7	1	0	2	9.5	3	3	2	2	3	.333	.667	0	0	SS-5
1974	4	17	3	0	0	0	0.0	0	3	0	3	1	.176	.176	0	0	SS-4
1975	3	11	0	0	0	0	0.0	1	0	1	1	0	.000	.000	0	0	SS-3
1979 CAL A	1	0	0	0	0	0	−	0	0	0	0	0	−	−	0	0	SS-1
6 yrs.	18	68	15	2	0	2	2.9	7	6	4	7	6	.221	.338	0	0	SS-18

WORLD SERIES

	G	AB	H	2B	3B	HR	HR%	R	RBI	BB	SO	SB	BA	SA	PH AB	PH H	G by POS
1972 OAK A	7	28	5	0	0	0	0.0	1	0	1	4	0	.179	.179	0	0	SS-7
1973	7	31	9	0	1	1	3.2	6	3	1	7	3	.290	.452	0	0	SS-7
1974	5	17	6	2	0	0	0.0	1	2	0	2	1	.353	.471	0	0	SS-5
3 yrs.	19	76	20	2	1	1	1.3	8	5	2	13	4	.263	.355	0	0	SS-19

Alex Campanis

CAMPANIS, ALEXANDER SEBASTIAN
Father of Jim Campanis.
B. Nov. 2, 1916, Kos, Greece

BB TR 6'   185 lbs.

	G	AB	H	2B	3B	HR	HR%	R	RBI	BB	SO	SB	BA	SA	PH AB	PH H	G by POS
1943 BKN N	7	20	2	0	0	0	0.0	3	0	4	5	0	.100	.100	0	0	2B-7

Jim Campanis

CAMPANIS, JAMES ALEXANDER
Son of Alex Campanis.
B. Feb. 9, 1944, New York, N. Y.

BR TR 6'   195 lbs.

	G	AB	H	2B	3B	HR	HR%	R	RBI	BB	SO	SB	BA	SA	PH AB	PH H	G by POS
1966 LA N	1	1	0	0	0	0	0.0	0	0	0	0	0	.000	.000	1	0	C-1
1967	41	62	10	1	0	2	3.2	3	2	9	14	0	.161	.274	24	5	C-23
1968	4	11	1	0	0	0	0.0	0	0	1	2	0	.091	.091	0	0	C-4
1969 KC A	30	83	13	5	0	0	0.0	4	5	5	19	0	.157	.217	7	1	C-26
1970	31	54	7	0	0	2	3.7	6	2	4	14	0	.130	.241	16	1	C-13, OF-1
1973 PIT N	6	6	1	0	0	0	0.0	0	0	0	0	0	.167	.167	6	1	
6 yrs.	113	217	32	6	0	4	1.8	13	9	19	49	0	.147	.230	54	8	C-67, OF-1

Count Campau

CAMPAU, CHARLES COLUMBUS
B. Oct. 17, 1863, Detroit, Mich.   D. Apr. 3, 1938, New Orleans, La.
Manager 1890.

BL TR 5'11"   160 lbs.

	G	AB	H	2B	3B	HR	HR%	R	RBI	BB	SO	SB	BA	SA	PH AB	PH H	G by POS
1888 DET N	70	251	51	5	3	1	0.4	28	18	19	36	27	.203	.259	0	0	OF-70
1890 STL AA	75	314	101	9	11	**10**	3.2	68		26		36	.322	.516	0	0	OF-74, 3B-1, 1B-1
1894 WAS N	2	7	1	0	0	0	0.0	1	0	1	4	0	.143	.143	0	0	OF-2
3 yrs.	147	572	153	14	14	11	1.9	97	18	46	40	63	.267	.399	0	0	OF-146, 3B-1, 1B-1

Bruce Campbell

CAMPBELL, BRUCE DOUGLAS
B. Oct. 20, 1909, Chicago, Ill.

BL TR 6'1"   185 lbs.

	G	AB	H	2B	3B	HR	HR%	R	RBI	BB	SO	SB	BA	SA	PH AB	PH H	G by POS
1930 CHI A	5	10	5	1	1	0	0.0	4	5	1	2	0	.500	.800	1	1	OF-4
1931	4	17	7	2	0	2	11.8	4	5	0	4	0	.412	.882	0	0	OF-4
1932 2 teams	CHI	A (9G − .154)		STL	A	(137G −	.289)										
" total	146	611	173	36	11	14	2.3	86	87	40	**104**	7	.283	.447	3	0	OF-143
1933 STL A	148	567	157	38	8	16	2.8	87	106	69	77	10	.277	.457	4	1	OF-144
1934	138	481	134	25	6	9	1.9	62	74	51	64	5	.279	.412	14	4	OF-123
1935 CLE A	80	308	100	26	3	7	2.3	54	54	31	33	2	.325	.497	4	1	OF-75
1936	76	172	64	15	2	6	3.5	35	30	19	17	2	.372	.587	25	9	OF-47
1937	134	448	135	42	11	4	0.9	82	61	67	49	4	.301	.471	11	5	OF-123
1938	133	511	148	27	12	12	2.3	90	72	53	57	11	.290	.460	11	2	OF-122
1939	130	450	129	23	13	8	1.8	84	72	67	48	7	.287	.449	14	2	OF-115
1940 DET A	103	297	84	15	5	8	2.7	56	44	45	28	2	.283	.448	23	9	OF-74
1941	141	512	141	28	10	15	2.9	72	93	68	67	3	.275	.457	5	2	OF-133
1942 WAS A	122	378	105	17	5	5	1.3	41	63	37	34	0	.278	.389	29	5	OF-87
13 yrs.	1360	4762	1382	295	87	106	2.2	759	766	548	584	53	.290	.455	144	41	OF-1194

WORLD SERIES

	G	AB	H	2B	3B	HR	HR%	R	RBI	BB	SO	SB	BA	SA	PH AB	PH H	G by POS
1940 DET A	7	25	9	1	0	1	4.0	4	5	4	4	0	.360	.520	0	0	OF-7

Dave Campbell

CAMPBELL, DAVID WILSON
B. Jan. 14, 1942, Manistee, Mich.

BR TR 6'1"   180 lbs.

	G	AB	H	2B	3B	HR	HR%	R	RBI	BB	SO	SB	BA	SA	PH AB	PH H	G by POS
1967 DET A	2	2	0	0	0	0	0.0	0	0	0	1	0	.000	.000	1	0	1B-1
1968	9	8	1	0	0	1	12.5	1	2	1	3	0	.125	.500	3	0	2B-5
1969	32	39	4	1	0	0	0.0	4	2	4	15	0	.103	.128	14	2	1B-13, 2B-5, 3B-1
1970 SD N	154	581	127	28	2	12	2.1	71	40	40	115	18	.219	.336	1	0	2B-153
1971	108	365	83	14	2	7	1.9	38	29	37	75	9	.227	.334	1	0	2B-69, 3B-40, SS-4, OF-2, 1B-2
1972	33	100	24	5	0	0	0.0	6	3	11	12	0	.240	.290	0	0	3B-31, 2B-1

	G	AB	H	2B	3B	HR	HR %	R	RBI	BB	SO	SB	BA	SA	Pinch Hit AB	H	G by POS

Dave Campbell continued

	G	AB	H	2B	3B	HR	HR %	R	RBI	BB	SO	SB	BA	SA	PH AB	PH H	G by POS
1973 3 teams	SD N (33G – .224)			STL N (13G – .000)				HOU N (9G – .267)									
" total	55	134	26	5	0	0	0.0	4	11	8	25	1	.194	.231	10	0	2B-33, 3B-7, 1B-5, OF-1
1974 HOU N	35	23	2	1	0	0	0.0	4	2	1	8	1	.087	.130	13	0	2B-9, 1B-6, 3B-2, OF-1
8 yrs.	428	1252	267	54	4	20	1.6	128	89	102	254	29	.213	.311	43	2	2B-275, 3B-81, 1B-27, OF-4, SS-4

Gilly Campbell

CAMPBELL, WILLIAM GILTHORPE
B. Feb. 13, 1908, Kansas City, Kans.　　D. Feb. 21, 1973, Los Angeles, Calif.　　BL TR 5'11" 176 lbs.

	G	AB	H	2B	3B	HR	HR %	R	RBI	BB	SO	SB	BA	SA	PH AB	PH H	G by POS
1933 CHI N	46	89	25	3	1	1	1.1	11	10	7	4	0	.281	.371	23	6	C-20
1935 CIN N	88	218	56	7	0	3	1.4	26	30	42	7	3	.257	.330	15	4	C-66, 1B-5, OF-1
1936	89	235	63	13	1	1	0.4	28	40	43	14	2	.268	.345	14	3	C-71, 1B-1
1937	18	40	11	2	0	0	0.0	3	2	5	1	0	.275	.325	1	0	C-17
1938 BKN N	54	126	31	5	0	0	0.0	10	11	19	9	0	.246	.286	10	2	C-44
5 yrs.	295	708	186	30	2	5	0.7	78	93	116	35	5	.263	.332	63	15	C-218, 1B-6, OF-1

Jim Campbell

CAMPBELL, JAMES ROBERT
B. June 24, 1937, Palo Alto, Calif.　　BR TR 6' 190 lbs.

	G	AB	H	2B	3B	HR	HR %	R	RBI	BB	SO	SB	BA	SA	PH AB	PH H	G by POS
1962 HOU N	27	86	19	4	0	3	3.5	6	6	6	23	0	.221	.372	2	1	C-25
1963	55	158	35	3	0	4	2.5	9	19	10	40	0	.222	.316	12	2	C-42
2 yrs.	82	244	54	7	0	7	2.9	15	25	16	63	0	.221	.336	14	3	C-67

Jim Campbell

CAMPBELL, JAMES ROBERT JR
B. Jan. 10, 1943, Hartsville, S. C.　　BL TR 6' 205 lbs.

	G	AB	H	2B	3B	HR	HR %	R	RBI	BB	SO	SB	BA	SA	PH AB	PH H	G by POS
1970 STL N	13	13	3	0	0	0	0.0	0	1	0	3	0	.231	.231	13	3	

Joe Campbell

CAMPBELL, JOSEPH EARL
B. Mar. 10, 1944, Louisville, Ky.　　BR TR 6'1" 175 lbs.

	G	AB	H	2B	3B	HR	HR %	R	RBI	BB	SO	SB	BA	SA	PH AB	PH H	G by POS
1967 CHI N	1	3	0	0	0	0	0.0	0	0	0	3	0	.000	.000	0	0	OF-1

Marc Campbell

CAMPBELL, MARC THADDEUS (Hutch)
B. Nov. 29, 1884, Punxsutawney, Pa.　　D. Feb. 13, 1946, New Bethlehem, Pa.　　BL TR 5'10" 155 lbs.

	G	AB	H	2B	3B	HR	HR %	R	RBI	BB	SO	SB	BA	SA	PH AB	PH H	G by POS
1907 PIT N	2	4	1	0	0	0	0.0	0		1		0	.250	.250	0	0	SS-2

Paul Campbell

CAMPBELL, PAUL McLAUGHLIN
B. Sept. 1, 1917, Paw Creek, N. C.　　BL TL 5'10" 185 lbs.

	G	AB	H	2B	3B	HR	HR %	R	RBI	BB	SO	SB	BA	SA	PH AB	PH H	G by POS
1941 BOS A	1	0	0	0	0	0	–	0	0	0	0	0	–	–	0	0	
1942	26	15	1	0	0	0	0.0	4	0	1	5	1	.067	.067	13	1	OF-4
1946	28	26	3	1	0	0	0.0	3	0	2	7	0	.115	.154	14	2	1B-5
1948 DET A	59	83	22	1	1	1	1.2	15	11	1	10	0	.265	.337	13	1	1B-27
1949	87	255	71	15	4	3	1.2	38	30	24	32	3	.278	.404	9	5	1B-74
1950	3	1	0	0	0	0	0.0	1	0	0	0	0	.000	.000	1	0	
6 yrs.	204	380	97	17	5	4	1.1	61	41	28	54	4	.255	.358	50	9	1B-106, OF-4

WORLD SERIES
| 1946 BOS A | 1 | 0 | 0 | 0 | 0 | 0 | – | 0 | 0 | 0 | 0 | 0 | – | – | 0 | 0 | |

Ron Campbell

CAMPBELL, RONALD THOMAS
B. Apr. 5, 1940, Chattanooga, Tenn.　　BR TR 6'1" 180 lbs.

	G	AB	H	2B	3B	HR	HR %	R	RBI	BB	SO	SB	BA	SA	PH AB	PH H	G by POS
1964 CHI N	26	92	25	6	1	1	1.1	7	10	1	21	0	.272	.391	0	0	2B-26
1965	2	2	0	0	0	0	0.0	0	0	0	0	0	.000	.000	2	0	
1966	24	60	13	1	0	0	0.0	4	4	6	5	1	.217	.233	5	1	SS-11, 3B-7
3 yrs.	52	154	38	7	1	1	0.6	11	14	7	26	1	.247	.325	7	1	2B-26, SS-11, 3B-7

Sam Campbell

CAMPBELL, SAMUEL
B. Philadelphia, Pa.　　Deceased.

	G	AB	H	2B	3B	HR	HR %	R	RBI	BB	SO	SB	BA	SA	PH AB	PH H	G by POS
1890 PHI AA	2	5	0	0	0	0	0.0	0		1		0	.000	.000	0	0	2B-2

Soup Campbell

CAMPBELL, CLARENCE
B. Mar. 7, 1915, Sparta, Va.　　BL TR 6'1" 188 lbs.

	G	AB	H	2B	3B	HR	HR %	R	RBI	BB	SO	SB	BA	SA	PH AB	PH H	G by POS
1940 CLE A	35	62	14	1	0	0	0.0	8	2	7	12	0	.226	.242	19	5	OF-16
1941	104	328	82	10	4	3	0.9	36	35	31	21	1	.250	.332	24	4	OF-78
2 yrs.	139	390	96	11	4	3	0.8	44	37	38	33	1	.246	.318	43	9	OF-94

Vin Campbell

CAMPBELL, ARTHUR VINCENT
B. Jan. 30, 1888, St. Louis, Mo.　　D. Nov. 16, 1969, Towson, Md.　　BL TR

	G	AB	H	2B	3B	HR	HR %	R	RBI	BB	SO	SB	BA	SA	PH AB	PH H	G by POS
1908 CHI N	1	1	0	0	0	0	0.0	0	0	0		0	.000	.000	1	0	
1910 PIT N	97	282	92	9	5	4	1.4	42	21	26	23	17	.326	.436	18	5	OF-74
1911	42	93	29	3	1	0	0.0	12	10	8	7	6	.312	.366	17	4	OF-21
1912 BOS N	145	624	185	32	9	3	0.5	102	48	32	44	19	.296	.391	1	0	OF-144
1914 IND F	134	544	173	23	11	7	1.3	92	44	37		26	.318	.439	1	0	OF-132
1915 NWK F	127	525	163	18	10	1	0.2	78	44	29		24	.310	.389	1	0	OF-126
6 yrs.	546	2069	642	85	36	15	0.7	326	167	132	74	92	.310	.408	39	9	OF-497

Frank Campos

CAMPOS, FRANCISCO JOSE LOPEZ
B. May 11, 1924, Havana, Cuba　　BL TL 5'10" 170 lbs.

	G	AB	H	2B	3B	HR	HR %	R	RBI	BB	SO	SB	BA	SA	PH AB	PH H	G by POS
1951 WAS A	8	26	11	3	1	0	0.0	4	3	0	1	0	.423	.615	1	0	OF-7
1952	53	112	29	6	1	0	0.0	9	8	1	13	0	.259	.330	27	2	OF-23
1953	10	9	1	0	0	0	0.0	0	2	1	0	0	.111	.111	9	1	
3 yrs.	71	147	41	9	2	0	0.0	13	13	2	14	0	.279	.367	37	3	OF-30

Jimmy Canavan

CANAVAN, JAMES EDWARD
B. Nov. 26, 1866, New Bedford, Mass.　　D. May 26, 1949, New Bedford, Mass.　　BR TR 5'8" 160 lbs.

	G	AB	H	2B	3B	HR	HR %	R	RBI	BB	SO	SB	BA	SA	PH AB	PH H	G by POS
1891 C-M AA	136	568	135	15	18	10	1.8	107	87	43	54	28	.238	.380	0	0	SS-112, 2B-24
1892 CHI N	118	439	73	10	11	0	0.0	48	32	48	48	33	.166	.239	0	0	2B-112, OF-4, SS-2
1893 CIN N	121	461	104	13	7	5	1.1	65	64	51	20	31	.226	.317	1	0	OF-116, 2B-5, 3B-1

	G	AB	H	2B	3B	HR	HR %	R	RBI	BB	SO	SB	BA	SA	Pinch Hit AB	Pinch Hit H	G by POS

Jimmy Canavan continued

	G	AB	H	2B	3B	HR	HR %	R	RBI	BB	SO	SB	BA	SA	AB	H	G by POS
1894	101	356	97	16	9	13	3.7	77	70	62	25	13	.272	.478	1	0	OF-95, SS-3, 3B-2, 2B-1, 1B-1
1897 BKN N	63	240	52	9	3	2	0.8	25	34	26		9	.217	.304	0	0	2B-63
5 yrs.	539	2064	461	63	48	30	1.5	322	287	230	147	114	.223	.344	2	0	OF-215, 2B-205, SS-117, 3B-3, 1B-1

Rip Cannell

CANNELL, VIRGIN WIRT   BL TR 5'10½" 180 lbs.
B. Jan. 23, 1880, S. Bridgton, Me.   D. Aug. 26, 1948, Bridgton, Me.

	G	AB	H	2B	3B	HR	HR %	R	RBI	BB	SO	SB	BA	SA	AB	H	G by POS
1904 BOS N	100	346	81	5	1	0	0.0	32	18	23		10	.234	.254	6	1	OF-93
1905	154	567	140	14	4	0	0.0	52	36	51		17	.247	.286	0	0	OF-154
2 yrs.	254	913	221	19	5	0	0.0	84	54	74		27	.242	.274	6	1	OF-247

Chris Cannizzaro

CANNIZZARO, CHRISTOPHER JOHN   BR TR 6' 190 lbs.
B. May 3, 1938, Oakland, Calif.

	G	AB	H	2B	3B	HR	HR %	R	RBI	BB	SO	SB	BA	SA	AB	H	G by POS
1960 STL N	7	9	2	0	0	0	0.0	0	1	1	3	0	.222	.222	0	0	C-6
1961	6	2	1	0	0	0	0.0	0	0	0	0	0	.500	.500	1	1	C-5
1962 NY N	59	133	32	2	1	0	0.0	9	9	19	26	1	.241	.271	3	1	C-56, OF-1
1963	16	33	8	1	0	0	0.0	4	4	1	8	0	.242	.273	1	1	C-15
1964	60	164	51	10	0	0	0.0	11	10	14	28	0	.311	.372	5	1	C-53
1965	114	251	46	8	2	0	0.0	17	7	28	60	0	.183	.231	2	0	C-112
1968 PIT N	25	58	14	2	2	1	1.7	5	7	9	13	0	.241	.397	2	0	C-25
1969 SD N	134	418	92	14	3	4	1.0	23	33	42	81	0	.220	.297	2	0	C-132
1970	111	341	95	13	3	5	1.5	27	42	48	49	2	.279	.378	2	0	C-110
1971 2 teams		SD N (21G – .190)				CHI N (71G – .213)											
" total	92	260	54	9	1	6	2.3	20	31	39	34	0	.208	.319	2	0	C-89
1972 LA N	73	200	48	6	0	2	1.0	14	18	31	38	0	.240	.300	5	2	C-72
1973	17	21	4	0	0	0	0.0	0	3	3	3	0	.190	.190	3	0	C-13
1974 SD N	26	60	11	1	0	0	0.0	2	4	6	11	0	.183	.200	0	0	C-26
13 yrs.	740	1950	458	66	12	18	0.9	132	169	241	354	3	.235	.309	26	6	C-714, OF-1

Joe Cannon

CANNON, JOSEPH JEROME   BL TR 6'2" 185 lbs.
B. July 13, 1953, Camp Lejeune, N. C.

	G	AB	H	2B	3B	HR	HR %	R	RBI	BB	SO	SB	BA	SA	AB	H	G by POS
1977 HOU N	9	17	2	2	0	0	0.0	3	1	0	5	1	.118	.235	4	1	OF-3
1978	8	18	4	0	0	0	0.0	1	1	0	1	0	.222	.222	3	0	OF-5
1979 TOR A	61	142	30	1	1	1	0.7	14	5	1	34	12	.211	.254	0	0	OF-50
1980	70	50	4	0	0	0	0.0	16	4	0	14	2	.080	.080	4	0	OF-33, DH-1
4 yrs.	148	227	40	3	1	1	0.4	34	11	1	54	15	.176	.211	11	1	OF-91, DH-1

Bart Cantz

CANTZ, BARTHOLOMEW L.   TR
B. Jan. 29, 1860, Philadelphia, Pa.   D. Feb. 12, 1943, Philadelphia, Pa.

	G	AB	H	2B	3B	HR	HR %	R	RBI	BB	SO	SB	BA	SA	AB	H	G by POS
1888 BAL AA	37	126	21	2	1	0	0.0	7	9	2		0	.167	.198	0	0	C-33, OF-4
1889	20	69	12	2	0	0	0.0	6	8	4	14	2	.174	.203	0	0	C-18, OF-2
1890 PHI AA	5	22	1	0	0	0	0.0	1		0		0	.045	.045	0	0	C-5
3 yrs.	62	217	34	4	1	0	0.0	14	17	6	14	2	.157	.184	0	0	C-56, OF-6

Nick Capra

CAPRA, NICK LEE   BR TR 5'7" 164 lbs.
B. Mar. 8, 1958, Denver, Colo.

	G	AB	H	2B	3B	HR	HR %	R	RBI	BB	SO	SB	BA	SA	AB	H	G by POS
1982 TEX A	13	15	4	0	0	1	6.7	2	1	3	4	2	.267	.467	0	0	OF-9
1983	8	2	0	0	0	0	0.0	2	0	0	0	0	.000	.000	2	0	OF-4
2 yrs.	21	17	4	0	0	1	5.9	4	1	3	4	2	.235	.412	2	0	OF-13

Pat Capri

CAPRI, PATRICK NICHOLAS   BR TR 6'½" 170 lbs.
B. Nov. 27, 1918, New York, N. Y.

	G	AB	H	2B	3B	HR	HR %	R	RBI	BB	SO	SB	BA	SA	AB	H	G by POS
1944 BOS N	7	1	0	0	0	0	0.0	1	0	0	1	0	.000	.000	0	0	2B-1

Ralph Capron

CAPRON, RALPH EARL (Cape)   BL TR 5'11½" 165 lbs.
B. June 16, 1889, Minneapolis, Minn.   D. Sept. 19, 1980, Los Angeles, Calif.

	G	AB	H	2B	3B	HR	HR %	R	RBI	BB	SO	SB	BA	SA	AB	H	G by POS
1912 PIT N	1	0	0	0	0	0		0	0	0	0	0	–	–	0	0	
1913 PHI N	2	1	0	0	0	0	0.0	1	0	0	0	0	.000	.000	0	0	OF-1
2 yrs.	3	1	0	0	0	0	0.0	1	0	0	0	0	.000	.000	0	0	OF-1

John Carbine

CARBINE, JOHN C.   6' 187 lbs.
B. Oct. 12, 1855, Syracuse, N. Y.   D. Sept. 11, 1915, Chicago, Ill.

	G	AB	H	2B	3B	HR	HR %	R	RBI	BB	SO	SB	BA	SA	AB	H	G by POS
1876 LOU N	7	25	4	0	0	0	0.0	3	1	0	0		.160	.160	0	0	1B-6, OF-1

Bernie Carbo

CARBO, BERNARDO   BL TR 5'11" 173 lbs.
B. Aug. 5, 1947, Detroit, Mich.

	G	AB	H	2B	3B	HR	HR %	R	RBI	BB	SO	SB	BA	SA	AB	H	G by POS
1969 CIN N	4	3	0	0	0	0	0.0	0	0	0	2	0	.000	.000	3	0	
1970	125	365	113	19	3	21	5.8	54	63	94	77	10	.310	.551	7	3	OF-119
1971	106	310	68	20	1	5	1.6	33	20	54	56	2	.219	.339	12	3	OF-90
1972 2 teams		CIN N (19G – .143)				STL N (99G – .258)											
" total	118	323	81	13	1	7	2.2	44	34	63	59	0	.251	.362	17	5	OF-96, 3B-1
1973 STL N	111	308	88	18	0	8	2.6	42	40	58	52	2	.286	.422	17	1	OF-94
1974 BOS A	117	338	84	20	0	12	3.6	40	61	58	90	4	.249	.414	12	6	OF-87, DH-15
1975	107	319	82	21	3	15	4.7	64	50	83	69	2	.257	.483	8	2	OF-85, DH-13
1976 2 teams		BOS A (17G – .236)				MIL N (69G – .235)											
" total	86	238	56	11	0	5	2.1	25	21	41	72	2	.235	.345	12	2	DH-39, OF-34
1977 BOS A	86	228	66	6	1	15	6.6	36	34	47	72	1	.289	.522	14	4	OF-67, DH-7
1978 2 teams		BOS A (17G – .261)				CLE N (60G – .287)											
" total	77	220	62	11	0	5	2.3	28	22	28	39	2	.282	.400	8	0	DH-57, OF-13
1979 STL N	52	64	18	1	0	3	4.7	6	12	10	22	1	.281	.438	32	6	OF-17
1980 2 teams		STL N (14G – .182)				PIT N (7G – .333)											
" total	21	17	4	0	0	0	0.0	0	1	2	1	0	.235	.235	17	4	
12 yrs.	1010	2733	722	140	9	96	3.5	372	358	538	611	26	.264	.427	159	36	OF-702, DH-131, 3B-1

LEAGUE CHAMPIONSHIP SERIES

	G	AB	H	2B	3B	HR	HR %	R	RBI	BB	SO	SB	BA	SA	AB	H	G by POS
1970 CIN N	2	6	0	0	0	0	0.0	0	0	0	3	0	.000	.000	0	0	OF-2

	G	AB	H	2B	3B	HR	HR %	R	RBI	BB	SO	SB	BA	SA	Pinch Hit AB	Pinch Hit H	G by POS

Bernie Carbo continued

WORLD SERIES

	G	AB	H	2B	3B	HR	HR %	R	RBI	BB	SO	SB	BA	SA	AB	H	G by POS
1970 CIN N	4	8	0	0	0	0	0.0	0	0	2	3	0	.000	.000	2	0	OF-2
1975 BOS A	4	7	3	1	0	2	28.6	3	4	1	1	0	.429	1.429	3	2	OF-2
2 yrs.	8	15	3	1	0	2	13.3	3	4	3	4	0	.200	.667	5	2	OF-4

Jose Cardenal

CARDENAL, JOSE DOMEC
B. Oct. 7, 1943, Matanzas, Cuba

BR TR 5'10"   150 lbs.

	G	AB	H	2B	3B	HR	HR %	R	RBI	BB	SO	SB	BA	SA	AB	H	G by POS
1963 SF N	9	5	1	0	0	0	0.0	1	2	1	1	0	.200	.200	4	1	OF-2
1964	20	15	0	0	0	0	0.0	3	0	2	3	2	.000	.000	2	0	OF-16
1965 CAL A	134	512	128	23	2	11	2.1	58	57	27	72	37	.250	.367	1	1	OF-129, 3B-2, 2B-1
1966	154	561	155	15	3	16	2.9	67	48	34	69	24	.276	.399	10	2	OF-146
1967	108	381	90	13	5	6	1.6	40	27	15	63	10	.236	.344	8	0	OF-101
1968 CLE A	157	583	150	21	7	7	1.2	78	44	39	74	40	.257	.353	7	1	OF-153
1969	146	557	143	26	3	11	2.0	75	45	49	58	36	.257	.373	4	1	OF-142, 3B-5
1970 STL N	148	552	162	32	6	10	1.8	73	74	45	70	26	.293	.428	16	8	OF-134
1971 2 teams	STL	N (89G –	.243)		MIL	A	(53G –	.258)									
" total	142	499	124	22	4	10	2.0	57	80	42	55	21	.248	.369	9	5	OF-135
1972 CHI N	143	533	155	24	6	17	3.2	96	70	55	58	25	.291	.454	5	2	OF-137
1973	145	522	158	33	2	11	2.1	80	68	58	62	19	.303	.437	2	1	OF-142
1974	143	542	159	35	3	13	2.4	75	72	56	67	23	.293	.441	8	2	OF-136
1975	154	574	182	30	2	9	1.6	85	68	77	50	34	.317	.423	5	1	OF-151
1976	136	521	156	25	2	8	1.5	64	47	32	39	23	.299	.401	8	1	OF-128
1977	100	226	54	12	1	3	1.3	33	18	28	30	5	.239	.341	31	10	OF-62, 3B-1, 2B-1
1978 PHI N	87	201	50	12	0	4	2.0	27	33	23	16	2	.249	.368	33	9	1B-50, OF-13
1979 2 teams	PHI	N (29G –	.208)		NY	N	(11G –	.297)									
" total	40	85	21	7	0	2	2.4	12	13	14	11	2	.247	.400	17	4	OF-21, 1B-3
1980 2 teams	NY	N (26G –	.167)		KC	A	(25G –	.340)									
" total	51	95	25	3	0	0	0.0	12	9	11	9	0	.263	.295	17	1	OF-29, 1B-5
18 yrs.	2017	6964	1913	333	46	138	2.0	936	775	608	807	329	.275	.395	187	50	OF-1777, 1B-58, 3B-8, 2B-2

LEAGUE CHAMPIONSHIP SERIES

	G	AB	H	2B	3B	HR	HR %	R	RBI	BB	SO	SB	BA	SA	AB	H	G by POS
1978 PHI N	2	6	1	0	0	0	0.0	0	0	1	1	0	.167	.167	0	0	1B-2

WORLD SERIES

	G	AB	H	2B	3B	HR	HR %	R	RBI	BB	SO	SB	BA	SA	AB	H	G by POS
1980 KC A	4	10	2	0	0	0	0.0	0	0	0	3	0	.200	.200	1	0	OF-4

Leo Cardenas

CARDENAS, LEONARDO LAZARO (Chico)
B. Dec. 17, 1938, Matanzas, Cuba

BR TR 5'11"   150 lbs.

	G	AB	H	2B	3B	HR	HR %	R	RBI	BB	SO	SB	BA	SA	AB	H	G by POS
1960 CIN N	48	142	33	2	4	1	0.7	13	12	6	32	0	.232	.324	1	0	SS-47
1961	74	198	61	18	1	5	2.5	23	24	15	39	1	.308	.485	12	1	SS-63
1962	153	589	173	31	4	10	1.7	77	60	39	99	2	.294	.411	3	1	SS-149
1963	158	565	133	22	4	7	1.2	42	48	23	101	3	.235	.326	2	1	SS-157
1964	163	597	150	32	2	9	1.5	61	69	41	110	4	.251	.357	0	0	SS-163
1965	156	557	160	25	11	11	2.0	65	57	60	100	1	.287	.431	1	0	SS-155
1966	160	568	145	25	4	20	3.5	59	81	45	87	9	.255	.419	0	0	SS-160
1967	108	379	97	14	3	2	0.5	30	21	34	77	4	.256	.325	0	0	SS-108
1968	137	452	106	13	2	7	1.5	45	41	36	83	2	.235	.319	1	0	SS-136
1969 MIN A	160	578	162	24	4	10	1.7	67	70	66	96	5	.280	.388	0	0	SS-160
1970	160	588	145	34	4	11	1.9	67	65	42	101	2	.247	.374	0	0	SS-160
1971	153	554	146	25	4	18	3.2	59	75	51	69	3	.264	.421	1	0	SS-153
1972 CAL A	150	551	123	11	2	6	1.1	25	42	35	73	1	.223	.283	0	0	SS-150
1973 CLE A	72	195	42	4	0	0	0.0	9	12	13	42	1	.215	.236	0	0	SS-67, 3B-5
1974 TEX A	34	92	25	3	0	0	0.0	5	7	2	14	1	.272	.304	1	0	3B-21, SS-10, DH-4
1975	55	102	24	2	0	1	1.0	15	5	14	12	0	.235	.284	9	1	3B-43, SS-5, 2B-3
16 yrs.	1941	6707	1725	285	49	118	1.8	662	689	522	1135	39	.257	.367	31	4	SS-1843, 3B-69, DH-4, 2B-3

LEAGUE CHAMPIONSHIP SERIES

	G	AB	H	2B	3B	HR	HR %	R	RBI	BB	SO	SB	BA	SA	AB	H	G by POS
1969 MIN A	3	13	2	0	1	0	0.0	0	0	0	7	0	.154	.308	0	0	SS-3
1970	3	11	2	0	0	0	0.0	1	1	1	1	0	.182	.182	0	0	SS-3
2 yrs.	6	24	4	0	1	0	0.0	1	1	1	8	0	.167	.250	0	0	SS-6

WORLD SERIES

	G	AB	H	2B	3B	HR	HR %	R	RBI	BB	SO	SB	BA	SA	AB	H	G by POS
1961 CIN N	3	3	1	1	0	0	0.0	0	0	0	1	0	.333	.667	3	1	

Rod Carew

CAREW, RODNEY CLINE
B. Oct. 1, 1945, Gaton, Panama

BL TR 6'   170 lbs.

	G	AB	H	2B	3B	HR	HR %	R	RBI	BB	SO	SB	BA	SA	AB	H	G by POS
1967 MIN A	137	514	150	22	7	8	1.6	66	51	37	91	5	.292	.409	1	1	2B-134
1968	127	461	126	27	2	1	0.2	46	42	26	71	12	.273	.347	9	2	2B-117, SS-4
1969	123	458	152	30	4	8	1.7	79	56	37	72	19	.332	.467	7	4	2B-118
1970	51	191	70	12	3	4	2.1	27	28	11	28	4	.366	.524	5	0	2B-45, 1B-1
1971	147	577	177	16	10	2	0.3	88	48	45	81	6	.307	.380	3	1	2B-142, 3B-2
1972	142	535	170	21	6	0	0.0	61	51	43	60	12	.318	.379	5	1	2B-139
1973	149	580	203	30	11	6	1.0	98	62	62	55	41	.350	.471	3	0	2B-147
1974	153	599	218	30	5	3	0.5	86	55	74	49	38	.364	.446	5	1	2B-148
1975	143	535	192	24	4	14	2.6	89	80	64	40	35	.359	.497	5	2	2B-123, 1B-14, DH-2
1976	156	605	200	29	12	9	1.5	97	90	67	52	49	.331	.463	5	3	1B-152, 2B-7
1977	155	616	239	38	16	14	2.3	128	100	69	55	23	.388	.570	6	3	1B-151, 2B-4, DH-1
1978	152	564	188	26	10	5	0.9	85	70	78	62	27	.333	.441	10	4	1B-148, 2B-4, OF-1
1979 CAL A	110	409	130	15	3	3	0.7	78	44	73	46	18	.318	.391	0	0	1B-103, DH-6
1980	144	540	179	34	7	3	0.6	74	59	59	38	23	.331	.437	11	4	1B-103, DH-32
1981	93	364	111	17	1	2	0.5	57	21	45	45	16	.305	.374	2	1	1B-90, DH-2
1982	138	523	167	25	5	3	0.6	88	44	67	49	10	.319	.403	5	1	1B-134
1983	129	472	160	24	2	2	0.4	66	44	57	48	6	.339	.411	17	6	1B-89, DH-24, 2B-2
1984	93	329	97	8	1	3	0.9	42	31	40	39	4	.295	.353	12	4	1B-83, DH-1
18 yrs.	2342	8872	2929	428	109	90	1.0	1355	976	954	981	348	.330	.433	111	38	2B-1130, 1B-1068, DH-68, SS-4, 3B-2, OF-1

	G	AB	H	2B	3B	HR	HR %	R	RBI	BB	SO	SB	BA	SA	Pinch Hit AB	Pinch Hit H	G by POS

Rod Carew continued

LEAGUE CHAMPIONSHIP SERIES

	G	AB	H	2B	3B	HR	HR %	R	RBI	BB	SO	SB	BA	SA	AB	H	G by POS
1969 MIN A	3	14	1	0	0	0	0.0	0	0	1	4	0	.071	.071	0	0	2B-3
1970	2	2	0	0	0	0	0.0	0	0	0	1	0	.000	.000	2	0	
1979 CAL A	4	17	7	3	0	0	0.0	4	1	0	0	1	.412	.588	0	0	1B-4
1982	5	17	3	1	0	0	0.0	2	0	4	4	1	.176	.235	0	0	1B-5
4 yrs.	14	50	11	4	0	0	0.0	6	1	5	9	2	.220	.300	2	0	1B-9, 2B-3

Andy Carey

CAREY, ANDREW ARTHUR   BR TR 6'1½" 190 lbs.
Born Andrew Arthur Nordstrom.
B. Oct. 18, 1931, Oakland, Calif.

	G	AB	H	2B	3B	HR	HR %	R	RBI	BB	SO	SB	BA	SA	AB	H	G by POS
1952 NY A	16	40	6	0	0	0	0.0	6	1	3	10	0	.150	.150	0	0	3B-14, SS-1
1953	51	81	26	5	0	4	4.9	14	8	9	12	2	.321	.531	7	1	3B-40, SS-2, 2B-1
1954	122	411	124	14	6	8	1.9	60	65	43	38	5	.302	.423	3	0	3B-120
1955	135	510	131	19	11	7	1.4	73	47	44	51	3	.257	.378	0	0	3B-135
1956	132	422	100	18	2	7	1.7	54	50	45	53	9	.237	.339	1	0	3B-131
1957	85	247	63	6	5	6	2.4	30	33	15	42	2	.255	.393	6	1	3B-81
1958	102	315	90	19	4	12	3.8	39	45	34	43	1	.286	.486	7	2	3B-99
1959	41	101	26	1	0	3	3.0	11	9	7	17	1	.257	.356	8	3	3B-34
1960 2 teams	NY	A (4G – .333)			KC	A	(102G – .233)										
" total	106	346	81	14	4	12	3.5	31	54	26	53	0	.234	.402	15	1	3B-93, OF-1
1961 2 teams	KC	A (39G – .244)			CHI	A	(56G – .266)										
" total	95	266	68	18	5	3	1.1	41	25	26	47	0	.256	.395	1	0	3B-93
1962 LA N	53	111	26	5	1	2	1.8	12	13	16	23	0	.234	.351	13	2	3B-42
11 yrs.	938	2850	741	119	38	64	2.2	371	350	268	389	23	.260	.396	61	10	3B-882, SS-3, OF-1, 2B-1

WORLD SERIES

	G	AB	H	2B	3B	HR	HR %	R	RBI	BB	SO	SB	BA	SA	AB	H	G by POS
1955 NY A	2	2	1	0	1	0	0.0	0	1	0	0	0	.500	1.500	2	1	
1956	7	19	3	0	0	0	0.0	2	0	1	6	0	.158	.158	0	0	3B-7
1957	2	7	2	1	0	0	0.0	0	1	1	0	0	.286	.429	0	0	3B-2
1958	5	12	1	0	0	0	0.0	1	0	0	3	0	.083	.083	0	0	3B-5
4 yrs.	16	40	7	1	1	0	0.0	3	2	2	9	0	.175	.250	2	1	3B-14

Max Carey

CAREY, MAX GEORGE (Scoops)   BB TR 5'11½" 170 lbs.
Also known as Maximilian Carnarius.
B. Jan. 11, 1890, Terre Haute, Ind.   D. May 30, 1976, Miami, Fla.
Manager 1932-33.
Hall of Fame 1961.

	G	AB	H	2B	3B	HR	HR %	R	RBI	BB	SO	SB	BA	SA	AB	H	G by POS
1910 PIT N	2	6	3	0	1	0	0.0	2	2	2	1	0	.500	.833	0	0	OF-2
1911	129	427	110	15	10	5	1.2	77	43	44	75	27	.258	.375	5	1	OF-122
1912	150	587	177	23	8	5	0.9	114	66	61	79	45	.302	.394	0	0	OF-150
1913	154	620	172	23	10	5	0.8	99	49	55	67	61	.277	.371	0	0	OF-154
1914	156	593	144	25	17	1	0.2	76	31	59	56	38	.243	.347	1	1	OF-154
1915	140	564	143	26	5	3	0.5	76	27	57	58	36	.254	.333	1	0	OF-140
1916	154	599	158	23	11	7	1.2	90	42	59	58	63	.264	.374	0	0	OF-154
1917	155	588	174	21	12	1	0.2	82	51	58	38	46	.296	.378	2	2	OF-153
1918	126	468	128	14	6	3	0.6	70	48	62	25	58	.274	.348	0	0	OF-126
1919	66	244	75	10	2	0	0.0	41	9	25	24	18	.307	.365	2	1	OF-63
1920	130	485	140	18	4	1	0.2	74	35	59	31	52	.289	.348	2	1	OF-129
1921	140	521	161	34	4	7	1.3	85	56	70	30	37	.309	.430	1	0	OF-139
1922	155	629	207	28	12	10	1.6	140	70	80	26	51	.329	.459	0	0	OF-155
1923	153	610	188	32	19	6	1.0	120	63	73	28	51	.308	.452	0	0	OF-153
1924	149	599	178	30	9	7	1.2	113	55	58	17	49	.297	.412	0	0	OF-149
1925	133	542	186	39	13	5	0.9	109	44	66	19	46	.343	.491	2	0	OF-130
1926 2 teams	PIT	N (86G – .222)			BKN	N	(27G – .260)										
" total	113	424	98	17	6	0	0.0	64	35	38	19	10	.231	.300	3	3	OF-109
1927 BKN N	144	538	143	30	10	1	0.2	70	54	64	18	32	.266	.364	2	1	OF-141
1928	108	296	73	11	0	2	0.7	41	19	47	24	18	.247	.304	10	3	OF-95
1929	19	23	7	0	0	0	0.0	2	1	3	2	0	.304	.304	11	4	OF-4
20 yrs.	2476	9363	2665	419	159	69	0.7	1545	800	1040	695	738 4th	.285	.385	42	17	OF-2422

WORLD SERIES

	G	AB	H	2B	3B	HR	HR %	R	RBI	BB	SO	SB	BA	SA	AB	H	G by POS
1925 PIT N	7	24	11	4	0	0	0.0	6	2	2	3	3	.458	.625	0	0	OF-7

Roger Carey

CAREY, ROGER J.
B. Unknown.

	G	AB	H	2B	3B	HR	HR %	R	RBI	BB	SO	SB	BA	SA	AB	H	G by POS
1887 NY N	1	4	0	0	0	0	0.0	0	2	0	1	0	.000	.000	0	0	2B-1

Scoops Carey

CAREY, GEORGE C.   BR TR
B. Dec. 4, 1870, East Liverpool, Ohio   D. Dec. 17, 1916, East Liverpool, Ohio

	G	AB	H	2B	3B	HR	HR %	R	RBI	BB	SO	SB	BA	SA	AB	H	G by POS
1895 BAL N	123	490	128	21	6	1	0.2	59	75	27	32	2	.261	.335	0	0	1B-123, OF-1, SS-1, 3B-1
1898 LOU N	8	32	6	1	1	0	0.0	1	1	1		0	.188	.281	0	0	1B-8
1902 WAS A	120	452	142	35	11	0	0.0	46	60	20		3	.314	.440	0	0	1B-120
1903	48	183	37	3	2	0	0.0	8	23	4		0	.202	.240	1	0	1B-47
4 yrs.	299	1157	313	60	20	1	0.1	114	159	52	32	5	.271	.360	1	0	1B-298, OF-1, SS-1, 3B-1

Tom Carey

CAREY, THOMAS FRANCIS (Scoops)   BR TR 5'8½" 170 lbs.
B. Oct. 11, 1908, Hoboken, N. J.   D. Feb. 21, 1970, Rochester, N. Y.

	G	AB	H	2B	3B	HR	HR %	R	RBI	BB	SO	SB	BA	SA	AB	H	G by POS
1935 STL A	76	296	86	18	4	0	0.0	29	42	13	11	0	.291	.378	0	0	2B-76
1936	134	488	133	27	6	1	0.2	58	57	27	25	2	.273	.359	6	2	2B-128, SS-1
1937	130	487	134	24	1	1	0.2	54	40	21	26	1	.275	.335	0	0	2B-87, SS-44, 3B-1
1939 BOS A	54	161	39	6	2	0	0.0	17	20	3	9	0	.242	.304	7	2	2B-35, SS-10
1940	43	62	20	4	0	0	0.0	4	7	2	1	0	.323	.387	10	3	SS-20, 3B-4, 2B-4
1941	24	20	4	0	0	0	0.0	7	2	0	2	0	.200	.200	3	1	2B-9, SS-8
1942	1	1	1	0	0	0	0.0	0	1	0	0	0	1.000	1.000	0	0	2B-1
1946	3	5	1	0	0	0	0.0	0	0	0	1	0	.200	.200	0	0	2B-3
8 yrs.	465	1520	418	79	13	2	0.1	169	169	66	75	3	.275	.348	26	8	2B-343, SS-83, 3B-5

	G	AB	H	2B	3B	HR	HR %	R	RBI	BB	SO	SB	BA	SA	Pinch Hit AB	Pinch Hit H	G by POS

Tom Carey

CAREY, THOMAS JOHN
Also known as J. J. Norton.
B. 1849, Brooklyn, N. Y.   D. Feb. 13, 1899, Los Angeles, Calif.
Manager 1873-74.
BR TR 5'8" 145 lbs.

	G	AB	H	2B	3B	HR	HR %	R	RBI	BB	SO	SB	BA	SA	AB	H	G by POS
1876 HAR N	68	289	78	7	0	0	0.0	51	26	3		4	.270	.294	0	0	SS-68
1877	60	274	70	3	2	1	0.4	38	20	0		9	.255	.292	0	0	SS-60
1878 PRO N	61	253	60	10	3	0	0.0	33	24	0		14	.237	.300	0	0	SS-61
1879 CLE N	80	335	80	14	1	0	0.0	30	32	5		20	.239	.287	0	0	SS-80
4 yrs.	269	1151	288	34	6	1	0.1	152	102	8		47	.250	.293	0	0	SS-269

Chick Cargo

CARGO, ROBERT J.
B. 1871, Pittsburgh, Pa.   D. Apr. 27, 1904, Atlanta, Ga.
BR TR

	G	AB	H	2B	3B	HR	HR %	R	RBI	BB	SO	SB	BA	SA	AB	H	G by POS
1892 PIT N	2	4	1	0	0	0	0.0	0	0	0		0	.250	.250	0	0	SS-2

Fred Carisch

CARISCH, FREDERICK BEHLMER
B. Nov. 14, 1881, Fountain City, Wis.   D. Apr. 19, 1977, San Gabriel, Calif.
BR TR 5'10½" 174 lbs.

	G	AB	H	2B	3B	HR	HR %	R	RBI	BB	SO	SB	BA	SA	AB	H	G by POS
1903 PIT N	5	18	6	4	0	1	5.6	4	5	0		0	.333	.722	1	0	C-4
1904	37	125	31	3	1	0	0.0	9	8	9		3	.248	.288	1	0	C-22, 1B-14
1905	32	107	22	0	3	0	0.0	7	8	2		1	.206	.262	2	0	C-30
1906	4	12	1	0	0	0	0.0	0	0	1		1	.083	.083	0	0	C-4
1912 CLE A	25	69	19	3	1	0	0.0	4	5	1		3	.275	.348	2	0	C-23
1913	81	222	48	4	2	0	0.0	11	26	21	19	6	.216	.252	2	0	C-79
1914	40	102	22	3	2	0	0.0	8	5	12	18	2	.216	.284	2	0	C-38
1923 DET A	1	0	0	0	0	0		0	0	0	0				0	0	C-2
8 yrs.	226	655	149	17	9	1	0.2	43	57	46	37	16	.227	.285	10	0	C-202, 1B-14

Fred Carl

CARL, FREDERICK E.
B. 1856, Washington, D. C.   D. May 4, 1919, Washington, D. C.

	G	AB	H	2B	3B	HR	HR %	R	RBI	BB	SO	SB	BA	SA	AB	H	G by POS
1889 LOU AA	25	99	20	2	2	0	0.0	13	13	16	22	0	.202	.263	0	0	OF-18, 2B-6, 3B-1

Jim Carlin

CARLIN, JAMES ARTHUR
B. Feb. 23, 1918, Wylam, Ala.
BL TR 5'11" 165 lbs.

	G	AB	H	2B	3B	HR	HR %	R	RBI	BB	SO	SB	BA	SA	AB	H	G by POS
1941 PHI N	16	21	3	1	0	1	4.8	2	2	3	4	0	.143	.333	4	0	OF-9, 3B-2

Walter Carlisle

CARLISLE, WALTER G. (Rosy)
B. July 6, 1883, Yorkshire, England   D. May 27, 1945, Los Angeles, Calif.
BB TR

	G	AB	H	2B	3B	HR	HR %	R	RBI	BB	SO	SB	BA	SA	AB	H	G by POS
1908 BOS A	3	10	1	0	0	0	0.0	0	0	1		1	.100	.100	0	0	OF-3

Swede Carlstrom

CARLSTROM, ALBIN OSCAR
B. Oct. 26, 1890, Elizabeth, N. J.   D. Apr. 23, 1935, Elizabeth, N. J.
BR TR 6' 167 lbs.

	G	AB	H	2B	3B	HR	HR %	R	RBI	BB	SO	SB	BA	SA	AB	H	G by POS
1911 BOS A	2	6	1	0	0	0	0.0	0	0	0		0	.167	.167	0	0	SS-2

Cleo Carlyle

CARLYLE, HIRAM CLEO
Brother of Roy Carlyle.
B. Sept. 7, 1902, Fairburn, Ga.   D. Nov. 12, 1967, Los Angeles, Calif.
BL TR 6' 170 lbs.

	G	AB	H	2B	3B	HR	HR %	R	RBI	BB	SO	SB	BA	SA	AB	H	G by POS
1927 BOS A	95	278	65	12	8	1	0.4	31	28	36	40	4	.234	.345	10	3	OF-83

Roy Carlyle

CARLYLE, ROY EDWARD (Dizzy)
Brother of Cleo Carlyle.
B. Dec. 10, 1900, Buford, Ga.   D. Nov. 22, 1956, Norcross, Ga.
BL TR 6'2½" 195 lbs.

	G	AB	H	2B	3B	HR	HR %	R	RBI	BB	SO	SB	BA	SA	AB	H	G by POS
1925 2 teams		WAS	A	(1G –	.000)		BOS	A	(93G –	.326)							
" total	94	277	90	20	3	7	2.5	36	49	16	30	1	.325	.495	22	8	OF-67
1926 2 teams		BOS	A	(45G –	.287)		NY	A	(35G –	.377)							
" total	80	217	67	11	3	2	0.9	25	27	8	27	0	.309	.415	25	10	OF-53
2 yrs.	174	494	157	31	6	9	1.8	61	76	24	57	1	.318	.460	47	18	OF-120

George Carman

CARMAN, GEORGE WARTMAN
B. Doylestown, Pa.   D. June 16, 1929, Lancaster, Pa.

	G	AB	H	2B	3B	HR	HR %	R	RBI	BB	SO	SB	BA	SA	AB	H	G by POS
1890 PHI AA	28	97	17	2	0	0	0.0	9		8		5	.175	.196	0	0	SS-15, OF-10, 2B-2, 3B-1

Duke Carmel

CARMEL, LEON JAMES
B. Apr. 23, 1937, New York, N. Y.
BL TL 6'3" 202 lbs.

	G	AB	H	2B	3B	HR	HR %	R	RBI	BB	SO	SB	BA	SA	AB	H	G by POS
1959 STL N	10	23	3	1	0	0	0.0	2	3	1	6	0	.130	.174	0	0	OF-10
1960	4	3	0	0	0	0	0.0	0	0	1	1	1	.000	.000	0	0	1B-2, OF-1
1963 2 teams		STL	N	(57G –	.227)		NY	N	(47G –	.235)							
" total	104	193	45	6	3	4	2.1	20	20	25	48	2	.233	.358	19	4	OF-59, 1B-19
1965 NY N	6	8	0	0	0	0	0.0	0	0	0	5	0	.000	.000	4	0	1B-2
4 yrs.	124	227	48	7	3	4	1.8	22	23	27	60	3	.211	.322	23	4	OF-70, 1B-23

Eddie Carnett

CARNETT, EDWIN ELLIOTT (Lefty)
B. Oct. 21, 1916, Springfield, Mo.
BL TL 6' 185 lbs.

	G	AB	H	2B	3B	HR	HR %	R	RBI	BB	SO	SB	BA	SA	AB	H	G by POS
1941 BOS A	2	0	0	0	0	0		0	0	0	0	0	–	–	0	0	P-2
1944 CHI A	126	457	126	18	8	1	0.2	51	60	26	35	5	.276	.357	10	1	OF-88, 1B-25, P-2
1945 CLE A	30	73	16	7	0	0	0.0	5	7	2	9	0	.219	.315	11	3	OF-16, P-2
3 yrs.	158	530	142	25	8	1	0.2	56	67	28	44	5	.268	.351	21	4	OF-104, 1B-25, P-6

Bill Carney

CARNEY, WILLIAM JOHN
B. Mar. 25, 1874, St. Paul, Minn.   D. July 31, 1938, Hopkins, Minn.
BB TR 5'10"

	G	AB	H	2B	3B	HR	HR %	R	RBI	BB	SO	SB	BA	SA	AB	H	G by POS
1904 CHI N	2	7	0	0	0	0	0.0	0	0	1		0	.000	.000	0	0	OF-2

Jack Carney

CARNEY, JOHN JOSEPH (Handsome Jack)
B. Nov. 10, 1867, Salem, Mass.   D. Oct. 19, 1925, Litchfield, N. H.
BR TR 6' 200 lbs.

	G	AB	H	2B	3B	HR	HR %	R	RBI	BB	SO	SB	BA	SA	AB	H	G by POS
1889 WAS N	69	273	63	7	0	1	0.4	25	29	14	14	12	.231	.267	0	0	1B-53, OF-16
1890 2 teams		BUF	P	(28G –	.271)		CLE	P	(25G –	.348)							
" total	53	196	60	8	3	0	0.0	26	34	21	19	8	.306	.378	0	0	1B-30, OF-23

	G	AB	H	2B	3B	HR	HR %	R	RBI	BB	SO	SB	BA	SA	Pinch Hit AB	Pinch Hit H	G by POS

Jack Carney continued

	G	AB	H	2B	3B	HR	HR%	R	RBI	BB	SO	SB	BA	SA	AB	H	G by POS
1891 C-M AA	130	477	135	15	10	6	1.3	69	66	48	26	20	.283	.394	0	0	1B-130
3 yrs.	252	946	258	30	13	7	0.7	120	129	83	59	40	.273	.354	0	0	1B-213, OF-39

Pat Carney

CARNEY, PATRICK JOSEPH (Doc)   BL TL 6'   200 lbs.
B. Aug. 7, 1876, Holyoke, Mass.   D. Jan. 9, 1953, Worcester, Mass.

	G	AB	H	2B	3B	HR	HR%	R	RBI	BB	SO	SB	BA	SA	AB	H	G by POS
1901 BOS N	13	55	16	2	1	0	0.0	6	6	3		0	.291	.364	0	0	OF-13
1902	137	522	141	17	4	2	0.4	75	65	42		27	.270	.330	0	0	OF-137, P-2
1903	110	392	94	12	4	1	0.3	37	49	28		10	.240	.298	8	0	OF-92, P-10, 1B-1
1904	78	279	57	5	2	0	0.0	24	11	12		6	.204	.237	1	0	OF-71, P-4, 1B-1
4 yrs.	338	1248	308	36	11	3	0.2	142	131	85		43	.247	.300	9	0	OF-313, P-16, 1B-2

Hick Carpenter

CARPENTER, WARREN WILLIAM   BR TL 5'11"   186 lbs.
B. Aug. 16, 1855, Grafton, Mass.   D. Apr. 18, 1937, San Diego, Calif.

	G	AB	H	2B	3B	HR	HR%	R	RBI	BB	SO	SB	BA	SA	AB	H	G by POS
1879 SYR N	65	261	53	6	0	0	0.0	30	20	2	15		.203	.226	0	0	1B-34, 3B-18, OF-11, 2B-3
1880 CIN N	77	300	72	6	4	0	0.0	32	23	2	15		.240	.287	0	0	3B-67, 1B-9, SS-1
1881 WOR N	83	347	75	12	2	2	0.6	40	31	3	19		.216	.280	0	0	3B-83
1882 CIN AA	80	351	120	15	5	1	0.3	78		10			.342	.422	0	0	3B-80
1883	95	436	129	18	4	3	0.7	99		18			.296	.376	0	0	3B-95
1884	108	474	121	16	2	4	0.8	80		6			.255	.323	0	0	3B-108, OF-1
1885	112	473	131	12	8	2	0.4	89		9			.277	.349	0	0	3B-112
1886	111	458	101	8	5	2	0.4	67		18			.221	.273	0	0	3B-111
1887	127	498	124	12	6	1	0.2	70		19		44	.249	.303	0	0	3B-127
1888	136	551	147	14	5	3	0.5	68	67	5		59	.267	.327	0	0	3B-136
1889	123	486	127	23	6	0	0.0	67	63	18	41	47	.261	.333	0	0	3B-121, 1B-2
1892 STL N	1	3	1	0	0	0	0.0	0	0	1	1	0	.333	.333	0	0	3B-1
12 yrs.	1118	4638	1201	142	47	18	0.4	720	204	111	91	150	.259	.321	0	0	3B-1059, 1B-45, OF-12, 2B-3, SS-1

Charlie Carr

CARR, CHARLES CARBITT   BR TR 6'2"   195 lbs.
B. Dec. 27, 1876, Coatesville, Pa.   D. Nov. 26, 1932, Memphis, Tenn.

	G	AB	H	2B	3B	HR	HR%	R	RBI	BB	SO	SB	BA	SA	AB	H	G by POS
1898 WAS N	20	73	14	2	0	0	0.0	6	4	2		2	.192	.219	0	0	1B-20
1901 PHI A	2	8	1	0	0	0	0.0	0	0	0		0	.125	.125	0	0	1B-2
1903 DET A	135	548	154	23	11	2	0.4	59	79	10		10	.281	.374	0	0	1B-135
1904 2 teams		DET	A	(92G –	.214)		CLE	A	(32G –	.225)							
" total	124	480	104	18	4	0	0.0	38	47	18		6	.217	.271	0	0	1B-124
1905 CLE A	89	306	72	12	4	1	0.3	29	31	13		12	.235	.310	2	1	1B-87
1906 CIN N	22	94	18	2	3	0	0.0	9	10	2		0	.191	.277	0	0	1B-22
1914 IND F	115	441	129	11	10	3	0.7	44	69	26		19	.293	.383	0	0	1B-505
7 yrs.	507	1950	492	68	32	6	0.3	185	240	71		49	.252	.329	2	1	1B-505

Lew Carr

CARR, LEWIS SMITH   BR TR 6'2"   200 lbs.
B. Aug. 15, 1872, Union Springs, N.Y.   D. June 15, 1954, Moravia, N.Y.

	G	AB	H	2B	3B	HR	HR%	R	RBI	BB	SO	SB	BA	SA	AB	H	G by POS
1901 PIT N	9	28	7	1	1	0	0.0	2	4	2		0	.250	.357	0	0	SS-9, 3B-1

Chico Carrasquel

CARRASQUEL, ALFONSO COLON   BR TR 6'   170 lbs.
B. Jan. 23, 1928, Caracas, Venezuela

	G	AB	H	2B	3B	HR	HR%	R	RBI	BB	SO	SB	BA	SA	AB	H	G by POS
1950 CHI A	141	524	148	21	5	4	0.8	72	46	66	46	0	.282	.365	0	0	SS-141
1951	147	538	142	22	4	2	0.4	41	58	46	39	14	.264	.331	0	0	SS-147
1952	100	359	89	7	4	1	0.3	36	42	33	27	2	.248	.298	1	1	SS-99
1953	149	552	154	30	4	2	0.4	72	47	38	47	5	.279	.359	0	0	SS-149
1954	155	620	158	28	3	12	1.9	106	62	85	67	7	.255	.368	0	0	SS-155
1955	145	523	134	11	2	11	2.1	83	52	61	59	1	.256	.348	4	1	SS-144
1956 CLE A	141	474	115	15	1	7	1.5	60	48	52	61	0	.243	.323	0	0	SS-141, 3B-1
1957	125	392	108	14	1	8	2.0	37	57	41	53	0	.276	.378	3	1	SS-122
1958 2 teams		CLE	A	(49G –	.256)		KC	A	(59G –	.213)							
" total	108	316	74	11	1	4	1.3	33	34	35	27	0	.234	.313	11	4	SS-54, 3B-46
1959 BAL A	114	346	77	13	0	4	1.2	28	28	34	41	2	.223	.295	6	2	SS-89, 2B-22, 3B-2, 1B-1
10 yrs.	1325	4644	1199	172	25	55	1.2	568	474	491	467	31	.258	.342	25	9	SS-1241, 3B-49, 2B-22, 1B-1

Cam Carreon

CARREON, CAMILO GARCIA   BR TR 6'1½"   190 lbs.
B. Aug. 6, 1937, Colton, Calif.

	G	AB	H	2B	3B	HR	HR%	R	RBI	BB	SO	SB	BA	SA	AB	H	G by POS
1959 CHI A	1	1	0	0	0	0	0.0	0	0	0	0	0	.000	.000	0	0	C-1
1960	8	17	4	0	0	0	0.0	2	2	1	3	0	.235	.235	1	0	C-7
1961	78	229	62	5	1	4	1.7	32	27	21	24	0	.271	.354	7	2	C-71
1962	106	313	80	19	1	4	1.3	31	37	33	37	1	.256	.361	11	5	C-93
1963	101	270	74	10	1	2	0.7	28	35	23	32	1	.274	.341	7	3	C-92
1964	37	95	26	5	0	0	0.0	12	4	7	13	0	.274	.326	3	0	C-34
1965 CLE A	19	52	12	2	1	1	1.9	6	7	9	6	1	.231	.365	0	0	C-19
1966 BAL A	4	9	2	2	0	0	0.0	2	2	3	2	0	.222	.444	1	1	C-3
8 yrs.	354	986	260	43	4	11	1.1	113	114	97	117	3	.264	.349	30	11	C-320

Bill Carrigan

CARRIGAN, WILLIAM FRANCIS (Rough)   BR TR 5'11"   175 lbs.
B. Oct. 22, 1883, Lewiston, Me.   D. July 8, 1969, Lewiston, Me.
Manager 1913-16, 1927-29.

	G	AB	H	2B	3B	HR	HR%	R	RBI	BB	SO	SB	BA	SA	AB	H	G by POS
1906 BOS A	37	109	23	0	0	0	0.0	5	10	5		3	.211	.211	2	1	C-35
1908	57	149	35	5	2	0	0.0	13	14	3		1	.235	.295	7	2	C-47, 1B-3
1909	94	280	83	13	2	1	0.4	27	36	17		2	.296	.368	6	0	C-77, 1B-8
1910	114	342	85	11	1	3	0.9	36	53	23		10	.249	.313	4	0	C-110
1911	72	232	67	6	1	1	0.4	29	30	26		5	.289	.336	4	2	C-62, 1B-6
1912	87	266	70	7	1	0	0.0	34	24	38		7	.263	.297	0	0	C-87
1913	85	256	62	15	5	0	0.0	17	28	27	26	6	.242	.340	4	0	C-81
1914	81	178	45	5	1	0	0.6	18	22	40	18	1	.253	.309	2	1	C-78
1915	46	95	19	3	0	0	0.0	10	7	16	12	0	.200	.232	2	1	C-44

	G	AB	H	2B	3B	HR	HR %	R	RBI	BB	SO	SB	BA	SA	Pinch Hit AB	Pinch Hit H	G by POS

Bill Carrigan continued

	G	AB	H	2B	3B	HR	HR%	R	RBI	BB	SO	SB	BA	SA	AB	H	G by POS
1916	33	63	17	2	1	0	0.0	7	11	11	3	2	.270	.333	5	1	C-27
10 yrs.	706	1970	506	67	14	6	0.3	196	235	206	59	37	.257	.314	36	6	C-648, 1B-17

WORLD SERIES

	G	AB	H	2B	3B	HR	HR%	R	RBI	BB	SO	SB	BA	SA	AB	H	G by POS
1912 BOS A	2	7	0	0	0	0	0.0	0	0	0	0	0	.000	.000	0	0	C-2
1915	1	2	0	0	0	0	0.0	0	0	1	1	0	.000	.000	0	0	C-1
1916	1	3	2	0	0	0	0.0	0	1	0	1	0	.667	.667	0	0	C-1
3 yrs.	4	12	2	0	0	0	0.0	0	1	1	2	0	.167	.167	0	0	C-4

Chick Carroll

CARROLL, EDWARD
B. 1868, Arkansas   D. July 13, 1908, Chicago, Ill.

	G	AB	H	2B	3B	HR	HR%	R	RBI	BB	SO	SB	BA	SA	AB	H	G by POS
1884 WAS U	4	16	4	0	0	0	0.0	1		0			.250	.250	0	0	OF-4

Cliff Carroll

CARROLL, SAMUEL CLIFFORD   BB TR 5'8"   163 lbs.
B. Oct. 18, 1859, Clay Grove, Iowa   D. June 12, 1923, Portland, Ore.

	G	AB	H	2B	3B	HR	HR%	R	RBI	BB	SO	SB	BA	SA	AB	H	G by POS
1882 PRO N	10	41	5	0	0	0	0.0	4		0	4		.122	.122	0	0	OF-10
1883	58	238	63	12	3	1	0.4	37		4	28		.265	.353	0	0	OF-58
1884	113	452	118	16	4	3	0.7	90		29	39		.261	.334	0	0	OF-113
1885	104	426	99	12	3	1	0.2	62	40	29	29		.232	.282	0	0	OF-104
1886 WAS N	111	433	99	11	6	2	0.5	73	22	44	26		.229	.296	0	0	OF-111
1887	103	420	104	17	4	4	1.0	79	37	17	30	40	.248	.336	0	0	OF-103
1888 PIT N	5	20	0	0	0	0	0.0	1	0	0	8	2	.000	.000	0	0	OF-5
1890 CHI N	136	582	166	16	6	7	1.2	134	65	53	34	34	.285	.369	0	0	OF-136
1891	130	515	132	20	8	7	1.4	87	80	50	42	31	.256	.367	0	0	OF-130
1892 STL N	101	407	111	14	8	4	1.0	82	49	47	22	30	.273	.376	0	0	OF-101
1893 BOS N	120	438	98	7	5	2	0.5	80	54	88	28	29	.224	.276	0	0	OF-120
11 yrs.	991	3972	995	125	47	31	0.8	729	346	361	290	166	.251	.329	0	0	OF-991

Dixie Carroll

CARROLL, DORSEY LEE   BL TR 5'11"   165 lbs.
B. May 19, 1891, Paducah, Ky.   D. Dec. 1, 1984, Jacksonville, Fla.

	G	AB	H	2B	3B	HR	HR%	R	RBI	BB	SO	SB	BA	SA	AB	H	G by POS
1919 BOS N	15	49	13	3	1	0	0.0	7		7	1	5	.265	.367	1	1	OF-13

Doc Carroll

CARROLL, RALPH ARTHUR (Red)   BR TR 6'   170 lbs.
B. Dec. 28, 1891, Worcester, Mass.

	G	AB	H	2B	3B	HR	HR%	R	RBI	BB	SO	SB	BA	SA	AB	H	G by POS
1916 PHI A	10	22	2	0	0	0	0.0	1	0	1	8	0	.091	.091	0	0	C-10

Fred Carroll

CARROLL, FREDERICK HERBERT   BR TR 5'11"   185 lbs.
B. July 2, 1864, Sacramento, Calif.   D. Nov. 7, 1904, San Rafael, Calif.

	G	AB	H	2B	3B	HR	HR%	R	RBI	BB	SO	SB	BA	SA	AB	H	G by POS
1884 COL AA	69	252	70	13	5	6	2.4	46		13			.278	.440	0	0	C-54, OF-15
1885 PIT AA	71	280	75	13	8	5	1.0	45		7			.268	.371	0	0	C-60, OF-12
1886	122	486	140	28	11	5	1.0	92		52			.288	.422	0	0	C-70, OF-27, 1B-25, SS-1
1887 PIT N	102	421	138	24	15	6	1.4	91	54	36	21	23	.328	.499	0	0	OF-46, C-40, 1B-17, SS-1
1888	97	366	91	14	5	2	0.5	62	48	32	31	18	.249	.331	0	0	C-54, OF-38, 1B-5, 3B-1
1889	91	318	105	21	11	2	0.6	80	51	85	26	19	.330	.484	0	0	C-43, OF-41, 1B-7, 3B-1
1890 PIT P	111	416	124	20	7	2	0.5	95	71	75	22	35	.298	.394	0	0	C-56, OF-49, 1B-7
1891 PIT N	91	353	77	13	4	4	1.1	55	48	48	36	22	.218	.312	0	0	OF-91
8 yrs.	754	2892	820	146	66	27	0.9	546	271	348	136	117	.284	.408	0		C-377, OF-319, 1B-61, SS-2, 3B-2

Pat Carroll

CARROLL, PATRICK
B. Philadelphia, Pa.   D. Feb. 14, 1916, Philadelphia, Pa.

	G	AB	H	2B	3B	HR	HR%	R	RBI	BB	SO	SB	BA	SA	AB	H	G by POS
1884 2 teams		ALT	U (11G – .265)		PHI	U (5G – .158)											
" total	16	68	16	2	0	0	0.0	5		1			.235	.265	0	0	C-13, OF-3

Scrappy Carroll

CARROLL, JOHN E.   5'7½"
B. Aug. 15, 1863, Buffalo, N.Y.   D. Nov. 14, 1942, Buffalo, N.Y.

	G	AB	H	2B	3B	HR	HR%	R	RBI	BB	SO	SB	BA	SA	AB	H	G by POS
1884 STP U	9	31	3	1	0	0	0.0	3		2			.097	.129	0	0	OF-8, 3B-2
1885 BUF N	13	40	3	0	0	0	0.0	1	1	2	8		.075	.075	0	0	OF-13
1887 CLE AA	57	216	43	5	1	0	0.0	30		15		19	.199	.231	0	0	OF-54, 3B-3, 2B-1
3 yrs.	79	287	49	6	1	0	0.0	34		19	8	19	.171	.199	0	0	OF-75, 3B-5, 2B-1

Tommy Carroll

CARROLL, THOMAS EDWARD   BR TR 6'3"   186 lbs.
B. Sept. 17, 1936, Jamaica, N.Y.

	G	AB	H	2B	3B	HR	HR%	R	RBI	BB	SO	SB	BA	SA	AB	H	G by POS
1955 NY A	14	6	2	0	0	0	0.0	3	0	0	2	0	.333	.333	0	0	SS-4
1956	36	17	6	0	0	0	0.0	11	0	1	3	1	.353	.353	3	2	3B-11, SS-1
1959 KC A	14	7	1	0	0	0	0.0	1	1	0	1	0	.143	.143	0	0	SS-9, 3B-3
3 yrs.	64	30	9	0	0	0	0.0	15	1	1	6	1	.300	.300	3	2	SS-14, 3B-14

WORLD SERIES

	G	AB	H	2B	3B	HR	HR%	R	RBI	BB	SO	SB	BA	SA	AB	H	G by POS
1955 NY A	2	0	0	0	0	0	–	0	0	0	0	0	–	–	0	0	

Kid Carsey

CARSEY, WILFRED   BR TR 5'7"   168 lbs.
B. Oct. 22, 1870, New York, N.Y.   D. Mar. 29, 1960, Miami, Fla.

	G	AB	H	2B	3B	HR	HR%	R	RBI	BB	SO	SB	BA	SA	AB	H	G by POS
1891 WAS AA	61	187	28	5	2	0	0.0	25	15	19	38	2	.150	.198	0	0	P-54, OF-7, SS-2
1892 PHI N	44	131	20	2	1	1	0.8	8	10	9	24	1	.153	.206	0	0	P-43, OF-2
1893	39	145	27	1	1	0	0.0	12	10	5	14	2	.186	.207	0	0	P-39
1894	35	125	34	2	2	0	0.0	30	18	16	11	3	.272	.320	0	0	P-35
1895	44	141	41	2	0	0	0.0	24	20	15	12	2	.291	.305	0	0	P-44
1896	27	81	18	2	2	0	0.0	13	7	11	12	1	.222	.296	0	0	P-27
1897 2 teams		PHI	N (4G – .231)		STL	N (13G – .302)											
" total	17	56	16	2	2	0	0.0	3	6	1		1	.286	.393	1	1	P-16
1898 STL N	38	105	21	0	1	1	1.0	8	10	10		3	.200	.248	0	0	P-20, 2B-10, OF-8
1899 3 teams		CLE	N (11G – .278)		WAS	N (4G – .000)		NY	N (5G – .333)								
" total	20	65	16	1	0	0	0.0	8	5	5		2	.246	.262	0	0	P-14, SS-3, 3B-3
1901 BKN N	2	2	0	0	0	0	0.0	0	0	0		0	.000	.000	0	0	P-2
10 yrs.	327	1038	221	17	11	2	0.2	131	101	91	111	17	.213	.256	1	1	P-294, OF-17, 2B-10, SS-5, 3B-3

	G	AB	H	2B	3B	HR	HR %	R	RBI	BB	SO	SB	BA	SA	Pinch Hit AB	Pinch Hit H	G by POS

Kit Carson

CARSON, WALTER LLOYD
B. Nov. 15, 1912, Colton, Calif.　D. June 21, 1983
BL TL 6'　180 lbs.

	G	AB	H	2B	3B	HR	HR %	R	RBI	BB	SO	SB	BA	SA	PH AB	PH H	G by POS
1934 CLE A	5	18	5	2	1	0	0.0	4	1	2	3	0	.278	.500	1	1	OF-4
1935	16	22	5	2	0	0	0.0	1	1	2	6	0	.227	.318	10	2	OF-4
2 yrs.	21	40	10	4	1	0	0.0	5	2	4	9	0	.250	.400	11	3	OF-8

Frank Carswell

CARSWELL, FRANK WILLIS (Tex, Wheels)
B. Nov. 6, 1919, Palestine, Tex.
BR TR 6'　195 lbs.

	G	AB	H	2B	3B	HR	HR %	R	RBI	BB	SO	SB	BA	SA	PH AB	PH H	G by POS
1953 DET A	16	15	4	0	0	0	0.0	2	2	3	1	0	.267	.267	12	4	OF-3

Blackie Carter

CARTER, OTIS LEONARD
B. Sept. 30, 1902, Langley, S. C.　D. Sept. 10, 1976, Greenville, S. C.
BR TR 5'10"　175 lbs.

	G	AB	H	2B	3B	HR	HR %	R	RBI	BB	SO	SB	BA	SA	PH AB	PH H	G by POS
1925 NY N	1	4	0	0	0	0	0.0	0	0	0	1	0	.000	.000	0	0	OF-1
1926	5	17	4	1	0	1	5.9	4	1	1	0	0	.235	.471	1	0	OF-4
2 yrs.	6	21	4	1	0	1	4.8	4	1	1	1	0	.190	.381	1	0	OF-5

Gary Carter

CARTER, GARY EDMUND
B. Apr. 8, 1954, Culver City, Calif.
BR TR 6'2"　205 lbs.

	G	AB	H	2B	3B	HR	HR %	R	RBI	BB	SO	SB	BA	SA	PH AB	PH H	G by POS
1974 MON N	9	27	11	0	1	1	3.7	5	6	1	2	2	.407	.593	1	1	C-6, OF-2
1975	144	503	136	20	1	17	3.4	58	68	72	83	5	.270	.416	5	1	OF-92, C-66, 3B-1
1976	91	311	68	8	1	6	1.9	31	38	30	43	0	.219	.309	2	0	C-60, OF-36
1977	154	522	148	29	2	31	5.9	86	84	58	103	5	.284	.525	6	3	C-146, OF-1
1978	157	533	136	27	1	20	3.8	76	72	62	70	10	.255	.422	6	0	C-152, 1B-1
1979	141	505	143	26	5	22	4.4	74	75	40	62	3	.283	.485	3	0	C-138
1980	154	549	145	25	5	29	5.3	76	101	58	78	3	.264	.486	4	0	C-149
1981	100	374	94	20	2	16	4.3	48	68	35	35	1	.251	.444	0	0	C-100, 1B-1
1982	154	557	163	32	1	29	5.2	91	97	78	64	2	.293	.510	3	0	C-153
1983	145	541	146	37	3	17	3.1	63	79	51	57	1	.270	.444	2	0	C-144, 1B-1
1984	159	596	175	32	1	27	4.5	75	106	64	57	2	.294	.487	2	0	C-143, 1B-25
11 yrs.	1408	5018	1365	256	23	215	4.3	683	794	549	654	34	.272	.461	34	5	C-1257, OF-131, 1B-28, 3B-1

DIVISIONAL PLAYOFF SERIES

	G	AB	H	2B	3B	HR	HR %	R	RBI	BB	SO	SB	BA	SA	PH AB	PH H	G by POS
1981 MON N	5	19	8	3	0	2	10.5	3	6	1	1	0	.421	.895	0	0	C-5

LEAGUE CHAMPIONSHIP SERIES

	G	AB	H	2B	3B	HR	HR %	R	RBI	BB	SO	SB	BA	SA	PH AB	PH H	G by POS
1981 MON N	5	16	7	1	0	0	0.0	3	0	4	2	0	.438	.500	0	0	C-5

Howard Carter

CARTER, JOHN HOWARD (Nick)
B. Oct. 13, 1904, New York, N. Y.
BR TR 5'10"　154 lbs.

	G	AB	H	2B	3B	HR	HR %	R	RBI	BB	SO	SB	BA	SA	PH AB	PH H	G by POS
1926 CIN N	5	1	0	0	0	0	0.0	0	0	0	0	0	.000	.000	0	0	2B-3, SS-1

Joe Carter

CARTER, JOSEPH
B. Mar. 7, 1960, Oklahoma City, Okla.
BR TR 6'3"　210 lbs.

	G	AB	H	2B	3B	HR	HR %	R	RBI	BB	SO	SB	BA	SA	PH AB	PH H	G by POS
1983 CHI N	23	51	9	1	1	0	0.0	6	1	0	21	1	.176	.235	5	1	OF-16
1984 CLE A	66	244	67	6	1	13	5.3	32	41	11	48	2	.275	.467	7	5	OF-59, 1B-7
2 yrs.	89	295	76	7	2	13	4.4	38	42	11	69	3	.258	.427	12	6	OF-75, 1B-7

Ed Cartwright

CARTWRIGHT, EDWARD CHARLES (Jumbo)
B. Oct. 3, 1859, Pittsburgh, Pa.　D. Sept. 3, 1933, St. Petersburg, Fla.
BR　5'10"　220 lbs.

	G	AB	H	2B	3B	HR	HR %	R	RBI	BB	SO	SB	BA	SA	PH AB	PH H	G by POS
1890 STL AA	75	300	90	12	4	8	2.7	70		29		26	.300	.447	0	0	1B-75
1894 WAS N	132	507	149	35	13	12	2.4	88	106	57	43	31	.294	.485	0	0	1B-132
1895	122	472	156	34	17	3	0.6	95	90	54	41	50	.331	.494	0	0	1B-122
1896	133	499	138	15	10	1	0.2	76	62	54	44	28	.277	.353	0	0	1B-133
1897	33	124	29	4	0	0	0.0	19	15	8		9	.234	.266	0	0	1B-33
5 yrs.	495	1902	562	100	44	24	1.3	348	272	202	128	144	.295	.432	0	0	1B-495

Rico Carty

CARTY, RICARDO ADOLFO JACABO
B. Sept. 1, 1941, San Pedro de Macoris, Dominican Republic
BR TR 6'3"　200 lbs.

	G	AB	H	2B	3B	HR	HR %	R	RBI	BB	SO	SB	BA	SA	PH AB	PH H	G by POS
1963 MIL N	2	2	0	0	0	0	0.0	0	0	0	2	0	.000	.000	2	0	
1964	133	455	150	28	4	22	4.8	72	88	43	78	1	.330	.554	12	3	OF-121
1965	83	271	84	18	1	10	3.7	37	35	17	44	1	.310	.494	11	3	OF-73
1966 ATL N	151	521	170	25	2	15	2.9	73	76	60	74	4	.326	.468	12	2	OF-126, C-17, 1B-2, 3B-1
1967	134	444	113	16	2	15	3.4	41	64	49	70	4	.255	.401	14	2	OF-112, 1B-9
1969	104	304	104	15	0	16	5.3	47	58	32	28	0	.342	.549	22	9	OF-79
1970	136	478	175	23	3	25	5.2	84	101	77	46	1	.366	.584	3	1	OF-133
1972	86	271	75	12	2	6	2.2	31	29	44	33	0	.277	.402	8	2	OF-78
1973 3 teams	TEX A	(86G –	.232)		CHI N	(22G –	.214)		OAK A	(7G –	.250)						
" total	115	384	88	13	0	5	1.3	29	42	44	50	2	.229	.302	7	2	OF-72, DH-32
1974 CLE A	33	91	33	5	0	1	1.1	6	16	5	9	0	.363	.451	11	2	DH-14, 1B-8
1975	118	383	118	19	1	18	4.7	57	64	45	31	2	.308	.504	8	6	DH-72, 1B-26, OF-12
1976	152	552	171	34	0	13	2.4	67	83	67	45	1	.310	.442	1	0	DH-137, 1B-12, OF-1
1977	127	461	129	23	1	15	3.3	50	80	56	51	1	.280	.432	2	1	DH-123, 1B-2
1978 2 teams	TOR A	(104G –	.284)		OAK A	(41G –	.277)										
" total	145	528	149	21	1	31	5.9	70	99	57	57	1	.282	.502	4	0	DH-142
1979 TOR A	132	461	118	26	0	12	2.6	48	55	46	45	3	.256	.390	9	4	DH-129
15 yrs.	1651	5606	1677	278	17	204	3.6	712	890	642	663	21	.299	.464	126	38	OF-807, DH-649, 1B-59, C-17, 3B-1

LEAGUE CHAMPIONSHIP SERIES

	G	AB	H	2B	3B	HR	HR %	R	RBI	BB	SO	SB	BA	SA	PH AB	PH H	G by POS
1969 ATL N	3	10	3	2	0	0	0.0	4	0	3	1	0	.300	.500	0	0	OF-3

Bob Caruthers

CARUTHERS, ROBERT LEE (Parisian Bob)
B. Jan. 5, 1864, Memphis, Tenn.　D. Aug. 5, 1911, Peoria, Ill.
BL TR 5'7"　138 lbs.

	G	AB	H	2B	3B	HR	HR %	R	RBI	BB	SO	SB	BA	SA	PH AB	PH H	G by POS
1884 STL AA	23	82	21	2	0	2	2.4	15		4			.256	.354	0	0	OF-16, P-13
1885	60	222	50	10	2	1	0.5	37		20			.225	.302	0	0	P-53, OF-7
1886	87	317	106	21	14	4	1.3	91		64			.334	.527	0	0	P-44, OF-43, 2B-2
1887	98	364	130	23	11	8	2.2	102		66		49	.357	.547	0	0	OF-54, P-39, 1B-7
1888 BKN AA	94	335	77	10	5	5	1.5	58	53	45		23	.230	.334	0	0	OF-51, P-44

	G	AB	H	2B	3B	HR	HR %	R	RBI	BB	SO	SB	BA	SA	Pinch Hit AB	Pinch Hit H	G by POS

Bob Caruthers continued

	G	AB	H	2B	3B	HR	HR%	R	RBI	BB	SO	SB	BA	SA	PH AB	PH H	G by POS
1889	59	172	43	8	3	2	1.2	45	31	44	17	9	.250	.366	0	0	P-56, OF-3, 1B-2
1890 BKN N	71	238	63	7	4	1	0.4	46	29	47	18	13	.265	.340	0	0	OF-39, P-37
1891	56	171	48	5	3	2	1.2	24	23	25	13	4	.281	.380	1	0	P-38, OF-17, 2B-1
1892 STL N	143	513	142	16	8	3	0.6	76	69	86	29	24	.277	.357	0	0	OF-122, P-16, 2B-6, 1B-4
1893 2 teams	CHI	N	(1G –	.000)		CIN	N	(13G –	.292)								
" total	14	51	14	2	0	1	2.0	14	8	16	2	4	.275	.373	0	0	OF-14
10 yrs.	705	2465	694	104	50	29	1.2	508	212	417	79	126	.282	.400	1	0	OF-366, P-340, 1B-13, 2B-9

Paul Casanova

CASANOVA, ORTIZ PAULINO
B. Dec. 31, 1941, Colon Matanzas, Cuba

BR TR 6'4" 180 lbs.

	G	AB	H	2B	3B	HR	HR%	R	RBI	BB	SO	SB	BA	SA	PH AB	PH H	G by POS
1965 WAS A	5	13	4	1	0	0	0.0	2	1	1	3	0	.308	.385	0	0	C-4
1966	122	429	109	16	5	13	3.0	45	44	14	78	1	.254	.406	3	0	C-119
1967	141	528	131	19	1	9	1.7	47	53	17	65	1	.248	.339	8	1	C-137
1968	96	322	63	6	0	4	1.2	19	25	7	52	0	.196	.252	7	1	C-92
1969	124	379	82	9	2	4	1.1	26	37	18	52	0	.216	.282	5	1	C-122
1970	104	328	75	17	3	6	1.8	25	30	10	47	0	.229	.354	9	1	C-100
1971	94	311	63	9	1	5	1.6	19	26	14	52	0	.203	.286	8	1	C-83
1972 ATL N	49	136	28	3	0	2	1.5	8	10	4	28	0	.206	.272	6	0	C-43
1973	82	236	51	7	0	7	3.0	18	18	11	36	0	.216	.335	4	1	C-78
1974	42	104	21	0	0	0	0.0	5	8	5	17	0	.202	.202	9	4	C-33
10 yrs.	859	2786	627	87	12	50	1.8	214	252	101	430	2	.225	.319	59	10	C-811

George Case

CASE, GEORGE WASHINGTON
B. Nov. 11, 1915, Trenton, N. J.

BR TR 6' 183 lbs.

	G	AB	H	2B	3B	HR	HR%	R	RBI	BB	SO	SB	BA	SA	PH AB	PH H	G by POS
1937 WAS A	22	90	26	6	2	0	0.0	14	11	3	5	2	.289	.400	0	0	OF-22
1938	107	433	132	27	3	2	0.5	69	40	39	28	11	.305	.395	8	1	OF-101
1939	128	530	160	20	7	2	0.4	103	35	56	36	51	.302	.377	2	0	OF-123
1940	154	656	192	29	5	5	0.8	109	56	52	39	35	.293	.375	0	0	OF-154
1941	153	649	176	32	8	2	0.3	95	53	51	37	33	.271	.354	2	0	OF-151
1942	125	513	164	26	2	5	1.0	101	43	44	30	44	.320	.407	1	0	OF-120
1943	141	613	180	36	5	1	0.2	102	52	40	27	61	.294	.374	0	0	OF-140
1944	119	465	116	14	2	2	0.4	63	32	49	22	49	.249	.301	0	0	OF-114
1945	123	504	148	19	5	1	0.2	72	31	49	27	30	.294	.357	0	0	OF-123
1946 CLE A	118	484	109	23	4	1	0.2	46	22	34	38	28	.225	.295	0	0	OF-118
1947 WAS A	36	80	12	1	0	0	0.0	11	2	8	8	5	.150	.163	3	0	OF-21
11 yrs.	1226	5017	1415	233	43	21	0.4	785	377	425	297	349	.282	.358	16	1	OF-1187

Bob Casey

CASEY, ORRIN ROBINSON
B. 1859, Canada   D. Nov. 28, 1936, Syracuse, N. Y.

5'11" 190 lbs.

	G	AB	H	2B	3B	HR	HR%	R	RBI	BB	SO	SB	BA	SA	PH AB	PH H	G by POS
1882 DET N	9	39	9	2	1	1	2.6	5	7	0	15		.231	.410	0	0	3B-8, 2B-1

Dennis Casey

CASEY, DENNIS PATRICK
Brother of Dan Casey.
B. Mar. 30, 1858, Binghamton, N. Y.   D. Jan. 19, 1909, Binghamton, N. Y.

BL TR 6' 180 lbs.

	G	AB	H	2B	3B	HR	HR%	R	RBI	BB	SO	SB	BA	SA	PH AB	PH H	G by POS
1884 2 teams	WIL	U	(2G –	.250)		BAL	AA	(37G –	.248)								
" total	39	157	39	8	4	3	1.9	21		5			.248	.408	0	0	OF-39
1885 BAL AA	63	264	76	10	5	3	1.1	50		21			.288	.398	0	0	OF-63
2 yrs.	102	421	115	18	9	6	1.4	71		26			.273	.401	0	0	OF-102

Doc Casey

CASEY, JAMES PETER
B. Mar. 15, 1871, Lawrence, Mass.   D. Dec. 30, 1936, Detroit, Mich.

BL TR

	G	AB	H	2B	3B	HR	HR%	R	RBI	BB	SO	SB	BA	SA	PH AB	PH H	G by POS
1898 WAS N	28	112	31	2	0	0	0.0	13	15	3		15	.277	.295	0	0	3B-22, SS-4, C-3
1899 2 teams	WAS	N	(9G –	.118)		BKN	N	(134G –	.269)								
" total	143	559	145	16	8	1	0.2	78	45	27		28	.259	.322	0	0	3B-143
1900 BKN N	1	3	1	0	0	0	0.0	0	1	0		0	.333	.333	0	0	3B-1
1901 DET A	128	540	153	16	9	2	0.4	105	46	32		34	.283	.357	1	0	3B-127
1902	132	520	142	18	7	3	0.6	69	55	44		22	.273	.352	0	0	3B-132
1903 CHI N	112	435	126	8	3	1	0.2	56	40	19		11	.290	.329	0	0	3B-112
1904	136	548	147	20	4	1	0.2	71	43	18		21	.268	.325	0	0	3B-134, C-2
1905	144	526	122	21	10	1	0.2	66	56	41		22	.232	.316	2	0	3B-142, SS-1
1906 BKN N	149	571	133	17	8	0	0.0	71	34	52		22	.233	.291	0	0	3B-149
1907	141	527	122	19	3	0	0.0	55	19	34		16	.231	.279	3	0	3B-138
10 yrs.	1114	4341	1122	137	52	9	0.2	584	354	270		191	.258	.320	6	0	3B-1100, SS-5, C-5

Joe Casey

CASEY, JOSEPH FELIX
B. Aug. 15, 1887, Boston, Mass.   D. June 2, 1966, Melrose, Mass.

BR TR

	G	AB	H	2B	3B	HR	HR%	R	RBI	BB	SO	SB	BA	SA	PH AB	PH H	G by POS
1909 DET A	3	5	0	0	0	0	0.0	1	0	1		0	.000	.000	0	0	C-3
1910	23	62	12	3	0	0	0.0	3	2	2		1	.194	.242	0	0	C-22
1911	15	33	5	0	0	0	0.0	2	3	3		0	.152	.152	0	0	C-12, OF-3
1918 WAS A	9	17	4	0	0	0	0.0	3	2	2	2	0	.235	.235	0	0	C-8
4 yrs.	50	117	21	3	0	0	0.0	9	7	8	2	1	.179	.205	0	0	C-45, OF-3

Dave Cash

CASH, DAVID
B. June 11, 1948, Utica, N. Y.

BR TR 5'11" 170 lbs.

	G	AB	H	2B	3B	HR	HR%	R	RBI	BB	SO	SB	BA	SA	PH AB	PH H	G by POS
1969 PIT N	18	61	17	3	1	0	0.0	8	4	9	9	2	.279	.361	0	0	2B-17
1970	64	210	66	7	6	1	0.5	30	28	17	25	5	.314	.419	4	1	2B-55
1971	123	478	138	17	4	2	0.4	79	34	46	33	13	.289	.354	4	2	2B-105, 3B-24, SS-3
1972	99	425	120	22	4	3	0.7	58	30	22	31	9	.282	.374	3	1	2B-97
1973	116	436	118	21	2	1	0.2	59	31	38	36	2	.271	.342	14	4	2B-92, 3B-17
1974 PHI N	162	687	206	26	11	2	0.3	89	58	46	33	20	.300	.378	0	0	2B-162
1975	162	699	213	40	3	4	0.6	111	57	56	34	13	.305	.388	0	0	2B-162
1976	160	666	189	14	12	1	0.2	92	56	54	13	10	.284	.345	1	0	2B-158
1977 MON N	153	650	188	42	7	0	0.0	91	43	52	33	21	.289	.375	0	0	2B-153
1978	159	658	166	26	3	3	0.5	66	43	37	29	12	.252	.315	0	0	2B-159

	G	AB	H	2B	3B	HR	HR %	R	RBI	BB	SO	SB	BA	SA	Pinch Hit AB	Pinch Hit H	G by POS

Dave Cash continued

	G	AB	H	2B	3B	HR	HR %	R	RBI	BB	SO	SB	BA	SA	PH AB	PH H	G by POS
1979	76	187	60	11	1	2	1.1	24	19	12	12	7	.321	.422	30	10	2B-47
1980 **SD** N	130	397	90	14	2	1	0.3	25	23	35	21	6	.227	.280	7	1	2B-123
12 yrs.	1422	5554	1571	243	56	21	0.4	732	426	424	309	120	.283	.358	63	19	2B-1330, 3B-41, SS-3

LEAGUE CHAMPIONSHIP SERIES
	G	AB	H	2B	3B	HR	HR %	R	RBI	BB	SO	SB	BA	SA	PH AB	PH H	G by POS
1970 **PIT** N	2	8	1	1	0	0	0.0	1	0	1	1	0	.125	.250	0	0	2B-2
1971	4	19	8	2	0	0	0.0	5	1	0	1	1	.421	.526	0	0	2B-4
1972	5	19	4	0	0	0	0.0	0	3	0	0	0	.211	.211	0	0	2B-5
1976 **PHI** N	3	13	4	1	0	0	0.0	1	1	0	0	0	.308	.385	0	0	2B-3
4 yrs.	14	59	17	4	0	0	0.0	7	5	1	2	1	.288	.356	0	0	2B-14

WORLD SERIES
	G	AB	H	2B	3B	HR	HR %	R	RBI	BB	SO	SB	BA	SA	PH AB	PH H	G by POS
1971 **PIT** N	7	30	4	1	0	0	0.0	2	1	3	1	1	.133	.167	0	0	2B-7

Norm Cash

CASH, NORMAN DALTON   BL TL 6'   185 lbs.
B. Nov. 10, 1934, Justiceburg, Tex.

	G	AB	H	2B	3B	HR	HR %	R	RBI	BB	SO	SB	BA	SA	PH AB	PH H	G by POS
1958 **CHI** A	13	8	2	0	0	0	0.0	2	0	0	1	0	.250	.250	5	1	OF-4
1959	58	104	25	0	1	4	3.8	16	16	18	9	1	.240	.375	19	5	1B-31
1960 **DET** A	121	353	101	16	3	18	5.1	64	63	65	58	4	.286	.501	23	9	1B-99, OF-4
1961	159	535	**193**	22	8	41	7.7	119	132	124	85	11	**.361**	.662	1	0	1B-157
1962	148	507	123	16	2	39	7.7	94	89	104	82	6	.243	.513	2	1	1B-146, OF-3
1963	147	493	133	19	1	26	5.3	67	79	89	76	2	.270	.471	7	0	1B-142
1964	144	479	123	15	5	23	4.8	63	83	70	66	2	.257	.453	10	1	1B-137
1965	142	467	124	23	1	30	6.4	79	82	77	62	6	.266	.512	5	0	1B-139
1966	160	603	168	18	3	32	5.3	98	93	66	91	2	.279	.478	3	1	1B-158
1967	152	488	118	16	5	22	4.5	64	72	81	100	3	.242	.430	7	1	1B-146
1968	127	411	108	15	1	25	6.1	50	63	39	70	1	.263	.487	15	2	1B-117
1969	142	483	135	15	4	22	4.6	81	74	63	80	2	.280	.464	9	2	1B-134
1970	130	370	96	18	2	15	4.1	58	53	72	58	0	.259	.441	17	6	1B-114
1971	135	452	128	10	3	32	7.1	72	91	59	86	1	.283	.531	7	1	1B-131
1972	137	440	114	16	0	22	5.0	51	61	50	64	0	.259	.445	11	0	1B-134
1973	121	363	95	19	0	19	5.2	51	40	47	73	1	.262	.471	8	2	1B-114, DH-3
1974	53	149	34	3	2	7	4.7	17	12	19	30	1	.228	.416	9	3	1B-44
17 yrs.	2089	6705	1820	241	41	377	5.6	1046	1103	1043	1091	43	.271	.488	158	35	1B-1943, OF-11, DH-3

LEAGUE CHAMPIONSHIP SERIES
	G	AB	H	2B	3B	HR	HR %	R	RBI	BB	SO	SB	BA	SA	PH AB	PH H	G by POS
1972 **DET** A	5	15	4	0	0	1	6.7	1	2	2	3	0	.267	.467	1	0	1B-5

WORLD SERIES
	G	AB	H	2B	3B	HR	HR %	R	RBI	BB	SO	SB	BA	SA	PH AB	PH H	G by POS
1959 **CHI** A	4	4	0	0	0	0	0.0	0	0	0	2	0	.000	.000	4	0	
1968 **DET** A	7	26	10	0	0	1	3.8	5	5	3	5	0	.385	.500	0	0	1B-7
2 yrs.	11	30	10	0	0	1	3.3	5	5	3	7	0	.333	.433	4	0	1B-7

Ron Cash

CASH, RONALD FORREST   BR TR 6'   180 lbs.
B. Nov. 20, 1949, Decatur, Ga.

	G	AB	H	2B	3B	HR	HR %	R	RBI	BB	SO	SB	BA	SA	PH AB	PH H	G by POS
1973 **DET** A	14	39	16	1	1	0	0.0	8	6	5	5	0	.410	.487	0	0	OF-7, 3B-6
1974	20	62	14	2	0	0	0.0	6	5	0	11	0	.226	.258	1	0	1B-15, 3B-4
2 yrs.	34	101	30	3	1	0	0.0	14	11	5	16	0	.297	.347	1	0	1B-15, 3B-10, OF-7

Jay Cashion

CASHION, JAY CARL   BL TR 6'2"   200 lbs.
B. June 6, 1891, Mecklenburg, N. C.   D. Nov. 17, 1935, Lake Millicent, Wis.

	G	AB	H	2B	3B	HR	HR %	R	RBI	BB	SO	SB	BA	SA	PH AB	PH H	G by POS
1911 **WAS** A	21	37	12	1	0	0	0.0	3	4	1		0	.324	.351	9	2	P-11
1912	43	103	22	5	1	2	1.9	7	12	8		2	.214	.340	8	1	P-26, OF-9
1913	7	12	3	0	0	0	0.0	1	2	1	1	0	.250	.250	0	0	P-4, OF-3
1914	2	1	0	0	0	0	0.0	0	0	0	1	0	.000	.000	0	0	P-2
4 yrs.	73	153	37	6	1	2	1.3	11	18	10	2	2	.242	.333	17	3	P-43, OF-12

Ed Caskin

CASKIN, EDWARD JAMES   6'   180 lbs.
B. Dec. 30, 1851, Danvers, Mass.   D. Oct. 9, 1924, Danvers, Mass.

	G	AB	H	2B	3B	HR	HR %	R	RBI	BB	SO	SB	BA	SA	PH AB	PH H	G by POS
1879 **TRO** N	70	304	78	13	2	0	0.0	32	21	2	14		.257	.313	0	0	SS-42, C-22, 2B-6
1880	82	333	75	5	4	0	0.0	36		7	24		.225	.264	0	0	SS-82, C-2
1881	63	234	53	7	1	0	0.0	33	21	13	29		.226	.265	0	0	SS-63
1883 **NY** N	95	383	91	11	2	1	0.3	47		14	25		.238	.285	0	0	SS-81, 2B-13, C-1
1884	100	351	81	10	1	2	0.6	49		34	55		.231	.282	0	0	SS-96, C-6
1885 **STL** N	71	262	47	3	0	0	0.0	31	12	12	22		.179	.191	0	0	3B-69, C-2, SS-1
1886 **NY** N	1	4	2	0	0	0	0.0	1	1	0	1		.500	.500	0	0	SS-1
7 yrs.	482	1871	427	49	10	3	0.2	229	55	82	170		.228	.270	0	0	SS-366, 3B-69, C-33, 2B-19

Harry Cassady

CASSADY, HARRY DELBERT   TL 5'8"   145 lbs.
B. July 20, 1880, Bellflower, Ill.   D. Apr. 19, 1969, Fresno, Calif.

	G	AB	H	2B	3B	HR	HR %	R	RBI	BB	SO	SB	BA	SA	PH AB	PH H	G by POS
1904 **PIT** N	12	44	9	0	0	0	0.0	8	3	2		2	.205	.205	0	0	OF-12
1905 **WAS** A	9	30	4	0	0	0	0.0	1	1	0		0	.133	.133	0	0	OF-9
2 yrs.	21	74	13	0	0	0	0.0	9	4	2		2	.176	.176	0	0	OF-21

Joe Cassidy

CASSIDY, JOSEPH PHILLIP   BR TR
B. Feb. 8, 1883, Chester, Pa.   D. Mar. 25, 1906, Chester, Pa.

	G	AB	H	2B	3B	HR	HR %	R	RBI	BB	SO	SB	BA	SA	PH AB	PH H	G by POS
1904 **WAS** A	152	581	140	12	19	1	0.2	63	33	15		17	.241	.332	0	0	SS-99, OF-32, 3B-23
1905	151	576	124	16	4	1	0.2	67	43	25		23	.215	.262	0	0	SS-151
2 yrs.	303	1157	264	28	23	2	0.2	130	76	40		40	.228	.297	0	0	SS-250, OF-32, 3B-23

John Cassidy

CASSIDY, JOHN P.   BR TL 5'8"   168 lbs.
B. 1857, Brooklyn, N. Y.   D. July 2, 1891, Brooklyn, N. Y.

	G	AB	H	2B	3B	HR	HR %	R	RBI	BB	SO	SB	BA	SA	PH AB	PH H	G by POS
1876 **HAR** N	12	47	13	2	0	0	0.0	6	8	1	0		.277	.319	0	0	OF-8, 1B-4
1877	60	251	95	10	5	0	0.0	43	27	3	3		.378	.458	0	0	OF-58, P-2
1878 **CHI** N	60	256	68	7	1	0	0.0	33	29	9	11		.266	.301	0	0	OF-60, C-1
1879 **TRO** N	9	37	7	1	0	0	0.0	4	1	2	4		.189	.216	0	0	OF-8, 1B-2

	G	AB	H	2B	3B	HR	HR %	R	RBI	BB	SO	SB	BA	SA	Pinch Hit AB	Pinch Hit H	G by POS

John Cassidy continued

	G	AB	H	2B	3B	HR	HR%	R	RBI	BB	SO	SB	BA	SA	PH AB	PH H	G by POS
1880	83	352	89	14	8	0	0.0	40		12	34		.253	.338	0	0	OF-82, 2B-1
1881	85	370	82	13	3	1	0.3	57	11	18	21		.222	.281	0	0	OF-84, SS-1
1882	29	121	21	3	1	0	0.0	14	9	3	16		.174	.215	0	0	OF-16, 3B-13
1883 PRO N	89	366	87	16	5	0	0.0	46		9	38		.238	.309	0	0	OF-88, 2B-1, 1B-1
1884 BKN AA	106	433	109	11	6	2	0.5	57		19			.252	.319	0	0	OF-100, 3B-5, SS-1
1885	54	221	47	6	2	1	0.5	36		8			.213	.271	0	0	OF-54
10 yrs.	587	2454	618	83	31	4	0.2	336	85	84	127		.252	.316	0	0	OF-558, 3B-18, 1B-7, SS-2, 2B-2, P-2, C-1

Pete Cassidy

CASSIDY, PETER FRANCIS
B. Apr. 8, 1873, Wilmington, Del.   D. July 9, 1929, Wilmington, Del.

BR TR 5'10"   165 lbs.

	G	AB	H	2B	3B	HR	HR%	R	RBI	BB	SO	SB	BA	SA	PH AB	PH H	G by POS
1896 LOU N	49	184	39	1		0	0.0	16	12	7	7	5	.212	.228	0	0	1B-38, SS-11
1899 2 teams		BKN N (6G – .150)				WAS N (46G – .315)											
" total	52	198	59	14		3	1.5	23	36	10		6	.298	.414	1	0	1B-37, 3B-9, SS-5
2 yrs.	101	382	98	15	1	3	0.8	39	48	17	7	11	.257	.325	1	0	1B-75, SS-16, 3B-9

Jack Cassini

CASSINI, JACK DEMPSEY (Scat)
B. Oct. 26, 1919, Dearborn, Mich.

BR TR 5'10"   175 lbs.

	G	AB	H	2B	3B	HR	HR%	R	RBI	BB	SO	SB	BA	SA	PH AB	PH H	G by POS
1949 PIT N	8	0	0	0	0	0	–	3	0	0	0	0	–	–	0	0	

Jim Castiglia

CASTIGLIA, JAMES VINCENT
B. Sept. 30, 1918, Passaic, N. J.

BL TR 5'11"   200 lbs.

	G	AB	H	2B	3B	HR	HR%	R	RBI	BB	SO	SB	BA	SA	PH AB	PH H	G by POS
1942 PHI A	16	18	7	0	0	0	0.0	2	1	3		0	.389	.389	13	4	C-3

Pete Castiglione

CASTIGLIONE, PETER PAUL
B. Feb. 13, 1921, Greenwich, Conn.

BR TR 5'11"   175 lbs.

	G	AB	H	2B	3B	HR	HR%	R	RBI	BB	SO	SB	BA	SA	PH AB	PH H	G by POS
1947 PIT N	13	50	14	0	0	0	0.0	6	1	2	5	0	.280	.280	0	0	SS-13
1948	4	2	0	0	0	0	0.0	0	0	0	0	0	.000	.000	1	0	SS-1
1949	118	448	120	20	2	6	1.3	57	43	20	43	2	.268	.362	5	1	3B-98, SS-17, OF-2
1950	94	263	67	10	3	3	1.1	29	22	23	23	1	.255	.350	22	7	3B-35, SS-29, 2B-9, 1B-3
1951	132	482	126	19	4	7	1.5	62	42	34	28	2	.261	.361	9	2	3B-99, SS-28
1952	67	214	57	9		4	1.9	27	18	17	8	3	.266	.374	9	2	3B-57, OF-1, 1B-1
1953 2 teams		PIT N (45G – .208)				STL N (67G – .173)											
" total	112	211	42	4	1	4	1.9	23	24	7	19	1	.199	.284	8	4	3B-94, 2B-9, SS-3
1954 STL N	5	0	0	0	0	0	–	1	0	0	0	0	–	–	0	0	3B-5
8 yrs.	545	1670	426	62	11	24	1.4	205	150	103	126	10	.255	.349	54	16	3B-388, SS-91, 2B-18, 1B-4, OF-3

Carmen Castillo

CASTILLO, MONTE CARMELO
B. June 8, 1958, San Pedro de Macoris, Dominican Republic

BR TR 6'1"   180 lbs.

	G	AB	H	2B	3B	HR	HR%	R	RBI	BB	SO	SB	BA	SA	PH AB	PH H	G by POS
1982 CLE A	47	120	25	4	0	2	1.7	11	11	6	17	0	.208	.292	3	0	OF-43, DH-2
1983	23	36	10	2	1	1	2.8	9	3	4	6	1	.278	.472	2	0	OF-19, DH-1
1984	87	211	55	9	2	10	4.7	36	36	21	32	1	.261	.464	18	3	OF-70, DH-2
3 yrs.	157	367	90	15	3	13	3.5	56	50	31	55	2	.245	.409	23	3	OF-132, DH-5

Manny Castillo

CASTILLO, ESTEBAN MANUEL
B. Apr. 1, 1957, Santo Domingo, Dominican Republic

BB TR 5'9"   160 lbs.

	G	AB	H	2B	3B	HR	HR%	R	RBI	BB	SO	SB	BA	SA	PH AB	PH H	G by POS
1980 KC A	7	10	2	0	0	0	0.0	1	0	0	0	0	.200	.200	2	1	3B-3, DH-2, 2B-1
1982 SEA A	138	506	130	29	1	3	0.6	49	49	22	35	2	.257	.336	11	1	3B-130, 2B-9
1983	91	203	42	6	3	0	0.0	13	24	7	20	1	.207	.266	29	7	3B-55, 1B-11, DH-6, 2B-5, P-1
3 yrs.	236	719	174	35	4	3	0.4	63	73	29	55	3	.242	.314	42	9	3B-188, 2B-15, 1B-11, DH-8, P-1

Marty Castillo

CASTILLO, MARTIN HORACE
B. Jan. 16, 1957, Long Beach, Calif.

BR TR 6'1"   190 lbs.

	G	AB	H	2B	3B	HR	HR%	R	RBI	BB	SO	SB	BA	SA	PH AB	PH H	G by POS
1981 DET A	6	8	1	0	0	0	0.0	1	0	0	2	0	.125	.125	0	0	3B-4, OF-1, C-1
1982	1	0	0	0	0	0	–	0	0	0	0	0	–	–	0	0	C-1
1983	67	119	23	4	0	2	1.7	10	10	7	22	2	.193	.277	2	0	3B-58, C-10
1984	70	141	33	5	2	4	2.8	16	17	10	33	1	.234	.383	1	0	C-36, 3B-33, DH-1
4 yrs.	144	268	57	9	2	6	2.2	27	27	17	57	3	.213	.328	3	0	3B-95, C-48, DH-1, OF-1
LEAGUE CHAMPIONSHIP SERIES																	
1984 DET A	3	8	2	0	0	0	0.0	0	2	0	3	1	.250	.250	0	0	3B-3
WORLD SERIES																	
1984 DET A	3	9	3	0	0	1	11.1	2	2	2	1	0	.333	.667	0	0	3B-3

Tony Castillo

CASTILLO, ANTHONY
B. June 14, 1957, San Jose, Calif.

BR TR 6'4"   190 lbs.

	G	AB	H	2B	3B	HR	HR%	R	RBI	BB	SO	SB	BA	SA	PH AB	PH H	G by POS
1978 SD N	5	8	1	0	0	0	0.0	0	1	0	2	0	.125	.125	0	0	C-5

John Castino

CASTINO, JOHN ANTHONY
B. Oct. 23, 1954, Evanston, Ill.

BR TR 5'11"   175 lbs.

	G	AB	H	2B	3B	HR	HR%	R	RBI	BB	SO	SB	BA	SA	PH AB	PH H	G by POS
1979 MIN A	148	393	112	13	8	5	1.3	49	52	27	72	5	.285	.397	8	3	3B-143, SS-5
1980	150	546	165	17	7	13	2.4	67	64	29	67	7	.302	.430	1	0	3B-138, SS-18
1981	101	381	102	13	9	6	1.6	41	36	18	52	4	.268	.396	0	0	3B-98, 2B-4
1982	117	410	99	12	6	6	1.5	48	37	36	51	2	.241	.344	0	0	2B-96, 3B-21, OF-6, DH-1
1983	142	563	156	30	4	11	2.0	83	57	62	54	4	.277	.403	2	0	2B-132, 3B-8, DH-1
1984	8	27	12	1	0	0	0.0	5	3	5	2	0	.444	.481	0	0	3B-8
6 yrs.	666	2320	646	86	34	41	1.8	293	249	177	298	22	.278	.398	11	3	3B-416, 2B-232, SS-23, OF-6, DH-2

	G	AB	H	2B	3B	HR	HR %	R	RBI	BB	SO	SB	BA	SA	Pinch Hit AB	Pinch Hit H	G by POS

Vince Castino

CASTINO, VINCENT CHARLES
B. Oct. 11, 1917, Willisville, Ill.   D. Mar. 6, 1967, Sacramento, Calif.
BR TR 5'9"   175 lbs.

	G	AB	H	2B	3B	HR	HR %	R	RBI	BB	SO	SB	BA	SA	AB	H	G by POS
1943 CHI A	33	101	23	1	0	2	2.0	14	16	12	11	0	.228	.297	3	0	C-30
1944	29	78	18	5	0	0	0.0	8	3	10	13	0	.231	.295	2	1	C-26
1945	26	37	8	1	0	0	0.0	2	4	3	7	0	.216	.243	1	0	C-25
3 yrs.	88	216	49	7	0	2	0.9	24	23	25	31	0	.227	.287	6	1	C-81

Don Castle

CASTLE, DONALD HARDY
B. Feb. 11, 1950, Kokomo, Ind.
BL TL 6'1"   205 lbs.

	G	AB	H	2B	3B	HR	HR %	R	RBI	BB	SO	SB	BA	SA	AB	H	G by POS
1973 TEX A	4	13	4	1	0	0	0.0	2	1	3	0	.308	.385	1	0	DH-3

John Castle

CASTLE, JOHN FRANCIS
B. June 1, 1883, Honeybrook, Pa.   D. Apr. 15, 1929, Philadelphia, Pa.

	G	AB	H	2B	3B	HR	HR %	R	RBI	BB	SO	SB	BA	SA	AB	H	G by POS
1910 PHI N	3	4	1	0	0	0	0.0	1	0	0	0	1	.250	.250	0	0	OF-2

Foster Castleman

CASTLEMAN, FOSTER EPHRAIM
B. Jan. 1, 1931, Nashville, Tenn.
BR TR 6'   175 lbs.

	G	AB	H	2B	3B	HR	HR %	R	RBI	BB	SO	SB	BA	SA	AB	H	G by POS
1954 NY N	13	12	3	0	0	0	0.0	0	1	0	3	0	.250	.250	11	3	2B-2
1955	15	28	6	1	0	2	7.1	3	4	2	4	0	.214	.464	7	1	2B-6, 3B-1
1956	124	385	87	16	3	14	3.6	33	45	15	50	2	.226	.392	17	3	3B-107, SS-2, 2B-1
1957	18	37	6	2	0	1	2.7	7	1	2	8	0	.162	.297	9	0	3B-7, SS-1, 2B-1
1958 BAL A	98	200	34	5	0	3	1.5	15	14	16	34	2	.170	.240	2	0	SS-91, 3B-4, 2B-4, OF-1
5 yrs.	268	662	136	24	3	20	3.0	58	65	35	99	4	.205	.341	46	8	3B-119, SS-94, 2B-14, OF-1

Louis Castro

CASTRO, LOUIS M. (Jud)
B. 1877, Colombia   D. Venezuela
BR TR 5'7"

	G	AB	H	2B	3B	HR	HR %	R	RBI	BB	SO	SB	BA	SA	AB	H	G by POS
1902 PHI A	42	143	35	8	1	1	0.7	18	15	4		2	.245	.336	2	0	2B-36, OF-3, SS-1

Danny Cater

CATER, DANNY ANDERSON
B. Feb. 25, 1940, Austin, Tex.
BR TR 6'   170 lbs.

	G	AB	H	2B	3B	HR	HR %	R	RBI	BB	SO	SB	BA	SA	AB	H	G by POS
1964 PHI N	60	152	45	9	1	1	0.7	13	13	7	15	1	.296	.388	18	6	OF-39, 1B-7, 3B-1
1965 CHI A	142	514	139	18	4	14	2.7	74	55	33	65	3	.270	.403	7	2	OF-127, 3B-11, 1B-3
1966 2 teams		CHI	A (21G – .183)			KC	A (116G – .292)										
" total	137	485	135	17	4	7	1.4	50	56	28	47	4	.278	.373	5	1	1B-53, 3B-42, OF-40
1967 KC A	142	529	143	17	4	4	0.8	55	46	34	56	4	.270	.340	2	1	3B-56, OF-55, 1B-44
1968 OAK A	147	504	146	28	3	6	1.2	53	62	35	43	8	.290	.393	11	4	1B-121, OF-20, 2B-1
1969	152	584	153	24	2	10	1.7	64	76	28	40	1	.262	.361	8	1	1B-132, OF-20, 2B-4
1970 NY A	155	582	175	26	5	6	1.0	64	76	34	44	4	.301	.393	3	0	1B-131, 3B-42, OF-7
1971	121	428	118	16	5	4	0.9	39	50	19	25	0	.276	.364	10	3	1B-78, 3B-52
1972 BOS A	92	317	75	17	1	8	2.5	32	39	15	33	0	.237	.372	6	1	1B-90
1973	63	195	61	12	0	1	0.5	30	24	10	22	0	.313	.390	7	2	1B-37, 3B-21, DH-3
1974	56	126	31	5	0	5	4.0	14	20	10	13	1	.246	.405	18	5	1B-23, DH-14
1975 STL N	22	35	8	2	0	0	0.0	3	2	1	3	0	.229	.286	13	2	1B-12
12 yrs.	1289	4451	1229	191	29	66	1.5	491	519	254	406	26	.276	.377	108	28	1B-731, OF-308, 3B-225, DH-17, 2B-5

Eli Cates

CATES, ELI ELDO
B. Jan. 26, 1877, Greensfork, Ind.   D. May 29, 1964, Richmond, Ind.
BR TR 5'9½"   175 lbs.

	G	AB	H	2B	3B	HR	HR %	R	RBI	BB	SO	SB	BA	SA	AB	H	G by POS
1908 WAS A	40	59	11	1	1	0	0.0	5	3	6		0	.186	.237	16	1	P-19, 2B-3

Ted Cather

CATHER, THEODORE P
B. May 20, 1889, Chester, Pa.   D. Apr. 9, 1945, Charlestown, Md.
BR TR 5'10½"   178 lbs.

	G	AB	H	2B	3B	HR	HR %	R	RBI	BB	SO	SB	BA	SA	AB	H	G by POS
1912 STL N	5	19	8	1	0	0	0.0	4	2	0	4	1	.421	.579	0	0	OF-5
1913	67	183	39	8	4	0	0.0	16	12	9	24	7	.213	.301	7	3	OF-57, 1B-1, P-1
1914 2 teams		STL	N (39G – .273)			BOS	N (50G – .297)										
" total	89	244	70	18	2	0	0.0	30	40	10	43	11	.287	.377	12	1	OF-76
1915 BOS N	40	102	21	3	1	2	2.0	10	18	15	19	2	.206	.314	7	1	OF-40
4 yrs.	201	548	138	30	8	2	0.4	60	72	34	90	21	.252	.347	26	5	OF-178, 1B-1, P-1
WORLD SERIES																	
1914 BOS N	1	5	0	0	0	0	0.0	0	0	0	1	0	.000	.000	0	0	OF-1

Buster Caton

CATON, JAMES HOWARD
B. July 16, 1896, Zanesville, Ohio   D. Jan. 8, 1948, Zanesville, Ohio
BR TR 5'6"   165 lbs.

	G	AB	H	2B	3B	HR	HR %	R	RBI	BB	SO	SB	BA	SA	AB	H	G by POS
1917 PIT N	14	57	12	1	2	0	0.0	6	4	6	7	0	.211	.298	0	0	SS-14
1918	80	303	71	5	7	0	0.0	37	17	32	16	12	.234	.297	1	0	SS-79
1919	39	102	18	1	2	0	0.0	13	5	12	10	2	.176	.225	6	1	SS-17, 3B-11, OF-1
1920	98	352	83	11	5	0	0.0	29	27	33	19	4	.236	.295	1	1	SS-96
4 yrs.	231	814	184	18	16	0	0.0	85	53	83	52	18	.226	.287	8	2	SS-206, 3B-11, OF-1

Tom Catterson

CATTERSON, THOMAS HENRY
B. Aug. 25, 1884, Warwick, R. I.   D. Feb. 5, 1920, Portland, Me.
BL TL 5'10"   170 lbs.

	G	AB	H	2B	3B	HR	HR %	R	RBI	BB	SO	SB	BA	SA	AB	H	G by POS
1908 BKN N	19	68	13	1	1	1	1.5	5	2	5		0	.191	.279	1	0	OF-18
1909	9	18	4	0	0	0	0.0	0	1	3		0	.222	.222	1	0	OF-6
2 yrs.	28	86	17	1	1	1	1.2	5	3	8		0	.198	.267	2	0	OF-24

John Caulfield

CAULFIELD, JOHN JOSEPH (Jake)
B. Nov. 23, 1918, Los Angeles, Calif.
BR TR 5'11"   170 lbs.

	G	AB	H	2B	3B	HR	HR %	R	RBI	BB	SO	SB	BA	SA	AB	H	G by POS
1946 PHI A	44	94	26	8	0	0	0.0	13	10	4	11	0	.277	.362	2	0	SS-31, 3B-1

Wayne Causey

CAUSEY, JAMES WAYNE
B. Dec. 26, 1936, Ruston, La.
BL TR 5'10½"   175 lbs.

	G	AB	H	2B	3B	HR	HR %	R	RBI	BB	SO	SB	BA	SA	AB	H	G by POS
1955 BAL A	68	175	34	2	1	1	0.6	14	9	17	25	0	.194	.234	8	0	3B-55, 2B-7, SS-1
1956	53	88	15	0	1	1	1.1	7	4	8	23	0	.170	.227	16	5	3B-30, 2B-7
1957	14	10	2	0	0	0	0.0	2	1	5	2	0	.200	.200	3	0	2B-6, 3B-5
1961 KC A	104	312	86	14	1	8	2.6	37	49	37	28	0	.276	.404	2	0	3B-88, SS-11, 2B-9

	G	AB	H	2B	3B	HR	HR %	R	RBI	BB	SO	SB	BA	SA	Pinch Hit AB	Pinch Hit H	G by POS

Wayne Causey continued

Year	Team	G	AB	H	2B	3B	HR	HR%	R	RBI	BB	SO	SB	BA	SA	PH AB	PH H	G by POS
1962		117	305	77	14	1	4	1.3	40	38	41	30	2	.252	.344	28	9	SS-51, 3B-26, 2B-9
1963		139	554	155	32	4	8	1.4	72	44	56	54	4	.280	.395	1	1	SS-135, 3B-2
1964		157	604	170	31	4	8	1.3	82	49	88	65	0	.281	.386	3	2	SS-131, 2B-17, 3B-9
1965		144	513	134	17	8	3	0.6	48	34	61	48	1	.261	.343	8	1	SS-62, 2B-45, 3B-35
1966 2 teams	KC A (28G – .228)			CHI A (78G – .244)														
" total		106	243	58	8	2	0	0.0	24	18	31	19	3	.239	.288	19	7	2B-60, 3B-16, SS-11
1967 CHI A		124	292	66	10	3	1	0.3	21	28	32	35	2	.226	.291	34	10	2B-96, SS-2
1968 3 teams	CHI A (59G – .180)			CAL A (4G – .000)				ATL N (16G – .108)										
" total		79	148	22	2	1	1	0.7	10	11	14	12	0	.149	.196	36	6	2B-51, SS-2, 3B-2
11 yrs.		1105	3244	819	130	26	35	1.1	357	285	390	341	12	.252	.341	158	41	SS-406, 2B-307, 3B-268

John Cavanaugh

CAVANAUGH, JOHN J.
B. June 5, 1900, Scranton, Pa.   D. Jan. 14, 1961, New Brunswick, N. J.   BR TR 5'9"   158 lbs.

Year	Team	G	AB	H	2B	3B	HR	HR%	R	RBI	BB	SO	SB	BA	SA	PH AB	PH H	G by POS
1919 PHI N		1	1	0	0	0	0	0.0	0	0	0	1	0	.000	.000	0	0	3B-1

Phil Cavarretta

CAVARRETTA, PHILIP JOSEPH
B. July 19, 1916, Chicago, Ill.   BL TL 5'11½" 175 lbs.
Manager 1951-53.

Year	Team	G	AB	H	2B	3B	HR	HR%	R	RBI	BB	SO	SB	BA	SA	PH AB	PH H	G by POS
1934 CHI N		7	21	8	0	1	1	4.8	5	6	2	3	1	.381	.619	2	0	1B-5
1935		146	589	162	28	12	8	1.4	85	82	39	61	4	.275	.404	1	0	1B-145
1936		124	458	125	18	1	9	2.0	55	56	17	36	8	.273	.376	8	4	1B-115
1937		106	329	94	18	7	5	1.5	43	56	32	35	7	.286	.429	11	4	OF-53, 1B-43
1938		92	268	64	11	4	1	0.4	29	28	14	27	4	.239	.321	13	1	OF-52, 1B-28
1939		22	55	15	3	1	0	0.0	4	0	4	3	2	.273	.364	7	3	1B-13, OF-1
1940		65	193	54	11	4	2	1.0	34	22	31	18	3	.280	.409	10	4	1B-52
1941		107	346	99	18	4	6	1.7	46	40	53	28	2	.286	.413	5	2	OF-66, 1B-33
1942		136	482	130	28	4	3	0.6	59	54	71	42	7	.270	.363	6	0	OF-70, 1B-61
1943		143	530	154	27	9	8	1.5	93	73	75	42	3	.291	.421	2	0	1B-134, OF-7
1944		152	614	197	35	15	5	0.8	106	82	67	42	4	.321	.451	0	0	1B-139, OF-13
1945		132	498	177	34	10	6	1.2	94	97	81	34	5	.355	.500	0	0	1B-120, OF-11
1946		139	510	150	28	10	8	1.6	89	78	88	54	2	.294	.435	2	0	OF-86, 1B-51
1947		127	459	144	22	5	2	0.4	56	63	58	35	2	.314	.397	3	2	1B-100, 1B-24
1948		111	334	93	16	5	3	0.9	41	40	35	29	4	.278	.383	23	3	1B-41, OF-40
1949		105	360	106	22	4	8	2.2	46	49	45	31	2	.294	.444	9	2	1B-70, OF-25
1950		82	256	70	11	1	10	3.9	49	31	40	31	1	.273	.441	9	2	1B-67, OF-3
1951		89	206	64	7	1	6	2.9	24	28	27	28	0	.311	.442	33	12	1B-53
1952		41	63	15	1	1	1	1.6	7	8	9	3	0	.238	.333	26	5	1B-13
1953		27	21	6	3	0	0	0.0	3	3	6	3	0	.286	.429	21	6	
1954 CHI A		71	158	50	6	0	3	1.9	21	24	26	12	4	.316	.411	16	2	1B-44, OF-9
1955		6	4	0	0	0	0	0.0	0	1	0	1	0	.000	.000	2	0	1B-3
22 yrs.		2030	6754	1977	347	99	95	1.4	990	920	820	598	65	.293	.416	209	48	1B-1254, OF-536

WORLD SERIES

Year	Team	G	AB	H	2B	3B	HR	HR%	R	RBI	BB	SO	SB	BA	SA	PH AB	PH H	G by POS
1935 CHI N		6	24	3	0	0	0	0.0	1	0	0	5	0	.125	.125	0	0	1B-6
1938		4	13	6	1	0	0	0.0	1	0	0	1	0	.462	.538	1	1	OF-3
1945		7	26	11	2	0	1	3.8	7	5	4	3	0	.423	.615	0	0	1B-7
3 yrs.		17	63	20	3	0	1	1.6	9	5	4	9	0	.317	.413	1	1	1B-13, OF-3

Ike Caveney

CAVENEY, JAMES CHRISTOPHER
B. Dec. 10, 1894, San Francisco, Calif.   D. July 6, 1949, San Francisco, Calif.   BR TR 5'9"   168 lbs.

Year	Team	G	AB	H	2B	3B	HR	HR%	R	RBI	BB	SO	SB	BA	SA	PH AB	PH H	G by POS
1922 CIN N		118	394	94	12	9	3	0.8	41	54	29	33	6	.239	.338	0	0	SS-118
1923		138	488	135	21	9	4	0.8	58	63	26	41	5	.277	.381	0	0	SS-138
1924		95	337	92	19	1	4	1.2	36	32	14	21	2	.273	.371	1	0	SS-90, 2B-5
1925		115	358	89	9	5	2	0.6	38	47	28	31	2	.249	.318	4	0	SS-111
4 yrs.		466	1577	410	61	24	13	0.8	173	196	97	126	15	.260	.354	5	0	SS-457, 2B-5

Cesar Cedeno

CEDENO, CESAR
B. Feb. 25, 1951, Santo Domingo, Dominican Republic   BR TR 6'2"   175 lbs.

Year	Team	G	AB	H	2B	3B	HR	HR%	R	RBI	BB	SO	SB	BA	SA	PH AB	PH H	G by POS
1970 HOU N		90	355	110	21	4	7	2.0	46	42	15	57	17	.310	.451	2	1	OF-90
1971		161	611	161	40	6	10	1.6	85	81	25	102	20	.264	.398	4	0	OF-157, 1B-2
1972		139	559	179	39	8	22	3.9	103	82	56	62	55	.320	.537	1	0	OF-137
1973		139	525	168	35	2	25	4.8	86	70	41	79	56	.320	.537	4	0	OF-136
1974		160	610	164	29	5	26	4.3	95	102	64	103	57	.269	.461	2	0	OF-157
1975		131	500	144	31	3	13	2.6	93	63	62	52	50	.288	.440	0	0	OF-131
1976		150	575	171	26	5	18	3.1	89	83	55	51	58	.297	.454	4	0	OF-146
1977		141	530	148	36	8	14	2.6	92	71	47	50	61	.279	.457	3	0	OF-137
1978		50	192	54	8	2	7	3.6	31	23	15	24	23	.281	.453	0	0	OF-50
1979		132	470	123	27	4	6	1.3	57	54	64	52	30	.262	.374	11	2	1B-91, OF-40
1980		137	499	154	32	8	10	2.0	71	73	66	72	48	.309	.465	1	0	OF-136
1981		82	306	83	19	0	5	1.6	42	34	24	31	12	.271	.382	2	0	1B-46, OF-34
1982 CIN N		138	492	142	35	1	8	1.6	52	57	41	41	16	.289	.413	7	2	OF-131, 1B-1
1983		98	332	77	16	0	9	2.7	40	39	33	53	13	.232	.361	10	2	OF-73, 1B-25
1984		110	380	105	24	2	10	2.6	59	47	25	54	19	.276	.429	14	2	OF-77, 1B-44
15 yrs.		1858	6936	1983	418	58	190	2.7	1041	921	633	883	535	.286	.445	65	9	OF-1632, 1B-201
												9th						

DIVISIONAL PLAYOFF SERIES

Year	Team	G	AB	H	2B	3B	HR	HR%	R	RBI	BB	SO	SB	BA	SA	PH AB	PH H	G by POS
1981 HOU N		4	13	3	1	0	0	0.0	0	0	2	2	2	.231	.308	0	0	1B-4

LEAGUE CHAMPIONSHIP SERIES

Year	Team	G	AB	H	2B	3B	HR	HR%	R	RBI	BB	SO	SB	BA	SA	PH AB	PH H	G by POS
1980 HOU N		3	11	2	0	0	0	0.0	1	1	1	0	0	.182	.182	0	0	OF-3

Orlando Cepeda

CEPEDA, ORLANDO MANUEL (The Baby Bull, Cha-Cha)
B. Sept. 17, 1937, Ponce, Puerto Rico   BR TR 6'2"   210 lbs.

Year	Team	G	AB	H	2B	3B	HR	HR%	R	RBI	BB	SO	SB	BA	SA	PH AB	PH H	G by POS
1958 SF N		148	603	188	38	4	25	4.1	88	96	29	84	15	.312	.512	1	0	1B-147
1959		151	605	192	35	4	27	4.5	92	105	33	100	23	.317	.522	0	0	1B-122, OF-44, 3B-4
1960		151	569	169	36	3	24	4.2	81	96	34	91	15	.297	.497	4	0	OF-91, 1B-63

	G	AB	H	2B	3B	HR	HR %	R	RBI	BB	SO	SB	BA	SA	Pinch Hit AB	Pinch Hit H	G by POS

Orlando Cepeda continued

	G	AB	H	2B	3B	HR	HR%	R	RBI	BB	SO	SB	BA	SA	AB	H	G by POS
1961	152	585	182	28	4	**46**	7.9	105	**142**	39	91	12	.311	.609	1	0	1B-81, OF-80
1962	162	625	191	26	1	35	5.6	105	114	37	97	10	.306	.518	4	1	1B-160, OF-2
1963	156	579	183	33	4	34	5.9	100	97	37	70	8	.316	.563	8	2	1B-150, OF-3
1964	142	529	161	27	2	31	5.9	75	97	43	83	9	.304	.539	2	0	1B-139, OF-1
1965	33	34	6	1	0	1	2.9	1	5	3	9	0	.176	.294	21	4	1B-4, OF-2
1966 2 teams	SF	N	(19G –	.286)		STL	N	(123G –	.303)								
" total	142	501	151	26	0	20	4.0	70	73	38	79	9	.301	.473	7	4	1B-126, OF-8
1967 STL N	151	563	183	37	0	25	4.4	91	111	62	75	11	.325	.524	1	1	1B-151
1968	157	600	149	26	2	16	2.7	71	73	43	96	8	.248	.378	3	1	1B-154
1969 ATL N	154	573	147	28	2	22	3.8	74	88	55	76	12	.257	.428	1	0	1B-153
1970	148	567	173	33	0	34	6.0	87	111	47	75	6	.305	.543	1	1	1B-148
1971	71	250	69	10	1	14	5.6	31	44	22	29	3	.276	.492	8	1	1B-63
1972 2 teams	ATL	N	(28G –	.298)		OAK	A	(3G –	.000)								
" total	31	87	25	3	0	4	4.6	6	9	7	17	0	.287	.460	8	0	1B-22
1973 BOS A	142	550	159	25	0	20	3.6	51	86	50	81	0	.289	.444	0	0	DH-142
1974 KC A	33	107	23	5	0	1	0.9	3	18	9	16	1	.215	.290	7	2	DH-26
17 yrs.	2124	7927	2351	417	27	379	4.8	1131	1365	588	1169	142	.297	.499	77	17	1B-1683, OF-231, DH-168, 3B-4

LEAGUE CHAMPIONSHIP SERIES

	G	AB	H	2B	3B	HR	HR%	R	RBI	BB	SO	SB	BA	SA	AB	H	G by POS
1969 ATL N	3	11	5	2	0	1	9.1	2	3	1	2	1	.455	.909	0	0	1B-3

WORLD SERIES

	G	AB	H	2B	3B	HR	HR%	R	RBI	BB	SO	SB	BA	SA	AB	H	G by POS
1962 SF N	5	19	3	1	0	0	0.0	1	2	0	4	0	.158	.211	0	0	1B-5
1967 STL N	7	29	3	2	0	0	0.0	1	1	0	4	0	.103	.172	0	0	1B-7
1968	7	28	7	0	0	2	7.1	2	6	2	3	0	.250	.464	0	0	1B-7
3 yrs.	19	76	13	3	0	2	2.6	4	9	2	11	0	.171	.289	0	0	1B-19

Ed Cermak

CERMAK, EDWARD HUGO
B. Mar. 10, 1882, Tex.　　D. Nov. 22, 1911, Cleveland, Ohio

BR TR 5'11" 170 lbs.

	G	AB	H	2B	3B	HR	HR%	R	RBI	BB	SO	SB	BA	SA	AB	H	G by POS
1901 CLE A	1	4	0	0	0	0	0.0	0		0		0	.000	.000	0	0	OF-1

Rick Cerone

CERONE, RICHARD ALDO
B. May 19, 1954, Newark, N. J.

BR TR 5'11" 192 lbs.

	G	AB	H	2B	3B	HR	HR%	R	RBI	BB	SO	SB	BA	SA	AB	H	G by POS
1975 CLE A	7	12	3	1	0	0	0.0	1	0	1	0	0	.250	.333	0	0	C-7
1976	7	16	2	0	0	0	0.0	1	1	0	2	0	.125	.125	1	1	C-6, DH-1
1977 TOR A	31	100	20	4	0	1	1.0	7	10	6	12	0	.200	.270	0	0	C-31
1978	88	282	63	8	2	3	1.1	25	20	23	32	0	.223	.298	4	1	C-84, DH-2
1979	136	469	112	27	4	7	1.5	47	61	37	40	1	.239	.358	2	0	C-136
1980 NY A	147	519	144	30	4	14	2.7	70	85	32	56	1	.277	.432	0	0	C-147
1981	71	234	57	13	2	2	0.9	23	21	12	24	0	.244	.342	2	2	C-69
1982	89	300	68	10	0	5	1.7	29	28	19	27	0	.227	.310	2	0	C-89
1983	80	246	54	7	0	2	0.8	18	22	15	29	0	.220	.272	2	0	C-78, 3B-1
1984	38	120	25	3	0	2	1.7	8	13	9	15	0	.208	.283	0	0	C-38
10 yrs.	694	2298	548	103	12	36	1.6	229	261	154	237	3	.238	.341	11	4	C-685, DH-3, 3B-1

DIVISIONAL PLAYOFF SERIES

	G	AB	H	2B	3B	HR	HR%	R	RBI	BB	SO	SB	BA	SA	AB	H	G by POS
1981 NY A	5	18	6	2	0	1	5.6	1	5	0	2	0	.333	.611	0	0	C-5

LEAGUE CHAMPIONSHIP SERIES

	G	AB	H	2B	3B	HR	HR%	R	RBI	BB	SO	SB	BA	SA	AB	H	G by POS
1980 NY A	3	12	4	0	0	1	8.3	1	2	0	1	0	.333	.583	0	0	C-3
1981	3	10	1	0	0	0	0.0	1	0	0	0	0	.100	.100	0	0	C-3
2 yrs.	6	22	5	0	0	1	4.5	2	2	0	1	0	.227	.364	0	0	C-6

WORLD SERIES

	G	AB	H	2B	3B	HR	HR%	R	RBI	BB	SO	SB	BA	SA	AB	H	G by POS
1981 NY A	6	21	4	1	0	1	4.8	2	3	4	2	0	.190	.381	0	0	C-6

Bob Cerv

CERV, ROBERT HENRY
B. May 5, 1926, Weston, Neb.

BR TR 6' 200 lbs.

	G	AB	H	2B	3B	HR	HR%	R	RBI	BB	SO	SB	BA	SA	AB	H	G by POS
1951 NY A	12	28	6	1	0	0	0.0	4	2	4	6	0	.214	.250	3	0	OF-9
1952	36	87	21	3	2	1	1.1	11	8	9	22	0	.241	.356	9	2	OF-27
1953	8	6	0	0	0	0	0.0	0	0	1	1	0	.000	.000	4	0	
1954	56	100	26	6	0	5	5.0	14	13	11	17	0	.260	.470	28	9	OF-24
1955	55	85	29	4	2	3	3.5	17	22	7	16	4	.341	.541	33	11	OF-20
1956	54	115	35	5	6	3	2.6	16	25	18	13	0	.304	.530	10	6	OF-44
1957 KC A	124	345	94	14	2	11	3.2	35	44	20	57	1	.272	.420	41	9	OF-89
1958	141	515	157	20	7	38	7.4	93	104	50	82	3	.305	.592	6	2	OF-136
1959	125	463	132	22	4	20	4.3	61	87	35	87	3	.285	.479	5	2	OF-119
1960 2 teams	KC	A	(23G –	.256)		NY	A	(87G –	.250)								
" total	110	294	74	12	2	14	4.8	46	40	40	53	0	.252	.449	30	8	OF-72, 1B-3
1961 2 teams	LA	A	(18G –	.158)		NY	A	(57G –	.271)								
" total	75	175	41	8	1	8	4.6	20	26	13	25	1	.234	.429	22	8	OF-45, 1B-3
1962 2 teams	NY	A	(14G –	.118)		HOU	A	(19G –	.226)								
" total	33	48	9	1	0	2	4.2	3	3	4	13	0	.188	.333	20	4	OF-9
12 yrs.	829	2261	624	96	26	105	4.6	320	374	212	392	12	.276	.481	213	55	OF-594, 1B-6

WORLD SERIES

	G	AB	H	2B	3B	HR	HR%	R	RBI	BB	SO	SB	BA	SA	AB	H	G by POS
1955 NY A	5	16	2	0	0	1	6.3	1	1	0	4	0	.125	.313	1	1	OF-4
1956	1	1	1	0	0	0	0.0	0	0	0	0	0	1.000	1.000	1	1	
1960	4	14	5	0	0	0	0.0	1	0	0	3	0	.357	.357	1	1	OF-3
3 yrs.	10	31	8	0	0	1	3.2	2	1	0	7	0	.258	.355	3	3	OF-7
															1st		

Ron Cey

CEY, RONALD CHARLES (Penguin)
B. Feb. 15, 1948, Tacoma, Wash.

BR TR 5'10" 185 lbs.

	G	AB	H	2B	3B	HR	HR%	R	RBI	BB	SO	SB	BA	SA	AB	H	G by POS
1971 LA N	2	2	0	0	0	0	0.0	0	0	0	2	0	.000	.000	2	0	
1972	11	37	10	1	0	1	2.7	3	3	7	10	0	.270	.378	0	0	3B-11
1973	152	507	124	18	4	15	3.0	60	80	74	77	1	.245	.385	7	1	3B-146
1974	159	577	151	20	2	18	3.1	88	97	76	68	1	.262	.397	0	0	3B-158
1975	158	566	160	29	2	25	4.4	72	101	78	74	5	.283	.473	0	0	3B-158

	G	AB	H	2B	3B	HR	HR %	R	RBI	BB	SO	SB	BA	SA	Pinch Hit AB	H	G by POS

Ron Cey continued

	G	AB	H	2B	3B	HR	HR%	R	RBI	BB	SO	SB	BA	SA	PH AB	PH H	G by POS
1976	145	502	139	18	3	23	4.6	69	80	89	74	0	.277	.462	1	0	3B-144
1977	153	564	136	22	3	30	5.3	77	110	93	106	3	.241	.450	0	0	3B-153
1978	159	555	150	32	0	23	4.1	84	84	96	96	2	.270	.452	1	0	3B-158
1979	150	487	137	20	1	28	5.7	77	81	86	85	3	.281	.499	0	0	3B-150
1980	157	551	140	25	0	28	5.1	81	77	69	92	2	.254	.452	0	0	3B-157
1981	85	312	90	15	2	13	4.2	42	50	40	55	0	.288	.474	1	1	3B-84
1982	150	556	141	23	1	24	4.3	62	79	57	99	3	.254	.428	1	0	3B-149
1983 CHI N	159	581	160	33	1	24	4.1	73	90	62	85	0	.275	.460	1	0	3B-157
1984	146	505	121	27	0	25	5.0	71	97	61	108	3	.240	.442	2	1	3B-144
14 yrs.	1786	6302	1659	283	19	277	4.4	859	1029	888	1031	23	.263	.446	16	3	3B-1769

LEAGUE CHAMPIONSHIP SERIES

	G	AB	H	2B	3B	HR	HR%	R	RBI	BB	SO	SB	BA	SA	PH AB	PH H	G by POS
1974 LA N	4	16	5	3	0	1	6.3	2	1	3	2	0	.313	.688	0	0	3B-4
1977	4	13	4	1	0	1	7.7	4	4	2	4	1	.308	.615	0	0	3B-4
1978	4	16	5	1	0	1	6.3	4	3	2	4	0	.313	.563	0	0	3B-4
1981	5	18	5	1	0	0	0.0	1	3	3	2	0	.278	.333	0	0	3B-5
1984 CHI N	5	19	3	1	0	1	5.3	3	3	3	3	0	.158	.368	0	0	3B-5
5 yrs.	22	82	22	7	0	4	4.9	14	14	13	15	1	.268	.500	0	0	3B-22

WORLD SERIES

	G	AB	H	2B	3B	HR	HR%	R	RBI	BB	SO	SB	BA	SA	PH AB	PH H	G by POS
1974 LA N	5	17	3	0	0	0	0.0	1	0	3	3	0	.176	.176	0	0	3B-5
1977	6	21	4	1	0	1	4.8	2	3	3	5	0	.190	.381	0	0	3B-6
1978	6	21	6	0	0	1	4.8	2	4	3	3	0	.286	.429	0	0	3B-6
1981	6	20	7	0	0	1	5.0	3	6	3	3	0	.350	.500	0	0	3B-6
4 yrs.	23	79	20	1	0	3	3.8	8	13	12	14	0	.253	.380	0	0	3B-23

Elio Chacon

CHACON, ELIO RODRIGUEZ
B. Oct. 26, 1936, Caracas, Venezuela
BR TR 5'9" 160 lbs.

	G	AB	H	2B	3B	HR	HR%	R	RBI	BB	SO	SB	BA	SA	PH AB	PH H	G by POS
1960 CIN N	49	116	21	1	0	0	0.0	14	7	14	23	7	.181	.190	3	0	2B-43, OF-2
1961	61	132	35	4	2	2	1.5	26	5	21	22	1	.265	.371	1	0	2B-42, OF-8
1962 NY N	118	368	87	10	3	2	0.5	49	27	76	64	12	.236	.296	3	0	SS-110, 2B-2, 3B-1
3 yrs.	228	616	143	15	5	4	0.6	89	39	111	109	20	.232	.292	7	0	SS-110, 2B-87, OF-10, 3B-1

WORLD SERIES

	G	AB	H	2B	3B	HR	HR%	R	RBI	BB	SO	SB	BA	SA	PH AB	PH H	G by POS
1961 CIN N	4	12	3	0	0	0	0.0	2	0	1	2	0	.250	.250	1	0	2B-3

Chet Chadbourne

CHADBOURNE, CHESTER JAMES (Pop)
B. Oct. 26, 1884, Parkman, Me. D. June 23, 1943, Los Angeles, Calif.
BL TR

	G	AB	H	2B	3B	HR	HR%	R	RBI	BB	SO	SB	BA	SA	PH AB	PH H	G by POS
1906 BOS A	11	43	13	1	0	0	0.0	7	3	3		1	.302	.326	0	0	2B-11, SS-1
1907	10	38	11	0	0	0	0.0	0	1	7		1	.289	.289	0	0	OF-10
1914 KC F	147	581	161	22	8	1	0.2	92	37	69		42	.277	.348	1	0	OF-146
1915	152	587	133	16	9	1	0.2	75	35	62		29	.227	.290	0	0	OF-152
1918 BOS N	27	104	27	2	1	0	0.0	9	6	5	5	5	.260	.298	0	0	OF-27
5 yrs.	347	1353	345	41	18	2	0.1	183	82	146	5	78	.255	.316	1	0	OF-335, 2B-11, SS-1

Dave Chalk

CHALK, DAVID LEE
B. Aug. 30, 1950, Del Rio, Tex.
BR TR 5'10" 175 lbs.

	G	AB	H	2B	3B	HR	HR%	R	RBI	BB	SO	SB	BA	SA	PH AB	PH H	G by POS
1973 CAL A	24	69	16	2	0	0	0.0	14	6	9	13	0	.232	.261	0	0	SS-22
1974	133	465	117	9	3	5	1.1	44	31	30	57	10	.252	.316	0	0	SS-99, 3B-38
1975	149	513	140	24	2	3	0.6	59	56	66	49	6	.273	.345	0	0	3B-149
1976	142	438	95	14	1	0	0.0	39	33	49	62	0	.217	.253	0	0	SS-102, 3B-49
1977	149	519	144	27	2	3	0.6	58	45	52	69	12	.277	.355	2	0	3B-141, 2B-7, SS-4
1978	135	470	119	12	0	1	0.2	42	34	38	34	5	.253	.285	0	0	SS-97, 2B-29, 3B-22, DH-1
1979 2 teams		TEX	A	(9G –	.250)		OAK	A	(66G –	.222)							
" total	75	220	49	6	0	2	0.9	15	13	29	14	2	.223	.277	8	3	2B-38, SS-19, 3B-16, DH-2
1980 KC A	69	167	42	10	1	1	0.6	19	20	18	27	1	.251	.341	14	2	3B-33, 2B-17, DH-6, SS-1
1981	27	49	11	3	0	0	0.0	2	5	4	2	0	.224	.286	4	2	3B-14, 2B-10, SS-1
9 yrs.	903	2910	733	107	9	15	0.5	292	243	295	327	36	.252	.310	28	7	3B-462, SS-345, 2B-101, DH-9

WORLD SERIES

	G	AB	H	2B	3B	HR	HR%	R	RBI	BB	SO	SB	BA	SA	PH AB	PH H	G by POS
1980 KC A	1	0	0	0	0	0	–	1	0	1	0	1	–	–	0	0	3B-1

Joe Chamberlain

CHAMBERLAIN, JOSEPH JEREMIAH
B. May 10, 1910, San Francisco, Calif.
BR TR 6'1" 175 lbs.

	G	AB	H	2B	3B	HR	HR%	R	RBI	BB	SO	SB	BA	SA	PH AB	PH H	G by POS
1934 CHI A	43	141	34	5	1	2	1.4	13	17	6	38	1	.241	.333	0	0	SS-26, 3B-14

Al Chambers

CHAMBERS, ALBERT EUGENE
B. Mar. 24, 1961, Harrisburg, Pa.
BL TL 6'4" 210 lbs.

	G	AB	H	2B	3B	HR	HR%	R	RBI	BB	SO	SB	BA	SA	PH AB	PH H	G by POS
1983 SEA A	31	67	14	3	0	1	1.5	11	7	18	20	0	.209	.299	7	0	DH-22, OF-3
1984	22	49	11	1	0	1	2.0	4	4	3	12	2	.224	.306	8	2	OF-13, DH-1
2 yrs.	53	116	25	4	0	2	1.7	15	11	21	32	2	.216	.302	15	2	DH-23, OF-16

Chris Chambliss

CHAMBLISS, CARROLL CHRISTOPHER
B. Dec. 26, 1948, Dayton, Ohio
BL TR 6'1" 195 lbs.

	G	AB	H	2B	3B	HR	HR%	R	RBI	BB	SO	SB	BA	SA	PH AB	PH H	G by POS
1971 CLE A	111	415	114	20	4	9	2.2	49	48	40	83	2	.275	.407	2	0	1B-108
1972	121	466	136	27	2	6	1.3	51	44	26	63	3	.292	.397	2	0	1B-119
1973	155	572	156	30	2	11	1.9	70	53	58	76	4	.273	.390	1	0	1B-154
1974 2 teams		CLE	A	(17G –	.328)		NY	A	(110G –	.243)							
" total	127	467	119	20	3	6	1.3	46	50	28	48	0	.255	.349	4	0	1B-123
1975 NY A	150	562	171	38	4	9	1.6	66	72	29	50	0	.304	.434	3	0	1B-147
1976	156	641	188	32	6	17	2.7	79	96	27	80	1	.293	.441	0	0	1B-155, DH-1
1977	157	600	172	32	6	17	2.8	90	90	45	73	4	.287	.445	2	0	1B-157
1978	162	625	171	26	3	12	1.9	81	90	41	60	2	.274	.382	1	0	1B-155, DH-7
1979	149	554	155	27	3	18	3.2	61	63	34	53	3	.280	.437	2	1	1B-134, DH-16

	G	AB	H	2B	3B	HR	HR %	R	RBI	BB	SO	SB	BA	SA	Pinch Hit AB	Pinch Hit H	G by POS

Chris Chambliss continued

	G	AB	H	2B	3B	HR	HR %	R	RBI	BB	SO	SB	BA	SA	PH AB	PH H	G by POS
1980 ATL N	158	602	170	37	2	18	3.0	83	72	49	73	7	.282	.440	0	0	1B-158
1981	107	404	110	25	2	8	2.0	44	51	44	41	4	.272	.403	0	0	1B-107
1982	157	534	144	25	2	20	3.7	57	86	57	57	7	.270	.436	11	5	1B-151
1983	131	447	125	24	3	20	4.5	59	78	63	68	2	.280	.481	8	5	1B-126
1984	133	389	100	14	0	9	2.3	47	44	58	54	1	.257	.362	24	4	1B-109
14 yrs.	1974	7278	2031	377	42	180	2.5	883	937	599	879	40	.279	.417	62	17	1B-1903, DH-24

LEAGUE CHAMPIONSHIP SERIES

	G	AB	H	2B	3B	HR	HR %	R	RBI	BB	SO	SB	BA	SA	PH AB	PH H	G by POS
1976 NY A	5	21	11	1	1	2	9.5	5	8	0	1	2	.524	.952	0	0	1B-5
1977	5	17	1	0	0	0	0.0	0	0	3	4	0	.059	.059	0	0	1B-5
1978	4	15	6	0	0	0	0.0	1	2	0	4	0	.400	.400	0	0	1B-4
1982 ATL N	3	10	0	0	0	0	0.0	0	0	1	0	0	.000	.000	0	0	1B-3
4 yrs.	17	63	18	1	1	2	3.2	6	10	4	9	2	.286	.429	0	0	1B-17

WORLD SERIES

	G	AB	H	2B	3B	HR	HR %	R	RBI	BB	SO	SB	BA	SA	PH AB	PH H	G by POS
1976 NY A	4	16	5	1	0	0	0.0	1	1	0	2	0	.313	.375	0	0	1B-4
1977	6	24	7	2	0	1	4.2	4	4	0	2	0	.292	.500	0	0	1B-6
1978	3	11	2	0	0	0	0.0	1	0	1	1	0	.182	.182	0	0	1B-3
3 yrs.	13	51	14	3	0	1	2.0	6	5	1	5	0	.275	.392	0	0	1B-13

Mike Champion

CHAMPION, ROBERT MICHAEL
B. Feb. 10, 1955, Montgomery, Ala.
BR TR 6'   185 lbs.

	G	AB	H	2B	3B	HR	HR %	R	RBI	BB	SO	SB	BA	SA	PH AB	PH H	G by POS
1976 SD N	11	38	9	2	0	1	2.6	4	2	1	3	0	.237	.368	0	0	2B-11
1977	150	507	116	14	6	1	0.2	35	43	27	85	3	.229	.286	1	1	2B-149
1978	32	53	12	0	2	0	0.0	3	4	5	13	0	.226	.302	6	2	2B-20, 3B-4
3 yrs.	193	598	137	16	8	2	0.3	42	49	33	101	3	.229	.293	7	3	2B-180, 3B-4

Bob Chance

CHANCE, ROBERT
B. Sept. 10, 1940, Statesboro, Ga.
BL TR 6'2"   196 lbs.

	G	AB	H	2B	3B	HR	HR %	R	RBI	BB	SO	SB	BA	SA	PH AB	PH H	G by POS
1963 CLE A	16	52	15	4	0	2	3.8	5	7	1	10	0	.288	.481	2	0	OF-14
1964	120	390	109	16	1	14	3.6	45	75	40	101	3	.279	.433	19	5	1B-81, OF-31
1965 WAS A	72	199	51	9	0	4	2.0	20	14	18	44	0	.256	.362	19	5	1B-48, OF-3
1966	37	57	10	3	0	1	1.8	1	8	2	23	0	.175	.281	24	4	1B-13
1967	27	42	9	2	0	3	7.1	5	7	7	13	0	.214	.476	13	3	1B-10
1969 CAL A	5	7	1	0	0	0	0.0	0	1	0	4	0	.143	.143	4	1	1B-1
6 yrs.	277	747	195	34	1	24	3.2	76	112	68	195	3	.261	.406	81	18	1B-153, OF-48

Frank Chance

CHANCE, FRANK LEROY (Husk, The Peerless Leader)
B. Sept. 9, 1877, Fresno, Calif.   D. Sept. 14, 1924, Los Angeles, Calif.
Manager 1905-14, 1923.
Hall of Fame 1946.
BR TR 6'   190 lbs.

	G	AB	H	2B	3B	HR	HR %	R	RBI	BB	SO	SB	BA	SA	PH AB	PH H	G by POS
1898 CHI N	53	147	42	4	3	1	0.7	32	14	7		7	.286	.374	2	1	C-33, OF-17, 1B-3
1899	64	192	55	6	2	1	0.5	37	22	15		10	.286	.354	3	0	C-57, OF-1, 1B-1
1900	56	151	46	8	4	0	0.0	26	13	15		8	.305	.411	4	1	C-51, 1B-1
1901	69	241	67	12	4	0	0.0	38	36	29		30	.278	.361	2	1	OF-50, C-13, 1B-6
1902	75	236	67	9	4	1	0.4	40	31	35		28	.284	.369	4	1	1B-38, C-29, OF-4
1903	125	441	144	24	10	2	0.5	83	81	78		67	.327	.440	2	1	1B-121, C-2
1904	124	451	140	16	10	6	1.3	89	49	36		42	.310	.430	0	0	1B-123, C-1
1905	118	392	124	16	12	2	0.5	92	70	78		38	.316	.434	3	0	1B-116
1906	136	474	151	24	10	3	0.6	103	71	70		57	.319	.430	0	0	1B-136
1907	111	382	112	19	2	1	0.3	58	49	51		35	.293	.361	2	1	1B-109
1908	129	452	123	27	4	2	0.4	65	55	37		27	.272	.363	4	2	1B-126
1909	93	324	88	16	4	0	0.0	53	46	30		29	.272	.346	0	0	1B-92
1910	88	295	88	12	8	0	0.0	54	36	37	15	16	.298	.393	1	0	1B-87
1911	31	88	21	6	3	1	1.1	23	17	25	13	9	.239	.409	1	0	1B-29
1912	2	5	1	0	0	0	0.0	2	0	3	0	1	.200	.200	0	0	1B-2
1913 NY A	11	24	5	0	0	0	0.0	3	6	8	1	1	.208	.208	3	0	1B-8
1914	1	0	0	0	0	0	—	0	0	0	0	0	—	—	0	0	1B-1
17 yrs.	1286	4295	1274	199	80	20	0.5	798	596	554	29	405	.297	.394	31	8	1B-998, C-186, OF-72

WORLD SERIES

	G	AB	H	2B	3B	HR	HR %	R	RBI	BB	SO	SB	BA	SA	PH AB	PH H	G by POS
1906 CHI N	6	21	5	1	0	0	0.0	3	0	2	1	2	.238	.286	0	0	1B-6
1907	4	14	3	1	0	0	0.0	3	0	3	2	3	.214	.286	0	0	1B-4
1908	5	19	8	0	0	0	0.0	4	2	3	1	5	.421	.421	0	0	1B-5
1910	5	17	6	1	1	0	0.0	1	4	0	2	0	.353	.529	0	0	1B-5
4 yrs.	20	71	22	3	1	0	0.0	11	6	8	6	10	.310	.380	0	0	1B-20
												3rd					

Darrel Chaney

CHANEY, DARREL LEE
B. Mar. 9, 1948, Hammond, Ind.
BB TR 6'2"   188 lbs.

	G	AB	H	2B	3B	HR	HR %	R	RBI	BB	SO	SB	BA	SA	PH AB	PH H	G by POS
1969 CIN N	93	209	40	5	2	0	0.0	21	15	24	75	1	.191	.234	1	1	SS-91
1970	57	95	22	3	0	1	1.1	7	4	3	26	1	.232	.295	9	2	SS-30, 2B-18, 3B-3
1971	10	24	3	0	0	0	0.0	2	1	1	3	0	.125	.125	1	0	SS-7, 3B-1, 2B-1
1972	83	196	49	7	2	2	1.0	29	19	29	28	1	.250	.337	3	2	SS-64, 2B-12, 3B-10
1973	105	227	41	7	1	0	0.0	27	14	26	50	4	.181	.220	3	2	SS-75, 2B-14, 3B-12
1974	117	135	27	6	1	2	1.5	27	16	26	33	1	.200	.304	3	0	3B-81, 2B-38, SS-12
1975	71	160	35	6	0	2	1.3	18	26	14	38	3	.219	.294	5	1	SS-34, 2B-23, 3B-13
1976 ATL N	153	496	125	20	8	1	0.2	42	50	54	92	5	.252	.331	4	2	SS-151, 3B-1, 2B-1
1977	74	209	42	7	2	3	1.4	22	15	17	44	0	.201	.297	14	3	SS-77, 3B-8, 2B-1
1978	89	245	55	9	1	3	1.2	27	20	25	48	1	.224	.306	15	6	SS-39, 2B-5, 3B-4, C-1
1979	63	117	19	5	0	0	0.0	15	10	19	34	2	.162	.205	12	2	SS-39, 2B-5, 3B-4, C-1
11 yrs.	915	2113	458	75	17	14	0.7	237	190	238	471	19	.217	.288	67	21	SS-621, 2B-137, 3B-133, C-1

LEAGUE CHAMPIONSHIP SERIES

	G	AB	H	2B	3B	HR	HR %	R	RBI	BB	SO	SB	BA	SA	PH AB	PH H	G by POS
1972 CIN N	5	16	3	0	0	0	0.0	3	1	1	1	1	.188	.188	0	0	SS-5
1973	5	9	0	0	0	0	0.0	0	0	3	4	0	.000	.000	0	0	SS-5
2 yrs.	10	25	3	0	0	0	0.0	3	1	4	5	1	.120	.120	0	0	SS-10

WORLD SERIES

	G	AB	H	2B	3B	HR	HR %	R	RBI	BB	SO	SB	BA	SA	PH AB	PH H	G by POS
1970 CIN N	3	1	0	0	0	0	0.0	0	0	0	1	0	.000	.000	0	0	SS-3

	G	AB	H	2B	3B	HR	HR %	R	RBI	BB	SO	SB	BA	SA	Pinch Hit AB	H	G by POS

Darrel Chaney continued

	G	AB	H	2B	3B	HR	HR %	R	RBI	BB	SO	SB	BA	SA	PH AB	PH H	G by POS
1972	4	7	0	0	0	0	0.0	0	0	2	2	0	.000	.000	0	0	SS-3
1975	2	2	0	0	0	0	0.0	0	0	0	1	0	.000	.000	2	0	
3 yrs.	9	10	0	0	0	0	0.0	0	0	2	4	0	.000	.000	2	0	SS-6

Les Channell

CHANNELL, LESTER CLARK (Dude)   BL TL
B. Mar. 3, 1886, Crestline, Ohio   D. May 7, 1954, Denver, Colo.

	G	AB	H	2B	3B	HR	HR %	R	RBI	BB	SO	SB	BA	SA	PH AB	PH H	G by POS
1910 NY A	6	19	6	0	0	0	0.0	3	3	2		2	.316	.316	0	0	OF-6
1914	1	1	1	1	0	0	0.0	0	0	0	0	0	1.000	2.000	1	1	
2 yrs.	7	20	7	1	0	0	0.0	3	3	2	0	2	.350	.400	1	1	OF-6

Charlie Chant

CHANT, CHARLES JOSEPH   BR TR 6'   190 lbs.
B. Aug. 7, 1951, Bell, Calif.

	G	AB	H	2B	3B	HR	HR %	R	RBI	BB	SO	SB	BA	SA	PH AB	PH H	G by POS
1975 OAK A	5	5	0	0	0	0	0.0	1	0	0	0	0	.000	.000	0	0	OF-5, DH-1
1976 STL N	15	14	2	0	0	0	0.0	0	0	0	4	0	.143	.143	1	0	OF-14
2 yrs.	20	19	2	0	0	0	0.0	1	0	0	4	0	.105	.105	1	0	OF-19, DH-1

Ed Chaplin

CHAPLIN, BERT EDGAR (Chappy)   BL TR 5'7"   158 lbs.
Also known as Bert Edgar Chapman.
B. Sept. 25, 1893, Pelzer, S. C.   D. Aug. 15, 1978, Sanford, Fla.

	G	AB	H	2B	3B	HR	HR %	R	RBI	BB	SO	SB	BA	SA	PH AB	PH H	G by POS
1920 BOS A	4	5	1	1	0	0	0.0	2	1	4	1	0	.200	.400	0	0	C-2
1921	3	2	0	0	0	0	0.0	0	0	0	1	0	.000	.000	2	0	C-1
1922	28	69	13	1	1	0	0.0	8	6	9	9	2	.188	.232	6	0	C-21
3 yrs.	35	76	14	2	1	0	0.0	10	7	13	11	2	.184	.237	8	0	C-24

Ben Chapman

CHAPMAN, WILLIAM BENJAMIN   BR TR 6'   190 lbs.
B. Dec. 25, 1908, Nashville, Tenn.
Manager 1945-48.

	G	AB	H	2B	3B	HR	HR %	R	RBI	BB	SO	SB	BA	SA	PH AB	PH H	G by POS
1930 NY A	138	513	162	31	10	10	1.9	74	81	43	58	14	.316	.474	2	0	3B-91, 2B-45
1931	149	600	189	28	11	17	2.8	120	122	75	77	61	.315	.483	1	0	OF-137, 2B-11
1932	150	581	174	41	15	10	1.7	101	107	71	55	38	.299	.433	1	0	OF-149
1933	147	565	176	36	4	9	1.6	112	98	72	45	27	.312	.437	0	0	OF-147
1934	149	588	181	21	13	5	0.9	82	86	67	68	26	.308	.413	0	0	OF-149
1935	140	553	160	38	8	8	1.4	118	74	61	39	17	.289	.430	2	0	OF-138
1936 2 teams	133	540	170	50	10	5	0.9	110	81	84	38	20	.315	.472	0	0	OF-133
" total NY A (36G – .266) WAS A (97G – .332)																	
1937 2 teams	148	553	164	30	12	7	1.3	99	69	83	42	35	.297	.432	2	1	OF-144, SS-1
" total WAS A (35G – .262) BOS A (113G – .307)																	
1938 BOS A	127	480	163	40	8	6	1.3	92	80	65	33	13	.340	.494	1	1	OF-126, 3B-1
1939 CLE A	149	545	158	31	9	6	1.1	101	82	87	30	18	.290	.413	2	1	OF-146
1940	143	548	157	40	6	4	0.7	82	50	78	45	13	.286	.403	3	1	OF-140
1941 2 teams	85	300	71	15	1	3	1.0	35	29	29	20	4	.237	.323	10	2	OF-75
" total WAS A (28G – .255) CHI A (57G – .226)																	
1944 BKN N	20	38	14	4	0	0	0.0	11	11	5	4	1	.368	.474	9	3	P-11
1945 2 teams	37	73	19	2	0	0	0.0	6	7	4	2	0	.260	.288	10	4	P-13, OF-10, 3B-4
" total BKN N (13G – .136) PHI N (24G – .314)																	
1946 PHI N	1	1	0	0	0	0	0.0	1	0	0	0	0	.000	.000	0	0	P-1
15 yrs.	1716	6478	1958	407	107	90	1.4	1144	977	824	556	287	.302	.440	43	13	OF-1494, 3B-96, 2B-56, P-25, SS-1

WORLD SERIES

	G	AB	H	2B	3B	HR	HR %	R	RBI	BB	SO	SB	BA	SA	PH AB	PH H	G by POS
1932 NY A	4	17	5	1	0	0	0.0	1	6	2	4	0	.294	.353	0	0	OF-4

Calvin Chapman

CHAPMAN, CALVIN LOUIS   BL TR 5'9"   160 lbs.
Brother of Ed Chapman.   BB 1935
B. Dec. 20, 1910, Courtland, Miss.

	G	AB	H	2B	3B	HR	HR %	R	RBI	BB	SO	SB	BA	SA	PH AB	PH H	G by POS
1935 CIN N	15	53	18	1	0	0	0.0	6	3	4	5	2	.340	.358	0	0	SS-12, 2B-4
1936	96	219	54	7	3	1	0.5	35	22	16	19	5	.247	.320	40	15	OF-31, 2B-23, 3B-1
2 yrs.	111	272	72	8	3	1	0.4	41	25	20	24	7	.265	.327	40	15	OF-31, 2B-27, SS-12, 3B-1

Fred Chapman

CHAPMAN, WILLIAM FRED (Chappie)   BR TR 6'1"   185 lbs.
B. July 17, 1916, Liberty, S. C.

	G	AB	H	2B	3B	HR	HR %	R	RBI	BB	SO	SB	BA	SA	PH AB	PH H	G by POS
1939 PHI A	15	49	14	1	1	0	0.0	5	1	1	3	1	.286	.347	0	0	SS-15
1940	26	69	11	1	0	0	0.0	6	4	6	10	1	.159	.174	0	0	SS-25
1941	35	69	11	1	0	0	0.0	1	4	4	15	1	.159	.174	2	1	SS-31, 3B-2, 2B-1
3 yrs.	76	187	36	3	1	0	0.0	12	9	11	28	3	.193	.219	2	1	SS-68, 3B-2, 2B-1

Glenn Chapman

CHAPMAN, GLENN JUSTICE (Pete)   BR TR 5'11½" 170 lbs.
B. Jan. 21, 1906, Cambridge City, Ind.

	G	AB	H	2B	3B	HR	HR %	R	RBI	BB	SO	SB	BA	SA	PH AB	PH H	G by POS
1934 BKN N	67	93	26	5	1	1	1.1	19	10	7	19	1	.280	.387	2	0	OF-40, 2B-14

Harry Chapman

CHAPMAN, HARRY E.   BR TR 5'11"   160 lbs.
B. Oct. 26, 1887, Severance, Kans.   D. Oct. 21, 1918, Nevada, Mo.

	G	AB	H	2B	3B	HR	HR %	R	RBI	BB	SO	SB	BA	SA	PH AB	PH H	G by POS
1912 CHI N	1	4	1	0	0	0	0.0	1	1	0	0	0	.250	.750	0	0	C-1
1913 CIN N	2	2	1	0	0	0	0.0	0	0	0	1	0	.500	.500	2	1	
1914 STL F	64	181	38	2	1	0	0.0	16	14	13		2	.210	.232	4	1	C-51, OF-1, 2B-1, 1B-1
1915	62	186	37	6	3	1	0.5	19	29	22		4	.199	.280	8	1	C-53
1916 STL A	18	31	3	0	0	0	0.0	2	0	2	5	0	.097	.097	3	0	C-14
5 yrs.	147	404	80	8	5	1	0.2	38	44	37	6	7	.198	.250	17	3	C-119, OF-1, 2B-1, 1B-1

Jack Chapman

CHAPMAN, JOHN CURTIS   TR 5'11"   170 lbs.
B. May 8, 1843, Brooklyn, N. Y.   D. June 10, 1916, Brooklyn, N. Y.
Manager 1877-78, 1882-85, 1889-92.

	G	AB	H	2B	3B	HR	HR %	R	RBI	BB	SO	SB	BA	SA	PH AB	PH H	G by POS
1876 LOU N	17	67	16	1	0	0	0.0	4	5	1	3		.239	.254	0	0	OF-17, 3B-1

	G	AB	H	2B	3B	HR	HR %	R	RBI	BB	SO	SB	BA	SA	Pinch Hit AB	Pinch Hit H	G by POS

John Chapman

CHAPMAN, JOHN JOSEPH   BR TR 5'10''   180 lbs.
B. Oct. 15, 1899, Centralia, Pa.   D. Nov. 3, 1953, Philadelphia, Pa.

	G	AB	H	2B	3B	HR	HR %	R	RBI	BB	SO	SB	BA	SA	AB	H	G by POS
1924 PHI A	19	71	20	4	1	0	0.0	7	7	4	8	0	.282	.366	0	0	SS-19

Kelvin Chapman

CHAPMAN, KELVIN KEITH   BR TR 5'11''   173 lbs.
B. June 2, 1956, Willits, Calif.

	G	AB	H	2B	3B	HR	HR %	R	RBI	BB	SO	SB	BA	SA	AB	H	G by POS
1979 NY N	35	80	12	1	2	0	0.0	7	4	5	15	0	.150	.213	10	2	2B-22, 3B-1
1984	75	197	57	13	0	3	1.5	27	23	19	30	8	.289	.401	14	5	2B-56, 3B-3, SS-1
2 yrs.	110	277	69	14	2	3	1.1	34	27	24	45	8	.249	.347	24	7	2B-78, 3B-4, SS-1

Ray Chapman

CHAPMAN, RAYMOND JOHNSON   BR TR 5'10''   170 lbs.
B. Jan. 15, 1891, Beaver Dam, Ky.   D. Aug. 17, 1920, New York, N. Y.

	G	AB	H	2B	3B	HR	HR %	R	RBI	BB	SO	SB	BA	SA	AB	H	G by POS
1912 CLE A	31	109	34	6	3	0	0.0	29	19	10		10	.312	.422	0	0	SS-31
1913	140	508	131	19	7	3	0.6	78	39	46	51	29	.258	.341	1	0	SS-138
1914	106	375	103	16	10	2	0.5	59	42	48	48	24	.275	.387	1	0	SS-72, 2B-33
1915	154	570	154	14	17	3	0.5	101	67	70	82	36	.270	.370	0	0	SS-154
1916	109	346	80	10	5	0	0.0	50	27	50	46	21	.231	.289	5	0	SS-52, 3B-36, 2B-16
1917	156	563	170	28	12	3	0.5	98	36	61	65	52	.302	.410	0	0	SS-156
1918	128	446	119	19	8	1	0.2	84	32	84	46	30	.267	.352	0	0	SS-128, OF-1
1919	115	433	130	23	10	3	0.7	75	53	31	38	18	.300	.420	0	0	SS-115
1920	111	435	132	27	8	3	0.7	97	49	52	38	13	.303	.423	0	0	SS-111
9 yrs.	1050	3785	1053	162	80	18	0.5	671	364	452	414	233	.278	.378	7	0	SS-957, 2B-49, 3B-36, OF-1

Sam Chapman

CHAPMAN, SAMUEL BLAKE   BR TR 6'   180 lbs.
B. Apr. 11, 1916, Tiburon, Calif.

	G	AB	H	2B	3B	HR	HR %	R	RBI	BB	SO	SB	BA	SA	AB	H	G by POS
1938 PHI A	114	406	105	17	7	17	4.2	60	63	55	94	3	.259	.461	3	1	OF-114
1939	140	498	134	24	6	15	3.0	74	64	51	62	11	.269	.432	7	1	OF-117, 1B-19
1940	134	508	140	26	3	23	4.5	88	75	46	96	2	.276	.474	5	2	OF-129
1941	143	552	178	29	9	25	4.5	97	106	47	49	6	.322	.543	2	0	OF-141
1945	9	30	6	2	0	0	0.0	3	1	2	4	0	.200	.267	0	0	OF-8
1946	146	545	142	22	5	20	3.7	77	67	54	66	1	.261	.429	1	0	OF-145
1947	149	551	139	18	5	14	2.5	84	83	65	70	3	.252	.379	4	1	OF-146
1948	123	445	115	18	6	13	2.9	58	70	55	50	5	.258	.413	4	0	OF-118
1949	154	589	164	24	4	24	4.1	89	108	80	68	3	.278	.455	0	0	OF-154
1950	144	553	139	20	6	23	4.2	93	95	67	79	3	.251	.434	0	0	OF-140
1951 2 teams	112	PHI A (18G – .169)				CLE A (94G – .228)											
" total	112	311	67	10	1	6	1.9	41	41	39	44	3	.215	.312	4	0	OF-101, 1B-1
11 yrs.	1368	4988	1329	210	52	180	3.6	754	773	561	682	40	.266	.438	33	5	OF-1313, 1B-20

Harry Chappas

CHAPPAS, HAROLD PERRY   BB TR 5'3''   150 lbs.
B. Oct. 26, 1957, Mt. Rainier, Md.

	G	AB	H	2B	3B	HR	HR %	R	RBI	BB	SO	SB	BA	SA	AB	H	G by POS
1978 CHI A	20	75	20	1	0	0	0.0	11	6	6	11	1	.267	.280	0	0	SS-20
1979	26	59	17	1	0	1	1.7	9	4	5	5	1	.288	.356	1	1	SS-23
1980	26	50	8	2	0	0	0.0	6	2	4	10	0	.160	.200	3	0	SS-19, DH-2, 2B-1
3 yrs.	72	184	45	4	0	1	0.5	26	12	15	26	2	.245	.283	4	1	SS-62, DH-2, 2B-1

Larry Chappell

CHAPPELL, LAVERNE ASHFORD   BL TL 6'2''   186 lbs.
B. Feb. 19, 1890, McCluskey, Ill.   D. Nov. 8, 1918, San Francisco, Calif.

	G	AB	H	2B	3B	HR	HR %	R	RBI	BB	SO	SB	BA	SA	AB	H	G by POS
1913 CHI A	60	208	48	8	1	0	0.0	21	15	18	22	7	.231	.279	1	0	OF-59
1914	21	39	9	0	0	0	0.0	3	1	4	11	0	.231	.231	10	1	OF-9
1915	1	1	0	0	0	0	0.0	0	0	0	0	0	.000	.000	1	0	
1916 2 teams		CLE A (3G – .000)				BOS N (20G – .226)											
" total	23	55	12	1	0	0	0.0	4	9	3	8	2	.218	.273	8	1	OF-14
1917 BOS N	4	2	0	0	0	0	0.0	0	1	0	1	0	.000	.000	2	0	OF-1
5 yrs.	109	305	69	9	2	0	0.0	28	26	25	42	9	.226	.269	22	2	OF-83

Joe Charboneau

CHARBONEAU, JOSEPH   BR TR 6'2''   205 lbs.
B. June 17, 1955, Belvedere, Ill.

	G	AB	H	2B	3B	HR	HR %	R	RBI	BB	SO	SB	BA	SA	AB	H	G by POS
1980 CLE A	131	453	131	17	2	23	5.1	76	87	49	70	2	.289	.488	8	5	OF-67, DH-57
1981	48	138	29	7	1	4	2.9	14	18	7	22	1	.210	.362	7	2	OF-27, DH-14
1982	22	56	12	2	1	2	3.6	7	9	5	7	0	.214	.393	6	2	OF-18, DH-1
3 yrs.	201	647	172	26	4	29	4.5	97	114	61	99	3	.266	.453	21	9	OF-112, DH-72

Chappy Charles

CHARLES, RAYMOND   BR TR
B. Mar. 25, 1881, Phillipsburg, N. J.   D. Aug. 4, 1959, Bethlehem, Pa.

	G	AB	H	2B	3B	HR	HR %	R	RBI	BB	SO	SB	BA	SA	AB	H	G by POS
1908 STL N	121	454	93	14	3	1	0.2	39	17	19		15	.205	.256	2	0	2B-65, SS-31, 3B-23
1909 2 teams		STL N (99G – .236)				CIN N (13G – .256)											
" total	112	382	91	9	3	0	0.0	36	34	35		9	.238	.277	0	0	2B-81, SS-31, 3B-2
1910 CIN N	4	15	2	0	1	0	0.0	1	0	0	1	0	.133	.267	0	0	SS-4
3 yrs.	237	851	186	23	7	1	0.1	76	51	54		24	.219	.266	2	0	2B-146, SS-66, 3B-25

Ed Charles

CHARLES, EDWIN DOUGLAS (The Glider)   BR TR 5'10''   170 lbs.
B. Apr. 29, 1935, Daytona Beach, Fla.

	G	AB	H	2B	3B	HR	HR %	R	RBI	BB	SO	SB	BA	SA	AB	H	G by POS
1962 KC A	147	535	154	24	7	17	3.2	81	74	54	70	20	.288	.454	7	0	3B-140, 2B-2
1963	158	603	161	28	2	15	2.5	82	79	58	79	15	.267	.395	0	0	3B-158
1964	150	557	134	25	2	16	2.9	69	63	64	92	12	.241	.379	5	1	3B-147
1965	134	480	129	19	7	8	1.7	55	56	44	72	13	.269	.388	5	1	3B-128, SS-1, 2B-1
1966	118	385	110	18	8	9	2.3	52	42	30	53	12	.286	.444	14	6	3B-104, OF-1, 1B-1
1967 2 teams		KC A (19G – .246)				NY N (101G – .238)											
" total	120	384	92	14	2	3	0.8	37	36	36	71	5	.240	.310	10	1	3B-107
1968 NY N	117	369	102	11	1	15	4.1	41	53	28	57	7	.276	.434	15	6	3B-106, 1B-2
1969	61	169	35	8	1	3	1.8	21	18	18	31	4	.207	.320	12	4	3B-52
8 yrs.	1005	3482	917	147	30	86	2.5	438	421	332	525	86	.263	.397	68	19	3B-942, 2B-3, 1B-3, OF-1, SS-1

WORLD SERIES																	
1969 NY N	4	15	2	1	0	0	0.0	1	0	0	2	0	.133	.200	0	0	3B-4

	G	AB	H	2B	3B	HR	HR %	R	RBI	BB	SO	SB	BA	SA	Pinch Hit AB	Pinch Hit H	G by POS

Mike Chartak

CHARTAK, MICHAEL GEORGE (Shotgun)   BL TL 6'2"   180 lbs.
B. Apr. 28, 1916, Brooklyn, N. Y.   D. July 25, 1967, Cedar Rapids, Iowa

	G	AB	H	2B	3B	HR	HR%	R	RBI	BB	SO	SB	BA	SA	PH AB	PH H	G by POS
1940 **NY A**	11	15	2	1	0	0	0.0	2	3	5	5	0	.133	.200	5	1	OF-3
1942 3 teams		NY A (5G – .000)			WAS A (24G – .217)			STL A (73G – .249)									
" total	102	334	79	15	4	10	3.0	48	51	54	43	3	.237	.395	12	3	OF-88
1943 **STL A**	108	344	88	16	2	10	2.9	38	37	39	55	1	.256	.401	18	3	OF-77, 1B-18
1944	35	72	17	2	1	1	1.4	8	7	6	9	0	.236	.333	17	3	1B-12, OF-7
4 yrs.	256	765	186	34	7	21	2.7	96	98	104	112	4	.243	.388	52	10	OF-175, 1B-30

WORLD SERIES

	G	AB	H	2B	3B	HR	HR%	R	RBI	BB	SO	SB	BA	SA	PH AB	PH H	G by POS
1944 **STL A**	2	2	0	0	0	0	0.0	0	0	0	2	0	.000	.000	2	0	

Hal Chase

CHASE, HAROLD HOMER (Prince Hal)   BR TL 6'   175 lbs.
B. Feb. 13, 1883, Los Gatos, Calif.   D. May 18, 1947, Colusa, Calif.
Manager 1910-11.

	G	AB	H	2B	3B	HR	HR%	R	RBI	BB	SO	SB	BA	SA	PH AB	PH H	G by POS
1905 **NY A**	126	465	116	16	6	3	0.6	60	49	15		22	.249	.329	1	1	1B-122, SS-1, 2B-1
1906	151	597	193	23	10	0	0.0	84	76	13		28	.323	.395	0	0	1B-150, 2B-1
1907	125	498	143	23	3	2	0.4	72	68	19		32	.287	.357	0	0	1B-121, OF-4
1908	106	405	104	11	3	1	0.2	50	36	15		27	.257	.306	1	1	1B-96, OF-3, 2B-3, 3B-1
1909	118	474	134	17	3	4	0.8	60	63	20		25	.283	.357	0	0	1B-118
1910	130	524	152	20	5	3	0.6	67	73	16		40	.290	.365	0	0	1B-130
1911	133	527	166	32	7	3	0.6	82	62	21		36	.315	.419	0	0	1B-124, OF-7, 2B-2, SS-1
1912	131	522	143	21	9	4	0.8	61	58	17		33	.274	.372	2	0	1B-121, 2B-8
1913 2 teams		NY A (39G – .212)			CHI A (102G – .286)												
" total	141	530	141	13	14	2	0.4	64	48	27	54	14	.266	.355	0		1B-131, OF-5, 2B-5
1914 2 teams		CHI A (58G – .267)			BUF F (75G – .347)												
" total	133	497	156	29	14	3	0.6	70	68	29	19	19	.314	.447	2	1	1B-131
1915 **BUF F**	145	567	165	31	10	**17**	**3.0**	85	89	20		23	.291	.471	1	0	1B-143, OF-1
1916 **CIN N**	142	542	**184**	29	12	4	0.7	66	82	19	48	22	**.339**	.459	7	2	1B-98, OF-25, 2B-16
1917	152	**602**	167	28	15	4	0.7	71	86	15	49	21	.277	.394	0	0	1B-151
1918	74	259	78	12	6	2	0.8	30	38	13	15	5	.301	.417	5	0	1B-67, OF-2
1919 **NY N**	110	408	116	17	7	5	1.2	58	45	17	40	16	.284	.397	2	1	1B-107
15 yrs.	1917	7417	2158	322	124	57	0.8	980	941	276	225	363	.291	.391	21	6	1B-1810, OF-47, 2B-36, SS-2, 3B-1

Buster Chatham

CHATHAM, CHARLES L.   BR TR 5'5"   150 lbs.
B. Dec. 25, 1901, West, Tex.   D. Dec. 15, 1975, Waco, Tex.

	G	AB	H	2B	3B	HR	HR%	R	RBI	BB	SO	SB	BA	SA	PH AB	PH H	G by POS
1930 **BOS N**	112	404	108	20	11	5	1.2	48	56	37	41	8	.267	.408	4	0	3B-92, SS-17
1931	17	44	10	1	0	1	2.3	4	3	6	6	0	.227	.318	3	0	SS-6, 3B-6
2 yrs.	129	448	118	21	11	6	1.3	52	59	43	47	8	.263	.400	7	0	3B-98, SS-23

Jim Chatterton

CHATTERTON, JAMES M.
B. Oct. 14, 1864, Brooklyn, N. Y.   D. Dec. 18, 1944, Malden, Mass.

	G	AB	H	2B	3B	HR	HR%	R	RBI	BB	SO	SB	BA	SA	PH AB	PH H	G by POS
1884 **KC U**	4	15	2	1	0	0	0.0	4		2			.133	.200	0	0	OF-2, 1B-2, P-1

Ossie Chavarria

CHAVARRIA, OSVALDO QUIJANO   BR TR 5'11"   155 lbs.
B. Aug. 5, 1940, Colon, Panama

	G	AB	H	2B	3B	HR	HR%	R	RBI	BB	SO	SB	BA	SA	PH AB	PH H	G by POS
1966 **KC A**	86	191	46	10	0	2	1.0	26	10	18	43	3	.241	.325	17	4	OF-26, SS-23, 2B-14, 1B-8, 3B-5
1967	38	59	6	2	0	0	0.0	2	4	7	16	1	.102	.136	8	1	2B-7, 3B-7, OF-3, SS-2
2 yrs.	124	250	52	12	0	2	0.8	28	14	25	59	4	.208	.280	25	5	2B-31, OF-29, SS-25, 3B-12, 1B-8

Harry Cheek

CHEEK, HARRY G.   TR
B. 1879, Sedalia, Mo.   D. June 25, 1956, Paramus, N. J.

	G	AB	H	2B	3B	HR	HR%	R	RBI	BB	SO	SB	BA	SA	PH AB	PH H	G by POS
1910 **PHI N**	2	4	2	1	0	0	0.0	0		0	0	0	.500	.750	0	0	C-2

Paul Chervinko

CHERVINKO, PAUL   BR TR 5'8"   185 lbs.
B. July 23, 1910, Trauger, Pa.   D. June 3, 1976, Danville, Ill.

	G	AB	H	2B	3B	HR	HR%	R	RBI	BB	SO	SB	BA	SA	PH AB	PH H	G by POS
1937 **BKN N**	30	48	7	0	1	0	0.0	1	2	3	16	0	.146	.188	3	0	C-26
1938	12	27	4	0	0	0	0.0	0	3	2	0	0	.148	.148	0	0	C-12
2 yrs.	42	75	11	0	1	0	0.0	1	5	5	16	0	.147	.173	3	0	C-38

Cupid Childs

CHILDS, CLARENCE ALGERNON   BL TR 5'8"   185 lbs.
B. Aug. 14, 1868, Calvert County, Md.   D. Nov. 8, 1912, Baltimore, Md.

	G	AB	H	2B	3B	HR	HR%	R	RBI	BB	SO	SB	BA	SA	PH AB	PH H	G by POS
1888 **PHI N**	2	4	0	0	0	0	0.0	0	0	0	0	0	.000	.000	0	0	2B-2
1890 **SYR AA**	136	493	170	33	14	2	0.4	109		72		56	.345	.481	0	0	2B-125, SS-1
1891 **CLE N**	141	551	155	21	12	2	0.4	120	83	97	32	39	.281	.374	0	0	2B-141
1892	145	558	177	14	11	3	0.5	**136**	53	117	20	26	.317	.398	0	0	2B-145
1893	124	485	158	19	10	3	0.6	145	65	120	12	23	.326	.425	0	0	2B-123
1894	118	479	169	21	12	4	0.8	143	52	107	11	17	.353	.459	0	0	2B-118
1895	119	462	133	15	3	4	0.9	96	90	74	24	20	.288	.359	0	0	2B-119
1896	132	498	177	24	9	1	0.2	106	106	100	18	25	.355	.446	0	0	2B-132
1897	114	444	150	15	9	1	0.2	105	61	74		25	.338	.419	0	0	2B-114
1898	110	422	122	9	4	1	0.2	91	31	69		9	.289	.336	0	0	2B-110
1899 **STL N**	125	465	124	11	11	1	0.2	73	48	74		11	.267	.344	0	0	2B-125
1900 **CHI N**	138	538	131	14	5	0	0.0	70	44	57		15	.243	.288	0	0	2B-137
1901	62	220	61	9	0	0	0.0	24	21	29		3	.257	.295	0	0	2B-62
13 yrs.	1467	5636	1727	205	100	20	0.4	1218	653	990	117	269	.306	.389	0	0	2B-1453, SS-1

Pete Childs

CHILDS, PETER PIERRE   TR
B. Nov. 15, 1871, Philadelphia, Pa.   D. Feb. 15, 1922, Philadelphia, Pa.

	G	AB	H	2B	3B	HR	HR%	R	RBI	BB	SO	SB	BA	SA	PH AB	PH H	G by POS
1901 2 teams		STL N (29G – .266)			CHI N (61G – .225)												
" total	90	292	69	6	1	0	0.0	35	22	41		4	.236	.264	6	1	2B-80, OF-2, SS-1
1902 **PHI N**	123	403	78	5	0	0	0.0	25	25	34		6	.194	.206	0	0	2B-123
2 yrs.	213	695	147	11	1	0	0.0	60	47	75		10	.212	.230	6	1	2B-203, OF-2, SS-1

	G	AB	H	2B	3B	HR	HR %	R	RBI	BB	SO	SB	BA	SA	Pinch Hit AB	Pinch Hit H	G by POS

Pearce Chiles

CHILES, PEARCE NUGET (What's the Use)
B. May 28, 1867, Deepwater, Mo.   Deceased.

	G	AB	H	2B	3B	HR	HR %	R	RBI	BB	SO	SB	BA	SA	PH AB	PH H	G by POS
1899 PHI N	97	338	108	28	7	2	0.6	57	76	16		6	.320	.462	10	2	OF-46, 1B-25, 2B-16
1900	33	111	24	6	2	1	0.9	13	23	6		4	.216	.333	2	0	1B-16, 2B-12, OF-3
2 yrs.	130	449	132	34	9	3	0.7	70	99	22		10	.294	.430	12	2	OF-49, 1B-41, 2B-28

Rich Chiles

CHILES, RICHARD FRANCIS   BL TL 5'11"   170 lbs.
B. Nov. 22, 1949, Sacramento, Calif.

	G	AB	H	2B	3B	HR	HR %	R	RBI	BB	SO	SB	BA	SA	PH AB	PH H	G by POS
1971 HOU N	67	119	27	5	1	2	1.7	12	15	6	20	0	.227	.336	38	11	OF-27
1972	9	11	3	1	0	0	0.0	0	2	1	1	0	.273	.364	6	2	OF-2
1973 NY N	8	25	3	2	0	0	0.0	2	1	0	2	0	.120	.200	0	0	OF-8
1976 HOU N	5	4	2	1	0	0	0.0	1	0	0	0	0	.500	.750	4	2	OF-1
1977 MIN A	108	261	69	16	1	3	1.1	31	36	23	17	0	.264	.368	29	8	DH-61, OF-22
1978	87	198	53	12	0	1	0.5	22	22	20	25	1	.268	.343	21	5	OF-61, DH-8
6 yrs.	284	618	157	37	2	6	1.0	68	76	50	65	1	.254	.350	98	28	OF-121, DH-69

Dino Chiozza

CHIOZZA, DINO JOSEPH (Dynamo)   BL TR 6'   170 lbs.
Brother of Lou Chiozza.
B. June 30, 1914, Memphis, Tenn.   D. Apr. 23, 1972, Memphis, Tenn.

	G	AB	H	2B	3B	HR	HR %	R	RBI	BB	SO	SB	BA	SA	PH AB	PH H	G by POS
1935 PHI N	2	0	0	0	0	0	–	1	0	0	0	0	–	–	0	0	SS-2

Lou Chiozza

CHIOZZA, LOUIS PEO   BL TR 6'   172 lbs.
Brother of Dino Chiozza.
B. May 11, 1910, Tallulah, La.   D. Feb. 28, 1971, Memphis, Tenn.

	G	AB	H	2B	3B	HR	HR %	R	RBI	BB	SO	SB	BA	SA	PH AB	PH H	G by POS
1934 PHI N	134	484	147	28	5	0	0.0	66	44	34	35	9	.304	.382	9	1	2B-85, 3B-26, OF-17
1935	124	472	134	26	6	3	0.6	71	47	33	44	5	.284	.383	1	0	2B-120, 3B-2
1936	144	572	170	32	6	1	0.2	83	48	37	39	17	.297	.379	2	1	OF-90, 2B-33, 3B-26
1937 NY N	117	439	102	11	2	4	0.9	49	29	20	30	6	.232	.294	9	2	3B-93, OF-12, 2B-2
1938	57	179	42	7	2	3	1.7	15	17	12	7	5	.235	.346	7	2	2B-34, OF-16, 3B-1
1939	40	142	38	3	1	3	2.1	19	12	9	10	3	.268	.366	0	0	3B-30, SS-8
6 yrs.	616	2288	633	107	22	14	0.6	303	197	145	165	45	.277	.361	28	6	2B-274, 3B-178, OF-135, SS-8

WORLD SERIES

	G	AB	H	2B	3B	HR	HR %	R	RBI	BB	SO	SB	BA	SA	PH AB	PH H	G by POS
1937 NY N	2	7	2	0	0	0	0.0	0	0	1	1	0	.286	.286	0	0	OF-2

Walt Chipple

CHIPPLE, WALTER JOHN   BR TR 6½"   168 lbs.
Born Walter John Chlipala.
B. Sept. 26, 1918, Utica, N. Y.

	G	AB	H	2B	3B	HR	HR %	R	RBI	BB	SO	SB	BA	SA	PH AB	PH H	G by POS
1945 WAS A	18	44	6	0	0	0	0.0	4	5	5	6	0	.136	.136	2	0	OF-13

Tom Chism

CHISM, THOMAS RAYMOND   BL TL 6'1"   195 lbs.
B. May 9, 1955, Chester, Pa.

	G	AB	H	2B	3B	HR	HR %	R	RBI	BB	SO	SB	BA	SA	PH AB	PH H	G by POS
1979 BAL A	6	3	0	0	0	0	0.0	0	0	0	0	0	.000	.000	0	0	1B-4

Harry Chiti

CHITI, HARRY DOMINICK   BR TR 6'2½"   221 lbs.
B. Nov. 16, 1932, Kincaid, Ill.

	G	AB	H	2B	3B	HR	HR %	R	RBI	BB	SO	SB	BA	SA	PH AB	PH H	G by POS
1950 CHI N	3	6	2	0	0	0	0.0	0	0	0	0	0	.333	.333	2	0	C-1
1951	9	31	11	2	0	0	0.0	1	5	2	2	0	.355	.419	1	0	C-8
1952	32	113	31	5	0	5	4.4	14	13	5	8	0	.274	.451	0	0	C-32
1955	113	338	78	6	1	11	3.3	24	41	25	68	0	.231	.352	1	0	C-113
1956	72	203	43	6	4	4	2.0	17	18	19	35	0	.212	.340	5	2	C-67
1958 KC A	103	295	79	11	3	9	3.1	32	44	18	48	3	.268	.417	19	3	C-83
1959	55	162	44	11	0	5	3.1	20	25	17	26	0	.272	.444	8	4	C-47
1960 2 teams			KC A (58G – .221)			DET A (37G – .163)											
" total	95	294	59	7	0	7	2.4	25	33	27	45	1	.201	.296	8	2	C-88
1961 DET A	5	12	1	0	0	0	0.0	0	0	1	2	0	.083	.083	0	0	C-5
1962 NY N	15	41	8	1	0	0	0.0	2	0	1	8	0	.195	.220	2	0	C-14
10 yrs.	502	1495	356	49	9	41	2.7	135	179	115	242	4	.238	.365	46	11	C-458

Felix Chouinard

CHOUINARD, FELIX GEORGE   BB TR
B. Oct. 5, 1887, Hines, Ill.   D. Apr. 28, 1955, Hines, Ill.

	G	AB	H	2B	3B	HR	HR %	R	RBI	BB	SO	SB	BA	SA	PH AB	PH H	G by POS
1910 CHI A	24	82	16	3	2	0	0.0	6	9	8		4	.195	.280	0	0	OF-23, 2B-1
1911	14	17	3	0	0	0	0.0	3	0	0		0	.176	.176	0	0	OF-4, 2B-4
1914 3 teams			PIT F (9G – .300)			BKN F (32G – .253)			BAL F (5G – .444)								
" total	46	118	33	2	1	1	0.8	12	12	4		4	.280	.356	11	2	OF-25, 2B-4, SS-1
1915 BKN F	4	4	2	0	0	0	0.0	1	2	0		0	.500	.500	1	0	OF-2
4 yrs.	88	221	54	5	4	1	0.5	23	23	12		8	.244	.317	12	2	OF-54, 2B-9, SS-1

Harry Chozen

CHOZEN, HARRY KENNETH   BR TR 5'9½"   190 lbs.
B. Sept. 27, 1915, Winnebago, Minn.

	G	AB	H	2B	3B	HR	HR %	R	RBI	BB	SO	SB	BA	SA	PH AB	PH H	G by POS
1937 CIN N	1	4	1	0	0	0	0.0	0	0	0	0	0	.250	.250	0	0	C-1

Neil Chrisley

CHRISLEY, BARBRA O'NEIL   BL TR 6'3"   187 lbs.
B. Dec. 16, 1931, Calhoun Falls, S. C.

	G	AB	H	2B	3B	HR	HR %	R	RBI	BB	SO	SB	BA	SA	PH AB	PH H	G by POS
1957 WAS A	26	51	8	2	1	0	0.0	6	3	7	7	0	.157	.235	13	2	OF-11
1958	105	233	50	7	4	5	2.1	19	26	16	18	1	.215	.343	38	10	OF-69, 3B-1
1959 DET A	65	106	14	3	0	6	5.7	7	11	12	10	0	.132	.330	43	5	OF-21
1960	96	220	56	10	3	5	2.3	27	24	19	26	2	.255	.395	44	10	OF-47, 1B-2
1961 MIL N	10	9	2	0	0	0	0.0	1	0	1	1	0	.222	.222	9	2	
5 yrs.	302	619	130	22	8	16	2.6	60	64	55	62	3	.210	.349	147	29	OF-148, 1B-2, 3B-1

Lloyd Christenbury

CHRISTENBURY, LLOYD REID (Low)   BL TR 5'7"   165 lbs.
B. Oct. 19, 1893, Mecklenburg County, N. C.   D. Dec. 13, 1944, Birmingham, Ala.

	G	AB	H	2B	3B	HR	HR %	R	RBI	BB	SO	SB	BA	SA	PH AB	PH H	G by POS
1919 BOS N	7	31	9	1	0	0	0.0	5	4	2	2	0	.290	.323	0	0	OF-7
1920	65	106	22	2	2	0	0.0	17	14	13	12	0	.208	.264	23	4	OF-14, SS-7, 2B-6, 3B-2
1921	62	125	44	6	2	3	2.4	34	16	21	7	3	.352	.504	17	6	2B-32, SS-2, 3B-2

	G	AB	H	2B	3B	HR	HR %	R	RBI	BB	SO	SB	BA	SA	Pinch Hit AB	H	G by POS

Lloyd Christenbury continued

	G	AB	H	2B	3B	HR	HR %	R	RBI	BB	SO	SB	BA	SA	AB	H	G by POS
1922	71	152	38	5	2	1	0.7	22	13	18	11	2	.250	.329	27	9	OF-32, 2B-5, 3B-2
4 yrs.	205	414	113	14	6	4	1.0	78	47	54	32	5	.273	.365	67	19	OF-53, 2B-43, SS-9, 3B-6

Bruce Christensen

CHRISTENSEN, BRUCE RAY
B. Feb. 22, 1948, Madison, Wis.   BL TR 5'11" 160 lbs.

	G	AB	H	2B	3B	HR	HR %	R	RBI	BB	SO	SB	BA	SA	AB	H	G by POS
1971 CAL A	29	63	17	1	0	0	0.0	4	3	6	5	0	.270	.286	7	2	SS-24

Cuckoo Christensen

CHRISTENSEN, WALTER NEILS (Seacap)
B. Oct. 24, 1899, San Francisco, Calif.   BL TL 5'6½" 156 lbs.

	G	AB	H	2B	3B	HR	HR %	R	RBI	BB	SO	SB	BA	SA	AB	H	G by POS
1926 CIN N	114	329	115	15	7	0	0.0	41	41	40	18	8	.350	.438	18	7	OF-93
1927	57	185	47	6	0	0	0.0	25	16	20	16	4	.254	.286	5	0	OF-50
2 yrs.	171	514	162	21	7	0	0.0	66	57	60	34	12	.315	.383	23	7	OF-143

John Christensen

CHRISTENSEN, JOHN LAWRENCE
B. Sept. 5, 1960, Downey, Calif.   BR TR 6'3" 205 lbs.

	G	AB	H	2B	3B	HR	HR %	R	RBI	BB	SO	SB	BA	SA	AB	H	G by POS
1984 NY N	5	11	3	2	0	0	0.0	2	3	1	2	0	.273	.455	1	1	OF-5

Bob Christian

CHRISTIAN, ROBERT CHARLES   BR TR 5'10" 180 lbs.
B. Oct. 17, 1945, Chicago, Ill.   D. Feb. 20, 1974, San Diego, Calif.

	G	AB	H	2B	3B	HR	HR %	R	RBI	BB	SO	SB	BA	SA	AB	H	G by POS
1968 DET A	3	3	1	1	0	0	0.0	0	0	0	0	0	.333	.667	1	0	OF-1, 1B-1
1969 CHI A	39	129	28	4	0	3	2.3	11	16	10	19	3	.217	.318	1	1	OF-38
1970	12	15	4	0	0	1	6.7	3	3	1	4	0	.267	.467	9	3	OF-4
3 yrs.	54	147	33	5	0	4	2.7	14	19	11	23	3	.224	.340	11	4	OF-43, 1B-1

Mark Christman

CHRISTMAN, MARK JOSEPH   BR TR 5'11" 175 lbs.
B. Oct. 21, 1913, Maplewood, Mo.   D. Oct. 9, 1976, St. Louis, Mo.

	G	AB	H	2B	3B	HR	HR %	R	RBI	BB	SO	SB	BA	SA	AB	H	G by POS
1938 DET A	95	318	79	6	4	1	0.3	35	44	27	21	5	.248	.302	0	0	3B-69, SS-21
1939 2 teams	85	238	52	8	3	0	0.0	27	20	20	12	2	.218	.277	11	0	SS-64, 3B-6, 2B-1
" total	DET A (6G – .250)			STL A (79G – .216)													
1943 STL A	98	336	91	11	5	2	0.6	31	35	19	19	0	.271	.351	3	0	3B-37, SS-24, 1B-20, 2B-14
1944	148	547	148	25	1	6	1.1	56	83	47	37	5	.271	.353	0	0	3B-145, 1B-3
1945	78	289	80	7	4	4	1.4	32	34	19	19	1	.277	.370	1	0	3B-77
1946	128	458	118	22	2	1	0.2	40	41	22	29	0	.258	.321	6	1	3B-77, SS-47
1947 WAS A	110	374	83	15	2	1	0.3	27	33	33	16	4	.222	.281	3	1	SS-106, 2B-1
1948	120	409	106	17	2	1	0.2	38	40	25	19	0	.259	.318	8	2	SS-102, 3B-9, 2B-3
1949	49	112	24	2	0	3	2.7	8	18	8	7	0	.214	.313	16	2	3B-23, 1B-6, SS-4, 2B-1
9 yrs.	911	3081	781	113	23	19	0.6	294	348	220	179	17	.253	.324	48	6	3B-443, SS-368, 1B-29, 2B-20

WORLD SERIES

	G	AB	H	2B	3B	HR	HR %	R	RBI	BB	SO	SB	BA	SA	AB	H	G by POS
1944 STL A	6	22	2	0	0	0	0.0	0	1	0	6	0	.091	.091	0	0	3B-6

Steve Christmas

CHRISTMAS, STEPHEN RANDALL   BL TR 6' 190 lbs.
B. Dec. 9, 1957, Orlando, Fla.

	G	AB	H	2B	3B	HR	HR %	R	RBI	BB	SO	SB	BA	SA	AB	H	G by POS
1983 CIN N	9	17	1	0	0	0	0.0	0	1	1	3	0	.059	.059	4	0	C-7
1984 CHI A	12	11	4	1	0	1	9.1	1	4	0	2	0	.364	.727	11	4	C-1
2 yrs.	21	28	5	1	0	1	3.6	1	5	1	5	0	.179	.321	15	4	C-8

Joe Christopher

CHRISTOPHER, JOSEPH O'NEAL   BR TR 5'10" 175 lbs.
B. Dec. 13, 1935, Frederiksted, Virgin Islands

	G	AB	H	2B	3B	HR	HR %	R	RBI	BB	SO	SB	BA	SA	AB	H	G by POS
1959 PIT N	15	12	0	0	0	0	0.0	6	0	1	4	0	.000	.000	0	0	OF-9
1960	50	56	13	2	0	1	1.8	21	3	5	8	1	.232	.321	6	0	OF-17
1961	76	186	49	7	3	0	0.0	25	14	18	24	6	.263	.333	11	3	OF-55
1962 NY N	119	271	66	10	2	6	2.2	36	32	35	42	11	.244	.362	18	3	OF-94
1963	64	149	33	5	1	1	0.7	19	8	13	21	1	.221	.289	21	3	OF-45
1964	154	543	163	26	8	16	2.9	78	76	48	92	6	.300	.466	9	3	OF-145
1965	148	437	109	18	3	5	1.1	38	40	35	82	4	.249	.339	34	10	OF-112
1966 BOS A	12	13	1	0	0	0	0.0	1	0	2	4	0	.077	.077	8	0	OF-2
8 yrs.	638	1667	434	68	17	29	1.7	224	173	157	277	29	.260	.374	107	22	OF-479

WORLD SERIES

	G	AB	H	2B	3B	HR	HR %	R	RBI	BB	SO	SB	BA	SA	AB	H	G by POS
1960 PIT N	3	0	0	0	0	0	–	0	0	0	0	0	–	–	0	0	

Lloyd Christopher

CHRISTOPHER, LLOYD EUGENE   BR TR 6'2" 190 lbs.
Brother of Russ Christopher.
B. Dec. 31, 1919, Richmond, Calif.

	G	AB	H	2B	3B	HR	HR %	R	RBI	BB	SO	SB	BA	SA	AB	H	G by POS
1945 2 teams	BOS A (8G – .286)			CHI N (1G – .000)													
" total	9	14	4	0	0	0	0.0	4	4	3	2	0	.286	.286	3	0	OF-4
1947 CHI A	7	23	5	0	1	0	0.0	1	0	2	4	0	.217	.304	0	0	OF-7
2 yrs.	16	37	9	0	1	0	0.0	5	4	5	6	0	.243	.297	3	0	OF-11

Hi Church

CHURCH, HIRAM LINCOLN
B. Central Square, N. Y.   Deceased.

	G	AB	H	2B	3B	HR	HR %	R	RBI	BB	SO	SB	BA	SA	AB	H	G by POS
1890 B-B AA	3	9	1	0	0	0	0.0	1		0		0	.111	.111	0	0	OF-3

John Churry

CHURRY, JOHN   BR TR 5'9" 172 lbs.
B. Nov. 26, 1900, Johnstown, Pa.   D. Feb. 8, 1970, Zanesville, Ohio

	G	AB	H	2B	3B	HR	HR %	R	RBI	BB	SO	SB	BA	SA	AB	H	G by POS
1924 CHI N	6	7	1	1	0	0	0.0	0	0	2	0	0	.143	.286	2	0	C-3
1925	3	6	3	0	0	0	0.0	1	1	0	0	0	.500	.500	0	0	C-3
1926	2	4	0	0	0	0	0.0	0	0	1	2	0	.000	.000	1	0	C-1
1927	1	1	1	0	0	0	0.0	0	0	0	0	0	1.000	1.000	0	0	C-1
4 yrs.	12	18	5	1	0	0	0.0	1	1	3	2	0	.278	.333	3	0	C-8

	G	AB	H	2B	3B	HR	HR %	R	RBI	BB	SO	SB	BA	SA	Pinch Hit AB	H	G by POS

Larry Ciaffone

CIAFFONE, LAWRENCE THOMAS (Symphony)
B. Aug. 17, 1924, Brooklyn, N. Y.   BR TR 5'9½" 185 lbs.

	G	AB	H	2B	3B	HR	HR %	R	RBI	BB	SO	SB	BA	SA	AB	H	G by POS
1951 STL N	5	5	0	0	0	0	0.0	0	0	1	2	0	.000	.000	3	0	OF-1

Darryl Cias

CIAS, DARRYL
B. Apr. 23, 1957, New York, N. Y.   BR TR 5'11" 188 lbs.

	G	AB	H	2B	3B	HR	HR %	R	RBI	BB	SO	SB	BA	SA	AB	H	G by POS
1983 OAK A	19	18	6	1	0	0	0.0	1	1	2	4	1	.333	.389	0	0	C-19

Joe Cicero

CICERO, JOSEPH FRANCIS (Dode)
B. Nov. 18, 1910, Atlantic City, N. J.   D. Mar. 30, 1983, Clearwater, Fla.   BR TR 5'8" 167 lbs.

	G	AB	H	2B	3B	HR	HR %	R	RBI	BB	SO	SB	BA	SA	AB	H	G by POS
1929 BOS A	10	32	10	2	2	0	0.0	6	4	0	2	0	.313	.500	3	2	OF-7
1930	18	30	5	1	2	0	0.0	5	4	1	5	0	.167	.333	11	1	OF-5, 3B-2
1945 PHI A	12	19	3	0	0	0	0.0	3	0	1	6	0	.158	.158	2	0	OF-7
3 yrs.	40	81	18	3	4	0	0.0	14	8	2	13	0	.222	.358	16	3	OF-19, 3B-2

Ted Cieslak

CIESLAK, THADDEUS WALTER
B. Nov. 22, 1916, Milwaukee, Wis.   BR TR 5'10" 175 lbs.

	G	AB	H	2B	3B	HR	HR %	R	RBI	BB	SO	SB	BA	SA	AB	H	G by POS
1944 PHI N	85	220	54	10	0	2	0.9	18	11	21	17	1	.245	.318	30	5	3B-48, OF-5

Al Cihocki

CIHOCKI, ALBERT JOSEPH
B. May 7, 1924, Nanticoke, Pa.   BR TR 5'11" 185 lbs.

	G	AB	H	2B	3B	HR	HR %	R	RBI	BB	SO	SB	BA	SA	AB	H	G by POS
1945 CLE A	92	283	60	9	3	0	0.0	21	24	11	48	2	.212	.265	0	0	SS-41, 3B-29, 2B-23

Ed Cihocki

CIHOCKI, EDWARD JOSEPH (Cy)
B. May 9, 1907, Wilmington, Del.   BR TR 5'8" 163 lbs.

	G	AB	H	2B	3B	HR	HR %	R	RBI	BB	SO	SB	BA	SA	AB	H	G by POS
1932 PHI A	1	1	0	0	0	0	0.0	0	0	0	0	0	.000	.000	1	0	SS-28, 3B-1, 2B-1
1933	33	97	14	2	3	0	0.0	6	9	7	16	0	.144	.227	2	0	SS-28, 3B-1, 2B-1
2 yrs.	34	98	14	2	3	0	0.0	6	9	7	16	0	.143	.224	3	0	SS-28, 3B-1, 2B-1

Gino Cimoli

CIMOLI, GINO NICHOLAS
B. Dec. 18, 1929, San Francisco, Calif.   BR TR 6'1" 180 lbs.

	G	AB	H	2B	3B	HR	HR %	R	RBI	BB	SO	SB	BA	SA	AB	H	G by POS
1956 BKN N	73	36	4	1	0	0	0.0	3	4	1	8	1	.111	.139	4	1	OF-62
1957	142	532	156	22	5	10	1.9	88	57	39	86	3	.293	.410	3	2	OF-138
1958 LA N	109	325	80	6	3	9	2.8	35	27	18	49	3	.246	.366	8	0	OF-104
1959 STL N	143	519	145	40	7	8	1.5	61	72	37	83	7	.279	.430	3	1	OF-141
1960 PIT N	101	307	82	14	4	0	0.0	36	28	32	43	1	.267	.339	10	2	OF-91
1961 2 teams			PIT N (21G – .299)			MIL N (37G – .197)											
" total	58	184	43	8	1	3	1.6	16	10	13	28	1	.234	.337	7	1	OF-50
1962 KC A	152	550	151	20	15	10	1.8	67	71	40	89	2	.275	.420	7	2	OF-147
1963	145	529	139	19	11	4	0.8	56	48	39	72	3	.263	.363	9	4	OF-136
1964 2 teams			KC A (4G – .000)			BAL A (38G – .138)											
" total	42	67	8	3	2	0	0.0	7	3	2	14	0	.119	.224	6	1	OF-39
1965 CAL A	4	5	0	0	0	0	0.0	1	0	1	2	0	.000	.000	3	0	OF-1
10 yrs.	969	3054	808	133	48	44	1.4	370	321	221	474	21	.265	.383	60	14	OF-909
WORLD SERIES																	
1956 BKN N	1	0	0	0	0	0	–	0	0	0	0	0	–	–	0	0	OF-1
1960 PIT N	7	20	5	0	0	0	0.0	4	1	2	4	0	.250	.250	1	0	OF-6
2 yrs.	8	20	5	0	0	0	0.0	4	1	2	4	0	.250	.250	1	0	OF-7

Frank Cipriani

CIPRIANI, FRANK DOMINICK
B. Apr. 14, 1941, Buffalo, N. Y.   BR TR 6' 180 lbs.

	G	AB	H	2B	3B	HR	HR %	R	RBI	BB	SO	SB	BA	SA	AB	H	G by POS
1961 KC A	13	36	9	0	0	0	0.0	2	2	2	4		.250	.250	2	0	OF-11

George Cisar

CISAR, GEORGE JOSEPH
B. Aug. 25, 1912, Chicago, Ill.   BR TR 6' 175 lbs.

	G	AB	H	2B	3B	HR	HR %	R	RBI	BB	SO	SB	BA	SA	AB	H	G by POS
1937 BKN N	20	29	6	0	0	0	0.0	8	4	2	6	3	.207	.207	1	0	OF-13

Bill Cissell

CISSELL, CHALMER WILLIAM
B. Jan. 3, 1904, Perryville, Mo.   D. Mar. 15, 1949, Chicago, Ill.   BR TR 5'11" 170 lbs.

	G	AB	H	2B	3B	HR	HR %	R	RBI	BB	SO	SB	BA	SA	AB	H	G by POS
1928 CHI A	125	443	115	22	3	1	0.2	66	60	29	41	18	.260	.330	1	1	SS-123
1929	152	618	173	27	12	5	0.8	83	62	28	53	26	.280	.387	0	0	SS-152
1930	141	561	152	28	9	2	0.4	82	48	28	32	16	.271	.364	1	0	2B-106, 3B-24, SS-10
1931	109	409	90	13	5	1	0.2	42	46	16	26	18	.220	.284	0	0	SS-83, 2B-23, 3B-1
1932 2 teams			CHI A (12G – .256)			CLE A (131G – .320)											
" total	143	584	184	36	7	7	1.2	85	98	29	25	18	.315	.437	0	0	2B-129, SS-18
1933 CLE A	112	409	94	21	3	6	1.5	53	33	31	29	6	.230	.340	2	1	2B-62, SS-46, 3B-1
1934 BOS A	102	416	111	13	4	4	1.0	71	44	28	23	11	.267	.346	2	1	2B-96, SS-7, 3B-2
1937 PHI A	34	117	31	7	0	1	0.9	15	14	17	10	0	.265	.350	1	0	2B-33
1938 NY N	38	149	40	6	0	2	1.3	19	18	6	11	1	.268	.349	0	0	2B-33, 3B-6
9 yrs.	956	3706	990	173	43	29	0.8	516	423	212	250	114	.267	.360	7	3	2B-482, SS-439, 3B-34

Moose Clabaugh

CLABAUGH, JOHN WILLIAM
B. Nov. 13, 1901, Albany, Mo.   BL TR 6' 185 lbs.

	G	AB	H	2B	3B	HR	HR %	R	RBI	BB	SO	SB	BA	SA	AB	H	G by POS
1926 BKN N	11	14	1	1	0	0	0.0	2	1	0	1	0	.071	.143	9	1	OF-2

Bobby Clack

CLACK, ROBERT S. (Gentlemanly Bobby)
Born Robert S. Clark.
B. 1851, Brooklyn, N. Y.   D. Oct. 22, 1933, Danvers, Mass.   BR TR 5'9" 153 lbs.

	G	AB	H	2B	3B	HR	HR %	R	RBI	BB	SO	SB	BA	SA	AB	H	G by POS
1876 CIN N	32	118	19	0	1	0	0.0	10	5	5	12		.161	.178	0	0	OF-17, 2B-8, 1B-5, 3B-3, P-1

Danny Claire

CLAIRE, DAVID MATTHEW
B. Nov. 18, 1897, Ludington, Mich.   D. Mar. 24, 1929, Battle Creek, Mich.   BR TR 5'8" 164 lbs.

	G	AB	H	2B	3B	HR	HR %	R	RBI	BB	SO	SB	BA	SA	AB	H	G by POS
1920 DET A	3	7	1	0	0	0	0.0	1	0	0	0	0	.143	.143	0	0	SS-3

	G	AB	H	2B	3B	HR	HR %	R	RBI	BB	SO	SB	BA	SA	Pinch Hit AB	Pinch Hit H	G by POS

Bill Clancey

CLANCEY, WILLIAM EDWARD
B. Apr. 12, 1878, Redfield, N. Y.   D. Feb. 10, 1948, Oriskany, N. Y.
TR

	G	AB	H	2B	3B	HR	HR%	R	RBI	BB	SO	SB	BA	SA	PH AB	PH H	G by POS
1905 PIT N	56	227	52	11	3	2	0.9	23	34	4		3	.229	.330	0	0	1B-52, OF-4

Al Clancy

CLANCY, ALBERT HARRISON
B. Aug. 14, 1888, Santa Fe, N. M.   D. Oct. 17, 1951, Las Cruces, N. M.
BR TR 5'10½" 175 lbs.

	G	AB	H	2B	3B	HR	HR%	R	RBI	BB	SO	SB	BA	SA	PH AB	PH H	G by POS
1911 STL A	3	5	0	0	0	0	0.0	0	0	0		0	.000	.000	1	0	3B-2

Bud Clancy

CLANCY, JOHN WILLIAM
B. Sept. 15, 1900, Odell, Ill.   D. Sept. 27, 1968, Ottumwa, Iowa
BL TL 6'   170 lbs.

	G	AB	H	2B	3B	HR	HR%	R	RBI	BB	SO	SB	BA	SA	PH AB	PH H	G by POS
1924 CHI A	13	35	9	1	0	0	0.0	5	6	3	2	3	.257	.286	4	1	1B-8
1925	4	3	0	0	0	0	0.0	0	0	1	0	0	.000	.000	3	0	
1926	12	38	13	2	2	0	0.0	3	7	1	1	0	.342	.500	2	0	1B-10
1927	130	464	139	21	2	3	0.6	46	53	24	24	4	.300	.373	5	1	1B-123
1928	130	487	132	19	11	2	0.4	64	37	42	25	6	.271	.368	2	0	1B-128
1929	92	290	82	14	6	3	1.0	36	45	16	19	3	.283	.403	16	4	1B-74
1930	68	234	57	8	3	3	1.3	28	27	12	18	3	.244	.342	7	1	1B-63
1932 BKN N	53	196	60	4	2	0	0.0	14	16	6	13	0	.306	.347	0	0	1B-53
1934 PHI N	20	49	12	0	0	1	2.0	8	7	6	4	0	.245	.306	9	2	1B-10
9 yrs.	522	1796	504	69	26	12	0.7	204	198	111	106	19	.281	.368	48	9	1B-469

Uke Clanton

CLANTON, UCAL (Cat)
B. Feb. 19, 1898, Powell, Mo.   D. Feb. 24, 1960, Antlers, Okla.
BL TL 5'8"   165 lbs.

	G	AB	H	2B	3B	HR	HR%	R	RBI	BB	SO	SB	BA	SA	PH AB	PH H	G by POS
1922 CLE A	1	1	0	0	0	0	0.0	0	0	0	1	0	.000	.000	0	0	1B-1

Aaron Clapp

CLAPP, AARON BRONSON
Brother of John Clapp.
B. July, 1856, Ithaca, N. Y.   D. Jan. 13, 1914, Sayre, Pa.
TR 5'8"   175 lbs.

	G	AB	H	2B	3B	HR	HR%	R	RBI	BB	SO	SB	BA	SA	PH AB	PH H	G by POS
1879 TRO N	36	146	39	9	3	0	0.0	24	18	6	10		.267	.370	0	0	1B-25, OF-11

John Clapp

CLAPP, JOHN EDGAR
Brother of Aaron Clapp.
B. July 17, 1851, Ithaca, N. Y.   D. Dec. 17, 1904, Ithaca, N. Y.
Manager 1878-80, 1883.
BR TR 5'7"   175 lbs.

	G	AB	H	2B	3B	HR	HR%	R	RBI	BB	SO	SB	BA	SA	PH AB	PH H	G by POS
1876 STL N	64	298	91	4	2	0	0.0	60	29	8	2		.305	.332	0	0	C-61, OF-4, 2B-1
1877	60	255	81	6	6	0	0.0	47	34	8	6		.318	.388	0	0	C-53, OF-10, 1B-1
1878 IND N	63	263	80	10	2	0	0.0	42	29	13	8		.304	.357	0	0	OF-44, 1B-12, C-9, SS-3, 2B-1
1879 BUF N	70	292	77	12	5	1	0.3	47	36	11	11		.264	.349	0	0	C-63, OF-7
1880 CIN N	80	323	91	16	4	1	0.3	33	20	21	10		.282	.365	0	0	C-73, OF-10
1881 CLE N	68	261	66	12	2	0	0.0	47	25	35	6		.253	.314	0	0	C-48, OF-21
1883 NY N	20	73	13	0	0	0	0.0	6		5	4		.178	.178	0	0	C-16, OF-5
7 yrs.	425	1765	499	60	21	2	0.1	282	173	101	47		.283	.344	0	0	C-323, OF-101, 1B-13, SS-3, 2B-2

Doug Clarey

CLAREY, DOUGLAS WILLIAM
B. Apr. 20, 1954, Los Angeles, Calif.
BR TR 6'   180 lbs.

	G	AB	H	2B	3B	HR	HR%	R	RBI	BB	SO	SB	BA	SA	PH AB	PH H	G by POS
1976 STL N	9	4	1	0	0	1	25.0	2	2	0	1	0	.250	1.000	2	1	2B-7

Allie Clark

CLARK, ALFRED ALOYSIUS
B. June 16, 1923, South Amboy, N. J.
BR TR 6'   185 lbs.

	G	AB	H	2B	3B	HR	HR%	R	RBI	BB	SO	SB	BA	SA	PH AB	PH H	G by POS
1947 NY A	24	67	25	5	0	1	1.5	9	14	5	2	0	.373	.493	7	2	OF-16
1948 CLE A	81	271	84	5	2	9	3.3	43	38	23	13	0	.310	.443	11	3	OF-65, 3B-5, 1B-1
1949	35	74	13	4	0	1	1.4	8	9	4	7	0	.176	.270	19	2	OF-17, 1B-1
1950	59	163	35	6	1	6	3.7	19	21	11	10	0	.215	.374	15	2	OF-41
1951 2 teams		CLE A (3G – .300)					PHI A (56G – .248)										
" total	59	171	43	12	1	5	2.9	23	25	16	9	2	.251	.421	13	4	OF-35, 3B-10
1952 PHI A	71	186	51	12	0	7	3.8	23	29	10	19	0	.274	.452	21	7	OF-48, 1B-2
1953 2 teams		PHI A (20G – .203)					CHI A (9G – .067)										
" total	29	89	16	4	0	3	3.4	6	13	3	10	0	.180	.326	9	1	OF-20, 1B-1
7 yrs.	358	1021	267	48	4	32	3.1	131	149	72	70	2	.262	.410	95	21	OF-242, 3B-15, 1B-5

WORLD SERIES

	G	AB	H	2B	3B	HR	HR%	R	RBI	BB	SO	SB	BA	SA	PH AB	PH H	G by POS
1947 NY A	3	2	1	0	0	0	0.0	1	1	1	0	0	.500	.500	2	1	OF-1
1948 CLE A	1	3	0	0	0	0	0.0	0	0	0	1	0	.000	.000	0	0	OF-1
2 yrs.	4	5	1	0	0	0	0.0	1	1	1	1	0	.200	.200	2	1	OF-2

Bill Clark

CLARK, WILLIAM WINFIELD (Win)
B. Apr. 11, 1875, Circleville, Ohio   D. Apr. 15, 1959, Los Angeles, Calif.
BR TR 5'10" 175 lbs.

	G	AB	H	2B	3B	HR	HR%	R	RBI	BB	SO	SB	BA	SA	PH AB	PH H	G by POS
1897 LOU N	7	26	6	0	0	0	0.0	2	2	1		1	.231	.231	0	0	2B-3, P-3, 3B-1

Bob Clark

CLARK, ROBERT H.
B. May 18, 1864, Covington, Ky.   D. Aug. 21, 1919, Covington, Ky.
BR TR 5'10" 175 lbs.

	G	AB	H	2B	3B	HR	HR%	R	RBI	BB	SO	SB	BA	SA	PH AB	PH H	G by POS
1886 BKN AA	71	269	58	8	2	0	0.0	37		17			.216	.260	0	0	C-44, OF-17, SS-12
1887	48	177	47	3	1	0	0.0	24		7		15	.266	.294	0	0	C-45, OF-3
1888	45	150	36	5	3	1	0.7	23	20	9			.240	.333	0	0	C-36, OF-8, 1B-1
1889	53	182	50	5	2	0	0.0	32	22	26	7	18	.275	.324	0	0	C-53
1890 BKN N	43	151	33	3	3	0	0.0	24	15	15	8	10	.219	.278	0	0	C-42, OF-1
1891 CIN N	16	54	6	0	0	0	0.0	2	3	6	9	3	.111	.111	0	0	C-16
1893 LOU N	12	28	3	1	0	0	0.0	3	3	5	5	0	.107	.143	0	0	C-10, OF-1, SS-1
7 yrs.	288	1011	233	25	11	1	0.1	145	62	85	29	57	.230	.280	0	0	C-246, OF-30, SS-13, 1B-1

Bobby Clark

CLARK, ROBERT CALE
B. June 13, 1955, North Highland, Calif.
BR TR 6'   190 lbs.

	G	AB	H	2B	3B	HR	HR%	R	RBI	BB	SO	SB	BA	SA	PH AB	PH H	G by POS
1979 CAL A	19	54	16	2	2	1	1.9	8	5	5	11	1	.296	.463	0	0	OF-19
1980	78	261	60	10	1	5	1.9	26	23	11	42	0	.230	.333	7	3	OF-77

	G	AB	H	2B	3B	HR	HR %	R	RBI	BB	SO	SB	BA	SA	Pinch Hit AB	Pinch Hit H	G by POS

Bobby Clark continued

	G	AB	H	2B	3B	HR	HR %	R	RBI	BB	SO	SB	BA	SA	AB	H	G by POS
1981	34	88	22	2	1	4	4.5	12	19	7	18	0	.250	.432	3	0	OF-34
1982	102	90	19	1	0	2	2.2	11	8	0	29	1	.211	.289	1	0	OF-102
1983	76	212	49	9	1	5	2.4	17	21	9	45	0	.231	.354	1	0	OF-72, DH-2, 3B-1
1984 **MIL A**	58	169	44	7	2	2	1.2	17	16	16	35	1	.260	.361	5	3	OF-56
6 yrs.	367	874	210	31	7	19	2.2	91	92	48	180	3	.240	.357	17	6	OF-360, DH-2, 3B-1

LEAGUE CHAMPIONSHIP SERIES

	G	AB	H	2B	3B	HR	HR %	R	RBI	BB	SO	SB	BA	SA	AB	H	G by POS
1979 **CAL A**	1	3	0	0	0	0	0.0	0	0	0	2	0	.000	.000	0	0	OF-1
1982	2	0	0	0	0	0	–	0	0	0	0	0	–	–	0	0	OF-2
2 yrs.	3	3	0	0	0	0	0.0	0	0	0	2	0	.000	.000	0	0	OF-3

Cap Clark

CLARK, JOHN CARROLL　　　　　　　　　　BL　TR　5'11"　180 lbs.
B. Sept. 19, 1906, Snow Camp, N. C.　D. Feb. 16, 1957, Fayetteville, N. C.

	G	AB	H	2B	3B	HR	HR %	R	RBI	BB	SO	SB	BA	SA	AB	H	G by POS
1938 **PHI N**	52	74	19	1	1	0	0.0	11	4	9	10	0	.257	.297	20	5	C-29

Danny Clark

CLARK, DANIEL CURRAN　　　　　　　　　　BL　TR　5'9"　167 lbs.
B. Jan. 18, 1895, Meridian, Miss.　D. May 23, 1937, Meridian, Miss.

	G	AB	H	2B	3B	HR	HR %	R	RBI	BB	SO	SB	BA	SA	AB	H	G by POS
1922 **DET A**	83	185	54	11	3	3	1.6	31	26	15	11	1	.292	.432	36	8	2B-38, OF-5, 3B-1
1924 **BOS A**	104	325	90	23	3	2	0.6	36	54	50	18	4	.277	.385	10	1	3B-93
1927 **STL N**	58	72	17	2	2	0	0.0	8	13	8	7	0	.236	.319	40	12	OF-9
3 yrs.	245	582	161	36	8	5	0.9	75	93	73	36	5	.277	.392	86	21	3B-94, 2B-38, OF-14

Earl Clark

CLARK, BAILEY EARL　　　　　　　　　　BR　TR　5'10"　160 lbs.
B. Nov. 6, 1907, Washington, D. C.　D. Jan. 16, 1938, Washington, D. C.

	G	AB	H	2B	3B	HR	HR %	R	RBI	BB	SO	SB	BA	SA	AB	H	G by POS
1927 **BOS N**	13	44	12	1	0	0	0.0	6	3	2	4	0	.273	.295	0	0	OF-13
1928	27	112	34	9	1	0	0.0	18	10	4	8	0	.304	.402	1	0	OF-27
1929	84	279	88	13	3	1	0.4	43	30	12	30	6	.315	.394	4	1	OF-74
1930	82	233	69	11	3	3	1.3	29	28	7	22	3	.296	.408	17	7	OF-63
1931	16	50	11	2	0	0	0.0	8	4	7	4	1	.220	.260	2	0	OF-14
1932	50	44	11	2	0	0	0.0	11	4	2	7	1	.250	.295	16	5	OF-16
1933	7	23	8	1	0	0	0.0	3	1	2	1	0	.348	.391	0	0	OF-7
1934 **STL A**	13	41	7	2	0	0	0.0	4	1	1	3	0	.171	.220	4	0	OF-9
8 yrs.	292	826	240	41	7	4	0.5	122	81	37	79	11	.291	.372	44	13	OF-223

Fred Clark

CLARK, ALFRED ROBERT　　　　　　　　　　TL
B. July 16, 1873, San Francisco, Calif.　D. July 26, 1956, Ogden, Utah

	G	AB	H	2B	3B	HR	HR %	R	RBI	BB	SO	SB	BA	SA	AB	H	G by POS
1902 **CHI N**	12	43	8	1	0	0	0.0	1	2	4		1	.186	.209	0	0	1B-12

Glen Clark

CLARK, GLEN ESTER　　　　　　　　　　BB　TR　6'1"　190 lbs.
B. Mar. 7, 1941, Austin, Tex.

	G	AB	H	2B	3B	HR	HR %	R	RBI	BB	SO	SB	BA	SA	AB	H	G by POS
1967 **ATL N**	4	4	0	0	0	0	0.0	0	0	0	1	0	.000	.000	4	0	

Jack Clark

CLARK, JACK ANTHONY　　　　　　　　　　BR　TR　6'2"　185 lbs.
B. Nov. 10, 1955, New Brighton, Pa.

	G	AB	H	2B	3B	HR	HR %	R	RBI	BB	SO	SB	BA	SA	AB	H	G by POS
1975 **SF N**	8	17	4	0	0	0	0.0	3	2	1	2	1	.235	.235	3	0	OF-3, 3B-2
1976	26	102	23	6	2	2	2.0	14	10	8	18	6	.225	.382	0	0	OF-26
1977	136	413	104	17	4	13	3.1	64	51	49	73	12	.252	.407	29	11	OF-114
1978	156	592	181	46	8	25	4.2	90	98	50	72	15	.306	.537	6	2	OF-152
1979	143	527	144	25	2	26	4.9	84	86	63	95	11	.273	.476	2	0	OF-140, 3B-2
1980	127	437	124	20	8	22	5.0	77	82	74	52	2	.284	.517	5	0	OF-120
1981	99	385	103	19	2	17	4.4	60	53	45	45	1	.268	.460	2	0	OF-98
1982	157	563	154	30	3	27	4.8	90	103	90	91	6	.274	.481	4	1	OF-155
1983	135	492	132	25	0	20	4.1	82	66	74	79	5	.268	.441	1	0	OF-133, 1B-2
1984	57	203	65	9	1	11	5.4	33	44	43	29	1	.320	.537	1	0	OF-54, 1B-4
10 yrs.	1044	3731	1034	197	30	163	4.4	597	595	497	556	60	.277	.477	53	14	OF-995, 1B-6, 3B-4

Jim Clark

CLARK, JAMES　　　　　　　　　　BL　TR　5'9"　150 lbs.
Born James Petrosky.
B. Sept. 21, 1927, Bagley, Pa.

	G	AB	H	2B	3B	HR	HR %	R	RBI	BB	SO	SB	BA	SA	AB	H	G by POS
1948 **WAS A**	9	12	3	0	0	0	0.0	1	0	1	2	0	.250	.250	6	2	SS-1, 3B-1

Jim Clark

CLARK, JAMES EDWARD　　　　　　　　　　BR　TR　6'1"　190 lbs.
B. Apr. 30, 1947, Kansas City, Kans.

	G	AB	H	2B	3B	HR	HR %	R	RBI	BB	SO	SB	BA	SA	AB	H	G by POS
1971 **CLE A**	13	18	3	0	1	0	0.0	2	0	2	7	0	.167	.278	5	1	OF-3, 1B-1

Jim Clark

CLARK, JAMES FRANCIS　　　　　　　　　　BR　TR　5'11"　175 lbs.
B. Dec. 26, 1887, Brooklyn, N. Y.　D. Mar. 20, 1969, Beaumont, Tex.

	G	AB	H	2B	3B	HR	HR %	R	RBI	BB	SO	SB	BA	SA	AB	H	G by POS
1911 **STL N**	14	18	3	0	1	0	0.0	2	3	3	4	2	.167	.278	6	1	OF-8
1912	2	1	0	0	0	0	0.0	0	0	0	1	0	.000	.000	1	0	
2 yrs.	16	19	3	0	1	0	0.0	2	3	3	5	2	.158	.263	7	1	OF-8

Mel Clark

CLARK, MELVIN EARL　　　　　　　　　　BR　TR　6'　180 lbs.
B. July 7, 1926, Letart, W. Va.

	G	AB	H	2B	3B	HR	HR %	R	RBI	BB	SO	SB	BA	SA	AB	H	G by POS
1951 **PHI N**	10	31	10	1	0	1	3.2	2	3	0	3	0	.323	.452	3	0	OF-7
1952	47	155	52	6	4	1	0.6	20	15	6	13	2	.335	.445	7	1	OF-38, 3B-1
1953	60	198	59	10	4	0	0.0	31	19	11	17	1	.298	.389	8	3	OF-51
1954	83	233	56	9	7	1	0.4	26	24	17	21	0	.240	.352	21	2	OF-63
1955	10	32	5	3	0	0	0.0	3	1	3	4	0	.156	.250	2	0	OF-8
1957 **DET A**	5	7	0	0	0	0	0.0	0	1	0	3	0	.000	.000	3	0	OF-2
6 yrs.	215	656	182	29	15	3	0.5	82	63	37	61	3	.277	.381	44	6	OF-169, 3B-1

Pep Clark

CLARK, HARRY　　　　　　　　　　BR　TR　5'7½"　175 lbs.
B. Mar. 18, 1883, Union City, Ohio　D. June 8, 1965, Milwaukee, Wis.

	G	AB	H	2B	3B	HR	HR %	R	RBI	BB	SO	SB	BA	SA	AB	H	G by POS
1903 **CHI A**	15	65	20	4	2	0	0.0	7	9	2		5	.308	.431	0	0	3B-15

	G	AB	H	2B	3B	HR	HR %	R	RBI	BB	SO	SB	BA	SA	Pinch Hit AB	Pinch Hit H	G by POS

Ron Clark

CLARK, RONALD BRUCE
B. Jan. 14, 1943, Fort Worth, Tex.   BR TR 5'10" 175 lbs.

	G	AB	H	2B	3B	HR	HR%	R	RBI	BB	SO	SB	BA	SA	PH AB	PH H	G by POS
1966 MIN A	5	1	1	0	0	0	0.0	1	1	0	0	0	1.000	1.000	0	0	3B-1
1967	20	60	10	3	1	2	3.3	7	11	4	9	0	.167	.350	3	0	3B-16
1968	104	227	42	5	1	1	0.4	14	13	16	44	3	.185	.229	12	1	3B-52, SS-43, 2B-10
1969 2 teams	MIN A (5G – .125)			SEA A (57G – .196)													
" total	62	171	33	5	0	0	0.0	9	12	13	29	1	.193	.222	3	1	SS-38, 3B-17, 2B-5, 1B-1
1971 OAK A	2	1	0	0	0	0	0.0	0	0	1	0	0	.000	.000	1	0	
1972 2 teams	OAK A (14G – .267)			MIL A (22G – .185)													
" total	36	69	14	3	1	2	2.9	9	6	7	15	0	.203	.362	7	1	2B-22, 3B-13
1975 PHI N	1	1	0	0	0	0	0.0	0	0	0	1	0	.000	.000	1	0	
7 yrs.	230	530	100	16	3	5	0.9	40	43	41	98	4	.189	.258	27	3	3B-99, SS-81, 2B-37, 1B-1

Royal Clark

CLARK, ROYAL ELLIOTT (Pepper)
B. May 11, 1874, New Haven, Conn.   D. Nov. 1, 1925, Bridgeport, Conn.   5'8½" 170 lbs.

	G	AB	H	2B	3B	HR	HR%	R	RBI	BB	SO	SB	BA	SA	PH AB	PH H	G by POS
1902 NY N	21	76	11	1	0	0	0.0	4	3	1		5	.145	.158	1	0	OF-20

Spider Clark

CLARK, OWEN F.
B. Sept. 16, 1867, Brooklyn, N. Y.   D. Feb. 8, 1892, Brooklyn, N. Y.   TR 5'10" 150 lbs.

	G	AB	H	2B	3B	HR	HR%	R	RBI	BB	SO	SB	BA	SA	PH AB	PH H	G by POS
1889 WAS N	38	145	37	7	2	3	2.1	19	22	6	18	8	.255	.393	0	0	C-14, SS-13, OF-9, 3B-2, 2B-2
1890 BUF P	69	260	69	11	1	1	0.4	45	25	20	16	8	.265	.327	0	0	OF-34, C-14, 2B-13, 1B-6, 3B-3, SS-1, P-1
2 yrs.	107	405	106	18	3	4	1.0	64	47	26	34	16	.262	.351	0	0	OF-43, C-28, 2B-15, SS-14, 1B-6, 3B-5, P-1

Willie Clark

CLARK, WILLIAM OTIS (Wee Willie)
B. Aug. 16, 1872, Pittsburgh, Pa.   D. Nov. 13, 1932, Pittsburgh, Pa.

	G	AB	H	2B	3B	HR	HR%	R	RBI	BB	SO	SB	BA	SA	PH AB	PH H	G by POS
1895 NY N	23	88	23	3	2	0	0.0	9	16	5	6	1	.261	.341	0	0	1B-22
1896	72	247	72	12	4	0	0.0	38	33	15	12	8	.291	.372	7	3	1B-65
1897	116	431	122	17	12	1	0.2	63	75	37		18	.283	.385	1	0	1B-107, OF-7, 3B-1
1898 PIT N	57	209	64	9	7	1	0.5	29	31	22		0	.306	.431	0	0	1B-57
1899	80	298	85	13	10	0	0.0	49	44	35		11	.285	.396	2	0	1B-78
5 yrs.	348	1273	366	54	35	2	0.2	188	199	114	18	38	.288	.390	10	3	1B-329, OF-7, 3B-1

Archie Clarke

CLARKE, ARTHUR FRANKLIN
B. May 6, 1865, Brookline, Mass.   D. Nov. 14, 1949, Brookline, Mass.   BR TR

	G	AB	H	2B	3B	HR	HR%	R	RBI	BB	SO	SB	BA	SA	PH AB	PH H	G by POS
1890 NY N	101	395	89	12	8	0	0.0	55	49	32	38	44	.225	.296	0	0	C-36, OF-33, 3B-16, 2B-15, SS-1
1891	48	174	33	2	2	0	0.0	17	21	15	16	5	.190	.224	0	0	C-42, 3B-5, OF-2
2 yrs.	149	569	122	14	10	0	0.0	72	70	47	54	49	.214	.274	0	0	C-78, OF-35, 3B-21, 2B-15, SS-1

Boileryard Clarke

CLARKE, WILLIAM JONES
B. Oct. 18, 1868, New York, N. Y.   D. July 29, 1959, Princeton, N. J.   BR TR 5'11" 170 lbs.

	G	AB	H	2B	3B	HR	HR%	R	RBI	BB	SO	SB	BA	SA	PH AB	PH H	G by POS
1893 BAL N	49	183	32	1	3	1	0.5	23	24	19	14	2	.175	.230	0	0	C-38, 1B-11
1894	28	100	24	8	0	1	1.0	18	19	16	14	2	.240	.350	0	0	C-23, 1B-5
1895	67	241	70	15	3	0	0.0	38	35	13	18	8	.290	.378	2	0	C-60, 1B-6
1896	80	300	89	14	7	2	0.7	48	71	14	12	7	.297	.410	1	0	C-67, 1B-14
1897	64	241	65	7	1	1	0.4	32	38	9		5	.270	.320	1	0	C-59, 1B-4
1898	82	285	69	5	2	0	0.0	26	27	4		2	.242	.274	3	0	C-70, 1B-10
1899 BOS N	60	223	50	3	2	2	0.9	25	32	10		2	.224	.283	0	0	C-60
1900	81	270	85	5	2	1	0.4	35	30	9		0	.315	.359	5	2	C-67, 1B-8
1901 WAS A	110	422	118	15	5	3	0.7	58	54	23		7	.280	.360	0	0	C-107, 1B-3
1902	87	291	78	15	0	7	2.4	31	42	23		1	.268	.392	0	0	C-87
1903	126	465	111	14	6	2	0.4	35	38	15		12	.239	.308	1	0	1B-88, C-37
1904	85	275	58	8	1	0	0.0	23	17	17		5	.211	.247	5	0	C-52, 1B-29
1905 NY N	31	50	9	0	0	1	2.0	2	4	4		1	.180	.240	4	1	1B-17, C-12
13 yrs.	950	3346	858	110	32	21	0.6	394	431	176	58	54	.256	.327	22	3	C-739, 1B-195

Dick Clarke

CLARKE, RICHARD GREY (Noisy)
B. Sept. 26, 1912, Fulton, Ala.   BR TR 5'9" 183 lbs.

	G	AB	H	2B	3B	HR	HR%	R	RBI	BB	SO	SB	BA	SA	PH AB	PH H	G by POS
1944 CHI A	63	169	44	10	1	0	0.0	14	27	22	6	0	.260	.331	15	1	3B-45

Fred Clarke

CLARKE, FRED CLIFFORD (Cap)
Brother of Josh Clarke.
B. Oct. 3, 1872, Winterset, Iowa   D. Aug. 14, 1960, Winfield, Kans.   BL TR 5'10½" 165 lbs.
Manager 1891915.
Hall of Fame 1945.

	G	AB	H	2B	3B	HR	HR%	R	RBI	BB	SO	SB	BA	SA	PH AB	PH H	G by POS
1894 LOU N	76	316	87	11	7	7	2.2	55	48	25	27	25	.275	.421	0	0	OF-76
1895	132	556	197	21	5	4	0.7	96	82	34	40	40	.354	.432	0	0	OF-132
1896	131	517	169	15	18	9	1.7	96	79	43	34	34	.327	.478	0	0	OF-131
1897	129	525	213	28	15	6	1.1	122	67	45		57	.406	.550	1	1	OF-128
1898	149	599	190	23	12	3	0.5	116	47	48		40	.317	.411	0	0	OF-149
1899	148	601	209	21	11	5	0.8	124	70	49		49	.348	.444	1	0	OF-144, SS-3
1900 PIT N	106	399	112	15	12	3	0.8	85	32	51		21	.281	.401	2	0	OF-104
1901	129	527	171	26	14	6	1.1	118	60	51		23	.324	.461	1	1	OF-127, SS-1, 3B-1
1902	114	461	148	27	14	2	0.4	104	53	51		29	.321	.453	0	0	OF-113
1903	104	427	150	32	15	5	1.2	88	70	41		21	.351	.532	2	1	OF-101, SS-2
1904	72	278	85	7	11	0	0.0	51	25	22		11	.306	.410	2	1	OF-70
1905	141	525	157	18	15	2	0.4	95	51	55		24	.299	.402	3	1	OF-137
1906	118	417	129	14	13	1	0.2	69	39	40		18	.309	.412	7	5	OF-110
1907	148	501	145	18	13	2	0.4	97	59	68		37	.289	.389	4	1	OF-144
1908	151	551	146	18	15	2	0.4	83	53	65		24	.265	.363	0	0	OF-151
1909	152	550	158	16	11	3	0.5	97	68	80		31	.287	.373	0	0	OF-152
1910	123	429	113	23	9	2	0.5	57	63	53	23	12	.263	.373	4	1	OF-118
1911	110	392	127	25	13	5	1.3	73	49	53	27	10	.324	.492	7	3	OF-101

	G	AB	H	2B	3B	HR	HR %	R	RBI	BB	SO	SB	BA	SA	Pinch Hit AB	Pinch Hit H	G by POS

Fred Clarke *continued*

	G	AB	H	2B	3B	HR	HR %	R	RBI	BB	SO	SB	BA	SA	PH AB	PH H	G by POS
1913	9	13	1	1	0	0	0.0	0	0	0	0	0	.077	.154	6	1	OF-2
1914	2	2	0	0	0	0	0.0	0	0	0	0	0	.000	.000	1	0	
1915	1	2	1	0	0	0	0.0	0	0	0	0	0	.500	.500	0	0	OF-1
21 yrs.	2245	8588	2708	359	223	67	0.8	1626	1015	874	135	506	.315	.432	41	16	OF-2191, SS-6, 3B-1
					6th												

WORLD SERIES

	G	AB	H	2B	3B	HR	HR %	R	RBI	BB	SO	SB	BA	SA	PH AB	PH H	G by POS
1903 PIT N	8	34	9	2	1	0	0.0	3	2	1	5	1	.265	.382	0	0	OF-8
1909	7	19	4	0	0	2	10.5	7	7	5	3	3	.211	.526	0	0	OF-7
2 yrs.	15	53	13	2	1	2	3.8	10	9	6	8	4	.245	.434	0	0	OF-15

Harry Clarke

CLARKE, HARRY CORSON
B. 1861   D. Mar. 3, 1923, Long Beach, Calif.

	G	AB	H	2B	3B	HR	HR %	R	RBI	BB	SO	SB	BA	SA	PH AB	PH H	G by POS
1889 WAS N	1	3	0	0	0	0	0.0	0	0	0	1	0	.000	.000	0	0	OF-1

Horace Clarke

CLARKE, HORACE MEREDITH
B. June 2, 1940, St. Croix, Virgin Islands   BB   TR   5'9''   170 lbs.

	G	AB	H	2B	3B	HR	HR %	R	RBI	BB	SO	SB	BA	SA	PH AB	PH H	G by POS
1965 NY A	51	108	28	1	0	1	0.9	13	9	6	6	2	.259	.296	26	9	3B-17, 2B-7, SS-1
1966	96	312	83	10	4	6	1.9	37	28	27	24	5	.266	.381	11	0	SS-63, 2B-16, 3B-4
1967	143	588	160	17	0	3	0.5	74	29	42	64	21	.272	.316	2	2	2B-140
1968	148	579	133	6	1	2	0.3	52	26	23	46	20	.230	.254	6	2	2B-139
1969	156	641	183	26	7	4	0.6	82	48	53	41	33	.285	.367	0	0	2B-156
1970	158	686	172	24	2	4	0.6	81	46	35	35	23	.251	.309	1	0	2B-157
1971	159	625	156	23	7	2	0.3	76	41	64	43	17	.250	.318	4	1	2B-156
1972	147	547	132	20	2	3	0.5	65	37	56	44	18	.241	.302	5	1	2B-143
1973	148	590	155	21	0	2	0.3	60	35	47	48	11	.263	.308	2	1	2B-147
1974 2 teams		NY A (24G – .234)			SD N (42G – .189)												
" total	66	137	28	2	0	0	0.0	8	5	12	11	1	.204	.219	34	5	2B-41, DH-1
10 yrs.	1272	4813	1230	150	23	27	0.6	548	304	365	362	151	.256	.313	91	21	2B-1102, SS-64, 3B-21, DH-1

Josh Clarke

CLARKE, JOSHUA BALDWIN (Pepper)
Brother of Fred Clarke.   BL   TR   5'10''   180 lbs.
B. Mar. 8, 1879, Winfield, Kans.   D. July 2, 1962, Ventura, Calif.

	G	AB	H	2B	3B	HR	HR %	R	RBI	BB	SO	SB	BA	SA	PH AB	PH H	G by POS
1898 LOU N	6	18	3	0	0	0	0.0	0	0	1		0	.167	.167	1	0	OF-5
1905 STL N	50	167	43	3	2	3	1.8	31	18	27		8	.257	.353	4	1	OF-26, 2B-16, SS-4
1908 CLE A	131	492	119	8	4	1	0.2	70	21	76		37	.242	.280	0	0	OF-131
1909	4	12	0	0	0	0	0.0	1	0	2		0	.000	.000	0	0	OF-4
1911 BOS N	32	120	28	7	3	1	0.8	16	4	29	22	6	.233	.367	2	0	OF-30
5 yrs.	223	809	193	18	9	5	0.6	118	43	135	22	51	.239	.302	7	1	OF-196, 2B-16, SS-4

Nig Clarke

CLARKE, JAY JUSTIN
B. Dec. 15, 1882, Amherstburg, Ont., Canada   D. June 15, 1949, Detroit, Mich.   BB   TR

	G	AB	H	2B	3B	HR	HR %	R	RBI	BB	SO	SB	BA	SA	PH AB	PH H	G by POS
1905 3 teams		CLE A (5G – .111)			DET A (3G – .429)				CLE A (37G – .202)								
" total	45	130	27	6	1	1	0.8	12	10	11		0	.208	.292	2	0	C-43
1906 CLE A	57	179	64	12	4	1	0.6	22	21	13		3	.358	.486	0	0	C-54
1907	120	390	105	19	6	3	0.8	44	33	35		3	.269	.372	5	0	C-115
1908	97	290	70	8	6	1	0.3	34	27	30		6	.241	.321	6	0	C-90
1909	55	164	45	4	2	0	0.0	15	14	9		1	.274	.323	10	0	C-44
1910	21	58	9	2	0	0	0.0	4	2	8		0	.155	.190	3	1	C-17
1911 STL A	82	256	55	10	1	0	0.0	22	18	26		2	.215	.262	4	0	C-73, 1B-4
1919 PHI N	26	62	15	3	0	0	0.0	4	2	4	5	1	.242	.290	4	0	C-22
1920 PIT N	3	7	0	0	0	0	0.0	0	0	2	4	0	.000	.000	1	0	C-3
9 yrs.	506	1536	390	64	20	6	0.4	157	127	138	9	16	.254	.333	35	1	C-461, 1B-4

Stu Clarke

CLARKE, WILLIAM STUART
B. Jan. 24, 1906, San Francisco, Calif.   BR   TR   5'8½''   160 lbs.

	G	AB	H	2B	3B	HR	HR %	R	RBI	BB	SO	SB	BA	SA	PH AB	PH H	G by POS
1929 PIT N	57	178	47	5	7	2	1.1	20	21	19	21	3	.264	.404	0	0	SS-41, 3B-15, 2B-1
1930	4	9	4	0	1	0	0.0	2	2	1	0	0	.444	.667	2	1	2B-2
2 yrs.	61	187	51	5	8	2	1.1	22	23	20	21	3	.273	.417	2	1	SS-41, 3B-15, 2B-3

Sumpter Clarke

CLARKE, SUMPTER MILLS
Brother of Rufe Clarke.   BR   TR   5'11''   170 lbs.
B. Oct. 18, 1897, Savannah, Ga.   D. Mar. 16, 1962, Knoxville, Tenn.

	G	AB	H	2B	3B	HR	HR %	R	RBI	BB	SO	SB	BA	SA	PH AB	PH H	G by POS
1920 CHI N	1	3	1	0	0	0	0.0	0	0	0	1	0	.333	.333	0	0	3B-1
1923 CLE A	1	3	0	0	0	0	0.0	0	0	0	0	0	.000	.000	0	0	OF-1
1924	45	104	24	6	1	0	0.0	17	11	6	12	0	.231	.308	2	1	OF-66
3 yrs.	47	110	25	6	1	0	0.0	17	11	6	13	0	.227	.300	2	1	OF-67, 3B-1

Tommy Clarke

CLARKE, THOMAS ALOYSIUS
B. May 9, 1888, New York, N. Y.   D. Aug. 14, 1945, Corona, N. Y.   BR   TR   5'11''   175 lbs.

	G	AB	H	2B	3B	HR	HR %	R	RBI	BB	SO	SB	BA	SA	PH AB	PH H	G by POS
1909 CIN N	18	52	13	3	2	0	0.0	8	10	6		3	.250	.385	1	0	C-17
1910	64	151	42	6	5	1	0.7	19	20	19	17	1	.278	.404	7	0	C-56
1911	86	203	49	6	7	1	0.5	20	25	25	22	4	.241	.355	4	0	C-81, 1B-1
1912	72	146	41	7	2	0	0.0	19	22	28	14	9	.281	.356	7	1	C-63
1913	114	330	87	11	8	1	0.3	29	38	39	40	2	.264	.355	13	5	C-100
1914	113	313	82	13	7	2	0.6	30	25	31	30	6	.262	.367	6	1	C-108
1915	96	226	65	7	2	0	0.0	23	21	33	22	7	.288	.336	20	5	C-72
1916	78	177	42	10	1	0	0.0	10	17	24	20	8	.237	.305	25	5	C-51
1917	29	110	32	3	3	1	0.9	11	13	11	12	2	.291	.400	27	9	C-29
1918 CHI N	1	0	0	0	0	0	–	0	0	0	0	0	–	–	0	0	C-1
10 yrs.	671	1708	453	66	37	6	0.4	169	191	216	177	42	.265	.358	110	26	C-578, 1B-1

	G	AB	H	2B	3B	HR	HR %	R	RBI	BB	SO	SB	BA	SA	Pinch Hit AB	Pinch Hit H	G by POS

Buzz Clarkson

CLARKSON, JAMES BUSTER
B. Mar. 13, 1918, Hopkins, S. C.

BR TR 5'11" 210 lbs.

	G	AB	H	2B	3B	HR	HR %	R	RBI	BB	SO	SB	BA	SA	AB	H	G by POS
1952 BOS N	14	25	5	0	0	0	0.0	3	1	3	3	0	.200	.200	5	1	SS-6, 3B-2

John Clarkson

CLARKSON, JOHN GIBSON
Brother of Dad Clarkson.   Brother of Walter Clarkson.
B. July 1, 1861, Cambridge, Mass.   D. Feb. 4, 1909, Cambridge, Mass.
Hall of Fame 1963.

BR TR 5'10" 150 lbs.

	G	AB	H	2B	3B	HR	HR %	R	RBI	BB	SO	SB	BA	SA	AB	H	G by POS
1882 WOR N	3	11	4	2	0	0	0.0	0	2	0	3		.364	.545	0	0	P-3, 1B-1
1884 CHI N	21	84	22	6	2	3	3.6	16		2	16		.262	.488	0	0	P-14, OF-8, 3B-2, 1B-1
1885	72	283	61	11	5	4	1.4	34	31	3	44		.216	.332	0	0	P-70, OF-3, 3B-1
1886	55	210	49	9	1	3	1.4	21	23	0	38		.233	.329	0	0	P-55, OF-5
1887	63	215	52	5	5	6	2.8	40	25	11	25	6	.242	.395	0	0	P-60, OF-5
1888 BOS N	55	205	40	9	1	1	0.5	20	17	7	48	5	.195	.263	0	0	P-54, OF-1
1889	73	262	54	9	3	2	0.8	36	23	11	59	8	.206	.286	0	0	P-73, OF-2, 3B-1
1890	45	173	43	6	3	2	1.2	18	26	8	31	2	.249	.353	0	0	P-44, OF-1
1891	55	187	42	7	4	0	0.0	28	26	18	51	2	.225	.305	0	0	P-55, OF-1
1892 2 teams	BOS	N	(16G –	.228)		CLE	N	(29G –	.139)								
" total	45	158	27	3	0	1	0.6	15	17	11	39	3	.171	.209	0	0	P-45
1893 CLE N	37	131	27	6	2	1	0.8	18	17	4	20	2	.206	.305	0	0	P-36, OF-1
1894	22	55	11	0	0	1	1.8	8	7	6	9	1	.200	.255	0	0	P-22
12 yrs.	546	1974	432	73	26	24	1.2	254	214	81	383	29	.219	.319	0	0	P-531, OF-27, 3B-4, 1B-2

Ellis Clary

CLARY, ELLIS (Cat)
B. Sept. 11, 1916, Valdosta, Ga.

BR TR 5'8" 160 lbs.

	G	AB	H	2B	3B	HR	HR %	R	RBI	BB	SO	SB	BA	SA	AB	H	G by POS
1942 WAS A	76	240	66	9	0	0	0.0	34	16	45	25	2	.275	.313	5	1	2B-69, 3B-2
1943 2 teams	WAS	A	(73G –	.256)		STL	A	(23G –	.275)								
" total	96	323	84	21	1	0	0.0	51	24	55	37	9	.260	.331	4	1	3B-82, 2B-3, SS-1
1944 STL A	25	49	13	1	1	0	0.0	6	4	12	9	1	.265	.327	9	1	3B-11, 2B-6
1945	26	38	8	1	0	1	2.6	6	2	2	3	0	.211	.316	4	0	3B-16, 2B-3
4 yrs.	223	650	171	32	2	1	0.2	97	46	114	74	12	.263	.323	22	3	3B-111, 2B-81, SS-1

WORLD SERIES

	G	AB	H	2B	3B	HR	HR %	R	RBI	BB	SO	SB	BA	SA	AB	H	G by POS
1944 STL A	1	1	0	0	0	0	0.0	0	0	0	0	0	.000	.000	1	0	

Bill Clay

CLAY, FREDERICK C.
B. Nov. 23, 1874, Baltimore, Md.   D. Oct. 12, 1917, York, Pa.

TR

	G	AB	H	2B	3B	HR	HR %	R	RBI	BB	SO	SB	BA	SA	AB	H	G by POS
1902 PHI N	3	8	2	0	0	0	0.0	1	1	0		0	.250	.250	0	0	OF-3

Dain Clay

CLAY, DAIN ELMER (Ding-a-Ling)
B. July 10, 1919, Hicksville, Ohio

BR TR 5'10½" 160 lbs.

	G	AB	H	2B	3B	HR	HR %	R	RBI	BB	SO	SB	BA	SA	AB	H	G by POS
1943 CIN N	49	93	25	2	4	0	0.0	19	9	8	14	1	.269	.376	10	3	OF-33
1944	110	356	89	15	0	0	0.0	51	17	17	18	8	.250	.292	5	1	OF-98
1945	153	656	184	29	2	1	0.2	81	50	37	58	19	.280	.335	0	0	OF-152
1946	121	435	99	17	0	2	0.5	52	22	53	40	11	.228	.280	0	0	OF-120
4 yrs.	433	1540	397	63	6	3	0.2	203	98	115	130	39	.258	.312	15	4	OF-403

Bob Clemens

CLEMENS, ROBERT BAXTER
B. Aug. 9, 1886, Mount Hebron, Mo.   D. Apr. 5, 1964, Los Angeles, Calif.

BR TR 5'11" 170 lbs.

	G	AB	H	2B	3B	HR	HR %	R	RBI	BB	SO	SB	BA	SA	AB	H	G by POS
1914 STL A	7	13	3	0	1	0	0.0	1	3	2	1	0	.231	.385	2	0	OF-5

Chet Clemens

CLEMENS, CHESTER SPURGEON
B. May 10, 1917, San Fernando, Calif.

BR TR 6' 175 lbs.

	G	AB	H	2B	3B	HR	HR %	R	RBI	BB	SO	SB	BA	SA	AB	H	G by POS
1939 BOS N	9	23	5	0	0	0	0.0	2	1	1	3	1	.217	.217	1	1	OF-7
1944	19	17	3	1	1	0	0.0	7	2	2	2	0	.176	.353	4	1	OF-7
2 yrs.	28	40	8	1	1	0	0.0	9	3	3	5	1	.200	.275	5	2	OF-14

Clem Clemens

CLEMENS, CLEMENT LAMBERT
Born Clement Lambert Ulatowski.
B. Nov. 21, 1886, Chicago, Ill.   D. Nov. 2, 1967, St. Petersburg, Fla.

BR TR 5'11" 176 lbs.

	G	AB	H	2B	3B	HR	HR %	R	RBI	BB	SO	SB	BA	SA	AB	H	G by POS
1914 CHI F	13	27	4	0	0	0	0.0	4	2	3		0	.148	.148	5	0	C-8
1915	11	22	3	1	0	0	0.0	3	3	1		0	.136	.182	0	0	C-9, 2B-2
1916 CHI N	10	15	0	0	0	0	0.0	0	0	1	6	0	.000	.000	1	0	C-9
3 yrs.	34	64	7	1	0	0	0.0	7	5	5	6	0	.109	.125	6	0	C-26, 2B-2

Doug Clemens

CLEMENS, DOUGLAS HORACE
B. June 9, 1939, Leesport, Pa.

BL TR 6' 180 lbs.

	G	AB	H	2B	3B	HR	HR %	R	RBI	BB	SO	SB	BA	SA	AB	H	G by POS
1960 STL N	1	0	0	0	0	0	–	0	0	0	0	0	–	–	0	0	OF-1
1961	6	12	2	1	0	0	0.0	1	0	3	1	0	.167	.250	3	1	OF-3
1962	48	93	22	1	1	1	1.1	12	12	17	19	0	.237	.301	15	5	OF-34
1963	5	6	1	0	0	1	16.7	1	2	1	2	0	.167	.667	1	0	OF-3
1964 2 teams	STL	N	(33G –	.205)		CHI	N	(54G –	.279)								
" total	87	218	55	14	5	3	1.4	31	21	24	38	0	.252	.404	19	3	OF-62
1965 CHI N	128	340	75	11	0	4	1.2	36	26	38	53	5	.221	.288	25	6	OF-105
1966 PHI N	79	121	31	1	0	1	0.8	10	15	16	25	1	.256	.289	49	12	OF-28, 1B-1
1967	69	73	13	5	0	0	0.0	2	4	8	15	0	.178	.247	54	11	OF-10
1968	29	57	12	1	1	2	3.5	6	8	7	13	0	.211	.368	13	3	OF-17
9 yrs.	452	920	211	34	7	12	1.3	99	88	114	166	6	.229	.321	179	41	OF-263, 1B-1

Wally Clement

CLEMENT, WALLACE OAKES
B. July 21, 1881, Auburn, Me.   D. Nov. 1, 1953, Coral Gables, Fla.

TR

	G	AB	H	2B	3B	HR	HR %	R	RBI	BB	SO	SB	BA	SA	AB	H	G by POS
1908 PHI N	16	36	8	3	0	0	0.0	0	1	0		2	.222	.306	8	2	OF-8
1909 2 teams	PHI	N	(3G –	.000)		BKN	N	(92G –	.256)								
" total	95	343	87	8	4	0	0.0	35	17	18		11	.254	.300	7	1	OF-88
2 yrs.	111	379	95	11	4	0	0.0	35	18	18		13	.251	.301	15	3	OF-96

	G	AB	H	2B	3B	HR	HR %	R	RBI	BB	SO	SB	BA	SA	Pinch Hit AB	Pinch Hit H	G by POS

Roberto Clemente

CLEMENTE, ROBERTO WALKER (Bob)   BR TR 5'11" 175 lbs.
B. Aug. 18, 1934, Carolina, Puerto Rico   D. Dec. 31, 1972, San Juan, Puerto Rico
Hall of Fame 1973.

	G	AB	H	2B	3B	HR	HR %	R	RBI	BB	SO	SB	BA	SA	AB	H	G by POS
1955 **PIT N**	124	474	121	23	11	5	1.1	48	47	18	60	2	.255	.382	8	2	OF-118
1956	147	543	169	30	7	7	1.3	66	60	13	58	6	.311	.431	11	4	OF-139, 2B-2, 3B-1
1957	111	451	114	17	7	4	0.9	42	30	23	45	0	.253	.348	2	1	OF-109
1958	140	519	150	24	10	6	1.2	69	50	31	41	8	.289	.408	5	1	OF-135
1959	105	432	128	17	7	4	0.9	60	50	15	51	2	.296	.396	0	0	OF-104
1960	144	570	179	22	6	16	2.8	89	94	39	72	4	.314	.458	3	0	OF-142
1961	146	572	201	30	10	23	4.0	100	89	35	59	4	**.351**	.559	2	1	OF-144
1962	144	538	168	28	9	10	1.9	95	74	35	73	6	.312	.454	2	0	OF-142
1963	152	600	192	23	8	17	2.8	77	76	31	64	12	.320	.470	3	1	OF-151
1964	155	622	**211**	40	7	12	1.9	95	87	51	87	5	**.339**	.484	1	0	OF-154
1965	152	589	194	21	14	10	1.7	91	65	43	78	8	**.329**	.463	8	2	OF-145
1966	154	638	202	31	11	29	4.5	105	119	46	109	7	.317	.536	1	0	OF-154
1967	147	585	**209**	26	10	23	3.9	103	110	41	103	9	**.357**	.554	2	0	OF-145
1968	132	502	146	18	12	18	3.6	74	57	51	77	2	.291	.482	2	0	OF-131
1969	138	507	175	20	**12**	19	3.7	87	91	56	73	4	.345	.544	3	2	OF-135
1970	108	412	145	22	10	14	3.4	65	60	38	66	3	.352	.556	4	1	OF-104
1971	132	522	178	29	8	13	2.5	82	86	26	65	1	.341	.502	9	3	OF-124
1972	102	378	118	19	7	10	2.6	68	60	29	49	0	.312	.479	7	1	OF-94
18 yrs.	2433	9454	3000	440	166	240	2.5	1416	1305	621	1230	83	.317	.475	73	19	OF-2370, 2B-2, 3B-1
LEAGUE CHAMPIONSHIP SERIES																	
1970 **PIT N**	3	14	3	0	0	0	0.0	1	1	0	4	0	.214	.214	0	0	OF-3
1971	4	18	6	0	0	0	0.0	2	4	1	6	0	.333	.333	0	0	OF-4
1972	5	17	4	1	0	1	5.9	1	2	3	5	0	.235	.471	0	0	OF-5
3 yrs.	12	49	13	1	0	1	2.0	4	7	4	15	0	.265	.347	0	0	OF-12
WORLD SERIES																	
1960 **PIT N**	7	29	9	0	0	0	0.0	1	3	0	4	0	.310	.310	0	0	OF-7
1971	7	29	12	2	1	2	6.9	3	4	2	2	0	.414	.759	0	0	OF-7
2 yrs.	14	58	21	2	1	2	3.4	4	7	2	6	0	.362	.534	0	0	OF-14
													6th				

Ed Clements

CLEMENTS, EDWARD
B. Philadelphia, Pa.   Deceased.

	G	AB	H	2B	3B	HR	HR %	R	RBI	BB	SO	SB	BA	SA	AB	H	G by POS
1890 **PIT N**	1	1	0	0	0	0	0.0	0	0	0	0	0	.000	.000	0	0	SS-1

Jack Clements

CLEMENTS, JOHN T.   BL TL 5'8½" 204 lbs.
B. June 24, 1864, Philadelphia, Pa.   D. May 23, 1941, Philadelphia, Pa.

	G	AB	H	2B	3B	HR	HR %	R	RBI	BB	SO	SB	BA	SA	AB	H	G by POS
1884 **2 teams**		**PHI U**	(41G –	.282)		**PHI N**	(9G –	.233)									
" total	50	207	57	13	2	3	1.4	40		13	8		.275	.401	0	0	C-29, OF-22, SS-1
1885 **PHI N**	52	188	36	11	3	1	0.5	14		2	30		.191	.298	0	0	C-41, OF-11
1886	54	185	38	5	1	0	0.0	15	11	7	34		.205	.243	0	0	C-47, OF-7
1887	66	246	69	13	7	1	0.4	48	47	9	24	7	.280	.402	0	0	C-59, 3B-4, SS-3
1888	86	326	80	8	4	1	0.3	26	32	10	36	3	.245	.304	0	0	C-85, OF-1
1889	78	310	88	17	1	4	1.3	51	35	29	21	3	.284	.384	0	0	C-78
1890	97	381	120	23	8	7	1.8	64	74	45	30	10	.315	.472	0	0	C-91, 1B-5
1891	107	423	131	29	4	4	0.9	58	75	43	19	3	.310	.426	0	0	C-107, 1B-2
1892	109	402	106	25	6	8	2.0	50	76	43	40	7	.264	.415	0	0	C-109
1893	94	376	107	20	3	17	4.5	64	80	39	29	3	.285	.489	2	0	C-92, 1B-1
1894	45	159	55	6	5	3	1.9	26	36	24	7	6	.346	.503	0	0	C-45
1895	88	322	127	27	2	13	**4.0**	64	75	22	7	3	.394	.612	0	0	C-88
1896	57	184	66	5	7	5	2.7	35	45	17	14	2	.359	.543	3	0	C-53
1897	55	185	44	4	2	6	3.2	18	36	12			.238	.378	5	1	C-49
1898 **STL N**	99	335	86	19	5	3	0.9	39	41	21		1	.257	.370	12	1	C-86
1899 **CLE N**	4	12	3	0	0	0	0.0	1	0	0		0	.250	.250	0	0	C-4
1900 **BOS N**	16	42	13	1	0	1	2.4	6	10	3		0	.310	.405	6	0	C-10
17 yrs.	1157	4283	1226	226	60	77	1.8	619	672	339	299	51	.286	.421	28	2	C-1073, OF-41, 1B-8, SS-4, 3B-4

Verne Clemons

CLEMONS, VERNE JAMES (Fats)   BR TR 5'9½" 190 lbs.
B. Sept. 8, 1891, Clemons, Iowa   D. May 5, 1959, Bay Pines, Fla.

	G	AB	H	2B	3B	HR	HR %	R	RBI	BB	SO	SB	BA	SA	AB	H	G by POS
1916 **STL A**	4	7	1	1	0	0	0.0	0	0	0	1	0	.143	.286	2	0	C-2
1919 **STL N**	88	239	63	13	2	0	0.8	14	22	26	13	4	.264	.360	10	5	C-75
1920	112	338	95	10	6	1	0.3	17	36	30	12	1	.281	.355	7	1	C-103
1921	117	341	109	16	2	2	0.6	29	48	33	17	0	.320	.396	8	2	C-109
1922	71	160	41	4	0	0	0.0	9	15	18	5	1	.256	.281	7	1	C-63
1923	57	130	37	9	1	0	0.0	6	13	10	11	0	.285	.369	13	4	C-41
1924	25	56	18	3	0	0	0.0	3	6	2	3	0	.321	.375	7	2	C-17
7 yrs.	474	1271	364	56	11	3	0.4	78	140	119	62	6	.286	.360	54	15	C-410

Donn Clendenon

CLENDENON, DONN ALVIN   BR TR 6'4" 209 lbs.
B. July 15, 1935, Neosho, Mo.

	G	AB	H	2B	3B	HR	HR %	R	RBI	BB	SO	SB	BA	SA	AB	H	G by POS
1961 **PIT N**	9	35	11	1	1	0	0.0	7	2	5	10	0	.314	.400	1	0	OF-8
1962	80	222	67	8	5	7	3.2	39	28	26	58	16	.302	.477	6	1	1B-52, OF-19
1963	154	563	155	28	7	15	2.7	65	57	39	**136**	22	.275	.430	5	0	1B-151
1964	133	457	129	23	8	12	2.6	53	64	26	96	12	.282	.446	15	7	1B-119
1965	162	612	184	32	14	14	2.3	89	96	48	128	9	.301	.467	3	1	1B-158, 3B-1
1966	155	571	171	22	10	28	4.9	80	98	52	142	8	.299	.520	4	1	1B-152
1967	131	478	119	15	2	13	2.7	46	56	34	107	4	.249	.370	8	1	1B-123
1968	158	584	150	20	6	17	2.9	63	87	47	**163**	10	.257	.399	2	1	1B-155
1969 **2 teams**		**MON N**	(38G –	.240)		**NY N**	(72G –	.252)									
" total	110	331	82	11	1	16	4.8	45	51	25	94	3	.248	.432	24	2	1B-82, OF-12
1970 **NY N**	121	396	114	18	3	22	5.6	65	97	39	91	4	.288	.515	22	5	1B-100
1971	88	263	65	10	0	11	4.2	29	37	21	78	1	.247	.411	27	2	1B-72

	G	AB	H	2B	3B	HR	HR %	R	RBI	BB	SO	SB	BA	SA	Pinch Hit AB	Pinch Hit H	G by POS

Donn Clendenon continued

	G	AB	H	2B	3B	HR	HR %	R	RBI	BB	SO	SB	BA	SA	AB	H	G by POS
1972 STL N	61	136	26	4	0	4	2.9	13	9	17	37	1	.191	.309	20	4	1B-36
12 yrs.	1362	4648	1273	192	57	159	3.4	594	682	379	1140	90	.274	.442	137	25	1B-1200, OF-39, 3B-1
WORLD SERIES																	
1969 NY N	4	14	5	1	0	3	21.4	4	4	2	6	0	.357	1.071	0	0	1B-4

Elmer Cleveland

CLEVELAND, ELMER ELLSWORTH
B. Sept. 15, 1862, Washington, D. C.   D. Oct. 8, 1913, Zimmerman, Pa.

	G	AB	H	2B	3B	HR	HR %	R	RBI	BB	SO	SB	BA	SA	AB	H	G by POS
1884 CIN U	29	115	37	9	1	1	0.9	24		4			.322	.443	0	0	3B-29
1888 2 teams	NY	N (9G – .235)				PIT	N (30G – .222)										
" total	39	142	32	2	3	4	2.8	16	16	8	24	4	.225	.366	0	0	3B-39
1891 COL AA	12	41	7	0	0	0	0.0	12	4	12	9	4	.171	.171	0	0	3B-12
3 yrs.	80	298	76	11	4	5	1.7	52	19	24	33	8	.255	.369	0	0	3B-80

Stan Cliburn

CLIBURN, STANLEY GENE
Brother of Stew Cliburn.
B. Dec. 19, 1956, Jackson, Miss.

BR TR 6'   195 lbs.

	G	AB	H	2B	3B	HR	HR %	R	RBI	BB	SO	SB	BA	SA	AB	H	G by POS
1980 CAL A	54	56	10	2	0	2	3.6	7	6	3	9	0	.179	.321	0	0	C-54

Harlond Clift

CLIFT, HARLOND BENTON (Darkie)
B. Aug. 12, 1912, El Reno, Okla.

BR TR 5'11"   180 lbs.

	G	AB	H	2B	3B	HR	HR %	R	RBI	BB	SO	SB	BA	SA	AB	H	G by POS
1934 STL A	147	572	149	30	10	14	2.4	104	56	84	100	7	.260	.421	5	1	3B-141
1935	137	475	140	26	4	11	2.3	101	69	83	39	0	.295	.436	5	1	3B-127, 2B-6
1936	152	576	174	40	11	20	3.5	145	73	115	68	12	.302	.514	0	0	3B-152
1937	155	571	175	36	7	29	5.1	103	118	98	80	8	.306	.546	0	0	3B-155
1938	149	534	155	25	7	34	6.4	119	118	118	67	10	.290	.554	0	0	3B-149
1939	151	526	142	25	2	15	2.9	90	84	111	55	4	.270	.411	0	0	3B-149
1940	150	523	143	29	5	20	3.8	92	87	104	62	9	.273	.463	2	1	3B-147
1941	154	584	149	33	9	17	2.9	108	84	113	93	6	.255	.430	0	0	3B-154
1942	143	541	148	39	4	7	1.3	108	55	106	48	6	.274	.399	1	0	3B-141, SS-1
1943 2 teams	STL	A (105G – .232)				WAS	A (8G – .300)										
" total	113	409	97	11	3	3	0.7	47	29	59	40	5	.237	.301	0	0	3B-112
1944 WAS A	12	44	7	3	0	0	0.0	4	3	3	3	0	.159	.227	0	0	3B-12
1945	119	375	79	12	0	8	2.1	49	53	76	58	2	.211	.307	8	0	3B-111
12 yrs.	1582	5730	1558	309	62	178	3.1	1070	829	1070	713	69	.272	.441	21	3	3B-1550, 2B-6, SS-1

Flea Clifton

CLIFTON, HERMAN EARL
B. Dec. 12, 1909, Cincinnati, Ohio

BR TR 5'10"   160 lbs.

	G	AB	H	2B	3B	HR	HR %	R	RBI	BB	SO	SB	BA	SA	AB	H	G by POS
1934 DET A	16	16	1	0	0	0	0.0	3	1	1	2	0	.063	.063	8	1	3B-4, 2B-1
1935	43	110	28	5	0	0	0.0	15	9	5	13	2	.255	.300	7	1	3B-21, 2B-5, SS-4
1936	13	26	5	1	0	0	0.0	5	1	4	3	0	.192	.231	1	1	SS-6, 3B-2, 2B-1
1937	15	43	5	1	0	0	0.0	4	2	7	10	3	.116	.140	0	0	3B-7, SS-4, 2B-3
4 yrs.	87	195	39	7	0	0	0.0	27	13	17	28	5	.200	.236	16	3	3B-34, SS-14, 2B-10
WORLD SERIES																	
1935 DET A	4	16	0	0	0	0	0.0	1	0	2	4	0	.000	.000	0	0	3B-4

Monk Cline

CLINE, JOHN
B. Mar. 3, 1858, Louisville, Ky.   D. Sept. 23, 1916, Louisville, Ky.

BL TL 5'3"   140 lbs.

	G	AB	H	2B	3B	HR	HR %	R	RBI	BB	SO	SB	BA	SA	AB	H	G by POS
1882 BAL AA	44	172	38	6	2	0	0.0	18		3			.221	.279	0	0	OF-39, SS-8, 2B-2, 3B-1
1884 LOU AA	94	396	115	16	7	2	0.5	91		27			.290	.381	0	0	OF-90, SS-6
1885	2	9	2	1	0	0	0.0	0		0			.222	.333	0	0	OF-1, 3B-1
1888 KC AA	73	293	69	13	2	0	0.0	45	19	20		29	.235	.294	0	0	OF-70, 2B-3, 3B-1
1891 LOU AA	21	76	23	3	1	0	0.0	13	12	19	3	2	.303	.368	0	0	OF-21
5 yrs.	234	946	247	39	12	2	0.2	167	30	69	3	31	.261	.334	0	0	OF-221, SS-14, 2B-5, 3B-3

Ty Cline

CLINE, TYRONE ALEXANDER
B. June 15, 1939, Hampton, S. C.

BL TL 6'½"   170 lbs.

	G	AB	H	2B	3B	HR	HR %	R	RBI	BB	SO	SB	BA	SA	AB	H	G by POS
1960 CLE A	7	26	8	1	1	0	0.0	2	2	0	4	0	.308	.423	1	0	OF-6
1961	12	43	9	2	1	0	0.0	9	1	6	1	1	.209	.302	0	0	OF-12
1962	118	375	93	15	5	2	0.5	53	28	28	50	5	.248	.331	10	1	OF-107
1963 MIL N	72	174	41	2	1	0	0.0	17	10	10	31	2	.236	.259	7	3	OF-62
1964	101	116	35	4	2	1	0.9	22	13	8	22	0	.302	.397	40	14	OF-54, 1B-6
1965	123	220	42	5	3	0	0.0	27	10	16	50	2	.191	.241	29	6	OF-86, 1B-5
1966 2 teams	CHI	N (7G – .353)				ATL	N (42G – .254)										
" total	49	88	24	0	0	0	0.0	15	8	3	13	3	.273	.273	22	6	OF-24, 1B-6
1967 2 teams	ATL	N (10G – .000)				SF	N (64G – .270)										
" total	74	130	33	5	5	0	0.0	18	4	9	16	2	.254	.369	24	4	OF-38
1968 SF N	116	291	65	6	3	1	0.3	37	28	11	26	0	.223	.275	26	5	OF-70, 1B-24
1969 MON N	101	209	50	5	3	2	1.0	26	12	32	22	4	.239	.321	42	9	OF-41, 1B-17
1970 2 teams	MON	N (2G – .500)				CIN	N (48G – .270)										
" total	50	65	18	7	1	0	0.0	13	8	12	11	1	.277	.415	26	7	OF-20, 1B-2
1971 CIN N	69	97	19	1	0	0	0.0	12	1	18	16	2	.196	.206	39	5	OF-28, 1B-2
12 yrs.	892	1834	437	53	25	6	0.3	251	125	153	262	22	.238	.304	266	60	OF-548, 1B-62
LEAGUE CHAMPIONSHIP SERIES																	
1970 CIN N	2	1	1	0	1	0	0.0	2	0	1	0	0	1.000	3.000	1	1	OF-1
WORLD SERIES																	
1970 CIN N	3	3	1	0	0	0	0.0	0	0	0	0	0	.333	.333	3	1	

Gene Clines

CLINES, EUGENE
B. Oct. 6, 1946, San Pablo, Calif.

BR TR 5'9"   170 lbs.

	G	AB	H	2B	3B	HR	HR %	R	RBI	BB	SO	SB	BA	SA	AB	H	G by POS
1970 PIT N	31	37	15	2	0	0	0.0	4	3	2	5	2	.405	.459	20	8	OF-7
1971	97	273	84	12	4	1	0.4	52	24	22	36	15	.308	.392	19	7	OF-74
1972	107	311	104	15	6	0	0.0	52	17	16	47	12	.334	.421	19	2	OF-83
1973	110	304	80	11	3	1	0.3	42	23	26	36	8	.263	.329	35	10	OF-77

	G	AB	H	2B	3B	HR	HR %	R	RBI	BB	SO	SB	BA	SA	Pinch Hit AB	Pinch Hit H	G by POS

Gene Clines continued

	G	AB	H	2B	3B	HR	HR%	R	RBI	BB	SO	SB	BA	SA	PH AB	PH H	G by POS
1974	107	276	62	5	1	0	0.0	29	14	30	40	14	.225	.250	27	6	OF-78
1975 NY N	82	203	46	6	3	0	0.0	25	10	11	21	4	.227	.286	18	2	OF-60
1976 TEX A	116	446	123	12	3	0	0.0	52	38	16	52	11	.276	.316	5	2	OF-103, DH-10
1977 CHI N	101	239	70	12	2	3	1.3	27	41	25	25	1	.293	.397	39	10	OF-63
1978	109	229	59	10	2	0	0.0	31	17	21	28	4	.258	.319	43	10	OF-66
1979	10	10	2	0	0	0	0.0	0	0	0	1	0	.200	.200	10	2	
10 yrs.	870	2328	645	85	24	5	0.2	314	187	169	291	71	.277	.341	235	59	OF-611, DH-10

LEAGUE CHAMPIONSHIP SERIES

	G	AB	H	2B	3B	HR	HR%	R	RBI	BB	SO	SB	BA	SA	PH AB	PH H	G by POS
1971 PIT N	1	3	1	0	0	1	33.3	1	1	0	1	0	.333	1.333	0	0	OF-1
1972	2	2	0	0	0	0	0.0	1	0	0	1	0	.000	.000	2	0	
1974	2	1	0	0	0	0	0.0	1	0	0	0	0	.000	.000	0	0	OF-2
3 yrs.	5	6	1	0	0	1	16.7	3	1	0	2	0	.167	.667	2	0	OF-3

WORLD SERIES

	G	AB	H	2B	3B	HR	HR%	R	RBI	BB	SO	SB	BA	SA	PH AB	PH H	G by POS
1971 PIT N	3	11	1	0	1	0	0.0	2	0	1	1	1	.091	.273	0	0	OF-3

Billy Clingman

CLINGMAN, WILLIAM FREDERICK   BB TR 5'11"   150 lbs.
B. Nov. 21, 1869, Cincinnati, Ohio   D. May 14, 1958, Cincinnati, Ohio

	G	AB	H	2B	3B	HR	HR%	R	RBI	BB	SO	SB	BA	SA	PH AB	PH H	G by POS
1890 CIN N	7	27	7	1	0	0	0.0	2	5	1	0	0	.259	.296	0	0	SS-6, 2B-1
1891 C-M AA	1	5	1	1	0	0	0.0	0	0	0	0	0	.200	.400	0	0	2B-1
1895 PIT N	106	382	99	16	4	0	0.0	69	45	41	43	19	.259	.322	0	0	3B-106
1896 LOU N	121	423	99	10	2	2	0.5	57	37	57	51	19	.234	.281	0	0	3B-121
1897	113	395	90	14	7	2	0.5	59	47	37		14	.228	.314	0	0	3B-113
1898	154	538	138	12	6	0	0.0	65	50	51		15	.257	.301	0	0	3B-79, SS-74, OF-1, 2B-1
1899	109	366	96	15	4	2	0.5	67	44	46		13	.262	.342	0	0	SS-109
1900 CHI N	47	159	33	6	0	0	0.0	15	11	17		6	.208	.245	0	0	SS-47
1901 WAS A	137	480	116	10	7	2	0.4	66	55	42		10	.242	.304	0	0	SS-137
1903 CLE A	21	64	18	1	1	0	0.0	10	7	11		2	.281	.328	0	0	2B-11, SS-7, 3B-3
10 yrs.	816	2839	697	86	31	8	0.3	410	301	303	94	98	.246	.306	0	0	3B-422, SS-380, 2B-14, OF-1

Jim Clinton

CLINTON, JAMES LAWRENCE (Big Jim)   BR TR 5'8½"   174 lbs.
B. Aug. 10, 1850, New York, N. Y.   D. Sept. 3, 1921, Brooklyn, N. Y.
Manager 1872.

	G	AB	H	2B	3B	HR	HR%	R	RBI	BB	SO	SB	BA	SA	PH AB	PH H	G by POS
1876 LOU N	16	65	22	2	0	0	0.0	8	0	0	0		.338	.369	0	0	OF-14, 1B-1, P-1
1882 WOR N	26	98	16	2	0	0	0.0	9	3	7	13		.163	.184	0	0	OF-26
1883 BAL AA	94	399	125	16	8	0	0.0	69		27			.313	.393	0	0	OF-92, 2B-2
1884	103	433	118	12	6	3	0.7	82		29			.273	.349	0	0	OF-103, 2B-1
1885 CIN AA	105	408	97	5	5	0	0.0	48		15			.238	.275	0	0	OF-105
1886 BAL AA	23	83	15	1	0	0	0.0	8		4			.181	.193	0	0	OF-23
6 yrs.	367	1486	393	38	19	3	0.2	224	3	82	13		.264	.322	0	0	OF-363, 2B-3, 1B-1, P-1

Lu Clinton

CLINTON, LUCIEAN LOUIS   BR TR 6'1"   185 lbs.
B. Oct. 13, 1937, Ponca City, Okla.

	G	AB	H	2B	3B	HR	HR%	R	RBI	BB	SO	SB	BA	SA	PH AB	PH H	G by POS
1960 BOS A	96	298	68	17	5	6	2.0	37	37	20	66	4	.228	.379	6	1	OF-89
1961	17	51	13	2	1	0	0.0	4	3	2	10	0	.255	.333	2	0	OF-13
1962	114	398	117	24	10	18	4.5	63	75	34	79	2	.294	.540	9	2	OF-103
1963	148	560	130	23	7	22	3.9	71	77	49	118	0	.232	.416	2	0	OF-146
1964 2 teams		BOS	A (37G – .258)			LA	A (91G – .248)										
" total	128	426	107	22	3	12	2.8	45	44	40	73	4	.251	.401	7	1	OF-121
1965 3 teams		CAL	A (89G – .243)			KC	A (1G – .000)			CLE	A (12G – .176)						
" total	102	257	60	13	3	2	0.8	31	10	26	44	2	.233	.331	16	5	OF-83
1966 NY A	80	159	35	10	2	5	3.1	18	21	16	27	0	.220	.403	14	6	OF-63
1967	6	4	2	1	0	0	0.0	1	2	1	1	0	.500	.750	4	2	OF-1
8 yrs.	691	2153	532	112	31	65	3.0	270	269	188	418	12	.247	.418	60	17	OF-619

Ed Clough

CLOUGH, EDGAR GEORGE (Spec)   BL TL 6'   188 lbs.
B. Oct. 11, 1905, Wiconisco, Pa.   D. Jan. 30, 1944, Harrisburg, Pa.

	G	AB	H	2B	3B	HR	HR%	R	RBI	BB	SO	SB	BA	SA	PH AB	PH H	G by POS
1924 STL N	7	14	1	0	0	0	0.0	0	1	0	3	0	.071	.071	1	0	OF-6
1925	3	4	1	0	0	0	0.0	0	0	0	0	0	.250	.250	0	0	P-3
1926	1	1	0	0	0	0	0.0	0	0	0	0	0	.000	.000	0	0	P-1
3 yrs.	11	19	2	0	0	0	0.0	0	1	0	3	0	.105	.105	1	0	OF-6, P-4

Bill Clymer

CLYMER, WILLIAM JOHNSTON (Derby Day)
B. Dec. 18, 1873, Philadelphia, Pa.   D. Dec. 26, 1936, Philadelphia, Pa.

	G	AB	H	2B	3B	HR	HR%	R	RBI	BB	SO	SB	BA	SA	PH AB	PH H	G by POS
1891 PHI AA	3	11	0	0	0	0	0.0	0	0	1	2	1	.000	.000	0	0	SS-3

Otis Clymer

CLYMER, OTIS EDGAR (Grump)   BB TR 6'   175 lbs.
B. Jan. 27, 1880, Pine Grove, Pa.   D. Feb. 27, 1926, St. Paul, Minn.

	G	AB	H	2B	3B	HR	HR%	R	RBI	BB	SO	SB	BA	SA	PH AB	PH H	G by POS
1905 PIT N	96	365	108	11	5	0	0.0	74	25	19		23	.296	.353	6	2	OF-89, 1B-1
1906	11	45	11	0	1	0	0.0	7	1	3		1	.244	.289	0	0	OF-11
1907 2 teams		PIT	N (22G – .227)			WAS	A (57G – .316)										
" total	79	272	80	7	5	1	0.4	38	20	23		22	.294	.368	9	3	OF-66, 1B-2
1908 WAS A	110	368	93	11	4	1	0.3	32	35	20		19	.253	.313	9	3	OF-82, 2B-13, 3B-2
1909	45	138	27	5	2	0	0.0	11	6	17		7	.196	.261	2	0	OF-41
1913 2 teams		CHI	N (30G – .229)			BOS	N (14G – .324)										
" total	44	142	36	8	2	0	0.0	20	13	17	21	11	.254	.338	6	2	OF-37
6 yrs.	385	1330	355	42	19	2	0.2	182	98	99	21	83	.267	.332	32	10	OF-326, 2B-13, 1B-3, 3B-2

Gil Coan

COAN, GILBERT FITZGERALD   BL TR 6'   180 lbs.
B. May 18, 1922, Monroe, N. C.

	G	AB	H	2B	3B	HR	HR%	R	RBI	BB	SO	SB	BA	SA	PH AB	PH H	G by POS
1946 WAS A	59	134	28	3	2	3	2.2	17	9	7	37	2	.209	.328	24	4	OF-29
1947	11	42	21	3	2	0	0.0	5	3	5	6	2	.500	.667	0	0	OF-11
1948	138	513	119	13	9	7	1.4	56	60	41	78	23	.232	.333	8	1	OF-131
1949	111	358	78	7	8	3	0.8	36	25	29	58	9	.218	.307	11	2	OF-97
1950	104	366	111	17	4	7	1.9	58	50	28	46	10	.303	.429	5	3	OF-98
1951	135	538	163	25	7	9	1.7	85	62	39	62	8	.303	.426	5	0	OF-132

	G	AB	H	2B	3B	HR	HR %	R	RBI	BB	SO	SB	BA	SA	Pinch Hit AB	Pinch Hit H	G by POS

Gil Coan continued

	G	AB	H	2B	3B	HR	HR%	R	RBI	BB	SO	SB	BA	SA	AB	H	G by POS
1952	107	332	68	11	6	5	1.5	50	20	32	35	9	.205	.319	16	3	OF-86
1953	68	168	33	1	4	2	1.2	28	17	22	23	7	.196	.286	22	4	OF-46
1954 BAL A	94	265	74	11	1	2	0.8	29	20	16	17	9	.279	.351	25	2	OF-67
1955 3 teams	BAL A (61G – .238)			CHI A (17G – .176)				NY N (9G – .154)									
" total	87	160	36	7	1	1	0.6	18	12	13	21	4	.225	.300	29	11	OF-51
1956 NY N	4	1	0	0	0	0	0.0	2	0	0	1	0	.000	.000	1	0	
11 yrs.	918	2877	731	98	44	39	1.4	384	278	232	384	83	.254	.359	146	30	OF-748

Joe Cobb

COBB, JOSEPH STANLEY   BR TR 5'9"   170 lbs.
Born Joseph Stanley Serafin.
B. Jan. 24, 1895, Hudson, Pa.   D. Dec. 24, 1947, Allentown, Pa.

	G	AB	H	2B	3B	HR	HR%	R	RBI	BB	SO	SB	BA	SA	AB	H	G by POS
1918 DET A	1	0	0	0	0	0	–	0	0	1	0	0	–	–	0	0	

Ty Cobb

COBB, TYRUS RAYMOND (The Georgia Peach)   BL TR 6'1"   175 lbs.
B. Dec. 18, 1886, Narrows, Ga.   D. July 17, 1961, Atlanta, Ga.
Manager 1921-26.
Hall of Fame 1936.

	G	AB	H	2B	3B	HR	HR%	R	RBI	BB	SO	SB	BA	SA	AB	H	G by POS
1905 DET A	41	150	36	6	0	1	0.7	19	15	10		2	.240	.300	0	0	OF-41
1906	98	350	112	13	7	1	0.3	45	41	19		23	.320	.406	1	0	OF-96
1907	150	605	212	29	15	5	0.8	97	116	24		49	.350	.473	0	0	OF-150
1908	150	581	188	36	20	4	0.7	88	108	34		39	.324	.475	0	0	OF-150
1909	156	573	216	33	10	9	1.6	116	107	48		76	.377	.517	0	0	OF-156
1910	140	509	196	36	13	8	1.6	106	91	64		65	.385	.554	3	1	OF-137
1911	146	591	248	47	24	8	1.4	147	144	44		83	.420	.621	0	0	OF-146
1912	140	553	227	30	23	7	1.3	119	90	43		61	.410	.586	0	0	OF-140
1913	122	428	167	18	16	4	0.9	70	67	58	31	52	.390	.535	2	0	OF-118
1914	97	345	127	22	11	2	0.6	69	57	57	22	35	.368	.513	0	0	OF-96
1915	156	563	208	31	13	3	0.5	144	99	118	43	96	.369	.487	0	0	OF-156
1916	145	542	201	31	10	5	0.9	113	68	78	39	68	.371	.493	0	0	OF-143, 1B-1
1917	152	588	225	44	23	7	1.2	107	102	61	34	55	.383	.571	0	0	OF-152
1918	111	421	161	19	14	3	0.7	83	64	41	21	34	.382	.515	3	1	OF-95, 1B-13, P-2, 3B-1, 2B-1
1919	124	497	191	36	13	1	0.2	92	70	38	22	28	.384	.515	0	0	OF-123
1920	112	428	143	28	8	2	0.5	86	63	58	28	14	.334	.451	0	0	OF-112
1921	128	507	197	37	16	12	2.4	124	101	56	19	22	.389	.596	7	1	OF-121
1922	137	526	211	42	16	4	0.8	99	99	55	24	9	.401	.565	3	0	OF-134
1923	145	556	189	40	7	6	1.1	103	88	66	14	9	.340	.469	2	1	OF-141
1924	155	625	211	38	10	4	0.6	115	74	85	18	23	.338	.450	0	0	OF-155
1925	121	415	157	31	12	12	2.9	97	102	65	12	13	.378	.598	12	2	OF-105, P-1
1926	79	233	79	18	5	4	1.7	48	62	26	2	9	.339	.511	18	6	OF-55
1927 PHI A	134	490	175	32	7	5	1.0	104	93	67	12	22	.357	.482	8	2	OF-126
1928	95	353	114	27	4	1	0.3	54	40	34	16	5	.323	.431	10	1	OF-95
24 yrs.	3034	11429	4191	724	297	118	1.0	2245	1961	1249	357	892	.367	.513	69	15	OF-2943, 1B-14, P-3, 3B-1, 2B-1
	4th	4th	1st	4th	2nd			1st	4th			2nd	1st				

WORLD SERIES

	G	AB	H	2B	3B	HR	HR%	R	RBI	BB	SO	SB	BA	SA	AB	H	G by POS
1907 DET A	5	20	4	0	1	0	0.0	1	1	0	3	0	.200	.300	0	0	OF-5
1908	5	19	7	1	0	0	0.0	3	4	1	2	2	.368	.421	0	0	OF-5
1909	7	26	6	3	0	0	0.0	3	6	2	2	2	.231	.346	0	0	OF-7
3 yrs.	17	65	17	4	1	0	0.0	7	11	3	7	4	.262	.354	0	0	OF-17

Dave Coble

COBLE, DAVID LAMAR   BR TR 6'1"   183 lbs.
B. Dec. 24, 1912, Monroe, N. C.   D. Oct. 15, 1971, Orlando, Fla.

	G	AB	H	2B	3B	HR	HR%	R	RBI	BB	SO	SB	BA	SA	AB	H	G by POS
1939 PHI N	15	25	7	1	0	0	0.0	2	0	3	0	0	.280	.320	2	0	C-13

George Cochran

COCHRAN, GEORGE LESLIE   TR
B. Feb. 12, 1889, Rusk, Tex.   D. May 21, 1960, Harbour City, Calif.

	G	AB	H	2B	3B	HR	HR%	R	RBI	BB	SO	SB	BA	SA	AB	H	G by POS
1918 BOS A	25	63	8	0	0	0	0.0	8	3	11	7	3	.127	.127	1	0	3B-23, SS-1

Mickey Cochrane

COCHRANE, GORDON STANLEY (Black Mike)   BL TR 5'10½" 180 lbs.
B. Apr. 6, 1903, Bridgewater, Mass.   D. June 28, 1962, Lake Forest, Ill.
Manager 1934-38.
Hall of Fame 1947.

	G	AB	H	2B	3B	HR	HR%	R	RBI	BB	SO	SB	BA	SA	AB	H	G by POS
1925 PHI A	134	420	139	21	5	6	1.4	69	55	44	19	7	.331	.448	1	1	C-133
1926	120	370	101	8	9	8	2.2	50	47	56	15	5	.273	.408	1	0	C-115
1927	126	432	146	20	6	12	2.8	80	80	50	7	9	.338	.495	3	1	C-123
1928	131	468	137	26	12	10	2.1	92	57	76	25	7	.293	.464	1	0	C-130
1929	135	514	170	37	8	7	1.4	113	95	69	8	7	.331	.475	0	0	C-135
1930	130	487	174	42	5	10	2.1	110	85	55	18	5	.357	.526	0	0	C-130
1931	122	459	160	31	6	17	3.7	87	89	56	21	2	.349	.553	5	0	C-117
1932	139	518	152	35	4	23	4.4	118	112	100	22	0	.293	.510	2	0	C-137, OF-1
1933	130	429	138	30	4	15	3.5	104	60	106	22	8	.322	.515	2	0	C-128
1934 DET A	129	437	140	32	1	2	0.5	74	76	78	26	8	.320	.412	8	1	C-124
1935	115	411	131	33	3	5	1.2	93	47	96	15	5	.319	.450	3	1	C-110
1936	44	126	34	8	0	2	1.6	24	17	46	15	1	.270	.381	1	0	C-42
1937	27	98	30	10	1	2	2.0	27	12	25	4	0	.306	.490	0	0	C-27
13 yrs.	1482	5169	1652	333	64	119	2.3	1041	832	857	217	64	.320	.478	27	4	C-1451, OF-1

WORLD SERIES

	G	AB	H	2B	3B	HR	HR%	R	RBI	BB	SO	SB	BA	SA	AB	H	G by POS
1929 PHI A	5	15	6	1	0	0	0.0	5	0	7	0	0	.400	.467	0	0	C-5
1930	6	18	4	1	0	2	11.1	5	3	5	2	0	.222	.611	0	0	C-6
1931	7	25	4	0	0	0	0.0	2	1	5	2	0	.160	.160	0	0	C-7
1934 DET A	7	28	6	1	0	0	0.0	2	1	4	3	0	.214	.250	0	0	C-7
1935	6	24	7	1	0	0	0.0	3	1	4	1	0	.292	.333	0	0	C-6
5 yrs.	31	110	27	4	0	2	1.8	17	6	25	8	0	.245	.336	0	0	C-31
										6th							

	G	AB	H	2B	3B	HR	HR %	R	RBI	BB	SO	SB	BA	SA	Pinch Hit AB	Pinch Hit H	G by POS

Jim Cockman

COCKMAN, JAMES
B. Apr. 26, 1873, Guelph, Ont., Canada   D. Sept. 28, 1947, Guelph, Ont., Canada   BR TR

	G	AB	H	2B	3B	HR	HR%	R	RBI	BB	SO	SB	BA	SA	PH AB	PH H	G by POS
1905 NY A	13	38	4	0	0	0	0.0	5	2	4		2	.105	.105	0	0	3B-13

Jack Coffey

COFFEY, JOHN FRANCIS
B. Jan. 28, 1887, New York, N.Y.   D. Feb. 14, 1966, Bronx, N.Y.   BR TR 5'11" 178 lbs.

	G	AB	H	2B	3B	HR	HR%	R	RBI	BB	SO	SB	BA	SA	PH AB	PH H	G by POS
1909 BOS N	73	257	48	4	4	0	0.0	21	20	11		2	.187	.233	0	0	SS-73
1918 2 teams	DET	A (22G – .209)		BOS	A (15G – .159)												
" total	37	111	21	1	2	1	0.9	12	6	11	8	4	.189	.261	0	0	2B-23, 3B-14
2 yrs.	110	368	69	5	6	1	0.3	33	26	22	8	6	.188	.242	0	0	SS-73, 2B-23, 3B-14

Frank Coggins

COGGINS, FRANKLIN (Swish)
B. May 22, 1944, Griffin, Ga.   BB TR 6'2" 187 lbs.

	G	AB	H	2B	3B	HR	HR%	R	RBI	BB	SO	SB	BA	SA	PH AB	PH H	G by POS
1967 WAS A	19	75	23	3	0	1	1.3	9	8	2	17	1	.307	.387	0	0	2B-19
1968	62	171	30	6	1	0	0.0	15	7	9	33	1	.175	.222	8	0	2B-52
1972 CHI N	6	1	0	0	0	0	0.0	1	0	1	0	0	.000	.000	1	0	
3 yrs.	87	247	53	9	1	1	0.4	25	15	12	50	2	.215	.271	9	0	2B-71

Rich Coggins

COGGINS, RICHARD ALLEN
B. Dec. 7, 1950, Indianapolis, Ind.   BL TL 5'8" 170 lbs.

	G	AB	H	2B	3B	HR	HR%	R	RBI	BB	SO	SB	BA	SA	PH AB	PH H	G by POS
1972 BAL A	16	39	13	4	0	0	0.0	5	1	1	6	0	.333	.436	2	1	OF-13
1973	110	389	124	19	9	7	1.8	54	41	28	24	17	.319	.468	7	1	OF-101, DH-1
1974	113	411	100	13	3	4	1.0	53	32	29	31	26	.243	.319	12	1	OF-105
1975 2 teams	MON	N (13G – .270)		NY	A (51G – .224)												
" total	64	144	34	4	1	1	0.7	8	10	8	23	3	.236	.299	5	1	OF-46, DH-9
1976 2 teams	NY	A (7G – .250)		CHI	A (32G – .156)												
" total	39	100	16	2	0	0	0.0	5	6	6	16	4	.160	.180	5	1	OF-28, DH-1
5 yrs.	342	1083	287	42	13	12	1.1	125	90	72	100	50	.265	.361	31	5	OF-293, DH-11

LEAGUE CHAMPIONSHIP SERIES

	G	AB	H	2B	3B	HR	HR%	R	RBI	BB	SO	SB	BA	SA	PH AB	PH H	G by POS
1973 BAL A	2	9	4	1	0	0	0.0	1	0	0	0	0	.444	.556	0	0	OF-2
1974	3	11	0	0	0	0	0.0	0	0	0	3	0	.000	.000	0	0	OF-3
2 yrs.	5	20	4	1	0	0	0.0	1	0	0	3	0	.200	.250	0	0	OF-5

Ed Cogswell

COGSWELL, EDWARD
B. Feb. 25, 1854, England   D. July 27, 1888, Fitchburg, Mass.   BR

	G	AB	H	2B	3B	HR	HR%	R	RBI	BB	SO	SB	BA	SA	PH AB	PH H	G by POS
1879 BOS N	49	236	76	8	1	0	0.4	51	18	8	5		.322	.377	0	0	1B-49
1880 TRO N	47	209	63	7	3	0	0.0	41		11	10		.301	.364	0	0	1B-47
1882 WOR N	13	51	7	1	0	0	0.0	10	1	6	6		.137	.157	0	0	1B-13
3 yrs.	109	496	146	16	4	0	0.2	102	19	25	21		.294	.349	0	0	1B-109

Alta Cohen

COHEN, ALBERT (Schoolboy)
B. Dec. 25, 1908, New York, N.Y.   BL TL 5'10½" 170 lbs.

	G	AB	H	2B	3B	HR	HR%	R	RBI	BB	SO	SB	BA	SA	PH AB	PH H	G by POS
1931 BKN N	1	3	2	0	0	0	0.0	0	0	0	0	0	.667	.667	0	0	OF-1
1932	9	32	5	1	0	0	0.0	1	1	3	7	0	.156	.188	0	0	OF-8
1933 PHI N	19	32	6	1	0	0	0.0	6	1	6	4	0	.188	.219	10	0	OF-7
3 yrs.	29	67	13	2	0	0	0.0	8	2	9	11	0	.194	.224	10	0	OF-16

Andy Cohen

COHEN, ANDREW HOWARD
Brother of Sid Cohen.
B. Oct. 25, 1904, Baltimore, Md.
Manager 1960.   BR TR 5'8" 155 lbs.

	G	AB	H	2B	3B	HR	HR%	R	RBI	BB	SO	SB	BA	SA	PH AB	PH H	G by POS
1926 NY N	32	35	9	0	1	0	0.0	4	8	1	2	0	.257	.314	7	1	SS-10, 2B-10, 3B-2
1928	129	504	138	24	7	9	1.8	64	59	31	17	3	.274	.403	0	0	2B-126, SS-3, 3B-1
1929	101	347	102	12	2	5	1.4	40	47	11	15	3	.294	.383	5	0	2B-94, SS-1, 3B-1
3 yrs.	262	886	249	36	10	14	1.6	108	114	43	34	6	.281	.392	12	1	2B-230, SS-14, 3B-4

Jimmie Coker

COKER, JIMMIE GOODWIN
B. Mar. 28, 1936, Holly Mill, S. C.   BR TR 5'11" 195 lbs.

	G	AB	H	2B	3B	HR	HR%	R	RBI	BB	SO	SB	BA	SA	PH AB	PH H	G by POS
1958 PHI N	2	6	1	0	0	0	0.0	0	0	0	0	0	.167	.167	0	0	C-2
1960	81	252	54	5	3	6	2.4	18	34	23	45	0	.214	.329	5	1	C-76
1961	11	25	10	1	0	1	4.0	3	4	7	4	1	.400	.560	1	1	C-11
1962	5	3	0	0	0	0	0.0	0	1	1	2	0	.000	.000	3	0	
1963 SF N	4	5	1	0	0	0	0.0	0	0	1	2	0	.200	.200	4	1	C-2
1964 CIN N	11	32	10	2	0	1	3.1	3	4	3	5	0	.313	.474	1	1	C-11
1965	24	61	15	2	0	2	3.3	3	9	8	16	0	.246	.377	6	1	C-19
1966	50	111	28	3	0	4	3.6	9	14	8	5	0	.252	.387	10	2	C-39, OF-2
1967	45	97	18	2	1	2	2.1	8	4	4	20	0	.186	.289	15	6	C-34
9 yrs.	233	592	137	15	4	16	2.7	44	70	55	99	1	.231	.351	45	13	C-194, OF-2

Rocky Colavito

COLAVITO, ROCCO DOMENICO
B. Aug. 10, 1933, New York, N. Y.   BR TR 6'3" 190 lbs

	G	AB	H	2B	3B	HR	HR%	R	RBI	BB	SO	SB	BA	SA	PH AB	PH H	G by POS
1955 CLE A	5	9	4	2	0	0	0.0	3	0	0	2	0	.444	.667	2	0	OF-2
1956	101	322	89	11	4	21	6.5	55	65	49	46	0	.276	.531	5	0	OF-98
1957	134	461	116	26	0	25	5.4	66	84	71	80	1	.252	.471	3	1	OF-130
1958	143	489	148	26	3	41	8.4	80	113	84	89	0	.303	.620	5	1	OF-129, 1B-11, P-1
1959	154	588	151	24	0	42	7.1	90	111	71	86	3	.257	.512	0	0	OF-154
1960 DET A	145	555	138	18	1	35	6.3	67	87	53	80	3	.249	.474	2	0	OF-144
1961	163	583	169	30	2	45	7.7	129	140	113	75	1	.290	.580	2	0	OF-161
1962	161	601	164	30	2	37	6.2	90	112	96	68	2	.273	.514	0	0	OF-161
1963	160	597	162	29	2	22	3.7	91	91	84	78	0	.271	.437	1	0	OF-159
1964 KC A	160	588	161	31	2	34	5.8	89	102	83	56	3	.274	.507	1	1	OF-159
1965 CLE A	162	592	170	25	2	26	4.4	92	108	93	63	1	.287	.468	0	0	OF-162

	G	AB	H	2B	3B	HR	HR %	R	RBI	BB	SO	SB	BA	SA	Pinch Hit AB	Pinch Hit H	G by POS

Rocky Colavito continued

	G	AB	H	2B	3B	HR	HR %	R	RBI	BB	SO	SB	BA	SA	AB	H	G by POS
1966	151	533	127	13	0	30	5.6	68	72	76	81	2	.238	.432	5	3	OF-146
1967 2 teams		CLE A (63G – .241)				CHI A (60G – .221)											
" total	123	381	88	13	1	8	2.1	30	50	49	41	3	.231	.333	12	3	OF-108
1968 2 teams		LA N (40G – .204)				NY A (39G – .220)											
" total	79	204	43	5	2	8	3.9	21	24	29	35	0	.211	.373	17	2	OF-61, P-1
14 yrs.	1841	6503	1730	283	21	374	5.8	971	1159	951	880	19	.266	.489	55	11	OF-1774, 1B-11, P-2

Mike Colbern

COLBERN, MICHAEL MALLOY
B. Apr. 19, 1955, Santa Monica, Calif.

BR TR 6'3" 205 lbs.

	G	AB	H	2B	3B	HR	HR %	R	RBI	BB	SO	SB	BA	SA	AB	H	G by POS
1978 CHI A	48	141	38	5	1	2	1.4	11	20	1	36	0	.270	.362	0	0	C-47, DH-1
1979	32	83	20	5	1	0	0.0	5	8	4	25	0	.241	.325	1	0	C-32
2 yrs.	80	224	58	10	2	2	0.9	16	28	5	61	0	.259	.348	1	0	C-79, DH-1

Nate Colbert

COLBERT, NATHAN
B. Apr. 9, 1946, St. Louis, Mo.

BR TR 6'2" 190 lbs.

	G	AB	H	2B	3B	HR	HR %	R	RBI	BB	SO	SB	BA	SA	AB	H	G by POS
1966 HOU N	19	7	0	0	0	0	0.0	3	0	0	4	0	.000	.000	7	0	
1968	20	53	8	1	0	0	0.0	5	4	1	23	1	.151	.170	2	0	OF-11, 1B-5
1969 SD N	139	483	123	20	9	24	5.0	64	66	45	123	6	.255	.482	4	0	1B-134
1970	156	572	148	17	6	38	6.6	84	86	56	150	3	.259	.509	4	0	1B-153, 3B-1
1971	156	565	149	25	3	27	4.8	81	84	63	119	5	.264	.462	3	1	1B-153
1972	151	563	141	27	2	38	6.7	87	111	70	127	15	.250	.508	2	0	1B-150
1973	145	529	143	25	2	22	4.2	73	80	54	146	9	.270	.450	1	0	1B-144
1974	119	368	76	16	0	14	3.8	53	54	62	108	10	.207	.364	12	4	1B-79, OF-48
1975 2 teams		DET A (45G – .147)				MON N (38G – .173)											
" total	83	237	37	8	3	8	3.4	26	29	22	83	0	.156	.316	19	3	1B-66, DH-1
1976 2 teams		MON N (14G – .200)				OAK N (2G – .000)											
" total	16	45	8	2	0	2	4.4	5	6	10	19	3	.178	.356	3	1	OF-7, 1B-6, DH-2
10 yrs.	1004	3422	833	141	25	173	5.1	481	520	383	902	52	.243	.451	57	9	1B-890, OF-66, DH-3, 3B-1

Dick Cole

COLE, RICHARD ROY
B. May 6, 1926, Long Beach, Calif.

BR TR 6'2" 175 lbs.

	G	AB	H	2B	3B	HR	HR %	R	RBI	BB	SO	SB	BA	SA	AB	H	G by POS
1951 2 teams		STL N (15G – .194)				PIT N (42G – .236)											
" total	57	142	32	5	0	1	0.7	13	14	21	14	0	.225	.282	0	0	2B-48, SS-8
1953 PIT N	97	235	64	13	1	0	0.0	29	23	38	26	2	.272	.336	9	6	SS-77, 2B-7, 1B-1
1954	138	486	131	22	5	1	0.2	40	40	41	48	0	.270	.342	7	1	SS-66, 3B-55, 2B-17
1955	77	239	54	8	3	0	0.0	16	21	18	22	0	.226	.285	11	2	3B-33, 2B-24, SS-12
1956	72	99	21	2	1	0	0.0	7	9	11	9	0	.212	.253	40	7	3B-18, 2B-12, SS-6
1957 MIL N	15	14	1	0	0	0	0.0	1	0	3	5	0	.071	.071	2	0	2B-10, 3B-1, 1B-1
6 yrs.	456	1215	303	50	10	2	0.2	106	107	132	124	2	.249	.312	69	16	SS-169, 2B-118, 3B-107, 1B-2

Willis Cole

COLE, WILLIS RUSSELL
B. Jan. 6, 1882, Milton Junction, Wis. D. Oct. 11, 1965, Madison, Wis.

BR TR 5'8" 170 lbs.

	G	AB	H	2B	3B	HR	HR %	R	RBI	BB	SO	SB	BA	SA	AB	H	G by POS
1909 CHI A	46	165	39	7	3	0	0.0	17	16	16		3	.236	.315	0	0	OF-46
1910	22	80	14	2	1	0	0.0	6	2	4		0	.175	.225	0	0	OF-22
2 yrs.	68	245	53	9	4	0	0.0	23	18	20		3	.216	.286	0	0	OF-68

Bob Coleman

COLEMAN, ROBERT HUNTER
B. Sept. 26, 1890, Huntingburg, Ind. D. July 16, 1959, Boston, Mass.
Manager 1944-45.

BR TR 6'2" 190 lbs.

	G	AB	H	2B	3B	HR	HR %	R	RBI	BB	SO	SB	BA	SA	AB	H	G by POS
1913 PIT N	24	50	9	2	0	0	0.0	5	9	7	8	0	.180	.220	0	0	C-24
1914	73	150	40	4	1	1	0.7	11	14	15	32	3	.267	.327	1	0	C-72
1916 CLE A	19	28	6	2	0	0	0.0	3	4	7	6	0	.214	.286	5	1	C-12
3 yrs.	116	228	55	8	1	1	0.4	19	27	29	46	3	.241	.298	6	1	C-108

Choo Choo Coleman

COLEMAN, CLARENCE
B. Aug. 25, 1937, Orlando, Fla.

BL TR 5'9" 165 lbs.

	G	AB	H	2B	3B	HR	HR %	R	RBI	BB	SO	SB	BA	SA	AB	H	G by POS
1961 PHI N	34	47	6	1	0	0	0.0	3	4	2	8	0	.128	.149	20	2	C-14
1962 NY N	55	152	38	7	2	6	3.9	24	17	11	24	2	.250	.441	14	2	C-44
1963	106	247	44	0	0	3	1.2	22	9	24	49	5	.178	.215	11	2	C-91, OF-1
1966	6	16	3	0	0	0	0.0	2	0	0	4	0	.188	.188	0	0	C-5
4 yrs.	201	462	91	8	2	9	1.9	51	30	37	85	7	.197	.281	45	6	C-154, OF-1

Curt Coleman

COLEMAN, CURTIS HANCOCK
B. Feb. 18, 1887, Salem, Ore. D. July 1, 1980, Newport, Ore.

BL TR 5'11" 180 lbs.

	G	AB	H	2B	3B	HR	HR %	R	RBI	BB	SO	SB	BA	SA	AB	H	G by POS
1912 NY A	12	37	9	4	0	0	0.0	8	4	7		0	.243	.351	2	0	3B-10

Dave Coleman

COLEMAN, DAVID LEE
B. Oct. 26, 1950, Dayton, Ohio

BR TR 6'3" 195 lbs.

	G	AB	H	2B	3B	HR	HR %	R	RBI	BB	SO	SB	BA	SA	AB	H	G by POS
1977 BOS A	11	12	0	0	0	0	0.0	1	0	1	3	0	.000	.000	4	0	OF-9

Ed Coleman

COLEMAN, PARKE EDWARD
B. Dec. 1, 1901, Canby, Ore. D. Aug. 5, 1964, Oregon City, Ore.

BL TR 6'2" 200 lbs.

	G	AB	H	2B	3B	HR	HR %	R	RBI	BB	SO	SB	BA	SA	AB	H	G by POS
1932 PHI A	26	73	25	7	1	1	1.4	13	13	1	6	1	.342	.507	10	2	OF-16
1933	102	388	109	26	3	6	1.5	48	68	19	51	0	.281	.410	12	2	OF-89
1934	101	329	92	14	6	14	4.3	53	60	29	34	0	.280	.486	15	8	OF-86
1935 2 teams		PHI A (10G – .077)				STL A (108G – .287)											
" total	118	410	115	15	9	17	4.1	66	71	53	44	0	.280	.485	14	1	OF-103
1936 STL A	92	137	40	5	4	2	1.5	13	34	15	17	0	.292	.431	62	20	OF-18
5 yrs.	439	1337	381	67	23	40	3.0	193	246	117	152	1	.285	.459	113	33	OF-312

	G	AB	H	2B	3B	HR	HR %	R	RBI	BB	SO	SB	BA	SA	Pinch Hit AB	Pinch Hit H	G by POS

Gordy Coleman

COLEMAN, GORDON CALVIN
B. July 5, 1934, Rockville, Md.
BL TR 6'3"   208 lbs.

	G	AB	H	2B	3B	HR	HR %	R	RBI	BB	SO	SB	BA	SA	PH AB	PH H	G by POS
1959 CLE A	6	15	8	0	1	0	0.0	5	2	1	2	0	.533	.667	2	2	1B-3
1960 CIN N	66	251	68	10	1	6	2.4	26	32	12	32	1	.271	.390	0	0	1B-66
1961	150	520	149	27	4	26	5.0	63	87	45	67	1	.287	.504	6	3	1B-150
1962	136	476	132	13	1	28	5.9	73	86	36	68	2	.277	.485	15	3	1B-128
1963	123	365	90	20	2	14	3.8	38	59	29	51	1	.247	.427	19	8	1B-107
1964	89	198	48	6	2	5	2.5	18	27	13	30	2	.242	.369	35	9	1B-49
1965	108	325	98	19	0	14	4.3	39	57	24	38	0	.302	.489	16	6	1B-89
1966	91	227	57	7	0	5	2.2	20	37	16	45	2	.251	.348	25	9	1B-65
1967	4	7	0	0	0	0	0.0	0	0	1	0	0	.000	.000	2	0	1B-2
9 yrs.	773	2384	650	102	11	98	4.1	282	387	177	333	9	.273	.448	120	40	1B-659
WORLD SERIES																	
1961 CIN N	5	20	5	0	0	1	5.0	2	2	0	1	0	.250	.400	0	0	1B-5

Jerry Coleman

COLEMAN, GERALD FRANCIS
B. Sept. 14, 1924, San Jose, Calif.
Manager 1980.
BR TR 6'   165 lbs.

	G	AB	H	2B	3B	HR	HR %	R	RBI	BB	SO	SB	BA	SA	PH AB	PH H	G by POS
1949 NY A	128	447	123	21	5	2	0.4	54	42	63	44	8	.275	.358	1	1	2B-122, SS-4
1950	153	522	150	19	6	6	1.1	69	69	67	38	3	.287	.381	1	0	2B-152, SS-6
1951	121	362	90	11	2	3	0.8	48	43	31	36	6	.249	.315	1	0	2B-102, SS-18
1952	11	42	17	2	1	0	0.0	6	4	5	4	0	.405	.500	0	0	2B-11
1953	8	10	2	0	0	0	0.0	1	0	0	2	0	.200	.200	0	0	2B-7, SS-1
1954	107	300	65	7	1	3	1.0	39	21	26	29	3	.217	.277	0	0	2B-79, SS-30, 3B-1
1955	43	96	22	5	0	0	0.0	12	8	11	11	0	.229	.281	1	0	SS-29, 2B-13, 3B-1
1956	80	183	47	5	1	0	0.0	15	18	12	33	1	.257	.295	2	0	2B-41, SS-24, 3B-18
1957	72	157	42	7	2	2	1.3	23	12	20	21	1	.268	.376	4	1	2B-45, 3B-21, SS-4
9 yrs.	723	2119	558	77	18	16	0.8	267	217	235	218	22	.263	.339	10	2	2B-572, SS-116, 3B-41
WORLD SERIES																	
1949 NY A	5	20	5	3	0	0	0.0	0	4	0	4	0	.250	.400	0	0	2B-5
1950	4	14	4	1	0	0	0.0	2	3	2	0	0	.286	.357	0	0	2B-4
1951	5	8	2	0	0	0	0.0	2	0	1	2	0	.250	.250	0	0	2B-5
1955	3	3	0	0	0	0	0.0	0	0	0	1	0	.000	.000	0	0	SS-3
1956	2	2	0	0	0	0	0.0	0	0	0	0	0	.000	.000	0	0	2B-2
1957	7	22	8	2	0	0	0.0	2	2	3	1	0	.364	.455	0	0	2B-7
6 yrs.	26	69	19	6	0	0	0.0	6	9	6	8	0	.275	.362	0	0	2B-23, SS-3

John Coleman

COLEMAN, JOHN FRANCIS
B. Mar. 6, 1863, Saratoga Springs, N. Y.
D. May 31, 1922, Detroit, Mich.
BL TR 5'9½" 165 lbs.
BB 1887

	G	AB	H	2B	3B	HR	HR %	R	RBI	BB	SO	SB	BA	SA	PH AB	PH H	G by POS
1883 PHI N	90	354	83	12	8	0	0.0	33		15	39		.234	.314	0	0	P-65, OF-31, 2B-1
1884 2 teams		PHI	N (43G –	.246)		PHI	AA (28G –	.206)									
" total	71	278	64	9	5	2	0.7	32		13	20		.230	.320	0	0	OF-51, P-24, 1B-4
1885 PHI N	96	398	119	15	12	2	0.5	71		25			.299	.412	0	0	OF-93, P-8
1886 2 teams		PHI	AA (121G –	.246)		PIT	AA (11G –	.349)									
" total	132	535	136	20	17	0	0.0	70		35			.254	.355	0	0	OF-126, 1B-6, P-3, 2B-1
1887 PIT N	115	475	139	21	11	2	0.4	75	54	31	40	25	.293	.396	0	0	OF-115, 1B-2
1888	116	438	101	11	4	0	0.0	49	26	29	52	15	.231	.274	0	0	OF-91, 1B-25
1889 PHI AA	6	19	1	0	0	0	0.0	1	1	1	3	1	.053	.053	0	0	P-5, OF-1
1890 PIT N	3	11	2	0	0	0	0.0	1	0	3		1	.182	.182	0	0	OF-2, P-2
8 yrs.	629	2508	645	88	57	6	0.2	332	80	152	154	42	.257	.345	0	0	OF-510, P-107, 1B-37, 2B-2

Ray Coleman

COLEMAN, RAYMOND LeROY
B. June 4, 1922, Dunsmuir, Calif.
BL TR 5'11"   170 lbs.

	G	AB	H	2B	3B	HR	HR %	R	RBI	BB	SO	SB	BA	SA	PH AB	PH H	G by POS
1947 STL A	110	343	89	9	7	2	0.6	34	30	26	32	2	.259	.344	18	3	OF-93
1948 2 teams		STL	A (17G –	.172)		PHI	A (68G –	.243)									
" total	85	239	56	6	7	0	0.0	34	23	33	22	5	.234	.318	24	2	OF-58
1950 STL A	117	384	104	25	6	8	2.1	54	55	32	37	7	.271	.430	17	6	OF-98
1951 2 teams		STL	A (91G –	.282)		CHI	A (51G –	.276)									
" total	142	522	146	24	12	8	1.5	62	76	39	46	5	.280	.418	6	2	OF-138
1952 2 teams		CHI	A (85G –	.215)		STL	A (20G –	.196)									
" total	105	241	51	10	1	2	0.8	24	15	18	21	0	.212	.286	16	1	OF-89
5 yrs.	559	1729	446	74	33	20	1.2	208	199	148	158	19	.258	.374	81	14	OF-476

Cad Coles

COLES, CADWALLADER R.
B. Jan. 17, 1889, Rock Hill, S. C.   D. June 30, 1942, At Sea Near Miami, Fla.
BL TR 6'½" 174 lbs.

	G	AB	H	2B	3B	HR	HR %	R	RBI	BB	SO	SB	BA	SA	PH AB	PH H	G by POS
1914 KC F	78	194	49	7	3	1	0.5	17	25	5		6	.253	.335	34	7	OF-39, 1B-3

Chuck Coles

COLES, CHARLES EDWARD
B. June 27, 1931, Fredericktown, Pa.
BL TL 5'9"   180 lbs.

	G	AB	H	2B	3B	HR	HR %	R	RBI	BB	SO	SB	BA	SA	PH AB	PH H	G by POS
1958 CIN N	5	11	2	1	0	0	0.0	2	2	2	6	0	.182	.273	1	0	OF-4

Darnell Coles

COLES, DARNELL
B. June 2, 1962, San Bernardino, Calif.
BR TR 6'2"   175 lbs.

	G	AB	H	2B	3B	HR	HR %	R	RBI	BB	SO	SB	BA	SA	PH AB	PH H	G by POS
1983 SEA A	27	92	26	7	0	1	1.1	9	6	7	12	0	.283	.391	1	0	3B-26
1984	48	143	23	3	1	0	0.0	15	6	17	26	2	.161	.196	0	0	3B-42, DH-3, OF-3
2 yrs.	75	235	49	10	1	1	0.4	24	12	24	38	2	.209	.272	1	0	3B-68, DH-3, OF-3

Chris Coletta

COLETTA, CHRISTOPHER MICHAEL
B. Aug. 2, 1944, Brooklyn, N. Y.
BL TL 5'11"   190 lbs.

	G	AB	H	2B	3B	HR	HR %	R	RBI	BB	SO	SB	BA	SA	PH AB	PH H	G by POS
1972 CAL A	14	30	9	1	0	1	3.3	5	7	1	4	0	.300	.433	8	3	OF-7

Bill Colgan

COLGAN, WILLIAM H.
B. East St. Louis, Ill.   D. Aug. 13, 1895, Great Falls, Mont.

	G	AB	H	2B	3B	HR	HR %	R	RBI	BB	SO	SB	BA	SA	PH AB	PH H	G by POS
1884 PIT AA	48	161	25	4	1	0	0.0	10		3			.155	.193	0	0	C-44, OF-4

	G	AB	H	2B	3B	HR	HR %	R	RBI	BB	SO	SB	BA	SA	Pinch Hit AB	Pinch Hit H	G by POS

Bill Coliver

COLIVER, WILLIAM J.
B. 1867, Detroit, Mich.   D. Mar. 24, 1888, Detroit, Mich.

	G	AB	H	2B	3B	HR	HR%	R	RBI	BB	SO	SB	BA	SA	AB	H	G by POS
1885 BOS N	1	4	0	0	0	0	0.0	0	0	0	1		.000	.000	0	0	OF-1

Bill Collins

COLLINS, WILLIAM J.   BR
B. 1867, Dublin, Ireland   D. June 8, 1893, Brooklyn, N. Y.

	G	AB	H	2B	3B	HR	HR%	R	RBI	BB	SO	SB	BA	SA	AB	H	G by POS
1889 PHI AA	1	4	1	0	0	0	0.0	0	1	1	0	1	.250	.250	0	0	C-1
1890	1	1	0	0	0	0	0.0	0		0	0	0	.000	.000	0	0	SS-1
1891 CLE N	2	3	0	0	0	0	0.0	0	0	0	0	0	.000	.000	0	0	OF-1, C-1
3 yrs.	4	8	1	0	0	0	0.0	0		1	0	1	.125	.125	0	0	C-2, OF-1, SS-1

Bill Collins

COLLINS, WILLIAM SHIRLEY   BR TR
B. Mar. 27, 1882, Chestertown, Ind.   D. June 26, 1961, San Bernardino, Calif.

	G	AB	H	2B	3B	HR	HR%	R	RBI	BB	SO	SB	BA	SA	AB	H	G by POS
1910 BOS N	151	584	141	6	7	3	0.5	67	40	43	48	36	.241	.291	0	0	OF-151
1911 2 teams		BOS	N (17G – .136)			CHI	N (7G – .200)										
" total	24	49	7	2	1	0	0.0	10	8	2	11	4	.143	.224	1	1	OF-17, 3B-1
1913 BKN N	32	95	18	1	0	0	0.0	8	4	8	11	2	.189	.200	4	0	OF-27
1914 BUF F	21	47	7	2	2	0	0.0	6	2	1		0	.149	.277	4	0	OF-15
4 yrs.	228	775	173	11	10	3	0.4	91	54	54	70	42	.223	.275	9	1	OF-210, 3B-1

Bob Collins

COLLINS, ROBERT JOSEPH   BR TR 5'11" 176 lbs.
B. Sept. 18, 1909, Pittsburgh, Pa.   D. Apr. 19, 1969, Pittsburgh, Pa.

	G	AB	H	2B	3B	HR	HR%	R	RBI	BB	SO	SB	BA	SA	AB	H	G by POS
1940 CHI N	47	120	25	3	0	1	0.8	11	14	14	18	4	.208	.258	4	1	C-42
1944 NY A	3	3	1	0	0	0	0.0	0	0	1	0	0	.333	.333	0	0	C-3
2 yrs.	50	123	26	3	0	1	0.8	11	14	15	18	4	.211	.260	4	1	C-45

Chub Collins

COLLINS, CHARLES
B. 1862, Dundas, Ont., Canada   D. May 21, 1914, Dundas, Ont., Canada

	G	AB	H	2B	3B	HR	HR%	R	RBI	BB	SO	SB	BA	SA	AB	H	G by POS
1884 2 teams		BUF	N (45G – .178)			IND	AA (38G – .225)										
" total	83	307	61	9	1	0	0.0	42		23	36		.199	.235	0	0	2B-80, SS-3
1885 DET N	14	55	10	0	2	0	0.0	8	6	0	11		.182	.255	0	0	SS-14
2 yrs.	97	362	71	9	3	0	0.0	50	5	23	47		.196	.238	0	0	2B-80, SS-17

Cyril Collins

COLLINS, CYRIL WILSON   BR TR 5'9½" 165 lbs.
B. May 7, 1889, Pulaski, Tenn.   D. Feb. 28, 1941, Knoxville, Tenn.

	G	AB	H	2B	3B	HR	HR%	R	RBI	BB	SO	SB	BA	SA	AB	H	G by POS
1913 BOS N	16	3	1	0	0	0	0.0	3	0	0	1	0	.333	.333	0	0	OF-9
1914	27	35	9	0	0	0	0.0	5	1	2	8	0	.257	.257	1	0	OF-19
2 yrs.	43	38	10	0	0	0	0.0	8	1	2	9	0	.263	.263	1	0	OF-28

Dan Collins

COLLINS, DANIEL THOMAS
B. July 12, 1854   D. Sept. 21, 1883, New Orleans, La.

	G	AB	H	2B	3B	HR	HR%	R	RBI	BB	SO	SB	BA	SA	AB	H	G by POS
1876 LOU N	7	28	4	1	0	0	0.0	3	9	0	2		.143	.179	0	0	OF-7

Dave Collins

COLLINS, DAVID S.   BB TL 5'10" 175 lbs.
B. Oct. 20, 1952, Rapid City, S. D.

	G	AB	H	2B	3B	HR	HR%	R	RBI	BB	SO	SB	BA	SA	AB	H	G by POS
1975 CAL A	93	319	85	13	4	3	0.9	41	29	36	55	24	.266	.361	5	4	OF-75, DH-12
1976	99	365	96	12	1	4	1.1	45	28	40	55	32	.263	.334	2	0	OF-71, DH-22
1977 SEA A	120	402	96	9	3	5	1.2	46	28	33	66	25	.239	.313	7	4	OF-73, DH-40
1978 CIN N	102	102	22	1	0	0	0.0	13	7	15	18	7	.216	.225	64	14	OF-24
1979	122	396	126	16	4	3	0.8	59	35	27	48	16	.318	.402	28	9	OF-91, 1B-10
1980	144	551	167	20	4	3	0.5	94	35	53	68	79	.303	.370	3	1	OF-141
1981	95	360	98	18	6	3	0.8	63	23	41	41	26	.272	.381	1	0	OF-94
1982 NY A	111	348	88	12	3	3	0.9	41	25	28	49	13	.253	.330	7	1	OF-60, 1B-52, DH-1
1983 TOR A	118	402	109	12	4	1	0.2	55	34	43	67	31	.271	.328	18	5	OF-112, 1B-5, DH-4
1984	128	441	136	24	15	2	0.5	59	44	33	41	60	.308	.444	14	6	OF-108, 1B-6, DH-4
10 yrs.	1132	3686	1023	137	44	27	0.7	516	288	349	508	313	.278	.361	149	44	OF-849, DH-80, 1B-73
LEAGUE CHAMPIONSHIP SERIES																	
1979 CIN N	3	14	5	1	0	0	0.0	0	1	0	2	2	.357	.429	0	0	OF-3

Eddie Collins

COLLINS, EDWARD TROWBRIDGE, SR. (Cocky)   BL TR 5'9" 175 lbs.
Played as Eddie Sullivan 1906.   Father of Eddie Collins.
B. May 2, 1887, Millerton, N. Y.   D. Mar. 25, 1951, Boston, Mass.
Manager 1925-26.
Hall of Fame 1939.

	G	AB	H	2B	3B	HR	HR%	R	RBI	BB	SO	SB	BA	SA	AB	H	G by POS
1906 PHI A	6	17	4	0	0	0	0.0	1	0	0		1	.235	.235	1	0	SS-3, 3B-1, 2B-1
1907	14	20	5	0	1	0	0.0	0	2	0		0	.250	.350	6	1	SS-6
1908	102	330	90	18	7	1	0.3	39	40	16		8	.273	.379	11	4	2B-47, SS-28, OF-10
1909	153	572	198	30	10	3	0.5	104	56	62		67	.346	.449	0	0	2B-152, SS-1
1910	153	583	188	16	15	3	0.5	81	81	49		81	.322	.417	0	0	2B-153
1911	132	493	180	22	13	3	0.6	92	73	62		38	.365	.481	0	0	2B-132
1912	153	543	189	25	11	0	0.0	137	64	101		63	.348	.435	0	0	2B-153
1913	148	534	184	23	13	3	0.6	125	73	85	37	55	.345	.453	0	0	2B-148
1914	152	526	181	23	14	2	0.4	122	85	97	31	58	.344	.452	0	0	2B-152
1915 CHI A	155	521	173	22	10	4	0.8	118	77	119	27	46	.332	.436	0	0	2B-155
1916	155	545	168	14	17	0	0.0	87	52	86	36	40	.308	.396	0	0	2B-155
1917	156	564	163	18	12	0	0.0	91	67	89	16	53	.289	.363	0	0	2B-156
1918	97	330	91	8	2	2	0.6	51	30	73	13	22	.276	.330	1	1	2B-96
1919	140	518	165	19	7	4	0.8	87	80	68	27	33	.319	.405	0	0	2B-140
1920	153	601	222	37	13	3	0.5	115	75	69	19	19	.369	.489	0	0	2B-153
1921	139	526	177	20	10	2	0.4	79	58	66	11	12	.337	.424	3	0	2B-136
1922	154	598	194	20	12	1	0.2	92	69	73	16	20	.324	.403	0	0	2B-154
1923	145	505	182	22	5	5	1.0	89	67	84	8	47	.360	.453	3	0	2B-142
1924	152	556	194	27	7	6	1.1	108	86	89	16	42	.349	.455	2	0	2B-150
1925	118	425	147	26	3	3	0.7	80	80	87	8	19	.346	.442	2	0	2B-116
1926	106	375	129	32	4	1	0.3	66	62	62	8	13	.344	.459	3	0	2B-101

	G	AB	H	2B	3B	HR	HR %	R	RBI	BB	SO	SB	BA	SA	Pinch Hit AB	Pinch Hit H	G by POS

Eddie Collins continued

	G	AB	H	2B	3B	HR	HR%	R	RBI	BB	SO	SB	BA	SA	AB	H	G by POS
1927 PHI A	95	225	76	12	1	1	0.4	50	15	60	9	6	.338	.413	34	12	2B-56, SS-1
1928	36	33	10	3	0	0	0.0	3	7	4	4	0	.303	.394	29	8	2B-2, SS-1
1929	9	7	0	0	0	0	0.0	0	0	2	0	0	.000	.000	7	0	
1930	3	2	1	0	0	0	0.0	1	0	0	0	0	.500	.500	2	1	
25 yrs.	2826	9949	3311	437	187	47	0.5	1818	1299	1503	286	743	.333	.428	104	27	2B-2650, SS-40, OF-10, 3B-1
		10th		8th								3rd					

WORLD SERIES																	
1910 PHI A	5	21	9	4	0	0	0.0	5	3	2	0	4	.429	.619	0	0	2B-5
1911	6	21	6	1	0	0	0.0	4	1	2	2	2	.286	.333	0	0	2B-6
1913	5	19	8	0	2	0	0.0	5	3	1	2	3	.421	.632	0	0	2B-5
1914	4	14	3	0	0	0	0.0	0	1	2	1	1	.214	.214	0	0	2B-4
1917 CHI A	6	22	9	1	0	0	0.0	4	2	2	3	3	.409	.455	0	0	2B-6
1919	8	31	7	1	0	0	0.0	2	1	1	2	1	.226	.258	0	0	2B-8
6 yrs.	34	128	42	7	2	0	0.0	20	11	10	10	14	.328	.414	0	0	2B-34
		10th	8th									1st					

Eddie Collins

COLLINS, EDWARD TROWBRIDGE, JR.
Son of Eddie Collins.
B. Nov. 23, 1916, Lansdowne, Pa.   BL TR 5'10" 175 lbs.

	G	AB	H	2B	3B	HR	HR%	R	RBI	BB	SO	SB	BA	SA	AB	H	G by POS
1939 PHI A	32	21	5	1	0	0	0.0	6	0	6	0	3	.238	.286	10	3	OF-6, 2B-1
1941	80	219	53	6	3	0	0.0	29	12	20	24	2	.242	.297	28	6	OF-50
1942	20	34	8	2	0	0	0.0	6	4	4	2	1	.235	.294	5	1	OF-9
3 yrs.	132	274	66	9	3	0	0.0	41	16	24	29	4	.241	.296	43	10	OF-65, 2B-1

Hub Collins

COLLINS, GEORGE HUBBERT
B. Apr. 15, 1864, Louisville, Ky.   D. May 21, 1892, Brooklyn, N. Y.   BR TR

	G	AB	H	2B	3B	HR	HR%	R	RBI	BB	SO	SB	BA	SA	AB	H	G by POS
1886 LOU AA	27	101	29	3	2	0	0.0	12		5			.287	.356	0	0	OF-24, 3B-2, SS-1, 2B-1, 1B-1
1887	130	559	162	22	8	1	0.2	122		39		71	.290	.363	0	0	OF-109, 2B-10, 1B-8, SS-4, 3B-1
1888 2 teams		LOU	AA (116G – .307)			BKN	AA (12G – .310)										
" total	128	527	162	31	12	2	0.4	133	53	50		71	.307	.423	0	0	OF-82, 2B-31, SS-15
1889 BKN AA	138	560	149	18	3	2	0.4	139	73	80	41	65	.266	.320	0	0	2B-138
1890 BKN N	129	510	142	32	7	3	0.6	148	69	85	47	85	.278	.386	0	0	2B-129
1891	107	435	120	16	5	3	0.7	82	31	59	63	32	.276	.356	0	0	2B-72, OF-35
1892	21	87	26	5	1	0	0.0	17	17	14	13	4	.299	.379	0	0	OF-21
7 yrs.	680	2779	790	127	38	11	0.4	653	242	332	164	328	.284	.369	0	0	2B-381, OF-271, SS-20, 1B-9, 3B-3

Hugh Collins

COLLINS, HUGH

	G	AB	H	2B	3B	HR	HR%	R	RBI	BB	SO	SB	BA	SA	AB	H	G by POS
1887 NY AA	1	4	1	0	0	0	0.0	0		0		0	.250	.250	0	0	C-1

Jimmy Collins

COLLINS, JAMES JOSEPH
B. Jan. 16, 1870, Buffalo, N. Y.   D. Mar. 6, 1943, Buffalo, N. Y.   BR TR 5'7½" 160 lbs.
Manager 1901-06.
Hall of Fame 1945.

	G	AB	H	2B	3B	HR	HR%	R	RBI	BB	SO	SB	BA	SA	AB	H	G by POS
1895 2 teams		BOS	N (11G – .211)			LOU	N (96G – .279)										
" total	107	411	112	20	5	7	1.7	75	57	37	20	12	.273	.397	0	0	3B-77, OF-28, 2B-2, SS-1
1896 BOS N	84	304	90	10	9	1	0.3	48	46	30	12	10	.296	.398	0	0	3B-80, SS-4
1897	134	529	183	28	13	6	1.1	103	132	41		14	.346	.482	0	0	3B-134
1898	152	597	196	35	5	15	2.5	107	111	40		12	.328	.479	0	0	3B-152
1899	151	599	166	28	11	4	0.7	98	91	40		12	.277	.381	0	0	3B-151
1900	142	586	178	25	5	6	1.0	104	95	34		23	.304	.394	0	0	3B-141, SS-1
1901 BOS A	138	564	187	42	16	6	1.1	109	94	34		19	.332	.495	0	0	3B-138
1902	108	429	138	21	10	6	1.4	71	61	24		18	.322	.459	0	0	3B-107
1903	130	540	160	33	17	5	0.9	87	72	24		23	.296	.448	0	0	3B-130
1904	156	631	168	33	13	3	0.5	85	67	27		19	.266	.374	0	0	3B-156
1905	131	508	140	25	5	4	0.8	66	65	37		18	.276	.368	0	0	3B-131
1906	37	142	39	8	4	1	0.7	17	16	4		1	.275	.408	5		3B-32
1907 2 teams		BOS	A (41G – .291)			PHI	A (102G – .274)										
" total	143	523	146	30	0	0	0.0	51	45	34		8	.279	.337	2	0	3B-141
1908 PHI A	115	433	94	13	3	0	0.0	34	30	20		5	.217	.263	0	0	3B-115
14 yrs.	1728	6796	1997	352	116	64	0.9	1055	982	426	32	194	.294	.408	7	1	3B-1685, OF-28, SS-6, 2B-2

WORLD SERIES																	
1903 BOS A	8	36	9	1	2	0	0.0	5	1	1	1	3	.250	.389	0	0	3B-8

Joe Collins

COLLINS, JOSEPH EDWARD
Born Joseph Edward Kollonige.
B. Dec. 3, 1922, Scranton, Pa.   BL TL 6' 185 lbs.

	G	AB	H	2B	3B	HR	HR%	R	RBI	BB	SO	SB	BA	SA	AB	H	G by POS
1948 NY A	5	5	1	1	0	0	0.0	0	2	0	1	0	.200	.400	5	1	
1949	7	10	1	0	0	0	0.0	2	4	6	2	0	.100	.100	0	0	1B-5
1950	108	205	48	8	3	8	3.9	47	28	31	34	5	.234	.420	4	0	1B-99, OF-2
1951	125	262	75	8	5	9	3.4	52	48	34	23	9	.286	.458	5	1	1B-114, OF-15
1952	122	428	120	16	8	18	4.2	69	59	55	47	4	.280	.481	1	0	1B-119
1953	127	387	104	11	2	17	4.4	72	44	59	36	2	.269	.439	11	2	1B-113, OF-4
1954	130	343	93	20	2	12	3.5	67	46	51	37	2	.271	.446	23	4	1B-117
1955	105	278	65	9	1	13	4.7	40	45	44	32	0	.234	.414	13	5	1B-73, OF-27
1956	100	262	59	5	3	7	2.7	38	43	34	33	3	.225	.347	16	4	OF-51, 1B-43
1957	79	149	30	1	0	2	1.3	17	10	24	18	2	.201	.248	32	6	1B-32, OF-15
10 yrs.	908	2329	596	79	24	86	3.7	404	329	338	263	27	.256	.421	110	21	1B-715, OF-114

WORLD SERIES																	
1950 NY A	1	0	0	0	0	0	–	0	0	0	0	0	–	–	0	0	1B-1
1951	6	18	4	0	0	1	5.6	2	3	2	1	0	.222	.389	0	0	1B-6

	G	AB	H	2B	3B	HR	HR %	R	RBI	BB	SO	SB	BA	SA	Pinch Hit AB	Pinch Hit H	G by POS

Joe Collins continued

	G	AB	H	2B	3B	HR	HR%	R	RBI	BB	SO	SB	BA	SA	PH AB	PH H	G by POS
1952	6	12	0	0	0	0	0.0	1	0	1	3	0	.000	.000	0	0	1B-6
1953	6	24	4	1	0	1	4.2	4	2	3	8	0	.167	.333	0	0	1B-6
1955	5	12	2	0	0	2	16.7	6	3	6	4	1	.167	.667	0	0	1B-5
1956	6	21	5	2	0	0	0.0	2	2	2	3	0	.238	.333	1	0	1B-5
1957	6	5	0	0	0	0	0.0	0	0	0	3	0	.000	.000	1	0	1B-5
7 yrs.	36	92	15	3	0	4	4.3	15	10	14	22	1	.163	.326	2	0	1B-34

Kevin Collins

COLLINS, KEVIN MICHAEL (Casey)   BL TR 6'1"   180 lbs.
B. Aug. 4, 1946, Springfield, Mass.

	G	AB	H	2B	3B	HR	HR%	R	RBI	BB	SO	SB	BA	SA	PH AB	PH H	G by POS
1965 NY N	11	23	4	1	0	0	0.0	3	0	1	9	0	.174	.217	3	1	3B-7, SS-3
1967	4	10	1	0	0	0	0.0	1	0	0	3	1	.100	.100	2	0	2B-2
1968	58	154	31	5	2	1	0.6	12	13	7	37	0	.201	.279	14	0	3B-40, 2B-6, SS-1
1969 2 teams	NY	N (16G – .150)		MON	N (52G – .240)												
" total	68	136	29	8	1	3	2.2	6	14	11	26	0	.213	.353	30	9	3B-30, 2B-20
1970 DET A	25	24	5	1	0	1	4.2	2	3	1	10	0	.208	.375	21	4	1B-1
1971	35	41	11	2	1	1	2.4	6	4	0	12	0	.268	.439	31	9	3B-4, OF-2, 2B-1
6 yrs.	201	388	81	17	4	6	1.5	30	34	20	97	1	.209	.320	101	23	3B-81, 2B-29, SS-4, OF-2, 1B-1

Orth Collins

COLLINS, ORTH STEIN (Buck)   BL TR 6'   150 lbs.
B. Apr. 27, 1880, Lafayette, Ind.   D. Dec. 13, 1949, Fort Lauderdale, Fla.

	G	AB	H	2B	3B	HR	HR%	R	RBI	BB	SO	SB	BA	SA	PH AB	PH H	G by POS
1904 NY N	5	17	6	1	1	0	0.0	3	1	1		0	.353	.529	0	0	OF-5
1909 WAS A	8	7	0	0	0	0	0.0	0	0	0		0	.000	.000	5	0	OF-2, P-1
2 yrs.	13	24	6	1	1	0	0.0	3	1	1		0	.250	.375	5	0	OF-7, P-1

Pat Collins

COLLINS, THARON LESLIE   BR TR 5'11½" 178 lbs.
B. Sept. 13, 1896, Sweet Springs, Mo.   D. May 20, 1960, Kansas City, Kans.

	G	AB	H	2B	3B	HR	HR%	R	RBI	BB	SO	SB	BA	SA	PH AB	PH H	G by POS
1919 STL A	10	20	3	1	0	0	0.0	2	1	4	2	0	.150	.200	4	0	C-5
1920	23	28	6	1	0	0	0.0	5	6	3	5	0	.214	.250	13	0	C-7
1921	58	111	27	3	0	1	0.9	9	10	16	17	1	.243	.297	22	7	C-31
1922	63	127	39	6	0	8	6.3	14	23	21	21	0	.307	.543	22	5	C-27, 1B-5
1923	85	181	32	8	0	3	1.7	9	30	15	45	0	.177	.271	32	6	C-47
1924	31	53	16	2	0	1	1.9	9	11	11	14	0	.302	.396	8	0	C-20
1926 NY A	102	290	83	11	3	7	2.4	41	35	73	55	3	.286	.417	1	0	C-100
1927	92	251	69	9	3	7	2.8	38	36	54	24	0	.275	.418	1	1	C-89
1928	70	136	30	5	0	6	4.4	18	14	35	16	0	.221	.390	0	0	C-70
1929 BOS N	7	5	0	0	0	0	0.0	1	2	3	1	0	.000	.000	1	0	C-6
10 yrs.	541	1202	305	46	6	33	2.7	146	168	235	200	4	.254	.384	104	19	C-402, 1B-5

WORLD SERIES

	G	AB	H	2B	3B	HR	HR%	R	RBI	BB	SO	SB	BA	SA	PH AB	PH H	G by POS
1926 NY A	3	2	0	0	0	0	0.0	0	0	0	1	0	.000	.000	0	0	C-3
1927	2	5	3	1	0	0	0.0	0	0	3	0	0	.600	.800	0	0	C-2
1928	1	1	1	1	0	0	0.0	0	0	0	0	0	1.000	2.000	0	0	C-1
3 yrs.	6	8	4	2	0	0	0.0	0	0	3	1	0	.500	.750	0	0	C-6

Ripper Collins

COLLINS, JAMES ANTHONY   BB TL 5'9"   165 lbs.
B. Mar. 30, 1904, Altoona, Pa.   D. Apr. 16, 1970, New Haven, N. Y.

	G	AB	H	2B	3B	HR	HR%	R	RBI	BB	SO	SB	BA	SA	PH AB	PH H	G by POS
1931 STL N	89	279	84	20	10	4	1.4	34	59	18	24	1	.301	.487	16	2	1B-68, OF-3
1932	149	549	153	28	8	21	3.8	82	91	38	67	4	.279	.474	8	2	1B-81, OF-60
1933	132	493	153	26	7	10	2.0	66	68	38	49	7	.310	.452	8	3	1B-123
1934	154	600	200	40	12	35	5.8	116	128	57	50	2	.333	.615	0	0	1B-154
1935	150	578	181	36	10	23	4.0	109	122	65	45	0	.313	.529	0	0	1B-150
1936	103	277	81	15	3	13	4.7	48	48	48	30	1	.292	.509	26	8	1B-61, OF-9
1937 CHI N	115	456	125	16	5	16	3.5	77	71	32	46	2	.274	.436	4	0	1B-111
1938	143	490	131	22	8	13	2.7	78	61	54	48	1	.267	.424	7	0	1B-135
1941 PIT N	49	62	13	2	2	0	0.0	5	11	6	14	0	.210	.306	32	4	1B-11, OF-3
9 yrs.	1084	3784	1121	205	65	135	3.6	615	659	356	373	18	.296	.492	101	19	1B-894, OF-75

WORLD SERIES

	G	AB	H	2B	3B	HR	HR%	R	RBI	BB	SO	SB	BA	SA	PH AB	PH H	G by POS
1931 STL N	2	2	0	0	0	0	0.0	0	0	0	1	0	.000	.000	2	0	
1934	7	30	11	1	0	0	0.0	4	4	1	2	0	.367	.400	0	0	1B-7
1938 CHI N	4	15	2	0	0	0	0.0	1	0	0	3	0	.133	.133	0	0	1B-4
3 yrs.	13	47	13	1	0	0	0.0	5	4	1	6	0	.277	.298	2	0	1B-11

Shano Collins

COLLINS, JOHN FRANCIS   BR TR 6'   185 lbs.
B. Dec. 4, 1885, Charlestown, Mass.   D. Sept. 10, 1955, Newton, Mass.
Manager 1931-32.

	G	AB	H	2B	3B	HR	HR%	R	RBI	BB	SO	SB	BA	SA	PH AB	PH H	G by POS
1910 CHI A	97	315	62	10	8	1	0.3	29	24	25		10	.197	.289	4	1	OF-65, 1B-27
1911	106	370	97	16	12	4	1.1	48	48	20		14	.262	.403	3	0	1B-97, OF-3, 2B-3
1912	153	575	168	34	10	2	0.3	75	81	29		26	.292	.397	2	0	OF-105, 1B-46
1913	148	535	128	26	9	1	0.2	53	47	32	60	22	.239	.327	1	1	OF-147
1914	154	598	164	34	9	3	0.5	61	65	27	49	30	.274	.376	0	0	OF-154
1915	153	576	148	24	17	2	0.3	73	85	28	50	38	.257	.368	2	0	OF-104, 1B-47
1916	143	527	128	28	12	0	0.0	74	42	59	51	16	.243	.342	3	0	OF-136, 1B-4
1917	82	252	59	13	3	1	0.4	38	14	10	27	14	.234	.321	8	2	OF-73
1918	103	365	100	18	11	1	0.3	30	56	17	19	7	.274	.392	5	1	OF-92, 1B-5, 2B-1
1919	63	179	50	6	3	1	0.6	21	16	7	11	3	.279	.363	9	2	OF-46, 1B-8
1920	133	495	150	21	9	1	0.2	70	63	23	24	12	.303	.392	4	0	1B-117, OF-12
1921 BOS A	141	542	155	29	12	4	0.7	63	65	18	38	15	.286	.406	0	0	OF-138, 1B-3
1922	135	472	128	24	7	1	0.2	33	52	7	16	7	.271	.358	16	5	OF-117, 1B-1
1923	97	342	79	10	5	0	0.0	41	18	11	29	7	.231	.289	6	1	OF-89
1924	88	240	70	16	6	0	0.0	36	28	18	17	4	.292	.400	20	7	OF-55, 1B-12
1925	2	3	1	0	0	0	0.0	0	1	0	0	0	.333	.333	1	0	OF-1
16 yrs.	1798	6386	1687	309	133	22	0.3	746	705	331	391	225	.264	.365	84	20	OF-1337, 1B-367, 2B-4

WORLD SERIES

	G	AB	H	2B	3B	HR	HR%	R	RBI	BB	SO	SB	BA	SA	PH AB	PH H	G by POS
1917 CHI A	6	21	6	1	0	0	0.0	2	0	1	2	0	.286	.333	0	0	OF-6

	G	AB	H	2B	3B	HR	HR %	R	RBI	BB	SO	SB	BA	SA	Pinch Hit AB	Pinch Hit H	G by POS

Shano Collins continued

1919	4	16	4	1	0	0	0.0	2	0	0	0	0	.250	.313	0	0	OF-4
2 yrs.	10	37	10	2	0	0	0.0	4	0	0	2	0	.270	.324	0	0	OF-10

Zip Collins

COLLINS, JOHN EDGAR   BL TL 5'11"   152 lbs.
B. May 2, 1892, Brooklyn, N. Y.   D. Dec. 19, 1983, Manassas, Va.

1914 PIT N	49	182	44	2	0	0	0.0	14	15	8	10	3	.242	.253	0	0	OF-49
1915 2 teams	PIT	N (106G –	.294)		BOS	N (5G –	.286)										
" total	111	368	108	9	6	1	0.3	54	23	26	39	7	.293	.359	11	2	OF-106
1916 BOS N	93	268	56	1	6	1	0.4	39	18	18	42	4	.209	.269	11	1	OF-78
1917	9	27	4	0	1	0	0.0	3	2	0	4	0	.148	.222	4	2	OF-5
1921 PHI A	24	71	20	5	1	0	0.0	14	5	6	5	1	.282	.380	3	1	OF-20
5 yrs.	286	916	232	17	14	2	0.2	124	63	58	100	15	.253	.309	29	6	OF-258

Frank Colman

COLMAN, FRANK LLOYD   BL TL 5'11"   186 lbs.
B. Mar. 2, 1918, London, Ont., Canada   D. Feb. 19, 1983, London, Ont., Canada

1942 PIT N	10	37	5	0	0	1	2.7	2	2	2	2	0	.135	.216	2	0	OF-8
1943	32	59	16	2	2	0	0.0	9	4	8	7	0	.271	.373	17	4	OF-11
1944	99	226	61	9	5	6	2.7	30	53	25	27	0	.270	.434	39	11	OF-53, 1B-6
1945	77	153	32	11	1	4	2.6	18	30	9	16	0	.209	.373	42	5	1B-22, OF-12
1946 2 teams	PIT	N (26G –	.170)		NY	A (5G –	.267)										
" total	31	68	13	3	0	2	2.9	5	11	3	8	0	.191	.324	13	2	OF-13, 1B-2
1947 NY A	22	28	3	0	0	2	7.1	2	6	2	6	0	.107	.321	14	3	OF-6
6 yrs.	271	571	130	25	8	15	2.6	66	106	49	66	0	.228	.378	127	25	OF-103, 1B-30

Bob Coluccio

COLUCCIO, ROBERT PASQUALI   BR TR 5'11"   183 lbs.
B. Oct. 2, 1951, Centralia, Wash.

1973 MIL A	124	438	98	21	8	15	3.4	64	58	54	92	13	.224	.411	5	0	OF-108, DH-11
1974	138	394	88	13	4	6	1.5	42	31	43	61	15	.223	.322	2	0	OF-131, DH-2
1975 2 teams	MIL	A (22G –	.194)		CHI	A (61G –	.205)										
" total	83	223	45	4	3	5	2.2	30	18	24	45	5	.202	.314	4	0	OF-81, DH-1
1977 CHI A	20	37	10	0	0	0	0.0	4	7	6	2	0	.270	.270	0	0	OF-19
1978 STL N	5	3	0	0	0	0	0.0	0	0	1	2	0	.000	.000	3	0	OF-2
5 yrs.	370	1095	241	38	15	26	2.4	140	114	128	202	33	.220	.353	14	0	OF-341, DH-14

Earle Combs

COMBS, EARLE BRYAN (The Kentucky Colonel)   BL TR 6'   185 lbs.
B. May 14, 1899, Pebworth, Ky.   D. July 21, 1976, Richmond, Ky.
Hall of Fame 1970.

1924 NY A	24	35	14	5	0	0	0.0	10	2	4	2	0	.400	.543	8	5	OF-11
1925	150	593	203	36	13	3	0.5	117	61	65	43	12	.342	.462	0	0	OF-150
1926	145	606	181	31	12	8	1.3	113	56	47	23	8	.299	.429	0	0	OF-145
1927	152	648	231	36	23	6	0.9	137	64	62	31	15	.356	.511	0	0	OF-152
1928	149	626	194	33	21	7	1.1	118	56	77	33	10	.310	.463	0	0	OF-149
1929	142	586	202	33	15	3	0.5	119	65	69	32	11	.345	.468	1	0	OF-141
1930	137	532	183	30	22	7	1.3	129	82	74	26	16	.344	.523	2	0	OF-135
1931	138	563	179	31	13	5	0.9	120	58	68	34	11	.318	.446	7	3	OF-129
1932	143	591	190	32	10	9	1.5	143	65	81	16	3	.321	.455	3	0	OF-138
1933	122	419	125	22	16	5	1.2	86	60	47	19	6	.298	.463	18	4	OF-104
1934	63	251	80	13	5	2	0.8	47	25	40	9	3	.319	.434	2	1	OF-62
1935	89	298	84	7	4	3	1.0	47	35	36	10	1	.282	.362	15	4	OF-70
12 yrs.	1454	5748	1866	309	154	58	1.0	1186	629	670	278	96	.325	.462	56	17	OF-1386

WORLD SERIES

1926 NY A	7	28	10	2	0	0	0.0	3	2	5	2	0	.357	.429	0	0	OF-7
1927	4	16	5	0	0	0	0.0	6	2	1	2	0	.313	.313	0	0	OF-4
1928	1	0	0	0	0	0		0	1	0	0	0	–	–	0	0	
1932	4	16	6	2	0	1	6.3	8	4	4	3	0	.375	.688	0	0	OF-4
4 yrs.	16	60	21	4	0	1	1.7	17	9	10	7	0	.350	.467	0	0	OF-15
													10th				

Merrill Combs

COMBS, MERRILL RUSSELL   BL TR 6'   172 lbs.
B. Dec. 11, 1919, Los Angeles, Calif.   D. July 8, 1981, Riverside, Calif.

1947 BOS A	17	68	15	1	0	1	1.5	8	6	9	9	0	.221	.279	0	0	3B-17
1949	14	24	5	1	0	0	0.0	5	1	9	0	0	.208	.250	1	0	3B-9, SS-1
1950 2 teams	BOS	A (1G –	.000)		WAS	A (37G –	.245)										
" total	38	102	25	1	0	0	0.0	19	6	23	16	0	.245	.255	5	1	SS-30
1951 CLE A	19	28	5	2	0	0	0.0	2	2	2	3	0	.179	.250	2	0	SS-16
1952	52	139	23	1	1	1	0.7	11	10	14	15	0	.165	.209	0	0	SS-49, 2B-3
5 yrs.	140	361	73	6	1	2	0.6	45	25	57	43	0	.202	.241	8	1	SS-96, 3B-26, 2B-3

Wayne Comer

COMER, HARRY WAYNE   BR TR 5'10"   175 lbs.
B. Feb. 3, 1944, Shenandoah, Va.

1967 DET A	4	3	1	0	0	0	0.0	0	0	0	0	0	.333	.333	1	1	OF-1
1968	48	8	6	0	1	1	2.1	8	3	2	7	0	.125	.229	18	2	OF-27, C-1
1969 SEA A	147	481	118	18	1	15	3.1	88	54	82	79	18	.245	.380	12	1	OF-139, 3B-1, C-1
1970 2 teams	MIL	A (13G –	.059)		WAS	A (77G –	.233)										
" total	90	146	31	4	0	0	0.0	22	9	22	19	4	.212	.240	26	3	OF-63, 3B-1
1972 DET A	27	9	1	0	0	0	0.0	1	1	0	1	0	.111	.111	6	1	OF-17
5 yrs.	316	687	157	22	2	16	2.3	119	67	106	106	22	.229	.336	63	8	OF-247, 3B-2, C-2

WORLD SERIES

1968 DET A	1	1	1	0	0	0	0.0	0	0	0	0	0	1.000	1.000	1	1	

Charlie Comiskey

COMISKEY, CHARLES ALBERT (Commy, The Old Roman)   BR TR 6'   180 lbs.
B. Aug. 15, 1859, Chicago, Ill.   D. Oct. 26, 1931, Eagle River, Wis.
Manager 1883, 1885-94.
Hall of Fame 1939.

1882 STL AA	78	329	80	9	5	1	0.3	58			4		.243	.310	0	0	1B-77, P-2

	G	AB	H	2B	3B	HR	HR %	R	RBI	BB	SO	SB	BA	SA	Pinch Hit AB	Pinch Hit H	G by POS

Charlie Comiskey continued

	G	AB	H	2B	3B	HR	HR%	R	RBI	BB	SO	SB	BA	SA	AB	H	G by POS
1883	96	401	118	17	9	2	0.5	87		11			.294	.397	0	0	1B-96, OF-1
1884	108	460	110	17	6	2	0.4	76		5			.239	.315	0	0	1B-108, 2B-1, P-1
1885	83	340	87	15	7	2	0.6	68		14			.256	.359	0	0	1B-83
1886	131	578	147	15	9	3	0.5	95		10			.254	.327	0	0	1B-122, 2B-9, OF-2
1887	125	538	180	22	5	4	0.7	139		27		117	.335	.416	0	0	1B-116, 2B-9, OF-3
1888	137	576	157	22	5	6	1.0	102	83	12		72	.273	.359	0	0	1B-133, OF-5, 2B-3
1889	137	587	168	28	10	3	0.5	105	102	19	19	65	.286	.383	0	0	1B-134, OF-3, 2B-3, P-1
1890 CHI P	88	377	92	11	3	0	0.0	53	59	14	17	34	.244	.289	0	0	1B-88
1891 STL AA	141	580	152	16	2	3	0.5	86	93	33	25	41	.262	.312	0	0	1B-141, OF-2
1892 CIN N	141	551	125	14	6	3	0.5	61	71	32	16	30	.227	.290	0	0	1B-141
1893	64	259	57	12	1	0	0.0	38	26	11	2	9	.220	.274	0	0	1B-64
1894	61	220	58	8	0	0	0.0	26	33	5	5	10	.264	.300	0	0	1B-60, OF-1
13 yrs.	1390	5796	1531	206	68	29	0.5	994	466	197	84	378	.264	.338	0	0	1B-1363, 2B-25, OF-17, P-4

Jim Command

COMMAND, JAMES DALTON (Igor)
B. Oct. 15, 1928, Grand Rapids, Mich.   BL TR 6'2" 200 lbs.

	G	AB	H	2B	3B	HR	HR%	R	RBI	BB	SO	SB	BA	SA	AB	H	G by POS
1954 PHI N	9	18	4	1	0	1	5.6	1	6	2	4	0	.222	.444	3	1	3B-6
1955	5	5	0	0	0	0	0.0	0	0	0	0	0	.000	.000	5	0	
2 yrs.	14	23	4	1	0	1	4.3	1	6	2	4	0	.174	.348	8	1	3B-6

Adam Comorosky

COMOROSKY, ADAM ANTHONY
B. Dec. 9, 1904, Swoyersville, Pa.   D. Mar. 2, 1951, Swoyersville, Pa.   BR TR 5'10" 167 lbs.

	G	AB	H	2B	3B	HR	HR%	R	RBI	BB	SO	SB	BA	SA	AB	H	G by POS
1926 PIT N	8	15	4	1	1	0	0.0	2	0	1	2	1	.267	.467	1	0	OF-6
1927	18	61	14	1	0	0	0.0	5	4	3	1	0	.230	.246	1	0	OF-16
1928	51	176	52	6	3	2	1.1	22	34	15	6	1	.295	.398	1	1	OF-49
1929	127	473	152	26	11	6	1.3	86	97	40	22	19	.321	.461	3	0	OF-121
1930	152	597	187	47	23	12	2.0	112	119	51	33	14	.313	.529	0	0	OF-152
1931	99	350	85	12	1	1	0.3	37	48	34	28	11	.243	.291	7	1	OF-90
1932	108	370	106	18	4	4	1.1	54	46	25	20	7	.286	.389	11	3	OF-92
1933	64	162	46	8	1	1	0.6	18	15	4	9	2	.284	.364	32	9	OF-30
1934 CIN N	127	446	115	12	6	0	0.0	46	40	34	23	1	.258	.312	4	0	OF-122
1935	59	137	34	3	1	2	1.5	22	14	7	14	1	.248	.328	7	2	OF-40
10 yrs.	813	2787	795	134	51	28	1.0	404	417	214	158	57	.285	.400	67	16	OF-718

Mike Compton

COMPTON, MICHAEL LYNN
B. Aug. 15, 1944, Stamford, Tex.   BR TR 5'10" 180 lbs.

	G	AB	H	2B	3B	HR	HR%	R	RBI	BB	SO	SB	BA	SA	AB	H	G by POS
1970 PHI N	47	110	18	0	1	1	0.9	8	7	9	22	0	.164	.209	1	0	C-40

Pete Compton

COMPTON, ANNA SEBASTIAN (Bash)
B. Sept. 28, 1889, San Marcos, Tex.   D. Feb. 3, 1978, Kansas City, Mo.   BL TL 5'11" 170 lbs.

	G	AB	H	2B	3B	HR	HR%	R	RBI	BB	SO	SB	BA	SA	AB	H	G by POS
1911 STL A	28	107	29	4	0	0	0.0	9	5	8		2	.271	.308	0	0	OF-28
1912	100	268	75	6	4	2	0.7	26	30	21		11	.280	.354	27	9	OF-72
1913	61	100	18	5	2	2	2.0	14	17	13	13	2	.180	.330	34	7	OF-21
1915 2 teams	STL	F (2G – .250)				BOS	N (35G – .241)										
" total	37	124	30	7	1	1	0.8	10	15	8	11	4	.242	.339	3	0	OF-37
1916 2 teams	BOS	N (34G – .204)				PIT	N (5G – .063)										
" total	39	114	21	2	0	0	0.0	14	8	9	12	5	.184	.202	3	0	OF-35
1918 NY N	21	60	13	0	1	0	0.0	5	5	5	4	2	.217	.250	2	0	OF-19
6 yrs.	286	773	186	24	8	5	0.6	78	80	64	40	26	.241	.312	69	16	OF-212

Clint Conatser

CONATSER, CLINTON ASTOR (Connie)
B. July 24, 1921, Los Angeles, Calif.   BR TR 5'11" 182 lbs.

	G	AB	H	2B	3B	HR	HR%	R	RBI	BB	SO	SB	BA	SA	AB	H	G by POS
1948 BOS N	90	224	62	9	3	3	1.3	30	23	32	27	0	.277	.384	11	1	OF-76
1949	53	152	40	6	0	3	2.0	10	16	14	19	0	.263	.362	10	3	OF-44
2 yrs.	143	376	102	15	3	6	1.6	40	39	46	46	0	.271	.375	21	4	OF-120

WORLD SERIES

	G	AB	H	2B	3B	HR	HR%	R	RBI	BB	SO	SB	BA	SA	AB	H	G by POS
1948 BOS N	2	4	0	0	0	0	0.0	0	1	0	0	0	.000	.000	1	0	OF-2

Dave Concepcion

CONCEPCION, DAVID ISMAEL BONITEZ
B. June 17, 1948, Aragua, Venezuela   BR TR 6'2" 155 lbs.

	G	AB	H	2B	3B	HR	HR%	R	RBI	BB	SO	SB	BA	SA	AB	H	G by POS
1970 CIN N	101	265	69	6	3	1	0.4	38	19	23	45	10	.260	.317	5	1	SS-93, 2B-3
1971	130	327	67	4	4	1	0.3	24	20	18	51	9	.205	.251	1	0	SS-112, 2B-10, 3B-7, OF-5
1972	119	378	79	13	2	2	0.5	40	29	32	65	13	.209	.270	0	0	SS-114, 3B-9, 2B-1
1973	89	328	94	18	3	8	2.4	39	46	21	55	22	.287	.433	2	0	SS-88, OF-2
1974	160	594	167	25	1	14	2.4	70	82	44	79	41	.281	.397	1	0	SS-160
1975	140	507	139	23	1	5	1.0	62	49	39	51	33	.274	.353	8	2	SS-130, 3B-6
1976	152	576	162	28	7	9	1.6	74	69	49	68	21	.281	.401	3	1	SS-150
1977	156	572	155	26	3	8	1.4	59	64	46	77	29	.271	.369	0	0	SS-156
1978	153	565	170	33	4	6	1.1	75	67	51	83	23	.301	.405	3	1	SS-152
1979	149	590	166	25	3	16	2.7	91	84	64	73	19	.281	.415	1	0	SS-148
1980	156	622	162	31	8	5	0.8	72	77	37	107	12	.260	.360	2	0	SS-155, 2B-1
1981	106	421	129	28	0	5	1.2	57	67	37	61	4	.306	.409	0	0	SS-106
1982	147	572	164	25	4	5	0.9	48	53	45	61	13	.287	.371	3	1	SS-145, 3B-1, 1B-1
1983	143	528	123	22	0	1	0.2	54	47	56	81	14	.233	.280	3	1	SS-139, 3B-6
1984	154	531	130	26	1	4	0.8	46	58	52	72	22	.245	.320	13	1	SS-104, 3B-54, 1B-6
15 yrs.	2055	7376	1976	333	44	90	1.2	849	831	614	1029	285	.268	.362	45	8	SS-1952, 3B-83, 2B-15, 1B-8, OF-7

LEAGUE CHAMPIONSHIP SERIES

	G	AB	H	2B	3B	HR	HR%	R	RBI	BB	SO	SB	BA	SA	AB	H	G by POS
1970 CIN N	3	0	0	0	0	0	–	0	0	0	0	0			0	0	SS-3
1972	3	2	0	0	0	0	0.0	0	0	0	0	0	.000	.000	1	0	SS-1
1975	3	11	5	0	0	1	9.1	2	1	1	2	2	.455	.727	0	0	SS-3
1976	3	10	2	1	0	0	0.0	4	0	2	1	0	.200	.300	0	0	SS-3

	G	AB	H	2B	3B	HR	HR %	R	RBI	BB	SO	SB	BA	SA	Pinch Hit AB	Pinch Hit H	G by POS

Dave Concepcion continued

	G	AB	H	2B	3B	HR	HR%	R	RBI	BB	SO	SB	BA	SA	AB	H	G by POS
1979	3	14	6	1	0	0	0.0	1	0	0	3	0	.429	.500	0	0	SS-3
5 yrs.	15	37	13	2	0	1	2.7	7	1	3	6	2	.351	.486	1	0	SS-13

WORLD SERIES

	G	AB	H	2B	3B	HR	HR%	R	RBI	BB	SO	SB	BA	SA	AB	H	G by POS
1970 CIN N	3	9	3	0	1	0	0.0	0	3	0	0	0	.333	.556	0	0	SS-3
1972	6	13	4	0	1	0	0.0	2	2	2	2	1	.308	.462	1	0	SS-5
1975	7	28	5	1	0	1	3.6	3	4	0	1	3	.179	.321	0	0	SS-7
1976	4	14	5	1	0	0	0.0	1	3	1	3	1	.357	.571	0	0	SS-4
4 yrs.	20	64	17	2	3	1	1.6	6	12	3	6	5	.266	.438	1	0	SS-19
					4th												

Onix Concepcion

CONCEPCION, ONIX
Also known as Onix Cardona.
B. Oct. 5, 1957, Dorado, Puerto Rico

BR TR 5'6" 160 lbs.

	G	AB	H	2B	3B	HR	HR%	R	RBI	BB	SO	SB	BA	SA	AB	H	G by POS
1980 KC A	12	15	2	0	0	0	0.0	1	2	0	1	0	.133	.133	2	1	SS-6
1981	2	0	0	0	0	0	–	0	0	0	0	0	–	–	0	0	SS-1
1982	74	205	48	9	1	0	0.0	17	15	5	18	2	.234	.288	3	0	SS-46, 2B-24, DH-1
1983	80	219	53	11	3	0	0.0	22	20	12	12	10	.242	.320	3	1	3B-31, 2B-28, SS-21, DH-1
1984	90	287	81	9	2	1	0.3	36	23	14	33	9	.282	.338	1	0	SS-85, 2B-6, 3B-1
5 yrs.	258	726	184	29	6	1	0.1	76	60	31	64	21	.253	.314	9	2	SS-159, 2B-58, 3B-32, DH-2

LEAGUE CHAMPIONSHIP SERIES

	G	AB	H	2B	3B	HR	HR%	R	RBI	BB	SO	SB	BA	SA	AB	H	G by POS
1984 KC A	3	7	0	0	0	0	0.0	0	0	0	0	0	.000	.000	0	0	SS-3

WORLD SERIES

	G	AB	H	2B	3B	HR	HR%	R	RBI	BB	SO	SB	BA	SA	AB	H	G by POS
1980 KC A	3	0	0	0	0	0	–	0	0	0	0	0	–	–	0	0	

Ramon Conde

CONDE, RAMON LUIS (Wito)
B. Dec. 29, 1934, Juana Diaz, Puerto Rico

BR TR 5'8" 172 lbs.

	G	AB	H	2B	3B	HR	HR%	R	RBI	BB	SO	SB	BA	SA	AB	H	G by POS
1962 CHI A	14	16	0	0	0	0	0.0	1	3	3	0	0	.000	.000	5	0	3B-7

Bunk Congalton

CONGALTON, WILLIAM MILLAR
B. Jan. 24, 1875, Guelph, Ont., Canada   D. Aug. 19, 1937, Cleveland, Ohio

BL 5'11" 190 lbs.

	G	AB	H	2B	3B	HR	HR%	R	RBI	BB	SO	SB	BA	SA	AB	H	G by POS
1902 CHI N	45	179	40	3	0	1	0.6	14	24	7		3	.223	.257	0	0	OF-45
1905 CLE A	12	47	17	0	0	0	0.0	4	5	2		3	.362	.362	0	0	OF-12
1906	117	419	134	13	5	2	0.5	51	50	24		12	.320	.389	3	0	OF-114
1907 2 teams		CLE A (9G – .182)			BOS A (127G – .286)												
" total	136	518	146	11	8	2	0.4	46	49	24		13	.282	.346	4	0	OF-132
4 yrs.	310	1163	337	27	13	5	0.4	115	128	57		31	.290	.348	7	0	OF-303

Billy Conigliaro

CONIGLIARO, WILLIAM MICHAEL
Brother of Tony Conigliaro.
B. Aug. 15, 1947, Revere, Mass.

BR TR 6' 180 lbs.

	G	AB	H	2B	3B	HR	HR%	R	RBI	BB	SO	SB	BA	SA	AB	H	G by POS
1969 BOS A	32	80	23	6	2	4	5.0	14	7	9	23	1	.288	.563	6	3	OF-24
1970	114	398	108	16	3	18	4.5	59	58	35	73	3	.271	.462	6	1	OF-108
1971	101	351	92	26	1	11	3.1	42	33	25	68	3	.262	.436	4	1	OF-100
1972 MIL A	52	191	44	6	2	7	3.7	22	16	8	54	1	.230	.393	3	1	OF-50
1973 OAK A	48	110	22	2	2	0	0.0	5	14	9	26	1	.200	.255	6	2	OF-40, 2B-1
5 yrs.	347	1130	289	56	10	40	3.5	142	128	86	244	9	.256	.429	25	8	OF-322, 2B-1

LEAGUE CHAMPIONSHIP SERIES

	G	AB	H	2B	3B	HR	HR%	R	RBI	BB	SO	SB	BA	SA	AB	H	G by POS
1973 OAK A	1	4	0	0	0	0	0.0	0	0	0	2	0	.000	.000	0	0	OF-1

WORLD SERIES

	G	AB	H	2B	3B	HR	HR%	R	RBI	BB	SO	SB	BA	SA	AB	H	G by POS
1973 OAK A	3	3	0	0	0	0	0.0	0	0	0	1	0	.000	.000	3	0	

Tony Conigliaro

CONIGLIARO, ANTHONY RICHARD
Brother of Billy Conigliaro.
B. Jan. 7, 1945, Revere, Mass.

BR TR 6'3" 185 lbs.

	G	AB	H	2B	3B	HR	HR%	R	RBI	BB	SO	SB	BA	SA	AB	H	G by POS
1964 BOS A	111	404	117	21	2	24	5.9	69	52	35	78	2	.290	.530	5	1	OF-106
1965	138	521	140	21	5	32	6.1	82	82	51	116	4	.269	.512	0	0	OF-137
1966	150	558	148	26	7	28	5.0	77	93	52	112	0	.265	.487	4	3	OF-146
1967	95	349	100	11	5	20	5.7	59	67	27	58	4	.287	.519	0	0	OF-95
1969	141	506	129	21	3	20	4.0	57	82	48	111	2	.255	.427	4	0	OF-137
1970	146	560	149	20	1	36	6.4	89	116	43	93	4	.266	.498	0	0	OF-146
1971 CAL A	74	266	59	18	0	4	1.5	23	15	23	52	3	.222	.335	2	1	OF-72
1975 BOS A	21	57	7	1	0	2	3.5	8	9	8	9	1	.123	.246	5	0	DH-15
8 yrs.	876	3221	849	139	23	166	5.2	464	516	287	629	20	.264	.476	20	5	OF-839, DH-15

Jocko Conlan

CONLAN, JOHN BERTRAND
B. Dec. 6, 1899, Chicago, Ill.
Hall of Fame 1974.

BL TL 5'7½" 165 lbs.

	G	AB	H	2B	3B	HR	HR%	R	RBI	BB	SO	SB	BA	SA	AB	H	G by POS
1934 CHI A	63	225	56	11	3	0	0.0	35	16	19	7	2	.249	.324	8	3	OF-54
1935	65	140	40	7	1	0	0.0	20	15	14	6	3	.286	.350	24	5	OF-37
2 yrs.	128	365	96	18	4	0	0.0	55	31	33	13	5	.263	.334	32	8	OF-91

Art Conlon

CONLON, ARTHUR JOSEPH (Jocko)
B. Dec. 10, 1897, Woburn, Mass.

BR TR 5'7" 145 lbs.

	G	AB	H	2B	3B	HR	HR%	R	RBI	BB	SO	SB	BA	SA	AB	H	G by POS
1923 BOS N	59	147	32	3	0	0	0.0	23	17	11	11	0	.218	.238	9	3	2B-36, SS-6, 3B-4

Bert Conn

CONN, ALBERT THOMAS
B. Sept. 22, 1879, Philadelphia, Pa.   D. Nov. 2, 1944, Philadelphia, Pa.

TR

	G	AB	H	2B	3B	HR	HR%	R	RBI	BB	SO	SB	BA	SA	AB	H	G by POS
1898 PHI N	1	3	1	0	0	0	0.0	1	1	0		0	.333	1.000	0	0	P-1
1900	6	9	3	1	0	0	0.0	4	1	0		0	.333	.444	2	0	P-4
1901	5	18	4	1	0	0	0.0	2	0	0		0	.222	.278	0	0	2B-5
3 yrs.	12	30	8	2	1	0	0.0	7	2	0		0	.267	.400	2	0	2B-5, P-5

	G	AB	H	2B	3B	HR	HR %	R	RBI	BB	SO	SB	BA	SA	Pinch Hit AB	Pinch Hit H	G by POS

Bud Connally

CONNALLY, MERVIN THOMAS (Mike)   BR TR 5'8"   154 lbs.
B. Apr. 25, 1901, San Francisco, Calif.   D. June 12, 1964, Berkeley, Calif.

	G	AB	H	2B	3B	HR	HR %	R	RBI	BB	SO	SB	BA	SA	AB	H	G by POS
1925 BOS A	43	107	28	7	1	0	0.0	12	21	23	9	0	.262	.346	8	4	SS-34, 3B-2

Fritzie Connally

CONNALLY, FRITZIE LEE   BR TR 6'4"   210 lbs.
B. May 9, 1958, Bryan, Tex.

	G	AB	H	2B	3B	HR	HR %	R	RBI	BB	SO	SB	BA	SA	AB	H	G by POS
1983 CHI N	8	10	1	0	0	0	0.0	0	0	0	5	0	.100	.100	7	1	3B-3

Bruce Connatser

CONNATSER, BROADUS MILBURN   BR TR 5'11½" 170 lbs.
B. Sept. 19, 1902, Sevierville, Tenn.   D. Jan. 27, 1971, Terre Haute, Ind.

	G	AB	H	2B	3B	HR	HR %	R	RBI	BB	SO	SB	BA	SA	AB	H	G by POS
1931 CLE A	12	49	14	3	0	0	0.0	5	4	2	3	0	.286	.347	0	0	1B-12
1932	23	60	14	3	1	0	0.0	8	4	4	8	1	.233	.317	8	1	1B-14
2 yrs.	35	109	28	6	1	0	0.0	13	8	6	11	1	.257	.330	8	1	1B-26

Frank Connaughton

CONNAUGHTON, FRANK H   BR TR 5'9"   165 lbs.
B. Jan. 1, 1869, Clinton, Mass.   D. Dec. 1, 1942, Boston, Mass.

	G	AB	H	2B	3B	HR	HR %	R	RBI	BB	SO	SB	BA	SA	AB	H	G by POS
1894 BOS N	46	171	59	9	2	2	1.2	42	33	16	8	3	.345	.456	2	2	SS-33, C-7, OF-4
1896 NY N	88	315	82	3	2	2	0.6	53	43	25	7	22	.260	.302	3	0	SS-54, OF-30
1906 BOS N	12	44	9	0	0	0	0.0	3	1	3		1	.205	.205	0	0	SS-11, 2B-1
3 yrs.	146	530	150	12	4	4	0.8	98	77	44	15	26	.283	.343	5	2	SS-98, OF-34, C-7, 2B-1

Gene Connell

CONNELL, EUGENE JOSEPH   BR TR 6'½"   180 lbs.
Brother of Joe Connell.
B. May 10, 1906, Hazleton, Pa.   D. Aug. 31, 1937, Waverly, N. Y.

	G	AB	H	2B	3B	HR	HR %	R	RBI	BB	SO	SB	BA	SA	AB	H	G by POS
1931 PHI N	6	12	3	0	0	0	0.0	0		0	3	0	.250	.250	0	0	C-6

Joe Connell

CONNELL, JOSEPH BERNARD   BL TL 5'8"   165 lbs.
Brother of Gene Connell.
B. Jan. 16, 1902, Bethlehem, Pa.   D. Sept. 21, 1977, Trexlertown, Pa.

	G	AB	H	2B	3B	HR	HR %	R	RBI	BB	SO	SB	BA	SA	AB	H	G by POS
1926 NY N	2	1	0	0	0	0	0.0	1		0	0	0	.000	.000	1	0	

Pete Connell

CONNELL, PETER J.
B. Brooklyn, N. Y.   Deceased.

	G	AB	H	2B	3B	HR	HR %	R	RBI	BB	SO	SB	BA	SA	AB	H	G by POS
1886 NY AA	1	5	0	0	0	0	0.0	0		0			.000	.000	0	0	3B-1

Tom Connelly

CONNELLY, THOMAS MARTIN   BL TR 5'11½" 165 lbs.
B. Oct. 20, 1897, Chicago, Ill.   D. Feb. 18, 1941, Hines, Ill.

	G	AB	H	2B	3B	HR	HR %	R	RBI	BB	SO	SB	BA	SA	AB	H	G by POS
1920 NY A	1	1	0	0	0	0	0.0	0		0	0	0	.000	.000	1	0	
1921	4	5	1	0	0	0	0.0	0	0	1	0	0	.200	.200	1	1	OF-3
2 yrs.	5	6	1	0	0	0	0.0	0	0	1	0	0	.167	.167	2	1	OF-3

Ed Connolly

CONNOLLY, EDWARD JOSEPH   BR TR 5'8½"   180 lbs.
Father of Ed Connolly.
B. July 17, 1908, Brooklyn, N. Y.   D. Nov. 12, 1963, Pittsfield, Mass.

	G	AB	H	2B	3B	HR	HR %	R	RBI	BB	SO	SB	BA	SA	AB	H	G by POS
1929 BOS A	5	8	0	0	0	0	0.0	0	0	0	2	0	.000	.000	0	0	C-5
1930	27	48	9	2	0	0	0.0	1	7	4	3	0	.188	.229	0	0	C-26
1931	42	93	7	1	0	0	0.0	3	3	5	18	0	.075	.086	1	0	C-41
1932	75	222	50	8	4	0	0.0	9	21	20	27	0	.225	.297	0	0	C-75
4 yrs.	149	371	66	11	4	0	0.0	13	31	29	50	0	.178	.229	1	0	C-147

Joe Connolly

CONNOLLY, JOSEPH ALOYSIUS   BL TR 5'7½"   165 lbs.
B. Feb. 12, 1888, N. Smithfield, R. I.   D. Sept. 1, 1943, Springfield, R. I.

	G	AB	H	2B	3B	HR	HR %	R	RBI	BB	SO	SB	BA	SA	AB	H	G by POS
1913 BOS N	126	427	120	18	11	5	1.2	79	57	66	47	18	.281	.410	1	0	OF-124
1914	120	399	122	28	10	9	2.3	64	65	49	36	12	.306	.494	1	0	OF-118
1915	104	305	91	14	8	0	0.0	48	23	39	35	13	.298	.397	9	1	OF-93
1916	62	110	25	5	2	0	0.0	11	12	14	13	5	.227	.309	25	6	OF-31
4 yrs.	412	1241	358	65	31	14	1.1	202	157	168	131	48	.288	.425	36	7	OF-366
WORLD SERIES																	
1914 BOS N	3	9	1	0	0	0	0.0	1	1	1	1	0	.111	.111	0	0	OF-3

Joe Connolly

CONNOLLY, JOSEPH GEORGE (Coaster Joe)   BR TR 6'   170 lbs.
B. June 4, 1896, San Francisco, Calif.   D. Mar. 30, 1960, San Francisco, Calif.

	G	AB	H	2B	3B	HR	HR %	R	RBI	BB	SO	SB	BA	SA	AB	H	G by POS
1921 NY N	2	4	0	0	0	0	0.0	0	0	1	1	0	.000	.000	1	0	OF-1
1922 CLE A	12	45	11	2	1	0	0.0	6	6	5	8	1	.244	.333	0	0	OF-12
1923	52	109	33	10	1	3	2.8	25	25	13	7	1	.303	.495	9	1	OF-39
1924 BOS A	14	10	1	0	0	0	0.0	1	1	2	2	0	.100	.100	10	1	OF-3
4 yrs.	80	168	45	12	2	3	1.8	32	32	21	18	2	.268	.417	20	2	OF-55

Red Connolly

CONNOLLY, JOHN M.
B. 1863, New York, N. Y.   D. Mar. 2, 1896, New York, N. Y.

	G	AB	H	2B	3B	HR	HR %	R	RBI	BB	SO	SB	BA	SA	AB	H	G by POS
1886 STL N	2	7	0	0	0	0	0.0	0	0	0	3		.000	.000	0	0	OF-2

Tom Connolly

CONNOLLY, THOMAS FRANCIS (Blackie)   BL TR 5'11"   175 lbs.
B. Dec. 30, 1892, Boston, Mass.   D. May 14, 1966, Boston, Mass.

	G	AB	H	2B	3B	HR	HR %	R	RBI	BB	SO	SB	BA	SA	AB	H	G by POS
1915 WAS A	50	141	26	3	2	0	0.0	14	7	14	19	5	.184	.234	3	0	3B-24, OF-19, SS-4

Jim Connor

CONNOR, JAMES MATTHEW
Born James Matthew O'Connor.
B. May 11, 1865, Port Jervis, N. Y.   D. Sept. 4, 1950, Providence, R. I.

	G	AB	H	2B	3B	HR	HR %	R	RBI	BB	SO	SB	BA	SA	AB	H	G by POS
1892 CHI N	9	34	2	0	0	0	0.0	0	0	1	7	0	.059	.059	0	0	2B-9
1897	77	285	83	10	5	3	1.1	40	38	24		10	.291	.393	2	1	2B-76
1898	138	505	114	9	9	0	0.0	51	67	42		11	.226	.279	0	0	2B-138
1899	69	234	48	7	1	0	0.0	26	24	18		6	.205	.244	0	0	2B-44, 3B-25
4 yrs.	293	1058	247	26	15	3	0.3	117	129	85	7	27	.233	.295	2	1	2B-267, 3B-25

	G	AB	H	2B	3B	HR	HR %	R	RBI	BB	SO	SB	BA	SA	Pinch Hit AB	Pinch Hit H	G by POS

Joe Connor

CONNOR, JOSEPH
Deceased.

	G	AB	H	2B	3B	HR	HR %	R	RBI	BB	SO	SB	BA	SA	AB	H	G by POS
1895 STL N	2	7	0	0	0	0	0.0	0	1	0	2	0	.000	.000	0	0	3B-2

Joe Connor

BR TR 6'2"   185 lbs.

CONNOR, JOSEPH FRANCIS
Brother of Roger Connor.
B. Dec. 8, 1874, Waterbury, Conn.   D. Nov. 8, 1957, Waterbury, Conn.

	G	AB	H	2B	3B	HR	HR %	R	RBI	BB	SO	SB	BA	SA	AB	H	G by POS
1900 BOS N	7	19	4	0	0	0	0.0	2	4	2		1	.211	.211	0	0	C-7
1901 2 teams		MIL	A (38G – .275)			CLE	A (37G – .140)										
" total	75	223	45	6	2	1	0.4	23	15	13		6	.202	.260	5	1	C-62, OF-5, SS-1, 3B-1, 2B-1
1905 NY A	8	22	5	1	0	0	0.0	4	2	3		1	.227	.273	0	0	C-6, 1B-2
3 yrs.	90	264	54	7	2	1	0.4	29	21	18		8	.205	.258	5	1	C-75, OF-5, 1B-2, SS-1, 3B-1, 2B-1

Roger Connor

BL TL 6'3"   220 lbs.

CONNOR, ROGER
Brother of Joe Connor.
B. July 1, 1857, Waterbury, Conn.   D. Jan. 4, 1931, Waterbury, Conn.
Manager 1896.
Hall of Fame 1976.

	G	AB	H	2B	3B	HR	HR %	R	RBI	BB	SO	SB	BA	SA	AB	H	G by POS
1880 TRO N	83	340	113	18	8	3	0.9	53		13	21		.332	.459	0	0	3B-83
1881	85	367	107	17	6	2	0.5	55	31	15	20		.292	.387	0	0	1B-85
1882	81	349	115	22	18	4	1.1	65	42	13	20		.330	.530	0	0	1B-43, OF-24, 3B-14
1883 NY N	98	409	146	28	15	1	0.2	80		25	16		.357	.506	0	0	1B-98
1884	116	477	151	28	4	4	0.8	98		38	32		.317	.417	0	0	2B-67, OF-37, 3B-12
1885	110	455	**169**	23	15	1	0.2	102		51	8		**.371**	.495	0	0	1B-110
1886	118	485	172	29	**20**	7	1.4	105	71	41	15		.355	.540	0	0	1B-118
1887	127	471	134	26	22	17	3.6	113	104	75	50	43	.285	.541	0	0	1B-127
1888	134	481	140	15	17	14	2.9	98	71	**73**	44	27	.291	.480	0	0	1B-133, 2B-1
1889	131	496	157	32	17	13	2.6	117	**130**	93	46	21	.317	**.528**	0	0	1B-131, 3B-1
1890 NY P	123	484	180	25	15	**13**	**2.7**	134	103	88	32	22	.372	**.566**	0	0	1B-123
1891 NY N	129	479	139	29	13	6	1.3	112	94	83	39	27	.290	.443	0	0	1B-129
1892 PHI N	155	564	166	**37**	11	12	2.1	123	73	116	39	22	.294	.463	0	0	1B-155
1893 NY N	135	511	158	25	8	11	2.2	111	105	91	26	24	.309	.454	0	0	1B-135, 3B-1
1894 2 teams		NY	N (22G – .293)			STL	N (99G – .321)										
" total	121	462	146	35	25	8	1.7	93	93	59	17	19	.316	.552	0	0	1B-120, OF-1
1895 STL N	104	402	131	29	9	8	2.0	78	77	63	10	9	.326	.502	0	0	1B-103
1896	126	483	137	21	9	11	2.3	71	72	52	14	10	.284	.433	0	0	1B-126
1897	22	83	19	3	1	1	1.2	13	12	13		3	.229	.325	0	0	1B-22
18 yrs.	1998	7798	2480	442	233	136	1.7	1621	1077	1002	449	227	.318	.487	0	0	1B-1758, 3B-111, 2B-68, OF-62
									5th								

Chuck Connors

BL TL 6'5"   190 lbs.

CONNORS, KEVIN JOSEPH
B. Apr. 10, 1921, Brooklyn, N. Y.

	G	AB	H	2B	3B	HR	HR %	R	RBI	BB	SO	SB	BA	SA	AB	H	G by POS
1949 BKN N	1	1	0	0	0	0	0.0	0	0	0	0	0	.000	.000	1	0	
1951 CHI N	66	201	48	5	1	2	1.0	16	18	12	25	4	.239	.303	10	1	1B-57
2 yrs.	67	202	48	5	1	2	1.0	16	18	12	25	4	.238	.302	11	1	1B-57

Jerry Connors

CONNORS, JEREMIAH
B. Philadelphia, Pa.   Deceased.

	G	AB	H	2B	3B	HR	HR %	R	RBI	BB	SO	SB	BA	SA	AB	H	G by POS
1892 PHI N	1	3	0	0	0	0	0.0	0		0	1	0	.000	.000	0	0	OF-1

Joe Connors

CONNORS, JOSEPH P.
B. Philadelphia, Pa.   Deceased.

	G	AB	H	2B	3B	HR	HR %	R	RBI	BB	SO	SB	BA	SA	AB	H	G by POS
1884 2 teams		ALT	U (3G – .091)			KC	U (3G – .091)										
" total	6	22	2	0	0	0	0.0	2		1			.091	.091	0	0	OF-3, P-3, 3B-1

Merv Connors

BR TR 6'2"   192 lbs.

CONNORS, MERVYN JAMES
B. Jan. 23, 1914, Berkeley, Calif.

	G	AB	H	2B	3B	HR	HR %	R	RBI	BB	SO	SB	BA	SA	AB	H	G by POS
1937 CHI A	28	103	24	4	1	2	1.9	12	12	14	19	2	.233	.350	0	0	3B-28
1938	24	62	22	4	0	6	9.7	14	13	9	17	0	.355	.710	7	2	1B-16
2 yrs.	52	165	46	8	1	8	4.8	26	25	23	36	2	.279	.485	7	2	3B-28, 1B-16

Ben Conroy

CONROY, BERNARD PATRICK
B. Mar. 14, 1871, Philadelphia, Pa.   D. Nov. 25, 1937, Philadelphia, Pa.

	G	AB	H	2B	3B	HR	HR %	R	RBI	BB	SO	SB	BA	SA	AB	H	G by POS
1890 PHI AA	117	404	69	13	1	0	0.0	45		45		17	.171	.208	0	0	SS-74, 2B-42, OF-1

Bill Conroy

BR TR 6'   185 lbs.

CONROY, WILLIAM GORDON
B. Feb. 26, 1915, Bloomington, Ill.

	G	AB	H	2B	3B	HR	HR %	R	RBI	BB	SO	SB	BA	SA	AB	H	G by POS
1935 PHI A	1	4	1	1	0	0	0.0	0	0	1	0	0	.250	.500	0	0	C-1
1936	1	2	1	0	0	0	0.0	0	0	0	1	0	.500	.500	0	0	C-1
1937	26	60	12	1	1	0	0.0	4	3	7	9	1	.200	.250	5	1	C-18, 1B-1
1942 BOS A	83	250	50	4	2	4	1.6	22	20	40	47	2	.200	.280	0	0	C-83
1943	39	89	16	5	0	1	1.1	13	6	18	19	0	.180	.270	3	1	C-38
1944	19	47	10	2	0	0	0.0	6	4	11	9	0	.213	.255	0	0	C-19
6 yrs.	169	452	90	13	3	5	1.1	45	33	77	85	3	.199	.274	8	2	C-160, 1B-1

Pep Conroy

BR TR 5'8½"   160 lbs.

CONROY, WILLIAM FREDERICK
B. Jan. 9, 1899, Chicago, Ill.   D. Jan. 23, 1970, Chicago, Ill.

	G	AB	H	2B	3B	HR	HR %	R	RBI	BB	SO	SB	BA	SA	AB	H	G by POS
1923 WAS A	18	60	8	2	2	0	0.0	4	2	4	9	0	.133	.233	1	0	3B-10, 1B-6, OF-1

Wid Conroy

BR TR 5'9"   158 lbs.

CONROY, WILLIAM EDWARD
B. Apr. 5, 1877, Camden, N. J.   D. Dec. 6, 1959, Mt. Holly, N. J.

	G	AB	H	2B	3B	HR	HR %	R	RBI	BB	SO	SB	BA	SA	AB	H	G by POS
1901 MIL A	131	503	129	20	6	5	1.0	74	64	36		21	.256	.350	1	0	SS-118, 3B-12
1902 PIT N	99	365	89	10	6	1	0.3	55	47	24		10	.244	.312	0	0	SS-95, OF-3
1903 NY A	126	503	137	23	12	1	0.2	74	45	32		33	.272	.372	0	0	3B-123, SS-4
1904	140	489	119	18	12	1	0.2	58	52	43		30	.243	.335	0	0	3B-110, SS-27, OF-3

	G	AB	H	2B	3B	HR	HR %	R	RBI	BB	SO	SB	BA	SA	Pinch Hit AB	Pinch Hit H	G by POS

Wid Conroy continued

	G	AB	H	2B	3B	HR	HR %	R	RBI	BB	SO	SB	BA	SA	AB	H	G by POS
1905	102	385	105	19	11	2	0.5	55	25	32		25	.273	.395	1	0	3B-48, OF-21, SS-18, 1B-9, 2B-3
1906	148	567	139	17	10	4	0.7	67	54	47		32	.245	.332	0	0	OF-97, SS-49, 3B-2
1907	140	530	124	12	11	3	0.6	58	51	30		41	.234	.315	2	0	OF-100, SS-38
1908	141	531	126	22	3	1	0.2	44	39	14		23	.237	.296	0	0	3B-119, 2B-12, OF-10
1909 WAS A	139	488	119	13	4	1	0.2	44	20	37		24	.244	.293	0	0	3B-120, 2B-13, OF-5, SS-1
1910	105	351	89	11	3	1	0.3	36	27	30		11	.254	.311	6	1	3B-48, OF-46, 2B-5
1911	106	349	81	11	4	2	0.6	40	28	20		12	.232	.304	4	2	3B-85, OF-15, 2B-1
11 yrs.	1377	5061	1257	176	82	22	0.4	605	452	345		262	.248	.329	14	3	3B-667, SS-350, OF-300, 2B-34, 1B-9

Billy Consolo

CONSOLO, WILLIAM ANGELO
B. Aug. 18, 1934, Cleveland, Ohio

BR TR 5'11" 180 lbs.

	G	AB	H	2B	3B	HR	HR %	R	RBI	BB	SO	SB	BA	SA	AB	H	G by POS
1953 BOS A	47	65	14	2	1	1	1.5	9	6	2	23	1	.215	.323	9	1	3B-16, 2B-11
1954	91	242	55	7	1	1	0.4	23	11	33	69	2	.227	.277	4	1	SS-50, 3B-18, 2B-12
1955	8	18	4	0	0	0	0.0	4	0	5	4	0	.222	.222	1	1	2B-4
1956	48	11	2	0	0	0	0.0	13	1	3	5	0	.182	.182	0	0	2B-25
1957	68	196	53	6	1	4	2.0	26	19	23	48	1	.270	.372	0	0	SS-42, 2B-16, 3B-2
1958	46	72	9	2	1	0	0.0	13	5	6	14	0	.125	.181	1	0	2B-13, SS-11, 3B-1
1959 2 teams		BOS A (10G – .214)				WAS A (79G – .213)											
" total	89	216	46	6	3	0	0.0	28	10	38	59	1	.213	.269	8	1	SS-77, 2B-4
1960 WAS A	100	174	36	4	2	3	1.7	23	15	25	29	1	.207	.305	7	2	SS-82, 2B-12, 3B-2
1961 MIN A	11	5	0	0	0	0	0.0	1	0	0	1	0	.000	.000	1	0	SS-3, 2B-3, 3B-1
1962 3 teams		PHI N (13G – .400)				LA A (28G – .100)						KC A (54G – .240)					
" total	95	179	41	4	2	0	0.0	18	16	26	45	3	.229	.274	13	4	SS-52, 3B-21, 2B-1
10 yrs.	603	1178	260	31	11	9	0.8	158	83	161	297	9	.221	.289	44	10	SS-317, 2B-101, 3B-61

Bill Conway

CONWAY, WILLIAM
Brother of Dick Conway.
B. Nov. 28, 1861, Lowell, Mass.   D. Dec. 18, 1943, Somerville, Mass.

BR TR 5'8½" 170 lbs.

	G	AB	H	2B	3B	HR	HR %	R	RBI	BB	SO	SB	BA	SA	AB	H	G by POS
1884 PHI N	1	4	0	0	0	0	0.0	0		0	1		.000	.000	0	0	C-1
1886 BAL AA	7	14	2	0	0	0	0.0	4		7			.143	.143	0	0	C-7
2 yrs.	8	18	2	0	0	0	0.0	4		7	1		.111	.111	0	0	C-8

Jack Conway

CONWAY, JACK CLEMENTS
B. July 30, 1919, Bryan, Tex.

BR TR 5'11" 175 lbs.

	G	AB	H	2B	3B	HR	HR %	R	RBI	BB	SO	SB	BA	SA	AB	H	G by POS
1941 CLE A	2	2	1	0	0	0	0.0	0	1	0	0	0	.500	.500	0	0	SS-2
1946	68	258	58	6	2	0	0.0	24	18	20	36	2	.225	.264	2	0	2B-50, SS-14, 3B-3
1947	34	50	9	2	0	0	0.0	3	5	3	8	0	.180	.220	2	0	SS-24, 2B-5, 3B-1
1948 NY N	24	49	12	2	1	1	2.0	8	3	5	10	0	.245	.388	2	0	2B-13, SS-6, 3B-3
4 yrs.	128	359	80	10	3	1	0.3	35	27	28	54	2	.223	.276	6	0	2B-68, SS-46, 3B-7

Owen Conway

CONWAY, OWEN SYLVESTER
B. Oct. 23, 1890, New York, N. Y.   D. Mar. 13, 1942, Philadelphia, Pa.

TR

	G	AB	H	2B	3B	HR	HR %	R	RBI	BB	SO	SB	BA	SA	AB	H	G by POS
1915 PHI A	4	15	1	0	0	0	0.0	2	0	0	3	0	.067	.067	0	0	3B-4

Pete Conway

CONWAY, PETER J.
Brother of Jim Conway.
B. Oct. 30, 1866, Burmont, Pa.   D. Jan. 13, 1903, Clifton Heights, Pa.

BR TR 5'10½"

	G	AB	H	2B	3B	HR	HR %	R	RBI	BB	SO	SB	BA	SA	AB	H	G by POS
1885 BUF N	29	90	10	5	0	1	1.1	7	7	5	28		.111	.200	0	0	P-27, OF-2, SS-1, 1B-1
1886 2 teams		KC N (51G – .242)				DET N (12G – .186)											
" total	63	237	55	9	2	3	1.3	32	21	6	42		.232	.325	0	0	P-34, OF-32
1887 DET N	24	95	22	5	1	1	1.1	16	7	2	9	0	.232	.337	0	0	P-17, OF-8
1888	45	167	46	4	2	3	1.8	28	23	8	25	1	.275	.377	0	0	P-45, OF-1
1889 PIT N	3	10	1	0	0	1	10.0	2	2	1	3	1	.100	.400	0	0	P-3, OF-1
5 yrs.	164	599	134	23	5	9	1.5	85	60	22	107	2	.224	.324	0	0	P-126, OF-44, SS-1, 1B-1

Rip Conway

CONWAY, RICHARD DANIEL
B. Apr. 18, 1896, White Bear, Minn.   D. Dec. 3, 1971, St. Paul, Minn.

BL TR 5'6" 160 lbs.

	G	AB	H	2B	3B	HR	HR %	R	RBI	BB	SO	SB	BA	SA	AB	H	G by POS
1918 BOS N	14	24	4	0	0	0	0.0	4	2	2	4	1	.167	.167	5	2	2B-5, 3B-1

Ed Conwell

CONWELL, EDWARD JAMES (Irish)
B. Jan. 29, 1890, Chicago, Ill.   D. May 1, 1980, Norwood Park, Ill.

BR TR 5'11" 155 lbs.

	G	AB	H	2B	3B	HR	HR %	R	RBI	BB	SO	SB	BA	SA	AB	H	G by POS
1911 STL N	1	1	0	0	0	0	0.0	0	0	0	1	0	.000	.000	0	0	3B-1

Herb Conyers

CONYERS, HERBERT LEROY
B. Jan. 8, 1921, Cowgill, Mo.   D. Sept. 16, 1964, Cleveland, Ohio

BL TR 6'5" 210 lbs.

	G	AB	H	2B	3B	HR	HR %	R	RBI	BB	SO	SB	BA	SA	AB	H	G by POS
1950 CLE A	7	9	3	0	0	1	11.1	2	1	1	2	1	.333	.667	4	2	1B-1

Dale Coogan

COOGAN, DALE ROGER
B. Aug. 14, 1930, Los Angeles, Calif.

BL TL 6'1" 190 lbs.

	G	AB	H	2B	3B	HR	HR %	R	RBI	BB	SO	SB	BA	SA	AB	H	G by POS
1950 PIT N	53	129	31	6	1	1	0.8	19	13	17	24	0	.240	.326	16	2	1B-32

Dan Coogan

COOGAN, DANIEL GEORGE
B. Feb. 16, 1875, Philadelphia, Pa.   D. Oct. 28, 1942, Philadelphia, Pa.

	G	AB	H	2B	3B	HR	HR %	R	RBI	BB	SO	SB	BA	SA	AB	H	G by POS
1895 WAS N	26	77	17	2	1	0	0.0	9	7	13	6	1	.221	.273	1	0	SS-18, C-5, OF-2, 3B-1

Cliff Cook

COOK, RAYMOND CLIFFORD
B. Aug. 20, 1936, Dallas, Tex.

BR TR 6' 185 lbs.

	G	AB	H	2B	3B	HR	HR %	R	RBI	BB	SO	SB	BA	SA	AB	H	G by POS
1959 CIN N	9	21	8	2	1	0	0.0	3	5	2	8	1	.381	.571	0	0	3B-9
1960	54	149	31	7	0	3	2.0	9	13	8	51	0	.208	.315	0	0	3B-47, OF-4
1961	4	5	0	0	0	0	0.0	0	0	0	4	0	.000	.000	3	0	3B-1

	G	AB	H	2B	3B	HR	HR %	R	RBI	BB	SO	SB	BA	SA	Pinch Hit AB	Pinch Hit H	G by POS

Cliff Cook continued

	G	AB	H	2B	3B	HR	HR %	R	RBI	BB	SO	SB	BA	SA	AB	H	G by POS
1962 **2 teams**	**CIN**	**N** (6G – .000)			**NY**	**N** (40G – .232)											
" total	46	117	26	6	1	2	1.7	12	9	4	36	1	.222	.342	14	4	3B-20, OF-10
1963 **NY N**	50	106	15	2	1	2	1.9	9	8	12	37	0	.142	.236	19	4	OF-21, 3B-9, 1B-5
5 yrs.	163	398	80	17	3	7	1.8	33	35	26	136	2	.201	.312	36	8	3B-86, OF-35, 1B-5

Doc Cook

COOK, LUTHER ALMUS　　　　　　　　　　　BL TR 6'　　170 lbs.
B. June 24, 1886, Witt, Tex.　　D. June 30, 1973, Lawrenceburg, Tenn.

	G	AB	H	2B	3B	HR	HR %	R	RBI	BB	SO	SB	BA	SA	AB	H	G by POS
1913 **NY A**	20	72	19	2	1	0	0.0	9	1	10	4	1	.264	.319	0	0	OF-20
1914	131	470	133	11	3	1	0.2	59	40	44	60	26	.283	.326	5	1	OF-126
1915	132	476	129	16	5	2	0.4	70	33	62	43	29	.271	.338	0	0	OF-131
1916	3	10	1	0	0	0	0.0	0	1	0	2	0	.100	.100	0	0	OF-3
4 yrs.	286	1028	282	29	9	3	0.3	138	75	116	109	56	.274	.329	5	1	OF-280

Jim Cook

COOK, JAMES FITCHIE　　　　　　　　　　　TR
B. Nov. 10, 1879, Dundee, Ill.　　D. June 17, 1949, St. Louis, Mo.

	G	AB	H	2B	3B	HR	HR %	R	RBI	BB	SO	SB	BA	SA	AB	H	G by POS
1903 **CHI N**	8	26	4	1	0	0	0.0	3	2	2		1	.154	.192	0	0	OF-5, 2B-2, 1B-1

Paul Cook

COOK, PAUL　　　　　　　　　　　BR TR
B. May 5, 1863, Caledonia, N. Y.　　D. May 26, 1905, Rochester, N. Y.

	G	AB	H	2B	3B	HR	HR %	R	RBI	BB	SO	SB	BA	SA	AB	H	G by POS
1884 **PHI N**	3	12	1	0	0	0	0.0	0		0	2		.083	.083	0	0	C-3
1886 **LOU AA**	66	262	54	5	2	0	0.0	28		10			.206	.240	0	0	1B-43, C-21, OF-2
1887	61	223	55	4	2	0	0.0	34		11		15	.247	.283	0	0	C-55, 1B-6
1888	57	185	34	2	0	0	0.0	20	13	5		9	.184	.195	0	0	C-53, OF-4, SS-1
1889	81	286	65	10	1	0	0.0	34	15	15	48	11	.227	.269	0	0	C-74, OF-7, SS-1, 1B-1
1890 **BKN P**	58	218	55	3	3	0	0.0	32	31	14	18	7	.252	.294	0	0	C-36, 1B-21, OF-1
1891 **2 teams**	52	**LOU**	**AA** (45G – .229)			**STL**	**AA** (7G – .200)										
" total	52	178	40	3	1	0	0.0	24	24	12	19	4	.225	.253	0	0	C-42, 1B-10
7 yrs.	378	1364	304	27	9	0	0.0	172	82	67	87	46	.223	.256	0	0	C-284, 1B-81, OF-14, SS-2

Dusty Cooke

COOKE, ALLEN LINDSEY　　　　　　　　　　　BB TR 6'1"　　205 lbs.
B. June 23, 1907, Swepsonville, N. C.
Manager 1948.

	G	AB	H	2B	3B	HR	HR %	R	RBI	BB	SO	SB	BA	SA	AB	H	G by POS
1930 **NY A**	92	216	55	12	3	6	2.8	43	29	32	61	4	.255	.421	10	1	OF-73
1931	27	39	13	1	0	1	2.6	10	6	8	11	4	.333	.436	2	0	OF-11
1932	3	0	0	0	0	0	–	1	0	1	0	0	–	–	0	0	
1933 **BOS A**	119	454	132	35	10	5	1.1	86	54	67	71	7	.291	.445	2	0	OF-118
1934	74	168	41	8	5	1	0.6	34	26	36	25	7	.244	.369	21	4	OF-44
1935	100	294	90	18	6	3	1.0	51	34	46	24	6	.306	.439	11	2	OF-82
1936	111	341	93	20	3	6	1.8	58	47	72	48	4	.273	.402	13	4	OF-91
1938 **CIN N**	82	233	64	15	1	2	0.9	41	33	28	36	0	.275	.373	27	5	OF-51
8 yrs.	608	1745	488	109	28	24	1.4	324	229	290	276	32	.280	.415	86	16	OF-470

Fred Cooke

COOKE, FREDERICK B.
B. Paulding, Ohio　　Deceased.

	G	AB	H	2B	3B	HR	HR %	R	RBI	BB	SO	SB	BA	SA	AB	H	G by POS
1897 **CLE N**	5	17	5	2	0	0	0.0	2	3	3		0	.294	.412	0	0	OF-5

Duff Cooley

COOLEY, DICK GORDON (Sir Richard)　　　　　　　BL TR
B. Mar. 14, 1873, Dallas, Tex.　　D. Aug. 9, 1937, Dallas, Tex.

	G	AB	H	2B	3B	HR	HR %	R	RBI	BB	SO	SB	BA	SA	AB	H	G by POS
1893 **STL N**	29	107	37	2	3	0	0.0	20	21	8	9	8	.346	.421	1	0	OF-15, C-10, SS-5
1894	54	206	61	3	1	1	0.5	35	21	12	16	7	.296	.335	0	0	OF-39, 3B-13, SS-1, 1B-1
1895	132	563	191	9	21	6	1.1	106	75	36	29	27	.339	.462	1	0	OF-124, 3B-5, SS-3, C-1
1896 **2 teams**	104	**STL**	**N** (40G – .307)			**PHI**	**N** (64G – .307)										
" total	104	453	139	11	7	2	0.4	92	35	25	19	30	.307	.375	0	0	OF-104
1897 **PHI N**	133	566	186	14	13	4	0.7	124	40	51		31	.329	.420	0	0	OF-131, 1B-2
1898	149	629	196	24	12	4	0.6	123	55	48		17	.312	.407	0	0	OF-149
1899	94	406	112	15	8	1	0.2	75	31	29		15	.276	.360	1	0	1B-79, OF-14, 2B-1
1900 **PIT N**	66	249	50	8	1	0	0.0	30	22	14		9	.201	.241	0	0	1B-66
1901 **BOS N**	63	240	62	13	3	0	0.0	27	27	14		5	.258	.338	0	0	OF-53, 1B-10
1902	135	548	162	26	8	0	0.0	73	58	34		27	.296	.372	1	0	OF-127, 1B-7
1903	138	553	160	26	10	1	0.2	76	70	44		27	.289	.378	0	0	OF-126, 1B-13
1904	122	467	127	18	7	5	1.1	41	70	24		14	.272	.373	0	0	OF-116, 1B-6
1905 **DET A**	99	377	93	11	9	1	0.3	25	32	26		7	.247	.332	1	0	OF-97
13 yrs.	1318	5364	1576	180	103	25	0.5	847	557	365	73	224	.294	.380	5	1	OF-1095, 1B-184, 3B-18, C-11, SS-9, 2B-1

Cecil Coombs

COOMBS, CECIL LYSANDER　　　　　　　　BR TR 5'9"　　160 lbs.
B. Mar. 18, 1888, Moweaqua, Ill.　　D. Nov. 25, 1975, Fort Worth, Tex.

	G	AB	H	2B	3B	HR	HR %	R	RBI	BB	SO	SB	BA	SA	AB	H	G by POS
1914 **CHI A**	7	23	4	1	0	0	0.0	1	1	1	7	0	.174	.217	0	0	OF-7

Jack Coombs

COOMBS, JOHN WESLEY (Colby Jack)　　　　　　BB TR 6'　　185 lbs.
B. Nov. 18, 1882, LeGrand, Iowa　　D. Apr. 15, 1957, LeGrand, Iowa
Manager 1919.

	G	AB	H	2B	3B	HR	HR %	R	RBI	BB	SO	SB	BA	SA	AB	H	G by POS
1906 **PHI A**	24	67	16	2	0	0	0.0	9	3	1		2	.239	.269	1	0	P-23
1907	24	48	8	0	0	1	2.1	4	4	0		1	.167	.229	1	0	P-23
1908	78	220	56	9	5	1	0.5	24	23	9		6	.255	.355	5	4	OF-47, P-26
1909	37	83	14	4	0	0	0.0	4	10	4		1	.169	.217	6	1	P-31
1910	46	132	29	3	0	0	0.0	20	9	7		3	.220	.242	1	0	P-45
1911	52	141	45	6	1	2	1.4	31	23	8		5	.319	.418	4	1	P-47
1912	55	110	28	2	0	0	0.0	10	13	14		1	.255	.273	14	4	P-40
1913	2	3	1	1	0	0	0.0	1	0	0		0	.333	.667	0	0	P-2
1914	5	11	3	1	0	0	0.0	0	2	1	1	0	.273	.364	1	0	OF-2, P-2
1915 **BKN N**	29	75	21	1	1	0	0.0	8	5	2	17	0	.280	.320	1	0	P-29
1916	27	61	11	2	0	0	0.0	2	3	2	10	0	.180	.213	0	0	P-27

	G	AB	H	2B	3B	HR	HR %	R	RBI	BB	SO	SB	BA	SA	Pinch Hit AB	Pinch Hit H	G by POS

Jack Coombs continued

	G	AB	H	2B	3B	HR	HR %	R	RBI	BB	SO	SB	BA	SA	AB	H	G by POS
1917	32	44	10	0	1	0	0.0	4	2	4	9	1	.227	.273	0	0	P-31
1918	46	113	19	3	2	0	0.0	6	3	7	5	1	.168	.230	3	1	P-27, OF-13
1920 DET A	2	2	0	0	0	0	0.0	0	0	0	0	0	.000	.000	0	0	P-2
14 yrs.	459	1110	261	34	10	4	0.4	123	100	59	44	21	.235	.295	36	11	P-355, OF-62
WORLD SERIES																	
1910 PHI A	3	13	5	1	0	0	0.0	0	3	0	3	0	.385	.462	0	0	P-3
1911	2	8	2	0	0	0	0.0	1	0	0	0	0	.250	.250	0	0	P-2
1916 BKN N	1	3	1	0	0	0	0.0	0	1	0	0	0	.333	.333	0	0	P-1
3 yrs.	6	24	8	1	0	0	0.0	1	4	0	3	0	.333	.375	0	0	P-6

Bill Cooney

COONEY, WILLIAM A.   TR
B. Apr. 4, 1887, Boston, Mass.   D. Nov. 6, 1928, Roxbury, Mass.

	G	AB	H	2B	3B	HR	HR %	R	RBI	BB	SO	SB	BA	SA	AB	H	G by POS
1909 BOS N	5	10	3	0	0	0	0.0	0	0	0		0	.300	.300	0	0	P-3, SS-1, 2B-1
1910	8	12	3	0	0	0	0.0	2	1	2	0	0	.250	.250	5	2	OF-2
2 yrs.	13	22	6	0	0	0	0.0	2	1	2	0	0	.273	.273	5	2	P-3, OF-2, SS-1, 2B-1

Jimmy Cooney

COONEY, JAMES EDWARD (Scoops)   BR TR 5'11" 160 lbs.
Son of Jimmy Cooney.   Brother of Johnny Cooney.
B. Aug. 24, 1894, Cranston, R. I.

	G	AB	H	2B	3B	HR	HR %	R	RBI	BB	SO	SB	BA	SA	AB	H	G by POS
1917 BOS A	11	36	8	1	0	0	0.0	4	3	6	2	0	.222	.250	0	0	2B-10, SS-1
1919 NY N	5	14	3	0	0	0	0.0	3	1	0	0	0	.214	.214	0	0	SS-4, 2B-1
1924 STL N	110	383	113	20	8	1	0.3	44	57	20	20	12	.295	.397	0	0	SS-99, 3B-7, 2B-1
1925	54	187	51	11	2	0	0.0	27	18	4	5	1	.273	.353	1	0	SS-37, 2B-15, OF-1
1926 CHI N	141	513	129	18	5	1	0.2	52	47	23	10	11	.251	.312	0	0	SS-141
1927 2 teams		CHI N (33G – .242)			PHI N (76G – .270)												
" total	109	391	102	14	1	0	0.0	49	21	21	16	5	.261	.302	1	0	SS-107
1928 BOS N	18	51	7	0	0	0	0.0	2	3	2	5	1	.137	.137	4	0	SS-11, 2B-4
7 yrs.	448	1575	413	64	16	2	0.1	181	150	76	58	30	.262	.327	6	0	SS-400, 2B-31, 3B-7, OF-1

Jimmy Cooney

COONEY, JAMES JOSEPH   BR TR 5'9" 155 lbs.
Father of Jimmy Cooney.   Father of Johnny Cooney.
B. July 9, 1865, Cranston, R. I.   D. July 1, 1903, Cranston, R. I.

	G	AB	H	2B	3B	HR	HR %	R	RBI	BB	SO	SB	BA	SA	AB	H	G by POS
1890 CHI N	135	574	156	19	10	4	0.7	114	52	73	23	45	.272	.361	0	0	SS-135, C-1
1891	118	465	114	15	3	0	0.0	84	42	48	17	21	.245	.290	0	0	SS-118
1892 2 teams		CHI N (65G – .172)			WAS N (6G – .160)												
" total	71	263	45	1	1	0	0.0	23	24	27	8	11	.171	.183	0	0	SS-71
3 yrs.	324	1302	315	35	14	4	0.3	221	118	148	48	77	.242	.300	0	0	SS-324, C-1

Johnny Cooney

COONEY, JOHN WALTER   BR TL 5'10" 165 lbs.
Son of Jimmy Cooney.   Brother of Jimmy Cooney.
B. Mar. 18, 1901, Cranston, R. I.

	G	AB	H	2B	3B	HR	HR %	R	RBI	BB	SO	SB	BA	SA	AB	H	G by POS
1921 BOS N	8	5	1	0	0	0	0.0	0	0	0	1	0	.200	.200	0	0	P-8
1922	4	8	0	0	0	0	0.0	0	0	0	1	0	.000	.000	0	0	P-4
1923	42	66	25	1	0	0	0.0	7	3	4	2	0	.379	.394	1	1	P-23, OF-11, 1B-1
1924	55	130	33	2	1	0	0.0	10	4	9	5	0	.254	.285	1	1	P-34, OF-14, 1B-1
1925	54	103	33	7	0	0	0.0	17	13	3	6	1	.320	.388	1	0	P-31, 1B-3, OF-1
1926	64	126	38	3	2	0	0.0	17	18	13	7	6	.302	.357	5	3	1B-32, P-19, OF-1
1927	10	1	0	0	0	0	0.0	3	0	0	0	0	.000	.000	1	0	
1928	33	41	7	0	0	0	0.0	2	2	4	3	0	.171	.171	3	0	P-24, 1B-3, OF-2
1929	41	72	23	4	1	0	0.0	10	6	3	3	1	.319	.403	5	3	OF-16, P-14
1930	4	3	0	0	0	0	0.0	0	0	0	0	0	.000	.000	1	0	P-2
1935 BKN N	10	29	9	0	1	0	0.0	3	1	3	2	0	.310	.379	0	0	OF-10
1936	130	507	143	17	5	0	0.0	71	30	24	15	3	.282	.335	0	0	OF-130
1937	120	430	126	18	5	0	0.0	61	37	22	10	5	.293	.358	5	1	OF-111, 1B-2
1938 BOS N	120	432	117	25	5	0	0.0	45	17	22	12	2	.271	.352	0	0	OF-110, 1B-13
1939	118	368	101	8	1	2	0.5	39	27	21	8	2	.274	.318	0	0	OF-116, 1B-2
1940	108	365	116	14	3	0	0.0	40	21	25	9	4	.318	.373	1	0	OF-99, 1B-7
1941	123	442	141	25	2	0	0.0	52	29	27	15	3	.319	.385	6	1	OF-111, 1B-4
1942	74	198	41	6	0	0	0.0	23	7	23	5	2	.207	.237	0	0	OF-54, 1B-23
1943 BKN N	37	34	7	0	0	0	0.0	7	2	4	3	1	.206	.206	22	4	1B-3, OF-2
1944 2 teams		BKN N (7G – .750)			NY A (10G – .125)												
" total	17	12	4	0	0	0	0.0	1	2	1	0	0	.333	.333	7	3	OF-4
20 yrs.	1172	3372	965	130	26	2	0.1	408	219	208	107	30	.286	.342	59	17	OF-792, P-159, 1B-94

Phil Cooney

COONEY, PHILLIP   BR TR
Born Phillip Cohn.
B. Sept. 14, 1886, Paterson, N. J.

	G	AB	H	2B	3B	HR	HR %	R	RBI	BB	SO	SB	BA	SA	AB	H	G by POS
1905 NY A	1	3	0	0	0	0	0.0	0	0	0		0	.000	.000	0	0	3B-1

William Coons

COONS, WILBUR K.
B. Mar. 21, 1855, Philadelphia, Pa.   D. Aug. 30, 1915, Burlington, N. J.

	G	AB	H	2B	3B	HR	HR %	R	RBI	BB	SO	SB	BA	SA	AB	H	G by POS
1876 PHI N	54	220	50	5	1	0	0.0	30	22	2	4		.227	.259	0	0	OF-29, C-18, 3B-4, 2B-4, P-2

Cecil Cooper

COOPER, CECIL CELESTER   BL TL 6'2" 165 lbs.
B. Dec. 20, 1949, Washington County, Tex.

	G	AB	H	2B	3B	HR	HR %	R	RBI	BB	SO	SB	BA	SA	AB	H	G by POS
1971 BOS A	14	42	13	4	1	0	0.0	9	3	5	4	1	.310	.452	3	2	1B-11
1972	12	17	4	1	0	0	0.0	0	2	2	5	0	.235	.294	9	1	1B-3
1973	30	101	24	2	0	3	3.0	12	11	7	12	1	.238	.347	1	0	1B-29
1974	121	414	114	24	1	8	1.9	55	43	32	74	2	.275	.396	7	1	1B-74, DH-41
1975	106	305	95	17	6	14	4.6	49	44	19	33	1	.311	.544	18	6	DH-54, 1B-35
1976	123	451	127	22	6	15	3.3	66	78	16	62	7	.282	.457	9	0	1B-66, DH-53
1977 MIL A	160	643	193	31	7	20	3.1	86	78	28	110	13	.300	.463	1	0	1B-148, DH-10
1978	107	407	127	23	2	13	3.2	60	54	32	72	3	.312	.474	4	1	1B-84, DH-19

	G	AB	H	2B	3B	HR	HR %	R	RBI	BB	SO	SB	BA	SA	Pinch Hit AB	Pinch Hit H	G by POS

Cecil Cooper continued

	G	AB	H	2B	3B	HR	HR%	R	RBI	BB	SO	SB	BA	SA	PH AB	PH H	G by POS
1979	150	590	182	**44**	1	24	4.1	83	106	56	77	15	.308	.508	2	1	1B-135, DH-15
1980	153	622	219	33	4	25	4.0	96	**122**	39	42	17	.352	.539	1	1	1B-142, DH-11
1981	106	416	133	**35**	1	12	2.9	70	60	28	30	5	.320	.495	2	0	1B-101, DH-5
1982	155	654	205	38	3	32	4.9	104	121	32	53	2	.313	.528	0	0	1B-154, DH-1
1983	160	661	203	37	3	30	4.5	106	**126**	37	63	2	.307	.508	1	1	1B-158, DH-2
1984	148	603	166	28	3	11	1.8	63	67	27	59	8	.275	.386	0	0	1B-122, DH-26
14 yrs.	1545	5926	1805	339	38	207	3.5	859	915	360	696	77	.305	.479	58	14	1B-1262, DH-237

DIVISIONAL PLAYOFF SERIES

	G	AB	H	2B	3B	HR	HR%	R	RBI	BB	SO	SB	BA	SA	PH AB	PH H	G by POS
1981 MIL A	5	18	4	0	0	0	0.0	1	3	1	3	0	.222	.222	0	0	1B-5

LEAGUE CHAMPIONSHIP SERIES

	G	AB	H	2B	3B	HR	HR%	R	RBI	BB	SO	SB	BA	SA	PH AB	PH H	G by POS
1975 BOS A	3	10	4	2	0	0	0.0	0	1	0	2	0	.400	.600	0	0	1B-3
1982 MIL A	5	20	3	2	0	0	0.0	1	4	0	6	0	.150	.250	0	0	1B-5
2 yrs.	8	30	7	4	0	0	0.0	1	5	0	8	0	.233	.367	0	0	1B-8

WORLD SERIES

	G	AB	H	2B	3B	HR	HR%	R	RBI	BB	SO	SB	BA	SA	PH AB	PH H	G by POS
1975 BOS A	5	19	1	1	0	0	0.0	0	1	0	3	0	.053	.105	1	0	1B-5
1982 MIL A	7	28	8	1	0	1	3.6	3	6	1	1	0	.286	.429	0	0	1B-7
2 yrs.	12	47	9	2	0	1	2.1	3	7	1	4	0	.191	.298	1	0	1B-12

Claude Cooper

COOPER, CLAUDE WILLIAM   BL TL 5'9"   158 lbs.
B. Apr. 1, 1893, Troupe, Tex.   D. Jan. 21, 1974, Plainview, Tex.

	G	AB	H	2B	3B	HR	HR%	R	RBI	BB	SO	SB	BA	SA	PH AB	PH H	G by POS
1913 NY N	27	30	9	4	0	0	0.0	11	4	4	6	3	.300	.433	2	0	OF-15
1914 BKN F	113	399	96	14	11	2	0.5	56	25	26		25	.241	.346	8	3	OF-101
1915	153	527	155	26	12	2	0.4	75	63	77		31	.294	.400	0	0	OF-121, 1B-32
1916 PHI N	56	104	20	2	0	0	0.0	9	11	7	15	1	.192	.212	22	6	OF-29, 1B-1
1917	24	29	3	1	0	0	0.0	5	1	5	4	0	.103	.138	8	0	OF-12
5 yrs.	373	1089	283	47	23	4	0.4	156	104	119	25	60	.260	.356	40	9	OF-278, 1B-33

WORLD SERIES

	G	AB	H	2B	3B	HR	HR%	R	RBI	BB	SO	SB	BA	SA	PH AB	PH H	G by POS
1913 NY N	2	0	0	0	0	0	—	0	0	0	0	1	—	—	0	0	

Gary Cooper

COOPER, GARY NATHANIEL   BB TR 6'3"   175 lbs.
B. Dec. 22, 1956, Savannah, Ga.

	G	AB	H	2B	3B	HR	HR%	R	RBI	BB	SO	SB	BA	SA	PH AB	PH H	G by POS
1980 ATL N	21	2	0	0	0	0	0.0	3	0	0	1	2	.000	.000	1	0	OF-13

Pat Cooper

COOPER, ORGE PATTERSON   BR TR 6'3"   180 lbs.
B. Nov. 26, 1917, Albemarle, N. C.

	G	AB	H	2B	3B	HR	HR%	R	RBI	BB	SO	SB	BA	SA	PH AB	PH H	G by POS
1946 PHI A	1	0	0	0	0	0	—	0	0	0	0	0	—	—	0	0	P-1
1947	13	16	4	2	0	0	0.0	0	3	0	5	0	.250	.375	12	3	1B-1
2 yrs.	14	16	4	2	0	0	0.0	0	3	0	5	0	.250	.375	12	3	1B-1, P-1

Walker Cooper

COOPER, WILLIAM WALKER   BR TR 6'3"   210 lbs.
Brother of Mort Cooper.
B. Jan. 8, 1915, Atherton, Mo.

	G	AB	H	2B	3B	HR	HR%	R	RBI	BB	SO	SB	BA	SA	PH AB	PH H	G by POS
1940 STL N	6	19	6	1	0	0	0.0	3	2	2	2	1	.316	.368	0	0	C-6
1941	68	200	49	9	1	1	0.5	19	20	13	14	1	.245	.315	5	2	C-63
1942	125	438	123	32	7	7	1.6	58	65	29	29	4	.281	.434	10	5	C-115
1943	122	449	143	30	4	9	2.0	52	81	19	19	1	.318	.463	10	1	C-112
1944	112	397	126	25	5	13	3.3	56	72	20	19	4	.317	.504	15	5	C-97
1945	4	18	7	0	0	0	0.0	3	1	0	1	0	.389	.389	0	0	C-4
1946 NY N	87	280	75	10	1	8	2.9	29	46	17	12	0	.268	.396	13	3	C-73
1947	140	515	157	24	8	35	6.8	79	122	24	43	2	.305	.586	6	1	C-132
1948	91	290	77	12	0	16	5.5	40	54	28	29	1	.266	.472	12	2	C-79
1949 2 teams		NY N (42G – .211)						CIN N (82G – .280)									
" total	124	454	117	13	4	20	4.4	48	83	28	32	0	.258	.436	5	1	C-117
1950 2 teams		CIN N (15G – .191)						BOS N (102G – .329)									
" total	117	384	120	22	3	14	3.6	55	64	30	31	1	.313	.495	12	6	C-101
1951 BOS N	109	342	107	14	1	18	5.3	42	59	28	18	1	.313	.518	18	2	C-90
1952	102	349	82	12	1	10	2.9	33	55	22	32	1	.235	.361	13	4	C-89
1953 MIL N	53	137	30	6	0	3	2.2	12	16	12	15	1	.219	.328	17	3	C-35
1954 2 teams		PIT N (14G – .200)						CHI N (57G – .310)									
" total	71	173	52	12	2	7	4.0	21	33	23	24	0	.301	.514	23	5	C-50
1955 CHI N	54	111	31	8	1	7	6.3	11	15	6	19	0	.279	.559	28	6	C-31
1956 STL N	40	68	18	5	1	2	2.9	5	14	3	8	0	.265	.456	22	3	C-16
1957	48	78	21	5	1	3	3.8	7	10	5	10	0	.269	.474	30	7	C-13
18 yrs.	1473	4702	1341	240	40	173	3.7	573	812	309	357	18	.285	.464	239	56	C-1223

WORLD SERIES

	G	AB	H	2B	3B	HR	HR%	R	RBI	BB	SO	SB	BA	SA	PH AB	PH H	G by POS
1942 STL N	5	21	6	1	0	0	0.0	3	4	0	1	0	.286	.333	0	0	C-5
1943	5	17	5	0	0	0	0.0	1	0	0	1	0	.294	.294	0	0	C-5
1944	6	22	7	2	1	0	0.0	1	2	3	2	0	.318	.500	0	0	C-6
3 yrs.	16	60	18	3	1	0	0.0	5	6	3	4	0	.300	.383	0	0	C-16

Gene Corbett

CORBETT, EUGENE LOUIS   BL TR 6'1½"   190 lbs.
B. Oct. 25, 1913, Winona, Minn.

	G	AB	H	2B	3B	HR	HR%	R	RBI	BB	SO	SB	BA	SA	PH AB	PH H	G by POS
1936 PHI N	6	21	3	0	0	0	0.0	1	2	2	3	0	.143	.143	0	0	1B-6
1937	7	12	4	2	0	0	0.0	4	1	0	0	0	.333	.500	3	1	3B-3, 2B-1
1938	24	75	6	1	0	2	2.7	7	7	6	11	0	.080	.173	1	0	1B-22
3 yrs.	37	108	13	3	0	2	1.9	12	10	8	14	0	.120	.204	4	1	1B-28, 3B-3, 2B-1

Claude Corbitt

CORBITT, CLAUDE ELLIOTT   BR TR 5'10"   170 lbs.
B. July 21, 1915, Sunbury, N. C.   D. May 1, 1978, Cincinnati, Ohio

	G	AB	H	2B	3B	HR	HR%	R	RBI	BB	SO	SB	BA	SA	PH AB	PH H	G by POS
1945 BKN N	2	4	2	0	0	0	0.0	1	0	1	0	0	.500	.500	0	0	3B-2
1946 CIN N	82	274	68	10	1	1	0.4	25	16	23	13	3	.248	.303	2	1	SS-77
1948	87	258	66	11	0	0	0.0	24	18	14	16	4	.256	.298	9	3	2B-52, 3B-16, SS-11
1949	44	94	17	1	0	0	0.0	10	3	9	1	1	.181	.191	3	0	SS-18, 2B-17, 3B-1
4 yrs.	215	630	153	22	1	1	0.2	60	37	47	30	8	.243	.286	14	4	SS-106, 2B-69, 3B-19

	G	AB	H	2B	3B	HR	HR %	R	RBI	BB	SO	SB	BA	SA	Pinch Hit AB	H	G by POS

Art Corcoran

CORCORAN, ARTHUR ANDREW (Bunny)   TR
B. Oct. 23, 1894, Roxbury, Mass.   D. July 27, 1958, Chelsea, Mass.

	G	AB	H	2B	3B	HR	HR %	R	RBI	BB	SO	SB	BA	SA	AB	H	G by POS
1915 PHI A	1	4	0	0	0	0	0.0	0	0	0	2	0	.000	.000	0	0	3B-1

John Corcoran

CORCORAN, JOHN A.
B. 1873, Cincinnati, Ohio   D. Nov. 1, 1901, Cincinnati, Ohio

	G	AB	H	2B	3B	HR	HR %	R	RBI	BB	SO	SB	BA	SA	AB	H	G by POS
1895 PIT N	6	20	3	0	0	0	0.0	0	1	0	2	0	.150	.150	0	0	SS-4, 3B-2

John Corcoran

CORCORAN, JOHN H.
B. Lowell, Mass.   Deceased.

	G	AB	H	2B	3B	HR	HR %	R	RBI	BB	SO	SB	BA	SA	AB	H	G by POS
1884 BKN AA	52	185	39	4	3	0	0.0	17		8			.211	.265	0	0	C-38, OF-9, 2B-4, SS-2, P-1

Larry Corcoran

CORCORAN, LAWRENCE J.
Brother of Mike Corcoran.   TR
B. Aug. 10, 1859, Brooklyn, N. Y.   D. Oct. 14, 1891, Newark, N. J.

	G	AB	H	2B	3B	HR	HR %	R	RBI	BB	SO	SB	BA	SA	AB	H	G by POS
1880 CHI N	72	286	66	11	1	0	0.0	41	25	10	33		.231	.276	0	0	P-63, OF-8, SS-8
1881	47	189	42	8	0	0	0.0	25	9	5	22		.222	.265	0	0	P-45, SS-2, OF-1
1882	40	169	35	10	2	1	0.6	23	24	6	18		.207	.308	0	0	P-39, 3B-1
1883	68	263	55	12	7	0	0.0	40		6	62		.209	.308	0	0	P-56, OF-13, SS-3, 2B-1
1884	64	251	61	3	4	1	0.4	43		10	33		.243	.299	0	0	P-60, OF-4, SS-2
1885 2 teams	CHI	N (7G –	.273)		NY	N (3G –	.357)										
" total	10	36	11	1	0	0	0.0	9	4	6	2		.306	.333	0	0	P-10, SS-1
1886 2 teams	NY	N (1G –	.000)		WAS	N (21G –	.185)										
" total	22	85	15	2	1	0	0.0	9	3	7	16		.176	.224	0	0	OF-12, SS-9, P-2
1887 IND N	3	10	2	0	0	0	0.0	2	0	2	1	2	.200	.200	0	0	OF-2, P-2
8 yrs.	326	1289	287	47	15	2	0.2	192	65	52	187	2	.223	.287	0	0	P-277, OF-40, SS-25, 3B-1, 2B-1

Mickey Corcoran

CORCORAN, MICHAEL JOSEPH   BR TR 5'8"   165 lbs.
B. Aug. 26, 1882, Buffalo, N. Y.   D. Dec. 9, 1950, Buffalo, N. Y.

	G	AB	H	2B	3B	HR	HR %	R	RBI	BB	SO	SB	BA	SA	AB	H	G by POS
1910 CIN N	14	46	10	3	0	0	0.0	3	7	5	9	0	.217	.283	0	0	2B-14

Tim Corcoran

CORCORAN, TIMOTHY MICHAEL   BL TL 5'11"   175 lbs.
B. Mar. 19, 1953, Glendale, Calif.

	G	AB	H	2B	3B	HR	HR %	R	RBI	BB	SO	SB	BA	SA	AB	H	G by POS
1977 DET A	55	103	29	3	0	3	2.9	13	15	6	9	0	.282	.398	32	10	OF-18, DH-3
1978	116	324	86	13	1	1	0.3	37	27	24	27	3	.265	.321	12	2	OF-109, DH-1
1979	18	22	5	1	0	0	0.0	4	6	4	2	1	.227	.273	2	1	OF-9, 1B-5, DH-2
1980	84	153	44	7	1	3	2.0	20	18	22	10	0	.288	.405	16	3	1B-48, OF-18, DH-5
1981 MIN A	22	51	9	3	0	0	0.0	4	4	6	7	0	.176	.235	4	0	1B-16, DH-3
1983 PHI N	3	0	0	0	0	0	–	0	0	0	0	0	–	–	0	0	1B-3
1984	102	208	71	13	1	5	2.4	30	36	37	27	0	.341	.486	37	10	1B-51, OF-17
7 yrs.	400	861	244	40	3	12	1.4	108	106	99	82	4	.283	.379	103	26	OF-171, 1B-123, DH-14

Tommy Corcoran

CORCORAN, THOMAS WILLIAM   BR TR 5'9"   164 lbs.
B. Jan. 4, 1869, New Haven, Conn.   D. June 25, 1960, Plainfield, Conn.

	G	AB	H	2B	3B	HR	HR %	R	RBI	BB	SO	SB	BA	SA	AB	H	G by POS
1890 PIT P	123	505	121	14	13	1	0.2	80	61	38	45	43	.240	.325	0	0	SS-123
1891 PHI AA	133	511	130	11	15	7	1.4	84	71	29	56	30	.254	.376	0	0	SS-133
1892 BKN N	151	615	146	12	6	1	0.2	77	74	34	51	39	.237	.281	0	0	SS-151
1893	115	459	126	11	10	2	0.4	61	58	27	12	14	.275	.355	0	0	SS-115
1894	129	576	173	21	20	5	0.9	123	92	25	17	33	.300	.432	0	0	SS-129
1895	128	541	150	17	10	2	0.4	85	69	23	11	17	.277	.357	0	0	SS-127
1896	132	532	154	15	7	3	0.6	63	73	15	13	16	.289	.361	0	0	SS-132
1897 CIN N	109	445	128	30	5	3	0.7	76	57	13		15	.288	.398	0	0	SS-63, 2B-47
1898	153	619	155	28	15	2	0.3	80	87	26		19	.250	.354	0	0	SS-153
1899	137	537	149	11	8	0	0.0	91	81	28		32	.277	.328	1	1	SS-123, 2B-14
1900	127	523	128	21	9	1	0.2	64	54	22		27	.245	.325	0	0	SS-124, 2B-5
1901	31	115	24	4	3	0	0.0	14	15	11		6	.209	.296	1	1	SS-30
1902	138	537	135	20	4	0	0.0	54	54	11		20	.251	.304	0	0	SS-137, 2B-1
1903	115	459	113	18	7	2	0.4	61	73	12		12	.246	.329	0	0	SS-115
1904	150	578	133	17	9	2	0.3	55	74	19		19	.230	.301	0	0	SS-150
1905	151	605	150	21	11	2	0.3	70	85	23		28	.248	.329	0	0	SS-151
1906	117	430	89	13	1	1	0.2	29	33	19		8	.207	.249	0	0	SS-117
1907 NY N	62	226	60	9	2	0	0.0	21	24	7		9	.265	.323	0	0	2B-62
18 yrs.	2201	8813	2264	293	155	34	0.4	1188	1135	382	205	387	.257	.337	2	2	SS-2073, 2B-129

Fred Corey

COREY, FREDERICK HARRISON   BR TR
B. 1857, S. Kingston, R. I.   D. Nov. 27, 1912, Providence, R. I.

	G	AB	H	2B	3B	HR	HR %	R	RBI	BB	SO	SB	BA	SA	AB	H	G by POS
1878 PRO N	7	21	3	0	0	0	0.0	3	1	0	2		.143	.143	0	0	P-5, 2B-2, 1B-1
1880 WOR N	41	138	24	8	1	0	0.0	11		4	27		.174	.246	0	0	OF-29, P-25, SS-3, 3B-1, 1B-1
1881	51	203	45	8	4	0	0.0	22	10	5	10		.222	.300	0	0	OF-25, P-23, SS-7
1882	64	255	63	7	12	0	0.0	33	29	5	31		.247	.369	0	0	SS-25, P-21, OF-15, 3B-6, 1B-5
1883 PHI AA	71	298	77	16	2	1	0.3	45		12			.258	.336	0	0	3B-34, P-18, OF-14, 2B-9, SS-1, C-1
1884	104	439	121	17	16	5	1.1	64		17			.276	.421	0	0	3B-104
1885	94	384	94	14	8	1	0.3	61		17			.245	.331	0	0	3B-92, SS-1, P-1
7 yrs.	432	1738	427	70	43	7	0.4	239	40	60	70		.246	.348	0	0	3B-237, P-93, OF-83, SS-38, 2B-11, 1B-7, C-1

Mark Corey

COREY, MARK MUNDELL   BR TR 6'2"   200 lbs.
B. Nov. 3, 1955, Tucumcari, N. M.

	G	AB	H	2B	3B	HR	HR %	R	RBI	BB	SO	SB	BA	SA	AB	H	G by POS
1979 BAL A	13	13	2	0	0	0	0.0	1	1	0	4	1	.154	.154	3	0	OF-11, DH-1
1980	36	36	10	2	0	1	2.8	7	2	5	7	0	.278	.417	4	1	OF-34
1981	10	8	0	0	0	0	0.0	2	0	2	2	0	.000	.000	1	0	OF-9
3 yrs.	59	57	12	2	0	1	1.8	10	3	7	13	1	.211	.298	8	1	OF-54, DH-1

	G	AB	H	2B	3B	HR	HR %	R	RBI	BB	SO	SB	BA	SA	Pinch Hit AB	Pinch Hit H	G by POS

Chuck Corgan

CORGAN, CHARLES HOWARD
B. Dec. 3, 1903, Wagoner, Okla.   D. June 13, 1928, Wagoner, Okla.
BB TR 5'11"   180 lbs.

	G	AB	H	2B	3B	HR	HR%	R	RBI	BB	SO	SB	BA	SA	PH AB	PH H	G by POS
1925 BKN N	14	47	8	1	1	0	0.0	4	0	3	9	0	.170	.234	0	0	SS-14
1927	19	57	15	1	0	0	0.0	3	1	4	4	0	.263	.281	2	0	2B-13, SS-3
2 yrs.	33	104	23	2	1	0	0.0	7	1	7	13	0	.221	.260	2	0	SS-17, 2B-13

Roy Corhan

CORHAN, ROY GEORGE (Irish)
B. Oct. 21, 1887, Indianapolis, Ind.   D. Nov. 24, 1958, San Francisco, Calif.
BR TR 5'9½"   165 lbs.

	G	AB	H	2B	3B	HR	HR%	R	RBI	BB	SO	SB	BA	SA	PH AB	PH H	G by POS
1911 CHI A	43	131	28	6	2	0	0.0	14	8	15		2	.214	.290	0	0	SS-43
1916 STL N	92	295	62	6	3	0	0.0	30	18	20	31	15	.210	.251	7	3	SS-84
2 yrs.	135	426	90	12	5	0	0.0	44	26	35	31	17	.211	.263	7	3	SS-127

Pop Corkhill

CORKHILL, JOHN STEWART
B. Apr. 11, 1858, Parkesburg, Pa.   D. Apr. 4, 1921, Pennsauken, N. J.
BL TR 5'10"   180 lbs.

	G	AB	H	2B	3B	HR	HR%	R	RBI	BB	SO	SB	BA	SA	PH AB	PH H	G by POS
1883 CIN AA	88	375	81	10	8	2	0.5	53		3			.216	.301	0	0	OF-85, SS-2, 2B-2, 1B-2
1884	110	452	124	13	11	4	0.9	85		6			.274	.378	0	0	OF-92, SS-11, 1B-6, 3B-3, P-1
1885	112	440	111	10	8	1	0.2	64		7			.252	.318	0	0	OF-110, P-8, 1B-3
1886	129	540	143	9	8	4	0.7	81		23			.265	.333	0	0	OF-112, 3B-12, 1B-7, SS-3, P-1
1887	128	541	168	19	11	5	0.9	79		14		30	.311	.414	0	0	OF-128, P-5
1888 2 teams	CIN	AA (118G – .271)				BKN	AA (19G – .380)										
" total	137	561	160	15	12	2	0.4	85	93	19		30	.285	.365	0	0	OF-135, P-2, 2B-1, 1B-1
1889 BKN AA	138	537	134	21	9	8	1.5	91	78	42	24	22	.250	.367	0	0	OF-138, SS-1, 1B-1
1890 BKN N	51	204	46	4	2	1	0.5	23	21	15	11	6	.225	.279	0	0	OF-48, 1B-6
1891 3 teams	PHI	AA (83G – .209)				CIN	N (1G – .000)			PIT	N (41G – .228)						
" total	125	498	106	8	8	3	0.6	66	51	33	26	19	.213	.279	0	0	OF-125
1892 PIT N	68	256	47	1	4	0	0.0	23	25	12	19	6	.184	.219	0	0	OF-68
10 yrs.	1086	4404	1120	110	81	30	0.7	650	267	174	80	113	.254	.337	0	0	OF-1041, 1B-26, SS-17, P-17, 3B-15, 2B-3

Pat Corrales

CORRALES, PATRICK
B. Mar. 20, 1941, Los Angeles, Calif.
Manager 1978-80, 1982-84.
BR TR 6'   180 lbs.

	G	AB	H	2B	3B	HR	HR%	R	RBI	BB	SO	SB	BA	SA	PH AB	PH H	G by POS
1964 PHI N	2	1	0	0	0	0	0.0	1	0	1	0	0	.000	.000	1	0	C-62
1965	63	174	39	8	1	2	1.1	16	15	25	42	0	.224	.316	2	0	C-62
1966 STL N	28	72	13	2	0	0	0.0	5	3	2	17	1	.181	.208	1	0	C-27
1968 CIN N	20	56	15	4	0	0	0.0	3	6	6	16	0	.268	.339	0	0	C-20
1969	29	72	19	5	0	1	1.4	10	5	8	17	0	.264	.375	0	0	C-29
1970	43	106	25	5	1	1	0.9	9	10	8	22	0	.236	.330	3	0	C-42
1971	40	94	17	2	0	0	0.0	6	6	6	17	0	.181	.202	1	0	C-39
1972 2 teams	CIN	N (2G – .000)				SD	N (44G – .193)										
" total	46	120	23	0	0	0	0.0	6	6	13	26	0	.192	.192	1	0	C-45
1973 SD N	29	72	15	2	1	0	0.0	7	3	6	10	0	.208	.264	1	0	C-28
9 yrs.	300	767	166	28	3	4	0.5	63	54	75	167	1	.216	.276	10	0	C-292

WORLD SERIES

	G	AB	H	2B	3B	HR	HR%	R	RBI	BB	SO	SB	BA	SA	PH AB	PH H	G by POS
1970 CIN N	1	1	0	0	0	0	0.0	0	0	0	0	0	.000	.000	1	0	

Vic Correll

CORRELL, VICTOR CROSBY
B. Feb. 5, 1946, Florence, S. C.
BR TR 5'10"   185 lbs.

	G	AB	H	2B	3B	HR	HR%	R	RBI	BB	SO	SB	BA	SA	PH AB	PH H	G by POS
1972 BOS A	1	4	2	0	0	0	0.0	1	1	0	1	0	.500	.500	0	0	C-1
1974 ATL N	73	202	48	15	1	4	2.0	20	29	21	38	0	.238	.381	14	2	C-59
1975	103	325	70	12	1	11	3.4	37	39	42	66	0	.215	.360	6	2	C-97
1976	69	200	45	6	2	5	2.5	26	16	21	37	0	.225	.350	8	3	C-65
1977	54	144	30	7	0	7	4.9	16	16	22	33	2	.208	.403	4	1	C-49
1978 CIN N	52	105	25	7	0	1	1.0	9	6	8	17	0	.238	.333	2	0	C-52
1979	48	133	31	12	0	1	0.8	14	15	14	26	0	.233	.346	1	1	C-47
1980	10	19	8	1	0	0	0.0	1	3	0	2	0	.421	.474	1	0	C-10
8 yrs.	410	1132	259	60	4	29	2.6	124	125	128	220	2	.229	.366	36	9	C-380

Phillip Corridan

CORRIDAN, PHILLIP
Deceased.

	G	AB	H	2B	3B	HR	HR%	R	RBI	BB	SO	SB	BA	SA	PH AB	PH H	G by POS
1884 C-P U	2	7	1	0	0	0	0.0	1		0			.143	.143	0	0	2B-2, OF-1

John Corriden

CORRIDEN, JOHN MICHAEL, JR.
Son of Red Corriden.
B. Oct. 6, 1918, Logansport, Ind.
BB TR 5'6"   160 lbs.

	G	AB	H	2B	3B	HR	HR%	R	RBI	BB	SO	SB	BA	SA	PH AB	PH H	G by POS
1946 BKN N	1	0	0	0	0	0	–	0		0	0	0	–	–	0	0	

Red Corriden

CORRIDEN, JOHN MICHAEL, SR.
Father of John Corriden.
B. Sept. 4, 1887, Logansport, Ind.   D. Sept. 28, 1959, Indianapolis, Ind.
Manager 1950.
BR TR 5'9"   165 lbs.

	G	AB	H	2B	3B	HR	HR%	R	RBI	BB	SO	SB	BA	SA	PH AB	PH H	G by POS
1910 STL A	26	84	13	3	0	1	1.2	19	4	13		5	.155	.226	0	0	SS-14, 3B-12
1912 DET A	38	138	28	6	0	0	0.0	22	5	15		4	.203	.246	3	0	3B-25, 2B-7, SS-3
1913 CHI N	45	97	17	3	0	2	2.1	13	9	9	14	4	.175	.268	4	1	SS-36, 2B-2, 3B-1
1914	107	318	73	9	5	3	0.9	42	29	35	33	13	.230	.318	6	2	SS-96, 3B-8, 2B-3
1915	6	3	0	0	0	0	0.0	1	0	2	1	0	.000	.000	2	0	OF-1, 3B-1
5 yrs.	222	640	131	21	5	6	0.9	97	47	74	48	26	.205	.281	15	3	SS-149, 3B-47, 2B-12, OF-1

Shine Cortazzo

CORTAZZO, JOHN FRANCIS
B. Sept. 26, 1904, Wilmerding, Pa.   D. Mar. 4, 1963, Braddock, Pa.
BR TR 5'3½"   142 lbs.

	G	AB	H	2B	3B	HR	HR%	R	RBI	BB	SO	SB	BA	SA	PH AB	PH H	G by POS
1923 CHI A	1	1	0	0	0	0	0.0	0	0	0	0	0	.000	.000	1	0	

	G	AB	H	2B	3B	HR	HR %	R	RBI	BB	SO	SB	BA	SA	Pinch Hit AB	Pinch Hit H	G by POS

Joe Coscarart

COSCARART, JOSEPH MARVIN
Brother of Pete Coscarart.
B. Nov. 18, 1909, Escondido, Calif.

BR TR 6' 185 lbs.

	G	AB	H	2B	3B	HR	HR %	R	RBI	BB	SO	SB	BA	SA	AB	H	G by POS
1935 BOS N	86	284	67	11	2	1	0.4	30	29	16	28	2	.236	.299	2	0	3B-41, SS-27, 2B-15
1936	104	367	90	11	2	2	0.5	28	44	19	37	0	.245	.302	1	1	3B-97, SS-6, 2B-1
2 yrs.	190	651	157	22	4	3	0.5	58	73	35	65	2	.241	.301	3	1	3B-138, SS-33, 2B-16

Pete Coscarart

COSCARART, PETER JOSEPH
Brother of Joe Coscarart.
B. June 16, 1913, Escondido, Calif.

BR TR 5'11½" 175 lbs.

	G	AB	H	2B	3B	HR	HR %	R	RBI	BB	SO	SB	BA	SA	AB	H	G by POS
1938 BKN N	32	79	12	3	0	0	0.0	10	6	9	18	0	.152	.190	2	0	2B-27
1939	115	419	116	22	2	4	1.0	59	43	46	56	10	.277	.368	0	0	2B-107, 3B-4, SS-2
1940	143	506	120	24	4	9	1.8	55	58	53	59	5	.237	.354	2	1	2B-140
1941	43	62	8	1	0	0	0.0	13	5	7	12	1	.129	.145	15	2	2B-19, SS-1
1942 PIT N	133	487	111	12	4	3	0.6	57	29	38	56	2	.228	.287	1	1	SS-108, 2B-25
1943	133	491	119	19	6	0	0.0	57	48	46	48	4	.242	.305	1	1	2B-85, SS-47, 3B-1
1944	139	554	146	30	4	4	0.7	89	42	41	57	10	.264	.354	1	0	2B-136, SS-4, OF-1
1945	123	392	95	17	2	8	2.0	59	38	55	55	2	.242	.357	1	0	2B-122, SS-1
1946	3	2	1	1	0	0	0.0	0	0	0	0	0	.500	1.000	2	1	SS-1
9 yrs.	864	2992	728	129	22	28	0.9	399	269	295	361	34	.243	.329	25	6	2B-661, SS-164, 3B-5, OF-1

WORLD SERIES
| 1941 BKN N | 3 | 7 | 0 | 0 | 0 | 0 | 0.0 | 1 | 0 | 1 | 2 | 0 | .000 | .000 | 0 | 0 | 2B-3 |

Ray Cosey

COSEY, DONALD RAY
B. Feb. 15, 1956, San Rafael, Calif.

BL TL 5'10" 185 lbs.

	G	AB	H	2B	3B	HR	HR %	R	RBI	BB	SO	SB	BA	SA	AB	H	G by POS
1980 OAK A	9	9	1	0	0	0	0.0	0	0	0	0	0	.111	.111	9	1	

Dan Costello

COSTELLO, DANIEL FRANCIS (Dashing Dan)
B. Sept. 9, 1895, Jessup, Pa. D. Mar. 26, 1936, Pittsburgh, Pa.

BL TR 6'½" 185 lbs.

	G	AB	H	2B	3B	HR	HR %	R	RBI	BB	SO	SB	BA	SA	AB	H	G by POS
1913 NY A	2	2	1	0	0	0	0.0	1	0	0	0	0	.500	.500	2	1	
1914 PIT N	21	64	19	1	0	0	0.0	7	5	8	16	2	.297	.313	1	0	OF-20
1915	71	125	27	4	1	0	0.0	16	11	7	23	7	.216	.264	46	14	OF-17
1916	60	159	38	1	3	0	0.0	11	8	6	23	3	.239	.283	18	5	OF-41
4 yrs.	154	350	85	6	4	0	0.0	35	24	21	62	12	.243	.283	67	20	OF-78

Henry Cote

COTE, HENRY JOSEPH
B. Dec. 20, 1864, Troy, N. Y. D. Apr. 28, 1940, Troy, N. Y.

TR

	G	AB	H	2B	3B	HR	HR %	R	RBI	BB	SO	SB	BA	SA	AB	H	G by POS
1894 LOU N	10	31	9	2	2	0	0.0	7	3	5	6	2	.290	.484	0	0	C-10
1895	10	33	10	0	0	0	0.0	10	5	3	3	2	.303	.303	0	0	C-10
2 yrs.	20	64	19	2	2	0	0.0	17	8	8	9	4	.297	.391	0	0	C-20

Pete Cote

COTE, WARREN PETER
B. Aug. 30, 1902, Cambridge, Mass.

BR TR 5'6" 148 lbs.

	G	AB	H	2B	3B	HR	HR %	R	RBI	BB	SO	SB	BA	SA	AB	H	G by POS
1926 NY N	2	1	0	0	0	0	0.0	0	0	0	0	0	.000	.000	1	0	

Dick Cotter

COTTER, RICHARD RAPHAEL
B. Oct. 12, 1889, Manchester, N. H. D. Apr. 4, 1945, Brooklyn, N. Y.

BR TR 5'11" 172 lbs.

	G	AB	H	2B	3B	HR	HR %	R	RBI	BB	SO	SB	BA	SA	AB	H	G by POS
1911 PHI N	20	46	13	0	0	0	0.0	2	5	5	7	1	.283	.283	2	0	C-17
1912 CHI N	26	54	15	0	2	0	0.0	6	10	6	13	1	.278	.352	1	0	C-24
2 yrs.	46	100	28	0	2	0	0.0	8	15	11	20	2	.280	.320	3	0	C-41

Ed Cotter

COTTER, EDWARD CHRISTOPHER
B. July 4, 1904, Hartford, Conn. D. June 14, 1959, Hartford, Conn.

BR TR 6' 185 lbs.

	G	AB	H	2B	3B	HR	HR %	R	RBI	BB	SO	SB	BA	SA	AB	H	G by POS
1926 PHI N	17	26	8	0	1	0	0.0	3	1	4	1	1	.308	.385	4	1	3B-8, SS-5

Harvey Cotter

COTTER, HARVEY LOUIS (Hooks)
B. May 22, 1900, Holden, Mo. D. Aug. 6, 1955, Los Angeles, Calif.

BL TL 5'10" 160 lbs.

	G	AB	H	2B	3B	HR	HR %	R	RBI	BB	SO	SB	BA	SA	AB	H	G by POS
1922 CHI N	1	1	1	0	0	0	0.0	0	0	0	0	0	1.000	2.000	1	1	
1924	98	310	81	16	4	4	1.3	39	33	36	31	3	.261	.377	7	2	1B-90
2 yrs.	99	311	82	17	4	4	1.3	39	33	36	31	3	.264	.383	8	3	1B-90

Tom Cotter

COTTER, THOMAS B.
B. Sept. 30, 1866, Waltham, Mass. D. Nov. 22, 1906, Brookline, Mass.

	G	AB	H	2B	3B	HR	HR %	R	RBI	BB	SO	SB	BA	SA	AB	H	G by POS
1891 BOS AA	6	12	3	0	0	0	0.0	1	4	1	2	0	.250	.250	1	0	C-5, OF-1

Chuck Cottier

COTTIER, CHARLES KEITH
B. Jan. 8, 1936, Delta, Colo.
Manager 1984.

BR TR 5'10½" 175 lbs.

	G	AB	H	2B	3B	HR	HR %	R	RBI	BB	SO	SB	BA	SA	AB	H	G by POS
1959 MIL N	10	24	3	1	0	0	0.0	1	1	3	7	0	.125	.167	0	0	2B-10
1960	95	229	52	8	0	3	1.3	29	19	14	21	1	.227	.301	1	1	2B-92
1961 2 teams	DET	A (10G –	.286)			WAS	A (101G –	.234)									
" total	111	344	81	14	4	2	0.6	39	35	31	52	9	.235	.317	1	0	2B-102, SS-8
1962 WAS A	136	443	107	14	6	6	1.4	50	40	44	57	14	.242	.341	0	0	2B-134
1963	113	337	69	16	4	5	1.5	30	21	24	63	2	.205	.320	2	0	2B-85, SS-24, 3B-1
1964	73	137	23	6	2	3	2.2	16	10	19	33	2	.168	.307	5	1	2B-53, 3B-3, SS-2
1965	7	1	0	0	0	0	0.0	1	0	0	0	0	.000	.000	1	0	
1968 CAL A	33	67	13	4	1	0	0.0	2	1	2	15	0	.194	.284	2	0	3B-27, 2B-4
1969	2	2	0	0	0	0	0.0	0	0	0	0	0	.000	.000	0	0	2B-2
9 yrs.	580	1584	348	63	17	19	1.2	168	127	137	248	28	.220	.317	12	2	2B-482, SS-34, 3B-31

Henry Cotto

COTTO, HENRY
B. Jan. 5, 1961, New York, N. Y.

BR TR 6'2" 180 lbs.

	G	AB	H	2B	3B	HR	HR %	R	RBI	BB	SO	SB	BA	SA	AB	H	G by POS
1984 CHI N	105	146	40	5	0	0	0.0	24	8	10	23	9	.274	.308	13	3	OF-88

LEAGUE CHAMPIONSHIP SERIES
| 1984 CHI N | 3 | 1 | 1 | 0 | 0 | 0 | 0.0 | 1 | 0 | 0 | 0 | 0 | 1.000 | 1.000 | 0 | 0 | OF-3 |

	G	AB	H	2B	3B	HR	HR %	R	RBI	BB	SO	SB	BA	SA	Pinch Hit AB	Pinch Hit H	G by POS

Bill Coughlin

COUGHLIN, WILLIAM PAUL   BR TR 5'9" 140 lbs.
B. Aug. 12, 1877, Scranton, Pa.   D. May 7, 1943, Scranton, Pa.

	G	AB	H	2B	3B	HR	HR %	R	RBI	BB	SO	SB	BA	SA	AB	H	G by POS
1899 WAS N	6	24	3	0	1	0	0.0	2	3	1		1	.125	.208	0	0	3B-6
1901 WAS A	137	506	139	17	13	6	1.2	75	68	25		16	.275	.395	0	0	3B-137
1902	123	469	141	27	4	6	1.3	84	71	26		29	.301	.414	0	0	3B-66, SS-31, 2B-26
1903	125	470	118	18	3	1	0.2	56	31	9		30	.251	.309	0	0	3B-119, SS-4, 2B-2
1904 2 teams		WAS	A	(65G –	.275)		DET	A	(56G –	.228)							
" total	121	471	120	21	4	0	0.0	50	34	14		11	.255	.316	1	1	3B-120
1905 DET A	138	489	123	20	6	0	0.0	48	44	34		16	.252	.317	1	0	3B-137
1906	147	498	117	15	5	2	0.4	54	60	36		31	.235	.297	0	0	3B-147
1907	134	519	126	10	2	0	0.0	80	46	35		15	.243	.270	0	0	3B-133
1908	119	405	87	5	1	0	0.0	32	23	23		10	.215	.232	0	0	3B-119
9 yrs.	1050	3851	974	133	39	15	0.4	481	380	203		159	.253	.319	2	1	3B-984, SS-35, 2B-28
WORLD SERIES																	
1907 DET A	5	20	5	0	0	0	0.0	0	0	1	4	1	.250	.250	0	0	3B-5
1908	3	8	1	0	0	0	0.0	0	1	0	1	0	.125	.125	0	0	3B-3
2 yrs.	8	28	6	0	0	0	0.0	0	1	1	5	1	.214	.214	0	0	3B-8

Marlan Coughtry

COUGHTRY, JAMES MARLAN   BL TR 6'1" 170 lbs.
B. Sept. 11, 1934, Hollywood, Calif.

	G	AB	H	2B	3B	HR	HR %	R	RBI	BB	SO	SB	BA	SA	AB	H	G by POS
1960 BOS A	15	19	3	0	0	0	0.0	3	0	5	8	0	.158	.158	2	0	2B-13, 3B-1
1962 3 teams		LA	A	(11G –	.182)		KC	A	(6G –	.182)		CLE	A	(3G –	.500)		
" total	20	35	7	0	0	0	0.0	2	4	5	10	0	.200	.200	8	1	3B-7, 2B-2
2 yrs.	35	54	10	0	0	0	0.0	5	4	10	18	0	.185	.185	10	1	2B-15, 3B-8

Bob Coulson

COULSON, ROBERT JACKSON   BR TR 5'10½" 175 lbs.
B. June 17, 1887, Courtney, Pa.   D. Sept. 11, 1953, Washington, Pa.

	G	AB	H	2B	3B	HR	HR %	R	RBI	BB	SO	SB	BA	SA	AB	H	G by POS
1908 CIN N	8	18	6	1	1	0	0.0	3	1	3		0	.333	.500	1	0	OF-6
1910 BKN N	25	89	22	3	4	1	1.1	14	13	6	14	9	.247	.404	0	0	OF-25
1911	146	521	122	23	7	0	0.0	52	50	42	78	32	.234	.305	1	1	OF-145
1914 PIT F	18	64	13	1	0	0	0.0	7	3	7		2	.203	.219	0	0	OF-18
4 yrs.	197	692	163	28	12	1	0.1	76	67	58	92	43	.236	.315	2	1	OF-194

Tom Coulter

COULTER, THOMAS LEE   BL TR 5'10" 172 lbs.
B. June 5, 1945, Steubenville, Ohio

	G	AB	H	2B	3B	HR	HR %	R	RBI	BB	SO	SB	BA	SA	AB	H	G by POS
1969 STL N	6	19	6	1	1	0	0.0	3	4	2	6	0	.316	.474	0	0	2B-6

Clint Courtney

COURTNEY, CLINTON DAWSON (Scrap Iron)   BL TR 5'8" 180 lbs.
B. Mar. 16, 1927, Hall Summit, La.   D. June 16, 1975, Rochester, N. Y.

	G	AB	H	2B	3B	HR	HR %	R	RBI	BB	SO	SB	BA	SA	AB	H	G by POS
1951 NY A	1	2	0	0	0	0	0.0	0	0	1	1	0	.000	.000	0	0	C-1
1952 STL A	119	413	118	24	3	5	1.2	38	50	39	26	0	.286	.395	6	0	C-113
1953	106	355	89	12	2	4	1.1	29	19	25	20	0	.251	.330	7	2	C-103
1954 BAL A	122	397	107	18	3	4	1.0	25	37	30	7	2	.270	.360	14	5	C-111
1955 2 teams		CHI	A	(19G –	.378)		WAS	A	(75G –	.298)							
" total	94	275	85	12	4	3	1.1	33	40	26	9	0	.309	.415	11	6	C-84
1956 WAS A	101	283	85	20	3	5	1.8	31	44	20	10	0	.300	.445	31	8	C-76
1957	91	232	62	14	1	6	2.6	23	27	16	11	0	.267	.414	27	11	C-59
1958	134	450	113	18	0	8	1.8	46	62	48	23	1	.251	.344	7	2	C-128
1959	72	189	44	4	1	2	1.1	19	18	20	19	0	.233	.296	19	3	C-53
1960 BAL A	83	154	35	3	0	1	0.6	14	12	30	14	0	.227	.266	18	7	C-58
1961 2 teams		KC	A	(1G –	.000)		BAL	A	(22G –	.267)							
" total	23	46	12	2	0	0	0.0	3	4	10	3	0	.261	.304	7	2	C-16
11 yrs.	946	2796	750	127	17	38	1.4	260	313	265	143	3	.268	.367	147	46	C-802

Ernie Courtney

COURTNEY, ERNEST E.   BL TR 5'10"
B. Jan. 20, 1875, Los Angeles, Calif.   D. Feb. 29, 1920, Buffalo, N. Y.

	G	AB	H	2B	3B	HR	HR %	R	RBI	BB	SO	SB	BA	SA	AB	H	G by POS
1902 2 teams		BOS	N	(48G –	.218)		BAL	A	(1G –	.500)							
" total	49	169	38	3	1	0	0.0	26	18	14		3	.225	.254	6	2	OF-39, SS-3, 3B-1
1903 2 teams		NY	A	(25G –	.266)		DET	A	(23G –	.230)							
" total	48	153	38	3	1	0	0.7	14	14	12		2	.248	.327	2	0	SS-28, 3B-13, 2B-4, 1B-1
1905 PHI N	155	601	165	14	7	2	0.3	77	77	47		17	.275	.331	0	0	3B-155
1906	116	398	94	12	2	0	0.0	53	42	45		6	.236	.276	4	0	3B-96, 1B-13, OF-3, SS-1
1907	130	440	107	17	4	2	0.5	42	43	55		6	.243	.314	0	0	3B-75, 1B-48, OF-4, SS-2, 2B-2
1908	60	160	29	3	0	0	0.0	14	6	15		1	.181	.200	17	3	3B-22, 1B-13, 2B-5, SS-2
6 yrs.	558	1921	471	52	17	5	0.3	226	200	188		35	.245	.298	29	5	3B-362, 1B-75, OF-46, SS-36, 2B-11

Dee Cousineau

COUSINEAU, EDWARD THOMAS   BR TR 6' 170 lbs.
B. Dec. 16, 1898, Watertown, Mass.   D. July 14, 1951, Watertown, Mass.

	G	AB	H	2B	3B	HR	HR %	R	RBI	BB	SO	SB	BA	SA	AB	H	G by POS
1923 BOS N	1	2	2	0	0	0	0.0	1	2	0	0	0	1.000	1.000	0	0	C-1
1924	3	2	0	0	0	0	0.0	0	0	0	0	0	.000	.000	0	0	C-3
1925	1	0	0	0	0	0	–	0	0	0	0	0	–	–	0	0	C-1
3 yrs.	5	4	2	0	0	0	0.0	1	2	0	0	0	.500	.500	0	0	C-5

John Coveney

COVENEY, JOHN PATRICK   TR
B. June 10, 1880, S. Natick, Mass.   D. Mar. 28, 1961, Wayrand, Mass.

	G	AB	H	2B	3B	HR	HR %	R	RBI	BB	SO	SB	BA	SA	AB	H	G by POS
1903 STL N	4	14	2	0	0	0	0.0	0		0		0	.143	.143	0	0	C-4

Sam Covington

COVINGTON, CLARENCE OTTO   BL TR 6'1" 190 lbs.
Brother of Tex Covington.
B. Dec. 17, 1892, Henryville, Tenn.   D. Jan. 4, 1963, Denison, Tex.

	G	AB	H	2B	3B	HR	HR %	R	RBI	BB	SO	SB	BA	SA	AB	H	G by POS
1913 STL A	20	60	9	0	1	0	0.0	3	4	4	6	3	.150	.183	4	0	1B-16
1917 BOS N	17	66	13	2	0	1	1.5	8	10	5	5	1	.197	.273	0	0	1B-17
1918	3	3	1	0	0	0	0.0	0	0	0	0	0	.333	.333	3	1	
3 yrs.	40	129	23	2	1	1	0.8	11	14	9	11	4	.178	.233	7	1	1B-33

	G	AB	H	2B	3B	HR	HR %	R	RBI	BB	SO	SB	BA	SA	Pinch Hit AB	Pinch Hit H	G by POS

Wes Covington

COVINGTON, JOHN WESLEY
B. Mar. 27, 1932, Laurinburg, N. C.

BL TR 6'1"   205 lbs.

	G	AB	H	2B	3B	HR	HR %	R	RBI	BB	SO	SB	BA	SA	AB	H	G by POS
1956 MIL N	75	138	39	4	0	2	1.4	17	16	16	20	1	.283	.355	31	10	OF-35
1957	96	328	93	4	8	21	6.4	51	65	29	44	4	.284	.537	8	1	OF-89
1958	90	294	97	12	1	24	8.2	43	74	20	35	0	.330	.622	7	0	OF-82
1959	103	373	104	17	3	7	1.9	38	45	26	41	0	.279	.397	9	2	OF-94
1960	95	281	70	16	1	10	3.6	25	35	15	37	1	.249	.420	22	5	OF-72
1961 4 teams	MIL N (9G – .190)				CHI A (22G – .288)			KC A (17G – .159)			PHI N (57G – .303)						
" total	105	289	78	11	0	12	4.2	34	47	25	33	0	.270	.433	28	6	OF-76
1962 PHI N	116	304	86	12	1	9	3.0	36	44	19	44	0	.283	.418	30	9	OF-88
1963	119	353	107	24	1	17	4.8	46	64	26	56	1	.303	.521	25	8	OF-101
1964	129	339	95	18	0	13	3.8	37	58	38	50	0	.280	.448	31	5	OF-108
1965	101	235	58	10	1	15	6.4	27	45	26	47	0	.247	.489	35	7	OF-64
1966 2 teams	CHI N (9G – .091)				LA N (37G – .121)												
" total	46	44	5	0	1	1	2.3	1	6	7	7	0	.114	.227	34	4	OF-3
11 yrs.	1075	2978	832	128	17	131	4.4	355	499	247	414	7	.279	.466	260	57	OF-812

WORLD SERIES

	G	AB	H	2B	3B	HR	HR %	R	RBI	BB	SO	SB	BA	SA	AB	H	G by POS
1957 MIL N	7	24	5	1	0	0	0.0	1	1	2	6	1	.208	.250	0	0	OF-7
1958	7	26	7	0	0	0	0.0	2	4	2	4	0	.269	.269	0	0	OF-7
1966 LA N	1	1	0	0	0	0	0.0	0	0	0	1	0	.000	.000	1	0	
3 yrs.	15	51	12	1	0	0	0.0	3	5	4	11	1	.235	.255	1	0	OF-14

Billy Cowan

COWAN, BILLY ROLAND
B. Aug. 28, 1938, Calhoun City, Miss.

BR TR 6'   170 lbs.

	G	AB	H	2B	3B	HR	HR %	R	RBI	BB	SO	SB	BA	SA	AB	H	G by POS
1963 CHI N	14	36	9	1	1	1	2.8	1	2	0	11	0	.250	.417	4	1	OF-10
1964	139	497	120	16	4	19	3.8	52	50	18	128	12	.241	.404	4	2	OF-134
1965 2 teams	NY N (82G – .179)				MIL N (19G – .185)												
" total	101	183	33	9	2	3	1.6	20	9	4	54	3	.180	.301	20	2	OF-71, 2B-2, SS-1
1967 PHI N	34	59	9	0	0	3	5.1	11	6	4	14	1	.153	.305	5	0	OF-20, 3B-1, 2B-1
1969 2 teams	NY A (32G – .167)				CAL A (28G – .304)												
" total	60	104	25	1	0	5	4.8	15	13	6	18	0	.240	.394	33	9	OF-27, 1B-6
1970 CAL A	68	134	37	9	1	5	3.7	20	25	11	29	0	.276	.470	39	11	OF-27, 1B-14, 3B-2
1971	74	174	48	8	0	4	2.3	12	20	7	41	1	.276	.391	34	8	OF-40, 1B-5
1972	3	3	0	0	0	0	0.0	0	0	0	2	0	.000	.000	3	0	
8 yrs.	493	1190	281	44	8	40	3.4	131	125	50	297	17	.236	.387	142	33	OF-329, 1B-25, 3B-3, 2B-3, SS-1

Al Cowens

COWENS, ALFRED EDWARD
B. Oct. 25, 1951, Los Angeles, Calif.

BR TR 6'1"   197 lbs.

	G	AB	H	2B	3B	HR	HR %	R	RBI	BB	SO	SB	BA	SA	AB	H	G by POS
1974 KC A	110	269	65	7	1	1	0.4	28	25	23	38	5	.242	.286	8	4	OF-102, DH-4, 3B-2
1975	120	328	91	13	8	4	1.2	44	42	28	36	12	.277	.402	7	2	OF-113, DH-2
1976	152	581	154	23	6	3	0.5	71	59	26	50	23	.265	.341	5	2	OF-148, DH-1
1977	162	606	189	32	14	23	3.8	98	112	41	64	16	.312	.525	6	2	OF-159, DH-1
1978	132	485	133	24	8	5	1.0	63	63	31	54	14	.274	.388	2	0	OF-127, 3B-5, DH-2
1979	136	516	152	18	7	9	1.7	69	73	40	44	10	.295	.409	3	2	OF-134, DH-1
1980 2 teams	CAL A (34G – .227)				DET A (108G – .280)												
" total	142	522	140	20	3	6	1.1	69	59	49	61	6	.268	.352	5	1	OF-137, DH-2
1981 DET A	85	253	66	11	4	1	0.4	27	18	22	36	3	.261	.348	12	3	OF-83
1982 SEA A	146	560	151	39	8	20	3.6	72	78	46	81	11	.270	.475	0	0	OF-145, DH-1
1983	110	356	73	19	2	7	2.0	39	35	23	38	10	.205	.329	6	1	OF-70, DH-34
1984	139	524	145	34	2	15	2.9	60	78	27	83	9	.277	.435	8	1	OF-130, DH-7
11 yrs.	1434	5000	1359	240	63	94	1.9	640	642	356	585	119	.272	.401	62	18	OF-1348, DH-55, 3B-7

LEAGUE CHAMPIONSHIP SERIES

	G	AB	H	2B	3B	HR	HR %	R	RBI	BB	SO	SB	BA	SA	AB	H	G by POS
1976 KC A	5	21	4	0	1	0	0.0	3	0	1	1	2	.190	.286	0	0	OF-5
1977	5	19	5	0	0	1	5.3	2	5	1	3	0	.263	.421	0	0	OF-5
1978	4	15	2	0	0	0	0.0	2	1	0	2	0	.133	.133	0	0	OF-4
3 yrs.	14	55	11	0	1	1	1.8	7	6	2	6	2	.200	.291	0	0	OF-14

Billy Cox

COX, WILLIAM RICHARD
B. Aug. 29, 1919, Newport, Pa.   D. Mar. 30, 1978, Harrisburg, Pa.

BR TR 5'10"   150 lbs.

	G	AB	H	2B	3B	HR	HR %	R	RBI	BB	SO	SB	BA	SA	AB	H	G by POS
1941 PIT N	10	37	10	3	1	0	0.0	4	2	3	2	1	.270	.405	0	0	SS-10
1946	121	411	119	22	6	2	0.5	32	36	26	15	4	.290	.387	3	1	SS-114
1947	132	529	145	30	7	15	2.8	75	54	29	28	5	.274	.442	2	1	SS-129
1948 BKN N	88	237	59	13	2	3	1.3	36	15	38	19	3	.249	.359	6	1	3B-70, SS-6, 2B-1
1949	100	390	91	18	2	8	2.1	48	40	30	18	5	.233	.351	0	0	3B-100
1950	119	451	116	17	2	8	1.8	62	44	35	24	6	.257	.357	1	0	3B-107, 2B-13, SS-9
1951	142	455	127	25	4	9	2.0	62	51	37	30	5	.279	.411	3	1	3B-139, SS-1
1952	116	455	118	12	3	6	1.3	56	34	25	32	10	.259	.338	4	1	3B-100, SS-10, 2B-9
1953	100	327	95	18	1	10	3.1	44	44	37	21	2	.291	.443	5	0	3B-89, SS-6, 2B-1
1954	77	226	53	9	2	2	0.9	26	17	21	13	0	.235	.319	4	1	3B-58, 2B-11, SS-8
1955 BAL A	53	194	41	7	2	3	1.5	25	14	17	16	1	.211	.314	3	1	3B-37, 2B-18, SS-6
11 yrs.	1058	3712	974	174	32	66	1.8	470	351	298	218	42	.262	.380	31	8	3B-700, SS-299, 2B-53

WORLD SERIES

	G	AB	H	2B	3B	HR	HR %	R	RBI	BB	SO	SB	BA	SA	AB	H	G by POS
1949 BKN N	2	3	1	0	0	0	0.0	0	0	0	1	0	.333	.333	2	1	3B-1
1952	7	27	8	2	0	0	0.0	4	0	3	4	0	.296	.370	0	0	3B-6
1953	6	23	7	3	0	1	4.3	3	6	1	4	0	.304	.565	0	0	3B-6
3 yrs.	15	53	16	5	0	1	1.9	7	6	4	9	0	.302	.453	2	1	3B-14

Bobby Cox

COX, ROBERT JOE
B. May 21, 1941, Tulsa, Okla.
Manager 1978-84.

BR TR 5'11"   180 lbs.

	G	AB	H	2B	3B	HR	HR %	R	RBI	BB	SO	SB	BA	SA	AB	H	G by POS
1968 NY A	135	437	100	15	1	7	1.6	33	41	41	85	3	.229	.316	3	0	3B-132
1969	85	191	41	7	1	2	1.0	17	17	34	41	0	.215	.293	20	4	3B-56, 2B-6
2 yrs.	220	628	141	22	2	9	1.4	50	58	75	126	3	.225	.309	23	4	3B-188, 2B-6

	G	AB	H	2B	3B	HR	HR %	R	RBI	BB	SO	SB	BA	SA	Pinch Hit AB	Pinch Hit H	G by POS

Dick Cox

COX, ELMER JOSEPH   BR TR 5'7½" 158 lbs.
B. Sept. 30, 1897, Pasadena, Calif.   D. June 1, 1966, Morro Bay, Calif.

	G	AB	H	2B	3B	HR	HR%	R	RBI	BB	SO	SB	BA	SA	PH AB	PH H	G by POS
1925 BKN N	122	434	143	23	10	7	1.6	68	64	37	29	4	.329	.477	8	3	OF-111
1926	124	398	118	17	4	1	0.3	53	45	46	20	6	.296	.367	6	3	OF-117
2 yrs.	246	832	261	40	14	8	1.0	121	109	83	49	10	.314	.424	14	6	OF-228

Frank Cox

COX, FRANK BERNHARDT (Runt)
B. Aug. 29, 1859, Waltham, Mass.   D. June 24, 1928, Hartford, Conn.

	G	AB	H	2B	3B	HR	HR%	R	RBI	BB	SO	SB	BA	SA	PH AB	PH H	G by POS
1884 DET N	27	102	13	3	1	0	0.0	6		2	36		.127	.176	0	0	SS-27

Jeff Cox

COX, JEFFREY LINDEN   BR TR 5'11" 170 lbs.
B. Nov. 9, 1955, Los Angeles, Calif.

	G	AB	H	2B	3B	HR	HR%	R	RBI	BB	SO	SB	BA	SA	PH AB	PH H	G by POS
1980 OAK A	59	169	36	3	0	0	0.0	20	9	14	23	8	.213	.231	0	0	2B-58
1981	2	0	0	0	0	0	–	0	0	0	0	0	–	–	0	0	2B-1
2 yrs.	61	169	36	3	0	0	0.0	20	9	14	23	8	.213	.231	0	0	2B-59

Jim Cox

COX, JAMES CHARLES   BR TR 5'11" 175 lbs.
B. May 28, 1950, Bloomington, Ill.

	G	AB	H	2B	3B	HR	HR%	R	RBI	BB	SO	SB	BA	SA	PH AB	PH H	G by POS
1973 MON N	9	15	2	1	0	0	0.0	1	0	1	4	0	.133	.200	2	0	2B-7
1974	77	236	52	9	1	2	0.8	29	26	23	36	2	.220	.292	1	1	2B-72
1975	11	27	7	1	0	1	3.7	1	5	1	2	1	.259	.407	3	0	2B-8
1976	13	29	5	0	1	0	0.0	2	2	2	2	0	.172	.241	1	0	2B-11
4 yrs.	110	307	66	11	2	3	1.0	33	33	27	44	3	.215	.293	7	1	2B-98

Larry Cox

COX, LARRY EUGENE   BR TR 5'10" 178 lbs.
B. Sept. 11, 1947, Bluffton, Ohio

	G	AB	H	2B	3B	HR	HR%	R	RBI	BB	SO	SB	BA	SA	PH AB	PH H	G by POS
1973 PHI N	1	0	0	0	0	0	–	0	0	0	0	0	–	–	0	0	C-1
1974	30	53	9	2	0	0	0.0	5	4	4	9	0	.170	.208	2	1	C-29
1975	11	5	1	0	0	0	0.0	0	1	1	0	1	.200	.200	1	0	C-10
1977 SEA A	35	93	23	6	0	2	2.2	6	6	10	12	1	.247	.376	0	0	C-35
1978 CHI N	59	121	34	5	0	2	1.7	10	18	12	16	0	.281	.372	0	0	C-58
1979 SEA A	100	293	63	11	3	4	1.4	32	36	22	39	2	.215	.314	8	0	C-99
1980	105	243	49	6	2	4	1.6	18	20	19	36	1	.202	.292	2	0	C-104
1981 TEX A	5	13	3	1	0	0	0.0	0	0	0	4	0	.231	.308	0	0	C-5
1982 CHI N	2	4	0	0	0	0	0.0	1	0	2	1	0	.000	.000	0	0	C-2
9 yrs.	348	825	182	31	5	12	1.5	72	85	70	117	5	.221	.314	13	1	C-343

Ted Cox

COX, WILLIAM TED   BR TR 6'3" 195 lbs.
B. Jan. 24, 1955, Midwest City, Okla.

	G	AB	H	2B	3B	HR	HR%	R	RBI	BB	SO	SB	BA	SA	PH AB	PH H	G by POS
1977 BOS A	13	58	21	3	1	1	1.7	11	6	3	6	0	.362	.500	0	0	DH-13
1978 CLE A	82	227	53	7	0	1	0.4	14	19	16	30	0	.233	.278	12	1	OF-38, 3B-20, DH-12, 1B-7, SS-1
1979	78	189	40	6	0	4	2.1	17	22	14	27	3	.212	.307	8	2	3B-52, OF-16, 2B-4, DH-1
1980 SEA A	83	247	60	9	0	2	0.8	17	23	19	25	0	.243	.304	4	3	3B-80
1981 TOR A	16	50	15	4	0	2	4.0	6	9	5	10	0	.300	.500	0	0	3B-14, DH-1, 1B-1
5 yrs.	272	771	189	29	1	10	1.3	65	79	57	98	3	.245	.324	24	6	3B-166, OF-54, DH-27, 1B-8, 2B-4, SS-1

Toots Coyne

COYNE,   TR
B. Unknown.

	G	AB	H	2B	3B	HR	HR%	R	RBI	BB	SO	SB	BA	SA	PH AB	PH H	G by POS
1914 PHI A	1	2	0	0	0	0	0.0	0	0	0	2	0	.000	.000	0	0	3B-1

Estel Crabtree

CRABTREE, ESTEL CRAYTON (Crabby)   BL TR 6' 168 lbs.
B. Aug. 19, 1903, Crabtree, Ohio   D. Jan. 4, 1967, Logan, Ohio

	G	AB	H	2B	3B	HR	HR%	R	RBI	BB	SO	SB	BA	SA	PH AB	PH H	G by POS
1929 CIN N	1	1	0	0	0	0	0.0	0	0	0	0	0	.000	.000	1	0	
1931	117	443	119	12	12	4	0.9	70	37	23	33	3	.269	.377	10	3	OF-101, 3B-4, 1B-2
1932	108	402	110	14	9	2	0.5	38	35	23	26	2	.274	.368	7	3	OF-95
1933 STL N	23	34	9	3	0	0	0.0	6	3	2	3	1	.265	.353	12	2	OF-7
1941	77	167	57	6	3	5	3.0	27	28	26	24	1	.341	.503	21	7	OF-50, 3B-1
1942	10	9	3	2	0	0	0.0	1	2	1	3	0	.333	.556	9	3	
1943 CIN N	95	254	70	12	0	2	0.8	25	26	25	17	1	.276	.346	24	10	OF-64
1944	58	98	28	4	1	0	0.0	7	11	13	3	0	.286	.347	32	9	OF-19, 1B-2
8 yrs.	489	1408	396	53	25	13	0.9	174	142	113	109	8	.281	.382	116	37	OF-336, 3B-5, 1B-4

Harry Craft

CRAFT, HARRY FRANCIS   BR TR 6'1" 185 lbs.
B. Apr. 19, 1915, Ellisville, Miss.
Manager 1957-59, 1961-64.

	G	AB	H	2B	3B	HR	HR%	R	RBI	BB	SO	SB	BA	SA	PH AB	PH H	G by POS
1937 CIN N	10	42	13	2	1	0	0.0	7	4	1	3	0	.310	.405	0	0	OF-10
1938	151	612	165	28	9	15	2.5	70	83	29	46	3	.270	.418	0	0	OF-151
1939	134	502	129	20	7	13	2.6	58	67	27	54	5	.257	.402	0	0	OF-134
1940	115	422	103	18	5	6	1.4	47	48	17	46	2	.244	.353	3	0	OF-109, 1B-2
1941	119	413	103	15	2	10	2.4	48	59	33	43	4	.249	.368	4	1	OF-115
1942	37	113	20	2	1	0	0.0	7	6	3	11	0	.177	.212	1	0	OF-33
6 yrs.	566	2104	533	85	25	44	2.1	237	267	110	203	14	.253	.380	8	1	OF-552, 1B-2

WORLD SERIES																	
1939 CIN N	4	11	1	0	0	0	0.0	0	0	0	6	0	.091	.091	0	0	OF-4
1940	2	1	0	0	0	0	0.0	0	0	0	0	0	.000	.000	1	0	
2 yrs.	6	12	1	0	0	0	0.0	0	0	0	6	0	.083	.083	1	0	OF-4

Rodney Craig

CRAIG, RODNEY PAUL   BB TR 6'1" 195 lbs.
B. Jan. 12, 1958, Los Angeles, Calif.

	G	AB	H	2B	3B	HR	HR%	R	RBI	BB	SO	SB	BA	SA	PH AB	PH H	G by POS
1979 SEA A	16	52	20	8	1	0	0.0	9	6	1	5	1	.385	.577	1	0	OF-15
1980	70	240	57	15	1	3	1.3	30	20	17	35	3	.238	.346	2	1	OF-63
1982 CLE A	49	65	15	2	0	0	0.0	7	1	4	6	3	.231	.262	19	2	OF-22, DH-4
3 yrs.	135	357	92	25	2	3	0.8	46	27	22	46	7	.258	.364	22	3	OF-100, DH-4

	G	AB	H	2B	3B	HR	HR %	R	RBI	BB	SO	SB	BA	SA	Pinch Hit AB	Pinch Hit H	G by POS

Dick Cramer

CRAMER, WILLIAM B.
B. Brooklyn, N. Y.   D. Aug. 12, 1885, Camden, N. J.

	G	AB	H	2B	3B	HR	HR %	R	RBI	BB	SO	SB	BA	SA	PH AB	PH H	G by POS
1883 NY N	2	6	0	0	0	0	0.0	0		1	5		.000	.000	0	0	OF-2

Doc Cramer

CRAMER, ROGER MAXWELL (Flit)   BL TR 6'2"   185 lbs.
B. July 22, 1905, Beach Haven, N. J.

	G	AB	H	2B	3B	HR	HR %	R	RBI	BB	SO	SB	BA	SA	PH AB	PH H	G by POS
1929 PHI A	2	6	0	0	0	0	0.0	0	0	0	2	0	.000	.000	1	0	OF-1
1930	30	82	19	1	1	0	0.0	12	6	2	8	0	.232	.268	8	0	OF-21, SS-1
1931	65	223	58	8	2	2	0.9	37	20	11	15	2	.260	.341	10	3	OF-55
1932	92	384	129	27	6	3	0.8	73	46	17	27	3	.336	.461	4	2	OF-86
1933	152	661	195	27	8	8	1.2	109	75	36	24	5	.295	.396	0	0	OF-152
1934	153	649	202	29	9	6	0.9	99	46	40	35	1	.311	.411	0	0	OF-152
1935	149	644	214	37	4	3	0.5	96	70	37	34	6	.332	.416	0	0	OF-149
1936 BOS A	154	643	188	31	7	0	0.0	99	41	49	20	4	.292	.362	0	0	OF-154
1937	133	560	171	22	11	0	0.0	90	51	35	14	8	.305	.384	0	0	OF-133
1938	148	658	198	36	8	0	0.0	116	71	51	19	4	.301	.380	0	0	OF-148, P-1
1939	137	589	183	30	6	0	0.0	110	56	36	17	3	.311	.382	2	1	OF-135
1940	150	661	200	27	12	1	0.2	94	51	36	29	3	.303	.384	0	0	OF-149
1941 WAS A	154	660	180	25	6	2	0.3	93	66	37	15	4	.273	.338	2	0	OF-152
1942 DET A	151	630	166	26	4	0	0.0	71	43	43	18	4	.263	.317	1	1	OF-150
1943	140	606	182	18	4	1	0.2	79	43	31	13	4	.300	.348	2	1	OF-138
1944	143	578	169	20	9	2	0.3	69	42	37	21	6	.292	.369	2	0	OF-141
1945	141	541	149	22	8	6	1.1	62	58	35	21	2	.275	.379	1	0	OF-140
1946	68	204	60	8	2	1	0.5	26	26	15	8	3	.294	.368	16	4	OF-50
1947	73	157	42	2	2	2	1.3	21	30	20	5	0	.268	.344	33	9	OF-35
1948	4	4	0	0	0	0	0.0	1	1	3	0	0	.000	.000	2	0	OF-1
20 yrs.	2239	9140	2705	396	109	37	0.4	1357	842	571	345	62	.296	.375	84	21	OF-2142, SS-1, P-1

WORLD SERIES

	G	AB	H	2B	3B	HR	HR %	R	RBI	BB	SO	SB	BA	SA	PH AB	PH H	G by POS
1931 PHI A	2	2	1	0	0	0	0.0	0	2	0	0	1	.500	.500	2	1	
1945 DET A	7	29	11	0	0	0	0.0	7	4	1	0	1	.379	.379	0	0	OF-7
2 yrs.	9	31	12	0	0	0	0.0	7	6	1	0	1	.387	.387	2	1	OF-7

Del Crandall

CRANDALL, DELMAR WESLEY   BR TR 6'1½"   180 lbs.
B. Mar. 5, 1930, Ontario, Calif.
Manager 1972-75, 1983-84.

	G	AB	H	2B	3B	HR	HR %	R	RBI	BB	SO	SB	BA	SA	PH AB	PH H	G by POS
1949 BOS N	67	228	60	10	1	4	1.8	21	34	9	18	2	.263	.368	2	1	C-63
1950	79	255	56	11	0	4	1.6	21	37	13	24	0	.220	.310	1	0	C-75, 1B-1
1953 MIL N	116	382	104	13	1	15	3.9	55	51	33	47	2	.272	.429	8	1	C-108
1954	138	463	112	18	2	21	4.5	60	64	40	56	0	.242	.425	3	1	C-136
1955	133	440	104	15	2	26	5.9	61	62	40	56	2	.236	.457	4	1	C-131
1956	112	311	74	14	2	16	5.1	37	48	35	30	1	.238	.450	5	2	C-109
1957	118	383	97	11	2	15	3.9	45	46	30	38	1	.253	.410	12	4	C-102, OF-9, 1B-1
1958	131	427	116	23	1	18	4.2	50	63	48	38	4	.272	.457	8	3	C-124
1959	150	518	133	19	2	21	4.1	65	72	46	48	5	.257	.423	4	0	C-146
1960	142	537	158	14	1	19	3.5	81	77	34	36	4	.294	.430	2	0	C-141
1961	15	30	6	3	0	0	0.0	3	1	1	0	0	.200	.300	8	0	C-5
1962	107	350	104	12	3	8	2.3	35	45	27	24	3	.297	.417	14	6	C-90, 1B-5
1963	86	259	52	4	0	3	1.2	18	28	18	22	1	.201	.251	6	0	C-75, 1B-7
1964 SF N	69	195	45	8	1	3	1.5	12	11	22	21	0	.231	.328	6	2	C-65
1965 PIT N	60	140	30	2	0	2	1.4	11	10	14	10	1	.214	.271	0	0	C-60
1966 CLE A	50	108	25	2	0	4	3.7	10	8	14	9	0	.231	.361	2	0	C-49
16 yrs.	1573	5026	1276	179	18	179	3.6	585	657	424	477	26	.254	.404	85	21	C-1479, 1B-14, OF-9

WORLD SERIES

	G	AB	H	2B	3B	HR	HR %	R	RBI	BB	SO	SB	BA	SA	PH AB	PH H	G by POS
1957 MIL N	6	19	4	0	0	1	5.3	1	1	1	1	0	.211	.368	0	0	C-6
1958	7	25	6	0	0	1	4.0	4	3	3	10	0	.240	.360	0	0	C-7
2 yrs.	13	44	10	0	0	2	4.5	5	4	4	11	0	.227	.364	0	0	C-13

Doc Crandall

CRANDALL, JAMES OTIS   BR TR 5'10½"   180 lbs.
B. Oct. 8, 1887, Wadena, Ind.   D. Aug. 17, 1951, Bell, Calif.

	G	AB	H	2B	3B	HR	HR %	R	RBI	BB	SO	SB	BA	SA	PH AB	PH H	G by POS
1908 NY N	34	72	16	4	0	2	2.8	4	8	6	4		0	.222	.361	2	0	P-32, 2B-1
1909	30	41	10	0	1	1	2.4	4	1	1			0	.244	.366	0	0	P-30
1910	45	73	25	2	4	1	1.4	10	13	5	7	0	.342	.521	1	0	P-42, SS-1
1911	61	113	27	1	4	2	1.8	12	21	8	16	2	.239	.372	11	1	P-41, SS-6, 2B-3
1912	50	80	25	6	2	0	0.0	9	19	6	7	0	.313	.438	10	4	P-37, 2B-2, 1B-1
1913 2 teams		NY N (46G – .319)			STL N (2G – .000)												
" total	48	49	15	4	1	0	0.0	7	4	3		0	.306	.429	10	2	P-35, 2B-1
1914 STL F	118	278	86	16	5	2	0.7	40	41	58		3	.309	.424	17	5	2B-63, P-27, OF-1, SS-1
1915	84	141	40	2	2	1	0.7	18	19	27		4	.284	.348	28	5	P-51
1916 STL A	16	12	1	0	0	0	0.0	0	0	2	4	0	.083	.083	12	1	P-2
1918 BOS N	14	28	8	0	0	0	0.0	1	2	4	3	0	.286	.286	5	2	P-5, OF-3
10 yrs.	500	887	253	35	19	9	1.0	109	126	118	47	9	.285	.398	96	22	P-302, 2B-70, SS-8, OF-4, 1B-1

WORLD SERIES

	G	AB	H	2B	3B	HR	HR %	R	RBI	BB	SO	SB	BA	SA	PH AB	PH H	G by POS
1911 NY N	3	2	1	1	0	0	0.0	1	2	0		0	.500	1.000	0	0	P-2
1912	1	1	0	0	0	0	0.0	0	0	1		0	.000	.000	0	0	P-1
1913	4	4	0	0	0	0	0.0	0	0	1	2	0	.000	.000	2	0	P-2
3 yrs.	8	7	1	1	0	0	0.0	1	1	2		0	.143	.286	2	0	P-5

Cannonball Crane

CRANE, EDWARD NICHOLAS   BR TR 5'10½"   204 lbs.
B. May, 1862, Boston, Mass.   D. Sept. 19, 1896, Rochester, N. Y.

	G	AB	H	2B	3B	HR	HR %	R	RBI	BB	SO	SB	BA	SA	PH AB	PH H	G by POS
1884 BOS U	101	428	122	23	6	12	2.8	83		14			.285	.451	0	0	OF-57, C-42, 1B-5, P-4
1885 2 teams		PRO N (1G – .000)			BUF N (13G – .275)												
" total	14	53	14	0	1	2	3.8	5	10	4	9	0	.264	.415	0	0	OF-14
1886 WAS N	80	292	50	11	3	0	0.0	20	20	13	54		.171	.229	0	0	OF-68, P-10, C-4
1888 NY N	12	37	6	2	0	1	2.7	3	2	3	11	1	.162	.297	0	0	P-12
1889	29	103	21	1	0	2	1.9	16	11	13	21	6	.204	.272	0	0	P-29, 1B-1
1890 NY P	43	146	46	5	4	0	0.0	27	16	10	26	5	.315	.404	0	0	P-43

	G	AB	H	2B	3B	HR	HR %	R	RBI	BB	SO	SB	BA	SA	Pinch Hit AB	Pinch Hit H	G by POS

Cannonball Crane continued

1891 2 teams	C-M AA (34G – .155)		CIN N (15G – .109)														
" total	49	156	22	0	0	1	0.6	16	9	11	40	7	.141	.160	0	0	P-47, OF-3
1892 NY N	48	163	40	1	1	0	0.0	20	14	11	30	2	.245	.264	0	0	P-47, OF-1
1893 2 teams	NY N (12G – .462)		BKN N (3G – .400)														
" total	15	31	14	2	0	0	0.0	9	3	7	0	0	.452	.516	0	0	P-12, OF-2, 1B-1
9 yrs.	391	1409	335	45	15	18	1.3	199	84	86	191	21	.238	.329	0	0	P-204, OF-145, C-46, 1B-7

Sam Crane

CRANE, SAMUEL BYREN (Red)   BR   TR   5'11½" 154 lbs.
B. Sept. 13, 1894, Harrisburg, Pa.   D. Nov. 12, 1955, Philadelphia, Pa.

	G	AB	H	2B	3B	HR	HR %	R	RBI	BB	SO	SB	BA	SA	Pinch Hit AB	Pinch Hit H	G by POS
1914 PHI A	2	6	0	0	0	0	0.0	0	0	2	3	0	.000	.000	0	0	SS-2
1915	8	23	2	2	0	0	0.0	3	1	0	4	0	.087	.174	1	0	SS-6, 2B-1
1916	2	4	1	0	0	0	0.0	1	0	2	1	0	.250	.250	0	0	SS-2
1917 WAS A	32	95	17	2	0	0	0.0	6	4	4	14	0	.179	.200	0	0	SS-32
1920 CIN N	54	144	31	4	0	0	0.0	20	9	7	9	5	.215	.243	7	0	SS-25, 3B-10, 2B-4, OF-3
1921	73	215	50	10	2	0	0.0	20	16	14	14	2	.233	.298	3	0	SS-63, 3B-2, OF-1
1922 BKN N	3	8	2	1	0	0	0.0	1	0	0	1	0	.250	.375	0	0	SS-3
7 yrs.	174	495	103	19	2	0	0.0	51	30	29	46	7	.208	.255	11	0	SS-133, 3B-12, 2B-5, OF-4

Sam Crane

CRANE, SAMUEL NEWHALL   BR   TR
B. Jan. 2, 1854, Springfield, Mass.   D. June 26, 1925, New York, N. Y.
Manager 1880, 1884.

	G	AB	H	2B	3B	HR	HR %	R	RBI	BB	SO	SB	BA	SA	Pinch Hit AB	Pinch Hit H	G by POS
1880 BUF N	10	31	4	0	0	0	0.0	4	2	1	8		.129	.129	0	0	2B-10, OF-1
1883 NY AA	96	349	82	8	5	0	0.0	57		13			.235	.287	0	0	2B-96, OF-1
1884 CIN U	80	309	72	9	3	1	0.3	56		11			.233	.291	0	0	2B-80
1885 DET N	68	245	47	4	5	2	0.8	23	20	13	45		.192	.273	0	0	2B-68
1886 2 teams	DET N (47G – .141)		STL N (39G – .172)														
" total	86	301	46	5	3	1	0.3	34	19	21	61		.153	.199	0	0	2B-77, SS-8, OF-4
1887 WAS N	7	30	9	1	1	0	0.0	6	1	1	6	5	.300	.400	0	0	SS-7
1890 3 teams	NY N (2G – .000)		PIT N (22G – .195)					CLE N (2G – .000)									
" total	26	94	16	3	0	0	0.0	3	3	0	7	6	.170	.202	0	0	2B-17, SS-7, OF-2, 1B-1
7 yrs.	373	1359	276	30	17	4	0.3	183	45	60	127	11	.203	.259	0	0	2B-348, SS-22, OF-8, 1B-1

Gavvy Cravath

CRAVATH, CLIFFORD CARLTON (Cactus)   BR   TR   5'10½" 186 lbs.
B. Mar. 23, 1881, Escondido, Calif.   D. May 23, 1963, Laguna Beach, Calif.
Manager 1919-20.

	G	AB	H	2B	3B	HR	HR %	R	RBI	BB	SO	SB	BA	SA	Pinch Hit AB	Pinch Hit H	G by POS
1908 BOS A	94	277	71	10	11	1	0.4	43	34	38		6	.256	.383	14	5	OF-77, 1B-5
1909 2 teams	CHI A (19G – .180)		WAS A (3G – .000)														
" total	22	55	9	0	0	1	1.8	7	9	20		3	.164	.218	2	0	OF-19
1912 PHI N	130	436	124	30	9	11	2.5	63	70	47	77	15	.284	.470	16	4	OF-113
1913	147	525	**179**	34	14	**19**	3.6	78	**128**	55	63	10	.341	**.568**	5	1	OF-141
1914	149	499	149	27	8	**19**	3.8	76	100	83	72	14	.299	.499	6	0	OF-143
1915	150	522	149	31	7	**24**	4.6	**89**	**115**	**86**	77	11	.285	**.510**	2	0	OF-150
1916	137	448	127	21	8	11	2.5	70	70	64	**89**	9	.283	.440	7	1	OF-130
1917	140	503	141	29	16	**12**	2.4	70	83	70	57	6	.280	.473	1	0	OF-139
1918	121	426	99	27	5	**8**	1.9	43	54	54	46	7	.232	.376	2	0	OF-118
1919	83	214	73	18	5	**12**	5.6	34	45	35	21	8	.341	.640	19	6	OF-56
1920	46	45	13	5	0	1	2.2	2	11	9	12	0	.289	.467	34	**12**	OF-5
11 yrs.	1219	3950	1134	232	83	119	3.0	575	719	561	514	89	.287	.478	106	32	OF-1091, 1B-5

WORLD SERIES

	G	AB	H	2B	3B	HR	HR %	R	RBI	BB	SO	SB	BA	SA	Pinch Hit AB	Pinch Hit H	G by POS
1915 PHI N	5	16	2	1	1	0	0.0	2	1	2	6	0	.125	.313	0	0	OF-5

Bill Craver

CRAVER, WILLIAM H.   BR   TR   5'9"   160 lbs.
B. 1844, Troy, N. Y.   D. June 17, 1901, Troy, N. Y.
Manager 1871-72, 1874.

	G	AB	H	2B	3B	HR	HR %	R	RBI	BB	SO	SB	BA	SA	Pinch Hit AB	Pinch Hit H	G by POS
1876 NY N	56	246	55	4	0	0	0.0	24	22	2	7		.224	.240	0	0	2B-42, C-11, SS-6
1877 LOU N	57	238	63	5	2	0	0.0	33	29	5	11		.265	.303	0	0	SS-57
2 yrs.	113	484	118	9	2	0	0.0	57	51	7	18		.244	.271	0	0	SS-63, 2B-42, C-11

Forrest Crawford

CRAWFORD, FORREST   TR
B. May 10, 1881, Rockdale, Tex.   D. Mar. 27, 1908, Austin, Tex.

	G	AB	H	2B	3B	HR	HR %	R	RBI	BB	SO	SB	BA	SA	Pinch Hit AB	Pinch Hit H	G by POS
1906 STL N	45	145	30	3	1	0	0.0	8	11	7		1	.207	.241	0	0	SS-39, 3B-6
1907	7	22	5	0	0	0	0.0	0	3	2		0	.227	.227	0	0	SS-7
2 yrs.	52	167	35	3	1	0	0.0	8	14	9		1	.210	.240	0	0	SS-46, 3B-6

George Crawford

CRAWFORD, GEORGE
Deceased.

	G	AB	H	2B	3B	HR	HR %	R	RBI	BB	SO	SB	BA	SA	Pinch Hit AB	Pinch Hit H	G by POS
1890 PHI AA	5	17	2	0	0	0	0.0	1		0		1	.118	.118	0	0	OF-4, SS-1

Glenn Crawford

CRAWFORD, GLENN MARTIN (Shorty)   BL   TR   5'9"   165 lbs.
B. Dec. 2, 1913, North Branch, Mich.   D. Jan. 2, 1972, Saginaw, Mich.

	G	AB	H	2B	3B	HR	HR %	R	RBI	BB	SO	SB	BA	SA	Pinch Hit AB	Pinch Hit H	G by POS
1945 2 teams	STL N (4G – .000)		PHI N (82G – .295)														
" total	86	305	89	13	2	2	0.7	41	24	37	15	5	.292	.367	4	0	OF-39, SS-34, 2B-14
1946 PHI N	1	1	0	0	0	0	0.0	0	0	0	0	0	.000	.000	1	0	
2 yrs.	87	306	89	13	2	2	0.7	41	24	37	15	5	.291	.366	5	0	OF-39, SS-34, 2B-14

Ken Crawford

CRAWFORD, KENNETH DANIEL   BL   TR
B. Oct. 31, 1894, South Bend, Ind.   D. Nov. 11, 1976, Pittsburgh, Pa.

	G	AB	H	2B	3B	HR	HR %	R	RBI	BB	SO	SB	BA	SA	Pinch Hit AB	Pinch Hit H	G by POS
1915 BAL F	23	82	20	2	1	0	0.0	4	7	1		0	.244	.293	5	0	1B-14, OF-4

	G	AB	H	2B	3B	HR	HR %	R	RBI	BB	SO	SB	BA	SA	Pinch Hit AB	H	G by POS

Pat Crawford

CRAWFORD, CLIFFORD RANKIN
B. Jan. 28, 1902, Society Hill, S. C.
BL TR 5'11" 170 lbs.

	G	AB	H	2B	3B	HR	HR %	R	RBI	BB	SO	SB	BA	SA	PH AB	PH H	G by POS
1929 NY N	65	57	17	3	0	3	5.3	13	24	11	5	1	.298	.509	44	10	1B-7, 3B-1
1930 2 teams		NY	N	(25G –	.276)		CIN	N	(76G –	.290)							
" total	101	300	86	10	3	6	2.0	35	43	30	12	2	.287	.400	14	3	2B-72, 1B-14
1933 STL N	91	224	60	8	2	0	0.0	24	21	14	9	1	.268	.321	38	9	1B-29, 2B-15, 3B-7
1934	61	70	19	2	0	0	0.0	3	16	5	3	0	.271	.300	43	11	3B-9, 2B-4
4 yrs.	318	651	182	23	5	9	1.4	75	104	60	29	4	.280	.372	139	33	2B-91, 1B-50, 3B-17

WORLD SERIES

	G	AB	H	2B	3B	HR	HR %	R	RBI	BB	SO	SB	BA	SA	PH AB	PH H	G by POS
1934 STL N	2	2	0	0	0	0	0.0	0	0	0	0	0	.000	.000	2	0	

Rufus Crawford

CRAWFORD, RUFUS (Jake)
B. Mar. 20, 1928, Campbell, Mo.
BR TR 6'1½" 185 lbs.

	G	AB	H	2B	3B	HR	HR %	R	RBI	BB	SO	SB	BA	SA	PH AB	PH H	G by POS
1952 STL A	7	11	2	1	0	0	0.0	1	0	1	5	1	.182	.273	4	1	OF-3

Sam Crawford

CRAWFORD, SAMUEL EARL (Wahoo Sam)
B. Apr. 18, 1880, Wahoo, Neb. D. June 15, 1968, Hollywood, Calif.
Hall of Fame 1957.
BL TL 6' 190 lbs.

	G	AB	H	2B	3B	HR	HR %	R	RBI	BB	SO	SB	BA	SA	PH AB	PH H	G by POS
1899 CIN N	31	127	39	2	8	1	0.8	25	20	2		6	.307	.472	0	0	OF-31
1900	101	389	104	14	15	7	1.8	68	59	28		14	.267	.434	6	1	OF-94
1901	131	515	170	22	16	16	3.1	91	104	37		13	.330	.528	4	2	OF-126
1902	140	555	185	16	23	3	0.5	94	78	47		16	.333	.461	0	0	OF-140
1903 DET A	137	550	184	23	25	4	0.7	88	89	25		18	.335	.489	0	0	OF-137
1904	150	571	143	21	17	2	0.4	49	73	44		20	.250	.357	0	0	OF-150
1905	154	575	171	40	10	6	1.0	73	75	50		22	.297	.433	0	0	OF-103, 1B-51
1906	145	563	166	25	16	2	0.4	65	72	38		24	.295	.407	0	0	OF-116, 1B-32
1907	144	582	188	34	17	4	0.7	102	81	37		18	.323	.460	0	0	OF-144, 1B-2
1908	152	591	184	33	16	7	1.2	102	80	37		15	.311	.457	1	0	OF-134, 1B-17
1909	156	589	185	35	14	6	1.0	83	97	47		30	.314	.452	0	0	OF-139, 1B-17
1910	154	588	170	26	19	5	0.9	83	120	37		20	.289	.423	0	0	OF-153, 1B-1
1911	146	574	217	36	14	7	1.2	109	115	61		37	.378	.526	0	0	OF-146
1912	149	581	189	30	21	4	0.7	81	109	42		41	.325	.470	0	0	OF-149
1913	153	610	193	32	23	9	1.5	78	83	52	28	13	.316	.489	0	0	OF-140, 1B-13
1914	157	582	183	22	26	8	1.4	74	104	69	31	25	.314	.483	0	0	OF-157
1915	156	612	183	31	19	4	0.7	81	112	66	29	24	.299	.431	0	0	OF-156
1916	100	322	92	11	13	0	0.0	41	42	37	10	10	.286	.401	15	8	OF-79, 1B-2
1917	61	104	18	4	0	2	1.9	6	12	4	6	0	.173	.269	38	7	1B-15, OF-3
19 yrs.	2517	9580	2964	457	312	97	1.0	1393	1525	760	104	366	.309	.453	64	18	OF-2297, 1B-150
					1st												

WORLD SERIES

	G	AB	H	2B	3B	HR	HR %	R	RBI	BB	SO	SB	BA	SA	PH AB	PH H	G by POS
1907 DET A	5	21	5	1	0	0	0.0	1	2	0	3	0	.238	.286	0	0	OF-5
1908	5	21	5	1	0	0	0.0	2	1	1	2	0	.238	.286	0	0	OF-5
1909	7	28	7	3	0	1	3.6	4	3	1	1	1	.250	.464	0	0	OF-7
3 yrs.	17	70	17	5	0	1	1.4	7	6	2	6	1	.243	.357	0	0	OF-17

Willie Crawford

CRAWFORD, WILLIE MURPHY
B. Sept. 7, 1946, Los Angeles, Calif.
BL TL 6'1" 197 lbs.

	G	AB	H	2B	3B	HR	HR %	R	RBI	BB	SO	SB	BA	SA	PH AB	PH H	G by POS
1964 LA N	10	16	5	1	0	0	0.0	3	0	1	7	1	.313	.375	3	1	OF-4
1965	52	27	4	0	0	0	0.0	10	0	2	8	2	.148	.148	13	0	OF-8
1966	6	0	0	0	0	0	–	1	0	0	0	0	–	–	0	0	
1967	4	4	1	0	0	0	0.0	0	0	1	3	0	.250	.250	3	1	OF-1
1968	61	175	44	12	1	4	2.3	25	14	20	64	1	.251	.400	12	2	OF-48
1969	129	389	96	17	5	11	2.8	64	41	49	85	4	.247	.401	21	6	OF-113
1970	109	299	70	8	6	8	2.7	48	40	33	88	4	.234	.381	15	3	OF-94
1971	114	342	96	16	6	9	2.6	64	40	28	49	5	.281	.442	19	8	OF-97
1972	96	243	61	7	3	8	3.3	28	27	35	55	4	.251	.403	18	4	OF-74
1973	145	457	135	26	2	14	3.1	75	66	78	91	12	.295	.453	7	2	OF-138
1974	139	468	138	23	4	11	2.4	73	61	64	88	7	.295	.432	8	1	OF-133
1975	124	373	98	15	2	9	2.4	46	46	49	43	5	.263	.386	16	3	OF-113
1976 STL N	120	391	119	17	5	9	2.3	49	50	37	53	2	.304	.441	16	5	OF-107
1977 2 teams		HOU	N	(42G –	.254)		OAK	A	(59G –	.184)							
" total	101	250	54	10	1	3	1.2	21	34	34	30	0	.216	.300	22	3	OF-52, DH-18
14 yrs.	1210	3435	921	152	35	86	2.5	507	419	431	664	47	.268	.408	173	39	OF-982, DH-18

LEAGUE CHAMPIONSHIP SERIES

	G	AB	H	2B	3B	HR	HR %	R	RBI	BB	SO	SB	BA	SA	PH AB	PH H	G by POS
1974 LA N	2	4	1	0	0	0	0.0	1	1	1	1	0	.250	.250	1	1	OF-2

WORLD SERIES

	G	AB	H	2B	3B	HR	HR %	R	RBI	BB	SO	SB	BA	SA	PH AB	PH H	G by POS
1965 LA N	2	2	1	0	0	0	0.0	0	0	0	1	0	.500	.500	2	1	
1974	3	6	2	0	0	1	16.7	1	0	1	0	0	.333	.833	2	1	OF-2
2 yrs.	5	8	3	0	0	1	12.5	1	0	1	1	0	.375	.750	4	2	OF-2

George Creamer

CREAMER, GEORGE W.
Born George W. Triebel.
B. 1855, Philadelphia, Pa. D. June 27, 1886, Philadelphia, Pa.
Manager 1884.
BR TR 6'2"

	G	AB	H	2B	3B	HR	HR %	R	RBI	BB	SO	SB	BA	SA	PH AB	PH H	G by POS
1878 MIL N	50	193	41	7	3	0	0.0	30	15	5	15		.212	.280	0	0	2B-28, OF-17, 3B-6
1879 SYR N	15	60	13	2	0	0	0.0	3	3	1	2		.217	.250	0	0	2B-10, SS-3, OF-2
1880 WOR N	85	306	61	6	3	0	0.0	40		4	21		.199	.239	0	0	2B-85
1881	80	309	64	9	2	0	0.0	42	25	11	27		.207	.249	0	0	2B-80
1882	81	286	65	16	6	1	0.3	27	29	14	24		.227	.336	0	0	2B-81
1883 PIT AA	91	369	94	7	9	0	0.0	54		20			.255	.322	0	0	2B-91
1884	98	339	62	8	5	0	0.0	38		16			.183	.236	0	0	2B-98
7 yrs.	500	1862	400	55	28	1	0.1	234	72	71	89		.215	.276	0	0	2B-473, OF-19, 3B-6, SS-3

	G	AB	H	2B	3B	HR	HR %	R	RBI	BB	SO	SB	BA	SA	Pinch Hit AB	Pinch Hit H	G by POS

Birdie Cree

CREE, WILLIAM FRANKLIN   BR TR 5'6''   150 lbs.
B. Oct. 22, 1882, Khedive, Pa.   D. Nov. 8, 1942, Sunbury, Pa.

	G	AB	H	2B	3B	HR	HR %	R	RBI	BB	SO	SB	BA	SA	PH AB	PH H	G by POS
1908 NY A	21	78	21	0	2	0	0.0	5	4	7		1	.269	.321	0	0	OF-21
1909	104	343	90	6	3	2	0.6	48	27	30		10	.262	.315	12	1	OF-77, SS-6, 2B-4, 3B-1
1910	134	467	134	19	16	4	0.9	58	73	40		28	.287	.422	0	0	OF-134
1911	137	520	181	30	22	4	0.8	90	88	56		48	.348	.513	1	1	OF-137, SS-4, 2B-1
1912	50	190	63	11	6	0	0.0	25	22	20		12	.332	.453	0	0	OF-50
1913	145	534	145	25	6	1	0.2	51	63	50	51	22	.272	.346	1	0	OF-144
1914	77	275	85	18	5	0	0.0	45	40	30	24	4	.309	.411	1	0	OF-76
1915	74	196	42	8	2	0	0.0	23	15	36	22	7	.214	.276	18	7	OF-53
8 yrs.	742	2603	761	117	62	11	0.4	345	332	269	97	132	.292	.398	33	9	OF-692, SS-10, 2B-5, 3B-1

Pat Creeden

CREEDEN, PATRICK FRANCIS (Whoops)   BL TR 5'8''   175 lbs.
B. May 23, 1906, Newburyport, Mass.

	G	AB	H	2B	3B	HR	HR %	R	RBI	BB	SO	SB	BA	SA	PH AB	PH H	G by POS
1931 BOS A	5	8	0	0	0	0	0.0	0	0	1	3	0	.000	.000	3	0	2B-2

Connie Creedon

CREEDON, CORNELIUS CURTIS   BL TR 6'1''   200 lbs.
B. July 21, 1915, Danvers, Mass.   D. Nov. 30, 1969, Santa Ana, Calif.

	G	AB	H	2B	3B	HR	HR %	R	RBI	BB	SO	SB	BA	SA	PH AB	PH H	G by POS
1943 BOS N	5	4	1	0	0	0	0.0	0	1	1	0	0	.250	.250	4	1	

Marty Creegan

CREEGAN, MARTIN
B. Ireland   D. Mar. 14, 1941, San Francisco, Calif.

	G	AB	H	2B	3B	HR	HR %	R	RBI	BB	SO	SB	BA	SA	PH AB	PH H	G by POS
1884 WAS U	9	33	5	0	0	0	0.0	4		1			.152	.152	0	0	OF-6, C-3, 3B-2, 1B-1

Gus Creely

CREELY, AUGUST L.   5'6''   150 lbs.
B. June 6, 1870, Florissant, Mo.   D. Apr. 22, 1934, St. Louis, Mo.

	G	AB	H	2B	3B	HR	HR %	R	RBI	BB	SO	SB	BA	SA	PH AB	PH H	G by POS
1890 STL AA	4	15	0	0	0	0	0.0	0		0		1	.000	.000	0	0	SS-4

Pete Cregan

CREGAN, PETER JAMES (Peekskill Pete)   BR TR 5'7½''   150 lbs.
B. Apr. 13, 1875, Kingston, N. Y.   D. May 18, 1945, New York, N. Y.

	G	AB	H	2B	3B	HR	HR %	R	RBI	BB	SO	SB	BA	SA	PH AB	PH H	G by POS
1899 NY N	1	2	0	0	0	0	0.0	0	0	0		0	.000	.000	0	0	OF-1
1903 CIN N	6	19	2	0	0	0	0.0	0	0	1		0	.105	.105	0	0	OF-6
2 yrs.	7	21	2	0	0	0	0.0	0	0	1		0	.095	.095	0	0	OF-7

Bernie Creger

CREGER, BERNARD ODELL   BR TR 6'   175 lbs.
B. Mar. 21, 1927, Wytheville, Va.

	G	AB	H	2B	3B	HR	HR %	R	RBI	BB	SO	SB	BA	SA	PH AB	PH H	G by POS
1947 STL N	15	16	3	1	0	0	0.0	3	0	1	3	1	.188	.250	0	0	SS-13

Creepy Crespi

CRESPI, FRANK ANGELO JOSEPH   BR TR 5'8½''   175 lbs.
B. Feb. 16, 1918, St. Louis, Mo.

	G	AB	H	2B	3B	HR	HR %	R	RBI	BB	SO	SB	BA	SA	PH AB	PH H	G by POS
1938 STL N	7	19	5	2	0	0	0.0	2	1	2	7	0	.263	.368	0	0	SS-7
1939	15	29	5	1	0	0	0.0	3	6	3	6	0	.172	.207	3	0	2B-6, SS-4
1940	3	11	3	1	0	0	0.0	2	0	1	2	1	.273	.364	0	0	3B-2, SS-1
1941	146	560	156	24	2	4	0.7	85	46	57	58	3	.279	.350	0	0	2B-145
1942	93	292	71	4	2	0	0.0	33	35	27	29	4	.243	.271	4	1	2B-83, SS-5
5 yrs.	264	911	240	32	4	4	0.4	125	88	90	102	8	.263	.321	7	1	2B-234, SS-17, 3B-2

WORLD SERIES

	G	AB	H	2B	3B	HR	HR %	R	RBI	BB	SO	SB	BA	SA	PH AB	PH H	G by POS
1942 STL N	1	0	0	0	0	0	–	1	0	0	0	0	–	–	0	0	

Lou Criger

CRIGER, LOUIS   BR TR 6'   150 lbs.
B. Feb. 6, 1872, Elkhart, Ind.   D. May 14, 1934, Tucson, Ariz.

	G	AB	H	2B	3B	HR	HR %	R	RBI	BB	SO	SB	BA	SA	PH AB	PH H	G by POS
1896 CLE N	2	5	0	0	0	0	0.0	0	0	1	0	1	.000	.000	1	0	C-1
1897	39	138	31	4	1	0	0.0	15	22	23		5	.225	.268	0	0	C-37, 1B-2
1898	84	287	80	13	4	1	0.3	43	32	40		2	.279	.362	1	0	C-82
1899 STL N	77	258	66	4	5	2	0.8	39	44	28		14	.256	.333	2	1	C-75
1900	80	288	78	8	6	2	0.7	31	38	4		5	.271	.361	4	1	C-75, 3B-1
1901 BOS A	76	268	62	6	3	0	0.0	26	24	11		7	.231	.276	0	0	C-68, 1B-8
1902	83	266	68	16	6	0	0.0	32	28	27		7	.256	.361	1	0	C-80, OF-1
1903	96	317	61	7	10	3	0.9	41	31	26		5	.192	.306	0	0	C-96
1904	98	299	63	10	5	2	0.7	34	34	27		1	.211	.298	3	1	C-95
1905	109	313	62	6	7	1	0.3	33	36	54		5	.198	.272	0	0	C-109
1906	7	17	3	1	0	0	0.0	0	1	1		1	.176	.235	0	0	C-6
1907	75	226	41	4	0	0	0.0	12	14	19		2	.181	.199	1	0	C-75
1908	84	237	45	4	2	0	0.0	12	25	13		1	.190	.224	0	0	C-84
1909 STL A	74	212	36	1	1	0	0.0	15	9	25		2	.170	.184	1	0	C-73
1910 NY A	27	69	13	2	0	0	0.0	3	4	10		0	.188	.217	0	0	C-27
1912 STL A	1	2	0	0	0	0	0.0	1	0	0		0	.000	.000	0	0	C-1
16 yrs.	1012	3202	709	86	50	11	0.3	337	342	309		58	.221	.290	15	3	C-984, 1B-10, OF-1, 3B-1

WORLD SERIES

	G	AB	H	2B	3B	HR	HR %	R	RBI	BB	SO	SB	BA	SA	PH AB	PH H	G by POS
1903 BOS A	8	26	6	0	0	0	0.0	1	4	2	3	0	.231	.231	0	0	C-8

Dave Cripe

CRIPE, DAVID GORDON   BR TR 6'   180 lbs.
B. Apr. 7, 1951, Ramona, Calif.

	G	AB	H	2B	3B	HR	HR %	R	RBI	BB	SO	SB	BA	SA	PH AB	PH H	G by POS
1978 KC A	7	13	2	0	0	0	0.0	0	1	0	2	0	.154	.154	2	0	3B-5

Dave Criscione

CRISCIONE, DAVE GERALD   BR TR 5'8''   185 lbs.
B. Sept. 2, 1951, Dunkirk, N. Y.

	G	AB	H	2B	3B	HR	HR %	R	RBI	BB	SO	SB	BA	SA	PH AB	PH H	G by POS
1977 BAL A	7	9	3	0	0	1	11.1	1	1	0	1	0	.333	.667	0	0	C-7

Tony Criscola

CRISCOLA, ANTHONY PAUL   BL TR 5'11½''   180 lbs.
B. July 9, 1915, Walla Walla, Wash.

	G	AB	H	2B	3B	HR	HR %	R	RBI	BB	SO	SB	BA	SA	PH AB	PH H	G by POS
1942 STL A	91	158	47	9	2	1	0.6	17	13	8	13	2	.297	.399	32	7	OF-52
1943	29	52	8	0	0	0	0.0	4	1	8	7	0	.154	.154	15	1	OF-13

	G	AB	H	2B	3B	HR	HR %	R	RBI	BB	SO	SB	BA	SA	Pinch Hit AB	Pinch Hit H	G by POS

Tony Criscola continued

	G	AB	H	2B	3B	HR	HR %	R	RBI	BB	SO	SB	BA	SA	AB	H	G by POS
1944 **CIN N**	64	157	36	3	2	0	0.0	14	14	14	12	0	.229	.274	24	4	OF-35
3 yrs.	184	367	91	12	4	1	0.3	35	28	30	32	2	.248	.311	71	12	OF-100

Pat Crisham

CRISHAM, PATRICK LEWIS
B. June 4, 1877, Amesbury, Mass.   D. June 12, 1915, Syracuse, N. Y.

	G	AB	H	2B	3B	HR	HR %	R	RBI	BB	SO	SB	BA	SA	AB	H	G by POS
1899 **BAL N**	53	172	50	5	3	0	0.0	23	20	4		4	.291	.355	4	0	1B-26, C-22

Joe Crisp

CRISP, JOSEPH SHELBY   BR TR 6'4"   200 lbs.
B. July 8, 1889, Higginsville, Mo.   D. Feb. 5, 1939, Kansas City, Mo.

	G	AB	H	2B	3B	HR	HR %	R	RBI	BB	SO	SB	BA	SA	AB	H	G by POS
1910 **STL A**	1	1	0	0	0	0	0.0	0	0	0		0	.000	.000	0	0	C-1
1911	1	1	1	0	0	0	0.0	0	0	0		0	1.000	1.000	1	1	
2 yrs.	2	2	1	0	0	0	0.0	0	0	0		0	.500	.500	1	1	C-1

Dode Criss

CRISS, DODE   BL TR 6'2"   200 lbs.
B. Mar. 12, 1885, Sherman, Miss.   D. Sept. 8, 1955, Sherman, Miss.

	G	AB	H	2B	3B	HR	HR %	R	RBI	BB	SO	SB	BA	SA	AB	H	G by POS
1908 **STL A**	64	82	28	6	0	0	0.0	15	14	9		1	.341	.415	41	12	P-9, OF-7, 1B-1
1909	35	48	14	6	1	0	0.0	2	7	0		0	.292	.458	24	7	P-11
1910	70	91	21	4	2	1	1.1	11	11	11		2	.231	.352	44	7	1B-12, P-6
1911	58	83	21	3	1	2	2.4	10	15	11		0	.253	.386	38	9	1B-14, P-4
4 yrs.	227	304	84	19	4	3	1.0	38	47	31		3	.276	.395	147	35	P-30, 1B-27, OF-7

Ches Crist

CRIST, CHESTER ARTHUR (Squack)   BR TR 5'11"   165 lbs.
B. Feb. 10, 1882, Cozaddale, Ohio   D. Jan. 7, 1957, Cincinnati, Ohio

	G	AB	H	2B	3B	HR	HR %	R	RBI	BB	SO	SB	BA	SA	AB	H	G by POS
1906 **PHI N**	6	11	0	0	0	0	0.0	1	0	1		0	.000	.000	0	0	C-6

Hughie Critz

CRITZ, HUGH MELVILLE   BR TR 5'8"   147 lbs.
B. Sept. 17, 1900, Starkville, Miss.   D. Jan. 10, 1980, Greenwood, Miss.

	G	AB	H	2B	3B	HR	HR %	R	RBI	BB	SO	SB	BA	SA	AB	H	G by POS
1924 **CIN N**	102	413	133	15	14	3	0.7	67	35	19	18	19	.322	.448	0	0	2B-96, SS-1
1925	144	541	150	14	8	2	0.4	74	51	34	17	13	.277	.344	0	0	2B-144
1926	155	607	164	24	14	3	0.5	96	79	39	25	7	.270	.371	0	0	2B-155
1927	113	396	110	10	8	4	1.0	50	49	16	18	7	.278	.374	0	0	2B-113
1928	153	641	190	21	11	5	0.8	95	52	37	24	18	.296	.387	0	0	2B-153
1929	107	425	105	17	9	1	0.2	55	50	27	21	9	.247	.336	0	0	2B-106, SS-1
1930 2 teams	CIN	N	(28G –	.231)		NY	N	(124G –	.265)								
" total	152	662	172	20	13	4	0.6	108	61	30	32	8	.260	.347	0	0	2B-152
1931 **NY N**	66	238	69	7	2	4	1.7	33	17	8	17	4	.290	.387	1	1	2B-54
1932	151	659	182	32	7	2	0.3	90	50	34	27	3	.276	.355	0	0	2B-151
1933	133	558	137	18	5	2	0.4	68	33	23	24	4	.246	.306	0	0	2B-133
1934	137	571	138	17	1	6	1.1	77	40	19	24	3	.242	.306	0	0	2B-137
1935	65	219	41	0	3	2	0.9	19	14	3	11	2	.187	.242	1	0	2B-59
12 yrs.	1478	5930	1591	195	95	38	0.6	832	531	289	258	97	.268	.352	2	1	2B-1453, SS-2

WORLD SERIES

	G	AB	H	2B	3B	HR	HR %	R	RBI	BB	SO	SB	BA	SA	AB	H	G by POS
1933 **NY N**	5	22	3	0	0	0	0.0	2	0	1	0	0	.136	.136	0	0	2B-5

Davey Crockett

CROCKETT, DAVID SOLOMON   6'1"   175 lbs.
B. Oct. 5, 1875, Roanoke, Va.   D. Feb. 23, 1961, Charlottesville, Va.

	G	AB	H	2B	3B	HR	HR %	R	RBI	BB	SO	SB	BA	SA	AB	H	G by POS
1901 **DET A**	28	102	29	2	2	0	0.0	10	14	6		1	.284	.343	1	0	1B-27

Art Croft

CROFT, ARTHUR F.
B. Jan. 23, 1855, St. Louis, Mo.   D. Mar. 16, 1884, St. Louis, Mo.

	G	AB	H	2B	3B	HR	HR %	R	RBI	BB	SO	SB	BA	SA	AB	H	G by POS
1877 **STL N**	54	220	51	5	2	0	0.0	23	27	1	15		.232	.273	0	0	1B-28, OF-25, 2B-1
1878 **IND N**	60	222	35	6	0	0	0.0	22	16	5	23		.158	.185	0	0	1B-51, OF-9
2 yrs.	114	442	86	11	2	0	0.0	45	43	6	38		.195	.229	0	0	1B-79, OF-34, 2B-1

Henry Croft

CROFT, HENRY T.
B. Aug. 1, 1875, Chicago, Ill.   D. Dec. 11, 1933, Oak Park, Ill.

	G	AB	H	2B	3B	HR	HR %	R	RBI	BB	SO	SB	BA	SA	AB	H	G by POS
1899 2 teams	LOU	N	(2G –	.000)		PHI	N	(2G –	.143)								
" total	4	9	1	0	0	0	0.0	0	0	1		0	.111	.111	2	0	2B-2
1901 **CHI N**	3	12	4	0	0	0	0.0	1	4	0		0	.333	.333	0	0	OF-3
2 yrs.	7	21	5	0	0	0	0.0	1	4	1		0	.238	.238	2	0	OF-3, 2B-2

Fred Crolius

CROLIUS, FRED JOSEPH
B. Dec. 16, 1876, Jersey City, N. J.   D. Aug. 25, 1960, Ormond Beach, Fla.

	G	AB	H	2B	3B	HR	HR %	R	RBI	BB	SO	SB	BA	SA	AB	H	G by POS
1901 **BOS N**	49	200	48	4	1	1	0.5	22	13	9		6	.240	.285	0	0	OF-49
1902 **PIT N**	9	38	10	2	1	0	0.0	4	7	0		0	.263	.368	0	0	OF-9
2 yrs.	58	238	58	6	2	1	0.4	26	20	9		6	.244	.298	0	0	OF-58

Warren Cromartie

CROMARTIE, WARREN LIVINGSTON   BL TL 6'   180 lbs.
B. Sept. 29, 1953, Miami, Fla.

	G	AB	H	2B	3B	HR	HR %	R	RBI	BB	SO	SB	BA	SA	AB	H	G by POS
1974 **MON N**	8	17	3	0	0	0	0.0	2	0	3	3	1	.176	.176	1	1	OF-6
1976	33	81	17	1	0	0	0.0	8	2	1	5	1	.210	.222	14	1	OF-20
1977	155	620	175	41	7	5	0.8	64	50	33	40	10	.282	.395	0	0	OF-155
1978	159	607	180	32	6	10	1.6	77	56	33	48	8	.297	.418	1	0	OF-158, 1B-4
1979	158	659	181	46	5	8	1.2	84	46	38	78	8	.275	.396	0	0	OF-158
1980	162	597	172	33	5	14	2.3	74	70	51	64	8	.288	.430	2	1	1B-158, OF-2
1981	99	358	109	19	2	6	1.7	41	42	39	27	2	.304	.419	1	1	1B-62, OF-38
1982	144	497	126	24	3	14	2.8	59	62	69	60	6	.254	.398	6	2	OF-136, 1B-9
1983	120	360	100	26	2	3	0.8	37	43	48	48	8	.278	.386	22	8	OF-101, 1B-1
9 yrs.	1038	3796	1063	222	30	60	1.6	446	371	310	385	49	.280	.402	47	14	OF-774, 1B-234

DIVISIONAL PLAYOFF SERIES

	G	AB	H	2B	3B	HR	HR %	R	RBI	BB	SO	SB	BA	SA	AB	H	G by POS
1981 **MON N**	5	22	5	2	0	0	0.0	1	1	0	9	0	.227	.318	0	0	1B-5

LEAGUE CHAMPIONSHIP SERIES

	G	AB	H	2B	3B	HR	HR %	R	RBI	BB	SO	SB	BA	SA	AB	H	G by POS
1981 **MON N**	5	18	3	1	0	0	0.0	0	2	0	2	0	.167	.222	0	0	1B-5

	G	AB	H	2B	3B	HR	HR %	R	RBI	BB	SO	SB	BA	SA	Pinch Hit AB	Pinch Hit H	G by POS

Herb Crompton

CROMPTON, HERBERT BRYAN (Workhorse)   BR TR 6'   185 lbs.
B. Nov. 7, 1911, Taylor Ridge, Ill.   D. Aug. 5, 1963, Moline, Ill.

	G	AB	H	2B	3B	HR	HR %	R	RBI	BB	SO	SB	BA	SA	AB	H	G by POS
1937 WAS A	2	3	1	0	0	0	0.0	0	0	0	0	0	.333	.333	0	0	C-2
1945 NY A	36	99	19	3	0	0	0.0	6	12	2	7	0	.192	.222	3	1	C-33
2 yrs.	38	102	20	3	0	0	0.0	6	12	2	7	0	.196	.225	3	1	C-35

Ned Crompton

CROMPTON, EDWARD   BL TR 5'10½" 175 lbs.
B. Feb. 12, 1889, Liverpool, England   D. Sept. 28, 1950, Aspinwall Pa.

	G	AB	H	2B	3B	HR	HR %	R	RBI	BB	SO	SB	BA	SA	AB	H	G by POS
1909 STL A	17	63	10	2	1	0	0.0	7	2	7		1	.159	.222	0	0	OF-17
1910 CIN N	1	2	0	0	0	0	0.0	0	0	0	2	0	.000	.000	0	0	OF-1
2 yrs.	18	65	10	2	1	0	0.0	7	2	7	2	1	.154	.215	0	0	OF-18

Bill Cronin

CRONIN, WILLIAM PATRICK (Crungy)   BR TR 5'8½" 167 lbs.
B. Dec. 26, 1902, West Newton, Mass.   D. Oct. 26, 1966, Newton, Mass.

	G	AB	H	2B	3B	HR	HR %	R	RBI	BB	SO	SB	BA	SA	AB	H	G by POS
1928 BOS N	3	2	0	0	0	0	0.0	1	0	1	0	0	.000	.000	0	0	C-3
1929	6	9	1	0	0	0	0.0	0	0	0	0	0	.111	.111	0	0	C-6
1930	66	178	45	9	1	0	0.0	19	17	4	8	0	.253	.315	2	1	C-64
1931	51	107	22	6	1	0	0.0	8	10	7	5	0	.206	.280	1	0	C-50
4 yrs.	126	296	68	15	2	0	0.0	28	27	12	13	0	.230	.294	3	1	C-123

Dan Cronin

CRONIN, DANIEL
B. 1857, Boston, Mass.   D. Nov. 30, 1885, Boston, Mass.

1884 2 teams	C-P	U (1G – .250)		STL	U (1G – .000)												
" total	2	9	1	0	0	0	0.0	1		0			.111	.111	0	0	OF-1, 2B-1

Jim Cronin

CRONIN, JAMES JOHN   BB TR 5'10½" 150 lbs.
B. Aug. 7, 1905, Richmond, Calif.   D. June 10, 1983, Concord, Calif.

	G	AB	H	2B	3B	HR	HR %	R	RBI	BB	SO	SB	BA	SA	AB	H	G by POS
1929 PHI A	25	56	13	2	1	0	0.0	7	4	5	7	0	.232	.304	0	0	2B-10, SS-9, 3B-4

Joe Cronin

CRONIN, JOSEPH EDWARD   BR TR 5'11½" 180 lbs.
B. Oct. 12, 1906, San Francisco, Calif.   D. Sept. 7, 1984, Osterville, Mass.
Manager 1933-47.
Hall of Fame 1956.

	G	AB	H	2B	3B	HR	HR %	R	RBI	BB	SO	SB	BA	SA	AB	H	G by POS
1926 PIT N	38	83	22	2	2	0	0.0	9	11	6	15	0	.265	.337	0	0	2B-27, SS-7
1927	12	22	5	1	0	0	0.0	2	3	2	3	2	.227	.273	2	0	2B-7, SS-4, 1B-1
1928 WAS A	63	227	55	10	4	0	0.0	23	25	22	27	4	.242	.322	0	0	SS-63
1929	145	494	139	29	8	8	1.6	72	61	85	37	5	.281	.421	1	0	SS-143, 2B-1
1930	154	587	203	41	9	13	2.2	127	126	72	36	17	.346	.513	0	0	SS-154
1931	156	611	187	44	13	12	2.0	103	126	81	52	10	.306	.480	0	0	SS-155
1932	143	557	177	43	18	6	1.1	95	116	66	45	7	.318	.492	1	1	SS-141
1933	152	602	186	45	11	5	0.8	89	118	87	49	5	.309	.445	0	0	SS-152
1934	127	504	143	30	9	7	1.4	68	101	53	28	8	.284	.421	0	0	SS-127
1935 BOS A	144	556	164	37	14	9	1.6	70	95	63	40	3	.295	.460	3	0	SS-139
1936	81	295	83	22	4	2	0.7	36	43	32	21	1	.281	.403	1	0	SS-60, 3B-21
1937	148	570	175	40	4	18	3.2	102	110	84	73	5	.307	.486	0	0	SS-148
1938	143	530	172	51	5	17	3.2	98	94	91	60	7	.325	.536	1	0	SS-142
1939	143	520	160	33	3	19	3.7	97	107	87	48	6	.308	.492	0	0	SS-142
1940	149	548	156	35	6	24	4.4	104	111	83	65	7	.285	.502	1	0	SS-146, 3B-2
1941	143	518	161	38	8	16	3.1	98	95	82	55	1	.311	.508	3	1	SS-119, 3B-22, OF-1
1942	45	79	24	3	0	4	5.1	7	24	15	21	0	.304	.494	25	6	3B-11, 1B-5, SS-1
1943	59	77	24	4	0	5	6.5	8	29	11	4	0	.312	.558	42	18	3B-10
1944	76	191	46	7	0	5	2.6	24	28	34	19	1	.241	.356	24	4	1B-49
1945	3	8	3	0	0	0	0.0	1	1	3	2	0	.375	.375	0	0	3B-3
20 yrs.	2124	7579	2285	515	118	170	2.2	1233	1424	1059	700	87	.301	.468	104	30	SS-1843, 3B-69, 1B-55, 2B-35, OF-1

WORLD SERIES

	G	AB	H	2B	3B	HR	HR %	R	RBI	BB	SO	SB	BA	SA	AB	H	G by POS
1933 WAS A	5	22	7	0	0	0	0.0	1	2	0	2	0	.318	.318	0	0	SS-5

John Crooks

CROOKS, JOHN CHARLES (Jack)
B. Nov. 9, 1865, St. Paul, Minn.   D. Feb. 2, 1918, St. Louis, Mo.

	G	AB	H	2B	3B	HR	HR %	R	RBI	BB	SO	SB	BA	SA	AB	H	G by POS
1889 COL AA	12	43	14	2	3	0	0.0	13	7	10	4	10	.326	.512	0	0	2B-12
1890	135	485	107	5	4	1	0.2	86		96		57	.221	.254	0	0	2B-133, 3B-2, OF-1
1891	138	519	127	19	13	0	0.0	110	46	103	47	50	.245	.331	0	0	2B-138
1892 STL N	128	445	95	7	4	7	1.6	82	38	136	52	23	.213	.294	0	0	2B-102, 3B-24, OF-2
1893	128	448	106	10	9	1	0.2	93	48	121	37	31	.237	.306	0	0	3B-123, SS-4, C-1
1895 WAS N	117	409	114	19	8	6	1.5	80	57	68	39	36	.279	.408	0	0	2B-117
1896 2 teams	WAS	N	(25G – .286)		LOU	N	(39G – .238)										
" total	64	206	53	8	1	5	2.4	39	35	36	16	10	.257	.379	1	0	2B-59, 3B-4
1898 STL N	72	225	52	4	2	1	0.4	33	20	40		3	.231	.280	0	0	2B-66, 3B-3, SS-2, OF-1
8 yrs.	794	2780	668	74	44	21	0.8	536	251	610	195	220	.240	.321	1	0	2B-627, 3B-156, SS-6, OF-4, C-1

Tom Crooks

CROOKS, THOMAS A.   TR
B. Washington, D. C.   D. Apr. 5, 1929, Quantico, Va.

	G	AB	H	2B	3B	HR	HR %	R	RBI	BB	SO	SB	BA	SA	AB	H	G by POS
1909 WAS A	3	7	2	1	0	0	0.0	2	2	2		1	.286	.429	0	0	1B-3
1910	8	21	4	1	0	0	0.0	1	1	1		0	.190	.238	2	1	1B-5
2 yrs.	11	28	6	2	0	0	0.0	3	3	3		1	.214	.286	2	1	1B-8

Ed Crosby

CROSBY, EDWARD CARLTON   BL TR 6'2" 175 lbs.
B. May 26, 1949, Long Beach, Calif.

	G	AB	H	2B	3B	HR	HR %	R	RBI	BB	SO	SB	BA	SA	AB	H	G by POS
1970 STL N	38	95	24	4	1	0	0.0	9	6	7	5	0	.253	.316	2	1	SS-35, 3B-3, 2B-2
1972	101	276	60	9	1	0	0.0	27	19	18	27	1	.217	.257	15	0	SS-43, 2B-38, 3B-14
1973 2 teams	STL	N	(22G – .128)		CIN	N	(36G – .216)										
" total	58	90	16	3	2	0	0.0	8	6	11	16	0	.178	.256	13	4	SS-36, 2B-10, 3B-4
1974 CLE A	37	86	18	3	0	0	0.0	11	6	6	12	0	.209	.244	9	3	3B-18, SS-13, 2B-3
1975	61	128	30	3	0	0	0.0	12	7	13	14	0	.234	.258	0	0	SS-30, 2B-19, 3B-13

	G	AB	H	2B	3B	HR	HR %	R	RBI	BB	SO	SB	BA	SA	Pinch Hit AB	Pinch Hit H	G by POS

Ed Crosby continued

	G	AB	H	2B	3B	HR	HR %	R	RBI	BB	SO	SB	BA	SA	AB	H	G by POS
1976	2	2	1	0	0	0	0.0	0	0	0	0	0	.500	.500	0	0	DH-1, 3B-1
6 yrs.	297	677	149	22	4	0	0.0	67	44	55	74	1	.220	.264	39	8	SS-157, 2B-72, 3B-53, DH-1

LEAGUE CHAMPIONSHIP SERIES

	G	AB	H	2B	3B	HR	HR %	R	RBI	BB	SO	SB	BA	SA	AB	H	G by POS
1973 CIN N	3	2	1	0	0	0	0.0	0	0	0	1	0	.500	.500	1	0	SS-2

Frankie Crosetti

CROSETTI, FRANK PETER JOSEPH (The Crow)
B. Oct. 4, 1910, San Francisco, Calif.   BR TR 5'10" 165 lbs.

	G	AB	H	2B	3B	HR	HR %	R	RBI	BB	SO	SB	BA	SA	AB	H	G by POS
1932 NY A	115	398	96	20	9	5	1.3	47	57	51	51	3	.241	.374	2	0	SS-83, 3B-33, 2B-1
1933	136	451	114	20	5	9	2.0	71	60	55	40	4	.253	.379	2	1	SS-133
1934	138	554	147	22	10	11	2.0	85	67	61	58	5	.265	.401	2	1	SS-119, 3B-23, 2B-1
1935	87	305	78	17	6	8	2.6	49	50	41	27	3	.256	.430	0	0	SS-87
1936	151	632	182	35	7	15	2.4	137	78	90	83	18	.288	.437	0	0	SS-151
1937	149	611	143	29	5	11	1.8	127	49	86	105	13	.234	.352	2	1	SS-147
1938	157	631	166	35	3	9	1.4	113	55	106	99	27	.263	.371	0	0	SS-157
1939	152	656	153	25	5	10	1.5	109	56	65	81	11	.233	.332	0	0	SS-152
1940	145	546	106	23	4	4	0.7	84	31	72	77	14	.194	.273	0	0	SS-145
1941	50	148	33	2	2	1	0.7	13	22	18	14	0	.223	.284	6	1	SS-32, 3B-13
1942	74	285	69	5	5	4	1.4	50	23	31	31	1	.242	.337	1	0	3B-62, SS-8, 2B-2
1943	95	348	81	8	1	2	0.6	36	20	36	47	4	.233	.279	4	1	SS-90
1944	55	197	47	4	2	5	2.5	20	30	11	21	3	.239	.355	1	0	SS-55
1945	130	441	105	12	0	4	0.9	57	48	59	65	7	.238	.293	3	1	SS-126
1946	28	59	17	3	0	0	0.0	4	3	8	2	0	.288	.339	2	0	SS-24
1947	3	1	0	0	0	0	0.0	0	0	0	0	0	.000	.000	1	0	SS-1, 2B-1
1948	17	14	4	0	1	0	0.0	4	0	2	0	0	.286	.429	5	1	2B-6, SS-5
17 yrs.	1682	6277	1541	260	65	98	1.6	1006	649	792	801	113	.245	.354	31	7	SS-1515, 3B-131, 2B-11

WORLD SERIES

	G	AB	H	2B	3B	HR	HR %	R	RBI	BB	SO	SB	BA	SA	AB	H	G by POS
1932 NY A	4	15	2	1	0	0	0.0	2	0	2	3	0	.133	.200	0	0	SS-4
1936	6	26	7	2	0	0	0.0	5	3	3	5	0	.269	.346	0	0	SS-6
1937	5	21	1	0	0	0	0.0	2	0	3	2	0	.048	.048	0	0	SS-5
1938	4	16	4	2	1	1	6.3	1	6	2	4	0	.250	.688	0	0	SS-4
1939	4	16	1	0	0	0	0.0	2	1	2	2	0	.063	.063	0	0	SS-4
1942	1	3	0	0	0	0	0.0	0	0	0	1	0	.000	.000	0	0	3B-1
1943	5	18	5	0	0	0	0.0	4	1	2	3	1	.278	.278	0	0	SS-5
7 yrs.	29	115	20	5	1	1	0.9	16	11	14	20	1	.174	.261	0	0	SS-28, 3B-1

Amos Cross

CROSS, AMOS C.
Brother of Lave Cross.   Brother of Frank Cross.
B. 1861, Czechoslovakia   D. July 16, 1888, Cleveland, Ohio

	G	AB	H	2B	3B	HR	HR %	R	RBI	BB	SO	SB	BA	SA	AB	H	G by POS
1885 LOU AA	35	130	37	2	1	0	0.0	11		0			.285	.315	0	0	C-35
1886	74	283	78	14	6	1	0.4	51		44			.276	.378	0	0	C-51, 1B-20, SS-2, OF-1
1887	8	28	3	0	0	0	0.0	0		1		0	.107	.107	0	0	C-5, 1B-2, OF-1
3 yrs.	117	441	118	16	7	1	0.2	62		45			.268	.342	0	0	C-91, 1B-22, OF-2, SS-2

Clarence Cross

CROSS, CLARENCE
Born Clarence Crause.
B. Mar. 4, 1856, St. Louis, Mo.   D. June 23, 1931, Seattle, Wash.

	G	AB	H	2B	3B	HR	HR %	R	RBI	BB	SO	SB	BA	SA	AB	H	G by POS
1884 3 teams	ALT U (2G – .571)			PHI U (2G – .222)			KC U (25G – .215)										
" total	29	109	26	2	0	0	0.0	14		8			.239	.257	0	0	SS-26, 3B-3
1887 NY AA	16	55	11	2	1	0	0.0	9		2		0	.200	.273	0	0	SS-13, 3B-4
2 yrs.	45	164	37	4	1	0	0.0	23		10			.226	.262	0	0	SS-39, 3B-7

Frank Cross

CROSS, FRANK ATWELL (Mickey)
Brother of Amos Cross.   Brother of Lave Cross.   TR
B. Jan. 20, 1873, Cleveland, Ohio   D. Nov. 2, 1932, Geauga Lake, Ohio

	G	AB	H	2B	3B	HR	HR %	R	RBI	BB	SO	SB	BA	SA	AB	H	G by POS
1901 CLE A	1	5	3	0	0	0	0.0	0	0	0		0	.600	.600	0	0	OF-1

Jeff Cross

CROSS, JOFFRE JAMES
B. Aug. 28, 1918, Tulsa, Okla.   BR TR 5'11" 160 lbs.

	G	AB	H	2B	3B	HR	HR %	R	RBI	BB	SO	SB	BA	SA	AB	H	G by POS
1942 STL N	1	4	1	0	0	0	0.0	0	1	0	0	0	.250	.250	0	0	SS-1
1946	49	69	15	3	0	0	0.0	17	6	10	8	4	.217	.261	3	0	SS-17, 2B-8, 3B-1
1947	51	49	5	1	0	0	0.0	4	3	10	6	0	.102	.122	1	0	3B-15, SS-14, 2B-2
1948 2 teams	STL N (2G – .000)			CHI N (16G – .100)													
" total	18	20	2	0	0	0	0.0	1	0	0	4	0	.100	.100	4	0	SS-9, 2B-1
4 yrs.	119	142	23	4	0	0	0.0	22	10	20	18	4	.162	.190	8	0	SS-41, 3B-16, 2B-11

Lave Cross

CROSS, LAFAYETTE NAPOLEON
Brother of Frank Cross.   Brother of Amos Cross.   BR TR 5'8½" 155 lbs.
B. May 11, 1867, Milwaukee, Wis.   D. Sept. 4, 1927, Toledo, Ohio
Manager 1899.

	G	AB	H	2B	3B	HR	HR %	R	RBI	BB	SO	SB	BA	SA	AB	H	G by POS
1887 LOU AA	54	203	54	8	3	0	0.0	32		15		15	.266	.335	0	0	C-44, OF-10
1888	47	181	41	3	0	0	0.0	20	15	2		10	.227	.243	0	0	C-37, OF-12, SS-2
1889 PHI AA	55	199	44	8	2	0	0.0	22	23	14	9	11	.221	.281	0	0	C-55
1890 PHI P	63	245	73	7	8	3	1.2	42	47	12	6	5	.298	.429	0	0	C-49, OF-15
1891 PHI AA	110	402	121	20	14	5	1.2	66	52	38	23	14	.301	.458	0	0	OF-43, C-43, 3B-24, SS-1, 2B-1
1892 PHI N	140	541	149	15	10	4	0.7	84	69	39	16	18	.275	.362	0	0	3B-65, C-39, OF-25, 2B-1, SS-1
1893	96	415	124	17	6	4	1.0	81	78	26	7	18	.299	.398	1	1	C-40, 3B-30, OF-10, SS-10, 1B-6
1894	119	529	204	34	9	7	1.3	123	125	29	7	21	.386	.524	0	0	3B-100, C-16, SS-7, 2B-1
1895	125	535	145	26	9	2	0.4	95	101	35	8	21	.271	.364	0	0	3B-125
1896	106	406	104	23	5	1	0.2	63	73	32	14	8	.256	.345	0	0	3B-61, SS-37, 2B-6, OF-2, C-1
1897	88	344	89	17	5	3	0.9	37	51	10		10	.259	.363	0	0	3B-47, 2B-38, OF-2, SS-1

	G	AB	H	2B	3B	HR	HR %	R	RBI	BB	SO	SB	BA	SA	Pinch Hit AB	Pinch Hit H	G by POS

Lave Cross continued

	G	AB	H	2B	3B	HR	HR %	R	RBI	BB	SO	SB	BA	SA	AB	H	G by POS
1898 STL N	151	602	191	28	8	3	0.5	71	79	28		14	.317	.405	0	0	3B-149, SS-2
1899 2 teams	CLE N (38G – .286)					STL N (103G – .303)											
" total	141	557	166	19	5	5	0.9	76	84	25		13	.298	.377	0	0	3B-141
1900 2 teams	STL N (16G – .295)					BKN N (117G – .293)											
" total	133	522	153	15	6	4	0.8	79	73	26		21	.293	.368	0	0	3B-133
1901 PHI A	100	420	139	28	12	2	0.5	82	73	19		23	.331	.469	0	0	3B-100
1902	137	559	191	39	8	0	0.0	90	108	27		25	.342	.440	0	0	3B-137
1903	137	559	163	22	4	2	0.4	61	90	10		14	.292	.356	0	0	3B-136, 1B-1
1904	155	607	176	31	10	1	0.2	73	71	13		10	.290	.379	0	0	3B-155
1905	147	583	155	29	5	0	0.0	68	77	26		8	.266	.333	0	0	3B-147
1906 WAS A	130	494	130	14	6	1	0.2	55	46	28		19	.263	.322	0	0	3B-130
1907	41	161	32	8	0	0	0.0	13	10	10		3	.199	.248	0	0	3B-41
21 yrs.	2275	9064	2644	411	135	47	0.5	1333	1344	464	90	301	.292	.382	1	1	3B-1721, C-324, OF-119, SS-65, 2B-60, 1B-7

WORLD SERIES

	G	AB	H	2B	3B	HR	HR %	R	RBI	BB	SO	SB	BA	SA	AB	H	G by POS
1905 PHI A	5	19	2	0	0	0	0.0	0	0	1	1	0	.105	.105	0	0	3B-5

Monte Cross

CROSS, MONTFORD MONTGOMERY   BR TR 6'2" 180 lbs.
B. Aug. 31, 1869, Philadelphia, Pa.   D. June 21, 1934, Philadelphia, Pa.

	G	AB	H	2B	3B	HR	HR %	R	RBI	BB	SO	SB	BA	SA	AB	H	G by POS
1892 BAL N	15	50	8	0	0	0	0.0	5	2	4	10	2	.160	.160	0	0	SS-15
1894 PIT N	13	43	19	1	5	2	4.7	14	13	5	4	6	.442	.837	0	0	SS-13
1895	108	393	101	14	13	3	0.8	67	54	38	38	39	.257	.382	0	0	SS-107, 2B-1
1896 STL N	125	427	104	10	6	6	1.4	66	52	58	48	40	.244	.337	0	0	SS-125
1897	131	462	132	17	11	4	0.9	59	55	62		38	.286	.396	0	0	SS-131
1898 PHI N	149	525	135	25	5	1	0.2	68	50	55		20	.257	.330	0	0	SS-149
1899	154	557	143	25	6	3	0.5	85	65	56		26	.257	.339	0	0	SS-154
1900	131	466	94	11	3	3	0.6	59	62	51		19	.202	.258	0	0	SS-131
1901	139	483	95	14	1	1	0.2	49	44	52		24	.197	.236	0	0	SS-139
1902 PHI A	137	497	115	22	2	3	0.6	72	59	32		17	.231	.302	0	0	SS-137
1903	137	470	116	21	2	3	0.6	44	45	49		31	.247	.319	0	0	SS-137, 2B-1
1904	153	503	95	23	4	1	0.2	33	38	46		19	.189	.256	0	0	SS-153
1905	78	248	67	17	2	0	0.0	28	24	19		8	.270	.355	0	0	SS-76, 2B-2
1906	134	445	89	23	3	1	0.2	32	40	50		22	.200	.272	0	0	SS-134
1907	77	248	51	9	5	0	0.0	37	18	39		17	.206	.282	1	0	SS-74
15 yrs.	1681	5817	1364	232	68	31	0.5	718	621	616	100	328	.234	.314	1	0	SS-1675, 2B-4

WORLD SERIES

	G	AB	H	2B	3B	HR	HR %	R	RBI	BB	SO	SB	BA	SA	AB	H	G by POS
1905 PHI A	5	17	3	0	0	0	0.0	0	0	0	7	0	.176	.176	0	0	SS-5

Frank Crossin

CROSSIN, FRANK PATRICK   BR TR 5'10" 160 lbs.
B. June 15, 1891, Avondale, Pa.   D. Dec. 6, 1965, Kingston, Pa.

	G	AB	H	2B	3B	HR	HR %	R	RBI	BB	SO	SB	BA	SA	AB	H	G by POS
1912 STL A	8	22	5	0	0	0	0.0	2	2	1		1	.227	.227	0	0	C-8
1913	4	4	1	0	0	0	0.0	1	0	1	1	0	.250	.250	2	1	C-2
1914	43	90	11	1	1	0	0.0	5	5	10	10	3	.122	.156	2	0	C-41
3 yrs.	55	116	17	1	1	0	0.0	8	7	12	11	4	.147	.172	4	1	C-51

Joe Crotty

CROTTY, JOSEPH P.   BR TR
B. Dec. 24, 1860, Cincinnati, Ohio   D. June 22, 1926, Minneapolis, Minn.

	G	AB	H	2B	3B	HR	HR %	R	RBI	BB	SO	SB	BA	SA	AB	H	G by POS
1882 2 teams	LOU AA (5G – .100)					STL AA (8G – .143)											
" total	13	48	6	1	0	0	0.0	3		3			.125	.146	0	0	C-12, OF-1
1884 CIN U	21	84	22	4	2	1	1.2	11		1			.262	.393	0	0	C-21
1885 LOU AA	39	129	20	2	0	0	0.0	14		3			.155	.171	0	0	C-38, 1B-1
1886 NY AA	14	47	8	0	1	0	0.0	6		4			.170	.213	0	0	C-14
4 yrs.	87	308	56	7	3	1	0.3	34		11			.182	.234	0	0	C-85, OF-1, 1B-1

Jack Crouch

CROUCH, JACK ALBERT (Roxy)   BR TR 5'9" 165 lbs.
B. Feb. 20, 1906, Salisbury, N. C.   D. Aug. 25, 1972, Leesburg, Fla.

	G	AB	H	2B	3B	HR	HR %	R	RBI	BB	SO	SB	BA	SA	AB	H	G by POS
1930 STL A	6	14	2	1	0	0	0.0	1	1	1	3	0	.143	.214	0	0	C-5
1931	8	12	0	0	0	0	0.0	0	1	0	4	0	.000	.000	1	0	C-7
1933 2 teams	STL A (19G – .167)					CIN N (10G – .125)											
" total	29	46	7	0	0	1	2.2	6	6	2	6	1	.152	.217	10	1	C-15
3 yrs.	43	72	9	1	0	1	1.4	7	8	3	13	1	.125	.181	11	1	C-27

Frank Croucher

CROUCHER, FRANK DONALD (Dingle)   BR TR 5'11" 165 lbs.
B. July 23, 1914, San Antonio, Tex.   D. May 21, 1980, Houston, Tex.

	G	AB	H	2B	3B	HR	HR %	R	RBI	BB	SO	SB	BA	SA	AB	H	G by POS
1939 DET A	97	324	87	15	0	5	1.5	38	40	16	42	2	.269	.361	2	2	SS-93, 2B-3
1940	37	57	6	0	0	0	0.0	3	2	4	5	0	.105	.105	5	0	SS-26, 2B-7, 3B-1
1941	136	489	124	21	4	2	0.4	51	39	33	72	2	.254	.325	0	0	SS-136
1942 WAS A	26	65	18	1	1	0	0.0	2	5	3	9	0	.277	.323	7	2	2B-18
4 yrs.	296	935	235	37	5	7	0.7	94	86	56	128	4	.251	.324	14	4	SS-255, 2B-28, 3B-1

WORLD SERIES

	G	AB	H	2B	3B	HR	HR %	R	RBI	BB	SO	SB	BA	SA	AB	H	G by POS
1940 DET A	1	0	0	0	0	0	–	0	0	0	0	0	–	–	0	0	SS-1

Buck Crouse

CROUSE, CLYDE ELLSWORTH   BL TR 5'8" 158 lbs.
B. Jan. 6, 1897, Anderson, Ind.   D. Oct. 23, 1983, Muncie, Ind.

	G	AB	H	2B	3B	HR	HR %	R	RBI	BB	SO	SB	BA	SA	AB	H	G by POS
1923 CHI A	23	70	18	2	1	1	1.4	6	7	3	4	0	.257	.357	0	0	C-22
1924	94	305	79	10	1	1	0.3	30	44	23	12	3	.259	.308	4	0	C-90
1925	54	131	46	7	0	2	1.5	18	25	12	4	1	.351	.450	6	2	C-48
1926	49	135	32	4	1	0	0.0	10	17	14	7	0	.237	.281	3	0	C-45
1927	85	222	53	11	0	0	0.0	22	20	21	10	4	.239	.288	4	2	C-81
1928	78	218	55	5	2	2	0.9	17	20	19	14	3	.252	.321	2	0	C-76
1929	45	107	29	7	0	2	1.9	11	12	5	7	2	.271	.393	4	0	C-40
1930	42	118	30	8	1	0	0.0	14	15	17	10	1	.254	.339	3	0	C-38
8 yrs.	470	1306	342	54	6	8	0.6	128	160	114	68	14	.262	.331	26	4	C-440

	G	AB	H	2B	3B	HR	HR %	R	RBI	BB	SO	SB	BA	SA	Pinch Hit AB	Pinch Hit H	G by POS

Don Crow

CROW, DONALD LEROY   BR TR 6'4" 185 lbs.
B. Aug. 18, 1958, Yakima, Wash.

	G	AB	H	2B	3B	HR	HR%	R	RBI	BB	SO	SB	BA	SA	AB	H	G by POS
1982 LA N	4	4	0	0	0	0	0.0	0	0	0	3	0	.000	.000	0	0	C-4

George Crowe

CROWE, GEORGE DANIEL   BL TL 6'2" 210 lbs.
B. Mar. 22, 1923, Whiteland, Ind.

	G	AB	H	2B	3B	HR	HR%	R	RBI	BB	SO	SB	BA	SA	AB	H	G by POS
1952 BOS N	73	217	56	13	1	4	1.8	25	20	18	25	0	.258	.382	17	5	1B-55
1953 MIL N	47	42	12	2	0	2	4.8	6	6	2	7	0	.286	.476	37	9	1B-9
1955	104	303	85	12	4	15	5.0	41	55	45	44	1	.281	.495	21	5	1B-79
1956 CIN N	77	144	36	2	1	10	6.9	22	23	11	28	0	.250	.486	43	11	1B-32
1957	133	494	134	20	1	31	6.3	71	92	32	62	1	.271	.504	13	5	1B-120
1958	111	345	95	12	5	7	2.0	31	61	41	51	1	.275	.400	20	8	1B-93, 2B-1
1959 STL N	77	103	31	6	0	8	7.8	14	29	5	12	0	.301	.592	63	17	1B-14
1960	73	72	17	3	0	4	5.6	5	13	5	16	0	.236	.444	61	15	1B-5
1961	7	7	1	0	0	0	0.0	0	0	0	1	0	.143	.143	7	1	
9 yrs.	702	1727	467	70	12	81	4.7	215	299	159	246	3	.270	.466	282	76	1B-407, 2B-1

Bill Crowley

CROWLEY, WILLIAM MICHAEL   BR TR 5'9" 175 lbs.
B. Apr. 8, 1857, Philadelphia, Pa.   D. July 14, 1891, Gloucester, Mass.

	G	AB	H	2B	3B	HR	HR%	R	RBI	BB	SO	SB	BA	SA	AB	H	G by POS
1877 LOU N	61	238	67	9	3	1	0.4	30	23	4	13		.282	.357	0	0	OF-58, SS-2, C-2, 3B-1, 2B-1
1879 BUF N	60	261	75	9	5	0	0.0	41	30	6	14		.287	.360	0	0	OF-43, C-10, 1B-7, 2B-3
1880	85	354	95	16	4	0	0.0	57	20	19	23		.268	.336	0	0	OF-74, C-22
1881 BOS N	72	279	71	12	0	0	0.0	33	31	14	15		.254	.297	0	0	OF-72
1883 2 teams		PHI	AA (23G –	.250)		CLE	N	(11G –	.293)								
" total	34	137	36	9	3	0	0.0	19		4	7		.263	.372	0	0	OF-33, 1B-1
1884 BOS N	108	407	110	14	6	6	1.5	50		33	74		.270	.378	0	0	OF-108
1885 BUF N	92	344	83	14	1	1	0.3	29	36	21	32		.241	.297	0	0	OF-92
7 yrs.	512	2020	537	83	22	8	0.4	259	140	101	178		.266	.341	0	0	OF-480, C-34, 1B-8, 2B-4, SS-2, 3B-1

Ed Crowley

CROWLEY, EDGAR JEWEL   BR TR 6'1" 180 lbs.
B. Aug. 6, 1906, Watkinsville, Ga.   D. Apr. 14, 1970, Birmingham, Ala.

	G	AB	H	2B	3B	HR	HR%	R	RBI	BB	SO	SB	BA	SA	AB	H	G by POS
1928 WAS A	2	1	0	0	0	0	0.0	0	0	0	0	0	.000	.000	0	0	3B-1

John Crowley

CROWLEY, JOHN A.
B. Jan. 12, 1862, Lawrence, Mass.   D. Sept. 23, 1896, Lawrence, Mass.

	G	AB	H	2B	3B	HR	HR%	R	RBI	BB	SO	SB	BA	SA	AB	H	G by POS
1884 PHI N	48	168	41	7	3	0	0.0	26		15	21		.244	.321	0	0	C-48

Terry Crowley

CROWLEY, TERRENCE MICHAEL   BL TL 6' 180 lbs.
B. Feb. 16, 1947, Staten Island, N. Y.

	G	AB	H	2B	3B	HR	HR%	R	RBI	BB	SO	SB	BA	SA	AB	H	G by POS
1969 BAL A	7	18	6	0	0	0	0.0	2	3	1	4	0	.333	.333	2	0	1B-3, OF-2
1970	83	152	39	5	0	5	3.3	25	20	35	26	2	.257	.388	31	9	OF-27, 1B-23
1971	18	23	4	0	0	0	0.0	2	1	3	4	0	.174	.174	9	4	OF-6, 1B-2
1972	97	247	57	10	0	11	4.5	30	29	32	26	0	.231	.405	19	4	OF-68, 1B-15
1973	54	131	27	4	0	3	2.3	16	15	16	14	0	.206	.305	14	3	DH-23, OF-10, 1B-7
1974 CIN N	84	125	30	12	0	1	0.8	11	20	10	16	1	.240	.360	52	10	OF-22, 1B-7
1975	66	71	19	6	0	1	1.4	8	11	7	6	0	.268	.394	49	13	OF-4, 1B-4
1976 2 teams		ATL	N (7G –	.000)		BAL	A	(33G –	.246)								
" total	40	67	15	1	0	0	0.0	5	6	7	11	0	.224	.239	23	4	DH-17, 1B-1
1977 BAL A	18	22	8	1	0	1	4.5	3	9	1	3	0	.364	.545	15	7	DH-2, 1B-1
1978	62	95	24	2	0	0	0.0	9	12	8	12	0	.253	.274	38	13	DH-17, OF-2, 1B-1
1979	61	63	20	5	1	1	1.6	8	8	14	13	0	.317	.476	39	11	DH-15, 1B-2
1980	92	233	67	8	0	12	5.2	33	50	29	21	0	.288	.476	37	11	DH-65, 1B-3
1981	68	134	33	6	0	4	3.0	12	25	29	12	0	.246	.381	21	6	DH-42, 1B-4
1982	65	93	22	2	0	3	3.2	8	17	21	9	0	.237	.355	35	7	DH-14, 1B-10
1983 MON N	50	44	8	0	0	0	0.0	2	3	9	4	0	.182	.182	35	6	1B-4
15 yrs.	865	1518	379	62	1	42	2.8	174	229	222	181	3	.250	.375	419 6th	108 6th	DH-195, OF-141, 1B-87

LEAGUE CHAMPIONSHIP SERIES

	G	AB	H	2B	3B	HR	HR%	R	RBI	BB	SO	SB	BA	SA	AB	H	G by POS
1973 BAL A	2	2	0	0	0	0	0.0	0	0	0	0	0	.000	.000	2	0	OF-1
1975 CIN N	1	0	0	0	0	0	–	0	0	0	0	0	–	–	0	0	
1979 BAL A	2	2	1	0	0	0	0.0	0	1	0	0	0	.500	.500	2	1	
3 yrs.	5	4	1	0	0	0	0.0	0	1	0	0	0	.250	.250	4	1	OF-1

WORLD SERIES

	G	AB	H	2B	3B	HR	HR%	R	RBI	BB	SO	SB	BA	SA	AB	H	G by POS
1970 BAL A	1	1	0	0	0	0	0.0	0	0	0	0	0	.000	.000	1	0	
1975 CIN N	2	2	1	0	0	0	0.0	0	0	0	1	0	.500	.500	2	1	
1979 BAL A	5	4	1	1	0	0	0.0	0	2	1	0	0	.250	.500	4	1	
3 yrs.	8	7	2	1	0	0	0.0	0	2	1	1	0	.286	.429	7 6th	2	

Walt Cruise

CRUISE, WALTON EDWIN   BL TR 6' 175 lbs.
B. May 6, 1890, Childersburg, Ala.   D. Jan. 9, 1975, Sylacauga, Ala.

	G	AB	H	2B	3B	HR	HR%	R	RBI	BB	SO	SB	BA	SA	AB	H	G by POS
1914 STL N	95	256	58	9	3	4	1.6	20	28	25	42	3	.227	.332	11	3	OF-81
1916	3	3	2	0	0	0	0.0	0	0	1	0	0	.667	.667	1	1	OF-2
1917	153	529	156	20	10	5	0.9	70	59	38	73	16	.295	.399	1	1	OF-152
1918	70	240	65	5	4	6	2.5	34	39	30	26	2	.271	.400	5	0	OF-65
1919 2 teams		STL	N (9G –	.095)		BOS	N	(73G –	.216)								
" total	82	262	54	8	0	1	0.4	23	21	18	35	8	.206	.248	9	2	OF-71, 1B-2
1920 BOS N	91	288	80	7	5	0	0.3	40	21	31	26	5	.278	.347	6	1	OF-82
1921	108	344	119	16	8	8	2.3	47	55	48	24	10	.346	.503	3	2	OF-102, 1B-2
1922	104	352	98	15	10	4	1.1	51	46	44	20	4	.278	.412	2	0	OF-100, 1B-2
1923	21	38	8	2	0	0	0.0	4	0	3	2	1	.211	.263	9	2	OF-9
1924	9	9	4	1	1	1	11.1	4	3	0	2	0	.444	.889	9	4	
10 yrs.	736	2321	644	83	39	30	1.3	293	272	238	250	49	.277	.386	56	16	OF-664, 1B-6

	G	AB	H	2B	3B	HR	HR %	R	RBI	BB	SO	SB	BA	SA	Pinch Hit AB	Pinch Hit H	G by POS

Gene Crumling

CRUMLING, EUGENE LEON
B. Apr. 5, 1922, Wrightsville, Pa.
BR TR 6'   180 lbs.

	G	AB	H	2B	3B	HR	HR%	R	RBI	BB	SO	SB	BA	SA	PH AB	PH H	G by POS
1945 STL N	6	12	1	0	0	0	0.0	0	1	0	1	0	.083	.083	0	0	C-6

Buddy Crump

CRUMP, ARTHUR ELLIOTT
B. Nov. 29, 1901, Norfolk, Va.   D. Sept. 7, 1976, Raleigh, N. C.
BL TL 5'10"   156 lbs.

	G	AB	H	2B	3B	HR	HR%	R	RBI	BB	SO	SB	BA	SA	PH AB	PH H	G by POS
1924 NY N	1	4	0	0	0	0	0.0	1	0	1	0	1	0	.000	.000	0	0	OF-1

Press Cruthers

CRUTHERS, CHARLES PRESTON
B. Sept. 8, 1890, Marshallton, Del.   D. Dec. 27, 1976, Kenosha, Wis.
BR TR 5'9"   152 lbs.

	G	AB	H	2B	3B	HR	HR%	R	RBI	BB	SO	SB	BA	SA	PH AB	PH H	G by POS
1913 PHI A	3	12	3	1	0	0	0.0	0	0	0	0	0	.250	.333	0	0	2B-3
1914	4	15	3	0	1	0	0.0	1	0	0	4	0	.200	.333	0	0	2B-4
2 yrs.	7	27	6	1	1	0	0.0	1	0	0	4	0	.222	.333	0	0	2B-7

Hector Cruz

CRUZ, HECTOR DILAN
Brother of Jose Cruz.   Brother of Tommy Cruz.
B. Apr. 2, 1953, Arroyo, Puerto Rico
BR TR 5'11"   170 lbs.

	G	AB	H	2B	3B	HR	HR%	R	RBI	BB	SO	SB	BA	SA	PH AB	PH H	G by POS
1973 STL N	11	11	0	0	0	0	0.0	1	0	1	3	0	.000	.000	4	0	OF-5
1975	23	48	7	2	0	0	0.0	7	6	2	4	0	.146	.271	6	1	3B-12, OF-6
1976	151	526	120	17	1	13	2.5	54	71	42	119	1	.228	.338	3	0	3B-148
1977	118	339	80	19	2	6	1.8	50	42	46	56	2	.236	.357	15	2	OF-106, 3B-2
1978 2 teams	CHI	N (30G – .237)		SF	N (79G – .223)												
" total	109	273	62	13	1	8	2.9	27	33	24	45	0	.227	.370	30	7	OF-67, 3B-21
1979 2 teams	SF	N (16G – .120)		CIN	N (74G – .242)												
" total	90	207	47	10	2	4	1.9	26	28	34	46	0	.227	.353	16	2	OF-75, 3B-2
1980 CIN N	52	75	16	4	1	1	1.3	5	5	8	16	0	.213	.333	22	1	OF-29
1981 CHI N	53	109	25	5	0	7	6.4	15	15	17	24	2	.229	.468	17	3	3B-18, OF-16
1982	17	19	4	1	0	0	0.0	1	0	2	4	0	.211	.263	15	3	OF-4
9 yrs.	624	1607	361	71	9	39	2.4	186	200	176	317	5	.225	.353	128	19	OF-308, 3B-203

LEAGUE CHAMPIONSHIP SERIES

	G	AB	H	2B	3B	HR	HR%	R	RBI	BB	SO	SB	BA	SA	PH AB	PH H	G by POS
1979 CIN N	2	5	1	1	0	0	0.0	1	0	0	1	0	.200	.400	1	1	OF-1

Henry Cruz

CRUZ, HENRY ACOSTA
B. Feb. 27, 1952, St Croix, Virgin Islands
BL TL 6'   175 lbs.

	G	AB	H	2B	3B	HR	HR%	R	RBI	BB	SO	SB	BA	SA	PH AB	PH H	G by POS
1975 LA N	53	94	25	3	1	0	0.0	8	5	7	6	1	.266	.319	14	2	OF-41
1976	49	88	16	2	1	4	4.5	8	14	9	11	0	.182	.364	20	3	OF-23
1977 CHI A	16	21	6	0	0	2	9.5	3	5	1	3	0	.286	.571	1	0	OF-9
1978	53	77	17	2	1	2	2.6	13	10	8	11	0	.221	.351	11	1	OF-40, DH-1
4 yrs.	171	280	64	7	3	8	2.9	32	34	25	31	1	.229	.361	46	6	OF-113, DH-1

Jose Cruz

CRUZ, JOSE DILAN
Brother of Tommy Cruz.   Brother of Hector Cruz.
B. Aug. 8, 1947, Arroyo, Puerto Rico
BL TL 6'   170 lbs.

	G	AB	H	2B	3B	HR	HR%	R	RBI	BB	SO	SB	BA	SA	PH AB	PH H	G by POS
1970 STL N	6	17	6	1	0	0	0.0	2	1	4	0	0	.353	.412	1	1	OF-4
1971	83	292	80	13	2	9	3.1	46	27	49	35	6	.274	.425	2	1	OF-83
1972	117	332	78	14	4	2	0.6	33	23	36	54	9	.235	.319	13	5	OF-102
1973	132	406	92	22	5	10	2.5	51	57	51	66	10	.227	.379	14	3	OF-118
1974	107	161	42	4	3	5	3.1	24	20	20	27	4	.261	.416	47	11	OF-53, 1B-1
1975 HOU N	120	315	81	15	2	9	2.9	44	49	52	44	6	.257	.403	28	6	OF-94
1976	133	439	133	21	5	4	0.9	49	61	53	46	28	.303	.401	10	3	OF-125
1977	157	579	173	31	10	17	2.9	87	87	69	67	44	.299	.475	4	1	OF-155
1978	153	565	178	34	9	10	1.8	79	83	57	57	37	.315	.460	1	0	OF-152, 1B-2
1979	157	558	161	33	7	9	1.6	73	72	72	66	36	.289	.421	1	0	OF-156
1980	160	612	185	29	7	11	1.8	79	91	60	66	36	.302	.426	2	0	OF-158
1981	107	409	109	16	5	13	3.2	53	55	35	49	5	.267	.425	2	1	OF-105
1982	155	570	157	27	2	9	1.6	62	68	60	67	21	.275	.377	2	0	OF-155
1983	160	594	189	28	8	14	2.4	85	92	65	86	30	.318	.463	2	1	OF-160
1984	160	600	187	28	13	12	2.0	96	95	73	68	22	.312	.462	1	0	OF-160
15 yrs.	1907	6449	1851	316	82	134	2.1	863	881	756	798	294	.287	.424	130	34	OF-1780, 1B-3

DIVISIONAL PLAYOFF SERIES

	G	AB	H	2B	3B	HR	HR%	R	RBI	BB	SO	SB	BA	SA	PH AB	PH H	G by POS
1981 HOU N	5	20	6	1	0	0	0.0	0	0	1	3	1	.300	.350	0	0	OF-5

LEAGUE CHAMPIONSHIP SERIES

	G	AB	H	2B	3B	HR	HR%	R	RBI	BB	SO	SB	BA	SA	PH AB	PH H	G by POS
1980 HOU N	5	15	6	1	1	0	0.0	3	4	8	1	0	.400	.600	0	0	OF-5

Julio Cruz

CRUZ, JULIO LUIS
B. Dec. 2, 1954, Brooklyn, N. Y.
BB TR 5'9"   165 lbs.

	G	AB	H	2B	3B	HR	HR%	R	RBI	BB	SO	SB	BA	SA	PH AB	PH H	G by POS
1977 SEA A	60	199	51	3	1	1	0.5	25	7	24	29	15	.256	.296	2	0	2B-54
1978	147	550	129	14	1	1	0.2	77	25	69	66	59	.235	.269	0	0	2B-141, SS-5, DH-1
1979	107	414	112	16	2	1	0.2	70	29	62	61	49	.271	.326	0	0	2B-107
1980	119	422	88	9	3	2	0.5	66	16	59	49	45	.209	.258	0	0	2B-115, DH-3
1981	94	352	90	12	3	2	0.6	57	24	39	40	43	.256	.324	1	0	2B-93, SS-1
1982	154	549	133	22	5	8	1.5	83	49	57	71	46	.242	.344	0	0	2B-151, DH-2, SS-2, 3B-1
1983 2 teams	SEA	A (61G – .254)		CHI	A (99G – .251)												
" total	160	515	130	19	5	3	0.6	71	52	49	66	57	.252	.326	1	1	2B-157, DH-1
1984 CHI A	143	415	92	14	4	5	1.2	42	43	45	58	14	.222	.311	0	0	2B-141
8 yrs.	984	3416	825	109	24	23	0.7	491	245	404	440	328	.242	.308	4	1	2B-958, SS-8, DH-7, 3B-1

LEAGUE CHAMPIONSHIP SERIES

	G	AB	H	2B	3B	HR	HR%	R	RBI	BB	SO	SB	BA	SA	PH AB	PH H	G by POS
1983 CHI A	4	12	4	0	0	0	0.0	0	0	3	4	2	.333	.333	0	0	2B-4

Todd Cruz

CRUZ, TODD RUBEN
B. Nov. 23, 1955, Highland Park, Mich.
BR TR 6'   175 lbs.

	G	AB	H	2B	3B	HR	HR%	R	RBI	BB	SO	SB	BA	SA	PH AB	PH H	G by POS
1978 PHI N	3	4	2	0	0	0	0.0	0	2	0	0	0	.500	.500	0	0	SS-2
1979 KC A	55	118	24	7	0	2	1.7	9	15	3	19	0	.203	.314	0	0	SS-48, 3B-9
1980 2 teams	CAL	A (18G – .275)		CHI	A (90G – .232)												
" total	108	333	79	14	1	3	0.9	28	23	14	62	2	.237	.312	2	1	SS-102, 3B-4, OF-1, 2B-1
1982 SEA A	136	492	113	20	2	16	3.3	44	57	12	95	2	.230	.376	0	0	SS-136

	G	AB	H	2B	3B	HR	HR %	R	RBI	BB	SO	SB	BA	SA	Pinch Hit AB	Pinch Hit H	G by POS

Todd Cruz continued

	G	AB	H	2B	3B	HR	HR%	R	RBI	BB	SO	SB	BA	SA	PH AB	PH H	G by POS
1983 2 teams		SEA A (65G – .190)				BAL A (81G – .208)											
" total	146	437	87	13	3	10	2.3	37	48	22	108	4	.199	.311	5	2	3B-79, SS-63, 2B-2
1984 BAL A	96	142	31	4	0	3	2.1	15	9	8	33	1	.218	.310	14	5	3B-89, DH-1, P-1
6 yrs.	544	1526	336	58	6	34	2.2	133	154	59	317	9	.220	.333	21	8	SS-351, 3B-181, 2B-3, DH-1, OF-1, P-1

LEAGUE CHAMPIONSHIP SERIES

	G	AB	H	2B	3B	HR	HR%	R	RBI	BB	SO	SB	BA	SA	PH AB	PH H	G by POS
1983 BAL A	4	15	2	0	0	0	0.0	0	1	0	5	0	.133	.133	0	0	3B-4

WORLD SERIES

	G	AB	H	2B	3B	HR	HR%	R	RBI	BB	SO	SB	BA	SA	PH AB	PH H	G by POS
1983 BAL A	5	16	2	0	0	0	0.0	1	0	1	3	0	.125	.125	0	0	3B-5

Tommy Cruz

CRUZ, CIRILIO DILAN
Brother of Jose Cruz. Brother of Hector Cruz.
B. Feb. 15, 1951, Arroyo, Puerto Rico
BL TL 5'9" 165 lbs.

	G	AB	H	2B	3B	HR	HR%	R	RBI	BB	SO	SB	BA	SA	PH AB	PH H	G by POS
1973 STL N	3	0	0	0	0	0	–	1	0	0	0	0	–	–	0	0	OF-1
1977 CHI A	4	2	0	0	0	0	0.0	1	0	0	0	0	.000	.000	1	0	OF-2
2 yrs.	7	2	0	0	0	0	0.0	2	0	0	0	0	.000	.000	1	0	OF-3

Mike Cubbage

CUBBAGE, MICHAEL LEE
B. July 21, 1950, Charlottesville, Va.
BL TR 6' 180 lbs.

	G	AB	H	2B	3B	HR	HR%	R	RBI	BB	SO	SB	BA	SA	PH AB	PH H	G by POS
1974 TEX A	9	15	0	0	0	0	0.0	0	0	0	4	0	.000	.000	4	0	3B-3, 2B-2
1975	58	143	32	6	0	4	2.8	12	21	18	14	0	.224	.350	16	1	2B-37, 3B-3, DH-2
1976 2 teams		TEX A (14G – .219)				MIN A (104G – .260)											
" total	118	374	96	19	5	3	0.8	42	49	49	44	1	.257	.358	8	3	3B-100, DH-8, 2B-7
1977 MIN A	129	417	110	16	5	9	2.2	60	55	37	49	1	.264	.391	13	2	3B-126, DH-1
1978	125	394	111	12	7	7	1.8	40	57	40	44	3	.282	.401	22	8	3B-115, 2B-5
1979	94	243	67	10	1	2	0.8	26	23	39	26	1	.276	.350	17	3	3B-63, DH-21, 2B-1, 1B-1
1980	103	285	70	9	0	8	2.8	29	42	23	37	0	.246	.361	9	4	1B-72, 3B-32, DH-1, 2B-1
1981 NY N	67	80	17	2	2	1	1.3	9	4	9	15	0	.213	.325	44	12	3B-12
8 yrs.	703	1951	503	74	20	34	1.7	218	251	215	233	6	.258	.369	133	33	3B-454, 1B-73, 2B-53, DH-33

Al Cuccinello

CUCCINELLO, ALFRED EDWARD
Brother of Tony Cuccinello.
B. Nov. 26, 1914, Long Island City, N. Y.
BR TR 5'10" 165 lbs.

	G	AB	H	2B	3B	HR	HR%	R	RBI	BB	SO	SB	BA	SA	PH AB	PH H	G by POS
1935 NY N	54	165	41	7	1	4	2.4	27	20	1	20	0	.248	.376	3	2	2B-48, 3B-2

Tony Cuccinello

CUCCINELLO, ANTHONY FRANCIS (Chick)
Brother of Al Cuccinello.
B. Nov. 8, 1907, Long Island City, N. Y.
BR TR 5'7" 160 lbs.

	G	AB	H	2B	3B	HR	HR%	R	RBI	BB	SO	SB	BA	SA	PH AB	PH H	G by POS
1930 CIN N	125	443	138	22	5	10	2.3	64	78	47	44	5	.312	.451	3	1	3B-109, 2B-15, SS-4
1931	154	575	181	39	11	2	0.3	67	93	54	28	1	.315	.431	0	0	2B-154
1932 BKN N	154	597	168	32	6	12	2.0	76	77	46	47	5	.281	.415	0	0	2B-154
1933	134	485	122	31	4	9	1.9	58	65	44	40	4	.252	.388	0	0	2B-120, 3B-14
1934	140	528	138	32	2	14	2.7	59	94	49	45	0	.261	.409	1	1	2B-101, 3B-43
1935	102	360	105	20	3	8	2.2	49	53	40	35	3	.292	.431	4	1	2B-64, 3B-36
1936 BOS N	150	565	174	26	3	7	1.2	68	86	58	49	1	.308	.402	0	0	2B-150
1937	152	575	156	36	4	11	1.9	77	80	61	40	2	.271	.405	1	0	2B-151
1938	147	555	147	25	2	9	1.6	62	76	52	32	4	.265	.366	0	0	2B-147
1939	81	310	95	17	1	2	0.6	42	40	26	26	5	.306	.387	1	0	2B-80
1940 2 teams		BOS N (34G – .270)				NY N (88G – .208)											
" total	122	433	98	18	2	5	1.2	40	55	24	51	2	.226	.312	6	1	3B-70, 2B-47
1942 BOS N	40	104	21	3	0	1	1.0	8	8	9	11	1	.202	.260	5	2	3B-20, 2B-14
1943 2 teams		BOS N (13G – .000)				CHI A (34G – .272)											
" total	47	122	28	5	0	2	1.6	5	13	16	14	3	.230	.320	7	1	3B-34, 2B-2, SS-1
1944 CHI A	38	130	34	3	0	0	0.0	5	17	8	16	0	.262	.285	2	0	3B-30, 2B-6
1945	118	402	124	25	3	2	0.5	50	49	45	19	6	.308	.400	6	1	3B-112
15 yrs.	1704	6184	1729	334	46	94	1.5	730	884	579	497	42	.280	.394	36	7	2B-1205, 3B-468, SS-5

Jim Cudworth

CUDWORTH, JAMES ALARIC
B. Aug. 22, 1858, Fairhaven, Mass.   D. Dec. 21, 1943, Middleboro, Mass.
BR TR 6' 165 lbs.

	G	AB	H	2B	3B	HR	HR%	R	RBI	BB	SO	SB	BA	SA	PH AB	PH H	G by POS
1884 KC U	32	116	17	3	1	0	0.0	7		2				.147	.190	0	0	1B-19, OF-12, P-2

Manuel Cueto

CUETO, MANUEL MELO
B. Feb. 8, 1892, Havana, Cuba   D. June 29, 1942, Havana, Cuba
BR TR 5'5" 157 lbs.

	G	AB	H	2B	3B	HR	HR%	R	RBI	BB	SO	SB	BA	SA	PH AB	PH H	G by POS
1914 STL F	19	43	4	0	0	0	0.0	2	2	5		0	.093	.093	1	0	3B-10, SS-5, 2B-2
1917 CIN N	56	140	28	3	0	1	0.7	10	11	16	17	4	.200	.243	5	0	OF-38, 2B-6, C-5
1918	46	108	32	5	1	0	0.0	14	14	19	5	4	.296	.361	2	0	OF-19, 2B-10, SS-9, C-6
1919	29	88	22	2	0	0	0.0	10	4	10	4	5	.250	.273	3	0	OF-25, 3B-1
4 yrs.	150	379	86	10	1	1	0.3	36	31	50	26	13	.227	.266	11	0	OF-82, 2B-18, SS-14, 3B-11, C-11

John Cuff

CUFF, JOHN J.
B. Jersey City, N. J.   Deceased.

	G	AB	H	2B	3B	HR	HR%	R	RBI	BB	SO	SB	BA	SA	PH AB	PH H	G by POS
1884 BAL U	3	11	1	1	0	0	0.0	1		1				.091	.182	0	0	C-3

Leon Culberson

CULBERSON, DELBERT LEON
B. Aug. 6, 1919, Hall's Station, Ga.
BR TR 5'11" 180 lbs.

	G	AB	H	2B	3B	HR	HR%	R	RBI	BB	SO	SB	BA	SA	PH AB	PH H	G by POS
1943 BOS A	80	312	85	16	6	3	1.0	36	34	30	35	13	.272	.391	1	0	OF-79
1944	75	282	67	11	5	2	0.7	41	21	20	20	6	.238	.333	1	0	OF-72
1945	97	331	91	21	6	6	1.8	26	45	20	37	4	.275	.429	6	1	OF-91
1946	59	179	56	10	1	3	1.7	34	18	16	19	3	.313	.430	4	0	OF-49, 3B-4
1947	47	84	20	1	0	0	0.0	10	11	12	10	1	.238	.250	20	3	OF-25, 3B-4
1948 WAS A	12	29	5	0	0	0	0.0	1	2	8	5	0	.172	.172	1	0	OF-11
6 yrs.	370	1217	324	59	18	14	1.2	148	131	106	126	27	.266	.379	33	4	OF-327, 3B-8

WORLD SERIES

	G	AB	H	2B	3B	HR	HR%	R	RBI	BB	SO	SB	BA	SA	PH AB	PH H	G by POS
1946 BOS A	5	9	2	0	0	1	11.1	1	1	1	2	1	.222	.556	2	0	OF-3

	G	AB	H	2B	3B	HR	HR %	R	RBI	BB	SO	SB	BA	SA	Pinch Hit AB	Pinch Hit H	G by POS

John Cullen

CULLEN, JOHN J.
B. New York, N. Y.　D. Apr. 19, 1941, San Francisco, Calif.

	G	AB	H	2B	3B	HR	HR %	R	RBI	BB	SO	SB	BA	SA	PH AB	PH H	G by POS
1884 WIL U	9	31	6	0	0	0	0.0	2		1			.194	.194	0	0	OF-6, SS-3

Tim Cullen

BR TR 6'1" 185 lbs.

CULLEN, TIMOTHY LEO
B. Feb. 16, 1942, San Francisco, Calif.

	G	AB	H	2B	3B	HR	HR %	R	RBI	BB	SO	SB	BA	SA	PH AB	PH H	G by POS
1966 WAS A	18	34	8	1	0	0	0.0	8	0	2	8	0	.235	.265	6	1	3B-8, 2B-5
1967	124	402	95	7	0	2	0.5	35	31	40	47	4	.236	.269	2	0	SS-69, 2B-46, 3B-15, OF-1
1968 2 teams		CHI	A	(72G –	.200)		WAS	A	(47G –	.272)							
" total	119	269	62	11	2	3	1.1	24	29	22	35	0	.230	.320	4	2	2B-87, SS-33, 3B-3
1969 WAS A	119	249	52	7	0	1	0.4	22	15	14	27	1	.209	.249	10	2	2B-105, SS-9, 3B-1
1970	123	262	56	10	2	1	0.4	22	18	31	38	3	.214	.279	12	1	2B-112, SS-6
1971	125	403	77	13	4	2	0.5	34	26	33	47	2	.191	.258	1	0	2B-78, SS-62
1972 OAK A	72	142	37	8	1	0	0.0	10	15	5	17	0	.261	.331	3	1	2B-65, 3B-4, SS-1
7 yrs.	700	1761	387	57	9	9	0.5	155	134	147	219	10	.220	.278	38	7	2B-498, SS-180, 3B-31, OF-1

LEAGUE CHAMPIONSHIP SERIES

	G	AB	H	2B	3B	HR	HR %	R	RBI	BB	SO	SB	BA	SA	PH AB	PH H	G by POS
1972 OAK A	2	1	0	0	0	0	0.0	0	0	0	0	0	.000	.000	0	0	SS-2

Roy Cullenbine

BB TR 6'1" 195 lbs.
BL 1938,1941

CULLENBINE, ROY JOSEPH
B. Oct. 18, 1915, Nashville, Tenn.

	G	AB	H	2B	3B	HR	HR %	R	RBI	BB	SO	SB	BA	SA	PH AB	PH H	G by POS
1938 DET A	25	67	19	1	3	0	0.0	12	9	12	9	2	.284	.388	7	2	OF-17
1939	75	179	43	9	2	6	3.4	31	23	34	29	0	.240	.413	25	7	OF-46, 1B-2
1940 2 teams		BKN	N	(22G –	.180)		STL	A	(86G –	.230)							
" total	108	318	70	12	2	8	2.5	49	40	73	45	2	.220	.346	21	3	OF-76, 1B-6
1941 STL A	149	501	159	29	9	9	1.8	82	98	121	43	6	.317	.465	9	3	OF-120, 1B-22
1942 3 teams		STL	A	(38G –	.193)		WAS	A	(64G –	.286)		NY	A	(21G –	.364)		
" total	123	427	118	33	1	6	1.4	61	66	92	40	1	.276	.400	6	1	OF-77, 3B-28, 1B-6
1943 CLE A	138	488	141	24	4	8	1.6	66	56	96	58	3	.289	.404	5	0	OF-121, 1B-13
1944	154	571	162	34	5	16	2.8	98	80	87	49	4	.284	.445	2	0	OF-151
1945 2 teams		CLE	A	(8G –	.077)		DET	A	(146G –	.277)							
" total	154	536	146	28	5	18	3.4	83	93	112	36	2	.272	.444	1	0	OF-150, 3B-3
1946 DET A	113	328	110	21	0	15	4.6	63	56	88	39	3	.335	.537	9	2	OF-81, 1B-21
1947	142	464	104	18	1	24	5.2	82	78	137	51	3	.224	.422	4	0	1B-138
10 yrs.	1181	3879	1072	209	32	110	2.8	627	599	852	399	26	.276	.432	89	18	OF-839, 1B-208, 3B-31

WORLD SERIES

	G	AB	H	2B	3B	HR	HR %	R	RBI	BB	SO	SB	BA	SA	PH AB	PH H	G by POS
1942 NY A	5	19	5	1	0	0	0.0	3	2	1	2	1	.263	.316	0	0	OF-5
1945 DET A	7	22	5	2	0	0	0.0	5	4	8	2	1	.227	.318	0	0	OF-7
2 yrs.	12	41	10	3	0	0	0.0	8	6	9	4	2	.244	.317	0	0	OF-12

Dick Culler

BR TR 5'9½" 155 lbs.

CULLER, RICHARD BROADUS
B. Jan. 25, 1915, High Point, N. C.　D. June 16, 1964, Chapel Hill, N. C.

	G	AB	H	2B	3B	HR	HR %	R	RBI	BB	SO	SB	BA	SA	PH AB	PH H	G by POS
1936 PHI A	9	38	9	0	0	0	0.0	3	1	1	3	0	.237	.237	0	0	2B-7, SS-2
1943 CHI A	53	148	32	5	1	0	0.0	9	11	16	11	4	.216	.264	0	0	3B-26, 2B-19, SS-3
1944 BOS N	8	28	2	0	0	0	0.0	2	0	4	2	0	.071	.071	0	0	SS-8
1945	136	527	138	12	1	2	0.4	87	30	50	35	7	.262	.300	1	0	SS-126, 3B-6
1946	134	482	123	15	3	0	0.0	70	33	62	18	7	.255	.299	2	1	SS-132
1947	77	214	53	5	1	0	0.0	20	19	19	15	1	.248	.280	1	1	SS-75
1948 CHI N	48	89	15	2	0	0	0.0	4	5	13	3	0	.169	.191	1	0	SS-43, 2B-2
1949 NY N	7	1	0	0	0	0	0.0	0	0	1	0	0	.000	.000	1	0	SS-5
8 yrs.	472	1527	372	39	6	2	0.1	199	99	166	87	19	.244	.281	5	2	SS-396, 3B-32, 2B-28

Nick Cullop

BR TR 6' 200 lbs.

CULLOP, HENRY NICHOLAS (Tomato Face)
B. Oct. 16, 1900, St. Louis, Mo.　D. Dec. 8, 1978, Westerville, Ohio

	G	AB	H	2B	3B	HR	HR %	R	RBI	BB	SO	SB	BA	SA	PH AB	PH H	G by POS
1926 NY A	2	2	1	0	0	0	0.0	0	0	0	1	0	.500	.500	2	1	
1927 2 teams		WAS	A	(15G –	.217)		CLE	A	(32G –	.235)							
" total	47	91	21	4	3	1	1.1	11	9	10	25	0	.231	.374	19	5	OF-25, 1B-1, P-1
1929 BKN N	13	41	8	2	1	1	2.4	7	5	8	7	0	.195	.415	1	0	OF-11, 1B-1
1930 CIN N	7	22	4	0	0	1	4.5	2	5	1	9	0	.182	.318	2	0	OF-5
1931	104	334	88	23	7	8	2.4	29	48	21	86	1	.263	.446	19	3	OF-83
5 yrs.	173	490	122	29	12	11	2.2	49	67	40	128	1	.249	.424	43	9	OF-124, 1B-2, P-1

Wil Culmer

BR TR 6'4" 210 lbs.

CULMER, WILFRED HILLARD
B. Nov. 11, 1958, Nassau, Bahamas

	G	AB	H	2B	3B	HR	HR %	R	RBI	BB	SO	SB	BA	SA	PH AB	PH H	G by POS
1983 CLE A	7	19	2	0	0	0	0.0	0	1	0	4	0	.105	.105	0	0	OF-4, DH-2

Benny Culp

BR TR 5'9" 175 lbs.

CULP, BENJAMIN BALDY
B. Jan. 19, 1914, Philadelphia, Pa.

	G	AB	H	2B	3B	HR	HR %	R	RBI	BB	SO	SB	BA	SA	PH AB	PH H	G by POS
1942 PHI N	1	0	0	0	0	0		0	0	0	0	0	–	–	0	0	C-1
1943	10	24	5	1	0	0	0.0	4	2	3	3	0	.208	.250	0	0	C-10
1944	4	2	0	0	0	0	0.0	0	0	0	0	0	.000	.000	1	0	C-1
3 yrs.	15	26	5	1	0	0	0.0	4	2	3	3	0	.192	.231	1	0	C-12

Jack Cummings

BR TR 6' 195 lbs.

CUMMINGS, JOHN WILLIAM
B. Apr. 1, 1904, Pittsburgh, Pa.　D. Oct. 5, 1962, Pittsburgh, Pa.

	G	AB	H	2B	3B	HR	HR %	R	RBI	BB	SO	SB	BA	SA	PH AB	PH H	G by POS
1926 NY N	7	16	5	3	0	0	0.0	3	4	4	2	0	.313	.500	1	0	C-6
1927	43	80	29	6	1	2	2.5	8	14	5	10	0	.363	.538	8	3	C-34
1928	33	27	9	2	0	2	7.4	4	9	3	4	0	.333	.630	25	8	C-4
1929 2 teams		NY	N	(3G –	.333)		BOS	N	(3G –	.167)							
" total	6	9	2	0	0	0	0.0	0	1	0	2	0	.222	.222	2	1	C-4
4 yrs.	89	132	45	11	1	4	3.0	15	28	12	18	0	.341	.530	36	12	C-48

Bill Cunningham

BR TR 5'8" 155 lbs.

CUNNINGHAM, WILLIAM ALOYSIUS
B. July 30, 1895, San Francisco, Calif.　D. Sept. 26, 1953, Colusa, Calif.

	G	AB	H	2B	3B	HR	HR %	R	RBI	BB	SO	SB	BA	SA	PH AB	PH H	G by POS
1921 NY N	40	76	21	2	1	1	1.3	10	12	3	3	0	.276	.368	18	5	OF-20
1922	85	229	75	15	2	2	0.9	37	33	7	4	4	.328	.437	13	3	OF-70, 3B-1

	G	AB	H	2B	3B	HR	HR %	R	RBI	BB	SO	SB	BA	SA	Pinch Hit AB	Pinch Hit H	G by POS

Bill Cunningham continued

	G	AB	H	2B	3B	HR	HR %	R	RBI	BB	SO	SB	BA	SA	AB	H	G by POS
1923	79	203	55	7	1	5	2.5	22	27	10	9	5	.271	.389	6	0	OF-68, 2B-4
1924 BOS N	114	437	119	15	8	1	0.2	44	40	32	27	8	.272	.350	5	0	OF-109
4 yrs.	318	945	270	39	12	9	1.0	113	112	52	48	17	.286	.381	42	8	OF-267, 2B-4, 3B-1
WORLD SERIES																	
1922 NY N	4	10	2	0	0	0	0.0	0	2	2	1	0	.200	.200	0	0	OF-4
1923	4	7	1	0	0	0	0.0	0	1	0	1	0	.143	.143	1	0	OF-3
2 yrs.	8	17	3	0	0	0	0.0	0	3	2	2	0	.176	.176	1	0	OF-7

Bill Cunningham

CUNNINGHAM, WILLIAM JOHN
B. June 9, 1888, Schenectady, N. Y. D. Feb. 21, 1946, Schenectady, N. Y. BR TR

	G	AB	H	2B	3B	HR	HR %	R	RBI	BB	SO	SB	BA	SA	AB	H	G by POS
1910 WAS A	22	74	22	5	1	0	0.0	3	14	12		4	.297	.392	0	0	2B-22
1911	94	331	63	10	5	3	0.9	34	37	19		10	.190	.278	1	0	2B-93
1912	7	27	5	1	0	1	3.7	5	8	3		2	.185	.333	0	0	2B-7
3 yrs.	123	432	90	16	6	4	0.9	42	59	34		16	.208	.301	1	0	2B-122

George Cunningham

CUNNINGHAM, GEORGE HAROLD
B. July 13, 1894, Sturgeon Lake, Minn. D. Mar. 10, 1972, Chattanooga, Tenn. BR TR 5'11" 185 lbs.

	G	AB	H	2B	3B	HR	HR %	R	RBI	BB	SO	SB	BA	SA	AB	H	G by POS
1916 DET A	35	41	11	2	2	0	0.0	7	3	8	12	0	.268	.415	0	0	P-35
1917	44	34	6	0	0	1	2.9	5	3	3	13	0	.176	.265	0	0	P-44
1918	56	112	25	4	1	0	0.0	11	2	16	34	2	.223	.277	8	3	P-27, OF-20
1919	26	23	5	0	0	0	0.0	4	5	9	8	0	.217	.217	6	1	P-17
1921	1	0	0	0	0	0	–	0	0	0	0	0	–	–	0	0	OF-1
5 yrs.	162	210	47	6	3	1	0.5	27	13	36	67	2	.224	.295	14	4	P-123, OF-21

Joe Cunningham

CUNNINGHAM, JOSEPH ROBERT
B. Aug. 27, 1931, Paterson, N. J. BL TL 6' 180 lbs.

	G	AB	H	2B	3B	HR	HR %	R	RBI	BB	SO	SB	BA	SA	AB	H	G by POS
1954 STL N	85	310	88	11	3	11	3.5	40	50	43	40	1	.284	.445	0	0	1B-85
1956	4	3	0	0	0	0	0.0	0	1	0	1	0	.000	.000	2	0	1B-1
1957	122	261	83	15	0	9	3.4	50	52	56	29	3	.318	.479	29	11	1B-57, OF-46
1958	131	337	105	20	3	12	3.6	61	57	82	23	4	.312	.496	19	5	1B-67, OF-66
1959	144	458	158	28	6	7	1.5	65	60	88	47	2	.345	.478	8	2	OF-121, 1B-35
1960	139	492	138	28	3	6	1.2	68	39	59	59	1	.280	.386	9	2	OF-116, 1B-15
1961	113	322	92	11	2	7	2.2	60	40	53	32	1	.286	.398	20	5	OF-86, 1B-10
1962 CHI A	149	526	155	32	7	8	1.5	91	70	101	59	3	.295	.428	3	1	1B-143, OF-5
1963	67	210	60	12	1	1	0.5	32	31	33	23	1	.286	.367	6	4	1B-58
1964 2 teams		CHI A	(40G –	.250)		WAS A	(49G –	.214)									
" total	89	234	54	11	0	0	0.0	28	17	37	27	0	.231	.278	14	1	1B-74
1965 WAS A	95	201	46	9	1	3	1.5	29	20	46	27	0	.229	.328	27	5	1B-59
1966	3	8	1	0	0	0	0.0	0	0	1	0	0	.125	.125	0	0	1B-3
12 yrs.	1141	3362	980	177	26	64	1.9	525	436	599	368	16	.291	.417	137	36	1B-607, OF-440

Ray Cunningham

CUNNINGHAM, RAYMOND LEE
B. Jan. 17, 1908, Mesquite, Tex. BR TR 5'7½" 150 lbs.

	G	AB	H	2B	3B	HR	HR %	R	RBI	BB	SO	SB	BA	SA	AB	H	G by POS
1931 STL N	3	4	0	0	0	0	0.0	0	1	0	0	0	.000	.000	0	0	3B-3
1932	11	22	4	1	0	0	0.0	4	0	3	4	0	.182	.227	1	0	3B-8, 2B-2
2 yrs.	14	26	4	1	0	0	0.0	4	1	3	4	0	.154	.192	1	0	3B-11, 2B-2

Doc Curley

CURLEY, WALTER JAMES
B. Mar. 12, 1874, Upton, Mass. D. Sept. 23, 1920, Worcester, Mass. BR TR

	G	AB	H	2B	3B	HR	HR %	R	RBI	BB	SO	SB	BA	SA	AB	H	G by POS
1899 CHI N	10	37	4	0	1	0	0.0	7	2	3		0	.108	.162	0	0	2B-10

Pete Curren

CURREN, PETER
B. Baltimore, Md. Deceased.

	G	AB	H	2B	3B	HR	HR %	R	RBI	BB	SO	SB	BA	SA	AB	H	G by POS
1876 PHI N	3	12	4	1	0	0	0.0	5	2	0	0		.333	.417	0	0	C-2, OF-1

Perry Currin

CURRIN, PERRY GILMORE
B. Sept. 27, 1928, Washington, D. C. BL TR 6' 175 lbs.

	G	AB	H	2B	3B	HR	HR %	R	RBI	BB	SO	SB	BA	SA	AB	H	G by POS
1947 STL A	3	2	0	0	0	0	0.0	0	0	1	0	0	.000	.000	1	0	SS-1

Jim Curry

CURRY, JAMES L.
B. Mar. 10, 1893, Camden, N. J. D. Aug. 1, 1938, Lakefield, N. J. BR TR 5'11" 160 lbs.

	G	AB	H	2B	3B	HR	HR %	R	RBI	BB	SO	SB	BA	SA	AB	H	G by POS
1909 PHI A	1	4	1	0	0	0	0.0	1	0	1		0	.250	.250	0	0	2B-1
1911 NY A	4	11	2	0	0	0	0.0	3	0	1		0	.182	.182	0	0	2B-4
1918 DET A	5	20	5	1	0	0	0.0	1	0	0	0	0	.250	.300	0	0	2B-5
3 yrs.	10	35	8	1	0	0	0.0	5	0	1	0	0	.229	.257	0	0	2B-10

Tony Curry

CURRY, GEORGE ANTHONY
B. Dec. 22, 1938, Nassau, Bahamas BL TL 5'11" 185 lbs.

	G	AB	H	2B	3B	HR	HR %	R	RBI	BB	SO	SB	BA	SA	AB	H	G by POS
1960 PHI N	95	245	64	14	2	6	2.4	26	34	16	53	0	.261	.408	31	7	OF-64
1961	15	36	7	2	0	0	0.0	3	3	1	8	0	.194	.250	7	3	OF-8
1966 CLE A	19	16	2	0	0	0	0.0	4	3	3	8	0	.125	.125	16	2	
3 yrs.	129	297	73	16	2	6	2.0	40	40	20	69	0	.246	.374	54	12	OF-72

Fred Curtis

CURTIS, FREDERICK MARION
B. Oct. 30, 1880, Beaver Lake, Mich. D. Apr. 5, 1939, Minneapolis, Minn. BR TR 6'1"

	G	AB	H	2B	3B	HR	HR %	R	RBI	BB	SO	SB	BA	SA	AB	H	G by POS
1905 NY A	2	9	2	1	0	0	0.0	0	2	1		1	.222	.333	0	0	1B-2

Gene Curtis

CURTIS, EUGENE HOLMES (Eude)
B. May 5, 1883, Bethany, W. Va. D. Jan. 1, 1919, Steubenville, Ohio BR TR 6'3" 220 lbs.

	G	AB	H	2B	3B	HR	HR %	R	RBI	BB	SO	SB	BA	SA	AB	H	G by POS
1903 PIT N	5	19	8	1	0	0	0.0	2	3	1		0	.421	.474	0	0	OF-5

	G	AB	H	2B	3B	HR	HR %	R	RBI	BB	SO	SB	BA	SA	Pinch Hit AB	Pinch Hit H	G by POS

Harry Curtis

CURTIS, HARRY ALBERT   TR
B. Feb. 19, 1883, Portland, Me.   D. Aug. 1, 1951, Evanston, Ill.

Year/Team	G	AB	H	2B	3B	HR	HR%	R	RBI	BB	SO	SB	BA	SA	PH AB	PH H	G by POS
1907 NY N	6	9	2	0	0	0	0.0	2	1	2		2	.222	.222	0	0	C-6

Jim Curtiss

CURTISS, JAMES D.   BL   5'8½"   157 lbs.
B. Dec. 27, 1861, Coldwater, Mich.   D. Feb. 14, 1945, North Adams, Mass.

Year/Team	G	AB	H	2B	3B	HR	HR%	R	RBI	BB	SO	SB	BA	SA	PH AB	PH H	G by POS
1891 2 teams	CIN	N	(27G –	.269)	WAS	AA	(29G –	.252)									
" total	56	211	55	6	5	1	0.5	28	25	22	35	5	.261	.351	0	0	OF-56

Guy Curtright

CURTRIGHT, GUY PAXTON   BR TR 5'11"   200 lbs.
B. Oct. 18, 1912, Holliday, Mo.

Year/Team	G	AB	H	2B	3B	HR	HR%	R	RBI	BB	SO	SB	BA	SA	PH AB	PH H	G by POS
1943 CHI A	138	488	142	20	7	3	0.6	67	48	69	60	13	.291	.379	9	2	OF-128
1944	72	198	50	8	2	2	1.0	22	23	23	21	4	.253	.343	22	6	OF-51
1945	98	324	91	15	7	4	1.2	51	32	39	29	3	.281	.407	13	5	OF-84
1946	23	55	11	2	0	0	0.0	7	5	11	14	0	.200	.236	4	2	OF-15
4 yrs.	331	1065	294	45	16	9	0.8	147	108	142	124	20	.276	.374	48	15	OF-278

Jack Cusick

CUSICK, JOHN PETER   BR TR 6'   170 lbs.
B. June 12, 1928, Weehawken, N. J.

Year/Team	G	AB	H	2B	3B	HR	HR%	R	RBI	BB	SO	SB	BA	SA	PH AB	PH H	G by POS
1951 CHI N	65	164	29	3	2	2	1.2	16	16	17	29	2	.177	.256	3	1	SS-56
1952 BOS N	49	78	13	1	0	0	0.0	5	6	6	9	0	.167	.179	9	1	SS-28, 3B-3
2 yrs.	114	242	42	4	2	2	0.8	21	22	23	38	2	.174	.231	12	2	SS-84, 3B-3

Tony Cusick

CUSICK, ANDREW DANIEL   BR TR 5'9½"   190 lbs.
Born Andrew Cusick.
B. 1867, Limerick, Ireland   D. Aug. 6, 1929, Chicago, Ill.

Year/Team	G	AB	H	2B	3B	HR	HR%	R	RBI	BB	SO	SB	BA	SA	PH AB	PH H	G by POS
1884 2 teams	WIL	U	(11G –	.147)	PHI	N	(9G –	.138)									
" total	20	63	9	0	0	0	0.0	2		1	3		.143	.143	0	0	C-15, OF-3, SS-3, 3B-1, 2B-1
1885 PHI N	39	141	25	1	0	0	0.0	12		1	24		.177	.184	0	0	C-38, OF-1
1886	29	104	23	5	1	0	0.0	10	4	3	14		.221	.288	0	0	C-25, OF-3, 1B-1
1887	7	24	7	1	0	0	0.0	3	5	3	1	0	.292	.333	0	0	C-4, 1B-3, 2B-1
4 yrs.	95	332	64	7	1	0	0.0	27	8	8	42	0	.193	.220	0	0	C-82, OF-7, 1B-4, SS-3, 2B-2, 3B-1

Ned Cuthbert

CUTHBERT, EDGAR EDWARD   BR TR 5'6"   140 lbs.
B. June 20, 1845, Philadelphia, Pa.   D. Feb. 6, 1905, St. Louis, Mo.
Manager 1882.

Year/Team	G	AB	H	2B	3B	HR	HR%	R	RBI	BB	SO	SB	BA	SA	PH AB	PH H	G by POS
1876 STL N	63	283	70	10	1	0	0.0	46	25	7	4		.247	.290	0	0	OF-63
1877 CIN N	12	56	10	5	0	0	0.0	6	2	1	2		.179	.268	0	0	OF-12
1882 STL AA	60	233	52	16	5	0	0.0	28		17			.223	.335	0	0	OF-60
1883	21	71	12	1	0	0	0.0	3		4			.169	.183	0	0	OF-20, 1B-1
1884 BAL U	44	168	34	5	0	0	0.0	29		10			.202	.232	0	0	OF-44
5 yrs.	200	811	178	37	6	0	0.0	112	27	39	6		.219	.280	0	0	OF-199, 1B-1

George Cutshaw

CUTSHAW, GEORGE WILLIAM (Clancy)   BR TR 5'9"   160 lbs.
B. July 29, 1887, Wilmington, Ill.   D. Aug. 22, 1973, San Diego, Calif.

Year/Team	G	AB	H	2B	3B	HR	HR%	R	RBI	BB	SO	SB	BA	SA	PH AB	PH H	G by POS
1912 BKN N	102	357	100	14	4	0	0.0	41	28	31	16	16	.280	.342	5	1	2B-91, 3B-5, SS-1
1913	147	592	158	23	13	7	1.2	72	80	39	22	39	.267	.385	0	0	2B-147
1914	153	583	150	22	12	0	0.3	69	78	30	32	34	.257	.346	0	0	2B-153
1915	154	566	139	18	9	0	0.0	68	62	34	35	28	.246	.309	0	0	2B-154
1916	154	581	151	21	4	2	0.3	58	63	25	32	27	.260	.320	0	0	2B-154
1917	135	487	126	17	7	4	0.8	42	49	21	26	22	.259	.347	1	0	2B-134
1918 PIT N	126	463	132	16	10	5	1.1	56	68	27	18	25	.285	.395	0	0	2B-126
1919	139	512	124	15	8	3	0.6	49	51	30	22	36	.242	.320	0	0	2B-139
1920	131	488	123	16	8	0	0.0	56	47	23	10	17	.252	.318	2	0	2B-129
1921	98	350	119	18	4	0	0.0	46	53	11	11	14	.340	.414	14	2	2B-84
1922 DET A	132	499	133	14	8	2	0.4	57	61	20	13	11	.267	.339	0	0	2B-132
1923	45	143	32	1	2	0	0.0	15	13	9	5	2	.224	.259	0	0	2B-43, 3B-2
12 yrs.	1516	5621	1487	195	89	25	0.4	629	653	300	242	271	.265	.344	22	3	2B-1486, 3B-7, SS-1

WORLD SERIES

Year/Team	G	AB	H	2B	3B	HR	HR%	R	RBI	BB	SO	SB	BA	SA	PH AB	PH H	G by POS
1916 BKN N	5	19	2	1	0	0	0.0	2	2	1	1	0	.105	.158	0	0	2B-5

Kiki Cuyler

CUYLER, HAZEN SHIRLEY   BR TR 5'10½" 180 lbs.
B. Aug. 30, 1899, Harrisville, Mich.   D. Feb. 11, 1950, Ann Arbor, Mich.
Hall of Fame 1968.

Year/Team	G	AB	H	2B	3B	HR	HR%	R	RBI	BB	SO	SB	BA	SA	PH AB	PH H	G by POS
1921 PIT N	1	3	0	0	0	0	0.0	0	0	0	1	0	.000	.000	0	0	OF-1
1922	1	0	0	0	0	0	–	0	0	0	0	0	–	–	0	0	
1923	11	40	10	1	1	0	0.0	4	2	5	3	2	.250	.325	0	0	OF-11
1924	117	466	165	27	16	9	1.9	94	85	30	62	32	.354	.539	3	1	OF-114
1925	153	617	220	43	26	17	2.8	144	102	58	56	41	.357	.593	0	0	OF-153
1926	157	614	197	31	15	8	1.3	113	92	50	66	35	.321	.459	0	0	OF-157
1927	85	285	88	13	7	3	1.1	60	31	37	36	20	.309	.435	11	2	OF-73
1928 CHI N	133	499	142	25	9	17	3.4	92	79	51	61	37	.285	.473	5	0	OF-127
1929	139	509	183	29	7	15	2.9	111	102	66	56	43	.360	.532	9	4	OF-129
1930	156	642	228	50	17	13	2.0	155	134	72	49	37	.355	.547	0	0	OF-156
1931	154	613	202	37	12	9	1.5	110	88	72	54	13	.330	.473	1	0	OF-153
1932	110	446	130	19	9	10	2.2	58	77	29	43	9	.291	.442	1	0	OF-109
1933	70	262	83	13	3	5	1.9	37	35	21	29	4	.317	.447	1	0	OF-69
1934	142	559	189	42	8	6	1.1	80	69	31	62	15	.338	.474	0	0	OF-142
1935 2 teams	CHI	N	(45G –	.268)	CIN	N	(62G –	.251)									
" total	107	380	98	13	4	6	1.6	58	40	37	34	8	.258	.361	6	2	OF-99
1936 CIN N	144	567	185	29	11	7	1.2	96	74	47	67	16	.326	.453	4	2	OF-140
1937	117	406	110	12	4	0	0.0	48	32	36	50	10	.271	.320	10	2	OF-106
1938 BKN N	82	253	69	10	8	2	0.8	45	23	34	23	6	.273	.399	11	1	OF-68
18 yrs.	1879	7161	2299	394	157	127	1.8	1305	1065	676	752	328	.321	.473	62	14	OF-1807

WORLD SERIES

Year/Team	G	AB	H	2B	3B	HR	HR%	R	RBI	BB	SO	SB	BA	SA	PH AB	PH H	G by POS
1925 PIT N	7	26	7	3	0	1	3.8	3	6	1	4	0	.269	.500	0	0	OF-7

	G	AB	H	2B	3B	HR	HR %	R	RBI	BB	SO	SB	BA	SA	Pinch Hit AB	Pinch Hit H	G by POS

Kiki Cuyler continued

	G	AB	H	2B	3B	HR	HR %	R	RBI	BB	SO	SB	BA	SA	PH AB	PH H	G by POS
1929 CHI N	5	20	6	1	0	0	0.0	4	4	1	7	0	.300	.350	0	0	OF-5
1932	4	18	5	1	1	1	5.6	2	2	0	3	1	.278	.611	0	0	OF-4
3 yrs.	16	64	18	5	1	2	3.1	9	12	2	14	1	.281	.484	0	0	OF-16

Al Cypert

CYPERT, ALFRED BOYD
B. Aug. 7, 1889, Little Rock, Ark. D. Jan. 9, 1973, Washington, D. C.
BR TR 5'10½" 150 lbs.

	G	AB	H	2B	3B	HR	HR %	R	RBI	BB	SO	SB	BA	SA	PH AB	PH H	G by POS
1914 CLE A	1	1	0	0	0	0	0.0	0	0	0	1	0	.000	.000	0	0	3B-1

Paul Dade

DADE, LONNIE PAUL
B. Dec. 7, 1951, Seattle, Wash.
BR TR 6'1" 185 lbs.

	G	AB	H	2B	3B	HR	HR %	R	RBI	BB	SO	SB	BA	SA	PH AB	PH H	G by POS
1975 CAL A	11	30	6	4	0	0	0.0	5	1	6	7	0	.200	.333	1	1	DH-7, OF-3, 3B-1
1976	13	9	1	0	0	0	0.0	2	1	3	3	0	.111	.111	5	1	OF-4, 2B-2, DH-1, 3B-1
1977 CLE A	134	461	134	15	3	3	0.7	65	45	32	58	16	.291	.356	10	2	OF-99, 3B-26, DH-7, 2B-1
1978	93	307	78	12	1	3	1.0	37	20	34	45	12	.254	.329	8	1	OF-81, DH-9
1979 2 teams			CLE A (44G – .282)			SD N (76G – .276)											
" total	120	453	126	23	3	4	0.9	60	37	26	70	25	.278	.369	6	2	3B-72, OF-41, DH-4
1980 SD N	68	53	10	0	0	0	0.0	17	3	12	10	4	.189	.189	11	1	3B-21, OF-8, 2B-1
6 yrs.	439	1313	355	54	7	10	0.8	186	107	113	193	57	.270	.345	41	8	OF-236, 3B-121, DH-28, 2B-4

Angie Dagres

DAGRES, ANGELO GEORGE (Junior)
B. Aug. 22, 1934, Newburyport, Mass.
BL TL 5'11" 175 lbs.

	G	AB	H	2B	3B	HR	HR %	R	RBI	BB	SO	SB	BA	SA	PH AB	PH H	G by POS
1955 BAL A	8	15	4	0	0	0	0.0	5	3	1	2	0	.267	.267	3	1	OF-5

Bill Dahlen

DAHLEN, WILLIAM FREDERICK (Bad Bill)
B. Jan. 5, 1870, Nelliston, N. Y. D. Dec. 5, 1950, Brooklyn, N. Y.
Manager 1910-13.
BR TR 5'9" 180 lbs.

	G	AB	H	2B	3B	HR	HR %	R	RBI	BB	SO	SB	BA	SA	PH AB	PH H	G by POS
1891 CHI N	135	551	145	20	13	9	1.6	116	76	67	60	29	.263	.396	0	0	3B-84, OF-37, SS-15
1892	143	587	173	23	19	5	0.9	116	58	45	56	60	.295	.424	0	0	SS-72, 3B-68, OF-2, 2B-1
1893	116	485	146	28	15	5	1.0	113	64	58	30	31	.301	.452	0	0	SS-88, OF-17, 2B-10, 3B-3
1894	121	508	184	32	14	15	3.0	150	107	76	33	42	.362	.569	0	0	SS-66, 3B-55
1895	129	509	139	19	10	7	1.4	107	62	61	51	38	.273	.391	0	0	SS-129, OF-1
1896	125	476	172	30	19	9	1.9	153	74	64	36	51	.361	.561	0	0	SS-125
1897	75	277	82	18	8	6	2.2	67	40	43		15	.296	.484	0	0	SS-75
1898	142	524	152	35	8	1	0.2	96	79	58		27	.290	.393	0	0	SS-142
1899 BKN N	121	428	121	22	7	4	0.9	87	76	67		29	.283	.395	0	0	SS-110, 3B-11
1900	133	483	125	16	11	1	0.2	87	69	73		31	.259	.344	0	0	SS-133
1901	131	513	134	17	10	4	0.8	69	82	30		23	.261	.357	0	0	SS-129, 2B-2
1902	138	527	139	26	7	2	0.4	67	74	43		20	.264	.351	0	0	SS-138
1903	138	474	124	17	9	1	0.2	71	64	82		34	.262	.342	0	0	SS-138
1904 NY N	145	523	140	26	2	2	0.4	70	80	44		47	.268	.337	0	0	SS-145
1905	148	520	126	20	4	7	1.3	67	81	62		37	.242	.337	0	0	SS-147, OF-1
1906	143	471	113	18	3	1	0.2	63	49	76		16	.240	.297	0	0	SS-143
1907	143	464	96	20	1	0	0.0	40	34	51		11	.207	.254	0	0	SS-143
1908 BOS N	144	524	125	23	2	3	0.6	50	48	35		10	.239	.307	0	0	SS-144
1909	69	197	46	6	1	2	1.0	22	16	29		4	.234	.305	8	2	SS-49, 2B-6, 3B-2
1910 BKN N	3	2	0	0	0	0	0.0	0	0	0	0	0	.000	.000	2	0	
1911	1	3	0	0	0	0	0.0	0	0	0		3	0	.000	.000	0	0	SS-1
21 yrs.	2443	9046	2482	416	163	84	0.9	1611	1233	1064	269	555	.274	.384	10	2	SS-2132, 3B-223, OF-58, 2B-19

WORLD SERIES

	G	AB	H	2B	3B	HR	HR %	R	RBI	BB	SO	SB	BA	SA	PH AB	PH H	G by POS
1905 NY N	5	15	0	0	0	0	0.0	1	1	3	2	2	.000	.000	0	0	SS-5

Babe Dahlgren

DAHLGREN, ELLSWORTH TENNEY
B. June 15, 1912, San Francisco, Calif.
BR TR 6' 190 lbs.

	G	AB	H	2B	3B	HR	HR %	R	RBI	BB	SO	SB	BA	SA	PH AB	PH H	G by POS
1935 BOS A	149	525	138	27	7	9	1.7	77	63	56	67	6	.263	.392	0	0	1B-149
1936	16	57	16	3	1	1	1.8	6	7	7	1	2	.281	.421	0	0	1B-16
1937 NY A	1	1	0	0	0	0	0.0	0	0	0	0	0	.000	.000	1	0	
1938	29	43	8	1	0	0	0.0	8	1	1	7	0	.186	.209	6	0	3B-8, 1B-6
1939	144	531	125	18	6	15	2.8	71	89	57	54	2	.235	.377	0	0	1B-144
1940	155	568	150	24	4	12	2.1	51	73	46	54	1	.264	.384	0	0	1B-155
1941 2 teams			BOS N (44G – .235)			CHI N (99G – .281)											
" total	143	525	140	28	2	23	4.4	70	89	59	52	2	.267	.459	1	0	1B-137, 3B-5
1942 3 teams			CHI N (17G – .214)			STL A (2G – .000)			BKN N (17G – .053)								
" total	36	77	13	1	0	0	0.0	6	6	8	7	0	.169	.182	8	0	1B-24
1943 PHI N	136	508	146	19	2	5	1.0	55	56	50	39	2	.287	.362	3	2	1B-73, 3B-35, SS-25, C-1
1944 PIT N	158	599	173	28	7	12	2.0	67	101	47	56	2	.289	.419	0	0	1B-158
1945	144	531	133	24	8	5	0.9	57	75	51	51	1	.250	.354	2	0	1B-142
1946 STL A	28	80	14	1	0	0	0.0	2	9	8	13	0	.175	.188	4	1	1B-24
12 yrs.	1139	4045	1056	174	37	82	2.0	470	569	390	401	18	.261	.383	25	3	1B-1028, 3B-48, SS-25, C-1

WORLD SERIES

	G	AB	H	2B	3B	HR	HR %	R	RBI	BB	SO	SB	BA	SA	PH AB	PH H	G by POS
1939 NY A	4	14	3	2	0	1	7.1	2	2	0	4	0	.214	.571	0	0	1B-4

Con Daily

DAILY, CORNELIUS F.
Brother of Ed Daily.
B. Sept. 11, 1864, Blackstone, Mass. D. June 14, 1928, Brooklyn, N. Y.
BL 6' 192 lbs.

	G	AB	H	2B	3B	HR	HR %	R	RBI	BB	SO	SB	BA	SA	PH AB	PH H	G by POS
1884 PHI U	2	8	0	0	0	0	0.0	0		0			.000	.000	0	0	C-2
1885 PRO N	60	223	58	6	1	0	0.0	20	19	12	20		.260	.296	0	0	C-48, 1B-7, OF-6
1886 BOS N	50	180	43	4	2	0	0.0	25	21	19	29		.239	.283	0	0	C-49
1887	36	120	19	5	0	0	0.0	12	13	9	8	7	.158	.200	0	0	C-36
1888 IND N	57	202	44	6	1	0	0.0	14	14	10	28	15	.218	.257	0	0	C-42, OF-5, 3B-5, 1B-5, 2B-1
1889	62	219	55	6	2	0	0.0	35	26	28	21	14	.251	.297	0	0	C-51, OF-6, 1B-6, 3B-1

	G	AB	H	2B	3B	HR	HR %	R	RBI	BB	SO	SB	BA	SA	Pinch Hit AB	Pinch Hit H	G by POS

Con Daily continued

	G	AB	H	2B	3B	HR	HR %	R	RBI	BB	SO	SB	BA	SA	AB	H	G by POS
1890 BKN P	46	168	42	6	3	0	0.0	20	35	15	14	6	.250	.321	0	0	C-40, 1B-6, OF-1
1891 BKN N	60	206	66	10	1	0	0.0	25	30	15	13	7	.320	.379	0	0	C-55, OF-3, SS-2, 1B-1
1892	80	278	65	10	1	0	0.0	38	28	38	21	18	.234	.277	0	0	C-68, OF-13
1893	61	215	57	4	2	1	0.5	33	32	20	12	13	.265	.316	1	1	C-51, OF-9
1894	67	234	60	14	7	0	0.0	40	32	31	22	8	.256	.376	0	0	C-60, 1B-7
1895	40	142	30	3	2	1	0.7	17	11	10	18	3	.211	.282	0	0	C-39, OF-1
1896 CHI N	9	27	2	0	0	0	0.0	1	1	1	2	1	.074	.074	0	0	C-9
13 yrs.	630	2222	541	74	22	2	0.1	280	261	208	208	92	.243	.299	1	1	C-550, OF-44, 1B-32, 3B-6, SS-2, 2B-1

Ed Daily

DAILY, EDWARD M.
Brother of Con Daily.
B. Sept. 7, 1862, Providence, R. I.   D. Oct. 21, 1891, Washington, D. C.

BR TR

	G	AB	H	2B	3B	HR	HR %	R	RBI	BB	SO	SB	BA	SA	AB	H	G by POS
1885 PHI N	50	184	38	8	2	1	0.5	22		0	25		.207	.288	0	0	P-50
1886	79	309	70	17	1	4	1.3	40	50	7	34		.227	.327	0	0	OF-56, P-27
1887 2 teams	PHI	N (26G –	.283)		WAS	N	(78G –	.251)									
" total	104	417	108	17	11	3	0.7	57	53	17	36	34	.259	.374	0	0	OF-99, P-7
1888 WAS N	110	453	102	8	4	8	1.8	56	39	7	42	44	.225	.313	0	0	OF-100, P-9, 1B-1
1889 COL AA	136	578	148	22	8	3	0.5	105	70	38	65	60	.256	.337	0	0	OF-136, P-2
1890 3 teams	B-B	AA (91G –	.239)		NY	N	(4G –	.133)		LOU	AA (23G –	.250)					
" total	118	489	116	16	9	1	0.2	93	1	37	4	62	.237	.313	0	0	OF-78, P-41
1891 2 teams	LOU	AA (22G –	.250)		WAS	AA	(21G –	.228)									
" total	43	143	34	4	0	0	0.0	23	14	19	16	12	.238	.266	0	0	OF-28, P-15
7 yrs.	640	2573	616	92	35	20	0.8	396	226	125	222	212	.239	.326	0	0	OF-497, P-151, 1B-1

Vince Daily

DAILY, VINCENT PERRY
B. Dec. 25, 1864, Osceola, Pa.   D. Nov. 14, 1919, Hornell, N. Y.

	G	AB	H	2B	3B	HR	HR %	R	RBI	BB	SO	SB	BA	SA	AB	H	G by POS
1890 CLE N	64	246	71	5	7	0	0.0	41	32	33	23	17	.289	.366	0	0	OF-64, P-2

George Daisey

DAISEY, GEORGE K.
B. Altoona, Pa.   Deceased.

5'11"   190 lbs.

	G	AB	H	2B	3B	HR	HR %	R	RBI	BB	SO	SB	BA	SA	AB	H	G by POS
1884 ALT U	1	4	0	0	0	0	0.0	0		0			.000	.000	0	0	OF-1

John Daley

DALEY, JOHN FRANCIS
B. May 25, 1889, Pittsburgh, Pa.

BR TR 5'7½" 155 lbs.

	G	AB	H	2B	3B	HR	HR %	R	RBI	BB	SO	SB	BA	SA	AB	H	G by POS
1912 STL A	17	52	9	0	0	1	1.9	7	3	9		4	.173	.231	0	0	SS-17

Jud Daley

DALEY, JUDSON LAWRENCE
B. Mar. 14, 1884, S. Coventry, Conn.   D. Jan. 26, 1967, East Gadsden, Ala.

BL TR 5'8" 172 lbs.

	G	AB	H	2B	3B	HR	HR %	R	RBI	BB	SO	SB	BA	SA	AB	H	G by POS
1911 BKN N	19	65	15	2	1	0	0.0	8	7	2	8	2	.231	.292	2	0	OF-16
1912	61	199	51	9	1	2	1.0	22	13	24	17	2	.256	.342	6	3	OF-55
2 yrs.	80	264	66	11	2	2	0.8	30	20	26	25	4	.250	.330	8	3	OF-71

Pete Daley

DALEY, PETER HARVEY
B. Jan. 14, 1930, Grass Valley, Calif.

BR TR 6' 195 lbs.

	G	AB	H	2B	3B	HR	HR %	R	RBI	BB	SO	SB	BA	SA	AB	H	G by POS
1955 BOS A	17	50	11	2	1	0	0.0	4	5	3	6	0	.220	.300	4	0	C-14
1956	59	187	50	11	3	5	2.7	22	29	18	30	1	.267	.439	3	1	C-57
1957	78	191	43	10	0	3	1.6	17	25	16	31	0	.225	.325	1	1	C-77
1958	27	56	18	2	1	2	3.6	10	8	7	11	0	.321	.500	0	0	C-27
1959	65	169	38	7	0	1	0.6	9	11	13	31	1	.225	.284	9	2	C-58
1960 KC A	73	228	60	10	2	5	2.2	19	25	16	41	0	.263	.390	14	5	C-61, OF-1
1961 WAS A	72	203	39	7	1	2	1.0	12	17	14	37	0	.192	.266	0	0	C-72
7 yrs.	391	1084	259	49	8	18	1.7	93	120	87	187	2	.239	.349	31	9	C-366, OF-1

Tom Daley

DALEY, THOMAS FRANCIS (Pete)
B. Nov. 13, 1884, DuBois, Pa.   D. Dec. 2, 1934, Los Angeles, Calif.

BL TR 5'5" 168 lbs.

	G	AB	H	2B	3B	HR	HR %	R	RBI	BB	SO	SB	BA	SA	AB	H	G by POS
1908 CIN N	14	46	5	0	0	0	0.0	5	1	3		1	.109	.109	0	0	OF-13
1913 PHI A	59	141	36	2	0	0	0.0	13	11	13	28	4	.255	.284	19	2	OF-38
1914 2 teams	PHI	A (29G –	.256)		NY	A	(67G –	.251)									
" total	96	277	70	7	0	0	0.0	53	16	50	27	12	.253	.329	12	3	OF-81
1915 NY A	10	8	2	0	0	0	0.0	2	1	2	2	1	.250	.250	4	1	OF-2
4 yrs.	179	472	113	9	8	0	0.0	73	29	68	57	18	.239	.292	35	6	OF-134

Dom Dallessandro

DALLESSANDRO, NICHOLAS DOMINIC (Dim Dom)
B. Oct. 3, 1913, Reading, Pa.

BL TL 5'6" 168 lbs.

	G	AB	H	2B	3B	HR	HR %	R	RBI	BB	SO	SB	BA	SA	AB	H	G by POS
1937 BOS A	68	147	34	7	1	0	0.0	18	11	27	16	2	.231	.293	26	7	OF-35
1940 CHI N	107	287	77	19	6	1	0.3	33	36	34	13	4	.268	.387	29	10	OF-74
1941	140	486	132	36	2	6	1.2	73	85	68	37	3	.272	.391	7	1	OF-131
1942	96	264	69	12	4	4	1.5	30	43	36	18	4	.261	.383	26	9	OF-66
1943	87	176	39	8	3	1	0.6	13	31	40	14	1	.222	.318	32	8	OF-45
1944	117	381	116	19	4	8	2.1	53	74	61	29	1	.304	.438	11	3	OF-106
1946	65	89	20	2	2	1	1.1	4	9	23	12	1	.225	.326	29	6	OF-20
1947	66	115	33	7	1	0	0.9	18	14	21	11	0	.287	.391	32	6	OF-28
8 yrs.	746	1945	520	110	23	22	1.1	242	303	310	150	16	.267	.381	192	52	OF-505

Abner Dalrymple

DALRYMPLE, ABNER FRANK
B. Sept. 9, 1857, Warren, Ill.   D. Jan. 25, 1939, Warren, Ill.

BL TR 5'10½" 175 lbs.

	G	AB	H	2B	3B	HR	HR %	R	RBI	BB	SO	SB	BA	SA	AB	H	G by POS
1878 MIL N	61	271	96	10	4	0	0.0	52	15	6	29		.354	.421	0	0	OF-61
1879 CHI N	71	333	97	25	1	0	0.0	47	23	4	29		.291	.372	0	0	OF-71
1880	86	382	126	25	12	0	0.0	91	36	3	18		.330	.458	0	0	OF-86
1881	82	362	117	22	4	1	0.3	72	37	15	22		.323	.414	0	0	OF-82
1882	84	397	117	25	11	1	0.3	96	36	14	18		.295	.421	0	0	OF-84
1883	80	363	108	24	4	2	0.6	78		11	29		.298	.402	0	0	OF-80
1884	111	521	161	18	9	22	4.2	111		14	39		.309	.505	0	0	OF-111

	G	AB	H	2B	3B	HR	HR %	R	RBI	BB	SO	SB	BA	SA	Pinch Hit AB	Pinch Hit H	G by POS

Abner Dalrymple continued

	G	AB	H	2B	3B	HR	HR %	R	RBI	BB	SO	SB	BA	SA	AB	H	G by POS
1885	113	**492**	135	27	12	**11**	**2.2**	109	58	46	42		.274	.445	0	0	OF-113
1886	82	331	77	7	12	3	0.9	62	26	33	44		.233	.353	0	0	OF-82
1887 PIT N	92	358	76	18	5	2	0.6	45	31	45	43	29	.212	.307	0	0	OF-92
1888	57	227	50	9	2	0	0.0	19	14	6	28	7	.220	.278	0	0	OF-57
1891 C-M AA	32	135	42	7	5	1	0.7	31	22	7	18	6	.311	.459	0	0	OF-32
12 yrs.	951	4172	1202	217	81	43	1.0	813	298	204	359	42	.288	.410	0	0	OF-951

Clay Dalrymple

DALRYMPLE, CLAYTON ERROL
B. Dec. 3, 1936, Chico, Calif.   BL TR 6'   190 lbs.

	G	AB	H	2B	3B	HR	HR %	R	RBI	BB	SO	SB	BA	SA	AB	H	G by POS
1960 PHI N	82	158	43	6	2	4	2.5	11	21	15	21	0	.272	.411	42	12	C-48
1961	129	378	83	11	1	5	1.3	23	42	30	30	0	.220	.294	9	1	C-122
1962	123	370	102	13	3	11	3.0	40	54	70	32	1	.276	.416	9	1	C-119
1963	142	452	114	15	3	10	2.2	40	40	45	55	0	.252	.365	3	1	C-142
1964	127	382	91	16	3	6	1.6	36	46	39	40	0	.238	.343	4	1	C-124
1965	103	301	64	5	4	4	1.3	14	23	34	37	0	.213	.302	5	0	C-102
1966	114	331	81	13	3	4	1.2	30	39	60	57	0	.245	.338	6	0	C-110
1967	101	268	46	7	1	3	1.1	12	21	36	49	1	.172	.239	8	3	C-97
1968	85	241	50	9	1	3	1.2	19	26	22	57	1	.207	.290	6	0	C-80
1969 BAL A	37	80	19	1	1	3	3.8	8	6	13	8	0	.238	.388	8	1	C-30
1970	13	32	7	1	0	1	3.1	4	3	7	4	0	.219	.344	2	0	C-11
1971	23	49	10	1	0	1	2.0	6	6	16	13	0	.204	.286	3	0	C-18
12 yrs.	1079	3042	710	98	23	55	1.8	243	327	387	403	3	.233	.335	105	20	C-1003

WORLD SERIES

	G	AB	H	2B	3B	HR	HR %	R	RBI	BB	SO	SB	BA	SA	AB	H	G by POS
1969 BAL A	2	2	2	0	0	0	0.0	0	0	0	0	0	1.000	1.000	2	2	

Mike Dalrymple

DALRYMPLE, MICHAEL
B. St. Louis, Mo.   TR

	G	AB	H	2B	3B	HR	HR %	R	RBI	BB	SO	SB	BA	SA	AB	H	G by POS
1915 STL A	2	2	0	0	0	0	0.0	0	0	0	0	0	.000	.000	1	0	3B-1

Jack Dalton

DALTON, TALBOT PERCY
B. July 3, 1885, Henderson, Tenn.   BR TR 5'10½" 187 lbs.

	G	AB	H	2B	3B	HR	HR %	R	RBI	BB	SO	SB	BA	SA	AB	H	G by POS
1910 BKN N	77	273	62	9	4	1	0.4	33	21	26	30	5	.227	.300	4	1	OF-72
1914	128	442	141	13	8	1	0.2	65	45	53	39	19	.319	.391	10	4	OF-116
1915 BUF F	132	437	128	17	3	2	0.5	68	46	50		28	.293	.359	12	4	OF-119
1916 DET A	8	11	2	0	0	0	0.0	1	0	0	5	0	.182	.182	2	1	OF-4
4 yrs.	345	1163	333	39	15	4	0.3	167	112	129	74	52	.286	.356	28	10	OF-311

Bert Daly

DALY, ALBERT JOSEPH
B. Apr. 8, 1881, Bayonne, N. J.   D. Sept. 3, 1952, Bayonne, N. J.   TR 5'9" 170 lbs.

	G	AB	H	2B	3B	HR	HR %	R	RBI	BB	SO	SB	BA	SA	AB	H	G by POS
1903 PHI A	10	21	4	0	2	0	0.0	2	4	1		0	.190	.381	2	0	2B-4, 3B-3, SS-1

Joe Daly

DALY, JOSEPH JOHN
Brother of Tom Daly.
B. Sept. 21, 1868, Philadelphia, Pa.   D. Mar. 20, 1943, Philadelphia, Pa.

	G	AB	H	2B	3B	HR	HR %	R	RBI	BB	SO	SB	BA	SA	AB	H	G by POS
1890 PHI AA	21	75	21	4	1	0	0.0	8		3		1	.280	.360	0	0	OF-14, C-9
1891 CLE N	1	3	0	0	0	0	0.0	0	0	0	2	0	.000	.000	0	0	OF-1
1892 BOS N	1	0	0	0	0	0	–	0	0	0	0	0	–	–	0	0	C-1
3 yrs.	23	78	21	4	1	0	0.0	8		3	2	1	.269	.346	0	0	OF-15, C-10

Sun Daly

DALY, JAMES J.
B. Jan. 6, 1865, Rutland, Vt.   D. Apr. 30, 1938, Albany, N. Y.

	G	AB	H	2B	3B	HR	HR %	R	RBI	BB	SO	SB	BA	SA	AB	H	G by POS
1892 BAL N	13	48	12	0	2	0	0.0	5	7	1	4	0	.250	.333	0	0	OF-13

Tom Daly

DALY, THOMAS DANIEL
B. Dec. 12, 1891, St. John, N. B., Canada   D. Nov. 7, 1946, Bedford, Mass.   BR TR 5'11½" 171 lbs.

	G	AB	H	2B	3B	HR	HR %	R	RBI	BB	SO	SB	BA	SA	AB	H	G by POS
1913 CHI A	1	3	0	0	0	0	0.0	0	0	0	0	0	.000	.000	0	0	C-1
1914	61	133	31	2	0	0	0.0	13	8	7	13	3	.233	.248	24	6	OF-23, 3B-5, C-4, 1B-2
1915	29	47	9	1	0	0	0.0	5	3	5	9	0	.191	.213	9	1	C-19, 1B-1
1916 CLE A	31	73	16	1	1	0	0.0	3	8	1	2	0	.219	.260	5	1	C-25, OF-1
1918 CHI N	1	1	0	0	0	0	0.0	0	0	0	0	0	.000	.000	0	0	C-1
1919	25	50	11	0	1	0	0.0	4	1	2	5	0	.220	.260	6	0	C-18
1920	44	90	28	6	0	0	0.0	12	13	2	6	1	.311	.378	14	4	C-29
1921	51	143	34	7	1	0	0.0	12	22	8	8	1	.238	.301	4	1	C-47
8 yrs.	243	540	129	17	3	0	0.0	49	55	25	43	5	.239	.281	62	13	C-144, OF-24, 3B-5, 1B-3

Tom Daly

DALY, THOMAS PETER (Tido)
Brother of Joe Daly.
B. Feb. 7, 1866, Philadelphia, Pa.   D. Oct. 29, 1939, Brooklyn, N. Y.   BB TR 5'7" 170 lbs.

	G	AB	H	2B	3B	HR	HR %	R	RBI	BB	SO	SB	BA	SA	AB	H	G by POS
1887 CHI N	74	256	53	10	4	2	0.8	45	17	22	25	29	.207	.301	0	0	C-64, OF-8, SS-2, 2B-2, 1B-2
1888	65	219	42	2	6	0	0.0	34	29	10	26	10	.192	.256	0	0	C-62, OF-4
1889 WAS N	71	250	75	13	5	1	0.4	39	40	38	28	18	.300	.404	0	0	C-57, 1B-8, 2B-4, OF-3, SS-1
1890 BKN N	82	292	71	9	4	5	1.7	55	43	32	43	20	.243	.353	0	0	C-69, 1B-12, OF-1
1891	58	200	50	11	5	2	1.0	29	27	21	34	7	.250	.385	0	0	C-26, 1B-15, SS-11, OF-7
1892	124	446	114	15	6	4	0.9	76	51	64	61	34	.256	.343	0	0	3B-57, OF-30, C-27, 2B-10
1893	126	470	136	21	14	8	1.7	94	70	76	**65**	32	.289	.445	0	0	2B-82, 3B-45
1894	123	492	168	22	10	8	1.6	135	82	77	42	51	.341	.476	0	0	2B-123
1895	120	455	128	17	8	2	0.4	89	68	52	52	28	.281	.367	0	0	2B-120
1896	67	224	63	13	6	3	1.3	43	29	33	25	19	.281	.433	0	0	2B-66, C-1
1898	23	73	24	3	1	0	0.0	11	11	14		6	.329	.397	0	0	2B-23
1899	141	498	156	24	9	5	1.0	95	88	69		43	.313	.428	0	0	2B-141
1900	97	343	107	17	3	4	1.2	72	55	46		27	.312	.414	0	0	2B-93, 1B-3, OF-2

	G	AB	H	2B	3B	HR	HR %	R	RBI	BB	SO	SB	BA	SA	Pinch Hit AB	H	G by POS

Tom Daly continued

	G	AB	H	2B	3B	HR	HR %	R	RBI	BB	SO	SB	BA	SA	AB	H	G by POS
1901	133	520	164	38	10	3	0.6	88	90	42		31	.315	.444	0	0	2B-133
1902 CHI A	137	489	110	22	3	1	0.2	57	54	55		19	.225	.288	0	0	2B-137
1903 2 teams		CHI	A	(43G –	.207)		CIN	N	(80G –	.293)							
" total	123	457	121	25	9	1	0.2	62	57	36		11	.265	.365	1	0	2B-122
16 yrs.	1564	5684	1582	262	103	49	0.9	1024	811	687	401	385	.278	.387	1	0	2B-1056, C-306, 3B-102, OF-55, 1B-40, SS-14

Bill Dam

DAM, ELBRIDGE RUST
B. Apr. 4, 1885, Cambridge, Mass.   D. June 22, 1930, Quincy, Mass.

	G	AB	H	2B	3B	HR	HR %	R	RBI	BB	SO	SB	BA	SA	AB	H	G by POS
1909 BOS N	1	2	1	1	0	0	0.0	1	0	1		0	.500	1.000	0	0	OF-1

Jack Damaska

BR TR 5'11" 168 lbs.
DAMASKA, JACK LLOYD
B. Aug. 21, 1937, Beaver Falls, Pa.

	G	AB	H	2B	3B	HR	HR %	R	RBI	BB	SO	SB	BA	SA	AB	H	G by POS
1963 STL N	5	5	1	0	0	0	0.0	1	1	0	4	0	.200	.200	4	1	OF-1, 2B-1

Harry Damrau

BR TR 5'10" 178 lbs.
DAMRAU, HARRY ROBERT
B. Sept. 11, 1890, Newburgh, N. Y.   D. Aug. 21, 1957, Staten Island, N. Y.

	G	AB	H	2B	3B	HR	HR %	R	RBI	BB	SO	SB	BA	SA	AB	H	G by POS
1915 PHI A	16	56	11	1	0	0	0.0	4	3	5	17	1	.196	.214	0	0	3B-16

Jake Daniel

BL TL 5'11" 175 lbs.
DANIEL, HANDLEY JACOB
B. Apr. 22, 1911, Roanoke, Ala.

	G	AB	H	2B	3B	HR	HR %	R	RBI	BB	SO	SB	BA	SA	AB	H	G by POS
1937 BKN N	12	27	5	1	0	0	0.0	3	3	3	4	0	.185	.222	2	0	1B-7

Bert Daniels

BR TR 5'9½" 180 lbs.
DANIELS, BERNARD ELMER
B. Oct. 31, 1882, Danville, Ill.   D. June 6, 1958, Cedar Grove, N. J.

	G	AB	H	2B	3B	HR	HR %	R	RBI	BB	SO	SB	BA	SA	AB	H	G by POS
1910 NY A	95	356	90	13	8	1	0.3	68	17	41		41	.253	.343	0	0	OF-85, 3B-6, 1B-4
1911	131	462	132	16	9	2	0.4	84	31	48		40	.286	.372	6	1	OF-120
1912	133	496	136	25	11	2	0.4	72	41	51		37	.274	.381	2	1	OF-131
1913	93	320	69	13	5	0	0.0	52	22	44	36	27	.216	.288	4	1	OF-87
1914 CIN N	71	269	59	9	7	0	0.0	29	19	19	40	14	.219	.305	0	0	OF-71
5 yrs.	523	1903	486	76	40	5	0.3	295	130	203	76	159	.255	.345	12	3	OF-494, 3B-6, 1B-4

Fred Daniels

BR TR 5'9½" 185 lbs.
DANIELS, FRED CLINTON (Tony)
B. Dec. 28, 1924, Gastonia, N. C.

	G	AB	H	2B	3B	HR	HR %	R	RBI	BB	SO	SB	BA	SA	AB	H	G by POS
1945 PHI N	76	230	46	3	2	0	0.0	15	10	12	22	1	.200	.230	0	0	2B-75, 3B-1

Jack Daniels

BL TL 5'10" 165 lbs.
DANIELS, HAROLD JACK (Sour Mash)
B. Dec. 21, 1927, Chester, Pa.

	G	AB	H	2B	3B	HR	HR %	R	RBI	BB	SO	SB	BA	SA	AB	H	G by POS
1952 BOS N	106	219	41	5	1	2	0.9	31	14	28	30	3	.187	.247	17	2	OF-87

Law Daniels

BR TR 5'10" 170 lbs.
DANIELS, LAWRENCE LONG
B. July 14, 1862, Newton, Mass.   D. Jan. 7, 1929, Waltham, Mass.

	G	AB	H	2B	3B	HR	HR %	R	RBI	BB	SO	SB	BA	SA	AB	H	G by POS
1887 BAL AA	48	165	41	5	1	0	0.0	23		8		7	.248	.291	0	0	C-26, OF-15, 1B-4, 2B-2, SS-1, 3B-1
1888 KC AA	61	218	44	2	0	1	0.5	32	28	14		20	.202	.225	0	0	OF-30, C-29, 3B-2, SS-1
2 yrs.	109	383	85	7	1	1	0.3	55	27	22		27	.222	.253	0	0	C-55, OF-45, 1B-4, 3B-3, SS-2, 2B-2

Buck Danner

BR TR 5'6½" 135 lbs.
DANNER, HENRY FREDERICK
B. June 8, 1891, Dedham, Mass.   D. Sept. 19, 1949, Boston, Mass.

	G	AB	H	2B	3B	HR	HR %	R	RBI	BB	SO	SB	BA	SA	AB	H	G by POS
1915 PHI A	3	12	3	0	0	0	0.0	1	0	0	1	1	.250	.250	0	0	SS-3

Harry Danning

BR TR 6'1" 190 lbs.
DANNING, HARRY (Harry The Horse)
Brother of Ike Danning.
B. Sept. 6, 1911, Los Angeles, Calif.

	G	AB	H	2B	3B	HR	HR %	R	RBI	BB	SO	SB	BA	SA	AB	H	G by POS
1933 NY N	3	2	0	0	0	0	0.0	0	0	1	0	0	.000	.000	2	0	C-1
1934	53	97	32	7	0	1	1.0	8	7	1	9	0	.330	.433	16	8	C-37
1935	65	152	37	11	1	2	1.3	16	20	9	15	0	.243	.368	19	2	C-44
1936	32	69	11	2	2	0	0.0	3	4	1	5	0	.159	.246	6	1	C-24
1937	93	292	84	12	4	8	2.7	30	51	18	20	0	.288	.438	11	2	C-86
1938	120	448	137	26	3	9	2.0	59	60	23	40	1	.306	.438	6	2	C-114
1939	135	520	163	28	5	16	3.1	79	74	35	42	4	.313	.479	3	0	C-132
1940	140	524	157	34	4	13	2.5	65	91	35	31	3	.300	.454	9	0	C-131
1941	130	459	112	22	4	7	1.5	58	56	30	25	1	.244	.355	11	3	C-116, 1B-1
1942	119	408	114	20	3	0	0.2	45	34	34	29	3	.279	.350	2	1	C-116
10 yrs.	890	2971	847	162	26	57	1.9	363	397	187	216	13	.285	.415	85	19	C-801, 1B-1

WORLD SERIES

	G	AB	H	2B	3B	HR	HR %	R	RBI	BB	SO	SB	BA	SA	AB	H	G by POS
1936 NY N	2	2	0	0	0	0	0.0	0	0	0	1	0	.000	.000	1	0	C-1
1937	3	12	3	1	0	0	0.0	0	2	0	2	0	.250	.333	0	0	C-3
2 yrs.	5	14	3	1	0	0	0.0	0	2	0	3	0	.214	.286	1	0	C-4

Ike Danning

BR TR 5'10" 160 lbs.
DANNING, IKE
Brother of Harry Danning.
B. Jan. 20, 1905, Los Angeles, Calif.

	G	AB	H	2B	3B	HR	HR %	R	RBI	BB	SO	SB	BA	SA	AB	H	G by POS
1928 STL A	2	6	3	0	0	0	0.0	0	1	1	2	0	.500	.500	0	0	C-2

Fats Dantonio

BR TR 5'8" 165 lbs.
DANTONIO, JOHN JAMES
B. Dec. 31, 1919, New Orleans, La.

	G	AB	H	2B	3B	HR	HR %	R	RBI	BB	SO	SB	BA	SA	AB	H	G by POS
1944 BKN N	3	7	1	0	0	0	0.0	0	0	0	1	0	.143	.143	0	0	C-3
1945	47	128	32	6	1	0	0.0	12	12	11	6	3	.250	.313	1	1	C-45
2 yrs.	50	135	33	6	1	0	0.0	12	12	11	7	3	.244	.304	1	1	C-48

	G	AB	H	2B	3B	HR	HR %	R	RBI	BB	SO	SB	BA	SA	Pinch Hit AB	Pinch Hit H	G by POS

Babe Danzig

DANZIG, HAROLD P.
B. Apr. 30, 1887, Binghamton, N. Y.   D. July 14, 1931, San Francisco, Calif.
BR TR 6'2"   205 lbs.

| 1909 BOS A | 6 | 13 | 2 | 0 | 0 | 0 | 0.0 | 0 | 0 | 2 | | 0 | .154 | .154 | 2 | 0 | 1B-3 |

Cliff Dapper

DAPPER, CLIFFORD ROLAND
B. Jan. 2, 1920, Los Angeles, Calif.
BR TR 6'2"   190 lbs.

| 1942 BKN N | 8 | 17 | 8 | 1 | 0 | 1 | 5.9 | 2 | 9 | 2 | 2 | 0 | .471 | .706 | 0 | 0 | C-8 |

Cliff Daringer

DARINGER, CLIFFORD CLARENCE (Shanty)
Brother of Rolla Daringer.
B. Apr. 10, 1885, Hayden, Ind.   D. Dec. 26, 1971, Sacramento, Calif.
BL TR 5'7½"   155 lbs.

| 1914 KC F | 64 | 160 | 42 | 2 | 1 | 0 | 0.0 | 12 | 16 | 11 | | 9 | .263 | .288 | 4 | 1 | SS-24, 3B-19, 2B-14 |

Rolla Daringer

DARINGER, ROLLA HARRISON
Brother of Cliff Daringer.
B. Nov. 15, 1889, North Vernon, Ind.   D. May 23, 1974, Seymour, Ind.
BL TR 5'10"   155 lbs.

1914 STL N	2	4	2	1	0	0	0.0	1	0	1	2	0	.500	.750	1	0	SS-1
1915	10	23	2	0	0	0	0.0	3	0	9	5	0	.087	.087	0	0	SS-10
2 yrs.	12	27	4	1	0	0	0.0	4	0	10	7	0	.148	.185	1	0	SS-11

Alvin Dark

DARK, ALVIN RALPH (Blackie)
B. Jan. 7, 1922, Comanche, Okla.
Manager 1961-64, 1966-71, 1974-75, 1977.
BR TR 5'11"   185 lbs.

1946 BOS N	15	13	3	3	0	0	0.0	0	1	0	3	0	.231	.462	0	0	SS-12, OF-1
1948	137	543	175	39	6	3	0.6	85	48	24	36	4	.322	.433	4	3	SS-133
1949	130	529	146	23	5	3	0.6	74	53	31	43	5	.276	.355	0	0	SS-125, 3B-4
1950 NY N	154	587	164	36	5	16	2.7	79	67	39	60	9	.279	.440	0	0	SS-154
1951	156	646	196	41	7	14	2.2	114	69	42	39	12	.303	.454	0	0	SS-156
1952	151	589	177	29	3	14	2.4	92	73	47	39	6	.301	.431	1	0	SS-150
1953	155	647	194	41	6	23	3.6	126	88	28	34	7	.300	.488	1	0	SS-110, 2B-26, OF-17, 3B-8, P-1
1954	154	644	189	26	6	20	3.1	98	70	27	40	5	.293	.446	0	0	SS-154
1955	115	475	134	20	9	9	1.9	77	45	22	32	2	.282	.394	1	0	SS-115
1956 2 teams	148	NY N (48G – .252)			STL N (100G – .286)												
" total	148	619	170	26	7	6	1.0	73	54	29	46	3	.275	.368	1	0	SS-147
1957 STL N	140	583	169	25	8	4	0.7	80	64	29	56	3	.290	.381	1	0	SS-139, 3B-1
1958 2 teams	132	STL N (18G – .297)			CHI N (114G – .295)												
" total	132	528	156	16	4	4	0.8	61	48	31	29	1	.295	.364	8	5	3B-119, SS-8
1959 CHI N	136	477	126	22	9	6	1.3	60	45	55	50	1	.264	.386	1	0	3B-131, 1B-4, SS-1
1960 2 teams	105	PHI N (55G – .242)			MIL N (50G – .298)												
" total	105	339	90	11	3	4	1.2	45	32	26	27	1	.265	.351	17	3	3B-57, OF-25, 1B-11, 2B-3
14 yrs.	1828	7219	2089	358	72	126	1.7	1064	757	430	534	59	.289	.411	35	11	SS-1404, 3B-320, OF-43, 2B-29, 1B-15, P-1

WORLD SERIES

1948 BOS N	6	24	4	1	0	0	0.0	2	0	0	2	0	.167	.208	0	0	SS-6
1951 NY N	6	24	10	3	0	1	4.2	5	4	2	3	0	.417	.667	0	0	SS-6
1954	4	17	7	0	0	0	0.0	2	0	1	1	0	.412	.412	0	0	SS-4
3 yrs.	16	65	21	4	0	1	1.5	9	4	3	6	0	.323	.431	0	0	SS-16

Dell Darling

DARLING, DELL CONRAD
B. Dec. 21, 1861, Erie, Pa.   D. Nov. 20, 1904, Erie, Pa.
BR TR 5'8"   170 lbs.

1883 BUF N	6	18	3	0	0	0	0.0	1			2	5		.167	.167	0	0	C-6
1887 CHI N	38	141	45	7	4	3	2.1	28	20	22	18	19	.319	.489	0	0	OF-20, C-20
1888	20	75	16	3	1	2	2.7	12	7	3	12	0	.213	.360	0	0	C-20
1889	36	120	23	1	1	0	0.0	14	7	25	22	5	.192	.217	0	0	C-36
1890 CHI P	58	221	57	12	4	2	0.9	45	39	29	28	5	.258	.376	0	0	1B-29, SS-15, C-9, OF-7, 2B-3, 3B-2
1891 STL AA	17	53	7	1	3	0	0.0	9	9	10	11	0	.132	.264	0	0	C-17, 2B-2, SS-1
6 yrs.	175	628	151	24	13	7	1.1	109	81	91	96	29	.240	.354	0	0	C-108, 1B-29, OF-27, SS-16, 2B-5, 3B-2

Jack Darragh

DARRAGH, JAMES S.
B. July 17, 1866, Ebensburg, Pa.   D. Aug. 12, 1939, Rochester, N. Y.

| 1891 LOU AA | 1 | 2 | 1 | 0 | 0 | 0 | 0.0 | 0 | 0 | 0 | | 0 | .500 | .500 | 0 | 0 | 1B-1 |

Bobby Darwin

DARWIN, ARTHUR BOBBY LEE
B. Feb. 16, 1943, Los Angeles, Calif.
BR TR 6'2"   190 lbs.

1962 LA A	1	1	0	0	0	0	0.0	0	0	0	1	0	.000	.000	0	0	P-1
1969 LA N	6	0	0	0	0	0	–	1	0	0	0	0	–	–	0	0	P-3
1971	11	20	5	1	0	1	5.0	2	4	2	9	0	.250	.450	7	2	OF-4
1972 MIN A	145	513	137	20	2	22	4.3	48	80	38	145	2	.267	.442	5	1	OF-142
1973	145	560	141	20	2	18	3.2	69	90	46	137	5	.252	.391	6	0	OF-140, DH-1
1974	152	575	152	13	7	25	4.3	67	94	37	127	1	.264	.442	9	4	OF-142
1975 2 teams	103	MIN A (48G – .219)			MIL A (55G – .247)												
" total	103	355	83	12	2	13	3.7	45	41	29	98	6	.234	.389	6	2	OF-70, DH-28
1976 2 teams	68	MIL A (25G – .247)			BOS A (43G – .179)												
" total	68	179	37	8	2	3	1.7	15	18	8	51	1	.207	.352	18	1	OF-38, DH-17
1977 2 teams	15	BOS A (4G – .222)			CHI N (11G – .167)												
" total	15	21	4	2	0	0	0.0	3	5	1	9	0	.190	.286	10	2	DH-2, OF-2
9 yrs.	646	2224	559	76	16	83	3.7	250	328	160	577	15	.251	.412	61	14	OF-538, DH-48, P-4

Wally Dashiell

DASHIELL, JOHN WALLACE
B. May 9, 1901, Jewett, Tex.   D. May 20, 1972, Pensacola, Fla.
BR TR 5'9½"   170 lbs.

| 1924 CHI A | 1 | 2 | 0 | 0 | 0 | 0 | 0.0 | 0 | 0 | 0 | 0 | 0 | .000 | .000 | 0 | 0 | SS-1 |

	G	AB	H	2B	3B	HR	HR%	R	RBI	BB	SO	SB	BA	SA	Pinch Hit AB	Pinch Hit H	G by POS

Harry Daubert

DAUBERT, HARRY J.
B. June 19, 1892, Columbus, Ohio   D. Jan. 8, 1944, Detroit, Mich.   BR TR 6'   160 lbs.

	G	AB	H	2B	3B	HR	HR%	R	RBI	BB	SO	SB	BA	SA	AB	H	G by POS
1915 PIT N	1	1	0	0	0	0	0.0	0	0	0	1	0	.000	.000	1	0	

Jake Daubert

DAUBERT, JACOB ELSWORTH
B. Apr. 7, 1884, Shamokin, Pa.   D. Oct. 9, 1924, Cincinnati, Ohio   BL TL 5'10½" 160 lbs.

	G	AB	H	2B	3B	HR	HR%	R	RBI	BB	SO	SB	BA	SA	AB	H	G by POS
1910 BKN N	144	552	146	15	15	8	1.4	67	50	47	53	23	.264	.389	0	0	1B-144
1911	149	573	176	17	8	5	0.9	89	45	51	56	32	.307	.391	0	0	1B-149
1912	145	559	172	19	16	3	0.5	81	66	48	45	29	.308	.415	1	0	1B-143
1913	139	508	178	17	7	2	0.4	76	52	44	40	25	.350	.423	1	0	1B-138
1914	126	474	156	17	7	6	1.3	89	45	30	34	25	.329	.432	0	0	1B-126
1915	150	544	164	21	8	2	0.4	62	47	57	48	11	.301	.381	0	0	1B-150
1916	127	478	151	16	7	3	0.6	75	33	38	39	21	.316	.397	1	0	1B-126
1917	125	468	122	4	4	2	0.4	59	30	51	30	11	.261	.299	0	0	1B-125
1918	108	396	122	12	15	2	0.5	50	47	27	18	10	.308	.429	2	0	1B-105
1919 CIN N	140	537	148	10	12	2	0.4	79	44	35	23	11	.276	.350	0	0	1B-140
1920	142	553	168	28	13	4	0.7	97	48	47	29	11	.304	.423	2	0	1B-140
1921	136	516	158	18	12	2	0.4	69	64	24	16	12	.306	.399	0	0	1B-136
1922	156	610	205	15	22	12	2.0	114	66	56	21	14	.336	.492	0	0	1B-156
1923	125	500	146	27	10	2	0.4	63	54	40	20	11	.292	.398	4	1	1B-121
1924	102	405	114	14	9	1	0.2	47	31	28	17	5	.281	.368	0	0	1B-102
15 yrs.	2014	7673	2326	250	165	56	0.7	1117	722	623	489	251	.303	.401	11	1	1B-2001

WORLD SERIES

	G	AB	H	2B	3B	HR	HR%	R	RBI	BB	SO	SB	BA	SA	AB	H	G by POS
1916 BKN N	4	17	3	0	1	0	0.0	1	0	2	3	0	.176	.294	0	0	1B-4
1919 CIN N	8	29	7	0	1	0	0.0	4	1	1	2	1	.241	.310	0	0	1B-8
2 yrs.	12	46	10	0	2	0	0.0	5	1	3	5	1	.217	.304	0	0	1B-12

Rich Dauer

DAUER, RICHARD FREMONT
B. July 27, 1952, San Bernardino, Calif.   BR TR 6'   180 lbs.

	G	AB	H	2B	3B	HR	HR%	R	RBI	BB	SO	SB	BA	SA	AB	H	G by POS
1976 BAL A	11	39	4	0	0	0	0.0	3	1	3	3	1	.103	.103	1	0	2B-10
1977	96	304	74	15	1	5	1.6	38	25	20	28	1	.243	.349	12	1	2B-83, 3B-9, DH-2
1978	133	459	121	23	0	6	1.3	57	46	26	22	0	.264	.353	3	1	2B-87, 3B-52, DH-1
1979	142	479	123	20	0	9	1.9	63	61	36	36	0	.257	.355	0	0	2B-103, 3B-44
1980	152	557	158	32	0	2	0.4	71	63	46	19	3	.284	.352	1	0	2B-137, 3B-35
1981	96	369	97	27	0	4	1.1	41	38	27	18	0	.263	.369	1	0	2B-94, 3B-4
1982	158	558	156	24	2	8	1.4	75	57	50	34	0	.280	.373	1	0	2B-123, 3B-61
1983	140	459	108	19	0	5	1.1	49	41	47	29	1	.235	.309	0	0	2B-131, 3B-17
1984	127	397	101	26	0	2	0.5	29	24	24	23	1	.254	.335	2	0	2B-123, 3B-3
9 yrs.	1055	3621	942	186	3	41	1.1	423	358	277	212	6	.260	.347	21	2	2B-891, 3B-225, DH-3

LEAGUE CHAMPIONSHIP SERIES

	G	AB	H	2B	3B	HR	HR%	R	RBI	BB	SO	SB	BA	SA	AB	H	G by POS
1979 BAL A	4	11	2	0	0	0	0.0	0	0	0	1	0	.182	.182	0	0	2B-4
1983	4	14	0	0	0	0	0.0	0	1	0	0	0	.000	.000	0	0	2B-4
2 yrs.	8	25	2	0	0	0	0.0	0	1	0	1	0	.080	.080	0	0	2B-8

WORLD SERIES

	G	AB	H	2B	3B	HR	HR%	R	RBI	BB	SO	SB	BA	SA	AB	H	G by POS
1979 BAL A	6	17	5	1	0	1	5.9	1	1	0	1	0	.294	.529	1	1	2B-5
1983	5	19	4	1	0	0	0.0	2	3	0	3	0	.211	.263	0	0	2B-5
2 yrs.	11	36	9	2	0	1	2.8	4	4	0	4	0	.250	.389	1	1	2B-10

Doc Daugherty

DAUGHERTY, HAROLD RAY
B. Oct. 12, 1927, Paris, Pa.   BR TR 6'   180 lbs.

	G	AB	H	2B	3B	HR	HR%	R	RBI	BB	SO	SB	BA	SA	AB	H	G by POS
1951 DET A	1	1	0	0	0	0	0.0	0	0	0	1	0	.000	.000	1	0	

Bob Daughters

DAUGHTERS, ROBERT FRANCIS (Red)
B. Aug. 5, 1914, Cincinnati, Ohio   BR TR 6'2"   185 lbs.

	G	AB	H	2B	3B	HR	HR%	R	RBI	BB	SO	SB	BA	SA	AB	H	G by POS
1937 BOS A	1	0	0	0	0	0	–	1	0	0	0	0	–	–	0	0	

Darren Daulton

DAULTON, DARREN ARTHUR
B. Jan. 3, 1962, Arkansas City, Kans.   BL TR 6'   170 lbs.

	G	AB	H	2B	3B	HR	HR%	R	RBI	BB	SO	SB	BA	SA	AB	H	G by POS
1983 PHI N	2	3	1	0	0	0	0.0	1	0	1	1	0	.333	.333	0	0	C-2

Vic Davalillo

DAVALILLO, VICTOR JOSE
Brother of Yo-Yo Davalillo.
B. July 31, 1939, Cabimas, Venezuela   BL TL 5'7"   150 lbs.

	G	AB	H	2B	3B	HR	HR%	R	RBI	BB	SO	SB	BA	SA	AB	H	G by POS
1963 CLE A	90	370	108	18	5	7	1.9	44	36	16	41	3	.292	.424	2	2	OF-89
1964	150	577	156	26	2	6	1.0	64	51	34	77	21	.270	.354	5	0	OF-143
1965	142	505	152	19	1	5	1.0	67	40	35	50	26	.301	.372	8	1	OF-134
1966	121	344	86	6	4	3	0.9	42	19	24	37	8	.250	.317	18	3	OF-108
1967	139	359	103	17	5	2	0.6	47	22	10	30	6	.287	.379	20	4	OF-125
1968 2 teams			CLE	A (51G –	.239)			CAL	A (93G –	.298)							
" total	144	519	144	17	7	3	0.6	49	31	18	53	25	.277	.355	7	3	OF-135
1969 2 teams			CAL	A (33G –	.155)			STL	N (63G –	.265)							
" total	96	169	37	4	1	2	1.2	25	11	13	13	4	.219	.290	43	10	OF-45, 1B-3, P-2
1970 STL N	111	183	57	14	3	1	0.5	29	33	13	19	4	.311	.437	73	24	OF-54
1971 PIT N	99	295	84	14	6	1	0.3	48	33	11	31	10	.285	.383	27	9	OF-61, 1B-16
1972	117	368	117	19	2	4	1.1	59	28	26	44	14	.318	.413	12	5	OF-97, 1B-8
1973 2 teams			PIT	N (59G –	.181)			OAK	A (38G –	.188)							
" total	97	147	27	2	0	1	0.7	14	7	5	11	0	.184	.218	49	10	OF-29, 1B-18, DH-2
1974 OAK A	17	23	4	0	0	0	0.0	0	1	2	2	0	.174	.174	6	1	OF-6, DH-4
1977 LA N	24	48	15	2	0	0	0.0	3	4	0	6	0	.313	.354	14	4	OF-12
1978	75	77	24	1	1	1	1.3	15	11	3	7	2	.312	.390	47	12	OF-25, 1B-2
1979	29	27	7	1	0	0	0.0	2	2	2	2	0	.259	.296	24	6	OF-3
1980	7	6	1	0	0	0	0.0	1	0	0	1	0	.167	.167	5	1	1B-1
16 yrs.	1458	4017	1122	160	37	36	0.9	509	329	212	422	125	.279	.364	360 **10th**	95	OF-1066, 1B-48, DH-6, P-2

LEAGUE CHAMPIONSHIP SERIES

	G	AB	H	2B	3B	HR	HR%	R	RBI	BB	SO	SB	BA	SA	AB	H	G by POS
1971 PIT N	2	2	0	0	0	0	0.0	0	0	0	1	0	.000	.000	2	0	

	G	AB	H	2B	3B	HR	HR %	R	RBI	BB	SO	SB	BA	SA	Pinch Hit AB	Pinch Hit H	G by POS

Vic Davalillo continued

	G	AB	H	2B	3B	HR	HR %	R	RBI	BB	SO	SB	BA	SA	Pinch Hit AB	Pinch Hit H	G by POS
1972	1	0	0	0	0	0	–	0	0	1	0	0	–	–	0	0	
1973 OAK A	4	8	5	1	1	0	0.0	2	1	1	0	0	.625	1.000	1	1	OF-2
1977 LA N	1	1	1	0	0	0	0.0	1	0	0	0	0	1.000	1.000	1	1	
4 yrs.	8	11	6	1	1	0	0.0	3	1	2	1	0	.545	.818	4	2	OF-2

WORLD SERIES

	G	AB	H	2B	3B	HR	HR %	R	RBI	BB	SO	SB	BA	SA	Pinch Hit AB	Pinch Hit H	G by POS
1971 PIT N	3	3	1	0	0	0	0.0	1	0	0	0	0	.333	.333	3	1	OF-2
1973 OAK A	6	11	1	0	0	0	0.0	0	0	2	1	0	.091	.091	2	0	1B-1
1977 LA N	3	3	1	0	0	0	0.0	0	1	0	0	0	.333	.333	3	1	
1978	2	3	1	0	0	0	0.0	0	0	0	0	0	.333	.333	1	0	DH-1
4 yrs.	14	20	4	0	0	0	0.0	1	1	2	1	0	.200	.200	9	2	OF-2, DH-1, 1B-1
															1st		

Yo-Yo Davalillo

DAVALILLO, POMPEYO ANTONIO
Brother of Vic Davalillo.
B. June 30, 1931, Caracas, Venezuela

BR TR 5'3" 140 lbs.

	G	AB	H	2B	3B	HR	HR %	R	RBI	BB	SO	SB	BA	SA	Pinch Hit AB	Pinch Hit H	G by POS
1953 WAS A	19	58	17	1	0	0	0.0	10	2	1	7	1	.293	.310	0	0	SS-17

Jerry DaVanon

DaVANON, FRANK GERALD
B. Aug. 21, 1945, Oceanside, Calif.

BR TR 5'11" 175 lbs.

	G	AB	H	2B	3B	HR	HR %	R	RBI	BB	SO	SB	BA	SA	Pinch Hit AB	Pinch Hit H	G by POS
1969 2 teams	SD	N	(24G –	.136)		STL	N	(16G –	.300)								
" total	40	99	20	4	0	1	1.0	11	10	9	20	0	.202	.273	2	0	SS-23, 2B-15
1970 STL N	11	18	2	1	0	0	0.0	2	0	2	5	0	.111	.167	3	0	3B-5, 2B-3
1971 BAL A	38	81	19	5	0	0	0.0	14	4	12	20	0	.235	.296	0	0	2B-20, SS-11, 3B-3, 1B-1
1973 CAL A	41	49	12	3	0	0	0.0	6	2	3	9	1	.245	.306	0	0	SS-14, 2B-12, 3B-7
1974 STL N	30	40	6	1	0	0	0.0	4	4	4	5	0	.150	.175	1	0	SS-14, 3B-8, 2B-7, OF-1
1975 HOU N	32	97	27	4	2	1	1.0	15	10	16	7	2	.278	.392	3	0	SS-21, 2B-9, 3B-3
1976	61	107	31	3	3	1	0.9	19	20	21	12	0	.290	.402	15	2	SS-17, 2B-17, 3B-9
1977 STL N	9	8	0	0	0	0	0.0	2	0	1	2	0	.000	.000	1	0	2B-5
8 yrs.	262	499	117	21	5	3	0.6	73	50	68	80	3	.234	.315	25	2	SS-100, 2B-88, 3B-35, OF-1, 1B-1

Jim Davenport

DAVENPORT, JAMES HOUSTON
B. Aug. 17, 1933, Siluria, Ala.

BR TR 5'11" 170 lbs.

	G	AB	H	2B	3B	HR	HR %	R	RBI	BB	SO	SB	BA	SA	Pinch Hit AB	Pinch Hit H	G by POS
1958 SF N	134	434	111	22	3	12	2.8	70	41	33	64	1	.256	.403	1	0	3B-130, SS-5
1959	123	469	121	16	3	6	1.3	65	38	28	65	0	.258	.343	3	0	3B-121, SS-1
1960	112	363	91	15	3	6	1.7	43	38	26	58	0	.251	.358	9	1	3B-103, SS-7
1961	137	436	121	28	4	12	2.8	64	65	45	65	4	.278	.443	5	1	3B-132
1962	144	485	144	25	5	14	2.9	83	58	45	76	2	.297	.456	3	1	3B-141
1963	147	460	116	19	3	4	0.9	40	36	32	87	5	.252	.333	13	2	3B-127, 2B-22, SS-1
1964	116	297	70	10	6	2	0.7	24	26	29	46	2	.236	.330	7	0	SS-64, 3B-41, 2B-30
1965	106	271	68	14	3	4	1.5	29	31	21	47	0	.251	.369	14	4	3B-39, SS-37, 2B-26
1966	111	305	76	6	2	9	3.0	42	30	22	40	1	.249	.370	20	5	SS-58, 3B-36, 2B-21, 1B-2
1967	124	295	81	10	3	5	1.7	42	30	39	50	1	.275	.380	27	10	3B-64, SS-28, 2B-12
1968	113	272	61	1	1	1	0.4	27	17	26	32	0	.224	.246	23	5	3B-82, SS-17, 2B-1
1969	112	303	73	10	1	2	0.7	20	42	29	37	0	.241	.300	14	4	3B-104, OF-1, SS-1, 1B-1
1970	22	37	9	1	0	0	0.0	3	4	7	6	0	.243	.270	11	3	3B-10
13 yrs.	1501	4427	1142	177	37	77	1.7	552	456	382	673	16	.258	.367	150	36	3B-1130, SS-219, 2B-112, 1B-3, OF-1

WORLD SERIES

	G	AB	H	2B	3B	HR	HR %	R	RBI	BB	SO	SB	BA	SA	Pinch Hit AB	Pinch Hit H	G by POS
1962 SF N	7	22	3	1	0	0	0.0	1	1	4	7	0	.136	.182	0	0	3B-7

Andre David

DAVID, ANDRE
B. May 18, 1958, Hollywood, Calif.

BL TL 6' 170 lbs.

	G	AB	H	2B	3B	HR	HR %	R	RBI	BB	SO	SB	BA	SA	Pinch Hit AB	Pinch Hit H	G by POS
1984 MIN A	33	48	12	2	0	1	2.1	5	5	7	11	0	.250	.354	15	2	OF-14, DH-2

Bill Davidson

DAVIDSON, WILLIAM J.
B. May 10, 1884, Lafayette, Ind.   D. May 23, 1954, Lincoln, Neb.

BR TR

	G	AB	H	2B	3B	HR	HR %	R	RBI	BB	SO	SB	BA	SA	Pinch Hit AB	Pinch Hit H	G by POS
1909 CHI N	2	7	1	0	0	0	0.0	2	0	1		1	.143	.143	0	0	OF-2
1910 BKN N	136	509	121	13	7	0	0.0	48	34	24	54	27	.238	.291	4	0	OF-131
1911	87	292	68	3	4	1	0.3	33	26	16	21	18	.233	.281	8	2	OF-74
3 yrs.	225	808	190	16	11	1	0.1	83	60	41	75	46	.235	.286	12	2	OF-207

Claude Davidson

DAVIDSON, CLAUDE BOUCHER (Davey)
B. Oct. 13, 1896, Boston, Mass.   D. Apr. 18, 1956, Weymouth, Mass.

BL TR 5'11" 155 lbs.

	G	AB	H	2B	3B	HR	HR %	R	RBI	BB	SO	SB	BA	SA	Pinch Hit AB	Pinch Hit H	G by POS
1918 PHI A	31	81	15	1	0	0	0.0	4	4	5	9	0	.185	.198	7	2	2B-15, OF-8, 3B-1
1919 WAS A	2	7	3	0	0	0	0.0	1	0	1	1	0	.429	.429	0	0	3B-2
2 yrs.	33	88	18	1	0	0	0.0	5	4	6	10	0	.205	.216	7	2	2B-15, OF-8, 3B-3

Homer Davidson

DAVIDSON, HOMER HURD (Divvy)
B. Oct. 14, 1884, Cleveland, Ohio   D. July 26, 1948, Detroit, Mich.

BR TR 5'10½" 155 lbs.

	G	AB	H	2B	3B	HR	HR %	R	RBI	BB	SO	SB	BA	SA	Pinch Hit AB	Pinch Hit H	G by POS
1908 CLE A	9	4	0	0	0	0						1	.000	.000	0	0	C-5, OF-1

Chick Davies

DAVIES, LLOYD GARRISON
B. Mar. 6, 1892, Peabody, Mass.   D. Sept. 5, 1973, Middletown, Conn.

BL TL 5'8" 145 lbs.

	G	AB	H	2B	3B	HR	HR %	R	RBI	BB	SO	SB	BA	SA	Pinch Hit AB	Pinch Hit H	G by POS
1914 PHI A	19	46	11	3	1	0	0.0	6	5	5	13	1	.239	.348	6	2	OF-10, P-1
1915	56	132	24	5	3	0	0.0	13	11	14	31	2	.182	.265	16	2	OF-32, P-4
1925 NY N	4	6	0	0	0	0	0.0	1	0	1	0	0	.000	.000	1	0	P-2, OF-1
1926	38	18	4	0	0	0	0.0	4	1	3	5	0	.222	.222	0	0	P-38
4 yrs.	117	202	39	8	4	0	0.0	24	17	22	50	3	.193	.272	23	4	P-45, OF-43

Alvin Davis

DAVIS, ALVIN GLENN
B. Sept. 9, 1960, Riverside, Calif.

BL TR 6'1" 190 lbs.

	G	AB	H	2B	3B	HR	HR %	R	RBI	BB	SO	SB	BA	SA	Pinch Hit AB	Pinch Hit H	G by POS
1984 SEA A	152	567	161	34	3	27	4.8	80	116	97	78	5	.284	.497	0	0	1B-147, DH-7

	G	AB	H	2B	3B	HR	HR%	R	RBI	BB	SO	SB	BA	SA	Pinch Hit AB	Pinch Hit H	G by POS

Bill Davis

DAVIS, ARTHUR WILLARD
B. June 6, 1942, Graceville, Minn.
BL TL 6'7"   215 lbs.

	G	AB	H	2B	3B	HR	HR%	R	RBI	BB	SO	SB	BA	SA	AB	H	G by POS
1965 CLE A	10	10	3	1	0	0	0.0	0	0	0	1	0	.300	.400	10	3	
1966	23	38	6	1	0	1	2.6	2	4	6	9	0	.158	.263	12	3	1B-9
1969 SD N	31	57	10	1	0	0	0.0	1	1	8	18	0	.175	.193	14	2	1B-14
3 yrs.	64	105	19	3	0	1	1.0	3	5	14	28	0	.181	.238	36	8	1B-23

Bob Davis

DAVIS, ROBERT JOHN EUGENE
B. Mar. 1, 1952, Pryor, Okla.
BR TR 6'   180 lbs.

	G	AB	H	2B	3B	HR	HR%	R	RBI	BB	SO	SB	BA	SA	AB	H	G by POS
1973 SD N	5	11	1	0	0	0	0.0	1	0	0	5	0	.091	.091	0	0	C-5
1975	43	128	30	3	2	0	0.0	6	7	11	31	0	.234	.289	2	0	C-43
1976	51	83	17	0	1	0	0.0	7	5	5	13	0	.205	.229	0	0	C-47
1977	48	94	17	2	0	1	1.1	9	10	5	24	0	.181	.234	2	1	C-46
1978	19	40	8	1	0	0	0.0	3	2	1	5	0	.200	.225	3	0	C-16
1979 TOR A	32	89	11	2	0	1	1.1	6	8	6	15	0	.124	.180	0	0	C-32
1980	91	218	47	11	0	4	1.8	18	19	12	25	0	.216	.321	4	1	C-89
1981 CAL A	1	2	0	0	0	0	0.0	0	0	0	0	0	.000	.000	0	0	C-1
8 yrs.	290	665	131	19	3	6	0.9	50	51	40	118	0	.197	.262	11	2	C-279

Brandy Davis

DAVIS, ROBERT BRANDON
B. Sept. 10, 1928, Newark, Del.
BR TR 6'   170 lbs.

	G	AB	H	2B	3B	HR	HR%	R	RBI	BB	SO	SB	BA	SA	AB	H	G by POS
1952 PIT N	55	95	17	1	1	0	0.0	14	1	11	28	9	.179	.211	11	2	OF-29
1953	12	39	8	2	0	0	0.0	5	2	0	3	0	.205	.256	0	0	OF-9
2 yrs.	67	134	25	3	1	0	0.0	19	3	11	31	9	.187	.224	11	2	OF-38

Brock Davis

DAVIS, BRYSHEAR BARNETT
B. Oct. 19, 1943, Oakland, Calif.
BL TL 5'10"   160 lbs.

	G	AB	H	2B	3B	HR	HR%	R	RBI	BB	SO	SB	BA	SA	AB	H	G by POS
1963 HOU N	34	55	11	2	0	1	1.8	7	2	4	10	0	.200	.291	17	3	OF-14
1964	1	3	0	0	0	0	0.0	0	0	1	1	0	.000	.000	0	0	OF-1
1966	10	27	4	1	0	0	0.0	2	1	5	4	1	.148	.185	3	1	OF-7
1970 CHI N	6	3	0	0	0	0	0.0	0	0	0	1	0	.000	.000	3	0	OF-1
1971	106	301	77	7	5	0	0.0	22	28	35	34	0	.256	.312	10	1	OF-93
1972 MIL A	85	154	49	2	0	0	0.0	17	12	12	23	6	.318	.331	36	8	OF-43
6 yrs.	242	543	141	12	5	1	0.2	48	43	57	73	7	.260	.306	69	13	OF-159

Butch Davis

DAVIS, WALLACE McARTHUR
B. June 19, 1958, Martin County, N. C.
BR TR 6'   185 lbs.

	G	AB	H	2B	3B	HR	HR%	R	RBI	BB	SO	SB	BA	SA	AB	H	G by POS
1983 KC A	33	122	42	2	6	2	1.6	13	18	4	19	4	.344	.508	0	0	OF-33
1984	41	116	17	3	0	2	1.7	11	12	10	19	4	.147	.224	4	0	OF-35, DH-2
2 yrs.	74	238	59	5	6	4	1.7	24	30	14	38	8	.248	.370	4	0	OF-68, DH-2

Chili Davis

DAVIS, CHARLES THEODORE
B. Jan. 17, 1960, Kingston, Jamaica
BB TR 6'3"   195 lbs.

	G	AB	H	2B	3B	HR	HR%	R	RBI	BB	SO	SB	BA	SA	AB	H	G by POS
1981 SF N	8	15	2	0	0	0	0.0	1	0	1	2	2	.133	.133	3	1	OF-6
1982	154	641	167	27	6	19	3.0	86	76	45	115	24	.261	.410	1	1	OF-153
1983	137	486	113	21	2	11	2.3	54	59	55	108	10	.233	.352	4	1	OF-133
1984	137	499	157	21	6	21	4.2	87	81	42	74	12	.315	.507	15	6	OF-123
4 yrs.	436	1641	439	69	14	51	3.1	228	216	143	299	48	.268	.420	23	9	OF-415

Crash Davis

DAVIS, LAWRENCE COLUMBUS
B. July 14, 1919, Canon, Ga.
BR TR 6'   173 lbs.

	G	AB	H	2B	3B	HR	HR%	R	RBI	BB	SO	SB	BA	SA	AB	H	G by POS
1940 PHI A	23	67	18	1	1	0	0.0	4	9	3	10	1	.269	.313	3	0	2B-19, SS-1
1941	39	105	23	3	0	0	0.0	8	8	11	16	0	.219	.248	7	2	2B-20, 1B-12
1942	86	272	61	8	1	2	0.7	31	26	21	30	1	.224	.283	4	1	2B-57, SS-26, 1B-3
3 yrs.	148	444	102	12	2	2	0.5	43	43	35	56	2	.230	.279	14	3	2B-96, SS-27, 1B-15

Dick Davis

DAVIS, RICHARD EARL
B. Sept. 25, 1953, Long Beach, Calif.
BR TR 6'3"   190 lbs.

	G	AB	H	2B	3B	HR	HR%	R	RBI	BB	SO	SB	BA	SA	AB	H	G by POS
1977 MIL A	22	51	14	2	0	0	0.0	7	6	1	8	0	.275	.314	2	1	OF-12, DH-6
1978	69	218	54	10	1	5	2.3	28	26	7	23	2	.248	.372	13	3	DH-34, OF-28
1979	91	335	89	13	1	12	3.6	51	41	16	46	3	.266	.418	6	2	DH-53, OF-35
1980	106	365	99	26	2	4	1.1	50	30	11	43	5	.271	.386	5	2	DH-63, OF-38
1981 PHI N	45	96	32	6	1	2	2.1	12	19	8	13	1	.333	.479	14	5	OF-32
1982 3 teams	PHI N (28G – .279)			TOR A (3G – .286)						PIT N (39G – .182)							
" total	70	152	35	5	2	4	2.6	12	19	7	19	2	.230	.368	26	5	OF-45, DH-1
6 yrs.	403	1217	323	62	7	27	2.2	160	141	50	152	13	.265	.394	66	18	OF-190, DH-157

DIVISIONAL PLAYOFF SERIES

	G	AB	H	2B	3B	HR	HR%	R	RBI	BB	SO	SB	BA	SA	AB	H	G by POS
1981 PHI N	1	2	0	0	0	0	0.0	0	0	0	1	0	.000	.000	1	0	OF-1

Eric Davis

DAVIS, ERIC KEITH
B. May 29, 1962, Los Angeles, Calif.
BR TR 6'3"   175 lbs.

	G	AB	H	2B	3B	HR	HR%	R	RBI	BB	SO	SB	BA	SA	AB	H	G by POS
1984 CIN N	57	174	39	10	1	10	5.7	33	30	24	48	10	.224	.466	6	1	OF-51

George Davis

DAVIS, GEORGE STACEY
B. Aug. 23, 1870, Cohoes, N. Y.   D. Oct. 17, 1940, Philadelphia, Pa.
Manager 1895, 1900-01.
BB TR 5'9"   180 lbs.

	G	AB	H	2B	3B	HR	HR%	R	RBI	BB	SO	SB	BA	SA	AB	H	G by POS
1890 CLE N	136	526	139	22	9	6	1.1	98	73	53	34	22	.264	.375	0	0	OF-133, 2B-2, SS-1
1891	136	571	167	35	12	3	0.5	115	89	53	29	42	.292	.412	0	0	OF-116, 3B-22, P-3
1892	144	597	151	27	12	5	0.8	96	82	58	51	36	.253	.363	0	0	3B-79, OF-44, SS-20, 2B-3
1893 NY N	133	549	199	22	27	11	2.0	112	119	42	20	37	.362	.561	0	0	3B-133, SS-1
1894	124	492	170	28	20	9	1.8	124	91	66	10	40	.346	.539	0	0	3B-124
1895	110	433	143	32	11	5	1.2	106	101	55	12	48	.330	.490	0	0	3B-81, 1B-14, 2B-10, OF-7
1896	124	494	158	25	12	6	1.2	98	99	50	24	48	.320	.455	0	0	3B-74, SS-45, OF-3, 1B-3
1897	131	525	188	34	11	9	1.7	114	134	41		65	.358	.516	0	0	SS-130
1898	121	486	149	20	5	2	0.4	80	86	32		26	.307	.381	0	0	SS-121
1899	108	416	144	21	5	1	0.2	68	57	37		34	.346	.428	0	0	SS-108

	G	AB	H	2B	3B	HR	HR %	R	RBI	BB	SO	SB	BA	SA	Pinch Hit AB	Pinch Hit H	G by POS

George Davis continued

	G	AB	H	2B	3B	HR	HR %	R	RBI	BB	SO	SB	BA	SA	PH AB	PH H	G by POS
1900	114	426	138	20	4	3	0.7	69	61	35		29	.324	.411	0	0	SS-114
1901	130	495	153	26	6	7	1.4	69	65	40		26	.309	.428	0	0	SS-113, 3B-17
1902 CHI A	132	485	145	27	7	3	0.6	76	93	65		31	.299	.402	1	1	SS-129, 1B-3
1903 NY N	4	15	4	0	0	0	0.0	2	1	1		0	.267	.267	0	0	SS-4
1904 CHI A	152	563	142	27	15	1	0.2	75	69	43		32	.252	.359	0	0	SS-152
1905	157	550	153	29	1	1	0.2	74	55	60		31	.278	.340	0	0	SS-157
1906	133	484	134	26	6	0	0.0	63	80	41		27	.277	.355	3	1	SS-129, 2B-1
1907	132	466	111	18	2	1	0.2	59	52	47		15	.238	.292	0	0	SS-131
1908	128	419	91	14	1	0	0.0	41	26	41		22	.217	.255	5	1	2B-95, SS-23, 1B-4
1909	28	68	9	1	0	0	0.0	5	2	10		4	.132	.147	14	1	1B-17, 2B-2
20 yrs.	2377	9060	2688	454	166	73	0.8	1544	1435	870	180	615	.297	.408	23	4	SS-1378, 3B-530, OF-303, 2B-113, 1B-41, P-3

WORLD SERIES

	G	AB	H	2B	3B	HR	HR %	R	RBI	BB	SO	SB	BA	SA	PH AB	PH H	G by POS
1906 CHI A	3	13	4	3	0	0	0.0	4	6	0	1	1	.308	.538	0	0	SS-3

Gerry Davis

DAVIS, GERALD EDWARD
B. Dec. 25, 1958, Trenton, N. J.   BR TR 6'   185 lbs.

	G	AB	H	2B	3B	HR	HR %	R	RBI	BB	SO	SB	BA	SA	PH AB	PH H	G by POS
1983 SD N	5	15	5	2	0	0	0.0	3	1	3	4	1	.333	.467	0	0	OF-5

Glenn Davis

DAVIS, GLENN EARL
B. Mar. 28, 1961, Jacksonville, Fla.   BR TR 6'3"   210 lbs.

	G	AB	H	2B	3B	HR	HR %	R	RBI	BB	SO	SB	BA	SA	PH AB	PH H	G by POS
1984 HOU N	18	61	13	5	0	2	3.3	6	8	4	12	0	.213	.393	2	0	1B-16

Harry Davis

DAVIS, HARRY ALBERT (Stinky)
B. May 7, 1908, Shreveport, La.   BL TL 5'10½" 175 lbs.

	G	AB	H	2B	3B	HR	HR %	R	RBI	BB	SO	SB	BA	SA	PH AB	PH H	G by POS
1932 DET A	140	590	159	32	13	4	0.7	92	74	60	53	12	.269	.388	0	0	1B-140
1933	66	173	37	8	2	0	0.0	24	14	22	8	2	.214	.283	19	3	1B-44
1937 STL A	120	450	124	25	3	3	0.7	89	35	71	26	7	.276	.364	7	2	1B-112, OF-1
3 yrs.	326	1213	320	65	18	7	0.6	205	123	153	87	21	.264	.364	26	5	1B-296, OF-1

Harry Davis

DAVIS, HARRY H (Jasper)
B. July 10, 1873, Philadelphia, Pa.   D. Aug. 11, 1947, Philadelphia, Pa.
Manager 1912.   BR TR 5'11"   180 lbs.

	G	AB	H	2B	3B	HR	HR %	R	RBI	BB	SO	SB	BA	SA	PH AB	PH H	G by POS
1895 NY N	7	24	7	0	1	0	0.0	1	6	2		1	.292	.375	0	0	1B-7
1896 2 teams								NY N (64G – .275)			PIT N (44G – .190)						
" total	108	401	96	16	16	2	0.5	67	73	44	41	25	.239	.374	1	0	1B-58, OF-50, SS-1
1897 PIT N	111	429	131	10	28	2	0.5	70	63	26		21	.305	.473	2	0	1B-64, 3B-32, OF-14, SS-1
1898 3 teams							PIT N (58G – .293)			LOU N (37G – .217)			WAS N (1G – .000)				
" total	96	363	95	14	15	2	0.6	49	40	19		13	.262	.399	0	0	1B-88, OF-7, 2B-2
1899 WAS N	18	64	12	2	3	0	0.0	3	8	8		2	.188	.313	0	0	1B-18
1901 PHI A	117	496	152	28	10	8	1.6	92	76	23		21	.306	.452	0	0	1B-117
1902	133	561	172	43	8	6	1.1	89	92	30		28	.307	.444	0	0	1B-128, OF-5
1903	106	420	125	29	7	5	1.2	75	55	24		24	.298	.436	0	0	1B-104, OF-2
1904	102	404	125	21	11	10	2.5	54	62	23		12	.309	.490	0	0	1B-102
1905	149	602	171	47	6	8	1.3	92	83	43		36	.284	.422	0	0	1B-149
1906	145	551	161	42	7	12	2.2	94	96	49		23	.292	.459	0	0	1B-145
1907	149	582	155	36	8	8	1.4	84	87	42		20	.266	.397	0	0	1B-149
1908	147	513	127	23	9	5	1.0	65	62	61		20	.248	.357	0	0	1B-147
1909	149	530	142	22	11	4	0.8	73	75	51		20	.268	.374	0	0	1B-149
1910	139	492	122	19	4	1	0.2	61	41	53		17	.248	.309	0	0	1B-139
1911	57	183	36	9	1	1	0.5	27	22	24		2	.197	.273	1	0	1B-53
1912 CLE A	2	5	0	0	0	0	0.0	0	0	0		0	.000	.000	0	0	1B-2
1913 PHI A	7	17	6	2	0	0	0.0	2	4	1	4	0	.353	.471	1	1	1B-6
1914	5	7	3	0	0	0	0.0	0	2	1	0	0	.429	.429	3	1	1B-1
1915	5	3	1	0	0	0	0.0	0	4	0	0	0	.333	.333	1	0	1B-1
1916	4	6	1	0	0	0	0.0	0	1	1	2	0	.167	.167	2	0	OF-1
1917	1	1	0	0	0	0	0.0	0	0	0	0	0	.000	.000	1	0	
22 yrs.	1757	6654	1840	363	145	74	1.1	998	952	525	47	285	.277	.408	14	3	1B-1627, OF-79, 3B-32, SS-2, 2B-2

WORLD SERIES

	G	AB	H	2B	3B	HR	HR %	R	RBI	BB	SO	SB	BA	SA	PH AB	PH H	G by POS
1905 PHI A	5	20	4	1	0	0	0.0	0	0	0	1	0	.200	.250	0	0	1B-5
1910	5	17	6	3	0	0	0.0	5	2	3	4	0	.353	.529	0	0	1B-5
1911	6	24	5	1	0	0	0.0	3	5	0	3	0	.208	.250	0	0	1B-6
3 yrs.	16	61	15	5	0	0	0.0	8	7	3	8	0	.246	.328	0	0	1B-16

Ike Davis

DAVIS, ISAAC MARION
B. June 14, 1895, Pueblo, Colo.   D. Apr. 2, 1984, Tucson, Ariz.   BR TR 5'7"   155 lbs.

	G	AB	H	2B	3B	HR	HR %	R	RBI	BB	SO	SB	BA	SA	PH AB	PH H	G by POS
1919 WAS A	8	14	0	0	0	0	0.0	0	0	0	6	0	.000	.000	0	0	SS-4
1924 CHI A	10	33	8	1	1	0	0.0	5	4	2	5	0	.242	.333	5	0	SS-10
1925	146	562	135	31	9	0	0.0	105	61	71	58	19	.240	.327	2	1	SS-144
3 yrs.	164	609	143	32	10	0	0.0	110	65	73	69	19	.235	.320	7	1	SS-158

Ira Davis

DAVIS, J. IRA (Slats)
B. July 8, 1870, Philadelphia, Pa.   D. Dec. 21, 1942, Brooklyn, N. Y.

	G	AB	H	2B	3B	HR	HR %	R	RBI	BB	SO	SB	BA	SA	PH AB	PH H	G by POS
1899 NY N	6	17	4	1	1	0	0.0	3	2	0		1	.235	.412	1	0	SS-3, 1B-2

Jacke Davis

DAVIS, JACKE SYLVESTER
B. Mar. 5, 1936, Carthage, Tex.   BR TR 5'11"   190 lbs.

	G	AB	H	2B	3B	HR	HR %	R	RBI	BB	SO	SB	BA	SA	PH AB	PH H	G by POS
1962 PHI N	48	75	16	0	1	1	1.3	9	6	4	20	1	.213	.280	16	4	OF-26

	G	AB	H	2B	3B	HR	HR %	R	RBI	BB	SO	SB	BA	SA	Pinch Hit AB	Pinch Hit H	G by POS

Jody Davis

DAVIS, JODY RICHARD　　　　　　　　　　　　　BR TR 6'4"　192 lbs.
B. Nov. 12, 1956, Gainesville, Ga.

	G	AB	H	2B	3B	HR	HR %	R	RBI	BB	SO	SB	BA	SA	AB	H	G by POS
1981 CHI N	56	180	46	5	1	4	2.2	14	21	21	28	0	.256	.361	0	0	C-56
1982	130	418	109	20	2	12	2.9	41	52	36	92	0	.261	.404	1	0	C-129
1983	151	510	138	31	2	24	4.7	56	84	33	93	0	.271	.480	2	0	C-150
1984	150	523	134	24	2	19	3.6	55	94	47	99	5	.256	.419	4	1	C-146
4 yrs.	487	1631	427	80	7	59	3.6	166	251	137	312	5	.262	.428	7	1	C-481

LEAGUE CHAMPIONSHIP SERIES

| 1984 CHI N | 5 | 18 | 7 | 2 | 0 | 2 | 11.1 | 3 | 6 | 0 | 3 | 0 | .389 | .833 | 0 | 0 | C-5 |

John Davis

DAVIS, JOHN HUMPHREY (Red)　　　　　　　　　　BR TR 5'11"　172 lbs.
B. July 15, 1915, Laurel Run, Pa.

1941 NY N	21	70	15	3	0	0	0.0	8	5	8	12	0	.214	.257	0	0	3B-21

Jumbo Davis

DAVIS, JAMES J.　　　　　　　　　　　　　　　　BL TR 5'11"　195 lbs.
B. Sept. 5, 1861, St. Louis, Mo.　D. Feb. 14, 1921, St. Louis, Mo.

	G	AB	H	2B	3B	HR	HR %	R	RBI	BB	SO	SB	BA	SA	AB	H	G by POS
1884 KC U	7	29	6	0	0	0	0.0	3		0			.207	.207	0	0	3B-7
1886 BAL AA	60	216	42	5	2	1	0.5	23		11			.194	.250	0	0	3B-60
1887	130	485	150	23	19	8	1.6	81		28		49	.309	.485	0	0	3B-87, SS-43
1888 KC AA	121	491	131	22	8	3	0.6	70	61	20		42	.267	.363	0	0	3B-113, SS-8
1889 2 teams	KC	AA (62G – .266)			STL	AA (2G – .000)											
" total	64	245	64	4	3	0	0.0	41	30	18	36	25	.261	.302	0	0	3B-62, OF-1, SS-1
1890 2 teams	STL	AA (21G – .254)			B-B	AA (38G – .303)											
" total	59	213	61	12	3	2	0.9	41		24		15	.286	.399	0	0	3B-59
1891 WAS AA	12	44	14	3	2	0	0.0	7	9	7	5	8	.318	.477	0	0	3B-12
7 yrs.	453	1723	468	69	37	14	0.8	266	99	108	41	139	.272	.379	0	0	3B-400, SS-52, OF-1

Kiddo Davis

DAVIS, GEORGE WILLIS　　　　　　　　　　　　BR TR 5'11"　178 lbs.
B. Feb. 12, 1902, Bridgeport, Conn.　D. Apr. 4, 1983, Bridgeport, Conn.

	G	AB	H	2B	3B	HR	HR %	R	RBI	BB	SO	SB	BA	SA	AB	H	G by POS
1926 NY A	1	0	0	0	0	0	–	0	0	0	0	0	–	–	0	0	OF-1
1932 PHI N	137	576	178	39	6	5	0.9	100	57	44	56	16	.309	.424	0	0	OF-133
1933 NY N	126	434	112	20	4	7	1.6	61	37	25	30	10	.258	.371	5	1	OF-120
1934 2 teams	STL	N (16G – .303)			PHI	N (100G – .293)											
" total	116	426	125	28	5	4	0.9	56	52	30	29	2	.293	.411	5	2	OF-109
1935 NY N	47	91	24	7	1	2	2.2	16	6	10	4	2	.264	.429	21	5	OF-21
1936	47	67	16	1	0	0	0.0	6	5	6	5	0	.239	.254	9	1	OF-22
1937 2 teams	NY	N (56G – .263)			CIN	N (40G – .257)											
" total	96	212	55	16	0	1	0.5	39	14	26	13	2	.259	.349	13	4	OF-72
1938 CIN N	5	18	5	0	0	0	0.0	3	0	1	4	0	.278	.333	0	0	OF-5
8 yrs.	575	1824	515	112	16	19	1.0	281	171	142	141	32	.282	.393	53	13	OF-483

WORLD SERIES

1933 NY N	5	19	7	1	0	0	0.0	1	0	0	3	0	.368	.421	0	0	OF-5
1936	4	2	1	0	0	0	0.0	2	0	0	0	0	.500	.500	2	1	
2 yrs.	9	21	8	1	0	0	0.0	3	0	0	3	0	.381	.429	2	1	OF-5

Lefty Davis

DAVIS, ALFONZO　　　　　　　　　　　　　　　BL TL 5'10"　170 lbs.
B. Feb. 4, 1875, Nashville, Tenn.　D. Feb. 4, 1919, Collins, N. Y.

	G	AB	H	2B	3B	HR	HR %	R	RBI	BB	SO	SB	BA	SA	AB	H	G by POS
1901 2 teams	BKN	N (25G – .209)			PIT	N (87G – .313)											
" total	112	426	124	10	11	2	0.5	98	40	66		26	.291	.380	1	0	OF-110, 2B-1
1902 PIT N	59	232	65	7	3	0	0.0	52	20	35		19	.280	.336	0	0	OF-59
1903 NY A	104	372	88	10	0	0	0.0	54	25	43		11	.237	.263	2	0	OF-102, SS-1
1907 CIN N	73	266	61	5	5	1	0.4	28	25	23		9	.229	.297	2	0	OF-70
4 yrs.	348	1296	338	32	19	3	0.2	232	110	167		65	.261	.322	5	0	OF-341, SS-1, 2B-1

Mike Davis

DAVIS, MICHAEL DWAYNE　　　　　　　　　　　BL TL 6'2"　175 lbs.
B. June 11, 1959, San Diego, Calif.

	G	AB	H	2B	3B	HR	HR %	R	RBI	BB	SO	SB	BA	SA	AB	H	G by POS
1980 OAK A	51	95	20	2	1	1	1.1	11	8	7	14	2	.211	.284	22	4	OF-18, 1B-7, DH-6
1981	17	20	1	1	0	0	0.0	2	4	0	2	0	.050	.100	10	0	DH-3, OF-2, 1B-1
1982	23	75	30	4	0	1	1.3	12	10	2	8	3	.400	.493	4	1	OF-13, 1B-7
1983	128	443	122	24	4	8	1.8	61	62	27	74	32	.275	.402	6	3	OF-121, DH-3
1984	134	382	88	18	3	9	2.4	47	46	31	66	14	.230	.364	6	2	OF-127, DH-4
5 yrs.	353	1015	261	49	8	19	1.9	131	126	69	166	51	.257	.377	48	10	OF-281, DH-16, 1B-15

LEAGUE CHAMPIONSHIP SERIES

| 1981 OAK A | 1 | 1 | 1 | 0 | 0 | 0 | 0.0 | 0 | 0 | 0 | 0 | 0 | 1.000 | 1.000 | 1 | 1 | |

Odie Davis

DAVIS, ODIE ERNEST　　　　　　　　　　　　　BR TR 6'1"　178 lbs.
B. Aug. 13, 1955, San Antonio, Tex.

1980 TEX A	17	8	1	0	0	0	0.0	0	0	0	2	0	.125	.125	1	1	SS-13, 3B-1

Otis Davis

DAVIS, OTIS ALLEN (Scat)　　　　　　　　　　　BL TR 6'　160 lbs.
B. Sept. 24, 1920, Charleston, Ark.

1946 BKN N	1	0	0	0	0	0	0.0	1	0	0	0	0	–	–	0	0	

Ron Davis

DAVIS, RONALD EVERETTE　　　　　　　　　　　BR TR 6'　175 lbs.
B. Oct. 21, 1941, Roanoke Rapids, N. C.

	G	AB	H	2B	3B	HR	HR %	R	RBI	BB	SO	SB	BA	SA	AB	H	G by POS
1962 HOU N	6	14	3	0	0	0	0.0	1	1	1	7	1	.214	.214	0	0	OF-5
1966	48	194	48	10	1	2	1.0	21	19	13	26	2	.247	.340	0	0	OF-48
1967	94	285	73	19	1	7	2.5	31	38	17	48	5	.256	.404	15	3	OF-80
1968 2 teams	HOU	N (52G – .212)			STL	N (33G – .177)											
" total	85	296	60	14	3	1	0.3	33	17	18	65	1	.203	.280	0	0	OF-77
1969 PIT N	62	64	15	1	1	0	0.0	10	4	7	14	0	.234	.281	8	3	OF-51
5 yrs.	295	853	199	44	6	10	1.2	96	79	56	160	9	.233	.334	23	6	OF-261

WORLD SERIES

| 1968 STL N | 2 | 7 | 0 | 0 | 0 | 0 | 0.0 | 0 | 0 | 0 | 2 | 0 | .000 | .000 | 0 | 0 | OF-2 |

	G	AB	H	2B	3B	HR	HR %	R	RBI	BB	SO	SB	BA	SA	Pinch Hit AB	H	G by POS

Spud Davis

DAVIS, VIRGIL LAWRENCE
B. Dec. 20, 1904, Birmingham, Ala.   D. Aug. 14, 1984, Birmingham, Ala.
Manager 1946.
BR TR 6'1"   197 lbs.

		G	AB	H	2B	3B	HR	HR%	R	RBI	BB	SO	SB	BA	SA	AB	H	G by POS
1928	2 teams	STL	N (2G – .200)			PHI	N (67G – .282)											
"	total	69	168	47	2	0	3	1.8	17	19	16	11	0	.280	.345	17	4	C-51
1929	PHI N	98	263	90	18	0	7	2.7	31	48	19	17	1	.342	.490	7	3	C-98
1930		106	329	103	16	1	14	4.3	41	65	17	20	1	.313	.495	9	2	C-96
1931		120	393	128	32	1	4	1.0	30	51	36	28	0	.326	.443	5	0	C-114
1932		125	402	135	23	5	14	3.5	44	70	40	39	1	.336	.522	5	3	C-120
1933		141	495	173	28	3	9	1.8	51	65	32	24	2	.349	.473	6	2	C-132
1934	STL N	107	347	104	22	4	9	2.6	45	65	34	27	0	.300	.464	11	3	C-94
1935		102	315	100	24	2	1	0.3	28	60	33	30	0	.317	.416	13	4	C-81, 1B-5
1936		112	363	99	26	2	4	1.1	24	59	35	34	0	.273	.388	7	2	C-103, 3B-2
1937	CIN N	76	209	56	10	1	3	1.4	19	33	23	15	0	.268	.368	13	5	C-59
1938	2 teams	CIN	N (12G – .167)			PHI	N (70G – .247)											
"	total	82	251	59	8	0	2	0.8	14	24	19	20	1	.235	.291	8	1	C-74
1939	PHI N	87	202	62	8	1	0	0.0	10	23	24	20	0	.307	.356	2	1	C-85
1940	PIT N	99	285	93	14	1	5	1.8	23	39	35	20	0	.326	.435	10	3	C-87
1941		57	107	27	4	1	0	0.0	3	6	11	11	0	.252	.308	7	2	C-49
1944		54	93	28	7	0	2	2.2	6	14	10	8	0	.301	.441	17	8	C-35
1945		23	33	8	2	0	0	0.0	2	6	2	2	0	.242	.303	9	2	C-13
16 yrs.		1458	4255	1312	244	22	77	1.8	388	647	386	326	6	.308	.430	146	45	C-1291, 1B-5, 3B-2

WORLD SERIES

| 1934 | STL N | 2 | 2 | 2 | 0 | 0 | 0 | 0.0 | 0 | 1 | 0 | 0 | 0 | 1.000 | 1.000 | 2 | 2 | |

Steve Davis

DAVIS, STEVEN MICHAEL
B. Dec. 30, 1953, Oakland, Calif.
BR TR 6'1"   200 lbs.

| 1979 | CHI N | 3 | 4 | 0 | 0 | 0 | 0 | 0.0 | 0 | 1 | 0 | 0 | 0 | .000 | .000 | 0 | 0 | 2B-2, 3B-1 |

Tod Davis

DAVIS, THOMAS OSCAR
B. July 24, 1924, Los Angeles, Calif.   D. Dec. 31, 1978, West Covina, Calif.
BR TR 6'2"   190 lbs.

1949	PHI A	31	75	20	0	1	1	1.3	7	6	9	16	0	.267	.333	7	3	SS-14, 3B-12, 2B-1
1951		11	15	1	0	0	0	0.0	0	0	1	3	0	.067	.067	7	1	2B-2, 3B-1
2 yrs.		42	90	21	0	1	1	1.1	7	6	10	19	0	.233	.289	14	3	SS-14, 3B-13, 2B-3

Tommy Davis

DAVIS, HERMAN THOMAS
B. Mar. 21, 1939, Brooklyn, N. Y.
BR TR 6'2"   195 lbs.

		G	AB	H	2B	3B	HR	HR%	R	RBI	BB	SO	SB	BA	SA	AB	H	G by POS
1959	LA N	1	1	0	0	0	0	0.0	0	0	0	1	0	.000	.000	1	0	
1960		110	352	97	18	1	11	3.1	43	44	13	35	6	.276	.426	21	7	OF-87, 3B-5
1961		132	460	128	13	2	15	3.3	60	58	32	53	10	.278	.413	10	3	OF-86, 3B-59
1962		163	665	230	27	9	27	4.1	120	153	33	65	18	.346	.535	2	0	OF-146, 3B-39
1963		146	556	181	19	3	16	2.9	69	88	29	59	15	.326	.457	3	0	OF-129, 3B-40
1964		152	592	163	20	5	14	2.4	70	86	29	68	11	.275	.397	4	2	OF-148
1965		17	60	15	1	1	0	0.0	3	9	2	4	2	.250	.300	1	0	OF-16
1966		100	313	98	11	1	3	1.0	27	27	16	36	3	.313	.383	22	5	OF-79, 3B-2
1967	NY N	154	577	174	32	0	16	2.8	72	73	31	71	9	.302	.440	4	0	OF-149, 1B-1
1968	CHI A	132	456	122	5	3	8	1.8	30	50	16	48	4	.268	.344	12	4	OF-116, 1B-6
1969	2 teams	SEA	A (123G – .271)			HOU	N (24G – .241)											
"	total	147	533	142	32	1	7	1.3	54	89	38	55	20	.266	.370	16	7	OF-133, 1B-1
1970	3 teams	HOU	N (57G – .282)			OAK	A (66G – .290)		CHI	N (11G – .262)								
"	total	134	455	129	23	3	6	1.3	45	65	16	44	10	.284	.387	23	5	OF-108, 1B-8
1971	OAK A	79	219	71	8	1	3	1.4	26	42	15	19	7	.324	.411	28	13	1B-35, OF-16, 2B-3, 3B-2
1972	2 teams	CHI	N (15G – .269)			BAL	A (26G – .256)											
"	total	41	108	28	4	0	0	0.0	12	12	8	21	2	.259	.296	15	3	OF-20, 1B-6
1973	BAL A	137	552	169	20	3	7	1.3	53	89	30	56	11	.306	.391	6	4	DH-127, 1B-4
1974		158	626	181	20	1	11	1.8	67	84	34	49	6	.289	.377	4	1	DH-155
1975		116	460	130	14	1	6	1.3	43	57	23	52	2	.283	.357	4	1	DH-111
1976	2 teams	CAL	A (72G – .265)			KC	A (8G – .263)											
"	total	80	238	63	5	0	3	1.3	17	26	16	18	0	.265	.324	21	8	DH-56, 1B-1
18 yrs.		1999	7223	2121	272	35	153	2.1	811	1052	381	754	136	.294	.405	197	63	OF-1233, DH-449, 3B-147, 1B-62, 2B-3

LEAGUE CHAMPIONSHIP SERIES

1971	OAK A	3	8	3	1	0	0	0.0	1	0	0	0	0	.375	.500	1	0	1B-2
1973	BAL A	5	21	6	1	0	0	0.0	1	2	1	0	0	.286	.333	0	0	DH-5
1974		4	15	4	0	0	0	0.0	0	1	0	1	0	.267	.267	0	0	DH-4
3 yrs.		12	44	13	2	0	0	0.0	2	3	1	1	0	.295	.341	1	0	DH-9, 1B-2

WORLD SERIES

1963	LA N	4	15	6	0	2	0	0.0	0	2	0	2	1	.400	.667	0	0	OF-4
1966		4	8	2	0	0	0	0.0	0	0	1	1	0	.250	.250	2	2	OF-3
2 yrs.		8	23	8	0	2	0	0.0	0	2	1	3	1	.348	.522	2	2	OF-7

Willie Davis

DAVIS, WILLIE HENRY
B. Apr. 15, 1940, Mineral Springs, Ark.
BL TL 5'11"   180 lbs.

		G	AB	H	2B	3B	HR	HR%	R	RBI	BB	SO	SB	BA	SA	AB	H	G by POS
1960	LA N	22	88	28	6	1	2	2.3	12	10	4	12	3	.318	.477	0	0	OF-22
1961		128	339	86	19	6	12	3.5	56	45	27	46	12	.254	.451	9	1	OF-114
1962		157	600	171	18	10	21	3.5	103	85	42	72	32	.285	.453	0	0	OF-156
1963		156	515	126	19	8	9	1.7	60	60	25	61	25	.245	.365	4	2	OF-153
1964		157	613	180	23	7	12	2.0	91	77	22	59	42	.294	.413	1	0	OF-155
1965		142	558	133	24	3	10	1.8	52	57	14	81	25	.238	.346	2	1	OF-141
1966		153	624	177	31	6	11	1.8	74	61	15	68	21	.284	.405	0	0	OF-152
1967		143	569	146	27	9	6	1.1	65	41	29	65	20	.257	.367	6	1	OF-138
1968		160	643	160	24	10	7	1.1	86	31	31	88	36	.250	.351	2	1	OF-158
1969		129	498	155	23	8	11	2.2	66	59	33	39	24	.311	.456	4	0	OF-125
1970		146	593	181	23	16	8	1.3	92	93	29	54	38	.305	.438	4	0	OF-143
1971		158	641	198	33	10	10	1.6	84	74	23	47	20	.309	.438	3	1	OF-157
1972		149	615	178	22	7	19	3.1	81	79	27	61	20	.289	.441	2	0	OF-146
1973		152	599	171	29	9	16	2.7	82	77	29	62	17	.285	.444	7	3	OF-146

	G	AB	H	2B	3B	HR	HR %	R	RBI	BB	SO	SB	BA	SA	Pinch Hit AB	Pinch Hit H	G by POS

Willie Davis continued

		G	AB	H	2B	3B	HR	HR %	R	RBI	BB	SO	SB	BA	SA	PH AB	PH H	G by POS
1974	MON N	153	611	180	27	9	12	2.0	86	89	27	69	25	.295	.427	5	2	OF-151
1975	2 teams		TEX A (42G – .249)				STL N (98G – .291)											
"	total	140	519	144	27	8	11	2.1	57	67	18	52	23	.277	.424	12	3	OF-131
1976	SD N	141	493	132	18	10	5	1.0	61	46	19	34	14	.268	.375	12	2	OF-128
1979	CAL A	43	56	14	2	1	0	0.0	9	2	4	7	1	.250	.321	24	5	OF-7, DH-6
18 yrs.		2429	9174	2561	395	138	182	2.0	1217	1053	418	977	398	.279	.412	97	23	OF-2323, DH-6

LEAGUE CHAMPIONSHIP SERIES

		G	AB	H	2B	3B	HR	HR %	R	RBI	BB	SO	SB	BA	SA	PH AB	PH H	G by POS
1979	CAL A	2	2	1	1	0	0	0.0	1	0	0	0	0	.500	1.000	2	1	

WORLD SERIES

		G	AB	H	2B	3B	HR	HR %	R	RBI	BB	SO	SB	BA	SA	PH AB	PH H	G by POS
1963	LA N	4	12	2	2	0	0	0.0	2	3	0	6	0	.167	.333	0	0	OF-4
1965		7	26	6	0	0	0	0.0	3	0	0	2	3	.231	.231	0	0	OF-7
1966		4	16	1	0	0	0	0.0	0	0	0	4	0	.063	.063	0	0	OF-4
3 yrs.		15	54	9	2	0	0	0.0	5	3	0	12	3	.167	.204	0	0	OF-15

Andre Dawson

DAWSON, ANDRE NOLAN (Hawk)
B. July 7, 1954, Miami, Fla.   BR TR 6'3"   180 lbs.

		G	AB	H	2B	3B	HR	HR %	R	RBI	BB	SO	SB	BA	SA	PH AB	PH H	G by POS
1976	MON N	24	85	20	4	1	0	0.0	9	7	5	13	1	.235	.306	0	0	OF-24
1977		139	525	148	26	9	19	3.6	64	65	34	93	21	.282	.474	5	0	OF-136
1978		157	609	154	24	8	25	4.1	84	72	30	128	28	.253	.442	5	2	OF-153
1979		155	639	176	24	12	25	3.9	90	92	27	115	35	.275	.468	0	0	OF-153
1980		151	577	178	41	7	17	2.9	96	87	44	69	34	.308	.492	3	1	OF-147
1981		103	394	119	21	3	24	6.1	71	64	35	50	26	.302	.553	0	0	OF-103
1982		148	608	183	37	7	23	3.8	107	83	34	96	39	.301	.498	0	0	OF-147
1983		159	633	189	36	10	32	5.1	104	113	38	81	25	.299	.539	1	1	OF-157
1984		138	533	132	23	6	17	3.2	73	86	41	80	13	.248	.409	4	0	OF-134
9 yrs.		1174	4603	1299	236	63	182	4.0	698	669	288	725	222	.282	.479	18	4	OF-1154

DIVISIONAL PLAYOFF SERIES

		G	AB	H	2B	3B	HR	HR %	R	RBI	BB	SO	SB	BA	SA	PH AB	PH H	G by POS
1981	MON N	5	20	6	0	1	0	0.0	1	0	1	6	2	.300	.400	0	0	OF-5

LEAGUE CHAMPIONSHIP SERIES

		G	AB	H	2B	3B	HR	HR %	R	RBI	BB	SO	SB	BA	SA	PH AB	PH H	G by POS
1981	MON N	5	20	3	0	0	0	0.0	2	0	0	4	0	.150	.150	0	0	OF-5

Boots Day

DAY, CHARLES FREDERICK
B. Aug. 31, 1947, Ilion, N. Y.   BL TL 5'9"   160 lbs.

		G	AB	H	2B	3B	HR	HR %	R	RBI	BB	SO	SB	BA	SA	PH AB	PH H	G by POS
1969	STL N	11	6	0	0	0	0	0.0	1	0	1	1	0	.000	.000	5	0	OF-1
1970	2 teams	52	CHI N (11G – .250)				MON N (41G – .269)											
"	total	52	116	31	4	0	0	0.0	16	5	6	21	3	.267	.302	13	4	OF-42
1971	MON N	127	371	105	10	2	4	1.1	53	33	33	39	9	.283	.353	15	5	OF-120
1972		128	386	90	7	4	0	0.0	32	30	29	44	3	.233	.272	17	5	OF-117
1973		101	207	57	7	0	4	1.9	36	28	21	28	0	.275	.367	48	13	OF-51
1974		52	65	12	0	0	0	0.0	8	2	5	8	0	.185	.185	31	3	OF-16
6 yrs.		471	1151	295	28	6	8	0.7	146	98	95	141	15	.256	.312	129	30	OF-347

Brian Dayett

DAYETT, BRIAN KELLY
B. Jan. 22, 1957, New London, Conn.   BR TR 5'10"   180 lbs.

		G	AB	H	2B	3B	HR	HR %	R	RBI	BB	SO	SB	BA	SA	PH AB	PH H	G by POS
1983	NY A	11	29	6	0	1	0	0.0	3	5	2	4	0	.207	.276	3	1	OF-9
1984		64	127	31	9	0	4	3.1	14	23	9	14	0	.244	.409	7	3	OF-62, DH-1
2 yrs.		75	156	37	9	1	4	2.6	17	28	11	18	0	.237	.385	10	4	OF-71, DH-1

Charlie Deal

DEAL, CHARLES ALBERT
B. Oct. 30, 1891, Wilkinsburg, Pa.   D. Sept. 16, 1979, Covina, Calif.   BR TR 5'11"   160 lbs.

		G	AB	H	2B	3B	HR	HR %	R	RBI	BB	SO	SB	BA	SA	PH AB	PH H	G by POS
1912	DET A	41	142	32	4	2	0	0.0	13	11	9		4	.225	.282	0	0	3B-41
1913	2 teams	26	DET A (16G – .220)				BOS N (10G – .306)											
"	total	26	86	22	1	2	0	0.0	9	6	3	8	3	.256	.314	1	0	3B-15, 2B-10
1914	BOS N	79	257	54	13	2	0	0.0	17	23	20	23	4	.210	.276	4	0	3B-74, SS-1
1915	STL F	65	223	72	12	4	1	0.4	21	27	12		10	.323	.426	0	0	3B-65
1916	2 teams	25	STL A (23G – .135)				CHI N (2G – .250)											
"	total	25	82	12	2	0	0	0.0	9	13	6	8	4	.146	.171	0	0	3B-24, 2B-1
1917	CHI N	135	449	114	11	3	0	0.0	46	47	19	18	10	.254	.292	5	1	3B-130
1918		119	414	99	9	3	2	0.5	43	34	21	13	11	.239	.290	1	0	3B-118
1919		116	405	117	23	5	2	0.5	37	52	12	12	11	.289	.385	0	0	3B-116
1920		129	450	108	10	5	3	0.7	48	39	20	14	5	.240	.304	1	1	3B-128
1921		115	422	122	19	8	3	0.7	52	66	13	9	3	.289	.393	2	0	3B-113
10 yrs.		850	2930	752	104	34	11	0.4	295	318	135	105	65	.257	.327	14	2	3B-824, 2B-11, SS-1

WORLD SERIES

		G	AB	H	2B	3B	HR	HR %	R	RBI	BB	SO	SB	BA	SA	PH AB	PH H	G by POS
1914	BOS N	4	16	2	2	0	0	0.0	1	0	0	0	2	.125	.250	0	0	3B-4
1918	CHI N	6	17	3	0	0	0	0.0	0	0	0	1	0	.176	.176	0	0	3B-6
2 yrs.		10	33	5	2	0	0	0.0	1	0	0	1	2	.152	.212	0	0	3B-10

Lindsay Deal

DEAL, LINDSAY FRED
B. Sept. 3, 1911, Lenoir, N. C.   D. Apr. 18, 1979, Little Rock, Ark.   BL TR 6'   175 lbs.

		G	AB	H	2B	3B	HR	HR %	R	RBI	BB	SO	SB	BA	SA	PH AB	PH H	G by POS
1939	BKN N	4	7	0	0	0	0	0.0	0	0	0	2	0	.000	.000	3	0	OF-1

Snake Deal

DEAL, JOHN WESLEY
B. Jan. 21, 1879, Lancaster, Pa.   D. May 9, 1944, Harrisburg, Pa.   BR TR 6'   164 lbs.

		G	AB	H	2B	3B	HR	HR %	R	RBI	BB	SO	SB	BA	SA	PH AB	PH H	G by POS
1906	CIN N	65	231	48	4	3	0	0.0	13	21	6		15	.208	.251	0	0	1B-65

Pat Dealy

DEALY, PATRICK E.
B. Moosup, Conn.   D. Dec. 17, 1924, Buffalo, N. Y.   BR TR

		G	AB	H	2B	3B	HR	HR %	R	RBI	BB	SO	SB	BA	SA	PH AB	PH H	G by POS
1884	STP U	5	15	2	0	0	0	0.0	2		0			.133	.133	0	0	C-4, OF-1
1885	BOS N	35	130	29	4	1	1	0.8	18	9	2	14		.223	.292	0	0	C-29, 3B-3, OF-2, SS-2, 1B-1
1886		15	46	15	1	1	0	0.0	9	3	4	4		.326	.391	0	0	C-14, OF-1
1887	WAS N	58	312	85	8	2	1	0.3	33	18	8	8	36	.272	.321	0	0	C-28, SS-23, OF-5, 3B-5

	G	AB	H	2B	3B	HR	HR %	R	RBI	BB	SO	SB	BA	SA	Pinch Hit AB	Pinch Hit H	G by POS

Pat Dealy continued

	G	AB	H	2B	3B	HR	HR %	R	RBI	BB	SO	SB	BA	SA	AB	H	G by POS
1890 SYR AA	18	66	12	1	0	0	0.0	9		5		4	.182	.197	0	0	C-10, 3B-6, OF-2
5 yrs.	131	569	143	14	4	2	0.4	71	29	19	26	40	.251	.301	0	0	C-85, SS-25, 3B-14, OF-11, 1B-1

Chubby Dean

DEAN, ALFRED LOVILL
B. Aug. 24, 1916, Mt. Airy, N. C.   D. Dec. 21, 1970, Riverside, N. J.   BL TL 5'11"   181 lbs.

	G	AB	H	2B	3B	HR	HR %	R	RBI	BB	SO	SB	BA	SA	AB	H	G by POS
1936 PHI A	111	342	98	21	3	1	0.3	41	48	24	24	3	.287	.374	34	13	1B-77
1937	104	309	81	14	4	2	0.6	36	31	42	10	2	.262	.353	23	6	1B-78, P-2
1938	16	20	6	2	0	0	0.0	3	1	1	4	0	.300	.400	9	2	P-6
1939	80	77	27	4	0	0	0.0	12	19	8	4	0	.351	.403	26	10	P-54
1940	67	90	26	2	0	0	0.0	6	6	16	9	0	.289	.311	28	9	P-30, 1B-1
1941 2 teams		PHI	A	(27G –	.237)		CLE	A	(17G –	.167)							
" total	44	62	13	3	0	0	0.0	2	11	7	5	0	.210	.258	14	2	P-26, 1B-1
1942 CLE A	70	101	27	1	0	0	0.0	4	7	11	7	0	.267	.277	37	5	P-27
1943	41	46	9	0	0	0	0.0	2	5	6	2	0	.196	.196	20	2	P-17
8 yrs.	533	1047	287	47	7	3	0.3	106	128	115	65	5	.274	.341	191	49	P-162, 1B-157

Tommy Dean

DEAN, TOMMY DOUGLAS
B. Aug. 30, 1945, Iuka, Miss.   BR TR 6'   165 lbs.

	G	AB	H	2B	3B	HR	HR %	R	RBI	BB	SO	SB	BA	SA	AB	H	G by POS
1967 LA N	12	28	4	1	0	0	0.0	1	2	0	9	0	.143	.179	0	0	SS-12
1969 SD N	101	273	48	9	2	2	0.7	14	9	27	54	0	.176	.245	0	0	SS-97, 2B-2
1970	61	158	35	5	1	2	1.3	18	13	11	29	2	.222	.304	1	1	SS-55
1971	41	70	8	0	0	0	0.0	2	1	4	13	1	.114	.114	2	1	SS-28, 3B-11, 2B-1
4 yrs.	215	529	95	15	3	4	0.8	35	25	42	105	3	.180	.242	3	2	SS-192, 3B-11, 2B-3

Wayland Dean

DEAN, WAYLAND OGDEN
B. June 20, 1903, Richwood, W. Va.
D. Apr. 10, 1930, Huntington, W. Va.   BB TR 6'2"   178 lbs.   BL 1926-27

	G	AB	H	2B	3B	HR	HR %	R	RBI	BB	SO	SB	BA	SA	AB	H	G by POS
1924 NY N	26	40	8	0	0	2	5.0	5	4	1	9	0	.200	.350	0	0	P-26
1925	33	51	12	2	1	1	2.0	7	7	3	12	0	.235	.373	0	0	P-33
1926 PHI N	63	102	27	4	0	3	2.9	11	19	5	26	0	.265	.392	26	6	P-33
1927 2 teams		PHI	N	(3G –	.667)		CHI	N	(2G –	.000)							
" total	5	3	2	0	0	0	0.0	1	1	0	0	0	.667	1.333	1	0	P-4
4 yrs.	127	196	49	6	2	6	3.1	24	31	9	47	0	.250	.393	27	6	P-96
WORLD SERIES																	
1924 NY N	1	0	0	0	0	0	–	0	0	0	0	0	–	–	0	0	P-1

Buddy Dear

DEAR, PAUL STANFORD
B. Dec. 1, 1905, Norfolk, Va.   BR TR 5'8"   143 lbs.

	G	AB	H	2B	3B	HR	HR %	R	RBI	BB	SO	SB	BA	SA	AB	H	G by POS
1927 WAS A	2	1	0	0	0	0	0.0	1	0	0	0	0	.000	.000	0	0	2B-1

Charlie DeArmond

DeARMOND, CHARLES HOMMER (Hummer)
B. Feb. 13, 1877, Okeana, Ohio   D. Dec. 17, 1933, Morning Sun, Ohio   BR TR 5'10"   165 lbs.

	G	AB	H	2B	3B	HR	HR %	R	RBI	BB	SO	SB	BA	SA	AB	H	G by POS
1903 CIN N	11	39	11	2	1	0	0.0	10	7	3		1	.282	.385	0	0	3B-11

Jim Deasley

DEASLEY, JOHN
Brother of Pat Deasley.
B. Philadelphia, Pa.   D. Dec. 25, 1910, Philadelphia, Pa.

	G	AB	H	2B	3B	HR	HR %	R	RBI	BB	SO	SB	BA	SA	AB	H	G by POS
1884 2 teams		WAS	U	(31G –	.216)		KC	U	(13G –	.175)							
" total	44	174	36	3	1	0	0.0	23		5			.207	.236	0	0	SS-44

Pat Deasley

DEASLEY, THOMAS H.
Brother of Jim Deasley.
B. Nov. 17, 1857, Ireland   D. Apr. 1, 1943, Philadelphia, Pa.   BR TR 5'8½"   154 lbs.

	G	AB	H	2B	3B	HR	HR %	R	RBI	BB	SO	SB	BA	SA	AB	H	G by POS
1881 BOS N	43	147	35	5	2	0	0.0	13	8	5	10		.238	.299	0	0	C-28, OF-7, SS-7, 1B-2
1882	67	264	70	8	0	0	0.0	36	29	7	22		.265	.295	0	0	C-56, OF-14, SS-1
1883 STL AA	58	206	53	2	1	0	0.0	27		6			.257	.277	0	0	C-56, OF-2
1884	75	254	52	5	4	0	0.0	27		7			.205	.256	0	0	C-75, OF-2, 1B-1
1885 NY N	54	207	53	5	1	0	0.0	22		9	20		.256	.290	0	0	C-54, OF-2, SS-1
1886	41	143	38	6	1	0	0.0	18	17	4	12		.266	.322	0	0	C-30, OF-15
1887	30	118	37	5	0	0	0.0	12	23	9	7	3	.314	.356	0	0	C-24, 3B-7, SS-1
1888 WAS N	34	127	20	1	0	0	0.0	6	4	2	18	2	.157	.165	0	0	C-31, OF-1, SS-1, 2B-1
8 yrs.	402	1466	358	37	9	0	0.0	161	81	49	89	5	.244	.282	0	0	C-354, OF-43, SS-11, 3B-7, 1B-3, 2B-1

Hank DeBerry

DeBERRY, JOHN HERMAN
B. Dec. 29, 1893, Savannah, Tenn.   D. Sept. 10, 1951, Savannah, Tenn.   BR TR 5'11"   195 lbs.

	G	AB	H	2B	3B	HR	HR %	R	RBI	BB	SO	SB	BA	SA	AB	H	G by POS
1916 CLE A	15	33	9	4	0	0	0.0	7	4	6	9	0	.273	.394	1	0	C-14
1917	25	33	9	2	0	0	0.0	3	1	2	7	0	.273	.333	14	3	C-9
1922 BKN N	85	259	78	10	1	3	1.2	29	35	20	9	4	.301	.382	3	1	C-81
1923	78	235	67	11	6	1	0.4	21	48	20	12	2	.285	.396	13	3	C-60
1924	77	218	53	10	3	3	1.4	20	26	20	21	0	.243	.358	12	2	C-63
1925	67	193	50	8	1	2	1.0	26	24	16	8	2	.259	.342	11	1	C-55
1926	48	115	33	11	0	0	0.0	6	13	8	5	0	.287	.383	10	2	C-37
1927	68	201	47	3	2	1	0.5	15	21	17	8	1	.234	.284	1	1	C-67
1928	82	258	65	8	2	0	0.0	19	23	18	15	3	.252	.298	2	0	C-80
1929	68	210	55	11	1	1	0.5	13	25	17	15	1	.262	.338	0	0	C-68
1930	35	95	28	3	0	0	0.0	11	14	4	10	0	.295	.326	0	0	C-35
11 yrs.	648	1850	494	81	16	11	0.6	170	234	148	119	13	.267	.346	67	13	C-569

Adam DeBus

DeBUS, ADAM JOSEPH
B. Oct. 7, 1892, Chicago, Ill.   D. May 13, 1977, Chicago, Ill.   BR TR 5'10½"   150 lbs.

	G	AB	H	2B	3B	HR	HR %	R	RBI	BB	SO	SB	BA	SA	AB	H	G by POS
1917 PIT N	38	131	30	5	4	0	0.0	9	7	7	14	2	.229	.328	0	0	SS-21, 3B-18

	G	AB	H	2B	3B	HR	HR %	R	RBI	BB	SO	SB	BA	SA	Pinch Hit AB	H	G by POS

Doug DeCinces

DeCINCES, DOUGLAS VERNON
B. Aug. 29, 1950, Burbank, Calif.　　　　　　　　BR TR 6'2"　190 lbs.

	G	AB	H	2B	3B	HR	HR %	R	RBI	BB	SO	SB	BA	SA	AB	H	G by POS
1973 BAL A	10	18	2	0	0	0	0.0	2	3	1	5	0	.111	.111	0	0	3B-8, 2B-2, SS-1
1974	1	1	0	0	0	0	0.0	0	0	1	0	0	.000	.000	0	0	3B-1
1975	61	167	42	6	3	4	2.4	20	23	13	32	0	.251	.395	7	1	3B-34, SS-13, 2B-11, 1B-2
1976	129	440	103	17	2	11	2.5	36	42	29	68	8	.234	.357	2	0	3B-109, 2B-17, 1B-11, SS-2, DH-1
1977	150	522	135	28	3	19	3.6	63	69	64	86	8	.259	.433	1	0	3B-148, DH-1, 2B-1, 1B-1
1978	142	511	146	37	1	28	5.5	72	80	46	81	7	.286	.526	0	0	3B-130, 2B-12
1979	120	422	97	27	1	16	3.8	67	61	54	68	5	.230	.412	0	0	3B-120
1980	145	489	122	23	2	16	3.3	64	64	49	83	11	.249	.403	3	0	3B-142, 1B-1
1981	100	346	91	23	2	13	3.8	49	55	41	32	0	.263	.454	1	0	3B-100, OF-1, 1B-1
1982 CAL A	153	575	173	42	5	30	5.2	94	97	66	80	7	.301	.548	0	0	3B-153, SS-2
1983	95	370	104	19	3	18	4.9	49	65	32	56	2	.281	.495	1	0	3B-84, DH-10
1984	146	547	147	23	3	20	3.7	77	82	53	79	4	.269	.431	1	0	3B-140, DH-5
12 yrs.	1252	4408	1162	245	25	175	4.0	593	641	449	670	52	.264	.450	16	1	3B-1169, 2B-43, SS-18, DH-17, 1B-16, OF-1

LEAGUE CHAMPIONSHIP SERIES

	G	AB	H	2B	3B	HR	HR %	R	RBI	BB	SO	SB	BA	SA	AB	H	G by POS
1979 BAL A	4	13	4	1	0	0	0.0	4	3	1	1	0	.308	.385	0	0	3B-4
1982 CAL A	5	19	6	2	0	0	0.0	5	0	1	5	0	.316	.421	0	0	3B-5
2 yrs.	9	32	10	3	0	0	0.0	9	3	2	6	0	.313	.406	0	0	3B-9

WORLD SERIES

	G	AB	H	2B	3B	HR	HR %	R	RBI	BB	SO	SB	BA	SA	AB	H	G by POS
1979 BAL A	7	25	5	0	0	1	4.0	2	3	5	5	1	.200	.320	0	0	3B-7

Frank Decker

DECKER, FRANK
B. Feb. 26, 1853, St. Louis, Mo.　　D. Feb. 5, 1940, St. Louis, Mo.　　BR TR

	G	AB	H	2B	3B	HR	HR %	R	RBI	BB	SO	SB	BA	SA	AB	H	G by POS
1879 SYR N	3	10	1	0	0	0	0.0	0		0	3		.100	.100	0	0	C-2, OF-1, 1B-1
1882 STL AA	2	8	2	0	0	0	0.0	0					.250	.250	0	0	2B-2
2 yrs.	5	18	3	0	0	0	0.0	0		0	3		.167	.167	0	0	2B-2, C-2, OF-1, 1B-1

George Decker

DECKER, GEORGE A.
B. June 1, 1869, York, Pa.　　D. June 9, 1909, Compton, Calif.

	G	AB	H	2B	3B	HR	HR %	R	RBI	BB	SO	SB	BA	SA	AB	H	G by POS
1892 CHI N	78	291	66	6	7	1	0.3	32	28	20	49	9	.227	.306	0	0	OF-62, 2B-16
1893	81	328	89	9	8	2	0.6	57	48	24	22	22	.271	.366	0	0	OF-33, 1B-27, 2B-20, SS-2
1894	91	384	120	17	6	8	2.1	74	92	24	17	23	.313	.451	4	1	1B-48, OF-29, 3B-7, 2B-2, SS-1
1895	73	297	82	9	7	2	0.7	51	41	17	22	11	.276	.374	0	0	OF-57, 1B-11, 3B-3, SS-1, 2B-1
1896	107	421	118	23	11	5	1.2	68	61	23	14	20	.280	.423	0	0	OF-71, 1B-36
1897	111	428	124	12	7	5	1.2	72	63	24		11	.290	.386	1	0	OF-75, 1B-38, 2B-1
1898 2 teams		STL N (76G – .259)				LOU N (42G – .297)											
" total	118	434	118	14	3	1	0.2	53	64	29		13	.272	.325	5	2	1B-107, OF-6
1899 2 teams		LOU N (38G – .267)				WAS N (4G – .000)											
" total	42	144	36	8	0	1	0.7	13	18	12		3	.250	.326	1	0	1B-40, OF-1
8 yrs.	701	2727	753	98	49	25	0.9	420	415	173	124	112	.276	.376	11	3	OF-334, 1B-307, 2B-40, 3B-10, SS-4

Harry Decker

DECKER, EARL HARRY
B. Sept. 3, 1854, Lockport, Ill.　　Deceased.　　　　BR TR

	G	AB	H	2B	3B	HR	HR %	R	RBI	BB	SO	SB	BA	SA	AB	H	G by POS
1884 2 teams		IND AA (4G – .267)				KC U (23G – .133)											
" total	27	90	14	3	0	0	0.0	9		6			.156	.189	0	0	OF-16, C-15
1886 2 teams		DET N (14G – .222)				WAS N (7G – .217)											
" total	21	77	17	2	1	0	0.0	2	7	3	14		.221	.273	0	0	C-18, 3B-2, OF-1, SS-1
1889 PHI N	11	30	3	0	0	0	0.0	4	2	2	5	1	.100	.100	0	0	2B-7, C-3, OF-1
1890 2 teams		PHI N (5G – .368)				PIT N (92G – .274)											
" total	97	373	104	15	3	5	1.3	57	40	30	37	12	.279	.375	0	0	C-71, 1B-18, OF-6, SS-1, 2B-1
4 yrs.	156	570	138	20	4	5	0.9	72	48	41	56	13	.242	.318	0	0	C-107, OF-24, 1B-18, 2B-8, SS-2, 3B-2

Artie Dede

DEDE, ARTHUR RICHARD
B. July 12, 1895, Brooklyn, N. Y.　　D. Sept. 6, 1971, Keene, N. H.　　BR TR 5'9"　155 lbs.

	G	AB	H	2B	3B	HR	HR %	R	RBI	BB	SO	SB	BA	SA	AB	H	G by POS
1916 BKN N	1	1	0	0	0	0	0.0	0	0	0	0	0	.000	.000	0	0	C-1

Raoul Dedeaux

DEDEAUX, RAOUL (Rod)
B. Feb. 17, 1915, New Orleans, La.　　　　BR TR 5'11"　160 lbs.

	G	AB	H	2B	3B	HR	HR %	R	RBI	BB	SO	SB	BA	SA	AB	H	G by POS
1935 BKN N	2	4	1	0	0	0	0.0	0	1	0	0	0	.250	.250	0	0	SS-2

Jim Dee

DEE, JAMES D.
B. Buffalo, N. Y.　　Deceased.

	G	AB	H	2B	3B	HR	HR %	R	RBI	BB	SO	SB	BA	SA	AB	H	G by POS
1884 PIT AA	12	40	5	0	0	0	0.0	0		1			.125	.125	0	0	SS-12

Shorty Dee

DEE, MAURICE LEO
B. Oct. 4, 1889, Halifax, Canada　　D. Aug. 12, 1971, Jamaica Plains, Mass.　　BR TR

	G	AB	H	2B	3B	HR	HR %	R	RBI	BB	SO	SB	BA	SA	AB	H	G by POS
1915 STL A	1	3	0	0	0	0	0.0	1	0	1	0	0	.000	.000	0	0	SS-1

Rob Deer

DEER, ROBERT GEORGE
B. Sept. 29, 1960, Orange, Calif.　　　　BR TR 6'3"　215 lbs.

	G	AB	H	2B	3B	HR	HR %	R	RBI	BB	SO	SB	BA	SA	AB	H	G by POS
1984 SF N	13	24	4	0	0	3	12.5	5	3	7	10	1	.167	.542	3	0	OF-9

Charlie Dees

DEES, CHARLES HENRY
B. June 24, 1935, Birmingham, Ala.　　　　BL TL 6'1"　173 lbs.

	G	AB	H	2B	3B	HR	HR %	R	RBI	BB	SO	SB	BA	SA	AB	H	G by POS
1963 LA A	60	202	62	11	1	3	1.5	23	27	11	31	3	.307	.416	4	1	1B-56
1964	26	26	2	1	0	0	0.0	3	1	1	4	1	.077	.115	6	1	1B-12
1965 CAL A	12	32	5	0	0	0	0.0	1	1	1	8	1	.156	.156	4	0	1B-8
3 yrs.	98	260	69	12	1	3	1.2	27	29	13	43	5	.265	.354	14	2	1B-76

	G	AB	H	2B	3B	HR	HR %	R	RBI	BB	SO	SB	BA	SA	Pinch Hit AB	Pinch Hit H	G by POS

Tony DeFate

DeFATE, CLYDE HERBERT — BR TR 5'8½" 158 lbs.
B. Feb. 22, 1898, Kansas City, Mo. D. Sept. 3, 1963, New Orleans, La.

	G	AB	H	2B	3B	HR	HR %	R	RBI	BB	SO	SB	BA	SA	AB	H	G by POS
1917 **2 teams**		STL N (14G – .143)				DET A (3G – .000)											
" total	17	16	2	0	0	0	0.0	1	1	4	6	0	.125	.125	6	1	3B-5, 2B-2

Art DeFreites

DeFREITES, ARTURO SIMON — BR TR 6'2" 195 lbs.
B. Apr. 26, 1953, San Pedro de Macoris, Dominican Republic

	G	AB	H	2B	3B	HR	HR %	R	RBI	BB	SO	SB	BA	SA	AB	H	G by POS
1978 CIN N	9	19	4	1	0	1	5.3	1	2	1	4	0	.211	.421	2	1	1B-6
1979	23	34	7	2	0	0	0.0	2	4	0	16	0	.206	.265	17	3	1B-6, OF-1
2 yrs.	32	53	11	3	0	1	1.9	3	6	1	20	0	.208	.321	19	4	1B-12, OF-1

Rube DeGroff

DeGROFF, EDWARD ARTHUR — 5'11"
B. Sept. 2, 1879, Hyde Park, N. Y. D. Dec. 17, 1955, Poughkeepsie, N. Y.

	G	AB	H	2B	3B	HR	HR %	R	RBI	BB	SO	SB	BA	SA	AB	H	G by POS
1905 STL N	15	56	14	2	1	0	0.0	3	5	5		1	.250	.321	0	0	OF-15
1906	1	4	0	0	0	0	0.0	1	0	0		0	.000	.000	0	0	OF-1
2 yrs.	16	60	14	2	1	0	0.0	4	5	5		1	.233	.300	0	0	OF-16

Herman Dehlman

DEHLMAN, HERMAN J.
B. 1850, Catasauqua, Pa. D. Mar. 13, 1885, Wilkes-Barre, Pa.
Manager 1876.

	G	AB	H	2B	3B	HR	HR %	R	RBI	BB	SO	SB	BA	SA	AB	H	G by POS
1876 STL N	64	245	45	6	0	0	0.0	40	9	9	10		.184	.208	0	0	1B-64
1877	32	119	22	4	0	0	0.0	24	11	7	21		.185	.218	0	0	1B-31, OF-1
2 yrs.	96	364	67	10	0	0	0.0	64	20	16	31		.184	.212	0	0	1B-95, OF-1

Jim Deidel

DEIDEL, JAMES LAWRENCE — BR TR 6'2" 195 lbs.
B. June 6, 1949, Denver, Colo.

	G	AB	H	2B	3B	HR	HR %	R	RBI	BB	SO	SB	BA	SA	AB	H	G by POS
1974 NY A	2	2	0	0	0	0	0.0	0	0	0	0	0	.000	.000	0	0	C-2

Pep Deininger

DEININGER, OTTO CHARLES — BL TL 5'8½" 180 lbs.
B. Oct. 10, 1877, Wasseralfingen, Germany D. Sept. 25, 1950, Boston, Mass.

	G	AB	H	2B	3B	HR	HR %	R	RBI	BB	SO	SB	BA	SA	AB	H	G by POS
1902 BOS A	2	6	2	1	0	0	0.0	0	0	0		0	.333	.833	0	0	P-2
1908 PHI N	1	0	0	0	0	0	–	0	0	0	0	0	–	–	0	0	OF-1
1909	55	169	44	9	0	0	0.0	22	16	11		5	.260	.314	6	0	OF-45, 2B-1
3 yrs.	58	175	46	10	0	0	0.0	22	16	11		5	.263	.331	6	0	OF-46, P-2, 2B-1

Pat Deisel

DEISEL, EDWARD — BR TR 5'10" 180 lbs.
B. Apr. 9, 1876, Ripley, Ohio D. Apr. 17, 1948, Cincinnati, Ohio

	G	AB	H	2B	3B	HR	HR %	R	RBI	BB	SO	SB	BA	SA	AB	H	G by POS
1902 BKN N	1	3	2	0	0	0	0.0	0	1	1		0	.667	.667	0	0	C-1
1903 CIN N	2	0	0	0	0	0	–	0	0	1		0	–	–	0	0	C-1
2 yrs.	3	3	2	0	0	0	0.0	0	1	2		0	.667	.667	0	0	C-2

Mike Dejan

DEJAN, MICHAEL DAN — BL TL 6'1" 185 lbs.
B. Jan. 13, 1915, Cleveland, Ohio D. Feb. 2, 1953, West Los Angeles, Calif.

	G	AB	H	2B	3B	HR	HR %	R	RBI	BB	SO	SB	BA	SA	AB	H	G by POS
1940 CIN N	12	16	3	0	1	0	0.0	1	2	3	3	0	.188	.313	8	1	OF-2

Ivan DeJesus

DeJESUS, IVAN — BR TR 5'11" 175 lbs.
Also known as Ivan Alvarez.
B. Jan. 9, 1953, Santurce, Puerto Rico

	G	AB	H	2B	3B	HR	HR %	R	RBI	BB	SO	SB	BA	SA	AB	H	G by POS
1974 LA N	3	3	1	0	0	0	0.0	1	0	0	2	0	.333	.333	1	0	SS-2
1975	63	87	16	2	1	0	0.0	10	2	11	15	1	.184	.230	2	0	SS-63
1976	22	41	7	2	0	0	0.0	4	2	4	9	0	.171	.268	1	0	SS-13, 3B-7
1977 CHI N	155	624	166	31	7	3	0.5	91	40	56	90	24	.266	.353	0	0	SS-154
1978	160	619	172	24	7	3	0.5	104	35	74	78	41	.278	.354	0	0	SS-160
1979	160	636	180	26	10	5	0.8	92	52	59	82	24	.283	.379	0	0	SS-160
1980	157	618	160	26	3	3	0.5	78	33	60	81	44	.259	.325	0	0	SS-156
1981	106	403	78	8	4	0	0.0	49	13	46	61	21	.194	.233	0	0	SS-106
1982 PHI N	161	536	128	21	5	3	0.6	53	59	54	70	14	.239	.313	0	0	SS-154, 3B-7
1983	158	497	126	15	7	4	0.8	60	45	53	77	11	.254	.336	0	0	SS-158
1984	144	435	112	15	3	0	0.0	40	35	43	76	12	.257	.306	2	0	SS-141
11 yrs.	1289	4499	1146	170	48	21	0.5	582	316	460	641	192	.255	.328	6	0	SS-1267, 3B-14
LEAGUE CHAMPIONSHIP SERIES																	
1983 PHI N	4	12	3	0	0	0	0.0	1	3	3	0		.250	.250	0	0	SS-4
WORLD SERIES																	
1983 PHI N	5	16	2	0	0	0	0.0	0	0	1	2	0	.125	.125	0	0	SS-5

Mark DeJohn

DeJOHN, MARK STEPHEN — BB TR 5'11" 170 lbs.
B. Sept. 18, 1953, Middletown, Conn.

	G	AB	H	2B	3B	HR	HR %	R	RBI	BB	SO	SB	BA	SA	AB	H	G by POS
1982 DET A	24	21	4	2	0	0	0.0	1	1	4	4	1	.190	.286	0	0	SS-20, 3B-4, 2B-1

Bill DeKoning

DeKONING, WILLIAM CALLAHAN — BR TR 5'11" 185 lbs.
B. Dec. 19, 1918, Brooklyn, N. Y. D. July 26, 1979, Palm Harbor, Fla.

	G	AB	H	2B	3B	HR	HR %	R	RBI	BB	SO	SB	BA	SA	AB	H	G by POS
1945 NY N	3	1	0	0	0	0	0.0	0	0	0	1	0	.000	.000	1	0	C-2

Ed Delahanty

DELAHANTY, EDWARD JAMES (Big Ed) — BR TR 6'1" 170 lbs.
Brother of Joe Delahanty. Brother of Frank Delahanty.
Brother of Jim Delahanty. Brother of Tom Delahanty.
B. Oct. 30, 1867, Cleveland, Ohio D. July 2, 1903, Niagara Falls, N. Y.
Hall of Fame 1945.

	G	AB	H	2B	3B	HR	HR %	R	RBI	BB	SO	SB	BA	SA	AB	H	G by POS
1888 PHI N	74	290	66	12	2	1	0.3	40	31	12	26	38	.228	.293	0	0	2B-56, OF-17
1889	56	246	72	13	3	0	0.0	37	27	14	17	19	.293	.370	0	0	OF-31, 2B-24, SS-1
1890 CLE P	115	517	154	26	13	3	0.6	107	64	24	30	25	.298	.416	0	0	SS-76, 2B-20, OF-18, 3B-3, 1B-1
1891 PHI N	128	543	132	19	9	4	0.7	92	86	33	50	25	.243	.333	0	0	OF-99, 1B-27, 2B-3
1892	123	477	146	30	21	6	1.3	79	91	31	32	29	.306	.495	0	0	OF-121, 3B-4
1893	132	595	219	35	18	19	3.2	145	146	47	20	37	.368	.583	0	0	OF-117, 2B-15, 1B-6
1894	114	497	199	36	16	4	0.8	149	131	60	16	21	.400	.561	0	0	OF-88, 1B-12, 3B-9, SS-8, 2B-6

	G	AB	H	2B	3B	HR	HR %	R	RBI	BB	SO	SB	BA	SA	Pinch Hit AB	H	G by POS

Ed Delahanty continued

	G	AB	H	2B	3B	HR	HR %	R	RBI	BB	SO	SB	BA	SA	AB	H	G by POS
1895	116	481	192	**49**	10	11	2.3	149	106	86	31	46	.399	.611	0	0	OF-103, SS-9, 2B-6, 3B-1
1896	123	499	198	**44**	17	13	2.6	131	**126**	62	22	37	.397	**.631**	1	1	OF-99, 1B-22, 2B-1
1897	129	530	200	40	15	5	0.9	109	96	60			26	.377	.538	0	0	OF-129, 1B-1
1898	144	548	183	36	9	4	0.7	115	92	77			58	.334	.454	0	0	OF-144
1899	145	573	**234**	56	9	9	1.6	133	**137**	55			31	**.408**	**.585**	3	2	OF-143
1900	131	539	174	32	10	2	0.4	82	109	41			16	.323	.430	1	0	1B-130
1901	139	538	192	**39**	16	8	1.5	106	108	65			29	.357	.533	0	0	OF-84, 1B-58
1902 WAS A	123	473	178	**43**	14	10	2.1	103	93	62			16	**.376**	**.590**	0	0	OF-111, 1B-13
1903	42	156	52	11	1	1	0.6	22	21	12			3	.333	.436	1	0	OF-40, 1B-1
16 yrs.	1834	7502	2591	521	183	100	1.3	1599	1464	741	244	456	.345 4th	.504	6	3	OF-1344, 1B-271, 2B-131, SS-94, 3B-17

Frank Delahanty

DELAHANTY, FRANK GEORGE (Pudgie)   BR TR 5'9" 160 lbs.
Brother of Jim Delahanty.   Brother of Ed Delahanty.
Brother of Tom Delahanty.   Brother of Joe Delahanty.
B. Dec. 29, 1885, Cleveland, Ohio   D. July 22, 1966, Cleveland, Ohio

	G	AB	H	2B	3B	HR	HR %	R	RBI	BB	SO	SB	BA	SA	AB	H	G by POS
1905 NY A	9	27	6	1	0	0	0.0	0	2	1		0	.222	.259	1	0	1B-5, OF-3
1906	92	307	73	11	8	2	0.7	37	41	16		11	.238	.345	5	2	OF-92
1907 CLE A	15	52	9	0	1	0	0.0	3	4	4		2	.173	.212	0	0	OF-15
1908 NY A	37	125	32	1	2	0	0.0	12	10	10		9	.256	.296	1	0	OF-36
1914 2 teams		BUF	F (79G – .201)			PIT	F (41G – .239)										
" total	120	433	93	8	11	3	0.7	54	34	34		28	.215	.305	1	0	OF-114, 2B-4
1915 PIT F	14	42	10	1	0	0	0.0	3	3	1		0	.238	.262	2	0	OF-11
6 yrs.	287	986	223	22	22	5	0.5	109	94	66		50	.226	.308	10	2	OF-271, 1B-5, 2B-4

Jim Delahanty

DELAHANTY, JAMES CHRISTOPHER   BR TR 5'10½" 170 lbs.
Brother of Ed Delahanty.   Brother of Frank Delahanty.
Brother of Tom Delahanty.   Brother of Joe Delahanty.
B. June 20, 1879, Cleveland, Ohio   D. Oct. 17, 1953, Cleveland, Ohio

	G	AB	H	2B	3B	HR	HR %	R	RBI	BB	SO	SB	BA	SA	AB	H	G by POS
1901 CHI N	17	63	12	2	0	0	0.0	4	4	3		5	.190	.222	0	0	3B-17, 2B-1
1902 NY N	7	26	6	1	0	0	0.0	3	3	1		0	.231	.269	0	0	OF-7
1904 BOS N	142	499	142	27	8	3	0.6	56	60	27		16	.285	.389	0	0	3B-113, 2B-18, OF-9, P-1
1905	125	461	119	11	8	5	1.1	50	55	28		12	.258	.349	1	0	OF-124, P-1
1906 CIN N	115	379	106	21	4	1	0.3	63	39	45		21	.280	.364	3	1	3B-105, SS-5, OF-2
1907 2 teams		STL	A (33G – .221)			WAS	A (109G – .292)										
" total	142	499	139	21	7	2	0.4	52	60	41		24	.279	.361	8	0	2B-70, 3B-48, OF-13, 1B-4
1908 WAS A	83	287	91	11	4	1	0.3	33	30	24		16	.317	.394	2	0	2B-79
1909 2 teams		WAS	A (90G – .222)			DET	A (46G – .253)										
" total	136	452	105	23	6	1	0.2	47	41	40		13	.232	.316	5	0	2B-131
1910 DET A	106	378	111	16	3	2	0.5	67	45	43		15	.294	.368	0	0	2B-106
1911	144	542	184	30	14	3	0.6	83	94	56		15	.339	.463	1	0	1B-72, 2B-59, 3B-12
1912	78	266	76	14	1	0	0.0	34	41	42		9	.286	.346	1	0	2B-44, OF-33
1914 BKN F	74	214	62	13	5	0	0.0	28	15	25		4	.290	.397	13	2	2B-55, 1B-5
1915	17	25	6	1	0	0	0.0	0	2	3		1	.240	.280	11	1	2B-4
13 yrs.	1186	4091	1159	191	60	18	0.4	520	489	378		151	.283	.373	45	4	2B-567, 3B-295, OF-188, 1B-81, SS-5, P-2

WORLD SERIES

	G	AB	H	2B	3B	HR	HR %	R	RBI	BB	SO	SB	BA	SA	AB	H	G by POS
1909 DET A	7	26	9	4	0	0	0.0	2	4	2	5	0	.346	.500	0	0	2B-7

Joe Delahanty

DELAHANTY, JOSEPH NICHOLAS   BR TR 5'9" 168 lbs.
Brother of Tom Delahanty.   Brother of Jim Delahanty.
Brother of Frank Delahanty.   Brother of Ed Delahanty.
B. Oct. 18, 1875, Cleveland, Ohio   D. Jan. 9, 1936, Cleveland, Ohio

	G	AB	H	2B	3B	HR	HR %	R	RBI	BB	SO	SB	BA	SA	AB	H	G by POS
1907 STL N	6	21	7	0	0	1	4.8	3	2	0		3	.333	.476	0	0	OF-6
1908	140	499	127	14	11	1	0.2	37	44	32		11	.255	.333	1	0	OF-138
1909	123	411	88	16	4	2	0.5	28	54	42		10	.214	.287	10	3	OF-63, 2B-48
3 yrs.	269	931	222	30	15	4	0.4	68	100	74		24	.238	.316	11	3	OF-207, 2B-48

Tom Delahanty

DELAHANTY, THOMAS JAMES   BR TR 5'8" 175 lbs.
Brother of Joe Delahanty.   Brother of Frank Delahanty.
Brother of Jim Delahanty.   Brother of Ed Delahanty.
B. Mar. 9, 1872, Cleveland, Ohio   D. Jan. 10, 1951, Sanford, Fla.

	G	AB	H	2B	3B	HR	HR %	R	RBI	BB	SO	SB	BA	SA	AB	H	G by POS
1894 PHI N	1	4	1	0	0	0	0.0	0	0	0	1	0	.250	.250	0	0	2B-1
1896 2 teams		CLE	N (16G – .232)			PIT	N (1G – .333)										
" total	17	59	14	4	0	0	0.0	12	4	8	4	4	.237	.305	0	0	3B-16, SS-1
1897 LOU N	1	4	1	1	0	0	0.0	1	2	0		0	.250	.500	0	0	2B-1
3 yrs.	19	67	16	5	0	0	0.0	13	6	8	5	4	.239	.313	0	0	3B-16, 2B-2, SS-1

Mike de la Hoz

de la HOZ, MIGUEL ANGEL   BR TR 5'11" 170 lbs.
B. Oct. 2, 1939, Havana, Cuba

	G	AB	H	2B	3B	HR	HR %	R	RBI	BB	SO	SB	BA	SA	AB	H	G by POS
1960 CLE A	49	160	41	6	2	6	3.8	20	23	9	12	0	.256	.431	2	1	SS-38, 3B-8
1961	61	173	45	10	0	3	1.7	20	23	7	10	0	.260	.370	16	2	SS-17, 2B-17, 3B-16
1962	12	12	1	0	0	0	0.0	0	0	0	3	0	.083	.083	12	1	2B-2
1963	67	150	40	10	0	5	3.3	15	25	9	29	0	.267	.433	26	1	2B-34, 3B-6, OF-2, SS-2
1964 MIL N	78	189	55	7	1	4	2.1	25	12	14	22	1	.291	.402	32	11	3B-25, 2B-25, SS-8
1965	81	176	45	3	2	2	1.1	15	11	8	21	0	.256	.330	38	4	SS-41, 3B-22, 2B-10, 1B-1
1966 ATL N	71	110	24	3	0	2	1.8	11	7	5	18	0	.218	.300	37	8	3B-30, 2B-8, SS-1
1967	74	143	29	3	0	3	2.1	10	14	4	14	1	.203	.287	34	8	2B-23, 3B-22, SS-1
1969 CIN N	1	0	0	0	0	0	0.0	0	0	0		0	.000	.000	1	0	
9 yrs.	494	1114	280	42	5	25	2.2	116	115	56	130	2	.251	.365	198	36	3B-129, 2B-119, SS-108, OF-2, 1B-1

Bill DeLancey

DeLANCEY, WILLIAM PINKNEY   BL TR 5'11½" 185 lbs.
B. Nov. 28, 1901, Greensboro, N. C.   D. Nov. 28, 1946, Phoenix, Ariz.

	G	AB	H	2B	3B	HR	HR %	R	RBI	BB	SO	SB	BA	SA	AB	H	G by POS
1932 STL N	8	26	5	0	2	0	0.0	1	2	2	1	0	.192	.346	0	0	C-8
1934	93	253	80	18	3	13	5.1	41	40	41	37	1	.316	.565	15	3	C-77

	G	AB	H	2B	3B	HR	HR %	R	RBI	BB	SO	SB	BA	SA	Pinch Hit AB	Pinch Hit H	G by POS

Bill DeLancey continued

	G	AB	H	2B	3B	HR	HR%	R	RBI	BB	SO	SB	BA	SA	AB	H	G by POS
1935	103	301	84	14	5	6	2.0	37	41	42	34	0	.279	.419	17	4	C-83
1940	15	18	4	0	0	0	0.0	0	2	0	2	0	.222	.222	1	0	C-12
4 yrs.	219	598	173	32	10	19	3.2	79	85	85	74	1	.289	.472	33	7	C-180
WORLD SERIES																	
1934 STL N	7	29	5	3	0	1	3.4	3	4	2	8	0	.172	.379	0	0	C-7

Bill Delaney

DELANEY, WILLIAM L.
B. Mar. 4, 1863, Cincinnati, Ohio   D. Mar. 1, 1942, Canton, Ohio   BR TR

	G	AB	H	2B	3B	HR	HR%	R	RBI	BB	SO	SB	BA	SA	AB	H	G by POS
1890 CLE N	36	116	22	1	1	1	0.9	16	7	21	19	5	.190	.241	0	0	2B-36

Jesus De La Rosa

De La ROSA, JESUS
B. Aug. 5, 1953, Santo Domingo, Dominican Republic   BR TR 6'1"   185 lbs.

	G	AB	H	2B	3B	HR	HR%	R	RBI	BB	SO	SB	BA	SA	AB	H	G by POS
1975 HOU N	3	3	1	1	0	0	0.0	1	0	0	0	0	.333	.667	3	1	

Luis Delgado

DELGADO, LUIS FELIPE
B. Feb. 2, 1954, Hatillo, Puerto Rico   BB TL 5'11"   170 lbs.

	G	AB	H	2B	3B	HR	HR%	R	RBI	BB	SO	SB	BA	SA	AB	H	G by POS
1977 SEA A	13	22	4	0	0	0	0.0	4	2	1	8	0	.182	.182	0	0	OF-13

Bobby Del Greco

DEL GRECO, ROBERT GEORGE
B. Apr. 7, 1933, Pittsburgh, Pa.   BR TR 5'10½"   185 lbs.

	G	AB	H	2B	3B	HR	HR%	R	RBI	BB	SO	SB	BA	SA	AB	H	G by POS
1952 PIT N	99	341	74	14	2	1	0.3	34	20	38	70	6	.217	.279	4	1	OF-93
1956 2 teams		PIT	N (14G –	.200)		STL	N (102G –	.215)									
" total	116	290	62	16	2	7	2.4	33	21	35	53	1	.214	.355	7	0	OF-107, 3B-3
1957 2 teams		CHI	N (20G –	.200)		NY	A (8G –	.429)									
" total	28	47	11	2	0	0	0.0	5	3	12	19	2	.234	.277	6	1	OF-22
1958 NY A	12	5	1	0	0	0	0.0	1	0	1	1	0	.200	.200	0	0	OF-12
1960 PHI N	100	300	71	16	4	10	3.3	48	26	54	64	1	.237	.417	11	3	OF-89
1961 2 teams		PHI	N (41G –	.259)		KC	A (74G –	.230)									
" total	115	351	84	19	1	7	2.0	48	32	42	48	1	.239	.359	9	1	OF-105, 3B-1, 2B-1
1962 KC A	132	338	86	21	1	9	2.7	61	38	49	62	4	.254	.402	6	1	OF-124
1963	121	306	65	7	1	8	2.6	40	29	40	52	1	.212	.320	8	2	OF-110, 3B-2
1965 PHI N	8	4	0	0	0	0	0.0	1	0	0	3	0	.000	.000	2	0	OF-4
9 yrs.	731	1982	454	95	11	42	2.1	271	169	271	372	16	.229	.352	53	9	OF-666, 3B-6, 2B-1

Juan Delis

DELIS, JUAN FRANCISCO
B. Feb. 27, 1928, Santiago, Cuba   BR TR 5'11"   170 lbs.

	G	AB	H	2B	3B	HR	HR%	R	RBI	BB	SO	SB	BA	SA	AB	H	G by POS
1955 WAS A	54	132	25	3	1	0	0.0	12	11	3	15	1	.189	.227	16	2	3B-24, OF-8, 2B-1

Eddie Delker

DELKER, EDWARD ALBERTS
B. Apr. 17, 1907, Palo Alto, Calif.   BR TR 5'10½"   170 lbs.

	G	AB	H	2B	3B	HR	HR%	R	RBI	BB	SO	SB	BA	SA	AB	H	G by POS
1929 STL N	22	40	6	0	0	0	0.0	5	3	2	12	0	.150	.200	2	0	SS-9, 2B-7, 3B-3
1931	1	2	1	1	0	0	0.0	0	2	0	0	0	.500	1.000	0	0	3B-1
1932 2 teams		STL	N (20G –	.119)		PHI	N (30G –	.161)									
" total	50	104	15	5	1	1	1.0	8	9	14	21	0	.144	.240	1	0	2B-37, 3B-5, SS-4
1933 PHI N	25	41	7	3	1	0	0.0	6	1	0	12	0	.171	.293	3	0	2B-17, 3B-4
4 yrs.	98	187	29	9	3	1	0.5	19	15	16	45	0	.155	.251	6	0	2B-61, SS-13, 3B-13

Bert Delmas

DELMAS, ALBERT CHARLES
B. May 20, 1911, San Francisco, Calif.   D. Dec. 4, 1979, Huntington Beach, Calif.   BL TR 5'11"   165 lbs.

	G	AB	H	2B	3B	HR	HR%	R	RBI	BB	SO	SB	BA	SA	AB	H	G by POS
1933 BKN N	12	28	7	0	0	0	0.0	4	0	1	7	0	.250	.250	1	0	2B-10

Garton Del Savio

DEL SAVIO, GARTON ORVILLE
B. Nov. 26, 1913, New York, N. Y.   BR TR 5'9½"   165 lbs.

	G	AB	H	2B	3B	HR	HR%	R	RBI	BB	SO	SB	BA	SA	AB	H	G by POS
1943 PHI N	4	11	1	0	0	0	0.0	0	0	1	0	0	.091	.091	0	0	SS-4

Jim Delsing

DELSING, JAMES HENRY
B. Nov. 13, 1925, Rudolph, Wis.   BL TR 5'10"   175 lbs.

	G	AB	H	2B	3B	HR	HR%	R	RBI	BB	SO	SB	BA	SA	AB	H	G by POS
1948 CHI A	20	63	12	0	0	0	0.0	5	5	5	12	0	.190	.190	4	0	OF-15
1949 NY A	9	20	7	0	1	1	5.0	5	3	1	2	0	.350	.550	4	2	OF-5
1950 2 teams		NY	A (12G –	.400)		STL	A (69G –	.263)									
" total	81	219	59	5	2	0	0.0	27	17	22	23	1	.269	.311	24	8	OF-53
1951 STL A	131	449	112	20	2	8	1.8	59	45	56	39	2	.249	.356	4	1	OF-124
1952 2 teams		STL	A (93G –	.255)		DET	A (33G –	.274)									
" total	126	411	107	15	7	4	1.0	48	49	36	37	4	.260	.360	11	4	OF-117
1953 DET A	138	479	138	26	6	11	2.3	77	62	66	39	1	.288	.436	6	1	OF-133
1954	122	371	92	24	2	6	1.6	39	38	49	38	4	.248	.372	13	5	OF-108
1955	114	356	85	14	2	10	2.8	49	60	48	40	2	.239	.374	14	3	OF-101
1956 2 teams		DET	A (10G –	.000)		CHI	A (55G –	.122)									
" total	65	53	5	3	0	0	0.0	11	2	13	16	1	.094	.151	21	3	OF-32
1960 KC A	16	40	10	3	0	0	0.0	2	5	3	5	0	.250	.325	6	1	OF-10
10 yrs.	822	2461	627	111	21	40	1.6	322	286	299	251	15	.255	.366	107	28	OF-698

Joe DeMaestri

DeMAESTRI, JOSEPH PAUL (Oats)
B. Dec. 9, 1928, San Francisco, Calif.   BR TR 6'   170 lbs.

	G	AB	H	2B	3B	HR	HR%	R	RBI	BB	SO	SB	BA	SA	AB	H	G by POS
1951 CHI A	56	74	15	0	2	1	1.4	8	3	5	11	0	.203	.297	6	1	SS-27, 2B-11, 3B-8
1952 STL A	81	186	42	9	1	1	0.5	13	18	8	25	0	.226	.301	1	0	SS-77, 3B-1, 2B-1
1953 PHI A	111	420	107	17	3	6	1.4	53	35	24	39	0	.255	.352	0	0	SS-108
1954	146	539	124	16	3	8	1.5	49	40	20	63	1	.230	.315	0	0	SS-142, 3B-1, 2B-1
1955 KC A	123	457	114	14	1	6	1.3	42	37	20	47	3	.249	.324	1	1	SS-122
1956	133	434	101	16	1	6	1.4	41	39	25	73	3	.233	.316	1	0	SS-132, 2B-2
1957	135	461	113	14	6	9	2.0	44	33	22	82	6	.245	.360	1	0	SS-134
1958	139	442	97	11	1	6	1.4	32	38	16	84	1	.219	.290	2	1	SS-137
1959	118	352	86	16	5	6	1.7	31	34	28	65	1	.244	.369	2	0	SS-115
1960 NY A	49	35	8	1	0	0	0.0	8	2	9	7	0	.229	.257	7	1	2B-19, SS-17

	G	AB	H	2B	3B	HR	HR %	R	RBI	BB	SO	SB	BA	SA	Pinch Hit AB	Pinch Hit H	G by POS

Joe DeMaestri continued

	G	AB	H	2B	3B	HR	HR%	R	RBI	BB	SO	SB	BA	SA	AB	H	G by POS
1961	30	41	6	0	0	0	0.0	1	2	0	13	0	.146	.146	0	0	SS-18, 2B-5, 3B-4
11 yrs.	1121	3441	813	114	23	49	1.4	322	281	168	511	15	.236	.325	24	4	SS-1029, 2B-39, 3B-14

WORLD SERIES

1960 NY A	4	2	1	0	0	0	0.0	1	0	0	1	0	.500	.500	0	0	SS-3

Frank Demaree

DEMAREE, JOSEPH FRANKLIN
Born Joseph Franklin Dimaria.
B. June 10, 1910, Winters, Calif.   D. Aug. 30, 1958, Los Angeles, Calif.

BR TR 5'11½" 185 lbs.

	G	AB	H	2B	3B	HR	HR%	R	RBI	BB	SO	SB	BA	SA	AB	H	G by POS
1932 CHI N	23	56	14	3	0	0	0.0	4	6	2	7	0	.250	.304	5	1	OF-17
1933	134	515	140	24	6	6	1.2	68	51	22	42	4	.272	.377	0	0	OF-133
1935	107	385	125	19	4	2	0.5	60	66	26	23	6	.325	.410	8	2	OF-98
1936	154	605	212	34	3	16	2.6	93	96	49	30	4	.350	.496	0	0	OF-154
1937	154	615	199	36	6	17	2.8	104	115	57	31	6	.324	.485	0	0	OF-154
1938	129	476	130	15	7	8	1.7	63	62	45	34	1	.273	.384	4	1	OF-125
1939 NY N	150	560	170	27	2	11	2.0	68	79	66	40	2	.304	.418	0	0	OF-150
1940	121	460	139	18	6	7	1.5	68	61	45	39	5	.302	.413	2	1	OF-119
1941 2 teams		NY	N (16G –	.171)		BOS	N	(48G –	.230)								
" total	64	148	32	5	2	2	1.4	23	16	16	6	2	.216	.318	22	3	OF-38
1942 BOS N	64	187	42	5	0	3	1.6	18	24	17	10	2	.225	.299	13	1	OF-49
1943 STL N	39	86	25	2	0	0	0.0	5	9	8	4	1	.291	.314	13	1	OF-23
1944 STL A	16	51	13	2	0	0	0.0	4	6	6	3	0	.255	.294	0	0	OF-16
12 yrs.	1155	4144	1241	190	36	72	1.7	578	591	359	269	33	.299	.415	67	10	OF-1076

WORLD SERIES

	G	AB	H	2B	3B	HR	HR%	R	RBI	BB	SO	SB	BA	SA	AB	H	G by POS
1932 CHI N	2	7	2	0	0	1	14.3	1	4	1	0	0	.286	.714	0	0	OF-2
1935	6	24	6	1	0	2	8.3	2	2	1	4	0	.250	.542	0	0	OF-6
1938	3	10	1	0	0	0	0.0	1	0	1	2	0	.100	.100	0	0	OF-3
1943 STL N	1	1	0	0	0	0	0.0	0	0	0	0	0	.000	.000	1	0	
4 yrs.	12	42	9	1	0	3	7.1	4	6	3	6	0	.214	.452	1	0	OF-11

Billy DeMars

DeMARS, WILLIAM LESTER (Kid)
B. Aug. 26, 1925, Brooklyn, N. Y.

BR TR 5'10" 160 lbs.

	G	AB	H	2B	3B	HR	HR%	R	RBI	BB	SO	SB	BA	SA	AB	H	G by POS
1948 PHI A	18	29	5	0	0	0	0.0	3	1	5	3	0	.172	.172	2	0	SS-9, 3B-1, 2B-1
1950 STL A	61	178	44	5	1	0	0.0	25	13	22	13	0	.247	.287	2	0	SS-54, 3B-5
1951	1	4	1	0	0	0	0.0	1	0	1	0	0	.250	.250	0	0	SS-1
3 yrs.	80	211	50	5	1	0	0.0	29	14	28	16	0	.237	.270	4	0	SS-64, 3B-6, 2B-1

John DeMerit

DeMERIT, JOHN STEPHEN (Thumper)
B. Jan. 8, 1936, West Bend, Wis.

BR TR 6'1½" 195 lbs.

	G	AB	H	2B	3B	HR	HR%	R	RBI	BB	SO	SB	BA	SA	AB	H	G by POS
1957 MIL N	33	34	5	0	0	0	0.0	8	1	0	8	1	.147	.147	6	1	OF-13
1958	3	3	2	0	0	0	0.0	1	0	0	0	0	.667	.667	0	0	OF-2
1959	11	5	1	0	0	0	0.0	4	0	1	2	0	.200	.200	0	0	OF-4
1961	32	74	12	3	0	2	2.7	5	5	5	19	0	.162	.284	6	1	OF-21
1962 NY N	14	16	3	0	0	1	6.3	3	1	2	4	0	.188	.375	1	0	OF-9
5 yrs.	93	132	23	3	0	3	2.3	21	7	8	33	1	.174	.265	13	2	OF-49

WORLD SERIES

	G	AB	H	2B	3B	HR	HR%	R	RBI	BB	SO	SB	BA	SA	AB	H	G by POS
1957 MIL N	1	0	0	0	0	0	–	0	0	0	0	0	–	–	0	0	

Don Demeter

DEMETER, DONALD LEE
B. June 25, 1935, Oklahoma City, Okla.

BR TR 6'4" 190 lbs.

	G	AB	H	2B	3B	HR	HR%	R	RBI	BB	SO	SB	BA	SA	AB	H	G by POS
1956 BKN N	3	3	1	0	0	1	33.3	1	1	0	1	0	.333	1.333	2	0	OF-1
1958 LA N	43	106	20	2	0	5	4.7	11	8	5	32	2	.189	.349	4	0	OF-39
1959	139	371	95	11	1	18	4.9	55	70	16	87	5	.256	.437	22	3	OF-124
1960	64	168	46	7	1	9	5.4	23	29	8	34	0	.274	.488	8	2	OF-62
1961 2 teams	121	LA	N (15G –	.172)		PHI	N	(106G –	.257)								
" total	121	411	103	18	4	21	5.1	57	70	22	80	2	.251	.467	13	2	OF-93, 1B-22
1962 PHI N	153	550	169	24	3	29	5.3	85	107	41	93	2	.307	.520	6	2	3B-105, OF-63, 1B-1
1963	154	515	133	20	2	22	4.3	63	83	31	93	1	.258	.433	11	2	OF-119, 3B-43, 1B-26
1964 DET A	134	441	113	22	1	22	5.0	57	80	17	85	4	.256	.460	27	5	OF-88, 1B-23
1965	122	389	108	16	4	16	4.1	50	58	23	65	4	.278	.463	15	6	OF-81, 1B-34
1966 2 teams	105	DET	A (32G –	.212)		BOS	A	(73G –	.292)								
" total	105	325	87	18	1	14	4.3	43	41	8	61	2	.268	.458	21	2	OF-84, 1B-6
1967 2 teams	71	BOS	A (20G –	.279)		CLE	A	(51G –	.207)								
" total	71	164	37	9	0	6	3.7	22	16	9	27	0	.226	.390	26	7	OF-47, 3B-2
11 yrs.	1109	3443	912	147	17	163	4.7	467	563	180	658	22	.265	.459	155	31	OF-801, 3B-150, 1B-112

WORLD SERIES

	G	AB	H	2B	3B	HR	HR%	R	RBI	BB	SO	SB	BA	SA	AB	H	G by POS
1959 LA N	6	12	3	0	0	0	0.0	2	0	1	3	0	.250	.250	0	0	OF-6

Steve Demeter

DEMETER, STEPHEN
B. Jan. 27, 1935, Homer City, Pa.

BR TR 5'9½" 185 lbs.

	G	AB	H	2B	3B	HR	HR%	R	RBI	BB	SO	SB	BA	SA	AB	H	G by POS
1959 DET A	11	18	2	1	0	0	0.0	1	1	0	1	0	.111	.167	9	1	3B-4
1960 CLE A	4	5	0	0	0	0	0.0	0	0	0	1	0	.000	.000	2	0	3B-3
2 yrs.	15	23	2	1	0	0	0.0	1	1	0	2	0	.087	.130	11	1	3B-7

Harry DeMiller

DeMILLER, HARRY
B. Nov. 12, 1867, Wooster, Ohio   D. Oct. 19, 1928, Santa Ana, Calif.

	G	AB	H	2B	3B	HR	HR%	R	RBI	BB	SO	SB	BA	SA	AB	H	G by POS
1892 STL N	1	4	0	0	0	0	0.0	0		0		0	.000	.000	0	0	3B-1

Ray Demmitt

DEMMITT, CHARLES RAYMOND
B. Feb. 2, 1884, Illiopolis, Ill.   D. Feb. 19, 1956, Glen Ellyn, Ill.

BL TR 5'8½" 170 lbs.

	G	AB	H	2B	3B	HR	HR%	R	RBI	BB	SO	SB	BA	SA	AB	H	G by POS
1909 NY A	123	427	105	12	12	4	0.9	68	30	55		16	.246	.358	0	0	OF-109
1910 STL A	10	23	4	1	0	0	0.0	4	2	3		0	.174	.217	2	0	OF-8
1914 2 teams		DET	A (1G –	.000)		CHI	A	(146G –	.258)								
" total	147	515	133	13	12	2	0.4	63	46	61	48	12	.258	.342	3	1	OF-142
1915 CHI A	9	6	0	0	0	0	0.0	0	0	1	2	0	.000	.000	6	0	OF-3
1917 STL A	14	53	15	1	2	0	0.0	6	7	0	8	1	.283	.377	0	0	OF-14

	G	AB	H	2B	3B	HR	HR %	R	RBI	BB	SO	SB	BA	SA	Pinch Hit AB	Pinch Hit H	G by POS

Ray Demmitt continued

	G	AB	H	2B	3B	HR	HR%	R	RBI	BB	SO	SB	BA	SA	AB	H	G by POS
1918	116	405	114	23	5	1	0.2	45	61	38	35	10	.281	.370	1	0	OF-114
1919	79	202	48	11	2	1	0.5	19	19	14	27	3	.238	.327	27	6	OF-49
7 yrs.	498	1631	419	61	33	8	0.5	205	165	172	120	42	.257	.349	39	7	OF-439

Gene DeMontreville

DeMONTREVILLE, EUGENE
Also appeared in box score as Demont   Brother of Lee DeMontreville.   BR TR 5'8"   165 lbs.
B. Mar. 26, 1874, St. Paul, Minn.   D. Feb. 18, 1935, Memphis, Tenn.

	G	AB	H	2B	3B	HR	HR%	R	RBI	BB	SO	SB	BA	SA	AB	H	G by POS
1894 PIT N	2	8	2	0	0	0	0.0	0	0	1	4	0	.250	.250	0	0	SS-2
1895 WAS N	12	46	10	1	3	0	0.0	7	9	3	4	5	.217	.370	0	0	SS-12
1896	133	533	183	24	5	8	1.5	94	77	29	27	28	.343	.452	0	0	SS-133
1897	133	566	197	27	8	3	0.5	92	93	21		30	.348	.440	1	1	SS-99, 2B-33
1898 BAL N	151	567	186	19	2	0	0.0	93	86	52		49	.328	.369	0	0	2B-123, SS-28
1899 2 teams	CHI	N	(82G –	.281)		BAL	N	(60G –	.279)								
" total	142	550	154	19	7	1	0.2	83	76	27		47	.280	.345	0	0	SS-82, 2B-60
1900 BKN N	69	234	57	8	1	0	0.0	34	28	10		21	.244	.286	1	0	2B-48, SS-12, 3B-7, OF-1, 1B-1
1901 BOS N	140	570	173	14	4	5	0.9	83	72	17		25	.304	.368	0	0	2B-120, 3B-20
1902	124	481	129	16	5	0	0.0	51	53	12		23	.268	.322	2	0	2B-112, SS-10
1903 WAS A	12	44	12	2	0	0	0.0	0	3	0		0	.273	.318	0	0	2B-11, SS-1
1904 STL A	4	9	1	0	0	0	0.0	0	0	0		2	.111	.111	1	0	2B-3
11 yrs.	922	3608	1104	130	35	17	0.5	537	497	174	35	228	.306	.376	5	1	2B-510, SS-379, 3B-27, OF-1, 1B-1

Lee DeMontreville

DeMONTREVILLE, LEON
Brother of Gene DeMontreville.   BR TR 5'7"   140 lbs.
B. Sept. 23, 1879, St. Paul, Minn.   D. Mar. 22, 1962, Pelham Manor, N. Y.

	G	AB	H	2B	3B	HR	HR%	R	RBI	BB	SO	SB	BA	SA	AB	H	G by POS
1903 STL N	26	70	17	3	1	0	0.0	8	7	8		3	.243	.314	5	1	SS-15, 2B-4, OF-1

Rick Dempsey

DEMPSEY, JOHN RIKARD   BR TR 6'   180 lbs.
B. Sept. 13, 1949, Fayetteville, Tenn.

	G	AB	H	2B	3B	HR	HR%	R	RBI	BB	SO	SB	BA	SA	AB	H	G by POS
1969 MIN A	5	6	3	1	0	0	0.0	1	0	1	0	0	.500	.667	1	0	C-3
1970	5	7	0	0	0	0	0.0	1	0	1	1	0	.000	.000	1	0	C-3
1971	6	13	4	1	0	0	0.0	2	0	1	1	0	.308	.385	0	0	C-6
1972	25	40	8	1	0	0	0.0	0	0	6	8	0	.200	.225	2	1	C-23
1973 NY A	6	11	2	0	0	0	0.0	0	0	1	3	0	.182	.182	0	0	C-5
1974	43	109	26	3	0	2	1.8	12	12	8	7	1	.239	.321	12	2	C-31, OF-2, DH-1
1975	71	145	38	8	0	1	0.7	18	11	21	15	0	.262	.338	23	5	C-19, DH-18, OF-8, 3B-1
1976 2 teams	NY	A	(21G –	.119)		BAL	A	(59G –	.213)								
" total	80	216	42	0	0	0	0.0	12	12	18	21	1	.194	.204	6	1	C-67, OF-7
1977 BAL A	91	270	61	7	4	3	1.1	27	34	34	34	2	.226	.315	1	1	C-91
1978	136	441	114	25	0	6	1.4	41	32	48	54	7	.259	.356	4	1	C-135
1979	124	368	88	23	0	6	1.6	48	41	38	37	0	.239	.351	39	11	C-124
1980	119	362	95	26	3	9	2.5	51	40	36	45	3	.262	.425	9	1	C-112, OF-6, 1B-2, DH-1
1981	92	251	54	10	1	6	2.4	24	25	32	36	0	.215	.335	7	0	C-90, DH-1
1982	125	344	88	15	1	5	1.5	35	36	46	37	0	.256	.349	8	3	C-124, DH-1
1983	128	347	80	16	2	4	1.2	33	32	40	54	1	.231	.323	7	0	C-128
1984	109	330	76	11	0	11	3.3	37	34	40	58	1	.230	.364	0	0	C-108
16 yrs.	1165	3260	779	149	11	53	1.6	342	299	371	411	16	.239	.340	120	26	C-1069, OF-23, DH-22, 1B-2, 3B-1

LEAGUE CHAMPIONSHIP SERIES
	G	AB	H	2B	3B	HR	HR%	R	RBI	BB	SO	SB	BA	SA	AB	H	G by POS
1979 BAL A	3	10	4	2	0	0	0.0	3	2	1	0	1	.400	.600	0	0	C-3
1983	4	12	2	0	0	0	0.0	1	0	1	1	0	.167	.167	0	0	C-4
2 yrs.	7	22	6	2	0	0	0.0	4	2	2	1	1	.273	.364	0	0	C-7

WORLD SERIES
	G	AB	H	2B	3B	HR	HR%	R	RBI	BB	SO	SB	BA	SA	AB	H	G by POS
1979 BAL A	7	21	6	2	0	0	0.0	1	0	1	3	0	.286	.381	0	0	C-6
1983	5	13	5	4	0	1	7.7	3	2	2	2	0	.385	.923	0	0	C-5
2 yrs.	12	34	11	6	0	1	2.9	6	2	3	5	0	.324	.588	0	0	C-11

Tod Dennehey

DENNEHEY, THOMAS FRANCIS   BL TL 5'10"   180 lbs.
B. May 12, 1899, Philadelphia, Pa.   D. Aug. 8, 1977, Philadelphia, Pa.

	G	AB	H	2B	3B	HR	HR%	R	RBI	BB	SO	SB	BA	SA	AB	H	G by POS
1923 PHI N	9	24	7	2	0	0	0.0	4	2	1	3	0	.292	.375	0	0	OF-9

Otto Denning

DENNING, OTTO GEORGE (Dutch)   BR TR 6'   180 lbs.
B. Dec. 28, 1912, Hays, Kans.

	G	AB	H	2B	3B	HR	HR%	R	RBI	BB	SO	SB	BA	SA	AB	H	G by POS
1942 CLE A	92	214	45	14	0	1	0.5	15	19	18	14	0	.210	.290	20	3	C-78, OF-2
1943	37	129	31	6	0	0	0.0	8	13	5	1	3	.240	.287	3	0	1B-34
2 yrs.	129	343	76	20	0	1	0.3	23	32	23	15	3	.222	.289	23	3	C-78, 1B-34, OF-2

Jerry Denny

DENNY, JEREMIAH DENNIS   BR TR 5'11½"   180 lbs.
Born Jeremiah Dennis Eldridge.
B. Mar. 16, 1859, New York, N. Y.   D. Aug. 16, 1927, Houston, Tex.

	G	AB	H	2B	3B	HR	HR%	R	RBI	BB	SO	SB	BA	SA	AB	H	G by POS
1881 PRO N	85	320	77	16	2	1	0.3	38	24	5	44		.241	.313	0	0	3B-85
1882	84	329	81	10	9	2	0.6	54		4	46		.246	.350	0	0	3B-84
1883	98	393	108	26	8	8	2.0	73		9	48		.275	.443	0	0	3B-98
1884	110	439	109	22	9	6	1.4	57		14	58		.248	.380	0	0	3B-99, 1B-9, 2B-3, C-1
1885	83	318	71	14	4	3	0.9	40	25	12	53		.223	.321	0	0	3B-83
1886 STL N	119	475	122	24	6	9	1.9	58	62	14	68		.257	.389	0	0	3B-117, SS-3
1887 IND N	122	510	165	34	12	11	2.2	86	97	13	22	29	.324	.502	0	0	3B-116, SS-4, OF-1, 2B-1
1888	126	524	137	27	7	12	2.3	92	63	9	79	32	.261	.408	0	0	3B-96, SS-25, 2B-5, OF-1, P-1
1889	133	578	163	24	18	18	3.1	96	112	27	63	22	.282	.417	0	0	3B-123, 2B-7, SS-5
1890 NY N	114	437	93	18	7	3	0.7	50	42	28	62	11	.213	.307	0	0	3B-106, SS-7, 2B-1
1891 3 teams	NY	(4G –	.250)		CLE	N	(36G –	.225)		PHI	N	(19G –	.288)				
" total	59	227	56	7	1	0	0.0	22	33	16	32	6	.247	.286	0	0	3B-40, 1B-12, OF-8
1893 LOU N	44	175	43	5	4	1	0.6	22	22	9	15	4	.246	.337	0	0	SS-42, 3B-2

	G	AB	H	2B	3B	HR	HR %	R	RBI	BB	SO	SB	BA	SA	Pinch Hit AB	Pinch Hit H	G by POS

Jerry Denny continued

	G	AB	H	2B	3B	HR	HR%	R	RBI	BB	SO	SB	BA	SA	AB	H	G by POS
1894	60	221	61	11	7	0	0.0	26	32	13	12	10	.276	.389	0	0	3B-60
13 yrs.	1237	4946	1286	238	76	74	1.5	714	512	173	602	114	.260	.384	0	0	3B-1109, SS-86, 1B-21, 2B-17, OF-10, C-1, P-1

Bucky Dent

DENT, RUSSELL EARL
Born Russell Earl O'Dey.
B. Nov. 25, 1951, Savannah, Ga.

BR TR 5'9"   170 lbs.

	G	AB	H	2B	3B	HR	HR%	R	RBI	BB	SO	SB	BA	SA	AB	H	G by POS
1973 CHI A	40	117	29	2	0	0	0.0	17	10	10	18	2	.248	.265	1	0	SS-36, 2B-3, 3B-1
1974	154	496	136	15	3	5	1.0	55	45	28	48	3	.274	.347	0	0	SS-154
1975	157	602	159	29	4	3	0.5	52	58	36	48	2	.264	.341	0	0	SS-157
1976	158	562	138	18	4	2	0.4	44	52	43	45	3	.246	.302	1	0	SS-158
1977 NY A	158	477	118	18	4	8	1.7	54	49	39	28	1	.247	.352	0	0	SS-157
1978	123	379	92	11	1	5	1.3	40	40	23	24	3	.243	.317	0	0	SS-123
1979	141	431	99	14	2	2	0.5	47	32	37	30	0	.230	.285	0	0	SS-141
1980	141	489	128	26	2	5	1.0	57	52	48	37	0	.262	.354	0	0	SS-141
1981	73	227	54	11	0	7	3.1	20	27	19	17	0	.238	.379	0	0	SS-73
1982 2 teams	NY	A (59G – .169)			TEX	A	(46G – .219)										
" total	105	306	59	10	1	1	0.3	27	23	21	21	0	.193	.242	2	0	SS-103
1983 TEX A	131	417	99	15	2	2	0.5	36	34	23	31	3	.237	.297	0	0	SS-129, DH-1
1984 KC A	11	9	3	0	0	0	0.0	2	1	1	2	0	.333	.333	0	0	SS-9, 3B-2
12 yrs.	1392	4512	1114	169	23	40	0.9	451	423	328	349	17	.247	.321	4	0	SS-1381, 3B-3, 2B-3, DH-1

LEAGUE CHAMPIONSHIP SERIES

	G	AB	H	2B	3B	HR	HR%	R	RBI	BB	SO	SB	BA	SA	AB	H	G by POS
1977 NY A	5	14	3	1	0	0	0.0	1	2	1	0	0	.214	.286	0	0	SS-5
1978	4	15	3	0	0	0	0.0	0	4	0	0	0	.200	.200	0	0	SS-4
1980	3	11	2	0	0	0	0.0	0	0	0	1	0	.182	.182	0	0	SS-3
3 yrs.	12	40	8	1	0	0	0.0	1	6	1	1	0	.200	.225	0	0	SS-12

WORLD SERIES

	G	AB	H	2B	3B	HR	HR%	R	RBI	BB	SO	SB	BA	SA	AB	H	G by POS
1977 NY A	6	19	5	0	0	0	0.0	0	2	2	1	0	.263	.263	0	0	SS-6
1978	6	24	10	1	0	0	0.0	3	7	1	2	0	.417	.458	0	0	SS-6
2 yrs.	12	43	15	1	0	0	0.0	3	9	3	3	0	.349	.372	0	0	SS-12

Sam Dente

DENTE, SAMUEL JOSEPH (Blackie)
B. Apr. 26, 1922, Harrison, N. J.

BR TR 5'11"   175 lbs.

	G	AB	H	2B	3B	HR	HR%	R	RBI	BB	SO	SB	BA	SA	AB	H	G by POS
1947 BOS A	46	168	39	4	2	0	0.0	14	11	19	15	0	.232	.280	0	0	3B-46
1948 STL A	98	267	72	11	2	0	0.0	26	22	22	8	1	.270	.326	17	5	SS-76, 3B-6
1949 WAS A	153	590	161	24	4	1	0.2	48	53	31	24	4	.273	.332	0	0	SS-153
1950	155	603	144	20	5	2	0.3	56	59	39	19	1	.239	.299	0	0	SS-128, 2B-29
1951	88	273	65	8	1	0	0.0	21	29	25	10	3	.238	.275	14	2	SS-65, 2B-10, 3B-5
1952 CHI A	62	145	32	0	1	0	0.0	12	11	5	8	0	.221	.234	12	1	SS-27, 3B-18, OF-6, 2B-6, 1B-2
1953	2	0	0	0	0	0	–	0	0	0	0	0	–	–	0	0	SS-1
1954 CLE A	68	169	45	7	1	1	0.6	18	19	14	4	0	.266	.337	1	1	SS-60, 2B-7
1955	73	105	27	4	0	0	0.0	10	10	12	8	0	.257	.295	3	1	SS-53, 3B-13, 2B-4
9 yrs.	745	2320	585	78	16	4	0.2	205	214	167	96	9	.252	.305	47	10	SS-563, 3B-88, 2B-56, OF-6, 1B-2

WORLD SERIES

	G	AB	H	2B	3B	HR	HR%	R	RBI	BB	SO	SB	BA	SA	AB	H	G by POS
1954 CLE A	3	3	0	0	0	0	0.0	1	0	1	0	0	.000	.000	0	0	SS-3

Tony DePhillips

DePHILLIPS, ANTHONY ANDREW
B. Sept. 20, 1912, New York, N. Y.

BR TR 6'2"   185 lbs.

	G	AB	H	2B	3B	HR	HR%	R	RBI	BB	SO	SB	BA	SA	AB	H	G by POS
1943 CIN N	35	20	2	1	0	0	0.0	0	2	1	5	0	.100	.150	0	0	C-35

Gene Derby

DERBY, EUGENE A.
B. Feb., 1860, New Hampshire   D. Oct. 12, 1928, Buffalo, N. Y.

	G	AB	H	2B	3B	HR	HR%	R	RBI	BB	SO	SB	BA	SA	AB	H	G by POS
1885 BAL AA	10	31	4	0	0	0	0.0	4		1				.129	.129	0	0	C-9, OF-1

Bob Dernier

DERNIER, ROBERT EUGENE
B. Jan. 5, 1957, Kansas City, Mo.

BR TR 6'   160 lbs.

	G	AB	H	2B	3B	HR	HR%	R	RBI	BB	SO	SB	BA	SA	AB	H	G by POS
1980 PHI N	10	7	4	0	0	0	0.0	5	1	1	0	3	.571	.571	0	0	OF-3
1981	10	4	3	0	0	0	0.0	0	0	0	0	2	.750	.750	0	0	OF-5
1982	122	370	92	10	2	4	1.1	56	21	36	69	42	.249	.319	1	0	OF-119
1983	122	221	51	10	0	1	0.5	41	15	18	21	35	.231	.290	3	0	OF-107
1984 CHI N	143	536	149	26	5	3	0.6	94	32	63	60	45	.278	.362	2	0	OF-140
5 yrs.	407	1138	299	46	7	8	0.7	196	69	118	150	127	.263	.337	6	0	OF-374

LEAGUE CHAMPIONSHIP SERIES

	G	AB	H	2B	3B	HR	HR%	R	RBI	BB	SO	SB	BA	SA	AB	H	G by POS
1983 PHI N	1	0	0	0	0	0	–	0	0	0	0	0	–	–	0	0	OF-1
1984 CHI N	5	17	4	2	0	1	5.9	5	1	5	4	2	.235	.529	0	0	OF-5
2 yrs.	6	17	4	2	0	1	5.9	5	1	5	4	2	.235	.529	0	0	OF-6

WORLD SERIES

	G	AB	H	2B	3B	HR	HR%	R	RBI	BB	SO	SB	BA	SA	AB	H	G by POS
1983 PHI N	1	0	0	0	0	0	–	1	0	0	0	0	–	–	0	0	

Claud Derrick

DERRICK, CLAUD LESTER (Deek)
B. June 11, 1886, Burton, Ga.   D. July 15, 1974, Clayton, Ga.

BR TR 6'   175 lbs.

	G	AB	H	2B	3B	HR	HR%	R	RBI	BB	SO	SB	BA	SA	AB	H	G by POS
1910 PHI A	1	1	0	0	0	0	0.0	0	0	0		0	.000	.000	0	0	SS-1
1911	36	100	23	1	2	0	0.0	14	5	7		7	.230	.280	1	0	2B-20, SS-6, 1B-3, 3B-2
1912	21	58	14	0	1	0	0.0	7	7	5		1	.241	.276	3	0	SS-18
1913 NY A	22	65	19	1	0	1	1.5	7	7	5	8	2	.292	.354	2	0	SS-14, 3B-4, 2B-1
1914 2 teams	CIN	N	(2G – .333)			CHI	N	(28G – .219)									
" total	30	102	23	4	1	0	0.0	7	14	5	13	3	.225	.284	1	0	SS-30
5 yrs.	110	326	79	6	4	1	0.3	35	33	22	21	13	.242	.294	7	0	SS-69, 2B-21, 3B-6, 1B-3

	G	AB	H	2B	3B	HR	HR %	R	RBI	BB	SO	SB	BA	SA	Pinch Hit AB	Pinch Hit H	G by POS

Jim Derrick

DERRICK, JAMES MICHAEL
B. Sept. 19, 1943, Columbia, S. C.   BL TR 6'   190 lbs.

	G	AB	H	2B	3B	HR	HR%	R	RBI	BB	SO	SB	BA	SA	PH AB	PH H	G by POS
1970 BOS A	24	33	7	1	0	0	0.0	3	5	0	11	0	.212	.242	21	2	OF-2, 1B-1

Russ Derry

DERRY, ALVA RUSSELL
B. Oct. 7, 1916, Princeton, Mo.   BL TR 6'1"   180 lbs.

	G	AB	H	2B	3B	HR	HR%	R	RBI	BB	SO	SB	BA	SA	PH AB	PH H	G by POS
1944 NY A	38	114	29	3	0	4	3.5	14	14	20	19	1	.254	.386	7	5	OF-28
1945	78	253	57	6	2	13	5.1	37	45	31	49	1	.225	.419	9	3	OF-68
1946 PHI A	69	184	38	8	5	0	0.0	17	14	27	54	0	.207	.304	16	3	OF-50
1949 STL N	2	2	0	0	0	0	0.0	0	0	0	2	0	.000	.000	2	0	
4 yrs.	187	553	124	17	7	17	3.1	68	73	78	124	2	.224	.373	34	11	OF-146

Joe DeSa

DeSA, JOSEPH
B. July 7, 1959, Honolulu, Hawaii   BL TL 5'11"   170 lbs.

	G	AB	H	2B	3B	HR	HR%	R	RBI	BB	SO	SB	BA	SA	PH AB	PH H	G by POS
1980 STL N	7	11	3	0	0	0	0.0	0	0	0	2	0	.273	.273	5	2	OF-1, 1B-1

Gene Desautels

DESAUTELS, EUGENE ABRAHAM (Red)
B. June 13, 1907, Worcester, Mass.   BR TR 5'11"   170 lbs.

	G	AB	H	2B	3B	HR	HR%	R	RBI	BB	SO	SB	BA	SA	PH AB	PH H	G by POS
1930 DET A	42	126	24	4	2	0	0.0	13	9	7	9	2	.190	.254	0	0	C-42
1931	3	11	1	0	0	0	0.0	1	0	1	1	0	.091	.091	0	0	C-3
1932	28	72	17	2	0	0	0.0	8	2	13	11	0	.236	.264	3	0	C-24
1933	30	42	6	1	0	0	0.0	5	4	4	6	0	.143	.167	0	0	C-30
1937 BOS A	96	305	74	10	3	0	0.0	33	27	36	26	1	.243	.295	1	1	C-94
1938	108	333	97	16	2	2	0.6	47	48	57	31	1	.291	.369	0	0	C-108
1939	76	226	55	14	0	0	0.0	26	21	33	13	3	.243	.305	2	1	C-73
1940	71	222	50	7	1	0	0.0	19	17	32	13	0	.225	.266	0	0	C-70
1941 CLE A	66	189	38	5	1	1	0.5	20	17	14	12	1	.201	.254	0	0	C-66
1942	62	162	40	5	0	0	0.0	14	9	12	13	1	.247	.278	1	0	C-61
1943	68	185	38	6	1	0	0.0	14	19	11	16	2	.205	.249	2	0	C-66
1945	10	9	1	0	0	0	0.0	1	0	1	1	0	.111	.111	0	0	C-10
1946 PHI A	52	130	28	3	1	0	0.0	10	13	12	16	1	.215	.254	0	0	C-52
13 yrs.	712	2012	469	73	11	3	0.1	211	186	233	168	12	.233	.285	9	2	C-699

Bob Detherage

DETHERAGE, ROBERT WAYNE
B. Sept. 20, 1954, Springfield, Mo.   BR TR 6'   180 lbs.

	G	AB	H	2B	3B	HR	HR%	R	RBI	BB	SO	SB	BA	SA	PH AB	PH H	G by POS
1980 KC A	26	26	8	2	0	1	3.8	2	7	1	4	1	.308	.500	0	0	OF-20

George Detore

DETORE, GEORGE FRANCIS
B. Nov. 11, 1906, Utica, N. Y.   BR TR 5'8"   170 lbs.

	G	AB	H	2B	3B	HR	HR%	R	RBI	BB	SO	SB	BA	SA	PH AB	PH H	G by POS
1930 CLE A	3	12	2	1	0	0	0.0	0	2	0	2	0	.167	.250	0	0	3B-3
1931	30	56	15	6	0	0	0.0	3	7	8	0	2	.268	.375	4	0	3B-13, SS-10, 2B-3
2 yrs.	33	68	17	7	0	0	0.0	3	9	8	2	2	.250	.353	4	0	3B-16, SS-10, 2B-3

Ducky Detweiler

DETWEILER, ROBERT STERLING
B. Feb. 15, 1919, Trumbauersville, Pa.   BR TR 5'11"   178 lbs.

	G	AB	H	2B	3B	HR	HR%	R	RBI	BB	SO	SB	BA	SA	PH AB	PH H	G by POS
1942 BOS N	12	44	14	2	1	0	0.0	3	5	2	7	0	.318	.409	0	0	3B-12
1946	1	1	0	0	0	0	0.0	0	0	0	0	0	.000	.000	1	0	
2 yrs.	13	45	14	2	1	0	0.0	3	5	2	7	0	.311	.400	1	0	3B-12

Mickey Devine

DEVINE, WILLIAM PATRICK
B. May 9, 1892, Albany, N. Y.   D. Oct. 1, 1937, Albany, N. Y.   BR TR 5'10"   165 lbs.

	G	AB	H	2B	3B	HR	HR%	R	RBI	BB	SO	SB	BA	SA	PH AB	PH H	G by POS
1918 PHI N	4	8	1	1	0	0	0.0	0	0	0	1	0	.125	.250	1	0	C-3
1920 BOS A	8	12	2	0	0	0	0.0	1	0	1	2	1	.167	.167	3	0	C-5
1925 NY N	21	33	9	3	0	0	0.0	6	4	2	3	0	.273	.364	4	1	C-11, 3B-1
3 yrs.	33	53	12	4	0	0	0.0	7	4	3	6	1	.226	.302	8	1	C-19, 3B-1

Bernie DeViveiros

DeVIVEIROS, BERNARD JOHN
B. Apr. 19, 1901, Oakland, Calif.   BR TR 5'7"   160 lbs.

	G	AB	H	2B	3B	HR	HR%	R	RBI	BB	SO	SB	BA	SA	PH AB	PH H	G by POS
1924 CHI A	1	1	0	0	0	0	0.0	0	0	0	0	0	.000	.000	0	0	SS-1
1927 DET A	24	22	5	1	0	0	0.0	4	2	2	8	1	.227	.273	2	0	SS-14, 3B-1
2 yrs.	25	23	5	1	0	0	0.0	4	2	2	8	1	.217	.261	2	0	SS-15, 3B-1

Art Devlin

DEVLIN, ARTHUR McARTHUR
B. Oct. 16, 1879, Washington, D. C.   D. Sept. 18, 1948, Jersey City, N. J.   BR TR 6'   175 lbs.

	G	AB	H	2B	3B	HR	HR%	R	RBI	BB	SO	SB	BA	SA	PH AB	PH H	G by POS
1904 NY N	130	474	133	16	8	1	0.2	81	66	62		33	.281	.354	0	0	3B-130
1905	153	525	129	14	7	2	0.4	74	61	66		59	.246	.310	0	0	3B-153
1906	148	498	149	23	8	2	0.4	76	65	74		54	.299	.390	0	0	3B-148
1907	143	491	136	16	2	1	0.2	61	54	63		38	.277	.324	0	0	3B-140, SS-3
1908	157	534	135	18	4	2	0.4	59	45	62		19	.253	.313	0	0	3B-157
1909	143	491	130	19	8	0	0.0	61	55	65		24	.265	.336	0	0	3B-142
1910	147	493	128	17	5	2	0.4	71	67	62	32	28	.260	.327	0	0	3B-147
1911	83	260	71	16	2	0	0.0	42	25	42	19	9	.273	.350	0	0	3B-79, SS-6, 2B-6, 1B-6
1912 BOS N	124	436	126	18	8	0	0.0	59	54	51	37	11	.289	.367	4	1	1B-69, SS-26, 3B-26, OF-1
1913	73	210	48	7	5	0	0.0	19	12	29	17	8	.229	.310	3	2	3B-69
10 yrs.	1301	4412	1185	164	57	10	0.2	603	504	576	105	283	.269	.338	7	3	3B-1191, 1B-75, SS-35, 2B-6, OF-1

WORLD SERIES

	G	AB	H	2B	3B	HR	HR%	R	RBI	BB	SO	SB	BA	SA	PH AB	PH H	G by POS
1905 NY N	5	16	4	1	0	0	0.0	0	1	1	3	3	.250	.313	0	0	3B-5

Jim Devlin

DEVLIN, JAMES RAYMOND
B. Aug. 25, 1922, Plains, Pa.   BL TR 5'11½"   165 lbs.

	G	AB	H	2B	3B	HR	HR%	R	RBI	BB	SO	SB	BA	SA	PH AB	PH H	G by POS
1944 CLE A	1	1	0	0	0	0	0.0	0	0	0	0	0	.000	.000	0	0	C-1

	G	AB	H	2B	3B	HR	HR %	R	RBI	BB	SO	SB	BA	SA	Pinch Hit AB	H	G by POS

Rex DeVogt

DeVOGT, REX EUGENE   BR TR 5'9"   170 lbs.
B. Jan. 4, 1889, Clare, Mich.   D. Nov. 9, 1935, East Lansing, Mich.

	G	AB	H	2B	3B	HR	HR %	R	RBI	BB	SO	SB	BA	SA	AB	H	G by POS
1913 BOS N	3	6	0	0	0	0	0.0	0	0	0	3	0	.000	.000	0	0	C-3

Josh Devore

DEVORE, JOSHUA   BL TR 5'6"   160 lbs.
B. Nov. 13, 1887, Murray City, Ohio   D. Oct. 5, 1954, Chillicothe, Ohio

	G	AB	H	2B	3B	HR	HR %	R	RBI	BB	SO	SB	BA	SA	AB	H	G by POS
1908 NY N	5	6	1	0	0	0	0.0	1	2	1			.167	.167	2	0	OF-2
1909	22	28	4	1	0	0	0.0	6	1	2		1	.143	.179	5	0	OF-12
1910	133	490	149	11	0	2	0.4	92	27	46	67	43	.304	.380	1	0	OF-130
1911	149	565	158	19	10	3	0.5	96	50	81	69	61	.280	.365	0	0	OF-149
1912	106	327	90	14	6	2	0.6	66	37	51	43	27	.275	.373	4	0	OF-96
1913 3 teams		NY N (16G – .190)			CIN N (66G – .267)				PHI N (23G – .282)								
" total	105	277	73	7	5	3	1.1	43	20	19	32	23	.264	.357	12	3	OF-79
1914 2 teams		PHI N (30G – .302)			BOS N (51G – .227)												
" total	81	181	45	6	0	1	0.6	27	12	22	19	2	.249	.298	25	11	OF-51
7 yrs.	601	1874	520	58	31	11	0.6	331	149	222	230	160	.277	.359	49	14	OF-519
WORLD SERIES																	
1911 NY N	6	24	4	1	0	0	0.0	1	3	1	8	0	.167	.208	0	0	OF-6
1912	7	24	6	0	0	0	0.0	4	0	0	7	5	4	.250	.250	0	0	OF-7
1914 BOS N	1	1	0	0	0	0	0.0	0	0	0	1	0	.000	.000	1	0	
3 yrs.	14	49	10	1	0	0	0.0	5	3	8	14	4	.204	.224	1	0	OF-13

Al DeVormer

DeVORMER, ALBERT E.   BR TR 6'½"   175 lbs.
B. Aug. 19, 1891, Grand Rapids, Mich.   D. Aug. 29, 1966, Grand Rapids, Mich.

	G	AB	H	2B	3B	HR	HR %	R	RBI	BB	SO	SB	BA	SA	AB	H	G by POS
1918 CHI A	8	19	5	2	0	0	0.0	2	0	0	4	1	.263	.368	1	0	C-6, OF-1
1921 NY A	22	49	17	4	0	0	0.0	6	7	2	4	2	.347	.429	5	1	C-17
1922	24	59	12	4	1	0	0.0	8	11	1	6	0	.203	.305	4	1	C-17, 1B-1
1923 BOS A	74	209	54	7	3	0	0.0	20	18	6	21	3	.258	.321	12	3	C-55, 1B-2
1927 NY N	68	141	35	3	1	2	1.4	14	21	11	11	1	.248	.326	8	4	C-54, 1B-3
5 yrs.	196	477	123	20	5	2	0.4	50	57	20	46	7	.258	.333	30	9	C-149, 1B-6, OF-1
WORLD SERIES																	
1921 NY A	2	1	0	0	0	0	0.0	0	0	0	0	0	.000	.000	0	0	C-1

Walt Devoy

DEVOY, WALTER JOSEPH   BR TR 5'7"   155 lbs.
B. Mar. 14, 1885, St. Louis, Mo.   D. Dec. 17, 1953, St. Louis, Mo.

	G	AB	H	2B	3B	HR	HR %	R	RBI	BB	SO	SB	BA	SA	AB	H	G by POS
1909 STL A	19	69	17	3	1	0	0.0	7	8	3		4	.246	.319	0	0	OF-16, 1B-3

Charlie Dexter

DEXTER, CHARLES DANA   TR 5'7"   155 lbs.
B. June 15, 1876, Evansville, Ind.   D. June 9, 1934, Cedar Rapids, Iowa

	G	AB	H	2B	3B	HR	HR %	R	RBI	BB	SO	SB	BA	SA	AB	H	G by POS
1896 LOU N	107	402	112	18	7	3	0.7	65	37	17	34	21	.279	.381	5	0	C-55, OF-47
1897	76	257	72	12	5	2	0.8	43	46	21		12	.280	.389	5	1	OF-32, C-23, 3B-14, SS-2
1898	112	421	132	13	5	1	0.2	76	66	26		44	.314	.375	3	1	OF-95, 2B-8, C-7
1899	80	295	76	7	1	1	0.3	47	33	21		21	.258	.298	3	0	OF-71, SS-6
1900 CHI N	40	125	25	5	0	2	1.6	7	20	1		2	.200	.288	4	1	C-22, OF-13, 2B-1
1901	116	460	123	9	5	1	0.2	46	66	16		22	.267	.315	2	0	1B-54, 3B-25, OF-21, 2B-13, C-3
1902 2 teams		CHI N (69G – .226)			BOS N (48G – .257)												
" total	117	449	107	15	0	3	0.7	63	44	35		29	.238	.292	0	0	3B-40, SS-22, 1B-22, 2B-19, OF-17
1903 BOS N	123	457	102	15	1	3	0.7	82	34	61		32	.223	.280	2	0	OF-106, SS-9, C-6
8 yrs.	771	2866	749	94	24	16	0.6	429	346	198	34	183	.261	.328	24	3	OF-402, C-116, 3B-79, 1B-76, 2B-41, SS-39

Bo Diaz

DIAZ, BAUDILIO JOSE   BR TR 5'11"   185 lbs.
B. Mar. 23, 1953, Cua Miranda, Venezuela

	G	AB	H	2B	3B	HR	HR %	R	RBI	BB	SO	SB	BA	SA	AB	H	G by POS
1977 BOS A	2	1	0	0	0	0	0.0	0	0	0	1	0	.000	.000	1	0	C-2
1978 CLE A	44	127	30	4	0	2	1.6	12	11	4	17	0	.236	.315	0	0	C-44
1979	15	32	5	2	0	0	0.0	0	1	2	6	0	.156	.219	0	0	C-15
1980	76	207	47	11	2	3	1.4	15	32	7	27	1	.227	.343	9	2	C-75
1981	63	182	57	19	0	7	3.8	25	38	13	23	2	.313	.533	12	3	C-51, DH-3
1982 PHI N	144	525	151	29	1	18	3.4	69	85	36	87	3	.288	.450	2	1	C-144
1983	136	471	111	17	0	15	3.2	49	64	38	57	1	.236	.367	4	2	C-134
1984	27	75	16	4	0	1	1.3	5	9	5	13	0	.213	.307	4	0	C-23
8 yrs.	507	1620	417	86	3	46	2.8	175	240	105	231	7	.257	.399	32	8	C-488, DH-3
LEAGUE CHAMPIONSHIP SERIES																	
1983 PHI N	4	13	2	1	0	0	0.0	0	2	1	0	0	.154	.231	0	0	C-4
WORLD SERIES																	
1983 PHI N	5	15	5	1	0	0	0.0	0	1	2	0	0	.333	.400	0	0	C-5

Mike Diaz

DIAZ, MICHAEL ANTHONY   BR TR 6'2"   205 lbs.
B. Apr. 15, 1960, San Francisco, Calif.

	G	AB	H	2B	3B	HR	HR %	R	RBI	BB	SO	SB	BA	SA	AB	H	G by POS
1983 CHI N	6	7	2	1	0	0	0.0	1	0	0	2	0	.286	.429	3	1	C-3

Paul Dicken

DICKEN, PAUL FRANKLIN   BR TR 6'5"   195 lbs.
B. Oct. 2, 1943, Deland, Fla.

	G	AB	H	2B	3B	HR	HR %	R	RBI	BB	SO	SB	BA	SA	AB	H	G by POS
1964 CLE A	11	11	0	0	0	0	0.0	0	0	0	5	0	.000	.000	11	0	
1966	2	2	0	0	0	0	0.0	0	0	0	1	0	.000	.000	2	0	
2 yrs.	13	13	0	0	0	0	0.0	0	0	0	6	0	.000	.000	13	0	

Buttercup Dickerson

DICKERSON, LOUIS PESSANO   BL TR 5'6"   140 lbs.
B. Oct. 11, 1858, Tyaskin, Md.   D. July 23, 1920, Baltimore, Md.

	G	AB	H	2B	3B	HR	HR %	R	RBI	BB	SO	SB	BA	SA	AB	H	G by POS
1878 CIN N	29	123	38	5	1	0	0.0	17	9	0	7			.309	.366	0	0	OF-29
1879	81	350	102	18	14	2	0.6	73	57	3	27			.291	.440	0	0	OF-81
1880 2 teams		TRO N (30G – .193)			WOR N (31G – .293)												
" total	61	252	62	10	8	0	0.0	37		3	5			.246	.349	0	0	OF-61, SS-1
1881 WOR N	80	367	116	18	6	1	0.3	48	31	8	8			.316	.406	0	0	OF-80

	G	AB	H	2B	3B	HR	HR %	R	RBI	BB	SO	SB	BA	SA	Pinch Hit AB	Pinch Hit H	G by POS

Buttercup Dickerson continued

	G	AB	H	2B	3B	HR	HR %	R	RBI	BB	SO	SB	BA	SA	AB	H	G by POS
1883 PIT AA	85	355	88	15	4	0	0.0	62		17			.248	.296	0	0	OF-78, SS-8, 2B-2
1884 3 teams	STL U (46G – .365)							BAL AA (13G – .214)			LOU AA (8G – .143)						
" total	67	295	93	17	4	1	0.3	64		15			.315	.410	0	0	OF-62, 3B-5
1885 BUF N	5	21	1	1	0	0	0.0	1		0	4		.048	.095	0	0	OF-5
7 yrs.	408	1763	500	84	34	4	0.2	302	97	47	51		.284	.377	0	0	OF-396, SS-9, 3B-5, 2B-2

Bill Dickey

DICKEY, WILLIAM MALCOLM
Brother of George Dickey.
B. June 6, 1907, Bastrop, La.
Manager 1946.
Hall of Fame 1954.

BL TR 6'1½" 185 lbs.

	G	AB	H	2B	3B	HR	HR %	R	RBI	BB	SO	SB	BA	SA	AB	H	G by POS
1928 NY A	10	15	3	1	1	0	0.0	1	2	0	2	0	.200	.400	0	0	C-10
1929	130	447	145	30	6	10	2.2	60	65	14	16	4	.324	.485	3	1	C-127
1930	109	366	124	25	7	5	1.4	55	65	21	14	7	.339	.486	5	3	C-101
1931	130	477	156	17	10	6	1.3	65	78	39	20	2	.327	.442	4	0	C-125
1932	108	423	131	20	4	15	3.5	66	84	34	13	2	.310	.482	0	0	C-108
1933	130	478	152	24	8	14	2.9	58	97	47	14	3	.318	.490	3	1	C-127
1934	104	395	127	24	4	12	3.0	56	72	38	18	0	.322	.494	0	0	C-104
1935	120	448	125	26	6	14	3.1	54	81	35	11	1	.279	.458	2	1	C-118
1936	112	423	153	26	8	22	5.2	99	107	46	16	0	.362	.617	6	2	C-107
1937	140	530	176	35	2	29	5.5	87	133	73	22	3	.332	.570	3	1	C-137
1938	132	454	142	27	4	27	5.9	84	115	75	22	3	.313	.568	6	1	C-126
1939	128	480	145	23	3	24	5.0	98	105	77	37	5	.302	.513	2	0	C-126
1940	106	372	92	11	1	9	2.4	45	54	48	32	0	.247	.355	4	0	C-102
1941	109	348	99	15	5	7	2.0	35	71	45	17	2	.284	.417	6	1	C-104
1942	82	268	79	13	1	2	0.7	28	37	26	11	2	.295	.373	2	0	C-80
1943	85	242	85	18	2	4	1.7	29	33	41	12	2	.351	.492	10	4	C-71
1946	54	134	35	8	0	2	1.5	10	10	19	12	0	.261	.366	11	3	C-39
17 yrs.	1789	6300	1969	343	72	202	3.2	930	1209	678	289	36	.313	.486	67	18	C-1712

WORLD SERIES

	G	AB	H	2B	3B	HR	HR %	R	RBI	BB	SO	SB	BA	SA	AB	H	G by POS
1932 NY A	4	16	7	0	0	0	0.0	2	4	2	1	0	.438	.438	0	0	C-4
1936	6	25	3	0	0	1	4.0	5	5	3	4	0	.120	.240	0	0	C-6
1937	5	19	4	0	1	0	0.0	3	3	2	2	0	.211	.316	0	0	C-5
1938	4	15	6	0	0	1	6.7	2	2	1	0	1	.400	.600	0	0	C-4
1939	4	15	4	0	0	2	13.3	2	5	1	2	0	.267	.667	0	0	C-4
1941	5	18	3	1	0	0	0.0	3	1	3	1	0	.167	.222	0	0	C-5
1942	5	19	5	0	0	0	0.0	1	0	1	0	0	.263	.263	0	0	C-5
1943	5	18	5	0	0	1	5.6	1	4	2	2	0	.278	.444	0	0	C-5
8 yrs.	38	145	37	1	1	5	3.4	19	24	15	12	1	.255	.379	0	0	C-38

8th

George Dickey

DICKEY, GEORGE WILLARD (Skeets)
Brother of Bill Dickey.
B. July 10, 1915, Kensett, Ark.   D. June 16, 1976, DeWitt, Ark.

BB TR 6'2" 180 lbs.

	G	AB	H	2B	3B	HR	HR %	R	RBI	BB	SO	SB	BA	SA	AB	H	G by POS
1935 BOS A	5	11	0	0	0	0	0.0	1	1	1	3	0	.000	.000	1	0	C-4
1936	10	23	1	1	0	0	0.0	0	0	2	3	0	.043	.087	0	0	C-10
1941 CHI A	32	55	11	1	0	2	3.6	6	8	5	7	0	.200	.327	14	3	C-17
1942	59	116	27	3	0	1	0.9	6	17	9	11	0	.233	.284	31	9	C-29
1946	37	78	15	1	0	0	0.0	8	1	12	13	0	.192	.205	8	3	C-30
1947	83	211	47	6	0	1	0.5	15	27	34	25	4	.223	.265	4	2	C-80
6 yrs.	226	494	101	12	0	4	0.8	36	54	63	62	4	.204	.253	58	17	C-170

Johnny Dickshot

DICKSHOT, JOHN OSCAR
Born John Oscar Dicksus.
B. Jan. 24, 1910, Waukegan, Ill.

BR TR 6' 195 lbs.

	G	AB	H	2B	3B	HR	HR %	R	RBI	BB	SO	SB	BA	SA	AB	H	G by POS
1936 PIT N	9	9	2	0	0	0	0.0	2	1	1	2	0	.222	.222	7	1	OF-1
1937	82	264	67	8	4	3	1.1	42	33	26	36	0	.254	.348	15	3	OF-64
1938	29	35	8	0	0	0	0.0	3	4	8	5	3	.229	.229	9	3	OF-10
1939 NY N	10	34	8	0	0	0	0.0	3	5	5	3	0	.235	.235	0	0	OF-10
1944 CHI A	62	162	41	8	5	0	0.0	18	15	13	10	2	.253	.364	20	5	OF-40
1945	130	486	147	19	10	4	0.8	74	58	48	41	18	.302	.407	5	1	OF-124
6 yrs.	322	990	273	35	19	7	0.7	142	116	101	97	23	.276	.371	56	13	OF-249

Bob Didier

DIDIER, ROBERT DANIEL
B. Feb. 16, 1949, Hattiesburg, Miss.

BB TR 6' 190 lbs.

	G	AB	H	2B	3B	HR	HR %	R	RBI	BB	SO	SB	BA	SA	AB	H	G by POS
1969 ATL N	114	352	90	16	1	0	0.0	30	32	34	39	1	.256	.307	0	0	C-114
1970	57	168	25	2	1	0	0.0	9	7	12	11	1	.149	.173	0	0	C-57
1971	51	155	34	4	1	0	0.0	9	5	6	17	0	.219	.258	2	1	C-50
1972	13	40	12	2	1	0	0.0	5	5	2	4	0	.300	.400	2	0	C-11
1973 DET A	7	22	10	1	0	0	0.0	3	1	3	0	0	.455	.500	0	0	C-7
1974 BOS A	5	14	1	0	0	0	0.0	0	1	2	1	0	.071	.071	0	0	C-5
6 yrs.	247	751	172	25	4	0	0.0	56	51	59	72	2	.229	.273	4	1	C-244

LEAGUE CHAMPIONSHIP SERIES

	G	AB	H	2B	3B	HR	HR %	R	RBI	BB	SO	SB	BA	SA	AB	H	G by POS
1969 ATL N	3	11	0	0	0	0	0.0	0	0	0	2	0	.000	.000	0	0	C-3

Ernie Diehl

DIEHL, ERNEST GUY
B. Oct. 2, 1874, Cincinnati, Ohio   D. Nov. 6, 1958, Miami, Fla.

TR

	G	AB	H	2B	3B	HR	HR %	R	RBI	BB	SO	SB	BA	SA	AB	H	G by POS
1903 PIT N	1	3	1	0	0	0	0.0	0		0		0	.333	.333	0	0	OF-1
1904	12	37	6	0	0	0	0.0	6	4	6		3	.162	.162	1	1	OF-7, SS-4
1906 BOS N	3	11	5	0	1	0	0.0	1	0	0		0	.455	.636	0	0	OF-2, SS-1
1909	1	4	2	1	0	0	0.0	1	0	0		0	.500	.750	0	0	OF-1
4 yrs.	17	55	14	1	1	0	0.0	8	4	6		3	.255	.309	1	1	OF-11, SS-5

	G	AB	H	2B	3B	HR	HR %	R	RBI	BB	SO	SB	BA	SA	Pinch Hit AB	Pinch Hit H	G by POS

Chuck Diering

DIERING, CHARLES EDWARD ALLEN
B. Feb. 5, 1923, St. Louis, Mo.   BR TR 5'10"   165 lbs.

	G	AB	H	2B	3B	HR	HR%	R	RBI	BB	SO	SB	BA	SA	PH AB	PH H	G by POS
1947 STL N	105	74	16	3	1	2	2.7	22	11	19	22	3	.216	.365	8	1	OF-75
1948	7	7	0	0	0	0	0.0	2	0	2	2	1	.000	.000	0	0	OF-5
1949	131	369	97	21	8	3	0.8	60	38	35	49	1	.263	.388	1	0	OF-124
1950	89	204	51	12	0	3	1.5	34	18	35	38	1	.250	.353	0	0	OF-81
1951	64	85	22	5	1	0	0.0	9	8	6	15	0	.259	.341	8	3	OF-44
1952 NY N	41	23	4	1	1	0	0.0	2	2	4	3	0	.174	.304	0	0	OF-36
1954 BAL A	128	418	108	14	1	2	0.5	35	29	56	57	3	.258	.311	6	2	OF-119
1955	137	371	95	16	2	3	0.8	38	31	57	45	5	.256	.334	4	1	OF-107, 3B-34, SS-12
1956	50	97	18	4	0	1	1.0	15	4	23	19	2	.186	.258	4	0	OF-40, 3B-2
9 yrs.	752	1648	411	76	14	14	0.8	217	141	237	250	16	.249	.338	31	7	OF-631, 3B-36, SS-12

Bill Dietrick

DIETRICK, WILLIAM ALEXANDER
B. Apr. 20, 1902, Hanover County, Va.   D. May 6, 1946, Bethesda, Md.   BR TR 5'10"   160 lbs.

	G	AB	H	2B	3B	HR	HR%	R	RBI	BB	SO	SB	BA	SA	PH AB	PH H	G by POS
1927 PHI N	5	6	1	0	0	0	0.0	1	0	0	0	0	.167	.167	0	0	SS-5
1928	52	100	20	6	0	0	0.0	13	7	17	10	1	.200	.260	15	5	OF-21, SS-8
2 yrs.	57	106	21	6	0	0	0.0	14	7	17	10	1	.198	.255	15	5	OF-21, SS-13

Dick Dietz

DIETZ, RICHARD ALLEN
B. Sept. 18, 1941, Crawfordsville, Ind.   BR TR 6'1"   195 lbs.

	G	AB	H	2B	3B	HR	HR%	R	RBI	BB	SO	SB	BA	SA	PH AB	PH H	G by POS
1966 SF N	13	23	1	0	0	0	0.0	1	0	0	9	0	.043	.043	7	0	C-6
1967	56	120	27	3	0	4	3.3	10	19	25	44	0	.225	.350	15	4	C-43
1968	98	301	82	14	2	6	2.0	21	38	34	68	1	.272	.392	12	6	C-90
1969	79	244	56	8	1	11	4.5	28	35	53	53	0	.230	.406	2	2	C-73
1970	148	493	148	36	2	22	4.5	82	107	109	106	0	.300	.515	9	1	C-139
1971	142	453	114	19	0	19	4.2	58	72	97	86	1	.252	.419	9	4	C-135
1972 LA N	27	56	9	1	0	1	1.8	4	6	14	11	2	.161	.232	7	0	C-22
1973 ATL N	83	139	41	8	1	3	2.2	22	24	49	25	0	.295	.432	18	6	1B-36, C-20
8 yrs.	646	1829	478	89	6	66	3.6	226	301	381	402	4	.261	.425	79	23	C-528, 1B-36

LEAGUE CHAMPIONSHIP SERIES

	G	AB	H	2B	3B	HR	HR%	R	RBI	BB	SO	SB	BA	SA	PH AB	PH H	G by POS
1971 SF N	4	15	1	0	0	0	0.0	0	0	2	5	0	.067	.067	0	0	C-4

Roy Dietzel

DIETZEL, LEROY LOUIS
B. Jan. 9, 1931, Baltimore, Md.   BR TR 6'   190 lbs.

	G	AB	H	2B	3B	HR	HR%	R	RBI	BB	SO	SB	BA	SA	PH AB	PH H	G by POS
1954 WAS A	9	21	5	0	0	0	0.0	1	1	5	4	0	.238	.238	0	0	2B-7, 3B-2

Jay Difani

DIFANI, CLARENCE JOSEPH
B. Dec. 21, 1923, Crystal City, Mo.   BR TR 6'   170 lbs.

	G	AB	H	2B	3B	HR	HR%	R	RBI	BB	SO	SB	BA	SA	PH AB	PH H	G by POS
1948 WAS A	2	2	0	0	0	0	0.0	0	0	0	2	0	.000	.000	2	0	
1949	2	1	1	1	0	0	0.0	0	0	0	0	0	1.000	2.000	1	1	2B-1
2 yrs.	4	3	1	1	0	0	0.0	0	0	0	2	0	.333	.667	3	1	2B-1

Steve Dignan

DIGNAN, STEPHEN E.
B. May 16, 1859, Boston, Mass.   D. July 11, 1881, Boston, Mass.

	G	AB	H	2B	3B	HR	HR%	R	RBI	BB	SO	SB	BA	SA	PH AB	PH H	G by POS
1880 2 teams	BOS N (8G – .324)			WOR N (3G – .300)													
" total	11	44	14	1	1	0	0.0	5	6	0	4		.318	.386	0	0	OF-11

Don Dillard

DILLARD, DAVID DONALD
B. Jan. 8, 1937, Greenville, S. C.   BL TR 6'1"   200 lbs.

	G	AB	H	2B	3B	HR	HR%	R	RBI	BB	SO	SB	BA	SA	PH AB	PH H	G by POS
1959 CLE A	10	10	4	0	0	0	0.0	0	1	0	2	0	.400	.400	10	4	
1960	6	7	1	0	0	0	0.0	0	0	1	3	0	.143	.143	5	1	OF-1
1961	74	147	40	5	0	7	4.8	27	17	15	28	0	.272	.449	35	15	OF-39
1962	95	174	40	5	1	5	2.9	22	14	11	25	0	.230	.356	45	11	OF-50
1963 MIL N	67	119	28	6	4	1	0.8	9	12	5	21	0	.235	.378	35	6	OF-30
1965	20	19	3	0	0	1	5.3	1	3	0	6	0	.158	.316	19	3	OF-1
6 yrs.	272	476	116	16	5	14	2.9	59	47	32	85	0	.244	.387	149	40	OF-121

Pat Dillard

DILLARD, ROBERT LEE
B. June 12, 1874, Chattanooga, Tenn.   D. July 22, 1907, Denver, Colo.

	G	AB	H	2B	3B	HR	HR%	R	RBI	BB	SO	SB	BA	SA	PH AB	PH H	G by POS
1900 STL N	57	183	42	5	2	0	0.0	24	12	13		7	.230	.279	8	1	OF-26, 3B-21, SS-3

Steve Dillard

DILLARD, STEPHEN BRADLEY
B. Dec. 8, 1951, Memphis, Tenn.   BR TR 6'1"   171 lbs.

	G	AB	H	2B	3B	HR	HR%	R	RBI	BB	SO	SB	BA	SA	PH AB	PH H	G by POS
1975 BOS A	1	5	2	0	0	0	0.0	2	0	0	0	1	.400	.400	0	0	2B-1
1976	57	167	46	14	0	1	0.6	22	15	17	20	6	.275	.377	3	1	3B-18, 2B-17, SS-12, DH-7
1977	66	141	34	7	0	1	0.7	22	13	7	13	4	.241	.312	7	1	2B-45, SS-9, DH-6
1978 DET A	56	130	29	5	2	0	0.0	21	7	6	11	1	.223	.292	1	0	2B-41, DH-4
1979 CHI N	89	166	47	6	1	5	3.0	31	24	17	24	1	.283	.422	17	6	2B-60, 3B-9
1980	100	244	55	8	1	4	1.6	31	27	20	54	2	.225	.316	13	3	3B-51, 2B-38, SS-2
1981	53	119	26	7	1	2	1.7	18	11	8	20	0	.218	.345	11	3	2B-32, 3B-7, SS-2
1982 CHI A	16	41	7	3	1	0	0.0	1	5	1	5	0	.171	.293	0	0	2B-16
8 yrs.	438	1013	246	50	6	13	1.3	148	102	76	147	15	.243	.343	52	14	2B-250, 3B-85, SS-25, DH-17

Pickles Dillhoefer

DILLHOEFER, WILLIAM MARTIN
B. Oct. 13, 1894, Cleveland, Ohio   D. Feb. 22, 1922, St. Louis, Mo.   BR TR 5'7"   154 lbs.

	G	AB	H	2B	3B	HR	HR%	R	RBI	BB	SO	SB	BA	SA	PH AB	PH H	G by POS
1917 CHI N	42	95	12	1	1	0	0.0	3	8	2	9	1	.126	.158	4	0	C-37
1918 PHI N	8	11	1	0	0	0	0.0	0	0	1	1	2	.091	.091	2	0	C-6
1919 STL N	45	108	23	3	2	0	0.0	11	12	8	6	5	.213	.278	1	1	C-39
1920	76	224	59	8	3	0	0.0	26	13	13	7	2	.263	.326	2	0	C-73
1921	76	162	39	4	4	0	0.0	19	15	11	7	2	.241	.315	4	0	C-69
5 yrs.	247	600	134	16	10	0	0.0	59	48	35	30	12	.223	.283	13	1	C-224

	G	AB	H	2B	3B	HR	HR %	R	RBI	BB	SO	SB	BA	SA	Pinch Hit AB	Pinch Hit H	G by POS

Bob Dillinger

DILLINGER, ROBERT BERNARD
B. Sept. 17, 1918, Glendale, Calif.
BR TR 5'11½" 170 lbs.

	G	AB	H	2B	3B	HR	HR%	R	RBI	BB	SO	SB	BA	SA	AB	H	G by POS
1946 STL A	83	225	63	6	3	0	0.0	33	11	19	32	8	.280	.333	18	8	3B-54, SS-1
1947	137	571	168	23	6	3	0.5	70	37	56	38	34	.294	.371	0	0	3B-137
1948	153	644	207	34	10	2	0.3	110	44	65	34	28	.321	.415	1	0	3B-153
1949	137	544	176	22	13	1	0.2	68	51	51	40	20	.324	.417	4	1	3B-133
1950 2 teams	PHI	A (84G –	.309)		PIT	N	(58G –	.288)									
" total	142	578	174	29	11	4	0.7	78	50	42	42	9	.301	.410	5	0	3B-135
1951 2 teams	PIT	N (12G –	.233)		CHI	A	(89G –	.301)									
" total	101	342	100	9	4	0	0.0	42	20	16	19	5	.292	.342	15	4	3B-80
6 yrs.	753	2904	888	123	47	10	0.3	401	213	249	205	104	.306	.391	43	13	3B-692, SS-1

Pop Dillon

DILLON, FRANK EDWARD
B. Oct. 17, 1873, Normal, Ill.   D. Sept. 12, 1931, Pasadena, Calif.
BL TR

	G	AB	H	2B	3B	HR	HR%	R	RBI	BB	SO	SB	BA	SA	AB	H	G by POS
1899 PIT N	30	121	31	5	0	0	0.0	21	20	5		5	.256	.298	0	0	1B-30
1900	5	18	2	1	0	0	0.0	3	1	0		0	.111	.167	0	0	1B-5
1901 DET A	74	281	81	14	6	1	0.4	40	42	15		14	.288	.391	0	0	1B-74
1902 2 teams	DET	A (66G –	.206)		BAL	A	(2G –	.286)									
" total	68	250	52	6	4	0	0.0	22	22	18		2	.208	.264	0	0	1B-68
1904 BKN N	135	511	132	18	6	0	0.0	60	31	40		13	.258	.317	0	0	1B-134
5 yrs.	312	1181	298	44	16	1	0.1	146	116	78		34	.252	.319	0	0	1B-311

Miguel Dilone

DILONE, MIGUEL ANGEL
Also known as Miguel Angel Reyes.
B. Nov. 1, 1954, Santiago, Dominican Republic
BB TR 6'   160 lbs.

	G	AB	H	2B	3B	HR	HR%	R	RBI	BB	SO	SB	BA	SA	AB	H	G by POS
1974 PIT N	12	2	0	0	0	0	0.0	3	0	1	0	2	.000	.000	2	0	OF-2
1975	18	6	0	0	0	0	0.0	8	0	0	1	2	.000	.000	1	0	OF-2
1976	16	17	4	0	0	0	0.0	7	0	0	0	5	.235	.235	4	0	OF-3
1977	29	44	6	0	0	0	0.0	5	0	2	3	12	.136	.136	10	1	OF-17
1978 OAK A	135	258	59	8	0	1	0.4	34	14	23	30	50	.229	.271	1	0	OF-99, 3B-3, DH-1
1979 2 teams	OAK	A (30G –	.187)		CHI	N	(43G –	.306)									
" total	73	127	28	1	2	1	0.8	29	7	8	12	21	.220	.283	2	1	OF-47
1980 CLE A	132	528	180	30	9	0	0.0	82	40	28	45	61	.341	.432	3	0	OF-118, DH-11
1981	72	269	78	5	5	0	0.0	33	19	18	28	29	.290	.346	4	2	OF-56, DH-11
1982	104	379	89	12	3	3	0.8	50	25	25	36	33	.235	.306	12	1	OF-97, DH-1
1983 3 teams	CLE	A (32G –	.191)		CHI	A	(4G –	.000)		PIT	N	(7G –	.000)				
" total	43	71	13	3	1	0	0.0	17	7	10	5	8	.183	.254	4	0	OF-21, DH-2
1984 MON N	88	169	47	8	2	1	0.6	28	10	17	18	27	.278	.367	37	9	OF-41
11 yrs.	722	1870	504	67	22	6	0.3	296	122	132	178	250	.270	.339	80	14	OF-503, DH-26, 3B-3

Dom DiMaggio

DiMAGGIO, DOMINIC PAUL (The Little Professor)
Brother of Vince DiMaggio.   Brother of Joe DiMaggio.
B. Feb. 12, 1917, San Francisco, Calif.
BR TR 5'9"   168 lbs.

	G	AB	H	2B	3B	HR	HR%	R	RBI	BB	SO	SB	BA	SA	AB	H	G by POS
1940 BOS A	108	418	126	32	6	8	1.9	81	46	41	46	7	.301	.464	10	4	OF-94
1941	144	584	165	37	6	8	1.4	117	58	90	57	13	.283	.408	0	0	OF-144
1942	151	622	178	36	8	14	2.3	110	48	70	52	16	.286	.437	0	0	OF-151
1946	142	534	169	24	7	7	1.3	85	73	66	58	10	.316	.427	0	0	OF-142
1947	136	513	145	21	5	8	1.6	75	71	74	62	10	.283	.390	1	0	OF-134
1948	155	648	185	40	4	9	1.4	127	87	101	58	10	.285	.401	0	0	OF-155
1949	145	605	186	34	5	8	1.3	126	60	96	55	9	.307	.420	1	0	OF-144
1950	141	588	193	30	11	7	1.2	131	70	82	68	15	.328	.452	1	1	OF-140
1951	146	639	189	34	4	12	1.9	113	72	73	53	4	.296	.418	0	0	OF-146
1952	128	486	143	20	1	6	1.2	81	33	57	61	6	.294	.377	5	2	OF-123
1953	3	3	1	0	0	0	0.0	0	0	0	1	0	.333	.333	3	1	
11 yrs.	1399	5640	1680	308	57	87	1.5	1046	618	750	571	100	.298	.419	21	8	OF-1373
WORLD SERIES																	
1946 BOS A	7	27	7	3	0	0	0.0	2	3	2	2	0	.259	.370	0	0	OF-7

Joe DiMaggio

DiMAGGIO, JOSEPH PAUL (Joltin' Joe, The Yankee Clipper)
Brother of Vince DiMaggio.   Brother of Dom DiMaggio.
B. Nov. 25, 1914, Martinez, Calif.
Hall of Fame 1955.
BR TR 6'2"   193 lbs.

	G	AB	H	2B	3B	HR	HR%	R	RBI	BB	SO	SB	BA	SA	AB	H	G by POS
1936 NY A	138	637	206	44	15	29	4.6	132	125	24	39	4	.323	.576	0	0	OF-138
1937	151	621	215	35	15	46	7.4	151	167	64	37	3	.346	.673	1	1	OF-150
1938	145	599	194	32	13	32	5.3	129	140	59	21	6	.324	.581	0	0	OF-145
1939	120	462	176	32	6	30	6.5	108	126	52	20	3	.381	.671	1	1	OF-117
1940	132	508	179	28	9	31	6.1	93	133	61	30	1	.352	.626	2	1	OF-130
1941	139	541	193	43	11	30	5.5	122	125	76	13	4	.357	.643	0	0	OF-139
1942	154	610	186	29	13	21	3.4	123	114	68	36	4	.305	.498	0	0	OF-154
1946	132	503	146	20	8	25	5.0	81	95	59	24	1	.290	.511	0	0	OF-131
1947	141	534	168	31	10	20	3.7	97	97	64	32	3	.315	.522	2	0	OF-139
1948	153	594	190	26	11	39	6.6	110	155	67	30	1	.320	.598	1	1	OF-152
1949	76	272	94	14	6	14	5.1	58	67	55	18	0	.346	.596	0	0	OF-76
1950	139	525	158	33	10	32	6.1	114	122	80	33	0	.301	.585	1	0	OF-137, 1B-1
1951	116	415	109	22	4	12	2.9	72	71	61	36	0	.263	.422	3	2	OF-113
13 yrs.	1736	6821	2214	389	131	361	5.3	1390	1537	790	369	30	.325	.579 6th	12	6	OF-1721, 1B-1
WORLD SERIES																	
1936 NY A	6	26	9	3	0	0	0.0	3	3	1	3	0	.346	.462	0	0	OF-6
1937	5	22	6	0	0	1	4.5	2	4	0	3	0	.273	.409	0	0	OF-5
1938	4	15	4	0	0	1	6.7	4	2	1	1	0	.267	.467	0	0	OF-4
1939	4	16	5	0	0	1	6.3	3	3	1	1	0	.313	.500	0	0	OF-4
1941	5	19	5	0	0	0	0.0	1	1	2	2	0	.263	.263	0	0	OF-5
1942	5	21	7	0	0	0	0.0	3	3	0	1	0	.333	.333	0	0	OF-5
1947	7	26	6	0	0	2	7.7	4	5	6	2	0	.231	.462	0	0	OF-7
1949	5	18	2	0	0	1	5.6	2	2	3	5	0	.111	.278	0	0	OF-5
1950	4	13	4	1	0	1	7.7	2	2	3	1	0	.308	.615	0	0	OF-4

	G	AB	H	2B	3B	HR	HR %	R	RBI	BB	SO	SB	BA	SA	Pinch Hit AB	Pinch Hit H	G by POS

Joe DiMaggio continued

	G	AB	H	2B	3B	HR	HR %	R	RBI	BB	SO	SB	BA	SA	AB	H	G by POS
1951	6	23	6	2	0	1	4.3	3	5	2	4	0	.261	.478	0	0	OF-6
10 yrs.	51	199	54	6	0	8	4.0	27	30	19	23	0	.271	.422	0	0	OF-51
		7th	3rd	4th				7th		5th	5th	10th	10th				

Vince DiMaggio

DiMAGGIO, VINCENT PAUL
Brother of Dom DiMaggio.   Brother of Joe DiMaggio.
B. Sept. 6, 1912, Martinez, Calif.

BR TR 5'11½" 185 lbs.

	G	AB	H	2B	3B	HR	HR %	R	RBI	BB	SO	SB	BA	SA	AB	H	G by POS
1937 BOS N	132	493	126	18	4	13	2.6	56	69	39	111	8	.256	.387	2	0	OF-130
1938	150	540	123	28	3	14	2.6	71	61	65	134	11	.228	.369	0	0	OF-149, 2B-1
1939 CIN N	8	14	1	1	0	0	0.0	1	2	2	10	0	.071	.143	1	0	OF-7
1940 2 teams		CIN	N	(2G –	.250)		PIT	N	(110G –	.289)							
" total	112	360	104	26	4	19	5.3	61	54	38	83	11	.289	.519	0	0	OF-109
1941 PIT N	151	528	141	27	5	21	4.0	73	100	68	100	10	.267	.456	0	0	OF-151
1942	143	496	118	22	3	15	3.0	57	75	52	87	10	.238	.385	4	1	OF-138
1943	157	580	144	41	2	15	2.6	64	88	70	126	11	.248	.403	0	0	OF-156, SS-1
1944	109	342	82	20	4	9	2.6	41	50	33	83	6	.240	.401	9	2	OF-101, 3B-1
1945 PHI N	127	452	116	25	3	19	4.2	64	84	43	91	12	.257	.451	5	1	OF-121
1946 2 teams		PHI	N	(6G –	.211)		NY	N	(15G –	.000)							
" total	21	44	4	1	0	0	0.0	3	1	2	12	0	.091	.114	1	0	OF-19
10 yrs.	1110	3849	959	209	24	125	3.2	491	584	412	837	79	.249	.413	22	4	OF-1081, SS-1, 3B-1, 2B-1

Mike Dimmel

DIMMEL, MICHAEL WAYNE
B. Oct. 18, 1954, Albert Lea, Minn.

BR TR 6' 180 lbs.

	G	AB	H	2B	3B	HR	HR %	R	RBI	BB	SO	SB	BA	SA	AB	H	G by POS
1977 BAL A	25	5	0	0	0	0	0.0	8	0	0	1	1	.000	.000	0	0	OF-23
1978	8	0	0	0	0	0	–	2	0	0	0	0	–	–	0	0	OF-7
1979 STL N	6	3	1	0	0	0	0.0	1	0	0	0	0	.333	.333	0	0	OF-5
3 yrs.	39	8	1	0	0	0	0.0	11	0	0	1	1	.125	.125	0	0	OF-35

Kerry Dineen

DINEEN, KERRY MICHAEL
B. July 1, 1952, Englewood, N. J.

BL TL 5'11" 165 lbs.

	G	AB	H	2B	3B	HR	HR %	R	RBI	BB	SO	SB	BA	SA	AB	H	G by POS
1975 NY A	7	22	8	1	0	0	0.0	3	1	2	1	0	.364	.409	0	0	OF-7
1976	4	7	2	0	0	0	0.0	0	1	1	2	1	.286	.286	0	0	OF-4
1978 PHI N	5	8	2	1	0	0	0.0	0	0	1	0	0	.250	.375	3	0	OF-1
3 yrs.	16	37	12	2	0	0	0.0	3	2	4	3	1	.324	.378	3	0	OF-12

Vance Dinges

DINGES, VANCE (George)
B. May 29, 1915, Elizabeth, N. J.

BL TL 6'2" 175 lbs.

	G	AB	H	2B	3B	HR	HR %	R	RBI	BB	SO	SB	BA	SA	AB	H	G by POS
1945 PHI N	109	397	114	15	4	1	0.3	46	36	35	17	5	.287	.353	2	1	OF-65, 1B-42
1946	50	104	32	5	1	1	1.0	7	10	9	12	2	.308	.404	22	3	1B-26, OF-1
2 yrs.	159	501	146	20	5	2	0.4	53	46	44	29	7	.291	.363	24	4	1B-68, OF-66

Bob DiPietro

DiPIETRO, ROBERT LOUIS PAUL
B. Sept. 1, 1927, San Francisco, Calif.

BR TR 5'11" 185 lbs.

	G	AB	H	2B	3B	HR	HR %	R	RBI	BB	SO	SB	BA	SA	AB	H	G by POS
1951 BOS A	4	11	1	0	0	0	0.0	0	0	1	1	0	.091	.091	0	0	OF-3

Benny Distefano

DISTEFANO, BENITO JAMES
B. Jan. 23, 1962, Brooklyn, N. Y.

BL TL 6'1" 195 lbs.

	G	AB	H	2B	3B	HR	HR %	R	RBI	BB	SO	SB	BA	SA	AB	H	G by POS
1984 PIT N	45	78	13	1	2	3	3.8	9	5	13	0	.167	.346	14	2	OF-20, 1B-17

Dutch Distel

DISTEL, GEORGE ADAM
B. Apr. 15, 1896, Madison, Ind.   D. Feb. 12, 1967, Madison, Ind.

BR TR 5'9" 165 lbs.

	G	AB	H	2B	3B	HR	HR %	R	RBI	BB	SO	SB	BA	SA	AB	H	G by POS
1918 STL N	8	17	3	1	1	0	0.0	3	1	2	3	0	.176	.353	1	0	2B-5, SS-2, OF-1

Jack Dittmer

DITTMER, JOHN DOUGLAS
B. Jan. 10, 1928, Elkader, Iowa

BL TR 6'1" 175 lbs.

	G	AB	H	2B	3B	HR	HR %	R	RBI	BB	SO	SB	BA	SA	AB	H	G by POS
1952 BOS N	93	326	63	7	2	7	2.1	26	41	26	26	1	.193	.291	3	0	2B-90
1953 MIL N	138	504	134	22	1	9	1.8	54	63	18	35	1	.266	.367	0	0	2B-138
1954	66	192	47	8	0	6	3.1	22	20	19	17	0	.245	.385	11	2	2B-55
1955	38	72	9	1	1	1	1.4	4	4	4	15	0	.125	.208	11	1	2B-28
1956	44	102	25	4	0	1	1.0	8	6	8	8	0	.245	.314	4	2	2B-42
1957 DET A	16	22	5	1	0	0	0.0	3	2	2	1	0	.227	.273	12	4	3B-3, 2B-1
6 yrs.	395	1218	283	43	4	24	2.0	117	136	77	102	2	.232	.333	41	9	2B-354, 3B-3

Leo Dixon

DIXON, LEO MICHAEL
B. Sept. 6, 1896, Chicago, Ill.

BR TR 5'11" 170 lbs.

	G	AB	H	2B	3B	HR	HR %	R	RBI	BB	SO	SB	BA	SA	AB	H	G by POS
1925 STL N	76	205	46	11	1	1	0.5	27	19	24	42	3	.224	.302	0	0	C-75
1926	33	89	17	3	1	0	0.0	7	8	11	14	1	.191	.247	0	0	C-33
1927	36	103	20	3	1	0	0.0	6	12	7	6	0	.194	.243	1	0	C-35
1929 CIN N	14	30	5	2	0	0	0.0	0	2	3	7	0	.167	.233	0	0	C-14
4 yrs.	159	427	88	19	3	1	0.2	40	41	45	69	4	.206	.272	1	0	C-157

Dan Dobbek

DOBBEK, DANIEL JOHN
B. Dec. 6, 1934, Ontonagon, Mich.

BL TR 6' 195 lbs.

	G	AB	H	2B	3B	HR	HR %	R	RBI	BB	SO	SB	BA	SA	AB	H	G by POS
1959 WAS A	16	60	15	1	2	1	1.7	8	5	5	13	0	.250	.383	0	0	OF-16
1960	110	248	54	8	2	10	4.0	32	30	35	41	4	.218	.387	32	5	OF-78
1961 MIN A	72	125	21	3	1	4	3.2	12	14	13	18	1	.168	.304	23	3	OF-48
3 yrs.	198	433	90	12	5	15	3.5	52	49	53	72	5	.208	.363	55	8	OF-142

John Dobbs

DOBBS, JOHN L.
B. June 3, 1876, Chattanooga, Tenn.   D. Sept. 9, 1934, Charlotte, N. C.

BL TR 5'9½" 170 lbs.

	G	AB	H	2B	3B	HR	HR %	R	RBI	BB	SO	SB	BA	SA	AB	H	G by POS
1901 CIN N	109	435	119	17	4	2	0.5	71	27	36		19	.274	.345	1	0	OF-100, 3B-8
1902 2 teams		CIN	N	(63G –	.297)		CHI	N	(59G –	.302)							
" total	122	491	147	16	5	1	0.2	70	51	37		10	.299	.358	0	0	OF-122

	G	AB	H	2B	3B	HR	HR %	R	RBI	BB	SO	SB	BA	SA	Pinch Hit AB	Pinch Hit H	G by POS

John Dobbs continued

	G	AB	H	2B	3B	HR	HR%	R	RBI	BB	SO	SB	BA	SA	PH AB	PH H	G by POS
1903 2 teams	CHI	N	(16G –	.230)		BKN	N	(111G –	.237)								
" total	127	475	112	16	8	2	0.4	69	63	55		23	.236	.316	1	1	OF-126
1904 BKN N	101	363	90	16	2	0	0.0	36	30	28		11	.248	.303	3	0	OF-92, SS-2, 2B-2
1905	123	460	117	21	4	2	0.4	59	36	31		15	.254	.330	0	0	OF-123
5 yrs.	582	2224	585	86	23	7	0.3	305	207	187		78	.263	.332	5	1	OF-563, 3B-8, SS-2, 2B-2

Larry Doby

DOBY, LAWRENCE EUGENE
B. Dec. 13, 1923, Camden, S. C.
Manager 1978. BL TR 6'1" 180 lbs.

	G	AB	H	2B	3B	HR	HR%	R	RBI	BB	SO	SB	BA	SA	PH AB	PH H	G by POS
1947 CLE A	29	32	5	1	0	0	0.0	3	2	1	11	0	.156	.188	21	4	2B-4, SS-1, 1B-1
1948	121	439	132	23	9	14	3.2	83	66	54	77	9	.301	.490	6	2	OF-114
1949	147	547	153	25	3	24	4.4	106	85	91	90	10	.280	.468	0	0	OF-147
1950	142	503	164	25	5	25	5.0	110	102	98	71	8	.326	.545	2	1	OF-140
1951	134	447	132	27	5	20	4.5	84	69	101	81	4	.295	.512	2	0	OF-132
1952	140	519	143	26	8	32	6.2	104	104	90	111	5	.276	.541	3	1	OF-136
1953	149	513	135	18	5	29	5.7	92	102	96	121	3	.263	.487	3	1	OF-146
1954	153	577	157	18	4	32	5.5	94	126	85	94	3	.272	.484	0	0	OF-153
1955	131	491	143	17	5	26	5.3	91	75	61	100	2	.291	.505	2	0	OF-129
1956 CHI A	140	504	135	22	3	24	4.8	89	102	102	105	0	.268	.466	3	1	OF-137
1957	119	416	120	27	2	14	3.4	57	79	56	79	2	.288	.464	9	1	OF-110
1958 CLE A	89	247	70	10	1	13	5.3	41	45	26	49	0	.283	.490	18	5	OF-68
1959 2 teams	DET	A	(18G –	.218)		CHI	A	(21G –	.241)								
" total	39	113	26	4	2	0	0.0	6	12	10	22	1	.230	.301	9	1	OF-28, 1B-2
13 yrs.	1533	5348	1515	243	52	253	4.7	960	969	871	1011	47	.283	.490	78	18	OF-1440, 2B-4, 1B-3, SS-1
WORLD SERIES																	
1948 CLE A	6	22	7	1	0	1	4.5	1	2	2	4	0	.318	.500	0	0	OF-6
1954	4	16	2	0	0	0	0.0	0	0	2	4	0	.125	.125	0	0	OF-4
2 yrs.	10	38	9	1	0	1	2.6	1	2	4	8	0	.237	.342	0	0	OF-10

Ona Dodd

DODD, ORAN A
B. Sept. 14, 1889, Bagwell, Tex. D. Mar. 31, 1929, Newport, Ark. BR TR 5'8" 150 lbs.

	G	AB	H	2B	3B	HR	HR%	R	RBI	BB	SO	SB	BA	SA	PH AB	PH H	G by POS
1912 PIT N	5	9	0	0	0	0	0.0	1		1	3	0	.000	.000	0	0	3B-4, 2B-1

John Dodge

DODGE, JOHN LEWIS
B. Apr. 27, 1889, Bolivar, Tenn. D. June 19, 1916, Mobile, Ala. BR TR 5'11½" 165 lbs.

	G	AB	H	2B	3B	HR	HR%	R	RBI	BB	SO	SB	BA	SA	PH AB	PH H	G by POS
1912 PHI N	30	92	11	1	0	0	0.0	3	3	4	11	2	.120	.130	0	0	3B-23, 2B-5, SS-1
1913 2 teams	PHI	N	(3G –	.333)		CIN	N	(94G –	.241)								
" total	97	326	79	8	8	4	1.2	35	45	12	34	11	.242	.353	2	0	3B-91, SS-3
2 yrs.	127	418	90	9	8	4	1.0	38	48	16	45	13	.215	.304	2	0	3B-114, 2B-5, SS-4

Bobby Doerr

DOERR, ROBERT PERSHING
B. Apr. 7, 1918, Los Angeles, Calif. BR TR 5'11" 175 lbs.

	G	AB	H	2B	3B	HR	HR%	R	RBI	BB	SO	SB	BA	SA	PH AB	PH H	G by POS
1937 BOS A	55	147	33	5	1	2	1.4	22	14	18	25	2	.224	.313	0	0	2B-47
1938	145	509	147	26	7	5	1.0	70	80	59	39	5	.289	.397	0	0	2B-145
1939	127	525	167	28	2	12	2.3	75	73	38	32	1	.318	.448	1	0	2B-126
1940	151	595	173	37	10	22	3.7	87	105	57	53	10	.291	.497	0	0	2B-151
1941	132	500	141	28	4	16	3.2	74	93	43	43	1	.282	.450	0	0	2B-132
1942	144	545	158	35	5	15	2.8	71	102	67	55	4	.290	.455	2	0	2B-142
1943	155	604	163	32	3	16	2.6	78	75	62	59	8	.270	.412	0	0	2B-155
1944	125	468	152	30	10	15	3.2	95	81	58	31	5	.325	.528	0	0	2B-125
1946	151	583	158	34	9	18	3.1	95	116	66	67	5	.271	.453	0	0	2B-151
1947	146	561	145	23	10	17	3.0	79	95	59	47	3	.258	.426	0	0	2B-146
1948	140	527	150	23	6	27	5.1	94	111	83	49	3	.285	.505	1	0	2B-138
1949	139	541	167	30	9	18	3.3	91	109	75	33	2	.309	.497	0	0	2B-139
1950	149	586	172	29	11	27	4.6	103	120	67	42	3	.294	.519	0	0	2B-149
1951	106	402	116	21	2	13	3.2	60	73	57	33	2	.289	.448	0	0	2B-106
14 yrs.	1865	7093	2042	381	89	223	3.1	1094	1247	809	608	54	.288	.461	4	0	2B-1852
WORLD SERIES																	
1946 BOS A	6	22	9	1	0	1	4.5	1	3	2	2	0	.409	.591	0	0	2B-6

John Doherty

DOHERTY, JOHN MICHAEL
B. Aug. 22, 1951, Woburn, Mass. BL TL 5'11" 185 lbs.

	G	AB	H	2B	3B	HR	HR%	R	RBI	BB	SO	SB	BA	SA	PH AB	PH H	G by POS
1974 CAL A	74	223	57	14	1	3	1.3	20	15	8	13	2	.256	.368	9	1	1B-70, DH-2
1975	30	94	19	3	0	1	1.1	7	12	8	12	1	.202	.266	2	1	1B-26, DH-1
2 yrs.	104	317	76	17	1	4	1.3	27	27	16	25	3	.240	.338	11	2	1B-96, DH-3

Biddy Dolan

DOLAN, E. L.
B. Unknown. BR TR

	G	AB	H	2B	3B	HR	HR%	R	RBI	BB	SO	SB	BA	SA	PH AB	PH H	G by POS
1914 IND F	32	103	23	4	2	1	1.0	13	15	12		5	.223	.330	0	0	1B-31

Cozy Dolan

DOLAN, ALBERT J
Born James Alberts.
B. Dec. 23, 1889, Chicago, Ill. D. Dec. 10, 1958, Chicago, Ill. BR TR 5'10" 160 lbs.

	G	AB	H	2B	3B	HR	HR%	R	RBI	BB	SO	SB	BA	SA	PH AB	PH H	G by POS
1909 CIN N	3	6	1	0	0	0	0.0	2	0	2		0	.167	.167	0	0	3B-3
1911 NY A	19	69	21	1	2	1	1.4	19	6	8		12	.304	.420	0	0	3B-19
1912 2 teams	NY	A	(17G –	.200)		PHI	N	(11G –	.280)								
" total	28	110	26	3	5	0	0.0	23	18	6	10	8	.236	.355	0	0	3B-28
1913 2 teams	PHI	N	(55G –	.262)		PIT	N	(35G –	.203)								
" total	90	259	60	9	2	0	0.0	37	17	16	35	23	.232	.282	13	3	3B-39, OF-12, SS-10, 2B-9, 1B-1
1914 STL N	126	421	101	16	3	4	1.0	76	32	55	74	42	.240	.321	1	1	OF-97, 3B-29
1915	111	322	90	14	9	2	0.6	53	38	34	37	17	.280	.398	3	1	OF-98

	G	AB	H	2B	3B	HR	HR %	R	RBI	BB	SO	SB	BA	SA	Pinch Hit AB	Pinch Hit H	G by POS

Cozy Dolan continued

	G	AB	H	2B	3B	HR	HR %	R	RBI	BB	SO	SB	BA	SA	AB	H	G by POS
1922 NY N	1	0	0	0	0	0	–	0	0	0	0	0	–	–	0	0	
7 yrs.	378	1187	299	43	21	7	0.6	210	111	121	156	102	.252	.341	17	5	OF-207, 3B-118, SS-10, 2B-9, 1B-1

Cozy Dolan

DOLAN, PATRICK HENRY   BL TL 5'10" 160 lbs.
B. Dec. 3, 1872, Cambridge, Mass.   D. Mar. 29, 1907, Louisville, Ky.

	G	AB	H	2B	3B	HR	HR %	R	RBI	BB	SO	SB	BA	SA	AB	H	G by POS
1895 BOS N	26	83	20	4	1	0	0.0	12	7	6	7	3	.241	.313	0	0	P-25, OF-1
1896	6	14	2	0	0	0	0.0	4	0	0	1	0	.143	.143	0	0	P-6
1900 CHI N	13	48	13	1	0	0	0.0	5	2	2		2	.271	.292	0	0	OF-13
1901 2 teams		CHI	N (43G – .263)			BKN	N (66G – .261)										
" total	109	424	111	12	3	0	0.0	62	45	24		10	.262	.304	4	1	OF-105
1902 BKN N	141	592	166	16	7	1	0.2	72	54	33		24	.280	.336	0	0	OF-141
1903 2 teams		CHI	A (27G – .260)			CIN	N (93G – .288)										
" total	120	489	138	25	4	0	0.0	80	65	34		16	.282	.350	4	0	OF-97, 1B-19
1904 CIN N	129	465	132	8	10	6	1.3	88	51	39		19	.284	.383	3	0	OF-102, 1B-24
1905 2 teams		CIN	N (22G – .234)			BOS	N (112G – .275)										
" total	134	510	137	13	8	3	0.6	51	52	34		23	.269	.343	0	0	OF-120, 1B-15, P-2
1906 BOS N	152	549	136	20	4	0	0.0	54	39	55		17	.248	.299	0	0	OF-144, 2B-7, P-2, 1B-1
9 yrs.	830	3174	855	99	37	10	0.3	428	315	227	8	114	.269	.333	11	1	OF-723, 1B-59, P-35, 2B-7

Joe Dolan

DOLAN, JOSEPH   TR 5'10½" 155 lbs.
B. Feb. 24, 1873, Baltimore, Md.   D. Mar. 24, 1938, Omaha, Neb.

	G	AB	H	2B	3B	HR	HR %	R	RBI	BB	SO	SB	BA	SA	AB	H	G by POS
1896 LOU N	44	165	35	2	1	3	1.8	14	18	9	12	6	.212	.291	0	0	SS-44
1897	36	133	28	2	2	0	0.0	10	7	8		6	.211	.256	0	0	SS-18, 2B-18
1899 PHI N	61	222	57	6	3	1	0.5	27	30	11		3	.257	.324	0	0	2B-61
1900	74	257	51	7	3	1	0.4	39	27	16		10	.198	.261	0	0	3B-31, 2B-29, SS-12
1901 2 teams		PHI	N (10G – .081)			PHI	A (98G – .216)										
" total	108	375	76	21	2	1	0.3	50	40	28		3	.203	.277	0	0	SS-61, 3B-35, 2B-11, OF-1
5 yrs.	323	1152	247	38	11	6	0.5	140	122	72	12	28	.214	.282	0	0	SS-135, 2B-119, 3B-66, OF-1

Tom Dolan

DOLAN, THOMAS J.   BR TR
B. Jan. 10, 1859, New York, N. Y.   D. Jan. 16, 1913, St. Louis, Mo.

	G	AB	H	2B	3B	HR	HR %	R	RBI	BB	SO	SB	BA	SA	AB	H	G by POS
1879 CHI N	1	4	0	0	0	0	0.0	0	0	0	2		.000	.000	0	0	C-1
1882 BUF N	22	89	14	0	1	0	0.0	12		2	11		.157	.180	0	0	C-18, OF-4, 3B-2
1883 STL AA	81	295	63	9	2	1	0.3	32		9			.214	.268	0	0	OF-82, P-1
1884 2 teams		STL	AA (35G – .263)			STL	U (19G – .188)										
" total	54	206	49	9	2	0	0.0	28		10			.238	.301	0	0	C-48, OF-4, 3B-3
1885 STL N	3	9	2	0	0	0	0.0	2	1	1			.222	.222	0	0	C-3
1886 2 teams		STL	N (15G – .250)			BAL	AA (38G – .152)										
" total	53	169	30	6	2	0	0.0	21	1	15	9		.178	.237	0	0	C-50, OF-3
1888 STL AA	11	36	7	1	0	0	0.0	1	1	1		1	.194	.222	0	0	C-11
7 yrs.	225	808	165	25	7	1	0.1	95	1	39	23	1	.204	.256	0	0	C-131, OF-93, 3B-5, P-1

Frank Doljack

DOLJACK, FRANK JOSEPH   BR TR 5'11" 175 lbs.
B. Oct. 5, 1907, Cleveland, Ohio   D. Jan. 23, 1948, Cleveland, Ohio

	G	AB	H	2B	3B	HR	HR %	R	RBI	BB	SO	SB	BA	SA	AB	H	G by POS
1930 DET A	20	74	19	5	1	3	4.1	10	17	2	11	0	.257	.473	0	0	OF-20
1931	63	187	52	13	3	4	2.1	20	20	15	17	3	.278	.444	7	0	OF-54
1932	8	26	10	1	0	1	3.8	5	7	2	2	1	.385	.538	1	0	OF-6
1933	42	147	42	5	2	0	0.0	18	22	14	13	2	.286	.347	5	1	OF-37
1934	56	120	28	7	1	1	0.8	15	19	13	15	2	.233	.333	22	4	OF-30, 1B-3
1943 CLE A	3	7	0	0	0	0	0.0	0	0	1	2	0	.000	.000	1	0	OF-3
6 yrs.	192	561	151	31	7	9	1.6	68	85	47	60	8	.269	.398	36	5	OF-150, 1B-3

WORLD SERIES
	G	AB	H	2B	3B	HR	HR %	R	RBI	BB	SO	SB	BA	SA	AB	H	G by POS
1934 DET A	2	2	0	0	0	0	0.0	0	0	0	0	0	.000	.000	1	0	OF-1

Jiggs Donahue

DONAHUE, JOHN AUGUSTUS   BL TL 6'1" 178 lbs.
Brother of Pat Donahue.
B. July 13, 1879, Springfield, Ohio   D. July 19, 1913, Columbus, Ohio

	G	AB	H	2B	3B	HR	HR %	R	RBI	BB	SO	SB	BA	SA	AB	H	G by POS
1900 PIT N	3	10	2	0	1	0	0.0	1	3	0		1	.200	.400	0	0	C-2, OF-1
1901 2 teams		PIT	N (2G – .000)			MIL	A (37G – .306)										
" total	39	108	33	5	4	0	0.0	10	16	10		4	.306	.426	5	0	C-20, 1B-13, OF-1
1902 STL A	30	89	21	1	1	1	1.1	11	7	12		2	.236	.303	2	0	C-23, 1B-5
1904 CHI A	102	367	91	9	7	1	0.3	46	48	25		18	.248	.319	1	1	1B-101
1905	149	533	153	22	4	1	0.2	71	76	44		32	.287	.349	0	0	1B-149
1906	154	556	143	17	7	1	0.2	70	57	48		36	.257	.318	0	0	1B-154
1907	157	609	158	16	5	1	0.2	75	68	28		27	.259	.307	0	0	1B-157
1908	93	304	62	8	2	0	0.0	22	22	25		14	.204	.243	10	1	1B-83
1909 2 teams		CHI	A (2G – .000)			WAS	A (84G – .237)										
" total	86	287	67	12	1	0	0.0	13	30	23		9	.233	.282	3	2	1B-83
9 yrs.	813	2863	730	90	32	5	0.2	319	327	215		143	.255	.314	21	4	1B-745, C-45, OF-2

WORLD SERIES
	G	AB	H	2B	3B	HR	HR %	R	RBI	BB	SO	SB	BA	SA	AB	H	G by POS
1906 CHI A	6	18	6	2	1	0	0.0	0	4	3	4	0	.333	.556	0	0	1B-6

Jim Donahue

DONAHUE, JAMES AUGUSTUS   BR TR
B. Jan. 8, 1862, Lockport, Ill.   D. Apr. 19, 1935, Lockport, Ill.

	G	AB	H	2B	3B	HR	HR %	R	RBI	BB	SO	SB	BA	SA	AB	H	G by POS
1886 NY AA	49	186	37	0	0	0	0.0	14		10			.199	.199	0	0	OF-32, C-19
1887	60	220	62	4	1	1	0.5	33		21		6	.282	.323	0	0	C-51, OF-5, 1B-4, 3B-1, 2B-1
1888 KC AA	88	337	79	11	3	1	0.3	29	28	21		12	.234	.294	0	0	C-67, OF-18, 3B-5, 2B-1
1889	67	252	59	5	4	0	0.0	30	32	21	20	12	.234	.286	0	0	C-46, OF-14, 3B-10
1891 COL AA	77	280	61	4	3	0	0.0	27	35	31	18	2	.218	.254	0	0	C-75, OF-1, 1B-1
5 yrs.	341	1275	298	24	11	2	0.2	133	94	104	38	32	.234	.275	0	0	C-258, OF-70, 3B-16, 1B-5, 2B-2

	G	AB	H	2B	3B	HR	HR %	R	RBI	BB	SO	SB	BA	SA	Pinch Hit AB	Pinch Hit H	G by POS

Pat Donahue

DONAHUE, PATRICK WILLIAM   BR TR 6' 175 lbs.
Brother of Jiggs Donahue.
B. Nov. 3, 1884, Springfield, Ohio   D. Jan. 31, 1966, Springfield, Ohio

	G	AB	H	2B	3B	HR	HR %	R	RBI	BB	SO	SB	BA	SA	PH AB	PH H	G by POS
1908 BOS A	35	86	17	2	0	1	1.2	8	6	9		0	.198	.256	0	0	C-32, 1B-3
1909	64	176	42	4	1	2	1.1	14	25	17		2	.239	.307	6	2	C-58
1910 3 teams	BOS	A (2G –	.000)		PHI	A (15G –	.162)		CLE	A (2G –	.000)						
" total	19	45	6	0	0	0	0.0	2	4	3		1	.133	.133	2	0	C-17
3 yrs.	118	307	65	6	1	3	1.0	24	35	29		3	.212	.267	8	2	C-107, 1B-3

She Donahue

DONAHUE, CHARLES MICHAEL   BR TR 5'9"
B. June 29, 1877, Oswego, N. Y.   D. Aug. 28, 1947, New York, N. Y.

	G	AB	H	2B	3B	HR	HR %	R	RBI	BB	SO	SB	BA	SA	PH AB	PH H	G by POS
1904 2 teams	STL	N (4G –	.267)		PHI	N (58G –	.215)										
" total	62	215	47	4	0	0	0.0	22	16	3		10	.219	.237	0	0	SS-30, 3B-24, 2B-5, 1B-3

Tim Donahue

DONAHUE, TIMOTHY CORNELIUS   BL TR
B. June 8, 1870, Raynham, Mass.   D. June 12, 1902, Taunton, Mass.

	G	AB	H	2B	3B	HR	HR %	R	RBI	BB	SO	SB	BA	SA	PH AB	PH H	G by POS
1891 BOS AA	4	7	0	0	0	0	0.0	0	0	0	5	0	.000	.000	0	0	C-4
1895 CHI N	63	219	59	9	1	2	0.9	29	36	20	25	5	.269	.347	0	0	C-63
1896	57	188	41	10	1	0	0.0	27	20	11	15	11	.218	.282	0	0	C-57
1897	58	188	45	7	3	0	0.0	28	21	9		3	.239	.309	1	1	C-55, SS-2, 1B-1
1898	122	396	87	12	3	0	0.0	52	39	49		17	.220	.265	0	0	C-122
1899	92	278	69	9	3	0	0.0	39	29	34		10	.248	.302	0	0	C-91, 1B-1
1900	67	216	51	10	1	0	0.0	21	17	19		8	.236	.292	0	0	C-66, 2B-1
1902 WAS A	3	8	2	0	0	0	0.0	0	1	0		0	.250	.250	0	0	C-3
8 yrs.	466	1500	354	57	12	2	0.1	196	163	142	45	54	.236	.294	1	1	C-461, SS-2, 1B-2, 2B-1

John Donaldson

DONALDSON, JOHN DAVID   BL TR 5'11" 160 lbs.
B. May 5, 1943, Charlotte, N. C.

	G	AB	H	2B	3B	HR	HR %	R	RBI	BB	SO	SB	BA	SA	PH AB	PH H	G by POS
1966 KC A	15	30	4	0	0	0	0.0	4	1	3	4	1	.133	.133	5	0	2B-9
1967	105	377	104	16	5	0	0.0	27	28	37	39	6	.276	.345	4	2	2B-101, SS-1
1968 OAK A	127	363	80	9	2	0	0.6	37	27	45	44	5	.220	.273	26	6	2B-98, 3B-5, SS-1
1969 2 teams	OAK	A (12G –	.077)		SEA	A (95G –	.234)										
" total	107	351	80	8	3	1	0.3	23	19	38	40	6	.228	.276	10	0	2B-91, 3B-2, SS-1
1970 OAK A	41	89	22	2	1	1	1.1	4	11	9	6	1	.247	.326	13	6	2B-21, SS-6, 3B-1
1974	10	15	2	0	0	0	0.0	1	0	0		0	.133	.133	1	0	2B-7, 3B-3
6 yrs.	405	1225	292	35	11	4	0.3	96	86	132	133	19	.238	.295	59	14	2B-327, 3B-11, SS-9

Len Dondero

DONDERO, LEONARD PETER (Mike)   BR TR 5'11" 178 lbs.
B. Sept. 12, 1903, Newark, Calif.

	G	AB	H	2B	3B	HR	HR %	R	RBI	BB	SO	SB	BA	SA	PH AB	PH H	G by POS
1929 STL A	19	31	6	0	0	1	3.2	2	8	0	4	0	.194	.290	4	0	3B-10, 2B-5

Mike Donlin

DONLIN, MICHAEL JOSEPH (Turkey Mike)   BL TL 5'9" 170 lbs.
B. May 30, 1878, Erie, Pa.   D. Sept. 24, 1933, Hollywood, Calif.

	G	AB	H	2B	3B	HR	HR %	R	RBI	BB	SO	SB	BA	SA	PH AB	PH H	G by POS
1899 STL N	66	267	88	9	6	6	2.2	49	27	17		20	.330	.476	0	0	OF-51, 1B-13, SS-3, P-3
1900	78	276	90	8	6	10	3.6	40	48	14		14	.326	.507	10	4	OF-47, 1B-21
1901 BAL A	122	481	164	23	13	5	1.0	108	67	53		33	.341	.474	1	1	OF-74, 1B-47
1902 CIN N	34	143	42	4	5	0	0.0	30	9	9		9	.294	.392	1	0	OF-32, SS-1, P-1
1903	126	496	174	25	18	7	1.4	110	67	56		26	.351	.516	2	1	OF-118, 1B-7
1904 2 teams	CIN	N (60G –	.356)		NY	N (42G –	.280)										
" total	102	368	121	18	10	3	0.8	59	52	28		22	.329	.457	6	0	OF-90, 1B-6
1905 NY N	150	606	216	31	16	7	1.2	124	80	56		33	.356	.495	0	0	OF-150
1906	37	121	38	5	1	1	0.8	15	14	11		9	.314	.397	6	0	OF-29, 1B-1
1908	155	593	198	26	13	6	1.0	71	106	23		30	.334	.452	0	0	OF-155
1911 2 teams	NY	N (12G –	.333)		BOS	N (56G –	.315)										
" total	68	234	74	16	1	3	1.3	36	35	22	18	9	.316	.432	9	2	OF-59
1912 PIT N	77	244	77	9	8	2	0.8	27	35	20	16	8	.316	.443	13	2	OF-62
1914 NY N	35	31	5	1	1	1	3.2	1	3	3	5	0	.161	.355	31	5	
12 yrs.	1050	3860	1287	175	98	51	1.3	670	543	312	39	213	.333	.469	79	15	OF-867, 1B-95, SS-4, P-4
WORLD SERIES																	
1905 NY N	5	19	6	1	0	0	0.0	4	1	2	1	2	.316	.368	0	0	OF-5

Jim Donnelly

DONNELLY, JAMES B.   BR TR
B. July 19, 1865, New Haven, Conn.   D. Mar. 5, 1915, Meriden, Conn.

	G	AB	H	2B	3B	HR	HR %	R	RBI	BB	SO	SB	BA	SA	PH AB	PH H	G by POS
1884 2 teams	KC	U (6G –	.130)		IND	AA (40G –	.254)										
" total	46	157	37	3	2	0	0.0	24		6			.236	.280	0	0	3B-29, SS-8, OF-6, 2B-2, C-1
1885 DET N	56	211	49	4	3	1	0.5	24	22	10	29		.232	.294	0	0	3B-55, 1B-1
1886 KC N	113	438	88	11	3	0	0.0	51	38	36	57		.201	.240	0	0	3B-113
1887 WAS N	117	425	85	9	6	1	0.2	51	46	16	26	42	.200	.256	0	0	3B-115, SS-2
1888	122	428	86	9	4	0	0.0	43	23	20	16	44	.201	.241	0	0	3B-117, SS-5
1889	4	13	2	0	0	0	0.0	3	0	2	0	1	.154	.154	0	0	3B-4
1890 STL AA	11	42	14	0	0	0	0.0	11		8		5	.333	.333	0	0	3B-11
1891 COL AA	17	54	13	0	1	0	0.0	6	9	13	5	7	.241	.241	0	0	3B-17
1896 BAL N	106	396	130	14	10	0	0.0	70	71	34	11	38	.328	.414	0	0	3B-106
1897 2 teams	PIT	N (44G –	.193)		NY	N (23G –	.188)										
" total	67	246	47	7	0	0	0.0	41	25	25		20	.191	.220	0	0	3B-67
1898 STL N	1	1	1	0	0	0	0.0	0	0	0		0	1.000	1.000	0	0	3B-1
11 yrs.	660	2411	552	57	28	2	0.1	324	233	170	144	157	.229	.278	0	0	3B-635, SS-15, OF-6, 2B-2, 1B-1, C-1

Joe Donohue

DONOHUE, JOSEPH F.
B. 1869, Syracuse, N. Y.   D. Nov. 12, 1894

	G	AB	H	2B	3B	HR	HR %	R	RBI	BB	SO	SB	BA	SA	PH AB	PH H	G by POS
1891 PHI N	6	22	7	1	0	0	0.0	2	2	1	3	0	.318	.364	0	0	OF-4, SS-2

	G	AB	H	2B	3B	HR	HR %	R	RBI	BB	SO	SB	BA	SA	Pinch Hit AB	Pinch Hit H	G by POS

John Donohue

DONOHUE, JOHN FREDERICK (Jiggs)
BL TR 5'8" 170 lbs.
B. Apr. 19, 1894, Boston, Mass.   D. Oct. 3, 1949, Boston, Mass.

	G	AB	H	2B	3B	HR	HR %	R	RBI	BB	SO	SB	BA	SA	AB	H	G by POS
1923 BOS A	10	36	10	4	0	0	0.0	5	1	4	5	0	.278	.389	1	1	OF-9

Tom Donohue

DONOHUE, THOMAS JAMES
BR TR 6' 185 lbs.
B. Nov. 15, 1952, Westbury, N. Y.

	G	AB	H	2B	3B	HR	HR %	R	RBI	BB	SO	SB	BA	SA	AB	H	G by POS
1979 CAL A	38	107	24	3	1	3	2.8	13	14	3	29	2	.224	.355	0	0	C-38
1980	84	218	41	4	1	2	0.9	18	14	7	63	5	.188	.243	0	0	C-84
2 yrs.	122	325	65	7	2	5	1.5	31	28	10	92	7	.200	.280	0	0	C-122

Fred Donovan

DONOVAN, FREDERICK MAURICE
B. July 4, 1864, New Hampshire   D. Mar. 7, 1916, Bloomington, Ill.

	G	AB	H	2B	3B	HR	HR %	R	RBI	BB	SO	SB	BA	SA	AB	H	G by POS
1895 CLE N	3	12	1	0	0	0	0.0	1	1	1	2	0	.083	.083	0	0	C-3

Jerry Donovan

DONOVAN, JEREMIAH FRANCIS
TR
Brother of Tom Donovan.
B. Aug. 24, 1875, Williamsport, Pa.   D. June 27, 1938, St. Petersburg, Fla.

	G	AB	H	2B	3B	HR	HR %	R	RBI	BB	SO	SB	BA	SA	AB	H	G by POS
1906 PHI N	61	166	33	4	0	0	0.0	11	15	6		2	.199	.223	7	1	C-52, OF-1, SS-1

Mike Donovan

DONOVAN, MICHAEL BERCHMAN
TR
B. Oct. 13, 1883, New York, N. Y.   D. Feb. 3, 1938, New York, N. Y.

	G	AB	H	2B	3B	HR	HR %	R	RBI	BB	SO	SB	BA	SA	AB	H	G by POS
1904 CLE A	2	2	0	0	0	0	0.0	0	0	0		0	.000	.000	1	0	SS-1
1908 NY A	5	19	5	1	0	0	0.0	2	2	0		0	.263	.316	0	0	3B-5
2 yrs.	7	21	5	1	0	0	0.0	2	2	0		0	.238	.286	1	0	3B-5, SS-1

Patsy Donovan

DONOVAN, PATRICK JOSEPH
BR TL 5'11½" 175 lbs.
B. Mar. 16, 1865, County Cork, Ireland   D. Dec. 25, 1953, Lawrence, Mass.
Manager 1897, 1899, 1901-04, 1906-08, 1910-11.

	G	AB	H	2B	3B	HR	HR %	R	RBI	BB	SO	SB	BA	SA	AB	H	G by POS
1890 2 teams	BOS N (32G – .179)					BKN N (28G – .352)											
" total	60	245	62	6	1	0	0.0	34	17	13	22	13	.253	.286	0	0	OF-60
1891 2 teams	LOU AA (105G – .321)					WAS AA (17G – .200)											
" total	122	509	155	11	3	2	0.4	82	56	34	23	28	.305	.350	0	0	OF-122
1892 2 teams	WAS N (40G – .239)					PIT N (90G – .294)											
" total	130	551	153	18	6	2	0.4	106	38	31	29	56	.278	.343	0	0	OF-130
1893 PIT N	113	499	158	5	8	2	0.4	114	56	42	8	46	.317	.371	1	0	OF-112
1894	132	576	174	21	10	4	0.7	145	76	33	12	41	.302	.394	0	0	OF-132
1895	125	519	160	17	6	1	0.2	114	58	47	19	36	.308	.370	0	0	OF-125
1896	131	573	183	20	5	3	0.5	113	59	35	18	48	.319	.387	0	0	OF-131
1897	120	479	154	16	7	0	0.0	82	57	25		34	.322	.384	0	0	OF-120
1898	147	610	184	16	9	0	0.0	112	37	34		41	.302	.357	0	0	OF-147
1899	121	531	156	11	7	1	0.2	82	55	17		26	.294	.347	0	0	OF-121
1900 STL N	126	503	159	11	1	0	0.0	78	61	38		45	.316	.342	2	1	OF-124
1901	130	527	154	23	5	1	0.2	92	73	27		28	.292	.361	0	0	OF-129
1902	126	502	158	12	4	0	0.0	70	35	28		34	.315	.355	0	0	OF-126
1903	105	410	134	15	3	0	0.0	63	39	25		25	.327	.378	0	0	OF-105
1904 WAS A	125	436	100	6	0	0	0.0	30	19	24		17	.229	.243	3	0	OF-122
1906 BKN N	7	21	5	0	0	0	0.0	1	0	0		0	.238	.238	1	0	OF-6
1907	1	1	0	0	0	0	0.0	0	0	0		0	.000	.000	0	0	OF-1
17 yrs.	1821	7492	2249	208	75	16	0.2	1318	736	453	131	518	.300	.354	7	1	OF-1813

Tom Donovan

DONOVAN, THOMAS JOSEPH
BR TR
Brother of Jerry Donovan.
B. July 7, 1879, Lock Haven, Pa.   D. Feb. 20, 1955, Williamsport, Pa.

	G	AB	H	2B	3B	HR	HR %	R	RBI	BB	SO	SB	BA	SA	AB	H	G by POS
1901 CLE A	18	71	18	3	1	0	0.0	9	5	0		1	.254	.324	0	0	OF-18, P-1

Wild Bill Donovan

DONOVAN, WILLIAM EDWARD
BR TR 5'11" 190 lbs.
B. Oct. 13, 1876, Lawrence, Mass.   D. Dec. 9, 1923, Forsyth, N. Y.
Manager 1915-17, 1921.

	G	AB	H	2B	3B	HR	HR %	R	RBI	BB	SO	SB	BA	SA	AB	H	G by POS
1898 WAS N	39	103	17	2	3	1	1.0	11	8	4		2	.165	.272	2	1	OF-20, P-17, SS-1, 2B-1
1899 BKN N	5	13	3	1	0	0	0.0	2	0	0		0	.231	.308	0	0	P-5
1900	5	13	0	0	0	0	0.0	0	0	2		0	.000	.000	0	0	P-5
1901	46	135	23	3	0	2	1.5	16	13	8		1	.170	.237	0	0	P-45
1902	48	161	27	3	2	1	0.6	16	16	9		7	.168	.230	0	0	P-35, 1B-8, OF-4, 2B-1
1903 DET A	40	124	30	3	2	0	0.0	11	12	4		3	.242	.298	2	0	P-35, SS-2, OF-1, 2B-1
1904	46	140	38	2	1	1	0.7	12	6	3		2	.271	.321	2	1	P-34, 1B-8, OF-1
1905	46	130	25	4	0	0	0.0	16	5	12		8	.192	.223	0	0	P-34, OF-8, 2B-2
1906	28	91	11	0	1	0	0.0	5	0	1		6	.121	.143	0	0	P-25, 2B-3, OF-1
1907	37	109	29	7	2	0	0.0	20	19	6		4	.266	.367	4	0	P-32
1908	30	82	13	1	0	0	0.0	5	2	10		2	.159	.171	0	0	P-29
1909	22	45	9	0	0	0	0.0	6	1	2		0	.200	.200	0	0	P-21
1910	26	69	10	1	0	0	0.0	6	2	5		0	.145	.159	0	0	P-26
1911	24	60	12	3	1	1	1.7	11	6	11		1	.200	.333	1	1	P-20
1912	6	13	1	0	0	0	0.0	3	0	1		0	.077	.077	0	0	P-3, OF-2, 1B-2
1915 NY A	10	12	1	0	0	0	0.0	1	0	1	6	0	.083	.083	0	0	P-9
1916	1	0	0	0	0	0	–	0	0	0	0	0	–	–	0	0	P-1
1918 DET A	2	2	1	0	0	0	0.0	0	1	0	0	0	.500	.500	0	0	P-2
18 yrs.	461	1302	250	30	12	6	0.5	142	93	77	6	36	.192	.247	11	3	P-378, OF-37, 1B-18, 2B-8, SS-3

WORLD SERIES

	G	AB	H	2B	3B	HR	HR %	R	RBI	BB	SO	SB	BA	SA	AB	H	G by POS
1907 DET A	2	8	0	0	0	0	0.0	0	0	0	3	0	.000	.000	0	0	P-2
1908	2	4	0	0	0	0	0.0	0	0	1	1	0	.000	.000	0	0	P-2
1909	2	4	0	0	0	0	0.0	0	0	0	1	0	.000	.000	0	0	P-2
3 yrs.	6	16	0	0	0	0	0.0	0	0	1	5	0	.000	.000	0	0	P-6

	G	AB	H	2B	3B	HR	HR %	R	RBI	BB	SO	SB	BA	SA	Pinch Hit AB	Pinch Hit H	G by POS

Red Dooin

DOOIN, CHARLES SEBASTIAN BR TR 5'9½" 165 lbs.
B. June 12, 1879, Cincinnati, Ohio   D. May 14, 1952, Rochester, N. Y.
Manager 1910-14.

	G	AB	H	2B	3B	HR	HR %	R	RBI	BB	SO	SB	BA	SA	AB	H	G by POS
1902 PHI N	94	333	77	7	3	0	0.0	20	35	10		8	.231	.270	4	1	C-84, OF-6
1903	62	188	41	5	1	0	0.0	18	14	8		9	.218	.255	9	3	C-51, OF-1, 1B-1
1904	108	355	86	11	4	6	1.7	41	36	8		15	.242	.346	5	0	C-96, 1B-4, OF-3, 3B-1
1905	113	380	95	13	5	0	0.0	45	36	10		12	.250	.311	5	3	C-107, 3B-1
1906	113	351	86	19	1	0	0.0	25	32	13		15	.245	.305	6	1	C-107
1907	101	313	66	8	4	0	0.0	18	14	15		10	.211	.262	5	1	C-94, OF-1, 2B-1
1908	133	435	108	17	4	0	0.0	28	41	17		20	.248	.306	1	0	C-132
1909	141	468	105	14	1	2	0.4	42	38	21		14	.224	.271	1	0	C-140
1910	103	331	80	13	4	0	0.0	30	30	22	17	10	.242	.305	8	3	C-91, OF-3
1911	74	247	81	15	1	1	0.4	18	16	14	12	6	.328	.409	0	0	C-74
1912	69	184	43	9	0	0	0.0	20	22	5	12	8	.234	.283	8	1	C-58
1913	55	129	33	4	1	0	0.0	6	13	3	9	1	.256	.302	5	2	C-50
1914	53	118	21	2	0	1	0.8	10	8	4	14	4	.178	.220	8	2	C-40
1915 2 teams	CIN	N (10G – .323)		NY	N	(46G – .218)											
" total	56	155	37	2	2	0	0.0	11	9	5	20	1	.239	.277	0	0	C-56
1916 NY N	15	17	2	0	0	0	0.0	1	0	1	3	0	.118	.118	0	0	C-15
15 yrs.	1290	4004	961	139	31	10	0.2	333	344	155	87	133	.240	.298	65	17	C-1195, OF-14, 1B-5, 3B-2, 2B-1

Mickey Doolan

DOOLAN, MICHAEL JOSEPH BR TR 5'10½" 170 lbs.
Born Michael Joseph Doolittle.
B. May 7, 1880, Ashland, Pa.   D. Nov. 1, 1951, Orlando, Fla.

	G	AB	H	2B	3B	HR	HR %	R	RBI	BB	SO	SB	BA	SA	AB	H	G by POS
1905 PHI N	136	492	125	27	11	1	0.2	53	48	24		17	.254	.360	1	0	SS-135
1906	154	535	123	19	7	1	0.2	41	55	27		16	.230	.297	0	0	SS-154
1907	145	509	104	19	7	1	0.2	33	47	25		18	.204	.275	0	0	SS-145
1908	129	445	104	25	4	2	0.4	29	49	17		5	.234	.321	0	0	SS-129
1909	147	493	108	12	10	1	0.2	39	35	37		10	.219	.290	0	0	SS-147
1910	148	536	141	31	6	2	0.4	58	57	35	56	16	.263	.354	0	0	SS-148
1911	146	512	122	23	6	1	0.2	51	49	44	65	14	.238	.313	1	0	SS-145
1912	146	532	137	26	6	1	0.2	47	62	34	59	6	.258	.335	0	0	SS-146
1913	151	518	113	12	6	1	0.2	32	43	29	68	17	.218	.270	0	0	SS-148, 2B-3
1914 BAL F	145	486	119	23	6	1	0.2	58	53	40		30	.245	.323	0	0	SS-145
1915 2 teams	BAL	F (119G – .186)		CHI	F	(24G – .267)											
" total	143	490	98	14	8	2	0.4	50	30	26		15	.200	.273	1	0	SS-143
1916 2 teams	CHI	N (28G – .214)		NY	N	(18G – .235)											
" total	46	121	27	5	2	1	0.8	8	8	10	11	1	.223	.322	3	0	SS-40, 2B-2
1918 BKN N	92	308	55	8	2	0	0.0	14	18	22	24	8	.179	.218	0	0	2B-91
13 yrs.	1728	5977	1376	244	81	15	0.3	513	554	370	283	173	.230	.306	5	0	SS-1625, 2B-96

Jack Dooms

DOOMS, HENRY E. (Harry)
B. Jan. 30, 1867, St. Louis, Mo.   D. Dec. 14, 1899, St. Louis, Mo.

	G	AB	H	2B	3B	HR	HR %	R	RBI	BB	SO	SB	BA	SA	AB	H	G by POS
1892 LOU N	1	4	0	0	0	0	0.0	0		0	1	0	.000	.000	0	0	OF-1

Bill Doran

DORAN, WILLIAM DONALD BR TR 5'11" 170 lbs.
B. May 28, 1958, Cincinnati, Ohio

	G	AB	H	2B	3B	HR	HR %	R	RBI	BB	SO	SB	BA	SA	AB	H	G by POS
1982 HOU N	26	97	27	3	0	0	0.0	11	6	4	11	5	.278	.309	0	0	2B-26
1983	154	535	145	12	7	8	1.5	70	39	86	67	12	.271	.364	3	1	2B-153
1984	147	548	143	18	11	4	0.7	92	41	66	69	21	.261	.356	2	0	2B-139, SS-13
3 yrs.	327	1180	315	33	18	12	1.0	173	86	156	147	38	.267	.356	5	1	2B-318, SS-13

Bill Doran

DORAN, WILLIAM JAMES BL TR 5'11½" 175 lbs.
B. June 14, 1898, San Francisco, Calif.   D. Mar. 9, 1978, Santa Monica, Calif.

	G	AB	H	2B	3B	HR	HR %	R	RBI	BB	SO	SB	BA	SA	AB	H	G by POS
1922 CLE A	3	2	1	0	0	0	0.0	0	1	0	1	0	.500	.500	0	0	3B-2

Tom Doran

DORAN, THOMAS J. TL
B. Feb. 2, 1880, Westchester County, N. Y.   D. June 22, 1910, New York, N. Y.

	G	AB	H	2B	3B	HR	HR %	R	RBI	BB	SO	SB	BA	SA	AB	H	G by POS
1904 BOS A	12	32	4	0	1	0	0.0	1	0	4		1	.125	.188	1	0	C-11
1905 2 teams	BOS	A (2G – .000)		DET	A	(34G – .160)											
" total	36	96	15	3	0	0	0.0	8	4	8		2	.156	.188	3	1	C-33
1906 BOS A	2	3	0	0	0	0	0.0	1	0	0		0	.000	.000	0	0	C-2
3 yrs.	50	131	19	3	1	0	0.0	10	4	12		3	.145	.183	4	1	C-46

Jerry Dorgan

DORGAN, JEREMIAH F.
Brother of Mike Dorgan.
B. 1856, Meriden, Conn.   D. June 10, 1891, New Haven, Conn.

	G	AB	H	2B	3B	HR	HR %	R	RBI	BB	SO	SB	BA	SA	AB	H	G by POS
1880 WOR N	10	35	7	1	0	0	0.0	2		0	1		.200	.229	0	0	OF-9, C-1
1882 PHI N	44	181	51	9	1	0	0.0	25		4			.282	.343	0	0	C-25, OF-22, 3B-1
1884 2 teams	IND	AA (34G – .298)		BKN	AA	(4G – .308)											
" total	38	154	46	6	1	0	0.0	24		2			.299	.351	0	0	OF-29, C-9
1885 DET N	39	161	46	6	2	0	0.0	23	23	8	10		.286	.348	0	0	OF-39
4 yrs.	131	531	150	22	4	0	0.0	74	23	14	11		.282	.339	0	0	OF-99, C-35, 3B-1

Mike Dorgan

DORGAN, MICHAEL CORNELIUS TR 5'9" 180 lbs.
Brother of Jerry Dorgan.
B. Oct. 2, 1853, Middletown, Conn.   D. Apr. 26, 1909, Hartford, Conn.
Manager 1879.

	G	AB	H	2B	3B	HR	HR %	R	RBI	BB	SO	SB	BA	SA	AB	H	G by POS
1877 STL N	60	266	82	9	7	0	0.0	45	23	9	13		.308	.395	0	0	OF-50, C-12, 3B-2, SS-1, 2B-1
1879 SYR N	59	270	72	11	5	1	0.4	38	17	4	13		.267	.356	0	0	1B-21, OF-16, 3B-11, SS-6, C-4, P-2, 2B-1
1880 PRO N	79	321	79	10	4	0	0.0	45	31	10	18		.246	.283	0	0	OF-77, 3B-2, P-1
1881 2 teams	WOR	N (51G – .277)		DET	N	(8G – .235)											
" total	59	254	69	6	0	0	0.0	41	23	9	4		.272	.295	0	0	OF-28, 1B-27, SS-2, 3B-2
1883 NY N	64	261	61	11	3	0	0.0	32		2	23		.234	.299	0	0	OF-59, C-6, P-1
1884	83	341	94	11	6	1	0.3	61		13	27		.276	.352	0	0	OF-64, P-14, C-6, 2B-3

	G	AB	H	2B	3B	HR	HR %	R	RBI	BB	SO	SB	BA	SA	Pinch Hit AB	Pinch Hit H	G by POS

Mike Dorgan continued

	G	AB	H	2B	3B	HR	HR %	R	RBI	BB	SO	SB	BA	SA	AB	H	G by POS
1885	89	347	113	17	8	0	0.0	60		11	24		.326	.421	0	0	OF-88, 1B-1
1886	118	442	129	19	3	3	0.7	61	79	29	37		.292	.369	0	0	OF-116, 1B-3
1887	71	283	73	10	0	0	0.0	41	34	15	20	22	.258	.293	0	0	OF-69, 1B-2
1890 SYR AA	33	139	30	8	0	0	0.0	19		16		8	.216	.273	0	0	OF-33
10 yrs.	715	2924	802	112	33	5	0.2	443	207	118	179	30	.274	.340	0	0	OF-600, 1B-54, C-28, P-18, 3B-17, SS-9, 2B-5

Curly Dorman

DORMAN, DWIGHT DEXTER (Red)
B. Oct. 3, 1905, Jacksonville, Ill.

BR TR 6'2"   185 lbs.

	G	AB	H	2B	3B	HR	HR %	R	RBI	BB	SO	SB	BA	SA	AB	H	G by POS
1923 CHI A	1	2	1	0	0	0	0.0	0	0	0	0	0	.500	.500	0	0	C-1
1928 CLE A	25	77	28	6	0	0	0.0	12	11	9	6	1	.364	.442	1	1	OF-24
2 yrs.	26	79	29	6	0	0	0.0	12	11	9	6	1	.367	.443	1	1	OF-24, C-1

Jerry Dorsey

DORSEY, JEREMIAH
B. 1885, Oakland, Calif.

	G	AB	H	2B	3B	HR	HR %	R	RBI	BB	SO	SB	BA	SA	AB	H	G by POS
1911 PIT N	2	6	0	0	0	0	0.0	0		0	1	0	.000	.000	1	0	OF-1

Herm Doscher

DOSCHER, JOHN HENRY, SR.
Father of Jack Doscher.
B. Dec. 20, 1852, New York, N. Y.   D. Mar. 30, 1934, Buffalo, N. Y.

5'10"   182 lbs.

	G	AB	H	2B	3B	HR	HR %	R	RBI	BB	SO	SB	BA	SA	AB	H	G by POS
1879 2 teams		TRO	N	(47G –	.220)		CHI	N	(3G –	.182)							
" total	50	202	44	8	0	0	0.0	17	19	2	13		.218	.257	0	0	3B-50
1881 CLE N	5	19	4	0	0	0	0.0	2	0	0	2		.211	.211	0	0	3B-5
1882	25	104	25	2	0	0	0.0	7	10	0	11		.240	.260	0	0	3B-22, OF-2, SS-1
3 yrs.	80	325	73	10	0	0	0.0	26	29	2	26		.225	.255	0	0	3B-77, OF-2, SS-1

Dutch Dotterer

DOTTERER, HENRY JOHN
B. Nov. 11, 1931, Syracuse, N. Y.

BR TR 6'   209 lbs.

	G	AB	H	2B	3B	HR	HR %	R	RBI	BB	SO	SB	BA	SA	AB	H	G by POS
1957 CIN N	4	12	1	0	0	0	0.0	0	2	1	2	0	.083	.083	1	0	C-4
1958	11	28	7	1	0	1	3.6	1	2	2	4	0	.250	.393	3	0	C-8
1959	52	161	43	7	0	2	1.2	21	17	16	23	0	.267	.348	1	0	C-51
1960	33	79	18	5	0	2	2.5	4	11	13	10	0	.228	.367	3	0	C-31
1961 WAS A	7	19	5	2	0	0	0.0	1	1	3	5	0	.263	.368	0	0	C-7
5 yrs.	107	299	74	15	0	5	1.7	27	33	35	44	0	.247	.348	8	0	C-101

Charlie Dougherty

DOUGHERTY, CHARLES WILLIAM
B. Feb. 7, 1862, Darlington, Wis.   D. Feb. 18, 1925, Milwaukee, Wis.

	G	AB	H	2B	3B	HR	HR %	R	RBI	BB	SO	SB	BA	SA	AB	H	G by POS
1884 ALT U	23	85	22	5	0	0	0.0	6		2			.259	.318	0	0	2B-16, OF-8, SS-1

Patsy Dougherty

DOUGHERTY, PATRICK HENRY
B. Oct. 27, 1876, Andover, N. Y.   D. Apr. 30, 1940, Bolivar, N. Y.

BL TR 6'2"   190 lbs.

	G	AB	H	2B	3B	HR	HR %	R	RBI	BB	SO	SB	BA	SA	AB	H	G by POS
1902 BOS A	108	438	150	12	6	0	0.0	77	34	42		20	.342	.397	3	2	OF-102, 3B-1
1903	139	590	195	19	12	4	0.7	108	59	33		35	.331	.424	0	0	OF-139
1904 2 teams		BOS	A	(49G –	.272)		NY	A	(106G –	.283)							
" total	155	647	181	18	14	6	0.9	113	26	44		21	.280	.379	0	0	OF-155
1905 NY A	116	418	110	9	6	3	0.7	56	29	28		17	.263	.335	5	1	OF-108, 3B-1
1906 2 teams		NY	A	(12G –	.192)		CHI	A	(75G –	.233)							
" total	87	305	69	11	4	1	0.3	33	31	19		11	.226	.298	0	0	OF-86
1907 CHI A	148	533	144	17	2	1	0.2	69	59	36		33	.270	.315	0	0	OF-148
1908	138	482	134	11	6	0	0.0	68	45	58		47	.278	.326	9	2	OF-138
1909	139	491	140	23	13	1	0.2	71	55	51		36	.285	.391	1	0	OF-138
1910	127	444	110	8	6	1	0.2	45	43	41		22	.248	.300	3	1	OF-121
1911	76	211	61	10	9	0	0.0	39	32	26		19	.289	.422	19	3	OF-56
10 yrs.	1233	4558	1294	138	78	17	0.4	679	413	378		261	.284	.360	40	9	OF-1191, 3B-2
WORLD SERIES																	
1903 BOS A	8	34	8	0	2	2	5.9	3	5	2	5	0	.235	.529	0	0	OF-8
1906 CHI A	6	20	2	0	0	0	0.0	1	1	3	3	2	.100	.100	0	0	OF-6
2 yrs.	14	54	10	0	2	2	3.7	4	6	5	8	2	.185	.370	0	0	OF-14

John Douglas

DOUGLAS, JOHN FRANKLIN
B. Sept. 14, 1917, Thayer, W. Va.

BL TL 6'2½"   195 lbs.

	G	AB	H	2B	3B	HR	HR %	R	RBI	BB	SO	SB	BA	SA	AB	H	G by POS
1945 BKN N	5	9	0	0	0	0	0.0	0	0	2	4	0	.000	.000	1	0	1B-4

Astyanax Douglass

DOUGLASS, ASTYANAX SAUNDERS
B. Sept. 19, 1897, Covington, Tex.   D. Jan. 26, 1975, El Paso, Tex.

BL TR 6'1"   190 lbs.

	G	AB	H	2B	3B	HR	HR %	R	RBI	BB	SO	SB	BA	SA	AB	H	G by POS
1921 CIN N	4	7	1	0	0	0	0.0	1	0	0	1	0	.143	.143	0	0	C-4
1925	7	17	3	0	0	0	0.0	1	1	1	3	0	.176	.176	0	0	C-7
2 yrs.	11	24	4	0	0	0	0.0	2	1	1	4	0	.167	.167	0	0	C-11

Klondike Douglass

DOUGLASS, WILLIAM BIGHAM
B. May 10, 1872, Boston, Pa.   D. Dec. 13, 1953, Bend, Ore.

BL TR 6'   200 lbs.

	G	AB	H	2B	3B	HR	HR %	R	RBI	BB	SO	SB	BA	SA	AB	H	G by POS
1896 STL N	81	296	78	6	4	1	0.3	42	28	35	15	18	.264	.321	1	0	OF-74, C-6, SS-2
1897	125	516	170	15	3	6	1.2	77	50	52		12	.329	.405	1	1	C-61, OF-43, 1B-17, 3B-7, SS-1
1898 PHI N	146	582	150	26	4	2	0.3	105	48	55		18	.258	.326	0	0	1B-146
1899	77	275	70	6	6	0	0.0	26	27	10		7	.255	.320	1	0	C-66, 3B-4, 1B-4, OF-1
1900	50	160	48	9	4	0	0.0	23	25	13		7	.300	.406	2	0	C-47, 3B-2
1901	51	173	56	6	1	0	0.0	14	23	11		10	.324	.370	3	0	C-41, 1B-6, OF-2
1902	109	408	95	12	3	0	0.0	37	37	23		6	.233	.277	1	0	1B-69, C-29, OF-10
1903	105	377	96	5	4	1	0.3	43	36	28		6	.255	.297	5	1	1B-97
1904	3	10	3	0	0	0	0.0	1	1	0		0	.300	.300	0	0	1B-3
9 yrs.	747	2797	766	85	29	10	0.4	368	275	227	15	84	.274	.336	14	3	1B-342, C-250, OF-130, 3B-13, SS-3

	G	AB	H	2B	3B	HR	HR %	R	RBI	BB	SO	SB	BA	SA	Pinch Hit AB	Pinch Hit H	G by POS

Taylor Douthit

DOUTHIT, TAYLOR LEE
B. Apr. 22, 1901, Little Rock, Ark.   BR TR 5'11½" 175 lbs.

	G	AB	H	2B	3B	HR	HR %	R	RBI	BB	SO	SB	BA	SA	AB	H	G by POS
1923 STL N	9	27	5	0	2	0	0.0	3	0	0	4	1	.185	.333	2	0	OF-7
1924	53	173	48	13	1	0	0.0	24	13	16	19	4	.277	.364	1	0	OF-50
1925	30	73	20	3	1	1	1.4	13	8	2	6	0	.274	.384	9	5	OF-21
1926	139	530	163	20	4	3	0.6	96	52	55	46	23	.308	.377	1	0	OF-138
1927	130	488	128	29	6	5	1.0	81	50	52	45	6	.262	.377	4	2	OF-125
1928	154	648	191	35	3	3	0.5	111	43	84	36	11	.295	.372	0	0	OF-154
1929	150	613	206	42	7	9	1.5	128	62	79	49	8	.336	.471	0	0	OF-150
1930	154	664	201	41	10	7	1.1	109	93	60	38	4	.303	.426	0	0	OF-154
1931 2 teams		STL	N	(36G –	.331)		CIN	N	(95G –	.262)							
" total	131	507	142	20	3	1	0.2	63	45	53	33	5	.280	.337	0	0	OF-131
1932 CIN N	96	333	81	12	1	0	0.0	28	25	31	29	3	.243	.285	2	0	OF-88
1933 2 teams		CIN	N	(1G –	.000)		CHI	N	(27G –	.225)							
" total	28	71	16	5	0	0	0.0	9	5	11	7	2	.225	.296	1	0	OF-18
11 yrs.	1074	4127	1201	220	38	29	0.7	665	396	443	312	67	.291	.384	20	7	OF-1036
WORLD SERIES																	
1926 STL N	4	15	4	2	0	0	0.0	3	1	3	2	0	.267	.400	0	0	OF-4
1928	3	11	1	0	0	0	0.0	1	0	1	1	0	.091	.091	0	0	OF-3
1930	6	24	2	0	0	1	4.2	1	2	0	2	0	.083	.208	0	0	OF-6
3 yrs.	13	50	7	2	0	1	2.0	5	3	4	5	0	.140	.240	0	0	OF-13

Clarence Dow

DOW, CLARENCE G.
B. Oct. 11, 1854, Charlestown, Mass.   D. Mar. 11, 1893, Somerville, Mass.

	G	AB	H	2B	3B	HR	HR %	R	RBI	BB	SO	SB	BA	SA	AB	H	G by POS
1884 BOS U	1	6	2	0	0	0	0.0	1					.333	.333	0	0	OF-1

Snooks Dowd

DOWD, RAYMOND BERNARD   BR TR 5'8" 163 lbs.
B. Dec. 20, 1897, Springfield, Mass.   D. Apr. 4, 1962, Springfield, Mass.

	G	AB	H	2B	3B	HR	HR %	R	RBI	BB	SO	SB	BA	SA	AB	H	G by POS
1919 2 teams		DET	A	(1G –	.000)		PHI	A	(13G –	.167)							
" total	14	18	3	0	0	0	0.0	4	6	0	5	2	.167	.167	1	0	2B-3, SS-2, OF-1, 3B-1
1926 BKN N	2	8	0	0	0	0	0.0	0	0	0	0	0	.000	.000	0	0	2B-2
2 yrs.	16	26	3	0	0	0	0.0	4	6	0	5	2	.115	.115	1	0	2B-5, SS-2, OF-1, 3B-1

Tommy Dowd

DOWD, THOMAS JEFFERSON (Buttermilk Tommy)   BR TR 5'8" 173 lbs.
B. Apr. 20, 1869, Holyoke, Mass.   D. July 2, 1933, Holyoke, Mass.
Manager 1896-97.

	G	AB	H	2B	3B	HR	HR %	R	RBI	BB	SO	SB	BA	SA	AB	H	G by POS
1891 2 teams		BOS	AA	(4G –	.091)		WAS	AA	(112G –	.259)							
" total	116	475	121	9	10	1	0.2	67	44	19	45	39	.255	.322	0	0	2B-107, OF-9
1892 WAS N	144	584	142	9	10	1	0.2	94	50	34	49	49	.243	.298	0	0	2B-98, OF-23, 3B-18, SS-6
1893 STL N	132	581	164	18	7	1	0.2	114	54	49	23	59	.282	.343	0	0	OF-132, 2B-1
1894	123	524	142	16	8	4	0.8	92	62	54	33	31	.271	.355	0	0	OF-117, 2B-7, 3B-1
1895	129	505	163	19	17	6	1.2	95	74	30	31	30	.323	.463	2	0	OF-115, 3B-17, 2B-2
1896	126	521	138	17	11	5	1.0	93	46	42	19	40	.265	.369	0	0	2B-78, OF-48
1897 2 teams		STL	N	(35G –	.262)		PHI	N	(91G –	.292)							
" total	126	536	152	23	5	0	0.0	93	52	25		41	.284	.345	0	0	OF-103, 2B-24
1898 STL N	139	586	143	17	7	0	0.0	70	32	30		16	.244	.297	0	0	OF-129, 2B-11
1899 CLE N	147	605	168	17	6	2	0.3	81	35	48		28	.278	.336	0	0	OF-147
1901 BOS A	138	594	159	18	7	3	0.5	104	52	38		33	.268	.337	0	0	OF-137, 1B-2, 3B-1
10 yrs.	1320	5511	1492	163	88	23	0.4	903	501	369	200	366	.271	.345	2	0	OF-960, 2B-328, 3B-37, SS-6, 1B-2

Joe Dowie

DOWIE, JOSEPH E.   5'8" 150 lbs.
B. 1866, New Orleans, La.   D. Sept. 3, 1893, New Orleans, La.

	G	AB	H	2B	3B	HR	HR %	R	RBI	BB	SO	SB	BA	SA	AB	H	G by POS
1889 BAL AA	20	75	17	5	0	0	0.0	12	8	2	10	5	.227	.293	0	0	OF-20

Red Downey

DOWNEY, ALEXANDER CUMMINGS   BL TL 5'11" 174 lbs.
B. Feb. 6, 1889, Aurora, Ind.   D. July 10, 1949, Detroit, Mich.

	G	AB	H	2B	3B	HR	HR %	R	RBI	BB	SO	SB	BA	SA	AB	H	G by POS
1909 BKN N	19	78	20	1	0	0	0.0	7	8	2		4	.256	.269	0	0	OF-19

Tom Downey

DOWNEY, THOMAS EDWARD   BR TR 6' 170 lbs.
B. Jan. 1, 1884, Lewiston, Mass.   D. Aug. 3, 1961, Passaic, N. J.

	G	AB	H	2B	3B	HR	HR %	R	RBI	BB	SO	SB	BA	SA	AB	H	G by POS
1909 CIN N	119	416	96	9	6	1	0.2	39	32	32		16	.231	.288	0	0	SS-119, C-1
1910	111	378	102	9	3	2	0.5	43	32	34	28	12	.270	.325	0	0	SS-68, 3B-41
1911	111	360	94	16	7	0	0.0	50	36	44	38	10	.261	.344	4	0	SS-93, 2B-6, 3B-5, 1B-2, OF-1
1912 2 teams		PHI	N	(54G –	.292)		CHI	N	(13G –	.182)							
" total	67	193	54	6	5	1	0.5	31	27	22	25	3	.280	.378	7	2	3B-49, SS-8, 2B-1
1914 BUF F	151	541	118	20	3	2	0.4	69	42	40	35	35	.218	.277	1	0	2B-129, SS-16, 3B-5
1915	92	282	56	9	1	1	0.4	24	19	26		11	.199	.248	5	1	2B-48, 3B-35, SS-2, 1B-1
6 yrs.	651	2170	520	69	25	7	0.3	256	188	198	91	87	.240	.304	17	3	SS-306, 2B-184, 3B-135, 1B-3, OF-1, C-1

Brian Downing

DOWNING, BRIAN JAY   BR TR 5'10" 170 lbs.
B. Oct. 9, 1950, Los Angeles, Calif.

	G	AB	H	2B	3B	HR	HR %	R	RBI	BB	SO	SB	BA	SA	AB	H	G by POS
1973 CHI A	34	73	13	1	0	2	2.7	4	4	10	17	0	.178	.274	8	2	OF-13, C-11, 3B-8
1974	108	293	66	12	1	10	3.4	41	39	51	72	0	.225	.375	5	0	C-63, OF-39, DH-9
1975	138	420	101	12	1	7	1.7	58	41	76	75	13	.240	.324	0	0	C-137, DH-1
1976	104	317	81	14	0	3	0.9	38	30	40	55	7	.256	.328	3	1	C-93, DH-11
1977	69	169	48	4	2	4	2.4	28	25	34	21	1	.284	.402	3	1	C-61, OF-3, DH-2
1978 CAL A	133	412	105	15	0	7	1.7	42	46	52	47	3	.255	.342	3	1	C-128, DH-2
1979	148	509	166	27	3	12	2.4	87	75	77	57	3	.326	.462	3	1	C-129, OF-16, 3B-5
1980	30	93	27	6	0	2	2.2	5	25	12	12	0	.290	.419	2	0	C-16, DH-13
1981	93	317	79	14	0	9	2.8	47	41	46	35	1	.249	.379	2	0	OF-56, C-37, DH-5
1982	158	623	175	37	2	28	4.5	109	84	86	58	2	.281	.482	1	0	OF-158
1983	113	403	99	15	1	19	4.7	68	53	62	59	1	.246	.429	3	1	OF-84, DH-26

	G	AB	H	2B	3B	HR	HR %	R	RBI	BB	SO	SB	BA	SA	Pinch Hit AB	Pinch Hit H	G by POS

Brian Downing continued

	G	AB	H	2B	3B	HR	HR%	R	RBI	BB	SO	SB	BA	SA	AB	H	G by POS
1984	156	539	148	28	2	23	4.3	66	91	70	66	0	.275	.462	3	1	OF-131, DH-21
12 yrs.	1284	4168	1108	185	12	126	3.0	593	554	616	574	31	.266	.407	36	8	C-675, OF-484, DH-108, 3B-8

LEAGUE CHAMPIONSHIP SERIES

	G	AB	H	2B	3B	HR	HR%	R	RBI	BB	SO	SB	BA	SA	AB	H	G by POS
1979 CAL A	4	15	3	0	0	0	0.0	1	1	1	1	0	.200	.200	0	0	C-4
1982	5	19	3	1	0	0	0.0	4	0	3	2	0	.158	.211	0	0	OF-5
2 yrs.	9	34	6	1	0	0	0.0	5	1	4	3	0	.176	.206	0	0	OF-5, C-4

Red Downs

DOWNS, JEROME WILLIS   BR TR
B. Aug. 23, 1883, Neola, Iowa   D. Oct. 19, 1939, Council Bluffs, Iowa

	G	AB	H	2B	3B	HR	HR%	R	RBI	BB	SO	SB	BA	SA	AB	H	G by POS
1907 DET A	105	374	82	13	5	1	0.3	28	42	13		3	.219	.289	4	1	2B-80, OF-20, SS-1, 3B-1
1908	84	289	64	10	3	1	0.3	29	35	5		2	.221	.287	1	0	2B-82, 3B-1
1912 2 teams	BKN	N	(9G –	.250)		CHI	N	(43G –	.263)								
" total	52	127	33	7	3	1	0.8	11	17	10	22	8	.260	.386	11	2	2B-25, SS-9, 3B-5
3 yrs.	241	790	179	30	11	3	0.4	68	94	28	22	13	.227	.304	16	3	2B-187, OF-20, SS-10, 3B-7

WORLD SERIES

	G	AB	H	2B	3B	HR	HR%	R	RBI	BB	SO	SB	BA	SA	AB	H	G by POS
1908 DET A	2	6	1	1	0	0	0.0	1	1	1	2	0	.167	.333	0	0	2B-2

Tom Dowse

DOWSE, THOMAS JOSEPH   BR TR 5'11"   175 lbs.
B. Aug. 12, 1867, Ireland   D. Dec. 14, 1946, Riverside, Calif.

	G	AB	H	2B	3B	HR	HR%	R	RBI	BB	SO	SB	BA	SA	AB	H	G by POS
1890 CLE N	40	159	33	2	1	0	0.0	20	9	12	22	3	.208	.233	0	0	OF-26, 1B-10, C-3, P-1
1891 COL AA	55	201	45	7	0	0	0.0	24	22	13	22	2	.224	.259	0	0	C-51, OF-5
1892 4 teams	LOU	N	(41G –	.145)		CIN	N	(1G –	.000)		PHI	N	(16G –	.185)		WAS	N	(7G –	.259)
" total	65	230	38	3	0	0	0.0	18	15	4	22	2	.165	.178	1	0	C-48, 1B-11, OF-7, 2B-1
3 yrs.	160	590	116	12	1	0	0.0	62	46	29	66	7	.197	.220	1	0	C-102, OF-38, 1B-21, 2B-1, P-1

Brian Doyle

DOYLE, BRIAN REED   BL TR 5'10"   160 lbs.
Brother of Denny Doyle.
B. Jan. 26, 1954, Cave City, Ky.

	G	AB	H	2B	3B	HR	HR%	R	RBI	BB	SO	SB	BA	SA	AB	H	G by POS
1978 NY A	39	52	10	0	0	0	0.0	6	0	0	3	0	.192	.192	0	0	2B-29, SS-7, 3B-5
1979	20	32	4	2	0	0	0.0	2	5	3	1	0	.125	.188	0	0	2B-13, 3B-6
1980	34	75	13	1	0	1	1.3	8	5	6	7	1	.173	.227	1	0	2B-20, SS-12, 3B-2
1981 OAK A	17	40	5	0	0	0	0.0	2	3	1	2	0	.125	.125	0	0	2B-17
4 yrs.	110	199	32	3	0	1	0.5	18	13	10	13	1	.161	.191	1	0	2B-79, SS-19, 3B-13

LEAGUE CHAMPIONSHIP SERIES

	G	AB	H	2B	3B	HR	HR%	R	RBI	BB	SO	SB	BA	SA	AB	H	G by POS
1978 NY A	3	7	2	0	0	0	0.0	0	1	1	1	0	.286	.286	0	0	2B-3

WORLD SERIES

	G	AB	H	2B	3B	HR	HR%	R	RBI	BB	SO	SB	BA	SA	AB	H	G by POS
1978 NY A	6	16	7	1	0	0	0.0	4	2	0	0	0	.438	.500	0	0	2B-6

Conny Doyle

DOYLE, CORNELIUS J.   5'10"   185 lbs.
B. Sept. 26, 1857, South Hampton, Mass.   D. Oct. 6, 1938, West Springfield, Mass.

	G	AB	H	2B	3B	HR	HR%	R	RBI	BB	SO	SB	BA	SA	AB	H	G by POS
1883 PHI N	16	68	15	3	2	0	0.0	3		0		15		.221	.324	0	0	OF-16

Danny Doyle

DOYLE, HOWARD JAMES   BR TR 6'1"   195 lbs.
B. Jan. 24, 1917, McLoud, Okla.

	G	AB	H	2B	3B	HR	HR%	R	RBI	BB	SO	SB	BA	SA	AB	H	G by POS
1943 BOS A	13	43	9	1	0	0	0.0	2	6	7	9	0	.209	.233	0	0	C-13

Denny Doyle

DOYLE, ROBERT DENNIS   BL TR 5'9"   175 lbs.
Brother of Brian Doyle.
B. Jan. 17, 1944, Glasgow, Ky.

	G	AB	H	2B	3B	HR	HR%	R	RBI	BB	SO	SB	BA	SA	AB	H	G by POS
1970 PHI N	112	413	86	10	7	2	0.5	43	16	33	64	6	.208	.281	7	0	2B-103
1971	95	342	79	12	1	3	0.9	34	24	19	31	4	.231	.298	3	0	2B-91
1972	123	442	110	14	2	1	0.2	33	26	31	33	6	.249	.296	1	0	2B-119
1973	116	370	101	9	3	3	0.8	45	26	31	32	1	.273	.338	6	1	2B-114
1974 CAL A	147	511	133	19	2	1	0.2	47	34	25	49	6	.260	.311	1	1	2B-146, SS-2
1975 2 teams	CAL	A	(8G –	.067)		BOS	A	(89G –	.310)								
" total	97	325	97	21	2	4	1.2	50	36	15	12	5	.298	.412	5	1	2B-90, 3B-7, SS-2
1976 BOS A	117	432	108	15	5	0	0.0	51	26	22	39	8	.250	.308	8	2	2B-113
1977	137	455	109	13	6	2	0.4	54	49	29	50	2	.240	.308	5	0	2B-118, 2B-1
8 yrs.	944	3290	823	113	28	16	0.5	357	237	205	310	38	.250	.316	36	5	2B-913, 3B-7, SS-4

LEAGUE CHAMPIONSHIP SERIES

	G	AB	H	2B	3B	HR	HR%	R	RBI	BB	SO	SB	BA	SA	AB	H	G by POS
1975 BOS A	3	11	3	0	0	0	0.0	3	1	0	1	0	.273	.273	0	0	2B-3

WORLD SERIES

	G	AB	H	2B	3B	HR	HR%	R	RBI	BB	SO	SB	BA	SA	AB	H	G by POS
1975 BOS A	7	30	8	1	1	0	0.0	3	0	2	1	0	.267	.367	0	0	2B-7

Jack Doyle

DOYLE, JOHN JOSEPH (Dirty Jack)   BR TR 5'9"   155 lbs.
B. Oct. 25, 1869, Killorgin, Ireland   D. Dec. 31, 1958, Holyoke, Mass.
Manager 1895, 1898.

	G	AB	H	2B	3B	HR	HR%	R	RBI	BB	SO	SB	BA	SA	AB	H	G by POS
1889 COL AA	11	36	10	1	1	0	0.0	6	3	6	6	9	.278	.361	0	0	C-7, OF-3, 2B-1
1890	77	298	80	17	7	2	0.7	48		13		27	.268	.393	0	0	C-38, SS-25, OF-9, 2B-6, 3B-3
1891 CLE N	69	250	69	14	4	0	0.0	43	43	26	44	24	.276	.364	0	0	C-29, OF-21, 3B-20, SS-1
1892 2 teams	CLE	N	(24G –	.295)		NY	N	(90G –	.298)								
" total	114	454	135	26	2	6	1.3	78	69	24	40	47	.297	.403	1	1	C-35, 2B-31, OF-29, 3B-13, SS-8, 1B-1
1893 NY N	82	318	102	17	5	1	0.3	56	51	27	12	40	.321	.415	0	0	C-48, OF-29, SS-4, 3B-3, 1B-1
1894	105	425	157	30	8	3	0.7	94	100	35	3	42	.369	.499	0	0	1B-99, C-6
1895	82	319	100	21	3	1	0.3	52	66	24	12	35	.313	.408	2	1	1B-58, 2B-13, 3B-6, C-4
1896 BAL N	118	487	168	29	4	1	0.2	116	101	42	15	73	.345	.427	0	0	1B-118, 2B-1
1897	114	463	165	29	4	1	0.2	93	87	29		62	.356	.443	0	0	1B-114

	G	AB	H	2B	3B	HR	HR %	R	RBI	BB	SO	SB	BA	SA	Pinch Hit AB	Pinch Hit H	G by POS

Jack Doyle continued

	G	AB	H	2B	3B	HR	HR%	R	RBI	BB	SO	SB	BA	SA	PH AB	PH H	G by POS
1898 **2 teams**	**WAS** **N** (43G – .305)				**NY** **N** (82G – .283)												
" total	125	474	138	17	5	3	0.6	68	69	19		23	.291	.367	1	1	1B-62, OF-38, SS-15, 3B-5, 2B-5, C-2
1899 **NY** **N**	118	454	140	15	7	3	0.7	57	76	33		35	.308	.392	1	0	1B-113, C-5
1900	133	505	138	24	1	1	0.2	69	66	34		34	.273	.331	0	0	1B-133
1901 **CHI** **N**	75	285	66	9	2	0	0.0	21	39	7		8	.232	.277	0	0	1B-75
1902 **2 teams**	**NY** **N** (49G – .301)				**WAS** **A** (78G – .247)												
" total	127	498	133	27	2	2	0.4	73	39	39		18	.267	.341	0	0	2B-68, 1B-56, OF-4, C-1
1903 **BKN** **N**	139	524	164	27	6	0	0.0	84	91	54		34	.313	.387	0	0	1B-139
1904 **2 teams**	**BKN** **N** (8G – .227)				**PHI** **N** (66G – .220)												
" total	74	258	57	11	3	1	0.4	22	24	25		5	.221	.298	0	0	1B-73, 2B-1
1905 **NY** **A**	1	3	0	0	0	0	0.0	0	0	0		0	.000	.000	0	0	1B-1
17 yrs.	1564	6051	1822	314	64	25	0.4	980	924	437	132	516	.301	.387	5	3	1B-1043, C-175, OF-133, 2B-127, SS-53, 3B-50

Jeff Doyle

DOYLE, JEFFREY DONALD
B. Oct. 2, 1956, Havre, Ill.   BB TR 5'8"   160 lbs.

	G	AB	H	2B	3B	HR	HR%	R	RBI	BB	SO	SB	BA	SA	PH AB	PH H	G by POS
1983 **STL** **N**	13	37	11	1	2	0	0.0	4	2	1	3	0	.297	.432	1	0	2B-12

Jim Doyle

DOYLE, JAMES FRANCIS
B. Dec. 25, 1881, Detroit, Mich.   D. Feb. 1, 1912, Syracuse, N. Y.   BR TR 5'10"   168 lbs.

	G	AB	H	2B	3B	HR	HR%	R	RBI	BB	SO	SB	BA	SA	PH AB	PH H	G by POS
1910 **CIN** **N**	7	13	2	2	0	0	0.0	1	1	0	2	0	.154	.308	1	0	3B-3, OF-1
1911 **CHI** **N**	130	472	133	23	12	5	1.1	69	62	40	54	19	.282	.413	3	1	3B-127
2 yrs.	137	485	135	25	12	5	1.0	70	63	40	56	19	.278	.410	4	1	3B-130, OF-1

John Doyle

DOYLE, JOHN A.
B. Nova Scotia   Deceased.

	G	AB	H	2B	3B	HR	HR%	R	RBI	BB	SO	SB	BA	SA	PH AB	PH H	G by POS
1884 **PIT** **AA**	15	58	17	3	2	0	0.0	8		2			.293	.414	0	0	OF-14, SS-1

Larry Doyle

DOYLE, LAWRENCE JOSEPH (Laughing Larry)
B. July 31, 1886, Caseyville, Ill.   D. Mar. 1, 1974, Saranac Lake, N. Y.   BL TR 5'10"   165 lbs.

	G	AB	H	2B	3B	HR	HR%	R	RBI	BB	SO	SB	BA	SA	PH AB	PH H	G by POS
1907 **NY** **N**	69	227	59	3	0	0	0.0	16	16	20		3	.260	.273	0	0	2B-69
1908	104	377	116	16	9	0	0.0	65	33	22		17	.308	.398	3	1	2B-102
1909	146	570	172	27	11	6	1.1	86	49	45		30	.302	.419	3	2	2B-143
1910	151	575	164	21	14	8	1.4	97	69	71	26	39	.285	.412	0	0	2B-151
1911	143	526	163	25	**25**	13	2.5	102	77	71	39	38	.310	.527	2	1	2B-141
1912	143	558	184	33	8	10	1.8	98	90	56	20	36	.330	.471	0	0	2B-143
1913	132	482	135	25	6	5	1.0	67	73	59	29	38	.280	.388	2	1	2B-130
1914	145	539	140	19	8	5	0.9	87	63	58	25	17	.260	.353	0	0	2B-145
1915	150	591	**189**	40	10	4	0.7	86	70	32	28	22	**.320**	.442	3	0	2B-150
1916 **2 teams**	**NY** **N** (113G – .268)				**CHI** **N** (9G – .395)												
" total	122	479	133	29	11	3	0.6	61	54	28	24	19	.278	.403	0	0	2B-122
1917 **CHI** **N**	135	476	121	19	5	6	1.3	48	61	48	28	5	.254	.353	7	3	2B-128
1918 **NY** **N**	75	257	67	7	4	3	1.2	38	36	37	10	10	.261	.354	2	0	2B-73
1919	113	381	110	14	10	7	1.8	61	52	31	17	12	.289	.433	11	1	2B-100
1920	137	471	134	21	2	4	0.8	48	50	47	28	11	.285	.363	4	0	2B-133
14 yrs.	1765	6509	1887	299	123	74	1.1	960	793	625	274	297	.290	.408	37	9	2B-1730
WORLD SERIES																	
1911 **NY** **N**	6	23	7	3	1	0	0.0	3	1	2	1	2	.304	.522	0	0	2B-6
1912	8	33	8	1	0	1	3.0	5	2	3	2	2	.242	.364	0	0	2B-8
1913	5	20	3	0	0	0	0.0	1	2	0	1	0	.150	.150	0	0	2B-5
3 yrs.	19	76	18	4	1	1	1.3	9	5	5	4	4	.237	.355	0	0	2B-19

Drake

DRAKE,
Deceased.

	G	AB	H	2B	3B	HR	HR%	R	RBI	BB	SO	SB	BA	SA	PH AB	PH H	G by POS
1884 **WAS** **AA**	2	7	2	1	0	0	0.0	0		0			.286	.429	0	0	OF-2

Delos Drake

DRAKE, DELOS DANIEL
B. Dec. 3, 1886, Girard, Ohio   D. Oct. 3, 1965, Findlay, Ohio   BR TL 5'11½"   170 lbs.

	G	AB	H	2B	3B	HR	HR%	R	RBI	BB	SO	SB	BA	SA	PH AB	PH H	G by POS
1911 **DET** **A**	91	315	88	9	9	1	0.3	37	36	17		20	.279	.375	9	3	OF-83, 1B-2
1914 **STL** **F**	138	514	129	18	8	3	0.6	51	42	31		17	.251	.335	4	0	OF-116, 1B-18
1915	102	343	91	23	4	1	0.3	32	41	23		6	.265	.364	4	0	OF-99, 1B-1
3 yrs.	331	1172	308	50	21	5	0.4	120	119	71		43	.263	.354	17	3	OF-298, 1B-21

Larry Drake

DRAKE, LARRY FRANCIS
B. May 4, 1921, McKinney, Tex.   BL TR 6'1½"   195 lbs.

	G	AB	H	2B	3B	HR	HR%	R	RBI	BB	SO	SB	BA	SA	PH AB	PH H	G by POS
1945 **PHI** **A**	1	2	0	0	0	0	0.0	0	0	0	2	0	.000	.000	0	0	OF-1
1948 **WAS** **A**	4	7	2	0	0	0	0.0	0	1	1	3	0	.286	.286	2	0	OF-2
2 yrs.	5	9	2	0	0	0	0.0	0	1	1	5	0	.222	.222	2	0	OF-3

Sammy Drake

DRAKE, SAMUEL HARRISON
Brother of Solly Drake.
B. Oct. 7, 1934, Little Rock, Ark.   BB TR 5'11"   175 lbs.

	G	AB	H	2B	3B	HR	HR%	R	RBI	BB	SO	SB	BA	SA	PH AB	PH H	G by POS
1960 **CHI** **N**	15	15	1	0	0	0	0.0	5	0	1	4	0	.067	.067	4	1	3B-6, 2B-2
1961	13	5	0	0	0	0	0.0	1	0	1	1	0	.000	.000	2	0	OF-1
1962 **NY** **N**	25	52	10	0	0	0	0.0	2	7	6	12	0	.192	.192	6	3	2B-10, 3B-6
3 yrs.	53	72	11	0	0	0	0.0	8	7	8	17	0	.153	.153	12	4	3B-12, 2B-12, OF-1

Solly Drake

DRAKE, SOLOMON LOUIS
Brother of Sammy Drake.
B. Oct. 23, 1930, Little Rock, Ark.   BB TR 6'   170 lbs.

	G	AB	H	2B	3B	HR	HR%	R	RBI	BB	SO	SB	BA	SA	PH AB	PH H	G by POS
1956 **CHI** **N**	65	215	55	9	1	2	0.9	29	15	23	35	9	.256	.335	8	3	OF-53
1959 **2 teams**	**LA** **N** (9G – .250)				**PHI** **N** (67G – .145)												
" total	76	70	11	1	0	0	0.0	12	3	9	18	6	.157	.171	22	0	OF-41
2 yrs.	141	285	66	10	1	2	0.7	41	18	32	53	15	.232	.295	30	3	OF-94

	G	AB	H	2B	3B	HR	HR %	R	RBI	BB	SO	SB	BA	SA	Pinch Hit AB	Pinch Hit H	G by POS

Jake Drauby

DRAUBY, JACOB C.   5'11"   180 lbs.
B. 1865, Harrisburg, Pa.   Deceased.

	G	AB	H	2B	3B	HR	HR%	R	RBI	BB	SO	SB	BA	SA	PH AB	PH H	G by POS
1892 WAS N	10	34	7	0	1	0	0.0	3	3	2	12	0	.206	.265	0	0	3B-10

Bill Dreesen

DREESEN, WILLIAM RICHARD   BL TR 5'7½" 160 lbs.
B. July 26, 1904, New York, N. Y.   D. Nov. 9, 1971, Mount Vernon, N. Y.

	G	AB	H	2B	3B	HR	HR%	R	RBI	BB	SO	SB	BA	SA	PH AB	PH H	G by POS
1931 BOS N	47	180	40	10	4	1	0.6	38	10	23	23	1	.222	.339	1	1	3B-47

Bill Drescher

DRESCHER, WILLIAM CLAYTON (Dutch, Moose)   BL TR 6'2" 190 lbs.
B. May 23, 1921, Congers, N. Y.   D. May 15, 1968, Haverstraw, N. Y.

	G	AB	H	2B	3B	HR	HR%	R	RBI	BB	SO	SB	BA	SA	PH AB	PH H	G by POS
1944 NY A	4	7	1	0	0	0	0.0	0	0	0	0	0	.143	.143	3	0	C-1
1945	48	126	34	3	1	0	0.0	10	15	8	5	0	.270	.310	14	2	C-33
1946	5	6	2	1	0	0	0.0	0	1	0	0	0	.333	.500	2	0	C-3
3 yrs.	57	139	37	4	1	0	0.0	10	16	8	5	0	.266	.309	19	2	C-37

Chuck Dressen

DRESSEN, CHARLES WALTER   BR TR 5'5½" 146 lbs.
B. Sept. 20, 1898, Decatur, Ill.   D. Aug. 10, 1966, Detroit, Mich.
Manager 1934-37, 1951-53, 1955-57, 1960-61, 1963-66.

	G	AB	H	2B	3B	HR	HR%	R	RBI	BB	SO	SB	BA	SA	PH AB	PH H	G by POS
1925 CIN N	76	215	59	8	2	3	1.4	35	19	12	4	5	.274	.372	10	0	3B-47, 2B-5, OF-4
1926	127	474	126	27	11	4	0.8	76	48	49	31	0	.266	.395	0	0	3B-123, OF-1, SS-1
1927	144	548	160	36	10	2	0.4	78	55	71	32	7	.292	.405	1	0	3B-142, SS-2
1928	135	498	145	26	3	1	0.2	72	59	43	22	10	.291	.361	0	0	3B-135
1929	110	401	98	22	3	1	0.2	49	36	41	21	8	.244	.322	5	0	3B-98, 2B-8
1930	33	19	4	0	0	0	0.0	0	1	1	3	0	.211	.211	13	2	3B-10, 2B-3
1931	5	15	1	0	0	0	0.0	0	0	1	1	0	.067	.067	0	0	3B-4
1933 NY N	16	45	10	4	0	0	0.0	3	3	1	4	0	.222	.311	0	0	3B-16
8 yrs.	646	2215	603	123	29	11	0.5	313	221	219	118	30	.272	.369	29	2	3B-575, 2B-16, OF-5, SS-3

Lee Dressen

DRESSEN, LEE AUGUST   BL TL 6' 165 lbs.
B. July 23, 1889, Ellinwood, Kans.   D. June 30, 1931, Diller, Neb.

	G	AB	H	2B	3B	HR	HR%	R	RBI	BB	SO	SB	BA	SA	PH AB	PH H	G by POS
1914 STL N	46	103	24	2	1	0	0.0	16	7	11	20	2	.233	.272	7	1	1B-38
1918 DET A	31	107	19	1	2	0	0.0	10	3	21	10	2	.178	.224	1	0	1B-30
2 yrs.	77	210	43	3	3	0	0.0	26	10	32	30	4	.205	.248	8	1	1B-68

Dave Drew

DREW, DAVID
Deceased.

	G	AB	H	2B	3B	HR	HR%	R	RBI	BB	SO	SB	BA	SA	PH AB	PH H	G by POS
1884 2 teams		PHI U (2G – .444)				WAS U (13G – .302)											
" total	15	62	20	1	2	0	0.0	9		1			.323	.403	0	0	SS-9, 1B-5, OF-1, 2B-1, P-1

Frank Drews

DREWS, FRANK JOHN   BR TR 5'10" 175 lbs.
B. May 25, 1916, Buffalo, N. Y.   D. Apr. 22, 1972, Buffalo, N. Y.

	G	AB	H	2B	3B	HR	HR%	R	RBI	BB	SO	SB	BA	SA	PH AB	PH H	G by POS
1944 BOS N	46	141	29	9	1	0	0.0	14	10	25	14	0	.206	.284	0	0	2B-46
1945	49	147	30	4	1	0	0.0	13	19	16	18	0	.204	.245	0	0	2B-48
2 yrs.	95	288	59	13	2	0	0.0	27	29	41	32	0	.205	.264	0	0	2B-94

Dan Driessen

DRIESSEN, DANIEL   BL TR 5'11" 187 lbs.
B. July 29, 1951, Hilton Head, S. C.

	G	AB	H	2B	3B	HR	HR%	R	RBI	BB	SO	SB	BA	SA	PH AB	PH H	G by POS
1973 CIN N	102	366	110	15	2	4	1.1	49	47	24	37	8	.301	.385	7	3	3B-87, 1B-35, OF-1
1974	150	470	132	23	6	7	1.5	63	56	48	62	10	.281	.400	14	5	3B-126, 1B-47, OF-3
1975	88	210	59	8	1	7	3.3	38	38	35	30	10	.281	.429	21	5	1B-41, OF-29
1976	98	219	54	11	1	7	3.2	32	44	43	32	14	.247	.402	34	6	1B-40, OF-20
1977	151	536	161	31	4	17	3.2	75	91	64	85	31	.300	.468	6	1	1B-148
1978	153	524	131	23	3	16	3.1	68	70	75	79	28	.250	.397	5	0	1B-151
1979	150	515	129	24	3	18	3.5	72	75	62	77	11	.250	.414	7	1	1B-143
1980	154	524	139	36	1	14	2.7	81	74	93	68	19	.265	.418	1	0	1B-151
1981	82	233	55	14	0	7	3.0	35	33	40	31	2	.236	.386	5	1	1B-74
1982	149	516	139	25	1	17	3.3	64	57	82	62	11	.269	.421	3	0	1B-144
1983	122	386	107	17	1	12	3.1	57	57	75	51	6	.277	.420	8	2	1B-112
1984 2 teams		CIN N (81G – .280)				MON N (51G – .254)											
" total	132	387	104	24	0	16	4.1	47	60	54	40	2	.269	.455	17	1	1B-115
12 yrs.	1531	4886	1320	251	23	142	2.9	681	702	695	654	152	.270	.418	128	25	1B-1201, 3B-213, OF-53
LEAGUE CHAMPIONSHIP SERIES																	
1973 CIN N	4	12	2	1	0	0	0.0	0	1	0	2	0	.167	.250	0	0	3B-4
1976	1	1	0	0	0	0	0.0	0	0	0	0	0	.000	.000	1	0	
1979	3	12	1	0	0	0	0.0	1	0	1	3	0	.083	.083	0	0	1B-3
3 yrs.	8	25	3	1	0	0	0.0	1	1	1	5	0	.120	.160	1	0	3B-4, 1B-3
WORLD SERIES																	
1975 CIN N	2	2	0	0	0	0	0.0	0	0	0	0	0	.000	.000	2	0	
1976	4	14	5	2	0	1	7.1	4	1	2	0	1	.357	.714	0	0	DH-4
2 yrs.	6	16	5	2	0	1	6.3	4	1	2	0	1	.313	.625	2	0	DH-4

Lew Drill

DRILL, LEWIS L   BR TR 5'6" 186 lbs.
B. May 9, 1877, Browerville, Minn.   D. July 4, 1969, St. Paul, Minn.

	G	AB	H	2B	3B	HR	HR%	R	RBI	BB	SO	SB	BA	SA	PH AB	PH H	G by POS
1902 2 teams		BAL A (2G – .250)				WAS A (71G – .262)											
" total	73	229	60	10	4	1	0.4	35	29	26		5	.262	.354	4	0	C-54, OF-8, 2B-5, 3B-1, 1B-1
1903 WAS A	51	154	39	9	3	0	0.0	11	23	15		4	.253	.351	1	0	C-47, 1B-3
1904 2 teams		WAS A (46G – .268)				DET A (51G – .244)											
" total	97	302	77	13	3	1	0.3	24	24	41		5	.255	.328	2	1	C-78, OF-14, 1B-2
1905 DET A	71	211	55	9	0	0	0.0	17	24	32		7	.261	.303	1	0	C-70
4 yrs.	292	896	231	41	10	2	0.2	87	100	114		21	.258	.333	8	1	C-249, OF-22, 1B-6, 2B-5, 3B-1

	G	AB	H	2B	3B	HR	HR %	R	RBI	BB	SO	SB	BA	SA	Pinch Hit AB	Pinch Hit H	G by POS

Denny Driscoll

DRISCOLL, JOHN F.
B. Nov. 19, 1855, Lowell, Mass.   D. July 11, 1886, Lowell, Mass.   5'10½" 160 lbs.

	G	AB	H	2B	3B	HR	HR %	R	RBI	BB	SO	SB	BA	SA	PH AB	PH H	G by POS
1880 BUF N	18	65	10	1	0	0	0.0	1	4	1	7		.154	.169	0	0	OF-14, P-6
1882 PIT AA	23	80	11	2	0	1	1.3	12		3			.138	.200	0	0	P-23
1883	41	148	27	2	1	0	0.0	19		4			.182	.209	0	0	P-41, OF-4, 3B-1
1884 LOU AA	13	48	9	1	0	0	0.0	5		2			.188	.208	0	0	P-13, OF-2
1885 BUF N	7	19	3	0	0	0	0.0	2	0	2	5		.158	.158	0	0	2B-7
5 yrs.	102	360	60	6	1	1	0.3	39	4	12	12		.167	.197	0	0	P-83, OF-20, 2B-7, 3B-1

Jim Driscoll

DRISCOLL, JAMES BERNARD
B. May 14, 1944, Medford, Mass.   BL TR 5'11" 175 lbs.

	G	AB	H	2B	3B	HR	HR %	R	RBI	BB	SO	SB	BA	SA	PH AB	PH H	G by POS
1970 OAK A	21	52	10	0	0	1	1.9	2	2	2	15	0	.192	.250	5	2	SS-7, 2B-7
1972 TEX A	15	18	0	0	0	0	0.0	0	0	2	3	0	.000	.000	11	0	2B-4, 3B-2
2 yrs.	36	70	10	0	0	1	1.4	2	2	4	18	0	.143	.186	16	2	2B-11, SS-7, 3B-2

Paddy Driscoll

DRISCOLL, JOHN LEO
B. Jan. 11, 1895, Evanston, Ill.   D. June 29, 1968, Chicago, Ill.   BR TR 5'8½" 155 lbs.

	G	AB	H	2B	3B	HR	HR %	R	RBI	BB	SO	SB	BA	SA	PH AB	PH H	G by POS
1917 CHI N	13	28	3	1	0	0	0.0	2	3	2	6	2	.107	.143	0	0	2B-8, 3B-2, SS-1

Mike Drissel

DRISSEL, NICHOLAS MICHAEL
B. Dec. 19, 1865, St. Louis, Mo.   D. Feb. 26, 1913, St. Louis, Mo.   BR TR

	G	AB	H	2B	3B	HR	HR %	R	RBI	BB	SO	SB	BA	SA	PH AB	PH H	G by POS
1885 STL AA	6	20	1	0	0	0	0.0	0		0			.050	.050	0	0	C-6

Walt Dropo

DROPO, WALTER (Moose)
B. Jan. 30, 1923, Moosup, Conn.   BR TR 6'5" 220 lbs.

	G	AB	H	2B	3B	HR	HR %	R	RBI	BB	SO	SB	BA	SA	PH AB	PH H	G by POS
1949 BOS A	11	41	6	2	0	0	0.0	3	1	3	7	0	.146	.195	0	0	1B-11
1950	136	559	180	28	8	34	6.1	101	144	45	75	0	.322	.583	2	0	1B-134
1951	99	360	86	14	0	11	3.1	37	57	38	52	0	.239	.369	2	2	1B-93
1952 2 teams	152			BOS	A (37G – .265)			DET	A (115G – .279)								
" total	152	591	163	24	4	29	4.9	69	97	37	85	2	.276	.477	2	0	1B-150
1953 DET A	152	606	150	30	3	13	2.1	61	96	29	69	2	.248	.371	2	1	1B-150
1954	107	320	90	14	2	4	1.3	27	44	24	41	0	.281	.375	18	5	1B-95
1955 CHI A	141	453	127	15	2	19	4.2	55	79	42	71	0	.280	.448	2	1	1B-140
1956	125	361	96	13	1	8	2.2	42	52	37	51	1	.266	.374	10	2	1B-117
1957	93	223	57	2	0	13	5.8	24	49	16	40	0	.256	.439	31	11	1B-69
1958 2 teams	91			CHI	A (28G – .192)			CIN	N (63G – .290)								
" total	91	214	57	8	2	9	4.2	21	39	17	42	0	.266	.449	31	7	1B-59
1959 2 teams	88			CIN	N (26G – .103)			BAL	A (62G – .278)								
" total	88	190	46	10	0	7	3.7	21	23	16	27	0	.242	.405	11	1	1B-77, 3B-2
1960 BAL A	79	179	48	8	0	4	2.2	16	21	20	19	0	.268	.380	14	2	1B-67, 3B-1
1961	14	27	7	0	0	1	3.7	1	2	4	3	0	.259	.370	2	1	1B-12
13 yrs.	1288	4124	1113	168	22	152	3.7	478	704	328	582	5	.270	.432	132	33	1B-1174, 3B-3

Keith Drumright

DRUMRIGHT, KEITH ALAN
B. Oct. 21, 1954, Springfield, Mo.   BL TR 5'10" 170 lbs.

	G	AB	H	2B	3B	HR	HR %	R	RBI	BB	SO	SB	BA	SA	PH AB	PH H	G by POS
1978 HOU N	17	55	9	0	0	0	0.0	5	2	3	4	0	.164	.164	0	0	2B-17
1981 OAK A	31	86	25	1	1	0	0.0	8	11	4	4	0	.291	.326	7	2	2B-19, DH-5
2 yrs.	48	141	34	1	1	0	0.0	13	13	7	8	0	.241	.262	7	2	2B-36, DH-5

DIVISIONAL PLAYOFF SERIES
| 1981 OAK A | 1 | 4 | 1 | 0 | 0 | 0 | 0.0 | 0 | 0 | 0 | 0 | 0 | .250 | .250 | 0 | 0 | DH-1 |

LEAGUE CHAMPIONSHIP SERIES
| 1981 OAK A | 3 | 4 | 0 | 0 | 0 | 0 | 0.0 | 0 | 0 | 1 | 0 | 0 | .000 | .000 | 3 | 0 | DH-1 |

Jean Dubuc

DUBUC, JEAN JOSEPH OCTAVE (Chauncey)
Born Jean Baptiste Arthur Dubuc.
B. Sept. 15, 1888, St. Johnsbury, Vt.   D. Aug. 29, 1958, Ft. Myers, Fla.   BR TR 5'10½" 185 lbs.

	G	AB	H	2B	3B	HR	HR %	R	RBI	BB	SO	SB	BA	SA	PH AB	PH H	G by POS
1908 CIN N	15	29	4	1	0	0	0.0	2	2	0		0	.138	.172	0	0	P-15
1909	19	18	3	0	0	0	0.0	1	0	2		0	.167	.167	0	0	P-19
1912 DET N	40	108	29	6	2	1	0.9	16	9	3		0	.269	.389	1	0	P-37, OF-2
1913	68	135	36	5	3	2	1.5	17	11	2	17	1	.267	.393	28	3	P-36, OF-3
1914	70	124	28	8	1	1	0.8	9	11	7	11	1	.226	.331	32	6	P-36
1915	60	112	23	2	1	0	0.0	7	14	8	15	0	.205	.241	17	5	P-39
1916	52	78	20	0	2	0	0.0	3	7	7	12	0	.256	.308	12	2	P-36
1918 BOS A	5	6	1	0	0	0	0.0	0	0	1	2	0	.167	.167	2	0	P-2
1919 NY N	36	42	6	1	1	0	0.0	2	2	0	6	0	.143	.214	1	0	P-36
9 yrs.	365	652	150	23	10	4	0.6	57	56	30	63	2	.230	.314	93	16	P-256, OF-5

WORLD SERIES
| 1918 BOS A | 1 | 1 | 0 | 0 | 0 | 0 | 0.0 | 0 | 0 | 0 | 1 | 0 | .000 | .000 | 1 | 0 | |

Dud Dudley

Playing record listed under Dud Lee

John Dudra

DUDRA, JOHN JOSEPH
B. May 27, 1916, Assumption, Ill.   D. Oct. 24, 1965, Pana, Ill.   BR TR 5'11½" 175 lbs.

	G	AB	H	2B	3B	HR	HR %	R	RBI	BB	SO	SB	BA	SA	PH AB	PH H	G by POS
1941 BOS N	14	25	9	3	1	0	0.0	3	3	3	4	0	.360	.560	1	0	3B-5, 2B-5, SS-1, 1B-1

Pat Duff

DUFF, PATRICK HENRY
B. May 6, 1875, Providence, R. I.   D. Sept. 11, 1925, Providence, R. I.   TR

	G	AB	H	2B	3B	HR	HR %	R	RBI	BB	SO	SB	BA	SA	PH AB	PH H	G by POS
1906 WAS A	1	1	0	0	0	0	0.0	0	0	0		0	.000	.000	1	0	

Charlie Duffee

DUFFEE, CHARLES EDWARD (Home Run)
B. Jan. 27, 1866, Mobile, Ala.   D. Dec. 24, 1894, Mobile, Ala.   BR TR

	G	AB	H	2B	3B	HR	HR %	R	RBI	BB	SO	SB	BA	SA	PH AB	PH H	G by POS
1889 STL AA	137	509	124	15	12	15	2.9	93	86	60	81	21	.244	.409	0	0	OF-132, 3B-5, 2B-2
1890	98	378	104	11	7	3	0.8	68		37		20	.275	.365	0	0	OF-66, 3B-33, SS-1
1891 COL AA	137	552	166	28	4	10	1.8	86	90	42	36	41	.301	.420	0	0	OF-128, 3B-7, SS-2

	G	AB	H	2B	3B	HR	HR %	R	RBI	BB	SO	SB	BA	SA	Pinch Hit AB	Pinch Hit H	G by POS

Charlie Duffee continued

		G	AB	H	2B	3B	HR	HR%	R	RBI	BB	SO	SB	BA	SA	AB	H	G by POS
1892	WAS N	132	492	122	12	11	6	1.2	64	51	36	33	28	.248	.354	0	0	OF-125, 3B-6, 1B-4
1893	CIN N	4	12	2	1	0	0	0.0	3	0	5	0	0	.167	.250	0	0	OF-4
5 yrs.		508	1943	518	67	34	34	1.7	314	227	180	150	110	.267	.389	0	0	OF-455, 3B-51, 1B-4, SS-3, 2B-2

Frank Duffy

DUFFY, FRANK THOMAS
B. Oct. 14, 1946, Oakland, Calif.

BR TR 6'1" 180 lbs.

		G	AB	H	2B	3B	HR	HR%	R	RBI	BB	SO	SB	BA	SA	AB	H	G by POS
1970	CIN N	6	11	2	2	0	0	0.0	1	0	1	2	1	.182	.364	2	0	SS-5
1971	2 teams	CIN	N (13G –	.188)		SF	N	(21G –	.179)									
"	total	34	44	8	1	0	0	0.0	4	3	1	12	0	.182	.205	9	2	SS-16, 3B-1, 2B-1
1972	CLE A	130	385	92	16	4	3	0.8	23	27	31	54	6	.239	.325	4	1	SS-126
1973		116	361	95	16	4	8	2.2	34	50	25	41	6	.263	.396	0	0	SS-115
1974		158	549	128	18	0	8	1.5	62	48	30	64	7	.233	.310	0	0	SS-158
1975		146	482	117	22	2	1	0.2	44	47	27	60	10	.243	.303	2	0	SS-145
1976		133	392	83	11	2	2	0.5	38	30	29	50	10	.212	.265	1	0	SS-132
1977		122	334	67	13	2	4	1.2	30	31	21	47	8	.201	.287	1	0	SS-121
1978	BOS A	64	104	27	5	0	0	0.0	12	4	6	11	1	.260	.308	2	1	3B-22, SS-21, 2B-12, DH-6
1979		6	3	0	0	0	0	0.0	0	0	1	0	0	.000	.000	0	0	2B-3, 1B-1
10 yrs.		915	2665	619	104	14	26	1.0	248	240	171	342	49	.232	.311	21	4	SS-839, 3B-23, 2B-16, DH-6, 1B-1

LEAGUE CHAMPIONSHIP SERIES

		G	AB	H	2B	3B	HR	HR%	R	RBI	BB	SO	SB	BA	SA	AB	H	G by POS
1971	SF N	1	1	0	0	0	0	0.0	0	0	0	1	0	.000	.000	1	0	

Hugh Duffy

DUFFY, HUGH
B. Nov. 26, 1866, Cranston, R. I.   D. Oct. 19, 1954, Boston, Mass.
Manager 1901, 1904-06, 1910-11, 1921-22.
Hall of Fame 1945.

BR TR 5'7" 168 lbs.

		G	AB	H	2B	3B	HR	HR%	R	RBI	BB	SO	SB	BA	SA	AB	H	G by POS
1888	CHI N	71	298	84	10	4	7	2.3	60	41	9	32	13	.282	.413	0	0	OF-67, SS-3, 3B-1
1889		136	584	182	21	7	12	2.1	144	89	46	30	52	.312	.433	0	0	OF-126, SS-10
1890	CHI P	137	596	194	36	16	7	1.2	161	82	59	20	79	.326	.475	0	0	OF-137
1891	BOS AA	127	536	180	20	8	8	1.5	134	108	61	29	85	.336	.448	0	0	OF-124, 3B-3, SS-1
1892	BOS N	147	612	184	28	12	5	0.8	125	81	60	37	61	.301	.410	0	0	OF-146, 3B-1
1893		131	560	203	23	7	6	1.1	147	118	50	13	50	.363	.461	0	0	OF-131
1894		124	539	236	50	13	18	3.3	160	145	66	15	49	.438¹	.679	0	0	OF-124, SS-2
1895		131	540	190	30	6	9	1.7	113	100	63	16	42	.352	.480	0	0	OF-130
1896		131	533	161	16	8	5	0.9	93	112	52	19	45	.302	.390	0	0	OF-126, 2B-9, SS-2
1897		134	554	189	25	10	11	2.0	131	129	52		45	.341	.482	0	0	OF-129, 2B-6, SS-2
1898		152	568	179	13	3	8	1.4	97	108	59		32	.315	.391	0	0	OF-152, 3B-1, 1B-1, C-1
1899		147	588	164	29	7	3	0.5	103	102	39		18	.279	.367	0	0	OF-147
1900		55	181	55	5	4	2	1.1	27	31	16		12	.304	.409	4	1	OF-49, 2B-1
1901	MIL A	79	286	88	15	9	2	0.7	41	45	16		13	.308	.444	2	0	OF-77
1904	PHI N	18	46	13	1	1	0	0.0	10	5	13		3	.283	.348	4	1	OF-14
1905		15	40	12	2	1	0	0.0	7	3	1		0	.300	.400	7	3	OF-8
1906		1	1	0	0	0	0	0.0	0	0	0		0	.000	.000	1	0	
17 yrs.		1736	7062	2314	324	116	103	1.5	1553	1299	662	211	599	.328	.450	18	5	OF-1687, SS-20, 2B-16, 3B-7, 1B-1, C-1

Bill Dugan

DUGAN, WILLIAM E.
Brother of Ed Dugan.
B. 1864, Kingston, N. Y.   Deceased.

		G	AB	H	2B	3B	HR	HR%	R	RBI	BB	SO	SB	BA	SA	AB	H	G by POS
1884	RIC AA	9	28	2	1	0	0	0.0	4		0			.071	.107	0	0	C-9

Joe Dugan

DUGAN, JOSEPH ANTHONY (Jumping Joe)
B. May 12, 1897, Mahanoy City, Pa.   D. July 7, 1982, Norwood, Mass.

BR TR 5'11" 160 lbs.

		G	AB	H	2B	3B	HR	HR%	R	RBI	BB	SO	SB	BA	SA	AB	H	G by POS
1917	PHI A	43	134	26	8	0	0	0.0	9	16	3	16	0	.194	.254	0	0	SS-39, 2B-2
1918		120	406	79	11	3	3	0.7	25	34	16	55	4	.195	.259	0	0	SS-85, 2B-35
1919		104	387	105	17	2	1	0.3	25	30	11	30	9	.271	.333	0	0	SS-98, 2B-4, 3B-2
1920		123	491	158	40	5	3	0.6	65	60	19	51	5	.322	.442	0	0	3B-59, SS-32, 2B-32
1921		119	461	136	22	6	10	2.2	54	58	28	45	5	.295	.434	0	0	3B-119
1922	2 teams	BOS	A (84G –	.287)		NY	A	(60G –	.286)									
"	total	144	593	170	31	4	6	1.0	89	63	22	49	3	.287	.383	1	0	3B-123, SS-20
1923	NY A	146	644	182	30	7	7	1.1	111	67	25	41	4	.283	.384	0	0	3B-146
1924		148	610	184	31	7	3	0.5	105	56	31	32	1	.302	.390	0	0	3B-148, 2B-2
1925		102	404	118	19	4	0	0.0	50	31	19	20	2	.292	.359	5	1	3B-96
1926		123	434	125	19	5	1	0.2	39	64	25	16	2	.288	.362	1	0	3B-122
1927		112	387	104	24	3	2	0.5	44	43	27	37	1	.269	.362	1	1	3B-111
1928		94	312	86	15	0	6	1.9	33	34	16	15	1	.276	.381	2	0	3B-91
1929	BOS A	60	125	38	10	0	0	0.0	14	15	8	8	0	.304	.384	26	9	3B-24, SS-5, OF-2, 2B-2
1931	DET A	8	17	4	0	0	0	0.0	1	0	1	3	0	.235	.235	3	1	3B-5
14 yrs.		1446	5405	1515	277	46	42	0.8	664	571	250	418	37	.280	.372	39	12	3B-1046, SS-279, 2B-77, OF-2

WORLD SERIES

		G	AB	H	2B	3B	HR	HR%	R	RBI	BB	SO	SB	BA	SA	AB	H	G by POS
1922	NY A	5	20	5	1	0	0	0.0	4	0	0	1	0	.250	.300	0	0	3B-6
1923		6	25	7	2	1	1	4.0	5	5	3	0	0	.280	.560	0	0	3B-7
1926		7	24	8	1	0	0	0.0	2	2	1	1	0	.333	.375	0	0	3B-7
1927		4	15	3	0	0	0	0.0	2	0	0	0	0	.200	.200	0	0	3B-4
1928		3	6	1	0	0	0	0.0	0	1	0	0	0	.167	.167	0	0	3B-3
5 yrs.		25	90	24	4	1	1	1.1	13	8	4	2	0	.267	.367	0	0	3B-25

Gus Dugas

DUGAS, AUGUSTIN JOSEPH
B. Mar. 24, 1907, St-Jean-de-Matha, Que., Canada

BL TL 5'9" 165 lbs.

		G	AB	H	2B	3B	HR	HR%	R	RBI	BB	SO	SB	BA	SA	AB	H	G by POS
1930	PIT N	9	31	9	2	0	0	0.0	8	1	7	4	0	.290	.355	0	0	OF-9
1932		55	97	23	3	3	3	3.1	13	12	7	11	0	.237	.423	33	5	OF-20
1933	PHI N	37	71	12	3	0	0	0.0	4	9	1	9	0	.169	.211	24	5	1B-11, OF-1

	G	AB	H	2B	3B	HR	HR %	R	RBI	BB	SO	SB	BA	SA	Pinch Hit AB	Pinch Hit H	G by POS

Gus Dugas continued

	G	AB	H	2B	3B	HR	HR%	R	RBI	BB	SO	SB	BA	SA	AB	H	G by POS
1934 **WAS A**	24	19	1	1	0	0	0.0	2	1	3	3	0	.053	.105	18	0	OF-2
4 yrs.	125	218	45	9	3	3	1.4	27	23	18	27	0	.206	.317	75	10	OF-32, 1B-11

Dan Dugdale

DUGDALE, DANIEL EDWARD
B. Oct. 28, 1864, Peoria, Ill.   D. Mar. 9, 1934, Seattle, Wash.

	G	AB	H	2B	3B	HR	HR%	R	RBI	BB	SO	SB	BA	SA	AB	H	G by POS
1886 **KC N**	12	40	7	0	0	0	0.0	4	2	2	13		.175	.175	0	0	C-7, OF-6
1894 **WAS N**	38	134	32	4	2	0	0.0	19	16	13	14	7	.239	.299	0	0	C-33, 3B-3, OF-2
2 yrs.	50	174	39	4	2	0	0.0	23	18	15	27	7	.224	.270	0	0	C-40, OF-8, 3B-3

Oscar Dugey

DUGEY, OSCAR JOSEPH
B. Oct. 25, 1887, Palestine, Tex.   D. Jan. 1, 1966, Dallas, Tex.   BR TR 5'8"   160 lbs.

	G	AB	H	2B	3B	HR	HR%	R	RBI	BB	SO	SB	BA	SA	AB	H	G by POS
1913 **BOS N**	5	8	2	0	0	0	0.0	1	0	1	1	0	.250	.250	1	0	3B-2, SS-1, 2B-1
1914	58	109	21	2	0	1	0.9	17	10	10	15	10	.193	.239	21	4	OF-17, 2B-16, 3B-1
1915 **PHI N**	42	39	6	1	0	0	0.0	4	0	7	5	2	.154	.179	16	1	2B-14
1916	41	50	11	3	0	0	0.0	9	1	9	8	3	.220	.280	9	1	2B-12
1917	44	72	14	4	1	0	0.0	12	9	4	9	2	.194	.278	19	4	2B-15, OF-4
1920 **BOS N**	5	0	0	0	0	0	–	2	0	0	0	0	–	–	0	0	
6 yrs.	195	278	54	10	1	1	0.4	45	20	31	38	17	.194	.248	66	10	2B-58, OF-21, 3B-3, SS-1
WORLD SERIES																	
1915 **PHI N**	2	0	0	0	0	0	–	0	0	0	0	1	–	–	0	0	

Jim Duggan

DUGGAN, JAMES ELMER
B. June 3, 1887, Franklin, Ind.   D. Dec. 5, 1951, Indianapolis, Ind.   BR TL

	G	AB	H	2B	3B	HR	HR%	R	RBI	BB	SO	SB	BA	SA	AB	H	G by POS
1911 **STL A**	1	4	0	0	0	0	0.0	1	1	1		0	.000	.000	0	0	1B-1

Tom Dunbar

DUNBAR, THOMAS JEROME
B. Nov. 24, 1959, Aiken, S. C.   BL TL 6'2"   185 lbs.

	G	AB	H	2B	3B	HR	HR%	R	RBI	BB	SO	SB	BA	SA	AB	H	G by POS
1983 **TEX A**	12	24	6	0	0	0	0.0	3	3	5	7	3	.250	.250	0	0	OF-9, DH-1
1984	34	97	25	2	0	2	2.1	9	10	6	16	1	.258	.340	10	2	OF-20, DH-5
2 yrs.	46	121	31	2	0	2	1.7	12	13	11	23	4	.256	.322	10	2	OF-29, DH-6

Dave Duncan

DUNCAN, DAVID EDWIN
B. Sept. 26, 1945, Dallas, Tex.   BR TR 6'2"   190 lbs.

	G	AB	H	2B	3B	HR	HR%	R	RBI	BB	SO	SB	BA	SA	AB	H	G by POS
1964 **KC A**	25	53	9	0	1	1	1.9	2	5	2	20	0	.170	.264	2	1	C-22
1967	34	101	19	4	0	5	5.0	9	11	4	50	0	.188	.376	2	0	C-32
1968 **OAK A**	82	246	47	4	0	7	2.8	15	28	25	68	1	.191	.293	3	2	C-79
1969	58	127	16	3	0	3	2.4	11	22	19	41	0	.126	.220	4	0	C-56
1970	86	232	60	7	0	10	4.3	21	29	22	38	0	.259	.418	10	4	C-73
1971	103	363	92	13	1	15	4.1	39	40	28	77	1	.253	.419	1	1	C-102
1972	121	403	88	13	0	19	4.7	39	59	34	68	0	.218	.392	8	1	C-113
1973 **CLE A**	95	344	80	11	1	17	4.9	43	43	35	86	3	.233	.419	0	0	C-86, DH-9
1974	136	425	85	10	1	16	3.8	45	46	42	91	0	.200	.341	1	0	C-134, 1B-3, DH-1
1975 **BAL A**	96	307	63	7	0	12	3.9	30	41	16	82	0	.205	.345	7	0	C-95
1976	93	284	58	7	0	4	1.4	20	17	25	56	0	.204	.271	7	0	C-93
11 yrs.	929	2885	617	79	4	109	3.8	274	341	252	677	5	.214	.357	39	9	C-885, DH-10, 1B-3
LEAGUE CHAMPIONSHIP SERIES																	
1971 **OAK A**	2	6	3	1	0	0	0.0	0	2	0	0	0	.500	.667	0	0	C-2
1972	2	2	0	0	0	0	0.0	0	0	1	1	0	.000	.000	1	0	C-2
2 yrs.	4	8	3	1	0	0	0.0	0	2	1	1	0	.375	.500	1	0	C-4
WORLD SERIES																	
1972 **OAK A**	3	5	1	0	0	0	0.0	0	0	1	3	0	.200	.200	2	1	C-1

Jim Duncan

DUNCAN, JAMES WILLIAM
B. July 1, 1871, Oil City, Pa.   D. Oct. 16, 1901, Foxburg, Pa.   BR TR

	G	AB	H	2B	3B	HR	HR%	R	RBI	BB	SO	SB	BA	SA	AB	H	G by POS
1899 2 teams	**WAS N** (15G – .234)				**CLE N**	(31G – .229)											
" total	46	152	35	4	3	2	1.3	14	14	8		1	.230	.336	2	0	C-28, 1B-17

Pat Duncan

DUNCAN, LOUIS BAIRD
B. Oct. 6, 1893, Coalton, Ohio   D. July 17, 1960, Jackson, Ohio   BR TR 5'10"   170 lbs.

	G	AB	H	2B	3B	HR	HR%	R	RBI	BB	SO	SB	BA	SA	AB	H	G by POS
1915 **PIT N**	3	5	1	0	0	0	0.0	0	0	0	1	0	.200	.200	2	1	OF-1
1919 **CIN N**	31	90	22	3	3	2	2.2	9	17	8	7	2	.244	.411	3	0	OF-27
1920	154	576	170	16	11	2	0.3	75	83	42	42	18	.295	.372	0	0	OF-154
1921	145	532	164	27	10	2	0.4	57	60	44	33	7	.308	.408	0	0	OF-145
1922	151	607	199	44	12	8	1.3	94	94	40	31	12	.328	.479	0	0	OF-151
1923	147	566	185	26	8	7	1.2	92	83	30	27	15	.327	.438	1	0	OF-146
1924	96	319	86	21	6	2	0.6	34	37	20	23	1	.270	.392	13	4	OF-83
7 yrs.	727	2695	827	137	50	23	0.9	361	374	184	164	55	.307	.420	19	5	OF-707
WORLD SERIES																	
1919 **CIN N**	8	26	7	2	0	0	0.0	3	8	2	2	0	.269	.346	0	0	OF-8

Taylor Duncan

DUNCAN, TAYLOR McDOWELL
B. May 12, 1953, Memphis, Tenn.   BR TR 6'   170 lbs.

	G	AB	H	2B	3B	HR	HR%	R	RBI	BB	SO	SB	BA	SA	AB	H	G by POS
1977 **STL N**	8	12	4	0	0	1	8.3	2	2	2	1	0	.333	.583	2	0	3B-5
1978 **OAK A**	104	319	82	15	2	2	0.6	25	37	19	38	1	.257	.335	13	1	3B-84, 2B-11, DH-7, SS-1
2 yrs.	112	331	86	15	2	3	0.9	27	39	21	39	1	.260	.344	15	1	3B-89, 2B-11, DH-7, SS-1

Vern Duncan

DUNCAN, VERNON VAN DUKE
B. Jan. 6, 1890, Clayton, N. C.   D. June 1, 1954, Daytona Beach, Fla.   BL TR 5'9"   155 lbs.

	G	AB	H	2B	3B	HR	HR%	R	RBI	BB	SO	SB	BA	SA	AB	H	G by POS
1913 **PHI N**	8	12	5	1	0	0	0.0	3	1	0	3	0	.417	.500	4	2	OF-3
1914 **BAL F**	157	557	160	20	8	2	0.4	99	53	67		13	.287	.363	2	0	OF-148, 3B-8, 2B-1
1915	146	531	142	18	4	2	0.4	68	43	54		19	.267	.328	4	0	OF-124, 3B-21, 2B-1
3 yrs.	311	1100	307	39	12	4	0.4	170	97	121	3	32	.279	.347	10	2	OF-275, 3B-29, 2B-2

	G	AB	H	2B	3B	HR	HR %	R	RBI	BB	SO	SB	BA	SA	Pinch Hit AB	H	G by POS

Ed Dundon

DUNDON, EDWARD JOSEPH (Dummy)
B. July 10, 1859, Columbus, Ohio   D. Aug. 18, 1893, Columbus, Ohio

	G	AB	H	2B	3B	HR	HR %	R	RBI	BB	SO	SB	BA	SA	AB	H	G by POS
1883 COL AA	26	93	15	1	0	0	0.0	8		3			.161	.172	0	0	P-20, OF-9, 2B-1
1884	26	86	12	2	2	0	0.0	6		5			.140	.209	0	0	OF-16, P-11, 1B-3
2 yrs.	52	179	27	3	2	0	0.0	14		8			.151	.190	0	0	P-31, OF-25, 1B-3, 2B-1

Gus Dundon

DUNDON, AUGUSTUS
B. July 10, 1874, Columbus, Ohio   D. Sept. 1, 1940, Pittsburgh, Pa.
TR 5'10" 165 lbs.

	G	AB	H	2B	3B	HR	HR %	R	RBI	BB	SO	SB	BA	SA	AB	H	G by POS
1904 CHI A	108	373	85	9	3	0	0.0	40	36	30		19	.228	.268	0	0	2B-103, 3B-3, SS-2
1905	106	364	70	7	3	0	0.0	30	22	23		14	.192	.228	0	0	2B-104, SS-2
1906	33	96	13	1	0	0	0.0	7	4	11		4	.135	.146	1	0	2B-18, SS-14
3 yrs.	247	833	168	17	6	0	0.0	77	62	64		37	.202	.236	1	0	2B-225, SS-18, 3B-3

Sam Dungan

DUNGAN, SAMUEL MORRISON
B. Jan. 29, 1866, Ferndale, Calif.   D. Mar. 16, 1939, Santa Ana, Calif.
BR 5'11" 180 lbs.

	G	AB	H	2B	3B	HR	HR %	R	RBI	BB	SO	SB	BA	SA	AB	H	G by POS
1892 CHI N	113	433	123	19	7	0	0.0	46	53	35	19	15	.284	.360	0	0	OF-113
1893	107	465	138	23	7	2	0.4	86	64	29	8	11	.297	.389	0	0	OF-107
1894 2 teams								CHI N (10G – .231)		LOU N (8G – .344)							
" total	18	71	20	3	0	0	0.0	11	6	11	2	3	.282	.324	0	0	OF-18
1900 CHI N	6	15	4	0	0	0	0.0	1	1	1		0	.267	.267	3	1	OF-3
1901 WAS A	138	559	179	26	12	1	0.2	70	73	40		9	.320	.415	0	0	OF-104, 1B-35
5 yrs.	382	1543	464	71	26	3	0.2	214	197	116	29	38	.301	.386	3	1	OF-345, 1B-35

Lee Dunham

DUNHAM, LELAND HUFFIELD
B. June 9, 1902, Atlanta, Ill.   D. May 11, 1961, Atlanta, Ill.
BL TL 5'11" 185 lbs.

	G	AB	H	2B	3B	HR	HR %	R	RBI	BB	SO	SB	BA	SA	AB	H	G by POS
1926 PHI N	5	4	1	0	0	0	0.0	0	1	0	1	0	.250	.250	3	0	1B-2

Bill Dunlap

DUNLAP, WILLIAM JAMES
B. May 1, 1909, Three Rivers, Mass.   D. Nov. 29, 1980, Reading, Pa.
BR TL 5'11" 170 lbs.

	G	AB	H	2B	3B	HR	HR %	R	RBI	BB	SO	SB	BA	SA	AB	H	G by POS
1929 BOS N	10	29	12	0	1	1	3.4	6	4	4	4	0	.414	.586	1	0	OF-9
1930	16	29	2	1	0	0	0.0	3	0	6	6	0	.069	.103	9	0	OF-7
2 yrs.	26	58	14	1	1	1	1.7	9	4	10	10	0	.241	.345	10	0	OF-16

Fred Dunlap

DUNLAP, FREDERICK C. (Sure Shot)
B. May 21, 1859, Philadelphia, Pa.   D. Dec. 1, 1902, Philadelphia, Pa.
Manager 1889.
BR TR 5'8" 165 lbs.

	G	AB	H	2B	3B	HR	HR %	R	RBI	BB	SO	SB	BA	SA	AB	H	G by POS
1880 CLE N	85	373	103	**27**	9	4	1.1	61		7	32		.276	.429	0	0	2B-85
1881	80	351	114	25	4	3	0.9	60	24	18	24		.325	.444	0	0	2B-79, 3B-1
1882	84	364	102	19	4	0	0.0	68	28	23	26		.280	.354	0	0	2B-84
1883	93	396	129	34	2	4	1.0	81		22	21		.326	.452	0	0	2B-93, OF-1
1884 STL U	101	449	**185**	39	8	**13**	**2.9**	**160**		29			**.412**	**.621**	0	0	2B-100, OF-1, P-1
1885 STL N	106	423	114	11	5	2	0.5	70	25	41	24		.270	.333	0	0	2B-106
1886 2 teams								STL N (71G – .267)		DET N (51G – .286)							
" total	122	481	132	23	5	7	1.5	85	69	44	51		.274	.387	0	0	2B-122, OF-1
1887 DET N	65	272	72	13	10	5	1.8	60	45	25	12	15	.265	.441	0	0	2B-65, P-1
1888 PIT N	82	321	84	12	4	1	0.3	41	36	16	30	24	.262	.333	0	0	2B-82
1889	121	451	106	19	0	2	0.4	59	65	46	33	21	.235	.290	0	0	2B-121
1890 2 teams								PIT N (17G – .172)		NY P (1G – .500)							
" total	18	68	13	1	1	0	0.0	10	3	7	6	2	.191	.235	0	0	2B-18
1891 WAS AA	8	25	5	1	1	0	0.0	4		4	4	3	.200	.320	0	0	2B-8
12 yrs.	965	3974	1159	224	53	41	1.0	759	298	283	263	65	.292	.406	0	0	2B-963, OF-3, P-2, 3B-1

Grant Dunlap

DUNLAP, GRANT LESTER (Snap)
B. Dec. 20, 1923, Stockton, Calif.
BR TR 6'2" 180 lbs.

	G	AB	H	2B	3B	HR	HR %	R	RBI	BB	SO	SB	BA	SA	AB	H	G by POS
1953 STL N	16	17	6	0	1	1	5.9	2	3	2		0	.353	.647	15	5	OF-1

Jack Dunleavy

DUNLEAVY, JOHN FRANCIS
B. Sept. 14, 1879, Harrison, N. J.   D. Apr. 12, 1944, South Norwalk, Conn.
5'6½" 145 lbs.

	G	AB	H	2B	3B	HR	HR %	R	RBI	BB	SO	SB	BA	SA	AB	H	G by POS
1903 STL N	61	193	48	3	3	0	0.0	23	10	13		10	.249	.295	9	4	OF-38, P-14
1904	51	172	40	7	3	1	0.6	23	14	16		8	.233	.326	0	0	OF-44, P-7
1905	119	435	105	8	8	1	0.2	52	25	55		15	.241	.303	0	0	OF-118, 2B-1
3 yrs.	231	800	193	18	14	2	0.3	98	49	84		33	.241	.306	9	4	OF-200, P-21, 2B-1

George Dunlop

DUNLOP, GEORGE HENRY
B. July 19, 1888, Meriden, Conn.   D. Dec. 12, 1972, Meriden, Conn.
BR TR 5'10" 170 lbs.

	G	AB	H	2B	3B	HR	HR %	R	RBI	BB	SO	SB	BA	SA	AB	H	G by POS
1913 CLE A	7	17	4	1	0	0	0.0	3	0	1	5	0	.235	.294	0	0	SS-4, 3B-3
1914	1	3	0	0	0	0	0.0	0	0	1	1	0	.000	.000	0	0	SS-1
2 yrs.	8	20	4	1	0	0	0.0	3	0	1	6	0	.200	.250	0	0	SS-5, 3B-3

Jack Dunn

DUNN, JOHN JOSEPH
B. Oct. 6, 1872, Meadville, Pa.   D. Oct. 22, 1928, Towson, Md.
BR TR 5'9"

	G	AB	H	2B	3B	HR	HR %	R	RBI	BB	SO	SB	BA	SA	AB	H	G by POS
1897 BKN N	36	131	29	4	0	0	0.0	20	17	4		2	.221	.252	0	0	P-25, 2B-4, OF-3, 3B-3, SS-1
1898	51	167	41	0	1	0	0.0	21	19	7		3	.246	.257	0	0	P-41, OF-4, SS-4, 3B-2
1899	43	122	30	2	1	0	0.0	21	16	3		3	.246	.279	1	0	P-41, SS-1
1900 2 teams								BKN N (10G – .231)		PHI N (10G – .303)							
" total	20	59	16	1	0	0	0.0	5	6	1		1	.271	.288	0	0	P-20
1901 2 teams								PHI N (2G – 1.000)		BAL A (96G – .249)							
" total	98	363	91	9	4	0	0.0	42	36	22		10	.251	.298	0	0	3B-67, SS-19, P-11, OF-1, 2B-1
1902 NY N	100	342	72	11	0	0	0.0	26	14	20		13	.211	.249	1	1	OF-43, SS-36, 3B-18, P-3, 2B-2
1903	78	257	62	15	1	0	0.0	35	37	15		12	.241	.307	6	1	SS-27, 3B-25, 2B-19, OF-1
1904	64	181	56	12	2	1	0.6	27	19	11		11	.309	.414	6	1	3B-28, SS-10, 2B-9, OF-7, P-1
8 yrs.	490	1622	397	54	10	1	0.1	197	164	83		55	.245	.292	14	3	3B-143, P-142, SS-98, OF-59, 2B-35

	G	AB	H	2B	3B	HR	HR %	R	RBI	BB	SO	SB	BA	SA	Pinch Hit AB	Pinch Hit H	G by POS

Joe Dunn

DUNN, JOSEPH EDWARD
B. Mar. 11, 1885, Springfield, Ohio   D. Mar. 19, 1944, Springfield, Ohio
BR TR

	G	AB	H	2B	3B	HR	HR %	R	RBI	BB	SO	SB	BA	SA	PH AB	PH H	G by POS
1908 BKN N	20	64	11	3	0	0	0.0	3	5	0		0	.172	.219	0	0	C-20
1909	10	25	4	1	0	0	0.0	1	2	0		0	.160	.200	3	0	C-7
2 yrs.	30	89	15	4	0	0	0.0	4	7	0		0	.169	.213	3	0	C-27

Ron Dunn

DUNN, RONALD RAY
B. Jan. 24, 1950, Oklahoma City, Okla.
BR TR 5'11" 180 lbs.

	G	AB	H	2B	3B	HR	HR %	R	RBI	BB	SO	SB	BA	SA	PH AB	PH H	G by POS
1974 CHI N	23	68	20	7	0	2	2.9	6	15	12	8	0	.294	.485	1	0	2B-21, 3B-6
1975	32	44	7	3	0	1	2.3	2	6	6	17	0	.159	.295	17	3	3B-11, OF-2, 2B-1
2 yrs.	55	112	27	10	0	3	2.7	8	21	18	25	0	.241	.411	18	3	2B-22, 3B-17, OF-2

Steve Dunn

DUNN, STEPHEN
B. Dec. 21, 1858, London, Ont., Canada   D. May 5, 1933, London, Ont., Canada

	G	AB	H	2B	3B	HR	HR %	R	RBI	BB	SO	SB	BA	SA	PH AB	PH H	G by POS
1884 STP U	9	32	8	2	0	0	0.0	2		0			.250	.313	0	0	1B-9, 3B-1

Mike Dupaugher

DUPAUGHER, MICHAEL H.
B. Sept. 11, 1858, Marysville, Calif.   D. July 7, 1915, San Francisco, Calif.
5'8" 190 lbs.

	G	AB	H	2B	3B	HR	HR %	R	RBI	BB	SO	SB	BA	SA	PH AB	PH H	G by POS
1884 PHI N	4	10	2	0	0	0	0.0	0		1	3		.200	.200	0	0	C-4

Dan Duran

DURAN, DANIEL JAMES
B. Mar. 16, 1954, Palo Alto, Calif.
BL TL 5'11" 190 lbs.

	G	AB	H	2B	3B	HR	HR %	R	RBI	BB	SO	SB	BA	SA	PH AB	PH H	G by POS
1981 TEX A	13	16	4	0	0	0	0.0	1	0	1	1	0	.250	.250	5	2	OF-7, 1B-1

Kid Durbin

DURBIN, BLAINE ALPHONSUS
B. Sept. 10, 1886, Lamar, Kans.   D. Sept. 11, 1943, Kirkwood, Mo.
BL TL 5'8" 155 lbs.

	G	AB	H	2B	3B	HR	HR %	R	RBI	BB	SO	SB	BA	SA	PH AB	PH H	G by POS
1907 CHI N	11	18	6	0	0	0	0.0	2	0	1		0	.333	.333	1	0	OF-5, P-5
1908	14	28	7	1	0	0	0.0	3	0	2		0	.250	.286	2	0	OF-11
1909 2 teams		CIN N (6G – .200)				PIT N (1G – .000)											
" total	7	5	1	0	0	0	0.0	1	0	1		0	.200	.200	5	1	
3 yrs.	32	51	14	1	0	0	0.0	6	0	4		0	.275	.294	8	1	OF-16, P-5

Joe Durham

DURHAM, JOSEPH VANN (Pop)
B. July 31, 1931, Newport News, Va.
BR TR 6'1" 186 lbs.

	G	AB	H	2B	3B	HR	HR %	R	RBI	BB	SO	SB	BA	SA	PH AB	PH H	G by POS
1954 BAL A	10	40	9	0	0	1	2.5	4	3	4	7	0	.225	.300	0	0	OF-10
1957	77	157	29	2	0	4	2.5	19	17	16	42	1	.185	.274	15	1	OF-59
1959 STL N	6	5	0	0	0	0	0.0	2	0	0	1	0	.000	.000	2	0	OF-1
3 yrs.	93	202	38	2	0	5	2.5	25	20	20	50	1	.188	.272	17	1	OF-70

Leon Durham

DURHAM, LEON (Bull)
B. July 31, 1957, Cincinnati, Ohio
BL TL 6'1" 185 lbs.

	G	AB	H	2B	3B	HR	HR %	R	RBI	BB	SO	SB	BA	SA	PH AB	PH H	G by POS
1980 STL N	96	303	82	15	4	8	2.6	42	42	18	55	8	.271	.426	16	5	OF-78, 1B-8
1981 CHI N	87	328	95	14	6	10	3.0	42	35	27	53	25	.290	.460	3	1	OF-83, 1B-3
1982	148	539	168	33	7	22	4.1	84	90	66	77	28	.312	.521	2	0	OF-143, 1B-1
1983	100	337	87	18	8	12	3.6	58	55	66	83	12	.258	.466	1	0	OF-95, 1B-6
1984	137	473	132	30	4	23	4.9	86	96	69	86	16	.279	.505	8	2	1B-130
5 yrs.	568	1980	564	110	29	75	3.8	312	318	246	354	89	.285	.483	33	10	OF-399, 1B-148

LEAGUE CHAMPIONSHIP SERIES

	G	AB	H	2B	3B	HR	HR %	R	RBI	BB	SO	SB	BA	SA	PH AB	PH H	G by POS
1984 CHI N	5	20	3	0	0	2	10.0	2	4	1	4	0	.150	.450	0	0	1B-5

Bobby Durnbaugh

DURNBAUGH, ROBERT EUGENE (Scroggy)
B. Jan. 15, 1933, Dayton, Ohio
BR TR 5'8" 170 lbs.

	G	AB	H	2B	3B	HR	HR %	R	RBI	BB	SO	SB	BA	SA	PH AB	PH H	G by POS
1957 CIN N	2	1	0	0	0	0	0.0	0	0	0	0	0	.000	.000	0	0	SS-2

George Durning

DURNING, GEORGE DEWEY
B. May 9, 1898, Philadelphia, Pa.
BR TR 5'11" 175 lbs.

	G	AB	H	2B	3B	HR	HR %	R	RBI	BB	SO	SB	BA	SA	PH AB	PH H	G by POS
1925 PHI N	5	14	5	0	0	0	0.0	3	1	2	1	0	.357	.357	1	0	OF-4

Leo Durocher

DUROCHER, LEO ERNEST (The Lip)
B. July 27, 1905, W. Springfield, Mass.
Manager 1939-46, 1948-55, 1966-73.
BR TR 5'10" 160 lbs.
BB 1929

	G	AB	H	2B	3B	HR	HR %	R	RBI	BB	SO	SB	BA	SA	PH AB	PH H	G by POS
1925 NY A	2	1	0	0	0	0	0.0	1	0	0	0	0	.000	.000	1	0	
1928	102	296	80	8	6	0	0.0	46	31	22	52	1	.270	.338	1	1	2B-66, SS-29
1929	106	341	84	4	5	0	0.0	53	32	34	33	3	.246	.287	1	0	SS-93, 2B-12
1930 CIN N	119	354	86	15	3	3	0.8	31	32	20	45	0	.243	.328	0	0	SS-103, 2B-13
1931	121	361	82	11	5	1	0.3	26	29	18	32	0	.227	.294	0	0	SS-120
1932	143	457	99	22	6	1	0.2	43	33	36	40	3	.217	.293	0	0	SS-142
1933 2 teams		CIN N (16G – .216)				STL N (123G – .258)											
" total	139	446	113	19	4	3	0.7	51	44	30	37	3	.253	.334	0	0	SS-139
1934 STL N	146	500	130	26	5	3	0.6	62	70	33	40	2	.260	.350	0	0	SS-146
1935	143	513	136	23	5	8	1.6	62	78	29	46	4	.265	.376	0	0	SS-142
1936	136	510	146	22	3	1	0.2	57	58	29	47	3	.286	.347	0	0	SS-136
1937	135	477	97	11	3	1	0.2	46	47	38	36	6	.203	.245	0	0	SS-134
1938 BKN N	141	479	105	18	5	1	0.2	41	56	47	30	3	.219	.284	0	0	SS-141
1939	116	390	108	21	6	1	0.3	42	34	27	24	2	.277	.369	2	0	SS-113, 3B-1
1940	62	160	37	9	1	1	0.6	10	14	12	13	1	.231	.319	1	0	SS-53, 2B-4
1941	18	42	12	1	0	0	0.0	2	6	1	3	0	.286	.310	5	1	SS-12, 2B-1
1943	6	18	4	0	0	0	0.0	1	1	1	2	0	.222	.222	0	0	SS-6
1945	2	5	1	0	0	0	0.0	1	2	0	0	0	.200	.200	0	0	2B-2
17 yrs.	1637	5350	1320	210	56	24	0.4	575	567	377	480	31	.247	.320	13	2	SS-1509, 2B-98, 3B-1

WORLD SERIES

	G	AB	H	2B	3B	HR	HR %	R	RBI	BB	SO	SB	BA	SA	PH AB	PH H	G by POS
1928 NY A	4	2	0	0	0	0	0.0	0	0	0	1	0	.000	.000	0	0	2B-4
1934 STL N	7	27	7	1	1	0	0.0	4	0	0	0	0	.259	.370	0	0	SS-7
2 yrs.	11	29	7	1	1	0	0.0	4	0	0	1	0	.241	.345	0	0	SS-7, 2B-4

	G	AB	H	2B	3B	HR	HR %	R	RBI	BB	SO	SB	BA	SA	Pinch Hit AB	Pinch Hit H	G by POS

Red Durrett

DURRETT, ELMER CHARLES
B. Feb. 3, 1921, Sherman, Tex.   BL TL 5'10" 170 lbs.

	G	AB	H	2B	3B	HR	HR %	R	RBI	BB	SO	SB	BA	SA	AB	H	G by POS
1944 BKN N	11	32	5	1	0	1	3.1	3	1	7	10	0	.156	.281	1	0	OF-9
1945	8	16	2	0	0	0	0.0	2	0	3	3	0	.125	.125	2	0	OF-4
2 yrs.	19	48	7	1	0	1	2.1	5	1	10	13	0	.146	.229	3	0	OF-13

Cedric Durst

DURST, CEDRIC MONTGOMERY
B. Aug. 23, 1896, Austin, Tex.   D. Feb. 16, 1971, San Diego, Calif.   BL TL 5'11" 160 lbs.

	G	AB	H	2B	3B	HR	HR %	R	RBI	BB	SO	SB	BA	SA	AB	H	G by POS
1922 STL A	15	12	4	1	0	0	0.0	5	0	0	1	0	.333	.417	3	1	OF-6
1923	45	85	18	2	0	5	5.9	11	11	8	14	0	.212	.412	20	3	OF-10, 1B-8
1926	80	219	52	7	5	3	1.4	32	16	22	19	0	.237	.356	15	3	OF-57, 1B-4
1927 NY A	65	129	32	4	3	0	0.0	18	25	6	7	0	.248	.326	21	4	OF-36, 1B-2
1928	74	135	34	2	1	2	1.5	18	10	7	9	1	.252	.326	33	3	OF-33, 1B-3
1929	92	202	52	3	4	2	2.0	32	31	15	25	3	.257	.361	16	5	OF-72, 1B-1
1930 2 teams		NY	A	(8G –	.158)			BOS	A	(102G –	.245)						
" total	110	321	77	20	5	1	0.3	29	29	17	25	3	.240	.343	25	7	OF-83
7 yrs.	481	1103	269	39	17	15	1.4	145	122	75	100	7	.244	.351	133	26	OF-297, 1B-18

WORLD SERIES

	G	AB	H	2B	3B	HR	HR %	R	RBI	BB	SO	SB	BA	SA	AB	H	G by POS
1927 NY A	1	1	0	0	0	0	0.0	0	0	0	0	0	.000	.000	1	0	
1928	4	8	3	0	0	1	12.5	3	2	0	1	0	.375	.750	0	0	OF-4
2 yrs.	5	9	3	0	0	1	11.1	3	2	0	1	0	.333	.667	1	0	OF-4

Erv Dusak

DUSAK, ERVIN FRANK (Four Sack)
B. July 29, 1920, Chicago, Ill.   BR TR 6'2" 185 lbs.

	G	AB	H	2B	3B	HR	HR %	R	RBI	BB	SO	SB	BA	SA	AB	H	G by POS
1941 STL N	6	14	2	0	0	0	0.0	1	3	2	6	1	.143	.143	2	0	OF-4
1942	12	27	5	3	0	0	0.0	4	3	3	7	0	.185	.296	1	0	OF-8, 3B-1
1946	100	275	66	9	1	9	3.3	38	42	33	63	7	.240	.378	7	2	OF-77, 3B-11, 2B-2
1947	111	328	93	7	3	6	1.8	56	28	50	34	1	.284	.378	13	1	OF-89, 3B-7
1948	114	311	65	9	2	6	1.9	60	19	49	55	3	.209	.309	9	3	OF-68, 2B-29, 3B-9, SS-1, P-1
1949	1	0	0	0	0	0	–	1	0	0	0	0	–	–	0	0	
1950	23	12	1	1	0	0	0.0	0	0	0	3	0	.083	.167	0	0	P-14, OF-2
1951 2 teams		STL	N	(5G –	.500)			PIT	N	(21G –	.308)						
" total	26	41	13	3	0	2	4.9	7	8	3	12	0	.317	.537	1	0	OF-12, P-8, 3B-2, 2B-2
1952 PIT N	20	27	6	0	0	1	3.7	1	3	2	8	0	.222	.333	11	2	OF-11
9 yrs.	413	1035	251	32	6	24	2.3	168	106	142	188	12	.243	.355	44	8	OF-271, 2B-33, 3B-30, P-23, SS-1

WORLD SERIES

	G	AB	H	2B	3B	HR	HR %	R	RBI	BB	SO	SB	BA	SA	AB	H	G by POS
1946 STL N	4	4	1	1	0	0	0.0	0	0	2	2	0	.250	.500	1	0	OF-4

Ward Dwight

DWIGHT, ALBERT WARD
B. Jan. 4, 1856, New York, N. Y.   D. Feb. 20, 1903, San Francisco, Calif.

	G	AB	H	2B	3B	HR	HR %	R	RBI	BB	SO	SB	BA	SA	AB	H	G by POS
1884 KC U	12	43	10	2	0	0	0.0	8		2			.233	.279	0	0	C-10, OF-1, 2B-1

Double Joe Dwyer

DWYER, JOSEPH MICHAEL
B. Mar. 27, 1904, Orange, N. J.   BL TL 5'9" 186 lbs.

	G	AB	H	2B	3B	HR	HR %	R	RBI	BB	SO	SB	BA	SA	AB	H	G by POS
1937 CIN N	12	11	3	0	0	0	0.0	2	1	1	0	0	.273	.273	11	3	

Frank Dwyer

DWYER, JOHN FRANCIS
B. Mar. 25, 1868, Lee, Mass.   D. Feb. 4, 1943, Pittsfield, Mass.   BR TR 5'8" 145 lbs.
Manager 1902.

	G	AB	H	2B	3B	HR	HR %	R	RBI	BB	SO	SB	BA	SA	AB	H	G by POS
1888 CHI N	5	21	4	1	0	0	0.0	2	2	0	5	0	.190	.238	0	0	P-5
1889	36	135	27	1	1	1	0.7	14	6	4	8	0	.200	.244	0	0	P-32, OF-3, SS-2
1890 CHI P	16	53	14	2	0	0	0.0	10	11	0	2	1	.264	.302	0	0	P-12, OF-4
1891 C-M AA	48	181	49	5	3	0	0.0	25	20	6	16	5	.271	.331	0	0	P-45, OF-4, 2B-2
1892 2 teams		STL	N	(10G –	.080)			CIN	N	(40G –	.163)						
" total	50	154	23	0	2	0	0.0	19	6	8	11	2	.149	.175	1	0	P-43, OF-6
1893 CIN N	38	120	24	1	2	1	0.8	22	17	9	5	2	.200	.267	0	0	P-37, OF-1, 1B-1
1894	54	172	46	9	2	2	1.2	31	28	15	13	0	.267	.378	1	0	P-45, OF-10, SS-2
1895	37	113	30	3	5	1	0.9	14	16	5	5	2	.265	.407	0	0	P-37
1896	36	110	29	4	4	0	0.0	17	15	11	15	3	.264	.373	0	0	P-36
1897	37	94	25	1	1	0	0.0	13	10	5		0	.266	.298	0	0	P-37
1898	31	85	12	1	1	0	0.0	11	5	7		1	.141	.176	0	0	P-31
1899	5	11	4	0	0	0	0.0	0	0	0		0	.364	.364	0	0	P-5
12 yrs.	393	1249	287	28	21	5	0.4	178	136	70	80	16	.230	.298	2	0	P-365, OF-28, SS-4, 2B-2, 1B-1

Jim Dwyer

DWYER, JAMES EDWARD
B. Jan. 3, 1950, Evergreen Park, Ill.   BL TL 5'10" 165 lbs.

	G	AB	H	2B	3B	HR	HR %	R	RBI	BB	SO	SB	BA	SA	AB	H	G by POS
1973 STL N	28	57	11	1	1	0	0.0	7	0	1	5	0	.193	.246	8	1	OF-20
1974	74	86	24	1	0	2	2.3	13	11	11	16	0	.279	.360	41	10	OF-25, 1B-3
1975 2 teams		STL	N	(21G –	.194)			MON	N	(60G –	.286)						
" total	81	206	56	8	1	3	1.5	26	21	27	36	4	.272	.364	21	6	OF-61
1976 2 teams		MON	N	(50G –	.185)			NY	N	(11G –	.154)						
" total	61	105	19	3	1	0	0.0	9	5	13	11	0	.181	.229	38	6	OF-21
1977 STL N	13	31	7	1	0	0	0.0	3	2	4	5	0	.226	.258	2	1	OF-12
1978 2 teams		STL	N	(34G –	.215)			SF	N	(73G –	.225)						
" total	107	238	53	12	2	6	2.5	30	26	37	32	7	.223	.366	24	5	OF-58, 1B-29
1979 BOS A	76	113	30	7	0	2	1.8	19	14	17	9	3	.265	.381	22	7	1B-25, OF-19, DH-4
1980	93	260	74	11	1	9	3.5	41	38	28	23	3	.285	.438	11	2	OF-65, DH-12, 1B-9
1981 BAL A	68	134	30	0	1	3	2.2	16	10	20	19	0	.224	.306	6	0	OF-59, 1B-3, DH-1
1982	71	148	45	4	3	6	4.1	28	15	27	24	2	.304	.493	23	6	OF-49, DH-1, 1B-1
1983	100	196	56	17	1	8	4.1	37	38	31	29	1	.286	.505	33	8	OF-52, DH-3
1984	76	161	41	9	1	2	1.2	22	21	23	24	0	.255	.360	27	7	OF-52, DH-3
12 yrs.	848	1735	446	74	12	41	2.4	251	201	239	233	20	.257	.384	256	59	OF-497, 1B-74, DH-21

LEAGUE CHAMPIONSHIP SERIES

	G	AB	H	2B	3B	HR	HR %	R	RBI	BB	SO	SB	BA	SA	AB	H	G by POS
1983 BAL A	2	4	1	1	0	0	0.0	1	0	1	0	0	.250	.500	1	0	OF-1

	G	AB	H	2B	3B	HR	HR %	R	RBI	BB	SO	SB	BA	SA	Pinch Hit AB	Pinch Hit H	G by POS

Jim Dwyer continued

WORLD SERIES
| 1983 BAL A | 2 | 8 | 3 | 1 | 0 | 1 | 12.5 | 3 | 1 | 0 | 0 | 0 | .375 | .875 | 0 | 0 | OF-2 |

John Dwyer

DWYER, JOHN E.
B. Lisbon, Ill. Deceased.

| 1882 CLE N | 1 | 3 | 0 | 0 | 0 | 0 | 0.0 | 0 | 1 | 0 | 0 | | .000 | .000 | 0 | 0 | OF-1, C-1 |

Jerry Dybzinski

DYBZINSKI, JEROME MATHEW
B. July 7, 1955, Cleveland, Ohio

BR TR 6'2" 180 lbs.

1980 CLE A	114	248	57	11	1	1	0.4	32	23	13	35	4	.230	.294	3	0	SS-73, 2B-29, 3B-4, DH-2
1981	48	57	17	0	0	0	0.0	10	6	5	8	7	.298	.298	1	0	SS-34, 3B-3, 2B-3, DH-1
1982	80	212	49	6	2	0	0.0	19	22	21	25	3	.231	.278	2	0	SS-77, 3B-3
1983 CHI A	127	256	59	10	1	1	0.4	30	32	18	29	11	.230	.289	1	0	SS-118, 3B-9
1984	94	132	31	5	1	1	0.8	17	10	13	12	7	.235	.311	0	0	SS-76, 3B-14, DH-1, 2B-1
5 yrs.	463	905	213	32	5	3	0.3	108	93	70	109	32	.235	.292	7	0	SS-378, 3B-33, 2B-33, DH-4

LEAGUE CHAMPIONSHIP SERIES
| 1983 CHI A | 2 | 4 | 1 | 0 | 0 | 0 | 0.0 | 0 | 0 | 0 | 0 | 0 | .250 | .250 | 0 | 0 | SS-2 |

Jim Dyck

DYCK, JAMES ROBERT
B. Feb. 3, 1922, Omaha, Neb.

BR TR 6'2" 200 lbs.

1951 STL A	4	15	1	0	0	0	0.0	1	0	1	1	0	.067	.067	0	0	3B-4
1952	122	402	108	22	3	15	3.7	60	64	50	68	0	.269	.450	9	3	3B-74, OF-48
1953	112	334	71	15	1	9	2.7	38	27	38	40	3	.213	.344	9	0	OF-55, 3B-51
1954 CLE A	2	1	1	0	0	0	0.0	0	1	1	0	0	1.000	1.000	1	1	
1955 BAL A	61	197	55	13	1	2	1.0	32	22	28	21	1	.279	.386	9	3	OF-45, 3B-17
1956 2 teams	BAL A (11G – .217)				CIN N (18G – .091)												
" total	29	34	6	2	0	0	0.0	8	0	13	10	0	.176	.235	9	0	OF-9, 3B-1, 1B-1
6 yrs.	330	983	242	52	5	26	2.6	139	114	131	140	4	.246	.389	37	7	OF-157, 3B-147, 1B-1

Ben Dyer

DYER, BENJAMIN FRANKLIN
B. Feb. 13, 1893, Chicago, Ill. D. Aug. 7, 1959, Kenosha, Wis.

BR TR 5'10" 170 lbs.

1914 NY N	7	4	1	0	0	0	0.0	1	0	0	1	1	.250	.250	0	0	SS-6, 2B-1
1915	7	19	4	0	1	0	0.0	4	0	4	3	0	.211	.316	0	0	3B-6, SS-1
1916 DET A	4	14	4	1	0	0	0.0	4	1	1	1	0	.286	.357	0	0	SS-4
1917	30	67	14	5	0	0	0.0	6	0	2	17	3	.209	.284	8	0	SS-14, 3B-8
1918	13	18	5	0	0	0	0.0	1	2	0	6	0	.278	.278	6	2	OF-2, 1B-2, P-2, 2B-1
1919	44	85	21	4	0	0	0.0	11	15	8	19	0	.247	.294	8	3	3B-23, SS-11, OF-1
6 yrs.	105	207	49	10	1	0	0.0	27	18	15	47	4	.237	.295	22	5	3B-37, SS-36, OF-3, 2B-2, 1B-2, P-2

Duffy Dyer

DYER, DON ROBERT
B. Aug. 15, 1945, Dayton, Ohio

BR TR 6' 187 lbs.

1968 NY N	1	3	1	0	0	0	0.0	0	1	1	0	0	.333	.333	0	0	C-1
1969	29	74	19	3	1	3	4.1	5	12	4	22	0	.257	.446	8	3	C-19
1970	59	148	31	1	0	2	1.4	8	12	21	32	1	.209	.257	1	1	C-57
1971	59	169	39	7	1	2	1.2	13	18	14	45	1	.231	.320	9	4	C-53
1972	94	325	75	17	3	8	2.5	33	36	28	71	0	.231	.375	3	2	C-91, OF-1
1973	70	189	35	6	1	1	0.5	9	9	13	40	0	.185	.243	10	2	C-60
1974	63	142	30	1	1	0	0.0	14	10	18	15	0	.211	.232	17	8	C-45
1975 PIT N	48	132	30	5	2	3	2.3	8	16	6	22	0	.227	.364	11	3	C-36
1976	69	184	41	8	0	3	1.6	12	9	29	35	0	.223	.315	12	5	C-58
1977	94	270	65	11	1	3	1.1	27	19	54	49	6	.241	.322	3	0	C-93
1978	58	175	37	8	1	0	0.0	7	13	18	32	2	.211	.269	3	2	C-55
1979 MON N	28	74	18	6	0	1	1.4	4	8	9	17	0	.243	.365	1	0	C-27
1980 DET A	48	108	20	1	0	4	3.7	11	11	13	34	0	.185	.306	3	0	C-37, DH-10
1981	2	0	0	0	0	0	–	0	0	0	0	0	–	–	0	0	C-2
14 yrs.	722	1993	441	74	11	30	1.5	151	173	228	415	10	.221	.315	81	30	C-634, DH-10, OF-1

LEAGUE CHAMPIONSHIP SERIES
| 1975 PIT N | 1 | 0 | 0 | 0 | 0 | 0 | – | 0 | 1 | 1 | 0 | 0 | – | – | 0 | 0 | |

WORLD SERIES
| 1969 NY N | 1 | 1 | 0 | 0 | 0 | 0 | 0.0 | 0 | 0 | 0 | 0 | 0 | .000 | .000 | 1 | 0 | |

Eddie Dyer

DYER, EDWIN HAWLEY
B. Oct. 11, 1900, Morgan City, La. D. Apr. 20, 1964, Houston, Tex.
Manager 1946-50.

BL TL 5'11½" 168 lbs.

1922 STL N	6	3	1	1	0	0	0.0	1	0	0	0	0	.333	.667	1	1	P-2
1923	35	45	12	3	0	2	4.4	17	5	3	5	1	.267	.467	14	3	P-8, P-4
1924	50	76	18	2	3	0	0.0	8	8	3	8	1	.237	.342	16	4	P-29, OF-1
1925	31	31	3	1	0	0	0.0	4	0	3	1	1	.097	.129	1	0	P-31
1926	6	2	1	0	0	0	0.0	1	0	0	0	0	.500	.500	0	0	P-6
1927	1	0	0	0	0	0	–	0	0	1	0	0	–	–	0	0	P-1
6 yrs.	129	157	35	7	3	2	1.3	31	13	10	14	3	.223	.344	32	8	P-73, OF-9

Jimmy Dykes

DYKES, JAMES JOSEPH
B. Nov. 10, 1896, Philadelphia, Pa. D. June 15, 1976, Philadelphia, Pa.
Manager 1934-46, 1951-54, 1958-61.

BR TR 5'9" 185 lbs.

1918 PHI A	59	186	35	3	3	0	0.0	13	13	19	32	3	.188	.237	2	0	2B-56, 3B-1
1919	17	49	9	1	0	0	0.0	4	1	7	11	0	.184	.204	0	0	2B-16
1920	142	546	140	25	4	8	1.5	81	35	52	73	6	.256	.361	0	0	2B-108, 3B-36
1921	155	613	168	32	13	17	2.8	88	77	60	75	6	.274	.452	0	0	2B-155
1922	145	501	138	23	7	12	2.4	66	68	55	98	6	.275	.421	0	0	3B-140, 2B-5
1923	124	416	105	28	1	4	1.0	50	43	35	40	6	.252	.353	0	0	2B-102, SS-20, 3B-2
1924	110	410	128	26	6	3	0.7	68	50	38	59	1	.312	.427	2	1	2B-78, 3B-27, SS-4

	G	AB	H	2B	3B	HR	HR %	R	RBI	BB	SO	SB	BA	SA	Pinch Hit AB	Pinch Hit H	G by POS

Jimmy Dykes continued

	G	AB	H	2B	3B	HR	HR %	R	RBI	BB	SO	SB	BA	SA	AB	H	G by POS
1925	122	465	150	32	11	5	1.1	93	55	46	49	3	.323	.471	3	2	3B-64, 2B-58, SS-2
1926	124	429	123	32	5	1	0.2	54	44	49	34	6	.287	.392	1	0	3B-77, 2B-44, SS-1
1927	121	417	135	33	6	3	0.7	61	60	44	23	2	.324	.453	5	3	1B-82, 3B-25, OF-5, SS-5, 2B-5, P-2
1928	85	242	67	11	0	5	2.1	39	30	27	21	2	.277	.384	3	0	2B-32, SS-23, 3B-20, 1B-8, OF-1
1929	119	401	131	34	6	13	3.2	76	79	51	25	8	.327	.539	2	0	SS-60, 3B-48, 2B-13
1930	125	435	131	28	4	6	1.4	69	73	74	53	3	.301	.425	1	0	3B-123, OF-1
1931	101	355	97	28	2	3	0.8	48	46	48	47	1	.273	.389	0	0	3B-87, SS-15
1932	153	558	148	29	5	7	1.3	71	90	77	65	8	.265	.373	1	0	3B-141, SS-10, 2B-1
1933 CHI A	151	554	144	22	6	1	0.2	49	68	69	37	3	.260	.327	0	0	3B-151
1934	127	456	122	17	4	7	1.5	52	82	64	28	1	.268	.368	1	1	3B-74, 2B-27, 1B-27
1935	117	403	116	24	2	4	1.0	45	61	59	28	4	.288	.387	1	0	3B-98, 1B-16, 2B-3
1936	127	435	116	16	3	7	1.6	62	60	61	36	1	.267	.366	1	0	3B-125
1937	30	85	26	5	0	1	1.2	10	23	9	7	0	.306	.400	4	2	1B-15, 3B-11
1938	26	89	27	4	2	2	2.2	9	13	10	8	0	.303	.461	1	0	2B-23, 3B-1
1939	2	1	0	0	0	0	0.0	0	0	0	0	0	.000	.000	0	0	3B-2
22 yrs.	2282	8046	2256	453	90	109	1.4	1108	1071	954	849	70	.280	.400	28	9	3B-1253, 2B-726, 1B-148, SS-140, OF-7, P-2

WORLD SERIES

	G	AB	H	2B	3B	HR	HR %	R	RBI	BB	SO	SB	BA	SA	AB	H	G by POS
1929 PHI A	5	19	8	1	0	0	0.0	2	4	1	1	0	.421	.474	0	0	3B-5
1930	6	18	4	3	0	1	5.6	2	5	5	3	0	.222	.556	0	0	3B-6
1931	7	22	5	0	0	0	0.0	2	2	5	1	0	.227	.227	0	0	3B-7
3 yrs.	18	59	17	4	0	1	1.7	6	11	11	5	0	.288	.407	0	0	3B-18

John Dyler

DYLER, JOHN F.
B. June, 1852, Louisville, Ky.   Deceased.
Manager 1882.

	G	AB	H	2B	3B	HR	HR %	R	RBI	BB	SO	SB	BA	SA	AB	H	G by POS
1882 LOU AA	1	4	0	0	0	0	0.0	0		0			.000	.000	0	0	OF-1

Don Eaddy

EADDY, DONALD JOHNSON   BR TR 5'11"   165 lbs.
B. Feb. 16, 1934, Grand Rapids, Mich.

	G	AB	H	2B	3B	HR	HR %	R	RBI	BB	SO	SB	BA	SA	AB	H	G by POS
1959 CHI N	15	1	0	0	0	0	0.0	3	0	0	1	0	.000	.000	0	0	3B-1

Bad Bill Eagan

EAGAN, WILLIAM
B. June 1, 1869, Camden, N. J.   D. Feb. 14, 1905, Denver, Colo.

	G	AB	H	2B	3B	HR	HR %	R	RBI	BB	SO	SB	BA	SA	AB	H	G by POS
1891 STL AA	83	302	65	11	4	4	1.3	49	43	44	54	21	.215	.318	0	0	2B-83
1893 CHI N	6	19	5	0	0	0	0.0	3	2	5	5	4	.263	.263	0	0	2B-6
1898 PIT N	19	61	20	2	3	0	0.0	14	5	8		1	.328	.459	0	0	2B-17
3 yrs.	108	382	90	13	7	4	1.0	66	50	57	59	26	.236	.338	0	0	2B-106

Truck Eagan

EAGAN, CHARLES EUGENE   BR TR 5'11"   190 lbs.
B. Aug. 10, 1876, San Francisco, Calif.   D. Mar. 19, 1949, San Francisco, Calif.

	G	AB	H	2B	3B	HR	HR %	R	RBI	BB	SO	SB	BA	SA	AB	H	G by POS
1901 2 teams	PIT	N (4G – .083)				CLE	A (5G – .167)										
" total	9	30	4	0	1	0	0.0	2	4	1		1	.133	.200	1	0	2B-5, SS-3, 3B-1

Bill Eagle

EAGLE, WILLIAM LYCURGUS
B. July 25, 1877, Rockville, Md.   D. Apr. 27, 1951, Churchtown, Md.

	G	AB	H	2B	3B	HR	HR %	R	RBI	BB	SO	SB	BA	SA	AB	H	G by POS
1898 WAS N	4	13	4	1	0	0	0.0	0	2	0		0	.308	.385	0	0	OF-4

Charlie Eakle

EAKLE, CHARLES EMORY
B. Sept. 27, 1887, Baltimore, Md.   D. June 15, 1959, Baltimore, Md.

	G	AB	H	2B	3B	HR	HR %	R	RBI	BB	SO	SB	BA	SA	AB	H	G by POS
1915 BAL F	2	7	2	1	0	0	0.0	0	0	0		1	.286	.429	0	0	2B-2

Howard Earl

EARL, HOWARD J. (Slim Jim)
B. Feb. 27, 1869, Palmyra, N. Y.   D. Dec. 22, 1916, North Bay, N. Y.

	G	AB	H	2B	3B	HR	HR %	R	RBI	BB	SO	SB	BA	SA	AB	H	G by POS
1890 CHI N	92	384	95	10	3	6	1.6	57	51	18	47	17	.247	.336	0	0	OF-49, 2B-39, SS-4, 1B-3
1891 C-M AA	31	129	32	5	2	1	0.8	21	17	5	13	3	.248	.341	0	0	OF-30, 1B-2
2 yrs.	123	513	127	15	5	7	1.4	78	68	23	60	20	.248	.337	0	0	OF-79, 2B-39, 1B-5, SS-4

Scottie Earl

EARL, WILLIAM SCOTT   BR TR 5'11"   165 lbs.
B. Sept. 18, 1960, Seymour, Ind.

	G	AB	H	2B	3B	HR	HR %	R	RBI	BB	SO	SB	BA	SA	AB	H	G by POS
1984 DET A	14	35	4	0	1	0	0.0	3	1	0	9	1	.114	.171	0	0	2B-14

Billy Earle

EARLE, WILLIAM MOFFAT (The Little Globetrotter)   BR TR 5'10½" 170 lbs.
B. Nov. 10, 1867, Philadelphia, Pa.   D. May 30, 1946, Omaha, Neb.

	G	AB	H	2B	3B	HR	HR %	R	RBI	BB	SO	SB	BA	SA	AB	H	G by POS
1889 CIN AA	53	169	45	4	7	4	2.4	37	31	30	24	26	.266	.444	0	0	OF-26, C-23, 1B-5
1890 STL AA	22	73	17	3	1	0	0.0	16		7		6	.233	.301	0	0	C-18, OF-3, SS-1, 3B-1, 2B-1
1892 PIT N	5	13	7	2	0	0	0.0	5	3	4	1	2	.538	.692	0	0	C-5
1893	27	95	24	4	4	2	2.1	21	15	7	6	1	.253	.442	0	0	C-27
1894 2 teams	LOU	N (21G – .354)				BKN	N (14G – .340)										
" total	35	115	40	7	0	0	0.0	23	13	15	5	6	.348	.409	1	0	C-30, 2B-2, OF-1, 3B-1, 1B-1
5 yrs.	142	465	133	20	12	6	1.3	102	62	63	36	41	.286	.419	1	0	C-103, OF-30, 1B-6, 2B-3, 3B-2, SS-1

Jake Early

EARLY, JACOB WILLARD   BL TR 5'11"   168 lbs.
B. May 19, 1915, King's Mountain, N. C.

	G	AB	H	2B	3B	HR	HR %	R	RBI	BB	SO	SB	BA	SA	AB	H	G by POS
1939 WAS A	32	84	22	7	2	0	0.0	14		5	14	0	.262	.393	6	2	C-24
1940	80	206	53	8	4	5	2.4	26	14	23	22	0	.257	.408	21	4	C-56
1941	104	355	102	20	7	10	2.8	42	54	24	38	0	.287	.468	6	3	C-100
1942	104	353	72	14	2	3	0.8	31	46	37	37	0	.204	.280	7	0	C-98
1943	126	423	109	23	3	5	1.2	37	60	52	43	5	.258	.362	4	0	C-122
1946	64	189	38	6	0	4	2.1	13	18	23	27	0	.201	.296	0	0	C-64

	G	AB	H	2B	3B	HR	HR %	R	RBI	BB	SO	SB	BA	SA	Pinch Hit AB	H	G by POS

Jake Early continued

		G	AB	H	2B	3B	HR	HR %	R	RBI	BB	SO	SB	BA	SA	Pinch AB	Hit H	G by POS
1947	STL A	87	214	48	9	3	3	1.4	25	19	54	34	0	.224	.336	3	1	C-85
1948	WAS A	97	246	54	7	2	1	0.4	22	28	36	33	2	.220	.276	5	2	C-92
1949		53	138	34	4	0	1	0.7	12	11	26	11	0	.246	.297	3	0	C-53
9 yrs.		747	2208	532	98	23	32	1.4	216	264	280	259	7	.241	.350	55	12	C-694

Mike Easler

EASLER, MICHAEL ANTHONY   BL TR 6'   190 lbs.
B. Nov. 29, 1950, Cleveland, Ohio

		G	AB	H	2B	3B	HR	HR %	R	RBI	BB	SO	SB	BA	SA	Pinch AB	Hit H	G by POS
1973	HOU N	6	7	0	0	0	0	0.0	1	0	2	4	0	.000	.000	2	0	OF-2
1974		15	15	1	0	0	0	0.0	0	0	0	5	0	.067	.067	15	1	
1975		5	5	0	0	0	0	0.0	0	0	0	1	0	.000	.000	5	0	
1976	CAL A	21	54	13	1	1	0	0.0	6	4	2	11	1	.241	.296	5	2	DH-16
1977	PIT N	10	18	8	2	0	1	5.6	3	5	0	1	0	.444	.722	6	2	OF-4
1979		55	54	15	1	1	2	3.7	8	11	8	13	0	.278	.444	44	10	OF-4
1980		132	393	133	27	3	21	5.3	66	74	43	65	5	.338	.583	12	4	OF-119
1981		95	339	97	18	5	7	2.1	43	42	24	45	4	.286	.431	6	2	OF-90
1982		142	475	131	27	2	15	3.2	52	58	40	85	1	.276	.436	10	5	OF-138
1983		115	381	117	17	2	10	2.6	44	54	22	64	4	.307	.441	17	8	OF-105
1984	BOS A	156	601	188	31	5	27	4.5	87	91	58	134	1	.313	.516	1	0	DH-126, 1B-29
11 yrs.		752	2342	703	124	19	83	3.5	310	339	199	428	16	.300	.476	123	34	OF-462, DH-142, 1B-29

LEAGUE CHAMPIONSHIP SERIES
| 1979 | PIT N | 1 | 1 | 0 | 0 | 0 | 0 | 0.0 | 0 | 0 | 0 | 0 | 0 | .000 | .000 | 1 | 0 | |

WORLD SERIES
| 1979 | PIT N | 2 | 1 | 0 | 0 | 0 | 0 | 0.0 | 0 | 0 | 0 | 1 | 0 | .000 | .000 | 1 | 0 | |

Carl East

EAST, CARLTON WILLIAM   BL TR 6'2"   178 lbs.
B. Aug. 27, 1894, Marietta, Ga.   D. Jan. 15, 1953, Whitesburg, Ga.

		G	AB	H	2B	3B	HR	HR %	R	RBI	BB	SO	SB	BA	SA	Pinch AB	Hit H	G by POS
1915	STL A	1	1	0	0	0	0	0.0	0	0	0	0	0	.000	.000	0	0	P-1
1924	WAS A	2	6	2	1	0	0	0.0	1	2	2	1	0	.333	.500	0	0	OF-2
2 yrs.		3	7	2	1	0	0	0.0	1	2	2	1	0	.286	.429	0	0	OF-2, P-1

Harry East

EAST, HARRY H.
B. Apr., 1863, St. Louis, Mo.   Deceased.

		G	AB	H	2B	3B	HR	HR %	R	RBI	BB	SO	SB	BA	SA	Pinch AB	Hit H	G by POS
1882	BAL AA	1	4	0	0	0	0	0.0	0				0	.000	.000	0	0	3B-1

Luke Easter

EASTER, LUSCIOUS LUKE   BL TR 6'4½"   240 lbs.
B. Aug. 4, 1915, St. Louis, Mo.   D. Mar. 29, 1979, Euclid, Ohio

		G	AB	H	2B	3B	HR	HR %	R	RBI	BB	SO	SB	BA	SA	Pinch AB	Hit H	G by POS
1949	CLE A	21	45	10	3	0	0	0.0	6	2	8	6	0	.222	.289	6	1	OF-12
1950		141	540	151	20	4	28	5.2	96	107	70	95	0	.280	.487	1	1	1B-128, OF-13
1951		128	486	131	12	5	27	5.6	65	103	37	71	0	.270	.481	3	0	1B-125
1952		127	437	115	10	3	31	7.1	63	97	44	84	1	.263	.513	9	2	1B-118
1953		68	211	64	9	0	7	3.3	26	31	15	35	0	.303	.445	11	4	1B-56
1954		6	6	1	0	0	0	0.0	0	0	0	2	0	.167	.167	6	1	
6 yrs.		491	1725	472	54	12	93	5.4	256	340	174	293	1	.274	.481	36	9	1B-427, OF-25

Henry Easterday

EASTERDAY, HENRY JR.   BR TR 5'6"   145 lbs.
B. Sept. 16, 1864, Philadelphia, Pa.   D. Mar. 30, 1895, Philadelphia, Pa.

		G	AB	H	2B	3B	HR	HR %	R	RBI	BB	SO	SB	BA	SA	Pinch AB	Hit H	G by POS
1884	PHI U	28	115	28	5	0	0	0.0	12		5			.243	.287	0	0	SS-28
1888	KC AA	115	401	76	7	6	3	0.7	42	37	31		23	.190	.259	0	0	SS-115
1889	COL AA	95	324	56	5	8	4	1.2	43	34	41	57	10	.173	.275	0	0	SS-89, 2B-5, 3B-1
1890	3 teams		COL	AA (58G – .157)		PHI	AA (19G – .147)			LOU	AA (7G – .083)							
"	total	84	289	43	6	2	1	0.3	44		35		10	.149	.194	0	0	SS-83, 3B-1
4 yrs.		322	1129	203	23	16	8	0.7	141	70	112	57	43	.180	.250	0	0	SS-315, 2B-5, 3B-2

Paul Easterling

EASTERLING, PAUL   BR TR 5'11"   180 lbs.
B. Sept. 28, 1905, Reidsville, Ga.

		G	AB	H	2B	3B	HR	HR %	R	RBI	BB	SO	SB	BA	SA	Pinch AB	Hit H	G by POS
1928	DET A	43	114	37	7	1	3	2.6	17	12	8	24	2	.325	.482	8	3	OF-34
1930		29	79	16	6	0	1	1.3	7	14	6	18	0	.203	.316	2	0	OF-25
1938	PHI A	4	7	2	0	0	0	0.0	1	0	1	2	0	.286	.286	3	0	OF-1
3 yrs.		76	200	55	13	1	4	2.0	25	26	15	44	2	.275	.410	13	3	OF-60

Ted Easterly

EASTERLY, THEODORE HARRISON   BL TR
B. Apr. 20, 1886, Lincoln, Neb.   D. July 6, 1951, Clear Lake, Calif.

		G	AB	H	2B	3B	HR	HR %	R	RBI	BB	SO	SB	BA	SA	Pinch AB	Hit H	G by POS
1909	CLE A	98	287	75	14	10	1	0.3	32	27	13		8	.261	.390	22	4	C-76
1910		110	363	111	16	6	0	0.0	34	55	21		10	.306	.383	14	4	C-66, OF-30
1911		99	287	93	19	5	1	0.3	34	37	8		6	.324	.436	23	8	OF-54, C-23
1912	2 teams		CLE	A (63G – .296)		CHI	A (30G – .364)											
"	total	93	241	75	6	0	1	0.4	22	35	9		4	.311	.349	30	13	C-61, OF-1
1913	CHI A	60	97	23	1	0	0	0.0	3	8	4	9	2	.237	.247	37	8	C-19
1914	KC F	134	436	146	20	12	1	0.2	58	67	31		10	.335	.443	6	0	C-128
1915		110	309	84	12	5	3	1.0	32	32	21		2	.272	.372	20	8	C-88
7 yrs.		704	2020	607	88	38	7	0.3	215	261	107	9	42	.300	.392	152	45	C-461, OF-85

Roy Easterwood

EASTERWOOD, ROY CHARLES (Shag)   BR TR 6'½"   196 lbs.
B. Jan. 12, 1915, Waxahachie, Tex.

		G	AB	H	2B	3B	HR	HR %	R	RBI	BB	SO	SB	BA	SA	Pinch AB	Hit H	G by POS
1944	CHI N	17	33	7	2	0	1	3.0	1	2	1	11	0	.212	.364	5	1	C-12

John Easton

EASTON, JOHN S. (Goose)   BR TR 6'2"   185 lbs.
B. Mar. 4, 1933, Trenton, N. J.

		G	AB	H	2B	3B	HR	HR %	R	RBI	BB	SO	SB	BA	SA	Pinch AB	Hit H	G by POS
1955	PHI N	1	0	0	0	0	0	–	0	0	0	0	0	–	–	0	0	
1959		3	3	0	0	0	0	0.0	0	0	0	3	0	.000	.000	3	0	
2 yrs.		4	3	0	0	0	0	0.0	0	0	0	3	0	.000	.000	3	0	

	G	AB	H	2B	3B	HR	HR %	R	RBI	BB	SO	SB	BA	SA	Pinch Hit AB	Pinch Hit H	G by POS

Eddie Eayrs

EAYRS, EDWIN BL TL 5'7" 160 lbs.
B. Nov. 10, 1890, Blackstone, Mass.   D. Nov. 30, 1969, Warwick, R. I.

	G	AB	H	2B	3B	HR	HR%	R	RBI	BB	SO	SB	BA	SA	AB	H	G by POS
1913 **PIT N**	4	6	1	0	0	0	0.0	0	0	0	1	0	.167	.167	2	0	P-2
1920 **BOS N**	87	244	80	5	2	1	0.4	31	24	30	18	4	.328	.377	16	5	OF-63, P-7
1921 **2 teams**		BOS	N	(15G –	.067)		BKN	N	(8G –	.167)							
" **total**	23	21	2	0	0	0	0.0	1	2	2	4	0	.095	.095	18	1	P-2, OF-1
3 yrs.	114	271	83	5	2	1	0.4	32	26	32	23	4	.306	.351	36	6	OF-64, P-11

Hi Ebright

EBRIGHT, HIRAM C. (Buck) BR TR
B. June 12, 1859, Lancaster County, Pa.   D. Oct. 24, 1916, Milwaukee, Wis.

	G	AB	H	2B	3B	HR	HR%	R	RBI	BB	SO	SB	BA	SA	AB	H	G by POS
1889 **WAS N**	16	59	15	2	2	1	1.7	7	6	3	8	1	.254	.407	0	0	C-9, OF-4, SS-3

Johnny Echols

ECHOLS, JOHN GRESHAM BR TR 5'10½" 175 lbs.
B. Jan. 9, 1917, Atlanta, Ga.   D. Nov. 13, 1972, Atlanta, Ga.

	G	AB	H	2B	3B	HR	HR%	R	RBI	BB	SO	SB	BA	SA	AB	H	G by POS
1939 **STL N**	2	0	0	0	0	0	–	0	0	0	0	0	–	–	0	0	

Ox Eckhardt

ECKHARDT, OSCAR GEORGE BL TR 6'1" 185 lbs.
B. Dec. 23, 1901, Yorktown, Tex.   D. Apr. 22, 1951, Yorktown, Tex.

	G	AB	H	2B	3B	HR	HR%	R	RBI	BB	SO	SB	BA	SA	AB	H	G by POS
1932 **BOS N**	8	8	2	0	0	0	0.0	1	1	0	1	0	.250	.250	8	2	
1936 **BKN N**	16	44	8	1	0	1	2.3	5	6	5	2	0	.182	.273	3	0	OF-10
2 yrs.	24	52	10	1	0	1	1.9	6	7	5	3	0	.192	.269	11	2	OF-10

Charlie Eden

EDEN, CHARLES M. BR TR
B. Jan. 18, 1855, Lexington, Ky.   D. Sept. 17, 1920, Cincinnati, Ohio

	G	AB	H	2B	3B	HR	HR%	R	RBI	BB	SO	SB	BA	SA	AB	H	G by POS
1877 **CHI N**	15	55	12	0	1	0	0.0	9	5	3	6		.218	.255	0	0	OF-15
1879 **CLE N**	81	353	96	31	7	3	0.8	40	34	6	20		.272	.425	0	0	OF-80, 1B-3, C-1
1884 **PIT AA**	32	122	33	7	4	1	0.8	12		7			.270	.418	0	0	OF-31, P-2
1885	98	405	103	18	6	0	0.0	57		17			.254	.328	0	0	OF-96, P-4, 3B-2
4 yrs.	226	935	244	56	18	4	0.4	118	39	33	26		.261	.372	0	0	OF-222, P-6, 1B-3, 3B-2, C-1

Mike Eden

EDEN, EDWARD MICHAEL BB TR 5'10" 170 lbs.
B. May 22, 1949, Fort Clayton, Canal Zone

	G	AB	H	2B	3B	HR	HR%	R	RBI	BB	SO	SB	BA	SA	AB	H	G by POS
1976 **ATL N**	5	8	0	0	0	0	0.0	0	0	0	0	0	.000	.000	2	0	2B-2
1978 **CHI A**	10	17	2	0	0	0	0.0	1	0	4	0	0	.118	.118	0	0	SS-5, 2B-4
2 yrs.	15	25	2	0	0	0	0.0	1	0	4	0	0	.080	.080	2	0	2B-6, SS-5

Stump Edington

EDINGTON, JACOB FRANK BL TL 5'6½" 180 lbs.
B. July 4, 1891, Koleen, Ind.   D. Nov. 29, 1969, Bastrop, La.

	G	AB	H	2B	3B	HR	HR%	R	RBI	BB	SO	SB	BA	SA	AB	H	G by POS
1912 **PIT N**	15	53	16	0	2	0	0.0	4	12	3	1	0	.302	.377	2	0	OF-14

Dave Edler

EDLER, DAVID DELMAR BR TR 6' 185 lbs.
B. Aug. 5, 1956, Sioux City, Iowa

	G	AB	H	2B	3B	HR	HR%	R	RBI	BB	SO	SB	BA	SA	AB	H	G by POS
1980 **SEA A**	28	89	20	1	0	3	3.4	11	9	8	16	2	.225	.337	0	0	3B-28
1981	29	78	11	3	0	0	0.0	7	5	11	13	3	.141	.179	3	1	3B-26, SS-1
1982	40	104	29	2	2	2	1.9	14	18	11	13	4	.279	.394	5	2	3B-31, DH-2, OF-2
1983	29	63	12	1	1	1	1.6	2	4	5	11	3	.190	.286	4	0	3B-13, DH-6, 1B-5, OF-1
4 yrs.	126	334	72	7	3	6	1.8	34	36	35	53	12	.216	.308	12	3	3B-98, DH-8, 1B-5, OF-3, SS-1

Eddie Edmonson

EDMONSON, EDWARD EARL (Axel) BL TR 6' 175 lbs.
B. Nov. 20, 1889, Hopewell, Pa.   D. May 10, 1971, Leesberg, Fla.

	G	AB	H	2B	3B	HR	HR%	R	RBI	BB	SO	SB	BA	SA	AB	H	G by POS
1913 **CLE A**	2	5	0	0	0	0	0.0	0	0	0	0	0	.000	.000	0	0	OF-1, 1B-1

Bob Edmundson

EDMUNDSON, ROBERT E. BL TR
B. Apr. 30, 1879, Paris, Ky.   D. Aug. 14, 1931, Lawrence, Kans.

	G	AB	H	2B	3B	HR	HR%	R	RBI	BB	SO	SB	BA	SA	AB	H	G by POS
1908 **WAS A**	26	80	15	4	1	0	0.0	5	2	7		0	.188	.263	2	1	OF-24

Al Edwards

EDWARDS, ALBERT TR
B. 1896, Freeport, N. Y.

	G	AB	H	2B	3B	HR	HR%	R	RBI	BB	SO	SB	BA	SA	AB	H	G by POS
1915 **PHI A**	2	5	0	0	0	0	0.0	0	0	0	3	0	.000	.000	1	0	2B-1

Bruce Edwards

EDWARDS, CHARLES BRUCE (Bull) BR TR 5'8" 180 lbs.
B. July 15, 1923, Quincy, Ill.   D. Apr. 25, 1975, Sacramento, Calif.

	G	AB	H	2B	3B	HR	HR%	R	RBI	BB	SO	SB	BA	SA	AB	H	G by POS
1946 **BKN N**	92	292	78	13	5	1	0.3	24	25	34	20	1	.267	.356	0	0	C-91
1947	130	471	139	15	8	9	1.9	53	80	49	55	2	.295	.418	2	0	C-128
1948	96	286	79	17	2	8	2.8	36	54	26	28	4	.276	.434	9	2	C-48, OF-21, 3B-14, 1B-1
1949	64	148	31	3	0	8	5.4	24	25	25	15	0	.209	.392	17	3	C-41, OF-4, 3B-1
1950	50	142	26	4	1	8	5.6	16	16	13	22	1	.183	.394	8	1	C-38, 1B-2
1951 **2 teams**		BKN	N	(17G –	.250)		CHI	N	(51G –	.234)							
" **total**	68	177	42	11	2	4	2.3	25	25	17	17	1	.237	.390	22	8	C-42, 1B-9
1952 **CHI N**	50	94	23	2	2	1	1.1	7	12	8	12	0	.245	.340	24	7	C-22, 2B-1
1954	4	3	0	0	0	0	0.0	1	1	2	2	0	.000	.000	3	0	
1955 **WAS A**	30	57	10	2	0	0	0.0	5	3	16	6	0	.175	.211	1	0	C-22, 3B-5
1956 **CIN N**	7	5	1	0	0	0	0.0	0	0	0	2	0	.200	.200	5	1	C-2, 3B-1, 2B-1
10 yrs.	591	1675	429	67	20	39	2.3	191	241	190	179	9	.256	.390	91	22	C-434, OF-25, 3B-21, 1B-12, 2B-2

WORLD SERIES	G	AB	H	2B	3B	HR	HR%	R	RBI	BB	SO	SB	BA	SA	AB	H	G by POS
1947 **BKN N**	7	27	6	1	0	0	0.0	3	2	2	7	0	.222	.259	0	0	C-7
1949	2	2	1	0	0	0	0.0	0	0	0	1	0	.500	.500	2	1	
2 yrs.	9	29	7	1	0	0	0.0	3	2	2	8	0	.241	.276	2	2	C-7

Dave Edwards

EDWARDS, DAVID LEONARD BR TR 6' 170 lbs.
Brother of Marshall Edwards.   Brother of Mike Edwards.
B. Feb. 24, 1954, Los Angeles, Calif.

	G	AB	H	2B	3B	HR	HR%	R	RBI	BB	SO	SB	BA	SA	AB	H	G by POS
1978 **MIN A**	15	44	11	3	0	1	2.3	7	3	7	13	1	.250	.386	1	0	OF-15

	G	AB	H	2B	3B	HR	HR %	R	RBI	BB	SO	SB	BA	SA	Pinch Hit AB	H	G by POS

Dave Edwards continued

	G	AB	H	2B	3B	HR	HR %	R	RBI	BB	SO	SB	BA	SA	AB	H	G by POS
1979	96	229	57	8	0	8	3.5	42	35	24	45	6	.249	.389	6	0	OF-86, DH-3
1980	81	200	50	9	1	2	1.0	26	20	12	51	2	.250	.335	5	2	OF-72, DH-3
1981 SD N	58	112	24	4	1	2	1.8	13	13	11	24	3	.214	.321	17	4	OF-49
1982	71	55	10	2	0	1	1.8	7	2	1	14	0	.182	.273	20	3	OF-45, 1B-1
5 yrs.	321	640	152	26	2	14	2.2	95	73	55	147	12	.238	.350	49	9	OF-267, DH-6, 1B-1

Doc Edwards

EDWARDS, HOWARD RODNEY
B. Dec. 10, 1937, Red Jacket, W. Va.

BR TR 6'2" 215 lbs.

	G	AB	H	2B	3B	HR	HR %	R	RBI	BB	SO	SB	BA	SA	AB	H	G by POS
1962 CLE A	53	143	39	6	0	3	2.1	13	9	9	14	0	.273	.378	11	2	C-39
1963 2 teams		CLE	A (10G –	.258)		KC	A (71G –	.250)									
" total	81	271	68	14	0	6	2.2	22	35	13	29	0	.251	.369	11	1	C-73
1964 KC A	97	294	66	10	0	5	1.7	25	28	13	40	0	.224	.310	12	4	C-79, 1B-7
1965 2 teams		KC	A (6G –	.150)		NY	A (45G –	.190)									
" total	51	120	22	3	0	1	0.8	4	9	14	16	1	.183	.233	2	0	C-49
1970 PHI N	35	78	21	0	0	0	0.0	5	6	4	10	0	.269	.269	1	0	C-34
5 yrs.	317	906	216	33	0	15	1.7	69	87	53	109	1	.238	.325	37	7	C-274, 1B-7

Hank Edwards

EDWARDS, HENRY ALBERT
B. Jan. 29, 1919, Elmwood Place, Ohio

BL TL 6' 190 lbs.

	G	AB	H	2B	3B	HR	HR %	R	RBI	BB	SO	SB	BA	SA	AB	H	G by POS
1941 CLE A	16	68	15	1	1	1	1.5	10	6	2	4	0	.221	.309	0	0	OF-16
1942	13	48	12	2	1	0	0.0	6	7	5	8	2	.250	.333	1	0	OF-12
1943	92	297	82	18	6	3	1.0	38	28	30	34	4	.276	.407	15	4	OF-74
1946	124	458	138	33	16	10	2.2	62	54	43	48	1	.301	.509	2	1	OF-123
1947	108	393	102	12	3	15	3.8	54	59	31	55	1	.260	.420	8	3	OF-100
1948	55	160	43	9	2	3	1.9	27	18	18	18	1	.269	.406	12	2	OF-41
1949 2 teams		CLE	A (5G –	.267)		CHI	N (58G –	.290)									
" total	63	191	55	8	4	8	4.2	28	22	20	24	0	.288	.497	6	1	OF-56
1950 CHI N	41	110	40	11	1	2	1.8	13	21	10	13	0	.364	.536	10	0	OF-29
1951 2 teams		BKN	N (35G –	.226)		CIN	N (41G –	.315)									
" total	76	158	47	12	1	3	1.9	15	23	17	26	0	.297	.443	37	8	OF-34
1952 2 teams		CIN	N (74G –	.283)		CHI	A (8G –	.333)									
" total	82	202	58	7	6	6	3.0	26	29	19	24	0	.287	.470	26	4	OF-54
1953 STL A	65	106	21	3	0	0	0.0	6	9	13	10	0	.198	.226	40	12	OF-21
11 yrs.	735	2191	613	116	41	51	2.3	285	276	208	264	9	.280	.440	157	35	OF-560

Johnny Edwards

EDWARDS, JOHN ALBAN
B. June 10, 1938, Columbus, Ohio

BL TR 6'4" 220 lbs.

	G	AB	H	2B	3B	HR	HR %	R	RBI	BB	SO	SB	BA	SA	AB	H	G by POS
1961 CIN N	52	145	27	5	0	2	1.4	14	14	18	28	1	.186	.262	2	0	C-52
1962	133	452	115	28	5	8	1.8	47	50	45	70	1	.254	.392	7	4	C-130
1963	148	495	128	19	4	11	2.2	46	67	45	93	1	.259	.380	2	2	C-148
1964	126	423	119	23	1	7	1.7	47	55	34	65	1	.281	.390	8	0	C-120
1965	114	371	99	22	2	17	4.6	47	51	50	45	0	.267	.474	11	5	C-110
1966	98	282	54	8	0	6	2.1	24	39	31	42	1	.191	.284	1	0	C-98
1967	80	209	43	6	0	2	1.0	10	20	16	28	1	.206	.263	7	1	C-73
1968 STL N	85	230	55	9	1	3	1.3	14	29	16	20	1	.239	.326	26	7	C-54
1969 HOU N	151	496	115	20	6	6	1.2	52	50	53	69	2	.232	.333	1	0	C-151
1970	140	458	101	16	4	7	1.5	46	49	51	63	1	.221	.319	2	2	C-139
1971	106	317	74	13	4	1	0.3	18	23	26	38	1	.233	.309	7	2	C-104
1972	108	332	89	16	2	5	1.5	33	40	50	39	2	.268	.373	6	0	C-105
1973	79	250	61	10	2	5	2.0	24	27	19	23	1	.244	.360	7	1	C-76
1974	50	117	26	7	1	1	0.9	8	10	11	12	1	.222	.325	17	5	C-32
14 yrs.	1470	4577	1106	202	32	81	1.8	430	524	465	635	15	.242	.353	104	29	C-1392

WORLD SERIES

	G	AB	H	2B	3B	HR	HR %	R	RBI	BB	SO	SB	BA	SA	AB	H	G by POS
1961 CIN N	3	11	4	2	0	0	0.0	1	2	0	0	0	.364	.545	0	0	C-3
1968 STL N	1	1	0	0	0	0	0.0	0	0	0	1	0	.000	.000	1	0	
2 yrs.	4	12	4	2	0	0	0.0	1	2	0	1	0	.333	.500	1	0	C-3

Marshall Edwards

EDWARDS, MARSHALL LYNN
Brother of Dave Edwards. Brother of Mike Edwards.
B. Aug. 27, 1952, Fort Lewis, Wash.

BL TL 5'9" 157 lbs.

	G	AB	H	2B	3B	HR	HR %	R	RBI	BB	SO	SB	BA	SA	AB	H	G by POS
1981 MIL A	40	58	14	1	1	0	0.0	10	4	0	2	6	.241	.293	0	0	OF-36, DH-1
1982	69	178	44	4	1	2	1.1	24	14	4	8	10	.247	.315	9	3	OF-54, DH-6
1983	51	74	22	1	1	0	0.0	14	5	1	9	5	.297	.338	3	1	OF-35, DH-4
3 yrs.	160	310	80	6	3	2	0.6	48	23	5	19	21	.258	.316	12	4	OF-125, DH-11

DIVISIONAL PLAYOFF SERIES

	G	AB	H	2B	3B	HR	HR %	R	RBI	BB	SO	SB	BA	SA	AB	H	G by POS
1981 MIL A	2	1	0	0	0	0	0.0	0	0	0	1	0	.000	.000	0	0	OF-2

LEAGUE CHAMPIONSHIP SERIES

	G	AB	H	2B	3B	HR	HR %	R	RBI	BB	SO	SB	BA	SA	AB	H	G by POS
1982 MIL A	3	1	0	0	0	0	0.0	2	0	0	0	1	.000	.000	0	0	OF-1

WORLD SERIES

	G	AB	H	2B	3B	HR	HR %	R	RBI	BB	SO	SB	BA	SA	AB	H	G by POS
1982 MIL A	1	0	0	0	0	0	–	0	0	0	0	0	–	–	0	0	OF-1

Mike Edwards

EDWARDS, MICHAEL LEWIS
Brother of Dave Edwards. Brother of Marshall Edwards.
B. Aug. 27, 1952, Fort Lewis, Wash.

BR TR 5'10" 154 lbs.

	G	AB	H	2B	3B	HR	HR %	R	RBI	BB	SO	SB	BA	SA	AB	H	G by POS
1977 PIT N	7	6	0	0	0	0	0.0	1	0	0	3	0	.000	.000	0	0	2B-4
1978 OAK A	142	414	113	16	2	1	0.2	48	23	16	32	27	.273	.329	0	0	2B-133, SS-9, DH-4
1979	122	400	93	12	2	1	0.3	35	23	15	37	10	.233	.280	3	1	2B-113, SS-3, DH-2
1980	46	59	14	0	0	0	0.0	10	3	1	5	1	.237	.237	2	1	2B-23, DH-5, OF-1
4 yrs.	317	879	220	28	4	2	0.2	94	49	32	77	38	.250	.298	5	2	2B-273, SS-12, DH-11, OF-1

	G	AB	H	2B	3B	HR	HR %	R	RBI	BB	SO	SB	BA	SA	Pinch Hit AB	Pinch Hit H	G by POS

Ben Egan

EGAN, ARTHUR AUGUSTUS
B. Nov. 20, 1883, Augusta, N. Y.   D. Feb. 18, 1968, Sherrill, N. Y.
BR TR 6'2"   185 lbs.

	G	AB	H	2B	3B	HR	HR %	R	RBI	BB	SO	SB	BA	SA	AB	H	G by POS
1908 PHI A	2	6	1	1	0	0	0.0	1	0	1		0	.167	.333	0	0	C-2
1912	48	138	24	3	4	0	0.0	9	13	6		3	.174	.254	2	1	C-46
1914 CLE A	29	88	20	2	1	0	0.0	7	11	3	20	0	.227	.273	2	1	C-27
1915	42	120	13	3	0	0	0.0	4	6	8	14	0	.108	.133	2	0	C-40
4 yrs.	121	352	58	9	5	0	0.0	21	30	18	34	3	.165	.219	6	2	C-115

Dick Egan

EGAN, RICHARD JOSEPH
B. June 23, 1884, Portland, Ore.   D. July 7, 1947, Oakland, Calif.
BR TR 5'11"   162 lbs.

	G	AB	H	2B	3B	HR	HR %	R	RBI	BB	SO	SB	BA	SA	AB	H	G by POS
1908 CIN N	18	68	14	3	1	0	0.0	8	5	2		7	.206	.279	0	0	2B-18
1909	127	480	132	14	3	2	0.4	59	53	37		39	.275	.329	1	0	2B-116, SS-10
1910	135	474	116	11	5	0	0.0	70	46	53	38	41	.245	.289	0	0	2B-131, SS-3
1911	153	558	139	11	5	1	0.2	80	56	59	50	37	.249	.292	1	1	2B-152
1912	149	507	125	14	5	0	0.0	69	52	56	26	24	.247	.294	0	0	2B-149
1913	60	195	55	7	3	0	0.0	15	22	15	13	6	.282	.349	4	0	2B-38, SS-17, 3B-2
1914 BKN N	106	337	76	10	3	1	0.3	30	21	22	25	8	.226	.282	6	5	SS-83, 3B-10, OF-3, 2B-2, 1B-1
1915 2 teams			BKN N (3G – .000)			BOS N (83G – .259)											
" total	86	223	57	9	1	0	0.0	20	21	28	18	3	.256	.305	15	3	OF-24, 2B-22, SS-10, 1B-9, 3B-4
1916 BOS N	83	238	53	8	3	0	0.0	23	16	19	21	2	.223	.282	11	5	2B-53, SS-12, 3B-8
9 yrs.	917	3080	767	87	29	4	0.1	374	292	291	191	167	.249	.300	38	14	2B-681, SS-135, OF-27, 3B-24, 1B-10

Jim Egan

EGAN, JAMES (Troy Terrier)
B. 1838, Ansonia, Conn.   D. Sept. 26, 1884, New Haven, Conn.
TB

	G	AB	H	2B	3B	HR	HR %	R	RBI	BB	SO	SB	BA	SA	AB	H	G by POS
1882 TRO N	30	115	23	3	2	0	0.0	15	10	1	21		.200	.261	0	0	OF-18, P-12, C-2

Tom Egan

EGAN, THOMAS PATRICK
B. June 9, 1946, Los Angeles, Calif.
BR TR 6'4"   218 lbs.

	G	AB	H	2B	3B	HR	HR %	R	RBI	BB	SO	SB	BA	SA	AB	H	G by POS
1965 CAL A	18	38	10	0	1	0	0.0	3	1	3	12	0	.263	.316	2	1	C-16
1966	7	11	0	0	0	0	0.0	0	1	5		0	.000	.000	0	0	C-6
1967	1	1	0	0	0	0	0.0	0	0	0	0	0	.000	.000	0	0	C-1
1968	16	43	5	1	0	1	2.3	2	4	2	15	0	.116	.209	3	0	C-14
1969	46	120	17	1	0	5	4.2	7	16	17	41	0	.142	.275	1	0	C-46
1970	79	210	50	6	0	4	1.9	14	20	14	67	0	.238	.324	1	0	C-79
1971 CHI A	85	251	60	11	1	10	4.0	29	34	26	94	1	.239	.410	10	5	C-77, 1B-1
1972	50	141	27	3	0	2	1.4	8	9	4	48	0	.191	.255	11	3	C-46
1974 CAL A	43	94	11	0	0	0	0.0	4	4	8	40	1	.117	.117	2	0	C-41
1975	28	70	16	3	1	0	0.0	7	3	5	14	0	.229	.300	0	0	C-28
10 yrs.	373	979	196	25	3	22	2.2	74	91	80	336	2	.200	.299	30	9	C-354, 1B-1

Elmer Eggert

EGGERT, ELMER ALBERT (Mose)
B. Jan. 29, 1902, Rochester, N. Y.   D. Apr. 9, 1971, Rochester, N. Y.
BR TR 5'9"   160 lbs.

	G	AB	H	2B	3B	HR	HR %	R	RBI	BB	SO	SB	BA	SA	AB	H	G by POS
1927 BOS A	5	3	0	0	0	0	0.0	0	0	1	1	0	.000	.000	2	0	2B-1

Dave Eggler

EGGLER, DAVID DANIEL
B. Apr. 30, 1851, Brooklyn, N. Y.   D. Apr. 5, 1902, Buffalo, N. Y.
BR TR 5'9"   165 lbs.

	G	AB	H	2B	3B	HR	HR %	R	RBI	BB	SO	SB	BA	SA	AB	H	G by POS
1876 PHI N	39	174	52	4	0	0	0.0	28	19	2	4		.299	.322	0	0	OF-39
1877 CHI N	33	136	36	3	0	0	0.0	20	20	1	5		.265	.287	0	0	OF-33
1879 BUF N	78	317	66	5	7	0	0.0	41	27	11	41		.208	.268	0	0	OF-78
1883 2 teams			BAL AA (53G – .188)			BUF N (38G – .248)											
" total	91	355	76	4	1	0	0.0	28		3	29		.214	.231	0	0	OF-91
1884 BUF N	63	241	47	3	1	0	0.0	25		6	54		.195	.216	0	0	OF-63
1885	6	24	2	0	0	0	0.0	0	0	2	4		.083	.083	0	0	OF-6
6 yrs.	310	1247	279	19	9	0	0.0	142	66	25	137		.224	.253	0	0	OF-310

Red Ehret

EHRET, PHILIP SYDNEY
B. Aug. 31, 1868, Louisville, Ky.   D. July 28, 1940, Cincinnati, Ohio
BR TR 6'   175 lbs.

	G	AB	H	2B	3B	HR	HR %	R	RBI	BB	SO	SB	BA	SA	AB	H	G by POS
1888 KC AA	17	63	12	4	0	0	0.0	4	4	1		1	.190	.254	0	0	OF-10, P-7, 2B-1, 1B-1
1889 LOU AA	67	258	65	6	6	1	0.4	27	31	4	23	4	.252	.333	0	0	P-45, OF-22, SS-1, 3B-1, 2B-1
1890	43	146	31	2	1	0	0.0	11		1		1	.212	.240	0	0	P-43
1891	26	91	22	1	0	0	0.0	9	9	5	15	3	.242	.286	0	0	P-26
1892 PIT N	40	132	34	2	0	0	0.0	12	19	7	22	1	.258	.273	1	0	P-39
1893	40	136	24	3	0	1	0.7	16	17	10	18	1	.176	.221	1	0	P-39
1894	46	135	23	4	1	0	0.0	6	11	8	22	0	.170	.215	0	0	P-46
1895 STL N	37	96	21	2	1	1	1.0	13	9	6	12	0	.219	.292	0	0	P-37
1896 CIN N	34	102	20	2	0	1	1.0	10	20	10	12	2	.196	.245	0	0	P-34, 1B-1
1897	34	66	13	2	0	0	0.0	6	6	4		2	.197	.227	0	0	P-34
1898 LOU N	13	40	9	3	1	0	0.0	3	4	1		0	.225	.350	1	0	P-12
11 yrs.	397	1265	274	32	11	4	0.3	117	130	57	124	15	.217	.269	2	0	P-362, OF-32, 2B-2, 1B-2, SS-1, 3B-1

Hack Eibel

EIBEL, HENRY H.
B. Dec. 6, 1893, Brooklyn, N. Y.   D. Oct. 16, 1945, Macon, Ga.
BL

	G	AB	H	2B	3B	HR	HR %	R	RBI	BB	SO	SB	BA	SA	AB	H	G by POS
1912 CLE A	1	3	0	0	0	0	0.0	0	0	0		0	.000	.000	0	0	OF-1
1920 BOS A	29	43	8	2	0	0	0.0	4	6	3	6	1	.186	.233	17	3	OF-5, P-3, 1B-1
2 yrs.	30	46	8	2	0	0	0.0	4	6	3	6	1	.174	.217	17	3	OF-6, P-3, 1B-1

Fred Eichrodt

EICHRODT, FREDERICK GEORGE (Ike)
B. Jan. 6, 1903, Chicago, Ill.   D. July 14, 1965, Indianapolis, Ind.
BR TR 5'11½"   167 lbs.

	G	AB	H	2B	3B	HR	HR %	R	RBI	BB	SO	SB	BA	SA	AB	H	G by POS
1925 CLE A	15	52	12	3	1	0	0.0	4	4	2	7	0	.231	.327	2	0	OF-13
1926	37	80	25	7	1	0	0.0	14	7	2	11	1	.313	.425	10	2	OF-27
1927	85	267	59	19	2	0	0.0	24	25	16	25	2	.221	.307	4	0	OF-81

	G	AB	H	2B	3B	HR	HR %	R	RBI	BB	SO	SB	BA	SA	Pinch Hit AB	Pinch Hit H	G by POS

Fred Eichrodt continued

	G	AB	H	2B	3B	HR	HR %	R	RBI	BB	SO	SB	BA	SA	AB	H	G by POS
1931 CHI A	34	117	25	5	1	0	0.0	9	15	1	8	0	.214	.274	2	1	OF-32
4 yrs.	171	516	121	34	5	0	0.0	51	51	21	51	3	.234	.320	18	3	OF-153

Jim Eisenreich

EISENREICH, JAMES M.
B. Apr. 18, 1959, St. Cloud, Minn.
BL TL 5'11" 175 lbs.

	G	AB	H	2B	3B	HR	HR %	R	RBI	BB	SO	SB	BA	SA	AB	H	G by POS
1982 MIN A	34	99	30	6	0	2	2.0	10	9	11	13	0	.303	.424	3	1	OF-30
1983	2	7	2	1	0	0	0.0	1	0	1	1	0	.286	.429	0	0	OF-2
1984	12	32	7	1	0	0	0.0	1	3	2	4	2	.219	.250	3	1	DH-6, OF-3
3 yrs.	48	138	39	8	0	2	1.4	12	12	14	18	2	.283	.384	6	2	OF-35, DH-6

Kid Elberfeld

ELBERFELD, NORMAN ARTHUR (The Tabasco Kid)
B. Apr. 13, 1875, Pomeroy, Ohio   D. Jan. 13, 1944, Chattanooga, Tenn.
Manager 1908.
BR TR 5'5½" 134 lbs.

	G	AB	H	2B	3B	HR	HR %	R	RBI	BB	SO	SB	BA	SA	AB	H	G by POS
1898 PHI N	14	38	9	4	0	0	0.0	1	7	5		0	.237	.342	0	0	3B-14
1899 CIN N	41	138	36	4	2	0	0.0	23	22	15		5	.261	.319	0	0	SS-24, 3B-18
1901 DET A	122	436	135	21	11	3	0.7	76	76	57		24	.310	.429	0	0	SS-121
1902	130	488	127	17	6	1	0.2	70	64	55		19	.260	.326	0	0	SS-130
1903 2 teams		DET	A (35G –	.341)		NY	A (90G –	.287)									
" total	125	481	145	23	8	0	0.0	78	64	33		22	.301	.383	0	0	SS-124, 3B-1
1904 NY A	122	445	117	13	5	2	0.4	55	46	37		18	.263	.328	0	0	SS-122
1905	111	390	102	18	2	0	0.0	48	53	23		18	.262	.318	2	0	SS-108
1906	99	346	106	11	5	2	0.6	59	31	30		19	.306	.384	0	0	SS-98
1907	120	447	121	17	6	0	0.0	61	51	36		22	.271	.336	2	2	SS-118
1908	19	56	11	3	0	0	0.0	11	5	6		1	.196	.250	2	0	SS-17
1909	106	379	90	9	5	0	0.0	47	26	28		23	.237	.288	2	0	SS-61, 3B-43
1910 WAS A	127	455	114	9	2	2	0.4	53	42	35		19	.251	.292	3	0	3B-113, 2B-10, SS-3
1911	127	404	110	19	4	0	0.0	58	47	65		24	.272	.339	7	1	2B-66, 3B-54
1914 BKN N	30	62	14	1	0	0	0.0	7	1	2	4	0	.226	.242	6	1	SS-18, 2B-1
14 yrs.	1293	4565	1237	169	56	10	0.2	647	535	427	4	214	.271	.339	24	4	SS-944, 3B-243, 2B-77

George Elder

ELDER, GEORGE REZIN
B. Mar. 10, 1921, Lebanon, Ky.
BL TR 5'11" 180 lbs.

	G	AB	H	2B	3B	HR	HR %	R	RBI	BB	SO	SB	BA	SA	AB	H	G by POS
1949 STL A	41	44	11	3	0	0	0.0	9	2	4	11	0	.250	.318	17	5	OF-10

Lee Elia

ELIA, LEE CONSTANTINE
B. July 16, 1937, Philadelphia, Pa.
Manager 1982-83.
BR TR 5'11" 175 lbs.

	G	AB	H	2B	3B	HR	HR %	R	RBI	BB	SO	SB	BA	SA	AB	H	G by POS
1966 CHI A	80	195	40	5	2	3	1.5	16	22	15	39	0	.205	.297	1	0	SS-75
1968 CHI N	15	17	3	0	0	0	0.0	1	3	0	6	0	.176	.176	10	2	SS-2, 3B-1, 2B-1
2 yrs.	95	212	43	5	2	3	1.4	17	25	15	45	0	.203	.288	11	2	SS-77, 3B-1, 2B-1

Pete Elko

ELKO, PETER (Piccolo Pete)
B. June 17, 1918, Wilkes-Barre, Pa.
BR TR 5'11" 185 lbs.

	G	AB	H	2B	3B	HR	HR %	R	RBI	BB	SO	SB	BA	SA	AB	H	G by POS
1943 CHI N	9	30	4	0	0	0	0.0	1	0	4	5	0	.133	.133	0	0	3B-9
1944	7	22	5	1	0	0	0.0	2	0	0	1	0	.227	.273	1	1	3B-6
2 yrs.	16	52	9	1	0	0	0.0	3	0	4	6	0	.173	.192	1	1	3B-15

Roy Ellam

ELLAM, ROY (Whitey, Slippery)
B. Feb. 8, 1886, Conshohocken, Pa.   D. Oct. 28, 1948, Conshohocken, Pa.
BR TR 5'10½" 203 lbs.

	G	AB	H	2B	3B	HR	HR %	R	RBI	BB	SO	SB	BA	SA	AB	H	G by POS
1909 CIN N	10	21	4	0	1	1	4.8	4	4	7		1	.190	.429	0	0	SS-9
1918 PIT N	26	77	10	1	1	0	0.0	9	2	17	17	2	.130	.169	0	0	SS-26
2 yrs.	36	98	14	1	2	1	1.0	13	6	24	17	3	.143	.224	0	0	SS-35

Frank Ellerbe

ELLERBE, FRANCIS ROGERS (Governor)
B. Dec. 25, 1895, Marion, S. C.
BR TR 5'10½" 165 lbs.

	G	AB	H	2B	3B	HR	HR %	R	RBI	BB	SO	SB	BA	SA	AB	H	G by POS
1919 WAS A	28	105	29	4	1	0	0.0	13	16	2	15	5	.276	.333	0	0	SS-28
1920	101	336	98	14	2	0	0.0	38	36	19	23	5	.292	.345	6	1	3B-75, SS-19, OF-1
1921 2 teams		WAS	A (10G –	.200)		STL	A (105G –	.288)									
" total	115	440	126	20	13	2	0.5	66	50	22	44	1	.286	.405	9	2	3B-106
1922 STL A	91	342	84	16	3	1	0.3	42	33	25	37	1	.246	.319	0	0	3B-91
1923	18	49	9	0	0	0	0.0	6	1	1	5	0	.184	.184	4	0	3B-14
1924 2 teams		STL	A (21G –	.197)		CLE	A (46G –	.258)									
" total	67	181	43	4	3	1	0.6	14	16	3	12	0	.238	.309	4	0	3B-60, 2B-2
6 yrs.	420	1453	389	58	22	4	0.3	179	152	72	136	12	.268	.346	23	3	3B-346, SS-47, 2B-2, OF-1

Joe Ellick

ELLICK, JOSEPH J.
B. Apr. 3, 1854, Cincinnati, Ohio   D. Apr. 21, 1923, Kansas City, Mo.
Manager 1884.

	G	AB	H	2B	3B	HR	HR %	R	RBI	BB	SO	SB	BA	SA	AB	H	G by POS
1878 MIL N	3	13	2	0	0	0	0.0	2	1	0	1		.154	.154	0	0	C-2, 3B-1, P-1
1880 WOR N	5	18	1	0	0	0	0.0	1		1	2		.056	.056	0	0	3B-5
1884 3 teams		C-P	U (92G –	.236)		KC	U (2G –	.000)		BAL	U (7G –	.148)					
" total	101	429	97	11	0	0	0.0	73		18			.226	.252	0	0	OF-59, SS-41, 2B-5
3 yrs.	109	460	100	11	0	0	0.0	76	1	19	3		.217	.241	0	0	OF-59, SS-41, 3B-6, 2B-5, C-2, P-1

Larry Elliot

ELLIOT, LAWRENCE LEE
B. Mar. 5, 1938, San Diego, Calif.
BL TL 6'2" 200 lbs.

	G	AB	H	2B	3B	HR	HR %	R	RBI	BB	SO	SB	BA	SA	AB	H	G by POS
1962 PIT N	8	10	3	0	0	1	10.0	2	2	0	1	0	.300	.600	5	2	OF-3
1963	4	4	0	0	0	0	0.0	0	0	0	3	0	.000	.000	4	0	
1964 NY N	80	224	51	8	0	9	4.0	27	22	28	55	1	.228	.384	15	3	OF-63
1966	65	199	49	14	2	5	2.5	24	32	17	46	0	.246	.412	10	2	OF-54
4 yrs.	157	437	103	22	2	15	3.4	53	56	45	105	1	.236	.398	34	7	OF-120

	G	AB	H	2B	3B	HR	HR %	R	RBI	BB	SO	SB	BA	SA	Pinch Hit AB	H	G by POS

Allen Elliott

ELLIOTT, ALLEN CLIFFORD (Ace)　　BL TR 6'　170 lbs.
B. Dec. 25, 1897, St. Louis, Mo.　D. May 6, 1979, St. Louis, Mo.

	G	AB	H	2B	3B	HR	HR %	R	RBI	BB	SO	SB	BA	SA	PH AB	H	G by POS
1923 CHI N	53	168	42	8	2	2	1.2	21	29	2	12	3	.250	.357	0	0	1B-52
1924	10	14	2	0	0	0	0.0	0	0	0	1	0	.143	.143	0	0	1B-10
2 yrs.	63	182	44	8	2	2	1.1	21	29	2	13	3	.242	.341	0	0	1B-62

Bob Elliott

ELLIOTT, ROBERT IRVING　　BR TR 6'　185 lbs.
B. Nov. 26, 1916, San Francisco, Calif.　D. May 4, 1966, San Diego, Calif.
Manager 1960.

	G	AB	H	2B	3B	HR	HR %	R	RBI	BB	SO	SB	BA	SA	PH AB	H	G by POS
1939 PIT N	32	129	43	10	3	3	2.3	18	19	9	4	0	.333	.527	2	0	OF-30
1940	148	551	161	34	11	5	0.9	88	64	45	28	13	.292	.421	1	0	OF-147
1941	141	527	144	24	10	3	0.6	74	76	64	52	6	.273	.374	2	0	OF-139
1942	143	560	166	26	7	9	1.6	75	89	52	35	2	.296	.416	1	0	3B-142, OF-1
1943	156	581	183	30	12	7	1.2	82	101	56	24	4	.315	.444	4	0	3B-151, 2B-2, SS-1
1944	143	538	160	28	16	10	1.9	85	108	75	42	9	.297	.465	3	0	3B-140, SS-1
1945	144	541	157	36	6	8	1.5	80	108	64	38	5	.290	.423	3	0	3B-81, OF-61
1946	140	486	128	25	3	5	1.0	50	68	64	44	6	.263	.358	4	2	OF-92, 3B-43
1947 BOS N	150	555	176	35	5	22	4.0	93	113	87	60	3	.317	.517	2	0	3B-148
1948	151	540	153	24	5	23	4.3	99	100	131	57	6	.283	.474	1	0	3B-150
1949	139	482	135	29	5	17	3.5	77	76	90	38	0	.280	.467	10	5	3B-130
1950	142	531	162	28	5	24	4.5	94	107	68	67	2	.305	.512	5	1	3B-137
1951	136	480	137	29	2	15	3.1	73	70	65	56	2	.285	.448	7	1	3B-127
1952 NY N	98	272	62	6	2	10	3.7	33	35	36	20	1	.228	.375	18	3	OF-65, 3B-13
1953 2 teams	STL	A (48G –	.250)		CHI	A (67G –	.260)										
" total	115	368	94	19	2	9	2.4	43	61	61	39	1	.255	.391	8	2	3B-103, OF-2
15 yrs.	1978	7141	2061	383	94	170	2.4	1064	1195	967	604	60	.289	.440	71	14	3B-1365, OF-537, SS-2, 2B-2

WORLD SERIES

	G	AB	H	2B	3B	HR	HR %	R	RBI	BB	SO	SB	BA	SA	PH AB	H	G by POS
1948 BOS N	6	21	7	0	0	2	9.5	4	5	2	2	0	.333	.619	0	0	3B-6

Carter Elliott

ELLIOTT, CARTER WARD　　BL TR 5'11"　165 lbs.
B. Nov. 29, 1893, Atchison, Kans.　D. May 21, 1959, Palm Springs, Calif.

	G	AB	H	2B	3B	HR	HR %	R	RBI	BB	SO	SB	BA	SA	PH AB	H	G by POS
1921 CHI N	12	28	7	2	0	0	0.0	5	0	5	3	0	.250	.321	0	0	SS-10

Gene Elliott

ELLIOTT, EUGENE BILLINGHOUSE　　BL TR 5'7"　150 lbs.
B. Feb. 8, 1889, Fayette City, Pa.　D. Jan. 5, 1976, Huntingdon, Pa.

	G	AB	H	2B	3B	HR	HR %	R	RBI	BB	SO	SB	BA	SA	PH AB	H	G by POS
1911 NY A	5	13	1	1	0	0	0.0	1	1	2		0	.077	.154	2	0	OF-2, 3B-1

Harry Elliott

ELLIOTT, HARRY LEWIS　　BR TR 5'9"　175 lbs.
B. Dec. 30, 1923, San Francisco, Calif.

	G	AB	H	2B	3B	HR	HR %	R	RBI	BB	SO	SB	BA	SA	PH AB	H	G by POS
1953 STL N	24	59	15	6	1	1	1.7	6	6	3	8	0	.254	.441	6	0	OF-17
1955	68	117	30	4	0	1	0.9	9	12	11	9	0	.256	.316	38	7	OF-28
2 yrs.	92	176	45	10	1	2	1.1	15	18	14	17	0	.256	.358	44	7	OF-45

Randy Elliott

ELLIOTT, RANDY LEE　　BR TR 6'2"　190 lbs.
B. June 5, 1951, Oxnard, Calif.

	G	AB	H	2B	3B	HR	HR %	R	RBI	BB	SO	SB	BA	SA	PH AB	H	G by POS
1972 SD N	14	49	10	3	1	0	0.0	5	6	2	11	0	.204	.306	2	1	OF-13
1974	13	33	7	1	0	1	3.0	5	2	7	9	0	.212	.333	2	0	OF-11, 1B-1
1977 SF N	73	167	40	5	1	7	4.2	17	26	8	24	0	.240	.407	31	11	OF-46
1980 OAK A	14	39	5	3	0	0	0.0	4	1	1	13	0	.128	.205	4	0	DH-11
4 yrs.	114	288	62	12	2	8	2.8	31	35	18	57	0	.215	.354	39	12	OF-70, DH-11, 1B-1

Rowdy Elliott

ELLIOTT, HAROLD B.　　BR TR 5'9½"　160 lbs.
B. July 8, 1890, Kokomo, Ind.　D. Feb. 12, 1934, San Francisco, Calif.

	G	AB	H	2B	3B	HR	HR %	R	RBI	BB	SO	SB	BA	SA	PH AB	H	G by POS
1910 BOS N	3	2	0	0	0	0	0.0	0	0	0	0	0	.000	.000	2	0	C-1
1916 CHI N	23	55	14	3	0	0	0.0	5	3	3	5	1	.255	.309	4	0	C-18
1917	85	223	56	8	5	0	0.0	18	28	11	11	4	.251	.332	12	2	C-73
1918	5	10	0	0	0	0	0.0	0	0	2	1	0	.000	.000	0	0	C-5
1920 BKN N	41	112	27	4	0	1	0.9	13	13	3	6	0	.241	.304	2	0	C-39
5 yrs.	157	402	97	15	5	1	0.2	36	44	19	23	5	.241	.311	20	2	C-136

Ben Ellis

ELLIS, BENJAMIN F.
B. Pottsville, Pa.　Deceased.

	G	AB	H	2B	3B	HR	HR %	R	RBI	BB	SO	SB	BA	SA	PH AB	H	G by POS
1896 PHI N	4	16	1	0	0	0	0.0	0	0	3	6	0	.063	.063	0	0	SS-2, 3B-2

John Ellis

ELLIS, JOHN CHARLES　　BR TR 6'2½"　225 lbs.
B. Aug. 21, 1948, New London, Conn.

	G	AB	H	2B	3B	HR	HR %	R	RBI	BB	SO	SB	BA	SA	PH AB	H	G by POS
1969 NY A	22	62	18	4	0	1	1.6	2	8	1	11	0	.290	.403	7	2	C-15
1970	78	226	56	12	1	7	3.1	24	29	18	47	0	.248	.403	20	2	1B-53, 3B-5, C-2
1971	83	238	58	12	1	3	1.3	16	34	23	42	0	.244	.340	15	4	1B-65, C-2
1972	52	136	40	5	1	5	3.7	13	25	8	22	0	.294	.456	17	4	C-25, 1B-8
1973 CLE A	127	437	118	12	2	14	3.2	59	68	46	57	0	.270	.403	5	1	C-72, DH-38, 1B-12
1974	128	477	136	23	6	10	2.1	58	64	32	53	1	.285	.421	3	1	1B-69, C-42, DH-21
1975	92	296	68	11	1	7	2.4	22	32	14	33	0	.230	.345	10	5	C-84, DH-3, 1B-2
1976 TEX A	11	31	13	2	0	1	3.2	4	8	0	4	0	.419	.581	4	1	C-7, DH-3
1977	49	119	28	7	0	4	3.4	7	15	8	26	0	.235	.395	16	2	C-16, DH-15, 1B-8
1978	34	94	23	4	0	3	3.2	7	17	6	20	0	.245	.383	5	2	C-22, DH-7
1979	111	316	90	12	0	12	3.8	33	61	15	55	2	.285	.437	26	7	DH-62, 1B-30, C-7
1980	73	182	43	9	1	1	0.5	12	23	14	23	3	.236	.313	15	4	1B-39, DH-20, C-3
1981	23	58	8	3	0	1	1.7	2	7	5	10	0	.138	.241	8	1	1B-18, DH-1
13 yrs.	883	2672	699	116	13	69	2.6	259	391	190	403	6	.262	.392	151	36	1B-304, C-297, DH-170, 3B-5

	G	AB	H	2B	3B	HR	HR %	R	RBI	BB	SO	SB	BA	SA	Pinch Hit AB	H	G by POS

Rob Ellis

ELLIS, ROBERT WALTER
B. July 3, 1950, Grand Rapids, Mich. BR TR 5'11" 180 lbs.

	G	AB	H	2B	3B	HR	HR %	R	RBI	BB	SO	SB	BA	SA	AB	H	G by POS
1971 MIL A	36	111	22	2	0	0	0.0	9	6	12	24	0	.198	.216	4	2	3B-19, OF-15
1974	22	48	14	2	0	0	0.0	4	4	4	11	0	.292	.333	1	0	OF-11, DH-9, 3B-1
1975	6	7	2	0	0	0	0.0	3	0	0	0	0	.286	.286	0	0	OF-5, DH-1
3 yrs.	64	166	38	4	0	0	0.0	16	10	16	35	0	.229	.253	5	2	OF-31, 3B-20, DH-10

Rube Ellis

ELLIS, GEORGE WILLIAM
B. Nov. 17, 1885, Dowley, Calif. D. Mar. 13, 1938, Rivera, Calif. BL TL 6' 160 lbs.

	G	AB	H	2B	3B	HR	HR %	R	RBI	BB	SO	SB	BA	SA	AB	H	G by POS
1909 STL N	149	575	154	10	9	3	0.5	76	46	54		16	.268	.332	4	1	OF-145
1910	142	550	142	18	8	4	0.7	87	54	62	70	25	.258	.342	0	0	OF-141
1911	155	555	139	20	10	3	0.5	69	66	66	64	9	.250	.339	6	1	OF-148
1912	109	305	82	18	2	4	1.3	47	33	34	36	6	.269	.380	27	8	OF-76
4 yrs.	555	1985	517	66	29	14	0.7	279	199	216	170	56	.260	.344	37	10	OF-510

Babe Ellison

ELLISON, HERBERT SPENCER
B. Nov. 15, 1896, Ola, Ark. D. Aug. 11, 1955, San Francisco, Calif. BR TR 5'11" 170 lbs.

	G	AB	H	2B	3B	HR	HR %	R	RBI	BB	SO	SB	BA	SA	AB	H	G by POS
1916 DET A	2	7	1	0	0	0	0.0	0	1	0	1	0	.143	.143	0	0	3B-2
1917	9	29	5	1	2	1	3.4	2	4	6	3	0	.172	.448	0	0	1B-9
1918	7	23	6	1	0	0	0.0	1	2	3	1	1	.261	.304	0	0	OF-4, 2B-3
1919	56	134	29	4	0	0	0.0	18	11	13	24	4	.216	.246	15	3	2B-25, OF-10, SS-1
1920	61	155	34	7	2	0	0.0	11	21	8	26	4	.219	.290	17	3	1B-38, OF-4, 3B-1
5 yrs.	135	348	75	13	4	1	0.3	32	39	30	55	9	.216	.284	32	6	1B-47, 2B-28, OF-18, 3B-3, SS-1

Verdo Elmore

ELMORE, VERDO WILSON
B. Dec. 10, 1899, Gordo, Ala. D. Aug. 5, 1969, Birmingham, Ala. BL TR 5'11" 185 lbs.

	G	AB	H	2B	3B	HR	HR %	R	RBI	BB	SO	SB	BA	SA	AB	H	G by POS
1924 STL A	7	17	3	3	0	0	0.0	2	0	1	3	0	.176	.353	4	1	OF-3

Roy Elsh

ELSH, EUGENE ROY
B. Mar. 1, 1892, Pennsgrove, N. J. D. Nov. 12, 1978, Philadelphia, Pa. BR TR 5'9" 165 lbs.

	G	AB	H	2B	3B	HR	HR %	R	RBI	BB	SO	SB	BA	SA	AB	H	G by POS
1923 CHI A	81	209	52	7	2	0	0.0	28	24	16	23	15	.249	.301	15	4	OF-57
1924	60	147	45	9	1	0	0.0	21	11	10	14	6	.306	.381	16	3	OF-38, 1B-2
1925	32	48	9	1	0	0	0.0	6	4	5	7	2	.188	.208	13	3	OF-16, 1B-3
3 yrs.	173	404	106	17	3	0	0.0	55	39	31	44	23	.262	.319	44	10	OF-111, 1B-5

Bones Ely

ELY, FREDERICK WILLIAM
B. June 7, 1863, Girard, Pa. D. Jan. 10, 1952, Berkeley, Calif. BR TR 6'1" 155 lbs.

	G	AB	H	2B	3B	HR	HR %	R	RBI	BB	SO	SB	BA	SA	AB	H	G by POS
1884 BUF N	1	4	0	0	0	0	0.0	0		0	2		.000	.000	0	0	OF-1, P-1
1886 LOU AA	10	32	5	0	0	0	0.0	5		0	2		.156	.156	0	0	P-6, OF-5
1890 SYR AA	119	496	130	16	6	0	0.0	72		31		44	.262	.319	0	0	OF-78, SS-36, 1B-4, 2B-2, 3B-1, P-1
1891 BKN N	31	111	17	0	1	0	0.0	9	11	7	9	4	.153	.171	0	0	SS-28, 3B-2, 2B-1
1893 STL N	44	178	45	1	6	0	0.0	25	16	17	13	2	.253	.326	0	0	SS-44
1894	127	510	156	20	12	12	2.4	85	89	30	34	23	.306	.463	0	0	SS-126, 2B-1, P-1
1895	117	467	121	16	2	1	0.2	68	46	19	17	28	.259	.308	0	0	SS-117
1896 PIT N	128	537	153	15	9	3	0.6	85	77	33	33	18	.285	.363	0	0	SS-128
1897	133	516	146	20	8	2	0.4	63	74	25		10	.283	.364	0	0	SS-133
1898	148	519	110	14	5	2	0.4	49	44	24		6	.212	.270	0	0	SS-148
1899	138	522	145	18	6	3	0.6	66	72	22		8	.278	.352	0	0	SS-132, 2B-6
1900	130	475	116	6	6	0	0.0	60	51	17		6	.244	.282	0	0	SS-130
1901 2 teams	PIT	N (65G – .208)						PHI	A (45G – .216)								
" total	110	411	87	12	5	0	0.0	29	44	9		11	.212	.265	1	0	SS-109, 3B-1
1902 WAS A	105	381	100	11	2	1	0.3	39	62	21		3	.262	.310	0	0	SS-105
14 yrs.	1341	5159	1331	149	68	24	0.5	655	585	257	108	163	.258	.327	1	0	SS-1236, OF-84, 2B-10, P-9, 3B-4, 1B-4

Chester Emerson

EMERSON, CHESTER ARTHUR (Chuck)
B. Oct. 27, 1889, Stow, Me. D. July 2, 1971, Augusta, Me. BL TR 5'9" 170 lbs.

	G	AB	H	2B	3B	HR	HR %	R	RBI	BB	SO	SB	BA	SA	AB	H	G by POS
1911 PHI A	7	18	4	0	0	0	0.0	2	0	6		1	.222	.222	0	0	OF-7
1912	1	1	0	0	0	0	0.0	0	0	0		0	.000	.000	1	0	P-1
2 yrs.	8	19	4	0	0	0	0.0	2	0	6		1	.211	.211	1	0	OF-7, P-1

Cal Emery

EMERY, CALVIN WAYNE
B. June 28, 1937, Centre Hall, Pa. BL TL 6'2" 205 lbs.

	G	AB	H	2B	3B	HR	HR %	R	RBI	BB	SO	SB	BA	SA	AB	H	G by POS
1963 PHI N	16	19	3	1	0	0	0.0	0	0	0	2	0	.158	.211	14	1	1B-2

Spoke Emery

EMERY, HERRICK SMITH
B. Dec. 10, 1898, Bay City, Mich. D. June 2, 1975, Cape Canaveral, Fla. BR TL 5'8" 162 lbs.

	G	AB	H	2B	3B	HR	HR %	R	RBI	BB	SO	SB	BA	SA	AB	H	G by POS
1924 PHI N	5	3	2	0	0	0	0.0	3	0	0	0	0	.667	.667	1	0	OF-1

Frank Emmer

EMMER, FRANK WILLIAM
B. Feb. 17, 1896, Crestline, Ohio D. Oct. 18, 1963, Homestead, Fla. BR TR 5'8" 150 lbs.

	G	AB	H	2B	3B	HR	HR %	R	RBI	BB	SO	SB	BA	SA	AB	H	G by POS
1916 CIN N	42	89	13	3	1	0	0.0	8	2	7	27	1	.146	.202	0	0	SS-29, OF-2, 3B-1, 2B-1
1926	80	224	44	7	6	0	0.0	22	18	13	30	1	.196	.281	0	0	SS-79
2 yrs.	122	313	57	10	7	0	0.0	30	20	20	57	2	.182	.259	0	0	SS-108, OF-2, 3B-1, 2B-1

Bob Emmerich

EMMERICH, ROBERT G.
B. Aug. 1, 1897, New York, N. Y. D. Nov. 22, 1948, Bridgeport, Conn. BR TR 5'3" 155 lbs.

	G	AB	H	2B	3B	HR	HR %	R	RBI	BB	SO	SB	BA	SA	AB	H	G by POS
1923 BOS N	13	24	2	0	0	0	0.0	3	0	2	3	1	.083	.083	0	0	OF-8

Bill Endicott

ENDICOTT, WILLIAM FRANKLIN
B. Sept. 4, 1918, Acorn, Mo. BL TL 5'11½" 175 lbs.

	G	AB	H	2B	3B	HR	HR %	R	RBI	BB	SO	SB	BA	SA	AB	H	G by POS
1946 STL N	20	20	4	3	0	0	0.0	2	3	4	4	0	.200	.350	14	3	OF-2

	G	AB	H	2B	3B	HR	HR %	R	RBI	BB	SO	SB	BA	SA	Pinch Hit AB	Pinch Hit H	G by POS

Charlie Engle

ENGLE, CHARLES AUGUST
B. Aug. 27, 1903, New York, N. Y.   D. Oct. 12, 1983, San Antonio, Tex.
BR TR 5'8''   145 lbs.

	G	AB	H	2B	3B	HR	HR %	R	RBI	BB	SO	SB	BA	SA	AB	H	G by POS
1925 PHI A	1	0	0	0	0	0	–	0	0	0	0	0	–	–	0	0	SS-1
1926	19	19	2	0	0	0	0.0	7	0	10	6	0	.105	.105	0	0	SS-16
1930 PIT N	67	216	57	10	1	0	0.0	34	15	22	20	1	.264	.319	7	2	3B-24, SS-23, 2B-10
3 yrs.	87	235	59	10	1	0	0.0	41	15	32	26	1	.251	.302	7	2	SS-40, 3B-24, 2B-10

Clyde Engle

ENGLE, ARTHUR CLYDE (Hack)
B. Mar. 19, 1884, Dayton, Ohio   D. Dec. 26, 1939, Boston, Mass.
BR TR

	G	AB	H	2B	3B	HR	HR %	R	RBI	BB	SO	SB	BA	SA	AB	H	G by POS
1909 NY A	135	492	137	20	5	3	0.6	66	71	47		18	.278	.358	1	1	OF-134
1910 2 teams			NY	A (5G – .231)		BOS	A (106G – .264)										
" total	111	376	99	18	7	2	0.5	59	38	33		13	.263	.364	7	0	3B-51, 2B-27, OF-18, SS-7
1911 BOS A	146	514	139	13	3	2	0.4	58	48	51		24	.270	.319	5	1	1B-65, 3B-51, 2B-13, OF-10
1912	57	171	40	5	3	0	0.0	32	18	28		12	.234	.298	3	0	1B-25, 2B-15, 3B-11, SS-2, OF-1
1913	143	498	144	17	12	2	0.4	75	50	53	41	28	.289	.384	7	0	1B-133, OF-2
1914 2 teams			BOS	A (55G – .194)		BUF	F (32G – .255)										
" total	87	244	54	6	1	0	0.0	26	21	25	11	9	.221	.254	18	5	1B-29, 3B-25, OF-9, 2B-5
1915 BUF F	141	501	131	22	8	3	0.6	56	71	34		24	.261	.355	5	2	OF-100, 2B-21, 3B-17, 1B-1
1916 CLE A	11	26	4	0	0	0	0.0	1	1	0	6	0	.154	.154	1	0	3B-7, 1B-2, OF-1
8 yrs.	831	2822	748	101	39	12	0.4	373	318	271	58	128	.265	.341	47	9	OF-275, 1B-255, 3B-162, 2B-81, SS-9

WORLD SERIES

	G	AB	H	2B	3B	HR	HR %	R	RBI	BB	SO	SB	BA	SA	AB	H	G by POS
1912 BOS A	3	3	1	1	0	0	0.0	1	2	0	0	0	.333	.667	3	1	

Dave Engle

ENGLE, RALPH DAVID
B. Nov. 30, 1956, San Diego, Calif.
BR TR 6'3''   210 lbs.

	G	AB	H	2B	3B	HR	HR %	R	RBI	BB	SO	SB	BA	SA	AB	H	G by POS
1981 MIN A	82	248	64	14	4	5	2.0	29	32	13	37	0	.258	.407	1	0	OF-76, DH-1, 3B-1
1982	58	186	42	7	2	4	2.2	20	16	10	22	0	.226	.349	13	3	OF-34, DH-20
1983	120	374	114	22	4	8	2.1	46	43	28	39	2	.305	.449	20	6	C-73, DH-29, OF-4
1984	109	391	104	20	1	4	1.0	56	38	26	22	0	.266	.353	6	0	C-86, DH-22
4 yrs.	369	1199	324	63	11	21	1.8	151	129	77	120	2	.270	.394	40	9	C-159, OF-114, DH-72, 3B-1

Charlie English

ENGLISH, CHARLES DEWIE
B. Apr. 8, 1910, Darlington, S. C.
BR TR 5'9½''   160 lbs.

	G	AB	H	2B	3B	HR	HR %	R	RBI	BB	SO	SB	BA	SA	AB	H	G by POS
1932 CHI A	24	63	20	3	1	1	1.6	7	8	3	7	0	.317	.444	9	2	3B-13, SS-1
1933	3	9	4	2	0	0	0.0	2	1	1	1	0	.444	.667	0	0	2B-3
1936 NY N	6	1	0	0	0	0	0.0	0	0	0	0	0	.000	.000	1	0	2B-1
1937 CIN N	17	63	15	3	1	0	0.0	1	4	0	2	0	.238	.317	0	0	3B-15, 2B-2
4 yrs.	50	136	39	8	2	1	0.7	10	13	4	10	0	.287	.397	10	2	3B-28, 2B-6, SS-1

Gil English

ENGLISH, GILBERT RAYMOND
B. July 2, 1909, Glenola, N. C.
BR TR 5'11''   180 lbs.

	G	AB	H	2B	3B	HR	HR %	R	RBI	BB	SO	SB	BA	SA	AB	H	G by POS
1931 NY N	3	8	0	0	0	0	0.0	0	0	1	3	0	.000	.000	0	0	3B-3
1932	59	204	46	7	5	2	1.0	22	19	5	20	0	.225	.338	1	0	3B-39, SS-23
1936 DET A	1	0	0	0	0	0	0.0	0	0	0	1	0	.000	.000	0	0	3B-1
1937 2 teams			DET	A (18G – .262)		BOS	N (79G – .290)										
" total	97	334	95	6	2	3	0.9	31	43	29	31	4	.284	.341	6	4	3B-77, 2B-12
1938 BOS N	53	165	41	6	0	2	1.2	17	21	15	16	1	.248	.321	4	2	3B-43, OF-3, SS-2, 2B-2
1944 BKN N	27	79	12	3	0	1	1.3	4	7	6	7	0	.152	.228	1	0	SS-13, 3B-11, 2B-2
6 yrs.	240	791	194	22	7	8	1.0	74	90	56	78	5	.245	.321	12	6	3B-174, SS-38, 2B-16, OF-3

Woody English

ENGLISH, ELWOOD GEORGE
B. Mar. 2, 1907, Fredonia, Ohio
BR TR 5'10''   155 lbs.

	G	AB	H	2B	3B	HR	HR %	R	RBI	BB	SO	SB	BA	SA	AB	H	G by POS
1927 CHI N	87	334	97	14	4	1	0.3	46	28	16	26	1	.290	.365	0	0	SS-84, 3B-1
1928	116	475	142	22	4	2	0.4	68	34	30	28	4	.299	.375	0	0	SS-114, 3B-2
1929	144	608	168	29	3	1	0.2	131	52	68	50	13	.276	.339	0	0	SS-144
1930	156	638	214	36	17	14	2.2	152	59	100	72	3	.335	.511	0	0	3B-83, SS-78
1931	156	634	202	38	8	2	0.3	117	53	68	80	12	.319	.413	0	0	SS-138, 3B-18
1932	127	522	142	23	7	3	0.6	70	47	55	73	5	.272	.360	1	0	3B-93, SS-38
1933	105	398	104	19	2	3	0.8	54	41	53	44	5	.261	.342	0	0	3B-103, SS-1
1934	109	421	117	26	5	3	0.7	65	31	48	65	6	.278	.385	0	0	SS-56, 3B-46, 2B-7
1935	34	84	17	2	0	2	2.4	11	8	20	4	1	.202	.298	4	2	3B-16, SS-12
1936	64	182	45	9	0	0	0.0	33	20	40	28	1	.247	.297	5	0	SS-42, 3B-17, 2B-1
1937 BKN N	129	378	90	16	2	1	0.3	45	42	65	55	4	.238	.299	2	0	SS-116, 2B-11
1938	34	72	18	2	0	0	0.0	9	7	8	11	2	.250	.278	7	1	3B-21, SS-3, 2B-3
12 yrs.	1261	4746	1356	236	52	32	0.7	801	422	571	536	57	.286	.378	19	3	SS-826, 3B-400, 2B-22

WORLD SERIES

	G	AB	H	2B	3B	HR	HR %	R	RBI	BB	SO	SB	BA	SA	AB	H	G by POS
1929 CHI N	5	21	4	2	0	0	0.0	1	0	1	6	0	.190	.286	0	0	SS-5
1932	4	17	3	0	0	0	0.0	2	1	2	2	0	.176	.176	0	0	3B-4
2 yrs.	9	38	7	2	0	0	0.0	3	1	3	8	0	.184	.237	0	0	SS-5, 3B-4

Del Ennis

ENNIS, DELMER
B. June 8, 1925, Philadelphia, Pa.
BR TR 6'   195 lbs.

	G	AB	H	2B	3B	HR	HR %	R	RBI	BB	SO	SB	BA	SA	AB	H	G by POS
1946 PHI N	141	540	169	30	6	17	3.1	70	73	39	65	5	.313	.485	3	0	OF-138
1947	139	541	149	25	6	12	2.2	71	81	37	51	9	.275	.410	4	1	OF-135
1948	152	589	171	40	4	30	5.1	86	95	47	58	2	.290	.525	2	1	OF-151
1949	154	610	184	39	11	25	4.1	92	110	59	61	0	.302	.525	0	0	OF-154
1950	153	595	185	34	8	31	5.2	92	126	56	59	2	.311	.551	4	0	OF-149
1951	144	532	142	20	5	15	2.8	76	73	68	42	4	.267	.408	8	2	OF-144
1952	151	592	171	30	10	20	3.4	90	107	47	65	6	.289	.475	2	0	OF-149
1953	152	578	165	22	3	29	5.0	79	125	57	53	1	.285	.484	2	0	OF-150

	G	AB	H	2B	3B	HR	HR %	R	RBI	BB	SO	SB	BA	SA	Pinch Hit AB	H	G by POS

Del Ennis continued

	G	AB	H	2B	3B	HR	HR %	R	RBI	BB	SO	SB	BA	SA	PH AB	PH H	G by POS
1954	145	556	145	23	2	25	4.5	73	119	50	60	2	.261	.444	1	0	OF-142, 1B-1
1955	146	564	167	24	7	29	5.1	82	120	46	46	4	.296	.518	1	0	OF-145
1956	153	630	164	23	3	26	4.1	80	95	33	62	7	.260	.430	0	0	OF-153
1957 STL N	136	490	140	24	3	24	4.9	61	105	37	50	1	.286	.494	8	3	OF-127
1958	106	329	86	18	1	3	0.9	22	47	15	35	0	.261	.350	22	2	OF-84
1959 2 teams	CIN	N (5G –	.333)		CHI	A	(26G –	.219)									
" total	31	108	25	6	0	2	1.9	11	8	6	12	0	.231	.343	3	1	OF-28
14 yrs.	1903	7254	2063	358	69	288	4.0	985	1284	597	719	45	.284	.472	60	10	OF-1849, 1B-1

WORLD SERIES

	G	AB	H	2B	3B	HR	HR %	R	RBI	BB	SO	SB	BA	SA	PH AB	PH H	G by POS
1950 PHI N	4	14	2	1	0	0	0.0	1	0	0	1	0	.143	.214	0	0	OF-4

Russ Ennis

ENNIS, RUSSELL ELWOOD (Hack) BR TR 5'11½" 160 lbs.
B. Mar. 10, 1897, Superior, Wis. D. Jan. 29, 1949, Superior, Wis.

	G	AB	H	2B	3B	HR	HR %	R	RBI	BB	SO	SB	BA	SA	PH AB	PH H	G by POS
1926 WAS A	1	0	0	0	0	0	0.0	0	0	0	0	0	–	–	0	0	C-1

George Enright

ENRIGHT, GEORGE ALBERT BR TR 5'11" 175 lbs.
B. May 9, 1954, New Britain, Conn.

	G	AB	H	2B	3B	HR	HR %	R	RBI	BB	SO	SB	BA	SA	PH AB	PH H	G by POS
1976 CHI A	2	1	0	0	0	0	0.0	0	0	0	0	0	.000	.000	0	0	C-2

Jewel Ens

ENS, JEWEL WILLOUGHBY BR TR 5'10½" 165 lbs.
Brother of Mutz Ens.
B. Aug. 24, 1889, St. Louis, Mo. D. Jan. 17, 1950, Syracuse, N. Y.
Manager 1929-31.

	G	AB	H	2B	3B	HR	HR %	R	RBI	BB	SO	SB	BA	SA	PH AB	PH H	G by POS
1922 PIT N	47	142	42	7	3	0	0.0	18	17	7	9	3	.296	.387	13	3	2B-29, 3B-3, 1B-2, SS-1
1923	12	29	8	1	1	0	0.0	3	5	0	3	2	.276	.379	5	2	1B-4, 3B-2, SS-1
1924	5	10	3	0	0	0	0.0	2	0	0	3	0	.300	.300	0	0	1B-5
1925	3	5	1	0	0	1	20.0	2	2	0	1	0	.200	.800	0	0	1B-3
4 yrs.	67	186	54	8	4	1	0.5	25	24	7	16	5	.290	.392	18	5	2B-29, 1B-14, 3B-5, SS-2

Mutz Ens

ENS, ANTON BL TL 6'1" 185 lbs.
Brother of Jewel Ens.
B. Nov. 8, 1884, St. Louis, Mo. D. June 28, 1950, St. Louis, Mo.

	G	AB	H	2B	3B	HR	HR %	R	RBI	BB	SO	SB	BA	SA	PH AB	PH H	G by POS
1912 CHI A	3	6	0	0	0	0	0.0	0	0	0		0	.000	.000	0	0	1B-3

Charlie Enwright

ENWRIGHT, CHARLES MASSEY BL TR 5'10"
B. Oct. 6, 1887, Sacramento, Calif. D. Jan. 19, 1917, Sacramento, Calif.

	G	AB	H	2B	3B	HR	HR %	R	RBI	BB	SO	SB	BA	SA	PH AB	PH H	G by POS
1909 STL N	3	7	1	0	0	0	0.0	1	1	2		0	.143	.143	1	0	SS-2

Jack Enzenroth

ENZENROTH, CLARENCE HERMAN BR TR 5'10" 164 lbs.
B. Nov. 4, 1885, Mineral Point, Wis. D. Feb. 21, 1944, Detroit, Mich.

	G	AB	H	2B	3B	HR	HR %	R	RBI	BB	SO	SB	BA	SA	PH AB	PH H	G by POS
1914 2 teams	STL	A (3G –	.167)		KC	F	(26G –	.179)									
" total	29	73	13	4	1	0	0.0	7	5	7	3	0	.178	.260	2	1	C-27
1915 KC F	14	19	3	0	0	0	0.0	3	3	6		0	.158	.158	1	1	C-8
2 yrs.	43	92	16	4	1	0	0.0	10	8	13	3	0	.174	.239	3	2	C-35

Aubrey Epps

EPPS, AUBREY LEE (Yo-Yo) BR TR 5'10" 170 lbs.
B. Mar. 3, 1912, Memphis, Tenn.

	G	AB	H	2B	3B	HR	HR %	R	RBI	BB	SO	SB	BA	SA	PH AB	PH H	G by POS
1935 PIT N	1	4	3	0	1	0	0.0	1	3	0	0	0	.750	1.250	0	0	C-1

Hal Epps

EPPS, HAROLD FRANKLIN BL TL 6' 175 lbs.
B. Mar. 26, 1914, Athens, Ga.

	G	AB	H	2B	3B	HR	HR %	R	RBI	BB	SO	SB	BA	SA	PH AB	PH H	G by POS
1938 STL N	17	50	15	0	0	1	2.0	8	3	2	4	2	.300	.360	7	0	OF-10
1940	11	15	3	0	0	0	0.0	6	1	0	3	0	.200	.200	2	0	OF-3
1943 STL A	8	35	10	4	0	0	0.0	2	1	1	3	1	.286	.400	0	0	OF-8
1944 2 teams	STL	A (22G –	.177)		PHI	A	(67G –	.262)									
" total	89	291	71	9	9	0	0.0	42	16	32	32	2	.244	.337	10	3	OF-78
4 yrs.	125	391	99	13	9	1	0.3	58	21	37	43	5	.253	.340	19	3	OF-99

Mike Epstein

EPSTEIN, MICHAEL PETER (Superjew) BL TL 6'3½" 230 lbs.
B. Apr. 4, 1943, Bronx, N. Y.

	G	AB	H	2B	3B	HR	HR %	R	RBI	BB	SO	SB	BA	SA	PH AB	PH H	G by POS
1966 BAL A	6	11	2	0	1	0	0.0	1	3	1	3	0	.182	.364	1	0	1B-4
1967 2 teams	BAL	A (9G –	.154)		WAS	A	(96G –	.229)									
" total	105	297	67	7	4	9	3.0	32	29	41	79	1	.226	.367	19	3	1B-83
1968 WAS A	123	385	90	8	2	13	3.4	40	33	48	91	1	.234	.366	13	2	1B-110
1969	131	403	112	18	1	30	7.4	73	85	85	99	2	.278	.551	12	3	1B-118
1970	140	430	110	15	3	20	4.7	55	56	73	117	2	.256	.444	18	2	1B-122
1971 2 teams	WAS	A (24G –	.247)		OAK	A	(104G –	.234)									
" total	128	414	98	14	1	19	4.6	49	60	74	102	1	.237	.413	9	1	1B-120
1972 OAK A	138	455	123	18	2	26	5.7	63	70	68	68	0	.270	.490	1	0	1B-137
1973 2 teams	TEX	A (27G –	.188)		CAL	A	(91G –	.215)									
" total	118	397	83	11	2	9	2.3	39	38	48	73	0	.209	.315	4	1	1B-111
1974 CAL A	18	62	10	2	0	4	6.5	10	6	10	13	0	.161	.387	0	0	1B-18
9 yrs.	907	2854	695	93	16	130	4.6	362	380	448	645	7	.244	.424	77	12	1B-823

LEAGUE CHAMPIONSHIP SERIES

	G	AB	H	2B	3B	HR	HR %	R	RBI	BB	SO	SB	BA	SA	PH AB	PH H	G by POS
1971 OAK A	2	5	1	0	0	0	0.0	0	0	0	3	0	.200	.200	1	0	1B-1
1972	5	16	3	0	0	1	6.3	1	1	4	5	0	.188	.375	0	0	1B-5
2 yrs.	7	21	4	0	0	1	4.8	1	1	4	8	0	.190	.333	1	0	1B-6

WORLD SERIES

	G	AB	H	2B	3B	HR	HR %	R	RBI	BB	SO	SB	BA	SA	PH AB	PH H	G by POS
1972 OAK A	6	16	0	0	0	0	0.0	1	0	1	5	0	.000	.000	0	0	1B-6

Joe Erautt

ERAUTT, JOSEPH MICHAEL (Stubby) BR TR 5'9" 175 lbs.
Brother of Eddie Erautt.
B. Sept. 1, 1921, Vibank, Sask., Canada

	G	AB	H	2B	3B	HR	HR %	R	RBI	BB	SO	SB	BA	SA	PH AB	PH H	G by POS
1950 CHI A	16	18	4	0	0	0	0.0	0	1	1	3	0	.222	.222	10	2	C-5

	G	AB	H	2B	3B	HR	HR %	R	RBI	BB	SO	SB	BA	SA	Pinch Hit AB	H	G by POS

Joe Erautt continued

	G	AB	H	2B	3B	HR	HR %	R	RBI	BB	SO	SB	BA	SA	AB	H	G by POS
1951	16	25	4	1	0	0	0.0	3	0	3	2	0	.160	.200	4	1	C-12
2 yrs.	32	43	8	1	0	0	0.0	3	1	4	5	0	.186	.209	14	3	C-17

Hank Erickson

ERICKSON, HENRY NELS (Popeye)   BR TR 6'1"   185 lbs.
B. Nov. 11, 1907, Chicago, Ill.   D. Dec. 3, 1964, Louisville, Ky.

	G	AB	H	2B	3B	HR	HR %	R	RBI	BB	SO	SB	BA	SA	AB	H	G by POS
1935 CIN N	37	88	23	3	2	1	1.1	9	4	6	4	0	.261	.375	12	2	C-25

Cal Ermer

ERMER, CALVIN COOLIDGE   BR TR 6'½"   175 lbs.
B. Nov. 10, 1923, Baltimore, Md.
Manager 1967-68.

	G	AB	H	2B	3B	HR	HR %	R	RBI	BB	SO	SB	BA	SA	AB	H	G by POS
1947 WAS A	1	3	0	0	0	0	0.0	0	0	0	0	0	.000	.000	0	0	2B-1

Frank Ernaga

ERNAGA, FRANK JOHN   BR TR 6'1"   195 lbs.
B. Aug. 22, 1930, Susanville, Calif.

	G	AB	H	2B	3B	HR	HR %	R	RBI	BB	SO	SB	BA	SA	AB	H	G by POS
1957 CHI N	20	35	11	3	2	2	5.7	9	7	9	14	0	.314	.686	7	1	OF-10
1958	9	8	1	0	0	0	0.0	0	0	0	2	0	.125	.125	8	1	
2 yrs.	29	43	12	3	2	2	4.7	9	7	9	16	0	.279	.581	15	2	OF-10

Tex Erwin

ERWIN, ROSS EMIL   BL TR 6'   185 lbs.
B. Dec. 22, 1885, Forney, Tex.   D. Apr. 5, 1953, Rochester, N. Y.

	G	AB	H	2B	3B	HR	HR %	R	RBI	BB	SO	SB	BA	SA	AB	H	G by POS
1907 DET A	4	5	1	0	0	0	0.0	0	1	1		0	.200	.200	0	0	C-4
1910 BKN N	81	202	38	3	1	1	0.5	15	10	24	12	3	.188	.228	12	1	C-68
1911	91	218	59	13	2	7	3.2	30	34	31	23	5	.271	.445	15	4	C-74
1912	59	133	28	3	0	2	1.5	14	14	18	16	1	.211	.278	12	2	C-41
1913	20	31	8	1	0	0	0.0	6	3	4	5	0	.258	.290	7	1	C-13
1914 2 teams		BKN	N (9G – .455)				CIN	N	(12G – .314)								
" total	21	46	16	3	0	1	2.2	5	8	4	4	1	.348	.478	6	3	C-16
6 yrs.	276	635	150	23	3	11	1.7	70	70	82	60	10	.236	.334	52	11	C-216

Nick Esasky

ESASKY, NICHOLAS ANDREW   BR TR 6'3"   190 lbs.
B. Feb. 24, 1960, Hialeah, Fla.

	G	AB	H	2B	3B	HR	HR %	R	RBI	BB	SO	SB	BA	SA	AB	H	G by POS
1983 CIN N	85	302	80	10	5	12	4.0	41	46	27	99	6	.265	.450	1	0	3B-84
1984	113	322	62	10	5	10	3.1	30	45	52	103	1	.193	.348	12	0	3B-82, 1B-25
2 yrs.	198	624	142	20	10	22	3.5	71	91	79	202	7	.228	.397	13	0	3B-166, 1B-25

Nino Escalera

ESCALERA, SATURNINO CUADRADO   BL TL 5'10"   165 lbs.
B. Dec. 1, 1929, Santurce, Puerto Rico

	G	AB	H	2B	3B	HR	HR %	R	RBI	BB	SO	SB	BA	SA	AB	H	G by POS
1954 CIN N	73	69	11	1	1	0	0.0	15	3	7	11	1	.159	.203	29	6	OF-14, 1B-8, SS-1

Jim Eschen

ESCHEN, JAMES GODRICH   BR TR 5'10½" 160 lbs.
Father of Larry Eschen.
B. Aug. 21, 1891, Brooklyn, N. Y.   D. Sept. 27, 1960, Sloatsburg, N. Y.

	G	AB	H	2B	3B	HR	HR %	R	RBI	BB	SO	SB	BA	SA	AB	H	G by POS
1915 CLE A	15	42	10	1	0	0	0.0	11	2	5	9	0	.238	.262	5	2	OF-10

Larry Eschen

ESCHEN, LAWRENCE EDWARD   BR TR 6'   180 lbs.
Son of Jim Eschen.
B. Sept. 22, 1920, Suffern, N. Y.

	G	AB	H	2B	3B	HR	HR %	R	RBI	BB	SO	SB	BA	SA	AB	H	G by POS
1942 PHI A	12	11	0	0	0	0	0.0	0	0	4	6	0	.000	.000	2	0	SS-7, 2B-1

Jimmy Esmond

ESMOND, JAMES J.   BR TR 5'11"   167 lbs.
B. Oct. 8, 1889, Albany, N. Y.   D. June 26, 1948, Troy, N. Y.

	G	AB	H	2B	3B	HR	HR %	R	RBI	BB	SO	SB	BA	SA	AB	H	G by POS
1911 CIN N	73	198	54	4	6	1	0.5	27	11	17	30	7	.273	.369	5	2	SS-44, 3B-14, 2B-2
1912	82	231	45	5	3	1	0.4	24	40	20	31	11	.195	.255	1	0	SS-74
1914 IND F	151	542	160	23	15	2	0.4	74	49	40		25	.295	.404	0	0	SS-151
1915 NWK F	155	569	147	20	10	5	0.9	79	62	59		18	.258	.355	0	0	SS-155
4 yrs.	461	1540	406	52	34	9	0.6	204	162	136	61	61	.264	.359	6	2	SS-424, 3B-14, 2B-2

Juan Espino

ESPINO, JUAN   BR TR 6'   175 lbs.
Also known as Juan Reyes.
B. Mar. 16, 1956, Bonao, Dominican Republic

	G	AB	H	2B	3B	HR	HR %	R	RBI	BB	SO	SB	BA	SA	AB	H	G by POS
1982 NY A	3	2	0	0	0	0	0.0	0	0	0	1	0	.000	.000	0	0	C-3
1983	10	23	6	0	0	1	4.3	1	3	1	5	0	.261	.391	0	0	C-10
2 yrs.	13	25	6	0	0	1	4.0	1	3	1	6	0	.240	.360	0	0	C-13

Sammy Esposito

ESPOSITO, SAMUEL   BR TR 5'9"   165 lbs.
B. Dec. 15, 1931, Chicago, Ill.

	G	AB	H	2B	3B	HR	HR %	R	RBI	BB	SO	SB	BA	SA	AB	H	G by POS
1952 CHI A	1	4	1	0	0	0	0.0	0	0	0	2	0	.250	.250	0	0	SS-1
1955	3	4	0	0	0	0	0.0	3	0	1	0	0	.000	.000	0	0	3B-2
1956	81	184	42	8	2	3	1.6	30	25	41	19	1	.228	.342	8	1	3B-61, SS-19, 2B-3
1957	94	176	36	3	0	2	1.1	26	15	38	27	5	.205	.256	11	3	3B-53, SS-22, 2B-4, OF-1
1958	98	81	20	3	0	0	0.0	16	3	12	6	1	.247	.284	7	1	3B-63, SS-22, 2B-2, OF-1
1959	69	66	11	1	0	1	1.5	12	5	11	16	0	.167	.227	5	1	3B-45, SS-14, 2B-2
1960	57	77	14	5	0	1	1.3	14	11	10	20	0	.182	.286	4	1	3B-37, SS-11, 2B-5
1961	63	94	16	5	0	1	1.1	12	8	12	21	0	.170	.255	2	0	3B-28, SS-20, 2B-11
1962	75	81	19	1	0	0	0.0	14	4	17	13	0	.235	.247	3	1	3B-41, SS-20, 2B-7
1963 2 teams		CHI	A (1G – .000)				KC	A	(18G – .200)								
" total	19	25	5	1	0	0	0.0	3	2	3	3	0	.200	.240	1	1	2B-7, SS-4, 3B-3
10 yrs.	560	792	164	27	2	8	1.0	130	73	145	127	7	.207	.277	41	9	3B-333, SS-133, 2B-41, OF-2

WORLD SERIES

	G	AB	H	2B	3B	HR	HR %	R	RBI	BB	SO	SB	BA	SA	AB	H	G by POS
1959 CHI A	2	2	0	0	0	0	0.0	0	0	0	1	0	.000	.000	0	0	3B-2

	G	AB	H	2B	3B	HR	HR %	R	RBI	BB	SO	SB	BA	SA	Pinch Hit AB	Pinch Hit H	G by POS

Cecil Espy

ESPY, CECIL EDWARD
B. Jan. 30, 1963, San Diego, Calif.

BB TR 6'3" 190 lbs.

	G	AB	H	2B	3B	HR	HR %	R	RBI	BB	SO	SB	BA	SA	PH AB	PH H	G by POS
1983 LA N	20	11	3	1	0	0	0.0	4	1	1	2	0	.273	.364	2	1	OF-15

Chuck Essegian

ESSEGIAN, CHARLES ABRAHAM
B. Aug. 9, 1931, Boston, Mass.

BR TR 5'11" 200 lbs.

	G	AB	H	2B	3B	HR	HR %	R	RBI	BB	SO	SB	BA	SA	PH AB	PH H	G by POS
1958 PHI N	39	114	28	5	2	5	4.4	15	16	12	34	0	.246	.456	9	2	OF-30
1959 2 teams		STL	N (17G –	.179)		LA	N	(24G –	.304)								
" total	41	85	21	8	1	1	1.2	8	10	5	24	0	.247	.400	22	5	OF-19
1960 LA N	52	79	17	3	0	3	3.8	8	11	8	24	0	.215	.367	37	8	OF-18
1961 3 teams		BAL	A (1G –	.000)		KC	A	(4G –	.333)		CLE	A	(60G –	.289)			
" total	65	173	50	8	1	12	6.9	26	36	11	35	0	.289	.555	20	7	OF-50
1962 CLE A	106	336	92	12	0	21	6.3	59	50	42	68	0	.274	.497	14	2	OF-90
1963 KC A	101	231	52	9	0	5	2.2	23	27	19	48	0	.225	.329	40	9	OF-53
6 yrs.	404	1018	260	45	4	47	4.6	139	150	97	233	0	.255	.446	142	33	OF-260
WORLD SERIES																	
1959 LA N	4	3	2	0	0	2	66.7	2	2	1	1	0	.667	2.667	4	2	

Jim Essian

ESSIAN, JAMES SARKIS
B. Jan. 2, 1951, Detroit, Mich.

BR TR 6'2" 195 lbs.

	G	AB	H	2B	3B	HR	HR %	R	RBI	BB	SO	SB	BA	SA	PH AB	PH H	G by POS
1973 PHI N	2	3	0	0	0	0	0.0	0	0	0	1	0	.000	.000	2	0	C-1
1974	17	20	2	0	0	0	0.0	1	0	2	1	0	.100	.100	1	0	C-15, 3B-1, 1B-1
1975	2	1	1	0	0	0	0.0	1	1	1	0	0	1.000	1.000	1	1	C-2
1976 CHI A	78	199	49	7	0	0	0.0	20	21	23	28	2	.246	.281	0	0	C-77, 1B-2, 3B-1
1977	114	322	88	18	2	10	3.1	50	44	52	35	1	.273	.435	0	0	C-111, 3B-2
1978 OAK A	126	278	62	9	4	3	1.1	21	26	44	22	2	.223	.295	4	0	C-119, 1B-3, 2B-1
1979	98	313	76	16	0	8	2.6	34	40	25	29	0	.243	.371	8	2	C-70, 3B-10, OF-4, 1B-4, DH-3
1980	87	285	66	11	0	5	1.8	19	29	30	18	1	.232	.323	8	1	C-68, DH-11, 1B-1
1981 CHI A	27	52	16	3	0	0	0.0	6	5	4	5	0	.308	.365	2	0	C-25, 3B-2
1982 SEA A	48	153	42	8	0	3	2.0	14	20	11	7	2	.275	.386	1	1	C-48
1983 CLE A	48	93	19	4	0	2	2.2	11	11	16	8	0	.204	.312	0	0	C-47, 3B-1
1984 OAK A	62	135	31	9	0	2	1.5	17	9	23	17	1	.230	.341	3	0	C-59, DH-1, 3B-1
12 yrs.	709	1854	452	85	6	33	1.8	194	206	231	171	9	.244	.346	30	5	C-642, 3B-18, DH-15, 1B-11, OF-4, 2B-1

Bobby Estalella

ESTALELLA, ROBERTO MENDEZ
B. Apr. 25, 1911, Cardenas, Cuba

BR TR 5'6" 185 lbs.

	G	AB	H	2B	3B	HR	HR %	R	RBI	BB	SO	SB	BA	SA	PH AB	PH H	G by POS
1935 WAS A	15	51	16	2	0	2	3.9	7	10	17	7	1	.314	.471	0	0	3B-15
1936	13	9	2	0	0	0	0.0	2	0	4	5	0	.222	.667	9	2	
1939	82	280	77	18	6	8	2.9	51	41	40	27	2	.275	.468	8	2	OF-74
1941 STL A	46	83	20	6	1	0	0.0	7	14	18	13	0	.241	.337	22	6	OF-17
1942 WAS A	133	429	119	24	5	8	1.9	68	65	85	42	5	.277	.413	18	4	3B-78, OF-36
1943 PHI A	117	367	95	14	4	11	3.0	43	63	52	44	1	.259	.409	20	7	OF-97
1944	140	506	151	17	9	7	1.4	54	60	59	60	3	.298	.409	11	4	OF-128, 1B-6
1945	126	451	135	25	6	8	1.8	45	52	74	46	1	.299	.435	2	1	OF-124
1949	8	20	5	0	0	0	0.0	2	3	1	2	0	.250	.250	1	0	OF-6
9 yrs.	680	2196	620	106	33	44	2.0	279	308	350	246	13	.282	.421	91	26	OF-482, 3B-93, 1B-6

Dude Esterbrook

ESTERBROOK, THOMAS JEFFERSON
B. June 20, 1860, Staten Island, N. Y.   D. Apr. 30, 1901, Middletown, N. Y.
Manager 1889.

BR TR 5'11" 167 lbs.

	G	AB	H	2B	3B	HR	HR %	R	RBI	BB	SO	SB	BA	SA	PH AB	PH H	G by POS
1880 BUF N	64	253	61	12	1	0	0.0	20	35	0	15		.241	.296	0	0	1B-47, OF-15, 2B-6, SS-1, C-1
1882 CLE N	45	179	44	4	3	0	0.0	13	19	5	12		.246	.302	0	0	OF-45, 1B-1
1883 NY AA	97	407	103	9	7	0	0.0	55		15			.253	.310	0	0	3B-97
1884	112	477	150	29	11	1	0.2	110		12			.314	.428	0	0	3B-112
1885 NY N	88	359	92	14	5	2	0.6	48		4	28		.256	.340	0	0	3B-84, OF-4
1886	123	473	125	20	6	3	0.6	62	43	8	43		.264	.351	0	0	3B-123
1887 NY AA	26	101	17	1	0	0	0.0	11		6		8	.168	.178	0	0	1B-9, OF-7, SS-5, 2B-5
1888 2 teams		IND	N (64G –	.220)		LOU	AA	(23G –	.226)								
" total	87	339	75	14	0	0	0.0	30	24	5	20	16	.221	.263	0	0	1B-84, 3B-3
1889 LOU AA	11	44	14	3	0	0	0.0	8	9	5	2	6	.318	.386	0	0	1B-8, OF-2, SS-1
1890 NY N	45	197	57	14	1	0	0.0	29	29	10	8	12	.289	.371	0	0	1B-45
1891 BKN N	3	8	3	0	0	0	0.0	1	0	0	1	0	.375	.375	0	0	OF-2, 2B-1
11 yrs.	701	2837	741	120	34	6	0.2	387	159	70	129	42	.261	.334	0	0	3B-419, 1B-194, OF-75, 2B-12, SS-7, C-1

Francisco Estrada

ESTRADA, FRANCISCO SOTO
B. Feb. 12, 1948, Navojoa, Mexico

BR TR 5'8" 182 lbs.

	G	AB	H	2B	3B	HR	HR %	R	RBI	BB	SO	SB	BA	SA	PH AB	PH H	G by POS
1971 NY N	1	2	1	0	0	0	0.0	0	0	0	0	0	.500	.500	0	0	C-1

Andy Etchebarren

ETCHEBARREN, ANDREW AUGUSTE
B. June 20, 1943, Whittier, Calif.

BR TR 6'1" 190 lbs.

	G	AB	H	2B	3B	HR	HR %	R	RBI	BB	SO	SB	BA	SA	PH AB	PH H	G by POS
1962 BAL A	2	6	2	0	0	0	0.0	0	1	0	2	0	.333	.333	0	0	C-2
1965	5	6	1	0	0	1	16.7	1	4	0	2	0	.167	.667	0	0	C-5
1966	121	412	91	14	6	11	2.7	49	50	38	106	0	.221	.364	0	0	C-121
1967	112	330	71	13	0	7	2.1	29	35	38	80	1	.215	.318	6	1	C-110
1968	74	189	44	11	2	5	2.6	20	20	19	46	0	.233	.392	6	2	C-70
1969	73	217	54	9	1	3	1.4	29	26	28	42	1	.249	.350	10	1	C-72
1970	78	230	56	10	1	4	1.7	19	28	21	41	4	.243	.348	8	1	C-76
1971	70	222	60	8	0	9	4.1	21	29	16	40	1	.270	.428	4	1	C-70
1972	71	188	38	6	1	2	1.1	11	21	17	43	0	.202	.277	10	3	C-70
1973	54	152	39	9	1	2	1.3	16	23	12	21	1	.257	.368	4	0	C-51
1974	62	180	40	8	0	2	1.1	13	15	6	26	1	.222	.300	3	1	C-60

	G	AB	H	2B	3B	HR	HR %	R	RBI	BB	SO	SB	BA	SA	Pinch Hit AB	Pinch Hit H	G by POS

Andy Etchebarren continued

1975 2 teams	BAL A (8G – .200)			CAL	A	(31G –	.280)										
" total	39	120	32	1	1	3	2.5	10	20	14	22	1	.267	.367	1	1	C-38
1976 CAL A	103	247	56	9	1	0	0.0	15	21	24	37	0	.227	.271	3	1	C-102
1977	80	114	29	2	2	0	0.0	11	14	12	19	3	.254	.307	0	0	C-80
1978 MIL A	4	5	2	1	0	0	0.0	1	2	1	2	0	.400	.600	0	0	C-4
15 yrs.	948	2618	615	101	17	49	1.9	245	309	246	529	13	.235	.343	55	15	C-931

LEAGUE CHAMPIONSHIP SERIES

	G	AB	H	2B	3B	HR	HR %	R	RBI	BB	SO	SB	BA	SA	PH AB	PH H	G by POS
1969 BAL A	2	4	0	0	0	0	0.0	0	0	0	0	0	.000	.000	0	0	C-2
1970	2	9	1	0	0	0	0.0	1	0	0	3	0	.111	.111	0	0	C-2
1971	2	5	0	0	0	0	0.0	0	0	0	0	0	.000	.000	1	0	C-2
1973	4	14	5	1	0	1	7.1	1	4	0	1	0	.357	.643	0	0	C-4
1974	2	6	2	0	0	0	0.0	0	0	0	0	0	.333	.333	0	0	C-2
5 yrs.	12	38	8	1	0	1	2.6	2	4	0	4	0	.211	.316	1	0	C-12

WORLD SERIES

	G	AB	H	2B	3B	HR	HR %	R	RBI	BB	SO	SB	BA	SA	PH AB	PH H	G by POS
1966 BAL A	4	12	1	0	0	0	0.0	2	0	2	4	0	.083	.083	0	0	C-4
1969	2	6	0	0	0	0	0.0	0	0	0	1	0	.000	.000	0	0	C-2
1970	2	7	1	0	0	0	0.0	1	0	2	3	0	.143	.143	0	0	C-2
1971	1	2	0	0	0	0	0.0	0	0	0	0	0	.000	.000	0	0	C-1
4 yrs.	9	27	2	0	0	0	0.0	3	0	4	8	0	.074	.074	0	0	C-9

Buck Etchison

ETCHISON, CLARENCE HAMPTON
B. Jan. 27, 1915, Baltimore, Md.   D. Jan. 24, 1980, East New Market, Md.
BL TL 6'1"   190 lbs.

	G	AB	H	2B	3B	HR	HR %	R	RBI	BB	SO	SB	BA	SA	PH AB	PH H	G by POS
1943 BOS N	10	19	6	3	0	0	0.0	2	2	2	2	0	.316	.474	4	2	1B-6
1944	109	308	66	16	0	8	2.6	30	33	33	50	1	.214	.344	21	3	1B-85
2 yrs.	119	327	72	19	0	8	2.4	32	35	35	52	1	.220	.352	25	5	1B-91

Bobby Etheridge

ETHERIDGE, BOBBY LAMAR (Luke)
B. Nov. 25, 1943, Greenville, Miss.
BR TR 5'9"   170 lbs.

	G	AB	H	2B	3B	HR	HR %	R	RBI	BB	SO	SB	BA	SA	PH AB	PH H	G by POS
1967 SF N	40	115	26	7	2	1	0.9	13	15	7	12	0	.226	.348	4	1	3B-37
1969	56	131	34	9	0	1	0.8	13	10	19	26	0	.260	.351	15	2	3B-39, SS-1
2 yrs.	96	246	60	16	2	2	0.8	26	25	26	38	0	.244	.350	19	3	3B-76, SS-1

Nick Etten

ETTEN, NICHOLAS RAYMOND THOMAS
B. Sept. 19, 1913, Spring Grove, Ill.
BL TL 6'2"   198 lbs.

	G	AB	H	2B	3B	HR	HR %	R	RBI	BB	SO	SB	BA	SA	PH AB	PH H	G by POS
1938 PHI A	22	81	21	6	2	0	0.0	6	11	9	7	1	.259	.383	0	0	1B-22
1939	43	155	39	11	2	3	1.9	20	29	16	11	0	.252	.406	2	0	1B-41
1941 PHI N	151	540	168	27	4	14	2.6	78	79	82	33	9	.311	.454	1	0	1B-150
1942	139	459	121	21	3	8	1.7	37	41	67	26	3	.264	.375	3	2	1B-135
1943 NY A	154	583	158	35	5	14	2.4	78	107	76	31	3	.271	.420	0	0	1B-154
1944	154	573	168	25	4	22	3.8	88	91	97	29	4	.293	.466	0	0	1B-154
1945	152	565	161	24	4	18	3.2	77	111	90	23	2	.285	.437	0	0	1B-152
1946	108	323	75	14	1	9	2.8	37	49	38	35	0	.232	.365	22	4	1B-84
1947 PHI N	14	41	10	4	0	1	2.4	5	8	5	4	0	.244	.415	3	0	1B-11
9 yrs.	937	3320	921	167	25	89	2.7	426	526	480	199	22	.277	.423	31	6	1B-903

WORLD SERIES

	G	AB	H	2B	3B	HR	HR %	R	RBI	BB	SO	SB	BA	SA	PH AB	PH H	G by POS
1943 NY A	5	19	2	0	0	0	0.0	0	2	1	2	0	.105	.105	0	0	1B-5

Ferd Eunick

EUNICK, FERNANDAS BOWEN
B. Apr. 22, 1896, Baltimore, Md.   D. Dec. 9, 1959, Baltimore, Md.
BR TR 5'6"   148 lbs.

	G	AB	H	2B	3B	HR	HR %	R	RBI	BB	SO	SB	BA	SA	PH AB	PH H	G by POS
1917 CLE A	1	2	0	0	0	0	0.0	0	0	0	0	0	.000	.000	0	0	3B-1

Frank Eustace

EUSTACE, FRANK JOHN
B. Nov. 7, 1873, New York, N. Y.   D. Oct. 20, 1932, Pottsville, Pa.
5'9"   160 lbs.

	G	AB	H	2B	3B	HR	HR %	R	RBI	BB	SO	SB	BA	SA	PH AB	PH H	G by POS
1896 LOU N	25	100	17	2	2	1	1.0	18	11	6	14	4	.170	.260	0	0	SS-22, 2B-3

Al Evans

EVANS, ALFRED HUBERT
B. Sept. 28, 1916, Kenly, N. C.   D. Apr. 6, 1979, Wilson, N. C.
BR TR 5'11"   190 lbs.

	G	AB	H	2B	3B	HR	HR %	R	RBI	BB	SO	SB	BA	SA	PH AB	PH H	G by POS
1939 WAS A	7	21	7	0	0	0	0.0	2	1	5	2	0	.333	.333	1	0	C-6
1940	14	25	8	2	0	0	0.0	1	7	6	7	1	.320	.400	4	1	C-9
1941	53	159	44	8	4	1	0.6	16	19	9	18	0	.277	.396	3	0	C-51
1942	74	223	51	4	1	0	0.0	22	10	25	36	3	.229	.256	10	1	C-67
1944	14	22	2	0	0	0	0.0	5	0	2	6	0	.091	.091	1	0	C-8
1945	51	150	39	11	2	2	1.3	19	19	17	22	2	.260	.400	7	0	C-41
1946	88	272	69	10	4	2	0.7	30	30	30	28	1	.254	.342	7	0	C-81
1947	99	319	77	8	3	2	0.6	17	23	28	25	2	.241	.304	5	1	C-94
1948	93	228	59	6	3	2	0.9	19	28	38	20	0	.259	.338	11	2	C-85
1949	109	321	87	12	3	2	0.6	32	42	50	19	4	.271	.346	3	1	C-107
1950	90	289	68	8	3	2	0.7	24	30	29	21	0	.235	.304	1	0	C-88
1951 BOS A	12	24	3	1	0	0	0.0	1	2	4	2	0	.125	.167	1	0	C-10
12 yrs.	704	2053	514	70	23	13	0.6	188	211	243	206	13	.250	.326	54	6	C-647

Barry Evans

EVANS, BARRY STEVEN
B. Nov. 30, 1956, Atlanta, Ga.
BR TR 6'1"   180 lbs.

	G	AB	H	2B	3B	HR	HR %	R	RBI	BB	SO	SB	BA	SA	PH AB	PH H	G by POS
1978 SD N	24	90	24	1	1	0	0.0	7	4	4	10	0	.267	.300	0	0	3B-24
1979	56	162	35	5	0	1	0.6	9	14	5	16	0	.216	.265	1	0	3B-53, SS-2, 2B-1
1980	73	125	29	3	2	1	0.8	11	14	17	21	1	.232	.312	1	0	3B-43, 2B-19, SS-4, 1B-1
1981	54	93	30	5	0	0	0.0	11	7	9	9	2	.323	.376	16	1	3B-24, 1B-10, 2B-6, SS-2
1982 NY A	17	31	8	3	0	0	0.0	2	2	6	6	0	.258	.355	1	0	2B-8, 3B-6, SS-4
5 yrs.	224	501	126	17	3	2	0.4	40	41	41	62	3	.251	.309	19	3	3B-150, 2B-34, SS-12, 1B-11

	G	AB	H	2B	3B	HR	HR %	R	RBI	BB	SO	SB	BA	SA	Pinch Hit AB	Pinch Hit H	G by POS

Darrell Evans

EVANS, DARRELL WAYNE
B. May 26, 1947, Pasadena, Calif.
BL TR 6'2" 200 lbs.

	G	AB	H	2B	3B	HR	HR %	R	RBI	BB	SO	SB	BA	SA	AB	H	G by POS
1969 ATL N	12	26	6	0	0	0	0.0	3	1	1	8	0	.231	.231	4	0	3B-6
1970	12	44	14	1	1	0	0.0	4	9	7	5	0	.318	.386	0	0	3B-12
1971	89	260	63	11	1	12	4.6	42	38	39	54	2	.242	.431	10	1	3B-72, OF-3
1972	125	418	106	12	0	19	4.5	67	71	90	58	4	.254	.419	1	0	3B-123
1973	161	595	167	25	8	41	6.9	114	104	124	104	6	.281	.556	2	0	3B-146, 1B-20
1974	160	571	137	21	3	25	4.4	99	79	126	88	4	.240	.419	0	0	3B-160
1975	156	567	138	22	2	22	3.9	82	73	105	106	12	.243	.406	3	1	3B-156, 1B-3
1976 2 teams			ATL	N	(44G –	.173)		SF	N	(92G –	.222)						
" total	136	396	81	9	1	11	2.8	53	46	72	71	9	.205	.316	7	0	1B-119, 3B-12
1977 SF N	144	461	117	18	3	17	3.7	64	72	69	50	9	.254	.416	16	4	OF-81, 1B-41, 3B-35
1978	159	547	133	24	2	20	3.7	82	78	105	64	4	.243	.404	5	1	3B-155
1979	160	562	142	23	2	17	3.0	68	70	91	80	6	.253	.391	2	1	3B-159
1980	154	556	147	23	0	20	3.6	69	78	83	65	17	.264	.414	4	1	3B-140, 1B-14
1981	102	357	92	13	4	12	3.4	51	48	54	33	2	.258	.417	2	0	3B-87, 1B-12
1982	141	465	119	20	4	16	3.4	64	61	77	64	5	.256	.419	12	2	3B-84, 1B-49, SS-13
1983	142	523	145	29	3	30	5.7	94	82	84	81	6	.277	.516	2	1	1B-113, 3B-32, SS-9
1984 DET A	131	401	93	11	1	16	4.0	60	63	77	70	2	.232	.384	18	3	DH-62, 1B-47, 3B-19
16 yrs.	1984	6749	1700	262	35	278	4.1	1016	973	1204	1001	88	.252	.425	88	15	3B-1398, 1B-418, OF-84, DH-62, SS-22

LEAGUE CHAMPIONSHIP SERIES

1984 DET A	3	10	3	1	0	0	0.0	1	1	1	0	1	.300	.400	0	0	1B-3

WORLD SERIES

1984 DET A	5	15	1	0	0	0	0.0	1	1	4	4	0	.067	.067	0	0	1B-4

Dwight Evans

EVANS, DWIGHT MICHAEL (Dewey)
B. Nov. 3, 1951, Santa Monica, Calif.
BR TR 6'2" 180 lbs.

	G	AB	H	2B	3B	HR	HR %	R	RBI	BB	SO	SB	BA	SA	AB	H	G by POS
1972 BOS A	18	57	15	3	1	1	1.8	2	6	7	13	0	.263	.404	1	1	OF-17
1973	119	282	63	13	1	10	3.5	46	32	40	52	5	.223	.383	3	0	OF-113
1974	133	463	130	19	8	10	2.2	60	70	38	77	4	.281	.421	12	2	OF-122, DH-7
1975	128	412	113	24	6	13	3.2	61	56	47	60	3	.274	.456	6	0	OF-115, DH-7
1976	146	501	121	34	5	17	3.4	61	62	57	92	6	.242	.431	2	1	OF-145, DH-1
1977	73	230	66	9	2	14	6.1	39	36	28	58	4	.287	.526	7	1	OF-63, DH-17
1978	147	497	123	24	2	24	4.8	75	63	65	119	8	.247	.449	4	1	OF-142, DH-4
1979	152	489	134	24	1	21	4.3	69	58	69	76	6	.274	.456	5	1	OF-149
1980	148	463	123	37	5	18	3.9	72	60	64	98	3	.266	.484	5	0	OF-144, DH-2
1981	108	412	122	19	4	22	5.3	84	71	85	85	3	.296	.522	0	0	OF-108
1982	162	609	178	37	7	32	5.3	122	98	112	125	3	.292	.534	0	0	OF-161, DH-1
1983	126	470	112	19	4	22	4.7	74	58	70	97	3	.238	.436	5	0	OF-99, DH-21
1984	162	630	186	37	8	32	5.1	121	104	96	115	3	.295	.532	0	0	OF-161, DH-1
13 yrs.	1622	5515	1486	299	54	236	4.3	886	774	778	1067	51	.269	.472	50	9	OF-1539, DH-61

LEAGUE CHAMPIONSHIP SERIES

1975 BOS A	3	10	1	1	0	0	0.0	1	1	1	2	0	.100	.200	0	0	OF-3

WORLD SERIES

1975 BOS A	7	24	7	1	1	1	4.2	3	5	3	4	0	.292	.542	0	0	OF-7

Jake Evans

EVANS, JACOB (Bloody Jake)
B. Baltimore, Md.   D. Feb. 3, 1907, Baltimore, Md.
5'8" 154 lbs.

	G	AB	H	2B	3B	HR	HR %	R	RBI	BB	SO	SB	BA	SA	AB	H	G by POS
1879 TRO N	72	280	65	9	5	0	0.0	30	17	5	18		.232	.300	0	0	OF-72
1880	47	180	46	8	1	0	0.0	31		7	15		.256	.311	0	0	OF-47, P-1
1881	83	315	76	11	5	0	0.0	35	28	14	30		.241	.308	0	0	OF-83
1882 WOR N	80	334	71	10	4	0	0.0	33	25	7	22		.213	.266	0	0	OF-68, SS-11, 3B-1, 2B-1, P-1
1883 CLE N	90	332	79	13	2	0	0.0	36		8	38		.238	.289	0	0	OF-86, SS-3, 3B-3, 2B-1, P-1
1884	80	313	81	18	3	1	0.3	32	39	15	49		.259	.345	0	0	OF-76, 2B-4, SS-2
1885 BAL AA	20	77	17	1	1	0	0.0	18		7			.221	.260	0	0	OF-20
7 yrs.	472	1831	435	70	21	1	0.1	215	109	63	172		.238	.300	0	0	OF-452, SS-16, 2B-6, 3B-4, P-3

Joe Evans

EVANS, JOSEPH PATTON (Doc)
B. May 15, 1895, Meridian, Miss.   D. Aug. 8, 1953, Gulfport, Miss.
BR TR 5'9" 160 lbs.

	G	AB	H	2B	3B	HR	HR %	R	RBI	BB	SO	SB	BA	SA	AB	H	G by POS
1915 CLE A	42	109	28	4	2	0	0.0	17	11	22	18	6	.257	.330	10	3	3B-30, 2B-2
1916	33	82	12	1	0	0	0.0	4	1	7	12	4	.146	.159	3	0	3B-28
1917	132	385	73	4	5	2	0.5	36	33	42	44	12	.190	.242	1	0	3B-127
1918	79	243	64	6	7	1	0.4	38	22	30	29	7	.263	.358	2	1	3B-74
1919	21	14	1	0	0	0	0.0	9	0	2	1	1	.071	.071	0	0	SS-6
1920	55	172	60	9	9	0	0.0	32	23	15	3	6	.349	.506	2	0	OF-43, SS-6
1921	57	153	51	11	0	0	0.0	36	21	19	5	4	.333	.405	1	0	OF-47
1922	75	145	39	6	2	0	0.0	35	22	8	5	11	.269	.338	0	0	OF-49
1923 WAS A	106	372	98	15	3	0	0.0	42	38	27	18	6	.263	.320	0	2	OF-72, 3B-21, 1B-5
1924 STL A	77	209	53	3	3	0	0.0	30	18	23	12	1	.254	.297	24	9	OF-48
1925	55	159	50	12	0	0	0.0	27	20	16	6	6	.314	.390	6	2	OF-47
11 yrs.	732	2043	529	71	31	3	0.1	306	209	211	152	64	.259	.328	55	17	OF-306, 3B-280, SS-12, 1B-5, 2B-2

WORLD SERIES

1920 CLE A	4	13	4	0	0	0	0.0	0	0	1	0	0	.308	.308	1	0	OF-4

Steve Evans

EVANS, LOUIS RICHARD
B. Feb. 17, 1885, Cleveland, Ohio   D. Dec. 28, 1943, Cleveland, Ohio
BL TL 5'10½" 175 lbs.

	G	AB	H	2B	3B	HR	HR %	R	RBI	BB	SO	SB	BA	SA	AB	H	G by POS
1908 NY N	2	2	1	0	0	0	0.0	0	0	0			.500	.500	1	0	OF-1
1909 STL N	143	498	129	17	6	2	0.4	67	56	66		14	.259	.329	0	0	OF-141, 1B-2
1910	151	506	122	21	8	2	0.4	73	73	78	63	10	.241	.326	0	0	OF-141, 1B-10
1911	154	547	161	24	13	5	0.9	74	71	46	52	13	.294	.413	3	1	OF-150
1912	135	491	139	23	9	6	1.2	59	72	36	51	11	.283	.403	1	0	OF-134

	G	AB	H	2B	3B	HR	HR %	R	RBI	BB	SO	SB	BA	SA	Pinch Hit AB	Pinch Hit H	G by POS

Steve Evans continued

	G	AB	H	2B	3B	HR	HR %	R	RBI	BB	SO	SB	BA	SA	AB	H	G by POS
1913	97	245	61	15	6	1	0.4	18	31	20	28	5	.249	.371	20	4	OF-74, 1B-1
1914 BKN F	145	514	179	41	15	12	2.3	93	96	50		18	.348	.556	7	1	OF-112, 1B-27
1915 2 teams		BKN F	(63G –	.296)			BAL F	(88G –	.315)								
" total	151	556	171	34	10	4	0.7	94	67	63		15	.308	.426	1	0	OF-149, 1B-5
8 yrs.	978	3359	963	175	67	32	1.0	478	466	359	194	86	.287	.407	33	6	OF-902, 1B-45

Bill Everett

EVERETT, WILLIAM L.
B. Dec. 13, 1868, Fort Wayne, Ind.   D. Jan. 19, 1938, Denver, Colo.
TR 6'½" 188 lbs.

	G	AB	H	2B	3B	HR	HR %	R	RBI	BB	SO	SB	BA	SA	AB	H	G by POS
1895 CHI N	133	550	197	16	10	3	0.5	129	88	33	42	47	.358	.440	0	0	3B-130, 2B-3
1896	132	575	184	16	13	2	0.3	130	46	41	43	46	.320	.403	0	0	3B-97, OF-35
1897	92	379	119	14	7	5	1.3	63	39	36		26	.314	.427	1	0	3B-83, OF-8
1898	149	596	190	15	6	0	0.0	102	69	53		28	.319	.364	0	0	1B-149
1899	136	536	166	17	5	1	0.2	87	74	31		30	.310	.366	0	0	1B-136
1900	23	91	24	4	0	0	0.0	10	17	3		2	.264	.308	0	0	1B-23
1901 WAS A	33	115	22	3	2	0	0.0	14	8	15		7	.191	.252	0	0	1B-33
7 yrs.	698	2842	902	85	43	11	0.4	535	341	212	85	186	.317	.389	1	0	1B-341, 3B-310, OF-43, 2B-3

Hoot Evers

EVERS, WALTER ARTHUR
B. Feb. 8, 1921, St. Louis, Mo.
BR TR 6'2" 180 lbs.

	G	AB	H	2B	3B	HR	HR %	R	RBI	BB	SO	SB	BA	SA	AB	H	G by POS
1941 DET A	1	4	0	0	0	0	0.0	0	0	0	2	0	.000	.000	0	0	OF-1
1946	81	304	81	8	4	4	1.3	42	33	34	43	7	.266	.359	2	0	OF-76
1947	126	460	136	24	5	10	2.2	67	67	45	49	8	.296	.435	2	1	OF-123
1948	139	538	169	33	6	10	1.9	81	103	51	31	3	.314	.454	1	0	OF-138
1949	132	432	131	21	6	7	1.6	68	72	70	38	6	.303	.428	10	2	OF-123
1950	143	526	170	35	11	21	4.0	100	103	71	40	5	.323	.551	1	0	OF-139
1951	116	393	88	15	2	11	2.8	47	46	40	47	5	.224	.356	8	2	OF-108
1952 2 teams		DET	A	(1G –	1.000)		BOS	A	(106G –	.262)							
" total	107	402	106	17	4	14	3.5	53	59	29	55	5	.264	.430	2	1	OF-105
1953 BOS N	99	300	72	10	1	11	3.7	39	31	23	41	2	.240	.390	7	1	OF-93
1954 3 teams		BOS	A	(6G –	.000)		NY	N	(12G –	.091)		DET	A	(30G –	.183)		
" total	48	79	12	4	0	1	1.3	7	8	5	16	1	.152	.241	17	1	OF-29
1955 2 teams		BAL	A	(60G –	.238)		CLE	A	(39G –	.288)							
" total	99	251	63	17	2	8	3.2	31	39	22	40	2	.251	.430	16	6	OF-80
1956 2 teams		CLE	A	(3G –	.000)		BAL	A	(48G –	.241)							
" total	51	112	27	3	0	1	0.9	21	4	25	18	1	.241	.295	10	2	OF-36
12 yrs.	1142	3801	1055	187	41	98	2.6	556	565	415	420	45	.278	.426	76	16	OF-1051

Joe Evers

EVERS, JOSEPH FRANCIS
Brother of Johnny Evers.
B. Sept. 10, 1891, Troy, N. Y.   D. Jan. 4, 1949, Albany, N. Y.
BL TR 5'9" 135 lbs.

	G	AB	H	2B	3B	HR	HR %	R	RBI	BB	SO	SB	BA	SA	AB	H	G by POS
1913 NY N	1	0	0	0	0	0	–	0	0	0	0	0	–	–	0	0	

Johnny Evers

EVERS, JOHN JOSEPH (The Trojan, The Crab)
Brother of Joe Evers.
B. July 21, 1881, Troy, N. Y.   D. Mar. 28, 1947, Albany, N. Y.
Manager 1913, 1921, 1924.
Hall of Fame 1946.
BL TR 5'9" 125 lbs.

	G	AB	H	2B	3B	HR	HR %	R	RBI	BB	SO	SB	BA	SA	AB	H	G by POS
1902 CHI N	26	89	20	0	0	0	0.0	7	2	3		1	.225	.225	0	0	2B-18, SS-8
1903	124	464	136	27	7	0	0.0	70	52	19		25	.293	.381	0	0	2B-110, SS-11, 3B-2
1904	152	532	141	14	7	0	0.0	49	47	28		26	.265	.318	0	0	2B-152
1905	99	340	94	11	2	1	0.3	44	37	27		19	.276	.329	0	0	2B-99
1906	154	533	136	17	6	1	0.2	65	51	36		49	.255	.315	0	0	2B-153, 3B-1
1907	151	508	127	18	4	2	0.4	66	51	38		46	.250	.313	0	0	2B-151
1908	126	416	125	19	6	0	0.0	83	37	66		36	.300	.375	2	1	2B-123
1909	127	463	122	19	6	1	0.2	88	24	73		28	.263	.337	0	0	2B-126
1910	125	433	114	11	7	0	0.0	87	28	108	18	28	.263	.321	0	0	2B-125
1911	46	155	35	4	3	0	0.0	29	7	34	10	6	.226	.290	2	0	2B-33, 3B-11
1912	143	478	163	23	11	1	0.2	73	63	74	18	16	.341	.441	0	0	2B-143
1913	135	444	126	20	5	3	0.7	81	49	50	14	11	.284	.372	0	0	2B-135
1914 BOS N	139	491	137	20	3	1	0.2	81	40	87	26	12	.279	.338	0	0	2B-139
1915	83	278	73	4	1	1	0.4	38	22	50	16	7	.263	.295	0	0	2B-83
1916	71	241	52	4	1	0	0.0	33	15	40	19	5	.216	.241	0	0	2B-71
1917 2 teams		BOS	N	(24G –	.193)		PHI	N	(56G –	.224)							
" total	80	266	57	5	1	0	0.0	4	25	12	43	21	9	.214	.252	0	0	2B-73, 3B-7
1922 CHI A	1	3	0	0	0	0	0.0	0	1	2	0	0	.000	.000	0	0	2B-1
1929 BOS N	1	0	0	0	0	0	–	0	0	0	0	0	–	–	0	0	2B-1
18 yrs.	1783	6134	1658	216	70	12	0.2	919	538	778	142	324	.270	.334	4	1	2B-1736, 3B-21, SS-19
WORLD SERIES																	
1906 CHI N	6	20	3	1	0	0	0.0	2	1	1	3	2	.150	.200	0	0	2B-6
1907	5	20	7	2	0	0	0.0	2	1	0	1	3	.350	.450	0	0	2B-5
1908	5	20	7	1	0	0	0.0	5	2	1	2	2	.350	.400	0	0	2B-5
1914 BOS N	4	16	7	0	0	0	0.0	2	2	2	2	1	.438	.438	0	0	2B-4
4 yrs.	20	76	24	4	0	0	0.0	11	6	4	8	8	.316	.368	0	0	2B-20
											8th						

Tom Evers

EVERS, THOMAS FRANCIS
B. Mar. 31, 1852, Troy, N. Y.   D. Mar. 23, 1925, Washington, D. C.

	G	AB	H	2B	3B	HR	HR %	R	RBI	BB	SO	SB	BA	SA	AB	H	G by POS
1882 BAL AA	1	4	0	0	0	0	0.0	0		0			.000	.000	0	0	2B-1
1884 WAS U	109	427	99	6	1	0	0.0	54		7			.232	.251	0	0	2B-109
2 yrs.	110	431	99	6	1	0	0.0	54		7			.230	.248	0	0	2B-110

	G	AB	H	2B	3B	HR	HR %	R	RBI	BB	SO	SB	BA	SA	Pinch Hit AB	H	G by POS

Buck Ewing

EWING, WILLIAM
Brother of John Ewing.
B. Oct. 17, 1859, Hoaglands, Ohio   D. Oct. 20, 1906, Cincinnati, Ohio
Manager 1890, 1895-1900.
Hall of Fame 1939.

BR TR 5'10"   188 lbs.

	G	AB	H	2B	3B	HR	HR %	R	RBI	BB	SO	SB	BA	SA	AB	H	G by POS
1880 TRO N	13	45	8	1	0	0	0.0			1	3		.178	.200	0	0	C-10, OF-4
1881	67	272	68	14	7	0	0.0	40	25	7	8		.250	.353	0	0	C-44, SS-22, OF-2, 3B-1
1882	74	328	89	16	11	2	0.6	67	29	10	15		.271	.405	0	0	3B-44, C-25, 2B-4, OF-1, 1B-1, P-1
1883 NY N	88	376	114	11	13	10	2.7	90		20	14		.303	.481	0	0	C-63, OF-14, 2B-11, SS-4, 3B-1
1884	94	382	106	15	20	3	0.8	90		28	22		.277	.445	0	0	C-80, OF-12, SS-3, 3B-1, P-1
1885	81	342	104	15	12	6	1.8	81		13	17		.304	.471	0	0	C-63, OF-14, 3B-8, SS-1, 1B-1, P-1
1886	73	275	85	11	7	4	1.5	59	31	16	17		.309	.444	0	0	C-50, OF-23, 1B-2
1887	77	318	97	17	13	6	1.9	83	44	30	33	26	.305	.497	0	0	3B-51, 2B-19, C-8
1888	103	415	127	18	15	6	1.4	83	58	24	28	53	.306	.465	0	0	C-78, 3B-21, SS-4, P-2
1889	99	407	133	23	13	4	1.0	91	87	37	32	34	.327	.477	0	0	C-97, P-3, OF-1
1890 NY P	83	352	119	19	15	8	2.3	98	72	39	12	36	.338	.545	0	0	C-81, 2B-1, P-1
1891 NY N	14	49	17	2	1	0	0.0	8	18	5	5	5	.347	.429	0	0	2B-8, C-6
1892	105	393	122	10	15	7	1.8	58	76	38	26	42	.310	.466	0	0	1B-73, C-30, 2B-2
1893 CLE N	116	500	172	28	15	6	1.2	117	122	41	18	47	.344	.496	0	0	OF-112, 2B-5, 1B-1, C-1
1894	53	211	53	12	4	2	0.9	32	39	24	9	18	.251	.374	0	0	OF-52, 2B-1
1895 CIN N	105	434	138	24	13	5	1.2	90	94	30	22	34	.318	.468	0	0	1B-105
1896	69	263	73	14	4	1	0.4	41	38	29	13	41	.278	.373	0	0	1B-69
1897	1	1	0	0	0	0	0.0	0	0	0		0	.000	.000	0	0	1B-1
18 yrs.	1315	5363	1625	250	178	70	1.3	1129	732	392	294	336	.303	.455	0	0	C-636, 1B-253, OF-235, 3B-127, 2B-51, SS-34, P-9

Reuben Ewing

EWING, REUBEN
Born Reuben Cohen.
B. Nov. 30, 1899, Odessa, Russia   D. Oct. 5, 1970, W. Hartford, Conn.

BR TR 5'4½"   150 lbs.

	G	AB	H	2B	3B	HR	HR %	R	RBI	BB	SO	SB	BA	SA	AB	H	G by POS
1921 STL N	3	1	0	0	0	0	0.0	0	0	0	1	0	.000	.000	1	0	SS-1

Sam Ewing

EWING, SAMUEL JAMES
B. Apr. 9, 1949, Nashville, Tenn.

BL TR 6'3"   200 lbs.

	G	AB	H	2B	3B	HR	HR %	R	RBI	BB	SO	SB	BA	SA	AB	H	G by POS
1973 CHI A	11	20	3	1	0	0	0.0	1	2	2	6	0	.150	.200	5	1	1B-4
1976	19	41	9	2	1	0	0.0	3	2	2	8	0	.220	.317	8	3	DH-12, 1B-1
1977 TOR A	97	244	70	8	2	4	1.6	24	34	19	42	1	.287	.385	27	9	OF-46, DH-27, 1B-2
1978	40	56	10	0	0	2	3.6	3	9	5	9	0	.179	.286	29	5	DH-9, OF-3
4 yrs.	167	361	92	11	3	6	1.7	31	47	28	65	1	.255	.352	69	18	OF-49, DH-48, 1B-7

Art Ewoldt

EWOLDT, ARTHUR LEE (Sheriff)
B. Jan. 8, 1892, Paullina, Iowa   D. Dec. 8, 1977, Des Moines, Iowa

BR TR 5'10"   165 lbs.

	G	AB	H	2B	3B	HR	HR %	R	RBI	BB	SO	SB	BA	SA	AB	H	G by POS
1919 PHI A	9	32	7	1	0	0	0.0	2	2	1		5	.219	.250	0	0	3B-9

Homer Ezzell

EZZELL, HOMER ESTELL
B. Feb. 28, 1896, Victoria, Tex.   D. Aug. 3, 1976, San Antonio, Tex.

BR TR 5'10"   158 lbs.

	G	AB	H	2B	3B	HR	HR %	R	RBI	BB	SO	SB	BA	SA	AB	H	G by POS
1923 STL A	89	279	68	6	0	0	0.0	32	14	15	20	4	.244	.265	2	0	3B-73, 2B-8
1924 BOS A	89	273	75	8	4	0	0.0	33	32	13	20	12	.275	.333	4	0	3B-62, SS-21, C-1
1925	58	186	53	6	4	0	0.0	40	15	19	18	9	.285	.360	0	0	3B-47, 2B-9
3 yrs.	236	738	196	20	8	0	0.0	105	61	47	58	25	.266	.314	6	0	3B-182, SS-21, 2B-17, C-1

Jay Faatz

FAATZ, JAYSON S.
B. Oct. 24, 1860, Weedsport, N. Y.   D. Apr. 10, 1923, Syracuse, N. Y.
Manager 1890.

BR TR

	G	AB	H	2B	3B	HR	HR %	R	RBI	BB	SO	SB	BA	SA	AB	H	G by POS
1884 PIT AA	29	112	27	2	3	0	0.0	18		1			.241	.313	0	0	1B-29
1888 CLE AA	120	470	124	10	2	0	0.0	73	51	12		64	.264	.294	0	0	1B-120
1889 CLE N	117	442	102	12	5	2	0.5	50	38	17	28	27	.231	.294	0	0	1B-117
1890 BUF P	32	111	21	0	2	1	0.9	18	16	9	5	2	.189	.252	0	0	1B-32
4 yrs.	298	1135	274	24	12	3	0.3	159	104	39	33	93	.241	.292	0	0	1B-298

Bunny Fabrique

FABRIQUE, ALBERT LaVERNE
B. Dec. 23, 1887, Clinton, Mich.   D. Jan. 10, 1960, Ann Arbor, Mich.

BB TR 5'8½"   150 lbs.

	G	AB	H	2B	3B	HR	HR %	R	RBI	BB	SO	SB	BA	SA	AB	H	G by POS
1916 BKN N	2	2	0	0	0	0	0.0	0	0	0	1	0	.000	.000	0	0	SS-2
1917	25	88	18	3	0	1	1.1	8	3	8	9	0	.205	.273	4	0	SS-21
2 yrs.	27	90	18	3	0	1	1.1	8	3	8	10	0	.200	.267	4	0	SS-23

Len Faedo

FAEDO, LEONARDO LAGO JR.
B. May 13, 1960, Tampa, Fla.

BR TR 6'   170 lbs.

	G	AB	H	2B	3B	HR	HR %	R	RBI	BB	SO	SB	BA	SA	AB	H	G by POS
1980 MIN A	5	8	2	1	0	0	0.0	1	0	0	0	0	.250	.375	0	0	SS-5
1981	12	41	8	0	1	0	0.0	3	6	1	5	0	.195	.244	0	0	SS-12
1982	90	255	62	8	0	3	1.2	16	22	16	22	1	.243	.310	1	0	SS-88, DH-1
1983	51	173	48	7	0	1	0.6	16	18	4	19	0	.277	.335	0	0	SS-51
1984	16	52	13	1	0	1	1.9	6	6	4	3	0	.250	.327	1	0	SS-15, DH-1
5 yrs.	174	529	133	17	1	5	0.9	42	52	25	49	1	.251	.316	2	0	SS-171, DH-2

Fred Fagin

FAGIN, FREDERICK H.
B. Cincinnati, Ohio   Deceased.

	G	AB	H	2B	3B	HR	HR %	R	RBI	BB	SO	SB	BA	SA	AB	H	G by POS
1895 STL N	1	3	1	0	0	0	0.0	2		0	0	0	.333	.333	0	0	C-1

Bill Fahey

FAHEY, WILLIAM ROGER
B. June 14, 1950, Detroit, Mich.

BL TR 6'   200 lbs.

	G	AB	H	2B	3B	HR	HR %	R	RBI	BB	SO	SB	BA	SA	AB	H	G by POS
1971 WAS A	2	8	0	0	0	0	0.0	0	0	0	0	0	.000	.000	0	0	C-2
1972 TEX A	39	119	20	2	0	1	0.8	8	10	12	23	4	.168	.210	1	1	C-39
1974	6	16	4	0	0	0	0.0	1	0	1	0	0	.250	.250	0	0	C-6

	G	AB	H	2B	3B	HR	HR %	R	RBI	BB	SO	SB	BA	SA	Pinch Hit AB	Pinch Hit H	G by POS

Bill Fahey continued

	G	AB	H	2B	3B	HR	HR%	R	RBI	BB	SO	SB	BA	SA	PH AB	PH H	G by POS
1975	21	37	11	1	1	0	0.0	3	3	1	10	0	.297	.378	2	0	C-21
1976	38	80	20	2	0	1	1.3	12	9	11	6	1	.250	.313	1	0	C-38
1977	37	68	15	4	0	0	0.0	3	5	1	8	0	.221	.279	1	0	C-34
1979 SD N	73	209	60	8	1	3	1.4	14	19	21	17	1	.287	.378	6	1	C-68
1980	93	241	62	4	0	1	0.4	18	22	21	16	2	.257	.286	11	2	C-85
1981 DET A	27	67	17	2	0	1	1.5	5	9	2	4	0	.254	.328	0	0	C-27
1982	28	67	10	2	0	0	0.0	7	4	0	5	1	.149	.179	2	0	C-18
1983	19	22	6	1	0	0	0.0	4	2	5	3	0	.273	.318	1	0	
11 yrs.	383	934	225	26	2	7	0.7	75	83	74	93	9	.241	.296	25	4	C-366

Frank Fahey

FAHEY, FRANCIS RAYMOND
B. Jan. 22, 1896, Milford, Mass. D. Mar. 19, 1954, Uxbridge, Mass.
BB TR 6'1" 190 lbs.

	G	AB	H	2B	3B	HR	HR%	R	RBI	BB	SO	SB	BA	SA	PH AB	PH H	G by POS
1918 PHI A	10	17	3	1	0	0	0.0	2	1	0	3	0	.176	.235	1	0	OF-5, P-3

Howard Fahey

FAHEY, HOWARD SIMPSON (Cap, Kid)
B. June 24, 1892, Medford, Mass. D. Oct. 24, 1971, Clearwater, Fla.
BR TR 5'7½" 145 lbs.

	G	AB	H	2B	3B	HR	HR%	R	RBI	BB	SO	SB	BA	SA	PH AB	PH H	G by POS
1912 PHI A	5	8	0	0	0	0	0.0	0	0	0		0	.000	.000	1	0	3B-2, SS-1, 2B-1

Ferris Fain

FAIN, FERRIS ROY (Burrhead)
B. Mar. 29, 1921, San Antonio, Tex.
BL TL 5'11" 180 lbs.

	G	AB	H	2B	3B	HR	HR%	R	RBI	BB	SO	SB	BA	SA	PH AB	PH H	G by POS
1947 PHI A	136	461	134	28	6	7	1.5	70	71	95	34	4	.291	.423	4	0	1B-132
1948	145	520	146	27	6	7	1.3	81	88	113	37	10	.281	.396	0	0	1B-145
1949	150	525	138	21	5	3	0.6	81	78	136	51	8	.263	.339	0	0	1B-150
1950	151	522	147	25	4	10	1.9	83	83	132	26	8	.282	.402	0	0	1B-108, OF-11
1951	117	425	146	30	3	6	1.4	63	57	80	20	0	**.344**	.471	0	0	1B-117
1952	145	538	176	**43**	3	2	0.4	82	59	105	26	3	.327	.429	1	0	1B-144
1953 CHI A	128	446	114	18	2	6	1.3	73	52	108	28	3	.256	.345	1	1	1B-127
1954	65	235	71	10	1	5	2.1	30	51	40	14	5	.302	.417	0	0	1B-64
1955 2 teams	DET A (58G – .264)						CLE A (56G – .254)										
" total	114	258	67	11	0	2	0.8	32	31	94	25	5	.260	.326	13	4	1B-95
9 yrs.	1151	3930	1139	213	30	48	1.2	595	570	903	261	46	.290	.396	19	5	1B-1116, OF-11

Jim Fairey

FAIREY, JAMES BURKE
B. Sept. 22, 1944, Orangeburg, S. C.
BL TL 5'10" 190 lbs.

	G	AB	H	2B	3B	HR	HR%	R	RBI	BB	SO	SB	BA	SA	PH AB	PH H	G by POS
1968 LA N	99	156	31	3	3	1	0.6	17	10	9	32	1	.199	.276	37	8	OF-63
1969 MON N	20	49	14	1	0	1	2.0	6	6	1	7	0	.286	.367	11	2	OF-13
1970	92	211	51	9	3	3	1.4	35	25	14	38	1	.242	.355	37	14	OF-59
1971	92	200	49	8	1	1	0.5	19	19	12	23	3	.245	.310	36	11	OF-58
1972	86	141	33	7	0	1	0.7	9	15	10	21	1	.234	.305	55	10	OF-37
1973 LA N	10	9	2	0	0	0	0.0	0	0	1	1	0	.222	.222	9	2	
6 yrs.	399	766	180	28	7	7	0.9	86	75	47	122	6	.235	.317	185	47	OF-230

Ron Fairly

FAIRLY, RONALD RAY
B. July 12, 1938, Macon, Ga.
BL TL 5'10" 175 lbs.

	G	AB	H	2B	3B	HR	HR%	R	RBI	BB	SO	SB	BA	SA	PH AB	PH H	G by POS
1958 LA N	15	53	15	1	0	2	3.8	6	8	6	7	0	.283	.415	0	0	OF-15
1959	118	244	58	12	1	4	1.6	27	23	31	29	0	.238	.344	31	7	OF-88
1960	14	37	4	0	3	1	2.7	6	3	7	12	0	.108	.351	1	0	OF-13
1961	111	245	79	15	2	10	4.1	42	48	48	22	0	.322	.522	20	6	OF-71, 1B-23
1962	147	460	128	15	7	14	3.0	80	71	75	59	1	.278	.433	7	0	1B-120, OF-48
1963	152	490	133	21	0	12	2.4	62	77	58	69	5	.271	.388	5	2	1B-119, OF-45
1964	150	454	116	19	5	10	2.2	62	74	65	59	4	.256	.385	9	2	1B-141
1965	158	555	152	28	1	9	1.6	73	70	76	72	2	.274	.377	3	0	OF-98, 1B-25
1966	117	351	101	20	0	14	4.0	53	61	52	38	3	.288	.464	6	1	OF-97, 1B-68
1967	153	486	107	19	0	10	2.1	45	55	54	51	1	.220	.321	9	1	OF-105, 1B-36
1968	141	441	103	15	1	4	0.9	32	43	41	61	0	.234	.299	12	4	
1969 2 teams	LA N (30G – .219)						MON N (70G – .289)										
" total	100	317	87	16	6	12	3.8	38	47	37	28	1	.274	.476	10	3	1B-64, OF-31
1970 MON N	119	385	111	19	0	15	3.9	54	61	72	64	10	.288	.455	7	2	1B-118, OF-4
1971	146	447	115	23	0	13	2.9	58	71	81	65	1	.257	.396	17	5	1B-135, OF-10
1972	140	446	124	15	1	17	3.8	51	68	46	45	3	.278	.430	13	4	OF-70, 1B-68
1973	142	413	123	13	1	17	4.1	70	49	86	33	2	.298	.458	25	3	OF-121, 1B-5
1974	101	282	69	9	1	12	4.3	35	43	57	28	2	.245	.411	15	1	1B-67, OF-20
1975 STL N	107	229	69	13	2	7	3.1	32	37	45	22	0	.301	.467	35	12	1B-56, OF-20
1976 2 teams	STL N (73G – .264)						OAK A (15G – .239)										
" total	88	156	40	5	0	3	1.9	22	31	32	24	0	.256	.346	47	11	1B-42
1977 TOR A	132	458	128	24	2	19	4.1	60	64	60	58	0	.279	.465	4	2	DH-58, 1B-40, OF-33
1978 CAL A	91	235	51	5	0	10	4.3	23	40	58	31	0	.217	.366	13	1	1B-78, DH-5
21 yrs.	2442	7184	1913	307	33	215	3.0	931	1044	1052	877	35	.266	.408	289	68	1B-1218, OF-1037, DH-63

WORLD SERIES

	G	AB	H	2B	3B	HR	HR%	R	RBI	BB	SO	SB	BA	SA	PH AB	PH H	G by POS
1959 LA N	3	6	0	0	0	0	0.0	0	0	0	1	0	.000	.000	2	0	OF-4
1963	4	1	0	0	0	0	0.0	0	0	3	0	0	.000	.000	0	0	OF-4
1965	7	29	11	3	0	2	6.9	7	6	0	4	0	.379	.690	0	0	OF-7
1966	3	7	1	0	0	0	0.0	0	0	2	1	0	.143	.143	1	0	OF-2
4 yrs.	20	40	12	3	0	2	5.0	7	6	5	6	0	.300	.525	3	0	OF-17

Anton Falch

FALCH, ANTON C.
B. Dec. 4, 1860, Milwaukee, Wis. D. Mar. 31, 1936, Wauwatosa, Wis.
6'6" 220 lbs.

	G	AB	H	2B	3B	HR	HR%	R	RBI	BB	SO	SB	BA	SA	PH AB	PH H	G by POS
1884 MIL U	5	18	2	0	0	0	0.0						.111	.111	0	0	OF-3, C-2

Bibb Falk

FALK, BIBB AUGUST (Jockey)
Brother of Chet Falk.
B. Jan. 27, 1899, Austin, Tex.
BL TL 6' 175 lbs.

	G	AB	H	2B	3B	HR	HR%	R	RBI	BB	SO	SB	BA	SA	PH AB	PH H	G by POS
1920 CHI A	7	17	5	1	1	0	0.0	1	2	0	5	0	.294	.471	3	1	OF-4
1921	152	585	167	31	11	5	0.9	62	82	37	69	4	.285	.402	3	1	OF-149

	G	AB	H	2B	3B	HR	HR %	R	RBI	BB	SO	SB	BA	SA	Pinch Hit AB	Pinch Hit H	G by POS

Bibb Falk continued

	G	AB	H	2B	3B	HR	HR%	R	RBI	BB	SO	SB	BA	SA	AB	H	G by POS
1922	131	483	144	27	1	12	2.5	58	79	27	55	2	.298	.433	1	0	OF-131
1923	87	274	84	18	6	5	1.8	44	38	25	12	4	.307	.471	7	2	OF-80
1924	138	526	185	37	8	6	1.1	77	99	47	21	6	.352	.487	3	1	OF-134
1925	154	602	181	35	9	4	0.7	80	99	51	25	4	.301	.409	0	0	OF-154
1926	155	566	195	43	4	8	1.4	86	108	66	22	9	.345	.477	0	0	OF-155
1927	145	535	175	35	6	9	1.7	76	83	52	19	5	.327	.465	0	0	OF-145
1928	98	286	83	18	4	1	0.3	42	37	25	16	5	.290	.392	16	3	OF-78
1929 CLE A	126	430	133	30	7	13	3.0	66	94	42	14	4	.309	.502	4	1	OF-121
1930	82	191	62	12	1	4	2.1	34	36	23	8	2	.325	.461	34	13	OF-42
1931	79	161	49	13	1	2	1.2	30	28	17	13	1	.304	.435	43	14	OF-33
12 yrs.	1354	4656	1463	300	59	69	1.5	656	785	412	279	46	.314	.448	114	36	OF-1226

George Fallon

FALLON, GEORGE DECATUR (Flash)
B. July 8, 1916, Jersey City, N. J.   BR TR 5'9"   155 lbs.

	G	AB	H	2B	3B	HR	HR%	R	RBI	BB	SO	SB	BA	SA	AB	H	G by POS
1937 BKN N	4	8	2	1	0	0	0.0	0	0	1	0	0	.250	.375	0	0	2B-4
1943 STL N	36	78	18	1	0	0	0.0	6	5	2	9	0	.231	.244	0	0	2B-36
1944	69	141	28	6	0	1	0.7	16	9	16	11	1	.199	.262	0	0	2B-38, SS-24, 3B-6
1945	24	55	13	2	1	0	0.0	4	7	6	6	1	.236	.309	0	0	SS-20, 2B-4
4 yrs.	133	282	61	10	1	1	0.4	26	21	25	26	2	.216	.270	0	0	2B-82, SS-44, 3B-6

WORLD SERIES

	G	AB	H	2B	3B	HR	HR%	R	RBI	BB	SO	SB	BA	SA	AB	H	G by POS
1944 STL N	2	2	0	0	0	0	0.0	0	0	0	1	0	.000	.000	0	0	2B-2

Pete Falsey

FALSEY, PETER JAMES
B. Apr. 24, 1891, New Haven, Conn.   D. May 23, 1976, Los Angeles, Calif.   BL TL 5'6½" 132 lbs.

	G	AB	H	2B	3B	HR	HR%	R	RBI	BB	SO	SB	BA	SA	AB	H	G by POS
1914 PIT N	3	1	0	0	0	0	0.0	0	0	0	1	0	.000	.000	1	0	

Jim Fanning

FANNING, WILLIAM JAMES
B. Sept. 14, 1927, Chicago, Ill.
Manager 1981-82, 1984.   BR TR 5'11"   180 lbs.

	G	AB	H	2B	3B	HR	HR%	R	RBI	BB	SO	SB	BA	SA	AB	H	G by POS
1954 CHI N	11	38	7	0	0	0	0.0	2	1	1	7	0	.184	.184	0	0	C-11
1955	5	10	0	0	0	0	0.0	0	0	1	2	0	.000	.000	0	0	C-5
1956	1	4	1	0	0	0	0.0	0	0	0	0	0	.250	.250	0	0	C-1
1957	47	89	16	2	0	0	0.0	3	4	4	17	0	.180	.202	12	1	C-35
4 yrs.	64	141	24	2	0	0	0.0	5	5	6	26	0	.170	.184	12	1	C-52

Carmen Fanzone

FANZONE, CARMEN RONALD
B. Aug. 30, 1941, Detroit, Mich.   BR TR 6'   200 lbs.

	G	AB	H	2B	3B	HR	HR%	R	RBI	BB	SO	SB	BA	SA	AB	H	G by POS
1970 BOS A	10	15	3	1	0	0	0.0	0	3	2	2	0	.200	.267	4	0	3B-5
1971 CHI N	12	43	8	2	0	2	4.7	5	5	2	7	0	.186	.372	2	1	OF-6, 3B-3, 1B-2
1972	86	222	50	11	0	8	3.6	26	42	35	45	2	.225	.383	15	4	3B-36, 1B-21, 2B-13, OF-1, SS-1
1973	64	150	41	7	0	6	4.0	22	22	20	38	1	.273	.440	15	5	3B-25, 1B-24, OF-6
1974	65	158	30	6	0	4	2.5	13	22	15	27	0	.190	.304	15	4	3B-35, 2B-10, 1B-7, OF-1
5 yrs.	237	588	132	27	0	20	3.4	66	94	74	119	3	.224	.372	51	14	3B-104, 1B-54, 2B-23, OF-14, SS-1

Bob Farley

FARLEY, ROBERT JACOB
B. Nov. 15, 1937, Watsontown, Pa.   BL TL 6'2"   200 lbs.

	G	AB	H	2B	3B	HR	HR%	R	RBI	BB	SO	SB	BA	SA	AB	H	G by POS
1961 SF N	13	20	2	0	0	0	0.0	3	1	3	5	0	.100	.100	8	1	OF-3, 1B-1
1962 2 teams		CHI A (35G – .189)				DET A (36G – .160)											
" total	71	103	18	3	1	2	1.9	16	8	27	23	0	.175	.282	33	4	1B-20, OF-6
2 yrs.	84	123	20	3	1	2	1.6	19	9	30	28	0	.163	.252	41	5	1B-21, OF-9

Tom Farley

FARLEY, THOMAS T.
B. Chicago, Ill. Deceased.

	G	AB	H	2B	3B	HR	HR%	R	RBI	BB	SO	SB	BA	SA	AB	H	G by POS
1884 WAS AA	14	52	11	4	0	0	0.0	5		1			.212	.288	0	0	OF-14

Alex Farmer

FARMER, ALEXANDER JOHNSON
B. May 9, 1880, New York, N. Y.   D. Mar. 5, 1920, New York, N. Y.   BR TR 6'   175 lbs.

	G	AB	H	2B	3B	HR	HR%	R	RBI	BB	SO	SB	BA	SA	AB	H	G by POS
1908 BKN N	12	30	5	1	0	0	0.0	1	2	1		0	.167	.200	1	0	C-11

Bill Farmer

FARMER, WILLIAM
B. Dec. 27, 1870, Dublin, Ireland Deceased.   BR TR 5'11½"

	G	AB	H	2B	3B	HR	HR%	R	RBI	BB	SO	SB	BA	SA	AB	H	G by POS
1888 2 teams		PIT N (2G – .000)				PHI AA (3G – .167)											
" total	5	16	2	0	0	0	0.0	0	1	0	1	0	.125	.125	0	0	C-4, OF-1

Jack Farmer

FARMER, FLOYD HASKELL
B. July 14, 1892, Granville, Tenn.   D. May 21, 1970, Columbia, La.   BR TR 6'   180 lbs.

	G	AB	H	2B	3B	HR	HR%	R	RBI	BB	SO	SB	BA	SA	AB	H	G by POS
1916 PIT N	55	166	45	6	4	0	0.0	10	14	7	24	1	.271	.355	7	0	2B-31, OF-15, SS-4, 3B-1
1918 CLE A	7	9	2	0	0	0	0.0	1	1	0	3	2	.222	.222	4	2	3B-5
2 yrs.	62	175	47	6	4	0	0.0	11	15	7	27	3	.269	.349	11	2	2B-31, OF-15, 3B-6, SS-4

Sid Farrar

FARRAR, SIDNEY DOUGLAS
B. Aug. 10, 1859, Paris Hill, Me.   D. May 7, 1935, New York, N. Y.   TR 5'10"

	G	AB	H	2B	3B	HR	HR%	R	RBI	BB	SO	SB	BA	SA	AB	H	G by POS
1883 PHI N	99	377	88	19	7	1	0.3	41		4	37		.233	.329	0	0	1B-99
1884	111	428	105	16	6	1	0.2	62		9	25		.245	.318	0	0	1B-111
1885	111	420	103	20	3	3	0.7	49		28	34		.245	.329	0	0	1B-111
1886	118	439	109	19	7	5	1.1	55	50	16	47		.248	.358	0	0	1B-118
1887	116	443	125	20	9	4	0.9	83	72	42	29	24	.282	.395	0	0	1B-116
1888	131	508	124	24	7	1	0.2	53	53	31	38	21	.244	.325	0	0	1B-131
1889	130	477	128	22	2	3	0.6	70	58	52	36	28	.268	.342	0	0	1B-130
1890 PHI P	127	481	122	17	11	1	0.2	84	69	51	23	9	.254	.341	0	0	1B-127
8 yrs.	943	3573	904	157	52	19	0.5	497	301	233	269	82	.253	.342	0	0	1B-943

	G	AB	H	2B	3B	HR	HR %	R	RBI	BB	SO	SB	BA	SA	Pinch Hit AB	Pinch Hit H	G by POS

Bill Farrell

FARRELL, WILLIAM
B. Bridgeport, Conn.   Deceased.

	G	AB	H	2B	3B	HR	HR %	R	RBI	BB	SO	SB	BA	SA	AB	H	G by POS
1882 PHI AA	2	7	2	1	0	0	0.0	2		1			.286	.429	0	0	OF-2, C-1
1883 BAL AA	2	7	0	0	0	0	0.0	0		1			.000	.000	0	0	SS-2
2 yrs.	4	14	2	1	0	0	0.0	2		2			.143	.214	0	0	OF-2, SS-2, C-1

Doc Farrell

FARRELL, EDWARD STEPHEN   BR TR 5'8"   160 lbs.
B. Dec. 26, 1901, Johnson City, N. Y.   D. Dec. 20, 1966, Livingston, N. J.

	G	AB	H	2B	3B	HR	HR %	R	RBI	BB	SO	SB	BA	SA	AB	H	G by POS
1925 NY N	27	56	12	0	0	0	0.0	6	4	4	6	0	.214	.232	3	0	SS-13, 3B-7, 2B-1
1926	67	171	49	10	1	2	1.2	19	23	12	17	4	.287	.392	8	2	SS-53, 2B-3
1927 2 teams		NY	N (42G – .387)		BOS	N	(110G – .292)										
" total	152	566	179	23	3	4	0.7	57	92	26	32	4	.316	.389	4	2	SS-93, 2B-40, 3B-20
1928 BOS N	134	483	104	14	2	3	0.6	36	43	26	26	3	.215	.271	1	0	SS-132, 2B-1
1929 2 teams		BOS	N (5G – .125)		NY	N	(63G – .213)										
" total	68	186	39	6	0	0	0.0	18	18	9	18	2	.210	.242	8	1	3B-28, 2B-26, SS-5
1930 2 teams		STL	N (23G – .213)		CHI	N	(46G – .292)										
" total	69	174	46	7	1	1	0.6	24	22	13	7	1	.264	.333	2	0	2B-16, SS-5, 3B-2, 3B-1
1932 NY A	26	63	11	1	1	0	0.0	4	4	2	8	0	.175	.222	0	0	SS-22, 2B-20
1933	44	93	25	0	0	0	0.0	16	6	16	6	0	.269	.269	0	0	2B-4
1935 BOS A	4	7	2	1	0	0	0.0	1	1	1	0	0	.286	.429	0	0	2B-4
9 yrs.	591	1799	467	63	8	10	0.6	181	213	109	120	14	.260	.320	26	5	SS-376, 2B-118, 3B-56, 1B-3

Duke Farrell

FARRELL, CHARLES ANDREW   BB TR 6'2"   180 lbs.
B. Aug. 31, 1866, Oakdale, Mass.   D. Feb. 15, 1925, Boston, Mass.

	G	AB	H	2B	3B	HR	HR %	R	RBI	BB	SO	SB	BA	SA	AB	H	G by POS
1888 CHI N	64	241	56	6	3	3	1.2	34	19	4	41	8	.232	.320	0	0	C-33, OF-31, 1B-1
1889	101	407	101	19	7	11	2.7	66	75	41	21	13	.248	.410	0	0	C-76, OF-25
1890 CHI P	117	451	131	21	12	2	0.4	79	84	42	28	8	.290	.404	0	0	C-90, 1B-22, OF-10
1891 BOS N	122	473	143	19	13	12	2.5	108	110	59	48	21	.302	.474	0	0	3B-66, C-37, OF-23, 1B-4
1892 PIT N	152	605	130	10	13	8	1.3	96	77	46	53	20	.215	.314	0	0	3B-133, OF-20
1893 WAS N	124	511	143	13	13	4	0.8	84	75	47	12	11	.280	.380	0	0	C-81, 3B-41, 1B-3
1894 NY N	114	401	114	20	12	4	1.0	47	66	35	15	9	.284	.424	1	0	C-104, 3B-5, 1B-4
1895	90	312	90	16	9	1	0.3	38	58	38	18	11	.288	.407	0	0	C-62, 3B-24, 1B-2
1896 2 teams		NY	N (58G – .283)		WAS	N	(37G – .300)										
" total	95	321	93	14	6	2	0.6	41	67	26	10	4	.290	.389	10	4	C-52, 3B-21, SS-13
1897 WAS N	78	261	84	9	6	0	0.0	41	53	17		5	.322	.402	14	8	C-63, 1B-1
1898	99	338	106	12	6	1	0.3	47	53	34		12	.314	.393	10	5	C-61, 1B-28
1899 2 teams		WAS	N (5G – .333)		BKN	N	(80G – .299)										
" total	85	266	80	11	7	2	0.8	42	56	37		7	.301	.417	3	1	C-82
1900 BKN N	76	273	75	11	5	0	0.0	33	39	11		3	.275	.352	2	0	C-74
1901	80	284	84	10	6	1	0.4	38	31	7		7	.296	.384	4	3	C-59, 1B-17
1902	74	264	64	5	2	0	0.0	14	24	12		6	.242	.277	2	0	C-49, 1B-24
1903 BOS A	17	52	21	5	1	0	0.0	5	8	5		1	.404	.538	0	0	C-17
1904	68	198	42	9	2	0	0.0	11	15	15		1	.212	.278	11	1	C-56
1905	7	21	6	1	0	0	0.0	2	2	1		0	.286	.333	0	0	C-7
18 yrs.	1563	5679	1563	211	123	51	0.9	826	912	477	246	150	.275	.383	59	23	C-1003, 3B-290, OF-109, 1B-106, SS-13

WORLD SERIES

	G	AB	H	2B	3B	HR	HR %	R	RBI	BB	SO	SB	BA	SA	AB	H	G by POS
1903 BOS A	2	2	0	0	0	0	0.0	0	1	0	0	0	.000	.000	2	0	

Jack Farrell

FARRELL, JOHN A. (Moose)   BR TR 5'9"   165 lbs.
B. July 5, 1857, Newark, N. J.   D. Feb. 10, 1914, Overbrook, N. J.

	G	AB	H	2B	3B	HR	HR %	R	RBI	BB	SO	SB	BA	SA	AB	H	G by POS
1879 2 teams		SYR	N (54G – .303)		PRO	N	(12G – .255)										
" total	66	292	86	8	2	1	0.3	45	26	3	13		.295	.346	0	0	2B-66
1880 PRO N	80	339	92	12	5	3	0.9	46	36	10	6		.271	.363	0	0	2B-80
1881	84	345	82	16	5	5	1.4	69	36	29	23		.238	.357	0	0	2B-82, OF-3
1882	84	366	93	21	6	2	0.5	67		16	23		.254	.361	0	0	2B-84
1883	95	420	128	24	11	3	0.7	92		15	21		.305	.436	0	0	2B-95
1884	111	469	102	13	6	1	0.2	70		35	44		.217	.277	0	0	2B-109, 3B-3
1885	68	257	53	7	1	1	0.4	27	19	10	25		.206	.253	0	0	2B-68
1886 2 teams		PHI	N (17G – .183)		WAS	N	(47G – .240)										
" total	64	231	52	11	5	2	0.9	31	21	18	23		.225	.342	0	0	2B-64
1887 WAS N	87	339	75	14	9	0	0.0	40	41	20	12	31	.221	.316	0	0	SS-48, 2B-40
1888 BAL AA	103	398	81	19	5	3	0.8	72	36	26		29	.204	.299	0	0	SS-54, 2B-52
1889	42	157	33	3	0	1	0.6	25	26	15	15	14	.210	.248	0	0	SS-42
11 yrs.	884	3613	877	148	55	22	0.6	584	241	197	205	74	.243	.332	0	0	2B-740, SS-144, OF-3, 3B-3

Jack Farrell

FARRELL, JOHN J   BB TR 5'8"   145 lbs.
B. June 16, 1892, Chicago, Ill.   D. Mar. 24, 1918, Chicago, Ill.

	G	AB	H	2B	3B	HR	HR %	R	RBI	BB	SO	SB	BA	SA	AB	H	G by POS
1914 CHI F	156	524	123	23	4	0	0.0	58	35	52		12	.235	.294	0	0	2B-155, SS-3
1915	70	222	48	10	1	0	0.0	27	14	25		8	.216	.270	0	0	2B-70, SS-1
2 yrs.	226	746	171	33	5	0	0.0	85	49	77		20	.229	.287	0	0	2B-225, SS-4

Joe Farrell

FARRELL, JOSEPH F.   5'6"   160 lbs.
B. 1858, Brooklyn, N. Y.   D. Apr. 18, 1893, Brooklyn, N. Y.

	G	AB	H	2B	3B	HR	HR %	R	RBI	BB	SO	SB	BA	SA	AB	H	G by POS
1882 DET N	69	283	70	12	2	1	0.4	34	24	4	20		.247	.314	0	0	3B-42, 2B-18, SS-9
1883	101	444	108	13	5	0	0.0	58		5	29		.243	.295	0	0	3B-101
1884	110	461	104	10	5	3	0.7	59		14	66		.226	.289	0	0	3B-110, OF-1
1886 BAL AA	73	301	63	8	3	1	0.3	36		12			.209	.266	0	0	2B-45, 3B-27, OF-1
4 yrs.	353	1489	345	43	15	5	0.3	187	24	35	115		.232	.291	0	0	3B-280, 2B-63, SS-9, OF-2

John Farrell

FARRELL, JOHN SEBASTIAN   BR TR 5'10"   160 lbs.
B. Dec. 4, 1876, Covington, Ky.   D. May 13, 1921, Kansas City, Mo.

	G	AB	H	2B	3B	HR	HR %	R	RBI	BB	SO	SB	BA	SA	AB	H	G by POS
1901 WAS A	135	555	151	32	11	3	0.5	100	63	52		25	.272	.386	0	0	2B-72, OF-62, 3B-1
1902 STL N	138	565	141	13	5	0	0.0	68	25	43		9	.250	.290	0	0	2B-118, SS-21
1903	130	519	141	25	8	1	0.2	83	32	48		17	.272	.356	0	0	2B-118, OF-12

	G	AB	H	2B	3B	HR	HR %	R	RBI	BB	SO	SB	BA	SA	Pinch Hit AB	Pinch Hit H	G by POS

John Farrell continued

	G	AB	H	2B	3B	HR	HR %	R	RBI	BB	SO	SB	BA	SA	AB	H	G by POS
1904	131	509	130	23	3	0	0.0	72	20	46		16	.255	.312	1	0	2B-130
1905	7	24	4	0	1	0	0.0	6	1	4		1	.167	.250	0	0	2B-7
5 yrs.	541	2172	567	93	28	4	0.2	329	141	193		68	.261	.335	1	0	2B-445, OF-74, SS-21, 3B-1

Kerby Farrell

FARRELL, MAJOR KERBY
B. Sept. 3, 1913, Leapwood, Tenn.   D. Dec. 17, 1975, Nashville, Tenn.
Manager 1957.
BL TL 5'11" 172 lbs.

	G	AB	H	2B	3B	HR	HR %	R	RBI	BB	SO	SB	BA	SA	AB	H	G by POS
1943 BOS N	85	280	75	14	1	0	0.0	11	21	16	15	1	.268	.325	11	2	1B-69, P-5
1945 CHI A	103	396	102	11	3	0	0.0	44	34	24	18	4	.258	.301	6	3	1B-97
2 yrs.	188	676	177	25	4	0	0.0	55	55	40	33	5	.262	.311	17	5	1B-166, P-5

John Farrow

FARROW, JOHN JACOB
B. 1852, Verplanck's Point, N. Y.   D. Dec. 31, 1914, Perth Amboy, N. J.
BL TR

	G	AB	H	2B	3B	HR	HR %	R	RBI	BB	SO	SB	BA	SA	AB	H	G by POS
1884 BKN AA	16	58	11	2	0	0	0.0	7		3			.190	.224	0	0	C-16

Buck Fausett

FAUSETT, ROBERT SHAW (Leaky)
B. Apr. 8, 1908, Sheridan, Ark.
BL TR 5'10" 170 lbs.

	G	AB	H	2B	3B	HR	HR %	R	RBI	BB	SO	SB	BA	SA	AB	H	G by POS
1944 CIN N	13	31	3	0	1	0	0.0	2	1	1	2	0	.097	.161	5	0	3B-6, P-2

Joe Fautsch

FAUTSCH, JOSEPH ROAMAN
B. Feb. 28, 1887, Minneapolis, Minn.   D. Mar. 16, 1971, Newhope, Minn.
BR TR 5'10" 162 lbs.

	G	AB	H	2B	3B	HR	HR %	R	RBI	BB	SO	SB	BA	SA	AB	H	G by POS
1916 CHI A	1	1	0	0	0	0	0.0	0	0	0	0	0	.000	.000	1	0	

Ernie Fazio

FAZIO, ERNEST JOSEPH
B. Jan. 25, 1942, Oakland, Calif.
BR TR 5'7" 165 lbs.

	G	AB	H	2B	3B	HR	HR %	R	RBI	BB	SO	SB	BA	SA	AB	H	G by POS
1962 HOU N	12	12	1	0	0	0	0.0	3	1	2	5	0	.083	.083	1	0	SS-10
1963	102	228	42	10	3	2	0.9	31	5	27	70	4	.184	.281	9	2	2B-84, SS-1, 3B-1
1966 KC A	27	34	7	0	1	0	0.0	3	2	4	10	1	.206	.265	12	1	2B-10, SS-4
3 yrs.	141	274	50	10	4	2	0.7	37	8	33	85	5	.182	.270	22	3	2B-94, SS-15, 3B-1

Al Federoff

FEDEROFF, ALFRED (Whitey)
B. July 11, 1924, Bairford, Pa.
BR TR 5'10½" 165 lbs.

	G	AB	H	2B	3B	HR	HR %	R	RBI	BB	SO	SB	BA	SA	AB	H	G by POS
1951 DET A	2	4	0	0	0	0	0.0	0	0	0	0	0	.000	.000	0	0	2B-1
1952	74	231	56	4	2	0	0.0	14	14	16	13	1	.242	.277	0	0	2B-70, SS-7
2 yrs.	76	235	56	4	2	0	0.0	14	14	16	13	1	.238	.272	0	0	2B-71, SS-7

Bill Fehring

FEHRING, WILLIAM PAUL (Dutch)
B. May 31, 1912, Columbus, Ind.
BB TR 6' 195 lbs.

	G	AB	H	2B	3B	HR	HR %	R	RBI	BB	SO	SB	BA	SA	AB	H	G by POS
1934 CHI A	1	1	0	0	0	0	0.0	0	0	0	1	0	.000	.000	0	0	C-1

Eddie Feinberg

FEINBERG, EDWARD (Itzy)
B. Sept. 29, 1918, Philadelphia, Pa.
BB TR 5'9" 165 lbs.

	G	AB	H	2B	3B	HR	HR %	R	RBI	BB	SO	SB	BA	SA	AB	H	G by POS
1938 PHI N	10	20	3	0	0	0	0.0	0	0	0	1	0	.150	.150	0	0	SS-4, OF-2
1939	6	18	4	1	0	0	0.0	2	0	2	0	0	.222	.278	0	0	2B-4, SS-1
2 yrs.	16	38	7	1	0	0	0.0	2	0	2	1	0	.184	.211	0	0	SS-5, 2B-4, OF-2

Marv Felderman

FELDERMAN, MARVIN WILFRED
B. Dec. 20, 1915, Bellevue, Iowa
BR TR 6'1" 187 lbs.

	G	AB	H	2B	3B	HR	HR %	R	RBI	BB	SO	SB	BA	SA	AB	H	G by POS
1942 CHI N	3	6	1	0	0	0	0.0	0	0	1	4	0	.167	.167	0	0	C-2

Gus Felix

FELIX, AUGUST GUENTHER
B. May 24, 1895, Cincinnati, Ohio   D. May 12, 1960, Montgomery, Ala.
BR TR 6' 180 lbs.

	G	AB	H	2B	3B	HR	HR %	R	RBI	BB	SO	SB	BA	SA	AB	H	G by POS
1923 BOS N	139	506	138	17	2	6	1.2	64	44	51	65	8	.273	.350	3	1	OF-123, 2B-5, 3B-4
1924	59	204	43	7	1	1	0.5	25	10	18	16	0	.211	.270	3	2	OF-51
1925	121	459	141	25	7	2	0.4	60	66	30	34	5	.307	.405	7	1	OF-114
1926 BKN N	134	432	121	21	7	3	0.7	64	53	51	32	9	.280	.382	8	1	OF-125
1927	130	445	118	21	8	0	0.0	43	57	39	47	6	.265	.348	11	4	OF-119
5 yrs.	583	2046	561	91	25	12	0.6	256	230	189	194	28	.274	.361	32	9	OF-532, 2B-5, 3B-4

Jack Feller

FELLER, JACK LELAND
B. Dec. 10, 1936, Adrian, Mich.
BR TR 5'10½" 185 lbs.

	G	AB	H	2B	3B	HR	HR %	R	RBI	BB	SO	SB	BA	SA	AB	H	G by POS
1958 DET A	1	0	0	0	0	0	–	0	0	0	0	0	–	–	0	0	C-1

Happy Felsch

FELSCH, OSCAR EMIL
B. Aug. 22, 1891, Milwaukee, Wis.   D. Aug. 17, 1964, Milwaukee, Wis.
BR TL 5'11" 175 lbs.

	G	AB	H	2B	3B	HR	HR %	R	RBI	BB	SO	SB	BA	SA	AB	H	G by POS
1915 CHI A	121	427	106	18	11	3	0.7	65	53	51	59	16	.248	.363	3	0	OF-118
1916	146	546	164	24	12	7	1.3	73	70	31	67	13	.300	.427	4	2	OF-141
1917	152	575	177	17	10	6	1.0	75	102	33	52	26	.308	.403	0	0	OF-152
1918	53	206	52	2	5	1	0.5	16	20	15	13	6	.252	.325	0	0	OF-53
1919	135	502	138	34	11	7	1.4	68	86	40	35	19	.275	.428	0	0	OF-135
1920	142	556	188	40	15	14	2.5	88	115	37	25	8	.338	.540	0	0	OF-142
6 yrs.	749	2812	825	135	64	38	1.4	385	446	207	251	88	.293	.427	7	2	OF-741

WORLD SERIES

	G	AB	H	2B	3B	HR	HR %	R	RBI	BB	SO	SB	BA	SA	AB	H	G by POS
1917 CHI A	6	22	6	1	0	1	4.5	4	3	1	5	0	.273	.455	0	0	OF-6
1919	8	26	5	1	0	0	0.0	2	3	1	4	0	.192	.231	0	0	OF-8
2 yrs.	14	48	11	2	0	1	2.1	6	6	2	9	0	.229	.333	0	0	OF-14

John Felske

FELSKE, JOHN FREDRICK
B. May 30, 1942, Chicago, Ill.
BR TR 6'3" 195 lbs.

	G	AB	H	2B	3B	HR	HR %	R	RBI	BB	SO	SB	BA	SA	AB	H	G by POS
1968 CHI N	4	2	0	0	0	0	0.0	0	0	0	1	0	.000	.000	1	0	C-3
1972 MIL A	37	80	11	3	0	1	1.3	6	5	8	23	0	.138	.213	8	2	C-23, 1B-8
1973	13	22	3	0	1	0	0.0	1	4	1	11	0	.136	.227	1	0	C-7, 1B-6
3 yrs.	54	104	14	3	1	1	1.0	7	9	9	35	0	.135	.212	10	2	C-33, 1B-14

	G	AB	H	2B	3B	HR	HR %	R	RBI	BB	SO	SB	BA	SA	Pinch Hit AB	Pinch Hit H	G by POS

Frank Fennelly

FENNELLY, FRANCIS JOHN   BR TR 5'8"   168 lbs.
B. Feb. 18, 1860, Fall River, Mass.   D. Aug. 4, 1920, Fall River, Mass.

	G	AB	H	2B	3B	HR	HR %	R	RBI	BB	SO	SB	BA	SA	AB	H	G by POS
1884 2 teams	WAS	AA	(62G –	.292)		CIN	AA	(28G –	.352)								
" total	90	379	118	22	15	4	1.1	94		31			.311	.480	0	0	SS-88, 2B-4
1885 CIN AA	112	454	124	14	17	10	2.2	82		38			.273	.445	0	0	SS-112
1886	132	497	124	13	17	6	1.2	113		60			.249	.380	0	0	SS-132
1887	134	526	140	15	16	8	1.5	133		82		74	.266	.401	0	0	SS-134
1888 2 teams	CIN	AA	(120G –	.196)		PHI	AA	(15G –	.234)								
" total	135	495	99	10	9	3	0.6	77	68	72		48	.200	.275	0	0	SS-127, OF-4, 2B-4
1889 PHI AA	138	513	132	20	5	1	0.2	70	64	65	78	15	.257	.322	0	0	SS-138
1890 B-B AA	45	178	44	8	3	2	1.1	40		30		6	.247	.360	0	0	SS-38, 3B-7
7 yrs.	786	3042	781	102	82	34	1.1	609	131	378	78	143	.257	.378	0	0	SS-769, 2B-8, 3B-7, OF-4

Bobby Fenwick

FENWICK, ROBERT RICHARD (Bloop)   BR TR 5'9"   165 lbs.
B. Dec. 10, 1946, Okinawa

	G	AB	H	2B	3B	HR	HR %	R	RBI	BB	SO	SB	BA	SA	AB	H	G by POS
1972 HOU N	36	50	9	3	0	0	0.0	7	4	3	13	0	.180	.240	5	0	2B-17, SS-4, 3B-2
1973 STL N	5	6	1	0	0	0	0.0	0	1	0	2	0	.167	.167	2	0	2B-3
2 yrs.	41	56	10	3	0	0	0.0	7	5	3	15	0	.179	.232	7	0	2B-20, SS-4, 3B-2

Bob Ferguson

FERGUSON, ROBERT V. (Death to Flying Things)   BB TR 5'9½"   149 lbs.
B. Jan. 31, 1845, Brooklyn, N.Y.   D. May 3, 1894, Brooklyn, N.Y.
Manager 1871-84, 1886-87.

	G	AB	H	2B	3B	HR	HR %	R	RBI	BB	SO	SB	BA	SA	AB	H	G by POS
1876 HAR N	69	310	82	8	5	0	0.0	48	32	2	11		.265	.323	0	0	3B-69
1877	58	254	65	7	2	0	0.0	40	35	3	10		.256	.299	0	0	3B-56, P-3
1878 CHI N	61	259	91	10	2	0	0.0	44	39	10	12		.351	.405	0	0	SS-57, 2B-4, C-1
1879 TRO N	30	123	31	5	2	0	0.0	18	4	4	3		.252	.325	0	0	3B-24, 2B-6
1880	82	332	87	9	0	0	0.0	55		24	24		.262	.289	0	0	2B-82
1881	85	339	96	13	5	1	0.3	56	35	29	12		.283	.360	0	0	2B-85
1882	81	319	82	15	2	0	0.0	44	33	23	21		.257	.317	0	0	2B-79, SS-2
1883 PHI N	86	329	85	9	2	0	0.0	39		18	21		.258	.298	0	0	2B-86, P-1
1884 PIT AA	10	41	6	0	0	0	0.0	2		0			.146	.146	0	0	OF-6, 1B-3, 3B-1
9 yrs.	562	2306	625	76	20	1	0.0	346	178	113	114		.271	.323	0	0	2B-342, 3B-150, SS-59, OF-6, P-4, 1B-3, C-1

Charlie Ferguson

FERGUSON, CHARLES J.   BB TR 6'   165 lbs.
B. Apr. 17, 1863, Charlottesville, Va.   D. Apr. 29, 1888, Philadelphia, Pa.

	G	AB	H	2B	3B	HR	HR %	R	RBI	BB	SO	SB	BA	SA	AB	H	G by POS
1884 PHI N	52	203	50	6	3	0	0.0	26		19	54		.246	.305	0	0	P-50, OF-5
1885	61	235	72	8	3	1	0.4	42		23	18		.306	.379	0	0	P-48, OF-15
1886	72	261	66	9	1	2	0.8	56	25	37	28		.253	.318	0	0	P-48, OF-27
1887	72	264	89	14	6	3	1.1	67	85	34	19	13	.337	.470	0	0	P-37, 2B-27, OF-6, 3B-5
4 yrs.	257	963	277	37	13	6	0.6	191	109	113	119	13	.288	.372	0	0	P-183, OF-53, 2B-27, 3B-5

Joe Ferguson

FERGUSON, JOE VANCE   BR TR 6'2"   200 lbs.
B. Sept. 19, 1946, San Francisco, Calif.

	G	AB	H	2B	3B	HR	HR %	R	RBI	BB	SO	SB	BA	SA	AB	H	G by POS
1970 LA N	5	4	1	0	0	0	0.0	0	1	2	2	0	.250	.250	0	0	C-3
1971	36	102	22	3	0	2	2.0	13	7	12	15	1	.216	.304	2	1	C-35
1972	8	24	7	3	0	1	4.2	2	5	2	4	0	.292	.542	0	0	C-7, OF-2
1973	136	487	128	26	0	25	5.1	84	88	87	81	1	.263	.470	1	1	C-122, OF-20
1974	111	349	88	14	1	16	4.6	54	57	75	73	2	.252	.436	6	0	C-82, OF-34
1975	66	202	42	2	1	5	2.5	15	23	35	47	2	.208	.302	8	4	C-35, OF-34
1976 2 teams	LA	N	(54G –	.222)		STL	N	(71G –	.201)								
" total	125	374	79	15	4	10	2.7	46	39	57	81	6	.211	.353	14	2	C-65, OF-53
1977 HOU N	132	421	108	21	3	16	3.8	59	61	85	79	6	.257	.435	12	2	C-122, 1B-1
1978 2 teams	HOU	N	(51G –	.207)		LA	N	(67G –	.237)								
" total	118	348	78	16	0	14	4.0	40	50	71	71	1	.224	.391	5	1	C-113, OF-3
1979 LA N	122	363	95	14	0	20	5.5	54	69	70	68	1	.262	.466	9	1	C-67, OF-52
1980	77	172	41	3	2	9	5.2	20	29	38	46	2	.238	.436	14	2	C-66, OF-1
1981 2 teams	LA	N	(17G –	.143)		CAL	A	(12G –	.233)								
" total	29	44	9	2	0	1	2.3	7	6	11	13	0	.205	.318	13	0	C-8, OF-5
1982 CAL A	36	84	19	2	0	3	3.6	10	8	12	19	0	.226	.357	0	0	C-32, OF-2
1983	12	27	2	0	0	0	0.0	3	2	5	8	0	.074	.074	0	0	C-9, OF-3
14 yrs.	1013	3001	719	121	11	122	4.1	407	445	562	607	22	.240	.409	84	14	C-766, OF-207, 1B-1
LEAGUE CHAMPIONSHIP SERIES																	
1974 LA N	4	13	3	0	0	0	0.0	3	2	5	1	0	.231	.231	0	0	OF-3
1978	2	2	0	0	0	0	0.0	0	0	0	1	0	.000	.000	2	0	
2 yrs.	6	15	3	0	0	0	0.0	3	2	5	2	0	.200	.200	2	0	OF-3
WORLD SERIES																	
1974 LA N	5	16	2	0	0	1	6.3	2	2	4	6	1	.125	.313	0	0	C-2
1978	2	4	2	2	0	0	0.0	1	0	0	1	0	.500	1.000	0	0	C-2
2 yrs.	7	20	4	2	0	1	5.0	3	2	4	7	1	.200	.450	0	0	C-4

Ed Fernandes

FERNANDES, EDWARD PAUL   BB TR 5'9"   185 lbs.
B. Mar. 11, 1918, Oakland, Calif.   D. Nov. 27, 1968, Hayward, Calif.

	G	AB	H	2B	3B	HR	HR %	R	RBI	BB	SO	SB	BA	SA	AB	H	G by POS
1940 PIT N	28	33	4	1	0	0	0.0	1	2	7	6	0	.121	.152	2	0	C-27
1946 CHI A	14	32	8	2	0	0	0.0	4	4	8	7	0	.250	.313	2	0	C-12
2 yrs.	42	65	12	3	0	0	0.0	5	6	15	13	0	.185	.231	3	0	C-39

Chico Fernandez

FERNANDEZ, HUMBERTO PEREZ   BR TR 6'   165 lbs.
B. Mar. 2, 1932, Havana, Cuba

	G	AB	H	2B	3B	HR	HR %	R	RBI	BB	SO	SB	BA	SA	AB	H	G by POS
1956 BKN N	34	66	15	2	0	1	1.5	11	9	3	10	2	.227	.303	1	0	SS-25
1957 PHI N	149	500	131	14	4	5	1.0	42	51	31	64	18	.262	.336	0	0	SS-149
1958	148	522	120	18	5	6	1.1	38	51	37	48	12	.230	.318	0	0	SS-148
1959	45	123	26	5	1	0	0.0	15	3	10	11	2	.211	.268	0	0	SS-40, 2B-2
1960 DET A	133	435	105	13	3	4	0.9	44	35	39	50	13	.241	.313	2	0	SS-130
1961	133	435	108	15	4	3	0.7	41	40	36	45	8	.248	.322	4	2	SS-121, 3B-8
1962	141	503	125	17	2	20	4.0	64	59	42	69	10	.249	.410	0	0	SS-138, 3B-2, 1B-1

	G	AB	H	2B	3B	HR	HR %	R	RBI	BB	SO	SB	BA	SA	Pinch Hit AB	Pinch Hit H	G by POS

Chico Fernandez continued

	G	AB	H	2B	3B	HR	HR %	R	RBI	BB	SO	SB	BA	SA	AB	H	G by POS
1963 2 teams	DET A (15G – .143)					NY N (58G – .200)											
" total	73	194	36	7	0	1	0.5	15	11	15	41	3	.186	.237	15	1	SS-59, 3B-5, 2B-3
8 yrs.	856	2778	666	91	19	40	1.4	270	259	213	338	68	.240	.329	23	3	SS-810, 3B-15, 2B-5, 1B-1

Chico Fernandez

FERNANDEZ, LORENZO MARTO
B. Apr. 23, 1939, Havana, Cuba
BR TR 5'10" 160 lbs.

	G	AB	H	2B	3B	HR	HR %	R	RBI	BB	SO	SB	BA	SA	AB	H	G by POS
1968 BAL A	24	18	2	0	0	0	0.0	0	0	1	2	0	.111	.111	9	2	SS-7, 2B-4

Frank Fernandez

FERNANDEZ, FRANK
B. Apr. 16, 1943, Staten Island, N. Y.
BR TR 6' 185 lbs.

	G	AB	H	2B	3B	HR	HR %	R	RBI	BB	SO	SB	BA	SA	AB	H	G by POS
1967 NY A	9	28	6	2	0	1	3.6	1	4	2	7	1	.214	.393	0	0	C-7, OF-2
1968	51	135	23	6	1	7	5.2	15	30	35	50	1	.170	.385	1	0	C-45, OF-4
1969	89	229	51	6	1	12	5.2	34	29	65	68	1	.223	.415	11	1	C-65, OF-14
1970 OAK A	94	252	54	5	0	15	6.0	30	44	40	76	1	.214	.413	14	5	C-76, OF-1
1971 3 teams	OAK A (4G – .111)					WAS A (18G – .100)				CHI N (17G – .171)							
" total	39	80	11	2	0	4	5.0	12	9	22	28	0	.138	.313	14	1	C-20, OF-6
1972 CHI N	3	3	0	0	0	0	0.0	0	0	0	2	0	.000	.000	2	0	C-1
6 yrs.	285	727	145	21	2	39	5.4	92	116	164	231	4	.199	.395	42	7	C-214, OF-27

Nanny Fernandez

FERNANDEZ, FROILAN
B. Oct. 25, 1918, Wilmington, Calif.
BR TR 5'9" 170 lbs.

	G	AB	H	2B	3B	HR	HR %	R	RBI	BB	SO	SB	BA	SA	AB	H	G by POS
1942 BOS N	145	577	147	29	3	6	1.0	63	55	38	61	15	.255	.347	3	1	3B-98, OF-44
1946	115	372	95	15	2	2	0.5	37	42	30	44	1	.255	.323	8	1	3B-81, SS-18, OF-14
1947	83	209	43	4	0	2	1.0	16	21	22	20	2	.206	.254	2	0	SS-62, OF-8, 3B-6
1950 PIT N	65	198	51	11	0	6	3.0	23	27	19	17	2	.258	.404	12	6	3B-52
4 yrs.	408	1356	336	59	5	16	1.2	139	145	109	142	20	.248	.334	25	8	3B-237, SS-80, OF-66

Tony Fernandez

FERNANDEZ, OCTAVIO ANTONIO
B. Aug. 6, 1962, San Pedro de Macoris, Dominican Republic
BB TR 6'1" 160 lbs.

	G	AB	H	2B	3B	HR	HR %	R	RBI	BB	SO	SB	BA	SA	AB	H	G by POS
1983 TOR A	15	34	9	1	1	0	0.0	5	2	2	2	0	.265	.353	2	1	SS-13, DH-1
1984	88	233	63	5	3	3	1.3	29	19	17	15	5	.270	.356	6	1	SS-73, 3B-10, DH-1
2 yrs.	103	267	72	6	4	3	1.1	34	21	19	17	5	.270	.356	8	2	SS-86, 3B-10, DH-2

Al Ferrara

FERRARA, ALFRED JOHN (The Bull)
B. Dec. 22, 1939, Brooklyn, N. Y.
BR TR 6'1" 200 lbs.

	G	AB	H	2B	3B	HR	HR %	R	RBI	BB	SO	SB	BA	SA	AB	H	G by POS
1963 LA N	21	44	7	0	0	1	2.3	2	1	6	9	0	.159	.227	8	1	OF-11
1965	41	81	17	2	1	1	1.2	5	10	9	20	0	.210	.296	12	3	OF-27
1966	63	115	31	4	0	5	4.3	15	23	9	35	0	.270	.435	31	5	OF-32
1967	122	347	96	16	1	16	4.6	41	50	33	73	0	.277	.467	28	5	OF-94
1968	2	7	1	0	0	0	0.0	0	0	0	2	0	.143	.143	0	0	OF-2
1969 SD N	138	366	95	22	4	14	3.8	39	56	45	69	0	.260	.440	38	7	OF-96
1970	138	372	103	15	4	13	3.5	44	51	46	63	0	.277	.444	36	9	OF-96
1971 2 teams	SD N (17G – .118)					CIN N (32G – .182)											
" total	49	50	8	1	0	1	2.0	2	7	8	15	0	.160	.240	37	6	OF-7
8 yrs.	574	1382	358	60	7	51	3.7	148	198	156	286	0	.259	.423	190	36	OF-365
WORLD SERIES																	
1966 LA N	1	1	1	0	0	0	0.0	0	0	0	0	0	1.000	1.000	1	1	

Mike Ferraro

FERRARO, MICHAEL DENNIS
B. Aug. 14, 1944, Kingston, N. Y.
Manager 1983.
BR TR 5'11" 175 lbs.

	G	AB	H	2B	3B	HR	HR %	R	RBI	BB	SO	SB	BA	SA	AB	H	G by POS
1966 NY A	10	28	5	0	0	0	0.0	4	0	3	3	0	.179	.179	0	0	3B-10
1968	23	87	14	0	1	0	0.0	5	1	2	17	0	.161	.184	1	0	3B-22
1969 SEA A	5	4	0	0	0	0	0.0	0	0	1	0	0	.000	.000	4	0	
1972 MIL A	124	381	97	18	1	2	0.5	19	29	17	41	0	.255	.323	9	2	3B-115, SS-1
4 yrs.	162	500	116	18	2	2	0.4	28	30	23	61	0	.232	.288	14	2	3B-147, SS-1

Rick Ferrell

FERRELL, RICHARD BENJAMIN
Brother of Wes Ferrell.
B. Oct. 12, 1905, Durham, N. C.
Hall of Fame 1984.
BR TR 5'10" 160 lbs.

	G	AB	H	2B	3B	HR	HR %	R	RBI	BB	SO	SB	BA	SA	AB	H	G by POS
1929 STL A	64	144	33	6	1	0	0.0	21	20	32	10	1	.229	.285	16	2	C-45
1930	101	314	84	18	4	1	0.3	43	41	46	10	1	.268	.360	0	0	C-101
1931	117	386	118	30	4	3	0.8	47	57	56	12	2	.306	.427	7	3	C-108
1932	126	438	138	30	5	2	0.5	67	65	66	18	5	.315	.420	6	1	C-120
1933 2 teams	STL A (22G – .250)					BOS A (118G – .297)											
" total	140	493	143	21	4	4	0.8	58	77	70	23	4	.290	.373	3	1	C-136
1934 BOS A	132	437	130	29	4	1	0.2	50	48	66	20	0	.297	.389	5	1	C-128
1935	133	458	138	34	4	3	0.7	54	61	65	15	5	.301	.413	4	0	C-131
1936	121	410	128	27	5	8	2.0	59	55	65	17	0	.312	.461	1	0	C-121
1937 2 teams	BOS A (18G – .308)					WAS A (86G – .229)											
" total	104	344	84	8	0	2	0.6	39	36	65	22	1	.244	.285	1	0	C-102
1938 WAS A	135	411	120	24	5	1	0.2	55	58	75	17	1	.292	.382	4	0	C-131
1939	87	274	77	13	1	0	0.0	32	31	41	12	1	.281	.336	4	0	C-83
1940	103	326	89	18	2	0	0.0	35	28	47	15	1	.273	.340	4	0	C-99
1941 2 teams	WAS A (21G – .273)					STL A (100G – .252)											
" total	121	387	99	19	3	2	0.5	38	36	67	26	3	.256	.336	3	0	C-119
1942 STL A	99	273	61	6	1	0	0.0	20	26	33	13	0	.223	.253	3	0	C-95
1943	74	209	50	7	0	0	0.0	12	20	34	14	0	.239	.273	3	1	C-70
1944 WAS A	99	339	94	11	1	0	0.0	14	25	46	13	2	.277	.316	1	0	C-96
1945	91	286	76	12	1	1	0.3	33	38	43	13	2	.266	.325	8	2	C-83
1947	37	99	30	11	0	0	0.0	10	12	14	7	0	.303	.414	0	0	C-37
18 yrs.	1884	6028	1692	324	45	28	0.5	687	734	931	277	29	.281	.363	73	11	C-1805

	G	AB	H	2B	3B	HR	HR %	R	RBI	BB	SO	SB	BA	SA	Pinch Hit AB	H	G by POS

Wes Ferrell

FERRELL, WESLEY CHEEK
Brother of Rick Ferrell.
B. Feb. 2, 1908, Greensboro, N. C.   D. Dec. 9, 1976, Sarasota, Fla.

BR TR 6'2"   195 lbs.

	G	AB	H	2B	3B	HR	HR %	R	RBI	BB	SO	SB	BA	SA	AB	H	G by POS
1927 CLE A	1	0	0	0	0	0	–	0	0	0	0	0	.250	.750	0	0	P-1
1928	2	4	1	0	1	0	0.0	0	0	0	0	0	.237	.387	0	0	P-2
1929	47	93	22	5	3	1	1.1	12	12	6	28	1	.237	.387	4	2	P-43
1930	53	118	35	8	3	0	0.0	19	14	12	15	0	.297	.415	7	3	P-43
1931	48	116	37	6	1	9	7.8	24	30	10	21	0	.319	.621	7	0	P-40
1932	55	128	31	5	2	2	1.6	14	18	6	21	0	.242	.359	17	4	P-38
1933	61	140	38	7	0	7	5.0	26	26	20	22	0	.271	.471	14	2	P-28, OF-13
1934 BOS A	34	78	22	4	0	4	5.1	12	17	7	15	1	.282	.487	8	3	P-26
1935	75	150	52	5	1	7	4.7	25	32	21	16	0	.347	.533	32	9	P-41
1936	61	135	36	6	1	5	3.7	20	24	14	10	0	.267	.437	19	0	P-39
1937 2 teams		BOS	A	(18G –	.364)			WAS	A	(53G –	.255)						
" total	71	139	39	7	0	1	0.7	14	25	16	21	0	.281	.353	28	8	P-37
1938 2 teams		WAS	A	(26G –	.224)			NY	A	(5G –	.167)						
" total	31	61	13	3	0	1	1.6	7	7	16	11	0	.213	.311	2	0	P-28
1939 NY A	3	8	1	1	0	0	0.0	0	1	0	2	0	.125	.250	0	0	P-3
1940 BKN N	2	2	0	0	0	0	0.0	0	0	0	2	0	.000	.000	1	0	P-1
1941 BOS N	4	4	2	0	0	1	25.0	2	2	1	1	0	.500	1.250	0	0	P-4
15 yrs.	548	1176	329	57	12	38	3.2	175	208	129	185	2	.280	.446	139	31	P-374, OF-13

Sergio Ferrer

FERRER, SERGIO MARRERO
B. Jan. 29, 1951, Santurce, Puerto Rico

BB TR 5'7"   145 lbs.

	G	AB	H	2B	3B	HR	HR %	R	RBI	BB	SO	SB	BA	SA	AB	H	G by POS
1974 MIN A	24	57	16	0	2	0	0.0	12	0	8	6	3	.281	.351	1	0	SS-20, 2B-1
1975	32	81	20	3	1	0	0.0	14	2	3	11	3	.247	.309	1	0	SS-18, 2B-10, DH-2
1978 NY N	37	33	7	0	1	0	0.0	8	1	4	7	1	.212	.273	0	0	SS-29, 2B-3, 3B-2
1979	32	7	0	0	0	0	0.0	7	0	2	3	0	.000	.000	0	0	3B-12, SS-5, 2B-4
4 yrs.	125	178	43	3	4	0	0.0	41	3	17	27	7	.242	.303	2	0	SS-72, 2B-18, 3B-14, DH-2

Hobe Ferris

FERRIS, ALBERT SAYLES
B. Dec. 7, 1877, Providence, R. I.   D. Mar. 18, 1938, Detroit, Mich.

BR TR

	G	AB	H	2B	3B	HR	HR %	R	RBI	BB	SO	SB	BA	SA	AB	H	G by POS
1901 BOS A	138	523	131	16	15	2	0.4	68	63	23		13	.250	.350	0	0	2B-138, SS-1
1902	134	499	122	16	14	8	1.6	57	63	21		11	.244	.381	0	0	2B-134
1903	141	525	132	19	7	1	1.7	69	66	25		11	.251	.366	0	0	2B-139, SS-2
1904	156	563	120	23	10	3	0.5	50	63	23		7	.213	.306	0	0	2B-156
1905	141	523	115	24	16	6	1.1	51	59	23		11	.220	.361	0	0	2B-140, OF-1
1906	130	495	121	25	13	2	0.4	47	44	10		8	.244	.360	0	0	2B-126, 3B-4
1907	150	561	135	25	2	4	0.7	41	60	10		11	.241	.314	0	0	2B-150
1908 STL A	148	555	150	26	7	2	0.4	54	74	14		6	.270	.353	0	0	3B-148
1909	148	556	120	18	5	3	0.5	36	58	12		11	.216	.282	0	0	3B-114, 2B-34
9 yrs.	1286	4800	1146	192	89	39	0.8	473	550	161		89	.239	.340	0	0	2B-1017, 3B-266, SS-3, OF-1

WORLD SERIES

	G	AB	H	2B	3B	HR	HR %	R	RBI	BB	SO	SB	BA	SA	AB	H	G by POS
1903 BOS A	8	31	9	0	1	0	0.0	3	7	0		5	0	.290	.355	0	0	2B-8

Boo Ferriss

FERRISS, DAVID MEADOW
B. Dec. 5, 1921, Shaw, Miss.

BL TR 6'2"   208 lbs.

	G	AB	H	2B	3B	HR	HR %	R	RBI	BB	SO	SB	BA	SA	AB	H	G by POS
1945 BOS A	61	120	32	7	1	1	0.8	16	19	19	11	0	.267	.367	20	5	P-35
1946	45	115	24	6	0	0	0.0	12	7	7	19	0	.209	.261	4	1	P-40
1947	52	99	27	5	3	0	0.0	11	19	7	10	0	.273	.384	17	4	P-33
1948	31	37	9	1	0	0	0.0	4	6	6	6	0	.243	.270	0	0	P-31
1949	4	1	1	1	0	0	0.0	1	1	0	0	0	1.000	2.000	0	0	P-4
1950	1	0	0	0	0	0	–	0	0	0	0	0	–	–	0	0	P-1
6 yrs.	194	372	93	20	4	1	0.3	44	52	39	46	0	.250	.333	41	10	P-144

WORLD SERIES

	G	AB	H	2B	3B	HR	HR %	R	RBI	BB	SO	SB	BA	SA	AB	H	G by POS
1946 BOS A	2	6	0	0	0	0	0.0	0	0	0	1	0	.000	.000	0	0	P-2

Willy Fetzer

FETZER, WILLIAM McKINNON
B. June 24, 1884, Concord, N. C.   D. May 3, 1959, Durham, N. C.

BL TR 5'10½" 180 lbs.

	G	AB	H	2B	3B	HR	HR %	R	RBI	BB	SO	SB	BA	SA	AB	H	G by POS
1906 PHI A	1	1	0	0	0	0	0.0	0	0	0	1	0	.000	.000	1	0	

Chick Fewster

FEWSTER, WILSON LLOYD
B. Nov. 10, 1895, Baltimore, Md.   D. Apr. 16, 1945, Baltimore, Md.

BR TR 5'11"   160 lbs.

	G	AB	H	2B	3B	HR	HR %	R	RBI	BB	SO	SB	BA	SA	AB	H	G by POS
1917 NY A	11	36	8	0	0	0	0.0	2	1	5	5	1	.222	.222	0	0	2B-11
1918	5	2	1	0	0	0	0.0	1	0	0	0	0	.500	.500	1	0	2B-2
1919	81	244	69	9	3	1	0.4	38	15	34	36	8	.283	.357	7	3	OF-41, SS-23, 2B-4, 3B-2
1920	21	21	6	1	0	0	0.0	8	1	7	2	0	.286	.333	4	1	SS-5, 2B-2
1921	66	207	58	19	0	1	0.5	44	19	28	43	4	.280	.386	4	0	OF-43, 2B-15
1922 2 teams		NY	A	(44G –	.242)			BOS	A	(23G –	.289)						
" total	67	215	56	8	2	1	0.5	28	18	22	33	10	.260	.330	1	0	OF-38, 3B-23, 2B-2
1923 BOS A	90	284	67	10	1	0	0.0	32	15	39	35	7	.236	.278	1	0	2B-94, 3B-5
1924 CLE A	101	322	86	12	2	0	0.0	36	36	24	36	12	.267	.317	0	0	2B-86, 3B-10, OF-1
1925	93	294	73	16	1	1	0.3	39	38	36	25	6	.248	.320	2	1	2B-103
1926 BKN N	105	337	82	16	3	2	0.6	53	24	45	49	9	.243	.326	1	0	
1927	4	1	0	0	0	0	0.0	0	0	0	0	0	.000	.000	1	0	
11 yrs.	644	1963	506	91	12	6	0.3	282	167	240	264	57	.258	.326	22	5	2B-367, OF-123, SS-64, 3B-40

WORLD SERIES

	G	AB	H	2B	3B	HR	HR %	R	RBI	BB	SO	SB	BA	SA	AB	H	G by POS
1921 NY A	4	10	2	0	0	1	10.0	3	2	3	3	0	.200	.500	0	0	OF-4

Neil Fiala

FIALA, NEIL STEPHEN
B. Aug. 24, 1956, St. Louis, Mo.

BL TR 6'1"   185 lbs.

	G	AB	H	2B	3B	HR	HR %	R	RBI	BB	SO	SB	BA	SA	AB	H	G by POS
1981 2 teams		STL	N	(3G –	.000)			CIN	N	(2G –	.500)						
" total	5	5	1	0	0	0	0.0	1	1	0	2	0	.200	.200	5	1	

	G	AB	H	2B	3B	HR	HR %	R	RBI	BB	SO	SB	BA	SA	Pinch Hit AB	H	G by POS

Jim Field
FIELD, JAMES C.
B. Apr. 24, 1863, Philadelphia, Pa.   D. May 13, 1953, Atlantic City, N. J.

	G	AB	H	2B	3B	HR	HR%	R	RBI	BB	SO	SB	BA	SA	AB	H	G by POS
1883 COL AA	76	295	75	10	6	1	0.3	31		7			.254	.339	0	0	1B-76
1884	105	417	97	9	7	4	1.0	74		23			.233	.317	0	0	1B-105
1885 2 teams	PIT	AA (56G —	.239)			BAL	AA (38G —	.208)									
" total	94	353	80	12	3	1	0.3	44		26			.227	.286	0	0	1B-94
1890 ROC AA	52	188	38	7	5	4	2.1	30		21		8	.202	.356	0	0	1B-51, P-2
1898 WAS N	5	21	2	0	0	0	0.0	1	0	0		1	.095	.095	0	0	1B-5
5 yrs.	332	1274	292	38	21	10	0.8	180		77		9	.229	.316	0	0	1B-331, P-2

Sam Field
FIELD, SAMUEL JAY
B. Oct. 12, 1848, Philadelphia, Pa.   D. Oct. 28, 1904, Sinking Spring, Pa.
BR TR 5'9½" 182 lbs.

	G	AB	H	2B	3B	HR	HR%	R	RBI	BB	SO	SB	BA	SA	AB	H	G by POS
1876 CIN N	4	14	0	0	0	0	0.0	2	0	1	3		.000	.000	0	0	C-3, 2B-2

Jocko Fields
FIELDS, JOHN JOSEPH
B. Oct. 20, 1864, Cork, Ireland   D. Oct. 14, 1950, Jersey City, N. J.
BR TR 5'10" 160 lbs.

	G	AB	H	2B	3B	HR	HR%	R	RBI	BB	SO	SB	BA	SA	AB	H	G by POS
1887 PIT N	43	164	44	9	2	0	0.0	26	17	7	13	7	.268	.348	0	0	OF-27, C-14, 1B-3, 3B-1, P-1
1888	45	169	33	7	2	1	0.6	22	15	8	19	9	.195	.278	0	0	OF-29, C-14, 3B-3
1889	75	289	90	22	5	2	0.7	41	43	29	30	7	.311	.443	0	0	OF-60, C-16
1890 PIT P	126	526	149	18	20	9	1.7	101	86	57	52	24	.283	.445	0	0	OF-80, 2B-30, C-15, SS-4
1891 2 teams	PIT	N (23G —	.240)			PHI	N (8G —	.233)									
" total	31	105	25	5	1	0	0.0	14	10	14	15	1	.238	.305	0	0	C-23, SS-8
1892 NY N	21	66	18	4	2	0	0.0	8	5	9	10	2	.273	.394	0	0	OF-11, C-10
6 yrs.	341	1319	359	65	32	12	0.9	212	176	124	139	50	.272	.397	0	0	OF-207, C-92, 2B-30, SS-12, 3B-4, 1B-3, P-1

Jesus Figueroa
FIGUEROA, JESUS MARIA
B. Feb. 20, 1957, Santo Domingo, Dominican Republic
BL TL 5'10" 160 lbs.

	G	AB	H	2B	3B	HR	HR%	R	RBI	BB	SO	SB	BA	SA	AB	H	G by POS
1980 CHI N	115	198	50	5	0	1	0.5	20	11	14	16	2	.253	.293	53	15	OF-57

Sam File
FILE, LAWRENCE SAMUEL
B. May 18, 1922, Chester, Pa.
BR TR 5'11" 160 lbs.

	G	AB	H	2B	3B	HR	HR%	R	RBI	BB	SO	SB	BA	SA	AB	H	G by POS
1940 PHI N	7	13	1	0	0	0	0.0	0	1	0	2	0	.077	.077	0	0	SS-6, 3B-1

Steve Filipowicz
FILIPOWICZ, STEPHEN CHARLES (Flip)
B. June 28, 1921, Donora, Pa.   D. Feb. 21, 1975, Wilkes-Barre, Pa.
BR TR 5'8" 195 lbs.

	G	AB	H	2B	3B	HR	HR%	R	RBI	BB	SO	SB	BA	SA	AB	H	G by POS
1944 NY N	15	41	8	2	1	0	0.0	10	7	3	7	0	.195	.293	1	0	OF-10, C-1
1945	35	112	23	5	0	2	1.8	14	16	4	13	0	.205	.304	3	0	OF-31
1948 CIN N	7	26	9	0	1	0	0.0	0	3	2	1	0	.346	.423	0	0	OF-7
3 yrs.	57	179	40	7	2	2	1.1	24	26	9	21	0	.223	.318	4	0	OF-48, C-1

Jack Fimple
FIMPLE, JOHN JOSEPH
B. Feb. 10, 1958, Darby, Pa.
BR TR 6'2" 185 lbs.

	G	AB	H	2B	3B	HR	HR%	R	RBI	BB	SO	SB	BA	SA	AB	H	G by POS
1983 LA N	54	148	37	8	1	2	1.4	16	22	11	39	1	.250	.358	0	0	C-54
1984	12	26	5	1	0	0	0.0	2	3	1	6	0	.192	.231	0	0	C-12
2 yrs.	66	174	42	9	1	2	1.1	18	25	12	45	1	.241	.339	0	0	C-66

LEAGUE CHAMPIONSHIP SERIES

	G	AB	H	2B	3B	HR	HR%	R	RBI	BB	SO	SB	BA	SA	AB	H	G by POS
1983 LA N	3	7	1	0	0	0	0.0	0	1	0	3	0	.143	.143	0	0	C-3

Jim Finigan
FINIGAN, JAMES LEROY
B. Aug. 19, 1928, Quincy, Ill.   D. May 16, 1981, Quincy, Ill.
BR TR 5'11" 175 lbs.

	G	AB	H	2B	3B	HR	HR%	R	RBI	BB	SO	SB	BA	SA	AB	H	G by POS
1954 PHI A	136	487	147	25	6	7	1.4	57	51	64	66	2	.302	.421	1	0	3B-136
1955 KC A	150	545	139	30	7	9	1.7	72	68	61	49	1	.255	.385	2	1	2B-90, 3B-59
1956	91	250	54	7	2	2	0.8	29	21	30	28	3	.216	.284	9	0	2B-52, 3B-32
1957 DET A	64	174	47	4	2	0	0.0	20	17	23	18	1	.270	.316	3	0	3B-59, 2B-3
1958 SF N	23	25	5	2	0	0	0.0	3	1	3	5	0	.200	.280	12	2	2B-8, 3B-4
1959 BAL A	48	119	30	6	0	1	0.8	14	10	9	10	1	.252	.328	5	2	3B-42, 2B-6, SS-2
6 yrs.	512	1600	422	74	17	19	1.2	195	168	190	176	8	.264	.367	32	5	3B-332, 2B-159, SS-2

Bill Finley
FINLEY, WILLIAM JAMES
B. Oct. 4, 1863, New York, N. Y.   D. Oct. 6, 1912, Asbury Park, N. J.

	G	AB	H	2B	3B	HR	HR%	R	RBI	BB	SO	SB	BA	SA	AB	H	G by POS
1886 NY N	13	44	8	0	0	0	0.0	2	5	1	8		.182	.182	0	0	OF-8, C-8

Bob Finley
FINLEY, ROBERT EDWARD
B. Nov. 25, 1915, Ennis, Tex.
BR TR 6'1" 200 lbs.

	G	AB	H	2B	3B	HR	HR%	R	RBI	BB	SO	SB	BA	SA	AB	H	G by POS
1943 PHI N	28	81	21	2	0	1	1.2	9	7	4	10	0	.259	.321	4	1	C-24
1944	94	281	70	11	1	1	0.4	18	21	12	25	1	.249	.306	20	4	C-74
2 yrs.	122	362	91	13	1	2	0.6	27	28	16	35	1	.251	.309	24	5	C-98

Mickey Finn
FINN, CORNELIUS FRANCIS
B. Jan. 24, 1904, New York, N. Y.   D. July 7, 1933, Altoona, Pa.
BR TR 5'11" 168 lbs.

	G	AB	H	2B	3B	HR	HR%	R	RBI	BB	SO	SB	BA	SA	AB	H	G by POS
1930 BKN N	87	273	76	13	0	3	1.1	42	30	26	18	3	.278	.359	2	0	2B-81
1931	118	413	113	22	2	0	0.0	46	45	21	42	2	.274	.337	4	1	2B-112
1932	65	189	45	5	2	0	0.0	22	14	11	15	2	.238	.286	3	2	3B-50, 2B-2, SS-1
1933 PHI N	51	169	40	4	1	0	0.0	15	13	10	14	2	.237	.272	0	0	2B-51
4 yrs.	321	1044	274	44	5	3	0.3	125	102	68	89	9	.262	.323	9	3	2B-246, 3B-50, SS-1

Hal Finney
FINNEY, HAROLD WILSON
Brother of Lou Finney.
B. July 7, 1905, Lafayette, Ala.
BR TR 5'11" 170 lbs.

	G	AB	H	2B	3B	HR	HR%	R	RBI	BB	SO	SB	BA	SA	AB	H	G by POS
1931 PIT N	10	26	8	1	0	0	0.0	2	2	0	1	1	.308	.346	4	0	C-6
1932	31	33	7	3	0	0	0.0	2	4	3	4	0	.212	.303	0	0	C-11
1933	56	133	31	4	1	1	0.8	17	18	3	19	0	.233	.301	7	3	C-47
1934	5	0	0	0	0	0	–	3	0	0	0	0			0	0	C-5
1936	21	35	0	0	0	0	0.0	3	3	0	8	0	.000	.000	0	0	C-14
5 yrs.	123	227	46	8	1	1	0.4	39	27	6	32	1	.203	.260	11	3	C-83

	G	AB	H	2B	3B	HR	HR %	R	RBI	BB	SO	SB	BA	SA	Pinch Hit AB	Pinch Hit H	G by POS

Lou Finney

FINNEY, LOUIS KLOPSCHE
Brother of Hal Finney.
B. Aug. 13, 1910, Buffalo, Ala.   D. Apr. 22, 1966, Lafayette, Ala.

BL TR 6'   180 lbs.

	G	AB	H	2B	3B	HR	HR %	R	RBI	BB	SO	SB	BA	SA	PH AB	PH H	G by POS
1931 PHI A	9	24	9	0	1	0	0.0	7	3	6	1	0	.375	.458	1	0	OF-8
1933	74	240	64	12	3		1.3	26	32	13	17	1	.267	.371	12	2	OF-63
1934	92	272	76	11	4	1	0.4	32	28	14	17	4	.279	.360	21	4	OF-54, 1B-15
1935	109	410	112	11	6	0	0.0	45	31	18	18	7	.273	.329	14	3	OF-76, 1B-73
1936	151	653	197	26	10	1	0.2	100	41	47	22	7	.302	.377	1	0	1B-50, OF-39, 2B-1
1937	92	379	95	14	9	1	0.3	53	20	20	16	2	.251	.343	3	0	1B-64, OF-46
1938	122	454	125	21	12	10	2.2	61	48	39	25	5	.275	.441	14	5	
1939 2 teams	PHI	A (9G – .136)		BOS	A (95G – .325)												
" total	104	271	84	18	3	1	0.4	44	47	26	11	2	.310	.410	40	13	1B-32, OF-28
1940 BOS A	130	534	171	31	15	5	0.9	73	73	33	13	5	.320	.463	9	1	OF-69, 1B-51
1941	127	497	143	24	10	4	0.8	83	53	38	17	2	.288	.400	10	5	OF-92, 1B-24
1942	113	397	113	16	7	3	0.8	58	61	29	11	3	.285	.383	15	3	OF-95, 1B-2
1944	68	251	72	11	2	0	0.0	37	32	23	7	1	.287	.347	6	1	1B-59, OF-2
1945 2 teams	BOS	A (2G – .000)		STL	A (57G – .277)												
" total	59	215	59	8	4	2	0.9	24	22	21	7	0	.274	.377	3	0	OF-36, 1B-22, 3B-1
1946 STL A	16	30	9	0	0	0	0.0	0	3	2	4	0	.300	.300	6	4	OF-7
1947 PHI N	4	0	0	0	0	0		0	0	0	0	0	.000	.000	4	0	
15 yrs.	1270	4631	1329	203	85	31	0.7	643	494	329	186	39	.287	.388	159	41	OF-688, 1B-415, 3B-1, 2B-1

Mike Fiore

FIORE, MICHAEL GARRY JOSEPH (Lefty)
B. Oct. 11, 1944, Brooklyn, N.Y.

BL TL 6'   175 lbs.

	G	AB	H	2B	3B	HR	HR %	R	RBI	BB	SO	SB	BA	SA	PH AB	PH H	G by POS
1968 BAL A	6	17	1	0	0	0	0.0	2	0	4	4	0	.059	.059	0	0	1B-5, OF-1
1969 KC A	107	339	93	14	1	12	3.5	53	35	84	63	4	.274	.428	5	4	1B-91, OF-13
1970 2 teams	KC	A (25G – .181)		BOS	A (41G – .140)												
" total	66	122	20	2	0	1	0.0	11	8	21	28	1	.164	.180	26	5	1B-37, OF-2
1971 BOS A	51	62	11	2	0	1	1.6	9	6	12	14	0	.177	.258	33	8	1B-12
1972 2 teams	STL	N (17G – .100)		SD	N (7G – .000)												
" total	24	16	1	0	0	0	0.0	0	1	3	6	0	.063	.063	16	1	1B-6, OF-1
5 yrs.	254	556	126	18	1	13	2.3	75	50	124	115	5	.227	.333	80	18	1B-151, OF-17

Dan Firova

FIROVA, DANIEL MICHAEL
B. Oct. 16, 1956, Refugio, Tex.

BR TR 6'   185 lbs.

	G	AB	H	2B	3B	HR	HR %	R	RBI	BB	SO	SB	BA	SA	PH AB	PH H	G by POS
1981 SEA A	13	2	0	0	0	0	0.0	0	0	0	1	0	.000	.000	0	0	C-13
1982	3	5	0	0	0	0	0.0	0	0	0	0	0	.000	.000	0	0	C-3
2 yrs.	16	7	0	0	0	0	0.0	0	0	0	1	0	.000	.000	0	0	C-16

Sam Fisburn

FISBURN, SAMUEL
B. May 18, 1893, Haverhill, Mass.   D. Apr. 11, 1965, Bethlehem, Pa.

BR TR 5'9"   157 lbs.

	G	AB	H	2B	3B	HR	HR %	R	RBI	BB	SO	SB	BA	SA	PH AB	PH H	G by POS
1919 STL N	9	6	2	1	1	0	0.0	0	2	0	0	0	.333	.500	1	1	2B-1, 1B-1

Bill Fischer

FISCHER, WILLIAM CHARLES
B. Mar. 2, 1891, New York, N.Y.   D. Sept. 4, 1945, Richmond, Va.

BL TR 6'   174 lbs.

	G	AB	H	2B	3B	HR	HR %	R	RBI	BB	SO	SB	BA	SA	PH AB	PH H	G by POS
1913 BKN N	62	165	44	9	4	1	0.6	16	12	10	5	0	.267	.388	1	0	C-51
1914	43	105	27	1	2	0	0.0	12	8	8	12	1	.257	.305	12	5	C-30
1915 CHI F	105	292	96	15	4	4	1.4	30	50	24		5	.329	.449	21	7	C-80
1916 2 teams	CHI	N (65G – .196)		PIT	N (42G – .257)												
" total	107	292	64	16	3	2	0.7	26	20	21	11	3	.219	.315	12	0	C-91
1917 PIT N	95	245	70	9	2	3	1.2	25	25	27	19	11	.286	.376	16	3	C-69, 1B-2
5 yrs.	412	1099	301	50	15	10	0.9	109	115	90	47	20	.274	.374	62	15	C-321, 1B-2

Mike Fischlin

FISCHLIN, MICHAEL THOMAS
B. Sept. 13, 1955, Sacramento, Calif.

BR TR 6'1"   165 lbs.

	G	AB	H	2B	3B	HR	HR %	R	RBI	BB	SO	SB	BA	SA	PH AB	PH H	G by POS
1977 HOU N	13	15	3	0	0	0	0.0	0	0	0	2	0	.200	.200	0	0	SS-12
1978	44	86	10	1	0	0	0.0	3	0	4	9	1	.116	.128	3	0	SS-41
1980	1	1	0	0	0	0	0.0	0	0	0	1	0	.000	.000	0	0	SS-1
1981 CLE A	22	43	10	1	0	0	0.0	3	5	3	6	3	.233	.256	0	0	SS-19, 2B-1
1982	112	276	74	12	1	0	0.0	34	21	34	36	9	.268	.319	2	2	SS-101, 3B-8, 2B-6, C-1
1983	95	225	47	5	2	2	0.9	31	23	26	32	9	.209	.276	1	1	2B-71, SS-15, 3B-4, DH-1
1984	85	133	30	4	2	1	0.8	17	14	12	20	2	.226	.308	1	1	2B-55, 3B-17, SS-15
7 yrs.	372	779	174	23	5	3	0.4	88	63	79	106	24	.223	.277	7	3	SS-204, 2B-133, 3B-29, DH-1, C-1

Fisher

FISHER,
B. Johnstown, Pa.   Deceased.

	G	AB	H	2B	3B	HR	HR %	R	RBI	BB	SO	SB	BA	SA	PH AB	PH H	G by POS
1884 2 teams	PHI	U (10G – .222)		WIL	U (8G – .069)												
" total	18	65	10	2	0	0	0.0	7		3			.154	.185	0	0	P-8, OF-6, SS-2, 1B-2
1885 BUF N	1	4	0	0	0	0	0.0	0	0	0	0		.000	.000	0	0	P-1
2 yrs.	19	69	10	2	0	0	0.0	7		3	0		.145	.174	0	0	P-9, OF-6, SS-2, 1B-2

Bob Fisher

FISHER, ROBERT TECUMSEH
Brother of Newt Fisher.
B. Nov. 3, 1887, Nashville, Tenn.   D. Aug. 4, 1963, Jacksonville, Fla.

BR TR 5'9½"   170 lbs.

	G	AB	H	2B	3B	HR	HR %	R	RBI	BB	SO	SB	BA	SA	PH AB	PH H	G by POS
1912 BKN N	82	257	60	10	3	0	0.0	27	26	14	32	7	.233	.296	4	0	SS-74, 3B-1, 2B-1
1913	132	474	124	11	10	4	0.8	42	54	10	43	16	.262	.352	11	2	SS-131
1914 CHI N	15	50	15	2	2	0	0.0	5	5	3	4	2	.300	.420	0	0	SS-15
1915	147	568	163	22	5	5	0.9	70	53	30	51	9	.287	.370	2	0	SS-29, 2B-6, OF-1
1916 CIN N	61	136	37	4	3	0	0.0	9	11	8	14	7	.272	.346	25	6	2B-63
1918 STL N	63	246	78	11	3	2	0.8	36	20	15	11	7	.317	.411	0	0	2B-3
1919	3	11	3	1	0	0	0.0	0	1	0	2	0	.273	.364	0	0	2B-3
7 yrs.	503	1742	480	61	26	11	0.6	189	170	80	157	48	.276	.359	42	8	SS-396, 2B-73, OF-1, 3B-3

	G	AB	H	2B	3B	HR	HR %	R	RBI	BB	SO	SB	BA	SA	Pinch Hit AB	H	G by POS

Gus Fisher

FISHER, AUGUSTUS HARRIS
B. Oct. 21, 1885, Pottsborough, Tex.   D. Apr. 9, 1970, Portland, Ore.   BL TR 5'10"   175 lbs.

	G	AB	H	2B	3B	HR	HR %	R	RBI	BB	SO	SB	BA	SA	AB	H	G by POS
1911 CLE A	70	203	53	6	3	0	0.0	20	12	7		6	.261	.320	10	2	C-58, 1B-1
1912 NY A	4	10	1	0	0	0	0.0	1	0	0		0	.100	.100	0	0	C-4
2 yrs.	74	213	54	6	3	0	0.0	21	12	7		6	.254	.310	10	2	C-62, 1B-1

Harry Fisher

FISHER, HARRY C.
B. Philadelphia, Pa.   Deceased.

	G	AB	H	2B	3B	HR	HR %	R	RBI	BB	SO	SB	BA	SA	AB	H	G by POS
1884 3 teams	KC	U	(10G –	.200)		C-P	U	(1G –	.667)		CLE	N	(6G –	.125)			
" total	17	67	13	2	0	0	0.0	6		1		3	.194	.224	0	0	3B-10, 2B-6, SS-1, C-1
1889 LOU AA	1	2	1	0	0	0	0.0	0		0		0	.500	.500	0	0	OF-1
2 yrs.	18	69	14	2	0	0	0.0	6		1		3	.203	.232	0	0	3B-10, 2B-6, OF-1, SS-1, C-1

Harry Fisher

FISHER, HARRY DEVEREUX
B. Jan. 3, 1926, Newbury, Ont., Canada   D. Sept. 20, 1981, Waterloo, Ont., Canada   BL TR 6'   180 lbs.

	G	AB	H	2B	3B	HR	HR %	R	RBI	BB	SO	SB	BA	SA	AB	H	G by POS
1951 PIT N	3	3	0	0	0	0	0.0	0	0	0	0	0	.000	.000	3	0	
1952	15	15	5	1	0	0	0.0	0	1	0	3	0	.333	.400	7	3	P-8
2 yrs.	18	18	5	1	0	0	0.0	0	1	0	3	0	.278	.333	10	3	P-8

Newt Fisher

FISHER, NEWTON
Brother of Bob Fisher.
B. July 28, 1874, Chattanooga, Tenn.   D. Feb. 28, 1947, Norwood Park, Ill.   5'9½"   171 lbs.

	G	AB	H	2B	3B	HR	HR %	R	RBI	BB	SO	SB	BA	SA	AB	H	G by POS
1898 PHI N	9	26	3	1	0	0	0.0	0	0	0		1	.115	.154	0	0	C-8, 3B-1

Red Fisher

FISHER, JOHN GUS
B. June 22, 1887, Pittsburgh, Pa.   D. Jan. 31, 1940, Louisville, Ky.   BL TR

	G	AB	H	2B	3B	HR	HR %	R	RBI	BB	SO	SB	BA	SA	AB	H	G by POS
1910 STL A	23	72	9	2	1	0	0.0	5	3	8		5	.125	.181	3	0	OF-19

Showboat Fisher

FISHER, GEORGE ALOYS
B. Jan. 16, 1899, Jennings, Iowa   BL TR 5'10"   170 lbs.

	G	AB	H	2B	3B	HR	HR %	R	RBI	BB	SO	SB	BA	SA	AB	H	G by POS
1923 WAS A	13	23	6	2	0	0	0.0	4	2	4	3	0	.261	.348	4	1	OF-5
1924	15	41	9	1	0	0	0.0	7	6	6	6	2	.220	.244	4	2	OF-11
1930 STL N	92	254	95	18	6	8	3.1	49	61	25	21	4	.374	.587	20	8	OF-67
1932 STL A	18	22	4	0	0	0	0.0	2	2	2	5	0	.182	.182	11	2	OF-5
4 yrs.	138	340	114	21	6	8	2.4	62	71	37	35	6	.335	.503	39	13	OF-88
WORLD SERIES																	
1930 STL N	2	2	1	1	0	0	0.0	0	0	0	1	0	.500	1.000	2	1	

Wilbur Fisher

FISHER, WILBUR McCULLOUGH (Levy, Hod)
B. July 18, 1894, Chesapeake, Ohio   D. Oct. 24, 1960, Pageton, W. Va.   BL TR 5'11½"   200 lbs.

	G	AB	H	2B	3B	HR	HR %	R	RBI	BB	SO	SB	BA	SA	AB	H	G by POS
1916 PIT N	1	1	0	0	0	0	0.0	0	0	0	0	0	.000	.000	1	0	

Carlton Fisk

FISK, CARLTON ERNEST (Pudge)
B. Dec. 26, 1948, Bellows Falls, Vt.   BR TR 6'3"   200 lbs.

	G	AB	H	2B	3B	HR	HR %	R	RBI	BB	SO	SB	BA	SA	AB	H	G by POS
1969 BOS A	2	5	0	0	0	0	0.0	0	0	0	2	0	.000	.000	1	0	C-1
1971	14	48	15	2	1	2	4.2	7	6	1	10	0	.313	.521	0	0	C-14
1972	131	457	134	28	9	22	4.8	74	61	52	83	5	.293	.538	0	0	C-131
1973	135	508	125	21	0	26	5.1	65	71	37	99	7	.246	.441	1	1	C-131, DH-3
1974	52	187	56	12	1	11	5.9	36	26	24	23	5	.299	.551	0	0	C-50, DH-2
1975	79	263	87	14	4	10	3.8	47	52	27	32	4	.331	.529	2	0	C-71, DH-6
1976	134	487	124	17	5	17	3.5	76	58	56	71	12	.255	.415	1	0	C-133, DH-1
1977	152	536	169	26	3	26	4.9	106	102	75	85	7	.315	.521	0	0	C-151
1978	157	571	162	39	5	20	3.5	94	88	71	83	7	.284	.475	2	1	C-154, DH-1, OF-1
1979	91	320	87	23	2	10	3.1	49	42	10	38	3	.272	.450	13	3	DH-42, C-39, OF-1
1980	131	478	138	25	3	18	3.8	73	62	36	62	11	.289	.467	0	0	C-115, DH-5, OF-5, 3B-3, 1B-3
1981 CHI A	96	338	89	12	0	7	2.1	44	45	38	37	3	.263	.361	0	0	C-95, OF-1, 3B-1, 1B-1
1982	135	476	127	17	3	14	2.9	66	65	46	60	17	.267	.403	3	1	C-133, 1B-2
1983	138	488	141	26	4	26	5.3	85	86	46	88	9	.289	.518	6	1	C-133, DH-2
1984	102	359	83	20	1	21	5.8	54	43	26	60	6	.231	.468	11	1	C-90, DH-5
15 yrs.	1549	5521	1537	282	41	230	4.2	876	807	545	833	96	.278	.469	42	8	C-1441, DH-67, OF-8, 1B-6, 3B-4
LEAGUE CHAMPIONSHIP SERIES																	
1975 BOS A	3	12	5	1	0	0	0.0	4	2	0	2	1	.417	.500	0	0	C-3
1983 CHI A	4	17	3	1	0	0	0.0	0	0	1	3	0	.176	.235	0	0	C-4
2 yrs.	7	29	8	2	0	0	0.0	4	2	1	5	1	.276	.345	0	0	C-7
WORLD SERIES																	
1975 BOS A	7	25	6	0	0	2	8.0	5	4	7	7	0	.240	.480	0	0	C-7

Wes Fisler

FISLER, WESTON DICKSON
B. July 5, 1841, Camden, N. J.   D. Dec. 25, 1922, Philadelphia, Pa.   5'6"   137 lbs.

	G	AB	H	2B	3B	HR	HR %	R	RBI	BB	SO	SB	BA	SA	AB	H	G by POS
1876 PHI N	59	278	80	15	1	1	0.4	42	30	2	4		.288	.360	0	0	OF-24, 2B-21, 1B-14, SS-1

Charlie Fitzberger

FITZBERGER, CHARLES CASPAR (Hon)
B. Feb. 13, 1904, Baltimore, Md.   D. Jan. 25, 1965, Baltimore, Md.   BL TL 6'1½"   170 lbs.

	G	AB	H	2B	3B	HR	HR %	R	RBI	BB	SO	SB	BA	SA	AB	H	G by POS
1928 BOS N	7	7	2	0	0	0	0.0	0	0	0	3	0	.286	.286	7	2	

Dennis Fitzgerald

FITZGERALD, DENNIS S.
B. Mar., 1865, England   D. Oct. 16, 1936, New Haven, Conn.

	G	AB	H	2B	3B	HR	HR %	R	RBI	BB	SO	SB	BA	SA	AB	H	G by POS
1890 PHI AA	2	8	2	0	0	0	0.0	0		0		0	.250	.250	0	0	SS-2

	G	AB	H	2B	3B	HR	HR%	R	RBI	BB	SO	SB	BA	SA	Pinch Hit AB	Pinch Hit H	G by POS

Ed Fitz Gerald

FITZ GERALD, EDWARD RAYMOND
B. May 21, 1924, Santa Ynez, Calif.   BR TR 6'   170 lbs.

	G	AB	H	2B	3B	HR	HR%	R	RBI	BB	SO	SB	BA	SA	AB	H	G by POS
1948 PIT N	102	262	70	9	3	1	0.4	31	35	32	37	3	.267	.336	6	2	C-96
1949	75	160	42	7	0	2	1.3	16	18	8	27	1	.263	.344	16	1	C-56
1950	6	15	1	1	0	0	0.0	1	0	0	3	0	.067	.133	4	1	C-5
1951	55	97	22	6	0	0	0.0	8	13	7	10	1	.227	.289	14	2	C-38
1952	51	73	17	1	0	1	1.4	4	7	7	15	0	.233	.288	29	6	C-18, 3B-2
1953 2 teams			PIT	N	(6G –	.118)		WAS	A	(88G –	.250)						
" total	94	305	74	14	0	3	1.0	25	40	19	36	2	.243	.318	9	2	C-90
1954 WAS A	115	360	104	13	5	4	1.1	33	40	33	22	0	.289	.386	6	2	C-107
1955	74	236	56	3	1	4	1.7	28	19	25	23	0	.237	.309	4	0	C-72
1956	64	148	45	8	0	2	1.4	15	12	20	16	0	.304	.399	16	3	C-50
1957	45	125	34	8	0	1	0.8	14	13	10	9	2	.272	.360	10	4	C-37
1958	58	114	30	3	0	0	0.0	7	11	8	15	0	.263	.289	33	12	C-21, 1B-5
1959 2 teams			WAS	A	(19G –	.194)		CLE	A	(49G –	.271)						
" total	68	191	47	9	1	1	0.5	17	9	16	22	0	.246	.319	5	1	C-61
12 yrs.	807	2086	542	82	10	19	0.9	199	217	185	235	9	.260	.336	148	35	C-651, 1B-5, 3B-2

Howie Fitzgerald

FITZGERALD, HOWARD CHUMNEY (Lefty)
B. May 16, 1902, Eagle Lake, Tex.   D. Feb. 27, 1959, Eagle Falls, Tex.   BL TL 5'11½" 163 lbs.

	G	AB	H	2B	3B	HR	HR%	R	RBI	BB	SO	SB	BA	SA	AB	H	G by POS
1922 CHI N	10	24	8	1	0	0	0.0	3	4	3	2	1	.333	.375	3	2	OF-10
1924	7	19	3	0	0	0	0.0	1	2	0	2	0	.158	.158	2	0	OF-5
1926 BOS A	31	97	25	2	0	0	0.0	11	8	5	7	1	.258	.278	8	2	OF-23
3 yrs.	48	140	36	3	0	0	0.0	15	14	8	11	2	.257	.279	13	4	OF-38

Matty Fitzgerald

FITZGERALD, MATTHEW WILLIAM
B. Aug. 31, 1880, Albany, N. Y.   D. Sept. 22, 1949, Albany, N. Y.   BR TR 6'   185 lbs.

	G	AB	H	2B	3B	HR	HR%	R	RBI	BB	SO	SB	BA	SA	AB	H	G by POS
1906 NY N	4	6	4	0	0	0	0.0	2	2	2		1	.667	.667	1	0	C-3
1907	7	15	2	1	0	0	0.0	1	1	0		0	.133	.200	1	0	C-6
2 yrs.	11	21	6	1	0	0	0.0	3	3	2		1	.286	.333	2	0	C-9

Mike Fitzgerald

FITZGERALD, JUSTIN HOWARD
B. June 22, 1890, San Mateo, Calif.   D. Jan. 17, 1945, San Mateo, Calif.   BL TR 5'8"   160 lbs.

	G	AB	H	2B	3B	HR	HR%	R	RBI	BB	SO	SB	BA	SA	AB	H	G by POS
1911 NY A	16	37	10	1	0	0	0.0	6	6	4		4	.270	.297	7	1	OF-9
1918 PHI N	66	133	39	8	0	0	0.0	21	6	13	6	3	.293	.353	30	8	OF-57
2 yrs.	82	170	49	9	0	0	0.0	27	12	17	6	7	.288	.341	37	9	OF-66

Mike Fitzgerald

FITZGERALD, MICHAEL ROY
B. July 13, 1960, Long Beach, Calif.   BR TR 6'   185 lbs.

	G	AB	H	2B	3B	HR	HR%	R	RBI	BB	SO	SB	BA	SA	AB	H	G by POS
1983 NY N	8	20	2	0	0	1	5.0	1	2	3	6	0	.100	.250	0	0	C-8
1984	112	360	87	15	1	2	0.6	20	33	24	71	1	.242	.306	7	1	C-107
2 yrs.	120	380	89	15	1	3	0.8	21	35	27	77	1	.234	.303	7	1	C-115

Ray Fitzgerald

FITZGERALD, RAYMOND FRANCIS
B. Dec. 5, 1904, Chicopee, Mass.   D. Sept. 6, 1977, Westfield, Mass.   BR TR 5'9"   168 lbs.

	G	AB	H	2B	3B	HR	HR%	R	RBI	BB	SO	SB	BA	SA	AB	H	G by POS
1931 CIN N	1	1	0	0	0	0	0.0	0	0	0	0	0	.000	.000	1	0	

Shaun Fitzmaurice

FITZMAURICE, SHAUN EARLE
B. Aug. 25, 1942, Worcester, Mass.   BR TR 6'   180 lbs.

	G	AB	H	2B	3B	HR	HR%	R	RBI	BB	SO	SB	BA	SA	AB	H	G by POS
1966 NY N	9	13	2	0	0	0	0.0	2	0	2	6	1	.154	.154	1	0	OF-5

Ed Fitzpatrick

FITZPATRICK, EDWARD HENRY
B. Dec. 9, 1889, Lewiston, Pa.   D. Oct. 23, 1965, Bethlehem, Pa.   BR TR 5'8"   165 lbs.

	G	AB	H	2B	3B	HR	HR%	R	RBI	BB	SO	SB	BA	SA	AB	H	G by POS
1915 BOS N	105	303	67	19	3	0	0.0	54	24	43	36	13	.221	.304	2	0	2B-71, OF-29
1916	83	216	46	8	0	1	0.5	17	18	15	26	5	.213	.264	8	2	2B-46, OF-28
1917	63	178	45	8	4	0	0.0	20	17	12	22	4	.253	.343	3	0	2B-22, OF-19, 3B-15
3 yrs.	251	697	158	35	7	1	0.1	91	59	70	84	22	.227	.301	13	2	2B-139, OF-76, 3B-15

Tom Fitzsimmons

FITZSIMMONS, THOMAS WILLIAM
B. Apr. 6, 1890, Oakland, Calif.   D. Dec. 20, 1971, Oakland, Calif.   BR TR 6'1"   190 lbs.

	G	AB	H	2B	3B	HR	HR%	R	RBI	BB	SO	SB	BA	SA	AB	H	G by POS
1919 BKN N	4	4	0	0	0	0	0.0	1	0	1	2	0	.000	.000	0	0	3B-4

Max Flack

FLACK, MAX JOHN
B. Feb. 5, 1890, Belleville, Ill.   D. July 31, 1975, Belleville, Ill.   BL TL 5'7"   148 lbs.

	G	AB	H	2B	3B	HR	HR%	R	RBI	BB	SO	SB	BA	SA	AB	H	G by POS
1914 CHI F	134	502	124	15	3	2	0.4	66	39	51		37	.247	.301	1	0	OF-133
1915	141	523	164	20	14	3	0.6	88	45	40		37	.314	.423	3	2	OF-138
1916 CHI N	141	465	120	14	3	3	0.6	65	20	42	43	24	.258	.320	3	0	OF-136
1917	131	447	111	18	7	0	0.0	65	21	51	34	17	.248	.320	10	3	OF-117
1918	123	478	123	17	10	4	0.8	74	41	56	19	17	.257	.360	0	0	OF-121
1919	116	469	138	20	4	6	1.3	71	35	34	13	18	.294	.392	0	0	OF-116
1920	135	520	157	30	6	4	0.8	85	49	52	15	13	.302	.406	2	0	OF-132
1921	133	572	172	31	4	6	1.0	80	37	32	15	12	.301	.400	3	0	OF-130
1922 2 teams			CHI	N	(17G –	.222)		STL	N	(66G –	.292)						
" total	83	321	90	13	1	2	0.6	53	27	33	15	5	.280	.346	1	0	OF-83
1923 STL N	128	505	147	16	9	3	0.6	82	28	41	16	7	.291	.376	6	3	OF-121
1924	67	209	55	11	3	2	1.0	31	21	21	5	3	.263	.373	13	3	OF-52
1925	79	241	60	7	8	0	0.0	23	28	21	9	5	.249	.344	19	3	OF-59
12 yrs.	1411	5252	1461	212	72	35	0.7	783	391	474	184	200	.278	.366	61	15	OF-1338
WORLD SERIES																	
1918 CHI N	6	19	5	0	0	0	0.0	2	1	4	1	1	.263	.263	0	0	OF-6

Wally Flager

FLAGER, WALTER LEONARD
B. Nov. 3, 1921, Chicago Heights, Ill.   BL TR 5'11"   160 lbs.

	G	AB	H	2B	3B	HR	HR%	R	RBI	BB	SO	SB	BA	SA	AB	H	G by POS
1945 2 teams			CIN	N	(21G –	.212)		PHI	N	(49G –	.250)						
" total	70	220	53	5	1	2	0.9	26	21	25	20	1	.241	.300	5	1	SS-63, 2B-1

	G	AB	H	2B	3B	HR	HR %	R	RBI	BB	SO	SB	BA	SA	Pinch Hit AB	Pinch Hit H	G by POS

Ira Flagstead

FLAGSTEAD, IRA JAMES (Pete)
B. Sept. 22, 1893, Montague, Mich.   D. Mar. 13, 1940, Olympia, Wash.   BR TR 5'9"   165 lbs.

	G	AB	H	2B	3B	HR	HR%	R	RBI	BB	SO	SB	BA	SA	PH AB	PH H	G by POS
1917 DET A	4	4	0	0	0	0	0.0	0	0	0	1	0	.000	.000	2	0	OF-2
1919	97	287	95	22	3	5	1.7	43	41	35	39	6	.331	.481	11	3	OF-83
1920	110	311	73	13	5	3	1.0	40	35	37	27	3	.235	.338	26	6	OF-82
1921	85	259	79	15	1	0	0.0	40	31	21	21	7	.305	.371	7	2	OF-82
1922	44	91	28	5	3	3	3.3	21	8	14	16	0	.308	.527	8	2	SS-55, OF-12, 2B-8, 3B-1
1923 2 teams	110	383	119	23	DET A (1G – .000)			BOS A (109G – .312)									OF-31
" total	110	383	119	23	4	8	2.1	55	53	37	26	8	.311	.454	6	0	OF-102
1924 BOS A	149	560	171	35	7	5	0.9	106	43	75	41	10	.305	.420	5	2	OF-143
1925	148	572	160	38	2	6	1.0	84	61	63	30	5	.280	.385	3	1	OF-144
1926	98	415	124	31	7	3	0.7	65	31	36	22	4	.299	.429	0	0	OF-98
1927	131	466	133	26	8	4	0.9	63	69	57	25	12	.285	.401	2	0	OF-129
1928	140	510	148	41	4	1	0.2	84	39	60	23	12	.290	.392	4	0	OF-135
1929 3 teams	58	125	32	5	BOS A (14G – .306)			WAS A (18G – .179)			PIT N (26G – .280)						OF-33
" total	58	125	32	5	1	0	0.0	22	18	13	8	3	.256	.312	23	9	OF-33
1930 PIT N	44	156	39	7	4	2	1.3	21	21	17	9	1	.250	.385	3	0	OF-40
13 yrs.	1218	4139	1201	261	49	40	1.0	644	450	465	288	71	.290	.406	100	25	OF-1034, SS-55, 2B-8, 3B-1

P. J. Flaherty

FLAHERTY, P. J.
B. Worcester, Mass.   Deceased.   BL TL

	G	AB	H	2B	3B	HR	HR%	R	RBI	BB	SO	SB	BA	SA	PH AB	PH H	G by POS
1881 WOR N	1	2	0	0	0	0	0.0	0	0	0	2		.000	.000	0	0	OF-1

Pat Flaherty

FLAHERTY, PATRICK HENRY
B. Jan. 31, 1876, St Louis, Mo.   D. Jan. 28, 1946, Chicago, Ill.   5'9"   166 lbs.

	G	AB	H	2B	3B	HR	HR%	R	RBI	BB	SO	SB	BA	SA	PH AB	PH H	G by POS
1894 LOU N	38	145	43	5	3	0	0.0	15	15	9	6	2	.297	.372	0	0	3B-38

Patsy Flaherty

FLAHERTY, PATRICK JOSEPH
B. June 29, 1876, Carnegie, Pa.   D. Jan. 23, 1968, Alexandria, La.   BL TL

	G	AB	H	2B	3B	HR	HR%	R	RBI	BB	SO	SB	BA	SA	PH AB	PH H	G by POS
1899 LOU N	7	24	5	1	1	0	0.0	3	6	3		0	.208	.333	0	0	P-5, OF-2
1900 PIT N	4	9	1	0	0	0	0.0	0	0	1		0	.111	.111	0	0	P-4
1903 CHI N	40	102	14	4	0	0	0.0	7	5	5		4	.137	.176	0	0	P-40
1904 2 teams	41	116	26	4	CHI A (5G – .333)			PIT N (36G – .212)									P-40
" total	41	116	26	4	2	1.7		10	19	12		0	.224	.379	5	1	P-34, OF-2
1905 PIT N	30	76	15	4	2	0	0.0	7	4	3		0	.197	.303	1	0	P-27, OF-2
1907 BOS N	41	115	22	3	2	1	1.7	9	11	2		1	.191	.304	4	1	P-27, OF-8
1908	32	86	12	0	0	0	0.0	8	5	6		2	.140	.186	1	0	P-31
1910 PHI N	2	2	1	0	0	0	0.0	0	0	0		0	.500	.500	0	0	OF-1, P-1
1911 BOS N	38	94	27	3	2	2	2.1	9	20	8	11	2	.287	.426	17	6	OF-19, P-4
9 yrs.	235	624	123	19	13	6	1.0	53	70	40	11	9	.197	.298	28	8	P-173, OF-34

Al Flair

FLAIR, ALBERT DELL (Broadway)
B. July 24, 1916, New Orleans, La.   BL TL 6'4"   195 lbs.

	G	AB	H	2B	3B	HR	HR%	R	RBI	BB	SO	SB	BA	SA	PH AB	PH H	G by POS
1941 BOS A	10	30	6	2	1	0	0.0	3	2	1	1	1	.200	.333	2	0	1B-8

Charlie Flanagan

FLANAGAN, CHARLES JAMES
B. Dec. 13, 1891, Oakland, Calif.   D. Jan. 8, 1930, San Francisco, Calif.   BR TR 6'   175 lbs.

	G	AB	H	2B	3B	HR	HR%	R	RBI	BB	SO	SB	BA	SA	PH AB	PH H	G by POS
1913 STL A	4	3	0	0	0	0	0.0	0	1	0	0	0	.000	.000	1	0	OF-1, 3B-1

Ed Flanagan

FLANAGAN, EDWARD J.
B. Sept. 15, 1861, Lowell, Mass.   D. Nov. 10, 1926, Lowell, Mass.   6'1"   190 lbs.

	G	AB	H	2B	3B	HR	HR%	R	RBI	BB	SO	SB	BA	SA	PH AB	PH H	G by POS
1887 PHI AA	19	80	20	5	0	1	1.3	12		3		3	.250	.350	0	0	1B-19
1889 LOU AA	23	88	22	7	3	0	0.0	11	8	7	11	1	.250	.398	0	0	1B-23
2 yrs.	42	168	42	12	3	1	0.6	23	7	10	11	4	.250	.375	0	0	1B-42

Steamer Flanagan

FLANAGAN, JAMES PAUL
B. Apr. 20, 1881, Kingston, Pa.   D. Apr. 21, 1947, Wilkes-Barre, Pa.   BL TL 6'1"   185 lbs.

	G	AB	H	2B	3B	HR	HR%	R	RBI	BB	SO	SB	BA	SA	PH AB	PH H	G by POS
1905 PIT N	7	25	7	1	1	0	0.0	7	3	1		3	.280	.400	2	0	OF-5

John Flannery

FLANNERY, JOHN MICHAEL
B. Jan. 25, 1957, Long Beach, Calif.   BR TR 6'3"   173 lbs.

	G	AB	H	2B	3B	HR	HR%	R	RBI	BB	SO	SB	BA	SA	PH AB	PH H	G by POS
1977 CHI A	7	2	0	0	0	0	0.0	0	0	1	1	0	.000	.000	0	0	SS-4, DH-1, 3B-1

Tim Flannery

FLANNERY, TIMOTHY EARL
B. Sept. 29, 1957, Tulsa, Okla.   BL TR 5'11"   175 lbs.

	G	AB	H	2B	3B	HR	HR%	R	RBI	BB	SO	SB	BA	SA	PH AB	PH H	G by POS
1979 SD N	22	65	10	0	1	0	0.0	2	4	4	5	0	.154	.185	0	0	2B-21
1980	95	292	70	12	0	0	0.0	15	25	18	30	2	.240	.281	12	5	2B-53, 3B-41
1981	37	67	17	4	1	0	0.0	4	6	2	4	1	.254	.343	16	6	3B-15, 2B-7
1982	122	379	100	11	7	0	0.0	40	30	30	32	1	.264	.330	16	3	2B-104, 3B-5, SS-2
1983	92	214	50	7	3	3	1.4	24	19	20	23	2	.234	.336	19	4	3B-52, 2B-21, SS-7
1984	86	128	35	3	3	2	1.6	24	10	12	17	4	.273	.391	40	7	2B-22, SS-14, 3B-14
6 yrs.	454	1145	282	37	15	5	0.4	109	94	86	111	10	.246	.318	103	25	2B-228, 3B-127, SS-23

LEAGUE CHAMPIONSHIP SERIES

	G	AB	H	2B	3B	HR	HR%	R	RBI	BB	SO	SB	BA	SA	PH AB	PH H	G by POS
1984 SD N	3	2	1	0	0	0	0.0	0	2	0	0	0	.500	.500	2	1	

WORLD SERIES

	G	AB	H	2B	3B	HR	HR%	R	RBI	BB	SO	SB	BA	SA	PH AB	PH H	G by POS
1984 SD N	1	1	1	0	0	0	0.0	0	0	0	0	0	1.000	1.000	1	1	2B-1

Ray Flaskamper

FLASKAMPER, RAY HAROLD (Flash)
B. Oct. 31, 1901, St. Louis, Mo.   D. Feb. 3, 1978, San Antonio, Tex.   BB TR 5'7"   140 lbs.

	G	AB	H	2B	3B	HR	HR%	R	RBI	BB	SO	SB	BA	SA	PH AB	PH H	G by POS
1927 CHI A	26	95	21	5	0	0	0.0	12	6	3	8	0	.221	.274	1	0	SS-25

Angel Fleitas

FLEITAS, ANGEL FELIX HUSTA
B. Nov. 10, 1914, Cienfuegos, Cuba   BR TR 5'9"   160 lbs.

	G	AB	H	2B	3B	HR	HR%	R	RBI	BB	SO	SB	BA	SA	PH AB	PH H	G by POS
1948 WAS A	15	13	1	0	0	0	0.0	1	1	5	0	.077	.077	3	1	SS-7

	G	AB	H	2B	3B	HR	HR %	R	RBI	BB	SO	SB	BA	SA	Pinch Hit AB	Pinch Hit H	G by POS

Les Fleming

FLEMING, LESLIE HARVEY (Moe)
B. Aug. 7, 1915, Singleton, Tex.   D. Mar. 5, 1980, Cleveland, Tex.
BL TL 5'10"   185 lbs.

	G	AB	H	2B	3B	HR	HR %	R	RBI	BB	SO	SB	BA	SA	AB	H	G by POS
1939 DET A	8	16	0	0	0	0	0.0	0	1	0	4	0	.000	.000	5	0	OF-3
1941 CLE A	2	8	2	1	0	0	0.0	0	2	0	0	0	.250	.375	0	0	1B-2
1942	156	548	160	27	4	14	2.6	71	82	106	57	6	.292	.432	0	0	1B-156
1945	42	140	46	10	2	3	2.1	18	22	11	5	0	.329	.493	3	1	OF-33, 1B-5
1946	99	306	85	17	5	8	2.6	40	42	50	42	1	.278	.444	17	5	1B-80, OF-1
1947	103	281	68	14	2	4	1.4	39	43	53	42	0	.242	.349	20	6	1B-77
1949 PIT N	24	31	8	0	2	0	0.0	0	7	6	2	0	.258	.387	16	4	1B-5
7 yrs.	434	1330	369	69	15	29	2.2	168	199	226	152	7	.277	.417	61	16	1B-325, OF-37

Tom Fleming

FLEMING, THOMAS VINCENT (Sleuth)
B. Nov. 20, 1873, Philadelphia, Pa.   D. Dec. 26, 1957, Boston, Mass.
5'11"   155 lbs.

	G	AB	H	2B	3B	HR	HR %	R	RBI	BB	SO	SB	BA	SA	AB	H	G by POS
1899 NY N	22	77	16	1	1	0	0.0	9	9	4		1	.208	.247	0	0	OF-22
1902 PHI N	5	16	6	0	0	0	0.0	2	2	1		0	.375	.375	0	0	OF-5
1904	3	6	0	0	0	0	0.0	0	0	0		0	.000	.000	2	0	OF-1
3 yrs.	30	99	22	1	1	0	0.0	11	6	2		1	.222	.253	2	0	OF-28

Art Fletcher

FLETCHER, ARTHUR
B. Jan. 5, 1885, Collinsville, Ill.   D. Feb. 6, 1950, Los Angeles, Calif.
Manager 1923-26, 1929.
BR TR 5'10½"   170 lbs.

	G	AB	H	2B	3B	HR	HR %	R	RBI	BB	SO	SB	BA	SA	AB	H	G by POS
1909 NY N	29	98	21	0	1	0	0.0	7	6	1		0	.214	.235	0	0	SS-19, 3B-5, 2B-5
1910	51	125	28	2	1	0	0.0	12	13	4	9	9	.224	.256	4	0	SS-22, 3B-11, 2B-11
1911	112	326	104	17	8	1	0.3	73	37	30	27	20	.319	.429	2	1	SS-74, 3B-21, 2B-13
1912	129	419	118	17	9	1	0.2	64	57	16	29	16	.282	.372	0	0	SS-126, 2B-2, 3B-1
1913	136	538	160	20	9	4	0.7	76	71	24	35	32	.297	.390	0	0	SS-136
1914	135	514	147	26	8	2	0.4	62	79	22	37	15	.286	.379	0	0	SS-135
1915	149	562	143	17	7	3	0.5	59	74	6	36	36	.254	.326	0	0	SS-149
1916	133	500	143	23	8	3	0.6	53	66	13	36	15	.286	.382	0	0	SS-133
1917	151	557	145	24	5	4	0.7	70	56	23	28	12	.260	.343	0	0	SS-151
1918	124	468	123	20	2	0	0.0	51	47	18	26	12	.263	.314	0	0	SS-124
1919	127	488	135	20	5	3	0.6	54	54	9	28	6	.277	.357	0	0	SS-127
1920 2 teams	NY	N (41G – .257)				PHI	N (102G – .296)										
" total	143	550	156	32	9	4	0.7	57	62	16	43	7	.284	.396	1	0	SS-142
1922 PHI N	110	396	111	20	5	7	1.8	46	53	21	14	3	.280	.409	4	1	SS-106
13 yrs.	1529	5541	1534	238	77	32	0.6	684	675	203	348	159	.277	.365	11	2	SS-1444, 3B-38, 2B-31

WORLD SERIES

	G	AB	H	2B	3B	HR	HR %	R	RBI	BB	SO	SB	BA	SA	AB	H	G by POS
1911 NY N	6	23	3	1	0	0	0.0	1	1	0	4	0	.130	.174	0	0	SS-6
1912	8	28	5	1	0	0	0.0	1	3	1	4	1	.179	.214	0	0	SS-8
1913	5	18	5	0	0	0	0.0	1	4	1	1	1	.278	.278	0	0	SS-5
1917	6	25	5	1	0	0	0.0	2	0	0	2	0	.200	.240	0	0	SS-6
4 yrs.	25	94	18	3	0	0	0.0	5	8	2	11	2	.191	.223	0	0	SS-25

Elbie Fletcher

FLETCHER, ELBURT PRESTON
B. Mar. 18, 1916, Milton, Mass.
BL TL 6'   180 lbs.

	G	AB	H	2B	3B	HR	HR %	R	RBI	BB	SO	SB	BA	SA	AB	H	G by POS
1934 BOS N	8	4	2	0	0	0	0.0	4	0	0	2	1	.500	.500	0	0	1B-1
1935	39	148	35	7	1	1	0.7	12	9	7	13	1	.236	.318	0	0	1B-39
1937	148	539	133	22	4	1	0.2	56	38	56	64	3	.247	.308	0	0	1B-148
1938	147	529	144	24	7	6	1.1	71	48	60	40	5	.272	.378	1	0	1B-146
1939 2 teams	BOS	N (35G – .245)				PIT	N (102G – .303)										
" total	137	476	138	25	4	12	2.5	63	77	67	33	4	.290	.435	4	1	1B-132
1940 PIT N	147	510	139	22	7	16	3.1	94	104	119	54	5	.273	.437	0	0	1B-147
1941	151	521	150	29	13	11	2.1	95	74	118	54	5	.288	.457	0	0	1B-151
1942	145	506	146	22	5	7	1.4	86	57	105	60	0	.289	.393	1	1	1B-144
1943	154	544	154	24	5	9	1.7	91	70	95	49	1	.283	.395	0	0	1B-154
1946	148	532	136	25	8	4	0.8	72	66	111	37	4	.256	.355	1	0	1B-147
1947	69	157	38	9	1	1	0.6	22	22	29	24	2	.242	.331	18	2	1B-50
1949 BOS N	122	413	108	19	3	11	2.7	57	51	84	65	1	.262	.402	25	4	1B-121
12 yrs.	1415	4879	1323	228	58	79	1.6	723	616	851	495	32	.271	.390			1B-1380

Scott Fletcher

FLETCHER, SCOTT BRIAN
B. July 30, 1958, Fort Walton Beach, Fla.
BR TR 5'11"   168 lbs.

	G	AB	H	2B	3B	HR	HR %	R	RBI	BB	SO	SB	BA	SA	AB	H	G by POS
1981 CHI N	19	46	10	4	0	0	0.0	6	1	2	4	0	.217	.304	0	0	2B-13, SS-4, 3B-1
1982	11	24	4	0	0	0	0.0	4	1	4	5	1	.167	.167	0	0	SS-11
1983 CHI A	114	262	62	16	5	3	1.1	42	31	29	22	5	.237	.370	0	0	SS-100, 2B-12, 3B-7, DH-1
1984	149	456	114	13	3	3	0.7	46	35	46	46	10	.250	.311	0	0	SS-134, 2B-28, 3B-3
4 yrs.	293	788	190	33	8	6	0.8	98	68	81	77	16	.241	.326	0	0	SS-249, 2B-53, 3B-11, DH-1

LEAGUE CHAMPIONSHIP SERIES

	G	AB	H	2B	3B	HR	HR %	R	RBI	BB	SO	SB	BA	SA	AB	H	G by POS
1983 CHI A	3	7	0	0	0	0	0.0	0	0	1	0	0	.000	.000	0	0	SS-3

Elmer Flick

FLICK, ELMER HARRISON
B. Jan. 11, 1876, Bedford, Ohio   D. Jan. 9, 1971, Bedford, Ohio
Hall of Fame 1963.
BL TR 5'9"   168 lbs.

	G	AB	H	2B	3B	HR	HR %	R	RBI	BB	SO	SB	BA	SA	AB	H	G by POS
1898 PHI N	134	453	142	16	14	7	1.5	84	81	86		23	.313	.457	1	0	OF-133
1899	127	485	166	22	14	2	0.4	98	98	42		31	.342	.458	2	1	OF-125
1900	138	547	207	33	16	11	2.0	106	110	56		35	.378	.558	0	0	OF-138
1901	138	542	182	31	17	8	1.5	112	88	52		30	.336	.500	0	0	OF-138
1902 2 teams	PHI	A (11G – .297)				CLE	A (110G – .297)										
" total	121	461	137	22	12	2	0.4	85	64	53		24	.297	.410	0	0	OF-121
1903 CLE A	142	529	158	23	16	2	0.4	84	51	51		24	.299	.414	0	0	OF-140
1904	150	579	177	31	18	6	1.0	97	56	51		42	.306	.453	0	0	OF-144, 2B-6
1905	131	496	152	29	19	1	0.2	71	64	53		35	.306	.466	0	0	OF-130, 2B-1
1906	157	624	194	33	22	1	0.2	98	62	54		39	.311	.439	0	0	OF-150, 2B-8
1907	147	549	166	15	18	3	0.5	78	58	64		41	.302	.412	0	0	OF-147
1908	9	35	8	1	1	0	0.0	4	2	3		0	.229	.314	0	0	OF-9

	G	AB	H	2B	3B	HR	HR %	R	RBI	BB	SO	SB	BA	SA	Pinch Hit AB	Pinch Hit H	G by POS

Elmer Flick continued

	G	AB	H	2B	3B	HR	HR %	R	RBI	BB	SO	SB	BA	SA	AB	H	G by POS
1909	66	235	60	10	2	0	0.0	28	15	22		9	.255	.315	5	2	OF-61
1910	24	68	18	2	1	1	1.5	5	7	10		1	.265	.368	4	0	OF-18
13 yrs.	1484	5603	1767	268	170	47	0.8	950	756	597		334	.315	.449	12	3	OF-1454, 2B-15

Lew Flick

FLICK, LEWIS MILLER
B. Feb. 18, 1915, Bristol, Tenn.

BL TL 5'9" 155 lbs.

	G	AB	H	2B	3B	HR	HR %	R	RBI	BB	SO	SB	BA	SA	AB	H	G by POS
1943 PHI A	1	5	3	0	0	0	0.0	2	0	0	0	0	.600	.600	0	0	OF-1
1944	19	35	4	0	0	0	0.0	1	2	1	2	1	.114	.114	13	0	OF-6
2 yrs.	20	40	7	0	0	0	0.0	3	2	1	2	1	.175	.175	13	0	OF-7

Don Flinn

FLINN, DON RAPHAEL
B. Nov. 17, 1892, Bluffdale, Tex. D. Mar. 9, 1959, Waco, Tex.

BR TR 6'1" 185 lbs.

	G	AB	H	2B	3B	HR	HR %	R	RBI	BB	SO	SB	BA	SA	AB	H	G by POS
1917 PIT N	14	37	11	1	1	0	0.0	1	1	1	6	1	.297	.378	2	1	OF-12

Silver Flint

FLINT, FRANK SYLVESTER
B. Aug. 3, 1855, Philadelphia, Pa. D. Jan. 14, 1892, Chicago, Ill.

BR TR 5'10" 170 lbs.

	G	AB	H	2B	3B	HR	HR %	R	RBI	BB	SO	SB	BA	SA	AB	H	G by POS
1878 IND N	63	254	57	7	0	0	0.0	23	18	2	15		.224	.252	0	0	C-59, OF-9
1879 CHI N	79	324	92	22	6	1	0.3	46	41	6	44		.284	.398	0	0	C-78, OF-1
1880	74	284	46	10	4	0	0.0	30	17	5	32		.162	.225	0	0	C-67, OF-13
1881	80	306	95	18	0	1	0.3	46	34	6	39		.310	.379	0	0	C-80, OF-8, 1B-1
1882	81	331	83	18	8	4	1.2	48	44	2	50		.251	.390	0	0	C-81, OF-10
1883	85	332	88	23	4	0	0.0	57		3	69		.265	.358	0	0	C-83, OF-23
1884	73	279	57	5	2	9	3.2	35		7	57		.204	.333	0	0	C-73
1885	68	249	52	8	2	1	0.4	27	19	2	52		.209	.269	0	0	C-68, OF-1
1886	54	173	35	6	2	1	0.6	30	13	12	36		.202	.277	0	0	C-54, 1B-3
1887	49	187	50	8	6	3	1.6	22	21	4	28	7	.267	.422	0	0	C-47, 1B-2
1888	22	77	14	3	0	0	0.0	6	3	1	21	1	.182	.221	0	0	C-22
1889	15	56	13	1	0	1	1.8	6	9	3	18	1	.232	.304	0	0	C-15
12 yrs.	743	2852	682	129	34	21	0.7	376	219	53	461	9	.239	.330	0	0	C-727, OF-65, 1B-6

Curt Flood

FLOOD, CURTIS CHARLES
B. Jan. 18, 1938, Houston, Tex.

BR TR 5'9" 165 lbs.

	G	AB	H	2B	3B	HR	HR %	R	RBI	BB	SO	SB	BA	SA	AB	H	G by POS
1956 CIN N	5	1	0	0	0	0	0.0	0	0	0	1	0	.000	.000	1	0	
1957	3	3	1	0	0	1	33.3	2	1	0	0	0	.333	1.333	1	0	3B-2, 2B-1
1958 STL N	121	422	110	17	2	10	2.4	50	41	31	56	2	.261	.382	0	0	OF-120, 3B-1
1959	121	208	53	7	3	7	3.4	24	26	16	35	2	.255	.418	10	5	OF-106, 2B-1
1960	140	396	94	20	1	8	2.0	37	38	35	54	0	.237	.354	2	0	OF-134, 3B-1
1961	132	335	108	15	5	2	0.6	53	21	35	33	6	.322	.415	12	4	OF-119
1962	151	635	188	30	5	12	1.9	99	70	42	57	8	.296	.416	0	0	OF-151
1963	158	662	200	34	9	5	0.8	112	63	42	57	17	.302	.403	1	0	OF-158
1964	162	679	211	25	3	5	0.7	97	46	43	53	8	.311	.378	1	0	OF-162
1965	156	617	191	30	3	11	1.8	90	83	51	50	9	.310	.421	1	0	OF-151
1966	160	626	167	21	5	10	1.6	64	78	26	50	14	.267	.364	0	0	OF-159
1967	134	514	172	24	1	5	1.0	68	50	37	46	2	.335	.414	8	4	OF-126
1968	150	618	186	17	4	5	0.8	71	60	33	58	11	.301	.366	2	0	OF-149
1969	153	606	173	31	3	4	0.7	80	57	48	57	9	.285	.366	2	1	OF-152
1971 WAS A	13	35	7	0	0	0	0.0	4	2	5	2	0	.200	.200	1	0	OF-10
15 yrs.	1759	6357	1861	271	44	85	1.3	851	636	444	609	88	.293	.389	46	14	OF-1697, 3B-4, 2B-2
WORLD SERIES																	
1964 STL N	7	30	6	0	1	0	0.0	5	3	3	1	0	.200	.267	0	0	OF-7
1967	7	28	5	1	0	0	0.0	2	3	3	3	0	.179	.214	0	0	OF-7
1968	7	28	8	1	0	0	0.0	4	2	2	2	3	.286	.321	0	0	OF-7
3 yrs.	21	86	19	2	1	0	0.0	11	8	8	6	3	.221	.267	0	0	OF-21

Tim Flood

FLOOD, TIMOTHY A.
B. Mar. 13, 1877, Montgomery City, Mo. D. June 15, 1929, St. Louis, Mo.

BR TR

	G	AB	H	2B	3B	HR	HR %	R	RBI	BB	SO	SB	BA	SA	AB	H	G by POS
1899 STL N	10	31	9	0	0	0	0.0	0	3	4		1	.290	.290	0	0	2B-10
1902 BKN N	132	476	104	11	4	3	0.6	43	50	23		8	.218	.277	0	0	2B-11, 1B-3, OF-1
1903	89	309	77	15	2	0	0.0	27	32	15		14	.249	.311	2	0	2B-84, SS-2, OF-1
3 yrs.	231	816	190	26	6	3	0.4	70	85	42		23	.233	.290	2	0	2B-226, OF-2, SS-2

Paul Florence

FLORENCE, PAUL ROBERT (Pep)
B. Apr. 22, 1900, Chicago, Ill.

BL TR 6'1" 185 lbs.

	G	AB	H	2B	3B	HR	HR %	R	RBI	BB	SO	SB	BA	SA	AB	H	G by POS
1926 NY N	76	188	43	4	3	2	1.1	19	14	23	12	2	.229	.314	0	0	C-76

Gil Flores

FLORES, GILBERTO
Also known as Gilberto Garcia.
B. Oct. 27, 1952, Ponce, Puerto Rico

BR TR 6' 185 lbs.

	G	AB	H	2B	3B	HR	HR %	R	RBI	BB	SO	SB	BA	SA	AB	H	G by POS
1977 CAL A	104	342	95	19	4	1	0.3	41	26	23	39	12	.278	.365	10	2	OF-85, DH-8
1978 NY N	11	29	8	0	1	0	0.0	8	1	3	5	1	.276	.345	1	0	OF-8
1979	70	93	18	1	1	1	1.1	9	10	8	17	2	.194	.258	39	7	OF-32
3 yrs.	185	464	121	20	6	2	0.4	58	37	34	61	15	.261	.343	50	9	OF-125, DH-8

Jake Flowers

FLOWERS, D'ARCY RAYMOND
B. Mar. 16, 1902, Cambridge, Md. D. Dec. 27, 1962, Clearwater, Fla.

BR TR 5'11½" 170 lbs.

	G	AB	H	2B	3B	HR	HR %	R	RBI	BB	SO	SB	BA	SA	AB	H	G by POS
1923 STL N	13	32	3	1	0	0	0.0	0	2	2	7	1	.094	.125	0	0	SS-7, 3B-2, 2B-2
1926	40	74	20	1	0	3	4.1	13	9	5	9	1	.270	.405	23	6	2B-11, 1B-3, SS-1
1927 BKN N	67	231	54	5	5	2	0.9	26	20	21	25	3	.234	.325	1	0	SS-65, 2B-1
1928	103	339	93	11	6	2	0.6	51	44	47	30	10	.274	.360	3	1	2B-94, SS-1
1929	46	130	26	6	0	1	0.8	16	16	22	6	9	.200	.269	5	2	2B-39
1930	89	253	81	18	3	2	0.8	37	50	21	18	5	.320	.439	16	6	2B-65, OF-1
1931 2 teams				BKN N	(22G –	.226)		STL N	(45G –	.248)							
" total	67	168	41	11	1	2	1.2	22	20	16	10	8	.244	.357	12	3	2B-26, SS-23, 3B-1
1932 STL N	67	247	63	11	1	2	0.8	35	18	31	18	7	.255	.332	4	2	3B-54, SS-7, 2B-2

	G	AB	H	2B	3B	HR	HR %	R	RBI	BB	SO	SB	BA	SA	Pinch Hit AB	Pinch Hit H	G by POS

Jake Flowers continued

	G	AB	H	2B	3B	HR	HR%	R	RBI	BB	SO	SB	BA	SA	PH AB	PH H	G by POS
1933 BKN N	78	210	49	11	2	2	1.0	28	22	24	15	13	.233	.333	7	2	SS-36, 2B-19, 3B-8, OF-1
1934 CIN N	13	9	3	0	0	0	0.0	1	0	1	1	1	.333	.333	9	3	
10 yrs.	583	1693	433	75	18	16	0.9	229	201	190	139	58	.256	.350	81	25	2B-259, SS-145, 3B-65, 1B-3, OF-2
WORLD SERIES																	
1926 STL N	3	3	0	0	0	0	0.0	0	0	0	1	0	.000	.000	3	0	
1931	5	11	1	1	0	0	0.0	1	0	1	0	0	.091	.182	1	0	3B-4
2 yrs.	8	14	1	1	0	0	0.0	1	0	1	1	0	.071	.143	4	0	3B-4

Bobby Floyd

FLOYD, ROBERT NATHAN
B. Oct. 20, 1943, Hawthorne, Calif.
BR TR 6'1" 180 lbs.

	G	AB	H	2B	3B	HR	HR%	R	RBI	BB	SO	SB	BA	SA	PH AB	PH H	G by POS
1968 BAL A	5	9	1	1	0	0	0.0	1	0	0	3	0	.111	.222	0	0	SS-4
1969	39	84	17	4	0	0	0.0	7	1	6	17	0	.202	.250	1	0	SS-15, 2B-15, 3B-9
1970 2 teams		BAL	A (3G – .000)			KC	A (14G – .326)										
" total	17	45	14	4	0	0	0.0	5	9	4	11	0	.311	.400	0	0	SS-10, 3B-6, 2B-1
1971 KC A	31	66	10	3	0	0	0.0	8	2	7	21	0	.152	.197	3	1	SS-15, 2B-8, 3B-1
1972	61	134	24	3	0	0	0.0	9	5	5	29	1	.179	.201	0	0	3B-30, SS-29, 2B-2
1973	51	78	26	3	1	0	0.0	10	8	4	14	1	.333	.397	0	0	2B-25, SS-24
1974	10	9	1	0	0	0	0.0	0	1	2	4	0	.111	.111	0	0	2B-5, 3B-2, SS-1
7 yrs.	214	425	93	18	1	0	0.0	40	26	28	99	2	.219	.266	4	1	SS-98, 2B-56, 3B-48

Bubba Floyd

FLOYD, LESLIE ROE
B. June 23, 1917, Dallas, Tex.
BR TR 5'11" 160 lbs.

	G	AB	H	2B	3B	HR	HR%	R	RBI	BB	SO	SB	BA	SA	PH AB	PH H	G by POS
1944 DET A	3	9	4	1	0	0	0.0	1	0	1	0	0	.444	.556	0	0	SS-3

John Fluhrer

FLUHRER, JOHN L.
Played as William Morris Part Of 1915.
B. Jan. 3, 1894, Adrian, Mich. D. July 17, 1946, Columbus, Ohio
BR TR 5'9" 165 lbs.

	G	AB	H	2B	3B	HR	HR%	R	RBI	BB	SO	SB	BA	SA	PH AB	PH H	G by POS
1915 CHI N	6	6	2	0	0	0	0.0	0	0	1	0	1	.333	.333	3	0	OF-2

Doug Flynn

FLYNN, ROBERT DOUGLAS
B. Apr. 18, 1951, Lexington, Ky.
BR TR 5'11" 165 lbs.

	G	AB	H	2B	3B	HR	HR%	R	RBI	BB	SO	SB	BA	SA	PH AB	PH H	G by POS
1975 CIN N	89	127	34	0	1	1	0.8	17	20	11	13	3	.268	.346	7	1	3B-40, 2B-30, SS-17
1976	93	219	62	5	2	1	0.5	20	20	10	24	2	.283	.338	1	0	2B-55, 3B-23, SS-20
1977 2 teams		CIN	N (36G – .250)			NY	N (90G – .191)										
" total	126	314	62	7	2	0	0.0	14	19	2	21	1	.197	.232	4	0	SS-69, 2B-38, 3B-27
1978 NY N	156	532	126	12	8	0	0.0	37	36	30	50	3	.237	.289	0	0	2B-128, SS-60
1979	157	555	135	19	5	4	0.7	35	61	17	46	0	.243	.317	1	1	2B-148, SS-20
1980	128	443	113	9	8	0	0.0	46	24	22	20	2	.255	.312	0	0	2B-128, SS-3
1981	105	325	72	12	4	1	0.3	24	20	11	19	1	.222	.292	0	0	2B-100, SS-5
1982 2 teams		TEX	A (88G – .211)			MON	N (58G – .244)										
" total	146	463	104	12	4	0	0.0	26	39	8	37	6	.225	.268	0	0	2B-113, SS-35
1983 MON N	143	452	107	18	4	0	0.0	44	26	19	38	2	.237	.294	0	0	2B-107, SS-37
1984	124	366	89	12	1	0	0.0	23	17	12	41	0	.243	.281	3	0	2B-88, SS-34
10 yrs.	1267	3796	904	113	38	7	0.2	286	282	142	309	20	.238	.293	16	4	2B-935, SS-300, 3B-90
LEAGUE CHAMPIONSHIP SERIES																	
1976 CIN N	1	1	0	0	0	0	–	0	0	0	0	0	–	–	0	0	2B-1

Ed Flynn

FLYNN, EDWARD J.
B. 1864, Chicago, Ill. Deceased.
5'9" 165 lbs.

	G	AB	H	2B	3B	HR	HR%	R	RBI	BB	SO	SB	BA	SA	PH AB	PH H	G by POS
1887 CLE AA	7	27	5	1	0	0	0.0	0		1		3	.185	.222	0	0	3B-6, OF-1

George Flynn

FLYNN, GEORGE A. (Dibby)
B. May 24, 1871, Chicago, Ill. D. Dec. 28, 1901, Chicago, Ill.

	G	AB	H	2B	3B	HR	HR%	R	RBI	BB	SO	SB	BA	SA	PH AB	PH H	G by POS
1896 CHI N	29	106	27	1	2	0	0.0	15	4	11	9	12	.255	.302	0	0	OF-29

Jocko Flynn

FLYNN, JOHN A.
B. June 30, 1864, Lawrence, Mass. D. Dec. 30, 1907, Lawrence, Mass.
5'6½" 143 lbs.

	G	AB	H	2B	3B	HR	HR%	R	RBI	BB	SO	SB	BA	SA	PH AB	PH H	G by POS
1886 CHI N	57	205	41	6	2	4	2.0	40	19	18	45	0	.200	.307	0	0	P-32, OF-28
1887	1	0	0	0	0	0	–	0	0	0	0	0	–	–	0	0	OF-1
2 yrs.	58	205	41	6	2	4	2.0	40	19	18	45	0	.200	.307	0	0	P-32, OF-29

Joe Flynn

FLYNN, JOSEPH
B. Philadelphia, Pa. Deceased.

	G	AB	H	2B	3B	HR	HR%	R	RBI	BB	SO	SB	BA	SA	PH AB	PH H	G by POS
1884 2 teams		PHI	U (52G – .249)			BOS	U (9G – .226)										
" total	61	240	59	11	4	4	1.7	42		13			.246	.375	0	0	OF-47, C-17, 1B-2, SS-1

John Flynn

FLYNN, JOHN ANTHONY
B. Sept. 7, 1883, Providence, R. I. D. Mar. 23, 1935, Providence, R. I.
BR TR 6'½" 175 lbs.

	G	AB	H	2B	3B	HR	HR%	R	RBI	BB	SO	SB	BA	SA	PH AB	PH H	G by POS
1910 PIT N	96	332	91	10	2	6	1.8	32	52	30	47	6	.274	.370	3	2	1B-93
1911	33	59	12	0	1	0	0.0	5	3	9	8	0	.203	.237	15	3	1B-13, OF-1
1912 WAS A	20	71	12	4	1	0	0.0	9	5	7		2	.169	.254	0	0	1B-20
3 yrs.	149	462	115	14	4	6	1.3	46	60	46	55	8	.249	.335	18	5	1B-126, OF-1

Mike Flynn

FLYNN, MICHAEL E.
B. Lowell, Mass. Deceased.

	G	AB	H	2B	3B	HR	HR%	R	RBI	BB	SO	SB	BA	SA	PH AB	PH H	G by POS
1891 BOS AA	1	2	0	0	0	0	0.0	0	0	0	1	0	.000	.000	0	0	C-1

Jim Fogarty

FOGARTY, JAMES G.
Brother of Joe Fogarty.
B. Feb. 12, 1864, San Francisco, Calif. D. May 20, 1891, Philadelphia, Pa.
Manager 1890.
BR TR 5'6½" 180 lbs.

	G	AB	H	2B	3B	HR	HR%	R	RBI	BB	SO	SB	BA	SA	PH AB	PH H	G by POS
1884 PHI N	97	378	80	12	6	1	0.3	42		20	54		.212	.283	0	0	OF-78, 3B-14, 2B-4, SS-3
1885	111	427	99	13	3	0	0.0	49		30	37		.232	.276	0	0	OF-88, 2B-10, SS-8, 3B-5

	G	AB	H	2B	3B	HR	HR %	R	RBI	BB	SO	SB	BA	SA	Pinch Hit AB	H	G by POS

Jim Fogarty continued

	G	AB	H	2B	3B	HR	HR%	R	RBI	BB	SO	SB	BA	SA	PH AB	PH H	G by POS
1886	77	280	82	13	5	3	1.1	54	47	42	16		.293	.407	0	0	OF-60, 2B-13, SS-3, 3B-3, P-1
1887	126	495	129	26	12	8	1.6	113	50	82	44	102	.261	.410	0	0	OF-123, SS-2, 3B-2, 2B-1, P-1
1888	121	454	107	14	6	1	0.2	72	35	53	66	58	.236	.300	0	0	OF-117, 3B-5, SS-1
1889	128	499	129	15	17	3	0.6	107	54	65	60	99	.259	.375	0	0	OF-128, P-4
1890 PHI P	91	347	83	17	6	4	1.2	71	58	59	50	36	.239	.357	0	0	OF-91, 3B-1
7 yrs.	751	2880	709	110	55	20	0.7	508	243	351	327	295	.246	.343	0	0	OF-685, 3B-30, 2B-28, SS-17, P-6

Joe Fogarty

FOGARTY, JOSEPH J.
Brother of Jim Fogarty.
B. San Francisco, Calif.   Deceased.

	G	AB	H	2B	3B	HR	HR%	R	RBI	BB	SO	SB	BA	SA	PH AB	PH H	G by POS
1885 STL N	2	8	1	0	0	0	0.0	1	0	0	1		.125	.125	0	0	OF-2

Lee Fohl

FOHL, LEO ALEXANDER   BL TR 5'10"   175 lbs.
B. Nov. 28, 1876, Lowell, Ohio   D. Oct. 30, 1965, Cleveland, Ohio
Manager 1915-19, 1921-26.

	G	AB	H	2B	3B	HR	HR%	R	RBI	BB	SO	SB	BA	SA	PH AB	PH H	G by POS
1902 PIT N	1	3	0	0	0	0	0.0	0	1	0		0	.000	.000	0	0	C-1
1903 CIN N	4	14	5	1	1	0	0.0	3	2	0		0	.357	.571	0	0	C-4
2 yrs.	5	17	5	1	1	0	0.0	3	3	0		0	.294	.471	0	0	C-5

Hank Foiles

FOILES, HENRY LEE   BR TR 6'   195 lbs.
B. June 10, 1929, Richmond, Va.

	G	AB	H	2B	3B	HR	HR%	R	RBI	BB	SO	SB	BA	SA	PH AB	PH H	G by POS
1953 2 teams			CIN N (5G – .154)			CLE A (7G – .143)											
" total	12	20	3	0	0	0	0.0	3	0	2	3	0	.150	.150	2	0	C-10
1955 CLE A	62	111	29	9	0	1	0.9	13	7	17	18	0	.261	.369	20	6	C-41
1956 2 teams			CLE A (1G – .000)			PIT N (79G – .212)											
" total	80	222	47	10	2	7	3.2	24	25	17	56	0	.212	.369	5	1	C-74
1957 PIT N	109	281	76	10	4	9	3.2	32	36	37	53	1	.270	.431	4	0	C-109
1958	104	264	54	10	2	8	3.0	31	30	45	53	0	.205	.348	4	0	C-103
1959	53	80	18	3	0	3	3.8	10	4	7	16	0	.225	.375	1	0	C-51
1960 3 teams			KC A (6G – .571)			CLE A (24G – .279)			DET A (26G – .250)								
" total	56	131	37	4	0	1	0.8	15	10	11	15	1	.282	.336	6	1	C-46
1961 BAL A	43	124	34	6	0	6	4.8	18	19	12	27	0	.274	.468	4	0	C-38
1962 CIN N	43	131	36	6	1	7	5.3	17	25	13	39	0	.275	.496	5	2	C-41
1963 2 teams			CIN N (1G – .000)			LA A (41G – .214)											
" total	42	87	18	1	1	4	4.6	8	10	9	13	1	.207	.379	11	2	C-31
1964 LA A	4	4	1	0	0	0	0.0	0	0	0	2	0	.250	.250	4	1	
11 yrs.	608	1455	353	59	10	46	3.2	171	166	170	295	3	.243	.392	62	13	C-544

Curry Foley

FOLEY, CHARLES JOSEPH   TL   180 lbs.
B. Jan. 14, 1856, Milltown, Ireland   D. Oct. 20, 1898, Boston, Mass.

	G	AB	H	2B	3B	HR	HR%	R	RBI	BB	SO	SB	BA	SA	PH AB	PH H	G by POS
1879 BOS N	35	146	46	3	1	0	0.0	16	17	3	4		.315	.349	0	0	P-21, OF-17, 1B-2
1880	80	332	97	13	2	2	0.6	44	31	8	14		.292	.361	0	0	P-36, OF-35, 1B-25
1881 BUF N	83	375	96	20	2	1	0.3	58	25	7	27		.256	.328	0	0	OF-55, 1B-27, P-10
1882	84	341	104	16	4	3	0.9	51		12	26		.305	.402	0	0	OF-84, P-1
1883	23	111	30	5	3	0	0.0	23		4	12		.270	.369	0	0	OF-23, P-1
5 yrs.	305	1305	373	57	12	6	0.5	192	73	34	83		.286	.362	0	0	OF-214, P-69, 1B-54

Marv Foley

FOLEY, MARVIS EDWIN   BL TR 6'   195 lbs.
B. Aug. 29, 1953, Stanford, Ky.

	G	AB	H	2B	3B	HR	HR%	R	RBI	BB	SO	SB	BA	SA	PH AB	PH H	G by POS
1978 CHI A	11	34	12	0	0	0	0.0	3	6	4	6	0	.353	.353	1	0	C-10
1979	34	97	24	3	0	2	2.1	6	10	7	5	0	.247	.340	2	1	C-33
1980	68	137	29	5	0	4	2.9	14	15	9	22	0	.212	.336	8	3	C-64, 1B-3
1982 TEX A	27	36	4	0	0	0	0.0	1	1	6	4	0	.111	.111	11	1	C-15, 3B-2, DH-1, 1B-1
1984 TEX A	63	115	25	2	0	6	5.2	13	19	15	24	0	.217	.391	28	7	C-36, DH-4, 3B-1, 1B-1
5 yrs.	203	419	94	10	0	12	2.9	37	51	41	61	0	.224	.334	50	12	C-158, DH-5, 1B-5, 3B-3

Pat Foley

Playing record listed under Willie Greene

Ray Foley

FOLEY, RAYMOND KIRWIN   BL TR 5'11"   173 lbs.
B. June 23, 1906, Naugatuck, Conn.   D. Mar. 22, 1980, Vero Beach, Fla.

	G	AB	H	2B	3B	HR	HR%	R	RBI	BB	SO	SB	BA	SA	PH AB	PH H	G by POS
1928 NY N	2	1	0	0	0	0	0.0	1	0	1	1	0	.000	.000	1	0	

Tom Foley

FOLEY, THOMAS MICHAEL   BL TR 6'1"   160 lbs.
B. Sept. 9, 1959, Columbus, Ga.

	G	AB	H	2B	3B	HR	HR%	R	RBI	BB	SO	SB	BA	SA	PH AB	PH H	G by POS
1983 CIN N	68	98	20	4	1	0	0.0	7	9	13	17	1	.204	.265	20	4	SS-37, 2B-5
1984	106	277	70	8	3	5	1.8	26	27	24	36	3	.253	.357	13	5	SS-83, 2B-10, 3B-1
2 yrs.	174	375	90	12	4	5	1.3	33	36	37	53	4	.240	.333	33	9	SS-120, 2B-15, 3B-1

Will Foley

FOLEY, WILLIAM BROWN   BR TR 5'9½"   150 lbs.
B. Nov. 15, 1855, Chicago, Ill.   D. Nov. 15, 1916, Chicago, Ill.

	G	AB	H	2B	3B	HR	HR%	R	RBI	BB	SO	SB	BA	SA	PH AB	PH H	G by POS
1876 CIN N	58	221	50	3	2	0	0.0	19	9	0	14		.226	.258	0	0	3B-46, C-20
1877	56	216	41	5	1	0	0.0	23	18	4	13		.190	.222	0	0	3B-56
1878 MIL N	56	229	62	3	5	0	0.0	33	22	7	14		.271	.349	0	0	3B-53, C-7
1879 CIN N	56	218	46	5	1	0	0.0	22	25	2	16		.211	.243	0	0	3B-29, OF-25, 2B-3
1881 DET N	5	15	2	0	0	0	0.0	0	1	2	3		.133	.133	0	0	3B-5
1884 C-P U	19	71	20	1	1	0	0.0	15			5		.282	.324	0	0	3B-19
6 yrs.	250	970	221	22	10	0	0.0	112	75	20	60		.228	.271	0	0	3B-208, C-27, OF-25, 2B-3

	G	AB	H	2B	3B	HR	HR %	R	RBI	BB	SO	SB	BA	SA	Pinch Hit AB	Pinch Hit H	G by POS

Tim Foli

FOLI, TIMOTHY JOHN
B. Dec. 8, 1950, Culver City, Calif.

BR TR 6'   179 lbs.

	G	AB	H	2B	3B	HR	HR %	R	RBI	BB	SO	SB	BA	SA	PH AB	PH H	G by POS
1970 NY N	5	11	4	0	0	0	0.0	0	1	0	2	0	.364	.364	1	1	SS-2, 3B-2
1971	97	288	65	12	2	0	0.0	32	24	18	50	5	.226	.281	2	0	2B-58, 3B-36, SS-12, OF-1
1972 MON N	149	540	130	12	2	2	0.4	45	35	25	43	11	.241	.281	1	0	SS-148, 2B-1
1973	126	458	110	11	0	2	0.4	37	36	28	40	6	.240	.277	0	0	SS-123, 2B-2, OF-1
1974	121	441	112	10	3	0	0.0	41	39	28	27	8	.254	.290	1	1	SS-120, OF-1
1975	152	572	136	25	2	1	0.2	64	29	36	49	13	.238	.294	3	0	SS-151, 3B-1
1976	149	546	144	36	1	6	1.1	41	54	16	33	6	.264	.366	1	0	SS-146, 3B-1
1977 2 teams	MON N	(13G –	.175)		SF N	(104G –	.228)										
" total	117	425	94	22	4	4	0.9	32	30	11	20	2	.221	.320	4	2	SS-115, OF-1, 3B-1, 2B-1
1978 NY N	113	413	106	21	1	1	0.2	37	27	14	30	2	.257	.320	1	0	SS-112
1979 2 teams	NY N	(3G –	.000)		PIT N	(133G –	.291)										
" total	136	532	153	23	1	1	0.2	70	65	28	14	6	.288	.340	1	0	SS-135
1980 PIT N	127	495	131	22	0	3	0.6	61	38	19	23	11	.265	.327	1	0	SS-125
1981	86	316	78	12	2	0	0.0	32	20	17	10	7	.247	.297	4	0	SS-81
1982 CAL A	150	480	121	14	2	3	0.6	46	56	14	22	2	.252	.308	1	0	SS-139, 2B-8, 3B-2
1983	88	330	83	10	0	2	0.6	29	29	5	18	2	.252	.300	0	0	SS-74, 3B-13
1984 NY A	61	163	41	11	0	0	0.0	8	16	2	16	0	.252	.319	4	0	SS-28, 2B-21, 3B-10, 1B-2
15 yrs.	1677	6010	1508	241	20	25	0.4	575	499	261	397	81	.251	.310	29	5	SS-1511, 2B-92, 3B-65, OF-4, 1B-2

LEAGUE CHAMPIONSHIP SERIES

	G	AB	H	2B	3B	HR	HR %	R	RBI	BB	SO	SB	BA	SA	PH AB	PH H	G by POS
1979 PIT N	3	12	4	1	0	0	0.0	1	3	0	0	0	.333	.417	0	0	SS-3
1982 CAL A	5	16	2	0	0	0	0.0	0	1	0	3	0	.125	.125	0	0	SS-5
2 yrs.	8	28	6	1	0	0	0.0	1	4	0	3	0	.214	.250	0	0	SS-8

WORLD SERIES

	G	AB	H	2B	3B	HR	HR %	R	RBI	BB	SO	SB	BA	SA	PH AB	PH H	G by POS
1979 PIT N	7	30	10	1	1	0	0.0	6	3	2	0	0	.333	.433	0	0	SS-7

Dee Fondy

FONDY, DEE VIRGIL
B. Oct. 31, 1924, Slaton, Tex.

BL TL 6'3"   195 lbs.

	G	AB	H	2B	3B	HR	HR %	R	RBI	BB	SO	SB	BA	SA	PH AB	PH H	G by POS
1951 CHI N	49	170	46	7	2	3	1.8	23	20	11	20	5	.271	.388	5	1	1B-44
1952	145	554	166	21	9	10	1.8	69	67	28	60	13	.300	.424	2	0	1B-143
1953	150	595	184	24	11	18	3.0	79	78	44	106	10	.309	.477	1	0	1B-149
1954	141	568	162	30	4	9	1.6	77	49	35	84	20	.285	.400	2	1	1B-138
1955	150	574	152	23	8	17	3.0	69	65	35	87	8	.265	.422	0	0	1B-147
1956	137	543	146	22	9	9	1.7	52	46	20	74	9	.269	.392	4	1	1B-133
1957 2 teams	CHI N	(11G –	.314)		PIT N	(95G –	.313)										
" total	106	374	117	16	3	2	0.5	45	37	25	68	12	.313	.388	23	6	1B-84
1958 CIN N	89	124	27	1	1	1	0.8	23	11	5	27	7	.218	.266	23	4	1B-36, OF-22
8 yrs.	967	3502	1000	144	47	69	2.0	437	373	203	526	84	.286	.413	60	13	1B-874, OF-22

Lew Fonseca

FONSECA, LEWIS ALBERT
B. Jan. 21, 1899, Oakland, Calif.
Manager 1932-34.

BR TR 5'10½" 180 lbs.

	G	AB	H	2B	3B	HR	HR %	R	RBI	BB	SO	SB	BA	SA	PH AB	PH H	G by POS
1921 CIN N	82	297	82	10	3	1	0.3	38	41	8	13	2	.276	.340	2	0	2B-50, OF-16, 1B-16
1922	91	291	105	20	3	4	1.4	55	45	14	18	7	.361	.491	18	8	2B-71
1923	65	237	66	11	4	3	1.3	33	28	9	16	4	.278	.397	6	2	2B-45, 1B-14
1924	20	57	13	2	1	0	0.0	5	9	4	4	1	.228	.298	4	0	2B-10, 1B-6
1925 PHI N	126	467	149	30	5	7	1.5	78	60	21	42	6	.319	.450	5	1	2B-69, 1B-55
1927 CLE A	112	428	133	20	7	2	0.5	60	40	12	17	12	.311	.404	0	0	2B-96, 1B-13
1928	75	263	86	19	4	3	1.1	38	36	13	17	4	.327	.464	0	0	1B-56, 3B-15, SS-4, 2B-1
1929	148	566	209	44	15	6	1.1	97	103	50	23	19	.369	.532	1	0	1B-147
1930	40	129	36	9	2	0	0.0	20	17	7	7	1	.279	.380	5	0	1B-28, 3B-6
1931 2 teams	CLE A	(26G –	.370)		CHI A	(121G –	.299)										
" total	147	573	179	35	6	3	0.5	86	85	40	29	7	.312	.410	4	1	OF-95, 1B-28, 2B-21, 3B-1
1932 CHI A	18	37	5	1	0	0	0.0	0	6	1	7	0	.135	.162	7	3	OF-8, P-1
1933	23	59	12	2	0	2	3.4	8	15	7	6	1	.203	.339	10	1	1B-12
12 yrs.	947	3404	1075	203	50	31	0.9	518	485	186	199	64	.316	.432	68	17	1B-375, 2B-363, OF-119, 3B-22, SS-4, P-1

Barry Foote

FOOTE, BARRY CLIFTON
B. Feb. 16, 1952, Smithfield, N. C.

BR TR 6'3"   205 lbs.

	G	AB	H	2B	3B	HR	HR %	R	RBI	BB	SO	SB	BA	SA	PH AB	PH H	G by POS
1973 MON N	6	6	4	0	1	0	0.0	0	1	0	0	0	.667	1.000	6	4	
1974	125	420	110	23	4	11	2.6	44	60	35	74	2	.262	.414	3	2	C-122
1975	118	387	75	16	1	7	1.8	25	30	17	48	0	.194	.295	6	3	C-115
1976	105	350	82	12	2	7	2.0	32	27	17	32	2	.234	.340	8	2	C-96, 3B-2, 1B-1
1977 2 teams	MON N	(15G –	.245)		PHI N	(18G –	.219)										
" total	33	81	19	4	1	3	3.7	7	11	7	16	0	.235	.420	4	0	C-30
1978 PHI N	39	57	9	0	1	1	1.8	4	4	1	11	0	.158	.211	13	1	C-31
1979 CHI N	132	429	109	26	0	16	3.7	47	56	34	49	5	.254	.427	5	0	C-129
1980	63	202	48	13	1	6	3.0	16	28	13	18	1	.238	.401	9	2	C-55
1981 2 teams	CHI N	(9G –	.000)		NY A	(40G –	.208)										
" total	49	147	26	4	0	6	4.1	12	11	11	28	0	.177	.327	4	0	C-42, DH-4, 1B-1
1982 NY A	17	48	7	5	0	0	0.0	4	2	1	11	0	.146	.250	0	0	C-17
10 yrs.	687	2127	489	103	10	57	2.7	191	230	136	287	10	.230	.368	58	14	C-637, DH-4, 3B-2, 1B-2

DIVISIONAL PLAYOFF SERIES

	G	AB	H	2B	3B	HR	HR %	R	RBI	BB	SO	SB	BA	SA	PH AB	PH H	G by POS
1981 NY A	1	0	0	0	0	0	–	0	0	0	0	0	–	–	0	0	

LEAGUE CHAMPIONSHIP SERIES

	G	AB	H	2B	3B	HR	HR %	R	RBI	BB	SO	SB	BA	SA	PH AB	PH H	G by POS
1978 PHI N	1	1	0	0	0	0	0.0	0	0	0	1	0	.000	.000	1	0	
1981 NY A	2	1	1	0	0	0	0.0	0	0	0	0	0	1.000	1.000	1	1	C-1
2 yrs.	3	2	1	0	0	0	0.0	0	0	0	1	0	.500	.500	2	1	C-1

WORLD SERIES

	G	AB	H	2B	3B	HR	HR %	R	RBI	BB	SO	SB	BA	SA	PH AB	PH H	G by POS
1981 NY A	1	1	0	0	0	0	0.0	0	0	0	1	0	.000	.000	1	0	

	G	AB	H	2B	3B	HR	HR %	R	RBI	BB	SO	SB	BA	SA	Pinch Hit AB	Pinch Hit H	G by POS

Davy Force

FORCE, DAVID W. (Tom Thumb)
B. July 27, 1849, New York, N. Y.   D. June 21, 1918, Englewood, N. J.   BR TR 5'4"   130 lbs.

	G	AB	H	2B	3B	HR	HR %	R	RBI	BB	SO	SB	BA	SA	PH AB	PH H	G by POS
1876 **2 teams**		PHI	N (60G – .232)			NY	N (1G – .000)										
" total	61	287	66	6	0	0	0.0	48	17	5	3		.230	.251	0	0	SS-61, 3B-2
1877 **STL N**	58	225	59	5	3	0	0.0	24	22	11	15		.262	.311	0	0	SS-50, 3B-8
1879 **BUF N**	79	316	66	5	2	0	0.0	36	8	13	37		.209	.237	0	0	SS-78, 3B-1
1880	81	290	49	10	0	0	0.0	22	17	10	35		.169	.203	0	0	2B-53, SS-30
1881	75	278	50	9	1	0	0.0	21	15	11	29		.180	.219	0	0	2B-51, SS-21, OF-3, 3B-1
1882	73	278	67	10	1	1	0.4	39		12	17		.241	.295	0	0	SS-61, 3B-11, 2B-1
1883	96	378	82	11	3	0	0.0	40		12	39		.217	.262	0	0	SS-78, 3B-13, 2B-7
1884	106	403	83	13	3	0	0.0	47		27	41		.206	.253	0	0	SS-105, 2B-1
1885	71	253	57	6	1	0	0.0	20	17	13	19		.225	.257	0	0	2B-42, SS-24, 3B-6
1886 **WAS N**	68	242	44	5	1	0	0.0	26	16	17	26		.182	.211	0	0	SS-56, 2B-8, 3B-4
10 yrs.	768	2950	623	80	15	1	0.0	323	112	131	261		.211	.249	0	0	SS-564, 2B-163, 3B-46, OF-3

Dan Ford

FORD, DARNELL GLENN (Disco Danny)
B. May 19, 1952, Los Angeles, Calif.   BR TR 6'1"   185 lbs.

	G	AB	H	2B	3B	HR	HR %	R	RBI	BB	SO	SB	BA	SA	PH AB	PH H	G by POS
1975 **MIN A**	130	440	123	21	1	15	3.4	72	59	30	79	6	.280	.434	6	2	OF-120, DH-3
1976	145	514	137	24	7	20	3.9	87	86	36	118	17	.267	.457	6	2	OF-139, DH-3
1977	144	453	121	25	7	11	2.4	66	60	41	79	6	.267	.426	20	7	OF-137, DH-3
1978	151	592	162	36	10	11	1.9	78	82	48	88	7	.274	.424	2	0	OF-149, DH-1
1979 **CAL A**	142	569	165	26	5	21	3.7	100	101	40	86	8	.290	.464	1	0	OF-141
1980	65	226	63	11	0	7	3.1	22	26	19	45	0	.279	.420	7	3	OF-45, DH-15
1981	97	375	104	14	1	15	4.0	53	48	23	71	2	.277	.440	0	0	OF-97
1982 **BAL A**	123	421	99	21	3	10	2.4	46	43	23	71	5	.235	.371	18	4	OF-119, DH-1
1983	103	407	114	30	4	9	2.2	63	55	29	55	9	.280	.440	2	1	OF-103
1984	25	91	21	4	0	1	1.1	7	5	7	13	1	.231	.308	1	0	OF-15, DH-8
10 yrs.	1125	4088	1109	212	38	120	2.9	594	565	296	705	61	.271	.430	63	19	OF-1065, DH-34

LEAGUE CHAMPIONSHIP SERIES

	G	AB	H	2B	3B	HR	HR %	R	RBI	BB	SO	SB	BA	SA	PH AB	PH H	G by POS
1979 **CAL A**	4	17	5	1	0	2	11.8	2	4	0	0	0	.294	.706	0	0	OF-4
1983 **BAL A**	2	5	1	1	0	0	0.0	0	0	0	1	0	.200	.400	1	0	OF-1
2 yrs.	6	22	6	2	0	2	9.1	2	4	0	1	0	.273	.636	1	0	OF-5

WORLD SERIES

	G	AB	H	2B	3B	HR	HR %	R	RBI	BB	SO	SB	BA	SA	PH AB	PH H	G by POS
1983 **BAL A**	5	12	2	0	0	1	8.3	1	1	1	5	0	.167	.417	2	0	OF-4

E. L. Ford

FORD, EDWARD L.
B. Richmond, Va.   Deceased.

	G	AB	H	2B	3B	HR	HR %	R	RBI	BB	SO	SB	BA	SA	PH AB	PH H	G by POS
1884 **RIC AA**	2	5	0	0	0	0	0.0	0		0			.000	.000	0	0	SS-1, 1B-1

Hod Ford

FORD, HORACE HILLS
B. July 23, 1897, New Haven, Conn.   D. Jan. 29, 1977, Winchester, Mass.   BR TR 5'10"   165 lbs.

	G	AB	H	2B	3B	HR	HR %	R	RBI	BB	SO	SB	BA	SA	PH AB	PH H	G by POS
1919 **BOS N**	10	28	6	0	1	0	0.0	4	3	2	6	0	.214	.286	0	0	SS-8, 3B-2
1920	88	257	62	12	5	1	0.4	16	30	18	25	3	.241	.339	0	0	2B-59, SS-18, 1B-4
1921	152	555	155	29	5	2	0.4	50	61	36	49	2	.279	.360	0	0	2B-119, SS-33
1922	143	515	140	23	9	2	0.4	58	60	30	36	2	.272	.363	0	0	SS-115, 2B-28
1923	111	380	103	16	7	2	0.5	27	50	31	30	1	.271	.366	0	0	2B-95, SS-19
1924 **PHI N**	145	530	144	27	5	3	0.6	58	53	27	40	1	.272	.358	0	0	2B-145
1925 **BKN N**	66	216	59	11	0	1	0.5	32	15	26	15	0	.273	.338	0	0	SS-66
1926 **CIN N**	57	197	55	6	1	0	0.0	14	18	14	12	1	.279	.320	0	0	SS-57
1927	115	409	112	16	2	1	0.2	45	46	33	34	0	.274	.330	0	0	SS-104, 2B-12
1928	149	506	122	17	4	0	0.0	49	54	47	31	1	.241	.291	0	0	SS-149
1929	148	529	146	14	6	3	0.6	68	50	41	25	8	.276	.342	0	0	SS-108, 2B-42
1930	132	424	98	16	7	1	0.2	36	34	24	28	2	.231	.309	1	0	SS-74, 2B-66
1931	84	175	40	8	1	0	0.0	18	13	13	13	0	.229	.286	7	1	SS-73, 2B-3, 3B-1
1932 **2 teams**		STL	N (1G – .000)			BOS	N (40G – .274)										
" total	41	97	26	5	2	0	0.0	9	6	6	9	0	.268	.361	2	0	2B-20, SS-17, 3B-2
1933 **BOS N**	5	15	1	0	0	0	0.0	0	1	3	3	0	.067	.067	0	0	SS-5
15 yrs.	1446	4833	1269	200	55	16	0.3	484	494	351	354	21	.263	.337	16	1	SS-846, 2B-589, 3B-5, 1B-4

Ted Ford

FORD, THEODORE HENRY
B. Feb. 7, 1947, Vineland, N. J.   BR TR 5'10"   180 lbs.

	G	AB	H	2B	3B	HR	HR %	R	RBI	BB	SO	SB	BA	SA	PH AB	PH H	G by POS
1970 **CLE A**	26	46	8	1	0	1	2.2	5	1	3	13	0	.174	.261	12	1	OF-12
1971	74	196	38	6	0	2	1.0	15	14	9	34	2	.194	.255	19	3	OF-55
1972 **TEX A**	129	429	101	19	1	14	3.3	43	50	37	80	4	.235	.382	10	2	OF-119
1973 **CLE A**	11	40	9	0	1	0	0.0	3	3	2	7	1	.225	.275	1	0	OF-10
4 yrs.	240	711	156	26	2	17	2.4	66	68	51	134	7	.219	.333	42	6	OF-196

Tom Forster

FORSTER, THOMAS W.
B. May 1, 1859, New York, N. Y.   D. July 17, 1946, New York, N. Y.

	G	AB	H	2B	3B	HR	HR %	R	RBI	BB	SO	SB	BA	SA	PH AB	PH H	G by POS
1882 **DET N**	21	76	7	0	0	0	0.0	5	2	5	12		.092	.092	0	0	2B-21
1884 **PIT AA**	35	126	28	5	0	0	0.0	10		7			.222	.262	0	0	SS-28, 3B-6, 2B-1
1885 **NY AA**	57	213	47	7	2	0	0.0	28		17			.221	.272	0	0	2B-52, OF-5
1886	67	251	49	3	2	1	0.4	33		20			.195	.235	0	0	2B-62, OF-4, SS-1
4 yrs.	180	666	131	15	4	1	0.2	76	2	49	12		.197	.236	0	0	2B-136, SS-29, OF-9, 3B-6

Clarence Forsythe

FORSYTHE, CLARENCE D.
B. 1888, St. Louis, Mo.   TR

	G	AB	H	2B	3B	HR	HR %	R	RBI	BB	SO	SB	BA	SA	PH AB	PH H	G by POS
1915 **BAL F**	1	3	0	0	0	0	0.0	0	1			0	.000	.000	0	0	3B-1

George Foss

FOSS, GEORGE DUEWARD (Deeby)
B. June 13, 1898, Register, Ga.   D. Nov. 10, 1969, Brandon, Fla.   BR TR 5'10½"   170 lbs.

	G	AB	H	2B	3B	HR	HR %	R	RBI	BB	SO	SB	BA	SA	PH AB	PH H	G by POS
1921 **WAS A**	4	7	0	0	0	0	0.0	0	0	0	1	0	.000	.000	2	0	3B-2

	G	AB	H	2B	3B	HR	HR %	R	RBI	BB	SO	SB	BA	SA	Pinch Hit AB	Pinch Hit H	G by POS

Ray Fosse

FOSSE, RAYMOND EARL
B. Apr. 4, 1947, Marion, Ill.　　　　　　　　　　　　BR TR 6'2" 215 lbs.

	G	AB	H	2B	3B	HR	HR %	R	RBI	BB	SO	SB	BA	SA	PH AB	PH H	G by POS
1967 CLE A	7	16	1	0	0	0	0.0	0	0	0	5	0	.063	.063	0	0	C-7
1968	1	0	0	0	0	0	–	0	0	0	0	0	–	–	0	0	C-1
1969	37	116	20	3	0	2	1.7	11	9	8	29	1	.172	.250	1	0	C-37
1970	120	450	138	17	1	18	4.0	62	61	39	55	1	.307	.469	0	0	C-120
1971	133	486	134	21	1	12	2.5	53	62	36	62	4	.276	.397	6	0	C-126, 1B-4
1972	134	457	110	20	1	10	2.2	42	41	45	46	5	.241	.354	8	3	C-124, 1B-3
1973 OAK A	143	492	126	23	2	7	1.4	37	52	25	62	2	.256	.354	0	0	C-141, DH-2
1974	69	204	40	8	3	4	2.0	20	23	11	31	1	.196	.324	0	0	C-68, DH-1
1975	82	136	19	3	2	0	0.0	14	12	8	19	0	.140	.191	2	0	C-82, 2B-1, 1B-1
1976 CLE A	90	276	83	9	1	2	0.7	26	30	20	20	1	.301	.362	4	0	C-85, 1B-3, DH-1
1977 2 teams		CLE A (78G – .265)				SEA A (11G – .353)											
" total	89	272	75	10	1	6	2.2	28	32	9	28	0	.276	.386	1	0	C-85, DH-3, 1B-1
1979 MIL A	19	52	12	3	1	0	0.0	6	2	2	6	0	.231	.327	3	1	C-13, DH-5, 1B-1
12 yrs.	924	2957	758	117	13	61	2.1	299	324	203	363	15	.256	.367	25	4	C-889, 1B-13, DH-12, 2B-1

LEAGUE CHAMPIONSHIP SERIES

	G	AB	H	2B	3B	HR	HR %	R	RBI	BB	SO	SB	BA	SA	PH AB	PH H	G by POS
1973 OAK A	5	11	1	1	0	0	0.0	2	3	2	2	0	.091	.182	0	0	C-5
1974	4	12	4	1	0	1	8.3	1	3	1	2	0	.333	.667	0	0	C-4
1975	1	2	0	0	0	0	0.0	0	0	0	1	0	.000	.000	0	0	C-1
3 yrs.	10	25	5	2	0	1	4.0	3	6	3	5	0	.200	.400	0	0	C-10

WORLD SERIES

	G	AB	H	2B	3B	HR	HR %	R	RBI	BB	SO	SB	BA	SA	PH AB	PH H	G by POS
1973 OAK A	7	19	3	1	0	0	0.0	0	1	1	4	0	.158	.211	0	0	C-7
1974	5	14	2	0	0	1	7.1	1	0	1	5	0	.143	.357	0	0	C-5
2 yrs.	12	33	5	1	0	1	3.0	1	1	2	9	0	.152	.273	0	0	C-12

Eddie Foster

FOSTER, EDWARD CUNNINGHAM (Kid)
B. Feb. 13, 1888, Chicago, Ill.　　D. Jan. 15, 1937, Washington, D. C.　　BR TR 5'6½" 145 lbs.

	G	AB	H	2B	3B	HR	HR %	R	RBI	BB	SO	SB	BA	SA	PH AB	PH H	G by POS
1910 NY A	30	83	11	2	0	0	0.0	5	1	8		2	.133	.157	7	1	SS-22
1912 WAS A	154	618	176	34	9	2	0.3	98	70	53		27	.285	.379	1	0	3B-154
1913	106	409	101	11	5	1	0.2	56	41	36	31	22	.247	.306	1	0	3B-105
1914	156	616	174	16	10	2	0.3	82	50	60	47	31	.282	.351	0	0	3B-156
1915	154	618	170	25	10	0	0.0	75	52	48	30	20	.275	.348	0	0	3B-79, 2B-75
1916	158	606	153	18	9	1	0.2	75	44	68	26	23	.252	.317	2	0	3B-84, 2B-72
1917	143	554	130	16	8	0	0.0	66	43	46	23	11	.235	.292	0	0	3B-86, 2B-57
1918	129	519	147	13	3	0	0.0	70	29	41	20	12	.283	.320	0	0	3B-127, 2B-2
1919	120	478	126	12	5	0	0.0	57	26	33	21	20	.264	.310	4	1	3B-115
1920 BOS A	117	386	100	17	6	0	0.0	48	41	42	17	10	.259	.334	6	1	3B-88, 2B-21
1921	119	412	117	18	6	0	0.0	51	30	57	15	13	.284	.357	3	2	3B-94, 2B-21
1922 2 teams		BOS A (48G – .211)				STL A (37G – .306)											
" total	85	253	67	7	0	0	0.0	40	15	29	18	4	.265	.292	15	5	3B-65, SS-2, C-2
1923 STL A	27	100	18	2	0	0	0.0	9	4	7	7	0	.180	.200	0	0	2B-20, 3B-7
13 yrs.	1498	5652	1490	191	71	6	0.1	732	446	528	255	195	.264	.326	38	10	3B-1160, 2B-268, SS-24, C-2

Elmer Foster

FOSTER, ELMER E.
B. Aug. 15, 1861, Minneapolis, Minn.　　D. July 22, 1946, Minneapolis, Minn.　　TR

	G	AB	H	2B	3B	HR	HR %	R	RBI	BB	SO	SB	BA	SA	PH AB	PH H	G by POS
1884 2 teams		PHI AA (4G – .182)				PHI U (1G – .333)											
" total	5	14	3	0	1	0	0.0	4		3			.214	.357	0	0	C-5, OF-1
1886 NY AA	35	125	23	0	1	0	0.0	16		7			.184	.200	0	0	2B-21, OF-14
1888 NY N	37	136	20	3	0	0	0.0	15	10	9	20	13	.147	.199	0	0	OF-37, 3B-1
1889	2	4	0	0	0	0	0.0	2	0	3	1	2	.000	.000	0	0	OF-2
1890 CHI N	27	105	26	4	2	5	4.8	20	23	9	21	18	.248	.467	0	0	OF-27
1891	4	16	3	0	0	1	6.3	3	1	1	2	1	.188	.375	0	0	OF-4
6 yrs.	110	400	75	7	6	6	1.5	60	33	32	44	34	.188	.280	0	0	OF-85, 2B-21, C-5, 3B-1

George Foster

FOSTER, GEORGE ARTHUR
B. Dec. 1, 1949, Tuscaloosa, Ala.　　　　　　　　　　BR TR 6'1½" 180 lbs.

	G	AB	H	2B	3B	HR	HR %	R	RBI	BB	SO	SB	BA	SA	PH AB	PH H	G by POS
1969 SF N	9	5	2	0	0	0	0.0	1	1	0	1	0	.400	.400	0	0	OF-8
1970	9	19	6	1	1	1	5.3	2	4	2	5	0	.316	.632	2	1	OF-7
1971 2 teams		SF N (36G – .267)				CIN N (104G – .234)											
" total	140	473	114	23	4	13	2.7	50	58	29	120	7	.241	.389	10	2	OF-132
1972 CIN N	59	145	29	4	1	2	1.4	15	12	5	44	2	.200	.283	12	4	OF-47
1973	17	39	11	3	0	4	10.3	6	9	4	7	0	.282	.667	4	0	OF-13
1974	106	276	73	18	0	7	2.5	31	41	30	52	3	.264	.406	17	3	OF-98
1975	134	463	139	24	4	23	5.0	71	78	40	73	2	.300	.518	9	4	OF-125, 1B-1
1976	144	562	172	21	9	29	5.2	86	121	52	89	17	.306	.530	6	0	OF-158
1977	158	615	197	31	2	52	8.5	124	149	61	107	6	.320	.631	0	0	OF-157
1978	158	604	170	26	7	40	6.6	97	120	70	138	4	.281	.546	1	0	OF-116
1979	121	440	133	18	3	30	6.8	68	98	59	105	0	.302	.561	4	1	OF-141
1980	144	528	144	21	5	25	4.7	79	93	75	99	1	.273	.473	3	0	OF-141
1981	108	414	122	23	2	22	5.3	64	90	51	75	4	.295	.519	0	0	OF-108
1982 NY N	151	550	136	23	2	13	2.4	64	70	50	123	1	.247	.367	11	2	OF-138
1983	157	601	145	19	2	28	4.7	74	90	38	111	4	.241	.419	5	1	OF-153
1984	146	553	149	22	1	24	4.3	67	86	30	122	2	.269	.484	5	1	OF-141
16 yrs.	1761	6287	1742	277	43	313	5.0	899	1120	596	1271	50	.277	.484	89	19	OF-1684, 1B-2

LEAGUE CHAMPIONSHIP SERIES

	G	AB	H	2B	3B	HR	HR %	R	RBI	BB	SO	SB	BA	SA	PH AB	PH H	G by POS
1972 CIN N	1	0	0	0	0	0	–	1	0	0	0	0	–	–	0	0	OF-3
1975	3	11	4	0	0	0	0.0	3	0	1	2	1	.364	.364	0	0	OF-3
1976	3	12	2	0	0	2	16.7	2	4	0	4	0	.167	.667	0	0	OF-3
1979	3	10	2	0	0	1	10.0	1	2	4	3	0	.200	.500	0	0	OF-3
4 yrs.	10	33	8	0	0	3	9.1	7	6	5	9	1	.242	.515	0	0	OF-9

WORLD SERIES

	G	AB	H	2B	3B	HR	HR %	R	RBI	BB	SO	SB	BA	SA	PH AB	PH H	G by POS
1972 CIN N	2	0	0	0	0	0	–	0	0	0	0	0	–	–	0	0	OF-1
1975	7	29	8	1	0	0	0.0	1	2	1	1	1	.276	.310	0	0	OF-7

	G	AB	H	2B	3B	HR	HR %	R	RBI	BB	SO	SB	BA	SA	Pinch Hit AB	H	G by POS

George Foster continued

| 1976 | 4 | 14 | 6 | 1 | 0 | 0 | 0.0 | 3 | 4 | 2 | 3 | 0 | .429 | .500 | 0 | 0 | OF-4 |
| 3 yrs. | 13 | 43 | 14 | 2 | 0 | 0 | 0.0 | 4 | 6 | 3 | 4 | 1 | .326 | .372 | 0 | 0 | OF-12 |

Leo Foster

FOSTER, LEONARD NORRIS
B. Feb. 2, 1951, Covington, Ky.

BR TR 5'11"   165 lbs.

1971 ATL N	9	10	0	0	0	0	0.0	1	0	0	1	0	.000	.000	2	0	SS-3
1973	3	6	1	1	0	0	0.0	1	0	0	2	0	.167	.333	1	0	SS-1
1974	72	112	22	2	0	1	0.9	16	5	9	22	1	.196	.241	10	2	SS-43, 2B-10, 3B-3, OF-1
1976 NY N	24	59	12	2	0	1	1.7	11	15	8	5	3	.203	.288	2	0	3B-9, SS-7, 2B-3
1977	36	75	17	3	0	0	0.0	6	6	5	14	3	.227	.267	5	1	2B-20, SS-8, 3B-2
5 yrs.	144	262	52	8	0	2	0.8	35	26	22	44	7	.198	.252	20	3	SS-62, 2B-33, 3B-14, OF-1

Pop Foster

FOSTER, CLARENCE FRANCIS
B. Apr. 8, 1878, New Haven, Conn.   D. Apr. 16, 1944, Princeton, N. J.

TR

1898 NY N	32	112	30	6	1	0	0.0	10	9	0		0	.268	.339	0	0	OF-21, 3B-10, SS-2
1899	84	301	89	9	7	3	1.0	48	57	20		7	.296	.402	0	0	OF-84, SS-1, 3B-1
1900	31	84	22	3	1	0	0.0	19	11	11		0	.262	.321	5	0	OF-12, SS-7, 2B-5
1901 2 teams	WAS A (103G — .278)					CHI A (12G — .286)											
" total	115	427	119	18	11	7	1.6	69	59	45		10	.279	.422	3	1	OF-111, SS-8
4 yrs.	262	924	260	36	20	10	1.1	146	136	76		17	.281	.396	8	1	OF-228, SS-12, 3B-11, 2B-5

Reddy Foster

FOSTER, OSCAR E.
B. 1867, Richmond, Va.   D. Dec. 19, 1908, Richmond, Va.

| 1896 NY N | 1 | 1 | 0 | 0 | 0 | 0 | 0.0 | 0 | 0 | 0 | | 0 | .000 | .000 | 1 | 0 | |

Roy Foster

FOSTER, ROY
B. July 29, 1945, Bixby, Okla.

BR TR 6'   185 lbs.

1970 CLE A	139	477	128	26	0	23	4.8	66	60	54	75	3	.268	.468	8	2	OF-131
1971	125	396	97	21	1	18	4.5	51	45	35	48	6	.245	.439	20	5	OF-107
1972	73	143	32	4	0	4	2.8	19	13	21	23	0	.224	.336	26	4	OF-45
3 yrs.	337	1016	257	51	1	45	4.4	136	118	110	146	9	.253	.438	54	11	OF-283

Bob Fothergill

FOTHERGILL, ROBERT ROY (Fat)
B. Aug. 16, 1897, Massillon, Ohio   D. Mar. 20, 1938, Detroit, Mich.

BR TR 5'10½" 230 lbs.

1922 DET A	42	152	49	12	4	0	0.0	29	29	8	9	1	.322	.454	3	1	OF-39
1923	101	241	76	18	2	1	0.4	34	49	12	19	4	.315	.419	30	9	OF-68
1924	54	166	50	8	3	0	0.0	28	15	5	13	2	.301	.386	9	3	OF-45
1925	71	204	72	14	0	2	1.0	38	28	6	3	2	.353	.451	11	5	OF-59
1926	110	387	142	31	7	3	0.8	63	73	33	23	4	.367	.506	6	4	OF-103
1927	143	527	189	38	9	9	1.7	93	114	47	31	9	.359	.516	5	2	OF-137
1928	111	347	110	28	10	3	0.9	49	63	24	19	8	.317	.481	19	4	OF-90
1929	115	277	98	24	9	6	2.2	42	62	11	11	3	.354	.570	4	0	OF-59
1930 2 teams	DET A (55G — .259)					CHI A (51G — .305)											
" total	106	274	77	18	3	2	0.7	24	38	10	18	1	.281	.391	34	6	OF-68
1931 CHI A	108	312	88	9	4	3	1.0	25	56	17	17	2	.282	.365	31	8	OF-74
1932	116	346	102	24	1	7	2.0	36	50	27	10	4	.295	.431	29	8	OF-86
1933 BOS A	28	32	11	1	0	0	0.0	2	5	2	4	0	.344	.375	23	7	OF-4
12 yrs.	1105	3265	1064	225	52	36	1.1	453	582	202	177	40	.326	.460	253	76	OF-832

Jack Fournier

FOURNIER, JOHN FRANK (Jacques)
B. Sept. 28, 1892, Au Sable, Mich.   D. Sept. 5, 1973, Tacoma, Wash.

BL TR 6'   195 lbs.

1912 CHI A	35	73	14	5	2	0	0.0	5	2	4		1	.192	.315	18	5	1B-17
1913	68	172	40	8	5	1	0.6	20	23	21	23	9	.233	.355	13	1	1B-29, OF-23
1914	109	379	118	14	9	6	1.6	44	44	31	44	10	.311	.443	6	0	1B-97, OF-6
1915	126	422	136	20	18	5	1.2	86	77	64	37	21	.322	.491	6	2	1B-65, OF-57
1916	105	313	75	13	9	3	1.0	36	44	36	40	19	.240	.367	14	2	1B-85, OF-1
1917	1	1	0	0	0	0	0.0	0	0	0	1	0	.000	.000	1	0	
1918 NY A	27	100	35	6	1	0	0.0	9	12	7	7	7	.350	.430	0	0	1B-27
1920 STL N	141	530	162	33	14	3	0.6	77	61	42	42	26	.306	.438	3	2	1B-138
1921	149	574	197	27	9	16	2.8	103	86	56	48	20	.343	.505	0	0	1B-149
1922	128	404	119	23	9	10	2.5	64	61	40	21	6	.295	.470	12	5	1B-109, P-1
1923 BKN N	133	515	181	30	13	22	4.3	91	102	43	28	11	.351	.588	0	0	1B-133
1924	154	563	188	25	4	27	4.8	93	116	83	46	7	.334	.536	1	0	1B-153
1925	145	545	191	21	16	22	4.0	99	130	86	39	4	.350	.569	0	0	1B-145
1926	87	243	69	9	2	11	4.5	39	48	30	16	0	.284	.473	18	4	1B-64
1927 BOS N	122	374	106	18	2	10	2.7	55	53	44	16	4	.283	.422	19	8	1B-102
15 yrs.	1530	5208	1631	252	113	136	2.6	821	859	587	408	145	.313	.483	109	29	1B-1313, OF-87, P-1

Bill Fouser

FOUSER, WILLIAM C.
B. 1855, Philadelphia, Pa.   D. Mar. 1, 1919, Philadelphia, Pa.

| 1876 PHI N | 21 | 89 | 12 | 0 | 0 | 1 | 1.1 | 2 | | 0 | 0 | | .135 | .157 | 0 | 0 | 2B-14, OF-7, 1B-1 |

Dave Foutz

FOUTZ, DAVID LUTHER (Scissors)
B. Sept. 7, 1856, Carroll County, Md.   D. Mar. 5, 1897, Waverly, Md.
Manager 1893-96.

BR TR 6'2"   161 lbs.

1884 STL AA	33	119	27	4	0	0	0.0	17		8		0	.227	.261	0	0	P-25, OF-14
1885	65	238	59	6	4	0	0.0	42		11		0	.248	.307	0	0	P-47, 1B-15, OF-4
1886	102	414	116	18	9	3	0.7	66		9		0	.280	.389	0	0	P-59, OF-34, 1B-11
1887	102	423	151	26	13	4	0.9	79		23		22	.357	.508	0	0	OF-50, P-40, 1B-15
1888 BKN AA	140	563	156	20	13	3	0.5	91	99	28		35	.277	.375	0	0	1B-42, P-23
1889	138	553	153	19	8	7	1.3	118	113	64	23	43	.277	.378	0	0	1B-134, P-12
1890 BKN N	129	509	154	25	13	5	1.0	106	98	52	25	42	.303	.432	0	0	1B-113, OF-13, P-5
1891	130	521	134	26	8	2	0.4	87	73	40	25	48	.257	.349	0	0	1B-124, P-6, SS-1

	G	AB	H	2B	3B	HR	HR %	R	RBI	BB	SO	SB	BA	SA	Pinch Hit AB	Pinch Hit H	G by POS

Dave Foutz continued

	G	AB	H	2B	3B	HR	HR %	R	RBI	BB	SO	SB	BA	SA	PH AB	PH H	G by POS
1892	61	220	41	5	3	1	0.5	33	26	14	14	19	.186	.250	1	0	OF-29, P-27, 1B-6
1893	130	557	137	20	10	7	1.3	91	67	32	34	39	.246	.355	0	0	OF-77, 1B-54, P-6
1894	72	293	90	12	9	0	0.0	40	51	14	13	14	.307	.410	0	0	1B-72, P-1
1895	31	115	34	4	1	0	0.0	14	21	4	2	1	.296	.348	3	0	OF-20, 1B-8
1896	2	8	2	1	0	0	0.0	0	0	1	0	0	.250	.375	0	0	OF-1, 1B-1
13 yrs.	1135	4533	1254	186	91	32	0.7	784	547	300	136	263	.277	.379	4	0	1B-595, OF-320, P-251, SS-1

Frank Foutz

FOUTZ, FRANK HAYES
B. Apr. 8, 1877, Baltimore, Md.   D. Dec. 25, 1961, Lima, Ohio
BR TR

	G	AB	H	2B	3B	HR	HR %	R	RBI	BB	SO	SB	BA	SA	PH AB	PH H	G by POS
1901 BAL A	20	72	17	4	1	2	2.8	13	14	8		0	.236	.403	0	0	1B-20

Boob Fowler

FOWLER, JOSEPH CHESTER
B. Nov. 11, 1900, Waco, Tex.
BL TR 5'11½" 180 lbs.

	G	AB	H	2B	3B	HR	HR %	R	RBI	BB	SO	SB	BA	SA	PH AB	PH H	G by POS
1923 CIN N	11	33	11	0	1	1	3.0	9	6	1	3	1	.333	.485	0	0	SS-10
1924	59	129	43	6	1	0	0.0	20	9	5	15	2	.333	.395	3	0	SS-32, 2B-4, 3B-2
1925	6	5	2	1	0	0	0.0	0	2	0	1	0	.400	.600	5	2	
1926 BOS A	2	8	1	0	0	0	0.0	1	1	0	0	0	.125	.125	0	0	3B-2
4 yrs.	78	175	57	7	2	1	0.6	30	18	6	19	3	.326	.406	8	2	SS-42, 3B-4, 2B-4

Bill Fox

FOX, WILLIAM H.
B. Jan. 15, 1872, Fiskdale, Mass.   D. May 7, 1946, Minneapolis, Minn.
BR TR 5'11½" 150 lbs.

	G	AB	H	2B	3B	HR	HR %	R	RBI	BB	SO	SB	BA	SA	PH AB	PH H	G by POS
1897 WAS N	4	14	4	0	0	0	0.0	4	0	1		0	.286	.286	0	0	SS-2, 2B-2
1901 CIN N	44	163	29	2	1	0	0.0	9	7	4		9	.178	.202	0	0	2B-44
2 yrs.	48	177	33	2	1	0	0.0	13	7	5		9	.186	.209	0	0	2B-46, SS-2

Charlie Fox

FOX, CHARLES FRANCIS (Irish)
B. Oct. 7, 1921, New York, N. Y.
Manager 1970-74, 1976, 1983.
BR TR 5'11" 180 lbs.

	G	AB	H	2B	3B	HR	HR %	R	RBI	BB	SO	SB	BA	SA	PH AB	PH H	G by POS
1942 NY N	3	7	3	0	0	0	0.0	1	1	1	2	0	.429	.429	0	0	C-3

Jack Fox

FOX, JOHN PAUL
B. May 21, 1885, Reading, Pa.   D. June 28, 1963, Reading, Pa.
BR TR 5'10" 185 lbs.

	G	AB	H	2B	3B	HR	HR %	R	RBI	BB	SO	SB	BA	SA	PH AB	PH H	G by POS
1908 PHI A	9	30	6	0	0	0	0.0	2	0	0		2	.200	.200	0	0	OF-8

Nellie Fox

FOX, JACOB NELSON
B. Dec. 25, 1927, St. Thomas, Pa.   D. Dec. 1, 1975, Baltimore, Md.
BL TR 5'10" 160 lbs.

	G	AB	H	2B	3B	HR	HR %	R	RBI	BB	SO	SB	BA	SA	PH AB	PH H	G by POS
1947 PHI A	7	3	0	0	0	0	0.0	2	0	1	0	0	.000	.000	2	0	2B-1
1948	3	13	2	0	0	0	0.0	0	0	-1	0	1	.154	.154	0	0	2B-3
1949	88	247	63	6	2	0	0.0	42	21	32	9	2	.255	.296	2	0	2B-77
1950 CHI A	130	457	113	12	7	0	0.0	45	30	35	17	4	.247	.304	8	2	2B-121
1951	147	604	189	32	12	4	0.7	93	55	43	11	9	.313	.425	0	0	2B-147
1952	152	648	192	25	10	0	0.0	76	39	34	14	5	.296	.366	1	0	2B-151
1953	154	624	178	31	8	3	0.5	92	72	49	18	4	.285	.375	0	0	2B-154
1954	155	631	201	24	8	2	0.3	111	47	51	12	16	.319	.391	0	0	2B-154
1955	154	636	198	28	7	6	0.9	100	59	38	15	7	.311	.406	0	0	2B-154
1956	154	649	192	20	10	4	0.6	109	52	44	14	8	.296	.376	0	0	2B-155
1957	155	619	196	27	8	6	1.0	110	61	75	13	5	.317	.415	0	0	2B-155
1958	155	623	187	21	6	0	0.0	82	49	47	11	5	.300	.353	0	0	2B-156
1959	156	624	191	34	6	2	0.3	84	70	71	13	5	.306	.389	0	0	2B-149
1960	150	605	175	24	10	2	0.3	85	59	50	13	2	.289	.372	1	0	2B-159
1961	159	606	152	11	5	2	0.3	67	51	59	12	2	.251	.295	2	1	2B-154
1962	157	621	166	27	7	2	0.3	79	54	38	12	1	.267	.343	3	0	2B-134
1963	137	539	140	19	0	2	0.4	54	42	24	17	0	.260	.306	6	2	2B-115
1964 HOU N	133	442	117	12	6	0	0.0	45	28	27	13	0	.265	.319	13	1	3B-6, 1B-2, 2B-1
1965	21	41	11	2	0	0	0.0	3	1	0	2	0	.268	.317	12	4	3B-6, 1B-2
19 yrs.	2367	9232	2663	355	112	35	0.4	1279	790	719	216	76	.288	.363	50	10	2B-2295, 3B-6, 1B-2

WORLD SERIES

	G	AB	H	2B	3B	HR	HR %	R	RBI	BB	SO	SB	BA	SA	PH AB	PH H	G by POS
1959 CHI A	6	24	9	3	0	0	0.0	4	0	4	1	0	.375	.500	0	1	2B-6

Paddy Fox

FOX, GEORGE B.
B. Dec. 1, 1868, Pottstown, Pa.   D. May 8, 1914, Philadelphia, Pa.

	G	AB	H	2B	3B	HR	HR %	R	RBI	BB	SO	SB	BA	SA	PH AB	PH H	G by POS
1891 LOU AA	6	19	2	0	1	0	0.0	1	2	2	3	0	.105	.211	0	0	3B-6
1899 PIT N	13	41	10	0	1	1	2.4	4	3	3		2	.244	.366	1	0	1B-9, C-3
2 yrs.	19	60	12	0	2	1	1.7	5	5	5	3	2	.200	.317	1	0	1B-9, 3B-6, C-3

Pete Fox

FOX, ERVIN
B. Mar. 8, 1909, Evansville, Ind.   D. July 5, 1966, Detroit, Mich.
BR TR 5'11" 165 lbs.

	G	AB	H	2B	3B	HR	HR %	R	RBI	BB	SO	SB	BA	SA	PH AB	PH H	G by POS
1933 DET A	128	535	154	26	13	7	1.3	82	57	23	38	9	.288	.424	3	0	OF-124
1934	128	516	147	31	2	2	0.4	101	45	49	53	25	.285	.364	6	1	OF-125
1935	131	517	166	38	8	15	2.9	116	73	45	52	14	.321	.513	6	3	OF-125
1936	73	220	67	12	1	4	1.8	46	26	34	23	1	.305	.423	15	2	OF-55
1937	148	628	208	39	8	12	1.9	116	82	41	43	12	.331	.476	3	2	OF-143
1938	155	634	186	35	10	7	1.1	91	96	31	39	16	.293	.413	0	0	OF-154
1939	141	519	153	24	6	7	1.3	69	66	35	41	23	.295	.405	14	2	OF-126
1940	93	350	101	17	4	5	1.4	49	48	21	30	7	.289	.403	9	1	OF-85
1941 BOS A	73	268	81	12	7	0	0.0	38	31	21	32	9	.302	.399	7	0	OF-62
1942	77	256	67	15	5	3	1.2	42	42	20	28	8	.262	.395	3	1	OF-71
1943	127	489	141	24	4	2	0.4	54	44	34	40	22	.288	.366	1	0	OF-125
1944	121	496	156	38	6	1	0.2	70	64	27	34	10	.315	.421	2	0	OF-57
1945	66	208	51	14	0	0	0.0	21	20	11	18	2	.245	.274	5	0	OF-57
13 yrs.	1461	5636	1678	315	75	65	1.2	895	694	392	471	158	.298	.415	74	12	OF-1367

WORLD SERIES

	G	AB	H	2B	3B	HR	HR %	R	RBI	BB	SO	SB	BA	SA	PH AB	PH H	G by POS
1934 DET A	7	28	8	6	0	0	0.0	1	2	1	4	0	.286	.500	0	0	OF-7

	G	AB	H	2B	3B	HR	HR %	R	RBI	BB	SO	SB	BA	SA	Pinch Hit AB	Pinch Hit H	G by POS

Pete Fox continued

	G	AB	H	2B	3B	HR	HR%	R	RBI	BB	SO	SB	BA	SA	AB	H	G by POS
1935	6	26	10	3	1	0	0.0	1	4	0	1	0	.385	.577	0	0	OF-6
1940	1	1	0	0	0	0	0.0	0	0	0	0	0	.000	.000	1	0	
3 yrs.	14	55	18	9 (3rd)	1	0	0.0	2	6	1	5	0	.327	.527	1	0	OF-13

Jimmie Foxx

FOXX, JAMES EMORY (Double X, The Beast)   BR TR 6'   195 lbs.
B. Oct. 22, 1907, Sudlersville, Md.   D. July 21, 1967, Miami, Fla.
Hall of Fame 1951.

	G	AB	H	2B	3B	HR	HR%	R	RBI	BB	SO	SB	BA	SA	AB	H	G by POS
1925 PHI A	10	9	6	1	0	0	0.0	2	0	0	1	0	.667	.778	9	6	C-1
1926	26	32	10	2	1	0	0.0	8	5	1	6	1	.313	.438	8	0	C-12, OF-3
1927	61	130	42	6	5	3	2.3	23	20	14	11	2	.323	.515	20	7	1B-32, C-5
1928	118	400	131	29	10	13	3.3	85	79	60	43	3	.328	.548	8	2	3B-61, 1B-30, C-20
1929	149	517	183	23	9	33	6.4	123	117	103	70	10	.354	.625	0	0	1B-142, 3B-7
1930	153	562	188	33	13	37	6.6	127	156	93	66	7	.335	.637	0	0	1B-153
1931	139	515	150	32	10	30	5.8	93	120	73	84	4	.291	.567	0	0	1B-112, 3B-20, OF-1
1932	154	585	213	33	9	58	9.9	151	169	116	96	3	.364	.749	0	0	1B-141, 3B-13
1933	149	573	204	37	9	48	8.4	125	163	96	93	2	.356	.703	0	0	1B-149, SS-1
1934	150	539	180	28	6	44	8.2	120	130	111	75	11	.334	.653	1	0	1B-140, 3B-9
1935	147	535	185	33	7	36	6.7	118	115	114	99	6	.346	.636	0	0	1B-121, C-26, 3B-2
1936 BOS A	155	585	198	32	8	41	7.0	130	143	105	119	13	.338	.631	0	0	1B-139, OF-16, 3B-1
1937	150	569	162	24	6	36	6.3	111	127	99	96	10	.285	.538	0	0	1B-150, C-1
1938	149	565	197	33	9	50	8.8	139	175	119	76	5	.349	.704	0	0	1B-149
1939	124	467	168	31	10	35	7.5	130	105	89	72	4	.360	.694	1	0	1B-123, P-1
1940	144	515	153	30	4	36	7.0	106	119	101	87	4	.297	.581	4	1	1B-95, C-42, 3B-1
1941	135	487	146	27	8	19	3.9	87	105	93	103	2	.300	.505	4	2	1B-124, 3B-5, OF-1
1942 2 teams		BOS A (30G – .270)				CHI N (70G – .205)											
" total	100	305	69	12	5	8	2.6	43	33	40	70	1	.226	.344	18	3	1B-79, C-1
1944 CHI N	15	20	1	1	0	0	0.0	0	2	2	5	0	.050	.100	11	0	3B-2, C-1
1945 PHI N	89	224	60	11	1	7	3.1	30	38	23	39	0	.268	.420	26	8	1B-40, 3B-14, P-9
20 yrs.	2317	8134	2646	458	125	534 (7th)	6.6 (8th)	1751	1921 (6th)	1452	1311	88	.325	.609 (4th)	112	30	1B-1919, 3B-135, C-109, OF-21, P-10, SS-1

WORLD SERIES

	G	AB	H	2B	3B	HR	HR%	R	RBI	BB	SO	SB	BA	SA	AB	H	G by POS
1929 PHI A	5	20	7	1	0	2	10.0	5	5	1	1	0	.350	.700	0	0	1B-5
1930	6	21	7	2	1	1	4.8	3	3	2	4	0	.333	.667	0	0	1B-6
1931	7	23	8	0	0	1	4.3	3	3	6	5	0	.348	.478	0	0	1B-7
3 yrs.	18	64	22	3	1	4	6.3	11	11	9	10	0	.344	.609 (9th)	0	0	1B-18

Joe Foy

FOY, JOSEPH ANTHONY   BR TR 6'   215 lbs.
B. Feb. 21, 1943, New York, N.Y.

	G	AB	H	2B	3B	HR	HR%	R	RBI	BB	SO	SB	BA	SA	AB	H	G by POS
1966 BOS A	151	554	145	23	8	15	2.7	97	63	91	80	2	.262	.413	1	0	3B-139, SS-13
1967	130	446	112	22	4	16	3.6	70	49	46	87	8	.251	.426	13	2	3B-118, OF-1
1968	150	515	116	18	2	10	1.9	65	60	84	91	26	.225	.326	1	0	3B-147, OF-3
1969 KC A	145	519	136	19	2	11	2.1	72	71	74	75	37	.262	.370	1	0	3B-113, OF-16, 1B-16, SS-5, 2B-3
1970 NY N	99	322	76	12	0	6	1.9	39	37	68	58	22	.236	.329	2	0	3B-97
1971 WAS A	41	128	30	8	0	0	0.0	12	11	27	14	4	.234	.297	4	0	3B-37, 2B-3, SS-1
6 yrs.	716	2484	615	102	16	58	2.3	355	291	390	405	99	.248	.372	22	2	3B-651, OF-20, SS-19, 1B-16, 2B-6

WORLD SERIES

	G	AB	H	2B	3B	HR	HR%	R	RBI	BB	SO	SB	BA	SA	AB	H	G by POS
1967 BOS A	6	15	2	1	0	0	0.0	2	1	1	5	0	.133	.200	3	0	3B-3

Julio Franco

FRANCO, JULIO CESAR   BB TR 5'11"   155 lbs.
B. Aug. 23, 1958, San Pedro de Macoris, Dominican Republic

	G	AB	H	2B	3B	HR	HR%	R	RBI	BB	SO	SB	BA	SA	AB	H	G by POS
1982 PHI N	16	29	8	1	0	0	0.0	3	3	2	4	0	.276	.310	0	0	SS-11, 3B-2
1983 CLE A	149	560	153	24	8	8	1.4	68	80	27	50	32	.273	.388	0	0	SS-149
1984	160	658	188	22	5	3	0.5	82	79	43	68	19	.286	.348	0	0	SS-159, DH-1
3 yrs.	325	1247	349	47	13	11	0.9	153	162	72	122	51	.280	.365	0	0	SS-319, 3B-2, DH-1

Terry Francona

FRANCONA, TERRY JON   BL TL 6'1"   190 lbs.
Son of Tito Francona.
B. Apr. 22, 1959, New Brighton, Pa.

	G	AB	H	2B	3B	HR	HR%	R	RBI	BB	SO	SB	BA	SA	AB	H	G by POS
1981 MON N	34	95	26	0	1	1	1.1	11	8	5	6	1	.274	.326	10	5	OF-26, 1B-1
1982	46	131	42	3	0	0	0.0	14	9	8	11	2	.321	.344	7	2	OF-33, 1B-16
1983	120	230	59	11	1	3	1.3	21	22	6	20	0	.257	.352	38	8	OF-51, 1B-47
1984	58	214	74	19	2	1	0.5	18	18	5	12	0	.346	.467	3	0	1B-50, OF-6
4 yrs.	258	670	201	33	4	5	0.7	64	57	24	49	3	.300	.384	58	15	OF-116, 1B-114

DIVISIONAL PLAYOFF SERIES

	G	AB	H	2B	3B	HR	HR%	R	RBI	BB	SO	SB	BA	SA	AB	H	G by POS
1981 MON N	5	12	4	0	0	0	0.0	0	0	2	2	2	.333	.333	0	0	OF-5

LEAGUE CHAMPIONSHIP SERIES

	G	AB	H	2B	3B	HR	HR%	R	RBI	BB	SO	SB	BA	SA	AB	H	G by POS
1981 MON N	2	1	0	0	0	0	0.0	0	0	0	1	0	.000	.000	1	0	OF-1

Tito Francona

FRANCONA, JOHN PATSY   BL TL 5'11"   190 lbs.
Father of Terry Francona.
B. Nov. 4, 1933, Aliquippa, Pa.

	G	AB	H	2B	3B	HR	HR%	R	RBI	BB	SO	SB	BA	SA	AB	H	G by POS
1956 BAL A	139	445	115	16	4	9	2.0	62	57	51	60	11	.258	.373	18	4	OF-122, 1B-21
1957	97	279	65	8	3	7	2.5	35	38	29	48	7	.233	.358	23	3	OF-73, 1B-4
1958 2 teams		CHI A (41G – .258)				DET A (45G – .246)											
" total	86	197	50	8	2	1	0.5	21	20	29	40	2	.254	.330	29	11	OF-53, 1B-1
1959 CLE A	122	399	145	17	2	20	5.0	68	79	35	42	2	.363	.566	20	5	OF-64, 1B-35
1960	147	544	159	36	2	17	3.1	84	79	67	67	4	.292	.460	3	0	OF-138, 1B-13
1961	155	592	178	30	8	16	2.7	87	85	56	52	2	.301	.459	7	1	OF-138, 1B-14
1962	158	621	169	28	5	14	2.3	82	70	47	74	3	.272	.401	0	0	1B-158
1963	142	500	114	29	0	10	2.0	57	41	47	77	9	.228	.346	13	4	OF-122, 1B-11

	G	AB	H	2B	3B	HR	HR%	R	RBI	BB	SO	SB	BA	SA	Pinch Hit AB	Pinch Hit H	G by POS

Tito Francona continued

	G	AB	H	2B	3B	HR	HR%	R	RBI	BB	SO	SB	BA	SA	PH AB	PH H	G by POS
1964	111	270	67	13	2	8	3.0	35	24	44	46	1	.248	.400	29	6	OF-69, 1B-17
1965 STL N	81	174	45	6	2	5	2.9	15	19	17	30	0	.259	.402	35	9	OF-34, 1B-13
1966	83	156	33	4	1	4	2.6	14	17	7	27	0	.212	.327	41	7	1B-30, OF-9
1967 2 teams			PHI N (27G – .205)			ATL N (82G – .248)											
" total	109	327	78	6	1	6	1.8	35	28	27	44	1	.239	.318	27	3	1B-80, OF-7
1968 ATL N	122	346	99	13	2	6	2.0	32	47	51	45	3	.286	.347	24	5	OF-65, 1B-33
1969 2 teams			ATL N (51G – .295)			OAK A (32G – .341)											
" total	83	173	55	7	1	5	2.9	17	42	25	21	0	.318	.457	32	8	1B-26, OF-16
1970 2 teams			OAK A (32G – .242)			MIL A (52G – .231)											
" total	84	98	23	3	0	1	1.0	6	10	12	21	1	.235	.296	64	15	1B-19, OF-1
15 yrs.	1719	5121	1395	224	34	125	2.4	650	656	544	694	46	.272	.403	365	81	OF-911, 1B-475

Charlie Frank

FRANK, CHARLES
B. May 30, 1870, Mobile, Ala.   D. May 24, 1922, Memphis, Tenn.

	G	AB	H	2B	3B	HR	HR%	R	RBI	BB	SO	SB	BA	SA	PH AB	PH H	G by POS
1893 STL N	40	164	55	6	3	1	0.6	29	17	18	8	8	.335	.427	0	0	OF-40
1894	80	319	89	12	7	4	1.3	52	42	44	13	14	.279	.398	0	0	OF-77, 1B-3, P-2
2 yrs.	120	483	144	18	10	5	1.0	81	59	62	21	22	.298	.408	0	0	OF-117, 1B-3, P-2

Fred Frank

FRANK, FREDERICK
B. Mar. 11, 1874, Dayton, Ohio   D. Mar. 27, 1950, Ashland, Ky.

	G	AB	H	2B	3B	HR	HR%	R	RBI	BB	SO	SB	BA	SA	PH AB	PH H	G by POS
1898 CLE N	17	53	11	1	1	0	0.0	3	3	4		1	.208	.264	0	0	OF-17

Franklin

FRANKLIN,
Deceased.

	G	AB	H	2B	3B	HR	HR%	R	RBI	BB	SO	SB	BA	SA	PH AB	PH H	G by POS
1884 WAS U	1	3	0	0	0	0	0.0	0		0			.000	.000	0	0	OF-1

Murray Franklin

FRANKLIN, MURRAY ASHER (Moe)   BR TR 6' 175 lbs.
B. Apr. 1, 1914, Chicago, Ill.   D. Mar. 16, 1978, Harbor City, Calif.

	G	AB	H	2B	3B	HR	HR%	R	RBI	BB	SO	SB	BA	SA	PH AB	PH H	G by POS
1941 DET A	13	10	3	1	0	0	0.0	1	0	2	2	0	.300	.400	7	2	SS-4, 3B-1
1942	48	154	40	7	0	2	1.3	24	16	7	5	0	.260	.344	5	0	SS-32, 2B-7
2 yrs.	61	164	43	8	0	2	1.2	25	16	9	7	0	.262	.348	12	2	SS-36, 2B-7, 3B-1

Fletcher Franks

FRANKS, FLETCHER O.   BR TR 5'10" 165 lbs.
B. Mar. 6, 1891, Hindreth, Ill.   D. Oct. 7, 1974, St. Petersburg, Fla.

	G	AB	H	2B	3B	HR	HR%	R	RBI	BB	SO	SB	BA	SA	PH AB	PH H	G by POS
1914 PHI N	1	1	0	0	0	0	0.0	0	0	1	0	0	.000	.000	1	0	

Herman Franks

FRANKS, HERMAN LOUIS   BL TR 5'10½" 187 lbs.
B. Jan. 4, 1914, Price, Utah
Manager 1965-68, 1977-79.

	G	AB	H	2B	3B	HR	HR%	R	RBI	BB	SO	SB	BA	SA	PH AB	PH H	G by POS
1939 STL N	17	17	1	0	0	0	0.0	3	3	3	3	0	.059	.059	2	0	C-13
1940 BKN N	65	131	24	4	0	1	0.8	11	14	20	6	2	.183	.237	19	3	C-43
1941	59	139	28	7	0	1	0.7	10	11	14	13	0	.201	.273	2	1	C-54, OF-1
1947 PHI A	8	15	3	0	1	0	0.0	2	1	4	4	0	.200	.333	2	0	C-4
1948	40	98	22	7	1	1	1.0	10	14	16	11	0	.224	.347	9	1	C-27
1949 NY N	1	3	2	0	0	0	0.0	1	0	0	0	0	.667	.667	0	0	C-1
6 yrs.	190	403	80	18	2	3	0.7	35	43	57	37	2	.199	.275	34	5	C-142, OF-1

WORLD SERIES

	G	AB	H	2B	3B	HR	HR%	R	RBI	BB	SO	SB	BA	SA	PH AB	PH H	G by POS
1941 BKN N	1	1	0	0	0	0	0.0	0	0	0	0	0	.000	.000	0	0	C-1

Joe Frazier

FRAZIER, JOSEPH FILMORE (Cobra Joe)   BL TR 6' 180 lbs.
B. Oct. 6, 1922, Liberty, N.C.
Manager 1976-77.

	G	AB	H	2B	3B	HR	HR%	R	RBI	BB	SO	SB	BA	SA	PH AB	PH H	G by POS
1947 CLE A	9	14	1	1	0	0	0.0	1	0	1	1	0	.071	.143	2	0	OF-5
1954 STL N	81	88	26	5	2	3	3.4	8	18	13	17	0	.295	.500	62	20	OF-11, 1B-1
1955	58	70	14	1	0	4	5.7	12	9	6	12	0	.200	.386	45	4	OF-14
1956 3 teams			STL N (14G – .211)			CIN N (10G – .235)			BAL A (45G – .257)								
" total	69	110	27	8	0	3	2.7	10	18	15	16	0	.245	.400	40	9	OF-26
4 yrs.	217	282	68	15	2	10	3.5	31	45	35	46	0	.241	.415	149	33	OF-56, 1B-1

Johnny Frederick

FREDERICK, JOHN HENRY   BL TL 5'11" 165 lbs.
B. Jan. 26, 1902, Denver, Colo.   D. June 18, 1977, Tigard, Ore.

	G	AB	H	2B	3B	HR	HR%	R	RBI	BB	SO	SB	BA	SA	PH AB	PH H	G by POS
1929 BKN N	148	628	206	52	6	24	3.8	127	75	39	34	6	.328	.545	5	2	OF-143
1930	142	616	206	44	11	17	2.8	120	76	46	34	1	.334	.524	0	0	OF-142
1931	146	611	165	34	8	17	2.8	81	71	31	46	2	.270	.435	1	0	OF-145
1932	118	384	115	28	2	16	4.2	54	56	25	35	1	.299	.508	29	9	OF-88
1933	147	556	171	22	7	7	1.3	65	64	36	14	9	.308	.410	9	2	OF-138
1934	104	307	91	20	1	4	1.3	51	35	33	13	4	.296	.407	18	6	OF-77, 1B-1
6 yrs.	805	3102	954	200	35	85	2.7	498	377	210	176	23	.308	.477	62	19	OF-733, 1B-1

Ed Freed

FREED, EDWIN CHARLES   BR TR 5'6" 165 lbs.
B. Aug. 22, 1919, Centre Valley, Pa.

	G	AB	H	2B	3B	HR	HR%	R	RBI	BB	SO	SB	BA	SA	PH AB	PH H	G by POS
1942 PHI N	13	33	10	3	1	0	0.0	3	1	4	3	1	.303	.455	2	0	OF-11

Roger Freed

FREED, ROGER VERNON   BR TR 6' 190 lbs.
B. June 2, 1946, Los Angeles, Calif.

	G	AB	H	2B	3B	HR	HR%	R	RBI	BB	SO	SB	BA	SA	PH AB	PH H	G by POS
1970 BAL A	4	13	2	0	0	0	0.0	0	0	3	4	0	.154	.154	0	0	1B-3, OF-1
1971 PHI N	118	348	77	12	1	6	1.7	23	37	44	86	0	.221	.313	14	2	OF-106, C-1
1972	73	129	29	4	0	6	4.7	10	18	23	39	0	.225	.395	27	4	OF-46
1974 CIN N	6	6	2	0	0	1	16.7	1	3	1	1	0	.333	.833	6	2	1B-1
1976 MON N	8	15	3	1	0	0	0.0	0	1	0	3	0	.200	.267	5	1	1B-3, OF-1
1977 STL N	49	83	33	2	1	5	6.0	10	21	11	9	0	.398	.627	23	9	1B-18, OF-6
1978	52	92	22	6	0	2	2.2	3	20	8	17	1	.239	.370	29	11	1B-15, OF-6
1979	34	31	8	2	0	2	6.5	2	8	5	7	0	.258	.516	27	6	1B-1
8 yrs.	344	717	176	27	2	22	3.1	49	109	95	166	1	.245	.381	131	35	1B-166, 1B-41, C-1

	G	AB	H	2B	3B	HR	HR %	R	RBI	BB	SO	SB	BA	SA	Pinch Hit AB	Pinch Hit H	G by POS

Bill Freehan

FREEHAN, WILLIAM ASHLEY
B. Nov. 29, 1941, Detroit, Mich.

BR TR 6'3" 203 lbs.

	G	AB	H	2B	3B	HR	HR %	R	RBI	BB	SO	SB	BA	SA	PH AB	PH H	G by POS
1961 DET A	4	10	4	0	0	0	0.0	1	4	1	0	0	.400	.400	0	0	C-3
1963	100	300	73	12	2	9	3.0	37	36	39	56	2	.243	.387	9	3	C-73, 1B-19
1964	144	520	156	14	8	18	3.5	69	80	36	68	5	.300	.462	6	1	C-141, 1B-1
1965	130	431	101	15	0	10	2.3	45	43	39	63	4	.234	.339	1	1	C-129
1966	136	492	115	22	0	12	2.4	47	46	40	72	5	.234	.352	1	1	C-132, 1B-5
1967	155	517	146	23	1	20	3.9	66	74	73	71	1	.282	.447	2	2	C-147, 1B-11
1968	155	540	142	24	2	25	4.6	73	84	65	64	0	.263	.454	3	1	C-138, 1B-21, OF-1
1969	143	489	128	16	3	16	3.3	61	49	53	55	1	.262	.405	8	1	C-120, 1B-20
1970	117	395	95	17	3	16	4.1	44	52	52	48	0	.241	.420	3	1	C-114
1971	148	516	143	26	4	21	4.1	57	71	54	48	2	.277	.465	4	1	C-144, OF-1
1972	111	374	98	18	2	10	2.7	51	56	48	51	0	.262	.401	8	3	C-105, 1B-1
1973	110	380	89	10	1	6	1.6	33	29	40	30	0	.234	.313	3	0	C-98, 1B-7
1974	130	445	132	17	5	18	4.0	58	60	42	44	2	.297	.479	1	0	1B-65, C-63, DH-1
1975	120	427	105	17	3	14	3.3	42	47	32	56	2	.246	.398	2	1	C-113, 1B-5
1976	71	237	64	10	1	5	2.1	22	27	12	27	0	.270	.384	6	0	C-61, DH-3, 1B-2
15 yrs.	1774	6073	1591	241	35	200	3.3	706	758	626	753	24	.262	.412	59	16	C-1581, 1B-157, DH-4, OF-2

LEAGUE CHAMPIONSHIP SERIES

	G	AB	H	2B	3B	HR	HR %	R	RBI	BB	SO	SB	BA	SA	PH AB	PH H	G by POS
1972 DET A	3	12	3	1	0	1	8.3	2	3	0	1	0	.250	.583	0	0	C-3

WORLD SERIES

	G	AB	H	2B	3B	HR	HR %	R	RBI	BB	SO	SB	BA	SA	PH AB	PH H	G by POS
1968 DET A	7	24	2	1	0	0	0.0	0	2	4	8	0	.083	.125	0	0	C-7

Buck Freeman

FREEMAN, JOHN FRANK
B. Oct. 30, 1871, Catasauqua, Pa. D. June 25, 1949, Wilkes-Barre, Pa.

BL TL 5'11" 160 lbs.

	G	AB	H	2B	3B	HR	HR %	R	RBI	BB	SO	SB	BA	SA	PH AB	PH H	G by POS
1891 WAS AA	5	18	4	1	0	0	0.0	1	1	2		0	.222	.278	0	0	P-5
1898 WAS N	29	107	39	2	3	3	2.8	19	21	7		2	.364	.523	0	0	OF-29
1899	155	588	187	19	25	25	4.3	107	122	23		21	.318	.563	0	0	OF-155, P-2
1900 BOS N	117	418	126	19	13	6	1.4	58	65	25		10	.301	.452	8	1	OF-91, 1B-19
1901 BOS A	129	490	169	23	15	12	2.4	88	114	44		17	.345	.527	0	0	1B-128, OF-1, 2B-1
1902	138	564	174	38	19	11	2.0	75	121	32		17	.309	.502	0	0	OF-138
1903	141	567	163	39	20	13	2.3	74	104	30		5	.287	.496	0	0	OF-141
1904	157	597	167	20	19	7	1.2	64	84	32		7	.280	.412	0	0	OF-157
1905	130	455	109	20	8	3	0.7	59	49	46		8	.240	.338	5	3	1B-72, OF-51, 3B-2
1906	121	392	98	18	9	1	0.3	42	30	28		5	.250	.349	8	3	OF-65, 1B-43, 3B-4
1907	4	11	2	0	0	1	9.1	1	2	3		0	.182	.455	1	0	OF-3
11 yrs.	1126	4207	1238	199	131	82	1.9	588	713	272	2	92	.294	.462	22	7	OF-831, 1B-262, P-7, 3B-6, 2B-1

WORLD SERIES

	G	AB	H	2B	3B	HR	HR %	R	RBI	BB	SO	SB	BA	SA	PH AB	PH H	G by POS
1903 BOS A	8	32	9	0	3	0	0.0	6	4	2	2	0	.281	.469	0	0	OF-8
4th																	

Jerry Freeman

FREEMAN, FRANK ELLSWORTH (Buck)
B. Jan. 26, 1879, Placerville, Calif. D. Sept. 30, 1952, Los Angeles, Calif.

6'2" 220 lbs.

	G	AB	H	2B	3B	HR	HR %	R	RBI	BB	SO	SB	BA	SA	PH AB	PH H	G by POS
1908 WAS A	154	531	134	15	5	1	0.2	45	45	36		6	.252	.305	0	0	1B-154
1909	19	48	8	0	1	0	0.0	2	3	4		3	.167	.208	4	0	1B-14, OF-1
2 yrs.	173	579	142	15	6	1	0.2	47	48	40		9	.245	.297	4	0	1B-168, OF-1

John Freeman

FREEMAN, JOHN EDWARD (Buck)
B. Jan. 24, 1901, Boston, Mass. D. Apr. 14, 1958, Washington, D. C.

BR TR 5'8" 160 lbs.

	G	AB	H	2B	3B	HR	HR %	R	RBI	BB	SO	SB	BA	SA	PH AB	PH H	G by POS
1927 BOS A	4	2	0	0	0	0	0.0	0	0	0	0	0	.000	.000	0	0	OF-3

Gene Freese

FREESE, EUGENE LEWIS (Augie)
Brother of George Freese.
B. Jan. 8, 1934, Wheeling, W. Va.

BR TR 5'11" 175 lbs.

	G	AB	H	2B	3B	HR	HR %	R	RBI	BB	SO	SB	BA	SA	PH AB	PH H	G by POS
1955 PIT N	134	455	115	21	8	14	3.1	69	44	34	57	5	.253	.426	12	3	3B-65, 2B-57
1956	65	207	43	9	0	3	1.4	17	14	16	45	2	.208	.295	10	0	3B-47, 2B-26
1957	114	346	98	18	2	6	1.7	44	31	17	42	9	.283	.399	30	9	3B-74, OF-10, 2B-10
1958 2 teams	PIT	N (17G —	.167)			STL	N (62G —	.257)									
'' total	79	209	52	11	1	7	3.3	29	18	11	34	1	.249	.411	29	6	3B-38, 2B-14, 3B-4
1959 PHI N	132	400	107	14	5	23	5.8	60	70	43	61	8	.268	.500	20	7	3B-109, 2B-6
1960 CHI N	127	455	124	32	6	17	3.7	60	79	29	65	10	.273	.481	6	1	3B-122
1961 CIN N	152	575	159	27	2	26	4.5	78	87	27	78	8	.277	.466	1	0	3B-151, 2B-1
1962	18	42	6	1	0	0	0.0	2	1	6	8	0	.143	.167	5	0	3B-10
1963	66	217	53	9	1	6	2.8	20	26	17	42	4	.244	.378	3	0	3B-62, OF-1
1964 PIT N	99	289	65	13	2	9	3.1	33	40	19	45	1	.225	.377	30	5	3B-72
1965 2 teams	PIT	N (43G —	.263)			CHI	A (17G —	.281)									
'' total	60	112	30	4	1	1	0.9	8	12	11	27	0	.268	.348	31	12	3B-27
1966 2 teams	CHI	A (48G —	.208)			HOU	N (21G —	.091)									
'' total	69	139	25	2	0	3	2.2	9	10	13	31	3	.180	.259	29	2	3B-38, 2B-3, OF-1
12 yrs.	1115	3446	877	161	28	115	3.3	429	432	243	535	51	.254	.418	206	45	3B-781, 2B-117, SS-28, OF-12

WORLD SERIES

	G	AB	H	2B	3B	HR	HR %	R	RBI	BB	SO	SB	BA	SA	PH AB	PH H	G by POS
1961 CIN N	5	16	1	1	0	0	0.0	0	0	3	4	0	.063	.125	0	0	3B-5

George Freese

FREESE, GEORGE WALTER (Bud)
Brother of Gene Freese.
B. Sept. 12, 1926, Wheeling, W. Va.

BR TR 6' 190 lbs.

	G	AB	H	2B	3B	HR	HR %	R	RBI	BB	SO	SB	BA	SA	PH AB	PH H	G by POS
1953 DET A	1	1	0	0	0	0	0.0	0	0	0	0	0	.000	.000	1	0	
1955 PIT N	51	179	46	8	2	3	1.7	17	22	17	18	1	.257	.374	1	0	3B-50
1961 CHI N	9	7	2	0	0	0	0.0	0	1	1	4	0	.286	.286	7	2	
3 yrs.	61	187	48	8	2	3	1.6	17	23	18	22	1	.257	.369	9	2	3B-50

	G	AB	H	2B	3B	HR	HR %	R	RBI	BB	SO	SB	BA	SA	Pinch Hit AB	Pinch Hit H	G by POS

Jim Fregosi

FREGOSI, JAMES LOUIS
B. Apr. 4, 1942, San Francisco, Calif.
Manager 1978-81.

BR TR 6'1" 190 lbs.

	G	AB	H	2B	3B	HR	HR %	R	RBI	BB	SO	SB	BA	SA	AB	H	G by POS
1961 LA A	11	27	6	0	0	0	0.0	7	3	1	4	0	.222	.222	0	0	SS-11
1962	58	175	51	3	4	3	1.7	15	23	18	27	2	.291	.406	0	0	SS-52
1963	154	592	170	29	12	9	1.5	83	50	36	104	2	.287	.422	1	0	SS-151
1964	147	505	140	22	9	18	3.6	86	72	72	87	8	.277	.463	9	3	SS-137
1965 CAL A	161	602	167	19	7	15	2.5	66	64	54	107	13	.277	.407	2	0	SS-160
1966	162	611	154	32	7	13	2.1	78	67	67	89	17	.252	.391	1	0	SS-162, 1B-1
1967	151	590	171	23	6	9	1.5	75	56	49	77	9	.290	.395	0	0	SS-151
1968	159	614	150	21	13	9	1.5	77	49	60	101	9	.244	.365	0	0	SS-159
1969	161	580	151	22	6	12	2.1	78	47	93	86	9	.260	.381	1	0	SS-160
1970	158	601	167	33	5	22	3.7	95	82	69	92	0	.278	.459	2	1	SS-150, 1B-6
1971	107	347	81	15	1	5	1.4	31	33	39	61	2	.233	.326	10	3	SS-74, 1B-18, OF-7
1972 NY N	101	340	79	15	4	5	1.5	31	32	38	71	0	.232	.344	7	1	3B-85, SS-6, 1B-3
1973 2 teams		NY	N (45G – .234)		TEX	A	(45G –	.268)									
" total	90	281	71	10	3	6	2.1	32	27	32	56	1	.253	.374	5	0	3B-34, SS-23, OF-17, 1B-13
1974 TEX A	78	230	60	5	0	12	5.2	31	34	22	41	0	.261	.439	7	2	1B-41, 3B-32
1975	77	191	50	5	0	7	3.7	25	33	20	39	0	.262	.398	20	1	1B-54, DH-13, 3B-4
1976	58	133	31	7	0	2	1.5	17	12	23	33	2	.233	.331	15	3	1B-26, DH-18, 3B-5
1977 2 teams		TEX	A (13G – .250)		PIT	N	(36G –	.286)									
" total	49	84	23	2	1	4	4.8	14	21	16	14	2	.274	.464	20	3	1B-20, DH-3, 3B-1
1978 PIT N	20	20	4	1	0	0	0.0	3	1	6	8	0	.200	.250	12	4	3B-5, 1B-2
18 yrs.	1902	6523	1726	264	78	151	2.3	844	706	715	1097	76	.265	.398	112	21	SS-1396, 1B-190, 3B-166, DH-34, OF-24

Vern Freiberger

FREIBERGER, VERNON DONALD
B. Nov. 19, 1923, Detroit, Mich.

BR TL 6'1" 170 lbs.

	G	AB	H	2B	3B	HR	HR %	R	RBI	BB	SO	SB	BA	SA	AB	H	G by POS
1941 CLE A	2	8	1	0	0	0	0.0	0	0	2	0	.125	.125	0	0	1B-2

Howard Freigau

FREIGAU, HOWARD EARL (Ty)
B. Aug. 1, 1902, Dayton, Ohio   D. July 18, 1932, Chattanooga, Tenn.

BR TR 5'10½" 160 lbs.

	G	AB	H	2B	3B	HR	HR %	R	RBI	BB	SO	SB	BA	SA	AB	H	G by POS
1922 STL N	3	1	0	0	0	0	0.0	0	0	0	0	0	.000	.000	0	0	SS-2, 3B-1
1923	113	358	94	18	1	1	0.3	30	35	25	36	5	.263	.327	0	0	SS-87, 2B-16, 1B-9, OF-1, 3B-1
1924	98	376	101	17	6	2	0.5	35	39	19	24	10	.269	.362	0	0	3B-98, SS-2
1925 2 teams		STL	N (9G – .154)		CHI	N	(117G –	.307)									
" total	126	502	150	22	10	8	1.6	79	71	32	32	10	.299	.430	0	0	3B-96, SS-24, 1B-7, 2B-1
1926 CHI N	140	508	137	27	7	3	0.6	51	51	43	42	6	.270	.368	4	2	3B-135, SS-2, OF-1
1927	30	86	20	5	0	0	0.0	12	10	9	10	0	.233	.291	0	0	3B-30
1928 2 teams		BKN	N (17G – .206)		BOS	N	(52G –	.257)									
" total	69	143	35	10	1	0	0.7	17	20	10	17	1	.245	.350	26	8	SS-15, 2B-11, 3B-10
7 yrs.	579	1974	537	99	25	15	0.8	224	226	138	161	32	.272	.370	30	10	3B-371, SS-132, 2B-28, 1B-16, OF-2

Charlie French

FRENCH, CHARLES CALVIN
B. Oct. 12, 1883, Indianapolis, Ind.   D. Mar. 30, 1962, Indianapolis, Ind.

BL TR 5'6" 140 lbs.

	G	AB	H	2B	3B	HR	HR %	R	RBI	BB	SO	SB	BA	SA	AB	H	G by POS
1909 BOS A	51	167	42	3	1	0	0.0	13	13	15		8	.251	.281	0	0	2B-28, SS-23
1910 2 teams		BOS	A (9G – .200)		CHI	A	(45G –	.165)									
" total	54	210	36	2	1	0	0.0	21	7	11		5	.171	.190	0	0	2B-36, OF-16
2 yrs.	105	377	78	5	2	0	0.0	34	20	26		13	.207	.231	0	0	2B-64, SS-23, OF-16

Jim French

FRENCH, RICHARD JAMES
B. Aug. 13, 1941, Warren, Ohio

BL TR 5'8" 180 lbs.

	G	AB	H	2B	3B	HR	HR %	R	RBI	BB	SO	SB	BA	SA	AB	H	G by POS
1965 WAS A	13	37	11	0	1	1	2.7	4	7	9	5	1	.297	.378	0	0	C-13
1966	10	24	5	1	0	0	0.0	0	3	4	5	0	.208	.250	0	0	C-10
1967	6	16	1	0	0	0	0.0	0	1	3	4	0	.063	.063	0	0	C-6
1968	59	165	32	5	0	1	0.6	9	10	19	19	1	.194	.242	8	1	C-53
1969	63	158	29	6	3	2	1.3	14	13	41	15	1	.184	.297	0	0	C-63
1970	69	166	35	3	1	1	0.6	20	13	38	23	0	.211	.259	7	1	C-62, OF-1
1971	14	41	6	2	0	0	0.0	6	4	7	7	0	.146	.195	0	0	C-14
7 yrs.	234	607	119	17	4	5	0.8	53	51	121	78	3	.196	.262	15	2	C-221, OF-1

Pat French

FRENCH, FRANK ALEXANDER
B. Sept. 22, 1893, Dover, N. H.   D. July 13, 1969, Bath, Me.

BR TR 6'1" 180 lbs.

	G	AB	H	2B	3B	HR	HR %	R	RBI	BB	SO	SB	BA	SA	AB	H	G by POS
1917 PHI A	3	2	0	0	0	0	0.0	0	0	0	0	0	.000	.000	0	0	OF-1

Ray French

FRENCH, WALTER EDWARD
B. Jan. 9, 1897, Alameda, Calif.   D. Apr. 3, 1978, Alameda, Calif.

BR TR 5'9½" 158 lbs.

	G	AB	H	2B	3B	HR	HR %	R	RBI	BB	SO	SB	BA	SA	AB	H	G by POS
1920 NY A	2	2	0	0	0	0	0.0	2	1	0	1	0	.000	.000	0	0	SS-1
1923 BKN N	43	73	16	2	1	0	0.0	14	7	4	7	0	.219	.274	1	0	SS-30
1924 CHI A	37	112	20	4	0	0	0.0	13	11	10	13	3	.179	.214	5	0	SS-28, 2B-3
3 yrs.	82	187	36	6	1	0	0.0	29	19	14	21	3	.193	.235	6	0	SS-59, 2B-3

Walter French

FRENCH, WALTER EDWARD (Fitz)
B. July 12, 1899, Moorestown, N. J.   D. May 13, 1984, Mountain Home, Ark.

BL TR 5'7½" 155 lbs.

	G	AB	H	2B	3B	HR	HR %	R	RBI	BB	SO	SB	BA	SA	AB	H	G by POS
1923 PHI A	16	39	9	3	0	0	0.0	7	2	5	7	0	.231	.308	3	0	OF-10
1925	67	100	37	9	0	0	0.0	20	14	1	9	1	.370	.460	37	13	OF-19
1926	112	397	121	18	7	1	0.3	51	36	18	24	2	.305	.393	11	4	OF-99
1927	109	326	99	10	5	0	0.0	48	41	16	14	9	.304	.365	7	0	OF-94
1928	49	74	19	4	0	0	0.0	9	7	2	5	1	.257	.311	27	5	OF-20
1929	45	45	12	1	1	1	2.2	7	9	2	3	0	.267	.400	28	6	OF-10
6 yrs.	398	981	297	45	13	2	0.2	142	109	44	62	13	.303	.381	113	28	OF-252

WORLD SERIES																	
1929 PHI A	1	1	0	0	0	0	0.0	0	0	0	1	0	.000	.000	1	0	

	G	AB	H	2B	3B	HR	HR %	R	RBI	BB	SO	SB	BA	SA	Pinch Hit AB	Pinch Hit H	G by POS

Lonny Frey

FREY, LINUS REINHARD (Junior)
B. Aug. 23, 1910, St. Louis, Mo.
BL TR 5'10" 160 lbs.
BB 1933-38

	G	AB	H	2B	3B	HR	HR %	R	RBI	BB	SO	SB	BA	SA	AB	H	G by POS
1933 BKN N	34	135	43	5	3	0	0.0	25	12	13	13	4	.319	.400	0	0	SS-34
1934	125	490	139	24	5	8	1.6	77	57	52	54	11	.284	.402	2	0	SS-109, 3B-13
1935	131	515	135	35	11	11	2.1	88	77	66	68	6	.262	.437	0	0	SS-127, 2B-4
1936	148	524	146	29	4	4	0.8	63	60	71	56	7	.279	.372	3	0	SS-117, 2B-30, OF-1
1937 CHI N	78	198	55	9	3	1	0.5	33	22	33	15	6	.278	.369	14	2	SS-30, 2B-13, 3B-9, OF-5
1938 CIN N	124	501	133	26	6	4	0.8	76	36	49	50	4	.265	.365	0	0	2B-121, SS-3
1939	125	484	141	27	9	11	2.3	95	55	72	46	5	.291	.452	1	0	2B-123
1940	150	563	150	23	6	8	1.4	102	54	80	48	22	.266	.371	0	0	2B-150
1941	146	543	138	29	5	6	1.1	78	59	72	37	16	.254	.359	1	0	2B-145
1942	141	523	139	23	6	2	0.4	66	39	87	38	9	.266	.344	1	0	2B-140
1943	144	586	154	20	8	2	0.3	78	43	76	56	7	.263	.334	0	0	2B-144
1946	111	333	82	10	3	3	0.9	46	24	63	31	5	.246	.321	17	4	2B-65, OF-28
1947 2 teams			CHI	N	(24G –	.209)		NY	A	(24G –	.179)						
" total	48	71	14	2	0	0	0.0	14	5	14	7	3	.197	.225	14	4	2B-32
1948 2 teams			NY	A	(1G –	.000)		NY	N	(29G –	.255)						
" total	30	51	13	1	0	1	2.0	7	6	4	6	0	.255	.333	14	2	2B-13
14 yrs.	1535	5517	1482	263	69	61	1.1	848	549	752	525	105	.269	.374	67	14	2B-980, SS-420, OF-34, 3B-22
WORLD SERIES																	
1939 CIN N	4	17	0	0	0	0	0.0	0	0	1	4	0	.000	.000	0	0	2B-4
1940	3	2	0	0	0	0	0.0	0	0	0	0	0	.000	.000	2	0	
1947 NY A	1	1	0	0	0	0	0.0	0	1	0	0	0	.000	.000	1	0	
3 yrs.	8	20	0	0	0	0	0.0	0	1	1	4	0	.000	.000	3	0	2B-4

Pepe Frias

FRIAS, JESUS MARIA
B. July 15, 1948, San Pedro de Macoris, Dominican Republic
BR TR 5'10" 159 lbs.

	G	AB	H	2B	3B	HR	HR %	R	RBI	BB	SO	SB	BA	SA	AB	H	G by POS
1973 MON N	100	225	52	10	1	0	0.0	19	22	10	24	1	.231	.284	2	0	SS-46, 2B-44, 3B-6, OF-1
1974	75	112	24	4	1	0	0.0	12	7	7	10	1	.214	.268	4	1	SS-30, 3B-27, 2B-15, OF-3
1975	51	64	8	2	0	0	0.0	4	4	3	13	0	.125	.156	4	0	SS-29, 3B-11, 2B-7
1976	76	113	28	5	0	0	0.0	7	8	4	14	1	.248	.292	1	0	SS-35, 2B-35, 3B-4
1977	53	70	18	1	0	0	0.0	10	5	0	10	1	.257	.271	4	2	2B-20, SS-14, 3B-1
1978	73	15	4	2	1	0	0.0	5	5	0	3	0	.267	.533	2	0	2B-61, SS-3
1979 ATL N	140	475	123	18	4	1	0.2	41	44	20	36	3	.259	.320	3	1	SS-137
1980 2 teams			TEX	A	(116G –	.242)		LA	N	(14G –	.222)						
" total	130	236	57	6	1	0	0.0	28	10	4	23	5	.242	.275	5	1	SS-117, 3B-7, 2B-2
1981 LA N	25	36	9	1	0	0	0.0	6	3	1	3	0	.250	.278	1	0	SS-15, 2B-6, 3B-1
9 yrs.	723	1346	323	49	8	1	0.1	132	108	49	136	12	.240	.290	35	5	SS-426, 2B-190, 3B-57, OF-4

Barney Friberg

FRIBERG, AUGUSTAF BERNHARDT
Also known as Bernard Albert Friberg.
B. Aug. 18, 1899, Manchester, N. H.   D. Dec. 8, 1958, Swampscott, Mass.
BR TR 5'11" 178 lbs.

	G	AB	H	2B	3B	HR	HR %	R	RBI	BB	SO	SB	BA	SA	AB	H	G by POS
1919 CHI N	8	20	4	1	0	0	0.0	0	1	0	0	0	.200	.250	1	0	OF-7
1920	50	114	24	5	1	0	0.0	11	7	6	20	2	.211	.272	2	0	OF-24, 2B-24
1922	97	296	92	8	2	0	0.0	51	23	37	37	8	.311	.351	12	2	OF-74, 1B-6, 3B-5, 2B-3
1923	146	547	174	27	11	12	2.2	91	88	45	49	13	.318	.473	0	0	3B-146
1924	142	495	138	19	3	5	1.0	67	82	66	53	19	.279	.360	0	0	3B-142
1925 2 teams			CHI	N	(44G –	.257)		PHI	N	(91G –	.270)						
" total	135	456	121	17	4	6	1.3	53	38	53	57	1	.265	.360	2	0	2B-77, 3B-40, OF-12, 1B-6, SS-2, C-1, P-1
1926 PHI N	144	478	128	21	3	1	0.2	38	51	57	77	2	.268	.331	0	0	2B-144
1927	111	335	78	8	2	1	0.3	31	28	41	49	3	.233	.278	4	2	3B-103, 2B-5
1928	52	94	19	3	0	1	1.1	11	7	12	16	0	.202	.266	6	1	SS-31, 3B-5, OF-3, 2B-3, 1B-2
1929	128	455	137	21	10	7	1.5	74	55	49	54	1	.301	.437	5	2	SS-73, OF-40, 2B-8, 1B-2
1930	105	331	113	21	1	4	1.2	62	42	47	35	1	.341	.447	7	3	OF-35, SS-12, 3B-8
1931	103	353	92	19	5	1	0.3	33	26	33	25	1	.261	.351	3	0	2B-64, 3B-25, 1B-5, SS-3
1932	61	154	37	8	2	0	0.0	17	14	19	23	0	.240	.318	2	0	2B-56
1933 BOS A	17	41	13	3	0	0	0.0	5	9	6	1	0	.317	.390	3	1	2B-6, 3B-5, SS-2
14 yrs.	1299	4169	1170	181	44	38	0.9	544	471	471	498	51	.281	.373	47	11	3B-479, 2B-434, OF-195, SS-123, 1B-21, C-1, P-1

Jim Fridley

FRIDLEY, JAMES RILEY (Big Jim)
B. Sept. 6, 1924, Phillippi, W. Va.
BR TR 6'2" 205 lbs.

	G	AB	H	2B	3B	HR	HR %	R	RBI	BB	SO	SB	BA	SA	AB	H	G by POS
1952 CLE A	62	175	44	2	0	4	2.3	23	16	14	40	3	.251	.331	6	1	OF-54
1954 BAL A	85	240	59	8	5	4	1.7	25	36	21	41	0	.246	.371	18	6	OF-67
1958 CIN N	5	9	2	2	0	0	0.0	2	1	0	2	0	.222	.444	4	1	OF-2
3 yrs.	152	424	105	12	5	8	1.9	50	53	35	83	3	.248	.356	28	8	OF-123

Bill Friel

FRIEL, WILLIAM EDWARD
Brother of Pat Friel.
B. Apr. 1, 1876, Renovo, Pa.   D. Dec. 24, 1959, St. Louis, Mo.
BL TR

	G	AB	H	2B	3B	HR	HR %	R	RBI	BB	SO	SB	BA	SA	AB	H	G by POS
1901 MIL A	106	376	100	13	7	4	1.1	51	35	23		15	.266	.370	3	2	3B-61, OF-28, 2B-9, SS-6
1902 STL A	80	267	64	9	2	2	0.7	26	20	14		4	.240	.311	5	2	OF-33, 2B-25, 1B-10, 3B-8, SS-3, C-1, P-1
1903	97	351	80	11	8	0	0.0	46	25	23		4	.228	.305	2	1	2B-63, 3B-24, OF-9
3 yrs.	283	994	244	33	17	6	0.6	123	80	60		23	.245	.331	10	5	2B-97, 3B-93, OF-70, 1B-10, SS-9, C-1, P-1

Pat Friel

FRIEL, PATRICK HENRY
Brother of Bill Friel.
B. June 11, 1860, Lewisburg, W. Va.   D. Jan. 15, 1924, Providence, R. I.

	G	AB	H	2B	3B	HR	HR %	R	RBI	BB	SO	SB	BA	SA	AB	H	G by POS
1890 SYR AA	62	261	65	8	2	3	1.1	51		17		34	.249	.330	0	0	OF-62
1891 PHI AA	2	8	2	1	0	0	0.0	2	0	0	0	0	.250	.375	0	0	OF-2
2 yrs.	64	269	67	9	2	3	1.1	53		17	0	34	.249	.331	0	0	OF-64

	G	AB	H	2B	3B	HR	HR %	R	RBI	BB	SO	SB	BA	SA	Pinch Hit AB	Pinch Hit H	G by POS

Frank Friend

FRIEND, FRANK B.
B. Washington, D. C.   D. Sept. 8, 1897, Atlantic City, N. J.

	G	AB	H	2B	3B	HR	HR %	R	RBI	BB	SO	SB	BA	SA	PH AB	PH H	G by POS
1896 LOU N	2	5	1	0	0	0	0.0	1	0	1	1	0	.200	.200	0	0	C-2

Owen Friend

FRIEND, OWEN LACEY (Red)
B. Mar. 21, 1927, Granite City, Ill.
BR TR 6'1" 180 lbs.

	G	AB	H	2B	3B	HR	HR %	R	RBI	BB	SO	SB	BA	SA	PH AB	PH H	G by POS
1949 STL A	2	8	3	0	0	0	0.0	1	1	0	0	0	.375	.375	0	0	2B-2
1950	119	372	88	15	2	8	2.2	48	50	40	68	2	.237	.352	1	1	2B-93, 3B-24, SS-3
1953 2 teams	DET A (31G – .177)			CLE A (34G – .235)													
" total	65	164	33	6	0	5	3.0	17	23	11	25	0	.201	.329	2	1	2B-45, SS-8, 3B-1
1955 2 teams	BOS A (14G – .262)			CHI N (6G – .100)													
" total	20	52	12	3	0	0	0.0	3	2	4	14	0	.231	.288	3	0	SS-15, 3B-2, 2B-1
1956 CHI N	2	2	0	0	0	0	0.0	0	0	0	2	0	.000	.000	2	0	
5 yrs.	208	598	136	24	2	13	2.2	69	76	55	109	2	.227	.339	8	2	2B-141, 3B-27, SS-26

Buck Frierson

FRIERSON, ROBERT LAWRENCE
B. July 29, 1917, Chicota, Tex.
BR TR 6'3" 195 lbs.

	G	AB	H	2B	3B	HR	HR %	R	RBI	BB	SO	SB	BA	SA	PH AB	PH H	G by POS
1941 CLE A	5	11	3	1	0	0	0.0	2	2	1	1	0	.273	.364	2	1	OF-3

Fred Frink

FRINK, FRED FERDINAND
B. Aug. 25, 1911, Macon, Ga.
BR TR 6'1" 180 lbs.

	G	AB	H	2B	3B	HR	HR %	R	RBI	BB	SO	SB	BA	SA	PH AB	PH H	G by POS
1934 PHI N	2	0	0	0	0	0	–	0	0	0	0	0	–	–	0	0	OF-1

Charlie Frisbee

FRISBEE, CHARLES AUGUSTUS (Bunt)
B. Feb. 2, 1874, Dows, Iowa   D. Nov. 7, 1954, Alden, Iowa
BB TR 5'9" 175 lbs.

	G	AB	H	2B	3B	HR	HR %	R	RBI	BB	SO	SB	BA	SA	PH AB	PH H	G by POS
1899 BOS N	42	152	50	4	2	0	0.0	22	20	9		10	.329	.382	1	0	OF-40
1900 NY N	4	13	2	1	0	0	0.0	2	3	2		0	.154	.231	0	0	OF-4
2 yrs.	46	165	52	5	2	0	0.0	24	23	11		10	.315	.370	1	0	OF-44

Frankie Frisch

FRISCH, FRANK FRANCIS (The Fordham Flash)
B. Sept. 9, 1898, Queens, N. Y.   D. Mar. 12, 1973, Wilmington, Del.
Manager 1933-38, 1940-46, 1949-51.
Hall of Fame 1947.
BB TR 5'11" 165 lbs.

	G	AB	H	2B	3B	HR	HR %	R	RBI	BB	SO	SB	BA	SA	PH AB	PH H	G by POS
1919 NY N	54	190	43	3	2	2	1.1	21	24	4	14	15	.226	.295	3	0	2B-29, 3B-28, SS-1
1920	110	440	123	10	10	4	0.9	57	77	20	18	34	.280	.375	1	0	3B-110, SS-2
1921	153	618	211	31	17	8	1.3	121	100	42	28	49	.341	.485	0	0	3B-93, 2B-61
1922	132	514	168	16	13	5	1.0	101	51	47	13	31	.327	.438	0	0	2B-85, 3B-53, SS-1
1923	151	641	223	32	10	12	1.9	116	111	46	12	29	.348	.485	0	0	2B-135, 3B-17
1924	145	603	198	33	15	7	1.2	121	69	56	24	22	.328	.468	0	0	2B-143, SS-10, 3B-2
1925	120	502	166	26	6	11	2.2	89	48	32	14	21	.331	.472	0	0	3B-46, 2B-42, SS-39
1926	135	545	171	29	4	5	0.9	75	44	33	16	23	.314	.409	1	1	2B-127, 3B-7
1927 STL N	153	617	208	31	11	10	1.6	112	78	43	10	48	.337	.472	0	0	2B-153, SS-1
1928	141	547	164	29	9	10	1.8	107	86	64	17	29	.300	.441	2	1	2B-139
1929	138	527	176	40	12	5	0.9	93	74	53	12	24	.334	.484	3	2	2B-121, 3B-13, SS-1
1930	133	540	187	46	9	10	1.9	121	114	55	16	15	.346	.520	2	0	2B-123, 3B-10
1931	131	518	161	24	4	4	0.8	96	82	45	13	28	.311	.396	2	0	2B-129
1932	115	486	142	26	2	3	0.6	59	60	25	13	18	.292	.372	0	0	2B-75, 3B-37, SS-4
1933	147	585	177	32	6	4	0.7	74	66	48	16	18	.303	.398	4	2	2B-132, SS-15
1934	140	550	168	30	6	3	0.5	74	75	45	10	11	.305	.398	2	0	2B-115, 3B-25
1935	103	354	104	16	2	1	0.3	52	55	33	16	2	.294	.359	9	1	2B-88, 3B-5
1936	93	303	83	10	0	1	0.3	40	26	36	10	2	.274	.317	8	3	2B-61, 3B-22, SS-1
1937	17	32	7	2	0	0	0.0	3	4	1	0	0	.219	.281	12	2	2B-17
19 yrs.	2311	9112	2880	466	138	105	1.2	1532	1244	728	272	419	.316	.432	47	12	2B-1775, 3B-468, SS-75

WORLD SERIES

	G	AB	H	2B	3B	HR	HR %	R	RBI	BB	SO	SB	BA	SA	PH AB	PH H	G by POS
1921 NY N	8	30	9	0	1	0	0.0	5	1	4	3	3	.300	.367	0	0	3B-8
1922	5	17	8	1	0	0	0.0	3	2	1	0	1	.471	.529	0	0	2B-5
1923	6	25	10	0	1	0	0.0	2	1	0	0	0	.400	.480	0	0	2B-6
1924	7	30	10	4	1	0	0.0	1	0	4	1	1	.333	.533	0	0	2B-7
1928 STL N	4	13	3	0	0	0	0.0	1	1	2	2	2	.231	.231	0	0	2B-4
1930	6	24	5	2	0	0	0.0	0	0	0	1	0	.208	.292	0	0	2B-6
1931	7	27	7	2	0	0	0.0	2	1	1	2	1	.259	.333	0	0	2B-7
1934	7	31	6	1	0	0	0.0	2	4	0	1	0	.194	.226	0	0	2B-7
8 yrs.	50	197	58	10	3	0	0.0	16	10	12	9	9	.294	.376	0	0	2B-42, 3B-8
	8th	4th	3rd	1st	4th							6th					

Emil Frisk

FRISK, JOHN EMIL
B. Oct. 15, 1874, Kalkaska, Mich.   D. Jan. 27, 1922, Seattle, Wash.
BL TR 6'1" 190 lbs.

	G	AB	H	2B	3B	HR	HR %	R	RBI	BB	SO	SB	BA	SA	PH AB	PH H	G by POS
1899 CIN N	9	25	7	1	0	0	0.0	5	2	2		0	.280	.320	0	0	P-9
1901 DET A	20	48	15	3	0	1	2.1	10	7	3		0	.313	.438	6	2	P-11, OF-2
1905 STL A	127	429	112	11	6	3	0.7	58	36	42		7	.261	.336	7	1	OF-116
1907	4	4	1	0	0	0	0.0	0	0	1		0	.250	.250	4	1	
4 yrs.	160	506	135	15	6	4	0.8	73	45	48		7	.267	.344	17	4	OF-118, P-20

Harry Fritz

FRITZ, HARRY KOCH (Dutchman)
B. Sept. 30, 1890, Philadelphia, Pa.   D. Nov. 4, 1974, Columbus, Ohio
BR TR 5'8" 170 lbs.

	G	AB	H	2B	3B	HR	HR %	R	RBI	BB	SO	SB	BA	SA	PH AB	PH H	G by POS
1913 PHI A	5	13	0	0	0	0	0.0	1	0	2	4	0	.000	.000	0	0	3B-5
1914 CHI F	65	174	37	5	1	0	0.0	16	13	18		2	.213	.253	5	1	3B-46, SS-9, 2B-1
1915	79	236	59	8	4	3	1.3	27	26	13		4	.250	.356	3	2	3B-70, 2B-6, SS-1
3 yrs.	149	423	96	13	5	3	0.7	44	39	33	4	6	.227	.303	8	3	3B-121, SS-10, 2B-7

Larry Fritz

FRITZ, LAWRENCE JOSEPH
B. Feb. 14, 1949, East Chicago, Ind.
BL TL 6'2" 225 lbs.

	G	AB	H	2B	3B	HR	HR %	R	RBI	BB	SO	SB	BA	SA	PH AB	PH H	G by POS
1975 PHI N	1	1	0	0	0	0	0.0	0	0	0	0	0	.000	.000	1	0	

	G	AB	H	2B	3B	HR	HR %	R	RBI	BB	SO	SB	BA	SA	Pinch Hit AB	Pinch Hit H	G by POS

Doug Frobel

FROBEL, DOUGLAS STEVEN
B. June 6, 1959, Ottawa, Canada
BL TR 6'3" 190 lbs.

	G	AB	H	2B	3B	HR	HR %	R	RBI	BB	SO	SB	BA	SA	AB	H	G by POS
1982 PIT N	16	34	7	2	0	2	5.9	5	3	1	11	1	.206	.441	4	1	OF-12
1983	32	60	17	4	1	3	5.0	10	11	4	17	1	.283	.533	5	1	OF-24
1984	126	276	56	9	3	12	4.3	33	28	24	84	7	.203	.388	17	3	OF-112
3 yrs.	174	370	80	15	4	17	4.6	48	42	29	112	9	.216	.416	26	5	OF-148

Ben Froelich

FROELICH, WILLIAM PALMER
B. Nov. 12, 1887, Pittsburgh, Pa.   D. Sept. 1, 1916, Pittsburgh, Pa.
BR TR

	G	AB	H	2B	3B	HR	HR %	R	RBI	BB	SO	SB	BA	SA	AB	H	G by POS
1909 PHI N	1	1	0	0	0	0	0.0	0	0	0		0	.000	.000	0	0	C-1

Jerry Fry

FRY, JERRY RAY
B. Feb. 29, 1956, Springfield, Ill.
BR TR 6' 185 lbs.

	G	AB	H	2B	3B	HR	HR %	R	RBI	BB	SO	SB	BA	SA	AB	H	G by POS
1978 MON N	4	9	0	0	0	0	0.0	0	0	1	5	0	.000	.000	0	0	C-4

Mike Fuentes

FUENTES, MICHAEL J.
B. July 11, 1958, Miami, Fla.
BR TR 6'3" 190 lbs.

	G	AB	H	2B	3B	HR	HR %	R	RBI	BB	SO	SB	BA	SA	AB	H	G by POS
1983 MON N	6	4	1	0	0	0	0.0	1	0	0	2	0	.250	.250	4	1	
1984	3	4	1	0	0	0	0.0	0	0	1	2	0	.250	.250	2	1	OF-1
2 yrs.	9	8	2	0	0	0	0.0	1	0	1	4	0	.250	.250	6	2	OF-1

Tito Fuentes

FUENTES, RIGOBERTO PEAT
B. Jan. 4, 1944, Havana, Cuba
BR TR 5'11" 175 lbs.
BB 1969

	G	AB	H	2B	3B	HR	HR %	R	RBI	BB	SO	SB	BA	SA	AB	H	G by POS
1965 SF N	26	72	15	1	0	0	0.0	12	1	5	14	0	.208	.222	0	0	SS-18, 2B-7, 3B-1
1966	133	541	141	21	3	9	1.7	63	40	9	57	6	.261	.360	1	0	SS-76, 2B-60
1967	133	344	72	12	1	5	1.5	27	29	27	61	4	.209	.294	0	0	2B-130, SS-5
1969	67	183	54	4	3	1	0.5	28	14	15	25	2	.295	.366	1	0	3B-36, SS-30
1970	123	435	116	13	7	2	0.5	49	32	36	52	4	.267	.343	7	0	2B-78, SS-36, 3B-24
1971	152	630	172	28	6	4	0.6	63	52	18	46	12	.273	.356	1	0	2B-152
1972	152	572	151	33	6	7	1.2	64	53	39	56	16	.264	.379	1	0	2B-152
1973	160	656	182	25	5	6	0.9	78	63	45	62	12	.277	.358	0	0	2B-160, 3B-1
1974	108	390	97	15	2	0	0.0	33	22	22	32	7	.249	.297	7	2	2B-103
1975 SD N	146	565	158	21	3	4	0.7	57	43	25	51	8	.280	.349	2	0	2B-142
1976	135	520	137	18	0	2	0.4	48	36	18	38	5	.263	.310	8	2	2B-127
1977 DET A	151	615	190	19	10	5	0.8	83	51	38	61	4	.309	.397	1	0	2B-151
1978 OAK A	13	43	6	1	0	0	0.0	5	2	1	6	0	.140	.163	2	0	2B-13
13 yrs.	1499	5566	1491	211	46	45	0.8	610	438	298	561	80	.268	.347	31	4	2B-1275, SS-165, 3B-62

LEAGUE CHAMPIONSHIP SERIES

	G	AB	H	2B	3B	HR	HR %	R	RBI	BB	SO	SB	BA	SA	AB	H	G by POS
1971 SF N	4	16	5	1	0	1	6.3	4	2	1	3	0	.313	.563	0	0	2B-4

Ollie Fuhrman

FUHRMAN, ALFRED GEORGE
B. July 20, 1896, Jordan, Minn.   D. Jan. 11, 1969, Peoria, Ill.
BB TR 5'11" 185 lbs.

	G	AB	H	2B	3B	HR	HR %	R	RBI	BB	SO	SB	BA	SA	AB	H	G by POS
1922 PHI A	6	6	2	1	0	0	0.0	1	0	0	0	0	.333	.500	2	0	C-4

Dot Fulghum

FULGHUM, JAMES LAVOISIER
B. July 4, 1900, Valdosta, Ga.   D. Nov. 1, 1967, Raleigh, N. C.
BR TR 5'8½" 165 lbs.

	G	AB	H	2B	3B	HR	HR %	R	RBI	BB	SO	SB	BA	SA	AB	H	G by POS
1921 PHI A	2	2	0	0	0	0	0.0	0	0	1		0	.000	.000	0	0	SS-1

Frank Fuller

FULLER, FRANK EDWARD (Rabbit)
B. Jan. 1, 1893, Detroit, Mich.   D. Oct. 29, 1965, Warren, Mich.
BB TR 5'7" 150 lbs.

	G	AB	H	2B	3B	HR	HR %	R	RBI	BB	SO	SB	BA	SA	AB	H	G by POS
1915 DET A	14	32	5	0	0	0	0.0	6	2	9	7	2	.156	.156	2	1	2B-9, SS-1
1916	20	10	1	0	0	0	0.0	2	1	1	4	3	.100	.100	1	0	2B-8, SS-1
1923 BOS A	6	21	5	0	0	0	0.0	3	0	1	1	1	.238	.238	0	0	2B-6
3 yrs.	40	63	11	0	0	0	0.0	11	3	11	12	6	.175	.175	3	1	2B-23, SS-2

Harry Fuller

FULLER, HENRY W.
Brother of Shorty Fuller.
B. Dec. 5, 1862, Cincinnati, Ohio   D. Dec. 12, 1895, Cincinnati, Ohio
BR TR

	G	AB	H	2B	3B	HR	HR %	R	RBI	BB	SO	SB	BA	SA	AB	H	G by POS
1891 STL AA	1	2	0	0	0	0	0.0	0	0	0		1	.000	.000	0	0	3B-1

Jim Fuller

FULLER, JAMES HARDY
B. Nov. 28, 1950, Bethesda, Md.
BR TR 6'3" 215 lbs.

	G	AB	H	2B	3B	HR	HR %	R	RBI	BB	SO	SB	BA	SA	AB	H	G by POS
1973 BAL A	9	26	3	0	0	2	7.7	2	4	1	17	0	.115	.346	3	1	OF-5, 1B-2, DH-1
1974	64	189	42	11	0	7	3.7	17	28	8	68	1	.222	.392	5	1	OF-59, 1B-4, DH-2
1977 HOU N	34	100	16	6	0	2	2.0	5	9	10	45	0	.160	.280	5	0	OF-27, 1B-1
3 yrs.	107	315	61	17	0	11	3.5	24	41	19	130	1	.194	.352	13	2	OF-91, 1B-7, DH-3

John Fuller

FULLER, JOHN EDWARD
B. Jan. 29, 1950, Lynwood, Calif.
BL TL 6'2" 180 lbs.

	G	AB	H	2B	3B	HR	HR %	R	RBI	BB	SO	SB	BA	SA	AB	H	G by POS
1974 ATL N	3	3	1	0	0	0	0.0	1	0	0	0	0	.333	.333	2	0	OF-1

Nig Fuller

FULLER, CHARLES F.
B. Feb. 17, 1886, Indiana   D. Apr. 2, 1931, Hartford, Mich.
BR TR

	G	AB	H	2B	3B	HR	HR %	R	RBI	BB	SO	SB	BA	SA	AB	H	G by POS
1902 BKN N	3	9	0	0	0	0	0.0	1	0	0		0	.000	.000	0	0	C-3

Shorty Fuller

FULLER, WILLIAM BENJAMIN
Brother of Harry Fuller.
B. Oct. 10, 1867, Cincinnati, Ohio   D. Apr. 11, 1904, Cincinnati, Ohio
BR TR

	G	AB	H	2B	3B	HR	HR %	R	RBI	BB	SO	SB	BA	SA	AB	H	G by POS
1888 WAS N	49	170	31	5	2	0	0.0	11	12	10	14	6	.182	.235	0	0	SS-47, 2B-2
1889 STL AA	140	517	117	18	6	0	0.0	91	51	52		38	.226	.284	0	0	SS-140
1890	130	526	146	9	9	1	0.2	118				60	.278	.335	0	0	SS-130
1891	137	586	127	15	7	2	0.3	107	63	67	28	42	.217	.276	0	0	SS-103, 2B-39
1892 NY N	141	508	115	11	4	1	0.2	74	48	52	22	37	.226	.270	0	0	SS-141
1893	130	474	112	14	8	0	0.0	78	51	60	21	26	.236	.300	0	0	SS-130
1894	93	368	104	14	4	2	0.5	81	46	52	16	32	.283	.359	0	0	SS-89, OF-2, 3B-2, 2B-1

	G	AB	H	2B	3B	HR	HR %	R	RBI	BB	SO	SB	BA	SA	Pinch Hit AB	H	G by POS

Shorty Fuller continued

	G	AB	H	2B	3B	HR	HR %	R	RBI	BB	SO	SB	BA	SA	Pinch Hit AB	H	G by POS
1895	126	458	103	11	3	0	0.0	82	32	64	34	15	.225	.262	0	0	SS-126
1896	18	72	12	0	0	0	0.0	10	7	14	5	4	.167	.167	0	0	SS-18
9 yrs.	964	3679	867	97	43	6	0.2	652	310	444	196	260	.236	.290	0	0	SS-924, 2B-42, OF-2, 3B-2

Vern Fuller

FULLER, VERN GORDON
B. Mar. 1, 1944, Menomonie, Wis.

BR TR 6'1"   170 lbs.

	G	AB	H	2B	3B	HR	HR %	R	RBI	BB	SO	SB	BA	SA	Pinch Hit AB	H	G by POS
1964 CLE A	2	1	0	0	0	0	0.0	0	0	0	0	0	.000	.000	1	0	
1966	16	47	11	2	1	2	4.3	7	2	7	6	0	.234	.447	0	0	2B-16
1967	73	206	46	10	0	7	3.4	18	21	19	55	2	.223	.374	6	1	2B-64, SS-2
1968	97	244	59	8	2	0	0.0	14	18	24	49	2	.242	.291	4	0	2B-73, 3B-23, SS-4
1969	108	254	60	11	1	4	1.6	25	22	20	53	2	.236	.335	5	2	2B-102, 3B-7
1970	29	33	6	2	0	1	3.0	3	2	3	9	0	.182	.333	8	1	2B-16, 3B-4, 1B-1
6 yrs.	325	785	182	33	4	14	1.8	67	65	73	172	6	.232	.338	24	4	2B-271, 3B-34, SS-6, 1B-1

Chick Fullis

FULLIS, CHARLES PHILIP
B. Feb. 27, 1904, Girardville, Pa.   D. Mar. 28, 1946, Ashland, Pa.

BR TR 5'9"   170 lbs.

	G	AB	H	2B	3B	HR	HR %	R	RBI	BB	SO	SB	BA	SA	Pinch Hit AB	H	G by POS
1928 NY N	11	1	0	0	0	0	0.0	5	0	1	1	0	.000	.000	1	0	
1929	86	274	79	11	1	7	2.6	67	29	30	26	7	.288	.412	2	0	OF-78
1930	13	6	0	0	0	0	0.0	2	0	0	1	1	.000	.000	5	0	OF-2
1931	89	302	99	15	2	3	1.0	61	28	23	13	13	.328	.421	6	3	OF-68, 2B-9
1932	96	235	70	14	3	1	0.4	35	21	11	12	1	.298	.396	32	7	OF-55, 2B-1
1933 PHI N	151	647	200	31	6	1	0.2	91	45	36	34	18	.309	.380	0	0	OF-151, 3B-1
1934 2 teams		PHI	N (28G –	.225)		STL	N (69G –	.261)									
" total	97	301	75	15	1	0	0.0	29	38	24	15	6	.249	.306	15	6	OF-83
1936 STL N	47	89	25	6	1	0	0.0	15	6	7	11	0	.281	.371	12	2	OF-26
8 yrs.	590	1855	548	92	14	12	0.6	305	167	132	113	46	.295	.380	73	18	OF-463, 2B-10, 3B-1
WORLD SERIES																	
1934 STL N	3	5	2	0	0	0	0.0	0	0	0	0	0	.400	.400	0	0	OF-3

Chick Fulmer

FULMER, CHARLES JOHN
B. Feb. 12, 1851, Philadelphia, Pa.   D. Feb. 15, 1940, Philadelphia, Pa.
Manager 1876.

BR TR 6'   158 lbs.

	G	AB	H	2B	3B	HR	HR %	R	RBI	BB	SO	SB	BA	SA	Pinch Hit AB	H	G by POS
1876 LOU N	66	267	73	9	5	1	0.4	28	29	1		10	.273	.356	0	0	SS-66
1879 BUF N	76	306	82	11	5	0	0.0	30	28	5		34	.268	.337	0	0	2B-76
1880	11	44	7	0	0	0	0.0	3	1	2		4	.159	.159	0	0	2B-11
1882 CIN AA	79	324	91	13	4	0	0.0	54		10			.281	.346	0	0	SS-79
1883	92	361	93	13	5	5	1.4	52		13			.258	.363	0	0	SS-92
1884 2 teams		CIN	AA (31G –	.175)		STL	AA (1G –	.000)									
" total	32	119	20	2	1	0	0.0	13		1			.168	.202	0	0	SS-29, OF-2, 3B-1, 2B-1
6 yrs.	356	1421	366	48	20	6	0.4	180	58	32		48	.258	.332	0	0	SS-266, 2B-88, OF-2, 3B-1

Chris Fulmer

FULMER, CHRISTOPHER
B. July 4, 1858, Tamaqua, Pa.   D. Nov. 9, 1931, Tamaqua, Pa.

BR TR 5'8"   165 lbs.

	G	AB	H	2B	3B	HR	HR %	R	RBI	BB	SO	SB	BA	SA	Pinch Hit AB	H	G by POS
1884 WAS U	48	181	50	9	0	0	0.0	39		11			.276	.326	0	0	C-34, OF-16, 1B-5
1886 BAL AA	80	270	66	9	3	1	0.4	54		48		35	.244	.311	0	0	C-68, OF-12, P-1
1887	56	201	54	11	4	0	0.0	52		36			.269	.363	0	0	C-48, OF-8
1888	52	166	31	5	1	0	0.0	20	10	21		10	.187	.229	0	0	C-45, OF-7
1889	16	58	15	3	1	0	0.0	11	13	6	12	2	.259	.345	0	0	OF-14, C-2
5 yrs.	252	876	216	37	9	1	0.1	176	22	122	12	47	.247	.313	0	0	C-197, OF-57, 1B-5, P-1

Dave Fultz

FULTZ, DAVID LEWIS
B. May 29, 1875, Staunton, Va.   D. Oct. 29, 1959, Deland, Fla.

BR TR 5'11"   170 lbs.

	G	AB	H	2B	3B	HR	HR %	R	RBI	BB	SO	SB	BA	SA	Pinch Hit AB	H	G by POS
1898 PHI N	19	55	10	2	2	0	0.0	7	5	6		1	.182	.291	1	0	OF-14, 2B-3, SS-1
1899 2 teams		PHI	N (2G –	.400)		BAL	N (57G –	.295)									
" total	59	215	64	3	2	0	0.0	31	18	13		18	.298	.330	2	0	OF-31, 3B-20, 2B-3, SS-1, 1B-1
1901 PHI A	132	561	164	17	9	0	0.0	95	52	32		36	.292	.355	0	0	OF-106, 2B-18, SS-9
1902	129	506	153	20	5	1	0.2	109	49	62		44	.302	.368	0	0	OF-114, 2B-16
1903 NY A	79	295	66	12	1	0	0.0	39	25	25		29	.224	.271	1	0	OF-90
1904	97	339	93	17	4	2	0.6	39	32	24		17	.274	.366	6	2	OF-77, 3B-2
1905	130	422	98	13	3	0	0.0	49	42	39		44	.232	.277	5	1	OF-122
7 yrs.	645	2393	648	84	26	3	0.1	369	223	201		189	.271	.331	15	3	OF-554, 2B-40, 3B-22, SS-11, 1B-1

Mark Funderburk

FUNDERBURK, MARK CLIFFORD
B. May 16, 1957, Charlotte, N. C.

BR TR 6'4"   226 lbs.

	G	AB	H	2B	3B	HR	HR %	R	RBI	BB	SO	SB	BA	SA	Pinch Hit AB	H	G by POS
1981 MIN A	8	15	3	1	0	0	0.0	2	2	2	1	0	.200	.267	2	0	OF-6, DH-1

Liz Funk

FUNK, ELIAS CALVIN
B. Oct. 28, 1904, La Cygne, Kans.   D. Jan. 16, 1968, Norman, Okla.

BL TL 5'8½"   160 lbs.

	G	AB	H	2B	3B	HR	HR %	R	RBI	BB	SO	SB	BA	SA	Pinch Hit AB	H	G by POS
1929 NY A	1	0	0	0	0	0	–	0	0	0	0	0	–	–	0	0	
1930 DET A	140	527	145	26	11	4	0.8	74	65	29	39	12	.275	.389	10	0	OF-129
1932 CHI A	122	440	114	21	5	2	0.5	59	40	43	19	17	.259	.343	1	0	OF-120
1933	10	9	2	0	0	0	0.0	1	0	1	0	0	.222	.222	8	2	OF-2
4 yrs.	273	976	261	47	16	6	0.6	134	105	73	58	29	.267	.367	19	2	OF-251

Carl Furillo

FURILLO, CARL ANTHONY (Skoonj, The Reading Rifle)
B. Mar. 8, 1922, Stony Creek Mills, Pa.

BR TR 6'   190 lbs.

	G	AB	H	2B	3B	HR	HR %	R	RBI	BB	SO	SB	BA	SA	Pinch Hit AB	H	G by POS
1946 BKN N	117	335	95	18	6	3	0.9	29	35	31	20	6	.284	.400	4	1	OF-112
1947	124	437	129	24	7	8	1.8	61	88	34	24	7	.295	.437	2	1	OF-121
1948	108	364	108	20	4	4	1.1	55	44	43	32	6	.297	.407	4	0	OF-104
1949	142	549	177	27	10	18	3.3	95	106	37	29	4	.322	.506	0	0	OF-142
1950	153	620	189	30	6	18	2.9	99	106	41	40	8	.305	.460	0	0	OF-153
1951	158	667	197	32	4	16	2.4	93	91	43	33	8	.295	.427	1	0	OF-157

	G	AB	H	2B	3B	HR	HR %	R	RBI	BB	SO	SB	BA	SA	Pinch Hit AB	Pinch Hit H	G by POS

Carl Furillo continued

	G	AB	H	2B	3B	HR	HR %	R	RBI	BB	SO	SB	BA	SA	AB	H	G by POS
1952	134	425	105	18	1	8	1.9	52	59	31	33	1	.247	.351	2	0	OF-131
1953	132	479	165	38	6	21	4.4	82	92	34	32	1	**.344**	.580	2	0	OF-131
1954	150	547	161	23	1	19	3.5	56	96	49	35	2	.294	.444	1	0	OF-149
1955	140	523	164	24	3	26	5.0	83	95	43	43	4	.314	.520	1	0	OF-140
1956	149	523	151	30	0	21	4.0	66	83	57	41	1	.289	.467	3	0	OF-146
1957	119	395	121	17	4	12	3.0	61	66	29	33	0	.306	.461	10	1	OF-107
1958 LA N	122	411	119	19	3	18	4.4	54	83	35	28	0	.290	.482	5	3	OF-119
1959	50	93	27	4	0	0	0.0	8	13	7	11	0	.290	.333	25	7	OF-25
1960	8	10	2	0	1	0	0.0	1	1	0	2	0	.200	.400	5	1	OF-2
15 yrs.	1806	6378	1910	324	56	192	3.0	895	1058	514	436	48	.299	.458	65	14	OF-1739
WORLD SERIES																	
1947 BKN N	6	17	6	2	0	0	0.0	2	3	3	0	0	.353	.471	2	2	OF-6
1949	3	8	1	0	0	0	0.0	0	0	1	0	0	.125	.125	1	0	OF-2
1952	7	23	4	2	0	0	0.0	1	0	3	3	0	.174	.261	0	0	OF-7
1953	6	24	8	2	0	1	4.2	4	4	1	3	0	.333	.542	0	0	OF-6
1955	7	27	8	1	0	1	3.7	4	3	3	5	0	.296	.444	0	0	OF-7
1956	7	25	6	2	0	0	0.0	2	1	2	3	0	.240	.320	0	0	OF-7
1959 LA N	4	4	1	0	0	0	0.0	0	2	0	1	0	.250	.250	4	1	OF-1
7 yrs.	40	128	34	9	0	2	1.6	13	13	13	15	0	.266	.383	7	3	OF-36
				3rd											6th	1st	

Eddie Fusselbach

FUSSELBACH, EDWARD L.
B. July 17, 1856, Philadelphia, Pa.   D. Apr. 14, 1926, Philadelphia, Pa.   5'6"   156 lbs.

	G	AB	H	2B	3B	HR	HR %	R	RBI	BB	SO	SB	BA	SA	AB	H	G by POS
1882 STL AA	35	136	31	2	0	0	0.0	13		5			.228	.243	0	0	C-19, OF-15, P-4
1884 BAL U	68	303	86	16	3	1	0.3	60		3			.284	.366	0	0	C-54, 3B-6, SS-5, OF-4
1885 PHI AA	5	19	6	1	0	0	0.0	2		0			.316	.368	0	0	C-5
1888 LOU AA	1	4	1	0	0	0	0.0	0	1	0		0	.250	.250	0	0	OF-1
4 yrs.	109	462	124	19	3	1	0.2	75	0	8		0	.268	.329	0	0	C-78, OF-20, 3B-6, SS-5, P-4

Les Fusselman

FUSSELMAN, LESTER LeROY
B. Mar. 7, 1921, Pryor, Okla.   D. May 21, 1970, Cleveland, Ohio   BR TR 6'1"   195 lbs.

	G	AB	H	2B	3B	HR	HR %	R	RBI	BB	SO	SB	BA	SA	AB	H	G by POS
1952 STL N	32	63	10	3	0	1	1.6	5	3	0	9	0	.159	.254	1	0	C-32
1953	11	8	2	1	0	0	0.0	1	0	0	0	0	.250	.375	0	0	C-11
2 yrs.	43	71	12	4	0	1	1.4	6	3	0	9	0	.169	.268	1	0	C-43

Bill Gabler

GABLER, WILLIAM LOUIS (Gabe)
B. Aug. 4, 1930, St. Louis, Mo.   BL TL 6'1"   190 lbs.

	G	AB	H	2B	3B	HR	HR %	R	RBI	BB	SO	SB	BA	SA	AB	H	G by POS
1958 CHI N	3	3	0	0	0	0	0.0	0	0	0	3	0	.000	.000	3	0	

Len Gabrielson

GABRIELSON, LEONARD GARY
Son of Len Gabrielson.
B. Feb. 14, 1940, Oakland, Calif.   BL TR 6'4"   210 lbs.

	G	AB	H	2B	3B	HR	HR %	R	RBI	BB	SO	SB	BA	SA	AB	H	G by POS
1960 MIL N	4	3	0	0	0	0	0.0	0	1	0	0	0	.000	.000	3	0	OF-1
1963	46	120	26	5	0	3	2.5	14	15	8	23	1	.217	.333	12	4	OF-22, 1B-16, 3B-3
1964 2 teams		MIL	N (24G – .184)				CHI	N (89G – .246)									
" total	113	310	74	13	2	5	1.6	22	24	20	45	10	.239	.342	25	8	OF-70, 1B-20
1965 2 teams		CHI	N (28G – .250)				SF	N (88G – .301)									
" total	116	317	93	6	5	7	2.2	40	31	33	64	4	.293	.410	22	4	OF-91, 1B-6
1966 SF N	94	240	52	7	0	4	1.7	27	16	21	51	0	.217	.296	25	5	OF-67, 1B-6
1967 2 teams		CAL	A (11G – .083)				LA	N (90G – .261)									
" total	101	250	63	10	3	7	2.8	22	31	17	45	3	.252	.400	34	6	OF-69
1968 LA N	108	304	82	16	1	10	3.3	38	35	32	47	1	.270	.428	27	7	OF-86
1969	83	178	48	5	1	1	0.6	13	18	12	25	1	.270	.326	36	13	OF-47, 1B-2
1970	43	42	8	2	0	0	0.0	1	6	1	15	0	.190	.238	38	8	OF-2, 1B-1
9 yrs.	708	1764	446	64	12	37	2.1	178	176	145	315	20	.253	.366	222	55	OF-455, 1B-51, 3B-3

Len Gabrielson

GABRIELSON, LEONARD HILBORNE
Father of Len Gabrielson.
B. Sept. 8, 1915, Oakland, Calif.   BL TL 6'3"   210 lbs.

	G	AB	H	2B	3B	HR	HR %	R	RBI	BB	SO	SB	BA	SA	AB	H	G by POS
1939 PHI N	5	18	4	0	0	0	0.0	3	1	2	3	0	.222	.222	0	0	1B-5

Eddie Gaedel

GAEDEL, EDWARD CARL
B. June 8, 1925, Chicago, Ill.   D. June 18, 1961, Chicago, Ill.   BR TL 3'7"   065 lbs.

	G	AB	H	2B	3B	HR	HR %	R	RBI	BB	SO	SB	BA	SA	AB	H	G by POS
1951 STL A	1	0	0	0	0	0	–	0	0	1	0	0	–	–	0	0	

Gary Gaetti

GAETTI, GARY JOSEPH
B. Aug. 19, 1958, Centralia, Ill.   BR TR 6'   180 lbs.

	G	AB	H	2B	3B	HR	HR %	R	RBI	BB	SO	SB	BA	SA	AB	H	G by POS
1981 MIN A	9	26	5	0	0	2	7.7	4	3	0	6	0	.192	.423	0	0	3B-8, DH-1
1982	145	508	117	25	4	25	4.9	59	84	37	107	0	.230	.443	1	0	3B-142, SS-2
1983	157	584	143	30	3	21	3.6	81	78	54	121	7	.245	.414	2	1	3B-154, SS-3, DH-1
1984	162	588	154	29	4	5	0.9	55	65	44	81	11	.262	.350	0	0	3B-154, OF-8, SS-2
4 yrs.	473	1706	419	84	11	53	3.1	199	230	135	315	18	.246	.401	3	1	3B-458, OF-8, SS-7, DH-2

Fabian Gaffke

GAFFKE, FABIAN SEBASTIAN
B. Aug. 5, 1913, Milwaukee, Wis.   BR TR 5'10"   185 lbs.

	G	AB	H	2B	3B	HR	HR %	R	RBI	BB	SO	SB	BA	SA	AB	H	G by POS
1936 BOS A	15	55	7	2	0	1	1.8	5	3	4	5	0	.127	.218	0	0	OF-15
1937	54	184	53	10	4	6	3.3	32	34	15	25	1	.288	.484	4	1	OF-50
1938	15	10	1	0	0	0	0.0	2	1	3	2	0	.100	.100	8	1	OF-2, C-1
1939	1	1	0	0	0	0	0.0	0	1	0	0	0	.000	.000	1	0	
1941 CLE A	4	4	1	0	0	0	0.0	0	2	0	2	0	.250	.250	2	1	OF-2
1942	40	67	11	2	0	0	0.0	4	3	6	13	1	.164	.194	24	4	OF-16
6 yrs.	129	321	73	14	4	7	2.2	43	42	30	47	2	.227	.361	39	7	OF-85, C-1

	G	AB	H	2B	3B	HR	HR %	R	RBI	BB	SO	SB	BA	SA	Pinch Hit AB	Pinch Hit H	G by POS

Phil Gagliano

GAGLIANO, PHILIP JOSEPH
Brother of Ralph Gagliano.
B. Dec. 27, 1941, Memphis, Tenn.
BR TR 6'1" 180 lbs.

	G	AB	H	2B	3B	HR	HR %	R	RBI	BB	SO	SB	BA	SA	PH AB	PH H	G by POS
1963 STL N	10	5	2	0	0	0	0.0	1	1	1	1	0	.400	.400	2	0	2B-3, 3B-1
1964	40	58	15	4	0	1	1.7	5	9	3	10	0	.259	.379	19	3	2B-12, OF-2, 3B-1, 1B-1
1965	122	363	87	14	2	8	2.2	46	53	40	45	2	.240	.355	26	5	2B-57, OF-25, 3B-19
1966	90	213	54	8	2	2	0.9	23	15	24	29	2	.254	.338	36	4	3B-41, 1B-8, OF-5, 2B-1
1967	73	217	48	7	0	2	0.9	20	21	19	26	0	.221	.281	17	0	2B-27, 3B-25, 1B-4, SS-2
1968	53	105	24	4	2	0	0.0	13	13	7	12	0	.229	.305	17	4	2B-17, 3B-10, OF-5
1969	62	128	29	2	0	1	0.8	7	10	14	12	0	.227	.266	21	2	2B-20, 3B-9, 1B-9, OF-2
1970 2 teams		STL	N (18G –	.188)		CHI	N (26G –	.150)									
" total	44	72	12	0	0	0	0.0	5	7	6	8	0	.167	.167	16	3	2B-18, 3B-7, 1B-4
1971 BOS A	47	68	22	5	0	0	0.0	11	13	11	5	0	.324	.397	22	8	OF-11, 2B-7, 3B-4
1972	52	82	21	4	1	0	0.0	9	10	10	13	1	.256	.329	26	9	OF-12, 3B-5, 2B-4, 1B-2
1973 CIN N	63	69	20	2	0	0	0.0	8	7	13	16	0	.290	.319	41	15	2B-4, 3B-2, OF-1, 1B-1
1974	46	31	2	0	0	0	0.0	2	0	15	7	0	.065	.065	29	2	2B-2, 3B-1, 1B-1
12 yrs.	702	1411	336	50	7	14	1.0	150	159	163	184	5	.238	.313	272	55	2B-172, 3B-125, OF-63, 1B-30, SS-2
LEAGUE CHAMPIONSHIP SERIES																	
1973 CIN N	3	3	0	0	0	0	0.0	0	0	0	2	0	.000	.000	3	0	
WORLD SERIES																	
1967 STL N	1	1	0	0	0	0	0.0	0	0	0	0	0	.000	.000	1	0	
1968	3	3	0	0	0	0	0.0	0	0	0	0	0	.000	.000	3	0	
2 yrs.	4	4	0	0	0	0	0.0	0	0	0	0	0	.000	.000	4	0	

Ralph Gagliano

GAGLIANO, RALPH MICHAEL
Brother of Phil Gagliano.
B. Oct. 18, 1946, Memphis, Tenn.
BL TR 5'11" 170 lbs.

	G	AB	H	2B	3B	HR	HR %	R	RBI	BB	SO	SB	BA	SA	PH AB	PH H	G by POS
1965 CLE A	1	0	0	0	0	0	–	0	0	0	0	0	–	–	0	0	

Greg Gagne

GAGNE, GREGORY CARPENTER
B. Nov. 12, 1961, Fall River, Mass.
BR TR 5'11" 175 lbs.

	G	AB	H	2B	3B	HR	HR %	R	RBI	BB	SO	SB	BA	SA	PH AB	PH H	G by POS
1983 MIN A	10	27	3	1	0	0	0.0	2	3	0	6	0	.111	.148	0	0	SS-10
1984	2	1	0	0	0	0	0.0	0	0	0	0	0	.000	.000	1	0	
2 yrs.	12	28	3	1	0	0	0.0	2	3	0	6	0	.107	.143	1	0	SS-10

Ed Gagnier

GAGNIER, EDWARD J.
B. Apr. 16, 1883, Paris, France   D. Sept. 13, 1946, Detroit, Mich.
BR TR 5'9" 170 lbs.

	G	AB	H	2B	3B	HR	HR %	R	RBI	BB	SO	SB	BA	SA	PH AB	PH H	G by POS
1914 BKN F	94	337	63	12	2	0	0.0	22	25	13		8	.187	.234	0	0	SS-88, 3B-6
1915 2 teams		BKN	F (20G –	.260)		BUF	F (1G –	.000)									
" total	21	52	13	1	0	0	0.0	8	4	10		2	.250	.269	0	0	SS-13, 2B-7
2 yrs.	115	389	76	13	2	0	0.0	30	29	23		10	.195	.239	0	0	SS-101, 2B-7, 3B-6

Chick Gagnon

GAGNON, HAROLD DENNIS
B. Sept. 27, 1897, Millbury, Mass.   D. Apr. 30, 1970, Wilmington, Del.
BR TR 5'7½" 158 lbs.

	G	AB	H	2B	3B	HR	HR %	R	RBI	BB	SO	SB	BA	SA	PH AB	PH H	G by POS
1922 DET A	10	4	1	0	0	0	0.0	2	0	0	2	0	.250	.250	2	1	SS-1, 3B-1
1924 WAS A	4	5	1	0	0	0	0.0	1	1	0	0	0	.200	.200	2	1	SS-2
2 yrs.	14	9	2	0	0	0	0.0	3	1	0	2	0	.222	.222	4	2	SS-3, 3B-1

Joe Gaines

GAINES, ARNESTA JOE
B. Nov. 22, 1936, Bryant, Tex.
BR TR 6'1" 190 lbs.

	G	AB	H	2B	3B	HR	HR %	R	RBI	BB	SO	SB	BA	SA	PH AB	PH H	G by POS
1960 CIN N	11	15	3	0	0	0	0.0	2	1	0	1	0	.200	.200	2	1	OF-3
1961	5	3	0	0	0	0	0.0	2	0	2	1	0	.000	.000	1	0	OF-3
1962	64	52	12	3	0	1	1.9	12	7	8	16	0	.231	.346	40	12	OF-13
1963 BAL A	66	126	36	4	1	6	4.8	24	20	20	39	2	.286	.476	25	5	OF-39
1964 2 teams		BAL	A (16G –	.154)		HOU	N (89G –	.254)									
" total	105	333	82	9	7	8	2.4	39	36	30	76	8	.246	.387	17	2	OF-86
1965 HOU N	100	229	52	8	1	6	2.6	21	31	18	59	4	.227	.349	32	8	OF-65
1966	11	13	1	0	0	0	0.0	4	0	3	5	0	.077	.154	6	0	OF-3
7 yrs.	362	771	186	25	9	21	2.7	104	95	81	197	14	.241	.379	123	28	OF-212

Del Gainor

GAINOR, DELOS CLINTON (Sheriff)
B. Nov. 10, 1886, Montrose, W. Va.   D. Jan. 29, 1947, Elkins, W. Va.
BR TR 6' 180 lbs.

	G	AB	H	2B	3B	HR	HR %	R	RBI	BB	SO	SB	BA	SA	PH AB	PH H	G by POS
1909 DET A	2	5	1	0	0	0	0.0	0	0	0		0	.200	.200	0	0	1B-2
1911	70	248	75	11	4	2	0.8	32	25	20		10	.302	.403	0	0	1B-69
1912	51	179	43	5	6	0	0.0	28	20	18		14	.240	.335	0	0	1B-50
1913	104	363	97	16	8	2	0.6	47	25	30	45	10	.267	.372	2	1	1B-102
1914 2 teams		DET	A (1G –	.000)		BOS	A (38G –	.238)									
" total	39	84	20	9	2	2	2.4	11	13	8	14	2	.238	.464	8	1	1B-19, 2B-11
1915 BOS A	82	200	59	5	8	1	0.5	30	29	21	31	7	.295	.415	14	4	1B-56, OF-6
1916	56	142	36	6	0	3	2.1	14	18	10	24	5	.254	.359	4	0	1B-48, 2B-2
1917	52	172	53	10	2	2	1.2	28	19	15	21	1	.308	.424	1	0	1B-50
1919	47	118	28	6	2	0	0.0	9	13	13	15	5	.237	.322	6	1	1B-21, OF-18
1922 STL N	43	97	26	7	4	2	2.1	19	23	14	6	0	.268	.485	9	1	1B-26, OF-10
10 yrs.	546	1608	438	75	36	14	0.9	218	185	149	156	54	.272	.390	44	8	1B-443, OF-34, 2B-13
WORLD SERIES																	
1915 BOS A	3	3	1	0	0	0	0.0	1	0	1	0	0	.333	.333	1	0	1B-1
1916	1	1	1	0	0	0	0.0	0	1	0	0	0	1.000	1.000	1	1	
2 yrs.	2	4	2	0	0	0	0.0	1	1	0	0	0	.500	.500	2	1	1B-1

Augie Galan

GALAN, AUGUST JOHN
B. May 25, 1912, Berkeley, Calif.
BB TR 6' 175 lbs.
BL 1945-49

	G	AB	H	2B	3B	HR	HR %	R	RBI	BB	SO	SB	BA	SA	PH AB	PH H	G by POS
1934 CHI N	66	192	50	6	2	5	2.6	31	22	16	15	4	.260	.391	12	5	2B-43, 3B-3, SS-1
1935	154	646	203	41	11	12	1.9	133	79	87	53	22	.314	.467	0	0	OF-154
1936	145	575	152	26	4	8	1.4	74	81	67	50	16	.264	.365	2	0	OF-145
1937	147	611	154	24	10	18	2.9	104	78	79	48	23	.252	.412	0	0	OF-140, 2B-8, SS-2
1938	110	395	113	16	9	6	1.5	52	69	49	17	8	.286	.418	6	0	OF-103

	G	AB	H	2B	3B	HR	HR %	R	RBI	BB	SO	SB	BA	SA	Pinch Hit AB	Pinch Hit H	G by POS

Augie Galan continued

	G	AB	H	2B	3B	HR	HR %	R	RBI	BB	SO	SB	BA	SA	Ph AB	Ph H	G by POS
1939	148	549	167	36	8	6	1.1	104	71	75	26	8	.304	.432	3	0	OF-145
1940	68	209	48	14	2	3	1.4	33	22	37	23	9	.230	.359	9	2	OF-54, 2B-2
1941 2 teams	CHI	N	(65G –	.208)		BKN	N	(17G –	.259)								
" total	82	147	32	6	0	1	0.7	21	17	25	11	0	.218	.279	40	7	OF-37
1942 BKN N	69	209	55	16	0	0	0.0	24	22	24	12	2	.263	.340	9	3	OF-55, 1B-4, 2B-3
1943	139	495	142	26	3	9	1.8	83	67	103	39	6	.287	.406	1	0	OF-124, 1B-13
1944	151	547	174	43	9	12	2.2	96	93	101	23	4	.318	.495	4	2	OF-147, 2B-2
1945	152	576	177	36	7	9	1.6	114	92	114	27	13	.307	.441	1	1	1B-66, OF-49, 3B-40
1946	99	274	85	22	5	3	1.1	53	38	68	21	8	.310	.460	7	1	OF-60, 3B-19, 1B-12
1947 CIN N	124	392	123	18	2	6	1.5	60	61	94	19	0	.314	.416	5	2	OF-118
1948	54	77	22	3	2	2	2.6	18	16	26	4	0	.286	.455	26	3	OF-18
1949 2 teams	NY	N	(22G –	.059)		PHI	A	(12G –	.308)								
" total	34	43	9	3	0	0	0.0	4	2	14	5	0	.209	.279	18	2	OF-10, 1B-3
16 yrs.	1742	5937	1706	336	74	100	1.7	1004	830	979	393	123	.287	.419	143	28	OF-1359, 1B-98, 3B-62, 2B-58, SS-3

WORLD SERIES

	G	AB	H	2B	3B	HR	HR %	R	RBI	BB	SO	SB	BA	SA	Ph AB	Ph H	G by POS
1935 CHI N	6	25	4	1	0	0	0.0	2	2	2	2	0	.160	.200	0	0	OF-6
1938	2	2	0	0	0	0	0.0	0	0	0	1	0	.000	.000	2	0	
1941 BKN N	2	2	0	0	0	0	0.0	0	0	0	1	0	.000	.000	2	0	
3 yrs.	10	29	4	1	0	0	0.0	2	2	2	4	0	.138	.172	4	0	OF-6

Milt Galatzer

GALATZER, MILTON
B. May 4, 1907, Chicago, Ill.   D. Jan. 29, 1976, San Francisco, Calif.
BL TL 5'10"   168 lbs.

	G	AB	H	2B	3B	HR	HR %	R	RBI	BB	SO	SB	BA	SA	Ph AB	Ph H	G by POS
1933 CLE A	57	160	38	2	1	1	0.6	19	17	23	21	2	.238	.281	12	2	OF-40, 1B-5
1934	49	196	53	10	2	0	0.0	29	15	21	8	3	.270	.342	0	0	OF-49
1935	93	259	78	9	3	0	0.0	45	19	35	8	4	.301	.359	11	1	OF-81
1936	49	97	23	4	1	0	0.0	12	6	13	8	1	.237	.299	3	0	OF-42, 1B-1, P-1
1939 CIN N	3	5	0	0	0	0	0.0	0	0	0	1	0	.000	.000	0	0	1B-2
5 yrs.	251	717	192	25	7	1	0.1	105	57	92	46	10	.268	.326	26	3	OF-212, 1B-8, P-1

Alan Gallagher

GALLAGHER, ALAN MITCHELL EDWARD GEORGE PATRICK HENRY (Dirty Al)
BR TR 6'   180 lbs.
B. Oct. 19, 1945, San Francisco, Calif.

	G	AB	H	2B	3B	HR	HR %	R	RBI	BB	SO	SB	BA	SA	Ph AB	Ph H	G by POS
1970 SF N	109	282	75	15	2	4	1.4	31	28	30	37	2	.266	.376	18	7	3B-91
1971	136	429	119	18	5	5	1.2	47	57	40	57	2	.277	.378	9	3	3B-128
1972	82	233	52	3	1	2	0.9	19	18	33	39	2	.223	.270	12	3	3B-69
1973 2 teams	SF	N	(5G –	.222)		CAL	A	(110G –	.273)								
" total	115	320	87	6	1	0	0.0	17	27	35	31	1	.272	.297	9	0	3B-103, SS-1, 2B-1
4 yrs.	442	1264	333	42	9	11	0.9	114	130	138	164	7	.263	.337	48	13	3B-391, SS-1, 2B-1

LEAGUE CHAMPIONSHIP SERIES

	G	AB	H	2B	3B	HR	HR %	R	RBI	BB	SO	SB	BA	SA	Ph AB	Ph H	G by POS
1971 SF N	4	10	1	0	0	0	0.0	0	0	0	2	0	.100	.100	0	0	3B-4

Bill Gallagher

GALLAGHER, WILLIAM H.
B. 1875, Lowell, Mass.   Deceased.

	G	AB	H	2B	3B	HR	HR %	R	RBI	BB	SO	SB	BA	SA	Ph AB	Ph H	G by POS
1896 PHI N	14	49	15	2	0	0	0.0	9	6	10	0	0	.306	.347	0	0	SS-14

Bill Gallagher

GALLAGHER, WILLIAM JOHN
B. Philadelphia, Pa.   Deceased.

	G	AB	H	2B	3B	HR	HR %	R	RBI	BB	SO	SB	BA	SA	Ph AB	Ph H	G by POS
1883 2 teams	BAL	AA	(16G –	.164)		PHI	N	(2G –	.000)								
" total	18	69	10	3	1	0	0.0	10		3	4		.145	.217	0	0	OF-11, P-7, SS-4
1884 PHI U	3	11	1	0	0	0	0.0	1		0			.091	.091	0	0	P-3
2 yrs.	21	80	11	3	1	0	0.0	11		3	4		.138	.200	0	0	OF-11, P-10, SS-4

Bob Gallagher

GALLAGHER, ROBERT COLLINS
B. July 7, 1948, Newton, Mass.
BL TL 6'3"   185 lbs.

	G	AB	H	2B	3B	HR	HR %	R	RBI	BB	SO	SB	BA	SA	Ph AB	Ph H	G by POS
1972 BOS A	7	5	0	0	0	0	0.0	0	0	0	3	0	.000	.000	5	0	
1973 HOU N	71	148	39	3	1	2	1.4	16	10	3	27	0	.264	.338	29	7	OF-42, 1B-1
1974	102	87	15	2	0	0	0.0	13	3	12	23	1	.172	.195	40	6	OF-62, 1B-4
1975 NY N	33	15	2	1	0	0	0.0	5	0	1	3	0	.133	.200	10	1	OF-16
4 yrs.	213	255	56	6	1	2	0.8	34	13	16	56	1	.220	.275	84	14	OF-120, 1B-5

D. F. Gallagher

GALLAGHER, D. F.
B. Unknown.

	G	AB	H	2B	3B	HR	HR %	R	RBI	BB	SO	SB	BA	SA	Ph AB	Ph H	G by POS
1901 CLE A	2	4	0	0	0	0	0.0	0	0	0		0	.000	.000	0	0	OF-2

Gil Gallagher

GALLAGHER, LAWRENCE KIRBY
B. Sept. 5, 1896, Washington, D. C.   D. Jan. 6, 1957, Washington, D. C.
BB TR 5'8"   155 lbs.

	G	AB	H	2B	3B	HR	HR %	R	RBI	BB	SO	SB	BA	SA	Ph AB	Ph H	G by POS
1922 BOS N	7	22	1	1	0	0	0.0	1	2	1	7	0	.045	.091	1	0	SS-6

Jackie Gallagher

GALLAGHER, JOHN LAURENCE
B. Jan. 28, 1902, Providence, R. I.
BL TL 5'10"   175 lbs.

	G	AB	H	2B	3B	HR	HR %	R	RBI	BB	SO	SB	BA	SA	Ph AB	Ph H	G by POS
1923 CLE A	1	1	1	0	0	0	0.0	1	0	0	0	0	1.000	1.000	0	0	OF-1

Jim Gallagher

GALLAGHER, JAMES E.
B. Findlay, Ohio   D. Mar. 29, 1894, Scranton, Pa.

	G	AB	H	2B	3B	HR	HR %	R	RBI	BB	SO	SB	BA	SA	Ph AB	Ph H	G by POS
1886 WAS N	1	5	1	0	0	0	0.0	0	1	0	2		.200	.200	0	0	SS-1

Joe Gallagher

GALLAGHER, JOSEPH EMMETT (Muscles)
B. Mar. 7, 1914, Buffalo, N. Y.
BR TR 6'2"   210 lbs.

	G	AB	H	2B	3B	HR	HR %	R	RBI	BB	SO	SB	BA	SA	Ph AB	Ph H	G by POS
1939 2 teams	NY	A	(14G –	.244)		STL	A	(71G –	.282)								
" total	85	307	85	17	3	11	3.6	49	49	20	50	1	.277	.459	5	2	OF-79

	G	AB	H	2B	3B	HR	HR %	R	RBI	BB	SO	SB	BA	SA	Pinch Hit AB	H	G by POS

Joe Gallagher continued

	G	AB	H	2B	3B	HR	HR %	R	RBI	BB	SO	SB	BA	SA	PH AB	PH H	G by POS
1940 2 teams	STL A	(23G –	.271)		BKN	N	(57G –	.264)									
" total	80	180	48	9	2	5	2.8	24	24	6	26	3	.267	.422	42	12	OF-46
2 yrs.	165	487	133	26	5	16	3.3	73	73	26	76	4	.273	.446	47	14	OF-125

John Gallagher

GALLAGHER, JOHN C.
B. 1894, Pittsburgh, Pa.   BR TR 5'10½" 156 lbs.

	G	AB	H	2B	3B	HR	HR %	R	RBI	BB	SO	SB	BA	SA	PH AB	PH H	G by POS
1915 BAL F	40	126	25	4	0	0	0.0	11	4	5		1	.198	.230	0	0	2B-37, SS-5, 3B-1

Stan Galle

GALLE, STANLEY JOSEPH
Born Stanley Joseph Galazewski.
B. Feb. 7, 1919, Milwaukee, Wis.   BR TR 5'7" 165 lbs.

	G	AB	H	2B	3B	HR	HR %	R	RBI	BB	SO	SB	BA	SA	PH AB	PH H	G by POS
1942 WAS A	13	18	2	0	0	0	0.0	3	1	1	0	0	.111	.111	10	2	3B-3

John Galligan

GALLIGAN, JOHN M.
B. 1868, Easton, Pa.   D. July 17, 1901, New York, N. Y.   5'10" 160 lbs.

	G	AB	H	2B	3B	HR	HR %	R	RBI	BB	SO	SB	BA	SA	PH AB	PH H	G by POS
1889 LOU AA	31	120	20	0	2	0	0.0	6	7	6	17	1	.167	.200	0	0	OF-31

Bad News Galloway

GALLOWAY, JAMES CATO
B. Sept. 16, 1887, Iredell, Tex.   D. May 3, 1950, Fort Worth, Tex.   BB TR 6'3" 187 lbs.

	G	AB	H	2B	3B	HR	HR %	R	RBI	BB	SO	SB	BA	SA	PH AB	PH H	G by POS
1912 STL N	21	54	10	2	0	0	0.0	4	4	5	8	2	.185	.222	3	0	2B-16, SS-1

Chick Galloway

GALLOWAY, CLARENCE EDWARD
B. Aug. 4, 1896, Manning, S. C.   D. Nov. 7, 1969, Clinton, S. C.   BR TR 5'8" 160 lbs.

	G	AB	H	2B	3B	HR	HR %	R	RBI	BB	SO	SB	BA	SA	PH AB	PH H	G by POS
1919 PHI A	17	63	9	0	0	0	0.0	2	4	1	8	0	.143	.143	0	0	SS-17
1920	98	298	60	9	3	0	0.0	28	18	22	22	2	.201	.252	6	0	SS-84, 2B-4, 3B-3
1921	131	465	123	28	5	3	0.6	42	47	29	43	12	.265	.366	0	0	SS-110, 3B-20, 2B-1
1922	155	571	185	26	9	6	1.1	83	69	39	38	10	.324	.433	0	0	SS-155
1923	134	504	140	18	9	2	0.4	64	62	37	30	12	.278	.361	0	0	SS-134
1924	129	464	128	16	4	2	0.4	41	48	23	23	11	.276	.341	0	0	SS-129
1925	149	481	116	11	4	3	0.6	52	71	59	28	16	.241	.299	1	0	SS-148
1926	133	408	98	13	6	0	0.0	37	49	31	20	8	.240	.301	0	0	SS-133
1927	77	181	48	10	4	0	0.0	15	22	18	9	9	.265	.365	9	6	SS-61, 3B-7
1928 DET A	53	148	39	5	2	1	0.7	17	17	15	3	7	.264	.345	4	2	SS-22, 3B-21, OF-1, 1B-1
10 yrs.	1076	3583	946	136	46	17	0.5	381	407	274	224	79	.264	.342	20	8	SS-993, 3B-51, 2B-5, OF-1, 1B-1

Jim Galvin

GALVIN, JAMES JOSEPH
B. Aug. 11, 1907, Somerville, Mass.   D. Sept. 30, 1969, Marietta, Ga.   BR TR 5'11½" 198 lbs.

	G	AB	H	2B	3B	HR	HR %	R	RBI	BB	SO	SB	BA	SA	PH AB	PH H	G by POS
1930 BOS A	2	2	0	0	0	0	0.0	0	0	0	0	0	.000	.000	2	0	

Pud Galvin

GALVIN, JAMES FRANCIS (Gentle Jeems, The Little Steam Engine)
                                                              BR TR 5'8" 190 lbs.
Brother of Lou Galvin.
B. Dec. 25, 1855, St. Louis, Mo.   D. Mar. 7, 1902, Pittsburgh, Pa.
Manager 1885.
Hall of Fame 1965.

	G	AB	H	2B	3B	HR	HR %	R	RBI	BB	SO	SB	BA	SA	PH AB	PH H	G by POS
1879 BUF N	67	265	66	11	6	0	0.0	34	27	1	56		.249	.336	0	0	P-66, SS-1
1880	66	241	51	9	2	0	0.0	25	12	5	57		.212	.266	0	0	P-58, OF-19
1881	62	236	50	12	4	0	0.0	19	21	3	70		.212	.297	0	0	P-56, OF-14, SS-1
1882	54	206	44	7	4	0	0.0	21		2	49		.214	.286	0	0	P-52, OF-6
1883	80	322	71	11	2	1	0.3	41		3	79		.220	.276	0	0	P-76, OF-8
1884	72	274	49	6	1	0	0.0	34		2	80		.179	.208	0	0	P-72, OF-1
1885 2 teams	BUF	N	(33G –	.189)		PIT	AA	(11G –	.105)								
" total	44	160	27	4	2	1	0.6	16	10	1	27		.169	.238	0	0	P-44, OF-1
1886 PIT AA	50	194	49	7	2	0	0.0	24		3			.253	.309	0	0	P-50
1887 PIT N	49	193	41	7	3	2	1.0	10	22	2	47	5	.212	.311	0	0	P-49, OF-1
1888	50	175	25	1	1	1	0.6	6	3	1	51	4	.143	.177	0	0	P-50, OF-1
1889	41	150	28	7	2	0	0.0	15	16	3	46	2	.187	.260	0	0	P-41
1890 PIT P	26	97	20	2	1	0	0.0	8	12	6	20	1	.206	.247	0	0	P-26
1891 PIT N	33	109	18	0	0	0	0.0	11	7	3	29	0	.165	.165	0	0	P-33
1892 2 teams	PIT	N	(12G –	.122)		STL	N	(12G –	.051)								
" total	24	80	7	1	0	0	0.0	6	5	3	19	0	.088	.100	0	0	P-24
14 yrs.	718	2702	546	85	30	5	0.2	290	135	38	630	12	.202	.261	0	0	P-697, OF-51, SS-2

John Gamble

GAMBLE, JOHN ROBERT JR.
B. Feb. 10, 1948, Reno, Nev.   BR TR 5'10" 165 lbs.

	G	AB	H	2B	3B	HR	HR %	R	RBI	BB	SO	SB	BA	SA	PH AB	PH H	G by POS
1972 DET A	6	3	0	0	0	0	0.0	0	0	0	0	0	.000	.000	1	0	SS-1
1973	7	0	0	0	0	0	–	1	0	0	0	0	–	–	0	0	SS-1
2 yrs.	13	3	0	0	0	0	0.0	1	0	0	0	0	.000	.000	1	0	SS-1

Lee Gamble

GAMBLE, LEE JESSE
B. June 28, 1910, Renovo, Pa.   BL TR 6'1" 170 lbs.

	G	AB	H	2B	3B	HR	HR %	R	RBI	BB	SO	SB	BA	SA	PH AB	PH H	G by POS
1935 CIN N	2	4	2	1	0	0	0.0	2	2	1	0	1	.500	.750	0	0	OF-2
1938	53	75	24	3	1	0	0.0	13	5	0	6	0	.320	.387	37	11	OF-9
1939	72	221	59	7	2	0	0.0	24	14	9	14	5	.267	.317	11	1	OF-56
1940	38	42	6	1	0	0	0.0	12	0	0	1	0	.143	.167	9	2	OF-10
4 yrs.	165	342	91	12	3	0	0.0	51	21	10	21	6	.266	.319	57	14	OF-77

| WORLD SERIES | | | | | | | | | | | | | | | | | |
| 1939 CIN N | 1 | 1 | 0 | 0 | 0 | 0 | 0.0 | 0 | 0 | 0 | 1 | 0 | .000 | .000 | 1 | 0 | |

Oscar Gamble

GAMBLE, OSCAR CHARLES
B. Dec. 20, 1949, Ramer, Ala.   BL TR 5'11" 160 lbs.

	G	AB	H	2B	3B	HR	HR %	R	RBI	BB	SO	SB	BA	SA	PH AB	PH H	G by POS
1969 CHI N	24	71	16	1	1	1	1.4	6	5	10	12	0	.225	.310	0	0	OF-24
1970 PHI N	88	275	72	12	4	1	0.4	31	19	27	37	5	.262	.345	14	4	OF-74

	G	AB	H	2B	3B	HR	HR %	R	RBI	BB	SO	SB	BA	SA	Pinch Hit AB	Pinch Hit H	G by POS

Oscar Gamble continued

	G	AB	H	2B	3B	HR	HR %	R	RBI	BB	SO	SB	BA	SA	AB	H	G by POS
1971	92	280	62	11	1	6	2.1	24	23	21	35	5	.221	.332	13	4	OF-80
1972	74	135	32	5	2	1	0.7	17	13	19	16	0	.237	.326	30	9	OF-35, 1B-1
1973 CLE A	113	390	104	11	3	20	5.1	56	44	34	37	3	.267	.464	8	2	DH-70, OF-37
1974	135	454	132	16	4	19	4.2	74	59	48	51	5	.291	.469	7	0	DH-115, OF-13
1975	121	348	91	16	3	15	4.3	60	45	53	39	11	.261	.454	11	2	OF-82, DH-29
1976 NY A	110	340	79	13	1	17	5.0	43	57	38	38	5	.232	.426	16	6	OF-104, DH-1
1977 CHI A	137	408	121	22	2	31	7.6	75	83	54	54	1	.297	.588	18	8	DH-79, OF-49
1978 SD N	126	375	103	15	3	7	1.9	46	47	51	45	1	.275	.387	13	6	OF-107
1979 2 teams	TEX	A	(64G –	.335)		NY	A	(36G –	.389)								
" total	100	274	98	10	1	19	6.9	48	64	50	28	2	.358	.609	18	5	OF-48, DH-43
1980 NY A	78	194	54	10	2	14	7.2	40	50	28	21	2	.278	.567	17	4	OF-49, DH-20
1981	80	189	45	8	0	10	5.3	24	27	35	23	0	.238	.439	15	5	OF-43, DH-33
1982	108	316	86	21	2	18	5.7	49	57	58	47	6	.272	.522	18	2	DH-74, OF-29
1983	74	180	47	10	2	7	3.9	26	26	25	23	0	.261	.456	20	6	OF-32, DH-21
1984	54	125	23	2	0	10	8.0	17	27	25	18	1	.184	.440	13	1	DH-26, OF-12
16 yrs.	1514	4354	1165	183	31	196	4.5	636	646	576	524	47	.268	.459	231	64	OF-818, DH-511, 1B-1

DIVISIONAL PLAYOFF SERIES

	G	AB	H	2B	3B	HR	HR %	R	RBI	BB	SO	SB	BA	SA	AB	H	G by POS
1981 NY A	4	9	5	1	0	2	22.2	2	3	1	2	0	.556	1.333	1	1	DH-4

LEAGUE CHAMPIONSHIP SERIES

	G	AB	H	2B	3B	HR	HR %	R	RBI	BB	SO	SB	BA	SA	AB	H	G by POS
1976 NY A	3	8	2	1	0	0	0.0	1	1	1	1	0	.250	.375	1	1	OF-3
1980	2	5	1	0	0	0	0.0	1	0	1	1	0	.200	.200	1	1	OF-1
1981	3	6	1	0	0	0	0.0	2	1	5	3	0	.167	.167	0	0	OF-1
3 yrs.	8	19	4	1	0	0	0.0	4	2	7	5	0	.211	.263	2	2	OF-5

WORLD SERIES

	G	AB	H	2B	3B	HR	HR %	R	RBI	BB	SO	SB	BA	SA	AB	H	G by POS
1976 NY A	3	8	1	0	0	0	0.0	0	1	0	0	0	.125	.125	1	1	OF-2
1981	3	6	2	0	0	0	0.0	1	1	1	0	0	.333	.333	0	0	OF-2
2 yrs.	6	14	3	0	0	0	0.0	1	2	1	0	0	.214	.214	1	1	OF-4

Daff Gammons

GAMMONS, JOHN ASHLEY BR TR 5'11" 170 lbs.
B. Mar. 17, 1876, New Bedford, Mass. D. Sept. 24, 1963, East Greenwich, R. I.

	G	AB	H	2B	3B	HR	HR %	R	RBI	BB	SO	SB	BA	SA	AB	H	G by POS
1901 BOS N	28	93	18	0	1	0	0.0	10	10	3		5	.194	.215	1	0	OF-23, 2B-2, 3B-1

Chick Gandil

GANDIL, CHARLES ARNOLD BR TR 6'1½" 190 lbs.
B. Jan. 19, 1888, St. Paul, Minn. D. Dec. 13, 1970, Calistoga, Calif.

	G	AB	H	2B	3B	HR	HR %	R	RBI	BB	SO	SB	BA	SA	AB	H	G by POS
1910 CHI A	77	275	53	7	3	2	0.7	21	21	24		12	.193	.262	0	0	1B-74, OF-2
1912 WAS A	117	443	135	20	15	2	0.5	59	81	27		21	.305	.431	0	0	1B-117
1913	148	550	175	25	8	1	0.2	61	72	36	33	22	.318	.398	3	0	1B-145
1914	145	526	136	24	10	3	0.6	48	75	44	44	30	.259	.359	0	0	1B-145
1915	136	485	141	20	15	2	0.4	53	64	29	33	20	.291	.406	2	1	1B-134
1916 CLE A	146	533	138	26	9	0	0.0	51	72	36	48	13	.259	.341	1	1	1B-145
1917 CHI A	149	553	151	9	7	0	0.0	53	57	30	36	16	.273	.315	0	0	1B-149
1918	114	439	119	18	4	0	0.0	49	55	27	19	9	.271	.330	0	0	1B-114
1919	115	441	128	24	7	1	0.2	54	60	20	20	10	.290	.383	0	0	1B-115
9 yrs.	1147	4245	1176	173	78	11	0.3	449	557	273	233	153	.277	.362	6	2	1B-1138, OF-2

WORLD SERIES

	G	AB	H	2B	3B	HR	HR %	R	RBI	BB	SO	SB	BA	SA	AB	H	G by POS
1917 CHI A	6	23	6	1	0	0	0.0	1	5	0	2	1	.261	.304	0	0	1B-6
1919	8	30	7	0	1	0	0.0	1	5	1	3	1	.233	.300	0	0	1B-8
2 yrs.	14	53	13	1	1	0	0.0	2	10	1	5	2	.245	.302	0	0	1B-14

Bob Gandy

GANDY, ROBERT BRINKLEY (String) BL TR 6'3" 180 lbs.
B. Aug. 25, 1893, Jacksonville, Fla. D. June 19, 1945, Jacksonville, Fla.

	G	AB	H	2B	3B	HR	HR %	R	RBI	BB	SO	SB	BA	SA	AB	H	G by POS
1916 PHI N	1	2	0	0	0	0	0.0	0	0	0	1	0	.000	.000	0	0	OF-1

Bob Ganley

GANLEY, ROBERT STEPHEN BL TL
B. Apr. 23, 1875, Lowell, Mass. D. Oct. 9, 1945, Lowell, Mass.

	G	AB	H	2B	3B	HR	HR %	R	RBI	BB	SO	SB	BA	SA	AB	H	G by POS
1905 PIT N	32	127	40	1	2	0	0.0	12	7	8		3	.315	.354	0	0	OF-32
1906	137	511	132	7	6	0	0.0	63	31	41		19	.258	.295	3	1	OF-134
1907 WAS A	154	605	167	10	5	1	0.2	73	35	54		40	.276	.314	0	0	OF-154
1908	150	549	131	19	9	1	0.2	61	36	45		30	.239	.311	0	0	OF-150
1909 2 teams	WAS	A	(19G –	.254)		PHI	A	(80G –	.197)								
" total	99	337	70	7	2	0	0.0	37	14	29		20	.208	.240	4	0	OF-94
5 yrs.	572	2129	540	44	24	2	0.1	246	123	177		112	.254	.300	7	1	OF-564

Bill Gannon

GANNON, WILLIAM G.
B. New Haven, Conn. D. Apr. 26, 1927, Ft. Worth, Tex.

	G	AB	H	2B	3B	HR	HR %	R	RBI	BB	SO	SB	BA	SA	AB	H	G by POS
1898 STL N	1	3	0	0	0	0	0.0	0	0	0		0	.000	.000	0	0	P-1
1901 CHI N	15	61	9	0	0	0	0.0	2	0	1		5	.148	.148	0	0	OF-15
2 yrs.	16	64	9	0	0	0	0.0	2	0	1		5	.141	.141	0	0	OF-15, P-1

Joe Gantenbein

GANTENBEIN, JOSEPH STEVEN (Sep) BL TR 5'9" 168 lbs.
B. Aug. 25, 1916, San Francisco, Calif.

	G	AB	H	2B	3B	HR	HR %	R	RBI	BB	SO	SB	BA	SA	AB	H	G by POS
1939 PHI A	111	348	101	14	4	4	1.1	47	36	32	22	1	.290	.388	16	6	2B-76, 3B-14, SS-5
1940	75	197	47	6	2	4	2.0	21	23	11	21	1	.239	.350	18	4	3B-45, 1B-6, SS-3, OF-1
2 yrs.	186	545	148	20	6	8	1.5	68	59	43	43	2	.272	.374	34	10	2B-76, 3B-59, SS-8, 1B-6, OF-1

Jim Gantner

GANTNER, JAMES ELMER BL TR 6' 180 lbs.
B. Jan. 5, 1953, Fond de Lac, Wis.

	G	AB	H	2B	3B	HR	HR %	R	RBI	BB	SO	SB	BA	SA	AB	H	G by POS
1976 MIL A	26	69	17	1	0	0	0.0	6	7	6	11	1	.246	.261	1	0	3B-24, DH-2
1977	14	47	14	1	0	1	2.1	4	2	2	5	2	.298	.383	1	1	3B-14
1978	43	97	21	1	0	1	1.0	14	8	5	10	2	.216	.258	4	1	2B-21, 3B-15, SS-1, 1B-1
1979	70	208	59	10	3	2	1.0	29	22	16	17	3	.284	.389	0	0	3B-42, 2B-22, SS-3, P-1
1980	132	415	117	21	3	4	1.0	47	40	30	29	11	.282	.376	2	0	3B-69, 2B-66, SS-1
1981	107	352	94	14	1	2	0.6	35	33	29	29	3	.267	.330	3	0	2B-107

	G	AB	H	2B	3B	HR	HR %	R	RBI	BB	SO	SB	BA	SA	Pinch Hit AB	Pinch Hit H	G by POS

Jim Gantner continued

	G	AB	H	2B	3B	HR	HR %	R	RBI	BB	SO	SB	BA	SA	AB	H	G by POS
1982	132	447	132	17	2	4	0.9	48	43	26	36	6	.295	.369	4	1	2B-131
1983	161	603	170	23	8	11	1.8	85	74	38	46	5	.282	.401	3	0	2B-158
1984	153	613	173	27	1	3	0.5	61	56	30	51	6	.282	.344	2	1	2B-153
9 yrs.	838	2851	797	115	18	28	1.0	329	285	182	234	39	.280	.362	20	4	2B-658, 3B-164, SS-5, DH-2, 1B-1, P-1

DIVISIONAL PLAYOFF SERIES
| 1981 MIL A | 4 | 14 | 2 | 1 | 0 | 0 | 0.0 | 1 | 0 | 0 | 2 | 0 | .143 | .214 | 0 | 0 | 2B-4 |

LEAGUE CHAMPIONSHIP SERIES
| 1982 MIL A | 5 | 16 | 3 | .000 | 0 | 0 | 0.0 | 1 | 2 | 1 | 1 | 0 | .188 | .188 | 0 | 0 | 2B-5 |

WORLD SERIES
| 1982 MIL A | 7 | 24 | 8 | 4 | 1 | 0 | 0.0 | 5 | 4 | 1 | 1 | 0 | .333 | .583 | 0 | 0 | 2B-7 |

Babe Ganzel

GANZEL, FOSTER PIRIE   BR TR 5'10½" 172 lbs.
Son of Charlie Ganzel.
B. May 22, 1901, Malden, Mass.   D. Feb. 6, 1978, Jacksonville, Fla.

	G	AB	H	2B	3B	HR	HR %	R	RBI	BB	SO	SB	BA	SA	AB	H	G by POS
1927 WAS A	13	48	21	4	2	1	2.1	7	13	7	3	0	.438	.667	0	0	OF-13
1928	10	26	2	1	0	0	0.0	2	4	1	4	0	.077	.115	3	0	OF-7
2 yrs.	23	74	23	5	2	1	1.4	9	17	8	7	0	.311	.473	3	0	OF-20

Charlie Ganzel

GANZEL, CHARLES WILLIAM   BR TR 6'1" 188 lbs.
Father of Babe Ganzel.   Brother of John Ganzel.
B. June 18, 1862, Waterford, Wis.   D. Apr. 7, 1914, Quincy, Mass.

	G	AB	H	2B	3B	HR	HR %	R	RBI	BB	SO	SB	BA	SA	AB	H	G by POS
1884 STP U	7	23	5	0	0	0	0.0	2		0			.217	.217	0	0	C-6, OF-1
1885 PHI N	34	125	21	3	1	0	0.0	15		4	13		.168	.208	0	0	C-33, OF-1
1886 2 teams		PHI	N (1G – .000)			DET	N (57G – .272)										
" total	58	216	58	7	2	1	0.5	28	31	7	23		.269	.333	0	0	C-46, OF-7, 1B-5
1887 DET N	57	227	59	6	5	0	0.0	40	20	8	2	3	.260	.330	0	0	C-51, OF-4, 1B-2, 3B-1
1888	95	386	96	13	5	1	0.3	45	46	14	15	12	.249	.316	0	0	2B-49, C-28, 3B-9, OF-5, SS-3, 1B-1
1889 BOS N	73	275	73	3	5	1	0.4	30	43	15	11	13	.265	.324	0	0	C-39, OF-26, 1B-7, SS-6, 3B-1
1890	38	163	44	7	3	0	0.0	21	24	5	6	1	.270	.350	0	0	C-22, OF-15, SS-3, 2B-1
1891	70	263	68	18	5	1	0.4	33	29	12	13	7	.259	.376	0	0	C-59, OF-13
1892	54	198	53	9	3	0	0.0	25	25	18	12	7	.268	.343	0	0	C-51, OF-2, 1B-1
1893	73	281	75	10	2	1	0.4	50	48	22	9	6	.267	.327	1	0	C-40, OF-23, 1B-10
1894	70	266	74	7	6	3	1.1	51	56	19	6	1	.278	.383	1	0	C-59, 1B-7, OF-3, SS-2, 2B-1
1895	80	277	73	2	5	1	0.4	38	52	24	6	1	.264	.318	1	0	C-76, SS-2, 1B-2
1896	47	179	47	2	0	1	0.6	28	18	9	5	2	.263	.291	1	1	C-41, 1B-3, SS-2
1897	30	105	28	4	3	0	0.0	15	14	4		2	.267	.362	2	0	C-27, 1B-2
14 yrs.	786	2984	774	91	45	10	0.3	421	405	161	121	55	.259	.330	6	1	C-578, OF-100, 2B-51, 1B-40, SS-18, 3B-11

John Ganzel

GANZEL, JOHN HENRY   BR TR 6'½" 195 lbs.
Brother of Charlie Ganzel.
B. Apr. 7, 1874, Kalamazoo, Mich.   D. Jan. 14, 1959, Orlando, Fla.
Manager 1908, 1915.

	G	AB	H	2B	3B	HR	HR %	R	RBI	BB	SO	SB	BA	SA	AB	H	G by POS
1898 PIT N	15	45	6	0	0	0	0.0	5	2	4		0	.133	.133	2	0	1B-12
1900 CHI N	78	284	78	14	4	4	1.4	29	32	10		5	.275	.394	0	0	1B-78
1901 NY N	138	526	113	13	3	2	0.4	42	66	20		6	.215	.262	0	0	1B-138
1903 NY A	129	476	132	25	7	3	0.6	62	71	30		9	.277	.378	0	0	1B-129
1904	130	465	121	16	10	6	1.3	50	48	24		13	.260	.376	4	2	1B-118, 2B-9, SS-1
1907 CIN N	145	531	135	20	16	2	0.4	61	64	29		9	.254	.363	2	0	1B-143
1908	112	388	97	16	10	1	0.3	32	53	19		6	.250	.351	5	1	1B-108
7 yrs.	747	2715	682	104	50	18	0.7	281	336	136		48	.251	.346	13	3	1B-726, 2B-9, SS-1

Joe Garagiola

GARAGIOLA, JOSEPH HENRY   BL TR 6' 190 lbs.
B. Feb. 12, 1926, St. Louis, Mo.

	G	AB	H	2B	3B	HR	HR %	R	RBI	BB	SO	SB	BA	SA	AB	H	G by POS
1946 STL N	74	211	50	4	1	3	1.4	21	22	23	25	0	.237	.308	4	2	C-70
1947	77	183	47	10	2	5	2.7	20	25	40	14	0	.257	.415	4	1	C-74
1948	24	56	6	1	0	2	3.6	9	7	12	9	0	.107	.232	1	0	C-23
1949	81	241	63	14	0	3	1.2	25	26	31	19	0	.261	.357	2	1	C-80
1950	34	88	28	6	1	2	2.3	8	20	10	7	0	.318	.477	4	0	C-30
1951 2 teams		STL	N (27G – .194)			PIT	N (72G – .255)										
" total	99	284	68	11	4	11	3.9	33	44	41	27	4	.239	.423	12	0	C-84
1952 PIT N	118	344	94	15	4	8	2.3	35	54	50	24	0	.273	.410	12	4	C-105
1953 2 teams		PIT	N (27G – .233)			CHI	N (74G – .272)										
" total	101	301	79	14	4	3	1.0	30	35	31	34	1	.262	.365	13	3	C-90
1954 2 teams		CHI	N (63G – .281)			NY	N (5G – .273)										
" total	68	164	46	7	0	5	3.0	17	22	29	14	0	.280	.415	11	2	C-58
9 yrs.	676	1872	481	82	16	42	2.2	198	255	267	173	5	.257	.385	63	13	C-614

WORLD SERIES
| 1946 STL N | 5 | 19 | 6 | 2 | 0 | 0 | 0.0 | 2 | 4 | 0 | 3 | 0 | .316 | .421 | 0 | 0 | C-5 |

Bob Garbark

GARBARK, ROBERT MICHAEL   BR TR 5'11" 178 lbs.
Also known as Robert Michael Garbach.   Brother of Mike Garbark.
B. Nov. 13, 1909, Houston, Tex.

	G	AB	H	2B	3B	HR	HR %	R	RBI	BB	SO	SB	BA	SA	AB	H	G by POS
1934 CLE A	5	11	0	0	0	0	0.0	1	0	1	3	0	.000	.000	0	0	C-5
1935	6	18	6	1	0	0	0.0	4	4	5	1	0	.333	.389	0	0	C-6
1937 CHI N	1	1	0	0	0	0	0.0	0	0	0	0	0	.000	.000	1	0	
1938	23	54	14	0	0	0	0.0	2	5	1	0	0	.259	.259	1	0	C-20, 1B-1
1939	24	21	3	0	0	0	0.0	1	0	0	3	0	.143	.143	2	0	C-21
1944 PHI A	18	23	6	2	0	0	0.0	2	2	1	0	0	.261	.348	3	0	C-15
1945 BOS A	68	199	52	6	0	0	0.0	21	17	18	10	0	.261	.291	1	0	C-67
7 yrs.	145	327	81	9	0	0	0.0	31	28	26	17	0	.248	.275	8	0	C-134, 1B-1

	G	AB	H	2B	3B	HR	HR %	R	RBI	BB	SO	SB	BA	SA	Pinch Hit AB	Pinch Hit H	G by POS

Mike Garbark

GARBARK, MICHAEL NATHANIEL
Also known as Michael Nathaniel Garbach. Brother of Bob Garbark.
B. Feb. 2, 1916, Houston, Tex.   BR TR 6'   200 lbs.

	G	AB	H	2B	3B	HR	HR%	R	RBI	BB	SO	SB	BA	SA	PH AB	PH H	G by POS
1944 NY A	89	299	78	9	4	1	0.3	23	33	25	27	0	.261	.328	4	1	C-85
1945	60	176	38	5	3	1	0.6	23	26	23	12	0	.216	.295	1	0	C-59
2 yrs.	149	475	116	14	7	2	0.4	46	59	48	39	0	.244	.316	5	1	C-144

Barbaro Garbey

GARBEY, BARBARO GARBEY
B. Dec. 4, 1956, Santiago, Cuba   BR TR 5'9''   165 lbs.

	G	AB	H	2B	3B	HR	HR%	R	RBI	BB	SO	SB	BA	SA	PH AB	PH H	G by POS
1984 DET A	110	327	94	17	1	5	1.5	45	52	17	35	6	.287	.391	25	8	1B-65, 3B-20, DH-18, OF-10, 2B-3

LEAGUE CHAMPIONSHIP SERIES

	G	AB	H	2B	3B	HR	HR%	R	RBI	BB	SO	SB	BA	SA	PH AB	PH H	G by POS
1984 DET A	3	9	3	0	0	0	0.0	1	0	0	1	0	.333	.333	1	0	DH-2

WORLD SERIES

	G	AB	H	2B	3B	HR	HR%	R	RBI	BB	SO	SB	BA	SA	PH AB	PH H	G by POS
1984 DET A	4	12	0	0	0	0	0.0	0	0	0	2	0	.000	.000	1	0	DH-3

Alex Garbowski

GARBOWSKI, ALEXANDER
B. June 25, 1925, Yonkers, N. Y.   BR TR 6'1''   185 lbs.

	G	AB	H	2B	3B	HR	HR%	R	RBI	BB	SO	SB	BA	SA	PH AB	PH H	G by POS
1952 DET A	2	0	0	0	0	0	–	0	0	0	0	0	–	–	0	0	

Chico Garcia

GARCIA, VINICIO UZCANGA
B. Dec. 24, 1924, Vera Cruz, Mexico   BR TR 5'8''   170 lbs.

	G	AB	H	2B	3B	HR	HR%	R	RBI	BB	SO	SB	BA	SA	PH AB	PH H	G by POS
1954 BAL A	39	62	7	2	0	0	0.0	6	5	8	3	0	.113	.177	5	1	2B-24

Damaso Garcia

GARCIA, DAMASO DOMINGO
B. Feb. 7, 1955, Moca, Dominican Republic   BR TR 6'1''   165 lbs.

	G	AB	H	2B	3B	HR	HR%	R	RBI	BB	SO	SB	BA	SA	PH AB	PH H	G by POS
1978 NY A	18	41	8	0	0	0	0.0	5	1	2	6	1	.195	.195	0	0	2B-16, SS-3
1979	11	38	10	1	0	0	0.0	3	4	0	2	2	.263	.289	0	0	SS-10, 3B-1
1980 TOR A	140	543	151	30	7	4	0.7	50	46	12	55	13	.278	.381	2	0	2B-138, DH-1
1981	64	250	63	8	1	1	0.4	24	13	9	32	13	.252	.304	1	0	2B-62, DH-1
1982	147	597	185	32	3	5	0.8	89	42	21	44	54	.310	.399	0	0	2B-141, DH-4
1983	131	525	161	23	6	3	0.6	84	38	24	34	31	.307	.390	2	0	2B-130
1984	152	633	180	32	5	5	0.8	79	46	16	46	46	.284	.374	2	2	2B-149, DH-1
7 yrs.	663	2627	758	126	22	18	0.7	334	190	84	219	160	.289	.374	7	2	2B-636, SS-13, DH-7, 3B-1

Danny Garcia

GARCIA, DANIEL RAPHAEL
B. Apr. 29, 1954, Brooklyn, N. Y.   BL TL 6'1''   182 lbs.

	G	AB	H	2B	3B	HR	HR%	R	RBI	BB	SO	SB	BA	SA	PH AB	PH H	G by POS
1981 KC A	12	14	2	0	0	0	0.0	4	0	0	2	0	.143	.143	1	0	OF-6, 1B-2

Kiko Garcia

GARCIA, ALFONSO RAFAEL
B. Oct. 14, 1953, Martinez, Calif.   BR TR 5'11''   180 lbs.

	G	AB	H	2B	3B	HR	HR%	R	RBI	BB	SO	SB	BA	SA	PH AB	PH H	G by POS
1976 BAL A	11	32	7	1	1	1	3.1	2	4	0	4	2	.219	.406	0	0	SS-11
1977	65	131	29	6	0	2	1.5	20	10	6	31	2	.221	.313	0	0	SS-61
1978	79	186	49	6	4	0	0.0	17	13	7	43	7	.263	.339	3	1	SS-74, 2B-3
1979	126	417	103	15	9	5	1.2	54	24	32	87	11	.247	.362	4	0	SS-113, 2B-25, OF-2, 3B-2
1980	111	311	62	8	0	1	0.3	27	27	24	57	8	.199	.235	0	0	SS-96, 2B-27, OF-1
1981 HOU N	48	136	37	6	1	0	0.0	9	15	10	16	2	.272	.331	2	1	SS-28, 3B-13, 2B-9
1982	34	76	16	5	0	1	1.3	5	5	3	15	1	.211	.316	9	1	SS-21, 3B-2, 2B-1
1983 PHI N	84	118	34	7	1	2	1.7	22	9	9	20	1	.288	.415	2	0	2B-52, SS-22, 3B-10
1984	57	60	14	2	0	0	0.0	6	5	4	11	0	.233	.267	3	0	SS-30, 3B-23, 2B-1
9 yrs.	615	1467	351	56	16	12	0.8	162	112	95	284	34	.239	.324	23	3	SS-456, 2B-118, 3B-50, OF-3

DIVISIONAL PLAYOFF SERIES

	G	AB	H	2B	3B	HR	HR%	R	RBI	BB	SO	SB	BA	SA	PH AB	PH H	G by POS
1981 HOU N	2	4	0	0	0	0	0.0	0	0	0	1	0	.000	.000	1	0	SS-1

LEAGUE CHAMPIONSHIP SERIES

	G	AB	H	2B	3B	HR	HR%	R	RBI	BB	SO	SB	BA	SA	PH AB	PH H	G by POS
1979 BAL A	3	11	3	0	0	0	0.0	1	2	2	4	0	.273	.273	0	0	SS-3

WORLD SERIES

	G	AB	H	2B	3B	HR	HR%	R	RBI	BB	SO	SB	BA	SA	PH AB	PH H	G by POS
1979 BAL A	6	20	8	2	1	0	0.0	4	6	1	3	0	.400	.600	0	0	SS-6

Pedro Garcia

GARCIA, PEDRO DELFI
B. Apr. 17, 1950, Guayama, Puerto Rico   BR TR 5'10''   175 lbs.

	G	AB	H	2B	3B	HR	HR%	R	RBI	BB	SO	SB	BA	SA	PH AB	PH H	G by POS
1973 MIL A	160	580	142	32	5	15	2.6	67	54	40	119	11	.245	.395	0	0	2B-160
1974	141	452	90	15	4	12	2.7	46	54	26	67	8	.199	.330	0	0	2B-140
1975	98	302	68	15	2	6	2.0	40	38	18	59	12	.225	.348	1	0	2B-94, DH-1
1976 2 teams	MIL	A (41G –	.217)		DET	A	(77G –	.198)									
" total	118	333	68	17	3	4	1.2	33	29	13	63	4	.204	.309	3	0	2B-116
1977 TOR A	41	130	27	10	1	0	0.0	10	9	5	21	0	.208	.300	2	0	2B-34, DH-4
5 yrs.	558	1797	395	89	15	37	2.1	196	184	102	329	35	.220	.348	6	0	2B-544, DH-5

Al Gardella

GARDELLA, ALFRED STEPHAN
Brother of Danny Gardella.
B. Jan. 11, 1918, New York, N. Y.   BL TL 5'10''   172 lbs.

	G	AB	H	2B	3B	HR	HR%	R	RBI	BB	SO	SB	BA	SA	PH AB	PH H	G by POS
1945 NY N	16	26	2	0	0	0	0.0	4	1	4	3	0	.077	.077	6	0	1B-8, OF-1

Danny Gardella

GARDELLA, DANIEL LEWIS
Brother of Al Gardella.
B. Feb. 26, 1920, New York, N. Y.   BL TL 5'7½''   160 lbs.

	G	AB	H	2B	3B	HR	HR%	R	RBI	BB	SO	SB	BA	SA	PH AB	PH H	G by POS
1944 NY N	47	112	28	2	2	6	5.4	20	14	11	13	0	.250	.464	16	4	OF-25
1945	121	430	117	10	1	18	4.2	54	71	46	55	2	.272	.426	11	4	OF-94, 1B-15
1950 STL N	1	1	0	0	0	0	0.0	0	0	0	0	0	.000	.000	1	0	
3 yrs.	169	543	145	12	3	24	4.4	74	85	57	68	2	.267	.433	28	8	OF-119, 1B-15

	G	AB	H	2B	3B	HR	HR %	R	RBI	BB	SO	SB	BA	SA	Pinch Hit AB	Pinch Hit H	G by POS

Ron Gardenhire
GARDNER, RONALD CLYDE
B. Oct. 24, 1957, Butzbach, Germany   BR TR 6' 175 lbs.

	G	AB	H	2B	3B	HR	HR%	R	RBI	BB	SO	SB	BA	SA	PH AB	PH H	G by POS
1981 NY N	27	48	13	1	0	0	0.0	2	3	5	9	2	.271	.292	0	0	SS-18, 2B-6, 3B-1
1982	141	384	92	17	1	3	0.8	29	33	23	55	5	.240	.313	2	1	SS-135, 3B-1, 2B-1
1983	17	32	2	0	0	0	0.0	1	1	1	4	0	.063	.063	1	0	SS-15
1984	74	207	51	7	1	1	0.5	20	10	9	43	6	.246	.304	5	2	SS-49, 2B-18, 3B-7
4 yrs.	259	671	158	25	2	4	0.6	52	47	38	111	13	.235	.297	8	3	SS-217, 2B-25, 3B-9

Alex Gardner
GARDNER, ALEXANDER
B. Apr. 28, 1861, Toronto, Ont., Canada   D. June 18, 1926, Danvers, Mass.

	G	AB	H	2B	3B	HR	HR%	R	RBI	BB	SO	SB	BA	SA	PH AB	PH H	G by POS
1884 WAS AA	1	3	0	0	0	0	0.0		0		0		.000	.000	0	0	C-1

Art Gardner
GARDNER, ARTHUR JUNIOR
B. Sept. 21, 1952, Madden, Miss.   BL TL 5'11" 175 lbs.

	G	AB	H	2B	3B	HR	HR%	R	RBI	BB	SO	SB	BA	SA	PH AB	PH H	G by POS
1975 HOU N	13	31	6	0	0	0	0.0	3	2	1	8	1	.194	.194	9	0	OF-8
1977	66	65	10	0	0	0	0.0	7	3	3	15	0	.154	.154	26	5	OF-26
1978 SF N	7	3	0	0	0	0	0.0	2	0	0	2	0	.000	.000	3	0	
3 yrs.	86	99	16	0	0	0	0.0	12	5	4	25	1	.162	.162	38	5	OF-34

Billy Gardner
GARDNER, WILLIAM FREDERICK (Shotgun)
B. July 19, 1927, Waterford, Conn.   BR TR 6' 170 lbs.
Manager 1981-84.

	G	AB	H	2B	3B	HR	HR%	R	RBI	BB	SO	SB	BA	SA	PH AB	PH H	G by POS
1954 NY N	62	108	23	5	0	1	0.9	10	7	6	19	0	.213	.287	3	1	3B-30, 2B-13, SS-5
1955	59	187	38	10	1	3	1.6	26	17	13	19	0	.203	.316	8	0	SS-38, 3B-10, 2B-4
1956 BAL A	144	515	119	16	2	11	2.1	53	50	29	53	5	.231	.334	1	0	2B-132, SS-25, 3B-6
1957	154	644	169	36	3	6	0.9	79	55	53	67	10	.262	.356	0	0	2B-148, SS-9
1958	151	560	126	28	2	3	0.5	32	33	34	53	2	.225	.298	0	0	2B-151, SS-13
1959	140	401	87	13	2	6	1.5	34	27	38	61	2	.217	.304	0	0	2B-139, SS-1, 3B-1
1960 WAS A	145	592	152	26	5	9	1.5	71	56	43	76	0	.257	.363	0	0	2B-145, SS-13
1961 2 teams			MIN A (45G – .234)			NY A (41G – .212)											
" total	86	253	57	14	0	2	0.8	24	13	16	32	0	.225	.304	3	1	2B-47, 3B-35
1962 2 teams			NY A (4G – .000)			BOS A (53G – .271)											
" total	57	200	54	9	2	0	0.0	23	12	10	40	0	.270	.335	3	1	2B-39, 3B-8, SS-4
1963 BOS N	36	84	16	2	1	0	0.0	4	1	4	19	0	.190	.238	12	2	2B-21, 3B-2
10 yrs.	1034	3544	841	159	18	41	1.2	356	271	246	439	19	.237	.327	30	5	2B-839, SS-108, 3B-92

WORLD SERIES

	G	AB	H	2B	3B	HR	HR%	R	RBI	BB	SO	SB	BA	SA	PH AB	PH H	G by POS
1961 NY A	1	1	0	0	0	0	0.0	0	0	0	0	0	.000	.000	1	0	

Earl Gardner
GARDNER, EARLE McCLURKIN
B. 1884, Sparta, Ill.   D. Mar. 2, 1943, Sparta, Ill.   BR TR

	G	AB	H	2B	3B	HR	HR%	R	RBI	BB	SO	SB	BA	SA	PH AB	PH H	G by POS
1908 NY A	20	75	16	2	0	0	0.0	7	4	1		0	.213	.240	0	0	2B-20
1909	22	85	28	4	0	0	0.0	12	15	3		4	.329	.376	0	0	2B-22
1910	86	271	66	4	2	1	0.4	36	24	21		9	.244	.284	14	4	2B-70
1911	102	357	94	13	2	0	0.0	36	39	20		14	.263	.311	1	0	2B-101
1912	43	160	45	3	1	0	0.0	14	26	5		11	.281	.313	0	0	2B-43
5 yrs.	273	948	249	26	5	1	0.1	105	108	50		38	.263	.304	15	4	2B-256

Gid Gardner
GARDNER, FRANKLIN W.
B. Aug. 1, 1859, Cambridge, Mass.   D. Aug. 1, 1914, Cambridge, Mass.

	G	AB	H	2B	3B	HR	HR%	R	RBI	BB	SO	SB	BA	SA	PH AB	PH H	G by POS
1879 TRO N	2	6	1	0	0	0	0.0	0		0	0		.167	.167	0	0	P-2
1880 CLE N	10	32	6	1	1	0	0.0	0		2	4		.188	.281	0	0	P-9, OF-1
1883 BAL AA	42	161	44	10	3	1	0.6	28		18			.273	.391	0	0	OF-35, 2B-4, 3B-3, P-2
1884 3 teams			BAL AA (41G – .214)			C-P U (38G – .255)			BAL U (1G – .250)								
" total	80	326	76	16	10	2	0.6	54		24			.233	.362	0	0	OF-69, 3B-8, 1B-2, SS-1, 2B-1, P-1
1885 BAL AA	44	170	37	5	4	0	0.0	22		12			.218	.294	0	0	2B-39, OF-5, 1B-1, P-1
1887 IND N	18	63	11	1	0	1	1.6	8	8	12	11	7	.175	.238	0	0	OF-11, 2B-7
1888 2 teams			WAS N (2G – .250)			PHI N (1G – .667)											
" total	3	7	3	0	0	0	0.0	0	1	1	1	0	.429	.429	0	0	2B-2, SS-1
7 yrs.	199	765	178	33	18	4	0.5	113	8	69	16	7	.233	.339	0	0	OF-121, 2B-53, P-15, 3B-11, 1B-3, SS-2

Larry Gardner
GARDNER, WILLIAM LAWRENCE
B. May 13, 1886, Enosburg Falls, Vt.   D. Mar. 11, 1976, St. George, Vt.   BL TR 5'8" 165 lbs.

	G	AB	H	2B	3B	HR	HR%	R	RBI	BB	SO	SB	BA	SA	PH AB	PH H	G by POS
1908 BOS A	2	6	3	0	0	0	0.0	0	1	0		0	.500	.500	0	0	3B-2
1909	19	37	11	1	2	0	0.0	8	5	4		1	.297	.432	5	1	3B-8, SS-5
1910	113	413	117	12	10	2	0.5	55	36	41		8	.283	.375	0	0	2B-113
1911	138	492	140	17	8	4	0.8	80	44	64		27	.285	.376	4	3	3B-72, 2B-62
1912	143	517	163	24	18	3	0.6	88	86	56		25	.315	.449	0	0	3B-143
1913	131	473	133	17	10	0	0.0	64	63	47	34	18	.281	.359	1	0	3B-130
1914	155	553	143	23	19	3	0.5	50	68	35	39	16	.259	.385	2	0	3B-153
1915	127	430	111	14	6	1	0.2	51	55	39	24	11	.258	.326	0	0	3B-127
1916	148	493	152	19	7	2	0.4	47	62	48	27	12	.308	.387	1	0	3B-147
1917	146	501	133	23	7	1	0.2	53	61	54	37	16	.265	.345	0	0	3B-146
1918 PHI A	127	463	132	22	6	1	0.2	50	52	43	29	9	.285	.365	0	0	3B-127
1919 CLE A	139	524	157	29	7	2	0.4	67	79	39	29	7	.300	.393	0	0	3B-139
1920	154	597	185	31	11	3	0.5	72	118	53	25	3	.310	.414	0	0	3B-154
1921	153	586	187	32	14	3	0.5	101	115	65	16	3	.319	.437	1	0	3B-153
1922	137	470	134	31	3	2	0.4	74	68	49	21	9	.285	.377	9	4	3B-128
1923	52	79	20	5	1	0	0.0	4	12	12	7	0	.253	.342	30	9	3B-19
1924	38	50	10	0	0	0	0.0	3	4	5	1	0	.200	.200	22	5	3B-8, 2B-6
17 yrs.	1922	6684	1931	300	129	27	0.4	867	929	654	282	165	.289	.385	75	22	3B-1655, 2B-181, SS-5

WORLD SERIES

	G	AB	H	2B	3B	HR	HR%	R	RBI	BB	SO	SB	BA	SA	PH AB	PH H	G by POS
1912 BOS A	8	28	5	2	1	1	3.6	4	4	2	5	0	.179	.429	0	0	3B-8
1915	5	17	4	0	1	0	0.0	2	0	1	0	0	.235	.353	0	0	3B-5
1916	5	17	3	0	0	2	11.8	2	6	0	2	0	.176	.529	0	0	3B-5

	G	AB	H	2B	3B	HR	HR %	R	RBI	BB	SO	SB	BA	SA	Pinch Hit AB	Pinch Hit H	G by POS

Larry Gardner continued

	G	AB	H	2B	3B	HR	HR %	R	RBI	BB	SO	SB	BA	SA	AB	H	G by POS
1920 CLE A	7	24	5	1	0	0	0.0	1	1	1	1	0	.208	.250	0	0	3B-7
4 yrs.	25	86	17	3	2	3	3.5	9	11	4	8	0	.198	.384	0	0	3B-25

Ray Gardner

GARDNER, RAYMOND VINCENT BR TR 5'8" 145 lbs.
B. Oct. 25, 1901, Frederick, Md. D. May 3, 1968, Frederick, Md.

	G	AB	H	2B	3B	HR	HR %	R	RBI	BB	SO	SB	BA	SA	AB	H	G by POS
1929 CLE A	82	256	67	3	2	1	0.4	28	24	29	16	10	.262	.301	0	0	SS-82
1930	33	13	1	0	0	0	0.0	7	1	0	1	0	.077	.077	1	0	SS-22
2 yrs.	115	269	68	3	2	1	0.4	35	25	29	17	10	.253	.290	1	0	SS-104

Art Garibaldi

GARIBALDI, ARTHUR EDWARD BR TR 5'8" 175 lbs.
B. Aug. 20, 1907, San Francisco, Calif. D. Oct. 19, 1967, Sacramento, Calif.

	G	AB	H	2B	3B	HR	HR %	R	RBI	BB	SO	SB	BA	SA	AB	H	G by POS
1936 STL N	71	232	64	12	0	1	0.4	30	20	16	30	3	.276	.341	1	0	3B-46, 2B-24

Debs Garms

GARMS, DEBS BL TR 5'8½" 165 lbs.
B. June 26, 1908, Bangs, Tex. D. Dec. 16, 1984, Glen Rose, Tex.

	G	AB	H	2B	3B	HR	HR %	R	RBI	BB	SO	SB	BA	SA	AB	H	G by POS
1932 STL A	34	134	38	7	1	1	0.7	20	8	17	7	4	.284	.373	1	0	OF-33
1933	78	189	60	10	2	4	2.1	35	24	30	21	2	.317	.455	23	5	OF-47
1934	91	232	68	14	4	0	0.0	25	31	27	19	0	.293	.388	27	7	OF-56
1935	10	15	4	0	0	0	0.0	1	0	2	2	0	.267	.267	6	1	OF-2
1937 BOS N	125	478	124	15	8	2	0.4	60	37	37	33	2	.259	.337	10	3	OF-81, 3B-36
1938	117	428	135	19	1	0	0.0	62	47	34	22	4	.315	.364	4	1	OF-63, 3B-54, 2B-1
1939	132	513	153	24	9	2	0.4	68	37	39	20	2	.298	.392	2	0	OF-96, 3B-37
1940 PIT N	103	358	127	23	7	5	1.4	76	57	23	6	3	**.355**	.500	18	5	3B-64, OF-19
1941	83	220	58	9	3	3	1.4	25	42	22	12	0	.264	.373	31	**10**	3B-29, OF-24
1943 STL N	90	249	64	10	2	0	0.0	26	22	13	8	1	.257	.313	20	6	OF-47, 3B-23, SS-1
1944	73	149	30	3	0	0	0.0	17	5	13	8	0	.201	.221	30	6	OF-23, 3B-21
1945	74	146	49	7	2	0	0.0	23	18	31	3	0	.336	.411	26	10	3B-32, OF-10
12 yrs.	1010	3111	910	141	39	17	0.5	438	328	288	161	18	.293	.379	198	54	OF-501, 3B-296, SS-1, 2B-1

WORLD SERIES

	G	AB	H	2B	3B	HR	HR %	R	RBI	BB	SO	SB	BA	SA	AB	H	G by POS
1943 STL N	2	5	0	0	0	0	0.0	0	0	0	2	0	.000	.000	1	0	OF-1
1944	2	2	0	0	0	0	0.0	0	0	0	0	0	.000	.000	2	0	
2 yrs.	4	7	0	0	0	0	0.0	0	0	0	2	0	.000	.000	3	0	OF-1

Phil Garner

GARNER, PHILIP MASON (Scrap Iron) BR TR 5'10" 175 lbs.
B. Apr. 30, 1948, Houston, Tex.

	G	AB	H	2B	3B	HR	HR %	R	RBI	BB	SO	SB	BA	SA	AB	H	G by POS
1973 OAK A	9	5	0	0	0	0	0.0	0	0	0	3	0	.000	.000	0	0	3B-9
1974	30	28	5	1	0	0	0.0	4	1	1	5	1	.179	.214	0	0	SS-8, 2B-3, DH-2
1975	160	488	120	21	5	6	1.2	46	54	30	65	4	.246	.346	0	0	2B-160, SS-1
1976	159	555	145	29	12	8	1.4	54	74	36	71	35	.261	.400	0	0	2B-159
1977 PIT N	153	585	152	35	10	17	2.9	99	77	55	65	32	.260	.441	2	0	3B-107, 2B-50, SS-12
1978	154	528	138	25	9	10	1.9	66	66	66	71	27	.261	.400	1	0	3B-81, 2B-81, SS-4
1979	150	549	161	32	8	11	2.0	76	59	55	74	17	.293	.441	0	0	2B-83, 3B-78, SS-14
1980	151	548	142	27	6	5	0.9	62	58	46	53	32	.259	.358	0	0	2B-151, SS-1
1981 2 teams	PIT N (56G – .254)			HOU N (31G – .239)													
" total	87	294	73	9	3	1	0.3	35	26	36	32	10	.248	.310	3	2	2B-81
1982 HOU N	155	588	161	33	8	13	2.2	65	83	40	92	24	.274	.423	1	0	2B-136, 3B-18
1983	154	567	135	24	2	14	2.5	76	79	63	84	18	.238	.362	0	0	2B-154
1984	128	374	104	17	4	4	1.1	60	45	43	63	3	.278	.388	24	6	3B-82, 2B-35
12 yrs.	1490	5109	1336	253	69	89	1.7	643	622	471	678	203	.261	.390	31	8	2B-939, 3B-529, SS-40, DH-2

DIVISIONAL PLAYOFF SERIES

	G	AB	H	2B	3B	HR	HR %	R	RBI	BB	SO	SB	BA	SA	AB	H	G by POS
1981 HOU N	5	18	2	0	0	0	0.0	1	0	3	3	0	.111	.111	0	0	2B-5

LEAGUE CHAMPIONSHIP SERIES

	G	AB	H	2B	3B	HR	HR %	R	RBI	BB	SO	SB	BA	SA	AB	H	G by POS
1975 OAK A	3	5	0	0	0	0	0.0	0	0	0	1	0	.000	.000	0	0	2B-3
1979 PIT N	3	12	5	0	1	1	8.3	4	1	1	0	0	.417	.833	0	0	2B-3
2 yrs.	6	17	5	0	1	1	5.9	4	1	1	1	0	.294	.588	0	0	2B-6

WORLD SERIES

	G	AB	H	2B	3B	HR	HR %	R	RBI	BB	SO	SB	BA	SA	AB	H	G by POS
1979 PIT N	7	24	12	4	0	0	0.0	4	5	3	1	0	.500	.667	0	0	2B-7

Ralph Garr

GARR, RALPH ALLEN BL TR 5'11" 185 lbs.
B. Dec. 12, 1945, Monroe, La.

	G	AB	H	2B	3B	HR	HR %	R	RBI	BB	SO	SB	BA	SA	AB	H	G by POS
1968 ATL N	11	7	2	0	0	0	0.0	3	0	1	0	1	.286	.286	7	2	
1969	22	27	6	1	0	0	0.0	6	2	2	4	1	.222	.259	5	2	OF-7
1970	37	96	27	3	0	0	0.0	18	8	5	12	5	.281	.313	10	1	OF-21
1971	154	639	219	24	6	9	1.4	101	44	30	68	30	.343	.441	1	1	OF-153
1972	134	554	180	22	0	12	2.2	87	53	25	41	25	.325	.430	3	0	OF-131
1973	148	668	200	32	6	11	1.6	94	55	22	64	35	.299	.415	0	0	OF-148
1974	143	606	**214**	24	17	11	1.8	87	54	28	52	26	**.353**	.503	1	1	OF-139
1975	151	625	174	26	11	6	1.0	74	31	44	50	14	.278	.384	3	2	OF-148
1976 CHI A	136	527	158	22	6	4	0.8	63	36	17	41	14	.300	.387	5	2	OF-125
1977	134	543	163	29	7	10	1.8	78	54	27	44	12	.300	.435	7	1	OF-126, DH-2
1978	118	443	122	18	9	3	0.7	67	29	24	41	7	.275	.377	2	0	OF-109, DH-9
1979 2 teams	CHI A (102G – .280)			CAL A (6G – .125)													
" total	108	331	89	10	2	9	2.7	34	39	17	22	2	.269	.393	23	6	OF-67, DH-23
1980 CAL A	21	42	8	1	0	0	0.0	5	3	4	6	0	.190	.214	9	1	DH-8, OF-2
13 yrs.	1317	5108	1562	212	64	75	1.5	717	408	246	445	172	.306	.416	76	19	OF-1176, DH-42

Adrian Garrett

GARRETT, HENRY ADRIAN BL TR 6'3" 185 lbs.
Brother of Wayne Garrett.
B. Jan. 3, 1943, Brooksville, Fla.

	G	AB	H	2B	3B	HR	HR %	R	RBI	BB	SO	SB	BA	SA	AB	H	G by POS
1966 ATL N	4	3	0	0	0	0	0.0	0	0	0	2	0	.000	.000	3	0	OF-1
1970 CHI N	3	3	0	0	0	0	0.0	0	0	0	3	0	.000	.000	3	0	

	G	AB	H	2B	3B	HR	HR %	R	RBI	BB	SO	SB	BA	SA	Pinch Hit AB	Pinch Hit H	G by POS

Adrian Garrett continued

	G	AB	H	2B	3B	HR	HR%	R	RBI	BB	SO	SB	BA	SA	AB	H	G by POS
1971 OAK A	14	21	3	0	0	1	4.8	1	2	5	7	0	.143	.286	7	0	OF-5
1972	14	11	0	0	0	0	0.0	0	0	1	4	0	.000	.000	11	0	OF-2
1973 CHI N	36	54	12	0	0	3	5.6	7	8	4	18	1	.222	.389	21	6	OF-7, C-6
1974	10	8	0	0	0	0	0.0	0	0	1	1	0	.000	.000	6	0	C-3, OF-1, 1B-1
1975 2 teams	CHI N (16G – .095)					CAL A (37G – .262)											
" total	53	128	30	5	0	7	5.5	18	24	15	36	3	.234	.438	9	0	DH-23, 1B-14, OF-2, C-1
1976 CAL A	29	48	6	3	0	0	0.0	4	3	5	16	0	.125	.188	12	2	C-15, DH-4, 1B-1
8 yrs.	163	276	51	8	0	11	4.0	30	37	31	87	4	.185	.333	72	8	DH-27, C-25, OF-18, 1B-16

Wayne Garrett

GARRETT, RONALD WAYNE
Brother of Adrian Garrett.
B. Dec. 3, 1947, Sarasota, Fla.   BL TR 5'11" 175 lbs.

	G	AB	H	2B	3B	HR	HR%	R	RBI	BB	SO	SB	BA	SA	AB	H	G by POS
1969 NY N	124	400	87	11	3	1	0.3	38	39	40	75	4	.218	.268	14	1	3B-72, 2B-47, SS-9
1970	114	366	93	17	4	12	3.3	74	45	81	60	5	.254	.421	5	0	3B-70, 2B-45, SS-1
1971	56	202	43	2	0	1	0.5	20	11	28	31	1	.213	.238	2	0	3B-53, 2B-9
1972	111	298	69	13	3	2	0.7	41	29	70	58	3	.232	.315	8	0	3B-82, 2B-22
1973	140	504	129	20	3	16	3.2	76	58	72	74	6	.256	.403	4	4	3B-130, SS-9, 2B-6
1974	151	522	117	14	3	13	2.5	55	53	89	96	4	.224	.337	3	2	3B-144, SS-9
1975	107	274	73	8	3	6	2.2	49	34	50	45	3	.266	.383	12	6	3B-94, SS-3
1976 2 teams	NY N (80G – .223)					MON N (59G – .243)											
" total	139	428	99	12	2	6	1.4	51	37	82	46	9	.231	.311	17	3	3B-66, 2B-64, SS-1
1977 MON N	68	159	43	6	1	2	1.3	17	22	30	18	2	.270	.358	18	1	3B-49, 2B-1
1978 2 teams	MON N (49G – .174)					STL N (33G – .333)											
" total	82	132	33	4	0	2	1.5	17	12	19	26	1	.250	.326	43	9	3B-32
10 yrs.	1092	3285	786	107	22	61	1.9	438	340	561	529	38	.239	.341	126	26	3B-792, 2B-194, SS-32

LEAGUE CHAMPIONSHIP SERIES

	G	AB	H	2B	3B	HR	HR%	R	RBI	BB	SO	SB	BA	SA	AB	H	G by POS
1969 NY N	3	13	5	2	0	1	7.7	3	3	2	2	1	.385	.769	0	0	3B-3
1973	5	23	2	1	0	0	0.0	1	1	0	5	0	.087	.130	0	0	3B-5
2 yrs.	8	36	7	3	0	1	2.8	4	4	2	7	1	.194	.361	0	0	3B-8

WORLD SERIES

	G	AB	H	2B	3B	HR	HR%	R	RBI	BB	SO	SB	BA	SA	AB	H	G by POS
1969 NY N	2	1	0	0	0	0	0.0	0	0	2	1	0	.000	.000	0	0	3B-2
1973	7	30	5	0	0	2	6.7	4	2	5	11	0	.167	.367	0	0	3B-7
2 yrs.	9	31	5	0	0	2	6.5	4	2	7	12	0	.161	.355	0	0	3B-9

Gil Garrido

GARRIDO, GIL GONZALO
B. June 26, 1941, Panama City, Panama   BR TR 5'9" 150 lbs.

	G	AB	H	2B	3B	HR	HR%	R	RBI	BB	SO	SB	BA	SA	AB	H	G by POS
1964 SF N	14	25	2	0	0	0	0.0	1	1	2	7	1	.080	.080	1	0	SS-14
1968 ATL N	18	53	11	0	0	0	0.0	5	2	2	2	0	.208	.208	1	0	SS-17
1969	82	227	50	5	1	0	0.0	18	10	16	11	0	.220	.251	0	0	SS-81
1970	101	367	97	5	4	1	0.3	38	19	15	16	0	.264	.308	1	1	SS-80, 2B-26
1971	79	125	27	3	0	0	0.0	8	12	15	12	0	.216	.240	8	3	SS-32, 3B-28, 2B-18
1972	40	75	20	1	0	0	0.0	11	7	11	6	1	.267	.280	3	1	2B-21, SS-10, 3B-3
6 yrs.	334	872	207	14	5	1	0.1	81	51	61	54	2	.237	.268	13	5	SS-234, 2B-65, 3B-31

LEAGUE CHAMPIONSHIP SERIES

	G	AB	H	2B	3B	HR	HR%	R	RBI	BB	SO	SB	BA	SA	AB	H	G by POS
1969 ATL N	3	10	2	0	0	0	0.0	0	0	1	1	0	.200	.200	0	0	SS-3

Rabbit Garriott

GARRIOTT, VIRGIL CECIL
B. Aug. 15, 1916, Harristown, Ill.   BB TR 5'8" 165 lbs.

	G	AB	H	2B	3B	HR	HR%	R	RBI	BB	SO	SB	BA	SA	AB	H	G by POS
1946 CHI N	6	5	0	0	0	0	0.0	1	0	0	2	0	.000	.000	5	0	

Ford Garrison

GARRISON, ROBERT FORD (Snapper, Rocky)
B. Aug. 29, 1915, Greenville, S. C.   BR TR 5'10½" 180 lbs.

	G	AB	H	2B	3B	HR	HR%	R	RBI	BB	SO	SB	BA	SA	AB	H	G by POS
1943 BOS A	36	129	36	5	1	1	0.8	13	11	5	14	0	.279	.357	2	0	OF-32
1944 2 teams	BOS A (13G – .245)					PHI A (121G – .269)											
" total	134	498	133	16	2	4	0.8	63	39	28	44	10	.267	.331	2	0	OF-131
1945 PHI A	6	23	7	1	0	1	4.3	3	6	4	3	1	.304	.478	1	0	OF-5
1946	9	37	4	0	0	0	0.0	1	0	0	6	0	.108	.108	1	0	OF-8
4 yrs.	185	687	180	22	3	6	0.9	80	56	37	67	11	.262	.329	6	1	OF-176

Hank Garrity

GARRITY, FRANCIS JOSEPH
B. Feb. 4, 1908, Boston, Mass.   D. Sept. 1, 1962, Boston, Mass.   BR TR 6'1" 185 lbs.

	G	AB	H	2B	3B	HR	HR%	R	RBI	BB	SO	SB	BA	SA	AB	H	G by POS
1931 CHI A	8	14	3	1	0	0	0.0	0	2	1	2	0	.214	.286	0	0	C-7

Steve Garvey

GARVEY, STEVEN PATRICK
B. Dec. 22, 1948, Tampa, Fla.   BR TR 5'10" 192 lbs.

	G	AB	H	2B	3B	HR	HR%	R	RBI	BB	SO	SB	BA	SA	AB	H	G by POS
1969 LA N	3	3	1	0	0	0	0.0	0	0	0	1	0	.333	.333	3	1	
1970	34	93	25	5	0	1	1.1	8	6	6	17	1	.269	.355	10	3	3B-27, 2B-1
1971	81	225	51	12	1	7	3.1	27	26	21	33	1	.227	.382	2	0	3B-79
1972	96	294	79	14	2	9	3.1	36	30	19	36	4	.269	.422	11	3	3B-85, 1B-3
1973	114	349	106	17	3	8	2.3	37	50	11	42	0	.304	.438	30	12	1B-76, OF-10
1974	156	642	200	32	3	21	3.3	95	111	31	66	5	.312	.469	0	0	1B-156
1975	160	659	210	38	6	18	2.7	85	95	33	66	11	.319	.476	0	0	1B-160
1976	162	631	200	37	4	13	2.1	85	80	50	69	19	.317	.450	0	0	1B-162
1977	162	646	192	25	3	33	5.1	91	115	38	90	9	.297	.498	1	0	1B-162
1978	162	639	202	36	9	21	3.3	89	113	40	70	10	.316	.499	0	0	1B-162
1979	162	648	204	32	1	28	4.3	92	110	37	59	3	.315	.497	0	0	1B-162
1980	163	658	200	27	1	26	4.0	78	106	36	67	6	.304	.467	1	0	1B-162
1981	110	431	122	23	1	10	2.3	63	64	25	49	3	.283	.411	0	0	1B-110
1982	162	625	176	35	1	16	2.6	66	86	20	86	5	.282	.418	5	0	1B-158
1983 SD N	100	388	114	22	0	14	3.6	76	59	29	39	4	.294	.459	0	0	1B-100
1984	161	617	175	27	2	8	1.3	72	86	24	64	1	.284	.373	1	1	1B-160
16 yrs.	1988	7548	2257	382	37	233	3.1	1000	1137	420	854	82	.299	.452	64	20	1B-1731, 3B-191, OF-10, 2B-1

DIVISIONAL PLAYOFF SERIES

	G	AB	H	2B	3B	HR	HR%	R	RBI	BB	SO	SB	BA	SA	AB	H	G by POS
1981 LA N	5	19	7	0	1	2	10.5	4	4	0	2	0	.368	.789	0	0	1B-5

	G	AB	H	2B	3B	HR	HR %	R	RBI	BB	SO	SB	BA	SA	Pinch Hit AB	Pinch Hit H	G by POS

Steve Garvey continued

LEAGUE CHAMPIONSHIP SERIES

	G	AB	H	2B	3B	HR	HR %	R	RBI	BB	SO	SB	BA	SA	AB	H	G by POS
1974 LA N	4	18	7	1	0	2	11.1	4	5	1	1	0	.389	.778	0	0	1B-4
1977	4	13	4	0	0	0	0.0	2	0	2	1	1	.308	.308	0	0	1B-4
1978	4	18	7	1	1	4	22.2	6	7	0	1	0	.389	1.222	0	0	1B-4
1981	5	21	6	0	1	1	4.8	2	2	0	4	0	.286	.429	0	0	1B-5
1984 SD N	5	20	8	1	0	1	5.0	1	7	1	2	0	.400	.600	0	0	1B-5
5 yrs.	22	90	32	3	1	8	8.9	15	21	4	9	1	.356	.678	0	0	1B-22

WORLD SERIES

	G	AB	H	2B	3B	HR	HR %	R	RBI	BB	SO	SB	BA	SA	AB	H	G by POS
1974 LA N	5	21	8	0	0	0	0.0	2	1	0	3	0	.381	.381	0	0	1B-5
1977	6	24	9	1	1	1	4.2	5	3	1	4	0	.375	.625	0	0	1B-6
1978	6	24	5	1	0	0	0.0	1	0	1	7	1	.208	.250	0	0	1B-6
1981	6	24	10	1	0	0	0.0	3	0	2	5	0	.417	.458	0	0	1B-6
1984 SD N	5	20	4	2	0	0	0.0	2	2	0	2	0	.200	.300	0	0	1B-5
5 yrs.	28	113	36	5	1	1	0.9	13	6	4	21	1	.319	.407	0	0	1B-28

Rod Gaspar

GASPAR, RODNEY EARL
B. Apr. 3, 1946, Long Beach, Calif.   BB TL 5'11" 165 lbs.

	G	AB	H	2B	3B	HR	HR %	R	RBI	BB	SO	SB	BA	SA	AB	H	G by POS
1969 NY N	118	215	49	6	1	1	0.5	26	14	25	19	7	.228	.279	25	4	OF-91
1970	11	14	0	0	0	0	0.0	4	0	1	4	1	.000	.000	1	0	OF-8
1971 SD N	16	17	2	0	0	0	0.0	1	2	3	3	0	.118	.118	11	1	OF-2
1974	33	14	3	0	0	0	0.0	4	1	4	3	0	.214	.214	12	3	OF-8, 1B-2
4 yrs.	178	260	54	6	1	1	0.4	35	17	33	29	8	.208	.250	49	8	OF-109, 1B-2

LEAGUE CHAMPIONSHIP SERIES

	G	AB	H	2B	3B	HR	HR %	R	RBI	BB	SO	SB	BA	SA	AB	H	G by POS
1969 NY N	3	0	0	0	0	0	–	0	0	0	0	0	–	–	0	0	OF-3

WORLD SERIES

	G	AB	H	2B	3B	HR	HR %	R	RBI	BB	SO	SB	BA	SA	AB	H	G by POS
1969 NY N	3	2	0	0	0	0	0.0	1	0	0	0	0	.000	.000	1	0	OF-1

Tommy Gastall

GASTALL, THOMAS EVERETT
B. June 13, 1932, Fall River, Mass.   D. Sept. 20, 1956, Riviera Beach, Md.   BR TR 6'2" 187 lbs.

	G	AB	H	2B	3B	HR	HR %	R	RBI	BB	SO	SB	BA	SA	AB	H	G by POS
1955 BAL A	20	27	4	1	0	0	0.0	4	0	3	5	0	.148	.185	5	1	C-15
1956	32	56	11	2	0	0	0.0	3	4	3	8	0	.196	.232	12	0	C-20
2 yrs.	52	83	15	3	0	0	0.0	7	4	6	13	0	.181	.217	17	1	C-35

Ed Gastfield

GASTFIELD, EDWARD
B. Aug. 1, 1865, Chicago, Ill.   D. Dec. 1, 1899, Chicago, Ill.

	G	AB	H	2B	3B	HR	HR %	R	RBI	BB	SO	SB	BA	SA	AB	H	G by POS
1884 DET N	23	82	6	1	0	0	0.0	6		2	34		.073	.085	0	0	C-19, OF-2, 1B-2
1885 2 teams				DET N (1G – .000)				CHI N (1G – .000)									
" total	2	6	0	0	0	0	0.0	0		0	3		.000	.000	0	0	C-2
2 yrs.	25	88	6	1	0	0	0.0	6		2	37		.068	.080	0	0	C-21, OF-2, 1B-2

Alex Gaston

GASTON, ALEXANDER NATHANIEL
Brother of Milt Gaston.
B. Mar. 12, 1893, New York, N. Y.   D. Feb. 8, 1979, Santa Monica, Calif.   BR TR 5'9" 170 lbs.

	G	AB	H	2B	3B	HR	HR %	R	RBI	BB	SO	SB	BA	SA	AB	H	G by POS
1920 NY N	4	10	1	0	0	0	0.0	2	1	1	2	0	.100	.100	1	0	C-3
1921	20	22	5	1	1	0	0.0	1	3	1	9	0	.227	.364	9	2	C-11
1922	16	26	5	0	0	0	0.0	1	1	0	3	1	.192	.192	3	1	C-14
1923	22	39	8	2	0	1	2.6	3	5	0	6	0	.205	.333	1	0	C-21
1926 BOS A	98	301	67	5	3	0	0.0	37	21	21	28	3	.223	.259	0	0	C-98
1929	55	116	26	5	2	2	1.7	14	9	6	8	1	.224	.353	4	1	C-49
6 yrs.	215	514	112	13	6	3	0.6	58	40	29	56	5	.218	.284	18	4	C-196

Clarence Gaston

GASTON, CLARENCE EDWIN (Cito)
B. Mar. 17, 1944, San Antonio, Tex.   BR TR 6'3" 190 lbs.

	G	AB	H	2B	3B	HR	HR %	R	RBI	BB	SO	SB	BA	SA	AB	H	G by POS
1967 ATL N	9	25	3	0	1	0	0.0	1	1	0	5	1	.120	.200	1	0	OF-7
1969 SD N	129	391	90	11	7	2	0.5	20	28	24	117	4	.230	.309	17	1	OF-113
1970	146	584	186	26	9	29	5.0	92	93	41	142	4	.318	.543	4	1	OF-142
1971	141	518	118	13	9	17	3.3	57	61	24	121	1	.228	.386	11	1	OF-133
1972	111	379	102	14	0	7	1.8	30	44	22	76	0	.269	.361	18	4	OF-94
1973	133	476	119	18	4	16	3.4	51	57	20	88	0	.250	.405	13	3	OF-119
1974	106	267	57	11	0	6	2.2	19	33	16	51	0	.213	.322	39	9	OF-63
1975 ATL N	64	141	34	4	0	6	4.3	17	15	17	33	1	.241	.397	25	7	OF-51, 1B-1
1976	69	134	39	4	0	4	3.0	15	25	13	21	1	.291	.410	40	12	OF-28, 1B-2
1977	56	85	23	4	0	3	3.5	6	21	5	19	1	.271	.424	37	12	OF-9, 1B-5
1978 2 teams	62	120	28	1	0	1	0.8	6	9	3	20	0	.233	.267	29	9	OF-30, 1B-4
" ATL N (61G – .229)				PIT N (1G – .500)													
11 yrs.	1026	3120	799	106	30	91	2.9	314	387	185	693	13	.256	.397	234	59	OF-773, 1B-12

Joe Gates

GATES, JOSEPH DANIEL
B. Oct. 3, 1954, Gary, Ind.   BL TR 5'7" 175 lbs.

	G	AB	H	2B	3B	HR	HR %	R	RBI	BB	SO	SB	BA	SA	AB	H	G by POS
1978 CHI A	8	24	6	0	0	0	0.0	6	1	4	6	1	.250	.250	0	0	2B-8
1979	16	16	1	0	1	0	0.0	5	1	2	3	1	.063	.188	3	0	2B-8, DH-1, 3B-1
2 yrs.	24	40	7	0	1	0	0.0	11	2	6	9	2	.175	.225	3	0	2B-16, DH-1, 3B-1

Mike Gates

GATES, MICHAEL GRANT
B. Sept. 20, 1956, Culver City, Calif.   BL TR 6' 165 lbs.

	G	AB	H	2B	3B	HR	HR %	R	RBI	BB	SO	SB	BA	SA	AB	H	G by POS
1981 MON N	1	2	1	0	1	0	0.0	1	1	0	1	0	.500	1.500	1	0	2B-1
1982	36	121	28	2	3	0	0.0	16	8	9	19	0	.231	.298	2	0	2B-36
2 yrs.	37	123	29	2	4	0	0.0	17	9	9	20	0	.236	.317	3	0	2B-37

Frank Gatins

GATINS, FRANK ANTHONY
B. Mar. 6, 1871, Johnstown, Pa.   D. Nov. 8, 1911, Johnstown, Pa.

	G	AB	H	2B	3B	HR	HR %	R	RBI	BB	SO	SB	BA	SA	AB	H	G by POS
1898 WAS N	17	58	13	2	0	0	0.0	6	5	3		2	.224	.259	0	0	SS-17
1901 BKN N	50	197	45	7	2	1	0.5	21	21	5		6	.228	.299	0	0	3B-46, SS-5
2 yrs.	67	255	58	9	2	1	0.4	27	26	8		8	.227	.290	0	0	3B-46, SS-22

	G	AB	H	2B	3B	HR	HR %	R	RBI	BB	SO	SB	BA	SA	Pinch Hit AB	Pinch Hit H	G by POS

Jim Gaudet

GAUDET, JAMES JENNINGS
B. June 3, 1955, New Orleans, La.
BR TR 6'   185 lbs.

	G	AB	H	2B	3B	HR	HR%	R	RBI	BB	SO	SB	BA	SA	PH AB	PH H	G by POS
1978 KC A	3	8	0	0	0	0	0.0	0	0	0	3	0	.000	.000	0	0	C-3
1979	3	6	1	0	0	0	0.0	0	0	0	0	0	.167	.167	0	0	C-3
2 yrs.	6	14	1	0	0	0	0.0	0	0	0	3	0	.071	.071	0	0	C-6

Mike Gaule

GAULE, MICHAEL JOHN
B. Aug. 4, 1869, Baltimore, Md.   D. Jan. 24, 1918, Baltimore, Md.
BL TL 6'2"

	G	AB	H	2B	3B	HR	HR%	R	RBI	BB	SO	SB	BA	SA	PH AB	PH H	G by POS
1889 LOU AA	1	2	0	0	0	0	0.0	0	0	0	1	0	.000	.000	0	0	OF-1

Doc Gautreau

GAUTREAU, WALTER PAUL
B. July 26, 1904, Cambridge, Mass.   D. Aug. 23, 1970, Salt Lake City, Utah
BR TR 5'4"   129 lbs.

	G	AB	H	2B	3B	HR	HR%	R	RBI	BB	SO	SB	BA	SA	PH AB	PH H	G by POS
1925 2 teams	PHI A (4G – .000)				BOS N (68G – .262)												
" total	72	286	73	13	3	0	0.0	45	23	35	16	11	.255	.322	0	0	2B-72
1926 BOS N	79	266	71	9	4	0	0.0	36	8	35	24	17	.267	.331	3	0	2B-74
1927	87	236	58	12	2	0	0.0	38	20	25	20	11	.246	.314	17	0	2B-57
1928	23	18	5	0	1	0	0.0	3	1	4	3	1	.278	.389	15	4	2B-4, SS-1
4 yrs.	261	806	207	34	10	0	0.0	122	52	99	63	40	.257	.324	35	4	2B-207, SS-1

Sid Gautreaux

GAUTREAUX, SIDNEY ALLEN (Pudge)
B. May 4, 1912, Schriever, La.   D. Apr. 19, 1980, Morgan City, La.
BR TR 5'8"   190 lbs.

	G	AB	H	2B	3B	HR	HR%	R	RBI	BB	SO	SB	BA	SA	PH AB	PH H	G by POS
1936 BKN N	75	71	19	3	0	0	0.0	8	16	9	7	0	.268	.310	55	16	C-15
1937	11	10	1	1	0	0	0.0	0	2	1	1	0	.100	.200	10	1	
2 yrs.	86	81	20	4	0	0	0.0	8	18	10	8	0	.247	.296	65	17	C-15

Mike Gazella

GAZELLA, MICHAEL
B. Oct. 13, 1896, Olyphant, Pa.   D. Sept. 11, 1978, Odessa, Tex.
BR TR 5'7½"   165 lbs.

	G	AB	H	2B	3B	HR	HR%	R	RBI	BB	SO	SB	BA	SA	PH AB	PH H	G by POS
1923 NY A	8	13	1	0	0	0	0.0	2	1	2	3	0	.077	.077	0	0	SS-4, 3B-2, 2B-2
1926	66	168	39	6	0	0	0.0	21	21	25	24	2	.232	.268	9	4	3B-45, SS-11
1927	54	115	32	8	4	0	0.0	17	9	23	16	4	.278	.417	0	0	3B-44, SS-6
1928	32	56	13	0	0	0	0.0	11	2	6	7	2	.232	.232	6	0	3B-14, 2B-4, SS-3
4 yrs.	160	352	85	14	4	0	0.0	51	33	56	50	8	.241	.304	15	4	3B-105, SS-24, 2B-6
WORLD SERIES																	
1926 NY A	1	0	0	0	0	0	–	0	0	0	0	0	–	–	0	0	3B-1

Dale Gear

GEAR, DALE DUDLEY
B. Feb. 2, 1872, Lone Elm, Kans.   D. Sept. 23, 1951, Topeka, Kans.
BR TR 5'11"   165 lbs.

	G	AB	H	2B	3B	HR	HR%	R	RBI	BB	SO	SB	BA	SA	PH AB	PH H	G by POS
1896 CLE N	4	15	6	1	1	0	0.0	5	3	1	1	0	.400	.600	0	0	P-3, 1B-1
1897	7	24	4	1	0	0	0.0	3	2	3		2	.167	.208	0	0	OF-6
1901 WAS A	58	199	47	9	2	0	0.0	17	20	4		2	.236	.302	2	0	OF-34, P-24
3 yrs.	69	238	57	11	3	0	0.0	25	25	8	1	4	.239	.311	2	0	OF-40, P-27, 1B-1

Lloyd Gearhart

GEARHART, LLOYD WILLIAM (Gary)
B. Aug. 10, 1923, New Lebanon, Ohio
BR TL 5'11"   180 lbs.

	G	AB	H	2B	3B	HR	HR%	R	RBI	BB	SO	SB	BA	SA	PH AB	PH H	G by POS
1947 NY N	73	179	44	9	0	6	3.4	26	17	17	30	1	.246	.397	20	5	OF-44

Huck Geary

GEARY, EUGENE FRANCIS
B. Jan. 22, 1917, Buffalo, N. Y.   D. Jan. 27, 1981, Cuba, N. Y.
BL TR 5'10½"   170 lbs.

	G	AB	H	2B	3B	HR	HR%	R	RBI	BB	SO	SB	BA	SA	PH AB	PH H	G by POS
1942 PIT N	9	22	5	0	0	0	0.0	3	2	2	3	0	.227	.227	1	1	SS-8
1943	46	166	25	4	0	1	0.6	17	13	18	6	3	.151	.193	0	0	SS-46
2 yrs.	55	188	30	4	0	1	0.5	20	15	20	9	3	.160	.197	1	1	SS-54

Elmer Gedeon

GEDEON, ELMER JOHN
B. Apr. 15, 1917, Cleveland, Ohio   D. Apr. 15, 1944, France
BR TR 6'4"   196 lbs.

	G	AB	H	2B	3B	HR	HR%	R	RBI	BB	SO	SB	BA	SA	PH AB	PH H	G by POS
1939 WAS A	5	15	3	0	0	0	0.0	1	1	2	5	0	.200	.200	0	0	OF-5

Joe Gedeon

GEDEON, ELMER JOSEPH
B. Dec. 5, 1893, Sacramento, Calif.   D. May 19, 1941, San Francisco, Calif.
BR TR 6'   167 lbs.

	G	AB	H	2B	3B	HR	HR%	R	RBI	BB	SO	SB	BA	SA	PH AB	PH H	G by POS
1913 WAS A	27	71	13	1	2	1	1.4	3	6	1	6	3	.183	.296	2	0	OF-14, 3B-8, 2B-2, SS-1, P-1
1914	3	2	0	0	0	0	0.0	0	1	0	1	0	.000	.000	0	0	OF-3
1916 NY A	122	435	92	14	4	0	0.0	50	27	40	61	14	.211	.262	0	0	2B-122
1917	33	117	28	7	0	0	0.0	15	8	7	13	4	.239	.299	2	0	2B-31
1918 STL A	123	441	94	14	3	1	0.2	39	41	27	29	7	.213	.265	0	0	2B-123
1919	120	437	111	13	4	0	0.0	57	27	50	35	4	.254	.302	1	0	2B-118
1920	153	606	177	33	6	0	0.0	95	61	55	36	1	.292	.366	0	0	2B-153
7 yrs.	581	2109	515	82	19	2	0.1	259	171	180	181	33	.244	.304	5	0	2B-549, OF-17, 3B-8, SS-1, P-1

Rich Gedman

GEDMAN, RICHARD LEO
B. Sept. 26, 1959, Boston, Mass.
BL TR 6'   210 lbs.

	G	AB	H	2B	3B	HR	HR%	R	RBI	BB	SO	SB	BA	SA	PH AB	PH H	G by POS
1980 BOS A	9	24	5	0	0	0	0.0	2	1	0	9	0	.208	.208	5	0	DH-4, C-2
1981	62	205	59	15	0	5	2.4	22	26	9	31	0	.288	.434	3	1	C-59
1982	92	289	72	17	2	4	1.4	30	26	10	37	0	.249	.363	9	2	C-86
1983	81	204	60	16	1	2	1.0	21	18	15	37	0	.294	.412	19	5	C-69
1984	133	449	121	26	4	24	5.3	54	72	29	72	0	.269	.506	15	5	C-125
5 yrs.	377	1171	317	74	7	35	3.0	129	143	63	182	0	.271	.436	51	13	C-341, DH-4

Billy Geer

TR 5'8"   160 lbs.

GEER, WILLIAM HENRY
B. Aug. 13, 1849, Syracuse, N. Y.   D. Jan. 5, 1922, Syracuse, N. Y.

	G	AB	H	2B	3B	HR	HR%	R	RBI	BB	SO	SB	BA	SA	PH AB	PH H	G by POS
1878 CIN N	61	237	52	13	2	0	0.0	31	20	10	18		.219	.291	0	0	SS-60, 2B-2
1880 WOR N	2	6	0	0	0	0	0.0	0		0	0		.000	.000	0	0	OF-1, SS-1
1884 2 teams	PHI U (9G – .250)				BKN AA (107G – .210)												
" total	116	427	91	17	8	0	0.0	75		42			.213	.290	0	0	SS-115, 2B-2, P-2, 1B-1
1885 LOU AA	14	51	6	2	0	0	0.0	2		2			.118	.157	0	0	SS-14
4 yrs.	193	721	149	32	10	0	0.0	108	20	54	18		.207	.279	0	0	SS-190, 2B-4, P-2, OF-1, 1B-1

	G	AB	H	2B	3B	HR	HR %	R	RBI	BB	SO	SB	BA	SA	Pinch Hit AB	Pinch Hit H	G by POS

Lou Gehrig

GEHRIG, HENRY LOUIS (The Iron Horse, Columbia Lou)   BL TL 6'   200 lbs.
B. June 19, 1903, New York, N. Y.   D. June 2, 1941, New York, N. Y.
Hall of Fame 1939.

	G	AB	H	2B	3B	HR	HR %	R	RBI	BB	SO	SB	BA	SA	AB	H	G by POS
1923 NY A	13	26	11	4	1	1	3.8	6	9	2	5	0	.423	.769	4	1	1B-9
1924	10	12	6	1	0	0	0.0	2	5	1	3	0	.500	.583	6	2	1B-2, OF-1
1925	126	437	129	23	10	20	4.6	73	68	46	49	6	.295	.531	6	1	1B-114, OF-6
1926	155	572	179	47	20	16	2.8	135	107	105	72	6	.313	.549	0	0	1B-155
1927	155	584	218	52	18	47	8.0	149	175	109	84	10	.373	.765	0	0	1B-155
1928	154	562	210	47	13	27	4.8	139	142	95	69	4	.374	.648	0	0	1B-154
1929	154	553	166	33	9	35	6.3	127	126	122	68	4	.300	.582	0	0	1B-154
1930	154	581	220	42	17	41	7.1	143	174	101	63	12	.379	.721	0	0	1B-153, OF-1
1931	155	619	211	31	15	46	7.4	163	184	117	56	17	.341	.662	0	0	1B-154, OF-1
1932	156	596	208	42	9	34	5.7	138	151	108	38	4	.349	.621	0	0	1B-155
1933	152	593	198	41	12	32	5.4	138	139	92	42	9	.334	.605	0	0	1B-152
1934	154	579	210	40	6	49	8.5	128	165	109	31	9	.363	.706	0	0	1B-153, SS-1
1935	149	535	176	26	10	30	5.6	125	119	132	38	8	.329	.583	0	0	1B-149
1936	155	579	205	37	7	49	8.5	167	152	130	46	3	.354	.696	0	0	1B-155
1937	157	569	200	37	9	37	6.5	138	159	127	49	4	.351	.643	0	0	1B-157
1938	157	576	170	32	6	29	5.0	115	114	107	75	6	.295	.523	0	0	1B-157
1939	8	28	4	0	0	0	0.0	1	1	5	1	0	.143	.143	0	0	1B-8
17 yrs.	2164	8001	2721	535	162	493	6.2	1888 7th	1990 3rd	1508 10th	789	102	.340	.632 3rd	16	4	1B-2136, OF-9, SS-1

WORLD SERIES
1926 NY A	7	23	8	2	0	0	0.0	1	3	5	4	0	.348	.435	0	0	1B-7
1927	4	13	4	2	2	0	0.0	2	5	3	3	0	.308	.769	0	0	1B-4
1928	4	11	6	1	0	4	36.4	5	9	6	0	0	.545	1.727	0	0	1B-4
1932	4	17	9	1	0	3	17.6	9	8	2	1	0	.529	1.118	0	0	1B-4
1936	6	24	7	1	0	2	8.3	5	7	3	2	0	.292	.583	0	0	1B-6
1937	5	17	5	1	1	1	5.9	4	3	5	4	0	.294	.647	0	0	1B-5
1938	4	14	4	0	0	0	0.0	4	0	2	3	0	.286	.286	0	0	1B-4
7 yrs.	34	119	43	8	3	10	8.4	30	35	26	17	0	.361	.731	0	0	1B-34
			9th	6th	4th	5th		4th	4th	3rd	5th			7th	3rd		

Charlie Gehringer

GEHRINGER, CHARLES LEONARD   BL TR 5'11"   180 lbs.
B. May 11, 1903, Fowlerville, Mich.
Hall of Fame 1949.

	G	AB	H	2B	3B	HR	HR %	R	RBI	BB	SO	SB	BA	SA	AB	H	G by POS
1924 DET A	5	13	6	0	0	0	0.0	2	1	0	2	1	.462	.462	0	0	2B-5
1925	8	18	3	0	0	0	0.0	3	0	2	0	0	.167	.167	2	0	2B-6
1926	123	459	127	19	17	1	0.2	62	48	30	42	9	.277	.399	6	0	2B-112, 3B-6
1927	133	508	161	29	11	4	0.8	110	61	52	31	17	.317	.441	9	3	2B-121
1928	154	603	193	29	16	6	1.0	108	74	69	22	15	.320	.451	0	0	2B-154
1929	155	634	215	45	19	13	2.1	131	106	64	19	28	.339	.532	1	0	2B-154
1930	154	610	201	47	15	16	2.6	144	98	69	17	19	.330	.534	0	0	2B-154
1931	101	383	119	24	5	4	1.0	67	53	29	15	13	.311	.431	12	1	2B-78, 1B-9
1932	152	618	184	44	11	19	3.1	112	107	68	34	9	.298	.497	0	0	2B-152
1933	155	628	204	42	6	12	1.9	103	105	68	27	5	.325	.468	0	0	2B-155
1934	154	601	214	50	7	11	1.8	134	127	99	25	11	.356	.517	0	0	2B-154
1935	150	610	201	32	8	19	3.1	123	108	79	16	11	.330	.502	2	1	2B-149
1936	154	641	227	60	12	15	2.3	144	116	83	13	4	.354	.555	0	0	2B-154
1937	144	564	209	40	1	14	2.5	133	96	90	25	11	.371	.520	1	0	2B-142
1938	152	568	174	32	5	20	3.5	133	107	112	21	14	.306	.486	0	0	2B-152
1939	118	406	132	29	6	16	3.9	86	86	68	16	4	.325	.544	9	4	2B-107
1940	139	515	161	33	3	10	1.9	108	81	101	17	10	.313	.447	1	0	2B-138
1941	127	436	96	19	4	3	0.7	65	46	95	26	1	.220	.303	10	3	2B-116
1942	45	45	12	0	0	1	2.2	6	7	7	4	0	.267	.333	38	11	2B-3
19 yrs.	2323	8860	2839	574 10th	146	184	2.1	1774	1427	1185	372	182	.320	.480	91	23	2B-2206, 1B-9, 3B-6

WORLD SERIES
1934 DET A	7	29	11	1	0	1	3.4	5	2	3	0	1	.379	.517	0	0	2B-7
1935	6	24	9	3	0	0	0.0	4	4	2	1	1	.375	.500	0	0	2B-6
1940	7	28	6	0	0	0	0.0	3	1	2	0	0	.214	.214	0	0	2B-7
3 yrs.	20	81	26	4	0	1	1.2	12	7	7	1	2	.321	.407	0	0	2B-20

Phil Geier

GEIER, LOUIS PHILLIP (Little Phil)   BR TR 5'7"   145 lbs.
B. Nov. 3, 1875, Washington, D. C.   D. Sept. 20, 1967, Spokane, Wash.

	G	AB	H	2B	3B	HR	HR %	R	RBI	BB	SO	SB	BA	SA	AB	H	G by POS
1896 PHI N	17	56	13	0	1	0	0.0	12	6	6	7	3	.232	.268	0	0	OF-12, 2B-3, C-2
1897	92	316	88	6	2	1	0.3	51	35	56		19	.278	.320	2	0	OF-45, 2B-37, SS-6, 3B-2
1900 CIN N	30	113	29	1	4	0	0.0	18	10	7		3	.257	.336	1	0	OF-27, 3B-2
1901 2 teams		PHI	A (50G – .232)			MIL	A (11G – .179)										
" total	61	250	56	6	3	0	0.0	46	24	29		11	.224	.272	0	0	OF-58, 3B-4, SS-2
1904 BOS N	149	580	141	17	2	1	0.2	70	27	56		18	.243	.284	1	0	OF-137, 3B-7, 2B-5, SS-1
5 yrs.	349	1315	327	30	12	2	0.2	197	102	154	7	54	.249	.294	4	0	OF-279, 2B-45, 3B-15, SS-9, C-2

Gary Geiger

GEIGER, GARY MERLE   BL TR 6'   168 lbs.
B. Apr. 4, 1937, Sand Ridge, Ill.

	G	AB	H	2B	3B	HR	HR %	R	RBI	BB	SO	SB	BA	SA	AB	H	G by POS
1958 CLE A	91	195	45	3	1	1	0.5	28	6	27	43	2	.231	.272	32	6	OF-53, 3B-2, P-1
1959 BOS A	120	335	82	10	4	11	3.3	45	48	21	55	9	.245	.397	24	9	OF-95
1960	77	245	74	13	3	9	3.7	32	33	23	38	2	.302	.490	12	5	OF-66
1961	140	499	116	21	6	18	3.6	82	64	87	91	16	.232	.407	5	2	OF-137
1962	131	466	116	18	4	16	3.4	67	54	67	66	18	.249	.408	8	2	OF-129
1963	121	399	105	13	5	16	4.0	67	44	36	63	9	.263	.441	23	3	OF-95, 1B-6
1964	5	13	5	0	1	0	0.0	3	1	2	2	0	.385	.538	1	1	OF-4
1965	24	45	9	3	0	1	2.2	5	2	13	10	3	.200	.333	7	0	OF-16
1966 ATL N	78	126	33	5	3	4	3.2	23	10	21	29	0	.262	.444	27	4	OF-49
1967	69	117	19	1	1	1	0.9	17	5	20	35	1	.162	.214	24	1	OF-38
1969 HOU N	93	125	28	4	1	0	0.0	19	16	24	34	2	.224	.272	26	7	OF-65

	G	AB	H	2B	3B	HR	HR %	R	RBI	BB	SO	SB	BA	SA	Pinch Hit AB	Pinch Hit H	G by POS

Gary Geiger continued

	G	AB	H	2B	3B	HR	HR%	R	RBI	BB	SO	SB	BA	SA	AB	H	G by POS
1970	5	4	1	0	0	0	0.0	0	0	0	0	0	.250	.250	2	0	OF-2
12 yrs.	954	2569	633	91	29	77	3.0	388	283	341	466	62	.246	.394	191	40	OF-749, 1B-6, 3B-2, P-1

Bill Geis

GEIS, WILLIAM J
Brother of Emil Geis.
B. Mar. 20, 1867, Chicago, Ill.   D. Oct. 4, 1911, Chicago, Ill.
5'10"   164 lbs.

	G	AB	H	2B	3B	HR	HR%	R	RBI	BB	SO	SB	BA	SA	AB	H	G by POS
1884 DET N	75	283	50	11	4	2	0.7	23		6	60		.177	.265	0	0	2B-73, OF-1, 1B-1, P-1

Emil Geis

GEIS, EMIL AUGUST
Brother of Bill Geis.
B. Chicago, Ill.   Deceased.
BR

	G	AB	H	2B	3B	HR	HR%	R	RBI	BB	SO	SB	BA	SA	AB	H	G by POS
1887 CHI N	3	12	1	0	0	0	0.0	0	0	0	7	0	.083	.083	0	0	2B-1, 1B-1, P-1

Charley Gelbert

GELBERT, CHARLES MAGNUS
B. Jan. 26, 1906, Scranton, Pa.   D. Jan. 13, 1967, Easton, Pa.
BR TR 5'11"   170 lbs.

	G	AB	H	2B	3B	HR	HR%	R	RBI	BB	SO	SB	BA	SA	AB	H	G by POS
1929 STL N	146	512	134	29	8	3	0.6	60	65	51	46	8	.262	.367	0	0	SS-146
1930	139	513	156	39	11	3	0.6	92	72	43	41	6	.304	.441	0	0	SS-139
1931	131	447	129	29	5	1	0.2	61	62	54	31	7	.289	.383	0	0	SS-131
1932	122	455	122	28	9	1	0.2	60	45	39	30	8	.268	.376	0	0	SS-122
1935	62	168	49	7	2	2	1.2	24	21	17	18	0	.292	.393	5	1	3B-37, SS-21, 2B-3
1936	93	280	64	15	2	3	1.1	33	27	25	26	2	.229	.329	2	0	3B-60, SS-28, 2B-8
1937 2 teams	CIN	N (43G – .193)			DET	A (20G – .085)											
" total	63	161	26	6	0	1	0.6	16	14	19	23	1	.161	.217	6	0	SS-53, 2B-9, 3B-1
1939 WAS A	68	188	48	7	5	3	1.6	36	29	30	11	2	.255	.394	16	2	SS-28, 3B-20, 2B-1
1940 2 teams	WAS	A (22G – .370)			BOS	A (30G – .198)											
" total	52	145	38	9	1	0	0.0	16	15	12	19	0	.262	.338	4	0	3B-29, SS-13, P-2, 2B-1
9 yrs.	876	2869	766	169	43	17	0.6	398	350	290	245	34	.267	.374	33	3	SS-681, 3B-147, 2B-22, P-2

WORLD SERIES

	G	AB	H	2B	3B	HR	HR%	R	RBI	BB	SO	SB	BA	SA	AB	H	G by POS
1930 STL N	6	17	6	0	1	0	0.0	2	2	3	3	0	.353	.471	0	0	SS-6
1931	7	23	6	1	0	0	0.0	0	3	0	4	0	.261	.304	0	0	SS-7
2 yrs.	13	40	12	1	1	0	0.0	2	5	3	7	0	.300	.375	0	0	SS-13

Frank Genins

GENINS, C. FRANK (Frenchy)
B. Nov. 2, 1866, St. Louis, Mo.   D. Sept. 30, 1922, St. Louis, Mo.
TR

	G	AB	H	2B	3B	HR	HR%	R	RBI	BB	SO	SB	BA	SA	AB	H	G by POS
1892 2 teams	CIN	N (35G – .182)			STL	N (15G – .196)											
" total	50	161	30	5	0	0	0.0	17	11	13	23	10	.186	.217	0	0	SS-31, OF-15, 3B-4
1895 PIT N	73	252	63	8	0	2	0.8	43	24	22	14	19	.250	.306	3	0	OF-29, 3B-16, 2B-16, SS-8, 1B-2
1901 CLE A	26	101	23	5	0	0	0.0	15	9	8		3	.228	.277	0	0	OF-26
3 yrs.	149	514	116	18	0	2	0.4	75	44	43	37	32	.226	.272	3	0	OF-70, SS-39, 3B-20, 2B-16, 1B-2

George Genovese

GENOVESE, GEORGE MICHAEL
B. Feb. 22, 1922, Staten Island, N. Y.
BL TR 5'6½"   160 lbs.

	G	AB	H	2B	3B	HR	HR%	R	RBI	BB	SO	SB	BA	SA	AB	H	G by POS
1950 WAS A	3	1	0	0	0	0	0.0	0	0	1	0	0	.000	.000	1	0	

Jim Gentile

GENTILE, JAMES EDWARD (Diamond Jim)
B. June 3, 1934, San Francisco, Calif.
BL TL 6'3½"   210 lbs.

	G	AB	H	2B	3B	HR	HR%	R	RBI	BB	SO	SB	BA	SA	AB	H	G by POS
1957 BKN N	4	6	1	0	0	1	16.7	1	1	1	1	0	.167	.667	1	0	1B-2
1958 LA N	12	30	4	1	0	0	0.0	0	4	4	6	0	.133	.167	4	1	1B-8
1960 BAL A	138	384	112	17	0	21	5.5	67	98	68	72	0	.292	.500	28	8	1B-124
1961	148	486	147	25	2	46	9.5	96	141	96	106	1	.302	.646	11	3	1B-144
1962	152	545	137	21	1	33	6.1	80	87	77	100	1	.251	.475	2	0	1B-150
1963	145	496	123	16	0	24	4.8	65	72	76	101	1	.248	.429	3	1	1B-143
1964 KC A	136	439	110	10	0	28	6.4	71	71	84	122	0	.251	.465	6	1	1B-128
1965 2 teams	KC	A (38G – .246)			HOU	N (81G – .242)											
" total	119	345	84	16	1	17	4.9	36	53	43	98	0	.243	.443	14	3	1B-103
1966 2 teams	HOU	N (49G – .243)			CLE	A (33G – .128)											
" total	82	191	41	7	1	9	4.7	18	22	26	57	0	.215	.403	30	6	1B-52
9 yrs.	936	2922	759	113	6	179	6.1	434	549	475	663	3	.260	.486	99	23	1B-854

Sam Gentile

GENTILE, SAMUEL CHRISTOPHER
B. Oct. 12, 1916, Charlestown, Mass.
BL TR 5'11"   180 lbs.

	G	AB	H	2B	3B	HR	HR%	R	RBI	BB	SO	SB	BA	SA	AB	H	G by POS
1943 BOS N	8	4	1	1	0	0	0.0	1	0	1	0	0	.250	.500	4	1	

Harvey Gentry

GENTRY, HARVEY WILLIAM
B. May 27, 1926, Winston-Salem, N. C.
BL TR 6'   170 lbs.

	G	AB	H	2B	3B	HR	HR%	R	RBI	BB	SO	SB	BA	SA	AB	H	G by POS
1954 NY N	5	4	1	0	0	0	0.0	0	1	1	0	0	.250	.250	4	1	

Alex George

GEORGE, ALEXANDER THOMAS
B. Sept. 27, 1938, Kansas City, Mo.
BL TR 5'11½" 170 lbs.

	G	AB	H	2B	3B	HR	HR%	R	RBI	BB	SO	SB	BA	SA	AB	H	G by POS
1955 KC A	5	10	1	0	0	0	0.0	0	0	1	7	0	.100	.100	2	0	SS-5

Greek George

GEORGE, CHARLES PETER
B. Dec. 25, 1912, Waycross, Ga.
BR TR 6'2"   200 lbs.

	G	AB	H	2B	3B	HR	HR%	R	RBI	BB	SO	SB	BA	SA	AB	H	G by POS
1935 CLE A	2	0	0	0	0	0	–	0	0	0	0	0	–	–	0	0	C-1
1936	23	77	15	3	0	0	0.0	3	5	9	16	0	.195	.234	1	0	C-22
1938 BKN N	7	20	4	0	1	0	0.0	0	2	0	4	0	.200	.300	0	0	C-7
1941 CHI N	35	64	10	2	0	0	0.0	4	6	2	10	0	.156	.188	17	0	C-18
1945 PHI A	51	138	24	4	1	0	0.0	8	11	17	29	0	.174	.217	5	0	C-46
5 yrs.	118	299	53	9	2	0	0.0	15	24	28	59	0	.177	.221	23	0	C-94

	G	AB	H	2B	3B	HR	HR %	R	RBI	BB	SO	SB	BA	SA	Pinch Hit AB	Pinch Hit H	G by POS

Ben Geraghty

GERAGHTY, BENJAMIN RAYMOND BR TR 5'11½" 155 lbs.
B. July 19, 1912, Jersey City, N. J. D. June 18, 1963, Jacksonville, Fla.

	G	AB	H	2B	3B	HR	HR %	R	RBI	BB	SO	SB	BA	SA	PH AB	PH H	G by POS
1936 BKN N	51	129	25	4	0	0	0.0	11	9	8	16	4	.194	.225	1	0	SS-31, 2B-9, 3B-5
1943 BOS N	8	1	0	0	0	0	0.0	2	0	0	0	0	.000	.000	0	0	SS-1, 3B-1, 2B-1
1944	11	16	4	0	0	0	0.0	3	0	1	2	0	.250	.250	0	0	2B-4, 3B-3
3 yrs.	70	146	29	4	0	0	0.0	16	9	9	18	4	.199	.226	1	0	SS-32, 2B-14, 3B-9

Wally Gerber

GERBER, WALTER (Spooks) BR TR 5'10" 152 lbs.
B. Aug. 18, 1891, Columbus, Ohio D. June 19, 1951, Columbus, Ohio

	G	AB	H	2B	3B	HR	HR %	R	RBI	BB	SO	SB	BA	SA	PH AB	PH H	G by POS
1914 PIT N	17	54	13	1	1	0	0.0	5	5	2	8	0	.241	.296	0	0	SS-17
1915	56	144	28	2	0	0	0.0	8	7	9	16	6	.194	.208	7	0	SS-23, 3B-23, 2B-2
1917 STL A	14	39	12	1	1	0	0.0	2	2	3	2	1	.308	.385	2	0	SS-12, 2B-2
1918	56	171	41	4	0	0	0.0	10	10	19	11	2	.240	.263	0	0	SS-56
1919	140	462	105	14	6	1	0.2	43	37	49	36	1	.227	.290	0	0	SS-140
1920	154	584	163	26	2	2	0.3	70	60	58	32	4	.279	.341	0	0	SS-154
1921	114	436	121	12	9	2	0.5	55	48	34	19	3	.278	.360	1	0	SS-113
1922	153	604	161	22	8	1	0.2	81	51	52	34	6	.267	.334	0	0	SS-153
1923	154	605	170	26	3	1	0.2	85	62	54	50	4	.281	.339	0	0	SS-154
1924	148	496	135	20	4	0	0.0	61	55	43	34	4	.272	.329	1	0	SS-146
1925	72	246	67	13	1	0	0.0	29	19	26	15	1	.272	.333	1	0	SS-71
1926	131	411	111	8	0	0	0.0	37	42	40	29	0	.270	.290	1	0	SS-129
1927	142	438	98	13	9	0	0.0	44	45	35	25	2	.224	.295	0	0	SS-141, 3B-1
1928 2 teams	STL A (6G – .278)			BOS	A	(104G –	.213)										
" total	110	318	69	7	1	0	0.0	22	28	33	34	6	.217	.245	0	0	SS-109
1929 BOS A	61	91	15	3	1	0	0.0	6	5	8	12	1	.165	.220	0	0	SS-30, 2B-22
15 yrs.	1522	5099	1309	172	46	7	0.1	558	476	465	357	41	.257	.313	11	0	SS-1448, 2B-26, 3B-24

Joe Gerhardt

GERHARDT, JOHN JOSEPH (Move Up Joe) BR TR 6' 160 lbs.
B. Feb. 14, 1855, Washington, D. C. D. Mar. 11, 1922, Middletown, N. Y.
Manager 1883-84.

	G	AB	H	2B	3B	HR	HR %	R	RBI	BB	SO	SB	BA	SA	PH AB	PH H	G by POS
1876 LOU N	65	292	76	10	3	2	0.7	33	18	3	5		.260	.336	0	0	1B-54, 2B-5, SS-3, OF-2, 3B-2
1877	59	250	76	6	5	1	0.4	41	35	5	8		.304	.380	0	0	2B-57, OF-1, SS-1, 1B-1
1878 CIN N	60	259	77	7	2	0	0.0	46	28	7	14		.297	.340	0	0	2B-60
1879	79	313	62	12	3	1	0.3	22	39	3	19		.198	.265	0	0	2B-55, SS-16, 1B-8, SS-1
1881 DET N	80	297	72	13	6	0	0.0	35	36	7	31		.242	.327	0	0	2B-79, 3B-1
1883 LOU AA	78	319	84	11	9	0	0.0	56		14			.263	.354	0	0	2B-78
1884	106	404	89	7	8	0	0.0	39		13			.220	.277	0	0	2B-105, SS-1
1885 NY N	112	399	62	12	2	0	0.0	43		24	47		.155	.195	0	0	2B-112
1886	123	426	81	11	7	0	0.0	44	40	22	63		.190	.249	0	0	2B-123
1887 2 teams	NY	N (1G –	.000)		NY	AA	(85G –	.221)									
" total	86	311	68	13	4	0	0.0	40		24		15	.219	.273	0		2B-84, 3B-2
1890 2 teams	B-B	AA (99G –	.203)		STL	AA	(37G –	.256)									
" total	136	494	107	10	3	4	0.8	49		39		14	.217	.273	0		2B-119, 3B-17
1891 LOU AA	2	6	0	0	0	0	0.0	0		1	0	0	.000	.000	0	0	2B-2
12 yrs.	986	3770	854	112	50	8	0.2	448	196	162	187	29	.227	.289	0		2B-879, 1B-63, 3B-38, SS-6, OF-3

George Gerken

GERKEN, GEORGE HERBERT (Pickles) BR TR 5'11½" 175 lbs.
B. July 28, 1903, Chicago, Ill. D. Oct. 23, 1977, Arcadia, Calif.

	G	AB	H	2B	3B	HR	HR %	R	RBI	BB	SO	SB	BA	SA	PH AB	PH H	G by POS
1927 CLE A	6	14	3	0	0	0	0.0	1	2	1	3	0	.214	.214	0	0	OF-5
1928	38	115	26	7	2	0	0.0	16	9	12	22	3	.226	.322	0	0	OF-34
2 yrs.	44	129	29	7	2	0	0.0	17	11	13	25	3	.225	.310	0	0	OF-39

John Gerlach

GERLACH, JOHN GLENN (Johnny) BR TR 5'9" 165 lbs.
B. May 11, 1917, Shullsburg, Wis.

	G	AB	H	2B	3B	HR	HR %	R	RBI	BB	SO	SB	BA	SA	PH AB	PH H	G by POS
1938 CHI A	9	25	7	0	0	0	0.0	2	1	4	2	0	.280	.280	0	0	SS-8
1939	3	2	2	0	0	0	0.0	0	0	0	0	0	1.000	1.000	1	1	3B-1
2 yrs.	12	27	9	0	0	0	0.0	2	1	4	2	0	.333	.333	1	1	SS-8, 3B-1

Dick Gernert

GERNERT, RICHARD EDWARD BR TR 6'3" 209 lbs.
B. Sept. 28, 1928, Reading, Pa.

	G	AB	H	2B	3B	HR	HR %	R	RBI	BB	SO	SB	BA	SA	PH AB	PH H	G by POS
1952 BOS A	102	367	89	20	2	19	5.2	58	67	35	83	4	.243	.463	4	1	1B-99
1953	139	494	125	15	1	21	4.3	73	71	88	82	0	.253	.415	3	0	1B-136
1954	14	23	6	2	0	0	0.0	2	1	6	4	0	.261	.348	7	1	1B-6
1955	7	20	4	2	0	0	0.0	6	1	1	5	0	.200	.300	1	0	1B-5
1956	106	306	89	11	0	16	5.2	53	68	56	57	1	.291	.484	22	4	OF-50, 1B-37
1957	99	316	75	13	3	14	4.4	45	58	39	62	1	.237	.430	18	6	1B-71, OF-16
1958	122	431	102	19	1	20	4.6	59	69	59	78	2	.237	.425	7	3	1B-114
1959	117	298	78	14	1	11	3.7	41	42	52	49	1	.262	.426	21	4	1B-75, OF-25
1960 2 teams	CHI	N (52G –	.250)		DET	A	(21G –	.300)									
" total	73	146	39	7	0	1	0.7	14	16	14	24	1	.267	.336	31	8	1B-31, OF-11
1961 2 teams	DET	A (6G –	.200)		CIN	N	(40G –	.302)									
" total	46	68	20	1	0	1	1.5	5	8	8	11	0	.294	.353	25	6	1B-21
1962 HOU N	10	24	5	0	0	0	0.0	1		5	7	0	.208	.208	1	0	1B-9
11 yrs.	835	2493	632	104	8	103	4.1	357	402	363	462	10	.254	.426	140	33	1B-604, OF-102

WORLD SERIES

	G	AB	H	2B	3B	HR	HR %	R	RBI	BB	SO	SB	BA	SA	PH AB	PH H	G by POS
1961 CIN N	4	4	0	0	0	0	0.0	0	0	0	1	0	.000	.000	4	0	

Cesar Geronimo

GERONIMO, CESAR FRANCISCO BL TL 6' 165 lbs.
B. Mar. 11, 1948, El Seybo, Dominican Republic

	G	AB	H	2B	3B	HR	HR %	R	RBI	BB	SO	SB	BA	SA	PH AB	PH H	G by POS
1969 HOU N	28	8	2	1	0	0	0.0	8	0	0	3	0	.250	.375	5	1	OF-9
1970	47	37	9	0	0	0	0.0	5	2	2	5	0	.243	.243	11	4	OF-26
1971	94	82	18	2	2	1	1.2	13	6	5	31	2	.220	.329	11	2	OF-64
1972 CIN N	120	255	70	9	7	4	1.6	32	29	24	64	2	.275	.412	12	1	OF-106
1973	139	324	68	14	3	4	1.2	35	33	23	74	5	.210	.309	7	1	OF-130
1974	150	474	133	17	8	7	1.5	73	54	46	96	9	.281	.395	7	0	OF-145

	G	AB	H	2B	3B	HR	HR %	R	RBI	BB	SO	SB	BA	SA	Pinch Hit AB	Pinch Hit H	G by POS

Cesar Geronimo continued

	G	AB	H	2B	3B	HR	HR%	R	RBI	BB	SO	SB	BA	SA	AB	H	G by POS
1975	148	501	129	25	5	6	1.2	69	53	48	97	13	.257	.363	3	1	OF-148
1976	149	486	149	24	11	2	0.4	59	49	56	95	22	.307	.414	4	2	OF-146
1977	149	492	131	22	4	10	2.0	54	52	35	89	10	.266	.388	7	3	OF-147
1978	122	296	67	15	1	5	1.7	28	27	43	67	8	.226	.334	11	5	OF-115
1979	123	356	85	17	4	4	1.1	38	38	37	56	1	.239	.343	9	2	OF-118
1980	103	145	37	5	0	2	1.4	16	9	14	24	2	.255	.331	21	5	OF-86
1981 KC A	59	118	29	0	2	2	1.7	14	13	11	16	6	.246	.331	2	2	OF-57
1982	53	119	32	6	3	4	3.4	14	23	8	16	2	.269	.471	10	2	OF-44, DH-1
1983	38	87	18	4	0	0	0.0	2	4	2	13	0	.207	.253	6	1	OF-35
15 yrs.	1522	3780	977	161	50	51	1.3	460	392	354	746	82	.258	.368	126	32	OF-1376, DH-1

DIVISIONAL PLAYOFF SERIES

	G	AB	H	2B	3B	HR	HR%	R	RBI	BB	SO	SB	BA	SA	AB	H	G by POS
1981 KC A	1	0	0	0	0	0	–	0	0	0	0	0	–	–	0	0	

LEAGUE CHAMPIONSHIP SERIES

	G	AB	H	2B	3B	HR	HR%	R	RBI	BB	SO	SB	BA	SA	AB	H	G by POS
1972 CIN N	5	20	2	0	0	1	5.0	2	1	0	2	0	.100	.250	0	0	OF-5
1973	4	15	1	0	0	0	0.0	0	0	0	7	0	.067	.067	0	0	OF-4
1975	3	10	0	0	0	0	0.0	0	1	1	7	0	.000	.000	0	0	OF-3
1976	3	11	2	0	1	0	0.0	0	2	1	3	0	.182	.364	0	0	OF-3
1979	2	7	1	0	0	0	0.0	0	0	0	5	0	.143	.143	0	0	OF-2
5 yrs.	17	63	6	0	1	1	1.6	2	4	2	24	0	.095	.175	0	0	OF-17

WORLD SERIES

	G	AB	H	2B	3B	HR	HR%	R	RBI	BB	SO	SB	BA	SA	AB	H	G by POS
1972 CIN N	7	19	3	0	0	0	0.0	1	3	1	4	1	.158	.158	0	0	OF-7
1975	7	25	7	0	1	2	8.0	3	3	3	5	0	.280	.600	0	0	OF-7
1976	4	13	4	2	0	0	0.0	3	1	2	2	2	.308	.462	0	0	OF-4
3 yrs.	18	57	14	2	1	2	3.5	7	7	6	11	3	.246	.421	0	0	OF-18

Lou Gertenrich

GERTENRICH, LOUIS WILHELM   BR TR 5'8"   175 lbs.
B. May 4, 1875, Chicago, Ill.   D. Oct. 23, 1933, Chicago, Ill.

	G	AB	H	2B	3B	HR	HR%	R	RBI	BB	SO	SB	BA	SA	AB	H	G by POS
1901 MIL A	2	3	1	0	0	0	0.0	1	0	0		0	.333	.333	1	0	OF-1
1903 PIT N	1	3	0	0	0	0	0.0	0	0	0		0	.000	.000	0	0	OF-1
2 yrs.	3	6	1	0	0	0	0.0	1	0	0		0	.167	.167	1	0	OF-2

Doc Gessler

GESSLER, HARRY HOMER   BL TR
B. Dec. 23, 1880, Indiana, Pa.   D. Dec. 26, 1924, Indiana, Pa.
Manager 1914.

	G	AB	H	2B	3B	HR	HR%	R	RBI	BB	SO	SB	BA	SA	AB	H	G by POS
1903 2 teams		DET A	(29G –	.238)		BKN N	(49G –	.247)									
" total	78	259	63	13	7	0	0.0	29	30	20		10	.243	.347	4	1	OF-71
1904 BKN N	104	341	99	18	4	2	0.6	41	28	30		13	.290	.384	12	2	OF-88, 2B-1, 1B-1
1905	126	431	125	17	4	3	0.7	44	46	38		26	.290	.369	7	2	1B-107, OF-12
1906 2 teams		BKN N	(9G –	.242)		CHI N	(34G –	.253)									
" total	43	116	29	4	2	0	0.0	11	14	15		7	.250	.319	11	2	OF-21, 1B-10
1908 BOS A	128	435	134	13	14	3	0.7	55	63	51		19	.308	.423	2	2	OF-126
1909 2 teams		BOS A	(111G –	.298)		WAS A	(17G –	.241)									
" total	128	440	128	26	2	0	0.0	66	54	43		20	.291	.359	1	0	OF-127, 1B-2
1910 WAS A	145	487	126	17	11	2	0.4	58	50	62		18	.259	.351	1	0	OF-144
1911	128	450	127	19	5	4	0.9	65	78	74		29	.282	.373	1	0	OF-126, 1B-1
8 yrs.	880	2959	831	127	49	14	0.5	369	363	333		142	.281	.371	39	9	OF-715, 1B-121, 2B-1

WORLD SERIES

	G	AB	H	2B	3B	HR	HR%	R	RBI	BB	SO	SB	BA	SA	AB	H	G by POS
1906 CHI N	2	1	0	0	0	0	0.0	0	0	1		0	.000	.000	1	0	

Charlie Gettig

GETTIG, CHARLES HENRY
Also known as Charles Henry Gettinger.   Brother of Tom Gettinger.
B. Dec., 1870, Cumberland, Md.   Deceased.

	G	AB	H	2B	3B	HR	HR%	R	RBI	BB	SO	SB	BA	SA	AB	H	G by POS
1896 NY N	6	9	3	1	0	0	0.0	3	0	0	0	0	.333	.444	2	0	P-4
1897	22	75	15	6	0	0	0.0	8	12	6		3	.200	.280	1	0	3B-7, 2B-6, OF-3, SS-3, P-3
1898	64	196	49	6	2	0	0.0	30	26	15		5	.250	.301	0	0	OF-21, P-17, 2B-12, SS-9, 3B-4, C-1
1899	34	97	24	3	0	0	0.0	7	9	7		4	.247	.278	1	0	P-18, 3B-8, 2B-3, 1B-3, OF-1
4 yrs.	126	377	91	16	2	0	0.0	48	47	28		12	.241	.294	4	0	P-42, OF-25, 2B-21, 3B-19, SS-12, 1B-5, C-1

Tom Gettinger

GETTINGER, THOMAS L   BL TL 5'10"   180 lbs.
Brother of Charlie Gettig.
B. 1870, Mobile, Ala.   Deceased.

	G	AB	H	2B	3B	HR	HR%	R	RBI	BB	SO	SB	BA	SA	AB	H	G by POS
1889 STL AA	4	16	7	0	0	1	6.3	2	2	2	1	0	.438	.625	0	0	OF-4
1890	58	227	54	7	5	3	1.3	31		20		8	.238	.352	0	0	OF-58
1895 LOU N	63	260	70	11	5	2	0.8	28	32	8	15	6	.269	.373	0	0	OF-63, P-2
3 yrs.	125	503	131	18	10	6	1.2	61	34	30	16	14	.260	.372	0	0	OF-125, P-2

Jake Gettman

GETTMAN, JACOB JOHN   BB TR 5'11"   185 lbs.
B. Oct. 25, 1875, Frank, Russia   D. Oct. 4, 1956, Denver, Colo.

	G	AB	H	2B	3B	HR	HR%	R	RBI	BB	SO	SB	BA	SA	AB	H	G by POS
1897 WAS N	36	143	45	7	3	3	2.1	28	29	7		8	.315	.469	0	0	OF-36
1898	142	567	157	16	5	5	0.9	75	47	29		32	.277	.349	0	0	OF-139, 1B-3
1899	19	62	13	1	0	0	0.0	5	2	4		4	.210	.226	1	1	OF-16, 1B-2
3 yrs.	197	772	215	24	8	8	1.0	108	78	40		44	.278	.361	1	1	OF-191, 1B-5

Gus Getz

GETZ, GUSTAVE (Gee-Gee)   BR TR 5'11"   165 lbs.
B. Aug. 3, 1889, Pittsburgh, Pa.   D. May 28, 1969, Keansburg, N. J.

	G	AB	H	2B	3B	HR	HR%	R	RBI	BB	SO	SB	BA	SA	AB	H	G by POS
1909 BOS N	40	148	33	2	0	0	0.0	6	9	1		2	.223	.236	0	0	3B-36, SS-2, 2B-2
1910	54	144	28	0	1	0	0.0	14	7	6	10	2	.194	.208	6	1	3B-22, 2B-13, OF-8, SS-4
1914 BKN N	55	210	52	8	1	0	0.0	13	20	2	15	9	.248	.295	0	0	3B-55
1915	130	477	123	10	5	2	0.4	39	46	8	14	19	.258	.312	0	0	3B-128, SS-2
1916	40	96	21	1	2	0	0.0	9	8	0	5	9	.219	.271	7	0	3B-20, SS-7, 1B-3
1917 CIN N	7	14	4	0	0	0	0.0	2	3	3	0	0	.286	.286	0	0	2B-4, 3B-3

	G	AB	H	2B	3B	HR	HR %	R	RBI	BB	SO	SB	BA	SA	Pinch Hit AB	Pinch Hit H	G by POS

Gus Getz continued

	G	AB	H	2B	3B	HR	HR%	R	RBI	BB	SO	SB	BA	SA	PH AB	PH H	G by POS
1918 2 teams	CLE A (6G – .133)				PIT N (7G – .200)												
" total	13	25	4	1	0	0	0.0	2	0	4	2	0	.160	.200	4	0	OF-3, 3B-2
7 yrs.	339	1114	265	22	9	2	0.2	85	93	24	46	41	.238	.279	17	1	3B-266, 2B-19, SS-15, OF-11, 1B-3

WORLD SERIES

	G	AB	H	2B	3B	HR	HR%	R	RBI	BB	SO	SB	BA	SA	PH AB	PH H	G by POS
1916 BKN N	1	1	0	0	0	0	0.0	0	0	0	0	0	.000	.000	1	0	

Chappie Geygan

GEYGAN, JAMES EDWARD
B. June 3, 1903, Ironton, Ohio   D. Mar. 15, 1966, Columbus, Ohio
BR TR 5'11" 170 lbs.

	G	AB	H	2B	3B	HR	HR%	R	RBI	BB	SO	SB	BA	SA	PH AB	PH H	G by POS
1924 BOS A	33	82	21	5	2	0	0.0	7	4	4	16	0	.256	.366	1	1	SS-32
1925	3	11	2	0	0	0	0.0	0	0	0	2	0	.182	.182	0	0	SS-3
1926	4	10	3	0	0	0	0.0	0	0	1	1	0	.300	.300	1	0	3B-3
3 yrs.	40	103	26	5	2	0	0.0	7	4	5	19	0	.252	.340	2	1	SS-35, 3B-3

Patsy Gharrity

GHARRITY, EDWARD PATRICK
B. Mar. 13, 1892, Parnell, Iowa   D. Oct. 10, 1966, Beloit, Wis.
BR TR 5'10" 170 lbs.

	G	AB	H	2B	3B	HR	HR%	R	RBI	BB	SO	SB	BA	SA	PH AB	PH H	G by POS
1916 WAS A	39	92	21	5	1	0	0.0	8	9	8	18	2	.228	.304	6	0	C-18, 1B-15
1917	76	176	50	5	0	0	0.0	15	18	14	18	7	.284	.313	20	3	1B-46, C-5, OF-1
1918	4	4	1	1	0	0	0.0	0	2	0	1	0	.250	.500	4	1	
1919	111	347	94	19	4	2	0.6	35	43	25	39	4	.271	.366	10	1	C-60, OF-33, 1B-7
1920	131	428	105	18	3	3	0.7	51	44	37	52	6	.245	.322	4	0	C-120, 1B-7, OF-1
1921	121	387	120	19	8	7	1.8	62	55	45	44	4	.310	.455	5	2	C-115
1922	96	273	70	16	6	5	1.8	40	45	36	30	3	.256	.414	8	1	C-87
1923	96	251	52	9	4	3	1.2	26	33	22	27	6	.207	.311	20	5	C-35, 1B-33
1929	3	2	0	0	0	0	0.0	0	0	1	2	0	.000	.000	2	0	
1930	2	1	0	0	0	0	0.0	0	0	0	0	0	.000	.000	1	0	1B-1
10 yrs.	679	1961	513	92	26	20	1.0	237	249	188	231	32	.262	.366	80	13	C-440, 1B-109, OF-35

Joe Giannini

GIANNINI, JOSEPH FRANCIS
B. Sept. 8, 1888, San Francisco, Calif.   D. Sept. 26, 1942, San Francisco, Calif.
BL TR 5'8" 155 lbs.

	G	AB	H	2B	3B	HR	HR%	R	RBI	BB	SO	SB	BA	SA	PH AB	PH H	G by POS
1911 BOS A	1	2	1	1	0	0	0.0	0	0	0		0	.500	1.000	0	0	SS-1

John Gibbons

GIBBONS, JOHN MICHAEL
B. June 8, 1962, Great Falls, Mont.
BR TR 5'11" 185 lbs.

	G	AB	H	2B	3B	HR	HR%	R	RBI	BB	SO	SB	BA	SA	PH AB	PH H	G by POS
1984 NY N	10	31	2	0	0	0	0.0	1	1	3	11	0	.065	.065	1	0	C-9

Jake Gibbs

GIBBS, JERRY DEAN
B. Nov. 7, 1938, Grenada, Miss.
BL TR 6' 180 lbs.

	G	AB	H	2B	3B	HR	HR%	R	RBI	BB	SO	SB	BA	SA	PH AB	PH H	G by POS
1962 NY A	2	0	0	0	0	0	–	2	0	0	0	0	–	–	0	0	3B-1
1963	4	8	2	0	0	0	0.0	1	0	0	1	0	.250	.250	3	2	C-1
1964	3	6	1	0	0	0	0.0	1	0	0	2	0	.167	.167	1	1	C-2
1965	37	68	15	1	0	2	2.9	6	7	4	20	0	.221	.324	16	3	C-21
1966	62	182	47	6	0	3	1.6	19	20	19	16	5	.258	.341	5	1	C-54
1967	116	374	87	7	1	4	1.1	33	25	28	57	7	.233	.289	17	3	C-99
1968	124	423	90	12	3	3	0.7	31	29	27	68	9	.213	.277	4	1	C-121
1969	71	219	49	9	2	0	0.0	18	18	23	30	3	.224	.283	2	0	C-66
1970	49	153	46	9	2	8	5.2	23	26	7	14	2	.301	.542	5	1	C-44
1971	70	206	45	9	0	5	2.4	23	21	12	23	2	.218	.335	16	1	C-51
10 yrs.	538	1639	382	53	8	25	1.5	157	146	120	231	28	.233	.321	69	13	C-459, 3B-1

Charlie Gibson

GIBSON, CHARLES ELLSWORTH
B. Nov. 17, 1879, Sharon, Pa.   D. Nov. 22, 1954, Sharon, Pa.
BR TR 6'

	G	AB	H	2B	3B	HR	HR%	R	RBI	BB	SO	SB	BA	SA	PH AB	PH H	G by POS
1905 STL A	1	3	0	0	0	0	0.0	0	0	0		0	.000	.000	0	0	C-1

Charlie Gibson

GIBSON, CHARLES GRIFFIN
B. Nov. 21, 1899, LaGrange, Ga.
BR TR 5'8" 160 lbs.

	G	AB	H	2B	3B	HR	HR%	R	RBI	BB	SO	SB	BA	SA	PH AB	PH H	G by POS
1924 PHI A	12	15	2	0	0	0	0.0	1	1	2	2	0	.133	.133	0	0	C-12

Frank Gibson

GIBSON, FRANK GILBERT
B. Sept. 27, 1890, Omaha, Neb.
D. Apr. 27, 1961, Austin, Tex.
BB TR 6½" 172 lbs.
BL 1921-22,1924

	G	AB	H	2B	3B	HR	HR%	R	RBI	BB	SO	SB	BA	SA	PH AB	PH H	G by POS
1913 DET A	20	57	8	1	0	0	0.0	8	2	3	9	2	.140	.158	0	0	C-19, OF-1
1921 BOS N	63	125	33	5	4	2	1.6	14	13	3	17	0	.264	.416	17	4	C-41
1922	66	164	49	7	2	3	1.8	15	20	10	27	4	.299	.421	15	2	C-29, 1B-20
1923	41	50	15	1	0	0	0.0	13	5	7	7	0	.300	.320	15	6	C-20
1924	90	229	71	15	6	1	0.4	25	30	10	23	1	.310	.441	31	0	C-46, 1B-10, 3B-2
1925	104	316	88	23	5	2	0.6	36	50	15	28	3	.278	.402	15	7	C-88, 1B-2
1926	24	47	16	4	0	0	0.0	3	7	4	6	0	.340	.426	12	6	C-12
1927	60	167	37	1	2	0	0.0	7	19	3	10	2	.222	.251	12	4	C-47
8 yrs.	468	1155	317	57	19	8	0.7	121	146	55	127	12	.274	.377	117	29	C-302, 1B-32, 3B-2, OF-1

George Gibson

GIBSON, GEORGE (Moon)
B. July 22, 1880, London, Ont., Canada   D. Jan. 25, 1967, London, Ont., Canada
Manager 1920-22, 1925, 1932-34.
BR TR 5'11½" 190 lbs.

	G	AB	H	2B	3B	HR	HR%	R	RBI	BB	SO	SB	BA	SA	PH AB	PH H	G by POS
1905 PIT N	46	135	24	2	2	0	1.5	14	14	15		2	.178	.267	1	0	C-44
1906	81	259	46	6	1	0	0.0	8	20	16		1	.178	.208	0	0	C-81
1907	113	382	84	8	7	3	0.8	28	35	18		2	.220	.301	3	1	C-109, 1B-1
1908	143	486	111	19	4	2	0.4	37	45	19		4	.228	.296	3	1	C-140
1909	150	510	135	25	9	2	0.4	42	52	44		9	.265	.361	0	0	C-150
1910	143	482	125	22	6	3	0.6	53	44	47	31	7	.259	.349	0	0	C-143
1911	100	311	65	12	2	0	0.0	32	19	29	16	3	.209	.260	1	1	C-98
1912	95	300	72	14	3	2	0.7	23	35	20	16	0	.240	.327	1	1	C-94
1913	48	118	33	4	2	0	0.0	6	12	10	8	2	.280	.347	1	0	C-48
1914	102	274	78	9	5	0	0.0	19	30	27	27	4	.285	.354	1	0	C-101

	G	AB	H	2B	3B	HR	HR %	R	RBI	BB	SO	SB	BA	SA	Pinch Hit AB	Pinch Hit H	G by POS

George Gibson continued

	G	AB	H	2B	3B	HR	HR %	R	RBI	BB	SO	SB	BA	SA	PH AB	PH H	G by POS
1915	120	351	88	15	6	1	0.3	28	30	31	25	5	.251	.336	2	0	C-120
1916	33	84	17	2	2	0	0.0	4	4	3	7	0	.202	.274	2	0	C-29
1917 NY N	35	82	14	3	0	0	0.0	1	5	7	2	1	.171	.207	0	0	C-35
1918	4	2	1	1	0	0	0.0	0	0	0	0	0	.500	1.000	0	0	C-4
14 yrs.	1213	3776	893	142	49	15	0.4	295	345	286	132	40	.236	.312	14	4	C-1196, 1B-1

WORLD SERIES

	G	AB	H	2B	3B	HR	HR %	R	RBI	BB	SO	SB	BA	SA	PH AB	PH H	G by POS
1909 PIT N	7	25	6	2	0	0	0.0	2	2	1	1	2	.240	.320	0	0	C-7

Kirk Gibson

GIBSON, KIRK HAROLD   BL TL 6'3"   215 lbs.
B. May 28, 1957, Pontiac, Mich.

	G	AB	H	2B	3B	HR	HR %	R	RBI	BB	SO	SB	BA	SA	PH AB	PH H	G by POS
1979 DET A	12	38	9	3	0	1	2.6	3	4	1	3	3	.237	.395	2	0	OF-10
1980	51	175	46	2	1	9	5.1	23	16	10	45	4	.263	.440	5	1	OF-49, DH-1
1981	83	290	95	11	3	9	3.1	41	40	18	64	17	.328	.479	8	1	OF-67, DH-9
1982	69	266	74	16	2	8	3.0	34	35	25	41	9	.278	.444	1	0	OF-64, DH-4
1983	128	401	91	12	9	15	3.7	60	51	53	96	14	.227	.414	20	5	DH-66, OF-54
1984	149	531	150	23	10	27	5.1	92	91	63	103	29	.282	.516	11	1	OF-139, DH-6
6 yrs.	492	1701	465	67	25	69	4.1	253	237	170	352	76	.273	.464	47	8	OF-383, DH-86

LEAGUE CHAMPIONSHIP SERIES

	G	AB	H	2B	3B	HR	HR %	R	RBI	BB	SO	SB	BA	SA	PH AB	PH H	G by POS
1984 DET A	3	12	5	1	0	1	8.3	2	2	2	1	1	.417	.750	0	0	OF-3

WORLD SERIES

	G	AB	H	2B	3B	HR	HR %	R	RBI	BB	SO	SB	BA	SA	PH AB	PH H	G by POS
1984 DET A	5	18	6	0	0	2	11.1	4	7	4	4	3	.333	.667	0	0	OF-5

Russ Gibson

GIBSON, JOHN RUSSELL   BR TR 6'1"   195 lbs.
B. May 6, 1939, Fall River, Mass.

	G	AB	H	2B	3B	HR	HR %	R	RBI	BB	SO	SB	BA	SA	PH AB	PH H	G by POS
1967 BOS A	49	138	28	7	1	1	0.7	8	15	12	31	0	.203	.275	4	0	C-48
1968	76	231	52	11	1	3	1.3	15	20	8	38	1	.225	.320	3	1	C-74, 1B-1
1969	85	287	72	9	1	3	1.0	21	27	15	25	1	.251	.321	4	1	C-83
1970 SF N	24	69	16	6	0	0	0.0	3	6	7	12	0	.232	.319	1	0	C-23
1971	25	57	11	1	1	1	1.8	2	7	2	13	0	.193	.298	2	0	C-22
1972	5	12	2	0	0	0	0.0	0	3	0	4	0	.167	.333	1	0	C-5
6 yrs.	264	794	181	34	4	8	1.0	49	78	44	123	2	.228	.311	15	2	C-255, 1B-1

WORLD SERIES

	G	AB	H	2B	3B	HR	HR %	R	RBI	BB	SO	SB	BA	SA	PH AB	PH H	G by POS
1967 BOS A	2	2	0	0	0	0	0.0	0	0	0	2	0	.000	.000	0	0	C-2

Whitey Gibson

GIBSON, LEIGHTON B.   TR 5'9"   178 lbs.
B. 1866, Lancaster, Pa.   D. Oct. 11, 1907, Talmadge, Pa.

	G	AB	H	2B	3B	HR	HR %	R	RBI	BB	SO	SB	BA	SA	PH AB	PH H	G by POS
1888 PHI AA	1	3	0	0	0	0	0.0	0	0	0		0	.000	.000	0	0	C-1

Joe Giebel

GIEBEL, JOSEPH HENRY   BR TR 5'10½" 175 lbs.
B. Nov. 30, 1891, Washington, D. C.   D. Mar. 17, 1981, Silver Springs, Md.

	G	AB	H	2B	3B	HR	HR %	R	RBI	BB	SO	SB	BA	SA	PH AB	PH H	G by POS
1913 PHI A	1	3	1	0	0	0	0.0	0	0	0	1	0	.333	.333	0	0	C-1

Norm Gigon

GIGON, NORMAN PHILLIP   BR TR 6'   195 lbs.
B. May 12, 1938, Teaneck, N. J.

	G	AB	H	2B	3B	HR	HR %	R	RBI	BB	SO	SB	BA	SA	PH AB	PH H	G by POS
1967 CHI N	34	70	12	3	1	1	1.4	8	6	4	14	0	.171	.286	15	2	2B-12, OF-4, 3B-1

Gus Gil

GIL, TOMAS GUSTAVO   BR TR 5'10"   180 lbs.
B. Apr. 19, 1940, Caracas, Venezuela

	G	AB	H	2B	3B	HR	HR %	R	RBI	BB	SO	SB	BA	SA	PH AB	PH H	G by POS
1967 CLE A	51	96	11	4	0	0	0.0	11	5	9	18	1	.115	.156	1	0	2B-49, 1B-1
1969 SEA A	92	221	49	7	0	0	0.0	20	17	16	28	2	.222	.253	36	10	3B-38, 2B-18, SS-12
1970 MIL A	64	119	22	4	0	1	0.8	12	12	21	12	2	.185	.244	11	3	2B-38, 3B-14
1971	14	32	5	1	0	0	0.0	3	3	10	5	1	.156	.188	4	0	2B-8, 3B-6
4 yrs.	221	468	87	16	0	1	0.2	46	37	56	63	5	.186	.226	52	13	2B-113, 3B-58, SS-12, 1B-1

Andy Gilbert

GILBERT, ANDREW   BR TR 6'1"   203 lbs.
B. July 18, 1914, Latrobe, Pa.

	G	AB	H	2B	3B	HR	HR %	R	RBI	BB	SO	SB	BA	SA	PH AB	PH H	G by POS
1942 BOS A	6	11	1	0	0	0	0.0	0	1	1	3	0	.091	.091	1	0	OF-5
1946	2	1	0	0	0	0	0.0	1	0	0	0	0	.000	.000	1	0	OF-1
2 yrs.	8	12	1	0	0	0	0.0	1	1	1	3	0	.083	.083	2	0	OF-6

Billy Gilbert

GILBERT, WILLIAM OLIVER   BR TR
B. June 21, 1876, Trenton, N. J.   D. Aug. 8, 1927, New York, N. Y.

	G	AB	H	2B	3B	HR	HR %	R	RBI	BB	SO	SB	BA	SA	PH AB	PH H	G by POS
1901 MIL A	127	492	133	14	7	0	0.0	77	43	31		19	.270	.327	0	0	2B-127
1902 BAL A	129	445	109	12	3	2	0.4	74	38	45		38	.245	.299	0	0	SS-129
1903 NY N	128	413	104	9	0	1	0.2	62	40	41		37	.252	.281	0	0	2B-128
1904	146	478	121	13	3	1	0.2	57	54	46		33	.253	.299	0	0	2B-146
1905	115	376	93	11	3	0	0.0	45	24	41		11	.247	.293	0	0	2B-115
1906	104	307	71	6	1	1	0.3	44	27	42		22	.231	.267	4	1	2B-98
1908 STL N	89	276	59	7	0	0	0.0	12	10	20		6	.214	.239	0	0	2B-89
1909	12	29	5	0	0	0	0.0	4	1	4		1	.172	.172	0	0	2B-12
8 yrs.	850	2816	695	72	17	5	0.2	375	237	270		167	.247	.290	4	1	2B-715, SS-129

WORLD SERIES

	G	AB	H	2B	3B	HR	HR %	R	RBI	BB	SO	SB	BA	SA	PH AB	PH H	G by POS
1905 NY N	5	17	4	0	0	0	0.0	1	1	0	2	1	.235	.235	0	0	2B-5

Buddy Gilbert

GILBERT, DREW EDWARD   BL TR 6'3"   195 lbs.
B. July 26, 1935, Knoxville, Tenn.

	G	AB	H	2B	3B	HR	HR %	R	RBI	BB	SO	SB	BA	SA	PH AB	PH H	G by POS
1959 CIN N	7	20	3	0	0	2	10.0	4	2	3	4	0	.150	.450	1	0	OF-6

Charlie Gilbert

GILBERT, CHARLES MADER
Son of Larry Gilbert.   Brother of Tookie Gilbert.   BL TL 5'9"   165 lbs.
B. July 8, 1919, New Orleans, La.   D. Aug., 1983

	G	AB	H	2B	3B	HR	HR %	R	RBI	BB	SO	SB	BA	SA	PH AB	PH H	G by POS
1940 BKN N	57	142	35	9	1	2	1.4	23	8	8	13	0	.246	.366	8	1	OF-43

	G	AB	H	2B	3B	HR	HR%	R	RBI	BB	SO	SB	BA	SA	Pinch Hit AB	Pinch Hit H	G by POS

Charlie Gilbert continued

	G	AB	H	2B	3B	HR	HR%	R	RBI	BB	SO	SB	BA	SA	PH AB	PH H	G by POS
1941 CHI N	39	86	24	2	1	0	0.0	11	12	11	6	1	.279	.326	14	2	OF-22
1942	74	179	33	6	3	0	0.0	18	7	25	24	1	.184	.251	23	2	OF-47
1943	8	20	3	0	0	0	0.0	1	0	3	3	1	.150	.150	2	0	OF-6
1946 2 teams			CHI N (15G – .077)			PHI N (88G – .242)											
" total	103	273	64	5	2	1	0.4	36	18	26	22	3	.234	.278	28	0	OF-71
1947 PHI N	83	152	36	5	2	2	1.3	20	10	13	14	1	.237	.336	40	9	OF-37
6 yrs.	364	852	195	27	9	5	0.6	109	55	86	82	7	.229	.299	115	14	OF-226

Harry Gilbert

GILBERT, HARRY
Brother of John Gilbert.
B. Pottstown, Pa.   D. Apr. 10, 1906, Pottstown, Pa.

	G	AB	H	2B	3B	HR	HR%	R	RBI	BB	SO	SB	BA	SA	PH AB	PH H	G by POS
1890 PIT N	2	8	2	0	0	0	0.0	1	0	0	3	0	.250	.250	0	0	2B-2

Jack Gilbert

GILBERT, JOHN ROBERT (Jackrabbit)
B. Sept. 7, 1875, Rhinecliff, N. Y.   D. July 7, 1941, Albany, N. Y.

	G	AB	H	2B	3B	HR	HR%	R	RBI	BB	SO	SB	BA	SA	PH AB	PH H	G by POS
1898 2 teams			WAS N (2G – .200)			NY N (1G – .250)											
" total	3	9	2	0	0	0	0.0	0	1	1		2	.222	.222	0	0	OF-3
1904 PIT N	25	87	21	0	0	0	0.0	13	3	12		3	.241	.241	0	0	OF-25
2 yrs.	28	96	23	0	0	0	0.0	13	4	13		5	.240	.240	0	0	OF-28

John Gilbert

GILBERT, JOHN G.
Brother of Harry Gilbert.
B. Jan. 8, 1864, Pottstown, Pa.   D. Nov. 12, 1903, Pottstown, Pa.

	G	AB	H	2B	3B	HR	HR%	R	RBI	BB	SO	SB	BA	SA	PH AB	PH H	G by POS
1890 PIT N	2	8	0	0	0	0	0.0	0	0	0		2	.000	.000	0	0	SS-2

Larry Gilbert

GILBERT, LAWRENCE WILLIAM   BL TL 5'8"   165 lbs.
Father of Charlie Gilbert.   Father of Tookie Gilbert.
B. Dec. 3, 1891, New Orleans, La.   D. Feb. 17, 1965, New Orleans, La.

	G	AB	H	2B	3B	HR	HR%	R	RBI	BB	SO	SB	BA	SA	PH AB	PH H	G by POS
1914 BOS N	72	224	60	6	1	5	2.2	32	25	26	34	3	.268	.371	10	1	OF-60
1915	45	106	16	4	0	0	0.0	11	4	11	13	4	.151	.189	14	3	OF-27
2 yrs.	117	330	76	10	1	5	1.5	43	29	37	47	7	.230	.312	24	4	OF-87

WORLD SERIES

	G	AB	H	2B	3B	HR	HR%	R	RBI	BB	SO	SB	BA	SA	PH AB	PH H	G by POS
1914 BOS N	1	0	0	0	0	0	–	0	0	1	0	0	–	–	0	0	

Pete Gilbert

GILBERT, PETER   TR
B. Sept. 6, 1867, Baltic, Conn.   D. Jan. 1, 1912, Springfield, Mass.

	G	AB	H	2B	3B	HR	HR%	R	RBI	BB	SO	SB	BA	SA	PH AB	PH H	G by POS
1890 B-B AA	29	100	28	2	1	1	1.0	25		10		12	.280	.350	0	0	3B-29
1891 BAL AA	139	513	118	15	7	3	0.6	81	72	37	77	31	.230	.304	0	0	3B-139
1892 BAL N	4	15	3	0	0	0	0.0	0	0	1	3	1	.200	.200	0	0	3B-4
1894 2 teams			BKN N (6G – .080)			LOU N (28G – .306)											
" total	34	133	35	3	1	1	0.8	14	15	6	7	4	.263	.323	0	0	3B-31, 2B-3
4 yrs.	206	761	184	20	9	5	0.7	120	86	54	87	48	.242	.311	0	0	3B-203, 2B-3

Tookie Gilbert

GILBERT, HAROLD JOSEPH   BL TR 6'2½"   185 lbs.
Son of Larry Gilbert.   Brother of Charlie Gilbert.
B. Apr. 4, 1929, New Orleans, La.   D. June 23, 1967, New Orleans, La.

	G	AB	H	2B	3B	HR	HR%	R	RBI	BB	SO	SB	BA	SA	PH AB	PH H	G by POS
1950 NY N	113	322	71	12	2	4	1.2	40	32	43	36	3	.220	.307	2	0	1B-111
1953	70	160	27	3	0	3	1.9	12	16	22	21	1	.169	.244	23	4	1B-44
2 yrs.	183	482	98	15	2	7	1.5	52	48	65	57	4	.203	.286	25	4	1B-155

Wally Gilbert

GILBERT, WALTER JOHN   BR TR 6'   180 lbs.
B. Dec. 19, 1901, Oscoda, Mich.   D. Sept. 8, 1958, Duluth, Minn.

	G	AB	H	2B	3B	HR	HR%	R	RBI	BB	SO	SB	BA	SA	PH AB	PH H	G by POS
1928 BKN N	39	153	31	4	0	0	0.0	26	3	14	8	2	.203	.229	0	0	3B-39
1929	143	569	173	31	4	3	0.5	88	58	42	29	7	.304	.388	1	0	3B-142
1930	150	623	183	34	5	3	0.5	92	67	47	33	7	.294	.379	0	0	3B-150
1931	145	552	147	25	6	0	0.0	60	46	39	38	3	.266	.333	0	0	3B-145
1932 CIN N	114	420	90	18	2	1	0.2	35	40	20	23	2	.214	.274	2	0	3B-111
5 yrs.	591	2317	624	112	17	7	0.3	301	214	162	131	21	.269	.341	3	1	3B-587

Rod Gilbreath

GILBREATH, RODNEY JOE   BR TR 6'2"   180 lbs.
B. Sept. 24, 1952, Laurel, Miss.

	G	AB	H	2B	3B	HR	HR%	R	RBI	BB	SO	SB	BA	SA	PH AB	PH H	G by POS
1972 ATL N	18	38	9	1	0	0	0.0	2	1	2	10	1	.237	.263	4	0	2B-7, 3B-4
1973	29	74	21	2	1	0	0.0	10	2	6	10	2	.284	.338	10	3	3B-22
1974	3	6	2	0	0	0	0.0	2	0	2	0	0	.333	.333	0	0	2B-2
1975	90	202	49	3	1	2	1.0	24	16	24	26	5	.243	.297	25	10	2B-52, 3B-10, SS-1
1976	116	383	96	11	8	1	0.3	57	32	42	36	7	.251	.329	5	1	2B-104, 3B-7, SS-1
1977	128	407	99	15	2	8	2.0	47	43	45	79	3	.243	.349	5	0	2B-122, 3B-1
1978	116	326	80	13	3	3	0.9	22	31	26	51	7	.245	.331	11	1	3B-62, 2B-39
7 yrs.	500	1436	356	45	15	14	1.0	164	125	147	212	25	.248	.329	60	15	2B-326, 3B-106, SS-2

Don Gile

GILE, DONALD LOREN (Bear)   BR TR 6'6"   220 lbs.
B. Apr. 19, 1935, Modesto, Calif.

	G	AB	H	2B	3B	HR	HR%	R	RBI	BB	SO	SB	BA	SA	PH AB	PH H	G by POS
1959 BOS A	3	10	2	1	0	0	0.0	1	1	0	2	0	.200	.300	0	0	C-3
1960	29	51	9	1	1	1	2.0	6	4	1	13	0	.176	.294	5	0	C-15, 1B-11
1961	8	18	5	0	0	1	5.6	2	1	1	5	0	.278	.444	2	0	1B-6, C-1
1962	18	41	2	0	0	1	2.4	3	3	3	15	0	.049	.122	2	0	1B-14
4 yrs.	58	120	18	2	1	3	2.5	12	9	5	35	0	.150	.258	8	0	1B-31, C-19

Brian Giles

GILES, BRIAN JEFFREY   BR TR 6'1"   165 lbs.
B. Apr. 27, 1960, Manhattan, Kans.

	G	AB	H	2B	3B	HR	HR%	R	RBI	BB	SO	SB	BA	SA	PH AB	PH H	G by POS
1981 NY N	9	7	0	0	0	0	0.0	0	0	0	3	0	.000	.000	2	0	SS-2, 2B-2
1982	45	138	29	5	0	3	2.2	14	10	12	29	6	.210	.312	0	0	2B-45, SS-2
1983	145	400	98	15	0	2	0.5	39	27	36	77	17	.245	.298	5	0	2B-140, SS-12
3 yrs.	199	545	127	20	0	5	0.9	53	37	48	109	23	.233	.297	7	0	2B-187, SS-16

	G	AB	H	2B	3B	HR	HR %	R	RBI	BB	SO	SB	BA	SA	Pinch Hit AB	Pinch Hit H	G by POS

George Gilham
GILHAM, GEORGE LOUIS   BR TR 5'11" 164 lbs.
B. Sept. 17, 1899, Shamokin, Pa.   D. Apr. 25, 1937, Lansdowne, Pa.

	G	AB	H	2B	3B	HR	HR %	R	RBI	BB	SO	SB	BA	SA	PH AB	PH H	G by POS
1920 STL N	1	3	0	0	0	0	0.0	0	0	0	1	0	.000	.000	0	0	C-1
1921	1	1	0	0	0	0	0.0	0	0	0	0	0	.000	.000	1	0	
2 yrs.	2	4	0	0	0	0	0.0	0	0	0	1	0	.000	.000	1	0	C-1

Frank Gilhooley
GILHOOLEY, FRANK PATRICK (Flash)   BL TR 5'8" 155 lbs.
B. June 10, 1892, Toledo, Ohio   D. July 11, 1959, Toledo, Ohio

	G	AB	H	2B	3B	HR	HR %	R	RBI	BB	SO	SB	BA	SA	PH AB	PH H	G by POS
1911 STL N	1	0	0	0	0	0	–	0	0	0	0	0	–	–	0	0	OF-1
1912	13	49	11	0	0	0	0.0	5	2	3	8	0	.224	.224	1	0	OF-11
1913 NY A	24	85	29	2	1	0	0.0	10	14	4	9	6	.341	.388	0	0	OF-24
1914	1	3	2	0	0	0	0.0	0	0	0	0	0	.667	.667	0	0	OF-1
1915	1	4	0	0	0	0	0.0	0	0	0	1	0	.000	.000	0	0	OF-1
1916	58	223	62	5	3	1	0.4	40	10	37	17	16	.278	.341	1	1	OF-57
1917	54	165	40	6	1	0	0.0	14	8	30	13	6	.242	.291	2	1	OF-46
1918	112	427	118	13	5	1	0.2	59	23	53	24	7	.276	.337	1	0	OF-111
1919 BOS A	48	112	27	4	0	0	0.0	14	1	12	8	2	.241	.277	10	2	OF-33
9 yrs.	312	1068	289	30	10	2	0.2	142	58	140	80	37	.271	.323	15	4	OF-285

Bob Gilks
GILKS, ROBERT JAMES   BR TR 5'8" 178 lbs.
B. July 2, 1867, Cincinnati, Ohio   D. Aug. 20, 1944, Brunswick, Ga.

	G	AB	H	2B	3B	HR	HR %	R	RBI	BB	SO	SB	BA	SA	PH AB	PH H	G by POS
1887 CLE AA	22	83	26	2	0	0	0.0	12		3		5	.313	.337	0	0	P-13, 1B-6, OF-3, 2B-1
1888	119	484	111	14	4	1	0.2	59	63	7		16	.229	.281	0	0	OF-87, 3B-28, SS-4, P-4, 2B-1
1889 CLE N	53	210	50	5	2	0	0.0	17	18	7	20	6	.238	.281	0	0	OF-29, SS-13, 1B-10, 2B-1
1890	130	544	116	10	3	0	0.0	65	41	32	38	17	.213	.243	0	0	OF-123, P-4, SS-3, 2B-2
1893 BAL N	15	64	17	2	0	0	0.0	10	7	0	3	3	.266	.297	0	0	OF-15
5 yrs.	339	1385	320	33	9	1	0.1	163	128	49	61	47	.231	.270	0	0	OF-257, 3B-28, P-21, SS-20, 1B-16, 2B-5

Jim Gill
GILL, JAMES C.
B. St. Louis, Mo.   Deceased.

	G	AB	H	2B	3B	HR	HR %	R	RBI	BB	SO	SB	BA	SA	PH AB	PH H	G by POS
1889 STL AA	2	8	2	1	0	0	0.0	2	1	1	2	1	.250	.375	0	0	OF-1, 2B-1

Johnny Gill
GILL, JOHN WESLEY (Patcheye)   BL TR 6'2" 190 lbs.
B. Mar. 27, 1905, Nashville, Tenn.

	G	AB	H	2B	3B	HR	HR %	R	RBI	BB	SO	SB	BA	SA	PH AB	PH H	G by POS
1927 CLE A	21	60	13	3	0	1	1.7	8	4	7	13	1	.217	.317	2	2	OF-17
1928	2	2	0	0	0	0	0.0	0	0	0	1	0	.000	.000	2	0	
1931 WAS A	8	30	8	2	1	0	0.0	2	5	1	6	0	.267	.400	0	0	OF-8
1934	13	53	13	3	0	2	3.8	7	7	2	3	0	.245	.415	0	0	OF-13
1935 CHI N	3	3	1	1	0	0	0.0	2	1	0	1	0	.333	.667	3	1	
1936	71	174	44	8	0	7	4.0	20	28	13	19	0	.253	.420	25	6	OF-41
6 yrs.	118	322	79	17	1	10	3.1	39	45	23	43	1	.245	.398	32	9	OF-79

Warren Gill
GILL, WARREN DARST   TR 6'1"
B. Dec. 21, 1878, Ladoga, Ind.   D. Nov. 26, 1952, Laguna Beach, Calif.

	G	AB	H	2B	3B	HR	HR %	R	RBI	BB	SO	SB	BA	SA	PH AB	PH H	G by POS
1908 PIT N	27	76	17	0	1	0	0.0	10	14	11		3	.224	.250	1	1	1B-25

Sam Gillen
GILLEN, SAMUEL
Born Samuel Gilleland.
B. 1870, Pittsburgh, Pa.   D. May 13, 1905, Pittsburgh, Pa.

	G	AB	H	2B	3B	HR	HR %	R	RBI	BB	SO	SB	BA	SA	PH AB	PH H	G by POS
1893 PIT N	3	6	0	0	0	0	0.0	0		0	1	0	.000	.000	0	0	SS-3
1897 PHI N	75	270	70	10	3	0	0.0	32	27	35		2	.259	.319	0	0	SS-69, 3B-6
2 yrs.	78	276	70	10	3	0	0.0	32	27	35	1	2	.254	.312	0	0	SS-72, 3B-6

Tom Gillen
GILLEN, THOMAS J.
B. May 18, 1862, Philadelphia, Pa.   D. Jan. 26, 1889, Philadelphia, Pa.

	G	AB	H	2B	3B	HR	HR %	R	RBI	BB	SO	SB	BA	SA	PH AB	PH H	G by POS
1884 PHI U	29	116	18	2	0	0	0.0	5		1			.155	.172	0	0	C-27, OF-3
1886 DET N	2	10	4	0	0	0	0.0	2	4	0		1	.400	.400	0	0	C-2
2 yrs.	31	126	22	2	0	0	0.0	7		1			.175	.190	0	0	C-29, OF-3

Carden Gillenwater
GILLENWATER, CLARAL LEWIS   BR TR 6'1" 175 lbs.
B. May 13, 1918, Riceville, Tenn.   D. Feb. 26, 1978, Bradenton, Fla.

	G	AB	H	2B	3B	HR	HR %	R	RBI	BB	SO	SB	BA	SA	PH AB	PH H	G by POS
1940 STL N	7	25	4	1	0	0	0.0	1	5	0	2	0	.160	.200	0	0	OF-7
1943 BKN N	8	17	3	0	0	0	0.0	1	2	2	3	0	.176	.176	3	0	OF-5
1945 BOS N	144	517	149	20	2	7	1.4	74	72	73	70	13	.288	.375	3	1	OF-140
1946	99	224	51	10	1	1	0.4	30	14	39	27	3	.228	.295	14	2	OF-78
1948 WAS A	77	221	54	10	4	3	1.4	23	21	39	36	4	.244	.367	11	0	OF-67
5 yrs.	335	1004	261	41	7	11	1.1	129	114	153	138	20	.260	.348	31	3	OF-297

Jim Gillespie
GILLESPIE, JAMES WHEATFIELD   BL TR
B. Buffalo, N. Y.   D. Sept. 5, 1921, North Tonawanda, N. Y.

	G	AB	H	2B	3B	HR	HR %	R	RBI	BB	SO	SB	BA	SA	PH AB	PH H	G by POS
1890 BUF P	1	3	0	0	0	0	0.0	0		0	2	0	.000	.000	0	0	OF-1

Paul Gillespie
GILLESPIE, PAUL ALLEN   BL TR 6'2" 180 lbs.
B. Sept. 18, 1920, Sugar Valley, Ga.   D. Aug. 11, 1970, Anniston, Ala.

	G	AB	H	2B	3B	HR	HR %	R	RBI	BB	SO	SB	BA	SA	PH AB	PH H	G by POS
1942 CHI N	5	16	4	0	0	2	12.5	3	4	1	2	0	.250	.625	1	0	C-4
1944	9	26	7	1	0	1	3.8	2	2	3	3	0	.269	.423	2	0	C-7
1945	75	163	47	6	0	3	1.8	12	25	18	9	2	.288	.380	24	7	C-45, OF-1
3 yrs.	89	205	58	7	0	6	2.9	17	31	22	14	2	.283	.405	27	7	C-56, OF-1

WORLD SERIES

	G	AB	H	2B	3B	HR	HR %	R	RBI	BB	SO	SB	BA	SA	PH AB	PH H	G by POS
1945 CHI N	3	6	0	0	0	0	0.0	0	0	0	0	0	.000	.000	2	0	C-1

	G	AB	H	2B	3B	HR	HR %	R	RBI	BB	SO	SB	BA	SA	Pinch Hit AB	H	G by POS

Pete Gillespie

GILLESPIE, PATRICK PETER
B. Nov. 30, 1851, Carbondale, Pa.   D. May 5, 1910, Carbondale, Pa.   BL   6'1½"   178 lbs.

	G	AB	H	2B	3B	HR	HR %	R	RBI	BB	SO	SB	BA	SA	PH AB	H	G by POS
1880 TRO N	82	346	84	20	5	2	0.6	50		17	35		.243	.347	0	0	OF-82
1881	84	348	96	14	3	0	0.0	43	41	9	24		.276	.333	0	0	OF-84
1882	74	298	82	5	4	2	0.7	46	32	9	14		.275	.339	0	0	OF-74
1883 NY N	98	411	129	23	12	1	0.2	64		9	27		.314	.436	0	0	OF-98
1884	101	413	109	7	4	2	0.5	75		19	35		.264	.315	0	0	OF-101
1885	102	420	123	17	6	0	0.0	67		15	32		.293	.362	0	0	OF-102
1886	97	396	108	13	8	0	0.0	65	58	16	30		.273	.346	0	0	OF-97
1887	76	295	78	9	3	3	1.0	40	37	12	21	37	.264	.346	0	0	OF-76, 3B-1
8 yrs.	714	2927	809	108	45	10	0.3	450	167	106	218	37	.276	.354	0	0	OF-714, 3B-1

Jim Gilliam

GILLIAM, JAMES (Junior)
B. Oct. 17, 1928, Nashville, Tenn.   D. Oct. 8, 1978, Los Angeles, Calif.   BB   TR   5'10½"   175 lbs.

	G	AB	H	2B	3B	HR	HR %	R	RBI	BB	SO	SB	BA	SA	PH AB	H	G by POS
1953 BKN N	151	605	168	31	17	6	1.0	125	63	100	38	21	.278	.415	2	1	2B-149
1954	146	607	171	28	8	13	2.1	107	52	76	30	8	.282	.418	2	0	2B-143, OF-5
1955	147	538	134	20	8	7	1.3	110	40	70	37	15	.249	.355	3	2	2B-99, OF-46
1956	153	594	178	23	8	6	1.0	102	43	95	39	21	.300	.396	1	0	2B-102, OF-56
1957	149	617	154	26	4	2	0.3	89	37	64	31	26	.250	.314	0	0	2B-148, OF-2
1958 LA N	147	555	145	25	5	2	0.4	81	43	78	22	18	.261	.335	5	1	OF-75, 3B-44, 2B-32
1959	145	553	156	18	4	3	0.5	91	34	96	25	23	.282	.345	7	1	3B-132, 2B-8, OF-4
1960	151	557	138	20	2	5	0.9	96	40	96	28	12	.248	.318	2	1	3B-130, 2B-30
1961	144	439	107	26	3	4	0.9	74	32	79	34	8	.244	.344	11	3	3B-74, 2B-71, OF-11
1962	160	588	159	24	1	4	0.7	83	43	93	35	17	.270	.335	2	0	2B-113, 3B-90, OF-1
1963	148	525	148	27	4	6	1.1	77	49	60	28	19	.282	.383	9	1	2B-119, 3B-55
1964	116	334	76	8	3	2	0.6	44	27	42	21	4	.228	.287	13	3	3B-86, 2B-25, OF-2
1965	111	372	104	19	4	4	1.1	54	39	53	31	9	.280	.384	7	1	3B-80, OF-22, 2B-5
1966	88	235	51	9	0	1	0.4	30	16	34	17	2	.217	.268	22	3	3B-70, 2B-2, 1B-2
14 yrs.	1956	7119	1889	304	71	65	0.9	1163	558	1036	416	203	.265	.355	89	18	2B-1046, 3B-761, OF-224, 1B-2

WORLD SERIES

	G	AB	H	2B	3B	HR	HR %	R	RBI	BB	SO	SB	BA	SA	PH AB	H	G by POS
1953 BKN N	6	27	8	3	0	2	7.4	4	4	0	2	0	.296	.630	0	0	2B-6
1955	7	24	7	1	0	0	0.0	2	3	8	1	1	.292	.333	0	0	2B-5
1956	7	24	2	0	0	0	0.0	2	2	7	3	1	.083	.083	0	0	2B-6
1959 LA N	6	25	6	0	0	0	0.0	2	0	2	2	2	.240	.240	0	0	3B-6
1963	4	13	2	0	0	0	0.0	3	0	3	1	0	.154	.154	0	0	3B-4
1965	7	28	6	1	0	0	0.0	2	2	1	0	0	.214	.250	0	0	3B-7
1966	2	6	0	0	0	0	0.0	0	1	2	0	0	.000	.000	0	0	3B-2
7 yrs.	39	147	31	5	0	2	1.4	15	12	23	9	4	.211	.286	0	0	3B-19, 2B-17
								7th									

Barney Gilligan

GILLIGAN, ANDREW BERNARD
B. Jan. 3, 1857, Cambridge, Mass.   D. Apr. 1, 1934, Lynn, Mass.   BR   TR   5'6½"   130 lbs.

	G	AB	H	2B	3B	HR	HR %	R	RBI	BB	SO	SB	BA	SA	PH AB	H	G by POS
1879 CLE N	52	205	35	6	2	0	0.0	20	11	0	13		.171	.220	0	0	C-27, OF-23, SS-2
1880	30	99	17	4	3	1	1.0	9		6	12		.172	.303	0	0	C-23, OF-4, SS-4
1881 PRO N	46	183	40	7	2	0	0.0	19	20	9	24		.219	.279	0	0	C-36, SS-10, OF-1
1882	56	201	45	7	6	0	0.0	32		4	26		.224	.318	0	0	C-54, SS-2
1883	74	263	52	13	3	0	0.0	34		26	32		.198	.270	0	0	C-74
1884	82	294	72	13	2	1	0.3	47		35	41		.245	.313	0	0	C-81, 3B-1, 1B-1
1885	71	252	54	7	3	0	0.0	23	12	23	33		.214	.266	0	0	C-65, SS-5, OF-1, 2B-1
1886 WAS N	81	273	52	9	2	0	0.0	23	17	39	35		.190	.238	0	0	C-71, OF-14, SS-1, 3B-1
1887	28	90	18	2	0	1	1.1	7	6	5	18	2	.200	.256	0	0	C-26, SS-3, OF-1
1888 DET N	1	5	1	0	0	0	0.0	1	0	0	1	0	.200	.200	0	0	C-1
10 yrs.	521	1865	386	68	23	3	0.2	215	66	147	235	2	.207	.273	0	0	C-458, OF-44, SS-27, 3B-2, 2B-1, 1B-1

Grant Gillis

GILLIS, GRANT
B. Jan. 24, 1901, Grove Hill, Ala.   D. Feb. 4, 1981, Thomasville, Ala.   BR   TR   5'10"   165 lbs.

	G	AB	H	2B	3B	HR	HR %	R	RBI	BB	SO	SB	BA	SA	PH AB	H	G by POS
1927 WAS A	10	36	8	3	1	0	0.0	8	2	2	0	0	.222	.361	0	0	SS-10
1928	24	87	22	5	1	0	0.0	13	10	4	5	0	.253	.333	0	0	SS-16, 2B-5, 3B-3
1929 BOS A	28	73	18	4	0	0	0.0	5	11	6	8	0	.247	.301	1	0	2B-25
3 yrs.	62	196	48	12	2	0	0.0	26	23	12	13	0	.245	.327	1	0	2B-30, SS-26, 3B-3

Jim Gilman

GILMAN, JAMES
B. Unknown.

	G	AB	H	2B	3B	HR	HR %	R	RBI	BB	SO	SB	BA	SA	PH AB	H	G by POS
1893 CLE N	2	7	2	0	0	0	0.0	1	1	0	2	0	.286	.286	0	0	2B-2

Pit Gilman

GILMAN, PITKIN CLARK
B. Mar. 14, 1864, Laporte, Ohio   D. Aug. 17, 1950, Elyria, Ohio   BL   TL

	G	AB	H	2B	3B	HR	HR %	R	RBI	BB	SO	SB	BA	SA	PH AB	H	G by POS
1884 CLE N	2	10	1	0	0	0	0.0	0	0	0	3		.100	.100	0	0	OF-2

Ernie Gilmore

GILMORE, ERNEST GROVER
B. Nov. 1, 1888, Chicago, Ill.   D. Nov. 25, 1919, Sioux City, Iowa   BL   TL   5'9½"   170 lbs.

	G	AB	H	2B	3B	HR	HR %	R	RBI	BB	SO	SB	BA	SA	PH AB	H	G by POS
1914 KC F	139	530	152	25	5	1	0.2	91	32	37		23	.287	.358	7	2	OF-132
1915	119	411	117	22	15	1	0.2	53	47	26		19	.285	.418	0	0	OF-119
2 yrs.	258	941	269	47	20	2	0.2	144	79	63		42	.286	.385	7	2	OF-251

Tinsley Ginn

GINN, TINSLEY RUCKER
B. Sept. 26, 1891, Royston, Ga.   D. Aug. 30, 1931, Atlanta, Ga.

	G	AB	H	2B	3B	HR	HR %	R	RBI	BB	SO	SB	BA	SA	PH AB	H	G by POS
1914 CLE A	2	1	0	0	0	0	0.0	0	0	0	0	0	.000	.000	0	0	OF-2

Joe Ginsberg

GINSBERG, MYRON NATHAN
B. Oct. 11, 1926, New York, N.Y.   BL   TR   5'11"   180 lbs.

	G	AB	H	2B	3B	HR	HR %	R	RBI	BB	SO	SB	BA	SA	PH AB	H	G by POS
1948 DET A	11	36	13	0	0	0	0.0	7	1	3	1	0	.361	.361	0	0	C-11
1950	36	95	22	6	0	0	0.0	12	12	11	6	1	.232	.295	4	1	C-31
1951	102	304	79	10	2	8	2.6	44	37	43	21	0	.260	.385	8	2	C-95

	G	AB	H	2B	3B	HR	HR %	R	RBI	BB	SO	SB	BA	SA	Pinch Hit AB	Pinch Hit H	G by POS

Joe Ginsberg continued

	G	AB	H	2B	3B	HR	HR %	R	RBI	BB	SO	SB	BA	SA	AB	H	G by POS
1952	113	307	68	13	2	6	2.0	29	36	51	21	1	.221	.336	16	2	C-101
1953 2 teams	DET	A (18G – .302)			CLE	A (46G – .284)											
" total	64	162	47	6	0	0	0.0	16	13	24	5	0	.290	.327	12	2	C-54
1954 CLE A	3	2	1	0	0	0	0.0	0	1	0	0	0	.500	1.500	2	1	C-1
1956 2 teams	KC	A (71G – .246)			BAL	A (15G – .071)											
" total	86	223	50	8	1	1	0.4	15	14	25	21	1	.224	.283	18	3	C-65
1957 BAL A	85	175	48	8	2	1	0.6	15	18	18	19	2	.274	.360	18	3	C-66
1958	61	109	23	1	0	3	2.8	4	16	13	14	0	.211	.303	20	4	C-39
1959	65	166	30	2	1	1	0.6	14	14	21	3	1	.181	.211	5	1	C-62
1960 2 teams	BAL	A (14G – .267)			CHI	A (28G – .253)											
" total	42	105	27	5	0	0	0.0	11	15	16	9	1	.257	.305	2	0	C-39
1961 2 teams	CHI	A (6G – .000)			BOS	A (19G – .250)											
" total	25	27	6	0	0	0	0.0	1	5	1	4	0	.222	.222	16	3	C-8
1962 NY N	2	5	0	0	0	0	0.0	0	0	0	1	0	.000	.000	0	0	C-2
13 yrs.	695	1716	414	59	8	20	1.2	168	182	226	125	7	.241	.320	121	22	C-574

Al Gionfriddo

GIONFRIDDO, ALBERT FRANCIS
B. Mar. 8, 1922, Dysart, Pa.
BL TL 5'6"   165 lbs.

	G	AB	H	2B	3B	HR	HR %	R	RBI	BB	SO	SB	BA	SA	AB	H	G by POS
1944 PIT N	4	6	1	0	0	0	0.0	0	0	1	1	0	.167	.167	3	1	OF-1
1945	122	409	116	18	9	2	0.5	74	42	60	22	12	.284	.386	14	2	OF-106
1946	64	102	26	2	2	0	0.0	11	10	14	5	1	.255	.314	24	5	OF-33
1947 2 teams	PIT	N (1G – .000)			BKN	N (37G – .177)											
" total	38	63	11	2	1	0	0.0	10	6	16	11	2	.175	.238	13	2	OF-17
4 yrs.	228	580	154	22	12	2	0.3	95	58	91	39	15	.266	.355	54	10	OF-157
WORLD SERIES																	
1947 BKN N	4	3	0	0	0	0	0.0	2	0	1	0	1	.000	.000	1	0	OF-1

Tommy Giordano

GIORDANO, THOMAS ARTHUR (T-Bone)
B. Oct. 9, 1925, Newark, N. J.
BR TR 6'   175 lbs.

	G	AB	H	2B	3B	HR	HR %	R	RBI	BB	SO	SB	BA	SA	AB	H	G by POS
1953 PHI A	11	40	7	2	0	2	5.0	6	5	5	6	0	.175	.375	0	0	2B-11

Tony Giuliani

GIULIANI, ANGELO JOHN
B. Nov. 24, 1912, St. Paul, Minn.
BR TR 5'11"   175 lbs.

	G	AB	H	2B	3B	HR	HR %	R	RBI	BB	SO	SB	BA	SA	AB	H	G by POS
1936 STL A	71	198	43	3	0	0	0.0	17	13	11	13	0	.217	.232	8	1	C-66
1937	19	53	16	1	0	0	0.0	6	3	3	3	0	.302	.321	0	0	C-19
1938 WAS A	46	115	25	4	0	0	0.0	10	15	8	3	1	.217	.252	0	0	C-46
1939	54	172	43	6	2	0	0.0	20	18	4	7	0	.250	.308	3	1	C-50
1940 BKN N	1	1	0	0	0	0	0.0	0	0	0	0	0	.000	.000	0	0	C-1
1941	3	2	0	0	0	0	0.0	0	0	0	0	0	.000	.000	0	0	C-3
1943 WAS A	49	133	30	4	1	0	0.0	5	20	12	14	0	.226	.271	0	0	C-49
7 yrs.	243	674	157	18	3	0	0.0	58	69	38	40	1	.233	.269	11	2	C-234

Jim Gladd

GLADD, JAMES WALTER
B. Oct. 2, 1922, Fort Gibson, Okla.   D. Nov. 8, 1977, Long Beach, Calif.
BR TR 6'2"   190 lbs.

	G	AB	H	2B	3B	HR	HR %	R	RBI	BB	SO	SB	BA	SA	AB	H	G by POS
1946 NY N	4	11	1	0	0	0	0.0	0	1	1	4	0	.091	.091	0	0	C-4

Dan Gladden

GLADDEN, CLINTON DANIEL III
B. July 7, 1957, San Jose, Calif.
BB TR 5'11"   175 lbs.

	G	AB	H	2B	3B	HR	HR %	R	RBI	BB	SO	SB	BA	SA	AB	H	G by POS
1983 SF N	18	63	14	2	0	1	1.6	6	9	5	11	4	.222	.302	1	0	OF-18
1984	86	342	120	17	2	4	1.2	71	31	33	37	31	.351	.447	2	0	OF-85
2 yrs.	104	405	134	19	2	5	1.2	77	40	38	48	35	.331	.425	3	0	OF-103

Buck Gladman

GLADMAN, JOHN H.
B. 1864, Washington, D. C.   Deceased.

	G	AB	H	2B	3B	HR	HR %	R	RBI	BB	SO	SB	BA	SA	AB	H	G by POS
1883 PHI N	1	4	0	0	0	0	0.0	1		0	2		.000	.000	0	0	3B-1
1884 WAS AA	56	224	35	5	3	1	0.4	17		3			.156	.219	0	0	3B-53, OF-2, SS-1
1886 WAS N	44	152	21	5	3	1	0.7	17	15	12	30		.138	.230	0	0	3B-44
3 yrs.	101	380	56	10	6	2	0.5	35	14	15	32		.147	.221	0	0	3B-98, OF-2, SS-1

Roland Gladu

GLADU, ROLAND EDOUARD
B. May 10, 1913, Montreal, Que., Canada
BL TR 5'8½"   185 lbs.

	G	AB	H	2B	3B	HR	HR %	R	RBI	BB	SO	SB	BA	SA	AB	H	G by POS
1944 BOS N	21	66	16	2	1	1	1.5	5	7	3	8	0	.242	.348	2	0	3B-15, OF-3

Jack Glasscock

GLASSCOCK, JOHN WESLEY (Pebbly Jack)
B. July 22, 1859, Wheeling, W. Va.   D. Feb. 24, 1947, Wheeling, W. Va.
Manager 1889.
BR TR 5'8"   160 lbs.

	G	AB	H	2B	3B	HR	HR %	R	RBI	BB	SO	SB	BA	SA	AB	H	G by POS
1879 CLE N	80	325	68	9	3	0	0.0	31	29	6	24		.209	.255	0	0	2B-66, 3B-14
1880	77	296	72	13	3	0	0.0	37		2	21		.243	.307	0	0	SS-77
1881	85	335	86	9	5	0	0.0	49	33	15	8		.257	.313	0	0	SS-79, 2B-6
1882	84	358	104	27	4	1	1.1	66	46	13	9		.291	.450	0	0	SS-83, 3B-1
1883	96	383	110	19	6	0	0.0	67		13	23		.287	.368	0	0	SS-93, 2B-3
1884 2 teams	CLE	N (72G – .249)			CIN	U (38G – .419)											
" total	110	453	142	13	9	3	0.7	93	22	33	16		.313	.402	0	0	SS-105, 2B-5, P-2
1885 STL N	111	446	125	18	3	1	0.2	66	40	29	10		.280	.341	0	0	SS-110, 2B-1
1886	121	486	158	29	7	3	0.6	96	40	38	13		.325	.432	0	0	SS-120, OF-1
1887 IND N	122	483	142	18	7	0	0.0	91	40	41	8	62	.294	.360	0	0	SS-122, P-1
1888	113	442	119	17	3	1	0.2	63	45	14	17	48	.269	.328	0	0	SS-110, 2B-3, P-1
1889	134	582	205	40	3	7	1.2	128	85	31	10	57	.352	.467	0	0	SS-132, 2B-2, P-1
1890 NY N	124	512	172	32	9	1	0.2	91	66	41	8	54	.336	.439	0	0	SS-124
1891	97	369	89	12	6	0	0.0	46	55	36	11	29	.241	.306	0	0	SS-97
1892 STL N	139	566	151	27	5	3	0.5	83	72	44	19	26	.267	.348	0	0	SS-139
1893 2 teams	STL	N (48G – .287)			PIT	N (66G – .341)											
" total	114	488	156	15	12	2	0.4	81	100	42	7	36	.320	.412	0	0	SS-114
1894 PIT N	86	332	93	10	7	1	0.3	46	63	31	4	18	.280	.361	1	0	SS-85

	G	AB	H	2B	3B	HR	HR %	R	RBI	BB	SO	SB	BA	SA	Pinch Hit AB	Pinch Hit H	G by POS

Jack Glasscock continued

	G	AB	H	2B	3B	HR	HR %	R	RBI	BB	SO	SB	BA	SA	AB	H	G by POS
1895 2 teams	LOU	N	(18G –	.338)		WAS	N	(25G –	.230)								
" total	43	174	48	5	1	1	0.6	29	16	10	4	4	.276	.333	0	0	SS-38, 1B-5
17 yrs.	1736	7030	2040	313	98	27	0.4	1163	752	439	212	334	.290	.374	1	0	SS-1628, 2B-86, 3B-15, 1B-5, P-5, OF-1

Tommy Glaviano

GLAVIANO, THOMAS GIATANO (Rabbit) BR TR 5'9" 175 lbs.
B. Oct. 26, 1923, Sacramento, Calif.

	G	AB	H	2B	3B	HR	HR %	R	RBI	BB	SO	SB	BA	SA	AB	H	G by POS
1949 STL N	87	258	69	16	1	6	2.3	32	36	41	35	0	.267	.407	7	3	3B-73, 2B-7
1950	115	410	117	29	2	11	2.7	92	44	90	74	6	.285	.446	4	0	3B-106, 2B-5, SS-1
1951	54	104	19	4	0	1	1.0	20	4	26	18	3	.183	.250	23	4	OF-35, 2B-9
1952	80	162	39	5	1	3	1.9	30	19	27	26	0	.241	.340	10	2	3B-52, 2B-1
1953 PHI N	53	74	15	1	2	3	4.1	17	5	24	20	2	.203	.392	20	2	3B-14, 2B-12, SS-1
5 yrs.	389	1008	259	55	6	24	2.4	191	108	208	173	11	.257	.395	64	11	3B-245, OF-35, 2B-34, SS-2

Bill Gleason

GLEASON, WILLIAM G. (Will) BR TR 5'8" 170 lbs.
Brother of Jack Gleason.
B. Nov. 12, 1858, St. Louis, Mo.   D. July 21, 1932, St. Louis, Mo.

	G	AB	H	2B	3B	HR	HR %	R	RBI	BB	SO	SB	BA	SA	AB	H	G by POS
1882 STL AA	79	347	100	11	6	1	0.3	63		6			.288	.363	0	0	SS-79
1883	98	425	122	21	9	2	0.5	81		16			.287	.393	0	0	SS-98
1884	110	472	127	21	7	1	0.2	97		28			.269	.350	0	0	SS-110, 3B-1
1885	112	472	119	9	5	3	0.6	79		29			.252	.311	0	0	SS-112
1886	125	524	141	18	5	0	0.0	97		43			.269	.323	0	0	SS-125
1887	135	598	172	19	1	0	0.0	135		41		23	.288	.323	0	0	SS-135
1888 PHI AA	123	499	112	10	2	0	0.0	55	61	12		27	.224	.253	0	0	SS-121, 3B-1, 1B-1
1889 LOU AA	16	58	14	2	0	0	0.0	6	5	4	1	1	.241	.276	0	0	SS-16
8 yrs.	798	3395	907	111	35	7	0.2	613	65	179	1	51	.267	.327	0	0	SS-796, 3B-2, 1B-1

Bill Gleason

GLEASON, WILLIAM PATRICK BR TR 5'6½" 157 lbs.
B. Sept. 6, 1894, Chicago, Ill.   D. Jan. 9, 1957, Holyoke, Mass.

	G	AB	H	2B	3B	HR	HR %	R	RBI	BB	SO	SB	BA	SA	AB	H	G by POS
1916 PIT N	1	2	0	0	0	0	0.0	0	0	0	0	0	.000	.000	0	0	2B-1
1917	13	42	7	1	0	0	0.0	3		5	5	1	.167	.190	0	0	2B-13
1921 STL A	26	74	19	0	1	0	0.0	6	8	6	6	0	.257	.284	0	0	2B-25
3 yrs.	40	118	26	1	1	0	0.0	9	8	11	11	1	.220	.246	0	0	2B-39

Harry Gleason

GLEASON, HARRY GILBERT BR TR 5'6" 150 lbs.
Brother of Kid Gleason.
B. Mar. 28, 1875, Camden, N. J.   D. Oct. 21, 1961, Camden, N. J.

	G	AB	H	2B	3B	HR	HR %	R	RBI	BB	SO	SB	BA	SA	AB	H	G by POS
1901 BOS A	1	1	1	0	0	0	0.0	0	0	0		1	1.000	1.000	0	0	3B-1
1902	71	240	54	5	5	2	0.8	30	25	10		6	.225	.313	8	3	3B-35, OF-23, 2B-4
1903	6	13	2	1	0	0	0.0	3	2	0		0	.154	.231	4	0	3B-2
1904 STL A	46	155	33	7	1	0	0.0	10	6	4		1	.213	.271	1	0	SS-20, 3B-20, 2B-5, OF-1
1905	150	535	116	11	5	1	0.2	45	57	34		23	.217	.262	0	0	3B-144, 2B-6
5 yrs.	274	944	206	24	11	3	0.3	88	90	48		31	.218	.276	13	3	3B-202, OF-24, SS-20, 2B-15

Jack Gleason

GLEASON, JOHN DAY BR TR 170 lbs.
Brother of Bill Gleason.
B. July 14, 1854, St. Louis, Mo.   D. Sept. 4, 1944, St. Louis, Mo.

	G	AB	H	2B	3B	HR	HR %	R	RBI	BB	SO	SB	BA	SA	AB	H	G by POS
1877 STL N	1	4	1	0	0	0	0.0	0		0	1		.250	.250	0	0	OF-1
1882 STL AA	78	331	84	10	1	2	0.6	53		27			.254	.308	0	0	3B-73, OF-6, 2B-1
1883 2 teams	STL	AA	(9G –	.235)		LOU	AA	(84G –	.296)								
" total	93	389	113	11	4	2	0.5	71		29			.290	.355	0	0	3B-84, OF-9, SS-1
1884 STL U	92	395	128	30	2	3	0.8	90		23			.324	.433	0	0	3B-92
1885 STL N	2	7	1	0	0	0	0.0	0	0	0		1	.143	.143	0	0	3B-2
1886 PHI AA	77	299	56	8	7	1	0.3	39		16			.187	.271	0	0	3B-77
6 yrs.	343	1425	383	59	14	8	0.6	253		95	2		.269	.347	0	0	3B-328, OF-16, SS-1, 2B-1

Kid Gleason

GLEASON, WILLIAM J. BL TR 5'7" 158 lbs.
Brother of Harry Gleason.
B. Oct. 26, 1866, Camden, N. J.   D. Jan. 2, 1933, Philadelphia, Pa.
Manager 1919-23.

	G	AB	H	2B	3B	HR	HR %	R	RBI	BB	SO	SB	BA	SA	AB	H	G by POS
1888 PHI N	24	83	17	2	0	0	0.0	4	5	3	16	3	.205	.229	0	0	P-24, OF-1
1889	30	99	25	5	0	0	0.0	11	8	8	12	4	.253	.303	0	0	P-28, OF-3, 2B-2
1890	63	224	47	3	0	0	0.0	22	17	12	21	10	.210	.223	0	0	P-60, 2B-2
1891	65	214	53	5	2	0	0.0	31	17	20	17	6	.248	.290	0	0	P-53, OF-9, SS-4
1892 STL N	66	233	50	4	2	3	1.3	35	25	34	23	7	.215	.288	0	0	P-47, OF-11, 2B-10, 1B-1, C-1
1893	59	199	51	6	4	0	0.0	25	20	19	8	2	.256	.327	2	1	P-48, OF-11, SS-1
1894 2 teams	STL	N	(9G –	.250)		BAL	N	(26G –	.349)								
" total	35	114	37	5	2	0	0.0	25	18	9	3	1	.325	.404	4	2	P-29, 1B-2
1895 BAL N	112	421	130	14	12	0	0.0	90	74	33	18	19	.309	.399	3	0	2B-85, 3B-12, P-9, OF-4
1896 NY N	133	541	162	17	5	4	0.7	79	89	42	13	46	.299	.372	0	0	2B-130, 3B-3, OF-1
1897	131	540	172	16	4	1	0.2	85	106	26		43	.319	.369	0	0	2B-129, SS-3
1898	150	570	126	8	5	0	0.0	78	62	39		21	.221	.253	0	0	2B-144, SS-6
1899	146	576	152	14	4	0	0.0	72	59	24		29	.264	.302	0	0	2B-146
1900	111	420	104	11	3	1	0.2	60	29	17		23	.248	.295	0	0	2B-111, SS-1
1901 DET A	135	547	150	16	12	3	0.5	82	75	41		32	.274	.364	0	0	2B-135
1902	118	441	109	11	4	1	0.2	42	38	25		17	.247	.297	0	0	2B-118
1903 PHI N	106	412	117	19	6	1	0.2	65	49	23		12	.284	.367	0	0	2B-102, OF-4
1904	153	587	161	23	6	0	0.0	61	42	37		17	.274	.334	0	0	2B-152, 3B-1
1905	155	608	150	17	7	1	0.2	95	50	45		16	.247	.303	0	0	2B-155
1906	135	494	112	17	2	0	0.0	47	34	36		17	.227	.269	0	0	2B-135
1907	36	126	18	3	0	0	0.0	11	6	7		3	.143	.167	1	0	2B-26, SS-4, 1B-4, OF-1
1908	2	1	0	0	0	0	0.0	0	0	0		0	.000	.000	0	0	OF-1, 2B-1

	G	AB	H	2B	3B	HR	HR %	R	RBI	BB	SO	SB	BA	SA	Pinch Hit AB	Pinch Hit H	G by POS

Kid Gleason continued

	G	AB	H	2B	3B	HR	HR %	R	RBI	BB	SO	SB	BA	SA	AB	H	G by POS
1912 CHI A	1	2	1	0	0	0	0.0	0	0	0		0	.500	.500	0	0	2B-1
22 yrs.	1966	7452	1944	216	80	15	0.2	1020	823	500	131	328	.261	.317	10	3	2B-1584, P-298, OF-46, SS-19, 3B-16, 1B-7, C-1

Roy Gleason

GLEASON, ROY WILLIAM   BB TR 6'5½" 220 lbs.
B. Apr. 9, 1943, Melrose Park, Ill.

	G	AB	H	2B	3B	HR	HR %	R	RBI	BB	SO	SB	BA	SA	AB	H	G by POS
1963 LA N	8	1	1	1	0	0	0.0	3	0	0	0	0	1.000	2.000	1	1	

Jim Gleeson

GLEESON, JAMES JOSEPH (Gee Gee)   BB TR 6'1" 191 lbs.
B. Mar. 5, 1912, Kansas City, Mo.

	G	AB	H	2B	3B	HR	HR %	R	RBI	BB	SO	SB	BA	SA	AB	H	G by POS
1936 CLE A	41	139	36	9	2	4	2.9	26	12	18	17	2	.259	.439	7	0	OF-33
1939 CHI N	111	332	74	19	6	4	1.2	43	45	39	46	7	.223	.352	17	4	OF-91
1940	129	485	152	39	11	5	1.0	76	61	54	52	4	.313	.470	5	1	OF-123
1941 CIN N	102	301	70	10	0	3	1.0	47	34	45	30	7	.233	.296	14	3	OF-84
1942	9	20	4	0	0	0	0.0	3	2	2	2	0	.200	.200	3	0	OF-5
5 yrs.	392	1277	336	77	19	16	1.3	195	154	158	147	20	.263	.391	46	8	OF-336

Frank Gleich

GLEICH, FRANK ELMER (Inch)   BL TR 5'11" 175 lbs.
B. Mar. 7, 1894, Columbus, Ohio   D. Mar. 27, 1949, Columbus, Ohio

	G	AB	H	2B	3B	HR	HR %	R	RBI	BB	SO	SB	BA	SA	AB	H	G by POS
1919 NY A	5	4	1	0	0	0	0.0	0	1	1	0	0	.250	.250	0	0	OF-4
1920	24	41	5	0	0	0	0.0	6	3	6	10	0	.122	.122	9	1	OF-15
2 yrs.	29	45	6	0	0	0	0.0	6	4	7	10	0	.133	.133	9	1	OF-19

Bob Glenalvin

GLENALVIN, ROBERT J.   TR
Born Rodney J. Dowling.
B. Apr. 7, 1874, Kalamazoo, Mich.   D. Mar. 24, 1944, Detroit, Mich.

	G	AB	H	2B	3B	HR	HR %	R	RBI	BB	SO	SB	BA	SA	AB	H	G by POS
1890 CHI N	66	250	67	10	3	4	1.6	43	26	19	31	30	.268	.380	0	0	2B-66
1893	16	61	21	3	1	0	0.0	11	12	7	3	7	.344	.426	0	0	2B-16
2 yrs.	82	311	88	13	4	4	1.3	54	38	26	34	37	.283	.389	0	0	2B-82

Ed Glenn

GLENN, EDWARD C.   TR 5'10" 160 lbs.
B. Sept. 19, 1860, Richmond, Va.   D. Feb. 10, 1892, Richmond, Va.

	G	AB	H	2B	3B	HR	HR %	R	RBI	BB	SO	SB	BA	SA	AB	H	G by POS
1884 RIC AA	43	175	43	2	4	1	0.6	26		5			.246	.320	0	0	OF-43
1886 PIT AA	71	277	53	6	5	0	0.0	32		17			.191	.249	0	0	OF-71
1888 2 teams		KC	AA (3G – .000)					BOS	N (20G – .154)								
" total	23	73	10	0	2	0	0.0	8	3	2	8	1	.137	.192	0	0	OF-22, 3B-1
3 yrs.	137	525	106	8	11	1	0.2	66	2	24	8	1	.202	.265	0	0	OF-136, 3B-1

Ed Glenn

GLENN, EDWARD D.
B. 1876, Ludlow, Ky.   D. Dec. 7, 1911, Ludlow, Ky.

	G	AB	H	2B	3B	HR	HR %	R	RBI	BB	SO	SB	BA	SA	AB	H	G by POS
1898 2 teams		WAS	N (1G – .000)					NY	N (2G – .250)								
" total	3	8	1	0	0	0	0.0	1	0	3		1	.125	.125	0	0	SS-3
1902 CHI N	2	7	0	0	0	0	0.0	0	0	1		0	.000	.000	0	0	SS-2
2 yrs.	5	15	1	0	0	0	0.0	1	0	4		1	.067	.067	0	0	SS-5

Harry Glenn

GLENN, HARRY MELVILLE   BL TR 6'1" 200 lbs.
B. June 9, 1890, Shelburn, Ind.   D. Oct. 12, 1918, St. Paul, Minn.

	G	AB	H	2B	3B	HR	HR %	R	RBI	BB	SO	SB	BA	SA	AB	H	G by POS
1915 STL N	6	16	5	0	0	0	0.0	1	1	3	0	0	.313	.313	1	0	C-5

Joe Glenn

GLENN, JOSEPH CHARLES (Gabber)   BR TR 5'11" 175 lbs.
Born Joseph Charles Gurzensky.
B. Nov. 19, 1908, Dickson City, Pa.

	G	AB	H	2B	3B	HR	HR %	R	RBI	BB	SO	SB	BA	SA	AB	H	G by POS
1932 NY A	6	16	2	0	0	0	0.0	0	0	1	5	0	.125	.125	1	0	C-5
1933	5	21	3	0	0	0	0.0	1	1	0	3	0	.143	.143	0	0	C-5
1935	17	43	10	4	0	0	0.0	7	6	4	1	0	.233	.326	1	0	C-16
1936	44	129	35	7	0	1	0.8	21	20	20	10	1	.271	.349	0	0	C-44
1937	25	53	15	2	2	0	0.0	6	4	10	11	0	.283	.396	1	0	C-24
1938	41	123	32	7	2	0	0.0	9	25	10	14	1	.260	.350	1	0	C-40
1939 STL A	88	286	78	13	1	4	1.4	29	29	31	40	4	.273	.367	4	3	C-82
1940 BOS A	22	47	6	1	0	0	0.0	3	4	5	7	0	.128	.149	4	1	C-19
8 yrs.	248	718	181	34	5	5	0.7	76	89	81	91	6	.252	.334	12	4	C-235

John Glenn

GLENN, JOHN   BR TR 6'3" 180 lbs.
B. July 10, 1928, Moultrie, Ga.

	G	AB	H	2B	3B	HR	HR %	R	RBI	BB	SO	SB	BA	SA	AB	H	G by POS
1960 STL N	32	31	8	0	1	0	0.0	4	5	0	9	0	.258	.323	3	0	OF-28

John Glenn

GLENN, JOHN W.   BR TR 5'8½" 169 lbs.
B. 1849, Rochester, N. Y.   D. Nov. 10, 1888, Glens Falls, N. Y.

	G	AB	H	2B	3B	HR	HR %	R	RBI	BB	SO	SB	BA	SA	AB	H	G by POS
1876 CHI N	66	276	84	9	2	0	0.0	55	32	12	6		.304	.351	0	0	OF-56, 1B-15
1877	50	202	46	6	1	0	0.0	31	20	8	16		.228	.267	0	0	OF-36, 1B-14
2 yrs.	116	478	130	15	3	0	0.0	86	52	20	22		.272	.316	0	0	OF-92, 1B-29

Norm Glockson

GLOCKSON, NORMAN STANLEY   BR TR 6'2" 200 lbs.
B. June 15, 1894, Blue Island, Ill.   D. Aug. 5, 1955, Maywood, Ill.

	G	AB	H	2B	3B	HR	HR %	R	RBI	BB	SO	SB	BA	SA	AB	H	G by POS
1914 CIN N	7	12	0	0	0	0	0.0	0	0	1	6	0	.000	.000	0	0	C-7

Al Glossop

GLOSSOP, ALBAN   BB TR 6' 170 lbs.
B. July 23, 1912, Christopher, Ill.

	G	AB	H	2B	3B	HR	HR %	R	RBI	BB	SO	SB	BA	SA	AB	H	G by POS
1939 NY N	10	32	6	0	0	1	3.1	3	3	4	2	0	.188	.281	0	0	2B-10
1940 2 teams		NY	N (27G – .209)					BOS	N (60G – .236)								
" total	87	239	54	5	1	7	2.9	33	22	27	38	2	.226	.343	25	5	2B-42, 3B-18, SS-10
1942 PHI N	121	454	102	15	1	4	0.9	33	40	29	35	3	.225	.289	3	1	2B-118, 3B-1
1943 BKN N	87	217	37	9	0	3	1.4	28	21	28	27	0	.171	.253	11	0	SS-33, 2B-24, 3B-17

	G	AB	H	2B	3B	HR	HR %	R	RBI	BB	SO	SB	BA	SA	Pinch Hit AB	Pinch Hit H	G by POS

Al Glossop continued

	G	AB	H	2B	3B	HR	HR%	R	RBI	BB	SO	SB	BA	SA	AB	H	G by POS
1946 CHI N	4	10	0	0	0	0	0.0	2	0	1	3	0	.000	.000	0	0	SS-2, 2B-2
5 yrs.	309	952	199	29	2	15	1.6	99	86	89	105	5	.209	.291	39	6	2B-196, SS-45, 3B-36

Bill Glynn

GLYNN, WILLIAM VINCENT
B. Jan. 30, 1925, Sussex, N. J. BL TL 6' 190 lbs.

	G	AB	H	2B	3B	HR	HR%	R	RBI	BB	SO	SB	BA	SA	AB	H	G by POS
1949 PHI N	8	10	2	0	0	0	0.0	0	1	0	3	0	.200	.200	6	2	1B-1
1952 CLE A	44	92	25	5	0	2	2.2	15	7	5	16	1	.272	.391	14	3	1B-32
1953	147	411	100	14	2	3	0.7	60	30	44	65	1	.243	.309	10	3	1B-135, OF-2
1954	111	171	43	3	2	5	2.9	19	18	12	21	3	.251	.380	17	2	1B-96, OF-1
4 yrs.	310	684	170	22	4	10	1.5	94	56	61	105	5	.249	.336	47	10	1B-264, OF-3

WORLD SERIES

	G	AB	H	2B	3B	HR	HR%	R	RBI	BB	SO	SB	BA	SA	AB	H	G by POS
1954 CLE A	2	2	1	1	0	0	0.0	1	0	0	1	0	.500	1.000	2	1	1B-1

John Gochnaur

GOCHNAUR, JOHN PETER
B. Sept. 12, 1875, Altoona, Pa.   D. Sept. 27, 1929, Altoona, Pa. BR TR 5'9" 160 lbs.

	G	AB	H	2B	3B	HR	HR%	R	RBI	BB	SO	SB	BA	SA	AB	H	G by POS
1901 BKN N	3	11	4	0	0	0	0.0	1	2	1		1	.364	.364	0	0	SS-3
1902 CLE A	127	459	85	16	4	0	0.0	45	37	38		7	.185	.237	0	0	SS-127
1903	134	438	81	16	4	0	0.0	48	48	48		10	.185	.240	0	0	SS-134
3 yrs.	264	908	170	32	8	0	0.0	94	87	87		18	.187	.240	0	0	SS-264

John Godar

GODAR, JOHN MICHAEL
B. Oct. 25, 1864, Cincinnati, Ohio   D. June 23, 1949, Park Ridge, Ill. BR TR 5'9" 170 lbs.

	G	AB	H	2B	3B	HR	HR%	R	RBI	BB	SO	SB	BA	SA	AB	H	G by POS
1892 BAL N	5	14	3	0	0	0	0.0	2	1	2	1	1	.214	.214	0	0	OF-5

Danny Godby

GODBY, DANNY RAY
B. Nov. 4, 1946, Logan, W. Va. BR TR 6' 185 lbs.

	G	AB	H	2B	3B	HR	HR%	R	RBI	BB	SO	SB	BA	SA	AB	H	G by POS
1974 STL N	13	13	2	0	0	0	0.0	2	1	3	4	0	.154	.154	6	1	OF-4

Joe Goddard

GODDARD, JOSEPH HAROLD
B. July 23, 1950, Beckley, W. Va. BR TR 5'11" 181 lbs.

	G	AB	H	2B	3B	HR	HR%	R	RBI	BB	SO	SB	BA	SA	AB	H	G by POS
1972 SD N	12	35	7	2	0	0	0.0	2	5	9		0	.200	.257	0	0	C-12

John Godwin

GODWIN, JOHN HENRY
B. Mar. 10, 1877, East Liverpool, Ohio   D. May 5, 1956, East Liverpool, Ohio TR

	G	AB	H	2B	3B	HR	HR%	R	RBI	BB	SO	SB	BA	SA	AB	H	G by POS
1905 BOS A	13	37	13	1	0	0	0.0	4	10	3		3	.351	.378	3	0	OF-6, 2B-5
1906	66	193	36	2	1	0	0.0	11	15	6		6	.187	.207	9	2	3B-27, SS-14, OF-10, 2B-3, 1B-1
2 yrs.	79	230	49	3	1	0	0.0	15	25	9		9	.213	.235	12	2	3B-27, OF-16, SS-14, 2B-8, 1B-1

Ed Goebel

GOEBEL, EDWIN
B. Sept. 1, 1899, Brooklyn, N. Y.   D. Aug. 12, 1959, Brooklyn, N. Y. BR TR 5'11" 170 lbs.

	G	AB	H	2B	3B	HR	HR%	R	RBI	BB	SO	SB	BA	SA	AB	H	G by POS
1922 WAS A	37	59	16	1	0	1	1.7	13	3	8	16	1	.271	.339	13	1	OF-17

Bill Goeckel

GOECKEL, WILLIAM JOHN
B. Sept. 3, 1871, Wilkes-Barre, Pa.   D. Nov. 1, 1922, Philadelphia, Pa. BL TL

	G	AB	H	2B	3B	HR	HR%	R	RBI	BB	SO	SB	BA	SA	AB	H	G by POS
1899 PHI N	37	141	37	3	1	0	0.0	17	16	1		6	.262	.298	1	0	1B-36

Chuck Goggin

GOGGIN, CHARLES FRANCIS III
B. July 7, 1945, Tampa, Fla. BB TR 5'11" 175 lbs.

	G	AB	H	2B	3B	HR	HR%	R	RBI	BB	SO	SB	BA	SA	AB	H	G by POS
1972 PIT N	5	7	2	0	0	0	0.0	0	0	1	1	0	.286	.286	3	0	2B-1
1973 2 teams		PIT N (1G – 1.000)						ATL N (64G – .289)									
" total	65	91	27	5	0	0	0.0	19	7	9	19	0	.297	.352	29	8	2B-19, OF-6, SS-5, C-2
1974 BOS A	2	1	0	0	0	0	0.0	0	0	0	1	0	.000	.000	0	0	2B-2
3 yrs.	72	99	29	5	0	0	0.0	19	7	10	21	0	.293	.343	32	8	2B-22, OF-6, SS-5, C-2

Mike Golden

GOLDEN, MICHAEL HENRY
B. Sept. 11, 1851, Shirley, Mass.   D. Jan. 11, 1929, Rockford, Ill. BR TR 5'7" 166 lbs.

	G	AB	H	2B	3B	HR	HR%	R	RBI	BB	SO	SB	BA	SA	AB	H	G by POS
1878 MIL N	55	214	44	6	3	0	0.0	16	20	3	35		.206	.262	0	0	OF-39, P-22, 1B-1

Jonah Goldman

GOLDMAN, JONAH JOHN
B. Aug. 29, 1906, New York, N. Y.   D. Aug. 17, 1980, Palm Beach, Fla. BR TR 5'7" 170 lbs.

	G	AB	H	2B	3B	HR	HR%	R	RBI	BB	SO	SB	BA	SA	AB	H	G by POS
1928 CLE A	7	21	5	1	0	0	0.0	1	2	3	0	0	.238	.286	0	0	SS-7
1930	111	306	74	18	0	1	0.3	32	44	28	25	3	.242	.310	0	0	SS-93, 3B-20
1931	30	62	8	1	0	0	0.0	0	3	4	6	1	.129	.145	0	0	SS-30
3 yrs.	148	389	87	20	0	1	0.3	33	49	35	31	4	.224	.283	0	0	SS-130, 3B-20

Gordon Goldsberry

GOLDSBERRY, GORDON FREDERICK
B. Aug. 30, 1927, Sacramento, Calif. BL TL 6' 170 lbs.

	G	AB	H	2B	3B	HR	HR%	R	RBI	BB	SO	SB	BA	SA	AB	H	G by POS
1949 CHI A	39	145	36	3	2	1	0.7	25	13	18	9	2	.248	.317	1	0	1B-38
1950	82	127	34	8	2	2	1.6	19	25	26	18	0	.268	.409	39	12	1B-40, OF-3
1951	10	11	1	0	0	0	0.0	4	1	2	2	0	.091	.091	2	0	1B-8
1952 STL A	86	227	52	9	3	3	1.3	30	17	34	37	0	.229	.335	10	2	1B-72, OF-2
4 yrs.	217	510	123	20	7	6	1.2	78	56	80	66	2	.241	.343	52	14	1B-158, OF-5

Walt Goldsby

GOLDSBY, WALTON HUGH
B. Jan. 1, 1862, Evansville, Ind.   D. Jan. 11, 1914, Dallas, Tex. BL

	G	AB	H	2B	3B	HR	HR%	R	RBI	BB	SO	SB	BA	SA	AB	H	G by POS
1884 3 teams	STL AA (5G – .200)			WAS AA (6G – .375)			RIC AA (11G – .225)										
" total	22	84	22	1	0	0	0.0	10		2			.262	.274	0	0	OF-22
1886 WAS N	6	18	4	0	0	0	0.0	0	1	2	3		.222	.278	0	0	OF-6
1888 BAL AA	45	165	39	1	1	0	0.0	13	14	8		17	.236	.255	0	0	OF-45
3 yrs.	73	267	65	3	1	0	0.0	23	14	12	3	17	.243	.262	0	0	OF-73

	G	AB	H	2B	3B	HR	HR %	R	RBI	BB	SO	SB	BA	SA	Pinch Hit AB	Pinch Hit H	G by POS

Fred Goldsmith

GOLDSMITH, FRED ERNEST
B. May 15, 1852, New Haven, Conn.   D. Mar. 28, 1939, Berkley, Mich.
BR TR 6'1" 195 lbs.

	G	AB	H	2B	3B	HR	HR %	R	RBI	BB	SO	SB	BA	SA	AB	H	G by POS
1879 TRO N	9	38	9	1	0	0	0.0	6	2	1	3		.237	.263	0	0	P-8, OF-2, 1B-1
1880 CHI N	35	142	37	4	2	0	0.0	24	15	2	15		.261	.317	0	0	P-26, OF-10, 1B-4
1881	42	158	38	3	4	0	0.0	24	16	6	17		.241	.310	0	0	P-39, OF-3
1882	45	183	42	11	1	0	0.0	23	19	4	29		.230	.301	0	0	P-45, 1B-1
1883	60	235	52	12	3	1	0.4	38		4	35		.221	.311	0	0	P-46, OF-16, 1B-2
1884 2 teams		CHI	N (22G – .136)		BAL	AA (4G – .143)											
" total	26	95	13	2	0	2	2.1	13		9	26		.137	.221	0	0	P-25, OF-2, 1B-1
6 yrs.	217	851	191	33	10	3	0.4	128	52	26	125		.224	.297	0	0	P-189, OF-33, 1B-9

Lonnie Goldstein

GOLDSTEIN, LESLIE ELMER
B. May 13, 1918, Austin, Tex.
BL TL 6'2½" 190 lbs.

	G	AB	H	2B	3B	HR	HR %	R	RBI	BB	SO	SB	BA	SA	AB	H	G by POS
1943 CIN N	5	5	1	0	0	0	0.0	1	0	2	1	0	.200	.200	3	1	1B-2
1946	6	5	0	0	0	0	0.0	1	0	1	1	0	.000	.000	5	0	
2 yrs.	11	10	1	0	0	0	0.0	2	0	3	2	0	.100	.100	8	1	1B-2

Purnal Goldy

GOLDY, PURNAL WILLIAM
B. Nov. 28, 1937, Camden, N. J.
BR TR 6'5" 200 lbs.

	G	AB	H	2B	3B	HR	HR %	R	RBI	BB	SO	SB	BA	SA	AB	H	G by POS
1962 DET A	20	70	16	1	1	3	4.3	8	12	0	12	0	.229	.400	3	1	OF-15
1963	9	8	2	0	0	0	0.0	1	0	0	4	0	.250	.250	8	2	
2 yrs.	29	78	18	1	1	3	3.8	9	12	0	16	0	.231	.385	11	3	OF-15

Stan Goletz

GOLETZ, STANLEY (Stash)
B. May 21, 1918, Crescent, Ohio
BL TL 6'3" 200 lbs.

	G	AB	H	2B	3B	HR	HR %	R	RBI	BB	SO	SB	BA	SA	AB	H	G by POS
1941 CHI A	5	5	3	0	0	0	0.0	0	0	0	2	0	.600	.600	5	3	

Mike Goliat

GOLIAT, MIKE MITCHELL
B. Nov. 3, 1919, Yatesboro, Pa.
BR TR 6' 180 lbs.

	G	AB	H	2B	3B	HR	HR %	R	RBI	BB	SO	SB	BA	SA	AB	H	G by POS
1949 PHI N	55	189	40	6	3	3	1.6	24	19	20	32	0	.212	.323	0	0	2B-50, 1B-5
1950	145	483	113	13	6	13	2.7	49	64	53	75	3	.234	.366	5	0	2B-139
1951 2 teams		PHI	N (41G – .225)		STL	A (5G – .182)											
" total	46	149	33	2	1	4	2.7	14	16	9	19	0	.221	.329	4	0	2B-39, 3B-2
1952 STL A	3	4	0	0	0	0	0.0	0	0	1	1	0	.000	.000	1	0	2B-3
4 yrs.	249	825	186	21	10	20	2.4	87	99	83	127	3	.225	.348	10	0	2B-231, 1B-5, 3B-2
WORLD SERIES																	
1950 PHI N	4	14	3	0	0	0	0.0	1	1	1	2	0	.214	.214	0	0	2B-4

Walt Golvin

GOLVIN, WALTER GEORGE
B. Feb. 1, 1894, Hershey, Neb.   D. June 11, 1973, Gardinia, Calif.
BL TL 6' 165 lbs.

	G	AB	H	2B	3B	HR	HR %	R	RBI	BB	SO	SB	BA	SA	AB	H	G by POS
1922 CHI N	2	2	0	0	0	0	0.0	0	1	0	1	0	.000	.000	0	0	1B-2

Chile Gomez

GOMEZ, JOSE LUIS RODRIGUEZ
B. May 23, 1909, Villaunion, Mexico
BR TR 5'10" 165 lbs.

	G	AB	H	2B	3B	HR	HR %	R	RBI	BB	SO	SB	BA	SA	AB	H	G by POS
1935 PHI N	67	222	51	3	0	0	0.0	24	16	17	34	2	.230	.243	0	0	SS-36, 2B-32
1936	108	332	77	4	1	0	0.0	24	28	14	32	0	.232	.250	0	0	2B-71, SS-40
1942 WAS A	25	73	14	2	2	0	0.0	8	6	9	7	1	.192	.274	1	0	2B-23, 3B-1
3 yrs.	200	627	142	9	3	0	0.0	56	50	40	73	3	.226	.250	1	0	2B-126, SS-76, 3B-1

Luis Gomez

GOMEZ, JOSE LUIS
Born Jose Luis Gomez Sanchez.
B. Aug. 19, 1951, Los Angeles, Calif.
BR TR 5'9" 150 lbs.

	G	AB	H	2B	3B	HR	HR %	R	RBI	BB	SO	SB	BA	SA	AB	H	G by POS
1974 MIN A	82	168	35	1	0	0	0.0	18	3	12	16	2	.208	.214	0	0	SS-74, 2B-2, DH-1
1975	89	72	10	0	0	0	0.0	7	5	4	12	0	.139	.139	0	0	SS-70, DH-7, 2B-6
1976	38	57	11	1	0	0	0.0	5	3	3	3	1	.193	.211	0	0	SS-24, 2B-8, 3B-4, DH-1, OF-1
1977	32	65	16	4	2	0	0.0	6	11	4	9	0	.246	.369	4	0	2B-19, SS-7, 3B-4, DH-2, OF-1
1978 TOR A	153	413	92	7	3	0	0.0	39	32	34	41	2	.223	.254	0	0	SS-153
1979	59	163	39	7	0	0	0.0	11	11	6	17	1	.239	.282	0	0	3B-22, 2B-20, SS-15
1980 ATL N	121	278	53	6	0	0	0.0	18	24	17	27	0	.191	.212	0	0	SS-119
1981	35	35	7	0	0	0	0.0	4	1	6	4	0	.200	.200	2	0	SS-21, 3B-9, 2B-3, P-1
8 yrs.	609	1251	263	26	5	0	0.0	108	90	86	129	6	.210	.239	6	0	SS-483, 2B-58, 3B-39, DH-11, OF-2, P-1

Preston Gomez

GOMEZ, PEDRO MARTINEZ
B. Apr. 20, 1923, Central Preston, Cuba
Manager 1969-72, 1974-75, 1980.
BR TR 5'11" 170 lbs.

	G	AB	H	2B	3B	HR	HR %	R	RBI	BB	SO	SB	BA	SA	AB	H	G by POS
1944 WAS A	8	7	2	1	0	0	0.0	2	2	0	4	0	.286	.429	0	0	SS-2, 2B-2

Randy Gomez

GOMEZ, RANDALL SCOTT
B. Feb. 4, 1958, San Mateo, Calif.
BR TR 5'9" 180 lbs.

	G	AB	H	2B	3B	HR	HR %	R	RBI	BB	SO	SB	BA	SA	AB	H	G by POS
1984 SF N	14	30	5	1	0	0	0.0	0	0	8	3	0	.167	.200	0	0	C-14

Jesse Gonder

GONDER, JESSE LEMAR
B. Jan. 20, 1936, Monticello, Ark.
BL TR 5'10" 180 lbs.

	G	AB	H	2B	3B	HR	HR %	R	RBI	BB	SO	SB	BA	SA	AB	H	G by POS
1960 NY A	7	7	2	0	0	1	14.3	1	3	1	1	0	.286	.714	5	1	C-1
1961	15	12	4	1	0	0	0.0	2	3	3	1	0	.333	.417	12	4	
1962 CIN N	4	4	0	0	0	0	0.0	0	0	0	3	0	.000	.000	4	0	
1963 2 teams		CIN	N (31G – .313)		NY	N (42G – .302)											
" total	73	158	48	6	0	6	3.8	17	20	7	37	1	.304	.456	34	10	C-38
1964 NY N	131	341	92	11	1	7	2.1	28	35	29	65	0	.270	.370	43	8	C-97
1965 2 teams		NY	N (53G – .238)		MIL	N (31G – .151)											
" total	84	158	33	6	0	5	3.2	8	14	15	29	0	.209	.342	52	13	C-44
1966 PIT N	59	160	36	3	1	7	4.4	13	16	12	39	0	.225	.388	12	2	C-52
1967	22	36	5	1	0	0	0.0	4	3	5	9	0	.139	.167	5	1	C-18
8 yrs.	395	876	220	28	2	26	3.0	73	94	72	184	1	.251	.377	167	39	C-250

	G	AB	H	2B	3B	HR	HR %	R	RBI	BB	SO	SB	BA	SA	Pinch Hit AB	Pinch Hit H	G by POS

Dan Gonzalez

GONZALEZ, DANIEL DAVID
B. Sept. 30, 1953, Whittier, Calif.   BL TR 6'1" 195 lbs.

	G	AB	H	2B	3B	HR	HR %	R	RBI	BB	SO	SB	BA	SA	AB	H	G by POS
1979 DET A	7	18	4	1	0	0	0.0	1	2	0	2	1	.222	.278	3	0	OF-3, DH-1
1980	2	7	1	0	0	0	0.0	1	0	0	1	0	.143	.143	1	0	DH-1, OF-1
2 yrs.	9	25	5	1	0	0	0.0	2	2	0	3	1	.200	.240	4	0	OF-4, DH-2

Denny Gonzalez

GONZALEZ, DENIO MARIANO
B. July 20, 1963, Grande Boya, Dominican Republic   BR TR 5'11" 165 lbs.

	G	AB	H	2B	3B	HR	HR %	R	RBI	BB	SO	SB	BA	SA	AB	H	G by POS
1984 PIT N	26	82	15	3	1	0	0.0	9	4	7	21	1	.183	.244	0	0	3B-11, SS-10, OF-3

Eusebio Gonzalez

GONZALEZ, EUSEBIO MIGUEL
B. July 13, 1892, Havana, Cuba   D. Feb. 14, 1976, Havana, Cuba   BR TR

	G	AB	H	2B	3B	HR	HR %	R	RBI	BB	SO	SB	BA	SA	AB	H	G by POS
1918 BOS A	2	2	1	0	1	0	0.0	1	0	0	0	0	.500	1.500	0	0	SS-2

Fernando Gonzalez

GONZALEZ, JOSE FERNANDO
B. June 19, 1950, Arecibo, Puerto Rico   BR TR 5'10" 165 lbs.

	G	AB	H	2B	3B	HR	HR %	R	RBI	BB	SO	SB	BA	SA	AB	H	G by POS
1972 PIT N	3	2	0	0	0	0	0.0	0	0	0	2	0	.000	.000	2	0	3B-1
1973	37	49	11	0	1	1	2.0	5	5	1	11	0	.224	.327	29	8	3B-5
1974 2 teams	KC	A (9G – .143)			NY	A	(51G – .215)										
" total	60	142	29	6	1	1	0.7	12	9	7	11	1	.204	.282	3	0	2B-42, 3B-15, SS-3, DH-1
1977 PIT N	80	181	50	10	0	4	2.2	17	27	13	21	3	.276	.398	27	10	3B-37, OF-16, 2B-6, SS-2
1978 2 teams	PIT	N (10G – .190)			SD	N	(100G – .250)										
" total	110	341	84	11	2	2	0.6	29	29	19	35	4	.246	.308	9	4	2B-98, 3B-3
1979 SD N	114	323	70	13	3	9	2.8	22	34	18	34	0	.217	.359	16	4	2B-103, 3B-3
6 yrs.	404	1038	244	40	7	17	1.6	85	104	58	114	8	.235	.336	86	26	2B-249, 3B-64, OF-16, SS-5, DH-1

Jose Gonzalez

GONZALEZ, JOSE ALTA
B. Jan. 21, 1958, San Cristobal, Dominican Republic   BB TR 5'10" 156 lbs.

	G	AB	H	2B	3B	HR	HR %	R	RBI	BB	SO	SB	BA	SA	AB	H	G by POS
1984 STL N	8	19	4	0	0	0	0.0	4	3	0	2	1	.211	.211	0	0	SS-5, 2B-1

Julio Gonzalez

GONZALEZ, JULIO CESAR
Also known as Julio Cesar Hernandez.
B. Dec. 25, 1953, Caguas, Puerto Rico   BR TR 5'11" 162 lbs.

	G	AB	H	2B	3B	HR	HR %	R	RBI	BB	SO	SB	BA	SA	AB	H	G by POS
1977 HOU N	110	383	94	18	3	1	0.3	34	27	19	45	3	.245	.316	7	1	SS-63, 2B-45
1978	78	223	52	3	1	1	0.4	24	16	8	31	6	.233	.269	12	1	2B-54, SS-17, 3B-4
1979	68	181	45	5	2	0	0.0	16	10	5	14	2	.249	.298	7	3	2B-32, SS-21, 3B-9
1980	40	52	6	1	0	0	0.0	5	1	1	8	1	.115	.135	10	0	SS-16, 3B-11, 2B-2
1981 STL N	20	22	7	1	0	1	4.5	2	3	1	3	0	.318	.500	10	2	SS-5, 2B-4, 3B-2
1982	42	87	21	3	2	1	1.1	9	7	1	24	1	.241	.356	12	1	3B-21, 2B-9, SS-1
1983 DET A	12	21	3	1	0	0	0.0	0	2	1	7	0	.143	.190	0	0	SS-6, 2B-5, 3B-1
7 yrs.	370	969	228	32	8	4	0.4	90	66	36	132	13	.235	.297	58	8	2B-151, SS-129, 3B-48

Mike Gonzalez

GONZALEZ, MIGUEL ANGEL
B. Sept. 24, 1890, Havana, Cuba   D. Feb. 19, 1977, Havana, Cuba   BR TR 6'1" 200 lbs.
Manager 1938, 1940.

	G	AB	H	2B	3B	HR	HR %	R	RBI	BB	SO	SB	BA	SA	AB	H	G by POS
1912 BOS N	1	2	0	0	0	0	0.0	0	0	1		0	.000	.000	0	0	C-1
1914 CIN N	95	176	41	6	0	0	0.0	19	10	13	16	2	.233	.267	9	2	C-83
1915 STL N	51	97	22	2	0	0	0.0	12	10	8	9	4	.227	.289	6	1	C-31, 1B-8
1916	118	331	79	15	4	0	0.0	33	29	28	18	5	.239	.308	10	0	C-93, 1B-13
1917	106	290	76	8	1	1	0.3	28	28	22	24	12	.262	.307	17	2	C-68, 1B-18, OF-1
1918	117	349	88	13	4	3	0.9	33	20	39	30	14	.252	.338	8	1	C-100, OF-5, 1B-2
1919 NY N	58	158	30	6	0	0	0.0	18	8	20	9	3	.190	.228	3	0	C-52, 1B-4
1920	11	13	3	0	0	0	0.0	1	0	3	1	1	.231	.231	2	0	C-8
1921	13	24	9	1	0	0	0.0	3	0	1	0	0	.375	.417	4	1	1B-6, C-2
1924 STL N	120	402	119	27	1	3	0.7	34	53	24	22	1	.296	.391	1	1	C-119
1925 2 teams	STL	(22G – .310)			CHI	N	(70G – .264)										
" total	92	268	74	16	1	3	1.1	35	22	19	17	3	.276	.377	9	2	C-72, 1B-9
1926 CHI N	80	253	63	13	3	1	0.4	24	23	13	17	3	.249	.336	2	0	C-78
1927	39	108	26	4	1	1	0.9	15	15	10	8	1	.241	.324	3	1	C-36
1928	49	158	43	9	2	1	0.6	12	21	11	7	2	.272	.373	4	0	C-45
1929	60	167	40	3	0	0	0.0	15	18	18	14	1	.240	.257	0	0	C-60
1931 STL N	15	19	2	0	0	0	0.0	1	3	0	3	0	.105	.105	3	0	C-12
1932	17	14	2	0	0	0	0.0	0	3	0	2	0	.143	.143	10	2	C-7
17 yrs.	1042	2829	717	123	19	13	0.5	283	263	231	198	52	.253	.324	91	13	C-867, 1B-60, OF-6

WORLD SERIES

	G	AB	H	2B	3B	HR	HR %	R	RBI	BB	SO	SB	BA	SA	AB	H	G by POS
1929 CHI N	2	1	0	0	0	0	0.0	0	0	0	1	0	.000	.000	1	0	C-1

Orlando Gonzalez

GONZALEZ, ORLANDO EUGENE
B. Nov. 15, 1951, Havana, Cuba   BR TR 6'2" 180 lbs.

	G	AB	H	2B	3B	HR	HR %	R	RBI	BB	SO	SB	BA	SA	AB	H	G by POS
1976 CLE A	28	68	17	2	0	0	0.0	5	4	5	7	1	.250	.279	6	2	1B-15, OF-7, DH-2
1978 PHI N	26	26	5	0	0	0	0.0	1	0	1	1	0	.192	.192	14	3	OF-11, 1B-3
1980 OAK A	25	70	17	0	0	0	0.0	10	1	9	8	0	.243	.243	4	0	1B-11, DH-8, OF-2
3 yrs.	79	164	39	2	0	0	0.0	16	5	15	16	1	.238	.250	24	5	1B-29, OF-20, DH-10

LEAGUE CHAMPIONSHIP SERIES

	G	AB	H	2B	3B	HR	HR %	R	RBI	BB	SO	SB	BA	SA	AB	H	G by POS
1978 PHI N	1	1	0	0	0	0	0.0	0	0	0	1	0	.000	.000	1	0	

Pedro Gonzalez

GONZALEZ, PEDRO
B. Dec. 12, 1938, San Pedro de Macoris, Dominican Republic   BR TR 6' 176 lbs.

	G	AB	H	2B	3B	HR	HR %	R	RBI	BB	SO	SB	BA	SA	AB	H	G by POS
1963 NY A	14	26	5	1	0	0	0.0	3	1	0	5	0	.192	.231	5	1	2B-7
1964	80	112	31	8	1	0	0.0	18	5	7	22	3	.277	.366	8	1	1B-31, OF-20, 3B-9, 2B-6
1965 2 teams	NY	A (7G – .400)			CLE	A	(116G – .253)										
" total	123	405	103	15	3	5	1.2	38	39	18	59	7	.254	.343	8	3	2B-112, OF-3, 3B-2
1966 CLE A	110	352	82	9	2	2	0.6	21	17	15	54	8	.233	.287	3	0	2B-104, OF-1, 3B-1
1967	80	189	43	6	0	1	0.5	19	8	12	36	4	.228	.275	7	3	2B-64, 3B-4, 1B-4, SS-3
5 yrs.	407	1084	264	39	6	8	0.7	99	70	52	176	22	.244	.313	31	8	2B-293, 1B-35, OF-24, 3B-16, SS-3

	G	AB	H	2B	3B	HR	HR %	R	RBI	BB	SO	SB	BA	SA	Pinch Hit AB	Pinch Hit H	G by POS

Pedro Gonzalez continued

WORLD SERIES

	G	AB	H	2B	3B	HR	HR %	R	RBI	BB	SO	SB	BA	SA	PH AB	PH H	G by POS
1964 NY A	1	1	0	0	0	0	0.0	0	0	0	0	0	.000	.000	0	0	3B-1

Rene Gonzalez

GONZALEZ, RENE ADRIAN
B. Sept. 23, 1961, Austin, Tex.   BR TR 6'3"   180 lbs.

	G	AB	H	2B	3B	HR	HR %	R	RBI	BB	SO	SB	BA	SA	PH AB	PH H	G by POS
1984 MON N	29	30	7	1	0	0	0.0	5	2	2	5	0	.233	.267	0	0	SS-27

Tony Gonzalez

GONZALEZ, ANDRES ANTONIO
B. Aug. 28, 1936, Camaguey, Cuba   BL TR 5'9"   170 lbs.

	G	AB	H	2B	3B	HR	HR %	R	RBI	BB	SO	SB	BA	SA	PH AB	PH H	G by POS
1960 2 teams	CIN N (39G – .212)					PHI N (78G – .299)											
" total	117	340	93	22	6	9	2.6	37	47	15	74	3	.274	.453	29	5	OF-98
1961 PHI N	126	426	118	16	8	12	2.8	58	58	49	66	15	.277	.437	16	6	OF-118
1962	118	437	132	16	4	20	4.6	76	63	40	82	17	.302	.494	4	1	OF-114
1963	155	555	170	36	12	4	0.7	78	66	53	68	13	.306	.436	7	0	OF-151
1964	131	421	117	25	3	4	1.0	55	40	44	74	0	.278	.380	16	3	OF-119
1965	108	370	109	19	1	13	3.5	48	41	31	52	3	.295	.457	11	2	OF-104
1966	132	384	110	20	4	6	1.6	53	40	26	60	2	.286	.406	19	5	OF-121
1967	149	508	172	23	9	9	1.8	74	59	47	58	10	.339	.472	17	7	OF-143
1968	121	416	110	13	4	3	0.7	45	38	40	42	6	.264	.337	8	3	OF-117
1969 2 teams	SD N (53G – .225)					ATL N (89G – .294)											
" total	142	502	135	19	2	12	2.4	68	58	46	46	4	.269	.386	13	2	OF-131
1970 2 teams	ATL N (123G – .265)					CAL A (26G – .304)											
" total	149	522	142	20	2	8	1.5	66	67	48	56	6	.272	.364	9	2	OF-143
1971 CAL A	111	314	77	9	2	3	1.0	32	38	28	28	0	.245	.315	29	10	OF-88
12 yrs.	1559	5195	1485	238	57	103	2.0	690	615	467	706	79	.286	.413	178	46	OF-1447

LEAGUE CHAMPIONSHIP SERIES

	G	AB	H	2B	3B	HR	HR %	R	RBI	BB	SO	SB	BA	SA	PH AB	PH H	G by POS
1969 ATL N	3	14	5	1	0	1	7.1	4	2	1	4	0	.357	.643	0	0	OF-3

Charlie Gooch

GOOCH, CHARLES FURMAN
B. June 5, 1902, Smyrna, Tenn.   D. May 30, 1982, Lanham, Md.   BR TR 5'9"   170 lbs.

	G	AB	H	2B	3B	HR	HR %	R	RBI	BB	SO	SB	BA	SA	PH AB	PH H	G by POS
1929 WAS A	39	57	16	2	1	0	0.0	6	5	7	8	0	.281	.351	22	7	3B-7, 1B-7, SS-1

Johnny Gooch

GOOCH, JOHN BEVERLEY
B. Nov. 9, 1897, Smyrna, Tenn.   D. May 15, 1975, Nashville, Tenn.   BB TR 5'11"   175 lbs.

	G	AB	H	2B	3B	HR	HR %	R	RBI	BB	SO	SB	BA	SA	PH AB	PH H	G by POS
1921 PIT N	13	38	9	0	0	0	0.0	2	3	3	3	1	.237	.237	0	0	C-13
1922	105	353	116	15	3	1	0.3	45	42	39	15	1	.329	.397	2	1	C-103
1923	66	202	56	10	2	1	0.5	16	20	17	13	2	.277	.361	0	0	C-66
1924	70	224	65	6	5	0	0.0	26	25	16	12	1	.290	.362	1	0	C-69
1925	79	215	64	8	4	0	0.0	24	30	20	16	1	.298	.372	3	0	C-76
1926	86	218	59	15	1	1	0.5	19	42	20	14	1	.271	.362	3	0	C-80
1927	101	291	75	17	2	2	0.7	22	48	19	21	0	.258	.351	9	1	C-91
1928 2 teams	PIT N (31G – .238)					BKN N (42G – .317)											
" total	73	181	51	3	3	0	0.0	16	17	10	15	0	.282	.331	4	1	C-69
1929 2 teams	BKN N (1G – .000)					CIN N (92G – .300)											
" total	93	288	86	13	5	0	0.0	22	34	24	10	4	.299	.378	7	1	C-86
1930 CIN N	92	276	67	10	3	2	0.7	29	30	27	15	0	.243	.322	2	0	C-79
1933 BOS A	37	77	14	1	1	0	0.0	6	2	11	7	0	.182	.221	8	1	C-26
11 yrs.	815	2363	662	98	29	7	0.3	227	293	206	141	11	.280	.355	39	5	C-758

WORLD SERIES

	G	AB	H	2B	3B	HR	HR %	R	RBI	BB	SO	SB	BA	SA	PH AB	PH H	G by POS
1925 PIT N	3	3	0	0	0	0	0.0	0	0	0	0	0	.000	.000	0	0	C-3
1927	3	5	0	0	0	0	0.0	0	0	1	1	0	.000	.000	0	0	C-3
2 yrs.	6	8	0	0	0	0	0.0	0	0	1	1	0	.000	.000	0	0	C-6

Lee Gooch

GOOCH, LEE CURRIN
B. Feb. 23, 1890, Oxford, N. C.   D. May 18, 1966, Raleigh, N. C.   BR TR 6'   190 lbs.

	G	AB	H	2B	3B	HR	HR %	R	RBI	BB	SO	SB	BA	SA	PH AB	PH H	G by POS
1915 CLE A	2	2	1	0	0	0	0.0	0	0	0	0	0	.500	.500	2	1	
1917 PHI A	17	59	17	2	0	1	1.7	4	8	4	10	0	.288	.373	1	0	OF-16
2 yrs.	19	61	18	2	0	1	1.6	4	8	4	10	0	.295	.377	3	1	OF-16

Gene Good

GOOD, EUGENE J.
B. Dec. 13, 1882, Roxbury, Mass.   D. Aug. 6, 1947, Boston, Mass.   BL TL 5'6"   130 lbs.

	G	AB	H	2B	3B	HR	HR %	R	RBI	BB	SO	SB	BA	SA	PH AB	PH H	G by POS
1906 BOS N	34	119	18	0	0	0	0.0	4	0	13		2	.151	.151	0	0	OF-34

Wilbur Good

GOOD, WILBUR DAVID (Lefty)
B. Sept. 28, 1885, Punxsutawney, Pa.   D. Dec. 30, 1963, Brooksville, Fla.   BL TL 5'6"   165 lbs.

	G	AB	H	2B	3B	HR	HR %	R	RBI	BB	SO	SB	BA	SA	PH AB	PH H	G by POS
1905 NY A	6	8	3	0	0	0	0.0	2	0	0		0	.375	.375	0	0	P-5
1908 CLE A	46	154	43	1	3	1	0.6	23	14	13		7	.279	.344	2	1	OF-42
1909	94	318	68	6	5	0	0.0	33	17	28		13	.214	.264	10	1	OF-80
1910 BOS N	23	86	29	5	4	0	0.0	15	11	6	13	5	.337	.488	0	0	OF-23
1911 2 teams	BOS N (43G – .267)					CHI N (58G – .269)											
" total	101	310	83	14	7	2	0.6	48	36	23	39	13	.268	.377	12	1	OF-83
1912 CHI N	39	35	5	0	0	0	0.0	7	1	3	7	3	.143	.143	21	3	OF-10
1913	49	91	23	3	2	1	1.1	11	12	11	16	5	.253	.363	16	4	OF-26
1914	154	580	158	24	7	2	0.3	70	40	53	74	31	.272	.348	0	0	OF-154
1915	128	498	126	18	9	2	0.4	66	27	34	65	19	.253	.337	2	1	OF-125
1916 PHI N	75	136	34	4	3	1	0.7	25	15	8	13	7	.250	.346	22	3	OF-46
1918 CHI A	35	148	37	9	4	0	0.0	24	11	11	16	1	.250	.365	0	0	OF-35
11 yrs.	750	2364	609	84	44	9	0.4	324	187	190	243	104	.258	.342	85	14	OF-624, P-5

Bill Goodenough

GOODENOUGH, WILLIAM B.
B. 1863, St. Louis, Mo.   D. May 24, 1905, St. Louis, Mo.   6'1"   170 lbs.

	G	AB	H	2B	3B	HR	HR %	R	RBI	BB	SO	SB	BA	SA	PH AB	PH H	G by POS
1893 STL N	10	31	5	1	0	0	0.0	4	2	3		2	.161	.194	0	0	OF-10

	G	AB	H	2B	3B	HR	HR %	R	RBI	BB	SO	SB	BA	SA	Pinch Hit AB	Pinch Hit H	G by POS

Mike Goodfellow

GOODFELLOW, MICHAEL J. BR TR 6' 180 lbs.
B. Oct. 3, 1866, Port Jervis, N. Y.   D. Feb. 12, 1920, Newark, N. J.

	G	AB	H	2B	3B	HR	HR %	R	RBI	BB	SO	SB	BA	SA	PH AB	PH H	G by POS
1887 STL AA	1	4	0	0	0	0	0.0	0		0		0	.000	.000	0	0	C-1
1888 CLE AA	68	269	66	7	0	0	0.0	24	29	11		7	.245	.271	0	0	OF-62, C-4, 1B-3, SS-1
2 yrs.	69	273	66	7	0	0	0.0	24	28	11		7	.242	.267	0	0	OF-62, C-5, 1B-3, SS-1

Billy Goodman

GOODMAN, WILLIAM DALE BL TR 5'11" 165 lbs.
B. Mar. 22, 1926, Concord, N. C.   D. Oct. 2, 1984, Sarasota, Fla.

	G	AB	H	2B	3B	HR	HR %	R	RBI	BB	SO	SB	BA	SA	PH AB	PH H	G by POS
1947 BOS A	12	11	2	0	0	0	0.0	1	1	1	2	0	.182	.182	9	1	OF-1
1948	127	445	138	27	2	1	0.2	65	66	74	44	5	.310	.387	4	2	1B-117, 3B-2, 2B-2
1949	122	443	132	23	3	0	0.0	54	56	58	21	2	.298	.363	3	2	1B-117
1950	110	424	150	25	3	4	0.9	91	68	52	25	2	.354	.455	11	2	OF-45, 3B-27, 1B-21, 2B-5, SS-1
1951	141	546	162	34	4	0	0.0	92	50	79	37	7	.297	.374	1		1B-62, 2B-44, OF-38, 3B-1
1952	138	513	157	27	3	4	0.8	79	56	48	23	8	.306	.394	6	1	2B-103, 1B-23, 3B-5, OF-4
1953	128	514	161	33	5	2	0.4	73	41	57	11	1	.313	.409	2	2	2B-112, 1B-20
1954	127	489	148	25	4	1	0.2	71	36	51	15	3	.303	.376	10	3	2B-72, 1B-27, OF-13, 3B-12
1955	149	599	176	31	2	0	0.0	100	52	99	44	5	.294	.352	0	0	2B-143, 1B-5, OF-1
1956	105	399	117	22	8	2	0.5	61	38	40	22	0	.293	.404	9	2	2B-95
1957 2 teams		BOS	A	(18G –	.063)		BAL	A	(73G –	.308)							
" total	91	279	82	11	3	3	1.1	37	33	23	19	0	.294	.387	22	2	3B-54, OF-9, 1B-8, SS-5, 2B-5
1958 CHI A	116	425	127	15	5	0	0.0	41	40	37	21	1	.299	.358	4	2	3B-111, 1B-3, SS-1, 2B-1
1959	104	268	67	14	1	1	0.4	21	28	19	20	3	.250	.321	31	7	3B-74, 2B-3
1960	30	77	18	4	0	0	0.0	5	6	12	8	0	.234	.286	6	0	3B-20, 2B-7
1961	41	51	13	4	0	1	2.0	4	10	7	6	0	.255	.392	27	9	3B-7, 1B-2, 2B-1
1962 HOU N	82	161	41	4	1	0	0.0	12	10	12	11	0	.255	.292	53	14	2B-31, 3B-17, 1B-1
16 yrs.	1623	5644	1691	299	44	19	0.3	807	591	669	329	37	.300	.378	198	49	2B-624, 1B-406, 3B-330, OF-111, SS-7
WORLD SERIES																	
1959 CHI A	5	13	3	0	0	0	0.0	1	1	0	5	0	.231	.231	2	0	3B-5

Ival Goodman

GOODMAN, IVAL RICHARD (Goodie) BL TR 5'11" 170 lbs.
B. July 23, 1908, Northview, Mo.   D. Nov. 25, 1984, Cincinnati, Ohio

	G	AB	H	2B	3B	HR	HR %	R	RBI	BB	SO	SB	BA	SA	PH AB	PH H	G by POS
1935 CIN N	148	592	159	23	18	12	2.0	86	72	35	50	14	.269	.429	2	0	OF-146
1936	136	489	139	15	14	17	3.5	81	71	38	53	6	.284	.476	15	5	OF-120
1937	147	549	150	25	12	12	2.2	86	55	55	58	10	.273	.428	3	1	OF-141
1938	145	568	166	27	10	30	5.3	103	92	53	51	3	.292	.533	3	1	OF-142
1939	124	470	152	37	16	7	1.5	85	84	54	32	2	.323	.515	1	1	OF-123
1940	136	519	134	20	6	12	2.3	78	63	60	54	9	.258	.389	0	0	OF-135
1941	42	149	40	5	2	1	0.7	14	12	16	15	1	.268	.349	1	0	OF-40
1942	87	226	55	18	1	0	0.0	21	15	24	32	0	.243	.332	23	6	OF-57
1943 CHI N	80	225	72	10	5	3	1.3	31	45	24	20	4	.320	.449	17	5	OF-61
1944	62	141	37	8	1	1	0.7	24	16	23	15	0	.262	.355	23	6	OF-35
10 yrs.	1107	3928	1104	188	85	95	2.4	609	525	382	380	49	.281	.445	88	25	OF-1000
WORLD SERIES																	
1939 CIN N	4	15	5	1	0	0	0.0	3	1	1	2	1	.333	.400	0	0	OF-4
1940	7	29	8	2	0	0	0.0	5	5	0	3	0	.276	.345	0	0	OF-7
2 yrs.	11	44	13	3	0	0	0.0	8	6	1	5	1	.295	.364	0	0	OF-11

Jake Goodman

GOODMAN, JACOB
B. Sept. 14, 1853, Lancaster, Pa.   D. Mar. 9, 1890, Reading, Pa.

	G	AB	H	2B	3B	HR	HR %	R	RBI	BB	SO	SB	BA	SA	PH AB	PH H	G by POS
1878 MIL N	60	252	62	4	3	1	0.4	28	27	7	33		.246	.298	0	0	1B-60
1882 PIT AA	10	41	13	2	2	0	0.0	5		2			.317	.463	0	0	1B-10
2 yrs.	70	293	75	6	5	1	0.3	33	27	9	33		.256	.321	0	0	1B-70

Ed Goodson

GOODSON, JAMES EDWARD BL TR 6'3" 180 lbs.
B. Jan. 25, 1948, Pulaski, Va.

	G	AB	H	2B	3B	HR	HR %	R	RBI	BB	SO	SB	BA	SA	PH AB	PH H	G by POS
1970 SF N	7	11	3	0	0	0	0.0	1	0	0	2	0	.273	.273	5	2	1B-2
1971	20	42	8	1	0	0	0.0	4	1	2	4	0	.190	.214	7	1	1B-14
1972	58	150	42	1	1	6	4.0	15	30	8	12	0	.280	.420	15	4	1B-42
1973	102	384	116	20	1	12	3.1	37	53	15	44	0	.302	.453	8	3	3B-93
1974	98	298	81	15	0	6	2.0	25	48	18	22	1	.272	.383	20	6	1B-73, 3B-8
1975 2 teams		SF	N	(39G –	.207)		ATL	N	(47G –	.211)							
" total	86	197	41	9	0	2	1.0	15	16	9	22	0	.208	.284	40	9	1B-29, 3B-14
1976 LA N	83	118	27	4	0	3	2.5	8	17	8	19	0	.229	.339	56	15	3B-16, 1B-3, OF-2, 2B-1
1977	61	66	11	1	0	1	1.5	3	5	3	10	0	.167	.227	45	8	1B-13, 3B-4
8 yrs.	515	1266	329	51	2	30	2.4	108	170	63	135	1	.260	.374	196	48	1B-176, 3B-135, OF-2, 2B-1
LEAGUE CHAMPIONSHIP SERIES																	
1977 LA N	1	1	0	0	0	0	0.0	0	0	0	0	0	.000	.000	1	0	
WORLD SERIES																	
1977 LA N	1	1	0	0	0	0	0.0	0	0	0	1	0	.000	.000	1	0	

Danny Goodwin

GOODWIN, DANNY KAY BL TR 6'1" 195 lbs.
B. Sept. 2, 1953, St. Louis, Mo.

	G	AB	H	2B	3B	HR	HR %	R	RBI	BB	SO	SB	BA	SA	PH AB	PH H	G by POS
1975 CAL A	4	10	1	0	0	0	0.0	0	0	0	5	0	.100	.100	1	0	DH-3
1977	35	91	19	6	1	1	1.1	5	8	5	19	0	.209	.330	12	1	DH-23
1978	24	58	16	5	0	2	3.4	9	10	10	13	0	.276	.466	8	2	DH-15
1979 MIN A	58	159	46	8	5	5	3.1	22	27	11	23	0	.289	.497	11	4	DH-51, 1B-8
1980	55	115	23	5	0	1	0.9	12	11	17	32	0	.200	.270	22	6	DH-38, 1B-13
1981	59	151	34	6	1	2	1.3	18	17	16	32	3	.225	.318	10	3	1B-40, DH-5, OF-1
1982 OAK A	17	52	11	2	1	2	3.8	6	8	2	13	0	.212	.404	2	1	DH-15
7 yrs.	252	636	150	32	8	13	2.0	72	81	61	137	3	.236	.373	66	17	DH-150, 1B-61, OF-1

	G	AB	H	2B	3B	HR	HR %	R	RBI	BB	SO	SB	BA	SA	Pinch Hit AB	Pinch Hit H	G by POS

Pep Goodwin

GOODWIN, CLAIRE VERNON BL TR 5'10½" 160 lbs.
B. Dec. 19, 1894, Pocatello, Ida.   D. Feb. 15, 1972, Oakland, Calif.

	G	AB	H	2B	3B	HR	HR %	R	RBI	BB	SO	SB	BA	SA	Pinch Hit AB	Pinch Hit H	G by POS
1914 KC F	112	374	88	15	6	1	0.3	38	32	27		4	.235	.316	6	2	SS-67, 3B-40, 1B-1
1915	81	229	54	5	1	0	0.0	22	16	15		6	.236	.266	14	2	SS-42, 2B-23
2 yrs.	193	603	142	20	7	1	0.2	60	48	42		10	.235	.297	20	4	SS-109, 3B-40, 2B-23, 1B-1

Ray Goolsby

GOOLSBY, RAYMOND DANIEL (Ox) BR TR 6'1" 185 lbs.
B. Sept. 5, 1919, Florala, Ala.

	G	AB	H	2B	3B	HR	HR %	R	RBI	BB	SO	SB	BA	SA	Pinch Hit AB	Pinch Hit H	G by POS
1946 WAS A	3	4	0	0	0	0	0.0	0	1	1	1	0	.000	.000	2	0	OF-1

Greg Goossen

GOOSSEN, GREGORY BRYANT BR TR 6'1½" 210 lbs.
B. Dec. 14, 1945, Los Angeles, Calif.

	G	AB	H	2B	3B	HR	HR %	R	RBI	BB	SO	SB	BA	SA	Pinch Hit AB	Pinch Hit H	G by POS
1965 NY N	11	31	9	0	0	1	3.2	2	2	1	5	0	.290	.387	2	0	C-8
1966	13	32	6	2	0	1	3.1	1	5	1	11	0	.188	.344	2	0	C-11
1967	37	69	11	1	0	0	0.0	2	3	4	26	0	.159	.174	20	4	C-23
1968	38	106	22	7	0	0	0.0	4	6	10	21	0	.208	.274	6	0	1B-30, C-2
1969 SEA A	52	139	43	8	1	10	7.2	19	24	14	29	1	.309	.597	19	2	1B-31, OF-2
1970 2 teams	MIL	A (21G – .255)			WAS	A	(21G – .222)										
" total	42	83	20	6	0	1	1.2	5	4	12	20	0	.241	.349	19	5	1B-17, OF-5
6 yrs.	193	460	111	24	1	13	2.8	33	44	42	112	1	.241	.383	68	11	1B-78, C-44, OF-7

Glen Gorbous

GORBOUS, GLEN EDWARD BL TR 6'2" 175 lbs.
B. July 8, 1930, Drumheller, Alta., Canada

	G	AB	H	2B	3B	HR	HR %	R	RBI	BB	SO	SB	BA	SA	Pinch Hit AB	Pinch Hit H	G by POS
1955 2 teams	CIN	N (6G – .333)			PHI	N	(91G – .237)										
" total	97	242	59	12	1	4	1.7	27	27	24	18	0	.244	.351	37	10	OF-62
1956 PHI N	15	33	6	0	0	0	0.0	1	1	0	1	0	.182	.182	6	1	OF-8
1957	3	2	1	1	0	0	0.0	1	1	1	0	0	.500	1.000	2	1	
3 yrs.	115	277	66	13	1	4	1.4	29	29	25	19	0	.238	.336	45	11	OF-70

Joe Gordon

GORDON, JOSEPH LOWELL (Flash) BR TR 5'10" 180 lbs.
B. Feb. 18, 1915, Los Angeles, Calif.   D. Apr. 14, 1978, Sacramento, Calif.
Manager 1958-61, 1969.

	G	AB	H	2B	3B	HR	HR %	R	RBI	BB	SO	SB	BA	SA	Pinch Hit AB	Pinch Hit H	G by POS
1938 NY A	127	458	117	24	7	25	5.5	83	97	56	72	11	.255	.502	1	1	2B-126
1939	151	567	161	32	5	28	4.9	92	111	75	57	11	.284	.506	0	0	2B-151
1940	155	616	173	32	10	30	4.9	112	103	52	57	18	.281	.511	0	0	2B-155
1941	156	588	162	26	7	24	4.1	104	87	72	80	10	.276	.466	0	0	2B-131, 1B-30
1942	147	538	173	29	4	18	3.3	88	103	79	95	12	.322	.491	0	0	2B-147
1943	152	543	135	28	5	17	3.1	82	69	98	75	4	.249	.413	0	0	2B-152
1946	112	376	79	15	0	11	2.9	35	47	49	72	2	.210	.338	4	0	2B-108
1947 CLE A	155	562	153	27	6	29	5.2	89	93	62	49	7	.272	.496	0	0	2B-155
1948	144	550	154	21	4	32	5.8	96	124	77	68	5	.280	.507	1	0	2B-144, SS-2
1949	148	541	136	18	3	20	3.7	74	84	83	33	5	.251	.407	3	0	2B-145
1950	119	368	87	12	1	19	5.2	59	57	56	44	4	.236	.429	12	1	2B-105
11 yrs.	1566	5707	1530	264	52	253	4.4	914	975	759	702	89	.268	.466	21	2	2B-1519, 1B-30, SS-2

WORLD SERIES

	G	AB	H	2B	3B	HR	HR %	R	RBI	BB	SO	SB	BA	SA	Pinch Hit AB	Pinch Hit H	G by POS
1938 NY A	4	15	6	2	0	1	6.7	3	6	1	3	1	.400	.733	0	0	2B-4
1939	4	14	2	0	0	0	0.0	1	1	0	2	0	.143	.143	0	0	2B-4
1941	5	14	7	1	1	1	7.1	2	5	7	0	0	.500	.929	0	0	2B-5
1942	5	21	2	1	0	0	0.0	1	0	0	7	0	.095	.143	0	0	2B-5
1943	5	17	4	1	0	1	5.9	2	2	3	3	0	.235	.471	0	0	2B-5
1948 CLE A	6	22	4	0	0	1	4.5	3	2	1	2	1	.182	.318	0	0	2B-6
6 yrs.	29	103	25	5	1	4	3.9	12	16	12	17	2	.243	.427	0	0	2B-29

Mike Gordon

GORDON, MICHAEL WILLIAM BB TR 6'3" 215 lbs.
B. Sept. 11, 1953, Leominister, Mass.

	G	AB	H	2B	3B	HR	HR %	R	RBI	BB	SO	SB	BA	SA	Pinch Hit AB	Pinch Hit H	G by POS
1977 CHI N	8	23	1	0	0	0	0.0	0	2	2	8	0	.043	.043	0	0	C-8
1978	4	5	1	0	0	0	0.0	0	0	3	2	0	.200	.200	0	0	C-4
2 yrs.	12	28	2	0	0	0	0.0	0	2	5	10	0	.071	.071	0	0	C-12

Sid Gordon

GORDON, SIDNEY BR TR 5'10" 185 lbs.
B. Aug. 13, 1917, Brooklyn, N. Y.   D. June 17, 1975, New York, N. Y.

	G	AB	H	2B	3B	HR	HR %	R	RBI	BB	SO	SB	BA	SA	Pinch Hit AB	Pinch Hit H	G by POS
1941 NY N	9	31	8	1	1	0	0.0	4	4	6	1	0	.258	.355	0	0	OF-9
1942	6	19	6	0	1	0	0.0	4	2	3	2	0	.316	.421	0	0	3B-6
1943	131	474	119	9	11	9	1.9	50	63	43	32	2	.251	.373	6	1	3B-53, 1B-41, OF-28, 2B-3
1946	135	450	132	15	4	5	1.1	64	45	60	27	1	.293	.378	5	2	OF-101, 3B-30
1947	130	437	119	19	8	13	3.0	57	57	50	21	2	.272	.442	4	1	OF-124, 3B-2
1948	142	521	156	26	4	30	5.8	100	107	74	39	8	.299	.537	5	0	3B-115, OF-23
1949	141	489	139	26	2	26	5.3	87	90	95	37	1	.284	.505	5	0	3B-123, OF-15, 1B-1
1950 BOS N	134	481	146	33	4	27	5.6	78	103	78	31	2	.304	.557	1	0	OF-123, 3B-10
1951	150	550	158	28	1	29	5.3	96	109	80	32	2	.287	.500	0	0	OF-122, 3B-34
1952	144	522	151	22	2	25	4.8	69	75	77	49	0	.289	.483	0	0	OF-142, 3B-2
1953 MIL N	140	464	127	22	4	19	4.1	67	75	71	40	1	.274	.461	3	1	OF-137
1954 PIT N	131	363	111	12	0	12	3.3	38	49	67	24	0	.306	.438	17	3	OF-73, 3B-40
1955 2 teams	PIT	N (16G – .170)			NY	N	(66G – .243)										
" total	82	191	43	7	1	7	3.7	21	26	27	21	0	.225	.382	21	1	3B-39, OF-21
13 yrs.	1475	4992	1415	220	43	202	4.0	735	805	731	356	19	.283	.466	67	9	OF-918, 3B-454, 1B-42, 2B-3

George Gore

GORE, GEORGE F. BL TR 5'11" 195 lbs.
B. 1855, Hartland, Me.   D. Sept. 16, 1933, Utica, N. Y.

	G	AB	H	2B	3B	HR	HR %	R	RBI	BB	SO	SB	BA	SA	Pinch Hit AB	Pinch Hit H	G by POS
1879 CHI N	63	266	70	17	4	0	0.0	43	32	8	30		.263	.357	0	0	OF-54, 1B-9
1880	77	322	116	23	2	2	0.6	70	47	21	10		**.360**	**.463**	0	0	OF-74, 1B-7
1881	73	309	92	18	9	1	0.3	86	44	27	23		.298	.424	0	0	OF-72, 3B-1, 1B-1
1882	84	367	117	15	7	3	0.8	99	51	29	19		.319	.422	0	0	OF-84
1883	92	392	131	30	9	2	0.5	105		27	13		.334	.472	0	0	OF-92
1884	103	422	134	18	4	5	1.2	104		61	26		.318	.415	0	0	OF-103

	G	AB	H	2B	3B	HR	HR %	R	RBI	BB	SO	SB	BA	SA	Pinch Hit AB	Pinch Hit H	G by POS

George Gore continued

	G	AB	H	2B	3B	HR	HR%	R	RBI	BB	SO	SB	BA	SA	AB	H	G by POS
1885	109	441	138	21	13	5	1.1	115	51	68	25		.313	.454	0	0	OF-109
1886	118	444	135	20	12	6	1.4	150	63	102	30		.304	.444	0	0	OF-118
1887 NY N	111	459	133	16	5	1	0.2	95	49	42	18	39	.290	.353	0	0	OF-111
1888	64	254	56	4	4	2	0.8	37	17	30	31	11	.220	.291	0	0	OF-64
1889	120	488	149	21	7	7	1.4	132	54	84	28	28	.305	.420	0	0	OF-120
1890 NY P	93	399	127	26	8	10	2.5	132	55	77	23	28	.318	.499	0	0	OF-93
1891 NY N	130	528	150	22	7	2	0.4	103	48	74	34	19	.284	.364	0	0	OF-130
1892 2 teams		NY	N (53G – .254)			STL	N (20G – .205)										
" total	73	266	64	11	3	0	0.0	56	15	67	22	22	.241	.305	0	0	OF-73
14 yrs.	1310	5357	1612	262	94	46	0.9	1327	526	717	332	147	.301	.411	0	0	OF-1297, 1B-17, 3B-1

Bob Gorinski

GORINSKI, ROBERT JOHN
B. Jan. 7, 1952, Latrobe, Pa.
BR TR 6'3" 215 lbs.

	G	AB	H	2B	3B	HR	HR%	R	RBI	BB	SO	SB	BA	SA	AB	H	G by POS
1977 MIN A	54	118	23	4	1	3	2.5	14	22	5	29	1	.195	.322	16	1	OF-37, DH-9

Herb Gorman

GORMAN, HERBERT ALLEN
B. Dec. 22, 1924, San Francisco, Calif. D. Apr. 5, 1953, San Diego, Calif.
BL TL 5'11" 180 lbs.

	G	AB	H	2B	3B	HR	HR%	R	RBI	BB	SO	SB	BA	SA	AB	H	G by POS
1952 STL N	1	1	0	0	0	0	0.0	0	0	0	0	0	.000	.000	1	0	

Howie Gorman

GORMAN, HOWARD PAUL (Lefty)
B. May 14, 1913, Pittsburgh, Pa. D. Apr. 29, 1984, Harrisburg, Pa.
BL TL 6'2" 160 lbs.

	G	AB	H	2B	3B	HR	HR%	R	RBI	BB	SO	SB	BA	SA	AB	H	G by POS
1937 PHI N	13	19	4	1	0	0	0.0	3	1	1	1	1	.211	.263	4	0	OF-7
1938	1	1	0	0	0	0	0.0	0	0	0	0	0	.000	.000	1	0	
2 yrs.	14	20	4	1	0	0	0.0	3	1	1	1	1	.200	.250	5	0	OF-7

Jack Gorman

GORMAN, JOHN F. (Stooping Jack)
B. 1859, St. Louis, Mo. D. Sept. 9, 1889, St. Louis, Mo.

	G	AB	H	2B	3B	HR	HR%	R	RBI	BB	SO	SB	BA	SA	AB	H	G by POS
1883 STL AA	1	4	0	0	0	0	0.0	0		0			.000	.000	0	0	OF-1
1884 2 teams		KC	U (33G – .277)			PIT	AA (8G – .148)										
" total	41	164	42	5	3	0	0.0	28		5			.256	.323	0	0	1B-24, OF-8, 3B-6, P-3
2 yrs.	42	168	42	5	3	0	0.0	28		5			.250	.315	0	0	1B-24, OF-9, 3B-6, P-3

John Goryl

GORYL, JOHN ALBERT
B. Oct. 21, 1933, Cumberland, R. I.
Manager 1980-81.
BR TR 5'10" 175 lbs.

	G	AB	H	2B	3B	HR	HR%	R	RBI	BB	SO	SB	BA	SA	AB	H	G by POS
1957 CHI N	9	38	8	2	0	0	0.0	7	1	5	9	0	.211	.263	0	0	3B-9
1958	83	219	53	9	3	4	1.8	27	14	27	34	0	.242	.365	10	4	3B-44, 2B-35
1959	25	48	9	1	1	1	2.1	1	6	5	3	1	.188	.354	8	1	2B-11, 3B-4
1962 MIN A	37	26	5	0	1	2	7.7	6	2	2	6	0	.192	.500	19	3	2B-4, SS-1
1963	64	150	43	5	3	9	6.0	29	24	15	29	0	.287	.540	12	2	3B-34, 3B-11, SS-7
1964	58	114	16	0	2	0	0.0	9	1	10	25	1	.140	.175	22	4	2B-28, 3B-13
6 yrs.	276	595	134	19	10	16	2.7	79	48	64	106	2	.225	.371	71	13	2B-112, 3B-81, SS-8

Jim Gosger

GOSGER, JAMES CHARLES
B. Nov. 6, 1942, Port Huron, Mich.
BL TL 5'11" 185 lbs.

	G	AB	H	2B	3B	HR	HR%	R	RBI	BB	SO	SB	BA	SA	AB	H	G by POS
1963 BOS A	19	16	1	0	0	0	0.0	3	0	3	5	0	.063	.063	6	1	OF-4
1965	81	324	83	15	4	9	2.8	45	35	29	61	3	.256	.410	0	0	OF-81
1966 2 teams		BOS	A (40G – .254)			KC	A (88G – .224)										
" total	128	398	93	18	1	10	2.5	50	44	52	73	5	.234	.359	23	6	OF-109
1967 KC A	134	356	86	14	5	5	1.4	31	36	53	69	5	.242	.351	26	7	OF-113
1968 OAK A	88	150	27	1	4	0	0.0	7	5	17	21	4	.180	.200	18	3	OF-64
1969 2 teams		SEA	A (39G – .109)			NY	N (10G – .133)										
" total	49	70	8	4	1	1	1.4	4	2	7	17	2	.114	.243	15	1	OF-31
1970 MON N	91	274	72	11	2	5	1.8	38	37	35	35	5	.263	.372	10	1	OF-71, 1B-19
1971	51	102	16	2	2	0	0.0	7	8	9	17	1	.157	.216	23	3	OF-23, 1B-6
1973 NY N	38	92	22	2	0	0	0.0	9	10	9	16	0	.239	.261	4	0	OF-35
1974	26	33	3	0	0	0	0.0	3	0	3	2	0	.091	.091	2	0	OF-24
10 yrs.	705	1815	411	67	16	30	1.7	197	177	217	316	25	.226	.331	127	22	OF-555, 1B-25

Goose Goslin

GOSLIN, LEON ALLEN
B. Oct. 16, 1900, Salem, N. J. D. May 15, 1971, Bridgeton, N. J.
Hall of Fame 1968.
BL TR 5'11½" 185 lbs.

	G	AB	H	2B	3B	HR	HR%	R	RBI	BB	SO	SB	BA	SA	AB	H	G by POS
1921 WAS A	14	50	13	1	1	1	2.0	8	6	6	5	0	.260	.380	0	0	OF-14
1922	101	358	116	19	7	3	0.8	44	53	25	26	4	.324	.441	5	0	OF-93
1923	150	600	180	29	18	9	1.5	86	99	40	53	7	.300	.453	1	1	OF-149
1924	154	579	199	30	17	12	2.1	100	129	68	29	16	.344	.516	0	0	OF-154
1925	150	601	201	34	20	18	3.0	116	113	53	50	26	.334	.547	0	0	OF-150
1926	147	567	201	26	15	17	3.0	105	108	63	38	8	.354	.543	0	0	OF-147
1927	148	581	194	37	15	13	2.2	96	120	50	28	21	.334	.516	0	0	OF-148
1928	135	456	173	36	10	17	3.7	80	102	48	19	16	.379	.614	7	2	OF-125
1929	145	553	159	28	7	18	3.3	82	91	66	33	10	.288	.461	3	3	OF-142
1930 2 teams		WAS	A (47G – .271)			STL	A (101G – .326)										
" total	148	584	180	36	12	37	6.3	115	138	67	54	17	.308	.601	0	0	OF-148
1931 STL A	151	591	194	42	10	24	4.1	114	105	80	41	9	.328	.555	0	0	OF-151
1932	150	572	171	28	9	17	3.0	88	104	92	35	12	.299	.469	0	0	OF-149, 3B-1
1933 WAS A	132	549	163	35	10	10	1.8	97	64	42	32	5	.297	.452	4	2	OF-128
1934 DET A	151	614	187	38	7	13	2.1	106	100	65	38	5	.305	.453	2	0	OF-149
1935	147	590	172	34	6	9	1.5	88	109	56	31	5	.292	.415	3	1	OF-144
1936	147	572	180	33	8	24	4.2	122	125	85	50	14	.315	.526	3	0	OF-144
1937	79	181	43	11	1	4	2.2	30	35	35	18	0	.238	.376	29	9	OF-40, 1B-1
1938 WAS A	38	57	9	3	0	2	3.5	6	8	8	5	0	.158	.316	18	4	OF-13
18 yrs.	2287	8655	2735	500	173	248	2.9	1483	1609	949	585	175	.316	.500	75	22	OF-2188, 3B-1, 1B-1
WORLD SERIES																	
1924 WAS A	7	32	11	1	0	3	9.4	4	7	0	7	0	.344	.656	0	0	OF-7
1925	7	26	8	1	0	3	11.5	6	5	3	3	1	.308	.692	0	0	OF-7

	G	AB	H	2B	3B	HR	HR %	R	RBI	BB	SO	SB	BA	SA	Pinch Hit AB	Pinch Hit H	G by POS

Goose Goslin continued

1933	5	20	5	1	0	1	5.0	2	1	1	3	0	.250	.450	0	0	OF-5
1934 DET A	7	29	7	1	0	0	0.0	2	2	3	1	0	.241	.276	0	0	OF-7
1935	6	22	6	1	0	0	0.0	2	3	5	0	0	.273	.318	0	0	OF-6
5 yrs.	32	129	37	5	0	7	5.4	16	18	12	14	1	.287	.488	0	0	OF-32
							10th										

Howie Goss

GOSS, HOWARD WAYNE
B. Nov. 1, 1934, Wewoka, Okla.

BR TR 6'4" 204 lbs.

	G	AB	H	2B	3B	HR	HR %	R	RBI	BB	SO	SB	BA	SA	AB	H	G by POS
1962 PIT N	89	111	27	6	0	2	1.8	19	10	9	36	5	.243	.351	8	2	OF-66
1963 HOU N	133	411	86	18	2	9	2.2	37	44	31	128	4	.209	.328	15	2	OF-123
2 yrs.	222	522	113	24	2	11	2.1	56	54	40	164	9	.216	.333	23	4	OF-189

Dick Gossett

GOSSETT, JOHN STAR
B. Aug. 21, 1891, Dennison, Ohio   D. Oct. 6, 1962, Massillon, Ohio

BR TR 5'11" 185 lbs.

	G	AB	H	2B	3B	HR	HR %	R	RBI	BB	SO	SB	BA	SA	AB	H	G by POS
1913 NY A	39	105	17	2	0	0	0.0	9	9	10	22	1	.162	.181	1	1	C-38
1914	9	21	3	0	0	0	0.0	3	1	5	5	0	.143	.143	0	0	C-9
2 yrs.	48	126	20	2	0	0	0.0	12	10	15	27	1	.159	.175	1	1	C-47

Julio Gotay

GOTAY, JULIO SANCHEZ
B. June 9, 1939, Fajardo, Puerto Rico

BR TR 6' 180 lbs.

	G	AB	H	2B	3B	HR	HR %	R	RBI	BB	SO	SB	BA	SA	AB	H	G by POS
1960 STL N	3	8	3	0	0	0	0.0	0	0	0	2	1	.375	.375	1	1	SS-2, 3B-1
1961	10	45	11	4	0	0	0.0	5	5	3	5	0	.244	.333	0	0	SS-10
1962	127	369	94	12	1	2	0.5	47	27	27	47	7	.255	.309	1	0	SS-120, 2B-8, OF-2, 3B-1
1963 PIT N	4	2	1	0	0	0	0.0	0	0	0	0	0	.500	.500	1	1	2B-1
1964	3	2	1	0	0	0	0.0	1	0	1	0	0	.500	.500	2	1	
1965 CAL A	40	77	19	4	0	1	1.3	6	3	4	9	0	.247	.338	8	2	2B-23, 3B-9, SS-1
1966 HOU N	4	5	0	0	0	0	0.0	0	0	0	0	0	.000	.000	3	0	3B-1
1967	77	234	66	10	2	2	0.9	30	15	15	30	1	.282	.368	19	6	2B-30, SS-20, 3B-3
1968	75	165	41	3	0	1	0.6	9	11	4	21	1	.248	.285	25	8	2B-48, 3B-1
1969	46	81	21	5	0	0	0.0	7	9	7	13	2	.259	.321	30	6	2B-16, 3B-1
10 yrs.	389	988	257	38	3	6	0.6	106	70	61	127	12	.260	.323	90	25	SS-153, 2B-126, 3B-17, OF-2

Charlie Gould

GOULD, CHARLES HARVEY
B. Aug. 21, 1847, Cincinnati, Ohio   D. Apr. 10, 1917, Flushing, N. Y.
Manager 1875-76.

BR TR 6' 172 lbs.

	G	AB	H	2B	3B	HR	HR %	R	RBI	BB	SO	SB	BA	SA	AB	H	G by POS
1876 CIN N	61	258	65	7	0	0	0.0	27	11	6	11		.252	.279	0	0	1B-61, P-2
1877	24	91	25	2	1	0	0.0	5	13	5	5		.275	.319	0	0	1B-24, OF-1
2 yrs.	85	349	90	9	1	0	0.0	32	24	11	16		.258	.289	0	0	1B-85, P-2, OF-1

Nick Goulish

GOULISH, NICHOLAS EDWARD
B. Nov. 13, 1917, Punxsutawney, Pa.   D. May 15, 1984, Youngstown, Ohio

BL TL 6'1" 179 lbs.

	G	AB	H	2B	3B	HR	HR %	R	RBI	BB	SO	SB	BA	SA	AB	H	G by POS
1944 PHI N	1	1	0	0	0	0	0.0	0	0	0	0	0	.000	.000	1	0	
1945	13	11	3	0	0	0	0.0	4	2	1	3	0	.273	.273	9	2	OF-2
2 yrs.	14	12	3	0	0	0	0.0	4	2	1	3	0	.250	.250	10	2	OF-2

Claude Gouzzie

GOUZZIE, CLYDE CLAUDE
B. 1871, Pa.   D. Sept. 21, 1907, Denver, Colo.

BR TR 5'9" 170 lbs.

	G	AB	H	2B	3B	HR	HR %	R	RBI	BB	SO	SB	BA	SA	AB	H	G by POS
1903 STL A	1	1	0	0	0	0	0.0	0	0	0		0	.000	.000	0	0	2B-1

Hank Gowdy

GOWDY, HENRY MORGAN
B. Aug. 24, 1889, Columbus, Ohio   D. Aug. 1, 1966, Columbus, Ohio

BR TR 6'2" 182 lbs.

	G	AB	H	2B	3B	HR	HR %	R	RBI	BB	SO	SB	BA	SA	AB	H	G by POS
1910 NY N	7	14	3	1	0	0	0.0	1	2	2	3	1	.214	.286	2	0	1B-5
1911 2 teams	NY	N (4G –	.250)		BOS	N (29G –	.289)										
" total	33	101	29	5	2	0	0.0	10	16	6	19	2	.287	.376	3	0	1B-28, C-1
1912 BOS N	44	96	26	6	1	3	3.1	16	10	16	13	3	.271	.448	14	3	C-22, 1B-7
1913	3	5	3	1	0	0	0.0	0	2	3	2	0	.600	.800	0	0	C-2
1914	128	366	89	17	6	3	0.8	42	46	48	40	14	.243	.347	3	1	C-115, 1B-9
1915	118	316	78	15	3	2	0.6	27	30	41	34	10	.247	.332	1	1	C-118
1916	118	349	88	12	1	1	0.3	32	34	24	33	8	.252	.301	2	0	C-116
1917	49	154	33	7	0	0	0.0	12	14	15	13	2	.214	.260	0	0	C-49
1919	78	219	61	8	1	1	0.5	18	22	19	16	5	.279	.338	2	0	C-74, 1B-1
1920	80	214	52	11	2	0	0.0	14	18	20	15	6	.243	.313	5	2	C-74
1921	64	164	49	7	2	2	1.2	17	17	16	11	2	.299	.402	8	3	C-53
1922	92	221	70	11	1	1	0.5	23	27	24	13	2	.317	.389	17	5	C-72, 1B-1
1923 2 teams	BOS	N (23G –	.125)		NY	N (53G –	.328)										
" total	76	170	46	7	4	1	0.6	18	23	36	14	3	.271	.376	12	3	C-58
1924 NY N	87	191	62	9	1	4	2.1	25	37	26	11	1	.325	.445	9	4	C-78
1925	47	114	37	4	3	3	2.6	14	19	12	7	0	.325	.491	6	3	C-41
1929 BOS N	10	16	7	0	0	0	0.0	1	3	0	2	0	.438	.438	1	0	C-9
1930	16	25	5	1	0	0	0.0	0	2	3	1	0	.200	.240	0	0	C-15
17 yrs.	1050	2735	738	122	27	21	0.8	270	322	311	247	59	.270	.357	85	25	C-897, 1B-51
WORLD SERIES																	
1914 BOS N	4	11	6	3	1	1	9.1	3	3	5	1	1	.545	1.273	0	0	C-4
1923 NY N	3	4	0	0	0	0	0.0	0	0	1	0	0	.000	.000	1	0	C-2
1924	7	27	7	0	0	0	0.0	4	1	2	2	0	.259	.259	0	0	C-7
3 yrs.	14	42	13	3	1	1	2.4	7	4	8	3	1	.310	.500	1	0	C-13

Billy Grabarkewitz

GRABARKEWITZ, BILLY CORDELL
B. Jan. 18, 1946, Lockhart, Tex.

BR TR 5'10" 165 lbs.

	G	AB	H	2B	3B	HR	HR %	R	RBI	BB	SO	SB	BA	SA	AB	H	G by POS
1969 LA N	34	65	6	1	1	0	0.0	4	5	4	19	1	.092	.138	3	0	SS-18, 3B-6, 2B-3
1970	156	529	153	20	8	17	3.2	92	84	95	149	19	.289	.454	2	1	3B-97, SS-50, 2B-20
1971	44	71	16	5	0	0	0.0	9	6	19	16	1	.225	.296	11	3	2B-13, 3B-10, SS-1
1972	53	144	24	4	0	4	2.8	17	16	18	53	3	.167	.278	5	1	3B-24, 2B-19, SS-2

	G	AB	H	2B	3B	HR	HR %	R	RBI	BB	SO	SB	BA	SA	Pinch Hit AB	Pinch Hit H	G by POS

Billy Grabarkewitz continued

	G	AB	H	2B	3B	HR	HR %	R	RBI	BB	SO	SB	BA	SA	PH AB	PH H	G by POS
1973 2 teams	CAL A (61G – .163)					PHI N (25G – .288)											
" total	86	195	40	8	1	5	2.6	39	16	40	45	5	.205	.333	16	6	2B-38, 3B-14, OF-2, SS-1
1974 2 teams	PHI N (34G – .133)					CHI N (53G – .248)											
" total	87	155	35	3	2	2	1.3	28	14	26	38	4	.226	.310	14	2	2B-45, SS-7, 3B-7, OF-5
1975 OAK A	6	2	0	0	0	0	0.0	0	0	0	1	0	.000	.000	2	0	2B-4, DH-1
7 yrs.	466	1161	274	41	12	28	2.4	189	141	202	321	33	.236	.364	53	13	3B-158, 2B-142, SS-79, OF-7, DH-1

Rod Graber

GRABER, RODNEY BLAINE
B. June 20, 1931, Marshallville, Ohio — BL TL 5'11" 175 lbs.

	G	AB	H	2B	3B	HR	HR %	R	RBI	BB	SO	SB	BA	SA	PH AB	PH H	G by POS
1958 CLE A	4	8	1	0	0	0	0.0	0	0	1	2	0	.125	.125	2	0	OF-2

Johnny Grabowski

GRABOWSKI, JOHN PATRICK (Nig)
B. Jan. 7, 1900, Ware, Mass. D. May 23, 1946, Albany, N. Y. — BR TR 5'10" 185 lbs.

	G	AB	H	2B	3B	HR	HR %	R	RBI	BB	SO	SB	BA	SA	PH AB	PH H	G by POS
1924 CHI A	20	56	14	3	0	0	0.0	10	3	2	4	0	.250	.304	0	0	C-19
1925	21	46	14	4	1	0	0.0	5	10	2	4	0	.304	.435	0	0	C-21
1926	48	122	32	1	1	1	0.8	6	11	4	15	0	.262	.311	8	4	C-38, 1B-1
1927 NY A	70	195	54	2	4	0	0.0	29	25	20	15	0	.277	.328	2	0	C-68
1928	75	202	48	7	1	1	0.5	21	21	10	21	0	.238	.297	0	0	C-75
1929	22	59	12	1	0	0	0.0	4	2	3	6	1	.203	.220	0	0	C-22
1931 DET A	40	136	32	7	1	0	0.7	9	14	6	19	0	.235	.324	1	1	C-39
7 yrs.	296	816	206	25	8	3	0.4	84	86	47	84	1	.252	.314	11	5	C-282, 1B-1
WORLD SERIES																	
1927 NY A	1	2	0	0	0	0	0.0	0	0	0	0	0	.000	.000	0	0	C-1

Earl Grace

GRACE, ROBERT EARL
B. Feb. 24, 1907, Barlow, Ky. D. Dec. 22, 1980, Phoenix, Ariz. — BL TR 6' 175 lbs.

	G	AB	H	2B	3B	HR	HR %	R	RBI	BB	SO	SB	BA	SA	PH AB	PH H	G by POS
1929 CHI N	27	80	20	1	0	2	2.5	7	17	9	7	0	.250	.338	0	0	C-27
1931 2 teams	CHI N (7G – .111)					PIT N (47G – .280)											
" total	54	159	43	6	1	0	0.6	10	21	17	6	0	.270	.340	6	0	C-47
1932 PIT N	115	390	107	17	5	7	1.8	41	55	14	23	0	.274	.397	1	0	C-114
1933	93	291	84	13	1	3	1.0	22	44	26	23	0	.289	.371	4	0	C-88
1934	95	289	78	17	1	4	1.4	27	24	20	19	0	.270	.377	10	5	C-83, 1B-1
1935	77	224	59	8	1	3	1.3	19	29	32	17	1	.263	.348	8	3	C-69
1936 PHI N	86	221	55	11	0	4	1.8	24	32	34	20	0	.249	.353	19	2	C-65
1937	80	223	47	10	1	6	2.7	19	29	33	15	0	.211	.345	13	0	C-64
8 yrs.	627	1877	493	83	10	30	1.6	169	251	185	130	1	.263	.365	61	10	C-557, 1B-1

Joe Grace

GRACE, JOSEPH LaVERNE
B. Jan. 5, 1914, Gorham, Ill. D. Sept. 18, 1969, Murphysboro, Ill. — BL TR 6'1" 180 lbs.

	G	AB	H	2B	3B	HR	HR %	R	RBI	BB	SO	SB	BA	SA	PH AB	PH H	G by POS
1938 STL A	12	47	16	1	0	0	0.0	7	4	2	3	0	.340	.362	0	0	OF-12
1939	74	207	63	11	2	3	1.4	35	22	19	24	3	.304	.420	15	5	OF-53
1940	80	229	59	14	2	5	2.2	45	25	26	23	2	.258	.402	17	4	OF-51, C-12
1941	115	362	112	17	4	6	1.7	53	60	57	31	1	.309	.428	15	6	OF-88, C-9
1946 2 teams	STL A (48G – .230)					WAS A (77G – .302)											
" total	125	482	134	24	6	3	0.6	60	44	40	39	2	.278	.371	7	2	OF-117
1947 WAS A	78	234	58	9	4	3	1.3	25	17	35	15	1	.248	.359	10	2	OF-67
6 yrs.	484	1561	442	76	18	20	1.3	225	172	179	135	9	.283	.393	64	19	OF-388, C-21

Mike Grace

GRACE, MICHAEL LEE
B. June 14, 1956, Pontiac, Mich. — BR TR 6' 175 lbs.

	G	AB	H	2B	3B	HR	HR %	R	RBI	BB	SO	SB	BA	SA	PH AB	PH H	G by POS
1978 CIN N	5	3	0	0	0	0	0.0	0	0	0	2	0	.000	.000	3	0	3B-2

John Grady

GRADY, JOHN J.
B. 1860, Lowell, Mass. D. July 15, 1893, Lowell, Mass. — 5'6½" 155 lbs.

	G	AB	H	2B	3B	HR	HR %	R	RBI	BB	SO	SB	BA	SA	PH AB	PH H	G by POS
1884 ALT U	9	36	11	3	0	0	0.0	5		2			.306	.389	0	0	1B-8, OF-1

Mike Grady

GRADY, MICHAEL WILLIAM
B. Dec. 23, 1869, Kennett Square, Pa. D. Dec. 3, 1943, Kennett Square, Pa. — BR TR 5'11" 190 lbs.

	G	AB	H	2B	3B	HR	HR %	R	RBI	BB	SO	SB	BA	SA	PH AB	PH H	G by POS
1894 PHI N	60	190	69	13	8	0	0.0	45	40	14	13	3	.363	.516	3	2	C-44, 1B-11, OF-2
1895	46	123	40	3	1	1	0.8	21	23	14	8	5	.325	.390	2	1	C-38, OF-5, 3B-1, 1B-1
1896	72	242	77	20	7	1	0.4	49	44	16	19	10	.318	.471	4	0	C-61, 3B-7
1897 2 teams	PHI N (4G – .154)					STL N (83G – .280)											
" total	87	335	92	11	3	7	2.1	49	55	27		7	.275	.388	1	0	1B-83, C-3, OF-1
1898 NY A	93	287	85	19	5	3	1.0	64	49	38		20	.296	.429	2	0	C-57, OF-30, 1B-7, SS-3
1899	86	311	104	18	8	2	0.6	47	54	29		20	.334	.463	1	1	C-43, 3B-35, OF-4, 1B-4
1900	83	251	55	8	4	0	0.0	36	27	34		9	.219	.283	6	2	C-41, 1B-12, SS-11, 3B-7, OF-5, 2B-2
1901 WAS A	94	347	99	17	10	9	2.6	57	56	27		14	.285	.470	2	0	1B-59, C-30, OF-3
1904 STL N	101	323	101	15	11	5	1.5	44	43	31		6	.313	.474	7	1	C-77, 1B-21, 2B-3, 3B-1
1905	100	311	89	20	7	4	1.3	41	41	33		15	.286	.434	9	2	C-71, 1B-20
1906	97	280	70	11	3	3	1.1	33	27	48		5	.250	.343	5	1	C-60, 1B-38
11 yrs.	919	3000	881	155	67	35	1.2	486	459	311	40	114	.294	.425	42	10	C-525, 1B-246, 3B-51, OF-50, SS-14, 2B-5

Fred Graff

GRAFF, FREDERICK GOTTLIEB
B. Aug. 25, 1889, Canton, Ohio D. Oct. 4, 1979, Chattanooga, Tenn. — BR TR 5'10½" 164 lbs.

	G	AB	H	2B	3B	HR	HR %	R	RBI	BB	SO	SB	BA	SA	PH AB	PH H	G by POS
1913 STL A	4	5	2	1	0	0	0.0	3		0	3	0	.400	.600	0	0	3B-4

Louis Graff

GRAFF, LOUIS GEORGE (Chappie)
B. July 25, 1866, Philadelphia, Pa. D. Apr. 16, 1955, Bryn Mawr, Pa.

	G	AB	H	2B	3B	HR	HR %	R	RBI	BB	SO	SB	BA	SA	PH AB	PH H	G by POS
1890 SYR AA	1	5	2	1	0	0	0.0	1		0			.400	.600	0	0	C-1

	G	AB	H	2B	3B	HR	HR %	R	RBI	BB	SO	SB	BA	SA	Pinch Hit AB	Pinch Hit H	G by POS

Milt Graff

GRAFF, MILTON EDWARD BL TR 5'7½" 158 lbs.
B. Dec. 30, 1930, Jefferson Center, Pa.

	G	AB	H	2B	3B	HR	HR%	R	RBI	BB	SO	SB	BA	SA	PH AB	PH H	G by POS
1957 KC A	56	155	28	4	3	0	0.0	16	10	15	10	2	.181	.245	1	1	2B-53
1958	5	1	0	0	0	0	0.0	0	0	0	0	0	.000	.000	1	0	2B-1
2 yrs.	61	156	28	4	3	0	0.0	16	10	15	10	2	.179	.244	2	1	2B-54

Barney Graham

GRAHAM, BARNEY
B. Philadelphia, Pa.   D. Dec. 31, 1896, Mobile, Ala.

1889 PHI AA	4	18	3	0	0	0	0.0	0	0	0	0	0	.167	.167	0	0	3B-4

Bernie Graham

GRAHAM, BERNARD
B. 1860, Beloit, Wis.   D. Oct. 31, 1886, Mobile, Ala.

1884 2 teams	C-P U (1G – .200)			BAL U (41G – .269)													
" total	42	172	46	11	0	0	0.0	23		2			.267	.331	0	0	OF-41, 1B-1

Bert Graham

GRAHAM, BERT BB TR 6'1" 187 lbs.
B. Apr. 3, 1886, Near Tilton, Ill.   D. June 19, 1971, Cottonwood, Ariz.

1910 STL A	8	26	3	2	0	0	0.0	1	5	1		0	.115	.269	1	0	1B-5, 2B-2

Charlie Graham

GRAHAM, CHARLES HENRY BR TR
B. Apr. 24, 1878, Santa Clara, Calif.   D. Aug. 29, 1948, San Francisco, Calif.

1906 BOS A	30	90	21	1	0	1	1.1	10	12	10		1	.233	.278	3	0	C-27

Dan Graham

GRAHAM, DANIEL JAY BL TR 6'1" 205 lbs.
B. July 19, 1954, Ray, Ariz.

1979 MIN A	2	4	0	0	0	0	0.0	0	0	0	0	0	.000	.000	1	0	DH-1
1980 BAL A	86	266	74	7	1	15	5.6	32	54	14	40	0	.278	.481	1	0	C-73, 3B-9, DH-2
1981	55	142	25	3	0	2	1.4	7	11	13	32	0	.176	.239	8	0	C-40, DH-6, 3B-4
3 yrs.	143	412	99	10	1	17	4.1	39	65	27	72	0	.240	.393	10	0	C-113, 3B-13, DH-9

Jack Graham

GRAHAM, JOHN BERNARD BL TL 6'2" 200 lbs.
Son of Peaches Graham.
B. Dec. 24, 1916, Minneapolis, Minn.

1946 2 teams	BKN N (2G – .200)			NY N (100G – .219)													
" total	102	275	60	6	4	14	5.1	34	47	23	37	1	.218	.422	25	4	OF-62, 1B-9
1949 STL A	137	500	119	22	1	24	4.8	71	79	61	62	0	.238	.430	1	1	1B-136
2 yrs.	239	775	179	28	5	38	4.9	105	126	84	99	1	.231	.427	26	5	1B-145, OF-62

Lee Graham

GRAHAM, LEE BL TL 5'10" 170 lbs.
B. Sept. 22, 1959, Summerfield, Fla.

1983 BOS A	5	6	0	0	0	0	0.0	2	1	0	0	0	.000	.000	0	0	OF-3

Moonlight Graham

GRAHAM, ARCHIBALD WRIGHT BL TR 5'10½" 170 lbs.
B. Nov. 9, 1879, Fayetteville, N. C.   D. Aug. 25, 1965, Chisholm, Minn.

1905 NY N	1	0	0	0	0	0	–	0	0	0		0	–	–	0	0	OF-1

Peaches Graham

GRAHAM, GEORGE FREDERICK BR TR 5'9" 180 lbs.
Father of Jack Graham.
B. Mar. 23, 1880, Aledo, Ill.   D. July 25, 1939, Long Beach, Calif.

1902 CLE A	2	6	2	0	0	0	0.0	0	1	1		0	.333	.333	1	0	2B-1
1903 CHI N	1	2	0	0	0	0	0.0	0	0	0		0	.000	.000	0	0	P-1
1908 BOS N	75	215	59	5	0	0	0.0	22	22	23		4	.274	.298	8	2	C-62, 2B-5
1909	92	267	64	6	3	0	0.0	27	17	24		7	.240	.285	10	1	C-76, OF-6, SS-1, 3B-1
1910	110	291	82	13	2	0	0.0	31	21	33	15	5	.282	.340	20	7	C-87, 3B-2, OF-1, 1B-1
1911 2 teams	BOS N (33G – .273)			CHI N (36G – .239)													
" total	69	159	41	9	1	0	0.0	13	20	25	13	4	.258	.327	13	3	C-54
1912 PHI N	24	59	17	1	0	1	1.7	6	4	8	5	1	.288	.356	2	2	C-19
7 yrs.	373	999	265	34	6	1	0.1	99	85	114	33	21	.265	.314	54	15	C-298, OF-7, 2B-6, 3B-3, SS-1, 1B-1, P-1

Roy Graham

GRAHAM, ROY VINCENT BR TR 5'10½" 175 lbs.
B. Feb. 22, 1895, San Francisco, Calif.   D. Apr. 26, 1933, Manila, Philippines

1922 CHI A	5	3	0	0	0	0	0.0	0	0	0	0	0	.000	.000	1	0	C-3
1923	36	82	16	2	0	0	0.0	3	6	9	6	0	.195	.220	2	0	C-33
2 yrs.	41	85	16	2	0	0	0.0	3	6	9	6	0	.188	.212	3	0	C-36

Skinny Graham

GRAHAM, ARTHUR WILLIAM JR. BL TR 5'7" 181 lbs.
B. Aug. 12, 1909, Somerville, Mass.   D. July 10, 1967, Cambridge, Mass.

1934 BOS A	13	47	11	2	1	0	0.0	7	3	6	13	1	.234	.319	0	0	OF-13
1935	8	10	3	0	0	0	0.0	1	1	1	3	1	.300	.300	3	1	OF-2
2 yrs.	21	57	14	2	1	0	0.0	8	4	7	16	3	.246	.316	3	1	OF-15

Tiny Graham

GRAHAM, DAWSON FRANK BR TR 6'2" 185 lbs.
B. Dec. 9, 1892, Nashville, Tenn.   D. Dec. 29, 1962, Nashville, Tenn.

1914 CIN N	25	61	14	1	0	0	0.0	5	3	3	10	1	.230	.246	0	0	1B-25

Wayne Graham

GRAHAM, WAYNE LEON BR TR 6' 200 lbs.
B. Apr. 6, 1937, Yoakum, Tex.

1963 PHI N	10	22	4	0	0	0	0.0	1	0	3	1	0	.182	.182	3	0	OF-6
1964 NY N	20	33	3	1	0	0	0.0	1	0	0	5	0	.091	.121	12	1	3B-11
2 yrs.	30	55	7	1	0	0	0.0	2	0	3	6	0	.127	.145	15	1	3B-11, OF-6

Alex Grammas

GRAMMAS, ALEXANDER PETER BR TR 6' 175 lbs.
B. Apr. 3, 1926, Birmingham, Ala.
Manager 1969, 1976-77.

1954 STL N	142	401	106	17	4	2	0.5	57	29	40	29	6	.264	.342	0	0	SS-142, 3B-1

	G	AB	H	2B	3B	HR	HR %	R	RBI	BB	SO	SB	BA	SA	Pinch Hit AB	Pinch Hit H	G by POS

Alex Grammas continued

	G	AB	H	2B	3B	HR	HR %	R	RBI	BB	SO	SB	BA	SA	PH AB	PH H	G by POS
1955	128	366	88	19	2	3	0.8	32	25	33	36	4	.240	.328	1	0	SS-126
1956 2 teams		STL	N	(6G –	.250)		CIN	N	(77G –	.243)							
" total	83	152	37	11	0	0	0.0	18	17	17	20	0	.243	.316	2	1	3B-58, SS-17, 2B-5
1957 CIN N	73	99	30	4	0	0	0.0	14	8	10	6	1	.303	.343	2	0	SS-42, 2B-20, 3B-9
1958	105	216	47	8	0	0	0.0	25	12	34	24	2	.218	.255	1	0	SS-61, 3B-38, 2B-14
1959 STL N	131	368	99	14	2	3	0.8	43	30	38	26	3	.269	.342	1	1	SS-130
1960	102	196	48	4	1	4	2.0	20	17	12	15	0	.245	.337	7	2	SS-40, 2B-38, 3B-13
1961	89	170	36	10	1	0	0.0	23	21	19	21	0	.212	.282	5	1	SS-65, 2B-18, 3B-3
1962 2 teams		STL	N	(21G –	.111)		CHI	N	(23G –	.233)							
" total	44	78	16	3	0	0	0.0	3	4	3	13	1	.205	.244	4	0	SS-29, 2B-5, 3B-1
1963 CHI N	16	27	5	0	0	0	0.0	1	0	3	3	0	.185	.185	3	0	SS-13
10 yrs.	913	2073	512	90	10	12	0.6	236	163	206	193	17	.247	.317	26	5	SS-665, 3B-123, 2B-100

Jack Graney

GRANEY, JOHN GLADSTONE
B. June 10, 1886, St. Thomas, Ont., Canada   D. Apr. 20, 1978, Louisiana, Mo.
BL TL 5'9" 180 lbs.

	G	AB	H	2B	3B	HR	HR %	R	RBI	BB	SO	SB	BA	SA	PH AB	PH H	G by POS
1908 CLE A	2	0	0	0	0	0	–	0	0	0		0	–	–	0	0	P-2
1910	116	454	107	13	9	1	0.2	62	31	37		18	.236	.311	2	1	OF-114
1911	146	527	142	25	5	1	0.2	84	45	66		21	.269	.342	4	2	OF-142
1912	78	264	64	13	2	0	0.0	44	20	50		9	.242	.307	3	0	OF-75
1913	148	517	138	18	12	3	0.6	56	68	48	55	27	.267	.366	0	0	OF-148
1914	130	460	122	17	10	1	0.2	63	39	67	46	20	.265	.352	3	2	OF-127
1915	116	404	105	20	7	1	0.2	42	56	59	29	12	.260	.351	1	0	OF-115
1916	155	589	142	41	14	5	0.8	106	54	102	72	10	.241	.384	1	1	OF-154
1917	146	535	122	29	7	3	0.6	87	35	94	49	16	.228	.325	1	0	OF-145
1918	71	177	42	7	4	0	0.0	27	9	28	13	3	.237	.322	18	7	OF-45
1919	128	461	108	22	8	1	0.2	79	30	105	39	7	.234	.323	1	1	OF-125
1920	62	152	45	11	1	0	0.0	31	13	27	21	4	.296	.382	12	6	OF-47
1921	68	107	32	3	1	2	1.9	19	18	20	9	1	.299	.383	27	8	OF-32
1922	37	58	9	0	0	0	0.0	6	2	9	12	0	.155	.155	19	1	OF-13
14 yrs.	1403	4705	1178	219	79	18	0.4	706	420	712	345	148	.250	.342	92	29	OF-1282, P-2

WORLD SERIES
	G	AB	H	2B	3B	HR	HR %	R	RBI	BB	SO	SB	BA	SA	PH AB	PH H	G by POS
1920 CLE A	3	3	0	0	0	0	0.0	0	0	0	2	0	.000	.000	3	0	OF-2

Eddie Grant

GRANT, EDWARD LESLIE (Harvard Eddie)
B. May 21, 1883, Franklin, Mass.   D. Oct. 5, 1918, Argonne Forest, France
BL TR 5'11½" 168 lbs.

	G	AB	H	2B	3B	HR	HR %	R	RBI	BB	SO	SB	BA	SA	PH AB	PH H	G by POS
1905 CLE A	2	8	3	0	0	0	0.0	1	0	0		0	.375	.375	0	0	2B-2
1907 PHI N	74	268	65	4	3	0	0.0	26	19	10		10	.243	.280	0	0	3B-74
1908	147	598	146	13	8	0	0.0	69	32	35		27	.244	.293	0	0	3B-134, SS-13
1909	154	631	170	18	4	1	0.2	75	37	35		28	.269	.315	0	0	3B-154
1910	152	579	155	15	2	0	0.2	70	67	39	54	25	.268	.316	0	0	3B-152
1911 CIN N	136	458	102	12	7	1	0.2	49	53	51	47	28	.223	.286	0	0	3B-122, SS-11
1912	96	255	61	6	1	2	0.8	37	20	18	27	11	.239	.294	5	1	SS-56, 3B-15
1913 2 teams		CIN	N	(27G –	.213)		NY	N	(27G –	.200)							
" total	54	114	24	2	0	0	0.0	20	10	13	12	8	.211	.228	5	1	3B-31, 2B-3, SS-1
1914 NY N	88	282	78	7	1	0	0.0	34	29	23	21	11	.277	.309	2	0	3B-52, SS-21, 2B-16
1915	57	192	40	2	1	0	0.0	18	10	9	20	5	.208	.229	32	1	3B-8, 2B-9, SS-1, 1B-1
10 yrs.	960	3385	844	79	30	5	0.1	399	277	233	181	153	.249	.295	44	9	3B-789, SS-103, 2B-30, 1B-1

WORLD SERIES
	G	AB	H	2B	3B	HR	HR %	R	RBI	BB	SO	SB	BA	SA	PH AB	PH H	G by POS
1913 NY N	2	1	0	0	0	0	0.0	1	0	0	0	0	.000	.000	1	0	

Jimmy Grant

GRANT, JAMES CHARLES
B. Oct. 6, 1918, Racine, Wis.   D. July 8, 1970, Rochester, Minn.
BL TR 5'8" 166 lbs.

	G	AB	H	2B	3B	HR	HR %	R	RBI	BB	SO	SB	BA	SA	PH AB	PH H	G by POS
1942 CHI A	12	36	6	1	1	0	0.0	0	1	5	6	1	.167	.250	1	0	3B-10
1943 2 teams		CHI	A	(58G –	.259)		CLE	A	(15G –	.136)							
" total	73	219	54	11	2	4	1.8	26	23	22	41	4	.247	.370	19	2	3B-56
1944 CLE A	61	99	27	4	3	1	1.0	12	12	11	20	1	.273	.404	32	5	2B-20, 3B-4
3 yrs.	146	354	87	16	6	5	1.4	38	36	38	67	5	.246	.367	52	7	3B-70, 2B-20

Tom Grant

GRANT, THOMAS R.
B. May 28, 1957, Mendon, Mass.
BL TR 6'2" 185 lbs.

	G	AB	H	2B	3B	HR	HR %	R	RBI	BB	SO	SB	BA	SA	PH AB	PH H	G by POS
1983 CHI N	16	20	3	1	0	0	0.0	3	2	1	4	0	.150	.200	5	0	OF-10

George Grantham

GRANTHAM, GEORGE FARLEY (Boots)
B. May 20, 1900, Galena, Kans.   D. Mar. 16, 1954, Kingman, Ariz.
BL TR 5'10" 170 lbs.

	G	AB	H	2B	3B	HR	HR %	R	RBI	BB	SO	SB	BA	SA	PH AB	PH H	G by POS
1922 CHI N	7	23	4	1	1	0	0.0	3	3	1	3	2	.174	.304	1	0	3B-5
1923	152	570	160	36	8	8	1.4	81	70	71	92	43	.281	.414	2	0	2B-150
1924	127	469	148	19	6	12	2.6	85	60	55	63	21	.316	.458	2	0	2B-118, 3B-6
1925 PIT N	114	359	117	24	6	8	2.2	74	52	50	29	14	.326	.493	9	1	1B-102
1926	141	449	143	27	13	8	1.8	66	70	60	42	6	.318	.490	6	2	1B-132
1927	151	531	162	33	11	8	1.5	96	66	74	39	9	.305	.454	0	0	2B-124, 1B-29
1928	124	440	142	24	9	10	2.3	93	85	59	37	9	.323	.486	4	0	1B-119, 3B-1, 2B-1
1929	110	349	107	23	10	12	3.4	85	59	93	38	10	.307	.533	5	0	2B-76, OF-19, 1B-12
1930	146	552	179	34	14	18	3.3	120	99	81	66	5	.324	.534	1	0	2B-141, 1B-4
1931	127	465	142	26	6	10	2.2	91	46	71	50	5	.305	.452	4	0	1B-78, 2B-51
1932 CIN N	126	493	144	29	6	6	1.2	81	39	56	40	4	.292	.412	0	0	2B-115, 1B-10
1933	87	260	53	14	3	4	1.5	32	28	38	21	4	.204	.327	7	2	2B-72, 1B-17
1934 NY N	32	29	7	2	0	1	3.4	5	4	8	6	0	.241	.414	21	6	1B-4, 3B-2
13 yrs.	1444	4989	1508	292	93	105	2.1	912	712	717	526	132	.302	.461	62	11	2B-848, 1B-507, OF-19, 3B-14

WORLD SERIES
	G	AB	H	2B	3B	HR	HR %	R	RBI	BB	SO	SB	BA	SA	PH AB	PH H	G by POS
1925 PIT N	5	15	2	0	0	0	0.0	0	0	0	3	1	.133	.133	1	0	1B-4
1927	3	11	4	1	0	0	0.0	0	1	0	1	0	.364	.455	0	0	2B-3
2 yrs.	8	26	6	1	0	0	0.0	0	1	0	4	1	.231	.269	1	0	1B-4, 2B-3

	G	AB	H	2B	3B	HR	HR %	R	RBI	BB	SO	SB	BA	SA	Pinch Hit AB	H	G by POS

Mickey Grasso

GRASSO, NEWTON MICHAEL   BR TR 6'   195 lbs.
B. May 10, 1920, Newark, N. J.   D. Oct. 15, 1975, Miami, Fla.

	G	AB	H	2B	3B	HR	HR %	R	RBI	BB	SO	SB	BA	SA	PH AB	H	G by POS
1946 NY N	7	22	3	0	0	0	0.0	1	1	0	3	0	.136	.136	0	0	C-7
1950 WAS A	75	195	56	4	1	1	0.5	25	22	25	31	1	.287	.333	6	1	C-69
1951	52	175	36	3	0	1	0.6	16	14	14	17	0	.206	.240	4	0	C-49
1952	115	361	78	9	0	0	0.0	22	27	29	36	1	.216	.241	1	0	C-114
1953	61	196	41	7	0	2	1.0	13	22	9	20	0	.209	.276	2	0	C-59
1954 CLE A	4	6	2	0	0	1	16.7	1	1	1	1	0	.333	.833	0	0	C-4
1955 NY N	8	2	0	0	0	0	0.0	0	0	3	0	0	.000	.000	0	0	C-8
7 yrs.	322	957	216	23	1	5	0.5	78	87	81	108	2	.226	.268	13	1	C-310

WORLD SERIES
| 1954 CLE A | 1 | 0 | 0 | 0 | 0 | 0 | – | 0 | 0 | 0 | 0 | 0 | – | – | 0 | 0 | C-1 |

Lew Graulich

GRAULICH, LEWIS
B. Camden, N. J.   Deceased.

	G	AB	H	2B	3B	HR	HR %	R	RBI	BB	SO	SB	BA	SA	PH AB	H	G by POS
1891 PHI N	7	26	8	0	0	0	0.0	2	3	1	2	0	.308	.308	0	0	C-4, 1B-3

Frank Graves

GRAVES, FRANK M.   6'   163 lbs.
B. Nov. 2, 1860, Cincinnati, Ohio   Deceased.

	G	AB	H	2B	3B	HR	HR %	R	RBI	BB	SO	SB	BA	SA	PH AB	H	G by POS
1886 STL N	43	138	21	2	0	0	0.0	7	9	7	48		.152	.167	0	0	C-41, OF-3, P-1

Joe Graves

GRAVES, JOSEPH EBENEZER   BL TR 5'10"   160 lbs.
Brother of Sid Graves.
B. Feb. 27, 1906, Marblehead, Mass.   D. Dec. 22, 1980, Salem, Mass.

	G	AB	H	2B	3B	HR	HR %	R	RBI	BB	SO	SB	BA	SA	PH AB	H	G by POS
1926 CHI N	2	5	0	0	0	0	0.0	0	0	0	1	0	.000	.000	0	0	3B-2

Sid Graves

GRAVES, SAMUEL SIDNEY (Whitey)   BR TR 6'   170 lbs.
Brother of Joe Graves.
B. Nov. 30, 1901, Marblehead, Mass.

	G	AB	H	2B	3B	HR	HR %	R	RBI	BB	SO	SB	BA	SA	PH AB	H	G by POS
1927 BOS N	7	20	5	1	1	0	0.0	5	2	0	1	1	.250	.400	1	0	OF-5

Dick Gray

GRAY, RICHARD BENJAMIN   BR TR 5'11"   165 lbs.
B. July 11, 1931, Jefferson, Pa.

	G	AB	H	2B	3B	HR	HR %	R	RBI	BB	SO	SB	BA	SA	PH AB	H	G by POS
1958 LA N	58	197	49	5	6	9	4.6	25	30	19	30	1	.249	.472	4	2	3B-55
1959 2 teams	57	LA N (21G – .154)				STL N (36G – .314)											
" total	57	103	24	2	0	3	2.9	17	10	12	20	3	.233	.340	25	5	3B-17, SS-13, 2B-2, OF-1
1960 STL N	9	5	0	0	0	0	0.0	1	1	2	2	0	.000	.000	3	0	2B-4, 3B-1
3 yrs.	124	305	73	7	6	12	3.9	43	41	33	52	4	.239	.420	32	7	3B-73, SS-13, 2B-6, OF-1

Gary Gray

GRAY, GARY GEORGE   BR TR 6'   187 lbs.
B. Sept. 21, 1952, New Orleans, La.

	G	AB	H	2B	3B	HR	HR %	R	RBI	BB	SO	SB	BA	SA	PH AB	H	G by POS
1977 TEX A	1	2	0	0	0	0	0.0	0	0	0	1	0	.000	.000	0	0	OF-1
1978	17	50	12	1	0	2	4.0	4	6	1	12	1	.240	.380	5	1	DH-11
1979	16	42	10	0	0	0	0.0	4	1	2	8	1	.238	.238	5	2	DH-13
1980 CLE A	28	54	8	1	0	2	3.7	4	4	3	13	0	.148	.278	12	1	DH-9, OF-6, 1B-6
1981 SEA A	69	208	51	7	1	13	6.3	27	31	4	44	2	.245	.476	19	5	1B-34, DH-15, OF-4
1982	80	269	69	14	2	7	2.6	26	29	24	59	1	.257	.401	7	2	1B-60, DH-14
6 yrs.	211	625	150	23	3	24	3.8	65	71	34	137	5	.240	.402	48	11	1B-100, DH-62, OF-11

Jim Gray

GRAY, JAMES W.
B. Aug. 7, 1862, Pittsburgh, Pa.   D. Jan. 31, 1938, Pittsburgh, Pa.

	G	AB	H	2B	3B	HR	HR %	R	RBI	BB	SO	SB	BA	SA	PH AB	H	G by POS
1884 PIT AA	1	2	1	0	0	0	0.0		0				.500	.500	0	0	3B-1

Lorenzo Gray

GRAY, LORENZO   BR TR 6'1"   180 lbs.
B. Mar. 4, 1958, Mound Bayou, Miss.

	G	AB	H	2B	3B	HR	HR %	R	RBI	BB	SO	SB	BA	SA	PH AB	H	G by POS
1982 CHI A	17	28	8	1	0	0	0.0	4	0	2	4	1	.286	.321	1	0	3B-16
1983	41	78	14	3	0	1	1.3	18	4	8	16	1	.179	.256	3	1	3B-31, DH-7
2 yrs.	58	106	22	4	0	1	0.9	22	4	10	20	2	.208	.274	4	1	3B-47, DH-7

Milt Gray

GRAY, MILTON MARSHALL   BR TR 6'1"   170 lbs.
B. Feb. 21, 1914, Louisville, Ky.   D. June 30, 1969, Quincy, Fla.

	G	AB	H	2B	3B	HR	HR %	R	RBI	BB	SO	SB	BA	SA	PH AB	H	G by POS
1937 WAS A	2	6	0	0	0	0	0.0	0	0	0	1	0	.000	.000	0	0	C-2

Pete Gray

GRAY, PETER   BL TL 6'1"   169 lbs.
Born Peter J. Wyshner.
B. Mar. 6, 1917, Nanticoke, Pa.

	G	AB	H	2B	3B	HR	HR %	R	RBI	BB	SO	SB	BA	SA	PH AB	H	G by POS
1945 STL A	77	234	51	6	2	0	0.0	26	13	13	11	5	.218	.261	12	1	OF-61

Reddy Gray

GRAY, JAMES D.
Deceased.

	G	AB	H	2B	3B	HR	HR %	R	RBI	BB	SO	SB	BA	SA	PH AB	H	G by POS
1890 2 teams		PIT P (2G – .222)				PIT N (1G – .000)											
" total	3	12	2	0	0	1	8.3	3	3	0	3	0	.167	.417	0	0	2B-2, SS-1
1893 PIT N	2	9	4	1	0	0	0.0	0	2	0	1	0	.444	.556	0	0	SS-2
2 yrs.	5	21	6	1	0	1	4.8	3	5	0	4	0	.286	.476	0	0	SS-3, 2B-2

Stan Gray

GRAY, STANLEY OSCAR (Dolly)   BR TR 6'1½"   184 lbs.
B. Dec. 10, 1888, Ladonia, Tex.   D. Oct. 11, 1964, Snyder, Tex.

	G	AB	H	2B	3B	HR	HR %	R	RBI	BB	SO	SB	BA	SA	PH AB	H	G by POS
1912 PIT N	6	20	5	0	1	0	0.0	4	2	0	3	0	.250	.350	1	0	1B-4

Danny Green

GREEN, EDWARD   BL
B. Nov. 6, 1876, Burlington, N. J.   D. Nov. 9, 1914, Camden, N. J.

	G	AB	H	2B	3B	HR	HR %	R	RBI	BB	SO	SB	BA	SA	PH AB	H	G by POS
1898 CHI N	47	188	59	4	3	4	2.1	26	27	7		12	.314	.431	0	0	OF-47
1899	117	475	140	12	11	6	1.3	90	56	35		18	.295	.404	2	0	OF-115
1900	103	389	116	5	5	5	1.3	63	49	17		28	.298	.416	2	1	OF-101
1901	133	537	168	16	12	6	1.1	82	60	40		31	.313	.421	0	0	OF-133

	G	AB	H	2B	3B	HR	HR %	R	RBI	BB	SO	SB	BA	SA	Pinch Hit AB	Pinch Hit H	G by POS

Danny Green continued

	G	AB	H	2B	3B	HR	HR %	R	RBI	BB	SO	SB	BA	SA	PH AB	PH H	G by POS
1902 CHI A	129	481	150	16	11	0	0.0	77	62	53		35	.312	.391	0	0	OF-129
1903	135	499	154	26	7	6	1.2	75	62	47		29	.309	.425	2	1	OF-133
1904	147	536	142	16	10	2	0.4	83	62	63		28	.265	.343	1	0	OF-146
1905	112	379	92	13	6	0	0.0	56	44	53		11	.243	.309	5	1	OF-107
8 yrs.	923	3484	1021	124	65	29	0.8	552	422	315		192	.293	.391	12	2	OF-911

David Green

GREEN, DAVID ALEJANDRO   BR TR 6'3"   170 lbs.
B. Dec. 4, 1960, Managua, Nicaragua

	G	AB	H	2B	3B	HR	HR %	R	RBI	BB	SO	SB	BA	SA	PH AB	PH H	G by POS
1981 STL N	21	34	5	1	0	0	0.0	4	2	6	5	0	.147	.176	2	0	OF-18
1982	76	166	47	7	1	2	1.2	21	23	8	29	11	.283	.373	12	4	OF-68
1983	146	422	120	14	10	8	1.9	52	69	26	76	34	.284	.422	20	6	OF-136
1984	126	452	121	14	4	15	3.3	49	65	20	105	17	.268	.416	5	1	1B-117, OF-14
4 yrs.	369	1074	293	36	15	25	2.3	128	159	60	215	62	.273	.404	39	11	OF-236, 1B-117

LEAGUE CHAMPIONSHIP SERIES

	G	AB	H	2B	3B	HR	HR %	R	RBI	BB	SO	SB	BA	SA	PH AB	PH H	G by POS
1982 STL N	2	1	1	0	0	0	0.0	1	0	0	0	0	1.000	1.000	0	0	OF-2

WORLD SERIES

	G	AB	H	2B	3B	HR	HR %	R	RBI	BB	SO	SB	BA	SA	PH AB	PH H	G by POS
1982 STL N	7	10	2	1	1	0	0.0	3	0	1	3	0	.200	.500	1	0	OF-5

Dick Green

GREEN, RICHARD LARRY   BR TR 5'10"   180 lbs.
B. Apr. 21, 1941, Sioux City, Iowa

	G	AB	H	2B	3B	HR	HR %	R	RBI	BB	SO	SB	BA	SA	PH AB	PH H	G by POS
1963 KC A	13	37	10	2	0	1	2.7	5	4	2	10	0	.270	.405	2	0	SS-6, 2B-4
1964	130	435	115	14	5	11	2.5	48	37	27	87	3	.264	.395	3	2	2B-120
1965	133	474	110	15	1	15	3.2	64	55	50	110	0	.232	.363	7	2	2B-126
1966	140	507	127	24	3	9	1.8	58	62	27	101	6	.250	.363	1	0	2B-137, 3B-2
1967	122	349	69	12	4	5	1.4	26	37	30	68	6	.198	.298	14	4	3B-59, 2B-50, SS-1, 1B-1
1968 OAK A	76	202	47	6	0	6	3.0	19	18	21	41	3	.233	.351	9	3	2B-61, 3B-1, C-1
1969	136	483	133	25	6	12	2.5	61	64	53	94	2	.275	.427	4	1	2B-131
1970	135	384	73	7	0	4	1.0	34	29	38	73	3	.190	.240	7	2	2B-127, 3B-5, C-1
1971	144	475	116	14	1	12	2.5	58	49	51	83	1	.244	.354	1	0	2B-143, SS-1
1972	26	42	12	1	1	0	0.0	1	3	3	5	0	.286	.357	0	0	2B-26
1973	133	332	87	17	0	3	0.9	33	42	21	63	0	.262	.340	0	0	2B-133, SS-1, 3B-1
1974	100	287	61	8	2	2	0.7	20	22	22	50	2	.213	.275	0	0	2B-100
12 yrs.	1288	4007	960	145	23	80	2.0	427	422	345	785	26	.240	.347	48	14	2B-1158, 3B-68, SS-9, C-2, 1B-1

LEAGUE CHAMPIONSHIP SERIES

	G	AB	H	2B	3B	HR	HR %	R	RBI	BB	SO	SB	BA	SA	PH AB	PH H	G by POS
1971 OAK A	3	7	2	0	0	0	0.0	0	0	1	1	0	.286	.286	0	0	2B-3
1972	5	8	1	1	0	0	0.0	0	0	0	0	0	.125	.250	0	0	2B-5
1973	5	13	1	1	0	0	0.0	0	1	1	4	0	.077	.154	0	0	2B-5
1974	4	9	2	0	0	0	0.0	0	0	2	1	0	.222	.222	0	0	2B-4
4 yrs.	17	37	6	2	0	0	0.0	0	1	4	6	0	.162	.216	0	0	2B-17

WORLD SERIES

	G	AB	H	2B	3B	HR	HR %	R	RBI	BB	SO	SB	BA	SA	PH AB	PH H	G by POS
1972 OAK A	7	18	6	2	0	0	0.0	0	1	0	4	0	.333	.444	0	0	2B-7
1973	7	16	1	0	0	0	0.0	0	0	1	6	0	.063	.063	0	0	2B-7
1974	5	13	0	0	0	0	0.0	1	1	1	4	0	.000	.000	0	0	2B-5
3 yrs.	19	47	7	2	0	0	0.0	1	2	2	14	0	.149	.191	0	0	2B-19

Gene Green

GREEN, GENE LEROY   BR TR 6'2½"   200 lbs.
B. June 26, 1933, Los Angeles, Calif.   D. May 23, 1981, St. Louis, Mo.

	G	AB	H	2B	3B	HR	HR %	R	RBI	BB	SO	SB	BA	SA	PH AB	PH H	G by POS
1957 STL N	6	15	3	1	0	0	0.0	0	2	0	3	0	.200	.267	3	0	OF-3
1958	137	442	124	18	3	13	2.9	47	55	37	48	2	.281	.423	13	1	OF-75, C-48
1959	30	74	14	6	0	1	1.4	8	3	5	18	0	.189	.311	2	0	OF-19, C-11
1960 BAL A	1	4	1	0	0	0	0.0	0	0	0	0	0	.250	.250	0	0	OF-1
1961 WAS A	110	364	102	16	3	18	4.9	52	62	35	65	0	.280	.489	11	2	C-79, OF-21
1962 CLE A	66	143	40	4	1	11	7.7	16	28	8	21	0	.280	.552	30	10	OF-33, 1B-2
1963 2 teams			CLE A (43G – .205)			CIN N (15G – .226)											
" total	58	109	23	4	0	3	2.8	7	10	4	30	0	.211	.330	31	5	OF-18, C-8
7 yrs.	408	1151	307	49	7	46	4.0	130	160	89	185	2	.267	.441	90	18	OF-170, C-146, 1B-2

Jim Green

GREEN, JAMES R.
B. Cleveland, Ohio   Deceased.

	G	AB	H	2B	3B	HR	HR %	R	RBI	BB	SO	SB	BA	SA	PH AB	PH H	G by POS
1884 WAS U	10	36	5	1	0	0	0.0	0		1			.139	.167	0	0	3B-9, OF-1

Joe Green

GREEN, JOSEPH HENRY (Tilly)   BR TR 6'2"   170 lbs.
B. Sept. 17, 1897, Philadelphia, Pa.   D. Feb. 4, 1972, Bryn Mawr, Pa.

	G	AB	H	2B	3B	HR	HR %	R	RBI	BB	SO	SB	BA	SA	PH AB	PH H	G by POS
1924 PHI A	1	1	0	0	0	0	0.0	0	0	0	0	0	.000	.000	1	0	

Julius Green

GREEN, JULIUS FOUST   BL TR 6'2½"   185 lbs.
Also known as Henry Green.
B. June 25, 1902, Greensboro, N. C.   D. Mar. 19, 1974, San Clemente, Calif.

	G	AB	H	2B	3B	HR	HR %	R	RBI	BB	SO	SB	BA	SA	PH AB	PH H	G by POS
1928 PHI N	11	6	3	0	0	0	0.0	0	3	1	0	0	.500	.500	6	3	P-1
1929	21	19	4	1	0	0	0.0	1	0	2	4	0	.211	.263	14	2	P-5
2 yrs.	32	25	7	1	0	0	0.0	1	0	5	5	0	.280	.320	20	5	P-6

Lenny Green

GREEN, LEONARD CHARLES   BL TL 5'11"   170 lbs.
B. Jan. 6, 1934, Detroit, Mich.

	G	AB	H	2B	3B	HR	HR %	R	RBI	BB	SO	SB	BA	SA	PH AB	PH H	G by POS
1957 BAL A	19	33	6	1	1	1	3.0	2	5	1	4	0	.182	.364	2	0	OF-15
1958	69	91	21	4	0	1	1.1	10	4	9	10	0	.231	.275	9	1	OF-53
1959 2 teams			BAL A (27G – .292)			WAS A (88G – .242)											
" total	115	214	53	6	4	3	1.4	32	17	21	18	9	.248	.327	35	11	OF-81
1960 WAS A	127	330	97	16	7	5	1.5	62	33	43	25	21	.294	.430	29	8	OF-100
1961 MIN A	156	600	171	28	7	9	1.5	92	50	81	50	17	.285	.400	2	1	OF-153
1962	158	619	168	33	3	14	2.3	97	63	88	36	8	.271	.402	3	1	OF-156
1963	145	280	67	10	1	4	1.4	41	27	31	21	11	.239	.325	23	4	OF-119

	G	AB	H	2B	3B	HR	HR %	R	RBI	BB	SO	SB	BA	SA	Pinch Hit AB	Pinch Hit H	G by POS

Lenny Green continued

GREEN, ELIJAH JERRY
B. Oct. 27, 1933, Oakland, Calif.   BB TR 6' 175 lbs.

	G	AB	H	2B	3B	HR	HR%	R	RBI	BB	SO	SB	BA	SA	PH AB	PH H	G by POS
1964 3 teams	MIN A (26G – .000)					LA A (39G – .250)			BAL A (14G – .190)								
" total	79	128	27	2	0	2	1.6	16	5	21	17	3	.211	.273	33	4	OF-38
1965 BOS A	119	373	103	24	6	7	1.9	69	24	48	43	8	.276	.429	24	7	OF-95
1966	85	133	32	6	0	1	0.8	18	12	15	19	0	.241	.308	52	14	OF-27
1967 DET A	58	151	42	8	1	1	0.7	22	13	9	17	1	.278	.364	11	1	OF-44
1968	6	4	1	0	0	0	0.0	0	0	1	0	0	.250	.250	3	1	OF-2
12 yrs.	1136	2956	788	138	27	47	1.6	461	253	368	260	78	.267	.379	226	53	OF-883

Pumpsie Green

GREEN, ELIJAH JERRY
B. Oct. 27, 1933, Oakland, Calif.   BB TR 6' 175 lbs.

	G	AB	H	2B	3B	HR	HR%	R	RBI	BB	SO	SB	BA	SA	PH AB	PH H	G by POS
1959 BOS A	50	172	40	6	3	1	0.6	30	10	29	22	4	.233	.320	4	0	2B-45, SS-1
1960	133	260	63	10	3	3	1.2	36	21	44	47	3	.242	.338	24	8	2B-69, SS-41
1961	88	219	57	12	3	6	2.7	33	27	42	32	4	.260	.425	25	7	SS-57, 2B-7
1962	56	91	21	2	1	2	2.2	12	11	11	18	1	.231	.341	35	8	2B-18, SS-5
1963 NY N	17	54	15	1	2	1	1.9	8	5	12	13	0	.278	.426	0	0	3B-16
5 yrs.	344	796	196	31	12	13	1.6	119	74	138	132	12	.246	.364	88	23	2B-139, SS-104, 3B-16

Hank Greenberg

GREENBERG, HENRY BENJAMIN (Hammerin' Hank)
B. Jan. 1, 1911, New York, N. Y.   BR TR 6'3½" 210 lbs.
Hall of Fame 1956.

	G	AB	H	2B	3B	HR	HR%	R	RBI	BB	SO	SB	BA	SA	PH AB	PH H	G by POS
1930 DET A	1	1	0	0	0	0	0.0	0	0	0	0	0	.000	.000	1	0	
1933	117	449	135	33	3	12	2.7	59	87	46	78	6	.301	.468	1	0	1B-117
1934	153	593	201	63	7	26	4.4	118	139	63	93	9	.339	.600	0	0	1B-153
1935	152	619	203	46	16	36	5.8	121	170	87	91	4	.328	.628	0	0	1B-152
1936	12	46	16	6	2	1	2.2	10	16	9	6	1	.348	.630	0	0	1B-12
1937	154	594	200	49	14	40	6.7	137	183	102	101	8	.337	.668	0	0	1B-154
1938	155	556	175	23	4	58	10.4	144	146	119	92	7	.315	.683	0	0	1B-155
1939	138	500	156	42	7	33	6.6	112	112	91	95	8	.312	.622	1	0	1B-136
1940	148	573	195	50	8	41	7.2	129	150	93	75	6	.340	.670	0	0	OF-148
1941	19	67	18	5	1	2	3.0	12	12	16	12	1	.269	.463	0	0	OF-19
1945	78	270	84	20	2	13	4.8	47	60	42	40	3	.311	.544	5	2	OF-72
1946	142	523	145	29	5	44	8.4	91	127	80	88	5	.277	.604	2	0	1B-140
1947 PIT N	125	402	100	13	2	25	6.2	71	74	104	73	0	.249	.478	6	1	1B-119
13 yrs.	1394	5193	1628	379	71	331	6.4 9th	1051	1276	852	844	58	.313	.605 5th	16	3	1B-1138, OF-239

WORLD SERIES																	
1934 DET A	7	28	9	2	1	1	3.6	4	7	4	9	1	.321	.571	0	0	1B-7
1935	2	6	1	0	0	1	16.7	1	2	1	0	0	.167	.667	0	0	1B-2
1940	7	28	10	2	1	1	3.6	5	6	2	5	0	.357	.607	0	0	OF-7
1945	7	23	7	3	0	2	8.7	7	7	6	5	0	.304	.696	0	0	OF-7
4 yrs.	23	85	27	7	2	5	5.9	17	22	13	19	1	.318 8th	.624	0	0	OF-14, 1B-9 7th

Al Greene

GREENE, ALTAR ALPHONSE
B. Nov. 9, 1954, Detroit, Mich.   BL TR 5'11" 190 lbs.

	G	AB	H	2B	3B	HR	HR%	R	RBI	BB	SO	SB	BA	SA	PH AB	PH H	G by POS
1979 DET A	29	59	8	1	0	3	5.1	9	6	10	15	0	.136	.305	6	2	DH-15, OF-6

Willie Greene

GREENE, PATRICK JOSEPH
Played as Pat Foley 1902.
B. Mar. 20, 1875, Providence, R. I.   D. Oct. 20, 1934, Providence, R. I.

	G	AB	H	2B	3B	HR	HR%	R	RBI	BB	SO	SB	BA	SA	PH AB	PH H	G by POS
1902 PHI N	19	65	11	1	0	0	0.0	6	1	2		2	.169	.185	0	0	3B-19
1903 2 teams	NY A (4G – .308)					DET A (1G – .000)											
" total	5	16	4	1	0	0	0.0	1	0	0		0	.250	.313	1	0	3B-3, SS-1
2 yrs.	24	81	15	2	0	0	0.0	7	1	2		2	.185	.210	1	0	3B-22, SS-1

Jim Greengrass

GREENGRASS, JAMES RAYMOND
B. Oct. 24, 1927, Addison, N. Y.   BR TR 6'1" 200 lbs.

	G	AB	H	2B	3B	HR	HR%	R	RBI	BB	SO	SB	BA	SA	PH AB	PH H	G by POS
1952 CIN N	18	68	21	2	1	5	7.4	10	24	7	12	0	.309	.588	1	0	OF-17
1953	154	606	173	22	7	20	3.3	86	100	47	83	6	.285	.444	1	0	OF-153
1954	139	542	152	27	4	27	5.0	79	95	41	81	0	.280	.494	2	0	OF-137
1955 2 teams	CIN N (13G – .103)					PHI N (94G – .272)											
" total	107	362	92	22	2	12	3.3	44	38	42	52	0	.254	.425	8	2	OF-94, 3B-2
1956 PHI N	86	215	44	9	2	5	2.3	24	25	28	43	0	.205	.335	22	6	OF-62
5 yrs.	504	1793	482	82	16	69	3.8	243	282	165	271	6	.269	.448	34	8	OF-463, 3B-2

Bill Greenwood

GREENWOOD, WILLIAM F.
B. 1857, Philadelphia, Pa.   D. May 2, 1902, Philadelphia, Pa.   BR TL 5'7½" 180 lbs.

	G	AB	H	2B	3B	HR	HR%	R	RBI	BB	SO	SB	BA	SA	PH AB	PH H	G by POS
1882 PHI AA	7	30	9	1	0	0	0.0	8		1			.300	.333	0	0	OF-7, 2B-2
1884 BKN AA	92	385	83	8	3	3	0.8	52		10			.216	.275	0	0	2B-92, SS-1
1887 BAL AA	118	495	130	16	6	0	0.0	114		54		71	.263	.319	0	0	2B-86, SS-28, OF-1
1888	115	409	78	13	1	0	0.0	69	29	30		46	.191	.227	0	0	2B-118
1889 COL AA	118	414	93	7	10	3	0.7	62	49	58	71	37	.225	.312	0	0	2B-118
1890 ROC AA	124	437	97	11	6	2	0.5	76		48		40	.222	.288	0	0	2B-123, SS-1
6 yrs.	574	2170	490	56	26	8	0.4	381	77	201	71	194	.226	.287	0	0	2B-538, SS-30, OF-9

Brian Greer

GREER, BRIAN KEITH
B. May 13, 1957, Lynwood, Calif.   BR TR 6'3" 210 lbs.

	G	AB	H	2B	3B	HR	HR%	R	RBI	BB	SO	SB	BA	SA	PH AB	PH H	G by POS
1977 SD N	1	1	0	0	0	0	0.0	0	0	0	1	0	.000	.000	1	0	
1979	4	3	0	0	0	0	0.0	0	0	0	1	0	.000	.000	0	0	OF-4
2 yrs.	5	4	0	0	0	0	0.0	0	0	0	2	0	.000	.000	1	0	OF-4

Ed Greer

GREER, EDWARD C.
B. 1865, Philadelphia, Pa.   D. Feb. 4, 1890, Philadelphia, Pa.   BR

	G	AB	H	2B	3B	HR	HR%	R	RBI	BB	SO	SB	BA	SA	PH AB	PH H	G by POS
1885 BAL AA	56	211	42	7	0	0	0.0	32		8			.199	.232	0	0	OF-47, C-12

	G	AB	H	2B	3B	HR	HR%	R	RBI	BB	SO	SB	BA	SA	Pinch Hit AB	Pinch Hit H	G by POS

Ed Greer continued

1886 2 teams	**BAL AA** (11G – .132)				**PHI AA** (71G – .193)												
" total	82	302	56	6	3	1	0.3	35		10			.185	.235	0	0	OF-79, C-3
1887 2 teams	**PHI AA** (3G – .182)				**BKN AA** (91G – .254)												
" total	94	338	85	13	2	2	0.6	50		25		35	.251	.320	0	0	OF-79, C-16
3 yrs.	232	851	183	26	5	3	0.4	117		25		35	.215	.268	0	0	OF-205, C-31

Tim Greisenbeck

GREISENBECK, CARLOS TIMOTHY   BR TR 5'10½" 190 lbs.
B. Dec. 10, 1898, San Antonio, Tex.   D. Mar. 25, 1953, San Antonio, Tex.

	G	AB	H	2B	3B	HR	HR%	R	RBI	BB	SO	SB	BA	SA			G by POS
1920 STL N	5	3	1	0	0	0	0.0	1	0	0	0	0	.333	.333	1	0	C-3

Ed Gremminger

GREMMINGER, LORENZO EDWARD (Battleship)   BR TR 6'1" 200 lbs.
B. Mar. 30, 1874, Canton, Ohio   D. May 26, 1942, Canton, Ohio

	G	AB	H	2B	3B	HR	HR%	R	RBI	BB	SO	SB	BA	SA			G by POS
1895 CLE N	20	78	21	1	0	0	0.0	10	15	5	13	0	.269	.282	0	0	3B-20
1902 BOS N	140	522	134	20	12	1	0.2	55	66	39		7	.257	.347	0	0	3B-140
1903	140	511	135	24	9	5	1.0	57	56	31		12	.264	.376	0	0	3B-140
1904 DET A	83	309	66	13	3	1	0.3	18	28	14		3	.214	.285	0	0	3B-83
4 yrs.	383	1420	356	58	24	7	0.5	140	165	89	13	22	.251	.340	0	0	3B-383

Buddy Gremp

GREMP, LOUIS EDWARD   BR TR 6'1" 175 lbs.
B. Aug. 5, 1919, Denver, Colo.

	G	AB	H	2B	3B	HR	HR%	R	RBI	BB	SO	SB	BA	SA			G by POS
1940 BOS N	4	9	2	0	0	0	0.0	0	2	0	0	0	.222	.222	1	0	1B-3
1941	37	75	18	3	0	0	0.0	7	10	5	3	0	.240	.280	8	1	1B-21, 2B-6, C-3
1942	72	207	45	11	0	3	1.4	12	19	13	21	1	.217	.314	8	3	1B-62, 3B-1
3 yrs.	113	291	65	14	0	3	1.0	19	31	18	24	1	.223	.302	17	4	1B-86, 2B-6, C-3, 3B-1

Bill Grey

GREY, WILLIAM TOBIN   5'11" 175 lbs.
B. Apr. 15, 1871, Philadelphia, Pa.   D. Dec. 8, 1932, Philadelphia, Pa.

	G	AB	H	2B	3B	HR	HR%	R	RBI	BB	SO	SB	BA	SA			G by POS
1890 PHI N	34	128	31	8	4	0	0.0	20	21	6	3	5	.242	.367	0	0	OF-10, 3B-8, 2B-8, C-7, 1B-1
1891	23	75	18	0	0	0	0.0	11	7	3	10	3	.240	.240	0	0	C-11, OF-10, SS-3, 3B-1
1895 CIN N	52	181	55	17	4	1	0.6	24	29	15	8	4	.304	.459	0	0	3B-27, 2B-16, SS-5, C-5, OF-1
1896	46	121	25	2	1	0	0.0	15	17	19	11	6	.207	.240	5	0	2B-12, C-11, SS-8, OF-3, 1B-2, 3B-1
1898 PIT N	137	528	121	17	5	0	0.0	56	67	28		5	.229	.280	0	0	3B-137
5 yrs.	292	1033	250	44	14	1	0.1	126	141	71	32	23	.242	.315	5	0	3B-174, 2B-36, C-34, OF-24, SS-16, 1B-3

Reddy Grey

GREY, ROMER CARL   5'11" 175 lbs.
Born Romer Carl Gray.
B. Jan. 4, 1875, Zanesville, Ohio   D. Nov. 9, 1934, Altadena, Calif.

	G	AB	H	2B	3B	HR	HR%	R	RBI	BB	SO	SB	BA	SA			G by POS
1903 PIT N	2	6	2	0	0	0	0.0	1	1	1		0	.333	.333	0	0	OF-2

Bobby Grich

GRICH, ROBERT ANTHONY   BR TR 6'2" 180 lbs.
B. Jan. 15, 1949, Muskegon, Mich.

	G	AB	H	2B	3B	HR	HR%	R	RBI	BB	SO	SB	BA	SA			G by POS
1970 BAL A	30	95	20	1	3	0	0.0	11	8	9	21	1	.211	.284	1	0	SS-20, 2B-9, 3B-1
1971	7	30	9	0	0	1	3.3	7	6	5	8	1	.300	.400	0	0	SS-5, 2B-2
1972	133	460	128	21	3	12	2.6	66	50	53	96	13	.278	.415	3	1	SS-81, 2B-45, 1B-16, 3B-8
1973	162	581	146	29	7	12	2.1	82	50	107	91	17	.251	.387	0	0	2B-162
1974	160	582	153	29	6	19	3.3	92	82	90	117	17	.263	.431	0	0	2B-160
1975	150	524	136	26	4	13	2.5	81	57	107	88	14	.260	.399	1	0	2B-150
1976	144	518	138	31	4	13	2.5	93	54	86	99	14	.266	.417	3	1	2B-140, 3B-2
1977 CAL A	52	181	44	6	0	7	3.9	24	23	37	40	6	.243	.392	0	0	SS-52
1978	144	487	122	16	2	6	1.2	68	42	75	83	4	.251	.329	0	0	2B-140
1979	153	534	157	30	5	30	5.6	78	101	59	84	1	.294	.537	1	0	2B-153
1980	150	498	135	22	2	14	2.8	60	62	84	108	3	.271	.408	4	2	2B-146, DH-3, 1B-3
1981	100	352	107	14	2	**22**	**6.3**	56	61	40	71	2	.304	**.543**	0	0	2B-100
1982	145	506	132	28	5	19	3.8	74	65	82	109	3	.261	.449	2	1	2B-142, DH-1
1983	120	387	113	17	0	16	4.1	65	62	76	62	2	.292	.460	3	2	2B-115, SS-1
1984	116	363	93	15	1	18	5.0	60	58	57	70	2	.256	.452	5	1	2B-91, 1B-25, 3B-21
15 yrs.	1766	6098	1633	285	44	202	3.3	917	781	967	1147	100	.268	.428	23	8	2B-1562, SS-159, 1B-44, 3B-32, DH-4
LEAGUE CHAMPIONSHIP SERIES																	
1973 BAL A	5	20	2	0	0	1	5.0	1	1	2	5	0	.100	.250	0	0	2B-5
1974	4	16	4	1	0	1	6.3	2	2	0	1	0	.250	.500	0	0	2B-4
1979 CAL A	4	13	2	1	0	0	0.0	0	2	1	1	0	.154	.231	0	0	2B-4
1982	5	15	3	1	0	0	0.0	1	1	2	7	0	.200	.267	0	0	2B-5
4 yrs.	18	64	11	3	0	2	3.1	4	6	5	14	0	.172	.313	0	0	2B-18

Tom Grieve

GRIEVE, THOMAS ALAN   BR TR 6'2" 190 lbs.
B. Mar. 4, 1948, Pittsfield, Mass.

	G	AB	H	2B	3B	HR	HR%	R	RBI	BB	SO	SB	BA	SA			G by POS
1970 WAS A	47	116	23	5	1	3	2.6	12	10	14	38	0	.198	.336	12	2	OF-39
1972 TEX A	64	142	29	2	1	3	2.1	12	11	11	39	1	.204	.296	17	4	OF-49
1973	66	123	38	6	0	7	5.7	22	21	7	25	1	.309	.528	5	2	OF-59, DH-1
1974	84	259	66	10	4	9	3.5	30	32	20	48	0	.255	.429	7	2	DH-40, OF-38, 1B-1
1975	118	369	102	17	1	14	3.8	46	61	22	74	0	.276	.442	14	1	OF-63, DH-45
1976	149	546	139	23	3	20	3.7	57	81	35	119	4	.255	.418	3	1	DH-96, OF-52
1977	79	236	53	9	0	7	3.0	24	30	13	57	1	.225	.352	12	4	OF-60, DH-13
1978 NY N	54	101	21	3	0	2	2.0	5	8	9	23	0	.208	.297	25	2	OF-26
1979 STL N	9	15	3	1	0	0	0.0	1	0	4	1	0	.200	.267	1	0	OF-5
9 yrs.	670	1907	474	76	10	65	3.4	209	254	135	424	7	.249	.401	96	18	OF-391, DH-195, 1B-1

	G	AB	H	2B	3B	HR	HR%	R	RBI	BB	SO	SB	BA	SA	Pinch Hit AB	Pinch Hit H	G by POS

Ken Griffey

GRIFFEY, GEORGE KENNETH
B. Apr. 10, 1950, Donora, Pa.
BL TL 5'11" 190 lbs.

	G	AB	H	2B	3B	HR	HR%	R	RBI	BB	SO	SB	BA	SA	PH AB	PH H	G by POS
1973 CIN N	25	86	33	5	1	3	3.5	19	14	6	10	4	.384	.570	3	2	OF-21
1974	88	227	57	9	5	2	0.9	24	19	27	43	9	.251	.361	15	4	OF-70
1975	132	463	141	15	9	4	0.9	95	46	67	67	16	.305	.402	10	2	OF-119
1976	148	562	189	28	9	6	1.1	111	74	62	65	34	.336	.450	10	3	OF-144
1977	154	585	186	35	8	12	2.1	117	57	69	84	17	.318	.467	4	1	OF-147
1978	158	614	177	33	8	10	1.6	90	63	54	70	23	.288	.417	6	3	OF-154
1979	95	380	120	27	4	8	2.1	62	32	36	39	12	.316	.471	1	1	OF-93
1980	146	544	160	28	10	13	2.4	89	85	62	77	23	.294	.454	7	4	OF-138
1981	101	396	123	21	6	2	0.5	65	34	39	42	12	.311	.409	1	0	OF-99
1982 NY A	127	484	134	23	2	12	2.5	70	54	39	58	10	.277	.407	7	1	OF-125
1983	118	458	140	21	3	11	2.4	60	46	34	45	6	.306	.437	5	1	1B-101, OF-14, DH-2
1984	120	399	109	20	1	7	1.8	44	56	29	32	2	.273	.381	18	5	OF-82, 1B-27, DH-2
12 yrs.	1412	5198	1569	265	66	90	1.7	846	580	524	632	168	.302	.430	87	27	OF-1206, 1B-128, DH-4
LEAGUE CHAMPIONSHIP SERIES																	
1973 CIN N	3	7	1	0	0	0	0.0	0	0	0	1	0	.143	.286	1	0	OF-2
1975	3	12	4	1	0	0	0.0	4	4	0	3	3	.333	.417	0	0	OF-3
1976	3	13	5	0	1	0	0.0	2	2	2	1	2	.385	.538	0	0	OF-3
3 yrs.	9	32	10	2	1	0	0.0	6	6	2	5	5	.313	.438	1	0	OF-8
WORLD SERIES																	
1975 CIN N	7	26	7	3	1	0	0.0	4	4	4	2	2	.269	.462	0	0	OF-7
1976	4	17	1	0	0	0	0.0	2	1	0	1	1	.059	.059	0	0	OF-4
2 yrs.	11	43	8	3	1	0	0.0	6	5	4	3	3	.186	.302	0	0	OF-11

Alfredo Griffin

GRIFFIN, ALFREDO CLAUDINO
B. Mar. 6, 1957, Dominican Republic City, Dominican Republic
BB TR 5'11" 160 lbs.

	G	AB	H	2B	3B	HR	HR%	R	RBI	BB	SO	SB	BA	SA	PH AB	PH H	G by POS
1976 CLE A	12	4	1	0	0	0	0.0	0	0	0	2	0	.250	.250	0	0	SS-6, DH-4
1977	14	41	6	1	0	0	0.0	5	3	3	5	2	.146	.171	0	0	SS-13, DH-1
1978	5	4	2	1	0	0	0.0	1	0	2	1	0	.500	.750	0	0	SS-2
1979 TOR A	153	624	179	22	10	2	0.3	81	31	40	59	21	.287	.364	0	0	SS-153
1980	155	653	166	26	15	2	0.3	63	41	24	58	18	.254	.349	0	0	SS-155
1981	101	388	81	19	6	0	0.0	30	21	17	38	8	.209	.289	0	0	SS-97, 3B-4, 2B-1
1982	162	539	130	20	8	1	0.2	57	48	22	48	10	.241	.314	0	0	SS-162
1983	162	528	132	22	9	4	0.8	62	47	27	44	8	.250	.348	0	0	SS-157, 2B-5, DH-1
1984	140	419	101	8	2	4	1.0	53	30	4	33	11	.241	.298	0	0	SS-115, 2B-21, DH-5
9 yrs.	904	3200	798	119	50	13	0.4	352	221	139	288	78	.249	.330	1	0	SS-860, 2B-27, DH-11, 3B-4

Doug Griffin

GRIFFIN, DOUGLAS LEE
B. June 4, 1947, South Gate, Calif.
BR TR 6' 160 lbs.

	G	AB	H	2B	3B	HR	HR%	R	RBI	BB	SO	SB	BA	SA	PH AB	PH H	G by POS
1970 CAL A	18	55	7	1	0	0	0.0	2	4	6	5	0	.127	.145	0	0	2B-11, 3B-8
1971 BOS A	125	483	118	23	2	3	0.6	51	27	31	45	11	.244	.319	1	0	2B-124
1972	129	470	122	12	1	2	0.4	43	35	45	48	9	.260	.302	0	0	2B-129
1973	113	396	101	14	5	1	0.3	43	33	21	42	7	.255	.323	0	0	2B-113
1974	93	312	83	12	4	0	0.0	35	33	28	21	2	.266	.330	2	1	2B-91, SS-1
1975	100	287	69	6	0	1	0.3	21	29	18	29	2	.240	.272	16	8	2B-99, SS-1
1976	49	127	24	2	0	0	0.0	14	4	9	14	2	.189	.205	3	0	2B-44, DH-2
1977	5	6	0	0	0	0	0.0	0	0	0	0	0	.000	.000	2	0	2B-3
8 yrs.	632	2136	524	70	12	7	0.3	209	165	158	204	33	.245	.299	24	9	2B-614, 3B-8, DH-2, SS-2
WORLD SERIES																	
1975 BOS A	1	1	0	0	0	0	0.0	0	0	0	0	0	.000	.000	0	0	

Ivy Griffin

GRIFFIN, IVY MOORE
B. Jan. 16, 1896, Thomasville, Ala.   D. Aug. 25, 1957, Gainesville, Fla.
BL TR 5'11" 180 lbs.

	G	AB	H	2B	3B	HR	HR%	R	RBI	BB	SO	SB	BA	SA	PH AB	PH H	G by POS
1919 PHI A	17	68	20	2	2	0	0.0	5	6	3	10	0	.294	.382	0	0	1B-17
1920	129	467	111	15	1	0	0.0	46	20	15	49	3	.238	.274	1	0	1B-126, 2B-2
1921	39	103	33	4	2	0	0.0	14	13	5	6	1	.320	.398	10	2	1B-28
3 yrs.	185	638	164	21	5	0	0.0	65	39	23	65	4	.257	.306	11	2	1B-171, 2B-2

Mike Griffin

GRIFFIN, MICHAEL JOSEPH
B. Mar. 20, 1865, Utica, N.Y.   D. Apr. 10, 1908, Utica, N.Y.
Manager 1898.
BL TR 5'7" 160 lbs.

	G	AB	H	2B	3B	HR	HR%	R	RBI	BB	SO	SB	BA	SA	PH AB	PH H	G by POS
1887 BAL AA	136	532	160	32	13	3	0.6	142		55		94	.301	.427	0	0	OF-136
1888	137	542	141	21	11	0	0.0	103	46	55		46	.260	.339	0	0	OF-137
1889	137	533	149	21	14	4	0.8	152	48	91	29	39	.280	.394	0	0	OF-109, SS-25, 2B-5
1890 PHI P	115	492	143	29	6	6	1.2	127	54	64	19	30	.291	.411	0	0	OF-115
1891 BKN N	134	521	141	36	9	3	0.6	106	65	57	31	65	.271	.392	0	0	OF-134
1892	129	459	127	18	11	3	0.7	103	66	68	36	49	.277	.383	0	0	OF-127, SS-2
1893	95	362	106	22	8	5	1.4	85	59	59	23	30	.293	.439	0	0	OF-93, 2B-2
1894	107	405	148	29	5	5	1.2	123	75	78	14	39	.365	.499	1	0	OF-106
1895	131	522	175	38	7	4	0.8	140	65	93	29	27	.335	.458	0	0	OF-131, SS-1
1896	122	493	155	28	9	4	0.8	101	51	48	25	23	.314	.432	0	0	OF-122
1897	134	534	170	25	11	2	0.4	136	56	81		16	.318	.418	0	0	OF-134
1898	134	544	161	18	6	2	0.4	88	40	60		15	.296	.362	0	0	OF-134
12 yrs.	1511	5939	1776	317	110	41	0.7	1406	624	809	206	473	.299	.410	1	0	OF-1478, SS-28, 2B-7

Pug Griffin

GRIFFIN, FRANCIS ARTHUR
B. Apr. 24, 1896, Lincoln, Neb.   D. Oct. 12, 1951, Colorado Springs, Colo.
BR TR 5'11½" 187 lbs.

	G	AB	H	2B	3B	HR	HR%	R	RBI	BB	SO	SB	BA	SA	PH AB	PH H	G by POS
1917 PHI A	18	25	5	1	0	1	4.0	4	3	1	9	1	.200	.360	13	2	1B-3
1920 NY N	5	4	1	0	0	0	0.0	0	0	1	2	0	.250	.250	2	0	OF-2
2 yrs.	23	29	6	1	0	1	3.4	4	3	2	11	1	.207	.345	15	2	1B-3, OF-2

	G	AB	H	2B	3B	HR	HR %	R	RBI	BB	SO	SB	BA	SA	Pinch Hit AB	Pinch Hit H	G by POS

Sandy Griffin

GRIFFIN, TOBIAS CHARLES   BR TR 5'10" 160 lbs.
B. July 19, 1858, Fayetteville, N. Y.   D. June 5, 1926, Fayetteville, N. Y.
Manager 1891.

	G	AB	H	2B	3B	HR	HR %	R	RBI	BB	SO	SB	BA	SA	AB	H	G by POS
1884 NY N	16	62	11	2	0	0	0.0	7		1	19		.177	.210	0	0	OF-16
1890 ROC AA	107	407	125	28	4	5	1.2	85		50		21	.307	.432	0	0	OF-107, 2B-1
1891 WAS AA	20	69	19	4	2	0	0.0	15	10	10	3	2	.275	.391	0	0	OF-20
1893 STL N	23	92	18	1	1	0	0.0	9	9	16	2	2	.196	.228	0	0	OF-23
4 yrs.	166	630	173	35	7	5	0.8	116	18	77	24	25	.275	.376	0	0	OF-166, 2B-1

Tom Griffin

GRIFFIN, THOMAS WILLIAM
B. Titusville, Pa.   D. Apr. 17, 1933, Rockford, Ill.

	G	AB	H	2B	3B	HR	HR %	R	RBI	BB	SO	SB	BA	SA	AB	H	G by POS
1884 MIL U	11	41	9	2	0	0	0.0	5		3			.220	.268	0	0	1B-11

Bert Griffith

GRIFFITH, BERT JOSEPH   BR TR 5'11" 185 lbs.
B. Mar. 3, 1897, St. Louis, Mo.   D. May 5, 1973, Bishop, Calif.

	G	AB	H	2B	3B	HR	HR %	R	RBI	BB	SO	SB	BA	SA	AB	H	G by POS
1922 BKN N	106	325	100	22	8	2	0.6	45	35	5	11	5	.308	.443	23	4	OF-77, 1B-6
1923	79	248	73	8	4	2	0.8	23	37	13	16	1	.294	.383	17	3	OF-62
1924 WAS A	6	8	1	0	0	0	0.0	1	0	0	1	0	.125	.125	4	0	OF-2
3 yrs.	191	581	174	30	12	4	0.7	69	72	18	28	6	.299	.413	44	7	OF-141, 1B-6

Clark Griffith

GRIFFITH, CLARK CALVIN (The Old Fox)   BR TR 5'6½" 156 lbs.
B. Nov. 20, 1869, Stringtown, Mo.   D. Oct. 27, 1955, Washington, D. C.
Manager 1901-20.
Hall of Fame 1946.

	G	AB	H	2B	3B	HR	HR %	R	RBI	BB	SO	SB	BA	SA	AB	H	G by POS
1891 2 teams	STL	AA (27G –	.156)		BOS	AA (10G –	.174)										
" total	37	100	16	2	1	2	2.0	17	11	14	20	3	.160	.260	1	0	P-34, OF-3
1893 CHI N	4	11	2	0	0	0	0.0	1	2	0	1	0	.182	.182	0	0	P-4
1894	46	142	33	5	4	0	0.0	27	15	23	9	6	.232	.324	2	1	P-36, OF-7, SS-1
1895	43	144	46	3	0	1	0.7	20	27	16	9	2	.319	.361	0	0	P-42, OF-1
1896	38	135	36	5	2	1	0.7	22	16	9	7	3	.267	.356	2	0	P-36
1897	46	162	38	8	4	0	0.0	27	21	18			.235	.333	0	0	P-41, OF-2, SS-2, 3B-1, 1B-1
1898	38	122	20	2	3	0	0.0	15	15	13		1	.164	.230	0	0	P-38
1899	39	120	31	5	0	0	0.0	15	14	14		2	.258	.300	0	0	P-38, SS-1
1900	30	95	24	4	1	1	1.1	16	7	8		2	.253	.347	0	0	P-30
1901 CHI A	35	89	27	3	1	2	2.2	21	14	23		0	.303	.427	0	0	P-35
1902	35	92	20	3	0	0	0.0	11	8	7		0	.217	.250	4	0	P-28, OF-3
1903 NY A	25	69	11	4	0	1	1.4	5	7	11		1	.159	.261	0	0	P-25
1904	16	42	6	2	0	0	0.0	2	1	4		0	.143	.190	0	0	P-16
1905	26	32	7	1	1	0	0.0	2	5	3		0	.219	.313	0	0	P-25, OF-1
1906	17	18	2	0	0	0	0.0	0	1	3		0	.111	.111	0	0	P-17
1907	4	2	0	0	0	0	0.0	0	0	0		0	.000	.000	0	0	P-4
1909 CIN N	1	2	0	0	0	0	0.0	0	0	0		0	.000	.000	0	0	P-1
1910	1	0	0	0	0	0	–	1	0	0	0	0	–	–	0	0	P-1
1912 WAS A	1	1	0	0	0	0	0.0	0	1	0	0	0	.000	.000	0	0	2B-1, P-1
1913	1	1	1	1	0	0	0.0	0	1	0	0	0	1.000	2.000	0	0	OF-1, P-1
1914	1	1	1	1	0	0	0.0	0	1	0	0	0	1.000	2.000	0	0	P-1
21 yrs.	484	1380	321	49	17	8	0.6	202	166	166	46	22	.233	.310	9	1	P-453, OF-18, SS-4, 3B-1, 2B-1, 1B-1

Derrell Griffith

GRIFFITH, ROBERT DERRELL   BL TR 6' 168 lbs.
B. Dec. 12, 1943, Anadarko, Okla.

	G	AB	H	2B	3B	HR	HR %	R	RBI	BB	SO	SB	BA	SA	AB	H	G by POS
1963 LA N	1	2	0	0	0	0	0.0	0	0	0	0	0	.000	.000	1	0	2B-1
1964	78	238	69	16	2	4	1.7	27	23	5	21	5	.290	.424	12	1	3B-35, OF-29
1965	22	41	7	0	0	1	2.4	3	2	0	9	0	.171	.244	8	1	OF-11
1966	23	15	1	0	0	0	0.0	3	2	2	3	0	.067	.067	9	1	OF-7
4 yrs.	124	296	77	16	2	5	1.7	33	27	7	33	5	.260	.378	30	4	OF-47, 3B-35, 2B-1

Tommy Griffith

GRIFFITH, THOMAS HERMAN   BL TR 5'10" 175 lbs.
B. Oct. 26, 1889, Prospect, Ohio   D. Apr. 13, 1967, Cincinnati, Ohio

	G	AB	H	2B	3B	HR	HR %	R	RBI	BB	SO	SB	BA	SA	AB	H	G by POS
1913 BOS N	37	127	32	4	1	1	0.8	16	12	9	8	1	.252	.323	1	0	OF-35
1914	16	48	5	0	0	0	0.0	3	1	2	6	0	.104	.104	2	2	OF-14
1915 CIN N	160	583	179	31	16	4	0.7	59	85	41	34	6	.307	.436	0	0	OF-160
1916	155	595	158	28	7	2	0.3	50	61	36	37	16	.266	.346	0	0	OF-155
1917	115	363	98	18	7	1	0.3	45	45	19	23	5	.270	.366	13	4	OF-100
1918	118	427	113	10	4	2	0.5	47	48	39	30	10	.265	.321	0	0	OF-118
1919 BKN N	125	484	136	18	4	6	1.2	65	57	23	32	8	.281	.372	0	0	OF-125
1920	93	334	87	9	4	2	0.6	41	30	15	18	3	.260	.329	1	0	OF-92
1921	129	455	142	21	6	12	2.6	66	71	36	13	3	.312	.464	4	1	OF-124
1922	99	329	104	17	8	4	1.2	44	49	23	10	7	.316	.453	14	4	OF-82
1923	131	481	141	21	9	8	1.7	70	66	50	19	8	.293	.424	2	0	OF-128
1924	140	482	121	19	5	3	0.6	43	67	34	19	0	.251	.330	0	0	OF-139
1925 2 teams	BKN	N (7G –	.000)		CHI	N (76G –	.285)										
" total	83	239	67	12	1	7	2.9	40	27	24	13	3	.280	.427	16	3	OF-62
13 yrs.	1401	4947	1383	208	72	52	1.1	589	619	351	262	70	.280	.382	53	15	OF-1334

WORLD SERIES

	G	AB	H	2B	3B	HR	HR %	R	RBI	BB	SO	SB	BA	SA	AB	H	G by POS
1920 BKN N	7	21	4	2	0	0	0.0	1	3	0	2	0	.190	.286	0	0	OF-7

Art Griggs

GRIGGS, ART CARLE   BR TR 5'11" 185 lbs.
B. Dec. 10, 1883, Topeka, Kans.   D. Dec. 19, 1938, Los Angeles, Calif.

	G	AB	H	2B	3B	HR	HR %	R	RBI	BB	SO	SB	BA	SA	AB	H	G by POS
1909 STL A	108	364	102	17	5	0	0.0	38	43	24		11	.280	.354	9	1	1B-49, OF-40, 2B-8, SS-1
1910	123	416	98	22	5	2	0.5	28	30	25		11	.236	.327	10	1	OF-49, 2B-41, 1B-17, SS-3, 3B-3
1911 CLE A	27	68	17	3	2	1	1.5	7	7	5		0	.250	.397	5	1	2B-11, OF-4, 3B-3, 1B-1
1912	89	273	83	16	7	0	0.0	29	39	33		10	.304	.414	18	3	1B-71
1914 BKN F	40	112	32	6	1	1	0.9	10	15	5		0	.286	.384	12	2	1B-27, OF-1
1915	27	38	11	1	0	1	2.6	4	2	3		0	.289	.395	16	5	1B-5, OF-1

	G	AB	H	2B	3B	HR	HR %	R	RBI	BB	SO	SB	BA	SA	Pinch Hit AB	Pinch Hit H	G by POS

Art Griggs continued

	G	AB	H	2B	3B	HR	HR %	R	RBI	BB	SO	SB	BA	SA	PH AB	PH H	G by POS
1918 DET A	28	99	36	8	0	0	0.0	11	16	10	5	2	.364	.444	2	2	1B-25
7 yrs.	442	1370	379	73	20	5	0.4	127	152	105	5	36	.277	.370	72	15	1B-195, OF-95, 2B-60, 3B-6, SS-4

Denver Grigsby

GRIGSBY, DENVER CLARENCE   BL TR 5'9"   155 lbs.
B. Mar. 24, 1901, Jackson, Ky.   D. Nov. 10, 1973, Sapulpa, Okla.

	G	AB	H	2B	3B	HR	HR %	R	RBI	BB	SO	SB	BA	SA	PH AB	PH H	G by POS
1923 CHI N	24	72	21	5	2	0	0.0	8	5	7	5	1	.292	.417	1	1	OF-22
1924	124	411	123	18	2	3	0.7	58	48	31	47	10	.299	.375	2	0	OF-121
1925	51	137	35	5	0	0	0.0	20	20	19	12	1	.255	.292	8	0	OF-39
3 yrs.	199	620	179	28	4	3	0.5	86	73	57	64	12	.289	.361	11	1	OF-182

John Grim

GRIM, JOHN HELM   BR TR 6'2"   175 lbs.
B. Aug. 9, 1867, Lebanon, Ky.   D. July 28, 1961, Indianapolis, Ind.

	G	AB	H	2B	3B	HR	HR %	R	RBI	BB	SO	SB	BA	SA	PH AB	PH H	G by POS
1888 PHI N	2	7	1	0	0	0	0.0	0	0	0	0	0	.143	.143	0	0	OF-1, 2B-1
1890 ROC AA	50	192	51	6	9	2	1.0	30		7		14	.266	.422	0	0	SS-21, C-15, 3B-8, 2B-4, OF-3, 1B-2, P-1
1891 C-M AA	29	119	28	5	1	1	0.8	14	14	2	5	1	.235	.319	0	0	C-16, 3B-10, 2B-3
1892 LOU N	97	370	90	16	4	1	0.3	40	36	13	24	18	.243	.316	0	0	C-69, 1B-11, 2B-10, OF-8, SS-1, 3B-1
1893	99	415	111	19	8	3	0.7	68	54	12	10	15	.267	.373	0	0	C-92, 1B-3, 2B-2, OF-1, SS-1
1894	108	410	122	27	7	7	1.7	66	70	16	15	14	.298	.449	1	0	C-77, 3B-24, 1B-7, 3B-1
1895 BKN N	93	329	92	17	5	0	0.0	54	44	13	9	9	.280	.362	0	0	C-91, OF-1, 1B-1
1896	81	281	75	13	1	2	0.7	32	35	12	14	7	.267	.342	0	0	C-77, 1B-5
1897	80	290	72	10	1	0	0.0	26	25	1		3	.248	.290	3	0	C-77
1898	52	178	50	5	1	0	0.0	17	11	8		1	.281	.320	3	0	C-52
1899	15	47	13	1	0	0	0.0	3	7	1		0	.277	.298	3	0	C-12
11 yrs.	706	2638	705	119	37	16	0.6	350	295	85	77	82	.267	.359	7	0	C-578, 2B-44, 1B-29, SS-23, 3B-20, OF-14, P-1

Ed Grimes

GRIMES, EDWARD EDELBERT   BR TR 5'10"   178 lbs.
B. Sept. 8, 1905, Chicago, Ill.   D. Oct. 5, 1974, Chicago, Ill.

	G	AB	H	2B	3B	HR	HR %	R	RBI	BB	SO	SB	BA	SA	PH AB	PH H	G by POS
1931 STL A	43	57	15	1	2	0	0.0	9	5	9	3	1	.263	.351	5	0	3B-22, 2B-4, SS-3
1932	31	68	16	0	1	0	0.0	7	13	6	12	0	.235	.265	3	0	3B-18, 2B-2, SS-1
2 yrs.	74	125	31	1	3	0	0.0	16	18	15	15	1	.248	.304	8	0	3B-40, 2B-6, SS-4

Oscar Grimes

GRIMES, OSCAR RAY, JR.   BR TR 5'11"   178 lbs.
Son of Ray Grimes.
B. Apr. 13, 1915, Minerva, Ohio

	G	AB	H	2B	3B	HR	HR %	R	RBI	BB	SO	SB	BA	SA	PH AB	PH H	G by POS
1938 CLE A	4	10	2	0	1	0	0.0	2	2	2	0	0	.200	.400	1	0	2B-2, 1B-1
1939	119	364	98	20	5	4	1.1	51	56	56	61	8	.269	.385	3	0	2B-48, 1B-43, SS-37
1940	11	13	0	0	0	0	0.0	3	0	0	5	0	.000	.000	1	0	1B-4, 3B-1
1941	77	244	58	9	3	4	1.6	28	24	39	47	4	.238	.348	1	0	1B-62, 2B-13, 3B-1
1942	51	84	15	2	0	0	0.0	10	2	13	17	3	.179	.202	9	1	2B-24, 3B-8, SS-1, 1B-1
1943 NY A	9	20	3	0	0	0	0.0	4	1	3	7	0	.150	.150	4	0	SS-3, 1B-1
1944	116	387	108	17	8	5	1.3	44	46	59	57	6	.279	.403	1	0	3B-97, SS-20
1945	142	480	127	19	7	4	0.8	64	45	97	73	7	.265	.358	1	0	3B-141, 1B-1
1946 2 teams																	
NY A (14G – .205)			PHI A (59G – .262)														
" total	73	230	58	6	0	1	0.4	29	24	28	36	2	.252	.291	7	2	2B-48, SS-11, 3B-6
9 yrs.	602	1832	469	73	24	18	1.0	235	200	297	303	30	.256	.352	28	3	3B-254, 2B-135, 1B-113, SS-72

Ray Grimes

GRIMES, OSCAR RAY, SR.   BR TR 5'11"   168 lbs.
Father of Oscar Grimes.   Brother of Roy Grimes.
B. Sept. 11, 1893, Bergholz, Ohio   D. May 25, 1953, Minerva, Ohio

	G	AB	H	2B	3B	HR	HR %	R	RBI	BB	SO	SB	BA	SA	PH AB	PH H	G by POS
1920 BOS A	1	4	1	0	0	0	0.0	1	0	1	0	0	.250	.250	0	0	1B-1
1921 CHI N	147	530	170	38	6	6	1.1	91	79	70	55	5	.321	.449	0	0	1B-147
1922	138	509	180	45	12	14	2.8	99	99	75	33	7	.354	.572	0	0	1B-138
1923	64	216	71	7	2	2	0.9	32	36	24	17	5	.329	.407	2	0	1B-62
1924	51	177	53	6	5	5	2.8	33	34	28	15	4	.299	.475	1	0	1B-50
1926 PHI N	32	101	30	5	0	0	0.0	13	15	6	13	0	.297	.347	3	0	1B-28
6 yrs.	433	1537	505	101	25	27	1.8	269	263	204	133	21	.329	.480	6	0	1B-426

Roy Grimes

GRIMES, ROY AUSTIN   BR TR 6'1"   185 lbs.
Brother of Ray Grimes.
B. Sept. 11, 1893, Bergholz, Ohio   D. Sept. 13, 1954, Gilford Lake, Ohio

	G	AB	H	2B	3B	HR	HR %	R	RBI	BB	SO	SB	BA	SA	PH AB	PH H	G by POS
1920 NY N	26	57	9	1	0	0	0.0	5	3	3	8	1	.158	.175	5	1	2B-21

Charlie Grimm

GRIMM, CHARLES JOHN (Jolly Cholly)   BL TL 5'11½" 173 lbs.
B. Aug. 28, 1898, St. Louis, Mo.   D. Nov. 15, 1983, Scottsdale, Ariz.
Manager 1932-38, 1944-49, 1952-56, 1960.

	G	AB	H	2B	3B	HR	HR %	R	RBI	BB	SO	SB	BA	SA	PH AB	PH H	G by POS
1916 PHI A	12	22	2	0	0	0	0.0	0	0	2	4	0	.091	.091	4	0	OF-7
1918 STL N	50	141	31	7	0	0	0.0	11	12	6	15	2	.220	.270	5	0	1B-42, OF-2, 3B-1
1919 PIT N	12	44	14	1	3	0	0.0	6	6	2	4	1	.318	.477	0	0	1B-11
1920	148	533	121	13	7	2	0.4	38	54	30	40	7	.227	.289	0	0	1B-148
1921	151	562	154	21	17	7	1.2	62	71	31	38	6	.274	.409	1	0	1B-150
1922	154	593	173	28	13	0	0.0	64	76	43	15	6	.292	.383	0	0	1B-154
1923	152	563	194	29	13	7	1.2	78	99	41	43	6	.345	.480	0	0	1B-152
1924	151	542	156	25	12	2	0.4	53	63	37	22	3	.288	.389	0	0	1B-151
1925 CHI N	141	519	159	29	5	10	1.9	73	76	38	25	4	.306	.439	2	0	1B-139
1926	147	524	145	30	6	8	1.5	58	82	49	25	3	.277	.403	0	0	1B-147
1927	147	543	169	29	6	2	0.4	68	74	45	21	3	.311	.398	0	0	1B-147
1928	147	547	161	25	5	5	0.9	67	62	39	20	7	.294	.386	0	0	1B-147
1929	120	463	138	28	3	10	2.2	66	91	42	25	3	.298	.436	0	0	1B-120
1930	114	429	124	27	2	6	1.4	58	66	41	26	1	.289	.403	1	0	1B-113
1931	146	531	176	33	11	4	0.8	65	66	53	29	1	.331	.458	1	0	1B-144

	G	AB	H	2B	3B	HR	HR %	R	RBI	BB	SO	SB	BA	SA	Pinch Hit AB	Pinch Hit H	G by POS

Charlie Grimm continued

	G	AB	H	2B	3B	HR	HR%	R	RBI	BB	SO	SB	BA	SA	PH AB	PH H	G by POS
1932	149	570	175	42	2	7	1.2	66	80	35	22	2	.307	.425	0	0	1B-149
1933	107	384	95	15	2	3	0.8	38	37	23	15	1	.247	.320	2	0	1B-104
1934	75	267	79	8	1	5	1.9	24	47	16	12	1	.296	.390	1	0	1B-74
1935	2	8	0	0	0	0	0.0	0	0	0	1	0	.000	.000	0	0	1B-2
1936	39	132	33	4	0	1	0.8	13	16	5	8	0	.250	.303	4	1	1B-35
20 yrs.	2164	7917	2299	394	108	79	1.0	908	1078	578	410	57	.290	.397	21	1	1B-2129, OF-9, 3B-1
WORLD SERIES																	
1929 CHI N	5	18	7	0	0	1	5.6	2	4	1	2	0	.389	.556	0	0	1B-5
1932	4	15	5	2	0	0	0.0	2	1	2	2	0	.333	.467	0	0	1B-4
2 yrs.	9	33	12	2	0	1	3.0	4	5	3	4	0	.364	.515	0	0	1B-9

Moose Grimshaw

GRIMSHAW, MYRON FREDERICK
B. Nov. 30, 1875, St. Johnsville, N. Y. D. Dec. 11, 1936, Canajoharie, N. Y.
BB TR 6'1" 173 lbs.

	G	AB	H	2B	3B	HR	HR%	R	RBI	BB	SO	SB	BA	SA	PH AB	PH H	G by POS
1905 BOS A	85	285	68	8	2	4	1.4	39	35	21		4	.239	.323	11	3	1B-74
1906	110	428	124	16	12	0	0.0	46	48	23		5	.290	.383	0	0	1B-110
1907	64	181	37	7	2	0	0.0	19	33	16		6	.204	.265	14	2	OF-23, 1B-15, SS-2
3 yrs.	259	894	229	31	16	4	0.4	104	116	60		15	.256	.340	25	5	1B-199, OF-23, SS-2

Dick Groat

GROAT, RICHARD MORROW
B. Nov. 4, 1930, Wilkinsburg, Pa.
BR TR 5'11½" 180 lbs.

	G	AB	H	2B	3B	HR	HR%	R	RBI	BB	SO	SB	BA	SA	PH AB	PH H	G by POS
1952 PIT N	95	384	109	6	1	1	0.3	38	29	19	27	2	.284	.313	1	0	SS-94
1955	151	521	139	28	2	4	0.8	45	51	38	26	0	.267	.351	1	0	SS-149
1956	142	520	142	19	3	0	0.0	40	37	35	25	0	.273	.321	0	0	SS-141, 3B-2
1957	125	501	158	30	5	7	1.4	58	54	27	28	0	.315	.437	0	0	SS-123, 3B-2
1958	151	584	175	36	9	3	0.5	67	66	23	32	2	.300	.408	1	0	SS-149
1959	147	593	163	22	7	5	0.8	74	51	32	35	0	.275	.361	2	0	SS-145
1960	138	573	186	26	4	2	0.3	85	50	39	35	0	.325	.394	1	0	SS-136
1961	148	596	164	25	6	6	1.0	71	55	40	44	0	.275	.367	2	0	SS-144, 3B-1
1962	161	678	199	34	3	2	0.3	76	61	31	61	2	.294	.361	0	0	SS-161
1963 STL N	158	631	201	43	11	6	1.0	85	73	56	58	3	.319	.450	1	0	SS-158
1964	161	636	186	35	6	1	0.2	70	70	44	42	2	.292	.371	1	0	SS-160
1965	153	587	149	26	5	0	0.0	55	52	56	50	1	.254	.315	6	3	SS-148, 3B-2
1966 PHI N	155	584	152	21	4	2	0.3	58	53	40	38	2	.260	.320	2	1	SS-139, 3B-20, 1B-1
1967 2 teams			PHI	N	(10G –	.115)		SF	N	(34G –	.171)						
" total	44	96	15	1	1	0	0.0	7	5	10	11	0	.156	.188	14	1	SS-30, 2B-1
14 yrs.	1929	7484	2138	352	67	39	0.5	829	707	490	512	14	.286	.366	32	5	SS-1877, 3B-27, 2B-1, 1B-1
WORLD SERIES																	
1960 PIT N	7	28	6	2	0	0	0.0	3	2	0	1	0	.214	.286	0	0	SS-7
1964 STL N	7	26	5	1	1	0	0.0	3	1	4	3	0	.192	.308	0	0	SS-7
2 yrs.	14	54	11	3	1	0	0.0	6	3	4	4	0	.204	.296	0	0	SS-14

Heinie Groh

GROH, HENRY KNIGHT
Brother of Lew Groh.
B. Sept. 18, 1889, Rochester, N. Y. D. Aug. 22, 1968, Cincinnati, Ohio
Manager 1918.
BR TR 5'8" 158 lbs.

	G	AB	H	2B	3B	HR	HR%	R	RBI	BB	SO	SB	BA	SA	PH AB	PH H	G by POS
1912 NY N	27	48	13	2	1	0	0.0	8	3	8	7	6	.271	.354	0	0	2B-12, SS-7, 3B-6
1913 2 teams		NY	N	(4G –	.000)			CIN	N	(117G –	.282)						
" total	121	399	112	19	5	3	0.8	51	48	38	37	24	.281	.376	0	0	2B-113, SS-5, 3B-2
1914 CIN N	139	455	131	18	4	2	0.4	59	32	64	28	24	.288	.358	2	0	2B-134, SS-2
1915	160	587	170	32	9	3	0.5	72	50	50	33	12	.290	.390	0	0	3B-131, 2B-29
1916	149	553	149	24	14	2	0.4	85	28	84	34	13	.269	.374	1	0	3B-110, 2B-33, SS-5
1917	156	599	182	39	11	1	0.2	91	53	71	30	15	.304	.411	1	0	3B-154, 2B-2
1918	126	493	158	28	3	1	0.2	88	37	54	24	11	.320	.396	0	0	3B-126
1919	122	448	139	17	11	5	1.1	79	63	56	26	21	.310	.431	0	0	3B-121
1920	145	550	164	28	12	0	0.0	86	49	60	29	16	.298	.393	1	0	3B-144, SS-1
1921	97	357	118	19	6	0	0.0	54	48	36	17	22	.331	.417	0	0	3B-97
1922 NY N	115	426	113	21	3	3	0.7	63	51	53	21	5	.265	.350	5	1	3B-110
1923	123	465	135	22	5	4	0.9	91	48	60	22	3	.290	.385	5	1	3B-118
1924	145	559	157	32	3	2	0.4	82	46	52	29	8	.281	.360	0	0	3B-145
1925	25	65	15	4	0	0	0.0	7	4	6	3	0	.231	.292	5	1	3B-16, 2B-2
1926	12	35	8	2	0	0	0.0	2	3	2	3	0	.229	.286	4	1	3B-7
1927 PIT N	14	35	10	1	0	0	0.0	2	3	2	2	0	.286	.314	2	1	3B-12
16 yrs.	1676	6074	1774	308	87	26	0.4	920	566	696	345	180	.292	.384	26	5	3B-1299, 2B-325, SS-20
WORLD SERIES																	
1919 CIN N	8	29	5	2	0	0	0.0	6	2	6	4	0	.172	.241	0	0	3B-8
1922 NY N	5	19	9	0	1	0	0.0	4	0	2	1	0	.474	.579	0	0	3B-5
1923	6	22	4	0	1	0	0.0	3	2	3	1	0	.182	.273	0	0	3B-6
1924	1	1	1	0	0	0	0.0	0	0	0	0	0	1.000	1.000	1	1	
1927 PIT N	1	1	0	0	0	0	0.0	0	0	0	0	0	.000	.000	1	0	
5 yrs.	21	72	19	2	2	0	0.0	13	4	11	6	0	.264	.347	2	1	3B-19

Lew Groh

GROH, LEWIS CARL (Silver)
Brother of Heinie Groh.
B. Oct. 16, 1883, Rochester, N. Y. D. Oct. 20, 1960, Rochester, N. Y.
BR TR

	G	AB	H	2B	3B	HR	HR%	R	RBI	BB	SO	SB	BA	SA	PH AB	PH H	G by POS
1919 PHI A	2	4	0	0	0	0	0.0	0	0	0		2	0	.000	.000	1	0	3B-1

George Grosart

GROSART, GEORGE ALBERT
B. 1879, Meadville, Pa. D. Apr. 18, 1902, Homestead, Pa.

	G	AB	H	2B	3B	HR	HR%	R	RBI	BB	SO	SB	BA	SA	PH AB	PH H	G by POS
1901 BOS N	7	26	3	0	0	0	0.0	4	1	0		0	.115	.115	0	0	OF-7

	G	AB	H	2B	3B	HR	HR %	R	RBI	BB	SO	SB	BA	SA	Pinch Hit AB	Pinch Hit H	G by POS

Emil Gross

GROSS, EMIL MICHAEL
B. 1859, Chicago, Ill.   D. Aug. 24, 1921, Eagle River, Wis.   6'   190 lbs.

	G	AB	H	2B	3B	HR	HR %	R	RBI	BB	SO	SB	BA	SA	AB	H	G by POS
1879 PRO N	30	132	46	9	5	0	0.0	31	24	4	8		.348	.492	0	0	C-30
1880	87	347	90	18	3	1	0.3	43	34	16	15		.259	.337	0	0	C-87
1881	51	182	50	9	4	1	0.5	15	24	13	11		.275	.385	0	0	C-50, OF-1
1883 PHI N	57	231	71	25	7	1	0.4	39		12	18		.307	.489	0	0	C-55, OF-2
1884 C-P U	23	95	34	6	2	4	4.2	13		6			.358	.589	0	0	C-15, OF-9
5 yrs.	248	987	291	67	21	7	0.7	141	82	51	52		.295	.427	0	0	C-237, OF-12

Greg Gross

GROSS, GREGORY EUGENE
B. Aug. 1, 1952, York, Pa.   BL TL 5'10"   160 lbs.

	G	AB	H	2B	3B	HR	HR %	R	RBI	BB	SO	SB	BA	SA	AB	H	G by POS
1973 HOU N	14	39	9	2	1	0	0.0	5	1	4	4	2	.231	.333	4	0	OF-9
1974	156	589	185	21	8	0	0.0	78	36	76	39	12	.314	.377	5	2	OF-151
1975	132	483	142	14	10	0	0.0	67	41	63	37	2	.294	.364	8	1	OF-121
1976	128	426	122	12	3	0	0.0	52	27	64	39	2	.286	.329	13	1	OF-115
1977 CHI N	115	239	77	10	4	5	2.1	43	32	33	19	0	.322	.460	39	10	OF-71
1978	124	347	92	12	7	1	0.3	34	39	33	19	3	.265	.349	20	5	OF-111
1979 PHI N	111	174	58	6	3	0	0.0	21	15	29	5	5	.333	.402	51	14	OF-73
1980	127	154	37	7	2	0	0.0	19	12	24	7	1	.240	.312	39	10	OF-91, 1B-1
1981	83	102	23	6	1	0	0.0	14	7	15	5	2	.225	.304	39	6	OF-55
1982	119	134	40	4	0	0	0.0	14	10	19	8	4	.299	.328	53	19	OF-71
1983	136	245	74	12	3	0	0.0	25	29	34	16	3	.302	.376	33	7	OF-110, 1B-1
1984	112	202	65	9	1	0	0.0	19	16	24	11	1	.322	.376	46	13	OF-48, 1B-28
12 yrs.	1357	3134	924	115	43	6	0.2	391	265	418	209	37	.295	.365	350	88	OF-1026, 1B-30

DIVISIONAL PLAYOFF SERIES

	G	AB	H	2B	3B	HR	HR %	R	RBI	BB	SO	SB	BA	SA	AB	H	G by POS
1981 PHI N	4	4	0	0	0	0	0.0	0	0	0	0	0	.000	.000	3	0	OF-2

LEAGUE CHAMPIONSHIP SERIES

	G	AB	H	2B	3B	HR	HR %	R	RBI	BB	SO	SB	BA	SA	AB	H	G by POS
1980 PHI N	4	4	3	0	0	0	0.0	2	1	0	0	0	.750	.750	2	2	OF-1
1983	4	5	0	0	0	0	0.0	1	0	2	2	0	.000	.000	0	0	OF-3
2 yrs.	8	9	3	0	0	0	0.0	3	1	2	2	0	.333	.333	2	2	OF-4

WORLD SERIES

	G	AB	H	2B	3B	HR	HR %	R	RBI	BB	SO	SB	BA	SA	AB	H	G by POS
1980 PHI N	4	2	0	0	0	0	0.0	0	0	0	0	0	.000	.000	1	0	OF-3
1983	2	6	0	0	0	0	0.0	0	0	0	0	0	.000	.000	0	0	OF-2
2 yrs.	6	8	0	0	0	0	0.0	0	0	0	0	0	.000	.000	1	0	OF-5

Turkey Gross

GROSS, EWELL
B. Feb. 23, 1896, Mesquite, Tex.   D. Jan. 22, 1936, Dallas, Tex.   BR TR 6'   165 lbs.

	G	AB	H	2B	3B	HR	HR %	R	RBI	BB	SO	SB	BA	SA	AB	H	G by POS
1925 BOS A	9	32	3	0	1	0	0.0	2	2	2	2	0	.094	.156	0	0	SS-9

Wayne Gross

GROSS, WAYNE DALE
B. Jan. 14, 1952, Riverside, Calif.   BL TR 6'2"   210 lbs.

	G	AB	H	2B	3B	HR	HR %	R	RBI	BB	SO	SB	BA	SA	AB	H	G by POS
1976 OAK A	10	18	4	0	0	0	0.0	0	1	2	1	0	.222	.222	5	2	DH-3, 1B-3, OF-2
1977	146	485	113	21	1	22	4.5	66	63	86	84	5	.233	.416	0	0	3B-145, 1B-1
1978	118	285	57	10	2	7	2.5	18	23	40	63	0	.200	.323	12	2	3B-106, 1B-15
1979	138	442	99	19	1	14	3.2	54	50	72	62	4	.224	.367	5	2	3B-120, 1B-18, OF-2
1980	113	366	103	20	3	14	3.8	45	61	44	39	5	.281	.467	13	3	3B-99, 1B-10, DH-1
1981	82	243	50	7	1	10	4.1	29	31	34	28	2	.206	.366	9	1	3B-73, 1B-2, DH-1
1982	129	386	97	14	0	9	2.3	43	41	53	50	3	.251	.358	20	6	3B-108, 1B-16, DH-1
1983	137	339	79	18	0	12	3.5	34	44	36	52	3	.233	.392	8	3	1B-74, 3B-67, DH-1, P-1
1984 BAL A	127	342	74	9	1	22	6.4	53	64	68	69	1	.216	.442	13	4	3B-117, 1B-3, DH-1
9 yrs.	1000	2906	676	118	9	110	3.8	342	378	435	448	23	.233	.393	85	23	3B-835, 1B-142, DH-8, OF-4, P-1

DIVISIONAL PLAYOFF SERIES

	G	AB	H	2B	3B	HR	HR %	R	RBI	BB	SO	SB	BA	SA	AB	H	G by POS
1981 OAK A	2	5	2	0	0	1	20.0	1	3	0	0	0	.400	1.000	1	0	3B-1

LEAGUE CHAMPIONSHIP SERIES

	G	AB	H	2B	3B	HR	HR %	R	RBI	BB	SO	SB	BA	SA	AB	H	G by POS
1981 OAK A	3	5	0	0	0	0	0.0	0	0	0	0	0	.000	.000	3	0	3B-3

Howdie Grosskloss

GROSSKLOSS, HOWARD HOFFMAN
B. Apr. 10, 1908, Pittsburgh, Pa.   BR TR 5'9"   176 lbs.

	G	AB	H	2B	3B	HR	HR %	R	RBI	BB	SO	SB	BA	SA	AB	H	G by POS
1930 PIT N	2	3	1	0	0	0	0.0	1	1	0	0	0	.333	.333	1	0	SS-1
1931	53	161	45	7	2	0	0.0	13	20	11	16	1	.280	.348	12	4	2B-39, SS-3
1932	17	20	2	0	0	0	0.0	1	0	0	3	0	.100	.100	16	2	SS-1
3 yrs.	72	184	48	7	2	0	0.0	14	21	11	19	1	.261	.321	29	6	2B-39, SS-5

Jerry Grote

GROTE, GERALD WAYNE
B. Oct. 6, 1942, San Antonio, Tex.   BR TR 5'10"   185 lbs.

	G	AB	H	2B	3B	HR	HR %	R	RBI	BB	SO	SB	BA	SA	AB	H	G by POS
1963 HOU N	3	5	1	0	0	0	0.0	0	1	1	3	0	.200	.200	0	0	C-3
1964	100	298	54	9	3	3	1.0	26	24	20	75	0	.181	.262	2	0	C-98
1966 NY N	120	317	75	12	2	3	0.9	26	31	40	81	4	.237	.315	5	1	C-115, 3B-2
1967	120	344	67	8	0	4	1.2	25	23	14	65	2	.195	.253	2	0	C-119
1968	124	404	114	18	0	3	0.7	29	31	44	81	1	.282	.349	8	2	C-115
1969	113	365	92	12	3	6	1.6	38	40	32	59	2	.252	.351	4	1	C-112
1970	126	415	106	14	1	2	0.5	38	34	36	39	2	.255	.308	0	0	C-125
1971	125	403	109	25	0	2	0.5	35	35	40	47	1	.270	.347	4	0	C-122
1972	64	205	43	5	1	3	1.5	15	21	26	27	1	.210	.288	2	0	C-59, 3B-3, OF-1
1973	84	285	73	10	2	1	0.4	17	32	13	23	0	.256	.316	1	0	C-81, 3B-2
1974	97	319	82	8	1	5	1.6	25	36	33	33	0	.257	.335	3	0	C-94
1975	119	386	114	14	5	2	0.5	28	39	38	23	0	.295	.373	8	2	C-111
1976	101	323	88	14	2	4	1.2	30	28	38	19	1	.272	.365	10	4	C-95, OF-2
1977 2 teams NY N (42G – .270) LA N (18G – .259)																	
" total	60	142	38	3	1	0	0.0	11	11	11	17	0	.268	.303	11	3	C-44, 3B-13
1978 LA N	41	70	19	5	0	0	0.0	5	9	10	5	0	.271	.343	2	1	C-32, 3B-7
1981 2 teams KC A (22G – .304) LA N (2G – .000)																	
" total	24	58	17	3	1	1	1.7	4	9	3	3	1	.293	.431	0	0	C-23
16 yrs.	1421	4339	1092	160	22	39	0.9	352	404	399	600	15	.252	.326	62	14	C-1348, 3B-27, OF-3

	G	AB	H	2B	3B	HR	HR %	R	RBI	BB	SO	SB	BA	SA	Pinch Hit AB	Pinch Hit H	G by POS

Jerry Grote continued

LEAGUE CHAMPIONSHIP SERIES

	G	AB	H	2B	3B	HR	HR %	R	RBI	BB	SO	SB	BA	SA	AB	H	G by POS
1969 NY N	3	12	2	1	0	0	0.0	3	1	1	4	0	.167	.250	0	0	C-3
1973	5	19	4	0	0	0	0.0	2	2	1	3	0	.211	.211	0	0	C-5
1977 LA N	2	0	0	0	0	0	–	0	0	1	0	0	–	–	0	0	C-1
1978	1	0	0	0	0	0	–	0	0	0	0	0	–	–	0	0	C-1
4 yrs.	11	31	6	1	0	0	0.0	5	3	3	7	0	.194	.226	0	0	C-10

WORLD SERIES

	G	AB	H	2B	3B	HR	HR %	R	RBI	BB	SO	SB	BA	SA	AB	H	G by POS
1969 NY N	5	19	4	2	0	0	0.0	1	1	1	3	0	.211	.316	0	0	C-5
1973	7	30	8	0	0	0	0.0	2	0	0	1	0	.267	.267	0	0	C-7
1977 LA N	1	1	0	0	0	0	0.0	0	0	0	0	0	.000	.000	0	0	C-1
1978	2	0	0	0	0	0	–	0	0	0	0	0	–	–	0	0	C-2
4 yrs.	15	50	12	2	0	0	0.0	3	1	1	4	0	.240	.280	0	0	C-15

Johnny Groth

GROTH, JOHN THOMAS
B. July 23, 1926, Chicago, Ill.
BR TR 6' 182 lbs.

	G	AB	H	2B	3B	HR	HR %	R	RBI	BB	SO	SB	BA	SA	AB	H	G by POS
1946 DET A	4	9	0	0	0	0	0.0	1	0	0	3	0	.000	.000	0	0	OF-4
1947	2	4	1	0	0	0	0.0	1	0	2	1	0	.250	.250	0	0	OF-1
1948	6	17	8	3	0	1	5.9	3	5	1	1	0	.471	.824	1	0	OF-4
1949	103	348	102	19	5	11	3.2	60	73	65	27	3	.293	.471	3	0	OF-99
1950	157	566	173	30	8	12	2.1	95	85	95	27	1	.306	.451	0	0	OF-157
1951	118	428	128	29	1	3	0.7	41	49	31	32	1	.299	.393	6	2	OF-112
1952	141	524	149	22	2	4	0.8	56	51	51	39	2	.284	.357	3	0	OF-139
1953 STL A	141	557	141	27	4	10	1.8	65	57	42	53	5	.253	.370	0	0	OF-141
1954 CHI A	125	422	116	20	0	7	1.7	41	60	42	37	3	.275	.372	1	0	OF-125
1955 2 teams		CHI	A	(32G –	.338)		WAS	A	(63G –	.219)							
" total	95	260	66	11	5	4	1.5	35	28	24	31	3	.254	.381	14	5	OF-74
1956 KC A	95	244	63	13	3	5	2.0	22	37	30	31	1	.258	.398	13	4	OF-84
1957 2 teams		KC	A	(55G –	.254)		DET	A	(38G –	.291)							
" total	93	162	45	10	0	0	0.0	21	18	13	13	0	.278	.340	4	0	OF-86
1958 DET A	88	146	41	5	2	2	1.4	24	11	13	19	0	.281	.384	16	6	OF-80
1959	55	102	24	1	1	1	1.0	12	10	7	14	0	.235	.353	13	4	OF-41
1960	25	19	7	1	0	0	0.0	3	2	3	1	0	.368	.421	8	3	OF-8
15 yrs.	1248	3808	1064	197	31	60	1.6	480	486	419	329	19	.279	.395	83	24	OF-1155

Roy Grover

GROVER, ROY ARTHUR
B. Jan. 17, 1892, Snohomish, Wash. D. Feb. 7, 1978, Milwaukie, Ore.
BR TR 5'8" 150 lbs.

	G	AB	H	2B	3B	HR	HR %	R	RBI	BB	SO	SB	BA	SA	AB	H	G by POS
1916 PHI A	20	77	21	1	2	0	0.0	8	7	6	10	5	.273	.338	0	0	2B-20
1917	141	482	108	15	7	0	0.0	45	34	43	53	12	.224	.284	1	0	2B-139
1919 2 teams		PHI	A	(22G –	.232)		WAS	A	(24G –	.187)							
" total	46	131	27	1	0	0	0.0	14	9	11	16	2	.206	.214	5	0	2B-36, 3B-3
3 yrs.	207	690	156	17	9	0	0.0	67	50	60	79	19	.226	.277	6	0	2B-195, 3B-3

Harvey Grubb

GRUBB, HARVEY HARRISON
B. Sept. 18, 1890, Lexington, N. C. D. Jan. 25, 1970, Corpus Christi, Tex.
BR TR 6' 165 lbs.

	G	AB	H	2B	3B	HR	HR %	R	RBI	BB	SO	SB	BA	SA	AB	H	G by POS
1912 CLE A	1	0	0	0	0	0	–	0	0	0	0	0	–	–	0	0	OF-1

Johnny Grubb

GRUBB, JOHN MAYWOOD JR.
B. Aug. 4, 1948, Richmond, Va.
BL TR 6'3" 175 lbs.

	G	AB	H	2B	3B	HR	HR %	R	RBI	BB	SO	SB	BA	SA	AB	H	G by POS
1972 SD N	7	21	7	1	1	0	0.0	4	1	1	3	0	.333	.476	1	0	OF-6
1973	113	389	121	22	3	8	2.1	52	37	37	50	9	.311	.445	12	7	OF-102, 3B-2
1974	140	444	127	20	4	8	1.8	53	42	46	47	4	.286	.403	17	3	OF-122, 3B-2
1975	144	553	149	36	2	4	0.7	72	38	59	59	2	.269	.363	6	0	OF-139
1976	109	384	109	22	1	5	1.3	54	27	65	53	1	.284	.385	5	0	OF-98, 1B-9, 3B-3
1977 CLE A	34	93	28	3	3	2	2.2	8	14	19	18	0	.301	.462	1	0	OF-28, DH-4
1978 2 teams		CLE	A	(113G –	.265)		TEX	A	(21G –	.394)							
" total	134	411	113	19	6	15	3.6	62	67	70	65	6	.275	.460	11	5	OF-123, DH-3
1979 TEX A	102	289	79	14	0	10	3.5	42	37	34	44	2	.273	.426	24	6	OF-82, DH-6
1980	110	274	76	12	1	9	3.3	40	32	42	35	2	.277	.427	28	7	OF-77, DH-8
1981	67	199	46	9	1	3	1.5	26	26	23	25	0	.231	.332	9	2	OF-58
1982	103	308	86	13	3	3	1.0	35	26	39	37	0	.279	.370	14	4	OF-77, DH-18
1983 DET A	57	134	34	5	2	4	3.0	20	22	28	17	0	.254	.410	10	4	OF-26, DH-18
1984	86	176	47	5	0	8	4.5	25	17	36	36	1	.267	.432	22	8	OF-36, DH-33
13 yrs.	1206	3675	1022	181	27	79	2.1	493	386	499	489	27	.278	.407	160	46	OF-974, DH-90, 1B-9, 3B-7

LEAGUE CHAMPIONSHIP SERIES

	G	AB	H	2B	3B	HR	HR %	R	RBI	BB	SO	SB	BA	SA	AB	H	G by POS
1984 DET A	1	4	1	1	0	0	0.0	0	2	0	0	0	.250	.500	0	0	

WORLD SERIES

	G	AB	H	2B	3B	HR	HR %	R	RBI	BB	SO	SB	BA	SA	AB	H	G by POS
1984 DET A	4	3	1	0	0	0	0.0	0	0	0	0	0	.333	.333	0	0	DH-2

Frank Grube

GRUBE, FRANKLIN THOMAS (Hans)
B. Jan. 7, 1905, Easton, Pa. D. July 2, 1945, New York, N. Y.
BR TR 5'9" 190 lbs.

	G	AB	H	2B	3B	HR	HR %	R	RBI	BB	SO	SB	BA	SA	AB	H	G by POS
1931 CHI A	88	265	58	13	2	1	0.4	29	24	22	21	2	.219	.294	6	1	C-81
1932	93	277	78	16	2	0	0.0	36	31	33	13	6	.282	.354	1	0	C-92
1933	85	256	59	13	0	0	0.0	23	23	38	20	1	.230	.281	1	0	C-83
1934 STL A	65	170	49	10	0	0	0.0	22	11	24	11	2	.288	.347	9	0	C-55
1935 2 teams		STL	A	(3G –	.333)		CHI	A	(9G –	.368)							
" total	12	25	9	3	0	0	0.0	4	6	3	3	0	.360	.480	0	0	C-12
1936 CHI A	33	93	15	2	1	0	0.0	6	11	9	15	1	.161	.204	2	0	C-32
1941 STL A	18	39	6	2	0	0	0.0	1	1	2	5	0	.154	.205	0	0	C-18
7 yrs.	394	1125	274	59	5	1	0.1	121	107	131	88	12	.244	.308	19	1	C-373

Kelly Gruber

GRUBER, KELLY WAYNE
B. Feb. 26, 1962, Bellaire, Tex.
BR TR 6' 175 lbs.

	G	AB	H	2B	3B	HR	HR %	R	RBI	BB	SO	SB	BA	SA	AB	H	G by POS
1984 TOR A	15	16	1	0	0	1	6.3	1	2	0	5	0	.063	.250	4	1	3B-12, OF-2, SS-1

	G	AB	H	2B	3B	HR	HR %	R	RBI	BB	SO	SB	BA	SA	Pinch Hit AB	Pinch Hit H	G by POS

Sig Gryska

GRYSKA, SIGMUND STANLEY
B. Nov. 4, 1915, Chicago, Ill.
BR TR 5'11½" 173 lbs.

	G	AB	H	2B	3B	HR	HR %	R	RBI	BB	SO	SB	BA	SA	PH AB	PH H	G by POS
1938 STL A	7	21	10	2	1	0	0.0	3	4	3	3	0	.476	.667	0	0	SS-7
1939	18	49	13	2	0	0	0.0	4	8	6	10	3	.265	.306	3	1	SS-14
2 yrs.	25	70	23	4	1	0	0.0	7	12	9	13	3	.329	.414	3	1	SS-21

Marv Gudat

GUDAT, MARVIN JOHN
B. Aug. 27, 1905, Coliad, Tex.   D. Mar. 1, 1954, Los Angeles, Calif.
BL TL 5'11" 176 lbs.

	G	AB	H	2B	3B	HR	HR %	R	RBI	BB	SO	SB	BA	SA	PH AB	PH H	G by POS
1929 CIN N	9	10	2	0	0	0	0.0	0	0	0	0	0	.200	.200	2	0	P-7
1932 CHI N	60	94	24	4	1	1	1.1	15	15	16	10	0	.255	.351	30	10	OF-14, 1B-8, P-1
2 yrs.	69	104	26	4	1	1	1.0	15	15	16	10	0	.250	.337	32	10	OF-14, 1B-8, P-8

WORLD SERIES

	G	AB	H	2B	3B	HR	HR %	R	RBI	BB	SO	SB	BA	SA	PH AB	PH H	G by POS
1932 CHI N	2	2	0	0	0	0	0.0	0	0	0	1	0	.000	.000	2	0	

Mike Guerra

GUERRA, FERMIN ROMERO
B. Oct. 11, 1912, Havana, Cuba
BR TR 5'10" 155 lbs.

	G	AB	H	2B	3B	HR	HR %	R	RBI	BB	SO	SB	BA	SA	PH AB	PH H	G by POS
1937 WAS A	1	3	0	0	0	0	0.0	0	0	0	2	0	.000	.000	0	0	C-1
1944	75	210	59	7	2	1	0.5	29	29	13	14	8	.281	.348	6	3	C-58, OF-1
1945	56	138	29	1	1	1	0.7	11	15	10	12	4	.210	.254	12	3	C-38
1946	41	83	21	2	1	0	0.0	3	4	5	6	1	.253	.301	10	1	C-27
1947 PHI A	72	209	45	2	2	0	0.0	20	18	10	15	1	.215	.244	7	1	C-62
1948	53	142	30	4	2	1	0.7	18	23	18	13	2	.211	.289	2	0	C-47
1949	98	298	79	14	1	3	1.0	41	31	37	26	3	.265	.349	1	0	C-95
1950	87	252	71	10	4	2	0.8	25	26	16	12	1	.282	.377	9	1	C-78
1951 2 teams		BOS	A	(10G –	.156)		WAS	A	(72G –	.201)							
" total	82	246	48	2	1	1	0.4	21	22	22	23	4	.195	.224	4	1	C-76
9 yrs.	565	1581	382	42	14	9	0.6	168	168	131	123	24	.242	.303	51	10	C-482, OF-1

Mario Guerrero

GUERRERO, MARIO MIGUEL
B. Sept. 28, 1949, Santo Domingo, Dominican Republic
BR TR 5'10" 155 lbs.

	G	AB	H	2B	3B	HR	HR %	R	RBI	BB	SO	SB	BA	SA	PH AB	PH H	G by POS
1973 BOS A	66	219	51	5	2	0	0.0	19	11	10	21	2	.233	.274	0	0	SS-46, 2B-24
1974	93	284	70	6	2	0	0.0	18	23	13	22	3	.246	.282	0	0	SS-93
1975 STL N	64	184	44	9	0	0	0.0	17	11	10	7	0	.239	.288	0	0	SS-64
1976 CAL A	83	268	76	12	0	1	0.4	24	18	7	12	0	.284	.340	1	0	SS-41, 2B-41, DH-7
1977	86	244	69	8	2	1	0.4	17	28	4	16	0	.283	.344	27	4	SS-31, DH-19, 2B-12
1978 OAK A	143	505	139	18	4	3	0.6	27	38	15	35	0	.275	.345	2	0	SS-142
1979	46	166	38	5	0	0	0.0	12	18	6	7	0	.229	.259	3	0	SS-43
1980	116	381	91	16	2	2	0.5	32	23	19	32	3	.239	.307	0	0	SS-116
8 yrs.	697	2251	578	79	12	7	0.3	166	170	84	152	8	.257	.312	33	4	SS-576, 2B-77, DH-26

Pedro Guerrero

GUERRERO, PEDRO
B. June 29, 1956, San Pedro de Macoris, Dominican Republic
BR TR 5'11" 176 lbs.

	G	AB	H	2B	3B	HR	HR %	R	RBI	BB	SO	SB	BA	SA	PH AB	PH H	G by POS
1978 LA N	5	8	5	0	0	0	0.0	3	1	0	0	0	.625	.875	1	1	1B-4
1979	25	62	15	2	0	2	3.2	7	9	1	14	2	.242	.371	7	3	OF-12, 1B-8, 3B-3
1980	75	183	59	9	1	7	3.8	27	31	12	31	2	.322	.497	17	11	OF-40, 2B-12, 3B-3, 1B-2
1981	98	347	104	17	2	12	3.5	46	48	34	57	5	.300	.464	4	1	OF-75, 3B-21, 1B-1
1982	150	575	175	27	5	32	5.6	87	100	65	89	22	.304	.536	0	0	OF-137, 3B-24
1983	160	584	174	28	6	32	5.5	87	103	72	110	23	.298	.531	1	1	3B-157, 1B-4
1984	144	535	162	29	4	16	3.0	85	72	49	105	9	.303	.462	7	1	3B-76, OF-58, 1B-16
7 yrs.	657	2294	694	112	19	101	4.4	342	364	233	406	63	.303	.500	37	18	OF-322, 3B-284, 1B-33, 2B-12

DIVISIONAL PLAYOFF SERIES

	G	AB	H	2B	3B	HR	HR %	R	RBI	BB	SO	SB	BA	SA	PH AB	PH H	G by POS
1981 LA N	5	17	3	1	0	1	5.9	1	1	2	4	1	.176	.412	0	0	3B-5

LEAGUE CHAMPIONSHIP SERIES

	G	AB	H	2B	3B	HR	HR %	R	RBI	BB	SO	SB	BA	SA	PH AB	PH H	G by POS
1981 LA N	5	19	2	0	0	1	5.3	1	2	1	4	0	.105	.263	0	0	OF-5
1983	4	12	3	1	1	0	0.0	1	2	3	3	0	.250	.500	0	0	3B-4
2 yrs.	9	31	5	1	1	1	3.2	2	4	4	7	0	.161	.355	0	0	OF-5, 3B-4

WORLD SERIES

	G	AB	H	2B	3B	HR	HR %	R	RBI	BB	SO	SB	BA	SA	PH AB	PH H	G by POS
1981 LA N	6	21	7	1	1	2	9.5	2	7	2	6	0	.333	.762	0	0	OF-6

Bob Guindon

GUINDON, ROBERT JOSEPH
B. Sept. 4, 1943, Brookline, Mass.
BL TL 6'2" 185 lbs.

	G	AB	H	2B	3B	HR	HR %	R	RBI	BB	SO	SB	BA	SA	PH AB	PH H	G by POS
1964 BOS A	5	8	1	1	0	0	0.0	0	0	1	4	0	.125	.250	0	0	OF-1, 1B-1

Ben Guiney

GUINEY, BENJAMIN FRANKLIN
B. Nov. 16, 1858, Detroit, Mich.   D. Dec. 5, 1930, Detroit, Mich.
BB TR 6' 170 lbs.

	G	AB	H	2B	3B	HR	HR %	R	RBI	BB	SO	SB	BA	SA	PH AB	PH H	G by POS
1883 DET N	1	5	1	0	0	0	0.0	1		0	1		.200	.200	0	0	OF-1
1884	2	7	0	0	0	0	0.0	0		0	3		.000	.000	0	0	C-2
2 yrs.	3	12	1	0	0	0	0.0	1		0	4		.083	.083	0	0	C-2, OF-1

Ben Guintini

GUINTINI, BENJAMIN JOHN
B. Jan. 13, 1920, Los Banos, Calif.
BR TR 6'1½" 190 lbs.

	G	AB	H	2B	3B	HR	HR %	R	RBI	BB	SO	SB	BA	SA	PH AB	PH H	G by POS
1946 PIT N	2	3	0	0	0	0	0.0	0	0	0	0	0	.000	.000	1	0	OF-1
1950 PHI A	3	4	0	0	0	0	0.0	0	0	0	1	0	.000	.000	2	0	OF-1
2 yrs.	5	7	0	0	0	0	0.0	0	0	0	1	0	.000	.000	3	0	OF-2

Lou Guisto

GUISTO, LOUIS JOSEPH
B. Jan. 16, 1894, Napa, Calif.
BR TR 5'11" 193 lbs.

	G	AB	H	2B	3B	HR	HR %	R	RBI	BB	SO	SB	BA	SA	PH AB	PH H	G by POS
1916 CLE A	6	19	3	0	0	0	0.0	2	2	4	3	1	.158	.158	0	0	1B-6
1917	73	200	37	4	2	0	0.0	9	29	25	18	3	.185	.225	11	2	1B-59
1921	2	2	1	0	0	0	0.0	0	1	0	1	0	.500	.500	1	1	1B-1
1922	35	84	21	10	1	0	0.0	7	9	2	7	0	.250	.393	10	3	1B-24
1923	40	144	26	5	0	0	0.0	17	18	15	15	1	.181	.215	0	0	1B-40
5 yrs.	156	449	88	19	3	0	0.0	35	59	46	44	5	.196	.252	22	6	1B-130

	G	AB	H	2B	3B	HR	HR %	R	RBI	BB	SO	SB	BA	SA	Pinch Hit AB	H	G by POS

Brad Gulden

GULDEN, BRADLEY LEE
B. June 10, 1956, New Ulm, Minn.　　　BL TR 5'10" 175 lbs.

	G	AB	H	2B	3B	HR	HR%	R	RBI	BB	SO	SB	BA	SA	AB	H	G by POS
1978 LA N	3	4	0	0	0	0	0.0	0	0	0	2	0	.000	.000	0	0	C-3
1979 NY A	40	92	15	4	0	0	0.0	10	6	9	16	0	.163	.207	0	0	C-40
1980	2	3	1	0	0	1	33.3	1	2	0	0	0	.333	1.333	0	0	C-2
1981 SEA A	8	16	3	2	0	0	0.0	0	1	0	2	0	.188	.313	4	0	C-6, DH-2
1982 MON N	5	6	0	0	0	0	0.0	1	0	1	1	0	.000	.000	3	0	C-2
1984 CIN N	107	292	66	8	2	4	1.4	31	33	33	35	2	.226	.308	20	3	C-100
6 yrs.	165	413	85	14	2	5	1.2	43	42	43	56	2	.206	.286	27	3	C-153, DH-2

Tom Gulley

GULLEY, THOMAS JEFFERSON
B. Dec. 25, 1899, Garner, N. C.　D. Nov. 24, 1966, St. Charles, Ark.　BL TR 5'11" 178 lbs.

	G	AB	H	2B	3B	HR	HR%	R	RBI	BB	SO	SB	BA	SA	AB	H	G by POS
1923 CLE A	2	3	1	1	0	0	0.0	1	0	0	0	0	.333	.667	1	0	OF-1
1924	8	20	3	0	1	0	0.0	4	1	3	2	0	.150	.250	3	0	OF-5
1926 CHI A	16	35	8	3	1	0	0.0	5	8	5	2	0	.229	.371	4	1	OF-12
3 yrs.	26	58	12	4	2	0	0.0	10	9	8	4	0	.207	.345	8	1	OF-18

Ted Gullic

GULLIC, TEDD JASPER
B. Jan. 2, 1907, Koshkonong, Mo.　　　BR TR 6'2" 175 lbs.

	G	AB	H	2B	3B	HR	HR%	R	RBI	BB	SO	SB	BA	SA	AB	H	G by POS
1930 STL A	92	308	77	7	5	4	1.3	39	44	27	43	4	.250	.344	6	0	OF-82, 1B-3
1933	104	304	74	18	3	5	1.6	34	35	15	38	3	.243	.372	24	4	OF-36, 3B-33, 1B-14
2 yrs.	196	612	151	25	8	9	1.5	73	79	42	81	7	.247	.358	30	4	OF-118, 3B-33, 1B-17

Glenn Gulliver

GULLIVER, GLENN JAMES
B. Oct. 15, 1954, Detroit, Mich.　　　BL TR 5'10" 180 lbs.

	G	AB	H	2B	3B	HR	HR%	R	RBI	BB	SO	SB	BA	SA	AB	H	G by POS
1982 BAL A	50	145	29	7	0	1	0.7	24	5	37	18	0	.200	.269	1	0	3B-50
1983	23	47	10	3	0	0	0.0	5	2	9	5	0	.213	.277	4	0	3B-21
2 yrs.	73	192	39	10	0	1	0.5	29	7	46	23	0	.203	.271	5	0	3B-71

Ad Gumbert

GUMBERT, ADDISON COURTNEY
Brother of Billy Gumbert.
B. Oct. 10, 1868, Pittsburgh, Pa.　D. Apr. 23, 1925, Pittsburgh, Pa.　BR TR 5'10" 200 lbs.

	G	AB	H	2B	3B	HR	HR%	R	RBI	BB	SO	SB	BA	SA	AB	H	G by POS
1888 CHI N	7	24	8	0	1	0	0.0	3	2	0	2	0	.333	.417	0	0	P-6, OF-2
1889	41	153	44	3	2	7	4.6	30	29	11	36	2	.288	.471	0	0	P-31, OF-13
1890 BOS P	44	145	35	7	1	3	2.1	23	20	18	26	5	.241	.366	0	0	P-39, OF-7
1891 CHI N	34	105	32	7	4	0	0.0	18	16	13	14	4	.305	.448	0	0	P-32, OF-1, 1B-1
1892	52	178	42	1	2	1	0.6	18	8	14	24	5	.236	.281	0	0	P-46, OF-7
1893 PIT N	29	95	21	3	3	0	0.0	17	10	10	16	0	.221	.316	0	0	P-22, OF-7
1894	38	113	33	4	5	1	0.9	19	6	20	1	0	.292	.442	1	0	P-37
1895 BKN N	34	97	35	6	0	2	2.1	21	13	7	10	0	.361	.485	0	0	P-33, OF-1
1896 2 teams		BKN	N	(5G –	.182)		PHI	N	(11G –	.265)							
" total	16	45	11	2	1	1	2.2	7	7	1	5	1	.244	.400	0	0	P-16
9 yrs.	295	955	261	33	19	15	1.6	155	124	80	153	18	.273	.395	1	0	P-262, OF-38, 1B-1

Fred Gunkle

GUNKLE, FREDERICK W.
B. Dubuque, Iowa　Deceased.

	G	AB	H	2B	3B	HR	HR%	R	RBI	BB	SO	SB	BA	SA	AB	H	G by POS
1879 CLE N	1	3	0	0	0	0	0.0	0		0	1		.000	.000	0	0	OF-1, C-1

Hy Gunning

GUNNING, HYLAND
B. Aug. 6, 1888, Maplewood, N. J.　D. Mar. 28, 1975, Togus, Me.　BL TR 6'1½" 189 lbs.

	G	AB	H	2B	3B	HR	HR%	R	RBI	BB	SO	SB	BA	SA	AB	H	G by POS
1911 BOS A	4	9	1	0	0	0	0.0	0	2	2		0	.111	.111	0	0	1B-4

Tom Gunning

GUNNING, THOMAS FRANCIS
B. Mar. 4, 1862, Newmarket, N. H.　D. Mar. 17, 1931, Fall River, Mass.

	G	AB	H	2B	3B	HR	HR%	R	RBI	BB	SO	SB	BA	SA	AB	H	G by POS
1884 BOS N	12	45	5	1	1	0	0.0	4		1	12		.111	.178	0	0	C-12
1885	48	174	32	3	0	0	0.0	17	15	5	29		.184	.201	0	0	C-48
1886	27	98	22	2	1	0	0.0	15	7	3	19		.224	.265	0	0	C-27
1887 PHI N	28	104	27	6	1	1	1.0	22	16	5	6	18	.260	.365	0	0	C-28
1888 PHI AA	23	92	18	0	0	0	0.0	18	5	2	14	14	.196	.196	0	0	C-23
1889	8	24	6	0	1	1	4.2	3	1	0	4	3	.250	.458	0	0	C-8
6 yrs.	146	537	110	12	4	2	0.4	79	43	16	70	35	.205	.253	0	0	C-146

Joe Gunson

GUNSON, JOSEPH BROOK
B. Mar. 23, 1863, Philadelphia, Pa.　D. Nov. 15, 1942, Philadelphia, Pa.　TR 5'6" 160 lbs.

	G	AB	H	2B	3B	HR	HR%	R	RBI	BB	SO	SB	BA	SA	AB	H	G by POS
1884 WAS U	45	166	23	2	0	0	0.0	15		3			.139	.151	0	0	C-33, OF-18
1889 KC AA	34	122	24	3	1	0	0.0	15	12	3	17	2	.197	.238	0	0	C-32, OF-1, 3B-1
1892 BAL N	89	314	67	10	5	0	0.0	35	32	16	17	2	.213	.277	0	0	C-67, OF-20, 1B-2, 2B-1
1893 2 teams	61		STL	N	(40G –	.272)		CLE	N	(21G –	.260)						
" total	61	224	60	6	0	0	0.0	31	24	12	6	0	.268	.295	2	1	C-55, OF-5
4 yrs.	229	826	174	21	6	0	0.0	96	67	34	40	4	.211	.251	2	1	C-187, OF-44, 1B-2, 3B-1, 2B-1

Ernie Gust

GUST, ERNEST HERMAN FRANK (Red)
B. Jan. 24, 1888, Bay City, Mich.　D. Oct. 26, 1945, Maupin, Ore.

	G	AB	H	2B	3B	HR	HR%	R	RBI	BB	SO	SB	BA	SA	AB	H	G by POS
1911 STL A	3	12	0	0	0	0	0.0					0	.000	.000	0	0	1B-3

Frankie Gustine

GUSTINE, FRANK WILLIAM
B. Feb. 20, 1920, Hoopeston, Ill.　　　BR TR 6' 175 lbs.

	G	AB	H	2B	3B	HR	HR%	R	RBI	BB	SO	SB	BA	SA	AB	H	G by POS
1939 PIT N	22	70	13	3	0	0	0.0	5	3	9	4	0	.186	.229	0	0	3B-22
1940	133	524	147	32	7	1	0.2	59	55	35	39	7	.281	.374	3	1	2B-130
1941	121	463	125	24	7	1	0.2	46	46	28	38	5	.270	.359	2	0	2B-104, 3B-15
1942	115	388	89	11	4	2	0.5	34	35	29	27	5	.229	.294	3	0	2B-108, SS-2, 3B-2, C-1
1943	112	414	120	21	3	0	0.0	40	43	32	36	12	.290	.355	5	1	SS-68, 2B-40, 1B-1
1944	127	405	93	18	3	2	0.5	42	42	33	41	1	.230	.304	1	0	SS-116, 2B-11, 3B-1
1945	128	478	134	27	5	2	0.4	67	66	37	33	8	.280	.370	1	0	SS-104, 2B-29, C-1
1946	131	495	128	23	6	8	1.6	60	52	40	52	2	.259	.378	1	0	2B-113, SS-13, 3B-7
1947	156	616	183	30	6	9	1.5	102	67	63	65	5	.297	.409	0	0	3B-156

	G	AB	H	2B	3B	HR	HR %	R	RBI	BB	SO	SB	BA	SA	Pinch Hit AB	Pinch Hit H	G by POS

Frankie Gustine continued

	G	AB	H	2B	3B	HR	HR %	R	RBI	BB	SO	SB	BA	SA	AB	H	G by POS
1948	131	449	120	19	2	9	2.0	68	42	42	62	5	.267	.379	10	2	3B-119
1949 CHI N	76	261	59	13	4	4	1.5	29	27	18	22	3	.226	.352	5	0	3B-55, 2B-16
1950 STL A	9	19	3	1	0	0	0.0		2	3	8	0	.158	.211	1	0	3B-6
12 yrs.	1261	4582	1214	222	47	38	0.8	553	480	369	427	60	.265	.359	32	4	2B-551, 3B-383, SS-303, C-2, 1B-1

GUTH, CHARLES HENRY
B. Aug. 18, 1947, Baltimore, Md.

BR TR 6'1" 180 lbs.

Bucky Guth

	G	AB	H	2B	3B	HR	HR %	R	RBI	BB	SO	SB	BA	SA	AB	H	G by POS
1972 MIN A	3	3	0	0	0	0	0.0	1	0	0		0	.000	.000	0	1	SS-1

GUTIERREZ, CESAR DARIO (Coca)
B. Jan. 26, 1943, Coro, Venezuela

BR TR 5'9" 155 lbs.

Cesar Gutierrez

	G	AB	H	2B	3B	HR	HR %	R	RBI	BB	SO	SB	BA	SA	AB	H	G by POS
1967 SF N	18	21	3	0	0	0	0.0	4	0	1	4	1	.143	.143	1	1	SS-15, 2B-1
1969 2 teams	SF N (15G – .217)						DET A (17G – .245)										
" total	32	72	17	2	0	0	0.0	9	0	11	5	2	.236	.264	2	1	SS-20, 3B-7
1970 DET A	135	415	101	11	6	0	0.0	40	22	18	39	4	.243	.299	0	0	SS-135
1971	38	37	7	0	0	0	0.0	8	4	0	3	0	.189	.189	9	3	SS-14, 3B-5, 2B-2
4 yrs.	223	545	128	13	6	0	0.0	61	26	30	51	7	.235	.281	12	5	SS-184, 3B-12, 2B-3

GUTIERREZ, JOAQUIN FERNANDO
B. June 27, 1960, Cartagena, Columbia

BR TR 5'11" 168 lbs.

Jackie Gutierrez

	G	AB	H	2B	3B	HR	HR %	R	RBI	BB	SO	SB	BA	SA	AB	H	G by POS
1983 BOS A	5	10	3	0	0	0	0.0	2	0	1	1	0	.300	.300	0	0	SS-4
1984	151	449	118	12	3	2	0.4	55	29	15	49	12	.263	.316	0	0	SS-150
2 yrs.	156	459	121	12	3	2	0.4	57	29	16	50	12	.264	.316	0	0	SS-154

GUTTERIDGE, DONALD JOSEPH
B. June 19, 1912, Pittsburg, Kans.
Manager 1969-70.

BR TR 5'10½" 165 lbs.

Don Gutteridge

	G	AB	H	2B	3B	HR	HR %	R	RBI	BB	SO	SB	BA	SA	AB	H	G by POS
1936 STL N	23	91	29	3	4	3	3.3	13	16	1	14	3	.319	.538	0	0	3B-23
1937	119	447	121	26	10	7	1.6	66	61	25	66	12	.271	.421	8	1	3B-105, SS-8
1938	142	552	141	21	15	9	1.6	61	64	29	49	14	.255	.397	2	0	3B-73, SS-68
1939	148	524	141	27	4	7	1.3	71	54	27	70	5	.269	.376	2	0	3B-143, SS-2
1940	69	108	29	5	0	3	2.8	19	14	5	15	3	.269	.398	20	2	3B-39
1942 STL A	147	616	157	27	11	1	0.2	90	50	59	54	16	.255	.339	1	1	2B-145, 3B-2
1943	132	538	147	35	6	1	0.2	77	36	50	46	10	.273	.366	1	0	2B-132
1944	148	603	148	27	11	3	0.5	89	36	51	63	20	.245	.342	1	0	2B-146
1945	143	543	129	24	3	2	0.4	72	49	43	46	9	.238	.304	1	0	2B-128, OF-14
1946 BOS A	22	47	11	3	0	1	2.1	8	6	2	7	0	.234	.362	1	0	2B-9, 3B-8
1947	54	131	22	2	0	2	1.5	20	5	17	13	3	.168	.229	5	1	2B-20, 3B-19
1948 PIT N	4	2	0	0	0	0	0.0	0	0	0	1	0	.000	.000	2	0	
12 yrs.	1151	4202	1075	200	64	39	0.9	586	391	309	444	95	.256	.362	44	5	2B-580, 3B-412, SS-78, OF-14

WORLD SERIES																	
1944 STL A	6	21	3	1	0	0	0.0	1	0	3	5	0	.143	.190	0	0	2B-6
1946 BOS A	3	5	2	0	0	0	0.0	1	1	0	0	0	.400	.400	0	0	2B-2
2 yrs.	9	26	5	1	0	0	0.0	2	1	3	5	0	.192	.231	0	0	2B-8

GWOSDZ, DOUGLAS WAYNE (Eyechart)
B. June 20, 1960, Houston, Tex.

BR TR 5'11" 180 lbs.

Doug Gwosdz

	G	AB	H	2B	3B	HR	HR %	R	RBI	BB	SO	SB	BA	SA	AB	H	G by POS
1981 SD N	16	24	4	2	0	0	0.0	1	3	3	6	0	.167	.250	4	0	C-13
1982	7	17	3	0	0	0	0.0	1	0	2	7	0	.176	.176	1	0	C-7
1983	39	55	6	1	0	1	1.8	7	4	7	19	0	.109	.182	5	1	C-32
1984	7	8	2	0	0	0	0.0	0	1	2	5	0	.250	.250	0	0	C-6
4 yrs.	69	104	15	3	0	1	1.0	9	8	14	37	0	.144	.202	10	1	C-58

GWYNN, ANTHONY KEITH
B. May 9, 1960, Los Angeles, Calif.

BL TL 5'11" 185 lbs.

Tony Gwynn

	G	AB	H	2B	3B	HR	HR %	R	RBI	BB	SO	SB	BA	SA	AB	H	G by POS
1982 SD N	54	190	55	12	2	1	0.5	33	17	14	16	8	.289	.389	4	1	OF-52
1983	86	304	94	12	2	1	0.3	34	37	23	21	7	.309	.372	6	1	OF-81
1984	158	606	213	21	10	5	0.8	88	71	59	23	33	.351	.444	2	1	OF-156
3 yrs.	298	1100	362	45	14	7	0.6	155	125	96	60	48	.329	.415	12	3	OF-289

LEAGUE CHAMPIONSHIP SERIES																	
1984 SD N	5	19	7	3	0	0	0.0	6	3	1	2	0	.368	.526	0	0	OF-5

WORLD SERIES																	
1984 SD N	5	19	5	0	0	0	0.0	1	0	3	2	1	.263	.263	0	0	OF-5

GYSELMAN, RICHARD RENALD
B. Apr. 6, 1908, San Francisco, Calif.

BR TR 6'2" 170 lbs.

Dick Gyselman

	G	AB	H	2B	3B	HR	HR %	R	RBI	BB	SO	SB	BA	SA	AB	H	G by POS
1933 BOS N	58	155	37	6	2	0	0.0	10	12	7	21	0	.239	.303	3	1	3B-42, 2B-5, SS-1
1934	24	36	6	1	1	0	0.0	7	4	2	11	0	.167	.250	4	1	3B-15, 2B-2
2 yrs.	82	191	43	7	3	0	0.0	17	16	9	32	0	.225	.293	7	2	3B-57, 2B-7, SS-1

HAAS, BERTHOLD JOHN
B. Feb. 8, 1914, Naperville, Ill.

BR TR 5'11" 178 lbs.

Bert Haas

	G	AB	H	2B	3B	HR	HR %	R	RBI	BB	SO	SB	BA	SA	AB	H	G by POS
1937 BKN N	16	25	10	3	0	0	0.0	2	2	1	1	0	.400	.520	9	4	OF-4, 1B-3
1938	1	0	0	0	0	0	–	0	0	0	0	0	–		0	0	
1942 CIN N	154	585	140	21	6	6	1.0	59	54	59	54	6	.239	.326	0	0	3B-146, 1B-6, OF-2
1943	101	332	87	17	6	4	1.2	39	44	22	26	6	.262	.386	16	4	1B-44, 3B-23, OF-18
1946	140	535	141	24	7	3	0.6	57	50	33	42	22	.264	.351	2	1	1B-131, 3B-6
1947	135	482	138	17	7	3	0.6	58	67	42	27	9	.286	.369	11	2	OF-69, 1B-53
1948 PHI N	95	333	94	9	2	4	1.2	35	34	36	25	8	.282	.357	9	2	3B-54, 1B-35
1949 2 teams	PHI N (2G – .000)						NY N (54G – .260)										
" total	56	105	27	2	3	1	1.0	12	10	6	9	0	.257	.362	19	4	1B-23, 3B-11

	G	AB	H	2B	3B	HR	HR %	R	RBI	BB	SO	SB	BA	SA	Pinch Hit AB	Pinch Hit H	G by POS

Bert Haas continued

	G	AB	H	2B	3B	HR	HR %	R	RBI	BB	SO	SB	BA	SA	AB	H	G by POS
1951 CHI A	25	43	7	0	1	1	2.3	1	2	5	4	0	.163	.279	11	3	1B-7, OF-4, 3B-1
9 yrs.	723	2440	644	93	32	22	0.9	263	263	204	188	51	.264	.355	77	20	1B-302, 3B-241, OF-97

Bruno Haas

HAAS, BRUNO PHILIP (Boon)
B. May 5, 1891, Worcester, Mass.   D. June 5, 1952, Sarasota, Fla.   BB TL 5'10"   180 lbs.

	G	AB	H	2B	3B	HR	HR %	R	RBI	BB	SO	SB	BA	SA	AB	H	G by POS
1915 PHI A	12	18	1	0	0	0	0.0	1	0	1	7	0	.056	.056	1	0	P-6, OF-3

Eddie Haas

HAAS, GEORGE EDWIN
B. May 26, 1935, Paducah, Ky.   BL TR 5'11"   178 lbs.

	G	AB	H	2B	3B	HR	HR %	R	RBI	BB	SO	SB	BA	SA	AB	H	G by POS
1957 CHI N	14	24	5	1	0	0	0.0	1	4	1	5	0	.208	.250	8	2	OF-4
1958 MIL N	9	14	5	0	0	0	0.0	2	1	2	1	0	.357	.357	4	3	OF-3
1960	32	32	7	2	0	1	3.1	4	5	5	14	0	.219	.375	25	6	OF-2
3 yrs.	55	70	17	3	0	1	1.4	7	10	8	20	0	.243	.329	37	11	OF-9

Mule Haas

HAAS, GEORGE WILLIAM
B. Oct. 15, 1903, Montclair, N. J.   D. June 30, 1974, New Orleans, La.   BL TR 6'1"   175 lbs.

	G	AB	H	2B	3B	HR	HR %	R	RBI	BB	SO	SB	BA	SA	AB	H	G by POS
1925 PIT N	4	3	0	0	0	0	0.0	1	0	0	1	0	.000	.000	1	0	OF-2
1928 PHI A	91	332	93	21	4	6	1.8	41	39	23	20	2	.280	.422	8	0	OF-82
1929	139	578	181	41	9	16	2.8	115	82	34	38	2	.313	.498	0	0	OF-139
1930	132	532	159	33	7	2	0.4	91	68	43	33	2	.299	.398	1	0	OF-131
1931	102	440	142	29	7	8	1.8	82	56	30	29	0	.323	.475	0	0	OF-102
1932	143	558	170	28	5	6	1.1	91	65	62	49	1	.305	.405	6	3	OF-137
1933 CHI N	146	585	168	33	4	1	0.2	97	51	65	41	0	.287	.362	0	0	OF-146
1934	106	351	94	16	3	2	0.6	54	22	47	22	1	.268	.348	13	4	OF-89
1935	92	327	95	22	1	2	0.6	44	40	37	17	4	.291	.382	7	2	OF-84
1936	119	408	116	26	2	0	0.0	75	46	64	29	1	.284	.358	15	3	OF-96, 1B-7
1937	54	111	23	3	3	0	0.0	8	15	16	10	1	.207	.288	16	2	1B-32, OF-2
1938 PHI A	40	78	16	2	0	0	0.0	7	12	12	10	0	.205	.231	20	1	OF-12, 1B-6
12 yrs.	1168	4303	1257	254	45	43	1.0	706	496	433	299	12	.292	.402	87	15	OF-1022, 1B-45
WORLD SERIES																	
1929 PHI A	5	21	5	0	0	2	9.5	3	6	1	3	0	.238	.524	0	0	OF-5
1930	6	18	2	0	1	0	0.0	1	1	1	3	0	.111	.222	0	0	OF-6
1931	7	23	3	1	0	0	0.0	1	2	3	5	0	.130	.174	0	0	OF-7
3 yrs.	18	62	10	1	1	2	3.2	5	9	5	11	0	.161	.306	0	0	OF-18

Emil Haberer

HABERER, EMIL KARL
B. Feb. 2, 1878, Cincinnati, Ohio   D. Oct. 19, 1951, Louisville, Ky.   BR TR 6'1"   204 lbs.

	G	AB	H	2B	3B	HR	HR %	R	RBI	BB	SO	SB	BA	SA	AB	H	G by POS
1901 CIN N	6	18	3	0	1	0	0.0	2	1	3		0	.167	.278	1	1	3B-3, 1B-2
1903	5	13	1	0	0	0	0.0	1	0	2		0	.077	.077	1	1	C-4
1909	5	16	3	1	0	0	0.0	1	2	0		0	.188	.250	1	0	C-4
3 yrs.	16	47	7	1	1	0	0.0	4	3	5		0	.149	.213	3	1	C-8, 3B-3, 1B-2

Irv Hach

HACH, IRVIN WILLIAM (Major)
B. June 6, 1873, Louisville, Ky.   D. Aug. 13, 1936, Louisville, Ky.   BR TR

	G	AB	H	2B	3B	HR	HR %	R	RBI	BB	SO	SB	BA	SA	AB	H	G by POS
1897 LOU N	16	51	11	2	0	0	0.0	5	3	5		1	.216	.255	0	0	2B-9, 3B-7

Stan Hack

HACK, STANLEY CAMFIELD (Smiling Stan)
B. Dec. 6, 1909, Sacramento, Calif.   D. Dec. 15, 1979, Dickson, Ill.   BL TR 6'   170 lbs.
Manager 1954-56, 1958.

	G	AB	H	2B	3B	HR	HR %	R	RBI	BB	SO	SB	BA	SA	AB	H	G by POS
1932 CHI N	72	178	42	5	6	2	1.1	32	19	17	16	5	.236	.365	14	2	3B-51
1933	20	60	21	3	1	1	1.7	10	2	8	3	4	.350	.483	0	0	3B-17
1934	111	402	116	16	6	1	0.2	54	21	45	42	11	.289	.366	0	0	3B-109
1935	124	427	133	23	9	4	0.9	75	64	65	39	14	.311	.436	5	2	3B-111, 1B-7
1936	149	561	167	27	4	6	1.1	102	78	89	39	17	.298	.392	0	0	3B-140, 1B-11
1937	154	582	173	27	6	2	0.3	106	63	83	42	16	.297	.375	1	0	3B-150, 1B-4
1938	152	609	195	34	11	4	0.7	109	67	94	39	16	.320	.432	0	0	3B-152
1939	156	641	191	28	6	8	1.2	112	56	65	35	17	.298	.398	0	0	3B-156
1940	149	603	191	38	6	8	1.3	101	40	75	24	21	.317	.439	0	0	3B-148, 1B-1
1941	151	586	186	33	5	7	1.2	111	45	99	40	10	.317	.427	0	0	3B-150, 1B-1
1942	140	553	166	36	3	6	1.1	91	39	94	40	9	.300	.409	0	0	3B-139
1943	144	533	154	24	4	3	0.6	78	35	82	27	5	.289	.366	7	0	3B-136
1944	98	383	108	16	1	3	0.8	65	32	53	21	5	.282	.352	4	1	3B-75, 1B-18
1945	150	597	193	29	7	2	0.3	110	43	99	30	12	.323	.405	0	0	3B-146, 1B-5
1946	92	323	92	13	4	0	0.0	55	26	83	32	3	.285	.350	2	0	3B-90
1947	76	240	65	11	2	0	0.0	28	12	41	19	0	.271	.333	0	2	3B-66
16 yrs.	1938	7278	2193	363	81	57	0.8	1239	642	1092	466	165	.301	.397	45	7	3B-1836, 1B-47
WORLD SERIES																	
1932 CHI N	1	0	0	0	0	0	—	0	0	0	0	0	—	—	0	0	
1935	6	22	5	1	1	0	0.0	2	0	2	1	0	.227	.364	0	0	SS-1
1938	4	17	8	1	0	0	0.0	3	1	1	2	0	.471	.529	0	0	3B-4
1945	7	30	11	3	0	0	0.0	1	4	4	2	0	.367	.467	0	0	3B-7
4 yrs.	18	69	24	5	1	0	0.0	6	5	7	6	1	.348	.449	0	0	3B-11, SS-1

Rich Hacker

HACKER, RICHARD WARREN
B. Oct. 6, 1947, Belleville, Ill.   BB TR 6'   160 lbs.

	G	AB	H	2B	3B	HR	HR %	R	RBI	BB	SO	SB	BA	SA	AB	H	G by POS
1971 MON N	16	33	4	1	0	0	0.0	2	2	3	12	0	.121	.152	0	0	SS-16

Jim Hackett

HACKETT, JAMES JOSEPH (Sunny Jim)
B. Oct. 1, 1877, Jacksonville, Ill.   D. Mar. 28, 1961, Douglas, Mich.   BR TR 6'2"   185 lbs.

	G	AB	H	2B	3B	HR	HR %	R	RBI	BB	SO	SB	BA	SA	AB	H	G by POS
1902 STL N	6	21	6	1	0	0	0.0	2	4	2		1	.286	.333	0	0	P-4, OF-2
1903	99	351	80	13	8	0	0.0	24	36	19		2	.228	.311	3	0	1B-89, P-7
2 yrs.	105	372	86	14	8	0	0.0	26	40	21		3	.231	.312	3	0	1B-89, P-11, OF-2

Player Register

	G	AB	H	2B	3B	HR	HR %	R	RBI	BB	SO	SB	BA	SA	Pinch Hit AB	Pinch Hit H	G by POS

Mert Hackett

HACKETT, MORTIMER MARTIN
Brother of Walter Hackett.
B. Nov. 11, 1859, Cambridge, Mass.   D. Feb. 22, 1938, Cambridge, Mass.

TR

	G	AB	H	2B	3B	HR	HR %	R	RBI	BB	SO	SB	BA	SA	AB	H	G by POS
1883 BOS N	46	179	42	8	6	2	1.1	20	24	1	48		.235	.380	0	0	C-44, OF-4
1884	72	268	55	13	2	1	0.4	28		2	66		.205	.280	0	0	C-71, 3B-1
1885	34	115	21	7	1	0	0.0	9	4	2	28		.183	.261	0	0	C-34
1886 KC N	62	230	50	8	3	3	1.3	18	25	4	59		.217	.317	0	0	C-40, OF-2, 1B-1
1887 IND N	42	147	35	6	3	2	1.4	12	10	7	24	4	.238	.361	0	0	C-241, OF-19, 3B-1, 1B-1
5 yrs.	256	939	203	42	15	8	0.9	87	63	16	225	4	.216	.318	0	0	

Walter Hackett

HACKETT, WALTER HENRY
Brother of Mert Hackett.
B. Aug. 15, 1857, Cambridge, Mass.   D. Oct. 2, 1920, Cambridge, Mass.

	G	AB	H	2B	3B	HR	HR %	R	RBI	BB	SO	SB	BA	SA	AB	H	G by POS
1884 BOS U	103	415	101	19	0	1	0.2	71		7			.243	.296	0	0	SS-103
1885 BOS N	35	125	23	3	0	0	0.0	8	9	3	22		.184	.208	0	0	2B-20, SS-15
2 yrs.	138	540	124	22	0	1	0.2	79	8	10	22		.230	.276	0	0	SS-118, 2B-20

Harvey Haddix

HADDIX, HARVEY (The Kitten)
B. Sept. 18, 1925, Medway, Ohio

BL TL 5'9½" 170 lbs.

	G	AB	H	2B	3B	HR	HR %	R	RBI	BB	SO	SB	BA	SA	AB	H	G by POS
1952 STL N	9	14	3	0	0	0	0.0	3	2	1	5	1	.214	.214	0	0	P-7, OF-1
1953	48	97	28	3	3	1	1.0	21	11	5	19	0	.289	.412	2	1	P-36
1954	61	93	18	4	2	0	0.0	16	4	5	11	2	.194	.280	0	0	P-43
1955	37	73	12	2	2	1	1.4	10	7	4	15	0	.164	.288	0	0	P-37
1956 2 teams		STL	N (5G –	.222)		PHI	N (46G –	.237)									
" total	51	102	24	5	0	0	0.0	7	11	7	13	0	.235	.284	15	4	P-35
1957 PHI N	41	68	21	3	1	0	0.0	6	6	3	12	1	.309	.382	7	1	P-27
1958 CIN N	42	61	11	4	0	1	1.6	11	1	8	18	0	.180	.295	2	0	P-29
1959 PIT N	31	83	12	4	0	0	0.0	3	5	3	17	0	.145	.193	0	0	P-31
1960	29	67	17	4	0	0	0.0	7	7	3	15	0	.254	.313	0	0	P-29
1961	31	56	8	3	0	0	0.0	2	3	6	14	0	.143	.196	0	0	P-29
1962	28	52	13	3	1	1	1.9	9	5	1	11	0	.250	.404	0	0	P-28
1963	50	11	2	0	0	0	0.0	0	2	0	1	0	.182	.364	1	0	P-49
1964 BAL A	49	19	0	0	0	0	0.0	0	0	1	10	0	.000	.000	0	0	P-49
1965	24	2	0	0	0	0	0.0	0	0	0	1	0	.000	.000	1	0	P-24
14 yrs.	531	798	169	37	9	4	0.5	95	64	46	162	4	.212	.296	28	7	P-453, OF-1

WORLD SERIES

	G	AB	H	2B	3B	HR	HR %	R	RBI	BB	SO	SB	BA	SA	AB	H	G by POS
1960 PIT N	2	3	1	0	0	0	0.0	0	1	0	1	0	.333	.333	0	0	P-2

George Haddock

HADDOCK, GEORGE SILAS (Gentleman George)
B. Dec. 25, 1866, Portsmouth, N. H.   D. Apr. 18, 1926, Boston, Mass.

TR 5'11" 155 lbs.

	G	AB	H	2B	3B	HR	HR %	R	RBI	BB	SO	SB	BA	SA	AB	H	G by POS
1888 WAS N	2	5	1	0	0	0	0.0	1	0	1	2	0	.200	.200	0	0	P-2
1889	34	112	25	3	0	2	1.8	13	14	19	27	3	.223	.304	0	0	P-33, OF-3
1890 BUF P	42	146	36	11	0	0	0.0	21	24	24	32	3	.247	.322	0	0	P-35, OF-7
1891 BOS AA	58	185	45	4	1	3	1.6	30	23	21	46	3	.243	.324	0	0	P-51, OF-8
1892 BKN N	47	158	28	6	1	0	0.0	23	11	12	31	2	.177	.228	0	0	P-46, OF-7
1893	29	85	24	1	2	1	1.2	21	7	8	15	2	.282	.376	0	0	P-23, OF-7
1894 2 teams		PHI	N (10G –	.172)		WAS	N (5G –	.188)									
" total	15	45	8	2	2	0	0.0	6	4	4	4	1	.178	.311	0	0	P-14, OF-1
7 yrs.	227	736	167	27	6	6	0.8	114	83	89	157	14	.227	.304	0	0	P-204, OF-27

Kent Hadley

HADLEY, KENT WILLIAM
B. Dec. 17, 1934, Pocatello, Ida.

BL TL 6'3" 190 lbs.

	G	AB	H	2B	3B	HR	HR %	R	RBI	BB	SO	SB	BA	SA	AB	H	G by POS
1958 KC A	3	11	2	0	0	0	0.0	1	0	0	4	0	.182	.182	1	0	1B-2
1959	113	288	73	11	0	10	3.5	40	39	24	74	1	.253	.403	16	2	1B-95
1960 NY A	55	64	13	2	0	4	6.3	8	11	6	19	0	.203	.422	29	6	1B-24
3 yrs.	171	363	88	13	0	14	3.9	49	50	30	97	1	.242	.399	46	8	1B-121

Bill Haeffner

HAEFFNER, WILLIAM BERNHARD
B. July 18, 1894, Philadelphia, Pa.   D. Jan. 27, 1982, Springfield, Pa.

BR TR 5'9" 165 lbs.

	G	AB	H	2B	3B	HR	HR %	R	RBI	BB	SO	SB	BA	SA	AB	H	G by POS
1915 PHI A	3	4	1	0	0	0	0.0	0	0	0	1	0	.250	.250	0	0	C-3
1920 PIT N	54	175	34	4	1	0	0.0	8	14	8	14	1	.194	.229	2	0	C-52
1928 NY N	2	1	0	0	0	0	0.0	0	0	0	0	0	.000	.000	0	0	C-2
3 yrs.	59	180	35	4	1	0	0.0	8	14	8	15	1	.194	.228	2	0	C-57

Bud Hafey

HAFEY, DANIEL ALBERT
Brother of Tom Hafey.
B. Aug. 6, 1912, Berkeley, Calif.

BR TR 6' 185 lbs.

	G	AB	H	2B	3B	HR	HR %	R	RBI	BB	SO	SB	BA	SA	AB	H	G by POS
1935 2 teams		CHI	A (2G –	.000)		PIT	N (58G –	.228)									
" total	60	184	42	11	2	6	3.3	30	16	16	48	0	.228	.408	5	1	OF-47
1936 PIT N	39	118	25	6	1	4	3.4	19	13	10	27	0	.212	.381	9	0	OF-29
1939 2 teams		CIN	N (6G –	.154)		PHI	N (18G –	.176)									
" total	24	64	11	2	0	0	0.0	4	4	4	16	2	.172	.203	5	1	OF-17, P-2
3 yrs.	123	366	78	19	3	10	2.7	53	33	30	91	2	.213	.363	19	2	OF-93, P-2

Chick Hafey

HAFEY, CHARLES JAMES
B. Feb. 12, 1903, Berkeley, Calif.   D. July 2, 1973, Calistoga, Calif.
Hall of Fame 1971.

BR TR 6' 185 lbs.

	G	AB	H	2B	3B	HR	HR %	R	RBI	BB	SO	SB	BA	SA	AB	H	G by POS
1924 STL N	24	91	23	5	2	2	2.2	10	22	4	8	1	.253	.418	0	0	OF-24
1925	93	358	108	25	2	5	1.4	36	57	10	29	3	.302	.425	5	1	OF-88
1926	78	225	61	19	2	4	1.8	30	38	11	36	2	.271	.427	22	7	OF-54
1927	103	346	114	26	5	18	5.2	62	63	36	41	12	.329	.590	9	5	OF-94
1928	138	520	175	46	6	27	5.2	101	111	40	53	8	.337	.604	4	0	OF-133
1929	134	517	175	47	9	29	5.6	101	125	45	42	7	.338	.632	3	0	OF-130
1930	120	446	150	39	12	26	5.8	108	107	46	51	12	.336	.652	4	1	OF-116
1931	122	450	157	35	8	16	3.6	94	95	39	43	11	.349	.569	18	5	OF-83
1932 CIN N	83	253	87	19	3	2	0.8	34	36	22	20	4	.344	.466	2	0	OF-83
1933	144	568	172	34	6	7	1.2	77	62	40	44	3	.303	.421	0	0	OF-144

	G	AB	H	2B	3B	HR	HR %	R	RBI	BB	SO	SB	BA	SA	Pinch Hit AB	Pinch Hit H	G by POS

Chick Hafey continued

	G	AB	H	2B	3B	HR	HR%	R	RBI	BB	SO	SB	BA	SA	PH AB	PH H	G by POS
1934	140	535	157	29	6	18	3.4	75	67	52	63	4	.293	.471	0	0	OF-140
1935	15	59	20	6	1	1	1.7	10	9	4	5	1	.339	.525	0	0	OF-15
1937	89	257	67	11	5	9	3.5	39	41	23	42	2	.261	.447	22	3	OF-64
13 yrs.	1283	4625	1466	341	67	164	3.5	777	833	372	477	70	.317	.526	88	22	OF-1203

WORLD SERIES

	G	AB	H	2B	3B	HR	HR%	R	RBI	BB	SO	SB	BA	SA	PH AB	PH H	G by POS
1926 STL N	7	27	5	0	0	0	0.0	2	0	0	7	0	.185	.259	0	0	OF-7
1928	4	15	3	0	0	0	0.0	0	0	1	4	0	.200	.200	0	0	OF-4
1930	6	22	6	5	0	0	0.0	2	2	1	3	0	.273	.500	0	0	OF-6
1931	6	24	4	0	0	0	0.0	1	0	0	5	1	.167	.167	0	0	OF-6
4 yrs.	23	88	18	7	0	0	0.0	5	2	2	19	1	.205	.284	0	0	OF-23
				8th													

Tom Hafey

HAFEY, THOMAS FRANCIS (The Arm)
Brother of Bud Hafey.
B. July 12, 1913, Berkeley, Calif.

BR TR 6'1" 180 lbs.

	G	AB	H	2B	3B	HR	HR%	R	RBI	BB	SO	SB	BA	SA	PH AB	PH H	G by POS
1939 NY N	70	256	62	10	1	6	2.3	37	26	10	44	1	.242	.359	0	0	3B-70
1944 STL A	8	14	5	2	0	0	0.0	1	2	1	4	0	.357	.500	3	1	OF-4, 1B-1
2 yrs.	78	270	67	12	1	6	2.2	38	28	11	48	1	.248	.367	3	1	3B-70, OF-4, 1B-1

Bill Hague

HAGUE, WILLIAM L.
Born William L. Haug.
B. 1852, Philadelphia, Pa.   Deceased.

BR TR 5'9" 164 lbs.

	G	AB	H	2B	3B	HR	HR%	R	RBI	BB	SO	SB	BA	SA	PH AB	PH H	G by POS
1876 LOU N	67	294	78	8	1	1	0.3	31	22	2	10		.265	.303	0	0	3B-67, SS-1
1877	59	263	70	7	1	1	0.4	38	24	7	18		.266	.312	0	0	3B-59
1878 PRO N	62	250	51	3	0	0	0.0	21	25	5	34		.204	.216	0	0	3B-62
1879	51	209	47	3	1	0	0.0	20	21	3	19		.225	.249	0	0	3B-51
4 yrs.	239	1016	246	21	2	2	0.2	110	92	17	81		.242	.273	0	0	3B-239, SS-1

Joe Hague

HAGUE, JOE CLARENCE
B. Apr. 25, 1944, Huntington, W. Va.

BL TL 6' 195 lbs.

	G	AB	H	2B	3B	HR	HR%	R	RBI	BB	SO	SB	BA	SA	PH AB	PH H	G by POS
1968 STL N	7	17	4	0	0	1	5.9	2	1	2	2	0	.235	.412	1	0	OF-3, 1B-2
1969	40	100	17	2	1	2	2.0	8	8	12	23	0	.170	.270	14	1	OF-17, 1B-9
1970	139	451	122	16	4	14	3.1	58	68	63	87	2	.271	.417	17	7	1B-82, OF-52
1971	129	380	86	9	3	16	4.2	46	54	58	69	0	.226	.392	17	2	1B-91, OF-36
1972 2 teams		STL	N	(27G –	.237)		CIN	N	(69G –	.246)							
" total	96	214	52	12	2	7	3.3	25	31	37	36	1	.243	.416	32	11	1B-44, OF-22
1973 CIN N	19	33	5	2	0	0	0.0	2	1	5	5	1	.152	.212	8	3	OF-5, 1B-4
6 yrs.	430	1195	286	41	10	40	3.3	141	163	177	222	4	.239	.391	89	24	1B-232, OF-135

LEAGUE CHAMPIONSHIP SERIES

	G	AB	H	2B	3B	HR	HR%	R	RBI	BB	SO	SB	BA	SA	PH AB	PH H	G by POS
1972 CIN N	3	1	0	0	0	0	0.0	0	0	2	1	0	.000	.000	1	0	

WORLD SERIES

	G	AB	H	2B	3B	HR	HR%	R	RBI	BB	SO	SB	BA	SA	PH AB	PH H	G by POS
1972 CIN N	3	3	0	0	0	0	0.0	0	0	0	0	0	.000	.000	3	0	OF-1

Dick Hahn

HAHN, RICHARD FREDERICK
B. July 24, 1916, Canton, Ohio

BR TR 5'11" 176 lbs.

	G	AB	H	2B	3B	HR	HR%	R	RBI	BB	SO	SB	BA	SA	PH AB	PH H	G by POS
1940 WAS A	1	3	0	0	0	0	0.0	0	0	0	0	0	.000	.000	0	0	C-1

Don Hahn

HAHN, DONALD ANTONE
B. Nov. 16, 1948, San Francisco, Calif.

BR TR 6'1" 180 lbs.

	G	AB	H	2B	3B	HR	HR%	R	RBI	BB	SO	SB	BA	SA	PH AB	PH H	G by POS
1969 MON N	4	9	1	0	0	0	0.0	0	2	0	5	0	.111	.111	0	0	OF-3
1970	82	149	38	8	0	0	0.0	22	8	27	27	4	.255	.309	18	5	OF-61
1971 NY N	98	178	42	5	1	1	0.6	16	11	21	32	2	.236	.292	8	2	OF-80
1972	17	37	6	0	0	0	0.0	0	1	4	12	0	.162	.162	6	0	OF-10
1973	93	262	60	10	0	2	0.8	22	21	22	43	2	.229	.290	9	2	OF-87
1974	110	323	81	14	4	1	1.2	34	28	37	34	2	.251	.337	8	3	OF-106
1975 3 teams	PHI	N	(9G –	.000)		STL	N	(7G –	.125)		SD	N	(34G –	.231)			
" total	50	39	7	1	2	0	0.0	10	3	11	5	1	.179	.308	5	0	OF-37
7 yrs.	454	997	235	38	4	7	0.7	104	74	122	158	11	.236	.303	54	12	OF-384

LEAGUE CHAMPIONSHIP SERIES

	G	AB	H	2B	3B	HR	HR%	R	RBI	BB	SO	SB	BA	SA	PH AB	PH H	G by POS
1973 NY N	5	17	4	0	0	0	0.0	2	1	2	4	0	.235	.235	0	0	OF-5

WORLD SERIES

	G	AB	H	2B	3B	HR	HR%	R	RBI	BB	SO	SB	BA	SA	PH AB	PH H	G by POS
1973 NY N	7	29	7	1	1	0	0.0	2	2	1	6	0	.241	.345	0	0	OF-7

Ed Hahn

HAHN, EDGAR WILLIAM
B. Aug. 27, 1875, Nevada, Ohio   D. Nov. 29, 1941, Des Moines, Iowa

BL TR

	G	AB	H	2B	3B	HR	HR%	R	RBI	BB	SO	SB	BA	SA	PH AB	PH H	G by POS
1905 NY A	43	160	51	5	0	0	0.0	32	11	25		1	.319	.350	0	0	OF-43
1906 2 teams	NY	A	(11G –	.091)		CHI	A	(130G –	.227)								
" total	141	506	112	8	5	0	0.0	82	28	72		21	.221	.257	1	0	OF-137
1907 CHI A	156	592	151	9	7	0	0.0	87	45	84		17	.255	.294	0	0	OF-156
1908	122	447	112	12	8	0	0.0	58	21	39		11	.251	.313	3	1	OF-118
1909	76	287	52	6	0	1	0.3	30	16	31		9	.181	.213	0	0	OF-76
1910	15	53	6	2	0	0	0.0	2	1	7		0	.113	.151	0	0	OF-15
6 yrs.	553	2045	484	42	20	1	0.0	291	122	258		59	.237	.278	4	1	OF-545

WORLD SERIES

	G	AB	H	2B	3B	HR	HR%	R	RBI	BB	SO	SB	BA	SA	PH AB	PH H	G by POS
1906 CHI A	6	22	6	0	0	0	0.0	4	0	1		1	.273	.273	0	0	OF-6

Ed Haigh

HAIGH, EDWARD E.
B. Feb. 7, 1867, Philadelphia, Pa.   D. Feb. 13, 1953, Atlantic City, N. J.

	G	AB	H	2B	3B	HR	HR%	R	RBI	BB	SO	SB	BA	SA	PH AB	PH H	G by POS
1892 STL N	1	4	1	0	0	0	0.0	0	0	0	2	0	.250	.250	0	0	OF-1

	G	AB	H	2B	3B	HR	HR %	R	RBI	BB	SO	SB	BA	SA	Pinch Hit AB	Pinch Hit H	G by POS

Hinkey Haines

HAINES, HENRY LUTHER   BR TR 5'10" 170 lbs.
B. Dec. 23, 1898, Sharon Hill, Pa.   D. Jan. 9, 1979, Sharon Hills, Pa.

	G	AB	H	2B	3B	HR	HR %	R	RBI	BB	SO	SB	BA	SA	PH AB	PH H	G by POS
1923 NY A	28	25	4	2	0	0	0.0	9	3	4	5	3	.160	.240	3	0	OF-14

WORLD SERIES
| 1923 NY A | 2 | 1 | 0 | 0 | 0 | 0 | 0.0 | 1 | 0 | 0 | 0 | 0 | .000 | .000 | 0 | 0 | OF-2 |

Jerry Hairston

HAIRSTON, JERRY WAYNE   BB TR 5'10" 170 lbs.
Brother of John Hairston.   Son of Sam Hairston.
B. Feb. 16, 1952, Birmingham, Ala.

	G	AB	H	2B	3B	HR	HR %	R	RBI	BB	SO	SB	BA	SA	PH AB	PH H	G by POS
1973 CHI A	60	210	57	11	1	0	0.0	25	23	33	30	0	.271	.333	2	0	OF-33, 1B-19, DH-8
1974	45	109	25	7	0	0	0.0	8	8	13	18	0	.229	.294	12	2	OF-22, DH-10
1975	69	219	62	8	0	0	0.0	26	23	46	23	1	.283	.320	3	0	OF-59, DH-8
1976	44	119	27	2	2	0	0.0	20	10	24	19	1	.227	.277	4	1	OF-40
1977 2 teams		CHI	A (13G –	.308)		PIT	N (51G –	.192)									
" total	64	78	18	4	0	2	2.6	8	10	11	17	0	.231	.359	34	7	OF-25, 2B-1
1981 CHI A	9	25	7	1	0	1	4.0	5	6	2	4	0	.280	.440	2	1	OF-7
1982	85	90	21	5	0	5	5.6	11	18	9	15	0	.233	.456	47	11	OF-36, DH-2
1983	101	126	37	9	1	5	4.0	17	22	23	16	0	.294	.500	62	17	OF-32, DH-4
1984	115	227	59	13	2	5	2.2	41	19	41	29	2	.260	.401	59	18	OF-37, DH-20
9 yrs.	592	1203	313	60	6	18	1.5	161	139	202	171	4	.260	.365	225	57	OF-291, DH-52, 1B-19, 2B-1

LEAGUE CHAMPIONSHIP SERIES
| 1983 CHI A | 2 | 3 | 0 | 0 | 0 | 0 | 0.0 | 0 | 0 | 1 | 1 | 0 | .000 | .000 | 2 | 0 | OF-2 |

John Hairston

HAIRSTON, JOHN LOUIS   BR TR 6'2" 200 lbs.
Son of Sam Hairston.   Brother of Jerry Hairston.
B. Aug. 29, 1945, Birmingham, Ala.

	G	AB	H	2B	3B	HR	HR %	R	RBI	BB	SO	SB	BA	SA	PH AB	PH H	G by POS
1969 CHI N	3	4	1	0	0	0	0.0	0	0	0	2	0	.250	.250	1	1	OF-1, C-1

Sam Hairston

HAIRSTON, SAMUEL   BR TR 5'10½" 187 lbs.
Father of Jerry Hairston.   Father of John Hairston.
B. Jan. 28, 1920, Crawford, Miss.

	G	AB	H	2B	3B	HR	HR %	R	RBI	BB	SO	SB	BA	SA	PH AB	PH H	G by POS
1951 CHI A	4	5	2	1	0	0	0.0	1	1	2	0	0	.400	.600	1	0	C-2

Chet Hajduk

HAJDUK, CHESTER   BR TR 6' 195 lbs.
B. July 21, 1918, Chicago, Ill.

	G	AB	H	2B	3B	HR	HR %	R	RBI	BB	SO	SB	BA	SA	PH AB	PH H	G by POS
1941 CHI A	1	1	0	0	0	0	0.0	0	0	0	0	0	.000	.000	1	0	

George Halas

HALAS, GEORGE STANLEY   BB TR 6' 164 lbs.
B. Feb. 2, 1895, Chicago, Ill.   D. Oct. 31, 1983, Chicago, Ill.

	G	AB	H	2B	3B	HR	HR %	R	RBI	BB	SO	SB	BA	SA	PH AB	PH H	G by POS
1919 NY A	12	22	2	0	0	0	0.0	0	0	0	8	0	.091	.091	4	0	OF-6

John Haldeman

HALDEMAN, JOHN AVERY   BR TR 5'10" 175 lbs.
B. Dec. 2, 1855, Pewee Valley, Ky.   D. Sept. 17, 1899, Louisville, Ky.

	G	AB	H	2B	3B	HR	HR %	R	RBI	BB	SO	SB	BA	SA	PH AB	PH H	G by POS
1877 LOU N	1	4	0	0	0	0	0.0	0	0	0		0	.000	.000	0	0	2B-1

Bob Hale

HALE, ROBERT HOUSTON   BL TL 5'10" 195 lbs.
B. Nov. 7, 1933, Sarasota, Fla.

	G	AB	H	2B	3B	HR	HR %	R	RBI	BB	SO	SB	BA	SA	PH AB	PH H	G by POS
1955 BAL A	67	182	65	7	1	0	0.0	13	29	5	19	0	.357	.407	26	10	1B-44
1956	85	207	49	10	1	1	0.5	18	24	11	10	0	.237	.309	36	6	1B-51
1957	42	44	11	0	0	0	0.0	2	7	2	2	0	.250	.250	35	9	1B-5
1958	19	20	7	2	0	0	0.0	2	3	2	1	0	.350	.450	15	5	1B-2
1959	40	54	10	3	0	0	0.0	2	7	2	6	0	.185	.241	30	7	1B-8
1960 CLE A	70	70	21	7	0	0	0.0	2	12	3	6	0	.300	.400	63	19	1B-5
1961 2 teams		CLE	A (42G –	.167)		NY	A (11G –	.154)									
" total	53	49	8	0	1	0	0.0	2	7	1	7	0	.163	.224	44	6	1B-5
7 yrs.	376	626	171	29	2	2	0.3	41	89	26	51	0	.273	.335	249	62	1B-120

George Hale

HALE, GEORGE WAGNER (Ducky)   BR TR 5'10" 160 lbs.
B. Aug. 3, 1894, Dexter, Kans.   D. Nov. 1, 1945, Wichita, Kans.

	G	AB	H	2B	3B	HR	HR %	R	RBI	BB	SO	SB	BA	SA	PH AB	PH H	G by POS
1914 STL A	6	11	2	0	0	0	0.0	1	0	0	3	0	.182	.182	0	0	C-6
1916	4	1	0	0	0	0	0.0	0	0	0	1	0	.000	.000	1	0	C-3
1917	38	61	12	2	1	0	0.0	4	8	10	12	0	.197	.262	7	2	C-28
1918	12	30	4	1	0	0	0.0	0	1	1	5	0	.133	.167	1	0	C-11
4 yrs.	60	103	18	3	1	0	0.0	5	9	11	21	0	.175	.223	9	2	C-48

John Hale

HALE, JOHN STEVEN   BL TR 6'2" 195 lbs.
B. Aug. 5, 1953, Fresno, Calif.

	G	AB	H	2B	3B	HR	HR %	R	RBI	BB	SO	SB	BA	SA	PH AB	PH H	G by POS
1974 LA N	4	4	4	1	0	0	0.0	2	2	0	0	0	1.000	1.250	1	1	OF-3
1975	71	204	43	7	0	6	2.9	20	22	26	51	0	.211	.333	7	2	OF-68
1976	44	91	14	2	1	0	0.0	4	8	16	14	4	.154	.198	6	0	OF-37
1977	79	108	26	4	1	2	1.9	10	11	15	28	2	.241	.352	5	1	OF-73
1978 SEA A	107	211	36	8	0	4	1.9	24	22	34	64	3	.171	.265	6	1	OF-98, DH-3
1979	54	63	14	3	0	2	3.2	6	7	12	26	0	.222	.365	8	0	OF-42, DH-2
6 yrs.	359	681	137	25	2	14	2.1	66	72	103	183	10	.201	.305	33	5	OF-321, DH-5

Odell Hale

HALE, ARVEL ODELL (Bad News)   BR TR 5'10" 175 lbs.
B. Aug. 10, 1908, Hosston, La.   D. June 9, 1980, El Dorado, Ark.

	G	AB	H	2B	3B	HR	HR %	R	RBI	BB	SO	SB	BA	SA	PH AB	PH H	G by POS
1931 CLE A	25	92	26	2	4	1	1.1	14	5	8	8	2	.283	.424	0	0	3B-15, 2B-10, SS-1
1933	98	351	97	19	8	10	2.8	49	64	30	37	2	.276	.462	3	1	2B-73, 3B-21
1934	143	563	170	44	6	13	2.3	82	101	48	50	8	.302	.471	3	1	2B-137, 3B-5
1935	150	589	179	37	11	16	2.7	80	101	52	55	15	.304	.486	1	0	3B-149, 2B-1
1936	153	620	196	50	13	14	2.3	126	87	64	43	8	.316	.506	2	0	3B-148, 2B-3
1937	154	561	150	32	4	6	1.1	74	82	56	41	9	.267	.371	1	1	3B-90, 2B-64
1938	130	496	138	32	2	8	1.6	69	69	44	39	8	.278	.399	3	1	2B-127
1939	108	253	79	16	2	4	1.6	36	48	25	18	4	.312	.439	35	10	2B-73, 3B-2

	G	AB	H	2B	3B	HR	HR %	R	RBI	BB	SO	SB	BA	SA	Pinch Hit AB	Pinch Hit H	G by POS

Odell Hale continued

	G	AB	H	2B	3B	HR	HR%	R	RBI	BB	SO	SB	BA	SA	PH AB	PH H	G by POS
1940	48	50	11	3	1	0	0.0	3	6	5	7	0	.220	.320	40	8	3B-3
1941 2 teams	BOS	A (12G –	.208)			NY	N	(41G –	.196)								
" total	53	126	25	5	0	1	0.8	18	10	21	17	1	.198	.262	12	1	2B-30, 3B-6
10 yrs.	1062	3701	1071	240	51	73	2.0	551	573	353	315	57	.289	.441	100	23	2B-518, 3B-439, SS-1

Sammy Hale

HALE, SAMUEL DOUGLAS
B. Sept. 10, 1896, Glen Rose, Tex.   D. Sept. 6, 1974, Wheeler, Tex.   BR TR 5'8½" 160 lbs.

	G	AB	H	2B	3B	HR	HR%	R	RBI	BB	SO	SB	BA	SA	PH AB	PH H	G by POS
1920 DET A	76	116	34	3	3	1	0.9	13	14	5	15	2	.293	.397	52	17	3B-16, OF-4, 2B-1
1921	9	2	0	0	0	0	0.0	2	0	0	1	0	.000	.000	2	0	
1923 PHI A	115	434	125	22	8	3	0.7	68	51	17	31	8	.288	.396	5	2	3B-107
1924	80	261	83	14	2	2	0.8	41	17	17	19	3	.318	.410	14	2	3B-55, OF-5, SS-1, C-1
1925	110	391	135	30	11	8	2.0	62	63	17	27	7	.345	.540	12	4	3B-96, 2B-1
1926	111	327	92	22	9	4	1.2	49	43	13	36	1	.281	.440	28	6	3B-77, OF-1
1927	131	501	157	24	8	5	1.0	77	81	32	32	11	.313	.423	1	0	3B-128
1928	88	314	97	20	9	4	1.3	38	58	9	21	2	.309	.468	8	3	3B-79
1929	101	379	105	14	3	1	0.3	51	40	12	18	6	.277	.338	0	0	3B-99, 2B-1
1930 STL A	62	190	52	8	1	2	1.1	21	25	8	18	1	.274	.358	12	2	3B-47
10 yrs.	883	2915	880	157	54	30	1.0	422	392	130	218	41	.302	.424	134	36	3B-704, OF-10, 2B-3, SS-1, C-1

Fred Haley

HALEY, FRED
B. Wheeling, W. Va.   Deceased.

	G	AB	H	2B	3B	HR	HR%	R	RBI	BB	SO	SB	BA	SA	PH AB	PH H	G by POS
1880 TRO N	2	7	0	0	0	0	0.0	0		1	2		.000	.000	0	0	C-2

Ray Haley

HALEY, RAYMOND TIMOTHY
B. Jan. 23, 1891, Danbury, Iowa   D. Oct. 8, 1973, Bradenton, Fla.   BR TR 5'11" 180 lbs.

	G	AB	H	2B	3B	HR	HR%	R	RBI	BB	SO	SB	BA	SA	PH AB	PH H	G by POS
1915 BOS A	5	7	1	1	0	0	0.0	2	0	1	0	0	.143	.286	0	0	C-4
1916 2 teams	BOS	A (1G –	.000)			PHI	A	(34G –	.231)								
" total	35	109	25	5	0	0	0.0	8	4	6	20	0	.229	.275	2	0	C-33
1917 PHI A	41	98	27	2	1	0	0.0	7	11	4	12	2	.276	.316	7	0	C-34
3 yrs.	81	214	53	8	1	0	0.0	17	15	11	32	2	.248	.294	9	0	C-71

Al Hall

HALL, ARCHIBALD W.
B. Worcester, Mass.   D. Feb. 10, 1885, Warren, Pa.

	G	AB	H	2B	3B	HR	HR%	R	RBI	BB	SO	SB	BA	SA	PH AB	PH H	G by POS
1879 TRO N	67	306	79	7	3	0	0.0	30	14	3	13		.258	.301	0	0	OF-67
1880 CLE N	3	8	1	0	0	0	0.0	1		0	0		.125	.125	0	0	OF-3
2 yrs.	70	314	80	7	3	0	0.0	31	14	3	13		.255	.296	0	0	OF-70

Albert Hall

HALL, ALBERT
B. Mar. 7, 1959, Birmingham, Ala.   BB TR 5'11" 155 lbs.

	G	AB	H	2B	3B	HR	HR%	R	RBI	BB	SO	SB	BA	SA	PH AB	PH H	G by POS
1981 ATL N	6	2	0	0	0	0	0.0	1		1	1	0	.000	.000	1	0	OF-2
1982	5	0	0	0	0	0	–	1	0	0	0	0	–	–	0	0	
1983	10	8	0	0	0	0	0.0	2	0	2	2	1	.000	.000	1	0	OF-4
1984	87	142	37	6	1	1	0.7	25	9	10	18	6	.261	.338	13	5	OF-66
4 yrs.	108	152	37	6	1	1	0.7	29	9	13	21	7	.243	.316	15	5	OF-72

Bill Hall

HALL, WILLIAM LEMUEL
B. July 30, 1928, Moultrie, Ga.   BL TR 5'11" 165 lbs.

	G	AB	H	2B	3B	HR	HR%	R	RBI	BB	SO	SB	BA	SA	PH AB	PH H	G by POS
1954 PIT N	5	7	0	0	0	0	0.0	0	0	0	0	0	.000	.000	3	0	C-1
1956	1	3	0	0	0	0	0.0	0	0	0	1	0	.000	.000	0	0	C-1
1958	51	116	33	6	0	1	0.9	15	15	15	13	0	.284	.362	1	0	C-51
3 yrs.	57	126	33	6	0	1	0.8	15	15	15	14	0	.262	.333	4	0	C-53

Bob Hall

HALL, ROBERT PRILL
B. Dec. 20, 1878, Baltimore, Md.   D. Dec. 1, 1950, Wellesley, Mass.   TR 5'10" 158 lbs.

	G	AB	H	2B	3B	HR	HR%	R	RBI	BB	SO	SB	BA	SA	PH AB	PH H	G by POS
1904 PHI N	46	163	26	4	0	0	0.0	11	17	14		5	.160	.184	0	0	3B-20, SS-15, 1B-11
1905 2 teams	NY	N (1G –	.333)			BKN	N	(56G –	.236)								
" total	57	206	49	4	1	2	1.0	22	15	11		8	.238	.296	4	0	OF-43, 2B-7, 1B-3
2 yrs.	103	369	75	8	1	2	0.5	33	32	25		13	.203	.247	4	0	OF-43, 3B-20, SS-15, 1B-14, 2B-7

Charley Hall

HALL, CHARLES LOUIS (Sea Lion)
Born Carlos Clolo.
B. July 27, 1885, Ventura, Calif.   D. Dec. 6, 1943, Ventura, Calif.   BL TR 6'2" 185 lbs.

	G	AB	H	2B	3B	HR	HR%	R	RBI	BB	SO	SB	BA	SA	PH AB	PH H	G by POS
1906 CIN N	17	47	6	2	0	0	0.0	7	2	2		0	.128	.170	1	0	P-14, 1B-2
1907	12	26	7	0	1	0	0.0	1	1	0		0	.269	.346	1	0	P-11
1909 BOS A	11	19	3	0	0	0	0.0	0	4	0		0	.158	.158	0	0	P-11
1910	47	82	17	2	4	0	0.0	6	8	6		0	.207	.329	8	1	P-35, OF-3
1911	39	64	9	1	1	1	1.6	6	8	4		0	.141	.234	7	1	P-32
1912	34	75	20	4	2	1	1.3	10	14	4		0	.267	.413	0	0	P-34
1913	43	42	9	1	1	0	0.0	2	2	1	10	0	.214	.286	7	0	P-35, 3B-1
1916 STL N	10	14	2	0	0	0	0.0	0	1	0	6	0	.143	.143	0	0	P-10
1918 DET A	6	2	0	0	0	0	0.0	0	0	0	0	0	.000	.000	0	0	P-6
9 yrs.	219	371	73	10	9	2	0.5	32	40	17	16	1	.197	.288	24	2	P-188, OF-3, 1B-2, 3B-1
WORLD SERIES																	
1912 BOS A	2	4	3	1	0	0	0.0	0	0	1		0	.750	1.000	0	0	P-2

Charlie Hall

HALL, CHARLES W. (Doc)
Deceased.

	G	AB	H	2B	3B	HR	HR%	R	RBI	BB	SO	SB	BA	SA	PH AB	PH H	G by POS
1887 NY AA	3	12	1	0	0	0	0.0	1		2		1	.083	.083	0	0	OF-3

	G	AB	H	2B	3B	HR	HR %	R	RBI	BB	SO	SB	BA	SA	Pinch Hit AB	Pinch Hit H	G by POS

Dick Hall

HALL, RICHARD WALLACE
B. Sept. 27, 1930, St. Louis, Mo.
BR TR 6'6"   200 lbs.

	G	AB	H	2B	3B	HR	HR %	R	RBI	BB	SO	SB	BA	SA	AB	H	G by POS
1952 PIT N	26	80	11	1	0	0	0.0	6	2	2	17	0	.138	.150	5	1	OF-14, 3B-5
1953	7	24	4	0	0	0	0.0	2	1	1	3	1	.167	.167	0	0	2B-7
1954	112	310	74	8	4	2	0.6	38	27	33	46	3	.239	.310	12	1	OF-102
1955	21	40	7	1	0	1	2.5	3	3	6	5	0	.175	.275	3	1	P-15, OF-3
1956	33	29	10	0	0	0	0.0	5	1	5	7	0	.345	.345	12	6	P-19, 1B-1
1957	10	1	0	0	0	0	0.0	0	0	0	1	0	.000	.000	0	0	P-8
1959	2	2	0	0	0	0	0.0	0	0	0	0	0	.000	.000	0	0	P-2
1960 KC A	32	56	6	0	0	0	0.0	5	4	4	15	1	.107	.107	0	0	P-29
1961 BAL A	30	36	5	0	0	0	0.0	4	1	3	13	0	.139	.139	0	0	P-29
1962	44	24	4	1	0	0	0.0	3	1	4	9	0	.167	.208	0	0	P-43
1963	48	28	13	1	0	1	3.6	7	4	0	8	0	.464	.607	0	0	P-47
1964	45	16	2	0	0	0	0.0	1	3	1	3	0	.125	.125	1	0	P-45
1965	49	15	5	2	0	0	0.0	1	4	1	4	0	.333	.467	0	0	P-48
1966	32	12	2	0	0	0	0.0	0	2	0	5	0	.167	.167	2	0	P-32
1967 PHI N	48	14	1	0	0	0	0.0	1	0	0	5	0	.071	.071	0	0	P-48
1968	32	3	1	0	0	0	0.0	0	0	0	1	0	.333	.333	0	0	P-32
1969 BAL A	39	7	2	0	0	0	0.0	1	2	1	1	1	.286	.286	0	0	P-39
1970	32	12	1	0	0	0	0.0	2	1	0	3	0	.083	.083	0	0	P-32
1971	27	5	2	1	0	0	0.0	0	0	0	1	0	.400	.600	0	0	P-27
19 yrs.	669	714	150	15	4	4	0.6	79	56	61	147	6	.210	.259	35	9	P-495, OF-119, 2B-7, 3B-5, 1B-1

LEAGUE CHAMPIONSHIP SERIES
1969 BAL A	1	0	0	0	0	0	–	0	0	0	0	0	–	–	0	0	P-1
1970	1	2	1	0	0	0	0.0	0	0	0	1	0	.500	.500	0	0	P-1
2 yrs.	2	2	1	0	0	0	0.0	0	0	0	1	0	.500	.500	0	0	P-2

WORLD SERIES
1969 BAL A	1	0	0	0	0	0	–	0	0	0	0	0	–	–	0	0	P-1
1970	1	1	0	0	0	0	0.0	0	0	0	1	0	.000	.000	0	0	P-1
1971	1	0	0	0	0	0	–	0	0	0	0	0	–	–	0	0	P-1
3 yrs.	3	1	0	0	0	0	0.0	0	0	0	1	0	.000	.000	0	0	P-3

George Hall

HALL, GEORGE WILLIAM
B. June 22, 1849, England D. June 11, 1923, Ridgewood, N. Y.
BL   5'7"   142 lbs.

	G	AB	H	2B	3B	HR	HR %	R	RBI	BB	SO	SB	BA	SA	AB	H	G by POS
1876 PHI N	60	268	98	7	13	5	1.9	51	45	8	4		.366	.545	0	0	OF-60
1877 LOU N	61	269	87	15	8	0	0.0	53	26	12	19		.323	.439	0	0	OF-61
2 yrs.	121	537	185	22	21	5	0.9	104	71	20	23		.345	.492	0	0	OF-121

Irv Hall

HALL, IRVIN GLADSTONE
B. Oct. 7, 1918, Alberton, Md.
BR TR 5'10½" 160 lbs.

	G	AB	H	2B	3B	HR	HR %	R	RBI	BB	SO	SB	BA	SA	AB	H	G by POS
1943 PHI A	151	544	139	15	4	0	0.0	37	54	22	42	10	.256	.298	1	1	SS-148, 3B-1, 2B-1
1944	143	559	150	20	8	0	0.0	60	45	31	46	2	.268	.333	2	0	2B-97, SS-40, 1B-4
1945	151	616	161	17	5	0	0.0	62	50	35	42	3	.261	.305	0	0	2B-151
1946	63	185	46	6	2	0	0.0	19	19	9	18	1	.249	.303	13	2	2B-40, SS-7
4 yrs.	508	1904	496	58	19	0	0.0	178	168	97	148	16	.261	.311	16	3	2B-289, SS-195, 1B-4, 3B-1

Jimmie Hall

HALL, JIMMIE RANDOLPH
B. Mar. 17, 1938, Mt. Holly, N. C.
BL TR 6'   175 lbs.

	G	AB	H	2B	3B	HR	HR %	R	RBI	BB	SO	SB	BA	SA	AB	H	G by POS
1963 MIN A	156	497	129	21	5	33	6.6	88	80	63	101	3	.260	.521	13	5	OF-143
1964	149	510	144	20	3	25	4.9	61	75	44	112	5	.282	.480	10	3	OF-137
1965	148	522	149	25	4	20	3.8	81	86	51	79	14	.285	.464	10	2	OF-141
1966	120	356	85	7	4	20	5.6	52	47	33	66	1	.239	.449	21	4	OF-103
1967 CAL A	129	401	100	8	3	16	4.0	54	55	42	65	4	.249	.404	14	8	OF-120
1968 2 teams	CAL A (46G – .214)							CLE A (58G – .198)									
" total	104	237	49	7	2	0.8		19	16	26	38	2	.207	.262	35	6	OF-68
1969 3 teams	CLE A (4G – .000)							NY A (80G – .236)			CHI N (11G – .208)						
" total	95	246	55	9	5	3	1.2	23	27	22	42	9	.224	.337	22	5	OF-58, 1B-7
1970 2 teams	CHI N (28G – .094)							ATL N (39G – .213)									
" total	67	79	13	3	0	2	2.5	9	5	6	26	0	.165	.278	29	4	OF-36
8 yrs.	968	2848	724	100	24	121	4.2	387	391	287	529	38	.254	.434	154	37	OF-806, 1B-7

WORLD SERIES
| 1965 MIN A | 2 | 7 | 1 | 0 | 0 | 0 | 0.0 | 0 | 0 | 1 | 5 | 0 | .143 | .143 | 0 | 0 | OF-2 |

Mel Hall

HALL, MELVIN, JR.
B. Sept. 16, 1960, Lyons, N. Y.
BL TL 6'   185 lbs.

	G	AB	H	2B	3B	HR	HR %	R	RBI	BB	SO	SB	BA	SA	AB	H	G by POS
1981 CHI N	10	11	1	0	0	1	9.1	1	2	1	4	0	.091	.364	7	1	OF-3
1982	24	80	21	3	2	0	0.0	6	4	5	17	0	.263	.350	1	0	OF-22
1983	112	410	116	23	5	17	4.1	60	56	42	101	6	.283	.488	2	0	OF-112
1984 2 teams	CHI N (48G – .280)							CLE A (83G – .257)									
" total	131	407	108	24	4	11	2.7	68	52	47	78	3	.265	.425	14	3	OF-115, DH-9
4 yrs.	277	908	246	50	11	29	3.2	135	114	95	200	9	.271	.446	24	5	OF-252, DH-9

Russ Hall

HALL, RUSSELL ROBERT
B. Sept. 29, 1871, Shelbyville, Ky.   D. July 1, 1937, Los Angeles, Calif.
TR

	G	AB	H	2B	3B	HR	HR %	R	RBI	BB	SO	SB	BA	SA	AB	H	G by POS
1898 STL N	39	143	35	2	1	0	0.0	13	10	7		1	.245	.273	0	0	SS-35, 3B-3, OF-1
1901 CLE A	1	4	2	0	0	0	0.0	2	0	0		0	.500	.500	0	0	SS-1
2 yrs.	40	147	37	2	1	0	0.0	15	10	7		1	.252	.279	0	0	SS-36, 3B-3, OF-1

Tom Haller

HALLER, THOMAS FRANK
B. June 23, 1937, Lockport, Ill.
BL TR 6'4"   195 lbs.

	G	AB	H	2B	3B	HR	HR %	R	RBI	BB	SO	SB	BA	SA	AB	H	G by POS
1961 SF N	30	62	9	1	0	2	3.2	5	8	9	23	0	.145	.258	4	0	C-25
1962	99	272	71	13	1	18	6.6	53	55	51	59	1	.261	.515	9	0	C-91
1963	98	298	76	8	1	14	4.7	32	44	34	45	4	.255	.430	8	2	C-85, OF-7
1964	117	388	98	14	3	16	4.1	43	48	55	51	4	.253	.428	7	1	C-113, OF-3
1965	134	422	106	4	3	16	3.8	40	49	47	67	0	.251	.389	3	1	C-133

	G	AB	H	2B	3B	HR	HR %	R	RBI	BB	SO	SB	BA	SA	Pinch Hit AB	Pinch Hit H	G by POS

Tom Haller continued

	G	AB	H	2B	3B	HR	HR %	R	RBI	BB	SO	SB	BA	SA	AB	H	G by POS
1966	142	471	113	19	2	27	5.7	74	67	53	74	1	.240	.461	10	1	C-136, 1B-4
1967	141	455	114	23	5	14	3.1	54	49	62	61	0	.251	.415	12	5	C-136, OF-1
1968 LA N	144	474	135	27	5	4	0.8	37	53	46	76	1	.285	.388	12	1	C-139
1969	134	445	117	18	3	6	1.3	46	39	48	58	0	.263	.357	7	3	C-132
1970	112	325	93	16	6	10	3.1	47	47	32	35	3	.286	.465	12	5	C-106
1971	84	202	54	5	0	5	2.5	23	32	25	30	0	.267	.366	17	6	C-67
1972 DET A	59	121	25	5	2	2	1.7	7	13	15	14	0	.207	.331	20	2	C-36
12 yrs.	1294	3935	1011	153	31	134	3.4	461	504	477	593	14	.257	.414	121	27	C-1199, OF-11, 1B-4

LEAGUE CHAMPIONSHIP SERIES
	G	AB	H	2B	3B	HR	HR %	R	RBI	BB	SO	SB	BA	SA	AB	H	G by POS
1972 DET A	1	1	0	0	0	0	0.0	0	0	0	0	0	.000	.000	1	0	

WORLD SERIES
	G	AB	H	2B	3B	HR	HR %	R	RBI	BB	SO	SB	BA	SA	AB	H	G by POS
1962 SF N	4	14	4	1	0	1	7.1	1	3	0	2	0	.286	.571	0	0	C-4

Newt Halliday

HALLIDAY, NEWTON REESE BR TR 6'1" 175 lbs.
B. June 18, 1896, Chicago, Ill. D. Apr. 6, 1918, Great Lakes, Ill.

	G	AB	H	2B	3B	HR	HR %	R	RBI	BB	SO	SB	BA	SA	AB	H	G by POS
1916 PIT N	1	1	0	0	0	0	0.0	0	0	0	1	0	.000	.000	0	0	1B-1

Jocko Halligan

HALLIGAN, WILLIAM E.
B. Dec. 8, 1867, Avon, N.Y. D. Feb. 13, 1945, Buffalo, N.Y.

	G	AB	H	2B	3B	HR	HR %	R	RBI	BB	SO	SB	BA	SA	AB	H	G by POS
1890 BUF P	57	211	53	9	2	3	1.4	28	33	20	19	7	.251	.355	0	0	OF-43, C-16
1891 CIN N	61	247	77	13	6	3	1.2	43	44	24	25	5	.312	.449	0	0	OF-61
1892 2 teams						CIN N (26G – .287)					BAL N (46G – .270)						
" total	72	279	77	8	7	4	1.4	52	55	42	33	11	.276	.398	1	0	OF-48, 1B-19, C-5
3 yrs.	190	737	207	30	15	10	1.4	123	132	86	77	23	.281	.403	1	0	OF-152, C-21, 1B-19

Ed Hallinan

HALLINAN, EDWARD S. BR TR 5'9" 168 lbs.
B. Aug. 23, 1888, San Francisco, Calif. D. Aug. 24, 1940, San Francisco, Calif.

	G	AB	H	2B	3B	HR	HR %	R	RBI	BB	SO	SB	BA	SA	AB	H	G by POS
1911 STL A	52	169	35	3	1	0	0.0	13	14	14		4	.207	.237	0	0	SS-34, 2B-15, 3B-3
1912	28	86	19	2	0	0	0.0	11	1	5		3	.221	.244	1	0	SS-26
2 yrs.	80	255	54	5	1	0	0.0	24	15	19		7	.212	.239	1	0	SS-60, 2B-15, 3B-3

Jimmy Hallinan

HALLINAN, JAMES H. BL TL 5'9" 172 lbs.
B. May 27, 1849, Ireland D. Oct. 28, 1879, Chicago, Ill.

	G	AB	H	2B	3B	HR	HR %	R	RBI	BB	SO	SB	BA	SA	AB	H	G by POS
1876 NY N	54	240	67	7	6	2	0.8	45	36	2	4		.279	.383	0	0	SS-50, 2B-4, OF-2
1877 2 teams						CIN N (16G – .370)					CHI N (19G – .281)						
" total	35	162	52	5	2	0	0.0	35	18	5	3		.321	.377	0	0	OF-19, 2B-16
1878 2 teams						CHI N (16G – .284)					IND N (3G – .250)						
" total	19	79	22	5	0	0	0.0	14	3	5	8		.278	.342	0	0	OF-14, 2B-5
3 yrs.	108	481	141	17	8	2	0.4	94	57	12	15		.293	.374	0	0	SS-50, OF-35, 2B-25

Bill Hallman

HALLMAN, WILLIAM HARRY
B. Mar. 15, 1876, Philadelphia, Pa. D. Apr. 23, 1950, Philadelphia, Pa.

	G	AB	H	2B	3B	HR	HR %	R	RBI	BB	SO	SB	BA	SA	AB	H	G by POS
1901 MIL A	139	549	135	27	6	2	0.4	70	47	41		12	.246	.328	0	0	OF-139
1903 CHI A	63	207	43	7	4	0	0.0	29	18	31		11	.208	.280	6	0	OF-57
1906 PIT N	23	89	24	3	1	1	1.1	12	6	15		3	.270	.360	0	0	OF-23
1907	94	302	67	6	2	0	0.0	39	15	33		21	.222	.255	9	2	OF-84
4 yrs.	319	1147	269	43	13	3	0.3	150	86	120		47	.235	.303	15	2	OF-303

Bill Hallman

HALLMAN, WILLIAM WILSON BR TR 5'8"
B. Mar. 30, 1867, Pittsburgh, Pa. D. Sept. 11, 1920, Philadelphia, Pa.
Manager 1897.

	G	AB	H	2B	3B	HR	HR %	R	RBI	BB	SO	SB	BA	SA	AB	H	G by POS
1888 PHI N	18	63	13	4	1	0	0.0	5	6	1	12	1	.206	.302	0	0	C-10, 2B-4, OF-3, SS-1, 3B-1
1889	119	462	117	21	8	2	0.4	67	60	36	54	20	.253	.346	0	0	SS-106, 2B-13, C-1
1890 PHI P	84	356	95	16	7	1	0.3	59	37	33	24	6	.267	.360	0	0	OF-34, C-26, 2B-14, 3B-10, SS-2
1891 PHI AA	141	587	166	21	13	6	1.0	112	69	38	56	18	.283	.394	0	0	2B-141
1892 PHI N	138	586	171	27	10	2	0.3	106	84	32	52	19	.292	.382	0	0	2B-138
1893	132	596	183	28	7	4	0.7	119	76	51	27	22	.307	.398	0	0	2B-120, 1B-12
1894	119	505	156	19	7	0	0.0	107	66	36	15	36	.309	.374	0	0	2B-119
1895	124	539	169	26	5	1	0.2	94	91	34	20	16	.314	.386	0	0	2B-122, SS-3
1896	120	469	150	21	3	2	0.4	82	83	45	23	16	.320	.390	0	0	2B-120, P-1
1897 2 teams						PHI N (31G – .262)					STL N (79G – .221)						
" total	110	424	99	9	2	0	0.0	47	41	32		13	.233	.264	0	0	2B-108, 1B-3
1898 BKN N	134	509	124	10	7	2	0.4	57	63	29		9	.244	.303	0	0	2B-124, 3B-10
1901 2 teams						CLE A (5G – .211)					PHI N (123G – .184)						
" total	128	464	86	13	5	0	0.0	48	41	28		13	.185	.235	0	0	2B-90, 3B-33, SS-5
1902 PHI N	73	254	63	8	4	0	0.0	14	35	14		9	.248	.311	1	1	3B-72
1903	63	198	42	11	2	0	0.0	20	17	16		2	.212	.288	6	0	2B-22, 3B-19, 1B-9, OF-4, SS-3
14 yrs.	1503	6012	1634	234	81	20	0.3	937	769	425	283	200	.272	.348	7	1	2B-1135, 3B-145, SS-120, OF-41, C-37, 1B-24, P-1

Jim Halpin

HALPIN, JAMES NATHANIEL
B. Oct. 4, 1863, England D. Jan. 4, 1893, Boston, Mass.

	G	AB	H	2B	3B	HR	HR %	R	RBI	BB	SO	SB	BA	SA	AB	H	G by POS
1882 WOR N	2	8	0	0	0	0	0.0	0	0	0			.000	.000	0	0	3B-2
1884 WAS U	46	168	31	3	0	0	0.0	24		2			.185	.202	0	0	SS-39, 3B-7
1885 DET N	15	54	7	2	0	0	0.0	3	1	1	12		.130	.167	0	0	SS-15
3 yrs.	63	230	38	5	0	0	0.0	27	0	3	12		.165	.187	0	0	SS-54, 3B-9

Al Halt

HALT, ALVA WILLIAM BL TR 6' 180 lbs.
B. Nov. 23, 1890, Sandusky, Ohio D. Jan. 22, 1973, Sandusky, Ohio

	G	AB	H	2B	3B	HR	HR %	R	RBI	BB	SO	SB	BA	SA	AB	H	G by POS
1914 BKN F	80	261	61	6	2	3	1.1	26	25	13		11	.234	.307	4	0	SS-71, 2B-3, OF-1
1915	151	524	131	22	7	3	0.6	41	64	39		20	.250	.336	0	0	3B-111, SS-40

	G	AB	H	2B	3B	HR	HR %	R	RBI	BB	SO	SB	BA	SA	Pinch Hit AB	Pinch Hit H	G by POS

Al Halt continued

	G	AB	H	2B	3B	HR	HR %	R	RBI	BB	SO	SB	BA	SA	AB	H	G by POS
1918 **CLE A**	26	69	12	2	0	0	0.0	9	1	9	12	4	.174	.203	1	0	3B-14, SS-4, 2B-4, 1B-2
3 yrs.	257	854	204	30	9	6	0.7	76	90	61	12	35	.239	.316	5		3B-125, SS-115, 2B-7, 1B-2, OF-1

Charlie Hamburg

HAMBURG, CHARLES M.
Also known as Charles M. Hambrick.
B. Nov. 22, 1863, Louisville, Ky.   D. May 18, 1931, Union, N. J.

6'   178 lbs.

	G	AB	H	2B	3B	HR	HR %	R	RBI	BB	SO	SB	BA	SA	AB	H	G by POS
1890 **LOU AA**	133	485	132	22	2	3	0.6	93		69		46	.272	.344	0	0	OF-133

Sam Hamby

HAMBY, JAMES SANFORD (Cracker)
B. July 29, 1897, Wilkesboro, N. C.

BR TR 6'   170 lbs.

	G	AB	H	2B	3B	HR	HR %	R	RBI	BB	SO	SB	BA	SA	AB	H	G by POS
1926 **NY N**	1	3	0	0	0	0	0.0	0	0	0	0	0	.000	.000	0	0	C-1
1927	21	52	10	0	1	0	0.0	6	5	7	7	1	.192	.231	1	0	C-19
2 yrs.	22	55	10	0	1	0	0.0	6	5	7	7	1	.182	.218	1	0	C-20

Billy Hamilton

HAMILTON, WILLIAM ROBERT (Sliding Billy)
B. Feb. 16, 1866, Newark, N. J.   D. Dec. 15, 1940, Worcester, Mass.
Hall of Fame 1961.

BL TL 5'6"   165 lbs.

	G	AB	H	2B	3B	HR	HR %	R	RBI	BB	SO	SB	BA	SA	AB	H	G by POS
1888 **KC AA**	35	129	34	4	4	0	0.0	21	11	4		23	.264	.357	0	0	OF-35
1889	137	534	161	17	12	3	0.6	144	77	87	41	117	.301	.395	0	0	OF-137
1890 **PHI N**	123	496	161	13	9	2	0.4	133	49	83	37	102	.325	.399	0	0	OF-123
1891	133	527	179	23	7	2	0.4	141	60	102	28	115	.340	.421	0	0	OF-133
1892	139	554	183	21	7	3	0.5	132	53	81	29	56	.330	.410	0	0	OF-139
1893	82	355	135	22	7	5	1.4	110	44	63	7	41	.380	.524	0	0	OF-82
1894	131	559	223	25	15	4	0.7	196¹	87	126	17	99	.399	.519	0	0	OF-129
1895	123	517	201	22	6	7	1.4	166	74	96	30	95	.389	.495	0	0	OF-123
1896 **BOS N**	131	523	191	24	9	3	0.6	152	52	110	29	93	.365	.463	0	0	OF-131
1897	127	507	174	17	5	3	0.6	152	61	105		70	.343	.414	0	0	OF-126
1898	110	417	154	16	5	3	0.7	110	50	87		59	.369	.453	0	0	OF-110
1899	84	297	92	7	1	1	0.3	63	33	72		19	.310	.350	2	0	OF-81
1900	136	520	173	20	5	1	0.2	102	47	107		29	.333	.396	0	0	OF-136
1901	102	349	102	11	2	3	0.9	70	38	64		19	.292	.361	3	2	OF-99
14 yrs.	1593	6284	2163	242	94	40	0.6	1692	736	1187	218	937	.344	.432	5	2	OF-1584
												8th					

Tom Hamilton

HAMILTON, THOMAS BALL (Ham)
B. Sept. 29, 1925, Altoona, Kans.   D. Nov. 29, 1973, Tyler, Tex.

BL TR 6'4"   213 lbs.

	G	AB	H	2B	3B	HR	HR %	R	RBI	BB	SO	SB	BA	SA	AB	H	G by POS
1952 **PHI A**	9	10	2	1	0	0	0.0	1	1	1	1	0	.200	.300	4	1	1B-5
1953	58	56	11	2	0	0	0.0	8	5	7	11	0	.196	.232	43	8	1B-7, OF-2
2 yrs.	67	66	13	3	0	0	0.0	9	6	8	12	0	.197	.242	47	9	1B-12, OF-2

Ken Hamlin

HAMLIN, KENNETH LEE
B. May 18, 1935, Detroit, Mich.

BR TR 5'10"   170 lbs.

	G	AB	H	2B	3B	HR	HR %	R	RBI	BB	SO	SB	BA	SA	AB	H	G by POS
1957 **PIT N**	2	1	0	0	0	0	0.0	0	0	0	0	0	.000	.000	0	0	SS-1
1959	3	8	1	0	0	0	0.0	1	0	2	1	0	.125	.125	0	0	SS-3
1960 **KC A**	140	428	96	10	2	2	0.5	51	24	44	48	1	.224	.271	1	1	SS-139
1961 **LA A**	42	91	19	3	0	1	1.1	4	5	11	9	0	.209	.275	2	1	SS-39
1962 **WAS A**	98	292	74	12	0	3	1.0	29	22	22	22	7	.253	.325	6	2	SS-87, 2B-2
1965	117	362	99	21	1	4	1.1	45	22	33	45	8	.273	.370	9	2	2B-77, SS-47, 3B-1
1966	66	158	34	7	1	1	0.6	13	16	13	21	1	.215	.291	18	1	2B-50, 3B-1
7 yrs.	468	1340	323	53	4	11	0.8	143	89	125	146	17	.241	.311	36	7	SS-316, 2B-129, 3B-2

Jack Hammond

HAMMOND, WALTER CHARLES (Wobby)
B. Feb. 26, 1891, Amsterdam, N. Y.   D. Mar. 4, 1942, Kenosha, Wis.

BR TR 5'11"   170 lbs.

	G	AB	H	2B	3B	HR	HR %	R	RBI	BB	SO	SB	BA	SA	AB	H	G by POS
1915 **CLE A**	35	84	18	2	1	0	0.0	9	4	1	19	0	.214	.262	9	1	2B-19
1922 **2 teams**		**CLE A** (1G – .250)					**PIT N** (9G – .273)										
" total	10	15	4	0	0	0	0.0	4	0	1	0	0	.267	.267	0	0	2B-5
2 yrs.	45	99	22	2	1	0	0.0	13	4	2	19	0	.222	.263	9	1	2B-24

Steve Hammond

HAMMOND, STEVEN BENJAMIN
B. Feb. 9, 1957, Atlanta, Ga.

BL TR 6'3"   190 lbs.

	G	AB	H	2B	3B	HR	HR %	R	RBI	BB	SO	SB	BA	SA	AB	H	G by POS
1982 **KC A**	46	126	29	5	1	1	0.8	14	11	4	18	0	.230	.310	11	2	OF-37, DH-1

Garvin Hamner

HAMNER, WESLEY GARVIN (Wes)
Brother of Granny Hamner.
B. Mar. 18, 1924, Richmond, Va.

BR TR 5'11"   172 lbs.

	G	AB	H	2B	3B	HR	HR %	R	RBI	BB	SO	SB	BA	SA	AB	H	G by POS
1945 **PHI N**	32	101	20	3	0	0	0.0	12	5	7	9	2	.198	.228	0	0	2B-21, SS-9, 3B-1

Granny Hamner

HAMNER, GRANVILLE WILBUR
Brother of Garvin Hamner.
B. Apr. 26, 1927, Richmond, Va.

BR TR 5'10"   163 lbs.

	G	AB	H	2B	3B	HR	HR %	R	RBI	BB	SO	SB	BA	SA	AB	H	G by POS
1944 **PHI N**	21	77	19	1	0	0	0.0	6	5	3	7	0	.247	.260	0	0	SS-21
1945	14	41	7	2	0	0	0.0	3	6	1	3	0	.171	.220	0	0	SS-13
1946	2	7	1	0	0	0	0.0	0	0	0	3	0	.143	.143	0	0	SS-2
1947	2	7	2	0	0	0	0.0	1	0	1	0	0	.286	.286	0	0	SS-2
1948	129	446	116	21	5	3	0.7	42	48	22	39	2	.260	.350	4	1	2B-87, SS-37, 3B-3
1949	154	662	174	32	5	6	0.9	83	53	25	47	6	.263	.353	0	0	SS-154
1950	157	637	172	27	5	11	1.7	78	82	39	35	2	.270	.380	0	0	SS-157
1951	150	589	150	23	7	9	1.5	61	72	29	32	10	.255	.363	0	0	SS-151
1952	151	596	164	30	5	17	2.9	74	87	27	51	7	.275	.428	1	0	SS-151
1953	154	609	168	38	8	21	3.4	90	92	32	28	2	.276	.455	0	0	2B-93, SS-71
1954	152	596	178	39	11	13	2.2	83	89	53	44	1	.299	.466	0	0	2B-152, SS-1
1955	104	405	104	12	4	5	1.2	57	43	41	30	0	.257	.343	1	0	2B-82, SS-32
1956	122	401	90	24	3	4	1.0	42	42	30	42	2	.224	.329	5	1	SS-110, 2B-11, P-3

	G	AB	H	2B	3B	HR	HR %	R	RBI	BB	SO	SB	BA	SA	Pinch Hit AB	H	G by POS

Granny Hamner continued

	G	AB	H	2B	3B	HR	HR%	R	RBI	BB	SO	SB	BA	SA	AB	H	G by POS
1957	133	502	114	19	5	10	2.0	59	62	34	42	3	.227	.345	8	0	2B-125, SS-5, P-1
1958	35	133	40	7	3	2	1.5	18	18	8	16	0	.301	.444	0	0	3B-22, 2B-11, SS-3
1959 2 teams	PHI	N	(21G –	.297)		CLE	A	(27G –	.164)								
" total	48	131	30	5	1	3	2.3	14	9	6	13	0	.229	.351	17	2	SS-25, 2B-7, 3B-6
1962 KC A	3	0	0	0	0	0	–	0	0	0	0	0	–	–	0	0	P-3
17 yrs.	1531	5839	1529	272	62	104	1.8	711	708	351	432	35	.262	.383	37	4	SS-934, 2B-568, 3B-31, P-7

WORLD SERIES

	G	AB	H	2B	3B	HR	HR%	R	RBI	BB	SO	SB	BA	SA	AB	H	G by POS
1950 PHI N	4	14	6	2	1	0	0.0	1	0	1	2	1	.429	.714	0	0	SS-4

Ike Hampton

HAMPTON, ISAAC BERNARD
B. Aug. 22, 1951, Camden, S. C.

BB TR 6' 165 lbs.

	G	AB	H	2B	3B	HR	HR%	R	RBI	BB	SO	SB	BA	SA	AB	H	G by POS
1974 NY N	4	4	0	0	0	0	0.0	0	1	0	1	0	.000	.000	3	0	C-1
1975 CAL A	31	66	10	3	0	0	0.0	8	4	7	19	0	.152	.197	0	0	C-28, SS-2, 3B-1
1976	3	2	0	0	0	0	0.0	0	0	0	0	0	.000	.000	0	0	C-2, DH-1, SS-1
1977	52	44	13	1	0	3	6.8	5	9	2	10	0	.295	.523	5	3	C-47
1978	19	14	3	0	1	1	7.1	2	4	2	7	1	.214	.571	1	0	C-13, DH-4, 1B-1
1979	4	5	2	0	0	0	0.0	0	0	0	1	0	.400	.400	1	0	1B-2
6 yrs.	113	135	28	4	1	4	3.0	15	18	11	38	1	.207	.341	10	3	C-91, DH-5, SS-3, 1B-3, 3B-1

Bert Hamric

HAMRIC, ODBERT HERMAN
B. Mar. 1, 1928, Clarksburg, W. Va.

BL TR 6' 165 lbs.

	G	AB	H	2B	3B	HR	HR%	R	RBI	BB	SO	SB	BA	SA	AB	H	G by POS
1955 BKN N	2	1	0	0	0	0	0.0	0	0	0	1	0	.000	.000	1	0	
1958 BAL A	8	8	1	0	0	0	0.0	0	0	0	6	0	.125	.125	8	1	
2 yrs.	10	9	1	0	0	0	0.0	0	0	0	7	0	.111	.111	9	1	

Ray Hamrick

HAMRICK, RAYMOND BERNARD
B. Aug. 1, 1921, Nashville, Tenn.

BR TR 5'11½" 160 lbs.

	G	AB	H	2B	3B	HR	HR%	R	RBI	BB	SO	SB	BA	SA	AB	H	G by POS
1943 PHI N	44	160	32	3	1	0	0.0	12	9	8	28	0	.200	.231	0	0	2B-31, SS-12
1944	74	292	60	10	1	1	0.3	22	23	23	34	1	.205	.257	0	0	SS-74
2 yrs.	118	452	92	13	2	1	0.2	34	32	31	62	1	.204	.248	0	0	SS-86, 2B-31

Buddy Hancken

HANCKEN, MORRIS MEDLOCK
B. Aug. 30, 1914, Birmingham, Ala.

BR TR 6'1" 175 lbs.

	G	AB	H	2B	3B	HR	HR%	R	RBI	BB	SO	SB	BA	SA	AB	H	G by POS
1940 PHI A	1	0	0	0	0	0	–	0	0	0	0	0	–	–	0	0	C-1

Fred Hancock

HANCOCK, FRED JAMES
B. Mar. 28, 1920, Allenport, Pa.

BR TR 5'8" 170 lbs.

	G	AB	H	2B	3B	HR	HR%	R	RBI	BB	SO	SB	BA	SA	AB	H	G by POS
1949 CHI A	39	52	7	2	0	0	0.0	7	9	8	9	0	.135	.212	5	1	SS-27, 3B-3, OF-1

Garry Hancock

HANCOCK, RONALD GARRY
B. Jan. 23, 1954, Tampa, Fla.

BL TL 6' 175 lbs.

	G	AB	H	2B	3B	HR	HR%	R	RBI	BB	SO	SB	BA	SA	AB	H	G by POS
1978 BOS A	38	80	18	3	0	0	0.0	10	4	1	12	0	.225	.263	8	3	OF-19, DH-13
1980	46	115	33	6	0	4	3.5	9	19	3	11	0	.287	.443	12	2	OF-27, DH-12
1981	26	45	7	3	0	0	0.0	4	3	2	4	0	.156	.222	12	1	OF-8, DH-4
1982	11	14	0	0	0	0	0.0	3	0	1	1	0	.000	.000	4	0	OF-7
1983 OAK A	101	256	70	7	3	8	3.1	29	30	5	13	2	.273	.418	14	7	OF-67, 1B-27, DH-9
1984	51	60	13	2	0	0	0.0	2	8	0	1	0	.217	.250	33	6	OF-18, DH-5, 1B-4, P-1
6 yrs.	273	570	141	21	3	12	2.1	57	64	12	42	2	.247	.358	83	19	OF-146, DH-43, 1B-31, P-1

Mike Handiboe

HANDIBOE, ALOYSIUS JAMES (Coalyard Mike)
B. July 21, 1887, Washington, D. C.   D. Jan. 31, 1953, Savannah, Ga.

BL TL 5'10" 155 lbs.

	G	AB	H	2B	3B	HR	HR%	R	RBI	BB	SO	SB	BA	SA	AB	H	G by POS
1911 NY A	5	15	1	0	0	0	0.0	2		0		2	.067	.067	0	0	OF-4

Gene Handley

HANDLEY, EUGENE LOUIS
Brother of Lee Handley.
B. Nov. 25, 1914, Kennett, Mo.

BR TR 5'10½" 165 lbs.

	G	AB	H	2B	3B	HR	HR%	R	RBI	BB	SO	SB	BA	SA	AB	H	G by POS
1946 PHI A	89	251	63	8	5	0	0.0	31	21	22	25	8	.251	.323	8	3	2B-68, 3B-4, SS-1
1947	36	90	23	2	1	0	0.0	10	8	10	2	1	.256	.300	3	0	2B-17, 3B-10, SS-1
2 yrs.	125	341	86	10	6	0	0.0	41	29	32	27	9	.252	.317	11	3	2B-85, 3B-14, SS-2

Lee Handley

HANDLEY, LEE ELMER (Jeep)
Brother of Gene Handley.
B. July 31, 1913, Clarion, Iowa   D. Apr. 8, 1970, Pittsburgh, Pa.

BR TR 5'7" 160 lbs.

	G	AB	H	2B	3B	HR	HR%	R	RBI	BB	SO	SB	BA	SA	AB	H	G by POS
1936 CIN N	24	78	24	1	0	2	2.6	10	8	7	16	3	.308	.397	1	0	2B-16, 3B-7
1937 PIT N	127	480	120	21	12	3	0.6	59	37	37	40	5	.250	.363	0	0	2B-126, 3B-1
1938	139	570	153	25	8	6	1.1	91	51	53	31	7	.268	.372	0	0	3B-136
1939	101	376	107	14	5	1	0.3	43	42	32	20	17	.285	.356	1	0	3B-100
1940	98	302	85	7	4	1	0.3	50	19	27	16	7	.281	.341	4	1	3B-80, 2B-7
1941	124	459	132	18	4	0	0.0	59	33	35	22	16	.288	.344	6	1	3B-114
1944	40	86	19	2	0	0	0.0	7	5	3	5	1	.221	.244	4	1	2B-19, 3B-11, SS-3
1945	98	312	93	16	2	1	0.3	39	32	20	16	7	.298	.372	11	5	3B-79
1946	116	416	99	8	7	1	0.2	43	28	29	20	4	.238	.298	5	0	3B-102, 2B-3
1947 PHI N	101	277	70	10	3	0	0.0	17	42	24	18	1	.253	.310	7	2	3B-83, 2B-3, SS-1
10 yrs.	968	3356	902	122	45	15	0.4	418	297	267	204	68	.269	.345	39	10	3B-713, 2B-174, SS-4

Harry Hanebrink

HANEBRINK, HARRY ALOYSIUS
B. Nov. 12, 1927, St. Louis, Mo.

BL TR 6' 165 lbs.

	G	AB	H	2B	3B	HR	HR%	R	RBI	BB	SO	SB	BA	SA	AB	H	G by POS
1953 MIL N	51	80	19	1	1	1	1.3	8	8	6	8	1	.238	.313	25	2	2B-21, 3B-1
1957	6	7	2	0	0	0	0.0	0	0	1	2	0	.286	.286	4	1	3B-2
1958	63	133	25	3	0	4	3.0	14	10	13	9	0	.188	.301	19	5	OF-33, 3B-7
1959 PHI N	57	97	25	3	1	1	1.0	10	7	2	12	0	.258	.340	41	11	2B-15, 3B-9, OF-1
4 yrs.	177	317	71	7	2	6	1.9	32	25	22	31	1	.224	.315	89	19	2B-36, OF-34, 3B-19

	G	AB	H	2B	3B	HR	HR%	R	RBI	BB	SO	SB	BA	SA	Pinch Hit AB	Pinch Hit H	G by POS

Harry Hanebrink continued

	G	AB	H	2B	3B	HR	HR%	R	RBI	BB	SO	SB	BA	SA	PH AB	PH H	G by POS
WORLD SERIES																	
1958 MIL N	2	2	0	0	0	0	0.0	0	0	0	0	0	.000	.000	2	0	

Fred Haney

HANEY, FRED GIRARD (Pudge)
B. Apr. 25, 1898, Albuquerque, N. M. D. Nov. 9, 1977, Beverly Hills, Calif.
Manager 1939-41, 1953-59.
BR TR 5'6" 170 lbs.

	G	AB	H	2B	3B	HR	HR%	R	RBI	BB	SO	SB	BA	SA	PH AB	PH H	G by POS
1922 DET A	81	213	75	7	4	0	0.0	41	25	32	14	3	.352	.423	9	3	3B-42, 1B-11, SS-2
1923	142	503	142	13	4	4	0.8	85	67	45	23	12	.282	.348	0	0	2B-69, 3B-55, SS-16
1924	86	256	79	11	1	1	0.4	54	30	39	13	7	.309	.371	13	4	3B-59, SS-4, 2B-3
1925	114	398	111	15	3	0	0.0	84	40	66	29	11	.279	.332	5	1	3B-107
1926 BOS A	138	462	102	15	7	0	0.0	47	52	74	28	13	.221	.284	1	0	3B-137
1927 2 teams	BOS A (47G – .276)					CHI N (4G – .000)											
" total	51	119	32	4	1	3	2.5	23	12	25	14	4	.269	.395	14	4	3B-34, OF-1
1929 STL N	10	26	3	1	1	0	0.0	4	2	1	2	0	.115	.231	2	1	3B-6
7 yrs.	622	1977	544	66	21	8	0.4	338	228	282	123	50	.275	.342	44	13	3B-440, 2B-72, SS-22, 1B-11, OF-1

Larry Haney

HANEY, WALLACE LARRY
B. Nov. 19, 1942, Charlottesville, Va.
BR TR 6'2" 195 lbs.

	G	AB	H	2B	3B	HR	HR%	R	RBI	BB	SO	SB	BA	SA	PH AB	PH H	G by POS
1966 BAL A	20	56	9	1	0	1	1.8	3	3	1	15	0	.161	.232	1	0	C-20
1967	58	164	44	11	0	3	1.8	13	20	6	28	1	.268	.390	1	0	C-57
1968	38	89	21	3	1	1	1.1	5	5	0	19	0	.236	.326	6	2	C-32
1969 2 teams	SEA A (22G – .254)					OAK A (53G – .151)											
" total	75	145	28	7	0	4	2.8	11	19	13	31	1	.193	.324	2	1	C-73
1970 OAK A	2	2	0	0	0	0	0.0	2	0	2	1	0	.000	.000	1	0	C-1
1972	5	4	0	0	0	0	0.0	0	0	0	1	0	.000	.000	1	0	C-4, 2B-1
1973 2 teams	OAK A (2G – .500)					STL N (2G – .000)											
" total	4	3	1	0	0	0	0.0	0	0	0	1	0	.333	.333	0	0	C-4
1974 OAK A	76	121	20	4	0	2	1.7	12	3	3	18	1	.165	.248	1	0	C-73, 3B-3, 1B-2
1975	47	26	5	0	0	1	3.8	3	2	1	4	0	.192	.308	1	0	C-43, 3B-4
1976	88	177	40	2	0	0	0.0	12	10	13	26	0	.226	.237	1	0	C-87
1977 MIL A	63	127	29	2	0	0	0.0	7	10	5	30	0	.228	.244	0	0	C-63
1978	4	5	1	0	0	0	0.0	0	1	0	1	0	.200	.200	0	0	C-4
12 yrs.	480	919	198	30	1	12	1.3	68	73	44	175	3	.215	.289	14	4	C-461, 3B-7, 1B-2, 2B-1
WORLD SERIES																	
1974 OAK A	2	0	0	0	0	0	–	0	0	0	0	0	–	–	0	0	C-2

Charlie Hanford

HANFORD, CHARLES JOSEPH
B. June 3, 1882, Tunstall, England D. July 19, 1963, Trenton, N. J.
BR TR 5'6½" 145 lbs.

	G	AB	H	2B	3B	HR	HR%	R	RBI	BB	SO	SB	BA	SA	PH AB	PH H	G by POS
1914 BUF F	155	597	174	28	13	13	2.2	83	90	32		37	.291	.447	0	0	OF-155
1915 CHI F	77	179	43	4	5	0	0.0	27	22	12		10	.240	.318	26	7	OF-43
2 yrs.	232	776	217	32	18	13	1.7	110	112	44		47	.280	.418	26	7	OF-198

Pat Hanifin

HANIFIN, PATRICK JAMES
B. 1873, Nova Scotia, Canada D. Nov. 5, 1908, Springfield, Mass.

	G	AB	H	2B	3B	HR	HR%	R	RBI	BB	SO	SB	BA	SA	PH AB	PH H	G by POS
1897 BKN N	10	20	5	0	0	0	0.0	4	2	1		4	.250	.250	3	1	OF-3, 2B-2

Jay Hankins

HANKINS, JAY NELSON
B. Nov. 7, 1935, St. Louis County, Mo.
BL TR 5'7" 170 lbs.

	G	AB	H	2B	3B	HR	HR%	R	RBI	BB	SO	SB	BA	SA	PH AB	PH H	G by POS
1961 KC A	76	173	32	0	3	3	1.7	23	6	8	17	2	.185	.272	3	1	OF-65
1963	10	34	6	0	1	1	2.9	2	4	0	3	0	.176	.324	1	1	OF-9
2 yrs.	86	207	38	0	4	4	1.9	25	10	8	20	2	.184	.280	4	2	OF-74

Frank Hankinson

HANKINSON, FRANK EDWARD
B. Apr. 29, 1856, New York, N. Y. D. Apr. 5, 1911, Palisades Park, N. J.
BR TR 5'11" 168 lbs.

	G	AB	H	2B	3B	HR	HR%	R	RBI	BB	SO	SB	BA	SA	PH AB	PH H	G by POS
1878 CHI N	58	240	64	8	3	1	0.4	38	27	5	36		.267	.338	0	0	3B-57, P-1
1879	44	171	31	4	0	0	0.0	14	8	2	14		.181	.205	0	0	P-26, OF-14, 3B-5
1880 CLE N	69	263	55	7	4	1	0.4	32		1	23		.209	.278	0	0	3B-56, OF-12, P-4
1881 TRO N	85	321	62	15	0	1	0.3	34	19	10	41		.193	.249	0	0	3B-84, SS-1
1883 NY N	94	337	74	13	6	2	0.6	40		19	38		.220	.312	0	0	3B-93, OF-1
1884	105	389	90	16	7	2	0.5	44		23	59		.231	.324	0	0	3B-105, OF-1
1885 NY AA	94	362	81	12	2	2	0.6	43		12			.224	.285	0	0	3B-94, P-1
1886	136	522	126	14	5	2	0.4	66		49			.241	.299	0	0	3B-136
1887	127	512	137	29	11	1	0.2	79		38		19	.268	.373	0	0	3B-127
1888 KC AA	37	155	27	4	1	1	0.6	20	20	11		2	.174	.232	0	0	2B-13, SS-9, OF-7, 3B-7, 1B-2
10 yrs.	849	3272	747	122	39	13	0.4	410	74	170	211	21	.228	.301	0	0	3B-764, OF-35, P-32, 2B-13, SS-10, 1B-2

Bill Hanlon

HANLON, WILLIAM HENRY (Big Bill)
B. Mar. 16, 1865, Sacramento, Calif. D. Mar. 18, 1951, Sacramento, Calif.

	G	AB	H	2B	3B	HR	HR%	R	RBI	BB	SO	SB	BA	SA	PH AB	PH H	G by POS
1903 CHI N	8	21	2	0	0	0	0.0	4	2	6		1	.095	.095	0	0	1B-8

Ned Hanlon

HANLON, EDWARD HUGH
B. Aug. 22, 1857, Montville, Conn. D. Apr. 14, 1937, Baltimore, Md.
Manager 1889-1907.
BL 5'9½" 170 lbs.

	G	AB	H	2B	3B	HR	HR%	R	RBI	BB	SO	SB	BA	SA	PH AB	PH H	G by POS
1880 CLE N	73	280	69	10	3	0	0.0	30		11	30		.246	.304	0	0	OF-69, SS-4
1881 DET N	76	305	85	14	8	2	0.7	63	28	22	11		.279	.397	0	0	OF-74, SS-2
1882	82	347	80	18	6	5	1.4	68	38	26	25		.231	.360	0	0	OF-82, 3B-1
1883	100	413	100	13	2	1	0.2	65		34	44		.242	.291	0	0	OF-90, 2B-11
1884	114	450	119	18	6	5	1.1	86		40	52		.264	.364	0	0	OF-114
1885	105	424	128	18	8	1	0.2	93	29	47	18		.302	.389	0	0	OF-105
1886	126	494	116	6	4	4	0.8	105	60	57	39		.235	.296	0	0	OF-126, 2B-1
1887	118	471	129	13	7	4	0.8	79	69	30	24	69	.274	.357	0	0	OF-118
1888	109	459	122	6	8	5	1.1	64	39	15	32	38	.266	.346	0	0	OF-109

	G	AB	H	2B	3B	HR	HR %	R	RBI	BB	SO	SB	BA	SA	Pinch Hit AB	Pinch Hit H	G by POS

Ned Hanlon continued

	G	AB	H	2B	3B	HR	HR%	R	RBI	BB	SO	SB	BA	SA	AB	H	G by POS
1889 PIT N	116	461	110	14	10	2	0.4	81	37	58	25	53	.239	.325	0	0	OF-116
1890 PIT P	118	472	131	16	6	1	0.2	106	44	80	24	65	.278	.343	0	0	OF-118
1891 PIT N	119	455	121	12	8	0	0.0	87	60	48	30	54	.266	.327	0	0	OF-119, SS-1
1892 BAL N	11	43	7	1	1	0	0.0	3	2	3	3	0	.163	.233	0	0	OF-11
13 yrs.	1267	5074	1317	159	79	30	0.6	930	405	471	357	279	.260	.340	0	0	OF-1251, 2B-13, SS-7

John Hanna

HANNA, JOHN
B. Nov. 3, 1863, Philadelphia, Pa. D. Nov. 7, 1930, Philadelphia, Pa.

	G	AB	H	2B	3B	HR	HR%	R	RBI	BB	SO	SB	BA	SA	AB	H	G by POS
1884 2 teams			WAS	AA	(23G –	.066)		RIC	AA	(22G –	.194)						
" total	45	143	18	2	1	0	0.0	14		6			.126	.154	0	0	C-39, OF-6, SS-1

Truck Hannah

HANNAH, JAMES HARRISON
B. June 5, 1889, Larimore, N. D. D. Apr., 1982, Fountain Valley, Calif.
BR TR 6'1" 190 lbs.

	G	AB	H	2B	3B	HR	HR%	R	RBI	BB	SO	SB	BA	SA	AB	H	G by POS
1918 NY A	90	250	55	6	0	2	0.8	24	21	51	25	5	.220	.268	2	0	C-88
1919	75	227	54	8	3	1	0.4	14	20	22	19	0	.238	.313	1	1	C-73, 1B-1
1920	79	259	64	11	1	2	0.8	24	25	24	35	2	.247	.320	1	0	C-78
3 yrs.	244	736	173	25	4	5	0.7	62	66	97	79	7	.235	.300	4	1	C-239, 1B-1

Jack Hannifin

HANNIFIN, JOHN JOSEPH
B. Feb. 25, 1883, Northampton, Mass. D. Oct. 27, 1945, Holyoke, Mass.
BR TR 5'10" 150 lbs.

	G	AB	H	2B	3B	HR	HR%	R	RBI	BB	SO	SB	BA	SA	AB	H	G by POS
1906 2 teams			PHI	A	(1G –	1.000)		NY	N	(10G –	.200)						
" total	11	31	7	0	1	0	0.0	4	3	2		1	.226	.290	0	0	SS-6, 3B-3, 2B-1
1907 NY N	56	149	34	7	3	1	0.7	16	15	15		6	.228	.336	7	1	1B-29, 3B-10, SS-9, OF-2
1908 2 teams			NY	N	(1G –	.000)		BOS	N	(74G –	.206)						
" total	75	259	53	6	2	2	0.8	30	22	28		7	.205	.266	11	2	3B-35, 2B-22, SS-15, OF-8
3 yrs.	142	439	94	13	6	3	0.7	50	40	45		14	.214	.292	18	3	3B-48, SS-30, 1B-29, 2B-23, OF-10

Bob Hansen

HANSEN, ROBERT JOSEPH
B. May 26, 1948, Winthrop, Mass.
BL TL 6' 195 lbs.

	G	AB	H	2B	3B	HR	HR%	R	RBI	BB	SO	SB	BA	SA	AB	H	G by POS
1974 MIL A	58	88	26	4	1	2	2.3	8	9	3	16	2	.295	.432	34	14	DH-18, 1B-3
1976	24	61	10	1	0	0	0.0	4	4	6	8	0	.164	.180	7	1	DH-14, 1B-1
2 yrs.	82	149	36	5	1	2	1.3	12	13	9	24	2	.242	.329	41	15	DH-32, 1B-4

Doug Hansen

HANSEN, DOUGLAS WILLIAM
B. Dec. 16, 1928, Los Angeles, Calif.
BR TR 6' 180 lbs.

	G	AB	H	2B	3B	HR	HR%	R	RBI	BB	SO	SB	BA	SA	AB	H	G by POS
1951 CLE A	3	0	0	0	0	0	–	2	0	0	0	0	–	–	0	0	

Ron Hansen

HANSEN, RONALD LAVERN
B. Apr. 5, 1938, Oxford, Neb.
BR TR 6'3" 190 lbs.

	G	AB	H	2B	3B	HR	HR%	R	RBI	BB	SO	SB	BA	SA	AB	H	G by POS
1958 BAL A	12	19	0	0	0	0	0.0	1	1	0	7	0	.000	.000	0	0	SS-12
1959	2	4	0	0	0	0	0.0	0	0	1	1	0	.000	.000	0	0	SS-2
1960	153	530	135	22	5	22	4.2	72	86	69	94	3	.255	.440	1	0	SS-153
1961	155	533	132	13	2	12	2.3	51	51	66	96	1	.248	.347	0	0	SS-149, 2B-7
1962	71	196	34	7	0	3	1.5	12	17	30	36	0	.173	.255	6	2	SS-64
1963 CHI A	144	482	109	17	2	13	2.7	55	67	78	74	1	.226	.351	0	0	SS-144
1964	158	575	150	25	3	20	3.5	85	68	73	73	1	.261	.419	0	0	SS-158
1965	162	587	138	23	4	11	1.9	61	66	60	73	1	.235	.344	0	0	SS-161, 2B-1
1966	23	74	13	1	0	0	0.0	3	4	15	10	0	.176	.189	0	0	SS-23
1967	157	498	116	20	0	8	1.6	35	51	64	51	0	.233	.321	0	0	SS-157
1968 2 teams			WAS	A	(86G –	.185)		CHI	A	(40G –	.230)						
" total	126	362	71	15	0	9	2.5	35	32	46	61	0	.196	.312	6	2	SS-88, 3B-34, 2B-2
1969 CHI A	85	185	48	6	1	2	1.1	15	22	18	25	2	.259	.335	25	6	2B-26, 1B-21, SS-8, 3B-7
1970 NY A	59	91	27	4	0	4	4.4	13	14	19	9	0	.297	.473	28	4	SS-15, 3B-11, 2B-1
1971	61	145	30	3	0	2	1.4	6	20	9	27	0	.207	.269	22	4	3B-30, 2B-9, SS-3
1972 KC A	16	30	4	0	0	0	0.0	2	2	3	6	0	.133	.133	7	1	SS-6, 3B-4, 2B-1
15 yrs.	1384	4311	1007	156	17	106	2.5	446	501	551	643	9	.234	.351	95	19	SS-1143, 3B-86, 2B-47, 1B-21

Don Hanski

HANSKI, DONALD THOMAS
Born Donald Thomas Hanyzewski.
B. Feb. 27, 1916, LaPorte, Ind. D. Sept. 2, 1957, Worth, Ill.
BL TL 5'11" 180 lbs.

	G	AB	H	2B	3B	HR	HR%	R	RBI	BB	SO	SB	BA	SA	AB	H	G by POS
1943 CHI A	9	21	5	1	0	0	0.0	1	2	0	5	0	.238	.286	3	1	1B-5, P-1
1944	2	1	0	0	0	0	0.0	0	0	0	0	0	.000	.000	0	0	P-2
2 yrs.	11	22	5	1	0	0	0.0	1	2	0	5	0	.227	.273	3	1	1B-5, P-3

Joe Hanson

HANSON, JOSEPH
B. St. Louis, Mo.
TR

	G	AB	H	2B	3B	HR	HR%	R	RBI	BB	SO	SB	BA	SA	AB	H	G by POS
1913 NY A	1	2	0	0	0	0	0.0	0	0	0	0	0	.000	.000	0	0	C-1

John Happenny

HAPPENNY, JOHN CLIFFORD (Cliff)
B. May 18, 1901, Waltham, Mass.
BR TR 5'11" 165 lbs.

	G	AB	H	2B	3B	HR	HR%	R	RBI	BB	SO	SB	BA	SA	AB	H	G by POS
1923 CHI A	32	86	19	5	0	0	0.0	7	10	3	13	0	.221	.279	1	0	2B-20, SS-8

Bill Harbidge

HARBIDGE, WILLIAM ARTHUR
B. Mar. 29, 1855, Philadelphia, Pa. D. Mar. 17, 1924, Philadelphia, Pa.
BL TL 162 lbs.

	G	AB	H	2B	3B	HR	HR%	R	RBI	BB	SO	SB	BA	SA	AB	H	G by POS
1876 HAR N	30	106	23	2	1	0	0.0	11	6	3	2		.217	.255	0	0	C-24, OF-6, 1B-2
1877	41	167	37	5	2	0	0.0	18	8	3	6		.222	.275	0	0	C-32, OF-5, 2B-4, 3B-1
1878 CHI N	54	240	71	12	0	0	0.0	32	37	6	13		.296	.346	0	0	C-50, OF-8
1879	4	18	2	0	0	0	0.0	2	1	0	5		.111	.111	0	0	OF-4
1880 TRO N	9	27	10	0	1	0	0.0	3		0	3		.370	.444	0	0	C-9, OF-1
1882	32	123	23	1	1	0	0.0	11	13	10	17		.187	.211	0	0	OF-23, 1B-6, C-3
1883 PHI N	73	280	62	12	3	0	0.0	32		24	20		.221	.286	0	0	OF-44, SS-11, 2B-9, C-7, 3B-5

	G	AB	H	2B	3B	HR	HR %	R	RBI	BB	SO	SB	BA	SA	Pinch Hit AB	Pinch Hit H	G by POS

Bill Harbidge continued

	G	AB	H	2B	3B	HR	HR %	R	RBI	BB	SO	SB	BA	SA	AB	H	G by POS
1884 CIN U	82	341	95	12	5	2	0.6	59		25			.279	.361	0	0	OF-80, SS-3, 1B-2
8 yrs.	325	1302	323	44	13	2	0.2	168	65	71	66		.248	.306	0	0	OF-171, C-125, SS-14, 2B-13, 1B-10, 3B-6

Scott Hardesty

HARDESTY, SCOTT DURBIN
B. Jan. 26, 1870, Belleville, Ohio   D. Oct. 29, 1944, Fostoria, Ohio

	G	AB	H	2B	3B	HR	HR %	R	RBI	BB	SO	SB	BA	SA	AB	H	G by POS
1899 NY N	22	72	16	0	0	0	0.0	4	4	1		2	.222	.222	0	0	SS-20, 1B-2

Pat Hardgrove

BR TR 5'10" 158 lbs.

HARDGROVE, WILLIAM HENRY
B. May 10, 1895, Palmyra, Kans.   D. Jan. 26, 1973, Jackson, Miss.

	G	AB	H	2B	3B	HR	HR %	R	RBI	BB	SO	SB	BA	SA	AB	H	G by POS
1918 CHI A	2	2	0	0	0	0	0.0	0	0	0	0	0	.000	.000	2	0	

Lew Hardie

HARDIE, LOUIS W.   5'11" 180 lbs.
B. Aug. 24, 1864, New York, N. Y.   D. Mar. 5, 1929, Oakland, Calif.

	G	AB	H	2B	3B	HR	HR %	R	RBI	BB	SO	SB	BA	SA	AB	H	G by POS
1884 PHI N	3	8	3	2	0	0	0.0	0		0	2		.375	.625	0	0	C-3
1886 CHI N	16	51	9	0	0	0	0.0	4	3	4	10		.176	.176	0	0	C-13, OF-2, 3B-1
1890 BOS N	47	185	42	8	0	3	1.6	17	17	18	36	4	.227	.319	0	0	C-25, OF-15, 3B-7, SS-1, 1B-1
1891 BAL AA	15	56	13	0	3	0	0.0	7	1	8	8	3	.232	.339	0	0	OF-15
4 yrs.	81	300	67	10	3	3	1.0	28	20	30	56	7	.223	.307	0	0	C-41, OF-32, 3B-8, SS-1, 1B-1

Bud Hardin

BR TR 5'10" 165 lbs.

HARDIN, WILLIAM EDGAR
B. June 14, 1922, Shelby, N. C.

	G	AB	H	2B	3B	HR	HR %	R	RBI	BB	SO	SB	BA	SA	AB	H	G by POS
1952 CHI N	3	7	1	0	0	0	0.0	1	0	0	0	0	.143	.143	1	0	SS-2, 2B-1

Lou Harding

HARDING, LOUIS EDWARD (Jumbo)   219 lbs.
B. San Francisco, Calif.   Deceased.

	G	AB	H	2B	3B	HR	HR %	R	RBI	BB	SO	SB	BA	SA	AB	H	G by POS
1886 STL AA	1	3	1	1	0	0	0.0	0		0			.333	.667	0	0	C-1

Carroll Hardy

BR TR 6' 185 lbs.

HARDY, CARROLL WILLIAM
B. May 18, 1933, Sturgis, S. D.

	G	AB	H	2B	3B	HR	HR %	R	RBI	BB	SO	SB	BA	SA	AB	H	G by POS
1958 CLE A	27	49	10	3	0	1	2.0	10	6	6	14	1	.204	.327	6	1	OF-17
1959	32	53	11	1	0	0	0.0	12	2	3	7	1	.208	.226	12	1	OF-15
1960 2 teams		CLE A	(29G –	.111)		BOS A	(73G –	.234)									
" total	102	163	36	6	2	2	1.2	33	16	19	42	3	.221	.319	7	2	OF-76
1961 BOS A	85	281	74	20	2	3	1.1	46	36	26	53	4	.263	.381	14	3	OF-76
1962	115	362	78	13	5	8	2.2	52	36	54	68	3	.215	.345	7	0	OF-105
1963 HOU N	15	44	10	3	0	0	0.0	5	3	3	7	1	.227	.295	4	0	OF-10
1964	46	157	29	1	1	2	1.3	13	12	8	30	0	.185	.242	5	1	OF-41
1967 MIN A	11	8	3	0	0	1	12.5	1	2	1	1	0	.375	.750	7	3	OF-4
8 yrs.	433	1117	251	47	10	17	1.5	172	113	120	222	13	.225	.330	62	11	OF-344

Jack Hardy

BR TR 6' 185 lbs.

HARDY, JOHN DOOLITTLE
B. June 23, 1877, Cleveland, Ohio   D. Oct. 20, 1921, Cleveland, Ohio

	G	AB	H	2B	3B	HR	HR %	R	RBI	BB	SO	SB	BA	SA	AB	H	G by POS
1903 CLE A	5	19	3	1	0	0	0.0	1	1		1		.158	.211	0	0	OF-5
1907 CHI N	1	4	1	0	0	0	0.0	0	0	0		0	.250	.250	0	0	C-1
1909 WAS A	10	24	4	0	0	0	0.0	3	4	1		0	.167	.167	0	0	C-9, 2B-1
1910	7	8	2	0	0	0	0.0	1	0	0		0	.250	.250	2	0	C-4, OF-1
4 yrs.	23	55	10	1	0	0	0.0	5	5	2		1	.182	.200	2	0	C-14, OF-6, 2B-1

Gary Hargis

BR TR 5'11" 165 lbs.

HARGIS, GARY LYNN
B. Nov. 2, 1956, Minneapolis, Minn.

	G	AB	H	2B	3B	HR	HR %	R	RBI	BB	SO	SB	BA	SA	AB	H	G by POS
1979 PIT N	1	0	0	0	0	0		0	0	0	0	0	–	–	0	0	

Bubbles Hargrave

BR TR 5'10½" 174 lbs.

HARGRAVE, EUGENE FRANKLIN
Brother of Pinky Hargrave.
B. July 15, 1892, New Haven, Ind.   D. Feb. 23, 1969, Cincinnati, Ohio

	G	AB	H	2B	3B	HR	HR %	R	RBI	BB	SO	SB	BA	SA	AB	H	G by POS
1913 CHI N	3	3	1	0	0	0	0.0	0	1	0	0	0	.333	.333	1	0	C-2
1914	23	36	8	2	0	0	0.0	3	2	0	4	2	.222	.278	7	1	C-16
1915	15	19	3	0	1	0	0.0	2	2	1	5	0	.158	.263	6	1	C-9
1921 CIN N	93	263	76	17	8	1	0.4	28	38	12	15	4	.289	.426	19	3	C-73
1922	98	320	101	22	10	7	2.2	49	57	26	18	7	.316	.513	10	0	C-87
1923	118	378	126	23	9	10	2.6	54	78	44	22	4	.333	.521	7	1	C-109
1924	98	312	94	19	10	3	1.0	42	33	30	20	2	.301	.455	6	2	C-91
1925	87	273	82	13	6	2	0.7	28	33	25	23	4	.300	.414	3	0	C-84
1926	105	326	115	22	8	6	1.8	42	62	25	17	2	.353	.525	11	3	C-93
1927	102	305	94	18	3	0	0.0	36	35	31	18	0	.308	.387	9	1	C-92
1928	65	190	56	12	3	0	0.0	19	23	13	14	4	.295	.389	6	2	C-57
1930 NY A	45	108	30	7	0	0	0.0	11	12	10	9	0	.278	.343	11	0	C-34
12 yrs.	852	2533	786	155	58	29	1.1	314	376	217	165	29	.310	.452	96	14	C-747

Pinky Hargrave

BB TR 5'8½" 180 lbs.
BR 1923-26, BL 1933

HARGRAVE, WILLIAM McKINLEY
Brother of Bubbles Hargrave.
B. Jan. 31, 1896, New Haven, Ind.   D. Oct. 3, 1942, Fort Wayne, Ind.

	G	AB	H	2B	3B	HR	HR %	R	RBI	BB	SO	SB	BA	SA	AB	H	G by POS
1923 WAS A	33	59	17	2	0	0	0.0	4	8	2	6	0	.288	.322	18	7	3B-8, C-5, OF-1
1924	24	33	5	1	1	0	0.0	3	5	1	4	0	.152	.242	14	1	C-8
1925 2 teams		WAS A	(5G –	.500)		STL A	(67G –	.284)									
" total	72	231	67	15	2	8	3.5	34	43	14	15	2	.290	.476	9	5	C-63
1926 STL A	92	235	66	16	3	7	3.0	20	37	10	38	3	.281	.464	33	9	C-59
1928 DET A	121	321	88	13	5	10	3.1	38	63	32	28	4	.274	.439	25	9	C-88
1929	76	185	61	12	0	3	1.6	26	26	20	24	2	.330	.443	26	5	C-48

	G	AB	H	2B	3B	HR	HR %	R	RBI	BB	SO	SB	BA	SA	Pinch Hit AB	Pinch Hit H	G by POS

Pinky Hargrave continued

	G	AB	H	2B	3B	HR	HR%	R	RBI	BB	SO	SB	BA	SA	AB	H	G by POS
1930 **2 teams**		DET	A	(55G –	.285)		**WAS**	**A**	(10G –	.194)							
" total	65	168	45	10	2	6	3.6	21	25	23	13	3	.268	.458	15	2	C-49
1931 **WAS A**	40	80	26	8	0	1	1.3	6	19	9	12	1	.325	.463	15	4	C-25
1932 **BOS N**	82	217	57	14	3	4	1.8	20	33	24	18	1	.263	.410	7	2	C-73
1933	45	73	13	0	0	0	0.0	5	6	5	7	1	.178	.178	18	1	C-25
10 yrs.	650	1602	445	91	16	39	2.4	177	265	140	165	17	.278	.428	180	45	C-443, 3B-8, OF-1

Charlie Hargreaves

HARGREAVES, CHARLES RUSSELL   BR TR 6'   170 lbs.
B. Dec. 14, 1896, Trenton, N. J.   D. May 9, 1979, Neptune, N. J.

	G	AB	H	2B	3B	HR	HR%	R	RBI	BB	SO	SB	BA	SA	AB	H	G by POS
1923 **BKN N**	20	57	16	0	0	0	0.0	5	4	1	2	0	.281	.281	5	1	C-15
1924	15	27	11	2	0	0	0.0	4	5	1	1	0	.407	.481	5	1	C-9
1925	45	83	23	3	1	0	0.0	9	13	6	1	1	.277	.337	22	5	C-18, 1B-2
1926	85	208	52	13	2	2	1.0	14	23	19	10	1	.250	.361	13	2	C-70
1927	44	133	38	3	1	0	0.0	9	11	14	7	1	.286	.323	2	0	C-44
1928 **2 teams**		**BKN**	**N**	(20G –	.197)		**PIT**	**N**	(79G –	.285)							
" total	99	321	86	10	2	1	0.3	18	37	18	15	2	.268	.321	2	0	C-97
1929 **PIT N**	102	328	88	12	5	1	0.3	33	44	16	12	1	.268	.345	1	0	C-102
1930	11	31	7	1	0	0	0.0	4	2	2	1	0	.226	.258	0	0	C-11
8 yrs.	421	1188	321	44	11	4	0.3	96	139	77	49	6	.270	.336	50	9	C-366, 1B-2

Mike Hargrove

HARGROVE, DUDLEY MICHAEL   BL TL 6'   195 lbs.
B. Oct. 26, 1949, Perryton, Tex.

	G	AB	H	2B	3B	HR	HR%	R	RBI	BB	SO	SB	BA	SA	AB	H	G by POS
1974 **TEX A**	131	415	134	18	6	4	1.0	57	66	49	42	0	.323	.424	10	3	1B-91, DH-32, OF-6
1975	145	519	157	22	2	11	2.1	82	62	79	66	4	.303	.416	8	4	OF-96, 1B-48, DH-12
1976	151	541	155	30	1	7	1.3	80	58	97	64	2	.287	.384	4	0	1B-141, DH-5
1977	153	525	160	28	4	18	3.4	98	69	103	59	2	.305	.474	2	0	1B-152
1978	146	494	124	24	1	7	1.4	63	40	107	47	2	.251	.346	2	0	1B-140, DH-4
1979 **2 teams**		**SD**	**N**	(52G –	.192)		**CLE**	**A**	(100G –	.325)							
" total	152	463	134	26	4	10	2.2	75	64	88	55	2	.289	.428	16	3	OF-65, 1B-65, DH-7
1980 **CLE A**	160	589	179	22	2	11	1.9	86	85	111	36	4	.304	.404	0	0	1B-160
1981	94	322	102	21	0	2	0.6	43	49	60	16	5	.317	.401	2	1	1B-88, DH-4
1982	160	591	160	26	1	4	0.7	67	65	101	58	2	.271	.338	0	0	1B-153, DH-5
1983	134	469	134	21	4	3	0.6	57	57	78	40	0	.286	.367	4	2	1B-131, DH-1
1984	133	352	94	14	2	2	0.6	44	44	53	38	0	.267	.335	12	1	1B-124
11 yrs.	1559	5280	1533	252	27	79	1.5	752	659	926	521	23	.290	.393	60	15	1B-1293, OF-167, DH-70

John Harkins

HARKINS, JOHN JOSEPH (Pa)   BR TR 6'1"   205 lbs.
B. Apr. 12, 1859, New Brunswick, N. J.   D. Nov. 18, 1940, New Brunswick, N. J.

	G	AB	H	2B	3B	HR	HR%	R	RBI	BB	SO	SB	BA	SA	AB	H	G by POS
1884 **CLE N**	61	229	47	4	2	0	0.0	24	20	7	45		.205	.240	0	0	P-46, OF-17, SS-1, 3B-1
1885 **BKN AA**	43	159	42	4	1	1	0.6	20	9				.264	.333	0	0	P-34, OF-9, 3B-1
1886	41	142	32	4	2	1	0.7	18	17				.225	.303	0	0	P-34, OF-8
1887	27	98	23	5	0	0	0.0	10	7			4	.235	.286	0	0	P-24, OF-4, 2B-1
1888 **BAL AA**	1	3	0	0	0	0	0.0	1	0			0	.000	.000	0	0	P-1
5 yrs.	173	631	144	17	6	2	0.3	73	20	41	45	4	.228	.284	0	0	P-139, OF-38, 3B-2, SS-1, 2B-1

Tim Harkness

HARKNESS, THOMAS WILLIAM   BL TL 6'2"   182 lbs.
B. Dec. 23, 1937, Lachine, Que., Canada

	G	AB	H	2B	3B	HR	HR%	R	RBI	BB	SO	SB	BA	SA	AB	H	G by POS
1961 **LA N**	5	8	4	2	0	0	0.0	4	0	3	1	1	.500	.750	2	1	1B-2
1962	92	62	16	2	0	2	3.2	9	7	10	20	1	.258	.387	30	8	1B-59
1963 **NY N**	123	375	79	12	3	10	2.7	35	41	36	79	4	.211	.339	16	1	1B-106
1964	39	117	33	2	1	2	1.7	11	13	9	18	1	.282	.368	9	0	1B-32
4 yrs.	259	562	132	18	4	14	2.5	59	61	58	118	7	.235	.356	57	10	1B-199

Dick Harley

HARLEY, RICHARD JOSEPH   BL TR 5'10½"   150 lbs.
B. Sept. 25, 1872, Blue Bell, Pa.   D. Apr. 3, 1952, Philadelphia, Pa.

	G	AB	H	2B	3B	HR	HR%	R	RBI	BB	SO	SB	BA	SA	AB	H	G by POS
1897 **STL N**	89	330	96	6	4	3	0.9	43	35	36		23	.291	.361	0	0	OF-89
1898	142	549	135	6	5	0	0.0	74	42	34		13	.246	.275	1	1	OF-141
1899 **CLE N**	142	567	142	15	7	1	0.2	70	50	40		15	.250	.307	0	0	OF-143
1900 **CIN N**	5	21	9	1	0	0	0.0	2	5	1		4	.429	.476	0	0	OF-5
1901	133	535	146	13	2	4	0.7	69	27	31		37	.273	.327	0	0	OF-133
1902 **DET A**	125	491	138	9	8	2	0.4	59	44	36		20	.281	.344	0	0	OF-125
1903 **CHI N**	104	386	89	9	1	0	0.0	72	33	45		27	.231	.259	2	2	OF-103
7 yrs.	740	2879	755	59	27	10	0.3	389	236	223		139	.262	.312	3	3	OF-739

Larry Harlow

HARLOW, LARRY DUANE   BL TL 6'2"   185 lbs.
B. Nov. 13, 1951, Colorado Springs, Colo.

	G	AB	H	2B	3B	HR	HR%	R	RBI	BB	SO	SB	BA	SA	AB	H	G by POS
1975 **BAL A**	4	3	1	0	0	0	0.0	1	0	0	1	0	.333	.333	0	0	OF-4
1977	46	48	10	0	1	0	0.0	4	0	5	8	6	.208	.250	3	0	OF-38
1978	147	460	112	25	1	8	1.7	67	26	55	72	14	.243	.354	9	1	OF-138, P-1
1979 **2 teams**		**BAL**	**A**	(38G –	.268)		**CAL**	**A**	(62G –	.233)							
" total	100	200	48	9	2	0	0.0	27	15	32	38	2	.240	.305	8	2	OF-89, DH-1
1980 **CAL A**	109	301	83	13	4	4	1.3	47	27	48	61	3	.276	.385	12	4	OF-94, DH-1, 1B-1
1981	43	82	17	1	0	0	0.0	13	4	16	25	1	.207	.220	7	0	OF-39
6 yrs.	449	1094	271	48	8	12	1.1	159	72	156	205	26	.248	.339	39	6	OF-402, DH-2, 1B-1, P-1

LEAGUE CHAMPIONSHIP SERIES

	G	AB	H	2B	3B	HR	HR%	R	RBI	BB	SO	SB	BA	SA	AB	H	G by POS
1979 **CAL A**	3	8	1	1	0	0	0.0	0	1	1	2	0	.125	.250	0	0	OF-2

Bill Harman

HARMAN, WILLIAM BELL   BR TR 6'4"   200 lbs.
B. Jan. 2, 1919, Bridgewater, Va.

	G	AB	H	2B	3B	HR	HR%	R	RBI	BB	SO	SB	BA	SA	AB	H	G by POS
1941 **PHI N**	15	14	1	0	0	0	0.0	1	0	1		3	0	.071	.071	5	0	C-5, P-5

Chuck Harmon

HARMON, CHARLES BYRON   BR TR 6'2"   175 lbs.
B. Apr. 23, 1926, Washington, Ind.

	G	AB	H	2B	3B	HR	HR%	R	RBI	BB	SO	SB	BA	SA	AB	H	G by POS
1954 **CIN N**	94	286	68	7	3	2	0.7	39	25	17	27	7	.238	.304	23	3	3B-67, 1B-3
1955	96	198	50	6	3	5	2.5	31	28	26	24	9	.253	.389	15	4	3B-39, OF-32, 1B-4

	G	AB	H	2B	3B	HR	HR %	R	RBI	BB	SO	SB	BA	SA	Pinch Hit AB	Pinch Hit H	G by POS

Chuck Harmon continued

		G	AB	H	2B	3B	HR	HR%	R	RBI	BB	SO	SB	BA	SA	AB	H	G by POS
1956	2 teams	CIN N (13G – .000)			STL N (20G – .000)													
"	total	33	19	0	0	0	0	0.0	4	0	2	2	1	.000	.000	3	0	OF-17, 1B-4, 3B-1
1957	2 teams	STL N (9G – .333)			PHI N (57G – .256)													
"	total	66	89	23	2	0	0	0.0	16	6	1	4	8	.258	.326	10	3	OF-33, 3B-5, 1B-2
4 yrs.		289	592	141	15	8	7	1.2	90	59	46	57	25	.238	.326	51	10	3B-112, OF-82, 1B-13

Terry Harmon

HARMON, TERRY WALTER   BR TR 6'2"   180 lbs.
B. Apr. 12, 1944, Toledo, Ohio

		G	AB	H	2B	3B	HR	HR%	R	RBI	BB	SO	SB	BA	SA	AB	H	G by POS
1967	PHI N	2	0	0	0	0	0	–	0	0	0	0	0	–	–	0	0	
1969		87	201	48	8	1	0	0.0	25	16	22	31	1	.239	.289	18	4	SS-38, 2B-19, 3B-2
1970		71	129	32	2	4	0	0.0	16	7	12	22	6	.248	.326	9	2	SS-37, 2B-14, 3B-2
1971		79	221	45	4	2	0	0.0	27	12	20	45	3	.204	.240	0	0	2B-58, SS-9, 3B-3, 1B-2
1972		73	218	62	8	2	2	0.9	35	13	29	28	3	.284	.367	8	1	2B-50, SS-15, 3B-5
1973		72	148	31	0	0	0	0.0	17	8	13	14	1	.209	.230	15	2	2B-43, SS-19, 3B-1
1974		27	15	2	0	0	0	0.0	5	0	3	3	0	.133	.133	9	2	SS-7, 2B-5
1975		48	72	13	1	2	0	0.0	14	5	9	13	0	.181	.250	0	0	SS-25, 2B-7, 3B-1
1976		42	61	18	4	1	0	0.0	12	6	3	10	3	.295	.393	7	2	SS-19, 2B-13, 3B-5
1977		46	60	11	1	0	2	3.3	13	5	6	9	0	.183	.300	3	0	2B-28, SS-16, 3B-5
10 yrs.		547	1125	262	31	12	4	0.4	164	72	117	175	17	.233	.292	69	13	2B-237, SS-185, 3B-22, 1B-2

LEAGUE CHAMPIONSHIP SERIES

		G	AB	H	2B	3B	HR	HR%	R	RBI	BB	SO	SB	BA	SA	AB	H	G by POS
1976	PHI N	1	0	0	0	0	0	–	1	0	0	0	0	–	–	0	0	

Brian Harper

HARPER, BRIAN DAVID   BR TR 6'2"   195 lbs.
B. Oct. 16, 1959, Los Angeles, Calif.

		G	AB	H	2B	3B	HR	HR%	R	RBI	BB	SO	SB	BA	SA	AB	H	G by POS
1979	CAL A	1	2	0	0	0	0	0.0	0	0	0	1	0	.000	.000	1	0	DH-1
1981		4	11	3	0	0	0	0.0	1	1	0	0	1	.273	.273	1	0	OF-2, DH-1
1982	PIT N	20	29	8	1	0	2	6.9	4	4	1	4	0	.276	.517	12	5	OF-8
1983		61	131	29	4	1	7	5.3	16	20	2	15	0	.221	.427	27	6	OF-35, 1B-1
1984		48	112	29	4	0	2	1.8	4	11	5	11	0	.259	.348	11	2	OF-37, C-2
5 yrs.		134	285	69	9	1	11	3.9	25	36	8	31	1	.242	.396	52	13	OF-82, DH-2, C-2, 1B-1

George Harper

HARPER, GEORGE WASHINGTON   BL TR 5'8"   167 lbs.
B. June 24, 1892, Arlington, Ky.   D. Aug. 18, 1978, Magnolia, Ark.

		G	AB	H	2B	3B	HR	HR%	R	RBI	BB	SO	SB	BA	SA	AB	H	G by POS
1916	DET A	44	56	9	1	0	0	0.0	4	3	5	8	0	.161	.179	24	4	OF-14
1917		47	117	24	3	0	0	0.0	6	12	11	15	2	.205	.231	16	4	OF-31
1918		69	227	55	5	2	0	0.0	19	16	18	14	3	.242	.282	3	0	OF-64
1922	CIN N	128	430	146	22	8	2	0.5	67	68	35	22	11	.340	.442	14	3	OF-109
1923		61	32	4	2	3	2.4	14	16	11	9	0	.256	.392	28	7	OF-29
1924	2 teams	CIN N (28G – .270)			PHI N (109G – .294)													
"	total	137	485	141	29	6	16	3.3	75	58	51	28	11	.291	.474	2	0	OF-131
1925	PHI N	132	495	173	35	7	18	3.6	86	97	28	32	10	.349	.558	6	3	OF-126
1926		56	194	61	6	5	7	3.6	32	38	16	7	6	.314	.505	1	1	OF-55
1927	NY N	145	483	160	19	6	16	3.3	85	87	84	27	7	.331	.495	3	1	OF-142
1928	2 teams	NY N (19G – .228)			STL N (99G – .305)													
"	total	118	329	96	9	2	19	5.8	52	65	61	19	3	.292	.505	13	4	OF-103
1929	BOS N	136	457	133	25	5	10	2.2	65	68	69	27	5	.291	.433	5	0	OF-130
11 yrs.		1073	3398	1030	158	43	91	2.7	505	528	389	208	58	.303	.455	115	27	OF-934

WORLD SERIES

		G	AB	H	2B	3B	HR	HR%	R	RBI	BB	SO	SB	BA	SA	AB	H	G by POS
1928	STL N	3	9	1	0	0	0	0.0	1	0	2	2	0	.111	.111	0	0	OF-3

Terry Harper

HARPER, TERRY JOE   BR TR 6'1"   195 lbs.
B. Aug. 19, 1955, Douglasville, Ga.

		G	AB	H	2B	3B	HR	HR%	R	RBI	BB	SO	SB	BA	SA	AB	H	G by POS
1980	ATL N	21	54	10	2	1	0	0.0	3	3	6	5	2	.185	.259	3	0	OF-18
1981		40	73	19	1	0	2	2.7	9	8	11	17	5	.260	.356	15	3	OF-27
1982		48	150	43	3	0	2	1.3	16	16	14	28	7	.287	.347	8	1	OF-41
1983		80	201	53	13	1	3	1.5	19	26	20	24	6	.264	.383	18	3	OF-60
1984		40	102	16	3	1	0	0.0	4	8	4	21	4	.157	.206	12	2	OF-29
5 yrs.		229	580	141	22	3	7	1.2	51	61	55	114	24	.243	.328	56	9	OF-175

LEAGUE CHAMPIONSHIP SERIES

		G	AB	H	2B	3B	HR	HR%	R	RBI	BB	SO	SB	BA	SA	AB	H	G by POS
1982	ATL N	1	1	0	0	0	0	0.0	1	0	0	0	0	.000	.000	0	0	OF-1

Tommy Harper

HARPER, TOMMY   BR TR 5'9"   165 lbs.
B. Oct. 14, 1940, Oakgrove, Ill.

		G	AB	H	2B	3B	HR	HR%	R	RBI	BB	SO	SB	BA	SA	AB	H	G by POS
1962	CIN N	6	23	4	0	0	0	0.0	1	1	2	6	1	.174	.174	0	0	3B-6
1963		129	408	106	12	3	10	2.5	67	37	44	72	12	.260	.377	6	2	OF-118, 3B-1
1964		102	317	77	5	2	4	1.3	42	22	39	56	24	.243	.309	10	3	OF-92, 3B-2
1965		159	646	166	28	3	18	2.8	126	64	78	127	35	.257	.393	0	0	OF-159, 3B-2, 2B-1
1966		149	553	154	22	5	5	0.9	85	31	57	85	29	.278	.363	3	1	OF-147
1967		103	365	82	17	3	7	1.9	55	22	43	51	23	.225	.345	1	0	OF-100
1968	CLE A	130	235	51	15	2	6	2.6	26	26	26	56	11	.217	.374	14	4	OF-115, 2B-2
1969	SEA A	148	537	126	10	2	9	1.7	78	41	95	90	73	.235	.311	5	1	3B-59, 2B-59, OF-26
1970	MIL A	154	604	179	35	4	31	5.1	104	82	77	107	38	.296	.522	2	1	3B-128, 2B-22, OF-13
1971		152	585	151	26	3	14	2.4	79	52	65	92	25	.258	.385	4	1	OF-90, 3B-70, 2B-1
1972	BOS A	144	556	141	29	2	14	2.5	92	49	67	104	25	.254	.388	0	0	OF-144
1973		147	566	159	23	3	17	3.0	92	71	61	93	54	.281	.422	0	0	OF-143, DH-1
1974		118	443	105	15	3	5	1.1	66	24	46	65	28	.237	.318	5	1	OF-61, DH-51
1975	2 teams	CAL A (89G – .239)			OAK A (34G – .319)													
"	total	123	354	90	14	1	4	1.1	51	38	43	60	26	.254	.342	7	3	DH-60, 1B-35, OF-18, 3B-2
1976	BAL A	46	77	18	5	0	1	1.3	8	7	10	16	4	.234	.338	10	4	DH-27, OF-1, 1B-1
15 yrs.		1810	6269	1609	256	36	146	2.3	972	567	753	1080	408	.257	.379	67	22	OF-1227, 3B-270, DH-139, 2B-85, 1B-36

LEAGUE CHAMPIONSHIP SERIES

		G	AB	H	2B	3B	HR	HR%	R	RBI	BB	SO	SB	BA	SA	AB	H	G by POS
1975	OAK A	1	0	0	0	0	0	–	0	0	1	0	0	–	–	0	0	

	G	AB	H	2B	3B	HR	HR %	R	RBI	BB	SO	SB	BA	SA	Pinch Hit AB	H	G by POS

Toby Harrah

HARRAH, COLBERT DALE
B. Oct. 26, 1948, Sissonville, W. Va.

BR TR 6' 175 lbs.

	G	AB	H	2B	3B	HR	HR %	R	RBI	BB	SO	SB	BA	SA	AB	H	G by POS
1969 WAS A	8	1	0	0	0	0	0.0	4	0	0	0	0	.000	.000	1	0	SS-1
1971	127	383	88	11	3	2	0.5	45	22	40	48	10	.230	.290	4	1	SS-116, 3B-7
1972 TEX A	116	374	97	14	3	1	0.3	47	31	34	31	16	.259	.321	3	2	SS-106
1973	118	461	120	16	1	10	2.2	64	50	46	49	10	.260	.364	0	0	SS-76, 3B-52
1974	161	573	149	23	2	21	3.7	79	74	50	65	15	.260	.417	0	0	SS-158, 3B-3
1975	151	522	153	24	1	20	3.8	81	93	98	71	23	.293	.458	0	0	SS-133, 3B-28, 2B-21
1976	155	584	152	21	1	15	2.6	64	67	91	59	8	.260	.377	1	1	SS-146, 3B-5, DH-4
1977	159	539	142	25	5	27	5.0	90	87	109	73	27	.263	.479	0	0	3B-159, SS-1
1978	139	450	103	17	3	12	2.7	56	59	83	66	31	.229	.360	2	2	3B-91, SS-49
1979 CLE A	149	527	147	25	1	20	3.8	99	77	89	60	20	.279	.444	1	0	3B-127, SS-33, DH-9
1980	160	561	150	22	4	11	2.0	100	72	98	60	17	.267	.380	1	0	3B-156, DH-3, SS-2
1981	103	361	105	12	4	5	1.4	64	44	57	44	12	.291	.388	1	1	3B-101, SS-3, DH-1
1982	162	602	183	29	4	25	4.2	100	78	84	52	17	.304	.490	1	0	3B-159, 2B-3, SS-2
1983	138	526	140	23	1	9	1.7	81	53	75	49	16	.266	.365	0	0	3B-137, DH-1, 2B-1
1984 NY A	88	253	55	9	4	1	0.4	40	27	42	28	3	.217	.296	11	2	3B-74, 2B-4, OF-1
15 yrs.	1934	6717	1784	271	37	179	2.7	1014	834	996	755	225	.266	.397	27	9	3B-1099, SS-811, 2B-29, DH-18, OF-1

Billy Harrell

HARRELL, WILLIAM
B. July 18, 1928, Norristown, Pa.

BR TR 6'1½" 180 lbs.

	G	AB	H	2B	3B	HR	HR %	R	RBI	BB	SO	SB	BA	SA	AB	H	G by POS
1955 CLE A	13	19	8	0	0	0	0.0	2	1	3	3	1	.421	.421	1	0	SS-11
1957	22	57	15	1	1	1	1.8	6	5	4	7	3	.263	.368	3	1	SS-14, 3B-6, 2B-1
1958	101	229	50	4	0	7	3.1	36	19	15	36	12	.218	.328	9	1	3B-46, SS-45, 2B-7, OF-1
1961 BOS A	37	37	6	2	0	0	0.0	10	1	1	8	1	.162	.216	6	0	3B-10, SS-7, 1B-2
4 yrs.	173	342	79	7	1	8	2.3	54	26	23	54	17	.231	.327	19	2	SS-77, 3B-62, 2B-8, 1B-2, OF-1

John Harrell

HARRELL, JOHN ROBERT
B. Nov. 27, 1947, Long Beach, Calif.

BR TR 6'2" 190 lbs.

	G	AB	H	2B	3B	HR	HR %	R	RBI	BB	SO	SB	BA	SA	AB	H	G by POS
1969 SF N	2	6	3	0	0	0	0.0	0	2	2	1	0	.500	.500	0	0	C-2

Bud Harrelson

HARRELSON, DERREL McKINLEY
B. June 6, 1944, Niles, Calif.

BB TR 5'11" 160 lbs.
BR 1965

	G	AB	H	2B	3B	HR	HR %	R	RBI	BB	SO	SB	BA	SA	AB	H	G by POS
1965 NY N	19	37	4	1	1	0	0.0	3	0	2	11	0	.108	.189	0	0	SS-18
1966	33	99	22	4	0	0	0.0	20	4	13	23	7	.222	.323	2	1	SS-29
1967	151	540	137	16	4	1	0.2	59	28	48	64	12	.254	.304	0	0	SS-149
1968	111	402	88	7	3	0	0.0	38	14	29	68	4	.219	.251	6	0	SS-106
1969	123	395	98	11	6	0	0.0	42	24	54	54	1	.248	.306	0	0	SS-119
1970	157	564	137	18	8	1	0.2	72	42	95	74	23	.243	.309	2	0	SS-156
1971	142	547	138	16	6	0	0.0	55	32	53	59	28	.252	.303	0	0	SS-140
1972	115	418	90	10	4	1	0.2	54	24	58	57	12	.215	.266	0	0	SS-115
1973	106	356	92	12	3	0	0.0	35	20	48	49	5	.258	.309	0	0	SS-103
1974	106	331	75	10	0	1	0.3	48	13	71	39	9	.227	.266	2	0	SS-97
1975	34	73	16	2	0	0	0.0	5	3	12	13	0	.219	.247	2	1	SS-34
1976	118	359	84	12	4	1	0.3	34	26	63	56	9	.234	.298	2	0	SS-117
1977	107	269	48	6	2	1	0.4	25	12	27	28	5	.178	.227	0	0	SS-98
1978 PHI N	71	103	22	1	0	0	0.0	16	9	18	21	5	.214	.223	7	0	2B-43, SS-15
1979	53	71	20	6	0	0	0.0	7	7	13	14	3	.282	.366	0	0	2B-25, SS-17, 3B-9, OF-1
1980 TEX A	87	180	49	6	0	1	0.6	26	9	29	23	4	.272	.322	0	0	SS-87, 2B-2
16 yrs.	1533	4744	1120	136	45	7	0.1	539	267	633	653	127	.236	.288	22	2	SS-1400, 2B-70, 3B-9, OF-1

LEAGUE CHAMPIONSHIP SERIES

	G	AB	H	2B	3B	HR	HR %	R	RBI	BB	SO	SB	BA	SA	AB	H	G by POS
1969 NY N	3	11	2	1	1	0	0.0	2	3	1	2	0	.182	.455	0	0	SS-3
1973	5	18	3	0	0	0	0.0	1	2	1	1	0	.167	.167	0	0	SS-5
2 yrs.	8	29	5	1	1	0	0.0	3	5	2	3	0	.172	.276	0	0	SS-8

WORLD SERIES

	G	AB	H	2B	3B	HR	HR %	R	RBI	BB	SO	SB	BA	SA	AB	H	G by POS
1969 NY N	5	17	3	0	0	0	0.0	1	0	3	4	0	.176	.176	0	0	SS-5
1973	7	24	6	1	0	0	0.0	2	1	5	3	0	.250	.292	0	0	SS-7
2 yrs.	12	41	9	1	0	0	0.0	3	1	8	7	0	.220	.244	0	0	SS-12

Ken Harrelson

HARRELSON, KENNETH SMITH (Hawk)
B. Sept. 4, 1941, Woodruff, S. C.

BR TR 6'2" 190 lbs.

	G	AB	H	2B	3B	HR	HR %	R	RBI	BB	SO	SB	BA	SA	AB	H	G by POS
1963 KC A	79	226	52	10	1	6	2.7	16	23	23	58	1	.230	.363	17	5	1B-34, OF-28
1964	49	139	27	5	0	7	5.0	15	12	13	34	0	.194	.381	12	4	OF-24, 1B-15
1965	150	483	115	17	3	23	4.8	61	66	66	112	9	.238	.429	21	5	1B-125, OF-4
1966 2 teams							KC A (63G – .224)					WAS A (71G – .248)					
" total	134	460	109	13	1	12	2.6	49	50	53	112	13	.237	.348	4	1	1B-128, OF-3
1967 3 teams							WAS A (26G – .203)					KC A (61G – .305)			BOS A (23G – .200)		
" total	110	333	85	15	1	12	3.6	42	54	29	44	10	.255	.414	24	5	1B-69, OF-23
1968 BOS A	150	535	147	17	4	35	6.5	79	109	69	90	2	.275	.518	2	1	OF-132, 1B-19
1969 2 teams							BOS A (10G – .217)					CLE A (149G – .222)					
" total	159	565	125	14	4	30	5.3	89	92	99	102	17	.221	.419	2	0	OF-144, 1B-26
1970 CLE A	17	39	11	1	0	1	2.6	3	1	6	4	0	.282	.385	4	1	1B-13
1971	52	161	32	2	0	5	3.1	20	14	24	21	1	.199	.304	5	2	1B-40, OF-7
9 yrs.	900	2941	703	94	14	131	4.5	374	421	382	577	53	.239	.414	91	24	1B-469, OF-365

WORLD SERIES

	G	AB	H	2B	3B	HR	HR %	R	RBI	BB	SO	SB	BA	SA	AB	H	G by POS
1967 BOS A	4	13	1	0	0	0	0.0	0	1	1	2	0	.077	.077	0	0	OF-4

Andy Harrington

HARRINGTON, ANDREW MATTHEW
B. Feb. 12, 1903, Mountain View, Calif. D. Jan. 29, 1979, Boise, Ida.

BR TR 5'11" 170 lbs.

	G	AB	H	2B	3B	HR	HR %	R	RBI	BB	SO	SB	BA	SA	AB	H	G by POS
1925 DET A	1	1	0	0	0	0	0.0	0	0	0	0	0	.000	.000	1	0	

	G	AB	H	2B	3B	HR	HR %	R	RBI	BB	SO	SB	BA	SA	Pinch Hit AB	Pinch Hit H	G by POS

Jerry Harrington

HARRINGTON, JEREMIAH PETER   BR TR 5'11" 220 lbs.
B. Aug. 12, 1869, Keokuk, Iowa   D. Apr. 16, 1913, Keokuk, Iowa

	G	AB	H	2B	3B	HR	HR %	R	RBI	BB	SO	SB	BA	SA	AB	H	G by POS
1890 CIN N	65	236	58	7	1	1	0.4	25	23	15	29	4	.246	.297	0	0	C-65
1891	92	333	76	10	5	2	0.6	25	41	19	34	4	.228	.306	0	0	C-92, 3B-1
1892	22	61	13	1	0	0	0.0	6	3	6	1	0	.213	.230	0	0	C-22, 1B-1
1893 LOU N	10	36	4	1	0	0	0.0	4	6	3	9	0	.111	.139	0	0	C-10
4 yrs.	189	666	151	19	6	3	0.5	60	73	43	73	8	.227	.287	0	0	C-189, 3B-1, 1B-1

Joe Harrington

HARRINGTON, JOSEPH C.   5'8½" 162 lbs.
Brother of Andy Harrington.
B. Dec. 21, 1869, Fall River, Mass.   D. Sept. 13, 1933, Fall River, Mass.

	G	AB	H	2B	3B	HR	HR %	R	RBI	BB	SO	SB	BA	SA	AB	H	G by POS
1895 BOS N	18	65	18	0	2	2	3.1	21	13	7	5	3	.277	.431	0	0	2B-18
1896	54	198	39	5	3	1	0.5	25	25	19	17	2	.197	.268	0	0	3B-49, SS-4, 2B-1
2 yrs.	72	263	57	5	5	3	1.1	46	38	26	22	5	.217	.308	0	0	3B-49, 2B-19, SS-4

Mike Harrington

HARRINGTON, CHARLES MICHAEL   BR TR 6'4" 205 lbs.
B. Oct. 8, 1934, Hattiesburg, Miss.

	G	AB	H	2B	3B	HR	HR %	R	RBI	BB	SO	SB	BA	SA	AB	H	G by POS
1963 PHI N	1	0	0	0	0	0	–	0	–	0	0	0	–	–	0	0	

Alonzo Harris

HARRIS, ALONZO (Candy)   BL TR 6' 160 lbs.
B. Sept. 17, 1947, Selma, Ala.

	G	AB	H	2B	3B	HR	HR %	R	RBI	BB	SO	SB	BA	SA	AB	H	G by POS
1967 HOU N	6	1	0	0	0	0	0.0	0	0	0	1	0	.000	.000	0	0	

Billy Harris

HARRIS, JAMES WILLIAM   BL TR 6' 175 lbs.
B. Nov. 24, 1943, Hamlet, N. C.

	G	AB	H	2B	3B	HR	HR %	R	RBI	BB	SO	SB	BA	SA	AB	H	G by POS
1968 CLE A	38	94	20	5	1	0	0.0	10	3	8	22	2	.213	.287	5	1	2B-27, 3B-10, SS-1
1969 KC A	5	7	2	1	0	0	0.0	1	0	0	1	0	.286	.429	4	1	2B-1
2 yrs.	43	101	22	6	1	0	0.0	11	3	8	23	2	.218	.297	9	2	2B-28, 3B-10, SS-1

Bob Harris

HARRIS, ROBERT NED   BL TL 5'11" 175 lbs.
B. July 9, 1916, Ames, Iowa   D. Dec. 18, 1976, West Palm Beach, Fla.

	G	AB	H	2B	3B	HR	HR %	R	RBI	BB	SO	SB	BA	SA	AB	H	G by POS
1941 DET A	26	61	13	3	1	1	1.6	11	4	6	13	1	.213	.344	11	1	OF-12
1942	121	398	108	16	10	9	2.3	53	45	49	35	5	.271	.430	15	6	OF-104
1943	114	354	90	14	3	6	1.7	43	32	47	29	6	.254	.362	18	5	OF-96
1946	1	1	0	0	0	0	0.0	0	0	0	0	0	.000	.000	1	0	
4 yrs.	262	814	211	33	14	16	2.0	107	81	102	77	12	.259	.393	45	12	OF-212

Bucky Harris

HARRIS, STANLEY RAYMOND   BR TR 5'9½" 156 lbs.
B. Nov. 8, 1896, Port Jervis, N. Y.   D. Nov. 8, 1977, Bethesda, Md.
Manager 1924-43, 1947-48, 1950-56.
Hall of Fame 1975.

	G	AB	H	2B	3B	HR	HR %	R	RBI	BB	SO	SB	BA	SA	AB	H	G by POS
1919 WAS A	8	28	6	2	0	0	0.0	4	4	1	3	0	.214	.286	0	0	2B-8
1920	137	506	152	26	6	1	0.2	76	68	41	36	16	.300	.381	1	1	2B-135
1921	154	584	169	22	8	0	0.0	82	54	54	39	29	.289	.354	0	0	2B-154
1922	154	602	162	24	8	2	0.3	95	40	52	38	25	.269	.346	0	0	2B-154
1923	145	532	150	21	13	2	0.4	60	70	50	29	23	.282	.382	0	0	2B-144, SS-1
1924	143	544	146	28	9	1	0.2	88	58	56	41	19	.268	.358	0	0	2B-143
1925	144	551	158	30	3	1	0.2	91	66	64	21	14	.287	.358	0	0	2B-144
1926	141	537	152	39	9	1	0.2	94	63	58	41	16	.283	.395	0	0	2B-141
1927	128	475	127	20	3	1	0.2	98	55	66	33	18	.267	.328	0	0	2B-128
1928	99	358	73	11	5	0	0.0	34	28	27	26	5	.204	.263	0	0	2B-96, OF-1, 3B-1
1929 DET A	7	11	1	0	0	0	0.0	3	0	2	1	1	.091	.091	0	0	2B-4, SS-1
1931	4	8	1	0	0	0	0.0	1	0	1	1	0	.125	.250	0	0	2B-3
12 yrs.	1264	4736	1297	224	64	9	0.2	722	506	472	310	166	.274	.354	1	1	2B-1254, SS-2, OF-1, 3B-1
WORLD SERIES																	
1924 WAS A	7	33	11	0	0	2	6.1	5	7	1	4	0	.333	.515	0	0	2B-7
1925	7	23	2	0	0	0	0.0	2	0	1	3	0	.087	.087	0	0	2B-7
2 yrs.	14	56	13	0	0	2	3.6	7	7	2	7	0	.232	.339	0	0	2B-14

Charlie Harris

HARRIS, CHARLES JENKINS   BR TR 5'8" 200 lbs.
B. Oct. 21, 1877, Macon, Ga.   D. Mar. 14, 1963, Gainesville, Fla.

	G	AB	H	2B	3B	HR	HR %	R	RBI	BB	SO	SB	BA	SA	AB	H	G by POS
1899 BAL N	30	68	19	3	0	0	0.0	16	1	3		4	.279	.324	1	1	3B-21, OF-3, 2B-2, SS-1

Dave Harris

HARRIS, DAVID STANLEY (Sheriff)   BR TR 5'11" 195 lbs.
B. July 27, 1900, Summerfield, N. C.   D. Sept. 18, 1973, Atlanta, Ga.

	G	AB	H	2B	3B	HR	HR %	R	RBI	BB	SO	SB	BA	SA	AB	H	G by POS
1925 BOS N	92	340	90	8	7	5	1.5	49	36	27	44	6	.265	.374	1	0	OF-90
1928	7	17	2	1	0	2	0	2	6	0	.118	.176	1	0	OF-6
1930 2 teams		CHI A (33G – .244)				WAS A (73G – .317)											
" total	106	291	86	21	9	9	3.1	56	57	35	57	6	.296	.522	21	9	OF-82, 2B-1
1931 WAS A	77	231	72	14	8	5	2.2	49	50	49	38	7	.312	.506	13	5	OF-60
1932	81	156	51	7	4	6	3.8	26	29	19	34	4	.327	.538	43	14	OF-34
1933	82	177	46	9	2	5	2.8	33	38	25	26	3	.260	.418	24	8	OF-45, 1B-6, 3B-2
1934	97	235	59	14	3	2	0.9	28	37	39	40	2	.251	.362	26	4	OF-64, 3B-5
7 yrs.	542	1447	406	74	33	32	2.2	243	247	196	245	28	.281	.444	129	40	OF-381, 3B-7, 1B-6, 2B-1
WORLD SERIES																	
1933 WAS A	3	2	0	0	0	0	0.0	0	0	2	0	0	.000	.000	1	0	OF-1

Frank Harris

HARRIS, WALTER FRANCIS   BR TR 6'7" 245 lbs.
B. Nov. 2, 1858, Pittsburgh, Pa.   D. Nov. 26, 1939, East Moline, Ill.

	G	AB	H	2B	3B	HR	HR %	R	RBI	BB	SO	SB	BA	SA	AB	H	G by POS
1884 ALT U	24	95	25	2	1	0	0.0	10		3				.263	.305	0	0	1B-17, OF-8

Gail Harris

HARRIS, BOYD GAIL   BL TL 6' 195 lbs.
B. Oct. 15, 1931, Abingdon, Va.

	G	AB	H	2B	3B	HR	HR %	R	RBI	BB	SO	SB	BA	SA	AB	H	G by POS
1955 NY N	79	263	61	9	0	12	4.6	27	36	20	46	0	.232	.403	4	2	1B-75
1956	12	38	5	0	1	1	2.6	2	1	3	10	0	.132	.263	1	0	1B-11

	G	AB	H	2B	3B	HR	HR %	R	RBI	BB	SO	SB	BA	SA	Pinch Hit AB	Pinch Hit H	G by POS

Gail Harris continued

	G	AB	H	2B	3B	HR	HR %	R	RBI	BB	SO	SB	BA	SA	AB	H	G by POS
1957	90	225	54	7	3	9	4.0	28	31	16	28	1	.240	.418	25	2	1B-61
1958 DET A	134	451	123	18	8	20	4.4	63	83	36	60	1	.273	.481	14	5	1B-122
1959	114	349	77	4	3	9	2.6	39	39	29	49	0	.221	.327	22	4	1B-93
1960	8	5	0	0	0	0	0.0	0	0	2	1	0	.000	.000	3	0	1B-5
6 yrs.	437	1331	320	38	15	51	3.8	159	190	106	194	2	.240	.406	69	13	1B-367

Joe Harris

HARRIS, JOSEPH (Moon)
B. May 20, 1891, Coulters, Pa.   D. Dec. 10, 1959, Plum Borough, Pa.
BR TR 5'9"   170 lbs.

	G	AB	H	2B	3B	HR	HR %	R	RBI	BB	SO	SB	BA	SA	AB	H	G by POS
1914 NY A	2	1	0	0	0	0	0.0	0	3	1	0	0	.000	.000	0	0	OF-1, 1B-1
1917 CLE A	112	369	112	22	4	0	0.0	40	65	55	32	11	.304	.385	8	0	1B-95, OF-5, 3B-1
1919	62	184	69	16	1	1	0.5	30	46	33	21	2	.375	.489	12	4	1B-46, SS-4
1922 BOS A	119	408	129	30	9	6	1.5	53	54	30	15	2	.316	.478	15	4	OF-83, 1B-21
1923	142	483	162	28	11	13	2.7	82	76	52	27	7	.335	.520	4	1	OF-132, 1B-9
1924	134	491	148	36	9	3	0.6	82	77	81	25	6	.301	.430	2	0	1B-127, OF-3
1925 2 teams		BOS	A	(8G –	.158)			WAS	A	(100G –	.323)						
" total	108	319	100	21	10	13	4.1	64	61	56	33	5	.313	.564	10	1	1B-63, OF-41
1926 WAS A	92	257	79	13	9	5	1.9	43	55	37	9	2	.307	.486	18	4	1B-36, OF-35
1927 PIT N	129	411	134	27	9	5	1.2	57	73	48	19	0	.326	.472	10	2	1B-116, OF-3
1928 2 teams		PIT	N	(16G –	.391)			BKN	N	(55G –	.236)						
" total	71	112	30	8	2	1	0.9	10	10	18	6	0	.268	.402	42	9	OF-16, 1B-6
10 yrs.	971	3035	963	201	64	47	1.5	461	517	413	188	35	.317	.472	121	25	1B-520, OF-319, SS-4, 3B-1

WORLD SERIES

	G	AB	H	2B	3B	HR	HR %	R	RBI	BB	SO	SB	BA	SA	AB	H	G by POS
1925 WAS A	7	25	11	2	0	3	12.0	5	6	3	4	0	.440	.880	0	0	OF-7
1927 PIT N	4	15	3	0	0	0	0.0	0	1	0	0	0	.200	.200	0	0	1B-4
2 yrs.	11	40	14	2	0	3	7.5	5	7	3	4	0	.350	.625	0	0	OF-7, 1B-4

John Harris

HARRIS, JOHN THOMAS JR.
B. Sept. 13, 1954, Portland, Ore.
BL TL 6'3"   205 lbs.

	G	AB	H	2B	3B	HR	HR %	R	RBI	BB	SO	SB	BA	SA	AB	H	G by POS
1979 CAL A	1	2	0	0	0	0	0.0	0	0	0	0	0	.000	.000	0	0	1B-1
1980	19	41	12	5	0	2	4.9	8	7	7	4	0	.293	.561	7	1	1B-10, OF-3
1981	36	77	19	3	0	3	3.9	5	9	3	11	0	.247	.403	19	3	1B-11, OF-10, DH-1
3 yrs.	56	120	31	8	0	5	4.2	13	16	10	15	0	.258	.450	26	4	1B-22, OF-13, DH-1

Spence Harris

HARRIS, ANTHONY SPENCER
B. Aug. 12, 1900, Duluth, Minn.   D. July 3, 1982, Minneapolis, Minn.
BL TL 5'9"   145 lbs.

	G	AB	H	2B	3B	HR	HR %	R	RBI	BB	SO	SB	BA	SA	AB	H	G by POS
1925 CHI A	56	92	26	2	0	1	1.1	12	13	14	13	1	.283	.337	24	7	OF-27
1926	80	222	56	11	3	2	0.9	36	27	20	15	8	.252	.356	14	2	OF-63
1929 WAS A	6	14	3	1	0	0	0.0	1	1	0	3	1	.214	.286	0	0	OF-4
1930 PHI A	22	49	9	1	0	0	0.0	4	5	5	2	0	.184	.204	7	1	OF-13
4 yrs.	164	377	94	15	3	3	0.8	53	46	39	33	10	.249	.329	45	10	OF-107

Vic Harris

HARRIS, VICTOR LANIER
B. Mar. 27, 1950, Los Angeles, Calif.
BB TR 5'11"   165 lbs.

	G	AB	H	2B	3B	HR	HR %	R	RBI	BB	SO	SB	BA	SA	AB	H	G by POS
1972 TEX A	61	186	26	5	1	0	0.0	8	10	12	39	7	.140	.177	4	0	2B-58, SS-1
1973	152	555	138	14	7	8	1.4	71	44	55	81	13	.249	.342	1	0	OF-113, 3B-25, 2B-18
1974 CHI N	62	200	39	6	3	0	0.0	18	11	29	26	9	.195	.255	4	0	2B-56
1975	51	56	10	0	0	0	0.0	6	5	6	7	0	.179	.179	24	4	OF-11, 3B-7, 2B-5
1976 STL N	97	259	59	12	3	1	0.4	21	19	16	55	1	.228	.309	23	4	2B-37, OF-35, 3B-12, SS-1
1977 SF N	69	165	43	12	0	2	1.2	28	14	19	36	2	.261	.370	25	3	2B-27, SS-11, 3B-9, OF-3
1978	53	100	15	4	0	1	1.0	8	11	11	24	0	.150	.220	16	1	SS-22, 2B-10, OF-6
1980 MIL A	34	89	19	4	1	1	1.1	8	7	12	13	4	.213	.315	1	0	OF-31, 3B-2, 2B-1
8 yrs.	579	1610	349	57	15	13	0.8	168	121	160	281	36	.217	.295	98	12	2B-212, OF-199, 3B-55, SS-35

Ben Harrison

HARRISON, LEO J.
B. Unknown.   Deceased.

	G	AB	H	2B	3B	HR	HR %	R	RBI	BB	SO	SB	BA	SA	AB	H	G by POS
1901 WAS A	1	2	0	0	0	0	0.0	0		1		0	.000	.000	0	0	OF-1

Chuck Harrison

HARRISON, CHARLES WILLIAM
B. Apr. 25, 1941, Abilene, Tex.
BR TR 5'10"   185 lbs.

	G	AB	H	2B	3B	HR	HR %	R	RBI	BB	SO	SB	BA	SA	AB	H	G by POS
1965 HOU N	15	45	9	4	0	1	2.2	2	9	8	9	0	.200	.356	2	0	1B-12
1966	119	434	111	23	2	9	2.1	52	52	37	69	2	.256	.380	5	0	1B-114
1967	70	177	43	7	3	2	1.1	13	26	13	30	0	.243	.350	11	4	1B-59
1969 KC A	75	213	47	5	1	3	1.4	18	18	16	20	1	.221	.296	20	4	1B-55
1971	49	143	31	4	0	2	1.4	9	21	11	19	0	.217	.287	11	1	1B-39
5 yrs.	328	1012	241	43	6	17	1.7	94	126	85	147	3	.238	.343	49	9	1B-279

Tom Harrison

HARRISON, THOMAS JAMES
B. Jan. 18, 1945, Trail, B. C., Canada
BR TR 6'3"   200 lbs.

	G	AB	H	2B	3B	HR	HR %	R	RBI	BB	SO	SB	BA	SA	AB	H	G by POS
1965 KC A	2	0	0	0	0	0	–	0	0	0	0	0	–	–	0	0	P-1

Sam Harshaney

HARSHANEY, SAMUEL
B. May 1, 1910, Madison, Ill.
BR TR 6'   180 lbs.

	G	AB	H	2B	3B	HR	HR %	R	RBI	BB	SO	SB	BA	SA	AB	H	G by POS
1937 STL A	5	11	1	1	0	0	0.0	0	3	0	0	0	.091	.182	0	0	C-4
1938	11	24	7	0	0	0	0.0	2	0	3	2	0	.292	.292	1	1	C-10
1939	42	145	35	2	0	0	0.0	15	15	9	8	0	.241	.255	6	3	C-36
1940	3	1	0	0	0	0	0.0	0	0	1	0	0	.000	.000	1	0	C-2
4 yrs.	61	181	43	3	0	0	0.0	17	15	16	10	0	.238	.254	8	4	C-52

Jack Harshman

HARSHMAN, JOHN ELVIN
B. July 12, 1927, San Diego, Calif.
BL TL 6'2"   178 lbs.

	G	AB	H	2B	3B	HR	HR %	R	RBI	BB	SO	SB	BA	SA	AB	H	G by POS
1948 NY N	5	8	2	0	0	0	0.0	0	1	1	3	0	.250	.250	2	0	1B-3
1950	9	32	4	0	0	2	6.3	3	4	3	6	0	.125	.313	0	0	1B-9

	G	AB	H	2B	3B	HR	HR %	R	RBI	BB	SO	SB	BA	SA	Pinch Hit AB	Pinch Hit H	G by POS

Jack Harshman continued

	G	AB	H	2B	3B	HR	HR%	R	RBI	BB	SO	SB	BA	SA	PH AB	PH H	G by POS
1952	3	2	0	0	0	0	0.0	0	0	0	0	0	.000	.000	1	0	P-2
1954 CHI A	36	56	8	1	0	2	3.6	6	5	12	21	0	.143	.268	0	0	P-35, 1B-1
1955	32	60	11	1	0	2	3.3	6	8	9	17	0	.183	.300	0	0	P-32
1956	36	71	12	1	0	6	8.5	8	19	11	21	0	.169	.437	1	0	P-34
1957	30	45	10	2	0	2	4.4	5	5	10	17	0	.222	.400	0	0	P-30
1958 BAL A	47	82	16	1	0	6	7.3	11	14	17	22	0	.195	.427	9	2	P-34, OF-1
1959 3 teams	BAL A (15G – .200)				BOS A (9G – .143)			CLE A (21G – .206)									
" total	45	51	10	1	0	1	2.0	7	8	9	8	0	.196	.275	9	1	P-35
1960 CLE A	15	17	3	1	0	0	0.0	0	1	0	4	0	.176	.235	0	0	P-15
10 yrs.	258	424	76	8	0	21	5.0	46	65	72	119	0	.179	.347	22	3	P-217, 1B-13, OF-1

Bill Hart

HART, WILLIAM FRANKLIN   6'   160 lbs.
B. July 19, 1865, Louisville, Ky.   D. Sept. 19, 1936, Cincinnati, Ohio

	G	AB	H	2B	3B	HR	HR%	R	RBI	BB	SO	SB	BA	SA	PH AB	PH H	G by POS
1886 PHI AA	22	73	10	1	1	0	0.0	3		3			.137	.178	0	0	P-22
1887	3	13	1	0	0	0	0.0	0		0		0	.077	.077	0	0	P-3
1892 BKN N	37	125	24	3	4	2	1.6	14	17	7	22	4	.192	.328	0	0	P-28, OF-12
1895 PIT N	36	106	25	5	2	0	0.0	8	11	1	12	1	.236	.321	0	0	P-36
1896 STL N	49	161	30	4	5	0	0.0	9	15	3	15	7	.186	.273	0	0	P-42, OF-8
1897	46	156	39	1	2	2	1.3	14	14	1		4	.250	.321	0	0	P-39, OF-6, 1B-1
1898 PIT N	16	50	12	0	1	0	0.0	4	3	1		1	.240	.280	0	0	P-16
1901 CLE A	20	64	14	0	0	0	0.0	7	6	1			.219	.219	0	0	P-20
8 yrs.	229	748	155	14	15	4	0.5	59	65	17	49	17	.207	.282	0	0	P-206, OF-26, 1B-1

Bill Hart

HART, WILLIAM WOODROW   BR TR 6'   175 lbs.
B. Mar. 4, 1913, Wiconisco, Pa.   D. July 29, 1968, Lykins, Pa.

	G	AB	H	2B	3B	HR	HR%	R	RBI	BB	SO	SB	BA	SA	PH AB	PH H	G by POS
1943 BKN N	8	19	3	0	0	0	0.0	1	1	1	2	0	.158	.158	1	0	3B-6, SS-1
1944	29	90	16	4	2	0	0.0	8	4	9	7	1	.178	.267	2	1	SS-25, 3B-2
1945	58	161	37	6	2	3	1.9	27	27	14	21	7	.230	.348	8	1	3B-39, SS-8
3 yrs.	95	270	56	10	4	3	1.1	35	32	24	30	8	.207	.307	11	2	3B-47, SS-34

Hub Hart

HART, JAMES HENRY   BL TR 5'11"   170 lbs.
B. Feb. 2, 1878, Everett, Mass.   D. Oct. 10, 1960, Fort Wayne, Ind.

	G	AB	H	2B	3B	HR	HR%	R	RBI	BB	SO	SB	BA	SA	PH AB	PH H	G by POS
1905 CHI A	10	17	2	0	0	0	0.0	2	4	3		0	.118	.118	4	1	C-6
1906	17	37	6	0	0	0	0.0	1	0	2		0	.162	.162	2	0	C-15
1907	29	70	19	1	0	0	0.0	6	7	5		1	.271	.286	4	0	C-25
3 yrs.	56	124	27	1	0	0	0.0	9	11	10		1	.218	.226	10	1	C-46

Jim Hart

HART, JAMES BURTON   BB 6'3"   200 lbs.
B. June 28, 1870, Brown County, Minn.   D. Jan. 29, 1921, Sacramento, Calif.

	G	AB	H	2B	3B	HR	HR%	R	RBI	BB	SO	SB	BA	SA	PH AB	PH H	G by POS
1901 BAL A	58	206	64	3	5	0	0.0	33	23	20		7	.311	.374	0	0	1B-58

Jim Ray Hart

HART, JAMES RAYMOND   BR TR 5'11"   185 lbs.
B. Oct. 30, 1941, Hookerton, N. C.

	G	AB	H	2B	3B	HR	HR%	R	RBI	BB	SO	SB	BA	SA	PH AB	PH H	G by POS
1963 SF N	7	20	4	1	0	0	0.0	1	2	3	6	0	.200	.250	0	0	3B-7
1964	153	566	162	15	6	31	5.5	71	81	47	94	5	.286	.498	2	0	3B-149, OF-6
1965	160	591	177	30	6	23	3.9	91	96	47	75	6	.299	.487	3	2	3B-144, OF-15
1966	156	578	165	23	4	33	5.7	88	93	48	75	2	.285	.510	4	1	3B-139, OF-17
1967	158	578	167	26	7	29	5.0	98	99	77	100	1	.289	.509	1	0	3B-89, OF-72
1968	136	480	124	14	3	23	4.8	67	78	46	74	3	.258	.444	3	1	3B-72, OF-65
1969	95	236	60	9	0	3	1.3	27	26	28	49	0	.254	.331	23	7	OF-68, 3B-3
1970	76	255	72	12	1	8	3.1	30	37	30	29	0	.282	.431	4	1	3B-56, OF-18
1971	31	39	10	0	0	2	5.1	5	5	6	8	0	.256	.410	23	6	OF-3, 3B-3
1972	24	79	24	5	0	5	6.3	10	8	6	10	0	.304	.557	3	0	3B-20
1973 2 teams	SF N (5G – .000)			NY A (114G – .254)													
" total	119	342	86	13	2	13	3.8	29	53	39	46	0	.251	.415	9	1	DH-106, 1B-1
1974 NY A	10	19	1	0	0	0	0.0	0	1	3	7	0	.053	.053	5	0	DH-4
12 yrs.	1125	3783	1052	148	29	170	4.5	518	578	380	573	17	.278	.467	80	19	3B-682, OF-264, DH-110, 1B-1

LEAGUE CHAMPIONSHIP SERIES

	G	AB	H	2B	3B	HR	HR%	R	RBI	BB	SO	SB	BA	SA	PH AB	PH H	G by POS
1971 SF N	3	5	0	0	0	0	0.0	0	0	0	2	0	.000	.000	1	0	3B-1

Mike Hart

HART, JAMES MICHAEL   BB TR 6'3"   185 lbs.
B. Dec. 20, 1951, Portage, Mich.

	G	AB	H	2B	3B	HR	HR%	R	RBI	BB	SO	SB	BA	SA	PH AB	PH H	G by POS
1980 TEX A	5	4	1	0	0	0	0.0	1	0	1	1	0	.250	.250	0	0	OF-2

Mike Hart

HART, MICHAEL LAWRENCE   BL TL 5'11"   185 lbs.
B. Feb. 12, 1958, Milwaukee, Wis.

	G	AB	H	2B	3B	HR	HR%	R	RBI	BB	SO	SB	BA	SA	PH AB	PH H	G by POS
1984 MIN A	13	29	5	0	0	0	0.0	3	5	1	2	0	.172	.172	3	0	OF-11

Tom Hart

HART, THOMAS HENRY   B. June 15, 1869, Canaan, N. Y.   D. Sept. 17, 1939, Gardner, Mass.

	G	AB	H	2B	3B	HR	HR%	R	RBI	BB	SO	SB	BA	SA	PH AB	PH H	G by POS
1891 WAS AA	8	24	3	0	0	0	0.0	1	2	2	1	1	.125	.125	0	0	C-5, OF-3

Bruce Hartford

HARTFORD, BRUCE DANIEL   BR TR 6'½"   190 lbs.
B. May 14, 1892, Chicago, Ill.   D. May 25, 1975, Los Angeles, Calif.

	G	AB	H	2B	3B	HR	HR%	R	RBI	BB	SO	SB	BA	SA	PH AB	PH H	G by POS
1914 CLE A	8	22	4	1	0	0	0.0	5	0	4	9	0	.182	.227	0	0	SS-8

Chris Hartje

HARTJE, CHRISTIAN HENRY   BR TR 5'11½" 180 lbs.
B. Mar. 25, 1915, San Francisco, Calif.   D. June 26, 1946, Seattle, Wash.

	G	AB	H	2B	3B	HR	HR%	R	RBI	BB	SO	SB	BA	SA	PH AB	PH H	G by POS
1939 BKN N	9	16	5	1	0	0	0.0	2	5	1	0	0	.313	.375	1	1	C-8

	G	AB	H	2B	3B	HR	HR %	R	RBI	BB	SO	SB	BA	SA	Pinch Hit AB	Pinch Hit H	G by POS

Chick Hartley

HARTLEY, WALTER SCOTT   BR TR
B. Aug. 22, 1880, Philadelphia, Pa.   D. July 18, 1948, Philadelphia, Pa.

	G	AB	H	2B	3B	HR	HR %	R	RBI	BB	SO	SB	BA	SA	AB	H	G by POS
1902 NY N	1	4	0	0	0	0	0.0	0	0	0		0	.000	.000	0	0	OF-1

Grover Hartley

HARTLEY, GROVER ALLEN (Slick)   BR TR 5'11"   175 lbs.
B. July 2, 1888, Osgood, Ind.   D. Oct. 19, 1964, Daytona Beach, Fla.

	G	AB	H	2B	3B	HR	HR %	R	RBI	BB	SO	SB	BA	SA	AB	H	G by POS
1911 NY N	11	18	4	2	0	0	0.0	1	1	1		1	.222	.333	0	0	C-10
1912	25	34	8	2	1	0	0.0	3	7	8	4	2	.235	.353	0	0	C-25
1913	23	19	6	0	0	0	0.0	4	0	1	2	4	.316	.316	1	1	C-21, 1B-1
1914 STL F	86	212	61	13	2	1	0.5	24	25	12		4	.288	.382	24	8	C-32, 2B-13, 1B-9, 3B-3, OF-2
1915	120	394	108	21	6	1	0.3	47	50	42		10	.274	.365	6	0	C-113, 1B-1
1916 STL A	89	222	50	8	0	0	0.0	19	12	30	24	4	.225	.261	9	2	C-75
1917	19	13	3	0	0	0	0.0	2		2	1	0	.231	.231	11	2	C-4, SS-1, 3B-1
1924 NY N	4	7	2	1	0	0	0.0	1	1	1	0	1	.286	.429	1	0	C-3
1925	46	95	30	1	1	0	0.0	9	8	8	3	2	.316	.347	1	0	C-37, 1B-8
1926	13	21	1	0	0	0	0.0	0	0	5	0	0	.048	.048	0	0	C-13
1927 BOS A	103	244	67	11	0	1	0.4	23	31	22	14	1	.275	.332	15	2	C-86
1929 CLE A	24	33	9	0	1	0	0.0	2	8	2	1	0	.273	.333	10	3	C-13
1930	1	4	3	0	0	0	0.0	0	1	0	0	0	.750	.750	0	0	C-1
1934 STL A	5	3	1	1	0	0	0.0	0	0	1	0	0	.333	.667	2	1	C-2
14 yrs.	569	1319	353	60	11	3	0.2	135	144	135	50	29	.268	.337	80	19	C-435, 1B-19, 2B-13, 3B-4, OF-2, SS-1

Fred Hartman

HARTMAN, FREDERICK ORRIN (Dutch)   TR
B. Apr. 25, 1868, Pittsburgh, Pa.   D. Nov. 11, 1938, McKeesport, Pa.

	G	AB	H	2B	3B	HR	HR %	R	RBI	BB	SO	SB	BA	SA	AB	H	G by POS
1894 PIT N	49	182	58	4	7	2	1.1	41	20	16	11	12	.319	.451	0	0	3B-49
1897 STL N	124	516	158	21	8	2	0.4	67	67	26		18	.306	.390	0	0	3B-124
1898 NY N	123	475	129	16	11	2	0.4	57	88	25		11	.272	.364	0	0	3B-123
1899	50	174	41	3	5	1	0.6	25	16	12		2	.236	.328	0	0	3B-50
1901 CHI A	120	473	146	23	13	3	0.6	77	89	25		31	.309	.431	1	1	3B-119
1902 STL N	114	416	90	10	3	0	0.0	30	52	14		14	.216	.255	2	1	3B-105, SS-4, 1B-3
6 yrs.	580	2236	622	77	47	10	0.4	297	332	118	11	88	.278	.368	3	2	3B-570, SS-4, 1B-3

J. C. Hartman

HARTMAN, J. C.   BR TR 6'   175 lbs.
B. Apr. 15, 1934, Cottonton, Ala.

	G	AB	H	2B	3B	HR	HR %	R	RBI	BB	SO	SB	BA	SA	AB	H	G by POS
1962 HOU N	51	148	33	5	0	0	0.0	11	5	4	16	1	.223	.257	2	0	SS-48
1963	39	90	11	1	0	0	0.0	2	3	2	13	1	.122	.133	7	2	SS-32
2 yrs.	90	238	44	6	0	0	0.0	13	8	6	29	2	.185	.210	9	2	SS-80

Gabby Hartnett

HARTNETT, CHARLES LEO   BR TR 6'1"   195 lbs.
B. Dec. 20, 1900, Woonsocket, R. I.   D. Dec. 20, 1972, Park Ridge, Ill.
Manager 1938-40.
Hall of Fame 1955.

	G	AB	H	2B	3B	HR	HR %	R	RBI	BB	SO	SB	BA	SA	AB	H	G by POS
1922 CHI N	31	72	14	1	1	0	0.0	4	4	6	8	1	.194	.236	4	1	C-27
1923	85	231	62	12	2	8	3.5	28	39	25	22	4	.268	.442	15	2	C-39, 1B-31
1924	111	354	106	17	7	16	4.5	56	67	39	37	10	.299	.523	4	0	C-105
1925	117	398	115	28	3	24	6.0	61	67	36	77	1	.289	.555	6	2	C-110
1926	93	284	78	25	3	8	2.8	35	41	32	37	0	.275	.468	3	1	C-88
1927	127	449	132	32	5	10	2.2	56	80	44	42	2	.294	.454	2	1	C-125
1928	120	388	117	26	9	14	3.6	61	57	65	32	3	.302	.523	2	0	C-118
1929	25	22	6	2	1	1	4.5	2	9	5	5	1	.273	.591	20	6	C-1
1930	141	508	172	31	3	37	7.3	84	122	55	62	0	.339	.630	3	2	C-136
1931	116	380	107	32	1	8	2.1	53	70	52	48	3	.282	.434	10	0	C-105
1932	121	406	110	25	3	12	3.0	52	52	51	59	0	.271	.436	2	1	C-117, 1B-1
1933	140	490	135	21	4	16	3.3	55	88	37	51	1	.276	.433	0	0	C-140
1934	130	438	131	21	1	22	5.0	58	90	37	46	0	.299	.502	1	0	C-129
1935	116	413	142	32	6	13	3.1	67	91	41	46	1	.344	.545	6	1	C-110
1936	121	424	130	25	6	7	1.7	49	64	30	36	0	.307	.443	7	0	C-114
1937	110	356	126	21	6	12	3.4	47	82	43	19	0	.354	.548	8	2	C-101
1938	88	299	82	19	1	10	3.3	40	59	48	17	1	.274	.445	4	2	C-83
1939	97	306	85	18	2	12	3.9	36	59	37	32	0	.278	.467	8	3	C-86
1940	37	64	17	3	0	1	1.6	3	12	8	7	0	.266	.359	13	5	C-22, 1B-1
1941 NY N	64	150	45	5	0	5	3.3	20	26	12	14	0	.300	.433	26	8	C-34
20 yrs.	1990	6432	1912	396	64	236	3.7	867	1179	703	697	28	.297	.489	144	37	C-1790, 1B-33

WORLD SERIES																	
1929 CHI N	3	3	0	0	0	0	0.0	0	0	0	3	0	.000	.000	3	0	
1932	4	16	5	2	0	1	6.3	2	1	1	3	0	.313	.625	0	0	C-4
1935	6	24	7	0	0	1	4.2	1	2	0	3	0	.292	.417	0	0	C-6
1938	3	11	1	0	1	0	0.0	0	0	0	2	0	.091	.273	0	0	C-3
4 yrs.	16	54	13	2	1	2	3.7	3	3	1	11	0	.241	.426	3	0	C-13

Pat Hartnett

HARTNETT, PATRICK J. (Happy)   6'1"   175 lbs.
B. Oct. 20, 1863, Boston, Mass.   D. Apr. 10, 1935, Boston, Mass.

	G	AB	H	2B	3B	HR	HR %	R	RBI	BB	SO	SB	BA	SA	AB	H	G by POS
1890 STL AA	14	53	10	2	1	0	0.0	6		6		1	.189	.264	0	0	1B-14

Greg Harts

HARTS, GREGORY RUDOLPH   BL TL 6'   168 lbs.
B. Apr. 21, 1950, Atlanta, Ga.

	G	AB	H	2B	3B	HR	HR %	R	RBI	BB	SO	SB	BA	SA	AB	H	G by POS
1973 NY N	3	2	1	0	0	0	0.0	0	0	0	0	0	.500	.500	2	1	

Topsy Hartsel

HARTSEL, TULLY FREDERICK   BL TL 5'5"   155 lbs.
B. June 26, 1874, Polk, Ohio   D. Oct. 14, 1944, Toledo, Ohio

	G	AB	H	2B	3B	HR	HR %	R	RBI	BB	SO	SB	BA	SA	AB	H	G by POS
1898 LOU N	22	71	23	0	0	0	0.0	11	9	11		2	.324	.324	0	0	OF-21
1899	30	75	18	1	1	1	1.3	8	7	11		1	.240	.320	6	2	OF-22
1900 CIN N	18	64	21	2	1	2	3.1	10	5	8		7	.328	.484	0	0	OF-18
1901 CHI N	140	558	187	25	16	7	1.3	111	54	74		41	.335	.475	0	0	OF-140
1902 PHI A	137	545	154	20	12	5	0.9	109	58	87		47	.283	.391	0	0	OF-137

	G	AB	H	2B	3B	HR	HR %	R	RBI	BB	SO	SB	BA	SA	Pinch Hit AB	Pinch Hit H	G by POS

Topsy Hartsel continued

	G	AB	H	2B	3B	HR	HR %	R	RBI	BB	SO	SB	BA	SA	AB	H	G by POS
1903	98	373	116	19	14	5	1.3	65	26	49		13	.311	.477	1	0	OF-96
1904	147	534	135	17	12	2	0.4	79	25	75		19	.253	.341	0	0	OF-147
1905	148	533	147	22	8	0	0.0	87	28	121		36	.276	.347	1	0	OF-147
1906	144	533	136	21	9	1	0.2	96	30	88		31	.255	.334	0	0	OF-143
1907	143	507	142	23	6	3	0.6	93	29	106		20	.280	.367	0	0	OF-143
1908	129	460	112	16	6	4	0.9	73	29	93		15	.243	.330	0	0	OF-129
1909	83	267	72	4	5	0	0.0	30	18	48		3	.270	.322	8	2	OF-74
1910	90	285	63	10	3	0	0.0	45	22	58		11	.221	.277	4	0	OF-83
1911	25	38	9	2	0	0	0.0	8	1	8		0	.237	.289	11	2	OF-10
14 yrs.	1354	4843	1335	182	93	30	0.6	825	341	837		246	.276	.370	31	6	OF-1311

WORLD SERIES																	
1905 PHI A	5	17	5	1	0	0	0.0	1	0	2	1	2	.294	.353	0	0	OF-5
1910	1	5	1	0	0	0	0.0	2	0	0	1	2	.200	.200	0	0	OF-1
2 yrs.	6	22	6	1	0	0	0.0	3	0	2	2	4	.273	.318	0	0	OF-6

Roy Hartsfield

HARTSFIELD, ROY THOMAS
B. Oct. 25, 1925, Chattahoochee, Ga.
Manager 1977-79.

BR TR 5'9" 165 lbs.

	G	AB	H	2B	3B	HR	HR %	R	RBI	BB	SO	SB	BA	SA	AB	H	G by POS
1950 BOS N	107	419	116	15	2	7	1.7	62	24	27	61	7	.277	.372	8	3	2B-96
1951	120	450	122	11	2	6	1.3	63	31	41	73	7	.271	.344	6	0	2B-114
1952	38	107	28	4	3	0	0.0	13	4	5	12	0	.262	.355	1	0	2B-29
3 yrs.	265	976	266	30	7	13	1.3	138	59	73	146	14	.273	.358	15	3	2B-239

Clint Hartung

HARTUNG, CLINTON CLARENCE (Floppy, The Hondo Hurricane)
B. Aug. 10, 1922, Hondo, Tex.

BR TR 6'5" 210 lbs.

	G	AB	H	2B	3B	HR	HR %	R	RBI	BB	SO	SB	BA	SA	AB	H	G by POS
1947 NY N	34	94	29	4	3	4	4.3	13	13	3	21	0	.309	.543	4	1	P-23, OF-7
1948	43	56	10	1	1	0	0.0	5	3	7	24	0	.179	.232	4	2	P-36
1949	38	63	12	0	0	4	6.3	7	7	4	21	0	.190	.381	4	0	P-33
1950	32	43	13	2	1	3	7.0	7	10	1	13	0	.302	.605	9	3	P-20, OF-2, 1B-1
1951	21	44	9	1	0	0	0.0	4	2	1	9	0	.205	.227	7	3	OF-12
1952	28	78	17	2	1	3	3.8	6	8	9	24	0	.218	.385	3	1	OF-24
6 yrs.	196	378	90	10	6	14	3.7	42	43	25	112	0	.238	.407	31	10	P-112, OF-45, 1B-1

WORLD SERIES																	
1951 NY N	2	4	0	0	0	0	0.0	0	0	0	0	0	.000	.000	0	0	OF-2

Roy Hartzell

HARTZELL, ROY ALLEN
B. July 6, 1881, Golden, Colo.   D. Nov. 6, 1961, Golden, Colo.

BL TR 5'8½" 155 lbs.

	G	AB	H	2B	3B	HR	HR %	R	RBI	BB	SO	SB	BA	SA	AB	H	G by POS
1906 STL A	113	404	86	7	0	0	0.0	43	24	19		21	.213	.230	1	0	3B-103, SS-6, 2B-2
1907	60	220	52	3	5	0	0.0	20	13	11		7	.236	.295	3	0	3B-38, 2B-15, OF-2, SS-2
1908	115	422	112	5	6	2	0.5	41	32	19		24	.265	.320	2	0	OF-82, SS-18, 3B-7, 2B-4
1909	152	595	161	12	5	0	0.0	64	32	29		14	.271	.308	1	0	OF-85, SS-65, 2B-1
1910	151	542	118	13	5	2	0.4	52	30	49		18	.218	.271	0	0	3B-89, SS-38, OF-23
1911 NY A	144	527	156	17	11	3	0.6	67	91	63		22	.296	.387	1	0	3B-124, SS-12, OF-8
1912	123	416	113	10	11	1	0.2	50	38	64		20	.272	.356	1	0	3B-56, OF-55, SS-10, 2B-2
1913	141	490	127	18	1	0	0.0	60	38	67	40	26	.259	.300	3	2	2B-81, OF-30, 3B-21, SS-4
1914	137	481	112	15	9	1	0.2	55	32	68	38	22	.233	.308	4	0	OF-128, 2B-5
1915	119	387	97	11	2	3	0.8	39	60	57	37	7	.251	.313	5	3	OF-107, 2B-5, 3B-2
1916	33	64	12	1	0	0	0.0	12	7	9	3	1	.188	.203	5	1	OF-28
11 yrs.	1288	4548	1146	112	55	12	0.3	503	397	455	118	182	.252	.309	26	6	OF-548, 3B-440, SS-155, 2B-115

Luther Harvel

HARVEL, LUTHER RAYMOND (Red)
B. Sept. 30, 1905, Cambria, Ill.

BR TR 5'11" 180 lbs.

	G	AB	H	2B	3B	HR	HR %	R	RBI	BB	SO	SB	BA	SA	AB	H	G by POS
1928 CLE A	40	136	30	6	1	0	0.0	12	12	4	17	1	.221	.279	1	0	OF-39

Erwin Harvey

HARVEY, ERWIN KING (Zaza)
B. Jan. 5, 1879, Saratoga, Calif.   D. June 3, 1954, Santa Monica, Calif.

TL

	G	AB	H	2B	3B	HR	HR %	R	RBI	BB	SO	SB	BA	SA	AB	H	G by POS
1900 CHI N	2	3	0	0	0	0	0.0	0	0	0		0	.000	.000	1	0	P-1
1901 2 teams	CHI A (17G – .250)				CLE A (45G – .353)												
" total	62	210	70	8	6	1	0.5	32	27	11		16	.333	.443	1	0	OF-45, P-16
1902 CLE A	12	46	16	2	0	0	0.0	5	5	3		1	.348	.391	0	0	OF-12
3 yrs.	76	259	86	10	6	1	0.4	37	32	14		17	.332	.429	2	0	OF-57, P-17

Ziggy Hasbrook

HASBROOK, ROBERT LYNDON
B. Nov. 21, 1893, Grundy Center, Iowa   D. Feb. 9, 1976, Garland, Tex.

BR TR 6'1" 180 lbs.

	G	AB	H	2B	3B	HR	HR %	R	RBI	BB	SO	SB	BA	SA	AB	H	G by POS
1916 CHI A	9	8	1	0	0	0	0.0	1	0	1	2	0	.125	.125	1	0	1B-7
1917	2	1	0	0	0	0	0.0	1	0	0	0	0	.000	.000	0	0	2B-1
2 yrs.	11	9	1	0	0	0	0.0	2	0	1	2	0	.111	.111	1	0	1B-7, 2B-1

Don Hasenmayer

HASENMAYER, DONALD IRVIN
B. Apr. 4, 1927, Roslyn, Pa.

BR TR 5'10½" 180 lbs.

	G	AB	H	2B	3B	HR	HR %	R	RBI	BB	SO	SB	BA	SA	AB	H	G by POS
1945 PHI N	5	18	2	0	0	0	0.0	1	1	2	1	0	.111	.111	0	0	2B-1, 3B-1
1946	6	12	1	1	0	0	0.0	0	0	0	2	0	.083	.167	1	0	3B-3
2 yrs.	11	30	3	1	0	0	0.0	1	1	2	3	0	.100	.133	1	0	3B-4, 2B-4

Mickey Haslin

HASLIN, MICHAEL JOSEPH
B. Oct. 31, 1910, Wilkes-Barre, Pa.

BR TR 5'8" 165 lbs.

	G	AB	H	2B	3B	HR	HR %	R	RBI	BB	SO	SB	BA	SA	AB	H	G by POS
1933 PHI N	26	89	21	2	0	0	0.0	9	3	3	5	1	.236	.258	0	0	2B-26
1934	72	166	44	8	2	1	0.6	28	11	16	13	1	.265	.355	16	5	3B-26, 2B-21, SS-4
1935	110	407	108	17	3	3	0.7	53	52	19	25	5	.265	.344	3	1	SS-87, 3B-11, 2B-9

	G	AB	H	2B	3B	HR	HR %	R	RBI	BB	SO	SB	BA	SA	Pinch Hit AB	Pinch Hit H	G by POS

Mickey Haslin continued

	G	AB	H	2B	3B	HR	HR %	R	RBI	BB	SO	SB	BA	SA	AB	H	G by POS
1936 **2 teams**				**PHI N** (16G – .344)				**BOS N** (36G – .279)								
" total	52	168	51	2	3	2	1.2	20	17	8	14	0	.304	.387	10	2	3B-22, 2B-19
1937 **NY N**	27	42	8	1	0	0	0.0	8	5	9	3	1	.190	.214	2	0	SS-9, 3B-4, 2B-4
1938	31	102	33	3	0	3	2.9	13	15	4	4	0	.324	.441	1	0	3B-15, 2B-13
6 yrs.	318	974	265	33	8	9	0.9	125	109	59	64	8	.272	.350	32	8	SS-100, 2B-92, 3B-78

Pete Hasney

HASNEY, PETER JAMES
B. May 26, 1865, England   D. May 24, 1908, Philadelphia, Pa.

	G	AB	H	2B	3B	HR	HR %	R	RBI	BB	SO	SB	BA	SA	AB	H	G by POS
1890 **PHI AA**	2	7	1	0	0	0	0.0	1		1		0	.143	.143	0	0	OF-2

Bill Hassamaer

HASSAMAER, WILLIAM LOUIS (Roaring Bill)   6'   180 lbs.
B. July 26, 1864, St. Louis, Mo.   D. May 29, 1910, St. Louis, Mo.

	G	AB	H	2B	3B	HR	HR %	R	RBI	BB	SO	SB	BA	SA	AB	H	G by POS
1894 **WAS N**	118	494	159	33	17	4	0.8	106	90	41	20	16	.322	.482	1	0	OF-68, 3B-31, 2B-14, SS-4
1895 **2 teams**				**WAS N** (85G – .279)				**LOU N** (23G – .208)								
" total	108	454	120	20	6	1	0.2	49	74	29	17	8	.264	.341	0	0	OF-75, 1B-30, SS-2, 3B-1, 2B-1
1896 **LOU N**	30	106	26	5	0	2	1.9	8	14	14	7	1	.245	.349	1	0	1B-29
3 yrs.	256	1054	305	58	23	7	0.7	163	178	84	44	25	.289	.408	2	0	OF-143, 1B-59, 3B-32, 2B-15, SS-6

Buddy Hassett

HASSETT, JOHN ALOYSIUS   BL TL 5'11"   180 lbs.
B. Sept. 5, 1911, New York, N. Y.

	G	AB	H	2B	3B	HR	HR %	R	RBI	BB	SO	SB	BA	SA	AB	H	G by POS
1936 **BKN N**	156	635	197	29	11	3	0.5	79	82	35	17	5	.310	.405	0	0	1B-156
1937	137	556	169	31	6	1	0.2	71	53	20	19	13	.304	.387	0	0	1B-131, OF-7
1938	115	335	98	11	6	0	0.0	49	40	32	19	3	.293	.382	32	12	OF-71, 1B-8
1939 **BOS N**	147	590	182	15	3	2	0.3	72	60	29	14	13	.308	.354	2	1	1B-127, OF-13
1940	124	458	107	19	4	0	0.0	59	27	25	16	4	.234	.293	12	0	1B-98, OF-13
1941	118	405	120	9	4	1	0.2	59	33	36	15	10	.296	.346	16	5	1B-99
1942 **NY A**	132	538	153	16	6	5	0.9	80	48	32	16	5	.284	.364	0	0	1B-132
7 yrs.	929	3517	1026	130	40	12	0.3	469	343	209	116	53	.292	.362	62	18	1B-751, OF-114
WORLD SERIES																	
1942 **NY A**	3	9	3	1	0	0	0.0	1	2	0	1	0	.333	.444	0	0	1B-3

Ron Hassey

HASSEY, RONALD WILLIAM   BL TR 6'2"   200 lbs.
B. Feb. 27, 1953, Tucson, Ariz.

	G	AB	H	2B	3B	HR	HR %	R	RBI	BB	SO	SB	BA	SA	AB	H	G by POS
1978 **CLE A**	25	74	15	0	0	2	2.7	5	9	5	7	2	.203	.284	1	0	C-24
1979	75	223	64	14	0	4	1.8	20	32	19	19	1	.287	.404	7	2	C-68, 1B-2, DH-1
1980	130	390	124	18	4	8	2.1	43	65	49	51	0	.318	.446	18	6	C-113, DH-7, 1B-3
1981	61	190	44	4	0	1	0.5	8	25	17	11	0	.232	.268	4	2	C-56, 1B-5, DH-1
1982	113	323	81	18	0	5	1.5	33	34	53	32	3	.251	.353	10	3	C-105, DH-2, 1B-2
1983	117	341	92	21	0	6	1.8	48	42	38	35	2	.270	.384	9	3	C-113, DH-1
1984 **2 teams**				**CLE A** (48G – .255)				**CHI N** (19G – .333)								
" total	67	182	49	5	1	2	1.1	16	24	19	32	1	.269	.341	9	2	C-50, 1B-5, DH-1
7 yrs.	588	1723	469	80	5	28	1.6	173	231	200	187	9	.272	.373	58	18	C-529, 1B-17, DH-13

Joe Hassler

HASSLER, JOSEPH FREDERICK   BR TR 6'   165 lbs.
B. Apr. 7, 1905, Fort Smith, Ark.   D. Sept. 4, 1971, Duncan, Okla.

	G	AB	H	2B	3B	HR	HR %	R	RBI	BB	SO	SB	BA	SA	AB	H	G by POS
1928 **PHI A**	28	34	9	2	0	0	0.0	5	3	2	4	0	.265	.324	0	0	SS-28
1929	4	4	0	0	0	0	0.0	1	0	0	2	0	.000	.000	2	0	SS-2
1930 **STL A**	5	8	2	0	0	0	0.0	3	1	0	1	0	.250	.250	0	0	SS-3
3 yrs.	37	46	11	2	0	0	0.0	9	4	2	7	0	.239	.283	2	0	SS-33

Gene Hasson

HASSON, CHARLES EUGENE   BL TL 6'   197 lbs.
B. July 20, 1915, Connellsville, Pa.

	G	AB	H	2B	3B	HR	HR %	R	RBI	BB	SO	SB	BA	SA	AB	H	G by POS
1937 **PHI A**	28	98	30	6	3	3	3.1	12	14	13	14	0	.306	.520	0	0	1B-28
1938	19	69	19	6	2	1	1.4	10	12	12	7	0	.275	.464	0	0	1B-19
2 yrs.	47	167	49	12	5	4	2.4	22	26	25	21	0	.293	.497	0	0	1B-47

Scott Hastings

HASTINGS, WINFIELD SCOTT   BR TR 5'8"   161 lbs.
B. Aug. 10, 1847, Hillsboro, Ohio   D. Aug. 15, 1907, Sawtelle, Calif.
Manager 1872.

	G	AB	H	2B	3B	HR	HR %	R	RBI	BB	SO	SB	BA	SA	AB	H	G by POS
1876 **LOU N**	67	283	73	6	1	0	0.0	36	21	5	11		.258	.286	0	0	OF-65, C-5
1877 **CIN N**	20	71	10	1	0	0	0.0	7	3	3	6		.141	.155	0	0	C-20, OF-1
2 yrs.	87	354	83	7	1	0	0.0	43	24	8	17		.234	.260	0	0	OF-66, C-25

Billy Hatcher

HATCHER, WILLIAM AUGUSTUS   BR TR 5'9"   175 lbs.
B. Oct. 4, 1960, Williams, Ohio

	G	AB	H	2B	3B	HR	HR %	R	RBI	BB	SO	SB	BA	SA	AB	H	G by POS
1984 **CHI N**	8	9	1	0	0	0	0.0	1	0	1	0	2	.111	.111	3	0	OF-4

Mickey Hatcher

HATCHER, MICHAEL VAUGHN, JR.   BR TR 6'2"   200 lbs.
B. Mar. 15, 1955, Cleveland, Ohio

	G	AB	H	2B	3B	HR	HR %	R	RBI	BB	SO	SB	BA	SA	AB	H	G by POS
1979 **LA N**	33	93	25	4	1	1	1.1	9	5	7	12	1	.269	.366	6	1	OF-19, 3B-17
1980	57	84	19	2	0	1	1.2	4	5	2	12	0	.226	.286	21	4	OF-25, 3B-18
1981 **MIN A**	99	377	96	23	2	3	0.8	36	37	15	29	3	.255	.350	2	1	OF-91, 1B-7, 3B-2, DH-1
1982	84	277	69	13	2	3	1.1	23	26	8	27	0	.249	.343	9	3	OF-47, DH-29, 3B-5
1983	105	375	119	15	3	9	2.4	50	47	14	19	2	.317	.445	15	6	OF-56, DH-39, 1B-7, 3B-1
1984	152	576	174	35	5	5	0.9	61	69	37	34	0	.302	.406	2	0	OF-100, DH-37, 1B-17, 3B-1
6 yrs.	530	1782	502	92	13	22	1.2	183	189	83	133	6	.282	.385	55	15	OF-338, DH-106, 3B-44, 1B-31

	G	AB	H	2B	3B	HR	HR %	R	RBI	BB	SO	SB	BA	SA	Pinch Hit AB	Pinch Hit H	G by POS

Fred Hatfield

HATFIELD, FRED JAMES
B. Mar. 18, 1925, Lanett, Ala.
BL TR 6'1" 171 lbs.

	G	AB	H	2B	3B	HR	HR %	R	RBI	BB	SO	SB	BA	SA	PH AB	PH H	G by POS
1950 BOS A	10	12	3	0	0	0	0.0	3	2	3	1	0	.250	.250	1	0	3B-3
1951	80	163	28	4	2	2	1.2	23	14	22	27	1	.172	.258	14	2	3B-49
1952 2 teams		BOS	A (19G – .320)			DET	A (112G – .236)										
" total	131	466	112	13	3	3	0.6	48	28	39	54	2	.240	.300	0	0	3B-124, SS-9
1953 DET A	109	311	79	11	1	3	1.0	41	19	40	34	3	.254	.325	19	7	3B-54, 2B-28, SS-1
1954	81	218	64	12	0	2	0.9	31	25	28	24	4	.294	.376	17	5	2B-54, 3B-15
1955	122	413	96	15	3	8	1.9	51	33	61	49	3	.232	.341	3	0	2B-92, 3B-16, SS-14
1956 2 teams		DET	A (8G – .250)			CHI	A (106G – .262)										
" total	114	333	87	9	1	7	2.1	48	35	39	37	1	.261	.357	12	2	3B-100, 2B-4, SS-3
1957 CHI A	69	114	23	3	0	0	0.0	14	8	15	20	1	.202	.228	23	4	3B-44
1958 2 teams		CLE	A (3G – .125)			CIN	N (3G – .000)										
" total	6	9	1	0	0	0	0.0	0	1	1	1	0	.111	.111	2	0	3B-2
9 yrs.	722	2039	493	67	10	25	1.2	259	165	248	247	15	.242	.321	91	20	3B-407, 2B-178, SS-27

Gil Hatfield

HATFIELD, GILBERT
Brother of John Hatfield.
B. Jan. 27, 1855, Hoboken, N. J. D. May 27, 1921, Hoboken, N. J.
TR 5'9" 168 lbs.

	G	AB	H	2B	3B	HR	HR %	R	RBI	BB	SO	SB	BA	SA	PH AB	PH H	G by POS
1885 BUF N	11	30	4	0	1	0	0.0	1	0	0	11		.133	.200	0	0	3B-8, 2B-3
1887 NY N	2	7	3	1	0	0	0.0	2	3	0	1	0	.429	.571	0	0	3B-2
1888	28	105	19	1	0	0	0.0	7	9	2	18	8	.181	.190	0	0	3B-14, SS-13, OF-1, 2B-1
1889	32	125	23	2	0	1	0.8	21	12	9	15	9	.184	.224	0	0	SS-24, P-6, 3B-2
1890 NY P	71	287	80	13	6	1	0.3	32	37	17	19	12	.279	.376	0	0	3B-42, SS-27, P-3, OF-1
1891 WAS AA	134	500	128	11	8	1	0.2	83	48	50	39	43	.256	.316	0	0	SS-105, 3B-27, P-4, OF-3
1893 BKN N	34	120	35	3	3	2	1.7	24	19	17	5	9	.292	.417	0	0	3B-34
1895 LOU N	5	16	3	0	0	0	0.0	3	1	1	1	0	.188	.188	0	0	3B-3, SS-2
8 yrs.	317	1190	295	31	18	5	0.4	173	129	96	109	81	.248	.317	0	0	SS-171, 3B-132, P-13, OF-5, 2B-4

John Hatfield

HATFIELD, JOHN VAN BUSKIRK
Brother of Gil Hatfield.
B. July 20, 1847, N. J. D. Feb. 20, 1909, Long Island City, N. Y.
5'10" 165 lbs.

	G	AB	H	2B	3B	HR	HR %	R	RBI	BB	SO	SB	BA	SA	PH AB	PH H	G by POS
1876 NY N	1	4	1	0	0	0	0.0	1		0	0		.250	.250	0	0	2B-1

Ray Hathaway

HATHAWAY, RAY WILSON
B. Oct. 13, 1916, Greenville, Ohio
BR TR 6' 165 lbs.

	G	AB	H	2B	3B	HR	HR %	R	RBI	BB	SO	SB	BA	SA	PH AB	PH H	G by POS
1945 BKN N	49	2	0	0	0	0	0.0	0	0	0	1	0	.000	.000	0	0	P-4

Grady Hatton

HATTON, GRADY EDGEBERT
B. Oct. 7, 1922, Beaumont, Tex.
Manager 1966-68.
BL TR 5'8½" 170 lbs.

	G	AB	H	2B	3B	HR	HR %	R	RBI	BB	SO	SB	BA	SA	PH AB	PH H	G by POS
1946 CIN N	116	436	118	18	3	14	3.2	56	69	66	53	6	.271	.422	0	0	3B-116, OF-2
1947	146	524	147	24	8	16	3.1	91	77	81	50	7	.281	.448	7	2	3B-136
1948	133	458	110	17	2	9	2.0	58	44	72	50	7	.240	.345	3	1	3B-123, 2B-3, SS-2, OF-1
1949	137	537	141	38	5	11	2.0	71	69	62	48	4	.263	.413	1	0	3B-136
1950	130	438	114	17	1	11	2.5	67	54	70	39	6	.260	.379	4	1	3B-126, SS-1, 2B-1
1951	96	331	84	9	3	4	1.2	41	37	33	32	4	.254	.335	7	2	3B-87, OF-2
1952	128	433	92	14	1	9	2.1	48	57	66	60	5	.212	.312	7	1	2B-120
1953	83	159	37	3	1	7	4.4	22	22	29	24	0	.233	.396	38	7	2B-35, 1B-10, 3B-5
1954 3 teams		CIN	N (1G – .000)			CHI	A (13G – .167)			BOS	A (99G – .281)						
" total	113	333	90	13	3	5	1.5	43	36	63	28	2	.270	.372	8	0	3B-103, 1B-4, SS-1
1955 BOS A	126	380	93	11	4	4	1.1	48	49	76	28	0	.245	.326	12	1	3B-111, 2B-1
1956 3 teams		BOS	A (5G – .400)			STL	N (44G – .247)			BAL	A (27G – .148)						
" total	76	139	29	2	1	0.7		14	12	26	13	1	.209	.273	35	9	2B-28, 3B-13
1960 CHI N	28	38	13	0	0	0	0.0	3	7	2	5	0	.342	.342	16	3	2B-8
12 yrs.	1312	4206	1068	166	33	91	2.2	562	533	646	430	42	.254	.374	138	27	3B-956, 2B-196, 1B-14, OF-5, SS-4

Art Haugher

HAUGHER, JOHN ARTHUR
B. Nov. 18, 1893, Delhi, Ohio D. Aug. 3, 1944, Redwood City, Calif.
BL TR 5'11" 168 lbs.

	G	AB	H	2B	3B	HR	HR %	R	RBI	BB	SO	SB	BA	SA	PH AB	PH H	G by POS
1912 CLE A	15	18	1	0	0	0	0.0	0	0	1		0	.056	.056	10	0	OF-5

Arnold Hauser

HAUSER, ARNOLD GEORGE (Pee Wee)
B. Sept. 25, 1888, Chicago, Ill. D. May 22, 1966, Aurora, Ill.
BR TR 5'7" 135 lbs.

	G	AB	H	2B	3B	HR	HR %	R	RBI	BB	SO	SB	BA	SA	PH AB	PH H	G by POS
1910 STL N	119	375	77	7	2	2	0.5	37	36	49	39	15	.205	.251	1	0	SS-117, 3B-1
1911	136	515	124	11	8	3	0.6	61	46	26	67	24	.241	.311	0	0	SS-134, 3B-2
1912	133	479	124	14	7	1	0.2	73	42	39	69	26	.259	.324	1	1	SS-132
1913	22	45	13	0	3	0	0.0	3	9	2	2	1	.289	.422	8	4	SS-8, 2B-4
1915 CHI F	23	54	11	1	0	0	0.0	6	4	5		2	.204	.222	0	0	SS-16, 3B-6
5 yrs.	433	1468	349	33	20	6	0.4	180	137	121	177	68	.238	.300	10	5	SS-407, 3B-9, 2B-4

Joe Hauser

HAUSER, JOSEPH JOHN (Unser Choe)
B. Jan. 12, 1899, Milwaukee, Wis.
BL TL 5'10½" 175 lbs.

	G	AB	H	2B	3B	HR	HR %	R	RBI	BB	SO	SB	BA	SA	PH AB	PH H	G by POS
1922 PHI A	111	368	119	21	5	9	2.4	61	43	30	37	1	.323	.481	16	6	1B-94
1923	146	537	165	21	10	16	3.0	93	94	69	52	6	.307	.473	0	0	1B-146
1924	149	562	162	31	8	27	4.8	97	115	56	52	7	.288	.516	1	0	1B-146
1926	91	229	44	10	0	8	3.5	31	36	39	34	1	.192	.341	22	5	1B-65
1928	95	300	78	19	5	16	5.3	61	59	52	45	4	.260	.517	7	0	1B-88
1929 CLE A	37	48	12	1	1	3	6.3	8	9	4	8	0	.250	.500	25	5	1B-8
6 yrs.	629	2044	580	103	29	79	3.9	351	356	250	228	19	.284	.478	71	16	1B-547

George Hausmann

HAUSMANN, GEORGE JOHN
B. Feb. 11, 1916, St. Louis, Mo.
BR TR 5'5" 145 lbs.

	G	AB	H	2B	3B	HR	HR %	R	RBI	BB	SO	SB	BA	SA	PH AB	PH H	G by POS
1944 NY N	131	466	124	20	4	1	0.2	70	30	40	25	3	.266	.333	1	0	2B-122
1945	154	623	174	15	8	2	0.3	98	45	73	46	7	.279	.339	0	0	2B-154
1949	16	47	6	0	1	0	0.0	5	3	7	6	0	.128	.170	1	0	2B-13
3 yrs.	301	1136	304	35	13	3	0.3	173	78	120	77	10	.268	.329	2	0	2B-289

	G	AB	H	2B	3B	HR	HR %	R	RBI	BB	SO	SB	BA	SA	Pinch Hit AB	H	G by POS

Charlie Hautz

HAUTZ, CHARLES M. 5'7" 150 lbs.
B. Feb. 5, 1852, St. Louis, Mo.　D. Jan. 24, 1929, St. Louis, Mo.

	G	AB	H	2B	3B	HR	HR%	R	RBI	BB	SO	SB	BA	SA	AB	H	G by POS
1884 PIT AA	7	24	5	0	0	0	0.0		3				.208	.208	0	0	1B-5, OF-2

Bill Hawes

HAWES, WILLIAM HILDRETH BR TR
B. Nov. 24, 1853, Nashua, N. H.　D. June 16, 1940, Lowell, Mass.

	G	AB	H	2B	3B	HR	HR%	R	RBI	BB	SO	SB	BA	SA	AB	H	G by POS
1879 BOS N	38	155	31	3	3	0	0.0	19	9	2	13		.200	.258	0	0	OF-34, C-5
1884 CIN U	79	349	97	7	4	4	1.1	80		5			.278	.355	0	0	OF-58, 1B-21
2 yrs.	117	504	128	10	7	4	0.8	99	9	7	13		.254	.325	0	0	OF-92, 1B-21, C-5

Roy Hawes

HAWES, ROY LEE BL TL 6'2" 190 lbs.
B. July 5, 1926, Shiloh, Ill.

	G	AB	H	2B	3B	HR	HR%	R	RBI	BB	SO	SB	BA	SA	AB	H	G by POS
1951 WAS A	3	6	1	0	0	0	0.0	0	0	0	1	0	.167	.167	2	1	1B-1

Thorny Hawkes

HAWKES, THORNDIKE PROCTOR 5'8" 135 lbs.
B. Oct. 15, 1852, Danvers, Mass.　D. Feb. 3, 1929, Danvers, Mass.

	G	AB	H	2B	3B	HR	HR%	R	RBI	BB	SO	SB	BA	SA	AB	H	G by POS
1879 TRO N	64	250	52	6	1	0	0.0	24	20	4	14		.208	.240	0	0	2B-64
1884 WAS AA	38	151	42	4	2	0	0.0	16		4			.278	.331	0	0	2B-38, OF-2
2 yrs.	102	401	94	10	3	0	0.0	40	20	8	14		.234	.274	0	0	2B-102, OF-2

Chicken Hawks

HAWKS, NELSON LOUIS BL TL 5'11" 167 lbs.
B. Feb. 3, 1896, San Francisco, Calif.　D. May 26, 1973, San Rafael, Calif.

	G	AB	H	2B	3B	HR	HR%	R	RBI	BB	SO	SB	BA	SA	AB	H	G by POS
1921 NY A	41	73	21	2	3	2	2.7	16	15	5	12	0	.288	.479	23	8	OF-15
1925 PHI N	105	320	103	15	5	5	1.6	52	45	32	33	3	.322	.447	13	5	1B-90
2 yrs.	146	393	124	17	8	7	1.8	68	60	37	45	3	.316	.453	36	13	1B-90, OF-15

Howie Haworth

HAWORTH, HOMER HOWARD (Cully) BR TR 5'10½" 165 lbs.
B. Aug. 27, 1893, Newburg, Ore.　D. Jan. 28, 1953, Troutdale, Ore.

	G	AB	H	2B	3B	HR	HR%	R	RBI	BB	SO	SB	BA	SA	AB	H	G by POS
1915 CLE A	7	7	1	0	0	0	0.0	0	1	2	2	0	.143	.143	1	0	C-5

Jack Hayden

HAYDEN, JOHN FRANCIS 5'9"
B. Oct. 21, 1880, Bryn Mawr, Pa.　D. Aug. 3, 1942, Haverford, Pa.

	G	AB	H	2B	3B	HR	HR%	R	RBI	BB	SO	SB	BA	SA	AB	H	G by POS
1901 PHI A	51	211	56	6	4	0	0.0	35	17	18		4	.265	.332	1	0	OF-50
1906 BOS A	85	322	90	6	4	1	0.3	22	13	17		6	.280	.332	0	0	OF-85
1908 CHI N	11	45	9	2	0	0	0.0	3	2	1		1	.200	.244	0	0	OF-11
3 yrs.	147	578	155	14	8	1	0.2	60	32	36		11	.268	.325	1	0	OF-146

Bill Hayes

HAYES, WILLIAM ERNEST BR TR 6' 195 lbs.
B. Oct. 24, 1957, Cheverly, Md.

	G	AB	H	2B	3B	HR	HR%	R	RBI	BB	SO	SB	BA	SA	AB	H	G by POS
1980 CHI N	4	9	2	1	0	0	0.0	0	0	0	3	0	.222	.333	1	0	C-3
1981	1	0	0	0	0	0	–	0	0	0	0	0	–	–	0	0	C-1
2 yrs.	5	9	2	1	0	0	0.0	0	0	0	3	0	.222	.333	1	0	C-4

Frankie Hayes

HAYES, FRANKLIN WITMAN (Blimp) BR TR 6'1" 190 lbs.
B. Oct. 13, 1914, Jamesburg, N. J.　D. June 22, 1955, Point Pleasant, N. J.

	G	AB	H	2B	3B	HR	HR%	R	RBI	BB	SO	SB	BA	SA	AB	H	G by POS
1933 PHI A	3	5	0	0	0	0	0.0	0	0	0	2	0	.000	.000	0	0	C-3
1934	92	248	56	10	0	6	2.4	24	30	20	44	2	.226	.339	4	3	C-89
1936	144	505	137	25	2	10	2.0	59	67	46	58	3	.271	.388	1	0	C-143
1937	60	188	49	11	1	10	5.3	24	38	29	34	0	.261	.489	4	1	C-56
1938	99	316	92	19	3	11	3.5	56	55	54	51	2	.291	.475	7	3	C-90
1939	124	431	122	28	5	20	4.6	66	83	40	55	4	.283	.510	10	5	C-114
1940	136	465	143	23	4	16	3.4	73	70	61	59	9	.308	.477	2	1	C-134, 1B-2
1941	126	439	123	27	4	12	2.7	66	63	62	56	2	.280	.442	3	0	C-123
1942 2 teams		PHI A (21G – .238)			STL A (56G – .252)												
" total	77	222	55	10	0	2	0.9	22	22	37	47	1	.248	.320	6	2	C-71
1943 STL A	88	250	47	7	0	5	2.0	16	30	30	36	1	.188	.276	9	3	C-76, 1B-1
1944 PHI A	155	581	144	18	6	13	2.2	62	78	57	59	2	.248	.367	0	0	C-155, 1B-1
1945 2 teams		PHI A (32G – .227)			CLE A (119G – .236)												
" total	151	495	116	17	7	9	1.8	51	57	71	66	2	.234	.352	0	0	C-151
1946 2 teams		CLE A (51G – .256)			CHI A (53G – .212)												
" total	104	335	78	18	0	5	1.5	26	34	50	59	2	.233	.331	2	1	C-100
1947 BOS A	5	13	2	0	0	0	0.0	0	1	0	1	0	.154	.154	1	0	C-4
14 yrs.	1364	4493	1164	213	32	119	2.6	545	628	564	627	30	.259	.400	49	19	C-1309, 1B-4

Jackie Hayes

HAYES, JOHN J. TR
B. June 27, 1861, Brooklyn, N. Y.　Deceased.

	G	AB	H	2B	3B	HR	HR%	R	RBI	BB	SO	SB	BA	SA	AB	H	G by POS
1882 WOR N	78	326	88	22	4	4	1.2	27	54	6	26		.270	.399	0	0	OF-58, C-15, 3B-5, SS-1
1883 PIT AA	85	351	92	23	5	3	0.9	41		15			.262	.382	0	0	C-62, OF-18, SS-5, 1B-5, 2B-1
1884 2 teams		PIT AA (33G – .226)			BKN AA (16G – .235)												
" total	49	175	40	9	1	0	0.0	15		7			.229	.291	0	0	C-38, OF-5, 1B-5, 2B-1
1885 BKN AA	42	137	18	3	0	0	0.0	10		5			.131	.153	0	0	C-42
1886 WAS N	26	89	17	3	0	3	3.4	8	9	4	23		.191	.326	0	0	C-14, OF-12, 2B-1
1887 BAL AA	8	28	4	3	0	0	0.0	2		0			.143	.250	0	0	OF-4, 3B-3, C-1
1890 BKN P	12	42	8	0	0	0	0.0	3	5	2	4	0	.190	.190	0	0	OF-6, SS-3, C-2, 2B-1
7 yrs.	300	1148	267	63	10	10	0.9	106	68	39	53	0	.233	.331	0	0	C-174, OF-103, 1B-10, SS-9, 3B-8, 2B-4

Jackie Hayes

HAYES, MINTER CARNEY BR TR 5'10½" 165 lbs.
B. July 19, 1906, Clanton, Ala.　D. Feb. 9, 1983, Birmingham, Ala.

	G	AB	H	2B	3B	HR	HR%	R	RBI	BB	SO	SB	BA	SA	AB	H	G by POS
1927 WAS A	10	29	7	0	0	0	0.0	2	1	2	0	0	.241	.241	0	0	SS-8, 3B-1
1928	60	210	54	7	3	0	0.0	30	22	5	10	3	.257	.319	2	1	2B-41, SS-15, 3B-2
1929	123	424	117	20	3	2	0.5	52	57	24	29	4	.276	.351	2	0	3B-63, 2B-56, SS-5
1930	51	166	47	7	2	1	0.6	25	20	7	8	2	.283	.367	5	1	2B-29, 3B-9, 1B-8
1931	38	108	24	2	1	0	0.0	11	8	6	4	2	.222	.259	7	1	2B-19, 3B-8, SS-3
1932 CHI A	117	475	122	20	5	2	0.4	53	54	30	28	7	.257	.333	0	0	2B-97, SS-10, 3B-10
1933	138	535	138	23	5	2	0.4	65	47	55	36	2	.258	.331	0	0	2B-138

	G	AB	H	2B	3B	HR	HR %	R	RBI	BB	SO	SB	BA	SA	Pinch Hit AB	Pinch Hit H	G by POS

Jackie Hayes continued

	G	AB	H	2B	3B	HR	HR%	R	RBI	BB	SO	SB	BA	SA	AB	H	G by POS
1934	62	226	58	9	1	1	0.4	19	31	23	20	3	.257	.319	0	0	2B-61
1935	89	329	88	14	0	4	1.2	45	45	29	15	3	.267	.347	5	0	2B-85
1936	108	417	130	34	3	5	1.2	53	84	35	25	4	.312	.444	3	0	2B-89, SS-13, 3B-2
1937	143	573	131	27	4	2	0.3	63	79	41	37	1	.229	.300	0	0	2B-143
1938	62	238	78	21	2	1	0.4	40	20	24	6	3	.328	.445	1	0	2B-61
1939	72	269	67	12	3	0	0.0	34	23	27	10	0	.249	.316	2	0	2B-69
1940	18	41	8	0	1	0	0.0	2	1	2	11	0	.195	.244	2	0	2B-15
14 yrs.	1091	4040	1069	196	33	20	0.5	494	493	309	241	34	.265	.344	29	3	2B-903, 3B-95, SS-51, 1B-8

Mike Hayes

HAYES, LAWRENCE MICHAEL
B. 1853, Cleveland, Ohio   Deceased.   5'7½" 170 lbs.

	G	AB	H	2B	3B	HR	HR%	R	RBI	BB	SO	SB	BA	SA	AB	H	G by POS
1876 NY N	5	21	3	0	2	0	0.0	1	2	0	0		.143	.333	0	0	OF-5

Von Hayes

HAYES, VON FRANCIS
B. Aug. 31, 1958, Stockton, Calif.   BL TR 6'5" 185 lbs.

	G	AB	H	2B	3B	HR	HR%	R	RBI	BB	SO	SB	BA	SA	AB	H	G by POS
1981 CLE A	43	109	28	8	2	1	0.9	21	17	14	10	8	.257	.394	9	4	DH-21, OF-13, 3B-5
1982	150	527	132	25	3	14	2.7	65	82	42	63	32	.250	.389	11	2	OF-139, 3B-5, 1B-4
1983 PHI N	124	351	93	9	5	6	1.7	45	32	36	55	20	.265	.370	21	5	OF-103
1984	152	561	164	27	6	16	2.9	85	67	59	84	48	.292	.447	12	2	OF-148
4 yrs.	469	1548	417	69	16	37	2.4	216	198	151	212	108	.269	.406	53	13	OF-403, DH-21, 3B-10, 1B-4

LEAGUE CHAMPIONSHIP SERIES

	G	AB	H	2B	3B	HR	HR%	R	RBI	BB	SO	SB	BA	SA	AB	H	G by POS
1983 PHI N	2	2	0	0	0	0	0.0	0	0	0	0	0	.000	.000	1	0	OF-1

WORLD SERIES

	G	AB	H	2B	3B	HR	HR%	R	RBI	BB	SO	SB	BA	SA	AB	H	G by POS
1983 PHI N	4	3	0	0	0	0	0.0	0	0	0	1	0	.000	.000	3	0	OF-1

Ray Hayworth

HAYWORTH, RAYMOND HALL
Brother of Red Hayworth.
B. Jan. 29, 1904, High Point, N. C.   BR TR 6' 180 lbs.

	G	AB	H	2B	3B	HR	HR%	R	RBI	BB	SO	SB	BA	SA	AB	H	G by POS
1926 DET A	12	11	3	0	0	0	0.0	1	5	1	1	0	.273	.273	3	0	C-8
1929	14	43	11	0	0	0	0.0	5	4	3	8	0	.256	.256	0	0	C-14
1930	77	227	63	15	4	0	0.0	24	22	20	19	0	.278	.379	0	0	C-76
1931	88	273	70	10	3	0	0.0	28	25	19	27	0	.256	.315	0	0	C-88
1932	108	338	99	20	2	2	0.6	41	44	31	22	1	.293	.382	3	1	C-105
1933	134	425	104	14	3	1	0.2	37	45	35	28	0	.245	.299	1	0	C-133
1934	54	167	49	5	2	0	0.0	20	27	16	22	0	.293	.347	1	0	C-54
1935	51	175	54	14	2	0	0.0	22	22	9	14	0	.309	.411	3	1	C-48
1936	81	250	60	10	0	1	0.4	31	30	39	18	0	.240	.292	1	0	C-81
1937	30	78	21	2	0	1	1.3	9	8	14	15	0	.269	.333	1	0	C-28
1938 2 teams		DET	A	(8G –	.211)			BKN	N	(5G –	.000)						
" total	13	23	4	0	0	0	0.0	1	5	4	5	1	.174	.174	2	1	C-10
1939 2 teams		BKN	N	(21G –	.154)			NY	N	(5G –	.231)						
" total	26	39	7	2	0	0	0.0	1	1	4	8	0	.179	.231	2	0	C-23
1942 STL A	1	1	1	0	0	0	0.0	0	0	0	0	0	1.000	1.000	1	1	
1944 BKN N	7	10	0	0	0	0	0.0	1	0	2	1	0	.000	.000	1	0	C-6
1945	2	2	0	0	0	0	0.0	0	0	1	0	0	.000	.000	0	0	C-2
15 yrs.	698	2062	546	92	16	5	0.2	221	238	198	188	2	.265	.332	19	4	C-676

WORLD SERIES

	G	AB	H	2B	3B	HR	HR%	R	RBI	BB	SO	SB	BA	SA	AB	H	G by POS
1934 DET A	1	0	0	0	0	0	–	0	0	0	0	0	–	–	0	0	C-1

Red Hayworth

HAYWORTH, MYRON CLAUDE
Brother of Ray Hayworth.
B. May 14, 1915, High Point, N. C.   BR TR 6'1½" 200 lbs.

	G	AB	H	2B	3B	HR	HR%	R	RBI	BB	SO	SB	BA	SA	AB	H	G by POS
1944 STL A	89	269	60	11	1	1	0.4	20	25	10	13	0	.223	.283	4	1	C-86
1945	56	160	31	4	0	0	0.0	7	17	7	6	0	.194	.219	2	0	C-55
2 yrs.	145	429	91	15	1	1	0.2	27	42	17	19	0	.212	.259	6	1	C-141

WORLD SERIES

	G	AB	H	2B	3B	HR	HR%	R	RBI	BB	SO	SB	BA	SA	AB	H	G by POS
1944 STL A	6	17	2	1	0	0	0.0	1	1	3	1	0	.118	.176	0	0	C-6

Drungo Hazewood

HAZEWOOD, DRUNGO LARUE
B. Sept. 1, 1959, Mobile, Ala.   BR TR 6'3" 210 lbs.

	G	AB	H	2B	3B	HR	HR%	R	RBI	BB	SO	SB	BA	SA	AB	H	G by POS
1980 BAL A	6	5	0	0	0	0	0.0	1	0	0	4	0	.000	.000	1	0	OF-3

Bob Hazle

HAZLE, ROBERT SIDNEY (Hurricane)
B. Dec. 9, 1930, Laurens, S. C.   BL TR 6' 190 lbs.

	G	AB	H	2B	3B	HR	HR%	R	RBI	BB	SO	SB	BA	SA	AB	H	G by POS
1955 CIN N	6	13	3	0	0	0	0.0	0	0	0	3	0	.231	.231	3	1	OF-4
1957 MIL N	41	134	54	12	0	7	5.2	26	27	18	15	1	.403	.649	1	1	OF-40
1958 2 teams		MIL	N	(20G –	.179)			DET	N	(43G –	.241)						
" total	63	114	24	2	0	2	1.8	11	10	14	17	0	.211	.281	29	6	OF-32
3 yrs.	110	261	81	14	0	9	3.4	37	37	32	35	1	.310	.467	33	8	OF-76

WORLD SERIES

	G	AB	H	2B	3B	HR	HR%	R	RBI	BB	SO	SB	BA	SA	AB	H	G by POS
1957 MIL N	4	13	2	0	0	0	0.0	2	0	1	2	0	.154	.154	0	0	OF-4

Doc Hazleton

HAZLETON, WILLARD CARPENTER
B. Aug. 28, 1876, Strafford, Vt.   D. Mar. 17, 1941, Burlington, Vt.

	G	AB	H	2B	3B	HR	HR%	R	RBI	BB	SO	SB	BA	SA	AB	H	G by POS
1902 STL N	7	23	3	0	0	0	0.0	0	2	2		0	.130	.130	0	0	1B-7

Fran Healy

HEALY, FRANCIS XAVIER
B. Sept. 6, 1946, Holyoke, Mass.   BR TR 6'5" 220 lbs.

	G	AB	H	2B	3B	HR	HR%	R	RBI	BB	SO	SB	BA	SA	AB	H	G by POS
1969 KC A	6	10	4	1	0	0	0.0	0	0	0	5	0	.400	.500	2	1	C-5
1971 SF N	47	93	26	3	0	2	2.2	10	11	15	24	1	.280	.376	22	5	C-22
1972	45	99	15	4	0	1	1.0	12	8	13	24	0	.152	.222	1	0	C-43

	G	AB	H	2B	3B	HR	HR %	R	RBI	BB	SO	SB	BA	SA	Pinch Hit AB	Pinch Hit H	G by POS

Fran Healy continued

	G	AB	H	2B	3B	HR	HR %	R	RBI	BB	SO	SB	BA	SA	AB	H	G by POS
1973 KC A	95	279	77	15	2	6	2.2	25	34	31	56	3	.276	.409	1	0	C-92, DH-1
1974	139	445	112	24	2	9	2.0	59	53	62	73	16	.252	.375	5	0	C-138
1975	56	188	48	5	2	2	1.1	16	18	14	19	4	.255	.335	2	2	C-51, DH-4
1976 2 teams	KC	A (8G – .125)			NY	A (46G – .267)											
" total	54	144	35	3	0	0	0.0	12	10	13	27	5	.243	.264	7	3	C-37, DH-2
1977 NY A	27	67	15	5	0	0	0.0	10	7	6	13	1	.224	.299	1	0	C-26
1978	1	1	0	0	0	0	0.0	0	0	0	1	0	.000	.000	0	0	C-1
9 yrs.	470	1326	332	60	6	20	1.5	144	141	154	242	30	.250	.350	41	11	C-415, DH-7

Francis Healy

HEALY, FRANCIS PAUL   BR TR 5'9½" 175 lbs.
B. June 29, 1910, Holyoke, Mass.

	G	AB	H	2B	3B	HR	HR %	R	RBI	BB	SO	SB	BA	SA	AB	H	G by POS
1930 NY N	7	2	0	0	0	0	0.0	2	0	0	0	0	.000	.000	2	0	C-1
1931	6	7	1	0	0	0	0.0	1	0	0	0	0	.143	.143	0	0	C-6
1932	14	32	8	2	0	0	0.0	5	4	2	8	0	.250	.313	2	0	C-11
1934 STL N	15	13	4	1	0	0	0.0	1	1	0	2	0	.308	.385	8	3	C-2, OF-1, 3B-1
4 yrs.	42	54	13	3	0	0	0.0	9	5	2	10	0	.241	.296	12	3	C-20, OF-1, 3B-1

Tom Healy

HEALY, THOMAS FITZGERALD   BR TR 6' 172 lbs.
B. Oct. 30, 1895, Altoona, Pa.   D. Jan. 15, 1979, Cleveland, Ohio

	G	AB	H	2B	3B	HR	HR %	R	RBI	BB	SO	SB	BA	SA	AB	H	G by POS
1915 PHI A	23	77	17	1	0	0	0.0	11	5	6	4	0	.221	.234	5	0	3B-17, SS-1
1916	6	23	6	1	1	0	0.0	4	2	1	2	1	.261	.391	0	0	3B-6
2 yrs.	29	100	23	2	1	0	0.0	15	7	7	6	1	.230	.270	5	0	3B-23, SS-1

Charlie Heard

HEARD, CHARLES H.   6'2" 190 lbs.
B. Jan. 30, 1872, Philadelphia, Pa.   D. Feb. 20, 1945, Philadelphia, Pa.

	G	AB	H	2B	3B	HR	HR %	R	RBI	BB	SO	SB	BA	SA	AB	H	G by POS
1890 PIT N	12	43	8	2	0	0	0.0	2	0	1	15	0	.186	.233	0	0	OF-6, P-6

Ed Hearn

HEARN, EDMUND   TR
B. Sept. 17, 1888, Ventura, Calif.   D. Sept. 8, 1952, Sawtelle, Calif.

	G	AB	H	2B	3B	HR	HR %	R	RBI	BB	SO	SB	BA	SA	AB	H	G by POS
1910 BOS A	2	2	0	0	0	0	0.0	0	0	0		0	.000	.000	0	0	SS-2

Hugh Hearne

HEARNE, HUGH JOSEPH   BR TR 5'8" 182 lbs.
B. Apr. 18, 1874, Troy, N. Y.   D. Sept. 22, 1932, Troy, N. Y.

	G	AB	H	2B	3B	HR	HR %	R	RBI	BB	SO	SB	BA	SA	AB	H	G by POS
1901 BKN N	2	5	2	0	0	0	0.0	1	3	0		0	.400	.400	0	0	C-2
1902	66	231	65	10	0	0	0.0	22	28	16		3	.281	.325	1	0	C-65
1903	26	57	16	3	2	0	0.0	8	4	3		2	.281	.404	6	1	C-17, 1B-2
3 yrs.	94	293	83	13	2	0	0.0	31	35	19		5	.283	.341	7	1	C-84, 1B-2

Bill Heath

HEATH, WILLIAM CHRIS   BL TR 5'8" 175 lbs.
B. Mar. 10, 1939, Yuba City, Calif.

	G	AB	H	2B	3B	HR	HR %	R	RBI	BB	SO	SB	BA	SA	AB	H	G by POS
1965 CHI A	1	1	0	0	0	0	0.0	0	0	0	0	0	.000	.000	1	0	
1966 HOU N	55	123	37	6	0	0	0.0	12	8	9	11	1	.301	.350	16	4	C-37
1967 2 teams	HOU	N (9G – .091)			DET	A (20G – .125)											
" total	29	43	5	0	0	0	0.0	0	4	5	7	0	.116	.116	19	2	C-12
1969 CHI N	27	32	5	0	1	0	0.0	1	1	12	4	0	.156	.219	12	2	C-9
4 yrs.	112	199	47	6	1	0	0.0	13	13	26	22	1	.236	.276	48	8	C-58

Jeff Heath

HEATH, JOHN GEOFFREY   BL TR 5'11½" 200 lbs.
B. Apr. 1, 1915, Ft. William, Ont., Canada   D. Dec. 9, 1975, Seattle, Wash.

	G	AB	H	2B	3B	HR	HR %	R	RBI	BB	SO	SB	BA	SA	AB	H	G by POS
1936 CLE A	12	41	14	3	3	1	2.4	6	8	3	4	1	.341	.634	0	0	OF-12
1937	20	61	14	1	4	0	0.0	8	8	0	9	0	.230	.377	6	1	OF-14
1938	126	502	172	31	18	21	4.2	104	112	33	55	3	.343	.602	3	1	OF-122
1939	121	431	126	31	7	14	3.2	64	69	41	64	8	.292	.494	13	3	OF-108
1940	100	356	78	16	3	14	3.9	55	50	40	62	5	.219	.399	10	1	OF-90
1941	151	585	199	32	20	24	4.1	89	123	50	69	18	.340	.586	0	0	OF-151
1942	147	568	158	37	13	10	1.8	82	76	62	66	9	.278	.442	0	0	OF-146
1943	118	424	116	22	6	18	4.2	58	79	63	58	5	.274	.481	7	1	OF-111
1944	60	151	50	5	2	5	3.3	20	33	18	12	0	.331	.490	22	9	OF-37
1945	102	370	113	16	7	15	4.1	60	61	56	39	3	.305	.508	1	0	OF-101
1946 2 teams	WAS	A (48G – .283)			STL	A (86G – .275)											
" total	134	482	134	32	7	16	3.3	69	84	73	73	0	.278	.473	4	1	OF-130
1947 STL A	141	491	123	20	7	27	5.5	81	85	88	87	2	.251	.485	1	0	OF-140
1948 BOS N	115	364	116	26	5	20	5.5	64	76	51	46	2	.319	.582	9	0	OF-106
1949	36	111	34	7	0	9	8.1	17	23	15	26	0	.306	.613	6	3	OF-31
14 yrs.	1383	4937	1447	279	102	194	3.9	777	887	593	670	56	.293	.509	82	20	OF-1299

Kelly Heath

HEATH, KELLY MARK   BR TR 5'7" 155 lbs.
B. Sept. 4, 1957, Plattsburg, N. Y.

	G	AB	H	2B	3B	HR	HR %	R	RBI	BB	SO	SB	BA	SA	AB	H	G by POS
1982 KC A	1	1	0	0	0	0	0.0	0	0	0	0	0	.000	.000	0	0	2B-1

Mickey Heath

HEATH, MINOR WILSON   BL TL 6' 175 lbs.
B. Oct. 30, 1904, Toledo, Ohio

	G	AB	H	2B	3B	HR	HR %	R	RBI	BB	SO	SB	BA	SA	AB	H	G by POS
1931 CIN N	7	26	7	0	0	0	0.0	2	3	2	5	0	.269	.269	0	0	1B-7
1932	39	134	27	1	3	0	0.0	14	15	20	23	0	.201	.254	0	0	1B-39
2 yrs.	46	160	34	1	3	0	0.0	16	18	22	28	0	.213	.256	0	0	1B-46

Mike Heath

HEATH, MICHAEL THOMAS   BR TR 5'11" 180 lbs.
B. Feb. 5, 1955, Tampa, Fla.

	G	AB	H	2B	3B	HR	HR %	R	RBI	BB	SO	SB	BA	SA	AB	H	G by POS
1978 NY A	33	92	21	3	1	0	0.0	6	8	8	9	0	.228	.283	0	0	C-33
1979 OAK A	74	258	66	8	0	3	1.2	19	27	17	18	1	.256	.322	5	3	OF-46, C-22, 3B-7, DH-3
1980	92	305	74	10	2	1	0.3	27	33	16	28	3	.243	.298	6	1	C-47, DH-31, OF-8
1981	84	301	71	7	1	8	2.7	26	30	13	36	3	.236	.346	4	2	C-78, OF-6
1982	101	318	77	18	4	3	0.9	43	39	27	36	8	.242	.352	2	1	C-90, OF-10, 3B-5
1983	96	345	97	17	0	6	1.7	45	33	18	59	3	.281	.383	3	1	C-80, OF-24, DH-2, 3B-2

	G	AB	H	2B	3B	HR	HR %	R	RBI	BB	SO	SB	BA	SA	Pinch Hit AB	Pinch Hit H	G by POS

Mike Heath continued

	G	AB	H	2B	3B	HR	HR %	R	RBI	BB	SO	SB	BA	SA	PH AB	PH H	G by POS
1984	139	472	118	21	5	13	2.8	48	64	26	72	7	.250	.398	10	1	C-108, OF-45, 3B-2, SS-1
7 yrs.	619	2091	524	84	13	34	1.6	214	234	121	258	25	.251	.352	30	9	C-458, OF-139, DH-36, 3B-16, SS-1

DIVISIONAL PLAYOFF SERIES

	G	AB	H	2B	3B	HR	HR %	R	RBI	BB	SO	SB	BA	SA	PH AB	PH H	G by POS
1981 OAK A	2	8	0	0	0	0	0.0	0	0	0	1	0	.000	.000	0	0	C-2

LEAGUE CHAMPIONSHIP SERIES

	G	AB	H	2B	3B	HR	HR %	R	RBI	BB	SO	SB	BA	SA	PH AB	PH H	G by POS
1981 OAK A	3	6	2	0	0	0	0.0	1	0	0	1	0	.333	.333	0	0	C-2

WORLD SERIES

	G	AB	H	2B	3B	HR	HR %	R	RBI	BB	SO	SB	BA	SA	PH AB	PH H	G by POS
1978 NY A	1	0	0	0	0	0	–	0	0	0	0	0	–	–	0	0	C-1

Tommy Heath

HEATH, THOMAS GEORGE
B. Aug. 18, 1913, Akron, Colo.   D. Feb. 26, 1967, Los Gatos, Calif.
BR TR 5'10½" 185 lbs.

	G	AB	H	2B	3B	HR	HR %	R	RBI	BB	SO	SB	BA	SA	PH AB	PH H	G by POS
1935 STL A	47	93	22	3	0	0	0.0	10	9	20	13	0	.237	.269	10	3	C-37
1937	17	43	10	0	2	1	2.3	4	3	10	3	0	.233	.395	2	1	C-14
1938	70	194	44	13	0	2	1.0	22	22	35	24	0	.227	.325	3	1	C-65
3 yrs.	134	330	76	16	2	3	0.9	36	34	65	40	0	.230	.318	15	5	C-116

Cliff Heathcote

HEATHCOTE, CLIFTON EARL
B. Jan. 24, 1898, Glen Rock, Pa.   D. Jan. 19, 1939, York, Pa.
BL TL 5'10½" 160 lbs.

	G	AB	H	2B	3B	HR	HR %	R	RBI	BB	SO	SB	BA	SA	PH AB	PH H	G by POS
1918 STL N	88	348	90	12	3	4	1.1	37	32	20	40	12	.259	.345	0	0	OF-88
1919	114	401	112	13	4	1	0.2	53	29	20	41	26	.279	.339	9	3	OF-101, 1B-2
1920	133	489	139	18	8	3	0.6	55	56	25	31	21	.284	.372	3	0	OF-129
1921	62	156	38	6	2	0	0.0	18	9	10	9	7	.244	.308	7	1	OF-51
1922 2 teams		STL	N (34G – .245)		CHI	N	(76G – .280)										
" total	110	341	92	13	9	1	0.3	48	48	27	19	5	.270	.370	12	3	OF-92
1923 CHI N	117	393	98	14	3	1	0.3	48	27	25	22	32	.249	.308	2	0	OF-112
1924	113	392	121	19	7	0	0.0	66	30	28	28	26	.309	.393	1	0	OF-111
1925	109	380	100	14	5	5	1.3	57	39	39	26	15	.263	.366	10	1	OF-99
1926	139	510	141	33	3	10	2.0	98	53	58	30	18	.276	.412	3	1	OF-133
1927	83	228	67	12	4	2	0.9	28	25	20	16	6	.294	.408	17	5	OF-57
1928	67	137	39	8	0	3	2.2	26	18	17	12	6	.285	.409	21	5	OF-39
1929	82	224	70	17	0	2	0.9	45	31	25	17	9	.313	.415	22	7	OF-52
1930	70	150	39	10	1	9	6.0	30	18	18	15	4	.260	.520	31	5	OF-35
1931 CIN N	90	252	65	15	6	0	0.0	24	28	32	16	3	.258	.365	25	6	OF-59
1932 2 teams		CIN	N (8G – .000)		PHI	N	(30G – .282)										
" total	38	42	11	2	0	1	2.4	10	5	3	3	0	.262	.381	20	4	1B-7
15 yrs.	1415	4443	1222	206	55	42	0.9	643	448	367	325	190	.275	.375	183	36	OF-1158, 1B-9

WORLD SERIES

	G	AB	H	2B	3B	HR	HR %	R	RBI	BB	SO	SB	BA	SA	PH AB	PH H	G by POS
1929 CHI N	2	1	0	0	0	0	0.0	0	0	0	0	0	.000	.000	1	0	

Richie Hebner

HEBNER, RICHARD JOSEPH
B. Nov. 26, 1947, Brighton, Mass.
BL TR 6'1" 195 lbs.

	G	AB	H	2B	3B	HR	HR %	R	RBI	BB	SO	SB	BA	SA	PH AB	PH H	G by POS
1968 PIT N	2	1	0	0	0	0	0.0	0	0	0	0	0	.000	.000	1	0	
1969	129	459	138	23	4	8	1.7	72	47	53	53	4	.301	.420	4	1	3B-124, 1B-1
1970	120	420	122	24	8	11	2.6	60	46	42	48	2	.290	.464	6	2	3B-117
1971	112	388	105	17	8	17	4.4	50	67	32	68	2	.271	.487	7	2	3B-108
1972	124	427	128	24	4	19	4.4	63	72	52	54	0	.300	.508	5	1	3B-121
1973	144	509	138	28	1	25	4.9	73	74	56	60	0	.271	.477	7	1	3B-139
1974	146	550	160	21	6	18	3.3	97	68	60	53	0	.291	.449	7	1	3B-141
1975	128	472	116	16	4	15	3.2	65	57	43	48	0	.246	.392	3	1	3B-126
1976	132	434	108	21	3	8	1.8	60	51	47	39	1	.249	.366	7	0	3B-126
1977 PHI N	118	397	113	17	4	18	4.5	67	62	61	46	7	.285	.484	10	3	1B-103, 3B-13, 2B-1
1978	137	435	123	22	3	17	3.9	61	71	53	58	4	.283	.464	9	5	1B-117, 3B-19, 2B-1
1979 NY N	136	473	127	25	2	10	2.1	54	79	59	59	3	.268	.393	4	1	3B-134, 1B-6
1980 DET A	104	341	99	10	7	12	3.5	48	82	38	45	0	.290	.466	11	6	1B-61, 3B-32, DH-5
1981	78	226	51	8	2	5	2.2	19	28	27	28	1	.226	.345	11	1	1B-61, DH-11
1982 2 teams		DET	A (68G – .274)		PIT	N	(25G – .300)										
" total	93	249	70	8	0	10	4.0	31	30	30	24	5	.281	.434	17	3	1B-44, OF-21, DH-20, 3B-1
1983 PIT N	78	162	43	4	1	5	3.1	23	26	17	28	8	.265	.395	27	7	3B-40, OF-7, 1B-7
1984 CHI N	44	81	27	3	0	2	2.5	12	8	10	15	1	.333	.444	26	8	3B-14, OF-3, 1B-3
17 yrs.	1825	6024	1668	271	57	200	3.3	855	868	680	726	38	.277	.440	162	43	3B-1255, 1B-403, DH-36, OF-31, 2B-2

LEAGUE CHAMPIONSHIP SERIES

	G	AB	H	2B	3B	HR	HR %	R	RBI	BB	SO	SB	BA	SA	PH AB	PH H	G by POS
1970 PIT N	2	6	4	2	0	0	0.0	0	0	2	1	0	.667	1.000	0	0	3B-2
1971	4	17	5	1	0	2	11.8	3	4	0	4	0	.294	.706	1	0	3B-4
1972	5	16	3	1	0	0	0.0	2	1	1	3	0	.188	.250	0	0	3B-5
1974	4	13	3	0	0	1	7.7	1	4	1	4	0	.231	.462	0	0	3B-4
1975	3	12	4	1	0	0	0.0	2	2	1	1	0	.333	.417	0	0	3B-3
1977 PHI N	4	14	5	2	0	0	0.0	2	0	1	0	1	.357	.500	1	0	1B-3
1978	3	9	1	0	0	0	0.0	0	0	1	0	0	.111	.111	1	0	1B-2
1984 CHI N	1	0	0	0	0	0	0.0	0	0	0	0	0	.000	.000	1	0	
8 yrs.	26	88	25	7	0	3	3.4	10	12	5	14	0	.284	.466	4	0	3B-18, 1B-5

WORLD SERIES

	G	AB	H	2B	3B	HR	HR %	R	RBI	BB	SO	SB	BA	SA	PH AB	PH H	G by POS
1971 PIT N	3	12	2	0	0	1	8.3	2	3	3	3	0	.167	.417	0	0	3B-3

Mike Hechinger

HECHINGER, MICHAEL VINCENT
B. Feb. 14, 1890, Chicago, Ill.   D. Aug. 13, 1967, Chicago, Ill.
BR TR 6' 175 lbs.

	G	AB	H	2B	3B	HR	HR %	R	RBI	BB	SO	SB	BA	SA	PH AB	PH H	G by POS
1912 CHI N	2	3	0	0	0	0	0.0	0	0	2	0	0	.000	.000	0	0	C-2
1913 2 teams		CHI	N (2G – .000)		BKN	N	(9G – .182)										
" total	11	13	2	1	0	0	0.0	1	0	0	2	0	.154	.231	7	1	C-4
2 yrs.	13	16	2	1	0	0	0.0	1	0	2	2	0	.125	.188	7	1	C-6

	G	AB	H	2B	3B	HR	HR %	R	RBI	BB	SO	SB	BA	SA	Pinch Hit AB	Pinch Hit H	G by POS

Guy Hecker

HECKER, GUY JACKSON (Blond Guy)
B. Apr. 3, 1856, Youngville, Pa.   D. Dec. 3, 1938, Wooster, Ohio
Manager 1890.

BR TR 5'10" 190 lbs.

	G	AB	H	2B	3B	HR	HR %	R	RBI	BB	SO	SB	BA	SA	PH AB	PH H	G by POS
1882 LOU AA	78	349	97	14	4	3	0.9	64		5				.278	.367	0	0	1B-66, P-13, OF-2
1883	81	334	90	6	6	1	0.3	59		10				.269	.332	0	0	P-51, OF-23, 1B-10
1884	79	321	95	14	8	4	1.2	53		10				.296	.427	0	0	P-75, OF-5
1885	72	299	81	9	2	2	0.7	48		5				.271	.334	0	0	P-53, 1B-17, OF-3
1886	84	345	118	14	5	4	1.2	76		32				**.342**	.446	0	0	P-49, 1B-22, OF-17
1887	91	370	118	21	6	4	1.1	89		31			48	.319	.441	0	0	1B-43, P-34, OF-16
1888	56	211	53	9	2	0	0.0	32	29	11			20	.251	.313	0	0	P-54, 1B-30
1889	82	327	93	17	5	1	0.3	42	36	18	27	17	.284	.376	0	0	1B-65, P-19, OF-1
1890 PIT N	86	340	77	13	9	0	0.0	43	38	19	17	13	.226	.318	0	0	1B-69, P-14, OF-7
9 yrs.	709	2896	822	117	47	19	0.7	506	102	141	44	98	.284	.376	0	0	P-362, 1B-322, OF-74

Danny Heep

HEEP, DANIEL WILLIAM
B. July 3, 1957, San Antonio, Tex.

BL TL 5'11" 185 lbs.

	G	AB	H	2B	3B	HR	HR %	R	RBI	BB	SO	SB	BA	SA	PH AB	PH H	G by POS
1979 HOU N	14	14	2	0	0	0	0.0	0	2	1	4	0	.143	.143	10	1	OF-2
1980	33	87	24	8	0	0	0.0	6	6	8	9	0	.276	.368	8	2	1B-22
1981	33	96	24	3	0	0	0.0	6	11	10	11	0	.250	.281	9	4	1B-22, OF-1
1982	85	198	47	14	1	4	2.0	16	22	21	31	0	.237	.379	23	6	OF-39, 1B-16
1983 NY N	115	253	64	12	0	8	3.2	30	21	29	40	3	.253	.395	40	11	OF-61, 1B-14
1984	99	199	46	9	2	1	0.5	36	12	27	22	3	.231	.312	38	8	OF-48, 1B-10
6 yrs.	379	847	207	46	3	13	1.5	94	74	96	117	6	.244	.352	128	32	OF-151, 1B-84

LEAGUE CHAMPIONSHIP SERIES

	G	AB	H	2B	3B	HR	HR %	R	RBI	BB	SO	SB	BA	SA	PH AB	PH H	G by POS
1980 HOU N	5	1	0	0	0	0	0.0	0	0	0	0	0	.000	.000	1	0	

Don Heffner

HEFFNER, DONALD HENRY (Jeep)
B. Feb. 8, 1911, Rouzerville, Pa.
Manager 1966.

BR TR 5'10" 155 lbs.

	G	AB	H	2B	3B	HR	HR %	R	RBI	BB	SO	SB	BA	SA	PH AB	PH H	G by POS
1934 NY A	72	241	63	8	3	0	0.0	29	25	25	18	1	.261	.320	2	2	2B-68
1935	10	36	11	3	1	0	0.0	3	8	4	1	0	.306	.444	0	0	2B-10
1936	19	48	11	2	1	0	0.0	7	6	6	5	0	.229	.313	2	1	3B-8, 2B-5, SS-3
1937	60	201	50	6	5	0	0.0	23	21	19	19	1	.249	.328	4	1	2B-38, SS-13, 3B-3, OF-1, 1B-1
1938 STL A	141	473	116	23	3	2	0.4	47	69	65	53	1	.245	.319	0	0	2B-141
1939	110	375	100	10	2	1	0.3	45	35	48	39	1	.267	.312	4	2	SS-73, 2B-32
1940	126	487	115	23	2	3	0.6	52	53	39	37	5	.236	.310	1	0	2B-125
1941	110	399	93	14	2	0	0.0	48	17	38	27	5	.233	.278	6	1	2B-105
1942	19	36	6	2	0	0	0.0	2	3	1	4	1	.167	.222	7	2	2B-6, 1B-4
1943 2 teams	STL A (18G – .121)			PHI A (52G – .208)													
" total	70	211	41	7	0	0	0.0	19	10	20	14	3	.194	.227	6	1	2B-60, 1B-2
1944 DET A	6	19	4	0	0	0	0.0	0	1	5	1	0	.211	.263	1	0	2B-5
11 yrs.	743	2526	610	99	19	6	0.2	275	248	270	218	18	.241	.303	33	10	2B-595, SS-89, 3B-11, 1B-7, OF-1

Jim Hegan

HEGAN, JAMES EDWARD
Father of Mike Hegan.
B. Aug. 3, 1920, Lynn, Mass.   D. June 17, 1984, Swampscott, Mass.

BR TR 6'2" 195 lbs.

	G	AB	H	2B	3B	HR	HR %	R	RBI	BB	SO	SB	BA	SA	PH AB	PH H	G by POS
1941 CLE A	16	47	15	2	0	1	2.1	4	5	4	7	0	.319	.426	0	0	C-16
1942	68	170	33	5	0	0	0.0	10	11	11	31	1	.194	.224	2	1	C-66
1946	88	271	64	11	5	0	0.0	29	17	17	44	1	.236	.314	0	0	C-87
1947	135	378	94	14	5	4	1.1	38	42	41	49	3	.249	.344	1	0	C-133
1948	144	472	117	21	6	14	3.0	60	61	48	74	6	.248	.407	3	0	C-142
1949	152	468	105	19	5	8	1.7	54	55	49	89	1	.224	.338	0	0	C-152
1950	131	415	91	16	5	14	3.4	53	58	42	52	1	.219	.383	0	0	C-129
1951	133	416	99	17	5	6	1.4	60	43	38	72	0	.238	.346	2	0	C-129
1952	112	333	75	17	2	4	1.2	39	41	29	47	0	.225	.324	3	0	C-107
1953	112	299	65	10	1	9	3.0	30	37	25	41	1	.217	.348	0	0	C-106
1954	139	423	99	12	7	11	2.6	56	40	34	48	0	.234	.374	2	0	C-137
1955	116	304	67	5	2	9	3.0	30	40	34	33	0	.220	.339	2	0	C-111
1956	122	315	70	15	2	6	1.9	42	34	49	54	1	.222	.340	3	1	C-118
1957	58	148	32	7	0	4	2.7	14	15	16	23	0	.216	.345	0	0	C-58
1958 2 teams	DET A (45G – .192)			PHI N (25G – .220)													
" total	70	189	38	12	0	1	0.5	19	13	14	48	0	.201	.280	0	0	C-70
1959 2 teams	PHI N (25G – .196)			SF N (21G – .133)													
" total	46	81	14	2	0	0	0.0	1	8	4	20	0	.173	.198	0	0	C-46
1960 CHI N	24	43	9	2	1	1	2.3	4	5	1	10	0	.209	.372	2	0	C-22
17 yrs.	1666	4772	1087	187	46	92	1.9	550	525	456	742	15	.228	.344	20	2	C-1629

WORLD SERIES

	G	AB	H	2B	3B	HR	HR %	R	RBI	BB	SO	SB	BA	SA	PH AB	PH H	G by POS
1948 CLE A	6	19	4	0	0	1	5.3	2	5	1	4	1	.211	.368	0	0	C-6
1954	4	13	2	1	0	0	0.0	1	0	1	1	0	.154	.231	0	0	C-4
2 yrs.	10	32	6	1	0	1	3.1	3	5	2	5	1	.188	.313	0	0	C-10

Mike Hegan

HEGAN, JAMES MICHAEL
Son of Jim Hegan.
B. July 21, 1942, Cleveland, Ohio

BL TL 6'1" 188 lbs.

	G	AB	H	2B	3B	HR	HR %	R	RBI	BB	SO	SB	BA	SA	PH AB	PH H	G by POS
1964 NY A	5	5	0	0	0	0	0.0	0	0	1	2	0	.000	.000	1	0	1B-2
1966	13	39	8	0	1	0	0.0	7	2	7	11	1	.205	.256	0	0	1B-13
1967	68	118	16	4	1	1	0.8	12	3	20	40	7	.136	.212	5	2	1B-54, OF-10
1969 SEA A	95	267	78	9	6	8	3.0	54	37	62	61	6	.292	.461	8	2	OF-64, 1B-19
1970 MIL A	148	476	116	21	2	11	2.3	70	52	67	116	9	.244	.366	14	5	1B-139, OF-8
1971 2 teams	MIL A (46G – .221)			OAK A (65G – .236)													
" total	111	177	40	7	1	4	2.3	24	14	31	32	2	.226	.345	22	8	1B-92, OF-2
1972 OAK A	98	79	26	3	1	1	1.3	13	5	7	20	1	.329	.430	31	7	1B-64, OF-3
1973 2 teams	OAK A (75G – .183)			NY A (37G – .275)													
" total	112	202	49	5	2	7	3.5	20	19	12	51	0	.243	.391	20	2	1B-93, DH-3, OF-3

	G	AB	H	2B	3B	HR	HR%	R	RBI	BB	SO	SB	BA	SA	Pinch Hit AB	Pinch Hit H	G by POS

Mike Hegan continued

		G	AB	H	2B	3B	HR	HR%	R	RBI	BB	SO	SB	BA	SA	PH AB	PH H	G by POS
1974	2 teams	NY	A (18G – .226)		MIL	A	(89G – .237)											
"	total	107	243	57	9	1	9	3.7	24	41	38	43	1	.235	.391	18	4	DH-37, 1B-34, OF-17
1975	MIL A	93	203	51	11	0	5	2.5	19	22	31	42	1	.251	.379	18	4	OF-42, 1B-27, DH-5
1976		80	218	54	4	3	5	2.3	30	31	25	54	0	.248	.362	10	1	DH-40, OF-20, 1B-10
1977		35	53	9	0	0	2	3.8	8	3	10	17	0	.170	.283	16	1	OF-8, DH-7, 1B-6
12 yrs.		965	2080	504	73	18	53	2.5	281	229	311	489	28	.242	.371	163	36	1B-553, OF-177, DH-92

LEAGUE CHAMPIONSHIP SERIES

		G	AB	H	2B	3B	HR	HR%	R	RBI	BB	SO	SB	BA	SA	PH AB	PH H	G by POS
1971	OAK A	1	1	0	0	0	0	0.0	0	0	0	1	0	.000	.000	1	0	
1972		3	1	0	0	0	0	0.0	1	0	0	0	0	.000	.000	1	0	1B-1
2 yrs.		4	2	0	0	0	0	0.0	1	0	0	1	0	.000	.000	2	0	1B-1

WORLD SERIES

		G	AB	H	2B	3B	HR	HR%	R	RBI	BB	SO	SB	BA	SA	PH AB	PH H	G by POS
1964	NY A	3	1	0	0	0	0	0.0	1	0	1	1	0	.000	.000	1	0	
1972	OAK A	6	5	1	0	0	0	0.0	0	0	0	2	0	.200	.200	1	0	1B-5
2 yrs.		9	6	1	0	0	0	0.0	1	0	1	3	0	.167	.167	2	0	1B-5

Jack Heidemann

HEIDEMANN, JACK SEALE
B. July 11, 1949, Brenham, Tex.   BR TR 6'   175 lbs.

		G	AB	H	2B	3B	HR	HR%	R	RBI	BB	SO	SB	BA	SA	PH AB	PH H	G by POS
1969	CLE A	3	3	0	0	0	0	0.0	0	0	0	2	0	.000	.000	0	0	SS-3
1970		133	445	94	14	2	6	1.3	44	37	34	88	2	.211	.292	1	0	SS-132
1971		81	240	50	7	0	0	0.0	16	9	12	46	1	.208	.238	0	0	SS-81
1972		10	20	3	0	0	0	0.0	0	0	2	3	0	.150	.150	0	0	SS-10
1974	2 teams	CLE	A (12G – .091)		STL	N	(47G – .271)											
"	total	59	81	20	1	0	0	0.0	10	3	5	12	0	.247	.259	5	0	SS-49, 3B-7, 2B-1, 1B-1
1975	NY N	61	145	31	4	2	1	0.7	12	16	17	28	1	.214	.290	18	1	SS-44, 3B-4, 2B-1
1976	2 teams	NY	N (5G – .083)		MIL	A	(69G – .219)											
"	total	74	158	33	1	0	2	1.3	11	10	7	24	1	.209	.253	6	0	3B-40, 2B-25, SS-3, DH-1
1977	MIL A	5	1	0	0	0	0	0.0	1	0	1	0	0	.000	.000	1	0	DH-3, 2B-1
8 yrs.		426	1093	231	27	4	9	0.8	94	75	78	203	5	.211	.268	31	1	SS-322, 3B-51, 2B-28, DH-4, 1B-1

Emmet Heidrick

HEIDRICK, R. EMMET (Snags)
B. July 9, 1876, Queenstown, Pa.   D. Jan. 20, 1916, Clarion, Pa.   BL TR 6'   185 lbs.

		G	AB	H	2B	3B	HR	HR%	R	RBI	BB	SO	SB	BA	SA	PH AB	PH H	G by POS
1898	CLE N	19	76	23	2	2	0	0.0	10	8	3			.303	.382	0	0	OF-19
1899	STL N	146	591	194	21	14	2	0.3	109	82	34		55	.328	.421	1	1	OF-145
1900		85	339	102	6	8	2	0.6	51	45	18		22	.301	.383	2	0	OF-83
1901		118	502	170	24	12	6	1.2	94	67	21		32	.339	.470	0	0	OF-118
1902	STL A	110	447	129	19	10	3	0.7	75	56	34		17	.289	.396	0	0	OF-109, SS-1, 3B-1, P-1
1903		120	461	129	20	15	1	0.2	55	42	19		19	.280	.395	1	0	OF-119, C-1
1904		133	538	147	14	10	1	0.2	66	36	16		35	.273	.342	3	0	OF-130
1908		26	93	20	2	2	1	1.1	8	6	1		3	.215	.312	1	0	OF-25
8 yrs.		757	3047	914	108	73	16	0.5	468	342	146		186	.300	.399	8	1	OF-748, SS-1, 3B-1, C-1, P-1

Chink Heileman

HEILEMAN, JOHN GEORGE
B. Aug. 10, 1872, Cincinnati, Ohio   D. July 19, 1940, Cincinnati, Ohio   BR TR 5'8"   155 lbs.

		G	AB	H	2B	3B	HR	HR%	R	RBI	BB	SO	SB	BA	SA	PH AB	PH H	G by POS
1901	CIN N	5	15	2	1	0	0	0.0	1	1	0		2	.133	.200	0	0	3B-4, 2B-1

Harry Heilmann

HEILMANN, HARRY EDWIN (Slug)
B. Aug. 3, 1894, San Francisco, Calif.   D. July 9, 1951, Southfield, Mich.   BR TR 6'1"   195 lbs.
Hall of Fame 1952.

		G	AB	H	2B	3B	HR	HR%	R	RBI	BB	SO	SB	BA	SA	PH AB	PH H	G by POS
1914	DET A	67	182	41	8	1	2	1.1	25	22	22	29	1	.225	.313	11	3	OF-29, 1B-16, 2B-6
1916		136	451	127	30	11	2	0.4	57	76	42	40	9	.282	.410	16	5	OF-77, 1B-30, 2B-9
1917		150	556	156	22	11	5	0.9	57	86	41	54	11	.281	.387	0	0	OF-123, 1B-27
1918		79	286	79	10	6	5	1.7	34	44	35	10	13	.276	.406	1	1	OF-40, 1B-37, 2B-2
1919		140	537	172	30	15	8	1.5	74	95	37	41	7	.320	.477	0	0	1B-140
1920		145	543	168	28	5	9	1.7	66	89	39	32	3	.309	.429	1	0	1B-122, OF-21
1921		149	602	237	43	14	19	3.2	114	139	53	37	2	.394	.606	1	0	OF-143, 1B-4
1922		118	455	162	27	10	21	4.6	92	92	58	28	8	.356	.598	0	0	OF-115, 1B-5
1923		144	524	211	44	11	18	3.4	121	115	74	40	8	.403	.632	1	0	OF-130, 1B-12
1924		153	570	197	45	16	10	1.8	107	113	78	41	13	.346	.533	2	0	OF-147, 1B-4
1925		150	573	225	40	11	13	2.3	97	133	67	27	6	.393	.569	2	1	OF-148
1926		141	502	184	41	8	9	1.8	90	103	67	19	6	.367	.534	6	1	OF-134
1927		141	505	201	50	9	14	2.8	106	120	72	16	11	.398	.616	5	1	OF-135
1928		151	558	183	38	10	14	2.5	83	107	57	45	7	.328	.507	1	0	OF-126, 1B-25
1929		125	453	156	41	7	15	3.3	86	120	50	39	5	.344	.565	7	1	OF-113, 1B-1
1930	CIN N	142	459	153	43	6	19	4.1	79	91	64	50	2	.333	.577	12	5	OF-106, 1B-19
1932		15	31	8	2	0	0	0.0	3	6	2	0	0	.258	.323	9	3	1B-6
17 yrs.		2146	7787	2660	542	151	183	2.4	1291	1551	856	550	112	.342	.520	75	23	OF-1587, 1B-448, 2B-17

Val Heim

HEIM, VAL RAYMOND
B. Nov. 4, 1920, Plymouth, Wis.   BL TR 5'11"   170 lbs.

		G	AB	H	2B	3B	HR	HR%	R	RBI	BB	SO	SB	BA	SA	PH AB	PH H	G by POS
1942	CHI A	13	45	9	1	1	0	0.0	6	7	5	3	1	.200	.267	1	0	OF-12

Fred Heimach

HEIMACH, FRED AMOS (Lefty)
B. Jan. 27, 1901, Camden, N. J.   D. June 1, 1973, Fort Myers, Fla.   BL TL 6'   175 lbs.

		G	AB	H	2B	3B	HR	HR%	R	RBI	BB	SO	SB	BA	SA	PH AB	PH H	G by POS
1920	PHI A	1	1	0	0	0	0	0.0	0	0	0	0	0	.000	.000	0	0	P-1
1921		1	4	1	0	0	0	0.0	0	1	0	1	0	.250	.250	0	0	P-1
1922		37	60	15	3	1	0	0.0	6	7	5	12	1	.250	.333	0	0	P-37
1923		63	118	30	4	1	1	0.8	14	11	4	18	0	.254	.331	12	4	P-40, 1B-6
1924		58	90	29	3	2	0	0.0	14	12	3	8	1	.322	.400	16	7	P-40
1925		15	6	1	0	0	0	0.0	0	2	0	2	0	.167	.167	1	0	P-10
1926	2 teams	PHI	A (14G – .100)		BOS	A	(26G – .295)											
"	total	40	54	14	1	0	0	0.0	2	4	3	13	0	.259	.278	6	4	P-33
1928	NY A	18	30	5	0	0	0	0.0	2	2	2	6	0	.167	.167	5	1	P-13

	G	AB	H	2B	3B	HR	HR %	R	RBI	BB	SO	SB	BA	SA	Pinch Hit AB	Pinch Hit H	G by POS

Fred Heimach continued

	G	AB	H	2B	3B	HR	HR%	R	RBI	BB	SO	SB	BA	SA	AB	H	G by POS
1929	36	49	9	2	0	1	2.0	5	2	3	12	0	.184	.286	0	0	P-35
1930 BKN N	13	4	1	0	0	0	0.0	0	0	0	1	0	.250	.250	4	1	P-9
1931	39	61	12	0	1	0	0.0	3	5	4	7	0	.197	.230	7	3	P-31
1932	37	55	9	2	0	1	1.8	9	4	4	18	0	.164	.255	1	0	P-36
1933	10	10	2	0	0	0	0.0	0	1	0	0	0	.200	.200	0	0	P-10
13 yrs.	368	542	128	15	5	3	0.6	58	49	28	98	2	.236	.299	52	20	P-296, 1B-6

Bud Heine

HEINE, WILLIAM HENRY BL TR 5'8" 145 lbs.
B. Sept. 22, 1900, Elmira, N. Y.   D. Sept. 2, 1976, Ft. Lauderdale, Fla.

	G	AB	H	2B	3B	HR	HR%	R	RBI	BB	SO	SB	BA	SA	AB	H	G by POS
1921 NY N	1	2	0	0	0	0	0.0	0	0	0	0	0	.000	.000	0	0	2B-1

Tom Heintzelman

HEINTZELMAN, THOMAS KENNETH BR TR 6'1" 180 lbs.
Son of Ken Heintzelman.
B. Nov. 3, 1946, St. Charles, Mo.

	G	AB	H	2B	3B	HR	HR%	R	RBI	BB	SO	SB	BA	SA	AB	H	G by POS
1973 STL N	23	29	9	0	0	0	0.0	5	0	3	3	0	.310	.310	15	4	2B-6
1974	38	74	17	4	0	1	1.4	10	6	9	14	0	.230	.324	7	1	2B-28, 3B-2, SS-1
1977 SF N	2	2	0	0	0	0	0.0	0	0	0	0	0	.000	.000	2	0	
1978	27	35	8	1	0	2	5.7	2	6	2	5	0	.229	.429	19	4	2B-5, 3B-3, 1B-2
4 yrs.	90	140	34	5	0	3	2.1	17	12	14	22	0	.243	.343	43	9	2B-39, 3B-5, 1B-2, SS-1

John Heinzman

HEINZMAN, JOHN PETER
B. Sept. 27, 1865, Louisville, Ky.   D. Nov. 10, 1914, Louisville, Ky.

	G	AB	H	2B	3B	HR	HR%	R	RBI	BB	SO	SB	BA	SA	AB	H	G by POS
1886 LOU AA	1	5	0	0	0	0	0.0	1		0			.000	.000	0	0	1B-1

Bob Heise

HEISE, ROBERT LOWELL BR TR 6' 175 lbs.
B. May 12, 1947, San Antonio, Tex.

	G	AB	H	2B	3B	HR	HR%	R	RBI	BB	SO	SB	BA	SA	AB	H	G by POS
1967 NY N	16	62	20	4	0	0	0.0	7	3	3	1	0	.323	.387	0	0	2B-12, SS-3, 3B-2
1968	6	23	5	0	0	0	0.0	3	1	1	1	0	.217	.217	0	0	SS-6, 2B-1
1969	4	10	3	1	0	0	0.0	1	0	3	2	0	.300	.400	1	1	SS-3
1970 SF N	67	154	36	5	1	1	0.6	15	22	5	13	0	.234	.299	7	2	SS-33, 2B-28, 3B-2
1971 2 teams		SF	N (13G – .000)			MIL	A (68G – .254)										
" total	81	200	48	7	0	0	0.0	12	7	7	16	1	.240	.275	10	1	SS-54, 3B-13, 2B-4, OF-1
1972 MIL A	95	271	72	10	1	0	0.0	23	12	12	14	1	.266	.310	18	5	2B-49, 3B-24, SS-9
1973	49	98	20	2	0	0	0.0	8	4	4	4	1	.204	.224	0	0	SS-29, 3B-9, 2B-4, 1B-4
1974 2 teams		STL	N (3G – .143)			CAL	A (29G – .267)										
" total	32	82	21	7	0	0	0.0	7	6	5	10	0	.256	.341	2	0	2B-20, 3B-6, SS-3
1975 BOS A	63	126	27	3	0	0	0.0	12	21	4	6	0	.214	.238	2	0	3B-45, 2B-14, SS-4, 1B-1
1976	32	56	15	2	0	0	0.0	5	5	1	2	0	.268	.304	0	0	3B-22, SS-9, 2B-1
1977 KC A	54	62	16	2	1	0	0.0	11	5	2	8	0	.258	.323	1	0	SS-21, 2B-21, 3B-12, 1B-1
11 yrs.	499	1144	283	43	3	1	0.1	104	86	47	77	3	.247	.293	41	9	SS-174, 2B-154, 3B-135, 1B-6, OF-1

Al Heist

HEIST, ALFRED MICHAEL BR TR 6'2" 185 lbs.
B. Oct. 5, 1927, Brooklyn, N. Y.

	G	AB	H	2B	3B	HR	HR%	R	RBI	BB	SO	SB	BA	SA	AB	H	G by POS
1960 CHI N	41	102	28	5	3	1	1.0	11	6	10	12	3	.275	.412	10	2	OF-33
1961	109	321	82	14	3	7	2.2	48	37	39	51	3	.255	.383	8	1	OF-99
1962 HOU N	27	72	16	1	0	0	0.0	4	3	3	9	0	.222	.236	4	0	OF-23
3 yrs.	177	495	126	20	6	8	1.6	63	46	52	72	6	.255	.368	22	3	OF-155

Heinie Heitmuller

HEITMULLER, WILLIAM FREDERICK BR TR
B. 1883, San Francisco, Calif.   D. Oct. 8, 1912, Los Angeles, Calif.

	G	AB	H	2B	3B	HR	HR%	R	RBI	BB	SO	SB	BA	SA	AB	H	G by POS
1909 PHI A	64	210	60	9	8	0	0.0	36	15	18		7	.286	.405	4	2	OF-60
1910	31	111	27	2	2	0	0.0	11	7	7		6	.243	.297	3	1	OF-28
2 yrs.	95	321	87	11	10	0	0.0	47	22	25		13	.271	.368	7	3	OF-88

Woodie Held

HELD, WOODSON GEORGE BR TR 5'10½" 167 lbs.
B. Mar. 25, 1932, Sacramento, Calif.

	G	AB	H	2B	3B	HR	HR%	R	RBI	BB	SO	SB	BA	SA	AB	H	G by POS
1954 NY A	4	3	0	0	0	0	0.0	2	0	2	1	0	.000	.000	0	0	SS-4, 3B-1
1957 2 teams		NY	A (1G – .000)			KC	A (92G – .239)										
" total	93	327	78	14	3	20	6.1	48	50	37	81	4	.239	.483	1	0	OF-92
1958 2 teams		KC	A (47G – .214)			CLE	A (67G – .194)										
" total	114	275	56	6	1	7	2.5	25	33	25	64	1	.204	.309	11	1	OF-84, SS-15, 3B-8
1959 CLE A	143	525	132	19	3	29	5.5	82	71	47	118	1	.251	.465	1	0	SS-103, 3B-40, OF-6, 2B-3
1960	109	376	97	15	1	21	5.6	45	67	44	73	0	.258	.471	0	0	SS-109
1961	146	509	136	23	5	23	4.5	67	78	69	111	0	.267	.468	2	1	SS-144
1962	139	466	116	12	2	19	4.1	55	58	73	107	5	.249	.406	3	1	SS-133, 3B-5, OF-1
1963	133	416	103	19	4	17	4.1	61	61	61	96	2	.248	.435	9	2	2B-96, OF-35, SS-5, 3B-3
1964	118	364	86	13	0	18	4.9	50	49	43	88	1	.236	.420	8	0	2B-52, OF-41, 3B-30
1965 WAS A	122	332	82	16	2	16	4.8	46	54	49	74	0	.247	.452	15	2	OF-106, 3B-5, 2B-4, SS-2
1966 BAL A	56	82	17	3	1	1	1.2	6	7	12	30	0	.207	.305	34	6	OF-10, 2B-5, SS-3, 3B-3
1967 2 teams		BAL	A (26G – .146)			CAL	A (58G – .220)										
" total	84	182	37	6	0	5	2.7	19	23	24	53	0	.203	.319	22	1	3B-24, OF-19, SS-13, 2B-12
1968 2 teams		CAL	A (33G – .111)			CHI	A (40G – .167)										
" total	73	99	14	2	0	2	2.0	10	29	6	24	0	.141	.162	22	3	OF-36, 3B-10, 2B-6, SS-5
1969 CHI A	56	63	9	2	0	3	4.8	9	6	13	19	0	.143	.317	19	2	OF-18, SS-3, 3B-3, 2B-1
14 yrs.	1390	4019	963	150	22	179	4.5	524	559	509	944	14	.240	.421	147	19	SS-539, OF-448, 2B-179, 3B-132

Hank Helf

HELF, HENRY HARTZ BR TR 6'1" 196 lbs.
B. Aug. 26, 1913, Austin, Tex.   D. Oct. 27, 1984, Austin, Tex.

	G	AB	H	2B	3B	HR	HR%	R	RBI	BB	SO	SB	BA	SA	AB	H	G by POS
1938 CLE A	6	13	1	0	0	0	0.0	1	1	1	1	0	.077	.077	1	0	C-5
1940	1	1	0	0	0	0	0.0	0	0	0	0	0	.000	.000	0	0	C-1
1946 STL A	71	182	35	11	0	6	3.3	17	21	9	40	0	.192	.352	1	0	C-69
3 yrs.	78	196	36	11	0	6	3.1	18	22	10	41	0	.184	.332	2	0	C-75

	G	AB	H	2B	3B	HR	HR %	R	RBI	BB	SO	SB	BA	SA	Pinch Hit AB	Pinch Hit H	G by POS

Ty Helfrich

HELFRICH, EMORY WILBUR BR TR 5'10" 178 lbs.
B. Oct. 9, 1890, Pleasantville, N. J. D. Mar. 18, 1955, Pleasantville, N. J.

	G	AB	H	2B	3B	HR	HR %	R	RBI	BB	SO	SB	BA	SA	PH AB	PH H	G by POS
1915 BKN F	43	104	25	6	0	0	0.0	12	5	15		2	.240	.298	5	0	2B-34, OF-1

Tony Hellman

HELLMAN, ANTHONY J.
B. 1861, Cincinnati, Ohio D. Mar. 29, 1898, Cincinnati, Ohio

	G	AB	H	2B	3B	HR	HR %	R	RBI	BB	SO	SB	BA	SA	PH AB	PH H	G by POS
1886 BAL AA	1	3	0	0	0	0	0.0	0		0			.000	.000	0	0	C-1

Tommy Helms

HELMS, TOMMY VAN BR TR 5'10" 165 lbs.
B. May 5, 1941, Charlotte, N. C.

	G	AB	H	2B	3B	HR	HR %	R	RBI	BB	SO	SB	BA	SA	PH AB	PH H	G by POS
1964 CIN N	2	1	0	0	0	0	0.0	0	0	0	1	0	.000	.000	0	0	
1965	21	42	16	2	2	0	0.0	4	6	3	7	1	.381	.524	10	3	SS-8, 3B-2, 2B-1
1966	138	542	154	23	1	9	1.7	72	49	24	31	3	.284	.380	5	3	3B-113, 2B-20
1967	137	497	136	27	4	2	0.4	40	35	24	41	5	.274	.356	3	1	2B-88, SS-46
1968	127	507	146	28	2	2	0.4	35	47	12	27	5	.288	.363	0	0	2B-127, SS-2, 3B-1
1969	126	480	129	18	1	1	0.2	38	40	18	33	4	.269	.317	1	0	2B-125, SS-4
1970	150	575	136	21	1	1	0.2	42	45	21	33	2	.237	.282	2	0	2B-148, SS-12
1971	150	547	141	26	1	3	0.5	40	52	26	33	3	.258	.325	1	0	2B-149
1972 HOU N	139	518	134	20	5	5	1.0	45	60	24	27	4	.259	.346	0	0	2B-139
1973	146	543	156	28	2	4	0.7	44	61	32	21	1	.287	.368	0	0	2B-145
1974	137	452	126	21	1	5	1.1	32	50	23	27	5	.279	.363	6	1	2B-133
1975	64	135	28	2	0	0	0.0	7	14	10	8	0	.207	.222	27	9	2B-42, 3B-3, SS-1
1976 PIT N	62	87	24	5	1	1	1.1	10	13	10	5	0	.276	.391	23	8	3B-22, 2B-11, SS-1
1977 2 teams	PIT N (15G – .000)		BOS A (21G – .271)														
" total	36	71	16	2	0	1	1.4	5	5	4	7	0	.225	.296	15	2	DH-13, 3B-2, 2B-1
14 yrs.	1435	4997	1342	223	21	34	0.7	414	477	231	301	33	.269	.342	93	27	2B-1129, 3B-143, SS-74, DH-13

LEAGUE CHAMPIONSHIP SERIES

	G	AB	H	2B	3B	HR	HR %	R	RBI	BB	SO	SB	BA	SA	PH AB	PH H	G by POS
1970 CIN N	3	11	3	0	0	0	0.0	0	0	0	1	0	.273	.273	0	0	2B-3

WORLD SERIES

	G	AB	H	2B	3B	HR	HR %	R	RBI	BB	SO	SB	BA	SA	PH AB	PH H	G by POS
1970 CIN N	5	18	4	0	0	0	0.0	1	0	1	1	0	.222	.222	0	0	2B-5

Heinie Heltzel

HELTZEL, WILLIAM WADE BR TR 5'10" 150 lbs.
B. Dec. 21, 1913, York, Pa.

	G	AB	H	2B	3B	HR	HR %	R	RBI	BB	SO	SB	BA	SA	PH AB	PH H	G by POS
1943 BOS N	29	86	13	3	0	0	0.0	6	5	7	13	0	.151	.186	0	0	3B-29
1944 PHI N	11	22	4	1	0	0	0.0	1	0	2	3	0	.182	.227	0	0	SS-10
2 yrs.	40	108	17	4	0	0	0.0	7	5	9	16	0	.157	.194	0	0	3B-29, SS-10

Ed Hemingway

HEMINGWAY, EDSON MARSHALL BB TR 5'11½" 165 lbs.
B. May 8, 1893, Sheridan, Mich. D. July 5, 1969, East Grand Rapids, Mich.

	G	AB	H	2B	3B	HR	HR %	R	RBI	BB	SO	SB	BA	SA	PH AB	PH H	G by POS
1914 STL A	3	5	0	0	0	0	0.0	0	0	1	1	0	.000	.000	0	0	3B-3
1917 NY N	7	25	8	1	1	0	0.0	3	1	2	1	2	.320	.440	0	0	3B-7
1918 PHI N	33	108	23	4	1	0	0.0	7	12	7	9	4	.213	.269	0	0	2B-25, 3B-3, 1B-1
3 yrs.	43	138	31	5	2	0	0.0	10	13	10	11	7	.225	.290	0	0	2B-25, 3B-13, 1B-1

Ducky Hemp

HEMP, WILLIAM H.
B. Dec. 27, 1867, St. Louis, Mo. D. Mar. 6, 1923, St. Louis, Mo.

	G	AB	H	2B	3B	HR	HR %	R	RBI	BB	SO	SB	BA	SA	PH AB	PH H	G by POS
1887 LOU AA	1	3	1	1	0	0	0.0	1		1		0	.333	.667	0	0	OF-1
1890 2 teams	PIT N (21G – .235)		SYR AA (9G – .152)														
" total	30	114	24	1	2	0	0.0	10	4	8	12	4	.211	.254	0	0	OF-30
2 yrs.	31	117	25	2	2	0	0.0	11	4	9	12	4	.214	.265	0	0	OF-31

Charlie Hemphill

HEMPHILL, CHARLES JUDSON (Eagle Eye) BL TL 5'9" 160 lbs.
Brother of Frank Hemphill.
B. Apr. 20, 1876, Greenville, Mich. D. June 22, 1953, Detroit, Mich.

	G	AB	H	2B	3B	HR	HR %	R	RBI	BB	SO	SB	BA	SA	PH AB	PH H	G by POS
1899 2 teams	STL N (11G – .243)		CLE N (55G – .277)														
" total	66	239	65	3	5	3	1.3	27	26	12		3	.272	.364	1	1	OF-64
1901 BOS A	136	545	142	10	10	3	0.6	71	62	39		11	.261	.332	0	0	OF-136
1902 2 teams	CLE A (25G – .266)		STL A (103G – .317)														
" total	128	510	157	16	11	6	1.2	81	69	49		27	.308	.418	6	2	OF-120, 2B-2
1903 STL A	105	383	94	6	3	3	0.8	36	29	23		16	.245	.300	1	0	OF-104
1904	114	438	112	13	2	2	0.5	47	45	35		23	.256	.308	4	1	OF-108, 2B-1
1906	154	585	169	19	12	4	0.7	90	62	43		33	.289	.383	0	0	OF-154
1907	153	603	156	20	9	0	0.0	66	38	51		14	.259	.322	0	0	OF-153
1908 NY A	142	505	150	12	9	0	0.0	62	44	59		42	.297	.356	0	0	OF-142
1909	73	181	44	5	1	0	0.0	23	10	32		10	.243	.282	24	6	OF-45
1910	102	351	84	9	4	0	0.0	45	21	55		19	.239	.288	4	1	OF-94
1911	69	201	57	4	2	1	0.5	32	15	37		9	.284	.338	9	0	OF-56
11 yrs.	1242	4541	1230	117	68	22	0.5	580	421	435		207	.271	.341	49	11	OF-1176, 2B-3

Frank Hemphill

HEMPHILL, FRANK VERNON BR TR 5'11" 165 lbs.
Brother of Charlie Hemphill.
B. May 13, 1878, Greenville, Mich. D. Nov. 16, 1950, Chicago, Ill.

	G	AB	H	2B	3B	HR	HR %	R	RBI	BB	SO	SB	BA	SA	PH AB	PH H	G by POS
1906 CHI A	13	40	3	0	0	0	0.0	0	2	9		1	.075	.075	0	0	OF-13
1909 WAS A	1	3	0	0	0	0	0.0	0	0	0		0	.000	.000	0	0	OF-1
2 yrs.	14	43	3	0	0	0	0.0	0	2	9		1	.070	.070	0	0	OF-14

Rollie Hemsley

HEMSLEY, RALSTON BURDETT BR TR 5'10" 170 lbs.
B. June 24, 1907, Syracuse, Ohio D. July 31, 1972, Washington, D. C.

	G	AB	H	2B	3B	HR	HR %	R	RBI	BB	SO	SB	BA	SA	PH AB	PH H	G by POS
1928 PIT N	50	133	36	2	3	0	0.0	14	18	4	10	1	.271	.331	6	0	C-49
1929	88	235	68	13	7	0	0.0	31	37	11	22	1	.289	.404	6	0	C-80
1930	104	324	82	19	6	2	0.6	45	45	22	21	3	.253	.367	5	1	C-98
1931 2 teams	PIT N (10G – .171)		CHI N (66G – .309)														
" total	76	239	69	20	4	3	1.3	31	32	20	33	4	.289	.444	9	3	C-75
1932 CHI N	60	151	36	10	3	4	2.6	27	20	10	16	2	.238	.424	8	3	C-47, OF-1

	G	AB	H	2B	3B	HR	HR %	R	RBI	BB	SO	SB	BA	SA	Pinch Hit AB	Pinch Hit H	G by POS

Rollie Hemsley continued

		G	AB	H	2B	3B	HR	HR %	R	RBI	BB	SO	SB	BA	SA	PH AB	PH H	G by POS
1933 2 teams	CIN N (49G – .190)						STL A (32G – .242)											
" total		81	211	45	10	1	1	0.5	16	22	17	20	0	.213	.284	7	1	C-68
1934 STL A		123	431	133	31	7	2	0.5	47	52	29	37	6	.309	.427	5	2	C-114, OF-6
1935		144	504	146	32	7	0	0.0	57	48	44	41	3	.290	.381	6	1	C-141
1936		116	377	99	24	2	2	0.5	43	39	46	30	2	.263	.353	8	2	C-114
1937		100	334	74	12	3	3	0.9	30	28	25	29	0	.222	.302	3	2	C-94, 1B-2
1938 CLE A		66	203	60	11	3	2	1.0	27	28	23	14	1	.296	.409	6	0	C-58
1939		107	395	104	17	4	2	0.5	58	36	26	26	2	.263	.342	0	0	C-106
1940		119	416	111	20	5	4	1.0	46	42	22	25	1	.267	.368	2	0	C-117
1941		98	288	69	10	5	2	0.7	29	24	18	19	2	.240	.330	2	0	C-96
1942 2 teams	CIN N (36G – .113)						NY A (31G – .294)											
" total		67	200	38	4	3	0	0.0	19	22	9	20	1	.190	.240	2	0	C-63
1943 NY A		62	180	43	6	3	2	1.1	12	24	13	9	0	.239	.339	10	1	C-52
1944		81	284	76	12	5	2	0.7	23	26	9	13	0	.268	.366	6	1	C-76
1946 PHI N		49	139	31	4	1	0	0.0	7	11	9	10	0	.223	.266	3	1	C-45
1947		2	3	1	0	0	0	0.0	0	1	0	0	0	.333	.333	0	0	C-2
19 yrs.		1593	5047	1321	257	72	31	0.6	562	555	357	395	29	.262	.360	89	18	C-1495, OF-7, 1B-2

WORLD SERIES

		G	AB	H	2B	3B	HR	HR %	R	RBI	BB	SO	SB	BA	SA	PH AB	PH H	G by POS
1932 CHI N		3	3	0	0	0	0	0.0	0	0	0	3	0	.000	.000	3	0	C-1

Solly Hemus

HEMUS, SOLOMON JOSEPH
B. Apr. 17, 1923, Phoenix, Ariz.
Manager 1959-61.

BL TR 5'9" 165 lbs.

		G	AB	H	2B	3B	HR	HR %	R	RBI	BB	SO	SB	BA	SA	PH AB	PH H	G by POS
1949 STL N		20	33	11	1	0	0	0.0	8	2	7	3	0	.333	.364	2	0	2B-16
1950		11	15	2	1	0	0	0.0	1	0	2	4	0	.133	.200	5	0	3B-5
1951		128	420	118	18	9	2	0.5	68	32	75	31	7	.281	.381	4	0	SS-105, 2B-12
1952		151	570	153	28	8	15	2.6	105	52	96	55	1	.268	.425	1	0	SS-148, 3B-2
1953		154	585	163	32	11	14	2.4	110	61	86	40	2	.279	.443	2	1	SS-150, 2B-3
1954		124	214	65	15	3	2	0.9	43	27	55	27	5	.304	.430	38	10	SS-66, 3B-27, 2B-12
1955		96	206	50	10	2	5	2.4	36	21	27	22	1	.243	.383	37	4	3B-43, 2B-40, SS-2
1956 2 teams	STL N (8G – .200)						PHI N (78G – .289)											
" total		86	192	55	10	4	5	2.6	25	26	29	21	1	.286	.458	33	9	2B-49, 3B-1
1957 PHI N		70	108	20	6	1	0	0.0	8	5	20	8	1	.185	.259	33	2	2B-24
1958		105	334	95	14	3	8	2.4	53	36	51	34	3	.284	.416	20	3	2B-84, 3B-1
1959 STL N		24	17	4	2	0	0	0.0	2	1	8	2	0	.235	.353	14	2	3B-1, 2B-1
11 yrs.		969	2694	736	137	41	51	1.9	459	263	456	247	21	.273	.411	189	31	SS-471, 2B-241, 3B-80

Dave Henderson

HENDERSON, DAVID LEE
B. July 21, 1958, Dos Palos, Calif.

BR TR 6'2" 210 lbs.

	G	AB	H	2B	3B	HR	HR %	R	RBI	BB	SO	SB	BA	SA	PH AB	PH H	G by POS
1981 SEA A	59	126	21	3	0	6	4.8	17	13	16	24	2	.167	.333	6	1	OF-58
1982	104	324	82	17	1	14	4.3	47	48	36	67	2	.253	.441	4	0	OF-101
1983	137	484	130	24	5	17	3.5	50	55	28	93	9	.269	.444	4	1	OF-133, DH-3
1984	112	350	98	23	0	14	4.0	42	43	19	56	5	.280	.466	5	1	OF-97, DH-10
4 yrs.	412	1284	331	67	6	51	4.0	156	159	99	240	18	.258	.438	19	3	OF-389, DH-13

Ken Henderson

HENDERSON, KENNETH JOSEPH
B. June 15, 1946, Carroll, Iowa

BB TR 6'2" 180 lbs.
BL 1967

		G	AB	H	2B	3B	HR	HR %	R	RBI	BB	SO	SB	BA	SA	PH AB	PH H	G by POS
1965 SF N		63	73	14	1	1	0	0.0	10	7	9	19	1	.192	.233	7	0	OF-48
1966		11	29	9	1	1	1	3.4	4	1	2	3	0	.310	.517	1	0	OF-10
1967		65	179	34	3	0	4	2.2	15	14	19	52	0	.190	.274	11	3	OF-52
1968		3	3	1	0	0	0	0.0	1	0	2	1	0	.333	.333	0	0	OF-2
1969		113	374	84	14	4	6	1.6	42	44	42	64	6	.225	.332	1	0	OF-111, 3B-3
1970		148	554	163	35	3	17	3.1	104	88	87	78	20	.294	.460	4	1	OF-140
1971		141	504	133	26	6	15	3.0	80	65	84	76	18	.264	.429	2	0	OF-138, 1B-1
1972		130	439	113	21	2	18	4.1	60	51	38	66	14	.257	.437	7	1	OF-123
1973 CHI A		73	262	68	13	0	6	2.3	31	32	27	49	3	.260	.378	1	1	OF-44, DH-26
1974		162	602	176	35	5	20	3.3	76	95	66	112	12	.292	.467	0	0	OF-162
1975		140	513	129	20	3	9	1.8	65	53	74	65	5	.251	.355	3	1	OF-137, DH-1
1976 ATL N		133	435	114	19	0	13	3.0	52	61	62	68	5	.262	.395	10	2	OF-122
1977 TEX A		75	244	63	14	0	5	2.0	23	23	18	37	2	.258	.377	9	2	OF-65, DH-3
1978 2 teams	NY N (7G – .227)						CIN N (64G – .167)											
" total		71	166	29	8	1	4	2.4	12	23	27	36	0	.175	.307	28	6	OF-45
1979 2 teams	CIN N (10G – .231)						CHI N (62G – .235)											
" total		72	94	22	3	0	2	2.1	12	10	15	18	0	.234	.330	50	9	OF-25
1980 CHI N		44	82	16	3	0	2	2.4	7	9	17	19	0	.195	.305	19	3	OF-22
16 yrs.		1444	4553	1168	216	26	122	2.7	594	576	589	763	86	.257	.396	153	29	OF-1246, DH-30, 3B-3, 1B-1

LEAGUE CHAMPIONSHIP SERIES

		G	AB	H	2B	3B	HR	HR %	R	RBI	BB	SO	SB	BA	SA	PH AB	PH H	G by POS
1971 SF N		4	16	5	1	0	0	0.0	3	2	2	1	1	.313	.375	0	0	OF-4

Rickey Henderson

HENDERSON, RICKEY HENLEY
B. Dec. 25, 1958, Chicago, Ill.

BR TL 5'10" 180 lbs.

	G	AB	H	2B	3B	HR	HR %	R	RBI	BB	SO	SB	BA	SA	PH AB	PH H	G by POS
1979 OAK A	89	351	96	13	3	1	0.3	49	26	34	39	33	.274	.336	0	0	OF-88
1980	158	591	179	22	4	9	1.5	111	53	117	54	100	.303	.399	0	0	OF-157, DH-1
1981	108	423	135	18	7	6	1.4	89	35	64	68	56	.319	.437	1	0	OF-107
1982	149	536	143	24	4	10	1.9	119	51	116	94	130	.267	.382	0	0	OF-144, DH-4
1983	145	513	150	25	7	9	1.8	105	48	103	80	108	.292	.421	6	1	OF-142, DH-1
1984	142	502	147	27	4	16	3.2	113	58	86	81	66	.293	.458	2	0	OF-140
6 yrs.	791	2916	850	129	29	51	1.7	586	271	520	416	493	.291	.408	9	1	OF-778, DH-6

DIVISIONAL PLAYOFF SERIES

	G	AB	H	2B	3B	HR	HR %	R	RBI	BB	SO	SB	BA	SA	PH AB	PH H	G by POS
1981 OAK A	3	11	2	0	0	0	0.0	3	0	2	0	2	.182	.182	0	0	OF-3

LEAGUE CHAMPIONSHIP SERIES

	G	AB	H	2B	3B	HR	HR %	R	RBI	BB	SO	SB	BA	SA	PH AB	PH H	G by POS
1981 OAK A	3	11	4	2	1	0	0.0	0	1	1	2	2	.364	.727	0	0	OF-3

	G	AB	H	2B	3B	HR	HR %	R	RBI	BB	SO	SB	BA	SA	Pinch Hit AB	Pinch Hit H	G by POS

Steve Henderson

HENDERSON, STEPHEN CURTIS
B. Nov. 18, 1952, Houston, Tex.
BR TR 6'2" 190 lbs.

	G	AB	H	2B	3B	HR	HR %	R	RBI	BB	SO	SB	BA	SA	PH AB	PH H	G by POS
1977 NY N	99	350	104	16	6	12	3.4	67	65	43	79	6	.297	.480	2	0	OF-97
1978	157	587	156	30	9	10	1.7	83	65	60	109	13	.266	.399	4	4	OF-155
1979	98	350	107	16	8	5	1.4	42	39	38	58	13	.306	.440	3	2	OF-94
1980	143	513	149	17	8	8	1.6	75	58	62	90	23	.290	.402	8	1	OF-136
1981 CHI N	82	287	84	9	5	5	1.7	32	35	42	61	5	.293	.411	4	0	OF-77
1982	92	257	60	12	4	2	0.8	23	29	22	64	6	.233	.335	25	6	OF-70
1983 SEA A	121	436	128	32	3	10	2.3	50	54	44	82	10	.294	.450	6	1	OF-112, DH-6
1984	109	325	85	12	3	10	3.1	42	35	38	62	2	.262	.409	15	4	OF-53, DH-51
8 yrs.	901	3105	873	144	46	62	2.0	414	380	349	605	78	.281	.417	67	18	OF-794, DH-57

George Hendrick

HENDRICK, GEORGE ANDREW
B. Oct. 18, 1949, Los Angeles, Calif.
BR TR 6'3" 195 lbs.

	G	AB	H	2B	3B	HR	HR %	R	RBI	BB	SO	SB	BA	SA	PH AB	PH H	G by POS
1971 OAK A	42	114	27	4	1	0	0.0	8	8	3	20	0	.237	.289	5	2	OF-36
1972	58	121	22	1	1	4	3.3	10	15	3	22	3	.182	.306	19	5	OF-41
1973 CLE A	113	440	118	18	0	21	4.8	64	61	25	71	7	.268	.452	3	1	OF-110
1974	139	495	138	23	1	19	3.8	65	67	33	73	6	.279	.444	5	0	OF-133, DH-1
1975	145	561	145	21	2	24	4.3	82	86	40	78	6	.258	.431	2	1	OF-143
1976	149	551	146	20	3	25	4.5	72	81	51	82	4	.265	.448	1	1	OF-146
1977 SD N	152	541	168	25	2	23	4.3	75	81	61	74	11	.311	.492	9	2	OF-142
1978 2 teams		SD N (36G – .243)			STL N (102G – .288)												
" total	138	493	137	31	1	20	4.1	64	75	40	60	2	.278	.467	5	3	OF-134
1979 STL N	140	493	148	27	1	16	3.2	67	75	49	62	2	.300	.456	7	2	OF-138
1980	150	572	173	33	2	25	4.4	73	109	32	67	6	.302	.498	3	0	OF-149
1981	101	394	112	19	3	18	4.6	67	61	41	44	4	.284	.485	0	0	OF-101
1982	136	515	145	20	5	19	3.7	65	104	37	80	3	.282	.450	1	1	OF-134
1983	144	529	168	33	3	18	3.4	73	97	51	76	3	.318	.493	5	1	1B-92, OF-51
1984	120	441	122	28	1	9	2.0	57	69	32	75	0	.277	.406	4	0	OF-116, 1B-1
14 yrs.	1727	6260	1769	303	26	241	3.8	842	989	498	884	57	.283	.455	70	19	OF-1574, 1B-93, DH-1

LEAGUE CHAMPIONSHIP SERIES

	G	AB	H	2B	3B	HR	HR %	R	RBI	BB	SO	SB	BA	SA	PH AB	PH H	G by POS
1972 OAK A	5	7	1	0	0	0	0.0	2	0	0	1	0	.143	.143	4	1	OF-1
1982 STL N	3	13	4	0	0	0	0.0	2	2	1	2	0	.308	.308	0	0	OF-3
2 yrs.	8	20	5	0	0	0	0.0	4	2	1	3	0	.250	.250	4	1	OF-4

WORLD SERIES

	G	AB	H	2B	3B	HR	HR %	R	RBI	BB	SO	SB	BA	SA	PH AB	PH H	G by POS
1972 OAK A	5	15	2	0	0	0	0.0	3	0	1	2	0	.133	.133	0	0	OF-5
1982 STL N	7	28	9	0	0	0	0.0	5	5	2	1	0	.321	.321	0	0	OF-7
2 yrs.	12	43	11	0	0	0	0.0	8	5	3	3	0	.256	.256	0	0	OF-12

Harvey Hendrick

HENDRICK, HARVEY LEE (Gink)
B. Nov. 9, 1897, Mason, Tenn.   D. Oct. 29, 1941, Covington, Tenn.
BL TR 6'2" 190 lbs.

	G	AB	H	2B	3B	HR	HR %	R	RBI	BB	SO	SB	BA	SA	PH AB	PH H	G by POS
1923 NY A	37	66	18	3	1	3	4.5	9	12	2	8	3	.273	.485	24	6	OF-12
1924	40	76	20	0	0	1	1.3	7	11	2	7	1	.263	.303	21	4	OF-17
1925 CLE A	25	28	8	1	2	0	0.0	2	9	3	5	0	.286	.464	16	6	1B-3
1927 BKN N	128	458	142	18	11	4	0.9	55	50	24	40	29	.310	.424	10	3	OF-64, 1B-53, 2B-1
1928	126	425	135	15	10	11	2.6	83	59	54	34	16	.318	.478	13	5	3B-91, OF-17
1929	110	384	136	25	6	14	3.6	69	82	31	20	14	.354	.560	13	7	OF-42, 3B-9, 2B-7, SS-4
1930	68	167	43	10	1	5	3.0	29	28	20	19	2	.257	.419	16	4	OF-42, 1B-7
1931 2 teams		BKN N (1G – .000)			CIN N (137G – .315)												
" total	138	531	167	32	9	1	0.2	74	75	53	40	3	.315	.414	1	0	1B-137
1932 2 teams		STL N (28G – .250)			CIN N (94G – .302)												
" total	122	470	138	32	3	5	1.1	64	45	28	38	3	.294	.406	9	3	1B-94, 3B-12, OF-5
1933 CHI N	69	189	55	13	3	4	2.1	30	23	13	17	4	.291	.455	19	6	1B-38, OF-8, 3B-1
1934 PHI N	59	116	34	8	0	0	0.0	12	19	9	15	0	.293	.362	31	7	OF-12, 3B-7, 1B-2
11 yrs.	922	2910	896	157	46	48	1.6	434	413	239	243	75	.308	.443	173	51	1B-378, OF-219, 3B-118, SS-4, 2B-1

WORLD SERIES

	G	AB	H	2B	3B	HR	HR %	R	RBI	BB	SO	SB	BA	SA	PH AB	PH H	G by POS
1923 NY A	1	1	0	0	0	0	0.0	0	0	0	0	0	.000	.000	1	0	

Ellie Hendricks

HENDRICKS, ELROD JEROME
B. Dec. 22, 1940, St. Thomas, Virgin Islands
BL TR 6'1" 175 lbs.

	G	AB	H	2B	3B	HR	HR %	R	RBI	BB	SO	SB	BA	SA	PH AB	PH H	G by POS
1968 BAL A	79	183	37	8	1	7	3.8	19	23	19	51	0	.202	.372	27	4	C-53
1969	105	295	72	5	0	12	4.1	36	38	39	44	0	.244	.383	16	5	C-87, 1B-4
1970	106	322	78	9	0	12	3.7	32	41	33	44	1	.242	.382	16	3	C-95
1971	101	316	79	14	1	9	2.8	33	42	39	38	0	.250	.386	11	3	C-90, 1B-3
1972 2 teams		BAL A (33G – .155)			CHI N (17G – .116)												
" total	50	127	18	5	0	2	1.6	13	10	25	27	0	.142	.228	4	0	C-44
1973 BAL A	41	101	18	5	1	3	3.0	9	15	10	22	0	.178	.337	2	0	C-38
1974	66	159	33	8	2	3	1.9	18	8	17	25	0	.208	.340	14	5	C-54, DH-1, 1B-1
1975	85	223	48	8	2	8	3.6	32	38	34	40	0	.215	.377	8	1	C-83
1976 2 teams		BAL A (28G – .139)			NY A (26G – .226)												
" total	54	132	23	2	0	4	3.0	8	9	10	23	0	.174	.280	12	2	C-45
1977 NY A	10	11	3	1	0	1	9.1	1	5	0	2	0	.273	.636	3	1	C-6
1978 BAL A	13	18	6	1	0	1	5.6	4	1	3	3	0	.333	.556	6	1	C-6, DH-1, P-1
1979	1	1	0	0	0	0	0.0	0	0	0	0	0	.000	.000	0	0	C-1
12 yrs.	711	1888	415	66	7	62	3.3	205	230	229	319	1	.220	.361	119	25	C-602, 1B-8, DH-2, P-1

LEAGUE CHAMPIONSHIP SERIES

	G	AB	H	2B	3B	HR	HR %	R	RBI	BB	SO	SB	BA	SA	PH AB	PH H	G by POS
1969 BAL A	3	8	2	2	0	0	0.0	2	3	1	3	0	.250	.500	0	0	C-3
1970	1	5	2	0	0	0	0.0	0	0	0	0	0	.400	.400	0	0	C-1
1971	2	4	2	0	0	1	25.0	1	2	1	1	0	.500	1.250	0	0	C-2
1974	3	6	1	0	0	0	0.0	1	0	1	3	0	.167	.167	0	0	C-3
1976 NY A	1	1	0	0	0	0	0.0	1	0	0	1	0	1.000	1.000	1	0	
5 yrs.	10	24	8	2	0	1	4.2	6	5	3	8	0	.333	.542	1	0	C-9

WORLD SERIES

	G	AB	H	2B	3B	HR	HR %	R	RBI	BB	SO	SB	BA	SA	PH AB	PH H	G by POS
1969 BAL A	3	10	1	0	0	0	0.0	1	1	1	1	0	.100	.100	0	0	C-3
1970	3	11	4	1	0	1	9.1	1	4	1	2	0	.364	.727	0	0	C-3
1971	6	19	5	1	0	0	0.0	3	1	3	3	0	.263	.316	0	0	C-6

	G	AB	H	2B	3B	HR	HR %	R	RBI	BB	SO	SB	BA	SA	Pinch Hit AB	Pinch Hit H	G by POS

Ellie Hendricks continued

	G	AB	H	2B	3B	HR	HR %	R	RBI	BB	SO	SB	BA	SA	AB	H	G by POS
1976 NY A	2	2	0	0	0	0	0.0	0	0	0	0	0	.000	.000	2	0	
4 yrs.	14	42	10	2	0	1	2.4	5	5	5	5	0	.238	.357	2	0	C-12

Jack Hendricks

HENDRICKS, JOHN CHARLES   BL TL 5'11½" 160 lbs.
B. Apr. 9, 1875, Joliet, Ill.   D. May 13, 1943, Chicago, Ill.
Manager 1918, 1924-29.

	G	AB	H	2B	3B	HR	HR %	R	RBI	BB	SO	SB	BA	SA	AB	H	G by POS
1902 2 teams	NY	N	(8G – .231)		CHI	N	(2G – .571)										
" total	10	33	10	2	1	0	0.0	1	0	2		2	.303	.424	1	0	OF-9
1903 WAS A	32	112	20	1	3	0	0.0	10	4	13		3	.179	.241	0	0	OF-32
2 yrs.	42	145	30	3	4	0	0.0	11	4	15		5	.207	.283	1	0	OF-41

Claude Hendrix

HENDRIX, CLAUDE RAYMOND   BR TR 6' 195 lbs.
B. Apr. 13, 1889, Olathe, Kans.   D. Mar. 22, 1944, Allentown, Pa.

	G	AB	H	2B	3B	HR	HR %	R	RBI	BB	SO	SB	BA	SA	AB	H	G by POS
1911 PIT N	22	41	4	1	1	0	0.0	2	2	1	15	0	.098	.171	0	0	P-22
1912	39	121	39	10	6	1	0.8	25	15	3	18	1	.322	.529	5	2	P-39
1913	53	99	27	5	4	1	1.0	13	8	3	16	0	.273	.434	8	0	P-42
1914 CHI F	52	130	30	3	0	2	1.5	15	13	7		3	.231	.300	2	1	P-49
1915	50	113	30	7	2	4	3.5	22	18	5		1	.265	.469	9	2	P-40
1916 CHI N	45	80	16	3	0	1	1.3	4	5	6	24	0	.200	.275	7	1	P-36
1917	48	86	22	3	1	0	0.0	7	7	5	20	1	.256	.314	5	1	P-40, OF-2
1918	35	91	24	3	3	3	3.3	14	17	4	11	1	.264	.462	3	1	P-32
1919	36	78	15	1	0	1	1.3	6	6	2	19	0	.192	.244	3	1	P-33
1920	34	83	15	3	0	0	0.0	10	6	3	11	2	.181	.217	7	1	P-27
10 yrs.	414	922	222	39	17	13	1.4	118	97	39	134	9	.241	.362	49	10	P-360, OF-2
WORLD SERIES																	
1918 CHI N	2	1	1	0	0	0	0.0	0	0	0	0	0	1.000	1.000	1	1	P-1

Tim Hendryx

HENDRYX, TIMOTHY GREEN   BR TR 5'9" 170 lbs.
B. Jan. 31, 1891, LeRoy, Ill.   D. Aug. 14, 1957, Corpus Christi, Tex.

	G	AB	H	2B	3B	HR	HR %	R	RBI	BB	SO	SB	BA	SA	AB	H	G by POS
1911 CLE A	2	4	1	0	0	0	0.0	0			0	0	.250	.250	0	0	3B-2
1912	23	70	17	2	4	1	1.4	9	14	8		3	.243	.429	1	0	OF-22
1915 NY A	13	40	8	2	0	0	0.0	4	1	4	2	0	.200	.250	1	0	OF-12
1916	15	62	18	7	1	0	0.0	10	5	8	6	4	.290	.435	0	0	OF-15
1917	125	393	98	14	7	5	1.3	43	44	62	45	6	.249	.359	16	4	OF-107
1918 STL A	88	219	61	14	3	0	0.0	22	33	37	35	5	.279	.370	18	0	OF-65
1920 BOS A	99	363	119	21	5	0	0.0	54	73	42	27	7	.328	.413	1	0	OF-98
1921	49	137	33	8	2	0	0.0	10	21	24	13	1	.241	.328	6	1	OF-41
8 yrs.	414	1288	355	68	22	6	0.5	152	191	185	128	26	.276	.377	43	5	OF-360, 3B-2

Moxie Hengle

HENGLE, EMERY J.
B. Oct. 7, 1857, Chicago, Ill.   D. Dec. 11, 1924, River Forest, Ill.

	G	AB	H	2B	3B	HR	HR %	R	RBI	BB	SO	SB	BA	SA	AB	H	G by POS
1884 2 teams	C-P	U	(19G – .203)		STP	U	(9G – .152)										
" total	28	107	20	3	2	0	0.0	11		3			.187	.252	0	0	2B-28
1885 BUF N	7	26	4	0	0	0	0.0	2	0	1	2		.154	.154	0	0	2B-5, OF-3
2 yrs.	35	133	24	3	2	0	0.0	13	0	4	2		.180	.233	0	0	2B-33, OF-3

Gail Henley

HENLEY, GAIL CURTICE   BL TR 5'9" 180 lbs.
B. Oct. 15, 1928, Wichita, Kans.

	G	AB	H	2B	3B	HR	HR %	R	RBI	BB	SO	SB	BA	SA	AB	H	G by POS
1954 PIT N	14	30	9	1	0	1	3.3	7	2	4	4	0	.300	.433	5	1	OF-9

Butch Henline

HENLINE, WALTER JOHN   BR TR 5'10" 175 lbs.
B. Dec. 20, 1894, Fort Wayne, Ind.   D. Oct. 9, 1957, Sarasota, Fla.

	G	AB	H	2B	3B	HR	HR %	R	RBI	BB	SO	SB	BA	SA	AB	H	G by POS
1921 2 teams	NY	N	(1G – .000)		PHI	N	(33G – .306)										
" total	34	112	34	2	0	0	0.0	8	8	2	7	1	.304	.321	2	0	C-32
1922 PHI N	125	430	136	20	4	14	3.3	57	64	36	33	2	.316	.479	4	2	C-119
1923	111	330	107	14	3	7	2.1	45	46	37	33	4	.324	.448	12	3	C-96, OF-1
1924	115	289	82	18	4	5	1.7	41	35	27	15	1	.284	.426	28	7	C-83, OF-1
1925	93	263	80	12	5	8	3.0	43	48	24	16	3	.304	.479	18	2	C-68, OF-1
1926	99	283	80	14	1	2	0.7	32	30	21	18	1	.283	.360	17	4	C-77, 1B-4, OF-2
1927 BKN N	67	177	47	10	3	1	0.6	12	18	17	10	1	.266	.373	7	1	C-60
1928	55	132	28	3	1	2	1.5	12	8	17	8	2	.212	.295	8	2	C-45
1929	27	62	15	2	0	1	1.6	5	7	9	9	0	.242	.323	5	0	C-21
1930 CHI A	3	8	1	0	0	0	0.0	1	2	0	3	0	.125	.125	0	0	C-3
1931	11	15	1	1	0	0	0.0	0	2	2	4	0	.067	.133	5	1	C-4
11 yrs.	740	2101	611	96	21	40	1.9	258	268	192	156	18	.291	.414	106	22	C-608, OF-6, 1B-4

Les Hennessy

HENNESSY, LESTER BAKER   BR TR 6' 190 lbs.
B. Dec. 12, 1893, Lynn, Mass.   D. Nov. 20, 1976, New York, N. Y.

	G	AB	H	2B	3B	HR	HR %	R	RBI	BB	SO	SB	BA	SA	AB	H	G by POS
1913 DET A	12	22	3	0	0	0	0.0	2	0	3	6	2	.136	.136	2	0	2B-9

Bobby Henrich

HENRICH, ROBERT EDWARD   BR TR 6'1" 185 lbs.
B. Dec. 24, 1938, Lawrence, Kans.

	G	AB	H	2B	3B	HR	HR %	R	RBI	BB	SO	SB	BA	SA	AB	H	G by POS
1957 CIN N	29	10	2	0	0	0	0.0	8	1	1	4	0	.200	.200	4	1	SS-7, OF-6, 3B-2, 2B-1
1958	5	3	0	0	0	0	0.0	2	0	0	2	0	.000	.000	0	0	SS-2
1959	14	3	0	0	0	0	0.0	3	0	0	1	0	.000	.000	1	0	SS-5, 3B-1
3 yrs.	48	16	2	0	0	0	0.0	13	1	1	7	0	.125	.125	5	1	SS-14, OF-6, 3B-3, 2B-1

Fritz Henrich

HENRICH, FRANK WILDE   BL TL 5'10" 160 lbs.
B. May 8, 1899, Cincinnati, Ohio   D. May 1, 1959, Philadelphia, Pa.

	G	AB	H	2B	3B	HR	HR %	R	RBI	BB	SO	SB	BA	SA	AB	H	G by POS
1924 PHI N	36	90	19	4	0	0	0.0	4	4	2	12	0	.211	.256	4	0	OF-32

	G	AB	H	2B	3B	HR	HR %	R	RBI	BB	SO	SB	BA	SA	Pinch Hit AB	Pinch Hit H	G by POS

Tommy Henrich

HENRICH, THOMAS DAVID (Old Reliable)
B. Feb. 20, 1913, Massillon, Ohio   BL TL 6'   180 lbs.

	G	AB	H	2B	3B	HR	HR %	R	RBI	BB	SO	SB	BA	SA	PH AB	PH H	G by POS
1937 NY A	67	206	66	14	5	8	3.9	39	42	35	17	4	.320	.553	7	1	OF-59
1938	131	471	127	24	7	22	4.7	109	91	92	32	6	.270	.490	1	0	OF-130
1939	99	347	96	18	4	9	2.6	64	57	51	23	7	.277	.429	11	4	OF-88, 1B-1
1940	90	293	90	28	5	10	3.4	57	53	48	30	1	.307	.539	12	4	OF-76, 1B-2
1941	144	538	149	27	5	31	5.8	106	85	81	40	3	.277	.519	4	1	OF-139
1942	127	483	129	30	5	13	2.7	77	67	58	42	4	.267	.431	3	1	OF-119, 1B-7
1946	150	565	142	25	4	19	3.4	92	83	87	63	5	.251	.411	0	0	OF-111, 1B-41
1947	142	550	158	35	13	16	2.9	109	98	71	54	3	.287	.485	5	1	OF-132, 1B-6
1948	146	588	181	42	14	25	4.3	138	100	76	42	2	.308	.554	1	0	OF-102, 1B-46
1949	115	411	118	20	3	24	5.8	90	85	86	34	2	.287	.526	2	0	OF-61, 1B-52
1950	73	151	41	6	8	6	4.0	20	34	27	6	0	.272	.536	33	7	1B-34
11 yrs.	1284	4603	1297	269	73	183	4.0	901	795	712	383	37	.282	.491	79	19	OF-1017, 1B-189
WORLD SERIES																	
1938 NY A	4	16	4	1	0	1	6.3	3	1	0	1	0	.250	.500	0	0	OF-4
1941	5	18	3	1	0	1	5.6	4	1	3	3	0	.167	.389	0	0	OF-5
1947	7	31	10	2	0	1	3.2	2	5	2	3	0	.323	.484	0	0	OF-7
1949	5	19	5	0	0	1	5.3	4	1	3	0	0	.263	.421	0	0	1B-5
4 yrs.	21	84	22	4	0	4	4.8	13	8	8	7	0	.262	.452	0	0	OF-16, 1B-5

Olaf Henriksen

HENRIKSEN, OLAF (Swede)
B. Apr. 26, 1888, Kirkerup, Denmark   D. Oct. 17, 1962, Canton, Mass.   BL TL 5'7½"   158 lbs.

	G	AB	H	2B	3B	HR	HR %	R	RBI	BB	SO	SB	BA	SA	PH AB	PH H	G by POS
1911 BOS A	27	93	34	2	1	0	0.0	17	8	14		4	.366	.409	2	0	OF-25
1912	37	56	18	3	1	0	0.0	20	8	14		0	.321	.411	25	6	OF-10
1913	30	40	15	1	0	0	0.0	8	2	7	5	3	.375	.400	17	6	OF-7
1914	61	95	25	2	1	1	1.1	16	5	22	12	5	.263	.337	26	5	OF-27
1915	73	92	18	2	2	0	0.0	9	13	18	7	1	.196	.261	31	7	OF-25
1916	68	99	20	2	2	0	0.0	13	11	19	15	2	.202	.263	21	4	OF-31
1917	15	12	1	0	0	0	0.0	1	1	3	4	0	.083	.083	12	1	
7 yrs.	311	487	131	12	7	1	0.2	84	48	97	43	15	.269	.329	134	29	OF-125
WORLD SERIES																	
1912 BOS A	2	1	1	1	0	0	0.0	0	1	0	0	0	1.000	2.000	1	1	
1915	2	2	0	0	0	0	0.0	0	0	0	0	0	.000	.000	2	0	
1916	1	0	0	0	0	0	–	1	0	1	0	0	–	–	0	0	
3 yrs.	5	3	1	1	0	0	0.0	1	1	1	0	0	.333	.667	3	1	

George Henry

HENRY, GEORGE WASHINGTON
B. Aug. 10, 1863, Philadelphia, Pa.   D. Dec. 30, 1934, Lynn, Mass.   BR TR 5'9"   180 lbs.

	G	AB	H	2B	3B	HR	HR %	R	RBI	BB	SO	SB	BA	SA	PH AB	PH H	G by POS
1893 CIN N	21	83	23	3	0	0	0.0	11	13	11	12		.277	.313	0	0	OF-21

John Henry

HENRY, JOHN MICHAEL
B. Sept. 2, 1864, Springfield, Mass.   D. June 11, 1939, Hartford, Conn.   TL

	G	AB	H	2B	3B	HR	HR %	R	RBI	BB	SO	SB	BA	SA	PH AB	PH H	G by POS
1884 CLE N	9	26	4	0	0	0	0.0	2	0	0	12		.154	.154	0	0	P-5, OF-4
1885 BAL AA	10	34	9	3	0	0	0.0	4		1			.265	.353	0	0	P-9, OF-1
1886 WAS N	4	14	5	0	0	0	0.0	3	0	0	3		.357	.357	0	0	P-4
1890 NY N	37	144	35	6	0	0	0.0	19	16	7	12	12	.243	.285	0	0	OF-37
4 yrs.	60	218	53	9	0	0	0.0	28	15	8	27	12	.243	.284	0	0	OF-42, P-18

John Henry

HENRY, JOHN T. (Bull)
B. Dec. 26, 1889, Amherst, Mass.   D. Nov. 24, 1941, Fort Huachuca, Ariz.   BR TR 6'   190 lbs.

	G	AB	H	2B	3B	HR	HR %	R	RBI	BB	SO	SB	BA	SA	PH AB	PH H	G by POS
1910 WAS A	28	87	13	1	1	0	0.0	2	5	2		2	.149	.184	0	0	C-18, 1B-10
1911	85	261	53	5	0	0	0.0	24	21	25		8	.203	.222	3	0	C-51, 1B-30
1912	63	191	37	4	1	0	0.0	23	9	31		10	.194	.225	0	0	C-63
1913	96	273	61	8	4	1	0.4	26	26	30	43	5	.223	.293	0	0	C-96
1914	91	261	44	7	4	0	0.0	22	20	37	47	7	.169	.226	0	0	C-91
1915	95	277	61	9	2	1	0.4	20	22	36	28	10	.220	.278	1	0	C-94
1916	117	305	76	12	3	0	0.0	28	46	49	40	12	.249	.308	1	0	C-116
1917	65	163	31	6	0	0	0.0	10	18	24	16	1	.190	.227	4	0	C-59
1918 BOS N	43	102	21	2	0	0	0.0	6	4	10	15	0	.206	.225	3	1	C-38
9 yrs.	683	1920	397	54	15	2	0.1	161	171	244	189	55	.207	.254	12	1	C-626, 1B-40

Ron Henry

HENRY, RONALD BAXTER
B. Aug. 7, 1936, Chester, Pa.   BR TR 6'1"   180 lbs.

	G	AB	H	2B	3B	HR	HR %	R	RBI	BB	SO	SB	BA	SA	PH AB	PH H	G by POS
1961 MIN A	20	28	4	0	0	0	0.0	1	3	2	7	0	.143	.143	14	3	C-5, 1B-1
1964	22	41	5	1	1	2	4.9	4	5	2	17	0	.122	.341	11	1	C-13
2 yrs.	42	69	9	1	1	2	2.9	5	8	4	24	0	.130	.261	25	4	C-18, 1B-1

Snake Henry

HENRY, FREDERICK MARSHALL
B. July 19, 1895, Waynesville, N. C.   BL TL 6'   170 lbs.

	G	AB	H	2B	3B	HR	HR %	R	RBI	BB	SO	SB	BA	SA	PH AB	PH H	G by POS
1922 BOS N	18	66	13	4	1	0	0.0	5	5	2	8	2	.197	.288	0	0	1B-18
1923	11	9	1	0	0	0	0.0	1	2	1	1	0	.111	.111	9	1	
2 yrs.	29	75	14	4	1	0	0.0	6	7	3	9	2	.187	.267	9	1	1B-18

Babe Herman

HERMAN, FLOYD CAVES
B. June 26, 1903, Buffalo, N. Y.   BL TL 6'4"   190 lbs.

	G	AB	H	2B	3B	HR	HR %	R	RBI	BB	SO	SB	BA	SA	PH AB	PH H	G by POS
1926 BKN N	137	496	158	35	11	11	2.2	64	81	44	53	8	.319	.500	6	2	1B-101, OF-35
1927	130	412	112	26	9	14	3.4	65	73	39	41	4	.272	.481	20	7	1B-105, OF-1
1928	134	486	165	37	6	12	2.5	64	91	38	36	1	.340	.514	6	1	OF-127
1929	146	569	217	42	13	21	3.7	105	113	55	45	21	.381	.612	3	2	OF-141, 1B-2
1930	153	614	241	48	11	35	5.7	143	130	66	56	18	.393	.678	0	0	OF-153
1931	151	610	191	43	16	18	3.0	93	97	50	65	17	.313	.525	0	0	OF-150
1932 CIN N	148	577	188	38	19	16	2.8	87	87	60	45	7	.326	.541	2	1	OF-146
1933 CHI N	137	508	147	36	12	16	3.1	77	93	50	57	6	.289	.502	5	4	OF-131
1934	125	467	142	34	5	14	3.0	65	84	35	71	1	.304	.488	6	2	OF-113, 1B-7

	G	AB	H	2B	3B	HR	HR %	R	RBI	BB	SO	SB	BA	SA	Pinch Hit AB	H	G by POS

Babe Herman continued

	G	AB	H	2B	3B	HR	HR %	R	RBI	BB	SO	SB	BA	SA	PH AB	PH H	G by POS
1935 2 teams	PIT N (26G – .235)				CIN N (92G – .335)												
" total	118	430	136	31	6	10	2.3	52	65	38	35	5	.316	.486	10	0	OF-91, 1B-17
1936 CIN N	119	380	106	25	2	13	3.4	59	71	39	36	4	.279	.458	19	4	OF-92, 1B-4
1937 DET A	17	20	6	3	0	0	0.0	2	3	1	6	2	.300	.450	14	3	OF-2
1945 BKN N	37	34	9	1	0	1	2.9	6	9	5	7	0	.265	.382	29	6	OF-3
13 yrs.	1552	5603	1818	399	110	181	3.2	882	997	520	553	94	.324	.532	120	32	OF-1185, 1B-236

Billy Herman

HERMAN, WILLIAM JENNINGS (Bryan)
B. July 7, 1909, New Albany, Ind.
Manager 1947, 1964-66.
Hall of Fame 1975.

BR TR 5'11"   180 lbs.

	G	AB	H	2B	3B	HR	HR %	R	RBI	BB	SO	SB	BA	SA	PH AB	PH H	G by POS
1931 CHI N	25	98	32	7	0	0	0.0	14	16	13	6	2	.327	.398	0	0	2B-25
1932	154	656	206	42	7	1	0.2	102	51	40	33	14	.314	.404	0	0	2B-154
1933	153	619	173	35	2	0	0.0	82	44	45	34	5	.279	.342	0	0	2B-153
1934	113	456	138	21	6	3	0.7	79	42	34	31	6	.303	.395	1	0	2B-111
1935	154	666	227	57	6	7	1.1	113	83	42	29	6	.341	.476	0	0	2B-154
1936	153	632	211	57	7	5	0.8	101	93	59	30	5	.334	.470	0	0	2B-153
1937	138	564	189	35	11	8	1.4	106	65	56	22	2	.335	.479	1	0	2B-137
1938	152	624	173	34	7	1	0.2	86	56	59	31	3	.277	.359	1	0	2B-151
1939	156	623	191	34	18	7	1.1	111	70	66	31	9	.307	.453	0	0	2B-156
1940	135	558	163	24	4	5	0.9	77	57	47	30	1	.292	.376	0	0	2B-135
1941 2 teams	CHI N (11G – .194)				BKN N (133G – .291)												
" total	144	572	163	30	5	3	0.5	81	41	67	43	1	.285	.371	0	0	2B-144
1942 BKN N	155	571	146	34	2	2	0.4	76	65	72	52	6	.256	.333	0	0	2B-153, 1B-3
1943	153	585	193	41	2	2	0.3	76	100	66	26	4	.330	.417	0	0	2B-117, 3B-37
1946 2 teams	BKN N (47G – .288)				BOS N (75G – .306)												
" total	122	436	130	31	5	3	0.7	56	50	69	23	3	.298	.413	4	1	2B-76, 3B-63, 1B-22
1947 PIT N	15	47	10	4	0	0	0.0	3	6	2	7	0	.213	.298	1	0	2B-10, 1B-2
15 yrs.	1922	7707	2345	486	82	47	0.6	1163	839	737	428	67	.304	.407	8	1	2B-1829, 3B-100, 1B-27
WORLD SERIES																	
1932 CHI N	4	18	4	1	0	0	0.0	5	1	1	3	0	.222	.278	0	0	2B-4
1935	6	24	8	2	1	1	4.2	3	6	0	2	0	.333	.625	0	0	2B-6
1938	4	16	3	0	0	0	0.0	1	0	1	4	0	.188	.188	0	0	2B-4
1941 BKN N	4	8	1	0	0	0	0.0	0	0	2	0	0	.125	.125	0	0	2B-4
4 yrs.	18	66	16	3	1	1	1.5	9	7	4	9	0	.242	.364	0	0	2B-18

Al Hermann

HERMANN, ALBERT BARTEL
B. Mar. 28, 1899, Milltown, N.J.   D. Aug. 20, 1980, Bethany Beach, Del.

BR TR 6'   180 lbs.

	G	AB	H	2B	3B	HR	HR %	R	RBI	BB	SO	SB	BA	SA	PH AB	PH H	G by POS
1923 BOS N	31	93	22	4	0	0	0.0	2	11	0	7	3	.237	.280	7	1	2B-15, 3B-5, 1B-4
1924	1	1	0	0	0	0	0.0	0	0	0	1	0	.000	.000	1	0	
2 yrs.	32	94	22	4	0	0	0.0	2	11	0	8	3	.234	.277	8	1	2B-15, 3B-5, 1B-4

Gene Hermanski

HERMANSKI, EUGENE VICTOR
B. May 11, 1920, Pittsfield, Mass.

BL TR 5'11½" 185 lbs.

	G	AB	H	2B	3B	HR	HR %	R	RBI	BB	SO	SB	BA	SA	PH AB	PH H	G by POS
1943 BKN N	18	60	18	2	1	0	0.0	6	12	11	7	1	.300	.367	0	0	OF-18
1946	64	110	22	2	0	0	0.0	15	8	17	10	2	.200	.255	24	2	OF-34
1947	79	189	52	7	1	7	3.7	36	39	28	7	5	.275	.434	12	4	OF-66
1948	133	400	116	22	7	15	3.8	63	60	64	46	15	.290	.493	12	3	OF-119
1949	87	224	67	12	3	8	3.6	48	42	47	21	12	.299	.487	13	5	OF-77
1950	94	289	86	17	3	7	2.4	36	34	36	26	2	.298	.450	12	3	OF-78
1951 2 teams	BKN N (31G – .250)				CHI N (75G – .281)												
" total	106	311	85	16	1	4	1.3	36	25	45	42	2	.273	.370	20	7	OF-94
1952 CHI N	99	275	70	6	0	4	1.5	28	34	29	32	2	.255	.320	21	10	OF-76
1953 2 teams	CHI N (18G – .150)				PIT N (41G – .177)												
" total	59	102	17	1	0	1	1.0	8	5	12	21	1	.167	.206	29	4	OF-26
9 yrs.	739	1960	533	85	18	46	2.3	276	259	289	212	43	.272	.404	143	38	OF-588
WORLD SERIES																	
1947 BKN N	7	19	3	0	1	0	0.0	4	1	3	3	0	.158	.263	0	0	OF-7
1949	4	13	4	0	1	0	0.0	1	2	3	3	0	.308	.462	0	0	OF-4
2 yrs.	11	32	7	0	2	0	0.0	5	3	6	6	0	.219	.344	0	0	OF-11

Angel Hermoso

HERMOSO, ANGEL REMIGIO (Remy)
B. Oct. 1, 1946, Carabobo, Venezuela

BR TR 5'8"   155 lbs.

	G	AB	H	2B	3B	HR	HR %	R	RBI	BB	SO	SB	BA	SA	PH AB	PH H	G by POS
1967 ATL N	11	26	8	0	0	0	0.0	3	0	2	4	1	.308	.308	0	0	SS-9, 2B-2
1969 MON N	28	74	12	0	0	0	0.0	6	3	5	10	3	.162	.162	3	0	2B-18, SS-6
1970	4	1	0	0	0	0	0.0	1	0	0	0	0	.000	.000	1	0	3B-1, 2B-1
1974 CLE A	48	122	27	3	1	0	0.0	15	5	7	7	2	.221	.262	1	0	2B-45
4 yrs.	91	223	47	3	1	0	0.0	25	8	14	21	6	.211	.233	5	0	2B-66, SS-15, 3B-1

Chico Hernandez

HERNANDEZ, SALVADOR JOSE RAMOS
B. Jan. 3, 1916, Havana, Cuba

BR TR 6'1"   195 lbs.

	G	AB	H	2B	3B	HR	HR %	R	RBI	BB	SO	SB	BA	SA	PH AB	PH H	G by POS
1942 CHI N	47	118	27	5	0	0	0.0	6	7	11	13	0	.229	.271	3	1	C-43
1943	43	126	34	4	0	0	0.0	10	9	9	9	0	.270	.302	2	0	C-41
2 yrs.	90	244	61	9	0	0	0.0	16	16	20	22	0	.250	.287	5	1	C-84

Enzo Hernandez

HERNANDEZ, ENZO OCTAVIO
B. Feb. 12, 1949, Valle de Guanape, Puerto Rico

BR TR 5'8"   155 lbs.

	G	AB	H	2B	3B	HR	HR %	R	RBI	BB	SO	SB	BA	SA	PH AB	PH H	G by POS
1971 SD N	143	549	122	9	3	0	0.0	58	12	54	34	21	.222	.250	0	0	SS-143
1972	114	329	64	11	2	1	0.3	33	15	22	25	24	.195	.249	1	0	SS-107, OF-3
1973	70	247	55	2	1	0	0.0	26	9	17	14	15	.223	.239	2	0	SS-67
1974	147	512	119	19	2	0	0.0	55	34	38	36	37	.232	.277	1	1	SS-145
1975	116	344	75	12	2	0	0.0	37	19	26	25	20	.218	.265	0	0	SS-111
1976	113	340	87	13	3	1	0.3	31	24	32	16	12	.256	.321	3	2	SS-101
1977	7	3	0	0	0	0	0.0	1	0	1	0	0	.000	.000	0	0	SS-7

	G	AB	H	2B	3B	HR	HR %	R	RBI	BB	SO	SB	BA	SA	Pinch Hit AB	Pinch Hit H	G by POS

Enzo Hernandez continued

	G	AB	H	2B	3B	HR	HR %	R	RBI	BB	SO	SB	BA	SA	AB	H	G by POS
1978 LA N	4	3	0	0	0	0	0.0	0	0	0	1	0	.000	.000	0	0	SS-2
8 yrs.	714	2327	522	66	13	2	0.1	241	113	189	151	129	.224	.266	7	3	SS-683, OF-3

Jackie Hernandez

HERNANDEZ, JACINTO ZULUETA
B. Sept. 11, 1940, Central Tinguaro, Cuba
    BR TR 5'11" 165 lbs.

	G	AB	H	2B	3B	HR	HR %	R	RBI	BB	SO	SB	BA	SA	AB	H	G by POS
1965 CAL A	6	6	2	1	0	0	0.0	2	1	0	1	1	.333	.500	0	0	SS-2, 3B-1
1966	58	23	1	0	0	0	0.0	19	2	1	4	1	.043	.043	2	0	3B-11, SS-8, 2B-8, OF-3
1967 MIN A	29	28	4	0	0	0	0.0	1	3	0	6	0	.143	.143	2	0	SS-15, 3B-13
1968	83	199	35	3	0	2	1.0	13	17	9	52	5	.176	.221	0	0	SS-79, 1B-1
1969 KC A	145	504	112	14	2	4	0.8	54	40	38	111	17	.222	.282	0	0	SS-144
1970	83	238	55	4	1	2	0.8	14	10	15	50	1	.231	.282	3	1	SS-77
1971 PIT N	88	233	48	7	3	3	1.3	30	26	17	45	0	.206	.300	1	0	SS-75, 3B-9
1972	72	176	33	7	1	1	0.6	12	14	9	43	0	.188	.256	0	0	SS-68, 3B-4
1973	54	73	18	1	2	0	0.0	8	8	4	12	0	.247	.315	2	1	SS-49
9 yrs.	618	1480	308	37	9	12	0.8	153	121	93	324	25	.208	.270	10	2	SS-517, 3B-38, 2B-8, OF-3, 1B-1

LEAGUE CHAMPIONSHIP SERIES
	G	AB	H	2B	3B	HR	HR %	R	RBI	BB	SO	SB	BA	SA	AB	H	G by POS
1971 PIT N	4	13	3	0	0	0	0.0	2	1	0	4	0	.231	.231	0	0	SS-4

WORLD SERIES
	G	AB	H	2B	3B	HR	HR %	R	RBI	BB	SO	SB	BA	SA	AB	H	G by POS
1971 PIT N	7	18	4	0	0	0	0.0	2	1	2	5	1	.222	.222	0	0	SS-7

Keith Hernandez

HERNANDEZ, KEITH
B. Oct. 20, 1953, San Francisco, Calif.
    BL TL 6' 180 lbs.

	G	AB	H	2B	3B	HR	HR %	R	RBI	BB	SO	SB	BA	SA	AB	H	G by POS
1974 STL N	14	34	10	1	2	0	0.0	3	2	7	8	0	.294	.441	3	1	1B-9
1975	64	188	47	8	2	3	1.6	20	20	17	26	0	.250	.362	9	3	1B-56
1976	129	374	108	21	5	7	1.9	54	46	49	53	4	.289	.428	17	4	1B-110
1977	161	560	163	41	4	15	2.7	90	91	79	88	7	.291	.459	6	1	1B-158
1978	159	542	138	32	4	11	2.0	90	64	82	68	13	.255	.389	5	1	1B-158
1979	161	610	210	48	11	11	1.8	116	105	80	78	11	.344	.513	2	2	1B-160
1980	159	595	191	39	8	16	2.7	111	99	86	73	14	.321	.494	2	0	1B-157
1981	103	376	115	27	4	8	2.1	65	48	61	45	12	.306	.463	2	0	1B-98, OF-3
1982	160	579	173	33	6	7	1.2	79	94	100	67	19	.299	.413	1	1	1B-158, OF-4
1983 2 teams	STL	N (55G – .284)			NY	N (95G – .306)											
" total	150	538	160	23	7	12	2.2	77	63	88	72	9	.297	.433	5	1	1B-144
1984 NY N	154	550	171	31	0	15	2.7	83	94	97	89	2	.311	.449	1	0	1B-153
11 yrs.	1414	4946	1486	304	53	105	2.1	788	726	746	667	91	.300	.447	53	14	1B-1361, OF-7

LEAGUE CHAMPIONSHIP SERIES
	G	AB	H	2B	3B	HR	HR %	R	RBI	BB	SO	SB	BA	SA	AB	H	G by POS
1982 STL N	3	12	4	0	0	0	0.0	3	1	2	3	0	.333	.333	0	0	1B-3

WORLD SERIES
	G	AB	H	2B	3B	HR	HR %	R	RBI	BB	SO	SB	BA	SA	AB	H	G by POS
1982 STL N	7	27	7	2	0	1	3.7	4	8	4	2	0	.259	.444	0	0	1B-7

Leo Hernandez

HERNANDEZ, LEONARDO JESUS
B. Nov. 6, 1959, Garagas, Venezuela
    BR TR 5'11" 170 lbs.

	G	AB	H	2B	3B	HR	HR %	R	RBI	BB	SO	SB	BA	SA	AB	H	G by POS
1982 BAL A	2	2	0	0	0	0	0.0	0	0	0	2	0	.000	.000	2	0	
1983	64	203	50	6	1	6	3.0	21	26	12	19	1	.246	.374	0	0	3B-64
2 yrs.	66	205	50	6	1	6	2.9	21	26	12	21	1	.244	.371	2	0	3B-64

Pedro Hernandez

HERNANDEZ, PEDRO JULIO
Also known as Pedro Julio Montas.
B. Apr. 4, 1959, La Romana, Dominican Republic
    BR TR 6'1" 160 lbs.

	G	AB	H	2B	3B	HR	HR %	R	RBI	BB	SO	SB	BA	SA	AB	H	G by POS
1979 TOR A	3	0	0	0	0	0	–	1	0	0	0	0	–	–	0	0	DH-2
1982	8	9	0	0	0	0	0.0	1	0	0	3	0	.000	.000	3	0	DH-3, 3B-2, OF-1
2 yrs.	11	9	0	0	0	0	0.0	2	0	0	3	0	.000	.000	3	0	DH-5, 3B-2, OF-1

Rudy Hernandez

HERNANDEZ, RODOLFO
Also known as Rodolfo Acosta.
B. Oct. 18, 1952, Empalme, Mexico
    BR TR 5'9" 150 lbs.

	G	AB	H	2B	3B	HR	HR %	R	RBI	BB	SO	SB	BA	SA	AB	H	G by POS
1972 CHI A	8	21	4	0	0	0	0.0	0	1	0	3	0	.190	.190	2	1	SS-6

Toby Hernandez

HERNANDEZ, TOBIAS RAFAEL ALVARADO
B. Nov. 30, 1958, Calabozo, Venezuela
    BR TR 6'1" 160 lbs.

	G	AB	H	2B	3B	HR	HR %	R	RBI	BB	SO	SB	BA	SA	AB	H	G by POS
1984 TOR A	3	2	1	0	0	0	0.0	1	0	1	0	0	.500	.500	0	0	C-3

Larry Herndon

HERNDON, LARRY DARNELL
B. Nov. 3, 1953, Sunflower, Miss.
    BR TR 6'3" 190 lbs.

	G	AB	H	2B	3B	HR	HR %	R	RBI	BB	SO	SB	BA	SA	AB	H	G by POS
1974 STL N	12	1	1	0	0	0	0.0	3	0	0	0	0	1.000	1.000	0	0	OF-1
1976 SF N	115	337	97	11	3	2	0.6	42	23	23	45	12	.288	.356	6	2	OF-110
1977	49	109	26	4	3	1	0.9	13	5	5	20	4	.239	.358	5	1	OF-44
1978	151	471	122	15	9	1	0.2	52	32	35	71	13	.259	.335	4	2	OF-149
1979	132	354	91	14	5	7	2.0	35	36	29	70	8	.257	.384	19	7	OF-122
1980	139	493	127	17	11	8	1.6	54	49	19	91	8	.258	.385	21	6	OF-122
1981	96	364	105	15	8	5	1.4	48	41	20	55	15	.288	.415	4	0	OF-93
1982 DET A	157	614	179	21	13	23	3.7	92	88	38	92	12	.292	.480	3	0	OF-155, DH-3
1983	153	603	182	28	9	20	3.3	88	92	46	95	9	.302	.478	5	1	OF-133, DH-19
1984	125	407	114	18	5	7	1.7	52	43	32	63	6	.280	.400	24	7	OF-117, DH-4
10 yrs.	1129	3753	1044	143	66	74	2.0	479	409	247	602	87	.278	.411	91	26	OF-1046, DH-26

LEAGUE CHAMPIONSHIP SERIES
	G	AB	H	2B	3B	HR	HR %	R	RBI	BB	SO	SB	BA	SA	AB	H	G by POS
1984 DET A	2	5	1	0	0	1	20.0	1	1	1	2	0	.200	.800	0	0	OF-2

WORLD SERIES
	G	AB	H	2B	3B	HR	HR %	R	RBI	BB	SO	SB	BA	SA	AB	H	G by POS
1984 DET A	5	15	5	0	0	1	6.7	1	3	3	2	0	.333	.533	2	0	OF-5

	G	AB	H	2B	3B	HR	HR %	R	RBI	BB	SO	SB	BA	SA	Pinch Hit AB	Pinch Hit H	G by POS

Tom Hernon

HERNON, THOMAS H.
B. Nov. 4, 1866, E. Bridgewater, Mass. D. Feb. 4, 1902, New Bedford, Mass.

	G	AB	H	2B	3B	HR	HR%	R	RBI	BB	SO	SB	BA	SA	PH AB	PH H	G by POS
1897 CHI N	4	16	1	0	0	0	0.0	2	2	0		1	.063	.063	0	0	OF-4

Ed Herr

HERR, EDWARD JOSEPH BR TR
B. May 18, 1862, St. Louis, Mo. D. July 18, 1943, St. Louis, Mo.

	G	AB	H	2B	3B	HR	HR%	R	RBI	BB	SO	SB	BA	SA	PH AB	PH H	G by POS
1887 CLE AA	11	44	12	2	0	0	0.0	6		6		2	.273	.318	0	0	3B-11
1888 STL AA	43	172	46	7	1	3	1.7	21	43	11		9	.267	.372	0	0	SS-28, OF-11, 3B-4
1890	12	41	9	2	1	0	0.0	5		5		2	.220	.317	0	0	2B-7, OF-4, 3B-1
3 yrs.	66	257	67	11	2	3	1.2	32	42	22		13	.261	.354	0	0	SS-28, 3B-16, OF-15, 2B-7

Tommy Herr

HERR, THOMAS MITCHELL BB TR 6' 175 lbs.
B. Apr. 4, 1956, Lancaster, Pa.

	G	AB	H	2B	3B	HR	HR%	R	RBI	BB	SO	SB	BA	SA	PH AB	PH H	G by POS
1979 STL N	14	10	2	0	0	0	0.0	4	1	2	2	1	.200	.200	1	0	2B-6
1980	76	222	55	12	5	0	0.0	29	15	16	21	9	.248	.347	9	2	2B-58, SS-14
1981	103	411	110	14	9	0	0.0	50	46	39	30	23	.268	.345	0	0	2B-103
1982	135	493	131	19	4	0	0.0	83	36	57	56	25	.266	.320	5	2	2B-128
1983	89	313	101	14	4	2	0.6	43	31	43	27	6	.323	.412	5	2	2B-86
1984	145	558	154	23	2	4	0.7	67	49	49	56	13	.276	.346	1	1	2B-144
6 yrs.	562	2007	553	82	24	6	0.3	276	178	206	192	77	.276	.349	21	7	2B-525, SS-14

LEAGUE CHAMPIONSHIP SERIES

	G	AB	H	2B	3B	HR	HR%	R	RBI	BB	SO	SB	BA	SA	PH AB	PH H	G by POS
1982 STL N	3	13	3	1	0	0	0.0	1	0	1	2	0	.231	.308	0	0	2B-3

WORLD SERIES

	G	AB	H	2B	3B	HR	HR%	R	RBI	BB	SO	SB	BA	SA	PH AB	PH H	G by POS
1982 STL N	7	25	4	2	0	0	0.0	2	5	3	3	0	.160	.240	0	0	2B-7

Jose Herrera

HERRERA, JOSE CONCEPCION (Loco) BR TR 5'8" 165 lbs.
B. Apr. 8, 1942, San Lorenzo, Venezuela

	G	AB	H	2B	3B	HR	HR%	R	RBI	BB	SO	SB	BA	SA	PH AB	PH H	G by POS
1967 HOU N	5	4	1	0	0	0	0.0	0	1	0	1	0	.250	.250	4	1	
1968	27	100	24	5	0	0	0.0	9	7	4	12	0	.240	.290	4	1	OF-17, 2B-7
1969 MON N	47	126	36	5	0	2	1.6	7	12	3	14	1	.286	.373	13	3	OF-31, 2B-2, 3B-1
1970	1	1	0	0	0	0	0.0	0	0	0	1	0	.000	.000	1	0	
4 yrs.	80	231	61	10	0	2	0.9	16	20	7	28	1	.264	.333	22	5	OF-48, 2B-9, 3B-1

Mike Herrera

HERRERA, RAMON (Mike) BR TR 5'6" 147 lbs.
B. Dec. 19, 1897, Havana, Cuba D. Feb. 3, 1978, Havana, Cuba

	G	AB	H	2B	3B	HR	HR%	R	RBI	BB	SO	SB	BA	SA	PH AB	PH H	G by POS
1925 BOS A	10	39	15	0	0	0	0.0	2	8	2	2	1	.385	.385	0	0	2B-10
1926	74	237	61	14	1	0	0.0	20	19	15	13	0	.257	.325	4	0	2B-48, 3B-16, SS-4
2 yrs.	84	276	76	14	1	0	0.0	22	27	17	15	1	.275	.333	4	0	2B-58, 3B-16, SS-4

Pancho Herrera

HERRERA, JUAN FRANCISCO BR TR 6'3" 220 lbs.
B. June 16, 1934, Santiago, Cuba

	G	AB	H	2B	3B	HR	HR%	R	RBI	BB	SO	SB	BA	SA	PH AB	PH H	G by POS
1958 PHI N	29	63	17	3	0	1	1.6	5	6	7	15	1	.270	.365	2	0	3B-16, 1B-11
1960	145	512	144	26	6	17	3.3	61	71	51	136	2	.281	.455	3	1	1B-134, 2B-17
1961	126	400	103	17	2	13	3.3	56	51	55	120	5	.258	.408	10	3	1B-115
3 yrs.	300	975	264	46	8	31	3.2	122	128	113	271	8	.271	.430	15	4	1B-260, 2B-17, 3B-16

Lefty Herring

HERRING, SILAS CLARKE BL TL 5'11" 160 lbs.
B. Mar. 4, 1880, Philadelphia, Pa. D. Feb. 11, 1965, Massapequa, N. Y.

	G	AB	H	2B	3B	HR	HR%	R	RBI	BB	SO	SB	BA	SA	PH AB	PH H	G by POS
1899 WAS N	2	1	1	0	0	0	0.0	1	0	1		0	1.000	1.000	0	0	P-2
1904 WAS A	15	46	8	1	0	0	0.0	3	2	7		0	.174	.196	0	0	1B-10, OF-5
2 yrs.	17	47	9	1	0	0	0.0	4	2	8		0	.191	.213	0	0	1B-10, OF-5, P-2

Ed Herrmann

HERRMANN, EDWARD MARTIN BL TR 6'1" 195 lbs.
B. Aug. 27, 1946, San Diego, Calif.

	G	AB	H	2B	3B	HR	HR%	R	RBI	BB	SO	SB	BA	SA	PH AB	PH H	G by POS
1967 CHI A	2	3	2	1	0	0	0.0	1	1	1	0	0	.667	1.000	0	0	C-2
1969	102	290	67	8	0	8	2.8	31	31	30	35	0	.231	.341	11	1	C-92
1970	96	297	84	9	0	19	6.4	42	52	31	41	0	.283	.505	7	1	C-88
1971	101	294	63	6	0	11	3.7	32	35	44	48	2	.214	.347	7	0	C-97
1972	116	354	88	9	0	10	2.8	23	40	43	37	0	.249	.359	5	2	C-112
1973	119	379	85	17	1	10	2.6	42	39	31	55	2	.224	.354	2	0	C-114, DH-2
1974	107	367	95	13	1	10	2.7	32	39	16	49	1	.259	.381	0	0	C-107
1975 NY A	80	200	51	9	2	6	3.0	16	30	16	23	0	.255	.410	19	3	DH-35, C-24
1976 2 teams		CAL A	(29G –	.174)				HOU	N	(79G –	.204)						
" total	108	311	62	11	0	5	1.6	19	33	29	48	0	.199	.283	4	0	C-106
1977 HOU N	56	158	46	7	0	1	0.6	7	17	15	18	1	.291	.354	7	2	C-49
1978 2 teams		HOU	N	(16G –	.111)			MON	N	(19G –	.175)						
" total	35	76	11	2	0	0	0.0	2	3	4	7	0	.145	.171	10	3	C-26
11 yrs.	922	2729	654	92	4	80	2.9	247	320	260	361	6	.240	.364	72	12	C-817, DH-37

John Herrnstein

HERRNSTEIN, JOHN ELLETT BL TL 6'3" 215 lbs.
B. Mar. 31, 1938, Hampton, Va.

	G	AB	H	2B	3B	HR	HR%	R	RBI	BB	SO	SB	BA	SA	PH AB	PH H	G by POS
1962 PHI N	6	5	1	0	0	0	0.0	0	1	1	3	0	.200	.200	5	1	OF-1
1963	15	12	2	0	0	1	8.3	1	1	1	5	0	.167	.417	10	1	OF-2, 1B-1
1964	125	303	71	12	4	6	2.0	38	25	22	67	1	.234	.360	21	7	OF-69, 1B-68
1965	63	85	17	2	0	1	1.2	8	5	2	18	0	.200	.259	30	5	1B-18, OF-14
1966 3 teams		PHI	N	(4G –	.100)			CHI	N	(9G –	.176)			ATL	N	(17G –	.222)
" total	30	45	8	0	0	0	0.0	5	2	3	22	0	.178	.178	20	4	OF-8, 1B-4
5 yrs.	239	450	99	14	4	8	1.8	52	34	29	115	1	.220	.322	86	18	OF-94, 1B-91

Rick Herrscher

HERRSCHER, RICHARD FRANKLIN BR TR 6'2½" 187 lbs.
B. Nov. 3, 1936, St. Louis, Mo.

	G	AB	H	2B	3B	HR	HR%	R	RBI	BB	SO	SB	BA	SA	PH AB	PH H	G by POS
1962 NY N	35	50	11	3	0	1	2.0	5	6	5	11	0	.220	.340	8	2	1B-10, 3B-6, OF-4, SS-3

	G	AB	H	2B	3B	HR	HR %	R	RBI	BB	SO	SB	BA	SA	Pinch Hit AB	Pinch Hit H	G by POS

Earl Hersh

HERSH, EARL WALTER
B. May 21, 1932, Ebbvale, Md.
BL TL 6' 205 lbs.

	G	AB	H	2B	3B	HR	HR %	R	RBI	BB	SO	SB	BA	SA	AB	H	G by POS
1956 MIL N	7	13	3	3	0	0	0.0	0	0	0	5	0	.231	.462	5	0	OF-2

Mike Hershberger

HERSHBERGER, NORMAN MICHAEL
B. Oct. 9, 1939, Massillon, Ohio
BR TR 5'10" 175 lbs.

	G	AB	H	2B	3B	HR	HR %	R	RBI	BB	SO	SB	BA	SA	AB	H	G by POS
1961 CHI A	15	55	17	3	0	0	0.0	9	5	2	1	1	.309	.364	1	0	OF-13
1962	148	427	112	14	2	4	0.9	54	46	37	36	10	.262	.333	13	3	OF-135
1963	135	476	133	26	2	3	0.6	64	45	39	39	9	.279	.361	14	2	OF-119
1964	141	452	104	15	3	2	0.4	55	31	48	47	8	.230	.290	10	1	OF-134
1965 KC A	150	494	114	15	5	5	1.0	43	48	37	42	7	.231	.312	9	5	OF-144
1966	146	538	136	27	7	2	0.4	55	57	47	37	13	.253	.340	5	0	OF-143
1967	142	480	122	25	1	1	0.2	55	49	38	40	10	.254	.317	12	5	OF-130
1968 OAK A	99	246	67	9	2	5	2.0	23	32	21	22	8	.272	.386	12	5	OF-90
1969	51	129	26	2	0	1	0.8	11	10	10	15	1	.202	.240	15	3	OF-35
1970 MIL A	49	98	23	5	0	1	1.0	7	6	10	8	1	.235	.316	16	3	OF-35
1971 CHI A	74	177	46	9	0	2	1.1	22	15	30	23	6	.260	.345	20	5	OF-59
11 yrs.	1150	3572	900	150	22	26	0.7	398	344	319	311	74	.252	.328	127	32	OF-1037

Willard Hershberger

HERSHBERGER, WILLARD McKEE
B. May 28, 1910, Lemon Cove, Calif.   D. Aug. 3, 1940, Boston, Mass.
BR TR 5'10½" 167 lbs.

	G	AB	H	2B	3B	HR	HR %	R	RBI	BB	SO	SB	BA	SA	AB	H	G by POS
1938 CIN N	49	105	29	3	1	0	0.0	12	12	5	6	1	.276	.324	7	1	C-39, 2B-1
1939	63	174	60	9	2	0	0.0	23	32	9	4	1	.345	.420	3	0	C-60
1940	48	123	38	4	2	0	0.0	6	26	6	6	0	.309	.374	9	4	C-37
3 yrs.	160	402	127	16	5	0	0.0	41	70	20	16	2	.316	.381	19	5	C-136, 2B-1

WORLD SERIES

	G	AB	H	2B	3B	HR	HR %	R	RBI	BB	SO	SB	BA	SA	AB	H	G by POS
1939 CIN N	3	2	1	0	0	0	0.0	0	1	0	0	0	.500	.500	1	1	C-2

Neal Hertweck

HERTWECK, NEAL CHARLES
B. Nov. 22, 1931, St. Louis, Mo.
BL TL 6'1½" 175 lbs.

	G	AB	H	2B	3B	HR	HR %	R	RBI	BB	SO	SB	BA	SA	AB	H	G by POS
1952 STL N	2	6	0	0	0	0	0.0	0	0	1	1	0	.000	.000	0	0	1B-2

Steve Hertz

HERTZ, STEPHEN ALLAN
B. Feb. 26, 1945, Dayton, Ohio
BR TR 6' 195 lbs.

	G	AB	H	2B	3B	HR	HR %	R	RBI	BB	SO	SB	BA	SA	AB	H	G by POS
1964 HOU N	5	4	0	0	0	0	0.0	2	0	0	3	0	.000	.000	2	0	3B-2

Buck Herzog

HERZOG, CHARLES LINCOLN
B. July 9, 1885, Baltimore, Md.   D. Sept. 4, 1953, Baltimore, Md.
Manager 1914-16.
BR TR 5'11" 160 lbs.

	G	AB	H	2B	3B	HR	HR %	R	RBI	BB	SO	SB	BA	SA	AB	H	G by POS
1908 NY N	64	160	48	6	2	0	0.0	38	11	36		16	.300	.363	3	0	2B-42, SS-11, 3B-3, OF-1
1909	42	130	24	2	0	0	0.0	16	8	13		2	.185	.200	1	0	OF-29, 3B-4, 2B-4, SS-1
1910 BOS N	106	380	95	20	3	3	0.8	51	32	30	34	13	.250	.342	1	0	3B-105
1911 2 teams		BOS N (79G – .310)			NY N (69G – .267)												
" total	148	541	157	33	9	6	1.1	90	67	47	40	48	.290	.418	1	0	SS-75, 3B-69, 2B-3
1912 NY N	140	482	127	20	9	2	0.4	72	47	57	34	37	.263	.355	0	0	3B-84, 2B-2
1913	96	290	83	15	3	3	1.0	46	31	22	12	23	.286	.390	2	1	3B-84, 2B-2
1914 CIN N	138	498	140	14	8	1	0.2	54	40	42	27	46	.281	.347	0	0	SS-137, 1B-2
1915	155	579	153	14	10	1	0.2	61	42	34	21	35	.264	.328	0	0	SS-153, 1B-2
1916 2 teams		CIN N (79G – .267)			NY N (77G – .261)												
" total	156	561	148	24	6	1	0.2	70	49	43	36	34	.264	.333	1	1	SS-74, 2B-44, 3B-39, OF-1
1917 NY N	114	417	98	10	8	2	0.5	69	31	31	36	12	.235	.312	0	0	2B-113
1918 BOS N	118	473	108	12	6	0	0.0	57	26	29	28	10	.228	.279	0	0	2B-99, 1B-12, SS-7
1919 2 teams		BOS N (73G – .280)			CHI N (52G – .275)												
" total	125	468	130	12	9	1	0.2	42	42	23	18	28	.278	.348	2	1	2B-122, 1B-1
1920 CHI N	91	305	59	9	2	0	0.0	39	19	20	21	6	.193	.236	2	0	2B-59, 3B-28, 1B-1
13 yrs.	1493	5284	1370	191	75	20	0.4	705	445	427	307	312	.259	.335	13	3	2B-488, 3B-472, SS-458, OF-31, 1B-18

WORLD SERIES

	G	AB	H	2B	3B	HR	HR %	R	RBI	BB	SO	SB	BA	SA	AB	H	G by POS
1911 NY N	6	21	4	2	0	0	0.0	3	0	2	3	2	.190	.286	0	0	3B-6
1912	8	30	12	4	1	0	0.0	6	4	1	3	2	.400	.600	0	0	3B-8
1913	5	19	1	0	0	0	0.0	1	0	0	1	0	.053	.053	0	0	3B-5
1917	6	24	6	0	1	0	0.0	1	2	0	4	0	.250	.333	0	0	2B-6
4 yrs.	25	94	23	6	2	0	0.0	11	6	3	11	4	.245	.351	0	0	3B-19, 2B-6

Whitey Herzog

HERZOG, DORREL NORMAN ELVERT
B. Nov. 9, 1931, New Athens, Ill.
Manager 1973, 1975-84.
BL TL 5'11" 182 lbs.

	G	AB	H	2B	3B	HR	HR %	R	RBI	BB	SO	SB	BA	SA	AB	H	G by POS
1956 WAS A	117	421	103	13	7	4	1.0	49	35	59	74	8	.245	.337	11	5	OF-103, 1B-5
1957	36	78	13	3	0	0	0.0	7	4	13	12	1	.167	.205	10	0	OF-28
1958 2 teams		WAS A (8G – .000)			KC A (88G – .240)												
" total	96	101	23	1	2	0	0.0	11	9	17	26	0	.228	.277	32	7	OF-44, 1B-22
1959 KC A	38	123	36	7	1	0	0.8	25	9	34	23	1	.293	.390	2	1	OF-34, 1B-1
1960	83	252	67	10	2	8	3.2	43	38	40	32	0	.266	.417	12	5	OF-69, 1B-2
1961 BAL A	113	323	94	11	6	5	1.5	39	35	50	41	1	.291	.409	18	6	OF-98
1962	99	263	70	13	1	7	2.7	34	35	41	36	2	.266	.403	26	5	OF-70
1963 DET A	52	53	8	2	1	0	0.0	5	7	11	17	0	.151	.226	35	4	1B-7, OF-4
8 yrs.	634	1614	414	60	20	25	1.5	213	172	241	261	13	.257	.365	146	33	OF-450, 1B-37

Otto Hess

HESS, OTTO C.
B. Nov. 13, 1878, Berne, Switzerland   D. Feb. 24, 1926, Tucson, Ariz.
BL TL

	G	AB	H	2B	3B	HR	HR %	R	RBI	BB	SO	SB	BA	SA	AB	H	G by POS
1902 CLE A	7	14	1	0	0	0	0.0	1		2		0	.071	.071	0	0	P-7
1904	34	100	12	2	1	0	0.0	4	5	3		0	.120	.160	1	0	P-21, OF-12
1905	54	175	44	8	1	2	1.1	15	13	7		2	.251	.343	0	0	OF-27, P-26
1906	53	154	31	5	2	0	0.0	13	11	2		1	.201	.260	5	0	P-43, OF-5
1907	19	30	4	0	0	0	0.0	4	0	4		1	.133	.133	1	0	P-17, OF-2
1908	8	14	0	0	0	0	0.0	0	0	1		0	.000	.000	0	0	OF-4, P-4

	G	AB	H	2B	3B	HR	HR %	R	RBI	BB	SO	SB	BA	SA	Pinch Hit AB	Pinch Hit H	G by POS

Otto Hess continued

	G	AB	H	2B	3B	HR	HR%	R	RBI	BB	SO	SB	BA	SA	PH AB	PH H	G by POS
1912 BOS N	33	94	23	4	4	0	0.0	10	10	0	26	0	.245	.372	0	0	P-33
1913	35	83	26	0	1	2	2.4	9	11	7	15	0	.313	.410	5	0	P-29
1914	31	47	11	1	0	1	2.1	5	6	1	11	0	.234	.319	12	2	P-14, 1B-5
1915	5	5	2	1	0	0	0.0	1	1	0	2	0	.400	.600	0	0	P-4, 1B-1
10 yrs.	279	716	154	21	9	5	0.7	63	58	27	54	4	.215	.291	24	2	P-198, OF-50, 1B-6

Tom Hess

HESS, THOMAS
Born Thomas Heslin.
B. Aug. 15, 1875, Brooklyn, N. Y.   D. Dec. 15, 1945, Albany, N. Y.

	G	AB	H	2B	3B	HR	HR%	R	RBI	BB	SO	SB	BA	SA	PH AB	PH H	G by POS
1892 BAL N	1	2	0	0	0	0	0.0	0	0	0	0	0	.000	.000	0	0	C-1

Gus Hetling

HETLING, AUGUST JULIUS   BR TR 5'10" 165 lbs.
B. Nov. 21, 1885, St. Louis, Mo.   D. Oct. 13, 1962, Wichita, Kans.

	G	AB	H	2B	3B	HR	HR%	R	RBI	BB	SO	SB	BA	SA	PH AB	PH H	G by POS
1906 DET A	2	7	1	0	0	0	0.0	0	0	0		0	.143	.143	0	0	3B-2

George Heuble

HEUBLE, GEORGE A.   5'11½" 178 lbs.
B. 1849, Paterson, N. J.   D. Jan. 22, 1896, Philadelphia, Pa.

	G	AB	H	2B	3B	HR	HR%	R	RBI	BB	SO	SB	BA	SA	PH AB	PH H	G by POS
1876 NY N	1	4	0	0	0	0	0.0	0	0	0			.000	.000	0	0	1B-1

Johnnie Heving

HEVING, JOHN ALOYS   BR TR 6' 175 lbs.
Brother of Joe Heving.
B. Apr. 29, 1896, Covington, Ky.   D. Dec. 24, 1968, Salisbury, N. C.

	G	AB	H	2B	3B	HR	HR%	R	RBI	BB	SO	SB	BA	SA	PH AB	PH H	G by POS
1920 STL A	1	1	0	0	0	0	0.0	0	0	0	0	0	.000	.000	1	0	
1924 BOS A	44	108	31	5	1	0	0.0	15	10	10	7	0	.287	.352	15	3	C-29
1925	45	119	20	7	0	0	0.0	14	6	12	6	0	.168	.227	10	3	C-34
1928	82	158	41	7	2	0	0.0	11	11	11	10	1	.259	.329	18	7	C-62
1929	76	188	60	4	3	0	0.0	26	23	8	7	1	.319	.372	19	4	C-55
1930	75	220	61	5	3	0	0.0	15	17	11	14	2	.277	.327	3	1	C-71
1931 PHI A	42	113	27	3	2	1	0.9	8	12	6	8	0	.239	.327	2	1	C-40
1932	33	77	21	6	1	0	0.0	14	10	7	6	0	.273	.377	5	1	C-28
8 yrs.	398	984	261	37	12	1	0.1	103	89	65	59	4	.265	.330	73	20	C-319

WORLD SERIES

	G	AB	H	2B	3B	HR	HR%	R	RBI	BB	SO	SB	BA	SA	PH AB	PH H	G by POS
1931 PHI A	1	1	0	0	0	0	0.0	0	0	0	0	0	.000	.000	1	0	

Mike Heydon

HEYDON, MICHAEL EDWARD   BL TR
B. July 15, 1874, Missouri   D. Oct. 13, 1913, Indianapolis, Ind.

	G	AB	H	2B	3B	HR	HR%	R	RBI	BB	SO	SB	BA	SA	PH AB	PH H	G by POS
1898 BAL N	3	9	1	0	0	0	0.0	2	1	2		0	.111	.111	0	0	C-3
1899 WAS N	3	3	0	0	0	0	0.0	0	0	0		0	.000	.000	1	0	C-2
1901 STL N	16	43	9	1	1	1	2.3	2	6	5		2	.209	.349	1	0	C-13, OF-1
1904 CHI A	4	10	1	1	0	0	0.0	0	1	1		0	.100	.200	0	0	C-4
1905 WAS A	77	245	47	7	4	1	0.4	20	26	21		5	.192	.265	0	0	C-77
1906	49	145	23	7	1	0	0.0	14	10	14		2	.159	.221	0	0	C-49
1907	62	164	30	3	0	0	0.0	14	9	25		3	.183	.201	4	0	C-57
7 yrs.	214	619	111	19	6	2	0.3	52	53	70		12	.179	.239	6	0	C-205, OF-1

Jack Hiatt

HIATT, JACK E.   BR TR 6'2" 190 lbs.
B. July 27, 1942, Bakersfield, Calif.

	G	AB	H	2B	3B	HR	HR%	R	RBI	BB	SO	SB	BA	SA	PH AB	PH H	G by POS
1964 LA A	9	16	6	0	0	0	0.0	2	2	2	3	0	.375	.375	4	3	C-3, 1B-2
1965 SF N	40	67	19	4	0	1	1.5	5	7	12	14	0	.284	.388	16	6	C-21, 1B-7
1966	18	23	7	2	0	0	0.0	2	1	4	5	0	.304	.391	9	3	1B-7
1967	73	153	42	6	0	6	3.9	24	26	27	37	0	.275	.431	31	8	1B-36, C-3, OF-2
1968	90	224	52	10	4	4	1.8	14	34	41	61	0	.232	.348	21	6	C-58, 1B-10
1969	69	194	38	4	0	7	3.6	18	34	48	58	0	.196	.325	2	0	C-60, 1B-3
1970 2 teams	83	221	57	14	1	2	0.9	23	29	45	62	0	.258	.357	7	0	C-75, 1B-4
" total	MON N (17G – .326)			CHI N (66G – .242)													
1971 HOU N	69	174	48	8	1	1	0.6	16	16	35	39	0	.276	.351	4	2	C-65, 1B-1
1972 2 teams	HOU N (10G – .200)			CAL A (22G – .289)													
" total	32	70	18	3	1	1	1.4	6	5	10	16	0	.257	.371	7	2	C-27
9 yrs.	483	1142	287	51	5	22	1.9	110	154	224	295	0	.251	.363	101	30	C-312, 1B-70, OF-2

Jim Hibbs

HIBBS, JAMES KERR   BR TR 6' 190 lbs.
B. Sept. 10, 1944, Klamath Falls, Ore.

	G	AB	H	2B	3B	HR	HR%	R	RBI	BB	SO	SB	BA	SA	PH AB	PH H	G by POS
1967 CAL A	3	3	0	0	0	0	0.0	0	0	0	2	0	.000	.000	3	0	

Mike Hickey

HICKEY, MICHAEL EDWARD   BR TR
B. Dec. 25, 1871, Chicopee, Mass.   D. June 11, 1918, Springfield, Mass.

	G	AB	H	2B	3B	HR	HR%	R	RBI	BB	SO	SB	BA	SA	PH AB	PH H	G by POS
1899 BOS N	1	3	1	0	0	0	0.0	0	0	0		0	.333	.333	0	0	2B-1
1901 CHI N	10	37	6	0	0	0	0.0	4	3	2		1	.162	.162	0	0	3B-10
2 yrs.	11	40	7	0	0	0	0.0	4	3	2		1	.175	.175	0	0	3B-10, 2B-1

Jim Hickman

HICKMAN, DAVID JAMES   BR TR 5'7½" 170 lbs.
B. May 19, 1894, Johnson City, Tenn.   D. Dec. 30, 1958, Brooklyn, N. Y.

	G	AB	H	2B	3B	HR	HR%	R	RBI	BB	SO	SB	BA	SA	PH AB	PH H	G by POS
1915 BAL F	20	81	17	4	1	1	1.2	7	7	4		5	.210	.321	0	0	OF-20
1916 BKN N	9	5	1	0	0	0	0.0	3	0	2	0	1	.200	.200	0	0	OF-3
1917	114	370	81	15	4	6	1.6	46	36	17	66	14	.219	.330	8	1	OF-101
1918	53	167	39	4	7	1	0.6	14	16	8	31	5	.234	.359	3	0	OF-46
1919	57	104	20	3	1	0	0.0	14	11	6	17	2	.192	.240	8	1	OF-29
5 yrs.	253	727	158	26	13	8	1.1	84	70	37	114	27	.217	.322	19	2	OF-199

Jim Hickman

HICKMAN, JAMES LUCIUS   BR TR 6'3" 192 lbs.
B. May 10, 1937, Henning, Tenn.

	G	AB	H	2B	3B	HR	HR%	R	RBI	BB	SO	SB	BA	SA	PH AB	PH H	G by POS
1962 NY N	140	392	96	18	2	13	3.3	54	46	47	96	4	.245	.401	13	3	OF-124
1963	146	494	113	21	6	17	3.4	53	51	44	120	0	.229	.399	11	1	OF-82, 3B-59
1964	139	409	105	14	1	11	2.7	48	57	36	90	0	.257	.377	31	8	OF-113, 3B-1

	G	AB	H	2B	3B	HR	HR %	R	RBI	BB	SO	SB	BA	SA	Pinch Hit AB	H	G by POS

Jim Hickman continued

	G	AB	H	2B	3B	HR	HR %	R	RBI	BB	SO	SB	BA	SA	AB	H	G by POS
1965	141	369	87	18	0	15	4.1	32	40	27	76	3	.236	.407	29	5	OF-91, 1B-30, 3B-14
1966	58	160	38	7	0	4	2.5	15	16	13	34	2	.238	.356	11	1	OF-45, 1B-17
1967 LA N	65	98	16	6	1	0	0.0	7	10	14	28	1	.163	.245	25	3	OF-37, 3B-2, 1B-2, P-1
1968 CHI N	75	188	42	6	3	5	2.7	22	23	18	38	1	.223	.367	12	2	OF-66
1969	134	338	80	11	2	21	6.2	38	54	47	74	2	.237	.467	18	5	OF-125
1970	149	514	162	33	4	32	6.2	102	115	93	99	0	.315	.582	2	0	OF-79, 1B-74
1971	117	383	98	13	2	19	5.0	50	60	50	61	0	.256	.449	12	2	OF-69, 1B-44
1972	115	368	100	15	2	17	4.6	65	64	52	64	3	.272	.462	13	3	1B-77, OF-27
1973	92	201	49	1	2	3	1.5	27	20	42	42	1	.244	.313	34	6	1B-51, OF-13
1974 STL N	50	60	16	0	0	2	3.3	5	4	8	10	0	.267	.367	30	6	1B-14, 3B-1
13 yrs.	1421	3974	1002	163	25	159	4.0	518	560	491	832	17	.252	.426	241	45	OF-871, 1B-309, 3B-77, P-1

Piano Legs Hickman

HICKMAN, CHARLES TAYLOR   BR TR 5'9"   185 lbs.
B. Mar. 4, 1876, Taylortown, Pa.   D. Apr. 19, 1934, Morgantown, W. Va.

	G	AB	H	2B	3B	HR	HR %	R	RBI	BB	SO	SB	BA	SA	AB	H	G by POS
1897 BOS N	2	3	2	0	0	1	33.3	1	2	0		0	.667	1.667	0	0	P-2
1898	19	58	15	2	0	0	0.0	4	7	1		0	.259	.293	0	0	OF-7, 1B-6, P-6
1899	19	63	25	2	7	0	0.0	15	15	2		1	.397	.651	0	0	P-11, OF-7, 1B-1
1900 NY N	127	473	148	19	17	9	1.9	65	91	17		10	.313	.482	0	0	3B-120, OF-7
1901	112	401	113	20	6	4	1.0	44	62	15		5	.282	.392	8	1	OF-50, SS-23, 3B-15, P-9, 2B-7, 1B-2
1902 2 teams		BOS A	(28G – .296)				CLE A	(102G – .380)									
" total	130	534	194	36	13	11	2.1	74	110	15		9	.363	.541	1	0	1B-98, OF-27, 2B-3, P-1
1903 CLE A	130	518	171	31	11	12	2.3	67	97	17		14	.330	.502	0	0	1B-125, 2B-7
1904 2 teams		CLE A	(86G – .288)				DET A	(42G – .243)									
" total	128	481	132	28	16	6	1.2	52	67	24		12	.274	.437	1	1	1B-79, 2B-45, OF-1
1905 2 teams		DET A	(59G – .221)				WAS A	(88G – .311)									
" total	147	573	159	37	12	4	0.7	69	66	21		6	.277	.405	0	0	2B-85, OF-47, 1B-15
1906 WAS A	120	451	128	25	5	9	2.0	53	57	14		9	.284	.421	1	0	OF-95, 1B-18, 3B-5, 2B-1
1907 2 teams		WAS A	(60G – .285)				CHI A	(21G – .261)									
" total	81	216	61	12	4	1	0.5	23	24	18		4	.282	.389	22	4	1B-30, OF-21, 2B-3, P-1
1908 CLE A	65	197	46	6	1	2	1.0	16	16	9		2	.234	.305	16	4	OF-28, 1B-20, 2B-1
12 yrs.	1080	3968	1194	218	92	59	1.5	483	614	153		72	.301	.447	49	10	1B-394, OF-290, 2B-152, 3B-140, P-30, SS-23

Buddy Hicks

HICKS, CLARENCE WALTER   BB TR 5'10"   170 lbs.
B. Feb. 15, 1927, Belvedere, Calif.

	G	AB	H	2B	3B	HR	HR %	R	RBI	BB	SO	SB	BA	SA	AB	H	G by POS
1956 DET A	26	47	10	2	0	0	0.0	5	5	3	2	0	.213	.255	2	0	SS-16, 2B-6, 3B-1

Jim Hicks

HICKS, JAMES EDWARD   BR TR 6'3"   205 lbs.
B. May 18, 1940, East Chicago, Ind.

	G	AB	H	2B	3B	HR	HR %	R	RBI	BB	SO	SB	BA	SA	AB	H	G by POS
1964 CHI A	2	0	0	0	0	0	–	0	0	0	0	0	–	–	0	0	
1965	13	19	5	1	0	1	5.3	2	2	0	9	0	.263	.474	8	2	OF-5
1966	18	26	5	0	1	0	0.0	3	1	1	5	0	.192	.269	2	0	OF-10, 1B-2
1969 2 teams		STL N	(19G – .182)				CAL A	(37G – .083)									
" total	56	92	12	0	2	4	4.3	11	11	17	32	0	.130	.304	17	0	OF-25, 1B-8
1970 CAL A	4	4	1	0	0	0	0.0	0	0	0	2	0	.250	.250	4	1	
5 yrs.	93	141	23	1	3	5	3.5	16	14	18	48	0	.163	.319	31	3	OF-40, 1B-10

Joe Hicks

HICKS, WILLIAM JOSEPH   BL TR 6'   180 lbs.
B. Apr. 7, 1933, Ivy, Va.

	G	AB	H	2B	3B	HR	HR %	R	RBI	BB	SO	SB	BA	SA	AB	H	G by POS
1959 CHI A	6	7	3	0	0	0	0.0	0	1	1	0	0	.429	.429	2	2	OF-4
1960	36	47	9	1	0	0	0.0	3	2	6	3	0	.191	.213	17	4	OF-14
1961 WAS A	12	29	5	0	0	1	3.4	2	1	0	4	0	.172	.276	6	2	OF-7
1962	102	174	39	4	2	6	3.4	20	14	15	34	3	.224	.374	61	9	OF-42
1963 NY N	56	159	36	6	1	5	3.1	16	22	7	31	0	.226	.371	16	3	OF-41
5 yrs.	212	416	92	11	3	12	2.9	41	39	29	73	3	.221	.349	102	20	OF-108

Nat Hicks

HICKS, NATHAN WOODHULL   BR TR 6'1"   186 lbs.
B. Apr. 19, 1845, Hempstead, N. Y.   D. Apr. 21, 1907, Hoboken, N. J.
Manager 1875.

	G	AB	H	2B	3B	HR	HR %	R	RBI	BB	SO	SB	BA	SA	AB	H	G by POS
1876 NY N	45	188	44	4	1	0	0.0	20	15	3	4		.234	.266	0	0	C-45
1877 CIN N	8	32	6	0	0	0	0.0	3	3	1	2		.188	.188	0	0	C-8
2 yrs.	53	220	50	4	1	0	0.0	23	18	4	6		.227	.255	0	0	C-53

Mahlon Higbee

HIGBEE, MAHLON JESSE   BR TR 5'11"   165 lbs.
B. Aug. 16, 1901, Louisville, Ky.   D. Apr. 7, 1968, DePauw, Ind.

	G	AB	H	2B	3B	HR	HR %	R	RBI	BB	SO	SB	BA	SA	AB	H	G by POS
1922 NY N	3	10	4	0	0	1	10.0	2	5	0	2	0	.400	.700	0	0	OF-3

Bill Higdon

HIGDON, WILLIAM TRAVIS   BL TR 6'2"   195 lbs.
B. Apr. 27, 1924, Camp Hill, Ala.

	G	AB	H	2B	3B	HR	HR %	R	RBI	BB	SO	SB	BA	SA	AB	H	G by POS
1949 CHI A	11	23	7	3	0	0	0.0	3	1	6	3	1	.304	.435	4	1	OF-6

Bill Higgins

HIGGINS, WILLIAM EDWARD   TR
B. Sept. 8, 1861, Wilmington, Del.   D. Apr. 25, 1919, Wilmington, Del.

	G	AB	H	2B	3B	HR	HR %	R	RBI	BB	SO	SB	BA	SA	AB	H	G by POS
1888 BOS N	14	54	10	1	0	0	0.0	5	4	1	3	1	.185	.204	0	0	2B-14
1890 2 teams		STL AA	(67G – .252)				SYR AA	(1G – .250)									
" total	68	262	66	7	2	0	0.0	40		24		7	.252	.294	0	0	2B-68
2 yrs.	82	316	76	8	2	0	0.0	45	4	25	3	8	.241	.278	0	0	2B-82

Bob Higgins

HIGGINS, ROBERT STONE   BR TR 5'8"   176 lbs.
B. Sept. 23, 1886, Fayetteville, Tenn.   D. May 25, 1941, Chattanooga, Tenn.

	G	AB	H	2B	3B	HR	HR %	R	RBI	BB	SO	SB	BA	SA	AB	H	G by POS
1909 CLE A	8	23	2	0	0	0	0.0	0	0	0		0	.087	.087	0	0	C-8
1911 BKN N	4	10	3	0	0	0	0.0	1	2	1	0	1	.300	.300	1	1	C-2, 3B-1
1912	1	2	0	0	0	0	0.0	0	0	0	1	0	.000	.000	0	0	C-1
3 yrs.	13	35	5	0	0	0	0.0	1	2	1	1	1	.143	.143	1	1	C-11, 3B-1

	G	AB	H	2B	3B	HR	HR%	R	RBI	BB	SO	SB	BA	SA	Pinch Hit AB	Pinch Hit H	G by POS

Pinky Higgins

HIGGINS, MICHAEL FRANKLIN BR TR 6'1" 185 lbs.
B. May 27, 1909, Red Oak, Tex. D. Mar. 21, 1969, Dallas, Tex.
Manager 1955-62.

	G	AB	H	2B	3B	HR	HR%	R	RBI	BB	SO	SB	BA	SA	AB	H	G by POS
1930 PHI A	14	24	6	2	0	0	0.0	1	0	4	5	0	.250	.333	4	0	3B-5, 2B-2, SS-1
1933	152	567	178	34	11	14	2.5	85	99	61	53	2	.314	.487	0	0	3B-152
1934	144	543	179	37	6	16	2.9	89	90	56	70	9	.330	.508	0	0	3B-144
1935	133	524	155	32	4	23	4.4	69	94	42	62	6	.296	.504	1	1	3B-131
1936	146	550	159	32	2	12	2.2	89	80	67	61	7	.289	.420	1	0	3B-145
1937 BOS A	153	570	172	33	5	9	1.6	88	106	76	51	2	.302	.425	1	1	3B-152
1938	139	524	159	29	5	5	1.0	77	106	71	55	10	.303	.406	1	0	3B-138
1939 DET A	132	489	135	23	2	8	1.6	57	76	56	41	7	.276	.380	2	1	3B-129
1940	131	480	130	24	3	13	2.7	70	76	61	31	4	.271	.415	1	0	3B-129
1941	147	540	161	28	3	11	2.0	79	73	67	45	5	.298	.422	2	0	3B-145
1942	143	499	133	34	2	11	2.2	65	79	72	21	3	.267	.409	5	0	3B-137
1943	138	523	145	20	1	10	1.9	62	84	57	31	2	.277	.377	0	0	3B-138
1944	148	543	161	32	4	7	1.3	79	76	81	34	4	.297	.409	2	1	3B-146
1946 2 teams	DET	A	(18G –	.217)		BOS	A	(64G –	.275)								
" total	82	260	68	14	2	2	0.8	20	36	29	30	0	.262	.354	5	1	3B-76
14 yrs.	1802	6636	1941	374	50	141	2.1	930	1075	800	590	61	.292	.428	25	5	3B-1768, 2B-2, SS-1
WORLD SERIES																	
1940 DET A	7	24	8	3	1	1	4.2	2 .	6	3	3	0	.333	.667	0	0	3B-7
1946 BOS A	7	24	5	1	0	0	0.0	1	2	2	0	0	.208	.250	0	0	3B-7
2 yrs.	14	48	13	4	1	1	2.1	3	8	5	3	0	.271	.458	0	0	3B-14

Andy High

HIGH, ANDREW AIRD (Handy Andy) BL TR 5'6" 155 lbs.
Brother of Charlie High. Brother of Hugh High.
B. Nov. 21, 1897, Ava, Ill. D. Feb. 22, 1981, Toledo, Ohio

	G	AB	H	2B	3B	HR	HR%	R	RBI	BB	SO	SB	BA	SA	AB	H	G by POS
1922 BKN N	153	579	164	27	10	6	1.0	82	65	59	26	3	.283	.396	0	0	3B-130, SS-22, 2B-1
1923	123	426	115	23	9	3	0.7	51	37	47	13	4	.270	.387	0	0	3B-80, SS-45, 2B-5
1924	144	582	191	26	13	6	1.0	98	61	57	16	3	.328	.448	0	0	2B-133, SS-17, 3B-1
1925 2 teams	BKN	N	(44G –	.200)		BOS	N	(60G –	.288)								
" total	104	334	86	15	2	4	1.2	42	34	38	7	3	.257	.350	17	5	3B-71, 2B-12, SS-3
1926 BOS N	130	476	141	17	10	2	0.4	55	66	39	9	4	.296	.387	4	2	3B-81, 2B-49
1927	113	384	116	15	9	4	1.0	59	46	26	11	4	.302	.419	13	6	3B-89, 2B-8, SS-2
1928 STL N	111	368	105	14	3	6	1.6	58	37	37	10	2	.285	.389	11	4	3B-73, 2B-19
1929	146	603	178	32	4	10	1.7	95	82	63	18	7	.295	.411	1	1	3B-123, 2B-22
1930	72	215	60	12	2	2	0.9	34	29	23	6	1	.279	.381	17	5	3B-48, 2B-3
1931	63	131	35	6	1	0	0.0	20	19	24	4	0	.267	.328	19	5	3B-23, 2B-19
1932 CIN N	84	191	36	4	2	0	0.0	16	12	23	6	1	.188	.230	23	7	3B-46, 2B-12
1933	24	43	9	2	0	1	2.3	4	6	5	1	0	.209	.326	10	2	3B-11, 2B-2
1934 PHI N	47	68	14	2	0	0	0.0	4	7	9	3	1	.206	.235	23	5	3B-14, 2B-2
13 yrs.	1314	4400	1250	195	65	44	1.0	618	482	425	130	33	.284	.388	144	42	3B-790, 2B-287, SS-89
WORLD SERIES																	
1928 STL N	4	17	5	2	0	0	0.0	1	1	1	3	0	.294	.412	0	0	3B-4
1930	1	2	1	0	0	0	0.0	1	0	0	0	0	.500	.500	0	0	3B-1
1931	4	15	4	0	0	0	0.0	3	0	0	2	0	.267	.267	0	0	3B-4
3 yrs.	9	34	10	2	0	0	0.0	5	1	1	5	0	.294	.353	0	0	3B-9

Charlie High

HIGH, CHARLES EDWIN BL TR 5'9" 170 lbs.
Brother of Andy High. Brother of Hugh High.
B. Dec. 1, 1898, Ava, Ill. D. Sept. 11, 1960, Oak Grove, Ore.

	G	AB	H	2B	3B	HR	HR%	R	RBI	BB	SO	SB	BA	SA	AB	H	G by POS
1919 PHI A	11	29	2	0	0	0	0.0	2	1	3	4	2	.069	.069	2	0	OF-9
1920	17	65	20	2	1	1	1.5	7	6	3	6	0	.308	.415	0	0	OF-17
2 yrs.	28	94	22	2	1	1	1.1	9	7	6	10	2	.234	.309	2	0	OF-26

Hugh High

HIGH, HUGH JENKEN (Bunny, Lefty) BL TL 5'7½" 155 lbs.
Brother of Andy High. Brother of Charlie High.
B. Oct. 24, 1887, Pottstown, Pa. D. Nov. 16, 1962, St. Louis, Mo.

	G	AB	H	2B	3B	HR	HR%	R	RBI	BB	SO	SB	BA	SA	AB	H	G by POS
1913 DET A	80	183	42	6	1	0	0.0	18	16	28	24	6	.230	.273	19	5	OF-50
1914	80	184	49	5	3	0	0.0	25	17	26	21	7	.266	.326	19	3	OF-53
1915 NY A	119	427	110	19	7	1	0.2	51	43	62	47	22	.258	.342	1	1	OF-117
1916	115	377	99	13	4	1	0.3	44	28	47	44	13	.263	.326	5	1	OF-109
1917	103	365	86	11	6	1	0.3	37	19	48	31	8	.236	.307	2	0	OF-100
1918	7	10	0	0	0	0	0.0	1	0	1	1	0	.000	.000	3	0	OF-4
6 yrs.	504	1546	386	54	21	3	0.2	176	123	212	168	56	.250	.318	49	10	OF-433

Dick Higham

HIGHAM, RICHARD BL TR
B. 1852, England D. Mar. 18, 1905, Chicago, Ill.
Manager 1874.

	G	AB	H	2B	3B	HR	HR%	R	RBI	BB	SO	SB	BA	SA	AB	H	G by POS
1876 HAR N	67	312	102	21	2	0	0.0	59	35	2	7		.327	.407	0	0	OF-59, C-13, SS-1, 2B-1
1878 PRO N	62	281	90	22	1	1	0.4	60	29	5	16		.320	.416	0	0	OF-62, C-1
1880 TRO N	1	5	1	0	0	0	0.0	1	0	0	0		.200	.200	0	0	OF-1, C-1
3 yrs.	130	598	193	43	3	1	0.2	120	64	7	23		.323	.410	0	0	OF-122, C-15, SS-1, 2B-1

John Hiland

HILAND, JOHN WILLIAM TL
B. 1861, Philadelphia, Pa. D. Apr. 10, 1901, Philadelphia, Pa.

	G	AB	H	2B	3B	HR	HR%	R	RBI	BB	SO	SB	BA	SA	AB	H	G by POS
1885 PHI N	3	9	0	0	0	0	0.0	0		0	4		.000	.000	0	0	2B-3

George Hildebrand

HILDEBRAND, GEORGE ALBERT BR TR 5'8" 170 lbs.
B. Sept. 6, 1878, San Francisco, Calif. D. May 30, 1960, Woodland Hills, Calif.

	G	AB	H	2B	3B	HR	HR%	R	RBI	BB	SO	SB	BA	SA	AB	H	G by POS
1902 BKN N	11	41	9	1	0	0	0.0	3	5	3		0	.220	.244	0	0	OF-11

Palmer Hildebrand

HILDEBRAND, PALMER MARION (Pete) BR TR 5'11" 180 lbs.
B. Dec. 23, 1884, Schauck, Ohio D. Jan. 25, 1960, North Canton, Ohio

	G	AB	H	2B	3B	HR	HR%	R	RBI	BB	SO	SB	BA	SA	AB	H	G by POS
1913 STL N	26	55	9	2	0	0	0.0	3	1	1	10	1	.164	.200	2	0	C-22, OF-1

	G	AB	H	2B	3B	HR	HR %	R	RBI	BB	SO	SB	BA	SA	Pinch Hit AB	Pinch Hit H	G by POS

R. E. Hildebrand

HILDEBRAND, R. E.
B. Unknown.

	G	AB	H	2B	3B	HR	HR %	R	RBI	BB	SO	SB	BA	SA	AB	H	G by POS
1902 CHI N	1	4	0	0	0	0	0.0	1	0	1		0	.000	.000	0	0	OF-1

Belden Hill

HILL, BELDEN L.
BL TR 6'
B. Aug. 24, 1864, Kewanee, Ill.   D. Oct. 23, 1934, Cedar Rapids, Iowa

	G	AB	H	2B	3B	HR	HR %	R	RBI	BB	SO	SB	BA	SA	AB	H	G by POS
1890 B-B AA	9	30	5	2	0	0	0.0	3		3		6	.167	.233	0	0	3B-9

Donny Hill

HILL, DONALD EARL
BB TR 5'10"   165 lbs.
B. Nov. 20, 1960, Westminster, Calif.

	G	AB	H	2B	3B	HR	HR %	R	RBI	BB	SO	SB	BA	SA	AB	H	G by POS
1983 OAK A	53	158	42	7	0	2	1.3	20	15	4	21	1	.266	.348	1	0	SS-53
1984	73	174	40	6	0	2	1.1	21	16	5	12	1	.230	.299	5	0	SS-66, 2B-4, DH-2, 3B-2
2 yrs.	126	332	82	13	0	4	1.2	41	31	9	33	2	.247	.322	6	0	SS-119, 2B-4, DH-2, 3B-2

Herman Hill

HILL, HERMAN ALEXANDER
BL TR 6'2"   190 lbs.
B. Oct. 12, 1945, Tuskegee, Ala.   D. Dec. 14, 1970, Magallanes, Venezuela.

	G	AB	H	2B	3B	HR	HR %	R	RBI	BB	SO	SB	BA	SA	AB	H	G by POS
1969 MIN A	16	2	0	0	0	0	0.0	4	0	0	1	1	.000	.000	1	0	OF-2
1970	27	22	2	0	0	0	0.0	8	0	0	6	0	.091	.091	4	0	OF-14
2 yrs.	43	24	2	0	0	0	0.0	12	0	0	7	1	.083	.083	5	0	OF-16

Hugh Hill

HILL, HUGH ELLIS
Brother of Still Bill Hill.
B. July 21, 1879, Ringgold, Ga.   D. Sept. 6, 1958, Cincinnati, Ohio

	G	AB	H	2B	3B	HR	HR %	R	RBI	BB	SO	SB	BA	SA	AB	H	G by POS
1903 CLE A	1	1	0	0	0	0	0.0	0	0	0		0	.000	.000	1	0	
1904 STL A	23	93	21	2	1	3	3.2	13	4	2		3	.226	.366	0	0	OF-23
2 yrs.	24	94	21	2	1	3	3.2	13	4	2		3	.223	.362	1	0	OF-23

Hunter Hill

HILL, HUNTER BENJAMIN
BR TR
B. June 21, 1879, Austin, Tex.   D. Feb. 22, 1959, Austin, Tex.

	G	AB	H	2B	3B	HR	HR %	R	RBI	BB	SO	SB	BA	SA	AB	H	G by POS
1903 STL A	86	317	77	11	3	0	0.0	30	25	8		2	.243	.297	0	0	3B-86
1904 2 teams		STL	A (58G – .215)		WAS	A	(77G – .197)										
" total	135	509	104	9	1	0	0.0	37	31	17		14	.204	.226	2	0	3B-127, OF-6
1905 WAS A	104	374	78	12	1	1	0.3	37	24	32		10	.209	.254	1	1	3B-103
3 yrs.	325	1200	259	32	5	1	0.1	104	80	57		26	.216	.253	3	1	3B-316, OF-6

Jesse Hill

HILL, JESSE TERRILL
BR TR 5'9"   165 lbs.
B. Jan. 20, 1907, Yates, Mo.

	G	AB	H	2B	3B	HR	HR %	R	RBI	BB	SO	SB	BA	SA	AB	H	G by POS
1935 NY A	107	392	115	20	3	4	1.0	69	33	42	32	14	.293	.390	7	2	OF-94
1936 WAS A	85	233	71	19	5	0	0.0	50	34	29	23	11	.305	.429	16	3	OF-60
1937 2 teams		WAS	A (33G – .217)		PHI	A	(70G – .293)										
" total	103	334	91	14	4	2	0.6	56	41	44	36	18	.272	.356	7	0	OF-89
3 yrs.	295	959	277	53	12	6	0.6	175	108	115	91	43	.289	.388	30	5	OF-243

John Hill

HILL, JOHN CLINTON
BL TR 5'11"   178 lbs.
B. Oct. 16, 1909, Powder Springs, Ga.   D. Sept. 20, 1970, Decatur, Ga.

	G	AB	H	2B	3B	HR	HR %	R	RBI	BB	SO	SB	BA	SA	AB	H	G by POS
1939 BOS N	2	2	1	1	0	0	0.0	1	0	0	0	0	.500	1.000	2	1	

Marc Hill

HILL, MARC KEVIN
BR TR 6'3"   205 lbs.
B. Feb. 18, 1952, Louisiana, Mo.

	G	AB	H	2B	3B	HR	HR %	R	RBI	BB	SO	SB	BA	SA	AB	H	G by POS
1973 STL N	1	3	0	0	0	0	0.0	0	0	0	1	0	.000	.000	0	0	C-1
1974	10	21	5	1	0	0	0.0	2	2	4	5	0	.238	.286	1	0	C-9
1975 SF N	72	182	39	4	0	5	2.7	14	23	25	27	0	.214	.319	16	3	C-60, 3B-1
1976	54	131	24	5	0	3	2.3	11	15	10	19	0	.183	.290	4	1	C-49, 1B-1
1977	108	320	80	10	0	9	2.8	28	50	34	34	0	.250	.366	7	2	C-102
1978	117	358	87	15	1	3	0.8	20	36	45	39	1	.243	.316	5	3	C-116, 1B-2
1979	63	169	35	3	0	3	1.8	20	15	26	25	0	.207	.278	6	1	C-58, 1B-1
1980 2 teams		SF	N (17G – .171)		SEA	A	(29G – .229)										
" total	46	111	23	4	1	2	1.8	9	9	4	17	0	.207	.315	3	0	C-43
1981 CHI A	16	6	0	0	0	0	0.0	0	0	0	1	0	.000	.000	3	0	C-14, 3B-1, 1B-1
1982	53	88	23	2	0	3	3.4	9	13	6	13	0	.261	.386	2	1	C-49, 3B-1, 1B-1
1983	58	133	30	6	0	1	0.8	11	11	9	24	0	.226	.293	4	2	C-55, DH-2, 1B-1
1984	77	193	45	10	1	5	2.6	15	20	9	26	0	.233	.373	5	0	C-72, 1B-2
12 yrs.	675	1715	391	60	3	34	2.0	139	194	172	231	1	.228	.326	56	13	C-628, 1B-9, 3B-3, DH-2

Homer Hillebrand

HILLEBRAND, HOMER HILLER
BR TL 5'8"   165 lbs.
Also known as Henry Hillebrand.
B. Oct. 10, 1879, Freeport, Ill.   D. Jan. 23, 1974, Elsinore, Calif.

	G	AB	H	2B	3B	HR	HR %	R	RBI	BB	SO	SB	BA	SA	AB	H	G by POS
1905 PIT N	39	110	26	3	2	0	0.0	9	7	6		1	.236	.300	1	0	1B-16, P-10, OF-7, C-3
1906	7	21	5	1	0	0	0.0	1	3	1		0	.238	.286	0	0	P-7
1908	1	0	0	0	0	0	–	0	0	0		0	–	–	0	0	P-1
3 yrs.	47	131	31	4	2	0	0.0	10	10	7		1	.237	.298	1	0	P-18, 1B-16, OF-7, C-3

Chuck Hiller

HILLER, CHARLES JOSEPH (Iron Hands)
BL TR 5'11"   170 lbs.
B. Oct. 1, 1935, Johnsburg, Ill.

	G	AB	H	2B	3B	HR	HR %	R	RBI	BB	SO	SB	BA	SA	AB	H	G by POS
1961 SF N	70	240	57	12	1	2	0.8	38	12	32	30	4	.238	.321	2	0	2B-67
1962	161	602	166	22	2	3	0.5	94	48	55	49	5	.276	.334	0	0	2B-161
1963	111	417	93	10	2	6	1.4	44	33	20	23	3	.223	.300	5	0	2B-109
1964	80	205	37	8	1	1	0.5	21	17	17	23	1	.180	.244	22	5	2B-60, 3B-1
1965 2 teams		SF	N (7G – .143)		NY	N	(100G – .238)										
" total	107	293	69	11	1	6	2.0	25	22	14	25	1	.235	.341	33	7	2B-82, OF-4, 3B-2
1966 NY N	108	254	71	8	2	2	0.8	25	14	15	22	0	.280	.350	45	15	2B-45, 3B-14, OF-9
1967 2 teams		NY	N (25G – .093)		PHI	N	(31G – .302)										
" total	56	97	18	4	0	0	0.0	4	5	4	15	0	.186	.227	38	7	2B-20
1968 PIT N	11	13	5	1	0	0	0.0	2	1	0	0	0	.385	.462	9	4	2B-2
8 yrs.	704	2121	516	76	9	20	0.9	253	152	157	187	14	.243	.316	154	38	2B-546, 3B-17, OF-13

WORLD SERIES																	
1962 SF N	7	26	7	3	0	1	3.8	4	5	3	4	0	.269	.500	0	0	2B-7

	G	AB	H	2B	3B	HR	HR %	R	RBI	BB	SO	SB	BA	SA	Pinch Hit AB	H	G by POS

Hob Hiller

HILLER, HARVEY MAX   BR TR 5'8"   162 lbs.
B. May 12, 1893, East Mauch Chunk, Pa.   D. Dec. 27, 1956, Lehighton, Pa.

	G	AB	H	2B	3B	HR	HR %	R	RBI	BB	SO	SB	BA	SA	AB	H	G by POS
1920 BOS A	17	29	5	1	1	0	0.0	4	2	2	5	0	.172	.276	0	0	3B-6, SS-5, 2B-2, OF-1
1921	1	1	0	0	0	0	0.0	0	0	0	0	0	.000	.000	1	0	
2 yrs.	18	30	5	1	1	0	0.0	4	2	2	5	0	.167	.267	1	0	3B-6, SS-5, 2B-2, OF-1

Ed Hilley

HILLEY, EDWARD GARFIELD (Whitey)   BR TR 5'10½" 170 lbs.
B. June 17, 1879, Cleveland, Ohio   D. Nov. 14, 1956, Cleveland, Ohio

	G	AB	H	2B	3B	HR	HR %	R	RBI	BB	SO	SB	BA	SA	AB	H	G by POS
1903 PHI A	1	3	1	0	0	0	0.0	1	0	1		0	.333	.333	0	0	3B-1

Mack Hillis

HILLIS, MALCOLM DAVID   BR TR 5'10"   165 lbs.
B. July 23, 1901, Cambridge, Mass.   D. June 16, 1961, Cambridge, Mass.

	G	AB	H	2B	3B	HR	HR %	R	RBI	BB	SO	SB	BA	SA	AB	H	G by POS
1924 NY A	1	1	0	0	0	0	0.0	1	0	0	0	0	.000	.000	0	0	2B-1
1928 PIT N	11	36	9	2	3	1	2.8	6	7	0	6	1	.250	.556	2	0	2B-8, 3B-1
2 yrs.	12	37	9	2	3	1	2.7	7	7	0	6	1	.243	.541	2	0	2B-9, 3B-1

Pat Hilly

HILLY, WILLIAM EDWARD   BR TR 5'11"   180 lbs.
Also known as William Edward Hilgerink.
B. Feb. 24, 1887, Fostoria, Ohio   D. July 25, 1953, Eureka, Mo.

	G	AB	H	2B	3B	HR	HR %	R	RBI	BB	SO	SB	BA	SA	AB	H	G by POS
1914 PHI N	8	10	3	0	0	0	0.0	2	1	1	5	0	.300	.300	1	1	OF-4

Dave Hilton

HILTON, JOHN DAVID   BR TR 5'11"   191 lbs.
B. Sept. 15, 1950, Uvalde, Tex.

	G	AB	H	2B	3B	HR	HR %	R	RBI	BB	SO	SB	BA	SA	AB	H	G by POS
1972 SD N	13	47	10	2	1	0	0.0	2	5	3	6	1	.213	.298	0	0	3B-13
1973	70	234	46	9	0	5	2.1	21	16	19	35	2	.197	.299	0	0	3B-47, 2B-23
1974	74	217	52	8	2	1	0.5	17	12	13	28	3	.240	.309	10	1	3B-55, 2B-15
1975	4	8	0	0	0	0	0.0	0	0	0	0	0	.000	.000	0	0	3B-4
4 yrs.	161	506	108	19	3	6	1.2	40	33	35	69	6	.213	.298	10	1	3B-119, 2B-38

Jack Himes

HIMES, JOHN HERB   BL TR 6'2"   180 lbs.
B. Sept. 22, 1878, Bryan, Ohio   D. Dec. 16, 1949, Joliet, Ill.

	G	AB	H	2B	3B	HR	HR %	R	RBI	BB	SO	SB	BA	SA	AB	H	G by POS
1905 STL N	12	41	6	0	0	0	0.0	3	0	1		0	.146	.146	1	0	OF-11
1906	40	155	42	5	2	0	0.0	10	14	7		4	.271	.329	0	0	OF-40
2 yrs.	52	196	48	5	2	0	0.0	13	14	8		4	.245	.291	1	0	OF-51

Bill Hinchman

HINCHMAN, WILLIAM WHITE   BR TR 5'11"   190 lbs.
Brother of Harry Hinchman.
B. Apr. 4, 1883, Philadelphia, Pa.   D. Feb. 21, 1963, Columbus, Ohio

	G	AB	H	2B	3B	HR	HR %	R	RBI	BB	SO	SB	BA	SA	AB	H	G by POS
1905 CIN N	17	51	13	4	1	0	0.0	10	10	13		4	.255	.373	0	0	OF-12, 3B-4, 1B-1
1906	18	54	11	1	1	0	0.0	7	1	8		2	.204	.259	1	1	OF-16
1907 CLE A	152	514	117	19	9	1	0.2	62	50	47		15	.228	.305	0	0	OF-150, 1B-4, 2B-1
1908	137	464	107	23	8	6	1.3	55	59	38		9	.231	.353	3	0	OF-75, SS-51, 1B-4
1909	139	457	118	20	13	2	0.4	57	53	41		22	.258	.372	2	1	OF-131, SS-6
1915 PIT N	156	577	177	33	14	5	0.9	72	77	48	75	17	.307	.438	0	0	OF-156
1916	152	555	175	18	16	4	0.7	64	76	54	61	10	.315	.427	1	0	OF-124, 1B-31
1917	69	244	46	5	5	2	0.8	27	29	33	27	5	.189	.275	4	0	OF-48, 1B-20
1918	50	111	26	5	2	0	0.0	10	13	15	8	1	.234	.315	19	6	OF-40, 1B-3
1920	18	16	3	0	0	0	0.0	0	1	1	1	3	.188	.188	16	3	
10 yrs.	908	3043	793	128	69	20	0.7	364	369	298	174	85	.261	.368	42	11	OF-752, 1B-63, SS-57, 3B-4, 2B-1

Harry Hinchman

HINCHMAN, HARRY SIBLEY   BB TR 5'11"   165 lbs.
Brother of Bill Hinchman.
B. Aug. 4, 1878, Philadelphia, Pa.   D. Jan. 19, 1933, Toledo, Ohio

	G	AB	H	2B	3B	HR	HR %	R	RBI	BB	SO	SB	BA	SA	AB	H	G by POS
1907 CLE A	15	51	11	3	1	0	0.0	3	9	5		2	.216	.314	0	0	2B-15

Hunkey Hines

HINES, HENRY FRED   5'7"   165 lbs.
B. Sept. 29, 1867, Elgin, Ill.   D. Jan. 2, 1928, Rockford, Ill.

	G	AB	H	2B	3B	HR	HR %	R	RBI	BB	SO	SB	BA	SA	AB	H	G by POS
1895 BKN N	2	8	2	0	0	0	0.0	3	1	2	0	0	.250	.250	0	0	OF-2

Mike Hines

HINES, MICHAEL P.   BR TL 5'10"   176 lbs.
B. 1864, Ireland   D. Mar. 14, 1910, New Bedford, Mass.

	G	AB	H	2B	3B	HR	HR %	R	RBI	BB	SO	SB	BA	SA	AB	H	G by POS
1883 BOS N	63	231	52	13	1	0	0.0	38	16	7	36		.225	.290	0	0	C-59, OF-7
1884	35	132	23	3	0	0	0.0	16		3	24		.174	.197	0	0	C-35
1885 3 teams	BOS	N (14G – .232)			BKN	AA (3G – .077)		PRO	N (1G – .000)								
" total	18	72	14	4	1	0	0.0	12	4	4	7		.194	.278	0	0	OF-14, C-4
1888 BOS N	4	16	2	0	1	0	0.0	3	2	2	0		.125	.250	0	0	OF-3, C-1
4 yrs.	120	451	91	20	3	0	0.0	69	22	16	67	0	.202	.259	0	0	C-99, OF-24

Paul Hines

HINES, PAUL A.   BR TR 5'9½"   173 lbs.
B. Mar. 1, 1852, Washington, D.C.   D. July 10, 1935, Hyattsville, Md.

	G	AB	H	2B	3B	HR	HR %	R	RBI	BB	SO	SB	BA	SA	AB	H	G by POS
1876 CHI N	64	305	101	21	3	2	0.7	62	59	1	3		.331	.439	0	0	OF-64, 2B-1
1877	60	261	73	11	7	0	0.0	44	23	1	8		.280	.375	0	0	OF-49, 2B-11
1878 PRO N	62	257	92	13	4	4	1.6	42	50	2	10		.358	.486	0	0	OF-61, SS-1
1879	85	409	146	25	10	2	0.5	81	52	8	16		.357	.482	0	0	OF-85
1880	85	374	115	20	2	3	0.8	64	35	13	17		.307	.396	0	0	OF-75, 2B-6, 1B-4
1881	80	361	103	27	5	2	0.6	65	31	13	12		.285	.404	0	0	OF-78, 2B-4, 1B-1
1882	84	379	117	28	10	4	1.1	73		10	14		.309	.467	0	0	OF-82, 1B-2
1883	97	442	132	32	4	4	0.9	94		18	23		.299	.416	0	0	OF-89, 1B-9
1884	114	490	148	36	10	3	0.6	94		44	28		.302	.435	0	0	OF-108, 1B-7, P-1
1885	98	411	111	20	4	1	0.2	63	35	19	18		.270	.345	0	0	OF-92, 1B-4, SS-1, 3B-1, 2B-1
1886 WAS N	121	487	152	30	8	9	1.8	80	56	35	21		.312	.462	0	0	OF-92, 2B-15, 1B-10, SS-5, 2B-3
1887	123	478	147	32	5	10	2.1	83	72	48	24	46	.308	.458	0	0	OF-109, 1B-7, 2B-5, SS-4
1888 IND N	133	513	144	26	3	4	0.8	84	58	41	45	31	.281	.366	0	0	OF-120, 1B-6, SS-2
1889	121	486	148	27	1	6	1.2	77	72	49	22	34	.305	.401	0	0	1B-109, OF-12

	G	AB	H	2B	3B	HR	HR %	R	RBI	BB	SO	SB	BA	SA	Pinch Hit AB	Pinch Hit H	G by POS

Paul Hines continued

	G	AB	H	2B	3B	HR	HR %	R	RBI	BB	SO	SB	BA	SA	AB	H	G by POS
1890 2 teams	PIT N (31G – .182)			BOS	N	(69G –	.264)										
" total	100	394	94	13	3	2	0.5	52	57	43	27	15	.239	.302	0	0	OF-83, 1B-18
1891 WAS AA	54	206	58	7	5	0	0.0	25	31	21	16	6	.282	.364	0	0	OF-47, 1B-8
16 yrs.	1481	6253	1881	368	84	56	0.9	1083	631	366	304	132	.301	.413	0	0	OF-1251, 1B-185, 2B-31, 3B-16, SS-13, P-1

Gordie Hinkle

HINKLE, DANIEL GORDON
B. Apr. 3, 1905, Toronto, Ohio   D. Mar. 19, 1972, Houston, Tex.   BR TR 6'   185 lbs.

	G	AB	H	2B	3B	HR	HR %	R	RBI	BB	SO	SB	BA	SA	AB	H	G by POS
1934 BOS A	27	75	13	6	1	0	0.0	7	9	7	23	0	.173	.280	0	0	C-26

George Hinshaw

HINSHAW, GEORGE ADDISON
B. Oct. 23, 1959, Los Angeles, Calif.   BR TR 6'   185 lbs.

	G	AB	H	2B	3B	HR	HR %	R	RBI	BB	SO	SB	BA	SA	AB	H	G by POS
1982 SD N	6	15	4	0	0	0	0.0	1	1	3	5	0	.267	.267	0	0	OF-6
1983	7	16	7	1	0	0	0.0	1	4	0	4	1	.438	.500	0	0	3B-5, 2B-1
2 yrs.	13	31	11	1	0	0	0.0	2	5	3	9	1	.355	.387	0	0	OF-6, 3B-5, 2B-1

Paul Hinson

HINSON, JAMES PAUL
B. May 9, 1904, Van Leer, Tenn.   D. Sept. 23, 1960, Muskogee, Okla.   BR TR 5'10"   150 lbs.

	G	AB	H	2B	3B	HR	HR %	R	RBI	BB	SO	SB	BA	SA	AB	H	G by POS
1928 BOS A	3	0	0	0	0	0	–	1	0	0	0	0	–	–	0	0	

Chuck Hinton

HINTON, CHARLES EDWARD
B. May 3, 1934, Rocky Mount, N. C.   BR TR 6'1"   180 lbs.

	G	AB	H	2B	3B	HR	HR %	R	RBI	BB	SO	SB	BA	SA	AB	H	G by POS
1961 WAS A	106	339	88	13	5	6	1.8	51	34	40	81	22	.260	.381	11	4	OF-92
1962	151	542	168	25	6	17	3.1	73	75	47	66	28	.310	.472	2	0	OF-136, 2B-12, SS-1
1963	150	566	152	20	12	15	2.7	80	55	64	79	25	.269	.426	0	0	OF-125, 3B-19, 1B-6, SS-2
1964	138	514	141	25	7	11	2.1	71	53	57	77	17	.274	.414	5	1	OF-131, 3B-2
1965 CLE A	133	431	110	11	6	18	4.2	59	54	53	65	17	.255	.448	16	2	OF-72, 1B-40, 2B-23, 3B-1
1966	123	348	89	9	3	12	3.4	46	50	35	66	10	.256	.402	17	4	OF-104, 1B-6, 2B-2
1967	147	498	122	19	3	10	2.0	55	37	43	100	6	.245	.355	12	4	OF-136, 2B-5
1968 CAL A	116	267	52	10	3	7	2.6	28	23	24	61	3	.195	.333	32	4	1B-48, OF-37, 3B-13, 2B-9
1969 CLE A	94	121	31	3	2	3	2.5	18	19	8	22	2	.256	.388	40	10	1B-40, OF-35, C-4, 2B-3, 3B-2
1970	107	195	62	4	0	9	4.6	24	29	25	34	0	.318	.477	37	11	OF-20, 1B-20, C-5
1971	88	147	33	7	0	5	3.4	13	14	20	34	0	.224	.374	43	5	OF-40, 3B-14
11 yrs.	1353	3968	1048	152	47	113	2.8	518	443	416	685	130	.264	.412	215	45	OF-928, 1B-160, 2B-54, 3B-51, C-9, SS-3

John Hinton

HINTON, JOHN ROBERT (Red)
B. June 20, 1876, Pittsburgh, Pa.   D. July 19, 1920, Braddock, Pa.   BR TR 6'   200 lbs.

	G	AB	H	2B	3B	HR	HR %	R	RBI	BB	SO	SB	BA	SA	AB	H	G by POS
1901 BOS N	4	13	1	0	0	0	0.0	0	0	2		0	.077	.077	0	0	3B-4

Gene Hiser

HISER, GENE TAYLOR
B. Dec. 11, 1948, Baltimore, Md.   BL TL 5'11"   175 lbs.

	G	AB	H	2B	3B	HR	HR %	R	RBI	BB	SO	SB	BA	SA	AB	H	G by POS
1971 CHI N	17	29	6	0	0	0	0.0	4	1	4	8	1	.207	.207	5	1	OF-9
1972	32	46	9	0	0	0	0.0	2	6	6	8	1	.196	.196	11	1	OF-15
1973	100	109	19	3	0	1	0.9	15	6	11	17	4	.174	.229	37	6	OF-64
1974	12	17	4	1	0	0	0.0	2	1	0	3	0	.235	.294	5	1	OF-8
1975	45	62	15	3	0	0	0.0	11	6	11	7	0	.242	.290	24	8	OF-18, 1B-1
5 yrs.	206	263	53	7	0	1	0.4	34	18	32	43	6	.202	.240	82	17	OF-114, 1B-1

Larry Hisle

HISLE, LARRY EUGENE
B. May 5, 1947, Portsmouth, Ohio   BR TR 6'2"   193 lbs.

	G	AB	H	2B	3B	HR	HR %	R	RBI	BB	SO	SB	BA	SA	AB	H	G by POS
1968 PHI N	7	11	4	1	0	0	0.0	1	1	1	4	0	.364	.455	1	0	OF-6
1969	145	482	128	23	5	20	4.1	75	56	48	152	18	.266	.459	2	0	OF-140
1970	126	405	83	22	4	10	2.5	52	44	53	139	5	.205	.353	3	0	OF-121
1971	36	76	15	3	0	0	0.0	7	3	6	22	1	.197	.237	5	1	OF-27
1973 MIN A	143	545	148	25	6	15	2.8	88	64	64	128	11	.272	.422	1	1	OF-143
1974	143	510	146	20	7	19	3.7	68	79	48	112	12	.286	.465	9	1	OF-137
1975	80	255	80	9	2	11	4.3	37	51	27	39	17	.314	.494	5	3	OF-58, DH-14
1976	155	581	158	19	5	14	2.4	81	96	56	93	31	.272	.394	1	0	OF-154
1977	141	546	165	36	3	28	5.1	95	119	56	106	21	.302	.533	2	1	OF-134, DH-6
1978 MIL A	142	520	151	24	5	34	6.5	96	115	67	90	10	.290	.533	4	1	OF-87, DH-51
1979	26	96	27	7	0	3	3.1	18	14	11	19	1	.281	.448	1	1	DH-15, OF-10
1980	17	60	17	0	0	6	10.0	16	16	14	7	1	.283	.583	0	0	DH-17
1981	27	87	20	4	0	4	4.6	11	11	6	17	0	.230	.414	4	1	DH-24
1982	9	31	4	0	0	2	6.5	7	5	5	13	0	.129	.323	1	0	DH-8
14 yrs.	1197	4205	1146	193	32	166	3.9	652	674	462	941	128	.273	.452	39	10	OF-1017, DH-135

Billy Hitchcock

HITCHCOCK, WILLIAM CLYDE
Brother of Jim Hitchcock.
B. July 31, 1916, Inverness, Ala.
Manager 1960, 1962-63, 1966-67.   BR TR 6'1½"   185 lbs.

	G	AB	H	2B	3B	HR	HR %	R	RBI	BB	SO	SB	BA	SA	AB	H	G by POS
1942 DET A	85	280	59	8	1	0	0.0	27	29	26	21	2	.211	.246	0	0	SS-80, 3B-1
1946 2 teams	DET	A	(3G –	.000)		WAS	A	(98G –	.212)								
" total	101	357	75	8	3	0	0.0	27	25	27	52	2	.210	.249	1	0	SS-53, 3B-46, 2B-1
1947 STL A	80	275	61	2	1	0	0.4	25	28	21	34	3	.222	.255	5	0	2B-46, 3B-17, SS-7, 1B-5
1948 BOS A	49	124	37	3	2	1	0.8	15	20	7	9	0	.298	.379	12	3	3B-15, 2B-15
1949	55	147	30	6	1	0	0.0	22	9	17	11	2	.204	.259	16	0	1B-29, 3B-8
1950 PHI A	115	399	109	22	5	1	0.3	35	54	44	32	3	.273	.361	8	3	2B-107, SS-1
1951	77	222	68	10	4	1	0.5	27	36	21	23	2	.306	.401	11	3	3B-45, 2B-23, 1B-1
1952	119	407	100	8	4	1	0.2	45	56	39	45	1	.246	.292	4	0	3B-117, 2B-1
1953 DET A	22	38	8	2	1	0	0.0	8	0	3	3	0	.211	.211	6	1	3B-12, SS-1, 2B-1
9 yrs.	703	2249	547	67	22	5	0.2	231	257	205	230	15	.243	.299	63	10	3B-240, 2B-201, SS-142, 1B-48

	G	AB	H	2B	3B	HR	HR %	R	RBI	BB	SO	SB	BA	SA	Pinch Hit AB	Pinch Hit H	G by POS

Jim Hitchcock

HITCHCOCK, JAMES FRANKLIN
Brother of Billy Hitchcock.
B. June 28, 1911, Inverness, Ala.   D. June 23, 1959, Montgomery, Ala.
BR TR 5'11" 175 lbs.

	G	AB	H	2B	3B	HR	HR %	R	RBI	BB	SO	SB	BA	SA	PH AB	PH H	G by POS
1938 BOS N	28	76	13	0	0	0	0.0	2	7	2	11	1	.171	.171	0	0	SS-24, 3B-2

Myril Hoag

HOAG, MYRIL OLIVER
B. Mar. 9, 1908, Davis, Calif.   D. July 28, 1971, High Springs, Fla.
BR TR 5'11" 180 lbs.

	G	AB	H	2B	3B	HR	HR %	R	RBI	BB	SO	SB	BA	SA	PH AB	PH H	G by POS
1931 NY A	44	28	4	2	0	0	0.0	6	3	1	8	0	.143	.214	10	1	OF-23, 3B-1
1932	46	54	20	5	0	1	1.9	18	7	7	13	1	.370	.519	3	1	OF-35, 1B-1
1934	97	251	67	8	2	3	1.2	45	34	21	21	1	.267	.351	7	0	OF-86
1935	48	110	28	4	1	1	0.9	13	13	12	19	4	.255	.336	5	0	OF-37
1936	45	156	47	9	4	3	1.9	23	34	7	16	3	.301	.468	3	1	OF-39
1937	106	362	109	19	8	3	0.8	48	46	33	33	4	.301	.423	7	2	OF-99
1938	85	267	74	14	3	0	0.0	28	48	25	31	4	.277	.352	15	3	OF-70
1939 STL A	129	482	142	23	4	10	2.1	58	75	24	35	9	.295	.421	12	4	OF-117, P-1
1940	76	191	50	11	0	3	1.6	20	26	13	30	2	.262	.366	28	5	OF-46
1941 2 teams		STL A (1G – .000)				CHI A	(106G – .255)										
" total	107	381	97	13	3	1	0.3	30	44	27	29	6	.255	.312	6	2	OF-99
1942 CHI A	113	412	99	18	2	2	0.5	47	37	36	21	17	.240	.308	1	1	OF-112
1944 2 teams		CHI A (17G – .229)				CLE A	(67G – .285)										
" total	84	325	90	10	3	1	0.3	38	31	35	24	7	.277	.335	4	0	OF-80
1945 CLE A	40	128	27	5	3	0	0.0	10	3	11	18	1	.211	.297	1	0	OF-33, P-2
13 yrs.	1020	3147	854	141	33	28	0.9	384	401	252	298	59	.271	.364	102	20	OF-876, P-3, 3B-1, 1B-1
WORLD SERIES																	
1932 NY A	1	0	0	0	0	0	–	1	0	0	0	0	–	–	0	0	
1937	5	20	6	1	0	1	5.0	4	2	0	1	0	.300	.500	0	0	OF-5
1938	2	5	2	1	0	0	0.0	3	1	0	0	0	.400	.600	1	0	OF-1
3 yrs.	8	25	8	2	0	1	4.0	8	3	0	1	0	.320	.520	1	0	OF-6

Don Hoak

HOAK, DONALD ALBERT (Tiger)
B. Feb. 5, 1928, Roulette, Pa.   D. Oct. 9, 1969, Pittsburgh, Pa.
BR TR 6'1" 170 lbs.

	G	AB	H	2B	3B	HR	HR %	R	RBI	BB	SO	SB	BA	SA	PH AB	PH H	G by POS
1954 BKN N	88	261	64	9	5	7	2.7	41	26	25	39	8	.245	.398	11	2	3B-75
1955	94	279	67	13	3	5	1.8	50	19	46	50	9	.240	.362	4	1	3B-78
1956 CHI N	121	424	91	18	4	5	1.2	51	37	41	46	8	.215	.311	5	1	3B-110
1957 CIN N	149	529	155	39	2	19	3.6	78	89	74	54	8	.293	.482	0	0	3B-149, 2B-1
1958	114	417	109	30	0	6	1.4	51	50	43	36	6	.261	.376	1	0	3B-112, SS-1
1959 PIT N	155	564	166	29	3	8	1.4	60	65	71	75	9	.294	.399	0	0	3B-155
1960	155	553	156	24	9	16	2.9	97	79	74	74	3	.282	.445	0	0	3B-155
1961	145	503	150	27	7	12	2.4	72	61	73	53	4	.298	.451	2	2	3B-143
1962	121	411	99	14	8	5	1.2	63	48	49	49	4	.241	.350	3	1	3B-116
1963 PHI N	115	377	87	11	3	6	1.6	35	24	27	52	5	.231	.324	9	2	3B-106
1964	6	4	0	0	0	0	0.0	0	0	0	2	0	.000	.000	4	0	
11 yrs.	1263	4322	1144	214	44	89	2.1	598	498	523	530	64	.265	.396	39	9	3B-1199, SS-1, 2B-1
WORLD SERIES																	
1955 BKN N	3	3	1	0	0	0	0.0	0	0	2	0	0	.333	.333	0	0	3B-1
1960 PIT N	7	23	5	2	0	0	0.0	3	3	4	1	0	.217	.304	0	0	3B-7
2 yrs.	10	26	6	2	0	0	0.0	3	3	6	1	0	.231	.308	0	0	3B-8

Bill Hobbs

HOBBS, WILLIAM LEE
B. May 7, 1893, Grant's Lick, Ky.   D. Jan. 5, 1945, Hamilton, Ohio
BR TR 5'9½" 155 lbs.

	G	AB	H	2B	3B	HR	HR %	R	RBI	BB	SO	SB	BA	SA	PH AB	PH H	G by POS
1913 CIN N	4	4	0	0	0	0	0.0	0	0	0	3	0	.000	.000	1	0	3B-1, 2B-1
1916	6	11	2	1	0	0	0.0	1	1	2	0	1	.182	.273	0	0	SS-6
2 yrs.	10	15	2	1	0	0	0.0	1	1	2	3	1	.133	.200	1	0	SS-6, 3B-1, 2B-1

Dick Hoblitzell

HOBLITZELL, RICHARD CARLETON
B. Oct. 26, 1888, Waverly, W. Va.   D. Nov. 14, 1962, Parkersburg, W. Va.
BL TL 6' 172 lbs.

	G	AB	H	2B	3B	HR	HR %	R	RBI	BB	SO	SB	BA	SA	PH AB	PH H	G by POS
1908 CIN N	32	114	29	3	2	0	0.0	8	8	7		2	.254	.316	0	0	1B-32
1909	142	517	159	23	11	4	0.8	59	67	44		17	.308	.418	0	0	1B-142
1910	155	611	170	24	13	4	0.7	85	70	47	32	28	.278	.380	0	0	1B-148, 2B-7
1911	158	622	180	19	13	11	1.8	81	97	42	44	32	.289	.415	0	0	1B-158
1912	148	558	164	32	12	2	0.4	73	85	48	28	23	.294	.405	0	0	1B-147
1913	137	502	143	23	7	3	0.6	59	68	35	26	18	.285	.376	3	2	1B-134
1914 2 teams		CIN N (78G – .210)				BOS A	(68G – .319)										
" total	146	477	125	18	10	0	0.0	62	62	45	47	19	.262	.342	1	0	1B-143
1915 BOS A	124	399	113	15	12	2	0.5	54	61	38	26	9	.283	.396	4	0	1B-117
1916	130	417	108	17	1	0	0.0	57	50	47	28	10	.259	.305	3	0	1B-126
1917	120	420	108	19	7	1	0.2	49	47	46	22	12	.257	.343	2	0	1B-118
1918	25	69	11	1	0	0	0.0	4	4	8	3	3	.159	.174	5	3	1B-19
11 yrs.	1317	4706	1310	194	88	27	0.6	591	619	407	256	173	.278	.374	18	5	1B-1284, 2B-7
WORLD SERIES																	
1915 BOS A	5	16	5	0	0	0	0.0	1	1	1	1	1	.313	.313	0	0	1B-5
1916	5	17	4	1	1	0	0.0	3	2	6	0	0	.235	.412	0	0	1B-5
2 yrs.	10	33	9	1	1	0	0.0	3	3	6	1	1	.273	.364	0	0	1B-10

Butch Hobson

HOBSON, CLELL LAVERN
B. Aug. 17, 1951, Tuscaloosa, Ala.
BR TR 6'1" 193 lbs.

	G	AB	H	2B	3B	HR	HR %	R	RBI	BB	SO	SB	BA	SA	PH AB	PH H	G by POS
1975 BOS A	2	4	1	0	0	0	0.0	0	0	0	2	0	.250	.250	0	0	3B-1
1976	76	269	63	7	5	8	3.0	34	34	15	62	0	.234	.387	0	0	3B-76
1977	159	593	157	33	5	30	5.1	77	112	27	162	5	.265	.489	0	0	3B-159
1978	147	512	128	26	2	17	3.3	65	80	50	122	1	.250	.408	0	0	3B-133, DH-14
1979	146	528	138	26	7	28	5.3	74	93	30	78	3	.261	.496	4	0	3B-132, 2B-11
1980	93	324	74	6	0	11	3.4	35	39	25	69	1	.228	.349	1	1	3B-57, DH-36
1981 CAL A	85	268	63	7	4	4	1.5	27	36	35	60	1	.235	.336	0	0	3B-83, DH-2
1982 NY A	30	58	10	2	0	2	3.4	9	3	1	14	0	.172	.207	12	3	DH-15, 1B-11
8 yrs.	738	2556	634	107	23	98	3.8	314	397	183	569	11	.248	.423	17	4	3B-651, DH-67, 1B-11, 2B-1

	G	AB	H	2B	3B	HR	HR %	R	RBI	BB	SO	SB	BA	SA	Pinch Hit AB	Pinch Hit H	G by POS

Ed Hock

HOCK, EDWARD FRANCIS
B. Mar. 27, 1899, Franklin Furnace, Ohio   D. Nov. 21, 1963, Portsmouth, Ohio   BL TR 5'10½" 165 lbs.

	G	AB	H	2B	3B	HR	HR %	R	RBI	BB	SO	SB	BA	SA	PH AB	PH H	G by POS
1920 STL N	1	0	0	0	0	0	–	0	0	0	0	0	–	–	0	0	OF-1
1923 CIN N	2	0	0	0	0	0	–	0	0	0	0	0	–	–	0	0	OF-2
1924	16	10	1	0	0	0	0.0	7	0	0	2	0	.100	.100	4	1	OF-3
3 yrs.	19	10	1	0	0	0	0.0	7	0	0	2	0	.100	.100	4	1	OF-3

Oris Hockett

HOCKETT, ORIS LEON
B. Sept. 29, 1909, Bluffton, Ind.   D. Mar. 23, 1969, Hawthorne, Calif.   BL TR 5'9" 182 lbs.

	G	AB	H	2B	3B	HR	HR %	R	RBI	BB	SO	SB	BA	SA	PH AB	PH H	G by POS
1938 BKN N	21	70	23	5	1	1	1.4	8	8	4	9	0	.329	.471	4	2	OF-17
1939	9	13	3	0	0	0	0.0	3	1	1	1	0	.231	.231	7	2	OF-1
1941 CLE A	2	6	2	0	0	0	0.0	0	1	2	0	0	.333	.333	0	0	OF-2
1942	148	601	150	22	7	7	1.2	85	48	45	45	12	.250	.344	1	0	OF-145
1943	141	601	166	33	4	2	0.3	70	51	45	45	13	.276	.354	2	0	OF-139
1944	124	457	132	29	5	1	0.2	47	50	35	27	8	.289	.381	14	2	OF-110
1945 CHI A	106	417	122	23	4	2	0.5	46	55	27	30	10	.293	.381	0	0	OF-106
7 yrs.	551	2165	598	112	21	13	0.6	259	214	159	157	43	.276	.365	28	6	OF-520

Johnny Hodapp

HODAPP, URBAN JOHN
B. Sept. 26, 1905, Cincinnati, Ohio   D. June 14, 1980, Cincinnati, Ohio   BR TR 6' 185 lbs.

	G	AB	H	2B	3B	HR	HR %	R	RBI	BB	SO	SB	BA	SA	PH AB	PH H	G by POS
1925 CLE A	37	130	31	5	1	0	0.0	12	14	11	7	2	.238	.292	0	0	3B-37
1926	3	5	1	0	0	0	0.0	0	0	0	1	0	.200	.200	0	0	3B-3
1927	75	240	73	15	3	5	2.1	25	40	14	23	2	.304	.454	7	3	3B-67, 1B-4
1928	116	449	145	31	6	2	0.4	51	73	20	20	2	.323	.432	3	2	3B-101, 1B-13
1929	90	294	96	12	7	4	1.4	30	51	15	14	3	.327	.456	16	4	2B-72
1930	154	635	225	51	8	9	1.4	111	121	32	29	6	.354	.502	0	0	2B-154
1931	122	468	138	19	4	2	0.4	71	56	27	23	1	.295	.365	1	0	2B-121
1932 2 teams			CLE	A	(7G –	.125)		CHI	A	(68G –	.227)						
" total	75	192	42	9	0	3	1.6	23	20	11	5	1	.219	.313	23	2	OF-31, 2B-12, 3B-4
1933 BOS A	115	413	129	27	5	3	0.7	55	54	33	14	1	.312	.424	6	3	3B-101, 1B-10
9 yrs.	787	2826	880	169	34	28	1.0	378	429	163	136	18	.311	.425	56	14	2B-460, 3B-212, OF-31, 1B-27

Mel Hoderlein

HODERLEIN, MELVIN ANTHONY
B. June 24, 1923, Mt. Carmel, Ohio   BR TR 5'10" 185 lbs.

	G	AB	H	2B	3B	HR	HR %	R	RBI	BB	SO	SB	BA	SA	PH AB	PH H	G by POS
1951 BOS A	9	14	5	1	1	0	0.0	1	1	6	2	0	.357	.571	1	0	3B-3, 2B-3
1952 WAS A	72	208	56	8	2	0	0.0	16	17	18	22	2	.269	.327	13	2	2B-58
1953	23	47	9	0	0	0	0.0	5	5	6	9	0	.191	.191	10	2	2B-11, SS-2
1954	14	25	4	1	0	0	0.0	0	1	1	4	0	.160	.200	3	0	SS-6, 2B-5
4 yrs.	118	294	74	10	3	0	0.0	22	24	31	37	2	.252	.306	27	4	2B-77, SS-8, 3B-3

Bert Hodge

HODGE, EDWARD BURTON
B. May 25, 1917, Knoxville, Tenn.   BL TR 5'11" 170 lbs.

	G	AB	H	2B	3B	HR	HR %	R	RBI	BB	SO	SB	BA	SA	PH AB	PH H	G by POS
1942 PHI N	8	11	2	0	0	0	0.0	1	0	1	0	0	.182	.182	6	2	3B-2

Gomer Hodge

HODGE, HAROLD MORRIS
B. Apr. 3, 1944, Rutherfordton, N. C.   BB TR 6'2" 185 lbs.

	G	AB	H	2B	3B	HR	HR %	R	RBI	BB	SO	SB	BA	SA	PH AB	PH H	G by POS
1971 CLE A	80	83	17	3	0	1	1.2	3	9	4	19	0	.205	.277	68	16	3B-3, 1B-3, 2B-2

Gil Hodges

HODGES, GILBERT RAYMOND
B. Apr. 4, 1924, Princeton, Ind.   D. Apr. 2, 1972, West Palm Beach, Fla.   BR TR 6'1½" 200 lbs.
Manager 1963-71.

	G	AB	H	2B	3B	HR	HR %	R	RBI	BB	SO	SB	BA	SA	PH AB	PH H	G by POS
1943 BKN N	1	2	0	0	0	0	0.0	0	0	1	2	1	.000	.000	0	0	3B-1
1947	28	77	12	3	1	1	1.3	9	7	14	19	0	.156	.260	4	1	C-24
1948	134	481	120	18	5	11	2.3	48	70	43	61	7	.249	.376	2	0	1B-96, C-38
1949	156	596	170	23	4	23	3.9	94	115	66	64	10	.285	.453	0	0	1B-156
1950	153	561	159	26	2	32	5.7	98	113	73	73	6	.283	.508	0	0	1B-153
1951	158	582	156	25	3	40	6.9	118	103	93	99	9	.268	.527	0	0	1B-158
1952	153	508	129	27	1	32	6.3	87	102	107	90	2	.254	.500	0	0	1B-153
1953	141	520	157	22	7	31	6.0	101	122	75	84	1	.302	.550	1	1	1B-127, OF-24
1954	154	579	176	23	5	42	7.3	106	130	74	84	3	.304	.579	0	0	1B-154
1955	150	546	158	24	5	27	4.9	75	102	80	91	2	.289	.500	0	0	1B-139, OF-16
1956	153	550	146	29	4	32	5.8	86	87	76	91	3	.265	.507	1	0	1B-150, 3B-2, 2B-1
1957	150	579	173	28	7	27	4.7	94	98	63	91	5	.299	.511	0	0	1B-122, 3B-15, OF-9, C-1
1958 LA N	141	475	123	15	1	22	4.6	68	64	52	87	8	.259	.434	9	1	1B-113, 3B-4
1959	124	413	114	19	2	25	6.1	57	80	58	92	3	.276	.513	7	1	1B-92, 3B-10
1960	101	197	39	8	1	8	4.1	22	30	26	37	0	.198	.371	15	0	1B-100
1961	109	215	52	4	0	8	3.7	25	31	24	43	3	.242	.372	28	7	1B-100
1962 NY N	54	127	32	1	0	9	7.1	15	17	15	27	0	.252	.472	9	2	1B-47
1963	11	22	5	0	0	0	0.0	2	3	3	2	0	.227	.227	1	0	1B-10
18 yrs.	2071	7030	1921	295	48	370	5.3	1105	1274	943	1137	63	.273	.487	77	13	1B-1908, OF-79, C-64, 3B-32, 2B-1

WORLD SERIES	G	AB	H	2B	3B	HR	HR %	R	RBI	BB	SO	SB	BA	SA	PH AB	PH H	G by POS
1947 BKN N	1	1	0	0	0	0	0.0	0	0	0	1	0	.000	.000	1	0	1B-5
1949	5	17	4	0	0	1	5.9	2	4	1	4	0	.235	.412	0	0	1B-7
1952	7	21	0	0	0	0	0.0	1	1	5	6	0	.000	.000	0	0	1B-6
1953	6	22	8	0	0	1	4.5	3	1	3	3	1	.364	.500	0	0	1B-7
1955	7	24	7	0	0	1	4.2	2	5	3	2	0	.292	.417	0	0	1B-7
1956	7	23	7	2	0	1	4.3	5	8	4	4	0	.304	.522	0	0	1B-6
1959 LA N	6	23	9	0	1	1	4.3	2	2	1	2	0	.391	.609	0	0	1B-6
7 yrs.	39	131	35	2	1	5	3.8	15	21	17	22	1	.267	.412	1	0	1B-38

Ron Hodges

HODGES, RONALD WRAY
B. June 22, 1949, Franklin County, Va.   BL TR 6'1" 185 lbs.

	G	AB	H	2B	3B	HR	HR %	R	RBI	BB	SO	SB	BA	SA	PH AB	PH H	G by POS
1973 NY N	45	127	33	2	0	1	0.8	5	18	11	19	0	.260	.299	5	2	C-40
1974	59	136	30	4	0	4	2.9	16	14	19	11	0	.221	.338	13	2	C-44

	G	AB	H	2B	3B	HR	HR %	R	RBI	BB	SO	SB	BA	SA	Pinch Hit AB	Pinch Hit H	G by POS

Ron Hodges continued

	G	AB	H	2B	3B	HR	HR %	R	RBI	BB	SO	SB	BA	SA	AB	H	G by POS
1975	9	34	7	1	0	2	5.9	3	4	1	6	0	.206	.412	0	0	C-9
1976	56	155	35	6	0	4	2.6	21	24	27	16	2	.226	.342	7	2	C-52
1977	66	117	31	4	0	1	0.9	6	5	9	17	0	.265	.325	39	9	C-27
1978	47	102	26	4	1	0	0.0	4	7	10	11	1	.255	.314	16	4	C-30
1979	59	86	14	4	0	0	0.0	4	5	19	16	0	.163	.209	29	3	C-22
1980	36	42	10	2	0	0	0.0	4	5	10	13	1	.238	.286	22	4	C-9
1981	35	43	13	2	0	1	2.3	5	6	5	8	1	.302	.419	25	6	C-7
1982	80	228	56	12	1	5	2.2	26	27	41	40	4	.246	.373	12	4	C-74
1983	110	250	65	12	0	0	0.0	20	21	49	42	0	.260	.308	14	6	C-96
1984	64	106	22	3	0	1	0.9	5	11	23	18	1	.208	.264	24	6	C-35
12 yrs.	666	1426	342	56	2	19	1.3	119	147	224	217	10	.240	.322	206	48	C-445

WORLD SERIES

	G	AB	H	2B	3B	HR	HR %	R	RBI	BB	SO	SB	BA	SA	AB	H	G by POS
1973 NY N	1	0	0	0	0	0	–	0	0	1	0	0	–	–	0	0	

Ralph Hodgin

HODGIN, ELMER RALPH
B. Feb. 10, 1916, Greensboro, N. C. BL TR 5'10'' 167 lbs.

	G	AB	H	2B	3B	HR	HR %	R	RBI	BB	SO	SB	BA	SA	AB	H	G by POS
1939 BOS N	32	48	10	1	0	0	0.0	4	4	3	4	0	.208	.229	20	4	OF-9
1943 CHI A	117	407	128	22	8	1	0.2	52	50	20	24	3	.314	.415	20	8	3B-56, OF-42
1944	121	465	137	25	7	1	0.2	56	51	21	14	3	.295	.385	6	2	3B-82, OF-33
1946	87	258	65	10	1	0	0.0	32	25	19	6	0	.252	.298	29	9	OF-57
1947	59	180	53	10	3	1	0.6	26	24	13	4	1	.294	.400	16	1	OF-41
1948	114	331	88	11	5	1	0.3	28	34	21	11	0	.266	.338	33	7	OF-79
6 yrs.	530	1689	481	79	24	4	0.2	198	188	97	63	7	.285	.367	124	31	OF-261, 3B-138

Paul Hodgson

HODGSON, PAUL JOSEPH
Also known as Denis Hodgson.
B. Apr. 14, 1960, Montreal, Que., Canada BR TR 6'2'' 190 lbs.

	G	AB	H	2B	3B	HR	HR %	R	RBI	BB	SO	SB	BA	SA	AB	H	G by POS
1980 TOR A	20	41	9	0	1	1	2.4	5	5	3	12	0	.220	.341	0	0	OF-11, DH-3

Art Hoelskoetter

HOELSKOETTER, ARTHUR H.
Played as Art Hostetter 1907-08.
B. Sept. 30, 1882, St. Louis, Mo. D. Aug. 3, 1954, St. Louis, Mo. TR

	G	AB	H	2B	3B	HR	HR %	R	RBI	BB	SO	SB	BA	SA	AB	H	G by POS
1905 STL N	24	83	20	2	1	0	0.0	7	5	3		1	.241	.289	0	0	3B-20, 2B-3, P-1
1906	94	317	71	6	3	0	0.0	21	14	4		2	.224	.262	0	0	3B-53, SS-16, OF-12, P-12, 2B-1
1907	119	396	98	6	3	2	0.5	21	28	27		5	.247	.293	2	0	2B-73, 1B-27, OF-8, C-8, 3B-2, P-2
1908	62	155	36	7	1	0	0.0	10	6	6		1	.232	.290	16	3	C-41, 3B-2, 2B-1, 1B-1
4 yrs.	299	951	225	21	8	2	0.2	59	53	40		9	.237	.282	18	3	2B-78, 3B-77, C-49, 1B-28, OF-20, SS-16, P-15

John Hoey

HOEY, JOHN B.
B. Nov. 10, 1881, Watertown, Mass. D. Nov. 11, 1947, Naugatuck, Conn.

	G	AB	H	2B	3B	HR	HR %	R	RBI	BB	SO	SB	BA	SA	AB	H	G by POS
1906 BOS A	94	361	88	8	4	0	0.0	27	24	14		10	.244	.288	0	0	OF-94
1907	39	96	21	2	1	0	0.0	7	8	1		2	.219	.260	18	8	OF-21
1908	13	43	7	0	0	0	0.0	5	3	0		1	.163	.163	2	1	OF-11
3 yrs.	146	500	116	10	5	0	0.0	39	35	15		13	.232	.272	20	9	OF-126

Stew Hofferth

HOFFERTH, STEWART EDWARD
B. Jan. 27, 1913, Logansport, Ind. BR TR 6'2'' 195 lbs.

	G	AB	H	2B	3B	HR	HR %	R	RBI	BB	SO	SB	BA	SA	AB	H	G by POS
1944 BOS N	66	180	36	8	0	1	0.6	14	26	11	5	0	.200	.261	16	1	C-47
1945	50	170	40	2	0	3	1.8	13	15	14	11	1	.235	.300	5	1	C-45
1946	20	58	12	1	1	0	0.0	3	10	3	6	0	.207	.259	5	0	C-15
3 yrs.	136	408	88	11	1	4	1.0	30	51	28	22	1	.216	.277	26	2	C-107

Danny Hoffman

HOFFMAN, DANIEL JOHN
B. Mar. 10, 1880, Canton, Conn. D. Mar. 14, 1922, Manchester, Conn. BL TL

	G	AB	H	2B	3B	HR	HR %	R	RBI	BB	SO	SB	BA	SA	AB	H	G by POS
1903 PHI A	74	248	61	5	7	3	0.8	29	22	6		7	.246	.347	11	5	OF-62, P-1
1904	53	204	61	7	5	3	1.5	31	24	5		9	.299	.426	2	0	OF-51
1905	119	454	119	10	10	1	0.2	64	35	33		46	.262	.335	1	0	OF-119
1906 2 teams		PHI	A (7G – .227)					NY	A (100G – .256)								
" total	107	342	87	10	6	0	0.0	38	23	30		33	.254	.319	2	0	OF-105
1907 NY A	136	517	131	10	3	4	0.8	81	46	42		30	.253	.308	1	0	OF-135
1908 STL A	99	363	91	9	7	1	0.3	41	25	23		17	.251	.322	0	0	OF-99
1909	110	387	104	6	7	2	0.5	44	26	41		24	.269	.336	0	0	OF-109
1910	106	380	90	11	5	0	0.0	20	27	34		16	.237	.292	0	0	OF-106
1911	24	81	17	3	2	0	0.0	11	7	12		3	.210	.296	0	0	OF-23
9 yrs.	828	2976	761	71	52	13	0.4	359	235	226		185	.256	.328	17	5	OF-809, P-1

WORLD SERIES

	G	AB	H	2B	3B	HR	HR %	R	RBI	BB	SO	SB	BA	SA	AB	H	G by POS
1905 PHI A	1	1	0	0	0	0	0.0	0	0	1		0	.000	.000	0		

Dutch Hoffman

HOFFMAN, CLARENCE CASPER
B. Jan. 28, 1904, Freeburg, Ill. D. Dec. 6, 1962, Beneville, Ill. BR TR 6' 175 lbs.

	G	AB	H	2B	3B	HR	HR %	R	RBI	BB	SO	SB	BA	SA	AB	H	G by POS
1929 CHI A	103	337	87	16	5	3	0.9	27	37	24	28	6	.258	.362	19	6	OF-89

Glenn Hoffman

HOFFMAN, GLENN EDWARD
B. July 7, 1958, Orange, Calif. BR TR 6'1'' 175 lbs.

	G	AB	H	2B	3B	HR	HR %	R	RBI	BB	SO	SB	BA	SA	AB	H	G by POS
1980 BOS A	114	312	89	15	4	4	1.3	37	42	19	41	2	.285	.397	2	1	3B-110, SS-5, 2B-2
1981	78	242	56	10	0	1	0.4	28	20	12	25	0	.231	.285	0	0	SS-78, 3B-1
1982	150	469	98	23	2	7	1.5	53	49	30	69	0	.209	.311	0	0	SS-150
1983	143	473	123	24	1	4	0.8	56	41	30	76	1	.260	.340	0	0	SS-143
1984	64	74	14	4	0	0	0.0	8	4	5	10	0	.189	.243	3	1	SS-56, 3B-4, 2B-2
5 yrs.	549	1570	380	76	7	16	1.0	182	156	96	221	3	.242	.330	5	3	SS-432, 3B-115, 2B-4

	G	AB	H	2B	3B	HR	HR %	R	RBI	BB	SO	SB	BA	SA	Pinch Hit AB	Pinch Hit H	G by POS

Hickey Hoffman

HOFFMAN, CHARLES
B. Oct. 27, 1856, Cleveland, Ohio   D. Oct. 27, 1915, Peoria, Ill.

	G	AB	H	2B	3B	HR	HR%	R	RBI	BB	SO	SB	BA	SA	AB	H	G by POS
1879 CLE N	2	6	0	0	0	0	0.0	0	0	0	3		.000	.000	0	0	C-2, OF-1

Izzy Hoffman

HOFFMAN, HARRY C.   BL TL
B. Jan. 5, 1875, Bridgeport, N. J.   D. Nov. 13, 1942, Philadelphia, Pa.

	G	AB	H	2B	3B	HR	HR%	R	RBI	BB	SO	SB	BA	SA	AB	H	G by POS
1904 WAS A	10	30	3	1	0	0	0.0	1	1	2		0	.100	.133	1	0	OF-9
1907 BOS N	19	86	24	3	1	0	0.0	17	3	6		2	.279	.337	0	0	OF-19
2 yrs.	29	116	27	4	1	0	0.0	18	4	8		2	.233	.284	1	0	OF-28

John Hoffman

HOFFMAN, JOHN EDWARD (Pork Chop)   BL TR 6'   190 lbs.
B. Oct. 31, 1943, Aberdeen, S. D.

	G	AB	H	2B	3B	HR	HR%	R	RBI	BB	SO	SB	BA	SA	AB	H	G by POS
1964 HOU N	6	15	1	0	0	0	0.0	1	0	1	7	0	.067	.067	1	0	C-5
1965	2	6	2	0	0	0	0.0	1	1	0	3	0	.333	.333	0	0	C-2
2 yrs.	8	21	3	0	0	0	0.0	2	1	1	10	0	.143	.143	1	0	C-7

Larry Hoffman

HOFFMAN, LAWRENCE CHARLES   BR TR
B. July 18, 1878, Chicago, Ill.   D. Dec. 29, 1948, Chicago, Ill.

	G	AB	H	2B	3B	HR	HR%	R	RBI	BB	SO	SB	BA	SA	AB	H	G by POS
1901 CHI N	6	22	7	1	0	0	0.0	2	6	0		1	.318	.364	0	0	3B-5, 2B-1

Ray Hoffman

HOFFMAN, RAYMOND LAMONT   BL TR 6'½"   175 lbs.
B. June 4, 1917, Detroit, Mich.

	G	AB	H	2B	3B	HR	HR%	R	RBI	BB	SO	SB	BA	SA	AB	H	G by POS
1942 WAS A	7	19	1	0	0	0	0.0	2	2	1	1	0	.053	.053	0	0	3B-6

Tex Hoffman

HOFFMAN, EDWARD ADOLPH   BL TR 6'1"   200 lbs.
B. Nov. 30, 1893, San Antonio, Tex.   D. May 19, 1947, New Orleans, La.

	G	AB	H	2B	3B	HR	HR%	R	RBI	BB	SO	SB	BA	SA	AB	H	G by POS
1915 CLE A	9	13	2	0	0	0	0.0	1	2	1	5	0	.154	.154	5	1	3B-3

Jesse Hoffmeister

HOFFMEISTER, JESSE H.
B. Toledo, Ohio   Deceased.

	G	AB	H	2B	3B	HR	HR%	R	RBI	BB	SO	SB	BA	SA	AB	H	G by POS
1897 PIT N	48	188	58	6	9	3	1.6	33	36	8		6	.309	.484	0	0	3B-48

Bobby Hofman

HOFMAN, ROBERT GEORGE   BR TR 5'10"   160 lbs.
B. Oct. 5, 1925, St. Louis, Mo.

	G	AB	H	2B	3B	HR	HR%	R	RBI	BB	SO	SB	BA	SA	AB	H	G by POS
1949 NY N	19	48	10	0	0	0	0.0	4	3	5	6	0	.208	.208	2	0	2B-16
1952	32	63	18	2	2	2	3.2	11	4	8	10	0	.286	.476	7	1	2B-21, 3B-2, 1B-1
1953	74	169	45	7	2	12	7.1	21	34	12	23	1	.266	.544	34	13	3B-23, 2B-17
1954	71	125	28	5	0	8	6.4	12	30	17	15	0	.224	.456	36	10	1B-21, 2B-10, 3B-8
1955	96	207	55	7	2	10	4.8	32	28	22	31	0	.266	.464	40	9	1B-24, 2B-19, C-19, 3B-5
1956	47	56	10	1	0	0	0.0	1	2	6	8	0	.179	.196	26	5	3B-7, C-7, 1B-3, 2B-2
1957	2	2	0	0	0	0	0.0	0	0	0	1	0	.000	.000	2	0	
7 yrs.	341	670	166	22	6	32	4.8	81	101	70	94	1	.248	.442	147	38	2B-85, 1B-49, 3B-45, C-26

Solly Hofman

HOFMAN, ARTHUR FREDERICK (Circus Solly)   BR TR 6'   160 lbs.
B. Oct. 29, 1882, St. Louis, Mo.   D. Mar. 10, 1956, St. Louis, Mo.

	G	AB	H	2B	3B	HR	HR%	R	RBI	BB	SO	SB	BA	SA	AB	H	G by POS
1903 PIT N	3	2	0	0	0	0	0.0	1	0	0			.000	.000	1	0	OF-2
1904 CHI N	7	26	7	0	0	1	3.8	7	4	1		2	.269	.385	2	0	OF-6, SS-1
1905	86	287	68	14	4	1	0.3	43	38	20		15	.237	.324	1	1	2B-59, SS-9, 1B-9, OF-3, 3B-3
1906	64	195	50	2	3	2	1.0	30	20	20		13	.256	.328	3	0	OF-23, 1B-21, SS-9, 3B-4, 2B-4
1907	134	470	126	11	3	1	0.2	67	36	41		29	.268	.311	0	0	OF-68, SS-42, 1B-18, 3B-4, 2B-3
1908	120	411	100	15	5	2	0.5	55	42	33		15	.243	.319	4	2	OF-50, 1B-37, 2B-22, 3B-9
1909	153	527	150	21	4	2	0.4	60	58	53		20	.285	.351	0	0	OF-153
1910	136	477	155	24	16	3	0.6	83	86	65	34	29	.325	.461	0	0	OF-110, 1B-24, 3B-1
1911	143	512	129	17	2	2	0.4	66	70	66	40	30	.252	.305	0	0	OF-107, 1B-36
1912 2 teams								CHI	N (36G – .272)		PIT	N	(17G – .283)				
" total	53	178	49	15	1	0	0.0	35	20	27	19	5	.275	.371	2	0	OF-42, 1B-9
1913 PIT N	28	83	19	5	2	0	0.0	11	7	8	6	3	.229	.337	4	1	OF-24
1914 BKN F	147	515	148	25	12	5	1.0	65	83	54		34	.287	.412	0	0	2B-108, 1B-22, OF-21, SS-1
1915 BUF F	109	346	81	10	6	0	0.0	29	27	30		12	.234	.298	13	5	OF-82, 1B-11, 3B-4, 2B-2, SS-1
1916 2 teams								NY	A (6G – .296)		CHI	N	(5G – .313)				
" total	11	43	13	3	2	0	0.0	2	4	3	3	1	.302	.465	1	0	OF-10
14 yrs.	1194	4072	1095	162	60	19	0.5	554	495	421	102	208	.269	.352	29	9	OF-701, 2B-198, 1B-187, SS-63, 3B-25
WORLD SERIES																	
1906 CHI N	6	23	7	1	0	0	0.0	3	2	3	4	1	.304	.348	0	0	OF-6
1908	5	19	6	0	1	0	0.0	2	4	1	4	2	.316	.421	1	0	OF-5
1910	5	15	4	0	0	0	0.0	2	2	4	3	0	.267	.267	0	0	OF-5
3 yrs.	16	57	17	1	1	0	0.0	7	8	8	11	3	.298	.351	1	0	OF-16

Fred Hofmann

HOFMANN, FRED (Bootnose)   BR TR 5'11½" 175 lbs.
B. June 10, 1894, St. Louis, Mo.   D. Nov. 19, 1964, St. Helena, Calif.

	G	AB	H	2B	3B	HR	HR%	R	RBI	BB	SO	SB	BA	SA	AB	H	G by POS
1919 NY A	1	1	0	0	0	0	0.0	0	0	0	0	0	.000	.000	0	0	C-1
1920	15	24	7	0	0	0	0.0	3	1	1	2	0	.292	.292	1	0	C-14
1921	23	62	11	1	1	1	1.6	7	5	5	13	0	.177	.274	3	1	C-18, 1B-1
1922	37	91	27	5	3	2	2.2	13	10	9	12	0	.297	.484	6	0	C-29
1923	72	238	69	10	4	3	1.3	24	26	18	27	2	.290	.403	2	2	C-70
1924	62	166	29	6	1	1	0.6	17	11	12	15	2	.175	.241	6	1	C-54
1925	3	2	0	0	0	0	0.0	0	0	0	0	0	.000	.000	2	0	C-1
1927 BOS A	87	217	59	19	1	0	0.0	20	24	21	26	2	.272	.369	5	1	C-81
1928	78	199	45	8	1	0	0.0	14	16	11	25	0	.226	.276	7	0	C-71
9 yrs.	378	1000	247	49	11	7	0.7	98	93	77	120	6	.247	.339	32	6	C-339, 1B-1
WORLD SERIES																	
1923 NY A	2	1	0	0	0	0	0.0	0	0	0	1	0	.000	.000	1	0	

	G	AB	H	2B	3B	HR	HR %	R	RBI	BB	SO	SB	BA	SA	Pinch Hit AB	Pinch Hit H	G by POS

Eddie Hogan

HOGAN, ROBERT EDWARD
B. Apr., 1860, St. Louis, Mo.   Deceased.
BR   5'7"   153 lbs.

	G	AB	H	2B	3B	HR	HR %	R	RBI	BB	SO	SB	BA	SA	PH AB	PH H	G by POS
1882 STL AA	1	3	1	0	0	0	0.0	1		0			.333	.333	0	0	P-1
1884 MIL U	11	37	3	1	0	0	0.0	6		7			.081	.108	0	0	OF-11
1887 NY AA	32	120	24	6	1	0	0.0	22		30		12	.200	.267	0	0	OF-29, SS-4, 3B-1
1888 CLE AA	78	269	61	16	6	0	0.0	60	24	50		30	.227	.331	0	0	OF-78
4 yrs.	122	429	89	23	7	0	0.0	89	37	87		42	.207	.294	0	0	OF-118, SS-4, 3B-1, P-1

Happy Hogan

HOGAN, WILLIAM HENRY
Brother of George Hogan.
B. Sept. 14, 1884, San Juan, Calif.   D. Sept. 28, 1974, San Jose, Calif.
BR   TR

	G	AB	H	2B	3B	HR	HR %	R	RBI	BB	SO	SB	BA	SA	PH AB	PH H	G by POS
1911 2 teams	PHI A (7G – .105)				STL A (123G – .260)												
" total	130	462	117	18	8	2	0.4	54	64	43		18	.253	.340	1	0	OF-123, 1B-5
1912 STL A	107	360	77	10	2	1	0.3	32	36	34		17	.214	.261	8	1	OF-99
2 yrs.	237	822	194	28	10	3	0.4	86	100	77		35	.236	.305	9	1	OF-222, 1B-5

Harry Hogan

HOGAN, HARRY S.
B. Nov. 1, 1875, Syracuse, N.Y.   D. Jan. 25, 1934, Syracuse, N.Y.

	G	AB	H	2B	3B	HR	HR %	R	RBI	BB	SO	SB	BA	SA	PH AB	PH H	G by POS
1901 CLE A	1	4	0	0	0	0	0.0	0	0	0		0	.000	.000	0	0	OF-1

Ken Hogan

HOGAN, KENNETH SYLVESTER
B. Oct. 9, 1902, Cleveland, Ohio   D. Jan. 2, 1980, Cleveland, Ohio
BL   TR   5'9"   145 lbs.

	G	AB	H	2B	3B	HR	HR %	R	RBI	BB	SO	SB	BA	SA	PH AB	PH H	G by POS
1921 CIN N	1	2	0	0	0	0	0.0	0	0	0	1	0	.000	.000	0	0	OF-1
1923 CLE A	1	0	0	0	0	0	–	0	0	0	0	0	–	–	0	0	
1924	2	1	0	0	0	0	0.0	0	0	0	0	0	.000	.000	1	0	
3 yrs.	4	3	0	0	0	0	0.0	0	0	0	1	0	.000	.000	1	0	OF-1

Marty Hogan

HOGAN, MARTIN F.
B. Oct. 15, 1869, Wensbury, England   D. Aug. 15, 1923, Youngstown, Ohio
5'8"   145 lbs.

	G	AB	H	2B	3B	HR	HR %	R	RBI	BB	SO	SB	BA	SA	PH AB	PH H	G by POS
1894 2 teams	CIN N (6G – .130)				STL N (29G – .280)												
" total	35	123	31	3	4	0	0.0	15	16	4	17	9	.252	.341	0	0	OF-35
1895 STL N	5	18	3	1	0	0	0.0	2	2	3	0	2	.167	.222	0	0	OF-5
2 yrs.	40	141	34	4	4	0	0.0	17	18	7	17	11	.241	.326	0	0	OF-40

Shanty Hogan

HOGAN, JAMES FRANCIS
B. Mar. 21, 1906, Somerville, Mass.   D. Apr. 7, 1967, Boston, Mass.
BR   TR   6'1"   240 lbs.

	G	AB	H	2B	3B	HR	HR %	R	RBI	BB	SO	SB	BA	SA	PH AB	PH H	G by POS
1925 BOS N	9	21	6	1	1	0	0.0	2	3	1	3	0	.286	.429	4	0	OF-5
1926	4	14	4	1	1	0	0.0	1	5	0	4	0	.286	.500	4	0	C-4
1927	71	229	66	17	1	3	1.3	24	32	9	23	2	.288	.410	9	1	C-61
1928 NY N	131	411	137	25	2	10	2.4	48	71	42	25	0	.333	.477	6	1	C-124
1929	102	317	95	13	0	5	1.6	19	45	25	22	1	.300	.388	9	2	C-93
1930	122	389	132	26	2	13	3.3	60	75	21	24	2	.339	.517	24	8	C-96
1931	123	396	119	17	1	12	3.0	42	65	29	29	1	.301	.439	10	0	C-113
1932	140	502	144	18	2	8	1.6	36	77	26	22	0	.287	.378	4	2	C-136
1933 BOS N	96	328	83	7	0	3	0.9	15	30	13	9	0	.253	.302	1	0	C-95
1934	92	279	73	5	2	4	1.4	20	34	16	13	0	.262	.337	2	0	C-90
1935	59	163	49	8	0	2	1.2	9	25	21	8	0	.301	.387	3	1	C-56
1936 WAS A	19	65	21	4	0	1	1.5	8	7	11	2	0	.323	.431	0	0	C-19
1937	21	66	10	4	0	0	0.0	4	5	6	8	0	.152	.212	0	0	C-21
13 yrs.	989	3180	939	146	12	61	1.9	288	474	220	188	6	.295	.406	72	15	C-908, OF-5

Bert Hogg

HOGG, WILBERT GEORGE
B. Apr. 21, 1913, Detroit, Mich.   D. Nov. 5, 1973, Detroit, Mich.
BR   TR   5'11½"   162 lbs.

	G	AB	H	2B	3B	HR	HR %	R	RBI	BB	SO	SB	BA	SA	PH AB	PH H	G by POS
1934 BKN N	2	1	0	0	0	0	0.0	0	0	0	0	0	.000	.000	0	0	3B-1

George Hogriever

HOGRIEVER, GEORGE C.
B. Mar. 17, 1869, Cincinnati, Ohio   D. Jan. 26, 1961, Appleton, Wis.
BR   TR   5'8"   160 lbs.

	G	AB	H	2B	3B	HR	HR %	R	RBI	BB	SO	SB	BA	SA	PH AB	PH H	G by POS
1895 CIN N	69	239	65	8	7	2	0.8	61	34	36	17	41	.272	.389	0	0	OF-66, 2B-3
1901 MIL A	54	221	52	10	2	0	0.0	25	16	30		7	.235	.299	0	0	OF-54
2 yrs.	123	460	117	18	9	2	0.4	86	50	66	17	48	.254	.346	0	0	OF-120, 2B-3

Bill Hohman

HOHMAN, WILLIAM HENRY
B. Nov. 27, 1903, Brooklyn, Md.   D. Oct. 29, 1968, Baltimore, Md.
BR   TR   6'   178 lbs.

	G	AB	H	2B	3B	HR	HR %	R	RBI	BB	SO	SB	BA	SA	PH AB	PH H	G by POS
1927 PHI N	7	18	5	0	0	0	0.0	1	0	2	3	0	.278	.278	0	0	OF-6

Eddie Hohnhurst

HOHNHURST, EDWARD HENRY
B. Jan. 31, 1885, Cincinnati, Ohio   D. Mar. 28, 1916, Covington, Ky.
BL   TL

	G	AB	H	2B	3B	HR	HR %	R	RBI	BB	SO	SB	BA	SA	PH AB	PH H	G by POS
1910 CLE A	17	62	20	3	1	0	0.0	8	6	4		3	.323	.403	0	0	1B-17
1912	14	54	11	1	0	0	0.0	5	2	2		5	.204	.222	0	0	1B-14
2 yrs.	31	116	31	4	1	0	0.0	13	8	6		8	.267	.319	0	0	1B-31

Bill Holbert

HOLBERT, WILLIAM H.
B. Mar. 14, 1855, Baltimore, Md.   D. Mar. 1, 1935, Laurel, Md.
TR

	G	AB	H	2B	3B	HR	HR %	R	RBI	BB	SO	SB	BA	SA	PH AB	PH H	G by POS
1876 LOU N	12	43	11	0	0	0	0.0	3	5	0	3		.256	.256	0	0	C-12
1878 MIL N	45	173	32	2	0	0	0.0	10	12	3	14		.185	.197	0	0	OF-30, C-21
1879 2 teams	SYR N (59G – .201)				TRO N (4G – .267)												
" total	63	244	50	0	0	0	0.0	12	23	1	21		.205	.205	0	0	C-60, OF-4
1880 TRO N	60	212	40	5	1	0	0.0	18		9	18		.189	.222	0	0	C-58, OF-3
1881	46	180	49	3	0	0	0.0	16	14	3	13		.272	.289	0	0	C-43, OF-3
1882	71	251	46	5	0	0	0.0	24	23	11	22		.183	.203	0	0	C-58, 3B-12, OF-3
1883 NY AA	73	299	71	9	1	0	0.0	26		1			.237	.274	0	0	C-68, OF-5, 2B-1
1884	65	255	53	5	0	0	0.0	28		7			.208	.227	0	0	C-59, OF-5, SS-1
1885	56	202	35	3	0	0	0.0	13		8			.173	.188	0	0	C-39, OF-13, 3B-5
1886	48	171	35	4	2	0	0.0	8		6			.205	.251	0	0	C-45, OF-3, SS-1
1887	69	255	58	4	3	0	0.0	20		7		12	.227	.267	0	0	C-60, 1B-8, SS-2, 2B-1

	G	AB	H	2B	3B	HR	HR %	R	RBI	BB	SO	SB	BA	SA	Pinch Hit AB	Pinch Hit H	G by POS

Bill Holbert continued

	G	AB	H	2B	3B	HR	HR %	R	RBI	BB	SO	SB	BA	SA	AB	H	G by POS
1888 BKN AA	15	50	6	1	0	0	0.0	4	1	2		0	.120	.140	0	0	C-15
12 yrs.	623	2335	486	41	7	0	0.0	182	78	58	91	12	.208	.232	0	0	C-538, OF-69, 3B-17, 1B-8, SS-4, 2B-2

Sammy Holbrook

HOLBROOK, JAMES MARBURY
B. July 17, 1910, Meridian, Miss.

BR TR 5'11" 189 lbs.

	G	AB	H	2B	3B	HR	HR %	R	RBI	BB	SO	SB	BA	SA	AB	H	G by POS
1935 WAS A	52	135	35	2	2	2	1.5	20	25	30	16	0	.259	.348	6	1	C-47

Bill Holden

HOLDEN, WILLIAM PAUL
B. Sept. 7, 1889, Birmingham, Ala.   D. Sept. 14, 1971, Pensacola, Fla.

BR TR 6' 170 lbs.

	G	AB	H	2B	3B	HR	HR %	R	RBI	BB	SO	SB	BA	SA	AB	H	G by POS
1913 NY A	18	53	16	3	1	0	0.0	6	8	8	5	0	.302	.396	2	1	OF-16
1914 2 teams	NY	A (50G –	.182)		CIN	N (11G –	.214)										
" total	61	193	36	3	2	0	0.0	14	13	19	31	2	.187	.223	5	0	OF-55
2 yrs.	79	246	52	6	3	0	0.0	20	21	27	36	2	.211	.260	7	1	OF-71

Joe Holden

HOLDEN, JOSEPH FRANCIS (Socks)
B. June 4, 1913, St. Clair, Pa.

BL TR 5'8" 175 lbs.

	G	AB	H	2B	3B	HR	HR %	R	RBI	BB	SO	SB	BA	SA	AB	H	G by POS
1934 PHI N	10	14	1	0	0	0	0.0	1	0	0	2	0	.071	.071	4	0	C-6
1935	6	9	1	0	0	0	0.0	0	0	0	3	1	.111	.111	2	0	C-4
1936	1	1	0	0	0	0	0.0	0	0	0	0	0	.000	.000	1	0	
3 yrs.	17	24	2	0	0	0	0.0	1	0	0	5	1	.083	.083	7	0	C-10

Jim Holdsworth

HOLDSWORTH, JAMES (Long Jim)
B. July 14, 1850, New York, N. Y.   D. Mar. 22, 1918, New York, N. Y.

BR TR

	G	AB	H	2B	3B	HR	HR %	R	RBI	BB	SO	SB	BA	SA	AB	H	G by POS
1876 NY N	52	241	64	3	2	0	0.0	23	19	1	2		.266	.295	0	0	OF-49, 2B-3
1877 HAR N	55	260	66	5	2	0	0.0	26	20	2	8		.254	.288	0	0	OF-55
1882 TRO N	1	3	0	0	0	0	0.0	0	0	0	1		.000	.000	0	0	OF-1
1884 IND AA	5	18	2	0	0	0	0.0	1			2		.111	.111	0	0	OF-5
4 yrs.	113	522	132	8	4	0	0.0	50	39	5	11		.253	.284	0	0	OF-110, 2B-3

Walter Holke

HOLKE, WALTER HENRY (Union Man)
B. Dec. 25, 1892, St. Louis, Mo.   D. Oct. 12, 1954, St. Louis, Mo.

BB TL 6'1½" 185 lbs.

	G	AB	H	2B	3B	HR	HR %	R	RBI	BB	SO	SB	BA	SA	AB	H	G by POS
1914 NY N	2	6	2	0	0	0	0.0	0	0	0	0	0	.333	.333	0	0	1B-2
1916	34	111	39	4	2	0	0.0	16	13	6	16	10	.351	.423	0	0	1B-34
1917	153	527	146	12	7	2	0.4	55	55	34	54	13	.277	.338	0	0	1B-153
1918	88	326	82	17	4	1	0.3	38	27	10	26	10	.252	.337	0	0	1B-88
1919 BOS N	137	518	151	14	6	0	0.0	48	48	21	25	19	.292	.342	1	0	1B-136
1920	144	551	162	15	11	3	0.5	53	64	28	31	4	.294	.377	1	1	1B-143
1921	150	579	151	15	10	3	0.5	60	63	17	41	8	.261	.337	0	0	1B-150
1922	105	395	115	9	4	0	0.0	35	46	14	23	6	.291	.334	0	0	1B-105
1923 PHI N	147	562	175	31	4	7	1.2	64	70	16	37	7	.311	.418	1	1	1B-146, P-1
1924	148	563	169	23	6	4	0.0	60	64	25	33	3	.300	.394	0	0	1B-148
1925 2 teams	PHI	N (39G –	.244)		CIN	N (65G –	.280)										
" total	104	318	86	13	4	2	0.6	35	37	20	18	1	.270	.355	15	4	1B-88
11 yrs.	1212	4456	1278	153	58	24	0.5	464	487	191	304	81	.287	.363	18	6	1B-1193, P-1
WORLD SERIES																	
1917 NY N	6	21	6	2	0	0	0.0	2	1	0	6	0	.286	.381	0	0	1B-6

Bill Hollahan

HOLLAHAN, WILLIAM JAMES (Happy)
B. Nov. 22, 1896, New York, N. Y.   D. Nov. 27, 1965, New York, N. Y.

BR TR 5'9" 165 lbs.

	G	AB	H	2B	3B	HR	HR %	R	RBI	BB	SO	SB	BA	SA	AB	H	G by POS
1920 WAS A	3	4	1	0	0	0	0.0	0	1	1	2	1	.250	.250	0	0	3B-3

Dutch Holland

HOLLAND, ROBERT CLYDE
B. Oct. 12, 1903, Middlesex, N. C.   D. June 16, 1967, Lumberton, N. C.

BR TR 6'1" 190 lbs.

	G	AB	H	2B	3B	HR	HR %	R	RBI	BB	SO	SB	BA	SA	AB	H	G by POS
1932 BOS N	39	156	46	11	1	1	0.6	15	18	12	20	0	.295	.397	0	0	OF-39
1933	13	31	8	3	0	0	0.0	3	3	3	8	1	.258	.355	6	1	OF-7
1934 CLE A	50	128	32	12	1	2	1.6	19	13	13	11	0	.250	.406	16	2	OF-31
3 yrs.	102	315	86	26	2	3	1.0	37	34	28	39	1	.273	.397	22	3	OF-77

Will Holland

HOLLAND, WILLARD A.
B. Georgetown, Del.   D. July 19, 1930, Philadelphia, Pa.

5'10" 180 lbs.

	G	AB	H	2B	3B	HR	HR %	R	RBI	BB	SO	SB	BA	SA	AB	H	G by POS
1889 BAL AA	40	143	27	1	2	0	0.0	13	16	9	28	4	.189	.224	0	0	SS-39, OF-1

Gary Holle

HOLLE, GARY CHARLES
B. Aug. 11, 1954, Albany, N. Y.

BR TL 6'6" 210 lbs.

	G	AB	H	2B	3B	HR	HR %	R	RBI	BB	SO	SB	BA	SA	AB	H	G by POS
1979 TEX A	5	6	1	1	0	0	0.0	0	0	1	0	0	.167	.333	4	1	1B-1

Bug Holliday

HOLLIDAY, JAMES WEAR
B. Feb. 8, 1867, St. Louis, Mo.   D. Feb. 15, 1910, Cincinnati, Ohio

BR TR 5'7" 165 lbs.

	G	AB	H	2B	3B	HR	HR %	R	RBI	BB	SO	SB	BA	SA	AB	H	G by POS
1889 CIN AA	135	563	193	28	7	19	3.4	107	104	43	59	46	.343	.519	0	0	OF-135
1890 CIN N	131	518	140	18	14	4	0.8	93	75	49	36	50	.270	.382	0	0	OF-111
1891	111	442	141	21	10	9	2.0	74	84	37	28	30	.319	.473	0	0	OF-152, P-1
1892	152	602	176	23	16	13	2.2	114	91	57	39	43	.292	.449	0	0	OF-125, 1B-1
1893	126	500	155	24	10	5	1.0	108	89	73	22	32	.310	.428	0	0	OF-119, 1B-1
1894	122	519	199	24	8	13	2.5	125	119	40	20	29	.383	.536	1	0	OF-32
1895	32	127	38	9	2	0	0.0	25	20	10	3	6	.299	.402	0	0	OF-16, 1B-5, SS-1, P-1
1896	29	84	27	4	0	0	0.0	17	8	9	4	6	.321	.369	6	1	OF-42, SS-4, 2B-3, 1B-3
1897	61	195	61	9	4	2	1.0	50	20	27		6	.313	.431	8	3	OF-28
1898	30	106	25	2	1	0	0.0	21	7	14		5	.236	.274	1	0	OF-28
10 yrs.	929	3656	1155	162	72	65	1.8	734	617	359	211	248	.316	.453	16	0	OF-891, 1B-10, SS-5, 2B-3, P-2

	G	AB	H	2B	3B	HR	HR %	R	RBI	BB	SO	SB	BA	SA	Pinch Hit AB	Pinch Hit H	G by POS

Stan Hollmig

HOLLMIG, STANLEY ERNEST (Hondo)
B. Jan. 2, 1926, Fredericksburg, Tex.   D. Dec. 4, 1981, San Antonio, Tex.   BR TR 6'2½" 190 lbs.

	G	AB	H	2B	3B	HR	HR %	R	RBI	BB	SO	SB	BA	SA	AB	H	G by POS
1949 PHI N	81	251	64	11	6	2	0.8	28	26	20	43	1	.255	.371	14	3	OF-66
1950	11	12	3	2	0	0	0.0	1	1	0	3	0	.250	.417	8	2	OF-3
1951	2	2	0	0	0	0	0.0	0	0	0	0	0	.000	.000	2	0	
3 yrs.	94	265	67	13	6	2	0.8	29	27	20	46	1	.253	.370	24	5	OF-69

Charlie Hollocher

HOLLOCHER, CHARLES JACOB
B. June 11, 1896, St. Louis, Mo.   D. Aug. 14, 1940, Frontenac, Mo.   BL TR 5'7½" 158 lbs.

	G	AB	H	2B	3B	HR	HR %	R	RBI	BB	SO	SB	BA	SA	AB	H	G by POS
1918 CHI N	131	509	161	23	6	2	0.4	72	38	47	30	26	.316	.397	0	0	SS-131
1919	115	430	116	14	5	3	0.7	51	26	44	19	16	.270	.347	0	0	SS-115
1920	80	301	96	17	2	0	0.0	53	22	41	15	20	.319	.389	0	0	SS-80
1921	140	558	161	28	8	3	0.5	71	37	43	13	5	.289	.384	3	1	SS-137
1922	152	592	201	37	8	3	0.5	90	69	58	5	19	.340	.444	0	0	SS-152
1923	66	260	89	14	2	1	0.4	46	28	26	5	9	.342	.423	1	0	SS-65
1924	76	286	70	12	4	2	0.7	28	21	18	7	4	.245	.336	5	1	SS-71
7 yrs.	760	2936	894	145	35	14	0.5	411	241	277	94	99	.304	.392	9	2	SS-751
WORLD SERIES																	
1918 CHI N	6	21	4	0	1	0	0.0	2	0	1	1	2	.190	.286	0	0	SS-6

Ed Holly

HOLLY, EDWARD WILLIAM
B. July 6, 1879, Chicago, Ill.   D. Nov. 27, 1973, Williamsport, Pa.   BR TR 5'10" 165 lbs.

	G	AB	H	2B	3B	HR	HR %	R	RBI	BB	SO	SB	BA	SA	AB	H	G by POS
1906 STL N	10	34	2	0	0	0	0.0	1	7	5		0	.059	.059	0	0	SS-10
1907	149	544	125	18	3	1	0.2	55	40	36		16	.230	.279	0	0	SS-147, 2B-3
1914 PIT F	100	350	86	9	4	0	0.0	28	26	17		14	.246	.294	3	2	SS-94, OF-2, 2B-1
1915	16	42	11	2	0	0	0.0	8	5	5		3	.262	.310	1	1	SS-11, 3B-3
4 yrs.	275	970	224	29	7	1	0.1	92	78	63		33	.231	.278	4	3	SS-262, 2B-4, 3B-3, OF-2

Billy Holm

HOLM, WILLIAM FREDERICK HENRY
B. July 21, 1912, Chicago, Ill.   D. July 27, 1977, Portage, Ind.   BR TR 5'10½" 168 lbs.

	G	AB	H	2B	3B	HR	HR %	R	RBI	BB	SO	SB	BA	SA	AB	H	G by POS
1943 CHI N	7	15	1	0	0	0	0.0	0	0	2	4	0	.067	.067	0	0	C-7
1944	54	132	18	2	0	0	0.0	10	6	16	19	1	.136	.152	3	0	C-50
1945 BOS A	58	135	25	2	1	0	0.0	12	9	23	17	1	.185	.215	1	0	C-57
3 yrs.	119	282	44	4	1	0	0.0	22	15	41	40	2	.156	.177	4	0	C-114

Wattie Holm

HOLM, ROSCOE ALBERT
B. Dec. 28, 1901, Peterson, Iowa   D. May 19, 1950, Everly, Iowa   BR TR 5'9½" 160 lbs.

	G	AB	H	2B	3B	HR	HR %	R	RBI	BB	SO	SB	BA	SA	AB	H	G by POS
1924 STL N	81	293	86	10	4	0	0.0	40	23	8	16	1	.294	.355	5	1	OF-64, C-9, 3B-4
1925	13	58	12	1	1	0	0.0	10	2	3	1	1	.207	.259	0	0	OF-13
1926	55	144	41	5	1	0	0.0	18	21	18	14	3	.285	.333	15	5	OF-39
1927	110	419	120	27	8	3	0.7	55	66	24	29	4	.286	.411	4	2	OF-97, 3B-9
1928	102	386	107	24	6	3	0.8	61	47	32	17	1	.277	.394	9	4	3B-83, OF-7
1929	64	176	41	5	6	0	0.0	21	14	12	8	1	.233	.330	17	3	OF-44, 3B-1
1932	11	17	3	1	0	0	0.0	2	1	3	1	0	.176	.235	5	1	OF-4
7 yrs.	436	1493	410	73	26	6	0.4	207	174	100	86	11	.275	.370	55	16	OF-268, 3B-97, C-9
WORLD SERIES																	
1926 STL N	5	16	2	0	0	0	0.0	1	1	1	2	0	.125	.125	1	0	OF-4
1928	3	6	1	0	0	0	0.0	0	1	0	1	0	.167	.167	2	0	OF-1
2 yrs.	8	22	3	0	0	0	0.0	1	2	1	3	0	.136	.136	3	0	OF-5

Gary Holman

HOLMAN, GARY RICHARD
B. Jan. 25, 1944, Long Beach, Calif.   BL TL 6'1" 200 lbs.

	G	AB	H	2B	3B	HR	HR %	R	RBI	BB	SO	SB	BA	SA	AB	H	G by POS
1968 WAS A	75	85	25	5	1	0	0.0	10	7	13	15	0	.294	.376	32	11	1B-33, OF-10
1969	41	31	5	1	0	0	0.0	1	2	4	7	0	.161	.194	26	5	1B-11, OF-3
2 yrs.	116	116	30	6	1	0	0.0	11	9	17	22	0	.259	.328	58	16	1B-44, OF-13

Ducky Holmes

HOLMES, HOWARD ELBERT
B. July 8, 1883, Dayton, Ohio   D. Sept. 18, 1945, Dayton, Ohio   TR

	G	AB	H	2B	3B	HR	HR %	R	RBI	BB	SO	SB	BA	SA	AB	H	G by POS
1906 STL N	9	27	5	0	0	0	0.0	2	2	2		0	.185	.185	0	0	C-9

Ducky Holmes

HOLMES, JAMES WILLIAM
B. Jan. 28, 1869, Des Moines, Iowa   D. Aug. 6, 1932, Truro, Iowa   BL TR 5'6" 170 lbs.

	G	AB	H	2B	3B	HR	HR %	R	RBI	BB	SO	SB	BA	SA	AB	H	G by POS
1895 LOU N	40	161	60	10	2	3	1.9	33	20	12	9	9	.373	.516	0	0	OF-29, SS-8, 3B-4, P-2
1896	47	141	38	3	2	0	0.0	22	18	13	5	8	.270	.319	0	0	OF-33, P-2, SS-1, 2B-1
1897 2 teams					LOU N (2G – .000)			NY N (79G – .268)									
" total	81	310	82	8	6	1	0.3	51	44	19		30	.265	.339	2	0	OF-77, SS-2
1898 2 teams					STL N (23G – .238)			BAL N (113G – .285)									
" total	136	543	150	11	10	1	0.2	63	64	25		29	.276	.339	1	1	OF-135
1899 BAL N	138	553	177	31	7	4	0.7	80	66	39		50	.320	.423	0	0	OF-138
1901 DET A	131	537	158	28	10	4	0.7	90	62	37		35	.294	.406	0	0	OF-131
1902	92	362	93	15	4	2	0.6	50	33	28		16	.257	.337	0	0	OF-92
1903 2 teams					WAS A (21G – .225)			CHI A (86G – .279)									
" total	107	415	112	10	6	1	0.2	66	26	30		35	.270	.330	3	0	OF-96, 3B-7, 2B-2
1904 CHI A	68	251	78	11	9	1	0.4	42	19	14		13	.311	.438	5	2	OF-63
1905	92	328	66	15	2	0	0.0	42	22	19		11	.201	.259	3	0	OF-89
10 yrs.	932	3601	1014	142	58	17	0.5	539	374	236	14	236	.282	.367	24	8	OF-883, SS-11, 3B-11, P-4, 2B-3

Fred Holmes

HOLMES, FREDERICK
B. July 1, 1878, Chicago, Ill.   D. Feb. 13, 1956, Norwood Park Tnshp., Ill.   BR TR

	G	AB	H	2B	3B	HR	HR %	R	RBI	BB	SO	SB	BA	SA	AB	H	G by POS
1903 NY A	1	0	0	0	0	0	–	0	0	1		0	–	–	0	0	1B-1
1904 CHI N	1	3	1	1	0	0	0.0	1	0	0		0	.333	.667	0	0	C-1
2 yrs.	2	3	1	1	0	0	0.0	1	0	1		0	.333	.667	0	0	1B-1, C-1

	G	AB	H	2B	3B	HR	HR %	R	RBI	BB	SO	SB	BA	SA	Pinch Hit AB	Pinch Hit H	G by POS

Tommy Holmes

HOLMES, THOMAS FRANCIS (Kelly)
B. Mar. 29, 1917, Brooklyn, N. Y.
Manager 1951-52.

BL TL 5'10" 180 lbs.

	G	AB	H	2B	3B	HR	HR %	R	RBI	BB	SO	SB	BA	SA	AB	H	G by POS
1942 BOS N	141	558	155	24	4	4	0.7	56	41	64	10	2	.278	.357	0	0	OF-140
1943	152	629	170	33	10	5	0.8	75	41	58	20	7	.270	.378	0	0	OF-152
1944	155	631	195	42	6	13	2.1	93	73	61	11	4	.309	.456	0	0	OF-155
1945	154	636	224	47	6	28	4.4	125	117	70	9	15	.352	.577	0	0	OF-154
1946	149	568	176	35	6	6	1.1	80	79	58	14	7	.310	.424	2	1	OF-146
1947	150	618	191	33	3	9	1.5	90	53	44	16	3	.309	.416	1	0	OF-147
1948	139	585	190	35	7	6	1.0	85	61	46	20	1	.325	.439	2	1	OF-137
1949	117	380	101	20	4	8	2.1	47	59	39	6	1	.266	.403	12	4	OF-103
1950	105	322	96	20	1	9	2.8	44	51	33	8	0	.298	.450	15	4	OF-88
1951	27	29	5	0	0	0	0.0	1	5	3	4	0	.172	.241	22	3	OF-3
1952 BKN N	31	36	4	1	0	0	0.0	2	1	4	4	0	.111	.139	23	2	OF-6
11 yrs.	1320	4992	1507	292	47	88	1.8	698	581	480	122	40	.302	.432	77	15	OF-1231
WORLD SERIES																	
1948 BOS N	6	26	5	0	0	0	0.0	3	1	0	0	0	.192	.192	0	0	OF-6
1952 BKN N	3	1	0	0	0	0	0.0	0	0	0	0	0	.000	.000	0	0	OF-3
2 yrs.	9	27	5	0	0	0	0.0	3	1	0	0	0	.185	.185	0	0	OF-9

Jim Holt

HOLT, JAMES WILLIAM
B. May 27, 1944, Graham, N. C.

BL TR 6' 180 lbs.

	G	AB	H	2B	3B	HR	HR %	R	RBI	BB	SO	SB	BA	SA	AB	H	G by POS
1968 MIN A	70	106	22	2	1	0	0.0	9	8	4	20	0	.208	.245	26	4	OF-38, 1B-1
1969	12	14	5	0	1	1	7.1	3	2	0	4	0	.357	.571	7	4	OF-5, 1B-1
1970	142	319	85	9	3	3	0.9	37	40	17	32	3	.266	.342	14	3	OF-130, 1B-2
1971	126	340	88	11	3	1	0.3	35	29	16	28	5	.259	.318	13	4	OF-106, 1B-3
1972	10	27	12	1	0	1	3.7	6	6	0	1	0	.444	.593	4	1	OF-7, 1B-1
1973	132	441	131	25	3	11	2.5	52	58	29	43	0	.297	.442	11	5	OF-102, 1B-33
1974 2 teams	109				MIN A (79G – .254)				OAK A (30G – .143)								
" total	109	239	56	11	0	0	0.0	25	16	15	25	0	.234	.280	24	0	1B-84, OF-5, DH-3
1975 OAK A	102	123	27	3	0	2	1.6	7	16	11	11	0	.220	.293	43	10	1B-52, DH-4, OF-2, C-1
1976	4	7	2	2	0	0	0.0	0	2	1	2	0	.286	.571	2	1	DH-2
9 yrs.	707	1616	428	64	10	19	1.2	174	177	93	166	8	.265	.352	144	32	OF-395, 1B-177, DH-9, C-1
LEAGUE CHAMPIONSHIP SERIES																	
1970 MIN A	3	5	0	0	0	0	0.0	0	0	0	2	0	.000	.000	1	0	OF-3
1974 OAK A	2	0	0	0	0	0	0.0	0	0	1	0	0	–	–	0	0	1B-1
1975	3	3	1	1	0	0	0.0	0	0	0	0	0	.333	.667	2	1	1B-1
3 yrs.	8	8	1	1	0	0	0.0	0	0	1	2	0	.125	.250	3	1	OF-3, 1B-2
WORLD SERIES																	
1974 OAK A	4	3	2	0	0	0	0.0	0	2	0	0	0	.667	.667	3	2	1B-1

Red Holt

HOLT, JAMES EMMETT MADISON
B. July 25, 1894, Dayton, Tenn.   D. Feb. 2, 1961, Birmingham, Ala.

BB TL 5'11" 175 lbs.

	G	AB	H	2B	3B	HR	HR %	R	RBI	BB	SO	SB	BA	SA	AB	H	G by POS
1925 PHI A	27	88	24	7	0	1	1.1	13	8	12	9	0	.273	.386	1	0	1B-25

Roger Holt

HOLT, ROGER BOYD
B. Apr. 8, 1956, Daytona Beach, Fla.

BB TR 5'11" 165 lbs.

	G	AB	H	2B	3B	HR	HR %	R	RBI	BB	SO	SB	BA	SA	AB	H	G by POS
1980 NY A	2	6	1	0	0	0	0.0	0	1	1	2	0	.167	.167	0	0	2B-2

Marty Honan

HONAN, MARTIN WELDON
B. 1870, Chicago, Ill.   D. Aug. 20, 1908, Chicago, Ill.

	G	AB	H	2B	3B	HR	HR %	R	RBI	BB	SO	SB	BA	SA	AB	H	G by POS
1890 CHI N	1	3	0	0	0	0	0.0	0	1	0	2	0	.000	.000	0	0	C-1
1891	5	12	2	0	0	1	8.3	1	3	1	3	0	.167	.417	0	0	C-5
2 yrs.	6	15	2	0	0	1	6.7	1	4	1	5	0	.133	.333	0	0	C-6

Abie Hood

HOOD, ALBIE LARRISON
B. Jan. 31, 1903, Sanford, N. C.

BL TR 5'8" 152 lbs.

	G	AB	H	2B	3B	HR	HR %	R	RBI	BB	SO	SB	BA	SA	AB	H	G by POS
1925 BOS N	5	21	6	2	0	1	4.8	2	1	0		0	.286	.524	0	0	2B-5

Wally Hood

HOOD, WALLACE JAMES, SR.
Father of Wally Hood.
B. Feb. 9, 1895, Whittier, Calif.   D. May 2, 1965, Hollywood, Calif.

BR TR 5'11½" 160 lbs.

	G	AB	H	2B	3B	HR	HR %	R	RBI	BB	SO	SB	BA	SA	AB	H	G by POS
1920 2 teams					BKN N (7G – .143)				PIT N (2G – .000)								
" total	9	15	2	1	0	0	0.0	5	1	5	4	3	.133	.200	1	0	OF-5
1921 BKN N	56	65	17	1	2	1	1.5	16	4	9	14	2	.262	.385	20	4	OF-20
1922	2	0	0	0	0	0	–	2	0	0	0	0	–	–	0	0	OF-2
3 yrs.	67	80	19	2	2	1	1.3	23	5	14	18	5	.238	.350	21	4	OF-25

Alex Hooks

HOOKS, ALEXANDER MARCUS
B. Aug. 29, 1906, Edgewood, Tex.

BL TL 6'1" 183 lbs.

	G	AB	H	2B	3B	HR	HR %	R	RBI	BB	SO	SB	BA	SA	AB	H	G by POS
1935 PHI A	15	44	10	3	0	0	0.0	4	4	3	10	0	.227	.295	4	1	1B-10

Harry Hooper

HOOPER, HARRY BARTHOLOMEW
B. Aug. 24, 1887, Bell Station, Calif.   D. Dec. 18, 1974, Santa Cruz, Calif.
Hall of Fame 1971.

BL TR 5'10" 168 lbs.

	G	AB	H	2B	3B	HR	HR %	R	RBI	BB	SO	SB	BA	SA	AB	H	G by POS
1909 BOS A	81	255	72	3	4	0	0.0	29	12	16		15	.282	.325	4	2	OF-84
1910	155	584	156	9	10	2	0.3	81	27	62		40	.267	.327	0	0	OF-155
1911	130	524	163	20	6	4	0.8	93	45	73		38	.311	.395	0	0	OF-130
1912	147	590	143	20	12	2	0.3	98	53	66		29	.242	.327	0	0	OF-147
1913	148	586	169	29	12	4	0.7	100	40	60	51	26	.288	.399	1	0	OF-147, P-1
1914	141	530	137	23	15	1	0.2	85	41	58	47	19	.258	.364	1	0	OF-140
1915	149	566	133	20	13	2	0.4	90	51	89	36	22	.235	.327	0	0	OF-147
1916	151	575	156	20	11	1	0.2	75	37	80	35	27	.271	.350	0	0	OF-151
1917	151	559	143	21	11	3	0.5	89	45	80	40	21	.256	.349	0	0	OF-151
1918	126	474	137	26	13	1	0.2	81	44	75	25	24	.289	.405	0	0	OF-126

	G	AB	H	2B	3B	HR	HR %	R	RBI	BB	SO	SB	BA	SA	Pinch Hit AB	Pinch Hit H	G by POS

Harry Hooper *continued*

	G	AB	H	2B	3B	HR	HR %	R	RBI	BB	SO	SB	BA	SA	AB	H	G by POS
1919	128	491	131	25	6	3	0.6	76	49	79	28	23	.267	.360	0	0	OF-128
1920	139	536	167	30	17	7	1.3	91	53	88	27	16	.312	.470	0	0	OF-139
1921 CHI A	108	419	137	26	5	8	1.9	74	58	55	21	13	.327	.470	0	0	OF-108
1922	152	602	183	35	8	11	1.8	111	80	68	33	16	.304	.444	3	0	OF-149
1923	145	576	166	32	4	10	1.7	87	65	68	22	18	.288	.410	2	1	OF-143
1924	130	476	156	27	8	10	2.1	107	62	65	26	16	.328	.481	5	2	OF-123
1925	127	442	117	23	5	6	1.4	62	55	54	21	12	.265	.380	2	0	OF-124
17 yrs.	2308	8785	2466	389	160	75	0.9	1429	817	1136	412	375	.281	.387	18	5	OF-2292, P-1
WORLD SERIES																	
1912 BOS A	8	31	9	2	1	0	0.0	3	2	4	4	2	.290	.419	0	0	OF-8
1915	5	20	7	0	0	2	10.0	4	3	2	4	0	.350	.650	0	0	OF-5
1916	5	21	7	1	1	0	0.0	6	1	3	1	1	.333	.476	0	0	OF-5
1918	6	20	4	0	0	0	0.0	0	0	2	2	0	.200	.200	0	0	OF-6
4 yrs.	24	92	27	3	2	2	2.2	13	6	11	11	3	.293	.435	0	0	OF-24

Buster Hoover

HOOVER, WILLIAM J.
B. 1863, Philadelphia, Pa.   Deceased.   BR TR 6'1" 178 lbs.

	G	AB	H	2B	3B	HR	HR %	R	RBI	BB	SO	SB	BA	SA	AB	H	G by POS
1884 2 teams		PHI U	(63G – .364)			PHI N	(10G – .190)										
" total	73	317	108	21	8	1	0.3	82		16	9		.341	.467	0	0	OF-47, SS-15, 2B-6, 1B-6, 3B-1
1886 BAL AA	40	157	34	2	6	0	0.0	25		16			.217	.306	0	0	OF-40
1892 CIN N	14	51	9	0	0	0	0.0	7	2	5	4	1	.176	.176	0	0	OF-14
3 yrs.	127	525	151	23	14	1	0.2	114		37	13	1	.288	.390	0	0	OF-101, SS-15, 2B-6, 1B-6, 3B-1

Charlie Hoover

HOOVER, CHARLES E.
B. Sept. 21, 1865, Mound City, Ill.   Deceased.

	G	AB	H	2B	3B	HR	HR %	R	RBI	BB	SO	SB	BA	SA	AB	H	G by POS
1888 KC AA	3	10	3	0	0	0	0.0	0	1	0			.300	.300	0	0	C-3
1889	71	258	64	2	5	1	0.4	44	25	29	38	9	.248	.306	0	0	C-66, 3B-4, OF-3
2 yrs.	74	268	67	2	5	1	0.4	44	26	29	38	9	.250	.306	0	0	C-69, 3B-4, OF-3

Joe Hoover

HOOVER, ROBERT JOE
B. Apr. 15, 1915, Brawley, Calif.   D. Sept. 2, 1965, Los Angeles, Calif.   BR TR 5'11" 175 lbs.

	G	AB	H	2B	3B	HR	HR %	R	RBI	BB	SO	SB	BA	SA	AB	H	G by POS
1943 DET A	144	575	140	15	8	4	0.7	78	38	36	101	6	.243	.318	0	0	SS-144
1944	120	441	104	20	2	0	0.0	67	29	35	66	7	.236	.290	0	0	SS-119, 2B-1
1945	74	222	57	10	5	1	0.5	33	17	21	35	6	.257	.360	0	0	SS-68
3 yrs.	338	1238	301	45	15	5	0.4	178	84	92	202	19	.243	.316	0	0	SS-331, 2B-1
WORLD SERIES																	
1945 DET A	1	3	1	0	0	0	0.0	1	1	0	0	0	.333	.333	0	0	SS-1

Don Hopkins

HOPKINS, DONALD
B. Jan. 9, 1952, West Point, Miss.   BL TR 6'1" 175 lbs.

	G	AB	H	2B	3B	HR	HR %	R	RBI	BB	SO	SB	BA	SA	AB	H	G by POS
1975 OAK A	82	6	1	0	0	0	0.0	25	0	2	0	21	.167	.167	3	0	DH-20, OF-5
1976	3	0	0	0	0	0		0	0	0	0	0	–	–	0	0	DH-2
2 yrs.	85	6	1	0	0	0	0.0	25	0	2	0	21	.167	.167	3	0	DH-22, OF-5
LEAGUE CHAMPIONSHIP SERIES																	
1975 OAK A	1	0	0	0	0	0	–	0	0	0	0	0	–	–	0	0	DH-1

Gail Hopkins

HOPKINS, GAIL EASON
B. Feb. 19, 1943, Tulsa, Okla.   BL TR 5'10" 198 lbs.

	G	AB	H	2B	3B	HR	HR %	R	RBI	BB	SO	SB	BA	SA	AB	H	G by POS
1968 CHI A	29	37	8	2	0	0	0.0	4	2	6	3	0	.216	.270	20	4	1B-7
1969	124	373	99	13	3	8	2.1	52	46	50	28	2	.265	.381	21	6	1B-101
1970	116	287	82	8	1	6	2.1	32	29	28	19	0	.286	.383	36	10	1B-77, C-8
1971 KC A	103	295	82	16	1	9	3.1	35	47	37	13	3	.278	.431	17	5	1B-83
1972	53	71	15	2	0	0	0.0	1	5	7	4	0	.211	.239	34	6	1B-13, 3B-1
1973	74	138	34	6	1	2	1.4	17	16	29	15	1	.246	.348	19	7	DH-36, 1B-10
1974 LA N	15	18	4	0	0	0	0.0	1	0	3	1	0	.222	.222	11	4	1B-2, C-2
7 yrs.	514	1219	324	47	6	25	2.1	142	145	160	83	6	.266	.376	158	42	1B-293, DH-36, C-10, 3B-1

Marty Hopkins

HOPKINS, MEREDITH HILLIARD
B. Feb. 22, 1907, Wolfe City, Tex.   D. Nov. 20, 1963, Dallas, Tex.   BR TR 5'11" 175 lbs.

	G	AB	H	2B	3B	HR	HR %	R	RBI	BB	SO	SB	BA	SA	AB	H	G by POS
1934 2 teams		PHI N	(10G – .120)			CHI A	(67G – .214)										
" total	77	235	48	9	0	2	0.9	28	31	49	31	0	.204	.268	1	0	3B-72
1935 CHI A	59	144	32	3	0	2	1.4	20	17	36	23	1	.222	.285	1	0	3B-49, 2B-5
2 yrs.	136	379	80	12	0	4	1.1	48	48	85	54	1	.211	.274	2	0	3B-121, 2B-5

Mike Hopkins

HOPKINS, MICHAEL JOSEPH
B. Nov. 1, 1872, Glasgow, Scotland   D. Feb. 5, 1952, Pittsburgh, Pa.   BR TR

	G	AB	H	2B	3B	HR	HR %	R	RBI	BB	SO	SB	BA	SA	AB	H	G by POS
1902 PIT N	1	2	2	1	0	0	0.0	0	0	0		0	1.000	1.500	0	0	C-1

Sis Hopkins

HOPKINS, JOHN WINTON (Buck)
B. Jan. 3, 1883, Grafton, Va.   D. Oct. 2, 1929, Phoebus, Va.   BR TR

	G	AB	H	2B	3B	HR	HR %	R	RBI	BB	SO	SB	BA	SA	AB	H	G by POS
1907 STL N	15	44	6	3	0	0	0.0	7	3	10		2	.136	.205	0	0	OF-15

Johnny Hopp

HOPP, JOHN LEONARD (Hippity)
B. July 18, 1916, Hastings, Neb.   BL TL 5'10" 170 lbs.

	G	AB	H	2B	3B	HR	HR %	R	RBI	BB	SO	SB	BA	SA	AB	H	G by POS
1939 STL N	6	4	2	1	0	0	0.0	1	2	1	1	0	.500	.750	3	2	1B-1
1940	80	152	41	7	4	1	0.7	24	14	9	21	3	.270	.388	23	4	OF-39, 1B-10
1941	134	445	135	25	11	4	0.9	83	50	50	63	15	.303	.436	6	1	OF-91, 1B-39
1942	95	314	81	16	7	3	1.0	41	37	36	40	14	.258	.382	3	1	1B-88
1943	91	241	54	10	2	2	0.8	33	25	24	22	8	.224	.307	4	0	OF-52, 1B-27
1944	139	527	177	35	9	11	2.1	106	72	58	47	15	.336	.499	2	0	OF-131, 1B-6

	G	AB	H	2B	3B	HR	HR %	R	RBI	BB	SO	SB	BA	SA	Pinch Hit AB	Pinch Hit H	G by POS

Johnny Hopp continued

	G	AB	H	2B	3B	HR	HR%	R	RBI	BB	SO	SB	BA	SA	PH AB	PH H	G by POS
1945	124	446	129	22	8	3	0.7	67	44	49	24	14	.289	.395	6	1	OF-104, 1B-15
1946 BOS N	129	445	148	23	8	3	0.7	71	48	34	34	21	.333	.440	8	3	1B-68, OF-58
1947	134	430	124	20	2	2	0.5	74	32	58	30	13	.288	.358	7	0	OF-125
1948 PIT N	120	392	109	15	12	1	0.3	64	31	40	25	5	.278	.385	14	7	OF-80, 1B-25
1949 2 teams	PIT	N (105G – .318)			BKN	N	(8G – .000)										
" total	113	385	118	14	5	5	1.3	55	39	37	32	9	.306	.408	13	5	1B-79, OF-20
1950 2 teams	PIT	N (106G – .340)			NY	A	(19G – .333)										
" total	125	345	117	26	6	9	2.6	60	55	52	18	7	.339	.528	28	8	1B-82, OF-13
1951 NY A	46	63	13	1	0	2	3.2	10	4	9	11	2	.206	.317	19	4	1B-25
1952 2 teams	NY	A (15G – .160)			DET	A	(42G – .217)										
" total	57	71	14	1	0	0	0.0	9	5	8	10	2	.197	.211	33	8	1B-13, OF-4
14 yrs.	1393	4260	1262	216	74	46	1.1	698	458	465	378	128	.296	.414	169	44	OF-717, 1B-478

WORLD SERIES	G	AB	H	2B	3B	HR	HR%	R	RBI	BB	SO	SB	BA	SA	PH AB	PH H	G by POS
1942 STL N	5	17	3	0	0	0	0.0	3	0	1	1	0	.176	.176	0	0	1B-5
1943	1	4	0	0	0	0	0.0	0	0	0	1	0	.000	.000	0	0	OF-1
1944	6	27	5	0	0	0	0.0	2	0	0	8	0	.185	.185	0	0	OF-6
1950 NY A	3	2	0	0	0	0	0.0	0	0	0	0	0	.000	.000	0	0	1B-3
1951	1	0	0	0	0	0	–	0	0	1	0	0	–	–	0	0	
5 yrs.	16	50	8	0	0	0	0.0	5	0	2	10	0	.160	.160	0	0	1B-8, OF-7

Shags Horan

HORAN, JOSEPH PATRICK   BR TR 5'10" 170 lbs.
B. Sept. 7, 1894, St. Louis, Mo.   D. Feb. 13, 1969, Los Angeles, Calif.

	G	AB	H	2B	3B	HR	HR%	R	RBI	BB	SO	SB	BA	SA	PH AB	PH H	G by POS
1924 NY A	22	31	9	1	0	0	0.0	4	7	1	5	0	.290	.323	7	2	OF-13

Bob Horner

HORNER, JAMES ROBERT   BR TR 6'1" 195 lbs.
B. Aug. 6, 1957, Junction City, Kans.

	G	AB	H	2B	3B	HR	HR%	R	RBI	BB	SO	SB	BA	SA	PH AB	PH H	G by POS
1978 ATL N	89	323	86	17	1	23	7.1	50	63	24	42	0	.266	.539	0	0	3B-89
1979	121	487	153	15	1	33	6.8	66	98	22	74	0	.314	.552	1	0	3B-82, 1B-45
1980	124	463	124	14	1	35	7.6	81	89	27	50	3	.268	.529	3	1	3B-121, 1B-1
1981	79	300	83	10	0	15	5.0	42	42	32	39	2	.277	.460	0	0	3B-79
1982	140	499	130	24	0	32	6.4	85	97	66	75	3	.261	.501	3	0	3B-137
1983	104	386	117	25	1	20	5.2	75	68	50	63	4	.303	.528	0	0	3B-104, 1B-1
1984	32	113	31	8	0	3	2.7	15	19	14	17	0	.274	.425	0	0	3B-32
7 yrs.	689	2571	724	113	4	161	6.3	414	476	235	360	12	.282	.517	7	1	3B-644, 1B-47

LEAGUE CHAMPIONSHIP SERIES	G	AB	H	2B	3B	HR	HR%	R	RBI	BB	SO	SB	BA	SA	PH AB	PH H	G by POS
1982 ATL N	3	11	1	0	0	0	0.0	0	0	0	2	0	.091	.091	0	0	3B-3

Rogers Hornsby

HORNSBY, ROGERS (Rajah)   BR TR 5'11" 175 lbs.
B. Apr. 27, 1896, Winters, Tex.   D. Jan. 5, 1963, Chicago, Ill.
Manager 1925-26, 1928, 1930-37, 1952-53.
Hall of Fame 1942.

	G	AB	H	2B	3B	HR	HR%	R	RBI	BB	SO	SB	BA	SA	PH AB	PH H	G by POS
1915 STL N	18	57	14	2	0	0	0.0	5	4	2	6	0	.246	.281	0	0	SS-18
1916	139	495	155	17	15	6	1.2	63	65	40	63	17	.313	.444	1	1	3B-83, SS-45, 1B-15, 2B-1
1917	145	523	171	24	17	8	1.5	86	66	45	34	17	.327	.484	1	0	SS-144
1918	115	416	117	19	11	5	1.2	51	60	40	43	8	.281	.416	4	2	SS-109, OF-2
1919	138	512	163	15	9	8	1.6	68	71	48	41	17	.318	.430	0	0	3B-72, SS-37, 2B-25, 1B-5
1920	149	589	218	44	20	9	1.5	96	94	60	50	12	.370	.559	0	0	2B-149
1921	154	592	235	44	18	21	3.5	131	126	60	48	13	.397	.639	0	0	2B-142, OF-6, SS-3, 3B-3, 1B-1
1922	154	623	250	46	14	42	6.7	141	152	65	50	17	.401	.722	0	0	2B-154
1923	107	424	163	32	10	17	4.0	89	83	55	29	3	.384	.627	1	0	2B-96, 1B-10
1924	143	536	227	43	14	25	4.7	121	94	89	32	5	.424	.696	0	0	2B-136
1925	138	504	203	41	10	39	7.7	133	143	83	39	5	.403	.756	0	0	2B-134
1926	134	527	167	34	5	11	2.1	96	93	61	39	3	.317	.463	0	0	2B-134
1927 NY N	155	568	205	32	9	26	4.6	133	125	86	38	9	.361	.586	0	0	2B-155
1928 BOS N	140	486	188	42	7	21	4.3	99	94	107	41	5	.387	.632	0	0	2B-140
1929 CHI N	156	602	229	47	8	39	6.5	156	149	87	65	2	.380	.679	0	0	2B-156
1930	42	104	32	5	1	2	1.9	15	18	12	12	0	.308	.433	15	2	2B-25
1931	100	357	118	37	1	16	4.5	64	90	56	23	1	.331	.574	4	2	2B-69, 3B-26
1932	19	58	13	2	0	1	1.7	10	7	10	4	0	.224	.310	3	1	OF-10, 3B-6
1933 2 teams	STL	N (46G – .325)			STL	A	(11G – .333)										
" total	57	92	30	7	0	3	3.3	11	23	14	7	1	.326	.500	35	11	2B-17
1934 STL A	24	23	7	2	0	1	4.3	2	11	7	4	0	.304	.522	15	5	OF-1, 3B-1
1935	10	24	5	3	0	0	0.0	1	3	3	6	0	.208	.333	3	1	1B-3, 2B-2, 3B-1
1936	2	5	2	0	0	0	0.0	1	2	1	0	0	.400	.400	1	1	1B-1
1937	20	56	18	3	0	1	1.8	7	11	7	5	0	.321	.429	3	0	2B-17
23 yrs.	2259	8173	2930	541	169	301	3.7	1579	1584	1038	679	135	.358 2nd	.577 7th	86	26	2B-1561, SS-356, 3B-192, 1B-35, OF-19

WORLD SERIES	G	AB	H	2B	3B	HR	HR%	R	RBI	BB	SO	SB	BA	SA	PH AB	PH H	G by POS
1926 STL N	7	28	7	1	0	0	0.0	2	4	2	2	1	.250	.286	0	0	2B-7
1929 CHI N	5	21	5	1	1	0	0.0	4	1	1	8	0	.238	.381	0	0	2B-5
2 yrs.	12	49	12	2	1	0	0.0	6	5	3	10	1	.245	.327	0	0	2B-12

Joe Hornung

HORNUNG, MICHAEL JOSEPH (Ubbo Ubbo)   BR TR 5'8½" 164 lbs.
B. June 12, 1857, Carthage, N.Y.   D. Oct. 30, 1931, Howard Beach, N.Y.

	G	AB	H	2B	3B	HR	HR%	R	RBI	BB	SO	SB	BA	SA	PH AB	PH H	G by POS
1879 BUF N	78	319	85	18	7	0	0.0	46	38	2	27		.266	.367	0	0	OF-77, 1B-1
1880	85	342	91	8	11	1	0.3	47	42	8	29		.266	.363	0	0	OF-67, 1B-18, 2B-5, P-1
1881 BOS N	83	324	78	12	8	2	0.6	40	25	5	25		.241	.346	0	0	OF-83
1882	85	388	117	14	11	1	0.3	67	50	2	25		.302	.402	0	0	OF-84, 1B-1
1883	98	446	124	25	13	8	1.8	107	66	8	54		.278	.446	0	0	OF-98, 3B-1
1884	115	518	139	27	10	7	1.4	119		17	80		.268	.400	0	0	OF-110, 1B-6
1885	25	109	22	4	1	1	0.9	14	7	1	20		.202	.284	0	0	OF-25
1886	94	424	109	12	2	2	0.5	67	40	10	62		.257	.309	0	0	OF-112
1887	98	437	118	10	6	5	1.1	85	49	17	28	41	.270	.355	0	0	OF-98
1888	107	431	103	11	7	3	0.7	61	53	16	39	29	.239	.318	0	0	OF-107

	G	AB	H	2B	3B	HR	HR%	R	RBI	BB	SO	SB	BA	SA	Pinch Hit AB	Pinch Hit H	G by POS

Joe Hornung continued

	G	AB	H	2B	3B	HR	HR%	R	RBI	BB	SO	SB	BA	SA	AB	H	G by POS
1889 BAL AA	135	533	122	13	9	1	0.2	73	78	22	72	34	.229	.293	0	0	OF-134, 3B-1
1890 NY N	120	513	122	18	5	0	0.0	62	65	12	37	39	.238	.292	0	0	OF-77, 1B-36, 3B-5, SS-2
12 yrs.	1123	4784	1230	172	90	31	0.6	788	513	120	498	143	.257	.350	0	0	OF-1072, 1B-62, 3B-7, 2B-5, SS-2, P-1

Tony Horton

HORTON, ANTHONY DARRIN
B. Dec. 6, 1944, Santa Monica, Calif.   BR TR 6'3"   210 lbs.

	G	AB	H	2B	3B	HR	HR%	R	RBI	BB	SO	SB	BA	SA	AB	H	G by POS
1964 BOS A	36	126	28	5	0	1	0.8	9	8	3	20	0	.222	.286	6	0	OF-24, 1B-8
1965	60	163	48	8	1	7	4.3	23	23	18	36	0	.294	.485	14	3	1B-44
1966	6	22	3	0	0	0	0.0	0	2	0	5	0	.136	.136	2	0	1B-6
1967 2 teams		BOS	A	(21G –	.308)		CLE	A	(106G –	.281)							
" total	127	402	114	16	4	10	2.5	37	53	18	57	3	.284	.418	31	10	1B-100
1968 CLE A	133	477	119	29	4	14	2.9	57	59	34	56	3	.249	.411	9	2	1B-128
1969	159	625	174	25	4	27	4.3	77	93	37	91	3	.278	.461	2	0	1B-157
1970	115	413	111	19	3	17	4.1	48	59	30	54	3	.269	.453	8	3	1B-112
7 yrs.	636	2228	597	102	15	76	3.4	251	297	140	319	12	.268	.430	72	18	1B-555, OF-24

Willie Horton

HORTON, WILLIE WATTERSON
B. Oct. 18, 1942, Arno, Va.   BR TR 5'11"   209 lbs.

	G	AB	H	2B	3B	HR	HR%	R	RBI	BB	SO	SB	BA	SA	AB	H	G by POS
1963 DET A	15	43	14	2	1	1	2.3	6	4	0	8	2	.326	.488	5	3	OF-9
1964	25	80	13	1	3	1	1.3	6	10	11	20	0	.163	.288	3	1	OF-23
1965	143	512	140	20	2	29	5.7	69	104	48	101	5	.273	.490	3	0	OF-141, 3B-1
1966	146	526	138	22	6	27	5.1	72	100	44	103	1	.262	.481	9	2	OF-137
1967	122	401	110	20	3	19	4.7	47	67	36	80	0	.274	.481	11	3	OF-110
1968	143	512	146	20	2	36	7.0	68	85	49	110	0	.285	.543	5	1	OF-139
1969	141	508	133	17	1	28	5.5	66	91	52	93	3	.262	.465	5	1	OF-136
1970	96	371	113	18	2	17	4.6	53	69	28	43	0	.305	.501	0	0	OF-96
1971	119	450	130	25	1	22	4.9	64	72	37	75	1	.289	.496	2	0	OF-118
1972	108	333	77	9	5	11	3.3	44	36	27	47	0	.231	.387	12	1	OF-98
1973	111	411	130	19	3	17	4.1	42	53	23	57	1	.316	.501	3	1	OF-107, DH-1
1974	72	238	71	8	1	15	6.3	32	47	21	36	0	.298	.529	6	3	OF-64, DH-1
1975	159	615	169	13	1	25	4.1	62	92	44	109	1	.275	.421	0	0	DH-159
1976	114	401	105	17	0	14	3.5	40	56	49	63	0	.262	.409	0	0	DH-105
1977 2 teams		DET	A	(1G –	.250)		TEX	A	(139G –	.289)							
" total	140	523	151	23	3	15	2.9	55	75	42	117	2	.289	.430	6	2	DH-128, OF-11
1978 3 teams		CLE	A	(50G –	.249)		OAK	A	(32G –	.314)		TOR	A	(33G –	.205)	
"	115	393	99	21	0	11	2.8	39	60	28	69	3	.252	.389	9	3	DH-105, OF-1
1979 SEA A	162	646	180	19	5	29	4.5	77	106	42	112	1	.279	.458	0	0	DH-162
1980	97	335	74	10	1	8	2.4	32	36	39	70	0	.221	.328	5	2	DH-92
18 yrs.	2028	7298	1993	284	40	325	4.5	873	1163	620	1313	20	.273	.457	90	24	OF-1190, DH-753, 3B-1

LEAGUE CHAMPIONSHIP SERIES
| 1972 DET A | 5 | 10 | 1 | 0 | 0 | 0 | 0.0 | 0 | 0 | 1 | 3 | 0 | .100 | .100 | 2 | 1 | OF-3 |

WORLD SERIES
| 1968 DET A | 7 | 23 | 7 | 1 | 1 | 1 | 4.3 | 6 | 3 | 5 | 6 | 0 | .304 | .565 | 0 | 0 | OF-7 |

Tim Hosley

HOSLEY, TIMOTHY KENNETH
B. May 10, 1947, Spartanburg, S. C.   BR TR 5'11"   185 lbs.

	G	AB	H	2B	3B	HR	HR%	R	RBI	BB	SO	SB	BA	SA	AB	H	G by POS
1970 DET A	7	12	2	0	0	1	8.3	1	2	0	6	0	.167	.417	4	1	C-4
1971	7	16	3	0	0	2	12.5	2	6	0	1	0	.188	.563	4	0	C-4, 1B-1
1973 OAK A	13	14	3	0	0	0	0.0	3	2	2	3	0	.214	.214	4	1	C-12
1974	11	7	2	0	0	0	0.0	3	1	1	2	0	.286	.286	4	1	C-8, 1B-1
1975 CHI N	62	141	36	7	0	6	4.3	22	20	27	25	1	.255	.433	10	2	C-53
1976 2 teams		CHI	N	(1G –	.000)		OAK	A	(37G –	.164)							
" total	38	56	9	0	1	4	4	8	12	0	.161	.250	12	2	C-37		
1977 OAK A	39	78	15	0	0	1	1.3	5	10	16	13	0	.192	.231	5	1	C-19, DH-12, 1B-3
1978	13	23	7	2	0	0	0.0	1	3	1	6	0	.304	.391	7	2	C-2, DH-1
1981	18	21	2	0	0	1	4.8	2	5	2	5	0	.095	.238	14	1	DH-4, 1B-1
9 yrs.	208	368	79	11	0	12	3.3	43	43	57	73	1	.215	.342	64	11	C-139, DH-17, 1B-6

Chuck Hostetler

HOSTETLER, CHARLES CLOYD
B. Sept. 22, 1903, McClellandtown, Pa.   D. Feb. 18, 1971, Fort Collins, Colo.   BL TR 6'   175 lbs.

	G	AB	H	2B	3B	HR	HR%	R	RBI	BB	SO	SB	BA	SA	AB	H	G by POS
1944 DET A	90	265	79	9	2	0	0.0	42	20	21	31	4	.298	.347	19	4	OF-65
1945	42	44	7	3	0	0	0.0	3	2	7	8	0	.159	.227	30	6	OF-8
2 yrs.	132	309	86	12	2	0	0.0	45	22	28	39	4	.278	.330	49	10	OF-73

WORLD SERIES
| 1945 DET A | 3 | 3 | 0 | 0 | 0 | 0 | 0.0 | 0 | 0 | 0 | 0 | 0 | .000 | .000 | 3 | 0 | |

Dave Hostetler

HOSTETLER, DAVID ALAN
B. Mar. 27, 1956, Pasadena, Calif.   BR TR 6'4"   215 lbs.

	G	AB	H	2B	3B	HR	HR%	R	RBI	BB	SO	SB	BA	SA	AB	H	G by POS
1981 MON N	5	6	3	0	0	1	16.7	1	1	0	2	0	.500	1.000	3	0	1B-2
1982 TEX A	113	418	97	12	3	22	5.3	53	67	42	113	2	.232	.433	1	0	1B-109, DH-3
1983	94	304	67	9	2	11	3.6	31	46	42	103	0	.220	.372	8	1	DH-88, 1B-2
1984	37	82	18	2	1	3	3.7	7	10	13	27	0	.220	.378	9	2	1B-14, DH-13
4 yrs.	249	810	185	23	6	37	4.6	92	124	97	245	2	.228	.409	21	3	1B-127, DH-104

Art Hostetter

Playing record listed under Art Hoelskoetter

Pete Hotaling

HOTALING, PETER JAMES (Monkey)
B. Dec. 16, 1856, Mohawk, N. Y.   D. July 3, 1928, Cleveland, Ohio   BL TR 5'8"   166 lbs.

	G	AB	H	2B	3B	HR	HR%	R	RBI	BB	SO	SB	BA	SA	AB	H	G by POS
1879 CIN N	81	369	103	20	9	1	0.3	64	27	12	17		.279	.390	0	0	OF-69, C-8, 2B-6, 3B-3
1880 CLE N	78	325	78	17	8	0	0.0	40		10	30		.240	.342	0	0	OF-78, C-2
1881 WOR N	77	317	98	15	3	1	0.3	51	35	18	12		.309	.385	0	0	OF-74, C-3
1882 BOS N	84	378	98	16	5	0	0.0	64	28	16	21		.259	.328	0	0	OF-84
1883 CLE N	100	417	108	20	8	0	0.0	54		12	31		.259	.345	0	0	OF-100

Pete Hotaling *continued*

	G	AB	H	2B	3B	HR	HR %	R	RBI	BB	SO	SB	BA	SA	PH AB	PH H	G by POS
1884	102	408	99	16	6	3	0.7	69	27	28	50		.243	.333	0	0	OF-102, 2B-1
1885 BKN AA	94	370	95	9	5	1	0.3	73		49			.257	.316	0	0	OF-94
1887 CLE AA	126	505	151	28	13	3	0.6	108		53		43	.299	.424	0	0	OF-126
1888	98	403	101	7	6	0	0.0	67	55	26		35	.251	.298	0	0	OF-98
9 yrs.	840	3492	931	148	63	9	0.3	590	172	224	161	78	.267	.353	0	0	OF-825, C-13, 2B-7, 3B-3

Ken Hottman

HOTTMAN, KENNETH ROGER   BR TR 5'11" 190 lbs.
B. May 7, 1948, Stockton, Calif.

	G	AB	H	2B	3B	HR	HR %	R	RBI	BB	SO	SB	BA	SA	PH AB	PH H	G by POS
1971 CHI A	6	16	2	0	0	0	0.0	1	0	1	2	0	.125	.125	1	0	OF-5

Sadie Houck

HOUCK, SARGENT PERRY   BR TR
Also known as Douglas Houck.
B. 1856, Washington, D. C.   D. May 26, 1919, Washington, D. C.

	G	AB	H	2B	3B	HR	HR %	R	RBI	BB	SO	SB	BA	SA	PH AB	PH H	G by POS
1879 BOS N	80	356	95	24	9	2	0.6	69	49	4	11		.267	.402	0	0	OF-47, SS-33
1880 2 teams	BOS N (12G - .149) PRO N (49G - .201)																OF-61
" total	61	231	44	7	7	1	0.4	29	24	3	12		.190	.294	0	0	
1881 DET N	75	308	86	16	6	1	0.3	43	36	6	6		.279	.380	0	0	SS-75
1883	101	416	105	18	12	0	0.0	52		9	18		.252	.353	0	0	SS-101
1884 PHI AA	108	472	140	19	14	0	0.0	93		7			.297	.396	0	0	SS-108, 2B-1
1885	93	388	99	10	9	0	0.0	74		10			.255	.327	0	0	SS-93
1886 2 teams	BAL AA (61G - .192) WAS N (52G - .215)																SS-106, 2B-6, OF-1
" total	113	455	92	11	1	0	0.0	43	14	6	28		.202	.231	0	0	
1887 NY AA	10	33	5	1	0	0	0.0	3		3		2	.152	.182	0	0	SS-10, 2B-1
8 yrs.	641	2659	666	106	58	4	0.2	406	123	48	75	2	.250	.338	0	0	SS-526, OF-109, 2B-8

Ralph Houk

HOUK, RALPH GEORGE (Major)   BR TR 5'11" 193 lbs.
B. Aug. 9, 1919, Lawrence, Kans.
Manager 1961-63, 1966-78, 1981-84.

	G	AB	H	2B	3B	HR	HR %	R	RBI	BB	SO	SB	BA	SA	PH AB	PH H	G by POS
1947 NY A	41	92	25	3	1	0	0.0	7	12	11	5	0	.272	.326	0	0	C-41
1948	14	29	8	2	0	0	0.0	3	3	0	0	0	.276	.345	0	0	C-14
1949	5	7	4	0	0	0	0.0	0	1	0	1	0	.571	.571	0	0	C-5
1950	10	9	1	1	0	0	0.0	0	1	0	2	0	.111	.222	1	1	C-9
1951	3	5	1	0	0	0	0.0	0	2	0	1	0	.200	.200	0	0	C-3
1952	9	6	2	0	0	0	0.0	0	0	1	0	0	.333	.333	0	0	C-9
1953	8	9	2	0	0	0	0.0	2	1	0	1	0	.222	.222	0	0	C-8
1954	1	1	0	0	0	0	0.0	0	0	0	0	0	.000	.000	1	0	
8 yrs.	91	158	43	6	1	0	0.0	12	20	12	10	0	.272	.323	2	1	C-89

WORLD SERIES	G	AB	H	2B	3B	HR	HR %	R	RBI	BB	SO	SB	BA	SA	PH AB	PH H	G by POS
1947 NY A	1	1	1	0	0	0	0.0	0	0	0	0	0	1.000	1.000	1	1	
1952	1	1	0	0	0	0	0.0	0	0	0	0	0	.000	.000	1	0	
2 yrs.	2	2	1	0	0	0	0.0	0	0	0	0	0	.500	.500	2	1	

Frank House

HOUSE, HENRY FRANKLIN (Pig)   BL TR 6'1½" 190 lbs.
B. Feb. 18, 1930, Bessemer, Ala.

	G	AB	H	2B	3B	HR	HR %	R	RBI	BB	SO	SB	BA	SA	PH AB	PH H	G by POS
1950 DET A	5	5	2	1	0	0	0.0	1	0	0	1	0	.400	.600	1	0	C-5
1951	18	41	9	2	0	1	2.4	3	4	6	2	1	.220	.341	0	0	C-18
1954	114	352	88	12	1	9	2.6	35	38	31	34	2	.250	.366	9	1	C-107
1955	102	328	85	11	1	15	4.6	37	53	22	25	0	.259	.436	12	3	C-93
1956	94	321	77	6	2	10	3.1	44	44	21	19	1	.240	.364	9	3	C-88
1957	106	348	90	9	0	7	2.0	31	36	35	26	1	.259	.345	7	2	C-97
1958 KC A	76	202	51	6	3	4	2.0	16	24	12	13	1	.252	.371	19	7	C-55
1959	98	347	82	14	3	1	0.3	32	30	20	23	0	.236	.303	4	1	C-95
1960 CIN N	23	28	5	2	0	0	0.0	0	3	0	2	0	.179	.250	17	3	C-8
1961 DET A	17	22	5	1	0	0	0.0	3	3	4	2	0	.227	.364	3	0	C-14
10 yrs.	653	1994	494	64	11	47	2.4	202	235	151	147	6	.248	.362	81	20	C-580

Charlie Householder

HOUSEHOLDER, CHARLES F.   BR TR
B. 1856, Harrisburg, Pa.   Deceased.

	G	AB	H	2B	3B	HR	HR %	R	RBI	BB	SO	SB	BA	SA	PH AB	PH H	G by POS
1884 C-P U	83	310	74	12	5	1	0.3	32			12		.239	.319	0	0	3B-41, OF-40, SS-3, P-2

Charlie Householder

HOUSEHOLDER, CHARLES W.   BL TL 5'11" 158 lbs.
B. 1856, Harrisburg, Pa.   D. Dec. 26, 1908, Harrisburg, Pa.

	G	AB	H	2B	3B	HR	HR %	R	RBI	BB	SO	SB	BA	SA	PH AB	PH H	G by POS
1882 BAL AA	74	307	78	10	7	1	0.3	42			4		.254	.342	0	0	1B-74, C-3
1884 BKN AA	76	273	66	15	3	3	1.1	28			12		.242	.352	0	0	1B-40, C-31, OF-6, 2B-1
2 yrs.	150	580	144	25	10	4	0.7	70			16		.248	.347	0	0	1B-114, C-34, OF-6, 2B-1

Ed Householder

HOUSEHOLDER, EDWARD H.   BB TR 6' 180 lbs.
B. Oct. 12, 1869, Pittsburgh, Pa.   D. July 3, 1924, Los Angeles, Calif.

	G	AB	H	2B	3B	HR	HR %	R	RBI	BB	SO	SB	BA	SA	PH AB	PH H	G by POS
1903 BKN N	12	43	9	0	0	0	0.0	5	9	2		3	.209	.209	0	0	OF-12

Paul Householder

HOUSEHOLDER, PAUL WESLEY   BB TR 6' 180 lbs.
B. Sept. 4, 1958, Columbus, Ohio

	G	AB	H	2B	3B	HR	HR %	R	RBI	BB	SO	SB	BA	SA	PH AB	PH H	G by POS
1980 CIN N	20	45	11	1	0	0	0.0	3	7	1	13	1	.244	.311	7	2	OF-14
1981	23	69	19	4	0	2	2.9	12	9	10	16	3	.275	.420	4	1	OF-19
1982	138	417	88	11	5	9	2.2	40	34	30	77	17	.211	.326	10	1	OF-131
1983	123	380	97	24	4	6	1.6	40	43	44	60	12	.255	.387	17	3	OF-112
1984 2 teams	CIN N (14G - .083) STL N (13G - .143)																
" total	27	26	3	1	0	0	0.0	0		3	6	1	.115	.154	10	1	OF-18
5 yrs.	331	937	218	41	10	17	1.8	99	93	88	172	34	.233	.352	48	8	OF-294

John Houseman

HOUSEMAN, JOHN FRANKLIN
B. Jan. 10, 1870, Holland   D. Nov. 4, 1922, Chicago, Ill.

	G	AB	H	2B	3B	HR	HR %	R	RBI	BB	SO	SB	BA	SA	PH AB	PH H	G by POS
1894 CHI N	4	15	6	3	0	0	0.0	5	4	3		2	.400	.733	0	0	SS-3, 2B-1
1897 STL N	80	278	68	6	6	0	0.0	34	21	28		16	.245	.309	2	1	2B-41, OF-33, SS-5, 3B-3
2 yrs.	84	293	74	9	7	0	0.0	39	25	33	3	18	.253	.331	2	1	2B-42, OF-33, SS-8, 3B-3

	G	AB	H	2B	3B	HR	HR %	R	RBI	BB	SO	SB	BA	SA	Pinch Hit AB	Pinch Hit H	G by POS

Ben Houser

HOUSER, BENJAMIN FRANKLIN
B. Nov. 30, 1883, Shenandoah, Pa.   D. Jan. 15, 1952, Augusta, Me.   BL TL 6'1"   185 lbs.

	G	AB	H	2B	3B	HR	HR %	R	RBI	BB	SO	SB	BA	SA	PH AB	PH H	G by POS
1910 PHI A	34	69	13	3	2	0	0.0	9	7	7		0	.188	.290	8	2	1B-26
1911 BOS N	20	71	18	1	0	1	1.4	11	9	8	6	2	.254	.310	0	0	1B-20
1912	83	332	95	17	3	8	2.4	38	52	22	29	1	.286	.428	24	9	1B-83
3 yrs.	137	472	126	21	5	9	1.9	58	68	37	35	3	.267	.390	32	11	1B-129

Fred Houtz

HOUTZ, FRED (Lefty)
B. Sept. 4, 1875, Connersville, Ind.   D. Feb. 15, 1959, Wapakoneta, Ohio   BL TL 5'10"   170 lbs.

	G	AB	H	2B	3B	HR	HR %	R	RBI	BB	SO	SB	BA	SA	PH AB	PH H	G by POS
1899 CIN N	5	17	4	0	1	0	0.0	1	0	1		1	.235	.353	0	0	OF-5

Steve Hovley

HOVLEY, STEPHEN EUGENE
B. Dec. 18, 1944, Ventura, Calif.   BL TL 5'10"   188 lbs.

	G	AB	H	2B	3B	HR	HR %	R	RBI	BB	SO	SB	BA	SA	PH AB	PH H	G by POS
1969 SEA A	91	329	91	14	3	3	0.9	41	20	30	34	10	.277	.365	7	0	OF-84
1970 2 teams		MIL A (40G – .281)					OAK A (72G – .190)										
" total	112	235	57	10	0	0	0.0	25	17	22	22	8	.243	.285	31	8	OF-80
1971 OAK A	24	27	3	2	0	0	0.0	3	3	7	9	2	.111	.185	10	2	OF-11
1972 KC A	105	196	53	5	1	3	1.5	24	24	24	29	3	.270	.352	37	9	OF-68
1973	104	232	59	8	1	2	0.9	29	24	33	34	6	.254	.323	13	2	OF-79, DH-15
5 yrs.	436	1019	263	39	5	8	0.8	122	88	116	128	29	.258	.330	98	21	OF-322, DH-15

Dave Howard

HOWARD, DAVID AUSTIN (Del)
B. May 1, 1889, Washington, D. C.   D. Jan. 26, 1956, Dallas, Tex.   BR TR 5'11"   165 lbs.

	G	AB	H	2B	3B	HR	HR %	R	RBI	BB	SO	SB	BA	SA	PH AB	PH H	G by POS
1912 WAS A	1	0	0	0	0	0	–	1	0	0	0	0			0	0	
1915 BKN F	24	36	8	1	0	0	0.0	5	1	1		0	.222	.250	1	1	2B-12, OF-2, SS-1, 3B-1
2 yrs.	25	36	8	1	0	0	0.0	6	1	1		0	.222	.250	1	1	2B-12, OF-2, SS-1, 3B-1

Del Howard

HOWARD, GEORGE ELMER
Brother of Ivan Howard.
B. Dec. 24, 1877, Kenney, Ill.   D. Dec. 24, 1956, Seattle, Wash.   BL TR 6'   180 lbs.

	G	AB	H	2B	3B	HR	HR %	R	RBI	BB	SO	SB	BA	SA	PH AB	PH H	G by POS
1905 PIT N	123	435	127	18	5	2	0.5	56	63	27		19	.292	.370	3	0	1B-90, OF-28, P-1
1906 BOS N	147	545	142	19	8	1	0.2	46	54	26		17	.261	.330	0	0	OF-87, 2B-45, SS-14, 1B-2
1907 2 teams		BOS N (50G – .273)					CHI N (51G – .230)										
" total	101	335	85	6	4	1	0.3	30	26	17		14	.254	.304	11	3	OF-53, 1B-33, 2B-3
1908 CHI N	96	315	88	7	3	1	0.3	42	26	23		11	.279	.330	6	2	OF-81, 1B-5
1909	69	203	40	4	2	1	0.5	25	24	18		6	.197	.251	8	0	1B-57
5 yrs.	536	1833	482	54	22	6	0.3	199	193	111		67	.263	.326	28	5	OF-249, 1B-187, 2B-48, SS-14, P-1
WORLD SERIES																	
1907 CHI N	2	5	1	0	0	0	0.0	0	0	0	2	1	.200	.200	1	0	1B-1
1908	1	1	0	0	0	0	0.0	0	0	0	0	0	.000	.000	1	0	
2 yrs.	3	6	1	0	0	0	0.0	0	0	0	2	1	.167	.167	2	0	1B-1

Doug Howard

HOWARD, DOUGLAS LYN
B. Feb. 6, 1948, Salt Lake City, Utah   BR TR 6'3"   185 lbs.

	G	AB	H	2B	3B	HR	HR %	R	RBI	BB	SO	SB	BA	SA	PH AB	PH H	G by POS
1972 CAL A	11	38	10	1	0	0	0.0	4	2	1	3	0	.263	.289	1	0	OF-8, 3B-1, 1B-1
1973	8	21	2	0	0	0	0.0	2	1	1	6	0	.095	.095	2	0	OF-6, 3B-1, 1B-1
1974	22	39	9	0	1	0	0.0	5	5	2	1	0	.231	.282	9	3	OF-8, 1B-5, DH-3
1975 STL N	17	29	6	0	0	1	3.4	1	1	0	7	0	.207	.310	10	3	1B-7
1976 CLE A	39	90	19	4	0	0	0.0	7	13	3	13	2	.211	.256	4	1	1B-32, DH-4, OF-2
5 yrs.	97	217	46	5	1	1	0.5	19	22	7	30	2	.212	.258	26	7	1B-46, OF-24, DH-7, 3B-2

Elston Howard

HOWARD, ELSTON GENE (Ellie)
B. Feb. 23, 1929, St. Louis, Mo.   D. Dec. 14, 1980, New York, N. Y.   BR TR 6'2"   196 lbs.

	G	AB	H	2B	3B	HR	HR %	R	RBI	BB	SO	SB	BA	SA	PH AB	PH H	G by POS
1955 NY A	97	279	81	8	7	10	3.6	33	43	20	36	0	.290	.477	21	4	OF-75, C-9
1956	98	290	76	8	3	5	1.7	35	34	21	30	0	.262	.362	12	5	OF-65, C-26
1957	110	356	90	13	4	8	2.2	33	44	16	43	2	.253	.379	9	3	OF-71, C-32, 1B-2
1958	103	376	118	19	5	11	2.9	45	66	22	60	1	.314	.479	9	5	C-67, OF-24, 1B-5
1959	125	443	121	24	6	18	4.1	59	73	20	57	0	.273	.476	11	3	1B-50, C-43, OF-28
1960	107	323	79	11	3	6	1.9	29	39	28	43	3	.245	.353	14	5	C-91, OF-1
1961	129	446	155	17	5	21	4.7	64	77	28	65	0	.348	.549	14	4	C-111, 1B-9
1962	136	494	138	23	5	21	4.3	63	91	31	76	1	.279	.474	7	1	C-129
1963	135	487	140	21	6	28	5.7	75	85	35	68	0	.287	.528	5	1	C-132
1964	150	550	172	27	3	15	2.7	63	84	48	73	1	.313	.455	6	1	C-146
1965	110	391	91	15	1	9	2.3	38	45	24	65	0	.233	.345	12	2	C-95, 1B-5, OF-1
1966	126	410	105	19	2	6	1.5	38	35	37	65	0	.256	.356	12	2	C-100, 1B-13
1967 2 teams		NY A (66G – .196)					BOS A (42G – .147)										
" total	108	315	56	9	0	4	1.3	22	28	21	60	0	.178	.244	19	2	C-89, 1B-1
1968 BOS A	71	203	49	4	0	5	2.5	22	18	22	45	0	.241	.335	3	0	C-68
14 yrs.	1605	5363	1471	218	50	167	3.1	619	762	373	786	9	.274	.427	154	38	C-1138, OF-265, 1B-85
WORLD SERIES																	
1955 NY A	7	26	5	0	0	1	3.8	3	3	1	8	0	.192	.308	0	0	OF-7
1956	1	5	2	1	0	1	20.0	1	1	0	0	0	.400	1.200	0	0	OF-1
1957	6	11	3	0	0	1	9.1	2	3	1	3	0	.273	.545	3	1	1B-3
1958	6	18	4	0	0	0	0.0	4	2	1	4	0	.222	.222	1	0	OF-6
1960	5	13	6	1	1	1	7.7	4	4	1	4	1	.462	.923	1	1	C-4
1961	5	20	5	3	0	1	5.0	5	1	2	3	0	.250	.550	0	0	C-5
1962	6	21	3	1	0	0	0.0	1	1	1	4	0	.143	.190	0	0	C-6
1963	4	15	5	0	0	0	0.0	0	1	0	3	0	.333	.333	0	0	C-4
1964	7	24	7	1	0	0	0.0	5	2	4	6	0	.292	.333	0	0	C-7
1967 BOS A	7	18	2	0	0	0	0.0	0	1	1	2	0	.111	.111	0	0	C-7
10 yrs.	54	171	42	7	1	5	2.9	25	19	12	37	1	.246	.386	5	2	C-33, OF-14, 1B-3
	3rd	8th	10th	8th				7th		2nd							

	G	AB	H	2B	3B	HR	HR %	R	RBI	BB	SO	SB	BA	SA	Pinch Hit AB	Pinch Hit H	G by POS

Frank Howard

HOWARD, FRANK OLIVER (The Capital Punisher, Hondo) BR TR 6'7" 255 lbs.
B. Aug. 8, 1936, Columbus, Ohio
Manager 1981, 1983.

	G	AB	H	2B	3B	HR	HR %	R	RBI	BB	SO	SB	BA	SA	AB	H	G by POS
1958 LA N	8	29	7	1	0	1	3.4	3	2	1	11	0	.241	.379	0	0	OF-8
1959	9	21	3	0	1	1	4.8	2	6	2	9	0	.143	.381	4	1	OF-6
1960	117	448	120	15	2	23	5.1	54	77	32	108	0	.268	.464	2	0	OF-115, 1B-4
1961	99	267	79	10	2	15	5.6	36	45	21	50	0	.296	.517	19	7	OF-65, 1B-7
1962	141	493	146	25	6	31	6.3	80	119	39	108	1	.296	.560	11	2	OF-131
1963	123	417	114	16	1	28	6.7	58	64	33	116	1	.273	.518	15	3	OF-111
1964	134	433	98	13	2	24	5.5	60	69	51	113	1	.226	.432	10	0	OF-122
1965 WAS A	149	516	149	22	6	21	4.1	53	84	55	112	0	.289	.477	10	1	OF-138
1966	146	493	137	19	4	18	3.7	52	71	53	104	1	.278	.442	9	1	OF-135
1967	149	519	133	20	2	36	6.9	71	89	60	155	0	.256	.511	5	0	OF-141, 1B-4
1968	158	598	164	28	3	**44**	7.4	79	106	54	141	0	.274	**.552**	1	1	OF-107, 1B-55
1969	161	592	175	17	2	48	8.1	111	111	102	96	1	.296	.574	0	0	OF-114, 1B-70
1970	161	566	160	15	1	**44**	7.8	90	126	**132**	125	1	.283	.546	0	0	OF-120, 1B-48
1971	153	549	153	25	2	26	4.7	60	83	77	121	1	.279	.474	5	0	OF-100, 1B-68
1972 2 teams	TEX A (95G – .244)					DET A (14G – .242)											
" total	109	320	78	10	0	10	3.1	29	38	46	63	1	.244	.369	17	3	1B-76, OF-22
1973 DET A	85	227	58	9	1	12	5.3	26	29	24	28	0	.256	.463	7	1	DH-76, 1B-2
16 yrs.	1902	6488	1774	245	35	382	5.9	864	1119	782	1460	8	.273	.499	116	20	OF-1435, 1B-334, DH-76
WORLD SERIES																	
1963 LA N	3	10	3	1	0	1	10.0	2	1	0	2	0	.300	.700	0	0	OF-3

Ivan Howard

HOWARD, IVAN CHESTER BB TR 5'10" 170 lbs.
Brother of Del Howard.
B. Oct. 12, 1882, Kenney, Ill.   D. Mar. 30, 1967, Medford, Ore.

	G	AB	H	2B	3B	HR	HR %	R	RBI	BB	SO	SB	BA	SA	AB	H	G by POS
1914 STL A	81	209	51	6	2	0	0.0	21	20	28	42	14	.244	.292	11	3	3B-33, 1B-28, OF-2, SS-1
1915	113	324	90	10	7	1	0.3	43	43	43	48	29	.278	.361	17	3	1B-48, 3B-23, OF-17, SS-2, 2B-1
1916 CLE A	81	246	46	11	5	0	0.0	20	23	30	34	9	.187	.272	6	0	2B-65, 1B-7
1917	27	39	4	0	0	0	0.0	7	0	3	5	1	.103	.103	6	0	3B-6, OF-4, 2B-4
4 yrs.	302	818	191	27	14	1	0.1	91	86	104	129	53	.233	.304	40	6	1B-83, 2B-70, 3B-62, OF-23, SS-3

Larry Howard

HOWARD, LARRY RAYFORD BR TR 6'3" 200 lbs.
B. June 6, 1945, Columbus, Ohio

	G	AB	H	2B	3B	HR	HR %	R	RBI	BB	SO	SB	BA	SA	AB	H	G by POS
1970 HOU N	31	88	27	6	0	2	2.3	11	16	10	23	0	.307	.443	4	2	C-26, 1B-2, OF-1
1971	24	64	15	3	0	2	3.1	6	14	3	17	0	.234	.375	5	1	C-22
1972	54	157	35	7	0	2	1.3	16	13	17	30	0	.223	.306	2	0	C-53, OF-1
1973 2 teams	HOU N (20G – .167)					ATL N (4G – .125)											
" total	24	56	9	3	0	0	0.0	3	4	7	15	0	.161	.214	2	0	C-22
4 yrs.	133	365	86	19	0	6	1.6	36	47	37	85	0	.236	.337	13	3	C-123, OF-2, 1B-2

Mike Howard

HOWARD, MICHAEL FREDRICK BB TR 6'2" 185 lbs.
B. Apr. 2, 1958, Seattle, Wash.

	G	AB	H	2B	3B	HR	HR %	R	RBI	BB	SO	SB	BA	SA	AB	H	G by POS
1981 NY N	14	24	4	1	0	0	0.0	4	3	4	6	2	.167	.208	0	0	OF-14
1982	33	39	7	0	0	1	2.6	5	3	6	7	2	.179	.256	5	2	OF-22, 2B-3
1983	1	3	1	0	0	0	0.0	0	1	0	1	0	.333	.333	0	0	OF-1
3 yrs.	48	66	12	1	0	1	1.5	9	7	10	14	4	.182	.242	5	2	OF-37, 2B-3

Paul Howard

HOWARD, PAUL JOSEPH (Del) BR TR 5'8" 170 lbs.
B. May 20, 1884, Boston, Mass.   D. Aug. 29, 1968, Miami, Fla.

	G	AB	H	2B	3B	HR	HR %	R	RBI	BB	SO	SB	BA	SA	AB	H	G by POS
1909 BOS A	6	15	3	1	0	0	0.0	2	3	2		0	.200	.267	0	0	OF-6

Wilbur Howard

HOWARD, WILBUR LEON BR TR 6'2" 170 lbs.
B. Jan. 8, 1949, Lowell, N. C.

	G	AB	H	2B	3B	HR	HR %	R	RBI	BB	SO	SB	BA	SA	AB	H	G by POS
1973 MIL A	16	39	8	0	0	0	0.0	3	1	2	10	0	.205	.205	0	0	OF-12, DH-1
1974 HOU N	64	111	24	4	0	2	1.8	19	5	5	18	4	.216	.306	9	2	OF-50
1975	121	392	111	16	8	0	0.0	62	21	21	67	32	.283	.365	23	6	OF-63, 2B-2
1976	94	191	42	7	2	1	0.5	26	18	7	28	7	.220	.293	24	6	OF-62, 2B-4
1977	87	187	48	6	0	1	1.1	22	13	5	30	11	.257	.321	24	7	OF-16, C-3, 2B-1
1978	84	148	34	4	1	1	0.7	17	13	5	22	6	.230	.291	51	12	OF-298, 2B-7, C-3, DH-1
6 yrs.	466	1068	267	37	11	6	0.6	149	71	45	175	60	.250	.322	131	33	OF-298, 2B-7, C-3, DH-1

Jim Howarth

HOWARTH, JAMES EUGENE JR. BL TL 5'11" 175 lbs.
B. Mar. 7, 1947, Biloxi, Miss.

	G	AB	H	2B	3B	HR	HR %	R	RBI	BB	SO	SB	BA	SA	AB	H	G by POS
1971 SF N	7	13	3	1	0	0	0.0	3	2	3	3	0	.231	.308	1	0	OF-6
1972	74	119	28	4	0	1	0.8	16	7	16	18	3	.235	.294	39	13	OF-25, 1B-4
1973	65	90	18	1	1	0	0.0	8	7	7	8	0	.200	.233	26	6	OF-33, 1B-1
1974	6	4	0	0	0	0	0.0	0	0	0	0	0	.000	.000	4	0	OF-1
4 yrs.	152	226	49	6	1	1	0.4	27	16	26	29	3	.217	.265	70	19	OF-65, 1B-5

Art Howe

HOWE, ARTHUR HENRY JR. BR TR 6'2" 190 lbs.
B. Dec. 15, 1946, Pittsburgh, Pa.

	G	AB	H	2B	3B	HR	HR %	R	RBI	BB	SO	SB	BA	SA	AB	H	G by POS
1974 PIT N	29	74	18	4	1	1	1.4	10	5	9	13	0	.243	.365	8	4	3B-20, SS-2
1975	63	146	25	9	0	1	0.7	13	10	15	15	1	.171	.253	18	4	3B-42, SS-3
1976 HOU N	21	29	4	0	0	0	0.0	0	0	6	6	0	.138	.172	7	1	3B-8, 2B-2
1977	125	413	109	23	7	8	1.9	44	58	41	60	0	.264	.412	6	3	2B-96, 3B-19, SS-11
1978	119	420	123	33	3	7	1.7	46	55	34	41	2	.293	.436	3	1	2B-107, 3B-11, 1B-1
1979	118	355	88	15	2	6	1.7	32	33	36	37	3	.248	.352	11	1	2B-68, 3B-59, 1B-3
1980	110	321	91	12	5	10	3.1	34	46	34	29	1	.283	.445	18	2	1B-77, 3B-25, SS-5, 2B-3
1981	103	361	107	22	4	3	0.8	43	36	41	23	1	.296	.404	3	1	3B-98, 1B-2
1982	110	365	87	15	1	5	1.4	29	38	41	45	2	.238	.326	3	0	3B-72, 1B-35
1984 STL N	89	139	30	5	0	2	1.4	17	12	18	18	0	.216	.295	21	6	3B-45, 1B-11, 2B-8, SS-5
10 yrs.	887	2623	682	139	23	43	1.6	268	293	275	287	10	.260	.380	98	23	3B-399, 2B-284, 1B-129, SS-26

	G	AB	H	2B	3B	HR	HR %	R	RBI	BB	SO	SB	BA	SA	Pinch Hit AB	Pinch Hit H	G by POS

Art Howe *continued*

DIVISIONAL PLAYOFF SERIES

	G	AB	H	2B	3B	HR	HR%	R	RBI	BB	SO	SB	BA	SA	AB	H	G by POS
1981 HOU N	5	17	4	0	0	1	5.9	1	1	2	1	0	.235	.412	0	0	3B-5

LEAGUE CHAMPIONSHIP SERIES

1974 PIT N	1	1	0	0	0	0	0.0	0	0	0	0	0	.000	.000	1	0	
1980 HOU N	5	15	3	1	1	0	0.0	0	2	2	2	0	.200	.400	0	0	1B-4
2 yrs.	6	16	3	1	1	0	0.0	0	2	2	2	0	.188	.375	1	0	1B-4

Shorty Howe

HOWE, JOHN
B. New York, N. Y.   Deceased.

1890 NY N	19	64	11	0	0	0	0.0	4	4	3	2	3	.172	.172	0	0	2B-18, 3B-1
1893	1	5	3	0	0	0	0.0	1	2	0	0	1	.600	.600	0	0	3B-1
2 yrs.	20	69	14	0	0	0	0.0	5	6	3	2	4	.203	.203	0	0	2B-18, 3B-2

Dixie Howell

HOWELL, HOMER ELLIOTT
B. Apr. 24, 1919, Louisville, Ky.   BR TR 5'11½" 190 lbs.
                                                 BB 1947

1947 PIT N	76	214	59	11	0	4	1.9	23	25	27	34	1	.276	.383	1	0	C-74
1949 CIN N	64	172	42	6	1	2	1.2	17	18	8	21	0	.244	.326	8	4	C-56
1950	82	224	50	9	1	2	0.9	30	22	32	31	0	.223	.299	1	0	C-81
1951	77	207	52	6	1	2	1.0	22	18	15	34	0	.251	.319	4	2	C-73
1952	17	37	7	1	1	2	5.4	4	4	3	9	0	.189	.432	5	0	C-12
1953 BKN N	1	1	0	0	0	0	0.0	0	0	0	1	0	.000	.000	1	0	
1955	16	42	11	4	0	0	0.0	2	5	1	7	0	.262	.357	4	1	C-13
1956	7	13	3	2	0	0	0.0	0	1	1	3	0	.231	.385	2	0	C-6
8 yrs.	340	910	224	39	4	12	1.3	98	93	87	140	1	.246	.337	26	7	C-315

Harry Howell

HOWELL, HENRY (Handsome Harry)
B. Nov. 14, 1876, New Jersey   D. May 22, 1956, Spokane, Wash.   BR TR 5'9"

1898 BKN N	2	8	2	0	0	0	0.0	1	1	1		0	.250	.250	0	0	P-2
1899 BAL N	28	82	12	2	2	0	0.0	4	3	3		0	.146	.220	0	0	P-28
1900 BKN N	22	42	12	2	0	1	2.4	6	6	6		1	.286	.405	0	0	P-21
1901 BAL A	53	188	41	10	5	2	1.1	26	26	5		6	.218	.356	0	0	P-37, OF-9, SS-6, 1B-2, 2B-1
1902	96	347	93	16	11	2	0.6	42	42	18		7	.268	.395	1	0	2B-26, P-26, OF-18, 3B-15, SS-11, 1B-1
1903 NY A	40	106	23	3	2	1	0.9	14	12	5		1	.217	.311	4	0	P-25, 3B-7, SS-5, 2B-1, 1B-1
1904 STL A	36	113	25	5	2	1	0.9	9	6	4		0	.221	.327	2	1	P-34
1905	41	135	26	6	2	1	0.7	9	10	3		0	.193	.289	0	0	P-38, OF-3
1906	35	104	13	3	1	0	0.0	5	6	6		2	.125	.173	0	0	P-35
1907	44	114	27	5	0	2	1.8	12	7	7		2	.237	.333	0	0	P-42, OF-2
1908	41	120	22	7	0	1	0.8	10	9	4		0	.183	.267	0	0	P-41
1909	18	34	6	1	0	0	0.0	5	3	2		0	.176	.206	0	0	P-10, 3B-7, OF-1
1910	1	2	0	0	0	0	0.0	0	0	0		0	.000	.000	0	0	P-1
13 yrs.	457	1395	302	60	25	11	0.8	143	131	64		19	.216	.319	7	1	P-340, OF-33, 3B-29, 2B-28, SS-22, 1B-4

Red Howell

HOWELL, MURRAY DONALD (Porky)
B. Jan. 29, 1909, Atlanta, Ga.   D. Oct. 1, 1950, Travelers Rest, S. C.   BR TR 6'   215 lbs.

1941 CLE A	11	7	2	0	0	0	0.0	0	2	4	2	0	.286	.286	7	2	

Roy Howell

HOWELL, ROY LEE
B. Dec. 18, 1953, Lompoc, Calif.   BL TR 6'1"   190 lbs.

1974 TEX A	13	44	11	1	0	1	2.3	2	3	2	10	0	.250	.341	1	0	3B-12
1975	125	383	96	15	2	10	2.6	43	51	39	79	2	.251	.379	12	4	3B-115, DH-5
1976	140	491	124	28	2	8	1.6	55	53	30	106	1	.253	.367	8	1	3B-130, DH-8
1977 2 teams	103	TEX A (7G – .000)				TOR A (96G – .316)											
" total	103	381	115	17	1	10	2.6	41	44	44	80	4	.302	.430	19	3	3B-88, DH-10, OF-2, 1B-1
1978 TOR A	140	551	149	28	3	8	1.5	67	61	44	78	0	.270	.376	2	0	3B-131, OF-5, DH-1
1979	138	511	126	28	4	15	2.9	60	72	42	91	0	.247	.405	2	0	3B-133, DH-4
1980	142	528	142	28	9	10	1.9	51	57	50	92	0	.269	.413	0	0	3B-138, DH-2
1981 MIL A	76	244	58	13	1	6	2.5	37	33	23	39	0	.238	.373	8	0	3B-53, DH-13, 1B-3, OF-1
1982	98	300	78	11	2	4	1.3	31	38	21	39	0	.260	.350	12	2	DH-84, 1B-4, OF-2
1983	69	194	54	9	6	4	2.1	23	25	15	29	1	.278	.448	16	4	DH-54, 1B-2
1984	68	164	38	5	1	4	2.4	12	17	8	31	0	.232	.348	16	2	3B-46, DH-8, 1B-4
11 yrs.	1112	3791	991	183	31	80	2.1	422	454	318	674	9	.261	.389	96	14	3B-846, DH-189, 1B-14, OF-10

DIVISIONAL PLAYOFF SERIES

1981 MIL A	4	5	2	0	0	0	0.0	0	0	2	2	0	.400	.400	1	1	DH-3

LEAGUE CHAMPIONSHIP SERIES

1982 MIL A	1	3	0	0	0	0	0.0	0	0	0	1	0	.000	.000	0	0	DH-1

WORLD SERIES

1982 MIL A	4	11	0	0	0	0	0.0	1	0	0	3	0	.000	.000	0	0	DH-4

Bill Howerton

HOWERTON, WILLIAM RAY (Hopalong)
B. Dec. 12, 1921, Lompoc, Calif.   BL TR 5'11"   185 lbs.

1949 STL N	9	13	4	1	0	0	0.0	1	0	2		0	.308	.385	3	1	OF-6
1950	110	313	88	20	8	10	3.2	50	59	47	60	0	.281	.492	17	5	OF-94
1951 2 teams		STL N (24G – .262)				PIT N (80G – .274)											
" total	104	284	77	16	3	12	4.2	39	41	36	56	1	.271	.475	29	4	OF-70, 3B-4
1952 2 teams		PIT N (13G – .320)				NY N (11G – .067)											
" total	24	40	9	2	1	0	0.0	5	5	9	7	0	.225	.325	13	2	OF-8, 3B-1
4 yrs.	247	650	178	39	12	22	3.4	95	106	92	125	1	.274	.472	62	12	OF-178, 3B-5

	G	AB	H	2B	3B	HR	HR %	R	RBI	BB	SO	SB	BA	SA	Pinch Hit AB	H	G by POS

Dan Howley

HOWLEY, DANIEL PHILIP (Dapper Dan)
B. Oct. 16, 1885, E. Weymouth, Mass. D. Mar. 10, 1944, E. Weymouth, Mass.
Manager 1927-32.

BR TR 6' 167 lbs.

	G	AB	H	2B	3B	HR	HR %	R	RBI	BB	SO	SB	BA	SA	AB	H	G by POS
1913 PHI N	26	32	4	2	0	0	0.0	5	2	4	4	3	.125	.188	0	0	C-22

Dick Howser

HOWSER, RICHARD DALTON
B. May 14, 1937, Miami, Fla.
Manager 1978, 1980-84.

BR TR 5'8" 155 lbs.

	G	AB	H	2B	3B	HR	HR %	R	RBI	BB	SO	SB	BA	SA	AB	H	G by POS
1961 KC A	158	611	171	29	6	3	0.5	108	45	92	38	37	.280	.362	1	0	SS-157
1962	83	286	68	8	3	6	2.1	53	34	38	8	19	.238	.350	0	0	SS-72
1963 2 teams		KC	A	(15G –	.195)		CLE	A	(49G –	.247)							SS-54
" total	64	203	48	5	0	1	0.5	29	11	29	21	9	.236	.276	7	1	SS-162
1964 CLE A	162	637	163	23	4	3	0.5	101	52	76	39	20	.256	.319	0	0	SS-73, 2B-17
1965	107	307	72	8	2	1	0.3	47	6	57	25	17	.235	.283	12	3	SS-26, 2B-26
1966	67	140	32	9	1	2	1.4	18	4	15	23	2	.229	.350	8	0	SS-26, 3B-12, SS-3
1967 NY A	63	149	40	6	0	0	0.0	18	10	25	15	1	.268	.309	17	4	2B-22, 3B-12, SS-3
1968	85	150	23	2	1	0	0.0	24	3	35	17	0	.153	.180	40	8	2B-29, 3B-2, SS-1
8 yrs.	789	2483	617	90	17	16	0.6	398	165	367	186	105	.248	.318	85	16	SS-548, 2B-94, 3B-14

Dummy Hoy

HOY, WILLIAM ELLSWORTH
B. May 23, 1862, Houckstown, Ohio D. Dec. 15, 1961, Cincinnati, Ohio

BL TR 5'4" 148 lbs.

	G	AB	H	2B	3B	HR	HR %	R	RBI	BB	SO	SB	BA	SA	AB	H	G by POS
1888 WAS N	136	503	138	10	8	2	0.4	77	29	69	48	82	.274	.338	0	0	OF-136
1889	127	507	139	11	6	0	0.0	98	39	75	30	35	.274	.320	0	0	OF-127
1890 BUF P	122	493	147	17	8	1	0.2	107	53	94	36	39	.298	.371	0	0	OF-122, 2B-1
1891 STL AA	141	567	165	14	5	5	0.9	136	66	119	25	59	.291	.360	0	0	OF-141
1892 WAS N	152	593	166	19	8	3	0.5	108	75	86	23	60	.280	.354	0	0	OF-152
1893	130	564	138	12	6	0	0.0	106	45	66	9	48	.245	.287	0	0	OF-128
1894 CIN N	128	506	158	22	13	5	1.0	114	70	87	18	30	.312	.437	0	0	OF-107
1895	107	429	119	21	12	3	0.7	93	55	52	8	50	.277	.403	0	0	OF-120
1896	121	443	132	23	7	4	0.9	120	57	65	13	50	.298	.409	1	1	OF-128
1897	128	497	145	24	6	2	0.4	87	42	54		37	.292	.376	0	0	OF-128
1898 LOU N	148	582	177	15	16	6	1.0	104	66	49		37	.304	.416	0	0	OF-154
1899	154	633	194	17	13	5	0.8	116	49	61		32	.306	.398	0	0	OF-132
1901 CHI A	132	527	155	28	11	2	0.4	112	60	86		27	.294	.400	0	0	OF-72
1902 CIN N	72	279	81	16	2	2	0.7	48	20	41		11	.290	.384	1	1	OF-72
14 yrs.	1798	7123	2054	249	121	40	0.6	1426	726	1004	210	597	.288	.374	1	1	OF-1797, 2B-1

Kent Hrbek

HRBEK, KENT ALLEN
B. May 21, 1960, Minneapolis, Minn.

BL TR 6'4" 200 lbs.

	G	AB	H	2B	3B	HR	HR %	R	RBI	BB	SO	SB	BA	SA	AB	H	G by POS
1981 MIN A	24	67	16	5	0	1	1.5	5	7	5	9	0	.239	.358	5	2	1B-13, DH-8
1982	140	532	160	21	4	23	4.3	82	92	54	80	3	.301	.485	1	0	1B-138, DH-2
1983	141	515	153	41	5	16	3.1	75	84	57	71	4	.297	.489	3	0	1B-137, DH-2
1984	149	559	174	31	3	27	4.8	80	107	65	87	1	.311	.522	1	1	1B-148, DH-1
4 yrs.	454	1673	503	98	12	67	4.0	242	290	181	247	8	.301	.494	10	3	1B-436, DH-13

Walt Hriniak

HRINIAK, WALTER JOHN
B. May 22, 1943, Natick, Mass.

BL TR 5'11" 180 lbs.

	G	AB	H	2B	3B	HR	HR %	R	RBI	BB	SO	SB	BA	SA	AB	H	G by POS
1968 ATL N	9	26	9	0	0	0	0.0	3	0	3	0	0	.346	.346	0	0	C-9
1969 2 teams		ATL	N	(7G –	.143)		SD	N	(31G –	.227)							C-25
" total	38	73	16	0	0	0	0.0	4	4	10	12	0	.219	.219	15	2	C-34
2 yrs.	47	99	25	0	0	0	0.0	4	4	10	15	0	.253	.253	15	2	C-34

Al Hubbard

HUBBARD, ALLEN
Played as Al West Part of 1883.
B. Dec. 9, 1860, Westfield, Mass. D. Dec. 14, 1930, Newton, Mass.

	G	AB	H	2B	3B	HR	HR %	R	RBI	BB	SO	SB	BA	SA	AB	H	G by POS
1883 PHI AA	2	6	2	0	0	0	0.0	2		1			.333	.333	0	0	SS-1, C-1

Glenn Hubbard

HUBBARD, GLENN DEE
B. Sept. 25, 1957, Hahn A. F. Base, Germany

BR TR 5'9" 150 lbs.

	G	AB	H	2B	3B	HR	HR %	R	RBI	BB	SO	SB	BA	SA	AB	H	G by POS
1978 ATL N	44	163	42	4	0	2	1.2	15	13	10	20	2	.258	.319	0	0	2B-44
1979	97	325	75	12	0	3	0.9	34	29	27	43	0	.231	.295	6	1	2B-91
1980	117	431	107	21	3	9	2.1	55	43	49	69	7	.248	.374	0	0	2B-117
1981	99	361	85	13	5	6	1.7	39	33	33	59	4	.235	.349	0	0	2B-98
1982	145	532	132	25	1	9	1.7	75	59	59	62	4	.248	.350	0	0	2B-144
1983	148	517	136	24	6	12	2.3	65	70	55	71	3	.263	.402	1	0	2B-148
1984	120	397	93	27	2	9	2.3	53	43	55	61	4	.234	.380	4	2	2B-117
7 yrs.	770	2726	670	126	17	50	1.8	336	290	288	385	24	.246	.360	11	3	2B-759

LEAGUE CHAMPIONSHIP SERIES

	G	AB	H	2B	3B	HR	HR %	R	RBI	BB	SO	SB	BA	SA	AB	H	G by POS
1982 ATL N	3	9	2	0	0	0	0.0	1	1	0	3	0	.222	.222	0	0	2B-3

Ken Hubbs

HUBBS, KENNETH DOUGLASS
B. Dec. 23, 1941, Riverside, Calif. D. Feb. 15, 1964, Utah Lake, Utah

BR TR 6'2" 175 lbs.

	G	AB	H	2B	3B	HR	HR %	R	RBI	BB	SO	SB	BA	SA	AB	H	G by POS
1961 CHI N	10	28	5	1	1	1	3.6	4	2	0	8	0	.179	.393	2	0	2B-8
1962	160	661	172	24	9	5	0.8	90	49	35	129	3	.260	.346	1	0	2B-159
1963	154	566	133	19	3	8	1.4	54	47	39	93	8	.235	.322	2	1	2B-152
3 yrs.	324	1255	310	44	13	14	1.1	148	98	74	230	11	.247	.336	5	1	2B-319

Clarence Huber

HUBER, CLARENCE BILL (Gilly)
B. Oct. 28, 1897, Tyler, Tex. D. Feb. 22, 1965, Laredo, Tex.

BR TR 5'10" 165 lbs.

	G	AB	H	2B	3B	HR	HR %	R	RBI	BB	SO	SB	BA	SA	AB	H	G by POS
1920 DET A	11	42	9	2	1	0	0.0	4	5	0	5	0	.214	.310	0	0	3B-11
1921	1	0	0	0	0	0	–	0	0	0	0	0	–	–	0	0	3B-1
1925 PHI N	124	436	124	28	5	5	1.1	46	54	17	33	3	.284	.406	4	2	3B-120
1926	118	376	92	17	7	1	0.3	45	34	42	29	9	.245	.335	2	2	3B-115
4 yrs.	254	854	225	47	13	6	0.7	95	93	59	67	12	.263	.370	6	4	3B-247

	G	AB	H	2B	3B	HR	HR%	R	RBI	BB	SO	SB	BA	SA	Pinch Hit AB	Pinch Hit H	G by POS

Otto Huber

HUBER, OTTO
B. Mar. 12, 1914, Garfield, N. J.

BR TR 5'10" 165 lbs.

	G	AB	H	2B	3B	HR	HR%	R	RBI	BB	SO	SB	BA	SA	PH AB	PH H	G by POS
1939 BOS N	11	22	6	1	0	0	0.0	2	3	0	1	0	.273	.318	2	1	3B-4, 2B-4

Dave Hudgens

HUDGENS, DAVID MARK
B. Dec. 5, 1956, Oroville, Calif.

BL TL 6'2" 200 lbs.

	G	AB	H	2B	3B	HR	HR%	R	RBI	BB	SO	SB	BA	SA	PH AB	PH H	G by POS
1983 OAK A	6	7	1	0	0	0	0.0	0	0	3	0	.143	.143	3	0	1B-3, DH-1

Jimmy Hudgens

HUDGENS, JAMES PRICE
B. Aug. 24, 1902, Newburg, Mo.   D. Aug. 26, 1955, St. Louis, Mo.

BL TL 6' 180 lbs.

	G	AB	H	2B	3B	HR	HR%	R	RBI	BB	SO	SB	BA	SA	PH AB	PH H	G by POS
1923 STL N	6	12	3	1	0	0	0.0	2		3	3	0	.250	.333	2	0	1B-3, 2B-1
1925 CIN N	3	7	3	1	1	0	0.0	0		1	1	0	.429	.857	0	0	1B-3
1926	17	20	5	1	0	0	0.0	2	1	1		0	.250	.300	10	3	1B-6
3 yrs.	26	39	11	3	1	0	0.0	4	1	5	4	0	.282	.410	12	3	1B-12, 2B-1

Rex Hudler

HUDLER, REX ALLEN
B. Sept. 2, 1960, Tempe, Ariz.

BR TR 6'1" 180 lbs.

	G	AB	H	2B	3B	HR	HR%	R	RBI	BB	SO	SB	BA	SA	PH AB	PH H	G by POS
1984 NY A	9	7	1	1	0	0	0.0	2	0	1	5	0	.143	.286	0	0	2B-9

Johnny Hudson

HUDSON, JOHN WILSON
B. June 30, 1912, Bryan, Tex.   D. Nov. 7, 1970, Bryan, Tex.

BR TR 5'10" 160 lbs.

	G	AB	H	2B	3B	HR	HR%	R	RBI	BB	SO	SB	BA	SA	PH AB	PH H	G by POS
1936 BKN N	6	12	2	0	0	0	0.0	1	0	2	1	0	.167	.167	0	0	SS-4, 2B-1
1937	13	27	5	4	0	0	0.0	3	2	3	9	0	.185	.333	1	0	SS-11, 2B-1
1938	135	498	130	21	5	2	0.4	59	37	39	76	7	.261	.335	1	0	2B-132, SS-3
1939	109	343	87	17	3	2	0.6	46	32	30	36	5	.254	.338	12	3	SS-50, 2B-45, 3B-1
1940	85	179	39	4	3	0	0.0	13	19	9	26	2	.218	.274	4	2	SS-38, 2B-27, 3B-1
1941 CHI N	50	99	20	4	0	0	0.0	8	6	3	15	3	.202	.242	11	0	SS-17, 2B-13, 3B-10
1945 NY N	28	11	0	0	0	0	0.0	8	0	1	1	0	.000	.000	4	0	3B-5, 2B-2
7 yrs.	426	1169	283	50	11	4	0.3	138	96	87	164	17	.242	.314	33	5	2B-221, SS-123, 3B-17

Nat Hudson

HUDSON, NATHANIEL P.
B. Jan. 12, 1859, Chicago, Ill.   D. Mar. 14, 1928, Chicago, Ill.

TR

	G	AB	H	2B	3B	HR	HR%	R	RBI	BB	SO	SB	BA	SA	PH AB	PH H	G by POS
1886 STL AA	43	150	35	4	1	0	0.0	16		11			.233	.273	0	0	P-29, OF-12, 1B-3
1887	13	48	12	2	1	0	0.0	7		4		0	.250	.333	0	0	P-9, OF-6
1888	56	196	50	7	0	2	1.0	27	28	18		9	.255	.321	0	0	P-39, OF-16, 1B-3, SS-1
1889	13	52	13	1	1	1	1.9	6	10	2	11	1	.250	.365	0	0	P-9, OF-6, 1B-3
4 yrs.	125	446	110	14	3	3	0.7	56	37	35	11	10	.247	.312	0	0	P-86, OF-40, 1B-9, SS-1

Frank Huelsman

HUELSMAN, FRANK ELMER
B. June 5, 1874, St. Louis, Mo.   D. June 9, 1959, Affton, Mo.

BR TR 6'2" 210 lbs.

	G	AB	H	2B	3B	HR	HR%	R	RBI	BB	SO	SB	BA	SA	PH AB	PH H	G by POS
1897 STL N	2	7	2	1	0	0	0.0	0	0	0		0	.286	.429	0	0	OF-2
1904 4 teams			CHI A (4G – .143)			DET A (4G – .333)			STL A (20G – .221)				WAS A (84G – .248)				
" total	112	396	97	23	5	2	0.5	28	35	31		7	.245	.343	4	0	OF-107
1905 WAS A	126	421	114	28	8	3	0.7	48	62	31		11	.271	.397	4	1	OF-123
3 yrs.	240	824	213	52	13	5	0.6	76	97	62		18	.258	.371	8	1	OF-232

Ben Huffman

HUFFMAN, BENJAMIN FRANKLIN
B. July 18, 1914, Rileyville, Va.

BB TR 5'11½" 175 lbs.

	G	AB	H	2B	3B	HR	HR%	R	RBI	BB	SO	SB	BA	SA	PH AB	PH H	G by POS
1937 STL A	76	176	48	9	0	1	0.6	18	24	10	7	1	.273	.341	32	7	C-42

Ed Hug

HUG, EDWARD AMBROSE
B. July 14, 1880, Fayetteville, Ohio   D. May 11, 1953, Cincinnati, Ohio

BR TR

	G	AB	H	2B	3B	HR	HR%	R	RBI	BB	SO	SB	BA	SA	PH AB	PH H	G by POS
1903 BKN N	1	0	0	0	0	0	–	0	0	1		0	–	–	0	0	C-1

Miller Huggins

HUGGINS, MILLER JAMES (Hug, The Mighty Mite)
B. Mar. 27, 1879, Cincinnati, Ohio   D. Sept. 25, 1929, New York, N. Y.
Manager 1913-29.
Hall of Fame 1964.

BB TR 5'6½" 140 lbs.

	G	AB	H	2B	3B	HR	HR%	R	RBI	BB	SO	SB	BA	SA	PH AB	PH H	G by POS
1904 CIN N	140	491	129	12	7	2	0.4	96	30	88		13	.263	.328	0	0	2B-140
1905	149	564	154	11	8	1	0.2	117	38	103		27	.273	.326	0	0	2B-149
1906	146	545	159	11	7	0	0.0	81	26	71		41	.292	.338	0	0	2B-146
1907	156	561	139	12	4	1	0.2	64	31	83		28	.248	.289	0	0	2B-156
1908	135	498	119	14	5	0	0.0	65	23	58		30	.239	.287	4	1	2B-135
1909	57	159	34	3	1	0	0.0	18	6	28		11	.214	.245	10	1	2B-31, 3B-15
1910 STL N	151	547	145	15	6	1	0.2	101	36	116	46	34	.265	.320	0	0	2B-151
1911	138	509	133	19	2	1	0.2	106	24	96	52	37	.261	.312	1	1	2B-136
1912	120	431	131	15	4	0	0.0	82	29	87	31	35	.304	.357	5	0	2B-114
1913	120	381	109	12	0	0	0.0	73	27	91	49	23	.286	.318	5	1	2B-112
1914	148	509	134	17	4	1	0.2	85	24	105	63	32	.263	.318	1	0	2B-147
1915	107	353	85	5	2	2	0.6	57	24	74	68	13	.241	.283	0	0	2B-107
1916	18	9	3	0	0	0	0.0	2		2	3		.333	.333	4	2	2B-7
13 yrs.	1585	5557	1474	146	50	9	0.2	947	318	1002	312	324	.265	.314	30	6	2B-1531, 3B-15

Bill Hughes

HUGHES, WILLIAM W.
B. Apr. 10, 1862, Leavenworth, Kans.   D. Aug. 25, 1943, Santa Ana, Calif.

	G	AB	H	2B	3B	HR	HR%	R	RBI	BB	SO	SB	BA	SA	PH AB	PH H	G by POS
1884 WAS U	14	49	6	0	0	0	0.0	5		2			.122	.122	0	0	1B-9, OF-6
1885 PHI AA	4	16	3	1	1	0	0.0	3		1			.188	.375	0	0	OF-2, P-2
2 yrs.	18	65	9	1	1	0	0.0	8		3			.138	.185	0	0	1B-9, OF-8, P-2

Ed Hughes

HUGHES, EDWARD
B. Unknown.

	G	AB	H	2B	3B	HR	HR%	R	RBI	BB	SO	SB	BA	SA	PH AB	PH H	G by POS
1902 CHI N	1	3	0	0	0	0	0.0	0	0	0		0	.000	.000	0	0	OF-1

	G	AB	H	2B	3B	HR	HR %	R	RBI	BB	SO	SB	BA	SA	Pinch Hit AB	H	G by POS

Roy Hughes

HUGHES, ROY JOHN (Sage, Jeep)
B. Jan. 11, 1911, Cincinnati, Ohio
BR TR 5'10½" 167 lbs.

	G	AB	H	2B	3B	HR	HR %	R	RBI	BB	SO	SB	BA	SA	AB	H	G by POS
1935 CLE A	82	266	78	15	3	0	0.0	40	14	18	17	13	.293	.372	6	0	2B-40, SS-29, 3B-1
1936	152	638	188	35	9	0	0.0	112	63	57	40	20	.295	.378	0	0	2B-152
1937	104	346	96	12	6	1	0.3	57	40	40	22	11	.277	.355	11	4	3B-58, 2B-32
1938 STL A	58	96	27	3	0	2	2.1	16	13	12	11	3	.281	.375	30	6	2B-21, 3B-5, SS-2
1939 2 teams	STL A (17G – .087)				PHI N (65G – .228)												
" total	82	260	56	5	1	1	0.4	28	17	25	22	4	.215	.254	5	1	2B-71, SS-1
1944 CHI N	126	478	137	16	6	1	0.2	86	28	35	30	16	.287	.351	7	4	3B-66, SS-52
1945	69	222	58	8	1	0	0.0	34	8	16	18	6	.261	.306	5	1	SS-36, 2B-21, 3B-9, 1B-2
1946 PHI N	89	276	65	11	1	0	0.0	23	22	19	15	7	.236	.283	12	3	SS-34, 3B-31, 2B-7, 1B-1
8 yrs.	762	2582	705	105	27	5	0.2	396	205	222	175	80	.273	.340	76	19	2B-344, 3B-170, SS-154, 1B-3
WORLD SERIES																	
1945 CHI N	6	17	5	1	0	0	0.0	1	3	4	5	0	.294	.353	0	0	SS-6

Terry Hughes

HUGHES, TERRY WAYNE
B. May 13, 1949, Spartanburg, S. C.
BR TR 6'1" 185 lbs.

	G	AB	H	2B	3B	HR	HR %	R	RBI	BB	SO	SB	BA	SA	AB	H	G by POS
1970 CHI N	2	3	1	0	0	0	0.0	0	0	0	0	0	.333	.333	1	1	OF-1, 3B-1
1973 STL N	11	14	3	1	0	0	0.0	1	1	1	4	0	.214	.286	4	1	3B-5, 1B-1
1974 BOS A	41	69	14	2	0	1	1.4	5	6	6	18	0	.203	.275	1	0	3B-36, DH-1
3 yrs.	54	86	18	3	0	1	1.2	6	7	7	22	0	.209	.279	6	2	3B-42, DH-1, OF-1, 1B-1

Tom Hughes

HUGHES, THOMAS FRANKLIN
B. Aug. 6, 1907, Emmet, Ark.
BL TR 6'1" 190 lbs.

	G	AB	H	2B	3B	HR	HR %	R	RBI	BB	SO	SB	BA	SA	AB	H	G by POS
1930 DET A	17	59	22	2	3	0	0.0	8	5	4	8	0	.373	.508	0	0	OF-16

Emil Huhn

HUHN, EMIL HUGO (Hap)
B. Mar. 10, 1892, North Vernon, Ind.   D. Sept. 5, 1925, Camden, S. C.
BR TR 6' 180 lbs.

	G	AB	H	2B	3B	HR	HR %	R	RBI	BB	SO	SB	BA	SA	AB	H	G by POS
1915 NWK F	124	415	94	18	1	0	0.2	34	41	28		13	.227	.282	8	1	1B-101, C-16
1916 CIN N	37	94	24	3	2	0	0.0	4	3	2	11	0	.255	.330	3	1	C-18, 1B-14, OF-1
1917	23	51	10	1	2	0	0.0	2	3	2	5	1	.196	.294	7	1	C-15
3 yrs.	184	560	128	22	5	0	0.2	40	47	32	16	14	.229	.291	18	3	1B-115, C-49, OF-1

Billy Hulen

HULEN, WILLIAM FRANKLIN
B. Mar. 12, 1870, Dixon, Calif.   D. Oct. 2, 1947, Santa Rosa, Calif.
BL TL 5'8" 148 lbs.

	G	AB	H	2B	3B	HR	HR %	R	RBI	BB	SO	SB	BA	SA	AB	H	G by POS
1896 PHI N	88	339	90	18	7	0	0.0	87	38	55	20	23	.265	.360	1	0	SS-73, OF-12, 2B-2
1899 WAS N	19	68	10	1	0	0	0.0	10	3	10		5	.147	.162	0	0	SS-19
2 yrs.	107	407	100	19	7	0	0.0	97	41	65	20	28	.246	.327	1	1	SS-92, OF-12, 2B-2

Tim Hulett

HULETT, TIMOTHY CRAIG
B. Jan. 12, 1960, Springfield, Ill.
BR TR 6'1" 180 lbs.

	G	AB	H	2B	3B	HR	HR %	R	RBI	BB	SO	SB	BA	SA	AB	H	G by POS
1983 CHI A	6	5	1	0	0	0	0.0	1	0	0	0	1	.200	.200	0	0	2B-6
1984	8	7	0	0	0	0	0.0	0	0	1	4	1	.000	.000	1	0	3B-4, 2B-3
2 yrs.	14	12	1	0	0	0	0.0	1	0	1	4	2	.083	.083	1	0	2B-9, 3B-4

Rudy Hulswitt

HULSWITT, RUDOLPH EDWARD
B. Feb. 23, 1877, Newport, Ky.   D. Jan. 16, 1950, Louisville, Ky.
BR TR 5'11" 165 lbs.

	G	AB	H	2B	3B	HR	HR %	R	RBI	BB	SO	SB	BA	SA	AB	H	G by POS
1899 LOU N	1	0	0	0	0	0	–	0	0	0		0	–	–	0	0	SS-1
1902 PHI N	128	497	135	11	7	0	0.0	59	38	30		12	.272	.322	0	0	SS-125, 3B-3
1903	138	519	128	22	9	1	0.2	56	58	28		10	.247	.329	0	0	SS-138
1904	113	406	99	11	4	1	0.2	36	36	16		8	.244	.298	0	0	SS-113
1908 CIN N	119	386	88	5	7	1	0.3	27	28	30		7	.228	.285	1	0	SS-118, 2B-1
1909 STL N	82	289	81	8	3	0	0.0	21	29	19		7	.280	.329	4	1	SS-65, 2B-12
1910	63	133	33	7	2	0	0.0	9	14	13	10	5	.248	.331	31	6	SS-30, 2B-2
7 yrs.	644	2230	564	64	32	3	0.1	208	203	136	10	49	.253	.314	35	7	SS-590, 2B-15, 3B-3

John Hummel

HUMMEL, JOHN EDWIN (Silent John)
B. Apr. 4, 1883, Bloomsburg, Pa.   D. May 18, 1959, Springfield, Mass.
BR TR 5'11" 160 lbs.

	G	AB	H	2B	3B	HR	HR %	R	RBI	BB	SO	SB	BA	SA	AB	H	G by POS
1905 BKN N	30	109	29	3	4	0	0.0	19	7	9		6	.266	.367	0	0	2B-30
1906	97	286	57	6	4	1	0.3	20	21	36		10	.199	.259	8	2	2B-50, OF-21, 1B-15
1907	107	342	80	12	3	3	0.9	41	31	26		8	.234	.313	10	2	2B-44, OF-33, 1B-12, SS-8
1908	154	594	143	11	12	4	0.7	51	41	34		20	.241	.320	0	0	OF-95, 2B-39, SS-9, 1B-8
1909	146	542	152	15	9	4	0.7	54	52	22		16	.280	.363	2	0	1B-54, 2B-38, SS-36, OF-17
1910	153	578	141	21	13	5	0.9	67	74	57	81	21	.244	.351	0	0	2B-153
1911	137	477	129	21	11	5	1.0	54	58	67	66	16	.270	.392	3	0	2B-127, 1B-4, SS-2
1912	122	411	116	21	7	5	1.2	55	54	49	55	7	.282	.404	9	2	2B-58, OF-44, 1B-11
1913	67	198	48	7	7	2	1.0	20	24	13	23	4	.242	.379	15	3	OF-28, SS-17, 1B-6, 2B-3
1914	73	208	55	8	9	0	0.0	25	20	16	25	5	.264	.389	17	2	1B-36, OF-19, SS-1, 2B-1
1915	53	100	23	2	3	0	0.0	6	8	6	11	1	.230	.310	12	2	OF-20, 1B-11, SS-1
1918 NY A	22	61	18	1	2	0	0.0	9	4	4	11	3	.295	.377	4	1	OF-15, 1B-3, 2B-1
12 yrs.	1161	3906	991	128	84	29	0.7	421	394	346	269	117	.254	.352	85	12	2B-548, OF-292, 1B-160, SS-74

Al Humphrey

HUMPHREY, ALBERT
B. Feb. 28, 1886, Ashtabula, Ohio   D. May 13, 1961, Ashtabula, Ohio
BL TR 5'11" 180 lbs.

	G	AB	H	2B	3B	HR	HR %	R	RBI	BB	SO	SB	BA	SA	AB	H	G by POS
1911 BKN N	8	27	5	0	0	0	0.0	4	0	3	7	0	.185	.185	0	0	OF-8

Terry Humphrey

HUMPHREY, TERRYAL GENE
B. Aug. 4, 1949, Chickasha, Okla.
BR TR 6'3" 185 lbs.

	G	AB	H	2B	3B	HR	HR %	R	RBI	BB	SO	SB	BA	SA	AB	H	G by POS
1971 MON N	9	26	5	1	0	0	0.0	1	1	0	4	0	.192	.231	1	0	C-9
1972	69	215	40	8	0	1	0.5	13	9	16	38	4	.186	.237	4	1	C-65
1973	43	90	15	2	0	1	1.1	5	9	5	16	0	.167	.222	5	0	C-35
1974	20	52	10	3	0	0	0.0	3	3	4	9	0	.192	.250	2	2	C-17
1975 DET A	18	41	10	0	0	0	0.0	0	1	2	6	0	.244	.244	1	0	C-18

	G	AB	H	2B	3B	HR	HR %	R	RBI	BB	SO	SB	BA	SA	Pinch Hit AB	Pinch Hit H	G by POS

Terry Humphrey continued

	G	AB	H	2B	3B	HR	HR%	R	RBI	BB	SO	SB	BA	SA	AB	H	G by POS
1976 CAL A	71	196	48	10	0	1	0.5	17	19	13	30	0	.245	.311	1	0	C-71
1977	123	304	69	11	0	2	0.7	17	34	21	58	1	.227	.283	0	0	C-123
1978	53	114	25	4	1	1	0.9	11	9	6	12	0	.219	.298	0	0	C-52, 3B-1, 2B-1
1979	9	17	1	0	0	0	0.0	2	0	1	2	0	.059	.059	0	0	C-9
9 yrs.	415	1055	223	39	1	6	0.6	69	85	68	175	5	.211	.267	13	3	C-399, 3B-1, 2B-1

John Humphries

HUMPHRIES, JOHN HENRY
B. Nov. 15, 1861, North Gower, Ont., Canada   D. Nov. 29, 1933, Salinas, Calif.   BL TL 6'   185 lbs.

	G	AB	H	2B	3B	HR	HR%	R	RBI	BB	SO	SB	BA	SA	AB	H	G by POS
1883 NY N	29	107	12	1	1	0	0.0	5		1	22		.112	.121	0	0	C-20, OF-16
1884 2 teams	WAS	AA	(49G –	.176)		NY	N	(20G –	.094)								
" total	69	257	40	2	0	0	0.0	29		18	19		.156	.163	0	0	C-55, OF-12, 1B-4
2 yrs.	98	364	52	3	0	0	0.0	34		19	41		.143	.151	0	0	C-75, OF-24, 1B-4

Randy Hundley

HUNDLEY, CECIL RANDOLPH
B. June 1, 1942, Martinsville, Va.   BR TR 5'11"   170 lbs.

	G	AB	H	2B	3B	HR	HR%	R	RBI	BB	SO	SB	BA	SA	AB	H	G by POS
1964 SF N	2	1	0	0	0	0	0.0	0	0	0	1	0	.000	.000	0	0	C-2
1965	6	15	1	0	0	0	0.0	0	0	0	4	0	.067	.067	0	0	C-6
1966 CHI N	149	526	124	22	3	19	3.6	50	63	35	113	1	.236	.397	0	0	C-149
1967	152	539	144	25	3	14	2.6	68	60	44	75	2	.267	.403	2	0	C-152
1968	160	553	125	18	4	7	1.3	41	65	39	69	1	.226	.311	0	0	C-160
1969	151	522	133	15	1	18	3.4	67	64	61	90	2	.255	.391	1	0	C-151
1970	73	250	61	5	0	7	2.8	13	36	16	52	0	.244	.348	0	0	C-73
1971	9	21	7	1	0	0	0.0	1	2	0	2	0	.333	.381	1	0	C-8
1972	114	357	78	12	0	5	1.4	23	30	22	62	1	.218	.294	2	1	C-113
1973	124	368	83	11	1	10	2.7	35	43	30	51	5	.226	.342	3	1	C-122
1974 MIN A	32	88	17	2	0	0	0.0	2	3	4	12	0	.193	.216	3	0	C-28
1975 SD N	74	180	37	5	1	2	1.1	7	14	19	29	0	.206	.278	18	4	C-51
1976 CHI N	13	18	3	2	0	0	0.0	3	1	1	4	0	.167	.278	4	0	C-9
1977	2	4	0	0	0	0	0.0	0	0	0	1	0	.000	.000	0	0	C-2
14 yrs.	1061	3442	813	118	13	82	2.4	311	381	271	565	12	.236	.350	34	6	C-1026

Bernie Hungling

HUNGLING, BERNARD HERMAN (Bud)
B. Mar. 5, 1896, Dayton, Ohio   D. Mar. 30, 1968, Dayton, Ohio   BR TR 6'2"   180 lbs.

	G	AB	H	2B	3B	HR	HR%	R	RBI	BB	SO	SB	BA	SA	AB	H	G by POS
1922 BKN N	39	102	23	1	2	1	1.0	9	13	6	20	2	.225	.304	3	0	C-36
1923	2	4	0	0	0	0	0.0	0	0	0	2	0	.000	.000	0	0	C-1
1930 STL A	10	31	10	2	0	0	0.0	4	2	5	3	0	.323	.387	0	0	C-10
3 yrs.	51	137	33	3	2	1	0.7	13	15	11	25	2	.241	.314	3	0	C-47

Bill Hunnefield

HUNNEFIELD, WILLIAM FENTON (Wild Bill)
B. Jan. 5, 1899, Dedham, Mass.   D. Aug. 28, 1976, Nantauket, Mass.   BB TR 5'10"   165 lbs.

	G	AB	H	2B	3B	HR	HR%	R	RBI	BB	SO	SB	BA	SA	AB	H	G by POS
1926 CHI A	131	470	129	26	4	3	0.6	81	48	37	28	24	.274	.366	2	0	SS-98, 3B-17, 2B-15
1927	112	365	104	25	1	2	0.5	45	36	25	24	13	.285	.375	13	3	SS-78, 2B-17, 3B-1
1928	94	333	98	8	3	2	0.6	42	24	26	24	16	.294	.354	7	3	2B-83, SS-3, 3B-1
1929	47	127	23	5	0	0	0.0	13	9	7	3	5	.181	.220	10	1	2B-26, SS-4, SS-2
1930	31	81	22	2	0	1	1.2	11	5	4	10	1	.272	.333	6	1	SS-22, 1B-1
1931 3 teams	CLE	A	(21G –	.239)		BOS	N	(11G –	.286)		NY	N	(64G –	.270)			
" total	96	288	76	9	1	1	0.3	38	22	18	22	6	.264	.313	1	0	2B-61, SS-26, 3B-5
6 yrs.	511	1664	452	75	9	9	0.5	230	144	117	111	65	.272	.344	39	8	SS-229, 2B-202, 3B-28, 1B-1

Joel Hunt

HUNT, OLIVER JOEL (Jodie)
B. Oct. 11, 1905, Texico, N. M.   D. July 24, 1978, Teague, Tex.   BR TR 5'10"   165 lbs.

	G	AB	H	2B	3B	HR	HR%	R	RBI	BB	SO	SB	BA	SA	AB	H	G by POS
1931 STL N	4	1	0	0	0	0	0.0	2	0	0	1	0	.000	.000	1	0	OF-1
1932	12	21	4	1	0	0	0.0	0	3	4	3	0	.190	.238	5	2	OF-5
2 yrs.	16	22	4	1	0	0	0.0	2	3	4	4	0	.182	.227	6	2	OF-6

Ken Hunt

HUNT, KENNETH LAWRENCE
B. July 13, 1934, Grand Forks, N. D.   BR TR 6'1"   205 lbs.

	G	AB	H	2B	3B	HR	HR%	R	RBI	BB	SO	SB	BA	SA	AB	H	G by POS
1959 NY A	6	12	4	1	0	0	0.0	2	1	0	3	0	.333	.417	1	1	OF-5
1960	25	22	6	2	0	0	0.0	4	1	4	4	0	.273	.364	1	0	OF-24
1961 LA A	149	479	122	29	3	25	5.2	70	84	49	120	8	.255	.484	20	2	OF-134, 2B-1
1962	13	11	2	0	0	1	9.1	4	1	1	5	1	.182	.455	4	0	1B-3
1963 2 teams	LA	A	(59G –	.183)		WAS	A	(7G –	.200)								
" total	66	162	30	6	1	6	3.7	18	20	17	55	0	.185	.346	11	1	OF-55
1964 WAS A	51	96	13	4	0	1	1.0	9	4	14	35	0	.135	.208	14	3	OF-37
6 yrs.	310	782	177	42	4	33	4.2	107	111	85	222	9	.226	.417	51	7	OF-255, 1B-3, 2B-1

Ron Hunt

HUNT, RONALD KENNETH
B. Feb. 23, 1941, St. Louis, Mo.   BR TR 6'   186 lbs.

	G	AB	H	2B	3B	HR	HR%	R	RBI	BB	SO	SB	BA	SA	AB	H	G by POS
1963 NY N	143	533	145	28	4	10	1.9	64	42	40	50	5	.272	.396	1	1	2B-142, 3B-1
1964	127	475	144	19	6	6	1.3	59	42	29	30	6	.303	.406	6	2	2B-109, 3B-12
1965	57	196	47	12	1	1	0.5	21	10	14	19	2	.240	.327	4	0	2B-46, 3B-6
1966	132	479	138	19	2	3	0.6	63	33	41	34	9	.288	.355	8	2	2B-123, SS-1, 3B-1
1967 LA N	110	388	102	17	3	3	0.8	44	33	39	24	2	.263	.345	10	1	2B-90, 3B-8
1968 SF N	148	529	132	19	0	2	0.4	79	28	78	41	6	.250	.297	2	1	2B-147
1969	128	478	125	23	3	3	0.6	72	41	51	47	9	.262	.341	0	0	2B-125, 3B-1
1970	117	367	103	17	1	6	1.6	70	41	44	29	1	.281	.381	23	7	2B-85, 3B-16
1971 MON N	152	520	145	20	0	5	1.0	89	38	58	41	5	.279	.358	5	1	2B-133, 3B-19
1972	129	443	112	20	0	0	0.0	56	18	51	29	9	.253	.298	5	1	2B-122, 3B-5
1973	113	401	124	14	0	0	0.0	61	18	52	19	10	.309	.344	6	2	2B-102, 3B-14
1974 2 teams	MON	N	(115G –	.268)		STL	N	(12G –	.174)								
" total	127	426	112	15	0	0	0.0	67	26	58	19	2	.263	.298	10	3	3B-75, 2B-36, SS-1
12 yrs.	1483	5235	1429	223	23	39	0.7	745	370	555	382	65	.273	.347	83	20	2B-1260, 3B-158, SS-2

	G	AB	H	2B	3B	HR	HR%	R	RBI	BB	SO	SB	BA	SA	Pinch Hit AB	Pinch Hit H	G by POS

Bill Hunter

HUNTER, WILLIAM ELLSWORTH
Brother of George Hunter.
B. July 8, 1886, Buffalo, N. Y.   D. Apr. 10, 1934, Buffalo, N. Y.

BL TL 5'7½"   155 lbs.

	G	AB	H	2B	3B	HR	HR%	R	RBI	BB	SO	SB	BA	SA	AB	H	G by POS
1912 CLE A	21	55	9	2	0	0	0.0	6	2	10		0	.164	.200	5	0	OF-16

Bill Hunter

HUNTER, WILLIAM ROBERT
B. St. Thomas, Ont., Canada   Deceased.

	G	AB	H	2B	3B	HR	HR%	R	RBI	BB	SO	SB	BA	SA	AB	H	G by POS
1884 LOU AA	2	7	1	0	0	0	0.0	1		0			.143	.143	0	0	C-2

Billy Hunter

HUNTER, GORDON WILLIAM
B. June 4, 1928, Punxsutawney, Pa.
Manager 1977-78.

BR TR 6'   180 lbs.

	G	AB	H	2B	3B	HR	HR%	R	RBI	BB	SO	SB	BA	SA	AB	H	G by POS
1953 STL A	154	567	124	18	1	1	0.2	50	37	24	45	3	.219	.259	0	0	SS-152
1954 BAL A	125	411	100	9	5	2	0.5	28	27	21	38	5	.243	.304	1	0	SS-124
1955 NY A	98	255	58	7	1	3	1.2	14	20	15	18	9	.227	.298	1	0	SS-32, 3B-4
1956	39	75	21	3	4	0	0.0	8	11	2	4	0	.280	.427	1	0	2B-64, SS-35, 3B-17
1957 KC A	116	319	61	10	4	8	2.5	39	29	27	43	1	.191	.323	4	0	2B-112, SS-2
1958 2 teams	KC	A (22G – .155)			CLE	A (76G – .195)											
" total	98	248	46	11	3	2	0.8	27	20	22	44	5	.185	.278	0	0	SS-87, 2B-8, 3B-3
6 yrs.	630	1875	410	58	18	16	0.9	166	144	111	192	23	.219	.294	7	0	SS-528, 2B-72, 3B-24

Buddy Hunter

HUNTER, HAROLD JAMES (Hunter)
B. Aug. 9, 1947, Omaha, Neb.

BR TR 5'10"   170 lbs.

	G	AB	H	2B	3B	HR	HR%	R	RBI	BB	SO	SB	BA	SA	AB	H	G by POS
1971 BOS A	8	9	2	1	0	0	0.0	2	0	2	1	0	.222	.333	1	0	2B-6
1973	13	7	3	1	0	0	0.0	3	2	3	1	0	.429	.571	0	0	3B-3, 2B-2, DH-1
1975	1	1	0	0	0	0	0.0	0	0	0	0	0	.000	.000	0	0	2B-1
3 yrs.	22	17	5	2	0	0	0.0	5	2	5	2	0	.294	.412	1	0	2B-9, 3B-3, DH-1

Eddie Hunter

HUNTER, EDISON FRANKLIN
B. Feb. 6, 1905, Bellevue, Ky.   D. Mar. 14, 1967, Colerain Township, Ohio

BR TR 5'7½"   150 lbs.

	G	AB	H	2B	3B	HR	HR%	R	RBI	BB	SO	SB	BA	SA	AB	H	G by POS
1933 CIN N	1	0	0	0	0	0	–	0	0	0	0	0	–	–	0	0	

George Hunter

HUNTER, GEORGE HENRY
Brother of Bill Hunter.
B. July 8, 1886, Buffalo, N. Y.   D. Jan. 11, 1968, Harrisburg, Pa.

BB TL 5'8½"   165 lbs.

	G	AB	H	2B	3B	HR	HR%	R	RBI	BB	SO	SB	BA	SA	AB	H	G by POS
1909 BKN N	44	123	28	7	0	0	0.0	8	8	9		1	.228	.285	3	0	OF-23, P-16
1910	1	0	0	0	0	0	–	0	0	0	0	0	–	–	0	0	OF-1
2 yrs.	45	123	28	7	0	0	0.0	8	8	9	0	1	.228	.285	3	0	OF-24, P-16

Herb Hunter

HUNTER, HERBERT HARRISON
B. Dec. 25, 1895, Boston, Mass.   D. July 25, 1970, Orlando, Fla.

BL TR 6'½"   165 lbs.

	G	AB	H	2B	3B	HR	HR%	R	RBI	BB	SO	SB	BA	SA	AB	H	G by POS
1916 2 teams	NY	N (21G – .250)			CHI	N (2G – .000)											
" total	23	32	7	0	0	1	3.1	3	4	0	5	0	.219	.313	11	2	3B-7, 1B-2
1917 CHI N	3	3	0	0	0	0	0.0	0	0	0	0	0	.000	.000	1	0	3B-1, 2B-1
1920 BOS A	4	12	1	0	0	0	0.0	2	0	1	1	0	.083	.083	0	0	OF-4
1921 STL N	9	2	0	0	0	0	0.0	3	0	1	0	0	.000	.000	1	0	1B-1
4 yrs.	39	49	8	0	0	1	2.0	8	4	2	6	0	.163	.224	13	2	3B-8, OF-4, 1B-3, 2B-1

Newt Hunter

HUNTER, FREDERICK CREIGHTON
B. Jan. 5, 1880, Chillicothe, Ohio   D. Oct. 26, 1963, Columbus, Ohio

BR TR 6'   180 lbs.

	G	AB	H	2B	3B	HR	HR%	R	RBI	BB	SO	SB	BA	SA	AB	H	G by POS
1911 PIT N	65	209	53	10	6	2	1.0	35	24	25	43	9	.254	.388	3	0	1B-61

Steve Huntz

HUNTZ, STEPHEN MICHAEL
B. Dec. 3, 1945, Cleveland, Ohio

BB TR 6'1"   204 lbs.

	G	AB	H	2B	3B	HR	HR%	R	RBI	BB	SO	SB	BA	SA	AB	H	G by POS
1967 STL N	3	6	1	0	0	0	0.0	1	0	1	2	0	.167	.167	1	1	2B-2
1969	71	139	27	4	0	3	2.2	13	13	27	34	0	.194	.288	3	0	SS-52, 2B-12, 3B-6
1970 SD N	106	352	77	8	0	11	3.1	54	37	66	69	0	.219	.335	9	1	SS-57, 3B-51
1971 CHI A	35	86	18	3	1	2	2.3	10	6	7	9	1	.209	.337	12	0	2B-14, SS-7, 3B-6
1975 SD N	22	53	8	4	0	0	0.0	3	4	7	8	0	.151	.226	6	0	3B-16, 2B-2
5 yrs.	237	636	131	19	1	16	2.5	81	60	108	122	1	.206	.314	31	2	SS-116, 3B-79, 2B-30

Dave Huppert

HUPPERT, DAVID BLAIN
B. Apr. 1, 1957, Southgate, Calif.

BR TR 6'1"   190 lbs.

	G	AB	H	2B	3B	HR	HR%	R	RBI	BB	SO	SB	BA	SA	AB	H	G by POS
1983 BAL A	2	0	0	0	0	0	–	0	0	0	0	0	–	–	0	0	C-2

Clint Hurdle

HURDLE, CLINTON MERRICK
B. July 30, 1957, Big Rapids, Mich.

BL TR 6'3"   195 lbs.

	G	AB	H	2B	3B	HR	HR%	R	RBI	BB	SO	SB	BA	SA	AB	H	G by POS
1977 KC A	9	26	8	0	0	2	7.7	5	7	2	7	0	.308	.538	0	0	OF-9
1978	133	417	110	25	5	7	1.7	48	56	56	84	1	.264	.398	8	5	OF-78, 1B-52, DH-1, 3B-1
1979	59	171	41	10	3	3	1.8	16	30	28	24	0	.240	.386	7	1	OF-50, DH-4, 3B-1
1980	130	395	116	31	2	10	2.5	50	60	34	61	0	.294	.458	9	3	OF-126
1981	28	76	25	3	1	4	5.3	12	15	13	10	0	.329	.553	2	1	OF-28
1982 CIN N	19	34	7	1	0	0	0.0	2	1	2	6	0	.206	.235	3	1	OF-17
1983 NY N	13	33	6	2	0	0	0.0	3	2	2	10	0	.182	.242	4	0	3B-9, OF-1
7 yrs.	391	1152	313	72	11	26	2.3	136	171	137	202	1	.272	.421	33	11	OF-309, 1B-52, 3B-11, DH-5

DIVISIONAL PLAYOFF SERIES																	
1981 KC A	3	11	3	0	0	0	0.0	1	1	1	1	0	.273	.273	0	0	OF-3

LEAGUE CHAMPIONSHIP SERIES																	
1978 KC A	4	8	3	1	0	1	0.0	1	1	2	3	0	.375	.625	1	0	OF-2
1980	3	2	0	0	0	0	0.0	0	0	0	1	0	.000	.000	0	0	OF-2
2 yrs.	7	10	3	1	0	1	0.0	1	1	2	4	0	.300	.500	1	0	OF-4

WORLD SERIES																	
1980 KC A	4	12	5	1	0	0	0.0	1	0	2	1	1	.417	.500	0	0	OF-4

	G	AB	H	2B	3B	HR	HR %	R	RBI	BB	SO	SB	BA	SA	Pinch Hit AB	Pinch Hit H	G by POS

Jerry Hurley

HURLEY, JEREMIAH JOSEPH
B. June 15, 1863, Boston, Mass.   D. Sept. 17, 1950, Boston, Mass.   TR 6'   190 lbs.

	G	AB	H	2B	3B	HR	HR %	R	RBI	BB	SO	SB	BA	SA	AB	H	G by POS
1889 BOS N	1	4	0	0	0	0	0.0	0	0	0	0	0	.000	.000	0	0	OF-1, C-1
1890 PIT P	8	22	6	1	0	0	0.0	5	2	2	5	0	.273	.318	0	0	C-7, OF-1
1891 C-M AA	24	66	14	3	2	0	0.0	10	6	12	13	2	.212	.318	0	0	C-24, OF-1, 1B-1
3 yrs.	33	92	20	4	2	0	0.0	15	8	14	18	2	.217	.304	0	0	C-32, OF-3, 1B-1

Pat Hurley

HURLEY, JERRY J. (Jerry)
B. Apr., 1875, New York, N. Y.   D. Dec. 27, 1919, New York, N. Y.   BR TR

	G	AB	H	2B	3B	HR	HR %	R	RBI	BB	SO	SB	BA	SA	AB	H	G by POS
1901 CIN N	9	21	1	0	0	0	0.0	1	0	1		1	.048	.048	2	0	C-7
1907 BKN N	1	2	0	0	0	0	0.0	0	0	1		0	.000	.000	0	0	C-1
2 yrs.	10	23	1	0	0	0	0.0	1	0	2		1	.043	.043	2	0	C-8

Don Hurst

HURST, FRANK O'DONNELL
B. Aug. 12, 1905, Maysville, Ky.   D. Dec. 6, 1952, Los Angeles, Calif.   BL TL 6'   215 lbs.

	G	AB	H	2B	3B	HR	HR %	R	RBI	BB	SO	SB	BA	SA	AB	H	G by POS
1928 PHI N	107	396	113	23	4	19	4.8	73	64	68	40	3	.285	.508	3	0	1B-104
1929	154	589	179	29	4	31	5.3	100	125	80	36	10	.304	.525	0	0	1B-154
1930	119	391	128	19	3	17	4.3	78	78	46	22	6	.327	.522	13	3	1B-96, OF-7
1931	137	489	149	37	5	11	2.2	63	91	64	28	8	.305	.468	2	0	1B-135
1932	150	579	196	41	4	24	4.1	109	143	65	27	10	.339	.547	0	0	1B-150
1933	147	550	147	27	8	8	1.5	58	76	48	32	3	.267	.389	5	1	1B-142
1934 2 teams		PHI N (40G – .262)			CHI N (51G – .199)												
" total	91	281	64	14	0	5	1.8	29	33	20	25	1	.228	.331	9	2	1B-87
7 yrs.	905	3275	976	190	28	115	3.5	510	610	391	210	41	.298	.478	32	6	1B-868, OF-7

Carl Husta

HUSTA, CARL LAWRENCE (Sox)
B. Apr. 8, 1902, Egg Harbor, N. J.   D. Nov. 6, 1951, Kingston, N. Y.   BR TR 5'11"   176 lbs.

	G	AB	H	2B	3B	HR	HR %	R	RBI	BB	SO	SB	BA	SA	AB	H	G by POS
1925 PHI A	6	22	3	0	0	0	0.0	2	2	2	3	0	.136	.136	0	0	SS-6

Harry Huston

HUSTON, HARRY EMANUEL
Also known as Kress Huston.
B. Oct. 14, 1883, DeGraff, Ohio   D. Oct. 13, 1969, Blackwell, Okla.   BR TR 5'9"   168 lbs.

	G	AB	H	2B	3B	HR	HR %	R	RBI	BB	SO	SB	BA	SA	AB	H	G by POS
1906 PHI N	2	4	0	0	0	0	0.0	0	0		1	0	.000	.000	0	0	C-2

Warren Huston

HUSTON, WARREN LLEWELLYN
B. Oct. 31, 1913, Newtonville, Mass.   BR TR 6'   170 lbs.

	G	AB	H	2B	3B	HR	HR %	R	RBI	BB	SO	SB	BA	SA	AB	H	G by POS
1937 PHI A	38	54	7	3	0	0	0.0	5	3	2	9	0	.130	.185	3	0	2B-16, SS-15, 3B-2
1944 BOS N	33	55	11	1	0	0	0.0	7	1	8	5	0	.200	.218	0	0	3B-20, 2B-5, SS-4
2 yrs.	71	109	18	4	0	0	0.0	12	4	10	14	0	.165	.202	3	0	3B-22, 2B-21, SS-19

Joe Hutcheson

HUTCHESON, JOSEPH JOHNSON (Poodles)
B. Feb. 5, 1905, Springtown, Tex.   BL TR 6'2"   200 lbs.

	G	AB	H	2B	3B	HR	HR %	R	RBI	BB	SO	SB	BA	SA	AB	H	G by POS
1933 BKN N	55	184	43	4	1	6	3.3	19	21	15	13	1	.234	.364	10	1	OF-45

Ed Hutchinson

HUTCHINSON, EDWARD F.
B. 1870, Pittsburgh, Pa.   Deceased.   5'11"   163 lbs.

	G	AB	H	2B	3B	HR	HR %	R	RBI	BB	SO	SB	BA	SA	AB	H	G by POS
1890 CHI N	4	17	1	1	0	0	0.0	0	0	0	0	0	.059	.118	0	0	2B-4

Fred Hutchinson

HUTCHINSON, FREDERICK CHARLES
B. Aug. 12, 1919, Seattle, Wash.   D. Nov. 12, 1964, Bradenton, Fla.   BL TR 6'2"   190 lbs.
Manager 1952-54, 1956-64.

	G	AB	H	2B	3B	HR	HR %	R	RBI	BB	SO	SB	BA	SA	AB	H	G by POS
1939 DET A	13	34	13	1	0	0	0.0	5	6	2	0	0	.382	.412	0	0	P-13
1940	17	30	8	1	0	0	0.0	1	2	0	0	0	.267	.300	0	0	P-17
1941	2	2	0	0	0	0	0.0	0	0	0	2	0	.000	.000	2	0	
1946	40	89	28	4	0	0	0.0	11	13	6	1	0	.315	.360	9	2	P-28
1947	56	106	32	5	2	2	1.9	8	15	6	6	2	.302	.443	22	6	P-33
1948	76	112	23	1	0	1	0.9	11	12	23	9	3	.205	.241	32	7	P-33
1949	38	73	18	2	1	0	0.0	12	7	8	5	1	.247	.301	4	1	P-33
1950	44	95	31	7	0	0	0.0	15	20	12	3	0	.326	.400	4	1	P-39
1951	47	85	16	2	0	0	0.0	7	7	7	4	0	.188	.212	13	2	P-31
1952	17	18	1	0	0	0	0.0	0	0	0	3	0	.056	.056	5	1	P-12
1953	4	6	1	0	0	1	16.7	1	1	0	0	0	.167	.667	0	0	P-3, 1B-1
11 yrs.	354	650	171	23	3	4	0.6	71	83	67	30	6	.263	.326	91	20	P-242, 1B-1
WORLD SERIES																	
1940 DET A	1	0	0	0	0	0	–	0	0	0	0	0	–	–	0	0	P-1

Roy Hutson

HUTSON, ROY LEE
B. Feb. 27, 1902, Luray, Mo.   D. May 20, 1957, La Mesa, Calif.   BL TR 5'9"   165 lbs.

	G	AB	H	2B	3B	HR	HR %	R	RBI	BB	SO	SB	BA	SA	AB	H	G by POS
1925 BKN N	7	8	4	0	0	0	0.0	1	1	1	1	0	.500	.500	0	0	OF-4

Jim Hutto

HUTTO, JAMES NEAMON JR
B. Oct. 17, 1947, Norfolk, Va.   BR TR 5'11"   195 lbs.

	G	AB	H	2B	3B	HR	HR %	R	RBI	BB	SO	SB	BA	SA	AB	H	G by POS
1970 PHI N	57	92	17	2	0	3	3.3	7	12	5	20	0	.185	.304	26	6	OF-22, 1B-12, C-5, 3B-1
1975 BAL A	4	5	0	0	0	0	0.0	0	0	0	2	0	.000	.000	1	0	C-3
2 yrs.	61	97	17	2	0	3	3.1	7	12	5	22	0	.175	.289	27	6	OF-22, 1B-12, C-8, 3B-1

Tom Hutton

HUTTON, THOMAS GEORGE
B. Apr. 20, 1946, Los Angeles, Calif.   BL TL 5'11"   180 lbs.

	G	AB	H	2B	3B	HR	HR %	R	RBI	BB	SO	SB	BA	SA	AB	H	G by POS
1966 LA N	3	2	0	0	0	0	0.0	0	0	0	0	0	.000	.000	0	0	1B-3
1969	16	48	13	0	0	0	0.0	2	4	5	7	0	.271	.271	0	0	1B-16
1972 PHI N	134	381	99	16	2	4	1.0	40	38	56	24	5	.260	.344	19	8	1B-87, OF-48
1973	106	247	65	11	0	5	2.0	31	29	32	31	3	.263	.368	37	10	1B-71
1974	96	208	50	6	3	4	1.9	32	33	30	13	2	.240	.356	22	8	1B-39, OF-33
1975	113	165	41	6	0	3	1.8	24	24	27	10	2	.248	.339	36	11	1B-71, OF-12

	G	AB	H	2B	3B	HR	HR %	R	RBI	BB	SO	SB	BA	SA	Pinch Hit AB	Pinch Hit H	G by POS

Tom Hutton continued

	G	AB	H	2B	3B	HR	HR %	R	RBI	BB	SO	SB	BA	SA	AB	H	G by POS
1976	95	124	25	5	1	1	0.8	15	13	27	11	1	.202	.282	19	5	1B-72, OF-1
1977	107	81	25	3	0	2	2.5	12	11	12	10	1	.309	.420	34	10	1B-73, OF-9
1978 2 teams		TOR	A	(64G –	.254)		MON	N	(39G –	.203)							
" total	103	232	56	12	0	2	0.9	23	14	29	16	1	.241	.319	24	4	OF-60, 1B-26
1979 MON N	86	83	21	2	1	1	1.2	14	13	10	7	0	.253	.337	43	11	1B-25, OF-9
1980	62	55	12	2	0	0	0.0	2	5	4	10	0	.218	.255	43	10	1B-7, OF-4, P-1
1981	31	29	3	0	0	0	0.0	1	2	2	1	0	.103	.103	17	2	1B-9, OF-2
12 yrs.	952	1655	410	63	7	22	1.3	196	186	234	140	15	.248	.334	294	79	1B-499, OF-178, P-1

LEAGUE CHAMPIONSHIP SERIES

	G	AB	H	2B	3B	HR	HR %	R	RBI	BB	SO	SB	BA	SA	AB	H	G by POS
1976 PHI N	1	1	0	0	0	0	0.0	0	0	0	0	0	.000	.000	1	0	
1977	3	3	0	0	0	0	0.0	0	0	0	0	0	.000	.000	2	0	1B-1
2 yrs.	4	4	0	0	0	0	0.0	0	0	0	0	0	.000	.000	3	0	1B-1

Ham Hyatt

HYATT, ROBERT HAMILTON
BL TR 6'1"   185 lbs.
B. Nov. 1, 1884, Buncombe County, N. C.   D. Sept. 11, 1963, Liberty Lake, Wash.

	G	AB	H	2B	3B	HR	HR %	R	RBI	BB	SO	SB	BA	SA	AB	H	G by POS
1909 PIT N	48	67	20	3	4	0	0.0	9	7	3		1	.299	.463	37	9	OF-6, 1B-2
1910	74	175	46	5	6	1	0.6	19	30	8	14	3	.263	.377	31	6	1B-38, OF-4
1912	46	97	28	3	1	0	0.0	13	22	6	8	2	.289	.340	27	6	OF-15, 1B-3
1913	63	81	27	6	2	4	4.9	8	16	3	8	0	.333	.605	52	15	OF-5, 1B-5
1914	74	79	17	3	1	1	1.3	2	15	7	14	1	.215	.316	58	14	1B-7, C-1
1915 STL N	106	295	79	8	9	2	0.7	23	46	28	24	3	.268	.376	14	3	1B-81, OF-25
1918 NY A	53	131	30	8	0	2	1.5	11	10	8	8	1	.229	.336	21	4	OF-25, 1B-5
7 yrs.	464	925	247	36	23	10	1.1	85	146	63	76	11	.267	.388	240	57	1B-141, OF-80, C-1

WORLD SERIES

	G	AB	H	2B	3B	HR	HR %	R	RBI	BB	SO	SB	BA	SA	AB	H	G by POS
1909 PIT N	2	4	0	0	0	0	0.0	1	1	1		0	.000	.000	1	0	OF-1

Pat Hynes

HYNES, PATRICK J.
TL
B. Mar. 12, 1884, St. Louis, Mo.   D. Mar. 12, 1907, St. Louis, Mo.

	G	AB	H	2B	3B	HR	HR %	R	RBI	BB	SO	SB	BA	SA	AB	H	G by POS
1903 STL N	1	3	0	0	0	0	0.0	0	0	0		0	.000	.000	0	0	P-1
1904 STL A	66	254	60	7	3	0	0.0	23	15	3		3	.236	.287	0	0	OF-63, P-5
2 yrs.	67	257	60	7	3	0	0.0	23	15	3		3	.233	.284	0	0	OF-63, P-6

Scotty Ingerton

INGERTON, WILLIAM JOHN
BR TR 6'1"   172 lbs.
B. Apr. 19, 1886, Peninsula, Ohio   D. June 15, 1956, Cleveland, Ohio

	G	AB	H	2B	3B	HR	HR %	R	RBI	BB	SO	SB	BA	SA	AB	H	G by POS
1911 BOS N	136	521	130	24	4	5	1.0	63	61	39	68	6	.250	.340	3	0	3B-58, OF-43, 1B-17, 2B-11, SS-4

Charlie Ingraham

INGRAHAM, CHARLES
5'11"   170 lbs.
B. Apr., 1860, Youngstown, Ohio   Deceased.

	G	AB	H	2B	3B	HR	HR %	R	RBI	BB	SO	SB	BA	SA	AB	H	G by POS
1883 BAL AA	1	4	1	0	0	0	0.0	0		0			.250	.250	0	0	C-1

Mel Ingram

INGRAM, MELVIN DAVID
BR TR 5'11½" 175 lbs.
B. July 4, 1904, Asheville, N. C.   D. Oct. 28, 1979, Medford, Ore.

	G	AB	H	2B	3B	HR	HR %	R	RBI	BB	SO	SB	BA	SA	AB	H	G by POS
1929 PIT N	3	0	0	0	0	0	–	1	0	0	0	0	–	–	0	0	

Dane Iorg

IORG, DANE CHARLES
BL TR 6'   180 lbs.
Brother of Garth Iorg.
B. May 11, 1950, Eureka, Calif.

	G	AB	H	2B	3B	HR	HR %	R	RBI	BB	SO	SB	BA	SA	AB	H	G by POS
1977 2 teams		PHI	N	(12G –	.167)		STL	N	(30G –	.313)							
" total	42	62	15	2	0	0	0.0	5	6	7	6	0	.242	.274	21	6	1B-9, OF-7
1978 STL N	35	85	23	4	1	0	0.0	6	4	4	10	0	.271	.341	11	2	OF-25
1979	79	179	52	11	1	1	0.6	12	21	12	28	1	.291	.380	39	11	OF-39, 1B-10
1980	105	251	76	23	1	3	1.2	33	36	20	34	1	.303	.438	38	10	OF-63, 1B-5, 3B-1
1981	75	217	71	11	2	2	0.9	23	39	7	9	2	.327	.424	14	4	OF-57, 1B-8, 3B-2
1982	102	238	70	14	1	0	0.0	17	34	23	23	0	.294	.361	27	7	OF-63, 1B-10, 3B-2
1983	58	116	31	9	1	0	0.0	6	11	10	11	1	.267	.362	20	6	OF-22, 1B-11
1984 2 teams		STL	N	(15G –	.143)		KC	A	(78G –	.255)							
" total	93	263	64	18	2	5	1.9	30	33	15	21	0	.243	.384	20	6	1B-49, OF-27, 3B-1
8 yrs.	589	1411	402	92	9	11	0.8	132	184	97	143	5	.285	.386	190	52	OF-303, 1B-102, 3B-6

LEAGUE CHAMPIONSHIP SERIES

	G	AB	H	2B	3B	HR	HR %	R	RBI	BB	SO	SB	BA	SA	AB	H	G by POS
1984 KC A	2	2	1	0	0	0	0.0	0	1	0	0	0	.500	.500	2	1	

WORLD SERIES

	G	AB	H	2B	3B	HR	HR %	R	RBI	BB	SO	SB	BA	SA	AB	H	G by POS
1982 STL N	5	17	9	4	1	0	0.0	4	1	0	0	0	.529	.882	0	0	DH-5

Garth Iorg

IORG, GARTH RAY
BR TR 5'11"   170 lbs.
Brother of Dane Iorg.
B. Oct. 12, 1954, Arcata, Calif.

	G	AB	H	2B	3B	HR	HR %	R	RBI	BB	SO	SB	BA	SA	AB	H	G by POS
1978 TOR A	19	49	8	0	0	0	0.0	3	3	3	4	0	.163	.163	0	0	2B-18
1980	80	222	55	10	1	2	0.9	24	14	12	39	2	.248	.329	7	2	2B-32, 3B-20, OF-14, 1B-11, DH-2, SS-1
1981	70	215	52	11	0	0	0.0	17	10	7	31	2	.242	.293	7	1	2B-46, 3B-17, SS-2, 1B-1
1982	129	417	119	20	5	1	0.2	45	36	12	38	3	.285	.365	22	9	3B-100, 2B-30, DH-1
1983	122	375	103	22	5	2	0.5	40	39	13	45	7	.275	.376	16	5	3B-85, 2B-39, SS-1
1984	121	247	56	10	3	1	0.4	24	25	5	16	1	.227	.304	25	4	3B-112, 2B-7, SS-2, DH-1
6 yrs.	541	1525	393	73	14	6	0.4	153	127	52	173	15	.258	.336	77	21	3B-334, 2B-172, OF-14, 1B-12, SS-6, DH-4

Happy Iott

IOTT, FRED JOHN (Dimples)
Also known as Frederick Iott.
B. July 7, 1876, Houlton, Me.   D. Feb. 17, 1941, Oakfield, Me.

	G	AB	H	2B	3B	HR	HR %	R	RBI	BB	SO	SB	BA	SA	AB	H	G by POS
1903 CLE A	3	10	2	0	0	0	0.0	1	0	2		1	.200	.200	0	0	OF-3

	G	AB	H	2B	3B	HR	HR %	R	RBI	BB	SO	SB	BA	SA	Pinch Hit AB	Pinch Hit H	G by POS

Hal Irelan

IRELAN, HAROLD (Grump)
B. Aug. 5, 1890, Burnettsville, Ind.   D. July 16, 1944, Carmel, Ind.   BB TR 5'7"   165 lbs.

	G	AB	H	2B	3B	HR	HR%	R	RBI	BB	SO	SB	BA	SA	AB	H	G by POS
1914 PHI N	67	165	39	8	0	1	0.6	16	16	21	22	3	.236	.303	12	6	2B-44, SS-3, 3B-2, 1B-2

Tim Ireland

IRELAND, TIMOTHY NEAL
B. Mar. 14, 1953, Oakland, Calif.   BB TR 6'   180 lbs.

	G	AB	H	2B	3B	HR	HR%	R	RBI	BB	SO	SB	BA	SA	AB	H	G by POS
1981 KC A	4	0	0	0	0	0	–	1	0	0	0	0	–	–	0	0	1B-4
1982	7	7	1	0	0	0	0.0	2	0	1	1	0	.143	.143	0	0	2B-4, OF-2, 3B-1
2 yrs.	11	7	1	0	0	0	0.0	3	0	1	1	0	.143	.143	0	0	2B-4, 1B-4, OF-2, 3B-1

Ed Irvin

IRVIN, WILLIAM EDWARD
B. 1882, Philadelphia, Pa.   D. Feb. 18, 1916, Philadelphia, Pa.   TR

	G	AB	H	2B	3B	HR	HR%	R	RBI	BB	SO	SB	BA	SA	AB	H	G by POS
1912 DET A	1	3	2	0	2	0	0.0					0	.667	2.000	0	0	3B-1

Monte Irvin

IRVIN, MONFORD MERRILL
B. Feb. 25, 1919, Columbia, Ala.   BR TR 6'1"   195 lbs.
Hall of Fame 1973.

	G	AB	H	2B	3B	HR	HR%	R	RBI	BB	SO	SB	BA	SA	AB	H	G by POS
1949 NY N	36	76	17	3	2	0	0.0	7	7	17	11	0	.224	.316	13	4	OF-10, 3B-5, 1B-5
1950	110	374	112	19	5	15	4.0	61	66	52	41	3	.299	.497	4	1	1B-59, OF-49, 3B-1
1951	151	558	174	19	11	24	4.3	94	121	89	44	12	.312	.514	1	1	OF-112, 1B-39
1952	46	126	39	2	1	4	3.2	10	21	10	11	0	.310	.437	14	2	OF-32
1953	124	444	146	21	5	21	4.7	72	97	55	34	2	.329	.541	8	5	OF-113
1954	135	432	113	13	3	19	4.4	62	64	70	23	7	.262	.438	9	3	OF-128, 3B-1, 1B-1
1955	51	150	38	7	1	1	0.7	16	17	17	15	3	.253	.333	6	1	OF-45
1956 CHI N	111	339	92	13	3	15	4.4	44	50	41	41	1	.271	.460	18	7	OF-96
8 yrs.	764	2499	731	97	31	99	4.0	366	443	351	220	28	.293	.475	73	17	OF-585, 1B-104, 3B-7
WORLD SERIES																	
1951 NY N	6	24	11	0	1	0	0.0	4	2	2	1	2	.458	.542	0	0	OF-6
1954	4	9	2	1	0	0	0.0	1	2	0	3	0	.222	.333	0	0	OF-4
2 yrs.	10	33	13	1	1	0	0.0	5	4	2	4	2	.394	.485	0	0	OF-10

Arthur Irwin

IRWIN, ARTHUR ALBERT
Brother of John Irwin.   BL TR 5'8½"   158 lbs.
B. Feb. 14, 1858, Toronto, Ont., Canada   D. July 16, 1921, Atlantic Ocean
Manager 1889, 1891-92, 1894-96, 1898-99.

	G	AB	H	2B	3B	HR	HR%	R	RBI	BB	SO	SB	BA	SA	AB	H	G by POS
1880 WOR N	85	352	91	19	4	1	0.3	53		11	27		.259	.344	0	0	SS-82, 3B-3, C-1
1881	50	206	55	8	2	0	0.0	27	24	7	4		.267	.325	0	0	SS-50
1882	84	333	73	12	4	0	0.0	30	30	14	34		.219	.279	0	0	3B-51, SS-33
1883 PRO N	98	406	116	22	7	0	0.0	67		12	38		.286	.374	0	0	SS-94, 2B-4
1884	102	404	97	14	3	2	0.5	73		28	52		.240	.304	0	0	SS-102, P-1
1885	59	218	39	2	1	0	0.0	16	14	14	29		.179	.197	0	0	SS-58, 3B-1, 2B-1
1886 PHI N	101	373	87	6	0	0	0.0	51	34	35	39		.233	.282	0	0	SS-100, 3B-1
1887	100	374	95	14	8	2	0.5	65	56	48	26	19	.254	.350	0	0	SS-100
1888	125	448	98	12	4	0	0.0	51	28	33	56	19	.219	.263	0	0	SS-122, 2B-3
1889 2 teams	103	386	89	15	5	PHI N (18G – .219)		WAS N (85G – .233)									
" total	103	386	89	15	5	0	0.0	58	42	48	43	15	.231	.295	0	0	SS-103, 2B-1, P-1
1890 BOS P	96	354	92	17	1	0	0.0	60	45	57	29	16	.260	.314	0	0	SS-96
1891 BOS AA	6	17	2	0	0	0	0.0	1	0	2	1	0	.118	.118	0	0	SS-6
1894 PHI N	1	0	0	0	0	0	–	0	0	0	0	0	–	–	0	0	SS-1
13 yrs.	1010	3871	934	141	45	5	0.1	552	272	309	378	69	.241	.305	0	0	SS-947, 3B-56, 2B-9, P-2, C-1

Charlie Irwin

IRWIN, CHARLES EDWIN
B. Feb. 15, 1869, Clinton, Ill.   D. Sept. 21, 1925, Chicago, Ill.   BR TR 5'10"   160 lbs.

	G	AB	H	2B	3B	HR	HR%	R	RBI	BB	SO	SB	BA	SA	AB	H	G by POS
1893 CHI N	21	82	25	6	2	0	0.0	14	13	10	1	4	.305	.427	0	0	SS-21
1894	128	498	144	24	9	8	1.6	84	95	63	23	35	.289	.422	0	0	3B-67, SS-61
1895	3	10	2	0	0	0	0.0	4	0	2	1	0	.200	.200	0	0	SS-3
1896 CIN N	127	476	141	16	6	1	0.2	77	67	26	17	31	.296	.361	0	0	3B-127
1897	134	505	146	26	6	0	0.0	89	74	47		27	.289	.364	0	0	3B-134
1898	136	501	120	14	5	3	0.6	77	55	31		18	.240	.305	0	0	3B-136
1899	90	314	73	4	8	1	0.3	42	52	26		26	.232	.306	0	0	3B-78, SS-6, 2B-3, 1B-1
1900	87	333	91	15	6	1	0.3	59	44	14		9	.273	.363	2	1	3B-61, SS-16, OF-6, 2B-3
1901 2 teams	132	502	114	25	4	CIN N (67G – .238)		BKN N (65G – .215)									
" total	132	502	114	25	4	0	0.0	50	45	28		17	.227	.293	0	0	3B-132
1902 BKN N	131	458	125	14	0	2	0.4	59	43	39		17	.273	.317	0	0	3B-130, SS-1
10 yrs.	989	3679	981	144	46	16	0.4	555	488	286	42	180	.267	.344	4	1	3B-865, SS-108, OF-6, 2B-6, 1B-1

John Irwin

IRWIN, JOHN
Brother of Arthur Irwin.   BL TR 5'10"   168 lbs.
B. July 21, 1861, Toronto, Ont., Canada   D. Feb. 28, 1934, Boston, Mass.

	G	AB	H	2B	3B	HR	HR%	R	RBI	BB	SO	SB	BA	SA	AB	H	G by POS
1882 WOR N	1	4	0	0	0	0	0.0	0	0	0	2		.000	.000	0	0	1B-1
1884 BOS U	105	432	101	22	6	1	0.2	81		15			.234	.319	0	0	3B-105
1886 PHI AA	3	13	3	1	0	0	0.0	4		0			.231	.308	0	0	SS-2, 3B-1
1887 WAS N	8	31	11	2	0	2	6.5	9	6	3			.355	.613	0	0	SS-5, 3B-4
1888	37	126	28	5	2	0	0.0	14	8	5	18	15	.222	.294	0	0	SS-27, 3B-10
1889	58	228	66	11	4	0	0.0	42	25	25	14	10	.289	.373	0	0	3B-58
1890 BUF P	77	308	72	11	4	0	0.0	62	34	43	19	18	.234	.295	0	0	3B-64, 1B-12, 2B-1
1891 2 teams	33	127	31	3	3	BOS AA (19G – .222)		LOU AA (14G – .273)									
" total	33	127	31	3	3	0	0.0	13	22	11	15	7	.244	.315	0	0	OF-17, 3B-16, SS-1
8 yrs.	322	1269	312	55	19	3	0.2	222	91	102	74	56	.246	.326	0	0	3B-258, SS-35, OF-17, 1B-13, 2B-1

Tommy Irwin

IRWIN, THOMAS ANDREW
B. Dec. 20, 1912, Altoona, Pa.   BR TR 5'11"   165 lbs.

	G	AB	H	2B	3B	HR	HR%	R	RBI	BB	SO	SB	BA	SA	AB	H	G by POS
1938 CLE A	3	9	1	0	0	0	0.0	1	0		3	0	.111	.111	0	0	SS-3

	G	AB	H	2B	3B	HR	HR %	R	RBI	BB	SO	SB	BA	SA	Pinch Hit AB	Pinch Hit H	G by POS

Walt Irwin

IRWIN, WALTER KINGSLEY (Lightning)
B. Sept. 23, 1897, Henrietta, Pa.   D. Aug. 18, 1976, Spring Lake, Mich.
BR TR 5'10½" 170 lbs.

	G	AB	H	2B	3B	HR	HR %	R	RBI	BB	SO	SB	BA	SA	PH AB	PH H	G by POS
1921 STL N	4	1	0	0	0	0	0.0	1	0	0	1	0	.000	.000	1	0	

Orlando Isales

ISALES, ORLANDO
Also known as Orlando Pizarro.
B. Dec. 22, 1959, Santurce, Puerto Rico
BR TR 5'9" 175 lbs.

	G	AB	H	2B	3B	HR	HR %	R	RBI	BB	SO	SB	BA	SA	PH AB	PH H	G by POS
1980 PHI N	3	5	2	0	1	0	0.0	1	3	1	0	0	.400	.800	0	0	OF-2

Frank Isbell

ISBELL, WILLIAM FRANK (Bald Eagle)
B. Aug. 21, 1875, Delavan, N. Y.   D. July 15, 1941, Wichita, Kans.
BL TR 5'11" 190 lbs.

	G	AB	H	2B	3B	HR	HR %	R	RBI	BB	SO	SB	BA	SA	PH AB	PH H	G by POS
1898 CHI N	45	159	37	4	0	0	0.0	17	8	3		3	.233	.258	0	0	OF-28, P-13, 3B-3, 2B-3, SS-2
1901 CHI A	137	556	143	15	8	3	0.5	93	70	36		52	.257	.329	0	0	1B-137, 2B-2, SS-1, 3B-1, P-1
1902	137	515	130	14	4	4	0.8	62	59	14		38	.252	.318	0	0	1B-133, SS-4, C-1, P-1
1903	138	546	132	25	9	2	0.4	52	59	12		26	.242	.332	0	0	1B-117, 3B-19, 2B-2, OF-1, SS-1
1904	96	314	66	10	3	1	0.3	27	34	16		19	.210	.271	3	0	1B-57, 2B-27, OF-5, SS-4
1905	94	341	101	21	11	2	0.6	55	45	15		15	.296	.440	0	0	2B-42, OF-40, 1B-9, SS-2
1906	143	549	153	18	11	0	0.0	71	57	30		37	.279	.352	0	0	2B-132, OF-14, C-1, P-1
1907	125	486	118	19	7	0	0.0	60	41	22		22	.243	.322	1	0	1B-119, OF-5, SS-1, P-1
1908	84	320	79	15	3	1	0.3	31	49	19		18	.247	.322	1	0	1B-65, 2B-18
1909	120	433	97	17	6	0	0.0	33	33	23		23	.224	.291	5	2	1B-101, OF-9, 2B-5
10 yrs.	1119	4219	1056	158	62	13	0.3	501	455	190		253	.250	.326	10	2	1B-619, 2B-350, OF-102, 3B-23, P-17, SS-15, C-2

	G	AB	H	2B	3B	HR	HR %	R	RBI	BB	SO	SB	BA	SA	PH AB	PH H	G by POS
WORLD SERIES 1906 CHI A	6	26	8	4	0	0	0.0	4	4	0	6	1	.308	.462	0	0	2B-6

Mike Ivie

IVIE, MICHAEL WILSON
B. Aug. 8, 1952, Atlanta, Ga.
BR TR 6'3" 205 lbs.

	G	AB	H	2B	3B	HR	HR %	R	RBI	BB	SO	SB	BA	SA	PH AB	PH H	G by POS
1971 SD N	6	17	8	0	0	0	0.0	0	3	1	1	0	.471	.471	1	0	C-6
1974	12	34	3	0	0	1	2.9	1	3	2	8	0	.088	.176	1	0	1B-11
1975	111	377	94	16	2	8	2.1	36	46	20	63	4	.249	.366	9	3	1B-78, 3B-61, C-1
1976	140	405	118	19	5	7	1.7	51	70	30	41	6	.291	.415	4	0	1B-135, 3B-2, C-2
1977	134	489	133	29	2	9	1.8	66	66	39	57	3	.272	.395	15	2	1B-105, 3B-25
1978 SF N	117	318	98	14	3	11	3.5	34	55	27	45	3	.308	.475	31	12	1B-76, OF-22
1979	133	402	115	18	3	27	6.7	58	89	47	80	5	.286	.547	23	9	1B-98, OF-24, 3B-4, 2B-1
1980	79	286	69	16	1	4	1.4	21	25	19	40	1	.241	.346	6	1	1B-72
1981 2 teams		SF	N	(7G –	.294)			HOU	N	(19G –	.238)						
" total	26	59	15	5	0	0	0.0	3	9	2	12	0	.254	.339	13	4	1B-15
1982 2 teams		HOU	N	(7G –	.333)			DET	A	(80G –	.232)						
" total	87	265	62	12	1	14	5.3	35	38	25	51	0	.234	.445	17	4	DH-79
1983 DET A	12	42	9	4	0	0	0.0	4	7	2	4	0	.214	.310	0	0	1B-12
11 yrs.	857	2694	724	133	17	81	3.0	309	411	214	402	22	.269	.421	120	35	1B-602, 3B-92, DH-79, OF-46, C-9, 2B-1

Hank Izquierdo

IZQUIERDO, ENRIQUE ROBERTO
B. Mar. 20, 1931, Matanzas, Cuba
BR TR 5'11" 175 lbs.

	G	AB	H	2B	3B	HR	HR %	R	RBI	BB	SO	SB	BA	SA	PH AB	PH H	G by POS
1967 MIN A	16	26	7	2	0	0	0.0	4	2	1	2	0	.269	.346	1	0	C-16

Pete Jablonowski

Playing record listed under Pete Appleton

Ray Jablonski

JABLONSKI, RAYMOND LEO (Jabbo)
B. Dec. 17, 1926, Chicago, Ill.
BR TR 5'10" 175 lbs.

	G	AB	H	2B	3B	HR	HR %	R	RBI	BB	SO	SB	BA	SA	PH AB	PH H	G by POS
1953 STL N	157	604	162	23	5	21	3.5	64	112	34	61	2	.268	.427	0	0	3B-157
1954	152	611	181	33	3	12	2.0	80	104	49	42	9	.296	.419	2	2	3B-149, 1B-1
1955 CIN N	74	221	53	9	0	9	4.1	28	28	13	35	0	.240	.403	17	4	OF-28, 3B-28
1956	130	407	104	25	1	15	3.7	42	66	37	57	2	.256	.432	14	5	3B-127, 2B-1
1957 NY N	107	305	88	15	1	9	3.0	37	57	31	47	0	.289	.433	28	6	3B-70, 1B-6, OF-1
1958 SF N	82	230	53	15	1	12	5.2	28	46	17	50	2	.230	.461	31	9	3B-57
1959 2 teams		STL	N	(60G –	.253)			KC	A	(25G –	.262)						
" total	85	152	39	5	0	5	3.3	15	22	11	30	1	.257	.388	53	8	3B-36, SS-1
1960 KC A	21	32	7	1	0	0	0.0	3	3	4	8	0	.219	.250	13	3	3B-6
8 yrs.	808	2562	687	126	11	83	3.2	297	438	196	330	16	.268	.423	158	37	3B-630, OF-29, 1B-7, SS-1, 2B-1

Fred Jacklitsch

JACKLITSCH, FREDERICK LAWRENCE
B. May 24, 1876, Brooklyn, N. Y.   D. July 18, 1937, Brooklyn, N. Y.
BR TR

	G	AB	H	2B	3B	HR	HR %	R	RBI	BB	SO	SB	BA	SA	PH AB	PH H	G by POS
1900 PHI N	5	11	2	1	0	0	0.0	0	3	0		0	.182	.273	2	0	C-3
1901	33	120	30	4	3	0	0.0	14	24	12		2	.250	.333	1	0	C-30, 3B-1
1902	38	114	23	4	0	0	0.0	8	8	9		2	.202	.237	8	2	C-29, OF-1
1903 BKN N	60	176	47	8	3	1	0.6	31	21	33		4	.267	.364	6	2	C-53, OF-1, 2B-1
1904	26	77	18	3	1	0	0.0	8	8	7		7	.234	.299	2	0	1B-11, 2B-8, C-5
1905 NY A	1	3	0	0	0	0	0.0	1	1	1		0	.000	.000	0	0	C-1
1907 PHI N	73	202	43	7	0	0	0.0	19	17	27		7	.213	.248	8	5	C-58, 1B-6, OF-1
1908	37	86	19	3	0	0	0.0	6	7	14		3	.221	.256	5	1	C-30
1909	20	32	10	1	1	0	0.0	6	6	10		1	.313	.406	7	0	C-11, 2B-1
1910	25	51	10	3	0	0	0.0	7	2	5	9	0	.196	.255	7	2	C-13, 1B-2, 3B-1, 2B-1
1914 BAL F	122	337	93	21	4	2	0.6	40	48	52		7	.276	.380	4	1	C-118
1915	49	135	32	9	1	2	1.5	20	13	31		2	.237	.348	2	0	C-45, SS-1

	G	AB	H	2B	3B	HR	HR %	R	RBI	BB	SO	SB	BA	SA	Pinch Hit AB	Pinch Hit H	G by POS

Fred Jacklitsch continued

	G	AB	H	2B	3B	HR	HR %	R	RBI	BB	SO	SB	BA	SA	PH AB	PH H	G by POS
1917 BOS N	1	0	0	0	0	0	–	0	0	0	0	0	–	–	0	0	C-1
13 yrs.	490	1344	327	64	12	5	0.4	160	153	201	9	35	.243	.320	52	8	C-397, 1B-19, 2B-11, OF-3, 3B-2, SS-1

Bill Jackson

JACKSON, WILLIAM RILEY BL TL 5'11½" 160 lbs.
B. Apr. 4, 1881, Pittsburgh, Pa.   D. Sept. 24, 1958, Peoria, Ill.

	G	AB	H	2B	3B	HR	HR %	R	RBI	BB	SO	SB	BA	SA	PH AB	PH H	G by POS
1914 CHI F	26	25	1	0	0	0	0.0	2	1	3		0	.040	.040	8	0	OF-6, 1B-4
1915	50	98	16	1	0	1	1.0	15	12	14		3	.163	.204	8	1	1B-36, OF-1
2 yrs.	76	123	17	1	0	1	0.8	17	13	17		3	.138	.171	16	1	1B-40, OF-7

Charlie Jackson

JACKSON, CHARLES HERBERT (Lefty) BL TL 5'9" 150 lbs.
B. Feb. 7, 1894, Granite City, Ill.   D. May 27, 1968, Radford, Va.

	G	AB	H	2B	3B	HR	HR %	R	RBI	BB	SO	SB	BA	SA	PH AB	PH H	G by POS
1915 CHI A	1	1	0	0	0	0	0.0	0	0	0	1	0	.000	.000	1	0	
1917 PIT N	41	121	29	3	2	0	0.0	7	1	10	22	4	.240	.298	2	0	OF-36
2 yrs.	42	122	29	3	2	0	0.0	7	1	10	23	4	.238	.295	3	0	OF-36

George Jackson

JACKSON, GEORGE CHRISTOPHER (Hickory) BR TR 6'½" 180 lbs.
B. Jan. 2, 1882, Springfield, Mo.   D. Nov. 26, 1972, Blum, Tex.

	G	AB	H	2B	3B	HR	HR %	R	RBI	BB	SO	SB	BA	SA	PH AB	PH H	G by POS
1911 BOS N	39	147	51	11	2	0	0.0	28	25	12	21	12	.347	.449	0	0	OF-39
1912	110	397	104	13	5	4	1.0	55	48	38	72	22	.262	.350	2	0	OF-107
1913	3	10	3	0	0	0	0.0	2	0	0	2	0	.300	.300	0	0	OF-3
3 yrs.	152	554	158	24	7	4	0.7	85	73	50	95	34	.285	.375	2	0	OF-149

Henry Jackson

JACKSON, HENRY EVERETT BR TR 6'2" 185 lbs.
B. June 23, 1861, Union City, Ind.   D. Sept. 14, 1932, Chicago, Ill.

	G	AB	H	2B	3B	HR	HR %	R	RBI	BB	SO	SB	BA	SA	PH AB	PH H	G by POS
1887 IND N	10	38	10	1	0	0	0.0	1	3	0	12	2	.263	.289	0	0	1B-10

Jim Jackson

JACKSON, JAMES BENNER BR TR
B. Nov. 28, 1877, Philadelphia, Pa.   D. Oct. 8, 1955, Philadelphia, Pa.

	G	AB	H	2B	3B	HR	HR %	R	RBI	BB	SO	SB	BA	SA	PH AB	PH H	G by POS
1901 BAL A	99	364	91	17	3	2	0.5	42	50	20		11	.250	.330	3	0	OF-96
1902 NY N	35	110	20	5	1	0	0.0	14	13	15		6	.182	.245	1	0	OF-34
1905 CLE A	108	421	108	12	4	2	0.5	58	31	34		15	.257	.318	0	0	OF-105, 3B-3
1906	105	374	80	13	4	0	0.0	44	38	38		25	.214	.270	1	0	OF-105
4 yrs.	347	1269	299	47	12	4	0.3	158	132	107		57	.236	.301	5	0	OF-340, 3B-3

Joe Jackson

JACKSON, JOSEPH JEFFERSON (Shoeless Joe) BL TR 6'1" 200 lbs.
B. July 16, 1887, Brandon Mills, S. C.   D. Dec. 5, 1951, Greenville, S. C.

	G	AB	H	2B	3B	HR	HR %	R	RBI	BB	SO	SB	BA	SA	PH AB	PH H	G by POS
1908 PHI A	5	23	3	0	0	0	0.0	0	3			0	.130	.130	0	0	OF-5
1909	5	17	5	0	0	0	0.0	3	3	1		0	.294	.294	1	0	OF-4
1910 CLE A	20	75	29	2	5	1	1.3	15	11	8		4	.387	.587	0	0	OF-20
1911	147	571	233	45	19	7	1.2	126	83	56		41	.408	.590	0	0	OF-147
1912	152	572	226	44	26	3	0.5	121	90	54		35	.395	.579	0	0	OF-150
1913	148	528	197	39	17	7	1.3	109	71	80	26	26	.373	.551	0	0	OF-148
1914	122	453	153	22	13	3	0.7	61	53	41	34	22	.338	.464	2	1	OF-119
1915 2 teams									CLE A (82G – .331)			CHI A (46G – .265)					
" total	128	461	142	20	14	5	1.1	63	81	52	23	16	.308	.445	4	2	OF-95, 1B-27
1916 CHI A	155	592	202	40	21	3	0.5	91	78	46	25	24	.341	.495	0	0	OF-155
1917	146	538	162	20	17	5	0.9	91	75	57	25	13	.301	.429	1	0	OF-145
1918	17	65	23	2	2	1	1.5	9	20	8	1	3	.354	.492	0	0	OF-17
1919	139	516	181	31	14	7	1.4	79	96	60	10	9	.351	.506	0	0	OF-139
1920	146	570	218	42	20	12	2.1	105	121	56	14	9	.382	.589	1	0	OF-145
13 yrs.	1330	4981	1774	307	168	54	1.1	873	785	519	158	202	.356 **3rd**	.518	11	4	OF-1289, 1B-27

WORLD SERIES

	G	AB	H	2B	3B	HR	HR %	R	RBI	BB	SO	SB	BA	SA	PH AB	PH H	G by POS
1917 CHI A	6	23	7	0	0	0	0.0	4	2	1	0	1	.304	.304	0	0	OF-6
1919	8	32	12	3	0	1	3.1	5	6	1	2	0	.375	.563	0	0	OF-8
2 yrs.	14	55	19	3	0	1	1.8	9	8	2	2	1	.345	.455	0	0	OF-14

Lou Jackson

JACKSON, LOUIS CLARENCE BL TR 5'10" 168 lbs.
B. July 26, 1935, Riverton, La.   D. May 27, 1969, Tokyo, Japan

	G	AB	H	2B	3B	HR	HR %	R	RBI	BB	SO	SB	BA	SA	PH AB	PH H	G by POS
1958 CHI N	24	35	6	2	1	1	2.9	5	6	1	9	0	.171	.371	14	1	OF-12
1959	6	4	1	0	0	0	0.0	2	1	0	2	0	.250	.250	4	1	
1964 BAL A	4	8	3	0	0	0	0.0	0	0	0	2	0	.375	.375	3	0	OF-1
3 yrs.	34	47	10	2	1	1	2.1	7	7	1	13	0	.213	.362	18	2	OF-13

Randy Jackson

JACKSON, RANSOM JOSEPH (Handsome Ransom) BR TR 6'1½" 180 lbs.
B. Feb. 10, 1926, Little Rock, Ark.

	G	AB	H	2B	3B	HR	HR %	R	RBI	BB	SO	SB	BA	SA	PH AB	PH H	G by POS
1950 CHI N	34	111	25	4	3	3	2.7	13	6	7	25	4	.225	.396	7	0	3B-27
1951	145	557	153	24	6	16	2.9	78	76	47	44	14	.275	.425	2	1	3B-143
1952	116	379	88	8	5	9	2.4	44	34	27	42	6	.232	.351	10	2	3B-104, OF-1
1953	139	498	142	22	8	19	3.8	61	66	42	61	8	.285	.476	7	0	3B-133
1954	126	484	132	17	6	19	3.9	77	67	44	55	2	.273	.450	2	0	3B-124
1955	138	499	132	13	7	21	4.2	73	70	58	58	0	.265	.445	3	1	3B-134
1956 BKN N	101	307	84	15	7	8	2.6	37	53	28	38	2	.274	.446	21	5	3B-80
1957	48	131	26	1	0	2	1.5	7	16	9	21	0	.198	.252	4	2	3B-34
1958 2 teams									LA N (35G – .185)			CLE A (29G – .242)					
" total	64	156	34	6	1	5	3.2	15	17	8	28	0	.218	.365	21	4	3B-41
1959 2 teams									CLE A (3G – .143)			CHI N (41G – .243)					
" total	44	81	19	5	1	1	1.2	7	10	11	11	0	.235	.358	16	1	3B-24, OF-1
10 yrs.	955	3203	835	115	44	103	3.2	412	415	281	382	36	.261	.421	93	16	3B-844, OF-2

WORLD SERIES

	G	AB	H	2B	3B	HR	HR %	R	RBI	BB	SO	SB	BA	SA	PH AB	PH H	G by POS
1956 BKN N	3	3	0	0	0	0	0.0	0	0	0	2	0	.000	.000	3	0	

	G	AB	H	2B	3B	HR	HR %	R	RBI	BB	SO	SB	BA	SA	Pinch Hit AB	Pinch Hit H	G by POS

JACKSON, REGINALD MARTINEZ (Mr. October)
B. May 18, 1946, Wyncote, Pa.

BL TL 6'   195 lbs.

Reggie Jackson

	G	AB	H	2B	3B	HR	HR %	R	RBI	BB	SO	SB	BA	SA	AB	H	G by POS
1967 KC A	35	118	21	4	4	1	0.8	13	6	10	46	1	.178	.305	2	0	OF-34
1968 OAK A	154	553	138	13	6	29	5.2	82	74	50	171	14	.250	.452	1	0	OF-151
1969	152	549	151	36	3	47	8.6	123	118	114	142	13	.275	.608	2	1	OF-150
1970	149	426	101	21	2	23	5.4	57	66	75	135	26	.237	.458	7	2	OF-142
1971	150	567	157	29	3	32	5.6	87	80	63	161	16	.277	.508	5	1	OF-145
1972	135	499	132	25	2	25	5.0	72	75	59	125	9	.265	.473	0	0	OF-135
1973	151	539	158	28	2	32	5.9	99	117	76	111	22	.293	.531	4	0	OF-145, DH-3
1974	148	506	146	25	1	29	5.7	90	93	86	105	25	.289	.514	3	0	OF-127, DH-19
1975	157	593	150	39	3	36	6.1	91	104	67	133	17	.253	.511	1	0	OF-147, DH-9
1976 BAL A	134	498	138	27	2	27	5.4	84	91	54	108	28	.277	.502	1	0	OF-121, DH-11
1977 NY A	146	525	150	39	2	32	6.1	93	110	74	129	17	.286	.550	3	1	OF-127, DH-18
1978	139	511	140	13	5	27	5.3	82	97	58	133	14	.274	.477	1	1	OF-104, DH-35
1979	131	465	138	24	2	29	6.2	78	89	65	107	9	.297	.544	3	1	OF-125, DH-11
1980	143	514	154	22	4	41	8.0	94	111	83	122	1	.300	.597	3	1	OF-61, DH-33
1981	94	334	79	17	1	15	4.5	33	54	46	82	0	.237	.428	5	1	OF-63
1982 CAL A	153	530	146	17	1	39	7.4	92	101	85	156	4	.275	.532	11	6	OF-139, DH-5
1983	116	397	77	14	1	14	3.5	43	49	52	140	0	.194	.340	10	2	DH-62, OF-47
1984	143	525	117	17	2	25	4.8	67	81	55	141	8	.223	.406	7	1	DH-134, OF-3
18 yrs.	2430	8649	2293	410	46	503	5.8	1380	1516	1172	2247	224	.265	.498	66	18	OF-1997, DH-386
																1st	

DIVISIONAL PLAYOFF SERIES

	G	AB	H	2B	3B	HR	HR %	R	RBI	BB	SO	SB	BA	SA	AB	H	G by POS
1981 NY A	5	20	6	0	0	2	10.0	4	4	1	5	0	.300	.600	0	0	OF-5

LEAGUE CHAMPIONSHIP SERIES

	G	AB	H	2B	3B	HR	HR %	R	RBI	BB	SO	SB	BA	SA	AB	H	G by POS
1971 OAK A	3	12	4	1	0	2	16.7	2	2	0	1	0	.333	.917	0	0	OF-3
1972	5	18	5	1	0	0	0.0	1	2	1	6	2	.278	.333	0	0	OF-5
1973	5	21	3	0	0	0	0.0	0	0	0	6	0	.143	.143	0	0	OF-5
1974	4	12	2	1	0	0	0.0	0	1	5	2	0	.167	.250	0	0	OF-1
1975	3	12	5	0	0	1	8.3	1	3	0	2	1	.417	.667	0	0	OF-3
1977 NY A	5	16	2	0	0	0	0.0	1	1	2	2	1	.125	.125	1	1	OF-4
1978	4	13	6	1	0	2	15.4	5	6	3	4	0	.462	1.000	0	0	OF-3
1980	3	11	3	1	0	0	0.0	0	0	1	4	0	.273	.364	0	0	OF-2
1981	2	4	0	0	0	0	0.0	1	1	1	0	0	.000	.000	0	0	OF-2
1982 CAL A	5	18	2	0	0	1	5.6	2	2	2	7	0	.111	.278	0	0	OF-5
10 yrs.	39	137	32	5	0	6	4.4	14	18	15	34	4	.234	.401	1	1	OF-32

WORLD SERIES

	G	AB	H	2B	3B	HR	HR %	R	RBI	BB	SO	SB	BA	SA	AB	H	G by POS
1973 OAK A	7	29	9	3	1	1	3.4	3	6	2	7	0	.310	.586	0	0	OF-7
1974	5	14	4	1	0	1	7.1	3	1	5	3	0	.286	.571	0	0	OF-5
1977 NY A	6	20	9	1	0	5	25.0	10	8	3	4	0	.450	1.250	0	0	OF-6
1978	6	23	9	1	0	2	8.7	2	8	3	7	0	.391	.696	0	0	DH-6
1981	3	12	4	1	0	1	8.3	3	1	2	3	1	.333	.667	0	0	OF-3
5 yrs.	27	98	35	7	1	10	10.2	21	24	15	24	1	.357	.755	0	0	OF-21, DH-6
				8th		5th		2nd	10th	8th			8th	1st			

JACKSON, RONALD HARRIS
B. Oct. 22, 1933, Kalamazoo, Mich.

BR TR 6'7"   225 lbs.

Ron Jackson

	G	AB	H	2B	3B	HR	HR %	R	RBI	BB	SO	SB	BA	SA	AB	H	G by POS
1954 CHI A	40	93	26	4	0	4	4.3	10	10	6	20	2	.280	.452	7	1	1B-35
1955	40	74	15	1	1	2	2.7	10	7	8	22	1	.203	.324	7	4	1B-29
1956	22	56	12	3	0	1	1.8	7	4	10	13	1	.214	.321	3	0	1B-19
1957	13	60	19	3	0	2	3.3	4	8	1	12	0	.317	.467	22	4	1B-13
1958	61	146	34	4	0	7	4.8	19	21	18	46	2	.233	.404	22	4	1B-38
1959	10	14	3	1	0	1	7.1	3	2	1	0	0	.214	.500	1	0	1B-5
1960 BOS A	10	31	7	2	0	0	0.0	1	0	1	6	0	.226	.290	1	0	1B-9
7 yrs.	196	474	116	18	1	17	3.6	54	52	45	119	6	.245	.395	45	10	1B-148

JACKSON, RONNIE DAMIEN
B. May 9, 1953, Birmingham, Ala.

BR TR 6'   200 lbs.

Ron Jackson

	G	AB	H	2B	3B	HR	HR %	R	RBI	BB	SO	SB	BA	SA	AB	H	G by POS
1975 CAL A	13	39	9	2	0	0	0.0	2	2	2	10	1	.231	.282	1	0	OF-9, 3B-1, DH-1
1976	127	410	93	18	3	8	2.0	44	40	30	58	5	.227	.344	5	8	3B-114, 2B-7, DH-6, OF-4
1977	106	292	71	15	2	8	2.7	38	28	24	42	3	.243	.390	20	8	1B-43, 3B-30, DH-20, OF-3, SS-1
1978	105	387	115	18	6	6	1.6	49	57	16	31	2	.297	.421	5	1	1B-75, 3B-31, DH-1, OF-1
1979 MIN A	159	583	158	40	5	14	2.4	85	68	51	59	3	.271	.429	4	0	1B-157, OF-1, SS-1, 3B-1
1980	131	396	105	29	3	5	1.3	48	42	28	41	1	.265	.391	21	4	1B-119, OF-15, 3B-2, DH-1
1981 2 teams		MIN A (54G – .263)						DET A (31G – .284)									
" total	85	270	73	17	1	5	1.9	29	40	18	26	6	.270	.396	10	1	1B-65, OF-7, DH-6, 3B-3
1982 CAL A	53	142	47	6	0	2	1.4	15	19	10	12	0	.331	.415	8	4	1B-37, 3B-9
1983	102	348	80	16	1	8	2.3	41	39	27	33	2	.230	.351	12	2	3B-38, 1B-35, DH-16, OF-15
1984 2 teams		CAL A (33G – .165)						BAL A (12G – .286)									
" total	45	119	23	4	0	0	0.0	5	7	7	17	0	.193	.244	8	1	1B-21, 3B-19, OF-1
10 yrs.	926	2986	774	165	22	56	1.9	356	342	213	329	23	.259	.385	94	22	1B-552, 3B-250, OF-56, DH-51, 2B-7, SS-2

LEAGUE CHAMPIONSHIP SERIES

	G	AB	H	2B	3B	HR	HR %	R	RBI	BB	SO	SB	BA	SA	AB	H	G by POS
1982 CAL A	1	1	1	0	0	0	0.0	0	0	0	0	0	1.000	1.000	1	1	

JACKSON, ROLAND THOMAS
B. July 9, 1944, Washington, D. C.

BL TR 5'9"   150 lbs.

Sonny Jackson

	G	AB	H	2B	3B	HR	HR %	R	RBI	BB	SO	SB	BA	SA	AB	H	G by POS
1963 HOU N	1	3	0	0	0	0	0.0	0	0	0	1	0	.000	.000	0	0	SS-1
1964	9	23	8	1	0	0	0.0	3	1	2	3	1	.348	.391	1	0	SS-7
1965	10	23	3	0	0	0	0.0	1	1	1	1	1	.130	.130	0	0	SS-8, 3B-1
1966	150	596	174	16	5	3	0.5	80	25	42	53	49	.292	.334	0	0	SS-150
1967	129	520	123	18	3	0	0.0	67	25	36	45	22	.237	.283	2	0	SS-128
1968 ATL N	105	358	81	8	2	1	0.3	37	19	25	35	16	.226	.268	2	1	SS-99

	G	AB	H	2B	3B	HR	HR %	R	RBI	BB	SO	SB	BA	SA	Pinch Hit AB	H	G by POS

Sonny Jackson continued

	G	AB	H	2B	3B	HR	HR %	R	RBI	BB	SO	SB	BA	SA	PH AB	PH H	G by POS
1969	98	318	76	3	5	1	0.3	41	27	35	33	12	.239	.289	2	0	SS-97
1970	103	328	85	14	3	0	0.0	60	20	45	27	11	.259	.320	8	1	SS-87
1971	149	547	141	20	5	2	0.0	58	25	35	45	7	.258	.324	2	0	OF-145
1972	60	126	30	6	3	0	0.0	20	8	7	9	1	.238	.333	23	8	SS-17, OF-10, 3B-6
1973	117	206	43	5	2	0	0.0	29	12	22	13	6	.209	.252	27	8	OF-56, SS-36
1974	5	7	3	0	0	0	0.0	0	0	0	0	0	.429	.429	4	2	OF-1
12 yrs.	936	3055	767	81	28	7	0.2	396	162	250	265	126	.251	.303	72	20	SS-630, OF-212, 3B-7

LEAGUE CHAMPIONSHIP SERIES

	G	AB	H	2B	3B	HR	HR %	R	RBI	BB	SO	SB	BA	SA	PH AB	PH H	G by POS
1969 ATL N	1	0	0	0	0	0	0.0	0	0	0	0	0	–	–	0	0	SS-1

Travis Jackson

JACKSON, TRAVIS CALVIN (Stonewall)
B. Nov. 2, 1903, Waldo, Ark.
Hall of Fame 1982.   BR TR 5'10½" 160 lbs.

	G	AB	H	2B	3B	HR	HR %	R	RBI	BB	SO	SB	BA	SA	PH AB	PH H	G by POS
1922 NY N	3	8	0	0	0	0	0.0	1	0	0	2	0	.000	.000	0	0	SS-3
1923	96	327	90	12	7	4	1.2	45	37	22	40	3	.275	.391	4	2	SS-60, 3B-31, 2B-1
1924	151	596	180	26	8	11	1.8	81	76	21	56	6	.302	.428	0	0	SS-151
1925	112	411	117	15	2	9	2.2	51	59	24	43	8	.285	.397	2	0	SS-110
1926	111	385	126	24	8	8	2.1	64	51	20	26	2	.327	.494	2	1	SS-108, OF-1
1927	127	469	149	29	4	14	3.0	67	98	32	30	8	.318	.486	1	0	SS-124, 3B-2
1928	150	537	145	35	6	14	2.6	73	77	56	46	8	.270	.436	1	0	SS-149
1929	149	551	162	21	12	21	3.8	92	94	64	56	10	.294	.490	0	0	SS-149
1930	116	431	146	27	8	13	3.0	70	82	32	25	6	.339	.529	2	0	SS-115
1931	145	555	172	26	10	5	0.9	65	71	36	23	13	.310	.420	0	0	SS-145
1932	52	195	50	17	1	4	2.1	23	38	13	16	1	.256	.415	0	0	SS-52
1933	53	122	30	5	0	0	0.0	11	12	8	11	2	.246	.287	9	1	SS-21, 3B-21
1934	137	523	140	26	7	16	3.1	75	101	37	71	1	.268	.436	0	0	SS-130, 3B-9
1935	128	511	154	20	12	9	1.8	74	80	29	64	3	.301	.440	0	0	3B-128
1936	126	465	107	8	1	7	1.5	41	53	18	56	0	.230	.297	3	1	3B-116, SS-9
15 yrs.	1656	6086	1768	291	86	135	2.2	833	929	412	565	71	.291	.433	23	5	SS-1326, 3B-307, OF-1, 2B-1

WORLD SERIES

	G	AB	H	2B	3B	HR	HR %	R	RBI	BB	SO	SB	BA	SA	PH AB	PH H	G by POS
1923 NY N	1	1	0	0	0	0	0.0	0	0	0	0	0	.000	.000	1	0	
1924	7	27	2	0	0	0	0.0	3	1	1	4	1	.074	.074	0	0	SS-7
1933	5	18	4	1	0	0	0.0	3	2	1	3	0	.222	.278	0	0	3B-5
1936	6	21	4	0	0	0	0.0	1	1	1	3	0	.190	.190	0	0	3B-6
4 yrs.	19	67	10	1	0	0	0.0	7	4	3	10	1	.149	.164	1	0	3B-11, SS-7

Lamar Jacobs

JACOBS, LAMAR GARY (Jake)
B. June 9, 1937, Youngstown, Ohio   BR TR 6'   175 lbs.

	G	AB	H	2B	3B	HR	HR %	R	RBI	BB	SO	SB	BA	SA	PH AB	PH H	G by POS
1960 WAS A	6	2	0	0	0	0	0.0	0	0	0	0	0	.000	.000	2	0	
1961 MIN A	4	8	2	0	0	0	0.0	0	0	0	2	0	.250	.250	1	0	OF-3
2 yrs.	10	10	2	0	0	0	0.0	0	0	0	2	0	.200	.200	3	0	OF-3

Mike Jacobs

JACOBS, MORRIS ELMORE
B. 1877,   D. Mar. 21, 1949, Louisville, Ky.

	G	AB	H	2B	3B	HR	HR %	R	RBI	BB	SO	SB	BA	SA	PH AB	PH H	G by POS
1902 CHI N	5	19	4	0	0	0	0.0	1	2	0		0	.211	.211	0	0	SS-5

Otto Jacobs

JACOBS, OTTO ALBERT
B. Apr. 19, 1889, Chicago, Ill.   D. Nov. 19, 1955, Chicago, Ill.   BR TR 5'9"   180 lbs.

	G	AB	H	2B	3B	HR	HR %	R	RBI	BB	SO	SB	BA	SA	PH AB	PH H	G by POS
1918 CHI A	29	73	15	3	0	0	0.0	4	3	5	8	0	.205	.274	7	1	C-21

Ray Jacobs

JACOBS, RAYMOND F.
B. Jan. 2, 1902, Salt Lake City, Utah   D. Apr. 5, 1952, Los Angeles, Calif.   BR TR 6'   160 lbs.

	G	AB	H	2B	3B	HR	HR %	R	RBI	BB	SO	SB	BA	SA	PH AB	PH H	G by POS
1928 CHI N	2	2	0	0	0	0	0.0	0	0	0	1	0	.000	.000	2	0	

Spook Jacobs

JACOBS, FORREST VANDERGRIFT
B. Nov. 4, 1925, Cheswold, Del.   BR TR 5'8½" 155 lbs.

	G	AB	H	2B	3B	HR	HR %	R	RBI	BB	SO	SB	BA	SA	PH AB	PH H	G by POS
1954 PHI A	132	508	131	11	1	0	0.0	63	26	60	22	17	.258	.283	0	0	2B-131
1955 KC A	13	23	6	0	0	0	0.0	7	1	3	0	1	.261	.261	1	0	2B-7
1956 2 teams	KC A (32G – .216)				PIT N (11G – .162)												
" total	43	134	27	5	0	0	0.0	17	6	17	10	4	.201	.239	0	0	2B-42
3 yrs.	188	665	164	16	1	0	0.0	87	33	80	32	22	.247	.274	1	0	2B-180

Baby Doll Jacobson

JACOBSON, WILLIAM CHESTER
B. Aug. 16, 1890, Cable, Ill.   D. Jan. 16, 1977, Orion, Ill.   BR TR 6'3"   215 lbs.

	G	AB	H	2B	3B	HR	HR %	R	RBI	BB	SO	SB	BA	SA	PH AB	PH H	G by POS
1915 2 teams	DET A (37G – .215)				STL A (34G – .209)												
" total	71	180	38	12	3	2	1.1	18	13	15	40	3	.211	.344	22	5	OF-39, 1B-10
1917 STL A	148	529	131	23	7	4	0.8	53	55	31	67	10	.248	.340	6	1	OF-131, 1B-11
1919	120	455	147	31	8	4	0.9	70	51	24	47	9	.323	.453	5	2	OF-105, 1B-8
1920	154	609	216	34	14	9	1.5	97	122	46	37	11	.355	.501	0	0	OF-154, 1B-1
1921	151	599	211	38	14	5	0.8	90	90	42	30	8	.352	.487	0	0	OF-141, 1B-11
1922	145	555	176	22	16	9	1.6	88	102	46	36	19	.317	.463	1	0	OF-137, 1B-7
1923	147	592	183	29	6	8	1.4	76	81	29	27	6	.309	.419	1	0	OF-146
1924	152	579	184	41	12	19	3.3	103	97	35	45	6	.318	.528	0	0	OF-151
1925	142	540	184	30	9	15	2.8	103	76	46	26	4	.341	.513	2	1	OF-139
1926 2 teams	STL A (50G – .286)				BOS A (98G – .305)												
" total	148	576	172	51	2	8	1.4	62	90	31	36	5	.299	.436	1	0	OF-148
1927 3 teams	BOS A (45G – .245)				CLE A (32G – .252)			PHI A (17G – .229)									
" total	94	293	72	17	3	1	0.3	27	42	11	19	1	.246	.334	9	0	OF-84
11 yrs.	1472	5507	1714	328	94	84	1.5	787	819	355	410	86	.311	.451	46	9	OF-1375, 1B-48

Merwin Jacobson

JACOBSON, MERWIN JOHN WILLIAM (Jake)
B. Mar. 7, 1894, New Britain, Conn.   D. Jan. 13, 1978, Baltimore, Md.   BL TL 5'11½" 165 lbs.

	G	AB	H	2B	3B	HR	HR %	R	RBI	BB	SO	SB	BA	SA	PH AB	PH H	G by POS
1915 NY N	8	24	2	0	0	0	0.0	0	0	1	5	0	.083	.083	2	0	OF-5
1916 CHI N	4	13	3	0	0	0	0.0	2	0	1	4	2	.231	.231	0	0	OF-4

	G	AB	H	2B	3B	HR	HR %	R	RBI	BB	SO	SB	BA	SA	Pinch Hit AB	H	G by POS

Merwin Jacobson continued

	G	AB	H	2B	3B	HR	HR %	R	RBI	BB	SO	SB	BA	SA	AB	H	G by POS
1926 BKN N	110	288	71	9	2	0	0.0	41	23	36	24	5	.247	.292	17	5	OF-86
1927	11	6	0	0	0	0	0.0	4	1	0	1	0	.000	.000	5	0	OF-3
4 yrs.	133	331	76	9	2	0	0.0	47	24	38	34	7	.230	.269	24	5	OF-98

Brook Jacoby

BR TR 5'11" 175 lbs.

JACOBY, BROOK WALLACE
B. Nov. 23, 1959, Philadelphia, Pa.

	G	AB	H	2B	3B	HR	HR %	R	RBI	BB	SO	SB	BA	SA	AB	H	G by POS
1981 ATL N	11	10	2	0	0	0	0.0	0	1	0	3	0	.200	.200	8	2	3B-3
1983	4	8	0	0	0	0	0.0	0	0	0	1	0	.000	.000	2	0	3B-2
1984 CLE A	126	439	116	19	3	7	1.6	64	40	32	73	3	.264	.369	0	0	3B-126, SS-1
3 yrs.	141	457	118	19	3	7	1.5	64	41	32	77	3	.258	.359	10	2	3B-131, SS-1

Harry Jacoby

JACOBY, HARRY
B. Philadelphia, Pa.   Deceased.

	G	AB	H	2B	3B	HR	HR %	R	RBI	BB	SO	SB	BA	SA	AB	H	G by POS
1882 BAL AA	31	121	21	1	1	1	0.8	17		7			.174	.223	0	0	3B-19, OF-13
1885	11	43	6	2	0	0	0.0	4		2			.140	.186	0	0	2B-11
2 yrs.	42	164	27	3	1	1	0.6	21		9			.165	.213	0	0	3B-19, OF-13, 2B-11

Art Jahn

BR TR 6' 180 lbs.

JAHN, ARTHUR CHARLES
B. Dec. 5, 1895, Struble, Iowa   D. Jan. 9, 1948, Little Rock, Ark.

	G	AB	H	2B	3B	HR	HR %	R	RBI	BB	SO	SB	BA	SA	AB	H	G by POS
1925 CHI N	58	226	68	10	8	0	0.0	30	37	11	20	2	.301	.416	0	0	OF-58
1928 2 teams		NY	N (10G –	.276)		PHI	N (36G –	.223)									
" total	46	123	29	5	0	1	0.8	15	18	6	16	0	.236	.301	8	1	OF-39
2 yrs.	104	349	97	15	8	1	0.3	45	55	17	36	2	.278	.375	8	1	OF-97

Art James

BL TL 6' 170 lbs.

JAMES, ARTHUR, JR.
B. Aug. 2, 1952, Detroit, Mich.

	G	AB	H	2B	3B	HR	HR %	R	RBI	BB	SO	SB	BA	SA	AB	H	G by POS
1975 DET A	11	40	9	2	0	0	0.0	2	1	1	3	1	.225	.275	0	0	OF-11

Bernie James

BB TR 5'9½" 150 lbs.
BR 1929, BL 1930

JAMES, ROBERT BYRNE
B. Sept. 2, 1905, Angleton, Tex.

	G	AB	H	2B	3B	HR	HR %	R	RBI	BB	SO	SB	BA	SA	AB	H	G by POS
1929 BOS N	46	101	31	3	2	0	0.0	12	9	9	13	3	.307	.376	7	1	2B-32, OF-1
1930	8	11	2	1	0	0	0.0	1	1	0	1	0	.182	.273	1	0	2B-7
1933 NY N	60	125	28	2	1	1	0.8	22	10	8	12	5	.224	.280	5	2	2B-26, SS-6, 3B-5
3 yrs.	114	237	61	6	3	1	0.4	35	20	17	26	8	.257	.321	13	3	2B-65, SS-6, 3B-5, OF-1

Bob James

BL TR 5'11" 185 lbs.

JAMES, BURTON HULON
B. July 7, 1884, Coopertown, Tenn.   D. Jan. 2, 1959, Adairville, Ky.

	G	AB	H	2B	3B	HR	HR %	R	RBI	BB	SO	SB	BA	SA	AB	H	G by POS
1909 STL N	6	21	6	0	0	0	0.0	0	4			1	.286	.286	0	0	OF-6

Charlie James

BR TR 6'1" 195 lbs.

JAMES, CHARLES WESLEY
B. Dec. 22, 1937, St. Louis, Mo.

	G	AB	H	2B	3B	HR	HR %	R	RBI	BB	SO	SB	BA	SA	AB	H	G by POS
1960 STL N	43	50	9	1	0	2	4.0	5	5	1	12	0	.180	.320	9	1	OF-37
1961	108	349	89	19	2	4	1.1	43	44	15	59	2	.255	.355	19	3	OF-90
1962	129	388	107	13	4	8	2.1	50	59	10	58	3	.276	.392	12	4	OF-116
1963	116	347	93	14	2	10	2.9	34	45	10	64	2	.268	.406	18	10	OF-101
1964	88	233	52	9	1	5	2.1	24	17	11	58	0	.223	.335	31	8	OF-60
1965 CIN N	26	39	8	0	0	0	0.0	2	2	1	9	0	.205	.205	19	4	OF-7
6 yrs.	510	1406	358	56	9	29	2.1	158	172	48	260	7	.255	.369	108	30	OF-411
WORLD SERIES																	
1964 STL N	3	3	0	0	0	0	0.0	0	0	0	1	0	.000	.000	3	0	

Cleo James

BR TR 5'10" 176 lbs.

JAMES, CLEO JOEL
B. Aug. 31, 1940, Clarksdale, Mich.

	G	AB	H	2B	3B	HR	HR %	R	RBI	BB	SO	SB	BA	SA	AB	H	G by POS
1968 LA N	10	10	2	1	0	0	0.0	2	0	0	6	0	.200	.300	6	1	OF-2
1970 CHI N	100	176	37	7	2	3	1.7	33	14	17	24	5	.210	.324	6	0	OF-90
1971	54	150	43	7	0	2	1.3	25	13	10	16	6	.287	.373	3	1	OF-48, 3B-2
1973	44	45	5	0	0	0	0.0	9	0	1	6	5	.111	.111	10	1	OF-22
4 yrs.	208	381	87	15	2	5	1.3	69	27	28	52	16	.228	.318	25	3	OF-162, 3B-2

Dion James

BL TL 6'1" 170 lbs.

JAMES, DION
B. Nov. 9, 1962, Philadelphia, Pa.

	G	AB	H	2B	3B	HR	HR %	R	RBI	BB	SO	SB	BA	SA	AB	H	G by POS
1983 MIL A	11	20	2	0	0	0	0.0	1	1	2	2	1	.100	.100	0	0	OF-9, DH-2
1984	128	387	114	19	5	1	0.3	52	30	32	41	10	.295	.377	17	3	OF-118
2 yrs.	139	407	116	19	5	1	0.2	53	31	34	43	11	.285	.364	17	3	OF-127, DH-2

Skip James

BL TL 6' 185 lbs.

JAMES, PHILIP ROBERT
B. Oct. 21, 1949, Elmhurst, Ill.

	G	AB	H	2B	3B	HR	HR %	R	RBI	BB	SO	SB	BA	SA	AB	H	G by POS
1977 SF N	10	15	4	1	0	0	0.0	3	3	2	3	0	.267	.333	2	1	1B-9
1978	41	21	2	1	0	0	0.0	5	3	4	5	1	.095	.143	10	1	1B-27
2 yrs.	51	36	6	2	0	0	0.0	8	6	6	8	1	.167	.222	12	2	1B-36

Charlie Jamieson

BL TL 5'8½" 165 lbs.

JAMIESON, CHARLES DEVINE
B. Feb. 7, 1893, Paterson, N. J.   D. Oct. 27, 1969, Paterson, N. J.

	G	AB	H	2B	3B	HR	HR %	R	RBI	BB	SO	SB	BA	SA	AB	H	G by POS
1915 WAS A	17	68	19	3	2	0	0.0	9	7	6	9	0	.279	.382	0	0	OF-17
1916	64	145	36	4	0	0	0.0	16	13	18	18	5	.248	.276	13	4	OF-41, 1B-4, P-1
1917 2 teams		WAS	A (20G –	.171)		PHI	A (85G –	.265)									
" total	105	382	98	8	2	0	0.0	45	29	43	41	8	.257	.288	12	5	OF-92, P-1
1918 PHI A	110	416	84	11	2	0	0.0	50	11	54	30	11	.202	.238	4	1	OF-102, P-5
1919 CLE A	26	17	6	2	1	0	0.0	3	2	0	2	2	.353	.588	9	3	P-4, OF-3
1920	108	370	118	17	7	1	0.3	69	40	41	26	7	.319	.411	2	0	OF-98, 1B-4
1921	140	536	166	33	10	1	0.2	94	45	67	27	8	.310	.414	2	2	OF-137
1922	145	567	183	29	11	3	0.5	87	57	54	22	15	.323	.429	1	0	OF-144, P-2
1923	152	644	222	36	12	2	0.3	130	51	80	37	19	.345	.447	0	0	OF-152
1924	143	594	213	34	8	3	0.5	98	53	47	15	21	.359	.458	1	0	OF-139

	G	AB	H	2B	3B	HR	HR%	R	RBI	BB	SO	SB	BA	SA	Pinch Hit AB	Pinch Hit H	G by POS

Charlie Jamieson continued

	G	AB	H	2B	3B	HR	HR%	R	RBI	BB	SO	SB	BA	SA	AB	H	G by POS
1925	138	557	165	24	5	4	0.7	109	42	72	26	14	.296	.379	3	1	OF-135
1926	143	555	166	33	7	2	0.4	89	45	53	22	9	.299	.395	0	0	OF-143
1927	127	489	151	23	6	0	0.0	73	36	64	14	7	.309	.380	0	0	OF-127
1928	112	433	133	18	4	1	0.2	63	37	56	20	3	.307	.374	0	0	OF-111
1929	102	364	106	22	1	0	0.0	56	26	50	12	2	.291	.357	4	2	OF-93
1930	103	366	110	22	1	1	0.3	64	52	36	20	5	.301	.374	6	1	OF-95
1931	28	43	13	2	1	0	0.0	7	4	5	1	1	.302	.395	19	6	OF-7
1932	16	16	1	1	0	0	0.0	0	2	3	0	.063	.125	11	0	OF-2
18 yrs.	1779	6562	1990	322	80	18	0.3	1062	550	748	345	132	.303	.385	87	25	OF-1638, P-13, 1B-8

WORLD SERIES

	G	AB	H	2B	3B	HR	HR%	R	RBI	BB	SO	SB	BA	SA	AB	H	G by POS
1920 CLE A	6	15	5	1	0	0	0.0	2	1	1	0	1	.333	.400	1	0	OF-5

Vic Janowicz

JANOWICZ, VICTOR FELIX
B. Feb. 26, 1930, Elyria, Ohio   BR TR 5'9" 185 lbs.

	G	AB	H	2B	3B	HR	HR%	R	RBI	BB	SO	SB	BA	SA	AB	H	G by POS
1953 PIT N	42	123	31	3	1	2	1.6	10	8	5	31	0	.252	.341	5	1	C-35
1954	41	73	11	3	0	0	0.0	10	2	7	24	0	.151	.192	11	2	3B-18, OF-1
2 yrs.	83	196	42	6	1	2	1.0	20	10	12	55	0	.214	.286	16	3	C-35, 3B-18, OF-1

Ray Jansen

JANSEN, RAYMOND WILLIAM
B. Jan. 16, 1889, St. Louis, Mo.   D. Mar. 19, 1934, St. Louis, Mo.   BR TR 5'11" 155 lbs.

	G	AB	H	2B	3B	HR	HR%	R	RBI	BB	SO	SB	BA	SA	AB	H	G by POS
1910 STL A	1	5	4	0	0	0	0.0	0	0	0		0	.800	.800	0	0	3B-1

Heinie Jantzen

JANTZEN, WALTER C.
B. Apr. 9, 1890, Chicago, Ill.   D. Apr. 1, 1948, Hines, Ill.   BR TR 5'11½" 170 lbs.

	G	AB	H	2B	3B	HR	HR%	R	RBI	BB	SO	SB	BA	SA	AB	H	G by POS
1912 STL A	31	119	22	0	1	1	0.8	10	8	4		3	.185	.227	0	0	OF-31

Hal Janvrin

JANVRIN, HAROLD CHANDLER (Childe Harold)
B. Aug. 27, 1892, Haverhill, Mass.   D. Mar. 2, 1962, Boston, Mass.   BR TR 5'11½" 168 lbs.

	G	AB	H	2B	3B	HR	HR%	R	RBI	BB	SO	SB	BA	SA	AB	H	G by POS
1911 BOS A	9	27	4	1	0	0	0.0	2	1	3		0	.148	.185	0	0	3B-5, 1B-4
1913	86	276	57	5	1	3	1.1	18	25	23	27	17	.207	.264	5	0	SS-48, 3B-19, 2B-8, 1B-6
1914	143	492	117	18	6	1	0.2	65	51	38	50	29	.238	.305	0	0	2B-57, 1B-56, SS-20, 3B-6
1915	99	316	85	9	4	0	0.0	41	37	14	27	8	.269	.304	3	1	SS-64, 3B-20, 2B-8
1916	117	310	69	11	4	0	0.0	32	26	32	32	6	.223	.284	7	1	SS-59, 2B-39, 1B-4, 3B-3
1917	55	127	25	3	0	0	0.0	21	8	11	13	2	.197	.220	4	1	2B-38, SS-10, 1B-1
1919 2 teams		WAS	A	(61G –	.178)			STL	N	(7G –	.214)						
" total	68	222	40	5	1	0	0.5	18	14	21	19	8	.180	.225	3	1	2B-58, SS-3, 3B-1
1920 STL N	87	270	74	8	4	1	0.4	33	28	17	19	5	.274	.344	4	1	SS-27, 1B-25, OF-20, 2B-6
1921 2 teams		STL	N	(18G –	.281)			BKN	N	(44G –	.196)						
" total	62	124	27	5	0	0	0.0	13	19	8	6	4	.218	.258	8	1	SS-17, 2B-11, 1B-8, 3B-5, OF-1
1922 BKN N	30	57	17	3	1	0	0.0	7	1	4		0	.298	.386	5	2	2B-15, SS-4, 3B-2, OF-1, 1B-1
10 yrs.	756	2221	515	68	18	6	0.3	250	210	171	197	79	.232	.287	39	8	SS-252, 2B-240, 1B-105, 3B-61, OF-22

WORLD SERIES

	G	AB	H	2B	3B	HR	HR%	R	RBI	BB	SO	SB	BA	SA	AB	H	G by POS
1915 BOS A	1	1	0	0	0	0	0.0	0	0	0	0	0	.000	.000	0	0	SS-1
1916	5	23	5	3	0	0	0.0	2	1	0	6	0	.217	.348	0	0	2B-5
2 yrs.	6	24	5	3	0	0	0.0	2	1	0	6	0	.208	.333	0	0	2B-5, SS-1

Roy Jarvis

JARVIS, LeROY GILBERT
B. June 7, 1926, Shawnee, Okla.   BR TR 5'9" 160 lbs.

	G	AB	H	2B	3B	HR	HR%	R	RBI	BB	SO	SB	BA	SA	AB	H	G by POS
1944 BKN N	1	1	0	0	0	0	0.0	0	0	0	0	0	.000	.000	0	0	C-1
1946 PIT N	2	4	1	0	0	0	0.0	0	0	1	1	0	.250	.250	1	0	C-1
1947	18	45	7	1	0	1	2.2	4	4	6	5	0	.156	.244	2	0	C-15
3 yrs.	21	50	8	1	0	1	2.0	4	4	7	7	0	.160	.240	3	0	C-17

Paul Jata

JATA, PAUL
B. Sept. 4, 1949, Astoria, N. Y.   BR TR 6'1" 190 lbs.

	G	AB	H	2B	3B	HR	HR%	R	RBI	BB	SO	SB	BA	SA	AB	H	G by POS
1972 DET A	32	74	17	2	0	0	0.0	8	3	7	14	0	.230	.257	12	4	1B-12, OF-10, C-1

Alfredo Javier

JAVIER, IGNACIO ALFREDO
B. Feb. 1, 1954, San Pedro, Venezuela   BR TR 5'11" 170 lbs.

	G	AB	H	2B	3B	HR	HR%	R	RBI	BB	SO	SB	BA	SA	AB	H	G by POS
1976 HOU N	8	24	5	0	0	0	0.0	1	0	2	5	0	.208	.208	1	0	OF-7

Julian Javier

JAVIER, MANUEL JULIAN LIRANZO (Hoolie, The Phantom)   BR TR 6'1" 175 lbs.
Father of Stan Javier.
B. Aug. 9, 1936, San Francisco De Macoris, Dominican Republic

	G	AB	H	2B	3B	HR	HR%	R	RBI	BB	SO	SB	BA	SA	AB	H	G by POS
1960 STL N	119	451	107	19	8	4	0.9	55	21	21	72	19	.237	.341	0	0	2B-119
1961	113	445	124	14	3	2	0.4	58	41	30	51	11	.279	.337	0	0	2B-113
1962	155	598	157	25	5	7	1.2	97	39	47	73	26	.263	.356	0	0	2B-151, SS-4
1963	161	609	160	27	9	9	1.5	82	46	24	86	18	.263	.381	0	0	2B-161
1964	155	535	129	19	5	12	2.2	66	65	30	82	9	.241	.363	0	0	2B-154
1965	77	229	52	6	4	2	0.9	34	23	8	44	5	.227	.314	0	0	2B-69
1966	147	460	105	13	5	7	1.5	52	31	26	63	11	.228	.324	0	0	2B-145
1967	140	520	146	16	3	14	2.7	68	64	25	92	6	.281	.404	2	0	2B-138
1968	139	519	135	25	4	4	0.8	54	52	24	61	10	.260	.347	0	0	2B-139
1969	143	493	139	28	2	10	2.0	59	42	40	74	8	.282	.408	4	1	2B-141
1970	139	513	129	16	3	0	0.4	62	42	24	70	6	.251	.306	3	2	2B-139
1971	90	259	67	6	4	3	1.2	32	28	9	33	5	.259	.347	9	2	2B-80, 3B-1
1972 CIN N	44	91	19	2	0	2	2.2	3	12	6	11	1	.209	.297	20	4	3B-19, 2B-5, 1B-1
13 yrs.	1622	5722	1469	216	55	78	1.4	722	506	314	812	135	.257	.355	38	9	2B-1552, 3B-20, SS-4, 1B-1

WORLD SERIES

	G	AB	H	2B	3B	HR	HR%	R	RBI	BB	SO	SB	BA	SA	AB	H	G by POS
1964 STL N	1	0	0	0	0	0	–	1	0	0	0	0	–	–	0	0	2B-1

	G	AB	H	2B	3B	HR	HR %	R	RBI	BB	SO	SB	BA	SA	Pinch Hit AB	Pinch Hit H	G by POS

Julian Javier continued

	G	AB	H	2B	3B	HR	HR %	R	RBI	BB	SO	SB	BA	SA	AB	H	G by POS
1967	7	25	9	3	0	1	4.0	2	4	0	6	0	.360	.600	0	0	2B-7
1968	7	27	9	1	0	0	0.0	1	3	3	4	1	.333	.370	0	0	2B-7
1972 CIN N	4	2	0	0	0	0	0.0	0	0	0	0	0	.000	.000	2	0	
4 yrs.	19	54	18	4	0	1	1.9	4	7	3	10	1	.333	.463	2	0	2B-15

Stan Javier

JAVIER, STANLEY JULIAN   BB TR 6'   180 lbs.
Son of Julian Javier.
B. Sept. 1, 1965, San Francisco Macoris, Dominican Republic

	G	AB	H	2B	3B	HR	HR %	R	RBI	BB	SO	SB	BA	SA	AB	H	G by POS
1984 NY A	7	7	1	0	0	0	0.0	1	0	0	1	0	.143	.143	0	0	OF-5

Tex Jeanes

JEANES, ERNEST LEE   BR TR 6'   176 lbs.
B. Dec. 19, 1900, Maypearl, Tex.   D. Apr. 5, 1973, Longview, Tex.

	G	AB	H	2B	3B	HR	HR %	R	RBI	BB	SO	SB	BA	SA	AB	H	G by POS
1921 CLE A	4	2	1	0	0	0	0.0	2	2	1	0	0	.500	.500	0	0	OF-4
1922	1	1	0	0	0	0	0.0	0	0	1	0	0	.000	.000	0	0	OF-1, P-1
1925 WAS A	15	19	5	1	0	1	5.3	2	4	3	2	1	.263	.474	2	1	OF-13
1926	21	30	7	2	0	0	0.0	6	3	0	3	0	.233	.300	7	2	OF-14
1927 NY N	11	20	6	0	0	0	0.0	5	0	2	2	0	.300	.300	3	1	OF-6, P-1
5 yrs.	52	72	19	3	0	1	1.4	15	9	7	7	1	.264	.347	12	4	OF-38, P-2

Hal Jeffcoat

JEFFCOAT, HAROLD BENTLEY   BR TR 5'10½" 185 lbs.
Brother of George Jeffcoat.
B. Sept. 6, 1924, West Columbia, S. C.

	G	AB	H	2B	3B	HR	HR %	R	RBI	BB	SO	SB	BA	SA	AB	H	G by POS
1948 CHI N	134	473	132	16	4	4	0.8	53	42	24	68	8	.279	.355	14	6	OF-119
1949	108	363	89	18	6	2	0.6	43	26	20	48	12	.245	.344	5	2	OF-101
1950	66	179	42	13	1	2	1.1	21	18	6	23	7	.235	.352	8	1	OF-53
1951	113	278	76	20	2	4	1.4	44	27	16	23	8	.273	.403	9	3	OF-87
1952	102	297	65	17	2	4	1.3	29	30	15	40	7	.219	.330	1	0	OF-95
1953	106	183	43	3	1	4	2.2	22	22	21	26	5	.235	.328	2	0	OF-100
1954	56	31	8	2	1	1	3.2	13	6	1	7	2	.258	.484	0	0	P-43, OF-3
1955	52	23	4	0	0	1	4.3	3	1	2	9	0	.174	.304	0	0	P-50
1956 CIN N	49	54	8	2	0	0	0.0	5	5	3	20	0	.148	.185	0	0	P-38
1957	53	69	14	3	1	4	5.8	13	11	5	20	0	.203	.449	0	0	P-37
1958	50	9	5	0	0	0	0.0	2	0	1	2	0	.556	.556	0	0	P-49, OF-1
1959 2 teams			CIN	N (17G – 1.000)				STL	N	(12G – .000)							
" total	29	4	1	1	0	0	0.0	1	0	0	3	0	.250	.500	0	0	P-28
12 yrs.	918	1963	487	95	18	26	1.3	249	188	114	289	49	.248	.355	39	12	OF-559, P-245

Irv Jeffries

JEFFRIES, IRVINE FRANKLIN   BR TR 5'10" 175 lbs.
B. Sept. 10, 1905, Louisville, Ky.   D. June 8, 1982, Louisville, Ky.

	G	AB	H	2B	3B	HR	HR %	R	RBI	BB	SO	SB	BA	SA	AB	H	G by POS
1930 CHI A	40	97	23	3	0	2	2.1	14	11	3	2	1	.237	.330	1	0	SS-13, 3B-10
1931	79	223	50	10	0	2	0.9	29	16	14	9	3	.224	.296	5	0	3B-61, 2B-6, SS-5
1934 PHI N	56	175	43	6	0	4	2.3	28	19	15	10	2	.246	.349	2	0	2B-52, 3B-1
3 yrs.	175	495	116	19	0	8	1.6	71	46	32	21	6	.234	.321	8	0	3B-72, 2B-58, SS-18

Frank Jelincich

JELINCICH, FRANK ANTHONY (Jelly)   BR TR 6'2" 198 lbs.
B. Sept. 3, 1919, San Jose, Calif.

	G	AB	H	2B	3B	HR	HR %	R	RBI	BB	SO	SB	BA	SA	AB	H	G by POS
1941 CHI N	4	8	1	0	0	0	0.0	0	2	1	2	0	.125	.125	2	0	OF-2

Steve Jeltz

JELTZ, LARRY STEVEN   BB TR 5'11" 175 lbs.
B. May 28, 1959, Paris, France

	G	AB	H	2B	3B	HR	HR %	R	RBI	BB	SO	SB	BA	SA	AB	H	G by POS
1983 PHI N	13	8	1	0	1	0	0.0	0	1	1	2	0	.125	.375	3	0	2B-4, SS-2, 3B-2
1984	28	68	14	0	1	1	1.5	7	7	7	11	2	.206	.279	0	0	SS-27, 3B-1
2 yrs.	41	76	15	0	2	1	1.3	7	8	8	13	2	.197	.289	3	0	SS-29, 2B-4, 3B-3

Joe Jenkins

JENKINS, JOSEPH DANIEL   BR TR 5'11" 170 lbs.
B. Oct. 12, 1890, Shelbyville, Tenn.   D. June 21, 1974, Fresno, Calif.

	G	AB	H	2B	3B	HR	HR %	R	RBI	BB	SO	SB	BA	SA	AB	H	G by POS
1914 STL A	19	32	4	1	1	0	0.0	0	0	1	11	2	.125	.219	9	1	C-9
1917 CHI A	10	9	1	0	0	0	0.0	0	2	0	5	0	.111	.111	9	1	
1919	11	19	3	1	0	0	0.0	0	1	1	1	1	.158	.211	7	1	C-4
3 yrs.	40	60	8	2	1	0	0.0	0	3	2	17	3	.133	.200	25	3	C-13

John Jenkins

JENKINS, JOHN ROBERT   BR TR 5'8" 160 lbs.
B. July 7, 1896, Bosworth, Mo.   D. Aug. 3, 1968, Columbia, Mo.

	G	AB	H	2B	3B	HR	HR %	R	RBI	BB	SO	SB	BA	SA	AB	H	G by POS
1922 CHI A	5	3	0	0	0	0	0.0	0	0	1	0	2	.000	.000	1	0	SS-1, 2B-1

Tom Jenkins

JENKINS, THOMAS GRIFFIN (Tut)   BL TR 6'1½" 174 lbs.
B. Apr. 10, 1898, Camden, Ala.   D. May 3, 1979, Weymouth, Mass.

	G	AB	H	2B	3B	HR	HR %	R	RBI	BB	SO	SB	BA	SA	AB	H	G by POS
1925 BOS A	15	64	19	2	1	0	0.0	9	5	3	4	0	.297	.359	0	0	OF-15
1926 2 teams			BOS	A (21G – .180)				PHI	A	(6G – .174)							
" total	27	73	13	3	1	0	0.0	6	6	3	9	0	.178	.247	8	2	OF-19
1929 STL A	21	22	4	0	1	0	0.0	1	0	4	8	0	.182	.273	15	2	OF-3
1930	2	8	2	1	1	0	0.0	3	0	1	0	0	.250	.625	0	0	OF-2
1931	81	230	61	7	2	3	1.3	20	25	17	25	1	.265	.352	23	7	OF-58
1932	25	62	20	1	0	0	0.0	5	5	1	6	0	.323	.339	13	5	OF-12
6 yrs.	171	459	119	14	6	3	0.7	42	44	28	53	1	.259	.336	59	16	OF-109

Alamazoo Jennings

JENNINGS, ALFRED
B. 1851, Newport, Ky.   D. Nov. 2, 1894, Cincinnati, Ohio

	G	AB	H	2B	3B	HR	HR %	R	RBI	BB	SO	SB	BA	SA	AB	H	G by POS
1878 MIL N	1	2	0	0	0	0	0.0	0	0	1	0		.000	.000	0	0	C-1

Bill Jennings

JENNINGS, WILLIAM MORLEY   BR TR 6'2" 175 lbs.
B. Sept. 28, 1925, St. Louis, Mo.

	G	AB	H	2B	3B	HR	HR %	R	RBI	BB	SO	SB	BA	SA	AB	H	G by POS
1951 STL A	64	195	35	10	2	0	0.0	20	13	26	42	1	.179	.251	0	0	SS-64

	G	AB	H	2B	3B	HR	HR %	R	RBI	BB	SO	SB	BA	SA	Pinch Hit AB	H	G by POS

Hughie Jennings

JENNINGS, HUGH AMBROSE (Ee-Yah)
B. Apr. 2, 1869, Pittston, Pa.   D. Feb. 1, 1928, Scranton, Pa.
Manager 1907-20.
Hall of Fame 1945.
BR TR 5'8½" 165 lbs.

Year	G	AB	H	2B	3B	HR	HR %	R	RBI	BB	SO	SB	BA	SA	PH AB	H	G by POS
1891 LOU AA	90	360	105	10	8	1	0.3	53	58	17	36	12	.292	.372	0	0	SS-70, 1B-17, 3B-3
1892 LOU N	152	594	132	16	4	2	0.3	65	61	30	30	28	.222	.273	0	0	SS-152
1893 2 teams			LOU N (23G – .136)			BAL N (16G – .255)											
" total	39	143	26	3	0	1	0.7	12	15	7	6	0	.182	.224	0	0	SS-38, OF-1
1894 BAL N	128	501	168	28	16	4	0.8	134	109	37	17	37	.335	.479	0	0	SS-128
1895	131	529	204	41	7	4	0.8	159	125	24	17	53	.386	.512	0	0	SS-131
1896	130	523	208	27	9	0	0.0	125	121	19	11	70	.398	.484	0	0	SS-130
1897	117	439	156	26	9	2	0.5	133	79	42		60	.355	.469	1	0	SS-116
1898	143	534	175	25	11	1	0.2	135	87	78		28	.328	.421	0	0	SS-115, 2B-27, OF-1
1899 2 teams			BAL N (2G – .375)			BKN N (67G – .296)											
" total	69	224	67	3	12	0	0.0	44	42	22		18	.299	.420	1	1	1B-50, SS-12, 2B-3
1900 BKN N	115	441	120	18	6	1	0.2	61	69	31		31	.272	.347	1	1	1B-112, 2B-2
1901 PHI N	82	302	83	21	2	1	0.3	38	39	25		13	.275	.368	0	0	1B-80, SS-1, 2B-1
1902	78	289	80	16	3	1	0.3	31	32	14		8	.277	.363	0	0	1B-69, SS-5, 2B-4
1903 BKN N	6	17	4	0	0	0	0.0	2	1	1		1	.235	.235	2	0	OF-4
1907 DET A	1	4	1	1	0	0	0.0	0	0	0		0	.250	.500	0	0	SS-1, 1B-1
1909	2	4	2	1	0	0	0.0	1	2	0		0	.500	.500	0	0	1B-2
1912	1	1	0	0	0	0	0.0	0	0	0		0	.000	.000	1	0	
1918	1	0	0	0	0	0	–	0	0	0	0	0	–	–	0	0	1B-1
17 yrs.	1285	4905	1531	235	87	18	0.4	993	840	347	117	359	.312	.407	6	2	SS-899, 1B-331, 2B-38, OF-6, 3B-3

Jackie Jensen

JENSEN, JACK EUGENE
B. Mar. 9, 1927, San Francisco, Calif.   D. July 14, 1982, Charlottesville, Va.
BR TR 5'11" 190 lbs.

Year	G	AB	H	2B	3B	HR	HR %	R	RBI	BB	SO	SB	BA	SA	PH AB	H	G by POS
1950 NY A	45	70	12	2	2	1	1.4	13	5	7	8	4	.171	.300	6	1	OF-23
1951	56	168	50	8	1	8	4.8	30	25	18	18	8	.298	.500	6	1	OF-48
1952 2 teams	151		NY A (7G – .105)			WAS A (144G – .286)											
" total	151	589	165	30	6	10	1.7	83	82	67	44	18	.280	.402	3	1	OF-148
1953 WAS A	147	552	147	32	8	10	1.8	87	84	73	51	18	.266	.408	1	0	OF-146
1954 BOS A	152	580	160	25	7	25	4.3	92	117	79	52	22	.276	.472	1	0	OF-151
1955	152	574	158	27	6	26	4.5	95	116	89	63	16	.275	.479	0	0	OF-150
1956	151	578	182	23	11	20	3.5	80	97	89	43	11	.315	.497	0	0	OF-151
1957	145	544	153	29	2	23	4.2	82	103	75	66	8	.281	.469	1	1	OF-144
1958	154	548	157	31	0	35	6.4	83	122	99	65	9	.286	.535	1	0	OF-153
1959	148	535	148	31	0	28	5.2	101	112	88	67	20	.277	.492	2	0	OF-146
1961	137	498	131	21	2	13	2.6	64	66	66	69	9	.263	.392	6	0	OF-131
11 yrs.	1438	5236	1463	259	45	199	3.8	810	929	750	546	143	.279	.460	27	4	OF-1391

WORLD SERIES

Year	G	AB	H	2B	3B	HR	HR %	R	RBI	BB	SO	SB	BA	SA	PH AB	H	G by POS
1950 NY A	1	0	0	0	0	0	0.0	0	0	0	0	0	–	–	0	0	

Woody Jensen

JENSEN, FORREST DOCENUS
B. Aug. 11, 1907, Bremerton, Wash.
BL TL 5'10½" 160 lbs.

Year	G	AB	H	2B	3B	HR	HR %	R	RBI	BB	SO	SB	BA	SA	PH AB	H	G by POS
1931 PIT N	73	267	65	5	4	3	1.1	43	17	10	18	4	.243	.326	3	1	OF-67
1932	7	5	0	0	0	0	0.0	2	0	0	2	0	.000	.000	5	0	OF-1
1933	70	196	58	7	3	0	0.0	29	15	8	2	1	.296	.362	23	6	OF-40
1934	88	283	82	13	4	0	0.0	34	27	4	13	2	.290	.364	21	6	OF-66
1935	143	627	203	28	7	8	1.3	97	62	15	14	9	.324	.429	3	2	OF-143
1936	153	696	197	34	10	10	1.4	98	58	16	19	2	.283	.404	0	0	OF-153
1937	124	509	142	23	9	5	1.0	77	45	15	29	2	.279	.389	3	1	OF-120
1938	68	125	25	4	0	0	0.0	12	10	1	3	0	.200	.232	23	4	OF-38
1939	12	12	2	0	0	0	0.0	0	1	0	0	0	.167	.167	6	1	OF-3
9 yrs.	738	2720	774	114	37	26	1.0	392	235	69	100	20	.285	.382	87	21	OF-631

Dan Jessee

JESSEE, DANIEL EDWARD
B. Feb. 22, 1901, Olive Hill, Ky.   D. Apr. 30, 1970, Venice, Fla.
BL TR 5'10" 165 lbs.

Year	G	AB	H	2B	3B	HR	HR %	R	RBI	BB	SO	SB	BA	SA	PH AB	H	G by POS
1929 CLE A	1	0	0	0	0	0	–	0	0	0	0	0	–	–	0	0	

Garry Jestadt

JESTADT, GARRY ARTHUR
B. Mar. 19, 1947, Chicago, Ill.
BR TR 6'2" 188 lbs.

Year	G	AB	H	2B	3B	HR	HR %	R	RBI	BB	SO	SB	BA	SA	PH AB	H	G by POS
1969 MON N	6	6	0	0	0	0	0.0	1	1	0	0	0	.000	.000	4	0	SS-1
1971 2 teams			CHI N (3G – .000)			SD N (75G – .291)											
" total	78	192	55	13	0	0	0.0	17	13	11	24	1	.286	.354	4	1	3B-50, 2B-23, SS-1
1972 SD N	92	256	63	5	1	6	2.3	15	22	13	21	0	.246	.344	23	5	2B-48, 3B-25, SS-3
3 yrs.	176	454	118	18	1	6	1.3	33	36	24	45	1	.260	.344	31	6	3B-75, 2B-71, SS-5

John Jeter

JETER, JOHN
B. Oct. 24, 1944, Shreveport, La.
BR TR 6'1" 180 lbs.

Year	G	AB	H	2B	3B	HR	HR %	R	RBI	BB	SO	SB	BA	SA	PH AB	H	G by POS
1969 PIT N	28	29	9	1	1	1	3.4	7	6	3	15	1	.310	.517	3	1	OF-20
1970	85	126	30	3	2	2	1.6	27	12	13	34	9	.238	.341	17	5	OF-56
1971 SD N	18	75	24	4	0	1	1.3	8	3	2	16	2	.320	.413	1	0	OF-17
1972	110	326	72	4	3	7	2.1	25	21	18	92	11	.221	.316	20	5	OF-91
1973 CHI A	89	300	72	14	4	7	2.3	38	26	9	74	6	.240	.383	8	1	OF-72, DH-3
1974 CLE A	6	17	6	1	0	0	0.0	3	1	1	6	1	.353	.412	0	0	OF-6
6 yrs.	336	873	213	27	10	18	2.1	108	69	46	237	28	.244	.360	50	12	OF-262, DH-3

LEAGUE CHAMPIONSHIP SERIES

Year	G	AB	H	2B	3B	HR	HR %	R	RBI	BB	SO	SB	BA	SA	PH AB	H	G by POS
1970 PIT N	3	2	0	0	0	0	0.0	0	0	0	2	0	.000	.000	1	0	OF-1

Sam Jethroe

JETHROE, SAMUEL (Jet)
B. Jan. 20, 1922, East St. Louis, Ill.
BB TR 6'1" 178 lbs.

Year	G	AB	H	2B	3B	HR	HR %	R	RBI	BB	SO	SB	BA	SA	PH AB	H	G by POS
1950 BOS N	141	582	159	28	8	18	3.1	100	58	52	93	35	.273	.442	0	0	OF-141
1951	148	572	160	29	10	18	3.1	101	65	57	88	35	.280	.460	5	2	OF-140
1952	151	608	141	23	7	13	2.1	79	58	68	112	28	.232	.357	0	0	OF-151

	G	AB	H	2B	3B	HR	HR %	R	RBI	BB	SO	SB	BA	SA	Pinch Hit AB	Pinch Hit H	G by POS

Sam Jethroe continued

	G	AB	H	2B	3B	HR	HR%	R	RBI	BB	SO	SB	BA	SA	AB	H	G by POS
1954 PIT N	2	1	0	0	0	0	0.0	0	0	0	0	0	.000	.000	1	0	OF-1
4 yrs.	442	1763	460	80	25	49	2.8	280	181	177	293	98	.261	.418	6	2	OF-433

Elvio Jimenez

JIMENEZ, FELIX ELVIO
Brother of Manny Jimenez.
B. Jan. 6, 1940, San Pedro de Macoris, Dominican Republic

BR TR 5'9" 170 lbs.

	G	AB	H	2B	3B	HR	HR%	R	RBI	BB	SO	SB	BA	SA	AB	H	G by POS
1964 NY A	1	6	2	0	0	0	0.0	0	0	0	0	0	.333	.333	0	0	OF-1

Houston Jimenez

JIMENEZ, ALFONSO
Also known as Alfonso Gonzalez.
B. Oct. 30, 1957, Navojoa, Mexico

BR TR 5'7" 140 lbs.

	G	AB	H	2B	3B	HR	HR%	R	RBI	BB	SO	SB	BA	SA	AB	H	G by POS
1983 MIN A	36	86	15	5	1	0	0.0	5	9	4	11	0	.174	.256	0	0	SS-36
1984	108	298	60	11	1	0	0.0	28	19	15	34	0	.201	.245	0	0	SS-107
2 yrs.	144	384	75	16	2	0	0.0	33	28	19	45	0	.195	.247	0	0	SS-143

Manny Jimenez

JIMENEZ, MANUEL EMILIO
Brother of Elvio Jimenez.
B. Nov. 19, 1938, San Pedro de Macoris, Dominican Republic

BL TR 6'1" 185 lbs.

	G	AB	H	2B	3B	HR	HR%	R	RBI	BB	SO	SB	BA	SA	AB	H	G by POS
1962 KC A	139	479	144	24	2	11	2.3	48	69	31	34	0	.301	.428	17	7	OF-122
1963	60	157	44	9	0	0	0.0	12	15	16	14	0	.280	.338	15	2	OF-40
1964	95	204	46	7	0	12	5.9	19	38	15	24	0	.225	.436	41	9	OF-49
1966	13	35	4	0	1	0	0.0	1	1	6	4	0	.114	.171	2	0	OF-12
1967 PIT N	50	56	14	2	0	2	3.6	3	10	1	4	0	.250	.393	42	12	OF-6
1968	66	66	20	1	1	1	1.5	7	11	6	15	0	.303	.394	53	10	OF-5
1969 CHI N	6	6	1	0	0	0	0.0	0	0	0	2	0	.167	.167	6	1	
7 yrs.	429	1003	273	43	4	26	2.6	90	144	75	97	0	.272	.401	176	41	OF-234

Pete Johns

JOHNS, WILLIAM R.
B. Jan. 17, 1889, Cleveland, Ohio D. Aug. 9, 1964, Cleveland, Ohio

BR TR 5'10" 165 lbs.

	G	AB	H	2B	3B	HR	HR%	R	RBI	BB	SO	SB	BA	SA	AB	H	G by POS
1915 CHI A	28	100	21	2	1	0	0.0	7	11	8	11	2	.210	.250	0	0	3B-28
1918 STL A	46	89	16	1	1	0	0.0	5	11	4	6	0	.180	.213	20	2	1B-10, OF-4, SS-4, 3B-4, 2B-2
2 yrs.	74	189	37	3	2	0	0.0	12	22	12	17	2	.196	.233	20	2	3B-32, 1B-10, OF-4, SS-4, 2B-2

Abbie Johnson

JOHNSON, ALBERT J.
B. July 26, 1872, Chicago, Ill. D. May 2, 1924, Oak Forest, Ill.

	G	AB	H	2B	3B	HR	HR%	R	RBI	BB	SO	SB	BA	SA	AB	H	G by POS
1896 LOU N	25	87	20	2	1	0	0.0	10	14	4	6	0	.230	.276	0	0	2B-25
1897	48	161	39	6	1	0	0.0	16	23	13		2	.242	.292	2	0	2B-33, SS-12
2 yrs.	73	248	59	8	2	0	0.0	26	37	17	6	2	.238	.286	2	0	2B-58, SS-12

Alex Johnson

JOHNSON, ALEXANDER
B. Dec. 7, 1942, Helena, Ark.

BR TR 6' 205 lbs.

	G	AB	H	2B	3B	HR	HR%	R	RBI	BB	SO	SB	BA	SA	AB	H	G by POS
1964 PHI N	43	109	33	7	1	4	3.7	18	18	6	26	1	.303	.495	7	2	OF-35
1965	97	262	77	9	3	8	3.1	27	28	15	60	4	.294	.443	27	8	OF-82
1966 STL N	25	86	16	0	1	2	2.3	7	6	5	18	1	.186	.279	2	0	OF-22
1967	81	175	39	9	2	1	0.6	20	12	9	26	6	.223	.314	20	5	OF-57
1968 CIN N	149	603	188	32	6	2	0.3	79	58	26	71	16	.312	.395	9	1	OF-140
1969	139	523	165	18	4	17	3.3	86	88	25	69	11	.315	.463	9	3	OF-132
1970 CAL A	156	614	202	26	6	14	2.3	85	86	35	68	17	.329	.459	3	0	OF-156
1971	65	242	63	8	0	2	0.8	19	21	15	34	5	.260	.318	5	0	OF-61
1972 CLE A	108	356	85	10	1	8	2.2	31	37	22	40	6	.239	.340	10	0	OF-95
1973 TEX A	158	624	179	26	3	8	1.3	62	68	32	82	10	.287	.377	1	1	DH-116, OF-47
1974 2 teams		TEX A (114G – .291)				NY A (10G – .214)											
" total	124	481	138	15	3	5	1.0	60	43	28	62	20	.287	.362	6	0	OF-82, DH-36
1975 NY A	52	119	31	5	1	1	0.8	15	15	7	21	2	.261	.345	14	5	DH-28, OF-7
1976 DET A	125	429	115	15	2	6	1.4	41	45	19	49	14	.268	.354	16	5	OF-90, DH-19
13 yrs.	1322	4623	1331	180	33	78	1.7	550	525	244	626	113	.288	.392	126	30	OF-1006, DH-199

Bill Johnson

JOHNSON, WILLIAM LAWRENCE
B. Oct. 18, 1892, Chicago, Ill. D. Nov. 5, 1950, Los Angeles, Calif.

BL TR 5'11" 170 lbs.

	G	AB	H	2B	3B	HR	HR%	R	RBI	BB	SO	SB	BA	SA	AB	H	G by POS
1916 PHI A	4	15	4	1	0	0	0.0	1	1	0	4	0	.267	.333	0	0	OF-4
1917	48	109	19	2	1	1	0.9	7	8	8	14	4	.174	.257	16	2	OF-30
2 yrs.	52	124	23	3	1	1	0.8	8	9	8	18	4	.185	.266	16	2	OF-34

Bill Johnson

JOHNSON, WILLIAM T. (Sleepy Bill)
B. Chester, Pa. D. 1921

BL TL

	G	AB	H	2B	3B	HR	HR%	R	RBI	BB	SO	SB	BA	SA	AB	H	G by POS
1884 PHI U	1	4	0	0	0	0	0.0	0		0			.000	.000	0	0	OF-1
1887 IND N	11	42	8	0	0	0	0.0	3	3	0	6	5	.190	.190	0	0	OF-11
1890 B-B AA	24	95	28	2	3	0	0.0	15		7		8	.295	.379	0	0	OF-24
1891 BAL AA	129	480	130	13	14	2	0.4	101	79	89	55	32	.271	.369	0	0	OF-129
1892 BAL N	4	15	2	0	0	0	0.0	2	2	2	0	0	.133	.133	0	0	OF-4
5 yrs.	169	636	168	15	17	2	0.3	121	83	98	61	45	.264	.351	0	0	OF-169

Billy Johnson

JOHNSON, WILLIAM RUSSELL (Bull)
B. Aug. 30, 1918, Montclair, N. J.

BR TR 5'10" 180 lbs.

	G	AB	H	2B	3B	HR	HR%	R	RBI	BB	SO	SB	BA	SA	AB	H	G by POS
1943 NY A	155	592	166	24	6	5	0.8	70	94	53	30	3	.280	.367	0	0	3B-155
1946	85	296	77	14	5	4	1.4	51	35	31	42	1	.260	.382	10	1	3B-74
1947	132	494	141	19	8	10	2.0	67	95	44	43	1	.285	.417	0	0	3B-132
1948	127	446	131	20	6	12	2.7	59	64	41	30	0	.294	.446	8	2	3B-118
1949	113	329	82	11	3	8	2.4	48	56	48	44	1	.249	.374	13	6	3B-81, 1B-21, 2B-1
1950	108	327	85	16	2	6	1.8	44	40	42	30	1	.260	.376	4	1	3B-100, 1B-5
1951 2 teams		NY A (15G – .300)				STL N (124G – .262)											
" total	139	482	128	26	1	14	2.9	57	68	53	49	5	.266	.411	1	0	3B-137
1952 STL N	94	282	71	10	2	2	0.7	23	34	34	21	1	.252	.323	5	0	3B-89

	G	AB	H	2B	3B	HR	HR %	R	RBI	BB	SO	SB	BA	SA	Pinch Hit AB	Pinch Hit H	G by POS

Billy Johnson continued

	G	AB	H	2B	3B	HR	HR%	R	RBI	BB	SO	SB	BA	SA	AB	H	G by POS
1953	11	5	1	1	0	0	0.0	0	1	1	1	0	.200	.400	0	0	3B-11
9 yrs.	964	3253	882	141	33	61	1.9	419	487	347	290	13	.271	.391	41	10	3B-897, 1B-26, 2B-1

WORLD SERIES

	G	AB	H	2B	3B	HR	HR%	R	RBI	BB	SO	SB	BA	SA	AB	H	G by POS
1943 NY A	5	20	6	1	1	0	0.0	3	3	0	3	0	.300	.450	0	0	3B-5
1947	7	26	7	0	3	0	0.0	8	2	3	4	0	.269	.500	0	0	3B-7
1949	2	7	1	0	0	0	0.0	0	0	0	2	1	.143	.143	0	0	3B-2
1950	4	6	0	0	0	0	0.0	0	0	0	3	0	.000	.000	0	0	3B-4
4 yrs.	18	59	14	1	4	0	0.0	11	5	3	12	1	.237	.390	0	0	3B-18

1st

Bob Johnson

JOHNSON, ROBERT LEE (Indian Bob) BR TR 6' 180 lbs.
Brother of Roy Johnson.
B. Nov. 26, 1906, Pryor, Okla.   D. July 6, 1982, Tacoma, Wash.

	G	AB	H	2B	3B	HR	HR%	R	RBI	BB	SO	SB	BA	SA	AB	H	G by POS
1933 PHI A	142	535	155	44	4	21	3.9	103	93	85	74	8	.290	.505	0	0	OF-142
1934	141	547	168	26	6	34	6.2	111	92	58	60	12	.307	.563	1	0	OF-139
1935	147	582	174	29	5	28	4.8	103	109	78	76	2	.299	.510	0	0	OF-147
1936	153	566	165	29	14	25	4.4	91	121	88	71	6	.292	.525	0	0	OF-131, 2B-22, 1B-1
1937	138	477	146	32	6	25	5.2	91	108	98	65	9	.306	.556	3	0	OF-133, 2B-2
1938	152	563	176	27	9	30	5.3	114	113	87	73	9	.313	.552	0	0	OF-150, 2B-3, 3B-1
1939	150	544	184	30	9	23	4.2	115	114	99	59	15	.338	.553	0	0	OF-150, 2B-1
1940	138	512	137	25	4	31	6.1	93	103	83	64	8	.268	.514	2	0	OF-136
1941	149	552	152	30	8	22	4.0	98	107	95	75	6	.275	.478	0	0	OF-122, 1B-28
1942	149	550	160	35	7	13	2.4	78	80	82	61	3	.291	.451	0	0	OF-149
1943 WAS A	117	438	116	22	8	7	1.6	65	63	62	50	11	.265	.400	0	0	OF-88, 3B-19, 1B-10
1944 BOS A	144	525	170	40	8	17	3.2	106	106	95	67	2	.324	.528	2	0	OF-142
1945	143	529	148	27	7	12	2.3	71	74	63	56	5	.280	.425	3	1	OF-140
13 yrs.	1863	6920	2051	396	95	288	4.2	1239	1283	1073	851	96	.296	.506	11	1	OF-1769, 1B-39, 2B-28, 3B-20

Bob Johnson

JOHNSON, ROBERT WALLACE BR TR 5'10" 175 lbs.
B. Mar. 4, 1936, Omaha, Neb.

	G	AB	H	2B	3B	HR	HR%	R	RBI	BB	SO	SB	BA	SA	AB	H	G by POS
1960 KC A	76	146	30	4	0	1	0.7	12	9	19	23	2	.205	.253	5	0	SS-30, 2B-27, 3B-11
1961 WAS A	61	224	66	13	1	6	2.7	27	28	19	26	4	.295	.442	1	0	SS-57, 3B-2, 2B-2
1962	135	466	134	20	2	12	2.6	58	43	32	50	9	.288	.416	12	4	3B-72, SS-50, 2B-3, OF-1
1963 BAL A	82	254	75	10	0	8	3.1	34	32	18	35	5	.295	.429	14	6	2B-50, 1B-8, SS-7, 3B-5
1964	93	210	52	8	2	3	1.4	18	29	9	37	0	.248	.348	45	15	SS-18, 2B-15, 1B-15, OF-1, 3B-1
1965	87	273	66	13	2	5	1.8	36	27	15	34	1	.242	.359	15	1	1B-34, SS-23, 3B-13, 2B-5
1966	71	157	34	5	0	1	0.6	13	10	12	24	0	.217	.268	30	7	2B-20, 1B-17, 3B-3
1967 2 teams		BAL	A	(4G –	.333)			NY	N	(90G –	.348)						
" total	94	233	81	8	5	2.1	27	27	13	30	1	.348	.472	34	13	2B-39, 1B-23, SS-14, 3B-1
1968 2 teams		CIN	N	(16G –	.267)			ATL	N	(59G –	.262)						
" total	75	202	53	5	1	0	0.0	17	12	11	22	0	.262	.297	18	3	3B-48, 2B-4, SS-2, 1B-1
1969 2 teams		STL	N	(19G –	.207)			OAK	A	(51G –	.343)						
" total	70	96	29	1	0	2	2.1	6	11	5	8	0	.302	.375	50	14	1B-8, 3B-4, 2B-2
1970 OAK A	30	46	8	0	0	1	2.2	6	2	3	2	1	.174	.261	19	3	3B-6, SS-2, 1B-1
11 yrs.	874	2307	628	88	11	44	1.9	254	230	156	291	24	.272	.377	243	66	SS-203, 2B-167, 3B-166, 1B-107, OF-2

Bobby Johnson

JOHNSON, BOBBY EARL BR TR 6'3" 195 lbs.
B. July 31, 1959, Dallas, Tex.

	G	AB	H	2B	3B	HR	HR%	R	RBI	BB	SO	SB	BA	SA	AB	H	G by POS
1981 TEX A	6	18	5	0	0	2	11.1	2	4	1	3	0	.278	.611	0	0	C-5, 1B-1
1982	20	56	7	2	0	2	3.6	4	7	3	22	0	.125	.268	4	0	C-14, 1B-3
1983	72	175	37	6	1	5	2.9	18	16	16	55	3	.211	.343	0	0	C-62, 1B-10
3 yrs.	98	249	49	8	1	9	3.6	24	27	20	80	3	.197	.345	4	0	C-81, 1B-14

Charlie Johnson

JOHNSON, CHARLES CLEVELAND (Home Run) BL TL 5'9" 150 lbs.
B. Mar. 12, 1885, Slatington, Pa.   D. Aug. 28, 1940, Marcus Hook, Pa.

	G	AB	H	2B	3B	HR	HR%	R	RBI	BB	SO	SB	BA	SA	AB	H	G by POS
1908 PHI N	6	16	4	0	1	0	0.0	1		1		0	.250	.375	2	0	OF-4

Cliff Johnson

JOHNSON, CLIFFORD, JR. BR TR 6'4" 215 lbs.
B. July 22, 1947, San Antonio, Tex.

	G	AB	H	2B	3B	HR	HR%	R	RBI	BB	SO	SB	BA	SA	AB	H	G by POS
1972 HOU N	5	4	1	0	0	0	0.0	0	0	2	0	0	.250	.250	3	0	C-1
1973	7	20	6	2	0	2	10.0	6	6	1	7	0	.300	.700	2	0	1B-5
1974	83	171	39	4	1	10	5.8	26	29	33	45	0	.228	.439	38	13	C-28, 1B-21
1975	122	340	94	16	1	20	5.9	52	65	46	64	1	.276	.568	33	5	1B-47, C-41, OF-1
1976	108	318	72	21	2	10	3.1	36	49	62	59	0	.226	.399	9	2	C-66, OF-20, 1B-16
1977 2 teams		HOU	N	(51G –	.299)			NY	A	(56G –	.296)						
" total	107	286	85	16	0	22	7.7	46	54	43	53	0	.297	.584	22	8	OF-34, DH-25, 1B-21, C-15
1978 NY A	76	174	32	9	1	6	3.4	20	19	30	32	0	.184	.351	15	2	DH-39, C-22, 1B-1
1979 2 teams		NY	A	(28G –	.266)			CLE	A	(72G –	.271)						
" total	100	304	82	16	0	20	6.6	48	67	34	46	2	.270	.520	17	4	DH-82, C-5
1980 2 teams		CLE	A	(54G –	.230)			CHI	N	(68G –	.235)						
" total	122	370	86	11	1	16	4.3	53	62	54	65	0	.232	.397	23	4	1B-46, DH-45, OF-3, C-1
1981 OAK A	84	273	71	8	0	17	6.2	40	59	28	60	5	.260	.476	17	2	DH-68, 1B-9
1982	73	214	51	10	0	7	3.3	19	31	26	41	1	.238	.383	20	5	DH-48, 1B-11
1983 TOR A	142	407	108	23	1	22	5.4	59	76	67	69	0	.265	.489	24	4	DH-130, 1B-6
1984	127	359	109	23	1	16	4.5	51	61	50	62	0	.304	.507	34	11	DH-109, 1B-2
13 yrs.	1156	3240	836	159	8	168	5.2	456	578	476	603	9	.258	.468	257	60	DH-546, 1B-185, C-179, OF-58

DIVISIONAL PLAYOFF SERIES

	G	AB	H	2B	3B	HR	HR%	R	RBI	BB	SO	SB	BA	SA	AB	H	G by POS
1981 OAK A	2	7	2	1	0	0	0.0	0	0	0	1	0	.286	.429	0	0	DH-2

LEAGUE CHAMPIONSHIP SERIES

	G	AB	H	2B	3B	HR	HR%	R	RBI	BB	SO	SB	BA	SA	AB	H	G by POS
1977 NY A	5	15	6	2	0	1	6.7	2	2	1	2	0	.400	.733	1	0	DH-4
1978	1	1	0	0	0	0	0.0	0	0	0	0	0	.000	.000	1	0	

	G	AB	H	2B	3B	HR	HR %	R	RBI	BB	SO	SB	BA	SA	Pinch Hit AB	H	G by POS

Cliff Johnson continued

	G	AB	H	2B	3B	HR	HR %	R	RBI	BB	SO	SB	BA	SA	AB	H	G by POS
1981 OAK A	2	6	0	0	0	0	0.0	0	0	2	2	0	.000	.000	0	0	DH-2
3 yrs.	8	22	6	2	0	1	4.5	2	2	3	4	0	.273	.500	2	0	DH-6

WORLD SERIES

	G	AB	H	2B	3B	HR	HR %	R	RBI	BB	SO	SB	BA	SA	AB	H	G by POS
1977 NY A	2	1	0	0	0	0	0.0	0	0	0	0	0	.000	.000	1	0	C-1
1978	2	2	0	0	0	0	0.0	0	0	0	1	0	.000	.000	2	0	
2 yrs.	4	3	0	0	0	0	0.0	0	0	0	1	0	.000	.000	3	0	C-1

Darrell Johnson

JOHNSON, DARRELL DEAN   BR TR 6'1"   180 lbs.
B. Aug. 25, 1928, Horace, Neb.
Manager 1974-80, 1982.

	G	AB	H	2B	3B	HR	HR %	R	RBI	BB	SO	SB	BA	SA	AB	H	G by POS
1952 2 teams		STL A (29G – .282)			CHI A (22G – .108)												
" total	51	115	26	2	1	0	0.0	12	10	16	13	1	.226	.261	10	4	C-43
1957 NY A	21	46	10	1	0	1	2.2	4	8	3	10	0	.217	.304	1	0	C-20
1958	5	16	4	0	0	0	0.0	1	0	0	2	0	.250	.250	1	0	C-4
1960 STL N	8	2	0	0	0	0	0.0	0	0	1	0	0	.000	.000	0	0	C-8
1961 2 teams		PHI N (21G – .230)			CIN N (20G – .315)												
" total	41	115	31	3	0	1	0.9	7	9	4	10	0	.270	.322	0	0	C-41
1962 2 teams		CIN N (2G – .000)			BAL A (6G – .182)												
" total	8	26	4	0	0	0	0.0	0	1	2	4	0	.154	.154	0	0	C-8
6 yrs.	134	320	75	6	1	2	0.6	24	28	26	39	1	.234	.278	12	4	C-124

WORLD SERIES

	G	AB	H	2B	3B	HR	HR %	R	RBI	BB	SO	SB	BA	SA	AB	H	G by POS
1961 CIN N	2	4	2	0	0	0	0.0	0	0	0	0	0	.500	.500	0	0	C-2

Davy Johnson

JOHNSON, DAVID ALLEN   BR TR 6'1"   170 lbs.
B. Jan. 30, 1943, Orlando, Fla.
Manager 1984.

	G	AB	H	2B	3B	HR	HR %	R	RBI	BB	SO	SB	BA	SA	AB	H	G by POS
1965 BAL A	20	47	8	3	0	0	0.0	5	1	5	6	3	.170	.234	4	1	3B-9, 2B-3, SS-2
1966	131	501	129	20	3	7	1.4	47	56	31	64	3	.257	.351	2	0	2B-126, SS-3
1967	148	510	126	30	3	10	2.0	62	64	59	82	4	.247	.376	2	0	2B-144, 3B-3
1968	145	504	122	24	4	9	1.8	50	56	44	80	7	.242	.359	2	1	2B-127, SS-34
1969	142	511	143	34	1	7	1.4	52	57	57	52	3	.280	.391	0	0	2B-142, SS-2
1970	149	530	149	27	1	10	1.9	68	53	66	68	2	.281	.392	0	0	2B-149, SS-2
1971	142	510	144	26	1	18	3.5	67	72	51	55	3	.282	.443	1	0	2B-140
1972	118	376	83	22	3	5	1.3	31	32	52	68	1	.221	.335	2	1	2B-116
1973 ATL N	157	559	151	25	0	43	7.7	84	99	81	93	5	.270	.546	2	1	2B-155
1974	136	454	114	18	0	15	3.3	56	62	75	59	1	.251	.390	4	2	1B-73, 2B-71
1975	1	1	1	1	0	0	0.0	0	1	0	0	0	1.000	2.000	1	1	
1977 PHI N	78	156	50	9	1	8	5.1	23	36	23	20	1	.321	.545	26	9	1B-43, 2B-9, 3B-6
1978 2 teams		PHI N (44G – .191)			CHI N (24G – .306)												
" total	68	138	32	3	1	4	2.9	19	20	15	28	0	.232	.355	30	10	3B-21, 2B-15, 1B-7
13 yrs.	1435	4797	1252	242	18	136	2.8	564	609	559	675	33	.261	.404	76	26	2B-1197, 1B-123, SS-43, 3B-39

LEAGUE CHAMPIONSHIP SERIES

	G	AB	H	2B	3B	HR	HR %	R	RBI	BB	SO	SB	BA	SA	AB	H	G by POS
1969 BAL A	3	13	3	0	0	0	0.0	2	0	2	1	0	.231	.231	0	0	2B-3
1970	3	11	4	0	0	2	18.2	4	4	1	1	0	.364	.909	0	0	2B-3
1971	3	10	3	2	0	0	0.0	2	0	3	1	0	.300	.500	0	0	2B-3
1977 PHI N	1	4	1	0	0	0	0.0	0	2	0	1	0	.250	.250	0	0	1B-1
4 yrs.	10	38	11	2	0	2	5.3	8	6	6	4	0	.289	.500	0	0	2B-9, 1B-1

WORLD SERIES

	G	AB	H	2B	3B	HR	HR %	R	RBI	BB	SO	SB	BA	SA	AB	H	G by POS
1966 BAL A	4	14	4	1	0	0	0.0	1	1	0	1	0	.286	.357	0	0	2B-4
1969	5	16	1	0	0	0	0.0	0	0	2	1	0	.063	.063	0	0	2B-5
1970	5	16	5	2	0	0	0.0	2	2	5	2	0	.313	.438	0	0	2B-5
1971	7	27	4	0	0	0	0.0	1	3	0	1	0	.148	.148	0	0	2B-7
4 yrs.	21	73	14	3	0	0	0.0	5	6	7	5	0	.192	.233	0	0	2B-21

Deron Johnson

JOHNSON, DERON ROGER   BR TR 6'2"   200 lbs.
B. July 17, 1938, San Diego, Calif.

	G	AB	H	2B	3B	HR	HR %	R	RBI	BB	SO	SB	BA	SA	AB	H	G by POS
1960 NY A	6	4	2	1	0	0	0.0	0	0	0	0	0	.500	.750	1	0	3B-5
1961 2 teams		NY A (13G – .105)			KC A (83G – .216)												
" total	96	302	63	11	3	8	2.6	32	44	16	49	0	.209	.344	10	2	OF-59, 3B-27, 1B-3
1962 KC A	17	19	2	1	0	0	0.0	1	0	3	8	0	.105	.158	9	0	OF-2, 3B-2, 1B-2
1964 CIN N	140	477	130	24	4	21	4.4	63	79	37	98	4	.273	.472	13	5	1B-131, OF-10, 3B-1
1965	159	616	177	30	7	32	5.2	92	130	52	97	0	.287	.515	0	0	3B-159
1966	142	505	130	25	3	24	4.8	75	81	39	87	1	.257	.461	5	1	OF-106, 1B-71, 3B-18
1967	108	361	81	18	1	13	3.6	39	53	22	104	0	.224	.388	10	3	1B-81, 3B-24
1968 ATL N	127	342	71	11	1	8	2.3	29	33	35	79	0	.208	.316	13	3	1B-97, 3B-21
1969 PHI N	138	475	121	19	4	17	3.6	51	80	60	111	4	.255	.419	6	1	OF-72, 3B-50, 1B-18
1970	159	574	147	28	0	27	4.7	66	93	72	132	0	.256	.456	5	2	1B-154, 3B-3
1971	158	582	154	29	0	34	5.8	74	95	72	146	0	.265	.490	3	1	1B-136, 3B-22
1972	96	230	49	4	1	9	3.9	19	31	26	69	0	.213	.357	30	6	1B-62
1973 2 teams		PHI N (12G – .167)			OAK A (131G – .246)												
" total	143	500	120	16	2	20	4.0	64	86	64	126	0	.240	.400	3	0	DH-107, 1B-33
1974 3 teams		OAK A (50G – .195)			MIL A (49G – .151)			BOS A (11G – .120)									
" total	110	351	60	4	2	13	3.7	30	43	32	84	2	.171	.305	2	0	DH-77, 1B-30
1975 2 teams		CHI A (148G – .232)			BOS A (3G – .600)												
" total	151	565	135	25	1	19	3.4	68	75	50	117	0	.239	.388	3	2	DH-94, 1B-57
1976 BOS A	15	38	5	1	0	0	0.0	3	0	5	10	0	.132	.211	3	0	OF-5
16 yrs.	1765	5941	1447	247	33	245	4.1	706	923	585	1318	11	.244	.420	120	26	1B-875, 3B-332, DH-278, OF-254

LEAGUE CHAMPIONSHIP SERIES

	G	AB	H	2B	3B	HR	HR %	R	RBI	BB	SO	SB	BA	SA	AB	H	G by POS
1973 OAK A	4	10	1	0	0	0	0.0	0	0	0	0	0	.100	.100	0	0	DH-4

WORLD SERIES

	G	AB	H	2B	3B	HR	HR %	R	RBI	BB	SO	SB	BA	SA	AB	H	G by POS
1973 OAK A	6	10	3	1	0	0	0.0	0	0	1	4	0	.300	.400	3	2	1B-2

	G	AB	H	2B	3B	HR	HR %	R	RBI	BB	SO	SB	BA	SA	Pinch Hit AB	Pinch Hit H	G by POS

Dick Johnson

JOHNSON, RICHARD ALLAN (Footer, Treads)
B. Feb. 15, 1932, Dayton, Ohio
BL TL 5'11" 175 lbs.

	G	AB	H	2B	3B	HR	HR%	R	RBI	BB	SO	SB	BA	SA	AB	H	G by POS
1958 CHI N	8	5	0	0	0	0	0.0	1	0	0	1	0	.000	.000	5	0	

Don Johnson

JOHNSON, DONALD SPORE (Pep)
Son of Ernie Johnson.
B. Dec. 7, 1911, Chicago, Ill.
BR TR 6' 170 lbs.

	G	AB	H	2B	3B	HR	HR%	R	RBI	BB	SO	SB	BA	SA	AB	H	G by POS
1943 CHI N	10	42	8	2	0	0	0.0	5	1	2	4	0	.190	.238	0	0	2B-10
1944	154	608	169	37	1	2	0.3	50	71	28	48	8	.278	.352	0	0	2B-154
1945	138	557	168	23	2	2	0.4	94	58	32	34	9	.302	.361	0	0	2B-138
1946	83	314	76	10	1	1	0.3	37	19	26	39	6	.242	.290	0	0	2B-83
1947	120	402	104	17	2	3	0.7	33	26	24	45	2	.259	.333	5	1	2B-108, 3B-6
1948	6	12	3	0	0	0	0.0	0	0	0	1	1	.250	.250	2	0	3B-2, 2B-2
6 yrs.	511	1935	528	89	6	8	0.4	219	175	112	171	26	.273	.337	7	1	2B-495, 3B-8
WORLD SERIES																	
1945 CHI N	7	29	5	2	1	0	0.0	4	0	0	8	0	.172	.310	0	0	2B-7

Ed Johnson

JOHNSON, EDWIN CYRIL
B. Mar. 31, 1899, Morganfield, Ky. D. July 3, 1975, Morganfield, Ky.
BL TR 5'9" 160 lbs.

	G	AB	H	2B	3B	HR	HR%	R	RBI	BB	SO	SB	BA	SA	AB	H	G by POS
1920 WAS A	2	8	2	0	0	0	0.0	0	1	0	0	0	.250	.250	0	0	OF-2

Elmer Johnson

JOHNSON, ELMER ELLSWORTH (Hickory)
B. June 12, 1884, Beard, Ind. D. Oct. 31, 1966, Hollywood, Fla.
BR TR 5'9" 185 lbs.

	G	AB	H	2B	3B	HR	HR%	R	RBI	BB	SO	SB	BA	SA	AB	H	G by POS
1914 NY N	11	12	2	1	0	0	0.0	0	1	3	0	1	.167	.250	0	0	C-11

Ernie Johnson

JOHNSON, ERNEST RUDOLPH
Father of Don Johnson.
B. Apr. 29, 1888, Chicago, Ill. D. May 1, 1952, Monrovia, Calif.
BL TR 5'9" 151 lbs.

	G	AB	H	2B	3B	HR	HR%	R	RBI	BB	SO	SB	BA	SA	AB	H	G by POS
1912 CHI A	18	42	11	0	1	0	0.0	7	5	1		0	.262	.310	1	1	SS-16
1915 STL F	152	512	123	18	10	7	1.4	58	67	46		32	.240	.355	0	0	SS-152
1916 STL A	74	236	54	9	3	0	0.0	29	19	30	23	13	.229	.292	1	0	SS-60, 3B-12
1917	80	199	49	6	2	2	1.0	28	20	12	16	13	.246	.327	2	0	SS-39, 2B-18, 3B-14
1918	29	34	9	1	0	0	0.0	7	0	0	2	4	.265	.294	9	2	SS-11, 3B-1
1921 CHI A	142	613	181	28	7	1	0.2	93	51	29	24	22	.295	.369	1	1	SS-141
1922	145	603	153	17	3	0	0.0	85	56	40	30	21	.254	.292	2	0	SS-141
1923 2 teams		CHI A (12G – .189)				NY A (17G – .354)											
" total	29	101	27	3	1	1	1.0	11	9	4	6	2	.267	.347	3	3	SS-24, 3B-1
1924 NY A	64	119	42	4	8	3	2.5	24	12	11	7	1	.353	.597	13	3	2B-27, SS-9, 3B-2
1925	76	170	48	5	1	5	2.9	30	17	8	10	6	.282	.412	14	1	2B-34, SS-28, 3B-2
10 yrs.	809	2629	697	91	36	19	0.7	372	256	181	118	114	.265	.349	46	11	SS-621, 2B-79, 3B-32
WORLD SERIES																	
1923 NY A	2	0	0	0	0	0	–	1	0	0	0	0	–	–	0	0	SS-1

Frank Johnson

JOHNSON, FRANK HERBERT
B. July 22, 1942, El Paso, Tex.
BR TR 6'1" 155 lbs.

	G	AB	H	2B	3B	HR	HR%	R	RBI	BB	SO	SB	BA	SA	AB	H	G by POS
1966 SF N	15	32	7	0	0	0	0.0	2	0	2	7	0	.219	.219	1	0	OF-13
1967	8	10	3	0	0	0	0.0	3	0	1	2	0	.300	.300	2	0	OF-3
1968	67	174	33	2	0	1	0.6	11	7	12	23	1	.190	.218	8	0	3B-36, OF-8, SS-5, 2B-3
1969	7	10	1	0	0	0	0.0	2	0	0	1	0	.100	.100	0	0	OF-7
1970	67	161	44	1	2	3	1.9	25	31	19	18	1	.273	.360	11	3	OF-33, 1B-27
1971	32	49	4	1	0	0	0.0	4	5	3	9	0	.082	.102	21	2	1B-9, OF-4
6 yrs.	196	436	92	4	2	4	0.9	47	43	37	60	2	.211	.257	43	5	OF-68, 3B-36, 1B-36, SS-5, 2B-3

Howard Johnson

JOHNSON, HOWARD MICHAEL
B. Nov. 29, 1960, Clearwater, Fla.
BB TR 5'11" 175 lbs.

	G	AB	H	2B	3B	HR	HR%	R	RBI	BB	SO	SB	BA	SA	AB	H	G by POS
1982 DET A	54	155	49	5	0	4	2.6	23	14	16	30	7	.316	.426	7	1	3B-33, DH-10, OF-9
1983	27	66	14	0	0	3	4.5	11	5	7	10	0	.212	.348	6	2	3B-21, DH-2
1984	116	355	88	14	1	12	3.4	43	50	40	67	10	.248	.394	7	2	3B-108, SS-9, DH-4, OF-1, 1B-1
3 yrs.	197	576	151	19	1	19	3.3	77	69	63	107	17	.262	.398	20	5	3B-162, DH-16, OF-10, SS-9, 1B-1
WORLD SERIES																	
1984 DET A	1	1	0	0	0	0	0.0	0	0	0	0	0	.000	.000	1	0	

Lamar Johnson

JOHNSON, LAMAR
B. Sept. 2, 1950, Bessemer, Ala.
BR TR 6'2" 215 lbs.

	G	AB	H	2B	3B	HR	HR%	R	RBI	BB	SO	SB	BA	SA	AB	H	G by POS
1974 CHI A	10	29	10	0	0	0	0.0	1	2	0	3	0	.345	.345	0	0	1B-7, DH-3
1975	8	30	6	3	0	1	3.3	2	1	1	5	0	.200	.400	1	0	1B-6, DH-2
1976	82	222	71	11	1	4	1.8	29	33	19	37	2	.320	.432	18	4	DH-35, 1B-34, OF-1
1977	118	374	113	12	5	18	4.8	52	65	24	53	1	.302	.505	26	10	DH-68, 1B-45
1978	148	498	136	23	2	8	1.6	52	72	43	46	6	.273	.376	10	2	1B-108, DH-36
1979	133	479	148	29	1	12	2.5	60	74	41	56	8	.309	.449	7	1	1B-94, DH-37
1980	147	541	150	26	3	13	2.4	51	81	47	53	2	.277	.409	5	1	1B-80, DH-66
1981	41	134	37	7	0	1	0.7	10	15	5	14	0	.276	.351	6	1	1B-36, DH-2
1982 TEX A	105	324	84	11	0	7	2.2	37	38	31	40	3	.259	.358	19	5	DH-77, 1B-19
9 yrs.	792	2631	755	122	12	64	2.4	294	381	211	307	22	.287	.415	92	24	1B-422, DH-326, OF-1

Larry Johnson

JOHNSON, LARRY DOBY
B. Aug. 19, 1950, Cleveland, Ohio
BR TR 6' 185 lbs.

	G	AB	H	2B	3B	HR	HR%	R	RBI	BB	SO	SB	BA	SA	AB	H	G by POS
1972 CLE A	1	2	1	0	0	0	0.0	0	0	0	1	0	.500	.500	1	0	C-1
1974	1	0	0	0	0	0	–	1	0	0	0	0	–	–	0	0	
1975 MON N	3	3	1	1	0	0	0.0	0	1	1	0	0	.333	.667	0	0	C-1
1976	6	13	2	1	0	0	0.0	0	0	0	2	0	.154	.231	0	0	C-5
1978 CHI A	3	8	1	0	0	0	0.0	0	0	1	4	0	.125	.125	1	0	C-2, DH-1
5 yrs.	12	26	5	2	0	0	0.0	1	1	2	8	0	.192	.269	2	0	C-9, DH-1

	G	AB	H	2B	3B	HR	HR %	R	RBI	BB	SO	SB	BA	SA	Pinch Hit AB	Pinch Hit H	G by POS

Lou Johnson

JOHNSON, LOUIS BROWN (Slick, Sweet Lou)
B. Sept. 22, 1934, Lexington, Ky.
BR TR 5'11" 170 lbs.

	G	AB	H	2B	3B	HR	HR%	R	RBI	BB	SO	SB	BA	SA	AB	H	G by POS
1960 CHI N	34	68	14	2	1	0	0.0	6	1	5	19	3	.206	.265	6	0	OF-25
1961 LA A	1	0	0	0	0	0	–	0	0	0	0	0	–	–	0	0	OF-1
1962 MIL N	61	117	33	4	5	2	1.7	22	13	11	27	6	.282	.453	9	1	OF-55
1965 LA N	131	468	121	24	1	12	2.6	57	58	24	81	15	.259	.391	2	0	OF-128
1966	152	526	143	20	2	17	3.2	71	73	21	75	8	.272	.414	1	0	OF-148
1967	104	330	89	14	1	11	3.3	39	41	24	52	4	.270	.418	16	5	OF-91
1968 2 teams	CHI	N (62G –	.244)		CLE	A	(65G –	.257)									
" total	127	407	102	25	4	6	1.5	39	37	15	47	9	.251	.376	14	7	OF-114
1969 CAL A	67	133	27	8	0	0	0.0	10	9	10	19	5	.203	.263	22	3	OF-44
8 yrs.	677	2049	529	97	14	48	2.3	244	232	110	320	50	.258	.389	70	16	OF-606

WORLD SERIES

	G	AB	H	2B	3B	HR	HR%	R	RBI	BB	SO	SB	BA	SA	AB	H	G by POS
1965 LA N	7	27	8	2	0	2	7.4	3	4	1	3	0	.296	.593	0	0	OF-7
1966	4	15	4	1	0	0	0.0	1	0	1	1	0	.267	.333	0	0	OF-4
2 yrs.	11	42	12	3	0	2	4.8	4	4	2	4	0	.286	.500	0	0	OF-11

Otis Johnson

JOHNSON, OTIS L.
B. Nov. 5, 1883, Fowler, Ind.   D. Nov. 9, 1915, Johnson City, N. Y.
BB TR

	G	AB	H	2B	3B	HR	HR%	R	RBI	BB	SO	SB	BA	SA	AB	H	G by POS
1911 NY A	71	209	49	9	6	3	1.4	21	36	39		12	.234	.378	4	0	SS-47, 2B-15, 3B-4

Paul Johnson

JOHNSON, PAUL OSCAR
B. Sept. 2, 1896, N. Grosvenordale, Conn.   D. Feb. 14, 1973, McAllen, Tex.
BR TR 5'8" 160 lbs.

	G	AB	H	2B	3B	HR	HR%	R	RBI	BB	SO	SB	BA	SA	AB	H	G by POS
1920 PHI A	18	72	15	0	0	0	0.0	6	5	4	8	1	.208	.208	0	0	OF-18
1921	48	127	40	6	2	1	0.8	17	10	9	17	1	.315	.417	14	7	OF-32
2 yrs.	66	199	55	6	2	1	0.5	23	15	13	25	2	.276	.342	14	7	OF-50

Randy Johnson

JOHNSON, RANDALL GLENN
B. June 10, 1956, Escondido, Calif.
BR TR 6'1" 185 lbs.

	G	AB	H	2B	3B	HR	HR%	R	RBI	BB	SO	SB	BA	SA	AB	H	G by POS
1982 ATL N	27	46	11	5	0	0	0.0	5	6	6	4	0	.239	.348	7	1	2B-13, 3B-4
1983	86	144	36	3	0	1	0.7	22	17	20	27	1	.250	.292	25	8	3B-53, 2B-4
1984	91	294	82	13	0	5	1.7	28	30	21	21	4	.279	.374	13	3	3B-81
3 yrs.	204	484	129	21	0	6	1.2	55	53	47	52	5	.267	.347	45	12	3B-138, 2B-17

Randy Johnson

JOHNSON, RANDALL STUART
B. Aug. 15, 1958, Miami, Fla.
BL TL 6'2" 195 lbs.

	G	AB	H	2B	3B	HR	HR%	R	RBI	BB	SO	SB	BA	SA	AB	H	G by POS
1980 CHI A	12	20	4	0	0	0	0.0	0	3	2	4	0	.200	.200	5	2	DH-4, OF-1, 1B-1
1982 MIN N	89	234	58	10	0	10	4.3	26	33	30	46	0	.248	.419	22	2	DH-67, OF-2
2 yrs.	101	254	62	10	0	10	3.9	26	36	32	50	0	.244	.402	27	4	DH-71, OF-3, 1B-1

Ron Johnson

JOHNSON, RONALD DAVID
B. Mar. 23, 1956, Long Beach, Calif.
BR TR 6'2" 223 lbs.

	G	AB	H	2B	3B	HR	HR%	R	RBI	BB	SO	SB	BA	SA	AB	H	G by POS
1982 KC A	8	14	4	2	0	0	0.0	2	0	4	3	0	.286	.429	0	0	1B-7
1983	9	27	7	0	0	0	0.0	2	1	3	1	0	.259	.259	0	0	1B-7, C-2
1984 MON N	5	5	1	0	0	0	0.0	0	1	0	2	0	.200	.200	2	0	1B-2, OF-1
3 yrs.	22	46	12	2	0	0	0.0	4	2	7	6	0	.261	.304	2	0	1B-16, C-2, OF-1

Roy Johnson

JOHNSON, ROY CLEVELAND
Brother of Bob Johnson.
B. Feb. 23, 1903, Pryor, Okla.   D. Sept. 11, 1973, Tacoma, Wash.
Manager 1944.
BL TR 5'9" 175 lbs.

	G	AB	H	2B	3B	HR	HR%	R	RBI	BB	SO	SB	BA	SA	AB	H	G by POS
1929 DET A	146	640	201	45	14	10	1.6	128	69	67	60	20	.314	.475	2	0	OF-146
1930	125	462	127	30	13	2	0.4	84	35	40	46	17	.275	.409	6	2	OF-118
1931	151	621	173	37	19	8	1.3	107	55	72	51	33	.279	.438	1	1	OF-150
1932 2 teams	DET	A (49G –	.251)		BOS	A	(94G –	.299)									
" total	143	543	153	38	6	14	2.6	103	69	64	67	20	.282	.451	9	4	OF-133
1933 BOS A	133	483	151	30	7	10	2.1	88	95	55	36	13	.313	.466	7	1	OF-125
1934	143	569	182	43	10	7	1.2	85	119	54	36	11	.320	.467	5	1	OF-137
1935	145	553	174	33	9	3	0.5	70	66	74	34	11	.315	.423	3	2	OF-142
1936 NY A	63	147	39	8	2	1	0.7	21	19	21	14	3	.265	.367	20	3	OF-33
1937 2 teams	NY	A (12G –	.294)		BOS	N	(85G –	.277)									
" total	97	311	87	11	3	3	1.0	29	28	41	31	6	.280	.363	20	4	OF-75, 3B-1
1938 BOS N	7	29	5	0	0	0	0.0	2	1	1	5	1	.172	.172	0	0	OF-7
10 yrs.	1153	4358	1292	275	83	58	1.3	717	556	489	380	135	.296	.438	73	18	OF-1066, 3B-1

WORLD SERIES

	G	AB	H	2B	3B	HR	HR%	R	RBI	BB	SO	SB	BA	SA	AB	H	G by POS
1936 NY A	2	1	0	0	0	0	0.0	0	0	0	1	0	.000	.000	1	0	

Roy Johnson

JOHNSON, ROY EDWARD
B. June 27, 1959, Parkin, Ark.
BL TL 6'5" 205 lbs.

	G	AB	H	2B	3B	HR	HR%	R	RBI	BB	SO	SB	BA	SA	AB	H	G by POS
1982 MON N	17	32	7	2	0	0	0.0	2	2	1	6	0	.219	.281	5	1	OF-11
1984	16	33	5	2	0	1	3.0	2	2	7	10	1	.152	.303	6	2	OF-10
2 yrs.	33	65	12	4	0	1	1.5	4	4	8	16	1	.185	.292	11	3	OF-21

Spud Johnson

JOHNSON, JOHN RALPH
B. 1860, Canada   Deceased.
BL TL 5'9" 175 lbs.

	G	AB	H	2B	3B	HR	HR%	R	RBI	BB	SO	SB	BA	SA	AB	H	G by POS
1889 COL AA	116	459	130	14	10	2	0.4	91	79	39	47	34	.283	.370	0	0	OF-69, 3B-44, 1B-2, SS-1
1890	135	538	186	23	18	1	0.2	106		48		43	.346	.461	0	0	OF-135
1891 CLE N	80	327	84	8	3	1	0.3	49	46	22	23	16	.257	.309	0	0	OF-79, 1B-1
3 yrs.	331	1324	400	45	31	4	0.3	246	125	109	70	93	.302	.392	0	0	OF-283, 3B-44, 1B-3, SS-1

Stan Johnson

JOHNSON, STANLEY LUCIUS
B. Feb. 12, 1937, Dallas, Tex.
BL TL 5'10" 180 lbs.

	G	AB	H	2B	3B	HR	HR%	R	RBI	BB	SO	SB	BA	SA	AB	H	G by POS
1960 CHI A	5	6	1	0	0	1	16.7	1	1	0	1	0	.167	.667	5	1	OF-2
1961 KC A	3	3	0	0	0	0	0.0	1	0	2	1	0	.000	.000	1	0	OF-2
2 yrs.	8	9	1	0	0	1	11.1	2	1	2	2	0	.111	.444	6	1	OF-4

	G	AB	H	2B	3B	HR	HR %	R	RBI	BB	SO	SB	BA	SA	Pinch Hit AB	Pinch Hit H	G by POS

Tim Johnson

JOHNSON, TIMOTHY EVALD
B. July 22, 1949, Grand Forks, N. D. BL TR 6'1" 170 lbs.

	G	AB	H	2B	3B	HR	HR %	R	RBI	BB	SO	SB	BA	SA	AB	H	G by POS
1973 MIL A	136	465	99	10	2	0	0.0	39	32	29	93	6	.213	.243	2	0	SS-135
1974	93	245	60	7	7	0	0.0	25	25	11	48	4	.245	.331	4	1	SS-64, 2B-26, DH-1, OF-1, 3B-1
1975	38	85	12	1	0	0	0.0	6	2	6	17	3	.141	.153	5	2	3B-11, 2B-11, SS-10, DH-3, 1B-2
1976	105	273	75	4	3	0	0.0	25	14	19	32	4	.275	.311	1	0	2B-100, 3B-17, SS-1, 1B-1
1977	30	33	2	1	0	0	0.0	5	2	5	10	1	.061	.091	10	1	2B-10, SS-6, DH-4, 3B-4, OF-1
1978 2 teams		MIL	A (3G –	.000)		TOR	A (68G –	.241)									
" total	71	82	19	2	0	0	0.0	10	3	10	16	0	.232	.256	4	0	SS-51, 2B-13
1979 TOR A	43	86	16	2	1	0	0.0	6	6	8	15	0	.186	.233	1	0	2B-25, 3B-9, 1B-7
7 yrs.	516	1269	283	27	13	0	0.0	116	84	88	231	18	.223	.265	27	4	SS-267, 2B-185, 3B-42, 1B-10, DH-8, OF-2

Tony Johnson

JOHNSON, ANTHONY CLAIR
B. June 23, 1956, Memphis, Tenn. BR TR 6'3" 195 lbs.

	G	AB	H	2B	3B	HR	HR %	R	RBI	BB	SO	SB	BA	SA	AB	H	G by POS
1981 MON N	2	1	0	0	0	0	0.0	0	0	0	0	0	.000	.000	0	0	OF-1
1982 TOR A	70	98	23	2	1	3	3.1	17	14	11	26	3	.235	.367	10	3	DH-28, OF-28
2 yrs.	72	99	23	2	1	3	3.0	17	14	11	26	3	.232	.364	10	3	OF-29, DH-28

Wallace Johnson

JOHNSON, WALLACE DORNELL
B. Dec. 25, 1956, Gary, Ind. BB TR 6' 173 lbs.

	G	AB	H	2B	3B	HR	HR %	R	RBI	BB	SO	SB	BA	SA	AB	H	G by POS
1981 MON N	11	9	2	0	1	0	0.0	1	3	1	1	1	.222	.444	7	2	2B-1
1982	36	57	11	0	2	0	0.0	5	2	5	5	4	.193	.263	21	4	2B-13
1983 2 teams		MON	N (3G –	.500)		SF	N (7G –	.125)									
" total	10	10	2	0	0	0	0.0	1	1	1	0	1	.200	.200	7	1	2B-1
1984 MON N	17	24	5	0	0	0	0.0	3	4	5	4	0	.208	.208	10	3	1B-4
4 yrs.	74	100	20	0	3	0	0.0	10	10	12	10	6	.200	.260	45	10	2B-15, 1B-4

DIVISIONAL PLAYOFF SERIES

| 1981 MON N | 2 | 2 | 1 | 0 | 0 | 0 | 0.0 | 0 | 1 | 0 | 0 | 0 | .500 | .500 | 2 | 1 | |

Walter Johnson

JOHNSON, WALTER PERRY (The Big Train, Barney)
B. Nov. 6, 1887, Humboldt, Kans. D. Dec. 10, 1946, Washington, D. C. BR TR 6'1" 200 lbs.
Manager 1929-35.
Hall of Fame 1936.

	G	AB	H	2B	3B	HR	HR %	R	RBI	BB	SO	SB	BA	SA	AB	H	G by POS
1907 WAS A	14	36	4	0	1	0	0.0	3	1	1			.111	.167	0	0	P-14
1908	36	79	13	3	2	0	0.0	7	5	6			0	.165	.253	0	0	P-36
1909	40	101	13	3	0	1	1.0	6	6	1			0	.129	.188	0	0	P-40
1910	45	137	24	6	1	2	1.5	14	12	4			2	.175	.277	0	0	P-45
1911	42	128	30	5	3	1	0.8	18	15	0			1	.234	.344	2	1	P-40
1912	55	144	38	6	4	2	1.4	16	20	7			2	.264	.403	5	0	P-50
1913	54	134	35	5	6	2	1.5	12	14	5	14	2	.261	.433	5	2	P-47, OF-1
1914	55	136	30	4	1	3	2.2	23	16	10	27	2	.221	.331	3	0	P-51, OF-1
1915	64	147	34	7	4	2	1.4	14	17	8	34	0	.231	.374	12	2	P-47, OF-4
1916	58	142	33	2	4	1	0.7	14	7	11	28	0	.232	.324	9	2	P-48
1917	57	130	33	12	1	0	0.0	15	15	9	30	1	.254	.362	9	1	P-47
1918	65	150	40	4	4	1	0.7	10	18	9	18	2	.267	.367	20	5	P-39, OF-4
1919	56	125	24	1	3	1	0.8	13	8	12	17	1	.192	.272	14	3	P-39, OF-3
1920	35	69	18	1	3	1	1.4	7	8	6	12	0	.261	.406	11	2	P-21, OF-2
1921	38	111	30	7	0	0	0.0	10	10	6	14	0	.270	.333	2	0	P-35
1922	43	108	22	3	0	1	0.9	8	15	2	12	0	.204	.259	2	0	P-41
1923	43	93	18	3	0	0	0.0	11	13	4	15	0	.194	.290	0	0	P-43
1924	39	113	32	9	0	1	0.9	18	14	3	11	0	.283	.389	1	0	P-38
1925	36	97	42	6	1	2	2.1	12	20	3	6	0	.433	.577	6	2	P-30
1926	35	103	20	5	0	1	1.0	6	12	3	11	0	.194	.272	2	0	P-33
1927	26	46	16	2	0	2	4.3	6	10	3	4	0	.348	.522	7	1	P-18
21 yrs.	936	2329	549	94	41	24	1.0	243	256	113	253	13	.236	.342	110	21	P-802, OF-15

WORLD SERIES

1924 WAS A	3	9	1	0	0	0	0.0	0	0	0	0	0	.111	.111	0	0	P-3
1925	3	11	1	0	0	0	0.0	0	0	0	3	0	.091	.091	0	0	P-3
2 yrs.	6	20	2	0	0	0	0.0	0	0	0	3	0	.100	.100	0	0	P-6

Dick Johnston

JOHNSTON, RICHARD FREDERICK
B. Apr. 6, 1863, Kingston, N. Y. D. Apr. 4, 1934, Detroit, Mich. BR TR 5'8" 155 lbs.

	G	AB	H	2B	3B	HR	HR %	R	RBI	BB	SO	SB	BA	SA	AB	H	G by POS
1884 RIC AA	39	146	41	5	5	2	1.4	23		2				.281	.425	0	0	OF-37, SS-2
1885 BOS N	26	111	26	6	3	1	0.9	17	23	0	15		.234	.369	0	0	OF-26
1886	109	413	99	18	9	1	0.2	48	57	3	70		.240	.334	0	0	OF-109
1887	127	507	131	13	20	5	1.0	87	77	16	35	52	.258	.393	0	0	OF-127
1888	135	585	173	31	18	12	2.1	102	68	15	33	35	.296	.472	0	0	OF-135
1889	132	539	123	16	4	5	0.9	80	67	41	60	34	.228	.301	0	0	OF-132
1890 2 teams		BOS	P (2G –	.111)		NY	P (77G –	.242)									
" total	79	315	75	9	7	1	0.3	37	43	18	26	7	.238	.321	0	0	OF-78, SS-2
1891 C-M AA	99	376	83	11	2	6	1.6	59	51	38	44	12	.221	.309	0	0	OF-99
8 yrs.	746	2992	751	109	68	33	1.1	453	385	133	283	140	.251	.366	0	0	OF-743, SS-4

Doc Johnston

JOHNSTON, WHEELER ROGER
Brother of Jimmy Johnston.
B. Sept. 9, 1887, Cleveland, Tenn. D. Feb. 17, 1961, Chattanooga, Tenn. BL TL 6' 170 lbs.

	G	AB	H	2B	3B	HR	HR %	R	RBI	BB	SO	SB	BA	SA	AB	H	G by POS
1909 CIN N	3	10	0	0	0	0	0.0	1	0	1			0	.000	.000	0	0	1B-3
1912 CLE A	43	164	46	7	4	1	0.6	22	11	11		8	.280	.390	2	0	1B-41
1913	133	530	135	19	12	2	0.4	74	39	35	65	19	.255	.347	0	0	1B-133
1914	103	340	83	15	1	0	0.0	43	23	28	46	14	.244	.294	7	2	1B-89, OF-2
1915 PIT N	147	543	144	19	12	5	0.9	71	64	38	40	26	.265	.372	0	0	1B-147
1916	114	404	86	10	10	0	0.0	33	39	20	42	17	.213	.287	3	0	1B-110
1918 CLE A	74	273	62	12	2	0	0.0	30	25	26	19	12	.227	.286	1	0	1B-73

	G	AB	H	2B	3B	HR	HR %	R	RBI	BB	SO	SB	BA	SA	Pinch Hit AB	Pinch Hit H	G by POS

Doc Johnston continued

	G	AB	H	2B	3B	HR	HR %	R	RBI	BB	SO	SB	BA	SA	AB	H	G by POS
1919	102	331	101	17	3	1	0.3	42	33	25	18	21	.305	.384	4	1	1B-98
1920	147	535	156	24	10	2	0.4	68	71	28	32	13	.292	.385	0	0	1B-147
1921	118	384	114	20	7	2	0.5	53	44	29	15	2	.297	.401	3	1	1B-116
1922 PHI A	71	260	65	11	7	1	0.4	41	29	24	15	7	.250	.358	6	0	1B-65
11 yrs.	1055	3774	992	154	68	14	0.4	478	379	264	292	139	.263	.351	26	4	1B-1022, OF-2

WORLD SERIES

	G	AB	H	2B	3B	HR	HR %	R	RBI	BB	SO	SB	BA	SA	AB	H	G by POS
1920 CLE A	5	11	3	0	0	0	0.0	1	0	2	1	1	.273	.273	1	0	1B-5

Fred Johnston

JOHNSTON, WILFRED IVY (Red Top)   BR TR 5'10½" 160 lbs.
B. July 9, 1900, Pineville, N. C.   D. July 14, 1959, Tyler, Tex.

	G	AB	H	2B	3B	HR	HR %	R	RBI	BB	SO	SB	BA	SA	AB	H	G by POS
1924 BKN N	4	4	1	0	0	0	0.0	1	0	0	1	0	.250	.250	0	0	3B-1, 2B-1

Greg Johnston

JOHNSTON, GREGORY BERNARD   BL TL 6'   175 lbs.
B. Feb. 12, 1955, Los Angeles, Calif.

	G	AB	H	2B	3B	HR	HR %	R	RBI	BB	SO	SB	BA	SA	AB	H	G by POS
1979 SF N	42	74	15	2	0	1	1.4	5	7	2	17	0	.203	.270	27	6	OF-18
1980 MIN A	14	27	5	3	0	0	0.0	3	1	2	4	0	.185	.296	3	1	OF-14
1981	7	16	2	0	0	0	0.0	2	0	2	5	0	.125	.125	0	0	OF-6
3 yrs.	63	117	22	5	0	1	0.9	10	8	6	26	0	.188	.256	30	7	OF-38

Jimmy Johnston

JOHNSTON, JAMES HARLE   BR TR 5'10"   160 lbs.
Brother of Doc Johnston.
B. Dec. 10, 1889, Cleveland, Tenn.   D. Feb. 14, 1967, Chattanooga, Tenn.

	G	AB	H	2B	3B	HR	HR %	R	RBI	BB	SO	SB	BA	SA	AB	H	G by POS
1911 CHI A	1	2	0	0	0	0	0.0	0	2	0		0	.000	.000	0	0	OF-1
1914 CHI N	50	101	23	3	2	1	1.0	9	8	4	9	3	.228	.327	11	4	OF-28, 2B-4
1916 BKN N	118	425	107	13	8	1	0.2	58	26	35	38	22	.252	.327	1	1	OF-106
1917	103	330	89	10	4	0	0.0	33	25	23	28	16	.270	.324	8	1	OF-92, 1B-14, SS-4, 3B-3, 2B-3
1918	123	484	136	16	8	0	0.0	54	27	33	31	22	.281	.347	1	0	OF-96, 1B-21, 3B-4, 2B-1
1919	117	405	114	11	4	1	0.2	56	23	29	26	11	.281	.336	9	1	2B-87, OF-14, 1B-2, SS-1
1920	155	635	185	17	12	1	0.2	87	52	43	23	19	.291	.361	0	0	3B-146, OF-7, SS-3
1921	152	624	203	41	14	5	0.8	104	56	45	26	28	.325	.460	0	0	3B-150, SS-3
1922	138	567	181	20	7	4	0.7	110	49	38	17	18	.319	.400	0	0	2B-62, SS-50, 3B-26
1923	151	625	203	29	11	4	0.6	111	60	53	15	16	.325	.426	1	0	2B-84, SS-52, 3B-14
1924	86	315	94	11	2	2	0.6	51	29	27	10	5	.298	.365	7	4	SS-63, 3B-10, 1B-4, OF-1
1925	123	431	128	13	3	2	0.5	63	43	45	15	7	.297	.355	12	4	3B-81, OF-20, 1B-8, SS-2
1926 2 teams		BOS	N (23G – .246)		NY	N	(37G – .232)										
" total	60	126	30	1	0	1	0.8	18	10	16	8	2	.238	.270	25	5	OF-15, 3B-14, 2B-2
13 yrs.	1377	5070	1493	185	75	22	0.4	754	410	391	246	169	.294	.374	75	18	3B-448, OF-380, 2B-243, SS-178, 1B-49

WORLD SERIES

	G	AB	H	2B	3B	HR	HR %	R	RBI	BB	SO	SB	BA	SA	AB	H	G by POS
1916 BKN N	3	10	3	0	1	0	0.0	1	0	1	0	0	.300	.500	1	1	OF-2
1920	4	14	3	0	0	0	0.0	2	0	0	2	1	.214	.214	0	0	3B-4
2 yrs.	7	24	6	0	1	0	0.0	3	0	1	2	1	.250	.333	1	1	3B-4, OF-2

Johnny Johnston

JOHNSTON, JOHN THOMAS   BL TR 5'11"   172 lbs.
B. Mar. 28, 1890, Longview, Tex.   D. Mar. 7, 1940, San Diego, Calif.

	G	AB	H	2B	3B	HR	HR %	R	RBI	BB	SO	SB	BA	SA	AB	H	G by POS
1913 STL A	109	380	85	14	4	2	0.5	37	27	42	51	11	.224	.297	3	0	OF-106

Rex Johnston

JOHNSTON, REX DAVID   BR TR 6'1½" 202 lbs.
B. Nov. 8, 1937, Colton, Calif.

	G	AB	H	2B	3B	HR	HR %	R	RBI	BB	SO	SB	BA	SA	AB	H	G by POS
1964 PIT N	14	7	0	0	0	0	0.0	1	0	3	0	0	.000	.000	3	0	OF-8

Jay Johnstone

JOHNSTONE, JOHN WILLIAM   BL TR 6'1"   175 lbs.
B. Nov. 20, 1945, Manchester, Conn.   BB 1966

	G	AB	H	2B	3B	HR	HR %	R	RBI	BB	SO	SB	BA	SA	AB	H	G by POS
1966 CAL A	61	254	67	12	4	3	1.2	35	17	11	36	3	.264	.378	0	0	OF-61
1967	79	230	48	7	1	2	0.9	18	10	5	37	3	.209	.274	21	5	OF-63
1968	41	115	30	4	1	0	0.0	11	3	7	15	2	.261	.313	8	0	OF-29
1969	148	540	146	20	5	10	1.9	64	59	38	75	3	.270	.381	4	1	OF-144
1970	119	320	76	10	5	11	3.4	34	39	24	53	1	.238	.403	23	5	OF-100
1971 CHI A	124	388	101	14	1	16	4.1	53	40	38	50	10	.260	.425	11	3	OF-119
1972	113	261	49	9	0	4	1.5	27	17	25	42	2	.188	.268	19	6	OF-97
1973 OAK A	23	28	3	1	0	0	0.0	1	3	2	4	0	.107	.143	11	0	OF-7, DH-4, 2B-2
1974 PHI N	64	200	59	10	4	6	3.0	30	30	24	28	5	.295	.475	6	4	OF-59
1975	122	350	115	19	2	7	2.0	50	54	42	39	7	.329	.454	25	10	OF-101
1976	129	440	140	38	4	5	1.1	62	53	41	39	5	.318	.457	12	2	OF-122, 1B-6
1977	112	363	103	18	4	15	4.1	64	59	38	38	3	.284	.479	14	5	OF-91, 1B-19
1978 2 teams		PHI	N (35G – .179)		NY	A	(36G – .262)										
" total	71	121	27	2	0	1	0.8	9	10	10	19	0	.223	.264	28	2	OF-29, 1B-8, DH-5
1979 2 teams		NY	A (23G – .208)		SD	N	(75G – .294)										
" total	98	249	69	9	2	1	0.4	17	39	20	28	2	.277	.341	25	6	OF-64, 1B-22, DH-3
1980 LA N	109	251	77	15	2	2	0.8	31	20	24	29	3	.307	.406	41	11	OF-61
1981	61	83	17	3	0	3	3.6	8	6	7	13	0	.205	.349	38	11	OF-16, 1B-2
1982 2 teams		LA	N (21G – .077)		CHI	N	(98G – .249)										
" total	119	282	68	14	1	10	3.5	40	45	45	43	0	.241	.404	26	3	OF-86
1983 CHI N	86	140	36	7	0	6	4.3	16	22	20	24	1	.257	.436	38	6	OF-44
1984	52	73	21	2	0	0	0.0	8	3	7	18	0	.288	.370	39	10	OF-15
19 yrs.	1731	4688	1252	214	38	102	2.2	578	529	428	630	50	.267	.394	389 9th	90	OF-1308, 1B-57, DH-12, 2B-2

DIVISIONAL PLAYOFF SERIES

	G	AB	H	2B	3B	HR	HR %	R	RBI	BB	SO	SB	BA	SA	AB	H	G by POS
1981 LA N	1	1	0	0	0	0	0.0	0	0	0	0	0	.000	.000	1	0	

LEAGUE CHAMPIONSHIP SERIES

	G	AB	H	2B	3B	HR	HR %	R	RBI	BB	SO	SB	BA	SA	AB	H	G by POS
1976 PHI N	3	9	7	1	1	0	0.0	1	2	1	0	0	.778	1.111	1	1	OF-2
1977	2	5	1	0	0	0	0.0	0	0	0	1	0	.200	.200	1	0	OF-2

	G	AB	H	2B	3B	HR	HR %	R	RBI	BB	SO	SB	BA	SA	Pinch Hit AB	Pinch Hit H	G by POS

Jay Johnstone continued

		G	AB	H	2B	3B	HR	HR %	R	RBI	BB	SO	SB	BA	SA	AB	H	G by POS
1981	LA N	2	2	0	0	0	0	0.0	0	0	0	0	0	.000	.000	2	0	
3 yrs.		7	16	8	1	1	0	0.0	1	2	1	1	0	.500	.688	4	1	OF-4
WORLD SERIES																		
1978	NY A	2	0	0	0	0	0	–	0	0	0	0	0	–	–	0	0	OF-2
1981	LA N	3	3	2	0	0	1	33.3	1	3	0	0	0	.667	1.667	3	2	
2 yrs.		5	3	2	0	0	1	33.3	1	3	0	0	0	.667	1.667	3	2	OF-2

Stan Jok

JOK, STANLEY EDWARD (Tucker)   BR TR 6'   190 lbs.
B. May 3, 1926, Buffalo, N. Y.   D. Mar. 6, 1972, Buffalo, N. Y.

		G	AB	H	2B	3B	HR	HR %	R	RBI	BB	SO	SB	BA	SA	AB	H	G by POS
1954	2 teams	PHI	N (3G – .000)		CHI	A (3G – .167)												
"	total	6	15	2	0	0	0	0.0	1	2	1	4	0	.133	.133	3	0	3B-3
1955	CHI A	6	4	1	0	0	1	25.0	3	2	1	1	0	.250	1.000	0	0	3B-3, OF-1
2 yrs.		12	19	3	0	0	1	5.3	4	4	2	5	0	.158	.316	3	0	3B-6, OF-1

Smead Jolley

JOLLEY, SMEAD POWELL (Smudge)   BL TR 6'3½" 210 lbs.
B. Jan. 14, 1902, Wesson, Ark.

		G	AB	H	2B	3B	HR	HR %	R	RBI	BB	SO	SB	BA	SA	AB	H	G by POS
1930	CHI A	152	616	193	38	12	16	2.6	76	114	28	52	3	.313	.492	1	1	OF-151
1931		54	110	33	11	0	3	2.7	5	28	7	4	0	.300	.482	30	14	OF-23
1932	2 teams	CHI	A (12G – .357)		BOS	A (137G – .309)												
"	total	149	573	179	30	5	18	3.1	60	106	30	29	1	.312	.476	6	1	OF-137, C-5
1933	BOS A	118	411	116	32	4	9	2.2	47	65	24	20	1	.282	.445	15	4	OF-102
4 yrs.		473	1710	521	111	21	46	2.7	188	313	89	105	5	.305	.475	52	20	OF-413, C-5

Bill Jones

JONES,
B. Syracuse, N. Y.

		G	AB	H	2B	3B	HR	HR %	R	RBI	BB	SO	SB	BA	SA	AB	H	G by POS
1882	BAL AA	4	15	1	0	0	0	0.0	1		0			.067	.067	0	0	OF-2, C-2
1884	PHI U	4	14	2	0	0	0	0.0	2		1			.143	.143	0	0	C-4, OF-1
2 yrs.		8	29	3	0	0	0	0.0	3		1			.103	.103	0	0	C-6, OF-3

Bill Jones

JONES, WILLIAM DENNIS (Midget)   BL TR 5'6½" 157 lbs.
B. Apr. 8, 1887, Hartland, N. B., Canada   D. Oct. 10, 1946, Boston, Mass.

		G	AB	H	2B	3B	HR	HR %	R	RBI	BB	SO	SB	BA	SA	AB	H	G by POS
1911	BOS N	24	51	11	2	1	0	0.0	6	3	15	7	1	.216	.294	3	1	OF-18
1912		3	2	1	0	0	0	0.0	0	2	0	1	0	.500	.500	2	1	
2 yrs.		27	53	12	2	1	0	0.0	6	5	15	8	1	.226	.302	5	2	OF-18

Binky Jones

JONES, JOHN JOSEPH   BR TR 5'9" 154 lbs.
B. July 11, 1899, St. Louis, Mo.   D. May 13, 1961, St. Louis, Mo.

		G	AB	H	2B	3B	HR	HR %	R	RBI	BB	SO	SB	BA	SA	AB	H	G by POS
1924	BKN N	10	37	4	1	0	0	0.0	0	2	0	3	0	.108	.135	0	0	SS-10

Bob Jones

JONES, ROBERT WALTER (Ducky)   BL TR 6' 170 lbs.
B. Dec. 2, 1889, Clayton, Calif.   D. Aug. 30, 1964, San Diego, Calif.

		G	AB	H	2B	3B	HR	HR %	R	RBI	BB	SO	SB	BA	SA	AB	H	G by POS
1917	DET A	46	77	12	1	2	0	0.0	16	9	4	8	3	.156	.221	10	2	2B-18, 3B-8
1918		74	287	79	14	4	0	0.0	43	21	17	16	7	.275	.352	3	1	3B-63, 1B-6
1919		127	439	114	18	6	1	0.2	37	57	34	39	11	.260	.335	0	0	3B-127
1920		81	265	66	6	3	1	0.4	35	18	22	13	3	.249	.306	5	0	3B-67, 2B-5, SS-1
1921		141	554	168	23	9	1	0.2	82	72	37	24	8	.303	.383	0	0	3B-141
1922		124	455	117	10	6	3	0.7	65	44	36	18	8	.257	.325	3	0	3B-119
1923		100	372	93	15	4	1	0.3	51	40	29	13	7	.250	.320	0	0	3B-97
1924		110	393	107	27	4	0	0.0	52	47	20	20	1	.272	.361	3	1	3B-106
1925		50	148	35	6	0	0	0.0	18	15	9	5	1	.236	.277	3	1	3B-46
9 yrs.		853	2990	791	120	38	7	0.2	399	316	208	156	49	.265	.337	27	5	3B-774, 2B-23, 1B-6, SS-1

Bobby Jones

JONES, ROBERT OLIVER   BL TL 6'2" 195 lbs.
B. Oct. 11, 1949, Elkton, Md.

		G	AB	H	2B	3B	HR	HR %	R	RBI	BB	SO	SB	BA	SA	AB	H	G by POS
1974	TEX A	2	5	0	0	0	0	0.0	0	0	0	1	0	.000	.000	0	0	OF-2
1975		9	11	1	0	0	0	0.0	2	0	3	3	0	.091	.091	1	0	OF-5, DH-1
1976	CAL A	78	166	35	6	0	6	3.6	22	17	14	30	3	.211	.355	17	2	OF-62, DH-2
1977		14	17	3	0	0	1	5.9	3	3	4	5	0	.176	.353	6	1	DH-6
1981	TEX A	10	34	9	1	0	3	8.8	4	7	1	7	0	.265	.529	0	0	OF-10
1983		41	72	16	4	0	1	1.4	5	11	5	17	0	.222	.319	23	4	DH-11, OF-11, 1B-1
1984		64	143	37	4	0	4	2.8	14	22	10	19	1	.259	.371	24	5	OF-22, 1B-15, DH-4
7 yrs.		218	448	101	15	0	15	3.3	50	60	37	82	4	.225	.359	71	12	OF-112, DH-24, 1B-16

Charley Jones

JONES, CHARLES WESLEY   BR TR 5'11½" 202 lbs.
Also known as Benjamin Wesley Rippay.
B. Apr. 3, 1850, Alamance County, N. C.   Deceased.

		G	AB	H	2B	3B	HR	HR %	R	RBI	BB	SO	SB	BA	SA	AB	H	G by POS
1876	CIN N	64	276	79	17	4	4	1.4	40	38	7	17		.286	.420	0	0	OF-64
1877	3 teams	CIN	N (17G – .304)		CHI	N (2G – .375)			CIN	N (38G – .313)								
"	total	57	240	75	12	10	2	0.8	53	38	15	25	0	.313	.471	0	0	OF-94, 1B-10
1878	CIN N	61	261	81	11	7	3	1.1	50	39	4	17		.310	.441	0	0	OF-61
1879	BOS N	83	355	112	22	10	9	2.5	85	62	29	38		.315	.510	0	0	OF-83
1880		66	280	84	15	3	5	1.8	44	37	11	27		.300	.429	0	0	OF-66
1883	CIN AA	90	391	115	15	11	11	2.8	84		20			.294	.473	0	0	OF-90
1884		113	472	148	19	17	7	1.5	117		37			.314	.470	0	0	OF-113
1885		112	487	157	19	17	4	0.8	108		21			.322	.456	0	0	OF-112
1886		127	500	135	22	11	5	1.0	87		61			.270	.388	0	0	OF-127
1887	2 teams	CIN	AA (41G – .314)		NY	AA (62G – .255)												
"	total	103	400	111	18	7	5	1.3	58		31		15	.278	.395	0	0	OF-103, P-2, 1B-1
1888	KC AA	6	25	4	0	1	0	0.0	2	5	1		1	.160	.240	0	0	OF-6
11 yrs.		882	3687	1101	170	98	55	1.5	728	219	237	124	16	.299	.443	0	0	OF-919, 1B-11, P-2

	G	AB	H	2B	3B	HR	HR %	R	RBI	BB	SO	SB	BA	SA	Pinch Hit AB	Pinch Hit H	G by POS

Charlie Jones

JONES, CHARLES C. (Casey)
B. June 2, 1876, Butler, Pa.   D. Apr. 2, 1947, Two Harbors, Minn.   TR

	G	AB	H	2B	3B	HR	HR %	R	RBI	BB	SO	SB	BA	SA	PH AB	PH H	G by POS
1901 BOS A	10	41	6	2	0	0	0.0	6	6	1		2	.146	.195	0	0	OF-10
1905 WAS A	142	544	113	18	4	2	0.4	68	41	31		24	.208	.267	0	0	OF-142
1906	131	497	120	11	11	3	0.6	56	42	24		34	.241	.326	2	0	OF-128, 2B-1
1907	121	437	116	14	10	0	0.0	48	37	22		26	.265	.343	2	0	OF-111, 2B-5, 1B-4, SS-2
1908 STL A	74	263	61	11	2	0	0.0	37	17	14		14	.232	.289	2	0	OF-72
5 yrs.	478	1782	416	56	27	5	0.3	215	143	92		100	.233	.304	6	0	OF-463, 2B-6, 1B-4, SS-2

Charlie Jones

JONES, CHARLES F.
B. New York, N. Y.   Deceased.

	G	AB	H	2B	3B	HR	HR %	R	RBI	BB	SO	SB	BA	SA	PH AB	PH H	G by POS
1884 BKN AA	25	90	16	1	0	0	0.0	10		5			.178	.189	0	0	2B-13, 3B-11, OF-2
1885 NY AA	1	4	1	0	0	0	0.0	0		0			.250	.250	0	0	3B-1
2 yrs.	26	94	17	1	0	0	0.0	10		5			.181	.191	0	0	2B-13, 3B-12, OF-2

Clarence Jones

JONES, CLARENCE WOODROW   BL TL 6'2"   185 lbs.
B. Nov. 7, 1942, Zanesville, Ohio

	G	AB	H	2B	3B	HR	HR %	R	RBI	BB	SO	SB	BA	SA	PH AB	PH H	G by POS
1967 CHI N	53	135	34	7	0	2	1.5	13	16	14	33	0	.252	.348	9	3	OF-31, 1B-13
1968	5	2	0	0	0	0	0.0	0	0	2	1	0	.000	.000	2	0	1B-1
2 yrs.	58	137	34	7	0	2	1.5	13	16	16	34	0	.248	.343	11	3	OF-31, 1B-14

Cleon Jones

JONES, CLEON JOSEPH   BR TL 6'   185 lbs.
B. Aug. 4, 1942, Plateau, Ala.

	G	AB	H	2B	3B	HR	HR %	R	RBI	BB	SO	SB	BA	SA	PH AB	PH H	G by POS
1963 NY N	6	15	2	0	0	0	0.0	1	1	0	4	0	.133	.133	2	0	OF-5
1965	30	74	11	1	0	1	1.4	2	9	2	23	1	.149	.203	9	2	OF-23
1966	139	495	136	16	4	8	1.6	74	57	30	62	16	.275	.372	11	0	OF-129
1967	129	411	101	10	5	5	1.2	46	30	19	57	12	.246	.331	13	2	OF-115
1968	147	509	151	29	4	14	2.8	63	55	31	98	23	.297	.452	10	1	OF-139
1969	137	483	164	25	4	12	2.5	92	75	64	60	16	.340	.482	4	2	OF-122, 1B-15
1970	134	506	140	25	8	10	2.0	71	63	57	87	12	.277	.417	5	0	OF-130
1971	136	505	161	24	6	14	2.8	63	69	53	87	6	.319	.473	5	1	OF-132
1972	106	375	92	15	1	5	1.3	39	52	30	83	1	.245	.331	3	0	OF-84, 1B-20
1973	92	339	88	13	0	11	3.2	48	48	28	51	1	.260	.395	4	3	OF-92
1974	124	461	130	23	1	13	2.8	62	60	38	79	3	.282	.421	6	1	OF-120
1975	21	50	12	1	0	0	0.0	2	2	3	6	0	.240	.260	9	3	OF-12
1976 CHI A	12	40	8	1	0	0	0.0	2	3	5	5	0	.200	.225	1	0	OF-8, DH-3
13 yrs.	1213	4263	1196	183	33	93	2.2	565	524	360	702	91	.281	.404	82	15	OF-1111, 1B-35, DH-3

LEAGUE CHAMPIONSHIP SERIES

	G	AB	H	2B	3B	HR	HR %	R	RBI	BB	SO	SB	BA	SA	PH AB	PH H	G by POS
1969 NY N	3	14	6	2	0	1	7.1	4	4	1	2	2	.429	.786	0	0	OF-3
1973	5	20	6	2	0	0	0.0	3	3	2	4	0	.300	.400	0	0	OF-5
2 yrs.	8	34	12	4	0	1	2.9	7	7	3	6	2	.353	.559	0	0	OF-8

WORLD SERIES

	G	AB	H	2B	3B	HR	HR %	R	RBI	BB	SO	SB	BA	SA	PH AB	PH H	G by POS
1969 NY N	5	19	3	1	0	0	0.0	2	0	0	1	0	.158	.211	0	0	OF-5
1973	7	28	8	2	0	1	3.6	5	1	4	2	0	.286	.464	0	0	OF-7
2 yrs.	12	47	11	3	0	1	2.1	7	1	4	3	0	.234	.362	0	0	OF-12

Cobe Jones

JONES, COBURN DYAS   BB TR 5'7"   155 lbs.
B. Aug. 21, 1907, Denver, Colo.   D. June 3, 1969, Denver, Colo.

	G	AB	H	2B	3B	HR	HR %	R	RBI	BB	SO	SB	BA	SA	PH AB	PH H	G by POS
1928 PIT N	2	2	1	0	0	0	0.0	0	0	0	0	0	.500	.500	0	0	SS-2
1929	25	63	16	5	1	0	0.0	6	4	1	5	1	.254	.365	9	2	SS-15
2 yrs.	27	65	17	5	1	0	0.0	6	4	1	5	1	.262	.369	9	2	SS-17

Dalton Jones

JONES, JAMES DALTON   BL TR 6'1"   180 lbs.
B. Dec. 10, 1943, McComb, Miss.

	G	AB	H	2B	3B	HR	HR %	R	RBI	BB	SO	SB	BA	SA	PH AB	PH H	G by POS
1964 BOS A	118	374	86	16	4	6	1.6	37	39	22	38	6	.230	.342	35	11	2B-85, SS-1, 3B-1
1965	112	367	99	13	5	5	1.4	41	37	28	45	8	.270	.373	28	4	3B-81, 2B-8
1966	115	252	59	11	5	4	1.6	26	23	22	27	1	.234	.365	48	13	2B-70, 3B-3
1967	89	159	46	6	2	3	1.9	18	25	11	23	0	.289	.409	47	13	3B-30, 2B-19, 1B-1
1968	111	354	83	13	0	5	1.4	38	29	17	53	1	.234	.314	28	11	1B-56, 2B-26, 3B-8
1969	111	336	74	18	3	3	0.9	50	33	39	36	1	.220	.318	18	3	1B-81, 3B-9, 2B-1
1970 DET A	89	191	42	7	0	6	3.1	29	21	33	33	1	.220	.351	29	11	2B-35, 3B-18, 1B-10
1971	83	138	35	5	0	5	3.6	15	11	9	21	1	.254	.399	45	13	OF-16, 3B-13, 1B-3, 2B-1
1972 2 teams	DET A (7G – .000)						TEX A (72G – .159)										
" total	79	158	24	7	0	4	2.5	14	19	10	33	1	.152	.241	32	2	3B-23, 2B-17, 1B-7, OF-2
9 yrs.	907	2329	548	91	19	41	1.8	268	237	191	309	20	.235	.343	310	81	2B-262, 3B-186, 1B-158, OF-18, SS-1

WORLD SERIES

	G	AB	H	2B	3B	HR	HR %	R	RBI	BB	SO	SB	BA	SA	PH AB	PH H	G by POS
1967 BOS A	6	18	7	0	0	0	0.0	2	1	1	3	0	.389	.389	1	1	3B-4

Darryl Jones

JONES, DARRYL LEE   BR TR 5'10"   175 lbs.
Brother of Lynn Jones.
B. June 5, 1951, Meadville, Pa.

	G	AB	H	2B	3B	HR	HR %	R	RBI	BB	SO	SB	BA	SA	PH AB	PH H	G by POS
1979 NY A	18	47	12	5	1	0	0.0	6	6	2	7	0	.255	.404	2	2	DH-15, OF-2

Davy Jones

JONES, DAVID JEFFERSON (Kangaroo)   BL TR 5'10"   165 lbs.
B. June 30, 1880, Cambria, Wis.   D. Mar. 30, 1972, Mankato, Minn.

	G	AB	H	2B	3B	HR	HR %	R	RBI	BB	SO	SB	BA	SA	PH AB	PH H	G by POS
1901 MIL A	14	52	9	0	0	3	5.8	12	5	11		4	.173	.346	0	0	OF-14
1902 2 teams	STL A (15G – .224)						CHI N (64G – .305)										
" total	79	292	85	13	4	0	0.0	45	17	44		17	.291	.363	0	0	OF-79
1903 CHI N	130	497	140	18	3	1	0.0	64	62	53		15	.282	.336	0	0	OF-130
1904	98	336	82	11	5	3	0.9	44	39	41		14	.244	.333	0	0	OF-97
1906 DET A	84	323	84	12	2	0	0.0	41	24	41		21	.260	.310	0	0	OF-84
1907	126	491	134	10	6	0	0.0	101	27	60		30	.273	.318	0	0	OF-126
1908	56	121	25	2	1	0	0.0	17	10	13		11	.207	.240	21	3	OF-32
1909	69	204	57	2	2	0	0.0	44	10	28		12	.279	.309	10	1	OF-57
1910	113	377	100	6	6	0	0.0	77	24	51		25	.265	.313	9	0	OF-101

	G	AB	H	2B	3B	HR	HR %	R	RBI	BB	SO	SB	BA	SA	Pinch Hit AB	Pinch Hit H	G by POS

Davy Jones continued

	G	AB	H	2B	3B	HR	HR %	R	RBI	BB	SO	SB	BA	SA	AB	H	G by POS
1911	98	341	93	10	0	0	0.0	78	19	41		25	.273	.302	4	1	OF-92
1912	97	316	93	5	2	0	0.0	54	24	38		16	.294	.323	15	4	OF-81
1913 CHI A	10	21	6	0	0	0	0.0	2	0	9	0	1	.286	.286	1	0	OF-8
1914 PIT F	97	352	96	9	8	2	0.6	58	24	42		15	.273	.361	4	2	OF-93
1915	14	49	16	0	1	0	0.0	6	4	6		1	.327	.367	0	0	OF-13
14 yrs.	1085	3772	1020	98	40	9	0.2	643	289	478		207	.270	.325	64	11	OF-1007

WORLD SERIES

	G	AB	H	2B	3B	HR	HR %	R	RBI	BB	SO	SB	BA	SA	AB	H	G by POS
1907 DET A	5	17	6	0	0	0	0.0	1	0	4	0	3	.353	.353	0	0	OF-5
1908	3	2	0	0	0	0	0.0	1	0	1	1	0	.000	.000	2	0	
1909	7	30	7	0	0	1	3.3	6	2	2	1	1	.233	.333	0	0	OF-7
3 yrs.	15	49	13	0	0	1	2.0	8	2	7	2	4	.265	.327	2	0	OF-12

Deacon Jones

JONES, GROVER WILLIAM
B. Apr. 18, 1934, White Plains, N. Y.   BL TR 5'10"   185 lbs.

	G	AB	H	2B	3B	HR	HR %	R	RBI	BB	SO	SB	BA	SA	AB	H	G by POS
1962 CHI A	18	28	9	2	0	0	0.0	3	8	4	6	0	.321	.393	8	4	1B-6
1963	17	16	3	0	1	1	6.3	4	2	2	2	0	.188	.500	12	1	1B-1
1966	5	5	2	0	0	0	0.0	0	0	0	0	0	.400	.400	5	2	
3 yrs.	40	49	14	2	1	1	2.0	7	10	6	8	0	.286	.429	25	7	1B-7

Fielder Jones

JONES, FIELDER ALLISON
B. Aug. 13, 1871, Shinglehouse, Pa.   D. Mar. 13, 1934, Portland, Ore.
Manager 1904-08, 1914-18.   BL TR 5'11"   180 lbs.

	G	AB	H	2B	3B	HR	HR %	R	RBI	BB	SO	SB	BA	SA	AB	H	G by POS
1896 BKN N	104	399	141	10	8	3	0.8	82	46	48	15	18	.353	.441	0	0	OF-103
1897	135	553	178	14	10	2	0.4	134	49	61		48	.322	.394	0	0	OF-135
1898	147	599	181	15	9	1	0.2	89	69	46		36	.302	.362	0	0	OF-144, SS-2
1899	102	365	104	8	2	2	0.5	75	38	54		18	.285	.334	5	2	OF-96
1900	136	556	172	26	4	4	0.7	108	54	57		33	.309	.392	0	0	OF-136
1901 CHI A	133	521	162	16	3	2	0.4	120	65	84		38	.311	.365	0	0	OF-133
1902	135	532	171	16	5	0	0.0	98	54	57		33	.321	.370	0	0	OF-135
1903	136	530	152	18	5	0	0.0	71	45	47		21	.287	.340	0	0	OF-136
1904	154	564	137	14	6	3	0.5	74	43	54		25	.243	.305	0	0	OF-154
1905	153	568	139	17	12	2	0.4	91	38	73		20	.245	.327	0	0	OF-153
1906	144	496	114	22	4	2	0.4	77	34	83		26	.230	.302	0	0	OF-144
1907	154	559	146	18	1	0	0.0	72	47	67		17	.261	.297	0	0	OF-154
1908	149	529	134	11	7	1	0.2	92	50	86		26	.253	.306	0	0	OF-149
1914 STL F	5	3	1	0	0	0	0.0	0	0	1		0	.333	.333	3	1	
1915	7	6	0	0	0	0	0.0	0	0	0		0	.000	.000	3	0	OF-3
15 yrs.	1794	6780	1932	205	76	22	0.3	1184	632	818	15	359	.285	.347	11	3	OF-1775, SS-2

WORLD SERIES

	G	AB	H	2B	3B	HR	HR %	R	RBI	BB	SO	SB	BA	SA	AB	H	G by POS
1906 CHI A	6	21	2	0	0	0	0.0	4	0	3	3	0	.095	.095	0	0	OF-6

Frank Jones

JONES, FRANK M.
B. Duluth, Minn.   Deceased.

	G	AB	H	2B	3B	HR	HR %	R	RBI	BB	SO	SB	BA	SA	AB	H	G by POS
1884 DET N	2	6	2	0	0	0	0.0	1	0	0	0	0	.333	.333	0	0	OF-1, SS-1

Hal Jones

JONES, HAROLD MARION
B. Apr. 9, 1936, Louisiana, Mo.   BR TR 6'2"   194 lbs.

	G	AB	H	2B	3B	HR	HR %	R	RBI	BB	SO	SB	BA	SA	AB	H	G by POS
1961 CLE A	12	35	6	0	0	2	5.7	2	4	2	12	0	.171	.343	2	0	1B-10
1962	5	16	5	1	0	0	0.0	2	1	0	4	0	.313	.375	1	0	1B-4
2 yrs.	17	51	11	1	0	2	3.9	4	5	2	16	0	.216	.353	3	0	1B-14

Henry Jones

JONES, HENRY M. (Baldy)
B. Cadillac, Mich.   Deceased.

	G	AB	H	2B	3B	HR	HR %	R	RBI	BB	SO	SB	BA	SA	AB	H	G by POS
1884 DET N	34	129	27	3	1	0	0.0	23		16	19		.209	.248	0	0	2B-16, OF-12, SS-8
1890 PIT N	5	9	2	0	0	0	0.0	0	0	0	0	1	.222	.222	0	0	P-5
2 yrs.	39	138	29	3	1	0	0.0	23		16	19	1	.210	.246	0	0	2B-16, OF-12, SS-8, P-5

Howie Jones

JONES, HOWARD (Cotton)
Born Howard Painter.
B. Mar. 1, 1897, Irwin, Pa.   D. July 15, 1972, Jeanette, Pa.   BL TL 5'11"   165 lbs.

	G	AB	H	2B	3B	HR	HR %	R	RBI	BB	SO	SB	BA	SA	AB	H	G by POS
1921 STL N	3	2	0	0	0	0	0.0	0	0	0		1	0	.000	.000	2	0	OF-1

Jack Jones

JONES, RYERSON L. (Angel Sleeves)
B. Cincinnati, Ohio   Deceased.

	G	AB	H	2B	3B	HR	HR %	R	RBI	BB	SO	SB	BA	SA	AB	H	G by POS
1883 LOU AA	2	7	0	0	0	0	0.0	1		0			.000	.000	0	0	OF-2, SS-1
1884 CIN U	69	272	71	5	1	2	0.7	36		12			.261	.309	0	0	SS-41, 2B-19, 3B-10
2 yrs.	71	279	71	5	1	2	0.7	37		12			.254	.301	0	0	SS-42, 2B-19, 3B-10, OF-2

Jake Jones

JONES, JAMES MURRELL
B. Nov. 23, 1920, Epps, La.   BR TR 6'3"   197 lbs.

	G	AB	H	2B	3B	HR	HR %	R	RBI	BB	SO	SB	BA	SA	AB	H	G by POS
1941 CHI A	3	11	0	0	0	0	0.0	0	0	0	4	0	.000	.000	0	0	1B-3
1942	7	20	3	1	0	0	0.0	0	0	2	2	0	.150	.200	2	0	1B-5
1946	24	79	21	5	1	3	3.8	10	13	2	13	0	.266	.468	4	0	1B-20
1947 2 teams	CHI A (45G – .240)			BOS A (109G – .235)													
" total	154	575	136	21	4	19	3.3	65	96	54	85	6	.237	.386	2	0	1B-152
1948 BOS A	36	105	21	4	0	1	1.0	3	8	11	26	1	.200	.267	4	0	1B-31
5 yrs.	224	790	181	31	5	23	2.9	80	117	69	130	8	.229	.368	12	0	1B-211

Jeff Jones

JONES, JEFFRY RAYMOND
B. Oct. 22, 1957, Philadelphia, Pa.   BR TR 6'2"   200 lbs.

	G	AB	H	2B	3B	HR	HR %	R	RBI	BB	SO	SB	BA	SA	AB	H	G by POS
1983 CIN N	16	44	10	3	0	0	0.0	6	5	11	13	2	.227	.295	2	0	OF-13, 1B-1

	G	AB	H	2B	3B	HR	HR %	R	RBI	BB	SO	SB	BA	SA	Pinch Hit AB	Pinch Hit H	G by POS

Jim Jones

JONES, JAMES TILFORD (Sheriff)   5'10"   150 lbs.
B. Dec. 25, 1876, London, Ky.   D. May 6, 1953, London, Ky.

	G	AB	H	2B	3B	HR	HR %	R	RBI	BB	SO	SB	BA	SA	PH AB	PH H	G by POS
1897 LOU N	2	4	1	1	0	0	0.0	2	0	1		0	.250	.500	1	0	P-1
1901 NY N	21	91	19	4	3	0	0.0	10	5	4		2	.209	.319	0	0	OF-20, P-1
1902	67	249	59	11	1	0	0.0	16	19	13		7	.237	.289	0	0	OF-67
3 yrs.	90	344	79	16	4	0	0.0	28	24	18		9	.230	.299	1	0	OF-87, P-2

John Jones

JONES, JOHN WILLIAM (Skins)   BL TL 5'11"   185 lbs.
B. May 13, 1901, Coatsville, Pa.   D. Nov. 3, 1956, Baltimore, Md.

	G	AB	H	2B	3B	HR	HR %	R	RBI	BB	SO	SB	BA	SA	PH AB	PH H	G by POS
1923 PHI A	1	4	1	0	0	0	0.0	0	1	0	1	0	.250	.250	0	0	OF-1
1932	4	6	1	0	0	0	0.0	0	0	0	3	0	.167	.167	3	0	OF-1
2 yrs.	5	10	2	0	0	0	0.0	0	1	0	4	0	.200	.200	3	0	OF-2

Lynn Jones

JONES, LYNN MORRIS   BR TR 5'9"   175 lbs.
Brother of Darryl Jones.
B. Jan. 1, 1953, Meadville, Pa.

	G	AB	H	2B	3B	HR	HR %	R	RBI	BB	SO	SB	BA	SA	PH AB	PH H	G by POS
1979 DET A	95	213	63	8	0	4	1.9	33	26	17	22	9	.296	.390	11	2	OF-84, DH-6
1980	30	55	14	2	2	0	0.0	9	6	10	5	1	.255	.364	4	1	OF-17, DH-6
1981	71	174	45	5	0	2	1.1	19	19	18	10	1	.259	.322	13	4	OF-60, DH-4
1982	58	139	31	3	1	0	0.0	15	14	7	14	0	.223	.259	7	2	OF-56, DH-1
1983	49	64	17	1	2	0	0.0	9	6	3	6	1	.266	.344	15	3	OF-31, DH-6
1984 KC A	47	103	31	6	0	1	1.0	11	10	4	9	1	.301	.388	7	2	OF-45
6 yrs.	350	748	201	25	5	7	0.9	96	81	59	66	13	.269	.344	57	14	OF-293, DH-23

LEAGUE CHAMPIONSHIP SERIES

	G	AB	H	2B	3B	HR	HR %	R	RBI	BB	SO	SB	BA	SA	PH AB	PH H	G by POS
1984 KC A	3	5	1	0	0	0	0.0	1	0	0	0	0	.200	.200	3	1	OF-2

Mack Jones

JONES, MACK (Mack The Knife)   BL TR 6'1"   180 lbs.
B. Nov. 6, 1938, Atlanta, Ga.

	G	AB	H	2B	3B	HR	HR %	R	RBI	BB	SO	SB	BA	SA	PH AB	PH H	G by POS
1961 MIL N	28	104	24	3	2	0	0.0	13	12	12	28	4	.231	.298	1	0	OF-26
1962	91	333	85	17	4	10	3.0	51	36	44	100	5	.255	.420	1	0	OF-91
1963	93	228	50	11	4	3	1.3	36	22	26	59	8	.219	.342	17	4	OF-80
1965	143	504	132	18	7	31	6.2	78	75	29	122	8	.262	.510	10	2	OF-133
1966 ATL N	118	417	110	14	1	23	5.5	60	66	39	85	16	.264	.468	5	1	OF-112, 1B-1
1967	140	454	115	23	4	17	3.7	72	50	64	108	10	.253	.434	13	4	OF-126
1968 CIN N	103	234	59	9	1	10	4.3	40	34	28	46	2	.252	.427	38	9	OF-60
1969 MON N	135	455	123	23	5	22	4.8	73	79	67	110	6	.270	.488	5	1	OF-129
1970	108	271	65	11	3	14	5.2	51	32	59	74	5	.240	.458	27	10	OF-87
1971	43	91	15	3	0	3	3.3	11	9	15	24	1	.165	.297	16	2	OF-27
10 yrs.	1002	3091	778	132	31	133	4.3	485	415	383	756	65	.252	.444	133	33	OF-871, 1B-1

Nippy Jones

JONES, VERNAL LEROY   BR TR 6'1"   185 lbs.
B. June 29, 1925, Los Angeles, Calif.

	G	AB	H	2B	3B	HR	HR %	R	RBI	BB	SO	SB	BA	SA	PH AB	PH H	G by POS
1946 STL N	16	12	4	0	0	0	0.0	3	1	2	2	0	.333	.333	9	4	2B-3
1947	23	73	18	4	0	1	1.4	6	5	2	10	0	.247	.342	7	1	2B-13, OF-2
1948	132	481	122	21	9	10	2.1	58	81	36	45	2	.254	.397	2	0	1B-128
1949	110	380	114	20	2	8	2.1	51	62	16	20	1	.300	.426	11	2	1B-98
1950	13	26	6	1	0	0	0.0	0	6	3	1	0	.231	.269	4	2	1B-8
1951	80	300	79	12	0	3	1.0	20	41	9	13	1	.263	.333	9	1	1B-71
1952 PHI N	8	30	5	0	0	1	3.3	3	5	0	4	0	.167	.267	0	0	1B-8
1957 MIL N	30	79	21	2	1	2	2.5	5	8	3	7	0	.266	.392	10	2	1B-20, OF-1
8 yrs.	412	1381	369	60	12	25	1.8	146	209	71	102	4	.267	.382	52	12	1B-333, 2B-16, OF-3

WORLD SERIES

	G	AB	H	2B	3B	HR	HR %	R	RBI	BB	SO	SB	BA	SA	PH AB	PH H	G by POS
1946 STL N	1	1	0	0	0	0	0.0	0	0	0	0	0	.000	.000	1	0	
1957 MIL N	3	2	0	0	0	0	0.0	0	0	0	0	0	.000	.000	2	0	
2 yrs.	4	3	0	0	0	0	0.0	0	0	0	1	0	.000	.000	3	0	

Red Jones

JONES, MAURICE MORRIS   BL TR 6'3"   190 lbs.
B. Nov. 2, 1914, Timpson, Tex.   D. June 30, 1975, Lincoln, Calif.

	G	AB	H	2B	3B	HR	HR %	R	RBI	BB	SO	SB	BA	SA	PH AB	PH H	G by POS
1940 STL N	12	11	1	0	0	0	0.0	0	1	1	2	0	.091	.091	10	1	OF-1

Ross Jones

JONES, ROSS A.   BR TR 6'2"   185 lbs.
B. Jan. 14, 1960, Miami, Fla.

	G	AB	H	2B	3B	HR	HR %	R	RBI	BB	SO	SB	BA	SA	PH AB	PH H	G by POS
1984 NY N	17	10	1	1	0	0	0.0	2	1	3	4	0	.100	.200	3	0	SS-7, 2B-1

Ruppert Jones

JONES, RUPPERT SANDERSON   BL TL 5'10"   170 lbs.
B. Mar. 12, 1955, Dallas, Tex.

	G	AB	H	2B	3B	HR	HR %	R	RBI	BB	SO	SB	BA	SA	PH AB	PH H	G by POS
1976 KC A	28	51	11	1	1	1	2.0	9	7	3	16	0	.216	.333	9	1	OF-17, DH-3
1977 SEA A	160	597	157	26	8	24	4.0	85	76	55	120	13	.263	.454	1	0	OF-155, DH-4
1978	129	472	111	24	3	6	1.3	48	46	55	85	22	.235	.337	1	0	OF-128
1979	162	622	166	29	9	21	3.4	109	78	85	78	33	.267	.444	1	0	OF-161
1980 NY A	83	328	73	11	3	9	2.7	38	42	34	50	18	.223	.357	0	0	OF-82
1981 SD N	105	397	99	34	1	4	1.0	53	39	43	66	7	.249	.370	0	0	OF-104
1982	116	424	120	20	2	12	2.8	69	61	62	90	18	.283	.425	2	0	OF-114
1983	133	335	78	12	3	12	3.6	42	49	35	58	11	.233	.394	18	3	OF-111, 1B-5
1984 DET A	79	215	61	12	1	12	5.6	26	37	21	47	2	.284	.516	15	6	OF-73, DH-2
9 yrs.	995	3441	876	169	31	101	2.9	479	435	393	610	124	.255	.410	47	10	OF-945, DH-9, 1B-5

LEAGUE CHAMPIONSHIP SERIES

	G	AB	H	2B	3B	HR	HR %	R	RBI	BB	SO	SB	BA	SA	PH AB	PH H	G by POS
1984 DET A	2	5	0	0	0	0	0.0	0	1	1	1	0	.000	.000	1	0	OF-2

WORLD SERIES

	G	AB	H	2B	3B	HR	HR %	R	RBI	BB	SO	SB	BA	SA	PH AB	PH H	G by POS
1984 DET A	2	3	0	0	0	0	0.0	0	0	0	1	0	.000	.000	0	0	OF-2

Tex Jones

JONES, WILLIAM RODERICK   BR TR 6'   192 lbs.
B. Aug. 4, 1885, Marion, Kans.   D. Feb. 26, 1938, Wichita, Kans.

	G	AB	H	2B	3B	HR	HR %	R	RBI	BB	SO	SB	BA	SA	PH AB	PH H	G by POS
1911 CHI A	9	31	6	1	0	0	0.0	4	4	3		1	.194	.226	0	0	1B-9

	G	AB	H	2B	3B	HR	HR %	R	RBI	BB	SO	SB	BA	SA	Pinch Hit AB	Pinch Hit H	G by POS

Tom Jones

JONES, THOMAS BR TR 6'1" 195 lbs.
B. Jan. 22, 1877, Honesdale, Pa. D. June 21, 1923, Danville, Pa.

	G	AB	H	2B	3B	HR	HR%	R	RBI	BB	SO	SB	BA	SA	PH AB	PH H	G by POS
1902 BAL A	37	159	45	8	4	0	0.0	22	14	2		1	.283	.384	0	0	1B-37, 2B-1
1904 STL A	156	625	152	15	10	2	0.3	53	68	15		16	.243	.309	0	0	1B-134, 2B-23, OF-4
1905	135	504	122	16	2	0	0.0	44	48	30		5	.242	.282	0	0	1B-135
1906	144	539	136	22	6	0	0.0	51	30	24		27	.252	.315	1	0	1B-143
1907	155	549	137	17	3	0	0.0	53	34	34		24	.250	.291	0	0	1B-155
1908	155	549	135	14	2	1	0.2	43	50	30		18	.246	.284	0	0	1B-155
1909 2 teams	STL A (97G – .249)			DET A (44G – .281)													
" total	141	490	127	18	3	0	0.0	43	47	23		22	.259	.308	0	0	1B-139, 3B-2
1910 DET A	135	432	110	13	4	0	0.0	32	45	35		22	.255	.303	0	0	1B-135
8 yrs.	1058	3847	964	123	34	3	0.1	341	336	193		135	.251	.303	1	0	1B-1033, 2B-24, OF-4, 3B-2

WORLD SERIES

	G	AB	H	2B	3B	HR	HR%	R	RBI	BB	SO	SB	BA	SA	PH AB	PH H	G by POS
1909 DET A	7	24	6	1	0	0	0.0	3	2	2	0	1	.250	.292	0	0	1B-7

Willie Jones

JONES, WILLIE EDWARD (Puddin' Head) BR TR 6'2" 205 lbs.
B. Aug. 16, 1925, Dillon, S. C. D. Oct. 18, 1983, Cincinnati, Ohio

	G	AB	H	2B	3B	HR	HR%	R	RBI	BB	SO	SB	BA	SA	PH AB	PH H	G by POS
1947 PHI N	18	62	14	0	1	0	0.0	5	10	7	0	2	.226	.258	1	0	3B-17
1948	17	60	20	2	0	2	3.3	9	9	3	5	0	.333	.467	0	0	3B-17
1949	149	532	130	35	1	19	3.6	71	77	65	66	3	.244	.421	3	0	3B-145
1950	157	610	163	28	6	25	4.1	100	88	61	40	5	.267	.456	0	0	3B-157
1951	148	564	161	28	5	22	3.9	79	81	60	47	6	.285	.470	0	0	3B-147
1952	147	541	135	12	3	18	3.3	60	72	53	36	5	.250	.383	0	0	3B-147
1953	149	481	108	16	2	19	4.0	61	70	85	45	1	.225	.385	1	1	3B-147
1954	142	535	145	28	3	12	2.2	64	56	61	54	4	.271	.402	1	1	3B-141
1955	146	516	133	20	3	16	3.1	65	81	77	51	6	.258	.401	0	0	3B-146
1956	149	520	144	20	4	17	3.3	88	78	92	49	5	.277	.429	0	0	3B-149
1957	133	440	96	19	2	9	2.0	58	47	61	41	1	.218	.332	7	2	3B-126
1958	118	398	108	15	1	14	3.5	52	60	49	45	1	.271	.420	5	2	3B-110, 1B-1
1959 3 teams	PHI N (47G – .269)			CLE A (11G – .222)				CIN N (72G – .249)									
" total	130	411	105	22	2	14	3.4	57	56	48	43	0	.255	.421	11	2	3B-118
1960 CIN N	79	149	40	7	0	3	2.0	16	27	31	16	1	.268	.376	27	10	3B-46, 2B-1
1961	9	7	0	0	0	0	0.0	1	0	2	3	0	.000	.000	6	0	3B-1
15 yrs.	1691	5826	1502	252	33	190	3.3	786	812	755	541	40	.258	.410	62	18	3B-1614, 2B-1, 1B-1

WORLD SERIES

	G	AB	H	2B	3B	HR	HR%	R	RBI	BB	SO	SB	BA	SA	PH AB	PH H	G by POS
1950 PHI N	4	14	4	1	0	0	0.0	1	0	3	0		.286	.357	0	0	3B-4

Bubber Jonnard

JONNARD, CLARENCE JAMES BR TR 6'1" 185 lbs.
Brother of Claude Jonnard.
B. Nov. 23, 1897, Nashville, Tenn. D. Aug. 23, 1977, New York, N. Y.

	G	AB	H	2B	3B	HR	HR%	R	RBI	BB	SO	SB	BA	SA	PH AB	PH H	G by POS
1920 CHI A	2	5	0	0	0	0	0.0	0	0	0	1	0	.000	.000	1	0	C-1
1922 PIT N	10	21	5	0	1	0	0.0	4	2	2	4	0	.238	.333	4	1	C-10
1926 PHI N	19	34	4	1	0	0	0.0	3	2	3	4	0	.118	.147	4	0	C-15
1927	53	143	42	6	0	0	0.0	18	14	7	7	0	.294	.336	7	5	C-41
1929 STL N	18	31	3	0	0	0	0.0	1	2	0	6	0	.097	.097	0	0	C-18
1935 PHI N	1	1	0	0	0	0	0.0	0	0	0	0	0	.000	.000	0	0	C-1
6 yrs.	103	235	54	7	1	0	0.0	26	20	12	23	0	.230	.268	12	5	C-86

Eddie Joost

JOOST, EDWIN DAVID BR TR 6' 175 lbs.
B. June 5, 1916, San Francisco, Calif.
Manager 1954.

	G	AB	H	2B	3B	HR	HR%	R	RBI	BB	SO	SB	BA	SA	PH AB	PH H	G by POS
1936 CIN N	13	26	4	1	0	0	0.0	1	1	2	5	0	.154	.192	0	0	SS-7, 2B-5
1937	6	12	1	0	0	0	0.0	0	0	0	0	0	.083	.083	0	0	2B-6
1939	42	143	36	6	3	0	0.0	23	14	12	15	1	.252	.336	4	0	2B-32, SS-6
1940	88	278	60	7	2	1	0.4	24	24	32	40	4	.216	.266	0	0	SS-78, 2B-7, 3B-4
1941	152	537	136	25	4	4	0.7	67	40	69	59	9	.253	.337	0	0	SS-147, 2B-4, 1B-2, 3B-1
1942	142	562	126	30	3	6	1.1	65	41	62	57	9	.224	.320	0	0	SS-130, 2B-15
1943 BOS N	124	421	78	16	3	2	0.5	34	20	68	80	5	.185	.252	0	0	3B-67, 2B-60, SS-1
1945	35	141	35	7	1	0	0.0	16	9	13	7	0	.248	.312	0	0	2B-19, 3B-16
1947 PHI A	151	540	111	22	3	13	2.4	76	64	114	110	6	.206	.330	0	0	SS-151
1948	135	509	127	22	2	16	3.1	99	55	119	87	2	.250	.395	0	0	SS-135
1949	144	525	138	25	3	23	4.4	128	81	149	80	2	.263	.453	0	0	SS-144
1950	131	476	111	12	3	18	3.8	79	58	101	68	5	.233	.384	0	0	SS-131
1951	140	553	160	28	5	19	3.4	107	78	106	70	10	.289	.461	0	0	SS-140
1952	146	540	132	26	3	20	3.7	94	75	122	94	5	.244	.415	0	0	SS-146
1953	51	177	44	6	0	6	3.4	39	15	45	24	3	.249	.384	0	0	SS-51
1954	19	47	17	3	0	1	2.1	7	9	10	10	0	.362	.489	2	0	SS-9, 3B-5, 2B-1
1955 BOS A	55	119	23	2	0	5	4.2	15	17	17	21	0	.193	.336	17	5	SS-20, 2B-17, 3B-2
17 yrs.	1574	5606	1339	238	35	134	2.4	874	601	1041	827	61	.239	.366	23	5	SS-1296, 2B-166, 3B-95, 1B-2

WORLD SERIES

	G	AB	H	2B	3B	HR	HR%	R	RBI	BB	SO	SB	BA	SA	PH AB	PH H	G by POS
1940 CIN N	7	25	5	0	0	0	0.0	0	2	1	2	0	.200	.200	0	0	2B-7

Buck Jordan

JORDAN, BAXTER BYERLY BL TR 6' 170 lbs.
B. Jan. 16, 1907, Cooleemee, N. C.

	G	AB	H	2B	3B	HR	HR%	R	RBI	BB	SO	SB	BA	SA	PH AB	PH H	G by POS
1927 NY N	5	5	1	0	0	0	0.0	0	0	0	3	0	.200	.200	5	1	
1929	2	2	1	1	0	0	0.0	1	0	0	0	0	.500	1.000	1	0	1B-1
1931 WAS A	9	18	4	2	0	0	0.0	3	1	1	3	0	.222	.333	1	0	1B-7
1932 BOS N	49	212	68	12	3	2	0.9	27	29	4	5	1	.321	.434	0	0	1B-49
1933	152	588	168	29	9	4	0.7	77	66	34	22	4	.286	.386	2	0	1B-150
1934	124	489	152	26	9	2	0.4	68	58	35	19	3	.311	.413	7	6	1B-117
1935	130	470	131	24	5	5	1.1	62	35	19	17	3	.279	.383	19	5	1B-95, 3B-8, OF-2
1936	138	555	179	27	5	3	0.5	81	66	45	22	2	.323	.405	2	0	1B-136

	G	AB	H	2B	3B	HR	HR %	R	RBI	BB	SO	SB	BA	SA	Pinch Hit AB	Pinch Hit H	G by POS

Buck Jordan continued

	G	AB	H	2B	3B	HR	HR %	R	RBI	BB	SO	SB	BA	SA	AB	H	G by POS
1937 2 teams		BOS	N	(8G –	.250)		CIN	N	(98G –	.282)							
" total	106	324	91	14	3	1	0.3	46	28	25	14	6	.281	.352	28	7	1B-76
1938 2 teams		CIN	N	(9G –	.286)		PHI	N	(87G –	.300)							
" total	96	317	95	18	1	0	0.0	31	18	19	4	1	.300	.363	19	6	3B-58, 1B-17
10 yrs.	811	2980	890	153	35	17	0.6	396	281	182	109	20	.299	.391	84	25	1B-648, 3B-66, OF-2

Dutch Jordan

BR TR

JORDAN, ADOLPH OTTO
B. Jan. 5, 1880, Pittsburgh, Pa.   D. Dec. 23, 1972, Pittsburgh, Pa.

	G	AB	H	2B	3B	HR	HR %	R	RBI	BB	SO	SB	BA	SA	AB	H	G by POS
1903 BKN N	78	267	63	11	1	0	0.0	27	21	19		9	.236	.285	1	0	2B-54, 3B-18, OF-4, 1B-1
1904	87	252	45	10	2	0	0.0	21	19	13		7	.179	.234	2	1	2B-70, 3B-11, 1B-4
2 yrs.	165	519	108	21	3	0	0.0	48	40	32		16	.208	.260	3	1	2B-124, 3B-29, 1B-5, OF-4

Jimmy Jordan

BR TR 5'9"   157 lbs.

JORDAN, JAMES WILLIAM (Lord)
B. Jan. 13, 1908, Tucapau, S. C.   D. Dec. 4, 1957, Charlotte, N. C.

	G	AB	H	2B	3B	HR	HR %	R	RBI	BB	SO	SB	BA	SA	AB	H	G by POS
1933 BKN N	70	211	54	12	1	0	0.0	16	17	4	6	3	.256	.322	2	1	SS-51, 2B-11
1934	97	369	98	17	2	0	0.0	34	43	9	32	1	.266	.322	1	0	SS-51, 2B-41, 3B-9
1935	94	295	82	7	0	0	0.0	26	30	9	17	3	.278	.302	14	5	2B-46, SS-28, 3B-5
1936	115	398	93	15	1	2	0.5	26	28	15	21	1	.234	.291	4	1	2B-98, 3B-6, SS-1
4 yrs.	376	1273	327	51	4	2	0.2	102	118	37	76	8	.257	.308	21	7	2B-196, SS-131, 3B-20

Mike Jordan

JORDAN, MICHAEL HENRY
B. Feb. 7, 1863, Lawrence, Mass.   D. Sept. 25, 1940, Lawrence, Mass.

	G	AB	H	2B	3B	HR	HR %	R	RBI	BB	SO	SB	BA	SA	AB	H	G by POS
1890 PIT N	37	125	12	1	0	0	0.0	8	6	15	19	5	.096	.104	0	0	OF-37

Slats Jordan

BL TL 6'1"   190 lbs.

JORDAN, CLARENCE VEASEY
B. Sept. 26, 1879, Baltimore, Md.   D. Dec. 7, 1953, Catonsville, Md.

	G	AB	H	2B	3B	HR	HR %	R	RBI	BB	SO	SB	BA	SA	AB	H	G by POS
1901 BAL A	1	3	0	0	0	0	0.0	0	0	0	0	0	.000	.000	0	0	1B-1
1902	1	4	0	0	0	0	0.0	0	0	0	0	0	.000	.000	0	0	OF-1
2 yrs.	2	7	0	0	0	0	0.0	0	0	0	0	0	.000	.000	0	0	OF-1, 1B-1

Tim Jordan

BL TR 6'1"   170 lbs.

JORDAN, TIMOTHY JOSEPH
B. Feb. 14, 1879, New York, N. Y.   D. Sept. 13, 1949, Bronx, N. Y.

	G	AB	H	2B	3B	HR	HR %	R	RBI	BB	SO	SB	BA	SA	AB	H	G by POS
1901 WAS A	6	20	4	1	0	0	0.0	2	3			0	.200	.250	0	0	1B-6
1903 NY A	2	8	1	0	0	0	0.0	2	0			0	.125	.125	0	0	1B-2
1906 BKN N	129	450	118	20	8	12	2.7	67	78	59		16	.262	.422	3	0	1B-126
1907	147	485	133	15	8	4	0.8	43	53	74		10	.274	.363	2	0	1B-143
1908	148	515	127	18	5	12	2.3	58	60	59		9	.247	.371	1	0	1B-146
1909	103	330	90	20	3	3	0.9	47	36	59		13	.273	.379	7	1	1B-95
1910	5	5	1	0	0	1	20.0	1	3	0		0	.200	.800	5	1	
7 yrs.	540	1813	474	74	24	32	1.8	229	232	254		48	.261	.382	19	2	1B-518

Tom Jordan

BR TR 6'1½"   195 lbs.

JORDAN, THOMAS JEFFERSON
B. Sept. 5, 1919, Lawton, Okla.

	G	AB	H	2B	3B	HR	HR %	R	RBI	BB	SO	SB	BA	SA	AB	H	G by POS
1944 CHI A	14	45	12	1	1	0	0.0	2	3	1	0	0	.267	.333	0	0	C-14
1946 2 teams		CHI	A	(10G –	.267)		CLE	A	(14G –	.200)							
" total	24	50	11	3	1	1	2.0	3	3	3	2	1	.220	.380	10	1	C-15
1948 STL A	1	1	0	0	0	0	0.0	0	0	0	0	0	.000	.000	1	0	
3 yrs.	39	96	23	4	2	1	1.0	5	6	4	2	1	.240	.354	11	1	C-29

Arndt Jorgens

BR TR 5'9"   160 lbs.

JORGENS, ARNDT LUDWIG
Brother of Orville Jorgens.
B. May 18, 1905, Modum, Norway   D. Mar. 1, 1980, Wilmette, Ill.

	G	AB	H	2B	3B	HR	HR %	R	RBI	BB	SO	SB	BA	SA	AB	H	G by POS
1929 NY A	18	34	11	3	0	0	0.0	6	4	6	7	0	.324	.412	2	0	C-15
1930	16	30	11	3	0	0	0.0	7	1	2	4	0	.367	.467	2	0	C-16
1931	46	100	27	1	2	0	0.0	12	14	9	3	0	.270	.320	4	0	C-40
1932	55	151	33	7	1	2	1.3	13	19	14	11	0	.219	.318	0	0	C-55
1933	21	50	11	3	0	2	4.0	9	13	12	3	1	.220	.400	3	0	C-19
1934	58	183	38	6	1	0	0.0	14	20	23	24	2	.208	.251	2	1	C-56
1935	36	84	20	2	0	0	0.0	6	8	12	10	0	.238	.262	4	0	C-33
1936	31	66	18	3	1	0	0.0	5	5	2	3	0	.273	.348	1	1	C-30
1937	13	23	3	1	0	0	0.0	3	3	2	5	0	.130	.174	1	0	C-11
1938	9	17	4	2	0	0	0.0	3	2	3	3	0	.235	.353	1	0	C-8
1939	3	0	0	0	0	0		1	0	0	0	0			0	0	C-2
11 yrs.	306	738	176	31	5	4	0.5	79	89	85	73	3	.238	.310	17	2	C-285

Mike Jorgensen

BL TL 6'   195 lbs.

JORGENSEN, MICHAEL
B. Aug. 16, 1948, Passaic, N. J.

	G	AB	H	2B	3B	HR	HR %	R	RBI	BB	SO	SB	BA	SA	AB	H	G by POS
1968 NY N	8	14	2	1	0	0	0.0	0	0	0	4	0	.143	.214	4	0	1B-4
1970	76	87	17	3	1	3	3.4	15	4	10	23	2	.195	.356	15	4	1B-50, OF-10
1971	45	118	26	1	1	5	4.2	16	11	11	24	1	.220	.373	13	2	OF-31, 1B-1
1972 MON N	113	372	86	12	3	13	3.5	48	47	53	75	12	.231	.384	10	2	1B-76, OF-28
1973	138	413	95	16	2	9	2.2	49	47	64	49	16	.230	.344	13	4	1B-123, OF-11
1974	131	287	89	16	1	11	3.8	45	59	70	39	3	.310	.488	26	8	1B-91, OF-29
1975	144	445	116	18	0	18	4.0	58	67	79	75	3	.261	.422	17	4	1B-133, OF-6
1976	125	343	87	13	0	6	1.7	36	23	52	48	7	.254	.344	14	0	1B-81, OF-41
1977 2 teams		MON	N	(19G –	.200)		OAK	A	(66G –	.246)							
" total	85	223	54	9	1	8	3.6	21	32	28	48	3	.242	.381	18	1	1B-53, OF-20, DH-2
1978 TEX A	96	97	19	3	0	1	1.0	20	9	18	10	3	.196	.258	3	0	1B-78, OF-9, DH-1
1979	90	157	35	7	0	6	3.8	21	16	14	29	0	.223	.382	19	2	1B-60, OF-20, DH-2
1980 NY N	119	321	82	11	0	7	2.2	43	43	46	55	0	.255	.355	19	2	1B-72, OF-31
1981	86	122	25	5	2	3	2.5	8	15	12	24	4	.205	.352	29	5	1B-40, OF-19
1982	120	114	29	6	0	2	1.8	16	14	21	24	2	.254	.360	48	15	1B-56, OF-16
1983 2 teams		NY	N	(38G –	.250)		ATL	N	(57G –	.250)							
" total	95	72	18	4	0	2	2.8	10	11	10	12	0	.250	.389	45	12	1B-38, OF-6

	G	AB	H	2B	3B	HR	HR %	R	RBI	BB	SO	SB	BA	SA	Pinch Hit AB	Pinch Hit H	G by POS

Mike Jorgensen continued

	G	AB	H	2B	3B	HR	HR %	R	RBI	BB	SO	SB	BA	SA	AB	H	G by POS
1984 2 teams	ATL N (31G – .269)			STL N (59G – .245)													
" total	90	124	31	2	1	0.8	9	17	13	23	0	.250	.347	38	10	1B-47, OF-4
16 yrs.	1561	3309	811	126	13	95	2.9	415	415	501	562	56	.245	.377	331	69	1B-1003, OF-281, DH-5

Pinky Jorgensen

JORGENSEN, CARL
B. Nov. 21, 1914, Laton, Calif.

BR TR 6'1" 195 lbs.

	G	AB	H	2B	3B	HR	HR %	R	RBI	BB	SO	SB	BA	SA	AB	H	G by POS
1937 CIN N	6	14	4	0	0	0	0.0	1	1	1	2	0	.286	.286	1	0	OF-4

Spider Jorgensen

JORGENSEN, JOHN DONALD
B. Nov. 3, 1919, Folsom, Calif.

BL TR 5'9" 155 lbs.

	G	AB	H	2B	3B	HR	HR %	R	RBI	BB	SO	SB	BA	SA	AB	H	G by POS
1947 BKN N	129	441	121	29	8	5	1.1	57	67	58	45	4	.274	.410	1	1	3B-128
1948	31	90	27	6	2	1	1.1	15	13	16	13	1	.300	.444	5	3	3B-24
1949	53	134	36	5	1	1	0.7	15	14	23	13	0	.269	.343	13	2	3B-36
1950 2 teams	BKN N (2G – .000)			NY N (24G – .135)													
" total	26	39	5	0	0	0	0.0	5	5	6	2	0	.128	.128	17	2	3B-6
1951 NY N	28	51	12	0	0	2	3.9	5	8	3	2	0	.235	.353	16	3	OF-11, 3B-1
5 yrs.	267	755	201	40	11	9	1.2	97	107	106	75	5	.266	.384	52	11	3B-195, OF-11

WORLD SERIES	G	AB	H	2B	3B	HR	HR %	R	RBI	BB	SO	SB	BA	SA	AB	H	G by POS
1947 BKN N	7	20	4	2	0	0	0.0	3	2	4	4	0	.200	.300	0	0	3B-7
1949	4	11	2	2	0	0	0.0	1	0	2	2	0	.182	.364	1	0	3B-3
2 yrs.	11	31	6	4	0	0	0.0	2	3	4	6	0	.194	.323	1	0	3B-10

Rick Joseph

JOSEPH, RICARDO EMELINO
B. Aug. 24, 1940, San Pedro de Macoris, Dominican Republic   D. Sept. 8, 1979, Santo Domingo, Dominican Republic

BR TR 6'1" 192 lbs.

	G	AB	H	2B	3B	HR	HR %	R	RBI	BB	SO	SB	BA	SA	AB	H	G by POS
1964 KC A	17	54	12	2	0	0	0.0	3	1	3	11	0	.222	.259	4	0	1B-12, 3B-3
1967 PHI N	17	41	9	2	0	1	2.4	4	5	4	10	0	.220	.341	5	1	1B-13
1968	66	155	34	5	0	3	1.9	20	12	16	35	0	.219	.310	24	7	1B-30, 3B-14, OF-1
1969	99	264	72	15	0	6	2.3	35	37	22	57	2	.273	.398	25	3	3B-58, 1B-17, 2B-1
1970	71	119	27	2	1	3	2.5	7	10	6	28	0	.227	.336	37	11	OF-12, 1B-10, 3B-9
5 yrs.	270	633	154	26	1	13	2.1	69	65	51	141	2	.243	.349	95	22	3B-84, 1B-82, OF-13, 2B-1

Duane Josephson

JOSEPHSON, DUANE CHARLES
B. June 3, 1942, New Hampton, Iowa

BR TR 6' 190 lbs.

	G	AB	H	2B	3B	HR	HR %	R	RBI	BB	SO	SB	BA	SA	AB	H	G by POS
1965 CHI A	4	9	1	0	0	0	0.0	2	0	2	4	0	.111	.111	0	0	C-4
1966	11	38	9	1	0	0	0.0	3	3	3	3	0	.237	.263	0	0	C-11
1967	62	189	45	5	1	1	0.5	11	9	6	24	0	.238	.291	5	0	C-59
1968	128	434	107	16	6	6	1.4	35	45	18	52	2	.247	.353	11	3	C-122
1969	52	162	39	6	2	1	0.6	19	20	13	17	0	.241	.321	7	3	C-47
1970	96	285	90	12	1	4	1.4	28	41	24	28	1	.316	.407	14	5	C-84
1971 BOS A	91	306	75	14	1	10	3.3	38	39	22	35	2	.245	.395	5	1	C-87
1972	26	82	22	4	1	1	1.2	11	7	4	11	0	.268	.378	4	1	1B-16, C-6
8 yrs.	470	1505	388	58	12	23	1.5	147	164	92	174	5	.258	.358	46	13	C-420, 1B-16

Von Joshua

JOSHUA, VON EVERETT
B. May 1, 1948, Oakland, Calif.

BL TL 5'10" 170 lbs.

	G	AB	H	2B	3B	HR	HR %	R	RBI	BB	SO	SB	BA	SA	AB	H	G by POS
1969 LA N	14	8	2	0	0	0	0.0	2	0	0	2	1	.250	.250	1	0	OF-8
1970	72	109	29	1	3	1	0.9	23	8	6	24	2	.266	.358	21	5	OF-41
1971	11	7	0	0	0	0	0.0	2	0	0	1	0	.000	.000	5	0	OF-5
1973	75	159	40	4	1	2	1.3	19	17	8	29	7	.252	.327	25	8	OF-46
1974	81	124	29	5	1	1	0.8	11	16	7	17	3	.234	.315	45	8	OF-35
1975 SF N	129	507	161	25	10	7	1.4	75	43	32	75	20	.318	.448	11	4	OF-117
1976 2 teams	SF N (42G – .263)			MIL A (107G – .267)													
" total	149	579	154	18	7	5	0.9	57	30	22	78	9	.266	.347	10	3	OF-140, DH-1
1977 MIL A	144	536	140	25	7	9	1.7	58	49	21	74	12	.261	.384	12	1	OF-140
1979 LA N	94	142	40	7	1	3	2.1	22	14	7	23	1	.282	.408	48	9	OF-46
1980 SD N	53	63	15	2	1	2	3.2	8	7	5	15	0	.238	.397	39	9	OF-12, 1B-2
10 yrs.	822	2234	610	87	31	30	1.3	277	184	108	338	55	.273	.380	217	47	OF-590, 1B-2, DH-1

LEAGUE CHAMPIONSHIP SERIES	G	AB	H	2B	3B	HR	HR %	R	RBI	BB	SO	SB	BA	SA	AB	H	G by POS
1974 LA N	1	0	0	0	0	0	–	0	0	1	0	0	–	–	0	0	

WORLD SERIES	G	AB	H	2B	3B	HR	HR %	R	RBI	BB	SO	SB	BA	SA	AB	H	G by POS
1974 LA N	4	4	0	0	0	0	0.0	0	0	0	0	0	.000	.000	4	0	

Ted Jourdan

JOURDAN, THEODORE CHARLES
B. Sept. 5, 1895, New Orleans, La.   D. Sept. 23, 1961, New Orleans, La.

BL TL 6' 175 lbs.

	G	AB	H	2B	3B	HR	HR %	R	RBI	BB	SO	SB	BA	SA	AB	H	G by POS
1916 CHI A	3	2	0	0	0	0	0.0	0	1	1	1	2	.000	.000	2	0	
1917	17	34	5	0	1	0	0.0	2	2	1	3	0	.147	.206	3	0	1B-14
1918	7	10	1	0	0	0	0.0	1	0	0	0	0	.100	.100	5	1	1B-2
1920	48	150	36	6	1	0	0.0	16	8	17	17	3	.240	.293	8	1	1B-40
4 yrs.	75	196	42	6	2	0	0.0	19	11	19	21	5	.214	.265	18	2	1B-56

Pop Joy

JOY, ALOYSIUS C.
B. June 11, 1860, Washington, D. C.   D. June 28, 1937, Washington, D. C.

	G	AB	H	2B	3B	HR	HR %	R	RBI	BB	SO	SB	BA	SA	AB	H	G by POS
1884 WAS U	36	130	28	0	0	0	0.0	12		2			.215	.215	0	0	1B-36

Joyce

JOYCE,
Deceased.

	G	AB	H	2B	3B	HR	HR %	R	RBI	BB	SO	SB	BA	SA	AB	H	G by POS
1884 WAS AA	4	17	5	0	0	0	0.0	2		1			.294	.294	0	0	OF-4
1886 WAS N	1	0	0	0	0	0	–	0	0	0	0	0			0	0	OF-1
2 yrs.	5	17	5	0	0	0	0.0	2		1	0		.294	.294	0	0	OF-5

	G	AB	H	2B	3B	HR	HR %	R	RBI	BB	SO	SB	BA	SA	Pinch Hit AB	Pinch Hit H	G by POS

Bill Joyce

JOYCE, WILLIAM MICHAEL (Scrappy Bill)
B. Sept. 21, 1865, St. Louis, Mo.   D. May 8, 1941, St. Louis, Mo.
BL TR 5'11''   185 lbs.
Manager 1896-98.

	G	AB	H	2B	3B	HR	HR %	R	RBI	BB	SO	SB	BA	SA	AB	H	G by POS
1890 BKN P	133	489	123	18	18	1	0.2	121	78	123	77	43	.252	.368	0	0	3B-133
1891 BOS AA	65	243	75	9	15	3	1.2	76	51	63	27	36	.309	.506	0	0	3B-64, 1B-1
1892 BKN N	97	372	91	15	12	6	1.6	89	45	82	55	23	.245	.398	0	0	3B-94, OF-3
1894 WAS N	99	355	126	25	14	17	4.8	103	89	87	33	21	.355	.648	0	0	3B-99
1895	126	474	148	25	13	17	3.6	110	95	96	54	29	.312	.527	0	0	3B-126
1896 2 teams		WAS	N	(81G –	.313)			NY	N	(49G –	.370)						
" total	130	475	158	25	12	14	2.9	121	94	101	34	45	.333	.524	0	0	3B-97, 2B-33
1897 NY N	110	396	121	15	13	3	0.8	110	64	78		33	.306	.432	0	0	3B-106, 1B-2
1898	145	508	131	20	9	10	2.0	91	91	88		34	.258	.392	0	0	1B-130, 3B-14, 2B-2
8 yrs.	905	3312	973	152	106	71	2.1	821	607	718	280	264	.294	.468	0	0	3B-733, 1B-133, 2B-35, OF-3

Mike Joyce

Playing record listed under Mike O'Neill

Oscar Judd

JUDD, THOMAS WILLIAM OSCAR (Ossie)
B. Feb. 14, 1908, Rebecca, Ont., Canada
BL TL 6'½''   180 lbs.

	G	AB	H	2B	3B	HR	HR %	R	RBI	BB	SO	SB	BA	SA	AB	H	G by POS
1941 BOS A	10	4	2	1	0	0	0.0	2	3	3	0	0	.500	.750	1	0	P-7
1942	36	67	18	2	1	2	3.0	10	4	3	7	0	.269	.418	5	1	P-31
1943	27	54	14	1	1	0	0.0	2	0	5	4	0	.259	.315	2	0	P-23
1944	10	11	2	0	0	0	0.0	1	3	0	1	0	.182	.182	1	0	P-9
1945 2 teams		BOS	A	(2G –	.500)			PHI	N	(27G –	.267)						
" total	29	32	9	2	0	0	0.0	4	2	4	4	0	.281	.344	3	0	P-25
1946 PHI N	46	79	25	2	1	1	1.3	7	8	4	4	0	.316	.405	14	2	P-30
1947	44	64	12	2	2	0	0.0	6	2	4	16	0	.188	.281	10	2	P-32
1948	4	6	1	1	0	0	0.0	1	0	1	2	0	.167	.333	0	0	P-4
8 yrs.	206	317	83	11	5	3	0.9	36	19	27	37	0	.262	.356	36	5	P-161

Frank Jude

JUDE, FRANK
B. 1885, Mahnomen County, Minn.   D. May 4, 1961, Brownsville, Tex.
BR TR 5'7''   150 lbs.

	G	AB	H	2B	3B	HR	HR %	R	RBI	BB	SO	SB	BA	SA	AB	H	G by POS
1906 CIN N	80	308	64	6	4	1	0.3	31	31	16		7	.208	.263	0	0	OF-80

Joe Judge

JUDGE, JOSEPH IGNATIUS
B. May 25, 1894, Brooklyn, N. Y.   D. Mar. 11, 1963, Washington, D. C.
BL TL 5'8½''   155 lbs.

	G	AB	H	2B	3B	HR	HR %	R	RBI	BB	SO	SB	BA	SA	AB	H	G by POS
1915 WAS A	12	41	17	2	0	0	0.0	7	9	4	6	2	.415	.463	0	0	1B-10, OF-2
1916	103	336	74	10	8	0	0.0	42	31	54	44	18	.220	.298	0	0	1B-103
1917	102	393	112	15	15	2	0.5	62	30	50	40	17	.285	.415	0	0	1B-100
1918	130	502	131	23	7	1	0.2	56	46	49	32	20	.261	.341	0	0	1B-130
1919	135	521	150	33	12	2	0.4	83	31	81	35	23	.288	.409	2	0	1B-133
1920	126	493	164	19	15	1	1.0	103	51	65	34	12	.333	.462	1	0	1B-124
1921	153	622	187	26	11	7	1.1	87	72	68	35	21	.301	.412	0	0	1B-152
1922	148	591	174	32	15	10	1.7	84	81	50	20	5	.294	.450	1	1	1B-148
1923	113	405	127	24	6	2	0.5	56	63	58	20	11	.314	.417	1	0	1B-112
1924	140	516	167	38	9	3	0.6	71	79	53	21	13	.324	.450	0	0	1B-140
1925	112	376	118	31	5	8	2.1	65	66	55	21	7	.314	.487	2	0	1B-109
1926	134	453	132	25	11	7	1.5	70	92	53	25	7	.291	.442	6	3	1B-128
1927	137	522	161	29	11	2	0.4	68	71	45	22	10	.308	.418	1	0	1B-136
1928	153	542	166	31	10	3	0.6	78	93	80	19	16	.306	.417	3	1	1B-149
1929	143	543	171	35	8	6	1.1	83	71	73	33	12	.315	.442	1	0	1B-142
1930	126	442	144	29	11	10	2.3	83	80	60	29	13	.326	.509	9	3	1B-117
1931	35	74	21	3	0	0	0.0	11	9	8	8	0	.284	.324	18	4	1B-15
1932	82	291	75	16	3	3	1.0	45	29	37	19	3	.258	.364	4	0	1B-78
1933 2 teams		BKN	N	(42G –	.214)			BOS	A	(34G –	.288)						
" total	76	216	54	10	2	0	0.0	27	31	20	14	3	.250	.315	18	4	1B-56
1934 BOS A	10	15	5	2	0	0	0.0	3	2	2	1	0	.333	.467	8	2	1B-2
20 yrs.	2170	7894	2350	433	159	71	0.9	1184	1037	965	478	213	.298	.420	75	18	1B-2084, OF-2

WORLD SERIES

	G	AB	H	2B	3B	HR	HR %	R	RBI	BB	SO	SB	BA	SA	AB	H	G by POS
1924 WAS A	7	26	10	1	0	0	0.0	4	0	5	2	0	.385	.423	0	0	1B-7
1925	7	23	4	1	0	1	4.3	2	4	3	2	0	.174	.348	0	0	1B-7
2 yrs.	14	49	14	2	0	1	2.0	6	4	8	4	0	.286	.388	0	0	1B-14

Walt Judnich

JUDNICH, WALTER FRANKLIN
B. Jan. 24, 1917, San Francisco, Calif.   D. July 12, 1971, Glendale, Calif.
BL TL 6'1''   205 lbs.

	G	AB	H	2B	3B	HR	HR %	R	RBI	BB	SO	SB	BA	SA	AB	H	G by POS
1940 STL A	137	519	157	27	7	24	4.6	97	89	54	71	8	.303	.520	4	1	OF-133
1941	146	546	155	40	6	14	2.6	90	83	80	45	5	.284	.456	6	3	OF-140
1942	132	457	143	22	6	17	3.7	78	82	74	41	3	.313	.499	9	4	OF-122
1946	142	511	134	23	4	15	2.9	60	72	60	54	0	.262	.411	3	0	OF-137
1947	144	500	129	24	3	18	3.6	58	64	60	62	2	.258	.426	2	1	1B-129, OF-15
1948 CLE A	79	218	56	13	3	2	0.9	36	29	56	23	2	.257	.372	10	2	OF-49, 1B-20
1949 PIT N	10	35	8	1	0	0	0.0	5	1	1	2	0	.229	.257	2	0	OF-8
7 yrs.	790	2786	782	150	29	90	3.2	424	420	385	298	20	.281	.452	36	11	OF-604, 1B-149

WORLD SERIES

	G	AB	H	2B	3B	HR	HR %	R	RBI	BB	SO	SB	BA	SA	AB	H	G by POS
1948 CLE A	4	13	1	0	0	0	0.0	1	1	1	4	0	.077	.077	0	0	OF-4

Lyle Judy

JUDY, LYLE LeROY (Punch)
B. Nov. 15, 1913, Lawrenceville, Ill.
BR TR 5'10''   150 lbs.

	G	AB	H	2B	3B	HR	HR %	R	RBI	BB	SO	SB	BA	SA	AB	H	G by POS
1935 STL N	8	11	0	0	0	0	0.0	2	0	2	2	2	.000	.000	0	0	2B-5

Red Juelich

JUELICH, JOHN SAMUEL
B. Sept. 20, 1916, St. Louis, Mo.   D. Dec. 25, 1970, St. Louis, Mo.
BR TR 5'11½''   168 lbs.

	G	AB	H	2B	3B	HR	HR %	R	RBI	BB	SO	SB	BA	SA	AB	H	G by POS
1939 PIT N	17	46	11	0	2	0	0.0	5	4	2	4	0	.239	.326	3	0	2B-10, 3B-2

	G	AB	H	2B	3B	HR	HR %	R	RBI	BB	SO	SB	BA	SA	Pinch Hit AB	Pinch Hit H	G by POS

George Jumonville

JUMONVILLE, GEORGE BENEDICT
B. May 16, 1917, Mobile, Ala.
BR TR 6' 175 lbs.

	G	AB	H	2B	3B	HR	HR %	R	RBI	BB	SO	SB	BA	SA	AB	H	G by POS
1940 PHI N	11	34	3	0	0	0	0.0	0	0	1	6	0	.088	.088	0	0	SS-10, 3B-1
1941	6	7	3	0	0	1	14.3	1	2	0	0	0	.429	.857	3	2	SS-1, 2B-1
2 yrs.	17	41	6	0	0	1	2.4	1	2	1	6	0	.146	.220	3	2	SS-11, 3B-1, 2B-1

Ed Jurak

JURAK, EDWARD JAMES (Lizard)
B. Oct. 24, 1957, Los Angeles, Calif.
BR TR 6'2" 165 lbs.

	G	AB	H	2B	3B	HR	HR %	R	RBI	BB	SO	SB	BA	SA	AB	H	G by POS
1982 BOS A	12	21	7	0	0	0	0.0	3	7	2	4	0	.333	.333	0	0	3B-11, OF-1
1983	75	159	44	8	4	0	0.0	19	18	18	25	1	.277	.377	4	2	SS-38, 1B-19, 3B-12, DH-5, 2B-1
1984	47	66	16	3	1	1	1.5	6	7	12	12	0	.242	.364	3	1	1B-19, 2B-14, 3B-9, SS-2
3 yrs.	134	246	67	11	5	1	0.4	28	32	32	41	1	.272	.370	7	3	SS-40, 1B-38, 3B-32, 2B-15, DH-5, OF-1

Bill Jurges

JURGES, WILLIAM FREDERICK
B. May 9, 1908, Bronx, N. Y.
Manager 1959-60.
BR TR 5'11" 175 lbs.

	G	AB	H	2B	3B	HR	HR %	R	RBI	BB	SO	SB	BA	SA	AB	H	G by POS
1931 CHI N	88	293	59	15	5	0	0.0	34	23	25	41	2	.201	.287	1	0	3B-54, 2B-33, SS-3
1932	115	396	100	24	4	2	0.5	40	52	19	26	1	.253	.348	1	0	SS-103, 3B-5
1933	143	487	131	17	6	5	1.0	49	50	26	39	3	.269	.359	0	0	SS-143
1934	100	358	88	15	2	8	2.2	43	33	19	34	1	.246	.366	2	1	SS-98
1935	146	519	125	33	1	1	0.2	69	59	42	39	3	.241	.314	0	0	SS-146
1936	118	429	120	25	1	1	0.2	51	42	23	25	4	.280	.350	0	0	SS-116
1937	129	450	134	18	10	1	0.2	53	65	42	41	2	.298	.389	0	0	SS-128
1938	137	465	114	18	3	1	0.2	53	47	58	53	3	.245	.303	0	0	SS-136
1939 NY N	138	543	155	21	11	6	1.1	84	63	47	34	3	.285	.398	0	0	SS-137
1940	63	214	54	3	3	2	0.9	23	36	25	14	2	.252	.322	0	0	SS-63
1941	134	471	138	25	2	5	1.1	50	61	47	36	0	.293	.386	0	0	SS-134
1942	127	464	119	7	1	2	0.4	45	30	43	42	1	.256	.289	3	1	SS-124
1943	136	481	110	8	2	4	0.8	46	29	53	38	2	.229	.279	8	3	SS-99, 3B-28
1944	85	246	52	2	1	1	0.4	28	23	23	20	4	.211	.240	14	2	3B-61, SS-10, 2B-1
1945	61	176	57	3	1	3	1.7	22	24	24	11	2	.324	.403	7	2	3B-44, SS-8
1946 CHI N	82	221	49	9	2	0	0.0	26	17	43	28	3	.222	.281	0	0	SS-73, 3B-7, 2B-2
1947	14	40	8	2	0	1	2.5	5	2	9	9	0	.200	.325	0	0	SS-14
17 yrs.	1816	6253	1613	245	55	43	0.7	721	656	568	530	36	.258	.335	36	9	SS-1535, 3B-199, 2B-36
WORLD SERIES																	
1932 CHI N	3	11	4	1	0	0	0.0	1	1	0	1	1	.364	.455	0	0	SS-3
1935	6	16	4	0	0	0	0.0	3	1	4	4	0	.250	.250	0	0	SS-6
1938	4	13	3	1	0	0	0.0	0	0	1	3	0	.231	.308	0	0	SS-4
3 yrs.	13	40	11	2	0	0	0.0	4	2	5	8	1	.275	.325	0	0	SS-13

Joe Just

JUST, JOSEPH ERWIN
Born Joseph Erwin Juszczak.
B. Jan. 8, 1916, Milwaukee, Wis.
BR TR 5'11" 185 lbs.

	G	AB	H	2B	3B	HR	HR %	R	RBI	BB	SO	SB	BA	SA	AB	H	G by POS
1944 CIN N	11	11	2	0	0	0	0.0	0	0	0	2	0	.182	.182	1	0	C-10
1945	14	34	5	0	0	0	0.0	2	2	4	7	0	.147	.147	0	0	C-14
2 yrs.	25	45	7	0	0	0	0.0	2	2	4	9	0	.156	.156	1	0	C-24

Skip Jutze

JUTZE, ALFRED HENRY
B. May 28, 1946, Bayside, N. Y.
BR TR 5'11" 190 lbs.

	G	AB	H	2B	3B	HR	HR %	R	RBI	BB	SO	SB	BA	SA	AB	H	G by POS
1972 STL N	21	71	17	2	0	0	0.0	1	5	1	16	0	.239	.268	4	0	C-17
1973 HOU N	90	278	62	6	0	0	0.0	18	18	19	37	0	.223	.245	3	0	C-86
1974	8	13	3	0	0	0	0.0	0	1	1	1	0	.231	.231	0	0	C-7
1975	51	93	21	2	0	0	0.0	9	6	2	4	1	.226	.247	2	0	C-47
1976	42	92	14	2	3	0	0.0	7	6	4	16	0	.152	.239	2	1	C-42
1977 SEA A	42	109	24	2	0	3	2.8	10	15	7	12	0	.220	.321	3	0	C-40
6 yrs.	254	656	141	14	3	3	0.5	45	51	34	86	1	.215	.259	14	1	C-239

Jack Kading

KADING, JOHN FREDERICK
B. Nov. 27, 1884, Waukesha, Wis. D. June 2, 1964, Chicago, Ill.
BR TR 6'3" 190 lbs.

	G	AB	H	2B	3B	HR	HR %	R	RBI	BB	SO	SB	BA	SA	AB	H	G by POS
1910 PIT N	8	23	7	2	1	0	0.0	5	4	4	5	0	.304	.478	0	0	1B-8
1914 CHI F	3	3	0	0	0	0	0.0	0	0	0		0	.000	.000	3	0	
2 yrs.	11	26	7	2	1	0	0.0	5	4	4	5	0	.269	.423	3	0	1B-8

Jake Kafora

KAFORA, FRANK JACOB (Tomatoes)
B. Oct. 16, 1888, Chicago, Ill. D. Mar. 23, 1928, Chicago, Ill.
BR TR 6' 180 lbs.

	G	AB	H	2B	3B	HR	HR %	R	RBI	BB	SO	SB	BA	SA	AB	H	G by POS
1913 PIT N	1	1	0	0	0	0	0.0	1	0	0	1	0	.000	.000	0	0	C-1
1914	21	23	3	0	0	0	0.0	2	0	0	6	0	.130	.130	3	0	C-17
2 yrs.	22	24	3	0	0	0	0.0	3	0	0	7	0	.125	.125	3	0	C-18

Ike Kahdot

KAHDOT, ISAAC LEONARD
B. Oct. 22, 1901, Georgetown, Okla.
BR TR 5'6" 160 lbs.

	G	AB	H	2B	3B	HR	HR %	R	RBI	BB	SO	SB	BA	SA	AB	H	G by POS
1922 CLE A	4	2	0	0	0	0	0.0	0	0	0	1	0	.000	.000	0	0	3B-2

Nick Kahl

KAHL, NICHOLAS ALEXANDER
B. Apr. 10, 1879, Coulterville, Ill. D. July 13, 1959, Sparta, Ill.
BR TR 5'9" 185 lbs.

	G	AB	H	2B	3B	HR	HR %	R	RBI	BB	SO	SB	BA	SA	AB	H	G by POS
1905 CLE A	39	131	29	4	1	0	0.0	16	21	4		1	.221	.267	6	1	2B-31, OF-1, SS-1

Bob Kahle

KAHLE, ROBERT WAYNE
B. Nov. 23, 1915, Newcastle, Ind.
BR TR 6' 170 lbs.

	G	AB	H	2B	3B	HR	HR %	R	RBI	BB	SO	SB	BA	SA	AB	H	G by POS
1938 BOS N	8	3	1	0	0	0	0.0	2	0	0	0	0	.333	.333	3	1	

	G	AB	H	2B	3B	HR	HR %	R	RBI	BB	SO	SB	BA	SA	Pinch Hit AB	Pinch Hit H	G by POS

Owen Kahn

KAHN, OWEN EARLE (Jack)   BR TR 5'11" 160 lbs.
B. June 5, 1905, Richmond, Va.   D. Jan. 17, 1981, Richmond, Va.

	G	AB	H	2B	3B	HR	HR%	R	RBI	BB	SO	SB	BA	SA	AB	H	G by POS
1930 BOS N	1	0	0	0	0	0	0	–	1	0	0	0	0	–	–	0	0

Mike Kahoe

KAHOE, MICHAEL JOSEPH   BR TR 6' 185 lbs.
B. Sept. 3, 1873, Yellow Springs, Ohio   D. May 14, 1949, Akron, Ohio

	G	AB	H	2B	3B	HR	HR%	R	RBI	BB	SO	SB	BA	SA	AB	H	G by POS
1895 CIN N	3	4	0	0	0	0	0.0	0	0	0	0	0	.000	.000	0	0	C-3
1899	14	42	7	1	1	0	0.0	2	4	0		1	.167	.238	1	0	C-13
1900	52	175	33	3	3	1	0.6	18	9	4		3	.189	.257	0	0	C-51, SS-1
1901 2 teams		CIN	N (4G – .308)		CHI	N (67G – .224)											
" total	71	250	57	12	2	1	0.4	21	21	9		5	.228	.304	0	0	C-67, 1B-6
1902 2 teams		CHI	N (7G – .222)		STL	A (55G – .244)											
" total	62	215	52	10	2	2	0.9	21	30	6		4	.242	.335	2	1	C-57, 3B-2, SS-1
1903 STL N	77	244	46	7	5	0	0.0	26	23	11		1	.189	.258	4	0	C-71, OF-2
1904	72	236	51	6	1	0	0.0	9	12	8		4	.216	.250	2	0	C-69
1905 PHI N	16	51	13	2	0	0	0.0	2	4	1		1	.255	.294	1	0	C-15
1907 2 teams		CHI	N (5G – .400)		WAS	A (17G – .191)											
" total	22	57	13	1	0	0	0.0	3	2	0		0	.228	.246	3	1	C-18, 1B-1
1908 WAS A	17	27	5	1	0	0	0.0	1	0	0		0	.185	.222	6	1	C-11
1909	4	8	1	0	0	0	0.0	0	0	0		2	.125	.125	1	0	C-3
11 yrs.	410	1309	278	43	14	4	0.3	103	105	39		21	.212	.276	20	3	C-378, 1B-7, OF-2, SS-2, 3B-2

Al Kaiser

KAISER, ALFRED EDWARD (Deerfoot)   BR TR 5'9" 165 lbs.
B. Aug. 3, 1886, Cincinnati, Ohio   D. Apr. 11, 1969, Cincinnati, Ohio

	G	AB	H	2B	3B	HR	HR%	R	RBI	BB	SO	SB	BA	SA	AB	H	G by POS
1911 2 teams		CHI	N (27G – .250)		BOS	N (65G – .203)											
" total	92	281	61	5	7	2	0.7	36	22	17	38	10	.217	.306	10	2	OF-81
1912 BOS N	4	13	0	0	0	0	0.0	0	0	0	3	0	.000	.000	0	0	OF-4
1914 IND F	59	187	43	10	0	1	0.5	22	16	17		6	.230	.299	7	2	OF-50, 1B-1
3 yrs.	155	481	104	15	7	3	0.6	58	38	34	41	16	.216	.295	17	4	OF-135, 1B-1

John Kalahan

KALAHAN, JOHN JOSEPH   BR TR 6' 165 lbs.
B. Sept. 30, 1878, Philadelphia, Pa.   D. June 20, 1952, Philadelphia, Pa.

	G	AB	H	2B	3B	HR	HR%	R	RBI	BB	SO	SB	BA	SA	AB	H	G by POS
1903 PHI A	1	5	0	0	0	0	0.0	0	0	0		0	.000	.000	0	0	C-1

Charlie Kalbfus

KALBFUS, CHARLES HENRY   5'11" 125 lbs.
B. Dec. 28, 1864, Washington, D. C.   D. Nov. 18, 1941, Washington, D. C.

	G	AB	H	2B	3B	HR	HR%	R	RBI	BB	SO	SB	BA	SA	AB	H	G by POS
1884 WAS U	1	5	1	0	0	0	0.0	1		0			.200	.200	0	0	OF-1

Frank Kalin

KALIN, FRANK BRUNO (Fats)   BR TR 6' 200 lbs.
Also known as Frank Bruno Kalinkiewicz.
B. Oct. 3, 1917, Steubenville, Ohio   D. Jan. 12, 1975, Weirtown, W. Va.

	G	AB	H	2B	3B	HR	HR%	R	RBI	BB	SO	SB	BA	SA	AB	H	G by POS
1940 PIT N	3	3	0	0	0	0	0.0	0	0	1	2	0	.000	.000	1	0	OF-2
1943 CHI A	4	4	0	0	0	0	0.0	0	0	0	0	0	.000	.000	4	0	
2 yrs.	7	7	0	0	0	0	0.0	0	0	1	2	0	.000	.000	5	0	OF-2

Al Kaline

KALINE, ALBERT WILLIAM   BR TR 6'1½" 175 lbs.
B. Dec. 19, 1934, Baltimore, Md.
Hall of Fame 1980.

	G	AB	H	2B	3B	HR	HR%	R	RBI	BB	SO	SB	BA	SA	AB	H	G by POS
1953 DET A	30	28	7	0	0	1	3.6	9	2	1	5	1	.250	.357	1	0	OF-20
1954	138	504	139	18	3	4	0.8	42	43	22	45	9	.276	.347	3	1	OF-135
1955	152	588	200	24	8	27	4.6	121	102	82	57	6	.340	.546	0	0	OF-152
1956	153	617	194	32	10	27	4.4	96	128	70	55	7	.314	.530	0	0	OF-153
1957	149	577	170	29	4	23	4.0	83	90	43	38	11	.295	.478	5	1	OF-145
1958	146	543	170	34	7	16	2.9	84	85	54	47	7	.313	.490	2	0	OF-145
1959	136	511	167	19	2	27	5.3	86	94	72	42	10	.327	.530	2	0	OF-136
1960	147	551	153	29	4	15	2.7	77	68	65	47	19	.278	.426	4	2	OF-142
1961	153	586	190	41	7	19	3.2	116	82	66	42	14	.324	.515	3	1	OF-147, 3B-1
1962	100	398	121	16	6	29	7.3	78	94	47	39	4	.304	.593	0	0	OF-100
1963	145	551	172	24	3	27	4.9	89	101	54	48	6	.312	.514	5	3	OF-140
1964	146	525	154	31	5	17	3.2	77	68	75	51	4	.293	.469	9	2	OF-136
1965	125	399	112	18	2	18	4.5	72	72	72	49	6	.281	.471	11	4	OF-112, 3B-1
1966	142	479	138	29	1	29	6.1	85	88	81	66	5	.288	.534	3	1	OF-136
1967	131	458	141	28	2	25	5.5	94	78	83	47	8	.308	.541	1	0	OF-130
1968	102	327	94	14	1	10	3.1	49	53	55	39	6	.287	.428	10	5	OF-74, 1B-22
1969	131	456	124	17	0	21	4.6	74	69	54	61	1	.272	.447	7	2	OF-118, 1B-9
1970	131	467	130	24	4	16	3.4	64	71	77	49	2	.278	.450	3	0	OF-91, 1B-52
1971	133	405	119	19	2	15	3.7	69	54	82	57	4	.294	.462	12	3	OF-129, 1B-5
1972	106	278	87	11	2	10	3.6	46	32	28	33	1	.313	.475	24	10	OF-84, 1B-11
1973	91	310	79	13	0	10	3.2	40	45	29	28	4	.255	.394	9	0	OF-63, 1B-36
1974	147	558	146	28	2	13	2.3	71	64	65	75	2	.262	.389	1	0	DH-146
22 yrs.	2834	10116	3007	498	75	399	3.9	1622	1583	1277	1020	137	.297	.480	115	37	OF-2488, DH-146, 1B-135, 3B-2
	9th																

LEAGUE CHAMPIONSHIP SERIES

	G	AB	H	2B	3B	HR	HR%	R	RBI	BB	SO	SB	BA	SA	AB	H	G by POS
1972 DET A	5	19	5	0	0	1	5.3	3	1	2	2	0	.263	.421	0	0	OF-5

WORLD SERIES

	G	AB	H	2B	3B	HR	HR%	R	RBI	BB	SO	SB	BA	SA	AB	H	G by POS
1968 DET A	7	29	11	2	0	2	6.9	6	8	0	7	0	.379	.655	0	0	OF-7

Willie Kamm

KAMM, WILLIAM EDWARD   BR TR 5'10½" 170 lbs.
B. Feb. 2, 1900, San Francisco, Calif.

	G	AB	H	2B	3B	HR	HR%	R	RBI	BB	SO	SB	BA	SA	AB	H	G by POS
1923 CHI A	149	544	159	39	9	6	1.1	57	87	62	82	17	.292	.430	0	0	3B-149
1924	147	528	134	28	6	6	1.1	58	93	64	59	9	.254	.364	0	0	3B-145
1925	152	509	142	32	4	6	1.2	82	83	90	36	11	.279	.393	0	0	3B-152
1926	143	480	141	24	10	0	0.0	63	62	77	24	14	.294	.385	1	0	3B-142
1927	148	540	146	32	13	0	0.0	85	59	70	18	7	.270	.378	2	0	3B-146
1928	155	552	170	30	12	1	0.2	70	84	73	22	17	.308	.411	0	0	3B-155

	G	AB	H	2B	3B	HR	HR %	R	RBI	BB	SO	SB	BA	SA	Pinch Hit AB	Pinch Hit H	G by POS

Willie Kamm continued

	G	AB	H	2B	3B	HR	HR%	R	RBI	BB	SO	SB	BA	SA	PH AB	PH H	G by POS
1929	147	523	140	32	6	3	0.6	72	63	75	23	12	.268	.369	2	1	3B-145
1930	111	331	89	21	6	3	0.9	49	47	51	20	5	.269	.396	5	0	3B-105
1931 2 teams		CHI	A	(18G –	.254)		CLE	A	(114G –	.295)							
" total	132	469	136	35	5	0	0.0	77	75	71	19	14	.290	.386	0	0	3B-132
1932 CLE A	148	524	150	34	9	3	0.6	76	83	75	36	6	.286	.403	0	0	3B-148
1933	133	447	126	17	2	1	0.2	59	47	54	27	7	.282	.336	2	0	3B-131
1934	121	386	104	23	3	0	0.0	52	42	62	38	7	.269	.345	4	2	3B-118
1935	6	18	6	0	0	0	0.0	2	1	0	1	0	.333	.333	2	0	3B-4
13 yrs.	1692	5851	1643	347	85	29	0.5	802	826	824	405	126	.281	.384	18	3	3B-1672

Alex Kampouris

KAMPOURIS, ALEX WILLIAM BR TR 5'8" 155 lbs.
B. Nov. 13, 1912, Sacramento, Calif.

	G	AB	H	2B	3B	HR	HR%	R	RBI	BB	SO	SB	BA	SA	PH AB	PH H	G by POS
1934 CIN N	19	66	13	1	0	0	0.0	6	3	3	18	2	.197	.212	2	0	2B-16
1935	148	499	123	26	5	7	1.4	46	62	32	84	8	.246	.361	2	0	2B-141, SS-6
1936	122	355	85	10	4	5	1.4	43	46	24	46	3	.239	.332	1	0	2B-119, OF-1
1937	146	458	114	21	4	17	3.7	62	71	60	65	2	.249	.424	0	0	2B-146
1938 2 teams		CIN	N	(21G –	.257)		NY	N	(82G –	.246)							
" total	103	342	85	10	1	7	2.0	48	44	37	63	0	.249	.345	3	0	2B-100
1939 NY N	74	201	50	12	2	5	2.5	23	29	30	41	0	.249	.403	1	0	2B-62, 3B-11
1941 BKN N	16	51	16	4	2	2	3.9	8	9	11	8	0	.314	.588	1	0	2B-15
1942	10	21	5	2	1	0	0.0	3	3	1	4	0	.238	.429	1	0	2B-9
1943 2 teams		BKN	N	(19G –	.227)		WAS	A	(51G –	.207)							
" total	70	189	40	8	1	2	1.1	33	17	47	31	7	.212	.296	6	2	3B-33, 2B-28, OF-1
9 yrs.	708	2182	531	94	20	45	2.1	272	284	244	360	22	.243	.367	17	2	2B-636, 3B-44, SS-6, OF-2

Frank Kane

KANE, FRANCIS THOMAS (Sugar) BL TR 5'11½" 175 lbs.
Born Francis Thomas Kiley.
B. Mar. 9, 1895, Whitman, Mass.   D. Dec. 2, 1962, Brockton, Mass.

	G	AB	H	2B	3B	HR	HR%	R	RBI	BB	SO	SB	BA	SA	PH AB	PH H	G by POS
1915 BKN F	3	10	2	0	1	0	0.0	2	2	0		0	.200	.400	1	0	OF-2
1919 NY A	1	1	0	0	0	0	0.0	0	0	0	0	0	.000	.000	1	0	
2 yrs.	4	11	2	0	1	0	0.0	2	2	0	0	0	.182	.364	2	0	OF-2

Jerry Kane

KANE, WILLIAM BR TR 6' 175 lbs.
B. 1867, Collinsville, Ill.   Deceased.

	G	AB	H	2B	3B	HR	HR%	R	RBI	BB	SO	SB	BA	SA	PH AB	PH H	G by POS
1890 STL AA	8	25	5	0	0	0	0.0	3		2		0	.200	.200	0	0	1B-5, C-4

Jim Kane

KANE, JAMES JOSEPH (Shamus) BL TL 6'2" 225 lbs.
B. Nov. 27, 1881, Scranton, Pa.   D. Oct. 2, 1947, Omaha, Neb.

	G	AB	H	2B	3B	HR	HR%	R	RBI	BB	SO	SB	BA	SA	PH AB	PH H	G by POS
1908 PIT N	55	145	35	3	3	0	0.0	16	22	12		5	.241	.303	14	1	1B-40

John Kane

KANE, JOHN FRANCIS BB TR 5'10½" 162 lbs.
B. Feb. 19, 1900, Chicago, Ill.   D. June 25, 1956, Chicago, Ill.

	G	AB	H	2B	3B	HR	HR%	R	RBI	BB	SO	SB	BA	SA	PH AB	PH H	G by POS
1925 CHI A	14	56	10	1	0	0	0.0	6	3	0	3	0	.179	.196	0	0	SS-8, 2B-6

Johnny Kane

KANE, JOHN FRANCIS BR TR 5'6" 138 lbs.
B. Sept. 24, 1882, Chicago, Ill.   D. Jan. 28, 1934, St. Anthony, Ida.

	G	AB	H	2B	3B	HR	HR%	R	RBI	BB	SO	SB	BA	SA	PH AB	PH H	G by POS
1907 CIN N	79	262	65	9	4	3	1.1	40	19	22		20	.248	.347	2	1	OF-42, 3B-25, SS-6, 2B-2
1908	130	455	97	11	7	3	0.7	61	23	43		30	.213	.288	1	0	OF-127, 2B-1
1909 CHI N	20	45	4	1	0	0	0.0	6	5	2		1	.089	.111	2	0	OF-8, SS-3, 3B-3, 2B-2
1910	32	62	15	0	0	1	1.6	11	12	9	10	2	.242	.290	0	0	OF-18, 2B-6, 3B-4, SS-2
4 yrs.	261	824	181	21	11	7	0.8	118	59	76	10	53	.220	.297	5	1	OF-195, 3B-32, SS-11, 2B-11

WORLD SERIES

	G	AB	H	2B	3B	HR	HR%	R	RBI	BB	SO	SB	BA	SA	PH AB	PH H	G by POS
1910 CHI N	1	0	0	0	0	0	–	0	0	0	0	0	–	–	0	0	

Tom Kane

KANE, THOMAS JOSEPH (Sugar) BR TR 5'10½" 160 lbs.
B. Dec. 15, 1906, Chicago, Ill.   D. Nov. 26, 1973, Chicago, Ill.

	G	AB	H	2B	3B	HR	HR%	R	RBI	BB	SO	SB	BA	SA	PH AB	PH H	G by POS
1938 BOS N	2	2	0	0	0	0	0.0	0	0	2	0	0	.000	.000	0	0	2B-2

Rod Kanehl

KANEHL, RODERICK EDWIN (Hot Rod) BR TR 6'1" 180 lbs.
B. Apr. 1, 1934, Wichita, Kans.

	G	AB	H	2B	3B	HR	HR%	R	RBI	BB	SO	SB	BA	SA	PH AB	PH H	G by POS
1962 NY N	133	351	87	10	2	4	1.1	52	27	23	36	8	.248	.322	11	3	2B-62, 3B-30, OF-20, 1B-3, SS-2
1963	109	191	46	6	0	1	0.5	26	9	5	26	6	.241	.288	21	5	OF-58, SS-13, 2B-12, 1B-3
1964	98	254	59	7	1	1	0.4	25	11	7	18	3	.232	.280	15	3	2B-34, OF-25, 3B-19, 1B-2
3 yrs.	340	796	192	23	3	6	0.8	103	47	35	80	17	.241	.300	47	11	2B-108, OF-103, 3B-62, 1B-8, SS-2

Heinie Kappel

KAPPEL, HENRY BR TR 5'8" 160 lbs.
Brother of Joe Kappel.
B. 1862, Philadelphia, Pa.   D. Aug. 27, 1905, Philadelphia, Pa.

	G	AB	H	2B	3B	HR	HR%	R	RBI	BB	SO	SB	BA	SA	PH AB	PH H	G by POS
1887 CIN AA	23	78	22	3	2	0	0.0	11		2		3	.282	.372	0	0	3B-9, OF-7, 2B-6, SS-1
1888	36	143	37	4	4	1	0.7	18	15	2		20	.259	.364	0	0	SS-25, 2B-10, 3B-1
1889 COL AA	46	173	47	7	5	3	1.7	25	21	21	28	10	.272	.422	0	0	SS-23, 3B-23
3 yrs.	105	394	106	14	11	4	1.0	54	35	25	28	33	.269	.391	0	0	SS-49, 3B-33, 2B-16, OF-7

Joe Kappel

KAPPEL, JOSEPH BR 5'10" 168 lbs.
Brother of Heinie Kappel.
B. 1857, Philadelphia, Pa.   D. July 8, 1929, Philadelphia, Pa.

	G	AB	H	2B	3B	HR	HR%	R	RBI	BB	SO	SB	BA	SA	PH AB	PH H	G by POS
1884 PHI N	4	15	1	0	0	0	0.0	1		0	2		.067	.067	0	0	C-4
1890 PHI AA	56	208	50	8	1	1	0.5	29		20		12	.240	.303	0	0	OF-23, SS-18, 3B-11, C-3, 2B-2
2 yrs.	60	223	51	8	1	1	0.4	30		20	2	12	.229	.287	0	0	OF-23, SS-18, 3B-11, C-7, 2B-2

	G	AB	H	2B	3B	HR	HR %	R	RBI	BB	SO	SB	BA	SA	Pinch Hit AB	Pinch Hit H	G by POS

Bill Karlon

KARLON, WILLIAM JOHN (Hank)
B. Jan. 21, 1909, Palmer, Mass.   D. Dec. 7, 1964, Monson, Mass.   BR TR 6'1" 190 lbs.

	G	AB	H	2B	3B	HR	HR %	R	RBI	BB	SO	SB	BA	SA	AB	H	G by POS
1930 NY A	2	5	0	0	0	0	0.0	0	0	0	1	0	.000	.000	1	0	OF-1

Marty Karow

KAROW, MARTIN GREGORY
B. July 18, 1904, Braddock, Pa.   BR TR 5'10½" 170 lbs.

	G	AB	H	2B	3B	HR	HR %	R	RBI	BB	SO	SB	BA	SA	AB	H	G by POS
1927 BOS A	6	10	2	1	0	0	0.0	0	0	0	2	0	.200	.300	1	1	SS-3, 3B-2

Benn Karr

KARR, BENJAMIN JOYCE (Baldy)
B. Nov. 28, 1893, Mt. Pleasant, Miss.   D. Dec. 8, 1968, Memphis, Tenn.   BL TR 6' 175 lbs.

	G	AB	H	2B	3B	HR	HR %	R	RBI	BB	SO	SB	BA	SA	AB	H	G by POS
1920 BOS A	57	75	21	5	0	1	1.3	8	15	6	18	0	.280	.387	29	9	P-26
1921	43	62	16	2	0	0	0.0	7	9	3	16	1	.258	.290	14	1	P-26
1922	66	98	21	2	0	0	0.0	7	4	4	7	1	.214	.235	22	2	P-41
1925 CLE A	46	92	24	5	0	1	1.1	11	17	7	8	0	.261	.348	13	3	P-32
1926	31	45	10	5	0	0	0.0	8	4	3	4	0	.222	.333	1	0	P-30
1927	22	20	4	1	0	0	0.0	2	0	4	6	1	.200	.250	0	0	P-22
6 yrs.	265	392	96	20	0	2	0.5	43	49	27	59	3	.245	.311	79	15	P-177

John Karst

KARST, JOHN GOTTLIEB (King)
B. Oct. 15, 1893, Philadelphia, Pa.   D. May 21, 1976, Cape May, N. J.   BL TR 5'11½" 175 lbs.

	G	AB	H	2B	3B	HR	HR %	R	RBI	BB	SO	SB	BA	SA	AB	H	G by POS
1915 BKN N	1	0	0	0	0	0	–	0	0	0	0	0	–	–	0	0	3B-1

Eddie Kasko

KASKO, EDWARD MICHAEL
B. June 27, 1932, Linden, N. J.   BR TR 6' 180 lbs.
Manager 1970-73.

	G	AB	H	2B	3B	HR	HR %	R	RBI	BB	SO	SB	BA	SA	AB	H	G by POS
1957 STL N	134	479	131	16	5	1	0.2	59	35	33	53	6	.273	.334	5	1	3B-120, SS-13, 2B-1
1958	104	259	57	8	1	2	0.8	20	22	21	25	1	.220	.282	10	3	SS-77, 2B-12, 3B-1
1959 CIN N	118	329	93	14	1	2	0.6	39	31	14	38	2	.283	.350	2	0	SS-84, 3B-31, 2B-2
1960	126	479	140	21	1	6	1.3	56	51	46	37	9	.292	.378	7	2	3B-86, 2B-33, SS-15
1961	126	469	127	22	1	2	0.4	64	27	32	36	4	.271	.335	7	2	SS-112, 3B-12, 2B-6
1962	134	533	148	26	2	4	0.8	74	41	35	44	3	.278	.356	4	1	3B-114, SS-21
1963	76	199	48	9	0	3	1.5	25	10	21	29	0	.241	.332	14	3	3B-48, SS-15, 2B-1
1964 HOU N	133	448	109	16	1	0	0.0	45	22	37	52	4	.243	.283	4	2	SS-128, 3B-2
1965	68	215	53	7	1	1	0.5	18	10	11	20	1	.247	.302	8	2	SS-59, 3B-2
1966 BOS A	58	136	29	7	0	1	0.7	11	12	15	19	1	.213	.287	20	3	SS-20, 3B-10, 2B-8
10 yrs.	1077	3546	935	146	13	22	0.6	411	261	265	353	31	.264	.331	81	19	SS-544, 3B-426, 2B-63

WORLD SERIES

	G	AB	H	2B	3B	HR	HR %	R	RBI	BB	SO	SB	BA	SA	AB	H	G by POS
1961 CIN N	5	22	7	0	0	0	0.0	1	1	0	2	0	.318	.318	0	0	SS-5

Ray Katt

KATT, RAYMOND FREDERICK
B. May 9, 1927, New Braunfels, Tex.   BR TR 6'2" 190 lbs.

	G	AB	H	2B	3B	HR	HR %	R	RBI	BB	SO	SB	BA	SA	AB	H	G by POS
1952 NY N	9	27	6	0	0	0	0.0	4	1	1	5	0	.222	.222	0	0	C-8
1953	8	29	5	1	0	0	0.0	2	1	1	3	0	.172	.207	0	0	C-8
1954	86	200	51	7	1	9	4.5	26	33	19	29	1	.255	.435	5	0	C-82
1955	124	326	70	7	2	7	2.1	27	28	22	38	0	.215	.313	3	2	C-122
1956 2 teams		NY	N (37G – .228)		STL	N (47G – .259)											
" total	84	259	64	8	0	13	5.0	21	34	12	40	0	.247	.429	0	0	C-84
1957 NY N	72	165	38	3	1	2	1.2	11	17	15	35	1	.230	.297	7	2	C-68
1958 STL N	19	41	7	1	0	1	2.4	1	4	4	6	0	.171	.268	5	0	C-14
1959	15	24	7	2	0	0	0.0	0	2	0	8	0	.292	.375	1	0	C-14
8 yrs.	417	1071	248	29	4	32	3.0	92	120	74	164	2	.232	.356	21	4	C-400

Benny Kauff

KAUFF, BENJAMIN MICHAEL
B. Jan. 5, 1890, Pomeroy, Ohio   D. Nov. 17, 1961, Columbus, Ohio   BL TL 5'8" 157 lbs.

	G	AB	H	2B	3B	HR	HR %	R	RBI	BB	SO	SB	BA	SA	AB	H	G by POS
1912 NY A	5	11	3	0	0	0	0.0	4	2	3		1	.273	.273	0	0	OF-4
1914 IND F	154	571	211	44	13	8	1.4	120	95	72		75	.370	.534	0	0	OF-154
1915 BKN F	136	483	165	23	11	12	2.5	92	83	85		55	.342	.509	0	0	OF-136
1916 NY N	154	552	146	22	15	9	1.6	71	74	68	65	40	.264	.408	0	0	OF-154
1917	153	559	172	22	4	5	0.9	89	68	59	54	30	.308	.388	0	0	OF-153
1918	67	270	85	19	4	2	0.7	41	39	16	30	9	.315	.437	0	0	OF-67
1919	135	491	136	27	7	10	2.0	73	67	39	45	21	.277	.422	1	1	OF-134
1920	55	157	43	12	3	3	1.9	31	26	25	14	3	.274	.446	3	1	OF-51
8 yrs.	859	3094	961	169	57	49	1.6	521	454	367	208	234	.311	.450	4	2	OF-853

WORLD SERIES

	G	AB	H	2B	3B	HR	HR %	R	RBI	BB	SO	SB	BA	SA	AB	H	G by POS
1917 NY N	6	25	4	1	0	2	8.0	2	5	0	2	1	.160	.440	0	0	OF-6

Dick Kauffman

KAUFFMAN, HOWARD RICHARD
B. June 22, 1888, East Lewisburg, Pa.   D. Apr. 16, 1948, Lewisburg, Pa.   BB TR 6'3" 190 lbs.

	G	AB	H	2B	3B	HR	HR %	R	RBI	BB	SO	SB	BA	SA	AB	H	G by POS
1914 STL A	7	15	4	1	0	0	0.0	1	2	0	3	0	.267	.333	1	0	1B-6
1915	37	124	32	8	2	0	0.0	9	14	5	27	0	.258	.355	4	1	1B-32, OF-1
2 yrs.	44	139	36	9	2	0	0.0	10	16	5	30	0	.259	.353	5	1	1B-38, OF-1

Charlie Kavanagh

KAVANAGH, CHARLES HUGH (Silk)
B. June 9, 1893, Chicago, Ill.   D. Sept. 6, 1973, Readsburg, Wis.   BR TR 5'10½" 170 lbs.

	G	AB	H	2B	3B	HR	HR %	R	RBI	BB	SO	SB	BA	SA	AB	H	G by POS
1914 CHI A	5	5	1	0	0	0	0.0	0	0	0	2	0	.200	.200	5	1	

Leo Kavanagh

KAVANAGH, LEO DANIEL
B. Aug. 9, 1894, Chicago, Ill.   D. Aug. 10, 1950, Chicago, Ill.   BR TR 5'9" 180 lbs.

	G	AB	H	2B	3B	HR	HR %	R	RBI	BB	SO	SB	BA	SA	AB	H	G by POS
1914 CHI F	5	11	3	0	0	0	0.0	0	1	1		0	.273	.273	0	0	SS-5

Marty Kavanagh

KAVANAGH, MARTIN JOSEPH
B. June 13, 1891, Harrison, N. J.   D. July 28, 1960, Taylor, Mich.   BR TR 6' 187 lbs.

	G	AB	H	2B	3B	HR	HR %	R	RBI	BB	SO	SB	BA	SA	AB	H	G by POS
1914 DET A	127	439	109	21	6	4	0.9	60	35	41	42	16	.248	.351	8	1	2B-115, 1B-4
1915	113	332	98	14	13	4	1.2	55	49	42	44	8	.295	.452	20	10	1B-44, 2B-42, OF-2, SS-2

	G	AB	H	2B	3B	HR	HR %	R	RBI	BB	SO	SB	BA	SA	Pinch Hit AB	Pinch Hit H	G by POS

Marty Kavanagh continued

	G	AB	H	2B	3B	HR	HR %	R	RBI	BB	SO	SB	BA	SA	AB	H	G by POS
1916 **2 teams**	DET A (58G – .141)			CLE A (19G – .250)													
" total	77	122	22	6	1	1	0.8	10	15	11	20	0	.180	.270	46	7	OF-11, 2B-11, 3B-3, 1B-1
1917 CLE A	14	14	0	0	0	0	0.0	1	0	3	2	0	.000	.000	9	0	OF-2
1918 **3 teams**	CLE A (13G – .211)			STL N (12G – .182)				DET A (13G – .273)									
" total	38	126	28	6	0	1	0.8	12	23	21	14	2	.222	.294	2	0	1B-24, OF-8, 2B-4
5 yrs.	369	1033	257	47	20	10	1.0	138	122	118	122	26	.249	.362	85	18	2B-172, 1B-73, OF-23, 3B-3, SS-2

Bill Kay

KAY, WALTER B. (King Bill)
B. Feb. 14, 1878, New Castle, Va.   D. Dec. 3, 1945, Roanoke, Va.

	G	AB	H	2B	3B	HR	HR %	R	RBI	BB	SO	SB	BA	SA	AB	H	G by POS
1907 WAS A	25	60	20	1	1	0	0.0	8	7	0			.333	.383	11	3	OF-12

Eddie Kazak

KAZAK, EDWARD TERRANCE
Born Edward Terrance Tkaczuk.
B. July 18, 1920, Steubenville, Ohio

BR TR 6'   175 lbs.

	G	AB	H	2B	3B	HR	HR %	R	RBI	BB	SO	SB	BA	SA	AB	H	G by POS
1948 STL N	6	22	6	3	0	0	0.0	1	2	0	2	0	.273	.409	0	0	3B-6
1949	92	326	99	15	3	6	1.8	43	42	29	17	0	.304	.423	7	2	3B-80, 2B-5
1950	93	207	53	2	2	5	2.4	21	23	18	19	0	.256	.357	42	10	3B-48
1951	11	33	6	2	0	0	0.0	2	4	5	5	0	.182	.242	1	0	3B-10
1952 **2 teams**	STL N (3G – .000)			CIN N (13G – .067)													
" total	16	17	1	0	1	0	0.0	2	0	0	2	0	.059	.176	9	1	3B-4, 1B-1
5 yrs.	218	605	165	22	6	11	1.8	69	71	52	45	0	.273	.383	59	13	3B-148, 2B-5, 1B-1

Ted Kazanski

KAZANSKI, THEODORE STANLEY
B. Jan. 25, 1934, Hamtramck, Mich.

BR TR 6'1"   175 lbs.

	G	AB	H	2B	3B	HR	HR %	R	RBI	BB	SO	SB	BA	SA	AB	H	G by POS
1953 PHI N	95	360	78	17	5	2	0.6	39	27	26	53	1	.217	.308	0	0	SS-95
1954	39	104	14	2	1	1	1.0	7	8	4	14	0	.135	.183	1	0	SS-38
1955	9	12	1	0	0	1	8.3	1	1	1	1	0	.083	.333	1	0	SS-4, 3B-4
1956	117	379	80	11	1	4	1.1	35	34	20	41	0	.211	.277	1	0	2B-116, SS-1
1957	62	185	49	7	1	3	1.6	15	11	17	20	1	.265	.362	5	1	3B-36, 2B-22, SS-3
1958	95	289	66	12	3	3	1.0	21	35	22	34	2	.228	.315	5	1	2B-59, SS-22, 3B-16
6 yrs.	417	1329	288	49	9	14	1.1	118	116	90	163	4	.217	.299	13	2	2B-197, SS-163, 3B-56

Bob Kearney

KEARNEY, ROBERT HENRY
B. Oct. 3, 1956, San Antonio, Tex.

BR TR 6'   190 lbs.

	G	AB	H	2B	3B	HR	HR %	R	RBI	BB	SO	SB	BA	SA	AB	H	G by POS
1979 SF N	2	0	0	0	0	0	–	0	0	0	0	0	–	–	0	0	C-1
1981 OAK A	1	0	0	0	0	0	–	0	0	0	0	0	–	–	0	0	C-1
1982	22	71	12	3	0	0	0.0	7	5	3	10	0	.169	.211	0	0	C-22
1983	108	298	76	11	0	8	2.7	33	32	21	50	1	.255	.372	8	0	C-101, DH-3
1984 SEA A	133	431	97	24	1	7	1.6	39	43	18	72	7	.225	.334	0	0	C-133
5 yrs.	266	800	185	38	1	15	1.9	79	80	43	132	8	.231	.338	8	0	C-258, DH-3

Ted Kearns

KEARNS, EDWARD JOSEPH
B. Jan. 1, 1900, Trenton, N. J.   D. Dec. 21, 1949, Trenton, N. J.

BR TR 5'11"   180 lbs.

	G	AB	H	2B	3B	HR	HR %	R	RBI	BB	SO	SB	BA	SA	AB	H	G by POS
1924 CHI N	4	16	4	0	1	0	0.0	0	1	1	1	0	.250	.375	0	0	1B-4
1925	3	2	1	0	0	0	0.0	0	0	0	0	0	.500	.500	0	0	1B-3
2 yrs.	7	18	5	0	1	0	0.0	0	1	1	1	0	.278	.389	0	0	1B-7

Tom Kearns

KEARNS, THOMAS J. (Dasher)
B. 1860, Rochester, N. Y.   D. Dec. 7, 1938, Buffalo, N. Y.

5'7"   160 lbs.

	G	AB	H	2B	3B	HR	HR %	R	RBI	BB	SO	SB	BA	SA	AB	H	G by POS
1880 BUF N	2	7	0	0	0	0	0.0	0		0	0		.000	.000	0	0	C-2
1882 DET N	4	13	4	2	0	0	0.0	2	1	0	4		.308	.462	0	0	2B-4
1884	21	79	16	0	1	0	0.0	9		2	10		.203	.228	0	0	2B-21
3 yrs.	27	99	20	2	1	0	0.0	11	1	2	14		.202	.242	0	0	2B-25, C-2

Eddie Kearse

KEARSE, EDWARD PAUL (Truck)
B. Feb. 23, 1916, San Francisco, Calif.   D. July 15, 1968, Eureka, Calif.

BR TR 6'1"   195 lbs.

	G	AB	H	2B	3B	HR	HR %	R	RBI	BB	SO	SB	BA	SA	AB	H	G by POS
1942 NY A	11	26	5	0	0	0	0.0	2	2	3	1	1	.192	.192	0	0	C-11

Chick Keating

KEATING, WALTER FRANCIS
B. Aug. 8, 1891, Philadelphia, Pa.   D. July 13, 1959, Philadelphia, Pa.

BR TR 5'9½"   155 lbs.

	G	AB	H	2B	3B	HR	HR %	R	RBI	BB	SO	SB	BA	SA	AB	H	G by POS
1913 CHI N	2	5	1	1	0	0	0.0	1	0	0	1	0	.200	.400	0	0	SS-2
1914	20	30	3	0	1	0	0.0	3	0	6	9	0	.100	.167	0	0	SS-16
1915	4	8	0	0	0	0	0.0	1	0	0	3	1	.000	.000	1	0	SS-2
1926 PHI N	4	2	0	0	0	0	0.0	0	0	0	0	0	.000	.000	0	0	SS-2, 2B-2, 3B-1
4 yrs.	30	45	4	1	1	0	0.0	5	0	6	13	1	.089	.156	1	0	SS-22, 2B-2, 3B-1

Greg Keatley

KEATLEY, GREGORY STEVEN
B. Sept. 12, 1953, Princeton, W. Va.

BR TR 6'2"   200 lbs.

	G	AB	H	2B	3B	HR	HR %	R	RBI	BB	SO	SB	BA	SA	AB	H	G by POS
1981 KC A	2	0	0	0	0	0	–	0	0	0	0	0	–	–	0	0	C-2

Willie Keeler

KEELER, WILLIAM HENRY (Wee Willie)
B. Mar. 3, 1872, Brooklyn, N. Y.   D. Jan. 1, 1923, Brooklyn, N. Y.
Hall of Fame 1939.

BL TL 5'4½"   140 lbs.

	G	AB	H	2B	3B	HR	HR %	R	RBI	BB	SO	SB	BA	SA	AB	H	G by POS
1892 NY N	14	53	17	3	0	0	0.0	7	6	3	3	5	.321	.377	0	0	3B-14
1893 **2 teams**	NY N (7G – .333)			BKN N (20G – .313)													
" total	27	104	33	3	2	2	1.9	19	16	9	5	5	.317	.442	0	0	3B-12, OF-11, SS-2, 2B-2
1894 BAL N	129	590	219	27	22	5	0.8	165	94	40	6	32	.371	.517	0	0	OF-128, 2B-1
1895	131	565	221	24	15	4	0.7	162	78	37	12	47	.391	.508	0	0	OF-131
1896	127	546	214	22	13	4	0.7	154	82	37	9	67	.392	.502	0	0	OF-126
1897	128	562	243	27	19	1	0.2	147	74	35		64	.432	.553	0	0	OF-129
1898	128	564	214	10	2	1	0.2	126	44	31		28	.379	.410	1	0	OF-128, 3B-1
1899 BKN N	143	571	215	13	14	1	0.2	140	61	37		45	.377	.454	0	0	OF-141
1900	137	565	208	11	14	4	0.7	106	68	30		41	.368	.458	0	0	OF-136, 2B-1
1901	136	589	209	16	15	2	0.3	123	43	21		23	.355	.443	0	0	OF-125, 3B-10, 2B-3

	G	AB	H	2B	3B	HR	HR %	R	RBI	BB	SO	SB	BA	SA	Pinch Hit AB	H	G by POS

Willie Keeler continued

		G	AB	H	2B	3B	HR	HR %	R	RBI	BB	SO	SB	BA	SA	AB	H	G by POS
1902		132	556	188	18	7	0	0.0	86	38	21		19	.338	.396	0	0	OF-132
1903	NY A	132	515	164	14	7	0	0.0	95	32	32		24	.318	.373	0	0	OF-128, 3B-4
1904		143	543	186	14	8	2	0.4	78	40	35		21	.343	.409	1	1	OF-142
1905		149	560	169	14	4	4	0.7	81	38	43		19	.302	.363	0	0	OF-139, 2B-12, 3B-3
1906		152	592	180	8	3	2	0.3	96	33	40		23	.304	.338	0	0	OF-152
1907		107	423	99	5	2	0	0.0	50	17	15		7	.234	.255	0	0	OF-107
1908		91	323	85	3	1	1	0.3	38	14	31		14	.263	.288	3	0	OF-88
1909		99	360	95	7	5	1	0.3	44	32	24		10	.264	.319	3	0	OF-95
1910	NY N	19	10	3	0	0	0	0.0	5	0	3	1	1	.300	.300	9	2	OF-2
19 yrs.		2124	8591	2962	239	153	34	0.4	1722	810	524	36	495	.345 5th	.420	17	3	OF-2040, 3B-44, 2B-19, SS-2

Bob Keely

KEELY, ROBERT WILLIAM   BR TR 6'   175 lbs.
B. Aug. 22, 1909, St. Louis, Mo.

		G	AB	H	2B	3B	HR	HR %	R	RBI	BB	SO	SB	BA	SA	AB	H	G by POS
1944	STL N	1	0	0	0	0	0	-	0	0	0	0	0	-	-	0	0	C-1
1945		1	1	0	0	0	0	0.0	0	0	0	0	0	.000	.000	0	0	C-1
2 yrs.		2	1	0	0	0	0	0.0	0	0	0	0	0	.000	.000	0	0	C-2

Bill Keen

KEEN, WILLIAM BROWN (Buster)   BR TR 6'   181 lbs.
B. Aug. 16, 1892, Oglethorpe, Ga.   D. July 16, 1947, South Point, Ohio

		G	AB	H	2B	3B	HR	HR %	R	RBI	BB	SO	SB	BA	SA	AB	H	G by POS
1911	PIT N	6	7	0	0	0	0	0.0	0	1	0	1	4	.000	.000	5	0	1B-1

Jim Keenan

KEENAN, JAMES WILLIAM   BR TR 5'10"   186 lbs.
B. May 25, 1898, New Haven, Conn.   D. Sept. 21, 1926, Cincinnati, Ohio

		G	AB	H	2B	3B	HR	HR %	R	RBI	BB	SO	SB	BA	SA	AB	H	G by POS
1880	BUF N	2	7	1	0	0	0	0.0	1		0	1	1	.143	.143	0	0	C-2
1882	PIT AA	25	96	21	7	0	1	1.0	10		1			.219	.323	0	0	C-22, OF-3, SS-1
1884	IND AA	68	249	73	14	4	3	1.2	36		16			.293	.418	0	0	C-59, 1B-6, OF-2, SS-1, P-1
1885	CIN AA	36	132	35	2	2	1	0.8	16		8			.265	.333	0	0	C-33, 1B-4, P-1
1886		44	148	40	4	3	3	2.0	31		18			.270	.399	0	0	C-30, OF-7, 3B-5, 1B-4, P-2
1887		47	174	44	4	1	0	0.0	19		11		7	.253	.287	0	0	C-38, 1B-11
1888		85	313	73	9	8	1	0.3	38	40	22		9	.233	.323	0	0	C-69, 1B-16
1889		87	300	86	10	11	6	2.0	52	60	48	35	18	.287	.453	0	0	C-66, 1B-21, 3B-1
1890	CIN N	54	202	28	4	2	3	1.5	21	19	19	36	5	.139	.223	0	0	C-50, 1B-2, OF-1, 3B-1
1891		75	252	51	7	5	4	1.6	30	33	33	39	2	.202	.317	0	0	1B-41, C-34, 3B-1
10 yrs.		523	1873	452	61	36	22	1.2	254	151	177	111	41	.241	.348	0	0	C-403, 1B-105, OF-13, 3B-8, P-4, SS-2

Jim Keesey

KEESEY, JAMES WARD   BR TR 6½"   170 lbs.
B. Oct. 27, 1902, Perryville, Md.   D. Sept. 5, 1951, Boise, Ida.

		G	AB	H	2B	3B	HR	HR %	R	RBI	BB	SO	SB	BA	SA	AB	H	G by POS
1925	PHI A	5	5	2	0	0	0	0.0	1	1	0	2	0	.400	.400	3	2	1B-2
1930		11	12	3	1	0	0	0.0	2	2	1	2	0	.250	.333	8	2	1B-3
2 yrs.		16	17	5	1	0	0	0.0	3	3	1	4	0	.294	.353	11	4	1B-5

Bill Keister

KEISTER, WILLIAM HOFFMAN (Wagon Tongue)   BR TR 5'5½"   168 lbs.
B. Aug. 17, 1874, Baltimore, Md.   D. Aug. 19, 1924, Baltimore, Md.

		G	AB	H	2B	3B	HR	HR %	R	RBI	BB	SO	SB	BA	SA	AB	H	G by POS
1896	BAL N	15	58	14	3	0	0	0.0	8	5	3	5	4	.241	.293	1	0	2B-8, 3B-6
1898	BOS N	10	30	5	2	0	0	0.0	5	4	0		0	.167	.233	1	0	SS-4, 2B-4, OF-1
1899	BAL N	136	523	172	22	16	3	0.6	96	73	16		33	.329	.449	0	0	SS-90, 2B-46, OF-1
1900	STL N	126	497	149	26	10	1	0.2	78	72	25		32	.300	.398	1	1	2B-116, SS-7, 3B-3
1901	BAL A	115	442	145	20	21	2	0.5	78	93	18		24	.328	.482	2	0	SS-112
1902	WAS A	119	483	145	33	9	9	1.9	82	90	14		27	.300	.462	1		OF-65, 2B-40, 3B-14, SS-2
1903	PHI N	100	400	128	27	7	3	0.8	53	63	14		11	.320	.445	0	0	OF-100
7 yrs.		621	2433	758	133	63	18	0.7	400	400	90	5	131	.312	.440	6	1	SS-215, 2B-214, OF-167, 3B-23

Mickey Keliher

KELIHER, MAURICE MICHAEL   BL TL 6'   175 lbs.
B. Jan. 11, 1890, Washington, D. C.   D. July 7, 1930, Washington, D. C.

		G	AB	H	2B	3B	HR	HR %	R	RBI	BB	SO	SB	BA	SA	AB	H	G by POS
1911	PIT N	2	7	0	0	0	0	0.0	0	0	0	5	0	.000	.000	1	0	1B-2
1912		2	0	0	0	0	0	-	1	0	0	0	0	-	-	0	0	
2 yrs.		4	7	0	0	0	0	0.0	1	0	0	5	0	.000	.000	1	0	1B-2

George Kell

KELL, GEORGE CLYDE   BR TR 5'9"   175 lbs.
Brother of Skeeter Kell.
B. Aug. 23, 1922, Swifton, Ark.
Hall of Fame 1983.

		G	AB	H	2B	3B	HR	HR %	R	RBI	BB	SO	SB	BA	SA	AB	H	G by POS
1943	PHI A	1	5	1	0	1	0	0.0	1	1	0	2	0	.200	.600	0	0	3B-1
1944		139	514	138	15	3	0	0.0	51	44	22	23	5	.268	.309	0	0	3B-139
1945		147	567	154	30	3	4	0.7	50	56	27	15	2	.272	.356	0	0	3B-147
1946	2 teams		PHI	A (26G – .299)					DET	A (105G – .327)								
"	total	131	521	168	25	10	4	0.8	70	52	40	20	3	.322	.432	0	0	3B-131, 1B-1
1947	DET A	152	588	188	29	5	5	0.9	75	93	61	16	9	.320	.412	0	0	3B-152
1948		92	368	112	24	3	2	0.5	47	44	33	15	2	.304	.402	0	0	3B-92
1949		134	522	179	38	9	3	0.6	97	59	71	13	7	.343	.467	0	0	3B-134
1950		157	641	218	56	6	8	1.2	114	101	66	18	3	.340	.484	0	0	3B-157
1951		147	598	191	36	3	2	0.3	92	59	61	18	10	.319	.400	0	0	3B-147
1952	2 teams		DET	A (39G – .296)					BOS	A (75G – .319)								
"	total	114	428	133	28	2	7	1.6	52	57	45	23	0	.311	.423	1	0	3B-112
1953	BOS A	134	460	141	41	2	12	2.6	68	73	52	22	5	.307	.483	8	4	3B-124, OF-7
1954	2 teams		BOS	A (26G – .258)					CHI	A (71G – .283)								
"	total	97	326	90	13	0	5	1.5	40	58	33	15	1	.276	.362	9	1	3B-56, 1B-32, OF-2
1955	CHI A	128	429	134	24	1	8	1.9	44	81	51	36	2	.312	.429	8	0	3B-105, 1B-24, OF-1

	G	AB	H	2B	3B	HR	HR %	R	RBI	BB	SO	SB	BA	SA	Pinch Hit AB	H	G by POS

George Kell continued

	G	AB	H	2B	3B	HR	HR %	R	RBI	BB	SO	SB	BA	SA	AB	H	G by POS
1956 2 teams	CHI A (21G – .313)					BAL A (102G – .261)											
" total	123	425	115	22	2	9	2.1	52	48	33	37	0	.271	.395	6	0	3B-115, 1B-6, 2B-1
1957 BAL A	99	310	92	9	0	9	2.9	28	44	25	16	2	.297	.413	11	4	3B-80, 1B-22
15 yrs.	1795	6702	2054	385	50	78	1.2	881	870	620	287	51	.306	.414	43	11	3B-1692, 1B-85, OF-10, 2B-1

Skeeter Kell

KELL, EVERETT LEE
Brother of George Kell.
B. Oct. 11, 1929, Swifton, Ark.

BR TR 5'9" 160 lbs.

	G	AB	H	2B	3B	HR	HR %	R	RBI	BB	SO	SB	BA	SA	AB	H	G by POS
1952 PHI A	75	213	47	8	3	0	0.0	24	17	14	18	5	.221	.286	1	0	2B-68

Duke Kelleher

KELLEHER, ALBERT ALOYSIUS
B. Sept. 30, 1893, New York, N. Y.   D. Sept. 28, 1947, Staten Island, N. Y.

TR

	G	AB	H	2B	3B	HR	HR %	R	RBI	BB	SO	SB	BA	SA	AB	H	G by POS
1916 NY N	1	0	0	0	0	0	–	0	0	0	0	0	–	–	0	0	C-1

Frankie Kelleher

KELLEHER, FRANCIS EUGENE
B. Aug. 22, 1916, San Francisco, Calif.   D. Apr. 13, 1979, Stockton, Calif.

BR TR 6'1" 195 lbs.

	G	AB	H	2B	3B	HR	HR %	R	RBI	BB	SO	SB	BA	SA	AB	H	G by POS
1942 CIN N	38	110	20	3	1	3	2.7	13	12	16	20	0	.182	.309	7	3	OF-30
1943	9	10	0	0	0	0	0.0	1	0	2	0	0	.000	.000	7	0	OF-1
2 yrs.	47	120	20	3	1	3	2.5	14	12	18	20	0	.167	.283	14	3	OF-31

John Kelleher

KELLEHER, JOHN PATRICK
B. Sept. 13, 1893, Brookline, Mass.   D. Aug. 21, 1960, Boston, Mass.

BR TR 5'11" 150 lbs.

	G	AB	H	2B	3B	HR	HR %	R	RBI	BB	SO	SB	BA	SA	AB	H	G by POS
1912 STL N	8	12	4	1	0	0	0.0	0	1	0	2	0	.333	.417	4	1	3B-3
1916 BKN N	2	3	0	0	0	0	0.0	0	0	0	0	0	.000	.000	0	0	SS-1, 3B-1
1921 CHI N	95	301	93	11	7	4	1.3	31	47	16	16	2	.309	.432	9	5	3B-37, 2B-27, SS-11, 1B-11, OF-1
1922	63	193	50	7	1	0	0.0	23	20	15	14	5	.259	.306	6	0	3B-46, SS-8, 1B-4
1923	66	193	59	10	0	6	3.1	27	21	14	9	2	.306	.451	15	6	1B-22, SS-14, 3B-11, 2B-6
1924 BOS N	1	1	0	0	0	0	0.0	0	0	0	1	0	.000	.000	1	0	
6 yrs.	235	703	206	29	8	10	1.4	81	89	45	42	9	.293	.400	35	12	3B-98, 1B-37, SS-33, 2B-33, OF-1

Mick Kelleher

KELLEHER, MICHAEL DENNIS
B. July 25, 1947, Seattle, Wash.

BR TR 5'9" 176 lbs.

	G	AB	H	2B	3B	HR	HR %	R	RBI	BB	SO	SB	BA	SA	AB	H	G by POS
1972 STL N	23	63	10	2	1	0	0.0	5	1	6	15	0	.159	.222	0	0	SS-23
1973	43	38	7	2	0	0	0.0	4	2	4	11	0	.184	.237	0	0	SS-42
1974 HOU N	19	57	9	0	0	0	0.0	4	2	5	10	1	.158	.158	0	0	SS-18
1975 STL N	7	4	0	0	0	0	0.0	0	0	0	1	0	.000	.000	0	0	SS-7
1976 CHI N	124	337	77	12	1	0	0.0	28	22	15	32	0	.228	.270	3	1	SS-101, 3B-22, 2B-5
1977	63	122	28	5	2	0	0.0	14	11	9	12	0	.230	.303	0	0	2B-40, SS-14, 3B-1
1978	68	95	24	1	0	0	0.0	8	6	7	11	4	.253	.263	3	1	3B-37, 2B-17, SS-10
1979	73	142	36	4	0	0	0.0	14	10	7	9	2	.254	.296	0	0	3B-32, 2B-29, SS-14
1980	105	96	14	1	1	0	0.0	12	4	9	17	1	.146	.177	3	1	2B-57, 3B-31, SS-17
1981 DET A	61	77	17	4	0	0	0.0	10	6	7	10	0	.221	.273	1	0	3B-29, 2B-11, SS-9
1982 2 teams	DET A (2G – .000)					CAL A (34G – .163)											
" total	36	50	8	1	0	0	0.0	9	1	5	5	1	.160	.180	1	0	SS-28, 3B-7, 2B-1
11 yrs.	622	1081	230	32	6	0	0.0	108	65	74	133	9	.213	.253	13	4	SS-283, 3B-169, 2B-160

Charlie Keller

KELLER, CHARLES ERNEST (King Kong)
Brother of Hal Keller.
B. Sept. 12, 1916, Middletown, Md.

BL TR 5'10" 185 lbs.

	G	AB	H	2B	3B	HR	HR %	R	RBI	BB	SO	SB	BA	SA	AB	H	G by POS
1939 NY A	111	398	133	21	6	11	2.8	87	83	81	49	6	.334	.500	4	2	OF-105
1940	138	500	143	18	15	21	4.2	102	93	106	65	8	.286	.508	0	0	OF-136
1941	140	507	151	24	10	33	6.5	102	122	102	65	6	.298	.580	3	0	OF-137
1942	152	544	159	24	9	26	4.8	106	108	114	61	14	.292	.513	0	0	OF-152
1943	141	512	139	15	11	31	6.1	97	86	106	60	7	.271	.525	0	0	OF-141
1945	44	163	49	7	4	10	6.1	26	34	31	21	0	.301	.577	0	0	OF-44
1946	150	538	148	29	10	30	5.6	98	101	113	101	1	.275	.533	1	0	OF-149
1947	45	151	36	6	1	13	8.6	36	36	41	18	0	.238	.550	2	0	OF-43
1948	83	247	66	15	2	6	2.4	41	44	41	25	1	.267	.417	15	2	OF-66
1949	60	116	29	4	1	3	2.6	17	16	25	15	2	.250	.379	27	3	OF-31
1950 DET A	50	51	16	1	3	2	3.9	7	16	13	6	0	.314	.569	32	9	OF-6
1951	54	62	16	2	0	3	4.8	6	21	11	12	0	.258	.435	38	9	OF-8
1952 NY A	2	1	0	0	0	0	0.0	0	0	0	1	0	.000	.000	1	0	OF-1
13 yrs.	1170	3790	1085	166	72	189	5.0	725	760	784	499	45	.286	.518	123	25	OF-1019
WORLD SERIES																	
1939 NY A	4	16	7	1	1	3	18.8	8	6	1	2	0	.438	1.188	0	0	OF-4
1941	5	18	7	2	0	0	0.0	5	5	3	1	0	.389	.500	0	0	OF-5
1942	5	20	4	0	0	2	10.0	2	5	1	3	0	.200	.500	0	0	OF-5
1943	5	18	4	0	1	0	0.0	3	2	2	5	1	.222	.333	0	0	OF-5
4 yrs.	19	72	22	3	2	5	6.9	18	18	7	11	1	.306	.611 **8th**	0	0	OF-19

Hal Keller

KELLER, HAROLD KEFAUVER
Brother of Charlie Keller.
B. July 7, 1927, Middletown, Md.

BL TR 6'1" 200 lbs.

	G	AB	H	2B	3B	HR	HR %	R	RBI	BB	SO	SB	BA	SA	AB	H	G by POS
1949 WAS A	3	3	1	0	0	0	0.0	1	0	1	0	0	.333	.333	3	1	C-8
1950	11	28	6	3	0	1	3.6	1	5	2	2	0	.214	.429	2	1	C-8
1952	11	23	4	2	0	0	0.0	2	0	1	1	0	.174	.261	0	0	C-11
3 yrs.	25	54	11	5	0	1	1.9	4	5	3	3	0	.204	.352	5	2	C-19

	G	AB	H	2B	3B	HR	HR %	R	RBI	BB	SO	SB	BA	SA	Pinch Hit AB	Pinch Hit H	G by POS

Frank Kellert

KELLERT, FRANK WILLIAM   BR TR 6'2½" 185 lbs.
B. July 6, 1924, Oklahoma City, Okla.   D. Nov. 19, 1976, Oklahoma City, Okla.

	G	AB	H	2B	3B	HR	HR %	R	RBI	BB	SO	SB	BA	SA	PH AB	PH H	G by POS
1953 STL A	2	4	0	0	0	0	0.0	0	0	0	0	0	.000	.000	1	0	1B-1
1954 BAL A	10	34	7	2	0	0	0.0	3	1	5	4	0	.206	.265	12	0	1B-9
1955 BKN N	39	80	26	4	2	4	5.0	12	19	9	10	0	.325	.575	13	3	1B-22
1956 CHI N	71	129	24	3	1	4	3.1	10	17	12	22	0	.186	.318	41	10	1B-27
4 yrs.	122	247	57	9	3	8	3.2	25	37	26	36	0	.231	.389	56	13	1B-59
WORLD SERIES																	
1955 BKN N	3	3	1	0	0	0	0.0	0	0	0	0	0	.333	.333	3	1	

Red Kellett

KELLETT, DONALD STAFFORD   BR TR 6' 185 lbs.
B. July 15, 1909, Brooklyn, N. Y.   D. Nov. 5, 1970, Ft. Lauderdale, Fla.

	G	AB	H	2B	3B	HR	HR %	R	RBI	BB	SO	SB	BA	SA	PH AB	PH H	G by POS
1934 BOS A	9	9	0	0	0	0	0.0	0	0	1	5	0	.000	.000	1	0	SS-4, 2B-2, 3B-1

Joe Kelley

KELLEY, JOSEPH JAMES   BR TR 5'11" 190 lbs.
B. Dec. 9, 1871, Cambridge, Mass.   D. Aug. 14, 1943, Baltimore, Md.
Manager 1902-05, 1908.
Hall of Fame 1971.

	G	AB	H	2B	3B	HR	HR %	R	RBI	BB	SO	SB	BA	SA	PH AB	PH H	G by POS
1891 2 teams		BOS	N (12G –	.244)		PIT	N (2G –	.143)									
" total	14	52	12	1	1	0	0.0	8	2	1	4	0	.231	.288	0	0	OF-14
1892 2 teams		PIT	N (56G –	.239)		BAL	N (10G –	.212)									
" total	66	238	56	7	7	0	0.0	29	32	21	28	10	.235	.324	0	0	OF-66
1893 BAL N	125	502	153	27	16	9	1.8	120	76	77	44	33	.305	.476	0	0	OF-125
1894	129	507	199	48	20	6	1.2	167	111	107	36	46	.393	.602	0	0	OF-129
1895	131	518	189	26	19	10	1.9	148	134	77	54	54	.365	.546	0	0	OF-131
1896	131	519	189	31	19	8	1.5	148	100	91	19	87	.364	.543	0	0	OF-130
1897	131	505	196	31	9	5	1.0	113	118	70		44	.388	.515	0	0	OF-130, SS-3, 3B-2
1898	124	467	153	18	15	2	0.4	71	110	56		24	.328	.443	1	0	OF-122, 3B-2
1899 BKN N	144	540	178	21	14	6	1.1	108	93	70		31	.330	.454	0	0	OF-143
1900	121	454	145	23	17	6	1.3	92	91	53		26	.319	.485	1	1	OF-77, 1B-32, 3B-13
1901	120	492	152	22	12	4	0.8	77	65	40		18	.309	.427	0	0	1B-115, 3B-5
1902 2 teams		BAL	A (60G –	.311)		CIN	N (40G –	.321)									
" total	100	378	119	24	9	2	0.5	74	46	49		15	.315	.442	1	1	OF-68, 3B-17, 2B-10, 1B-5, SS-2
1903 CIN N	105	383	121	22	4	3	0.8	85	45	51		18	.316	.418	1	0	OF-67, SS-12, 2B-11, 3B-8, 1B-6
1904	123	449	126	21	13	0	0.0	75	63	49		15	.281	.385	0	0	1B-117, OF-6, 2B-1
1905	90	321	89	7	6	1	0.3	43	37	27		8	.277	.346	3	0	OF-85, 1B-2
1906	129	465	106	19	11	1	0.2	43	53	44		9	.228	.323	2	1	OF-122, 1B-3, SS-1, 3B-1
1908 BOS N	62	228	59	8	2	0	0.9	25	17	27		5	.259	.338	10	1	OF-38, 1B-10
17 yrs.	1845	7018	2242	356	194 9th	65	0.9	1426	1193	910	160	443	.319	.453	19	4	OF-1453, 1B-290, 3B-48, 2B-22, SS-18

Mike Kelley

KELLEY, MICHAEL JOSEPH   BR TR 6' 210 lbs.
B. Dec. 2, 1876, Otter River, Mass.   D. June 6, 1955, Minneapolis, Minn.

	G	AB	H	2B	3B	HR	HR %	R	RBI	BB	SO	SB	BA	SA	PH AB	PH H	G by POS
1899 LOU N	76	282	68	11	2	3	1.1	48	33	21		10	.241	.326	0	0	1B-76

Frank Kelliher

KELLIHER, FRANK MORTIMER (Yucca)   BL TL 5'9½" 175 lbs.
B. May 23, 1899, Somerville, Mass.   D. Mar. 4, 1956, Somerville, Mass.

	G	AB	H	2B	3B	HR	HR %	R	RBI	BB	SO	SB	BA	SA	PH AB	PH H	G by POS
1919 WAS A	1	1	0	0	0	0	0.0	0	0	0	0	0	.000	.000	1	0	

Bill Kellogg

KELLOGG, WILLIAM DEARSTYNE   BR TR 5'10" 153 lbs.
B. May 25, 1884, Albany, N. Y.   D. Dec. 12, 1971, Baltimore, Md.

	G	AB	H	2B	3B	HR	HR %	R	RBI	BB	SO	SB	BA	SA	PH AB	PH H	G by POS
1914 CIN N	71	126	22	0	1	0	0.0	14	7	14	28	7	.175	.190	7	1	1B-38, 2B-11, OF-2, 3B-1

Nat Kellogg

KELLOGG, NATHANIEL MONROE
B. Sept. 28, 1858, Rochester, Iowa   D. 1915

	G	AB	H	2B	3B	HR	HR %	R	RBI	BB	SO	SB	BA	SA	PH AB	PH H	G by POS
1885 DET N	5	17	2	1	0	0	0.0	4	0	1	5		.118	.176	0	0	SS-5

Bill Kelly

KELLY, WILLIAM HENRY (Big Bill)   BR TR 6' 190 lbs.
B. Dec. 28, 1899, Syracuse, N. Y.

	G	AB	H	2B	3B	HR	HR %	R	RBI	BB	SO	SB	BA	SA	PH AB	PH H	G by POS
1920 PHI A	9	13	3	1	0	0	0.0	0	0	0	2	0	.231	.308	7	2	1B-2
1928 PHI N	23	71	12	1	1	0	0.0	6	5	7	20	0	.169	.211	0	0	1B-23
2 yrs.	32	84	15	2	1	0	0.0	6	5	7	22	0	.179	.226	7	2	1B-25

Bill Kelly

KELLY, WILLIAM JOSEPH   BR TR 6'½" 183 lbs.
B. May 1, 1886, Baltimore, Md.   D. June 3, 1940, Detroit, Mich.

	G	AB	H	2B	3B	HR	HR %	R	RBI	BB	SO	SB	BA	SA	PH AB	PH H	G by POS
1910 STL N	2	2	0	0	0	0	0.0	1	0	1	0	0	.000	.000	1	0	C-1
1911 PIT N	6	8	1	0	0	0	0.0	0	0	0	2	0	.125	.125	5	1	C-1
1912	48	132	42	3	2	1	0.8	20	11	2	16	8	.318	.394	3	0	C-39
1913	48	82	22	2	2	0	0.0	11	9	2	12	1	.268	.341	5	2	C-40
4 yrs.	104	224	65	5	4	1	0.4	32	20	5	30	9	.290	.362	14	3	C-81

Bob Kelly

KELLY, R B (Speed)   BR TR 6'2" 185 lbs.
B. Aug. 12, 1884, Brian, Ohio   D. May 6, 1949, Goshen, Ind.

	G	AB	H	2B	3B	HR	HR %	R	RBI	BB	SO	SB	BA	SA	PH AB	PH H	G by POS
1909 WAS A	17	42	6	2	1	0	0.0	3	1	3		1	.143	.238	2	0	3B-10, 2B-3, OF-1

Charlie Kelly

KELLY, CHARLES H.
Deceased.

	G	AB	H	2B	3B	HR	HR %	R	RBI	BB	SO	SB	BA	SA	PH AB	PH H	G by POS
1883 PHI N	2	7	1	0	1	0	0.0	1		0	3		.143	.429	0	0	3B-2
1886 PHI AA	1	3	0	0	0	0	0.0	0		0	0		.000	.000	0	0	SS-1
2 yrs.	3	10	1	0	1	0	0.0	1		0	3		.100	.300	0	0	3B-2, SS-1

	G	AB	H	2B	3B	HR	HR %	R	RBI	BB	SO	SB	BA	SA	Pinch Hit AB	Pinch Hit H	G by POS

Dale Kelly

KELLY, DALE PATRICK
B. Aug. 27, 1955, Santa Barbara, Calif.
BR TR 6'3" 210 lbs.

	G	AB	H	2B	3B	HR	HR %	R	RBI	BB	SO	SB	BA	SA	AB	H	G by POS
1980 TOR A	3	7	2	0	0	0	0.0	0	0		4	0	.286	.286	0	0	C-3

George Kelly

KELLY, GEORGE LANGE (Highpockets)
Brother of Ren Kelly.
B. Sept. 10, 1895, San Francisco, Calif.   D. Oct. 13, 1984, San Francisco, Calif.
Hall of Fame 1973.
BR TR 6'4" 190 lbs.

	G	AB	H	2B	3B	HR	HR %	R	RBI	BB	SO	SB	BA	SA	AB	H	G by POS
1915 NY N	17	38	6	0	0	1	2.6	2	4	1	9	0	.158	.237	2	0	1B-9, OF-4
1916	49	76	12	2	1	0	0.0	4	3	6	24	1	.158	.211	23	5	1B-13, OF-12, 3B-1
1917 2 teams	NY	N (11G – .000)		PIT	N	(8G –	.087)										
" total	19	30	2	0	1	0	0.0	2	0	1	12	0	.067	.133	3	0	1B-9, OF-3, 2B-1, P-1
1919 NY N	32	107	31	6	2	1	0.9	12	14	3	15	1	.290	.411	0	0	1B-32
1920	155	590	157	22	11	11	1.9	69	94	41	92	6	.266	.397	0	0	1B-155
1921	149	587	181	42	9	23	3.9	95	122	40	73	4	.308	.528	0	0	1B-149
1922	151	592	194	33	8	17	2.9	96	107	30	65	12	.328	.497	0	0	1B-151
1923	145	560	172	23	5	16	2.9	82	103	47	64	14	.307	.452	0	0	1B-145
1924	144	571	185	37	9	21	3.7	91	136	38	52	7	.324	.531	2	0	1B-125, OF-14, 2B-5, 3B-1
1925	147	586	181	29	3	20	3.4	87	99	35	54	5	.309	.471	0	0	2B-108, 1B-25, OF-17
1926	136	499	151	24	4	13	2.6	70	80	36	52	4	.303	.445	5	0	1B-114, 2B-18
1927 CIN N	61	222	60	16	4	5	2.3	27	21	11	23	1	.270	.446	1	0	1B-49, 2B-13, OF-2
1928	116	402	119	33	7	3	0.7	46	58	28	35	2	.296	.435	2	0	1B-99, OF-13
1929	147	577	169	45	9	5	0.9	73	103	33	61	7	.293	.428	0	0	1B-147
1930 2 teams	CIN	N (51G – .287)		CHI	N	(39G –	.331)										
" total	90	354	109	16	2	8	2.3	40	54	14	36	1	.308	.432	1	0	1B-89
1932 BKN N	64	202	49	9	1	4	2.0	23	22	22	27	0	.243	.356	1	0	1B-62, OF-1
16 yrs.	1622	5993	1778	337	76	148	2.5	819	1020	386	694	65	.297	.452	40	5	1B-1373, 2B-145, OF-66, 3B-2, P-1

WORLD SERIES

	G	AB	H	2B	3B	HR	HR %	R	RBI	BB	SO	SB	BA	SA	AB	H	G by POS
1921 NY N	8	30	7	1	0	0	0.0	3	3	3	10	0	.233	.267	0	0	1B-8
1922	5	18	5	0	0	0	0.0	0	2	0	3	0	.278	.278	0	0	1B-5
1923	6	22	4	0	0	0	0.0	1	1	1	2	0	.182	.182	0	0	1B-6
1924	7	31	9	1	0	1	3.2	7	4	1	8	0	.290	.419	0	0	1B-4
4 yrs.	26	101	25	2	0	1	1.0	11	10	5	23	0	.248	.297	0	0	1B-23
									10th								

Honest John Kelly

KELLY, JOHN C.
B. 1856, New York, N. Y.   D. Mar. 27, 1926, New York, N. Y.

	G	AB	H	2B	3B	HR	HR %	R	RBI	BB	SO	SB	BA	SA	AB	H	G by POS
1879 2 teams	SYR	N (10G – .111)		TRO	N	(6G –	.227)										
" total	16	58	9	1	0	0	0.0	5	2	0	7		.155	.172	0	0	C-11, OF-2, 1B-2, 3B-1

Joe Kelly

KELLY, JOSEPH HENRY
B. Sept. 23, 1886, Weir City, Kans.   D. Aug. 16, 1977, St. Joseph, Mo.
BR TR 5'9" 172 lbs.

	G	AB	H	2B	3B	HR	HR %	R	RBI	BB	SO	SB	BA	SA	AB	H	G by POS
1914 PIT N	141	508	113	19	9	1	0.2	47	48	39	59	21	.222	.301	2	0	OF-138
1916 CHI N	54	169	43	7	1	2	1.2	18	15	9	16	10	.254	.343	8	1	OF-46
1917 BOS N	116	445	99	9	8	3	0.7	41	36	26	45	21	.222	.299	0	0	OF-116
1918	47	155	36	2	4	0	0.0	20	15	6	12	12	.232	.297	2	1	OF-45
1919	18	64	9	1	0	0	0.0	3	3	0	11	2	.141	.156	2	1	OF-16
5 yrs.	376	1341	300	38	22	6	0.4	129	117	80	143	66	.224	.298	14	3	OF-361

Joe Kelly

KELLY, JOSEPH JAMES
B. Apr. 23, 1900, New York, N. Y.   D. Nov. 24, 1967, Lynbrook, N. Y.
BL TL 6' 180 lbs.

	G	AB	H	2B	3B	HR	HR %	R	RBI	BB	SO	SB	BA	SA	AB	H	G by POS
1926 CHI N	65	176	59	15	3	0	0.0	16	32	7	11	0	.335	.455	24	9	OF-39
1928	32	52	11	1	0	1	1.9	3	7	1	3	0	.212	.288	21	3	1B-10
2 yrs.	97	228	70	16	3	1	0.4	19	39	8	14	0	.307	.417	45	12	OF-39, 1B-10

John Kelly

KELLY, JOHN B.
B. Mar. 13, 1879, Clifton Heights, Pa.   D. Mar. 19, 1944, Baltimore, Md.
5'9" 165 lbs.

	G	AB	H	2B	3B	HR	HR %	R	RBI	BB	SO	SB	BA	SA	AB	H	G by POS
1907 STL N	53	197	37	5	0	0	0.0	12	6	13		7	.188	.213	1	0	OF-52

Kick Kelly

KELLY, JOHN FRANCIS (Father)
B. 1859, Patterson, N. J.   D. Apr. 13, 1908, Patterson, N. J.
BR TR 6' 185 lbs.

	G	AB	H	2B	3B	HR	HR %	R	RBI	BB	SO	SB	BA	SA	AB	H	G by POS
1882 CLE N	30	104	14	2	0	0	0.0	6	5	1	24		.135	.154	0	0	C-30
1883 2 teams	BAL	AA (48G – .228)		PHI	N	(1G –	.000)										
" total	49	205	46	9	2	0	0.0	18		3	2		.224	.288	0	0	C-38, OF-14
1884 2 teams	CIN	U (38G – .282)		WAS	U	(4G –	.357)										
" total	42	156	45	6	1	1	0.6	24		6			.288	.359	0	0	C-40, OF-3
3 yrs.	121	465	105	17	3	1	0.2	48	5	10	26		.226	.282	0	0	C-108, OF-17

King Kelly

KELLY, MICHAEL JOSEPH
B. Dec. 31, 1857, Troy, N. Y.   D. Nov. 8, 1894, Boston, Mass.
Manager 1890-91.
Hall of Fame 1945.
BR TR 5'10" 180 lbs.

	G	AB	H	2B	3B	HR	HR %	R	RBI	BB	SO	SB	BA	SA	AB	H	G by POS
1878 CIN N	60	237	67	7	1	0	0.0	29	27	7	7		.283	.321	0	0	OF-47, C-17, 3B-1
1879	77	345	120	20	12	2	0.6	78	47	8	14		.348	.493	0	0	3B-33, OF-29, C-21, 2B-1
1880 CHI N	84	344	100	17	9	1	0.3	72	60	12	22		.291	.401	0	0	OF-64, C-17, 3B-14, SS-1, 2B-1, P-1
1881	82	353	114	27	3	2	0.6	84	55	16	14		.323	.433	0	0	OF-72, C-11, 3B-8
1882	84	377	115	37	4	1	0.3	81	55	10	27		.305	.432	0	0	SS-42, OF-38, C-12, 3B-3, 1B-1
1883	98	428	109	28	10	3	0.7	92		16	35		.255	.388	0	0	OF-82, C-38, 2B-3, 3B-2, P-1
1884	108	452	160	28	5	13	2.9	120		46	24		.354	.524	0	0	OF-63, C-28, SS-12, 3B-10, 1B-2, P-2
1885	107	438	126	24	7	9	2.1	124	74	46	24		.288	.436	0	0	OF-69, C-37, 2B-6, 3B-2, 1B-2
1886	118	451	175	32	11	4	0.9	155	79	83	33		.388	.534	0	0	OF-56, C-53, 1B-9, 3B-8, 2B-6, SS-5

King Kelly continued

	G	AB	H	2B	3B	HR	HR%	R	RBI	BB	SO	SB	BA	SA	PH AB	PH H	G by POS
1887 BOS N	116	484	156	34	11	8	1.7	120	63	55	40	84	.322	.488	0	0	OF-61, 2B-30, C-24, P-3, SS-2, 3B-2
1888	107	440	140	22	11	9	2.0	85	71	31	39	56	.318	.480	0	0	C-76, OF-34
1889	125	507	149	41	5	9	1.8	120	78	65	40	68	.294	.448	0	0	OF-113, C-23
1890 BOS P	89	340	111	18	6	4	1.2	83	66	52	22	51	.326	.450	0	0	C-56, SS-27, OF-6, 1B-4, 3B-2, P-1
1891 3 teams	C-M AA (82G – .297)						BOS AA (4G – .267)			BOS N (24G – .235)							
" total	110	379	107	17	7	2	0.5	71	63	58	43	29	.282	.380	0	0	C-80, OF-22, 3B-8, 2B-6, 1B-5, P-3, SS-1
1892 BOS N	78	281	53	7	0	2	0.7	40	41	39	31	24	.189	.235	0	0	C-72, OF-2, 3B-2, 1B-2, P-1
1893 NY N	20	67	18	1	0	0	0.0	9	15	6	5	3	.269	.284	2	0	C-17, OF-1
16 yrs.	1463	5923	1820	360	102	69	1.2	1363	794	550	420	315	.307	.437	2	0	OF-759, C-582, 3B-96, SS-90, 2B-53, 1B-25, P-12

Pat Kelly

KELLY, HAROLD PATRICK   B. July 30, 1944, Philadelphia, Pa.   BL TL 6'1" 185 lbs.

	G	AB	H	2B	3B	HR	HR%	R	RBI	BB	SO	SB	BA	SA	PH AB	PH H	G by POS
1967 MIN A	8	1	0	0	0	0	0.0	1	0	1	0	1	.000	.000	1	0	
1968	12	35	4	2	0	1	2.9	2	2	3	10	0	.114	.257	2	0	OF-10
1969 KC A	112	417	110	20	4	8	1.9	61	32	49	70	40	.264	.388	3	0	OF-107
1970	136	452	106	16	1	6	1.3	56	38	76	105	34	.235	.314	17	1	OF-118
1971 CHI A	67	213	62	6	3	3	1.4	32	22	36	29	14	.291	.390	7	4	OF-61
1972	119	402	105	14	7	5	1.2	57	24	55	69	32	.261	.368	17	3	OF-109
1973	144	550	154	24	5	1	0.2	77	44	65	91	22	.280	.347	7	2	OF-141, DH-1
1974	122	424	119	16	3	4	0.9	60	21	46	58	18	.281	.361	3	0	DH-67, OF-53
1975	133	471	129	21	7	9	1.9	73	45	58	69	18	.274	.406	5	1	OF-115, DH-14
1976	107	311	79	20	3	5	1.6	42	34	45	45	15	.254	.386	20	7	DH-63, OF-26
1977 BAL A	120	360	92	13	0	10	2.8	50	49	53	75	25	.256	.375	11	5	OF-109, DH-5
1978	100	274	75	12	1	11	4.0	38	40	34	58	10	.274	.445	18	6	OF-80, DH-2
1979	68	153	44	11	0	9	5.9	25	25	20	25	4	.288	.536	23	11	OF-24, DH-18
1980	89	200	52	10	1	3	1.5	38	26	34	54	16	.260	.365	29	8	OF-36, DH-30
1981 CLE A	48	75	16	4	0	1	1.3	8	16	14	9	2	.213	.307	24	3	DH-18, OF-8
15 yrs.	1385	4338	1147	189	35	76	1.8	620	418	588	768	250	.264	.377	187	51	OF-997, DH-214

LEAGUE CHAMPIONSHIP SERIES

	G	AB	H	2B	3B	HR	HR%	R	RBI	BB	SO	SB	BA	SA	PH AB	PH H	G by POS
1979 BAL A	3	11	4	0	0	1	9.1	3	4	1	3	2	.364	.636	0		OF-2

WORLD SERIES

	G	AB	H	2B	3B	HR	HR%	R	RBI	BB	SO	SB	BA	SA	PH AB	PH H	G by POS
1979 BAL A	5	4	1	0	0	0	0.0	0	0	1	1	0	.250	.250	4	1	

R. J. Kelly

KELLY, ROBERT JOHN   Born Robert John Taggert.   B. Feb. 1, 1884, Bloomfield, N. J.   D. Apr. 10, 1961, Kingsport, Tenn.   BL TR 5'11" 180 lbs.

	G	AB	H	2B	3B	HR	HR%	R	RBI	BB	SO	SB	BA	SA	PH AB	PH H	G by POS
1914 PIT N	32	44	10	2	1	0	0.0	4	3	2	3	0	.227	.318	22	7	OF-7
1915 PIT F	148	524	154	12	17	4	0.8	68	50	35		38	.294	.405	0	0	OF-148
1918 BOS N	35	146	48	1	4	0	0.0	19	4	9		4	.329	.390	0	0	OF-35
3 yrs.	215	714	212	15	22	4	0.6	91	57	46	12	42	.297	.396	22	7	OF-190

Red Kelly

KELLY, ALBERT MICHAEL   B. Nov. 15, 1884, Union, Ill.   D. Feb. 4, 1961, Zephyr Hills, Fla.   BR TR 5'11½" 165 lbs.

	G	AB	H	2B	3B	HR	HR%	R	RBI	BB	SO	SB	BA	SA	PH AB	PH H	G by POS
1910 CHI A	14	45	7	0	1	0	0.0	6	1	7		0	.156	.200	0	0	OF-14

Tom Kelly

KELLY, JAY THOMAS   B. Aug. 15, 1950, Graceville, Minn.   BL TL 5'11" 188 lbs.

	G	AB	H	2B	3B	HR	HR%	R	RBI	BB	SO	SB	BA	SA	PH AB	PH H	G by POS
1975 MIN A	49	127	23	5	0	1	0.8	11	11	15	22	0	.181	.244	5	1	1B-43, OF-2

Van Kelly

KELLY, VAN HOWARD   B. Mar. 18, 1946, Charlotte, N. C.   BL TR 5'11" 180 lbs.

	G	AB	H	2B	3B	HR	HR%	R	RBI	BB	SO	SB	BA	SA	PH AB	PH H	G by POS
1969 SD N	73	209	51	7	1	3	1.4	16	15	12	24	0	.244	.330	16	4	3B-49, 2B-10
1970	38	89	15	3	0	1	1.1	9	9	15	21	0	.169	.236	11	1	3B-27, 2B-1
2 yrs.	111	298	66	10	1	4	1.3	25	24	27	45	0	.221	.302	27	5	3B-76, 2B-11

Billy Kelsey

KELSEY, GEORGE WILLIAM   B. Aug. 24, 1881, Covington, Ohio   D. Apr. 25, 1968, Springfield, Ohio   BR TR 5'10" 150 lbs.

	G	AB	H	2B	3B	HR	HR%	R	RBI	BB	SO	SB	BA	SA	PH AB	PH H	G by POS
1907 PIT N	2	5	2	0	0	0	0.0	0	0	0		0	.400	.400	0	0	C-2

Ken Keltner

KELTNER, KENNETH FREDERICK   B. Oct. 31, 1916, Milwaukee, Wis.   BR TR 6' 190 lbs.

	G	AB	H	2B	3B	HR	HR%	R	RBI	BB	SO	SB	BA	SA	PH AB	PH H	G by POS
1937 CLE A	1	1	0	0	0	0	0.0	0	1	0	0	0	.000	.000	0	0	3B-1
1938	149	576	159	31	9	26	4.5	86	113	33	75	4	.276	.497	0	0	3B-149
1939	154	587	191	35	11	13	2.2	84	97	51	41	6	.325	.489	0	0	3B-154
1940	149	543	138	24	10	15	2.8	67	77	51	56	10	.254	.418	1	0	3B-149
1941	149	581	156	31	13	23	4.0	83	84	51	56	2	.269	.485	0	0	3B-149
1942	152	624	179	34	4	6	1.0	72	78	20	36	4	.287	.383	1	0	3B-151
1943	110	427	111	31	3	4	0.9	47	39	36	20	2	.260	.375	3	1	3B-107
1944	149	573	169	41	9	13	2.3	74	91	53	29	4	.295	.466	0	0	3B-149
1946	116	398	96	17	1	13	3.3	47	45	30	38	0	.241	.387	4	1	3B-112
1947	151	541	139	29	3	11	2.0	49	76	59	45	5	.257	.383	1	0	3B-150
1948	153	558	166	24	4	31	5.6	91	119	89	52	2	.297	.522	0	0	3B-153
1949	80	246	57	9	2	8	3.3	35	30	38	26	0	.232	.382	10	2	3B-69
1950 BOS A	13	28	9	2	0	0	0.0	2	2	3	6	0	.321	.393	4	1	3B-8, 1B-1
13 yrs.	1526	5683	1570	308	69	163	2.9	737	852	514	480	39	.276	.441	24	5	3B-1500, 1B-1

WORLD SERIES

	G	AB	H	2B	3B	HR	HR%	R	RBI	BB	SO	SB	BA	SA	PH AB	PH H	G by POS
1948 CLE A	6	21	2	0	0	0	0.0	3	0	2	3	0	.095	.095	0	0	3B-6

	G	AB	H	2B	3B	HR	HR %	R	RBI	BB	SO	SB	BA	SA	Pinch Hit AB	Pinch Hit H	G by POS

John Kelty

KELTY, JOHN E. JOSEPH (Chief)
B. 1867, Jersey City, N. J.   Deceased.
5'10"   175 lbs.

	G	AB	H	2B	3B	HR	HR %	R	RBI	BB	SO	SB	BA	SA	PH AB	PH H	G by POS
1890 PIT N	59	207	49	10	2	1	0.5	24	27	22	42	10	.237	.319	0	0	OF-59

Bill Kemmer

KEMMER, WILLIAM E.
Deceased.
TR

	G	AB	H	2B	3B	HR	HR %	R	RBI	BB	SO	SB	BA	SA	PH AB	PH H	G by POS
1895 LOU N	11	38	7	0	0	1	2.6	5	3	2	4	0	.184	.263	0	0	3B-9, 1B-2

Rudy Kemmler

KEMMLER, RUDOLPH
B. 1860, Chicago, Ill.   D. June 20, 1909, Chicago, Ill.
BR TR

	G	AB	H	2B	3B	HR	HR %	R	RBI	BB	SO	SB	BA	SA	PH AB	PH H	G by POS
1879 PRO N	2	7	1	0	0	0	0.0	0	0	0	1		.143	.143	0	0	C-2
1881 CLE N	1	3	0	0	0	0	0.0	0	0	0	1		.000	.000	0	0	C-1
1882 2 teams	CIN	AA (3G – .091)			PIT	AA (24G – .253)											
" total	27	110	26	5	0	0		7			1		.236	.282	0	0	C-26, OF-2
1883 COL AA	84	318	66	6	2	0	0.0	27		13			.208	.239	0	0	C-82, OF-2
1884	61	211	42	3	3	0	0.0	28		15			.199	.242	0	0	C-58, 1B-2, OF-1
1885 PIT AA	18	64	13	2	1	0	0.0	2		2			.203	.266	0	0	C-18
1886 STL AA	35	123	17	2	0	0	0.0	13		8			.138	.154	0	0	C-32, 1B-3
1889 COL AA	8	26	3	0	0	0	0.0	2	0	3	3	0	.115	.115	0	0	C-8
8 yrs.	236	862	168	18	6	0	0.0	79		42	5	0	.195	.230	0	0	C-227, OF-5, 1B-5

Steve Kemp

KEMP, STEVEN F.
B. Aug. 7, 1954, San Angelo, Tex.
BL TL 6'   195 lbs.

	G	AB	H	2B	3B	HR	HR %	R	RBI	BB	SO	SB	BA	SA	PH AB	PH H	G by POS
1977 DET A	151	552	142	29	4	18	3.3	75	88	71	93	3	.257	.422	3	0	OF-148
1978	159	582	161	18	4	15	2.6	75	79	97	87	2	.277	.399	2	1	OF-157
1979	134	490	156	26	3	26	5.3	88	105	68	70	5	.318	.543	4	1	OF-120, DH-11
1980	135	508	149	23	4	21	4.1	88	101	69	64	5	.293	.474	6	2	OF-85, DH-46
1981	105	372	103	18	4	9	2.4	52	49	70	48	9	.277	.419	3	1	OF-92, DH-12
1982 CHI A	160	580	166	23	1	19	3.3	91	98	89	83	7	.286	.428	3	1	OF-154, DH-2
1983 NY A	109	373	90	17	3	12	3.2	53	49	41	37	1	.241	.399	9	2	OF-101, DH-2
1984	94	313	91	12	1	7	2.2	37	41	40	54	4	.291	.403	9	2	OF-75, DH-12
8 yrs.	1047	3770	1058	166	23	127	3.4	559	610	545	536	36	.281	.438	39	10	OF-932, DH-85

Fred Kendall

KENDALL, FRED LYN
B. Jan. 31, 1949, Torrance, Calif.
BR TR 6'1"   185 lbs.

	G	AB	H	2B	3B	HR	HR %	R	RBI	BB	SO	SB	BA	SA	PH AB	PH H	G by POS
1969 SD N	10	26	4	0	0	0	0.0	2	0	2	5	0	.154	.154	1	0	C-9
1970	4	9	0	0	0	0	0.0	0	1	0	0	0	.000	.000	1	0	C-2, OF-1, 1B-1
1971	49	111	19	1	0	1	0.9	7	7	7	16	1	.171	.207	7	1	C-39, 3B-1, 1B-1
1972	91	273	59	3	4	6	2.2	18	18	11	42	0	.216	.322	8	1	C-82, 1B-1
1973	145	507	143	22	3	10	2.0	39	59	30	35	3	.282	.396	5	1	C-138
1974	141	424	98	15	2	8	1.9	32	45	49	33	0	.231	.325	21	6	C-133
1975	103	286	57	12	1	0	0.0	16	24	26	28	0	.199	.248	18	4	C-85
1976	146	456	112	17	0	2	0.4	30	39	36	42	1	.246	.296	1	0	C-146
1977 CLE A	103	317	79	13	1	3	0.9	18	39	16	27	0	.249	.325	1	0	C-102, DH-1
1978 BOS A	20	41	8	1	0	0	0.0	3	4	1	2	0	.195	.220	2	0	1B-13, C-5
1979 SD N	46	102	17	2	0	1	1.0	8	6	11	7	0	.167	.216	8	4	C-40, 1B-2
1980	19	24	7	0	0	0	0.0	2	2	0	3	0	.292	.292	5	2	C-14, 1B-1
12 yrs.	877	2576	603	86	11	31	1.2	170	244	189	240	5	.234	.312	78	19	C-795, 1B-19, DH-1, OF-1, 3B-1

Al Kenders

KENDERS, ALBERT DANIEL GEORGE
B. Apr. 4, 1937, Barrington, N. J.
BR TR 6'   185 lbs.

	G	AB	H	2B	3B	HR	HR %	R	RBI	BB	SO	SB	BA	SA	PH AB	PH H	G by POS
1961 PHI N	10	23	4	1	0	0	0.0	0	1	1	0	0	.174	.217	0	0	C-10

Ed Kenna

KENNA, EDWARD ALOYISIUS (Scrap Iron)
B. Sept. 30, 1897, San Francisco, Calif.   D. Aug. 21, 1972, San Francisco, Calif.
BR TR 5'7½"   150 lbs.

	G	AB	H	2B	3B	HR	HR %	R	RBI	BB	SO	SB	BA	SA	PH AB	PH H	G by POS
1928 WAS A	41	118	35	4	2	1	0.8	14	20	14	8	1	.297	.390	7	2	C-34

Bob Kennedy

KENNEDY, ROBERT DANIEL
Father of Terry Kennedy.
B. Aug. 18, 1920, Chicago, Ill.
Manager 1963-65, 1968.
BR TR 6'2"   193 lbs.

	G	AB	H	2B	3B	HR	HR %	R	RBI	BB	SO	SB	BA	SA	PH AB	PH H	G by POS
1939 CHI A	3	8	2	0	0	0	0.0	0	1	0	0	0	.250	.250	1	0	3B-2
1940	154	606	153	23	3	3	0.5	74	52	42	58	3	.252	.315	0	0	3B-154
1941	76	257	53	9	3	1	0.4	16	29	17	23	5	.206	.276	0	0	3B-71
1942	113	412	95	18	5	0	0.0	37	38	22	41	11	.231	.299	1	0	3B-96, OF-16
1946	113	411	106	13	5	5	1.2	43	34	24	42	6	.258	.350	5	2	OF-75, 3B-29
1947	115	428	112	19	3	6	1.4	47	48	18	38	3	.262	.362	4	0	OF-106, 3B-1
1948 2 teams	CHI	A (30G – .248)			CLE	A (66G – .301)											
" total	96	186	50	11	3	0	0.0	14	19	8	23	0	.269	.360	12	6	OF-80, 2B-2, 1B-1
1949 CLE A	121	424	117	23	5	9	2.1	49	57	37	40	5	.276	.417	2	0	OF-98, 3B-21
1950	146	540	157	27	5	9	1.7	79	54	53	31	3	.291	.409	2	0	OF-144
1951	108	321	79	15	4	7	2.2	30	29	34	33	4	.246	.383	4	0	OF-106
1952	22	40	12	3	1	0	0.0	6	12	9	5	1	.300	.425	5	1	OF-13, 3B-3
1953	100	161	38	5	0	3	1.9	22	22	19	11	0	.236	.323	6	2	OF-89
1954 2 teams	CLE	A (1G – .000)			BAL	A (106G – .251)											
" total	107	323	81	13	2	6	1.9	37	45	28	43	2	.251	.359	17	4	3B-71, OF-22
1955 2 teams	BAL	A (26G – .143)			CHI	A (83G – .304)											
" total	109	284	75	11	2	9	3.2	38	48	26	26	0	.264	.412	23	4	3B-56, OF-34, 1B-9
1956 2 teams	CHI	A (8G – .077)			DET	A (69G – .232)											
" total	77	190	42	5	0	4	2.1	17	22	26	23	2	.221	.311	19	2	3B-33, OF-29
1957 2 teams	CHI	A (4G – .000)			BKN	N (19G – .129)											
" total	23	33	4	1	0	1	3.0	5	4	1	6	0	.121	.242	7	1	OF-9, 3B-3
16 yrs.	1483	4624	1176	196	47	63	1.4	514	514	364	443	45	.254	.355	108	21	OF-821, 3B-540, 1B-10, 2B-2

WORLD SERIES

	G	AB	H	2B	3B	HR	HR %	R	RBI	BB	SO	SB	BA	SA	PH AB	PH H	G by POS
1948 CLE A	3	2	1	0	0	0	0.0	0	1	0	1	0	.500	.500	0	0	OF-3

Doc Kennedy

KENNEDY, MICHAEL JOSEPH
B. Aug. 11, 1855, Brooklyn, N. Y.　D. May 25, 1920, Swains, N. Y.

	G	AB	H	2B	3B	HR	HR%	R	RBI	BB	SO	SB	BA	SA	Pinch Hit AB	Pinch Hit H	G by POS
1879 CLE N	49	193	56	8	2	1	0.5	19	18	2	10		.290	.368	0	0	C-46, 1B-4
1880	66	250	50	10	1	0	0.0	26		5	12		.200	.248	0	0	C-65, OF-2
1881	39	150	47	7	1	0	0.0	19	15	5	13		.313	.373	0	0	C-35, OF-3, 3B-1
1882	1	3	1	0	0	0	0.0	0	0	1	0		.333	.333	0	0	C-1
1883 BUF N	5	19	6	0	0	0	0.0	3		2	2		.316	.316	0	0	OF-4, 1B-1
5 yrs.	160	615	160	25	4	1	0.2	67	33	15	37		.260	.319	0	0	C-147, OF-9, 1B-5, 3B-1

Ed Kennedy

KENNEDY, EDWARD
B. Apr. 1, 1856, Carbondale, Pa.　D. May 20, 1905, New York, N. Y.

	G	AB	H	2B	3B	HR	HR%	R	RBI	BB	SO	SB	BA	SA	Pinch Hit AB	Pinch Hit H	G by POS
1883 NY AA	94	356	78	6	7	2	0.6	57		17			.219	.292	0	0	OF-94
1884	103	378	72	6	2	1	0.3	49		16			.190	.225	0	0	OF-100, SS-1, 2B-1, C-1
1885	96	349	71	8	4	2	0.6	35		12			.203	.266	0	0	OF-96
1886 BKN AA	6	22	4	0	0	0	0.0	1		2			.182	.182	0	0	OF-6
4 yrs.	299	1105	225	20	13	5	0.5	142		47			.204	.259	0	0	OF-296, SS-1, 2B-1, C-1

Ed Kennedy

KENNEDY, WILLIAM EDWARD　　　　　　　　　　　　BR TR 5'7" 160 lbs.
B. Apr. 5, 1861, Bellevue, Ky.　D. Dec. 22, 1912, Cheyenne, Wyo.

	G	AB	H	2B	3B	HR	HR%	R	RBI	BB	SO	SB	BA	SA	Pinch Hit AB	Pinch Hit H	G by POS
1884 CIN U	13	48	10	1	1	0	0.0	6		1			.208	.271	0	0	3B-8, SS-4, OF-1

Jim Kennedy

KENNEDY, JAMES EARL　　　　　　　　　　　　　BL TR 5'9" 160 lbs.
Brother of Junior Kennedy.
B. Nov. 1, 1946, Tulsa, Okla.

	G	AB	H	2B	3B	HR	HR%	R	RBI	BB	SO	SB	BA	SA	Pinch Hit AB	Pinch Hit H	G by POS
1970 STL N	12	24	3	0	0	0	0.0	1	0	0	0	0	.125	.125	1	0	SS-7, 2B-5

John Kennedy

KENNEDY, JOHN EDWARD　　　　　　　　　　　　BR TR 6' 185 lbs.
B. May 29, 1941, Chicago, Ill.

	G	AB	H	2B	3B	HR	HR%	R	RBI	BB	SO	SB	BA	SA	Pinch Hit AB	Pinch Hit H	G by POS
1962 WAS A	14	42	11	0	1	1	2.4	6	2	2	7	0	.262	.381	3	2	SS-9, 3B-2
1963	36	62	11	1	1	0	0.0	3	4	6	22	2	.177	.226	3	0	3B-26, SS-5
1964	148	482	111	16	4	7	1.5	55	35	29	119	3	.230	.324	3	0	3B-106, SS-49, 2B-2
1965 LA N	104	105	18	3	0	1	1.0	12	5	8	33	1	.171	.229	3	0	3B-95, SS-5
1966	125	274	55	9	2	3	1.1	15	24	10	64	1	.201	.281	1	0	3B-87, SS-25, 2B-15
1967 NY A	78	179	35	4	0	1	0.6	22	17	17	35	2	.196	.235	5	2	SS-36, 3B-34, 2B-2
1969 SEA A	61	128	30	3	1	4	3.1	18	14	14	25	4	.234	.367	5	0	SS-33, 3B-23
1970 2 teams		MIL A (25G – .255)				BOS A (43G – .256)											
" total	68	184	47	9	1	6	3.3	23	23	11	23	0	.255	.413	8	1	3B-38, 2B-18, SS-4, 1B-1
1971 BOS A	74	272	75	12	5	5	1.8	41	22	14	42	1	.276	.412	2	1	2B-37, SS-33, 3B-5
1972	71	212	52	11	1	2	0.9	22	22	18	40	0	.245	.335	5	0	2B-32, SS-27, 3B-11
1973	67	155	28	9	1	1	0.6	17	16	12	45	0	.181	.271	1	0	2B-31, 3B-24, DH-9
1974	10	15	2	0	0	1	6.7	3	1	1	6	0	.133	.333	0	0	2B-6, 3B-4
12 yrs.	856	2110	475	77	17	32	1.5	237	185	142	461	14	.225	.323	39	6	3B-455, SS-226, 2B-143, DH-9, 1B-1

WORLD SERIES

	G	AB	H	2B	3B	HR	HR%	R	RBI	BB	SO	SB	BA	SA	Pinch Hit AB	Pinch Hit H	G by POS
1965 LA N	4	1	0	0	0	0	0.0	0	0	0	0	0	.000	.000	0	0	3B-4
1966	2	5	1	0	0	0	0.0	0	0	0	0	0	.200	.200	0	0	3B-2
2 yrs.	6	6	1	0	0	0	0.0	0	0	0	0	0	.167	.167	0	0	3B-6

John Kennedy

KENNEDY, JOHN IRVIN　　　　　　　　　　　　　BR TR 5'10" 175 lbs.
B. Nov. 23, 1934, Sumter, S. C.

	G	AB	H	2B	3B	HR	HR%	R	RBI	BB	SO	SB	BA	SA	Pinch Hit AB	Pinch Hit H	G by POS
1957 PHI N	5	2	0	0	0	0	0.0	1	0		1	0	.000	.000	0	0	3B-2

Junior Kennedy

KENNEDY, JUNIOR RAYMOND　　　　　　　　　　BR TR 5'11" 175 lbs.
Brother of Jim Kennedy.
B. Aug. 9, 1950, Fort Gibson, Okla.

	G	AB	H	2B	3B	HR	HR%	R	RBI	BB	SO	SB	BA	SA	Pinch Hit AB	Pinch Hit H	G by POS
1974 CIN N	22	19	3	0	0	0	0.0	2	0	4	4	0	.158	.158	2	0	2B-17, 3B-5
1978	89	157	40	2	2	0	0.0	22	11	31	28	4	.255	.293	13	2	2B-71, 3B-4
1979	83	220	60	7	0	1	0.5	29	17	28	31	4	.273	.318	17	4	2B-59, SS-5, 3B-4
1980	104	337	88	16	3	1	0.3	31	34	36	34	3	.261	.335	1	0	2B-103
1981	27	44	11	1	0	0	0.0	5	5	1	5	0	.250	.273	6	1	2B-16, 3B-5
1982 CHI N	105	242	53	3	1	2	0.8	22	25	21	34	1	.219	.264	4	0	2B-71, SS-28, 3B-7
1983	17	22	3	0	0	0	0.0	3	3	1	6	0	.136	.136	2	0	2B-7, 3B-4, SS-1
7 yrs.	447	1041	258	29	6	4	0.4	114	95	124	142	12	.248	.299	45	7	2B-344, SS-34, 3B-29

Ray Kennedy

KENNEDY, RAYMOND LINCOLN　　　　　　　　　BR TR 5'9" 165 lbs.
B. May 19, 1895, Pittsburgh, Pa.　D. Jan. 18, 1969, Casselberry, Fla.

	G	AB	H	2B	3B	HR	HR%	R	RBI	BB	SO	SB	BA	SA	Pinch Hit AB	Pinch Hit H	G by POS
1916 STL A	1	1	0	0	0	0	0.0	0	0	0	0	0	.000	.000	1	0	

Snapper Kennedy

KENNEDY, SHERMAN MONTGOMERY　　　　　　　BB TR 5'10" 165 lbs.
B. Nov. 1, 1878, Conneaut, Ohio　D. Aug. 15, 1945, Pasadena, Tex.

	G	AB	H	2B	3B	HR	HR%	R	RBI	BB	SO	SB	BA	SA	Pinch Hit AB	Pinch Hit H	G by POS
1902 CHI N	1	5	0	0	0	0	0.0	0	0	0	0	0	.000	.000	0	0	OF-1

Terry Kennedy

KENNEDY, TERRENCE EDWARD　　　　　　　　　BL TR 6'3" 220 lbs.
Son of Bob Kennedy.
B. June 4, 1956, Euclid, Ohio

	G	AB	H	2B	3B	HR	HR%	R	RBI	BB	SO	SB	BA	SA	Pinch Hit AB	Pinch Hit H	G by POS
1978 STL N	10	29	5	0	0	0	0.0	2	4		3	0	.172	.172	1	0	C-10
1979	33	109	31	7	0	2	1.8	11	17	6	20	0	.284	.404	5	1	C-32
1980	84	248	63	12	3	4	1.6	28	34	28	34	0	.254	.375	12	2	C-41, OF-28
1981 SD N	101	382	115	24	1	2	0.5	32	41	22	53	0	.301	.385	3	0	C-100
1982	153	562	166	42	1	21	3.7	75	97	26	91	1	.295	.486	5	2	C-139, 1B-12
1983	149	549	156	27	2	17	3.1	47	98	51	89	1	.284	.434	4	2	C-143, 1B-4
1984	148	530	127	16	1	14	2.6	54	57	33	99	1	.240	.353	5	0	C-147
7 yrs.	678	2409	663	128	8	60	2.5	247	346	170	389	3	.275	.410	35	7	C-612, OF-28, 1B-16

LEAGUE CHAMPIONSHIP SERIES

	G	AB	H	2B	3B	HR	HR%	R	RBI	BB	SO	SB	BA	SA	Pinch Hit AB	Pinch Hit H	G by POS
1984 SD N	5	18	4	0	0	0	0.0	1	1	1	3	0	.222	.222	0	0	C-5

WORLD SERIES

	G	AB	H	2B	3B	HR	HR%	R	RBI	BB	SO	SB	BA	SA	Pinch Hit AB	Pinch Hit H	G by POS
1984 SD N	5	19	4	1	0	1	5.3	2	3	1	1	0	.211	.421	0	0	C-5

	G	AB	H	2B	3B	HR	HR %	R	RBI	BB	SO	SB	BA	SA	Pinch Hit AB	Pinch Hit H	G by POS

Jerry Kenney

KENNEY, GERALD TENNYSON, JR.
B. June 30, 1945, St. Louis, Mo.   BL TR 6'1"   170 lbs.

	G	AB	H	2B	3B	HR	HR %	R	RBI	BB	SO	SB	BA	SA	PH AB	PH H	G by POS
1967 NY A	20	58	18	2	0	1	1.7	4	5	10	8	2	.310	.397	2	0	SS-18
1969	130	447	115	14	2	2	0.4	49	34	48	36	25	.257	.311	11	4	3B-83, OF-31, SS-10
1970	140	404	78	10	7	4	1.0	46	35	52	44	20	.193	.282	1	0	3B-135, 2B-2
1971	120	325	85	10	3	0	0.0	50	20	56	38	9	.262	.311	4	0	3B-109, SS-5, 1B-1
1972	50	119	25	2	0	0	0.0	16	7	16	13	3	.210	.227	4	1	SS-45, 3B-1
1973 CLE A	5	16	4	0	1	0	0.0	0	2	2	0	0	.250	.375	0	0	2B-5
6 yrs.	465	1369	325	38	13	7	0.5	165	103	184	139	59	.237	.299	22	5	3B-328, SS-78, OF-31, 2B-7, 1B-1

Dick Kenworthy

KENWORTHY, RICHARD LEE
B. Apr. 1, 1941, Red Oak, Iowa   BR TR 5'9"   170 lbs.

	G	AB	H	2B	3B	HR	HR %	R	RBI	BB	SO	SB	BA	SA	PH AB	PH H	G by POS
1962 CHI A	3	4	0	0	0	0	0.0	0	0	0	3	0	.000	.000	1	0	2B-2
1964	2	2	0	0	0	0	0.0	0	0	0	1	0	.000	.000	2	0	
1965	3	1	0	0	0	0	0.0	0	0	1	0	0	.000	.000	1	0	
1966	9	25	5	0	0	0	0.0	1	0	0	0	0	.200	.200	3	1	3B-6
1967	50	97	22	4	1	4	4.1	9	11	4	17	0	.227	.412	15	0	3B-35
1968	58	122	27	2	0	0	0.0	2	2	5	21	0	.221	.238	19	5	3B-38
6 yrs.	125	251	54	6	1	4	1.6	12	13	10	42	0	.215	.295	41	6	3B-79, 2B-2

Duke Kenworthy

KENWORTHY, WILLIAM JENNINGS
B. July 3, 1886, Hopewell, Ohio   D. Sept. 21, 1950, Eureka, Calif.   BB TR 5'7"   165 lbs.

	G	AB	H	2B	3B	HR	HR %	R	RBI	BB	SO	SB	BA	SA	PH AB	PH H	G by POS
1912 WAS A	12	38	9	1	0	0	0.0	6	2	2		3	.237	.263	2	0	OF-10
1914 KC F	146	545	173	40	14	15	2.8	93	91	36		37	.317	.525	1	0	2B-145
1915	122	396	118	30	7	3	0.8	59	52	28		20	.298	.432	6	1	2B-108, OF-7
1917 STL A	5	10	1	0	0	0	0.0	1	1	1	1	1	.100	.100	1	0	2B-4
4 yrs.	285	989	301	71	21	18	1.8	159	146	67	1	61	.304	.473	10	1	2B-257, OF-17

Joe Keough

KEOUGH, JOSEPH WILLIAM
Brother of Marty Keough.
B. Jan. 7, 1946, Pomona, Calif.   BL TL 6'   185 lbs.

	G	AB	H	2B	3B	HR	HR %	R	RBI	BB	SO	SB	BA	SA	PH AB	PH H	G by POS
1968 OAK A	34	98	21	2	1	2	2.0	7	18	8	11	1	.214	.316	3	1	OF-29, 1B-1
1969 KC A	70	166	31	2	0	0	0.0	17	7	13	13	5	.187	.199	20	3	OF-49, 1B-1
1970	57	183	59	6	2	4	2.2	28	21	23	18	1	.322	.443	8	2	OF-34, 1B-18
1971	110	351	87	14	2	3	0.9	34	30	35	26	0	.248	.325	11	4	OF-100
1972	56	64	14	2	0	0	0.0	8	5	8	7	2	.219	.250	31	6	OF-16
1973 CHI A	5	1	0	0	0	0	0.0	1	0	0	0	0	.000	.000	1	0	
6 yrs.	332	863	212	26	5	9	1.0	95	81	87	75	9	.246	.319	74	18	OF-228, 1B-20

Marty Keough

KEOUGH, RICHARD MARTIN
Father of Matt Keough.   Brother of Joe Keough.
B. Apr. 14, 1935, Oakland, Calif.   BL TL 6'   180 lbs.

	G	AB	H	2B	3B	HR	HR %	R	RBI	BB	SO	SB	BA	SA	PH AB	PH H	G by POS
1956 BOS A	3	2	0	0	0	0	0.0	1		1	0	0	.000	.000	2	0	
1957	9	17	1	0	0	0	0.0	1	0	4	3	0	.059	.059	1	0	OF-7
1958	68	118	26	3	3	1	0.8	21	9	7	29	1	.220	.322	34	5	OF-25, 1B-2
1959	96	251	61	13	5	7	2.8	40	27	26	40	3	.243	.418	27	7	OF-69, 1B-3
1960 2 teams	BOS A (38G – .248)				CLE A (65G – .248)												
" total	103	254	63	11	1	4	1.6	34	20	17	31	4	.248	.346	32	5	OF-71
1961 WAS A	135	390	97	18	9	9	2.3	57	34	32	60	12	.249	.410	17	4	OF-100, 1B-10
1962 CIN N	111	230	64	8	2	7	3.0	34	27	21	31	3	.278	.422	20	4	OF-71, 1B-29
1963	95	172	39	8	2	6	3.5	21	21	25	37	1	.227	.401	24	4	1B-46, OF-28
1964	109	276	71	9	1	9	3.3	29	28	22	58	1	.257	.395	34	9	OF-81, 1B-4
1965	62	43	5	0	0	0	0.0	14	3	3	14	0	.116	.116	21	4	1B-32, OF-4
1966 2 teams	ATL N (17G – .059)				CHI N (33G – .231)												
" total	50	43	7	1	0	0	0.0	4	6	6	15	1	.163	.186	31	5	OF-8, 1B-4
11 yrs.	841	1796	434	71	23	43	2.4	256	176	164	318	26	.242	.379	243	47	OF-464, 1B-130

John Kerins

KERINS, JOHN NELSON
B. Dec. 22, 1858, Indianapolis, Ind.   D. Sept. 15, 1919, Louisville, Ky.
Manager 1888.   BR TR 5'10"   177 lbs.

	G	AB	H	2B	3B	HR	HR %	R	RBI	BB	SO	SB	BA	SA	PH AB	PH H	G by POS
1884 IND AA	93	361	78	10	3	6	1.7	58		6			.216	.310	0	0	1B-87, C-5, OF-4, 3B-1
1885 LOU AA	112	456	111	9	16	3	0.7	65		20			.243	.353	0	0	1B-96, C-19, OF-3, 3B-1
1886	120	487	131	19	9	4	0.8	113		66			.269	.370	0	0	C-65, 1B-47, OF-7, SS-1
1887	112	476	140	18	19	5	1.1	101		38		49	.294	.443	0	0	1B-74, C-35, OF-5
1888	83	319	75	11	4	2	0.6	38	41	25		16	.235	.313	0	0	OF-47, C-33, 1B-4, 3B-2, 2B-1
1889 2 teams	LOU AA (2G – .333)				BAL AA (16G – .283)												
"	18	62	18	3	0	0	0.0	9	15	2	5	2	.290	.339	0	0	1B-9, C-5, OF-4, SS-1
1890 STL AA	18	63	8	2	0	0	0.0	8		8		2	.127	.159	0	0	1B-17, C-1
7 yrs.	556	2224	561	72	51	20	0.9	392	55	165	5	69	.252	.357	0	0	1B-334, C-163, OF-70, 3B-4, SS-2, 2B-1

Orie Kerlin

KERLIN, ORIE MILTON (Cy)
B. Jan. 23, 1891, Summerfield, La.   D. Oct. 29, 1974, Shreveport, La.   BL TR 5'7"   149 lbs.

	G	AB	H	2B	3B	HR	HR %	R	RBI	BB	SO	SB	BA	SA	PH AB	PH H	G by POS
1915 PIT F	3	1	0	0	0	0	0.0	0	0	0		0	.000	.000	0	0	C-3

Bill Kern

KERN, WILLIAM GEORGE
B. Feb. 28, 1935, Coplay, Pa.   BR TR 6'2"   184 lbs.

	G	AB	H	2B	3B	HR	HR %	R	RBI	BB	SO	SB	BA	SA	PH AB	PH H	G by POS
1962 KC A	8	16	4	0	0	1	6.3	1	1	0	3	0	.250	.438	5	2	OF-3

George Kernek

KERNEK, GEORGE BOYD
B. Jan. 12, 1940, Holdenville, Okla.   BL TL 6'3"   170 lbs.

	G	AB	H	2B	3B	HR	HR %	R	RBI	BB	SO	SB	BA	SA	PH AB	PH H	G by POS
1965 STL N	10	31	9	3	1	0	0.0	6	3	2	4	0	.290	.452	3	0	1B-7
1966	20	50	12	0	1	0	0.0	5	3	4	9	1	.240	.280	4	1	1B-16
2 yrs.	30	81	21	3	2	0	0.0	11	6	6	13	1	.259	.346	7	1	1B-23

	G	AB	H	2B	3B	HR	HR %	R	RBI	BB	SO	SB	BA	SA	Pinch Hit AB	H	G by POS

Dan Kerns

KERNS, DANIEL P.
B. Philadelphia, Pa.

	G	AB	H	2B	3B	HR	HR%	R	RBI	BB	SO	SB	BA	SA	PH AB	H	G by POS
1920 PHI A	1	1	0	0	0	0	0.0	0	0	0	0	0	.000	.000	1	0	

Russ Kerns

KERNS, RUSSELL ELDON
B. Nov. 10, 1920, Fremont, Ohio

BL TR 6' 188 lbs.

	G	AB	H	2B	3B	HR	HR%	R	RBI	BB	SO	SB	BA	SA	PH AB	H	G by POS
1945 DET A	1	1	0	0	0	0	0.0	0	0	0	0	0	.000	.000	1	0	

Buddy Kerr

KERR, JOHN JOSEPH
B. Nov. 6, 1922, Astoria, N. Y.

BR TR 6'2" 175 lbs.

	G	AB	H	2B	3B	HR	HR%	R	RBI	BB	SO	SB	BA	SA	PH AB	H	G by POS
1943 NY N	27	98	28	3	0	2	2.0	14	12	8	5	1	.286	.378	0	0	SS-27
1944	150	548	146	31	4	9	1.6	68	63	37	32	14	.266	.387	0	0	SS-149
1945	149	546	136	20	3	4	0.7	53	40	41	34	5	.249	.319	1	0	SS-148
1946	145	497	124	20	3	6	1.2	50	40	53	31	7	.249	.338	1	1	SS-126, 3B-18
1947	138	547	157	23	5	7	1.3	73	49	36	49	2	.287	.386	0	0	SS-138
1948	144	496	119	16	4	0	0.0	41	46	56	36	9	.240	.288	1	1	SS-143
1949	90	220	46	4	0	0	0.0	16	19	21	23	0	.209	.227	0	0	SS-89
1950 BOS N	155	507	115	24	6	2	0.4	45	46	50	50	0	.227	.310	0	0	SS-155
1951	69	172	32	4	0	1	0.6	18	18	22	20	0	.186	.227	0	0	SS-63, 2B-5
9 yrs.	1067	3631	903	145	25	31	0.9	378	333	324	280	38	.249	.328	3	2	SS-1038, 3B-18, 2B-5

Doc Kerr

KERR, JOHN JONAS
B. Jan. 17, 1882, Del Roy, Ohio   D. June 9, 1937, Baltimore, Md.

BR TR 5'10½" 190 lbs.

	G	AB	H	2B	3B	HR	HR%	R	RBI	BB	SO	SB	BA	SA	PH AB	H	G by POS
1914 2 teams	PIT F (42G – .239)				BAL F (14G – .265)												
" total	56	105	26	5	3	1	1.0	7	8	11		1	.248	.381	20	4	C-31, 1B-1
1915 BAL F	3	6	2	0	0	0	0.0	1	0	1		0	.333	.333	0	0	C-2, 1B-1
2 yrs.	59	111	28	5	3	1	0.9	8	8	12		1	.252	.378	20	4	C-33, 1B-2

John Kerr

KERR, JOHN FRANCIS
B. Nov. 26, 1898, San Francisco, Calif.

BR TR 5'8" 158 lbs.
BB 1923-24

	G	AB	H	2B	3B	HR	HR%	R	RBI	BB	SO	SB	BA	SA	PH AB	H	G by POS
1923 DET A	19	42	9	1	0	0	0.0	4	1	4	5	0	.214	.238	1	0	SS-15
1924	17	11	3	0	0	0	0.0	3	1	0	0	0	.273	.273	7	2	3B-3, OF-2
1929 CHI A	127	419	108	20	4	1	0.2	50	39	31	24	9	.258	.332	1	1	2B-122
1930	70	266	77	11	6	3	1.1	37	27	21	23	4	.289	.410	0	0	2B-51, SS-19
1931	128	444	119	17	2	2	0.5	51	50	35	22	9	.268	.329	4	1	2B-117, 3B-7, SS-1
1932 WAS A	51	132	36	6	1	0	0.0	14	15	13	3	3	.273	.333	10	1	2B-17, SS-14, 3B-8
1933	28	40	8	0	0	0	0.0	5	0	3	2	0	.200	.200	5	1	2B-16, 3B-1
1934	31	103	28	4	0	0	0.0	8	12	8	13	1	.272	.311	1	0	3B-17, 2B-13
8 yrs.	471	1457	388	59	13	6	0.4	172	145	115	92	26	.266	.337	29	7	2B-336, SS-49, 3B-36, OF-2

WORLD SERIES

	G	AB	H	2B	3B	HR	HR%	R	RBI	BB	SO	SB	BA	SA	PH AB	H	G by POS
1933 WAS A	1	0	0	0	0	0	–	0	0	0	0	0	–	–	0	0	

Mel Kerr

KERR, JOHN MELVILLE
B. May 22, 1903, Souris, Man., Canada   D. Aug. 9, 1980, Vero Beach, Fla.

BL TL 5'11½" 155 lbs.

	G	AB	H	2B	3B	HR	HR%	R	RBI	BB	SO	SB	BA	SA	PH AB	H	G by POS
1925 CHI N	1	0	0	0	0	0	–	0	0	0	0	0	–	–	0	0	

Dan Kerwin

KERWIN, DANIEL PATRICK
B. July 9, 1879, Philadelphia, Pa.   D. July 13, 1960, Philadelphia, Pa.

BL TL 5'9" 164 lbs.

	G	AB	H	2B	3B	HR	HR%	R	RBI	BB	SO	SB	BA	SA	PH AB	H	G by POS
1903 CIN N	2	6	4	1	0	0	0.0	1	1	2		0	.667	.833	0	0	OF-2

Don Kessinger

KESSINGER, DONALD EULON
B. July 17, 1942, Forrest City, Ark.
Manager 1979.

BB TR 6'1" 170 lbs.
BR 1964-65

	G	AB	H	2B	3B	HR	HR%	R	RBI	BB	SO	SB	BA	SA	PH AB	H	G by POS
1964 CHI N	4	12	2	0	0	0	0.0	1	0	0	1	0	.167	.167	2	0	SS-4
1965	106	309	62	4	3	0	0.0	19	14	20	44	1	.201	.233	0	0	SS-105
1966	150	533	146	8	2	1	0.2	50	43	26	46	13	.274	.302	0	0	SS-148
1967	145	580	134	10	7	0	0.0	61	42	33	80	6	.231	.272	0	0	SS-143
1968	160	655	157	14	7	1	0.2	63	32	38	86	9	.240	.287	1	0	SS-159
1969	158	664	181	38	6	4	0.6	109	53	61	70	11	.273	.366	1	0	SS-157
1970	154	631	168	21	14	1	0.2	100	39	66	59	12	.266	.349	0	0	SS-154
1971	155	617	159	18	6	2	0.3	77	38	52	54	15	.258	.316	2	0	SS-154
1972	149	577	158	20	6	1	0.2	77	39	67	44	8	.274	.334	3	0	SS-146
1973	160	577	151	22	3	0	0.0	52	43	57	44	6	.262	.310	2	0	SS-158
1974	153	599	155	20	7	0	0.2	83	42	62	54	7	.259	.321	3	0	SS-150
1975	154	601	146	26	10	0	0.0	77	46	68	47	4	.243	.319	2	0	SS-140, 3B-13
1976 STL N	145	502	120	22	6	1	0.2	55	40	61	51	3	.239	.313	1	0	SS-113, 2B-31, 3B-2
1977 2 teams	STL N (59G – .239)				CHI A (39G – .235)												
" total	98	253	60	7	2	0	0.0	26	18	27	33	2	.237	.281	15	0	SS-47, 2B-37, 3B-13
1978 CHI A	131	431	110	18	1	1	0.2	35	31	36	34	2	.255	.309	1	0	SS-123, 2B-9
1979	56	110	22	6	0	0	0.9	14	7	10	12	1	.200	.282	0	0	SS-54, 2B-1, 1B-1
16 yrs.	2078	7651	1931	254	80	14	0.2	899	527	684	759	100	.252	.312	33	0	SS-1955, 2B-78, 3B-28, 1B-1

Henry Kessler

KESSLER, HENRY (Lucky)
B. 1847, Brooklyn, N.Y.   D. Jan. 9, 1900, Franklin, Pa.

BR TR 5'10" 144 lbs.

	G	AB	H	2B	3B	HR	HR%	R	RBI	BB	SO	SB	BA	SA	PH AB	H	G by POS
1876 CIN N	59	248	64	5	0	0	0.0	26	11	7		10	.258	.278	0	0	SS-46, OF-16
1877	6	20	2	0	0	0	0.0	0	0	2		1	.100	.100	0	0	C-5, 1B-1
2 yrs.	65	268	66	5	0	0	0.0	26	11	9		11	.246	.265	0	0	SS-46, OF-16, C-5, 1B-1

Fred Ketcham

KETCHAM, FREDERICK L.
B. July 27, 1875, Elmira, N.Y.   D. Mar. 12, 1908, Cortland, N.Y.

BL TR

	G	AB	H	2B	3B	HR	HR%	R	RBI	BB	SO	SB	BA	SA	PH AB	H	G by POS
1899 LOU N	15	61	18	1	0	0	0.0	13	5	0		2	.295	.311	0	0	OF-15
1901 PHI A	5	22	5	0	0	0	0.0	5	2	0		2	.227	.227	0	0	OF-5
2 yrs.	20	83	23	1	0	0	0.0	18	7	0		2	.277	.289	0	0	OF-20

	G	AB	H	2B	3B	HR	HR %	R	RBI	BB	SO	SB	BA	SA	Pinch Hit AB	Pinch Hit H	G by POS

Phil Ketter

KETTER, PHILIP
B. Hutchinson, Kans.

TR

	G	AB	H	2B	3B	HR	HR%	R	RBI	BB	SO	SB	BA	SA	AB	H	G by POS
1912 STL A	2	6	2	0	0	0	0.0	1	0	0		0	.333	.333	0	0	C-2

Hod Kibbie

KIBBIE, HORACE KENT
B. July 18, 1903, Fort Worth, Tex.   D. Oct. 19, 1975, Fort Worth, Tex.

BR TR 5'10"   150 lbs.

	G	AB	H	2B	3B	HR	HR%	R	RBI	BB	SO	SB	BA	SA	AB	H	G by POS
1925 BOS N	11	41	11	2	0	0	0.0	5	2	5	6	0	.268	.317	0	0	2B-8, SS-3

Jack Kibble

KIBBLE, JOHN WESLEY (Happy)
B. Jan. 2, 1892, Seatonville, Ill.   D. Dec. 13, 1969, Roundup, Mont.

BB TR 5'9½"   154 lbs.

	G	AB	H	2B	3B	HR	HR%	R	RBI	BB	SO	SB	BA	SA	AB	H	G by POS
1912 CLE A	5	8	0	0	0	0	0.0	1	0	0		0	.000	.000	0	0	3B-4, 2B-1

Steve Kiefer

KIEFER, STEPHEN
B. Oct. 18, 1960, Chicago, Ill.

BR TR 6'1"   175 lbs.

	G	AB	H	2B	3B	HR	HR%	R	RBI	BB	SO	SB	BA	SA	AB	H	G by POS
1984 OAK A	23	40	7	1	2	0	0.0	7	2	2	10	2	.175	.300	1	1	SS-17, DH-3, 3B-2

Bill Kienzle

KIENZLE, WILLIAM H.
B. Philadelphia, Pa.   Deceased.

BL TL

	G	AB	H	2B	3B	HR	HR%	R	RBI	BB	SO	SB	BA	SA	AB	H	G by POS
1882 PHI AA	9	33	11	3	2	0	0.0	8		5			.333	.545	0	0	OF-9
1884 PHI U	67	299	76	13	8	0	0.0	76		21			.254	.351	0	0	OF-67
2 yrs.	76	332	87	16	10	0	0.0	84		26			.262	.370	0	0	OF-76

Pete Kilduff

KILDUFF, PETER JOHN
B. Apr. 4, 1893, Weir City, Kans.   D. Feb. 14, 1930, Pittsburg, Kans.

BR TR 5'7"   155 lbs.

	G	AB	H	2B	3B	HR	HR%	R	RBI	BB	SO	SB	BA	SA	AB	H	G by POS
1917 2 teams	NY N (31G – .205)					CHI N (56G – .277)											
" total	87	280	72	12	5	1	0.4	35	27	16	30	13	.257	.346	0	0	SS-56, 2B-26, 3B-1
1918 CHI N	30	93	19	2	2	0	0.0	7	13	7	7	1	.204	.269	0	0	2B-30
1919 2 teams	CHI N (31G – .273)					BKN N (32G – .301)											
" total	63	161	46	7	3	0	0.0	14	16	22	16	6	.286	.366	2	1	3B-40, 2B-9, SS-7
1920 BKN N	141	478	130	26	8	0	0.0	62	58	58	43	2	.272	.360	2	1	2B-134, 3B-5
1921	107	372	107	15	10	3	0.8	45	45	31	36	6	.288	.406	1	0	2B-105, 3B-1
5 yrs.	428	1384	374	62	28	4	0.3	163	159	134	132	28	.270	.364	5	2	2B-304, SS-63, 3B-47

WORLD SERIES

	G	AB	H	2B	3B	HR	HR%	R	RBI	BB	SO	SB	BA	SA	AB	H	G by POS
1920 BKN N	7	21	2	0	0	0	0.0	0	0	1	4	0	.095	.095	0	0	2B-7

Frank Kiley

Playing record listed under Frank Kane

John Kiley

KILEY, JOHN FREDERICK
B. July, 1859, South Dedham, Mass.   D. Dec. 18, 1940, Norwood, Mass.

BL TL

	G	AB	H	2B	3B	HR	HR%	R	RBI	BB	SO	SB	BA	SA	AB	H	G by POS
1884 WAS AA	14	56	12	2	2	0	0.0	9		3			.214	.321	0	0	OF-14
1891 BOS N	1	2	0	0	0	0	0.0	0		1	1	0	.000	.000	0	0	P-1
2 yrs.	15	58	12	2	2	0	0.0	9		4	1	0	.207	.310	0	0	OF-14, P-1

Pat Kilhullen

KILHULLEN, JOSEPH ISADORE
B. July 10, 1890, Carbondale, Pa.   D. Nov. 2, 1922, Oakland, Calif.

BR TR 5'9"   175 lbs.

	G	AB	H	2B	3B	HR	HR%	R	RBI	BB	SO	SB	BA	SA	AB	H	G by POS
1914 PIT N	1	1	0	0	0	0	0.0	0	0	0	0	0	.000	.000	0	0	C-1

Harmon Killebrew

KILLEBREW, HARMON CLAYTON (Killer)
B. June 29, 1936, Payette, Ida.
Hall of Fame 1984.

BR TR 6'   195 lbs.

	G	AB	H	2B	3B	HR	HR%	R	RBI	BB	SO	SB	BA	SA	AB	H	G by POS
1954 WAS A	9	13	4	1	0	0	0.0	1	3	2	3	0	.308	.385	2	0	2B-3
1955	38	80	16	1	0	4	5.0	12	7	9	31	0	.200	.363	13	1	3B-23, 2B-3
1956	44	99	22	2	0	5	5.1	10	13	10	39	0	.222	.394	21	2	3B-20, 2B-4
1957	9	31	9	2	0	2	6.5	4	5	2	8	0	.290	.548	2	1	3B-7, 2B-1
1958	13	31	6	0	0	0	0.0	2	2	0	12	0	.194	.194	4	1	3B-9
1959	153	546	132	20	2	42	7.7	98	105	90	116	3	.242	.516	0	0	3B-150, OF-4
1960	124	442	122	19	1	31	7.0	84	80	71	106	1	.276	.534	4	2	1B-71, 3B-65
1961 MIN A	150	541	156	20	7	46	8.5	94	122	107	109	1	.288	.606	0	0	1B-119, 3B-45, OF-2
1962	155	552	134	21	1	48	8.7	85	126	106	142	1	.243	.545	1	1	OF-151, 1B-4
1963	142	515	133	18	0	45	8.7	88	96	72	105	0	.258	.555	3	1	OF-137
1964	158	577	156	11	1	49	8.5	95	111	93	135	0	.270	.548	1	0	OF-157
1965	113	401	108	16	1	25	6.2	78	75	72	69	0	.269	.501	2	1	1B-72, 3B-44, OF-1
1966	162	569	160	27	1	39	6.9	89	110	103	98	0	.281	.538	1	0	3B-108, 1B-42, OF-18
1967	163	547	147	24	1	44	8.0	105	113	131	111	1	.269	.558	0	0	1B-160, 3B-3
1968	100	295	62	7	2	17	5.8	40	40	70	70	0	.210	.420	9	1	1B-77, 3B-11
1969	162	555	153	20	2	49	8.8	106	140	145	84	8	.276	.584	0	0	3B-105, 1B-80
1970	157	527	143	20	1	41	7.8	96	113	128	84	0	.271	.546	2	0	3B-138, 1B-28
1971	147	500	127	19	1	28	5.6	61	119	114	96	3	.254	.464	4	1	1B-90, 3B-64
1972	139	433	100	13	2	26	6.0	53	74	94	91	0	.231	.450	8	0	1B-130
1973	69	248	60	9	1	5	2.0	29	32	41	59	0	.242	.347	2	0	1B-57, DH-9
1974	122	333	74	7	0	13	3.9	28	54	45	61	0	.222	.360	30	11	DH-57, 1B-33
1975 KC A	106	312	62	13	0	14	4.5	25	44	54	70	1	.199	.375	9	1	DH-92, 1B-6
22 yrs.	2435	8147	2086	290	24	573	7.0	1283	1584	1559	1699	19	.256	.509	118	24	1B-969, 3B-792, OF-470, DH-158, 2B-11
						5th	3rd			9th	7th						

LEAGUE CHAMPIONSHIP SERIES

	G	AB	H	2B	3B	HR	HR%	R	RBI	BB	SO	SB	BA	SA	AB	H	G by POS
1969 MIN A	3	8	1	1	0	0	0.0	2	0	6	2	0	.125	.250	0	0	3B-3
1970	3	11	3	0	0	2	18.2	2	4	2	4	0	.273	.818	0	0	3B-2
2 yrs.	6	19	4	1	0	2	10.5	4	4	8	6	0	.211	.579	0	0	3B-5

WORLD SERIES

	G	AB	H	2B	3B	HR	HR%	R	RBI	BB	SO	SB	BA	SA	AB	H	G by POS
1965 MIN A	7	21	6	0	0	1	4.8	2	2	6	4	0	.286	.429	0	0	3B-7

	G	AB	H	2B	3B	HR	HR %	R	RBI	BB	SO	SB	BA	SA	Pinch Hit AB	Pinch Hit H	G by POS

Bill Killefer

KILLEFER, WILLIAM LAVIER (Reindeer Bill)   BR TR 5'10½" 200 lbs.
Brother of Red Killefer.
B. Oct. 10, 1887, Bloomingdale, Mich.   D. July 2, 1960, Elsmere, Del.
Manager 1921-25, 1930-33.

	G	AB	H	2B	3B	HR	HR %	R	RBI	BB	SO	SB	BA	SA	PH AB	PH H	G by POS
1909 STL A	11	29	4	0	0	0	0.0	0	1	0		2	.138	.138	0	0	C-11
1910	74	193	24	2	2	0	0.0	14	7	12		0	.124	.155	1	0	C-73
1911 PHI N	6	16	3	0	0	0	0.0	3	2	0		2	.188	.188	0	0	C-6
1912	85	268	60	6	3	1	0.4	18	21	4	14	6	.224	.280	0	0	C-85
1913	120	360	88	14	3	0	0.0	25	24	4	17	2	.244	.300	1	0	C-118, 1B-1
1914	98	299	70	10	1	0	0.0	27	27	8	17	3	.234	.274	8	3	C-90
1915	105	320	76	9	2	0	0.0	26	24	18	14	5	.238	.278	1	0	C-105
1916	97	286	62	5	4	3	1.0	22	27	8	14	2	.217	.294	4	0	C-91
1917	125	409	112	12	0	0	0.0	28	31	15	21	4	.274	.303	4	0	C-120
1918 CHI N	104	331	77	10	3	0	0.0	30	22	17	10	5	.233	.281	0	0	C-104
1919	103	315	90	10	2	0	0.0	17	22	15	8	5	.286	.330	3	0	C-100
1920	62	191	42	7	1	0	0.0	16	16	8	5	2	.220	.267	1	0	C-61
1921	45	133	43	1	0	0	0.0	11	16	4	4	3	.323	.331	3	1	C-42
13 yrs.	1035	3150	751	86	21	4	0.1	237	240	113	126	39	.238	.283	26	4	C-1006, 1B-1
WORLD SERIES																	
1915 PHI N	1	1	0	0	0	0	0.0	0	0	0	0	0	.000	.000	1	0	
1918 CHI N	6	17	2	1	0	0	0.0	2	2	2	0	0	.118	.176	0	0	C-6
2 yrs.	7	18	2	1	0	0	0.0	2	2	2	0	0	.111	.167	1	0	C-6

Red Killefer

KILLEFER, WADE (Lollypop)   BR TR 5'9½" 175 lbs.
Brother of Bill Killefer.
B. Apr. 13, 1884, Bloomingdale, Mich.   D. Sept. 4, 1958, Los Angeles, Calif.

	G	AB	H	2B	3B	HR	HR %	R	RBI	BB	SO	SB	BA	SA	PH AB	PH H	G by POS
1907 DET A	1	4	0	0	0	0	0.0	0	0	0		0	.000	.000	0	0	OF-1
1908	28	75	16	1	0	0	0.0	9	11	3		4	.213	.227	0	0	2B-16, SS-7, 3B-4
1909 2 teams		DET	A (23G –	.279)		WAS	A (40G –	.174)									
" total	63	182	38	3	2	1	0.5	17	9	16		6	.209	.264	7	3	OF-25, 2B-20, 3B-6, C-3, SS-1
1910 WAS A	106	345	79	17	0	0	0.0	35	24	29		17	.229	.284	4	1	2B-88, OF-12
1914 CIN N	42	141	39	6	0	0	0.0	16	12	20	18	11	.277	.333	1	0	OF-37, 2B-5, 3B-1
1915	155	555	151	25	11	1	0.2	75	41	38	33	12	.272	.362	2	0	OF-153, 1B-2
1916 2 teams		CIN	N (70G –	.244)		NY	N (2G –	1.000)									
" total	72	235	58	9	1	1	0.4	29	19	22	8	7	.247	.306	3	2	OF-68
7 yrs.	467	1537	381	61	16	3	0.2	181	116	128	59	57	.248	.314	17	6	OF-296, 2B-129, 3B-11, SS-8, C-3, 1B-2

Matt Kilroy

KILROY, MATTHEW ALOYSIUS (Matches)   BL TL 5'9" 175 lbs.
Brother of Mike Kilroy.
B. June 21, 1866, Philadelphia, Pa.   D. Mar. 2, 1940, Philadelphia, Pa.

	G	AB	H	2B	3B	HR	HR %	R	RBI	BB	SO	SB	BA	SA	PH AB	PH H	G by POS
1886 BAL AA	68	218	38	3	1	0	0.0	33		21			.174	.197	0	0	P-68, OF-2
1887	72	239	59	5	6	0	0.0	46		31		12	.247	.318	0	0	P-69, OF-4, SS-1
1888	43	145	26	5	2	0	0.0	13	19	11		10	.179	.241	0	0	P-40, OF-7
1889	65	208	57	3	6	1	0.5	32	26	23	26	13	.274	.361	0	0	P-59, OF-8
1890 BOS P	31	93	20	1	1	0	0.0	11	8	12	9	11	.215	.247	0	0	P-30, OF-2, SS-1, 3B-1
1891 C-M AA	8	20	3	0	0	0	0.0	2	0	4	2	0	.150	.150	0	0	P-7, OF-1
1892 WAS N	4	10	2	0	0	0	0.0	0	0	1	0	0	.200	.200	0	0	P-4
1893 LOU N	5	16	7	3	0	0	0.0	4	3	1	3	0	.438	.625	0	0	P-5
1894	8	17	2	0	0	0	0.0	2	1	1	6	1	.118	.118	0	0	P-8
1898 CHI N	26	96	22	4	1	0	0.0	20	10	13			.229	.292	1	0	P-13, OF-12
10 yrs.	330	1062	236	24	17	1	0.1	163	66	118	46	47	.222	.280	1	0	P-303, OF-36, SS-2, 3B-1

Dick Kimble

KIMBLE, RICHARD LOUIS   BL TR 5'9" 160 lbs.
B. July 27, 1915, Buchtel, Ohio

	G	AB	H	2B	3B	HR	HR %	R	RBI	BB	SO	SB	BA	SA	PH AB	PH H	G by POS
1945 WAS A	20	49	12	1	1	0	0.0	5	1	5	2	0	.245	.306	4	0	SS-15

Bruce Kimm

KIMM, BRUCE EDWARD   BR TR 5'11" 175 lbs.
B. June 29, 1951, Norway, Iowa

	G	AB	H	2B	3B	HR	HR %	R	RBI	BB	SO	SB	BA	SA	PH AB	PH H	G by POS
1976 DET A	63	152	40	8	0	1	0.7	13	6	15	20	4	.263	.336	0	0	C-61, DH-2
1977	14	25	2	1	0	0	0.0	2	1	0	4	0	.080	.120	0	0	C-12, DH-2
1979 CHI N	9	11	1	0	0	0	0.0	0	0	0	0	0	.091	.091	0	0	C-9
1980 CHI A	100	251	61	10	1	0	0.0	20	19	17	26	1	.243	.291	3	0	C-98
4 yrs.	186	439	104	19	1	1	0.2	35	26	32	50	5	.237	.292	3	0	C-180, DH-4

Wally Kimmick

KIMMICK, WALTER LYONS   BR TR 5'11" 174 lbs.
B. May 30, 1897, Turtle Creek, Pa.

	G	AB	H	2B	3B	HR	HR %	R	RBI	BB	SO	SB	BA	SA	PH AB	PH H	G by POS
1919 STL N	2	1	0	0	0	0	0.0	1	0	1	0	1	.000	.000	1	0	SS-1
1921 CIN N	3	6	1	0	0	0	0.0	0	1	0	1	0	.167	.167	1	0	3B-2
1922	39	89	22	2	1	0	0.0	11	12	3	12	0	.247	.292	3	0	SS-30, 2B-3, 3B-1
1923	29	80	18	2	1	0	0.0	11	6	5	15	3	.225	.275	2	0	2B-17, 3B-4, SS-1
1925 PHI N	70	141	43	3	2	1	0.7	16	10	22	26	0	.305	.376	11	4	SS-28, 3B-21, 2B-13
1926	20	28	6	2	1	0	0.0	0	2	3	7	0	.214	.357	6	1	1B-5, SS-4, 3B-4, 2B-1
6 yrs.	163	345	90	9	5	1	0.3	39	31	34	61	4	.261	.325	24	5	SS-64, 2B-34, 3B-32, 1B-5

Chad Kimsey

KIMSEY, CLYDE ELIAS   BL TR 6'3½" 200 lbs.
B. Aug. 6, 1905, Copperhill, Tenn.   D. Dec. 3, 1942, Pryor, Okla.

	G	AB	H	2B	3B	HR	HR %	R	RBI	BB	SO	SB	BA	SA	PH AB	PH H	G by POS
1929 STL A	29	30	8	2	0	2	6.7	6	4	1	8	0	.267	.533	5	1	P-24
1930	60	70	24	4	1	2	2.9	14	14	5	16	1	.343	.514	16	2	P-42
1931	47	37	10	1	0	2	5.4	5	5	8	11	1	.270	.459	4	0	P-42
1932 2 teams		STL	A (34G –	.333)		CHI	A (7G –	.000)									
" total	41	20	6	1	0	0	0.0	1	1	1	4	0	.300	.350	1	0	P-40
1933 CHI A	28	33	5	0	0	0	0.0	1	1	0	9	0	.152	.152	1	0	P-28
1936 DET A	22	16	5	1	1	0	0.0	3	1	1	5	0	.313	.500	0	0	P-22
6 yrs.	227	206	58	9	2	6	2.9	30	26	16	53	2	.282	.432	27	3	P-198

	G	AB	H	2B	3B	HR	HR %	R	RBI	BB	SO	SB	BA	SA	PH AB	PH H	G by POS

Jerry Kindall
KINDALL, GERALD DONALD (Slim)
B. May 27, 1935, St. Paul, Minn.
BR TR 6'2½" 175 lbs.
BB 1960

	G	AB	H	2B	3B	HR	HR %	R	RBI	BB	SO	SB	BA	SA	PH AB	PH H	G by POS
1956 CHI N	32	55	9	1	1	0	0.0	7	0	6	17	1	.164	.218	0	0	SS-18
1957	72	181	29	3	0	6	3.3	18	12	8	48	1	.160	.276	10	2	2B-28, 3B-19, SS-9
1958	3	6	1	1	0	0	0.0	0	0	0	3	0	.167	.333	0	0	2B-3
1960	89	246	59	16	2	2	0.8	17	23	5	52	4	.240	.346	3	0	2B-82, SS-2
1961	96	310	75	22	3	9	2.9	37	44	18	89	2	.242	.419	7	1	2B-50, SS-47
1962 CLE A	154	530	123	21	1	13	2.5	51	55	45	107	4	.232	.349	0	0	2B-154
1963	86	234	48	4	1	5	2.1	27	20	18	71	3	.205	.295	3	1	SS-46, 2B-37, 1B-4
1964 2 teams		CLE A (23G – .360)						MIN A (62G – .148)									
" total	85	153	28	3	0	3	2.0	13	8	9	51	0	.183	.261	0	0	2B-51, 1B-24, SS-7
1965 MIN A	125	342	67	12	1	6	1.8	41	36	36	97	2	.196	.289	2	1	2B-106, 3B-10, SS-7
9 yrs.	742	2057	439	83	9	44	2.1	211	198	145	535	17	.213	.327	25	5	2B-511, SS-136, 3B-29, 1B-28

Ralph Kiner
KINER, RALPH McPHERRAN
B. Oct. 27, 1922, Santa Rita, N. M.
Hall of Fame 1975.
BR TR 6'2" 195 lbs.

	G	AB	H	2B	3B	HR	HR %	R	RBI	BB	SO	SB	BA	SA	PH AB	PH H	G by POS
1946 PIT N	144	502	124	17	3	23	4.6	63	81	74	109	3	.247	.430	3	0	OF-140
1947	152	565	177	23	4	51	9.0	118	127	98	81	1	.313	.639	0	0	OF-152
1948	156	555	147	19	5	40	7.2	104	123	112	61	1	.265	.533	1	1	OF-154
1949	152	549	170	19	5	54	9.8	116	127	117	61	6	.310	.658	0	0	OF-152
1950	150	547	149	21	6	47	8.6	112	118	122	79	2	.272	.590	0	0	OF-150
1951	151	531	164	31	6	42	7.9	124	109	137	57	2	.309	.627	0	0	OF-94, 1B-58
1952	149	516	126	17	2	37	7.2	90	87	110	77	3	.244	.500	0	0	OF-149
1953 2 teams		PIT N (41G – .270)						CHI N (117G – .283)									
" total	158	562	157	20	3	35	6.2	100	116	100	88	2	.279	.512	1	0	OF-157
1954 CHI N	147	557	159	36	5	22	3.9	88	73	76	90	2	.285	.487	0	0	OF-147
1955 CLE A	113	321	78	13	0	18	5.6	56	54	65	46	0	.243	.452	28	11	OF-87
10 yrs.	1472	5205	1451	216	39	369	7.1	971	1015	1011	749	22	.279	.548	33	12	OF-1382, 1B-58
							2nd										

Charlie King
KING, CHARLES GILBERT (Chick)
B. Nov. 10, 1930, Paris, Tenn.
BR TR 6'2" 190 lbs.

	G	AB	H	2B	3B	HR	HR %	R	RBI	BB	SO	SB	BA	SA	PH AB	PH H	G by POS
1954 DET A	11	28	6	0	1	0	0.0	4	3	3	8	0	.214	.286	4	0	OF-7
1955	7	21	5	0	0	0	0.0	3	0	1	2	0	.238	.238	0	0	OF-6
1956	7	9	2	0	0	0	0.0	0	0	1	4	0	.222	.222	2	0	OF-4
1958 CHI N	8	8	2	0	0	0	0.0	1	1	3	1	0	.250	.250	1	0	OF-7
1959 2 teams		CHI N (7G – .000)						STL N (5G – .429)									
" total	12	10	3	0	0	0	0.0	3	1	0	3	0	.300	.300	0	0	OF-5
5 yrs.	45	76	18	0	1	0	0.0	11	5	8	18	0	.237	.263	7	0	OF-29

Hal King
KING, HAROLD
B. Feb. 1, 1944, Oviedo, Fla.
BL TR 6'1" 200 lbs.

	G	AB	H	2B	3B	HR	HR %	R	RBI	BB	SO	SB	BA	SA	PH AB	PH H	G by POS
1967 HOU N	15	44	11	1	2	0	0.0	2	6	2	9	0	.250	.364	4	1	C-11
1968	27	55	8	2	1	0	0.0	4	2	7	16	0	.145	.218	11	1	C-19
1970 ATL N	89	204	53	8	0	11	5.4	29	30	32	41	1	.260	.461	26	6	C-62
1971	86	198	41	9	0	5	2.5	14	19	29	43	0	.207	.328	26	6	C-60
1972 TEX A	50	122	22	5	0	4	3.3	12	12	25	35	0	.180	.320	12	0	C-38
1973 CIN N	35	43	8	0	0	4	9.3	5	10	6	10	0	.186	.465	26	5	C-9
1974	20	17	3	1	0	0	0.0	1	3	3	4	0	.176	.235	14	3	C-5
7 yrs.	322	683	146	26	3	24	3.5	67	82	104	158	1	.214	.366	119	22	C-204
LEAGUE CHAMPIONSHIP SERIES																	
1973 CIN N	3	2	1	0	0	0	0.0	0	0	1	1	0	.500	.500	2	1	

Jim King
KING, JAMES HUBERT
B. Aug. 27, 1932, Elkins, Ark.
BL TR 6' 185 lbs.

	G	AB	H	2B	3B	HR	HR %	R	RBI	BB	SO	SB	BA	SA	PH AB	PH H	G by POS
1955 CHI N	113	301	77	12	3	11	3.7	43	45	24	39	2	.256	.425	18	4	OF-93
1956	118	317	79	13	2	15	4.7	32	54	30	40	1	.249	.445	34	6	OF-82
1957 STL N	22	35	11	0	0	0	0.0	1	2	4	2	0	.314	.314	16	4	OF-8
1958 SF N	34	56	12	2	1	2	3.6	8	8	10	8	0	.214	.393	14	3	OF-15
1961 WAS A	110	263	71	12	1	11	4.2	43	46	38	45	4	.270	.449	17	1	OF-91, C-1
1962	132	333	81	15	0	11	3.3	39	35	55	37	4	.243	.387	31	8	OF-101
1963	136	459	106	16	5	24	5.2	61	62	45	43	3	.231	.444	22	4	OF-123
1964	134	415	100	15	1	18	4.3	46	56	55	65	3	.241	.412	22	7	OF-121
1965	120	258	55	10	2	14	5.4	46	49	44	50	1	.213	.430	37	8	OF-88
1966	117	310	77	14	2	10	3.2	41	30	38	41	4	.248	.403	34	7	OF-85
1967 3 teams		WAS A (47G – .210)						CHI A (23G – .120)					CLE A (19G – .143)				
" total	89	171	30	3	2	1	0.6	14	14	20	31	1	.175	.234	42	11	OF-44, C-1
11 yrs.	1125	2918	699	112	19	117	4.0	374	401	363	401	23	.240	.411	287	63	OF-851, C-2

Lee King
KING, EDWARD LEE
B. Jan. 24, 1894, New Britain, Conn.   D. Sept. 7, 1938, Newton Centre, Mass.
BR TR 5'10" 150 lbs.

	G	AB	H	2B	3B	HR	HR %	R	RBI	BB	SO	SB	BA	SA	PH AB	PH H	G by POS
1916 PHI A	42	144	27	1	2	0	0.0	13	8	7	15	4	.188	.222	2	0	OF-22, SS-11, 3B-5, 2B-2
1919 BOS N	2	1	0	0	0	0	0.0	0	0	0	0	0	.000	.000	1	0	
2 yrs.	44	145	27	1	2	0	0.0	13	8	7	15	4	.186	.221	3	0	OF-22, SS-11, 3B-5, 2B-2

Lee King
KING, LEE
B. Dec. 26, 1892, Hundred, W. Va.   D. Sept. 16, 1967, Shinnstown, W. Va.
BR TR 5'10" 175 lbs.

	G	AB	H	2B	3B	HR	HR %	R	RBI	BB	SO	SB	BA	SA	PH AB	PH H	G by POS
1916 PIT N	8	18	2	0	0	0	0.0	0	1	0	7	0	.111	.111	2	0	OF-8
1917	111	381	95	14	5	1	0.3	32	35	15	58	8	.249	.320	9	3	OF-102
1918	36	112	26	3	2	1	0.9	9	11	11	15	3	.232	.321	0	0	OF-36
1919 NY N	21	20	2	1	0	0	0.0	5	1	1	6	0	.100	.150	9	1	OF-7
1920	93	261	72	11	4	7	2.7	32	42	19	38	3	.276	.429	12	2	OF-84
1921 2 teams		NY N (39G – .223)						PHI N (64G – .269)									
" total	103	310	79	23	6	4	1.3	42	39	21	43	1	.255	.406	7	2	OF-92, 1B-1

	G	AB	H	2B	3B	HR	HR %	R	RBI	BB	SO	SB	BA	SA	Pinch Hit AB	Pinch Hit H	G by POS

Lee King continued

		G	AB	H	2B	3B	HR	HR%	R	RBI	BB	SO	SB	BA	SA	PH AB	PH H	G by POS
1922 2 teams	PHI N (19G – .226)			NY N (20G – .176)														
" total	39	87	18	8	1	2	2.3	14	15	13	8	1	.207	.391	7	1	OF-20, 1B-5
7 yrs.	411	1189	294	60	18	15	1.3	134	144	82	175	16	.247	.366	46	9	OF-349, 1B-6

WORLD SERIES
| 1922 NY N | 2 | 1 | 1 | 0 | 0 | 0 | 0.0 | 0 | 1 | 0 | 0 | 0 | 1.000 | 1.000 | 0 | 0 | OF-2 |

Lynn King

KING, LYNN PAUL (Dig)
B. Nov. 28, 1907, Villisca, Iowa   D. May 11, 1972, Atlantic, Iowa
BL TR 5'9"   165 lbs.

1935 STL N	8	22	4	0	0	0	0.0	6	0	4	1	2	.182	.182	1	0	OF-6
1936	78	100	19	2	1	0	0.0	12	10	9	14	2	.190	.230	25	5	OF-34
1939	89	85	20	2	0	0	0.0	10	11	15	3	2	.235	.259	35	10	OF-44
3 yrs.	175	207	43	4	1	0	0.0	28	21	28	18	6	.208	.237	61	15	OF-84

Sam King

KING, SAMUEL WARREN
B. May 17, 1852, Peabody, Mass.   D. Aug. 11, 1922, Peabody, Mass.

| 1884 WAS AA | 12 | 45 | 8 | 2 | 0 | 0 | 0.0 | | 3 | | | | .178 | .222 | 0 | 0 | 1B-12 |

Silver King

KING, CHARLES FREDERICK
Born Charles Frederick Koenig.
B. Jan. 11, 1868, St. Louis, Mo.   D. May 19, 1938, St. Louis, Mo.
BR TR 6'   170 lbs.

1886 KC N	7	22	1	0	0	0	0.0	0	1	2	12		.045	.045	0	0	P-5, OF-2
1887 STL AA	62	222	46	6	1	0	0.0	28		24		10	.207	.243	0	0	P-46, OF-17
1888	66	207	43	4	6	1	0.5	25	14	40		6	.208	.300	0	0	P-66, OF-2
1889	56	189	43	7	3	0	0.0	37	30	22	40	3	.228	.296	0	0	P-56, 1B-2, OF-1
1890 CHI P	58	185	31	2	5	1	0.5	24	16	13	22	3	.168	.249	0	0	P-56, OF-1, 1B-1
1891 PIT N	49	148	25	2	3	0	0.0	12	9	14	31	0	.169	.223	0	0	P-48, 3B-1
1892 NY N	52	167	35	3	4	2	1.2	27	23	16	26	1	.210	.311	0	0	P-52
1893 2 teams	NY N (7G – .176)			CIN N (17G – .162)														
" total	24	54	9	1	1	0	0.0	13	4	15	16	0	.167	.222	0	0	P-24
1896 WAS N	22	58	16	6	0	0	0.0	9	12	8	15	1	.276	.379	0	0	P-22
1897	24	57	11	2	0	0	0.0	8	7	12		0	.193	.228	0	0	P-23
10 yrs.	420	1309	260	33	23	4	0.3	183	116	166	162	24	.199	.268	0	0	P-398, OF-23, 1B-3, 3B-1

Wes Kingdon

KINGDON, WESCOTT WILLIAM
B. July 4, 1900, Los Angeles, Calif.   D. Apr. 19, 1975, Capistrano, Calif.
BR TR 5'8"   148 lbs.

| 1932 WAS A | 18 | 34 | 11 | 3 | 1 | 0 | 0.0 | 10 | 3 | 5 | 2 | 0 | .324 | .471 | 5 | 1 | 3B-8, SS-4 |

Dave Kingman

KINGMAN, DAVID ARTHUR
B. Dec. 21, 1948, Pendleton, Ore.
BR TR 6'6"   210 lbs.

1971 SF N	41	115	32	10	2	6	5.2	17	24	9	35	5	.278	.557	7	1	1B-20, OF-14
1972	135	472	106	17	4	29	6.1	65	83	51	140	16	.225	.462	5	0	3B-59, 1B-56, OF-22
1973	112	305	62	10	1	24	7.9	54	55	41	122	8	.203	.479	7	1	3B-60, 1B-46, P-2
1974	121	350	78	18	2	18	5.1	41	55	37	125	8	.223	.440	11	3	OF-71, 1B-58, 3B-12
1975 NY N	134	502	116	22	1	36	7.2	65	88	34	153	7	.231	.494	5	0	OF-111, 1B-16
1976	123	474	113	14	1	37	7.8	70	86	28	135	7	.238	.506	1	0	OF-111, 1B-16
1977 4 teams	NY N (58G – .209)			SD N (56G – .238)			CAL A (10G – .194)			NY A (8G – .250)								
" total	132	439	97	20	0	26	5.9	47	78	28	143	5	.221	.444	23	4	OF-75, 1B-38, DH-6, 3B-2
1978 CHI N	119	395	105	17	4	28	7.1	65	79	39	111	8	.266	.542	8	1	OF-100, 1B-6
1979	145	532	153	19	5	48	9.0	97	115	45	131	4	.288	.613	5	3	OF-139
1980	81	255	71	8	0	18	7.1	31	57	21	44	2	.278	.522	16	6	OF-61, 1B-2
1981 NY N	100	353	78	11	3	22	6.2	40	59	55	105	6	.221	.456	1	0	1B-56, OF-48
1982	149	535	109	9	1	37	6.9	80	99	59	156	4	.204	.432	5	0	1B-143
1983	100	248	49	7	0	13	5.2	25	29	22	57	2	.198	.383	39	7	1B-50, OF-5
1984 OAK A	147	549	147	23	1	35	6.4	68	118	44	119	2	.268	.505	0	0	DH-139, 1B-9
14 yrs.	1639	5524	1316	205	25	377	6.8	765	1025	513	1576	79	.238	.489	133	26	OF-648, 1B-591, 3B-154, DH-145, P-2
							5th				8th						

LEAGUE CHAMPIONSHIP SERIES
| 1971 SF N | 4 | 9 | 1 | 0 | 0 | 0 | 0.0 | 0 | 0 | 1 | 3 | 0 | .111 | .111 | 1 | 0 | OF-2 |

Henry Kingman

KINGMAN, HARRY LEES
B. Apr. 3, 1892, Tientsin, China   D. Dec. 27, 1982, Oakland, Calif.
BL TL 6'1½"   165 lbs.

| 1914 NY A | 4 | 3 | 0 | 0 | 0 | 0 | 0.0 | 0 | 0 | 1 | 2 | 0 | .000 | .000 | 3 | 0 | 1B-1 |

Walt Kinlock

KINLOCK, WALTER
B. 1878, St. Joseph, Mo.   Deceased.

| 1895 STL N | 1 | 3 | 1 | 0 | 0 | 0 | 0.0 | 0 | 0 | 0 | 2 | 0 | .333 | .333 | 0 | 0 | 3B-1 |

Bob Kinsella

KINSELLA, ROBERT FRANCIS (Red)
B. Jan. 5, 1899, Springfield, Ill.   D. Dec. 30, 1951, Los Angeles, Calif.
BL TR 5'9½"   165 lbs.

1919 NY N	3	9	2	0	0	0	0.0	1	0	0	3	0	.222	.222	0	0	OF-3
1920	1	3	1	0	0	0	0.0	0	1	0	2	0	.333	.333	0	0	OF-1
2 yrs.	4	12	3	0	0	0	0.0	1	1	0	5	1	.250	.250	0	0	OF-4

Kinsler

KINSLER,
B. Staten Island, N. Y.   Deceased.

| 1893 NY N | 1 | 3 | 0 | 0 | 0 | 0 | 0.0 | 1 | 0 | 1 | 1 | 0 | .000 | .000 | 0 | 0 | OF-1 |

Tom Kinslow

KINSLOW, THOMAS F.
B. Jan. 12, 1866, Washington, D. C.   D. Feb. 22, 1901, Washington, D. C.
TR   160 lbs.

1886 WAS N	3	8	2	0	0	0	0.0	1	1	0	1		.250	.250	0	0	C-3
1887 NY AA	2	6	0	0	0	0	0.0	0		0		0	.000	.000	0	0	C-2
1890 BKN P	64	242	64	11	6	4	1.7	30	46	10	22	2	.264	.409	0	0	C-64
1891 BKN N	61	228	54	6	0	0	0.0	22	33	9	22	3	.237	.263	0	0	C-61

	G	AB	H	2B	3B	HR	HR %	R	RBI	BB	SO	SB	BA	SA	Pinch Hit AB	H	G by POS

Tom Kinslow continued

		G	AB	H	2B	3B	HR	HR%	R	RBI	BB	SO	SB	BA	SA	AB	H	G by POS
1892		66	246	75	6	11	2	0.8	37	40	13	16	4	.305	.443	0	0	C-66
1893		78	312	76	8	4	4	1.3	38	45	11	13	4	.244	.333	0	0	C-76, OF-2
1894		62	223	68	5	6	2	0.9	39	41	20	11	4	.305	.408	0	0	C-61, 1B-1
1895 PIT N		19	62	14	2	0	0	0.0	10	5	2	2	1	.226	.258	1	0	C-18
1896 LOU N		8	25	7	0	1	0	0.0	4	7	1	5	0	.280	.360	2	1	C-5, 1B-1
1898 2 teams	WAS N (3G – .111)					STL N (14G – .283)												
" total		17	62	16	2	1	0	0.0	5	4	1	0		.258	.323	0	0	C-17, 1B-1
10 yrs.		380	1414	376	40	29	12	0.8	186	222	67	92	18	.266	.361	3	0	C-373, 1B-3, OF-2

Walt Kinzie

KINZIE, WALTER H.
B. Mar., 1856, Kansas   D. Nov. 5, 1909

5'10½" 161 lbs.

		G	AB	H	2B	3B	HR	HR%	R	RBI	BB	SO	SB	BA	SA	AB	H	G by POS
1882 DET N		13	53	5	0	1	0	0.0	5	2	0	8		.094	.132	0	0	SS-13
1884 2 teams	CHI N (19G – .159)					STL AA (2G – .111)												
" total		21	91	14	3	0	2	2.2	4		0	13		.154	.253	0	0	SS-17, 3B-2, 2B-2
2 yrs.		34	144	19	3	1	2	1.4	9	2	0	21		.132	.208	0	0	SS-30, 3B-2, 2B-2

Ed Kippert

KIPPERT, EDWARD AUGUST
B. Jan. 3, 1880, Detroit, Mich.   D. June 3, 1960, Detroit, Mich.

BR TR 5'10½" 180 lbs.

		G	AB	H	2B	3B	HR	HR%	R	RBI	BB	SO	SB	BA	SA	AB	H	G by POS
1914 CIN N		2	2	0	0	0	0	0.0	0	0	0	0	0	.000	.000	0	0	OF-2

Jim Kirby

KIRBY, JAMES HERSCHEL
B. May 5, 1923, Nashville, Tenn.

BR TR 5'11" 175 lbs.

		G	AB	H	2B	3B	HR	HR%	R	RBI	BB	SO	SB	BA	SA	AB	H	G by POS
1949 CHI N		3	2	1	0	0	0	0.0	0	0	0	0	0	.500	.500	2	1	

LaRue Kirby

KIRBY, LaRUE
B. Dec. 30, 1889, Eureka, Mich.   D. June 10, 1961, Lansing, Mich.

BB TR 6' 185 lbs.

		G	AB	H	2B	3B	HR	HR%	R	RBI	BB	SO	SB	BA	SA	AB	H	G by POS
1912 NY N		3	5	1	1	0	0	0.0	1	0	0	0	0	.200	.400	0	0	P-3
1914 STL F		52	195	48	6	3	2	1.0	21	18	14		5	.246	.338	0	0	OF-50
1915		61	178	38	7	2	0	0.0	15	16	17		3	.213	.275	5	1	OF-52, P-1
3 yrs.		116	378	87	14	5	2	0.5	37	34	31		8	.230	.310	5	1	OF-102, P-4

Tom Kirk

KIRK, THOMAS DANIEL
B. Sept. 27, 1927, Philadelphia, Pa.   D. Aug. 1, 1974, Philadelphia, Pa.

BL TL 5'10½" 182 lbs.

		G	AB	H	2B	3B	HR	HR%	R	RBI	BB	SO	SB	BA	SA	AB	H	G by POS
1947 PHI A		1	1	0	0	0	0	0.0	0	0	0	0	0	.000	.000	1	0	

Jay Kirke

KIRKE, JUDSON FABIAN
B. June 16, 1888, Fleichmans, N.Y.   D. Aug. 31, 1968, New Orleans, La.

BL TR 6' 195 lbs.

		G	AB	H	2B	3B	HR	HR%	R	RBI	BB	SO	SB	BA	SA	AB	H	G by POS
1910 DET A		8	25	5	1	0	0	0.0	3	3	1		1	.200	.240	0	0	2B-7, OF-1
1911 BOS N		20	89	32	5	5	0	0.0	9	12	2	6	3	.360	.528	0	0	OF-14, 1B-3, SS-1, 3B-1, 2B-1
1912		103	359	115	11	4	4	1.1	53	62	9	46	7	.320	.407	17	4	OF-71, 3B-32, 1B-1
1913		18	38	9	2	0	0	0.0	3	3	1	6	0	.237	.289	5	1	OF-13
1914 CLE A		67	242	66	10	2	1	0.4	18	25	7	30	5	.273	.343	7	3	OF-42, 1B-18
1915		87	339	105	19	2	2	0.6	35	40	14	21	5	.310	.395	0	0	1B-87
1918 NY N		17	56	14	1	0	0	0.0	1	3	1	3	0	.250	.268	1	0	1B-16
7 yrs.		320	1148	346	49	13	7	0.6	122	148	35	112	21	.301	.385	30	8	OF-141, 1B-125, 3B-33, 2B-8, SS-1

Willie Kirkland

KIRKLAND, WILLIE CHARLES
B. Feb. 17, 1934, Siluria, Ala.

BL TR 6'1" 206 lbs.

		G	AB	H	2B	3B	HR	HR%	R	RBI	BB	SO	SB	BA	SA	AB	H	G by POS
1958 SF N		122	418	108	25	6	14	3.3	48	56	43	69	3	.258	.447	9	3	OF-115
1959		126	463	126	22	3	22	4.8	64	68	42	84	5	.272	.475	8	2	OF-117
1960		146	515	130	21	10	21	4.1	59	65	44	86	12	.252	.454	4	1	OF-143
1961 CLE A		146	525	136	22	5	27	5.1	84	95	48	77	7	.259	.474	13	2	OF-138
1962		137	419	84	9	1	21	5.0	56	72	43	62	9	.200	.377	13	1	OF-125
1963		127	427	98	13	2	15	3.5	51	47	45	99	8	.230	.375	21	4	OF-112
1964 2 teams	BAL A (66G – .200)					WAS A (32G – .216)												
" total		98	252	52	11	0	8	3.2	22	35	23	56	3	.206	.345	13	2	OF-85
1965 WAS A		123	312	72	9	1	14	4.5	38	54	19	65	3	.231	.401	35	6	OF-92
1966		124	163	31	2	1	6	3.7	21	17	16	50	2	.190	.325	52	12	OF-68
9 yrs.		1149	3494	837	134	29	148	4.2	443	509	323	648	52	.240	.422	168	36	OF-995

Ed Kirkpatrick

KIRKPATRICK, EDGAR LEON
B. Oct. 8, 1944, Spokane, Wash.

BL TR 5'11½" 195 lbs.

		G	AB	H	2B	3B	HR	HR%	R	RBI	BB	SO	SB	BA	SA	AB	H	G by POS
1962 LA A		3	6	0	0	0	0	0.0	0	0	0	2	0	.000	.000	2	0	C-1
1963		34	77	15	5	0	2	2.6	4	7	6	19	1	.195	.338	14	1	C-14, OF-10
1964		75	219	53	13	2	2	0.9	20	22	23	30	2	.242	.356	13	4	OF-63
1965 CAL A		19	73	19	5	0	3	4.1	8	8	3	9	1	.260	.452	0	0	OF-19
1966		117	312	60	7	4	9	2.9	31	44	51	67	7	.192	.327	17	5	OF-102, 1B-3
1967		3	8	0	0	0	0	0.0	0	0	0	2	0	.000	.000	1	0	C-2, OF-1
1968		89	161	37	4	0	1	0.6	23	15	25	32	1	.230	.273	43	14	OF-45, C-4, 1B-2
1969 KC A		120	315	81	11	4	14	4.4	40	49	43	42	3	.257	.451	34	5	OF-82, C-8, 3B-2, 1B-2, 2B-1
1970		134	424	97	17	2	18	4.2	59	62	55	65	4	.229	.406	21	4	C-89, OF-19, 1B-16
1971		120	365	80	12	1	9	2.5	46	46	48	60	3	.219	.332	9	5	OF-61, C-59
1972		113	364	100	15	1	9	2.5	43	43	51	50	3	.275	.396	5	2	C-108, 1B-1
1973		126	429	113	24	5	6	1.4	61	45	46	48	3	.263	.375	2	0	OF-108, C-14, DH-8
1974 PIT N		116	271	67	9	0	6	2.2	32	38	51	30	1	.247	.347	33	5	OF-14, C-6
1975		89	144	34	5	0	5	3.5	15	16	18	22	1	.236	.375	42	13	1B-28, OF-14
1976		83	146	34	9	0	0	0.0	14	16	14	15	1	.233	.295	40	6	1B-25, OF-9, 3B-1
1977 3 teams	PIT N (21G – .143)					TEX A (20G – .188)				MIL A (29G – .273)								
" total		70	153	34	7	0	1	0.7	15	13	22	25	3	.222	.288	18	7	OF-30, 1B-13, DH-8, 3B-2, C-1
16 yrs.		1311	3467	824	143	18	85	2.5	411	424	456	518	34	.238	.363	294	71	OF-577, C-306, 1B-149, DH-16, 3B-5, 2B-1

	G	AB	H	2B	3B	HR	HR %	R	RBI	BB	SO	SB	BA	SA	Pinch Hit AB	Pinch Hit H	G by POS

Ed Kirkpatrick continued

LEAGUE CHAMPIONSHIP SERIES

	G	AB	H	2B	3B	HR	HR %	R	RBI	BB	SO	SB	BA	SA	PH AB	PH H	G by POS
1974 PIT N	3	9	0	0	0	0	0.0	0	0	2	0	0	.000	.000	0	0	1B-3
1975	2	2	0	0	0	0	0.0	0	0	0	0	0	.000	.000	2	0	
2 yrs.	5	11	0	0	0	0	0.0	0	0	2	0	0	.000	.000	2	0	1B-3

Enos Kirkpatrick

KIRKPATRICK, ENOS CLAIRE   BR TR 5'10" 175 lbs.
B. Dec. 8, 1885, Pittsburgh, Pa.   D. Apr. 14, 1964, Pittsburgh, Pa.

	G	AB	H	2B	3B	HR	HR %	R	RBI	BB	SO	SB	BA	SA	PH AB	PH H	G by POS
1912 BKN N	32	94	18	1	1	0	0.0	13	6	9	15	5	.191	.223	0	0	3B-29, SS-3
1913	48	89	22	4	1	1	1.1	13	5	3	18	5	.247	.348	13	2	SS-10, 1B-8, 2B-6, 3B-4
1914 BAL F	55	174	44	7	2	2	1.1	22	16	18		10	.253	.351	2	1	3B-36, SS-11, OF-3, 1B-1
1915	68	171	41	8	2	0	0.0	22	19	24		12	.240	.310	5	1	3B-28, 2B-21, SS-5, 1B-5
4 yrs.	203	528	125	20	6	3	0.6	70	46	54	33	32	.237	.314	21	4	3B-97, SS-29, 2B-27, 1B-14, OF-3

Joe Kirrene

KIRRENE, JOSEPH JOHN   BR TR 6'2" 195 lbs.
B. Oct. 4, 1931, San Francisco, Calif.

	G	AB	H	2B	3B	HR	HR %	R	RBI	BB	SO	SB	BA	SA	PH AB	PH H	G by POS
1950 CHI A	1	4	1	0	0	0	0.0	0	0	0	1	0	.250	.250	0	0	3B-1
1954	9	23	7	1	0	0	0.0	4	4	5	2	1	.304	.348	1	0	3B-9
2 yrs.	10	27	8	1	0	0	0.0	4	4	5	3	1	.296	.333	1	0	3B-10

Ernie Kish

KISH, ERNEST ALEXANDER   BL TR 5'9½" 170 lbs.
B. Feb. 6, 1918, Washington, D. C.

	G	AB	H	2B	3B	HR	HR %	R	RBI	BB	SO	SB	BA	SA	PH AB	PH H	G by POS
1945 PHI A	43	110	27	5	1	0	0.0	10	10	9	9	0	.245	.309	9	2	OF-30

Frank Kitson

KITSON, FRANK L   BL TR 5'11" 165 lbs.
B. Apr. 11, 1872, Hopkins, Mich.   D. Apr. 14, 1930, Allegan, Mich.

	G	AB	H	2B	3B	HR	HR %	R	RBI	BB	SO	SB	BA	SA	PH AB	PH H	G by POS
1898 BAL N	31	86	27	1	3	0	0.0	13	16	5		2	.314	.395	3	2	P-17, OF-11
1899	45	134	27	7	1	0	0.0	13	8	6		7	.201	.269	4	0	P-40
1900 BKN N	43	109	32	5	1	0	0.0	20	16	6		2	.294	.358	2	0	P-40, OF-1
1901	47	133	35	5	2	1	0.8	22	16	4		6	.263	.353	6	2	P-38, OF-2, 1B-1
1902	39	113	30	3	4	1	0.9	9	11	3		0	.265	.389	7	3	P-31
1903 DET A	36	116	21	0	2	0	0.0	12	4	2		1	.181	.216	0	0	P-31, OF-5
1904	27	72	15	0	0	1	1.4	9	4	1		0	.208	.250	1	0	P-26
1905	33	87	16	2	0	0	0.0	8	4	3		0	.184	.207	0	0	P-33
1906 WAS A	31	90	22	4	4	1	1.1	9	12	8		1	.244	.411	1	0	P-30
1907 2 teams		WAS A (5G – .125)				NY A (12G – .261)											
" total	17	31	7	0	0	0	0.0	4	4	1		0	.226	.226	0	0	P-17
10 yrs.	349	971	232	27	17	4	0.4	119	95	39		14	.239	.314	24	7	P-303, OF-19, 1B-1

Chris Kitsos

KITSOS, CHRISTOPHER ANESTOS   BB TR 5'9" 165 lbs.
B. Feb. 11, 1928, New York, N. Y.

	G	AB	H	2B	3B	HR	HR %	R	RBI	BB	SO	SB	BA	SA	PH AB	PH H	G by POS
1954 CHI N	1	0	0	0	0	0	0.0	0	0	0	0	0	–	–	0	0	SS-1

Ron Kittle

KITTLE, RONALD DALE   BR TR 6'3" 195 lbs.
B. Jan. 5, 1958, Gary, Ind.

	G	AB	H	2B	3B	HR	HR %	R	RBI	BB	SO	SB	BA	SA	PH AB	PH H	G by POS
1982 CHI A	20	29	7	2	0	1	3.4	3	7	3	12	0	.241	.414	13	2	OF-5, DH-3
1983	145	520	132	19	3	35	6.7	75	100	39	150	8	.254	.504	6	0	OF-139, DH-2
1984	139	466	100	15	0	32	6.9	67	74	49	137	3	.215	.453	13	4	OF-124, DH-7
3 yrs.	304	1015	239	36	3	68	6.7	145	181	91	299	11	.235	.478	32	6	OF-268, DH-12

LEAGUE CHAMPIONSHIP SERIES

	G	AB	H	2B	3B	HR	HR %	R	RBI	BB	SO	SB	BA	SA	PH AB	PH H	G by POS
1983 CHI A	3	7	2	1	0	0	0.0	1	0	1	2	0	.286	.429	0	0	OF-3

Malachi Kittredge

KITTREDGE, MALACHI J.   BR TR 5'10"
B. Oct. 12, 1869, Clinton, Mass.   D. June 23, 1928, Gary, Ind.
Manager 1904.

	G	AB	H	2B	3B	HR	HR %	R	RBI	BB	SO	SB	BA	SA	PH AB	PH H	G by POS
1890 CHI N	96	333	67	8	3	3	0.9	46	35	39	53	7	.201	.270	0	0	C-96
1891	79	296	62	8	5	2	0.7	26	27	17	28	4	.209	.291	0	0	C-79
1892	69	229	41	5	0	0	0.0	19	10	11	27	2	.179	.201	0	0	C-69
1893	70	255	59	9	5	2	0.8	32	30	17	15	3	.231	.329	0	0	C-70
1894	51	168	53	8	2	0	0.0	36	23	26	20	2	.315	.387	0	0	C-51
1895	60	212	48	6	3	3	1.4	30	29	16	9	6	.226	.325	0	0	C-59
1896	65	215	48	4	1	1	0.5	17	19	14	14	6	.223	.265	0	0	C-64, P-1
1897	79	262	53	5	5	1	0.4	25	30	22		9	.202	.271	0	0	C-79
1898 LOU N	86	287	70	8	5	1	0.3	27	31	15		7	.244	.317	0	0	C-86
1899 2 teams		LOU N (45G – .202)				WAS N (44G – .150)											
" total	89	262	46	5	1	0	0.0	25	23	36		5	.176	.202	3	1	C-86
1901 BOS N	114	381	96	14	0	2	0.5	24	40	32		2	.252	.304	0	0	C-113
1902	80	255	60	7	0	2	0.8	18	30	24		4	.235	.286	7	1	C-72
1903 2 teams		BOS N (32G – .212)				WAS A (60G – .214)											
" total	92	291	62	6	1	0	0.0	18	22	21		2	.213	.241	2	0	C-90
1904 WAS A	81	265	64	7	0	0	0.0	11	24	8		2	.242	.268	2	0	C-79
1905	76	238	39	8	0	0	0.0	16	14	15		1	.164	.197	0	0	C-75
1906 2 teams		WAS A (27G – .179)				CLE A (1G – .000)											
" total	28	81	14	0	0	0	0.0	5	3	1		0	.173	.173	0	0	C-28
16 yrs.	1215	4030	882	108	31	16	0.4	375	390	314	166	64	.219	.274	14	2	C-1196, P-1

Billy Klaus

KLAUS, WILLIAM JOSEPH   BL TR 5'9" 160 lbs.
Brother of Bobby Klaus.
B. Dec. 9, 1928, Fox Lake, Ill.

	G	AB	H	2B	3B	HR	HR %	R	RBI	BB	SO	SB	BA	SA	PH AB	PH H	G by POS
1952 BOS N	7	4	0	0	0	0	0.0	3	0	1	1	0	.000	.000	3	0	SS-4
1953 MIL N	2	2	0	0	0	0	0.0	1	1	0	1	0	.000	.000	2	0	
1955 BOS A	135	541	153	26	2	7	1.3	83	60	60	44	1	.283	.377	2	0	SS-126, 3B-8
1956	135	520	141	29	5	7	1.3	91	59	90	43	1	.271	.387	5	1	3B-106, SS-26
1957	127	477	120	18	4	10	2.1	76	42	55	53	2	.252	.369	8	2	SS-118
1958	61	88	14	4	0	1	1.1	5	7	5	16	0	.159	.239	39	6	SS-27

	G	AB	H	2B	3B	HR	HR %	R	RBI	BB	SO	SB	BA	SA	Pinch Hit AB	Pinch Hit H	G by POS

Billy Klaus continued

	G	AB	H	2B	3B	HR	HR%	R	RBI	BB	SO	SB	BA	SA	PH AB	PH H	G by POS
1959 BAL A	104	321	80	11	0	3	0.9	33	25	51	38	2	.249	.312	4	0	SS-59, 3B-49, 2B-1
1960	46	43	9	2	0	1	2.3	8	6	9	9	0	.209	.326	3	0	2B-30, SS-12, 3B-2
1961 WAS A	91	251	57	8	2	7	2.8	26	30	30	34	2	.227	.359	18	3	3B-51, SS-18, OF-1, 2B-1
1962 PHI N	102	248	51	8	2	4	1.6	30	20	29	43	1	.206	.302	28	5	3B-53, SS-30, 2B-11
1963	11	18	1	0	0	0	0.0	1	0	1	4	0	.056	.056	8	1	SS-5, 3B-3
11 yrs.	821	2513	626	106	15	40	1.6	357	250	331	285	14	.249	.351	120	18	SS-425, 3B-272, 2B-43, OF-1

Bobby Klaus

KLAUS, ROBERT FRANCIS
Brother of Billy Klaus.
B. Dec. 27, 1937, Spring Grove, Ill.

BR TR 5'10" 170 lbs.

	G	AB	H	2B	3B	HR	HR%	R	RBI	BB	SO	SB	BA	SA	PH AB	PH H	G by POS
1964 2 teams		CIN	N (40G –	.183)		NY	N (56G –	.244)									
" total	96	302	68	13	4	4	1.3	35	17	29	43	4	.225	.334	7	0	2B-43, 3B-39, SS-8
1965 NY N	119	288	55	12	0	2	0.7	30	12	45	49	1	.191	.253	4	1	2B-72, SS-28, 3B-25
2 yrs.	215	590	123	25	4	6	1.0	65	29	74	92	5	.208	.295	11	1	2B-115, 3B-64, SS-36

Ollie Klee

KLEE, OLLIE CHESTER (Babe)
B. May 20, 1900, Piqua, Ohio   D. Feb. 9, 1977, Toledo, Ohio

BL TR 5'9½" 160 lbs.

	G	AB	H	2B	3B	HR	HR%	R	RBI	BB	SO	SB	BA	SA	PH AB	PH H	G by POS
1925 CIN N	3	1	0	0	0	0	0.0	0	0	0	1	0	.000	.000	0	0	OF-1

Chuck Klein

KLEIN, CHARLES HERBERT
B. Oct. 7, 1904, Indianapolis, Ind.   D. Mar. 28, 1958, Indianapolis, Ind.
Hall of Fame 1980.

BL TR 6' 185 lbs.

	G	AB	H	2B	3B	HR	HR%	R	RBI	BB	SO	SB	BA	SA	PH AB	PH H	G by POS
1928 PHI N	64	253	91	14	4	11	4.3	41	34	14	22	0	.360	.577	1	0	OF-63
1929	149	616	219	45	6	43	7.0	126	145	54	61	5	.356	.657	0	0	OF-149
1930	156	648	250	59	8	40	6.2	158	170	54	50	4	.386	.687	0	0	OF-156
1931	148	594	200	34	10	31	5.2	121	121	59	49	7	.337	.584	0	0	OF-148
1932	154	650	226	50	15	38	5.8	152	137	60	49	20	.348	.646	0	0	OF-154
1933	152	606	223	44	7	28	4.6	101	120	56	36	15	.368	.602	0	0	OF-152
1934 CHI N	115	435	131	27	2	20	4.6	78	80	47	38	3	.301	.510	5	2	OF-110
1935	119	434	127	14	4	21	4.8	71	73	41	42	4	.293	.488	6	1	OF-111
1936 2 teams	146	CHI	N (29G –	.294)		PHI	N (117G –	.309)									
" total	146	601	184	35	7	25	4.2	102	104	49	59	6	.306	.512	0	0	OF-146
1937 PHI N	115	406	132	20	2	15	3.7	74	57	39	21	3	.325	.495	13	3	OF-102
1938	129	458	113	22	2	8	1.7	53	61	38	30	7	.247	.356	10	1	OF-119
1939 2 teams		PHI	N (25G –	.191)		PIT	N (85G –	.300)									
" total	110	317	90	18	5	12	3.8	45	56	36	21	2	.284	.486	26	11	OF-77, 1B-1
1940 PHI N	116	354	77	16	2	7	2.0	39	37	44	30	2	.218	.333	18	2	OF-116
1941	50	73	9	0	0	1	1.4	6	3	10	6	0	.123	.164	31	5	OF-14
1942	14	14	1	0	0	0	0.0	0	0	0	2	0	.071	.071	14	1	
1943	12	20	2	0	0	0	0.0	0	3	0	3	1	.100	.100	10	1	OF-2
1944	4	7	1	0	0	0	0.0	1	0	0	2	0	.143	.143	3	1	OF-1
17 yrs.	1753	6486	2076	398	74	300	4.6	1168	1201	601	521	79	.320	.543	137	28	OF-1620, 1B-1

WORLD SERIES

	G	AB	H	2B	3B	HR	HR%	R	RBI	BB	SO	SB	BA	SA	PH AB	PH H	G by POS
1935 CHI N	5	12	4	0	0	1	8.3	2	2	0	2	0	.333	.583	3	1	OF-3

Lou Klein

KLEIN, LOUIS FRANK
B. Oct. 22, 1918, New Orleans, La.   D. June 20, 1976, Metairie, La.
Manager 1961-62, 1965.

BR TR 5'11" 167 lbs.

	G	AB	H	2B	3B	HR	HR%	R	RBI	BB	SO	SB	BA	SA	PH AB	PH H	G by POS
1943 STL N	154	627	180	28	14	7	1.1	91	62	50	70	9	.287	.410	0	0	2B-126, SS-51
1945	19	57	13	4	1	1	1.8	12	6	14	9	0	.228	.386	0	0	OF-7, SS-7, 3B-4, 2B-2
1946	23	93	18	3	0	1	1.1	12	4	9	7	1	.194	.258	0	0	2B-23
1949	58	114	25	6	0	2	1.8	25	12	22	20	0	.219	.325	18	3	SS-21, 2B-9, 3B-7
1951 2 teams		CLE	A (2G –	.000)		PHI	A (49G –	.229)									
" total	51	146	33	7	0	5	3.4	22	17	10	13	0	.226	.377	9	0	2B-42
5 yrs.	305	1037	269	48	15	16	1.5	162	101	105	119	10	.259	.381	27	3	2B-202, SS-79, 3B-11, OF-7

WORLD SERIES

	G	AB	H	2B	3B	HR	HR%	R	RBI	BB	SO	SB	BA	SA	PH AB	PH H	G by POS
1943 STL N	5	22	3	0	0	0	0.0	0	0	1	2	0	.136	.136	0	0	2B-5

Red Kleinow

KLEINOW, JOHN PETER
B. July 20, 1879, Milwaukee, Wis.   D. Oct. 9, 1929, New York, N.Y.

BR TR

	G	AB	H	2B	3B	HR	HR%	R	RBI	BB	SO	SB	BA	SA	PH AB	PH H	G by POS
1904 NY A	68	209	43	8	4	0	0.0	12	16	15		4	.206	.282	2	0	C-62, 3B-2, OF-1
1905	88	253	56	6	3	1	0.4	23	24	20		7	.221	.281	2	0	C-83, 1B-3
1906	96	268	59	9	3	0	0.0	30	31	24		8	.220	.276	0	0	C-95, 1B-1
1907	90	269	71	6	4	0	0.0	30	26	24		5	.264	.316	3	0	C-86, 1B-1
1908	96	279	47	3	2	1	0.4	16	13	22		5	.168	.204	5	2	C-89, 2B-2
1909	78	206	47	11	4	0	0.0	24	15	25		7	.228	.320	1	0	C-77
1910 2 teams		NY	A (6G –	.417)		BOS	A (50G –	.150)									
" total	56	159	27	1	0	1	0.6	11	10	21		5	.170	.195	3	0	C-54
1911 2 teams		BOS	A (8G –	.214)		PHI	N (4G –	.125)									
" total	12	22	4	1	0	0	0.0	0	0	2	1	1	.182	.227	0	0	C-12
8 yrs.	584	1665	354	45	20	3	0.2	146	135	153	1	42	.213	.269	16	2	C-558, 1B-5, 3B-2, 2B-2, OF-1

Jay Kleven

KLEVEN, JAY ALLEN
B. Dec. 2, 1949, Oakland, Calif.

BR TR 6'2" 190 lbs.

	G	AB	H	2B	3B	HR	HR%	R	RBI	BB	SO	SB	BA	SA	PH AB	PH H	G by POS
1976 NY N	2	5	1	0	0	0	0.0	0	2	0	1	0	.200	.200	0	0	C-2

Lou Klimchock

KLIMCHOCK, LOUIS STEPHEN
B. Oct. 15, 1939, Hostetter, Pa.

BL TR 5'11" 180 lbs.

	G	AB	H	2B	3B	HR	HR%	R	RBI	BB	SO	SB	BA	SA	PH AB	PH H	G by POS
1958 KC A	2	10	2	0	0	1	10.0	2	1	0	1	0	.200	.500	0	0	2B-2
1959	17	66	18	1	0	4	6.1	10	13	1	6	0	.273	.470	1	0	2B-16
1960	10	10	3	0	0	0	0.0	0	0	0	0	0	.300	.300	9	2	2B-1
1961	57	121	26	4	1	1	0.8	8	16	5	13	0	.215	.289	32	6	1B-11, OF-7, 3B-6, 2B-1

	G	AB	H	2B	3B	HR	HR %	R	RBI	BB	SO	SB	BA	SA	Pinch Hit AB	Pinch Hit H	G by POS

Lou Klimchock continued

	G	AB	H	2B	3B	HR	HR%	R	RBI	BB	SO	SB	BA	SA	AB	H	G by POS
1962 MIL N	8	8	0	0	0	0	0.0	0	0	0	2	0	.000	.000	8	0	
1963 2 teams		WAS	A	(9G –	.143)		MIL	N	(24G –	.196)							
" total	33	60	11	1	0	0	0.0	7	3	0	13	0	.183	.200	20	3	1B-12, 2B-3
1964 MIL N	10	21	7	2	0	0	0.0	3	2	1	2	0	.333	.429	5	2	3B-4, 2B-2
1965	34	39	3	0	0	0	0.0	3	3	2	8	0	.077	.077	29	2	1B-4
1966 NY N	5	5	0	0	0	0	0.0	0	0	0	3	0	.000	.000	5	0	
1968 CLE A	11	15	2	0	0	0	0.0	0	3	1	0	0	.133	.133	7	0	3B-4, 2B-1, 1B-1
1969	90	258	74	13	2	6	2.3	26	26	18	14	0	.287	.422	15	2	3B-56, 2B-21, C-1
1970	41	56	9	0	0	1	1.8	5	2	3	9	0	.161	.214	30	4	2B-5, 1B-5
12 yrs.	318	669	155	21	3	13	1.9	64	69	31	71	0	.232	.330	161	21	3B-70, 2B-52, 1B-33, OF-7, C-1

Bobby Kline

KLINE, JOHN ROBERT   BR TR 6'   179 lbs.
B. Jan. 27, 1929, St. Petersburg, Fla.

	G	AB	H	2B	3B	HR	HR%	R	RBI	BB	SO	SB	BA	SA	AB	H	G by POS
1955 WAS A	77	140	31	5	0	0	0.0	12	9	11	27	0	.221	.257	0	0	SS-69, 2B-4, 3B-3, P-1

Johnny Kling

KLING, JOHN (Noisy)   BR TR 5'9½"   160 lbs.
Brother of Bill Kling.
B. Feb. 25, 1875, Kansas City, Mo.   D. Jan. 31, 1947, Kansas City, Mo.
Manager 1912.

	G	AB	H	2B	3B	HR	HR%	R	RBI	BB	SO	SB	BA	SA	AB	H	G by POS
1900 CHI N	15	51	15	3	1	0	0.0	8	7	2		0	.294	.392	0	0	C-15
1901	74	253	70	6	3	0	0.0	26	21	9		7	.277	.324	4	1	C-69, OF-1, 1B-1
1902	114	434	124	19	3	0	0.0	50	57	29		23	.286	.343	1	0	C-112, SS-1
1903	132	491	146	29	13	3	0.6	67	68	22		23	.297	.428	0	0	C-132
1904	123	452	110	18	0	2	0.4	41	46	16		7	.243	.296	2	0	C-104, OF-10, 1B-6
1905	111	380	83	8	6	1	0.3	26	52	28		13	.218	.279	1	0	C-106, OF-4, 1B-1
1906	107	343	107	15	8	2	0.6	45	46	23		14	.312	.420	7	2	C-96, OF-3
1907	104	334	95	15	8	1	0.3	44	43	27		9	.284	.386	3	0	C-98, 1B-2
1908	126	424	117	23	5	4	0.9	51	59	21		16	.276	.382	2	0	C-117, OF-6, 1B-2
1910	91	297	80	17	2	2	0.7	31	32	37	27	3	.269	.360	4	0	C-86
1911 2 teams		CHI	N	(27G –	.175)		BOS	N	(75G –	.224)							
" total	102	321	68	11	3	3	0.9	40	29	38	43	1	.212	.293	4	1	C-96, 3B-1
1912 BOS N	81	252	80	10	3	2	0.8	26	30	15	30	3	.317	.405	7	2	C-74
1913 CIN N	80	209	57	7	6	0	0.0	20	23	14	14	2	.273	.364	15	3	C-63
13 yrs.	1260	4241	1152	181	61	20	0.5	475	513	281	114	121	.272	.357	50	9	C-1168, OF-24, 1B-12, SS-1, 3B-1

WORLD SERIES																	
1906 CHI N	6	17	3	1	0	0	0.0	2	0	4	3	0	.176	.235	0	0	C-6
1907	5	19	4	0	0	0	0.0	2	1	1	4	0	.211	.211	0	0	C-5
1908	5	16	4	1	0	0	0.0	2	1	2	2	0	.250	.313	0	0	C-5
1910	5	13	1	0	0	0	0.0	0	1	1	2	0	.077	.077	2	0	C-3
4 yrs.	21	65	12	2	0	0	0.0	6	3	8	11	0	.185	.215	2	0	C-19

Rudy Kling

KLING, RUDOLPH A.   BR TR
B. Mar. 23, 1870, St. Louis, Mo.   D. Mar. 14, 1937, St. Louis, Mo.

	G	AB	H	2B	3B	HR	HR%	R	RBI	BB	SO	SB	BA	SA	AB	H	G by POS
1902 STL N	4	10	2	0	0	0	0.0	0	4		1	0	.200	.200	0	0	SS-4

Joe Klinger

KLINGER, JOSEPH JOHN   BR TR 6'   190 lbs.
B. Aug. 2, 1902, Canonsburg, Pa.   D. July 31, 1960, Little Rock, Ark.

	G	AB	H	2B	3B	HR	HR%	R	RBI	BB	SO	SB	BA	SA	AB	H	G by POS
1927 NY N	3	5	2	0	0	0	0.0	0	0	0	2	0	.400	.400	2	0	OF-1
1930 CHI A	4	8	3	0	0	0	0.0	0	1	0	0	0	.375	.375	0	0	1B-2, C-2
2 yrs.	7	13	5	0	0	0	0.0	0	1	0	2	0	.385	.385	2	0	1B-2, C-2, OF-1

Nap Kloza

KLOZA, JOHN CLARENCE   BR TR 5'11"   180 lbs.
B. Sept. 2, 1903, Poland   D. June 11, 1962, Milwaukee, Wis.

	G	AB	H	2B	3B	HR	HR%	R	RBI	BB	SO	SB	BA	SA	AB	H	G by POS
1931 STL A	3	7	1	0	0	0	0.0	1	0	1	4	0	.143	.143	0	0	OF-3
1932	19	13	2	0	1	0	0.0	4	2	4	4	0	.154	.308	10	1	OF-3
2 yrs.	22	20	3	0	1	0	0.0	5	2	5	8	0	.150	.250	10	1	OF-6

Joe Klugman

KLUGMAN, JOSIE   BR TR 5'11"   175 lbs.
B. Mar. 26, 1895, St. Louis, Mo.   D. July 18, 1951, Moberly, Mo.

	G	AB	H	2B	3B	HR	HR%	R	RBI	BB	SO	SB	BA	SA	AB	H	G by POS
1921 CHI N	6	21	6	0	0	0	0.0	3	2	1	2	0	.286	.286	1	1	2B-5
1922	2	2	0	0	0	0	0.0	0	0	0	0	0	.000	.000	0	0	2B-2
1924 BKN N	31	79	13	2	1	0	0.0	7	3	2	9	0	.165	.215	1	0	2B-28, SS-1
1925 CLE A	38	85	28	9	2	0	0.0	12	12	8	4	3	.329	.482	3	1	2B-29, 1B-4, 3B-2
4 yrs.	77	187	47	11	3	0	0.0	22	17	11	15	3	.251	.342	5	2	2B-64, 1B-4, 3B-2, SS-1

Elmer Klumpp

KLUMPP, ELMER EDWARD   BR TR 6'   184 lbs.
B. Aug. 26, 1906, St. Louis, Mo.

	G	AB	H	2B	3B	HR	HR%	R	RBI	BB	SO	SB	BA	SA	AB	H	G by POS
1934 WAS A	12	15	2	0	0	0	0.0	2	0	0	1	0	.133	.133	1	0	C-11
1937 BKN N	5	11	1	0	0	0	0.0	0	2	1	4	0	.091	.091	1	0	C-3
2 yrs.	17	26	3	0	0	0	0.0	2	2	1	5	0	.115	.115	2	0	C-14

Billy Klusman

KLUSMAN, WILLIAM F.   BR TR 5'10½"   185 lbs.
B. Mar. 24, 1865, Cincinnati, Ohio   D. June 24, 1907, Cincinnati, Ohio

	G	AB	H	2B	3B	HR	HR%	R	RBI	BB	SO	SB	BA	SA	AB	H	G by POS
1888 BOS N	28	107	18	4	0	2	1.9	9	11	5	13	3	.168	.262	0	0	2B-28
1890 STL AA	15	65	18	4	1	1	1.5	9		1		1	.277	.415	0	0	2B-15
2 yrs.	43	172	36	8	1	3	1.7	18	11	6	13	4	.209	.320	0	0	2B-43

Ted Kluszewski

KLUSZEWSKI, THEODORE BERNARD (Klu)   BL TL 6'2"   225 lbs.
B. Sept. 10, 1924, Argo, Ill.

	G	AB	H	2B	3B	HR	HR%	R	RBI	BB	SO	SB	BA	SA	AB	H	G by POS
1947 CIN N	9	10	1	0	0	0	0.0	1	2	1	2	0	.100	.100	5	0	1B-2
1948	113	379	104	23	4	12	3.2	49	57	18	32	1	.274	.451	15	5	1B-98
1949	136	531	164	26	2	8	1.5	63	68	19	24	3	.309	.411	2	1	1B-134
1950	134	538	165	37	0	25	4.6	76	111	33	28	3	.307	.515	2	0	1B-131

	G	AB	H	2B	3B	HR	HR%	R	RBI	BB	SO	SB	BA	SA	Pinch Hit AB	Pinch Hit H	G by POS

Ted Kluszewski continued

	G	AB	H	2B	3B	HR	HR%	R	RBI	BB	SO	SB	BA	SA	AB	H	G by POS
1951	154	607	157	35	2	13	2.1	74	77	35	33	6	.259	.387	1	0	1B-154
1952	135	497	159	24	11	16	3.2	62	86	47	28	3	.320	.509	3	1	1B-133
1953	149	570	180	25	0	40	7.0	97	108	55	34	2	.316	.570	1	0	1B-147
1954	149	573	187	28	3	49	8.6	104	141	78	35	0	.326	.642	0	0	1B-149
1955	153	612	192	25	0	47	7.7	116	113	66	40	1	.314	.585	0	0	1B-153
1956	138	517	156	14	1	35	6.8	91	102	49	31	1	.302	.536	7	1	1B-131
1957	69	127	34	7	0	6	4.7	12	21	5	5	0	.268	.465	47	12	1B-23
1958 PIT N	100	301	88	13	4	4	1.3	29	37	26	16	0	.292	.402	24	9	1B-72
1959 2 teams	PIT	N (60G –	.262)		CHI	A	(31G –	.297)									
" total	91	223	62	12	2	4	1.8	22	27	14	24	0	.278	.404	39	7	1B-49
1960 CHI A	81	181	53	9	0	5	2.8	20	39	22	10	0	.293	.425	34	8	1B-39
1961 LA A	107	263	64	12	0	15	5.7	32	39	24	23	0	.243	.460	43	9	1B-66
15 yrs.	1718	5929	1766	290	29	279	4.7	848	1028	492	365	20	.298	.498	223	53	1B-1481

WORLD SERIES

	G	AB	H	2B	3B	HR	HR%	R	RBI	BB	SO	SB	BA	SA	AB	H	G by POS
1959 CHI A	6	23	9	1	0	3	13.0	5	10	2	0	0	.391	.826	0	0	1B-6

Mickey Klutts

KLUTTS, GENE ELLIS   BR TR 5'11" 170 lbs.
B. Sept. 30, 1954, Montebello, Calif.

	G	AB	H	2B	3B	HR	HR%	R	RBI	BB	SO	SB	BA	SA	AB	H	G by POS
1976 NY A	2	3	0	0	0	0	0.0	0	0	0	1	0	.000	.000	0	0	SS-2
1977	5	15	4	1	0	1	6.7	3	4	2	1	0	.267	.533	0	0	3B-4, SS-1
1978	1	2	2	1	0	0	0.0	1	0	0	0	0	1.000	1.500	0	0	3B-1
1979 OAK A	24	73	14	2	1	1	1.4	3	4	7	20	0	.192	.288	0	0	SS-10, 2B-8, 3B-6
1980	75	197	53	14	0	4	2.0	20	21	13	41	1	.269	.401	5	3	3B-62, SS-8, 2B-7, DH-1
1981	15	46	17	0	0	5	10.9	9	11	2	9	0	.370	.696	1	1	3B-14
1982	55	157	28	8	0	0	0.0	10	14	9	18	0	.178	.229	9	2	3B-49
1983 TOR A	22	43	11	0	0	3	7.0	3	5	1	11	0	.256	.465	7	3	3B-17, DH-2
8 yrs.	199	536	129	26	1	14	2.6	49	59	34	101	1	.241	.371	22	9	3B-153, SS-21, 2B-15, DH-3

DIVISIONAL PLAYOFF SERIES

	G	AB	H	2B	3B	HR	HR%	R	RBI	BB	SO	SB	BA	SA	AB	H	G by POS
1981 OAK A	2	7	1	0	0	0	0.0	0	0	0	1	0	.143	.143	0	0	3B-2

LEAGUE CHAMPIONSHIP SERIES

	G	AB	H	2B	3B	HR	HR%	R	RBI	BB	SO	SB	BA	SA	AB	H	G by POS
1981 OAK A	3	7	3	0	0	0	0.0	1	0	0	1	0	.429	.429	0	0	3B-3

Clyde Kluttz

KLUTTZ, CLYDE FRANKLIN   BR TR 6' 193 lbs.
B. Dec. 12, 1917, Rockwell, N. C.   D. May 12, 1979, Salisbury, N. C.

	G	AB	H	2B	3B	HR	HR%	R	RBI	BB	SO	SB	BA	SA	AB	H	G by POS
1942 BOS N	72	210	56	10	1	1	0.5	21	31	7	13	0	.267	.338	15	6	C-57
1943	66	207	51	7	0	0	0.0	13	20	15	9	0	.246	.280	9	1	C-55
1944	81	229	64	12	2	2	0.9	20	19	13	14	0	.279	.376	23	4	C-58
1945 2 teams	BOS	N (25G –	.296)		NY	N	(73G –	.279)									
" total	98	303	86	18	1	4	1.3	34	31	17	16	1	.284	.389	20	3	C-76
1946 2 teams	NY	N (5G –	.375)		STL	N	(52G –	.265)									
" total	57	144	39	7	0	0	0.0	8	15	10	11	0	.271	.319	5	3	C-51
1947 PIT N	73	232	70	9	2	6	2.6	26	42	17	18	1	.302	.435	4	1	C-69
1948	94	271	60	12	2	4	1.5	26	20	20	19	3	.221	.325	3	1	C-91
1951 2 teams	STL	A (4G –	.500)		WAS	A	(53G –	.308)									
" total	57	163	51	10	0	1	0.6	17	23	21	8	0	.313	.393	9	2	C-47
1952 WAS A	58	144	33	5	0	1	0.7	7	11	12	11	0	.229	.285	6	1	C-52
9 yrs.	656	1903	510	90	8	19	1.0	172	212	132	119	5	.268	.354	94	22	C-556

Otto Knabe

KNABE, FRANZ OTTO (Dutch)   BR TR 5'8" 175 lbs.
B. June 12, 1884, Carrick, Pa.   D. May 17, 1961, Philadelphia, Pa.
Manager 1914-15.

	G	AB	H	2B	3B	HR	HR%	R	RBI	BB	SO	SB	BA	SA	AB	H	G by POS
1905 PIT N	3	10	3	1	0	0	0.0	0	2	3		0	.300	.400	0	0	3B-3
1907 PHI N	129	444	113	16	9	1	0.2	67	34	52		18	.255	.338	2	0	2B-121, OF-5
1908	151	555	121	26	8	0	0.0	63	27	49		27	.218	.294	0	0	2B-151
1909	114	402	94	13	3	0	0.0	40	33	35		9	.234	.281	2	0	2B-109, OF-1
1910	137	510	133	18	6	1	0.2	73	44	47	42	15	.261	.325	1	0	2B-136
1911	142	528	125	15	6	1	0.2	99	42	94	35	23	.237	.294	0	0	2B-142
1912	126	426	120	11	4	0	0.0	56	46	55	20	16	.282	.326	3	1	2B-123
1913	148	571	150	25	7	2	0.4	70	53	45	26	14	.263	.342	0	0	2B-148
1914 BAL F	147	469	106	26	2	2	0.4	45	42	53		10	.226	.303	3	1	2B-144
1915	103	320	81	16	2	1	0.3	38	25	37			.253	.325	8	2	2B-94, OF-1
1916 2 teams	PIT	N (28G –	.191)		CHI	N	(57G –	.276)									
" total	85	234	57	11	1	0	0.0	21	16	15	24	4	.244	.299	5	2	2B-70, OF-1, SS-1, 3B-1
11 yrs.	1285	4469	1103	178	48	8	0.2	572	364	485	147	143	.247	.313	24	6	2B-1238, OF-8, 3B-4, SS-1

Cotton Knaupp

KNAUPP, HENRY ANTONE   BR TR 5'9" 165 lbs.
B. Aug. 13, 1889, San Antonio, Tex.   D. July 6, 1967, New Orleans, La.

	G	AB	H	2B	3B	HR	HR%	R	RBI	BB	SO	SB	BA	SA	AB	H	G by POS
1910 CLE A	18	59	14	3	1	0	0.0	3	11	8		1	.237	.322	0	0	SS-18
1911	13	39	4	1	0	0	0.0	2	0	0		3	.103	.128	0	0	SS-13
2 yrs.	31	98	18	4	1	0	0.0	5	11	8		4	.184	.245	0	0	SS-31

Alan Knicely

KNICELY, ALAN LEE   BR TR 6' 190 lbs.
B. May 19, 1955, Harrisonburg, Va.

	G	AB	H	2B	3B	HR	HR%	R	RBI	BB	SO	SB	BA	SA	AB	H	G by POS
1979 HOU N	7	6	0	0	0	0	0.0	0	0	2	3	0	.000	.000	3	0	C-3
1980	1	1	0	0	0	0	0.0	0	0	0	1	0	.000	.000	1	0	
1981	3	7	4	0	0	2	28.6	2	2	0	1	0	.571	1.429	1	1	C-2, OF-1
1982	59	133	25	2	0	2	1.5	10	12	14	30	0	.188	.248	17	1	C-23, OF-16, 3B-1
1983 CIN N	59	98	22	3	0	2	2.0	11	10	16	28	0	.224	.316	19	4	C-31, OF-8, 1B-2
1984	10	29	4	0	0	0	0.0	0	5	3	6	0	.138	.138	0	0	1B-8, C-1
6 yrs.	139	274	55	5	0	6	2.2	23	29	35	69	0	.201	.285	41	6	C-60, OF-25, 1B-10, 3B-1

	G	AB	H	2B	3B	HR	HR %	R	RBI	BB	SO	SB	BA	SA	Pinch Hit AB	Pinch Hit H	G by POS

Austin Knickerbocker

KNICKERBOCKER, AUSTIN JAY
B. Oct. 15, 1918, Bangall, N. Y.
BR TR 5'11"   185 lbs.

	G	AB	H	2B	3B	HR	HR %	R	RBI	BB	SO	SB	BA	SA	PH AB	PH H	G by POS
1947 PHI A	21	48	12	3	2	0	0.0	8	2	3	4	0	.250	.396	2	2	OF-14

Bill Knickerbocker

KNICKERBOCKER, WILLIAM HART
B. Dec. 29, 1911, Los Angeles, Calif.   D. Sept. 8, 1963, Sebastopol, Calif.
BR TR 5'11"   170 lbs.

	G	AB	H	2B	3B	HR	HR %	R	RBI	BB	SO	SB	BA	SA	PH AB	PH H	G by POS
1933 CLE A	80	279	63	16	3	2	0.7	20	32	11	30	1	.226	.326	1	0	SS-80
1934	146	593	188	32	5	4	0.7	82	67	25	40	6	.317	.408	0	0	SS-146
1935	132	540	161	34	5	0	0.0	77	55	27	31	2	.298	.380	3	0	SS-128
1936	155	618	182	35	3	8	1.3	81	73	56	30	5	.294	.400	0	0	SS-155
1937 STL A	121	491	128	29	5	4	0.8	53	61	30	32	3	.261	.365	0	0	SS-115, 2B-6
1938 NY A	46	128	32	8	3	1	0.8	15	21	11	10	0	.250	.383	9	1	2B-34, SS-3
1939	6	13	2	1	0	0	0.0	2	1	0	0	0	.154	.231	2	0	SS-2, 2B-2
1940	45	124	30	8	1	1	0.8	17	10	14	8	1	.242	.347	7	2	SS-19, 3B-17
1941 CHI A	89	343	84	23	2	7	2.0	51	29	41	27	6	.245	.385	1	0	2B-88
1942 PHI A	87	289	73	12	0	1	0.3	25	19	29	30	1	.253	.304	6	0	2B-81, SS-1
10 yrs.	907	3418	943	198	27	28	0.8	423	368	244	238	25	.276	.374	29	3	SS-649, 2B-211, 3B-17

Joe Knight

KNIGHT, JONAS WILLIAM (Quiet Joe)
B. Sept. 26, 1859, Point Stanley, Ont., Canada   D. Oct. 18, 1938, St. Thomas, Ont., Canada
BL TL 5'11"   185 lbs.

	G	AB	H	2B	3B	HR	HR %	R	RBI	BB	SO	SB	BA	SA	PH AB	PH H	G by POS
1884 PHI N	6	24	6	3	0	0	0.0		0		2		.250	.375	0	0	P-6
1890 CIN N	127	481	150	26	8	4	0.8	67	67	38	31	17	.312	.424	0	0	OF-127
2 yrs.	133	505	156	29	8	4	0.8	69	66	38	33	17	.309	.422	0	0	OF-127, P-6

John Knight

KNIGHT, JOHN WESLEY (Schoolboy)
B. Oct. 6, 1885, Philadelphia, Pa.   D. Dec. 19, 1965, Walnut Creek, Calif.
BR TR 6'2½"   180 lbs.

	G	AB	H	2B	3B	HR	HR %	R	RBI	BB	SO	SB	BA	SA	PH AB	PH H	G by POS
1905 PHI A	88	325	66	12	1	3	0.9	28	29	9		4	.203	.274	5	0	SS-81, 3B-2
1906	74	253	49	7	2	3	1.2	29	20	19		6	.194	.273	0	0	3B-67, 2B-7
1907 2 teams		PHI	A (38G – .222)			BOS	A (100G – .212)										
" total	138	499	107	16	4	2	0.4	37	41	29		9	.214	.275	2	0	3B-134, SS-4
1909 NY A	116	360	85	8	5	0	0.0	46	40	37		15	.236	.286	1	0	SS-78, 1B-19, 2B-18
1910	117	414	129	25	4	3	0.7	59	45	34		23	.312	.413	2	1	SS-79, 1B-23, 2B-7, 3B-4, OF-1
1911	132	470	126	16	7	3	0.6	69	62	42		18	.268	.351	1	0	SS-82, 1B-27, 2B-21, 3B-1
1912 WAS A	32	93	15	2	1	0	0.0	10	9	16		4	.161	.204	0	0	2B-27, 1B-5
1913 NY A	70	250	59	10	0	0	0.0	24	24	25	27	7	.236	.276	0	0	1B-50, 2B-21
8 yrs.	767	2664	636	96	24	14	0.5	301	270	211	27	86	.239	.309	11	1	SS-324, 3B-208, 1B-124, 2B-101, OF-1

Lon Knight

KNIGHT, ALONZO P.
B. June 16, 1853, Philadelphia, Pa.   D. Apr. 23, 1932, Philadelphia, Pa.
Manager 1885.
BR TR 5'11½"   165 lbs.

	G	AB	H	2B	3B	HR	HR %	R	RBI	BB	SO	SB	BA	SA	PH AB	PH H	G by POS
1876 PHI N	55	240	60	9	3	0	0.0	32	24	2	2		.250	.313	0	0	P-34, 1B-13, OF-9, 2B-6
1880 WOR N	49	201	48	11	3	0	0.0	31		5	8		.239	.323	0	0	OF-49
1881 DET N	83	340	92	16	3	1	0.3	67	52	23	21		.271	.344	0	0	OF-82, 2B-1, 1B-1
1882	86	347	72	12	6	0	0.0	39	24	16	21		.207	.277	0	0	OF-84, 1B-2
1883 PHI AA	97	429	108	23	9	1	0.2	98		21			.252	.354	0	0	OF-93, 3B-3, 2B-2
1884	108	484	131	18	12	1	0.2	94		10			.271	.364	0	0	OF-108, P-2, 1B-1
1885 2 teams		PHI	AA (29G – .210)			PRO	N (25G – .160)										
" total	54	200	38	2	1	0	0.0	25	8	20	17		.190	.210	0	0	OF-54, P-2
7 yrs.	532	2241	549	91	37	3	0.1	386	108	97	69		.245	.323	0	0	OF-479, P-38, 1B-17, 2B-9, 3B-3

Ray Knight

KNIGHT, CHARLES RAY
B. Dec. 28, 1952, Albany, Ga.
BR TR 6'1"   185 lbs.

	G	AB	H	2B	3B	HR	HR %	R	RBI	BB	SO	SB	BA	SA	PH AB	PH H	G by POS
1974 CIN N	14	11	2	1	0	0	0.0	1	2	1	2	0	.182	.273	0	0	3B-14
1977	80	92	24	5	1	1	1.1	8	13	9	16	1	.261	.370	26	6	3B-37, 2B-17, OF-5, SS-3
1978	83	65	13	3	0	1	1.5	7	4	3	13	0	.200	.292	16	2	3B-60, 2B-4, OF-3, SS-1, 1B-1
1979	150	551	175	37	4	10	1.8	64	79	38	57	4	.318	.454	1	0	3B-149
1980	162	618	163	39	7	14	2.3	71	78	36	62	1	.264	.417	1	0	3B-162
1981	106	386	100	23	1	6	1.6	43	34	33	51	2	.259	.370	1	0	3B-105
1982 HOU N	158	609	179	36	6	6	1.0	72	70	48	58	2	.294	.402	0	0	1B-96, 3B-67
1983	145	507	154	36	4	9	1.8	43	70	42	62	0	.304	.444	4	0	1B-143
1984 2 teams		HOU	N (88G – .223)			NY	N (27G – .280)										
" total	115	371	88	14	0	3	0.8	28	35	21	43	0	.237	.299	10	4	3B-81, 1B-27
9 yrs.	1013	3210	898	194	23	50	1.6	337	385	231	364	10	.280	.401	59	12	3B-675, 1B-267, 2B-21, OF-8, SS-4

LEAGUE CHAMPIONSHIP SERIES

	G	AB	H	2B	3B	HR	HR %	R	RBI	BB	SO	SB	BA	SA	PH AB	PH H	G by POS
1979 CIN N	3	14	4	1	0	0	0.0	0	0	0	2	1	.286	.357	0	0	3B-3

Pete Knisely

KNISELY, PETER COLE
B. Aug. 11, 1883, Waynesburg, Pa.   D. July 1, 1948, Brownsville, Pa.
BR TR 5'9"   185 lbs.

	G	AB	H	2B	3B	HR	HR %	R	RBI	BB	SO	SB	BA	SA	PH AB	PH H	G by POS
1912 CIN N	21	67	22	7	3	0	0.0	10	7	4	5	3	.328	.522	3	0	OF-13, 2B-3, SS-1
1913 CHI N	2	2	0	0	0	0	0.0	0	0	0	1	0	.000	.000	2	0	
1914	37	69	9	0	1	0	0.0	5	5	5	6	0	.130	.159	19	4	OF-16
1915	64	134	33	9	0	0	0.0	12	17	15	18	1	.246	.313	17	4	OF-34, 2B-9
4 yrs.	124	272	64	16	4	0	0.0	27	29	24	30	4	.235	.324	41	8	OF-63, 2B-12, SS-1

Mike Knode

KNODE, KENNETH THOMSON
Brother of Ray Knode.
B. Nov. 8, 1895, Westminster, Md.   D. Dec. 20, 1980, South Bend, Ind.
BL TR 5'10"   160 lbs.

	G	AB	H	2B	3B	HR	HR %	R	RBI	BB	SO	SB	BA	SA	PH AB	PH H	G by POS
1920 STL N	42	65	15	1	1	0	0.0	11	12	5	6	0	.231	.277	18	4	OF-9, 2B-4, SS-2, 3B-2

	G	AB	H	2B	3B	HR	HR %	R	RBI	BB	SO	SB	BA	SA	Pinch Hit AB	Pinch Hit H	G by POS

Ray Knode

KNODE, ROBERT TROXELL (Bob)
Brother of Mike Knode.
B. Jan. 28, 1901, Westminster, Md.   D. Apr. 13, 1982, Battle Creek, Mich.
BL TL 5'10"   160 lbs.

	G	AB	H	2B	3B	HR	HR %	R	RBI	BB	SO	SB	BA	SA	AB	H	G by POS
1923 CLE A	22	38	11	0	0	2	5.3	7	4	2	4	1	.289	.447	0	0	1B-21
1924	11	37	9	1	0	0	0.0	6	4	3	0	2	.243	.270	0	0	1B-10
1925	45	108	27	5	0	0	0.0	13	11	10	4	3	.250	.296	3	0	1B-34
1926	31	24	8	1	1	0	0.0	6	2	2	3	0	.333	.458	5	2	1B-11
4 yrs.	109	207	55	7	1	2	1.0	32	21	17	11	6	.266	.338	8	2	1B-76

Punch Knoll

KNOLL, CHARLES ELMER
B. Oct. 7, 1881, Evansville, Ind.   D. Feb. 7, 1960, Evansville, Ind.
BR TR 5'7½"   170 lbs.

	G	AB	H	2B	3B	HR	HR %	R	RBI	BB	SO	SB	BA	SA	AB	H	G by POS
1905 WAS A	85	244	52	10	5	0	0.0	24	29	9		3	.213	.295	8	3	OF-70, C-5, 1B-2

Bobby Knoop

KNOOP, ROBERT FRANK
B. Oct. 18, 1938, Sioux City, Iowa
BR TR 6'1"   170 lbs.

	G	AB	H	2B	3B	HR	HR %	R	RBI	BB	SO	SB	BA	SA	AB	H	G by POS
1964 LA A	162	486	105	8	1	7	1.4	42	38	46	109	3	.216	.280	1	0	2B-161
1965 CAL A	142	465	125	24	4	7	1.5	47	43	31	101	3	.269	.383	0	0	2B-142
1966	161	590	137	18	11	17	2.9	54	72	43	144	1	.232	.386	0	0	2B-161
1967	159	511	125	18	5	9	1.8	51	38	44	136	2	.245	.352	0	0	2B-159
1968	152	494	123	20	4	3	0.6	48	39	35	128	3	.249	.324	1	1	2B-151
1969 2 teams		CAL	A	(27G –	.197)		CHI	A	(104G –	.229)							
" total	131	416	93	15	1	7	1.7	39	47	48	84	3	.224	.315	1	0	2B-131
1970 CHI A	130	402	92	13	2	5	1.2	34	36	34	79	0	.229	.308	3	1	2B-126
1971 KC A	72	161	33	8	1	1	0.6	14	11	15	36	1	.205	.286	16	3	2B-52, 3B-1
1972	44	97	23	5	0	0	0.0	8	7	9	16	0	.237	.289	9	2	2B-33, 3B-4
9 yrs.	1153	3622	856	129	29	56	1.5	337	331	304	833	16	.236	.334	31	7	2B-1116, 3B-5

Fritz Knothe

KNOTHE, WILFRED EDGAR
Brother of George Knothe.
B. May 1, 1903, Passaic, N. J.   D. Mar. 27, 1963, Passaic, N. J.
BR TR 5'10½"   180 lbs.

	G	AB	H	2B	3B	HR	HR %	R	RBI	BB	SO	SB	BA	SA	AB	H	G by POS
1932 BOS N	89	344	82	19	1	1	0.3	45	36	39	37	5	.238	.308	1	1	3B-87
1933 2 teams		BOS	N	(44G –	.228)		PHI	N	(41G –	.150)							
" total	85	271	53	7	2	1	0.4	25	17	19	44	3	.196	.247	5	0	3B-65, SS-9, 2B-4
2 yrs.	174	615	135	26	3	2	0.3	70	53	58	81	8	.220	.281	6	1	3B-152, SS-9, 2B-4

George Knothe

KNOTHE, GEORGE BERTRAM
Brother of Fritz Knothe.
B. Jan. 12, 1900, Bayonne, N. J.   D. July 3, 1981, Dover, N. J.
BR TR 5'10"   165 lbs.

	G	AB	H	2B	3B	HR	HR %	R	RBI	BB	SO	SB	BA	SA	AB	H	G by POS
1932 PHI N	6	12	1	1	0	0	0.0	2	0	0	0	0	.083	.167	0	0	2B-5

Joe Knotts

KNOTTS, JOSEPH STEVEN
B. Mar. 3, 1884, Greensboro, Pa.   D. Sept. 15, 1950, Philadelphia, Pa.
BR TR

	G	AB	H	2B	3B	HR	HR %	R	RBI	BB	SO	SB	BA	SA	AB	H	G by POS
1907 BOS N	3	8	0	0	0	0	0.0	0	0	1		0	.000	.000	0	0	C-3

Jake Knowdell

KNOWDELL, JACOB AUGUSTUS
B. Brooklyn, N. Y.   Deceased.
5'7½"   148 lbs.

	G	AB	H	2B	3B	HR	HR %	R	RBI	BB	SO	SB	BA	SA	AB	H	G by POS
1878 MIL N	4	14	3	1	0	0	0.0	2	2	0	3		.214	.286	0	0	C-2, OF-1, SS-1

Jim Knowles

KNOWLES, JAMES
B. 1859, Toronto, Ont., Canada   D. Feb., 1912, New York, N. Y.

	G	AB	H	2B	3B	HR	HR %	R	RBI	BB	SO	SB	BA	SA	AB	H	G by POS
1884 2 teams		PIT	AA	(46G –	.231)		BKN	AA	(41G –	.235)							
" total	87	335	78	10	8	1	0.3	38		8			.233	.319	0	0	1B-75, 3B-11, SS-1
1886 WAS N	115	443	94	16	11	3	0.7	43	35	15	73		.212	.318	0	0	2B-62, 3B-53
1887 NY AA	16	60	15	1	1	0	0.0	12		1			.250	.300	0	0	2B-16, 3B-1
1890 ROC AA	123	491	138	12	8	5	1.0	83		59		6	.281	.369	0	0	3B-123
1892 NY N	16	59	9	1	0	0	0.0	9	7	6	8	55	.153	.169	0	0	3B-15, SS-1
5 yrs.	357	1388	334	40	28	9	0.6	185	41	89	81	63	.241	.329	0	0	3B-203, 2B-78, 1B-75, SS-2

Andy Knox

KNOX, ANDREW JACKSON (Dasher)
B. Jan. 5, 1864, Philadelphia, Pa.   D. Sept. 14, 1940, Philadelphia, Pa.
BR TR

	G	AB	H	2B	3B	HR	HR %	R	RBI	BB	SO	SB	BA	SA	AB	H	G by POS
1890 PHI AA	21	75	19	3	0	0	0.0	6		9		5	.253	.293	0	0	1B-21

Cliff Knox

KNOX, CLIFFORD HIRAM (Bud)
B. Jan. 7, 1902, Coalville, Iowa   D. Sept. 24, 1965, Oskaloosa, Iowa
BB TR 5'11½"   178 lbs.

	G	AB	H	2B	3B	HR	HR %	R	RBI	BB	SO	SB	BA	SA	AB	H	G by POS
1924 PIT N	6	18	4	0	0	0	0.0	1	2	2	0	0	.222	.222	0	0	C-6

John Knox

KNOX, JOHN CLINTON
B. July 26, 1948, Newark, N. J.
BL TR 6'   170 lbs.

	G	AB	H	2B	3B	HR	HR %	R	RBI	BB	SO	SB	BA	SA	AB	H	G by POS
1972 DET A	14	13	1	1	0	0	0.0	1	0	1	2	0	.077	.154	9	1	2B-4
1973	12	32	9	1	0	0	0.0	1	3	3	3	1	.281	.313	0	0	2B-9
1974	55	88	27	1	1	0	0.0	11	6	6	13	5	.307	.341	4	1	2B-33, DH-1, 3B-1
1975	43	86	23	1	0	0	0.0	8	2	10	9	1	.267	.279	5	2	2B-23, DH-3, 3B-3
4 yrs.	124	219	60	4	1	0	0.0	21	11	20	27	7	.274	.301	18	4	2B-69, DH-4, 3B-4
LEAGUE CHAMPIONSHIP SERIES																	
1972 DET A	1	0	0	0	0	0	–	0	0	0	0	0	–	–	0	0	

Nick Koback

KOBACK, NICHOLAS NICHOLIE
B. July 19, 1935, Hartford, Conn.
BR TR 6'   187 lbs.

	G	AB	H	2B	3B	HR	HR %	R	RBI	BB	SO	SB	BA	SA	AB	H	G by POS
1953 PIT N	7	16	2	0	1	0	0.0	1	0	1	4	0	.125	.250	1	1	C-6
1954	4	10	0	0	0	0	0.0	0	0	0	8	0	.000	.000	0	0	C-4
1955	5	7	2	0	0	0	0.0	0	0	0	1	0	.286	.286	3	1	C-2
3 yrs.	16	33	4	0	1	0	0.0	1	0	1	13	0	.121	.182	4	2	C-12

	G	AB	H	2B	3B	HR	HR %	R	RBI	BB	SO	SB	BA	SA	Pinch Hit AB	H	G by POS

Barney Koch

KOCH, BARNETT   BR TR 5'8"   140 lbs.
B. Mar. 23, 1923, Campbell, Neb.

	G	AB	H	2B	3B	HR	HR%	R	RBI	BB	SO	SB	BA	SA	PH AB	H	G by POS
1944 BKN N	33	96	21	2	0	0	0.0	11	1	3	9	0	.219	.240	1	1	2B-29, SS-1

Brad Kocher

KOCHER, BRADLEY WILSON   BR TR 5'11"   188 lbs.
B. Jan. 16, 1888, White Haven, Pa.   D. Feb. 13, 1965, White Haven, Pa.

	G	AB	H	2B	3B	HR	HR%	R	RBI	BB	SO	SB	BA	SA	PH AB	H	G by POS
1912 DET A	24	63	13	3	1	0	0.0	5	9	2		0	.206	.286	1	0	C-23
1915 NY N	4	11	5	0	1	0	0.0	3	2	0	1	0	.455	.636	1	0	C-3
1916	34	65	7	2	0	0	0.0	1	1	2	10	0	.108	.138	4	1	C-30
3 yrs.	62	139	25	5	2	0	0.0	9	12	4	11	0	.180	.245	6	1	C-56

Pete Koegel

KOEGEL, PETER JOHN   BR TR 6'6½"   230 lbs.
B. July 31, 1947, Mineola, N. Y.

	G	AB	H	2B	3B	HR	HR%	R	RBI	BB	SO	SB	BA	SA	PH AB	H	G by POS
1970 MIL A	7	8	2	0	0	1	12.5	2	1	1	3	0	.250	.625	6	2	OF-1
1971 2 teams		MIL	A (2G –	.000)		PHI	N (12G –	.231)									
" total	14	29	6	1	0	0	0.0	1	3	4	9	0	.207	.241	4	1	C-7, OF-1, 1B-1
1972 PHI N	41	49	7	2	0	0	0.0	3	1	6	16	0	.143	.184	21	2	1B-8, C-5, 3B-4, OF-2
3 yrs.	62	86	15	3	0	1	1.2	6	5	11	28	0	.174	.244	31	5	C-12, 1B-9, OF-4, 3B-4

Ben Koehler

KOEHLER, BERNARD JAMES   BR TR 5'10½"   175 lbs.
B. Jan. 26, 1877, Schoerndorn, Germany   D. May 21, 1961, South Bend, Ind.

	G	AB	H	2B	3B	HR	HR%	R	RBI	BB	SO	SB	BA	SA	PH AB	H	G by POS
1905 STL A	142	536	127	14	6	2	0.4	55	47	32		22	.237	.297	0	0	OF-127, 1B-12, 2B-6
1906	66	186	41	1	1	0	0.0	27	15	24		9	.220	.237	5	1	OF-52, 2B-7, SS-1, 3B-1
2 yrs.	208	722	168	15	7	2	0.3	82	62	56		31	.233	.281	5	1	OF-179, 2B-13, 1B-12, SS-1, 3B-1

Pip Koehler

KOEHLER, HORACE LEVERING   BR TR 5'10"   165 lbs.
B. Jan. 16, 1902, Gilbert, Pa.

	G	AB	H	2B	3B	HR	HR%	R	RBI	BB	SO	SB	BA	SA	PH AB	H	G by POS
1925 NY N	12	2	0	0	0	0	0.0	1	0	0	1	0	.000	.000	0	0	OF-3

Len Koenecke

KOENECKE, LEONARD GEORGE   BL TR 5'11½"   192 lbs.
B. Jan. 18, 1904, Baraboo, Wis.   D. Sept. 17, 1935, Toronto, Ont., Canada

	G	AB	H	2B	3B	HR	HR%	R	RBI	BB	SO	SB	BA	SA	PH AB	H	G by POS
1932 NY N	42	137	35	5	0	4	2.9	33	14	11	13	3	.255	.380	1	0	OF-35
1934 BKN N	123	460	147	31	7	14	3.0	79	73	70	38	8	.320	.509	2	0	OF-121
1935	100	325	92	13	2	4	1.2	43	27	43	45	0	.283	.372	8	0	OF-91
3 yrs.	265	922	274	49	9	22	2.4	155	114	124	96	11	.297	.441	11	0	OF-247

Mark Koenig

KOENIG, MARK ANTHONY   BB TR 6'   180 lbs.   BL 1928
B. July 19, 1902, San Francisco, Calif.

	G	AB	H	2B	3B	HR	HR%	R	RBI	BB	SO	SB	BA	SA	PH AB	H	G by POS
1925 NY A	28	110	23	6	1	0	0.0	14	4	5	4	0	.209	.282	0	0	SS-28
1926	147	617	167	26	8	5	0.8	93	62	43	37	4	.271	.363	6	1	SS-141
1927	123	526	150	20	11	3	0.6	99	62	25	21	3	.285	.382	1	0	SS-122
1928	132	533	170	19	10	4	0.8	89	63	32	19	3	.319	.415	7	3	SS-125
1929	116	373	109	27	5	3	0.8	44	41	23	17	1	.292	.416	16	1	SS-61, 3B-37, 2B-1
1930 2 teams	NY	A (21G –	.230)		DET	A	(76G –	.240)									
" total	97	341	81	14	2	1	0.3	46	25	26	20	2	.238	.299	4	0	SS-89, 3B-2, P-2, OF-1
1931 DET A	106	364	92	24	4	1	0.3	33	39	14	12	8	.253	.349	15	4	2B-55, SS-35, P-3
1932 CHI N	33	102	36	5	1	3	2.9	15	11	3	5	0	.353	.510	2	0	SS-33
1933	80	218	62	12	1	3	1.4	32	25	15	9	5	.284	.390	15	4	3B-37, SS-26, 2B-2
1934 CIN N	151	633	172	26	6	1	0.2	60	67	15	24	5	.272	.336	2	0	3B-64, SS-58, 2B-26, 1B-4
1935 NY N	107	396	112	12	0	3	0.8	40	37	13	18	0	.283	.336	9	1	2B-64, SS-21, 3B-15
1936	42	58	16	4	0	1	1.7	7	7	8	4	0	.276	.397	17	4	SS-10, 2B-8, 3B-3
12 yrs.	1162	4271	1190	195	49	28	0.7	572	443	222	190	31	.279	.367	94	18	SS-749, 3B-158, 2B-156, P-5, 1B-4, OF-1
WORLD SERIES																	
1926 NY A	7	32	4	1	0	0	0.0	2	2	0	6	0	.125	.156	0	0	SS-7
1927	4	18	9	2	0	0	0.0	5	2	0	2	0	.500	.611	0	0	SS-4
1928	4	19	3	0	0	0	0.0	1	0	0	1	0	.158	.158	0	0	SS-4
1932 CHI N	2	4	1	0	1	0	0.0	1	1	1	0	0	.250	.750	0	0	SS-1
1936 NY N	3	3	1	0	0	0	0.0	0	0	0	1	0	.333	.333	3	1	2B-1
5 yrs.	20	76	18	3	1	0	0.0	9	5	1	10	0	.237	.303	3	1	SS-16, 2B-1

Dick Kokos

KOKOS, RICHARD JEROME   BL TL 5'8½"   170 lbs.
Born Richard Jerome Kokoszka.
B. Feb. 28, 1928, Chicago, Ill.

	G	AB	H	2B	3B	HR	HR%	R	RBI	BB	SO	SB	BA	SA	PH AB	H	G by POS
1948 STL A	71	258	77	15	3	4	1.6	40	40	28	32	4	.298	.426	1	0	OF-71
1949	143	501	131	28	1	23	4.6	80	77	66	91	3	.261	.459	6	2	OF-138
1950	143	490	128	27	5	18	3.7	77	67	88	73	8	.261	.447	14	2	OF-127
1953	107	299	72	12	0	13	4.3	41	38	56	53	0	.241	.411	25	6	OF-83
1954 BAL A	11	10	2	0	0	1	10.0	1	1	4	3	0	.200	.500	8	2	OF-1
5 yrs.	475	1558	410	82	9	59	3.8	239	223	242	252	15	.263	.441	54	12	OF-420

Gary Kolb

KOLB, GARY ALAN   BL TR 6'   194 lbs.
B. Mar. 13, 1940, Rock Falls, Ill.

	G	AB	H	2B	3B	HR	HR%	R	RBI	BB	SO	SB	BA	SA	PH AB	H	G by POS
1960 STL N	9	3	0	0	0	0	0.0	1	0	0	0	0	.000	.000	0	0	OF-2
1962	6	14	5	0	0	0	0.0	1	0	1	3	0	.357	.357	0	0	OF-6
1963	75	96	26	1	5	3	3.1	23	10	22	26	2	.271	.479	6	0	OF-58, 3B-1, C-1
1964 MIL N	36	64	12	1	0	0	0.0	7	2	6	10	3	.188	.203	5	0	OF-14, 3B-7, 2B-6, C-2
1965 2 teams	MIL	N (24G –	.259)		NY	N	(40G –	.167)									
" total	64	117	22	2	0	1	0.9	11	8	4	34	3	.188	.231	20	5	OF-42, 3B-1, 1B-1
1968 PIT N	74	119	26	4	1	2	1.7	16	6	11	17	2	.218	.319	31	6	OF-25, C-10, 3B-4, 2B-1
1969	29	37	3	1	0	0	0.0	4	3	2	14	0	.081	.108	20	1	C-7
7 yrs.	293	450	94	9	6	6	1.3	63	29	46	104	10	.209	.296	82	12	OF-147, C-20, 3B-13, 2B-7, 1B-1

	G	AB	H	2B	3B	HR	HR %	R	RBI	BB	SO	SB	BA	SA	Pinch Hit AB	Pinch Hit H	G by POS

Don Kolloway

KOLLOWAY, DONALD MARTIN (Butch, Cab)
B. Aug. 4, 1918, Posen, Ill.   BR TR 6'3"   200 lbs.

	G	AB	H	2B	3B	HR	HR %	R	RBI	BB	SO	SB	BA	SA	PH AB	PH H	G by POS
1940 CHI A	10	40	9	1	0	0	0.0	5	3	0	3	1	.225	.250	0	0	2B-10
1941	71	280	76	8	3	3	1.1	33	24	6	12	11	.271	.354	3	1	2B-62, 1B-4
1942	147	601	164	40	4	3	0.5	72	60	30	39	16	.273	.368	0	0	2B-116, 1B-33
1943	85	348	75	14	4	1	0.3	29	33	9	30	11	.216	.287	0	0	2B-85
1946	123	482	135	23	4	3	0.6	45	53	9	29	14	.280	.363	1	0	2B-90, 3B-31
1947	124	485	135	25	4	2	0.4	49	35	17	34	11	.278	.359	7	2	2B-99, 1B-11, 3B-8
1948	119	417	114	14	4	6	1.4	60	38	18	18	2	.273	.369	12	3	2B-83, 3B-18
1949 2 teams	CHI	A (4G – .000)				DET	A	(126G – .294)									
" total	130	487	142	19	3	2	0.4	71	47	49	26	7	.292	.355	12	2	2B-62, 1B-57, 3B-9
1950 DET A	125	467	135	20	4	6	1.3	55	62	29	28	1	.289	.388	5	1	1B-118, 2B-1
1951	78	212	54	7	0	1	0.5	28	17	15	12	2	.255	.302	17	4	1B-59
1952	65	173	42	9	0	2	1.2	19	21	7	19	0	.243	.329	25	5	1B-32, 2B-8
1953 PHI A	2	1	0	0	0	0	0.0	0	0	0	1	0	.000	.000	1	0	3B-1
12 yrs.	1079	3993	1081	180	30	29	0.7	466	393	189	251	76	.271	.353	83	18	2B-616, 1B-314, 3B-67

Karl Kolsth

KOLSTH, KARL DICKEY
B. Dec. 25, 1892, Somerville, Mass.   D. May 3, 1956, Cumberland, Md.   BL TR 6'   182 lbs.

	G	AB	H	2B	3B	HR	HR %	R	RBI	BB	SO	SB	BA	SA	PH AB	PH H	G by POS
1915 BAL F	6	23	6	1	1	0	0.0	1	1	1		0	.261	.391	0	0	1B-6

Fred Kommers

KOMMERS, FRED RAYMOND (Bugs)
B. Mar. 31, 1886, Chicago, Ill.   D. June 14, 1943, Chicago, Ill.   BL TR 6'   175 lbs.

	G	AB	H	2B	3B	HR	HR %	R	RBI	BB	SO	SB	BA	SA	PH AB	PH H	G by POS
1913 PIT N	40	155	36	5	4	0	0.0	14	22	10	29	1	.232	.316	0	0	OF-40
1914 2 teams	STL	F (76G – .307)				BAL	F	(16G – .214)									
" total	92	286	84	10	8	4	1.4	38	42	31		7	.294	.427	10	4	OF-79
2 yrs.	132	441	120	15	12	4	0.9	52	64	41	29	8	.272	.388	10	4	OF-119

Brad Komminsk

KOMMINSK, BRAD LYNN
B. Apr. 4, 1961, Lima, Ohio   BR TR 6'3"   187 lbs.

	G	AB	H	2B	3B	HR	HR %	R	RBI	BB	SO	SB	BA	SA	PH AB	PH H	G by POS
1983 ATL N	19	36	8	2	0	0	0.0	2	4	5	7	0	.222	.278	7	2	OF-13
1984	90	301	61	10	0	8	2.7	37	36	29	77	18	.203	.316	10	4	OF-80
2 yrs.	109	337	69	12	0	8	2.4	39	40	34	84	18	.205	.312	17	6	OF-93

Ed Konetchy

KONETCHY, EDWARD JOSEPH (Big Ed)
Also appeared in box score as Koney
B. Sept. 3, 1885, LaCrosse, Wis.   D. May 27, 1947, Fort Worth, Tex.   BR TR 6'2½"   195 lbs.

	G	AB	H	2B	3B	HR	HR %	R	RBI	BB	SO	SB	BA	SA	PH AB	PH H	G by POS
1907 STL N	90	330	83	11	8	3	0.9	34	30	26		13	.252	.361	0	0	1B-90
1908	154	545	135	19	12	5	0.9	46	50	38		16	.248	.354	0	0	1B-154
1909	152	576	165	23	14	4	0.7	88	80	65		25	.286	.396	0	0	1B-152
1910	144	520	157	23	16	3	0.6	87	78	78	59	18	.302	.425	0	0	1B-144, P-1
1911	158	571	165	38	13	6	1.1	90	88	81	63	27	.289	.433	0	0	1B-158
1912	143	538	169	26	13	8	1.5	81	82	62	66	25	.314	.455	0	0	1B-142, OF-1
1913	139	502	137	18	17	7	1.4	74	68	53	41	27	.273	.418	0	0	1B-139, P-1
1914 PIT N	154	563	140	23	9	4	0.7	56	51	32	48	20	.249	.343	0	0	1B-154
1915 PIT F	152	576	181	31	18	10	1.7	79	93	41		27	.314	.483	0	0	1B-152
1916 BOS N	158	566	147	29	13	3	0.5	76	70	43	46	13	.260	.373	0	0	1B-158
1917	130	474	129	19	13	2	0.4	56	54	36	40	16	.272	.380	1	0	1B-129
1918	119	437	103	15	5	2	0.5	33	56	32	35	5	.236	.307	0	0	1B-112, OF-6, P-1
1919 BKN N	132	486	145	24	9	1	0.2	46	47	29	39	14	.298	.391	0	0	1B-132
1920	131	497	153	22	12	5	1.0	62	63	33	18	3	.308	.431	0	0	1B-130
1921 2 teams	BKN	N (55G – .269)				PHI	N	(72G – .321)									
" total	127	465	139	23	9	11	2.4	63	82	40	38	6	.299	.458	2	0	1B-125
15 yrs.	2083	7646	2148	344	181	74	1.0	971	992	689	493	255	.281	.402	4	0	1B-2071, OF-7, P-3
WORLD SERIES																	
1920 BKN N	7	23	4	0	1	0	0.0	0	2	3	2	0	.174	.261	0	0	1B-7

Mike Konnick

KONNICK, MICHAEL ALOYSIUS
B. Jan. 13, 1889, Glen Lyon, Pa.   D. July 9, 1971, Wilkes-Barre, Pa.   BR TR 5'9"   180 lbs.

	G	AB	H	2B	3B	HR	HR %	R	RBI	BB	SO	SB	BA	SA	PH AB	PH H	G by POS
1909 CIN N	2	5	2	1	0	0	0.0	0	1	1	0	0	.400	.600	0	0	C-2
1910	1	3	0	0	0	0	0.0	0	0	1	0	0	.000	.000	0	0	SS-1
2 yrs.	3	8	2	1	0	0	0.0	0	1	1	0	0	.250	.375	0	0	C-2, SS-1

Bruce Konopka

KONOPKA, BRUNO BRUCE
B. Sept. 16, 1919, Hammond, Ind.   BL TL 6'2"   190 lbs.

	G	AB	H	2B	3B	HR	HR %	R	RBI	BB	SO	SB	BA	SA	PH AB	PH H	G by POS
1942 PHI A	5	10	3	0	0	0	0.0	2	1	1	1	0	.300	.300	2	1	1B-3
1943	2	2	0	0	0	0	0.0	0	0	0	1	0	.000	.000	2	0	
1946	38	93	22	4	1	0	0.0	7	9	4	8	0	.237	.301	17	5	1B-20, OF-1
3 yrs.	45	105	25	4	1	0	0.0	9	10	5	10	0	.238	.295	21	6	1B-23, OF-1

Harry Koons

KOONS, HENRY M.
B. 1863, Philadelphia, Pa.   Deceased.   5'8"   174 lbs.

	G	AB	H	2B	3B	HR	HR %	R	RBI	BB	SO	SB	BA	SA	PH AB	PH H	G by POS
1884 2 teams	ALT	U (21G – .231)				C-P	U	(1G – .000)									
" total	22	81	18	2	1	0	0.0	8		2			.222	.272	0	0	3B-22, C-1

George Kopacz

KOPACZ, GEORGE FELIX (Sonny)
B. Feb. 26, 1941, Chicago, Ill.   BL TL 6'1"   195 lbs.

	G	AB	H	2B	3B	HR	HR %	R	RBI	BB	SO	SB	BA	SA	PH AB	PH H	G by POS
1966 ATL N	6	9	0	0	0	0	0.0	1	0	1	5	0	.000	.000	4	0	1B-2
1970 PIT N	10	16	3	0	0	0	0.0	0	1	0	5	0	.188	.188	7	1	1B-3
2 yrs.	16	25	3	0	0	0	0.0	1	1	1	10	0	.120	.120	11	1	1B-5

Larry Kopf

KOPF, WILLIAM LORENZ
Played as Fred Brady 1913.   Brother of Wally Kopf.
B. Nov. 3, 1890, Bristol, Conn.   BB TR 5'9"   160 lbs.

	G	AB	H	2B	3B	HR	HR %	R	RBI	BB	SO	SB	BA	SA	PH AB	PH H	G by POS
1913 CLE A	5	9	2	0	0	0	0.0	1	1	0	0	0	.222	.222	0	0	2B-3, 3B-1
1914 PHI A	35	69	13	2	2	0	0.0	8	12	8	14	6	.188	.275	5	1	SS-13, 3B-8, 2B-5

	G	AB	H	2B	3B	HR	HR %	R	RBI	BB	SO	SB	BA	SA	Pinch Hit AB	Pinch Hit H	G by POS

Larry Kopf continued

	G	AB	H	2B	3B	HR	HR%	R	RBI	BB	SO	SB	BA	SA	PH AB	PH H	G by POS
1915	118	386	87	10	2	1	0.3	39	33	41	45	5	.225	.269	0	0	SS-74, 3B-42, 2B-2
1916 CIN N	11	40	11	2	0	0	0.0	2	5	1	8	1	.275	.325	0	0	SS-11
1917	148	573	146	19	8	2	0.3	81	26	28	48	17	.255	.326	2	1	SS-145
1919	135	503	136	18	5	0	0.0	51	58	28	27	18	.270	.326	0	0	SS-135
1920	126	458	112	15	6	0	0.0	56	59	35	24	14	.245	.303	1	1	SS-123, 3B-2, 2B-2, OF-1
1921	107	367	80	8	3	1	0.3	36	25	43	20	3	.218	.264	6	1	SS-93, 2B-4, 3B-3, OF-1
1922 BOS N	126	466	124	6	3	1	0.2	59	37	45	22	8	.266	.298	1	1	2B-78, SS-33, 3B-13
1923	39	138	38	3	1	0	0.0	15	10	13	6	0	.275	.312	0	0	SS-37, 2B-4
10 yrs.	850	3009	749	83	30	5	0.2	348	266	242	214	72	.249	.301	15	5	SS-664, 2B-98, 3B-69, OF-2

WORLD SERIES

	G	AB	H	2B	3B	HR	HR%	R	RBI	BB	SO	SB	BA	SA	PH AB	PH H	G by POS
1919 CIN N	8	27	6	0	2	0	0.0	3	2	3	2	0	.222	.370	0	0	SS-8

Wally Kopf

KOPF, WALTER HENRY   BL TR 5'11" 168 lbs.
Brother of Larry Kopf.
B. July 10, 1899, Stonington, Conn.   D. Apr. 30, 1979, Cincinnati, Ohio

	G	AB	H	2B	3B	HR	HR%	R	RBI	BB	SO	SB	BA	SA	PH AB	PH H	G by POS
1921 NY N	2	3	1	0	0	0	0.0	0	0	1	1	0	.333	.333	0	0	3B-2

Merlin Kopp

KOPP, MERLIN HENRY   BB TR 5'6" 170 lbs.
B. Jan. 2, 1892, Toledo, Ohio   D. May 6, 1960, Sacramento, Calif.

	G	AB	H	2B	3B	HR	HR%	R	RBI	BB	SO	SB	BA	SA	PH AB	PH H	G by POS
1915 WAS A	16	32	8	0	0	0	0.0	2	0	5	7	1	.250	.250	6	2	OF-9
1918 PHI A	96	363	85	7	7	0	0.0	60	18	42	55	22	.234	.292	0	0	OF-96
1919	75	235	53	2	4	1	0.4	34	12	42	43	16	.226	.281	4	0	OF-65
3 yrs.	187	630	146	9	11	1	0.2	96	30	89	105	39	.232	.286	10	2	OF-170

Joe Koppe

KOPPE, JOSEPH   BR TR 5'10" 165 lbs.
Born Joseph Kopchia.
B. Oct. 19, 1930, Detroit, Mich.

	G	AB	H	2B	3B	HR	HR%	R	RBI	BB	SO	SB	BA	SA	PH AB	PH H	G by POS
1958 MIL N	16	9	4	0	0	0	0.0	3	0	1	1	0	.444	.444	0	0	SS-3
1959 PHI N	126	422	110	18	7	7	1.7	68	28	41	80	7	.261	.386	0	0	SS-113, 2B-11
1960	58	170	29	6	1	1	0.6	13	13	23	47	3	.171	.235	1	0	SS-55, 3B-2
1961 2 teams	PHI N (6G – .000)			LA A (91G – .251)													
" total	97	341	85	12	2	5	1.5	47	40	45	77	3	.249	.340	0	0	SS-93, 2B-3, 3B-1
1962 LA A	128	375	85	16	0	4	1.1	47	40	73	84	2	.227	.301	2	0	SS-118, 2B-5, 3B-4
1963	76	143	30	4	1	1	0.7	11	12	9	30	0	.210	.273	20	4	SS-19, 3B-18, 2B-14, OF-3
1964	54	113	29	4	1	0	0.0	10	6	14	16	0	.257	.310	3	1	SS-31, 2B-13, 3B-3
1965 CAL A	23	33	7	1	0	1	3.0	3	2	3	10	1	.212	.333	3	1	2B-10, SS-4, 3B-4
8 yrs.	578	1606	379	61	12	19	1.2	202	141	209	345	16	.236	.324	29	6	SS-436, 2B-56, 3B-32, OF-3

George Kopshaw

KOPSHAW, GEORGE KARL   BR TR 5'11½" 176 lbs.
B. July 5, 1895, Passaic, N. J.   D. Dec. 26, 1934, Lynchburg, Va.

	G	AB	H	2B	3B	HR	HR%	R	RBI	BB	SO	SB	BA	SA	PH AB	PH H	G by POS
1923 STL N	2	5	1	1	0	0	0.0	1	0	1	0	0	.200	.400	0	0	C-1

Steve Korcheck

KORCHECK, STEPHEN JOSEPH (Hoss)   BR TR 6'1" 205 lbs.
B. Aug. 11, 1932, McClellandtown, Pa.

	G	AB	H	2B	3B	HR	HR%	R	RBI	BB	SO	SB	BA	SA	PH AB	PH H	G by POS
1954 WAS A	2	7	1	0	0	0	0.0	0	0	0	2	0	.143	.143	0	0	C-2
1955	13	36	10	2	0	0	0.0	3	2	0	5	0	.278	.333	3	1	C-12
1958	21	51	4	2	0	0	0.0	6	1	1	16	0	.078	.157	1	0	C-20
1959	22	51	8	2	0	0	0.0	3	4	5	13	0	.157	.196	0	0	C-22
4 yrs.	58	145	23	6	1	0	0.0	12	7	6	36	0	.159	.214	4	1	C-56

Art Kores

KORES, ARTHUR EMIL (Dutch)   BR TR 5'9" 167 lbs.
B. July 22, 1886, Milwaukee, Wis.   D. Nov. 26, 1974, Milwaukee, Wis.

	G	AB	H	2B	3B	HR	HR%	R	RBI	BB	SO	SB	BA	SA	PH AB	PH H	G by POS
1915 STL F	60	201	47	9	2	1	0.5	18	22	21		6	.234	.313	0	0	3B-60

Andy Kosco

KOSCO, ANDREW JOHN   BR TR 6'3" 205 lbs.
B. Oct. 5, 1941, Youngstown, Ohio

	G	AB	H	2B	3B	HR	HR%	R	RBI	BB	SO	SB	BA	SA	PH AB	PH H	G by POS
1965 MIN A	23	55	13	4	0	1	1.8	3	6	1	15	0	.236	.364	8	3	OF-14, 1B-2
1966	57	158	35	5	0	2	1.3	11	13	7	31	0	.222	.291	14	6	OF-40, 1B-5
1967	9	28	4	1	0	0	0.0	4	4	2	4	0	.143	.179	3	1	OF-7
1968 NY N	131	466	112	19	1	15	3.2	47	59	16	71	2	.240	.382	11	4	OF-95, 1B-28
1969 LA N	120	424	105	13	2	19	4.5	51	74	21	66	0	.248	.422	13	5	OF-109, 1B-3
1970	74	224	51	12	0	8	3.6	21	27	1	40	1	.228	.388	16	2	OF-58, 1B-1
1971 MIL A	98	264	60	6	2	10	3.8	27	39	24	57	1	.227	.424	19	8	OF-45, 1B-29, 3B-12
1972 2 teams	CAL A (49G – .239)			BOS A (17G – .213)													
" total	66	189	44	6	3	9	4.8	20	19	7	32	0	.233	.439	18	3	OF-48
1973 CIN N	47	118	33	7	0	9	7.6	17	21	13	26	0	.280	.568	13	3	OF-36, 1B-1
1974	33	37	7	2	0	0	0.0	3	5	7	8	0	.189	.243	20	4	3B-8, OF-1
10 yrs.	658	1963	464	75	8	73	3.7	204	267	99	350	5	.236	.394	144	39	OF-453, 1B-69, 3B-20

LEAGUE CHAMPIONSHIP SERIES

	G	AB	H	2B	3B	HR	HR%	R	RBI	BB	SO	SB	BA	SA	PH AB	PH H	G by POS
1973 CIN N	3	10	3	0	0	0	0.0	0	0	2	3	0	.300	.300	0	0	OF-3

Clem Koshorek

KOSHOREK, CLEMENT JOHN (Scooter)   BR TR 5'6" 165 lbs.
B. June 20, 1926, Royal Oak, Mich.

	G	AB	H	2B	3B	HR	HR%	R	RBI	BB	SO	SB	BA	SA	PH AB	PH H	G by POS
1952 PIT N	98	322	84	17	0	0	0.0	27	15	26	39	4	.261	.314	8	1	SS-33, 2B-27, 3B-26
1953	1	1	0	0	0	0	0.0	0	0	0	1	0	.000	.000	1	0	
2 yrs.	99	323	84	17	0	0	0.0	27	15	26	40	4	.260	.313	9	1	SS-33, 2B-27, 3B-26

Mike Kosman

KOSMAN, MICHAEL THOMAS   BR TR 5'9" 160 lbs.
B. Dec. 10, 1917, Hamtramck, Mich.

	G	AB	H	2B	3B	HR	HR%	R	RBI	BB	SO	SB	BA	SA	PH AB	PH H	G by POS
1944 CIN N	1	0	0	0	0	0	–	0	0	0	0	0	–	–	0	0	

	G	AB	H	2B	3B	HR	HR%	R	RBI	BB	SO	SB	BA	SA	Pinch Hit AB	Pinch Hit H	G by POS

Fred Koster

KOSTER, FREDERICK CHARLES (Fritz)
B. Dec. 21, 1905, Louisville, Ky.   D. Apr. 24, 1979, St. Matthews, Ky.   BL TL 5'10½" 165 lbs.

	G	AB	H	2B	3B	HR	HR%	R	RBI	BB	SO	SB	BA	SA	PH AB	PH H	G by POS
1931 PHI N	76	151	34	2	2	0	0.0	21	8	14	21	4	.225	.265	19	3	OF-41

Frank Kostro

KOSTRO, FRANK JERRY
B. Aug. 4, 1937, Windber, Pa.   BR TR 6'2" 190 lbs.

	G	AB	H	2B	3B	HR	HR%	R	RBI	BB	SO	SB	BA	SA	PH AB	PH H	G by POS
1962 DET A	16	41	11	3	0	0	0.0	5	3	1	6	0	.268	.341	4	1	3B-11
1963 2 teams		DET A (31G – .231)				LA A (43G – .222)											
" total	74	151	34	3	1	2	1.3	10	10	15	30	0	.225	.298	36	7	3B-25, 1B-8, OF-6
1964 MIN A	59	103	28	5	0	3	2.9	10	12	4	21	0	.272	.408	35	10	3B-12, 2B-7, OF-2, 1B-1
1965	20	31	5	2	0	0	0.0	2	1	4	5	0	.161	.226	6	0	2B-7, 3B-6, OF-2
1967	32	31	10	0	0	0	0.0	4	2	3	2	0	.323	.323	23	9	OF-3, 3B-1
1968	63	108	26	4	1	0	0.0	9	9	6	20	0	.241	.296	36	7	OF-24, 1B-5
1969	2	2	0	0	0	0	0.0	0	0	0	1	0	.000	.000	2	0	
7 yrs.	266	467	114	17	2	5	1.1	40	37	33	85	0	.244	.321	142	34	3B-55, OF-37, 2B-14, 1B-14

Ernie Koy

KOY, ERNEST ANYZ (Chief)
B. Sept. 17, 1909, Sealy, Tex.   BR TR 6' 200 lbs.

	G	AB	H	2B	3B	HR	HR%	R	RBI	BB	SO	SB	BA	SA	PH AB	PH H	G by POS
1938 BKN N	142	521	156	29	13	11	2.1	78	76	38	76	15	.299	.468	3	1	OF-135, 3B-1
1939	123	425	118	37	5	8	1.9	57	67	39	64	11	.278	.445	9	1	OF-114
1940 2 teams		BKN N (24G – .229)				STL N (93G – .310)											
" total	117	396	119	21	6	9	2.3	53	60	31	62	13	.301	.452	7	0	OF-110
1941 2 teams		STL N (13G – .200)				CIN N (67G – .250)											
" total	80	244	59	12	2	4	1.6	29	31	15	30	1	.242	.357	13	3	OF-61
1942 2 teams		CIN N (3G – .000)				PHI N (91G – .244)											
" total	94	260	63	9	3	4	1.5	21	26	14	52	0	.242	.346	9	2	OF-78
5 yrs.	556	1846	515	108	29	36	2.0	238	260	137	284	40	.279	.427	41	7	OF-498, 3B-1

Al Kozar

KOZAR, ALBERT KENNETH
B. July 5, 1922, McKees Rocks, Pa.   BR TR 5'9½" 173 lbs.

	G	AB	H	2B	3B	HR	HR%	R	RBI	BB	SO	SB	BA	SA	PH AB	PH H	G by POS
1948 WAS A	150	577	144	25	8	1	0.2	61	58	66	52	4	.250	.326	0	0	2B-149
1949	105	350	94	15	2	4	1.1	46	31	25	23	2	.269	.357	4	0	2B-102
1950 2 teams		WAS A (20G – .200)				CHI A (10G – .300)											
" total	30	65	14	1	0	1	1.5	11	5	5	11	0	.215	.277	6	1	2B-19, 3B-1
3 yrs.	285	992	252	41	10	6	0.6	118	94	96	86	6	.254	.334	10	1	2B-270, 3B-1

Joe Kracher

KRACHER, JOSEPH PETER (Jug)
B. Nov. 4, 1915, Philadelphia, Pa.   D. Dec. 24, 1981, San Angelo, Tex.   BR TR 5'11" 185 lbs.

	G	AB	H	2B	3B	HR	HR%	R	RBI	BB	SO	SB	BA	SA	PH AB	PH H	G by POS
1939 PHI N	5	5	1	0	0	0	0.0	0	1	0	0	0	.200	.200	2	1	C-2

Clarence Kraft

KRAFT, CLARENCE OTTO (Big Boy)
B. June 9, 1887, Evansville, Ind.   D. Mar. 26, 1958, Fort Worth, Tex.   BR TR 6' 190 lbs.

	G	AB	H	2B	3B	HR	HR%	R	RBI	BB	SO	SB	BA	SA	PH AB	PH H	G by POS
1914 BOS N	3	3	1	0	0	0	0.0	0	0	0	1	0	.333	.333	2	0	1B-1

Ed Kranepool

KRANEPOOL, EDWARD EMIL
B. Nov. 8, 1944, New York, N. Y.   BL TL 6'3" 205 lbs.

	G	AB	H	2B	3B	HR	HR%	R	RBI	BB	SO	SB	BA	SA	PH AB	PH H	G by POS
1962 NY N	3	6	1	1	0	0	0.0	0	0	0	1	0	.167	.333	0	0	1B-3
1963	86	273	57	12	2	2	0.7	22	14	18	50	4	.209	.289	13	3	OF-55, 1B-20
1964	119	420	108	19	4	10	2.4	47	45	32	50	0	.257	.393	10	2	1B-104, OF-6
1965	153	525	133	24	4	10	1.9	44	53	39	71	1	.253	.371	11	4	1B-147
1966	146	464	118	15	2	16	3.4	51	57	41	66	1	.254	.399	7	1	1B-132, OF-11
1967	141	469	126	17	1	10	2.1	37	54	37	51	0	.269	.373	9	1	1B-139
1968	127	373	86	13	1	3	0.8	29	20	19	39	0	.231	.295	16	3	1B-113, OF-2
1969	112	353	84	9	2	11	3.1	36	49	37	32	3	.238	.368	7	1	1B-106, OF-2
1970	43	47	8	0	0	0	0.0	2	3	5	2	0	.170	.170	31	4	1B-8
1971	122	421	118	20	4	14	3.3	61	58	38	33	0	.280	.447	8	2	1B-108, OF-11
1972	122	327	88	15	1	8	2.4	28	34	34	35	1	.269	.394	16	4	1B-108, OF-1
1973	100	284	68	12	2	1	0.4	28	35	30	28	1	.239	.306	16	2	1B-51, OF-32
1974	94	217	65	11	1	4	1.8	20	24	18	14	1	.300	.415	35	17	OF-33, 1B-24
1975	106	325	105	16	0	4	1.2	42	43	27	21	1	.323	.409	20	8	1B-82, OF-4
1976	123	415	121	17	1	10	2.4	47	49	35	38	1	.292	.410	10	4	1B-86, OF-31
1977	108	281	79	17	0	10	3.6	28	40	23	20	1	.281	.448	29	13	OF-42, 1B-41
1978	66	81	17	2	0	3	3.7	7	19	8	12	0	.210	.346	50	15	OF-12, 1B-3
1979	82	155	36	5	0	2	1.3	7	17	13	18	0	.232	.303	37	6	1B-29, OF-8
18 yrs.	1853	5436	1418	225	25	118	2.2	536	614	454	581	15	.261	.377	325	90	1B-1304, OF-250

LEAGUE CHAMPIONSHIP SERIES

	G	AB	H	2B	3B	HR	HR%	R	RBI	BB	SO	SB	BA	SA	PH AB	PH H	G by POS
1969 NY N	3	12	3	1	0	0	0.0	2	1	1	2	0	.250	.333	0	0	1B-3
1973	1	2	1	0	0	0	0.0	0	2	0	0	0	.500	.500	0	0	OF-1
2 yrs.	4	14	4	1	0	0	0.0	2	3	1	2	0	.286	.357	0	0	1B-3, OF-1

WORLD SERIES

	G	AB	H	2B	3B	HR	HR%	R	RBI	BB	SO	SB	BA	SA	PH AB	PH H	G by POS
1969 NY N	1	4	1	0	0	1	25.0	1	1	0	0	0	.250	1.000	0	0	1B-1
1973	4	3	0	0	0	0	0.0	0	0	0	0	0	.000	.000	3	0	
2 yrs.	5	7	1	0	0	1	14.3	1	1	0	0	0	.143	.571	3	0	1B-1

Danny Kravitz

KRAVITZ, DANIEL (Dusty, Beak)
B. Dec. 21, 1930, Lopez, Pa.   BL TR 5'11" 195 lbs.

	G	AB	H	2B	3B	HR	HR%	R	RBI	BB	SO	SB	BA	SA	PH AB	PH H	G by POS
1956 PIT N	32	68	18	2	2	2	2.9	6	10	5	9	1	.265	.441	12	0	C-26, 3B-2
1957	19	41	6	1	0	0	0.0	2	4	2	10	0	.146	.171	9	1	C-15
1958	45	100	24	3	2	1	1.0	9	5	11	10	0	.240	.340	8	1	C-37
1959	52	162	41	9	3	3	1.9	18	21	5	14	0	.253	.377	8	3	C-45
1960 2 teams		PIT N (8G – .000)				KC A (59G – .234)											
" total	67	181	41	7	2	4	2.2	17	14	12	21	0	.227	.354	18	4	C-48
5 yrs.	215	552	130	22	7	10	1.8	52	54	35	64	1	.236	.355	55	9	C-171, 3B-2

	G	AB	H	2B	3B	HR	HR %	R	RBI	BB	SO	SB	BA	SA	Pinch Hit AB	Pinch Hit H	G by POS

Mike Kreevich

KREEVICH, MICHAEL ANDREAS
B. June 10, 1908, Mount Olive, Ill.
BR TR 5'7½" 168 lbs.

	G	AB	H	2B	3B	HR	HR %	R	RBI	BB	SO	SB	BA	SA	AB	H	G by POS
1931 CHI N	5	12	2	0	0	0	0.0	0	0	0	6	1	.167	.167	1	0	OF-4
1935 CHI A	6	23	10	2	0	0	0.0	3	2	1	0	1	.435	.522	0	0	3B-6
1936	137	550	169	32	11	5	0.9	99	69	61	46	10	.307	.433	3	2	OF-133
1937	144	583	176	29	16	12	2.1	94	73	43	45	10	.302	.468	3	1	OF-138
1938	129	489	145	26	12	6	1.2	73	73	55	23	13	.297	.436	3	0	OF-127
1939	145	541	175	30	8	5	0.9	85	77	59	40	23	.323	.436	3	0	OF-139, 3B-4
1940	144	582	154	27	10	8	1.4	86	55	34	49	15	.265	.387	0	0	OF-144
1941	121	436	101	16	8	0	0.0	44	37	35	26	17	.232	.305	7	4	OF-113
1942 PHI A	116	444	113	19	1	1	0.2	57	30	47	31	7	.255	.309	6	2	OF-107
1943 STL A	60	161	41	6	0	0	0.0	24	10	26	13	4	.255	.292	7	1	OF-51
1944	105	402	121	15	6	5	1.2	55	44	27	24	3	.301	.405	5	0	OF-100
1945 2 teams	STL A (81G – .237)					WAS A (45G – .278)											
" total	126	453	114	19	3	3	0.7	56	44	58	38	11	.252	.327	7	2	OF-118
12 yrs.	1238	4676	1321	221	75	45	1.0	676	514	446	341	115	.283	.391	45	12	OF-1174, 3B-10
WORLD SERIES																	
1944 STL A	6	26	6	3	0	0	0.0	0	0	0	5	0	.231	.346	0	0	OF-6

Charlie Krehmeyer

KREHMEYER, CHARLES L
B. July 5, 1857, St. Louis, Mo.   D. Feb. 10, 1926, St. Louis, Mo.

	G	AB	H	2B	3B	HR	HR %	R	RBI	BB	SO	SB	BA	SA	AB	H	G by POS
1884 STL AA	21	70	16	0	1	0	0.0	3		2			.229	.257	0	0	OF-15, C-7, 1B-1
1885 2 teams	LOU AA (7G – .226)					STL N (1G – .000)											
" total	8	34	7	1	1	0	0.0	4		1	2		.206	.294	0	0	C-5, OF-2, 1B-1
2 yrs.	29	104	23	1	2	0	0.0	7		3	2		.221	.269	0	0	OF-17, C-12, 1B-2

Ralph Kreitz

KREITZ, RALPH WESLEY (Red)
B. Nov. 13, 1885, Plum Creek, Neb.   D. July 20, 1941, Portland, Ore.
BR TR 5'9½" 175 lbs.

	G	AB	H	2B	3B	HR	HR %	R	RBI	BB	SO	SB	BA	SA	AB	H	G by POS
1911 CHI A	7	17	4	1	0	0	0.0	0	0	2		0	.235	.294	0	0	C-7

Wayne Krenchicki

KRENCHICKI, WAYNE RICHARD
B. Sept. 17, 1954, Trenton, N. J.
BL TR 6'1" 180 lbs.

	G	AB	H	2B	3B	HR	HR %	R	RBI	BB	SO	SB	BA	SA	AB	H	G by POS
1979 BAL A	16	21	4	1	0	0	0.0	1	1	0	0	0	.190	.238	0	0	SS-7, 2B-6
1980	9	14	2	0	0	0	0.0	1	0	1	3	0	.143	.143	1	0	SS-6, DH-1, 2B-1
1981	33	56	12	4	0	0	0.0	7	6	4	9	0	.214	.286	1	0	SS-16, 2B-7, 3B-6, DH-1
1982 CIN N	94	187	53	6	1	2	1.1	19	21	13	23	5	.283	.358	28	7	3B-70, 2B-9
1983 2 teams	CIN N (51G – .273)					DET A (59G – .278)											
" total	110	210	58	9	0	1	0.5	24	27	19	31	0	.276	.333	18	2	3B-87, 2B-7, SS-6, 1B-3
1984 CIN N	97	181	54	9	2	6	3.3	18	22	19	23	0	.298	.470	36	7	3B-62, 2B-3, 1B-3
6 yrs.	359	669	183	29	3	9	1.3	70	76	56	89	5	.274	.366	84	16	3B-225, SS-35, 2B-33, 1B-6, DH-2

Charlie Kress

KRESS, CHARLES STEVEN (Chuck)
B. Dec. 9, 1921, Philadelphia, Pa.
BL TL 6' 190 lbs.

	G	AB	H	2B	3B	HR	HR %	R	RBI	BB	SO	SB	BA	SA	AB	H	G by POS
1947 CIN N	11	27	4	0	0	0	0.0	4	0	6	4	0	.148	.148	2	1	1B-8
1949 2 teams	CIN N (27G – .207)					CHI A (97G – .278)											
" total	124	382	104	20	6	1	0.3	48	47	42	49	6	.272	.364	11	3	1B-111
1950 CHI A	3	8	0	0	0	0	0.0	0	0	0	2	0	.000	.000	1	0	1B-2
1954 2 teams	DET A (24G – .189)					BKN N (13G – .083)											
" total	37	49	8	0	1	0	0.0	5	5	1	4	0	.163	.204	27	3	1B-8, OF-1
4 yrs.	175	466	116	20	7	1	0.2	57	52	49	59	6	.249	.328	41	7	1B-129, OF-1

Red Kress

KRESS, RALPH
B. Jan. 2, 1907, Columbia, Calif.   D. Nov. 29, 1962, Los Angeles, Calif.
BR TR 5'11½" 165 lbs.

	G	AB	H	2B	3B	HR	HR %	R	RBI	BB	SO	SB	BA	SA	AB	H	G by POS
1927 STL A	7	23	7	2	1	1	4.3	3	3	3	3	0	.304	.609	0	0	SS-7
1928	150	560	153	26	10	3	0.5	78	81	48	70	5	.273	.371	0	0	SS-150
1929	147	557	170	38	4	9	1.6	82	107	52	54	5	.305	.436	1	0	SS-146
1930	154	614	192	43	8	16	2.6	94	112	50	56	3	.313	.487	0	0	SS-123, 3B-31
1931	150	605	188	46	8	16	2.6	87	114	46	48	3	.311	.493	1	0	3B-84, OF-40, SS-38, 1B-10
1932 2 teams	STL A (14G – .173)					CHI A (135G – .285)											
" total	149	567	156	42	5	11	1.9	85	66	51	42	7	.275	.425	0	0	OF-64, SS-53, 3B-33
1933 CHI A	129	467	116	20	5	10	2.1	47	78	37	40	4	.248	.377	12	6	1B-111, OF-8
1934 2 teams	CHI A (8G – .286)					WAS A (56G – .228)											
" total	64	185	43	4	3	4	2.2	21	25	20	22	3	.232	.351	9	2	1B-30, OF-10, 2B-9, SS-1, 3B-1
1935 WAS A	84	252	75	13	4	2	0.8	32	42	25	16	3	.298	.405	18	4	SS-53, 1B-5, P-3, OF-2, 2B-1
1936	109	391	111	20	6	8	2.0	51	51	39	25	6	.284	.427	5	0	SS-64, 2B-33, 1B-5
1938 STL A	150	595	171	33	7	7	1.2	74	79	69	47	5	.302	.408	1	1	SS-150
1939 2 teams	STL A (13G – .279)					DET A (51G – .242)											
" total	64	200	50	8	0	1	0.5	24	30	23	18	3	.250	.350	6	4	SS-38, 2B-16, 3B-4
1940 DET A	33	99	22	3	1	1	1.0	13	11	10	12	0	.222	.303	5	3	3B-17, SS-12
1946 NY N	1	1	0	0	0	0	0.0	0	0	1	0	0	.000	.000	0	0	P-1
14 yrs.	1391	5087	1454	298	58	89	1.7	691	799	474	453	47	.286	.420	58	20	SS-835, 3B-170, 1B-161, OF-124, 2B-59, P-4

Paul Krichell

KRICHELL, PAUL BERNARD
B. Dec. 19, 1882, New York, N. Y.   D. June 4, 1957, New York, N. Y.
BR TR

	G	AB	H	2B	3B	HR	HR %	R	RBI	BB	SO	SB	BA	SA	AB	H	G by POS
1911 STL A	28	82	19	3	0	0	0.0	6	8	4		2	.232	.268	3	0	C-25
1912	57	161	35	6	0	0	0.0	19	8	19		2	.217	.255	0	0	C-57
2 yrs.	85	243	54	9	0	0	0.0	25	16	23		4	.222	.259	3	0	C-82

Bill Krieg

KRIEG, WILLIAM FREDERICK
B. Jan. 29, 1859, Petersburg, Ill.   D. Mar. 25, 1930, Chillicothe, Ill.
BR TR 5'8" 180 lbs.

	G	AB	H	2B	3B	HR	HR %	R	RBI	BB	SO	SB	BA	SA	AB	H	G by POS
1884 C-P U	71	279	69	15	4	0	0.0	35		11			.247	.330	0	0	C-52, OF-20, SS-1, 1B-1

	G	AB	H	2B	3B	HR	HR %	R	RBI	BB	SO	SB	BA	SA	Pinch Hit AB	Pinch Hit H	G by POS

Bill Krieg continued

1885 2 teams	CHI	N (1G – .000)			BKN	AA (17G – .150)											
" total	18	63	9	4	0	1	1.6	7		2	2		.143	.254	0	0	C-12, 1B-5, OF-1
1886 WAS N	27	98	25	6	3	1	1.0	11	15	3	12		.255	.408	0	0	1B-27
1887	25	95	24	4	1	2	2.1	9	17	7	5	2	.253	.379	0	0	1B-16, OF-9
4 yrs.	141	535	127	29	8	4	0.7	62	31	23	19	2	.237	.344	0	0	C-64, 1B-49, OF-30, SS-1

Mickey Krietner

KRIETNER, ALBERT JOSEPH
B. Oct. 10, 1922, Nashville, Tenn.

BR TR 6'3" 190 lbs.

1943 CHI N	3	8	3	0	0	0	0.0	0	2	1	2	0	.375	.375	0	0	C-3
1944	39	85	13	2	0	0	0.0	3	1	8	16	0	.153	.176	0	0	C-39
2 yrs.	42	93	16	2	0	0	0.0	3	3	9	18	0	.172	.194	0	0	C-42

John Kroner

KRONER, JOHN HAROLD
B. Nov. 13, 1908, St. Louis, Mo.　D. Aug. 26, 1968, St. Louis, Mo.

BR TR 6' 165 lbs.

1935 BOS A	2	4	1	0	0	0	0.0	1	0	1	1	0	.250	.250	0	0	3B-2
1936	84	298	87	17	8	4	1.3	40	62	26	24	2	.292	.443	1	0	2B-38, 3B-28, SS-18, OF-1
1937 CLE A	86	283	67	14	1	2	0.7	29	26	22	25	1	.237	.314	9	2	2B-64, 3B-11
1938	51	117	29	16	0	1	0.9	13	17	19	6	0	.248	.410	7	1	2B-31, 1B-7, 3B-3, SS-1
4 yrs.	223	702	184	47	9	7	1.0	83	105	68	56	3	.262	.385	17	3	2B-133, 3B-44, SS-19, 1B-7, OF-1

Mike Krsnich

KRSNICH, MICHAEL
Brother of Rocky Krsnich.
B. Sept. 24, 1931, West Allis, Wis.

BR TR 6'1" 190 lbs.

1960 MIL N	4	9	3	1	0	0	0.0	0	2	0	0	0	.333	.444	2	1	OF-3
1962	11	12	1	1	0	0	0.0	0	2	0	4	0	.083	.167	6	1	OF-3, 3B-1, 1B-1
2 yrs.	15	21	4	2	0	0	0.0	0	4	0	4	0	.190	.286	8	2	OF-6, 3B-1, 1B-1

Rocky Krsnich

KRSNICH, ROCCO PETER
Brother of Mike Krsnich.
B. Aug. 5, 1927, West Allis, Wis.

BR TR 6'1" 174 lbs.

1949 CHI A	16	55	12	3	1	1	1.8	..	7	9	6	4	0	.218	.364	0	0	2B-16
1952	40	91	21	7	2	1	1.1	11	15	12	9	0	.231	.385	2	0	3B-37
1953	64	129	26	8	0	1	0.8	9	14	12	11	0	.202	.287	6	1	3B-57
3 yrs.	120	275	59	18	3	3	1.1	27	38	30	24	0	.215	.335	8	1	3B-94, 2B-16

Art Krueger

KRUEGER, ARTHUR T.
B. Mar. 16, 1881, San Antonio, Tex.　D. Nov. 28, 1949, Hondo, Calif.

BR TR 6' 185 lbs.

1907 CIN N	100	317	74	10	8	0	0.0	25	28	18		10	0	.233	.322	4	0	OF-96
1910 2 teams	CLE	A (62G – .170)			BOS	N (1G – .000)											
" total	63	224	38	6	3	0	0.0	19	14	20		12	0	.170	.223	1	0	OF-62
1914 KC F	122	441	114	24	7	4	0.9	45	47	23		11	0	.259	.372	2	0	OF-120
1915	80	240	57	9	2	2	0.8	24	26	12		5	0	.238	.317	14	4	OF-66
4 yrs.	365	1222	283	49	21	6	0.5	113	115	73		38	0	.232	.321	21	4	OF-344

Ernie Krueger

KRUEGER, ERNEST GEORGE
B. Dec. 27, 1890, Chicago, Ill.　D. Apr. 22, 1976, Waukegan, Ill.

BR TR 5'10½" 185 lbs.

1913 CLE A	5	6	0	0	0	0	0.0	0	0	0	2	0	.000	.000	1	0	C-4
1915 NY A	10	29	5	1	0	0	0.0	3	0	0	5	0	.172	.207	2	0	C-8
1917 2 teams	NY	N (8G – .000)			BKN	N (31G – .272)											
" total	39	91	22	2	2	1	1.1	10	6	5	11	1	.242	.341	9	1	C-29
1918 BKN N	30	87	25	4	2	0	0.0	4	7	4	9	2	.287	.379	7	2	C-23
1919	80	226	56	7	4	5	2.2	24	36	19	25	4	.248	.381	10	2	C-66
1920	52	146	42	4	2	1	0.7	21	17	16	13	2	.288	.363	5	1	C-46
1921	65	163	43	11	4	3	1.8	18	20	14	12	2	.264	.436	14	3	C-52
1925 CIN N	37	88	27	4	0	1	1.1	7	7	6	8	1	.307	.386	6	0	C-30
8 yrs.	318	836	220	33	14	11	1.3	87	93	64	85	12	.263	.376	54	9	C-258

WORLD SERIES																	
1920 BKN N	4	6	1	0	0	0	0.0	0	0	0	0	0	.167	.167	1	0	C-3

Otto Krueger

KRUEGER, ARTHUR WILLIAM (Oom Paul)
B. Sept. 17, 1876, Chicago, Ill.　D. Feb. 20, 1961, St. Louis, Mo.

BR TR 5'7" 165 lbs.

1899 CLE N	13	44	10	1	0	0	0.0	4	2	8		1	.227	.250	0	0	3B-9, SS-2, 2B-2
1900 STL N	12	35	14	3	2	1	2.9	8	3	10		0	.400	.686	0	0	2B-12
1901	142	520	143	16	12	2	0.4	77	79	50		19	.275	.363	0	0	3B-142
1902	128	467	124	7	8	0	0.0	55	46	29		14	.266	.315	3	0	SS-107, 3B-18
1903 PIT N	80	256	63	6	8	1	0.4	42	28	21		5	.246	.344	4	1	SS-29, OF-28, 3B-13, 2B-3
1904	86	268	52	6	2	1	0.4	34	26	29		8	.194	.243	8	1	OF-33, SS-32, 3B-10
1905 PHI N	46	114	21	1	1	0	0.0	10	12	13		1	.184	.211	16	3	SS-23, OF-6, 3B-1
7 yrs.	507	1704	427	40	33	5	0.3	230	196	160		48	.251	.322	31	5	SS-193, 3B-193, OF-67, 2B-17

Chris Krug

KRUG, EVERETT BEN
B. Dec. 25, 1939, Los Angeles, Calif.

BR TR 6'4" 200 lbs.

1965 CHI N	60	169	34	5	0	5	3.0	16	24	13	52	0	.201	.320	3	0	C-58
1966	11	28	6	1	0	0	0.0	1	1	1	8	0	.214	.250	1	0	C-10
1969 SD N	8	17	1	0	0	0	0.0	0	0	1	6	0	.059	.059	1	0	C-7
3 yrs.	79	214	41	6	0	5	2.3	17	25	15	66	0	.192	.290	5	0	C-75

Gary Krug

KRUG, GARY EUGENE
B. Feb. 12, 1955, Garden City, Kans.

BL TL 6'4" 225 lbs.

1981 CHI N	7	5	2	0	0	0	0.0	0	0	1	1	0	.400	.400	5	2	

	G	AB	H	2B	3B	HR	HR %	R	RBI	BB	SO	SB	BA	SA	Pinch Hit AB	Pinch Hit H	G by POS

Henry Krug

KRUG, HENRY C.
B. Dec. 4, 1876, San Francisco, Calif.   D. Jan. 14, 1908, San Francisco, Calif.
BR TR

	G	AB	H	2B	3B	HR	HR %	R	RBI	BB	SO	SB	BA	SA	AB	H	G by POS
1902 PHI N	53	198	45	3	3	0	0.0	20	14	7		2	.227	.273	0	0	OF-28, 2B-13, SS-9, 3B-6

Marty Krug

KRUG, MARTIN JOHN
B. Sept. 10, 1888, Coblenz, Germany   D. June 27, 1966, Glendale, Calif.
BR TR 5'9" 165 lbs.

	G	AB	H	2B	3B	HR	HR %	R	RBI	BB	SO	SB	BA	SA	AB	H	G by POS
1912 BOS A	16	39	12	2	1	0	0.0	6	7	5		2	.308	.410	2	0	SS-9, 2B-4
1922 CHI N	127	450	124	23	4	4	0.9	67	60	43	43	7	.276	.371	0	0	3B-104, 2B-23, SS-1
2 yrs.	143	489	136	25	5	4	0.8	73	67	48	43	9	.278	.374	2	0	3B-104, 2B-27, SS-10

Dick Kryhoski

KRYHOSKI, RICHARD DAVID
B. Mar. 24, 1925, Leonia, N. J.
BL TL 6'2" 182 lbs.

	G	AB	H	2B	3B	HR	HR %	R	RBI	BB	SO	SB	BA	SA	AB	H	G by POS
1949 NY A	54	177	52	10	3	1	0.6	18	27	9	17	2	.294	.401	2	0	1B-51
1950 DET A	53	169	37	10	0	4	2.4	20	19	8	11	0	.219	.349	5	2	1B-47
1951	119	421	121	19	4	12	2.9	58	57	28	29	1	.287	.437	10	4	1B-112
1952 STL A	111	342	83	13	1	11	3.2	38	42	23	42	2	.243	.383	25	8	1B-86
1953	104	338	94	18	4	16	4.7	35	50	26	33	0	.278	.497	19	4	1B-88
1954 BAL A	100	300	78	13	2	1	0.3	32	34	19	24	0	.260	.327	23	3	1B-69
1955 KC A	28	47	10	2	0	0	0.0	2	2	6	7	0	.213	.255	13	3	1B-14
7 yrs.	569	1794	475	85	14	45	2.5	203	231	119	163	5	.265	.403	97	24	1B-467

Tony Kubek

KUBEK, ANTHONY CHRISTOPHER
B. Oct. 12, 1936, Milwaukee, Wis.
BL TR 6'3" 190 lbs.

	G	AB	H	2B	3B	HR	HR %	R	RBI	BB	SO	SB	BA	SA	AB	H	G by POS
1957 NY A	127	431	128	21	3	3	0.7	56	39	24	48	6	.297	.381	8	1	OF-50, SS-41, 3B-38, 2B-1
1958	138	559	148	21	1	2	0.4	66	48	25	57	5	.265	.317	1	0	SS-134, OF-3, 2B-1, 1B-1
1959	132	512	143	25	7	6	1.2	67	51	24	46	3	.279	.391	4	1	SS-67, OF-53, 3B-17, 2B-1
1960	147	568	155	25	3	14	2.5	77	62	31	42	3	.273	.401	6	2	SS-136, OF-29
1961	153	617	170	38	6	8	1.3	84	46	27	60	1	.276	.395	8	3	SS-145
1962	45	169	53	6	1	4	2.4	28	17	12	17	2	.314	.432	2	1	SS-35, OF-6
1963	135	557	143	21	3	7	1.3	72	44	28	68	4	.257	.343	1	0	SS-132, OF-1
1964	106	415	95	16	3	8	1.9	46	31	26	55	4	.229	.340	2	0	SS-99
1965	109	339	74	5	3	5	1.5	26	35	20	48	1	.218	.295	12	4	SS-93, OF-3, 1B-1
9 yrs.	1092	4167	1109	178	30	57	1.4	522	373	217	441	29	.266	.364	44	12	SS-882, OF-145, 3B-55, 2B-3, 1B-2

WORLD SERIES

	G	AB	H	2B	3B	HR	HR %	R	RBI	BB	SO	SB	BA	SA	AB	H	G by POS
1957 NY A	7	28	8	0	0	2	7.1	4	4	0	4	0	.286	.500	0	0	OF-5
1958	7	21	1	0	0	0	0.0	0	1	1	7	0	.048	.048	0	0	SS-7
1960	7	30	10	1	0	0	0.0	6	3	2	2	0	.333	.367	0	0	SS-7
1961	5	22	5	0	0	0	0.0	3	1	1	4	0	.227	.227	0	0	SS-5
1962	7	29	8	1	0	0	0.0	2	1	1	3	0	.276	.310	0	0	SS-7
1963	4	16	3	0	0	0	0.0	1	0	0	3	0	.188	.188	0	0	SS-4
6 yrs.	37	146	35	2	0	2	1.4	16	10	5	23	0	.240	.295	0	0	SS-30, OF-5
											10th						

Ted Kubiak

KUBIAK, THEODORE RODGER
B. May 12, 1942, New Brunswick, N. J.
BL TR 6' 175 lbs.
BB 1968

	G	AB	H	2B	3B	HR	HR %	R	RBI	BB	SO	SB	BA	SA	AB	H	G by POS
1967 KC A	53	102	16	2	1	0	0.0	6	5	12	20	0	.157	.196	15	2	SS-20, 2B-10, 3B-5
1968 OAK A	48	120	30	5	2	0	0.0	10	8	8	18	1	.250	.325	13	2	2B-24, SS-12
1969	92	305	76	9	1	2	0.7	38	27	25	35	2	.249	.305	14	3	SS-42, 2B-33
1970 MIL A	158	540	136	9	6	4	0.7	63	41	72	51	4	.252	.313	0	0	2B-91, SS-73
1971 2 teams		MIL A (89G – .227)						STL N (32G – .250)									
" total	121	332	77	9	7	4	1.2	34	27	52	43	1	.232	.337	12	2	2B-62, SS-56
1972 2 teams		TEX A (46G – .224)						OAK A (51G – .181)									
" total	97	210	43	7	1	0	0.0	19	15	21	23	0	.205	.248	9	1	2B-74, SS-15, 3B-2
1973 OAK A	106	182	40	6	1	3	1.6	15	17	12	19	1	.220	.313	4	1	2B-83, SS-26, 3B-2
1974	99	220	46	3	0	0	0.0	22	18	18	15	1	.209	.223	4	0	2B-71, SS-19, 3B-14, DH-2
1975 2 teams		OAK A (20G – .250)						SD N (87G – .224)									
" total	107	224	51	6	0	0	0.0	15	18	26	20	3	.228	.254	13	2	3B-71, 2B-17, SS-7, 1B-1
1976 SD N	96	212	50	5	2	0	0.0	16	26	25	28	0	.236	.278	39	2	3B-27, 2B-25, SS-6, 1B-1
10 yrs.	977	2447	565	61	21	13	0.5	238	202	271	272	13	.231	.289	123	15	2B-490, SS-276, 3B-121, DH-2, 1B-2

LEAGUE CHAMPIONSHIP SERIES

	G	AB	H	2B	3B	HR	HR %	R	RBI	BB	SO	SB	BA	SA	AB	H	G by POS
1972 OAK A	4	4	2	0	0	0	0.0	0	1	0	0	0	.500	.500	0	0	2B-3
1973	3	2	0	0	0	0	0.0	0	0	0	1	0	.000	.000	0	0	2B-3
2 yrs.	7	6	2	0	0	0	0.0	0	1	0	1	0	.333	.333	0	0	2B-6

WORLD SERIES

	G	AB	H	2B	3B	HR	HR %	R	RBI	BB	SO	SB	BA	SA	AB	H	G by POS
1972 OAK A	4	3	1	0	0	0	0.0	0	0	0	0	0	.333	.333	0	0	2B-4
1973	4	3	0	0	0	0	0.0	1	0	1	1	0	.000	.000	0	0	2B-4
2 yrs.	8	6	1	0	0	0	0.0	1	0	1	1	0	.167	.167	0	0	2B-8

Jack Kubiszyn

KUBISZYN, JACK JOSEPH
B. Dec. 19, 1936, Buffalo, N. Y.
BR TR 5'11" 170 lbs.

	G	AB	H	2B	3B	HR	HR %	R	RBI	BB	SO	SB	BA	SA	AB	H	G by POS
1961 CLE A	25	42	9	0	0	0	0.0	4	0	2	5	0	.214	.214	6	0	3B-8, SS-7, 2B-2
1962	25	59	10	2	0	1	1.7	3	2	5	7	0	.169	.254	5	1	SS-18, 3B-1
2 yrs.	50	101	19	2	0	1	1.0	7	2	7	12	0	.188	.238	11	1	SS-25, 3B-9, 2B-2

Gil Kubski

KUBSKI, GILBERT THOMAS
B. Oct. 12, 1954, Longview, Tex.
BL TR 6'3" 185 lbs.

	G	AB	H	2B	3B	HR	HR %	R	RBI	BB	SO	SB	BA	SA	AB	H	G by POS
1980 CAL A	22	63	16	3	0	0	0.0	11	6	6	10	1	.254	.302	1	0	OF-20

Steve Kuczek

KUCZEK, STANISLAW LEO
B. Dec. 28, 1924, Amsterdam, N. Y.
BR TR 6' 160 lbs.

	G	AB	H	2B	3B	HR	HR %	R	RBI	BB	SO	SB	BA	SA	AB	H	G by POS
1949 BOS N	1	1	1	1	0	0	0.0	0	0	0	0	0	1.000	2.000	1	1	

	G	AB	H	2B	3B	HR	HR %	R	RBI	BB	SO	SB	BA	SA	Pinch Hit AB	Pinch Hit H	G by POS

Willie Kuehne

KUEHNE, WILLIAM J.
Also known as William J. Knelme.
B. Oct. 24, 1858, Leipzig, Germany   D. Oct. 27, 1921, Sulphur Springs, Ohio
TR   185 lbs.

	G	AB	H	2B	3B	HR	HR%	R	RBI	BB	SO	SB	BA	SA	PH AB	PH H	G by POS
1883 COL AA	95	374	85	8	14	1	0.3	38		2			.227	.332	0	0	3B-69, 2B-18, SS-7, OF-3
1884	110	415	98	13	16	5	1.2	48		9			.236	.381	0	0	3B-109, OF-1
1885 PIT AA	104	411	93	9	19	0	0.0	54		15			.226	.341	0	0	3B-97, SS-7
1886	117	481	98	16	17	1	0.2	73		19			.204	.314	0	0	OF-54, 3B-47, 1B-18
1887 PIT N	102	402	120	18	15	1	0.2	68	41	14	39	17	.299	.425	0	0	SS-91, 3B-4, 1B-4, OF-3
1888	138	524	123	22	11	3	0.6	60	62	9	68	34	.235	.336	0	0	3B-75, SS-63
1889	97	390	96	20	5	5	1.3	43	57	9	36	15	.246	.362	0	0	3B-75, OF-13, 2B-5, SS-2, 1B-2
1890 PIT P	126	528	126	21	12	5	0.9	66	73	28	37	21	.239	.352	0	0	3B-126
1891 2 teams		COL	AA	(68G –	.215)			LOU	AA	(41G –	.277)						
" total	109	420	100	12	1	3	0.7	60	40	18	35	31	.238	.293			3B-109
1892 3 teams		LOU	N	(76G –	.167)			STL	N	(7G –	.143)		CIN	N	(6G –	.208)	
" total	89	339	57	6	5	1	0.3	26	40	14	45	7	.168	.224	0	0	3B-86, 2B-2, SS-1
10 yrs.	1087	4284	996	145	115	25	0.6	536	312	137	260	125	.232	.338	0	0	3B-797, SS-171, OF-74, 2B-25, 1B-24

Harvey Kuenn

KUENN, HARVEY EDWARD
B. Dec. 4, 1930, Milwaukee, Wis.
Manager 1975, 1982-83.
BR TR 6'2"   187 lbs.

	G	AB	H	2B	3B	HR	HR%	R	RBI	BB	SO	SB	BA	SA	PH AB	PH H	G by POS
1952 DET A	19	80	26	2	2	0	0.0	2	8	2	1	2	.325	.400	0	0	SS-19
1953	155	679	209	33	7	2	0.3	94	48	50	31	6	.308	.386	0	0	SS-155
1954	155	656	201	28	6	5	0.8	81	48	29	13	9	.306	.390	0	0	SS-155
1955	145	620	190	38	5	8	1.3	101	62	40	27	8	.306	.423	4	1	SS-141
1956	146	591	196	32	7	12	2.0	96	88	55	34	9	.332	.470	6	1	SS-141, OF-1
1957	151	624	173	30	6	9	1.4	74	44	47	28	5	.277	.388	1	0	SS-136, 3B-17, 1B-1
1958	139	561	179	39	3	8	1.4	73	54	51	34	5	.319	.442	1	1	OF-138
1959	139	561	198	42	7	9	1.6	99	71	48	37	7	.353	.501	1	0	OF-137
1960 CLE A	126	474	146	24	0	9	1.9	65	54	55	25	3	.308	.416	4	1	OF-119, 3B-5
1961 SF N	131	471	125	22	4	5	1.1	60	46	47	34	5	.265	.361	10	4	OF-93, 3B-32, SS-1
1962	130	487	148	23	5	10	2.1	73	68	49	37	3	.304	.433	9	2	OF-105, 3B-30
1963	120	417	121	13	2	6	1.4	61	31	44	38	2	.290	.374	15	2	OF-64, 3B-53
1964	139	351	92	16	2	4	1.1	42	22	35	32	0	.262	.353	17	5	OF-88, 1B-11, 3B-2
1965 2 teams		SF	N	(23G –	.237)			CHI	N	(54G –	.217)						
" total	77	179	40	5	0	0	0.0	15	12	32	16	4	.223	.251	25	7	OF-49, 1B-8
1966 2 teams		CHI	N	(3G –	.333)			PHI	N	(86G –	.296)						
" total	89	162	48	9	0	0	0.0	15	15	10	17	0	.296	.352	48	11	OF-32, 1B-13, 3B-1
15 yrs.	1833	6913	2092	356	56	87	1.3	951	671	594	404	68	.303	.408	141	35	OF-826, SS-748, 3B-140, 1B-33

WORLD SERIES

	G	AB	H	2B	3B	HR	HR%	R	RBI	BB	SO	SB	BA	SA	PH AB	PH H	G by POS
1962 SF N	4	12	1	0	0	0	0.0	1	0	1	1	0	.083	.083	0	0	OF-4

Joe Kuhel

KUHEL, JOSEPH ANTHONY
B. June 25, 1906, Kansas City, Kans.   D. Feb. 26, 1984, Kansas City, Mo.
Manager 1948-49.
BL TL 6'   180 lbs.

	G	AB	H	2B	3B	HR	HR%	R	RBI	BB	SO	SB	BA	SA	PH AB	PH H	G by POS
1930 WAS A	18	63	18	3	3	0	0.0	9	17	5	6	1	.286	.429	1	0	1B-16
1931	139	524	141	34	8	8	1.5	70	85	47	45	7	.269	.410	0	0	1B-139
1932	101	347	101	21	5	4	1.2	52	52	32	19	5	.291	.415	9	1	1B-85
1933	153	602	194	34	10	11	1.8	89	107	59	48	17	.322	.467	0	0	1B-153
1934	63	263	76	12	3	3	1.1	49	25	30	14	2	.289	.392	0	0	1B-63
1935	151	633	165	25	9	2	0.3	99	74	78	44	5	.261	.338	0	0	1B-151
1936	149	588	189	42	8	16	2.7	107	118	64	30	15	.321	.502	0	0	1B-149, 3B-1
1937	136	547	155	24	11	6	1.1	73	61	63	39	6	.283	.400	0	0	1B-136
1938 CHI A	117	412	110	27	4	8	1.9	67	51	72	35	9	.267	.410	6	0	1B-111
1939	139	546	164	24	9	15	2.7	107	56	64	51	18	.300	.460	3	0	1B-136
1940	155	603	169	28	8	27	4.5	111	94	87	59	12	.280	.488	0	0	1B-155
1941	153	600	150	39	5	12	2.0	99	63	70	55	20	.250	.392	1	0	1B-151
1942	115	413	103	14	4	4	1.0	60	52	60	22	22	.249	.332	3	0	1B-112
1943	153	531	113	21	1	5	0.9	55	46	76	45	14	.213	.284	0	0	1B-153
1944 WAS A	139	518	144	26	7	4	0.8	90	51	68	40	11	.278	.378	1	1	1B-138
1945	142	533	152	29	13	2	0.4	73	75	79	31	10	.285	.400	1	0	1B-141
1946 2 teams		WAS	A	(14G –	.150)			CHI	A	(64G –	.273)						
" total	78	258	68	9	3	4	1.6	26	22	26	26	4	.264	.368	8	2	1B-68
1947 CHI A	4	4	0	0	0	0	0.0	0	0	0	3	0	.000	.000	4	0	
18 yrs.	2105	7985	2212	412	111	131	1.6	1236	1049	980	612	178	.277	.406	37	4	1B-2057, 3B-1

WORLD SERIES

	G	AB	H	2B	3B	HR	HR%	R	RBI	BB	SO	SB	BA	SA	PH AB	PH H	G by POS
1933 WAS A	5	20	3	0	0	0	0.0	1	1	1	4	0	.150	.150	0	0	1B-5

Kenny Kuhn

KUHN, KENNETH HAROLD
B. Mar. 20, 1937, Louisville, Ky.
BL TR 5'10½" 175 lbs.

	G	AB	H	2B	3B	HR	HR%	R	RBI	BB	SO	SB	BA	SA	PH AB	PH H	G by POS
1955 CLE A	4	6	2	0	0	0	0.0	0	0	1	0	1	.333	.333	0	0	SS-4
1956	27	22	6	1	0	0	0.0	7	2	0	4	0	.273	.318	4	1	SS-17, 2B-5
1957	40	53	9	0	0	0	0.0	5	5	4	9	0	.170	.170	14	1	2B-19, 3B-2, SS-1
3 yrs.	71	81	17	1	0	0	0.0	12	7	5	13	1	.210	.222	18	2	SS-22, 2B-19, 3B-2

Walt Kuhn

KUHN, WALTER CHARLES (Red)
B. Feb. 2, 1884, Fresno, Calif.   D. June 14, 1935, Fresno, Calif.
BR TR

	G	AB	H	2B	3B	HR	HR%	R	RBI	BB	SO	SB	BA	SA	PH AB	PH H	G by POS
1912 CHI A	75	178	36	7	0	0	0.0	16	10	20		5	.202	.242	0	0	C-75
1913	26	50	8	1	0	0	0.0	5	5	13	8	1	.160	.180	2	0	C-24
1914	17	40	11	1	0	0	0.0	4	0	8	11	2	.275	.300	0	0	C-16
3 yrs.	118	268	55	9	0	0	0.0	25	15	41	19	8	.205	.239	2	0	C-115

	G	AB	H	2B	3B	HR	HR %	R	RBI	BB	SO	SB	BA	SA	Pinch Hit AB	Pinch Hit H	G by POS

Charlie Kuhns

KUHNS, CHARLES B.
B. Freeport, Pa.   D. July 15, 1922, Pittsburgh, Pa.

	G	AB	H	2B	3B	HR	HR %	R	RBI	BB	SO	SB	BA	SA	AB	H	G by POS
1897 PIT N	1	3	0	0	0	0	0.0	0	0	1		0	.000	.000	0	0	3B-1
1899 BOS N	7	18	5	0	0	0	0.0	2	3	2		0	.278	.278	0	0	SS-3, 3B-3
2 yrs.	8	21	5	0	0	0	0.0	2	3	3		0	.238	.238	0	0	3B-4, SS-3

Duane Kuiper

KUIPER, DUANE EUGENE
B. June 19, 1950, Racine, Wis.   BL TR 6'   175 lbs.

	G	AB	H	2B	3B	HR	HR %	R	RBI	BB	SO	SB	BA	SA	AB	H	G by POS
1974 CLE A	10	22	11	2	0	0	0.0	7	4	2	2	1	.500	.591	1	1	2B-8
1975	90	346	101	11	1	0	0.0	42	25	30	26	19	.292	.329	0	0	2B-87, DH-1
1976	135	506	133	13	6	0	0.0	47	37	30	42	10	.263	.312	4	0	2B-128, 1B-5, DH-2
1977	148	610	169	15	8	1	0.2	62	50	37	55	11	.277	.333	0	0	2B-148
1978	149	547	155	18	6	0	0.0	52	43	19	35	4	.283	.338	0	0	2B-149
1979	140	479	122	9	5	0	0.0	46	39	37	27	4	.255	.294	0	0	2B-140
1980	42	149	42	5	0	0	0.0	10	9	13	8	0	.282	.315	0	0	2B-42
1981	72	206	53	6	0	0	0.0	15	14	8	13	1	.257	.286	4	2	2B-72
1982 SF N	107	218	61	9	1	0	0.0	26	17	32	24	2	.280	.330	44	14	2B-51
1983	72	176	44	2	2	0	0.0	14	14	27	13	0	.250	.284	10	2	2B-64
1984	83	115	23	1	0	0	0.0	8	11	12	10	0	.200	.209	47	9	2B-31, 1B-1
11 yrs.	1048	3374	914	91	29	1	0.0	329	263	247	255	52	.271	.316	110	28	2B-920, 1B-6, DH-3

Jeff Kunkel

KUNKEL, JEFFREY WILLIAM
Son of Bill Kunkel.
B. Mar. 25, 1962, Leonardo, N. J.   BR TR 6'2"   175 lbs.

	G	AB	H	2B	3B	HR	HR %	R	RBI	BB	SO	SB	BA	SA	AB	H	G by POS
1984 TEX A	50	142	29	2	3	3	2.1	13	7	2	35	4	.204	.324	0	0	SS-48, DH-1

Rusty Kuntz

KUNTZ, RUSSELL JAY
B. Feb. 4, 1955, Orange, Calif.   BR TR 6'3"   190 lbs.

	G	AB	H	2B	3B	HR	HR %	R	RBI	BB	SO	SB	BA	SA	AB	H	G by POS
1979 CHI A	5	11	1	0	0	0	0.0	0	0	2	6	0	.091	.091	0	0	OF-5
1980	36	62	14	4	0	0	0.0	5	3	5	13	1	.226	.290	3	2	OF-34
1981	67	55	14	2	0	0	0.0	15	4	6	8	1	.255	.291	3	0	OF-51, DH-5
1982	21	26	5	1	0	0	0.0	4	3	2	8	0	.192	.231	0	0	OF-21, P-1
1983 2 teams		CHI	A (28G –	.262)		MIN	A	(31G –	.190)								
" total	59	142	30	4	0	3	2.1	19	6	18	41	1	.211	.303	4	1	OF-57, DH-1
1984 DET A	84	140	40	12	0	2	1.4	32	22	25	28	2	.286	.414	12	5	OF-67, DH-10
6 yrs.	272	436	104	23	0	5	1.1	75	38	58	104	5	.239	.326	22	8	OF-235, DH-16, P-1

LEAGUE CHAMPIONSHIP SERIES

	G	AB	H	2B	3B	HR	HR %	R	RBI	BB	SO	SB	BA	SA	AB	H	G by POS
1984 DET A	1	1	0	0	0	0	0.0	0	0	0	0	0	.000	.000	1	0	OF-1

WORLD SERIES

	G	AB	H	2B	3B	HR	HR %	R	RBI	BB	SO	SB	BA	SA	AB	H	G by POS
1984 DET A	2	1	0	0	0	0	0.0	0	1	0	1	0	.000	.000	1	0	

Whitey Kurowski

KUROWSKI, GEORGE JOHN
B. Apr. 19, 1918, Reading, Pa.   BR TR 5'11"   193 lbs.

	G	AB	H	2B	3B	HR	HR %	R	RBI	BB	SO	SB	BA	SA	AB	H	G by POS
1941 STL N	5	9	3	2	0	0	0.0	1	2	0	2	0	.333	.556	1	0	3B-4
1942	115	366	93	17	3	9	2.5	51	42	33	60	7	.254	.391	9	0	3B-104, OF-1, SS-1
1943	139	522	150	24	8	13	2.5	69	70	31	54	3	.287	.439	1	0	3B-137, SS-2
1944	149	555	150	25	7	20	3.6	95	87	58	40	2	.270	.449	2	0	3B-146, 2B-9, SS-1
1945	133	511	165	27	3	21	4.1	84	102	45	45	1	.323	.511	1	0	3B-131, SS-6
1946	142	519	156	32	5	14	2.7	76	89	72	47	3	.301	.462	3	1	3B-138
1947	146	513	159	27	6	27	5.3	108	104	87	56	4	.310	.544	4	1	3B-141
1948	77	220	47	8	0	2	0.9	34	33	42	28	0	.214	.277	9	1	3B-65
1949	10	14	2	0	0	0	0.0	0	0	1	0	0	.143	.143	8	2	3B-2
9 yrs.	916	3229	925	162	32	106	3.3	518	529	369	332	19	.286	.455	38	5	3B-868, SS-10, 2B-9, OF-1

WORLD SERIES

	G	AB	H	2B	3B	HR	HR %	R	RBI	BB	SO	SB	BA	SA	AB	H	G by POS
1942 STL N	5	15	4	0	1	1	6.7	3	5	2	3	0	.267	.600	0	0	3B-5
1943	5	18	4	1	0	0	0.0	2	1	0	3	0	.222	.278	0	0	3B-5
1944	6	23	5	1	0	0	0.0	2	1	1	4	0	.217	.261	0	0	3B-6
1946	7	27	8	3	0	0	0.0	5	2	0	3	0	.296	.407	0	0	3B-7
4 yrs.	23	83	21	5	1	1	1.2	12	9	3	13	0	.253	.373	0	0	3B-23

Craig Kusick

KUSICK, CRAIG ROBERT
B. Sept. 30, 1948, Milwaukee, Wis.   BR TR 6'3"   210 lbs.

	G	AB	H	2B	3B	HR	HR %	R	RBI	BB	SO	SB	BA	SA	AB	H	G by POS
1973 MIN A	15	48	12	2	0	0	0.0	4	4	7	9	0	.250	.292	1	0	1B-11, DH-2, OF-2
1974	76	201	48	7	1	8	4.0	36	26	35	36	0	.239	.403	7	2	1B-75
1975	57	156	37	8	0	6	3.8	14	27	21	23	0	.237	.404	9	3	1B-51
1976	109	266	69	13	0	11	4.1	33	36	35	44	5	.259	.432	35	3	DH-79, 1B-23
1977	115	268	68	12	0	12	4.5	34	45	49	60	3	.254	.433	38	10	DH-85, 1B-23
1978	77	191	33	3	2	4	2.1	23	20	37	38	3	.173	.272	24	4	DH-35, 1B-27, OF-9
1979 2 teams		MIN	A	(24G –	.241)		TOR	A	(24G –	.204)							
" total	48	108	24	0	0	5	4.6	11	13	10	18	0	.222	.407	10	1	1B-28, DH-13, P-1
7 yrs.	497	1238	291	50	3	46	3.7	155	171	194	228	11	.235	.392	124	23	1B-238, DH-214, OF-11, P-1

Art Kusnyer

KUSNYER, ARTHUR WILLIAM
B. Dec. 19, 1945, Akron, Ohio   BR TR 6'2"   197 lbs.

	G	AB	H	2B	3B	HR	HR %	R	RBI	BB	SO	SB	BA	SA	AB	H	G by POS
1970 CHI A	4	10	1	0	0	0	0.0	0	0	0	4	0	.100	.100	1	0	C-3
1971 CAL A	6	13	2	0	0	0	0.0	0	0	0	3	0	.154	.154	0	0	C-6
1972	64	179	37	2	1	2	1.1	13	13	16	33	0	.207	.263	2	0	C-63
1973	41	64	8	2	0	0	0.0	5	3	2	12	0	.125	.156	0	0	C-41
1976 MIL A	15	34	4	1	0	0	0.0	2	3	1	5	1	.118	.147	0	0	C-14
1978 KC A	9	13	3	1	0	1	7.7	1	2	2	4	0	.231	.538	0	0	C-9
6 yrs.	139	313	55	6	1	3	1.0	21	21	21	61	1	.176	.230	3	0	C-136

	G	AB	H	2B	3B	HR	HR %	R	RBI	BB	SO	SB	BA	SA	Pinch Hit AB	H	G by POS

Joe Kustus

KUSTUS, JOSEPH JULIUS
B. Sept. 5, 1882, Detroit, Mich.   D. Apr. 27, 1916, Eloise, Mich.
BR TR 5'10"

	G	AB	H	2B	3B	HR	HR%	R	RBI	BB	SO	SB	BA	SA	PH AB	PH H	G by POS
1909 BKN N	53	173	25	5	0	1	0.6	12	11	11		9	.145	.191	3	0	OF-50

Joe Kutina

KUTINA, JOSEPH PETER
B. Jan. 16, 1885, Chicago, Ill.   D. Apr. 13, 1945, Chicago, Ill.
BR TR 6'2"   205 lbs.

	G	AB	H	2B	3B	HR	HR%	R	RBI	BB	SO	SB	BA	SA	PH AB	PH H	G by POS
1911 STL A	26	101	26	6	2	3	3.0	12	15	2		2	.257	.446	0	0	1B-26
1912	67	205	42	9	3	1	0.5	18	18	13		0	.205	.293	15	2	1B-51, OF-1
2 yrs.	93	306	68	15	5	4	1.3	30	33	15		2	.222	.343	15	2	1B-77, OF-1

Al Kvasnak

KVASNAK, ALEXANDER
B. Jan. 11, 1921, Sagamore, Pa.
BR TR 6'1"   170 lbs.

	G	AB	H	2B	3B	HR	HR%	R	RBI	BB	SO	SB	BA	SA	PH AB	PH H	G by POS
1942 WAS A	5	11	2	0	0	0	0.0	3	0	2	1	0	.182	.182	2	1	OF-3

Cass Kwietniewski

Playing record listed under Cass Michaels

Andy Kyle

KYLE, ANDREW EWING
B. Oct. 29, 1889, Toronto, Ont., Canada   D. Sept. 6, 1971, Toronto, Ont., Canada
BL TL 5'8"   160 lbs.

	G	AB	H	2B	3B	HR	HR%	R	RBI	BB	SO	SB	BA	SA	PH AB	PH H	G by POS
1912 CIN N	9	21	7	1	0	0	0.0	3	4	4	2	0	.333	.381	2	0	OF-7

Chet Laabs

LAABS, CHESTER PETER
B. Apr. 30, 1912, Milwaukee, Wis.   D. Jan. 26, 1983, Warren, Mich.
BR TR 5'8"   175 lbs.

	G	AB	H	2B	3B	HR	HR%	R	RBI	BB	SO	SB	BA	SA	PH AB	PH H	G by POS
1937 DET A	72	242	58	13	5	8	3.3	31	37	24	66	6	.240	.434	9	2	OF-62
1938	64	211	50	7	3	7	3.3	26	37	15	52	3	.237	.398	11	3	OF-53
1939 2 teams		DET A (5G – .313)						STL A (95G – .300)									
" total	100	333	100	21	6	10	3.0	53	64	35	62	4	.300	.489	16	4	OF-84
1940 STL A	105	218	59	11	5	10	4.6	32	40	34	59	3	.271	.505	35	14	OF-63
1941	118	392	109	23	6	15	3.8	64	59	51	59	5	.278	.482	16	5	OF-100
1942	144	520	143	21	7	27	5.2	90	99	88	88	0	.275	.498	3	1	OF-139
1943	151	580	145	27	7	17	2.9	83	85	73	105	5	.250	.409	1	0	OF-150
1944	66	201	47	10	2	5	2.5	28	23	29	33	3	.234	.378	11	0	OF-55
1945	35	109	26	4	3	1	0.9	15	8	16	17	0	.239	.358	0	0	OF-35
1946	80	264	69	13	0	16	6.1	40	52	20	50	3	.261	.492	6	0	OF-72
1947 PHI A	15	32	7	1	0	1	3.1	5	5	4	4	0	.219	.344	7	1	OF-7
11 yrs.	950	3102	813	151	44	117	3.8	467	509	389	595	32	.262	.452	115	30	OF-820
WORLD SERIES																	
1944 STL A	5	15	3	1	1	0	0.0	1	0	2	6	0	.200	.400	1	0	OF-4

Coco Laboy

LABOY, JOSE ALBERTO
B. July 3, 1939, Ponce, Puerto Rico
BR TR 5'10"   165 lbs.

	G	AB	H	2B	3B	HR	HR%	R	RBI	BB	SO	SB	BA	SA	PH AB	PH H	G by POS
1969 MON N	157	562	145	29	1	18	3.2	53	83	40	96	0	.258	.409	1	0	3B-156
1970	137	432	86	26	1	5	1.2	37	53	31	81	0	.199	.299	7	0	3B-132, 2B-3
1971	76	151	38	4	0	1	0.7	10	14	11	19	0	.252	.298	15	5	3B-65, 2B-2
1972	28	69	18	2	0	3	4.3	6	14	10	16	0	.261	.420	2	0	3B-24, 2B-3, SS-2
1973	22	33	4	1	0	1	3.0	2	2	5	8	0	.121	.242	3	0	3B-20, OF-1, 2B-1
5 yrs.	420	1247	291	62	2	28	2.2	108	166	97	220	0	.233	.354	28	5	3B-397, 2B-9, SS-2, OF-1

Candy LaChance

LaCHANCE, GEORGE JOSEPH
B. Feb. 15, 1870, Waterbury, Conn.   D. Aug. 18, 1932, Waterbury, Conn.
BB TR 6'2"

	G	AB	H	2B	3B	HR	HR%	R	RBI	BB	SO	SB	BA	SA	PH AB	PH H	G by POS
1893 BKN N	11	35	6	1	0	0	0.0	1	6	2	12	0	.171	.200	0	0	C-6, OF-5
1894	68	257	83	13	8	5	1.9	48	52	16	32	20	.323	.494	0	0	1B-56, C-10, OF-3
1895	127	536	167	22	8	8	1.5	99	108	29	48	37	.312	.427	0	0	1B-125, OF-3
1896	89	348	99	10	13	7	2.0	60	58	23	32	17	.284	.448	0	0	1B-89
1897	126	520	160	28	16	4	0.8	86	90	15		26	.308	.446	0	0	1B-126
1898	136	526	130	23	7	5	1.0	62	65	31		23	.247	.346	1	0	1B-74, SS-48, OF-13
1899 BAL N	125	472	145	23	10	1	0.2	65	75	21		31	.307	.405	0	0	1B-125
1901 CLE A	133	548	166	22	9	1	0.2	81	75	7		11	.303	.381	0	0	1B-133
1902 BOS A	138	541	151	13	4	6	1.1	60	56	18		8	.279	.351	0	0	1B-138
1903	141	522	134	22	6	1	0.2	60	53	28		12	.257	.328	0	0	1B-141
1904	157	573	130	19	5	1	0.2	55	47	23		7	.227	.283	0	0	1B-157
1905	12	41	6	1	0	0	0.0	1	5	6		0	.146	.171	0	0	1B-12
12 yrs.	1263	4919	1377	197	86	39	0.8	678	690	219	124	192	.280	.379	1	0	1B-1176, SS-48, OF-24, C-16
WORLD SERIES																	
1903 BOS A	8	27	6	2	1	0	0.0	5	4	3	2	0	.222	.370	0	0	1B-8

Rene Lachemann

LACHEMANN, RENE GEORGE
Brother of Marcel Lachemann.
B. May 4, 1945, Los Angeles, Calif.
Manager 1981-84.
BR TR 6'   198 lbs.

	G	AB	H	2B	3B	HR	HR%	R	RBI	BB	SO	SB	BA	SA	PH AB	PH H	G by POS
1965 KC A	92	216	49	7	1	9	4.2	20	29	12	57	0	.227	.394	23	4	C-75
1966	7	5	1	1	0	0	0.0	0	0	0	1	0	.200	.400	1	0	C-6
1968 OAK A	19	60	9	1	0	0	0.0	3	4	1	11	0	.150	.167	4	0	C-16
3 yrs.	118	281	59	9	1	9	3.2	23	33	13	69	0	.210	.345	28	4	C-97

Pete LaCock

LaCOCK, RALPH PIERRE II
B. Jan. 17, 1952, Burbank, Calif.
BL TL 6'2"   200 lbs.

	G	AB	H	2B	3B	HR	HR%	R	RBI	BB	SO	SB	BA	SA	PH AB	PH H	G by POS
1972 CHI N	5	6	3	0	0	0	0.0	3	4	0	1	1	.500	.500	1	1	OF-3
1973	11	16	4	1	0	0	0.0	1	3	1	2	0	.250	.313	7	0	OF-5
1974	35	110	20	4	1	1	0.9	9	8	12	16	0	.182	.264	4	1	OF-22, 1B-11
1975	106	249	57	8	1	6	2.4	30	30	37	27	0	.229	.341	26	9	1B-53, OF-26
1976	106	244	54	9	2	8	3.3	34	28	42	37	1	.221	.373	39	7	1B-54, OF-19
1977 KC A	88	218	66	12	1	3	1.4	25	29	15	25	2	.303	.408	22	8	1B-29, DH-26, OF-12
1978	118	322	95	21	2	5	1.6	44	48	21	27	1	.295	.419	23	3	1B-106

	G	AB	H	2B	3B	HR	HR %	R	RBI	BB	SO	SB	BA	SA	Pinch Hit AB	Pinch Hit H	G by POS

Pete LaCock continued

	G	AB	H	2B	3B	HR	HR%	R	RBI	BB	SO	SB	BA	SA	PH AB	PH H	G by POS
1979	132	408	113	25	4	3	0.7	54	56	37	26	2	.277	.380	18	3	1B-108, DH-16
1980	114	156	32	6	0	1	0.6	14	18	17	10	1	.205	.263	12	5	1B-86, OF-29
9 yrs.	715	1729	444	86	11	27	1.6	214	224	182	171	8	.257	.366	152	40	1B-447, OF-116, DH-42

LEAGUE CHAMPIONSHIP SERIES

	G	AB	H	2B	3B	HR	HR%	R	RBI	BB	SO	SB	BA	SA	PH AB	PH H	G by POS
1977 KC A	1	1	0	0	0	0	0.0	0	0	1	1	1	.000	.000	1	0	1B-1
1978	4	11	4	2	1	0	0.0	1	1	3	1	1	.364	.727	1	0	1B-3
1980	1	0	0	0	0	0	–	0	0	0	0	0	–	–	0	0	1B-1
3 yrs.	6	12	4	2	1	0	0.0	1	1	4	2	1	.333	.667	2	0	1B-5

WORLD SERIES

	G	AB	H	2B	3B	HR	HR%	R	RBI	BB	SO	SB	BA	SA	PH AB	PH H	G by POS
1980 KC A	1	0	0	0	0	0	–	0	0	0	0	0	–	–	0	0	1B-1

Guy Lacy

LACY, OSCEOLA GUY
B. June 12, 1897, Cleveland, Tenn.   D. Nov. 19, 1953, Cleveland, Tenn.   BL TR 5'11½" 170 lbs.

	G	AB	H	2B	3B	HR	HR%	R	RBI	BB	SO	SB	BA	SA	PH AB	PH H	G by POS
1926 CLE A	13	24	4	0	0	1	4.2	2	2	2	2	0	.167	.292	0	0	2B-11, 3B-2

Lee Lacy

LACY, LEONDAUS
B. Apr. 10, 1948, Longview, Tex.   BR TR 6'1" 175 lbs.

	G	AB	H	2B	3B	HR	HR%	R	RBI	BB	SO	SB	BA	SA	PH AB	PH H	G by POS
1972 LA N	60	243	63	7	3	0	0.0	34	12	19	37	5	.259	.313	2	1	2B-58
1973	57	135	28	2	0	0	0.0	14	8	15	34	2	.207	.222	13	1	2B-41
1974	48	78	22	6	0	0	0.0	13	8	2	14	2	.282	.359	11	3	2B-34, 3B-1
1975	101	306	96	11	5	7	2.3	44	40	22	29	5	.314	.451	21	4	OF-43, 2B-43, SS-1
1976 2 teams		ATL N (50G – .272)				LA N (53G – .266)											
" total	103	338	91	11	3	3	0.9	42	34	22	25	3	.269	.346	17	5	2B-46, OF-42, 3B-4
1977 LA N	75	169	45	7	0	6	3.6	28	21	10	21	4	.266	.414	24	6	OF-32, 2B-22, 3B-12
1978	103	245	64	16	4	13	5.3	29	40	27	30	7	.261	.518	34	13	OF-44, 2B-24, 3B-9, SS-1
1979 PIT N	84	182	45	9	3	5	2.7	17	15	22	36	6	.247	.412	33	6	OF-41, 2B-5
1980	109	278	93	20	4	7	2.5	45	33	28	33	18	.335	.511	16	5	OF-88, 3B-3
1981	78	213	57	11	4	2	0.9	31	10	11	29	24	.268	.385	13	3	OF-63, 3B-1
1982	121	359	112	16	3	5	1.4	66	31	32	57	40	.312	.415	13	3	OF-113, 3B-2
1983	108	288	87	12	3	4	1.4	40	13	22	36	31	.302	.406	20	6	OF-98
1984	138	474	152	26	3	12	2.5	66	70	32	61	21	.321	.464	8	0	OF-127, 2B-2
13 yrs.	1185	3308	955	154	35	64	1.9	469	335	264	442	168	.289	.414	225	56	OF-691, 2B-275, 3B-32, SS-2

LEAGUE CHAMPIONSHIP SERIES

	G	AB	H	2B	3B	HR	HR%	R	RBI	BB	SO	SB	BA	SA	PH AB	PH H	G by POS
1974 LA N	1	0	0	0	0	0	–	0	0	0	0	0	–	–	0	0	
1977	1	1	1	0	0	0	0.0	1	0	0	0	0	1.000	1.000	1	1	
1978	2	2	0	0	0	0	0.0	0	0	0	0	0	.000	.000	2	0	
3 yrs.	4	3	1	0	0	0	0.0	1	0	0	0	0	.333	.333	3	1	

WORLD SERIES

	G	AB	H	2B	3B	HR	HR%	R	RBI	BB	SO	SB	BA	SA	PH AB	PH H	G by POS
1974 LA N	1	1	0	0	0	0	0.0	0	0	0	1	0	.000	.000	1	0	
1977	4	7	3	0	0	0	0.0	1	2	1	1	0	.429	.429	2	1	OF-2
1978	4	14	2	0	0	0	0.0	0	1	1	3	0	.143	.143	0	0	DH-4
1979 PIT N	4	4	1	0	0	0	0.0	0	0	0	1	0	.250	.250	4	1	
4 yrs.	13	26	6	0	0	0	0.0	1	3	2	6	0	.231	.231	7 (6th)	2	DH-4, OF-2

Hi Ladd

LADD, ARTHUR CLIFFORD HIRAM
B. Feb. 9, 1870, Willimantic, Conn.   D. May 7, 1948, Cranston, R. I.   BL TR 6'4" 180 lbs.

	G	AB	H	2B	3B	HR	HR%	R	RBI	BB	SO	SB	BA	SA	PH AB	PH H	G by POS
1898 2 teams		PIT N (1G – .000)				BOS N (1G – .250)											
" total	2	5	1	0	0	0	0.0	1	0	0		0	.200	.200	1	0	OF-1

Steve Ladew

LADEW, STEPHEN
B. St. Louis, Mo.   Deceased.

	G	AB	H	2B	3B	HR	HR%	R	RBI	BB	SO	SB	BA	SA	PH AB	PH H	G by POS
1889 KC AA	2	4	0	0	0	0	0.0	0	0		3	0	.000	.000	0	0	OF-1, P-1

Joe Lafata

LAFATA, JOSEPH JOSEPH
B. Aug. 3, 1921, Detroit, Mich.   BL TL 6' 163 lbs.

	G	AB	H	2B	3B	HR	HR%	R	RBI	BB	SO	SB	BA	SA	PH AB	PH H	G by POS
1947 NY N	62	95	21	1	0	2	2.1	13	18	15	18	1	.221	.295	31	6	OF-19, 1B-2
1948	1	1	0	0	0	0	0.0	0	0	0	1	0	.000	.000	1	0	
1949	64	140	33	2	2	3	2.1	18	16	9	23	1	.236	.343	14	6	1B-47
3 yrs.	127	236	54	3	2	5	2.1	31	34	24	42	2	.229	.322	46	12	1B-49, OF-19

Flip Lafferty

LAFFERTY, FRANK BERNARD
B. May 4, 1854, Scranton, Pa.   D. Feb. 8, 1910, Wilmington, Del.   TR

	G	AB	H	2B	3B	HR	HR%	R	RBI	BB	SO	SB	BA	SA	PH AB	PH H	G by POS
1876 PHI N	1	3	0	0	0	0	0.0	0	0	0	0		.000	.000	0	0	P-1
1877 LOU N	4	17	1	1	0	0	0.0	2	0	0	4		.059	.118	0	0	OF-4
2 yrs.	5	20	1	1	0	0	0.0	2	0	0	4		.050	.100	0	0	OF-4, P-1

Ty LaForest

LaFOREST, BYRON JOSEPH
B. Apr. 18, 1919, Edmondston, N. B., Canada   D. May 5, 1947, Arlington, Mass.   BR TR 5'8" 160 lbs.

	G	AB	H	2B	3B	HR	HR%	R	RBI	BB	SO	SB	BA	SA	PH AB	PH H	G by POS
1945 BOS A	52	204	51	7	4	2	1.0	25	16	10	35	4	.250	.353	0	0	3B-45, OF-5

Roger LaFrancois

LaFRANCOIS, ROGER VICTOR
B. Aug. 2, 1954, Norwich, Conn.   BL TR 6'2" 202 lbs.

	G	AB	H	2B	3B	HR	HR%	R	RBI	BB	SO	SB	BA	SA	PH AB	PH H	G by POS
1982 BOS A	8	10	4	1	0	0	0.0	1	1	0	0	0	.400	.500	2	1	C-8

Mike Laga

LAGA, MICHAEL RUSSELL
B. June 4, 1960, Ridgewood, N. J.   BL TL 6'3" 198 lbs.

	G	AB	H	2B	3B	HR	HR%	R	RBI	BB	SO	SB	BA	SA	PH AB	PH H	G by POS
1982 DET A	27	88	23	9	0	3	3.4	6	11	4	23	1	.261	.466	4	1	1B-19, DH-8
1983	12	21	4	0	0	0	0.0	2	2	1	9	0	.190	.190	3	1	DH-6, 1B-5
1984	9	11	6	0	0	0	0.0	1	1	1	2	0	.545	.545	3	3	DH-4, 1B-4
3 yrs.	48	120	33	9	0	3	2.5	9	14	6	34	1	.275	.425	10	5	1B-28, DH-18

	G	AB	H	2B	3B	HR	HR%	R	RBI	BB	SO	SB	BA	SA	Pinch Hit AB	Pinch Hit H	G by POS

Joe Lahoud

LAHOUD, JOSEPH MICHAEL (Duck)
B. Apr. 14, 1947, Danbury, Conn.   BL TL 6'1" 198 lbs.

Year/Team	G	AB	H	2B	3B	HR	HR%	R	RBI	BB	SO	SB	BA	SA	PH AB	PH H	G by POS
1968 BOS A	29	78	15	1	0	1	1.3	5	6	16	16	0	.192	.244	6	2	OF-25
1969	101	218	41	5	0	9	4.1	32	21	40	43	2	.188	.335	25	2	OF-66, 1B-1
1970	17	49	12	1	0	2	4.1	6	5	7	6	0	.245	.388	4	2	OF-13
1971	107	256	55	9	3	14	5.5	39	32	40	45	2	.215	.438	29	8	OF-69
1972 MIL A	111	316	75	9	3	12	3.8	35	34	45	54	3	.237	.399	11	4	OF-97
1973	96	225	46	9	0	5	2.2	29	26	27	36	5	.204	.311	15	4	DH-41, OF-40
1974 CAL A	127	325	88	16	3	13	4.0	46	44	47	57	4	.271	.458	14	4	OF-106, DH-10
1975	76	192	41	6	2	6	3.1	21	33	48	33	2	.214	.359	9	2	DH-35, OF-29
1976 2 teams	CAL A (42G – .177)					TEX A (38G – .225)											
" total	80	185	37	7	1	1	0.5	18	9	28	32	1	.200	.265	21	3	DH-50, OF-31
1977 KC A	34	65	17	5	0	2	3.1	8	8	11	16	1	.262	.431	12	3	OF-15, DH-4
1978	13	16	2	0	0	0	0.0	0	0	0	1	0	.125	.125	12	2	DH-1, OF-1
11 yrs.	791	1925	429	68	12	65	3.4	239	218	309	339	20	.223	.372	158	36	OF-492, DH-141, 1B-1

LEAGUE CHAMPIONSHIP SERIES

1977 KC A	1	1	0	0	0	0	0.0	2	0	2	0	0	.000	.000	0	0	DH-1

Dick Lajeskie

LAJESKIE, RICHARD EDWARD
B. Jan. 8, 1926, Passaic, N. J.   D. Aug. 15, 1976, Ramsey, N. J.   BR TR 5'11" 175 lbs.

1946 NY N	6	10	2	0	0	0	0.0	3	0	3	2	0	.200	.200	0	0	2B-4

Nap Lajoie

LAJOIE, NAPOLEON (Larry)
B. Sept. 5, 1875, Woonsocket, R. I.   D. Feb. 7, 1959, Daytona Beach, Fla.   BR TR 6'1" 195 lbs.
Manager 1905-09.
Hall of Fame 1937.

Year/Team	G	AB	H	2B	3B	HR	HR%	R	RBI	BB	SO	SB	BA	SA	PH AB	PH H	G by POS
1896 PHI N	39	174	57	11	6	4	2.3	37	42	1	11	6	.328	.529	0	0	1B-39
1897	126	545	198	37	25	10	1.8	107	127	15		22	.363	.578	0	0	1B-108, OF-19, 3B-2
1898	147	610	200	40	10	5	0.8	113	127	21		33	.328	.451	0	0	2B-146, 1B-1
1899	72	308	117	17	11	5	1.6	70	70	12		14	.380	.555	4	2	2B-67, OF-5
1900	102	451	156	32	12	7	1.6	95	92	10		25	.346	.517	0	0	2B-102, 3B-1
1901 PHI A	131	543	229	48	13	14	2.6	145	125	24		27	.422	.635	0	0	2B-119, SS-12
1902 2 teams	PHI A (1G – .250)					CLE A (86G – .368)											
" total	87	352	129	34	5	7	2.0	81	65	19		19	.366	.551	0	0	2B-87
1903 CLE A	126	488	173	40	13	7	1.4	90	93	24		22	.355	.533	1	0	2B-123, 3B-1, 1B-1
1904	140	554	211	50	14	6	1.1	92	102	27		31	.381	.554	0	0	2B-95, SS-44, 1B-2
1905	65	249	82	13	2	2	0.8	29	41	17		11	.329	.422	1	0	2B-59, 1B-5
1906	152	602	214	49	7	0	0.0	88	91	30		20	.355	.460	0	0	2B-130, 3B-15, SS-7
1907	137	509	152	30	6	2	0.4	53	63	30		24	.299	.393	0	0	2B-128, 1B-9
1908	157	581	168	32	6	2	0.3	77	74	47		15	.289	.375	0	0	2B-156, 1B-1
1909	128	469	152	33	7	1	0.2	56	47	35		13	.324	.431	0	0	2B-120, 1B-8
1910	159	591	227	51	7	4	0.7	92	76	60		26	.384	.514	0	0	2B-149, 1B-10, SS-4
1911	90	315	115	20	1	2	0.6	36	60	26		13	.365	.454	9	4	1B-41, 2B-37
1912	117	448	165	34	4	0	0.0	66	90	28		18	.368	.462	0	0	2B-97, 1B-20
1913	137	465	156	25	2	1	0.2	67	68	33	17	17	.335	.404	9	2	2B-126
1914	121	419	108	14	3	0	0.0	37	50	32	15	14	.258	.305	9	1	2B-80, 1B-31
1915 PHI A	129	490	137	24	5	1	0.2	40	61	11	16	10	.280	.355	1	0	2B-110, SS-10, 1B-5, 3B-2
1916	113	426	105	14	4	2	0.5	33	35	14	26	15	.246	.312	1	0	2B-105, 1B-5, OF-2
21 yrs.	2475	9589	3251 (10th)	648	163	82	0.9	1504	1599	516	85	395	.339	.466	35	9	2B-2036, 1B-286, SS-77, OF-26, 3B-21

(6th under H)

Eddie Lake

LAKE, EDWARD ERVING
B. Mar. 18, 1916, Antioch, Calif.   BR TR 5'7" 159 lbs.

Year/Team	G	AB	H	2B	3B	HR	HR%	R	RBI	BB	SO	SB	BA	SA	PH AB	PH H	G by POS
1939 STL N	2	4	1	0	0	0	0.0	0	0	1	0	0	.250	.250	0	0	SS-2
1940	32	66	14	3	0	2	3.0	12	7	12	17	1	.212	.348	5	0	2B-17, SS-6
1941	45	76	8	2	0	0	0.0	9	0	15	22	3	.105	.132	6	1	SS-15, 3B-15, 2B-5
1943 BOS A	75	216	43	10	0	3	1.4	26	16	47	35	3	.199	.287	2	0	SS-63
1944	57	126	26	5	0	0	0.0	21	8	23	22	5	.206	.246	1	0	SS-41, P-6, 2B-3, 3B-1
1945	133	473	132	27	1	11	2.3	81	51	106	37	9	.279	.410	1	0	SS-130, 2B-1
1946 DET A	155	587	149	24	1	8	1.4	105	31	103	69	15	.254	.339	0	0	SS-155
1947	158	602	127	19	6	12	2.0	96	46	120	54	11	.211	.322	0	0	SS-158
1948	64	198	52	6	0	2	1.0	51	18	57	20	3	.263	.323	0	0	SS-45, 3B-17
1949	94	240	47	9	1	1	0.4	38	15	61	33	2	.196	.254	12	2	SS-38, 2B-19, 3B-18
1950	20	7	0	0	0	0	0.0	3	1	1	3	0	.000	.000	7	0	SS-1, 3B-1
11 yrs.	835	2595	599	105	9	39	1.5	442	193	546	312	52	.231	.323	34	3	SS-609, 2B-90, 3B-52, P-6

Fred Lake

LAKE, FREDERICK LOVETT
B. Oct. 16, 1866, Nova Scotia, Canada   D. Nov. 24, 1931, Boston, Mass.   BR TR
Manager 1908-10.

Year/Team	G	AB	H	2B	3B	HR	HR%	R	RBI	BB	SO	SB	BA	SA	PH AB	PH H	G by POS
1891 BOS N	5	7	1	0	0	0	0.0	1	0	2	4	0	.143	.143	0	0	C-4, OF-1
1894 LOU N	16	42	12	2	0	1	2.4	8	10	11	6	2	.286	.405	0	0	2B-6, SS-5, C-5
1897 BOS N	19	62	15	4	0	0	0.0	2	5	1		2	.242	.306	1	0	C-18
1898 PIT N	5	13	1	0	0	0	0.0	1	1	2		0	.077	.077	1	0	1B-3
1910 BOS N	3	1	0	0	0	0	0.0	0	0	1	0	0	.000	.000	1	0	1B-1
5 yrs.	48	125	29	6	0	1	0.8	12	16	17	10	4	.232	.304	3	0	C-27, 2B-6, SS-5, 1B-3, OF-1

Steve Lake

LAKE, STEVEN MICHAEL
B. Mar. 14, 1957, Inglewood, Calif.   BR TR 6'1" 180 lbs.

Year/Team	G	AB	H	2B	3B	HR	HR%	R	RBI	BB	SO	SB	BA	SA	PH AB	PH H	G by POS
1983 CHI N	38	85	22	4	1	1	1.2	9	7	2	6	0	.259	.365	5	0	C-32
1984	25	54	12	4	0	2	3.7	4	7	0	7	0	.222	.407	1	0	C-24
2 yrs.	63	139	34	8	1	3	2.2	13	14	2	13	0	.245	.381	6	0	C-56

LEAGUE CHAMPIONSHIP SERIES

1984 CHI N	1	1	1	1	0	0	0.0	0	0	0	0	0	1.000	2.000	0	0	C-1

	G	AB	H	2B	3B	HR	HR %	R	RBI	BB	SO	SB	BA	SA	Pinch Hit AB	Pinch Hit H	G by POS

Al Lakeman

LAKEMAN, ALBERT WESLEY (Moose)   BR TR 6'2"   195 lbs.
B. Dec. 31, 1918, Cincinnati, Ohio   D. May 25, 1976, Spartanburg, S. C.

	G	AB	H	2B	3B	HR	HR %	R	RBI	BB	SO	SB	BA	SA	PH AB	PH H	G by POS
1942 CIN N	20	38	6	1	0	0	0.0	0	2	3	10	0	.158	.184	2	0	C-17
1943	22	55	14	2	1	0	0.0	5	6	3	11	0	.255	.327	1	0	C-21
1944	1	1	0	0	0	0	0.0	0	0	0	1	0	.000	.000	1	0	
1945	76	258	66	9	4	8	3.1	22	31	17	45	0	.256	.415	2	1	C-74
1946	23	30	4	0	0	0	0.0	0	4	2	7	0	.133	.133	16	1	C-6
1947 2 teams	CIN	N (2G – .000)		PHI	N	(55G –	.159)										
" total	57	184	29	3	0	6	3.3	11	19	5	40	0	.158	.272	5	0	1B-29, C-23
1948 PHI N	32	68	11	2	0	1	1.5	2	4	5	22	0	.162	.235	9	1	C-22, P-1
1949 BOS N	3	6	1	0	0	0	0.0	0	0	1	0	0	.167	.167	1	0	1B-2
1954 DET A	5	6	0	0	0	0	0.0	0	0	0	1	0	.000	.000	1	0	C-4
9 yrs.	239	646	131	17	5	15	2.3	40	66	36	137	0	.203	.314	38	3	C-167, 1B-31, P-1

Bud Lally

LALLY, DANIEL J.   BR TR 5'11½" 210 lbs.
B. Aug. 12, 1867, Jersey City, N. J.   D. Apr. 14, 1936, Milwaukee, Wis.

	G	AB	H	2B	3B	HR	HR %	R	RBI	BB	SO	SB	BA	SA	PH AB	PH H	G by POS
1891 PIT N	41	143	32	6	2	1	0.7	24	17	16	20	0	.224	.315	0	0	OF-41
1897 STL N	87	355	99	15	5	2	0.6	56	42	9		12	.279	.366	0	0	OF-84, 1B-3
2 yrs.	128	498	131	21	7	3	0.6	80	59	25	20	12	.263	.351	0	0	OF-125, 1B-3

Ray Lamanno

LAMANNO, RAYMOND SIMOND   BR TR 6'   185 lbs.
B. Nov. 17, 1919, Oakland, Calif.

	G	AB	H	2B	3B	HR	HR %	R	RBI	BB	SO	SB	BA	SA	PH AB	PH H	G by POS
1941 CIN N	1	0	0	0	0	0	–	0	0	0	0	0	–	–	0	0	C-1
1942	111	371	98	12	2	12	3.2	40	43	31	54	0	.264	.404	7	1	C-104
1946	85	239	58	12	0	1	0.4	18	30	11	26	0	.243	.305	21	4	C-61
1947	118	413	106	21	3	5	1.2	33	50	28	39	0	.257	.358	9	2	C-109
1948	127	385	93	12	0	0	0.0	31	27	48	32	2	.242	.273	3	0	C-125
5 yrs.	442	1408	355	57	5	18	1.3	122	150	118	151	2	.252	.338	40	7	C-400

Bill Lamar

LAMAR, WILLIAM HARMONG (Good Time Bill)   BL TR 6'1" 185 lbs.
B. Mar. 21, 1897, Rockville, Md.   BB 1927
D. May 24, 1970, Rockport, Mass.

	G	AB	H	2B	3B	HR	HR %	R	RBI	BB	SO	SB	BA	SA	PH AB	PH H	G by POS
1917 NY A	11	41	10	0	0	0	0.0	2	3	0	2	1	.244	.244	0	0	OF-11
1918	28	110	25	3	0	0	0.0	12	2	6	2	2	.227	.255	1	1	OF-27
1919 2 teams	59	NY	A (11G –	.188)		BOS	A	(48G –	.291)								
" total	59	164	46	6	1	0	0.0	19	14	7	10	4	.280	.329	19	3	OF-39, 1B-1
1920 BKN N	24	44	12	4	0	0	0.0	5	4	0	1	0	.273	.364	10	3	OF-12
1921	3	3	1	0	0	0	0.0	2	0	0	0	0	.333	.333	2	1	OF-1
1924 PHI A	87	367	121	22	5	7	1.9	68	48	18	21	8	.330	.474	0	0	OF-87
1925	138	568	202	39	8	3	0.5	85	77	21	17	2	.356	.468	6	1	OF-131
1926	116	419	119	17	6	5	1.2	62	50	18	15	4	.284	.389	8	3	OF-105
1927	84	324	97	23	3	4	1.2	48	47	16	10	4	.299	.426	5	1	OF-79
9 yrs.	550	2040	633	114	23	19	0.9	303	245	86	78	25	.310	.417	51	13	OF-492, 1B-1

WORLD SERIES

	G	AB	H	2B	3B	HR	HR %	R	RBI	BB	SO	SB	BA	SA	PH AB	PH H	G by POS
1920 BKN N	3	3	0	0	0	0	0.0	0	0	0	0	0	.000	.000	3	0	

Lyman Lamb

LAMB, LYMAN RAYMOND   BR TR 5'7"   150 lbs.
B. Mar. 17, 1895, Lincoln, Neb.   D. Oct. 5, 1955, Fayetteville, Ark.

	G	AB	H	2B	3B	HR	HR %	R	RBI	BB	SO	SB	BA	SA	PH AB	PH H	G by POS
1920 STL A	9	24	9	2	0	0	0.0	4	4	0	7	2	.375	.458	2	1	OF-7
1921	45	134	34	9	2	1	0.7	18	17	4	12	0	.254	.373	5	1	3B-23, 2B-7, OF-6
2 yrs.	54	158	43	11	2	1	0.6	22	21	4	19	2	.272	.386	7	2	3B-23, OF-13, 2B-7

Pete Lamer

LAMER, PIERRE   TR
B. 1874, Hoboken, N. J.   D. Oct. 24, 1931, Brooklyn, N. Y.

	G	AB	H	2B	3B	HR	HR %	R	RBI	BB	SO	SB	BA	SA	PH AB	PH H	G by POS
1902 CHI N	2	9	2	0	0	0	0.0	2	0	0		0	.222	.222	0	0	C-2
1907 CIN N	1	2	0	0	0	0	0.0	0	0	0		0	.000	.000	0	0	C-1
2 yrs.	3	11	2	0	0	0	0.0	2	0	0		0	.182	.182	0	0	C-3

Gene Lamont

LAMONT, GENE WILLIAM   BL TR 6'1" 195 lbs.
B. Dec. 25, 1946, Rockford, Ill.

	G	AB	H	2B	3B	HR	HR %	R	RBI	BB	SO	SB	BA	SA	PH AB	PH H	G by POS
1970 DET A	15	44	13	3	1	1	2.3	3	4	2	9	0	.295	.477	0	0	C-15
1971	7	15	1	0	0	0	0.0	2	1	0	5	0	.067	.067	0	0	C-7
1972	1	0	0	0	0	0	–	0	0	0	0	0	–	–	0	0	C-1
1974	60	92	20	4	0	3	3.3	9	8	7	19	0	.217	.359	0	0	C-60
1975	4	8	3	1	0	0	0.0	1	1	0	2	0	.375	.500	0	0	C-4
5 yrs.	87	159	37	8	1	4	2.5	15	14	9	35	1	.233	.371	0	0	C-87

Bobby LaMotte

LaMOTTE, ROBERT EUGENE   BR TR 5'11" 160 lbs.
B. Feb. 15, 1898, Savannah, Ga.   D. Nov. 2, 1970, Chatham, Ga.

	G	AB	H	2B	3B	HR	HR %	R	RBI	BB	SO	SB	BA	SA	PH AB	PH H	G by POS
1920 WAS A	4	3	0	0	0	0	0.0	0	0	1	1	0	.000	.000	0	0	SS-1, 3B-1
1921	16	41	8	0	0	0	0.0	5	2	5	0	0	.195	.195	0	0	SS-12
1922	68	214	54	10	2	1	0.5	22	23	15	21	6	.252	.332	0	0	3B-62, SS-6
1925 STL A	97	356	97	20	4	2	0.6	61	51	34	22	5	.272	.368	2	0	SS-93, 3B-3
1926	36	79	16	4	3	0	0.0	11	9	11	6	0	.203	.329	4	0	SS-30, 3B-1
5 yrs.	221	693	175	34	9	3	0.4	99	85	66	50	11	.253	.341	6	0	SS-142, 3B-67

Keith Lampard

LAMPARD, CHRISTOPHER KEITH   BL TR 6'2" 197 lbs.
B. Dec. 20, 1945, Warrington, England

	G	AB	H	2B	3B	HR	HR %	R	RBI	BB	SO	SB	BA	SA	PH AB	PH H	G by POS
1969 HOU N	9	12	3	0	0	1	8.3	2	2	0	3	0	.250	.500	7	3	OF-1
1970	53	72	17	8	1	0	0.0	8	5	5	24	0	.236	.375	38	9	OF-16, 1B-2
2 yrs.	62	84	20	8	1	1	1.2	10	7	5	27	0	.238	.393	45	12	OF-17, 1B-2

Rick Lancellotti

LANCELLOTTI, RICHARD ANTHONY   BL TL 6'3" 195 lbs.
B. July 5, 1956, Providence, R. I.

	G	AB	H	2B	3B	HR	HR %	R	RBI	BB	SO	SB	BA	SA	PH AB	PH H	G by POS
1982 SD N	17	39	7	2	0	0	0.0	2	4	2	8	0	.179	.231	8	1	1B-7, OF-3

	G	AB	H	2B	3B	HR	HR %	R	RBI	BB	SO	SB	BA	SA	Pinch Hit AB	H	G by POS

Doc Land
LAND, WILLIAM GILBERT   BL TL 5'11" 165 lbs.
B. May 14, 1903, Binnsville, Mass.

| 1929 WAS A | 1 | 3 | 0 | 0 | 0 | 0 | 0.0 | 0 | 0 | 1 | 0 | 0 | .000 | .000 | 0 | 0 | OF-1 |

Grover Land
LAND, GROVER CLEVELAND   BR TR 6' 190 lbs.
B. Sept. 22, 1884, Frankfort, Ky.   D. July 22, 1958, Phoenix, Ariz.

1908 CLE A	8	16	3	0	0	0	0.0		2	0			0	.188	.188	0	0	C-8
1910	34	111	23	0	0	0	0.0	4	7	2			1	.207	.207	0	0	C-33
1911	35	107	15	1	2	0	0.0	5	10	3			2	.140	.187	0	0	C-34, 1B-1
1913	17	47	11	1	0	0	0.0	3	9	4		1	1	.234	.255	1	1	C-17
1914 BKN F	102	335	92	6	2	0	0.0	24	29	12			7	.275	.304	5	1	C-97
1915	96	290	75	13	2	0	0.0	25	22	6			3	.259	.317	14	3	C-81
6 yrs.	292	906	219	21	6	0	0.0	62	79	27		1	14	.242	.278	20	5	C-270, 1B-1

Ken Landenberger
LANDENBERGER, KENNETH HENRY (Red)   BL TL 6'3" 200 lbs.
B. July 29, 1928, Lyndhurst, Ohio   D. July 28, 1960, Cleveland, Ohio

| 1952 CHI A | 2 | 5 | 1 | 0 | 0 | 0 | 0.0 | 0 | 0 | 2 | 2 | 0 | .200 | .200 | 1 | 0 | 1B-1 |

Rafael Landestoy
LANDESTOY, RAFAEL SILVIALDO   BR TR 5'10" 165 lbs.
Also known as Rafael Silvialdo Santana.
B. May 28, 1953, Bani, Dominican Republic

1977 LA N	15	18	5	0	0	0	0.0	6	0	3	2	2	.278	.278	0	0	2B-8, SS-3
1978 HOU N	59	218	58	5	1	0	0.0	18	9	8	23	7	.266	.298	9	1	SS-50, 2B-2
1979	129	282	76	9	6	0	0.0	33	30	29	24	13	.270	.344	14	2	2B-114, SS-3
1980	149	393	97	13	8	1	0.3	42	27	31	37	23	.247	.328	26	3	2B-94, SS-65, 3B-3
1981 2 teams	HOU	N	(35G – .149)		CIN	N	(12G – .182)										
" total	47	85	13	1	1	0	0.0	8	5	17	9	5	.153	.188	10	1	2B-34
1982 CIN N	73	111	21	3		0	1	0.9	11	9	8	14	2	.189	.243	35	11	3B-21, 2B-16, OF-3, SS-2
1983 2 teams	CIN	N	(7G – .000)		LA	N	(64G – .172)										
" total	71	69	11	1	1	1	1.4	6	1	3	8	0	.159	.246	33	4	2B-14, OF-11, 3B-11, 1B-2, SS-1
1984 LA N	53	54	10	0	0	1	1.9	10	2	1	6	2	.185	.241	18	3	2B-14, 3B-11, OF-5
8 yrs.	596	1230	291	32	17	4	0.3	134	83	100	123	54	.237	.300	145	25	2B-296, SS-124, 3B-46, OF-19, 1B-2

LEAGUE CHAMPIONSHIP SERIES
1980 HOU N	5	9	2	0	0	0	0.0	3	2	1	0	1	.222	.222	0	0	2B-3
1983 LA N	2	2	0	0	0	0	0.0	0	0	0	1	0	.000	.000	2	0	
2 yrs.	7	11	2	0	0	0	0.0	3	2	1	1	1	.182	.182	2	0	2B-3

WORLD SERIES
| 1977 LA N | 1 | 0 | 0 | 0 | 0 | 0 | – | 0 | 0 | 0 | 0 | 0 | – | – | 0 | 0 | |

Jim Landis
LANDIS, JAMES HENRY   BR TR 6'1" 180 lbs.
B. Mar. 9, 1934, Fresno, Calif.

1957 CHI A	96	274	58	11	3	2	0.7	38	16	45	61	14	.212	.296	4	1	OF-90
1958	142	523	145	23	7	15	2.9	72	64	52	80	19	.277	.434	1	0	OF-142
1959	149	515	140	26	7	5	1.0	78	60	78	68	20	.272	.379	0	0	OF-148
1960	148	494	125	25	6	10	2.0	89	49	80	84	23	.253	.389	1	0	OF-147
1961	140	534	151	18	8	22	4.1	87	85	65	71	19	.283	.470	2	0	OF-139
1962	149	534	122	21	6	15	2.8	82	61	80	105	19	.228	.375	4	1	OF-144
1963	133	396	89	6	6	13	3.3	56	45	47	75	8	.225	.369	11	3	OF-124
1964	106	298	62	8	4	1	0.3	30	18	36	64	5	.208	.272	7	1	OF-101
1965 KC A	118	364	87	15	1	3	0.8	46	36	57	84	8	.239	.310	13	3	OF-108
1966 CLE A	85	158	35	5	1	3	1.9	23	14	20	25	2	.222	.323	22	4	OF-61
1967 3 teams	HOU	N	(50G – .252)		DET	A	(25G – .208)			BOS	A	(5G – .143)					
" total	80	198	47	11	1	4	2.0	24	19	28	50	2	.237	.364	16	1	OF-61
11 yrs.	1346	4288	1061	169	50	93	2.2	625	467	588	767	139	.247	.375	80	14	OF-1265

WORLD SERIES
| 1959 CHI A | 6 | 24 | 7 | 0 | 0 | 0 | 0.0 | 6 | 1 | 1 | 7 | 1 | .292 | .292 | 0 | 0 | OF-6 |

Ken Landreaux
LANDREAUX, KENNETH FRANCIS   BL TR 5'10" 165 lbs.
B. Dec. 22, 1954, Los Angeles, Calif.

1977 CAL A	23	76	19	5	1	0	0.0	6	5	5	15	1	.250	.342	0	0	OF-22
1978	93	260	58	7	5	5	1.9	37	23	20	20	7	.223	.346	7	2	OF-83, DH-1
1979 MIN A	151	564	172	27	5	15	2.7	81	83	37	57	10	.305	.450	7	1	OF-147
1980	129	484	136	23	11	7	1.4	56	62	39	42	8	.281	.417	3	2	OF-120, DH-6
1981 LA N	99	390	98	16	4	7	1.8	48	41	25	42	18	.251	.367	4	1	OF-95
1982	129	461	131	23	7	7	1.5	71	50	39	54	31	.284	.410	11	4	OF-117
1983	141	481	135	25	3	17	3.5	63	66	34	52	30	.281	.451	4	1	OF-137
1984	134	438	110	11	5	11	2.5	39	47	29	35	10	.251	.374	16	3	OF-129
8 yrs.	899	3154	859	137	41	69	2.2	401	377	228	317	115	.272	.407	52	11	OF-850, DH-7

DIVISIONAL PLAYOFF SERIES
| 1981 LA N | 5 | 20 | 4 | 1 | 0 | 0 | 0.0 | 1 | 1 | 0 | 1 | 0 | .200 | .250 | 0 | 0 | OF-5 |

LEAGUE CHAMPIONSHIP SERIES
1981 LA N	5	10	1	1	0	0	0.0	0	1	3	2	0	.100	.200	0	0	OF-5
1983	4	14	2	0	0	0	0.0	0	1	1	3	0	.143	.143	0	0	OF-4
2 yrs.	9	24	3	1	0	0	0.0	0	1	4	5	0	.125	.167	0	0	OF-9

WORLD SERIES
| 1981 LA N | 5 | 6 | 1 | 1 | 0 | 0 | 0.0 | 1 | 0 | 0 | 2 | 1 | .167 | .333 | 2 | 1 | OF-3 |

Hobie Landrith
LANDRITH, HOBERT NEAL   BL TR 5'10" 170 lbs.
B. Mar. 16, 1930, Decatur, Ill.

1950 CIN N	4	14	3	0	0	0	0.0	1	1	2	1	0	.214	.214	0	0	C-4
1951	4	13	5	1	0	0	0.0	3	0	1	1	0	.385	.462	0	0	C-4
1952	15	50	13	4	0	0	0.0	1	4	0	4	0	.260	.340	1	1	C-14
1953	52	154	37	3	1	3	1.9	15	16	12	8	2	.240	.331	4	2	C-47
1954	48	81	16	0	0	5	6.2	12	14	18	9	1	.198	.383	5	2	C-42

	G	AB	H	2B	3B	HR	HR %	R	RBI	BB	SO	SB	BA	SA	Pinch Hit AB	Pinch Hit H	G by POS

Hobie Landrith continued

		G	AB	H	2B	3B	HR	HR%	R	RBI	BB	SO	SB	BA	SA	AB	H	G by POS
1955		43	87	22	3	0	4	4.6	9	7	10	14	0	.253	.425	16	3	C-27
1956 CHI N		111	312	69	10	3	4	1.3	22	32	39	38	0	.221	.311	15	4	C-99
1957 STL N		75	214	52	6	0	3	1.4	18	26	25	27	1	.243	.313	10	1	C-67
1958		70	144	31	4	0	3	2.1	9	13	26	21	0	.215	.306	24	5	C-45
1959 SF N		109	283	71	14	0	3	1.1	30	29	43	23	0	.251	.332	2	1	C-109
1960		71	190	46	10	0	1	0.5	18	20	23	11	1	.242	.311	2	0	C-70
1961		43	71	17	4	0	2	2.8	11	10	12	7	0	.239	.380	13	2	C-30
1962 2 teams	NY	N (23G – .289)			BAL	A	(60G – .222)											
" total	83	212	50	7	1	5	2.4	24	24	27	12	0	.236	.349	2	0	C-81
1963 2 teams	BAL	A (2G – .000)			WAS	A	(42G – .175)											
" total	44	104	18	3	0	1	1.0	6	7	15	12	0	.173	.231	7	0	C-38
14 yrs.	772	1929	450	69	5	34	1.8	179	203	253	188	5	.233	.327	101	21	C-677

Don Landrum

LANDRUM, DONALD LeROY   BL TR 6'   180 lbs.
B. Feb. 16, 1936, Santa Rosa, Calif.

		G	AB	H	2B	3B	HR	HR%	R	RBI	BB	SO	SB	BA	SA	AB	H	G by POS
1957 PHI N		2	7	1	1	0	0	0.0	1	0	2	1	0	.143	.286	0	0	OF-2
1960 STL N		13	49	12	0	1	2	4.1	7	3	4	6	3	.245	.408	0	0	OF-13
1961		28	66	11	2	0	1	1.5	5	3	5	14	1	.167	.242	1	0	OF-25, 2B-1
1962 2 teams	STL	N (32G – .314)			CHI	N	(83G – .282)											
" total	115	273	78	5	2	1	0.4	40	18	34	33	11	.286	.330	20	2	OF-85
1963 CHI N		84	227	55	4	1	1	0.4	27	10	13	42	6	.242	.282	24	3	OF-57
1964		11	11	0	0	0	0	0.0	2	0	1	2	0	.000	.000	8	0	OF-1
1965		131	425	96	20	4	6	1.4	60	34	36	84	14	.226	.334	15	2	OF-115
1966 SF N		72	102	19	4	0	1	1.0	9	7	9	18	1	.186	.255	18	2	OF-54
8 yrs.	456	1160	272	36	8	12	1.0	151	75	104	200	36	.234	.310	86	9	OF-352, 2B-1

Jesse Landrum

LANDRUM, JESSE GLENN   BR TR 5'11½" 175 lbs.
B. July 31, 1912, Crockett, Tex.   D. June 27, 1983, Beaumont, Tex.

	G	AB	H	2B	3B	HR	HR%	R	RBI	BB	SO	SB	BA	SA	AB	H	G by POS
1938 CHI A	4	6	0	0	0	0	0.0	0	1	0	2	0	.000	.000	1	0	2B-3

Tito Landrum

LANDRUM, TERRY LEE   BR TR 5'11"   175 lbs.
B. Oct. 25, 1954, Joplin, Mo.

		G	AB	H	2B	3B	HR	HR%	R	RBI	BB	SO	SB	BA	SA	AB	H	G by POS
1980 STL N		35	77	19	2	2	0	0.0	6	7	6	17	3	.247	.325	5	1	OF-29
1981		81	119	31	5	4	0	0.0	13	10	6	14	4	.261	.370	11	3	OF-67
1982		79	72	20	3	0	2	2.8	12	14	8	18	0	.278	.403	18	4	OF-56
1983 2 teams	STL	N (6G – .200)			BAL	A	(26G – .310)											
" total	32	47	14	2	1	1	2.1	8	4	2	13	1	.298	.447	9	2	OF-31
1984 STL N		105	173	47	9	1	3	1.7	21	26	10	27	3	.272	.387	23	9	OF-88
5 yrs.	332	488	131	21	8	6	1.2	60	61	32	89	11	.268	.381	66	19	OF-271

LEAGUE CHAMPIONSHIP SERIES

	G	AB	H	2B	3B	HR	HR%	R	RBI	BB	SO	SB	BA	SA	AB	H	G by POS
1983 BAL A	4	10	2	0	0	1	10.0	2	1	0	2	0	.200	.500	1	0	OF-3

WORLD SERIES

	G	AB	H	2B	3B	HR	HR%	R	RBI	BB	SO	SB	BA	SA	AB	H	G by POS
1983 BAL A	3	0	0	0	0	0	–	0	0	0	0	1	–	–	0	0	OF-3

Chappy Lane

LANE, GEORGE M.
B. Pittsburgh, Pa.   D. Mar. 8, 1896, Pittsburgh, Pa.

	G	AB	H	2B	3B	HR	HR%	R	RBI	BB	SO	SB	BA	SA	AB	H	G by POS
1882 PIT AA	57	214	38	8	2	3	1.4	26		5				.178	.276	0	0	1B-43, OF-13, C-2
1884 TOL AA	57	215	49	9	5	1	0.5	26		2				.228	.330	0	0	1B-46, OF-9, 3B-2, C-1
2 yrs.	114	429	87	17	7	4	0.9	52		7				.203	.303	0	0	1B-89, OF-22, C-3, 3B-2

Dick Lane

LANE, RICHARD HARRISON   BR TR 5'11"   178 lbs.
B. June 28, 1927, Highland Park, Mich.

	G	AB	H	2B	3B	HR	HR%	R	RBI	BB	SO	SB	BA	SA	AB	H	G by POS
1949 CHI A	12	42	5	0	0	0	0.0	4	4	5	3	0	.119	.119	1	0	OF-11

Hunter Lane

LANE, JAMES HUNTER (Dodo)   BR TR 5'11"   165 lbs.
B. July 20, 1900, Pulaski, Tenn.

	G	AB	H	2B	3B	HR	HR%	R	RBI	BB	SO	SB	BA	SA	AB	H	G by POS
1924 BOS N	7	15	1	0	0	0	0.0	0	0	1	1	0	.067	.067	2	0	3B-4, 2B-1

Marv Lane

LANE, MARVIN   BR TR 5'11"   180 lbs.
B. Jan. 18, 1950, Sandersville, Ga.

	G	AB	H	2B	3B	HR	HR%	R	RBI	BB	SO	SB	BA	SA	AB	H	G by POS
1971 DET A	8	14	2	0	0	0	0.0	0	1	1	3	0	.143	.143	2	0	OF-6
1972	8	6	0	0	0	0	0.0	2	0	0	2	0	.000	.000	1	0	OF-3
1973	6	8	2	0	0	1	12.5	2	2	2	2	0	.250	.625	0	0	OF-4
1974	50	103	24	4	1	2	1.9	16	9	19	24	2	.233	.350	5	3	OF-46, DH-1
1976	18	48	9	1	0	0	0.0	3	5	6	11	0	.188	.208	3	0	OF-15
5 yrs.	90	179	37	5	1	3	1.7	23	17	28	42	2	.207	.296	11	3	OF-74, DH-1

Don Lang

LANG, DONALD CHARLES   BR TR 6'   175 lbs.
B. Mar. 15, 1915, Selma, Calif.

	G	AB	H	2B	3B	HR	HR%	R	RBI	BB	SO	SB	BA	SA	AB	H	G by POS
1938 CIN N	21	50	13	3	1	1	2.0	5	11	2	7	0	.260	.420	2	2	3B-15, SS-1, 2B-1
1948 STL N	117	323	87	14	1	4	1.2	30	31	47	38	2	.269	.356	16	1	3B-95, 2B-2
2 yrs.	138	373	100	17	2	5	1.3	35	42	49	45	2	.268	.365	18	3	3B-110, 2B-3, SS-1

Bill Lange

LANGE, WILLIAM ALEXANDER (Little Eva)   BR TR 6'1"   180 lbs.
B. June 6, 1871, San Francisco, Calif.   D. July 23, 1950, San Francisco, Calif.

	G	AB	H	2B	3B	HR	HR%	R	RBI	BB	SO	SB	BA	SA	AB	H	G by POS
1893 CHI N	117	469	132	8	7	8	1.7	92	88	52	20	47	.281	.380	0	0	2B-57, OF-40, 3B-8, SS-7, C-7
1894	111	442	145	16	9	6	1.4	84	90	56	18	65	.328	.446	0	0	OF-109, SS-2, 3B-1
1895	123	478	186	27	16	10	2.1	120	98	55	24	67	.389	.575	0	0	OF-123
1896	122	469	153	21	16	4	0.9	114	92	65	24	84	.326	.465	0	0	OF-121, C-1
1897	118	479	163	24	14	5	1.0	119	83	48		73	.340	.480	0	0	OF-118
1898	113	442	141	16	10	6	1.4	79	69	36		22	.319	.441	0	0	OF-111, 1B-2
1899	107	416	135	21	7	1	0.2	81	59	38		41	.325	.416	0	0	OF-94, 1B-14
7 yrs.	811	3195	1055	133	79	40	1.3	689	578	350	86	399	.330	.459	0	0	OF-716, 2B-57, 1B-16, SS-9, 3B-9, C-8

	G	AB	H	2B	3B	HR	HR%	R	RBI	BB	SO	SB	BA	SA	Pinch Hit AB	H	G by POS

Frank Lange

LANGE, FRANK HERMAN (Seagan)
B. Oct. 28, 1883, Columbus, Wis. D. Dec. 26, 1945, Madison, Wis.
BR TR 5'11" 180 lbs.

	G	AB	H	2B	3B	HR	HR%	R	RBI	BB	SO	SB	BA	SA	AB	H	G by POS
1910 CHI A	23	51	13	4	0	0	0.0	3	8	2		0	.255	.333	0	0	P-23
1911	54	76	22	6	2	0	0.0	7	16	7		0	.289	.421	19	8	P-29
1912	40	65	14	4	1	0	0.0	4	7	4		0	.215	.308	9	2	P-31
1913	17	18	3	1	0	0	0.0	1	1	3	5	0	.167	.222	5	1	P-12
4 yrs.	134	210	52	15	3	0	0.0	15	32	16	5	0	.248	.348	33	11	P-95

Sam Langford

LANGFORD, ELTON L.
B. May 21, 1900, Briggs, Tex.
BL TR 6' 180 lbs.

	G	AB	H	2B	3B	HR	HR%	R	RBI	BB	SO	SB	BA	SA	AB	H	G by POS
1926 BOS A	1	1	0	0	0	0	0.0	1	0	0	0	0	.000	.000	1	0	
1927 CLE A	20	67	18	5	0	1	1.5	10	7	5	7	0	.269	.388	0	0	OF-20
1928	110	427	118	17	8	4	0.9	50	50	21	35	3	.276	.382	3	1	OF-107
3 yrs.	131	495	136	22	8	5	1.0	61	57	26	42	3	.275	.382	4	1	OF-127

Bob Langsford

LANGSFORD, ROBERT WILLIAM
Also known as Robert William Lankswert.
B. Aug. 5, 1865, Louisville, Ky. D. Jan. 10, 1907, Louisville, Ky.
BR TR

	G	AB	H	2B	3B	HR	HR%	R	RBI	BB	SO	SB	BA	SA	AB	H	G by POS
1899 LOU N	1	4	0	0	0	0	0.0	0	0	0		0	.000	.000	0	0	SS-1

Hal Lanier

LANIER, HAROLD CLIFTON
Son of Max Lanier.
B. July 4, 1942, Denton, N. C.
BR TR 6'2" 180 lbs.
BB 1967

	G	AB	H	2B	3B	HR	HR%	R	RBI	BB	SO	SB	BA	SA	AB	H	G by POS
1964 SF N	98	383	105	16	3	2	0.5	40	28	5	44	2	.274	.347	2	0	2B-98, SS-3
1965	159	522	118	15	9	0	0.0	41	39	21	67	2	.226	.289	1	0	2B-158, SS-1
1966	149	459	106	14	2	3	0.7	37	37	16	49	1	.231	.290	1	0	2B-112, SS-41
1967	151	525	112	16	3	0	0.0	37	42	16	61	2	.213	.255	0	0	SS-137, 2B-34
1968	151	486	100	14	1	0	0.0	37	27	12	57	2	.206	.239	1	0	SS-150
1969	150	495	113	9	1	0	0.0	37	35	25	68	0	.228	.251	0	0	SS-150
1970	134	438	101	13	1	2	0.5	33	41	21	41	1	.231	.279	0	0	SS-130, 2B-4, 1B-2
1971	109	206	48	8	0	1	0.5	21	13	15	26	0	.233	.286	3	0	3B-83, 2B-13, SS-8, 1B-3
1972 NY A	60	103	22	3	0	0	0.0	5	6	2	13	1	.214	.243	3	2	3B-47, SS-9, 2B-3
1973	35	86	18	3	0	0	0.0	9	5	3	10	0	.209	.244	0	0	SS-26, 2B-8, 3B-1
10 yrs.	1196	3703	843	111	20	8	0.2	297	273	136	436	11	.228	.275	11	2	SS-655, 2B-430, 3B-131, 1B-5

LEAGUE CHAMPIONSHIP SERIES

	G	AB	H	2B	3B	HR	HR%	R	RBI	BB	SO	SB	BA	SA	AB	H	G by POS
1971 SF N	1	1	0	0	0	0	0.0	0	0	0	0	0	.000	.000	0	0	3B-1

Rimp Lanier

LANIER, LORENZO
B. Oct. 19, 1948, Tuskegee, Ala.
BL TR 5'8" 150 lbs.

	G	AB	H	2B	3B	HR	HR%	R	RBI	BB	SO	SB	BA	SA	AB	H	G by POS
1971 PIT N	6	4	0	0	0	0	0.0	0	0	0	1	0	.000	.000	4	0	

Les Lanning

LANNING, LESTER ALFRED (Red)
B. May 13, 1895, Harvard, Ill. D. June 13, 1962, Bristol, Conn.
BL TL 5'9" 165 lbs.

	G	AB	H	2B	3B	HR	HR%	R	RBI	BB	SO	SB	BA	SA	AB	H	G by POS
1916 PHI A	19	33	6	2	0	0	0.0	5	1	10	9	0	.182	.242	3	0	OF-9, P-6

Carney Lansford

LANSFORD, CARNEY RAY
Brother of Joe Lansford.
B. Feb. 7, 1957, San Jose, Calif.
BR TR 6'2" 195 lbs.

	G	AB	H	2B	3B	HR	HR%	R	RBI	BB	SO	SB	BA	SA	AB	H	G by POS
1978 CAL A	121	453	133	23	2	8	1.8	63	52	31	67	20	.294	.406	2	0	3B-117, SS-2, DH-1
1979	157	654	188	30	5	19	2.9	114	79	39	115	20	.287	.436	0	0	3B-157
1980	151	602	157	27	3	15	2.5	87	80	50	93	14	.261	.390	1	1	3B-150
1981 BOS A	102	399	134	23	3	4	1.0	61	52	34	28	15	.336	.439	1	0	3B-86, DH-16
1982	128	482	145	28	4	11	2.3	65	63	46	48	9	.301	.444	1	0	3B-114, DH-13
1983 OAK A	80	299	92	16	2	10	3.3	43	45	22	33	3	.308	.475	3	1	3B-78, SS-1
1984	151	597	179	31	5	14	2.3	70	74	40	62	9	.300	.439	0	0	3B-151
7 yrs.	890	3486	1028	178	24	81	2.3	503	445	262	446	90	.295	.429	8	2	3B-853, DH-30, SS-3

LEAGUE CHAMPIONSHIP SERIES

	G	AB	H	2B	3B	HR	HR%	R	RBI	BB	SO	SB	BA	SA	AB	H	G by POS
1979 CAL A	4	17	5	0	0	0	0.0	2	3	1	2	1	.294	.294	0	0	3B-4

Joe Lansford

LANSFORD, JOSEPH DALE
Brother of Carney Lansford.
B. Jan. 15, 1961, San Jose, Calif.
BR TR 6'5" 225 lbs.

	G	AB	H	2B	3B	HR	HR%	R	RBI	BB	SO	SB	BA	SA	AB	H	G by POS
1982 SD N	13	22	4	0	0	0	0.0	6	3	6	4	0	.182	.182	3	0	1B-9
1983	12	8	2	0	0	1	12.5	1	2	0	3	0	.250	.625	6	1	1B-8
2 yrs.	25	30	6	0	0	1	3.3	7	5	6	7	0	.200	.300	9	1	1B-17

Pete Lapan

LAPAN, PETER NELSON
B. June 25, 1891, Easthampton, Mass. D. Jan. 5, 1953, Norwalk, Calif.
BR TR 5'7" 165 lbs.

	G	AB	H	2B	3B	HR	HR%	R	RBI	BB	SO	SB	BA	SA	AB	H	G by POS
1922 WAS A	11	34	11	1	0	1	2.9	7	6	3	4	1	.324	.441	0	0	C-11
1923	2	2	0	0	0	0	0.0	0	0	0	0	0	.000	.000	2	0	
2 yrs.	13	36	11	1	0	1	2.8	7	6	3	4	1	.306	.417	2	0	C-11

Ralph LaPointe

LaPOINTE, RALPH ROBERT
B. Jan. 8, 1922, Winooski, Vt. D. Sept. 13, 1967, Burlington, Vt.
BR TR 5'11" 185 lbs.

	G	AB	H	2B	3B	HR	HR%	R	RBI	BB	SO	SB	BA	SA	AB	H	G by POS
1947 PHI N	56	211	65	7	0	1	0.5	33	15	17	15	8	.308	.355	2	1	SS-54
1948 STL N	87	222	50	3	0	0	0.0	27	15	18	19	1	.225	.239	2	0	2B-44, SS-25, 3B-1
2 yrs.	143	433	115	10	0	1	0.2	60	30	35	34	9	.266	.296	4	1	SS-79, 2B-44, 3B-1

Frank LaPorte

LaPORTE, FRANK BREYFOGLE (Pot)
B. Feb. 6, 1880, Uhrichsville, Ohio D. Sept. 25, 1939, Newcomerstown, Ohio
BR TR 5'8" 175 lbs.

	G	AB	H	2B	3B	HR	HR%	R	RBI	BB	SO	SB	BA	SA	AB	H	G by POS
1905 NY A	11	40	16	1	0	1	2.5	4	12	1		1	.400	.500	0	0	2B-11
1906	123	454	120	23	9	2	0.4	60	54	22		10	.264	.368	3	1	3B-114, 2B-5, OF-1
1907	130	470	127	20	11	0	0.0	56	48	27		10	.270	.360	2	0	3B-64, OF-63, 1B-1

	G	AB	H	2B	3B	HR	HR %	R	RBI	BB	SO	SB	BA	SA	Pinch Hit AB	Pinch Hit H	G by POS

Frank LaPorte continued

	G	AB	H	2B	3B	HR	HR%	R	RBI	BB	SO	SB	BA	SA	PH AB	PH H	G by POS
1908 2 teams	BOS A (62G – .237)			NY A (39G – .262)													
" total	101	301	75	4	8	0	0.0	21	30	20		6	.249	.316	19	5	2B-53, OF-16, 3B-12
1909 NY A	89	309	92	19	3	0	0.0	35	31	18		5	.298	.379	5	2	2B-83
1910	124	432	114	14	6	2	0.5	43	67	33		16	.264	.338	6	1	2B-79, OF-24, 3B-15
1911 STL A	136	507	159	37	12	2	0.4	71	82	34		4	.314	.446	0	0	2B-133, 3B-3
1912 2 teams	STL A (80G – .312)			WAS A (39G – .309)													
" total	119	402	125	20	5	1	0.2	45	55	32		10	.311	.393	11	0	2B-76, OF-32
1913 WAS A	79	242	61	5	4	0	0.0	25	18	17	16	10	.252	.306	8	1	3B-46, 2B-13, OF-12
1914 IND F	133	505	157	27	12	4	0.8	86	107	36		15	.311	.436	1	0	2B-132
1915 NWK F	148	550	139	28	10	2	0.4	55	56	48		14	.253	.351	2	0	2B-146
11 yrs.	1193	4212	1185	198	80	14	0.3	501	560	288	16	101	.281	.376	57	10	2B-731, 3B-254, OF-148, 1B-1

Jack Lapp

LAPP, JOHN WALKER BL TR 5'8"
B. Sept. 10, 1884, Frazer, Pa.   D. Feb. 6, 1920, Philadelphia, Pa.

	G	AB	H	2B	3B	HR	HR%	R	RBI	BB	SO	SB	BA	SA	PH AB	PH H	G by POS
1908 PHI A	13	35	5	0	1	0	0.0	4	1	5		0	.143	.200	0	0	C-13
1909	21	56	19	3	1	0	0.0	8	10	3		1	.339	.429	2	0	C-19
1910	71	192	45	4	3	0	0.0	18	17	20		0	.234	.286	7	3	C-63
1911	68	167	59	10	3	1	0.6	35	26	24		4	.353	.467	6	3	C-57, 1B-4
1912	90	281	82	15	6	1	0.4	26	35	19		3	.292	.399	8	4	C-82
1913	81	238	54	4	4	1	0.4	23	20	37	26	1	.227	.290	2	0	C-77, 1B-1
1914	69	199	46	7	2	0	0.0	22	19	31	14	1	.231	.286	3	1	C-67
1915	112	312	85	16	5	2	0.6	26	31	30	29	5	.272	.375	10	4	C-89, 1B-12
1916 CHI A	40	101	21	0	1	0	0.0	6	7	8	10	1	.208	.228	4	0	C-34
9 yrs.	565	1581	416	59	26	5	0.3	168	166	177	79	16	.263	.343	42	15	C-501, 1B-17

WORLD SERIES																	
1910 PHI A	1	4	1	0	0	0	0.0	0	1	0		2	0	.250	.250	0	0	C-1
1911	2	8	2	0	0	0	0.0	1	0	0		1	0	.250	.250	0	0	C-2
1913	1	4	1	0	0	0	0.0	0	0	0		1	0	.250	.250	0	0	C-1
1914	1	1	0	0	0	0	0.0	0	0	0		0	0	.000	.000	0	0	C-1
4 yrs.	5	17	4	0	0	0	0.0	1	1	0		4	0	.235	.235	0	0	C-5

Norm Larker

LARKER, NORMAN HOWARD JOHN BL TL 6'   185 lbs.
B. Dec. 27, 1930, Beaver Meadows, Pa.

	G	AB	H	2B	3B	HR	HR%	R	RBI	BB	SO	SB	BA	SA	PH AB	PH H	G by POS
1958 LA N	99	253	70	16	5	4	1.6	32	29	29	21	1	.277	.427	29	7	OF-43, 1B-25
1959	108	311	90	14	1	8	2.6	37	49	26	25	0	.289	.418	24	7	1B-55, OF-30
1960	133	440	142	26	3	5	1.1	56	78	36	24	1	.323	.430	15	6	1B-119, OF-2
1961	97	282	76	16	1	5	1.8	29	38	24	22	0	.270	.387	10	2	1B-86, OF-1
1962 HOU N	147	506	133	19	5	9	1.8	58	63	70	47	1	.263	.374	10	6	1B-135, OF-6
1963 2 teams	MIL N (64G – .177)			SF N (19G – .071)													
" total	83	161	27	6	0	1	0.6	15	14	26	26	0	.168	.224	30	4	1B-53
6 yrs.	667	1953	538	97	15	32	1.6	227	271	211	165	3	.275	.390	118	32	1B-473, OF-82

WORLD SERIES																	
1959 LA N	6	16	3	0	0	0	0.0	2	0	2	3	0	.188	.188	0	0	OF-6

Ed Larkin

LARKIN, EDWARD FRANCIS BR TR 5'8"
B. July 1, 1885, Wyalusing, Pa.   D. Mar. 28, 1934, Wyalusing, Pa.

	G	AB	H	2B	3B	HR	HR%	R	RBI	BB	SO	SB	BA	SA	PH AB	PH H	G by POS
1909 PHI A	2	6	1	0	0	0	0.0	1	1	1		0	.167	.167	0	0	C-2

Henry Larkin

LARKIN, HENRY E. (Ted) BR TR 5'10"   170 lbs.
B. Jan. 12, 1860, Reading, Pa.   D. Jan. 31, 1942, Reading, Pa.
Manager 1890.

	G	AB	H	2B	3B	HR	HR%	R	RBI	BB	SO	SB	BA	SA	PH AB	PH H	G by POS
1884 PHI AA	85	326	90	21	9	3	0.9	59		15			.276	.423	0	0	OF-85, 2B-2
1885	108	453	149	37	14	8	1.8	114		26			.329	.525	0	0	OF-108
1886	139	565	180	36	16	2	0.4	133		59			.319	.450	0	0	OF-139
1887	126	497	154	22	12	3	0.6	105		48		37	.310	.421	0	0	OF-93, 1B-23, 2B-10
1888	135	546	147	28	12	7	1.3	92	101	33		20	.269	.403	0	0	1B-122, 2B-14
1889	133	516	164	23	12	3	0.6	105	74	83	41	11	.318	.426	0	0	1B-131, 3B-1, 2B-1
1890 CLE P	125	506	168	32	15	5	1.0	93	112	65	18	5	.332	.484	0	0	1B-125, OF-1
1891 PHI AA	133	526	147	27	14	10	1.9	94	93	66	56	2	.279	.441	0	0	1B-111, OF-23
1892 WAS N	119	464	130	13	7	8	1.7	76	96	39	21	21	.280	.390	0	0	1B-117, OF-2
1893	81	319	101	20	3	4	1.3	54	73	50	5	1	.317	.436	0	0	1B-81
10 yrs.	1184	4718	1430	259	114	53	1.1	925	548	484	141	97	.303	.440	0	0	1B-710, OF-451, 2B-27, 3B-1

Terry Larkin

LARKIN, FRANK BR TR
B. New York, N. Y.   Deceased.

	G	AB	H	2B	3B	HR	HR%	R	RBI	BB	SO	SB	BA	SA	PH AB	PH H	G by POS
1876 NY N	1	4	0	0	0	0	0.0	0	0	0	0		.000	.000	0	0	P-1
1877 HAR N	58	228	52	6	5	1	0.4	28	18	5	23		.228	.311	0	0	P-56, 3B-2, 2B-1
1878 CHI N	58	226	65	9	4	0	0.0	33	32	17	17		.288	.363	0	0	P-56, OF-1, 3B-1
1879	60	228	50	12	2	0	0.0	26	18	8	24		.219	.289	0	0	P-58, OF-3
1880 TRO N	6	20	3	1	0	0	0.0	1		3	4		.150	.200	0	0	P-5, OF-2, SS-1
1884 2 teams	WAS U (17G – .243)			RIC AA (40G – .201)													
" total	57	209	45	1	4	0	0.0	28		13			.215	.258	0	0	2B-40, 3B-17
6 yrs.	240	915	215	29	15	1	0.1	116	68	46	68		.235	.303	0	0	P-176, 2B-41, 3B-20, OF-6, SS-1

Bob Larmore

LARMORE, ROBERT McCAHAN (Red) BR TR 5'10½" 185 lbs.
B. Dec. 6, 1896, Anderson, Ind.   D. Jan. 15, 1964, St. Louis, Mo.

	G	AB	H	2B	3B	HR	HR%	R	RBI	BB	SO	SB	BA	SA	PH AB	PH H	G by POS
1918 STL N	4	7	2	0	0	0	0.0	0	1	0	2	0	.286	.286	2	2	SS-2

Sam LaRoque

LaROQUE, SAMUEL H J 5'11"   190 lbs.
B. Feb. 26, 1864, St. Mathias, Que., Canada   Deceased.

	G	AB	H	2B	3B	HR	HR%	R	RBI	BB	SO	SB	BA	SA	PH AB	PH H	G by POS
1888 DET N	2	9	4	0	0	0	0.0	1	2	1	1	0	.444	.444	0	0	2B-2
1890 PIT N	111	434	105	20	4	1	0.2	59	40	35	29	27	.242	.313	0	0	2B-78, SS-31, 1B-2, OF-1

	G	AB	H	2B	3B	HR	HR %	R	RBI	BB	SO	SB	BA	SA	Pinch Hit AB	Pinch Hit H	G by POS

Sam LaRoque continued

1891 2 teams	PIT	N	(1G – .000)		LOU	AA	(10G – .314)										
" total	11	39	11	2	1	1	2.6	6	8	5	9	1	.282	.462	0	0	2B-10, 3B-1, 1B-1
3 yrs.	124	482	120	22	5	2	0.4	66	50	41	39	28	.249	.328	0	0	2B-90, SS-31, 1B-3, OF-1, 3B-1

Vic LaRose

LaROSE, VICTOR RAYMOND
B. Dec. 23, 1944, Los Angeles, Calif.
BR TR 5'11" 180 lbs.

1968 CHI N	4	2	0	0	0	0	0.0	0	0	0	1	0	.000	.000	0	0	SS-2, 2B-2

Harry LaRoss

LaROSS, HARRY RAYMOND (Spike)
B. Jan. 12, 1888, Easton, Pa.   D. May 22, 1954, Hines, Ill.
BR TR 5'11½" 170 lbs.

1914 CIN N	22	48	11	1	0	0	0.0	7	5	2	10	4	.229	.250	0	0	OF-20

Don Larsen

LARSEN, DONALD JAMES
B. Aug. 7, 1929, Michigan City, Ind.
BR TR 6'4" 215 lbs.

1953 STL A	50	81	23	3	1	3	3.7	11	10	4	14	0	.284	.457	10	1	P-38, OF-1
1954 BAL A	44	88	22	5	3	1	1.1	6	4	5	15	0	.250	.409	15	0	P-29
1955 NY A	21	41	6	1	0	2	4.9	4	7	4	13	0	.146	.317	3	1	P-19
1956	45	79	19	5	0	2	2.5	10	12	6	17	0	.241	.380	7	2	P-38
1957	31	56	14	5	0	0	0.0	6	5	6	11	0	.250	.339	1	0	P-27
1958	28	49	15	1	0	4	8.2	9	13	5	9	0	.306	.571	7	2	P-19
1959	29	47	12	2	0	0	0.0	8	8	7	15	0	.255	.298	3	1	P-25
1960 KC A	23	29	6	1	0	0	0.0	3	3	0	11	0	.207	.241	1	0	P-22
1961 2 teams	KC	A	(18G – .300)		CHI	A	(25G – .320)										
" total	43	45	14	0	0	2	4.4	4	8	1	10	0	.311	.444	12	5	P-33, OF-1
1962 SF N	52	25	5	0	1	0	0.0	3	1	0	7	0	.200	.280	4	0	P-49
1963	46	11	2	0	0	0	0.0	1	0	1	1	0	.182	.182	0	0	P-46
1964 2 teams	SF	N	(6G – .000)		HOU	N	(31G – .097)										
" total	37	32	3	1	0	0	0.0	0	4	10	0	.094	.125	3	0	P-36		
1965 2 teams	HOU	N	(1G – .000)		BAL	A	(27G – .273)										
" total	28	13	3	1	0	0	0.0	0	1	0	5	0	.231	.308	0	0	P-28
1967 CHI N	3	0	0	0	0	0	–	0	0	0	0	0	–	–	0	0	P-3
14 yrs.	480	596	144	25	5	14	2.3	65	72	43	138	0	.242	.371	66	12	P-412, OF-2

WORLD SERIES																	
1955 NY A	1	2	0	0	0	0	0.0	0	0	0	0	0	.000	.000	0	0	P-1
1956	2	3	1	0	0	0	0.0	1	1	0	1	0	.333	.333	0	0	P-2
1957	2	2	0	0	0	0	0.0	1	0	2	1	0	.000	.000	0	0	P-2
1958	2	2	0	0	0	0	0.0	0	0	1	0	0	.000	.000	0	0	P-2
1962 SF N	3	0	0	0	0	0	0.0	0	0	0	0	0	–	–	0	0	P-3
5 yrs.	10	9	1	0	0	0	0.0	2	1	3	2	0	.111	.111	0	0	P-10

Swede Larsen

LARSEN, ERLING ADELI
B. Nov. 15, 1913, Jersey City, N. J.
BR TR 5'11" 175 lbs.

1936 BOS N	3	1	0	0	0	0	0.0	0	0	0	0	0	.000	.000	0	0	2B-2

Tony LaRussa

LaRUSSA, ANTHONY
B. Oct. 4, 1944, Tampa, Fla.
Manager 1979-84.
BR TR 6' 175 lbs.

1963 KC A	34	44	11	1	1	0	0.0	1	7	12	0	.250	.318	1	1	SS-14, 2B-3	
1968 OAK A	5	3	1	0	0	0	0.0	0	0	0	0	0	.333	.333	3	1	
1969	8	8	0	0	0	0	0.0	0	0	0	1	0	.000	.000	8	0	
1970	52	106	21	4	1	0	0.0	6	6	15	19	0	.198	.255	11	2	2B-44
1971 2 teams	OAK	A	(23G – .000)		ATL	N	(9G – .286)										
" total	32	15	2	0	0	0	0.0	4	0	1	5	0	.133	.133	6	0	2B-16, SS-4, 3B-2
1973 CHI N	1	0	0	0	0	0	–	1	0	0	0	0	–	–	0	0	
6 yrs.	132	176	35	5	2	0	0.0	15	7	23	37	0	.199	.250	29	4	2B-63, SS-18, 3B-2

Lyn Lary

LARY, LYNFORD HOBART
B. Jan. 28, 1906, Armona, Calif.   D. Jan. 9, 1973, Downey, Calif.
BR TR 6' 165 lbs.

1929 NY A	80	236	73	9	2	5	2.1	48	26	24	15	4	.309	.428	7	0	3B-55, SS-14, 2B-2
1930	117	464	134	20	8	3	0.6	93	52	45	40	14	.289	.386	3	0	SS-113
1931	155	610	171	35	9	10	1.6	100	107	88	54	13	.280	.416	0	0	SS-155
1932	91	280	65	14	4	3	1.1	56	39	52	28	9	.232	.343	1	0	SS-80, 1B-5, 3B-2, 2B-2, OF-1
1933	52	127	28	3	3	0	0.0	25	13	28	17	2	.220	.291	4	0	3B-28, SS-16, 1B-3, OF-1
1934 2 teams	NY	A	(1G – .000)		BOS	A	(129G – .241)										
" total	130	419	101	20	4	2	0.5	58	54	67	51	12	.241	.322	0	0	SS-129, 1B-1
1935 2 teams	WAS	A	(39G – .194)		STL	A	(93G – .288)										
" total	132	474	127	29	7	2	0.4	86	42	76	53	28	.268	.371	3	1	SS-123
1936 STL A	155	620	179	30	6	2	0.3	112	52	117	54	37	.289	.366	0	0	SS-155
1937 CLE A	156	644	187	46	7	8	1.2	110	77	88	64	18	.290	.421	0	0	SS-156
1938	141	568	152	36	4	3	0.5	94	51	88	65	23	.268	.361	0	0	SS-141
1939 3 teams	CLE	A	(3G – .000)		BKN	N	(29G – .161)		STL	N	(34G – .187)						
" total	66	108	19	4	1	0	0.0	18	10	28	22	2	.176	.231	3	0	SS-44, 3B-10
1940 STL A	27	54	3	1	0	0	0.0	5	3	4	7	0	.056	.111	6	0	SS-19
12 yrs.	1302	4604	1239	247	56	38	0.8	805	526	705	470	162	.269	.372	27	1	SS-1138, 3B-95, 1B-9, 2B-5, OF-2

Don Lassetter

LASSETTER, DONALD O'NEAL
B. Mar. 27, 1933, Newnan, Ga.
BR TR 6'3" 200 lbs.

1957 STL N	4	13	2	0	1	0	0.0	2	0	1	3	0	.154	.308	1	0	OF-3

Arlie Latham

LATHAM, WALTER ARLINGTON (The Freshest Man on Earth) BR TR 5'8" 150 lbs.
B. Mar. 15, 1859, W. Lebanon, N. H.   D. Nov. 29, 1952, Garden City, N. Y.
Manager 1896.

1880 BUF N	22	79	10	3	1	0	0.0	9	3	1	8		.127	.190	0	0	SS-12, OF-10, C-1

		G	AB	H	2B	3B	HR	HR %	R	RBI	BB	SO	SB	BA	SA	Pinch Hit AB	Pinch Hit H	G by POS

Arlie Latham continued

Year	Team	G	AB	H	2B	3B	HR	HR%	R	RBI	BB	SO	SB	BA	SA	PH AB	PH H	G by POS
1883	STL AA	98	406	96	12	7	0	0.0	86		18			.236	.300	0	0	3B-98, C-1
1884		110	474	130	17	12	1	0.2	115		19			.274	.367	0	0	3B-110, C-1
1885		110	485	100	15	3	1	0.2	84		18			.206	.256	0	0	3B-109, C-2
1886		134	578	174	23	8	1	0.2	152		55			.301	.374	0	0	3B-133, 2B-1
1887		136	627	198	35	10	2	0.3	163		45		129	.316	.413	0	0	3B-132, 2B-5, C-2
1888		133	570	151	19	5	2	0.4	119	31	43		109	.265	.326	0	0	3B-133, SS-1
1889		118	512	126	13	3	4	0.8	110	49	42	30	69	.246	.307	0	0	3B-116, 2B-3
1890	2 teams	CHI P (52G – .229)							CIN N (41G – .250)									
"	total	93	378	90	13	4	1	0.3	82	35	45	40	52	.238	.302	0	0	3B-93, C-1
1891	CIN N	135	533	145	20	10	7	1.3	119	53	74	35	87	.272	.386	0	0	3B-135, C-1
1892		152	622	148	20	4	0	0.0	111	44	60	54	66	.238	.283	0	0	3B-142, 2B-9, OF-1
1893		127	531	150	18	6	2	0.4	101	49	62	20	57	.282	.350	0	0	3B-127
1894		129	524	164	23	6	4	0.8	129	60	60	24	59	.313	.403	0	0	3B-127, 2B-2
1895		112	460	143	14	6	2	0.4	93	69	42	25	48	.311	.380	0	0	3B-108, 1B-3, 2B-1
1896	STL N	8	35	7	0	0	0	0.0	3	5	4	3	2	.200	.200	0	0	3B-8
1899	WAS N	6	6	1	0	0	0	0.0	1	0	1			.167	.167	2	1	OF-1, 2B-1
1909	NY N	4	2	0	0	0	0	0.0	0				1	.000	.000	0	0	2B-2
17 yrs.		1627	6822	1833	245	85	27	0.4	1478	398	589	239	679	.269	.341	3	1	3B-1571, 2B-24, OF-13, SS-13, C-8, 1B-3

Juice Latham

LATHAM, GEORGE WARREN (Jumbo)
B. Sept. 6, 1852, Utica, N.Y.   D. May 26, 1914, Utica, N.Y.   BR TR   240 lbs.

Year	Team	G	AB	H	2B	3B	HR	HR%	R	RBI	BB	SO	SB	BA	SA	PH AB	PH H	G by POS
1877	LOU N	59	278	81	10	6	0	0.0	42	22	5		6	.291	.371	0	0	1B-59
1882	PHI AA	74	323	92	10	2	0	0.0	47		10			.285	.328	0	0	1B-74
1883	LOU AA	88	368	92	7	6	0	0.0	60		12			.250	.302	0	0	1B-67, 2B-14, SS-9
1884		77	308	52	3	3	0	0.0	31		8			.169	.198	0	0	1B-76, 3B-1
4 yrs.		298	1277	317	30	17	0	0.0	180	22	35		6	.248	.298	0	0	1B-276, 2B-14, SS-9, 3B-1

Chick Lathers

LATHERS, CHARLES TEN EYCK
B. Oct. 22, 1888, Detroit, Mich.   D. July 26, 1971, Petoskey, Mich.   BL TR 6'   180 lbs.

Year	Team	G	AB	H	2B	3B	HR	HR%	R	RBI	BB	SO	SB	BA	SA	PH AB	PH H	G by POS
1910	DET A	41	82	19	2	0	0	0.0	4	3	8		0	.232	.256	14	3	3B-13, 2B-7, SS-4
1911		29	45	10	1	0	0	0.0	5	4	5		0	.222	.244	4	2	2B-9, 3B-8, SS-4, 1B-3
2 yrs.		70	127	29	3	0	0	0.0	9	7	13		0	.228	.252	18	5	3B-21, 2B-16, SS-8, 1B-3

Tacks Latimer

LATIMER, CLIFFORD WESLEY
B. Nov. 30, 1877, Loveland, Ohio   D. Apr. 24, 1936, Loveland, Ohio   TR 6'   180 lbs.

Year	Team	G	AB	H	2B	3B	HR	HR%	R	RBI	BB	SO	SB	BA	SA	PH AB	PH H	G by POS
1898	NY N	5	17	5	1	0	0	0.0	1	1	0		0	.294	.353	0	0	C-4, OF-2
1899	LOU N	9	29	8	1	0	0	0.0	3	4	2		1	.276	.310	0	0	C-8, 1B-1
1900	PIT N	4	12	4	1	0	0	0.0	1	2	0		0	.333	.417	0	0	C-4
1901	BAL A	1	4	1	0	0	0	0.0	0	0	0		0	.250	.250	0	0	C-1
1902	BKN N	8	24	1	0	0	0	0.0	0	0	0		0	.042	.042	0	0	C-8
5 yrs.		27	86	19	3	0	0	0.0	5	7	2		1	.221	.256	0	0	C-25, OF-2, 1B-1

Charlie Lau

LAU, CHARLES RICHARD
B. Apr. 12, 1933, Romulus, Mich.   D. Mar. 18, 1984, Key Colony Beach, Fla.   BL TR 6'   190 lbs.

Year	Team	G	AB	H	2B	3B	HR	HR%	R	RBI	BB	SO	SB	BA	SA	PH AB	PH H	G by POS
1956	DET A	3	9	2	0	0	0	0.0	1	0	0	1	0	.222	.222	0	0	C-3
1958		30	68	10	1	2	0	0.0	8	6	12	15	0	.147	.221	4	1	C-27
1959		2	6	1	0	0	0	0.0	0	0	0	2	0	.167	.167	1	0	C-2
1960	MIL N	21	53	10	2	0	0	0.0	4	2	6	10	0	.189	.226	7	0	C-16
1961	2 teams	MIL N (28G – .207)							BAL A (17G – .170)									
"	total	45	129	25	5	0	1	0.8	6	9	15	14	1	.194	.256	2	0	C-42
1962	BAL A	81	197	58	11	2	6	3.0	21	37	7	11	1	.294	.462	30	11	C-56
1963	2 teams	BAL A (29G – .188)							KC A (62G – .294)									
"	total	91	235	64	13	0	3	1.3	19	32	15	22	1	.272	.366	29	4	C-58
1964	2 teams	KC A (43G – .271)							BAL A (62G – .259)									
"	total	105	276	73	22	2	3	1.1	27	27	27	45	0	.264	.391	28	7	C-82
1965	BAL A	68	132	39	5	2	2	1.5	15	18	17	18	0	.295	.409	29	8	C-35
1966		18	12	6	2	0	0	0.0	1	5	4	1	0	.500	.833	12	6	
1967	2 teams	BAL A (11G – .125)							ATL N (52G – .200)									
"	total	63	53	10	2	0	1	1.9	3	8	6	11	0	.189	.283	53	10	
11 yrs.		527	1170	298	63	9	16	1.4	105	140	109	150	3	.255	.365	195	47	C-321

Billy Lauder

LAUDER, WILLIAM
B. Feb. 23, 1874, New York, N.Y.   D. May 20, 1933, Norwalk, Conn.   BR TR 5'10"   160 lbs.

Year	Team	G	AB	H	2B	3B	HR	HR%	R	RBI	BB	SO	SB	BA	SA	PH AB	PH H	G by POS
1898	PHI N	97	361	95	14	7	2	0.6	42	67	19		6	.263	.357	0	0	3B-97
1899		151	583	156	17	6	3	0.5	74	90	34		15	.268	.333	0	0	3B-151
1901	PHI A	2	8	1	0	0	0	0.0	1	0	0		0	.125	.125	0	0	3B-2
1902	NY N	125	482	114	20	1	1	0.2	41	44	10		19	.237	.288	0	0	3B-121, OF-4
1903		108	395	111	13	0	0	0.0	52	53	14		19	.281	.314	0	0	3B-108
5 yrs.		483	1829	477	64	14	6	0.3	210	254	77		59	.261	.321	0	0	3B-479, OF-4

Tim Laudner

LAUDNER, TIMOTHY JON
B. June 7, 1958, Mason City, Iowa   BR TR 6'3"   212 lbs.

Year	Team	G	AB	H	2B	3B	HR	HR%	R	RBI	BB	SO	SB	BA	SA	PH AB	PH H	G by POS
1981	MIN A	14	43	7	2	0	2	4.7	4	5	3	17	0	.163	.349	0	0	C-12, DH-2
1982		93	306	78	19	1	7	2.3	37	33	34	74	0	.255	.392	0	0	C-57, DH-4
1983		62	168	31	9	0	6	3.6	20	18	15	49	0	.185	.345	8	2	C-81, DH-2
1984		87	262	54	16	1	10	3.8	31	35	18	78	0	.206	.389	4	2	C-243, DH-8
4 yrs.		256	779	170	46	2	25	3.2	92	91	70	218	0	.218	.379	12	4	

Bill Lauterborn

LAUTERBORN, WILLIAM BERNARD
B. June 9, 1879, Hornell, N.Y.   D. Apr. 19, 1965, Andover, N.Y.   BR TR 5'6"   140 lbs.

Year	Team	G	AB	H	2B	3B	HR	HR%	R	RBI	BB	SO	SB	BA	SA	PH AB	PH H	G by POS
1904	BOS N	20	69	19	2	0	0	0.0	7	2	1		1	.275	.304	0	0	2B-20
1905		67	200	37	1	1	0	0.0	11	9	12		1	.185	.200	9	2	3B-29, 2B-23, SS-3, OF-2
2 yrs.		87	269	56	3	1	0	0.0	18	11	13		2	.208	.227	9	2	2B-43, 3B-29, SS-3, OF-2

	G	AB	H	2B	3B	HR	HR %	R	RBI	BB	SO	SB	BA	SA	Pinch Hit AB	Pinch Hit H	G by POS

Cookie Lavagetto

LAVAGETTO, HARRY ARTHUR
B. Dec. 1, 1912, Oakland, Calif.
Manager 1957-61.

BR TR 6' 170 lbs.

	G	AB	H	2B	3B	HR	HR %	R	RBI	BB	SO	SB	BA	SA	AB	H	G by POS
1934 PIT N	87	304	67	16	3	3	1.0	41	46	32	39	6	.220	.322	2	1	2B-83
1935	78	231	67	9	4	0	0.0	27	19	18	15	1	.290	.364	16	3	2B-42, 3B-15
1936	60	197	48	15	2	2	1.0	21	26	15	13	0	.244	.371	9	0	2B-37, 3B-13, SS-1
1937 BKN N	149	503	142	26	6	8	1.6	64	70	74	41	13	.282	.406	4	0	2B-100, 3B-45
1938	137	487	133	34	6	6	1.2	68	79	68	31	15	.273	.405	3	0	3B-132, 2B-4
1939	153	587	176	28	5	10	1.7	93	87	78	30	14	.300	.416	4	2	3B-149
1940	118	448	115	21	3	4	0.9	56	43	70	32	4	.257	.344	1	0	3B-116
1941	132	441	122	24	7	1	0.2	75	78	80	21	7	.277	.370	10	0	3B-120
1946	88	242	57	9	1	3	1.2	36	27	38	17	3	.236	.318	11	2	3B-67
1947	41	69	18	1	0	3	4.3	6	11	12	5	0	.261	.406	17	4	3B-18, 1B-3
10 yrs.	1043	3509	945	183	37	40	1.1	487	486	485	244	63	.269	.377	77	12	3B-675, 2B-266, 1B-3, SS-1

WORLD SERIES

	G	AB	H	2B	3B	HR	HR %	R	RBI	BB	SO	SB	BA	SA	AB	H	G by POS
1941 BKN N	3	10	1	0	0	0	0.0	1	0	2	0	0	.100	.100	0	0	3B-3
1947	5	7	1	1	0	0	0.0	0	3	0	2	0	.143	.286	5	1	3B-3
2 yrs.	8	17	2	1	0	0	0.0	1	3	2	2	0	.118	.176	5	1	3B-6

Mike Lavalliere

LAVALLIERE, MICHAEL
B. Aug. 18, 1960, Charlotte, N. C.

BL TR 5'10" 180 lbs.

	G	AB	H	2B	3B	HR	HR %	R	RBI	BB	SO	SB	BA	SA	AB	H	G by POS
1984 PHI N	6	7	0	0	0	0	0.0	0	0	2	2	0	.000	.000	0	0	C-6

Doc Lavan

LAVAN, JOHN LEONARD
B. Oct. 28, 1890, Grand Rapids, Mich.   D. May 29, 1952, Detroit, Mich.

BR TR 5'8½" 151 lbs.

	G	AB	H	2B	3B	HR	HR %	R	RBI	BB	SO	SB	BA	SA	AB	H	G by POS
1913 2 teams	STL	A (46G –	.141)		PHI	A (5G –	.071)										
" total	51	163	22	2	2	0	0.0	9	5	10	46	3	.135	.172	0	0	SS-51
1914 STL A	74	239	63	7	4	1	0.4	21	21	17	39	6	.264	.339	0	0	SS-73
1915	157	514	112	17	7	1	0.2	44	48	42	83	13	.218	.284	0	0	SS-157
1916	110	343	81	13	1	0	0.0	32	19	32	38	7	.236	.280	3	1	SS-106
1917	118	355	85	8	5	0	0.0	19	30	19	34	5	.239	.290	1	0	SS-110, 2B-7
1918 WAS A	117	464	129	17	2	0	0.0	44	45	14	21	12	.278	.323	0	0	SS-117, OF-1
1919 STL N	100	356	86	12	2	1	0.3	25	25	11	30	4	.242	.295	0	0	SS-99
1920	142	516	149	21	10	1	0.2	52	63	19	38	11	.289	.374	4	1	SS-138
1921	150	560	145	23	11	2	0.4	58	82	23	30	7	.259	.350	0	0	SS-150
1922	89	264	60	8	1	0	0.0	24	27	13	10	3	.227	.265	1	0	SS-82, 3B-5
1923	50	111	22	6	0	1	0.9	10	12	9	7	0	.198	.279	2	1	SS-40, 3B-4, 1B-3, 2B-1
1924	4	6	0	0	0	0	0.0	0	0	0	0	0	.000	.000	0	0	SS-2, 2B-2
12 yrs.	1162	3891	954	134	45	7	0.2	338	377	209	376	71	.245	.308	12	3	SS-1125, 2B-10, 3B-9, 1B-3, OF-1

Chuck Laver

LAVER, JOHN CHARLES
B. 1865, Pittsburgh, Pa.   Deceased.

TR

	G	AB	H	2B	3B	HR	HR %	R	RBI	BB	SO	SB	BA	SA	AB	H	G by POS
1884 PIT AA	13	44	5	0	0	0	0.0	5		0			.114	.114	0	0	OF-10, P-3, 1B-1
1889 PIT N	4	16	3	0	0	0	0.0	2	1	0	5	0	.188	.188	0	0	C-3, OF-1
1890 CHI N	2	8	2	1	0	0	0.0	1	2	0	0	0	.250	.375	0	0	C-2
3 yrs.	19	68	10	1	0	0	0.0	8	2	0	5	0	.147	.162	0	0	OF-11, C-5, P-3, 1B-1

Art LaVigne

LaVIGNE, ARTHUR DAVID
B. Jan. 26, 1885, Worcester, Mass.   D. July 18, 1950, Worcester, Mass.

BR TR 5'10" 162 lbs.

	G	AB	H	2B	3B	HR	HR %	R	RBI	BB	SO	SB	BA	SA	AB	H	G by POS
1914 BUF F	51	90	14	2	0	0	0.0	10	4	7		0	.156	.178	7	1	C-34, 1B-3

Johnny Lavin

LAVIN, JOHN
B. Bay City, Mich.   Deceased.

	G	AB	H	2B	3B	HR	HR %	R	RBI	BB	SO	SB	BA	SA	AB	H	G by POS
1884 STL AA	16	52	11	2	0	0	0.0	9		3			.212	.250	0	0	OF-16

Rudy Law

LAW, RUDY KARL
B. Oct. 7, 1956, Waco, Tex.

BL TL 6'1" 165 lbs.

	G	AB	H	2B	3B	HR	HR %	R	RBI	BB	SO	SB	BA	SA	AB	H	G by POS
1978 LA N	11	12	3	0	0	0	0.0	2	1	1	2	3	.250	.250	1	0	OF-6
1980	128	388	101	5	4	1	0.3	55	23	23	27	40	.260	.302	16	4	OF-106
1982 CHI A	121	336	107	15	8	3	0.9	55	32	23	41	36	.318	.438	17	3	OF-94, DH-3
1983	141	501	142	20	7	3	0.6	95	34	42	36	77	.283	.369	13	4	OF-132, DH-3
1984	136	487	122	14	7	6	1.2	68	37	39	42	29	.251	.345	11	5	OF-130
5 yrs.	537	1724	475	54	26	13	0.8	275	127	128	148	185	.276	.360	58	16	OF-468, DH-6

LEAGUE CHAMPIONSHIP SERIES

	G	AB	H	2B	3B	HR	HR %	R	RBI	BB	SO	SB	BA	SA	AB	H	G by POS
1983 CHI A	4	18	7	1	0	0	0.0	1	0	0	1	2	.389	.444	0	0	OF-4

Vance Law

LAW, VANCE AARON
Son of Vern Law.
B. Oct. 1, 1956, Boise, Ida.

BR TR 6'2" 185 lbs.

	G	AB	H	2B	3B	HR	HR %	R	RBI	BB	SO	SB	BA	SA	AB	H	G by POS
1980 PIT N	25	74	17	2	2	0	0.0	11	3	3	7	2	.230	.311	3	1	2B-11, SS-8, 3B-1
1981	30	67	9	0	1	0	0.0	1	3	2	15	1	.134	.164	2	0	2B-19, SS-7, 3B-2
1982 CHI A	114	359	101	20	1	5	1.4	40	54	26	46	4	.281	.384	1	1	SS-85, 3B-39, 2B-10, OF-1
1983	145	408	99	21	5	4	1.0	55	42	51	56	3	.243	.348	0	0	3B-139, 2B-3, SS-2, DH-1, OF-1
1984	151	481	121	18	2	17	3.5	60	59	41	75	4	.252	.403	4	2	3B-127, 2B-22, OF-5, SS-4
5 yrs.	465	1389	347	61	11	26	1.9	167	161	123	199	14	.250	.366	10	4	3B-318, SS-106, 2B-65, OF-7, DH-1

LEAGUE CHAMPIONSHIP SERIES

	G	AB	H	2B	3B	HR	HR %	R	RBI	BB	SO	SB	BA	SA	AB	H	G by POS
1983 CHI A	4	11	2	0	0	0	0.0	0	1	1	3	0	.182	.182	0	0	3B-4

	G	AB	H	2B	3B	HR	HR %	R	RBI	BB	SO	SB	BA	SA	Pinch Hit AB	Pinch Hit H	G by POS

Garland Lawing
LAWING, GARLAND FRED (Knobby)
B. Aug. 26, 1919, Gastonia, N. C.　　　　　　　　BR TR 6'1"　180 lbs.

	G	AB	H	2B	3B	HR	HR %	R	RBI	BB	SO	SB	BA	SA	AB	H	G by POS
1946 2 teams	CIN N (2G – .000)					NY N (8G – .167)											
" total	10	15	2	0	0	0	0.0	2	0	0	5	0	.133	.133	3	1	OF-4, P-1

Tom Lawless
LAWLESS, THOMAS JAMES
B. Dec. 19, 1956, Erie, Pa.　　　　　　　　BR TR 6'　165 lbs.

	G	AB	H	2B	3B	HR	HR %	R	RBI	BB	SO	SB	BA	SA	AB	H	G by POS
1982 CIN N	49	165	35	6	0	0	0.0	19	4	9	30	16	.212	.248	1	0	2B-47
1984 2 teams	CIN N (43G – .250)					MON N (11G – .176)											
" total	54	97	23	3	0	1	1.0	11	2	8	16	7	.237	.299	5	1	2B-32, 3B-6
2 yrs.	103	262	58	9	0	1	0.4	30	6	17	46	23	.221	.267	6	1	2B-79, 3B-6

Mike Lawlor
LAWLOR, MICHAEL H.
B. Mar. 11, 1854, Troy, N. Y.　　D. Aug. 3, 1918, Troy, N. Y.

	G	AB	H	2B	3B	HR	HR %	R	RBI	BB	SO	SB	BA	SA	AB	H	G by POS
1880 TRO N	4	9	1	0	0	0	0.0	1		1	1		.111	.111	0	0	C-4
1884 WAS U	2	7	0	0	0	0	0.0	0		0			.000	.000	0	0	C-2
2 yrs.	6	16	1	0	0	0	0.0	1		1	1		.063	.063	0	0	C-6

Bill Lawrence
LAWRENCE, WILLIAM HENRY
B. Mar. 11, 1906, San Mateo, Calif.　　　　　　BR TR 6'4"　194 lbs.

	G	AB	H	2B	3B	HR	HR %	R	RBI	BB	SO	SB	BA	SA	AB	H	G by POS
1932 DET A	25	46	10	1	0	0	0.0	10	3	5	5	0	.217	.239	2	0	OF-15

Jim Lawrence
LAWRENCE, JAMES ROSS
B. Feb. 12, 1939, Hamilton, Ont., Canada　　　　BL TR 6'1"　185 lbs.

	G	AB	H	2B	3B	HR	HR %	R	RBI	BB	SO	SB	BA	SA	AB	H	G by POS
1963 CLE A	2	0	0	0	0	0	–	0	0	0	0	0	–	–	0	0	C-2

Otis Lawry
LAWRY, OTIS CARROLL (Rabbit)
B. Nov. 1, 1893, Fairfield, Me.　　D. Oct. 23, 1965, China, Me.　　BL TR 5'8"　133 lbs.

	G	AB	H	2B	3B	HR	HR %	R	RBI	BB	SO	SB	BA	SA	AB	H	G by POS
1916 PHI A	41	123	25	0	0	0	0.0	10	4	9	21	4	.203	.203	5	0	2B-29, OF-5
1917	30	55	9	1	0	0	0.0	7	1	2	9	1	.164	.182	4	1	2B-17, OF-1
2 yrs.	71	178	34	1	0	0	0.0	17	5	11	30	5	.191	.197	9	1	2B-46, OF-6

Gene Layden
LAYDEN, EUGENE FRANCIS
B. Mar. 14, 1894, Pittsburgh, Pa.　　　　　　BL TL 5'10"　160 lbs.

	G	AB	H	2B	3B	HR	HR %	R	RBI	BB	SO	SB	BA	SA	AB	H	G by POS
1915 NY A	3	7	2	0	0	0	0.0	2	0	0	1	0	.286	.286	0	0	OF-2

Pete Layden
LAYDEN, PETER JOHN
B. Dec. 30, 1919, Dallas, Tex.　　D. July 18, 1982, Edna, Tex.　　BR TR 5'11"　185 lbs.

	G	AB	H	2B	3B	HR	HR %	R	RBI	BB	SO	SB	BA	SA	AB	H	G by POS
1948 STL A	41	104	26	2	1	0	0.0	11	4	6	10	4	.250	.288	8	2	OF-30

Herman Layne
LAYNE, HERMAN
B. Feb. 13, 1901, New Haven, W. Va.　　D. Aug. 27, 1973, Gallipolis, Ohio　　BR TR 5'11"　165 lbs.

	G	AB	H	2B	3B	HR	HR %	R	RBI	BB	SO	SB	BA	SA	AB	H	G by POS
1927 PIT N	11	6	0	0	0	0	0.0	3	0	1	0	0	.000	.000	1	0	OF-2

Hilly Layne
LAYNE, IVORIA HILLIS (Tony)
B. Feb. 23, 1918, Whitewell, Tenn.　　　　　　BL TR 6'　170 lbs.

	G	AB	H	2B	3B	HR	HR %	R	RBI	BB	SO	SB	BA	SA	AB	H	G by POS
1941 WAS A	13	50	14	2	0	0	0.0	8	6	4	5	1	.280	.320	0	0	3B-13
1944	33	87	17	2	0	0	0.0	6	8	6	10	2	.195	.218	13	2	3B-18, 2B-3
1945	61	147	44	5	4	1	0.7	23	14	10	7	0	.299	.408	23	4	3B-33
3 yrs.	107	284	75	9	4	1	0.4	37	28	20	22	3	.264	.335	36	6	3B-64, 2B-3

Les Layton
LAYTON, LESTER LEE
B. Nov. 18, 1921, Nardin, Okla.　　　　　　BR TR 6'　165 lbs.

	G	AB	H	2B	3B	HR	HR %	R	RBI	BB	SO	SB	BA	SA	AB	H	G by POS
1948 NY N	63	91	21	4	4	2	2.2	14	12	6	21	1	.231	.429	32	8	OF-20

Johnny Lazor
LAZOR, JOHN PAUL
B. Sept. 9, 1912, Taylor, Wash.　　　　　　BL TR 5'9½"　180 lbs.

	G	AB	H	2B	3B	HR	HR %	R	RBI	BB	SO	SB	BA	SA	AB	H	G by POS
1943 BOS A	83	208	47	10	2	0	0.0	21	13	21	25	5	.226	.293	17	2	OF-63
1944	16	24	2	1	0	0	0.0	0	0	1	0	0	.083	.125	8	1	OF-6, C-1
1945	101	335	104	19	2	5	1.5	35	45	18	17	3	.310	.424	17	5	OF-81
1946	23	29	4	0	0	1	3.4	1	4	0	11	0	.138	.241	16	1	OF-7
4 yrs.	223	596	157	30	4	6	1.0	57	62	40	53	8	.263	.357	58	9	OF-157, C-1

Tony Lazzeri
LAZZERI, ANTHONY MICHAEL (Poosh 'Em Up)　　　　　　BR TR 5'11½"　170 lbs.
B. Dec. 6, 1903, San Francisco, Calif.　　D. Aug. 6, 1946, San Francisco, Calif.

	G	AB	H	2B	3B	HR	HR %	R	RBI	BB	SO	SB	BA	SA	AB	H	G by POS
1926 NY A	155	589	162	28	14	18	3.1	79	114	54	96	16	.275	.462	0	0	2B-149, SS-5, 3B-1
1927	153	570	176	29	8	18	3.2	92	102	69	82	22	.309	.482	0	0	2B-113, SS-38, 3B-9
1928	116	404	134	30	11	10	2.5	62	82	43	50	15	.332	.535	4	1	2B-116
1929	147	545	193	37	11	18	3.3	101	106	69	45	9	.354	.561	0	0	2B-147, SS-61
1930	143	571	173	34	15	9	1.6	109	121	60	62	4	.303	.462	1	0	2B-77, 3B-60, SS-8, OF-1, 1B-1
1931	135	484	129	27	7	8	1.7	67	83	79	80	18	.267	.401	7	5	2B-90, 3B-39
1932	141	510	153	28	16	15	2.9	79	113	82	64	11	.300	.506	3	1	2B-133, 3B-5
1933	139	523	154	22	12	18	3.4	94	104	73	62	15	.294	.486	1	0	2B-138
1934	123	438	117	24	6	14	3.2	59	67	71	64	11	.267	.445	1	1	2B-92, 3B-30
1935	130	477	130	18	6	13	2.7	72	83	63	75	11	.273	.417	5	3	2B-118, SS-9
1936	150	537	154	29	6	14	2.6	82	109	97	65	8	.287	.441	0	0	2B-148, SS-2
1937	126	446	109	21	3	14	3.1	56	70	71	76	7	.244	.399	1	0	2B-125
1938 CHI N	54	120	32	5	0	5	4.2	21	23	22	30	0	.267	.433	14	2	SS-25, 3B-7, 2B-4, OF-1
1939 2 teams	BKN N (14G – .282)					NY N (13G – .295)											
" total	27	83	24	2	0	4	4.8	13	14	17	13	1	.289	.458	1	0	3B-15, 2B-11
14 yrs.	1739	6297	1840	334	115	178	2.8	986	1191	870	864	148	.292	.467	38	13	2B-1461, 3B-166, SS-148, OF-2, 1B-1

WORLD SERIES																	
1926 NY A	7	26	5	1	0	0	0.0	2	3	1	6	0	.192	.231	0	0	2B-7
1927	4	15	4	1	0	0	0.0	1	2	1	4	0	.267	.333	0	0	2B-4

	G	AB	H	2B	3B	HR	HR %	R	RBI	BB	SO	SB	BA	SA	Pinch Hit AB	Pinch Hit H	G by POS

Tony Lazzeri continued

	G	AB	H	2B	3B	HR	HR %	R	RBI	BB	SO	SB	BA	SA	PH AB	PH H	G by POS
1928	4	12	3	1	0	0	0.0	2	0	1	0	2	.250	.333	0	0	2B-4
1932	4	17	5	0	0	2	11.8	4	5	2	1	0	.294	.647	0	0	2B-4
1936	6	20	5	0	0	1	5.0	4	7	4	4	0	.250	.400	0	0	2B-6
1937	5	15	6	0	1	1	6.7	3	2	3	3	0	.400	.733	0	0	2B-5
1938 CHI N	2	2	0	0	0	0	0.0	0	0	0	1	0	.000	.000	2	0	
7 yrs.	32	107	28	3	1	4	3.7	16	19	12	19	2	.262	.421	2	0	2B-30

Freddy Leach

LEACH, FREDERICK
B. Nov. 23, 1897, Springfield, Mo.   D. Dec. 10, 1981, Ida.   BL TR 5'11" 183 lbs.

	G	AB	H	2B	3B	HR	HR %	R	RBI	BB	SO	SB	BA	SA	PH AB	PH H	G by POS
1923 PHI N	52	104	27	4	0	1	1.0	5	16	3	14	1	.260	.327	23	4	OF-26
1924	8	28	13	2	1	2	7.1	6	7	2	1	0	.464	.821	0	0	OF-7
1925	65	292	91	15	4	5	1.7	47	28	5	21	1	.312	.442	0	0	OF-65
1926	129	492	162	29	7	11	2.2	73	71	16	33	6	.329	.484	5	1	OF-123
1927	140	536	164	30	4	12	2.2	69	83	21	32	2	.306	.444	1	0	OF-139
1928	145	588	179	36	11	13	2.2	83	96	30	30	4	.304	.469	0	0	OF-120, 1B-25
1929 NY N	113	411	119	22	6	8	1.9	74	47	17	14	10	.290	.431	17	5	OF-95
1930	126	544	178	19	13	13	2.4	90	71	22	25	3	.327	.482	2	0	OF-124
1931	129	515	159	30	5	6	1.2	75	61	29	9	4	.309	.421	2	0	OF-125
1932 BOS N	84	223	55	9	2	1	0.4	21	29	18	10	1	.247	.318	30	8	OF-50
10 yrs.	991	3733	1147	196	53	72	1.9	543	509	163	189	32	.307	.446	80	18	OF-874, 1B-25

Rick Leach

LEACH, RICHARD MAX
B. May 4, 1957, Ann Arbor, Mich.   BL TL 6'1" 180 lbs.

	G	AB	H	2B	3B	HR	HR %	R	RBI	BB	SO	SB	BA	SA	PH AB	PH H	G by POS
1981 DET A	54	83	16	3	1	1	1.2	9	11	16	15	0	.193	.289	10	2	1B-32, OF-15, DH-2
1982	82	218	52	7	2	3	1.4	23	12	21	29	4	.239	.330	14	2	1B-56, OF-14, DH-4
1983	99	242	60	17	0	3	1.2	22	26	19	21	2	.248	.355	18	4	1B-73, OF-13, DH-3
1984 TOR A	65	88	23	6	2	0	0.0	11	7	8	14	0	.261	.375	22	8	OF-23, 1B-15, DH-6, P-1
4 yrs.	300	631	151	33	5	7	1.1	65	56	64	79	6	.239	.341	64	16	1B-176, OF-65, DH-15, P-1

Tommy Leach

LEACH, THOMAS WILLIAM
B. Nov. 4, 1877, French Creek, N. Y.   D. Sept. 29, 1969, Haines City, Fla.   BR TR 5'6½" 150 lbs.

	G	AB	H	2B	3B	HR	HR %	R	RBI	BB	SO	SB	BA	SA	PH AB	PH H	G by POS
1898 LOU N	3	10	3	0	0	0	0.0	0	0	0		0	.300	.300	0	0	3B-3, 2B-1
1899	106	406	117	10	6	5	1.2	75	57	37		19	.288	.379	0	0	3B-80, SS-25, 2B-2
1900 PIT N	51	160	34	1	2	1	0.6	20	16	21		8	.213	.263	1	0	3B-31, SS-8, 2B-7, OF-4
1901	98	374	112	13	13	1	0.3	64	44	20		16	.299	.412	2	1	3B-92, SS-4
1902	135	514	144	21	22	6	1.2	97	85	45		25	.280	.442	1	0	3B-134
1903	127	507	151	16	17	7	1.4	97	87	40		22	.298	.438	0	0	3B-127
1904	146	579	149	15	12	2	0.3	92	56	45		23	.257	.335	0	0	3B-146
1905	131	499	128	10	14	2	0.4	71	53	37		17	.257	.345	0	0	OF-71, 3B-58, SS-2, 2B-2
1906	133	476	136	10	7	1	0.2	66	39	33		21	.286	.342	6	3	3B-65, OF-60, SS-1
1907	149	547	166	19	12	4	0.7	102	43	40		43	.303	.404	0	0	OF-111, 3B-33, SS-6, 2B-1
1908	152	583	151	24	16	5	0.9	93	41	54		24	.259	.381	0	0	3B-150, OF-2
1909	151	587	153	29	8	6	1.0	126	43	66		27	.261	.368	0	0	OF-138, 3B-13
1910	135	529	143	24	5	4	0.8	83	52	38	62	18	.270	.357	1	0	OF-131, SS-2, 2B-1
1911	108	386	92	12	6	3	0.8	60	43	46	50	19	.238	.324	4	0	OF-89, SS-13, 3B-1
1912 2 teams	PIT	N (28G – .299)		CHI	N (82G – .242)												
" total	110	362	93	14	5	2	0.6	74	51	67	29	20	.257	.340	4	2	OF-97, 3B-4
1913 CHI N	130	454	131	23	10	6	1.3	99	32	77	44	21	.289	.423	7	3	OF-119, 3B-2
1914	153	577	152	24	9	7	1.2	80	46	79	50	16	.263	.373	1	0	OF-137, 3B-16
1915 CIN N	107	335	75	7	5	0	0.0	42	17	56	38	20	.224	.275	9	1	OF-96
1918 PIT N	30	72	14	2	3	0	0.0	14	5	19	5	2	.194	.306	2	0	OF-23, SS-3
19 yrs.	2155	7957	2144	274	172	62	0.8	1355	810	820	278	361	.269	.370	38	10	OF-1078, 3B-955, SS-64, 2B-14

WORLD SERIES

	G	AB	H	2B	3B	HR	HR %	R	RBI	BB	SO	SB	BA	SA	PH AB	PH H	G by POS
1903 PIT N	8	33	9	0	4	0	0.0	3	7	1	4	2	.273	.515	0	0	3B-8
1909	7	25	8	4	0	0	0.0	8	2	2	1	1	.320	.480	0	0	OF-6
2 yrs.	15	58	17	4	4	0	0.0	11	9	3	5	3	.293	.500	0	0	3B-8, OF-6

1st

Dan Leahy

LEAHY, DANIEL C.
B. Aug. 8, 1870, Knoxville, Tenn.   D. Dec. 30, 1903, Knoxville, Tenn.

	G	AB	H	2B	3B	HR	HR %	R	RBI	BB	SO	SB	BA	SA	PH AB	PH H	G by POS
1896 PHI N	2	6	2	1	0	0	0.0	0	1	1	2	0	.333	.500	0	0	SS-2

Tom Leahy

LEAHY, THOMAS JOSEPH
B. June 2, 1869, New Haven, Conn.   D. June 12, 1951, New Haven, Conn.   TR

	G	AB	H	2B	3B	HR	HR %	R	RBI	BB	SO	SB	BA	SA	PH AB	PH H	G by POS
1897 2 teams	PIT	N (24G – .261)		WAS	N (19G – .385)												
" total	43	144	44	5	4	0	0.0	22	19	16		9	.306	.396	0	0	OF-23, 3B-11, C-7, 2B-3
1898 WAS N	15	55	10	2	0	0	0.0	10	5	8		6	.182	.218	0	0	3B-12, 2B-3
1901 2 teams	MIL	A (33G – .242)		PHI	A (5G – .333)												
" total	38	114	29	7	2	0	0.0	19	11	12		3	.254	.351	3	2	C-29, OF-4, SS-1, 2B-1
1905 STL N	35	97	22	1	3	0	0.0	3	7	8		3	.227	.299	6	1	C-29
4 yrs.	131	410	105	15	9	0	0.0	54	42	44		18	.256	.337	9	3	C-65, OF-27, 3B-23, 2B-7, SS-1

Fred Lear

LEAR, FREDRICK FRANCIS (King)
B. Apr. 7, 1894, New York, N.Y.   D. Oct. 13, 1955, East Orange, N. J.   BR TR 6'½" 180 lbs.

	G	AB	H	2B	3B	HR	HR %	R	RBI	BB	SO	SB	BA	SA	PH AB	PH H	G by POS
1915 PHI A	2	2	0	0	0	0	0.0	0	0	0	2	0	.000	.000	0	0	3B-2
1918 CHI N	2	1	0	0	0	0	0.0	0	0	1	0	0	.000	.000	1	0	
1919	40	76	17	3	1	1	1.3	8	11	8	11	0	.224	.329	14	2	2B-9, 1B-9, SS-3
1920 NY N	31	87	22	0	1	1	1.1	12	7	8	15	0	.253	.310	4	1	3B-24, 2B-1
4 yrs.	75	166	39	3	2	2	1.2	20	18	17	28	2	.235	.313	19	3	3B-26, 2B-10, 1B-9, SS-3

	G	AB	H	2B	3B	HR	HR %	R	RBI	BB	SO	SB	BA	SA	Pinch Hit AB	Pinch Hit H	G by POS

Bill Leard

LEARD, WILLIAM WALLACE (Wild Bill)   BR TR 5'10"   155 lbs.
B. Oct. 14, 1885, Oneida, N. Y.   D. Jan. 15, 1970, San Francisco, Calif.

	G	AB	H	2B	3B	HR	HR %	R	RBI	BB	SO	SB	BA	SA	PH AB	PH H	G by POS
1917 BKN N	3	3	0	0	0	0	0.0	0	0	0	1	0	.000	.000	1	0	2B-1

Jack Leary

LEARY, JOHN J.   TL
B. 1858, New Haven, Conn.   Deceased.

	G	AB	H	2B	3B	HR	HR %	R	RBI	BB	SO	SB	BA	SA	PH AB	PH H	G by POS
1880 BOS N	1	3	0	0	0	0	0.0	1	0	1	0		.000	.000	0	0	OF-1, P-1
1881 DET N	3	11	3	1	1	0	0.0	2	4	1	1		.273	.545	0	0	OF-2, P-2
1882 2 teams	PIT	AA (60G –	.292)		BAL	AA (4G –	.222)										
" total	64	275	79	8	3	2	0.7	35		5			.287	.360	0	0	3B-33, OF-28, P-6, 2B-1, 1B-1
1883 2 teams	LOU	AA (40G –	.188)		BAL	AA (3G –	.182)										
" total	43	176	33	1	5	3	1.7	17		2			.188	.301	0	0	SS-40, 2B-3
1884 2 teams	ALT	U (8G –	.091)		C-P	U (10G –	.175)										
" total	18	73	10	1	0	0	0.0	1		1			.137	.151	0	0	OF-9, P-5, 3B-4, 2B-4
5 yrs.	129	538	125	11	9	5	0.9	56	4	10	1		.232	.314	0	0	OF-40, SS-40, 3B-37, P-14, 2B-8, 1B-1

John Leary

LEARY, JOHN LOUIS (Jack)   BR TR 5'11½" 180 lbs.
B. May 2, 1891, Waltham, Mass.   D. Aug. 18, 1961, Waltham, Mass.

	G	AB	H	2B	3B	HR	HR %	R	RBI	BB	SO	SB	BA	SA	PH AB	PH H	G by POS
1914 STL A	144	533	141	28	7	0	0.0	35	45	10	71	9	.265	.343	2	1	1B-130, C-15
1915	75	227	55	10	0	0	0.0	19	15	5	36	2	.242	.286	11	4	1B-53, C-11
2 yrs.	219	760	196	38	7	0	0.0	54	60	15	107	11	.258	.326	13	5	1B-183, C-26

Hal Leathers

LEATHERS, HAROLD LANGFORD   BL TR 5'7"   152 lbs.
B. Dec. 2, 1898, Los Angeles, Calif.   D. Apr. 12, 1977, Modesto, Calif.

	G	AB	H	2B	3B	HR	HR %	R	RBI	BB	SO	SB	BA	SA	PH AB	PH H	G by POS
1920 CHI N	9	23	7	1	0	1	4.3	3	1	1	1	1	.304	.478	1	0	SS-6, 2B-3

Emil Leber

LEBER, EMIL BOHMIEL   BR TR 5'11"   170 lbs.
B. May 15, 1881, Cleveland, Ohio   D. Nov. 6, 1924, Cleveland, Ohio

	G	AB	H	2B	3B	HR	HR %	R	RBI	BB	SO	SB	BA	SA	PH AB	PH H	G by POS
1905 CLE A	2	6	0	0	0	0	0.0	0	1	0			.000	.000	0	0	3B-2

Bevo LeBourveau

LeBOURVEAU, DeWITT WILEY   BL TR 5'11"   175 lbs.
B. Aug. 24, 1894, Dana, Calif.   D. Dec. 9, 1947, Nevada City, Calif.

	G	AB	H	2B	3B	HR	HR %	R	RBI	BB	SO	SB	BA	SA	PH AB	PH H	G by POS
1919 PHI N	17	63	17	0	0	0	0.0	4	0	10	8	2	.270	.270	0	0	OF-17
1920	84	261	67	7	2	3	1.1	29	12	11	36	9	.257	.333	8	1	OF-72
1921	93	281	83	12	5	6	2.1	42	35	29	51	4	.295	.438	16	9	OF-76
1922	74	167	45	8	3	2	1.2	24	20	24	29	0	.269	.389	25	4	OF-42
1929 PHI A	12	16	5	0	1	0	0.0	1	2	5	1	0	.313	.438	9	1	OF-3
5 yrs.	280	788	217	27	11	11	1.4	100	69	79	125	15	.275	.379	58	15	OF-210

Bill Lee

LEE, WILLIAM JOSEPH   BR TR 5'9"   165 lbs.
B. Jan. 9, 1892, Bayonne, N. J.   D. Jan. 6, 1984, West Hazleton, Pa.

	G	AB	H	2B	3B	HR	HR %	R	RBI	BB	SO	SB	BA	SA	PH AB	PH H	G by POS
1915 STL A	18	59	11	1	0	0	0.0	2	4	6	5	1	.186	.203	2	1	OF-15, 3B-1
1916	7	11	2	0	0	0	0.0	1	0	1	1	0	.182	.182	3	2	OF-3
2 yrs.	25	70	13	1	0	0	0.0	3	4	7	6	1	.186	.200	5	3	OF-18, 3B-1

Cliff Lee

LEE, CLIFFORD WALKER   BR TR 6'1"   175 lbs.
B. Aug. 4, 1896, Lexington, Neb.   D. Aug. 25, 1980, Denver, Colo.

	G	AB	H	2B	3B	HR	HR %	R	RBI	BB	SO	SB	BA	SA	PH AB	PH H	G by POS
1919 PIT N	42	112	22	2	4	0	0.0	5	2	6	8	2	.196	.286	8	1	C-28, OF-6
1920	37	76	18	2	2	0	0.0	9	8	4	14	0	.237	.316	16	3	C-19, OF-2
1921 PHI N	88	286	88	14	4	4	1.4	31	29	13	34	5	.308	.427	10	6	1B-48, OF-27, C-2
1922	122	422	136	29	6	17	4.0	65	77	32	43	2	.322	.540	13	3	OF-89, 1B-18, 3B-1
1923	107	355	114	20	4	11	3.1	54	47	20	39	3	.321	.493	12	1	OF-83, 1B-16
1924 2 teams	PHI	N (21G –	.250)		CIN	N (6G –	.333)										
" total	27	62	16	4	2	1	1.6	5	9	2	7	0	.258	.435	7	2	OF-14, 1B-4
1925 CLE A	77	230	74	15	6	4	1.7	43	42	21	33	2	.322	.491	7	2	OF-70
1926	21	40	7	1	0	1	2.5	4	2	6	8	0	.175	.275	8	1	OF-9, C-3
8 yrs.	521	1583	475	87	28	38	2.4	216	216	104	186	14	.300	.462	81	19	OF-300, 1B-86, C-52, 3B-1

Dud Lee

LEE, ERNEST DUDLEY   BL TR 5'9"   150 lbs.
Played as Dud Dudley 1920-21.
B. Aug. 22, 1899, Denver, Colo.   D. Jan. 7, 1971, Denver, Colo.

	G	AB	H	2B	3B	HR	HR %	R	RBI	BB	SO	SB	BA	SA	PH AB	PH H	G by POS
1920 STL A	1	2	2	0	0	0	0.0	2	1	0	0	1	1.000	1.000	0	0	SS-1
1921	72	180	30	4	2	0	0.0	18	11	14	34	1	.167	.211	0	0	SS-31, 2B-30, 3B-3
1924 BOS A	94	288	73	9	4	0	0.0	36	29	40	17	8	.253	.313	3	0	SS-90
1925	84	255	57	7	3	0	0.0	22	19	34	19	2	.224	.275	0	0	SS-84
1926	2	7	1	0	0	0	0.0	2	0	0	0	0	.143	.143	0	0	SS-2
5 yrs.	253	732	163	20	9	0	0.0	80	60	88	70	12	.223	.275	3	0	SS-208, 2B-30, 3B-3

Hal Lee

LEE, HAROLD BURNHAM (Sheriff)   BR TR 5'11"   180 lbs.
B. Feb. 15, 1905, Ludlow, Miss.

	G	AB	H	2B	3B	HR	HR %	R	RBI	BB	SO	SB	BA	SA	PH AB	PH H	G by POS
1930 BKN N	22	37	6	0	0	1	2.7	5	4	4	5	0	.162	.243	7	1	OF-12
1931 PHI N	44	131	29	10	2	2	1.5	13	12	10	18	0	.221	.344	5	1	OF-38
1932	149	595	180	42	10	18	3.0	76	85	36	45	6	.303	.497	0	0	OF-148
1933 2 teams	PHI	N (46G –	.287)		BOS	N (88G –	.221)										
" total	134	479	117	27	11	1	0.2	57	60	40	39	2	.244	.353	1	0	OF-132
1934 BOS N	139	521	152	23	6	8	1.5	70	79	47	43	3	.292	.405	7	1	OF-128, 2B-4
1935	112	422	128	18	6	0	0.0	49	39	18	25	0	.303	.374	2	0	OF-110
1936	152	565	143	24	7	3	0.5	46	46	52	50	4	.253	.336	1	0	OF-150
7 yrs.	752	2750	755	144	40	33	1.2	316	323	203	225	15	.275	.392	23	3	OF-718, 2B-4

Leonidas Lee

LEE, LEONIDAS PYRRHUS
Born Leonidas Pyrrhus Funkhouser.
B. Dec. 13, 1860, St. Louis, Mo.   D. June 11, 1912, Hendersonville, N. C.

	G	AB	H	2B	3B	HR	HR %	R	RBI	BB	SO	SB	BA	SA	PH AB	PH H	G by POS
1877 STL N	4	18	5	1	0	0	0.0	0	0	0	1		.278	.333	0	0	OF-4, SS-1

	G	AB	H	2B	3B	HR	HR %	R	RBI	BB	SO	SB	BA	SA	Pinch Hit AB	Pinch Hit H	G by POS

Leron Lee

LEE, LERON B. Mar. 4, 1948, Bakersfield, Calif.   BL TR 6' 196 lbs.

Year/Team	G	AB	H	2B	3B	HR	HR%	R	RBI	BB	SO	SB	BA	SA	PH AB	PH H	G by POS
1969 STL N	7	23	5	1	0	0	0.0	3	0	3	8	0	.217	.261	0	0	OF-7
1970	121	264	60	13	1	6	2.3	28	23	24	66	5	.227	.352	38	9	OF-77
1971 2 teams	STL N (25G – .179)			SD N (79G – .273)													
" total	104	284	75	21	2	5	1.8	32	23	22	57	4	.264	.405	26	3	OF-76
1972 SD N	101	370	111	23	7	12	3.2	50	47	29	58	2	.300	.497	4	2	OF-96
1973	118	333	79	7	2	3	0.9	36	30	33	61	4	.237	.297	30	7	OF-84
1974 CLE A	79	232	54	13	0	5	2.2	18	25	15	42	3	.233	.353	17	2	OF-62, DH-2
1975 2 teams	CLE A (13G – .130)			LA N (48G – .256)													
" total	61	66	14	5	0	0	0.0	5	2	5	14	1	.212	.288	46	10	OF-9, DH-3
1976 LA N	23	45	6	0	1	0	0.0	1	2	2	9	0	.133	.178	14	3	OF-10
8 yrs.	614	1617	404	83	13	31	1.9	173	152	133	315	19	.250	.375	175	36	OF-421, DH-5

Watty Lee

LEE, WYATT ARNOLD B. Aug. 12, 1879, Lynch's Station, Va. D. Mar. 6, 1936, Washington, D. C.   BL TL 5'10½" 171 lbs.

Year/Team	G	AB	H	2B	3B	HR	HR%	R	RBI	BB	SO	SB	BA	SA	PH AB	PH H	G by POS
1901 WAS A	43	129	33	6	3	0	0.0	15	12	7		0	.256	.349	2	0	P-36, OF-7
1902	109	391	100	21	5	4	1.0	61	45	33		8	.256	.366	3	0	OF-95, P-13
1903	75	231	48	8	4	0	0.0	17	13	18		5	.208	.277	5	1	OF-47, P-22
1904 PIT N	8	12	4	0	1	0	0.0	1	0	0		0	.333	.500	3	2	P-5
4 yrs.	235	763	185	35	13	4	0.5	94	70	58		13	.242	.338	13	3	OF-149, P-76

Gene Leek

LEEK, EUGENE HAROLD B. July 15, 1936, San Diego, Calif.   BR TR 6' 185 lbs.

Year/Team	G	AB	H	2B	3B	HR	HR%	R	RBI	BB	SO	SB	BA	SA	PH AB	PH H	G by POS
1959 CLE A	13	36	8	3	0	1	2.8	7	5	2	7	0	.222	.389	0	0	3B-13, SS-1
1961 LA A	57	199	45	9	1	5	2.5	16	20	7	54	0	.226	.357	0	0	3B-49, SS-7, OF-1
1962	7	14	2	0	0	0	0.0	0	0	0	6	0	.143	.143	2	1	3B-4
3 yrs.	77	249	55	12	1	6	2.4	23	25	9	67	0	.221	.349	2	1	3B-66, SS-8, OF-1

Dave Leeper

LEEPER, DAVID DALE B. Oct. 30, 1960, Santa Ana, Calif.   BL TL 5'11" 170 lbs.

Year/Team	G	AB	H	2B	3B	HR	HR%	R	RBI	BB	SO	SB	BA	SA	PH AB	PH H	G by POS
1984 KC A	4	6	0	0	0	0	0.0	1	0	0	1	0	.000	.000	1	0	OF-2, DH-1

George Lees

LEES, GEORGE EDWARD B. Feb. 2, 1895, Bethlehem, Pa. D. Jan. 2, 1980, Harrisburg, Pa.   BR TR 5'9" 150 lbs.

Year/Team	G	AB	H	2B	3B	HR	HR%	R	RBI	BB	SO	SB	BA	SA	PH AB	PH H	G by POS
1921 CHI A	20	42	9	2	0	0	0.0	3	4	0	3	0	.214	.262	4	0	C-16

Bill LeFebvre

LeFEBVRE, WILFRID HENRY (Lefty) B. Nov. 11, 1915, Natick, R. I.   BL TL 5'11½" 180 lbs.

Year/Team	G	AB	H	2B	3B	HR	HR%	R	RBI	BB	SO	SB	BA	SA	PH AB	PH H	G by POS
1938 BOS A	1	1	1	0	0	1	0.0	1	0	0	0	0	1.000	4.000	0	0	P-1
1939	7	10	3	0	0	0	0.0	3	1	2	2	0	.300	.300	2	1	P-5
1943 WAS A	7	14	4	3	0	0	0.0	0	1	1	0	0	.286	.500	1	1	P-6
1944	60	62	16	2	2	0	0.0	4	8	12	9	0	.258	.355	29	10	P-24, 1B-2
4 yrs.	75	87	24	5	2	1	1.1	8	11	15	11	0	.276	.414	32	12	P-36, 1B-2

Jim Lefebvre

LEFEBVRE, JAMES KENNETH B. Jan. 7, 1943, Hawthorne, Calif.   BB TR 6' 180 lbs.

Year/Team	G	AB	H	2B	3B	HR	HR%	R	RBI	BB	SO	SB	BA	SA	PH AB	PH H	G by POS
1965 LA N	157	544	136	21	4	12	2.2	57	69	71	92	3	.250	.369	2	1	2B-156
1966	152	544	149	23	3	24	4.4	69	74	48	72	1	.274	.460	3	1	2B-119, 3B-40
1967	136	494	129	18	5	8	1.6	51	50	44	64	1	.261	.366	7	0	3B-92, 2B-34, 1B-5
1968	84	286	69	12	1	5	1.7	23	31	26	55	0	.241	.343	5	1	2B-62, 3B-16, OF-5, 1B-3
1969	95	275	65	15	2	4	1.5	29	44	48	37	2	.236	.349	11	4	3B-44, 2B-37, 1B-6
1970	109	314	79	15	1	4	1.3	33	44	29	42	1	.252	.344	17	3	2B-70, 3B-20, 1B-1
1971	119	388	95	14	2	12	3.1	40	68	39	55	0	.245	.384	15	4	2B-102, 3B-7
1972	70	169	34	8	0	5	3.0	11	24	17	30	0	.201	.337	25	6	2B-33, 3B-11
8 yrs.	922	3014	756	126	18	74	2.5	313	404	322	447	8	.251	.378	85	20	2B-613, 3B-230, 1B-15, OF-5

WORLD SERIES

Year/Team	G	AB	H	2B	3B	HR	HR%	R	RBI	BB	SO	SB	BA	SA	PH AB	PH H	G by POS
1965 LA N	3	10	4	0	0	0	0.0	2	0	0	0	0	.400	.400	0	0	2B-3
1966	4	12	2	0	0	1	8.3	1	1	3	4	0	.167	.417	0	0	2B-4
2 yrs.	7	22	6	0	0	1	4.5	3	1	3	4	0	.273	.409	0	0	2B-7

Joe Lefebvre

LEFEBVRE, JOSEPH HENRY B. Feb. 22, 1956, Concord, N. H.   BL TR 5'10" 170 lbs.

Year/Team	G	AB	H	2B	3B	HR	HR%	R	RBI	BB	SO	SB	BA	SA	PH AB	PH H	G by POS
1980 NY A	74	150	34	1	1	8	5.3	26	21	27	30	0	.227	.407	4	2	OF-71
1981 SD N	86	246	63	13	4	8	3.3	31	31	35	33	6	.256	.439	5	2	OF-84
1982	102	239	57	9	0	4	1.7	25	21	18	50	0	.238	.326	34	8	3B-39, OF-36, C-3
1983 2 teams	SD N (18G – .250)			PHI N (101G – .310)													
" total	119	278	85	20	8	8	2.9	35	39	33	49	5	.306	.522	40	11	OF-80, 3B-13, C-5
1984 PHI N	52	160	40	9	0	3	1.9	22	18	23	37	0	.250	.363	8	4	OF-47, 3B-1
5 yrs.	433	1073	279	52	13	31	2.9	139	130	136	199	11	.260	.419	91	27	OF-318, 3B-53, C-8

LEAGUE CHAMPIONSHIP SERIES

Year/Team	G	AB	H	2B	3B	HR	HR%	R	RBI	BB	SO	SB	BA	SA	PH AB	PH H	G by POS
1980 NY A	1	0	0	0	0	0	–	0	0	0	0	0	–	–	0	0	OF-1
1983 PHI N	2	2	0	0	0	0	0.0	0	1	0	1	0	.000	.000	1	0	OF-1
2 yrs.	3	2	0	0	0	0	0.0	0	1	0	1	0	.000	.000	1	0	OF-2

WORLD SERIES

Year/Team	G	AB	H	2B	3B	HR	HR%	R	RBI	BB	SO	SB	BA	SA	PH AB	PH H	G by POS
1983 PHI N	3	5	1	1	0	0	0.0	0	2	0	1	0	.200	.400	0	0	OF-2

Al Lefevre

LEFEVRE, ALFREDO MODESTO B. Sept. 16, 1898, New York, N. Y. D. Jan. 21, 1982, Glen Cove, N. Y.   BR TR 5'10½" 160 lbs.

Year/Team	G	AB	H	2B	3B	HR	HR%	R	RBI	BB	SO	SB	BA	SA	PH AB	PH H	G by POS
1920 NY N	17	27	4	0	1	0	0.0	5	0	0	13	0	.148	.222	1	0	SS-9, 2B-6, 3B-1

	G	AB	H	2B	3B	HR	HR %	R	RBI	BB	SO	SB	BA	SA	Pinch Hit AB	Pinch Hit H	G by POS

Wade Lefler

LEFLER, WADE HAMPTON   BL TR 5'11" 162 lbs.
B. June 5, 1896, Cooleemee, N. C.   D. Mar. 6, 1981, Hickory, N. C.

	G	AB	H	2B	3B	HR	HR %	R	RBI	BB	SO	SB	BA	SA	PH AB	PH H	G by POS
1924 2 teams		BOS	N	(1G –	.000)		WAS	A	(5G –	.625)							
" total	6	9	5	3	0	0	0.0	0	4	0	1	0	.556	.889	5	3	OF-1

Ron LeFlore

LeFLORE, RONALD   BR TR 6' 200 lbs.
B. June 16, 1948, Detroit, Mich.

	G	AB	H	2B	3B	HR	HR %	R	RBI	BB	SO	SB	BA	SA	PH AB	PH H	G by POS
1974 DET A	59	254	66	8	1	2	0.8	37	13	13	58	23	.260	.323	0	0	OF-59
1975	136	550	142	13	6	8	1.5	66	37	33	139	28	.258	.347	0	0	OF-134
1976	135	544	172	23	8	4	0.7	93	39	51	111	58	.316	.410	1	0	OF-132, DH-1
1977	154	652	212	30	10	16	2.5	100	57	37	121	39	.325	.475	3	2	OF-154
1978	155	666	198	30	3	12	1.8	126	62	65	104	68	.297	.405	0	0	OF-155
1979	148	600	180	22	10	9	1.5	110	57	52	95	78	.300	.415	1	1	OF-113, DH-34
1980 MON N	139	521	134	21	11	4	0.8	95	39	62	99	97	.257	.363	1	1	OF-130
1981 CHI A	82	337	83	10	4	0	0.0	46	24	28	70	36	.246	.300	0	0	OF-82
1982	91	334	96	15	4	4	1.2	58	25	22	91	28	.287	.392	5	1	OF-83, DH-2
9 yrs.	1099	4458	1283	172	57	59	1.3	731	353	363	888	455	.288	.392	11	5	OF-1042, DH-37

Lou Legett

LEGETT, LOUIS ALFRED (Doc)   BR TR 5'10" 166 lbs.
B. June 1, 1901, New Orleans, La.

	G	AB	H	2B	3B	HR	HR %	R	RBI	BB	SO	SB	BA	SA	PH AB	PH H	G by POS
1929 BOS N	39	81	13	2	0	0	0.0	7	6	3	18	2	.160	.185	9	2	C-28
1933 BOS A	8	5	1	1	0	0	0.0	1	1	0	0	0	.200	.400	2	0	C-2
1934	19	38	11	0	0	0	0.0	4	1	2	4	0	.289	.289	1	1	C-17
1935	2	0	0	0	0	0	–	1	0	0	0	0	–	–	0	0	
4 yrs.	68	124	25	3	0	0	0.0	13	8	5	22	2	.202	.226	12	3	C-47

Mike Lehane

LEHANE, MICHAEL PATRICK   BR 6'1½" 187 lbs.
B. R. I. Deceased.

	G	AB	H	2B	3B	HR	HR %	R	RBI	BB	SO	SB	BA	SA	PH AB	PH H	G by POS
1884 WAS U	3	12	4	2	0	0	0.0	1		0				.333	.500	0	0	SS-3, OF-1, 3B-1
1890 COL AA	140	512	108	19	5	0	0.0	54		43		13		.211	.268	0	0	1B-140
1891	137	511	110	12	7	1	0.2	59	52	34	77	16	.215	.272	0	0	1B-137
3 yrs.	280	1035	222	33	12	1	0.1	114	51	77	77	29	.214	.272	0	0	1B-277, SS-3, OF-1, 3B-1

Paul Lehner

LEHNER, PAUL EUGENE (Gulliver)   BL TL 5'9" 160 lbs.
B. July 1, 1920, Dolomite, Ala.   D. Dec. 27, 1967, Birmingham, Ala.

	G	AB	H	2B	3B	HR	HR %	R	RBI	BB	SO	SB	BA	SA	PH AB	PH H	G by POS
1946 STL A	16	45	10	1	2	0	0.0	6	5	1	5	0	.222	.333	4	1	OF-12
1947	135	483	120	25	9	7	1.4	59	48	28	29	5	.248	.381	6	2	OF-127
1948	103	333	92	15	4	2	0.6	23	46	30	19	0	.276	.363	13	6	OF-89, 1B-2
1949	104	297	68	13	0	3	1.0	25	37	16	20	0	.229	.303	26	7	OF-55, 1B-18
1950 PHI A	114	427	132	17	5	9	2.1	48	52	31	33	1	.309	.436	8	3	OF-101
1951 4 teams		PHI	A	(9G –	.143)		CHI	A	(23G –	.208)		STL	A	(21G –	.134)		CLE A	(12G – .231)
" total	65	180	31	9	1	1	0.6	14	7	18	12	0	.172	.250	19	4	OF-45
1952 BOS A	3	3	2	0	0	0	0.0	0	2	2	0	0	.667	.667	1	1	OF-2
7 yrs.	540	1768	455	80	21	22	1.2	175	197	126	118	6	.257	.364	77	24	OF-431, 1B-20

Clarence Lehr

LEHR, CLARENCE EMANUEL (King)   BR TR 5'11" 165 lbs.
B. May 16, 1886, Escanaba, Mich.   D. Jan. 31, 1948, Detroit, Mich.

	G	AB	H	2B	3B	HR	HR %	R	RBI	BB	SO	SB	BA	SA	PH AB	PH H	G by POS
1911 PHI N	23	27	4	0	0	0	0.0	2	0	7		0	.148	.148	6	1	OF-5, SS-4, 2B-4

Hank Leiber

LEIBER, HENRY EDWARD   BR TR 6'1½" 205 lbs.
B. Jan. 17, 1911, Phoenix, Ariz.

	G	AB	H	2B	3B	HR	HR %	R	RBI	BB	SO	SB	BA	SA	PH AB	PH H	G by POS
1933 NY N	6	10	2	0	0	0	0.0	1	0	0	2	0	.200	.200	5	0	OF-1
1934	63	187	45	5	3	2	1.1	17	25	4	13	1	.241	.332	12	2	OF-51
1935	154	613	203	37	4	22	3.6	110	107	48	29	0	.331	.512	0	0	OF-154
1936	101	337	94	19	7	9	2.7	44	67	37	41	1	.279	.457	12	1	OF-86, 1B-1
1937	51	184	54	7	3	4	2.2	24	32	15	27	1	.293	.429	5	1	OF-46
1938	98	360	97	18	4	12	3.3	50	65	31	45	0	.269	.442	8	3	OF-89
1939 CHI N	112	365	113	16	1	24	6.6	65	88	59	42	1	.310	.556	8	1	OF-98
1940	117	440	133	24	2	17	3.9	68	86	45	68	1	.302	.482	3	0	OF-103, 1B-12
1941	53	162	35	5	0	7	4.3	20	25	16	25	0	.216	.377	9	0	OF-29, 1B-15
1942 NY N	58	147	32	6	0	4	2.7	11	23	19	27	0	.218	.340	14	4	OF-41, P-1
10 yrs.	813	2805	808	137	24	101	3.6	410	518	274	319	5	.288	.462	76	12	OF-698, 1B-28, P-1

WORLD SERIES																	
1936 NY N	2	6	0	0	0	0	0.0	0	0	2	2	0	.000	.000	0	0	OF-2
1937	3	11	4	0	0	0	0.0	2	2	1	1	0	.364	.364	0	0	OF-3
2 yrs.	5	17	4	0	0	0	0.0	2	2	3	3	0	.235	.235	0	0	OF-5

Nemo Leibold

LEIBOLD, HARRY LORAN   BL TR 5'6½" 157 lbs.
B. Feb. 17, 1892, Butler, Ind.   D. Feb. 4, 1977, Detroit, Mich.

	G	AB	H	2B	3B	HR	HR %	R	RBI	BB	SO	SB	BA	SA	PH AB	PH H	G by POS
1913 CLE A	84	286	74	11	6	0	0.0	37	12	21	43	16	.259	.339	10	1	OF-72
1914	114	402	106	13	0	0	0.0	46	32	54	56	12	.264	.311	6	1	OF-107
1915 2 teams		CLE	A	(57G –	.256)		CHI	A	(36G –	.230)							
" total	93	281	70	6	4	0	0.0	38	15	39	27	6	.249	.299	14	5	OF-75
1916 CHI A	45	82	20	1	2	0	0.0	5	13	7	7	7	.244	.305	20	4	OF-24
1917	125	428	101	12	6	0	0.0	59	29	74	34	27	.236	.292	3	0	OF-122
1918	116	440	110	14	6	1	0.2	57	31	63	32	13	.250	.316	1	0	OF-114
1919	122	434	131	18	2	0	0.0	81	26	72	30	17	.302	.353	0	0	OF-122
1920	108	413	91	16	3	1	0.2	61	28	55	30	7	.220	.281	3	1	OF-108
1921 BOS A	123	467	143	26	6	0	0.0	88	30	41	27	13	.306	.388	5	0	OF-117
1922	81	271	70	8	1	1	0.4	42	18	41	14	1	.258	.306	9	3	OF-71
1923 2 teams		BOS	A	(12G –	.111)		WAS	A	(95G –	.305)							
" 1924 WAS A	107	333	98	13	4	1	0.3	69	22	54	18	7	.294	.366	9	2	OF-94
1924 WAS A	84	246	72	6	4	0	0.0	41	20	42	10	6	.293	.350	11	1	OF-70
1925	56	84	23	1	1	0	0.0	14	7	8	7	1	.274	.310	19	3	OF-26, 3B-1
13 yrs.	1258	4167	1109	145	48	4	0.1	638	283	571	335	133	.266	.327	110	21	OF-1122, 3B-1

WORLD SERIES																	
1917 CHI A	2	5	2	0	0	0	0.0	0	1	2	1	0	.400	.400	2	0	OF-2

	G	AB	H	2B	3B	HR	HR %	R	RBI	BB	SO	SB	BA	SA	Pinch Hit AB	Pinch Hit H	G by POS

Nemo Leibold continued

	G	AB	H	2B	3B	HR	HR %	R	RBI	BB	SO	SB	BA	SA	PH AB	PH H	G by POS
1919	5	18	1	0	0	0	0.0	0	0	2	3	1	.056	.056	1	0	OF-5
1924 WAS A	3	6	1	0	0	0	0.0	1	0	1	0	0	.167	.333	2	1	OF-1
1925	3	2	1	1	0	0	0.0	1	0	1	0	0	.500	1.000	2	1	
4 yrs.	13	31	5	2	0	0	0.0	3	2	5	4	1	.161	.226	7 6th	2	OF-8

Elmer Leifer

LEIFER, ELMER EDWIN   BL TR 5'9½" 170 lbs.
B. May 23, 1893, Clarington, Ohio   D. Sept. 26, 1948, Everett, Wash.

	G	AB	H	2B	3B	HR	HR %	R	RBI	BB	SO	SB	BA	SA	PH AB	PH H	G by POS
1921 CHI A	9	10	3	0	0	0	0.0	0	1	0	4	0	.300	.300	7	2	OF-1, 3B-1

John Leighton

LEIGHTON, JOHN ATKINSON   5'11" 170 lbs.
B. Oct. 4, 1861, Peabody, Mass.   D. Oct. 31, 1956, Lynn, Mass.

	G	AB	H	2B	3B	HR	HR %	R	RBI	BB	SO	SB	BA	SA	PH AB	PH H	G by POS
1890 SYR AA	7	27	8	2	0	0	0.0	6		3		2	.296	.370	0	0	OF-7

Bill Leinhauser

LEINHAUSER, WILLIAM CHARLES   BR TR 5'10" 150 lbs.
B. Nov. 4, 1893, Philadelphia, Pa.   D. Apr. 14, 1978, Elkins Park, Pa.

	G	AB	H	2B	3B	HR	HR %	R	RBI	BB	SO	SB	BA	SA	PH AB	PH H	G by POS
1912 DET A	1	4	0	0	0	0	0.0	0	0	0	1	0	.000	.000	0	0	OF-1

Ed Leip

LEIP, EDGAR ELLSWORTH   BR TR 5'9" 160 lbs.
B. Nov. 29, 1910, Trenton, N. J.   D. Nov. 24, 1983, Zephyrhills, Fla.

	G	AB	H	2B	3B	HR	HR %	R	RBI	BB	SO	SB	BA	SA	PH AB	PH H	G by POS
1939 WAS A	9	32	11	0	0	0	0.0	4	2	2	4	0	.344	.375	1	0	2B-8
1940 PIT N	3	5	1	0	0	0	0.0	2	0	0	0	0	.200	.200	0	0	2B-2
1941	15	25	5	0	2	0	0.0	1	3	1	2	1	.200	.360	3	0	2B-7, 3B-1
1942	3	0	0	0	0	0	–	0	0	0	0	0	–	–	0	0	
4 yrs.	30	62	17	1	2	0	0.0	7	5	3	6	1	.274	.355	4	0	2B-17, 3B-1

Frank Leja

LEJA, FRANK JOHN   BL TL 6'4" 205 lbs.
B. Feb. 7, 1936, Holyoke, Mass.

	G	AB	H	2B	3B	HR	HR %	R	RBI	BB	SO	SB	BA	SA	PH AB	PH H	G by POS
1954 NY A	12	5	1	0	0	0	0.0	2	0	0	1	0	.200	.200	3	0	1B-6
1955	7	2	0	0	0	0	0.0	1	0	0	1	0	.000	.000	1	0	1B-2
1962 LA A	7	16	0	0	0	0	0.0	0	0	1	6	0	.000	.000	2	0	1B-4
3 yrs.	26	23	1	0	0	0	0.0	3	0	1	8	0	.043	.043	6	0	1B-12

Larry LeJeune

LeJEUNE, SHELDON ALDENBERT   BR TR 6' 180 lbs.
B. July 22, 1885, Chicago, Ill.   D. Apr. 21, 1952, Eloise, Mich.

	G	AB	H	2B	3B	HR	HR %	R	RBI	BB	SO	SB	BA	SA	PH AB	PH H	G by POS
1911 BKN N	6	19	3	0	0	0	0.0	2	2	2	8	2	.158	.158	0	0	OF-6
1915 PIT N	18	65	11	0	1	0	0.0	4	2	2	7	4	.169	.200	0	0	OF-18
2 yrs.	24	84	14	0	1	0	0.0	6	4	4	15	6	.167	.190	0	0	OF-24

Don LeJohn

LeJOHN, DONALD EVERETT   BR TR 5'10" 175 lbs.
B. May 13, 1934, Daisytown, Pa.

	G	AB	H	2B	3B	HR	HR %	R	RBI	BB	SO	SB	BA	SA	PH AB	PH H	G by POS
1965 LA N	34	78	20	2	0	0	0.0	2	7	5	13	0	.256	.282	10	2	3B-26
WORLD SERIES																	
1965 LA N	1	1	0	0	0	0	0.0	0	0	0	1	0	.000	.000	1	0	

Jack Lelivelt

LELIVELT, JOHN FRANK   BL TL 5'11" 175 lbs.
Brother of Bill Lelivelt.
B. Nov. 14, 1885, Chicago, Ill.   D. Jan. 20, 1941, Seattle, Wash.

	G	AB	H	2B	3B	HR	HR %	R	RBI	BB	SO	SB	BA	SA	PH AB	PH H	G by POS
1909 WAS A	91	318	93	8	6	0	0.0	25	24	19		8	.292	.355	0	0	OF-91
1910	110	347	92	10	3	0	0.0	40	33	40		20	.265	.311	13	2	OF-89, 1B-7
1911	72	225	72	12	4	0	0.0	29	22	22		7	.320	.409	16	6	OF-49, 1B-7
1912 NY A	36	149	54	6	7	2	1.3	12	23	4		7	.362	.537	0	0	OF-36
1913 2 teams	NY A (17G – .214)					CLE A (23G – .391)											
" total	40	51	15	2	1	0	0.0	2	11	2	5	2	.294	.373	35	12	OF-5
1914 CLE A	32	64	21	5	1	0	0.0	6	13	2	10	2	.328	.438	19	5	OF-12, 1B-1
6 yrs.	381	1154	347	43	22	2	0.2	114	126	89	15	46	.301	.381	83	25	OF-282, 1B-15

Johnnie LeMaster

LeMASTER, JOHNNIE LEE   BR TR 6'2" 165 lbs.
B. June 19, 1954, Portsmouth, Ohio

	G	AB	H	2B	3B	HR	HR %	R	RBI	BB	SO	SB	BA	SA	PH AB	PH H	G by POS
1975 SF N	22	74	14	4	0	2	2.7	4	9	4	15	2	.189	.324	0	0	SS-22
1976	33	100	21	3	2	0	0.0	9	9	2	21	2	.210	.280	2	0	SS-31
1977	68	134	20	5	1	0	0.0	13	8	13	27	2	.149	.201	2	0	SS-54, 3B-2
1978	101	272	64	18	3	1	0.4	23	14	21	45	6	.235	.335	0	0	SS-96, 2B-2
1979	108	343	87	11	2	3	0.9	42	29	23	55	9	.254	.324	2	0	SS-106
1980	135	405	87	16	6	3	0.7	33	31	25	57	0	.215	.306	0	0	SS-134
1981	104	324	82	9	1	0	0.0	27	28	24	46	3	.253	.287	0	0	SS-103
1982	130	436	94	14	1	2	0.5	34	30	31	78	13	.216	.266	0	0	SS-130
1983	141	534	128	16	1	6	1.1	81	30	60	96	39	.240	.307	1	0	SS-139
1984	132	451	98	13	2	4	0.9	46	32	31	97	17	.217	.282	1	1	SS-129
10 yrs.	974	3073	695	109	19	21	0.7	312	220	234	537	93	.226	.295	8	1	SS-944, 3B-2, 2B-2

Steve Lembo

LEMBO, STEPHEN NEAL   BR TR 6'1" 185 lbs.
B. Nov. 13, 1926, Brooklyn, N. Y.

	G	AB	H	2B	3B	HR	HR %	R	RBI	BB	SO	SB	BA	SA	PH AB	PH H	G by POS
1950 BKN N	5	6	1	0	0	0	0.0	0	0	1	0	0	.167	.167	0	0	C-5
1952	2	5	1	0	0	0	0.0	0	1	0	1	0	.200	.200	0	0	C-2
2 yrs.	7	11	2	0	0	0	0.0	0	1	1	1	0	.182	.182	0	0	C-7

Bob Lemon

LEMON, ROBERT GRANVILLE   BL TR 6' 180 lbs.
B. Sept. 22, 1920, San Bernardino, Calif.
Manager 1970-72, 1977-79, 1981-82.
Hall of Fame 1976.

	G	AB	H	2B	3B	HR	HR %	R	RBI	BB	SO	SB	BA	SA	PH AB	PH H	G by POS
1941 CLE A	5	4	1	0	0	0	0.0	0	0	0	1	0	.250	.250	3	1	3B-1
1942	5	5	0	0	0	0	0.0	0	0	0	3	0	.000	.000	3	0	3B-1
1946	55	89	16	3	0	1	1.1	9	4	7	18	0	.180	.247	7	1	P-32, OF-12

	G	AB	H	2B	3B	HR	HR %	R	RBI	BB	SO	SB	BA	SA	Pinch Hit AB	Pinch Hit H	G by POS

Bob Lemon continued

	G	AB	H	2B	3B	HR	HR %	R	RBI	BB	SO	SB	BA	SA	PH AB	PH H	G by POS
1947	47	56	18	4	3	2	3.6	11	5	6	9	0	.321	.607	3	1	P-37, OF-2
1948	52	119	34	9	0	5	4.2	20	21	8	23	0	.286	.487	4	1	P-43
1949	46	108	29	6	2	7	6.5	17	19	10	20	0	.269	.556	8	4	P-37
1950	72	136	37	9	1	6	4.4	21	26	13	25	0	.272	.485	26	6	P-44
1951	56	102	21	4	1	3	2.9	11	13	9	22	0	.206	.353	14	4	P-42
1952	54	124	28	5	0	2	1.6	14	9	4	21	0	.226	.315	8	1	P-42
1953	51	112	26	9	1	2	1.8	12	17	7	20	2	.232	.384	6	1	P-41
1954	40	98	21	4	1	2	2.0	11	10	6	24	0	.214	.337	3	1	P-36
1955	49	78	19	0	0	1	1.3	11	9	13	16	0	.244	.282	9	4	P-35
1956	43	93	18	0	0	5	5.4	8	12	9	21	0	.194	.355	5	3	P-39
1957	25	46	3	1	0	1	2.2	2	1	0	14	0	.065	.152	4	0	P-21
1958	15	13	3	0	0	0	0.0	1	1	1	4	0	.231	.231	6	3	P-11
15 yrs.	615	1183	274	54	9	37	3.1	148	147	93	241	2	.232	.386	109	31	P-460, OF-14, 3B-2
WORLD SERIES																	
1948 CLE A	2	7	0	0	0	0	0.0	0	0	0	0	0	.000	.000	0	0	P-2
1954	3	6	0	0	0	0	0.0	0	0	1	1	0	.000	.000	1	0	P-2
2 yrs.	5	13	0	0	0	0	0.0	0	0	1	1	0	.000	.000	1	0	P-4

Chet Lemon

LEMON, CHESTER EARL   BR TR 6'   190 lbs.
B. Feb. 12, 1955, Jackson, Miss.

	G	AB	H	2B	3B	HR	HR %	R	RBI	BB	SO	SB	BA	SA	PH AB	PH H	G by POS
1975 CHI A	9	35	9	2	0	0	0.0	2	1	2	6	1	.257	.314	1	0	3B-6, DH-2, OF-1
1976	132	451	111	15	5	4	0.9	46	38	28	65	13	.246	.328	1	0	OF-131
1977	150	553	151	38	4	19	3.4	99	67	52	88	8	.273	.459	0	0	OF-149
1978	105	357	107	24	6	13	3.6	51	55	39	46	5	.300	.510	1	0	OF-95, DH-10
1979	148	556	177	44	2	17	3.1	79	86	56	68	7	.318	.496	0	0	OF-147, DH-1
1980	147	514	150	32	6	11	2.1	76	51	71	56	6	.292	.442	1	0	OF-139, DH-6, 2B-1
1981	94	328	99	23	6	9	2.7	50	50	33	48	5	.302	.491	0	0	OF-93
1982 DET A	125	436	116	20	1	19	4.4	75	52	56	69	1	.266	.447	2	1	OF-121, DH-1
1983	145	491	125	21	5	24	4.9	78	69	54	70	0	.255	.464	2	1	OF-145
1984	141	509	146	34	6	20	3.9	77	76	51	83	5	.287	.495	3	1	OF-140, DH-1
10 yrs.	1196	4230	1191	253	41	136	3.2	633	545	442	599	51	.282	.457	11	3	OF-1161, DH-21, 3B-6, 2B-1
LEAGUE CHAMPIONSHIP SERIES																	
1984 DET A	3	13	0	0	0	0	0.0	1	0	0	1	0	.000	.000	0	0	OF-3
WORLD SERIES																	
1984 DET A	5	17	5	0	0	0	0.0	1	1	2	2	2	.294	.294	0	0	OF-5

Jim Lemon

LEMON, JAMES ROBERT   BR TR 6'4"   200 lbs.
B. Mar. 23, 1928, Covington, Va.
Manager 1968.

	G	AB	H	2B	3B	HR	HR %	R	RBI	BB	SO	SB	BA	SA	PH AB	PH H	G by POS
1950 CLE A	12	34	6	1	0	1	2.9	4	1	3	12	0	.176	.294	3	1	OF-10
1953	16	46	8	1	0	1	2.2	5	5	3	15	0	.174	.261	3	0	OF-11, 1B-2
1954 WAS A	37	128	30	2	3	2	1.6	12	13	9	34	0	.234	.344	4	1	OF-33
1955	10	25	5	2	0	1	4.0	3	3	3	4	0	.200	.400	3	2	OF-6
1956	146	538	146	21	11	27	5.0	77	96	65	138	2	.271	.502	4	1	OF-141
1957	137	518	147	22	6	17	3.3	58	64	49	94	1	.284	.448	4	1	OF-131, 1B-3
1958	142	501	123	15	9	26	5.2	65	75	50	120	2	.246	.467	8	3	OF-137
1959	147	531	148	18	3	33	6.2	73	100	46	99	5	.279	.510	5	1	OF-142
1960	148	528	142	10	1	38	7.2	81	100	67	114	2	.269	.508	5	1	OF-145
1961 MIN A	129	423	109	26	1	14	3.3	57	52	44	98	1	.258	.423	10	2	OF-120
1962	12	17	3	0	1	1	5.9	1	5	3	4	0	.176	.353	8	3	OF-3
1963 3 teams		MIN	N	(7G –	.118)			PHI	N	(31G –	.271)		CHI	A	(36G –	.200)	
" total	74	156	34	2	1	3	1.9	10	15	21	55	0	.218	.301	26	6	1B-25, OF-22
12 yrs.	1010	3445	901	120	35	164	4.8	446	529	363	787	13	.262	.460	83	22	OF-901, 1B-30

Don Lenhardt

LENHARDT, DONALD EUGENE (Footsie)   BR TR 6'3"   190 lbs.
B. Oct. 4, 1922, Alton, Ill.

	G	AB	H	2B	3B	HR	HR %	R	RBI	BB	SO	SB	BA	SA	PH AB	PH H	G by POS
1950 STL A	139	480	131	22	6	22	4.6	75	81	90	94	3	.273	.481	10	3	1B-86, OF-39, 3B-10
1951 2 teams		STL	A	(31G –	.262)			CHI	A	(64G –	.266)						
" total	95	302	80	12	1	15	5.0	32	63	30	38	2	.265	.460	13	3	OF-80, 1B-3
1952 3 teams		BOS	A	(30G –	.295)			DET	A	(45G –	.188)		STL	A	(18G –	.271)	
" total	93	297	71	10	2	11	3.7	41	42	47	44	0	.239	.397	10	2	OF-81, 1B-2
1953 STL A	97	303	96	15	0	10	3.3	37	35	41	41	1	.317	.465	17	4	OF-77, 3B-6
1954 2 teams		BAL	A	(13G –	.152)			BOS	A	(44G –	.273)						
" total	57	99	23	5	0	3	3.0	7	18	6	18	0	.232	.374	35	6	OF-20, 1B-2, 3B-1
5 yrs.	481	1481	401	64	9	61	4.1	192	239	214	235	6	.271	.450	85	18	OF-297, 1B-93, 3B-17

Bob Lennon

LENNON, ROBERT ALBERT (Arch)   BL TL 6'   200 lbs.
B. Sept. 15, 1928, Brooklyn, N. Y.

	G	AB	H	2B	3B	HR	HR %	R	RBI	BB	SO	SB	BA	SA	PH AB	PH H	G by POS
1954 NY N	3	3	0	0	0	0	0.0	0	0	0	0	0	.000	.000	3	0	
1956	26	55	10	1	0	0	0.0	3	1	4	17	0	.182	.200	3	0	OF-21
1957 CHI N	9	21	3	1	0	1	4.8	2	3	1	9	0	.143	.333	5	0	OF-4
3 yrs.	38	79	13	2	0	1	1.3	5	4	5	26	0	.165	.228	11	0	OF-25

Ed Lennox

LENNOX, JAMES EDGAR (Eggie)   BR TR 5'10"   174 lbs.
B. Nov. 3, 1885, Camden, N. J.   D. Oct. 26, 1939, Camden, N. J.

	G	AB	H	2B	3B	HR	HR %	R	RBI	BB	SO	SB	BA	SA	PH AB	PH H	G by POS
1906 PHI A	6	17	1	1	0	0	0.0	1	0	1		0	.059	.118	0	0	3B-6
1909 BKN N	126	435	114	18	9	2	0.5	33	44	47		11	.262	.359	5	1	3B-121
1910	110	367	95	19	4	3	0.8	19	32	36	39	7	.259	.357	10	1	3B-100
1912 CHI N	27	81	19	4	1	1	1.2	13	16	12	10	1	.235	.346	2	1	3B-24
1914 PIT F	124	430	134	25	10	11	2.6	71	84	71		19	.312	.493	1	0	3B-123
1915	55	53	16	3	1	1	1.9	1	9	7		0	.302	.453	45	14	3B-3
6 yrs.	448	1383	379	70	25	18	1.3	138	185	174	49	38	.274	.400	63	17	3B-377

	G	AB	H	2B	3B	HR	HR %	R	RBI	BB	SO	SB	BA	SA	Pinch Hit AB	Pinch Hit H	G by POS

Jim Lentine

LENTINE, JAMES MATTHEW
B. July 16, 1954, Los Angeles, Calif.

BR TR 6' 175 lbs.

	G	AB	H	2B	3B	HR	HR %	R	RBI	BB	SO	SB	BA	SA	AB	H	G by POS
1978 STL N	8	11	2	0	0	0	0.0	1	1	0	0	1	.182	.182	1	0	OF-3
1979	11	23	9	1	0	0	0.0	2	1	3	6	0	.391	.435	3	2	OF-8
1980 2 teams	STL	N (9G – .100)		DET	A	(67G –	.261)										
" total	76	171	43	8	1	1	0.6	20	18	28	32	2	.251	.327	10	2	OF-61, DH-9
3 yrs.	95	205	54	9	1	1	0.5	23	20	31	38	3	.263	.332	14	4	OF-72, DH-9

Eddie Leon

LEON, EDUARDO ANTONIO
B. Aug. 11, 1946, Tucson, Ariz.

BR TR 6' 170 lbs.

	G	AB	H	2B	3B	HR	HR %	R	RBI	BB	SO	SB	BA	SA	AB	H	G by POS
1968 CLE A	6	1	0	0	0	0	0.0	0	0	0	1	0	.000	.000	0	0	SS-6
1969	64	213	51	6	0	3	1.4	20	19	19	37	2	.239	.310	0	0	SS-64
1970	152	549	136	20	4	10	1.8	58	56	47	89	1	.248	.353	0	0	2B-141, SS-23, 3B-1
1971	131	429	112	12	2	4	0.9	35	35	34	69	3	.261	.326	4	1	2B-107, SS-24
1972	89	225	45	2	1	4	1.8	14	16	20	47	0	.200	.271	23	5	2B-36, SS-35
1973 CHI A	127	399	91	10	3	3	0.8	37	30	34	103	1	.228	.291	2	0	SS-122, 2B-3
1974	31	46	5	1	0	0	0.0	1	3	2	12	0	.109	.130	0	0	SS-21, 2B-7, 3B-2, DH-1
1975 NY A	0	0	0	0	0	0	–	0	0	0	0	0	–	–	0	0	SS-1
8 yrs.	601	1862	440	51	10	24	1.3	165	159	156	358	7	.236	.313	29	6	SS-296, 2B-294, 3B-3, DH-1

Andy Leonard

LEONARD, ANDREW JACKSON
B. June 1, 1846, County Cavan, Ireland   D. Aug. 22, 1903, Roxbury, Mass.

BR TR 5'7" 155 lbs.

	G	AB	H	2B	3B	HR	HR %	R	RBI	BB	SO	SB	BA	SA	AB	H	G by POS
1876 BOS N	64	303	85	10	2	0	0.0	53	27	4	6		.281	.327	0	0	OF-35, 2B-30
1877	58	272	78	5	0	0	0.0	46	27	5	5		.287	.305	0	0	OF-37, SS-21
1878	60	262	68	8	5	0	0.0	41	16	3	19		.260	.328	0	0	OF-60
1880 CIN N	33	133	28	3	0	1	0.8	15	17	8	11		.211	.256	0	0	SS-23, 3B-10
4 yrs.	215	970	259	26	7	1	0.1	155	87	20	41		.267	.311	0	0	OF-132, SS-44, 2B-30, 3B-10

Jeff Leonard

LEONARD, JEFFREY N.
B. Sept. 22, 1955, Philadelphia, Pa.

BR TR 6'4" 210 lbs.

	G	AB	H	2B	3B	HR	HR %	R	RBI	BB	SO	SB	BA	SA	AB	H	G by POS
1977 LA N	11	10	3	0	1	0	0.0	1	2	1	4	0	.300	.500	3	0	OF-10
1978 HOU N	8	26	10	2	0	0	0.0	2	4	1	2	0	.385	.462	1	0	OF-8
1979	134	411	119	15	5	0	0.0	47	47	46	68	23	.290	.350	11	2	OF-123
1980	88	216	46	7	5	3	1.4	29	20	19	46	4	.213	.333	24	6	OF-56, 1B-11
1981 2 teams	HOU	N	(7G –	.167)		SF	N	(37G –	.307)								
" total	44	145	42	12	4	4	2.8	21	29	12	25	5	.290	.510	6	1	1B-30, OF-7
1982 SF N	80	278	72	16	1	9	3.2	32	49	19	65	18	.259	.421	2	1	OF-74, 1B-1
1983	139	516	144	17	7	21	4.1	74	87	35	116	26	.279	.461	4	2	OF-136
1984	136	514	155	27	2	21	4.1	76	86	47	123	17	.302	.484	4	0	OF-131
8 yrs.	640	2116	591	96	25	58	2.7	282	324	180	449	93	.279	.431	55	12	OF-545, 1B-42

LEAGUE CHAMPIONSHIP SERIES

	G	AB	H	2B	3B	HR	HR %	R	RBI	BB	SO	SB	BA	SA	AB	H	G by POS
1980 HOU N	3	3	0	0	0	0	0.0	0	0	0	2	0	.000	.000	2	0	OF-1

Joe Leonard

LEONARD, JOSEPH HOWARD
B. Nov. 14, 1893, Chicago, Ill.   D. May 4, 1920, Washington, D. C.

BL TR 5'7½" 156 lbs.

	G	AB	H	2B	3B	HR	HR %	R	RBI	BB	SO	SB	BA	SA	AB	H	G by POS
1914 PIT N	53	126	25	2	2	0	0.0	17	4	12	21	4	.198	.246	7	0	3B-38, SS-1
1916 2 teams	CLE	A	(3G –	.000)		WAS	A	(42G –	.274)								
" total	45	170	46	7	0	0	0.0	21	14	22	24	4	.271	.312	1	0	3B-42, 2B-1
1917 WAS A	99	297	57	6	7	0	0.0	30	23	45	40	6	.192	.259	9	3	3B-67, 1B-20, OF-1, SS-1
1919	71	198	51	8	3	2	1.0	26	20	20	28	3	.258	.359	6	1	2B-28, 3B-25, 1B-4, OF-1
1920	1	0	0	0	0	0	–	0		0			–	–	0	0	
5 yrs.	269	791	179	23	12	2	0.3	94	61	99	113	17	.226	.293	23	4	3B-172, 2B-29, 1B-24, OF-2, SS-2

John Leovich

LEOVICH, JOHN JOSEPH
B. May 5, 1918, Portland, Ore.

BR TR 6'½" 200 lbs.

	G	AB	H	2B	3B	HR	HR %	R	RBI	BB	SO	SB	BA	SA	AB	H	G by POS
1941 PHI A	1	2	1	1	0	0	0.0	0	0	0	0	0	.500	1.000	0	0	C-1

Ted Lepcio

LEPCIO, THADDEUS STANLEY
B. July 28, 1930, Utica, N. Y.

BR TR 5'10" 177 lbs.

	G	AB	H	2B	3B	HR	HR %	R	RBI	BB	SO	SB	BA	SA	AB	H	G by POS
1952 BOS A	84	274	72	17	2	5	1.8	34	26	24	41	3	.263	.394	0	0	2B-57, 3B-25, SS-1
1953	66	161	38	4	2	4	2.5	17	11	17	24	0	.236	.360	4	1	2B-34, SS-20, 3B-11
1954	116	398	102	19	4	8	2.0	42	45	42	62	3	.256	.384	2	0	2B-80, 3B-24, SS-14
1955	51	134	31	9	0	6	4.5	19	15	13	36	1	.231	.433	4	0	3B-45
1956	83	284	74	10	0	15	5.3	34	51	30	77	1	.261	.454	9	3	2B-57, 3B-22
1957	79	232	56	10	2	9	3.9	24	37	29	61	0	.241	.418	10	2	2B-68
1958	50	136	27	3	0	6	4.4	10	14	12	47	0	.199	.353	10	3	2B-40
1959 2 teams	BOS	A	(3G –	.333)		DET	A	(76G –	.279)								
" total	79	218	61	9	0	7	3.2	26	25	17	51	2	.280	.417	16	5	SS-35, 2B-25, 3B-11
1960 PHI N	69	141	32	7	0	2	1.4	16	8	17	41	0	.227	.319	9	1	3B-50, SS-14, 2B-5
1961 2 teams	CHI	A	(5G –	.000)		MIN	A	(47G –	.170)								
" total	52	114	19	3	1	7	6.1	11	19	9	31	1	.167	.395	5	0	3B-36, 2B-22, SS-6
10 yrs.	729	2092	512	91	11	69	3.3	233	251	210	471	11	.245	.398	69	15	2B-388, 3B-224, SS-90

Pete LePine

LePINE, LOUIS JOSEPH
B. Sept. 5, 1876, Montreal, Que., Canada   D. Dec. 4, 1949, Woonsocket, R. I.

BL TL

	G	AB	H	2B	3B	HR	HR %	R	RBI	BB	SO	SB	BA	SA	AB	H	G by POS
1902 DET A	30	96	20	3	2	1	1.0	8	19	8		1	.208	.313	2	0	OF-19, 1B-8

Don Leppert

LEPPERT, DON EUGENE (Tiger)
B. Nov. 20, 1930, Memphis, Tenn.

BL TR 5'8" 175 lbs.

	G	AB	H	2B	3B	HR	HR %	R	RBI	BB	SO	SB	BA	SA	AB	H	G by POS
1955 BAL A	40	70	8	0	1	0	0.0	6	2	9	10	1	.114	.143	2	0	2B-35

	G	AB	H	2B	3B	HR	HR %	R	RBI	BB	SO	SB	BA	SA	Pinch Hit AB	H	G by POS

Don Leppert

LEPPERT, DONALD GEORGE
B. Oct. 19, 1931, Indianapolis, Ind.

BL TR 6'2" 220 lbs.

	G	AB	H	2B	3B	HR	HR %	R	RBI	BB	SO	SB	BA	SA	AB	H	G by POS
1961 **PIT N**	22	60	16	2	1	3	5.0	6	5	1	11	0	.267	.483	2	0	C-21
1962	45	139	37	6	1	3	2.2	14	18	12	21	0	.266	.388	1	0	C-44
1963 **WAS A**	73	211	50	11	0	6	2.8	20	24	20	29	0	.237	.374	14	6	C-60
1964	50	122	19	3	0	3	2.5	6	12	11	32	0	.156	.254	7	1	C-43
4 yrs.	190	532	122	22	2	15	2.8	46	59	44	93	0	.229	.363	24	7	C-168

Dutch Lerchen

LERCHEN, BERTRAM ROE
Father of George Lerchen.
B. Apr. 4, 1889, Detroit, Mich.   D. Jan. 7, 1962, Detroit, Mich.

BR TR 5'8" 160 lbs.

	G	AB	H	2B	3B	HR	HR %	R	RBI	BB	SO	SB	BA	SA	AB	H	G by POS
1910 **BOS A**	6	15	0	0	0	0	0.0	1	0	1		0	.000	.000	0	0	SS-6

George Lerchen

LERCHEN, GEORGE EDWARD
Son of Dutch Lerchen.
B. Dec. 1, 1922, Detroit, Mich.

BB TR 5'11" 175 lbs.
BL 1953

	G	AB	H	2B	3B	HR	HR %	R	RBI	BB	SO	SB	BA	SA	AB	H	G by POS
1952 **DET A**	14	32	5	1	0	1	3.1	1	3	7	10	1	.156	.281	7	2	OF-7
1953 **CIN N**	22	17	5	1	0	0	0.0	2	2	5	6	0	.294	.353	17	6	OF-1
2 yrs.	36	49	10	2	0	1	2.0	3	5	12	16	1	.204	.306	24	8	OF-8

Walt Lerian

LERIAN, WALTER IRVIN (Peck)
B. Feb. 10, 1903, Baltimore, Md.   D. Oct. 22, 1929, Baltimore, Md.

BR TR 6' 190 lbs.

	G	AB	H	2B	3B	HR	HR %	R	RBI	BB	SO	SB	BA	SA	AB	H	G by POS
1928 **PHI N**	96	239	65	16	2	2	0.8	28	25	41	29	1	.272	.381	17	4	C-74
1929	105	273	61	13	2	7	2.6	28	25	53	37	0	.223	.363	2	0	C-103
2 yrs.	201	512	126	29	4	9	1.8	56	50	94	66	1	.246	.371	19	4	C-177

Roy Leslie

LESLIE, ROY REID
B. Aug. 23, 1894, Bailey, Tex.   D. Apr. 10, 1972, Sherman, Tex.

BR TR 6'1" 175 lbs.

	G	AB	H	2B	3B	HR	HR %	R	RBI	BB	SO	SB	BA	SA	AB	H	G by POS
1917 **CHI N**	7	19	4	0	0	0	0.0	1	1	1	5	0	.211	.211	1	0	1B-6
1919 **STL N**	12	24	5	1	0	0	0.0	2	4	4	3	0	.208	.250	1	0	1B-9
1922 **PHI N**	141	513	139	23	2	6	1.2	44	50	37	49	3	.271	.359	2	2	1B-139
3 yrs.	160	556	148	24	2	6	1.1	47	55	42	57	4	.266	.349	4	2	1B-154

Sam Leslie

LESLIE, SAMUEL ANDREW (Sambo)
B. July 26, 1905, Pascagoula, Fla.   D. Jan. 21, 1979, Pascagula, Fla.

BL TL 6' 192 lbs.

	G	AB	H	2B	3B	HR	HR %	R	RBI	BB	SO	SB	BA	SA	AB	H	G by POS
1929 **NY N**	1	1	0	0	0	0	0.0	0	1	0	0	0	.000	.000	0	0	OF-1
1930	2	2	1	0	0	0	0.0	0	0	0	1	0	.500	.500	2	1	
1931	53	53	16	4	0	3	5.7	11	5	1	2	3	.302	.547	45	12	1B-6
1932	77	75	22	4	0	1	1.3	5	15	2	5	0	.293	.387	72	22	1B-2
1933 **2 teams**	**NY**	**N** (40G –	.321)		**BKN**	**N**	(96G –	.286)									
" total	136	501	148	23	7	8	1.6	62	73	35	23	1	.295	.417	6	3	1B-130
1934 **BKN N**	146	546	181	29	6	9	1.6	75	102	69	34	5	.332	.456	6	1	1B-138
1935	142	520	160	30	7	5	1.0	72	93	55	19	4	.308	.421	4	1	1B-138
1936 **NY N**	117	417	123	19	5	6	1.4	49	54	23	16	0	.295	.408	15	5	1B-99
1937	72	191	59	7	2	3	1.6	25	30	20	12	1	.309	.414	26	8	1B-44
1938	76	154	39	7	1	1	0.6	12	16	11	6	0	.253	.331	40	6	1B-32
10 yrs.	822	2460	749	123	28	36	1.5	311	389	216	118	14	.304	.421	216	59	1B-589, OF-1

WORLD SERIES																	
1936 **NY N**	3	3	2	0	0	0	0.0	0	0	0	0	0	.667	.667	3	2	
1937	2	1	0	0	0	0	0.0	0	0	1	0	0	.000	.000	1	0	
2 yrs.	5	4	2	0	0	0	0.0	0	0	1	0	0	.500	.500	4	2	

Charlie Letchas

LETCHAS, CHARLIE
B. Oct. 3, 1915, Thomasville, Ga.

BR TR 5'10" 150 lbs.

	G	AB	H	2B	3B	HR	HR %	R	RBI	BB	SO	SB	BA	SA	AB	H	G by POS
1939 **PHI N**	12	44	10	2	0	1	2.3	2	3	1	2	0	.227	.341	0	0	2B-12
1941 **WAS A**	2	8	1	0	0	0	0.0	0	1	1	1	0	.125	.125	0	0	2B-2
1944 **PHI N**	116	396	94	8	0	0	0.0	29	33	32	27	0	.237	.258	9	2	2B-47, 3B-32, SS-29
1946	6	13	3	0	0	0	0.0	1	0	1	1	0	.231	.231	1	0	2B-4
4 yrs.	136	461	108	10	0	1	0.2	32	37	35	31	0	.234	.262	10	2	2B-65, 3B-32, SS-29

Tom Letcher

LETCHER, THOMAS F.
B. 1868, Grand Rapids, Mich.   Deceased.

	G	AB	H	2B	3B	HR	HR %	R	RBI	BB	SO	SB	BA	SA	AB	H	G by POS
1891 **C-M AA**	6	21	4	1	0	0	0.0	3	2	0	1	1	.190	.238	0	0	OF-6

Jesse Levan

LEVAN, JESSE ROY
B. July 15, 1926, Reading, Pa.

BL TR 6' 172 lbs.

	G	AB	H	2B	3B	HR	HR %	R	RBI	BB	SO	SB	BA	SA	AB	H	G by POS
1947 **PHI N**	2	9	4	0	0	0	0.0	3	1	0	0	0	.444	.444	0	0	OF-2
1954 **WAS A**	7	10	3	0	0	0	0.0	1	0	0	0	0	.300	.300	2	1	3B-4, 1B-1
1955	16	16	3	0	0	1	6.3	1	4	0	2	0	.188	.375	16	3	
3 yrs.	25	35	10	0	0	1	2.9	5	5	0	2	0	.286	.371	18	4	3B-4, OF-2, 1B-1

Jim Levey

LEVEY, JAMES JULIUS
B. Sept. 13, 1906, Pittsburgh, Pa.
D. Mar. 14, 1970, Dallas, Tex.

BB TR 5'10½" 154 lbs.
BR 1930-31

	G	AB	H	2B	3B	HR	HR %	R	RBI	BB	SO	SB	BA	SA	AB	H	G by POS
1930 **STL A**	8	37	9	2	0	0	0.0	7	3	3	2	0	.243	.297	0	0	SS-8
1931	139	498	104	19	2	5	1.0	53	38	35	83	13	.209	.285	0	0	SS-139
1932	152	568	159	30	8	4	0.7	59	63	21	48	6	.280	.382	0	0	SS-152
1933	141	529	103	10	4	2	0.4	43	36	26	68	4	.195	.240	2	0	SS-138
4 yrs.	440	1632	375	61	14	11	0.7	162	140	85	201	23	.230	.305	2	0	SS-437

Charlie Levis

LEVIS, CHARLES H.
B. June 21, 1860, St. Louis, Mo.   D. Oct. 16, 1926, St. Louis, Mo.
Manager 1884.

	G	AB	H	2B	3B	HR	HR %	R	RBI	BB	SO	SB	BA	SA	AB	H	G by POS
1884 **3 teams**	**BAL**	**U** (87G –	.228)		**WAS**	**U**	(1G –	.000)		**IND**	**AA** (3G –	.200)					
" total	91	386	87	11	4	6	1.6	59		3			.225	.321	0	0	1B-91
1885 **BAL AA**	1	4	1	0	0	0	0.0	2		0			.250	.250	0	0	1B-1
2 yrs.	92	390	88	11	4	6	1.5	61		3			.226	.321	0	0	1B-92

	G	AB	H	2B	3B	HR	HR %	R	RBI	BB	SO	SB	BA	SA	Pinch Hit AB	Pinch Hit H	G by POS

Ed Levy

LEVY, EDWARD CLARENCE
Born Edward Clarence Whitner.
B. Oct. 28, 1916, Birmingham, Ala.   BR TR 6'5½" 190 lbs.

	G	AB	H	2B	3B	HR	HR %	R	RBI	BB	SO	SB	BA	SA	AB	H	G by POS
1940 PHI N	1	1	0	0	0	0	0.0	0	0	0	0	0	.000	.000	1	0	
1942 NY A	13	41	5	0	0	0	0.0	5	3	4	5	1	.122	.122	0	0	1B-13
1944	40	153	37	11	2	4	2.6	12	29	6	19	1	.242	.418	4	2	OF-36
3 yrs.	54	195	42	11	2	4	2.1	17	32	10	24	2	.215	.354	5	2	OF-36, 1B-13

Allan Lewis

LEWIS, ALLAN SYDNEY
B. Dec. 12, 1941, Colon, Panama   BB TR 6' 170 lbs.

	G	AB	H	2B	3B	HR	HR %	R	RBI	BB	SO	SB	BA	SA	AB	H	G by POS
1967 KC A	34	6	1	0	0	0	0.0	7	0	0	3	14	.167	.167	6	1	
1968 OAK A	26	4	1	0	0	0	0.0	9	0	1	0	8	.250	.250	3	1	OF-1
1969	12	1	0	0	0	0	0.0	2	0	0	0	0	.000	.000	1	0	
1970	25	8	2	0	0	1	12.5	8	1	0	0	7	.250	.625	0	0	OF-2
1972	24	10	2	1	0	0	0.0	5	2	0	1	8	.200	.300	0	0	OF-6
1973	35	0	0	0	0	0	–	16	0	0	0	7	–	–	0	0	DH-6, OF-1
6 yrs.	156	29	6	1	0	1	3.4	47	3	1	4	44	.207	.345	10	2	OF-10, DH-6
LEAGUE CHAMPIONSHIP SERIES																	
1973 OAK A	2	0	0	0	0	0	–	1	0	0	0	0	–	–	0	0	
WORLD SERIES																	
1972 OAK A	6	0	0	0	0	0	–	2	0	0	0	0	–	–	0	0	
1973	3	0	0	0	0	0	–	1	0	0	0	0	–	–	0	0	
2 yrs.	9	0	0	0	0	0	–	3	0	0	0	0	–	–	0	0	

Bill Lewis

LEWIS, WILLIAM HENRY (Buddy)
B. Oct. 15, 1904, Ripley, Tenn.   D. Oct. 24, 1977, Memphis, Tenn.   BR TR 5'9" 165 lbs.

	G	AB	H	2B	3B	HR	HR %	R	RBI	BB	SO	SB	BA	SA	AB	H	G by POS
1933 STL N	15	35	14	1	0	1	2.9	8	8	2	3	0	.400	.514	6	2	C-8
1935 BOS N	6	4	0	0	0	0	0.0	1	0	1	1	0	.000	.000	4	0	C-1
1936	29	62	19	2	0	0	0.0	11	3	12	7	0	.306	.339	8	2	C-21
3 yrs.	50	101	33	3	0	1	1.0	20	11	15	11	0	.327	.386	18	4	C-30

Buddy Lewis

LEWIS, JOHN KELLY
B. Aug. 10, 1916, Gastonia, N. C.   BL TR 6'1" 175 lbs.

	G	AB	H	2B	3B	HR	HR %	R	RBI	BB	SO	SB	BA	SA	AB	H	G by POS
1935 WAS A	8	28	3	0	0	0	0.0	0	2	0	5	0	.107	.107	1	0	3B-6
1936	143	601	175	21	13	6	1.0	100	67	47	46	6	.291	.399	1	0	3B-139
1937	156	668	210	32	6	10	1.5	107	79	52	44	11	.314	.425	0	0	3B-156
1938	151	656	194	35	9	12	1.8	122	91	58	35	17	.296	.431	0	0	3B-151
1939	140	536	171	23	16	10	1.9	87	75	72	27	10	.319	.478	4	1	3B-134
1940	148	600	190	38	10	6	1.0	101	63	74	36	15	.317	.443	0	0	OF-112, 3B-36
1941	149	569	169	29	11	9	1.6	97	72	82	30	10	.297	.434	4	3	OF-96, 3B-49
1945	69	258	86	14	7	2	0.8	42	37	37	15	1	.333	.465	0	0	OF-69
1946	150	582	170	28	13	7	1.2	82	45	59	26	5	.292	.421	5	1	OF-145
1947	140	506	132	15	4	6	1.2	67	48	51	27	6	.261	.342	9	2	OF-130
1949	95	257	63	14	4	3	1.2	25	28	41	12	2	.245	.366	24	9	OF-67
11 yrs.	1349	5261	1563	249	93	71	1.3	830	607	573	303	83	.297	.420	48	16	3B-671, OF-619

Duffy Lewis

LEWIS, GEORGE EDWARD
B. Apr. 18, 1888, San Francisco, Calif.   D. June 17, 1979, Salem, N. H.   BR TR 5'10½" 165 lbs.

	G	AB	H	2B	3B	HR	HR %	R	RBI	BB	SO	SB	BA	SA	AB	H	G by POS
1910 BOS A	151	541	153	29	7	8	1.5	64	68	32		10	.283	.407	2	1	OF-149
1911	130	469	144	32	4	7	1.5	64	86	25		11	.307	.437	4	1	OF-125
1912	154	581	165	36	9	6	1.0	85	109	52		9	.284	.408	0	0	OF-154
1913	149	551	164	31	12	0	0.0	54	90	30	55	12	.298	.397	6	1	OF-142, P-1
1914	146	510	142	37	9	2	0.4	53	79	57	41	22	.278	.398	2	0	OF-142
1915	152	557	162	31	7	2	0.4	69	76	45	63	14	.291	.382	0	0	OF-152
1916	152	563	151	29	5	1	0.2	56	56	33	56	16	.268	.343	1	0	OF-151
1917	150	553	167	29	9	1	0.2	55	65	29	54	8	.302	.392	0	0	OF-150
1919 NY A	141	559	152	23	4	7	1.3	67	89	17	42	8	.272	.365	0	0	OF-141
1920	107	365	99	8	1	4	1.1	34	61	24	32	2	.271	.332	7	1	OF-99
1921 WAS A	27	102	19	4	1	0	0.0	11	14	8	10	1	.186	.245	0	0	OF-27
11 yrs.	1459	5351	1518	289	68	38	0.7	612	793	352	353	113	.284	.384	22	4	OF-1432, P-1
WORLD SERIES																	
1912 BOS A	8	32	5	3	0	0	0.0	4	2	2	2	0	.156	.250	0	0	OF-8
1915	5	18	8	1	0	1	5.6	1	5	1	4	0	.444	.667	0	0	OF-5
1916	5	17	6	2	1	0	0.0	3	1	2	1	0	.353	.588	0	0	OF-5
3 yrs.	18	67	19	6	1	1	1.5	8	8	5	7	0	.284	.448	0	0	OF-18

Fred Lewis

LEWIS, FREDERICK MILLER
B. Oct. 13, 1858, Utica, N. Y.   D. June 5, 1945, Utica, N. Y.   BB TR 5'10½" 194 lbs.

	G	AB	H	2B	3B	HR	HR %	R	RBI	BB	SO	SB	BA	SA	AB	H	G by POS
1881 BOS N	27	114	25	6	0	0	0.0	17	9	7	5		.219	.272	0	0	OF-27
1883 2 teams	PHI N (38G – .250)					STL AA (49G – .301)											
" total	87	369	103	15	4	1	0.3	58		5	13		.279	.350	0	0	OF-87
1884 2 teams	STL AA (73G – .323)					STL U (8G – .300)											
" total	81	330	106	26	3	0	0.0	65		19			.321	.418	0	0	OF-81
1885 STL N	45	181	53	9	0	1	0.6	12	27	9	10		.293	.359	0	0	OF-45
1886 CIN AA	77	324	103	14	6	2	0.6	72		20			.318	.417	0	0	OF-76, 3B-1
5 yrs.	317	1318	390	70	13	4	0.3	224	36	60	28		.296	.378	0	0	OF-316, 3B-1

Jack Lewis

LEWIS, JOHN DAVID
B. Feb. 14, 1884, Pittsburgh, Pa.   D. Feb. 25, 1956, Steubenville, Ohio   BR TR 5'8" 158 lbs.

	G	AB	H	2B	3B	HR	HR %	R	RBI	BB	SO	SB	BA	SA	AB	H	G by POS
1911 BOS A	18	59	16	0	0	0	0.0	7	6	7		2	.271	.271	0	0	2B-18
1914 PIT F	117	394	92	14	5	0	0.0	32	48	17		9	.234	.302	1	0	2B-115, SS-1
1915	82	231	61	6	5	0	0.0	24	26	8		7	.264	.333	13	2	2B-45, SS-11, OF-6, 1B-5, 3B-1
3 yrs.	217	684	169	20	10	0	0.1	63	80	32		18	.247	.310	14	2	2B-178, SS-12, OF-6, 1B-5, 3B-1

	G	AB	H	2B	3B	HR	HR %	R	RBI	BB	SO	SB	BA	SA	Pinch Hit AB	Pinch Hit H	G by POS

Johnny Lewis

LEWIS, JOHNNY JOE
B. Aug. 10, 1939, Greenville, Ala.
BL TR 6'1" 189 lbs.

	G	AB	H	2B	3B	HR	HR %	R	RBI	BB	SO	SB	BA	SA	AB	H	G by POS
1964 STL N	40	94	22	2	2	2	2.1	10	7	13	23	2	.234	.362	3	0	OF-36
1965 NY N	148	477	117	15	3	15	3.1	64	45	59	117	4	.245	.384	14	4	OF-142
1966	65	166	32	6	1	5	3.0	21	20	21	43	2	.193	.331	16	2	OF-49
1967	13	34	4	1	0	0	0.0	2	2	2	11	0	.118	.147	4	0	OF-10
4 yrs.	266	771	175	24	6	22	2.9	97	74	95	194	8	.227	.359	37	6	OF-237

Phil Lewis

LEWIS, PHILIP
B. Oct. 7, 1883, Pittsburgh, Pa.   D. Aug. 8, 1959, Port Wentworth, Ga.
BR TR 6' 195 lbs.

	G	AB	H	2B	3B	HR	HR %	R	RBI	BB	SO	SB	BA	SA	AB	H	G by POS
1905 BKN N	118	433	110	9	2	3	0.7	32	33	16		16	.254	.305	0	0	SS-118
1906	136	452	110	8	4	0	0.0	40	37	43		14	.243	.279	1	1	SS-135
1907	136	475	118	11	1	0	0.0	52	30	23		16	.248	.276	0	0	SS-136
1908	118	415	91	5	6	1	0.2	22	30	13		9	.219	.267	3	0	SS-116
4 yrs.	508	1775	429	33	13	4	0.2	146	130	95		55	.242	.282	4	1	SS-505

Carlos Lezcano

LEZCANO, CARLOS MANUEL
B. Sept. 30, 1955, Arecibo, Puerto Rico
BR TR 6'2" 185 lbs.

	G	AB	H	2B	3B	HR	HR %	R	RBI	BB	SO	SB	BA	SA	AB	H	G by POS
1980 CHI N	42	88	18	4	1	3	3.4	15	12	11	29	1	.205	.375	2	0	OF-39
1981	7	14	1	0	0	0	0.0	1	2	0	4	0	.071	.071	2	0	OF-5
2 yrs.	49	102	19	4	1	3	2.9	16	14	11	33	1	.186	.333	4	0	OF-44

Sixto Lezcano

LEZCANO, SIXTO
B. Nov. 28, 1953, Manati, Puerto Rico
BR TR 5'10" 165 lbs.

	G	AB	H	2B	3B	HR	HR %	R	RBI	BB	SO	SB	BA	SA	AB	H	G by POS
1974 MIL A	15	54	13	2	0	2	3.7	5	9	4	9	1	.241	.389	0	0	OF-15
1975	134	429	106	19	3	11	2.6	55	43	46	93	5	.247	.382	4	0	OF-129, DH-2
1976	145	513	146	19	5	7	1.4	53	56	51	112	14	.285	.382	0	0	OF-142, DH-3
1977	109	400	109	21	4	21	5.3	50	49	52	78	6	.273	.503	0	0	OF-108
1978	132	442	129	21	4	15	3.4	62	61	64	83	3	.292	.459	2	1	OF-127, DH-3
1979	138	473	152	29	3	28	5.9	84	101	77	74	4	.321	.573	1	0	OF-135, DH-1
1980	112	394	91	19	3	18	4.4	51	55	39	75	1	.229	.421	0	0	OF-108, DH-4
1981 STL N	72	214	57	8	2	5	2.3	26	28	40	40	0	.266	.393	4	1	OF-65
1982 SD N	138	470	136	26	4	16	3.4	73	84	78	69	2	.289	.472	2	0	OF-134
1983 2 teams	SD N (97G – .233)								PHI N	(18G – .282)							
" total	115	356	85	12	2	8	2.2	49	56	52	75	1	.239	.351	14	5	OF-106
1984 PHI N	109	256	71	6	2	14	5.5	36	40	38	43	0	.277	.480	27	6	OF-87
11 yrs.	1219	4018	1098	182	34	145	3.6	544	582	541	751	37	.273	.444	54	13	OF-1156, DH-13

LEAGUE CHAMPIONSHIP SERIES

	G	AB	H	2B	3B	HR	HR %	R	RBI	BB	SO	SB	BA	SA	AB	H	G by POS
1983 PHI N	4	13	4	0	0	1	7.7	2	2	1	1	0	.308	.538	1	0	OF-4

WORLD SERIES

	G	AB	H	2B	3B	HR	HR %	R	RBI	BB	SO	SB	BA	SA	AB	H	G by POS
1983 PHI N	4	8	1	0	0	0	0.0	0	0	0	2	0	.125	.125	1	0	OF-3

Steve Libby

LIBBY, STEPHEN AUGUSTUS
B. Dec. 8, 1853, Scarborough, Me.   Deceased.
6'½" 168 lbs.

	G	AB	H	2B	3B	HR	HR %	R	RBI	BB	SO	SB	BA	SA	AB	H	G by POS
1879 BUF N	1	2	0	0	0	0	0.0	0	0	0	1		.000	.000	0	0	1B-1

Al Libke

LIBKE, ALBERT WALTER (Big Al)
B. Sept. 12, 1918, Tacoma, Wash.
BL TR 6'4" 215 lbs.

	G	AB	H	2B	3B	HR	HR %	R	RBI	BB	SO	SB	BA	SA	AB	H	G by POS
1945 CIN N	130	449	127	23	5	4	0.9	41	53	34	62	6	.283	.383	15	3	OF-108, P-4, 1B-2
1946	124	431	109	22	1	5	1.2	32	42	43	50	0	.253	.343	8	2	OF-115, P-1
2 yrs.	254	880	236	45	6	9	1.0	73	95	77	112	6	.268	.364	23	5	OF-223, P-5, 1B-2

Francisco Libran

LIBRAN, ROSAS FRANCISCO
B. May 6, 1948, Mayaguez, Puerto Rico
BR TR 6' 168 lbs.

	G	AB	H	2B	3B	HR	HR %	R	RBI	BB	SO	SB	BA	SA	AB	H	G by POS
1969 SD N	10	10	1	1	0	0	0.0	1	1	1	2	0	.100	.200	0	0	SS-9

John Lickert

LICKERT, JOHN WILBUR
B. Apr. 4, 1960, Pittsburgh, Pa.
BR TR 5'11" 175 lbs.

	G	AB	H	2B	3B	HR	HR %	R	RBI	BB	SO	SB	BA	SA	AB	H	G by POS
1981 BOS A	1	0	0	0	0	0	–	0	0	0	0	0	–	–	0	0	C-1

Fred Liese

LIESE, FREDERICK RICHARD
B. Oct. 7, 1885, Wis.   D. June 30, 1967, Los Angeles, Calif.

	G	AB	H	2B	3B	HR	HR %	R	RBI	BB	SO	SB	BA	SA	AB	H	G by POS
1910 BOS N	5	4	0	0	0	0	0.0	0	0	1	2	0	.000	.000	4	0	

Bill Lillard

LILLARD, WILLIAM BEVERLEY
Brother of Gene Lillard.
B. Jan. 10, 1918, Goleta, Calif.
BR TR 5'10" 170 lbs.

	G	AB	H	2B	3B	HR	HR %	R	RBI	BB	SO	SB	BA	SA	AB	H	G by POS
1939 PHI A	7	19	6	1	0	0	0.0	4	1	3	1	0	.316	.368	0	0	SS-7
1940	73	206	49	8	2	1	0.5	26	21	28	28	0	.238	.311	1	0	SS-69, 2B-1
2 yrs.	80	225	55	9	2	1	0.4	30	22	31	29	0	.244	.316	1	0	SS-76, 2B-1

Gene Lillard

LILLARD, ROBERT EUGENE
Brother of Bill Lillard.
B. Nov. 12, 1913, Santa Barbara, Calif.
BR TR 5'10½" 178 lbs.

	G	AB	H	2B	3B	HR	HR %	R	RBI	BB	SO	SB	BA	SA	AB	H	G by POS
1936 CHI N	19	34	7	1	0	0	0.0	6	2	3	8	0	.206	.235	10	3	SS-4, 3B-3
1939	23	10	1	0	0	0	0.0	3	0	6	3	0	.100	.100	0	0	P-20
1940 STL N	2	0	0	0	0	0	–	0	0	0	0	0	–	–	0	0	P-2
3 yrs.	44	44	8	1	0	0	0.0	9	2	9	11	0	.182	.205	10	3	P-22, SS-4, 3B-3

Jim Lillie

LILLIE, JAMES J. (Grasshopper)
B. 1862, New Haven, Conn.   D. Nov. 9, 1890, Kansas City, Mo.

	G	AB	H	2B	3B	HR	HR %	R	RBI	BB	SO	SB	BA	SA	AB	H	G by POS
1883 BUF N	50	201	47	7	3	1	0.5	25			31		.234	.313	0	0	OF-47, P-3, C-2, SS-1, 3B-1, 1B-1
1884	114	471	105	12	5	3	0.6	68		5	71		.223	.289	0	0	OF-114, P-2
1885	112	430	107	13	3	2	0.5	49	30	6	39		.249	.307	0	0	OF-112, SS-3, 1B-1

	G	AB	H	2B	3B	HR	HR %	R	RBI	BB	SO	SB	BA	SA	Pinch Hit AB	Pinch Hit H	G by POS

Jim Lillie continued

	G	AB	H	2B	3B	HR	HR%	R	RBI	BB	SO	SB	BA	SA	PH AB	PH H	G by POS
1886 KC N	114	416	73	9	0	0	0.0	37	22	11	80		.175	.197	0	0	OF-114, P-1
4 yrs.	390	1518	332	41	11	6	0.4	179	51	23	221		.219	.272	0	0	OF-387, P-6, SS-4, C-2, 3B-1, 2B-1, 1B-1

Bob Lillis

LILLIS, ROBERT PERRY (Flea)
B. June 2, 1930, Altadena, Calif.
Manager 1982-84.

BR TR 5'11" 160 lbs.

	G	AB	H	2B	3B	HR	HR%	R	RBI	BB	SO	SB	BA	SA	PH AB	PH H	G by POS
1958 LA N	20	69	27	3	1	1	1.4	10	5	4	2	1	.391	.507	1	1	SS-19
1959	30	48	11	2	0	0	0.0	7	2	3	4	0	.229	.271	1	1	SS-20
1960	48	60	16	4	0	0	0.0	6	6	2	6	2	.267	.333	3	0	SS-23, 3B-14, 2B-1
1961 2 teams	LA	N (19G – .111)			STL	N	(86G – .217)										
" total	105	239	51	4	0	0	0.0	24	22	8	14	3	.213	.230	3	0	SS-57, 2B-25, 3B-12
1962 HOU N	129	457	114	12	4	1	0.2	38	30	28	23	7	.249	.300	1	1	SS-99, 2B-33, 3B-9
1963	147	469	93	13	1	1	0.2	31	19	15	35	3	.198	.237	3	0	SS-124, 2B-19, 3B-6
1964	109	332	89	11	2	0	0.0	31	17	11	10	4	.268	.313	13	3	2B-52, SS-43, 3B-12
1965	124	408	90	12	1	0	0.0	34	20	20	10	2	.221	.255	5	3	SS-104, 3B-9, 2B-6
1966	68	164	38	6	0	0	0.0	14	11	7	4	1	.232	.268	8	1	2B-35, SS-18, 3B-6
1967	37	82	20	1	0	0	0.0	3	5	1	8	0	.244	.256	9	1	SS-23, 2B-3, 3B-2
10 yrs.	817	2328	549	68	9	3	0.1	198	137	99	116	23	.236	.277	47	11	SS-530, 2B-174, 3B-70

Lou Limmer

LIMMER, LOUIS
B. Mar. 10, 1925, New York, N. Y.

BL TL 6'2" 190 lbs.

	G	AB	H	2B	3B	HR	HR%	R	RBI	BB	SO	SB	BA	SA	PH AB	PH H	G by POS
1951 PHI A	94	214	34	9	1	5	2.3	25	30	28	40	1	.159	.280	31	5	1B-58
1954	115	316	73	10	3	14	4.4	41	32	35	37	2	.231	.415	30	8	1B-79
2 yrs.	209	530	107	19	4	19	3.6	66	62	63	77	3	.202	.360	61	13	1B-137

Rufino Linares

LINARES, RUFINO
B. Feb. 28, 1955, San Pedro de Macoris, Dominican Republic

BR TR 6' 170 lbs.

	G	AB	H	2B	3B	HR	HR%	R	RBI	BB	SO	SB	BA	SA	PH AB	PH H	G by POS
1981 ATL N	78	253	67	9	2	5	2.0	27	25	9	28	8	.265	.375	24	5	OF-60
1982	77	191	57	7	1	2	1.0	28	17	7	29	5	.298	.377	31	8	OF-53
1984	34	58	12	3	0	1	1.7	4	10	6	12	0	.207	.310	20	5	OF-13
3 yrs.	189	502	136	19	3	8	1.6	59	52	22	69	13	.271	.369	75	18	OF-126

Carl Lind

LIND, HENRY CARL
B. Sept. 19, 1904, New Orleans, La.   D. Aug. 4, 1946, New York, N. Y.

BR TR 6' 160 lbs.

	G	AB	H	2B	3B	HR	HR%	R	RBI	BB	SO	SB	BA	SA	PH AB	PH H	G by POS
1927 CLE A	12	37	5	0	0	0	0.0	2	1	5	7	1	.135	.135	0	0	2B-11, SS-1
1928	154	650	191	42	4	1	0.2	102	54	36	48	8	.294	.375	0	0	2B-154
1929	66	224	54	8	1	0	0.0	19	13	13	17	0	.241	.286	1	0	2B-64, 3B-1
1930	24	69	17	3	0	0	0.0	8	6	3	7	0	.246	.290	1	0	SS-22, 2B-1
4 yrs.	256	980	267	53	5	1	0.1	131	74	57	79	9	.272	.340	2	0	2B-230, SS-23, 3B-1

Jack Lind

LIND, JACKSON HUGH
B. June 8, 1946, Denver, Colo.

BB TR 6' 170 lbs.

	G	AB	H	2B	3B	HR	HR%	R	RBI	BB	SO	SB	BA	SA	PH AB	PH H	G by POS
1974 MIL A	9	17	4	2	0	0	0.0	4	1	3	2	0	.235	.353	0	0	SS-5, 2B-4
1975	17	20	1	0	0	0	0.0	1	0	2	12	1	.050	.050	0	0	SS-9, 3B-6, 1B-1
2 yrs.	26	37	5	2	0	0	0.0	5	1	5	14	1	.135	.189	0	0	SS-14, 3B-6, 2B-4, 1B-1

Em Lindbeck

LINDBECK, EMERIT DESMOND
B. Aug. 27, 1935, Kewanee, Ill.

BL TR 6' 185 lbs.

	G	AB	H	2B	3B	HR	HR%	R	RBI	BB	SO	SB	BA	SA	PH AB	PH H	G by POS
1960 DET A	2	1	0	0	0	0	0.0	0	0	1	0	0	.000	.000	1	0	

Johnny Lindell

LINDELL, JOHN HARLAN
B. Aug. 30, 1916, Greeley, Colo.

BR TR 6'4½" 217 lbs.

	G	AB	H	2B	3B	HR	HR%	R	RBI	BB	SO	SB	BA	SA	PH AB	PH H	G by POS
1941 NY A	1	1	0	0	0	0	0.0	0	0	0	0	0	.000	.000	1	0	
1942	27	24	6	1	0	0	0.0	1	4	0	5	0	.250	.292	5	2	P-23
1943	122	441	108	17	12	4	0.9	53	51	51	55	2	.245	.365	1	0	OF-122
1944	149	594	178	33	16	18	3.0	91	103	44	56	5	.300	.500	0	0	OF-149
1945	41	159	45	6	3	1	0.6	26	20	17	10	2	.283	.377	0	0	OF-41
1946	102	332	86	10	5	10	3.0	41	40	32	47	4	.259	.410	14	3	OF-74, 1B-14
1947	127	476	131	18	7	11	2.3	66	67	32	70	1	.275	.412	7	3	OF-118
1948	88	309	98	17	2	13	4.2	58	55	35	50	0	.317	.511	7	0	OF-79
1949	78	211	51	10	0	6	2.8	33	27	35	27	3	.242	.374	13	2	OF-65
1950 2 teams	NY	A (7G – .190)			STL	N	(36G – .186)										
" total	43	134	25	5	2	5	3.7	18	18	19	26	0	.187	.366	4	0	OF-39
1953 2 teams	PIT	N (58G – .286)			PHI	N	(11G – .389)										
" total	69	109	33	7	1	4	3.7	14	17	22	17	0	.303	.495	26	8	P-32, OF-2, 1B-2
1954 PHI N	7	5	1	0	0	0	0.0	0	2	2	3	0	.200	.200	5	1	
12 yrs.	854	2795	762	124	48	72	2.6	401	404	289	366	17	.273	.429	83	19	OF-689, P-55, 1B-16

WORLD SERIES

	G	AB	H	2B	3B	HR	HR%	R	RBI	BB	SO	SB	BA	SA	PH AB	PH H	G by POS
1943 NY A	4	9	1	0	0	0	0.0	1	0	1	4	0	.111	.111	0	0	OF-4
1947	6	18	9	3	1	0	0.0	3	7	5	2	0	.500	.778	0	0	OF-6
1949	2	7	1	0	0	0	0.0	0	0	0	2	0	.143	.143	0	0	OF-2
3 yrs.	12	34	11	3	1	0	0.0	4	7	6	8	0	.324	.471	0	0	OF-12

Bob Lindemann

LINDEMANN, JOHN FREDERICK MANN
B. Chester, Pa.   D. Dec. 19, 1951, Williamsport, Pa.

BR TR

	G	AB	H	2B	3B	HR	HR%	R	RBI	BB	SO	SB	BA	SA	PH AB	PH H	G by POS
1901 PHI A	3	9	1	0	0	0	0.0	0	0	0		0	.111	.111	0	0	OF-3

Walt Linden

LINDEN, WALTER CHARLES
B. Mar. 27, 1924, Chicago, Ill.

BR TR 6'1" 190 lbs.

	G	AB	H	2B	3B	HR	HR%	R	RBI	BB	SO	SB	BA	SA	PH AB	PH H	G by POS
1950 BOS N	3	5	2	1	0	0	0.0	0	0	1	0	0	.400	.600	0	0	C-3

	G	AB	H	2B	3B	HR	HR%	R	RBI	BB	SO	SB	BA	SA	Pinch Hit AB	Pinch Hit H	G by POS

Bill Lindsay

LINDSAY, WILLIAM GIBBONS   BL TR 5'10½" 165 lbs.
B. Feb. 24, 1881, Madison, N. C.   D. July 14, 1963, Greensboro, N. C.

	G	AB	H	2B	3B	HR	HR%	R	RBI	BB	SO	SB	BA	SA	AB	H	G by POS
1911 CLE A	19	66	16	2	0	0	0.0	6	5	1		2	.242	.273	2	1	3B-15, 2B-1

Pinky Lindsay

LINDSAY, CHRISTIAN HALLER
B. July 24, 1878, Moon Township, Pa.   D. Jan. 25, 1941, Cleveland, Ohio

	G	AB	H	2B	3B	HR	HR%	R	RBI	BB	SO	SB	BA	SA	AB	H	G by POS
1905 DET A	88	329	88	14	1	0	0.0	38	31	18		10	.267	.316	0	0	1B-88
1906	141	499	112	16	2	0	0.0	59	33	45		18	.224	.265	2	0	1B-122, 2B-17, 3B-1
2 yrs.	229	828	200	30	3	0	0.0	97	64	63		28	.242	.285	2	0	1B-210, 2B-17, 3B-1

Charlie Lindstrom

LINDSTROM, CHARLES WILLIAM (Chuck)   BR TR 5'11" 175 lbs.
Son of Freddie Lindstrom.
B. Sept. 7, 1936, Chicago, Ill.

	G	AB	H	2B	3B	HR	HR%	R	RBI	BB	SO	SB	BA	SA	AB	H	G by POS
1958 CHI A	1	1	1	0	1	0	0.0	1	1	0		0	1.000	3.000	0	0	C-1

Freddie Lindstrom

LINDSTROM, FRED CHARLES (Lindy)   BR TR 5'11" 170 lbs.
Born Frederick Anthony Lindstrom.   Father of Charlie Lindstrom.
B. Nov. 21, 1905, Chicago, Ill.   D. Oct. 4, 1981, Chicago, Ill.
Hall of Fame 1976.

	G	AB	H	2B	3B	HR	HR%	R	RBI	BB	SO	SB	BA	SA	AB	H	G by POS
1924 NY N	52	79	20	3	1	0	0.0	19	4	6	10	3	.253	.316	6	2	2B-23, 3B-11
1925	104	356	102	15	12	4	1.1	43	33	22	20	5	.287	.430	2	1	3B-96, SS-1, 2B-1
1926	140	543	164	19	9	9	1.7	90	76	39	21	11	.302	.420	1	1	3B-138, OF-1
1927	138	562	172	36	8	7	1.2	107	58	40	40	10	.306	.436	1	0	3B-87, OF-51
1928	153	646	231	39	9	14	2.2	99	107	25	21	15	.358	.511	0	0	3B-153
1929	130	549	175	23	6	15	2.7	99	91	30	28	10	.319	.464	2	0	3B-128
1930	148	609	231	39	7	22	3.6	127	106	48	33	15	.379	.575	0	0	3B-148
1931	78	303	91	12	6	5	1.7	38	36	26	12	5	.300	.429	1	0	OF-73, 2B-4
1932	144	595	161	26	5	15	2.5	83	92	27	28	6	.271	.407	0	0	OF-128, 3B-15
1933 PIT N	138	538	167	39	10	5	0.9	70	55	33	22	1	.310	.448	8	3	OF-130
1934	97	383	111	24	4	4	1.0	59	49	23	21	1	.290	.405	4	1	OF-92
1935 CHI N	90	342	94	22	4	3	0.9	49	62	10	13	1	.275	.389	6	1	OF-50, 3B-33
1936 BKN N	26	106	28	4	0	0	0.0	12	10	5	7	1	.264	.302	0	0	OF-26
13 yrs.	1438	5611	1747	301	81	103	1.8	895	779	334	276	84	.311	.449	31	9	3B-809, OF-551, 2B-28, SS-1

WORLD SERIES
	G	AB	H	2B	3B	HR	HR%	R	RBI	BB	SO	SB	BA	SA	AB	H	G by POS
1924 NY N	7	30	10	2	0	0	0.0	1	4	3	6	0	.333	.400	0	0	3B-7
1935 CHI N	4	15	3	1	0	0	0.0	0	0	1	1	0	.200	.267	0	0	3B-1
2 yrs.	11	45	13	3	0	0	0.0	1	4	4	7	0	.289	.356	0	0	3B-8

Carl Linhart

LINHART, CARL JAMES   BL TR 5'11" 184 lbs.
B. Dec. 14, 1929, Zborov, Czechoslovakia

	G	AB	H	2B	3B	HR	HR%	R	RBI	BB	SO	SB	BA	SA	AB	H	G by POS
1952 DET A	3	2	0	0	0	0	0.0	0	0	0	0	0	.000	.000	2	0	

Bob Linton

LINTON, CLAUD CLARENCE   BL TR 6' 185 lbs.
B. Apr. 18, 1902, Emerson, Ark.   D. Apr. 3, 1980, Destin, Fla.

	G	AB	H	2B	3B	HR	HR%	R	RBI	BB	SO	SB	BA	SA	AB	H	G by POS
1929 PIT N	17	18	2	0	0	0	0.0	0	1	1	2	0	.111	.111	8	1	C-8

Larry Lintz

LINTZ, LARRY   BR TR 5'9" 150 lbs.
B. Oct. 10, 1949, Martinez, Calif.

	G	AB	H	2B	3B	HR	HR%	R	RBI	BB	SO	SB	BA	SA	AB	H	G by POS
1973 MON N	52	116	29	1	0	0	0.0	20	3	17	18	12	.250	.259	2	1	2B-34, SS-15
1974	113	319	76	10	1	0	0.0	60	20	44	50	50	.238	.276	2	0	2B-67, SS-31, 3B-1
1975 2 teams	MON N (46G – .197)					STL N (27G – .278)											
" total	73	150	31	1	0	0	0.0	24	4	26	20	21	.207	.213	0	0	2B-45, SS-8
1976 OAK A	68	1	0	0	0	0	0.0	21	0	2	0	31	.000	.000	0	0	DH-19, 2B-5, OF-3
1977	41	30	4	1	0	0	0.0	11	0	8	13	13	.133	.167	0	0	2B-28, DH-5, SS-2, 3B-1
1978 CLE A	3	0	0	0	0	0	–	1	0	0	0	1	–	–	0	0	DH-1
6 yrs.	350	616	140	13	1	0	0.0	137	27	97	101	128	.227	.252	2	1	2B-179, SS-56, DH-25, OF-3, 3B-2

Phil Linz

LINZ, PHILIP FRANCIS (Supersub)   BR TR 6'1" 180 lbs.
B. June 4, 1939, Baltimore, Md.

	G	AB	H	2B	3B	HR	HR%	R	RBI	BB	SO	SB	BA	SA	AB	H	G by POS
1962 NY A	71	129	37	8	0	1	0.8	28	14	6	17	6	.287	.372	16	7	SS-21, 3B-8, 2B-5, OF-2
1963	72	186	50	9	0	2	1.1	22	12	15	18	1	.269	.349	15	2	SS-22, 3B-13, OF-12, 2B-6
1964	112	368	92	21	3	5	1.4	63	25	43	61	3	.250	.364	9	0	SS-55, 3B-41, 2B-5, OF-3
1965	99	285	59	12	1	2	0.7	37	16	30	33	2	.207	.277	8	1	SS-71, OF-4, 3B-4, 2B-1
1966 PHI N	40	70	14	3	0	0	0.0	4	6	2	14	0	.200	.243	15	0	3B-14, SS-6, 2B-3
1967 2 teams	PHI N (23G – .222)					NY N (24G – .207)											
" total	47	76	16	4	0	1	1.3	12	6	6	11	0	.211	.303	15	2	SS-15, 2B-11, 3B-2, OF-1
1968 NY N	78	258	54	7	0	0	0.0	19	17	10	41	1	.209	.236	9	1	2B-71
7 yrs.	519	1372	322	64	4	11	0.8	185	96	112	195	13	.235	.311	87	13	SS-190, 2B-102, 3B-82, OF-22

WORLD SERIES
	G	AB	H	2B	3B	HR	HR%	R	RBI	BB	SO	SB	BA	SA	AB	H	G by POS
1963 NY A	3	3	1	0	0	0	0.0	0	0	0	1	0	.333	.333	3	1	
1964	7	31	7	1	0	2	6.5	5	2	2	5	0	.226	.452	0	0	SS-7
2 yrs.	10	34	8	1	0	2	5.9	5	2	2	6	0	.235	.441	3	1	SS-7

Johnny Lipon

LIPON, JOHN JOSEPH (Skids)   BR TR 6' 175 lbs.
B. Nov. 10, 1922, Martin's Ferry, Ohio
Manager 1971.

	G	AB	H	2B	3B	HR	HR%	R	RBI	BB	SO	SB	BA	SA	AB	H	G by POS
1942 DET A	34	131	25	2	0	0	0.0	5	9	7	7	1	.191	.206	0	0	SS-34
1946	14	20	6	0	0	0	0.0	4	1	5	3	0	.300	.300	1	0	SS-8, 3B-1
1948	121	458	133	18	8	5	1.1	65	52	68	22	4	.290	.397	1	0	SS-117, 3B-1, 2B-1
1949	127	439	110	14	6	3	0.7	57	59	75	24	2	.251	.330	5	0	SS-120
1950	147	601	176	27	6	2	0.3	104	63	81	26	9	.293	.368	0	0	SS-147
1951	129	487	129	15	1	0	0.0	56	38	49	27	7	.265	.300	2	0	SS-125

	G	AB	H	2B	3B	HR	HR %	R	RBI	BB	SO	SB	BA	SA	Pinch Hit AB	Pinch Hit H	G by POS

Johnny Lipon continued

1952 2 teams	DET A (39G – .221)			BOS A (79G – .205)													
" total	118	370	78	12	3	0	0.0	42	30	48	26	4	.211	.259	1	0	SS-108, 3B-7
1953 2 teams	BOS A (60G – .214)			STL A (7G – .222)													
" total	67	154	33	7	0	0	0.0	18	14	14	17	1	.214	.260	2	0	SS-58, 3B-6, 2B-1
1954 CIN N	1	1	0	0	0	0	0.0	0	0	0	0	0	.000	.000	1	0	
9 yrs.	758	2661	690	95	24	10	0.4	351	266	347	152	28	.259	.324	13	0	SS-717, 3B-15, 2B-2

Nig Lipscomb

LIPSCOMB, GERARD
B. Feb. 24, 1911, Rutherfordton, N. C.   D. Feb. 27, 1978, Huntersville, N. C.
BR TR 6'   175 lbs.

1937 STL A	36	96	31	9	1	0	0.0	11	8	11	10	0	.323	.438	4	1	2B-27, P-3, 3B-1

Bob Lipski

LIPSKI, ROBERT PETER
B. July 7, 1938, Scranton, Pa.
BL TR 6'1"   180 lbs.

1963 CLE A	2	1	0	0	0	0	0.0	0	0	0	1	0	.000	.000	0	0	C-2

Joe Lis

LIS, JOSEPH ANTHONY
B. Aug. 15, 1946, Somerville, N. J.
BR TR 6'   195 lbs.

1970 PHI N	13	37	7	2	0	1	2.7	1	4	5	11	0	.189	.324	4	0	OF-9
1971	59	123	26	6	0	6	4.9	16	10	16	43	0	.211	.407	22	3	OF-35
1972	62	140	34	6	0	6	4.3	13	18	30	34	0	.243	.414	19	4	1B-30, OF-14
1973 MIN A	103	253	62	11	1	9	3.6	37	25	28	66	0	.245	.403	4	1	1B-96, DH-1
1974 2 teams	MIN A (24G – .195)			CLE A (57G – .202)													
" total	81	150	30	3	0	6	4.0	20	19	19	42	1	.200	.340	15	4	1B-49, DH-9, 3B-9, OF-1
1975 CLE A	9	13	4	2	0	2	15.4	4	8	3	3	0	.308	.923	0	0	1B-8, DH-1
1976	20	51	16	1	0	2	3.9	4	7	8	8	0	.314	.451	3	0	1B-17, DH-1
1977 SEA A	9	13	3	0	0	0	0.0	1	1	1	2	0	.231	.231	2	1	1B-4, C-1
8 yrs.	356	780	182	31	1	32	4.1	96	92	110	209	1	.233	.399	69	13	1B-204, OF-59, DH-12, 3B-9, C-1

Rick Lisi

LISI, RICCARDO PATRICK
B. Mar. 17, 1956, Halifax, Nova Scotia, Canada
BR TR 6'   175 lbs.

1981 TEX A	9	16	5	0	0	0	0.0	6	1	4	0	0	.313	.313	2	0	OF-8

Pete Lister

LISTER, MORRIS ELMER
B. July 21, 1881, Savanna, Ill.   D. Feb. 27, 1947, St. Petersburg, Fla.

1907 CLE A	22	65	18	2	0	0	0.0	5	4	3		2	.277	.308	0	0	1B-22

Bryan Little

LITTLE, RICHARD BRYAN
B. Oct. 8, 1959, Houston, Tex.
BB TR 5'11"   155 lbs.

1982 MON N	29	42	9	0	0	0	0.0	6	3	4	6	2	.214	.214	2	0	2B-16, SS-10
1983	106	350	91	15	3	1	0.3	48	36	50	22	4	.260	.329	4	1	SS-66, 2B-51
1984	85	266	65	11	1	0	0.0	31	9	34	19	2	.244	.293	7	3	2B-77, SS-2
3 yrs.	220	658	165	26	4	1	0.2	85	48	88	47	8	.251	.307	13	4	2B-144, SS-78

Harvey Little

LITTLE, HARRY A.
B. St. Louis, Mo.   D. Jan. 25, 1892
TR

1877 2 teams	STL N (3G – .167)			LOU N (1G – .000)													
" total	4	15	2	0	0	0	0.0	2	0	2	7		.133	.133	0	0	OF-3, 2B-1

Jack Little

LITTLE, WILLIAM ARTHUR
B. Mar. 12, 1891, Mart, Tex.   D. July 27, 1961, Dallas, Tex.
BR TR 5'11"   175 lbs.

1912 NY A	3	12	3	0	0	0	0.0	2	0	1	0	2	.250	.250	0	0	OF-3

Dennis Littlejohn

LITTLEJOHN, DENNIS GERALD
B. Oct. 4, 1954, Santa Monica, Calif.
BR TR 6'2"   200 lbs.

1978 SF N	2	0	0	0	0	0	–	0	0	0	0	0	–	–	0	0	C-2
1979	63	193	38	6	1	1	0.5	15	13	21	46	0	.197	.254	0	0	C-63
1980	13	29	7	1	0	0	0.0	2	2	7	7	0	.241	.276	3	0	C-10
3 yrs.	78	222	45	7	1	1	0.5	17	15	28	53	0	.203	.257	3	0	C-75

Larry Littleton

LITTLETON, LARRY MARVIN
B. Apr. 3, 1954, Charlotte, N. C.
BR TR 6'1"   185 lbs.

1981 CLE A	26	23	0	0	0	0	0.0	2	1	3	6	0	.000	.000	4	0	OF-24

Jack Littrell

LITTRELL, JACK NAPIER
B. Jan. 22, 1929, Louisville, Ky.
BR TR 6'   179 lbs.

1952 PHI A	4	2	0	0	0	0	0.0	0	0	1	2	0	.000	.000	1	0	SS-2, 3B-1
1954	9	30	9	2	0	1	3.3	7	3	6	3	1	.300	.467	0	0	SS-9
1955 KC A	37	70	14	0	1	0	0.0	7	1	4	12	0	.200	.229	6	0	SS-22, 1B-6, 2B-4
1957 CHI N	61	153	29	4	2	1	0.7	8	13	9	43	0	.190	.261	2	1	SS-47, 2B-6, 3B-5
4 yrs.	111	255	52	6	3	2	0.8	22	17	20	60	1	.204	.275	9	1	SS-80, 2B-10, 3B-6, 1B-6

Danny Litwhiler

LITWHILER, DANIEL WEBSTER
B. Aug. 31, 1916, Ringtown, Pa.
BR TR 5'10½"   198 lbs.

1940 PHI N	36	142	49	2	2	5	3.5	10	17	3	13	1	.345	.493	2	0	OF-36
1941	151	590	180	29	6	18	3.1	72	66	39	43	1	.305	.466	1	0	OF-150
1942	151	591	160	25	9	9	1.5	59	56	27	42	2	.271	.389	0	0	OF-151
1943 2 teams	PHI N (36G – .259)			STL N (80G – .279)													
" total	116	397	108	20	3	12	3.0	63	48	30	45	2	.272	.428	8	0	OF-104
1944 STL N	140	492	130	25	4	15	3.0	53	82	37	56	2	.264	.427	3	1	OF-136
1946 2 teams	STL N (6G – .000)			BOS N (79G – .291)													
" total	85	252	72	12	2	8	3.2	29	38	20	24	1	.286	.444	17	5	OF-65, 3B-2
1947 BOS N	91	226	59	5	2	7	3.1	38	31	25	43	1	.261	.394	23	4	OF-66

	G	AB	H	2B	3B	HR	HR %	R	RBI	BB	SO	SB	BA	SA	Pinch Hit AB	Pinch Hit H	G by POS

Danny Litwhiler continued

		G	AB	H	2B	3B	HR	HR%	R	RBI	BB	SO	SB	BA	SA	AB	H	G by POS
1948	**2 teams**		**BOS**	**N**	(13G –	.273)		**CIN**	**N**	(106G –	.275)							
"	total	119	371	102	21	2	14	3.8	51	50	52	43	1	.275	.456	15	5	OF-91, 3B-15
1949	CIN N	102	292	85	18	1	11	3.8	35	48	44	42	0	.291	.473	14	3	OF-82, 3B-3
1950		54	112	29	4	0	6	5.4	15	12	20	21	0	.259	.455	19	4	OF-29
1951		12	29	8	1	0	2	6.9	3	3	2	5	0	.276	.517	4	2	OF-7
11 yrs.		1057	3494	982	162	32	107	3.1	428	451	299	377	11	.281	.438	106	24	OF-917, 3B-20

WORLD SERIES

		G	AB	H	2B	3B	HR	HR%	R	RBI	BB	SO	SB	BA	SA	AB	H	G by POS
1943	STL N	5	15	4	1	0	0	0.0	0	2	2	4	0	.267	.333	1	1	OF-4
1944		5	20	4	1	0	1	5.0	2	1	2	7	0	.200	.400	0	0	OF-5
2 yrs.		10	35	8	2	0	1	2.9	2	3	4	11	0	.229	.371	1	1	OF-9

Mickey Livingston

LIVINGSTON, THOMPSON ORVILLE   BR TR 6'1½"   185 lbs.
B. Nov. 15, 1914, Newberry, S. C.   D. Apr. 3, 1983, Newberry, S. C.

		G	AB	H	2B	3B	HR	HR%	R	RBI	BB	SO	SB	BA	SA	AB	H	G by POS
1938	WAS A	2	4	3	2	0	0	0.0	0	1	0	1	0	.750	1.250	0	0	C-2
1941	PHI N	95	207	42	6	1	0	0.0	16	18	20	38	2	.203	.242	18	4	C-71, 1B-1
1942		89	239	49	6	1	2	0.8	20	22	25	20	0	.205	.264	6	2	C-78, 1B-6
1943	**2 teams**		**PHI**	**N**	(84G –	.249)		**CHI**	**N**	(36G –	.261)							
"	total	120	376	95	14	3	7	1.9	36	34	31	26	2	.253	.362	2	0	C-115, 1B-6
1945	CHI N	71	224	57	4	2	2	0.9	19	23	19	6	2	.254	.317	2	0	C-68, 1B-1
1946		66	176	45	14	0	2	1.1	14	20	20	19	0	.256	.369	8	1	C-56
1947	**2 teams**		**CHI**	**N**	(19G –	.212)		**NY**	**N**	(5G –	.167)							
"	total	24	39	8	2	0	0	0.0	2	3	2	7	0	.205	.256	14	5	C-9
1948	NY N	45	99	21	4	1	2	2.0	9	12	21	11	1	.212	.333	3	1	C-42
1949	**2 teams**		**NY**	**N**	(19G –	.298)		**BOS**	**N**	(28G –	.234)							
"	total	47	121	32	4	1	4	3.3	12	18	5	13	0	.264	.413	6	0	C-41
1951	BKN N	2	5	2	0	0	0	0.0	0	2	1	0	0	.400	.400	0	0	C-2
10 yrs.		561	1490	354	56	9	19	1.3	128	153	144	141	7	.238	.326	59	13	C-484, 1B-14

WORLD SERIES

		G	AB	H	2B	3B	HR	HR%	R	RBI	BB	SO	SB	BA	SA	AB	H	G by POS
1945	CHI N	6	22	8	3	0	0	0.0	3	4	1	1	0	.364	.500	0	0	C-6

Paddy Livingston

LIVINGSTON, PATRICK JOSEPH   BR TR 5'8"   197 lbs.
B. Jan. 14, 1880, Cleveland, Ohio   D. Sept. 19, 1977, Cleveland, Ohio

		G	AB	H	2B	3B	HR	HR%	R	RBI	BB	SO	SB	BA	SA	AB	H	G by POS
1901	CLE A	1	2	0	0	0	0	0.0	0	0	0		0	.000	.000	0	0	C-1
1906	CIN N	50	139	22	1	4	0	0.0	8	8	12		0	.158	.223	3	0	C-47
1909	PHI A	64	175	41	6	4	0	0.0	15	15	15		4	.234	.314	0	0	C-64
1910		37	120	25	4	3	0	0.0	11	9	6		2	.208	.292	0	0	C-37
1911		27	71	17	4	0	0	0.0	9	8	7		1	.239	.296	1	0	C-26
1912	CLE A	19	47	11	2	1	0	0.0	5	3	1		0	.234	.319	6	0	C-13
1917	STL N	7	20	4	0	0	0	0.0	0	2	0		2	.200	.200	1	0	C-6
7 yrs.		205	574	120	17	12	0	0.0	48	45	41		9	.209	.280	11	0	C-194

Abel Lizotte

LIZOTTE, ABEL
B. Apr. 13, 1870, Lewiston, Me.   D. Dec. 4, 1926, Wilkes-Barre, Pa.

		G	AB	H	2B	3B	HR	HR%	R	RBI	BB	SO	SB	BA	SA	AB	H	G by POS
1896	PIT N	7	29	3	0	0	0	0.0	3	3	2	2	1	.103	.103	0	0	1B-7

Winston Llenas

LLENAS, WINSTON ENRIQUILLO (Chilote)   BR TR 5'10"   165 lbs.
B. Sept. 23, 1943, Santiago, Dominican Republic

		G	AB	H	2B	3B	HR	HR%	R	RBI	BB	SO	SB	BA	SA	AB	H	G by POS
1968	CAL A	16	39	5	1	0	0	0.0	5	1	2	5	0	.128	.154	7	0	3B-9
1969		34	47	8	2	0	0	0.0	4	0	2	10	0	.170	.213	26	7	3B-9
1972		44	64	17	3	0	0	0.0	3	7	3	8	0	.266	.313	28	7	3B-10, OF-2, 2B-2
1973		78	130	35	1	0	1	0.8	16	25	10	16	0	.269	.300	56	16	2B-20, 3B-11, OF-4
1974		72	138	36	6	0	2	1.4	16	17	11	19	0	.261	.348	33	7	OF-32, 2B-15, DH-10, 3B-2
1975		56	113	21	4	0	0	0.0	6	11	10	11	0	.186	.221	24	7	2B-12, OF-10, DH-6, 1B-6, 3B-3
6 yrs.		300	531	122	17	0	3	0.6	50	61	38	69	0	.230	.279	174	44	2B-49, OF-48, 3B-44, DH-16, 1B-6

Mike Loan

LOAN, WILLIAM JOSEPH   BR TR 5'11"   185 lbs.
B. Sept. 27, 1894, Philadelphia, Pa.   D. Nov. 21, 1966, Springfield, Pa.

		G	AB	H	2B	3B	HR	HR%	R	RBI	BB	SO	SB	BA	SA	AB	H	G by POS
1912	PHI N	1	2	1	0	0	0	0.0	1	0	0	0	0	.500	.500	0	0	C-1

Bobby Loane

LOANE, ROBERT KENNETH   BR TR 6'   190 lbs.
B. Aug. 6, 1914, Berkeley, Calif.

		G	AB	H	2B	3B	HR	HR%	R	RBI	BB	SO	SB	BA	SA	AB	H	G by POS
1939	WAS A	3	9	0	0	0	0	0.0	2	1	4	4	0	.000	.000	0	0	OF-3
1940	BOS N	13	22	5	3	0	0	0.0	4	1	2	5	2	.227	.364	1	1	OF-10
2 yrs.		16	31	5	3	0	0	0.0	6	2	6	9	2	.161	.258	1	1	OF-13

Frank Lobert

LOBERT, FRANK JOHN   BR TR 6'   180 lbs.
Brother of Hans Lobert.
B. Nov. 26, 1883, Williamsport, Pa.   D. May 29, 1932, Pittsburgh, Pa.

		G	AB	H	2B	3B	HR	HR%	R	RBI	BB	SO	SB	BA	SA	AB	H	G by POS
1914	BAL F	11	30	6	0	1	0	0.0	3	2	0		0	.200	.267	1	0	3B-7, 2B-1

Hans Lobert

LOBERT, JOHN BERNARD (Honus)   BR TR 5'9"   170 lbs.
Brother of Frank Lobert.
B. Oct. 18, 1881, Wilmington, Del.   D. Sept. 14, 1968, Philadelphia, Pa.
Manager 1938, 1942.

		G	AB	H	2B	3B	HR	HR%	R	RBI	BB	SO	SB	BA	SA	AB	H	G by POS
1903	PIT N	5	13	1	1	0	0	0.0	1	0	1		1	.077	.154	0	0	3B-3, SS-1, 2B-1
1905	CHI N	14	46	9	2	0	0	0.0	7	1	3		4	.196	.239	0	0	3B-13, OF-1
1906	CIN N	79	268	83	5	5	0	0.0	39	19	19		20	.310	.366	4	1	3B-35, SS-31, 2B-10, OF-1
1907		148	537	132	9	12	1	0.2	61	41	37		30	.246	.313	1	0	SS-142, 3B-5
1908		155	570	167	17	18	4	0.7	71	63	46		47	.293	.407	0	0	3B-99, SS-35, OF-21
1909		122	425	90	13	5	4	0.9	50	52	48		30	.212	.294	0	0	3B-122
1910		93	314	97	6	6	3	1.0	43	40	30	9	41	.309	.395	0	0	3B-90

	G	AB	H	2B	3B	HR	HR %	R	RBI	BB	SO	SB	BA	SA	Pinch Hit AB	Pinch Hit H	G by POS

Hans Lobert continued

	G	AB	H	2B	3B	HR	HR%	R	RBI	BB	SO	SB	BA	SA	AB	H	G by POS
1911 PHI N	147	541	154	20	9	9	1.7	94	72	56	31	40	.285	.405	0	0	3B-147
1912	65	257	84	12	5	2	0.8	37	33	19	13	13	.327	.436	1	0	3B-64
1913	150	573	172	28	11	7	1.2	98	55	42	34	41	.300	.424	1	0	3B-145, SS-3, 2B-1
1914	135	505	139	24	5	1	0.2	83	52	49	32	31	.275	.349	0	0	3B-133, SS-2
1915 NY N	106	386	97	18	4	0	0.0	46	38	25	24	14	.251	.319	3	1	3B-106
1916	48	76	17	3	2	0	0.0	6	11	5	8	2	.224	.316	24	6	3B-20
1917	50	52	10	1	0	1	1.9	4	5	5	5	2	.192	.269	24	3	3B-21
14 yrs.	1317	4563	1252	159	82	32	0.7	640	482	395	156	316	.274	.366	58	11	3B-1003, SS-214, OF-23, 2B-12

Harry Lochhead

LOCHHEAD, HARRY ROBERT
B. Mar. 29, 1876, Stockton, Calif.   D. Aug. 22, 1909, Stockton, Calif.

TR

	G	AB	H	2B	3B	HR	HR%	R	RBI	BB	SO	SB	BA	SA	AB	H	G by POS
1899 CLE N	148	541	129	7	1	1	0.2	52	43	21		23	.238	.261	0	0	SS-146, 2B-1, P-1
1901 2 teams		DET	A (1G – .500)			PHI	A (9G – .088)										
" total	10	38	5	0	0	0	0.0	5	2	3		0	.132	.132	0	0	SS-10
2 yrs.	158	579	134	7	1	1	0.2	57	45	24		23	.231	.252	0	0	SS-156, 2B-1, P-1

Don Lock

LOCK, DON WILSON
B. July 27, 1936, Wichita, Kans.

BR TR 6'2" 195 lbs.

	G	AB	H	2B	3B	HR	HR%	R	RBI	BB	SO	SB	BA	SA	AB	H	G by POS
1962 WAS A	71	225	57	6	2	12	5.3	30	37	30	63	4	.253	.458	3	1	OF-67
1963	149	531	134	20	1	27	5.1	71	82	70	151	7	.252	.446	5	2	OF-146
1964	152	512	127	17	4	28	5.5	73	80	79	137	4	.248	.461	6	1	OF-149
1965	143	418	90	15	1	16	3.8	52	39	57	115	1	.215	.371	8	3	OF-136
1966	138	386	90	13	1	16	4.1	52	48	57	126	2	.233	.396	13	5	OF-129
1967 PHI N	112	313	79	13	1	14	4.5	46	51	43	98	9	.252	.435	25	2	OF-97
1968	99	248	52	7	2	8	3.2	27	34	26	64	3	.210	.351	25	3	OF-78
1969 2 teams		PHI	N (4G – .000)			BOS	A (53G – .224)										
" total	57	62	13	1	0	1	1.6	8	2	11	22	0	.210	.274	22	2	OF-29, 1B-4
8 yrs.	921	2695	642	92	12	122	4.5	359	373	373	776	30	.238	.417	107	19	OF-831, 1B-4

Marshall Locke

LOCKE, MARSHALL
B. Indianapolis, Ind.   Deceased.

	G	AB	H	2B	3B	HR	HR%	R	RBI	BB	SO	SB	BA	SA	AB	H	G by POS
1884 IND AA	7	29	7	0	1	0	0.0	5		0			.241	.310	0	0	OF-7

Gene Locklear

LOCKLEAR, GENE
B. July 19, 1949, Lumberton, N. C.

BL TR 5'10" 165 lbs.

	G	AB	H	2B	3B	HR	HR%	R	RBI	BB	SO	SB	BA	SA	AB	H	G by POS
1973 2 teams		CIN	N (29G – .192)			SD	N (67G – .240)										
" total	96	180	42	6	1	3	1.7	26	25	23	27	9	.233	.328	44	9	OF-42
1974 SD N	39	74	20	3	2	1	1.4	7	3	4	12	0	.270	.405	25	7	OF-12
1975	100	237	76	11	1	5	2.1	31	27	22	26	4	.321	.439	48	14	OF-51
1976 2 teams		SD	N (43G – .224)			NY	A (13G – .219)										
" total	56	99	22	4	0	0	0.0	11	9	6	22	0	.222	.263	33	9	OF-14, DH-6
1977 NY A	1	5	3	0	0	0	0.0	1	2	0	0	0	.600	.600	0	0	OF-1
5 yrs.	292	595	163	24	4	9	1.5	76	66	55	87	13	.274	.373	150	39	OF-120, DH-6

Stu Locklin

LOCKLIN, STUART CARLTON
B. July 22, 1928, Appleton, Wis.

BL TL 6'1½" 190 lbs.

	G	AB	H	2B	3B	HR	HR%	R	RBI	BB	SO	SB	BA	SA	AB	H	G by POS
1955 CLE A	16	18	3	1	0	0	0.0	4	0	3	4	0	.167	.222	6	1	OF-7
1956	9	6	1	0	0	0	0.0	0	0	0	1	0	.167	.167	4	0	OF-1
2 yrs.	25	24	4	1	0	0	0.0	4	0	3	5	0	.167	.208	10	1	OF-8

Whitey Lockman

LOCKMAN, CARROLL WALTER
B. July 25, 1926, Lowell, N. C.
Manager 1972-74.

BL TR 6'1" 175 lbs.

	G	AB	H	2B	3B	HR	HR%	R	RBI	BB	SO	SB	BA	SA	AB	H	G by POS
1945 NY N	32	129	44	9	0	3	2.3	16	18	13	10	1	.341	.481	0	0	OF-32
1947	2	2	1	0	0	0	0.0	0	1	0	0	0	.500	.500	2	1	
1948	146	584	167	24	10	18	3.1	117	59	68	63	8	.286	.454	1	0	OF-144
1949	151	617	186	32	7	11	1.8	97	65	62	31	12	.301	.429	0	0	OF-151
1950	129	532	157	28	5	6	1.1	72	52	42	29	1	.295	.400	1	0	OF-128
1951	153	614	173	27	7	12	2.0	85	73	50	32	4	.282	.407	0	0	1B-119, OF-34
1952	154	606	176	17	4	13	2.1	99	58	67	52	2	.290	.396	0	0	1B-154
1953	150	607	179	22	4	9	1.5	85	61	52	36	3	.295	.389	3	1	1B-120, OF-30
1954	148	570	143	17	3	16	2.8	73	60	59	31	2	.251	.375	1	0	1B-145, OF-2
1955	147	576	157	19	0	15	2.6	76	49	39	34	3	.273	.384	2	0	OF-81, 1B-68
1956 2 teams		NY	N (48G – .272)			STL	N (70G – .249)										
" total	118	362	94	7	3	1	0.3	27	20	34	25	2	.260	.304	17	4	OF-96, 1B-9
1957 NY N	133	456	113	9	4	7	1.5	51	30	39	19	5	.248	.331	8	0	1B-102, OF-27
1958 SF N	92	122	29	5	0	2	1.6	15	7	13	8	0	.238	.328	45	11	OF-25, 2B-15, 1B-7
1959 2 teams		BAL	A (38G – .217)			CIN	N (52G – .262)										
" total	90	153	37	6	2	0	0.0	17	9	12	10	0	.242	.307	33	4	1B-42, 2B-11, OF-2, 3B-1
1960 CIN N	21	10	2	0	0	1	10.0	6	1	2	3	0	.200	.500	8	1	1B-5
15 yrs.	1666	5940	1658	222	49	114	1.9	836	563	552	383	43	.279	.391	121	22	1B-771, OF-752, 2B-26, 3B-1

WORLD SERIES

	G	AB	H	2B	3B	HR	HR%	R	RBI	BB	SO	SB	BA	SA	AB	H	G by POS
1951 NY N	6	25	6	2	0	1	4.0	1	4	1	2	0	.240	.440	0	0	1B-6
1954	4	18	2	0	0	0	0.0	2	0	1	2	0	.111	.111	0	0	1B-4
2 yrs.	10	43	8	2	0	1	2.3	3	4	2	4	0	.186	.302	0	0	1B-10

Skip Lockwood

LOCKWOOD, CLAUDE EDWARD
B. Aug. 17, 1946, Roslindale, Mass.

BR TR 6'1" 175 lbs.

	G	AB	H	2B	3B	HR	HR%	R	RBI	BB	SO	SB	BA	SA	AB	H	G by POS
1965 KC A	42	33	4	0	0	0	0.0	4	0	7	11	0	.121	.121	25	3	3B-7
1969 SEA A	6	7	0	0	0	0	0.0	1	0	0	2	0	.000	.000	0	0	P-6
1970 MIL A	27	53	12	1	0	1	1.9	2	2	1	11	0	.226	.302	0	0	P-27
1971	36	62	5	0	1	1	1.6	2	4	5	20	0	.081	.145	0	0	P-33
1972	31	53	7	0	0	0	0.0	3	0	3	12	0	.132	.132	0	0	P-29

	G	AB	H	2B	3B	HR	HR %	R	RBI	BB	SO	SB	BA	SA	Pinch Hit AB	H	G by POS

Skip Lockwood continued

	G	AB	H	2B	3B	HR	HR %	R	RBI	BB	SO	SB	BA	SA	PH AB	H	G by POS
1973	37	0	0	0	0	0	–	0	0	0	0	0	–	–	0	0	P-37
1974 CAL A	37	0	0	0	0	0	–	0	0	0	0	0	–	–	0	0	P-37
1975 NY N	24	6	1	0	0	0	0.0	0	1	0	0	0	.167	.167	0	0	P-24
1976	56	18	6	1	0	0	0.0	2	2	2	3	0	.333	.389	0	0	P-56
1977	63	15	3	0	0	0	0.0	1	1	0	1	0	.200	.200	0	0	P-63
1978	57	11	2	1	0	1	9.1	1	1	0	5	0	.182	.545	0	0	P-57
1979	28	2	0	0	0	0	0.0	0	0	0	1	0	.000	.000	0	0	P-27
1980 BOS A	24	0	0	0	0	0	–	0	0	0	0	0	–	–	0	0	P-24
13 yrs.	468	260	40	4	0	3	1.2	15	11	18	66	0	.154	.204	25	3	P-420, 3B-7

Dario Lodigiani

LODIGIANI, DARIO ANTHONY (Lodi)   BR TR 5'8"   150 lbs.
B. June 6, 1916, San Francisco, Calif.

	G	AB	H	2B	3B	HR	HR %	R	RBI	BB	SO	SB	BA	SA	PH AB	H	G by POS
1938 PHI A	93	325	91	15	1	6	1.8	36	44	34	25	3	.280	.388	0	0	2B-80, 3B-13
1939	121	393	102	22	4	6	1.5	46	44	42	18	2	.260	.382	4	1	3B-89, 2B-28
1940	1	1	0	0	0	0	0.0	0	0	0	0	0	.000	.000	1	0	
1941 CHI A	87	322	77	19	2	4	1.2	39	40	31	19	0	.239	.348	0	0	3B-86
1942	59	168	47	7	0	0	0.0	9	15	18	10	3	.280	.321	5	1	3B-43, 2B-7
1946	44	155	38	8	0	0	0.0	12	13	16	14	4	.245	.297	0	0	3B-44
6 yrs.	405	1364	355	71	7	16	1.2	142	156	141	86	12	.260	.358	10	2	3B-275, 2B-115

George Loepp

LOEPP, GEORGE HERBERT   BR TR 5'11"   170 lbs.
B. Sept. 11, 1901, Detroit, Mich.   D. Sept. 4, 1967, Los Angeles, Calif.

	G	AB	H	2B	3B	HR	HR %	R	RBI	BB	SO	SB	BA	SA	PH AB	H	G by POS
1928 BOS A	15	51	9	3	1	0	0.0	6	3	5	12	0	.176	.275	1	0	OF-14
1930 WAS A	50	134	37	7	1	0	0.0	23	14	20	9	0	.276	.343	1	0	OF-48
2 yrs.	65	185	46	10	2	0	0.0	29	17	25	21	0	.249	.324	2	0	OF-62

Dick Loftus

LOFTUS, RICHARD JOSEPH   BL TR 6'   155 lbs.
B. Mar. 7, 1901, Concord, Mass.   D. Jan. 21, 1972, Concord, Mass.

	G	AB	H	2B	3B	HR	HR %	R	RBI	BB	SO	SB	BA	SA	PH AB	H	G by POS
1924 BKN N	46	81	22	6	0	0	0.0	18	8	7	2	1	.272	.346	7	3	OF-29, 1B-1
1925	51	131	31	6	0	0	0.0	16	13	5	5	2	.237	.282	10	1	OF-38
2 yrs.	97	212	53	12	0	0	0.0	34	21	12	7	3	.250	.307	17	4	OF-67, 1B-1

Tom Loftus

LOFTUS, THOMAS JOSEPH   BR   168 lbs.
B. Nov. 15, 1856, Jefferson City, Mo.   D. Apr. 16, 1910, Concord, Mass.
Manager 1884, 1888-91, 1900-03.

	G	AB	H	2B	3B	HR	HR %	R	RBI	BB	SO	SB	BA	SA	PH AB	H	G by POS
1877 STL N	3	11	2	0	0	0	0.0	2	0	0	1		.182	.182	0	0	OF-3
1883 STL AA	6	22	4	0	0	0	0.0	1		0	2		.182	.182	0	0	OF-6
2 yrs.	9	33	6	0	0	0	0.0	3		2	1		.182	.182	0	0	OF-9

Johnny Logan

LOGAN, JOHN (Yatcha)   BR TR 5'11"   175 lbs.
B. Mar. 23, 1927, Endicott, N. Y.

	G	AB	H	2B	3B	HR	HR %	R	RBI	BB	SO	SB	BA	SA	PH AB	H	G by POS
1951 BOS N	62	169	37	7	1	0	0.0	14	16	18	13	0	.219	.272	3	0	SS-58
1952	117	456	129	21	3	4	0.9	56	42	31	33	1	.283	.368	0	0	SS-117
1953 MIL N	150	611	167	27	8	11	1.8	100	73	41	33	2	.273	.398	0	0	SS-150
1954	154	560	154	17	7	8	1.4	66	66	51	51	2	.275	.373	0	0	SS-154
1955	154	595	177	37	5	13	2.2	95	83	58	58	3	.297	.442	0	0	SS-154
1956	148	545	153	27	5	15	2.8	69	46	46	49	3	.281	.431	0	0	SS-148
1957	129	494	135	19	7	10	2.0	59	49	31	49	5	.273	.401	1	1	SS-129
1958	145	530	120	20	0	11	2.1	54	53	40	57	1	.226	.326	1	1	SS-144
1959	138	470	137	17	0	13	2.8	59	50	57	45	1	.291	.411	0	0	SS-138
1960	136	482	118	14	4	7	1.5	52	42	43	40	1	.245	.334	0	0	SS-136
1961 2 teams		MIL N (18G – .105)				PIT N (27G – .231)											
" total	45	71	14	5	0	0	0.0	5	6	5	11	0	.197	.268	30	8	SS-8, 3B-7
1962 PIT N	44	80	24	3	0	1	1.3	7	12	7	6	0	.300	.375	23	3	3B-19
1963	81	181	42	2	1	0	0.0	15	9	23	27	0	.232	.254	30	7	SS-44, 3B-4
13 yrs.	1503	5244	1407	216	41	93	1.8	651	547	451	472	19	.268	.378	88	20	SS-1380, 3B-30

WORLD SERIES

	G	AB	H	2B	3B	HR	HR %	R	RBI	BB	SO	SB	BA	SA	PH AB	H	G by POS
1957 MIL N	7	27	5	1	0	1	3.7	5	2	3	6	0	.185	.333	0	0	SS-7
1958	7	25	3	2	0	0	0.0	3	2	2	4	0	.120	.200	0	0	SS-7
2 yrs.	14	52	8	3	0	1	1.9	8	4	5	10	0	.154	.269	0	0	SS-14

Pete Lohman

LOHMAN, GEORGE F.
B. Oct. 21, 1864, Lake Elmo, Minn.   D. Nov. 21, 1928, Los Angeles, Calif.

	G	AB	H	2B	3B	HR	HR %	R	RBI	BB	SO	SB	BA	SA	PH AB	H	G by POS
1891 WAS AA	32	109	21	1	4	1	0.9	18	11	16	17	1	.193	.303	0	0	C-21, OF-8, 3B-4, SS-1, 2B-1

Howard Lohr

LOHR, HOWARD SYLVESTER   BR TR 6'   165 lbs.
B. June 3, 1892, Philadelphia, Pa.   D. June 9, 1977, Philadelphia, Pa.

	G	AB	H	2B	3B	HR	HR %	R	RBI	BB	SO	SB	BA	SA	PH AB	H	G by POS
1914 CIN N	18	47	10	1	1	0	0.0	6	7	0	8	2	.213	.277	1	0	OF-17
1916 CLE A	3	7	1	0	0	0	0.0	0	1	0	1	1	.143	.143	0	0	OF-3
2 yrs.	21	54	11	1	1	0	0.0	6	8	0	9	3	.204	.259	1	0	OF-20

Lucky Lohrke

LOHRKE, JACK WAYNE   BR TR 6'   180 lbs.
B. Feb. 25, 1924, Los Angeles, Calif.

	G	AB	H	2B	3B	HR	HR %	R	RBI	BB	SO	SB	BA	SA	PH AB	H	G by POS
1947 NY N	112	329	79	12	4	11	3.3	44	35	46	29	3	.240	.401	1	0	3B-111
1948	97	280	70	15	1	5	1.8	35	31	30	30	3	.250	.364	9	0	3B-50, 2B-36
1949	55	180	48	11	4	5	2.8	32	22	16	12	3	.267	.456	3	1	2B-23, 3B-19, SS-15
1950	30	43	8	0	0	0	0.0	4	4	4	8	0	.186	.186	13	2	3B-17, SS-1
1951	23	40	8	0	0	1	2.5	3	3	10	2	0	.200	.275	5	0	3B-17, SS-1
1952 PHI N	25	29	6	0	0	0	0.0	4	1	4	3	0	.207	.207	12	4	SS-5, 3B-3, 2B-1
1953	12	13	2	0	0	0	0.0	3	0	1	2	0	.154	.154	5	2	SS-2, 2B-2, 3B-1
7 yrs.	354	914	221	38	9	22	2.4	125	96	111	86	9	.242	.375	48	9	3B-217, 2B-63, SS-23

WORLD SERIES

	G	AB	H	2B	3B	HR	HR %	R	RBI	BB	SO	SB	BA	SA	PH AB	H	G by POS
1951 NY N	2	2	0	0	0	0	0.0	0	0	0	1	0	.000	.000	2	0	

	G	AB	H	2B	3B	HR	HR %	R	RBI	BB	SO	SB	BA	SA	Pinch Hit AB	Pinch Hit H	G by POS

Al Lois

LOIS, ALBERTO
B. May 6, 1956, Hato Mayor, Dominican Republic   BR TR 5'9" 175 lbs.

	G	AB	H	2B	3B	HR	HR %	R	RBI	BB	SO	SB	BA	SA	PH AB	PH H	G by POS
1978 PIT N	3	4	1	0	1	0	0.0	0	0	0	1	0	.250	.750	0	0	OF-2
1979	11	0	0	0	0	0	–	6	0	0	0	1	–	–	0	0	
2 yrs.	14	4	1	0	1	0	0.0	6	0	0	1	1	.250	.750	0	0	OF-2

Ron Lolich

LOLICH, RONALD JOHN
B. Sept. 19, 1946, Portland, Ore.   BR TR 6'1" 185 lbs.

	G	AB	H	2B	3B	HR	HR %	R	RBI	BB	SO	SB	BA	SA	PH AB	PH H	G by POS
1971 CHI A	2	8	1	1	0	0	0.0	0	0	0	2	0	.125	.250	0	0	OF-2
1972 CLE A	24	80	15	1	0	2	2.5	4	8	4	20	0	.188	.275	3	0	OF-22
1973	61	140	32	7	0	2	1.4	16	15	7	27	0	.229	.321	19	4	OF-32, DH-12
3 yrs.	87	228	48	9	0	4	1.8	20	23	11	49	0	.211	.303	22	4	OF-56, DH-12

Sherm Lollar

LOLLAR, JOHN SHERMAN
B. Aug. 23, 1924, Durham, Ark.   D. Sept. 24, 1977, Springfield, Mo.   BR TR 6' 185 lbs.

	G	AB	H	2B	3B	HR	HR %	R	RBI	BB	SO	SB	BA	SA	PH AB	PH H	G by POS
1946 CLE A	28	62	15	6	0	1	1.6	7	9	5	9	0	.242	.387	4	1	C-24
1947 NY A	11	32	7	0	1	1	3.1	4	6	1	5	0	.219	.375	2	0	C-9
1948	22	38	8	0	0	0	0.0	0	4	1	6	0	.211	.211	12	4	C-10
1949 STL A	109	284	74	9	1	8	2.8	28	49	32	22	0	.261	.384	15	2	C-93
1950	126	396	111	22	3	13	3.3	55	65	64	25	2	.280	.449	13	4	C-109
1951	98	310	78	21	0	8	2.6	44	44	43	26	1	.252	.397	10	2	C-85, 3B-1
1952 CHI A	132	375	90	15	0	13	3.5	35	50	54	34	1	.240	.384	11	2	C-120
1953	113	334	96	19	0	8	2.4	46	54	47	29	1	.287	.416	5	1	C-107, 1B-1
1954	107	316	77	13	0	7	2.2	31	34	37	28	0	.244	.351	15	3	C-93
1955	138	426	111	13	1	16	3.8	67	61	68	34	2	.261	.408	4	1	C-136
1956	136	450	132	28	2	11	2.4	55	75	53	34	2	.293	.438	5	2	C-132
1957	101	351	90	11	2	11	3.1	33	70	35	24	2	.256	.393	9	3	C-96
1958	127	421	115	16	0	20	4.8	53	84	57	37	2	.273	.454	13	5	C-116
1959	140	505	134	22	3	22	4.4	63	84	55	49	4	.265	.451	5	3	C-122, 1B-24
1960	129	421	106	23	0	7	1.7	43	46	42	39	2	.252	.356	7	2	C-123
1961	116	337	95	10	1	7	2.1	38	41	37	22	0	.282	.380	10	4	C-107
1962	84	220	59	12	0	2	0.9	17	26	32	23	1	.268	.350	19	2	C-66
1963	35	73	17	4	0	0	0.0	4	6	8	7	0	.233	.288	11	2	C-23, 1B-2
18 yrs.	1752	5351	1415	244	14	155	2.9	623	808	671	453	20	.264	.402	170	43	C-1571, 1B-27, 3B-1

WORLD SERIES

	G	AB	H	2B	3B	HR	HR %	R	RBI	BB	SO	SB	BA	SA	PH AB	PH H	G by POS
1947 NY A	2	4	3	2	0	0	0.0	3	1	0	0	0	.750	1.250	0	0	C-2
1959 CHI A	6	22	5	0	0	1	4.5	3	5	1	3	0	.227	.364	0	0	C-6
2 yrs.	8	26	8	2	0	1	3.8	6	6	1	3	0	.308	.500	0	0	C-8

Doug Loman

LOMAN, DOUGLAS EDWARD
B. May 9, 1958, Bakersfield, Calif.   BL TL 5'11½" 185 lbs.

	G	AB	H	2B	3B	HR	HR %	R	RBI	BB	SO	SB	BA	SA	PH AB	PH H	G by POS
1984 MIL A	23	76	21	4	0	2	2.6	13	12	15	7	0	.276	.408	0	0	OF-23

Ernie Lombardi

LOMBARDI, ERNEST NATALI (Schnozz, Bocci)
B. Apr. 6, 1908, Oakland, Calif.   D. Sept. 26, 1977, Santa Cruz, Calif.   BR TR 6'3" 230 lbs.

	G	AB	H	2B	3B	HR	HR %	R	RBI	BB	SO	SB	BA	SA	PH AB	PH H	G by POS
1931 BKN N	73	182	54	7	1	4	2.2	20	23	12	12	1	.297	.412	21	7	C-50
1932 CIN N	118	413	125	22	9	11	2.7	43	68	41	19	0	.303	.479	7	2	C-108
1933	107	350	99	21	1	4	1.1	30	47	16	17	2	.283	.383	10	2	C-95
1934	132	417	127	19	4	9	2.2	42	62	16	22	0	.305	.434	19	4	C-111
1935	120	332	114	23	3	12	3.6	36	64	16	6	0	.343	.539	36	8	C-82
1936	121	387	129	23	2	12	3.1	42	68	19	16	1	.333	.496	15	3	C-105
1937	120	368	123	22	1	9	2.4	41	59	14	17	1	.334	.473	28	5	C-90
1938	129	489	167	30	1	19	3.9	60	95	40	14	0	.342	.524	6	3	C-123
1939	130	450	129	26	2	20	4.4	43	85	35	19	0	.287	.487	8	1	C-120
1940	109	376	120	22	0	14	3.7	50	74	31	14	0	.319	.489	7	2	C-101
1941	117	398	105	12	1	10	2.5	33	60	36	14	1	.264	.374	1	0	C-116
1942 BOS N	105	309	102	14	0	11	3.6	32	46	37	12	1	.330	.482	16	2	C-85
1943 NY N	104	295	90	7	0	10	3.4	19	51	16	11	1	.305	.431	28	7	C-73
1944	117	373	95	13	0	10	2.7	37	58	33	25	0	.255	.370	14	3	C-100
1945	115	368	113	7	1	19	5.2	46	70	43	11	0	.307	.486	18	4	C-96
1946	88	238	69	4	1	12	5.0	19	39	18	24	0	.290	.466	24	6	C-63
1947	48	110	31	5	0	4	3.6	8	21	7	9	0	.282	.436	23	7	C-24
17 yrs.	1853	5855	1792	277	27	190	3.2	601	990	430	262	8	.306	.460	281	66	C-1542

WORLD SERIES

	G	AB	H	2B	3B	HR	HR %	R	RBI	BB	SO	SB	BA	SA	PH AB	PH H	G by POS
1939 CIN N	4	14	3	0	0	0	0.0	0	2	0	1	0	.214	.214	0	0	C-4
1940	2	3	1	1	0	0	0.0	0	0	1	0	0	.333	.667	0	0	C-1
2 yrs.	6	17	4	1	0	0	0.0	0	2	1	1	0	.235	.294	0	0	C-5

Walt Lonergan

LONERGAN, WALTER E.
B. Sept. 22, 1885, Boston, Mass.   D. Jan. 23, 1958, Lexington, Mass.   BR TR 5'7" 156 lbs.

	G	AB	H	2B	3B	HR	HR %	R	RBI	BB	SO	SB	BA	SA	PH AB	PH H	G by POS
1911 BOS A	10	26	7	0	0	0	0.0	2	1	1		1	0	.269	.269	0	0	2B-7, SS-1, 3B-1

Dale Long

LONG, RICHARD DALE
B. Feb. 6, 1926, Springfield, Mo.   BL TL 6'4" 205 lbs.

	G	AB	H	2B	3B	HR	HR %	R	RBI	BB	SO	SB	BA	SA	PH AB	PH H	G by POS
1951 2 teams	PIT N (10G – .167)							STL A (34G – .238)									
" total	44	117	27	5	1	3	2.6	12	12	10	25	0	.231	.368	13	1	1B-29, OF-1
1955 PIT N	131	419	122	19	13	16	3.8	59	79	48	72	0	.291	.513	13	4	1B-119
1956	148	517	136	20	7	27	5.2	64	91	54	85	1	.263	.485	12	2	1B-138
1957 2 teams	PIT N (7G – .182)							CHI N (123G – .305)									
" total	130	419	125	20	0	21	5.0	55	67	56	73	1	.298	.496	18	6	1B-111
1958 CHI N	142	480	130	26	4	20	4.2	68	75	66	64	2	.271	.467	5	2	1B-137, C-2
1959	110	296	70	10	3	14	4.7	34	37	31	53	0	.236	.432	27	6	1B-85
1960 2 teams	SF N (37G – .167)							NY A (26G – .366)									
" total	63	95	24	3	1	6	6.3	10	16	12	13	0	.253	.495	39	11	1B-21
1961 WAS A	123	377	94	20	4	17	4.5	52	49	39	41	0	.249	.459	24	3	1B-95

	G	AB	H	2B	3B	HR	HR %	R	RBI	BB	SO	SB	BA	SA	Pinch Hit AB	Pinch Hit H	G by POS

Dale Long continued

	G	AB	H	2B	3B	HR	HR%	R	RBI	BB	SO	SB	BA	SA	AB	H	G by POS
1962 2 teams	WAS A (67G – .241)				NY A (41G – .298)												
" total	108	285	74	12	0	8	2.8	29	41	36	31	6	.260	.386	28	3	1B-82
1963 NY A	14	15	3	0	0	0	0.0	1	0	1	3	0	.200	.200	11	2	1B-2
10 yrs.	1013	3020	805	135	33	132	4.4	384	467	353	460	10	.267	.464	190	40	1B-819, C-2, OF-1
WORLD SERIES																	
1960 NY A	3	3	1	0	0	0	0.0	0	0	0	0	0	.333	.333	3	1	
1962	2	5	1	0	0	0	0.0	0	1	0	1	0	.200	.200	0	0	1B-2
2 yrs.	5	8	2	0	0	0	0.0	0	1	0	1	0	.250	.250	3	1	1B-2

Dan Long

LONG, DANIEL W.
B. Aug. 27, 1867, Boston, Mass.   D. Apr. 30, 1929, Sausalito, Calif.

	G	AB	H	2B	3B	HR	HR%	R	RBI	BB	SO	SB	BA	SA	AB	H	G by POS
1888 LOU AA	1	2	0	0	0	0	0.0	0	0	1		0	.000	.000	0	0	OF-1
1890 B-B AA	21	77	12	0	0	0	0.0	19		14		16	.156	.156	0	0	OF-21
2 yrs.	22	79	12	0	0	0	0.0	19		15		16	.152	.152	0	0	OF-22

Herman Long

LONG, HERMAN C. (Germany)   BL TR 5'8½" 160 lbs.
B. Apr. 13, 1866, Chicago, Ill.   D. Sept. 17, 1909, Denver, Colo.

	G	AB	H	2B	3B	HR	HR%	R	RBI	BB	SO	SB	BA	SA	AB	H	G by POS
1889 KC AA	136	574	160	32	6	3	0.5	137	60	64	63	89	.279	.371	0	0	SS-128, 2B-8, OF-1
1890 BOS N	101	431	108	15	3	8	1.9	95	52	40	34	49	.251	.355	0	0	SS-101
1891	139	577	166	21	12	10	1.7	129	74	80	51	60	.288	.418	0	0	SS-139
1892	151	647	185	33	6	6	0.9	115	77	44	36	57	.286	.383	0	0	SS-141, OF-12, 3B-1
1893	128	552	159	22	6	6	1.1	149	58	73	32	38	.288	.382	0	0	SS-123, 2B-5
1894	104	475	154	28	11	12	2.5	137	79	35	17	24	.324	.505	0	0	SS-98, OF-5, 2B-3
1895	124	540	172	23	10	9	1.7	110	75	31	12	35	.319	.448	0	0	SS-122, 2B-2
1896	120	508	172	26	8	6	1.2	108	100	26	16	36	.339	.457	0	0	SS-120
1897	107	452	148	32	7	3	0.7	89	69	23		22	.327	.449	0	0	SS-107, OF-1
1898	144	589	156	21	10	6	1.0	99	99	39		20	.265	.365	0	0	SS-142, 2B-2
1899	145	578	153	30	8	6	1.0	91	100	45		20	.265	.375	0	0	SS-143, 1B-2
1900	125	486	127	19	4	12	2.5	80	66	44		26	.261	.391	0	0	SS-125
1901	138	518	118	14	6	3	0.6	55	68	25		20	.228	.295	0	0	SS-138
1902	118	429	98	11	0	2	0.5	39	44	31		24	.228	.268	0	0	SS-105, 2B-13
1903 2 teams	NY A (22G – .188)				DET A (69G – .222)												
" total	91	319	68	15	0	0	0.0	27	31	12		14	.213	.260	1	1	SS-60, 2B-31
1904 PHI N	1	4	1	0	0	0	0.0	0	0	0		0	.250	.250	0	0	2B-1
16 yrs.	1872	7679	2145	342	97	92	1.2	1460	1052	612	261	534	.279	.385	1	1	SS-1792, 2B-65, OF-19, 1B-2, 3B-1

Jeoff Long

LONG, JEOFFREY KEITH   BR TR 6'1" 200 lbs.
B. Oct. 9, 1941, Covington, Ky.

	G	AB	H	2B	3B	HR	HR%	R	RBI	BB	SO	SB	BA	SA	AB	H	G by POS
1963 STL N	5	5	1	0	0	0	0.0	0	0	0	1	0	.200	.200	5	1	
1964 2 teams	STL N (28G – .233)				CHI A (23G – .143)												
" total	51	78	15	1	0	1	1.3	5	9	10	33	0	.192	.244	28	4	OF-9, 1B-8
2 yrs.	56	83	16	1	0	1	1.2	5	9	10	34	0	.193	.241	33	5	OF-9, 1B-8

Jim Long

LONG, JAMES ALBERT   BR TR 5'11" 160 lbs.
B. June 29, 1898, Fort Dodge, Iowa   D. Sept. 14, 1970, Fort Dodge, Iowa

	G	AB	H	2B	3B	HR	HR%	R	RBI	BB	SO	SB	BA	SA	AB	H	G by POS
1922 CHI A	3	3	0	0	0	0	0.0	0	0	1	0	0	.000	.000	1	0	C-2

Jim Long

LONG, JAMES M.
B. Nov. 15, 1862, Louisville, Ky.   D. Dec. 12, 1932, Louisville, Ky.

	G	AB	H	2B	3B	HR	HR%	R	RBI	BB	SO	SB	BA	SA	AB	H	G by POS
1891 LOU AA	6	25	6	0	0	0	0.0	5	4	3	6	1	.240	.240	0	0	OF-6
1893 BAL N	55	226	48	8	1	2	0.9	31	25	16	27	23	.212	.283	0	0	OF-55
2 yrs.	61	251	54	8	1	2	0.8	36	29	19	33	24	.215	.279	0	0	OF-61

Red Long

LONG, NELSON   BR TR 6'1" 190 lbs.
B. Sept. 28, 1876, Burlington, Ont., Canada   D. Aug. 11, 1929, Hamilton, Ont., Canada

	G	AB	H	2B	3B	HR	HR%	R	RBI	BB	SO	SB	BA	SA	AB	H	G by POS
1902 BOS N	3	11	3	0	0	0	0.0	1	0	0		0	.273	.273	0	0	SS-2, P-1

Tommy Long

LONG, THOMAS AUGUSTUS   BR TR 5'10½" 165 lbs.
B. June 1, 1890, Mitchum, Ala.   D. June 15, 1972, Jackson, Ala.

	G	AB	H	2B	3B	HR	HR%	R	RBI	BB	SO	SB	BA	SA	AB	H	G by POS
1911 WAS A	14	48	11	3	0	0	0.0	1	5	1		4	.229	.292	1	0	OF-13
1912	1	1	0	0	0	0	0.0	0	0	0		0	.000	.000	1	0	
1915 STL N	140	507	149	21	25	2	0.4	61	61	31	50	19	.294	.446	4	2	OF-140
1916	119	403	118	11	10	1	0.2	37	33	10	43	21	.293	.377	12	2	OF-106
1917	144	530	123	12	14	3	0.6	49	41	37	44	21	.232	.325	7	1	OF-137
5 yrs.	418	1489	401	47	49	6	0.4	148	140	79	137	65	.269	.379	25	5	OF-396

Joe Lonnett

LONNETT, JOSEPH PAUL   BR TR 5'10" 180 lbs.
B. Feb. 7, 1927, Beaver Falls, Pa.

	G	AB	H	2B	3B	HR	HR%	R	RBI	BB	SO	SB	BA	SA	AB	H	G by POS
1956 PHI N	16	22	4	0	0	0	0.0	2	0	2	7	0	.182	.182	8	1	C-7
1957	67	160	27	5	0	5	3.1	12	15	22	39	0	.169	.294	2	0	C-65
1958	17	50	7	2	0	0	0.0	0	2	2	11	0	.140	.180	2	0	C-15
1959	43	93	16	1	0	1	1.1	8	10	14	17	0	.172	.215	0	0	C-43
4 yrs.	143	325	54	8	0	6	1.8	22	27	40	74	0	.166	.246	12	1	C-130

Bruce Look

LOOK, BRUCE MICHAEL   BL TR 5'11" 183 lbs.
Brother of Dean Look.
B. June 9, 1943, Lansing, Mich.

	G	AB	H	2B	3B	HR	HR%	R	RBI	BB	SO	SB	BA	SA	AB	H	G by POS
1968 MIN A	59	118	29	4	0	0	0.0	7	9	20	24	0	.246	.280	16	3	C-41

Dean Look

LOOK, DEAN ZACHARY   BR TR 5'11" 185 lbs.
Brother of Bruce Look.
B. July 23, 1937, Lansing, Mich.

	G	AB	H	2B	3B	HR	HR%	R	RBI	BB	SO	SB	BA	SA	AB	H	G by POS
1961 CHI A	3	6	0	0	0	0	0.0	0	0	0	1	0	.000	.000	2	0	OF-1

	G	AB	H	2B	3B	HR	HR %	R	RBI	BB	SO	SB	BA	SA	Pinch Hit AB	Pinch Hit H	G by POS

Stan Lopata

LOPATA, STANLEY EDWARD
B. Sept. 12, 1925, Delray, Mich.

BR TR 6'2" 210 lbs.

	G	AB	H	2B	3B	HR	HR %	R	RBI	BB	SO	SB	BA	SA	Pinch Hit AB	Pinch Hit H	G by POS
1948 PHI N	6	15	2	1	0	0	0.0	2	2	0	4	0	.133	.200	2	0	C-4
1949	83	240	65	9	2	8	3.3	31	27	21	44	1	.271	.425	19	4	C-58
1950	58	129	27	2	2	1	0.8	10	11	22	25	1	.209	.279	5	1	C-51
1951	3	5	0	0	0	0	0.0	0	0	0	0	0	.000	.000	2	0	C-1
1952	57	179	49	9	1	4	2.2	25	27	36	33	1	.274	.402	3	0	C-55
1953	81	234	56	12	3	8	3.4	34	31	28	39	3	.239	.419	1	0	C-80
1954	86	259	75	14	5	14	5.4	42	42	33	37	1	.290	.544	8	3	C-75, 1B-1
1955	99	303	82	9	3	22	7.3	49	58	58	62	4	.271	.538	8	2	C-66, 1B-24
1956	146	535	143	33	7	32	6.0	96	95	75	93	5	.267	.535	5	2	C-102, 1B-39
1957	116	388	92	18	2	18	4.6	50	67	56	81	2	.237	.433	7	2	C-108
1958	86	258	64	9	0	9	3.5	36	33	60	63	0	.248	.388	6	2	C-80
1959 MIL N	25	48	5	0	0	0	0.0	0	4	3	13	0	.104	.104	11	2	C-11, 1B-2
1960	7	8	1	0	0	0	0.0	0	0	1	3	0	.125	.125	3	1	C-4
13 yrs.	853	2601	661	116	25	116	4.5	375	397	393	497	18	.254	.452	80	19	C-695, 1B-66

WORLD SERIES

	G	AB	H	2B	3B	HR	HR %	R	RBI	BB	SO	SB	BA	SA	Pinch Hit AB	Pinch Hit H	G by POS
1950 PHI N	2	1	0	0	0	0	0.0	0	0	0	1	0	.000	.000	1	0	C-1

Davey Lopes

LOPES, DAVID EARL
B. May 3, 1946, Providence, R. I.

BR TR 5'9" 170 lbs.

	G	AB	H	2B	3B	HR	HR %	R	RBI	BB	SO	SB	BA	SA	Pinch Hit AB	Pinch Hit H	G by POS
1972 LA N	11	42	9	4	0	0	0.0	6	1	7	6	4	.214	.310	0	0	2B-11
1973	142	535	147	13	5	6	1.1	77	37	62	77	36	.275	.351	1	0	2B-135, OF-5, SS-2, 3B-1
1974	145	530	141	26	3	10	1.9	95	35	66	71	59	.266	.383	0	0	2B-143
1975	155	618	162	24	6	8	1.3	108	41	91	93	77	.262	.359	0	0	2B-137, OF-24, SS-14
1976	117	427	103	17	7	4	0.9	72	20	56	49	63	.241	.342	0	0	2B-100, OF-19
1977	134	502	142	19	5	11	2.2	85	53	73	69	47	.283	.406	1	1	2B-130
1978	151	587	163	25	4	17	2.9	93	58	71	70	45	.278	.421	1	1	2B-147, OF-2
1979	153	582	154	20	6	28	4.8	109	73	97	88	44	.265	.464	1	0	2B-152
1980	141	553	139	15	3	10	1.8	79	49	58	71	23	.251	.344	0	0	2B-140
1981	58	214	44	2	0	5	2.3	35	17	22	35	20	.206	.285	3	0	2B-55
1982 OAK A	128	450	109	19	3	11	2.4	58	42	40	51	28	.242	.371	0	0	2B-125, OF-6
1983	147	494	137	13	4	17	3.4	64	67	51	61	22	.277	.423	10	3	2B-123, DH-12, OF-7, 3B-5
1984 2 teams	OAK	A (72G – .257)		CHI	N	(16G – .235)											
" total	88	247	63	12	1	9	3.6	37	36	37	41	15	.255	.421	7	2	OF-51, 2B-19, DH-9, 3B-5
13 yrs.	1570	5781	1513	209	47	136	2.4	918	529	731	782	483	.262	.385	24	7	2B-1417, OF-114, DH-21, SS-16, 3B-11

DIVISIONAL PLAYOFF SERIES

	G	AB	H	2B	3B	HR	HR %	R	RBI	BB	SO	SB	BA	SA	Pinch Hit AB	Pinch Hit H	G by POS
1981 LA N	5	20	4	1	0	0	0.0	1	0	3	7	1	.200	.250	0	0	2B-5

LEAGUE CHAMPIONSHIP SERIES

	G	AB	H	2B	3B	HR	HR %	R	RBI	BB	SO	SB	BA	SA	Pinch Hit AB	Pinch Hit H	G by POS
1974 LA N	4	15	4	0	1	0	0.0	4	3	5	1	3	.267	.400	0	0	2B-4
1977	4	17	4	0	0	0	0.0	2	3	2	0	0	.235	.235	0	0	2B-4
1978	4	18	7	1	1	2	11.1	3	5	0	1	1	.389	.889	0	0	2B-4
1981	5	18	5	0	0	0	0.0	0	0	1	3	5	.278	.278	0	0	2B-5
1984 CHI N	2	1	0	0	0	0	0.0	0	0	0	0	0	.000	.000	1	0	OF-1
5 yrs.	19	69	20	1	2	2	2.9	9	11	8	5	9	.290	.449	1	0	2B-17, OF-1

WORLD SERIES

	G	AB	H	2B	3B	HR	HR %	R	RBI	BB	SO	SB	BA	SA	Pinch Hit AB	Pinch Hit H	G by POS
1974 LA N	5	18	2	0	0	0	0.0	2	0	3	4	2	.111	.111	0	0	2B-5
1977	6	24	4	0	1	1	4.2	3	2	4	3	2	.167	.375	0	0	2B-6
1978	6	26	8	0	0	3	11.5	7	7	2	1	2	.308	.654	0	0	2B-6
1981	6	22	5	1	0	0	0.0	6	2	4	3	4	.227	.273	0	0	2B-6
4 yrs.	23	90	19	1	1	4	4.4	18	11	13	11	10 (3rd)	.211	.378	0	0	2B-23

Al Lopez

LOPEZ, ALFONSO RAYMOND
B. Aug. 20, 1908, Tampa, Fla.
Manager 1951-65, 1968-69.
Hall of Fame 1977.

BR TR 5'11" 165 lbs.

	G	AB	H	2B	3B	HR	HR %	R	RBI	BB	SO	SB	BA	SA	Pinch Hit AB	Pinch Hit H	G by POS
1928 BKN N	3	12	0	0	0	0	0.0	0	0	0	0	0	.000	.000	0	0	C-3
1930	128	421	130	20	4	6	1.4	60	57	33	35	3	.309	.418	1	1	C-126
1931	111	360	97	13	4	0	0.0	38	40	28	33	1	.269	.328	5	1	C-105
1932	126	404	111	18	6	1	0.2	44	43	34	35	3	.275	.356	1	0	C-125
1933	126	372	112	11	4	3	0.8	39	41	21	39	10	.301	.376	1	1	C-124, 3B-1
1934	140	439	120	23	2	7	1.6	58	54	49	44	2	.273	.383	1	0	C-137, 3B-2, 2B-2
1935	128	379	95	12	4	3	0.8	50	39	35	36	2	.251	.327	1	0	C-126
1936 BOS N	128	426	103	12	4	8	1.9	46	50	41	41	1	.242	.345	1	0	C-127, 1B-1
1937	105	334	68	11	1	3	0.9	31	38	35	57	3	.204	.269	1	1	C-102
1938	71	236	63	6	1	1	0.4	19	14	11	24	5	.267	.314	0	0	C-71
1939	131	412	104	22	1	8	1.9	32	49	40	45	1	.252	.369	0	0	C-129
1940 2 teams	BOS	N (36G – .294)		PIT	N	(59G – .259)											
" total	95	293	80	9	3	3	1.0	35	41	19	21	6	.273	.355	0	0	C-95
1941 PIT N	114	317	84	9	1	5	1.6	33	43	31	23	0	.265	.347	0	0	C-114
1942	103	289	74	8	2	1	0.3	17	26	34	17	0	.256	.308	2	2	C-99
1943	118	372	98	9	4	1	0.3	40	39	49	25	2	.263	.317	1	0	C-116, 3B-1
1944	115	331	76	12	1	1	0.3	27	34	34	24	4	.230	.281	0	0	C-115
1945	91	243	53	8	0	0	0.0	22	18	35	12	1	.218	.251	0	0	C-91
1946	56	150	46	2	0	0	0.0	13	12	23	14	1	.307	.340	0	0	C-56
1947 CLE A	61	126	33	1	0	0	0.0	9	14	9	13	1	.262	.270	4	0	C-57
19 yrs.	1950	5916	1547	206	42	52	0.9	613	652	561	538	46	.261	.337	19	6	C-1918, 3B-3, 2B-3, 1B-1

Art Lopez

LOPEZ, ARTURO
B. May 8, 1937, Mayaguez, Puerto Rico

BL TL 5'9" 170 lbs.

	G	AB	H	2B	3B	HR	HR %	R	RBI	BB	SO	SB	BA	SA	Pinch Hit AB	Pinch Hit H	G by POS
1965 NY A	38	49	7	0	0	0	0.0	5	0	1	6	0	.143	.143	13	1	OF-16

Carlos Lopez

LOPEZ, CARLOS ANTONIO
Also known as Carlos Antonio Morales.
B. Sept. 27, 1950, Mazatlan, Mexico.
BR TR 6' 190 lbs.

	G	AB	H	2B	3B	HR	HR %	R	RBI	BB	SO	SB	BA	SA	Pinch Hit AB	Pinch Hit H	G by POS
1976 CAL A	9	10	0	0	0	0	0.0	1	0	2	3	2	.000	.000	0	0	OF-4, DH-1
1977 SEA A	99	297	84	18	1	8	2.7	39	34	14	61	16	.283	.431	5	1	OF-90, DH-2
1978 BAL A	129	193	46	6	0	4	2.1	21	20	9	34	5	.238	.332	14	1	OF-114
3 yrs.	237	500	130	24	1	12	2.4	61	54	25	98	23	.260	.384	19	2	OF-208, DH-3

Hector Lopez

LOPEZ, HECTOR HEADLEY
B. July 8, 1932, Colon, Panama.
BR TR 5'11½" 174 lbs.

	G	AB	H	2B	3B	HR	HR %	R	RBI	BB	SO	SB	BA	SA	Pinch Hit AB	Pinch Hit H	G by POS
1955 KC A	128	483	140	15	2	15	3.1	50	68	33	58	1	.290	.422	1	0	3B-93, 2B-36
1956	151	561	153	27	3	18	3.2	91	69	63	73	4	.273	.428	5	2	3B-121, OF-20, 2B-8, SS-4
1957	121	391	115	19	4	11	2.8	51	35	41	66	1	.294	.448	8	3	3B-111, 2B-4, OF-3
1958	151	564	147	28	4	17	3.0	84	73	49	61	2	.261	.415	4	1	2B-96, 3B-55, OF-1, SS-1
1959 2 teams	KC A (36G – .281)			NY A (112G – .283)													
" total	148	541	153	26	5	22	4.1	82	93	36	77	4	.283	.471	5	0	3B-76, OF-35, 2B-33
1960 NY A	131	408	116	14	6	9	2.2	66	42	46	64	1	.284	.414	26	2	OF-106, 2B-5, 3B-1
1961	93	243	54	7	2	3	1.2	27	22	24	38	1	.222	.305	16	4	OF-72
1962	106	335	92	19	1	6	1.8	45	48	33	53	0	.275	.391	24	5	OF-84, 3B-1, 2B-1
1963	130	433	108	13	4	14	3.2	54	52	35	71	1	.249	.395	9	2	OF-124, 2B-1
1964	127	285	74	9	3	10	3.5	34	34	24	54	1	.260	.418	22	7	OF-103, 3B-1
1965	111	283	74	12	2	7	2.5	25	39	26	61	0	.261	.392	28	5	OF-75, 1B-2
1966	54	117	25	4	1	4	3.4	14	16	8	20	0	.214	.368	20	7	OF-29
12 yrs.	1451	4644	1251	193	37	136	2.9	623	591	418	696	16	.269	.415	168	38	OF-652, 3B-459, 2B-184, SS-5, 1B-2

WORLD SERIES

	G	AB	H	2B	3B	HR	HR %	R	RBI	BB	SO	SB	BA	SA	Pinch Hit AB	Pinch Hit H	G by POS
1960 NY A	3	7	3	0	0	0	0.0	0	0	0	0	0	.429	.429	2	2	OF-1
1961	4	9	3	0	1	1	11.1	3	7	2	3	0	.333	.889	0	0	OF-3
1962	2	2	0	0	0	0	0.0	0	0	0	0	0	.000	.000	2	0	
1963	3	8	2	2	0	0	0.0	1	0	0	1	0	.250	.500	1	0	OF-2
1964	3	2	0	0	0	0	0.0	0	0	0	2	0	.000	.000	2	0	OF-1
5 yrs.	15	28	8	2	1	1	3.6	4	7	2	6	0	.286	.536 (6th)	7	2	OF-7

Bris Lord

LORD, BRISTOL ROBOTHAM (The Human Eyeball)
B. Sept. 21, 1883, Upland, Pa.   D. Nov. 13, 1964, Annapolis, Md.
BR TR 5'9" 185 lbs.

	G	AB	H	2B	3B	HR	HR %	R	RBI	BB	SO	SB	BA	SA	Pinch Hit AB	Pinch Hit H	G by POS
1905 PHI A	66	238	57	14	0	0	0.0	38	13	14		3	.239	.298	5	1	OF-60, 3B-1
1906	118	434	101	13	7	1	0.2	50	44	27		12	.233	.302	2	1	OF-115
1907	57	170	31	3	0	1	0.6	12	11	14		2	.182	.218	4	1	OF-53, P-1
1909 CLE A	69	249	67	7	3	1	0.4	26	25	8		10	.269	.333	2	0	OF-69
1910 2 teams	CLE A (56G – .219)			PHI A (72G – .278)													
" total	128	489	124	21	18	1	0.2	76	37	35		10	.254	.376	2	1	OF-126
1911 PHI A	134	574	178	37	11	3	0.5	92	55	35		15	.310	.429	2	1	OF-132
1912	96	378	90	12	9	0	0.0	63	25	34		15	.238	.317	0	0	OF-96
1913 BOS N	73	235	59	12	1	6	2.6	22	26	8	22	7	.251	.387	11	1	OF-62
8 yrs.	741	2767	707	119	49	13	0.5	379	236	175	22	74	.256	.348	28	6	OF-713, 3B-1, P-1

WORLD SERIES

	G	AB	H	2B	3B	HR	HR %	R	RBI	BB	SO	SB	BA	SA	Pinch Hit AB	Pinch Hit H	G by POS
1905 PHI A	5	20	2	0	0	0	0.0	0	2	0	5	0	.100	.100	0	0	OF-5
1910	5	22	4	2	0	0	0.0	3	1	1	3	0	.182	.273	0	0	OF-5
1911	6	27	5	2	0	0	0.0	2	1	0	5	0	.185	.259	0	0	OF-6
3 yrs.	16	69	11	4	0	0	0.0	5	4	1	13	0	.159	.217	0	0	OF-16

Carlton Lord

LORD, WILLIAM CARLTON
B. Jan. 7, 1900, Philadelphia, Pa.   D. Aug. 15, 1947, Chester, Pa.
BR TR 5'11" 170 lbs.

	G	AB	H	2B	3B	HR	HR %	R	RBI	BB	SO	SB	BA	SA	Pinch Hit AB	Pinch Hit H	G by POS
1923 PHI N	17	47	11	2	0	0	0.0	2	2	2	3	0	.234	.277	3	1	3B-14

Harry Lord

LORD, HARRY DONALD
B. Mar. 8, 1882, Porter, Me.   D. Aug. 9, 1948, Westbrook, Me.
Manager 1915.
BL TR 5'10½" 165 lbs.

	G	AB	H	2B	3B	HR	HR %	R	RBI	BB	SO	SB	BA	SA	Pinch Hit AB	Pinch Hit H	G by POS
1907 BOS A	10	38	6	1	0	0	0.0	4	3	1		1	.158	.184	0	0	3B-10
1908	145	558	145	15	6	2	0.4	61	37	22		23	.260	.319	1	0	3B-143
1909	136	534	166	12	7	0	0.0	85	31	20		36	.311	.360	1	0	3B-134
1910 2 teams	BOS A (77G – .250)			CHI A (44G – .297)													
" total	121	453	121	11	8	1	0.2	51	42	28		34	.267	.333	3	1	3B-114, SS-1
1911 CHI A	141	561	180	18	18	1	0.2	103	61	32		43	.321	.433	2	0	3B-138
1912	151	570	152	19	12	5	0.9	81	54	52		28	.267	.368	0	0	3B-106, OF-45
1913	150	547	144	18	12	1	0.2	62	42	45	39	24	.263	.346	0	0	3B-150
1914	21	69	13	1	1	1	1.4	8	3	5	3	2	.188	.275	0	0	3B-19, OF-1
1915 BUF F	97	359	97	12	6	1	0.3	50	21	21		15	.270	.345	3	1	3B-92, OF-1
9 yrs.	972	3689	1024	107	70	14	0.4	505	294	226	42	206	.278	.356	10	2	3B-906, OF-47, SS-1

Scott Loucks

LOUCKS, SCOTT GREGORY
B. Nov. 11, 1956, Anchorage, Alaska.
BR TR 6' 178 lbs.

	G	AB	H	2B	3B	HR	HR %	R	RBI	BB	SO	SB	BA	SA	Pinch Hit AB	Pinch Hit H	G by POS
1980 HOU N	8	3	1	0	0	0	0.0	4	0	0	2	0	.333	.333	2	1	OF-4
1981	10	7	4	0	0	0	0.0	2	0	1	3	1	.571	.571	0	0	OF-5
1982	44	49	11	2	0	0	0.0	6	3	3	17	4	.224	.265	5	0	OF-37
1983	7	14	3	0	0	0	0.0	2	0	1	4	2	.214	.214	1	0	OF-6
4 yrs.	69	73	19	2	0	0	0.0	14	3	5	26	7	.260	.288	8	1	OF-52

Baldy Louden

LOUDEN, WILLIAM
B. Aug. 27, 1885, Piedmont, W. Va.   D. Dec. 8, 1935, Piedmont, W. Va.
BR TR 5'11" 175 lbs.

	G	AB	H	2B	3B	HR	HR %	R	RBI	BB	SO	SB	BA	SA	Pinch Hit AB	Pinch Hit H	G by POS
1907 NY A	5	9	1	0	0	0	0.0	4	0	2		1	.111	.111	0	0	3B-3
1912 DET A	121	403	97	12	4	1	0.2	57	36	58		28	.241	.298	2	1	2B-86, 3B-26, SS-5
1913	72	191	46	4	5	0	0.0	28	23	24	22	6	.241	.314	2	0	2B-32, 3B-26, SS-6, OF-5
1914 BUF F	126	431	135	11	4	6	1.4	73	63	52	35	4	.313	.399	10	4	SS-115
1915	141	469	132	18	5	4	0.9	67	48	64		30	.281	.367	2	0	2B-88, SS-27, 3B-19

	G	AB	H	2B	3B	HR	HR %	R	RBI	BB	SO	SB	BA	SA	Pinch Hit AB	Pinch Hit H	G by POS

Baldy Louden continued

	G	AB	H	2B	3B	HR	HR %	R	RBI	BB	SO	SB	BA	SA	PH AB	PH H	G by POS
1916 CIN N	134	439	96	16	4	1	0.2	38	32	54	54	12	.219	.280	5	0	2B-108, SS-23
6 yrs.	599	1942	507	61	22	12	0.6	267	202	254	76	112	.261	.334	21	5	2B-314, SS-176, 3B-74, OF-5

Charlie Loudenslager

LOUDENSLAGER, CHARLES EDWARD   TR 5'9" 186 lbs.
B. May 21, 1881, Baltimore, Md.   D. Oct. 31, 1933, Baltimore, Md.

	G	AB	H	2B	3B	HR	HR %	R	RBI	BB	SO	SB	BA	SA	PH AB	PH H	G by POS
1904 BKN N	1	2	0	0	0	0	0.0	0	0	0		0	.000	.000	0	0	2B-1

Bill Loughlin

LOUGHLIN, WILLIAM H.
B. Baltimore, Md.   Deceased.

	G	AB	H	2B	3B	HR	HR %	R	RBI	BB	SO	SB	BA	SA	PH AB	PH H	G by POS
1883 BAL AA	1	5	2	0	0	0	0.0	0		0			.400	.400	0	0	OF-1

Loughran

LOUGHRAN,
B. New York, N. Y.   Deceased.

	G	AB	H	2B	3B	HR	HR %	R	RBI	BB	SO	SB	BA	SA	PH AB	PH H	G by POS
1884 NY N	9	29	3	1	1	0	0.0	4		7	11		.103	.207	0	0	C-9, OF-1

Tom Lovelace

LOVELACE, THOMAS RIVERS   BR TR 5'11" 170 lbs.
B. Oct. 19, 1897, Wolfe City, Tex.   D. July 12, 1979, Dallas, Tex.

	G	AB	H	2B	3B	HR	HR %	R	RBI	BB	SO	SB	BA	SA	PH AB	PH H	G by POS
1922 PIT N	1	1	0	0	0	0	0.0	0	0	0	0	0	.000	.000	1	0	

Mem Lovett

LOVETT, MERRITT MARWOOD   BR TR 5'9½" 165 lbs.
B. June 15, 1912, Chicago, Ill.

	G	AB	H	2B	3B	HR	HR %	R	RBI	BB	SO	SB	BA	SA	PH AB	PH H	G by POS
1933 CHI A	1	1	0	0	0	0	0.0	0	0	0	0	0	.000	.000	1	0	

Jay Loviglio

LOVIGLIO, JOHN PAUL   BR TR 5'9" 160 lbs.
B. May 30, 1956, Freeport, N. Y.

	G	AB	H	2B	3B	HR	HR %	R	RBI	BB	SO	SB	BA	SA	PH AB	PH H	G by POS
1980 PHI N	16	5	0	0	0	0	0.0	7	0	1	0	1	.000	.000	0	0	2B-1
1981 CHI A	14	15	4	0	0	0	0.0	5	2	1	1	2	.267	.267	0	0	3B-4, 2B-3, DH-2
1982	15	31	6	0	0	0	0.0	5	2	1	4	2	.194	.194	0	0	2B-13, DH-2
1983 CHI N	1	1	0	0	0	0	0.0	0	0	0	1	0	.000	.000	1	0	
4 yrs.	46	52	10	0	0	0	0.0	17	4	3	6	5	.192	.192	1	0	2B-17, DH-4, 3B-4

Joe Lovitto

LOVITTO, JOSEPH JR.   BB TR 6' 185 lbs.
B. Jan. 6, 1951, San Pedro, Calif.

	G	AB	H	2B	3B	HR	HR %	R	RBI	BB	SO	SB	BA	SA	PH AB	PH H	G by POS
1972 TEX A	117	330	74	9	1	1	0.3	23	19	37	54	13	.224	.267	7	1	OF-103
1973	26	44	6	1	0	0	0.0	3	0	5	7	1	.136	.159	0	0	3B-20, OF-3
1974	113	283	63	9	3	2	0.7	27	26	25	36	6	.223	.297	1	0	OF-107, 1B-5
1975	50	106	22	3	0	1	0.9	17	8	13	16	2	.208	.264	7	1	OF-38, DH-2, 1B-1, C-1
4 yrs.	306	763	165	22	4	4	0.5	70	53	80	113	22	.216	.271	15	2	OF-251, 3B-20, 1B-6, DH-2, C-1

Fletcher Low

LOW, FLETCHER   BR TR 5'10½" 175 lbs.
B. Apr. 7, 1893, Essex, Mass.   D. June 6, 1973, Hanover, N. H.

	G	AB	H	2B	3B	HR	HR %	R	RBI	BB	SO	SB	BA	SA	PH AB	PH H	G by POS
1915 BOS N	1	4	1	0	1	0	0.0	1	1	0	0	0	.250	.750	0	0	3B-1

Lowe

LOWE,
Deceased.

	G	AB	H	2B	3B	HR	HR %	R	RBI	BB	SO	SB	BA	SA	PH AB	PH H	G by POS
1884 DET N	1	3	1	0	0	0	0.0	0		0		1		.333	.333	0	0	C-1

Bobby Lowe

LOWE, ROBERT LINCOLN (Link)   BR TR 5'10" 150 lbs.
B. July 10, 1868, Pittsburgh, Pa.   D. Dec. 8, 1951, Detroit, Mich.
Manager 1904.

	G	AB	H	2B	3B	HR	HR %	R	RBI	BB	SO	SB	BA	SA	PH AB	PH H	G by POS
1890 BOS N	52	207	58	13	2	2	1.0	35	21	26	32	15	.280	.391	0	0	SS-24, OF-15, 3B-12
1891	125	497	129	19	5	6	1.2	92	74	53	54	43	.260	.354	1	0	OF-107, 2B-17, SS-2, 3B-1, P-1
1892	124	475	115	16	7	3	0.6	79	57	37	46	36	.242	.324	0	0	OF-90, 3B-14, SS-13, 2B-10
1893	126	526	157	19	5	13	2.5	130	89	55	29	22	.298	.428	0	0	2B-121, SS-5
1894	133	613	212	34	11	17	2.8	158	115	50	25	23	.346	.520	0	0	2B-130, SS-2, 3B-1
1895	99	412	122	12	7	7	1.7	101	62	40	16	24	.296	.410	0	0	2B-99
1896	73	305	98	11	4	2	0.7	59	48	20	11	15	.321	.403	0	0	2B-73
1897	123	499	154	24	8	5	1.0	87	106	32		16	.309	.419	0	0	2B-123
1898	149	566	154	18	7	4	0.7	69	94	29		12	.272	.341	0	0	2B-145, SS-5
1899	152	559	152	5	9	4	0.7	81	88	35		17	.272	.335	0	0	2B-148, SS-4
1900	127	474	132	11	5	3	0.6	65	71	26		15	.278	.342	0	0	2B-127
1901	129	491	125	11	1	3	0.6	47	47	17		22	.255	.299	0	0	3B-111, 2B-18
1902 CHI N	121	472	116	13	3	0	0.0	41	31	11		16	.246	.286	0	0	2B-117, 3B-2
1903	32	105	28	5	3	0	0.0	14	15	4		5	.267	.371	1	1	2B-22, 1B-6, 3B-1
1904 2 teams		PIT	N (1G – .000)			DET	A	(140G – .208)									
" total	141	507	105	14	6	0	0.0	47	40	17		15	.207	.258	1	0	2B-140
1905 DET A	60	181	35	7	2	0	0.0	17	9	13		3	.193	.254	2	0	OF-25, 3B-22, 2B-6, SS-4, 1B-1
1906	41	145	30	3	0	1	0.7	11	12	4		3	.207	.248	2	0	SS-19, 2B-17, 3B-5
1907	17	37	9	2	0	0	0.0	2	5	4		0	.243	.297	2	0	3B-10, OF-4, SS-2
18 yrs.	1824	7071	1931	232	85	70	1.0	1135	984	473	213	302	.273	.360	9	1	2B-1313, OF-241, 3B-179, SS-77, 1B-7, P-1

John Lowenstein

LOWENSTEIN, JOHN LEE   BL TR 6' 175 lbs.
B. Jan. 27, 1947, Wolf Point, Mont.

	G	AB	H	2B	3B	HR	HR %	R	RBI	BB	SO	SB	BA	SA	PH AB	PH H	G by POS
1970 CLE A	17	43	11	3	1	1	2.3	5	6	1	9	1	.256	.442	3	0	2B-10, OF-2, 3B-2, SS-1
1971	58	140	26	5	0	4	2.9	15	9	16	28	1	.186	.307	9	2	2B-29, OF-18, SS-3
1972	68	151	32	8	1	6	4.0	16	21	20	43	2	.212	.397	11	3	OF-58, 1B-2
1973	98	305	89	16	1	6	2.0	42	40	23	41	5	.292	.410	20	7	OF-51, DH-25, 2B-25, 3B-8, 1B-1

	G	AB	H	2B	3B	HR	HR %	R	RBI	BB	SO	SB	BA	SA	Pinch Hit AB	Pinch Hit H	G by POS

John Lowenstein continued

	G	AB	H	2B	3B	HR	HR %	R	RBI	BB	SO	SB	BA	SA	PH AB	PH H	G by POS
1974	140	508	123	14	2	8	1.6	65	48	53	85	36	.242	.325	2	1	OF-100, 3B-28, 1B-12, 2B-4
1975	91	265	64	5	1	12	4.5	37	33	28	28	15	.242	.404	14	4	OF-36, DH-31, 3B-8, 2B-2
1976	93	229	47	8	2	2	0.9	33	14	25	35	11	.205	.284	16	2	OF-61, DH-11, 1B-9
1977	81	149	36	6	1	4	2.7	24	12	21	29	1	.242	.376	25	4	OF-39, DH-19, 1B-1
1978 TEX A	77	176	39	8	3	5	2.8	28	21	37	29	16	.222	.386	22	4	3B-25, DH-21, OF-16
1979 BAL A	97	197	50	8	2	11	5.6	33	34	30	37	16	.254	.482	23	5	OF-72, DH-3, 3B-1, 1B-1
1980	104	196	61	8	0	4	2.0	38	27	32	29	7	.311	.413	12	5	OF-91, DH-3
1981	83	189	47	7	0	6	3.2	19	20	22	32	7	.249	.381	10	3	OF-73, DH-4
1982	122	322	103	15	2	24	7.5	69	66	54	59	7	.320	.602	17	5	OF-111
1983	122	310	87	13	2	15	4.8	52	60	49	55	2	.281	.481	16	4	OF-107, DH-1, 2B-1
1984	105	270	64	13	0	8	3.0	34	28	33	54	1	.237	.374	26	6	OF-67, DH-22, 1B-2
15 yrs.	1356	3450	879	137	18	116	3.4	510	439	444	593	128	.255	.406	226	55	OF-902, DH-140, 3B-72, 2B-71, 1B-28, SS-4

LEAGUE CHAMPIONSHIP SERIES

	G	AB	H	2B	3B	HR	HR %	R	RBI	BB	SO	SB	BA	SA	PH AB	PH H	G by POS
1979 BAL A	4	6	1	0	0	1	16.7	2	3	2	2	0	.167	.667	2	1	OF-3
1983	2	6	1	1	0	0	0.0	0	2	1	2	0	.167	.333	0	0	OF-2
2 yrs.	6	12	2	1	0	1	8.3	2	5	3	4	0	.167	.500	2	1	OF-5

WORLD SERIES

	G	AB	H	2B	3B	HR	HR %	R	RBI	BB	SO	SB	BA	SA	PH AB	PH H	G by POS
1979 BAL A	6	13	3	0	0	0	0.0	2	3	1	3	0	.231	.308	3	2	OF-3
1983	4	13	5	1	0	1	7.7	2	1	0	3	0	.385	.692	0	0	OF-4
2 yrs.	10	26	8	2	0	1	3.8	4	4	1	6	0	.308	.500	3	2	OF-7

Peanuts Lowrey

LOWREY, HARRY LEE
B. Aug. 27, 1918, Culver City, Calif.   BR TR 5'8½" 170 lbs.

	G	AB	H	2B	3B	HR	HR %	R	RBI	BB	SO	SB	BA	SA	PH AB	PH H	G by POS
1942 CHI N	27	58	11	0	0	1	1.7	4	4	4	4	0	.190	.241	3	0	OF-19
1943	130	480	140	25	12	1	0.2	59	63	35	24	13	.292	.400	4	1	OF-113, SS-16, 2B-3
1945	143	523	148	22	7	7	1.3	72	89	48	27	11	.283	.392	5	1	OF-138, SS-2
1946	144	540	139	24	5	4	0.7	75	54	56	22	10	.257	.343	0	0	OF-126, 3B-20
1947	115	448	126	17	5	5	1.1	56	37	38	26	2	.281	.375	1	0	3B-91, OF-25, 2B-6
1948	129	435	128	12	3	2	0.5	47	54	34	31	2	.294	.349	13	3	OF-103, 3B-9, 2B-2, SS-1
1949 2 teams		CHI	N	(38G –	.270)			CIN	N	(89G –	.275)						
" total	127	420	115	21	2	4	1.0	66	35	46	19	4	.274	.362	16	6	OF-109, 3B-1
1950 2 teams		CIN	N	(91G –	.227)			STL	N	(17G –	.268)						
" total	108	320	75	14	0	2	0.6	44	15	42	8	0	.234	.297	14	2	OF-76, 2B-7, 3B-5
1951 STL N	114	370	112	19	5	5	1.4	52	40	35	12	0	.303	.422	19	5	OF-85, 3B-11, 2B-3
1952	132	374	107	18	2	1	0.3	48	48	34	13	3	.286	.353	27	13	OF-106, 3B-6
1953	104	182	49	9	2	5	2.7	26	27	15	21	1	.269	.423	59	22	OF-38, 2B-10, 3B-1
1954	74	61	7	1	2	0	0.0	6	5	9	9	0	.115	.197	53	7	OF-12
1955 PHI N	54	106	20	4	0	0	0.0	9	8	7	10	2	.189	.226	16	2	OF-28, 2B-2, 1B-1
13 yrs.	1401	4317	1177	186	45	37	0.9	564	479	403	226	48	.273	.362	230	62	OF-978, 3B-144, 2B-33, SS-19, 1B-1

WORLD SERIES

	G	AB	H	2B	3B	HR	HR %	R	RBI	BB	SO	SB	BA	SA	PH AB	PH H	G by POS
1945 CHI N	7	29	9	1	0	0	0.0	4	0	1	2	1	.310	.345	0	0	OF-7

Dwight Lowry

LOWRY, DWIGHT
B. Oct. 23, 1957, Robeson County, N. C.   BL TR 6'3" 210 lbs.

	G	AB	H	2B	3B	HR	HR %	R	RBI	BB	SO	SB	BA	SA	PH AB	PH H	G by POS
1984 DET A	32	45	11	2	0	2	4.4	8	7	3	11	0	.244	.422	4	1	C-31

Willie Lozado

LOZADO, WILLIAM
B. May 12, 1959, Brooklyn, N. Y.   BR TR 6'1" 170 lbs.

	G	AB	H	2B	3B	HR	HR %	R	RBI	BB	SO	SB	BA	SA	PH AB	PH H	G by POS
1984 MIL A	43	107	29	8	2	1	0.9	15	20	12	23	0	.271	.411	2	0	3B-36, SS-6, DH-1, 2B-1

Steve Lubratich

LUBRATICH, STEVEN GEORGE
B. May 1, 1955, Oakland, Calif.   BR TR 6' 170 lbs.

	G	AB	H	2B	3B	HR	HR %	R	RBI	BB	SO	SB	BA	SA	PH AB	PH H	G by POS
1981 CAL A	7	21	3	1	0	0	0.0	2	1	0	2	1	.143	.190	0	0	3B-6
1983	57	156	34	9	0	0	0.0	12	7	4	17	0	.218	.276	0	0	SS-23, 3B-22, 2B-14
2 yrs.	64	177	37	10	0	0	0.0	14	8	4	19	1	.209	.266	0	0	3B-28, SS-23, 2B-14

Hugh Luby

LUBY, HUGH MAX (Hal)
B. June 13, 1913, Blackfoot, Ida.   BR TR 5'10" 185 lbs.

	G	AB	H	2B	3B	HR	HR %	R	RBI	BB	SO	SB	BA	SA	PH AB	PH H	G by POS
1936 PHI A	9	38	7	1	0	0	0.0	3	3	0	7	2	.184	.211	0	0	2B-9
1944 NY N	111	323	82	10	2	2	0.6	30	35	52	15	2	.254	.316	2	0	3B-65, 2B-45, 1B-1
2 yrs.	120	361	89	11	2	2	0.6	33	38	52	22	4	.247	.305	2	0	3B-65, 2B-54, 1B-1

Pat Luby

LUBY, JOHN PERKINS
B. 1868, Charleston, S. C.   D. Apr. 24, 1899, Charleston, S. C.   TR 6' 185 lbs.

	G	AB	H	2B	3B	HR	HR %	R	RBI	BB	SO	SB	BA	SA	PH AB	PH H	G by POS
1890 CHI N	36	116	31	5	3	3	2.6	27	17	9	6	3	.267	.440	0	0	P-34, 1B-2
1891	32	98	24	2	4	2	2.0	19	24	8	16	3	.245	.408	0	0	P-30, OF-2, 1B-1
1892	45	163	31	3	2	2	1.2	14	20	12	27	3	.190	.270	0	0	P-31, OF-16
1895 LOU N	19	53	15	2	2	0	0.0	6	9	8	3	2	.283	.396	0	0	P-11, 1B-5, OF-2
4 yrs.	132	430	101	12	11	7	1.6	66	70	37	52	11	.235	.363	0	0	P-106, OF-20, 1B-8

Johnny Lucadello

LUCADELLO, JOHN
B. Feb. 22, 1919, Thurber, Tex.   BB TR 5'11" 160 lbs.

	G	AB	H	2B	3B	HR	HR %	R	RBI	BB	SO	SB	BA	SA	PH AB	PH H	G by POS
1938 STL A	7	20	3	1	0	0	0.0	1	0	0	0	0	.150	.200	1	0	3B-6
1939	9	30	7	2	0	0	0.0	0	4	2	4	0	.233	.300	2	1	2B-7
1940	17	63	20	4	2	2	3.2	15	10	6	4	1	.317	.540	1	0	2B-16
1941	107	351	98	22	4	2	0.6	58	31	48	23	5	.279	.382	22	2	2B-70, SS-12, 3B-6, OF-1
1946	87	210	52	7	1	1	0.5	21	15	36	20	0	.248	.305	25	7	3B-37, 2B-19
1947 NY A	12	12	1	0	0	0	0.0	0	0	1	5	0	.083	.083	7	1	2B-5
6 yrs.	239	686	181	36	7	5	0.7	95	60	93	56	6	.264	.359	58	11	2B-117, 3B-49, SS-12, OF-1

	G	AB	H	2B	3B	HR	HR %	R	RBI	BB	SO	SB	BA	SA	Pinch Hit AB	Pinch Hit H	G by POS

Fred Lucas

LUCAS, FREDERICK WARRINGTON   BR TR 5'10" 165 lbs.
B. Jan. 19, 1903, Vineland, N. J.

	G	AB	H	2B	3B	HR	HR %	R	RBI	BB	SO	SB	BA	SA	PH AB	PH H	G by POS
1935 PHI N	20	34	9	0	0	0	0.0	1	2	3	6	0	.265	.265	8	1	OF-10

Johnny Lucas

LUCAS, JOHN CHARLES (Buster)   BR TL 5'10" 186 lbs.
B. Feb. 10, 1903, Glen Carbon, Ill.   D. Oct. 31, 1970, Maryville, Ill.

	G	AB	H	2B	3B	HR	HR %	R	RBI	BB	SO	SB	BA	SA	PH AB	PH H	G by POS
1931 BOS A	3	2	0	0	0	0	0.0	0	0	0	1	0	.000	.000	0	0	OF-2
1932	1	1	0	0	0	0	0.0	0	0	0	0	0	.000	.000	1	0	
2 yrs.	4	3	0	0	0	0	0.0	0	0	0	1	0	.000	.000	1	0	OF-2

Red Lucas

LUCAS, CHARLES FRED (The Nashville Narcissus)   BL TR 5'9½" 170 lbs.
B. Apr. 28, 1902, Columbia, Tenn.

	G	AB	H	2B	3B	HR	HR %	R	RBI	BB	SO	SB	BA	SA	PH AB	PH H	G by POS
1923 NY N	3	2	0	0	0	0	0.0	0	0	0	1	0	.000	.000	0	0	P-3
1924 BOS N	33	33	11	1	0	0	0.0	5	5	1	4	0	.333	.364	3	0	P-27, 3B-2
1925	6	20	3	0	0	0	0.0	1	2	2	4	0	.150	.150	0	0	2B-6
1926 CIN N	66	76	23	4	4	0	0.0	15	14	10	13	0	.303	.461	21	5	P-39, 2B-1
1927	80	150	47	5	2	0	0.0	14	28	12	10	0	.313	.373	27	6	P-37, 2B-5, SS-3, OF-1
1928	39	73	23	2	1	0	0.0	8	7	4	6	0	.315	.370	12	4	P-27
1929	76	140	41	6	0	0	0.0	15	13	13	15	1	.293	.336	42	13	P-32
1930	80	113	38	4	1	2	1.8	18	19	17	4	0	.336	.442	39	14	P-33
1931	97	153	43	4	0	0	0.0	15	17	12	9	0	.281	.307	60	15	P-29
1932	76	150	43	11	2	0	0.0	13	19	10	9	0	.287	.387	42	10	P-31
1933	75	122	35	6	1	1	0.8	14	15	12	6	0	.287	.377	41	13	P-29
1934 PIT N	68	105	23	5	1	0	0.0	11	8	6	16	1	.219	.286	34	8	P-29
1935	47	66	21	6	0	0	0.0	6	10	7	11	0	.318	.409	22	8	P-20
1936	69	108	26	4	1	0	0.0	11	14	8	17	0	.241	.296	40	9	P-27
1937	59	82	22	3	0	0	0.0	8	17	7	6	0	.268	.305	37	9	P-20
1938	33	46	5	0	0	0	0.0	1	2	3	2	0	.109	.109	17	0	P-13
16 yrs.	907	1439	404	61	13	3	0.2	155	190	124	133	2	.281	.347	437	114	P-396, 2B-12, SS-3, 3B-2,
													5th	**5th**			OF-1

Frank Luce

LUCE, FRANK EDWARD   BL TR 5'11" 180 lbs.
B. Dec. 6, 1896, Spencer, Ohio   D. Feb. 3, 1942, Milwaukee, Wis.

	G	AB	H	2B	3B	HR	HR %	R	RBI	BB	SO	SB	BA	SA	PH AB	PH H	G by POS
1923 PIT N	9	12	6	0	0	0	0.0	2	3	2	2	2	.500	.500	3	0	OF-5

Fred Luderus

LUDERUS, FREDERICK WILLIAM   BL TR 5'11½" 185 lbs.
B. Sept. 12, 1885, Milwaukee, Wis.   D. Jan. 4, 1961, Milwaukee, Wis.

	G	AB	H	2B	3B	HR	HR %	R	RBI	BB	SO	SB	BA	SA	PH AB	PH H	G by POS
1909 CHI N	11	37	11	1	1	1	2.7	8	9	3		0	.297	.459	0	0	1B-11
1910 2 teams	CHI N (24G – .204)			PHI N (21G – .294)													
" total	45	122	31	6	3	0	0.0	15	17	13	8	2	.254	.352	8	2	1B-36
1911 PHI N	146	551	166	24	11	16	2.9	69	99	40	76	6	.301	.472	0	0	1B-146
1912	148	572	147	31	5	10	1.7	77	69	44	65	8	.257	.381	2	0	1B-146
1913	155	588	154	32	7	18	3.1	67	86	34	51	5	.262	.432	0	0	1B-155
1914	121	443	110	16	5	12	2.7	55	55	33	31	2	.248	.388	0	0	1B-121
1915	141	499	157	36	7	7	1.4	55	62	42	36	9	.315	.457	0	0	1B-141
1916	146	508	143	26	3	5	1.0	52	53	41	32	8	.281	.374	0	0	1B-146
1917	154	522	136	24	4	5	1.0	57	72	65	35	5	.261	.351	0	0	1B-154
1918	125	468	135	23	2	5	1.1	54	67	42	33	4	.288	.378	0	0	1B-125
1919	138	509	149	30	6	5	1.0	60	54	54	48	6	.293	.405	0	0	1B-138
1920	16	32	5	2	0	0	0.0	1	4	3	6	0	.156	.219	9	2	1B-7
12 yrs.	1346	4851	1344	251	54	84	1.7	570	647	414	421	55	.277	.403	19	4	1B-1326

WORLD SERIES

	G	AB	H	2B	3B	HR	HR %	R	RBI	BB	SO	SB	BA	SA	PH AB	PH H	G by POS
1915 PHI N	5	16	7	2	0	1	6.3	1	6	1	4	0	.438	.750	0	0	1B-5

Bill Ludwig

LUDWIG, WILLIAM LAWRENCE   BR TR
B. May 27, 1882, Louisville, Ky.   D. Sept. 5, 1947, Louisville, Ky.

	G	AB	H	2B	3B	HR	HR %	R	RBI	BB	SO	SB	BA	SA	PH AB	PH H	G by POS
1908 STL N	66	187	34	2	2	0	0.0	15	8	16		3	.182	.214	4	0	C-62

Roy Luebbe

LUEBBE, ROY JOHN   BB TR 6' 175 lbs.
B. Sept. 17, 1901, Parkersburg, Iowa

	G	AB	H	2B	3B	HR	HR %	R	RBI	BB	SO	SB	BA	SA	PH AB	PH H	G by POS
1925 NY A	8	15	0	0	0	0	0.0	0	1	3	2	6	0	.000	.000	0	0	C-8

Henry Luff

LUFF, HENRY T.
B. Sept. 14, 1856, Philadelphia, Pa.   D. Oct. 11, 1916, Philadelphia, Pa.

	G	AB	H	2B	3B	HR	HR %	R	RBI	BB	SO	SB	BA	SA	PH AB	PH H	G by POS
1882 2 teams	DET N (3G – .273)			CIN AA (28G – .233)													
" total	31	131	31	4	2	0	0.0	17	1		2			.237	.298	0	0	1B-27, 2B-3, OF-2
1883 LOU AA	6	23	4	0	0	0	0.0	1			0			.174	.174	0	0	1B-4, OF-2
1884 2 teams	PHI U (26G – .270)			KC U (5G – .053)													
" total	31	130	31	4	2	0	0.0	9			5			.238	.300	0	0	OF-16, 3B-9, 1B-6, 2B-3
3 yrs.	68	284	66	8	4	0	0.0	27	1		7			.232	.289	0	0	1B-37, OF-20, 3B-9, 2B-6

Eddie Lukon

LUKON, EDWARD PAUL (Mongoose)   BL TL 5'10" 168 lbs.
B. Aug. 5, 1920, Burgettstown, Pa.

	G	AB	H	2B	3B	HR	HR %	R	RBI	BB	SO	SB	BA	SA	PH AB	PH H	G by POS
1941 CIN N	23	86	23	3	0	0	0.0	6	3	6	6	1	.267	.302	0	0	OF-22
1945	2	8	1	0	0	0	0.0	1	0	0	1	0	.125	.125	0	0	OF-2
1946	102	312	78	8	8	12	3.8	31	34	26	29	3	.250	.442	18	2	OF-83
1947	86	200	41	6	1	11	5.5	26	33	28	36	0	.205	.410	28	6	OF-55
4 yrs.	213	606	143	17	9	23	3.8	64	70	60	72	4	.236	.408	46	8	OF-162

Mike Lum

LUM, MICHAEL KEN-WAI   BL TL 6' 180 lbs.
B. Oct. 27, 1945, Honolulu, Hawaii

	G	AB	H	2B	3B	HR	HR %	R	RBI	BB	SO	SB	BA	SA	PH AB	PH H	G by POS
1967 ATL N	9	26	6	0	0	0	0.0	1	1	1	4	0	.231	.231	3	1	OF-6
1968	122	232	52	7	3	3	1.3	22	21	14	35	3	.224	.319	27	8	OF-95
1969	121	168	45	8	0	1	0.6	20	22	16	18	0	.268	.333	31	9	OF-89
1970	123	291	74	17	2	7	2.4	25	28	17	43	3	.254	.399	28	9	OF-98
1971	145	454	122	14	1	13	2.9	56	55	47	43	0	.269	.390	14	2	OF-125, 1B-1

	G	AB	H	2B	3B	HR	HR %	R	RBI	BB	SO	SB	BA	SA	Pinch Hit AB	Pinch Hit H	G by POS

Mike Lum continued

	G	AB	H	2B	3B	HR	HR %	R	RBI	BB	SO	SB	BA	SA	PH AB	PH H	G by POS
1972	123	369	84	14	2	9	2.4	40	38	50	52	1	.228	.350	15	6	OF-109, 1B-2
1973	138	513	151	26	6	16	3.1	74	82	41	89	2	.294	.462	9	0	1B-84, OF-64
1974	106	361	84	11	2	11	3.0	50	50	45	49	0	.233	.366	10	1	1B-60, OF-50
1975	124	364	83	8	2	8	2.2	32	36	39	38	2	.228	.327	26	4	1B-60, OF-38
1976 CIN N	84	136	31	5	1	3	2.2	15	20	22	24	0	.228	.346	39	10	OF-38
1977	81	125	20	1	0	5	4.0	14	16	9	33	2	.160	.288	47	5	OF-24, 1B-8
1978	86	146	39	7	1	6	4.1	15	23	22	18	0	.267	.452	36	11	1B-43, OF-7
1979 ATL N	111	217	54	6	0	6	2.8	27	27	18	34	0	.249	.359	52	17	1B-51, OF-3
1980	93	83	17	3	0	0	0.0	7	5	18	19	0	.205	.241	50	12	OF-19, 1B-10
1981 2 teams	ATL	N (10G –	.091)		CHI	N	(41G –	.241)									
" total	51	69	15	1	0	2	2.9	6	7	7	7	0	.217	.319	31	8	OF-15, 1B-1
15 yrs.	1517	3554	877	128	20	90	2.5	404	431	366	506	13	.247	.370	418	103	OF-816, 1B-284
															7th	8th	

LEAGUE CHAMPIONSHIP SERIES

	G	AB	H	2B	3B	HR	HR %	R	RBI	BB	SO	SB	BA	SA	PH AB	PH H	G by POS
1969 ATL N	2	2	2	1	0	0	0.0	0	0	0	0	0	1.000	1.500	1	1	OF-1
1976 CIN N	1	1	0	0	0	0	0.0	0	0	0	0	0	.000	.000	1	0	
2 yrs.	3	3	2	1	0	0	0.0	0	0	0	0	0	.667	1.000	2	1	OF-1

Harry Lumley

LUMLEY, HARRY G   BL TR
B. Sept. 29, 1880, Forest City, Pa.   D. May 22, 1938, Binghamton, N. Y.
Manager 1909.

	G	AB	H	2B	3B	HR	HR %	R	RBI	BB	SO	SB	BA	SA	PH AB	PH H	G by POS
1904 BKN N	150	577	161	23	18	9	1.6	79	78	41		30	.279	.428	0	0	OF-150
1905	130	505	148	19	10	7	1.4	50	47	36		22	.293	.412	1	1	OF-129
1906	133	484	157	23	12	9	1.9	72	61	48		35	.324	.477	2	0	OF-131
1907	127	454	121	23	11	9	2.0	47	66	31		18	.267	.425	9	1	OF-118
1908	127	440	95	13	12	4	0.9	36	39	29		4	.216	.327	11	2	OF-116
1909	55	172	43	8	3	0	0.0	13	14	16		1	.250	.331	3	1	OF-52
1910	8	21	3	0	0	0	0.0	3	0	3	6	0	.143	.143	2	0	OF-4
7 yrs.	730	2653	728	109	66	38	1.4	300	305	204	6	110	.274	.408	28	5	OF-700

Jerry Lumpe

LUMPE, JERRY DEAN   BL TR 6'2"   185 lbs.
B. June 2, 1933, Lincoln, Mo.

	G	AB	H	2B	3B	HR	HR %	R	RBI	BB	SO	SB	BA	SA	PH AB	PH H	G by POS
1956 NY A	20	62	16	3	0	0	0.0	12	4	5	11	1	.258	.306	4	0	SS-17, 3B-1
1957	40	103	35	6	2	0	0.0	15	11	9	13	2	.340	.437	7	2	3B-30, SS-6
1958	81	232	59	8	4	3	1.3	34	32	23	21	1	.254	.362	16	4	3B-65, SS-5
1959 2 teams	NY	A (18G –	.222)		KC	A	(108G –	.243)									
" total	126	448	108	11	5	3	0.7	49	30	47	39	2	.241	.308	4	1	2B-62, SS-60, 3B-16
1960 KC A	146	574	156	19	3	8	1.4	69	53	48	49	1	.272	.357	5	0	2B-134, SS-15
1961	148	569	167	29	9	3	0.5	81	54	48	39	1	.293	.392	1	0	2B-147
1962	156	641	193	34	10	10	1.6	89	83	44	38	0	.301	.432	1	1	2B-156, SS-2
1963	157	595	161	26	7	5	0.8	75	59	58	44	3	.271	.363	2	0	2B-155
1964 DET A	158	624	160	21	6	6	1.0	75	46	50	61	2	.256	.338	0	0	2B-158
1965	145	502	129	15	3	4	0.8	72	39	56	34	7	.257	.323	10	1	2B-139
1966	113	385	89	14	3	1	0.3	30	26	24	44	0	.231	.291	20	2	2B-95
1967	81	177	41	4	0	4	2.3	19	17	16	18	0	.232	.322	29	3	2B-54, 3B-6
12 yrs.	1371	4912	1314	190	52	47	1.0	620	454	428	411	20	.268	.356	99	14	2B-1100, 3B-118, SS-105

WORLD SERIES

	G	AB	H	2B	3B	HR	HR %	R	RBI	BB	SO	SB	BA	SA	PH AB	PH H	G by POS
1957 NY A	6	14	4	0	0	0	0.0	0	2	1	1	0	.286	.286	3	2	3B-3
1958	6	12	2	0	0	0	0.0	0	0	1	2	0	.167	.167	3	0	3B-3
2 yrs.	12	26	6	0	0	0	0.0	0	2	2	3	0	.231	.231	6	2	3B-6

Don Lund

LUND, DONALD ANDREW   BR TR 6'   200 lbs.
B. May 18, 1923, Detroit, Mich.

	G	AB	H	2B	3B	HR	HR %	R	RBI	BB	SO	SB	BA	SA	PH AB	PH H	G by POS
1945 BKN N	4	3	0	0	0	0	0.0	0	0	1	1	0	.000	.000	3	0	
1947	11	20	6	2	0	2	10.0	5	5	3	7	0	.300	.700	5	2	OF-5
1948 2 teams	BKN	N (27G –	.188)		STL	A	(63G –	.248)									
" total	90	230	53	11	4	4	1.7	30	30	15	33	1	.230	.365	16	0	OF-70
1949 DET A	2	2	0	0	0	0	0.0	0	0	0	1	0	.000	.000	2	0	
1952	8	23	7	0	0	0	0.0	1	1	3	3	0	.304	.304	1	0	OF-7
1953	131	421	108	21	4	9	2.1	51	47	39	65	3	.257	.390	8	2	OF-123
1954	35	54	7	2	0	0	0.0	4	3	4	3	1	.130	.167	9	1	OF-31
7 yrs.	281	753	181	36	8	15	2.0	91	86	65	113	5	.240	.369	44	5	OF-236

Gordon Lund

LUND, GORDON THOMAS   BR TR 5'11"   170 lbs.
B. Feb. 23, 1941, Iron Mountain, Mich.

	G	AB	H	2B	3B	HR	HR %	R	RBI	BB	SO	SB	BA	SA	PH AB	PH H	G by POS
1967 CLE A	3	8	2	1	0	0	0.0	1	0	0	2	0	.250	.375	1	0	SS-2
1969 SEA A	20	38	10	0	0	0	0.0	4	1	5	7	1	.263	.263	0	0	SS-17, 3B-1, 2B-1
2 yrs.	23	46	12	1	0	0	0.0	5	1	5	9	1	.261	.283	1	0	SS-19, 3B-1, 2B-1

Tom Lundstedt

LUNDSTEDT, THOMAS ROBERT   BR TR 6'4"   195 lbs.
B. Apr. 10, 1949, Davenport, Iowa

	G	AB	H	2B	3B	HR	HR %	R	RBI	BB	SO	SB	BA	SA	PH AB	PH H	G by POS
1973 CHI N	4	5	0	0	0	0	0.0	0	0	0	1	0	.000	.000	0	0	C-4
1974	22	32	3	0	0	0	0.0	1	0	5	7	0	.094	.094	0	0	C-22
1975 MIN A	18	28	3	0	0	0	0.0	2	1	4	5	0	.107	.107	3	1	C-14, DH-2
3 yrs.	44	65	6	0	0	0	0.0	3	1	9	13	0	.092	.092	3	1	C-40, DH-2

Harry Lunte

LUNTE, HARRY AUGUST   BR TR 5'11½" 165 lbs.
B. Sept. 15, 1892, St. Louis, Mo.   D. July 27, 1965, St. Louis, Mo.

	G	AB	H	2B	3B	HR	HR %	R	RBI	BB	SO	SB	BA	SA	PH AB	PH H	G by POS
1919 CLE A	26	77	15	2	0	0	0.0	2	2	1	7	0	.195	.221	2	0	SS-24
1920	28	71	14	0	0	0	0.0	6	7	5	6	0	.197	.197	0	0	SS-21, 2B-3
2 yrs.	54	148	29	2	0	0	0.0	8	9	6	13	0	.196	.209	2	0	SS-45, 2B-3

WORLD SERIES

	G	AB	H	2B	3B	HR	HR %	R	RBI	BB	SO	SB	BA	SA	PH AB	PH H	G by POS
1920 CLE A	1	0	0	0	0	0	–	0	0	0	0	0	–	–	0	0	SS-1

	G	AB	H	2B	3B	HR	HR %	R	RBI	BB	SO	SB	BA	SA	Pinch Hit AB	Pinch Hit H	G by POS

Tony Lupien

LUPIEN, ULYSSES JOHN
B. Apr. 23, 1917, Chelmsford, Mass.　　　BL TL 5'10½" 185 lbs.

	G	AB	H	2B	3B	HR	HR%	R	RBI	BB	SO	SB	BA	SA	PH AB	PH H	G by POS
1940 BOS A	10	19	9	3	2	0	0.0	5	4	1	1	0	.474	.842	2	1	1B-8
1942	128	463	130	25	7	3	0.6	63	70	50	20	10	.281	.384	6	0	1B-121
1943	154	608	155	21	9	4	0.7	65	47	54	23	16	.255	.339	1	0	1B-153
1944 PHI N	153	597	169	23	9	5	0.8	82	52	56	29	18	.283	.377	1	1	1B-151
1945	15	54	17	1	0	0	0.0	1	3	6	0	2	.315	.333	0	0	1B-15
1948 CHI A	154	617	152	19	3	6	1.0	69	54	74	38	11	.246	.316	0	0	1B-154
6 yrs.	614	2358	632	92	30	18	0.8	285	230	241	111	57	.268	.355	10	2	1B-602

Al Luplow

LUPLOW, ALVIN DAVID
B. Mar. 13, 1939, Saginaw, Mich.　　　BL TR 5'10" 175 lbs.

	G	AB	H	2B	3B	HR	HR%	R	RBI	BB	SO	SB	BA	SA	PH AB	PH H	G by POS
1961 CLE A	5	18	1	0	0	0	0.0	0	0	2	6	0	.056	.056	0	0	OF-5
1962	97	318	88	15	3	14	4.4	54	45	36	44	1	.277	.475	13	4	OF-86
1963	100	295	69	6	2	7	2.4	34	27	33	62	4	.234	.339	18	1	OF-85
1964	19	18	2	0	0	0	0.0	1	1	1	8	0	.111	.111	15	1	OF-5
1965	53	45	6	2	0	1	2.2	3	4	3	14	0	.133	.244	44	6	OF-6
1966 NY N	111	334	84	9	1	7	2.1	31	31	38	46	2	.251	.347	19	5	OF-101
1967 2 teams		NY N (41G – .205)				PIT N (55G – .184)											
" total	96	215	42	2	0	4	1.9	24	17	14	33	1	.195	.260	41	7	OF-58
7 yrs.	481	1243	292	34	6	33	2.7	147	125	127	213	8	.235	.352	150	24	OF-346

Billy Lush

LUSH, WILLIAM LUCAS
Brother of Ernie Lush.
B. Nov. 10, 1873, Bridgeport, Conn.　　D. Aug. 28, 1951, Hawthorne, N. Y.　　BB TR 5'8" 165 lbs.

	G	AB	H	2B	3B	HR	HR%	R	RBI	BB	SO	SB	BA	SA	PH AB	PH H	G by POS
1895 WAS N	5	18	6	0	0	0	0.0	2	2	2	1	0	.333	.333	0	0	OF-5
1896	97	352	87	9	11	4	1.1	74	45	66	49	28	.247	.369	3	1	OF-91, 2B-3
1897	3	12	0	0	0	0	0.0	1	0	2		0	.000	.000	0	0	OF-3
1901 BOS N	7	27	5	1	1	0	0.0	2	3	3		0	.185	.296	0	0	OF-7
1902	120	413	92	8	1	2	0.5	68	19	76		30	.223	.262	3	1	OF-116, 3B-1
1903 DET A	119	423	116	18	14	1	0.2	71	33	70		14	.274	.390	1	0	OF-101, 3B-12, SS-3, 2B-3
1904 CLE A	138	477	123	13	8	1	0.2	76	50	72		12	.258	.325	0	0	OF-138
7 yrs.	489	1722	429	49	35	8	0.5	294	152	291	50	84	.249	.332	7	2	OF-461, 3B-13, 2B-6, SS-3

Ernie Lush

LUSH, ERNEST BENJAMIN
Brother of Billy Lush.
B. Oct. 31, 1884, Bridgeport, Conn.　　D. Feb. 26, 1937, Detroit, Mich.　　TL

	G	AB	H	2B	3B	HR	HR%	R	RBI	BB	SO	SB	BA	SA	PH AB	PH H	G by POS
1910 STL N	1	4	0	0	0	0	0.0	0	0	1	1	0	.000	.000	0	0	OF-1

Johnny Lush

LUSH, JOHN CHARLES
B. Oct. 8, 1885, Williamsport, Pa.　　D. Nov. 18, 1946, Beverly Hills, Calif.　　BL TL 5'9½" 165 lbs.

	G	AB	H	2B	3B	HR	HR%	R	RBI	BB	SO	SB	BA	SA	PH AB	PH H	G by POS
1904 PHI N	106	369	102	22	3	2	0.5	39	42	27		12	.276	.369	4	1	1B-62, OF-33, P-7
1905	6	16	5	0	0	0	0.0	3	1	1		0	.313	.313	1	1	OF-3, P-2
1906	76	212	56	7	1	0	0.0	28	15	14		6	.264	.307	14	1	P-37, OF-22, 1B-2
1907 2 teams		PHI N (17G – .200)				STL N (27G – .280)											
" total	44	122	31	3	4	0	0.0	11	10	6		5	.254	.344	13	2	P-28, OF-11
1908 STL N	45	89	15	2	0	0	0.0	7	2	7		1	.169	.191	6	1	P-38
1909	45	92	22	5	0	0	0.0	11	14	6		2	.239	.293	7	0	P-34, OF-3
1910	47	93	21	1	3	0	0.0	8	10	8	11	2	.226	.301	10	4	P-36
7 yrs.	369	993	252	40	11	2	0.2	107	94	69	11	28	.254	.322	55	10	P-182, OF-72, 1B-64

Charlie Luskey

LUSKEY, CHARLES MELTON
B. Apr. 6, 1876, Washington, D. C.　　D. Dec. 20, 1962, Bethesda, Md.　　BR TR 5'7" 165 lbs.

	G	AB	H	2B	3B	HR	HR%	R	RBI	BB	SO	SB	BA	SA	PH AB	PH H	G by POS
1901 WAS A	11	41	8	3	1	0	0.0	8	3	2		0	.195	.317	0	0	OF-8, C-3

Luke Lutenberg

LUTENBERG, CHARLES WILLIAM
B. Oct. 4, 1864, Quincy, Ill.　　D. Dec. 24, 1938, Quincy, Ill.

	G	AB	H	2B	3B	HR	HR%	R	RBI	BB	SO	SB	BA	SA	PH AB	PH H	G by POS
1894 LOU N	69	250	48	10	4	0	0.0	42	23	23	21	4	.192	.264	0	0	1B-67, 2B-2

Lyle Luttrell

LUTTRELL, LYLE KENNETH
B. Feb. 22, 1930, Bloomington, Ill.　　D. July 11, 1984, Chattanooga, Tenn.　　BR TR 6' 180 lbs.

	G	AB	H	2B	3B	HR	HR%	R	RBI	BB	SO	SB	BA	SA	PH AB	PH H	G by POS
1956 WAS A	38	122	23	5	3	2	1.6	17	9	8	19	5	.189	.328	1	0	SS-37
1957	19	45	9	4	0	0	0.0	4	5	3	8	0	.200	.289	2	0	SS-17
2 yrs.	57	167	32	9	3	2	1.2	21	14	11	27	5	.192	.317	3	0	SS-54

Joe Lutz

LUTZ, ROLLIN JOSEPH
B. Feb. 18, 1925, Keokuk, Iowa　　　BL TL 6' 195 lbs.

	G	AB	H	2B	3B	HR	HR%	R	RBI	BB	SO	SB	BA	SA	PH AB	PH H	G by POS
1951 STL A	14	36	6	0	1	0	0.0	7	2	6	9	0	.167	.222	3	1	1B-11

Red Lutz

LUTZ, LOUIS WILLIAM
B. Dec. 17, 1898, Cincinnati, Ohio　　　BR TR 5'10" 170 lbs.

	G	AB	H	2B	3B	HR	HR%	R	RBI	BB	SO	SB	BA	SA	PH AB	PH H	G by POS
1922 CIN N	1	1	1	1	0	0	0.0	0	0	0	0	0	1.000	2.000	0	0	C-1

Rube Lutzke

LUTZKE, WALTER JOHN
B. Nov. 17, 1897, Milwaukee, Wis.　　D. Mar. 6, 1938, Milwaukee, Wis.　　BR TR 5'11" 175 lbs.

	G	AB	H	2B	3B	HR	HR%	R	RBI	BB	SO	SB	BA	SA	PH AB	PH H	G by POS
1923 CLE A	143	511	131	20	6	3	0.6	71	65	59	57	10	.256	.337	0	0	3B-143
1924	106	341	83	18	3	0	0.0	37	42	38	46	4	.243	.314	0	0	3B-103, 2B-3
1925	81	238	52	9	0	1	0.4	31	16	26	29	2	.218	.269	2	1	3B-69, 2B-10
1926	142	475	124	28	6	0	0.0	42	59	34	35	6	.261	.345	0	0	3B-142
1927	100	311	78	12	3	0	0.0	35	41	22	29	2	.251	.309	2	0	3B-98
5 yrs.	572	1876	468	87	18	4	0.2	216	223	179	196	24	.249	.321	4	1	3B-555, 2B-13

	G	AB	H	2B	3B	HR	HR %	R	RBI	BB	SO	SB	BA	SA	Pinch Hit AB	Pinch Hit H	G by POS

Greg Luzinski

LUZINSKI, GREGORY MICHAEL   BR TR 6'1"   220 lbs.
B. Nov. 22, 1950, Chicago, Ill.

	G	AB	H	2B	3B	HR	HR %	R	RBI	BB	SO	SB	BA	SA	Pinch Hit AB	Pinch Hit H	G by POS
1970 PHI N	8	12	2	0	0	0	0.0	0	0	3	5	0	.167	.167	5	1	1B-3
1971	28	100	30	8	0	3	3.0	13	15	12	32	2	.300	.470	0	0	1B-28
1972	150	563	158	33	5	18	3.2	66	68	42	114	0	.281	.453	4	1	OF-145, 1B-2
1973	161	610	174	26	4	29	4.8	76	97	51	135	3	.285	.484	4	2	OF-159
1974	85	302	82	14	1	7	2.3	29	48	29	76	3	.272	.394	4	0	OF-82
1975	161	596	179	35	3	34	5.7	85	120	89	151	3	.300	.540	2	0	OF-159
1976	149	533	162	28	1	21	3.9	74	95	50	107	1	.304	.478	5	0	OF-144
1977	149	554	171	35	3	39	7.0	99	130	80	140	1	.309	.594	1	0	OF-148
1978	155	540	143	32	2	35	6.5	85	101	100	135	8	.265	.526	1	0	OF-154
1979	137	452	114	23	1	18	4.0	47	81	56	103	3	.252	.427	9	1	OF-125
1980	106	368	84	19	1	19	5.2	44	56	60	100	3	.228	.440	1	0	OF-105
1981 CHI A	104	378	100	15	1	21	5.6	55	62	58	80	0	.265	.476	0	0	DH-103
1982	159	583	170	37	1	18	3.1	87	102	89	120	1	.292	.451	2	1	DH-156
1983	144	502	128	26	1	32	6.4	73	95	70	117	2	.255	.502	2	0	DH-139, 1B-2
1984	125	412	98	13	0	13	3.2	47	58	56	80	5	.238	.364	11	3	DH-114
15 yrs.	1821	6505	1795	344	24	307	4.7	880	1128	845	1495	37	.276	.478	51	9	OF-1221, DH-512, 1B-35
LEAGUE CHAMPIONSHIP SERIES																	
1976 PHI N	3	11	3	2	0	1	9.1	2	3	1	4	0	.273	.727	0	0	OF-3
1977	4	14	4	1	0	1	7.1	2	2	3	3	1	.286	.571	0	0	OF-4
1978	4	16	6	0	1	2	12.5	3	3	1	2	0	.375	.875	0	0	OF-4
1980	5	17	5	2	0	1	5.9	3	4	0	6	0	.294	.588	1	1	OF-4
1983 CHI A	4	15	2	1	0	0	0.0	0	0	1	5	0	.133	.200	0	0	DH-4
5 yrs.	20	73	20	6	1	5	6.8	10	12	6	20	1	.274	.589	1	1	OF-15, DH-4
WORLD SERIES																	
1980 PHI N	3	9	0	0	0	0	0.0	0	0	1	5	0	.000	.000	0	0	OF-1

Dummy Lynch

LYNCH, MATTHEW DANIEL   BR TR 5'11"   174 lbs.
B. Feb. 7, 1927, Dallas, Tex.   D. June 30, 1978, Plano, Tex.

	G	AB	H	2B	3B	HR	HR %	R	RBI	BB	SO	SB	BA	SA	Pinch Hit AB	Pinch Hit H	G by POS
1948 CHI N	7	7	2	0	0	1	14.3	3	1	1	1	0	.286	.714	4	1	2B-1

Henry Lynch

LYNCH, HENRY W.   5'7"   143 lbs.
B. 1866, Worcester, Mass.   D. Nov. 23, 1925, Worcester, Mass.

	G	AB	H	2B	3B	HR	HR %	R	RBI	BB	SO	SB	BA	SA	Pinch Hit AB	Pinch Hit H	G by POS
1893 CHI N	4	14	3	2	0	0	0.0	0	2	1	1	0	.214	.357	0	0	OF-4

Jerry Lynch

LYNCH, GERALD THOMAS   BL TR 6'1"   185 lbs.
B. July 17, 1930, Bay City, Mich.

	G	AB	H	2B	3B	HR	HR %	R	RBI	BB	SO	SB	BA	SA	Pinch Hit AB	Pinch Hit H	G by POS
1954 PIT N	98	284	68	4	5	8	2.8	27	36	20	43	2	.239	.373	15	2	OF-83
1955	88	282	80	18	6	5	1.8	43	28	22	33	2	.284	.443	18	4	OF-71, C-2
1956	19	19	3	0	1	0	0.0	1	0	1	4	0	.158	.263	16	3	OF-1
1957 CIN N	67	124	32	4	1	4	3.2	11	13	6	18	0	.258	.403	42	8	OF-24, C-2
1958	122	420	131	20	5	16	3.8	58	68	18	54	1	.312	.498	25	9	OF-101
1959	117	379	102	16	3	17	4.5	49	58	29	50	2	.269	.462	19	7	OF-98
1960	102	159	46	8	2	6	3.8	23	27	16	25	0	.289	.478	66	19	OF-32
1961	96	181	57	13	2	13	7.2	33	50	27	25	2	.315	.624	47	19	OF-44
1962	114	288	81	15	4	12	4.2	41	57	24	38	3	.281	.486	38	9	OF-73
1963 2 teams	CIN	N (22G –	.250)		PIT	N (88G –	.266)										
" total	110	269	71	9	3	12	4.5	31	45	23	33	0	.264	.454	37	12	OF-71
1964 PIT N	114	297	81	14	2	16	5.4	35	66	26	57	0	.273	.495	34	7	OF-78
1965	73	121	34	1	0	5	4.1	7	16	8	26	0	.281	.413	41	7	OF-26
1966	64	56	12	1	0	1	1.8	5	6	4	10	0	.214	.286	49	10	OF-4
13 yrs.	1184	2879	798	123	34	115	4.0	364	470	224	416	12	.277	.463	447 3rd	116 4th	OF-706, C-4
WORLD SERIES																	
1961 CIN N	4	3	0	0	0	0	0.0	0	0	1	1	0	.000	.000	3	0	

Mike Lynch

LYNCH, MICHAEL JOSEPH
B. June 28, 1875, St. Paul, Minn.   D. Apr. 1, 1947, Jennings Lodge, Ore.

	G	AB	H	2B	3B	HR	HR %	R	RBI	BB	SO	SB	BA	SA	Pinch Hit AB	Pinch Hit H	G by POS
1902 CHI N	7	28	4	0	0	0	0.0	4	0	2		0	.143	.143	0	0	OF-7

Tom Lynch

LYNCH, THOMAS JAMES   BL TR 5'10½" 170 lbs.
B. Apr. 3, 1860, Bennington, Vt.   D. Mar. 28, 1955, Cohoes, N. Y.

	G	AB	H	2B	3B	HR	HR %	R	RBI	BB	SO	SB	BA	SA	Pinch Hit AB	Pinch Hit H	G by POS
1884 2 teams	WIL	U (16G –	.276)		PHI	N (13G –	.313)										
" total	29	106	31	7	3	0	0.0	13		9		5	.292	.415	0	0	OF-15, C-15, 1B-1
1885 PHI N	13	53	10	3	0	0	0.0	7		10		3	.189	.245	0	0	OF-13
2 yrs.	42	159	41	10	3	0	0.0	20		19		8	.258	.358	0	0	OF-28, C-15, 1B-1

Walt Lynch

LYNCH, WALTER EDWARD   BR TR 6'   176 lbs.
B. Apr. 15, 1897, Buffalo, N. Y.   D. Dec. 21, 1976, Daytona Beach, Fla.

	G	AB	H	2B	3B	HR	HR %	R	RBI	BB	SO	SB	BA	SA	Pinch Hit AB	Pinch Hit H	G by POS
1922 BOS A	3	2	1	0	0	0	0.0	1	0	0	0	0	.500	.500	0	0	C-3

Byrd Lynn

LYNN, BYRD   BR TR 5'11"   165 lbs.
B. Mar. 13, 1889, Unionville, Ill.   D. Feb. 5, 1940, Napa, Calif.

	G	AB	H	2B	3B	HR	HR %	R	RBI	BB	SO	SB	BA	SA	Pinch Hit AB	Pinch Hit H	G by POS
1916 CHI A	31	40	9	1	0	0	0.0	4	3	4	7	2	.225	.250	15	3	C-13
1917	35	72	16	2	0	0	0.0	7	5	7	11	1	.222	.250	6	1	C-29
1918	5	8	2	0	0	0	0.0	0	0	2	1	0	.250	.250	1	1	C-4
1919	29	66	15	4	0	0	0.0	4	4	4	9	0	.227	.288	1	1	C-28
1920	16	25	8	2	1	0	0.0	0	3	1	3	0	.320	.480	2	2	C-14
5 yrs.	116	211	50	9	1	0	0.0	15	15	18	31	3	.237	.289	25	8	C-88
WORLD SERIES																	
1917 CHI A	1	1	0	0	0	0	0.0	0	0	0	1	0	.000	.000	1	0	
1919	1	1	0	0	0	0	0.0	0	0	0	0	0	.000	.000	0	0	C-1
2 yrs.	2	2	0	0	0	0	0.0	0	0	0	1	0	.000	.000	1	0	C-1

	G	AB	H	2B	3B	HR	HR %	R	RBI	BB	SO	SB	BA	SA	Pinch Hit AB	Pinch Hit H	G by POS

Fred Lynn

LYNN, FREDRIC MICHAEL   BL TL 6'1"   185 lbs.
B. Feb. 3, 1952, Chicago, Ill.

	G	AB	H	2B	3B	HR	HR %	R	RBI	BB	SO	SB	BA	SA	AB	H	G by POS
1974 BOS A	15	43	18	2	2	2	4.7	5	10	6	6	0	.419	.698	2	0	OF-15, DH-1
1975	145	528	175	**47**	7	21	4.0	**103**	105	62	90	10	.331	**.566**	2	1	OF-144
1976	132	507	159	32	8	10	2.0	76	65	48	67	14	.314	.467	1	0	OF-128, DH-5
1977	129	497	129	29	5	18	3.6	81	76	51	63	2	.260	.447	3	0	OF-125, DH-1
1978	150	541	161	33	3	22	4.1	75	82	75	50	3	.298	.492	0	0	OF-149
1979	147	531	177	42	1	39	7.3	116	122	82	79	2	**.333**	**.637**	4	1	OF-143, DH-1
1980	110	415	125	32	3	12	2.9	67	61	58	39	12	.301	.480	0	0	OF-110
1981 CAL A	76	256	56	8	1	5	2.0	28	31	38	42	1	.219	.316	9	1	OF-69
1982	138	472	141	38	1	21	4.4	89	86	58	72	7	.299	.517	10	5	OF-133
1983	117	437	119	20	3	22	5.0	56	74	55	83	2	.272	.483	3	0	OF-113, DH-2
1984	142	517	140	28	4	23	4.4	84	79	77	98	2	.271	.474	5	2	OF-140
11 yrs.	1301	4744	1400	311	38	195	4.1	780	791	610	689	55	.295	.500	39	10	OF-1269, DH-10
LEAGUE CHAMPIONSHIP SERIES																	
1975 BOS A	3	11	4	1	0	0	0.0	1	3	0	0	0	.364	.455	0	0	OF-3
1982 CAL A	5	18	11	2	0	1	5.6	4	5	2	3	0	.611	.889	0	0	OF-5
2 yrs.	8	29	15	3	0	1	3.4	5	8	2	3	0	.517	.724	0	0	OF-8
WORLD SERIES																	
1975 BOS A	7	25	7	1	0	1	4.0	3	5	3	5	0	.280	.440	0	0	OF-7

Jerry Lynn

LYNN, JEROME EDWARD   BR TR 5'10"   164 lbs.
B. Apr. 14, 1916, Scranton, Pa.   D. Sept. 25, 1972, Scranton, Pa.

	G	AB	H	2B	3B	HR	HR %	R	RBI	BB	SO	SB	BA	SA	AB	H	G by POS
1937 WAS A	1	3	2	1	0	0	0.0	0	0	0	0	0	.667	1.000	0	0	2B-1

Russ Lyon

LYON, RUSSELL MAYO   BR TR 6'1"   230 lbs.
B. June 26, 1913, Ball Ground, Ga.

	G	AB	H	2B	3B	HR	HR %	R	RBI	BB	SO	SB	BA	SA	AB	H	G by POS
1944 CLE A	7	11	2	0	0	0	0.0	1	0	1	1	0	.182	.182	4	0	C-3

Danny Lyons

LYONS, WILLIAM ALLEN   BR TR 6'1"   175 lbs.
B. Apr. 6, 1958, Alton, Ill.

	G	AB	H	2B	3B	HR	HR %	R	RBI	BB	SO	SB	BA	SA	AB	H	G by POS
1983 STL N	42	60	10	1	1	0	0.0	3	3	1	11	3	.167	.217	11	1	2B-23, 3B-8, SS-2
1984	46	73	16	3	0	0	0.0	13	3	9	13	3	.219	.260	8	1	2B-25, SS-11, 3B-3
2 yrs.	88	133	26	4	1	0	0.0	16	6	10	24	6	.195	.241	19	2	2B-48, SS-13, 3B-11

Denny Lyons

LYONS, DENNIS PATRICK ALOYSIUS   BR TR 5'10"   185 lbs.
B. Mar. 12, 1866, Cincinnati, Ohio   D. Jan. 2, 1929, West Covington, Ky.

	G	AB	H	2B	3B	HR	HR %	R	RBI	BB	SO	SB	BA	SA	AB	H	G by POS
1885 PRO N	4	16	2	1	0	0	0.0	3	1	0	3		.125	.188	0	0	3B-4
1886 PHI AA	32	123	26	3	1	0	0.0	22		8			.211	.252	0	0	3B-32
1887	137	570	209	43	14	6	1.1	128		47		73	.367	.523	0	0	3B-137
1888	111	456	135	22	5	6	1.3	93	83	41		39	.296	.406	0	0	3B-111
1889	131	510	168	36	4	9	1.8	135	82	79	44	10	.329	.469	0	0	3B-130, 1B-1
1890	88	339	120	29	5	7	2.1	79		57		21	.354	.531	0	0	3B-88
1891 STL AA	120	451	142	24	3	11	2.4	124	84	88	58	9	.315	.455	0	0	3B-120
1892 NY N	108	389	100	16	7	8	2.1	71	51	59	36	11	.257	.396	0	0	3B-108
1893 PIT N	131	490	150	19	16	3	0.6	103	105	97	29	19	.306	.429	0	0	3B-131
1894	71	254	82	14	4	4	1.6	51	50	42	12	14	.323	.457	0	0	3B-71
1895 STL N	33	129	38	6	0	2	1.6	24	25	14	5	3	.295	.388	0	0	3B-33
1896 PIT N	118	436	134	25	6	4	0.9	77	71	67	25	13	.307	.420	2	0	3B-116
1897	37	131	27	6	4	2	1.5	22	17	22		5	.206	.359	0	0	1B-35, 3B-2
13 yrs.	1121	4294	1333	244	69	62	1.4	932	569	621	212	217	.310	.443	2	0	3B-1083, 1B-36

Ed Lyons

LYONS, EDWARD HOYTE (Mouse)   BR TR 5'9"   165 lbs.
B. May 12, 1923, Winston-Salem, N. C.

	G	AB	H	2B	3B	HR	HR %	R	RBI	BB	SO	SB	BA	SA	AB	H	G by POS
1947 WAS A	7	26	4	0	0	0	0.0	2	0	2	2	0	.154	.154	0	0	2B-7

Harry Lyons

LYONS, HARRY P.   BR TR 5'8½"   195 lbs.
B. Mar. 25, 1866, Chester, Pa.   D. June 30, 1912, Mauricetown, N. J.

	G	AB	H	2B	3B	HR	HR %	R	RBI	BB	SO	SB	BA	SA	AB	H	G by POS
1887 2 teams	PHI	N (1G –	.000)		STL	AA	(2G –	.125)									
" total	3	12	1	0	0	0	0.0	2		1		2	.083	.083	0	0	OF-2, 2B-1
1888 STL AA	123	499	97	10	5	4	0.8	66	63	20		36	.194	.259	0	0	OF-122, 3B-2, SS-1, 2B-1
1889 NY N	5	20	2	0	1	0	0.0	1	2	2	0	0	.100	.200	0	0	OF-5
1890 ROC AA	133	584	152	11	11	3	0.5	83		27		47	.260	.332	0	0	OF-132, 3B-2, C-1, P-1
1892 NY N	96	411	98	5	2	0	0.0	67	53	33	29	25	.238	.260	0	0	OF-96
1893	47	187	51	5	2	0	0.0	27	21	14	6	10	.273	.321	0	0	OF-47
6 yrs.	407	1713	401	31	21	7	0.4	246	138	97	35	120	.234	.289	0	0	OF-404, 3B-4, 2B-2, SS-1, C-1, P-1

Pat Lyons

LYONS, PATRICK JERRY
B. 1860, Canada   D. Jan. 20, 1914, Springfield, Ohio

	G	AB	H	2B	3B	HR	HR %	R	RBI	BB	SO	SB	BA	SA	AB	H	G by POS
1890 CLE N	11	38	2	1	0	0	0.0	2	1	4	4	0	.053	.079	0	0	2B-11

Ted Lyons

LYONS, THEODORE AMAR   BB TR 5'11"   200 lbs.
B. Dec. 28, 1900, Lake Charles, La.
Manager 1946-48.
Hall of Fame 1955.   BR 1925-27

	G	AB	H	2B	3B	HR	HR %	R	RBI	BB	SO	SB	BA	SA	AB	H	G by POS
1923 CHI A	9	5	1	0	0	0	0.0	0	1	1	3	0	.200	.200	0	0	P-9
1924	41	77	17	0	1	0	0.0	10	6	5	13	0	.221	.247	0	0	P-41
1925	43	97	18	3	0	0	0.0	6	7	3	13	0	.186	.216	0	0	P-43
1926	41	104	22	1	1	0	0.0	7	3	1	10	0	.212	.240	1	0	P-39
1927	41	110	28	6	2	1	0.9	16	9	6	17	0	.255	.373	0	0	P-39
1928	49	91	23	2	0	0	0.0	10	8	1	9	0	.253	.275	0	0	P-39
1929	40	91	20	4	0	0	0.0	7	11	9	13	0	.220	.264	0	0	P-37, OF-1
1930	57	122	38	6	3	1	0.8	20	15	2	18	0	.311	.434	9	3	P-42
1931	42	33	5	0	0	0	0.0	6	3	2	1	0	.152	.152	2	1	P-22
1932	49	73	19	2	1	1	1.4	11	10	4	10	0	.260	.356	1	0	P-33

	G	AB	H	2B	3B	HR	HR %	R	RBI	BB	SO	SB	BA	SA	Pinch Hit AB	Pinch Hit H	G by POS

Ted Lyons continued

	G	AB	H	2B	3B	HR	HR %	R	RBI	BB	SO	SB	BA	SA	AB	H	G by POS
1933	51	91	26	2	1	1	1.1	11	11	4	6	0	.286	.363	7	1	P-36
1934	50	97	20	4	0	1	1.0	9	16	3	19	0	.206	.278	17	3	P-30
1935	29	82	18	4	0	0	0.0	5	6	3	4	0	.220	.268	6	1	P-23
1936	26	70	11	0	0	0	0.0	2	5	5	12	0	.157	.157	0	0	P-26
1937	23	57	12	0	0	0	0.0	6	3	9	14	0	.211	.211	0	0	P-22
1938	24	72	14	2	0	0	0.0	9	4	2	9	0	.194	.222	1	0	P-23
1939	21	61	18	3	0	0	0.0	5	8	5	7	0	.295	.344	0	0	P-21
1940	22	75	18	4	0	0	0.0	4	7	2	7	0	.240	.293	0	0	P-22
1941	22	74	20	2	0	0	0.0	8	6	2	6	0	.270	.297	0	0	P-22
1942	20	67	16	4	0	0	0.0	10	10	3	7	0	.239	.299	0	0	P-20
1946	5	14	0	0	0	0	0.0	0	0	1	3	0	.000	.000	0	0	P-5
21 yrs.	705	1563	364	49	9	5	0.3	162	149	73	201	0	.233	.285	44	9	P-594, OF-1

Terry Lyons

LYONS, TERENCE HILBERT   BR TR 6'½"   165 lbs.
B. Dec. 14, 1908, New Holland, Ohio   D. Sept. 9, 1959, Dayton, Ohio

	G	AB	H	2B	3B	HR	HR %	R	RBI	BB	SO	SB	BA	SA	AB	H	G by POS
1929 PHI N	1	0	0	0	0	0	–	0	0	0	0	0	–	–	0	0	1B-1

Pop Lytle

LYTLE, EDWARD BENSON (Dad)   BR TR 5'11"   160 lbs.
B. Mar. 10, 1862, Racine, Wis.   D. Dec. 21, 1950, Long Beach, Calif.

	G	AB	H	2B	3B	HR	HR %	R	RBI	BB	SO	SB	BA	SA	AB	H	G by POS
1890 2 teams		CHI N (1G – .000)				PIT N (15G – .145)											
" total	16	59	8	1	0	0	0.0	3	0	8	10	0	.136	.153	0	0	OF-8, 2B-8

Jim Lyttle

LYTTLE, JAMES LAWRENCE   BL TR 6'   180 lbs.
B. May 20, 1946, Hamilton, Ohio

	G	AB	H	2B	3B	HR	HR %	R	RBI	BB	SO	SB	BA	SA	AB	H	G by POS
1969 NY A	28	83	15	4	0	0	0.0	7	4	4	19	1	.181	.229	1	0	OF-28
1970	87	126	39	7	1	3	2.4	20	14	10	26	3	.310	.452	7	3	OF-70
1971	49	86	17	5	0	1	1.2	7	7	8	18	0	.198	.291	15	1	OF-29
1972 CHI A	44	82	19	5	2	0	0.0	8	5	1	28	0	.232	.341	21	6	OF-21
1973 MON N	49	116	30	5	1	4	3.4	12	19	9	14	0	.259	.422	11	2	OF-36
1974	25	9	3	0	0	0	0.0	1	2	1	3	0	.333	.333	6	2	OF-18
1975	44	55	15	4	0	0	0.0	7	6	13	6	0	.273	.345	19	4	OF-16
1976 2 teams		MON N (42G – .271)				LA N (23G – .221)											
" total	65	153	38	7	1	1	0.7	9	13	15	25	0	.248	.327	20	5	OF-47
8 yrs.	391	710	176	37	5	9	1.3	71	70	61	139	4	.248	.352	100	23	OF-265

Harvey MacDonald

MacDONALD, HARVEY FORSYTH   BL TL 5'11"   170 lbs.
B. May 18, 1898, New York, N. Y.   D. Oct. 4, 1965, Philadelphia, Pa.

	G	AB	H	2B	3B	HR	HR %	R	RBI	BB	SO	SB	BA	SA	AB	H	G by POS
1928 PHI N	13	16	4	0	0	0	0.0	0	2	2	3	0	.250	.250	9	4	OF-2

Macey

MACEY,
B. Columbus, Ohio   Deceased.

	G	AB	H	2B	3B	HR	HR %	R	RBI	BB	SO	SB	BA	SA	AB	H	G by POS
1890 PHI AA	1	1	0	0	0	0	0.0	0		0		0	.000	.000	0	0	C-1

Ken Macha

MACHA, KENNETH EDWARD   BR TR 6'2"   215 lbs.
Brother of Mike Macha.
B. Sept. 29, 1950, Monroeville, Pa.

	G	AB	H	2B	3B	HR	HR %	R	RBI	BB	SO	SB	BA	SA	AB	H	G by POS
1974 PIT N	5	5	3	1	0	0	0.0	1	1	0	0	0	.600	.800	5	3	C-1
1977	35	95	26	4	0	0	0.0	2	11	6	17	1	.274	.316	6	0	3B-17, 1B-11, OF-4
1978	29	52	11	1	1	0	0.0	5	5	12	10	2	.212	.269	7	1	3B-21
1979 MON N	25	36	10	3	1	0	0.0	8	4	2	9	0	.278	.417	7	1	3B-13, OF-2, 1B-2, C-1
1980	49	107	31	5	1	1	0.9	10	8	11	17	0	.290	.383	11	2	3B-33, 1B-2, OF-1, C-1
1981 TOR A	37	85	17	2	0	0	0.0	4	6	8	15	1	.200	.224	1	0	3B-19, 1B-16, DH-2, C-1
6 yrs.	180	380	98	16	3	1	0.3	30	35	39	68	4	.258	.324	37	7	3B-103, 1B-31, OF-7, C-4, DH-2

Mike Macha

MACHA, MICHAEL WILLIAM   BR TR 5'11"   180 lbs.
Brother of Ken Macha.
B. Feb. 17, 1954, Victoria, Tex.

	G	AB	H	2B	3B	HR	HR %	R	RBI	BB	SO	SB	BA	SA	AB	H	G by POS
1979 ATL N	6	13	2	0	0	0	0.0	2	1	1	5	0	.154	.154	2	0	3B-3
1980 TOR A	5	8	0	0	0	0	0.0	0	0	0	1	0	.000	.000	2	0	3B-2, C-1
2 yrs.	11	21	2	0	0	0	0.0	2	1	1	6	0	.095	.095	4	0	3B-5, C-1

Dave Machemer

MACHEMER, DAVID RITCHIE   BR TR 5'11½" 180 lbs.
B. May 24, 1951, St. Joseph, Mich.

	G	AB	H	2B	3B	HR	HR %	R	RBI	BB	SO	SB	BA	SA	AB	H	G by POS
1978 CAL A	10	22	6	1	0	1	4.5	6	2	2	1	0	.273	.455	0	0	2B-5, 3B-3, SS-1
1979 DET A	19	26	5	1	0	0	0.0	8	2	3	2	0	.192	.231	0	0	2B-11, DH-1, OF-1
2 yrs.	29	48	11	2	0	1	2.1	14	4	5	3	0	.229	.333	0	0	2B-16, 3B-3, DH-1, OF-1, SS-1

Connie Mack

MACK, CORNELIUS (The Tall Tactician)   BR TR 6'1"   170 lbs.
Born Cornelius McGillicuddy.   Father of Earle Mack.
B. Dec. 22, 1862, E. Brookfield, Mass.   D. Feb. 8, 1956, Philadelphia, Pa.
Manager 1894-96, 1901-50.
Hall of Fame 1937.

	G	AB	H	2B	3B	HR	HR %	R	RBI	BB	SO	SB	BA	SA	AB	H	G by POS
1886 WAS N	10	36	13	2	1	0	0.0	4	5	0	2		.361	.472	0	0	C-10
1887	82	314	63	6	1	0	0.0	35	20	8	17	26	.201	.226	0	0	C-76, OF-5, 2B-2
1888	85	300	56	5	6	3	1.0	49	29	17	18	31	.187	.273	0	0	C-79, OF-4, SS-1, 1B-1
1889	98	386	113	16	1	0	0.0	51	42	15	12	26	.293	.339	0	0	C-45, OF-34, 1B-22
1890 BUF P	123	503	134	15	12	0	0.0	95	53	47	13	16	.266	.344	0	0	C-112, OF-9, 1B-5
1891 PIT N	75	280	60	10	0	0	0.0	43	29	19	11	4	.214	.250	0	0	C-72, 1B-3
1892	97	346	84	9	4	1	0.3	39	31	21	22	11	.243	.301	1	1	C-92, OF-3, 1B-1
1893	37	133	38	3	1	0	0.0	22	15	10	9	4	.286	.323	0	0	C-37
1894	69	228	57	7	1	1	0.4	32	21	20	14	8	.250	.303	0	0	C-69
1895	14	49	15	2	0	0	0.0	12	4	7	1	1	.306	.347	1	0	C-12, 1B-1

	G	AB	H	2B	3B	HR	HR %	R	RBI	BB	SO	SB	BA	SA	Pinch Hit AB	Pinch Hit H	G by POS

Connie Mack continued

	G	AB	H	2B	3B	HR	HR %	R	RBI	BB	SO	SB	BA	SA	PH AB	PH H	G by POS
1896	33	120	26	4	1	0	0.0	9	16	5	8	0	.217	.267	0	0	1B-28, C-5
11 yrs.	723	2695	659	79	28	5	0.2	391	265	169	127	127	.245	.300	2	1	C-609, 1B-61, OF-55, 2B-2, SS-1

Denny Mack

MACK, DENNIS JOSEPH   5'7"   164 lbs.
Born Dennis Joseph McGee.
B. 1851, Easton, Pa.   D. Apr. 10, 1888, Wilkes-Barre, Pa.

	G	AB	H	2B	3B	HR	HR %	R	RBI	BB	SO	SB	BA	SA	PH AB	PH H	G by POS
1876 STL N	48	180	39	5	0	1	0.6	32	7	11	5		.217	.261	0	0	SS-41, 2B-5, OF-2
1880 BUF N	17	59	12	0	0	0	0.0	5	3	5	7		.203	.203	0	0	SS-16, 2B-1
1882 LOU AA	72	264	48	3	1	0	0.0	41		16			.182	.201	0	0	SS-49, 2B-24, OF-5
1883 PIT AA	60	224	44	5	3	0	0.0	26		13			.196	.246	0	0	SS-38, 1B-25, 2B-1
4 yrs.	197	727	143	13	4	1	0.1	104	10	45	12		.197	.230	0	0	SS-144, 2B-31, 1B-25, OF-7

Earle Mack

MACK, EARLE THADDEUS   BL TR   5'8"   140 lbs.
Born Earle Thaddeus McGillicuddy. Son of Connie Mack.
B. Feb. 1, 1890, Philadelphia, Pa.   D. Feb. 5, 1967, Upper Darby Twp., Pa.

	G	AB	H	2B	3B	HR	HR %	R	RBI	BB	SO	SB	BA	SA	PH AB	PH H	G by POS
1910 PHI A	1	4	2	0	1	0	0.0	0	0	0		0	.500	1.000	0	0	C-1
1911	2	4	0	0	0	0	0.0	0	0	0		0	.000	.000	0	0	3B-2
1914	2	8	0	0	0	0	0.0	0	1	0	0	1	.000	.000	0	0	1B-2
3 yrs.	5	16	2	0	1	0	0.0	0	1	0	0	1	.125	.250	0	0	3B-2, 1B-2, C-1

Joe Mack

MACK, JOE JOHN   BB TL   5'11½"   185 lbs.
Also known as Joe John Maciarz.
B. Jan. 4, 1912, Chicago, Ill.

	G	AB	H	2B	3B	HR	HR %	R	RBI	BB	SO	SB	BA	SA	PH AB	PH H	G by POS
1945 BOS N	66	260	60	13	1	3	1.2	30	44	34	39	1	.231	.323	1	0	1B-65

Ray Mack

MACK, RAYMOND JAMES   BR TR   6'   200 lbs.
Born Raymond James Mlckovsky.
B. Aug. 31, 1916, Cleveland, Ohio   D. May 7, 1969, Columbus, Ohio

	G	AB	H	2B	3B	HR	HR %	R	RBI	BB	SO	SB	BA	SA	PH AB	PH H	G by POS
1938 CLE A	2	6	2	0	1	0	0.0	2	2	0	1	0	.333	.667	0	0	2B-2
1939	36	112	17	4	1	1	0.9	12	6	12	19	0	.152	.232	2	0	2B-34, 3B-1
1940	146	530	150	21	5	12	2.3	60	69	51	77	4	.283	.409	0	0	2B-146
1941	145	501	114	22	4	9	1.8	54	44	54	69	8	.228	.341	0	0	2B-145
1942	143	481	108	14	6	2	0.4	43	45	41	51	9	.225	.291	0	0	2B-143
1943	153	545	120	25	2	7	1.3	56	62	47	61	8	.220	.312	0	0	2B-153
1944	83	284	66	15	3	0	0.0	24	29	28	45	4	.232	.306	0	0	2B-83
1946	61	171	35	6	2	1	0.6	13	9	23	27	2	.205	.281	0	0	2B-61
1947 2 teams	NY	A (1G – .000)		CHI	N	(21G –	.218)										
" total	22	78	17	6	0	2	2.6	9	12	5	15	0	.218	.372	0	0	2B-21
9 yrs.	791	2708	629	113	24	34	1.3	273	278	261	365	35	.232	.329	2	0	2B-788, 3B-1

Reddy Mack

MACK, JOSEPH
Born Joseph McNamara.
B. May 2, 1866, Ireland   D. Dec. 30, 1916, Newport, Ky.

	G	AB	H	2B	3B	HR	HR %	R	RBI	BB	SO	SB	BA	SA	PH AB	PH H	G by POS
1885 LOU AA	11	41	10	1	0	0	0.0	7		2			.244	.268	0	0	2B-11
1886	137	483	118	23	11	1	0.2	82		68			.244	.344	0	0	2B-137
1887	128	478	147	23	8	1	0.2	117		83		22	.308	.395	0	0	2B-128
1888	112	446	97	13	5	3	0.7	77	34	52		18	.217	.289	0	0	2B-112
1889 BAL AA	136	519	125	24	7	1	0.2	84	87	60	69	23	.241	.320	0	0	2B-135, OF-1
1890 B-B AA	26	95	27	3	5	0	0.0	14		10		7	.284	.421	0	0	2B-26
6 yrs.	550	2062	524	87	36	6	0.3	381	120	275	69	70	.254	.340	0	0	2B-549, OF-1

Pete Mackanin

MACKANIN, PETER, JR.   BR TR   6'2"   190 lbs.
B. Aug. 1, 1951, Chicago, Ill.

	G	AB	H	2B	3B	HR	HR %	R	RBI	BB	SO	SB	BA	SA	PH AB	PH H	G by POS
1973 TEX A	44	90	9	2	0	0	0.0	3	2	4	26	0	.100	.122	2	0	SS-33, 3B-10
1974	2	6	1	0	1	0	0.0	0	0	0	2	0	.167	.500	1	0	SS-2
1975 MON N	130	448	101	19	6	12	2.7	59	44	31	99	11	.225	.375	4	0	2B-127, SS-1, 3B-1
1976	114	380	85	15	2	8	2.1	36	33	15	66	6	.224	.337	4	1	2B-100, 3B-8, SS-3, OF-1
1977	55	85	19	2	2	1	1.2	9	6	4	17	3	.224	.329	29	7	2B-9, SS-8, 3B-5, OF-4
1978 PHI N	8	8	2	0	0	0	0.0	0	1	0	4	0	.250	.250	4	1	3B-1, 1B-1
1979	13	9	1	0	0	1	11.1	2	2	1	2	0	.111	.444	6	0	SS-2, 3B-2, 2B-2
1980 MIN A	108	319	85	18	0	4	1.3	31	35	14	34	6	.266	.361	15	5	2B-71, SS-30, 1B-4, 3B-3
1981	77	225	52	7	1	4	1.8	21	18	7	40	1	.231	.324	9	2	2B-31, SS-28, 1B-10, DH-6, 3B-4
9 yrs.	548	1570	355	63	12	30	1.9	161	141	76	290	27	.226	.339	74	16	2B-340, SS-107, 3B-34, 1B-15, DH-6, OF-5

Eric MacKenzie

MacKENZIE, ERIC HUGH   BL TR   6'   185 lbs.
B. Aug. 29, 1932, Glendon, Alta., Canada

	G	AB	H	2B	3B	HR	HR %	R	RBI	BB	SO	SB	BA	SA	PH AB	PH H	G by POS
1955 KC A	1	1	0	0	0	0	0.0	0	0	0	0	0	.000	.000	0	0	C-1

Gordon MacKenzie

MacKENZIE, HENRY GORDON   BR TR   5'11"   175 lbs.
B. July 9, 1937, St. Petersburg, Fla.

	G	AB	H	2B	3B	HR	HR %	R	RBI	BB	SO	SB	BA	SA	PH AB	PH H	G by POS
1961 KC A	11	24	3	0	0	0	0.0	1	1	1	6	0	.125	.125	6	1	C-7

Felix Mackiewicz

MACKIEWICZ, FELIX THADDEUS   BR TR   6'2"   195 lbs.
B. Nov. 20, 1917, Chicago, Ill.

	G	AB	H	2B	3B	HR	HR %	R	RBI	BB	SO	SB	BA	SA	PH AB	PH H	G by POS
1941 PHI A	5	14	4	0	1	0	0.0	3	0	1	0	0	.286	.429	1	0	OF-3
1942	6	14	3	2	0	0	0.0	3	2	0	4	0	.214	.357	3	1	OF-3
1943	9	16	1	0	0	0	0.0	1	0	2	8	0	.063	.063	3	0	OF-3
1945 CLE A	120	359	98	14	7	2	0.6	42	37	44	41	5	.273	.368	7	0	OF-112
1946	78	258	67	15	4	0	0.0	35	16	16	32	5	.260	.349	5	1	OF-72

	G	AB	H	2B	3B	HR	HR %	R	RBI	BB	SO	SB	BA	SA	Pinch Hit AB	H	G by POS

Felix Mackiewicz continued

	G	AB	H	2B	3B	HR	HR %	R	RBI	BB	SO	SB	BA	SA	AB	H	G by POS
1947 2 teams	CLE	A	(2G –	.000)		WAS	A	(3G –	.167)								OF-5
" total	5	11	1	1	0	0	0.0	1	0	0	3	0	.091	.182	0	0	OF-5
6 yrs.	223	672	174	32	12	2	0.3	85	55	63	88	10	.259	.351	19	2	OF-198

MACKO, STEVEN JOSEPH
B. Sept. 6, 1954, Burlington, Iowa   D. Nov. 15, 1981, Arlington, Tex.   BL TR 5'10" 160 lbs.

Steve Macko

	G	AB	H	2B	3B	HR	HR %	R	RBI	BB	SO	SB	BA	SA	AB	H	G by POS
1979 CHI N	19	40	9	1	0	0	0.0	2	3	4	8	0	.225	.250	5	0	2B-10, 3B-4
1980	6	20	6	2	0	0	0.0	2	2	0	3	0	.300	.400	0	0	SS-3, 3B-2, 2B-1
2 yrs.	25	60	15	3	0	0	0.0	4	5	4	11	0	.250	.300	5	0	2B-11, 3B-6, SS-3

MACON, MAX CULLEN
B. Oct. 14, 1915, Pensacola, Fla.   BL TL 6'3" 175 lbs.

Max Macon

	G	AB	H	2B	3B	HR	HR %	R	RBI	BB	SO	SB	BA	SA	AB	H	G by POS
1938 STL N	46	36	11	0	0	0	0.0	5	3	2	4	0	.306	.306	2	0	P-38, OF-1
1940 BKN N	2	1	1	0	0	0	0.0	0	0	0	0	0	1.000	1.000	0	0	P-2
1942	26	43	12	2	1	0	0.0	4	1	2	4	1	.279	.372	11	5	P-14
1943	45	55	9	0	0	0	0.0	7	6	0	1	1	.164	.164	13	1	P-25, 1B-3
1944 BOS N	106	366	100	15	3	3	0.8	38	36	12	23	7	.273	.355	10	2	1B-72, OF-22, P-1
1947	1	1	0	0	0	0	0.0	0	0	0	0	0	.000	.000	0	0	P-1
6 yrs.	226	502	133	17	4	3	0.6	54	46	16	32	9	.265	.333	36	8	P-81, 1B-75, OF-23

MacPHEE, WALTER SCOTT
B. Dec. 23, 1899, Brooklyn, N. Y.   D. Jan. 20, 1980, Charlotte, N. C.   BR TR 5'8" 140 lbs.

Waddy MacPhee

	G	AB	H	2B	3B	HR	HR %	R	RBI	BB	SO	SB	BA	SA	AB	H	G by POS
1922 NY N	2	7	2	0	1	0	0.0	2	0	1	0	0	.286	.571	0	0	3B-2

MACULLAR, JAMES F. (Little Mac)
B. Jan. 16, 1855, Boston, Mass.   D. Apr. 8, 1924, Baltimore, Md.   BR TL

Jimmy Macullar

	G	AB	H	2B	3B	HR	HR %	R	RBI	BB	SO	SB	BA	SA	AB	H	G by POS
1879 SYR N	64	246	52	9	0	0	0.0	24	13	3	27		.211	.248	0	0	SS-37, OF-26, 2B-4, 3B-1
1882 CIN AA	79	299	70	6	6	0	0.0	44		14			.234	.294	0	0	OF-79
1883	14	48	8	2	0	0	0.0	4		4			.167	.208	0	0	OF-14, SS-1
1884 BAL AA	106	358	73	16	6	4	1.1	73		35			.204	.316	0	0	SS-107
1885	100	320	61	7	6	3	0.9	52		49			.191	.278	0	1	SS-98, OF-2
1886	85	268	55	7	1	0	0.0	49		49			.205	.239	0	0	SS-82, OF-2, 2B-1, P-1
6 yrs.	448	1539	319	47	19	7	0.5	246	13	154	27		.207	.276	0	0	SS-325, OF-123, 2B-5, 3B-1, P-1

MADDEN,
B. Pittsburgh, Pa.

Madden

	G	AB	H	2B	3B	HR	HR %	R	RBI	BB	SO	SB	BA	SA	AB	H	G by POS
1914 PIT F	2	2	1	0	0	0	0.0	0	1	0		0	.500	.500	1	0	C-1

MADDEN, THOMAS JOSEPH
B. July 31, 1883, Philadelphia, Pa.   D. July 26, 1930, Philadelphia, Pa.   BL TL 5'11" 160 lbs.

Bunny Madden

	G	AB	H	2B	3B	HR	HR %	R	RBI	BB	SO	SB	BA	SA	AB	H	G by POS
1906 BOS N	4	15	4	0	0	0	0.0	1	0	1		0	.267	.267	0	0	OF-4
1910 NY A	1	1	0	0	0	0	0.0	0	0	0		0	.000	.000	1	0	
2 yrs.	5	16	4	0	0	0	0.0	1	0	1		0	.250	.250	1	0	OF-4

MADDEN, EUGENE
B. June 5, 1890, Elm Grove, W. Va.   D. Apr. 6, 1949, Utica, N. Y.   BL TR 5'10" 155 lbs.

Gene Madden

	G	AB	H	2B	3B	HR	HR %	R	RBI	BB	SO	SB	BA	SA	AB	H	G by POS
1916 PIT N	1	1	0	0	0	0	0.0	0	0	0	0	0	.000	.000	1	0	

MADDEN, THOMAS FRANCIS
B. Sept. 14, 1882, Boston, Mass.   D. Jan. 20, 1954, Cambridge, Mass.   BR TR

Tom Madden

	G	AB	H	2B	3B	HR	HR %	R	RBI	BB	SO	SB	BA	SA	AB	H	G by POS
1909 BOS A	10	17	4	0	0	0	0.0	0	1	0		0	.235	.235	3	1	C-7
1910	14	35	13	3	0	0	0.0	4	4	3		0	.371	.457	2	1	C-12
1911 2 teams		BOS	A	(4G –	.200)		PHI	N	(28G –	.276)								C-26
" total	32	91	24	1	1	0	0.0	6	6	2	13	0	.264	.297	1	1	C-26
3 yrs.	56	143	41	4	1	0	0.0	10	11	5	13	0	.287	.329	6	3	C-45

MADDERN, CLARENCE JAMES
B. Sept. 26, 1921, Bisbee, Ariz.   BR TR 6'1" 185 lbs.

Clarence Maddern

	G	AB	H	2B	3B	HR	HR %	R	RBI	BB	SO	SB	BA	SA	AB	H	G by POS
1946 CHI N	3	3	0	0	0	0	0.0	0	0	0	0	0	.000	.000	1	0	OF-2
1948	80	214	54	12	1	4	1.9	16	27	10	25	0	.252	.374	23	5	OF-55
1949	10	9	3	0	0	1	11.1	1	2	2	0	0	.333	.667	7	1	1B-1
1951 CLE A	11	12	2	0	0	0	0.0	0	0	0	1	0	.167	.167	9	1	OF-1
4 yrs.	104	238	59	12	1	5	2.1	17	29	12	26	0	.248	.370	40	7	OF-58, 1B-1

MADDOX, ELLIOTT
B. Dec. 21, 1947, Orange, N. J.   BR TR 5'11" 180 lbs.

Elliott Maddox

	G	AB	H	2B	3B	HR	HR %	R	RBI	BB	SO	SB	BA	SA	AB	H	G by POS
1970 DET A	109	258	64	13	4	3	1.2	30	24	30	42	2	.248	.364	20	2	3B-40, OF-37, SS-19, 2B-1
1971 WAS A	128	258	56	8	2	1	0.4	38	18	51	42	10	.217	.275	19	7	OF-103, 3B-12
1972 TEX A	98	294	74	7	2	0	0.0	40	10	49	53	20	.252	.289	1	0	OF-94
1973	100	172	41	1	0	1	0.6	24	17	29	28	5	.238	.262	3	0	OF-89, 3B-7, DH-1
1974 NY A	137	466	141	26	2	3	0.6	75	45	69	48	6	.303	.386	3	1	OF-135, 2B-2, 3B-1
1975	55	218	67	10	3	1	0.5	36	23	21	24	9	.307	.394	0	0	OF-55, 2B-1
1976	18	46	10	2	0	0	0.0	4	3	4	3	0	.217	.261	2	1	OF-13, DH-2
1977 BAL A	49	107	28	7	0	2	1.9	14	9	13	9	2	.262	.383	2	0	OF-45, 3B-1
1978 NY N	119	389	100	18	2	2	0.5	43	39	71	38	2	.257	.329	7	0	OF-79, 3B-43, 1B-1
1979	86	224	60	13	0	1	0.4	21	12	20	27	3	.268	.339	21	8	OF-65, 3B-11
1980	130	411	101	16	1	4	1.0	35	34	52	44	1	.246	.319	11	2	3B-115, OF-4, 1B-2
11 yrs.	1029	2843	742	121	16	18	0.6	360	234	409	358	60	.261	.334	89	22	OF-719, 3B-230, SS-19, 2B-4, DH-3, 1B-3

LEAGUE CHAMPIONSHIP SERIES

	G	AB	H	2B	3B	HR	HR %	R	RBI	BB	SO	SB	BA	SA	AB	H	G by POS
1976 NY A	3	9	2	1	0	0	0.0	0	1	0	1	0	.222	.333	0	0	OF-3

WORLD SERIES

	G	AB	H	2B	3B	HR	HR %	R	RBI	BB	SO	SB	BA	SA	AB	H	G by POS
1976 NY A	2	5	1	0	1	0	0.0	0	0	1	2	0	.200	.600	0	0	OF-1

	G	AB	H	2B	3B	HR	HR %	R	RBI	BB	SO	SB	BA	SA	Pinch Hit AB	Pinch Hit H	G by POS

Garry Maddox

MADDOX, GARRY LEE
B. Sept. 1, 1949, Cincinnati, Ohio
BR TR 6'3" 175 lbs.

	G	AB	H	2B	3B	HR	HR %	R	RBI	BB	SO	SB	BA	SA	AB	H	G by POS
1972 SF N	125	458	122	26	7	12	2.6	62	58	14	97	13	.266	.432	2	0	OF-121
1973	144	587	187	30	10	11	1.9	81	76	24	73	24	.319	.460	2	1	OF-140
1974	135	538	153	31	3	8	1.5	74	50	29	64	21	.284	.398	6	2	OF-131
1975 2 teams		SF	N (17G –	.135)		PHI	N	(99G –	.291)								
" total	116	426	116	26	8	5	1.2	54	50	42	57	25	.272	.406	5	0	OF-110
1976 PHI N	146	531	175	37	6	6	1.1	75	68	42	59	29	.330	.456	2	0	OF-144
1977	139	571	167	27	10	14	2.5	85	74	24	58	22	.292	.448	2	0	OF-138
1978	155	598	172	34	3	11	1.8	62	68	39	89	33	.288	.410	1	0	OF-154
1979	148	548	154	28	6	13	2.4	70	61	17	71	26	.281	.425	6	1	OF-140
1980	143	549	142	31	3	11	2.0	59	73	18	52	25	.259	.386	1	0	OF-143
1981	94	323	85	7	1	5	1.5	37	40	17	42	9	.263	.337	1	0	OF-94
1982	119	412	117	27	2	8	1.9	39	61	12	32	7	.284	.417	9	2	OF-111
1983	97	324	89	14	2	4	1.2	27	32	17	31	7	.275	.367	11	3	OF-95
1984	77	241	68	11	0	5	2.1	29	19	13	29	3	.282	.390	14	0	OF-69
13 yrs.	1638	6106	1747	329	61	113	1.9	754	730	308	754	244	.286	.415	62	9	OF-1590

DIVISIONAL PLAYOFF SERIES

	G	AB	H	2B	3B	HR	HR %	R	RBI	BB	SO	SB	BA	SA	AB	H	G by POS
1981 PHI N	2	3	1	1	0	0	0.0	0	0	0	0	0	.333	.667	0	0	OF-2

LEAGUE CHAMPIONSHIP SERIES

	G	AB	H	2B	3B	HR	HR %	R	RBI	BB	SO	SB	BA	SA	AB	H	G by POS
1976 PHI N	3	13	3	1	0	0	0.0	2	1	1	0	0	.231	.308	0	0	OF-3
1977	4	7	3	0	0	0	0.0	1	2	0	1	0	.429	.429	0	0	OF-2
1978	4	19	5	0	0	0	0.0	1	2	0	3	0	.263	.263	0	0	OF-4
1980	5	20	6	2	0	0	0.0	2	3	2	2	2	.300	.400	0	0	OF-5
1983	3	11	3	1	0	0	0.0	0	1	0	1	0	.273	.364	0	0	OF-3
5 yrs.	19	70	20	4	0	0	0.0	6	9	3	7	2	.286	.343	0	0	OF-17

WORLD SERIES

	G	AB	H	2B	3B	HR	HR %	R	RBI	BB	SO	SB	BA	SA	AB	H	G by POS
1980 PHI N	6	22	5	2	0	0	0.0	1	1	1	3	0	.227	.318	0	0	OF-6
1983	4	12	3	1	0	1	8.3	1	1	0	2	0	.250	.583	1	0	OF-3
2 yrs.	10	34	8	3	0	1	2.9	2	2	1	5	0	.235	.412	1	0	OF-9

Jerry Maddox

MADDOX, GERALD GLENN
B. July 28, 1953, Whittier, Calif.
BR TR 6'2" 200 lbs.

	G	AB	H	2B	3B	HR	HR %	R	RBI	BB	SO	SB	BA	SA	AB	H	G by POS
1978 ATL N	7	14	3	0	0	0	0.0	1	1	2	0	.214	.214	2	1	3B-5

Art Madison

MADISON, ARTHUR M.
B. Jan. 14, 1872, Clarksburg, Mass.   D. Jan. 27, 1933, North Adams, Mass.
5'9" 165 lbs.

	G	AB	H	2B	3B	HR	HR %	R	RBI	BB	SO	SB	BA	SA	AB	H	G by POS
1895 PHI N	11	34	12	3	0	0	0.0	6	8	1	1	4	.353	.441	0	0	SS-6, 2B-3, 3B-2
1899 PIT N	42	118	32	2	4	0	0.0	20	19	11	1	.271	.356	6	3	2B-19, SS-15, 3B-2
2 yrs.	53	152	44	5	4	0	0.0	26	27	12	1	5	.289	.375	6	3	2B-22, SS-21, 3B-4

Ed Madjeski

MADJESKI, EDWARD WILLIAM
Born Edward William Majewski.
B. July 24, 1909, Far Rockaway, N. Y.
BR TR 5'11" 178 lbs.

	G	AB	H	2B	3B	HR	HR %	R	RBI	BB	SO	SB	BA	SA	AB	H	G by POS
1932 PHI A	17	35	8	0	0	0	0.0	4	3	3	6	0	.229	.229	8	2	C-8
1933	51	142	40	4	0	0	0.0	17	17	4	21	0	.282	.310	12	4	C-41
1934 2 teams		PHI	A (8G –	.375)		CHI	A	(85G –	.221)								
" total	93	289	65	15	2	5	1.7	37	34	14	32	2	.225	.343	11	3	C-80
1937 NY N	5	15	3	0	0	0	0.0	0	2	0	2	0	.200	.200	0	0	C-5
4 yrs.	166	481	116	19	2	5	1.0	58	56	21	61	2	.241	.320	31	9	C-134

Bill Madlock

MADLOCK, BILL JR.
B. Jan. 12, 1951, Memphis, Tenn.
BR TR 5'11" 180 lbs.

	G	AB	H	2B	3B	HR	HR %	R	RBI	BB	SO	SB	BA	SA	AB	H	G by POS
1973 TEX A	21	77	27	5	3	1	1.3	16	5	7	9	3	.351	.532	0	0	3B-21
1974 CHI N	128	453	142	21	5	9	2.0	65	54	42	39	11	.313	.442	8	4	3B-121
1975	130	514	182	29	7	7	1.4	77	64	42	34	9	.354	.479	0	0	3B-128
1976	142	514	174	36	1	15	2.9	68	84	56	27	15	.339	.500	5	1	3B-136
1977 SF N	140	533	161	28	1	12	2.3	70	46	43	33	13	.302	.426	8	1	3B-126, 2B-6
1978	122	447	138	26	3	15	3.4	76	44	48	39	16	.309	.481	8	1	2B-114, 1B-3
1979 2 teams		SF	N (69G –	.261)		PIT	N	(85G –	.328)								
" total	154	560	167	26	5	14	2.5	85	85	52	41	32	.298	.438	5	2	3B-85, 2B-63, 1B-5
1980 PIT N	137	494	137	22	4	10	2.0	62	53	45	33	16	.277	.399	3	1	3B-127, 1B-12
1981	82	279	95	23	1	6	2.2	35	45	34	17	18	.341	.495	4	0	3B-78
1982	154	568	181	33	3	19	3.3	92	95	48	39	18	.319	.488	7	2	3B-146, 1B-3
1983	130	473	153	21	0	12	2.5	68	68	49	24	3	.323	.444	4	1	3B-126
1984	103	403	102	16	0	4	1.0	38	44	26	29	3	.253	.323	3	0	3B-98, 1B-1
12 yrs.	1443	5315	1659	286	33	124	2.3	752	687	492	364	157	.312	.448	55	13	3B-1192, 2B-183, 1B-24

LEAGUE CHAMPIONSHIP SERIES

	G	AB	H	2B	3B	HR	HR %	R	RBI	BB	SO	SB	BA	SA	AB	H	G by POS
1979 PIT N	3	12	3	0	0	1	8.3	1	2	2	0	2	.250	.500	0	0	3B-3

WORLD SERIES

	G	AB	H	2B	3B	HR	HR %	R	RBI	BB	SO	SB	BA	SA	AB	H	G by POS
1979 PIT N	9	24	9	1	0	0	0.0	2	3	5	1	0	.375	.417	0	0	3B-7

Sal Madrid

MADRID, SALVADOR
B. June 19, 1920, El Paso, Tex.   D. Feb. 24, 1977, Fort Wayne, Ind.
BR TR 5'9" 165 lbs.

	G	AB	H	2B	3B	HR	HR %	R	RBI	BB	SO	SB	BA	SA	AB	H	G by POS
1947 CHI N	8	24	3	1	0	0	0.0	0	1	1	6	0	.125	.167	0	0	SS-8

Lee Magee

MAGEE, LEO CHRISTOPHER
Born Leopold Christopher Hoernschemeyer.
B. June 4, 1889, Cincinnati, Ohio   D. Mar. 14, 1966, Columbus, Ohio
Manager 1915.
BB TR 5'11" 165 lbs.

	G	AB	H	2B	3B	HR	HR %	R	RBI	BB	SO	SB	BA	SA	AB	H	G by POS
1911 STL N	26	69	18	1	1	0	0.0	9	8	8	8	4	.261	.304	2	0	2B-18, SS-3
1912	128	458	133	13	8	0	0.0	60	40	39	29	16	.290	.354	8	3	OF-85, 2B-23, 1B-6, SS-1
1913	136	529	140	13	7	2	0.4	53	31	34	30	23	.265	.327	0	0	OF-107, 2B-21, 1B-6, SS-2
1914	162	529	150	23	4	2	0.4	59	40	42	24	36	.284	.353	0	0	OF-102, 1B-40, 2B-6
1915 BKN F	121	452	146	19	10	4	0.9	87	49	22		34	.323	.436	4	0	2B-115, 1B-2

	G	AB	H	2B	3B	HR	HR %	R	RBI	BB	SO	SB	BA	SA	Pinch Hit AB	Pinch Hit H	G by POS

Lee Magee continued

	G	AB	H	2B	3B	HR	HR%	R	RBI	BB	SO	SB	BA	SA	AB	H	G by POS
1916 NY A	131	510	131	18	4	3	0.6	57	45	50	31	29	.257	.325	1	0	OF-128, 2B-2
1917 2 teams	NY	A (51G – .220)				STL	A (36G – .170)										
" total	87	285	57	5	1	0	0.0	28	12	19	24	6	.200	.225	3	1	OF-51, 3B-20, 2B-6, 1B-5
1918 CIN N	119	459	133	22	13	0	0.0	62	28	28	19	19	.290	.394	1	0	2B-114, 3B-3
1919 2 teams	BKN	N (45G – .238)				CHI	N (79G – .292)										
" total	124	448	121	19	6	1	0.2	52	24	23	24	19	.270	.346	7	2	OF-44, 2B-43, 3B-19, SS-13
9 yrs.	1034	3739	1029	133	54	12	0.3	467	277	265	189	186	.275	.349	26	6	OF-517, 2B-348, 1B-59, 3B-42, SS-19

Sherry Magee

MAGEE, SHERWOOD ROBERT
B. Aug. 6, 1884, Clarendon, Pa.   D. Mar. 13, 1929, Philadelphia, Pa.
BR TR 5'11"   179 lbs.

	G	AB	H	2B	3B	HR	HR%	R	RBI	BB	SO	SB	BA	SA	AB	H	G by POS
1904 PHI N	95	364	101	15	12	3	0.8	51	57	14		11	.277	.409	0	0	OF-94, 1B-1
1905	155	603	180	24	17	5	0.8	100	98	44		48	.299	.420	0	0	OF-155
1906	154	563	159	36	8	6	1.1	77	67	52		55	.282	.407	0	0	OF-154
1907	140	503	165	28	12	4	0.8	75	85	53		46	.328	.455	1	0	OF-139
1908	143	508	144	30	16	2	0.4	79	57	49		40	.283	.417	1	0	OF-142
1909	143	522	141	33	14	2	0.4	60	66	43		38	.270	.398	0	0	OF-143
1910	154	519	172	39	17	6	1.2	110	123	94	36	49	.331	.507	0	0	OF-154
1911	121	445	128	32	5	15	3.4	79	94	49	33	22	.288	.483	1	0	OF-120
1912	132	464	142	25	9	6	1.3	79	72	55	54	30	.306	.438	5	2	OF-124, 1B-6
1913	138	470	144	36	6	11	2.3	92	70	38	36	23	.306	.479	3	3	OF-123, 1B-4
1914	146	544	171	39	11	15	2.8	96	103	55	42	25	.314	.509	2	2	OF-67, SS-39, 1B-32, 2B-8
1915 BOS N	156	571	160	34	12	2	0.4	72	87	54	39	15	.280	.392	0	0	OF-134, 1B-22
1916	120	419	101	17	5	3	0.7	44	54	44	52	10	.241	.327	1	0	OF-120, 1B-2, SS-1
1917 2 teams	BOS	N (72G – .256)				CIN	N (45G – .321)										
" total	117	383	107	16	8	1	0.3	41	52	29	30	11	.279	.371	5	1	OF-106, 1B-4
1918 CIN N	115	400	119	15	13	2	0.5	46	76	37	18	14	.298	.415	5	1	1B-66, OF-38, 2B-6
1919	56	163	35	6	1	0	0.0	11	21	26	19	4	.215	.264	6	2	OF-47, 3B-1, 2B-1
16 yrs.	2085	7441	2169	425	166	83	1.1	1112	1182	736	359	441	.291	.427	39	11	OF-1860, 1B-137, SS-40, 2B-15, 3B-1

WORLD SERIES
	G	AB	H	2B	3B	HR	HR%	R	RBI	BB	SO	SB	BA	SA	AB	H	G by POS
1919 CIN N	2	2	1	0	0	0	0.0	0	0	0	0	0	.500	.500	2	1	

Harl Maggert

MAGGERT, HARL VESS
Father of Harl Maggert.
B. Feb. 13, 1883, Cromwell, Ind.   D. Jan. 7, 1963, Fresno, Calif.
BL TR

	G	AB	H	2B	3B	HR	HR%	R	RBI	BB	SO	SB	BA	SA	AB	H	G by POS
1907 PIT N	3	6	0	0	0	0	0.0	1	0	2		1	.000	.000	1	0	OF-2
1912 PHI A	72	242	62	8	6	1	0.4	39	13	36		10	.256	.351	11	3	OF-61
2 yrs.	75	248	62	8	6	1	0.4	40	13	38		11	.250	.343	12	3	OF-63

Harl Maggert

MAGGERT, HARL WARREN
Son of Harl Maggert.
B. May 4, 1914, Los Angeles, Calif.
BR TR 6'   190 lbs.

	G	AB	H	2B	3B	HR	HR%	R	RBI	BB	SO	SB	BA	SA	AB	H	G by POS
1938 BOS N	66	89	25	3	0	3	3.4	12	19	10	20	0	.281	.416	43	10	OF-10, 3B-8

John Magner

MAGNER, JOHN T.
B. Jan. 5, 1844, England   D. July 20, 1923, St. Louis, Mo.

	G	AB	H	2B	3B	HR	HR%	R	RBI	BB	SO	SB	BA	SA	AB	H	G by POS
1879 CIN N	1	4	0	0	0	0	0.0	0		0		1	.000	.000	0	0	OF-1

Stubby Magner

MAGNER, EDMUND BURKE
B. Feb. 20, 1888, Kalamazoo, Mich.   D. Sept. 6, 1956, Chillicothe, Ohio
BR TR 5'3"   135 lbs.

	G	AB	H	2B	3B	HR	HR%	R	RBI	BB	SO	SB	BA	SA	AB	H	G by POS
1911 NY A	13	33	7	0	0	0	0.0	3	4	4		1	.212	.212	0	0	SS-6, 2B-5

George Magoon

MAGOON, GEORGE HENRY (Topsy)
B. Mar. 27, 1875, St. Albans, Me.   D. Dec. 6, 1943, Rochester, N. H.
BR TR 5'9"   165 lbs.

	G	AB	H	2B	3B	HR	HR%	R	RBI	BB	SO	SB	BA	SA	AB	H	G by POS
1898 BKN N	93	343	77	7	0	1	0.3	35	39	30		7	.224	.254	0	0	SS-93
1899 2 teams	BAL	N (62G – .256)				CHI	N (59G – .228)										
" total	121	396	96	13	4	0	0.0	50	52	50		12	.242	.295	0	0	SS-121
1901 CIN N	127	460	116	16	7	1	0.2	47	53	52		15	.252	.324	0	0	SS-112, 2B-15
1902	45	162	44	9	2	0	0.0	29	23	13		7	.272	.352	1	0	2B-41, SS-3
1903 2 teams	CIN	N (42G – .216)				CHI	A (94G – .228)										
" total	136	473	106	17	3	0	0.0	38	34	49		6	.224	.273	1	0	2B-126, 3B-9
5 yrs.	522	1834	439	62	16	2	0.1	199	201	194		47	.239	.294	2	0	SS-329, 2B-182, 3B-9

Freddie Maguire

MAGUIRE, FRED EDWARD
B. May 10, 1899, Roxbury, Mass.   D. Nov. 3, 1961, Brighton, Mass.
BR TR 5'11"   155 lbs.

	G	AB	H	2B	3B	HR	HR%	R	RBI	BB	SO	SB	BA	SA	AB	H	G by POS
1922 NY N	5	12	4	0	0	0	0.0	4	1	0	1	1	.333	.333	1	0	2B-3
1923	41	30	6	1	0	0	0.0	11	2	2	4	1	.200	.233	1	0	2B-16, 3B-1
1928 CHI N	140	574	160	24	7	1	0.2	67	41	25	38	6	.279	.350	2	1	2B-138
1929 BOS N	138	496	125	26	8	0	0.0	54	41	19	40	8	.252	.337	0	0	2B-138, SS-1
1930	146	516	138	21	5	0	0.0	54	52	20	22	4	.267	.328	0	0	2B-146
1931	148	492	112	18	2	0	0.0	36	26	16	26	3	.228	.272	0	0	2B-148
6 yrs.	618	2120	545	90	22	1	0.0	226	163	82	131	23	.257	.322	4	1	2B-589, SS-1, 3B-1

WORLD SERIES
	G	AB	H	2B	3B	HR	HR%	R	RBI	BB	SO	SB	BA	SA	AB	H	G by POS
1923 NY N	2	0	0	0	0	0	–	1	0	0	0	0	–	–	0	0	

Jack Maguire

MAGUIRE, JACK
B. Feb. 5, 1925, St. Louis, Mo.
BR TR 5'11"   165 lbs.

	G	AB	H	2B	3B	HR	HR%	R	RBI	BB	SO	SB	BA	SA	AB	H	G by POS
1950 NY N	29	40	7	2	0	0	0.0	3	3	3	13	0	.175	.225	16	3	OF-9, 1B-2
1951 3 teams	NY	N (16G – .400)			PIT	N (8G – .000)			STL	A (41G – .244)							
" total	65	152	39	3	2	2	1.3	22	18	15	23	1	.257	.342	13	2	OF-34, 3B-6, 2B-3
2 yrs.	94	192	46	5	2	2	1.0	25	21	18	36	1	.240	.318	29	5	OF-43, 3B-6, 2B-3, 1B-2

	G	AB	H	2B	3B	HR	HR %	R	RBI	BB	SO	SB	BA	SA	Pinch Hit AB	Pinch Hit H	G by POS

Jim Maguire

MAGUIRE, JAMES A.
B. Feb. 4, 1875, Dunkirk, N. Y.   D. Jan. 27, 1917, Buffalo, N. Y.   TR

	G	AB	H	2B	3B	HR	HR %	R	RBI	BB	SO	SB	BA	SA	Pinch Hit AB	Pinch Hit H	G by POS
1901 CLE A	18	69	16	2	0	0	0.0	4	3	0		0	.232	.261	0	0	SS-18

Jim Mahady

MAHADY, JAMES BERNARD   BR TR 5'11" 170 lbs.
B. Apr. 22, 1901, Cortland, N. Y.   D. Aug. 9, 1936, Cortland, N. Y.

	G	AB	H	2B	3B	HR	HR %	R	RBI	BB	SO	SB	BA	SA	Pinch Hit AB	Pinch Hit H	G by POS
1921 NY N	1	0	0	0	0	0	–	0	0	0	0	0	–	–	0	0	2B-1

Art Mahan

MAHAN, ARTHUR LEO   BL TL 5'11" 178 lbs.
B. June 8, 1913, Somerville, Mass.

	G	AB	H	2B	3B	HR	HR %	R	RBI	BB	SO	SB	BA	SA	Pinch Hit AB	Pinch Hit H	G by POS
1940 PHI N	146	544	133	24	5	2	0.4	55	39	40	37	4	.244	.318	0	0	1B-145, P-1

Billy Maharg

MAHARG, WILLIAM JOSEPH   BR TR 5'4½"
Also known as William Joseph Graham.
B. Mar. 19, 1881, Philadelphia, Pa.   D. Nov. 20, 1953, Philadelphia, Pa.

	G	AB	H	2B	3B	HR	HR %	R	RBI	BB	SO	SB	BA	SA	Pinch Hit AB	Pinch Hit H	G by POS
1912 DET A	1	1	0	0	0	0	0.0	0	0	0		0	.000	.000	0	0	3B-1
1916 PHI N	1	1	0	0	0	0	0.0	0	0	0	0	0	.000	.000	0	0	OF-1
2 yrs.	2	2	0	0	0	0	0.0	0	0	0	0	0	.000	.000	0	0	OF-1, 3B-1

Frank Maher

MAHER, FRANK   TR
Brother of Tom Maher.
B. Philadelphia, Pa.

	G	AB	H	2B	3B	HR	HR %	R	RBI	BB	SO	SB	BA	SA	Pinch Hit AB	Pinch Hit H	G by POS
1902 PHI N	1	1	0	0	0	0	0.0	0	0	0		0	.000	.000	1	0	

Tom Maher

MAHER, THOMAS FRANCIS
Brother of Frank Maher.
B. July 6, 1870, Philadelphia, Pa.   D. Aug. 25, 1929

	G	AB	H	2B	3B	HR	HR %	R	RBI	BB	SO	SB	BA	SA	Pinch Hit AB	Pinch Hit H	G by POS
1902 PHI N	1	0	0	0	0	0	–	0	0	0		0	–	–	0	0	

Greg Mahlberg

MAHLBERG, GREGORY JAMES   BR TR 5'10" 180 lbs.
B. Aug. 8, 1951, Milwaukee, Wis.

	G	AB	H	2B	3B	HR	HR %	R	RBI	BB	SO	SB	BA	SA	Pinch Hit AB	Pinch Hit H	G by POS
1978 TEX A	1	1	0	0	0	0	0.0	0	0	0	0	0	.000	.000	0	0	C-1
1979	7	17	2	0	0	1	5.9	2	1	2	4	0	.118	.294	0	0	C-7
2 yrs.	8	18	2	0	0	1	5.6	2	1	2	4	0	.111	.278	0	0	C-8

Dan Mahoney

MAHONEY, DANIEL J.   5'9½" 165 lbs.
B. Mar. 20, 1864, Springfield, Mass.   D. Feb. 1, 1904, Springfield, Mass.

	G	AB	H	2B	3B	HR	HR %	R	RBI	BB	SO	SB	BA	SA	Pinch Hit AB	Pinch Hit H	G by POS
1892 CIN N	5	21	4	0	1	0	0.0	1	1	4		0	.190	.286	0	0	C-5
1895 WAS N	6	12	2	0	0	0	0.0	2	1	0	0	0	.167	.167	3	1	C-2, 1B-1
2 yrs.	11	33	6	0	1	0	0.0	3	2	4	0	0	.182	.242	3	1	C-7, 1B-1

Danny Mahoney

MAHONEY, DANIEL JOSEPH   BR TR 5'7" 140 lbs.
B. Sept. 6, 1888, Haverhill, Mass.   D. Sept. 28, 1960, Utica, N. Y.

	G	AB	H	2B	3B	HR	HR %	R	RBI	BB	SO	SB	BA	SA	Pinch Hit AB	Pinch Hit H	G by POS
1911 CIN N	1	0	0	0	0	0	–	0	0	0	0	0	–	–	0	0	

Jim Mahoney

MAHONEY, JAMES THOMAS (Moe)   BR TR 6' 175 lbs.
B. May 26, 1934, Englewood, N. J.

	G	AB	H	2B	3B	HR	HR %	R	RBI	BB	SO	SB	BA	SA	Pinch Hit AB	Pinch Hit H	G by POS
1959 BOS A	31	23	3	0	0	1	4.3	10	4	3	7	0	.130	.261	0	0	SS-30
1961 WAS A	43	108	26	0	1	0	0.0	10	6	5	23	1	.241	.259	1	0	SS-31, 2B-2
1962 CLE A	41	74	18	4	0	3	4.1	12	5	3	14	0	.243	.419	1	0	SS-23, 2B-8, 3B-1
1965 HOU N	5	5	1	0	0	0	0.0	0	0	0	3	0	.200	.200	0	0	SS-5
4 yrs.	120	210	48	4	1	4	1.9	32	15	11	47	1	.229	.314	2	0	SS-89, 2B-10, 3B-1

Mike Mahoney

MAHONEY, GEORGE W.
B. Dec. 5, 1873, Boston, Mass.   D. Jan. 3, 1940, Boston, Mass.

	G	AB	H	2B	3B	HR	HR %	R	RBI	BB	SO	SB	BA	SA	Pinch Hit AB	Pinch Hit H	G by POS
1897 BOS N	2	2	1	0	0	0	0.0	1	1	0		0	.500	.500	0	0	C-1, P-1
1898 STL N	2	7	0	0	0	0	0.0	0	0	0		0	.000	.000	0	0	1B-2
2 yrs.	4	9	1	0	0	0	0.0	1	1	0		0	.111	.111	0	0	1B-2, C-1, P-1

Bob Maier

MAIER, ROBERT PHILLIP   BR TR 5'8" 180 lbs.
B. Sept. 5, 1915, Dunellen, N. J.

	G	AB	H	2B	3B	HR	HR %	R	RBI	BB	SO	SB	BA	SA	Pinch Hit AB	Pinch Hit H	G by POS
1945 DET A	132	486	128	25	7	1	0.2	58	34	37	32	7	.263	.350	2	1	3B-124, OF-5
WORLD SERIES																	
1945 DET A	1	1	1	0	0	0	0.0	0	0	0	0	0	1.000	1.000	1	1	

Emil Mailho

MAILHO, EMIL PIERRE (Lefty)   BL TL 5'10" 165 lbs.
B. Dec. 16, 1909, Berkeley, Calif.

	G	AB	H	2B	3B	HR	HR %	R	RBI	BB	SO	SB	BA	SA	Pinch Hit AB	Pinch Hit H	G by POS
1936 PHI A	21	18	1	0	0	0	0.0	0	0	5	5	3	.056	.056	16	1	OF-1

Fritz Maisel

MAISEL, FREDERICK CHARLES (Flash)   BR TR 5'7½" 170 lbs.
Brother of George Maisel.
B. Dec. 23, 1889, Catonsville, Md.   D. Apr. 22, 1967, Baltimore, Md.

	G	AB	H	2B	3B	HR	HR %	R	RBI	BB	SO	SB	BA	SA	Pinch Hit AB	Pinch Hit H	G by POS
1913 NY A	51	187	48	4	3	0	0.0	33	12	34	20	25	.257	.310	0	0	3B-51
1914	149	548	131	23	9	2	0.4	78	47	76	69	74	.239	.325	0	0	3B-148
1915	135	530	149	16	6	4	0.8	77	46	48	35	51	.281	.357	1	1	3B-134
1916	53	158	36	5	0	0	0.0	18	7	20	18	4	.228	.259	6	1	OF-26, 3B-11, 2B-4
1917	113	404	80	4	4	0	0.0	46	20	36	18	29	.198	.228	5	2	2B-100, 3B-7
1918 STL A	90	284	66	4	2	0	0.0	43	16	46	17	11	.232	.261	5	0	3B-79, OF-1
6 yrs.	591	2111	510	56	24	6	0.3	295	148	260	177	194	.242	.299	17	4	3B-430, 2B-104, OF-27

George Maisel

MAISEL, GEORGE JOHN   BR TR 5'10½" 180 lbs.
Brother of Fritz Maisel.
B. Mar. 12, 1892, Catonsville, Md.   D. Nov. 20, 1968, Baltimore, Md.

	G	AB	H	2B	3B	HR	HR %	R	RBI	BB	SO	SB	BA	SA	Pinch Hit AB	Pinch Hit H	G by POS
1913 STL A	11	18	3	2	0	0	0.0	2	1	1	7	0	.167	.278	5	1	OF-5
1916 DET A	7	5	0	0	0	0	0.0	1	0	0	2	0	.000	.000	0	0	3B-3

	G	AB	H	2B	3B	HR	HR %	R	RBI	BB	SO	SB	BA	SA	Pinch Hit AB	Pinch Hit H	G by POS

George Maisel continued

	G	AB	H	2B	3B	HR	HR%	R	RBI	BB	SO	SB	BA	SA	AB	H	G by POS
1921 CHI N	111	393	122	7	2	0	0.0	54	43	11	13	17	.310	.338	1	1	OF-108
1922	38	84	16	1	1	0	0.0	9	6	8	2	1	.190	.226	5	1	OF-38
4 yrs.	167	500	141	10	3	0	0.0	67	50	20	24	18	.282	.314	11	3	OF-151, 3B-3

Hank Majeski

MAJESKI, HENRY (Heeney)
B. Dec. 13, 1916, Staten Island, N. Y.

BR TR 5'9''   174 lbs.

	G	AB	H	2B	3B	HR	HR%	R	RBI	BB	SO	SB	BA	SA	AB	H	G by POS
1939 BOS N	106	367	100	16	1	7	1.9	35	54	18	30	2	.272	.379	7	2	3B-99
1940	3	3	0	0	0	0	0.0	0	0	0	0	0	.000	.000	3	0	
1941	19	55	8	5	0	0	0.0	5	3	1	13	0	.145	.236	8	1	3B-11
1946 2 teams	NY	A (8G –	.083)		PHI	A (78G –	.250)										3B-74
" total	86	276	67	14	4	1	0.4	26	25	26	16	3	.243	.333	11	0	3B-74
1947 PHI A	141	479	134	26	5	8	1.7	54	72	53	31	1	.280	.405	2	0	3B-134, SS-4, 2B-1
1948	148	590	183	41	4	12	2.0	88	120	48	43	2	.310	.454	0	0	3B-142, SS-8
1949	114	448	124	26	5	9	2.0	62	67	29	23	0	.277	.417	1	0	3B-113
1950 CHI A	122	414	128	18	2	6	1.4	47	46	42	34	1	.309	.406	9	1	3B-112
1951 2 teams	CHI	A (12G –	.257)		PHI	A (89G –	.285)										3B-97
" total	101	358	101	23	4	5	1.4	45	48	36	24	1	.282	.411	5	2	3B-97
1952 2 teams	PHI	A (34G –	.256)		CLE	A (36G –	.296)										3B-45, 2B-3
" total	70	171	46	4	2	2	1.2	21	29	26	17	0	.269	.351	6	3	3B-45, 2B-3
1953 CLE A	50	50	15	1	0	2	4.0	6	12	3	8	0	.300	.440	31	11	2B-10, 3B-7, OF-1
1954	57	121	34	4	0	3	2.5	10	17	7	14	0	.281	.388	26	8	2B-25, 3B-10
1955 2 teams	CLE	A (36G –	.188)		BAL	A (16G –	.171)										3B-17, 2B-9
" total	52	89	16	3	0	2	2.2	5	8	10	7	0	.180	.281	23	1	3B-17, 2B-9
13 yrs.	1069	3421	956	181	27	57	1.7	404	501	299	260	10	.279	.398	149	32	3B-861, 2B-48, SS-12, OF-1

WORLD SERIES

	G	AB	H	2B	3B	HR	HR%	R	RBI	BB	SO	SB	BA	SA	AB	H	G by POS
1954 CLE A	4	6	1	0	0	1	16.7	1	3	0	1	0	.167	.667	2	1	3B-1

Charlie Malay

MALAY, CHARLES FRANCIS
Father of Joe Malay.
B. June 13, 1879, Brooklyn, N. Y.   D. Sept. 18, 1949, Brooklyn, N. Y.

BB TR 5'11½'' 175 lbs.

	G	AB	H	2B	3B	HR	HR%	R	RBI	BB	SO	SB	BA	SA	AB	H	G by POS
1905 BKN N	102	349	88	7	2	1	0.3	33	31	22		13	.252	.292	1	0	2B-75, OF-25, SS-1

Joe Malay

MALAY, JOSEPH CHARLES
Son of Charlie Malay.
B. Oct. 25, 1905, Brooklyn, N. Y.

BL TL 6'   175 lbs.

	G	AB	H	2B	3B	HR	HR%	R	RBI	BB	SO	SB	BA	SA	AB	H	G by POS
1933 NY N	8	24	3	0	0	0	0.0	0	2	0	0	0	.125	.125	0	0	1B-8
1935	1	1	1	0	0	0	0.0	0	0	0	0	0	1.000	1.000	1	1	
2 yrs.	9	25	4	0	0	0	0.0	0	2	0	0	0	.160	.160	1	1	1B-8

Candy Maldonado

MALDONADO, CANDIDO
Also known as Candido Guadarrama.
B. Sept. 5, 1960, Humacao, Puerto Rico

BR TR 6'   185 lbs.

	G	AB	H	2B	3B	HR	HR%	R	RBI	BB	SO	SB	BA	SA	AB	H	G by POS
1981 LA N	11	12	1	0	0	0	0.0	0	0	0	5	0	.083	.083	4	0	OF-9
1982	6	4	0	0	0	0	0.0	0	0	1	2	0	.000	.000	2	0	OF-3
1983	42	62	12	1	1	1	1.6	5	6	5	14	0	.194	.290	9	2	OF-33
1984	116	254	68	14	0	5	2.0	25	28	19	29	0	.268	.382	31	9	OF-102, 3B-4
4 yrs.	175	332	81	15	1	6	1.8	30	34	25	50	0	.244	.349	46	11	OF-147, 3B-4

LEAGUE CHAMPIONSHIP SERIES

	G	AB	H	2B	3B	HR	HR%	R	RBI	BB	SO	SB	BA	SA	AB	H	G by POS
1983 LA N	2	2	0	0	0	0	0.0	0	0	0	1	0	.000	.000	2	0	

Jim Maler

MALER, JAMES MICHAEL
B. Aug. 16, 1958, New York, N. Y.

BR TR 6'4''   230 lbs.

	G	AB	H	2B	3B	HR	HR%	R	RBI	BB	SO	SB	BA	SA	AB	H	G by POS
1981 SEA A	12	23	8	1	0	0	0.0	1	2	2	1	1	.348	.391	7	3	1B-5, DH-2
1982	64	221	50	8	3	4	1.8	18	26	12	35	0	.226	.344	5	1	1B-57, DH-5
1983	26	66	12	1	0	1	1.5	5	3	5	11	0	.182	.242	4	1	1B-19, DH-5
3 yrs.	102	310	70	10	3	5	1.6	24	31	19	47	1	.226	.326	16	5	1B-81, DH-12

Tony Malinosky

MALINOSKY, ANTHONY FRANCIS
B. Oct. 5, 1909, Collinsville, Ill.

BR TR 5'10½'' 165 lbs.

	G	AB	H	2B	3B	HR	HR%	R	RBI	BB	SO	SB	BA	SA	AB	H	G by POS
1937 BKN N	35	79	18	2	0	0	0.0	7	3	9	11	0	.228	.253	9	1	3B-13, SS-11

Bobby Malkmus

MALKMUS, ROBERT EDWARD
B. July 4, 1931, Newark, N. J.

BR TR 5'9''   175 lbs.

	G	AB	H	2B	3B	HR	HR%	R	RBI	BB	SO	SB	BA	SA	AB	H	G by POS
1957 MIL N	13	22	2	0	0	0	0.0	6	0	3	3	0	.091	.182	3	0	2B-7
1958 WAS A	41	70	13	2	1	0	0.0	5	3	4	15	0	.186	.243	11	4	2B-26, 3B-2, SS-1
1959	6	0	0	0	0	0	–	0	0	0	0	0	–	–	0	0	
1960 PHI N	79	133	28	4	1	1	0.8	16	12	11	28	0	.211	.278	5	0	2B-58, SS-34, 3B-25
1961	121	342	79	8	2	7	2.0	39	31	20	43	1	.231	.327	6	0	2B-114, SS-65, 3B-39
1962	8	5	1	1	0	0	0.0	3	0	0	1	0	.200	.400	3	0	SS-1
6 yrs.	268	572	123	15	5	8	1.4	69	46	38	90	3	.215	.301	28	4	2B-114, SS-65, 3B-39

Jerry Mallett

MALLETT, GERALD GORDON
B. Sept. 18, 1935, Bonne Terre, Mo.

BR TR 6'5''   208 lbs.

	G	AB	H	2B	3B	HR	HR%	R	RBI	BB	SO	SB	BA	SA	AB	H	G by POS
1959 BOS A	4	15	4	0	0	0	0.0	1	1	1	3	0	.267	.267	0	0	OF-4

Les Mallon

MALLON, LESLIE CLYDE
B. Nov. 21, 1905, Sweetwater, Tex.   Deceased.

BR TR 5'8''   160 lbs.

	G	AB	H	2B	3B	HR	HR%	R	RBI	BB	SO	SB	BA	SA	AB	H	G by POS
1931 PHI N	122	375	116	19	2	1	0.3	41	45	29	40	0	.309	.379	9	2	2B-97, 1B-5, SS-3, 3B-3
1932	103	347	90	16	0	5	1.4	44	31	28	28	1	.259	.349	9	3	2B-88, 3B-5
1934 BOS N	42	166	49	6	1	0	0.0	23	18	15	12	0	.295	.343	0	0	2B-42
1935	116	412	113	24	2	2	0.5	48	25	28	37	3	.274	.357	5	3	2B-73, 3B-36, OF-1
4 yrs.	383	1300	368	65	5	8	0.6	156	119	100	117	4	.283	.359	23	8	2B-300, 3B-44, 1B-5, SS-3, OF-1

	G	AB	H	2B	3B	HR	HR %	R	RBI	BB	SO	SB	BA	SA	Pinch Hit AB	Pinch Hit H	G by POS

Jule Mallonee

MALLONEE, JULIUS NORRIS   BL TR 6'2" 180 lbs.
B. Apr. 4, 1900, Charlotte, N. C.   D. Dec. 26, 1934, Charlotte, N. C.

	G	AB	H	2B	3B	HR	HR%	R	RBI	BB	SO	SB	BA	SA	PH AB	PH H	G by POS
1925 CHI A	2	3	0	0	0	0	0.0	1	0	1	0	0	.000	.000	1	0	OF-1

Ben Mallonnee

MALLONNEE, HOWARD BENNETT (Lefty)   BL TL 5'6" 150 lbs.
B. Mar. 31, 1894, Baltimore, Md.   D. Feb. 19, 1978, Baltimore, Md.

	G	AB	H	2B	3B	HR	HR%	R	RBI	BB	SO	SB	BA	SA	PH AB	PH H	G by POS
1921 PHI A	6	24	6	1	0	0	0.0	2		1	1	1	.250	.292	0	0	OF-6

Jim Mallory

MALLORY, JAMES BAUGH (Sunny Jim)   BR TR 6'1" 170 lbs.
B. Sept. 1, 1918, Lawrenceville, Va.

	G	AB	H	2B	3B	HR	HR%	R	RBI	BB	SO	SB	BA	SA	PH AB	PH H	G by POS
1940 WAS A	4	12	2	0	0	0	0.0	2	0	1	1	0	.167	.167	0	0	OF-3
1945 2 teams	STL N (13G – .233)				NY N (37G – .298)												
" total	50	137	38	3	0	0	0.0	13	14	6	9	1	.277	.299	11	3	OF-32
2 yrs.	54	149	40	3	0	0	0.0	15	14	7	10	1	.268	.289	11	3	OF-35

Sheldon Mallory

MALLORY, SHELDON   BL TL 6'2" 175 lbs.
B. July 16, 1953, Argo, Ill.

	G	AB	H	2B	3B	HR	HR%	R	RBI	BB	SO	SB	BA	SA	PH AB	PH H	G by POS
1977 OAK A	64	126	27	4	1	0	0.0	19	5	11	18	12	.214	.262	7	2	OF-45, DH-7, 1B-4

Harry Malmberg

MALMBERG, HARRY WILLIAM (Swede)   BR TR 6'1" 170 lbs.
B. July 31, 1926, Fairfield, Ala.   D. Oct. 29, 1976, San Francisco, Calif.

	G	AB	H	2B	3B	HR	HR%	R	RBI	BB	SO	SB	BA	SA	PH AB	PH H	G by POS
1955 DET A	67	208	45	5	2	0	0.0	25	19	29	19	0	.216	.260	0	0	2B-65

Eddie Malone

MALONE, EDWARD RUSSELL   BR TR 5'10" 175 lbs.
B. June 16, 1920, Chicago, Ill.

	G	AB	H	2B	3B	HR	HR%	R	RBI	BB	SO	SB	BA	SA	PH AB	PH H	G by POS
1949 CHI A	55	170	46	7	2	1	0.6	17	16	29	19	2	.271	.353	3	1	C-51
1950	31	71	16	2	0	0	0.0	2	10	10	8	0	.225	.254	10	2	C-21
2 yrs.	86	241	62	9	2	1	0.4	19	26	39	27	2	.257	.324	13	3	C-72

Fergy Malone

MALONE, FERGUSON G.   BL TL 5'8" 156 lbs.
B. 1842, Ireland   D. Jan. 18, 1905, Seattle, Wash.
Manager 1884.

	G	AB	H	2B	3B	HR	HR%	R	RBI	BB	SO	SB	BA	SA	PH AB	PH H	G by POS
1876 PHI N	22	96	22	2	0	0	0.0	14	6	0		1	.229	.250	0	0	C-20, OF-3, SS-1
1884 PHI U	1	4	1	0	0	0	0.0	0		0			.250	.250	0	0	C-1
2 yrs.	23	100	23	2	0	0	0.0	14	6	0		1	.230	.250	0	0	C-21, OF-3, SS-1

Lew Malone

MALONE, LEWIS ALOYSIUS   BR TR 5'11" 175 lbs.
Played as Lew Ryan Part of 1915.
B. Mar. 13, 1897, Baltimore, Md.   D. Feb. 17, 1973, Brooklyn, N. Y.

	G	AB	H	2B	3B	HR	HR%	R	RBI	BB	SO	SB	BA	SA	PH AB	PH H	G by POS
1915 PHI A	76	201	41	4	4	1	0.5	17	17	21	40	7	.204	.279	12	3	2B-43, 3B-12, OF-4, SS-2
1916	5	4	0	0	0	0	0.0	1	0	1	2	0	.000	.000	3	0	SS-1
1917 BKN N	1	0	0	0	0	0	–	1	0	0	0	0	–	–	1	0	
1919	51	162	33	7	3	0	0.0	9	11	6	18	1	.204	.284	0	0	3B-47, SS-2, 2B-2
4 yrs.	133	367	74	11	7	1	0.3	28	28	28	60	8	.202	.278	16	3	3B-59, 2B-45, SS-5, OF-4

Billy Maloney

MALONEY, WILLIAM ALPHONSE   BL TR 5'10" 177 lbs.
B. June 5, 1878, Lewiston, Me.   D. Sept. 2, 1960, Breckenridge, Tex.

	G	AB	H	2B	3B	HR	HR%	R	RBI	BB	SO	SB	BA	SA	PH AB	PH H	G by POS
1901 MIL A	86	290	85	3	4	0	0.0	42	22	7		11	.293	.331	5	2	C-72, OF-8
1902 2 teams	STL A (30G – .205)				CIN N (27G – .247)												
" total	57	201	45	7	0	1	0.5	21	18	8		8	.224	.274	3	0	OF-41, C-14
1905 CHI N	145	558	145	17	14	2	0.4	78	56	43		59	.260	.351	0	0	OF-145
1906 BKN N	151	566	125	15	7	0	0.0	71	32	49		38	.221	.272	0	0	OF-151
1907	144	502	115	7	10	0	0.0	51	32	31		25	.229	.283	0	0	OF-144
1908	113	359	70	5	7	3	0.8	31	17	24		14	.195	.273	6	1	OF-103, C-4
6 yrs.	696	2476	585	54	42	6	0.2	294	177	162		155	.236	.299	14	3	OF-592, C-90

John Maloney

MALONEY, JOHN   D. July 21, 1890

	G	AB	H	2B	3B	HR	HR%	R	RBI	BB	SO	SB	BA	SA	PH AB	PH H	G by POS
1876 NY N	2	7	2	0	1	0	0.0	2		0			.286	.571	0	0	OF-2
1877 HAR N	1	4	1	0	0	0	0.0	0	0	0	0	0	.250	.250	0	0	OF-1
2 yrs.	3	11	3	0	1	0	0.0	2		0		1	.273	.455	0	0	OF-3

Pat Maloney

MALONEY, PATRICK WILLIAM   BR TR 6' 150 lbs.
B. Jan. 19, 1888, Grosvenordale, Conn.   D. June 27, 1979, Pawtucket, R. I.

	G	AB	H	2B	3B	HR	HR%	R	RBI	BB	SO	SB	BA	SA	PH AB	PH H	G by POS
1912 NY A	22	79	17	1	0	0	0.0	9	4		3		.215	.228	0	0	OF-20

Frank Malzone

MALZONE, FRANK JAMES   BR TR 5'10" 180 lbs.
B. Feb. 28, 1930, Bronx, N. Y.

	G	AB	H	2B	3B	HR	HR%	R	RBI	BB	SO	SB	BA	SA	PH AB	PH H	G by POS
1955 BOS A	6	20	7	1	0	0	0.0	2	1	1	3	0	.350	.400	1	0	3B-4
1956	27	103	17	3	1	2	1.9	15	11	9	8	1	.165	.272	0	0	3B-26
1957	153	634	185	31	5	15	2.4	82	103	31	41	2	.292	.427	0	0	3B-153
1958	155	627	185	30	2	15	2.4	76	87	33	53	1	.295	.421	0	0	3B-155
1959	154	604	169	34	2	19	3.1	90	92	42	58	6	.280	.437	0	0	3B-154
1960	152	595	161	30	2	14	2.4	60	79	36	42	2	.271	.398	1	0	3B-151
1961	151	590	157	21	4	14	2.4	74	87	44	49	1	.266	.386	2	0	3B-149
1962	156	619	175	20	3	21	3.4	74	95	35	43	0	.283	.426	0	0	3B-156
1963	151	580	169	25	2	15	2.6	66	71	31	45	0	.291	.419	3	0	3B-148
1964	148	537	142	19	0	13	2.4	62	56	37	43	0	.264	.372	5	1	3B-143
1965	106	364	87	20	0	3	0.8	40	34	28	38	1	.239	.319	16	3	3B-96
1966 CAL A	82	155	32	5	0	2	1.3	6	12	10	11	0	.206	.277	43	10	3B-35
12 yrs.	1441	5428	1486	239	21	133	2.5	647	728	337	434	14	.274	.399	71	14	3B-1370

Frank Mancuso

MANCUSO, FRANK OCTAVIUS   BR TR 6' 195 lbs.
Brother of Gus Mancuso.
B. May 23, 1918, Houston, Tex.

	G	AB	H	2B	3B	HR	HR%	R	RBI	BB	SO	SB	BA	SA	PH AB	PH H	G by POS
1944 STL A	88	244	50	11	0	1	0.4	19	24	20	32	1	.205	.262	1	0	C-87

	G	AB	H	2B	3B	HR	HR %	R	RBI	BB	SO	SB	BA	SA	Pinch Hit AB	Pinch Hit H	G by POS

Frank Mancuso continued

	G	AB	H	2B	3B	HR	HR %	R	RBI	BB	SO	SB	BA	SA	PH AB	PH H	G by POS
1945	119	365	98	13	3	1	0.3	39	38	46	44	0	.268	.329	3	0	C-115
1946	87	262	63	8	3	3	1.1	22	23	30	31	1	.240	.328	1	0	C-85
1947 WAS A	43	131	30	5	1	0	0.0	5	13	5	11	0	.229	.282	7	2	C-35
4 yrs.	337	1002	241	37	7	5	0.5	85	98	101	118	2	.241	.306	12	2	C-322

WORLD SERIES

	G	AB	H	2B	3B	HR	HR %	R	RBI	BB	SO	SB	BA	SA	PH AB	PH H	G by POS
1944 STL A	2	3	2	0	0	0	0.0	0	1	0	0	0	.667	.667	1	1	C-1

Gus Mancuso

MANCUSO, AUGUST RODNEY (Blackie)   BR TR 5'10" 185 lbs.
Brother of Frank Mancuso.
B. Dec. 5, 1905, Galveston, Tex.   D. Oct. 26, 1984, Houston, Tex.

	G	AB	H	2B	3B	HR	HR %	R	RBI	BB	SO	SB	BA	SA	PH AB	PH H	G by POS
1928 STL N	11	38	7	0	1	0	0.0	2	3	0	5	0	.184	.237	0	0	C-11
1930	76	227	83	17	2	7	3.1	39	59	18	16	1	.366	.551	12	3	C-61
1931	67	187	49	16	1	1	0.5	13	23	18	13	2	.262	.374	10	1	C-56
1932	103	310	88	23	1	5	1.6	25	43	30	15	0	.284	.413	19	6	C-82
1933 NY N	144	481	127	17	2	6	1.2	39	56	48	21	0	.264	.345	2	1	C-142
1934	122	383	94	14	0	7	1.8	32	46	27	19	0	.245	.337	0	0	C-122
1935	128	447	133	18	2	5	1.1	33	56	30	16	1	.298	.380	2	0	C-126
1936	139	519	156	21	3	9	1.7	55	63	39	28	0	.301	.405	1	0	C-138
1937	86	287	80	17	1	4	1.4	30	39	17	20	1	.279	.387	5	0	C-81
1938	52	158	55	8	0	2	1.3	19	15	17	13	0	.348	.437	8	2	C-44
1939 CHI N	80	251	58	10	0	2	0.8	17	17	24	19	0	.231	.295	3	0	C-76
1940 BKN N	60	144	33	8	0	0	0.0	16	16	13	7	0	.229	.285	4	1	C-56
1941 STL N	106	328	75	13	1	2	0.6	25	37	37	19	0	.229	.293	1	0	C-105
1942 2 teams	STL N (5G – .077)			NY N (39G – .193)													
" total	44	122	22	1	1	0	0.0	4	9	14	7	1	.180	.205	3	0	C-41
1943 NY N	94	252	50	5	0	2	0.8	11	20	28	16	0	.198	.242	15	3	C-77
1944	78	195	49	4	1	1	0.5	15	25	30	20	0	.251	.297	4	2	C-72
1945 PHI N	70	176	35	5	0	0	0.0	11	16	28	10	2	.199	.227	0	0	C-70
17 yrs.	1460	4505	1194	197	16	53	1.2	386	543	418	264	8	.265	.351	89	19	C-1360

WORLD SERIES

	G	AB	H	2B	3B	HR	HR %	R	RBI	BB	SO	SB	BA	SA	PH AB	PH H	G by POS
1930 STL N	2	7	2	0	0	0	0.0	1	0	1	2	0	.286	.286	0	0	C-2
1931	2	1	0	0	0	0	0.0	0	0	0	0	0	.000	.000	1	0	C-1
1933 NY N	5	17	2	1	0	0	0.0	2	2	3	0	0	.118	.176	0	0	C-5
1936	6	19	5	2	0	0	0.0	3	1	3	3	0	.263	.368	0	0	C-6
1937	3	8	0	0	0	0	0.0	0	1	0	1	0	.000	.000	1	0	C-2
5 yrs.	18	52	9	3	0	0	0.0	6	4	7	6	0	.173	.231	2	0	C-16

Carl Manda

MANDA, CARL ALAN   BR TR 5'10" 170 lbs.
B. Nov. 16, 1886, Little River, Kans.   D. Mar. 9, 1983, Artesia, N. M.

	G	AB	H	2B	3B	HR	HR %	R	RBI	BB	SO	SB	BA	SA	PH AB	PH H	G by POS
1914 CHI A	9	15	4	0	0	0	0.0	2	1	3	3	1	.267	.267	0	0	2B-7

Jim Mangan

MANGAN, JAMES DANIEL   BR TR 5'10" 190 lbs.
B. Sept. 24, 1929, San Francisco, Calif.

	G	AB	H	2B	3B	HR	HR %	R	RBI	BB	SO	SB	BA	SA	PH AB	PH H	G by POS
1952 PIT N	11	13	2	0	0	0	0.0	1	2	1	3	0	.154	.154	7	0	C-4
1954	14	26	5	0	0	0	0.0	2	2	4	9	0	.192	.192	7	1	C-7
1956 NY N	20	20	2	0	0	0	0.0	2	1	4	6	0	.100	.100	3	1	C-15
3 yrs.	45	59	9	0	0	0	0.0	5	5	9	18	0	.153	.153	17	2	C-26

Angel Mangual

MANGUAL, ANGEL LUIS   BR TR 5'10" 178 lbs.
Brother of Pepe Mangual.
B. Mar. 19, 1947, Juana Diaz, Puerto Rico

	G	AB	H	2B	3B	HR	HR %	R	RBI	BB	SO	SB	BA	SA	PH AB	PH H	G by POS
1969 PIT N	6	4	1	1	0	0	0.0	1	0	0	0	0	.250	.500	3	1	OF-3
1971 OAK A	94	287	82	8	1	4	1.4	32	30	17	27	1	.286	.362	14	2	OF-81
1972	91	272	67	13	2	5	1.8	19	32	14	48	0	.246	.364	16	6	OF-74
1973	74	192	43	4	1	3	1.6	20	13	8	34	1	.224	.302	13	0	OF-50, 1B-2, 2B-1
1974	115	365	85	14	4	9	2.5	37	43	17	59	3	.233	.367	11	3	OF-74, DH-37, 3B-1
1975	62	109	24	3	0	1	0.9	13	6	3	18	0	.220	.275	17	4	OF-39, DH-15
1976	8	12	2	1	0	0	0.0	0	1	0	1	0	.167	.250	1	0	OF-7
7 yrs.	450	1241	304	44	8	22	1.8	122	125	59	187	5	.245	.346	75	16	OF-328, DH-52, 1B-2, 3B-1, 2B-1

LEAGUE CHAMPIONSHIP SERIES

	G	AB	H	2B	3B	HR	HR %	R	RBI	BB	SO	SB	BA	SA	PH AB	PH H	G by POS
1971 OAK A	3	12	2	1	1	0	0.0	1	2	0	1	0	.167	.417	0	0	OF-3
1972	3	3	0	0	0	0	0.0	0	0	0	1	0	.000	.000	3	0	
1973	3	9	1	0	0	0	0.0	1	0	0	3	0	.111	.111	1	0	OF-3
1974	1	4	1	0	0	0	0.0	0	0	0	0	0	.250	.250	0	0	DH-1
4 yrs.	10	28	4	1	1	0	0.0	2	2	0	5	0	.143	.250	4	0	OF-6, DH-1

WORLD SERIES

	G	AB	H	2B	3B	HR	HR %	R	RBI	BB	SO	SB	BA	SA	PH AB	PH H	G by POS
1972 OAK A	4	10	3	0	0	0	0.0	1	1	0	0	0	.300	.300	2	1	OF-2
1973	5	6	0	0	0	0	0.0	0	0	0	3	0	.000	.000	5	0	OF-1
1974	1	1	0	0	0	0	0.0	0	0	0	1	0	.000	.000	1	0	
3 yrs.	10	17	3	0	0	0	0.0	1	1	0	4	0	.176	.176	3rd	8	1	OF-3

Pepe Mangual

MANGUAL, JOSE MANUEL   BR TR 5'10" 157 lbs.
Brother of Angel Mangual.
B. May 23, 1952, Ponce, Puerto Rico

	G	AB	H	2B	3B	HR	HR %	R	RBI	BB	SO	SB	BA	SA	PH AB	PH H	G by POS
1972 MON N	8	11	3	0	0	0	0.0	2	0	1	5	0	.273	.273	1	0	OF-3
1973	33	62	11	2	1	3	4.8	9	7	6	18	2	.177	.387	7	1	OF-22
1974	23	61	19	3	0	0	0.0	10	4	5	15	5	.311	.361	2	1	OF-22
1975	140	514	126	16	2	9	1.8	84	45	74	115	33	.245	.337	6	3	OF-138
1976 2 teams	MON N (66G – .260)			NY N (41G – .186)													
" total	107	317	75	14	3	4	1.3	49	25	60	81	24	.237	.338	4	0	OF-100
1977 NY N	8	7	1	0	0	0	0.0	1	2	1	4	0	.143	.143	0	0	OF-4
6 yrs.	319	972	235	35	6	16	1.6	155	83	147	238	64	.242	.340	20	5	OF-289

	G	AB	H	2B	3B	HR	HR %	R	RBI	BB	SO	SB	BA	SA	Pinch Hit AB	Pinch Hit H	G by POS

George Mangus

MANGUS, GEORGE GRAHAM   BL TR 5'11½" 165 lbs.
B. May 22, 1890, Red Creek, N. Y.   D. Aug. 10, 1933, Rutland, Mass.

	G	AB	H	2B	3B	HR	HR %	R	RBI	BB	SO	SB	BA	SA	AB	H	G by POS
1912 PHI N	10	25	5	3	0	0	0.0	2	3	1	6	0	.200	.320	4	0	OF-5

Clyde Manion

MANION, CLYDE JENNINGS (Pete)   BR TR 5'11" 175 lbs.
B. Oct. 30, 1896, Jefferson City, Mo.   D. Sept. 4, 1967, Detroit, Mich.

	G	AB	H	2B	3B	HR	HR %	R	RBI	BB	SO	SB	BA	SA	AB	H	G by POS
1920 DET A	32	80	22	4	1	0	0.0	4	8	4	7	0	.275	.350	2	1	C-30
1921	12	18	2	0	0	0	0.0	0	2	2	2	0	.111	.111	6	1	C-4
1922	42	69	19	4	1	0	0.0	9	12	4	6	0	.275	.362	13	4	C-21, 1B-1
1923	23	22	3	0	0	0	0.0	0	2	2	2	0	.136	.136	17	2	C-3, 1B-1
1924	14	13	3	0	0	0	0.0	1	2	1	1	0	.231	.231	9	3	C-3, 1B-1
1926	75	176	35	4	0	0	0.0	15	14	24	16	1	.199	.222	1	0	C-74
1927	1	0	0	0	0	0	–	0	0	1	0	0	–	–	1	0	C
1928 STL A	76	243	55	5	1	2	0.8	25	31	15	18	3	.226	.280	5	2	C-71
1929	35	111	27	2	0	0	0.0	16	11	15	3	1	.243	.261	1	0	C-34
1930	57	148	32	1	0	1	0.7	12	11	24	17	0	.216	.243	1	0	C-56
1932 CIN N	49	135	28	4	0	0	0.0	7	12	14	16	0	.207	.237	1	0	C-47
1933	36	84	14	1	0	0	0.0	3	3	8	7	0	.167	.179	2	0	C-34
1934	25	54	10	0	0	0	0.0	4	4	4	7	0	.185	.185	1	0	C-24
13 yrs.	477	1153	250	25	3	3	0.3	96	112	118	102	5	.217	.252	60	13	C-401, 1B-3

Phil Mankowski

MANKOWSKI, PHILLIP ANTHONY   BL TR 6' 180 lbs.
B. Jan. 9, 1953, Buffalo, N. Y.

	G	AB	H	2B	3B	HR	HR %	R	RBI	BB	SO	SB	BA	SA	AB	H	G by POS
1976 DET A	24	85	23	2	1	1	1.2	9	4	4	8	0	.271	.353	1	0	3B-23
1977	94	286	79	7	3	3	1.0	21	27	16	41	1	.276	.353	10	3	3B-85, 2B-1
1978	88	222	61	8	0	4	1.8	28	20	22	28	2	.275	.365	9	2	3B-80, DH-1
1979	42	99	22	4	0	0	0.0	11	8	10	16	0	.222	.263	9	1	3B-36, DH-1
1980 NY N	8	12	2	1	0	0	0.0	1	1	2	4	0	.167	.250	4	0	3B-3
1982	13	35	8	1	0	0	0.0	2	4	1	6	0	.229	.257	0	0	3B-13
6 yrs.	269	739	195	23	4	8	1.1	72	64	55	103	3	.264	.338	33	6	3B-240, DH-2, 2B-1

Charlie Manlove

MANLOVE, CHARLES HALE   TR 5'9" 165 lbs.
B. Oct. 8, 1862, Philadelphia, Pa.   D. Feb. 12, 1952, Altoona, Pa.

	G	AB	H	2B	3B	HR	HR %	R	RBI	BB	SO	SB	BA	SA	AB	H	G by POS
1884 2 teams		ALT U (2G – .429)			NY	N (3G – .000)											
" total	5	17	3	0	0	0	0.0	1		0	4		.176	.176	0	0	C-4, OF-2

Ben Mann

MANN, BEN GARTH (Red)   BR TR 6' 155 lbs.
B. Nov. 16, 1915, Brandon, Tex.

	G	AB	H	2B	3B	HR	HR %	R	RBI	BB	SO	SB	BA	SA	AB	H	G by POS
1944 CHI N	1	0	0	0	0	0	–	1	0	0	0	0	–	–	0	0	

Fred Mann

MANN, FRED J.   BL 5'10½" 178 lbs.
B. Apr. 1, 1858, Sutton, Vt.   D. Apr. 16, 1916, Springfield, Mass.

	G	AB	H	2B	3B	HR	HR %	R	RBI	BB	SO	SB	BA	SA	AB	H	G by POS
1882 2 teams		WOR N (19G – .234)			PHI	AA (29G – .231)											
" total	48	198	46	12	4	0	0.0	25		6	15		.232	.333	0	0	3B-47, 1B-1
1883 COL AA	96	394	98	18	13	1	0.3	61		18			.249	.368	0	0	OF-82, 1B-9, 3B-6, SS-1
1884	99	366	101	12	18	7	1.9	70		25			.276	.464	0	0	OF-97, 2B-2
1885 PIT AA	99	391	99	17	6	0	0.0	60		31			.253	.327	0	0	OF-97, 3B-3
1886	116	440	110	16	14	2	0.5	85		45			.250	.364	0	0	OF-116
1887 2 teams		CLE AA (64G – .309)			PHI	AA (55G – .275)											
" total	119	488	143	29	13	2	0.4	87		38		41	.293	.418	0	0	OF-119
6 yrs.	577	2277	597	104	68	12	0.5	388		163	15	41	.262	.383	0	0	OF-511, 3B-56, 1B-10, 2B-2, SS-1

Johnny Mann

MANN, JOHN LEO   BR TR 5'11" 160 lbs.
B. Feb. 4, 1898, Fontanet, Ind.   D. Mar. 31, 1977, Terre Haute, Ind.

	G	AB	H	2B	3B	HR	HR %	R	RBI	BB	SO	SB	BA	SA	AB	H	G by POS
1928 CHI A	6	6	2	0	0	0	0.0	0	1	1	0	0	.333	.333	6	2	3B-2

Les Mann

MANN, LESLIE   BR TR 5'9" 172 lbs.
B. Nov. 18, 1893, Lincoln, Neb.   D. Jan. 14, 1962, Pasadena, Calif.

	G	AB	H	2B	3B	HR	HR %	R	RBI	BB	SO	SB	BA	SA	AB	H	G by POS
1913 BOS N	120	407	103	24	7	3	0.7	54	51	18	73	7	.253	.369	0	0	OF-120
1914	126	389	96	16	11	4	1.0	44	40	24	50	9	.247	.375	3	0	OF-123
1915 CHI F	135	470	144	12	19	4	0.9	74	59	36		18	.306	.438	4	2	OF-130, SS-1
1916 CHI N	127	415	113	13	9	2	0.5	46	29	19	31	11	.272	.361	9	1	OF-115
1917	117	444	121	19	10	1	0.2	63	44	27	44	14	.273	.367	1	0	OF-116
1918	129	489	141	27	7	2	0.4	69	55	38	45	21	.288	.384	0	0	OF-129
1919 2 teams		CHI N (80G – .227)			BOS	N (40G – .283)											
" total	120	444	109	14	12	4	0.9	46	42	20	43	19	.245	.358	1	0	OF-118
1920 BOS N	110	424	117	7	8	3	0.7	48	32	38	42	7	.276	.351	3	0	OF-110
1921 STL N	97	256	84	12	7	7	2.7	57	30	23	28	5	.328	.512	5	1	OF-79
1922	84	147	51	14	1	2	1.4	42	20	16	12	0	.347	.497	2	0	OF-57
1923 2 teams		STL N (38G – .371)			CIN	N (8G – .000)											
" total	46	90	33	5	2	5	5.6	21	11	9	5	0	.367	.633	1	0	OF-26
1924 BOS N	32	102	28	7	4	0	0.0	13	10	8	10	1	.275	.422	1	0	OF-28
1925	60	184	63	11	4	2	1.1	27	20	5	11	6	.342	.478	2	1	OF-57
1926	50	129	39	8	2	1	0.8	23	20	9	9	5	.302	.419	3	0	OF-46
1927 2 teams		BOS N (29G – .258)			NY	N (29G – .328)											
" total	58	133	39	7	2	2	1.5	21	16	16	10	4	.293	.421	5	1	OF-46
1928 NY N	82	193	51	7	1	2	1.0	29	25	18	9	2	.264	.342	1	0	OF-68
16 yrs.	1493	4716	1332	203	106	44	0.9	677	503	324	424	129	.282	.398	43	7	OF-1368, SS-1
WORLD SERIES																	
1914 BOS N	3	7	2	0	0	0	0.0	0	1	0	1	0	.286	.286	1	0	OF-2
1918 CHI N	6	22	5	2	0	0	0.0	0	2	0	0	0	.227	.318	0	0	OF-6
2 yrs.	9	29	7	2	0	0	0.0	1	3	0	1	0	.241	.310	1	0	OF-8

	G	AB	H	2B	3B	HR	HR %	R	RBI	BB	SO	SB	BA	SA	Pinch Hit AB	H	G by POS

Jack Manning

MANNING, JOHN E.
B. Dec. 20, 1853, Braintree, Mass.   D. Aug. 15, 1929, Boston, Mass.
BR TR 5'8½" 158 lbs.

	G	AB	H	2B	3B	HR	HR %	R	RBI	BB	SO	SB	BA	SA	AB	H	G by POS
1876 BOS N	70	288	76	13	0	2	0.7	52	25	7	5		.264	.330	0	0	OF-56, P-34, SS-1, 2B-1
1877 CIN N	57	252	80	16	7	0	0.0	47	36	5	6		.317	.437	0	0	SS-26, 1B-17, OF-12, P-10, 2B-2
1878 BOS N	60	248	63	10	1	0	0.0	41	23	10	16		.254	.302	0	0	OF-59, P-3
1880 CIN N	48	190	41	6	3	2	1.1	20	17	7	15		.216	.311	0	0	OF-47, 1B-1
1881 BUF N	1	1	0	0	0	0	0.0	0	0	0	0		.000	.000	0	0	OF-1
1883 PHI N	98	420	112	31	5	0	0.0	60		20	37		.267	.364	0	0	OF-98
1884	104	424	115	29	4	5	1.2	71		40	67		.271	.394	0	0	OF-104
1885	107	445	114	24	4	3	0.7	61		37	27		.256	.348	0	0	OF-107
1886 BAL AA	137	556	124	18	7	1	0.2	78		50			.223	.286	0	0	OF-137
9 yrs.	682	2824	725	147	31	13	0.5	430	101	176	173		.257	.345	0	0	OF-621, P-47, SS-27, 1B-18, 2B-3

Jimmy Manning

MANNING, JAMES H.
B. Jan. 31, 1862, Fall River, Mass.   D. Oct. 22, 1929, Edinburg, Tex.
Manager 1901.
TR   157 lbs.

	G	AB	H	2B	3B	HR	HR %	R	RBI	BB	SO	SB	BA	SA	AB	H	G by POS
1884 BOS N	89	345	83	8	6	2	0.6	52		19	47		.241	.316	0	0	OF-73, SS-9, 2B-9, 3B-3
1885 2 teams		BOS	N (84G – .206)					DET	N (20G – .269)								
" total	104	384	84	12	9	3	0.8	49	36	23	46		.219	.320	0	0	OF-83, SS-21
1886 DET N	26	97	18	2	3	0	0.0	14	7	6	10		.186	.268	0	0	OF-26, SS-1
1887	13	52	10	1	0	0	0.0	5	3	5	4	3	.192	.212	0	0	OF-10, SS-3
1889 KC AA	132	506	103	16	7	3	0.6	68	68	54	61	58	.204	.281	0	0	OF-69, 2B-63, SS-1, 3B-1
5 yrs.	364	1384	298	39	25	8	0.6	188	113	107	168	61	.215	.297	0	0	OF-261, 2B-72, SS-35, 3B-4

Rick Manning

MANNING, RICHARD EUGENE
B. Sept. 2, 1954, Niagara Falls, N. Y.
BL TR 6'1" 180 lbs.

	G	AB	H	2B	3B	HR	HR %	R	RBI	BB	SO	SB	BA	SA	AB	H	G by POS
1975 CLE A	120	480	137	16	5	3	0.6	69	35	44	62	19	.285	.358	1	0	OF-118, DH-1
1976	138	552	161	24	7	6	1.1	73	43	41	75	16	.292	.393	2	1	OF-136
1977	68	252	57	7	3	5	2.0	33	18	21	35	9	.226	.337	0	0	OF-68
1978	148	566	149	27	3	3	0.5	65	50	38	62	12	.263	.337	7	2	OF-144
1979	144	560	145	12	2	3	0.5	67	51	55	48	30	.259	.304	3	1	OF-141, DH-1
1980	140	471	110	17	4	3	0.6	55	52	63	66	12	.234	.306	0	0	OF-139
1981	103	360	88	15	3	4	1.1	47	33	40	57	25	.244	.336	0	0	OF-103
1982	152	562	152	18	2	8	1.4	71	44	54	60	12	.270	.352	0	0	OF-152
1983 2 teams		CLE	A (50G – .278)					MIL	A (108G – .229)								
" total	158	569	140	20	4	4	0.7	60	43	38	62	18	.246	.316	0	0	OF-158
1984 MIL A	119	341	85	10	5	7	2.1	53	31	34	32	5	.249	.370	11	3	OF-114, DH-1
10 yrs.	1290	4713	1224	166	38	46	1.0	593	400	428	559	158	.260	.340	24	7	OF-1273, DH-3

Tim Manning

MANNING, TIMOTHY E.
B. Aug. 3, 1853, Henley, England   D. June 11, 1934, Oak Park, Ill.
BR TR 5'10" 170 lbs.

	G	AB	H	2B	3B	HR	HR %	R	RBI	BB	SO	SB	BA	SA	AB	H	G by POS
1882 PRO N	21	76	8	0	0	0	0.0	7		5	13		.105	.105	0	0	SS-17, C-4
1883 BAL AA	35	121	26	5	0	0	0.0	23		14			.215	.256	0	0	2B-35
1884	91	341	70	14	5	2	0.6	49		26			.205	.293	0	0	2B-91
1885 2 teams		BAL	AA (43G – .204)					PRO	N (10G – .057)								
" total	53	192	34	9	1	0	0.0	20		11	11		.177	.234	0	0	2B-41, SS-10, 3B-3
4 yrs.	200	730	138	28	6	2	0.3	99		56	24		.189	.252	0	0	2B-167, SS-27, C-4, 3B-3

Don Manno

MANNO, DONALD D.
B. May 15, 1915, Williamsport, Pa.
BR TR 6'1" 190 lbs.

	G	AB	H	2B	3B	HR	HR %	R	RBI	BB	SO	SB	BA	SA	AB	H	G by POS
1940 BOS N	3	7	2	0	0	1	14.3	1	4	0	2	0	.286	.714	1	0	OF-2
1941	22	30	5	1	0	0	0.0	2	4	3	7	0	.167	.200	13	2	OF-5, 3B-3, 1B-1
2 yrs.	25	37	7	1	0	1	2.7	3	8	3	9	0	.189	.297	14	2	OF-7, 3B-3, 1B-1

Fred Manrique

MANRIQUE, FRED ELOY
B. Nov. 5, 1961, Bolivar, Venezuela
BR TR 6'1" 175 lbs.

	G	AB	H	2B	3B	HR	HR %	R	RBI	BB	SO	SB	BA	SA	AB	H	G by POS
1981 TOR A	14	28	4	0	0	0	0.0	1	1	0	12	0	.143	.143	2	1	SS-11, 3B-2, DH-1
1984	10	9	3	0	0	0	0.0	0	1	0	1	0	.333	.333	1	0	2B-9, DH-1
2 yrs.	24	37	7	0	0	0	0.0	1	2	0	13	0	.189	.189	3	1	SS-11, 2B-9, DH-2, 3B-2

John Mansell

MANSELL, JOHN
Brother of Tom Mansell.   Brother of Mike Mansell.
B. 1861, Auburn, N. Y.   D. Feb. 20, 1925, Willard, N. Y.
BL

	G	AB	H	2B	3B	HR	HR %	R	RBI	BB	SO	SB	BA	SA	AB	H	G by POS
1882 PHI AA	31	126	30	3	1	0	0.0	17		4			.238	.278	0	0	OF-31

Mike Mansell

MANSELL, MICHAEL R.
Brother of John Mansell.   Brother of Tom Mansell.
B. Jan. 15, 1858, Auburn, N. Y.   D. Dec. 4, 1902, Auburn, N. Y.
BL

	G	AB	H	2B	3B	HR	HR %	R	RBI	BB	SO	SB	BA	SA	AB	H	G by POS
1879 SYR N	67	242	52	4	2	1	0.4	24	13	5	45		.215	.260	0	0	OF-67
1880 CIN N	53	187	36	6	2	2	1.1	22	12	4	37		.193	.278	0	0	OF-53
1882 PIT AA	79	347	96	18	16	2	0.6	59		7			.277	.438	0	0	OF-79
1883	96	412	106	12	13	3	0.7	90		25			.257	.371	0	0	OF-96
1884 3 teams		PIT	AA (27G – .140)					PHI	AA (20G – .200)			RIC	AA (29G – .301)				
" total	76	283	62	3	9	1	0.4	42		20			.219	.304	0	0	OF-76, 1B-1
5 yrs.	371	1471	352	43	42	9	0.6	237	25	61	82		.239	.344	0	0	OF-371, 1B-1

Tom Mansell

MANSELL, THOMAS E.
Brother of Mike Mansell.   Brother of John Mansell.
B. Jan. 1, 1855, Auburn, N. Y.   D. Oct. 6, 1934, Auburn, N. Y.
BL 5'8" 160 lbs.

	G	AB	H	2B	3B	HR	HR %	R	RBI	BB	SO	SB	BA	SA	AB	H	G by POS
1879 2 teams		TRO	N (40G – .243)					SYR	N (1G – .250)								
" total	41	181	44	6	0	0	0.0	29	11	3	9		.243	.276	0	0	OF-41
1883 2 teams		DET	N (34G – .221)					STL	AA (28G – .402)								
" total	62	243	74	12	2	0	0.0	45		15	13		.305	.370	0	0	OF-62, P-1

	G	AB	H	2B	3B	HR	HR %	R	RBI	BB	SO	SB	BA	SA	Pinch Hit AB	H	G by POS

Tom Mansell continued

	G	AB	H	2B	3B	HR	HR%	R	RBI	BB	SO	SB	BA	SA	AB	H	G by POS
1884 2 teams	CIN AA (65G – .248)				COL AA (23G – .195)												
" total	88	343	81	5	9	0	0.0	58		21			.236	.303	0	0	OF-88, 3B-1
3 yrs.	191	767	199	23	11	0	0.0	132	11	39	22		.259	.318	0	0	OF-191, 3B-1, P-1

Felix Mantilla

MANTILLA, FELIX LAMELA
B. July 29, 1934, Isabela, Puerto Rico

BR TR 6' 160 lbs.

	G	AB	H	2B	3B	HR	HR%	R	RBI	BB	SO	SB	BA	SA	AB	H	G by POS
1956 MIL N	35	53	15	1	1	0	0.0	9	3	1	8	0	.283	.340	5	2	SS-15, 3B-3
1957	71	182	43	9	1	4	2.2	28	21	14	34	2	.236	.363	7	0	SS-35, 2B-13, 3B-7, OF-1
1958	85	226	50	5	1	7	3.1	37	19	20	20	2	.221	.345	7	1	OF-43, 2B-21, SS-5, 3B-2
1959	103	251	54	5	0	3	1.2	26	19	16	31	6	.215	.271	4	0	2B-60, SS-23, 3B-9, OF-7
1960	63	148	38	7	0	3	2.0	21	11	7	16	3	.257	.365	7	2	2B-26, SS-25, OF-8
1961	45	93	20	3	0	1	1.1	13	5	10	16	1	.215	.280	5	0	SS-19, OF-10, 2B-10, 3B-6
1962 NY N	141	466	128	17	4	11	2.4	54	59	37	51	3	.275	.399	17	3	3B-95, SS-25, 2B-14
1963 BOS A	66	178	56	8	0	6	3.4	27	15	20	14	2	.315	.461	16	2	SS-27, OF-11, 2B-5
1964	133	425	123	20	1	30	7.1	69	64	41	46	0	.289	.553	25	6	OF-48, 2B-45, 3B-7, SS-6
1965	150	534	147	17	2	18	3.4	60	92	79	84	7	.275	.416	1	1	2B-123, OF-27, 1B-2
1966 HOU N	77	151	33	5	0	6	4.0	16	22	11	32	1	.219	.371	38	10	3B-14, 1B-14, 2B-9, OF-1
11 yrs.	969	2707	707	97	10	89	3.3	360	330	256	352	27	.261	.403	132	27	2B-326, SS-180, OF-156, 3B-143, 1B-16
WORLD SERIES																	
1957 MIL N	4	10	0	0	0	0	0.0	1	0	1	0	0	.000	.000	0	0	2B-3
1958	4	0	0	0	0	0	–	0	0	0	0	0	–	–	0	0	
2 yrs.	8	10	0	0	0	0	0.0	1	0	1	0	0	.000	.000	0	0	2B-3

Mickey Mantle

MANTLE, MICKEY CHARLES (The Commerce Comet)
B. Oct. 20, 1931, Spavinaw, Okla.
Hall of Fame 1974.

BB TR 5'11½" 195 lbs.

	G	AB	H	2B	3B	HR	HR%	R	RBI	BB	SO	SB	BA	SA	AB	H	G by POS
1951 NY A	96	341	91	11	5	13	3.8	61	65	43	74	8	.267	.443	8	1	OF-86
1952	142	549	171	37	7	23	4.2	94	87	75	111	4	.311	.530	1	0	OF-141, 3B-1
1953	127	461	136	24	3	21	4.6	105	92	79	90	8	.295	.497	8	4	OF-121, SS-1
1954	146	543	163	17	12	27	5.0	129	102	102	107	5	.300	.525	1	0	OF-144, SS-4, 2B-1
1955	147	517	158	25	11	37	7.2	121	99	113	97	8	.306	.611	3	1	OF-145, SS-2
1956	150	533	188	22	5	52	9.8	132	130	112	99	10	.353	.705	4	1	OF-144
1957	144	474	173	28	6	34	7.2	121	94	146	75	16	.365	.665	4	1	OF-139
1958	150	519	158	21	1	42	8.1	127	97	129	120	18	.304	.592	0	0	OF-150
1959	144	541	154	23	4	31	5.7	104	75	94	126	21	.285	.514	0	0	OF-143
1960	153	527	145	17	6	40	7.6	119	94	111	125	14	.275	.558	2	0	OF-150
1961	153	514	163	16	6	54	10.5	132	128	126	112	12	.317	.687	2	0	OF-150
1962	123	377	121	15	1	30	8.0	96	89	122	78	9	.321	.605	6	1	OF-117
1963	65	172	54	8	0	15	8.7	40	35	40	32	2	.314	.622	10	3	OF-52
1964	143	465	141	25	2	35	7.5	92	111	99	102	6	.303	.591	11	2	OF-132
1965	122	361	92	12	1	19	5.3	44	46	73	76	4	.255	.452	14	0	OF-108
1966	108	333	96	12	1	23	6.9	40	56	57	76	1	.288	.538	11	2	OF-97
1967	144	440	108	17	0	22	5.0	63	55	107	113	1	.245	.434	12	5	1B-131
1968	144	435	103	14	1	18	4.1	57	54	106	97	6	.237	.398	9	4	1B-131
18 yrs.	2401	8102	2415	344	72	536	6.6	1677	1509	1734	1710	153	.298	.557	106	25	OF-2019, 1B-262, SS-7, 3B-1, 2B-1
							6th	7th		5th	6th						
WORLD SERIES																	
1951 NY A	2	5	1	0	0	0	0.0	1	0	2	1	0	.200	.200	0	0	OF-2
1952	7	29	10	1	1	2	6.9	5	3	3	4	0	.345	.655	0	0	OF-7
1953	6	24	5	0	0	2	8.3	3	7	3	8	0	.208	.458	0	0	OF-6
1955	3	10	2	0	0	1	10.0	1	1	0	2	0	.200	.500	1	0	OF-2
1956	7	24	6	1	0	3	12.5	6	4	6	5	1	.250	.667	0	0	OF-7
1957	6	19	5	0	0	1	5.3	3	2	3	1	0	.263	.421	0	0	OF-5
1958	7	24	6	0	1	2	8.3	4	3	7	4	0	.250	.583	0	0	OF-7
1960	7	25	10	1	0	3	12.0	8	11	8	9	0	.400	.800	0	0	OF-7
1961	2	6	1	0	0	0	0.0	0	0	0	2	0	.167	.167	0	0	OF-2
1962	7	25	3	1	0	0	0.0	2	0	4	5	2	.120	.160	0	0	OF-7
1963	4	15	2	0	0	1	6.7	1	1	1	5	0	.133	.333	0	0	OF-4
1964	7	24	8	2	0	3	12.5	8	8	6	8	0	.333	.792	0	0	OF-7
12 yrs.	65	230	59	6	2	18	7.8	42	40	43	54	3	.257	.535	1	0	OF-63
	2nd	2nd	2nd			1st	8th	1st	1st	1st	1st						

Chuck Manuel

MANUEL, CHARLES FUQUA
B. Jan. 4, 1944, North Fork, W. Va.

BL TR 6'4" 195 lbs.

	G	AB	H	2B	3B	HR	HR%	R	RBI	BB	SO	SB	BA	SA	AB	H	G by POS
1969 MIN A	83	164	34	6	0	2	1.2	14	24	28	33	1	.207	.280	37	3	OF-46
1970	59	64	12	0	0	1	1.6	4	7	6	17	0	.188	.234	43	9	OF-11
1971	18	16	2	1	0	0	0.0	1	1	1	8	0	.125	.188	16	2	OF-1
1972	63	122	25	5	0	1	0.8	6	8	4	16	0	.205	.270	33	7	OF-28
1974 LA N	4	3	1	0	0	0	0.0	0	1	1	0	0	.333	.333	3	1	
1975	15	15	2	0	0	0	0.0	0	2	0	3	0	.133	.133	15	2	
6 yrs.	242	384	76	12	0	4	1.0	25	43	40	77	1	.198	.260	147	24	OF-86
LEAGUE CHAMPIONSHIP SERIES																	
1969 MIN A	1	0	0	0	0	0	–	0	0	1	0	0	–	–	0	0	
1970	1	1	0	0	0	0	0.0	0	0	0	1	0	.000	.000	0	0	
2 yrs.	2	1	0	0	0	0	0.0	0	0	1	1	0	.000	.000	1	0	

Jerry Manuel

MANUEL, JERRY
B. Dec. 23, 1953, Hahira, Ga.

BB TR 6' 158 lbs.

	G	AB	H	2B	3B	HR	HR%	R	RBI	BB	SO	SB	BA	SA	AB	H	G by POS
1975 DET A	6	18	1	0	0	0	0.0	0	0	0	4	0	.056	.056	0	0	2B-6
1976	54	43	6	1	0	0	0.0	4	2	3	9	1	.140	.163	0	0	2B-47, SS-4, DH-1
1980 MON N	7	6	0	0	0	0	0.0	0	0	0	2	0	.000	.000	0	0	SS-7
1981	27	55	11	5	0	3	5.5	10	10	6	11	0	.200	.455	0	0	2B-23, SS-2

	G	AB	H	2B	3B	HR	HR %	R	RBI	BB	SO	SB	BA	SA	Pinch Hit AB	Pinch Hit H	G by POS

Jerry Manuel continued

	G	AB	H	2B	3B	HR	HR %	R	RBI	BB	SO	SB	BA	SA	AB	H	G by POS
1982 SD N	2	5	1	0	1	0	0.0	0	1	1	0	0	.200	.600	0	0	SS-1, 3B-1, 2B-1
5 yrs.	96	127	19	6	1	3	2.4	14	13	10	26	1	.150	.283	0	0	2B-77, SS-14, DH-1, 3B-1

DIVISIONAL PLAYOFF SERIES

	G	AB	H	2B	3B	HR	HR %	R	RBI	BB	SO	SB	BA	SA	AB	H	G by POS
1981 MON N	5	14	1	0	0	0	0.0	0	0	2	5	0	.071	.071	0	0	2B-5

LEAGUE CHAMPIONSHIP SERIES

	G	AB	H	2B	3B	HR	HR %	R	RBI	BB	SO	SB	BA	SA	AB	H	G by POS
1981 MON N	1	0	0	0	0	0	—	0	0	0	0	0	—	—	0	0	

Frank Manush

MANUSH, FRANK BENJAMIN
Brother of Heinie Manush.
B. Sept. 18, 1883, Tuscumbia, Ala.   D. Jan. 5, 1965, Laguna Beach, Calif.

BR   TR   5'10½"   175 lbs.

	G	AB	H	2B	3B	HR	HR %	R	RBI	BB	SO	SB	BA	SA	AB	H	G by POS
1908 PHI A	23	77	12	2	1	0	0.0	6	0	2	2		.156	.208	1	0	3B-20, 2B-2

Heinie Manush

MANUSH, HENRY EMMETT
Brother of Frank Manush.
B. July 20, 1901, Tuscumbia, Ala.   D. May 12, 1971, Sarasota, Fla.
Hall of Fame 1964.

BL   TL   6'1"   200 lbs.

	G	AB	H	2B	3B	HR	HR %	R	RBI	BB	SO	SB	BA	SA	AB	H	G by POS
1923 DET A	109	308	103	20	5	4	1.3	59	54	20	21	3	.334	.471	27	6	OF-79
1924	120	422	122	24	8	9	2.1	83	68	27	30	14	.289	.448	11	1	OF-106, 1B-1
1925	99	277	84	14	3	5	1.8	46	47	24	21	8	.303	.430	22	6	OF-73
1926	136	498	188	35	8	14	2.8	95	86	31	28	11	.378	.564	14	5	OF-120
1927	152	593	177	31	18	6	1.0	102	80	47	29	12	.298	.442	1	1	OF-150
1928 STL A	154	638	241	47	20	13	2.0	104	108	39	14	17	.378	.575	0	0	OF-154
1929	142	574	204	45	10	6	1.0	85	81	43	24	9	.355	.500	1	0	OF-141
1930 2 teams		STL	A (49G – .328)			WAS	A (88G – .362)										
" total	137	554	194	49	12	9	1.6	100	94	31	24	7	.350	.531	3	0	OF-134
1931 WAS A	146	616	189	41	11	6	1.0	110	70	36	27	3	.307	.438	3	0	OF-143
1932	149	625	214	41	14	14	2.2	121	116	36	29	7	.342	.520	3	1	OF-146
1933	153	658	221	32	17	5	0.8	115	95	36	18	6	.336	.459	3	2	OF-150
1934	137	556	194	42	11	11	2.0	88	89	36	23	7	.349	.523	7	1	OF-131
1935	119	479	131	26	9	4	0.8	68	56	35	17	2	.273	.390	7	1	OF-111
1936 BOS A	82	313	91	15	5	0	0.0	43	45	17	11	1	.291	.371	9	4	OF-72
1937 BKN N	132	466	155	25	7	4	0.9	57	73	40	24	6	.333	.442	9	3	OF-123
1938 2 teams		BKN	N (17G – .235)			PIT	N (15G – .308)										
" total	32	64	16	4	2	0	0.0	11	10	7	4	1	.250	.375	18	5	OF-12
1939 PIT N	10	12	0	0	0	0	0.0	0	1	1	1	0	.000	.000	8	0	OF-1
17 yrs.	2009	7653	2524	491	160	110	1.4	1287	1173	506	345	114	.330	.479	146	36	OF-1846, 1B-1

WORLD SERIES

	G	AB	H	2B	3B	HR	HR %	R	RBI	BB	SO	SB	BA	SA	AB	H	G by POS
1933 WAS A	5	18	2	0	0	0	0.0	2	0	2	1	0	.111	.111	0	0	OF-5

Cliff Mapes

MAPES, CLIFF FRANKLIN (Tiger)
B. Mar. 13, 1922, Sutherland, Neb.

BL   TR   6'3"   205 lbs.

	G	AB	H	2B	3B	HR	HR %	R	RBI	BB	SO	SB	BA	SA	AB	H	G by POS
1948 NY A	53	88	22	11	1	1	1.1	19	12	6	13	1	.250	.432	26	4	OF-21
1949	111	304	75	13	3	7	2.3	56	38	58	50	6	.247	.378	4	0	OF-108
1950	108	356	88	14	6	12	3.4	60	61	47	61	1	.247	.421	6	2	OF-102
1951 2 teams		NY	A (45G – .216)			STL	A (56G – .274)										
" total	101	252	66	10	3	9	3.6	38	38	30	47	0	.262	.433	13	5	OF-87
1952 DET A	86	193	38	7	0	9	4.7	26	23	27	42	0	.197	.373	23	6	OF-62
5 yrs.	459	1193	289	55	13	38	3.2	199	172	168	213	8	.242	.406	72	17	OF-380

WORLD SERIES

	G	AB	H	2B	3B	HR	HR %	R	RBI	BB	SO	SB	BA	SA	AB	H	G by POS
1949 NY A	4	10	1	1	0	0	0.0	3	2	2	4	0	.100	.200	0	0	OF-4
1950	1	4	0	0	0	0	0.0	0	0	0	1	0	.000	.000	0	0	OF-1
2 yrs.	5	14	1	1	0	0	0.0	3	2	2	5	0	.071	.143	0	0	OF-5

Howard Maple

MAPLE, HOWARD ALBERT
B. July 20, 1903, Adrian, Mo.   D. Nov. 9, 1970, Portland, Ore.

BL   TR   5'8½"   175 lbs.

	G	AB	H	2B	3B	HR	HR %	R	RBI	BB	SO	SB	BA	SA	AB	H	G by POS
1932 WAS A	44	41	10	0	1	0	0.0	6	7	7	7	0	.244	.293	2	0	C-41

George Mappis

MAPPIS, GEORGE RICHARD (Dick)
B. Dec. 25, 1865, St. Louis, Mo.   D. Feb. 20, 1934, St. Louis, Mo.

	G	AB	H	2B	3B	HR	HR %	R	RBI	BB	SO	SB	BA	SA	AB	H	G by POS
1885 BAL AA	6	19	4	0	1	0	0.0	2		1		5	.211	.316	0	0	2B-6
1886 STL N	6	14	2	0	0	0	0.0	1	0	1		5	.143	.143	0	0	C-3, 3B-2, 2B-1
2 yrs.	12	33	6	0	1	0	0.0	3		2		5	.182	.242	0	0	2B-7, C-3, 3B-2

Rabbit Maranville

MARANVILLE, WALTER JAMES VINCENT
B. Nov. 11, 1891, Springfield, Mass.   D. Jan. 5, 1954, New York, N. Y.
Manager 1925.
Hall of Fame 1954.

BR   TR   5'5"   155 lbs.

	G	AB	H	2B	3B	HR	HR %	R	RBI	BB	SO	SB	BA	SA	AB	H	G by POS
1912 BOS N	26	86	18	2	0	0	0.0	8	8	9	14	1	.209	.233	0	0	SS-26
1913	143	571	141	13	8	2	0.4	68	48	68	62	25	.247	.308	0	0	SS-143
1914	156	586	144	23	6	4	0.7	74	78	45	56	28	.246	.326	0	0	SS-156
1915	149	509	124	23	6	2	0.4	51	43	45	65	18	.244	.324	0	0	SS-149
1916	155	604	142	16	13	4	0.7	79	38	50	69	32	.235	.325	0	0	SS-155
1917	142	561	146	19	13	3	0.5	69	43	40	47	27	.260	.357	0	0	SS-142
1918	11	38	12	0	1	0	0.0	3	3	4	0	0	.316	.368	0	0	SS-11
1919	131	480	128	18	10	5	1.0	44	43	36	23	12	.267	.377	0	0	SS-131
1920	134	493	131	19	15	1	0.2	48	43	28	24	14	.266	.371	1	0	SS-133
1921 PIT N	153	612	180	25	12	1	0.2	90	70	47	38	25	.294	.379	0	0	SS-153
1922	155	672	198	26	15	0	0.0	115	63	61	43	24	.295	.378	0	0	SS-138, 2B-18
1923	141	581	161	19	9	1	0.2	78	41	42	34	14	.277	.346	0	0	SS-141
1924	152	594	158	33	20	2	0.3	62	71	35	53	18	.266	.399	0	0	2B-152
1925 CHI N	75	266	62	10	3	0	0.0	37	23	29	20	6	.233	.293	1	0	SS-74
1926 BKN N	78	234	55	8	5	0	0.0	32	24	26	24	7	.235	.312	0	0	SS-60, 2B-18
1927 STL N	9	29	7	1	0	0	0.0	0	0	2	0	0	.241	.276	0	0	SS-9

	G	AB	H	2B	3B	HR	HR %	R	RBI	BB	SO	SB	BA	SA	Pinch Hit AB	Pinch Hit H	G by POS

Rabbit Maranville continued

	G	AB	H	2B	3B	HR	HR%	R	RBI	BB	SO	SB	BA	SA	AB	H	G by POS
1928	112	366	88	14	10	1	0.3	40	34	36	27	3	.240	.342	0	0	SS-112, 2B-2
1929 BOS N	146	560	159	26	10	0	0.0	87	55	47	33	13	.284	.366	0	0	SS-146, 2B-1
1930	142	558	157	26	8	2	0.4	85	43	48	23	9	.281	.367	0	0	SS-138, 3B-4
1931	145	562	146	22	5	0	0.0	69	33	56	34	9	.260	.317	1	0	SS-137, 2B-11
1932	149	571	134	20	4	0	0.0	67	37	46	28	4	.235	.284	0	0	2B-149
1933	143	478	104	15	4	0	0.0	46	38	36	34	2	.218	.266	1	1	2B-142
1935	23	67	10	2	0	0	0.0	3	5	3	3	0	.149	.179	3	0	2B-20
23 yrs.	2670	10078	2605	380	177	28	0.3	1255	884	839	756	291	.258	.340	7	1	SS-2154, 2B-513, 3B-4
WORLD SERIES																	
1914 BOS N	4	13	4	0	0	0	0.0	1	3	1	1	2	.308	.308	0	0	SS-4
1928 STL N	4	13	4	1	0	0	0.0	2	0	1	1	1	.308	.385	0	0	SS-4
2 yrs.	8	26	8	1	0	0	0.0	3	3	2	2	3	.308	.346	0	0	SS-8

Johnny Marcum

MARCUM, JOHN ALFRED (Footsie)
B. Sept. 9, 1908, Campbellsburg, Ky. D. Sept. 10, 1984, Louisville, Ky.　BL TR 5'11" 197 lbs.

	G	AB	H	2B	3B	HR	HR%	R	RBI	BB	SO	SB	BA	SA	AB	H	G by POS
1933 PHI A	5	12	2	0	0	0	0.0	2	0	2	1	0	.167	.167	0	0	P-4
1934	58	112	30	4	0	1	0.9	10	13	3	5	0	.268	.330	20	3	P-37
1935	64	119	37	2	1	2	1.7	13	17	9	5	0	.311	.395	23	7	P-39
1936 BOS A	48	88	18	3	0	2	2.3	6	7	3	5	0	.205	.307	18	0	P-31
1937	51	86	23	8	0	0	0.0	12	13	7	4	0	.267	.360	13	2	P-37
1938	19	37	5	0	0	0	0.0	3	3	6	9	0	.135	.135	3	0	P-15
1939 2 teams	STL	A (16G –	.455)		CHI	A (38G –	.281)										
" total	54	79	26	1	0	0	0.0	10	17	6	3	0	.329	.342	22	5	P-31
7 yrs.	299	533	141	18	1	5	0.9	56	70	36	32	0	.265	.330	99	17	P-194

Marty Marion

MARION, MARTIN WHITFORD (Slats, The Octopus)　BR TR 6'2" 170 lbs.
Brother of Red Marion.
B. Dec. 1, 1917, Richburg, S. C.
Manager 1951-56.

	G	AB	H	2B	3B	HR	HR%	R	RBI	BB	SO	SB	BA	SA	AB	H	G by POS
1940 STL N	125	435	121	18	1	3	0.7	44	46	21	34	9	.278	.345	0	0	SS-125
1941	155	547	138	22	3	3	0.5	50	58	42	48	8	.252	.320	0	0	SS-155
1942	147	485	134	38	5	0	0.0	66	54	48	50	8	.276	.375	0	0	SS-147
1943	129	418	117	15	3	1	0.2	38	52	32	37	1	.280	.337	1	0	SS-128
1944	144	506	135	26	2	6	1.2	50	63	43	50	1	.267	.362	0	0	SS-144
1945	123	430	119	27	5	1	0.2	63	59	39	39	2	.277	.370	0	0	SS-122
1946	146	498	116	29	4	3	0.6	51	46	59	53	1	.233	.325	1	0	SS-145
1947	149	540	147	19	6	4	0.7	57	74	49	58	3	.272	.352	0	0	SS-149
1948	144	567	143	26	4	4	0.7	70	43	37	54	1	.252	.333	2	0	SS-142
1949	134	515	140	31	2	5	1.0	61	70	37	42	0	.272	.369	0	0	SS-134
1950	106	372	92	10	2	4	1.1	36	40	44	55	1	.247	.317	5	1	SS-101
1952 STL A	67	186	46	11	0	2	1.1	16	19	19	17	0	.247	.339	4	2	SS-63
1953	3	7	0	0	0	0	0.0	0	0	0	0	0	.000	.000	1	0	3B-2
13 yrs.	1572	5506	1448	272	37	36	0.7	602	624	470	537	35	.263	.345	14	3	SS-1555, 3B-2
WORLD SERIES																	
1942 STL N	5	18	2	0	1	0	0.0	2	3	1	2	0	.111	.222	0	0	SS-5
1943	5	14	5	2	0	1	7.1	1	2	3	1	1	.357	.714	0	0	SS-5
1944	6	22	5	3	0	0	0.0	1	2	2	3	0	.227	.364	0	0	SS-6
1946	7	24	6	2	0	0	0.0	1	4	1	1	0	.250	.333	0	0	SS-7
4 yrs.	23	78	18	7	1	1	1.3	5	11	7	7	1	.231	.385	0	0	SS-23
				8th													

Red Marion

MARION, JOHN WYETH　BR TR 6'2" 175 lbs.
Brother of Marty Marion.
B. Mar. 14, 1914, Richburg, S. C. D. Mar. 13, 1975, San Jose, Calif.

	G	AB	H	2B	3B	HR	HR%	R	RBI	BB	SO	SB	BA	SA	AB	H	G by POS
1935 WAS A	4	11	2	1	0	1	9.1	1	1	0	2	0	.182	.545	0	0	OF-3
1943	14	17	3	0	0	0	0.0	2	1	3	1	0	.176	.176	9	1	OF-4
2 yrs.	18	28	5	1	0	1	3.6	3	2	3	3	0	.179	.321	9	1	OF-7

Roger Maris

MARIS, ROGER EUGENE　BL TR 6' 197 lbs.
B. Sept. 10, 1934, Fargo, N. D.

	G	AB	H	2B	3B	HR	HR%	R	RBI	BB	SO	SB	BA	SA	AB	H	G by POS
1957 CLE A	116	358	84	9	5	14	3.9	61	51	60	79	8	.235	.405	5	2	OF-112
1958 2 teams	CLE	A (51G –	.225)		KC	A (99G –	.247)										
" total	150	583	140	19	4	28	4.8	87	80	45	85	4	.240	.431	6	0	OF-146
1959 KC A	122	433	118	21	7	16	3.7	69	72	58	53	2	.273	.464	5	2	OF-117
1960 NY A	136	499	141	18	7	39	7.8	98	112	70	65	2	.283	.581	4	1	OF-131
1961	161	590	159	16	4	61¹	10.3	132	142	94	67	0	.269	.620	1	0	OF-160
1962	157	590	151	34	1	33	5.6	92	100	87	78	1	.256	.485	3	0	OF-154
1963	90	312	84	14	1	23	7.4	53	53	35	40	1	.269	.542	5	2	OF-86
1964	141	513	144	12	2	26	5.1	86	71	62	78	3	.281	.464	6	1	OF-137
1965	46	155	37	7	0	8	5.2	22	27	29	29	0	.239	.439	4	1	OF-43
1966	119	348	81	9	2	13	3.7	37	43	36	60	0	.233	.382	20	6	OF-95
1967 STL N	125	410	107	18	7	9	2.2	64	55	52	61	0	.261	.405	19	2	OF-118
1968	100	310	79	18	2	5	1.6	25	45	24	38	0	.255	.374	21	6	OF-84
12 yrs.	1463	5101	1325	195	42	275	5.4	826	851	652	733	21	.260	.476	99	23	OF-1383
WORLD SERIES																	
1960 NY A	7	30	8	1	0	2	6.7	6	2	2	4	0	.267	.500	0	0	OF-7
1961	5	19	2	1	0	1	5.3	4	2	4	6	0	.105	.316	0	0	OF-5
1962	7	23	4	1	0	1	4.3	4	5	5	2	0	.174	.348	0	0	OF-7
1963	2	5	0	0	0	0	0.0	0	0	0	1	0	.000	.000	0	0	OF-2
1964	7	30	6	0	0	1	3.3	4	1	1	4	0	.200	.300	0	0	OF-7
1967 STL N	7	26	10	1	0	1	3.8	3	7	3	1	0	.385	.538	0	0	OF-7
1968	6	19	3	1	0	0	0.0	5	1	3	3	0	.158	.211	1	0	OF-5
7 yrs.	41	152	33	5	0	6	3.9	26	18	18	21	0	.217	.368	1	0	OF-40
	10th	10th							6th								

	G	AB	H	2B	3B	HR	HR %	R	RBI	BB	SO	SB	BA	SA	Pinch Hit AB	Pinch Hit H	G by POS

Gene Markland

MARKLAND, CLENETH EUGENE (Mousey)
B. Dec. 26, 1919, Detroit, Mich.
BR TR 5'10" 160 lbs.

	G	AB	H	2B	3B	HR	HR%	R	RBI	BB	SO	SB	BA	SA	AB	H	G by POS
1950 PHI A	5	8	1	0	0	0	0.0	2	0	3	0	0	.125	.125	0	0	2B-5

Hal Marnie

MARNIE, HARRY SYLVESTER
B. July 6, 1918, Philadelphia, Pa.
BR TR 6'1" 178 lbs.

	G	AB	H	2B	3B	HR	HR%	R	RBI	BB	SO	SB	BA	SA	AB	H	G by POS
1940 PHI N	11	34	6	0	0	0	0.0	4	4	4	2	0	.176	.176	0	0	2B-11
1941	61	158	38	3	3	0	0.0	12	11	13	25	0	.241	.297	2	0	2B-39, SS-16, 3B-3
1942	24	30	5	0	0	0	0.0	3	0	1	1	1	.167	.167	2	0	2B-11, SS-7, 3B-1
3 yrs.	96	222	49	3	3	0	0.0	19	15	18	28	1	.221	.261	4	0	2B-61, SS-23, 3B-4

Fred Marolewski

MAROLEWSKI, FRED DANIEL (Fritz)
B. Oct. 6, 1928, Chicago, Ill.
BR TR 6'2½" 205 lbs.

	G	AB	H	2B	3B	HR	HR%	R	RBI	BB	SO	SB	BA	SA	AB	H	G by POS
1953 STL N	1	0	0	0	0	0	–	0	0	0	0	0	–	–	0	0	1B-1

Ollie Marquardt

MARQUARDT, ALBERT LUDWIG
B. Sept. 22, 1902, Toledo, Ohio   D. Feb. 7, 1968, Port Clinton, Ohio
BR TR 5'9" 156 lbs.

	G	AB	H	2B	3B	HR	HR%	R	RBI	BB	SO	SB	BA	SA	AB	H	G by POS
1931 BOS A	17	39	7	1	0	0	0.0	4	2	3	4	0	.179	.205	1	0	2B-13

Gonzalo Marquez

MARQUEZ, GONZALO ENRIQUE
B. Mar. 31, 1946, Carupano, Venezuela   D. Dec. 19, 1984, Caracas, Venezuela
BL TL 5'11" 180 lbs.

	G	AB	H	2B	3B	HR	HR%	R	RBI	BB	SO	SB	BA	SA	AB	H	G by POS
1972 OAK A	23	21	8	0	0	0	0.0	2	4	3	4	1	.381	.381	16	7	1B-2
1973 2 teams		OAK	A	(23G –	.240)		CHI	N	(19G –	.224)							
" total	42	83	19	3	0	1	1.2	6	6	3	8	0	.229	.301	20	5	1B-19, 2B-2
1974 CHI N	11	11	0	0	0	0	0.0	1	0	1	2	0	.000	.000	10	0	1B-1
3 yrs.	76	115	27	3	0	1	0.9	9	10	7	14	1	.235	.287	46	12	1B-22, 2B-2

LEAGUE CHAMPIONSHIP SERIES

	G	AB	H	2B	3B	HR	HR%	R	RBI	BB	SO	SB	BA	SA	AB	H	G by POS
1972 OAK A	3	3	2	0	0	0	0.0	1	1	0	0	0	.667	.667	3	2	

WORLD SERIES

	G	AB	H	2B	3B	HR	HR%	R	RBI	BB	SO	SB	BA	SA	AB	H	G by POS
1972 OAK A	5	5	3	0	0	0	0.0	0	1	0	0	0	.600	.600	5	3 1st	

Luis Marquez

MARQUEZ, LUIS ANGEL (Canena)
B. Oct. 28, 1925, Aguadilla, Puerto Rico
BR TR 5'10½" 174 lbs.

	G	AB	H	2B	3B	HR	HR%	R	RBI	BB	SO	SB	BA	SA	AB	H	G by POS
1951 BOS N	68	122	24	5	1	0	0.0	19	11	10	20	4	.197	.254	9	2	OF-43
1954 2 teams		CHI	N	(17G –	.083)		PIT	N	(14G –	.111)							
" total	31	21	2	0	0	0	0.0	5	0	6	4	3	.095	.095	5	1	OF-18
2 yrs.	99	143	26	5	1	0	0.0	24	11	16	24	7	.182	.231	14	3	OF-61

Bob Marquis

MARQUIS, ROBERT RUDOLPH
B. Dec. 23, 1924, Oklahoma City, Okla.
BL TL 6'1" 170 lbs.

	G	AB	H	2B	3B	HR	HR%	R	RBI	BB	SO	SB	BA	SA	AB	H	G by POS
1953 CIN N	40	44	12	1	1	2	4.5	9	3	4	11	0	.273	.477	26	5	OF-10

Roger Marquis

MARQUIS, ROGER JULIAN (Noonie)
B. Apr. 5, 1937, Holyoke, Mass.
BL TL 6' 190 lbs.

	G	AB	H	2B	3B	HR	HR%	R	RBI	BB	SO	SB	BA	SA	AB	H	G by POS
1955 BAL A	1	1	0	0	0	0	0.0	0	0	0	0	0	.000	.000	0	0	OF-1

Lefty Marr

MARR, CHARLES W.
B. Sept. 19, 1862, Cincinnati, Ohio   D. Jan. 11, 1912, New Britain, Conn.
BL TL

	G	AB	H	2B	3B	HR	HR%	R	RBI	BB	SO	SB	BA	SA	AB	H	G by POS
1886 CIN AA	8	29	8	1	1	0	0.0	2		1			.276	.379	0	0	OF-8
1889 COL AA	139	546	167	26	15	1	0.2	110	75	87	32	29	.306	.414	0	0	3B-66, OF-47, SS-26, 1B-1, C-1
1890 CIN N	130	527	158	17	12	2	0.4	91	73	46	29	44	.300	.389	0	0	OF-64, 3B-63, SS-3
1891 2 teams		CIN	N	(72G –	.259)		C-M	AA	(14G –	.193)							
" total	86	343	85	10	7	0	0.0	41	36	32	19	18	.248	.318	0	0	OF-86
4 yrs.	363	1445	418	54	35	3	0.2	244	183	166	80	91	.289	.381	0	0	OF-205, 3B-129, SS-29, 1B-1, C-1

Bill Marriott

MARRIOTT, WILLIAM EARL
B. Apr. 18, 1893, Pratt, Kans.   D. Aug. 11, 1969, Berkeley, Calif.
BL TR 6' 170 lbs.

	G	AB	H	2B	3B	HR	HR%	R	RBI	BB	SO	SB	BA	SA	AB	H	G by POS
1917 CHI N	2	6	0	0	0	0	0.0	0	0	0	1	0	.000	.000	2	0	OF-1
1920	14	43	12	4	2	0	0.0	7	5	6	5	1	.279	.465	0	0	2B-14
1921	30	38	12	1	1	0	0.0	3	7	4	1	0	.316	.395	20	4	2B-6, OF-1, SS-1, 3B-1
1925 BOS N	103	370	99	9	1	1	0.3	37	40	28	26	3	.268	.305	8	1	3B-89, OF-1
1926 BKN N	109	360	96	13	9	3	0.8	39	42	17	20	12	.267	.378	4	0	3B-104
1927	6	9	1	0	1	0	0.0	0	1	2	2	0	.111	.333	4	0	3B-2
6 yrs.	264	826	220	27	14	4	0.5	86	95	57	55	16	.266	.347	38	5	3B-196, 2B-20, OF-3, SS-1

Armando Marsans

MARSANS, ARMANDO
B. Oct. 3, 1887, Matanzas, Cuba   D. Sept. 3, 1960, Havana, Cuba
BR TR 5'10" 157 lbs.

	G	AB	H	2B	3B	HR	HR%	R	RBI	BB	SO	SB	BA	SA	AB	H	G by POS
1911 CIN N	58	138	36	2	2	0	0.0	17	11	15	11	11	.261	.304	19	3	OF-34, 3B-1, 1B-1
1912	110	416	132	19	7	1	0.2	59	38	35	20	17	.317	.404	2	2	OF-98, 1B-6
1913	118	435	129	7	6	0	0.0	49	38	17	25	37	.297	.340	1	0	OF-94, 1B-22, 3B-2, SS-1
1914 2 teams		CIN	N	(36G –	.298)		STL	F	(9G –	.350)							
" total	45	164	51	3	2	0	0.0	21	24	17	6	17	.311	.354	0	0	OF-36, 2B-7, SS-2
1915 STL F	36	124	22	3	0	0	0.0	16	6	14		5	.177	.202	1	0	OF-35
1916 STL A	151	528	134	12	1	1	0.2	51	60	57	41	46	.254	.286	1	1	OF-150
1917 2 teams		STL	A	(75G –	.230)		NY	A	(25G –	.227)							
" total	100	345	79	16	0	0	0.0	41	35	28	9	17	.229	.275	1	1	OF-92, 3B-5, 2B-1
1918 NY A	37	123	29	5	1	0	0.0	13	9	5	3	3	.236	.293	1	0	OF-36
8 yrs.	655	2273	612	67	19	2	0.1	267	221	173	112	171	.269	.318	26	7	OF-575, 1B-29, 3B-8, 2B-8, SS-3

Freddie Marsh

MARSH, FRED FRANCIS
B. Jan. 5, 1924, Valley Falls, Kans.
BR TR 5'10" 180 lbs.

	G	AB	H	2B	3B	HR	HR%	R	RBI	BB	SO	SB	BA	SA	Pinch Hit AB	Pinch Hit H	G by POS
1949 CLE A	1	0	0	0	0	0	–	0	0	0	0	0	–	–	0	0	
1951 STL A	130	445	108	21	4	4	0.9	44	43	36	56	4	.243	.335	10	2	3B-117, SS-3, 2B-2
1952 3 teams	STL A (11G – .217)			WAS A (9G – .042)				STL A (76G – .286)									
" total	96	271	70	9	1	2	0.7	29	28	28	37	3	.258	.321	3	2	SS-60, 3B-21, 2B-14, OF-2
1953 CHI A	67	95	19	1	0	2	2.1	22	2	13	26	0	.200	.274	11	3	3B-32, SS-17, 1B-5, 2B-2
1954	62	98	30	5	2	0	0.0	21	4	9	16	4	.306	.398	2	0	3B-36, SS-3, 1B-2, OF-1
1955 BAL A	89	303	66	7	1	2	0.7	30	19	35	33	1	.218	.267	1	0	2B-76, 3B-18, SS-16
1956	20	24	3	0	0	0	0.0	2	0	4	3	1	.125	.125	0	0	SS-8, 3B-8, 2B-5
7 yrs.	465	1236	296	43	8	10	0.8	148	96	125	171	13	.239	.311	27	6	3B-232, SS-107, 2B-99, 1B-7, OF-3

Bill Marshall

MARSHALL, WILLIAM HENRY
B. Feb. 14, 1912, Dorchester, Mass. D. May 5, 1977, Sacramento, Calif.
BR TR 5'9" 160 lbs.

	G	AB	H	2B	3B	HR	HR%	R	RBI	BB	SO	SB	BA	SA	Pinch Hit AB	Pinch Hit H	G by POS
1931 BOS A	1	0	0	0	0	0	–	1	0	0	0	0	–	–	0	0	
1934 CIN N	6	8	1	0	0	0	0.0	0	0	0	2	0	.125	.125	3	1	2B-2
2 yrs.	7	8	1	0	0	0	0.0	1	0	0	2	0	.125	.125	3	1	2B-2

Charlie Marshall

MARSHALL, CHARLES ANTHONY
Born Charles Anthony Marczlewicz.
B. Aug. 28, 1919, Wilmington, Del.
BR TR 5'10½" 178 lbs.

	G	AB	H	2B	3B	HR	HR%	R	RBI	BB	SO	SB	BA	SA	Pinch Hit AB	Pinch Hit H	G by POS
1941 STL N	1	0	0	0	0	0	–	0	0	0	0	0	–	–	0	0	C-1

Dave Marshall

MARSHALL, DAVID LEWIS
B. Jan. 14, 1943, Artesia, Calif.
BL TR 6'1" 182 lbs.

	G	AB	H	2B	3B	HR	HR%	R	RBI	BB	SO	SB	BA	SA	Pinch Hit AB	Pinch Hit H	G by POS
1967 SF N	1	0	0	0	0	0	–	0	0	0	0	0	–	–	0	0	
1968	76	174	46	5	1	1	0.6	17	16	20	37	2	.264	.322	23	7	OF-50
1969	110	267	62	7	1	2	0.7	32	33	40	68	1	.232	.288	20	4	OF-87
1970 NY N	92	189	46	10	1	6	3.2	21	29	17	43	4	.243	.402	44	11	OF-43
1971	100	214	51	9	1	3	1.4	28	21	26	54	1	.238	.332	36	8	OF-64
1972	72	156	39	5	0	4	2.6	21	11	22	28	3	.250	.359	29	3	OF-42
1973 SD N	39	49	14	5	0	0	0.0	4	4	8	9	0	.286	.388	24	5	OF-8
7 yrs.	490	1049	258	41	4	16	1.5	123	114	133	239	13	.246	.338	176	38	OF-294

Doc Marshall

MARSHALL, EDWARD HERBERT
B. June 4, 1906, New Albany, Miss.
BR TR 5'11" 150 lbs.

	G	AB	H	2B	3B	HR	HR%	R	RBI	BB	SO	SB	BA	SA	Pinch Hit AB	Pinch Hit H	G by POS
1929 NY N	5	15	6	2	0	0	0.0	6	2	1	0	0	.400	.533	0	0	2B-5
1930	78	223	69	5	3	0	0.0	33	21	13	9	0	.309	.359	5	3	SS-45, 2B-17, 3B-5
1931	68	194	39	6	2	0	0.0	15	10	8	8	1	.201	.253	3	1	2B-47, SS-11, 3B-3
1932	68	226	56	8	1	0	0.0	18	28	6	11	1	.248	.292	0	0	SS-63
4 yrs.	219	658	170	21	6	0	0.0	72	61	28	28	2	.258	.309	8	4	SS-119, 2B-69, 3B-8

Doc Marshall

MARSHALL, WILLIAM RIDDLE
B. Sept. 22, 1875, Butler, Pa. D. Dec. 11, 1959, Clinton, Ill.
BR TR 6'1" 185 lbs.

	G	AB	H	2B	3B	HR	HR%	R	RBI	BB	SO	SB	BA	SA	Pinch Hit AB	Pinch Hit H	G by POS
1904 3 teams	PHI N (8G – .100)			NY N (11G – .353)				BOS N (13G – .209)									
" total	32	80	17	1	0	0	0.0	7	5	3			2	.213	.250	7	0	C-20, OF-3, 2B-1
1906 2 teams	NY N (38G – .167)			STL N (39G – .276)													
" total	77	225	51	7	3	0	0.0	14	17	13			8	.227	.284	9	1	C-51, OF-16, 1B-2
1907 STL N	84	268	54	8	2	2	0.7	19	18	12			2	.201	.269	1	0	C-83
1908 2 teams	STL N (6G – .071)			CHI N (12G – .300)													
" total	18	34	7	0	1	0	0.0	4	4	0				.206	.265	2	1	C-10, OF-3
1909 BKN N	50	149	30	7	1	0	0.0	7	10	6			3	.201	.262	1	0	C-49, OF-1
5 yrs.	261	756	159	23	8	2	0.3	51	54	34			15	.210	.270	20	2	C-213, OF-23, 1B-2, 2B-1

Jim Marshall

MARSHALL, RUFUS JAMES
B. May 25, 1932, Danville, Ill.
Manager 1974-76, 1979.
BL TL 6'1" 190 lbs.

	G	AB	H	2B	3B	HR	HR%	R	RBI	BB	SO	SB	BA	SA	Pinch Hit AB	Pinch Hit H	G by POS
1958 2 teams	BAL A (85G – .215)			CHI N (26G – .272)													
" total	111	272	63	6	3	10	3.7	29	30	30	43	4	.232	.386	36	6	1B-67, OF-19
1959 CHI N	108	294	74	10	1	11	3.7	39	40	33	39	0	.252	.405	33	8	1B-72, OF-8
1960 SF N	75	118	28	2	2	2	1.7	19	13	17	24	0	.237	.339	38	8	1B-28, OF-6
1961	44	36	8	0	0	1	2.8	5	7	3	8	0	.222	.306	32	7	1B-4, OF-2
1962 2 teams	NY N (17G – .344)			PIT N (55G – .220)													
" total	72	132	33	6	1	5	3.8	19	16	18	25	1	.250	.424	32	6	1B-31, OF-1
5 yrs.	410	852	206	24	7	29	3.4	111	106	101	139	5	.242	.388	171	35	1B-202, OF-36

Joe Marshall

MARSHALL, JOSEPH HANLEY (Home Run Joe)
B. Feb. 19, 1876, Audubon, Minn. D. Sept. 11, 1931, Norwalk, Calif.
BR TR

	G	AB	H	2B	3B	HR	HR%	R	RBI	BB	SO	SB	BA	SA	Pinch Hit AB	Pinch Hit H	G by POS
1903 PIT N	10	23	6	1	2	0	0.0	2	2	0			0	.261	.478	3	0	OF-3, SS-3, 2B-1
1906 STL N	33	95	15	1	2	0	0.0	2	7	6			0	.158	.211	5	1	OF-23, 1B-4
2 yrs.	43	118	21	2	4	0	0.0	4	9	6			0	.178	.263	8	1	OF-26, 1B-4, SS-3, 2B-1

Keith Marshall

MARSHALL, KEITH ALAN
B. July 2, 1951, San Francisco, Calif.
BR TR 6'2" 175 lbs.

	G	AB	H	2B	3B	HR	HR%	R	RBI	BB	SO	SB	BA	SA	Pinch Hit AB	Pinch Hit H	G by POS
1973 KC A	8	9	2	1	0	0	0.0	0	3	1	4	0	.222	.333	0	0	OF-8

Max Marshall

MARSHALL, MILO MAX
B. Sept. 18, 1913, Shenandoah, Iowa
BL TR 6'1" 180 lbs.

	G	AB	H	2B	3B	HR	HR%	R	RBI	BB	SO	SB	BA	SA	Pinch Hit AB	Pinch Hit H	G by POS
1942 CIN N	131	530	135	17	6	7	1.3	49	43	34	38	4	.255	.349	1	0	OF-129
1943	132	508	120	11	8	4	0.8	55	39	34	52	8	.236	.313	3	1	OF-129
1944	66	229	56	13	2	4	1.7	36	23	21	10	3	.245	.371	7	1	OF-59
3 yrs.	329	1267	311	41	16	15	1.2	140	105	89	100	15	.245	.339	11	2	OF-317

	G	AB	H	2B	3B	HR	HR%	R	RBI	BB	SO	SB	BA	SA	Pinch Hit AB	Pinch Hit H	G by POS

Mike Marshall

MARSHALL, MICHAEL ALLEN
B. Jan. 12, 1960, Libertyville, Ill.   BR TR 6'5"   215 lbs.

	G	AB	H	2B	3B	HR	HR%	R	RBI	BB	SO	SB	BA	SA	PH AB	PH H	G by POS
1981 LA N	14	25	5	3	0	0	0.0	2	1	1	4	0	.200	.320	7	3	3B-3, 1B-3, OF-2
1982	49	95	23	3	0	5	5.3	10	9	13	23	2	.242	.432	20	3	OF-19, 1B-13
1983	140	465	132	17	1	17	3.7	47	65	43	127	7	.284	.434	6	1	OF-109, 1B-33
1984	134	495	127	27	0	21	4.2	69	65	40	93	4	.257	.438	7	2	OF-118, 1B-15
4 yrs.	337	1080	287	50	1	43	4.0	128	140	97	247	13	.266	.433	40	9	OF-248, 1B-64, 3B-3

DIVISIONAL PLAYOFF SERIES

	G	AB	H	2B	3B	HR	HR%	R	RBI	BB	SO	SB	BA	SA	PH AB	PH H	G by POS
1981 LA N	1	1	0	0	0	0	0.0	0	0	0	1	0	.000	.000	1	0	

LEAGUE CHAMPIONSHIP SERIES

	G	AB	H	2B	3B	HR	HR%	R	RBI	BB	SO	SB	BA	SA	PH AB	PH H	G by POS
1983 LA N	4	15	2	1	0	1	6.7	1	2	1	6	0	.133	.400	0	0	1B-3

Willard Marshall

MARSHALL, WILLARD WARREN
B. Feb. 8, 1921, Richmond, Va.   BL TR 6'1"   205 lbs.

	G	AB	H	2B	3B	HR	HR%	R	RBI	BB	SO	SB	BA	SA	PH AB	PH H	G by POS
1942 NY N	116	401	103	9	2	11	2.7	41	59	26	20	1	.257	.372	8	2	OF-107
1946	131	510	144	18	3	13	2.5	63	48	33	29	3	.282	.406	7	2	OF-125
1947	155	587	171	19	6	36	6.1	102	107	67	30	3	.291	.528	0	0	OF-155
1948	143	537	146	21	8	14	2.6	72	86	64	34	2	.272	.419	0	0	OF-142
1949	141	499	153	19	3	12	2.4	81	70	78	20	4	.307	.429	3	1	OF-138
1950 BOS N	105	298	70	10	2	5	1.7	38	40	36	5	1	.235	.332	20	4	OF-85
1951	136	469	132	24	7	11	2.3	65	62	48	18	0	.281	.433	7	1	OF-127
1952 2 teams	BOS N (21G – .227)			CIN N (107G – .267)													
" total	128	463	121	27	2	10	2.2	57	57	41	25	0	.261	.393	9	0	OF-121
1953 CIN N	122	357	95	14	6	17	4.8	51	62	41	28	0	.266	.482	33	4	OF-95
1954 CHI A	47	71	18	2	0	1	1.4	7	7	11	9	0	.254	.324	19	4	OF-29
1955	22	41	7	0	0	0	0.0	6	6	13	1	0	.171	.171	7	0	OF-12
11 yrs.	1246	4233	1160	163	39	130	3.1	583	604	458	219	14	.274	.423	113	18	OF-1136

Marty Martel

MARTEL, LEON ALPHONSE (Doc)
B. Jan. 29, 1883, Weymouth, Mass.   D. Oct. 11, 1947, Washington, D. C.   BR TR 6'   185 lbs.

	G	AB	H	2B	3B	HR	HR%	R	RBI	BB	SO	SB	BA	SA	PH AB	PH H	G by POS
1909 PHI N	24	41	11	3	1	0	0.0	1	7	4		0	.268	.390	10	3	C-12, 1B-10
1910 BOS N	10	31	4	0	0	0	0.0	0	1	2	3	0	.129	.129	1	0	1B-10
2 yrs.	34	72	15	3	1	0	0.0	1	8	6	3	0	.208	.278	11	3	C-12, 1B-10

Babe Martin

MARTIN, BORIS MICHAEL
Born Boris Michael Martinovich.
B. Mar. 28, 1920, Seattle, Wash.   BR TR 5'11½"   194 lbs.

	G	AB	H	2B	3B	HR	HR%	R	RBI	BB	SO	SB	BA	SA	PH AB	PH H	G by POS
1944 STL A	2	4	3	1	0	0	0.0	0	1	0	0	0	.750	1.000	1	1	OF-1
1945	54	185	37	5	2	2	1.1	13	16	11	24	0	.200	.281	1	1	OF-48, 1B-6
1946	3	9	2	0	0	0	0.0	0	1	1	2	0	.222	.222	1	1	C-2
1948 BOS A	4	4	2	0	0	0	0.0	0	0	0	1	0	.500	.500	3	1	C-1
1949	2	2	0	0	0	0	0.0	0	0	0	0	0	.000	.000	2	0	C-1
1953 STL A	4	2	0	0	0	0	0.0	0	0	1	0	0	.000	.000	1	0	C-1
6 yrs.	69	206	44	6	2	2	1.0	13	18	13	27	0	.214	.291	9	4	OF-49, 1B-6, C-5

Bill Martin

MARTIN, WILLIAM GLOYD
B. Feb. 13, 1894, Washington, D. C.   D. Sept. 15, 1949, Washington, D. C.   BR TR 5'8½"   170 lbs.

	G	AB	H	2B	3B	HR	HR%	R	RBI	BB	SO	SB	BA	SA	PH AB	PH H	G by POS
1914 BOS N	1	3	0	0	0	0	0.0	0	0	0	0	0	.000	.000	0	0	SS-1

Billy Martin

MARTIN, ALFRED MANUEL
B. May 16, 1928, Berkeley, Calif.
Manager 1969, 1971-82.   BR TR 5'11½"   165 lbs.

	G	AB	H	2B	3B	HR	HR%	R	RBI	BB	SO	SB	BA	SA	PH AB	PH H	G by POS
1950 NY A	34	36	9	1	0	1	2.8	10	8	3	3	0	.250	.361	10	2	2B-22, 3B-1
1951	51	58	15	1	2	0	0.0	10	2	4	9	0	.259	.345	10	0	2B-23, SS-6, 3B-2, OF-1
1952	109	363	97	13	3	3	0.8	32	33	22	31	3	.267	.344	1	0	2B-107
1953	149	587	151	24	6	15	2.6	72	75	43	56	6	.257	.395	1	0	2B-146, SS-18
1955	20	70	21	2	0	1	1.4	8	9	7	9	1	.300	.371	0	0	2B-17, SS-3
1956	121	458	121	24	5	9	2.0	76	49	30	56	1	.264	.397	1	0	2B-105, 3B-16
1957 2 teams	NY A (43G – .241)			KC A (73G – .257)													
" total	116	410	103	14	5	10	2.4	45	39	15	34	9	.251	.383	5	0	2B-78, 3B-33, SS-2
1958 DET A	131	498	127	19	1	7	1.4	56	42	16	62	5	.255	.339	2	0	2B-67, 3B-4
1959 CLE A	73	242	63	7	0	9	3.7	37	24	7	18	0	.260	.401	1	0	2B-97
1960 CIN N	103	317	78	17	1	3	0.9	34	16	27	34	0	.246	.334	4	0	2B-97
1961 2 teams	MIL N (6G – .000)			MIN A (108G – .246)													
" total	114	380	92	15	5	6	1.6	45	36	13	43	3	.242	.355	9	1	2B-105, SS-1
11 yrs.	1021	3419	877	137	28	64	1.9	425	333	187	355	34	.257	.369	44	3	2B-767, SS-118, 3B-97, OF-1

WORLD SERIES

	G	AB	H	2B	3B	HR	HR%	R	RBI	BB	SO	SB	BA	SA	PH AB	PH H	G by POS
1951 NY A	1	0	0	0	0	0	–	1	0	0	0	0	–	–	0	0	
1952	7	23	5	0	0	1	4.3	2	4	2	2	0	.217	.348	0	0	2B-7
1953	6	24	12	1	2	2	8.3	5	8	1	2	1	.500	.958	0	0	2B-6
1955	7	25	8	1	1	0	0.0	2	4	1	5	0	.320	.440	0	0	2B-7
1956	7	27	8	0	0	2	7.4	5	3	1	6	0	.296	.519	0	0	2B-7
5 yrs.	28	99	33	2	3	5	5.1	15	19	5	15	1	.333	.566	0	0	2B-27

4th

Frank Martin

MARTIN, FRANK
B. 1877, Chicago, Ill.   Deceased.

	G	AB	H	2B	3B	HR	HR%	R	RBI	BB	SO	SB	BA	SA	PH AB	PH H	G by POS
1897 LOU N	2	8	2	0	0	0	0.0	1	0	0		0	.250	.250	0	0	2B-2
1898 CHI N	1	4	0	0	0	0	0.0	0	0	0		0	.000	.000	0	0	2B-1
1899 NY N	17	54	14	2	0	0	0.0	5	1	2		0	.259	.296	0	0	3B-17
3 yrs.	20	66	16	2	0	0	0.0	6	1	2		0	.242	.273	0	0	3B-17, 2B-3

	G	AB	H	2B	3B	HR	HR %	R	RBI	BB	SO	SB	BA	SA	Pinch Hit AB	Pinch Hit H	G by POS

Gene Martin

MARTIN, THOMAS EUGENE
B. Jan. 12, 1947, Americus, Ga.
BL TR 6'½" 190 lbs.

	G	AB	H	2B	3B	HR	HR %	R	RBI	BB	SO	SB	BA	SA	AB	H	G by POS
1968 WAS A	9	11	4	1	0	1	9.1	1	1	0	1	0	.364	.727	7	3	OF-2

Herschel Martin

MARTIN, HERSCHEL RAY
B. Sept. 19, 1909, Birmingham, Ala. D. Nov. 17, 1980, Cuba, Mo.
BB TR 6'2" 190 lbs.

	G	AB	H	2B	3B	HR	HR %	R	RBI	BB	SO	SB	BA	SA	AB	H	G by POS
1937 PHI N	141	579	164	35	7	8	1.4	102	49	69	66	11	.283	.409	2	0	OF-139
1938	120	466	139	36	6	3	0.6	58	39	34	48	8	.298	.421	4	3	OF-116
1939	111	393	111	28	5	1	0.3	59	22	42	27	4	.282	.387	14	3	OF-95
1940	33	83	21	6	1	0	0.0	10	5	9	9	1	.253	.349	10	4	OF-23
1944 NY A	85	328	99	12	4	9	2.7	49	47	34	26	5	.302	.445	5	1	OF-80
1945	117	408	109	18	6	7	1.7	53	53	65	31	4	.267	.392	14	5	OF-102
6 yrs.	607	2257	643	135	29	28	1.2	331	215	253	207	33	.285	.408	49	16	OF-555

J. C. Martin

MARTIN, JOSEPH CLIFTON
B. Dec. 13, 1936, Axton, Va.
BL TR 6'2" 188 lbs.

	G	AB	H	2B	3B	HR	HR %	R	RBI	BB	SO	SB	BA	SA	AB	H	G by POS
1959 CHI A	3	4	1	0	0	0	0.0	0	1	0	1	0	.250	.250	1	0	3B-2
1960	4	20	2	1	0	0	0.0	0	2	0	6	0	.100	.150	0	0	3B-5, 1B-1
1961	110	274	63	8	3	5	1.8	26	32	21	31	1	.230	.336	11	2	1B-60, 3B-36
1962	18	26	2	0	0	0	0.0	0	2	0	3	0	.077	.077	11	0	C-6, 3B-1, 1B-1
1963	105	259	53	11	1	5	1.9	25	28	26	35	0	.205	.313	12	3	C-98, 1B-3, 3B-1
1964	122	294	58	10	1	4	1.4	23	22	16	30	0	.197	.279	6	0	C-120
1965	119	230	60	12	0	2	0.9	21	21	24	29	2	.261	.339	15	3	C-112, 1B-4, 3B-2
1966	67	157	40	5	3	2	1.3	13	20	14	24	0	.255	.363	4	1	C-63
1967	101	252	59	12	1	4	1.6	22	22	30	41	4	.234	.337	6	1	C-96, 1B-1
1968 NY N	78	244	55	9	2	3	1.2	20	31	21	31	0	.225	.316	8	1	C-53, 1B-14
1969	66	177	37	5	1	4	2.3	12	21	12	32	0	.209	.316	18	3	C-48, 1B-2
1970 CHI N	40	77	12	1	0	1	1.3	11	4	20	11	0	.156	.208	3	0	C-36, 1B-3
1971	47	125	33	5	0	2	1.6	13	17	12	16	1	.264	.352	5	0	C-43, OF-1
1972	25	50	12	3	0	0	0.0	3	7	5	9	1	.240	.300	9	2	C-17
14 yrs.	905	2189	487	82	12	32	1.5	189	230	201	299	9	.222	.315	109	16	C-692, 1B-89, 3B-47, OF-1

LEAGUE CHAMPIONSHIP SERIES

	G	AB	H	2B	3B	HR	HR %	R	RBI	BB	SO	SB	BA	SA	AB	H	G by POS
1969 NY N	2	2	1	0	0	0	0.0	0	2	0	0	0	.500	.500	2	1	

WORLD SERIES

	G	AB	H	2B	3B	HR	HR %	R	RBI	BB	SO	SB	BA	SA	AB	H	G by POS
1969 NY N	1	0	0	0	0	0	–	0	0	0	0	0	–	–	0	0	

Jack Martin

MARTIN, JOHN CHRISTOPHER
B. Apr. 19, 1887, Plainfield, N. J. D. July 4, 1980, Plainfield, N. J.
BR TR 5'9" 159 lbs.

	G	AB	H	2B	3B	HR	HR %	R	RBI	BB	SO	SB	BA	SA	AB	H	G by POS
1912 NY A	69	231	52	6	1	0	0.0	30	17	37		14	.225	.260	0	0	SS-64, 3B-4, 2B-1
1914 2 teams	BOS N (33G – .212)							PHI N (83G – .253)									
" total	116	377	92	7	3	0	0.0	36	26	33	36	6	.244	.279	3	0	SS-83, 3B-27, 2B-1, 1B-1
2 yrs.	185	608	144	13	4	0	0.0	66	43	70	36	20	.237	.271	3	0	SS-147, 3B-31, 2B-2, 1B-1

Jerry Martin

MARTIN, JERRY LINDSEY
Son of Barney Martin.
B. May 11, 1949, Columbia, S. C.
BR TR 6'1" 195 lbs.

	G	AB	H	2B	3B	HR	HR %	R	RBI	BB	SO	SB	BA	SA	AB	H	G by POS
1974 PHI N	13	14	3	1	0	0	0.0	2	1	1	5	0	.214	.286	4	1	OF-11
1975	57	113	24	7	1	2	1.8	15	11	11	16	2	.212	.345	9	1	OF-49
1976	130	121	30	7	0	2	1.7	30	15	7	28	3	.248	.355	22	6	OF-110, 1B-1
1977	116	215	56	16	3	6	2.8	34	28	18	42	6	.260	.447	18	5	OF-106, 1B-1
1978	128	266	72	13	4	9	3.4	40	36	28	65	9	.271	.451	24	5	OF-112
1979 CHI N	150	534	145	34	3	19	3.6	74	73	38	85	8	.272	.453	8	1	OF-144
1980	141	494	112	22	2	23	4.7	57	73	38	107	8	.227	.419	11	2	OF-129
1981 SF N	72	241	58	5	3	4	1.7	23	25	21	52	6	.241	.336	7	0	OF-64
1982 KC A	147	519	138	22	1	15	2.9	52	65	38	138	1	.266	.399	7	2	OF-142, DH-3
1983	13	44	14	2	0	2	4.5	4	13	1	7	1	.318	.500	0	0	OF-13
1984 NY N	51	91	14	1	0	3	3.3	6	5	6	29	0	.154	.264	24	4	OF-30, 1B-3
11 yrs.	1018	2652	666	130	17	85	3.2	337	345	207	574	38	.251	.409	134	26	OF-910, 1B-5, DH-3

LEAGUE CHAMPIONSHIP SERIES

	G	AB	H	2B	3B	HR	HR %	R	RBI	BB	SO	SB	BA	SA	AB	H	G by POS
1976 PHI N	1	1	0	0	0	0	0.0	1	0	0	0	0	.000	.000	0	0	OF-1
1977	3	4	0	0	0	0	0.0	0	0	0	2	0	.000	.000	1	0	OF-1
1978	4	9	2	1	0	1	11.1	1	2	1	3	0	.222	.667	2	1	OF-3
3 yrs.	8	14	2	1	0	1	7.1	2	2	1	5	0	.143	.429	3	1	OF-5

Joe Martin

MARTIN, JOSEPH SAMUEL (Silent Joe)
B. Jan. 1, 1876, Hollidaysburg, Pa. D. May 25, 1964, Altoona, Pa.
BL TR 5'9½" 155 lbs.

	G	AB	H	2B	3B	HR	HR %	R	RBI	BB	SO	SB	BA	SA	AB	H	G by POS
1903 2 teams	WAS A (35G – .227)							STL A (44G – .214)									
" total	79	292	64	10	9	0	0.0	29	14	11		2	.219	.315	1	1	OF-45, 2B-21, 3B-14

Joe Martin

MARTIN, WILLIAM JOSEPH (Smokey Joe)
B. Aug. 28, 1911, Seymour, Mo. D. Sept. 28, 1960, Buffalo, N. Y.
BR TR 5'11½" 181 lbs.

	G	AB	H	2B	3B	HR	HR %	R	RBI	BB	SO	SB	BA	SA	AB	H	G by POS
1936 NY N	7	15	4	1	0	0	0.0	0	2	0	4	0	.267	.333	0	0	3B-7
1938 CHI A	1	0	0	0	0	0	–	0	0	0	0	0	–	–	0	0	
2 yrs.	8	15	4	1	0	0	0.0	0	2	0	4	0	.267	.333	0	0	3B-7

Pepper Martin

MARTIN, JOHNNY LEONARD ROOSEVELT (The Wild Hoss Of The Osage)
B. Feb. 29, 1904, Temple, Okla. D. Mar. 5, 1965, McAlester, Okla.
BR TR 5'8" 170 lbs.

	G	AB	H	2B	3B	HR	HR %	R	RBI	BB	SO	SB	BA	SA	AB	H	G by POS
1928 STL N	39	13	4	0	0	0	0.0	11	0	1	2	2	.308	.308	12	3	OF-4
1930	6	1	0	0	0	0	0.0	5	0	0	0	0	.000	.000	1	0	
1931	123	413	124	32	8	7	1.7	68	75	30	40	16	.300	.467	7	4	OF-110
1932	85	323	77	19	6	4	1.2	47	34	30	31	9	.238	.372	0	0	OF-69, 3B-15
1933	145	599	189	36	12	8	1.3	122	57	67	46	26	.316	.456	0	0	3B-145
1934	110	454	131	25	11	5	1.1	76	49	32	41	23	.289	.425	1	0	3B-107, P-1
1935	135	539	161	41	6	9	1.7	121	54	33	58	20	.299	.447	5	0	3B-114, OF-16

	G	AB	H	2B	3B	HR	HR %	R	RBI	BB	SO	SB	BA	SA	Pinch Hit AB	Pinch Hit H	G by POS

Pepper Martin continued

	G	AB	H	2B	3B	HR	HR %	R	RBI	BB	SO	SB	BA	SA	AB	H	G by POS
1936	143	572	177	36	11	11	1.9	121	76	58	66	23	.309	.469	1	0	OF-127, 3B-15, P-1
1937	98	339	103	27	8	5	1.5	60	38	33	50	9	.304	.475	9	2	OF-82, 3B-5
1938	91	269	79	18	2	2	0.7	34	38	18	34	4	.294	.398	23	5	OF-62, 3B-4
1939	88	281	86	17	7	3	1.1	48	37	30	35	6	.306	.448	10	0	OF-51, 3B-22
1940	86	228	72	15	4	3	1.3	28	39	22	24	6	.316	.456	17	4	OF-63, 3B-2
1944	40	86	24	4	0	2	2.3	15	4	15	11	2	.279	.395	5	1	OF-29
13 yrs.	1189	4117	1227	270	75	59	1.4	756	501	369	438	146	.298	.443	91	19	OF-613, 3B-429, P-2

WORLD SERIES

	G	AB	H	2B	3B	HR	HR %	R	RBI	BB	SO	SB	BA	SA	AB	H	G by POS
1928 STL N	1	0	0	0	0	0	—	1	0	0	0	0			0	0	OF-7
1931	7	24	12	4	0	1	4.2	5	5	2	3	5	.500	.792	0	0	3B-7
1934	7	31	11	3	1	0	0.0	8	3	3	3	2	.355	.516	0	0	OF-7, 3B-7
3 yrs.	15	55	23	7	1	1	1.8	14	8	5	6	7	.418	.636	0	0	
				8th							9th	1st		6th			

Stu Martin

MARTIN, STUART McGUIRE
B. Nov. 17, 1913, Rich Square, N. C.

BL TR 6' 155 lbs.

	G	AB	H	2B	3B	HR	HR %	R	RBI	BB	SO	SB	BA	SA	AB	H	G by POS
1936 STL N	92	332	99	21	4	6	1.8	63	41	29	27	17	.298	.440	4	0	2B-83, SS-3
1937	90	223	58	6	1	1	0.4	34	17	32	18	3	.260	.309	28	6	2B-48, 1B-9, SS-1
1938	114	417	116	26	2	1	0.2	54	27	30	28	4	.278	.357	15	3	2B-99
1939	120	425	114	26	7	3	0.7	60	30	33	40	4	.268	.384	11	0	2B-107, 1B-1
1940	112	369	88	12	6	4	1.1	45	32	33	35	4	.238	.336	9	1	3B-73, 2B-33
1941 PIT N	88	233	71	13	2	0	0.0	37	19	10	17	2	.305	.378	28	6	2B-53, 3B-2, 1B-1
1942	42	120	27	4	2	1	0.8	16	12	8	10	1	.225	.317	10	0	2B-30, SS-1, 1B-2
1943 CHI N	64	118	26	4	0	0	0.0	13	5	15	10	1	.220	.254	25	5	2B-22, 3B-8, 1B-2
8 yrs.	722	2237	599	112	24	16	0.7	322	183	190	185	36	.268	.361	130	21	2B-475, 3B-83, 1B-14, SS-5

Buck Martinez

MARTINEZ, JOHN ALBERT
B. Nov. 7, 1948, Redding, Calif.

BR TR 5'10" 190 lbs.

	G	AB	H	2B	3B	HR	HR %	R	RBI	BB	SO	SB	BA	SA	AB	H	G by POS
1969 KC A	72	205	47	6	1	4	2.0	14	23	8	25	0	.229	.327	18	4	C-55, OF-1
1970	6	9	1	0	0	0	0.0	1	0	2	1	0	.111	.111	1	0	C-5
1971	22	46	7	2	0	0	0.0	3	1	5	9	0	.152	.196	1	0	C-21
1973	14	32	8	1	0	1	3.1	2	6	4	5	0	.250	.375	0	0	C-14
1974	43	107	23	3	1	1	0.9	10	8	14	19	0	.215	.290	4	2	C-38
1975	80	226	51	9	2	3	1.3	15	23	21	28	1	.226	.323	1	0	C-79
1976	95	267	61	13	3	5	1.9	24	34	16	45	0	.228	.356	4	1	C-94
1977	29	80	18	4	0	1	1.3	3	9	3	12	0	.225	.313	2	0	C-29
1978 MIL A	89	256	56	10	1	1	0.4	26	20	14	42	1	.219	.277	0	0	C-89
1979	69	196	53	8	0	4	2.0	17	26	8	25	0	.270	.372	0	0	C-68, P-1
1980	76	219	49	9	0	3	1.4	16	17	12	33	1	.224	.306	0	0	C-76
1981 TOR A	45	128	29	8	1	4	3.1	13	21	11	16	1	.227	.398	0	0	C-45
1982	96	260	63	17	0	10	3.8	26	37	24	34	1	.242	.423	10	4	C-93
1983	88	221	56	14	0	10	4.5	27	33	29	39	0	.253	.452	12	4	C-85
1984	102	232	51	13	1	5	2.2	24	37	29	49	0	.220	.349	18	1	C-98, DH-1
15 yrs.	926	2484	573	117	10	52	2.1	221	295	200	382	5	.231	.349	71	16	C-889, DH-1, OF-1, P-1

LEAGUE CHAMPIONSHIP SERIES

	G	AB	H	2B	3B	HR	HR %	R	RBI	BB	SO	SB	BA	SA	AB	H	G by POS
1976 KC A	5	15	5	0	0	0	0.0	0	4	1	3	0	.333	.333	0	0	C-5

Carmelo Martinez

MARTINEZ, CARMELO
Also known as Carmelo Salgado.
B. July 28, 1960, Dorado, Puerto Rico

BR TR 6'2" 185 lbs.

	G	AB	H	2B	3B	HR	HR %	R	RBI	BB	SO	SB	BA	SA	AB	H	G by POS
1983 CHI N	29	89	23	3	0	6	6.7	8	16	4	19	0	.258	.494	4	1	1B-26, OF-1, 3B-1
1984 SD N	149	488	122	28	2	13	2.7	64	66	68	82	1	.250	.395	4	0	OF-142, 1B-2
2 yrs.	178	577	145	31	2	19	3.3	72	82	72	101	1	.251	.411	8	1	OF-143, 1B-28, 3B-1

LEAGUE CHAMPIONSHIP SERIES

	G	AB	H	2B	3B	HR	HR %	R	RBI	BB	SO	SB	BA	SA	AB	H	G by POS
1984 SD N	5	17	3	0	0	0	0.0	1	0	2	4	0	.176	.176	0	0	OF-5

WORLD SERIES

	G	AB	H	2B	3B	HR	HR %	R	RBI	BB	SO	SB	BA	SA	AB	H	G by POS
1984 SD N	5	17	3	0	0	0	0.0	0	0	1	9	0	.176	.176	0	0	OF-5

Hector Martinez

MARTINEZ, RODOLFO HECTOR
B. May 11, 1939, Las Villas, Cuba

BR TR 5'10" 160 lbs.

	G	AB	H	2B	3B	HR	HR %	R	RBI	BB	SO	SB	BA	SA	AB	H	G by POS
1962 KC A	1	1	0	0	0	0	0.0	0	0	0	1	0	.000	.000	1	0	
1963	6	14	4	0	0	1	7.1	2	3	1	3	0	.286	.500	3	0	OF-3
2 yrs.	7	15	4	0	0	1	6.7	2	3	1	4	0	.267	.467	4	0	OF-3

Jose Martinez

MARTINEZ, JOSE AZCUIZ
B. July 26, 1942, Cardenas, Matanzas, Cuba

BR TR 6' 178 lbs.

	G	AB	H	2B	3B	HR	HR %	R	RBI	BB	SO	SB	BA	SA	AB	H	G by POS
1969 PIT N	77	168	45	6	0	1	0.6	20	16	9	32	1	.268	.321	6	2	2B-42, SS-20, 3B-5, OF-2
1970	19	20	1	0	0	0	0.0	1	0	1	5	0	.050	.050	3	0	3B-7, 2B-4, SS-1
2 yrs.	96	188	46	6	0	1	0.5	21	16	10	37	1	.245	.293	9	2	2B-46, SS-21, 3B-12, OF-2

Marty Martinez

MARTINEZ, ORLANDO OLIVO
B. Aug. 23, 1941, Havana, Cuba

BB TR 6' 170 lbs.
BR 1962

	G	AB	H	2B	3B	HR	HR %	R	RBI	BB	SO	SB	BA	SA	AB	H	G by POS
1962 MIN A	37	18	3	0	1	0	0.0	13	3	3	4	0	.167	.278	0	0	SS-11, 3B-1
1967 ATL N	44	73	21	2	1	0	0.0	14	5	11	11	0	.288	.342	0	0	SS-25, 2B-9, C-3, 3B-2, 1B-1
1968	113	356	82	5	3	0	0.0	34	12	29	28	6	.230	.261	1	0	SS-54, 3B-37, 2B-16, C-14
1969 HOU N	78	198	61	5	4	0	0.0	14	15	10	21	0	.308	.374	18	4	OF-21, SS-17, 3B-15, C-7, 2B-1, P-1
1970	75	150	33	3	0	0	0.0	12	12	9	22	0	.220	.240	38	9	SS-29, 3B-10, C-6, 2B-4
1971	32	62	16	3	1	0	0.0	4	4	3	6	1	.258	.339	13	4	2B-9, SS-7, 1B-4, 3B-3

	G	AB	H	2B	3B	HR	HR %	R	RBI	BB	SO	SB	BA	SA	Pinch Hit AB	Pinch Hit H	G by POS

Marty Martinez continued

	G	AB	H	2B	3B	HR	HR %	R	RBI	BB	SO	SB	BA	SA	AB	H	G by POS
1972 3 teams	STL N (9G – .429)							TEX A (26G – .146)				OAK A (22G – .125)					
" total	57	88	14	1	1	0	0.0	6	6	5	15	0	.159	.193	19	4	2B-20, SS-14, 3B-6
7 yrs.	436	945	230	19	11	0	0.0	97	57	70	107	7	.243	.287	89	21	SS-157, 3B-74, 2B-59, C-30, OF-21, 1B-5, P-1

Teddy Martinez

MARTINEZ, TEODORO NOEL
B. Dec. 10, 1947, Central Barahona, Dominican Republic

BR TR 6' 165 lbs.

	G	AB	H	2B	3B	HR	HR %	R	RBI	BB	SO	SB	BA	SA	AB	H	G by POS
1970 NY N	4	16	1	0	0	0	0.0	0	0	0	3	0	.063	.063	0	0	2B-4, SS-1
1971	38	125	36	5	2	1	0.8	16	10	4	22	6	.288	.384	1	0	SS-23, 2B-13, 3B-3, OF-1
1972	103	330	74	5	5	1	0.3	22	19	12	49	7	.224	.279	4	0	2B-47, SS-42, OF-15, 3B-2
1973	92	263	67	11	0	1	0.4	34	14	13	38	3	.255	.308	1	0	SS-44, OF-21, 3B-14, 2B-5
1974	116	334	73	15	7	2	0.6	32	43	14	40	3	.219	.323	8	1	SS-75, 3B-12, 2B-11, OF-10
1975 2 teams	STL N (16G – .190)							OAK A (86G – .172)									
" total	102	108	19	2	0	0	0.0	8	5	2	11	1	.176	.194	11	1	SS-46, 2B-33, 3B-15, OF-7
1977 LA N	67	137	41	6	1	1	0.7	21	10	2	20	3	.299	.380	4	0	2B-27, SS-13, 3B-12
1978	54	55	14	1	0	1	1.8	13	5	4	14	3	.255	.327	4	0	SS-17, 3B-16, 2B-10
1979	81	112	30	5	1	0	0.0	19	2	4	16	3	.268	.330	4	0	3B-23, SS-21, 2B-18
9 yrs.	657	1480	355	50	16	7	0.5	165	108	55	213	29	.240	.309	37	2	SS-282, 2B-168, 3B-97, OF-54

LEAGUE CHAMPIONSHIP SERIES

	G	AB	H	2B	3B	HR	HR %	R	RBI	BB	SO	SB	BA	SA	AB	H	G by POS
1975 OAK A	3	0	0	0	0	0	–	0	0	0	0	0	–	–	0	0	2B-3

WORLD SERIES

	G	AB	H	2B	3B	HR	HR %	R	RBI	BB	SO	SB	BA	SA	AB	H	G by POS
1973 NY N	2	0	0	0	0	0	–	0	0	0	0	0	–	–	0	0	

Tony Martinez

MARTINEZ, GABRIEL ANTONIO
B. Mar. 18, 1941, Perico, Cuba

BR TR 5'10" 165 lbs.

	G	AB	H	2B	3B	HR	HR %	R	RBI	BB	SO	SB	BA	SA	AB	H	G by POS
1963 CLE A	43	141	22	4	0	0	0.0	10	8	5	18	1	.156	.184	0	0	SS-41
1964	9	14	3	1	0	0	0.0	1	2	0	2	0	.214	.286	1	0	2B-4, SS-1
1965	4	3	0	0	0	0	0.0	0	0	0	0	0	.000	.000	3	0	
1966	17	17	5	0	0	0	0.0	2	0	1	6	1	.294	.294	6	3	SS-5, 2B-4
4 yrs.	73	175	30	5	0	0	0.0	13	10	6	26	2	.171	.200	10	3	SS-47, 2B-8

Joe Marty

MARTY, JOSEPH ANTON
B. Sept. 1, 1913, Sacramento, Calif.   D. Oct. 4, 1984, Sacramento, Calif.

BR TR 6' 182 lbs.

	G	AB	H	2B	3B	HR	HR %	R	RBI	BB	SO	SB	BA	SA	AB	H	G by POS
1937 CHI N	88	290	84	17	2	5	1.7	41	44	28	30	3	.290	.414	3	2	OF-84
1938	76	235	57	8	3	7	3.0	32	35	18	26	0	.243	.391	7	0	OF-68
1939 2 teams	CHI N (23G – .132)							PHI N (91G – .254)									
" total	114	375	86	13	6	11	2.9	38	54	28	40	3	.229	.384	12	3	OF-100, P-1
1940 PHI N	123	455	123	21	8	13	2.9	52	50	17	50	2	.270	.437	4	1	OF-118
1941	137	477	128	19	3	8	1.7	60	39	51	41	6	.268	.371	5	0	OF-132
5 yrs.	538	1832	478	78	22	44	2.4	223	222	142	187	14	.261	.400	31	6	OF-502, P-1

WORLD SERIES

	G	AB	H	2B	3B	HR	HR %	R	RBI	BB	SO	SB	BA	SA	AB	H	G by POS
1938 CHI N	3	12	6	1	0	1	8.3	1	5	0	2	0	.500	.833	0	0	OF-3

Bob Martyn

MARTYN, ROBERT GORDON
B. Aug. 15, 1930, Weiser, Ida.

BL TR 6' 176 lbs.

	G	AB	H	2B	3B	HR	HR %	R	RBI	BB	SO	SB	BA	SA	AB	H	G by POS
1957 KC A	58	131	35	2	4	1	0.8	10	12	11	20	1	.267	.366	8	0	OF-49
1958	95	226	59	10	7	2	0.9	25	23	26	36	1	.261	.394	28	7	OF-63
1959	1	1	0	0	0	0	0.0	0	0	0	0	0	.000	.000	1	0	
3 yrs.	154	358	94	12	11	3	0.8	35	35	37	56	2	.263	.383	37	7	OF-112

Gary Martz

MARTZ, GARY ARTHUR
B. Jan. 10, 1951, Spokane, Wash.

BR TR 6'4" 210 lbs.

	G	AB	H	2B	3B	HR	HR %	R	RBI	BB	SO	SB	BA	SA	AB	H	G by POS
1975 KC A	1	1	0	0	0	0	0.0	0	0	0	0	0	.000	.000	1	0	OF-1

Clyde Mashore

MASHORE, CLYDE WAYNE
B. May 29, 1945, Concord, Calif.

BR TR 6' 182 lbs.

	G	AB	H	2B	3B	HR	HR %	R	RBI	BB	SO	SB	BA	SA	AB	H	G by POS
1969 CIN N	2	1	0	0	0	0	0.0	1	0	0	0	0	.000	.000	1	0	
1970 MON N	13	25	4	0	0	1	4.0	2	3	4	11	0	.160	.280	4	0	OF-10
1971	66	114	22	5	0	1	0.9	20	7	10	22	1	.193	.263	12	2	OF-47, 3B-1
1972	93	176	40	7	1	3	1.7	23	23	14	41	6	.227	.330	19	3	OF-74
1973	67	103	21	3	0	3	2.9	12	14	15	28	4	.204	.320	15	3	OF-44, 2B-1
5 yrs.	241	419	87	15	1	8	1.9	58	47	43	102	11	.208	.305	51	8	OF-175, 3B-1, 2B-1

Phil Masi

MASI, PHILIP SAMUEL
B. Jan. 6, 1917, Chicago, Ill.

BR TR 5'10" 177 lbs.

	G	AB	H	2B	3B	HR	HR %	R	RBI	BB	SO	SB	BA	SA	AB	H	G by POS
1939 BOS N	46	114	29	7	2	1	0.9	14	14	9	15	0	.254	.377	3	0	C-42
1940	63	138	27	4	1	1	0.7	11	14	14	14	0	.196	.261	9	3	C-52
1941	87	180	40	8	2	3	1.7	17	18	16	13	4	.222	.339	3	1	C-83
1942	57	87	19	3	1	0	0.0	14	9	12	4	2	.218	.276	1	0	C-39, OF-4
1943	80	238	65	9	1	2	0.8	27	28	27	20	7	.273	.345	1	1	C-73
1944	89	251	69	13	5	3	1.2	33	23	31	20	4	.275	.402	8	1	C-63, 1B-12, 3B-2
1945	111	371	101	25	4	7	1.9	55	46	42	32	9	.272	.418	9	1	C-95, 1B-7
1946	133	397	106	17	5	3	0.8	52	62	55	41	5	.267	.358	5	2	C-124
1947	126	411	125	22	4	9	2.2	54	50	47	27	2	.304	.443	3	1	C-123
1948	113	376	95	19	0	5	1.3	43	44	35	26	2	.253	.343	1	0	C-109
1949 2 teams	BOS N (37G – .210)							PIT N (48G – .274)									
" total	85	240	59	8	2	1	0.8	29	19	31	26	2	.246	.313	3	0	C-81, 1B-2
1950 CHI A	122	377	105	17	2	7	1.9	38	55	49	36	2	.279	.390	9	1	C-114
1951	84	225	61	11	2	4	1.8	24	28	32	27	1	.271	.391	3	0	C-78

	G	AB	H	2B	3B	HR	HR %	R	RBI	BB	SO	SB	BA	SA	Pinch Hit AB	Pinch Hit H	G by POS

Phil Masi continued

	G	AB	H	2B	3B	HR	HR %	R	RBI	BB	SO	SB	BA	SA	AB	H	G by POS
1952	30	63	16	1	1	0	0.0	9	7	10	10	0	.254	.302	3	1	C-25
14 yrs.	1226	3468	917	164	31	47	1.4	420	417	410	311	45	.264	.370	61	12	C-1101, 1B-21, OF-4, 3B-2

WORLD SERIES

	G	AB	H	2B	3B	HR	HR %	R	RBI	BB	SO	SB	BA	SA	AB	H	G by POS
1948 BOS N	5	8	1	1	0	0	0.0	1	1	0	0	0	.125	.250	1	1	C-5

Harry Maskrey

MASKREY, HARRY H.
Brother of Leech Maskrey.
B. Dec. 21, 1861, Mercer, Pa.   D. Aug. 17, 1930, Mercer, Pa.

	G	AB	H	2B	3B	HR	HR %	R	RBI	BB	SO	SB	BA	SA	AB	H	G by POS
1882 LOU AA	1	4	0	0	0	0	0.0	0		0			.000	.000	0	0	OF-1

Leech Maskrey

MASKREY, SAMUEL LEECH
Brother of Harry Maskrey.
B. Feb. 16, 1856, Mercer, Pa.   D. Apr. 1, 1922, Mercer, Pa.
Manager 1882-83.

	G	AB	H	2B	3B	HR	HR %	R	RBI	BB	SO	SB	BA	SA	AB	H	G by POS
1882 LOU AA	76	288	65	14	2	0	0.0	30		9			.226	.288	0	0	OF-76, 2B-1
1883	96	361	73	13	8	1	0.3	50		10			.202	.291	0	0	OF-96, SS-1
1884	105	412	103	13	4	0	0.0	48		17			.250	.301	0	0	OF-103, 3B-3, SS-1
1885	109	423	97	8	11	1	0.2	54		19			.229	.307	0	0	OF-108, 3B-3
1886 2 teams		LOU	AA (5G −	.158)		CIN	AA (27G −	.194)									
" total	32	117	22	4	1	0	0.0	8		6			.188	.239	0	0	OF-31, 3B-2
5 yrs.	418	1601	360	52	26	2	0.1	190		61			.225	.294	0	0	OF-414, 3B-8, SS-2, 2B-1

Charlie Mason

MASON, CHARLES E.
B. June 25, 1853, New Orleans, La.   D. Oct. 21, 1936, Philadelphia, Pa.
Manager 1882, 1884-85.

	G	AB	H	2B	3B	HR	HR %	R	RBI	BB	SO	SB	BA	SA	AB	H	G by POS
1883 PHI AA	1	2	1	0	0	0	0.0	0		0			.500	.500	0	0	OF-1

Don Mason

MASON, DONALD STETSON   BL TR 5'11"   160 lbs.
B. Dec. 20, 1944, Boston, Mass.

	G	AB	H	2B	3B	HR	HR %	R	RBI	BB	SO	SB	BA	SA	AB	H	G by POS
1966 SF N	42	25	3	0	0	1	4.0	8	1	0	2	0	.120	.240	13	1	2B-9
1967	4	3	0	0	0	0	0.0	0	0	0	0	0	.000	.000	0	0	2B-2
1968	10	19	3	0	0	0	0.0	3	1	1	4	1	.158	.158	0	0	2B-5, SS-4, 3B-2
1969	104	250	57	4	2	0	0.0	43	13	36	29	1	.228	.260	18	5	2B-51, 2B-21, SS-7
1970	46	36	5	0	0	0	0.0	4	1	5	7	0	.139	.139	20	1	2B-14
1971 SD N	113	344	73	12	1	2	0.6	43	11	27	35	6	.212	.270	17	6	2B-90, 3B-3
1972	9	11	2	0	0	0	0.0	1	0	1	1	0	.182	.182	4	1	2B-3
1973	8	8	0	0	0	0	0.0	0	0	0	2	0	.000	.000	6	0	2B-1
8 yrs.	336	696	143	16	3	3	0.4	102	27	70	80	8	.205	.250	78	14	2B-175, 3B-26, SS-11

Jim Mason

MASON, JAMES PERCY   BL TR 6'2"   185 lbs.
B. Aug. 14, 1950, Mobile, Ala.

	G	AB	H	2B	3B	HR	HR %	R	RBI	BB	SO	SB	BA	SA	AB	H	G by POS
1971 WAS A	3	9	3	0	0	0	0.0	0	1	3	3	0	.333	.333	0	0	SS-3
1972 TEX A	46	147	29	3	0	0	0.0	10	10	9	39	0	.197	.218	3	0	SS-32, 3B-10
1973	92	238	49	7	2	3	1.3	23	19	23	48	0	.206	.290	1	0	SS-74, 2B-19, 3B-1
1974 NY A	152	440	110	18	6	5	1.1	41	37	35	87	1	.250	.352	0	0	SS-152
1975	94	223	34	3	2	2	0.9	17	16	22	49	0	.152	.211	0	0	SS-93, 2B-1
1976	93	217	39	7	1	1	0.5	17	14	9	37	0	.180	.235	0	0	SS-93
1977 2 teams		TOR	A (22G −	.165)		TEX	A (36G −	.218)									
" total	58	134	25	6	0	1	0.7	19	9	13	20	1	.187	.254	1	0	SS-54, DH-3, 3B-1
1978 TEX A	55	105	20	4	0	0	0.0	10	3	5	17	0	.190	.229	2	0	SS-42, 3B-11, 2B-1
1979 MON N	40	71	13	5	1	0	0.0	3	6	7	16	0	.183	.282	4	0	SS-33, 3B-6
9 yrs.	633	1584	322	53	12	12	0.8	140	114	124	316	2	.203	.275	11	0	SS-576, 3B-29, 2B-21, DH-3

LEAGUE CHAMPIONSHIP SERIES

	G	AB	H	2B	3B	HR	HR %	R	RBI	BB	SO	SB	BA	SA	AB	H	G by POS
1976 NY A	2	0	0	0	0	0	−	0	0	0	0	0	−	−	0	0	SS-2

WORLD SERIES

	G	AB	H	2B	3B	HR	HR %	R	RBI	BB	SO	SB	BA	SA	AB	H	G by POS
1976 NY A	3	1	1	0	0	1	0.0	1	1	0	0	0	1.000	4.000	0	0	SS-3

Gordon Massa

MASSA, GORDON RICHARD (Moose, Duke)   BL TR 6'3"   210 lbs.
B. Sept. 2, 1935, Cincinnati, Ohio

	G	AB	H	2B	3B	HR	HR %	R	RBI	BB	SO	SB	BA	SA	AB	H	G by POS
1957 CHI N	6	15	7	1	0	0	0.0	2	3	4	3	0	.467	.533	0	0	C-6
1958	2	2	0	0	0	0	0.0	0	0	0	2	0	.000	.000	2	0	
2 yrs.	8	17	7	1	0	0	0.0	2	3	4	5	0	.412	.471	2	0	C-6

Bill Massey

MASSEY, WILLIAM HARRY (Big Bill)   6'   195 lbs.
B. Jan., 1871, Philadelphia, Pa.   D. Oct. 9, 1940, Manila, Philippines

	G	AB	H	2B	3B	HR	HR %	R	RBI	BB	SO	SB	BA	SA	AB	H	G by POS
1894 CIN N	13	53	15	3	0	0	0.0	7	5	3	2	0	.283	.340	0	0	1B-10, 2B-2, 3B-1

Mike Massey

MASSEY, WILLIAM HERBERT   BB TR 5'11"   168 lbs.
B. Sept. 28, 1893, Galveston, Tex.   D. Oct. 17, 1971, Shreveport, La.

	G	AB	H	2B	3B	HR	HR %	R	RBI	BB	SO	SB	BA	SA	AB	H	G by POS
1917 BOS N	31	91	18	0	0	0	0.0	12	2	15	15	2	.198	.198	0	0	2B-25

Roy Massey

MASSEY, ROY HARDEE (Red)   BB TR 5'11"   170 lbs.
B. Oct. 9, 1890, Sevierville, Tenn.   D. June 23, 1954, Atlanta, Ga.

	G	AB	H	2B	3B	HR	HR %	R	RBI	BB	SO	SB	BA	SA	AB	H	G by POS
1918 BOS N	66	203	59	6	2	0	0.0	20	18	23	20	1	.291	.340	12	0	OF-45, 1B-4, SS-1, 3B-1

Vic Mata

MATA, VICTOR J.   BR TR 6'1"   165 lbs.
B. June 17, 1961, Santiago, Dominican Republic

	G	AB	H	2B	3B	HR	HR %	R	RBI	BB	SO	SB	BA	SA	AB	H	G by POS
1984 NY A	30	70	23	5	0	1	1.4	8	6	0	12	1	.329	.443	4	2	OF-28

	G	AB	H	2B	3B	HR	HR %	R	RBI	BB	SO	SB	BA	SA	Pinch Hit AB	Pinch Hit H	G by POS

Tommy Matchick

MATCHICK, JOHN THOMAS
B. Sept. 7, 1943, Hazelton, Pa.
BL TR 6'1" 173 lbs.

	G	AB	H	2B	3B	HR	HR%	R	RBI	BB	SO	SB	BA	SA	PH AB	PH H	G by POS
1967 DET A	8	6	1	0	0	0	0.0	0	0	0	2	0	.167	.167	5	0	SS-1
1968	80	227	46	6	2	3	1.3	18	14	10	46	0	.203	.286	13	5	SS-59, 2B-13, 1B-6
1969	94	298	72	11	2	0	0.0	25	32	15	51	3	.242	.292	16	8	2B-47, 3B-27, SS-6, 1B-2
1970 2 teams	KC	A (55G – .196)				BOS	A (10G – .071)										
" total	65	172	32	3	2	0	0.0	13	11	7	25	0	.186	.227	12	0	SS-44, 2B-11, 3B-3
1971 MIL A	42	114	25	1	0	1	0.9	6	7	7	23	3	.219	.254	0	0	3B-41, 2B-1
1972 BAL A	3	9	2	0	0	0	0.0	0	0	0	1	0	.222	.222	0	0	3B-3
6 yrs.	292	826	178	21	6	4	0.5	63	64	39	148	6	.215	.270	46	13	SS-110, 3B-74, 2B-72, 1B-8

WORLD SERIES
| 1968 DET A | 3 | 3 | 0 | 0 | 0 | 0 | 0.0 | 0 | 0 | 0 | 1 | 0 | .000 | .000 | 3 | 0 | |

Joe Mathes

MATHES, JOSEPH JOHN
B. July 28, 1891, Milwaukee, Wis. D. Dec. 21, 1978, St. Louis, Mo.
BB TR 6'½" 180 lbs.

	G	AB	H	2B	3B	HR	HR%	R	RBI	BB	SO	SB	BA	SA	PH AB	PH H	G by POS
1912 PHI A	4	14	2	0	0	0	0.0	0	0	0		0	.143	.143	0	0	3B-4
1914 STL F	26	85	25	3	0	0	0.0	10	6	9		1	.294	.329	1	1	2B-23
1916 BOS N	2	0	0	0	0	0	–	0	0	0	0	0	–	–	0	0	2B-2
3 yrs.	32	99	27	3	0	0	0.0	10	6	9		1	.273	.303	1	1	2B-25, 3B-4

Bobby Mathews

MATHEWS, ROBERT T.
B. Nov. 21, 1851, Baltimore, Md. D. Apr. 17, 1898, Baltimore, Md.
BR TR 5'5½" 145 lbs.

	G	AB	H	2B	3B	HR	HR%	R	RBI	BB	SO	SB	BA	SA	PH AB	PH H	G by POS
1876 NY N	56	218	40	4	1	0	0.0	19	9	3	2		.183	.211	0	0	P-56, OF-1
1877 CIN N	15	59	10	0	0	0	0.0	5	0	1	2		.169	.169	0	0	P-15, OF-1, SS-1
1879 PRO N	43	173	35	2	0	1	0.6	25	10	7	12		.202	.231	0	0	P-27, OF-21, 3B-5
1881 2 teams	PRO	N (16G – .193)				BOS	N (19G – .169)										
" total	35	128	23	3	0	0	0.0	8	8	5	11		.180	.203	0	0	OF-23, P-19
1882 BOS N	45	169	38	6	0	0	0.0	17	13	8	18		.225	.260	0	0	P-34, OF-13, SS-1
1883 PHI AA	45	167	31	2	0	0	0.0	15		4			.186	.198	0	0	P-44, OF-3
1884	49	184	34	5	1	0	0.0	26		7			.185	.223	0	0	P-49, OF-1
1885	48	179	30	3	0	0	0.0	22		10			.168	.184	0	0	P-48, OF-1
1886	24	88	21	0	0	0	0.0	16		3			.239	.273	0	0	P-24, OF-1
1887	7	25	5	0	0	0	0.0	5		4		0	.200	.200	0	0	P-7
10 yrs.	367	1390	267	28	2	1	0.1	158	40	52	45	0	.192	.217	0	0	P-323, OF-65, 3B-5, SS-2

Eddie Mathews

MATHEWS, EDWIN LEE
B. Oct. 13, 1931, Texarkana, Tex.
Manager 1972-74.
Hall of Fame 1978.
BL TR 6'1" 190 lbs.

	G	AB	H	2B	3B	HR	HR%	R	RBI	BB	SO	SB	BA	SA	PH AB	PH H	G by POS
1952 BOS N	145	528	128	23	5	25	4.7	80	58	59	115	6	.242	.447	2	0	3B-142
1953 MIL N	154	579	175	31	8	47	8.1	110	135	99	83	1	.302	.627	0	0	3B-157
1954	138	476	138	21	4	40	8.4	96	103	113	61	10	.290	.603	2	0	3B-127, OF-10
1955	141	499	144	23	5	41	8.2	108	101	109	98	3	.289	.601	2	1	3B-137
1956	151	552	150	21	2	37	6.7	103	95	91	86	6	.272	.518	2	0	3B-150
1957	148	572	167	28	9	32	5.6	109	94	90	79	3	.292	.540	0	0	3B-147
1958	149	546	137	18	1	31	5.7	97	77	85	85	5	.251	.458	0	0	3B-149
1959	148	594	182	16	8	46	7.7	118	114	80	71	2	.306	.593	0	0	3B-148
1960	153	548	152	19	7	39	7.1	108	124	111	113	7	.277	.551	0	0	3B-153
1961	152	572	175	23	6	32	5.6	103	91	93	95	12	.306	.535	1	0	3B-151
1962	152	536	142	25	6	29	5.4	106	90	101	90	4	.265	.496	3	0	3B-140, 1B-7
1963	158	547	144	27	4	23	4.2	82	84	124	119	3	.263	.453	1	0	3B-121, OF-42
1964	141	502	117	19	1	23	4.6	83	74	85	100	2	.233	.412	6	1	3B-128, 1B-7
1965	156	546	137	23	0	32	5.9	77	95	73	110	1	.251	.469	8	1	3B-153
1966 ATL N	134	452	113	21	4	16	3.5	72	53	63	82	1	.250	.420	12	4	3B-127
1967 2 teams	HOU	N (101G – .238)				DET	A (36G – .231)										
" total	137	436	103	16	2	16	3.7	53	57	63	88	2	.236	.392	15	2	1B-92, 3B-45
1968 DET A	31	52	11	0	0	3	5.8	4	8	5	12	0	.212	.385	16	3	3B-6, 1B-6
17 yrs.	2388	8537	2315	354	72	512	6.0	1509	1453	1444	1487	68	.271	.509	70	12	3B-2181, 1B-112, OF-52
							10th										

WORLD SERIES
1957 MIL N	7	22	5	3	0	1	4.5	4	4	8	5	0	.227	.500	0	0	3B-7
1958	7	25	4	2	0	0	0.0	3	3	6	11	1	.160	.240	0	0	3B-7
1968 DET A	2	3	1	0	0	0	0.0	0	0	1	1	0	.333	.333	1	0	3B-1
3 yrs.	16	50	10	5	0	1	2.0	7	7	15	17	1	.200	.360	1	0	3B-15

Nelson Mathews

MATHEWS, NELSON ELMER
B. July 21, 1941, Columbia, Ill.
BR TR 6'4" 195 lbs.

	G	AB	H	2B	3B	HR	HR%	R	RBI	BB	SO	SB	BA	SA	PH AB	PH H	G by POS
1960 CHI N	3	8	2	0	0	0	0.0	1	0	0	2	0	.250	.250	1	1	OF-2
1961	3	9	1	0	0	0	0.0	0	0	0	2	0	.111	.111	1	0	OF-2
1962	15	49	15	2	0	2	4.1	5	13	5	4	3	.306	.469	1	0	OF-14
1963	61	155	24	3	2	4	2.6	12	10	16	48	3	.155	.277	8	0	OF-46
1964 KC A	157	573	137	27	5	14	2.4	58	60	43	143	7	.239	.377	1	0	OF-154
1965	67	184	39	7	7	2	1.1	17	15	24	49	0	.212	.359	10	1	OF-57
6 yrs.	306	978	218	39	14	22	2.2	93	98	88	248	8	.223	.359	22	2	OF-275

I. I. Mathison

MATHISON, I. I.
B. Baltimore, Md.
TR

	G	AB	H	2B	3B	HR	HR%	R	RBI	BB	SO	SB	BA	SA	PH AB	PH H	G by POS
1902 BAL A	29	91	24	2	1	0	0.0	12	7	9		2	.264	.308	0	0	3B-28, SS-1

John Matias

MATIAS, JOHN ROY
B. Aug. 15, 1944, Honolulu, Hawaii
BL TL 5'11" 170 lbs.

	G	AB	H	2B	3B	HR	HR%	R	RBI	BB	SO	SB	BA	SA	PH AB	PH H	G by POS
1970 CHI A	58	117	22	2	0	2	1.7	7	6	3	22	1	.188	.256	27	5	OF-22, 1B-18

	G	AB	H	2B	3B	HR	HR %	R	RBI	BB	SO	SB	BA	SA	Pinch Hit AB	Pinch Hit H	G by POS

Bob Matthews

MATTHEWS, ROBERT
B. Camden, N. J.   Deceased.

	G	AB	H	2B	3B	HR	HR%	R	RBI	BB	SO	SB	BA	SA	PH AB	PH H	G by POS
1891 PHI AA	1	3	1	0	0	0	0.0	1	0	0	1	0	.333	.333	0	0	OF-1

Gary Matthews

MATTHEWS, GARY NATHANIEL
B. July 5, 1950, San Fernando, Calif.
BR TR 6'2" 185 lbs.

	G	AB	H	2B	3B	HR	HR%	R	RBI	BB	SO	SB	BA	SA	PH AB	PH H	G by POS
1972 SF N	20	62	18	1	1	4	6.5	11	14	7	13	0	.290	.532	1	0	OF-19
1973	148	540	162	22	10	12	2.2	74	58	58	83	17	.300	.444	1	1	OF-145
1974	154	561	161	27	6	16	2.9	87	82	70	69	11	.287	.442	4	0	OF-151
1975	116	425	119	22	3	12	2.8	67	58	65	53	13	.280	.431	3	1	OF-113
1976	156	587	164	28	4	20	3.4	79	84	75	94	12	.279	.443	1	0	OF-156
1977 ATL N	148	555	157	25	5	17	3.1	89	64	67	90	22	.283	.438	2	1	OF-145
1978	129	474	135	20	5	18	3.8	75	62	61	92	8	.285	.462	3	0	OF-127
1979	156	631	192	34	5	27	4.3	97	90	60	75	18	.304	.502	0	0	OF-156
1980	155	571	159	17	3	19	3.3	79	75	42	93	11	.278	.419	8	2	OF-143
1981 PHI N	101	359	108	21	3	9	2.5	62	67	59	42	15	.301	.451	2	0	OF-100
1982	162	616	173	31	1	19	3.1	89	83	66	87	21	.281	.427	1	0	OF-162
1983	132	446	115	18	2	10	2.2	66	50	69	81	13	.258	.374	9	2	OF-122
1984 CHI N	147	491	143	21	2	14	2.9	101	82	**103**	97	17	.291	.428	3	0	OF-145
13 yrs.	1724	6318	1806	287	50	197	3.1	976	869	802	969	178	.286	.441	38	7	OF-1684

DIVISIONAL PLAYOFF SERIES
	G	AB	H	2B	3B	HR	HR%	R	RBI	BB	SO	SB	BA	SA	PH AB	PH H	G by POS
1981 PHI N	5	20	8	0	1	1	5.0	3	1	0	2	0	.400	.650	0	0	OF-5

LEAGUE CHAMPIONSHIP SERIES
	G	AB	H	2B	3B	HR	HR%	R	RBI	BB	SO	SB	BA	SA	PH AB	PH H	G by POS
1983 PHI N	4	14	6	0	0	3	21.4	4	8	2	1	1	.429	1.071	0	0	OF-4
1984 CHI N	5	15	3	0	0	2	13.3	4	5	6	4	1	.200	.600	0	0	OF-5
2 yrs.	9	29	9	0	0	5	17.2	8	13	8	5	2	.310	.828	0	0	OF-9

WORLD SERIES
	G	AB	H	2B	3B	HR	HR%	R	RBI	BB	SO	SB	BA	SA	PH AB	PH H	G by POS
1983 PHI N	5	16	4	0	0	1	6.3	1	1	2	2	0	.250	.438	0	0	OF-5

Wid Matthews

MATTHEWS, WID CURRY
B. Oct. 20, 1896, Raleigh, Ill.   D. Oct. 5, 1965, W. Hollywood, Calif.
BL TL 5'8½" 155 lbs.

	G	AB	H	2B	3B	HR	HR%	R	RBI	BB	SO	SB	BA	SA	PH AB	PH H	G by POS
1923 PHI A	129	485	133	11	6	1	0.2	52	25	50	27	16	.274	.328	1	0	OF-127
1924 WAS A	53	169	51	10	4	0	0.0	25	13	11	4	3	.302	.408	6	4	OF-44
1925	10	9	4	0	0	0	0.0	2	1	0	1	0	.444	.444	7	3	OF-1
3 yrs.	192	663	188	21	10	1	0.2	79	39	61	32	19	.284	.350	14	7	OF-172

Steve Matthias

MATTHIAS, STEPHEN J.
B. Mitchellville, Md.   Deceased.

	G	AB	H	2B	3B	HR	HR%	R	RBI	BB	SO	SB	BA	SA	PH AB	PH H	G by POS
1884 C-P U	37	142	39	7	1	0	0.0	24		5			.275	.338	0	0	SS-36, OF-2

Bobby Mattick

MATTICK, ROBERT JAMES
Son of Wally Mattick.
B. Dec. 5, 1915, Sioux City, Iowa
Manager 1980-81.
BR TR 5'11" 178 lbs.

	G	AB	H	2B	3B	HR	HR%	R	RBI	BB	SO	SB	BA	SA	PH AB	PH H	G by POS
1938 CHI N	1	1	1	0	0	0	0.0	0	1	0	0	0	1.000	1.000	0	0	SS-1
1939	51	178	51	12	1	0	0.0	16	23	6	19	1	.287	.365	1	0	SS-48
1940	128	441	96	15	0	0	0.0	30	33	19	33	5	.218	.252	1	0	SS-126, 3B-1
1941 CIN N	20	60	11	3	0	0	0.0	8	7	8	7	1	.183	.233	2	0	SS-12, 3B-5, 2B-1
1942	6	10	2	1	0	0	0.0	0	0	0	1	0	.200	.300	0	0	SS-3
5 yrs.	206	690	161	31	1	0	0.0	54	64	33	60	7	.233	.281	4	0	SS-190, 3B-6, 2B-1

Wally Mattick

MATTICK, WALTER JOSEPH (Chick)
Father of Bobby Mattick.
B. Mar. 12, 1887, St. Louis, Mo.   D. Nov. 5, 1968, Los Altos, Calif.
BR TR 5'10" 180 lbs.

	G	AB	H	2B	3B	HR	HR%	R	RBI	BB	SO	SB	BA	SA	PH AB	PH H	G by POS
1912 CHI A	88	285	74	7	9	1	0.4	45	35	27		15	.260	.358	8	3	OF-78
1913	68	207	39	8	1	0	0.0	15	11	18	16	3	.188	.237	3	1	OF-63
1918 STL N	8	14	2	0	0	0	0.0	0	1	2	3	0	.143	.143	5	1	OF-3
3 yrs.	164	506	115	15	10	1	0.2	60	47	47	19	18	.227	.302	16	5	OF-144

Mike Mattimore

MATTIMORE, MICHAEL JOSEPH
B. 1859, Renovo, Pa.   D. Apr. 29, 1931, Butte, Mont.
BL TR 5'8½" 160 lbs.

	G	AB	H	2B	3B	HR	HR%	R	RBI	BB	SO	SB	BA	SA	PH AB	PH H	G by POS
1887 NY N	8	32	8	1	0	0	0.0	5	4	0	6	1	.250	.281	0	0	P-7, OF-2
1888 PHI AA	41	142	38	6	5	0	0.0	22	12	12		16	.268	.380	0	0	P-26, OF-16
1889 2 teams	PHI	AA (23G – .233)						KC		AA (19G – .160)							
" total	42	148	29	2	3	1	0.7	16	13	12	23	6	.196	.270	0	0	OF-31, 1B-7, P-6
1890 B-B AA	33	129	17	1	0	0	0.0	14		16		11	.132	.155	0	0	P-19, OF-14
4 yrs.	124	451	92	10	9	1	0.2	57	29	40	29	34	.204	.273	0	0	OF-63, P-58, 1B-7

Don Mattingly

MATTINGLY, DONALD ARTHUR
B. Apr. 21, 1961, Evansville, Ind.
BL TL 6' 185 lbs.

	G	AB	H	2B	3B	HR	HR%	R	RBI	BB	SO	SB	BA	SA	PH AB	PH H	G by POS
1982 NY A	7	12	2	0	0	0	0.0	0	1	0	1	0	.167	.167	1	0	OF-6, 1B-1
1983	91	279	79	15	4	4	1.4	34	32	21	31	0	.283	.409	8	1	OF-48, 1B-42, 2B-1
1984	153	603	**207**	44	2	23	3.8	91	110	41	33	1	**.343**	.537	3	0	1B-133, OF-19
3 yrs.	251	894	288	59	6	27	3.0	125	143	62	65	1	.322	.492	12	2	1B-176, OF-73, 2B-1

Ralph Mattis

MATTIS, RALPH (Matty)
B. Aug. 24, 1890, Roxborough, Pa.   D. Sept. 13, 1960, Williamsport, Pa.
BR TR 5'11" 172 lbs.

	G	AB	H	2B	3B	HR	HR%	R	RBI	BB	SO	SB	BA	SA	PH AB	PH H	G by POS
1914 PIT F	36	85	21	4	2	0	0.0	14	8	9		2	.247	.318	11	3	OF-24

Cloy Mattox

MATTOX, CLOY MITCHELL (Monk)
Brother of Jim Mattox.
B. Nov. 21, 1902, Leesville, Va.
BL TR 5'8" 168 lbs.

	G	AB	H	2B	3B	HR	HR%	R	RBI	BB	SO	SB	BA	SA	PH AB	PH H	G by POS
1929 PHI A	3	6	1	0	0	0	0.0	0	0	1	1	0	.167	.167	0	0	C-3

	G	AB	H	2B	3B	HR	HR %	R	RBI	BB	SO	SB	BA	SA	Pinch Hit AB	Pinch Hit H	G by POS

Jim Mattox

MATTOX, JAMES POWELL
Brother of Cloy Mattox.
B. Dec. 17, 1896, Leesville, Va.   D. Oct. 12, 1973, Myrtle Beach, S. C.
BL TR 5'9½" 168 lbs.

	G	AB	H	2B	3B	HR	HR %	R	RBI	BB	SO	SB	BA	SA	PH AB	PH H	G by POS
1922 PIT N	29	51	15	1	1	0	0.0	11	3	1	3	0	.294	.353	4	3	C-21
1923	22	32	6	1	1	0	0.0	4	1	0	5	0	.188	.281	14	2	C-8
2 yrs.	51	83	21	2	2	0	0.0	15	4	1	8	0	.253	.325	18	5	C-29

Len Matuszek

MATUSZEK, LEONARD JAMES
B. Sept. 27, 1954, Toledo, Ohio
BL TR 6'2" 190 lbs.

	G	AB	H	2B	3B	HR	HR %	R	RBI	BB	SO	SB	BA	SA	PH AB	PH H	G by POS
1981 PHI N	13	11	3	1	0	0	0.0	1	1	3	1	0	.273	.364	9	3	3B-1, 1B-1
1982	25	39	3	1	0	0	0.0	1	3	1	10	0	.077	.103	17	1	3B-8, 1B-3
1983	28	80	22	6	1	4	5.0	12	16	4	14	0	.275	.525	6	1	1B-21
1984	101	262	65	17	1	12	4.6	40	43	39	54	4	.248	.458	24	10	1B-81, OF-1
4 yrs.	167	392	93	25	2	16	4.1	54	63	47	79	4	.237	.434	56	15	1B-106, 3B-9, OF-1

Gene Mauch

MAUCH, GENE WILLIAM (Skip)
B. Nov. 18, 1925, Salina, Kans.
Manager 1960-82.
BR TR 5'10" 165 lbs.

	G	AB	H	2B	3B	HR	HR %	R	RBI	BB	SO	SB	BA	SA	PH AB	PH H	G by POS
1944 BKN N	5	15	2	1	0	0	0.0	2	2	2	3	0	.133	.200	0	0	SS-5
1947 PIT N	16	30	9	0	0	0	0.0	8	1	7	6	0	.300	.300	0	0	2B-6, SS-4
1948 2 teams			BKN	N	(12G –	.154)		CHI	N	(53G –	.203)						
" total	65	151	30	3	2	1	0.7	19	7	27	14	1	.199	.265	11	4	2B-33, SS-20
1949 CHI N	72	150	37	6	1	1	0.7	15	7	21	15	3	.247	.333	13	4	2B-25, SS-19, 3B-7
1950 BOS N	48	121	28	5	0	1	0.8	17	15	14	9	1	.231	.298	3	2	2B-28, 3B-7, SS-5
1951	19	20	2	0	0	0	0.0	5	1	7	4	0	.100	.100	2	0	SS-10, 3B-3, 2B-2
1952 STL N	7	3	0	0	0	0	0.0	0	0	1	2	0	.000	.000	1	0	SS-2
1956 BOS A	7	25	8	0	0	0	0.0	4	1	3	3	0	.320	.320	1	0	2B-6
1957	65	222	60	10	3	2	0.9	23	28	22	26	1	.270	.369	7	3	2B-58
9 yrs.	304	737	176	25	7	5	0.7	93	62	104	82	6	.239	.312	38	9	2B-158, SS-65, 3B-17

Al Maul

MAUL, ALBERT JOSEPH (Smiling Al)
B. Oct. 9, 1865, Philadelphia, Pa.   D. May 3, 1958, Philadelphia, Pa.
BR TR 6' 175 lbs.

	G	AB	H	2B	3B	HR	HR %	R	RBI	BB	SO	SB	BA	SA	PH AB	PH H	G by POS
1884 PHI U	1	4	0	0	0	0	0.0	0		0			.000	.000	0	0	P-1
1887 PHI N	16	56	17	2	2	1	1.8	15	4	15	10	5	.304	.464	0	0	OF-8, P-7, 1B-2
1888 PIT N	74	259	54	9	4	0	0.0	21	31	21	45	9	.208	.274	0	0	1B-38, OF-34, P-3
1889	68	257	71	6	6	4	1.6	37	44	29	41	18	.276	.393	0	0	OF-64, P-6
1890 PIT P	45	162	42	6	2	0	0.0	31	21	22	12	5	.259	.321	0	0	P-30, OF-15, SS-1
1891 PIT N	47	149	28	2	4	0	0.0	15	14	20	28	4	.188	.255	0	0	OF-40, P-8
1893 WAS N	44	134	34	8	4	0	0.0	10	12	33	14	1	.254	.373	2	0	P-37, OF-7
1894	41	124	30	3	3	2	1.6	23	20	14	11	1	.242	.363	2	0	P-28, OF-12
1895	22	72	18	5	2	0	0.0	9	16	6	7	0	.250	.375	2	1	P-16, OF-4
1896	8	28	8	1	1	0	0.0	6	5	3	2	0	.286	.393	0	0	P-8
1897 2 teams			WAS	N	(1G –	.000)		BAL	N	(2G –	.333)						
" total	3	4	1	0	0	0	0.0	0		0			.250	.250	0	0	P-3
1898 BAL N	29	93	19	3	2	0	0.0	21	10	16		1	.204	.280	0	0	P-28, OF-1
1899 BKN N	4	11	3	0	0	0	0.0	2	0	1		0	.273	.273	0	0	P-4
1900 PHI N	5	15	3	0	0	0	0.0	2	1	2		0	.200	.200	0	0	P-5
1901 NY N	3	8	3	0	0	0	0.0	1	1	0		0	.375	.375	0	0	P-3
15 yrs.	410	1376	331	45	30	7	0.5	193	178	182	170	44	.241	.332	6	1	P-187, OF-185, 1B-40, SS-1

Mark Mauldin

MAULDIN, MARSHALL REESE
B. Nov. 5, 1914, Atlanta, Ga.
BR TR 5'11" 170 lbs.

	G	AB	H	2B	3B	HR	HR %	R	RBI	BB	SO	SB	BA	SA	PH AB	PH H	G by POS
1934 CHI A	10	38	10	2	0	1	2.6	3	3	0	3	0	.263	.395	0	0	3B-10

Carmen Mauro

MAURO, CARMEN LOUIS
B. Nov. 10, 1926, St. Paul, Minn.
BL TR 6' 167 lbs.

	G	AB	H	2B	3B	HR	HR %	R	RBI	BB	SO	SB	BA	SA	PH AB	PH H	G by POS
1948 CHI N	3	5	1	0	0	1	20.0	2	1	2	0	0	.200	.800	0	0	OF-2
1950	62	185	42	4	3	1	0.5	19	10	13	31	3	.227	.297	9	0	OF-49
1951	13	29	5	1	0	0	0.0	3	3	2	6	0	.172	.207	6	1	OF-6
1953 3 teams			BKN	N	(8G –	.000)		WAS	A	(17G –	.174)		PHI	A	(64G –	.267)	
" total	89	197	48	4	5	0	0.0	16	19	20	28	3	.244	.315	31	8	OF-56, 3B-1
4 yrs.	167	416	96	9	8	2	0.5	40	33	37	65	6	.231	.305	46	10	OF-113, 3B-1

Bob Mavis

MAVIS, ROBERT HENRY
B. Apr. 8, 1918, Milwaukee, Wis.
BL TR 5'7" 160 lbs.

	G	AB	H	2B	3B	HR	HR %	R	RBI	BB	SO	SB	BA	SA	PH AB	PH H	G by POS
1949 DET A	1	0	0	0	0	0	–	0	0	0	0	0	–	–	0	0	

Dal Maxvill

MAXVILL, CHARLES DALLAN
B. Feb. 18, 1939, Granite City, Ill.
BR TR 5'11" 157 lbs.

	G	AB	H	2B	3B	HR	HR %	R	RBI	BB	SO	SB	BA	SA	PH AB	PH H	G by POS
1962 STL N	79	189	42	3	1	1	0.5	20	18	17	39	1	.222	.265	3	0	SS-76, 3B-1
1963	53	51	12	2	0	0	0.0	12	3	6	11	0	.235	.275	3	0	SS-24, 2B-9, 3B-3
1964	37	26	6	0	0	0	0.0	4	4	0	7	1	.231	.231	1	0	2B-15, SS-13, OF-1, 3B-1
1965	68	89	12	2	2	0	0.0	10	10	7	15	0	.135	.202	2	0	2B-49, SS-12
1966	134	394	96	14	3	0	0.0	25	24	37	61	3	.244	.294	2	0	SS-128, 2B-5, OF-1
1967	152	476	108	14	4	1	0.2	37	41	48	66	0	.227	.279	0	0	SS-148, 2B-7
1968	151	459	116	8	5	1	0.2	51	24	52	71	0	.253	.298	0	0	SS-151
1969	132	372	65	10	2	2	0.5	27	32	44	52	1	.175	.228	0	0	SS-131
1970	132	399	80	5	2	0	0.0	35	28	51	56	0	.201	.223	0	0	SS-136, 2B-22
1971	142	356	80	10	1	0	0.0	31	24	43	45	1	.225	.258	1	0	SS-140
1972 2 teams			STL	N	(105G –	.221)		OAK	A	(27G –	.250)						
" total	132	312	70	7	1	0	0.3	24	24	32	58	0	.224	.263	1	0	SS-99, 2B-35
1973 2 teams			OAK	A	(29G –	.211)		PIT	N	(74G –	.189)						
" total	103	236	45	4	3	0	0.0	19	18	23	43	0	.191	.233	2	0	SS-92, 2B-11, 3B-1
1974 2 teams			PIT	N	(8G –	.182)		OAK	A	(60G –	.192)						
" total	68	74	14	0	0	0	0.0	6	2	10	14	0	.189	.189	0	0	SS-37, 2B-30, 3B-1
1975 OAK A	20	10	2	0	0	0	0.0	1	0	0	0	0	.200	.200	0	0	SS-20, 2B-2
14 yrs.	1423	3443	748	79	24	6	0.2	302	252	370	538	7	.217	.259	15	0	SS-1207, 2B-185, 3B-7, OF-2

	G	AB	H	2B	3B	HR	HR %	R	RBI	BB	SO	SB	BA	SA	Pinch Hit AB	Pinch Hit H	G by POS

Dal Maxvill continued

LEAGUE CHAMPIONSHIP SERIES

	G	AB	H	2B	3B	HR	HR %	R	RBI	BB	SO	SB	BA	SA	AB	H	G by POS
1972 OAK A	5	8	1	0	0	0	0.0	0	0	1	2	1	.125	.125	0	0	SS-4
1974	1	1	0	0	0	0	0.0	0	0	0	1	0	.000	.000	0	0	2B-1
2 yrs.	6	9	1	0	0	0	0.0	0	0	1	3	1	.111	.111	0	0	SS-4, 2B-1

WORLD SERIES

	G	AB	H	2B	3B	HR	HR %	R	RBI	BB	SO	SB	BA	SA	AB	H	G by POS
1964 STL N	7	20	4	1	0	0	0.0	0	1	1	4	0	.200	.250	0	0	2B-7
1967	7	19	3	0	1	0	0.0	1	1	4	1	0	.158	.263	0	0	SS-7
1968	7	22	0	0	0	0	0.0	1	0	3	5	0	.000	.000	0	0	SS-7
1974 OAK A	2	0	0	0	0	0	–	0	0	0	0	0	–	–	0	0	2B-2
4 yrs.	23	61	7	1	1	0	0.0	2	2	8	10	0	.115	.164	0	0	SS-14, 2B-9

Charlie Maxwell

MAXWELL, CHARLES RICHARD (Smokey)
B. Apr. 28, 1927, Lawton, Mich.

BL TL 5'11"   185 lbs.

	G	AB	H	2B	3B	HR	HR %	R	RBI	BB	SO	SB	BA	SA	AB	H	G by POS
1950 BOS A	3	8	0	0	0	0	0.0	1	0	1	3	0	.000	.000	1	0	OF-2
1951	49	80	15	1	0	3	3.8	8	12	9	18	0	.188	.313	31	7	OF-13
1952	8	15	1	1	0	0	0.0	0	0	3	11	0	.067	.133	3	0	OF-3, 1B-3
1954	74	104	26	4	1	0	0.0	9	5	12	21	3	.250	.308	45	12	OF-27
1955 2 teams			BAL A (4G – .000)				DET	A	(55G – .266)								
" total	59	113	29	7	1	7	6.2	19	18	8	21	0	.257	.522	30	7	OF-26, 1B-2
1956 DET A	141	500	163	14	3	28	5.6	96	87	79	74	1	.326	.534	7	4	OF-136
1957	138	492	136	23	3	24	4.9	75	82	76	84	3	.276	.482	3	3	OF-137
1958	131	397	108	14	4	13	3.3	56	65	64	54	6	.272	.426	8	1	OF-114, 1B-14
1959	145	518	130	12	2	31	6.0	81	95	81	91	0	.251	.461	8	3	OF-136
1960	134	482	114	16	5	24	5.0	70	81	58	75	5	.237	.440	14	1	OF-120
1961	79	131	30	4	2	5	3.8	11	18	20	24	0	.229	.405	45	12	OF-25
1962 2 teams			DET A (30G – .194)				CHI	A	(69G – .296)								
" total	99	273	74	10	3	10	3.7	35	52	42	42	0	.271	.440	20	3	OF-71, 1B-7
1963 CHI A	71	130	30	4	2	3	2.3	17	17	31	27	0	.231	.362	21	3	OF-24, 1B-17
1964	2	2	0	0	0	0	0.0	0	0	0	0	0	.000	.000	2	0	
14 yrs.	1133	3245	856	110	26	148	4.6	478	532	484	545	18	.264	.451	238	56	OF-834, 1B-43

Carlos May

MAY, CARLOS
Brother of Lee May.
B. May 17, 1948, Birmingham, Ala.

BL TR 5'11"   200 lbs.

	G	AB	H	2B	3B	HR	HR %	R	RBI	BB	SO	SB	BA	SA	AB	H	G by POS
1968 CHI A	17	67	12	1	0	0	0.0	4	1	3	15	0	.179	.194	0	0	OF-17
1969	100	367	103	18	2	18	4.9	62	62	58	66	1	.281	.488	2	1	OF-100
1970	150	555	158	28	4	12	2.2	83	68	79	96	12	.285	.414	2	0	OF-141, 1B-7
1971	141	500	147	21	7	7	1.4	64	70	62	61	16	.294	.406	5	2	1B-130, OF-9
1972	148	523	161	26	3	12	2.3	83	68	79	70	23	.308	.438	0	0	OF-145, 1B-5
1973	149	553	148	20	0	20	3.6	62	96	53	73	8	.268	.412	2	0	DH-75, OF-70, 1B-2
1974	149	551	137	19	2	8	1.5	66	58	46	76	8	.249	.334	10	0	OF-129, DH-13
1975	128	454	123	19	2	8	1.8	55	53	67	46	12	.271	.374	1	0	1B-63, OF-46, DH-19
1976 2 teams			CHI A (20G – .175)				NY	A	(87G – .278)								
" total	107	351	91	13	2	3	0.9	45	43	43	37	5	.259	.333	15	5	DH-81, OF-16, 1B-1
1977 2 teams			NY A (65G – .227)				CAL	A	(11G – .333)								
" total	76	199	47	7	1	2	1.0	21	17	22	25	0	.236	.312	14	6	DH-54, OF-4, 1B-3
10 yrs.	1165	4120	1127	172	23	90	2.2	545	536	512	565	85	.274	.392	51	14	OF-677, DH-242, 1B-211

LEAGUE CHAMPIONSHIP SERIES

	G	AB	H	2B	3B	HR	HR %	R	RBI	BB	SO	SB	BA	SA	AB	H	G by POS
1976 NY A	3	10	2	1	0	0	0.0	1	0	1	4	0	.200	.300	1	0	DH-3

WORLD SERIES

	G	AB	H	2B	3B	HR	HR %	R	RBI	BB	SO	SB	BA	SA	AB	H	G by POS
1976 NY A	4	9	0	0	0	0	0.0	0	0	0	1	0	.000	.000	2	0	DH-4

Dave May

MAY, DAVID LaFRANCE
B. Dec. 23, 1943, New Castle, Del.

BL TR 5'10½"   186 lbs.

	G	AB	H	2B	3B	HR	HR %	R	RBI	BB	SO	SB	BA	SA	AB	H	G by POS
1967 BAL A	36	85	20	1	1	1	1.2	12	7	6	13	0	.235	.306	15	3	OF-19
1968	84	152	29	6	3	0	0.0	15	7	19	27	3	.191	.270	26	3	OF-61
1969	78	120	29	6	0	3	2.5	8	10	9	23	2	.242	.367	32	8	OF-40
1970 2 teams			BAL A (25G – .194)				MIL	A	(101G – .240)								
" total	126	373	88	8	2	8	2.1	42	37	48	60	8	.236	.332	15	1	OF-108
1971 MIL A	144	501	139	20	3	16	3.2	74	65	50	59	15	.277	.425	3	0	OF-142
1972	143	500	119	20	2	9	1.8	49	45	47	56	11	.238	.340	7	3	OF-138
1973	156	624	189	23	4	25	4.0	96	93	44	78	6	.303	.473	3	1	OF-152, DH-2
1974	135	477	108	15	1	10	2.1	56	42	28	73	4	.226	.325	8	1	OF-121, DH-8
1975 ATL N	82	203	56	8	0	12	5.9	28	40	25	27	1	.276	.493	26	7	OF-53
1976	105	214	46	5	3	3	1.4	27	23	26	31	5	.215	.308	44	8	OF-60
1977 TEX A	120	340	82	14	1	7	2.1	46	42	32	43	4	.241	.350	11	2	OF-111, DH-5
1978 2 teams			MIL A (39G – .195)				PIT	N	(5G – .000)								
" total	44	81	15	4	0	2	2.5	9	11	10	11	1	.185	.309	18	4	OF-16, DH-8
12 yrs.	1253	3670	920	130	20	96	2.6	462	422	344	501	60	.251	.375	208	43	OF-1021, DH-23

LEAGUE CHAMPIONSHIP SERIES

	G	AB	H	2B	3B	HR	HR %	R	RBI	BB	SO	SB	BA	SA	AB	H	G by POS
1969 BAL A	1	1	0	0	0	0	0.0	0	0	0	0	0	.000	.000	1	0	

WORLD SERIES

	G	AB	H	2B	3B	HR	HR %	R	RBI	BB	SO	SB	BA	SA	AB	H	G by POS
1969 BAL A	2	1	0	0	0	0	0.0	0	0	1	0	0	.000	.000	1	0	

Jerry May

MAY, JERRY LEE
B. Dec. 14, 1943, Parnassus, Va.

BR TR 6'2"   190 lbs.

	G	AB	H	2B	3B	HR	HR %	R	RBI	BB	SO	SB	BA	SA	AB	H	G by POS
1964 PIT N	11	31	8	0	0	0	0.0	3	3	3	9	0	.258	.258	0	0	C-11
1965	4	2	1	0	0	0	0.0	0	1	0	0	0	.500	.500	0	0	C-4
1966	42	52	13	4	0	1	1.9	6	2	2	15	0	.250	.385	4	0	C-41
1967	110	325	88	13	2	3	0.9	23	22	36	55	1	.271	.351	1	0	C-110
1968	137	416	91	15	2	1	0.2	26	33	41	80	0	.219	.272	1	0	C-135
1969	62	190	44	8	0	7	3.7	21	23	9	53	1	.232	.384	11	2	C-52
1970	51	139	29	4	2	1	0.7	13	16	21	25	0	.209	.288	4	2	C-45
1971 KC A	71	218	55	13	2	1	0.5	16	24	27	37	0	.252	.344	2	0	C-71

	G	AB	H	2B	3B	HR	HR %	R	RBI	BB	SO	SB	BA	SA	Pinch Hit AB	H	G by POS

Jerry May continued

	G	AB	H	2B	3B	HR	HR %	R	RBI	BB	SO	SB	BA	SA	PH AB	PH H	G by POS
1972	53	116	22	5	1	1	0.9	10	4	14	13	0	.190	.276	11	1	C-41
1973 2 teams	KC	A (11G –	.133)		NY	N (4G –	.250)										
" total	15	38	6	1	1	0	0.0	4	2	4	6	0	.158	.237	0	0	C-15
10 yrs.	556	1527	357	63	10	15	1.0	120	130	157	293	1	.234	.318	34	5	C-525

Lee May

MAY, LEE ANDREW
Brother of Carlos May.
B. Mar. 23, 1943, Birmingham, Ala.

BR TR 6'3" 195 lbs.

	G	AB	H	2B	3B	HR	HR %	R	RBI	BB	SO	SB	BA	SA	PH AB	PH H	G by POS
1965 CIN N	5	4	0	0	0	0	0.0	1	0	0	1	0	.000	.000	4	0	
1966	25	75	25	5	1	2	2.7	14	10	0	14	0	.333	.507	9	1	1B-16
1967	127	438	116	29	2	12	2.7	54	57	19	80	4	.265	.422	8	0	1B-81, OF-48
1968	146	559	162	32	1	22	3.9	78	80	34	100	4	.290	.469	3	1	1B-122, OF-33
1969	158	607	169	32	3	38	6.3	85	110	45	142	5	.278	.529	1	0	1B-156, OF-7
1970	153	605	153	34	2	34	5.6	78	94	38	125	1	.253	.484	0	0	1B-153
1971	147	553	154	17	3	39	7.1	85	98	42	135	3	.278	.532	4	1	1B-143
1972 HOU N	148	592	168	31	2	29	4.9	87	98	52	145	3	.284	.490	2	1	1B-146
1973	148	545	147	24	3	28	5.1	65	105	34	122	1	.270	.479	4	0	1B-144
1974	152	556	149	26	0	24	4.3	59	85	17	97	1	.268	.444	8	1	1B-145
1975 BAL A	146	580	152	28	3	20	3.4	67	99	36	91	1	.262	.424	1	1	1B-144, DH-2
1976	148	530	137	17	4	25	4.7	61	109	41	104	4	.258	.447	4	1	1B-94, DH-52
1977	150	585	148	16	2	27	4.6	75	99	38	119	2	.253	.447	2	0	1B-110, DH-39
1978	148	556	137	16	1	25	4.5	56	80	31	110	5	.246	.426	6	1	DH-140, 1B-4
1979	124	456	116	15	0	19	4.2	59	69	28	100	3	.254	.412	7	3	DH-117, 1B-2
1980	78	222	54	10	2	7	3.2	20	31	15	53	2	.243	.401	27	11	DH-58, 1B-7
1981 KC A	26	55	16	3	0	0	0.0	3	8	3	14	0	.291	.345	13	4	1B-8, DH-4
1982	42	91	28	5	2	3	3.3	12	12	14	18	0	.308	.505	9	1	1B-32, DH-2
18 yrs.	2071	7609	2031	340	31	354	4.7	959	1244	487	1570 9th	39	.267	.459	112	27	1B-1507, DH-414, OF-88

DIVISIONAL PLAYOFF SERIES

	G	AB	H	2B	3B	HR	HR %	R	RBI	BB	SO	SB	BA	SA	PH AB	PH H	G by POS
1981 KC A	1	0	0	0	0	0	–	0	0	0	0	0	–	–	0	0	1B-1

LEAGUE CHAMPIONSHIP SERIES

	G	AB	H	2B	3B	HR	HR %	R	RBI	BB	SO	SB	BA	SA	PH AB	PH H	G by POS
1970 CIN N	3	12	2	1	0	0	0.0	0	2	0	2	0	.167	.250	0	0	1B-3
1979 BAL A	2	7	1	0	0	0	0.0	0	1	1	3	0	.143	.143	0	0	DH-2
2 yrs.	5	19	3	1	0	0	0.0	0	3	1	5	0	.158	.211	0	0	1B-3, DH-2

WORLD SERIES

	G	AB	H	2B	3B	HR	HR %	R	RBI	BB	SO	SB	BA	SA	PH AB	PH H	G by POS
1970 CIN N	5	18	7	2	0	2	11.1	6	8	2	2	0	.389	.833	0	0	1B-5
1979 BAL A	2	1	0	0	0	0	0.0	0	0	1	1	0	.000	.000	1	0	
2 yrs.	7	19	7	2	0	2	10.5	6	8	3	3	0	.368	.789	1	0	1B-5

Milt May

MAY, MILTON SCOTT
Son of Pinky May.
B. Aug. 1, 1950, Gary, Ind.

BL TR 6' 190 lbs.

	G	AB	H	2B	3B	HR	HR %	R	RBI	BB	SO	SB	BA	SA	PH AB	PH H	G by POS
1970 PIT N	5	4	2	1	0	0	0.0	1	2	0	0	0	.500	.750	6	3	
1971	49	126	35	1	0	6	4.8	15	25	9	16	0	.278	.429	17	3	C-31
1972	57	139	39	10	0	0	0.0	12	14	10	13	0	.281	.353	18	4	C-33
1973	101	283	76	8	1	7	2.5	29	31	34	26	0	.269	.378	18	2	C-79
1974 HOU N	127	405	117	17	4	7	1.7	47	54	39	33	0	.289	.402	9	2	C-116
1975	111	386	93	15	1	4	1.0	29	52	26	41	1	.241	.316	8	3	C-102
1976 DET A	6	25	7	1	0	0	0.0	2	1	0	1	0	.280	.320	0	0	C-6
1977	115	397	99	9	3	12	3.0	32	46	26	31	0	.249	.378	5	2	C-111
1978	105	352	88	9	0	10	2.8	24	37	27	26	0	.250	.361	12	1	C-94
1979 2 teams	DET	A (6G –	.273)		CHI	A (65G –	.252)										
" total	71	213	54	15	0	7	3.3	24	31	15	28	0	.254	.423	2	0	C-70
1980 SF N	111	358	93	16	2	6	1.7	27	50	25	40	0	.260	.366	15	6	C-103
1981	97	316	98	17	0	2	0.6	20	33	34	29	1	.310	.383	9	5	C-93
1982	114	395	104	19	0	9	2.3	29	39	28	38	0	.263	.380	13	6	C-110
1983 2 teams	SF	N (66G –	.247)		PIT	N (7G –	.250)										
" total	73	198	49	6	0	6	3.0	18	20	22	24	2	.247	.369	13	3	C-60
1984 PIT N	50	96	17	3	0	1	1.0	4	8	10	15	0	.177	.240	18	3	C-26
15 yrs.	1192	3693	971	147	11	77	2.1	313	443	305	361	4	.263	.371	163	43	C-1034

LEAGUE CHAMPIONSHIP SERIES

	G	AB	H	2B	3B	HR	HR %	R	RBI	BB	SO	SB	BA	SA	PH AB	PH H	G by POS
1971 PIT N	1	1	0	0	0	0	0.0	0	0	0	0	0	.000	.000	1	0	
1972	1	2	1	0	0	0	0.0	0	1	0	0	0	.500	.500	0	0	C-1
2 yrs.	2	3	1	0	0	0	0.0	0	1	0	0	0	.333	.333	1	0	C-1

WORLD SERIES

	G	AB	H	2B	3B	HR	HR %	R	RBI	BB	SO	SB	BA	SA	PH AB	PH H	G by POS
1971 PIT N	2	2	1	0	0	0	0.0	0	1	0	0	0	.500	.500	2	1	

Pinky May

MAY, MERRILL GLEND
Father of Milt May.
B. Jan. 18, 1911, Laconia, Ind.

BR TR 5'11½" 165 lbs.

	G	AB	H	2B	3B	HR	HR %	R	RBI	BB	SO	SB	BA	SA	PH AB	PH H	G by POS
1939 PHI N	135	464	133	27	3	2	0.4	49	62	41	20	4	.287	.371	3	1	3B-132
1940	136	501	147	24	2	1	0.2	59	48	58	33	2	.293	.355	0	0	3B-135, SS-1
1941	142	490	131	17	4	0	0.0	46	39	55	30	2	.267	.318	2	1	3B-140
1942	115	345	82	15	0	0	0.0	25	18	51	17	3	.238	.281	7	0	3B-107
1943	137	415	117	19	2	1	0.2	31	48	56	21	2	.282	.345	5	3	3B-132
5 yrs.	665	2215	610	102	11	4	0.2	210	215	261	121	13	.275	.337	17	5	3B-646, SS-1

John Mayberry

MAYBERRY, JOHN CLAIBORN
B. Feb. 18, 1950, Detroit, Mich.

BL TL 6'3" 215 lbs.

	G	AB	H	2B	3B	HR	HR %	R	RBI	BB	SO	SB	BA	SA	PH AB	PH H	G by POS
1968 HOU N	4	9	0	0	0	0	0.0	0	0	0	2	0	.000	.000	2	0	1B-2
1969	5	4	0	0	0	0	0.0	0	0	0	1	0	.000	.000	3	0	
1970	50	148	32	3	2	5	3.4	23	14	21	33	1	.216	.365	6	1	1B-45
1971	46	137	25	0	1	7	5.1	16	14	13	32	0	.182	.350	10	4	1B-37
1972 KC A	149	503	150	24	3	25	5.0	65	100	78	74	0	.298	.507	4	2	1B-146

	G	AB	H	2B	3B	HR	HR %	R	RBI	BB	SO	SB	BA	SA	Pinch Hit AB	H	G by POS

John Mayberry continued

	G	AB	H	2B	3B	HR	HR %	R	RBI	BB	SO	SB	BA	SA	AB	H	G by POS
1973	152	510	142	20	2	26	5.1	87	100	**122**	79	3	.278	.478	4	2	1B-149, DH-1
1974	126	427	100	13	1	22	5.2	63	69	77	72	4	.234	.424	7	2	1B-106, DH-16
1975	156	554	161	38	1	34	6.1	95	106	119	73	5	.291	.547	0	0	1B-131, DH-27
1976	161	594	138	22	2	13	2.2	76	95	82	73	3	.232	.342	1	0	1B-160, DH-9
1977	153	543	125	22	1	23	4.2	73	82	83	86	1	.230	.401	2	1	1B-145, DH-8
1978 TOR A	152	515	129	15	2	22	4.3	51	70	60	57	1	.250	.416	10	2	1B-139, DH-7
1979	137	464	127	22	1	21	4.5	61	74	69	60	1	.274	.461	6	2	1B-135
1980	149	501	124	19	2	30	6.0	62	82	77	80	0	.248	.473	5	1	1B-136, DH-8
1981	94	290	72	6	1	17	5.9	34	43	44	45	1	.248	.452	7	2	1B-80, DH-10
1982 2 teams	TOR	A	(17G –	.273)			NY	A	(69G –	.209)							
" total	86	248	54	7	0	10	4.0	27	30	35	43	0	.218	.367	6	1	1B-67, DH-17
15 yrs.	1620	5447	1379	211	19	255	4.7	733	879	881	810	20	.253	.439	73	20	1B-1478, DH-103
LEAGUE CHAMPIONSHIP SERIES																	
1976 KC A	5	18	4	0	0	1	5.6	4	3	1	0	0	.222	.389	0	0	1B-5
1977	4	12	2	1	0	1	8.3	1	3	1	2	0	.167	.500	0	0	1B-4
2 yrs.	9	30	6	1	0	2	6.7	5	6	2	2	0	.200	.433	0	0	1B-9

Lee Maye

MAYE, ARTHUR LEE
B. Dec. 11, 1934, Tuscaloosa, Ala.

BL TR 6'2"   190 lbs.

	G	AB	H	2B	3B	HR	HR %	R	RBI	BB	SO	SB	BA	SA	AB	H	G by POS
1959 MIL N	51	140	42	5	1	4	2.9	17	16	7	26	2	.300	.436	7	4	OF-44
1960	41	83	25	6	0	0	0.0	14	2	7	21	5	.301	.373	17	2	OF-19
1961	110	373	101	11	5	14	3.8	68	41	36	50	10	.271	.440	17	5	OF-96
1962	99	349	85	10	0	10	2.9	40	41	25	58	9	.244	.358	8	1	OF-94
1963	124	442	120	22	7	11	2.5	67	34	36	52	14	.271	.428	18	3	OF-111
1964	153	588	179	**44**	5	10	1.7	96	74	34	54	5	.304	.447	13	2	OF-135, 3B-5
1965 2 teams	MIL	N	(15G –	.302)			HOU	N	(108G –	.251)							
" total	123	468	120	19	7	5	1.1	46	49	22	43	1	.256	.359	8	1	OF-116
1966 HOU N	115	358	103	12	4	9	2.5	38	36	20	26	4	.288	.419	20	4	OF-97
1967 CLE A	115	297	77	20	4	9	3.0	43	27	26	47	3	.259	.444	42	10	OF-77, 2B-1
1968	109	299	84	13	4	4	1.3	20	26	15	24	0	.281	.378	30	9	OF-80, 1B-1
1969 2 teams	CLE	A	(43G –	.250)			WAS	A	(71G –	.290)							
" total	114	346	96	14	3	10	2.9	50	41	28	40	2	.277	.422	24	4	OF-93, 3B-1
1970 2 teams	WAS	A	(96G –	.263)			CHI	A	(6G –	.167)							
" total	102	261	68	12	1	7	2.7	28	31	21	33	4	.261	.395	39	7	OF-68, 3B-1
1971 CHI A	32	44	9	2	0	1	2.3	6	7	5	7	0	.205	.318	17	5	OF-10
13 yrs.	1288	4048	1109	190	39	94	2.3	533	419	282	481	59	.274	.410	260	57	OF-1040, 3B-7, 2B-1, 1B-1

Ed Mayer

MAYER, EDWARD H
B. Aug. 16, 1866, Marshall, Ill.   D. May 18, 1913, Chicago, Ill.

5'8½"   155 lbs.

	G	AB	H	2B	3B	HR	HR %	R	RBI	BB	SO	SB	BA	SA	AB	H	G by POS
1890 PHI N	117	484	117	25	5	1	0.2	49	70	22	36	20	.242	.320	0	0	3B-117
1891	68	268	50	2	4	0	0.0	24	31	14	29	7	.187	.224	0	0	3B-31, OF-29, SS-7, 2B-1
2 yrs.	185	752	167	27	9	1	0.1	73	101	36	65	27	.222	.286	0	0	3B-148, OF-29, SS-7, 2B-1

Sam Mayer

MAYER, SAMUEL FRANKEL
Born Samuel Frankel Erskine.   Brother of Erskine Mayer.
B. Feb. 28, 1893, Atlanta, Ga.   D. July 1, 1962, Atlanta, Ga.

BR TL 5'10"   164 lbs.

	G	AB	H	2B	3B	HR	HR %	R	RBI	BB	SO	SB	BA	SA	AB	H	G by POS
1915 WAS A	11	29	7	0	0	1	3.4	5	4	4	2	1	.241	.345	0	0	OF-9, 1B-1, P-1

Wally Mayer

MAYER, WALTER A.
B. July 8, 1890, Cincinnati, Ohio   D. Nov. 18, 1951, Minneapolis, Minn.

BR TR 5'11"   168 lbs.

	G	AB	H	2B	3B	HR	HR %	R	RBI	BB	SO	SB	BA	SA	AB	H	G by POS
1911 CHI A	1	3	0	0	0	0	0.0	0	0	2		0	.000	.000	0	0	C-1
1912	7	9	0	0	0	0	0.0	1	0	1		0	.000	.000	1	0	C-6
1914	39	85	14	3	1	0	0.0	7	5	14	23	1	.165	.224	5	0	C-33, 3B-1
1915	22	54	12	3	1	0	0.0	3	5	5	8	0	.222	.315	2	0	C-20
1917 BOS A	4	12	2	0	0	0	0.0	2	0	5	2	0	.167	.167	0	0	C-4
1918	26	49	11	4	0	0	0.0	7	5	7	7	0	.224	.306	3	0	C-23
1919 STL A	30	62	14	1	0	0	0.0	2	5	8	11	0	.226	.323	5	1	C-25
7 yrs.	129	274	53	14	3	0	0.0	22	20	42	51	1	.193	.266	16	1	C-112, 3B-1

Paddy Mayes

MAYES, ADAIR BUSHYHEAD
B. Mar. 17, 1885, Locust Grove, Okla.   D. May 28, 1962, Fayetteville, Ark.

BL TR 5'11"   160 lbs.

	G	AB	H	2B	3B	HR	HR %	R	RBI	BB	SO	SB	BA	SA	AB	H	G by POS
1911 PHI N	5	5	0	0	0	0	0.0	1	0	1	2	0	.000	.000	1	0	OF-2

Buster Maynard

MAYNARD, JAMES WALTER
B. Mar. 25, 1913, Henderson, N. C.   D. Sept. 7, 1977, Durham, N. C.

BR TR 5'11"   170 lbs.

	G	AB	H	2B	3B	HR	HR %	R	RBI	BB	SO	SB	BA	SA	AB	H	G by POS
1940 NY N	7	29	8	2	2	1	3.4	6	2	2	6	0	.276	.586	0	0	OF-7
1942	89	190	47	4	1	4	2.1	17	32	19	19	3	.247	.342	15	3	OF-58, 3B-10, 2B-1
1943	121	393	81	8	2	9	2.3	43	32	24	27	3	.206	.305	19	1	OF-74, 3B-22
1946	7	4	0	0	0	0	0.0	2	0	1	1	0	.000	.000	1	0	OF-3
4 yrs.	224	616	136	14	5	14	2.3	68	66	46	53	6	.221	.328	35	4	OF-142, 3B-32, 2B-1

Chick Maynard

MAYNARD, LEROY EVANS
B. Nov. 2, 1896, Turner Falls, Mass.   D. Jan. 31, 1957, Bangor, Me.

BR TR 5'9"   150 lbs.

	G	AB	H	2B	3B	HR	HR %	R	RBI	BB	SO	SB	BA	SA	AB	H	G by POS
1922 BOS A	12	24	3	0	0	0	0.0	1	0	3	2	0	.125	.125	0	0	SS-12

Eddie Mayo

MAYO, EDWARD JOSEPH
Born Edward Joseph Mayoski.
B. Apr. 15, 1910, Holyoke, Mass.

BL TR 5'11"   178 lbs.

	G	AB	H	2B	3B	HR	HR %	R	RBI	BB	SO	SB	BA	SA	AB	H	G by POS
1936 NY N	46	141	28	4	1	1	0.7	11	8	11	12	0	.199	.262	3	1	3B-40
1937 BOS N	65	172	39	6	1	1	0.6	19	18	15	20	1	.227	.291	14	4	3B-50
1938	8	14	3	0	0	1	7.1	2	4	1	0	0	.214	.429	0	0	3B-6, SS-2
1943 PHI A	128	471	103	10	1	0	0.0	49	28	34	32	2	.219	.244	5	0	3B-123
1944 DET A	154	607	151	18	3	5	0.8	76	63	57	23	9	.249	.313	0	0	2B-143, SS-11
1945	134	501	143	24	3	10	2.0	71	54	48	29	7	.285	.405	9	4	2B-124

	G	AB	H	2B	3B	HR	HR %	R	RBI	BB	SO	SB	BA	SA	Pinch Hit AB	Pinch Hit H	G by POS

Eddie Mayo continued

	G	AB	H	2B	3B	HR	HR%	R	RBI	BB	SO	SB	BA	SA	AB	H	G by POS
1946	51	202	51	9	2	0	0.0	21	22	14	12	6	.252	.317	2	0	2B-49
1947	142	535	149	28	4	6	1.1	66	48	48	28	3	.279	.379	1	1	2B-142
1948	106	370	92	20	1	2	0.5	35	42	30	19	1	.249	.324	10	2	2B-86, 3B-10
9 yrs.	834	3013	759	119	16	26	0.9	350	287	258	175	29	.252	.328	44	12	2B-544, 3B-229, SS-13

WORLD SERIES

	G	AB	H	2B	3B	HR	HR%	R	RBI	BB	SO	SB	BA	SA	AB	H	G by POS
1936 NY N	1	1	0	0	0	0	0.0	0	0	0	0	0	.000	.000	0	0	3B-1
1945 DET A	7	28	7	1	0	0	0.0	4	2	2	2	0	.250	.286	0	0	2B-7
2 yrs.	8	29	7	1	0	0	0.0	4	2	2	2	0	.241	.276	0	0	2B-7, 3B-1

Jackie Mayo

MAYO, JOHN LEWIS
B. July 26, 1925, Litchfield, Ill.

BL TR 6'1" 190 lbs.

	G	AB	H	2B	3B	HR	HR%	R	RBI	BB	SO	SB	BA	SA	AB	H	G by POS
1948 PHI N	12	35	8	2	1	0	0.0	7	3	7	7	1	.229	.343	1	0	OF-11
1949	45	39	5	0	0	0	0.0	3	2	4	5	0	.128	.128	15	1	OF-25
1950	18	36	8	3	0	0	0.0	1	3	2	5	0	.222	.306	3	0	OF-15
1951	9	7	1	0	0	0	0.0	1	0	0	0	0	.143	.143	4	0	OF-5
1952	50	119	29	5	0	1	0.8	13	4	12	17	1	.244	.311	15	0	OF-27, 1B-6
1953	5	4	0	0	0	0	0.0	0	0	0	1	0	.000	.000	4	0	OF-1
6 yrs.	139	240	51	10	1	1	0.4	25	12	25	35	2	.213	.275	42	1	OF-84, 1B-6

WORLD SERIES

	G	AB	H	2B	3B	HR	HR%	R	RBI	BB	SO	SB	BA	SA	AB	H	G by POS
1950 PHI N	3	0	0	0	0	0	—	0	0	1	0	0	—	—	0	0	OF-1

Willie Mays

MAYS, WILLIE HOWARD (Say Hey)
B. May 6, 1931, Westfield, Ala.
Hall of Fame 1979.

BR TR 5'10½" 170 lbs.

	G	AB	H	2B	3B	HR	HR%	R	RBI	BB	SO	SB	BA	SA	AB	H	G by POS
1951 NY N	121	464	127	22	5	20	4.3	59	68	56	60	7	.274	.472	0	0	OF-121
1952	34	127	30	2	4	4	3.1	17	23	16	17	4	.236	.409	0	0	OF-34
1954	151	565	195	33	13	41	7.3	119	110	66	57	8	.345	**.667**	0	0	OF-151
1955	152	580	185	18	13	51	8.8	123	127	79	60	24	.319	**.659**	0	0	OF-152
1956	152	578	171	27	8	36	6.2	101	84	68	65	40	.296	.557	0	0	OF-152
1957	152	585	195	26	**20**	35	6.0	112	97	76	62	**38**	.333	**.626**	1	0	OF-150
1958 SF N	152	600	208	33	11	29	4.8	**121**	96	78	56	**31**	.347	.583	2	0	OF-151
1959	151	575	180	43	5	34	5.9	125	104	65	58	**27**	.313	.583	4	2	OF-147
1960	153	595	**190**	29	12	29	4.9	107	103	61	70	25	.319	.555	1	0	OF-152
1961	154	572	176	32	3	40	7.0	**129**	123	81	77	18	.308	.584	1	1	OF-153
1962	162	621	189	36	5	**49**	**7.9**	130	141	78	85	18	.304	.615	1	0	OF-161
1963	157	596	187	32	7	38	6.4	115	103	66	83	8	.314	.582	2	0	OF-157, SS-1
1964	157	578	171	21	9	**47**	**8.1**	121	111	82	72	19	.296	**.607**	3	1	OF-155, SS-1, 3B-1, 1B-1
1965	157	558	177	21	3	**52**	**9.3**	118	112	76	71	9	.317	**.645**	6	0	OF-151
1966	152	552	159	29	4	37	6.7	99	103	70	81	5	.288	.556	4	1	OF-150
1967	141	486	128	22	2	22	4.5	83	70	51	92	6	.263	.453	11	1	OF-134
1968	148	498	144	20	5	23	4.6	84	79	67	81	12	.289	.488	3	2	OF-142, 1B-1
1969	117	403	114	17	3	13	3.2	64	58	49	71	6	.283	.437	12	3	OF-109, 1B-1
1970	139	478	139	15	2	28	5.9	94	83	79	90	5	.291	.506	10	2	OF-129, 1B-5
1971	136	417	113	24	5	18	4.3	82	61	**112**	123	23	.271	.482	15	4	OF-84, 1B-48
1972 2 teams	SF	N	(19G –	.184)				NY	N	(69G –	.267)						
" total	88	244	61	11	1	8	3.3	35	22	60	48	4	.250	.402	11	4	OF-63, 1B-11
1973 NY N	66	209	44	10	0	6	2.9	24	25	27	47	1	.211	.344	7	2	OF-45, 1B-17
22 yrs.	2992	10881	3283	523	140	660	6.1	2062	1903	1463	1526	338	.302	.557	94	23	OF-2843, 1B-84, SS-2, 3B-1
	6th	6th	9th		3rd			5th	7th					10th			

LEAGUE CHAMPIONSHIP SERIES

	G	AB	H	2B	3B	HR	HR%	R	RBI	BB	SO	SB	BA	SA	AB	H	G by POS
1971 SF N	4	15	4	2	0	1	6.7	2	3	3	3	1	.267	.600	0	0	OF-4
1973 NY N	1	3	1	0	0	0	0.0	1	1	0	0	0	.333	.333	1	1	OF-1
2 yrs.	5	18	5	2	0	1	5.6	3	4	3	3	1	.278	.556	1	1	OF-5

WORLD SERIES

	G	AB	H	2B	3B	HR	HR%	R	RBI	BB	SO	SB	BA	SA	AB	H	G by POS
1951 NY N	6	22	4	0	0	0	0.0	1	1	2	2	0	.182	.182	0	0	OF-6
1954	4	14	4	1	0	0	0.0	4	3	4	1	1	.286	.357	0	0	OF-4
1962 SF N	7	28	7	2	0	0	0.0	3	1	1	5	1	.250	.321	0	0	OF-7
1973 NY N	3	7	2	0	0	0	0.0	1	1	0	1	0	.286	.286	1	0	OF-2
4 yrs.	20	71	17	3	0	0	0.0	9	6	7	9	2	.239	.282	1	0	OF-19

Bill Mazeroski

MAZEROSKI, WILLIAM STANLEY (Maz)
B. Sept. 5, 1936, Wheeling, W. Va.

BR TR 5'11½" 183 lbs.

	G	AB	H	2B	3B	HR	HR%	R	RBI	BB	SO	SB	BA	SA	AB	H	G by POS
1956 PIT N	81	255	62	8	1	3	1.2	30	14	18	24	0	.243	.318	0	0	2B-81
1957	148	526	149	27	7	8	1.5	59	54	27	49	3	.283	.407	4	1	2B-144
1958	152	567	156	24	6	19	3.4	69	68	25	71	1	.275	.439	0	0	2B-152
1959	135	493	119	15	6	7	1.4	50	59	29	54	1	.241	.339	2	0	2B-133
1960	151	538	147	21	5	11	2.0	58	64	40	50	4	.273	.392	1	0	2B-151
1961	152	558	148	21	2	13	2.3	71	59	26	55	2	.265	.380	0	0	2B-152
1962	159	572	155	24	9	14	2.4	55	81	37	47	0	.271	.418	0	0	2B-159
1963	142	534	131	22	3	8	1.5	43	52	32	46	2	.245	.343	3	1	2B-138
1964	162	601	161	22	8	10	1.7	66	64	29	52	1	.268	.381	0	0	2B-162
1965	130	494	134	17	1	6	1.2	52	54	18	34	2	.271	.346	4	0	2B-127
1966	162	621	163	22	7	16	2.6	56	82	31	62	4	.262	.398	0	0	2B-162
1967	163	639	167	25	3	9	1.4	62	77	30	55	1	.261	.352	0	0	2B-163
1968	143	506	127	18	2	3	0.6	36	42	38	38	2	.251	.312	1	0	2B-142
1969	67	227	52	7	1	3	1.3	13	25	22	16	1	.229	.308	2	0	2B-65
1970	112	367	84	14	0	7	1.9	29	39	27	40	2	.229	.324	9	4	2B-102
1971	70	193	49	3	1	1	0.5	17	16	15	8	0	.254	.295	20	6	2B-46, 3B-7
1972	34	64	12	4	0	0	0.0	3	3	3	5	0	.188	.250	14	1	2B-15, 3B-3
17 yrs.	2163	7755	2016	294	62	138	1.8	769	853	447	706	27	.260	.367	60	13	2B-2094, 3B-10

LEAGUE CHAMPIONSHIP SERIES

	G	AB	H	2B	3B	HR	HR%	R	RBI	BB	SO	SB	BA	SA	AB	H	G by POS
1970 PIT N	1	2	0	0	0	0	0.0	0	0	2	0	0	.000	.000	0	0	2B-1
1971	1	1	1	0	0	0	0.0	1	0	0	0	0	1.000	1.000	1	1	

	G	AB	H	2B	3B	HR	HR %	R	RBI	BB	SO	SB	BA	SA	Pinch Hit AB	Pinch Hit H	G by POS

Bill Mazeroski continued

	G	AB	H	2B	3B	HR	HR %	R	RBI	BB	SO	SB	BA	SA	AB	H	G by POS
1972	2	2	1	0	0	0	0.0	0	0	0	1	0	.500	.500	2	1	
3 yrs.	4	5	2	0	0	0	0.0	1	0	2	1	0	.400	.400	3	2	2B-1
WORLD SERIES																	
1960 PIT N	7	25	8	2	0	2	8.0	4	5	0	3	0	.320	.640	0	0	2B-7
1971	1	1	0	0	0	0	0.0	0	0	0	0	0	.000	.000	1	0	
2 yrs.	8	26	8	2	0	2	7.7	4	5	0	3	0	.308	.615	1	0	2B-7

Mel Mazzera

MAZZERA, MELVIN LEONARD (Mike)
B. Jan. 31, 1914, Stockton, Calif.   BL TL 5'11" 180 lbs.

	G	AB	H	2B	3B	HR	HR %	R	RBI	BB	SO	SB	BA	SA	AB	H	G by POS
1935 STL A	12	30	7	2	0	1	3.3	4	2	4	9	0	.233	.400	2	0	OF-10
1937	7	7	2	2	0	0	0.0	1	0	0	2	0	.286	.571	7	2	OF-47
1938	86	204	57	8	2	6	2.9	33	29	12	25	1	.279	.426	37	9	OF-25
1939	34	111	33	5	2	3	2.7	21	22	10	20	0	.297	.459	6	1	OF-42, 1B-11
1940 PHI N	69	156	37	5	4	0	0.0	16	13	19	15	1	.237	.321	17	3	OF-42, 1B-11
5 yrs.	208	508	136	22	8	10	2.0	75	66	45	71	2	.268	.402	69	15	OF-124, 1B-11

Lee Mazzilli

MAZZILLI, LEE LOUIS
B. Mar. 25, 1955, Brooklyn, N. Y.   BB TR 6'1" 180 lbs.

	G	AB	H	2B	3B	HR	HR %	R	RBI	BB	SO	SB	BA	SA	AB	H	G by POS
1976 NY N	24	77	15	2	0	2	2.6	9	7	14	10	5	.195	.299	2	1	OF-23
1977	159	537	134	24	3	6	1.1	66	46	72	72	22	.250	.339	5	2	OF-156
1978	148	542	148	28	5	16	3.0	78	61	69	82	20	.273	.432	5	1	OF-144
1979	158	597	181	34	4	15	2.5	78	79	93	74	34	.303	.449	1	0	OF-143, 1B-15
1980	152	578	162	31	4	16	2.8	82	76	82	92	41	.280	.431	2	0	1B-92, OF-66
1981	95	324	74	14	5	6	1.9	36	34	46	53	17	.228	.358	6	2	OF-89
1982 2 teams		TEX A (58G – .241)				NY N	(37G – .266)										
" total	95	323	81	10	0	3	3.1	43	34	43	41	13	.251	.375	11	1	DH-33, OF-28, 1B-23
1983 PIT N	109	246	59	9	0	5	2.0	37	24	49	43	15	.240	.337	41	6	OF-57, 1B-7
1984	111	266	63	11	1	4	1.5	37	21	40	42	8	.237	.331	32	6	OF-74, 1B-5
9 yrs.	1051	3490	917	163	22	80	2.3	466	382	508	509	175	.263	.391	105	19	OF-780, 1B-142, DH-33

Jimmy McAleer

McALEER, JAMES ROBERT
B. July 10, 1864, Youngstown, Ohio   D. Apr. 29, 1931, Youngstown, Ohio
Manager 1901-11.   BR TR 6' 175 lbs.

	G	AB	H	2B	3B	HR	HR %	R	RBI	BB	SO	SB	BA	SA	AB	H	G by POS
1889 CLE N	110	447	105	6	6	1	0.2	66	35	30	49	37	.235	.282	0	0	OF-110
1890 CLE P	86	341	91	8	7	1	0.3	58	42	37	33	21	.267	.340	0	0	OF-86
1891 CLE N	136	565	134	16	10	2	0.4	97	61	49	47	51	.237	.312	0	0	OF-149
1892	149	571	136	26	7	4	0.7	92	70	63	54	40	.238	.329	0	0	OF-149
1893	91	350	83	5	1	2	0.6	63	41	35	21	32	.237	.274	0	0	OF-91
1894	64	253	73	15	1	2	0.8	36	40	13	17	14	.289	.379	0	0	OF-64
1895	132	531	152	15	6	2	0.4	84	68	38	37	32	.286	.348	0	0	OF-132
1896	116	455	131	16	4	1	0.2	70	54	47	32	24	.288	.347	0	0	OF-116
1897	24	91	20	2	0	0	0.0	6	10	7		4	.220	.242	0	0	OF-24
1898	106	366	87	3	0	0	0.0	47	48	46		7	.238	.246	0	0	OF-104, 2B-2
1901 CLE A	3	7	1	0	0	0	0.0	0	0	0		0	.143	.143	0	0	OF-2, 3B-1, P-1
1902 STL A	2	3	2	0	0	0	0.0	0	0	0		0	.667	.667	0	0	OF-2
1907	2	0	0	0	0	0	—	0	0	0	0	0	—	—	0	0	
13 yrs.	1021	3980	1015	112	42	15	0.4	619	469	365	290	262	.255	.316	0	0	OF-1016, 2B-2, 3B-1, P-1

John McAleese

McALEESE, JOHN JAMES
B. Aug. 22, 1877, Sharon, Pa.   D. Nov. 15, 1950, New York, N. Y.   BR TR 5'8"

	G	AB	H	2B	3B	HR	HR %	R	RBI	BB	SO	SB	BA	SA	AB	H	G by POS
1901 CHI A	1	1	0	0	0	0	0.0	0	0	0		0	.000	.000	0	0	P-1
1909 STL A	85	267	57	7	0	0	0.0	33	12	32		18	.213	.240	2	0	OF-79, 3B-2
2 yrs.	86	268	57	7	0	0	0.0	33	12	32		18	.213	.239	2	0	OF-79, 3B-2, P-1

Bill McAllester

McALLESTER, WILLIAM LUSK
B. Dec. 29, 1889, Chattanooga, Tenn.   D. Mar. 3, 1970, Chattanooga, Tenn.   BR TR 5'11½" 170 lbs.

	G	AB	H	2B	3B	HR	HR %	R	RBI	BB	SO	SB	BA	SA	AB	H	G by POS
1913 STL A	47	85	13	4	0	0	0.0	3	6	11	12	2	.153	.200	8	2	C-37

Jack McAllister

Playing record listed under Andy Coakley

Sport McAllister

McALLISTER, LEWIS WILLIAM
B. July 23, 1874, Austin, Miss.   D. July 18, 1962, Detroit, Mich.   BB TR 5'11" 180 lbs.

	G	AB	H	2B	3B	HR	HR %	R	RBI	BB	SO	SB	BA	SA	AB	H	G by POS
1896 CLE N	8	27	6	2	0	0	0.0	2	1	0	2	1	.222	.296	0	0	OF-4, C-2, P-1
1897	43	137	30	5	1	0	0.0	23	11	12		3	.219	.270	0	0	OF-28, SS-4, P-4, 1B-3, C-2, 2B-1
1898	17	57	13	3	1	0	0.0	8	9	5		0	.228	.316	2	0	P-9, OF-8
1899	113	418	99	6	8	1	0.2	29	31	19		5	.237	.297	2	0	OF-79, C-17, 3B-7, 1B-6, SS-3, P-3, 2B-1
1901 DET A	90	306	92	9	4	3	1.0	45	57	15		17	.301	.386	4	2	C-35, 1B-28, OF-11, 3B-10, SS-3
1902 2 teams		DET A (66G – .210)			BAL A	(3G – .091)											
" total	69	240	49	5	2	1	0.4	19	33	6		1	.204	.254	5	0	1B-27, OF-12, C-9, SS-6, 3B-6, 2B-5
1903 DET A	78	265	69	8	2	0	0.0	31	22	10		5	.260	.306	5	1	SS-46, C-18, OF-5, 3B-4, 1B-1
7 yrs.	418	1450	358	38	18	5	0.3	157	164	67	2	32	.247	.308	16	3	OF-147, C-83, 1B-65, SS-52, 3B-27, P-17, 2B-7

Jim McAnany

McANANY, JAMES
B. Sept. 4, 1936, Los Angeles, Calif.   BR TR 5'10" 196 lbs.

	G	AB	H	2B	3B	HR	HR %	R	RBI	BB	SO	SB	BA	SA	AB	H	G by POS
1958 CHI A	5	13	0	0	0	0	0.0	0	0	0	5	0	.000	.000	1	0	OF-3
1959	67	210	58	9	3	0	0.0	22	27	19	26	2	.276	.348	6	0	OF-67
1960	3	2	0	0	0	0	0.0	0	0	0	2	0	.000	.000	2	0	
1961 CHI N	11	10	3	1	0	0	0.0	1	0	1	3	0	.300	.400	10	3	OF-1

	G	AB	H	2B	3B	HR	HR %	R	RBI	BB	SO	SB	BA	SA	Pinch Hit AB	Pinch Hit H	G by POS

Jim McAnany continued

	G	AB	H	2B	3B	HR	HR %	R	RBI	BB	SO	SB	BA	SA	AB	H	G by POS
1962	7	6	0	0	0	0	0.0	0	0		2	0	.000	.000	6	0	
5 yrs.	93	241	61	10	3	0	0.0	23	27	21	38	2	.253	.320	19	3	OF-71
WORLD SERIES																	
1959 CHI A	3	5	0	0	0	0	0.0	0	0	1	0	0	.000	.000	0	0	OF-3

Ike McAuley

McAULEY, JAMES EARL
B. Aug. 19, 1891, Wichita, Kans.   D. Apr. 6, 1928, Des Moines, Iowa   BR TR 5'9½" 150 lbs.

	G	AB	H	2B	3B	HR	HR %	R	RBI	BB	SO	SB	BA	SA	AB	H	G by POS
1914 PIT N	15	24	3	0	0	0	0.0	3	0	8	0	0	.125	.125	1	0	SS-5, 3B-3, 2B-2
1915	5	15	2	1	0	0	0.0	0	0	0	6	0	.133	.200	2	0	SS-5
1916	4	8	2	0	0	0	0.0	1	1	0	1	0	.250	.250	0	0	SS-4
1917 STL N	3	7	2	0	0	0	0.0	0	1	0	1	0	.286	.286	0	0	SS-3
1925 CHI N	37	125	35	7	2	0	0.0	10	11	11	12	1	.280	.368	0	0	SS-37
5 yrs.	64	179	44	8	2	0	0.0	14	13	11	28	1	.246	.313	3	0	SS-54, 3B-3, 2B-2

Dick McAuliffe

McAULIFFE, RICHARD JOHN
B. Nov. 29, 1939, Hartford, Conn.   BL TR 5'11" 176 lbs.

	G	AB	H	2B	3B	HR	HR %	R	RBI	BB	SO	SB	BA	SA	AB	H	G by POS
1960 DET A	8	27	7	0	1	0	0.0	2	1	2	6	0	.259	.333	0	0	SS-7
1961	80	285	73	12	4	6	2.1	36	33	24	39	2	.256	.389	7	3	SS-55, 3B-22
1962	139	471	124	20	5	12	2.5	50	63	64	76	4	.263	.403	6	1	2B-70, 3B-49, SS-16
1963	150	568	149	18	6	13	2.3	77	61	64	75	11	.262	.384	2	1	SS-133, 2B-15
1964	162	557	134	18	7	24	4.3	85	66	77	96	8	.241	.427	2	1	SS-160
1965	113	404	105	13	6	15	3.7	61	54	49	62	6	.260	.433	2	0	SS-112
1966	124	430	118	16	8	23	5.3	83	56	66	80	5	.274	.509	8	2	SS-105, 3B-15
1967	153	557	133	16	7	22	3.9	92	65	105	118	6	.239	.411	0	0	2B-145, SS-43
1968	151	570	142	24	10	16	2.8	95	56	82	99	8	.249	.411	3	2	2B-148, SS-5
1969	74	271	71	10	5	11	4.1	49	33	47	41	2	.262	.458	2	1	2B-72
1970	146	530	124	21	1	12	2.3	73	50	101	62	5	.234	.345	8	0	2B-127, SS-15, 3B-12
1971	128	477	99	16	6	18	3.8	67	57	53	67	4	.208	.379	4	2	2B-123, SS-7
1972	122	408	98	16	3	8	2.0	47	30	59	59	0	.240	.353	8	0	2B-116, SS-3, 3B-1
1973	106	343	94	18	1	12	3.5	39	47	49	52	0	.274	.437	6	2	2B-102, SS-2, DH-1
1974 BOS A	100	272	57	13	1	5	1.8	32	24	39	40	2	.210	.320	9	1	2B-53, 3B-40, DH-3, SS-3
1975	7	15	2	0	0	0	0.0	0	1	1	2	0	.133	.133	0	0	3B-7
16 yrs.	1763	6185	1530	231	71	197	3.2	888	697	882	974	63	.247	.403	67	16	2B-971, SS-666, 3B-146, DH-4
LEAGUE CHAMPIONSHIP SERIES																	
1972 DET A	5	20	4	0	0	1	5.0	3	1	1	4	0	.200	.350	0	0	SS-4
WORLD SERIES																	
1968 DET A	7	27	6	0	0	1	3.7	5	3	4	6	0	.222	.333	0	0	2B-7

Gene McAuliffe

McAULIFFE, EUGENE LEO
B. Feb. 28, 1872, Randolph, Mass.   D. Apr. 29, 1953, Randolph, Mass.   BR TR 6'1" 180 lbs.

	G	AB	H	2B	3B	HR	HR %	R	RBI	BB	SO	SB	BA	SA	AB	H	G by POS
1904 BOS N	1	2	1	0	0	0	0.0	0	0			0	.500	.500	0	0	C-1

George McAvoy

McAVOY, GEORGE H.
B. Unknown.

	G	AB	H	2B	3B	HR	HR %	R	RBI	BB	SO	SB	BA	SA	AB	H	G by POS
1914 PHI N	1	1	0	0	0	0	0.0	0	0	0	0	0	.000	.000	1	0	

Wickey McAvoy

McAVOY, JAMES EUGENE
B. Oct. 20, 1894, Rochester, N. Y.   D. July 1, 1973, Rochester, N. Y.   BR TR 5'11" 172 lbs.

	G	AB	H	2B	3B	HR	HR %	R	RBI	BB	SO	SB	BA	SA	AB	H	G by POS
1913 PHI A	4	9	1	0	0	0	0.0	0	0	0	4	0	.111	.111	0	0	C-4
1914	8	16	2	0	1	0	0.0	1	0	0	4	0	.125	.250	0	0	C-8
1915	68	184	35	7	2	0	0.0	12	6	11	32	0	.190	.250	4	0	C-64
1917	10	24	6	1	0	1	4.2	1	4	0	3	0	.250	.417	2	0	C-8
1918	83	271	66	5	3	0	0.0	14	32	13	23	5	.244	.284	6	1	C-74, OF-1, 1B-1, P-1
1919	62	170	24	5	2	0	0.0	10	11	14	21	1	.141	.194	4	0	C-57
6 yrs.	235	674	134	18	8	1	0.1	38	53	38	87	6	.199	.254	16	1	C-215, OF-1, 1B-1, P-1

Algie McBride

McBRIDE, ALGERNON G
B. May 23, 1869, Washington, D. C.   D. Jan. 10, 1956, Georgetown, Ohio   BL TL 5'9" 152 lbs.

	G	AB	H	2B	3B	HR	HR %	R	RBI	BB	SO	SB	BA	SA	AB	H	G by POS
1896 CHI N	9	29	7	1	1	1	3.4	2	7	7	3	0	.241	.448	0	0	OF-9
1898 CIN N	120	486	147	14	12	2	0.4	94	43	51		16	.302	.393	0	0	OF-120
1899	64	251	87	12	5	1	0.4	57	23	30		5	.347	.446	0	0	OF-64
1900	112	436	120	15	8	4	0.9	59	59	25		12	.275	.374	3	0	OF-109
1901 2 teams			CIN N (30G – .236)						NY N (68G – .280)								
" total	98	387	103	18	0	4	1.0	46	47	19		3	.266	.344	5	2	OF-93
5 yrs.	403	1589	464	60	26	12	0.8	258	179	132		36	.292	.385	8	2	OF-395

Bake McBride

McBRIDE, ARNOLD RAY
B. Feb. 3, 1949, Fulton, Mo.   BL TR 6'2" 190 lbs.

	G	AB	H	2B	3B	HR	HR %	R	RBI	BB	SO	SB	BA	SA	AB	H	G by POS
1973 STL N	40	63	19	3	0	0	0.0	8	5	4	10	0	.302	.349	17	6	OF-17
1974	150	559	173	19	5	6	1.1	81	56	43	57	30	.309	.394	7	3	OF-144
1975	116	413	124	10	9	5	1.2	70	36	34	52	26	.300	.404	11	3	OF-107
1976	72	272	91	13	4	3	1.1	40	24	18	28	10	.335	.445	7	2	OF-66
1977 2 teams			STL N (43G – .262)						PHI N (85G – .339)								
" total	128	402	127	25	4	6	1.5	76	61	32	44	34	.316	.520	24	5	OF-106
1978 PHI N	122	472	127	20	4	15	3.7	68	61	28	68	21	.269	.392	6	1	OF-119
1979	151	582	163	16	12	12	2.1	82	60	41	77	25	.280	.411	9	3	OF-147
1980	137	554	171	33	10	9	1.6	68	87	26	58	13	.309	.453	3	1	OF-133
1981	58	221	60	17	1	2	0.9	26	21	11	25	5	.271	.385	9	3	OF-56
1982 CLE A	27	85	31	3	3	0	0.0	8	13	2	12	2	.365	.471	5	2	OF-22
1983	70	230	67	8	1	1	0.4	21	18	9	26	8	.291	.348	10	2	OF-46, DH-15
11 yrs.	1071	3853	1153	167	55	63	1.6	548	430	248	457	183	.299	.420	105	32	OF-963, DH-15
DIVISIONAL PLAYOFF SERIES																	
1981 PHI N	4	15	3	1	0	0	0.0	1	0	0	5	0	.200	.267	0	0	OF-4

	G	AB	H	2B	3B	HR	HR %	R	RBI	BB	SO	SB	BA	SA	Pinch Hit AB	Pinch Hit H	G by POS

Bake McBride continued

LEAGUE CHAMPIONSHIP SERIES

	G	AB	H	2B	3B	HR	HR%	R	RBI	BB	SO	SB	BA	SA	AB	H	G by POS
1977 PHI N	4	18	4	0	0	1	5.6	2	2	0	2	0	.222	.389	0	0	OF-4
1978	3	9	2	0	0	1	11.1	2	1	0	2	0	.222	.556	1	1	OF-2
1980	5	21	5	0	0	0	0.0	0	0	1	5	2	.238	.238	0	0	OF-5
3 yrs.	12	48	11	0	0	2	4.2	4	3	1	9	2	.229	.354	1	1	OF-11

WORLD SERIES

	G	AB	H	2B	3B	HR	HR%	R	RBI	BB	SO	SB	BA	SA	AB	H	G by POS
1980 PHI N	6	23	7	1	0	1	4.3	3	5	2	1	0	.304	.478	0	0	OF-6

George McBride

McBRIDE, GEORGE FLORIAN
B. Nov. 20, 1880, Milwaukee, Wis.   D. July 2, 1973, Milwaukee, Wis.
Manager 1921.
BR TR 5'11"   170 lbs.

	G	AB	H	2B	3B	HR	HR%	R	RBI	BB	SO	SB	BA	SA	AB	H	G by POS
1901 MIL A	3	12	2	0	0	0	0.0	0	0		1	0	.167	.167	0	0	SS-3
1905 2 teams		PIT N (27G – .218)				STL N (81G – .217)											
" total	108	368	80	5	2	2	0.5	31	41	20		12	.217	.258	2	0	SS-88, 3B-17, 1B-1
1906 STL N	90	313	53	8	2	0	0.0	24	13	17		5	.169	.208	0	0	SS-90
1908 WAS A	155	518	120	10	6	0	0.0	47	34	41		12	.232	.274	0	0	SS-155
1909	155	504	118	16	0	0	0.0	38	34	36		17	.234	.266	0	0	SS-155
1910	154	514	118	19	4	1	0.2	54	55	61		11	.230	.288	0	0	SS-154
1911	154	557	131	11	4	0	0.0	58	59	52		15	.235	.269	0	0	SS-154
1912	152	521	118	13	7	1	0.2	56	52	38		17	.226	.284	0	0	SS-152
1913	150	499	107	18	7	1	0.2	52	52	43	46	12	.214	.285	0	0	SS-150
1914	156	503	102	12	4	0	0.0	49	24	43	70	12	.203	.243	0	0	SS-156
1915	146	476	97	8	6	1	0.2	54	30	29	60	10	.204	.252	0	0	SS-146
1916	139	466	106	15	4	1	0.2	36	36	23	58	8	.227	.283	0	0	SS-41, 3B-6, 2B-2
1917	50	141	27	3	0	0	0.0	6	9	10	17	1	.191	.213	1	0	SS-14, 2B-2
1918	18	53	7	0	0	0	0.0	2	1	11	1	1	.132	.132	1	0	SS-15
1919	15	40	8	1	1	0	0.0	3	4	3	6	0	.200	.275	0	0	SS-13
1920	13	41	9	1	0	0	0.0	6	3	2	3	0	.220	.244	0	0	SS-13
16 yrs.	1658	5526	1203	140	47	7	0.1	516	447	419	271	133	.218	.264	4	0	SS-1625, 3B-23, 2B-4, 1B-1

John McBride

McBRIDE, JOHN F.
Deceased.

	G	AB	H	2B	3B	HR	HR%	R	RBI	BB	SO	SB	BA	SA	AB	H	G by POS
1890 PHI AA	1	2	0	0	0	0	0.0		1		0		.000	.000	0	0	OF-1

Tom McBride

McBRIDE, THOMAS RAYMOND
B. Nov. 2, 1914, Bonham, Tex.
BR TR 6'½"   188 lbs.

	G	AB	H	2B	3B	HR	HR%	R	RBI	BB	SO	SB	BA	SA	AB	H	G by POS
1943 BOS A	26	96	23	3	1	0	0.0	11	7	7	3	2	.240	.292	2	0	OF-24
1944	71	216	53	7	3	0	0.0	29	24	8	13	4	.245	.306	7	3	OF-57, 1B-5
1945	100	344	105	11	7	1	0.3	38	47	26	17	2	.305	.387	9	2	OF-81, 1B-11
1946	61	153	46	5	2	0	0.0	21	19	9	6	0	.301	.359	17	5	OF-43
1947 2 teams		BOS A (2G – .200)				WAS A (56G – .271)											
" total	58	171	46	4	2	0	0.0	19	15	15	9	3	.269	.316	8	2	OF-52, 3B-1
1948 WAS A	92	206	53	9	1	1	0.5	22	29	28	15	2	.257	.325	33	5	OF-55
6 yrs.	408	1186	326	39	16	2	0.2	140	141	93	63	13	.275	.340	76	17	OF-312, 1B-16, 3B-1

WORLD SERIES

	G	AB	H	2B	3B	HR	HR%	R	RBI	BB	SO	SB	BA	SA	AB	H	G by POS
1946 BOS A	5	12	2	0	0	0	0.0	0	1	0	1	0	.167	.167	3	0	OF-2

Bill McCabe

McCABE, WILLIAM FRANCIS
B. Oct. 28, 1892, Chicago, Ill.   D. July 2, 1968, Chicago, Ill.
BB TR 5'9½"   180 lbs.

	G	AB	H	2B	3B	HR	HR%	R	RBI	BB	SO	SB	BA	SA	AB	H	G by POS
1918 CHI N	29	45	8	0	1	0	0.0	9	5	4	7	2	.178	.222	6	1	2B-13, OF-4
1919	33	84	13	3	1	0	0.0	8	5	9	15	3	.155	.214	3	0	OF-19, SS-4, 3B-1
1920 2 teams		CHI N (3G – .500)				BKN N (41G – .147)											
" total	44	70	11	0	0	0	0.0	11	3	2	6	1	.157	.157	4	1	SS-13, OF-6, 2B-4, 3B-3
3 yrs.	106	199	32	3	2	0	0.0	28	13	15	28	6	.161	.196	13	2	OF-29, SS-17, 2B-17, 3B-4

WORLD SERIES

	G	AB	H	2B	3B	HR	HR%	R	RBI	BB	SO	SB	BA	SA	AB	H	G by POS
1918 CHI N	3	1	0	0	0	0	0.0	1	0	0	0	0	.000	.000	1	0	
1920 BKN N	1	0	0	0	0	0	–	0	0	0	0	0			0	0	
2 yrs.	4	1	0	0	0	0	0.0	1	0	0	0	0	.000	.000	1	0	

Joe McCabe

McCABE, JOSEPH ROBERT
B. Aug. 27, 1938, Indianapolis, Ind.
BR TR 6'   190 lbs.

	G	AB	H	2B	3B	HR	HR%	R	RBI	BB	SO	SB	BA	SA	AB	H	G by POS
1964 MIN A	14	19	3	0	0	0	0.0	1	2	0	8	0	.158	.158	1	0	C-12
1965 WAS A	14	27	5	0	0	1	3.7	1	5	4	13	1	.185	.296	4	2	C-11
2 yrs.	28	46	8	0	0	1	2.2	2	7	4	21	1	.174	.239	5	2	C-23

Swat McCabe

McCABE, JAMES ARTHUR
B. Nov. 20, 1881, Towanda, Pa.   D. Dec. 9, 1944, Bristol, Conn.
BL   5'10"

	G	AB	H	2B	3B	HR	HR%	R	RBI	BB	SO	SB	BA	SA	AB	H	G by POS
1909 CIN N	3	11	6	1	0	0	0.0	2	0	0		1	.545	.636	0	0	OF-3
1910	13	35	9	1	0	0	0.0	3	5	1	2	0	.257	.286	4	1	OF-9
2 yrs.	16	46	15	2	0	0	0.0	5	5	1	2	1	.326	.370	4	1	OF-12

Harry McCaffrey

McCAFFREY, HARRY CHARLES
B. Nov. 25, 1858, St. Louis, Mo.   D. Apr. 19, 1928, St. Louis, Mo.

	G	AB	H	2B	3B	HR	HR%	R	RBI	BB	SO	SB	BA	SA	AB	H	G by POS
1882 2 teams		STL AA (38G – .275)				LOU AA (1G – .250)											
" total	39	157	43	8	6	0	0.0	24		3				.274	.401	0	0	OF-23, 2B-9, 3B-7, 1B-1
1883 STL AA	5	18	1	0	0	0	0.0	0		1				.056	.056	0	0	OF-5
1885 CIN AA	1	5	0	0	0	0	0.0	0		0				.000	.000	0	0	P-1
3 yrs.	45	180	44	8	6	0	0.0	24		4				.244	.356	0	0	OF-28, 2B-9, 3B-7, 1B-1, P-1

	G	AB	H	2B	3B	HR	HR %	R	RBI	BB	SO	SB	BA	SA	Pinch Hit AB	Pinch Hit H	G by POS

Sparrow McCaffrey

McCAFFREY, CHARLES P.
B. Philadelphia, Pa.   D. Apr. 29, 1894, Philadelphia, Pa.

	G	AB	H	2B	3B	HR	HR%	R	RBI	BB	SO	SB	BA	SA	AB	H	G by POS
1889 COL AA	2	1	1	0	0	0	0.0	1	0	1		0	1.000	1.000	0	0	C-2

Brian McCall

McCALL, BRIAN ALLEN (Bam)
B. Jan. 25, 1943, Kentfield, Calif.
BL TL 5'10"   170 lbs.

	G	AB	H	2B	3B	HR	HR%	R	RBI	BB	SO	SB	BA	SA	AB	H	G by POS
1962 CHI A	4	8	3	0	0	2	25.0	2	3	0	2	0	.375	1.125	3	1	OF-1
1963	3	7	0	0	0	0	0.0	1	0	1	2	0	.000	.000	0	0	OF-2
2 yrs.	7	15	3	0	0	2	13.3	3	3	1	4	0	.200	.600	3	1	OF-3

John McCandless

McCANDLESS, JOHN SCOTT (Cook)
B. May 5, 1891, Pittsburgh, Pa.   D. Aug. 17, 1961, Pittsburgh, Pa.
BL TR 6'   170 lbs.

	G	AB	H	2B	3B	HR	HR%	R	RBI	BB	SO	SB	BA	SA	AB	H	G by POS
1914 BAL F	11	31	8	0	1	0	0.0	5	1	3		0	.258	.323	2	0	OF-8
1915	117	406	87	6	7	5	1.2	47	34	41		9	.214	.300	9	1	OF-105
2 yrs.	128	437	95	6	8	5	1.1	52	35	44		9	.217	.302	11	1	OF-113

Emmett McCann

McCANN, ROBERT EMMETT
B. Mar. 4, 1902, Philadelphia, Pa.   D. Apr. 15, 1937, Philadelphia, Pa.
BR TR 6'   175 lbs.

	G	AB	H	2B	3B	HR	HR%	R	RBI	BB	SO	SB	BA	SA	AB	H	G by POS
1920 PHI A	13	34	9	1	1	0	0.0	4	3	3	1	0	.265	.353	1	0	SS-11
1921	52	157	35	5	0	0	0.0	15	15	4	6	2	.223	.255	6	1	SS-32, 3B-9, 2B-2, 1B-1, C-1
1926 BOS A	6	3	0	0	0	0	0.0	0	0	1		0	.000	.000	1	0	SS-1, 3B-1
3 yrs.	71	194	44	6	1	0	0.0	19	18	8	8	2	.227	.268	8	1	SS-44, 3B-10, 2B-2, 1B-1, C-1

Roger McCardell

McCARDELL, ROGER MORTON
B. Aug. 29, 1932, Gorsuch Mills, Md.
BR TR 6'   200 lbs.

	G	AB	H	2B	3B	HR	HR%	R	RBI	BB	SO	SB	BA	SA	AB	H	G by POS
1959 SF N	4	4	0	0	0	0	0.0	0	0	0	0	0	.000	.000	1	0	C-3

Bill McCarren

McCARREN, WILLIAM JOSEPH
B. Nov. 4, 1895, Honesdale, Pa.   D. Sept. 11, 1983, Denver, Colo.
BR TR 5'11½"   170 lbs.

	G	AB	H	2B	3B	HR	HR%	R	RBI	BB	SO	SB	BA	SA	AB	H	G by POS
1923 BKN N	69	216	53	10	1	3	1.4	28	27	22	39	0	.245	.343	1	0	3B-66, OF-1

Alex McCarthy

McCARTHY, ALEXANDER GEORGE
B. May 12, 1888, Chicago, Ill.   D. Mar. 12, 1978, Salisbury, Md.
BR TR 5'9"   150 lbs.

	G	AB	H	2B	3B	HR	HR%	R	RBI	BB	SO	SB	BA	SA	AB	H	G by POS
1910 PIT N	3	12	1	0	1	0	0.0	1	0	0	2	0	.083	.250	0	0	SS-3
1911	50	150	36	5	1	2	1.3	18	31	14	24	4	.240	.327	0	0	SS-33, 2B-11, OF-1, 3B-1
1912	111	401	111	12	4	1	0.2	53	41	30	36	8	.277	.334	2	0	2B-105, 3B-4
1913	31	74	15	5	0	0	0.0	7	10	7	7	1	.203	.270	1	0	SS-12, 3B-12, 2B-6
1914	57	173	26	0	1	1	0.6	14	14	6	17	2	.150	.179	1	0	3B-36, 2B-10, SS-6
1915 2 teams	44	PIT N (21G – .204)				CHI N (23G – .264)											
" total	44	121	29	3	1	1	0.8	7	9	10	17	3	.240	.306	2	1	2B-21, 3B-16, SS-6, 1B-1
1916 2 teams	87	CHI N (37G – .243)				PIT N (50G – .199)											
" total	87	253	55	5	3	0	0.0	21	9	26	17	4	.217	.261	2	1	3B-26, 2B-41, 3B-5
1917 PIT N	49	151	33	4	0	0	0.0	15	8	11	13	1	.219	.245	0	0	3B-26, 2B-13, SS-9
8 yrs.	432	1335	306	34	11	5	0.4	136	122	104	133	23	.229	.282	10	1	2B-207, SS-111, 3B-100, OF-1, 1B-1

Bill McCarthy

McCARTHY, WILLIAM JOHN
B. Boston, Mass.   D. Feb. 4, 1928, Washington, D. C.
TR

	G	AB	H	2B	3B	HR	HR%	R	RBI	BB	SO	SB	BA	SA	AB	H	G by POS
1905 BOS N	1	3	0	0	0	0	0.0	0	0	0		0	.000	.000	0	0	C-1
1907 CIN N	3	8	1	0	0	0	0.0	1	0	0		0	.125	.125	0	0	C-3
2 yrs.	4	11	1	0	0	0	0.0	1	0	0		0	.091	.091	0	0	C-4

Jack McCarthy

McCARTHY, JOHN A.
B. Mar. 26, 1869, Gilbertville, Mass.   D. Sept. 11, 1931, Chicago, Ill.
BL TL 5'9"   155 lbs.

	G	AB	H	2B	3B	HR	HR%	R	RBI	BB	SO	SB	BA	SA	AB	H	G by POS
1893 CIN N	49	195	55	8	3	0	0.0	28	22	22	7	6	.282	.354	0	0	OF-47, 1B-2
1894	40	167	45	9	1	0	0.0	29	21	17	6	3	.269	.335	0	0	OF-25, 1B-15
1898 PIT N	137	537	155	13	12	4	0.7	75	78	34		7	.289	.380	0	0	OF-137
1899	138	560	171	22	17	3	0.5	108	67	39		28	.305	.421	0	0	OF-138
1900 CHI N	124	503	148	16	7	0	0.0	68	48	24		22	.294	.354	1	0	OF-123
1901 CLE A	86	343	110	14	7	0	0.0	60	32	30		9	.321	.402	0	0	OF-86
1902	95	359	102	31	5	0	0.0	45	41	24		12	.284	.398	0	0	OF-95
1903 2 teams	132	CLE A (108G – .265)				CHI N (24G – .277)											
" total	132	516	138	25	8	0	0.0	58	57	23		23	.267	.347	0	0	OF-132
1904 CHI N	115	432	114	14	2	0	0.0	36	51	23		14	.264	.306	0	0	OF-115
1905	59	167	47	4	3	0	0.0	16	14	10		8	.276	.335	15	6	OF-37, 1B-6
1906 BKN N	91	322	98	13	1	0	0.0	23	35	20		9	.304	.351	5	1	OF-86
1907	25	91	20	2	0	0	0.0	4	8	2		4	.220	.242	0	0	OF-25
12 yrs.	1091	4195	1203	171	66	7	0.2	550	474	268	13	145	.287	.364	21	7	OF-1046, 1B-23

Jerry McCarthy

McCARTHY, JEROME FRANCIS
B. May 23, 1923, Brooklyn, N. Y.   D. Oct. 3, 1965, Oceanside, N. Y.
BL TL 6'1"   205 lbs.

	G	AB	H	2B	3B	HR	HR%	R	RBI	BB	SO	SB	BA	SA	AB	H	G by POS
1948 STL A	2	3	1	0	0	0	0.0	0	0	0	0	0	.333	.333	1	0	1B-2

Joe McCarthy

McCARTHY, JOSEPH N.
B. Dec. 25, 1881, Syracuse, N. Y.   D. Jan. 12, 1937, Syracuse, N. Y.
BR TR

	G	AB	H	2B	3B	HR	HR%	R	RBI	BB	SO	SB	BA	SA	AB	H	G by POS
1905 NY A	1	2	0	0	0	0	0.0	0	0	0		0	.000	.000	0	0	C-1
1906 STL N	15	37	9	2	0	0	0.0	3	2	2		0	.243	.297	0	0	C-15
2 yrs.	16	39	9	2	0	0	0.0	3	2	2		0	.231	.282	0	0	C-16

Johnny McCarthy

McCARTHY, JOHN JOSEPH
B. Jan. 7, 1910, Chicago, Ill.   D. Sept. 13, 1973, Mundelein, Ill.
BL TL 6'1½"   185 lbs.

	G	AB	H	2B	3B	HR	HR%	R	RBI	BB	SO	SB	BA	SA	AB	H	G by POS
1934 BKN N	17	39	7	2	0	1	2.6	7	5	2	2	0	.179	.308	3	0	1B-13
1935	22	48	12	1	1	0	0.0	9	4	2	9	0	.250	.313	3	0	1B-19
1936 NY N	4	16	7	0	0	1	6.3	1	2	0	1	1	.438	.625	0	0	1B-4
1937	114	420	117	19	3	10	2.4	53	65	24	37	2	.279	.410	4	0	1B-110

	G	AB	H	2B	3B	HR	HR %	R	RBI	BB	SO	SB	BA	SA	Pinch Hit AB	Pinch Hit H	G by POS

Johnny McCarthy continued

	G	AB	H	2B	3B	HR	HR %	R	RBI	BB	SO	SB	BA	SA	AB	H	G by POS
1938	134	470	128	13	4	8	1.7	55	59	39	28	3	.272	.368	8	3	1B-125
1939	50	80	21	6	1	1	1.3	12	11	3	8	0	.263	.400	33	8	1B-12, OF-4, P-1
1940	51	67	16	4	0	0	0.0	6	5	2	8	0	.239	.299	43	11	1B-6
1941	14	40	13	3	0	0	0.0	1	12	3	0	0	.325	.400	5	2	1B-8, OF-1
1943 BOS N	78	313	95	24	6	2	0.6	32	33	10	19	1	.304	.438	0	0	1B-78
1946	2	7	1	0	0	0	0.0	0	1	2	0	0	.143	.143	0	0	1B-2
1948 NY N	56	57	15	0	1	2	3.5	6	12	3	2	0	.263	.404	45	13	1B-6
11 yrs.	542	1557	432	72	16	25	1.6	182	209	90	114	7	.277	.392	144	37	1B-383, OF-5, P-1
WORLD SERIES																	
1937 NY N	5	19	4	1	0	0	0.0	1	1	1	2	0	.211	.263	0	0	1B-5

Tommy McCarthy

McCARTHY, THOMAS FRANCIS MICHAEL   BR TR 5'7"   170 lbs.
B. July 24, 1864, Boston, Mass.   D. Aug. 5, 1922, Boston, Mass.
Manager 1890.
Hall of Fame 1946.

	G	AB	H	2B	3B	HR	HR %	R	RBI	BB	SO	SB	BA	SA	AB	H	G by POS
1884 BOS U	53	209	45	3	2	0	0.0	37		6			.215	.249	0	0	OF-48, P-7
1885 BOS N	40	148	27	2	0	0	0.0	16	11	5	25		.182	.196	0	0	OF-40
1886 PHI N	8	27	5	2	1	0	0.0	6	3	2	3		.185	.333	0	0	OF-8, P-1
1887	18	70	13	4	0	0	0.0	7	6	2	5	15	.186	.243	0	0	OF-8, 2B-5, SS-3, 3B-2
1888 STL AA	131	511	140	20	3	1	0.2	107	68	38		93	.274	.331	0	0	OF-131, P-2
1889	140	604	176	24	7	2	0.3	136	63	46	26	57	.291	.364	0	0	OF-140, 2B-2, P-1
1890	133	548	192	28	9	6	1.1	137		66	83	83	.350	.467	0	0	OF-112, 3B-32, 2B-1
1891	136	578	179	21	8	8	1.4	127	95	50	19	37	.310	.415	0	0	OF-113, 2B-14, SS-12, 3B-3, P-1
1892 BOS N	152	603	146	18	6	4	0.7	119	63	93	29	53	.242	.312	0	0	OF-152
1893	116	462	160	28	6	5	1.1	107	111	64	10	46	.346	.465	0	0	OF-108, 2B-7, SS-3
1894	127	539	188	21	8	13	2.4	118	126	59	17	43	.349	.490	0	0	OF-127, SS-2, 2B-1, P-1
1895	117	452	131	13	2	2	0.4	90	73	72	12	18	.290	.341	0	0	OF-109, 2B-9
1896 BKN N	104	377	94	8	6	3	0.8	62	47	34	17	22	.249	.326	0	0	OF-103
13 yrs.	1275	5128	1496	192	58	44	0.9	1069	665	537	163	467	.292	.378	0	0	OF-1189, 2B-39, 3B-37, SS-20, P-13

Lew McCarty

McCARTY, GEORGE LEWIS   BR TR 5'11½" 192 lbs.
B. Nov. 17, 1888, Milton, Pa.   D. June 9, 1930, Reading, Pa.

	G	AB	H	2B	3B	HR	HR %	R	RBI	BB	SO	SB	BA	SA	AB	H	G by POS
1913 BKN N	9	26	6	0	0	0	0.0	1	2	2	0	0	.231	.231	0	0	C-9
1914	90	284	72	14	2	0	0.4	20	30	14	22	1	.254	.327	6	2	C-84
1915	84	276	66	9	4	0	0.0	19	19	7	23	7	.239	.301	3	1	C-84
1916 2 teams		BKN N (55G – .313)						NY N (25G – .397)									
" total	80	218	74	9	5	0	0.0	23	22	21	25	4	.339	.427	10	4	C-51, 1B-17
1917 NY N	56	162	40	3	2	2	1.2	15	19	14	6	1	.247	.327	2	1	C-54
1918	86	257	69	7	3	0	0.0	16	24	17	13	3	.268	.319	7	2	C-75
1919	85	210	59	5	4	0	0.0	17	21	18	15	2	.281	.371	24	7	C-59
1920 2 teams		NY N (36G – .132)						STL N (5G – .286)									
" total	41	45	7	0	0	0	0.0	2	0	9	2	2	.156	.156	29	5	C-8
1921 STL N	1	1	0	0	0	0	0.0	0	0	0	1	0	.000	.000	1	0	
9 yrs.	532	1479	393	47	20	5	0.3	113	137	102	109	20	.266	.335	82	22	C-424, 1B-17
WORLD SERIES																	
1917 NY N	3	5	2	1	0	0	0.0	1	1	0	0	0	.400	.800	1	0	C-2

Tim McCarver

McCARVER, JAMES TIMOTHY   BL TR 6'   183 lbs.
B. Oct. 16, 1941, Memphis, Tenn.

	G	AB	H	2B	3B	HR	HR %	R	RBI	BB	SO	SB	BA	SA	AB	H	G by POS
1959 STL N	8	24	4	1	0	0	0.0	3	0	2	1	0	.167	.208	1	0	C-6
1960	10	10	2	0	0	0	0.0	3	0	0	2	0	.200	.200	4	1	C-5
1961	22	67	16	2	1	1	1.5	5	5	0	5	0	.239	.343	2	2	C-20
1963	127	405	117	12	7	4	1.0	39	51	27	43	5	.289	.383	5	1	C-126
1964	143	465	134	19	3	9	1.9	53	52	40	44	2	.288	.400	7	1	C-137
1965	113	409	113	17	2	11	2.7	48	48	31	26	5	.276	.408	5	2	C-111
1966	150	543	149	19	13	12	2.2	50	68	36	38	9	.274	.424	5	1	C-148
1967	138	471	139	26	3	14	3.0	68	69	54	32	6	.295	.452	11	4	C-130
1968	128	434	110	15	6	5	1.2	35	48	26	31	4	.253	.350	19	4	C-109
1969	138	515	134	27	3	7	1.4	46	51	49	26	4	.260	.365	4	1	C-136
1970 PHI N	44	164	47	11	1	4	2.4	16	14	14	10	2	.287	.439	0	0	C-44
1971	134	474	132	20	5	8	1.7	51	46	43	26	5	.278	.392	14	3	C-125
1972 2 teams		PHI N (45G – .237)						MON N (77G – .251)									
" total	122	391	96	13	1	7	1.8	33	34	36	29	5	.246	.338	18	2	C-85, OF-14, 3B-6
1973 STL N	130	331	88	16	4	3	0.9	30	49	38	31	2	.266	.366	39	8	1B-77, C-11
1974 2 teams		STL N (74G – .217)						BOS A (11G – .250)									
" total	85	134	30	1	1	0	0.0	16	12	26	7	1	.224	.246	43	7	C-29, 1B-6, DH-2
1975 2 teams		BOS A (12G – .381)						PHI N (47G – .254)									
" total	59	80	23	4	1	1	1.3	7	10	15	10	0	.288	.400	39	10	C-17, 1B-2
1976 PHI N	90	155	43	11	2	3	1.9	26	29	35	14	2	.277	.432	42	9	C-41, 1B-3
1977	93	169	54	13	2	6	3.6	28	30	28	11	3	.320	.527	36	9	C-34, 1B-11
1978	90	146	36	9	1	1	0.7	18	14	28	24	2	.247	.342	39	10	C-31, OF-1
1979	79	137	33	5	1	1	0.7	13	12	19	12	2	.241	.314	41	9	1B-2
1980	6	5	1	1	0	0	0.0	2	2	1	0	0	.200	.400	2	0	
21 yrs.	1909	5529	1501	242	57	97	1.8	590	645	548	422	61	.271	.388	373	82	C-1387, 1B-103, OF-15, 3B-6, DH-2
LEAGUE CHAMPIONSHIP SERIES																	
1976 PHI N	2	4	0	0	0	0	0.0	0	0	0	1	0	.000	.000	1	0	C-1
1977	3	6	1	0	0	0	0.0	1	0	1	3	0	.167	.167	1	0	C-2
1978	2	4	0	0	0	0	0.0	2	1	2	0	0	.000	.000	1	0	C-1
3 yrs.	7	14	1	0	0	0	0.0	3	1	3	4	0	.071	.071	3	0	C-4
WORLD SERIES																	
1964 STL N	7	23	11	1	1	1	4.3	4	5	5	1	1	.478	.739	0	0	C-7
1967	7	24	3	1	0	0	0.0	3	2	2	2	0	.125	.167	0	0	C-7

	G	AB	H	2B	3B	HR	HR %	R	RBI	BB	SO	SB	BA	SA	Pinch Hit AB	Pinch Hit H	G by POS

Tim McCarver continued

	G	AB	H	2B	3B	HR	HR%	R	RBI	BB	SO	SB	BA	SA	PH AB	PH H	G by POS
1968	7	27	9	0	2	1	3.7	3	4	3	2	0	.333	.593	0	0	C-7
3 yrs.	21	74	23	2	3	2	2.7	10	11	10	5	1	.311	.500	0	0	C-21
					4th												

Al McCauley

McCAULEY, ALLEN A.
B. Mar. 4, 1863, Indianapolis, Ind.   D. Aug. 24, 1917, Indianapolis, Ind.   BL TL 6'   180 lbs.

	G	AB	H	2B	3B	HR	HR%	R	RBI	BB	SO	SB	BA	SA	PH AB	PH H	G by POS
1884 IND AA	17	53	10	0	1	0	0.0	7		12			.189	.226	0	0	P-10, 1B-5, OF-3
1890 PHI N	112	418	102	25	7	1	0.2	63	42	57	38	8	.244	.344	0	0	1B-112
1891 WAS AA	59	206	58	5	8	1	0.5	36	31	30	13	9	.282	.398	0	0	1B-59
3 yrs.	188	677	170	30	16	2	0.3	106	72	99	51	17	.251	.352	0	0	1B-176, P-10, OF-3

F. F. McCauley

McCAULEY, WILLIAM H.
B. Dec. 20, 1869, Washington, D. C.   D. Jan. 27, 1926, Washington, D. C.

	G	AB	H	2B	3B	HR	HR%	R	RBI	BB	SO	SB	BA	SA	PH AB	PH H	G by POS
1895 WAS N	1	2	0	0	0	0	0.0	0	0	0	0	0	.000	.000	0	0	SS-1

Jim McCauley

McCAULEY, JAMES A.
B. Mar. 24, 1863, Stanley, N. Y.   D. Sept. 14, 1930, Canandaigua, N. Y.   5'11"   170 lbs.

	G	AB	H	2B	3B	HR	HR%	R	RBI	BB	SO	SB	BA	SA	PH AB	PH H	G by POS
1884 STL AA	1	2	0	0	0	0	0.0	0					.000	.000	0	0	C-1
1885 2 teams		BUF N (24G – .179)						CHI N (3G – .167)									
" total	27	90	16	2	1	0	0.0	5	7	13	15		.178	.222	0	0	C-23, OF-6
1886 BKN AA	11	30	7	1	0	0	0.0	5		11			.233	.267	0	0	C-11
3 yrs.	39	122	23	3	1	0	0.0	10	6	24	15		.189	.230	0	0	C-35, OF-6

Pat McCauley

McCAULEY, PATRICK M.
B. June 10, 1870, Ware, Mass.   D. Jan. 23, 1917, Newark, N. J.   TR

	G	AB	H	2B	3B	HR	HR%	R	RBI	BB	SO	SB	BA	SA	PH AB	PH H	G by POS
1893 STL N	5	16	1	0	0	0	0.0	0	0	0	1	0	.063	.063	0	0	C-5
1896 WAS N	26	84	21	3	0	2	2.4	14	11	7	8	3	.250	.357	1	0	C-24, OF-1
1903 NY A	6	19	1	0	0	0	0.0	0	1	0		0	.053	.053	0	0	C-6
3 yrs.	37	119	23	3	0	2	1.7	14	12	7	9	3	.193	.269	1	0	C-35, OF-1

Harry McChesney

McCHESNEY, HARRY VINCENT (Pud)
B. June 1, 1880, Pittsburgh, Pa.   D. Aug. 11, 1960, Pittsburgh, Pa.   BR TR 5'9"   165 lbs.

	G	AB	H	2B	3B	HR	HR%	R	RBI	BB	SO	SB	BA	SA	PH AB	PH H	G by POS
1904 CHI N	22	88	23	6	2	0	0.0	9	11	4		2	.261	.375	0	0	OF-22

Pete McClanahan

McCLANAHAN, PETE
B. Oct. 24, 1906, Coldspring, Tex.   BR TR 5'9"   170 lbs.

	G	AB	H	2B	3B	HR	HR%	R	RBI	BB	SO	SB	BA	SA	PH AB	PH H	G by POS
1931 PIT N	7	4	2	0	0	0	0.0	2	0	2	0	0	.500	.500	4	2	

Bill McClellan

McCLELLAN, WILLIAM HENRY
B. Mar. 22, 1856, Chicago, Ill.   D. July 2, 1929, Chicago, Ill.   BL TL   156 lbs.

	G	AB	H	2B	3B	HR	HR%	R	RBI	BB	SO	SB	BA	SA	PH AB	PH H	G by POS
1878 CHI N	48	205	46	6	1	0	0.0	26	29	2	13		.224	.263	0	0	2B-42, SS-5, OF-1
1881 PRO N	68	259	43	3	1	0	0.0	30	16	15	21		.166	.185	0	0	SS-50, OF-17, 2B-1
1883 PHI N	80	326	75	21	4	1	0.3	42		19	18		.230	.328	0	0	SS-78, OF-2, 3B-1
1884	111	450	116	13	2	3	0.7	71		28	43		.258	.316	0	0	SS-111, OF-1
1885 BKN AA	112	464	124	22	7	0	0.0	85		28			.267	.345	0	0	3B-57, 2B-55
1886	141	595	152	33	9	1	0.2	131		56			.255	.346	0	0	2B-141
1887	136	548	144	24	6	1	0.2	109		80		70	.263	.334	0	0	2B-136
1888 2 teams		BKN AA (74G – .205)						CLE AA (22G – .222)									
" total	96	350	73	7	3	0	0.0	39	26	46	19	19	.209	.246	0	0	2B-61, OF-33, SS-2
8 yrs.	792	3197	773	129	33	6	0.2	533	71	274	95	89	.242	.308	0	0	2B-436, SS-246, 3B-58, OF-54

Harvey McClellan

McCLELLAN, HARVEY McDOWELL
B. Dec. 22, 1894, Cynthiana, Ky.   D. Nov. 6, 1925, Cynthiana, Ky.   BR TR 5'10½" 150 lbs.

	G	AB	H	2B	3B	HR	HR%	R	RBI	BB	SO	SB	BA	SA	PH AB	PH H	G by POS
1919 CHI A	7	12	4	0	0	0	0.0	2	1	1	1	0	.333	.333	1	0	3B-3, SS-2
1920	10	18	6	1	0	0	0.0	4	5	4	1	2	.333	.500	2	0	SS-4, 3B-2
1921	63	196	35	4	1	1	0.5	20	14	14	18	2	.179	.224	3	0	2B-20, OF-15, SS-15, 3B-5
1922	91	301	68	17	3	2	0.7	28	28	16	32	3	.226	.322	5	4	3B-71, SS-8, 2B-2, OF-1
1923	141	550	129	29	3	1	0.2	67	41	27	44	14	.235	.304	1	1	SS-138, 2B-2
1924	32	85	15	3	0	0	0.0	9	9	6	7	2	.176	.212	1	0	SS-21, 2B-7, OF-1, 3B-1
6 yrs.	344	1162	257	54	8	4	0.3	130	98	68	103	23	.221	.292	13	5	SS-188, 3B-82, 2B-31, OF-17

Bill McCloskey

McCLOSKEY, WILLIAM GEORGE
B. Philadelphia, Pa.   Deceased.

	G	AB	H	2B	3B	HR	HR%	R	RBI	BB	SO	SB	BA	SA	PH AB	PH H	G by POS
1884 WIL U	9	30	3	0	0	0	0.0	0		0			.100	.100	0	0	OF-5, C-5

Jeff McCloskey

McCLOSKEY, JEFFERSON LAMAR
B. Nov. 6, 1891, Americus, Ga.   D. May 21, 1971, Americus, Ga.   BL TR 5'11"   160 lbs.

	G	AB	H	2B	3B	HR	HR%	R	RBI	BB	SO	SB	BA	SA	PH AB	PH H	G by POS
1913 BOS N	2	3	0	0	0	0	0.0	0	0	1	0	0	.000	.000	0	0	3B-2

Hal McClure

McCLURE, HAROLD MURRAY (Mac)
B. Aug. 8, 1859, Lewisburg, Pa.   D. Mar. 1, 1919, Lewisburg, Pa.   BR TR 6'   165 lbs.

	G	AB	H	2B	3B	HR	HR%	R	RBI	BB	SO	SB	BA	SA	PH AB	PH H	G by POS
1882 BOS N	2	6	2	0	0	0	0.0	0		1			.333	.333	0	0	OF-2

Larry McClure

McCLURE, LAWRENCE LEDWITH
B. Oct. 3, 1885, Wayne, W. Va.   D. Aug. 31, 1949, Huntington, W. Va.   BR TR 5'6½" 130 lbs.

	G	AB	H	2B	3B	HR	HR%	R	RBI	BB	SO	SB	BA	SA	PH AB	PH H	G by POS
1910 NY A	1	1	0	0	0	0	0.0	0		0		0	.000	.000	0	0	OF-1

Amby McConnell

McCONNELL, AMBROSE MOSES
B. Apr. 29, 1883, N. Pownal, Vt.   D. May 20, 1942, Utica, N. Y.   BL TR

	G	AB	H	2B	3B	HR	HR%	R	RBI	BB	SO	SB	BA	SA	PH AB	PH H	G by POS
1908 BOS A	140	502	140	10	6	2	0.4	77	43	38	31		.279	.335	10	5	2B-126, SS-3
1909	121	453	108	7	8	0	0.0	59	36	34	26		.238	.289	0	0	2B-121

	G	AB	H	2B	3B	HR	HR %	R	RBI	BB	SO	SB	BA	SA	Pinch Hit AB	Pinch Hit H	G by POS

Amby McConnell continued

	G	AB	H	2B	3B	HR	HR%	R	RBI	BB	SO	SB	BA	SA	PH AB	PH H	G by POS
1910 2 teams	BOS A (12G – .167)				CHI A (32G – .277)												
" total	44	155	39	2	3	0	0.0	19	6	12			8	.252	.303	2	0	2B-42
1911 CHI A	104	396	111	11	5	1	0.3	45	34	23			7	.280	.341	1	0	2B-103
4 yrs.	409	1506	398	30	22	3	0.2	200	119	107			72	.264	.319	13	5	2B-392, SS-3

George McConnell

McCONNELL, GEORGE NEELY   BR TR 6'3"   190 lbs.
B. Sept. 16, 1877, Shelbyville, Tenn.   D. May 10, 1964, Chattanooga, Tenn.

	G	AB	H	2B	3B	HR	HR%	R	RBI	BB	SO	SB	BA	SA	PH AB	PH H	G by POS
1909 NY A	13	43	9	0	1	0	0.0	4	5	1			1	.209	.256	0	0	1B-11, P-2
1912	42	91	27	4	2	0	0.0	11	8	4			0	.297	.385	17	6	P-23, 1B-2
1913	39	67	12	2	0	0	0.0	4	2	0	11		0	.179	.209	3	0	P-35, 1B-1
1914 CHI N	1	2	0	0	0	0	0.0	0	0	0			1	.000	.000	0	0	P-1
1915 CHI F	53	125	31	6	2	1	0.8	14	18	0			2	.248	.352	8	2	P-44
1916 CHI N	48	57	9	0	0	0	0.0	2	0	2	4		0	.158	.158	0	0	P-28
6 yrs.	196	385	88	12	5	1	0.3	35	33	7	16		3	.229	.294	28	8	P-133, 1B-14

Sammy McConnell

McCONNELL, SAMUEL FAULKNER   BL TR 5'6½"   150 lbs.
B. June 8, 1895, Philadelphia, Pa.   D. June 27, 1981, Phoenixville, Pa.

	G	AB	H	2B	3B	HR	HR%	R	RBI	BB	SO	SB	BA	SA	PH AB	PH H	G by POS
1915 PHI A	6	11	2	1	0	0	0.0	1	0	1	3		0	.182	.273	0	0	3B-5

Don McCormack

McCORMACK, DONALD ROSS   BR TR 6'3"   205 lbs.
B. Sept. 18, 1955, Omak, Wash.

	G	AB	H	2B	3B	HR	HR%	R	RBI	BB	SO	SB	BA	SA	PH AB	PH H	G by POS
1980 PHI N	2	1	1	0	0	0	0.0	0	0	0	0		0	1.000	1.000	0	0	C-2
1981	3	4	1	0	0	0	0.0	0	0	0	1		0	.250	.250	0	0	C-3
2 yrs.	5	5	2	0	0	0	0.0	0	0	0	1		0	.400	.400	0	0	C-5

Barry McCormick

McCORMICK, WILLIAM J.   TR 5'9"
B. Dec. 25, 1874, Maysville, Ky.   D. Jan. 28, 1956, Cincinnati, Ohio

	G	AB	H	2B	3B	HR	HR%	R	RBI	BB	SO	SB	BA	SA	PH AB	PH H	G by POS
1895 LOU N	3	12	3	0	1	0	0.0	2	0	0			1	.250	.417	0	0	SS-2, 2B-1
1896 CHI N	45	168	37	3	1	1	0.6	22	23	14		30	9	.220	.268	0	0	3B-35, SS-6, 2B-3, OF-1
1897	101	419	112	8	10	2	0.5	87	55	33			44	.267	.348	0	0	3B-56, SS-46, 2B-1
1898	137	530	131	15	9	2	0.4	76	78	47			15	.247	.321	0	0	2B-99, SS-3
1899	102	376	97	15	2	2	0.5	48	52	25			14	.258	.324	0	0	SS-84, 3B-21, 2B-5
1900	110	379	83	13	5	3	0.8	35	48	38			8	.219	.303	0	0	SS-112, 3B-3
1901	115	427	100	15	6	1	0.2	45	32	31			12	.234	.304	0	0	3B-132, SS-7, OF-1
1902 STL A	139	504	124	14	4	3	0.6	55	51	37			10	.246	.308	0	0	2B-91, 3B-28, SS-4
1903 2 teams	STL A (61G – .217)				WAS A (63G – .215)												
" total	124	426	92	16	3	2	0.5	28	40	28			8	.216	.282	0	0	2B-113
1904 WAS A	113	404	88	11	1	0	0.0	36	39	27			9	.218	.250	0	0	3B-411, 2B-314, SS-265, OF-2
10 yrs.	989	3645	867	110	42	16	0.4	434	418	280		30	130	.238	.304	0	0	

Frank McCormick

McCORMICK, FRANK ANDREW (Buck)   BR TR 6'4"   205 lbs.
B. June 9, 1911, New York, N. Y.   D. Nov. 21, 1982, Manhasset, N. Y.

	G	AB	H	2B	3B	HR	HR%	R	RBI	BB	SO	SB	BA	SA	PH AB	PH H	G by POS
1934 CIN N	12	16	5	2	1	0	0.0	1	5	0	1		0	.313	.563	10	4	1B-2
1937	24	83	27	5	0	0	0.0	5	9	2	4		1	.325	.386	0	0	1B-20, 2B-4, OF-1
1938	151	640	209	40	4	5	0.8	89	106	18	17		1	.327	.425	0	0	1B-151
1939	156	630	209	41	4	18	2.9	99	128	40	16		1	.332	.495	0	0	1B-156
1940	155	618	191	44	3	19	3.1	93	127	52	26		2	.309	.482	0	0	1B-155
1941	154	603	162	31	5	17	2.8	77	97	40	13		2	.269	.421	0	0	1B-154
1942	145	564	156	24	0	13	2.3	58	89	45	18		1	.277	.388	1	0	1B-144
1943	126	472	143	28	0	8	1.7	56	59	29	15		2	.303	.413	6	0	1B-120
1944	153	581	177	37	3	20	3.4	85	102	57	17		7	.305	.482	1	0	1B-153
1945	152	580	160	33	0	10	1.7	68	81	56	22		6	.276	.384	1	0	1B-151
1946 PHI N	135	504	143	20	2	11	2.2	46	66	36	21		2	.284	.397	1	0	1B-134
1947 2 teams	PHI N (15G – .225)				BOS N (81G – .354)												
" total	96	252	84	20	2	3	1.2	31	51	14	10		2	.333	.464	36	13	1B-60
1948 BOS N	75	180	45	9	2	4	2.2	14	34	10	9		0	.250	.389	22	4	1B-50
13 yrs.	1534	5723	1711	334	26	128	2.2	722	954	399	189		27	.299	.434	77	21	1B-1450, 2B-4, OF-1
WORLD SERIES																	
1939 CIN N	4	15	6	1	0	0	0.0	1	1	0	1		0	.400	.467	0	0	1B-4
1940	7	28	6	1	0	0	0.0	2	0	1	0		0	.214	.250	0	0	1B-7
1948 BOS N	3	5	1	0	0	0	0.0	0	0	0	2		0	.200	.200	2	0	1B-1
3 yrs.	14	48	13	2	0	0	0.0	3	1	1	4		0	.271	.313	2	0	1B-12

Jerry McCormick

McCORMICK, JOHN
B. Philadelphia, Pa.   D. Sept. 19, 1905, Philadelphia, Pa.

	G	AB	H	2B	3B	HR	HR%	R	RBI	BB	SO	SB	BA	SA	PH AB	PH H	G by POS
1883 BAL AA	93	389	102	16	6	0	0.0	40		2				.262	.334	0	0	3B-93
1884 2 teams	PHI U (67G – .285)				WAS U (42G – .217)												
" total	109	452	118	20	4	0	0.0	64		5				.261	.323	0	0	3B-92, SS-7, OF-5, 2B-5, P-1
2 yrs.	202	841	220	36	10	0	0.0	104		7				.262	.328	0	0	3B-185, SS-7, OF-5, 2B-5, P-1

Jim McCormick

McCORMICK, JAMES   BR TR 5'10½" 195 lbs.
B. 1856, Glasgow, Scotland   D. Mar. 10, 1918, Paterson, N. J.
Manager 1879-80.

	G	AB	H	2B	3B	HR	HR%	R	RBI	BB	SO	SB	BA	SA	PH AB	PH H	G by POS
1878 IND N	15	56	8	1	0	0	0.0	5		0	2			.143	.161	0	0	P-14, OF-3
1879 CLE N	75	282	62	10	2	0	0.0	35	20	1	9			.220	.270	0	0	P-62, OF-13, 1B-4
1880	78	289	71	11	0	0	0.0	34		5	5			.246	.284	0	0	P-74, OF-5
1881	70	309	79	9	4	0	0.0	45	26	5	16			.256	.311	0	0	P-59, OF-10, 3B-1, 2B-1
1882	70	262	57	7	3	2	0.8	35	15	2	22			.218	.290	0	0	P-68, OF-4
1883	43	157	37	2	2	0	0.0	21		2	14			.236	.274	0	0	P-42, OF-1, 1B-1
1884 2 teams	CLE N (49G – .263)				CIN U (27G – .245)												
" total	76	300	77	8	5	0	0.0	27	23	1	11			.257	.317	0	0	P-66, OF-11

	G	AB	H	2B	3B	HR	HR %	R	RBI	BB	SO	SB	BA	SA	Pinch Hit AB	H	G by POS

Jim McCormick continued

1885 2 teams	PRO N (4G – .214)					CHI N (25G – .223)											
" total	29	117	26	2	4	0	0.0	15	16	2	18		.222	.308	0	0	P-28, OF-1
1886 CHI N	42	174	41	9	2	2	1.1	17	21	2	30		.236	.345	0	0	P-42, OF-4
1887 PIT N	36	136	33	7	0	0	0.0	12	18	2	0	9	.243	.294	0	0	P-36
10 yrs.	534	2082	491	66	22	4	0.2	246	139	22	127	9	.236	.294	0	0	P-491, OF-52, 1B-5, 3B-1, 2B-1

Jim McCormick

McCORMICK, JAMES AMBROSE BR TR 6'1" 160 lbs.
B. Nov. 2, 1868, Spencer, Mass.　D. Feb. 1, 1948, Saco, Me.

	G	AB	H	2B	3B	HR	HR %	R	RBI	BB	SO	SB	BA	SA	AB	H	G by POS
1892 STL N	3	11	0	0	0	0	0.0	0	0	1	5	0	.000	.000	0	0	2B-2, 3B-1

Mike McCormick

McCORMICK, MICHAEL J. BR TR 5'9"
B. 1883, Jersey City, N. J.　D. Nov. 18, 1953, Jersey City, N. J.

	G	AB	H	2B	3B	HR	HR %	R	RBI	BB	SO	SB	BA	SA	AB	H	G by POS
1904 BKN N	105	347	64	5	4	0	0.0	28	27	43		22	.184	.222	0	0	3B-104, 2B-1

Mike McCormick

McCORMICK, MYRON WINTHROP BR TR 6' 195 lbs.
B. May 6, 1917, Angels Camp, Calif.　D. Apr. 14, 1976, Los Angeles, Calif.

	G	AB	H	2B	3B	HR	HR %	R	RBI	BB	SO	SB	BA	SA	AB	H	G by POS
1940 CIN N	110	417	125	20	0	1	0.2	48	30	13	36	8	.300	.355	2	0	OF-107
1941	110	369	106	17	3	4	1.1	52	31	30	24	4	.287	.382	4	0	OF-101
1942	40	135	32	2	3	1	0.7	18	11	13	7	0	.237	.319	1	0	OF-38
1943	4	15	2	0	0	0	0.0	0	0	2	0	0	.133	.133	0	0	OF-4
1946 2 teams	CIN N (23G – .216)					BOS N (59G – .262)											
" total	82	238	59	8	2	1	0.4	33	21	19	12	0	.248	.311	10	2	OF-69
1947 BOS N	92	284	81	13	7	3	1.1	42	36	20	21	1	.285	.412	12	4	OF-79
1948	115	343	104	22	7	1	0.3	45	39	32	34	1	.303	.417	14	6	OF-100
1949 BKN N	55	139	29	5	1	2	1.4	17	14	14	12	1	.209	.302	6	2	OF-49
1950 2 teams	NY N (4G – .000)					CHI A (55G – .232)											
" total	59	142	32	4	3	0	0.0	16	10	16	8	0	.225	.296	11	1	OF-44
1951 WAS A	81	243	70	9	3	1	0.4	31	23	29	20	1	.288	.362	15	7	OF-62
10 yrs.	748	2325	640	100	29	14	0.6	302	215	188	174	16	.275	.361	75	22	OF-653

WORLD SERIES

	G	AB	H	2B	3B	HR	HR %	R	RBI	BB	SO	SB	BA	SA	AB	H	G by POS
1940 CIN N	7	29	9	3	0	0	0.0	1	2	1	6	0	.310	.414	0	0	OF-7
1948 BOS N	6	23	6	0	0	0	0.0	1	2	0	4	0	.261	.261	0	0	OF-6
1949 BKN N	1	0	0	0	0	0	0.0	0	0	0	0	0	–	–	0	0	OF-1
3 yrs.	14	52	15	3	0	0	0.0	2	4	1	10	0	.288	.346	0	0	OF-14

Moose McCormick

McCORMICK, HARRY ELWOOD BL TL 5'11" 180 lbs.
B. Feb. 28, 1881, Philadelphia, Pa.　D. July 9, 1962, Lewisburg, Pa.

	G	AB	H	2B	3B	HR	HR %	R	RBI	BB	SO	SB	BA	SA	AB	H	G by POS
1904 2 teams	NY N (59G – .266)					PIT N (66G – .290)											
" total	125	441	123	19	11	3	0.7	53	49	26		19	.279	.392	4	2	OF-121
1908 2 teams	PHI N (11G – .091)					NY N (73G – .302)											
" total	84	274	78	16	3	0	0.0	31	34	6		6	.285	.365	10	3	OF-70
1909 NY N	110	413	120	21	8	3	0.7	68	27	49		4	.291	.402	10	2	OF-109
1912	42	39	13	4	1	0	0.0	4	8	6	9	1	.333	.487	30	11	OF-6, 1B-1
1913	57	80	22	2	3	0	0.0	9	15	5	13	0	.275	.375	39	10	OF-15
5 yrs.	418	1247	356	62	26	6	0.5	165	133	92	22	30	.285	.391	93	28	OF-321, 1B-1

WORLD SERIES

	G	AB	H	2B	3B	HR	HR %	R	RBI	BB	SO	SB	BA	SA	AB	H	G by POS
1912 NY N	5	4	1	0	0	0	0.0	0	1	0	0	0	.250	.250	4	1	
1913	2	2	1	0	0	0	0.0	1	0	0	0	0	.500	.500	2	1	
2 yrs.	7	6	2	0	0	0	0.0	1	1	0	0	0	.333	.333	6	2	

Barney McCosky

McCOSKY, WILLIAM BARNEY BL TR 6'1" 184 lbs.
B. Apr. 11, 1918, Coal Run, Pa.

	G	AB	H	2B	3B	HR	HR %	R	RBI	BB	SO	SB	BA	SA	AB	H	G by POS
1939 DET A	147	611	190	33	14	4	0.7	120	58	70	45	20	.311	.430	2	1	OF-145
1940	143	589	200	39	19	4	0.7	123	57	67	41	13	.340	.491	2	1	OF-141
1941	127	494	160	25	8	3	0.6	80	55	61	33	8	.324	.425	4	4	OF-122
1942	154	600	176	28	11	7	1.2	75	50	68	37	11	.293	.412	0	0	OF-154
1946 2 teams	DET A (25G – .198)					PHI A (92G – .354)											
" total	117	399	127	22	4	2	0.5	44	45	60	22	2	.318	.409	5	1	OF-109
1947 PHI A	137	546	179	22	7	1	0.2	77	52	57	29	1	.328	.399	1	0	OF-136
1948	135	515	168	21	5	0	0.0	95	46	68	22	1	.326	.386	1	1	OF-134
1950	66	179	43	10	1	0	0.0	19	11	22	12	0	.240	.307	23	5	OF-42
1951 3 teams	PHI A (12G – .296)					CIN N (25G – .320)					CLE A (31G – .213)						
" total	68	138	37	7	1	2	1.4	14	14	15	11	1	.268	.377	32	7	OF-34
1952 CLE A	54	80	17	4	1	1	1.3	14	8	8	5	1	.213	.325	30	9	OF-19
1953	22	21	4	3	0	0	0.0	3	3	1	4	0	.190	.333	21	4	
11 yrs.	1170	4172	1301	214	71	24	0.6	664	397	497	261	58	.312	.414	121	33	OF-1036

WORLD SERIES

	G	AB	H	2B	3B	HR	HR %	R	RBI	BB	SO	SB	BA	SA	AB	H	G by POS
1940 DET A	7	23	7	1	0	0	0.0	5	1	7	0	0	.304	.348	0	0	OF-7

Willie McCovey

McCOVEY, WILLIE LEE (Stretch) BL TL 6'4" 198 lbs.
B. Jan. 10, 1938, Mobile, Ala.

	G	AB	H	2B	3B	HR	HR %	R	RBI	BB	SO	SB	BA	SA	AB	H	G by POS
1959 SF N	52	192	68	9	5	13	6.8	32	38	22	35	2	.354	.656	2	2	1B-51
1960	101	260	62	15	3	13	5.0	37	51	45	53	1	.238	.469	32	7	1B-71
1961	106	328	89	12	3	18	5.5	59	50	37	60	1	.271	.491	21	4	1B-84
1962	91	229	67	6	1	20	8.7	41	54	29	35	3	.293	.590	17	4	OF-57, 1B-17
1963	152	564	158	19	5	44	7.8	103	102	50	119	1	.280	.566	5	0	OF-135, 1B-23
1964	130	364	80	14	1	18	4.9	55	54	61	73	2	.220	.412	23	4	OF-83, 1B-26
1965	160	540	149	17	4	39	7.2	93	92	88	118	0	.276	.539	6	1	1B-156
1966	150	502	148	26	6	36	7.2	85	96	76	100	2	.295	.586	7	2	1B-145
1967	135	456	126	17	4	31	6.8	73	91	71	110	3	.276	.535	9	2	1B-127
1968	148	523	153	16	4	36	6.9	81	105	72	71	4	.293	.545	2	1	1B-146
1969	149	491	157	26	2	45	9.2	101	126	121	66	0	.320	.656	1	0	1B-148
1970	152	495	143	39	2	39	7.9	98	126	137	75	0	.289	.612	4	0	1B-146
1971	105	329	91	13	0	18	5.5	45	70	64	57	0	.277	.480	8	3	1B-95

	G	AB	H	2B	3B	HR	HR %	R	RBI	BB	SO	SB	BA	SA	Pinch Hit AB	Pinch Hit H	G by POS

Willie McCovey continued

	G	AB	H	2B	3B	HR	HR %	R	RBI	BB	SO	SB	BA	SA	AB	H	G by POS
1972	81	263	56	8	0	14	5.3	30	35	38	45	0	.213	.403	7	2	1B-74
1973	130	383	102	14	3	29	7.6	52	75	105	78	1	.266	.546	8	2	1B-117
1974 SD N	128	344	87	19	1	22	6.4	53	63	96	76	1	.253	.506	18	7	1B-104
1975	122	413	104	17	0	23	5.6	43	68	57	80	1	.252	.460	4	2	1B-115
1976 2 teams	SD	N	(71G –	.203)		OAK	A	(11G –	.208)								
" total	82	226	46	9	0	7	3.1	20	36	24	43	0	.204	.336	21	6	1B-51, DH-9
1977 SF N	141	478	134	21	0	28	5.9	54	86	67	106	3	.280	.500	4	0	1B-136
1978	108	351	80	19	2	12	3.4	32	64	36	57	1	.228	.396	9	2	1B-97
1979	117	353	88	9	0	15	4.2	34	57	36	70	0	.249	.402	28	11	1B-89
1980	48	113	23	8	0	1	0.9	8	16	13	23	0	.204	.301	17	2	1B-27
22 yrs.	2588	8197	2211	353	46	521	6.4	1229	1555	1345	1550	26	.270	.515	254	66	1B-2045, OF-275, DH-9
							8th	10th									

LEAGUE CHAMPIONSHIP SERIES																	
1971 SF N	4	14	6	0	0	2	14.3	2	6	4	2	0	.429	.857	0	0	1B-4

WORLD SERIES																	
1962 SF N	4	15	3	0	1	1	6.7	2	1	1	3	0	.200	.533	0	0	OF-2

Art McCoy

McCOY, ARTHUR GRAY
B. 1865, Danville, Pa.   D. Mar. 22, 1904, Danville, Pa.

168 lbs.

	G	AB	H	2B	3B	HR	HR %	R	RBI	BB	SO	SB	BA	SA	AB	H	G by POS
1889 WAS N	2	6	0	0	0	0	0.0	0		2	1	0	.000	.000	0	0	2B-2

Benny McCoy

McCOY, BENJAMIN JENISON
B. Nov. 9, 1915, Jenison, Mich.

BL TR 5'9"   170 lbs.

	G	AB	H	2B	3B	HR	HR %	R	RBI	BB	SO	SB	BA	SA	AB	H	G by POS
1938 DET A	7	15	3	1	0	0	0.0	2	0	1	2	0	.200	.267	0	0	2B-6, 3B-1
1939	55	192	58	13	6	1	0.5	38	33	29	26	3	.302	.448	5	0	2B-34, SS-16
1940 PHI A	134	490	126	26	5	7	1.4	56	62	65	44	2	.257	.373	4	2	2B-130, 3B-1
1941	141	517	140	12	7	8	1.5	86	61	95	50	3	.271	.368	5	0	2B-135
4 yrs.	337	1214	327	52	18	16	1.3	182	156	190	122	8	.269	.381	14	2	2B-305, SS-16, 3B-2

Tom McCraw

McCRAW, THOMAS LEE
B. Nov. 21, 1941, Malvern, Ark.

BL TL 6'   183 lbs.

	G	AB	H	2B	3B	HR	HR %	R	RBI	BB	SO	SB	BA	SA	AB	H	G by POS
1963 CHI A	102	280	71	11	3	6	2.1	38	33	21	46	15	.254	.379	3	1	1B-97
1964	125	368	96	11	5	6	1.6	47	36	32	65	15	.261	.367	20	2	1B-84, OF-36
1965	133	273	65	12	1	5	1.8	38	21	25	48	12	.238	.344	22	7	1B-72, OF-64
1966	151	389	89	16	4	5	1.3	49	48	29	40	20	.229	.329	7	1	1B-121, OF-41
1967	125	453	107	18	3	11	2.4	55	45	33	55	24	.236	.362	2	0	1B-123, OF-6
1968	136	477	112	16	12	9	1.9	51	44	36	58	20	.235	.375	3	0	1B-135
1969	93	240	62	12	2	2	0.8	21	25	21	24	1	.258	.350	17	4	1B-44, OF-41
1970	129	332	73	11	2	6	1.8	39	31	21	50	12	.220	.319	32	8	1B-59, OF-49
1971 WAS A	122	207	44	6	4	7	3.4	33	25	19	38	3	.213	.382	40	9	OF-60, 1B-30
1972 CLE A	129	391	101	13	5	7	1.8	43	33	41	47	12	.258	.371	12	2	OF-84, 1B-38
1973 CAL A	99	264	70	7	0	3	1.1	25	24	30	42	3	.265	.326	23	5	OF-34, 1B-25, DH-8
1974 2 teams	CAL	A	(56G –	.286)		CLE	A	(45G –	.304)								
" total	101	231	68	16	0	6	2.6	38	34	17	24	2	.294	.442	23	6	1B-67, OF-13, DH-2
1975 CLE A	23	51	14	1	1	2	3.9	7	5	7	4	0	.275	.451	4	2	1B-16, OF-3
13 yrs.	1468	3956	972	150	42	75	1.9	484	404	332	544	143	.246	.362	208	47	1B-911, OF-431, DH-10

Frank McCrea

McCREA, FRANCIS WILLIAM
B. Sept. 6, 1896, Jersey City, N. J.   D. Feb. 25, 1981, Dover, N. J.

BR TR 5'9"   155 lbs.

	G	AB	H	2B	3B	HR	HR %	R	RBI	BB	SO	SB	BA	SA	AB	H	G by POS
1925 CLE A	1	5	1	0	0	0	0.0	1	0	0	0	0	.200	.200	0	0	C-1

Judge McCreedie

McCREEDIE, WALTER HENRY
B. Nov. 29, 1876, Manchester, Iowa   D. July 29, 1934, Portland, Ore.

	G	AB	H	2B	3B	HR	HR %	R	RBI	BB	SO	SB	BA	SA	AB	H	G by POS
1903 BKN N	56	213	69	5	0	0	0.0	40	24		10	1	.324	.347	0	0	OF-56

Tom McCreery

McCREERY, THOMAS LIVINGSTON
B. Oct. 19, 1874, Beaver, Pa.   D. July 3, 1941, Beaver, Pa.

BB TR 5'11"   180 lbs.

	G	AB	H	2B	3B	HR	HR %	R	RBI	BB	SO	SB	BA	SA	AB	H	G by POS
1895 LOU N	31	108	35	3	1	0	0.0	18	10	8	15	3	.324	.370	0	0	OF-18, P-8, SS-4, 3B-1, 1B-1
1896	115	441	155	23	21	7	1.6	87	65	42	58	26	.351	.546	2	1	OF-111, 2B-1, P-1
1897 2 teams	LOU	N	(89G –	.284)		NY	N	(49G –	.299)								
" total	138	515	149	13	11	5	1.0	91	68	60		28	.289	.386	2	0	OF-134, 2B-3
1898 2 teams	NY	N	(35G –	.198)		PIT	N	(53G –	.311)								
" total	88	311	83	9	10	3	1.0	48	37	45		6	.267	.389	2	1	OF-86
1899 PIT N	118	455	147	21	9	2	0.4	76	64	47		11	.323	.422	5	2	OF-97, SS-9, 2B-7
1900	43	132	29	4	3	1	0.8	20	13	16		2	.220	.318	5	0	OF-35, P-1
1901 BKN N	91	335	97	11	14	3	0.9	47	53	32		13	.290	.433	3	1	OF-82, 1B-4, SS-2
1902	112	430	105	8	4	4	0.9	49	57	29		16	.244	.309	0	0	1B-108, OF-4
1903 2 teams	BKN	N	(40G –	.262)		BOS	N	(23G –	.217)								
" total	63	224	55	7	3	1	0.4	28	20	29		11	.246	.317	2	2	OF-61
9 yrs.	799	2951	855	99	76	26	0.9	464	387	308	73	116	.290	.401	21	7	OF-628, 1B-113, SS-15, 2B-11, P-10, 3B-1

Frank McCue

McCUE, FRANK ALOYSIUS
B. Oct. 4, 1897, Chicago, Ill.   D. July 5, 1953, Chicago, Ill.

BB TR 5'9"   150 lbs.

	G	AB	H	2B	3B	HR	HR %	R	RBI	BB	SO	SB	BA	SA	AB	H	G by POS
1922 PHI A	2	5	0	0	0	0	0.0	0	0	0	0	0	.000	.000	0	0	3B-2

Clyde McCullough

McCULLOUGH, CLYDE EDWARD
B. Mar. 4, 1917, Nashville, Tenn.   D. Sept. 18, 1982, San Francisco, Calif.

BR TR 5'11½"   180 lbs.

	G	AB	H	2B	3B	HR	HR %	R	RBI	BB	SO	SB	BA	SA	AB	H	G by POS
1940 CHI N	9	26	4	1	0	0	0.0	4	1	5	5	0	.154	.192	2	0	C-7
1941	125	418	95	9	2	9	2.2	41	53	34	67	5	.227	.323	5	1	C-119
1942	109	337	95	22	1	5	1.5	39	31	25	47	7	.282	.398	8	2	C-97
1943	87	266	63	5	2	2	0.8	20	23	24	33	6	.237	.293	4	0	C-81
1946	95	307	88	18	5	4	1.3	38	34	22	39	2	.287	.417	5	0	C-89
1947	86	234	59	12	4	3	1.3	25	30	20	20	1	.252	.376	17	3	C-64

	G	AB	H	2B	3B	HR	HR %	R	RBI	BB	SO	SB	BA	SA	Pinch Hit AB	Pinch Hit H	G by POS

Clyde McCullough continued

	G	AB	H	2B	3B	HR	HR %	R	RBI	BB	SO	SB	BA	SA	AB	H	G by POS
1948	69	172	36	4	2	1	0.6	10	7	15	25	0	.209	.273	15	2	C-51
1949 PIT N	91	241	57	9	3	4	1.7	30	21	24	30	1	.237	.349	0	0	C-90
1950	103	279	71	16	4	6	2.2	28	34	31	35	3	.254	.405	2	0	C-100
1951	92	259	77	9	2	8	3.1	26	39	27	31	2	.297	.440	7	4	C-86
1952	66	172	40	5	1	1	0.6	10	15	10	18	0	.233	.291	5	1	C-61, 1B-1
1953 CHI N	77	229	59	3	2	6	2.6	21	23	15	23	0	.258	.367	4	1	C-73
1954	31	81	21	7	0	3	3.7	9	17	5	5	0	.259	.457	2	0	C-26, 3B-3
1955	44	81	16	0	0	0	0.0	7	10	8	15	0	.198	.198	7	3	C-37
1956	14	19	4	1	0	0	0.0	0	1	0	15	0	.211	.263	7	1	C-7
15 yrs.	1098	3121	785	121	28	52	1.7	308	339	265	398	27	.252	.358	90	18	C-988, 3B-3, 1B-1
WORLD SERIES																	
1945 CHI N	1	1	0	0	0	0	0.0	0	0	0	0	0	.000	.000	1	0	

Harry McCurdy

McCURDY, HARRY HENRY
B. Sept. 15, 1900, Stevens Point, Wis.   D. July 21, 1972, Houston, Tex.   BL TR 5'11" 187 lbs.

	G	AB	H	2B	3B	HR	HR %	R	RBI	BB	SO	SB	BA	SA	AB	H	G by POS
1922 STL N	13	27	8	2	2	0	0.0	3	5	1	1	0	.296	.519	3	0	C-9, 1B-2
1923	67	185	49	11	2	0	0.0	17	15	11	11	3	.265	.346	9	0	C-58
1926 CHI A	44	86	28	7	2	1	1.2	16	11	6	10	0	.326	.488	11	2	C-25, 1B-8
1927	86	262	75	19	3	1	0.4	34	27	32	24	6	.286	.393	3	0	C-82
1928	49	103	27	10	0	2	1.9	12	13	8	15	1	.262	.417	14	3	C-34
1930 PHI N	80	148	49	6	2	1	0.7	23	25	15	12	0	.331	.419	32	8	C-41
1931	66	150	43	9	0	1	0.7	21	25	23	16	2	.287	.367	17	7	C-45
1932	62	136	32	6	1	1	0.7	13	14	17	13	0	.235	.316	15	2	C-42
1933	73	54	15	1	0	2	3.7	9	12	16	6	0	.278	.407	52	15	C-2
1934 CIN N	3	6	0	0	0	0	0.0	0	1	0	0	0	.000	.000	2	0	1B-3
10 yrs.	543	1157	326	71	12	9	0.8	148	148	129	108	12	.282	.387	158	37	C-338, 1B-13

Mickey McDermott

McDERMOTT, MAURICE JOSEPH
B. Aug. 29, 1928, Poughkeepsie, N. Y.   BL TL 6'2" 170 lbs.

	G	AB	H	2B	3B	HR	HR %	R	RBI	BB	SO	SB	BA	SA	AB	H	G by POS
1948 BOS A	7	8	3	1	0	0	0.0	2	0	0	0	0	.375	.500	0	0	P-7
1949	13	33	7	3	0	0	0.0	3	6	3	6	0	.212	.303	0	0	P-12
1950	39	44	16	5	0	0	0.0	11	12	9	3	0	.364	.477	0	0	P-38
1951	43	66	18	1	1	1	1.5	8	6	3	14	0	.273	.364	3	0	P-34
1952	36	62	14	1	1	1	1.6	10	7	4	11	0	.226	.323	1	0	P-30
1953	45	93	28	8	0	1	1.1	9	13	2	13	0	.301	.419	12	1	P-32
1954 WAS A	54	95	19	3	0	0	0.0	7	4	7	12	0	.200	.232	19	3	P-30
1955	70	95	25	4	0	1	1.1	10	10	6	16	1	.263	.337	38	9	P-31
1956 NY A	46	52	11	0	0	1	1.9	4	4	8	13	0	.212	.269	19	4	P-23
1957 KC A	58	49	12	1	0	4	8.2	6	7	9	16	0	.245	.510	24	5	P-29, 1B-2
1958 DET A	4	3	1	0	0	0	0.0	0	1	0	2	0	.333	.333	2	1	P-2
1961 2 teams	STL N (22G – .071)				KC A (7G – .200)												
" total	29	19	2	2	0	0	0.0	1	4	1	6	0	.105	.211	9	2	P-23
12 yrs.	444	619	156	29	2	9	1.5	71	74	52	112	1	.252	.349	127	25	P-291, 1B-2
WORLD SERIES																	
1956 NY A	1	1	1	0	0	0	0.0	0	0	0	0	0	1.000	1.000	0	0	P-1

Red McDermott

McDERMOTT, FRANK S.
B. Nov. 12, 1889, Philadelphia, Pa.   D. Sept. 11, 1964, Philadelphia, Pa.   BR TR 5'6" 150 lbs.

	G	AB	H	2B	3B	HR	HR %	R	RBI	BB	SO	SB	BA	SA	AB	H	G by POS
1912 DET A	5	15	4	1	0	0	0.0	2	0			1	.267	.333	0	0	OF-5

Terry McDermott

McDERMOTT, TERRENCE MICHAEL
B. Mar. 20, 1951, Rockville Center, N. Y.   BR TR 6'3" 205 lbs.

	G	AB	H	2B	3B	HR	HR %	R	RBI	BB	SO	SB	BA	SA	AB	H	G by POS
1972 LA N	9	23	3	0	0	0	0.0	0	2	2	8	0	.130	.130	3	1	1B-7

Tom McDermott

McDERMOTT, THOMAS NATHANIEL
B. Zanesville, Ohio   D. Nov. 23, 1922, Mansfield, Ohio

	G	AB	H	2B	3B	HR	HR %	R	RBI	BB	SO	SB	BA	SA	AB	H	G by POS
1885 BAL AA	1	0	0	0	0	0	–	0		0			–	–	0	0	2B-1

Dave McDonald

McDONALD, DAVID BRUCE
B. May 20, 1943, New Albany, Ind.   BL TR 6'3" 215 lbs.

	G	AB	H	2B	3B	HR	HR %	R	RBI	BB	SO	SB	BA	SA	AB	H	G by POS
1969 NY A	9	23	5	1	0	0	0.0	0	2	2	5	0	.217	.261	3	0	1B-7
1971 MON N	24	39	4	2	0	1	2.6	3	4	4	14	0	.103	.231	17	1	1B-8, OF-1
2 yrs.	33	62	9	3	0	1	1.6	3	6	6	19	0	.145	.242	20	1	1B-15, OF-1

Ed McDonald

McDONALD, EDWARD C.
B. Oct. 28, 1886, Albany, N. Y.   D. Mar. 11, 1946, Albany, N. Y.   BR TR 6' 180 lbs.

	G	AB	H	2B	3B	HR	HR %	R	RBI	BB	SO	SB	BA	SA	AB	H	G by POS
1911 BOS N	54	175	36	7	3	1	0.6	28	21	40	39	11	.206	.297	0	0	3B-53, SS-1
1912	121	459	119	23	6	2	0.4	70	34	70	91	22	.259	.349	3	1	3B-118
1913 CHI N	1	0	0	0	0	0	–	0	0	0	0	0	–	–	0	0	
3 yrs.	176	634	155	30	9	3	0.5	98	55	110	130	33	.244	.334	3	1	3B-171, SS-1

Jim McDonald

McDONALD, JAMES
B. Philadelphia, Pa.

	G	AB	H	2B	3B	HR	HR %	R	RBI	BB	SO	SB	BA	SA	AB	H	G by POS
1902 NY N	2	9	3	0	0	0	0.0	0	1	0		0	.333	.333	0	0	OF-2

Jim McDonald

McDONALD, JAMES A.
B. Aug. 6, 1860, San Francisco, Calif.   D. Sept. 14, 1914, San Francisco, Calif.

	G	AB	H	2B	3B	HR	HR %	R	RBI	BB	SO	SB	BA	SA	AB	H	G by POS
1884 2 teams	PIT AA (38G – .159)				WAS U (2G – .167)												
" total	40	151	24	3	0	0	0.0	11		2			.159	.179	0	0	3B-22, OF-16, 2B-1, C-1
1885 BUF N	5	14	0	0	0	0	0.0	0		0	4		.000	.000	0	0	SS-4, OF-1
2 yrs.	45	165	24	3	0	0	0.0	11		2	4		.145	.164	0	0	3B-22, OF-17, SS-4, 2B-1, C-1

	G	AB	H	2B	3B	HR	HR %	R	RBI	BB	SO	SB	BA	SA	Pinch Hit AB	Pinch Hit H	G by POS

Joe McDonald

McDONALD, JOSEPH MALCOLM (Tex)
B. Apr. 9, 1888, Galveston, Tex.   D. May 30, 1963, Baytown, Tex.
BR TR 5'11"   175 lbs.

	G	AB	H	2B	3B	HR	HR %	R	RBI	BB	SO	SB	BA	SA	PH AB	PH H	G by POS
1910 STL A	10	32	5	0	0	0	0.0	4	1	1		0	.156	.156	0	0	3B-10

Tex McDonald

McDONALD, CHARLES E.
Born Charles C. Crabtree.
B. Jan. 31, 1891, Farmersville, Tex.   D. Mar. 31, 1943, Houston, Tex.
BL TR 5'10"   160 lbs.

	G	AB	H	2B	3B	HR	HR %	R	RBI	BB	SO	SB	BA	SA	PH AB	PH H	G by POS
1912 CIN N	61	140	36	3	4	1	0.7	16	15	13	24	5	.257	.357	15	5	SS-42
1913 2 teams	CIN	N (11G –	.300)		BOS	N	(62G –	.359)									
" total	73	155	55	4	0	0	0.0	25	20	15	18	4	.355	.432	26	9	3B-31, 2B-6, OF-1, SS-1
1914 2 teams	PIT	F (67G –	.318)		BUF	F	(69G –	.296)									
" total	136	473	145	29	13	6	1.3	59	61	33		20	.307	.461	8	1	OF-90, 2B-37, SS-5
1915 BUF F	87	251	68	9	6	6	2.4	31	39	27		5	.271	.426	20	7	OF-65
4 yrs.	357	1019	304	45	27	13	1.3	131	135	88	42	34	.298	.434	69	22	OF-156, SS-48, 2B-43, 3B-31

Jim McDonnell

McDONNELL, JAMES WILLIAM (Mack)
B. Aug. 15, 1922, Gagetown, Mich.
BL TR 5'11"   165 lbs.

	G	AB	H	2B	3B	HR	HR %	R	RBI	BB	SO	SB	BA	SA	PH AB	PH H	G by POS
1943 CLE A	2	1	0	0	0	0	0.0	1	0	2	1	0	.000	.000	0	0	C-1
1944	20	43	10	0	0	0	0.0	5	4	4	3	0	.233	.233	7	0	C-13
1945	28	51	10	2	0	0	0.0	3	8	2	4	0	.196	.235	5	0	C-23
3 yrs.	50	95	20	2	0	0	0.0	9	12	8	8	0	.211	.232	12	0	C-37

Ed McDonough

McDONOUGH, EDWARD SEBASTIAN
B. Sept. 11, 1886, Elgin, Ill.   D. Sept. 2, 1926, Elgin, Ill.
TR 6'   160 lbs.

	G	AB	H	2B	3B	HR	HR %	R	RBI	BB	SO	SB	BA	SA	PH AB	PH H	G by POS
1909 PHI N	1	1	0	0	0	0	0.0	0	0	0		0	.000	.000	0	0	C-1
1910	5	9	1	0	0	0	0.0	1	0	0	1	0	.111	.111	1	0	C-4
2 yrs.	6	10	1	0	0	0	0.0	1	0	0	1	0	.100	.100	1	0	C-5

Gil McDougald

McDOUGALD, GILBERT JAMES
B. May 19, 1928, San Francisco, Calif.
BR TR 6'   175 lbs.

	G	AB	H	2B	3B	HR	HR %	R	RBI	BB	SO	SB	BA	SA	PH AB	PH H	G by POS
1951 NY A	131	402	123	23	4	14	3.5	72	63	56	54	14	.306	.488	4	0	3B-82, 2B-55
1952	152	555	146	16	5	11	2.0	65	78	57	73	6	.263	.369	1	0	3B-117, 2B-38
1953	141	541	154	27	7	10	1.8	82	83	60	65	3	.285	.416	1	0	3B-136, 2B-26
1954	126	394	102	22	2	12	3.0	66	48	62	64	3	.259	.416	4	0	2B-92, 3B-35
1955	141	533	152	10	8	13	2.4	79	53	65	77	6	.285	.407	0	0	2B-126, 3B-17
1956	120	438	136	13	3	13	3.0	79	56	68	59	3	.311	.443	2	0	SS-92, 2B-31, 3B-5
1957	141	539	156	25	9	13	2.4	87	62	59	71	2	.289	.442	1	0	SS-121, 2B-21, 3B-7
1958	138	503	126	19	1	14	2.8	69	65	59	75	6	.250	.376	6	1	2B-115, SS-19
1959	127	434	109	16	8	4	0.9	44	34	35	40	0	.251	.353	2	0	2B-53, SS-52, 3B-25
1960	119	337	87	16	4	8	2.4	54	34	38	45	2	.258	.401	20	9	3B-84, 2B-42
10 yrs.	1336	4676	1291	187	51	112	2.4	697	576	559	623	45	.276	.410	41	10	2B-599, 3B-508, SS-284
WORLD SERIES																	
1951 NY A	6	23	6	1	0	1	4.3	2	7	2	2	0	.261	.435	0	0	2B-4
1952	7	25	5	0	0	1	4.0	5	3	5	2	1	.200	.320	0	0	3B-7
1953	6	24	4	0	1	2	8.3	2	4	1	3	0	.167	.500	0	0	3B-6
1955	7	27	7	0	0	1	3.7	2	1	2	6	0	.259	.370	0	0	SS-7
1956	7	21	3	0	0	0	0.0	0	1	3	6	0	.143	.143	0	0	SS-7
1957	7	24	6	0	0	0	0.0	3	2	3	3	1	.250	.250	0	0	SS-7
1958	7	28	9	2	0	2	7.1	5	4	2	4	0	.321	.607	0	0	2B-7
1960	6	18	5	1	0	0	0.0	4	2	2	3	0	.278	.333	0	0	3B-6
8 yrs.	53	190	45	4	1	7	3.7	23	24	20	29	2	.237	.379	0	0	3B-26, SS-14, 2B-11
	4th	5th	7th			10th		8th	8th	9th	5th						

Pryor McElveen

McELVEEN, PRYOR MYNATT (Humpy)
B. Nov. 5, 1883, Atlanta, Ga.   D. Oct. 27, 1951, Pleasant Hill, Tenn.
TR 5'10"   168 lbs.

	G	AB	H	2B	3B	HR	HR %	R	RBI	BB	SO	SB	BA	SA	PH AB	PH H	G by POS
1909 BKN N	81	258	51	8	1	3	1.2	22	25	14		6	.198	.271	13	4	3B-37, OF-13, SS-10, 2B-5, 1B-5
1910	74	213	48	8	3	1	0.5	19	26	22	47	6	.225	.305	9	3	3B-54, SS-6, 2B-3, C-1
1911	16	31	6	0	0	0	0.0	1	5	0	3	0	.194	.194	10	3	2B-5, SS-1
3 yrs.	171	502	105	16	4	4	0.8	42	56	36	50	12	.209	.281	32	10	3B-91, SS-17, OF-13, 2B-13, 1B-5, C-1

Lee McElwee

McELWEE, LELAND STANFORD (Mac)
B. May 23, 1894, La Mesa, Calif.   D. Feb. 8, 1957, Union, Me.
BR TR 5'10½" 160 lbs.

	G	AB	H	2B	3B	HR	HR %	R	RBI	BB	SO	SB	BA	SA	PH AB	PH H	G by POS
1916 PHI A	54	155	41	3	0	0	0.0	9	10	8	17	0	.265	.284	9	1	3B-30, OF-9, 2B-2, SS-1, 1B-1

Frank McElyea

McELYEA, FRANK
B. Aug. 4, 1918, Carmi, Ill.
BR TR 6'6"   221 lbs.

	G	AB	H	2B	3B	HR	HR %	R	RBI	BB	SO	SB	BA	SA	PH AB	PH H	G by POS
1942 BOS N	7	4	0	0	0	0	0.0	2	0	0	2	0	.000	.000	1	0	OF-1

Guy McFadden

McFADDEN, GUY
Deceased.

	G	AB	H	2B	3B	HR	HR %	R	RBI	BB	SO	SB	BA	SA	PH AB	PH H	G by POS
1895 STL N	4	14	3	0	0	0	0.0	1	2	0	2	0	.214	.214	0	0	1B-4

Leon McFadden

McFADDEN, LEON
B. Apr. 26, 1944, Little Rock, Ark.
BR TR 6'2"   195 lbs.

	G	AB	H	2B	3B	HR	HR %	R	RBI	BB	SO	SB	BA	SA	PH AB	PH H	G by POS
1968 HOU N	16	47	13	1	0	0	0.0	2	1	6	10	1	.277	.298	1	1	SS-16
1969	44	74	13	2	0	0	0.0	3	3	4	9	1	.176	.203	11	1	OF-17, SS-8
1970	2	0	0	0	0	0	–	0	0	0	0	0	–	–	0	0	
3 yrs.	62	121	26	3	0	0	0.0	5	4	10	19	2	.215	.240	12	2	SS-24, OF-17

	G	AB	H	2B	3B	HR	HR %	R	RBI	BB	SO	SB	BA	SA	Pinch Hit AB	Pinch Hit H	G by POS

Alex McFarlan

McFARLAN, ALEXANDER SHEPERD
Brother of Dan McFarlan.
B. Nov. 11, 1866, Kentucky   D. Mar. 2, 1939, Pewee Valley, Ky.

	G	AB	H	2B	3B	HR	HR%	R	RBI	BB	SO	SB	BA	SA	PH AB	PH H	G by POS
1892 LOU N	14	42	7	0	0	0	0.0	2	1	8	11	1	.167	.167	0	0	OF-12, 2B-2

Claude McFarland

McFARLAND, CLAUDE   5'9"   170 lbs.
B. Aug. 17, 1861, Fall River, Mass.   D. May 24, 1918, New Bedford, Mass.

	G	AB	H	2B	3B	HR	HR%	R	RBI	BB	SO	SB	BA	SA	PH AB	PH H	G by POS
1884 BAL U	3	14	3	1	0	0	0.0	2		1	0		.214	.286	0	0	OF-3, P-1

Ed McFarland

McFARLAND, EDWARD WILLIAM   BR TR 5'10"   180 lbs.
B. Aug. 3, 1874, Cleveland, Ohio   D. Nov. 28, 1959, Cleveland, Ohio

	G	AB	H	2B	3B	HR	HR%	R	RBI	BB	SO	SB	BA	SA	PH AB	PH H	G by POS
1893 CLE N	8	22	9	2	1	0	0.0	5	6	1	2	0	.409	.591	0	0	OF-5, 3B-2, C-1
1896 STL N	83	290	70	13	4	3	1.0	48	36	15	17	7	.241	.345	1	0	C-80, OF-2
1897 2 teams		STL	N	(31G –	.327)	PHI	N	(38G –	.223)								
" total	69	237	64	8	7	2	0.8	32	33	22		4	.270	.388	2	0	C-60, OF-3, 1B-3, 2B-1
1898 PHI N	121	429	121	21	5	3	0.7	65	71	44		4	.282	.375	0	0	C-121
1899	96	324	108	22	10	1	0.3	59	57	36		9	.333	.472	2	0	C-94
1900	94	344	105	14	8	0	0.0	50	38	29		9	.305	.392	1	0	C-93, 3B-1
1901	74	295	84	14	2	1	0.3	33	32	18		11	.285	.356	0	0	C-74
1902 CHI A	73	244	56	9	2	1	0.4	29	25	19		8	.230	.295	2	0	C-69, 1B-1
1903	61	201	42	7	2	1	0.5	15	19	14		3	.209	.279	4	1	C-56, 1B-1
1904	50	160	44	11	3	0	0.0	22	20	17		2	.275	.381	1	1	C-49
1905	80	250	70	13	4	0	0.0	24	31	23		5	.280	.364	9	4	C-70
1906	7	22	3	1	0	0	0.0	0	3	3		0	.136	.182	3	1	C-3
1907	52	138	39	9	1	0	0.0	11	8	12		3	.283	.362	7	2	C-43
1908 BOS A	19	48	10	2	1	0	0.0	5	4	1		0	.208	.292	6	2	C-13
14 yrs.	887	3004	825	146	50	12	0.4	398	383	254	19	65	.275	.369	38	11	C-826, OF-10, 1B-5, 3B-3, 2B-1

WORLD SERIES

	G	AB	H	2B	3B	HR	HR%	R	RBI	BB	SO	SB	BA	SA	PH AB	PH H	G by POS
1906 CHI A	1	1	0	0	0	0	0.0	0	0	0	0	0	.000	.000	1	0	

Herm McFarland

McFARLAND, HERMAS WALTER   BL TR 5'6"   150 lbs.
B. Mar. 11, 1870, Des Moines, Iowa   D. Sept. 21, 1935, Richmond, Va.

	G	AB	H	2B	3B	HR	HR%	R	RBI	BB	SO	SB	BA	SA	PH AB	PH H	G by POS
1896 LOU N	30	110	21	4	1	1	0.9	11	12	9	14	4	.191	.273	1	0	OF-28, C-1
1898 CIN N	19	64	18	1	3	0	0.0	10	11	7		3	.281	.391	1	0	OF-17
1901 CHI A	132	473	130	21	9	4	0.8	83	59	75		33	.275	.383	0	0	OF-132
1902 2 teams		CHI	A	(9G –	.172)	BAL	A	(61G –	.322)								
" total	70	271	83	19	6	3	1.1	59	40	38		11	.306	.454	2	0	OF-68
1903 NY A	103	362	88	16	9	5	1.4	41	45	46		13	.243	.378	0	0	OF-103
5 yrs.	354	1280	340	61	28	13	1.0	204	167	175	14	64	.266	.388	4	0	OF-348, C-1

Howie McFarland

McFARLAND, HOWARD ALEXANDER   BR TR 6'   175 lbs.
B. Mar. 7, 1911, El Reno, Okla.

	G	AB	H	2B	3B	HR	HR%	R	RBI	BB	SO	SB	BA	SA	PH AB	PH H	G by POS
1945 WAS A	6	11	1	0	0	0	0.0	0	0	3	0	0	.091	.091	3	0	OF-3

Orlando McFarlane

McFARLANE, ORLANDO JESUS   BR TR 6'   180 lbs.
B. June 28, 1938, Oriente, Cuba

	G	AB	H	2B	3B	HR	HR%	R	RBI	BB	SO	SB	BA	SA	PH AB	PH H	G by POS
1962 PIT N	8	23	2	0	0	0	0.0	0	1	1	4	0	.087	.087	0	0	C-8
1964	37	78	19	5	0	0	0.0	5	1	4	27	0	.244	.308	3	1	C-35, OF-1
1966 DET A	49	138	35	7	0	5	3.6	16	13	9	46	0	.254	.413	15	2	C-33
1967 CAL A	12	22	5	0	0	0	0.0	0	3	1	7	0	.227	.227	5	1	C-6
1968	18	31	9	0	0	0	0.0	1	2	5	9	0	.290	.290	10	3	C-9
5 yrs.	124	292	70	12	0	5	1.7	22	20	20	93	0	.240	.332	33	7	C-91, OF-1

Patsy McGaffigan

McGAFFIGAN, MARK ANDREW   BR TR 5'8"   140 lbs.
B. Sept. 22, 1888, Carlyle, Ill.   D. Dec. 22, 1940, Carlyle, Ill.

	G	AB	H	2B	3B	HR	HR%	R	RBI	BB	SO	SB	BA	SA	PH AB	PH H	G by POS
1917 PHI N	19	60	10	1	0	0	0.0	5	6	0	7	1	.167	.183	0	0	SS-17, OF-1
1918	54	192	39	3	2	1	0.5	17	8	16	23	3	.203	.255	0	0	2B-53, SS-1
2 yrs.	73	252	49	4	2	1	0.4	22	14	16	30	4	.194	.238	0	0	2B-53, SS-18, OF-1

Ed McGah

McGAH, EDWARD JOSEPH   BR TR 6'   183 lbs.
B. Sept. 30, 1921, Oakland, Calif.

	G	AB	H	2B	3B	HR	HR%	R	RBI	BB	SO	SB	BA	SA	PH AB	PH H	G by POS
1946 BOS A	15	37	8	1	1	0	0.0	2	1	7	7	0	.216	.297	1	0	C-14
1947	9	14	0	0	0	0	0.0	1	2	3	0	0	.000	.000	1	0	C-7
2 yrs.	24	51	8	1	1	0	0.0	3	3	10	7	0	.157	.216	2	0	C-21

Ed McGamwell

McGAMWELL, EDWARD M.   BB TR 6'   190 lbs.
B. Jan. 10, 1879, Buffalo, N. Y.   D. May 26, 1924, Albany, N. Y.

	G	AB	H	2B	3B	HR	HR%	R	RBI	BB	SO	SB	BA	SA	PH AB	PH H	G by POS
1905 BKN N	4	16	4	0	0	0	0.0	0	0	1		0	.250	.250	0	0	1B-4

Dan McGann

McGANN, DENNIS L.   BB TR 6'   190 lbs.
B. July 15, 1872, Shelbyville, Ky.   D. Dec. 13, 1910, Louisville, Ky.

	G	AB	H	2B	3B	HR	HR%	R	RBI	BB	SO	SB	BA	SA	PH AB	PH H	G by POS
1895 LOU N	20	73	21	5	2	0	0.0	9	9	8	6	6	.288	.411	1	0	SS-8, 3B-6, OF-5
1896 BOS N	43	171	55	6	7	2	1.2	25	30	12	10	2	.322	.474	0	0	2B-43
1898 BAL N	145	535	161	18	8	5	0.9	99	106	53		33	.301	.393	0	0	1B-145
1899 2 teams		BKN	N	(63G –	.243)	WAS	N	(76G –	.343)								
" total	139	494	148	20	12	7	1.4	114	90	35		27	.300	.431	2	0	1B-137
1900 STL N	124	450	136	14	9	4	0.9	79	58	32		26	.302	.400	0	0	1B-121, 2B-1
1901	103	426	123	14	10	6	1.4	73	56	16		17	.289	.411	0	0	1B-103
1902 2 teams		BAL	A	(68G –	.316)	NY	N	(61G –	.300)								
" total	129	477	147	15	15	0	0.0	67	63	31		29	.308	.403	0	0	1B-129
1903 NY N	129	482	130	21	6	3	0.6	75	50	32		36	.270	.357	0	0	1B-129
1904	141	517	148	22	6	6	1.2	81	71	36		42	.286	.387	0	0	1B-141
1905	136	491	147	23	14	5	1.0	88	75	55		22	.299	.434	0	0	1B-136
1906	134	451	107	14	8	0	0.0	62	37	60		30	.237	.304	1	0	1B-133
1907	81	262	78	9	1	2	0.8	29	36	29		9	.298	.363	0	0	1B-81

	G	AB	H	2B	3B	HR	HR %	R	RBI	BB	SO	SB	BA	SA	Pinch Hit AB	Pinch Hit H	G by POS

Dan McGann continued

1908 BOS N	135	475	114	8	5	2	0.4	52	55	38		9	.240	.291	5	1	1B-121, 2B-9
13 yrs.	1459	5304	1515	189	103	42	0.8	853	736	437	16	288	.286	.384	9	1	1B-1376, 2B-53, SS-8, 3B-6, OF-5

WORLD SERIES																	
1905 NY N	5	17	4	2	0	0	0.0	1	4	2	7	0	.235	.353	0	0	1B-5

Chippy McGarr

McGARR, JAMES B.
B. May 10, 1863, Worcester, Mass.   D. June 6, 1904, Worcester, Mass.   BR TR

	G	AB	H	2B	3B	HR	HR %	R	RBI	BB	SO	SB	BA	SA	PH AB	PH H	G by POS
1884 C-P U	19	70	11	2	0	0	0.0	10		0			.157	.186	0	0	2B-13, OF-6
1886 PHI AA	71	267	71	9	3	2	0.7	41		9			.266	.345	0	0	SS-71
1887	137	536	158	23	6	1	0.2	93		23		84	.295	.366	0	0	SS-137
1888 STL AA	34	132	31	1	0	0	0.0	17	13	6		25	.235	.242	0	0	2B-33, SS-1
1889 2 teams	KC	AA (25G – .287)							BAL	AA (3G – .143)							3B-11, OF-6, SS-6, 2B-5
" total	28	115	32	3	0	0	0.0	23	16	7	12	12	.278	.304	0	0	3B-115, SS-5, OF-1
1890 BOS N	121	487	115	12	7	1	0.2	68	51	34	38	39	.236	.296	0	0	3B-63
1893 CLE N	63	249	77	12	0	0	0.0	38	28	20	15	24	.309	.357	0	0	3B-128
1894	128	523	144	24	6	2	0.4	94	74	28	29	31	.275	.356	0	0	3B-108, 2B-4
1895	112	419	111	14	2	2	0.5	85	59	34	33	19	.265	.322	0	0	3B-113, C-1
1896	113	455	122	16	4	1	0.2	68	53	22	30	16	.268	.327	0	0	3B-113, C-1
10 yrs.	826	3253	872	116	28	9	0.3	537	293	183	157	250	.268	.329	0	0	3B-538, SS-220, 2B-55, OF-13, C-1

Jim McGarr

McGARR, JAMES VINCENT (Reds)
B. Nov. 9, 1888, Philadelphia, Pa.   D. July 21, 1981, Miami, Fla.   BR TR 5'9½" 170 lbs.

	G	AB	H	2B	3B	HR	HR %	R	RBI	BB	SO	SB	BA	SA	PH AB	PH H	G by POS
1912 DET A	1	4	0	0	0	0	0.0	0	0	0		0	.000	.000	0	0	2B-1

Dan McGarvey

McGARVEY, DANIEL
B. Unknown.

	G	AB	H	2B	3B	HR	HR %	R	RBI	BB	SO	SB	BA	SA	PH AB	PH H	G by POS
1912 DET A	1	3	0	0	0	0	0.0	0	0	1		0	.000	.000	0	0	OF-1

Jack McGeachy

McGEACHY, JOHN CHARLES
B. May 23, 1864, Clinton, Mass.   D. Apr. 5, 1930, Cambridge, Mass.   BR TR 5'8" 165 lbs.

	G	AB	H	2B	3B	HR	HR %	R	RBI	BB	SO	SB	BA	SA	PH AB	PH H	G by POS
1886 2 teams	DET	N (6G – .333)							STL	N (59G – .204)							OF-61, 3B-2, 2B-2
" total	65	253	55	12	4	2	0.8	34	28	1	40		.217	.320	0	0	OF-98, 3B-1, P-1
1887 IND N	99	405	109	17	3	1	0.2	49	56	5	16	27	.269	.333	0	0	OF-117, SS-1, P-1
1888	118	452	99	15	2	0	0.0	45	30	5	21	49	.219	.261	0	0	OF-131, P-3
1889	131	532	142	32	1	2	0.4	83	63	9	39	37	.267	.342	0	0	OF-104
1890 BKN P	104	443	108	24	4	1	0.2	84	65	19	12	21	.244	.323	0	0	OF-104
1891 2 teams	PHI	AA (50G – .229)							BOS	AA (41G – .253)							OF-91
" total	91	379	91	6	4	3	0.8	50	34	18	20	20	.240	.301	0	0	OF-602, P-5, 3B-3, 2B-2, SS-1
6 yrs.	608	2464	604	106	18	9	0.4	345	276	57	148	154	.245	.314	0	0	

Mike McGeary

McGEARY, MICHAEL HENRY
B. 1851, Philadelphia, Pa.   Deceased.
Manager 1881.   BR TR 5'7" 138 lbs.

	G	AB	H	2B	3B	HR	HR %	R	RBI	BB	SO	SB	BA	SA	PH AB	PH H	G by POS
1876 STL N	61	276	72	3	0	0	0.0	48	30	2	1		.261	.272	0	0	2B-56, C-5, OF-1, 3B-1
1877	57	258	65	3	2	0	0.0	35	20	2	6		.252	.279	0	0	2B-39, 3B-19
1879 PRO N	85	374	103	7	2	0	0.0	62	35	5	13		.275	.305	0	0	2B-73, 3B-12
1880 2 teams	PRO	N (18G – .136)							CLE	N (31G – .252)							3B-46, OF-2, 2B-2, SS-1
" total	49	170	36	2	1	0	0.0	19	1	4	9		.212	.235	0	0	3B-11
1881 CLE N	11	41	9	0	0	0	0.0	1	5	0	6		.220	.220	0	0	SS-33, 2B-3
1882 DET N	34	133	19	4	1	0	0.0	14	2	2	20		.143	.188	0	0	2B-173, 3B-89, SS-34, C-5, OF-3
6 yrs.	297	1252	304	19	6	0	0.0	179	93	15	55		.243	.268	0	0	

Dan McGee

McGEE, DANIEL ALOYSIUS
B. Sept. 29, 1913, New York, N. Y.   BR TR 5'8½" 152 lbs.

	G	AB	H	2B	3B	HR	HR %	R	RBI	BB	SO	SB	BA	SA	PH AB	PH H	G by POS
1934 BOS N	7	22	3	0	0	0	0.0	2	1	3	6	0	.136	.136	0	0	SS-7

F. McGee

McGEE, F.
B. Unknown.

	G	AB	H	2B	3B	HR	HR %	R	RBI	BB	SO	SB	BA	SA	PH AB	PH H	G by POS
1884 WAS U	1	4	0	0	0	0	0.0	0		0			.000	.000	0	0	OF-1, C-1

Tubby McGee

McGEE, FRANCIS DeSALES
B. Apr. 28, 1899, Columbus, Ohio   D. Jan. 30, 1934, Columbus, Ohio   BR TR 5'11½" 175 lbs.

	G	AB	H	2B	3B	HR	HR %	R	RBI	BB	SO	SB	BA	SA	PH AB	PH H	G by POS
1925 WAS A	2	3	0	0	0	0	0.0	0	0	0	1	0	.000	.000	0	0	1B-2

Willie McGee

McGEE, WILLIE DEAN
B. Nov. 2, 1958, San Francisco, Calif.   BB TR 6'1" 176 lbs.

	G	AB	H	2B	3B	HR	HR %	R	RBI	BB	SO	SB	BA	SA	PH AB	PH H	G by POS
1982 STL N	123	422	125	12	8	4	0.9	43	56	12	58	24	.296	.391	15	6	OF-117
1983	147	601	172	22	8	5	0.8	75	75	26	98	39	.286	.374	3	2	OF-145
1984	145	571	166	19	11	6	1.1	82	50	29	80	43	.291	.394	5	0	OF-141
3 yrs.	415	1594	463	53	27	15	0.9	200	181	67	236	106	.290	.386	23	8	OF-403

LEAGUE CHAMPIONSHIP SERIES																	
1982 STL N	3	13	4	0	2	1	7.7	4	5	0	5	0	.308	.846	0	0	OF-3

WORLD SERIES																	
1982 STL N	6	25	6	0	0	2	8.0	6	5	1	3	2	.240	.480	0	0	OF-6

Dan McGeehan

McGEEHAN, DANIEL DeSALES
Brother of Connie McGeehan.
B. June 7, 1885, Jeddo, Pa.   D. July 12, 1955, Hazleton, Pa.   BR TR 5'6" 135 lbs.

	G	AB	H	2B	3B	HR	HR %	R	RBI	BB	SO	SB	BA	SA	PH AB	PH H	G by POS
1911 STL N	3	9	2	0	0	0	0.0	0	1	0	1	0	.222	.222	0	0	2B-3

	G	AB	H	2B	3B	HR	HR %	R	RBI	BB	SO	SB	BA	SA	Pinch Hit AB	Pinch Hit H	G by POS

Bill McGhee

McGHEE, WILLIAM MAC (Fibber)
B. Sept. 5, 1908, Shawmut, Ala.
BL TL 5'10½" 185 lbs.

	G	AB	H	2B	3B	HR	HR %	R	RBI	BB	SO	SB	BA	SA	AB	H	G by POS
1944 PHI A	77	287	83	12	0	1	0.3	27	19	21	20	2	.289	.341	2	0	1B-75
1945	93	250	63	6	1	0	0.0	24	19	24	16	3	.252	.284	31	9	OF-48, 1B-8
2 yrs.	170	537	146	18	1	1	0.2	51	38	45	36	5	.272	.315	33	9	1B-83, OF-48

Ed McGhee

McGHEE, WARREN EDWARD
B. Sept. 29, 1924, Perry, Ark.
BR TR 5'11" 170 lbs.

	G	AB	H	2B	3B	HR	HR %	R	RBI	BB	SO	SB	BA	SA	AB	H	G by POS
1950 CHI A	3	6	1	0	1	0	0.0	0	0	0	1	0	.167	.500	1	0	OF-1
1953 PHI A	104	358	94	11	4	1	0.3	36	29	32	43	4	.263	.324	7	2	OF-99
1954 2 teams		PHI A (21G – .208)			CHI A (42G – .227)												
" total	63	128	28	3	0	2	1.6	17	14	16	16	5	.219	.289	11	1	OF-47
1955 CHI A	26	13	1	0	0	0	0.0	6	0	6	1	2	.077	.077	2	1	OF-17
4 yrs.	196	505	124	14	5	3	0.6	59	43	54	61	11	.246	.311	21	4	OF-164

Bill McGilvray

McGILVRAY, WILLIAM ALEXANDER (Big Bill)
B. Apr. 29, 1883, Portland, Ore. D. May 23, 1952, Denver, Colo.
BL TL 6' 160 lbs.

	G	AB	H	2B	3B	HR	HR %	R	RBI	BB	SO	SB	BA	SA	AB	H	G by POS
1908 CIN N	2	2	0	0	0	0	0.0	0		0		0	.000	.000	2	0	

Tim McGinley

McGINLEY, TIMOTHY S.
B. Philadelphia, Pa. D. Nov. 2, 1899, Oakland, Calif.
5'9½" 155 lbs.

	G	AB	H	2B	3B	HR	HR %	R	RBI	BB	SO	SB	BA	SA	AB	H	G by POS
1876 BOS N	9	40	6	0	0	0	0.0	5	2	0	1		.150	.150	0	0	OF-6, C-3

Frank McGinn

McGINN, FRANK J.
B. Cincinnati, Ohio D. Nov. 19, 1897, Cincinnati, Ohio

	G	AB	H	2B	3B	HR	HR %	R	RBI	BB	SO	SB	BA	SA	AB	H	G by POS
1890 PIT N	1	4	0	0	0	0	0.0	0	0	0	2	0	.000	.000	0	0	OF-1

John McGlone

McGLONE, JOHN T.
B. 1864, Brooklyn, N. Y. D. Nov. 24, 1927, Brooklyn, N. Y.

	G	AB	H	2B	3B	HR	HR %	R	RBI	BB	SO	SB	BA	SA	AB	H	G by POS
1886 WAS N	4	15	1	0	0	0	0.0	2	1	0	3		.067	.067	0	0	3B-4
1887 CLE AA	21	79	20	2	1	0	0.0	14		7		15	.253	.304	0	0	3B-21
1888	55	203	37	1	3	1	0.5	22	22	16		26	.182	.232	0	0	3B-48, OF-7
3 yrs.	80	297	58	3	4	1	0.3	38	23	23	3	41	.195	.242	0	0	3B-73, OF-7

Art McGovern

McGOVERN, ARTHUR JOHN
B. Feb. 27, 1882, St. John, N. B., Canada D. Nov. 14, 1915, Thornton, R. I.
BR TR 160 lbs.

	G	AB	H	2B	3B	HR	HR %	R	RBI	BB	SO	SB	BA	SA	AB	H	G by POS
1905 BOS A	15	44	5	1	0	0	0.0	1	1	4		0	.114	.136	0	0	C-15

Frank McGowan

McGOWAN, FRANK BERNARD (Beauty)
B. Nov. 8, 1901, Branford, Conn. D. May 6, 1982, Hamden, Conn.
BL TR 5'11" 190 lbs.

	G	AB	H	2B	3B	HR	HR %	R	RBI	BB	SO	SB	BA	SA	AB	H	G by POS
1922 PHI A	99	300	69	10	5	1	0.3	36	20	40	46	6	.230	.307	12	4	OF-82
1923	95	287	73	9	1	1	0.3	41	19	36	25	4	.254	.303	7	0	OF-79
1928 STL A	47	168	61	13	4	2	1.2	35	18	16	15	2	.363	.524	0	0	OF-47
1929	125	441	112	26	6	2	0.5	62	51	61	34	5	.254	.354	7	0	OF-117
1937 BOS N	9	12	1	0	0	0	0.0	0	0	1	2	0	.083	.083	6	0	OF-2
5 yrs.	375	1208	316	58	16	6	0.5	174	108	154	122	17	.262	.351	32	4	OF-327

John McGraw

McGRAW, JOHN JOSEPH (Little Napoleon)
B. Apr. 7, 1873, Truxton, N. Y. D. Feb. 25, 1934, New Rochelle, N. Y.
Manager 1899, 1901-32.
Hall of Fame 1937.
BL TR 5'7" 155 lbs.

	G	AB	H	2B	3B	HR	HR %	R	RBI	BB	SO	SB	BA	SA	AB	H	G by POS
1891 BAL AA	33	115	31	3	5	0	0.0	17	14	12	17		.270	.383	0	0	SS-21, OF-9, 2B-3
1892 BAL N	79	286	77	14	2	1	0.3	41	26	32	21	15	.269	.343	0	0	OF-34, 2B-34, SS-8, 3B-3
1893	127	480	154	10	8	5	1.0	123	64	101	11	38	.321	.406	0	0	SS-117, OF-11
1894	124	512	174	20	14	1	0.2	156	92	91	12	78	.340	.439	0	0	3B-118, 2B-6
1895	96	388	143	15	6	2	0.5	110	48	60	9	61	.369	.454	0	0	3B-95, 2B-1
1896	23	77	25	2	2	0	0.0	20	14	11	4	13	.325	.403	3	0	3B-18, 1B-1
1897	106	391	127	15	3	0	0.0	90	48	99		44	.325	.379	1	0	3B-105
1898	143	515	176	8	10	0	0.0	143	53	112		43	.342	.396	1	0	3B-137, OF-3
1899	117	399	156	13	3	1	0.3	140	33	124		73	.391	.446	0	0	3B-117
1900 STL N	99	334	115	10	4	2	0.6	84	33	85		29	.344	.416	0	0	3B-99
1901 BAL A	73	230	81	14	9	0	0.0	73	28	61		24	.352	.491	0	0	3B-69
1902 2 teams		BAL A (20G – .286)			NY N (35G – .224)												
" total	55	170	42	3	2	1	0.6	27	8	43		12	.247	.306	2	0	SS-34, 3B-19
1903 NY N	12	11	3	0	0	0	0.0	2	1	1		1	.273	.273	6	2	OF-2, 2B-2, SS-1, 3B-1
1904	5	12	4	0	0	0	0.0	0	0	3		0	.333	.333	1	0	SS-2, 2B-2
1905	3	0	0	0	0	0	–	0	0	0		1	–	–	0	0	OF-1
1906	4	2	0	0	0	0	0.0	0	0	0		0	.000	.000	2	0	3B-1
16 yrs.	1099	3922	1308	127	68	13	0.3	1026	462	836	74	436	.334	.411	19	2	3B-782, SS-183, OF-60, 2B-48, 1B-1

Mark McGrillis

McGRILLIS, MARK A.
B. Oct. 22, 1872, Philadelphia, Pa. D. May 16, 1935, Philadelphia, Pa.

	G	AB	H	2B	3B	HR	HR %	R	RBI	BB	SO	SB	BA	SA	AB	H	G by POS
1892 STL N	1	3	0	0	0	0	0.0	0	0	0	1	0	.000	.000	0	0	3B-1

Joe McGuckin

McGUCKIN, JOSEPH W.
B. 1862, Paterson, N. J. D. Dec. 31, 1903, Yonkers, N. Y.

	G	AB	H	2B	3B	HR	HR %	R	RBI	BB	SO	SB	BA	SA	AB	H	G by POS
1890 B-B AA	11	37	4	0	0	0	0.0	2		6		3	.108	.108	0	0	OF-11

John McGuinness

McGUINNESS, JOHN JAMES
B. 1857, Ireland D. Dec. 19, 1916, Binghamton, N. Y.

	G	AB	H	2B	3B	HR	HR %	R	RBI	BB	SO	SB	BA	SA	AB	H	G by POS
1876 NY N	1	4	0	0	0	0	0.0	0	0	0		0	.000	.000	0	0	2B-1, C-1
1879 SYR N	12	51	15	1	1	0	0.0	7	4	0	6		.294	.353	0	0	1B-12
1884 PHI U	53	220	52	8	1	0	0.0	25		5			.236	.282	0	0	1B-48, 2B-5, SS-1
3 yrs.	66	275	67	9	2	0	0.0	32	4	5	6		.244	.291	0	0	1B-60, 2B-6, SS-1, C-1

	G	AB	H	2B	3B	HR	HR %	R	RBI	BB	SO	SB	BA	SA	Pinch Hit AB	Pinch Hit H	G by POS

Deacon McGuire

McGUIRE, JAMES THOMAS
B. Nov. 2, 1865, Youngstown, Ohio   D. Oct. 31, 1936, Albion, Mich.
Manager 1898, 1907-11.
BR TR 6'1" 185 lbs.

	G	AB	H	2B	3B	HR	HR %	R	RBI	BB	SO	SB	BA	SA	PH AB	PH H	G by POS
1884 TOL AA	45	151	28	7	0	1	0.7	12			5		.185	.252	0	0	C-41, OF-4, SS-3
1885 DET N	34	121	23	4	2	0	0.0	11	9		5	23	.190	.256	0	0	C-31, OF-3
1886 PHI N	50	167	33	7	1	2	1.2	25	18		19	25	.198	.287	0	0	C-49, OF-1
1887	41	150	46	6	6	2	1.3	22	23		11	8	3	.307	.467	0	0	C-41
1888 3 teams	PHI N (12G – .333)			DET N (3G – .000)				CLE AA (26G – .255)									
" total	41	158	41	5	5	1	0.6	22	24		11	13	2	.259	.373	0	0	C-30, 1B-6, OF-3, 3B-2
1890 ROC AA	87	331	99	16	4	4	1.2	46		21		8	.299	.408	0	0	C-71, 1B-15, OF-3, P-1
1891 WAS AA	114	413	125	22	10	3	0.7	55	66	43	34	10	.303	.426	0	0	C-98, 1B-18, 3B-3, 1B-1
1892 WAS N	97	315	73	14	4	4	1.3	46	43	61	48	7	.232	.340	0	0	C-89, 1B-8, OF-1
1893	63	237	62	14	3	1	0.4	29	26	26	12	3	.262	.359	0	0	C-50, 1B-12
1894	104	425	130	18	6	6	1.4	67	78	33	19	11	.306	.419	0	0	C-132, SS-1
1895	132	533	179	30	8	10	1.9	89	97	40	18	16	.336	.478	9	2	C-98, 1B-1
1896	108	389	125	25	3	2	0.5	60	70	30	14	12	.321	.416	9	2	C-73, 1B-6
1897	93	327	112	17	7	4	1.2	51	53	21		9	.343	.474	11	3	C-93, 1B-37
1898	131	489	131	18	3	1	0.2	59	57	24		10	.268	.323	3	2	C-102, 1B-1
1899 2 teams	WAS N (59G – .271)			BKN N (46G – .318)													
" total	105	356	104	15	5	1	0.3	47	35	28		7	.292	.371	2	0	C-69
1900 BKN N	71	241	69	15	2	0	0.0	20	34	19		2	.286	.365	2	1	C-69
1901	85	301	89	16	4	0	0.0	28	40	18		4	.296	.375	1	0	C-81, 1B-3
1902 DET N	73	229	52	14	1	2	0.9	27	23	24		0	.227	.323	2	0	C-70
1903	72	248	62	12	1	0	0.0	15	21	19		3	.250	.306	2	2	C-69, 1B-1
1904 NY A	101	322	67	12	2	0	0.0	17	20	27		2	.208	.258	2	2	C-97, 1B-1
1905	72	228	50	7	2	0	0.0	9	33	18		3	.219	.268	1	1	C-71
1906	51	144	43	5	0	0	0.0	11	14	12		3	.299	.333	1	0	C-49, 1B-1
1907 2 teams	NY A (1G – .000)			BOS A (6G – .750)													
" total	7	5	3	0	0	1	20.0	1	1	0		0	.600	1.200	4	3	C-1
1908 2 teams	BOS A (1G – .000)			CLE A (1G – .250)													
" total	2	5	1	1	0	0	0.0	0	2	0		0	.200	.400	1	0	1B-1
1910 CLE A	1	3	1	0	0	0	0.0	0	0	0		0	.333	.333	0	0	C-1
1912 DET A	1	2	1	0	0	0	0.0	1	0	0		0	.500	.500	0	0	C-1
26 yrs.	1781	6290	1749	300	79	45	0.7	770	786	515	214	115	.278	.372	41	14	C-1611, 1B-94, OF-33, 3B-5, SS-4, P-1

Mickey McGuire

McGUIRE, M. C. ADOLFUS
B. Jan. 18, 1941, Dayton, Ohio
BR TR 5'10" 170 lbs.

	G	AB	H	2B	3B	HR	HR %	R	RBI	BB	SO	SB	BA	SA	PH AB	PH H	G by POS
1962 BAL A	6	4	0	0	0	0	0.0	0	0	0	0	0	.000	.000	1	0	SS-5
1967	10	17	4	0	0	0	0.0	2	2	0	2	0	.235	.235	6	1	2B-4
2 yrs.	16	21	4	0	0	0	0.0	2	2	0	2	0	.190	.190	7	1	SS-5, 2B-4

Bill McGunnigle

McGUNNIGLE, WILLIAM HENRY (Gunner)
B. Jan. 1, 1855, E. Stoughton, Mass.   D. Mar. 9, 1899, Brockton, Mass.
Manager 1880, 1888-91, 1896.
BR TR 5'9" 155 lbs.

	G	AB	H	2B	3B	HR	HR %	R	RBI	BB	SO	SB	BA	SA	PH AB	PH H	G by POS
1879 BUF N	47	171	30	0	1	0	0.0	22	5	5	24		.175	.187	0	0	OF-34, P-14
1880 2 teams	BUF N (7G – .182)			WOR N (1G – .000)													
" total	8	26	4	0	0	0	0.0	0	1	0	6		.154	.154	0	0	OF-1
1882 CLE N	1	5	1	0	0	0	0.0	2	0	0	1		.200	.200	0	0	OF-39, P-19
3 yrs.	56	202	35	0	1	0	0.0	24	6	5	31		.173	.183	0	0	

Bob McHale

McHALE, ROBERT EMMET
B. Feb. 25, 1872, Michigan Bluff, Calif.   D. June 9, 1952, Sacramento, Calif.
BR TR

	G	AB	H	2B	3B	HR	HR %	R	RBI	BB	SO	SB	BA	SA	PH AB	PH H	G by POS
1898 WAS N	11	33	6	2	0	0	0.0	5	7	1		1	.182	.242	0	0	OF-9, SS-1, 1B-1

Jim McHale

McHALE, JAMES BERNARD
B. Dec. 17, 1875, Miners Mills, Pa.   D. June 18, 1959, Los Angeles, Calif.
BR TR

	G	AB	H	2B	3B	HR	HR %	R	RBI	BB	SO	SB	BA	SA	PH AB	PH H	G by POS
1908 BOS A	21	67	15	2	2	0	0.0	9	7	4		4	.224	.313	0	0	OF-19

John McHale

McHALE, JOHN JOSEPH
B. Sept. 21, 1921, Detroit, Mich.
BL TR 6' 200 lbs.

	G	AB	H	2B	3B	HR	HR %	R	RBI	BB	SO	SB	BA	SA	PH AB	PH H	G by POS
1943 DET A	4	3	0	0	0	0	0.0	0	0	1	1	0	.000	.000	3	0	
1944	1	1	0	0	0	0	0.0	0	0	0	0	0	.000	.000	1	1	
1945	19	14	2	0	0	0	0.0	0	1	1	4	0	.143	.143	14	2	1B-3
1947	39	95	20	1	0	3	3.2	10	11	7	24	1	.211	.316	15	4	1B-25
1948	1	1	0	0	0	0	0.0	0	0	0	0	0	.000	.000	1	0	
5 yrs.	64	114	22	1	0	3	2.6	10	12	9	29	1	.193	.281	34	7	1B-28
WORLD SERIES 1945 DET A	3	3	0	0	0	0	0.0	0	0	0	1	0	.000	.000	3	0	

Austin McHenry

McHENRY, AUSTIN BUSH (Mac)
B. Sept. 22, 1895, Wrightsville, Ohio   D. Nov. 27, 1922, Jefferson Township, Ohio
BR TR 6' 175 lbs.

	G	AB	H	2B	3B	HR	HR %	R	RBI	BB	SO	SB	BA	SA	PH AB	PH H	G by POS
1918 STL N	80	272	71	12	6	1	0.4	32	29	21	24	8	.261	.360	0	0	OF-80
1919	110	371	106	19	11	1	0.3	41	47	19	57	7	.286	.404	4	0	OF-103
1920	137	504	142	19	11	10	2.0	66	65	25	73	8	.282	.423	3	1	OF-133
1921	152	574	201	37	8	17	3.0	92	102	38	48	10	.350	.531	0	0	OF-152
1922	64	238	72	18	3	5	2.1	31	43	14	27	2	.303	.466	2	1	OF-61
5 yrs.	543	1959	592	105	39	34	1.7	262	286	117	229	35	.302	.448	9	2	OF-529

Vance McHenry

McHENRY, VANCE LOREN
B. July 10, 1956, Chico, Calif.
BR TR 5'9" 165 lbs.

	G	AB	H	2B	3B	HR	HR %	R	RBI	BB	SO	SB	BA	SA	PH AB	PH H	G by POS
1981 SEA A	15	18	4	0	0	0	0.0	3	2	1	1	0	.222	.222	2	1	SS-13, DH-1
1982	3	1	0	0	0	0	0.0	0	0	0	0	0	.000	.000	1	0	DH-1, SS-1
2 yrs.	18	19	4	0	0	0	0.0	3	2	1	1	0	.211	.211	3	1	SS-14, DH-2

	G	AB	H	2B	3B	HR	HR %	R	RBI	BB	SO	SB	BA	SA	Pinch Hit AB	H	G by POS

Irish McIlveen

McILVEEN, HENRY COOKE
B. July 27, 1880, Belfast, Ireland   D. July 18, 1960, Lorain, Ohio   BL TL 5'11½" 180 lbs.

	G	AB	H	2B	3B	HR	HR %	R	RBI	BB	SO	SB	BA	SA	Pinch Hit AB	H	G by POS
1906 PIT N	5	5	2	0	0	0	0.0	1	0	0		0	.400	.400	2	1	P-2
1908 NY A	44	169	36	3	3	0	0.0	17	8	14		6	.213	.266	0	0	OF-44
1909	4	3	0	0	0	0	0.0	0	0	1		0	.000	.000	3	0	
3 yrs.	53	177	38	3	3	0	0.0	18	8	15		6	.215	.266	5	1	OF-44, P-2

Stuffy McInnis

McINNIS, JOHN PHALEN
B. Sept. 19, 1890, Gloucester, Mass.   D. Feb. 16, 1960, Ipswich, Mass.   BR TR 5'9½" 162 lbs.
Manager 1927.

	G	AB	H	2B	3B	HR	HR %	R	RBI	BB	SO	SB	BA	SA	Pinch Hit AB	H	G by POS
1909 PHI A	19	46	11	0	0	1	2.2	4	4	2		0	.239	.304	5	2	SS-14
1910	38	73	22	2	4	0	0.0	10	12	7		3	.301	.438	10	3	SS-17, 2B-5, 3B-4, OF-1
1911	126	468	150	20	10	3	0.6	76	77	25		23	.321	.425	4	1	1B-97, SS-24
1912	153	568	186	25	13	3	0.5	83	101	49		27	.327	.433	0	0	1B-153
1913	148	543	177	30	4	4	0.7	79	90	45	31	16	.326	.418	0	0	1B-148
1914	149	576	181	12	8	1	0.2	74	95	19	27	25	.314	.368	0	0	1B-149
1915	119	456	143	14	4	0	0.0	44	49	14	17	8	.314	.362	0	0	1B-119
1916	140	512	151	25	3	1	0.2	42	60	25	19	7	.295	.361	0	0	1B-140
1917	150	567	172	19	4	0	0.0	50	44	33	19	11	.303	.351	0	0	1B-150
1918 BOS A	117	423	115	11	5	0	0.0	40	56	19	10	10	.272	.322	0	0	1B-94, 3B-23
1919	120	440	134	12	5	1	0.2	32	58	23	11	8	.305	.361	2	1	1B-118
1920	148	559	166	21	3	2	0.4	50	71	18	19	6	.297	.356	0	0	1B-148
1921	152	584	179	31	10	0	0.0	72	74	21	9	2	.307	.394	0	0	1B-152
1922 CLE A	142	537	164	28	7	1	0.2	58	78	15	5	1	.305	.389	0	0	1B-140, C-1
1923 BOS N	154	607	191	23	9	2	0.3	70	95	26	12	7	.315	.392	0	0	1B-154
1924	146	581	169	23	7	1	0.2	57	59	15	6	9	.291	.360	0	0	1B-146
1925 PIT N	59	155	57	10	4	0	0.0	19	24	17	1	1	.368	.484	13	4	1B-46
1926	47	127	38	6	1	0	0.0	12	13	7	3	1	.299	.362	7	2	1B-40
1927 PHI N	1	0	0	0	0	0	0.0	0	0	0		0	—	—	0	0	1B-1
19 yrs.	2128	7822	2406	312	101	20	0.3	872	1060	380	189	172	.308	.381	42	13	1B-1995, SS-55, 3B-27, 2B-5, OF-1, C-1

WORLD SERIES

	G	AB	H	2B	3B	HR	HR %	R	RBI	BB	SO	SB	BA	SA	Pinch Hit AB	H	G by POS
1911 PHI A	1	0	0	0	0	0	—	0	0	0	0	0	—	—	0	0	1B-1
1913	5	17	2	1	0	0	0.0	1	2	0	2	0	.118	.176	0	0	1B-5
1914	4	14	2	1	0	0	0.0	2	0	3	3	0	.143	.214	0	0	1B-4
1918 BOS A	6	20	5	0	0	0	0.0	2	1	1	1	0	.250	.250	0	0	1B-6
1925 PIT N	4	14	4	0	0	0	0.0	0	1	0	2	0	.286	.286	1	0	1B-3
5 yrs.	20	65	13	2	0	0	0.0	5	4	4	8	0	.200	.231	1	0	1B-19

Matty McIntyre

McINTYRE, MATTHEW W.
B. June 12, 1880, Stonington, Conn.   D. Apr. 2, 1920, Detroit, Mich.   BL TL

	G	AB	H	2B	3B	HR	HR %	R	RBI	BB	SO	SB	BA	SA	Pinch Hit AB	H	G by POS
1901 PHI A	82	308	85	12	4	0	0.0	38	46	30		11	.276	.341	0	0	OF-82
1904 DET A	152	578	146	11	10	2	0.3	74	46	44		11	.253	.317	0	0	OF-152
1905	131	495	130	21	5	0	0.0	59	30	48		9	.263	.325	0	0	OF-131
1906	133	493	128	19	11	0	0.0	63	39	56		29	.260	.343	0	0	OF-133
1907	20	81	23	1	1	0	0.0	6	9	7		3	.284	.321	0	0	OF-20
1908	151	569	168	24	13	0	0.0	105	28	83		20	.295	.383	0	0	OF-151
1909	125	476	116	18	9	1	0.2	65	34	54		13	.244	.326	2	0	OF-122
1910	83	305	72	15	5	0	0.0	40	25	39		4	.236	.318	6	1	OF-77
1911 CHI A	146	569	184	19	11	1	0.2	102	52	64		17	.323	.401	0	0	OF-146
1912	45	84	14	0	0	0	0.0	10	10	14		3	.167	.167	0	0	OF-45
10 yrs.	1068	3958	1066	140	69	4	0.1	562	319	439		120	.269	.343	8	1	OF-1059

WORLD SERIES

	G	AB	H	2B	3B	HR	HR %	R	RBI	BB	SO	SB	BA	SA	Pinch Hit AB	H	G by POS
1908 DET A	5	18	4	1	0	0	0.0	2	0	3	2	1	.222	.278	0	0	OF-5
1909	4	3	0	0	0	0	0.0	0	0	0	1	0	.000	.000	3	0	OF-1
2 yrs.	9	21	4	1	0	0	0.0	2	0	3	3	1	.190	.238	3	0	OF-6

Otto McIver

McIVER, EDWARD OTTO
B. July 26, 1884, Greenville, Tex.   D. May 4, 1954, Dallas, Tex.   BB TL 5'11½" 175 lbs.

	G	AB	H	2B	3B	HR	HR %	R	RBI	BB	SO	SB	BA	SA	Pinch Hit AB	H	G by POS
1911 STL N	30	62	14	2	1	1	1.6	11	9	9	14	0	.226	.339	7	0	OF-17

Dave McKay

McKAY, DAVID LAWRENCE
B. Mar. 14, 1950, Vancouver, B. C., Canada   BB TR 6'1" 195 lbs.

	G	AB	H	2B	3B	HR	HR %	R	RBI	BB	SO	SB	BA	SA	Pinch Hit AB	H	G by POS
1975 MIN A	33	125	32	4	1	2	1.6	8	16	6	14	1	.256	.352	0	0	3B-33
1976	45	138	28	2	0	0	0.0	8	8	9	27	1	.203	.217	3	1	3B-41, SS-2, DH-1
1977 TOR A	95	274	54	4	3	3	1.1	18	22	7	51	2	.197	.266	0	0	2B-40, 3B-32, SS-20, DH-2
1978	145	504	120	20	8	7	1.4	59	45	20	91	4	.238	.351	0	0	2B-140, SS-3, 3B-2, DH-1
1979	47	156	34	9	0	0	0.0	19	12	7	19	1	.218	.276	0	0	3B-46, 2B-3
1980 OAK A	123	295	72	16	1	1	0.3	29	29	10	57	1	.244	.315	1	1	2B-62, 3B-54, SS-10
1981	79	224	59	11	1	4	1.8	25	21	16	43	4	.263	.375	0	0	3B-43, 2B-38, SS-7
1982	78	212	42	4	1	4	1.9	25	17	11	35	6	.198	.283	2	0	2B-39, 3B-16, SS-3
8 yrs.	645	1928	441	70	15	21	1.1	191	170	86	337	20	.229	.313	9	2	2B-385, 3B-223, SS-45, DH-4

DIVISIONAL PLAYOFF SERIES

	G	AB	H	2B	3B	HR	HR %	R	RBI	BB	SO	SB	BA	SA	Pinch Hit AB	H	G by POS
1981 OAK A	3	11	3	0	0	1	9.1	1	1	1	1	0	.273	.545	0	0	2B-3

LEAGUE CHAMPIONSHIP SERIES

	G	AB	H	2B	3B	HR	HR %	R	RBI	BB	SO	SB	BA	SA	Pinch Hit AB	H	G by POS
1981 OAK A	3	11	3	0	0	0	0.0	0	1	0	2	0	.273	.273	0	0	2B-3

Ed McKean

McKEAN, EDWARD JOHN (Mack)
B. June 6, 1864, Grafton, Ohio   D. Aug. 16, 1919, Cleveland, Ohio   BR TR 5'9" 160 lbs.

	G	AB	H	2B	3B	HR	HR %	R	RBI	BB	SO	SB	BA	SA	Pinch Hit AB	H	G by POS
1887 CLE AA	132	539	154	16	13	2	0.4	97		60			.286	.375	0	0	SS-123, 2B-8, OF-4
1888	131	548	164	21	15	6	1.1	94	68	28	76		.299	.425	0	0	SS-78, OF-48, 2B-9, 3B-1
1889 CLE N	123	500	159	22	8	4	0.8	88	75	42	25	35	.318	.418	0	0	SS-122, 2B-1
1890	136	530	157	15	14	7	1.3	95	61	87	25	23	.296	.417	0	0	SS-134, 2B-3
1891	141	603	170	13	12	6	1.0	115	69	64	19	14	.282	.373	0	0	SS-141

	G	AB	H	2B	3B	HR	HR %	R	RBI	BB	SO	SB	BA	SA	Pinch Hit AB	Pinch Hit H	G by POS

Ed McKean continued

	G	AB	H	2B	3B	HR	HR%	R	RBI	BB	SO	SB	BA	SA	PH AB	PH H	G by POS
1892	129	531	139	14	10	0	0.0	76	93	49	28	19	.262	.326	0	0	SS-129
1893	125	545	169	29	24	4	0.7	103	133	50	14	16	.310	.473	0	0	SS-130
1894	130	554	198	30	15	8	1.4	116	128	49	12	33	.357	.509	0	0	SS-131
1895	131	565	193	32	17	8	1.4	131	119	45	25	12	.342	.501	0	0	SS-133
1896	133	571	193	29	12	7	1.2	100	112	45	9	13	.338	.468	0	0	SS-125
1897	125	523	143	21	14	2	0.4	83	78	40		15	.273	.379	0	0	SS-125
1898	151	604	172	23	1	9	1.5	89	94	56		11	.285	.371	0	0	SS-151
1899 STL N	67	277	72	7	3	3	1.1	40	40	20		4	.260	.339	0	0	SS-42, 1B-15, 2B-10
13 yrs.	1654	6890	2083	272	158	66	1.0	1227	1069	635	157	323	.302	.416	0	0	SS-1564, OF-52, 2B-31, 1B-15, 3B-1

Bill McKechnie

McKECHNIE, WILLIAM BOYD (Deacon)
B. Aug. 7, 1886, Wilkinsburg, Pa.   D. Oct. 29, 1965, Bradenton, Fla.
Manager 1915, 1922-26, 1928-46.
Hall of Fame 1962.
BB TR 5'10" 160 lbs.

	G	AB	H	2B	3B	HR	HR%	R	RBI	BB	SO	SB	BA	SA	PH AB	PH H	G by POS
1907 PIT N	3	8	1	0	0	0	0.0	0	0	0		0	.125	.125	0	0	3B-2, 2B-1
1910	71	212	46	1	2	0	0.0	23	12	11	23	4	.217	.241	8	2	2B-36, SS-14, 3B-8, 1B-4
1911	104	321	73	8	7	2	0.6	40	37	28	18	9	.227	.315	5	2	1B-57, 2B-17, SS-12, 3B-6
1912	24	73	18	0	1	0	0.0	8	4	2	1	2	.247	.274	1	0	3B-15, SS-4, 2B-3, 1B-2
1913 2 teams	BOS	N (1G –	.000)		NY	A	(44G –	.134)									
" total	45	116	15	0	0	0	0.0	8	8	8	18	2	.129	.129	4	0	2B-27, SS-7, 3B-2, OF-1
1914 IND F	149	570	173	24	6	2	0.4	107	38	53		47	.304	.377	0	0	3B-149
1915 NWK F	127	451	113	22	5	1	0.2	49	43	41		28	.251	.328	8	3	3B-117, OF-1
1916 2 teams	NY	N (71G –	.246)		CIN	N	(37G –	.277)									
" total	108	390	100	12	1	0	0.0	26	27	10	32	11	.256	.292	2	0	3B-106
1917 CIN N	48	134	34	3	1	0	0.0	11	15	7	7	5	.254	.291	4	1	2B-26, SS-13, 3B-4
1918 PIT N	126	435	111	13	9	2	0.5	34	43	24	22	12	.255	.340	0	0	3B-126
1920	40	133	29	3	1	0	0.8	13	13	4	7	7	.218	.278	3	0	3B-20, SS-10, 2B-6, 1B-1
11 yrs.	845	2843	713	86	33	8	0.3	319	240	188	128	127	.251	.313	35	8	3B-555, 2B-116, 1B-64, SS-60, OF-2

McKee

McKEE,
B. Philadelphia, Pa.   Deceased.

	G	AB	H	2B	3B	HR	HR%	R	RBI	BB	SO	SB	BA	SA	PH AB	PH H	G by POS
1884 WAS U	3	13	3	0	0	0	0.0	2		1			.231	.231	0	0	OF-2, 3B-2

Red McKee

McKEE, RAYMOND ELLIS
B. July 20, 1890, Shawnee, Ohio   D. Aug. 5, 1972, Saginaw, Mich.
BL TR 5'11" 180 lbs.

	G	AB	H	2B	3B	HR	HR%	R	RBI	BB	SO	SB	BA	SA	PH AB	PH H	G by POS
1913 DET A	67	187	53	3	4	1	0.5	18	20	21	21	7	.283	.358	6	0	C-61
1914	32	64	12	1	1	0	0.0	7	8	14	16	1	.188	.234	5	1	C-27
1915	55	106	29	5	0	1	0.9	10	17	13	16	1	.274	.349	15	2	C-35
1916	32	76	16	1	2	0	0.0	3	4	6	11	0	.211	.276	6	2	C-26
4 yrs.	186	433	110	10	7	2	0.5	38	49	54	64	9	.254	.323	32	5	C-149

Jim McKeever

McKEEVER, JAMES
B. Apr. 19, 1861, Newfoundland, Canada   D. Aug. 19, 1897, Boston, Mass.

	G	AB	H	2B	3B	HR	HR%	R	RBI	BB	SO	SB	BA	SA	PH AB	PH H	G by POS
1884 BOS U	16	66	9	0	0	0	0.0	13		1		0	.136	.136	0	0	C-12, OF-4

Russ McKelvey

McKELVEY, RUSSELL ERRETT
B. Sept. 8, 1856, Meadville, Pa.   D. Oct. 19, 1915, Omaha, Neb.
TR

	G	AB	H	2B	3B	HR	HR%	R	RBI	BB	SO	SB	BA	SA	PH AB	PH H	G by POS
1878 IND N	63	253	57	4	3	2	0.8	33	36	5	38		.225	.289	0	0	OF-62, P-4
1882 PIT AA	1	4	0	0	0	0	0.0	0		0			.000	.000	0	0	OF-1
2 yrs.	64	257	57	4	3	2	0.8	33	36	5	38		.222	.284	0	0	OF-63, P-4

Ed McKenna

McKENNA, EDWARD J.
B. St. Louis, Mo.   Deceased.

	G	AB	H	2B	3B	HR	HR%	R	RBI	BB	SO	SB	BA	SA	PH AB	PH H	G by POS
1877 STL N	1	5	1	0	0	0	0.0	0	0	0		1	.200	.200	0	0	OF-1
1884 WAS U	32	117	22	1	0	0	0.0	19		4			.188	.197	0	0	C-23, OF-10, 3B-7
2 yrs.	33	122	23	1	0	0	0.0	19		4		1	.189	.197	0	0	C-23, OF-11, 3B-7

Dave McKeough

McKEOUGH, DAVID J.
B. 1865, Utica, N.Y.   D. July 10, 1901, Utica, N.Y.
5'7" 140 lbs.

	G	AB	H	2B	3B	HR	HR%	R	RBI	BB	SO	SB	BA	SA	PH AB	PH H	G by POS
1890 ROC AA	62	218	49	5	0	0	0.0	38		29		14	.225	.248	0	0	C-47, SS-13, 2B-2, 3B-1
1891 PHI AA	15	54	14	1	1	0	0.0	4	3	8	6	0	.259	.315	0	0	C-14, SS-1
2 yrs.	77	272	63	6	1	0	0.0	42		37	6	14	.232	.261	0	0	C-61, SS-14, 2B-2, 3B-1

Bob McKinney

McKINNEY, ROBERT FRANCIS
B. Oct. 4, 1875, McSherrystown, Pa.   D. Aug. 19, 1946, Hanover, Pa.

	G	AB	H	2B	3B	HR	HR%	R	RBI	BB	SO	SB	BA	SA	PH AB	PH H	G by POS
1901 PHI A	2	2	0	0	0	0	0.0	0	0	0		0	.000	.000	0	0	3B-1, 2B-1

Rich McKinney

McKINNEY, CHARLES RICHARD
B. Nov. 22, 1946, Piqua, Ohio
BR TR 5'11" 185 lbs.

	G	AB	H	2B	3B	HR	HR%	R	RBI	BB	SO	SB	BA	SA	PH AB	PH H	G by POS
1970 CHI A	43	119	20	5	0	4	3.4	12	17	11	25	3	.168	.311	8	1	3B-23, SS-11
1971	114	369	100	11	2	8	2.2	35	46	35	37	0	.271	.377	19	11	2B-67, OF-25, 3B-5
1972 NY A	37	121	26	2	0	1	0.8	10	7	7	13	1	.215	.256	4	0	3B-33
1973 OAK A	48	65	16	3	0	1	1.5	9	7	7	4	0	.246	.338	19	2	3B-17, 2B-7, DH-6, OF-3
1974	5	7	1	0	0	0	0.0	0	0	0	0	0	.143	.143	3	0	2B-3
1975	8	7	1	0	0	0	0.0	0	2	1	2	0	.143	.143	4	0	DH-2, 1B-1
1977	86	198	35	7	0	6	3.0	13	21	16	43	0	.177	.303	31	6	1B-32, DH-18, 3B-7, OF-5, 2B-3
7 yrs.	341	886	199	28	2	20	2.3	79	100	77	124	4	.225	.328	88	20	3B-85, 2B-80, OF-33, 1B-33, DH-26, SS-11

	G	AB	H	2B	3B	HR	HR %	R	RBI	BB	SO	SB	BA	SA	Pinch Hit AB	H	G by POS

Alex McKinnon

McKINNON, ALEXANDER J.
B. Aug. 14, 1856, Boston, Mass.　　D. July 24, 1887, Charlestown, Mass.　　5'11½"

	G	AB	H	2B	3B	HR	HR %	R	RBI	BB	SO	SB	BA	SA	AB	H	G by POS
1884 NY N	116	470	128	21	12	4	0.9	66		8	62		.272	.394	0	0	1B-116
1885 STL N	100	411	121	21	6	1	0.2	42	44	8	31		.294	.382	0	0	1B-100
1886	122	491	148	24	7	8	1.6	75	72	21	23		.301	.428	0	0	1B-119, OF-3
1887 PIT N	48	200	68	16	4	1	0.5	26	30	8	9	6	.340	.475	0	0	1B-48
4 yrs.	386	1572	465	82	29	14	0.9	209	145	45	125	6	.296	.412	0	0	1B-383, OF-3

Jim McKnight

McKNIGHT, JAMES ARTHUR
B. July 1, 1936, Bee Branch, Ark.　　BR TR 6'1"　　185 lbs.

	G	AB	H	2B	3B	HR	HR %	R	RBI	BB	SO	SB	BA	SA	AB	H	G by POS
1960 CHI N	3	6	2	0	0	0	0.0	0	1	0	1	0	.333	.333	1	0	OF-1, 2B-1
1962	60	85	19	0	1	0	0.0	6	5	2	13	0	.224	.247	49	11	3B-9, OF-5, 2B-2
2 yrs.	63	91	21	0	1	0	0.0	6	6	2	14	0	.231	.253	50	11	3B-9, OF-6, 2B-3

Ed McLane

McLANE, EDWARD CAMERON
B. Aug. 20, 1881, Weston, Mass.

	G	AB	H	2B	3B	HR	HR %	R	RBI	BB	SO	SB	BA	SA	AB	H	G by POS
1907 BKN N	1	2	0	0	0	0	0.0	0	0	0		0	.000	.000	0	0	OF-1

Art McLarney

McLARNEY, ARTHUR JAMES
B. Dec. 20, 1908, Ft. Worden, Wash.　　BB TR 6'　　168 lbs.

	G	AB	H	2B	3B	HR	HR %	R	RBI	BB	SO	SB	BA	SA	AB	H	G by POS
1932 NY N	9	23	3	1	0	0	0.0	2	3	1	3	0	.130	.174	0	0	SS-9

Polly McLarry

McLARRY, HOWARD BELL
B. Mar. 25, 1891, Leonard, Tex.　　D. Nov. 4, 1971, Bonham, Tex.　　BL TR 6'　　185 lbs.

	G	AB	H	2B	3B	HR	HR %	R	RBI	BB	SO	SB	BA	SA	AB	H	G by POS
1912 CHI A	2	2	0	0	0	0	0.0	0	0	0		0	.000	.000	2	0	
1915 CHI N	68	127	25	3	0	1	0.8	16	12	14	20	2	.197	.244	21	2	1B-25, 2B-20
2 yrs.	70	129	25	3	0	1	0.8	16	12	14	20	2	.194	.240	23	2	1B-25, 2B-20

Barney McLaughlin

McLAUGHLIN, BERNARD
Brother of Frank McLaughlin.
B. 1857, Ireland　　D. Feb. 13, 1921, Lowell, Mass.　　5'8"　　163 lbs.

	G	AB	H	2B	3B	HR	HR %	R	RBI	BB	SO	SB	BA	SA	AB	H	G by POS
1884 KC U	42	162	37	7	3	0	0.0	15		9			.228	.309	0	0	OF-24, 2B-12, P-7, SS-2
1887 PHI N	50	205	45	8	3	1	0.5	26	26	11	27	2	.220	.302	0	0	2B-50
1890 SYR AA	86	329	87	8	1	2	0.6	43		47		13	.264	.313	0	0	SS-86
3 yrs.	178	696	169	23	7	3	0.4	84	25	67	27	15	.243	.309	0	0	SS-88, 2B-62, OF-24, P-7

Frank McLaughlin

McLAUGHLIN, FRANCIS EDWARD
Brother of Barney McLaughlin.
B. June 19, 1856, Lowell, Mass.　　D. Apr. 5, 1917, Lowell, Mass.　　BR TR 5'9"　　160 lbs.

	G	AB	H	2B	3B	HR	HR %	R	RBI	BB	SO	SB	BA	SA	AB	H	G by POS
1882 WOR N	15	55	12	0	2	1	1.8	7	4	0	11		.218	.345	0	0	SS-14, OF-1
1883 PIT N	29	114	25	2	0	1	0.9	15		6			.219	.263	0	0	SS-25, OF-4, 2B-2, P-2
1884 3 teams	CIN U (16G – .239)					C-P U (15G – .239)				KC U (32G – .228)							
" total	63	257	60	19	2	3	1.2	38		12			.233	.358	0	0	2B-24, SS-22, OF-11, 3B-9, P-2
3 yrs.	107	426	97	21	4	5	1.2	60	4	18	11		.228	.331	0	0	SS-61, 2B-26, OF-16, 3B-9, P-4

Jim McLaughlin

McLAUGHLIN, JAMES C.
B. 1860, Cleveland, Ohio　　D. Nov. 16, 1895, Cleveland, Ohio　　TL

	G	AB	H	2B	3B	HR	HR %	R	RBI	BB	SO	SB	BA	SA	AB	H	G by POS
1884 2 teams	WAS U (10G – .189)					BAL AA (5G – .227)											
" total	15	59	12	4	1	0	0.0	6		0			.203	.305	0	0	SS-9, OF-3, P-3, 3B-1

Jim McLaughlin

McLAUGHLIN, JAMES ROBERT
B. Jan. 3, 1902, St. Louis, Mo.　　D. Dec. 18, 1968, Mount Vernon, Ill.　　BR TR 5'10½"　170 lbs.

	G	AB	H	2B	3B	HR	HR %	R	RBI	BB	SO	SB	BA	SA	AB	H	G by POS
1932 STL A	1	1	0	0	0	0	0.0	0	1	0	0	0	.000	.000	0	0	3B-1

Kid McLaughlin

McLAUGHLIN, JAMES ANSON (Sunshine)
B. Apr. 12, 1888, Randolph, N. Y.　　D. Nov. 17, 1934, Allegany, N. Y.　　BL TR 5'8½"　　158 lbs.

	G	AB	H	2B	3B	HR	HR %	R	RBI	BB	SO	SB	BA	SA	AB	H	G by POS
1914 CIN N	3	2	0	0	0	0	0.0	1	0	0	0	0	.000	.000	1	0	OF-2

Tom McLaughlin

McLAUGHLIN, THOMAS
B. Louisville, Ky.　　Deceased.

	G	AB	H	2B	3B	HR	HR %	R	RBI	BB	SO	SB	BA	SA	AB	H	G by POS
1883 LOU AA	42	146	28	1	2	0	0.0	16		5			.192	.226	0	0	SS-19, OF-17, 1B-5, 3B-2, 2B-2
1884	98	335	67	11	5	1	0.3	41		22			.200	.272	0	0	SS-93, 3B-4, 2B-2
1885	112	411	87	13	9	2	0.5	49		15			.212	.302	0	0	2B-93, SS-19
1886 NY N	74	250	34	3	1	0	0.0	27		26			.136	.156	0	0	SS-63, 2B-10, OF-1
1891 WAS AA	14	41	11	0	1	0	0.0	9	3	7	6	3	.268	.317	0	0	SS-14
5 yrs.	340	1183	227	28	18	3	0.3	142	2	75	6	3	.192	.254	0	0	SS-208, 2B-107, OF-18, 3B-6, 1B-5

Ralph McLaurin

McLAURIN, RALPH EDGAR
B. May 23, 1885, Kissimmee, Fla.　　D. Feb. 11, 1943, McColl, S. C.

	G	AB	H	2B	3B	HR	HR %	R	RBI	BB	SO	SB	BA	SA	AB	H	G by POS
1908 STL N	8	22	5	0	0	0	0.0	2	0	0		0	.227	.227	2	0	OF-6

Larry McLean

McLEAN, JOHN BANNERMAN
B. July 18, 1881, Cambridge, Mass.　　D. Mar. 14, 1921, Boston, Mass.　　BR TR 6'5"　　228 lbs.

	G	AB	H	2B	3B	HR	HR %	R	RBI	BB	SO	SB	BA	SA	AB	H	G by POS
1901 BOS A	9	19	4	1	0	0	0.0	4	2	0		1	.211	.263	4	2	1B-5
1903 CHI N	1	4	0	0	0	0	0.0	0	1	1		0	.000	.000	0	0	C-1
1904 STL N	27	84	14	2	1	0	0.0	5	4	4		0	.167	.214	2	0	C-24
1906 CIN N	12	35	7	2	0	0	0.0	3	2	4		0	.200	.257	0	0	C-12
1907	113	374	108	9	9	0	0.0	35	54	13		4	.289	.361	11	2	C-89, 1B-13
1908	99	309	67	9	4	1	0.3	24	28	15		2	.217	.282	10	2	C-69, 1B-19
1909	95	324	83	12	2	0	0.6	26	36	21		1	.256	.324	0	0	C-95
1910	127	423	126	14	7	2	0.5	27	71	26	23	4	.298	.378	9	2	C-119
1911	107	328	94	7	2	0	0.0	24	34	20	18	1	.287	.320	8	0	C-98

	G	AB	H	2B	3B	HR	HR %	R	RBI	BB	SO	SB	BA	SA	Pinch Hit AB	Pinch Hit H	G by POS

Larry McLean continued

	G	AB	H	2B	3B	HR	HR%	R	RBI	BB	SO	SB	BA	SA	AB	H	G by POS
1912	102	333	81	15	1	1	0.3	17	27	18	15	1	.243	.303	4	2	C-98
1913 2 teams		STL N	(48G –	.270)		NY N	(30G –	.320)									C-70
" total	78	227	65	13	0	0	0.0	10	21	10	13	1	.286	.344	8	2	C-74
1914 NY N	79	154	40	6	0	0	0.0	8	14	4	9	4	.260	.299	4	0	C-12
1915	13	33	5	0	0	0	0.0	0	4	0	1	0	.152	.152	1	0	C-761, 1B-37
13 yrs.	862	2647	694	90	26	6	0.2	183	298	136	79	20	.262	.323	61	12	

WORLD SERIES																	
1913 NY N	5	12	6	0	0	0	0.0	0	2	0	0	0	.500	.500	1	0	C-4

Jim McLeod

McLEOD, SOULE JAMES
B. Sept. 12, 1908, Jones, La. D. Aug. 3, 1981, Little Rock, Ark.
BR TR 6' 187 lbs.

	G	AB	H	2B	3B	HR	HR%	R	RBI	BB	SO	SB	BA	SA	AB	H	G by POS
1930 WAS A	18	34	9	1	0	0	0.0	3	1	1	5	0	.265	.294	0	0	3B-10, SS-7
1932	7	0	0	0	0	0	–	1	0	1	0	0	–	–	0	0	SS-1
1933 PHI N	67	232	45	6	1	0	0.0	20	15	12	25	1	.194	.228	0	0	3B-67, SS-1
3 yrs.	92	266	54	7	1	0	0.0	24	16	14	30	2	.203	.237	0	0	3B-77, SS-9

Ralph McLeod

McLEOD, RALPH ALTON
B. Oct. 19, 1916, North Quincy, Mass.
BL TL 6' 170 lbs.

	G	AB	H	2B	3B	HR	HR%	R	RBI	BB	SO	SB	BA	SA	AB	H	G by POS
1938 BOS N	6	7	2	1	0	0	0.0	1	0	0	2	0	.286	.429	5	2	OF-1

Jack McMahon

McMAHON, JOHN HENRY
B. Oct. 15, 1869, Waterbury, Conn. D. Dec. 30, 1894, Bridgeport, Conn.
TR 5'10" 165 lbs.

	G	AB	H	2B	3B	HR	HR%	R	RBI	BB	SO	SB	BA	SA	AB	H	G by POS
1892 NY N	40	147	33	5	7	1	0.7	21	24	10	9	3	.224	.374	0	0	1B-36, C-5
1893	11	30	10	2	1	0	0.0	5	4	2	0	0	.333	.467	0	0	C-11
2 yrs.	51	177	43	7	8	1	0.6	26	28	12	9	3	.243	.390	0	0	1B-36, C-16

Frank McManus

McMANUS, FRANCIS E.
B. Sept. 21, 1875, Lawrence, Mass. D. Sept. 1, 1923, Syracuse, N. Y.
TR 5'10"

	G	AB	H	2B	3B	HR	HR%	R	RBI	BB	SO	SB	BA	SA	AB	H	G by POS
1899 WAS N	7	21	8	1	0	0	0.0	3	2	2		3	.381	.429	0	0	C-7
1903 BKN N	2	7	0	0	0	0	0.0	0	0	0		0	.000	.000	0	0	C-2
1904 2 teams		DET A	(1G –	.000)		NY A	(4G –	.000)									C-5
" total	5	7	0	0	0	0	0.0	0	0	0		0	.000	.000	0	0	C-14
3 yrs.	14	35	8	1	0	0	0.0	3	2	2		3	.229	.257	0	0	C-14

Jim McManus

McMANUS, JAMES MICHAEL
B. July 20, 1936, Brookline, Mass.
BL TL 6'4" 215 lbs.

	G	AB	H	2B	3B	HR	HR%	R	RBI	BB	SO	SB	BA	SA	AB	H	G by POS
1960 KC A	5	13	4	0	0	1	7.7	3	2	1	2	0	.308	.538	2	0	1B-3

Marty McManus

McMANUS, MARTIN JOSEPH
B. Mar. 14, 1900, Chicago, Ill. D. Feb. 18, 1966, St. Louis, Mo.
Manager 1932-33.
BR TR 5'10½" 160 lbs.

	G	AB	H	2B	3B	HR	HR%	R	RBI	BB	SO	SB	BA	SA	AB	H	G by POS
1920 STL A	1	3	1	0	1	0	0.0	0	1	0	0	0	.333	1.000	0	0	3B-1
1921	121	412	107	19	8	3	0.7	49	64	27	30	5	.260	.367	0	0	2B-96, 3B-13, 1B-10, SS-2
1922	154	606	189	34	11	11	1.8	88	109	38	41	9	.312	.459	0	0	2B-153, 1B-1
1923	154	582	180	35	10	15	2.6	86	94	49	50	14	.309	.481	1	0	2B-133, 1B-20
1924	123	442	147	23	5	5	1.1	71	80	54	40	13	.333	.441	4	1	2B-118
1925	154	587	169	44	8	13	2.2	108	90	73	69	5	.288	.457	0	0	2B-154, OF-1
1926	149	549	156	30	10	9	1.6	102	68	55	62	5	.284	.424	0	0	3B-84, 2B-61, 1B-4
1927 DET A	108	369	99	19	7	9	2.4	60	69	34	38	8	.268	.431	9	4	SS-39, 3B-35, 3B-22, 1B-6
1928	139	500	144	37	5	8	1.6	78	73	51	32	11	.288	.430	4	1	3B-92, 1B-45, SS-1
1929	154	599	168	32	8	18	3.0	99	90	60	52	17	.280	.451	0	0	3B-150, SS-9
1930	132	484	155	40	4	9	1.9	74	89	59	28	23	.320	.475	0	0	3B-130, SS-3, 1B-1
1931 2 teams		DET A	(107G –	.271)		BOS A	(17G –	.290)									3B-90, 2B-28, 1B-1
" total	124	424	116	21	3	4	0.9	47	62	57	23	8	.274	.366	5	0	2B-49, 3B-30, SS-2, 1B-1
1932 BOS A	93	302	71	19	4	5	1.7	39	24	36	30	1	.235	.374	15	1	3B-76, 2B-26, 1B-4
1933	106	366	104	30	4	3	0.8	51	36	49	21	3	.284	.413	3	1	2B-73, 3B-37
1934 BOS N	119	435	120	18	0	8	1.8	56	47	32	42	5	.276	.372	8	2	2B-73, 3B-37
15 yrs.	1831	6660	1926	401	88	120	1.8	1008	996	674	558	127	.289	.430	49	10	2B-926, 3B-725, 1B-93, SS-56, OF-1

Jimmy McMath

McMATH, JIMMY LEE
B. Aug. 10, 1949, Tuscaloosa, Ala.
BL TL 6'1½" 195 lbs.

	G	AB	H	2B	3B	HR	HR%	R	RBI	BB	SO	SB	BA	SA	AB	H	G by POS
1968 CHI N	6	14	2	0	0	0	0.0	0	2	0	6	0	.143	.143	3	0	OF-3

George McMillan

McMILLAN, GEORGE A. (Reddy)
B. Evansville, Ind. Deceased.
5'8" 175 lbs.

	G	AB	H	2B	3B	HR	HR%	R	RBI	BB	SO	SB	BA	SA	AB	H	G by POS
1890 NY N	10	35	5	0	0	0	0.0	4	1	7	4	1	.143	.143	0	0	OF-10

Norm McMillan

McMILLAN, NORMAN ALEXIS (Bub)
B. Oct. 5, 1895, Latta, S. C. D. Sept. 28, 1969, Marion, S. C.
BR TR 6' 175 lbs.

	G	AB	H	2B	3B	HR	HR%	R	RBI	BB	SO	SB	BA	SA	AB	H	G by POS
1922 NY A	33	78	20	1	2	0	0.0	7	11	6	10	4	.256	.321	1	0	OF-23, 3B-5
1923 BOS A	131	459	116	24	5	0	0.0	37	42	28	44	13	.253	.327	2	0	3B-67, 2B-35, SS-28
1924 STL A	76	201	56	12	2	0	0.0	25	27	12	17	6	.279	.358	8	4	2B-37, 3B-17, SS-6, 1B-2
1928 CHI N	49	123	27	2	2	1	0.8	11	12	13	19	0	.220	.293	9	1	2B-19, 3B-18
1929	124	495	134	35	5	5	1.0	77	55	36	43	13	.271	.392	3	2	3B-120
5 yrs.	413	1356	353	74	16	6	0.4	157	147	95	133	36	.260	.352	23	7	3B-227, 2B-91, SS-34, OF-23, 1B-2

WORLD SERIES																	
1922 NY A	1	2	0	0	0	0	0.0	0	0	0	0	0	.000	.000	1	0	OF-1
1929 CHI N	5	20	2	0	0	0	0.0	0	0	2	6	1	.100	.100	1	0	3B-5
2 yrs.	6	22	2	0	0	0	0.0	0	0	2	6	1	.091	.091	1	0	3B-5, OF-1

	G	AB	H	2B	3B	HR	HR %	R	RBI	BB	SO	SB	BA	SA	Pinch Hit AB	H	G by POS

Roy McMillan

McMILLAN, ROY DAVID
B. July 17, 1930, Bonham, Tex.
Manager 1972, 1975.

BR TR 5'11" 170 lbs.

	G	AB	H	2B	3B	HR	HR %	R	RBI	BB	SO	SB	BA	SA	AB	H	G by POS
1951 CIN N	85	199	42	4	0	1	0.5	21	8	17	26	0	.211	.246	8	3	SS-54, 3B-12, 2B-1
1952	154	540	132	32	2	7	1.3	60	57	45	81	4	.244	.350	0	0	SS-154
1953	155	557	130	15	4	5	0.9	51	43	43	52	2	.233	.302	0	0	SS-155
1954	154	588	147	21	2	4	0.7	86	42	47	54	4	.250	.313	0	0	SS-154
1955	151	470	126	21	2	1	0.2	50	37	66	33	4	.268	.328	0	0	SS-150
1956	150	479	126	16	7	3	0.6	51	62	76	54	4	.263	.344	0	0	SS-150
1957	151	448	122	25	5	1	0.2	50	55	66	44	5	.272	.357	0	0	SS-151
1958	145	393	90	18	3	1	0.3	48	25	47	33	5	.229	.298	0	0	SS-145
1959	79	246	65	14	2	9	3.7	38	24	27	27	0	.264	.447	0	0	SS-73
1960	124	399	94	12	2	10	2.5	42	42	35	40	2	.236	.351	0	0	SS-116, 2B-10
1961 MIL N	154	505	111	16	0	7	1.4	42	48	61	86	2	.220	.293	0	0	SS-154
1962	137	468	115	13	0	12	2.6	66	41	60	53	2	.246	.350	2	1	SS-135
1963	100	320	80	10	1	4	1.3	35	29	17	25	1	.250	.325	4	2	SS-94
1964 2 teams		MIL N (8G – .308)						NY	N	(113G –	.211)						
" total	121	392	84	8	2	1	0.3	31	27	14	18	4	.214	.253	2	0	SS-119
1965 NY N	157	528	128	19	2	1	0.2	44	42	24	60	1	.242	.292	4	0	SS-153
1966	76	220	47	9	1	1	0.5	24	12	20	25	1	.214	.277	5	2	SS-71
16 yrs.	2093	6752	1639	253	35	68	1.0	739	594	665	711	41	.243	.321	25	8	SS-2028, 3B-12, 2B-11

Tommy McMillan

McMILLAN, THOMAS ERWIN
B. Sept. 13, 1951, Richmond, Va.

BR TR 5'9" 165 lbs.

	G	AB	H	2B	3B	HR	HR %	R	RBI	BB	SO	SB	BA	SA	AB	H	G by POS
1977 SEA A	2	5	0	0	0	0	0.0	0	0	0	0	0	.000	.000	0	0	SS-2

Tommy McMillan

McMILLAN, THOMAS LAW (Rebel)
B. Apr. 17, 1888, Pittston, Pa.   D. July 15, 1966, Orlando, Fla.

BR TR 5'5" 130 lbs.

	G	AB	H	2B	3B	HR	HR %	R	RBI	BB	SO	SB	BA	SA	AB	H	G by POS
1908 BKN N	43	147	35	3	0	0	0.0	9	3	9		5	.238	.259	0	0	SS-29, OF-14
1909	108	373	79	15	1	0	0.0	18	24	20		11	.212	.257	1	0	SS-105, 2B-2, 3B-1
1910 2 teams		BKN N (23G – .176)						CIN	N	(82G –	.185)						
" total	105	322	59	1	3	0	0.0	22	15	37	33	11	.183	.205	0	0	SS-105
1912 NY N	41	149	34	2	0	0	0.0	24	12	15		18	.228	.242	0	0	SS-41
4 yrs.	297	991	207	21	4	0	0.0	73	54	81	33	45	.209	.238	1	0	SS-280, OF-14, 2B-2, 3B-1

Hugh McMullen

McMULLEN, HUGH RAPHAEL
B. Dec. 16, 1901, La Cygne, Kans.

BR TR 6'1" 180 lbs.
BB 1928-29

	G	AB	H	2B	3B	HR	HR %	R	RBI	BB	SO	SB	BA	SA	AB	H	G by POS
1925 NY N	5	15	2	1	0	0	0.0	1	0	0	3	0	.133	.200	0	0	C-5
1926	57	91	17	2	0	0	0.0	5	6	2	18	1	.187	.209	1	0	C-56
1928 WAS A	1	1	0	0	0	0	0.0	0	0	0	1	0	.000	.000	1	0	C-1
1929 CIN N	1	1	0	0	0	0	0.0	0	0	0	0	0	.000	.000	0	0	C-1
4 yrs.	64	108	19	3	0	0	0.0	6	6	2	22	1	.176	.204	2	0	C-62

Ken McMullen

McMULLEN, KENNETH LEE
B. June 1, 1942, Oxnard, Calif.

BR TR 6'3" 190 lbs.

	G	AB	H	2B	3B	HR	HR %	R	RBI	BB	SO	SB	BA	SA	AB	H	G by POS
1962 LA N	6	11	3	0	0	0	0.0	0	0	0	3	0	.273	.273	4	1	OF-2
1963	79	233	55	9	0	5	2.1	16	28	20	46	1	.236	.339	8	1	3B-71, OF-1, 2B-1
1964	24	67	14	0	0	1	1.5	3	2	3	7	0	.209	.254	6	0	1B-13, 3B-4, OF-3
1965 WAS A	150	555	146	18	6	18	3.2	75	54	47	90	2	.263	.414	5	0	3B-142, OF-8, 1B-1
1966	147	524	122	19	4	13	2.5	48	54	44	89	3	.233	.359	2	1	3B-141, 1B-8, OF-1
1967	146	563	138	22	2	16	2.8	73	67	46	84	5	.245	.377	0	0	3B-145
1968	151	557	138	11	2	20	3.6	66	62	63	66	1	.248	.382	5	1	3B-145, SS-11
1969	156	562	153	25	2	19	3.4	83	87	70	103	4	.272	.425	5	1	3B-154
1970 2 teams		WAS A (15G – .203)						CAL	A	(124G –	.232)						
" total	139	481	110	11	3	14	2.9	55	64	64	91	1	.229	.351	4	1	3B-137
1971 CAL A	160	593	148	19	2	21	3.5	63	68	53	74	1	.250	.395	3	0	3B-158
1972	137	472	127	18	1	9	1.9	36	34	48	59	1	.269	.369	0	0	3B-137
1973 LA N	42	85	21	5	0	5	5.9	6	18	14	13	0	.247	.482	19	6	3B-24
1974	44	60	15	1	0	3	5.0	5	12	2	12	0	.250	.417	35	9	3B-7, 2B-3
1975	39	46	11	1	1	2	4.3	4	14	7	12	0	.239	.435	25	6	3B-11, 1B-3
1976 OAK A	98	186	41	6	2	5	2.7	20	23	22	33	1	.220	.355	31	9	3B-35, 1B-26, DH-23, OF-5, 2B-1
1977 MIL A	63	136	31	7	1	5	3.7	15	19	15	33	0	.228	.404	24	5	DH-29, 1B-11, 3B-7
16 yrs.	1583	5131	1273	172	26	156	3.0	568	606	510	815	20	.248	.383	176	41	3B-1318, 1B-62, DH-52, OF-20, SS-11, 2B-5

LEAGUE CHAMPIONSHIP SERIES

	G	AB	H	2B	3B	HR	HR %	R	RBI	BB	SO	SB	BA	SA	AB	H	G by POS
1974 LA N	1	1	0	0	0	0	0.0	0	0	0	1	0	.000	.000	1	0	

Fred McMullin

McMULLIN, FREDERICK WILLIAM
B. Oct. 13, 1891, Scammon, Kans.   D. Nov. 21, 1952, Los Angeles, Calif.

BR TR 5'11" 170 lbs.

	G	AB	H	2B	3B	HR	HR %	R	RBI	BB	SO	SB	BA	SA	AB	H	G by POS
1914 DET A	1	1	0	0	0	0	0.0	0	0	0	1	0	.000	.000	0	0	SS-1
1916 CHI A	68	187	48	3	0	0	0.0	8	10	19	30	9	.257	.273	0	0	3B-63, SS-2, 2B-1
1917	59	194	46	2	1	0	0.0	35	12	27	17	7	.237	.258	5	1	3B-52, SS-2
1918	70	235	65	7	0	1	0.4	32	16	25	26	7	.277	.319	0	0	3B-69, 2B-1
1919	60	170	50	8	4	0	0.0	31	19	11	18	4	.294	.388	4	0	3B-46, 2B-5
1920	46	127	25	1	4	0	0.0	14	13	9	13	1	.197	.268	11	5	3B-29, 2B-3, SS-1
6 yrs.	304	914	234	21	9	1	0.1	120	70	91	105	30	.256	.302	26	7	3B-259, 2B-10, SS-6

WORLD SERIES

	G	AB	H	2B	3B	HR	HR %	R	RBI	BB	SO	SB	BA	SA	AB	H	G by POS
1917 CHI A	6	24	3	1	0	0	0.0	1	2	1	6	0	.125	.167	0	0	3B-6
1919	2	2	1	0	0	0	0.0	0	0	0	0	0	.500	.500	2	1	
2 yrs.	8	26	4	1	0	0	0.0	1	2	1	6	0	.154	.192	2	1	3B-6

Carl McNabb

McNABB, CARL MAC (Skinny)
B. Jan. 25, 1917, Stevenson, Ala.

BR TR 5'9" 155 lbs.

	G	AB	H	2B	3B	HR	HR %	R	RBI	BB	SO	SB	BA	SA	AB	H	G by POS
1945 DET A	1	1	0	0	0	0	0.0	0	0	0	1	0	.000	.000	1	0	

	G	AB	H	2B	3B	HR	HR %	R	RBI	BB	SO	SB	BA	SA	Pinch Hit AB	Pinch Hit H	G by POS

Eric McNair

McNAIR, DONALD ERIC (Boob)
B. Apr. 12, 1909, Meridian, Miss.   D. Mar. 11, 1949, Meridian, Miss.
BR TR 5'8" 160 lbs.

	G	AB	H	2B	3B	HR	HR %	R	RBI	BB	SO	SB	BA	SA	AB	H	G by POS
1929 PHI A	4	8	4	1	0	0	0.0	2	3	0	0	1	.500	.625	0	0	SS-4
1930	78	237	63	12	2	0	0.0	27	34	9	19	5	.266	.333	7	1	SS-31, 3B-29, 2B-5, OF-1
1931	79	280	76	10	1	5	1.8	41	33	11	19	1	.271	.368	3	1	3B-47, 2B-16, SS-13
1932	135	554	158	47	3	18	3.2	87	95	28	29	8	.285	.478	2	0	SS-133
1933	89	310	81	15	4	7	2.3	57	48	15	32	2	.261	.403	16	5	SS-46, 2B-28
1934	151	599	168	20	4	17	2.8	80	82	35	42	7	.280	.412	0	0	SS-151
1935	137	526	142	22	2	4	0.8	55	57	35	33	3	.270	.342	3	0	SS-121, 3B-11, 1B-2
1936 BOS A	128	494	141	36	2	4	0.8	68	74	27	34	3	.285	.391	0	0	SS-84, 2B-35, 3B-1
1937	126	455	133	29	4	12	2.6	60	76	30	33	10	.292	.453	9	2	2B-106, SS-9, 3B-4, 1B-1
1938	46	96	15	1	1	0	0.0	9	7	3	6	0	.156	.188	14	5	SS-15, 2B-14, 3B-3
1939 CHI A	129	479	155	18	5	7	1.5	62	82	38	41	17	.324	.426	1	0	3B-103, 2B-19, SS-9
1940	66	251	57	13	1	7	2.8	26	31	12	26	1	.227	.371	0	0	2B-65, 3B-1
1941 DET A	23	59	11	1	0	0	0.0	5	3	4	4	0	.186	.203	9	3	3B-11, SS-3
1942 2 teams		DET A	(26G –	.162)		PHI A	(34G –	.243)									
" total	60	171	36	4	0	1	0.6	13	8	14	10	1	.211	.251	8	1	SS-50, 2B-1
14 yrs.	1251	4519	1240	229	29	82	1.8	592	633	261	328	59	.274	.392	72	15	SS-669, 2B-289, 3B-220, 1B-3, OF-1

WORLD SERIES																	
1930 PHI A	1	1	0	0	0	0	0.0	0	0	0	0	0	.000	.000	1	0	2B-1
1931	2	2	0	0	0	0	0.0	1	0	0	1	0	.000	.000	1	0	
2 yrs.	3	3	0	0	0	0	0.0	1	0	0	1	0	.000	.000	2	0	2B-1

Mike McNally

McNALLY, MICHAEL JOSEPH
B. Sept. 13, 1893, Minooka, Pa.   D. May 29, 1965, Bethlehem, Pa.
BR TR 5'11" 150 lbs.

	G	AB	H	2B	3B	HR	HR %	R	RBI	BB	SO	SB	BA	SA	AB	H	G by POS
1915 BOS A	23	53	8	1	0	0	0.0	7	0	3	7	0	.151	.189	0	0	3B-18, 2B-5
1916	87	135	23	0	0	0	0.0	28	9	10	19	9	.170	.170	2	0	2B-35, 3B-14, SS-7, OF-1
1917	42	50	15	1	0	0	0.0	9	2	6	3	3	.300	.320	1	1	3B-14, SS-9, 2B-6
1919	33	42	11	4	0	0	0.0	10	6	1	2	4	.262	.357	1	1	SS-11, 3B-11, 2B-3
1920	93	312	80	5	1	0	0.0	42	23	31	24	13	.256	.279	1	1	2B-76, SS-8, 1B-6
1921 NY A	71	215	56	4	2	1	0.5	36	24	14	15	5	.260	.312	1	0	3B-48, 2B-16
1922	52	143	36	2	2	0	0.0	20	18	16	14	2	.252	.294	0	0	3B-32, 2B-9, SS-4, 1B-1
1923	30	38	8	0	0	0	0.0	5	1	3	4	2	.211	.211	3	0	SS-13, 3B-7, 2B-5
1924	49	69	17	0	0	0	0.0	11	2	7	5	1	.246	.246	2	1	2B-25, 3B-13, SS-6
1925 WAS A	12	21	3	0	0	0	0.0	1	0	1	4	0	.143	.143	0	0	3B-7, SS-2, 2B-1
10 yrs.	492	1078	257	16	6	1	0.1	169	85	92	97	39	.238	.267	11	0	2B-181, 3B-164, SS-60, 1B-7, OF-1

WORLD SERIES																	
1916 BOS A	1	0	0	0	0	0	–	1	0	0	0	0	–	–	0	0	3B-7
1921 NY A	7	20	4	1	0	0	0.0	3	1	1	3	2	.200	.250	0	0	2B-1
1922	1	0	0	0	0	0	–	0	0	0	0	0	–	–	0	0	3B-7, 2B-1
3 yrs.	9	20	4	1	0	0	0.0	4	1	1	3	2	.200	.250	0	0	

Bob McNamara

McNAMARA, ROBERT MAXEY
B. Sept. 19, 1916, Denver, Colo.
BR TR 5'10" 170 lbs.

	G	AB	H	2B	3B	HR	HR %	R	RBI	BB	SO	SB	BA	SA	AB	H	G by POS
1939 PHI A	9	9	2	1	0	0	0.0	0	3	1	1	0	.222	.333	0	0	3B-5, SS-2, 2B-1, 1B-1

Dinny McNamara

McNAMARA, JOHN RAYMOND
B. Sept. 16, 1905, Lexington, Mass.   D. Dec. 20, 1963, Lexington, Mass.
BL TR 5'9" 165 lbs.

	G	AB	H	2B	3B	HR	HR %	R	RBI	BB	SO	SB	BA	SA	AB	H	G by POS
1927 BOS N	11	9	0	0	0	0	0.0	3	0	0	3	0	.000	.000	0	0	OF-3
1928	9	4	1	0	0	0	0.0	2	0	0	1	0	.250	.250	1	0	OF-3
2 yrs.	20	13	1	0	0	0	0.0	5	0	0	4	0	.077	.077	1	0	OF-6

George McNamara

McNAMARA, GEORGE FRANCIS
B. Jan. 11, 1903, Chicago, Ill.
BL TR 6' 175 lbs.

	G	AB	H	2B	3B	HR	HR %	R	RBI	BB	SO	SB	BA	SA	AB	H	G by POS
1922 WAS A	3	11	3	0	0	0	0.0	3	1	1	2	0	.273	.273	0	0	OF-3

Tom McNamara

McNAMARA, THOMAS HENRY
B. Nov. 5, 1895, Roxbury, Mass.   D. May 5, 1974, Danvers, Mass.
BR TR 6'2" 200 lbs.

	G	AB	H	2B	3B	HR	HR %	R	RBI	BB	SO	SB	BA	SA	AB	H	G by POS
1922 PIT N	1	1	0	0	0	0	0.0	0	0	0	0	0	.000	.000	1	0	

Rusty McNealy

McNEALY, ROBERT LEE
B. Aug. 12, 1958, Sacramento, Calif.
BL TL 5'8" 160 lbs.

	G	AB	H	2B	3B	HR	HR %	R	RBI	BB	SO	SB	BA	SA	AB	H	G by POS
1983 OAK A	15	4	0	0	0	0	0.0	5	0	0	0	0	.000	.000	0	0	DH-7, OF-5

Earl McNeely

McNEELY, GEORGE EARL
B. May 12, 1899, Sacramento, Calif.   D. July 16, 1971, Sacramento, Calif.
BR TR 5'9" 155 lbs.

	G	AB	H	2B	3B	HR	HR %	R	RBI	BB	SO	SB	BA	SA	AB	H	G by POS
1924 WAS A	43	179	59	5	6	0	0.0	31	15	5	21	1	.330	.425	1	0	OF-42
1925	122	385	110	14	2	3	0.8	76	37	48	54	14	.286	.356	1	0	OF-112, 1B-1
1926	124	442	134	20	12	0	0.0	84	48	44	28	18	.303	.403	2	0	OF-120
1927	73	185	51	10	4	0	0.0	40	16	11	13	11	.276	.373	11	2	OF-47, 1B-4
1928 STL A	127	496	117	27	7	0	0.0	66	44	37	39	8	.236	.319	7	2	OF-120
1929	69	230	56	8	1	1	0.4	27	18	7	13	2	.243	.300	6	0	OF-62
1930	76	235	64	19	1	0	0.0	33	20	22	14	8	.272	.362	3	1	OF-38, 1B-27
1931	49	102	23	4	0	0	0.0	12	15	9	5	4	.225	.265	4	0	OF-36
8 yrs.	683	2254	614	107	33	4	0.2	369	213	183	187	68	.272	.354	35	5	OF-577, 1B-32

WORLD SERIES																	
1924 WAS A	7	27	6	3	0	0	0.0	4	1	4	4	1	.222	.333	1	0	OF-6
1925	4	0	0	0	0	0	–	2	0	0	0	1	–	–	0	0	OF-2
2 yrs.	11	27	6	3	0	0	0.0	6	1	4	4	2	.222	.333	1	0	OF-8

	G	AB	H	2B	3B	HR	HR %	R	RBI	BB	SO	SB	BA	SA	Pinch Hit AB	Pinch Hit H	G by POS

Norm McNeil

McNEIL, NORMAN FRANCIS
B. Oct. 22, 1892, Chicago, Ill. D. Apr. 11, 1942, Buffalo, N. Y.
BR TR 5'11" 180 lbs.

	G	AB	H	2B	3B	HR	HR %	R	RBI	BB	SO	SB	BA	SA	PH AB	PH H	G by POS
1919 BOS A	5	9	3	0	0	0	0.0	0	1	1	0	0	.333	.333	0	0	C-5

Jerry McNertney

McNERTNEY, GERALD EDWARD
B. Aug. 7, 1936, Boone, Iowa
BR TR 6' 180 lbs.

	G	AB	H	2B	3B	HR	HR %	R	RBI	BB	SO	SB	BA	SA	PH AB	PH H	G by POS
1964 CHI A	73	186	40	5	0	3	1.6	16	23	19	24	0	.215	.290	6	0	C-69
1966	44	59	13	0	0	0	0.0	3	1	7	6	1	.220	.220	5	0	C-37
1967	56	123	28	6	0	3	2.4	8	13	6	14	0	.228	.350	1	1	C-52
1968	74	169	37	4	1	3	1.8	18	18	18	29	0	.219	.308	3	3	C-64, 1B-1
1969 SEA A	128	410	99	18	1	8	2.0	39	55	29	63	1	.241	.349	7	3	C-122
1970 MIL A	111	296	72	11	1	6	2.0	27	22	22	33	1	.243	.348	18	4	C-94, 1B-13
1971 STL N	56	128	37	4	2	4	3.1	15	22	12	14	0	.289	.445	16	5	C-36
1972	39	48	10	3	1	0	0.0	3	9	6	16	0	.208	.313	28	4	C-10
1973 PIT N	9	4	1	0	0	0	0.0	0	0	0	0	0	.250	.250	9	0	C-9
9 yrs.	590	1423	337	51	6	27	1.9	129	163	119	199	3	.237	.338	92	20	C-493, 1B-14

Bill McNulty

McNULTY, WILLIAM FRANCIS
B. Aug. 29, 1946, Sacramento, Calif.
BR TR 6'4" 205 lbs.

	G	AB	H	2B	3B	HR	HR %	R	RBI	BB	SO	SB	BA	SA	PH AB	PH H	G by POS
1969 OAK A	5	17	0	0	0	0	0.0	0	0	0	10	0	.000	.000	0	0	OF-5
1972	4	10	1	0	0	0	0.0	0	0	2	1	0	.100	.100	1	0	3B-3
2 yrs.	9	27	1	0	0	0	0.0	0	0	2	11	0	.037	.037	1	0	OF-5, 3B-3

Pat McNulty

McNULTY, PATRICK HOWARD
B. Feb. 27, 1899, Cleveland, Ohio D. May 4, 1963, Hollywood, Calif.
BL TR 5'11" 160 lbs.

	G	AB	H	2B	3B	HR	HR %	R	RBI	BB	SO	SB	BA	SA	PH AB	PH H	G by POS
1922 CLE A	22	59	16	2	1	0	0.0	10	5	9	5	4	.271	.339	0	0	OF-22
1924	101	291	78	13	5	0	0.0	46	26	33	22	10	.268	.347	15	3	OF-75
1925	118	373	117	18	2	6	1.6	70	43	47	23	7	.314	.421	5	3	OF-111
1926	48	56	14	2	1	0	0.0	3	6	5	9	0	.250	.321	31	7	OF-9
1927	19	41	13	1	0	0	0.0	3	4	4	3	1	.317	.341	5	2	OF-12
5 yrs.	308	820	238	36	9	6	0.7	132	84	98	62	22	.290	.378	56	15	OF-229

Bid McPhee

McPHEE, JOHN ALEXANDER
B. Nov. 1, 1859, Massena, N. Y. D. Jan. 3, 1943, San Diego, Calif.
Manager 1901-02.
BR TR 5'8" 152 lbs.

	G	AB	H	2B	3B	HR	HR %	R	RBI	BB	SO	SB	BA	SA	PH AB	PH H	G by POS
1882 CIN AA	78	311	71	8	7	1	0.3	43		11			.228	.309	0	0	2B-78
1883	96	367	90	10	10	2	0.5	61		18			.245	.343	0	0	2B-96
1884	113	462	135	10	7	5	1.1	107		27			.292	.377	0	0	2B-112
1885	110	440	121	14	5	0	0.0	78		19			.275	.330	0	0	2B-110
1886	140	562	153	23	12	7	1.2	139		59			.272	.393	0	0	2B-140
1887	129	540	156	20	19	2	0.4	137		55		95	.289	.407	0	0	2B-129
1888	111	458	110	12	10	4	0.9	88	51	43		54	.240	.336	0	0	2B-109, OF-1, 3B-1
1889	135	543	146	25	7	5	0.9	109	57	60	29	63	.269	.368	0	0	2B-135, 3B-1
1890 CIN N	132	528	135	16	22	3	0.6	125	39	82	26	55	.256	.386	0	0	2B-132
1891	138	562	144	14	16	6	1.1	107	38	74	35	33	.256	.370	0	0	2B-138
1892	144	573	167	19	12	4	0.7	111	60	84	44	44	.291	.387	0	0	2B-144
1893	127	491	138	17	11	3	0.6	101	68	94	20	25	.281	.379	0	0	2B-127
1894	128	481	154	21	9	5	1.0	113	88	90	23	33	.320	.432	0	0	2B-126
1895	115	432	129	24	12	1	0.2	107	75	73	30	30	.299	.417	0	0	2B-115
1896	117	433	132	18	7	1	0.2	81	87	51	18	48	.305	.386	0	0	2B-117
1897	81	282	85	13	7	1	0.4	45	39	35		9	.301	.408	0	0	2B-81
1898	133	486	121	26	9	1	0.2	72	60	66		21	.249	.346	0	0	2B-130, OF-3
1899	111	373	104	17	7	1	0.3	60	65	40		18	.279	.370			2B-106
18 yrs.	2138	8324	2291	307	189	52	0.6	1684	726	981	229	528	.275	.376	5	3	2B-2125, OF-4, 3B-2

Jim McQuaid

McQUAID, JAMES H.
B. Chicago, Ill. Deceased.

	G	AB	H	2B	3B	HR	HR %	R	RBI	BB	SO	SB	BA	SA	PH AB	PH H	G by POS
1898 WAS N	1	4	0	0	0	0	0.0	0	0	0		0	.000	.000	0	0	OF-1

Martin McQuaid

McQUAID, MORTIMER MARTIN
B. June 28, 1861, Chicago, Ill. D. Mar. 5, 1928, Chicago, Ill.

	G	AB	H	2B	3B	HR	HR %	R	RBI	BB	SO	SB	BA	SA	PH AB	PH H	G by POS
1891 STL AA	4	11	4	2	0	0	0.0	1	1	0	1	1	.364	.545	0	0	2B-3, OF-1

Jerry McQuaig

McQUAIG, GERALD JOSEPH
B. Jan. 31, 1912, Douglas, Ga.
BR TR 5'11" 183 lbs.

	G	AB	H	2B	3B	HR	HR %	R	RBI	BB	SO	SB	BA	SA	PH AB	PH H	G by POS
1934 PHI A	7	16	1	0	0	0	0.0	2	1	2	4	0	.063	.063	0	0	OF-6

Mox McQuery

McQUERY, WILLIAM THOMAS
B. June 28, 1861, Garrard County, Ky. D. June 12, 1900, Covington, Ky.
6'4"

	G	AB	H	2B	3B	HR	HR %	R	RBI	BB	SO	SB	BA	SA	PH AB	PH H	G by POS
1884 CIN U	35	132	37	5	0	2	1.5	31		8			.280	.364	0	0	1B-35
1885 DET N	70	278	76	15	4	3	1.1	34	30	8	29		.273	.388	0	0	1B-69, OF-1
1886 KC N	122	449	111	27	4	4	0.9	62	38	36	44		.247	.352	0	0	1B-122
1890 SYR AA	122	461	142	17	6	2	0.4	64		53		26	.308	.384	0	0	1B-122
1891 WAS AA	68	261	63	9	4	2	0.8	40	37	18	19	3	.241	.330	0	0	1B-68
5 yrs.	417	1581	429	73	18	13	0.8	231	104	123	92	29	.271	.365	0	0	1B-416, OF-1

Glenn McQuillen

McQUILLEN, GLENN RICHARD (Red)
B. Apr. 19, 1915, Strasburg, Va.
BR TR 6' 198 lbs.

	G	AB	H	2B	3B	HR	HR %	R	RBI	BB	SO	SB	BA	SA	PH AB	PH H	G by POS
1938 STL A	43	116	33	4	0	0	0.0	14	13	4	12	0	.284	.319	12	3	OF-30
1941	7	21	7	2	1	0	0.0	4	3	1	2	0	.333	.524	1	0	OF-6
1942	100	339	96	15	12	3	0.9	40	47	10	17	1	.283	.425	23	4	OF-77
1946	59	166	40	3	3	1	0.6	24	12	19	18	0	.241	.313	9	1	OF-48
1947	1	1	0	0	0	0	0.0	0	0	0	0	0	.000	.000	1	0	
5 yrs.	210	643	176	24	16	4	0.6	82	75	34	49	1	.274	.379	46	8	OF-161

	G	AB	H	2B	3B	HR	HR %	R	RBI	BB	SO	SB	BA	SA	Pinch Hit AB	H	G by POS

George McQuinn

McQUINN, GEORGE HARTLEY   BL TL 5'11"   165 lbs.
B. May 29, 1909, Arlington, Va.   D. Dec. 24, 1978, Little Rock, Ark.

	G	AB	H	2B	3B	HR	HR %	R	RBI	BB	SO	SB	BA	SA	AB	H	G by POS
1936 CIN N	38	134	27	3	4	0	0.0	5	13	10	22	0	.201	.284	0	0	1B-38
1938 STL A	148	602	195	42	7	12	2.0	100	82	58	49	4	.324	.477	0	0	1B-148
1939	154	617	195	37	13	20	3.2	101	94	65	42	6	.316	.515	0	0	1B-154
1940	151	594	166	39	10	16	2.7	78	84	57	58	3	.279	.460	1	0	1B-150
1941	130	495	147	28	4	18	3.6	93	80	74	30	5	.297	.479	4	0	1B-125
1942	145	554	145	32	5	12	2.2	86	78	60	77	1	.262	.403	1	0	1B-144
1943	125	449	109	19	2	12	2.7	53	74	56	65	4	.243	.374	3	0	1B-122
1944	146	516	129	26	3	11	2.1	83	72	85	74	4	.250	.376	0	0	1B-146
1945	139	483	134	31	3	7	1.4	69	61	65	51	1	.277	.398	4	4	1B-134
1946 PHI A	136	484	109	23	6	3	0.6	47	35	64	62	4	.225	.316	2	1	1B-142
1947 NY A	144	517	157	24	3	13	2.5	84	80	78	66	0	.304	.437	2	1	1B-142
1948	94	302	75	11	4	11	3.6	33	41	40	38	0	.248	.421	7	1	1B-90
12 yrs.	1550	5747	1588	315	64	135	2.3	832	794	712	634	32	.276	.424	24	7	1B-1529

WORLD SERIES

	G	AB	H	2B	3B	HR	HR %	R	RBI	BB	SO	SB	BA	SA	AB	H	G by POS
1944 STL A	6	16	7	2	0	1	6.3	2	5	7	2	0	.438	.750	0	0	1B-6
1947 NY A	7	23	3	0	0	0	0.0	3	1	5	8	0	.130	.130	0	0	1B-7
2 yrs.	13	39	10	2	0	1	2.6	5	6	12	10	0	.256	.385	0	0	1B-13

Hal McRae

McRAE, HAROLD ABRAHAM   BR TR 5'11"   180 lbs.
B. July 11, 1946, Avon Park, Fla.

	G	AB	H	2B	3B	HR	HR %	R	RBI	BB	SO	SB	BA	SA	AB	H	G by POS
1968 CIN N	17	51	10	1	0	0	0.0	1	2	4	14	1	.196	.216	1	0	2B-16
1970	70	165	41	6	1	8	4.8	18	23	15	23	0	.248	.442	19	5	OF-46, 3B-6, 2B-1
1971	99	337	89	24	2	9	2.7	39	34	11	35	3	.264	.427	13	2	OF-91
1972	61	97	27	4	0	5	5.2	9	26	2	10	0	.278	.474	40	10	OF-12, 3B-11
1973 KC A	106	338	79	18	3	9	2.7	36	50	34	38	2	.234	.385	10	2	OF-64, DH-37, 3B-2
1974	148	539	167	36	4	15	2.8	71	88	54	68	11	.310	.475	2	0	DH-90, OF-56, 3B-1
1975	126	480	147	38	6	5	1.0	58	71	47	47	11	.306	.442	0	0	OF-114, DH-12, 3B-1
1976	149	527	175	34	5	8	1.5	75	73	64	43	22	.332	.461	3	1	DH-117, OF-31
1977	162	641	191	54	11	21	3.3	104	92	59	43	18	.298	.515	1	1	DH-116, OF-46
1978	156	623	170	39	5	16	2.6	90	72	51	62	17	.273	.429	0	0	DH-153, OF-3
1979	101	393	113	32	4	10	2.5	55	74	38	46	5	.288	.466	2	1	DH-110, OF-9
1980	124	489	145	39	5	14	2.9	73	83	29	56	10	.297	.483	4	2	DH-97, OF-4
1981	101	389	106	23	2	7	1.8	38	36	34	33	3	.272	.396	0	0	DH-97, OF-1
1982	159	613	189	46	8	27	4.4	91	133	55	61	4	.308	.542	0	0	DH-158, OF-1
1983	157	589	183	41	6	12	2.0	84	82	50	68	2	.311	.462	1	0	DH-156
1984	106	317	96	13	4	3	0.9	30	42	34	47	0	.303	.397	20	4	DH-94
16 yrs.	1842	6588	1928	448	66	169	2.6	872	981	581	694	109	.293	.458	116	28	DH-1240, OF-477, 3B-21, 2B-17

DIVISIONAL PLAYOFF SERIES

	G	AB	H	2B	3B	HR	HR %	R	RBI	BB	SO	SB	BA	SA	AB	H	G by POS
1981 KC A	3	11	1	1	0	0	0.0	0	0	1	1	0	.091	.182	0	0	DH-3

LEAGUE CHAMPIONSHIP SERIES

	G	AB	H	2B	3B	HR	HR %	R	RBI	BB	SO	SB	BA	SA	AB	H	G by POS
1970 CIN N	2	4	0	0	0	0	0.0	0	0	0	1	0	.000	.000	1	0	OF-1
1972	1	0	0	0	0	0	—	0	0	0	0	0	—	—	0	0	
1976 KC A	5	17	2	1	1	0	0.0	2	1	1	4	0	.118	.294	0	0	OF-2
1977	5	18	8	3	0	1	5.6	6	2	3	1	0	.444	.778	0	0	OF-2
1978	4	14	3	0	0	0	0.0	0	2	2	2	1	.214	.214	0	0	DH-4
1980	3	10	2	0	0	0	0.0	0	0	1	3	0	.200	.200	0	0	DH-3
1984	2	2	2	1	0	0	0.0	0	1	0	0	0	1.000	1.500	2	2	
7 yrs.	22	65	17	5	1	1	1.5	8	6	7	11	0	.262	.415	3	2	DH-7, OF-5

WORLD SERIES

	G	AB	H	2B	3B	HR	HR %	R	RBI	BB	SO	SB	BA	SA	AB	H	G by POS
1970 CIN N	3	11	5	2	0	0	0.0	1	3	0	1	0	.455	.636	0	0	OF-3
1972	5	9	4	1	0	0	0.0	1	2	0	1	0	.444	.556	2	2	OF-2
1980 KC A	6	24	9	3	0	0	0.0	3	1	2	2	0	.375	.500	0	0	DH-6
3 yrs.	14	44	18	6	0	0	0.0	5	6	2	4	0	.409	.545	2	2	DH-6, OF-5

McRemer

McREMER,
Deceased.

	G	AB	H	2B	3B	HR	HR %	R	RBI	BB	SO	SB	BA	SA	AB	H	G by POS
1884 WAS U	1	3	0	0	0	0	0.0	0		0			.000	.000	0	0	OF-1

Kevin McReynolds

McREYNOLDS, WALTER KEVIN   BR TR 6'1"   205 lbs.
B. Oct. 16, 1959, Little Rock, Ark.

	G	AB	H	2B	3B	HR	HR %	R	RBI	BB	SO	SB	BA	SA	AB	H	G by POS
1983 SD N	39	140	31	3	1	4	2.9	15	14	12	29	2	.221	.343	2	1	OF-38
1984	147	525	146	26	6	20	3.8	68	75	34	69	3	.278	.465	5	1	OF-143
2 yrs.	186	665	177	29	7	24	3.6	83	89	46	98	5	.266	.439	7	2	OF-181

LEAGUE CHAMPIONSHIP SERIES

	G	AB	H	2B	3B	HR	HR %	R	RBI	BB	SO	SB	BA	SA	AB	H	G by POS
1984 SD N	4	10	3	0	0	1	10.0	2	4	3	1	0	.300	.600	0	0	OF-4

Pete McShannic

McSHANNIC, PETER ROBERT   BB TR 5'7"   190 lbs.
B. Mar. 20, 1864, Pittsburgh, Pa.   D. Nov. 30, 1946, Toledo, Ohio

	G	AB	H	2B	3B	HR	HR %	R	RBI	BB	SO	SB	BA	SA	AB	H	G by POS
1888 PIT N	26	98	19	1	0	0	0.0	5	5	1	9	3	.194	.204	0	0	3B-26

Trick McSorley

McSORLEY, JOHN BERNARD   5'4"   142 lbs.
B. Dec. 6, 1858, St. Louis, Mo.   D. Feb. 9, 1936, St. Louis, Mo.

	G	AB	H	2B	3B	HR	HR %	R	RBI	BB	SO	SB	BA	SA	AB	H	G by POS
1884 TOL AA	21	68	17	1	0	0	0.0	12		3				.250	.265	0	0	1B-16, OF-5, 3B-1, P-1
1885 STL N	2	6	3	1	0	0	0.0	2	1	2	1		.500	.667	0	0	3B-2
1886 STL AA	5	20	3	3	0	0	0.0	1		0				.150	.300	0	0	SS-5
3 yrs.	28	94	23	5	0	0	0.0	15		5	1		.245	.298	0	0	1B-16, OF-5, SS-5, 3B-3, P-1

Paul McSweeney

McSWEENEY, PAUL A.
B. Apr. 3, 1867, St. Louis, Mo.   D. Aug. 12, 1951, St. Louis, Mo.

	G	AB	H	2B	3B	HR	HR %	R	RBI	BB	SO	SB	BA	SA	AB	H	G by POS
1891 STL AA	3	12	3	1	0	0	0.0	2	2	0		1	.250	.333	0	0	2B-3, 3B-1

	G	AB	H	2B	3B	HR	HR %	R	RBI	BB	SO	SB	BA	SA	Pinch Hit AB	Pinch Hit H	G by POS

Jim McTamany

McTAMANY, JAMES EDWARD
B. July 4, 1863, Philadelphia, Pa.   D. Apr. 16, 1916, Lenni, Pa.   BR TR 5'8"   190 lbs.

	G	AB	H	2B	3B	HR	HR %	R	RBI	BB	SO	SB	BA	SA	PH AB	PH H	G by POS
1885 BKN AA	35	131	36	7	2	1	0.8	21		9			.275	.382	0	0	OF-35
1886	111	418	106	23	10	2	0.5	86		54			.254	.371	0	0	OF-111
1887	134	520	134	22	10	1	0.2	123		76		66	.258	.344	0	0	OF-134
1888 KC AA	130	516	127	12	10	4	0.8	94	41	67		55	.246	.331	0	0	OF-130
1889 COL AA	139	529	146	21	7	4	0.8	113	52	116	66	40	.276	.365	0	0	OF-139
1890	125	466	120	27	7	1	0.2	**140**		**112**		43	.258	.352	0	0	OF-125
1891 2 teams	COL	AA (81G –	.250)		PHI	AA (58G –	.225)										
" total	139	522	125	23	12	6	1.1	116	56	101	92	33	.239	.364	0	0	OF-139
7 yrs.	813	3102	794	135	58	19	0.6	693	148	535	158	237	.256	.355	0	0	OF-813

Cal McVey

McVEY, CALVIN ALEXANDER
B. Aug. 30, 1850, Montrose Lee County, Iowa   D. Aug. 20, 1926, San Francisco, Calif.   BR TR 5'9"   170 lbs.
Manager 1873, 1878-79.

	G	AB	H	2B	3B	HR	HR %	R	RBI	BB	SO	SB	BA	SA	PH AB	PH H	G by POS
1876 CHI N	63	308	107	15	0	1	0.3	62	53	2	4		.347	.406	0	0	1B-55, P-11, C-6, OF-1, 3B-1
1877	60	266	98	9	7	0	0.0	58	36	8	11		.368	.455	0	0	C-40, 3B-17, P-17, 2B-1, 1B-1
1878 CIN N	61	271	83	10	4	2	0.7	43	28	5	10		.306	.395	0	0	3B-61, C-3
1879	81	354	105	18	6	0	0.0	64	55	8	13		.297	.381	0	0	1B-72, OF-7, P-3, 3B-1, C-1
4 yrs.	265	1199	393	52	17	3	0.3	227	172	23	38		.328	.407	0	0	1B-128, 3B-80, C-50, P-31, OF-8, 2B-1

George McVey

McVEY, GEORGE W.
B. 1864, Port Jervis, N.Y.   D. May 3, 1896, Quincy, Ill.   6'1"   185 lbs.

	G	AB	H	2B	3B	HR	HR %	R	RBI	BB	SO	SB	BA	SA	PH AB	PH H	G by POS
1885 BKN AA	6	21	3	0	0	0	0.0	2		2			.143	.143	0	0	1B-3, C-3

Bill McWilliams

McWILLIAMS, WILLIAM HENRY
B. Nov. 28, 1910, Dubuque, Iowa   BR TR 6'   185 lbs.

	G	AB	H	2B	3B	HR	HR %	R	RBI	BB	SO	SB	BA	SA	PH AB	PH H	G by POS
1931 BOS A	2	2	0	0	0	0	0.0	0	0	0	1	0	.000	.000	2	0	

Bobby Meacham

MEACHAM, ROBERT ANDRES
B. Aug. 25, 1960, Los Angeles, Calif.   BR TR 6'1"   180 lbs.

	G	AB	H	2B	3B	HR	HR %	R	RBI	BB	SO	SB	BA	SA	PH AB	PH H	G by POS
1983 NY A	22	51	12	2	0	0	0.0	5	4	4	10	8	.235	.275	0	0	SS-18, 3B-4
1984	99	360	91	13	4	2	0.6	62	25	32	70	9	.253	.328	0	0	SS-96, 2B-2
2 yrs.	121	411	103	15	4	2	0.5	67	29	36	80	17	.251	.321	0	0	SS-114, 3B-4, 2B-2

Charlie Mead

MEAD, CHARLES RICHARD
B. Apr. 9, 1921, Vermilion Alta., Canada   BL TR 6'1"   185 lbs.

	G	AB	H	2B	3B	HR	HR %	R	RBI	BB	SO	SB	BA	SA	PH AB	PH H	G by POS
1943 NY N	37	146	40	6	1	1	0.7	9	13	10	15	3	.274	.349	0	0	OF-37
1944	39	78	14	1	0	1	1.3	5	8	5	7	0	.179	.231	14	2	OF-23
1945	11	37	10	1	0	1	2.7	4	6	5	2	0	.270	.378	0	0	OF-11
3 yrs.	87	261	64	8	1	3	1.1	18	27	20	24	3	.245	.318	14	2	OF-71

Pat Meaney

MEANEY, PATRICK J.
B. 1892, Philadelphia, Pa.   D. Oct. 20, 1922, Philadelphia, Pa.   TR

	G	AB	H	2B	3B	HR	HR %	R	RBI	BB	SO	SB	BA	SA	PH AB	PH H	G by POS
1912 DET A	1	2	0	0	0	0	0.0	0	0	1		0	.000	.000	0	0	SS-1

Charlie Meara

MEARA, CHARLES EDWARD (Goggy)
B. Apr. 16, 1891, New York, N.Y.   D. Feb. 8, 1962, Kingsbridge, N.Y.   BL TR 5'10"   160 lbs.

	G	AB	H	2B	3B	HR	HR %	R	RBI	BB	SO	SB	BA	SA	PH AB	PH H	G by POS
1914 NY A	4	7	2	0	0	0	0.0	2	1	2	2	0	.286	.286	0	0	OF-3

Ray Medeiros

MEDEIROS, RAY ANTONE (Pep)
B. May 9, 1926, Oakland, Calif.   BR TR 5'10"   163 lbs.

	G	AB	H	2B	3B	HR	HR %	R	RBI	BB	SO	SB	BA	SA	PH AB	PH H	G by POS
1945 CIN N	1	0	0	0	0	0	–	0	0	0	0	0	–	–	0	0	

Joe Medwick

MEDWICK, JOSEPH MICHAEL (Ducky, Muscles)
B. Nov. 24, 1911, Carteret, N.J.   D. Mar. 21, 1975, St. Petersburg, Fla.   BR TR 5'10"   187 lbs.
Hall of Fame 1968.

	G	AB	H	2B	3B	HR	HR %	R	RBI	BB	SO	SB	BA	SA	PH AB	PH H	G by POS
1932 STL N	26	106	37	12	1	2	1.9	13	12	2	10	3	.349	.538	0	0	OF-26
1933	148	595	182	40	10	18	3.0	92	98	26	56	5	.306	.497	1	0	OF-147
1934	149	620	198	40	**18**	18	2.9	110	106	21	83	3	.319	.529	0	0	OF-149
1935	154	634	224	46	13	23	3.6	132	126	30	59	4	.353	.576	0	0	OF-154
1936	155	636	**223**	64	13	18	2.8	115	**138**	34	33	3	.351	.577	0	0	OF-155
1937	156	**633**	237	56	10	**31**	4.9	111	**154**	41	50	4	**.374**	**.641**	0	0	OF-156
1938	146	590	190	**47**	8	21	3.6	100	**122**	42	41	0	.322	.536	2	0	OF-144
1939	150	606	201	48	8	14	2.3	98	117	45	44	6	.332	.507	1	0	OF-149
1940 2 teams	STL	N (37G –	.304)		BKN	N (106G –	.300)										
" total	143	581	175	30	12	17	2.9	83	86	32	36	2	.301	.482	3	0	OF-140
1941 BKN N	133	538	171	33	10	18	3.3	100	88	38	35	2	.318	.517	2	1	OF-131
1942	142	553	166	37	4	4	0.7	69	96	32	25	2	.300	.403	2	0	OF-140
1943 2 teams	BKN	N (48G –	.272)		NY	N (78G –	.281)										
" total	126	497	138	30	3	5	1.0	54	70	19	22	1	.278	.380	6	2	OF-117, 1B-3
1944 NY N	128	490	165	24	3	7	1.4	64	85	38	24	2	.337	.441	6	1	OF-122
1945 2 teams	NY	N (26G –	.304)		BOS	N (66G –	.284)										
" total	92	310	90	17	0	3	1.0	31	37	14	14	5	.290	.374	17	3	OF-61, 1B-15
1946 BKN N	41	77	24	4	0	2	2.6	7	18	6	5	0	.312	.442	18	4	OF-18, 1B-1
1947 STL N	75	150	46	12	0	4	2.7	19	28	16	12	0	.307	.467	31	7	OF-43
1948	20	19	4	0	0	0	0.0	0	2	1	2	0	.211	.211	18	4	OF-1
17 yrs.	1984	7635	2471	540	113	205	2.7	1198	1383	437	551	42	.324	.505	107	22	OF-1853, 1B-19
WORLD SERIES																	
1934 STL N	7	29	11	0	1	1	3.4	4	5	1	7	0	.379	.552	0	0	OF-7
1941 BKN N	5	17	4	1	0	0	0.0	1	0	1	2	0	.235	.294	0	0	OF-5
2 yrs.	12	46	15	1	1	1	2.2	5	5	2	9	0	.326	.457	0	0	OF-12

	G	AB	H	2B	3B	HR	HR %	R	RBI	BB	SO	SB	BA	SA	Pinch Hit AB	Pinch Hit H	G by POS

Tommy Mee

MEE, THOMAS WILLIAM (Judge)   BR TR 5'8" 165 lbs.
B. Mar. 18, 1890, Chicago, Ill.   D. May 16, 1981, Chicago, Ill.

| 1910 STL A | 8 | 19 | 3 | 2 | 0 | 0 | 0.0 | 1 | 1 | 0 | | 0 | .158 | .263 | 0 | 0 | SS-6, 3B-1, 2B-1 |

Dad Meek

MEEK, FRANK J.
B. St. Louis, Mo.   D. Dec. 26, 1922, St. Louis, Mo.

1889 STL AA	2	2	1	0	0	0	0.0	2	1	0	0	1	.500	.500	0	0	C-2
1890	4	16	5	0	0	0	0.0	3		0		1	.313	.313	0	0	C-4
2 yrs.	6	18	6	0	0	0	0.0	5	1	0		2	.333	.333	0	0	C-6

Sammy Meeks

MEEKS, SAMUEL MACK   BR TR 5'9" 160 lbs.
B. Apr. 23, 1923, Anderson, S. C.

1948 WAS A	24	33	4	1	0	0	0.0	4	2	1	12	0	.121	.152	9	0	SS-10, 2B-1
1949 CIN N	16	36	11	2	0	2	5.6	10	6	2	6	1	.306	.528	3	1	2B-8, SS-3
1950	39	95	27	5	0	1	1.1	7	8	6	14	1	.284	.368	7	3	SS-29, 3B-2
1951	23	35	8	0	0	0	0.0	4	2	0	4	1	.229	.229	18	3	3B-4, SS-1
4 yrs.	102	199	50	8	0	3	1.5	25	18	9	36	3	.251	.337	37	7	SS-43, 2B-9, 3B-6

Dave Meier

MEIER, DAVID KEITH   BR TR 6' 185 lbs.
B. Aug. 8, 1959, Helena, Mont.

| 1984 MIN A | 59 | 147 | 35 | 8 | 1 | 0 | 0.0 | 18 | 13 | 6 | 9 | 0 | .238 | .306 | 9 | 1 | OF-50, DH-4, 3B-1 |

Dutch Meier

MEIER, ARTHUR ERNST   BR TR 6' 180 lbs.
B. Mar. 30, 1879, St. Louis, Mo.   D. Mar. 23, 1948, Chicago, Ill.

| 1906 PIT N | 82 | 273 | 70 | 11 | 4 | 0 | 0.0 | 32 | 16 | 13 | | 4 | .256 | .326 | 13 | 2 | OF-52, SS-17 |

Walt Meinert

MEINERT, WALTER HENRY   BL TL 5'7½" 150 lbs.
B. Dec. 11, 1890, New York, N. Y.   D. Nov. 9, 1958, Decatur, Ill.

| 1913 STL A | 4 | 8 | 3 | 0 | 0 | 0 | 0.0 | 0 | 1 | 3 | 1 | .375 | .375 | 1 | 1 | OF-2 |

Bob Meinke

MEINKE, ROBERT BERNARD   BR TR 5'10" 135 lbs.
Son of Frank Meinke.
B. June 25, 1887, Chicago, Ill.   D. Dec. 29, 1952, Chicago, Ill.

| 1910 CIN N | 2 | 1 | 0 | 0 | 0 | 0 | 0.0 | 0 | 0 | 1 | 0 | 0 | .000 | .000 | 0 | 0 | SS-2 |

Frank Meinke

MEINKE, FRANK LOUIS   170 lbs.
Father of Bob Meinke.
B. Oct. 18, 1862, Chicago, Ill.   D. Nov. 8, 1931, Chicago, Ill.

1884 DET N	92	341	56	5	7	6	1.8	28		6	89		.164	.273	0	0	SS-51, P-35, OF-4, 3B-3, 2B-3
1885	1	3	0	0	0	0	0.0	0		0	1		.000	.000	0	0	OF-1, P-1
2 yrs.	93	344	56	5	7	6	1.7	28		6	90		.163	.270	0	0	SS-51, P-36, OF-5, 3B-3, 2B-3

Charlie Meisel

MEISEL, CHARLES LOUIS   TR
B. Apr. 21, 1894, Cantonsville, Md.   D. Aug. 25, 1953, Baltimore, Md.

| 1915 BAL F | 1 | 4 | 0 | 0 | 0 | 0 | 0.0 | 0 | 0 | 0 | | 0 | .000 | .000 | 0 | 0 | C-1 |

George Meister

MEISTER, GEORGE B.
B. June 5, 1864, Germany   D. Aug. 24, 1908, Pittsburgh, Pa.

| 1884 TOL AA | 34 | 119 | 23 | 6 | 0 | 0 | 0.0 | 9 | | 3 | | | .193 | .244 | 0 | 0 | 3B-34 |

John Meister

MEISTER, JOHN F.
B. May 10, 1863, Allenton, Pa.   D. Jan. 17, 1923, Philadelphia, Pa.

1886 NY AA	45	186	44	7	3	2	1.1	35		4			.237	.339	0	0	OF-22, 2B-14, 3B-3, SS-1
1887	39	158	35	6	2	1	0.6	24		16		9	.222	.304	0	0	2B-59, OF-22, 3B-3, SS-1
2 yrs.	84	344	79	13	5	3	0.9	59		20		9	.230	.323	0	0	

Karl Meister

MEISTER, KARL DANIEL (Dutch)   BR TR 6' 178 lbs.
B. May 15, 1891, Marietta, Ohio   D. Aug. 13, 1967, Marietta, Ohio

| 1913 CIN N | 4 | 7 | 2 | 1 | 0 | 0 | 0.0 | 1 | 2 | 0 | 4 | 0 | .286 | .429 | 0 | 0 | OF-4 |

Moxie Meixel

MEIXEL, MERTON MERRILL   BL TR 5'10" 168 lbs.
B. Oct. 18, 1887, Lake Crystal, Minn.   D. Aug. 17, 1982, Los Angeles, Calif.

| 1912 CLE A | 2 | 2 | 1 | 0 | 0 | 0 | 0.0 | 0 | | 0 | | 0 | .500 | .500 | 2 | 1 | |

Roman Mejias

MEJIAS, ROMAN GOMEZ   BR TR 6' 175 lbs.
B. Aug. 9, 1930, Abreus, Las Villas, Cuba

1955 PIT N	71	167	36	8	1	3	1.8	14	21	9	13	1	.216	.329	20	4	OF-43
1957	58	142	39	7	4	2	1.4	12	15	6	13	2	.275	.423	17	3	OF-42
1958	76	157	42	3	2	5	3.2	17	19	2	27	0	.268	.408	21	5	OF-57
1959	96	276	65	6	1	7	2.5	28	28	21	48	1	.236	.341	4	1	OF-85
1960	3	1	0	0	0	0	0.0	0	1	0	0	0	.000	.000	1	0	
1961	4	1	0	0	0	0	0.0	1	0	0	1	0	.000	.000	1	0	OF-2
1962 HOU N	146	566	162	12	3	24	4.2	82	76	30	83	12	.286	.445	5	0	OF-142
1963 BOS A	111	357	81	18	0	11	3.1	43	39	14	36	4	.227	.370	24	4	OF-86
1964	62	101	24	3	1	2	2.0	14	4	7	16	0	.238	.347	16	4	OF-37
9 yrs.	627	1768	449	57	12	54	3.1	212	202	89	238	20	.254	.391	109	21	OF-494

Sam Mejias

MEJIAS, SAMUEL ELIAS   BR TR 6' 170 lbs.
B. May 9, 1953, Santiago, Dominican Republic

1976 STL N	18	21	3	1	0	0	0.0	1	1	2	2	2	.143	.190	1	0	OF-17
1977 MON N	74	101	23	4	1	3	3.0	14	8	2	17	1	.228	.376	20	4	OF-56
1978	67	56	13	1	0	0	0.0	9	6	2	5	0	.232	.250	10	3	OF-52, P-1

	G	AB	H	2B	3B	HR	HR %	R	RBI	BB	SO	SB	BA	SA	Pinch Hit AB	Pinch Hit H	G by POS

Sam Mejias continued

	G	AB	H	2B	3B	HR	HR%	R	RBI	BB	SO	SB	BA	SA	PH AB	PH H	G by POS
1979 2 teams	CHI	N	(31G – .182)		CIN	N	(7G – .500)										
" total	38	13	3	0	0	0	0.0	5	0	2	5	0	.231	.231	7	1	OF-28
1980 CIN N	71	108	30	5	1	1	0.9	16	10	6	13	4	.278	.370	7	2	OF-67
1981	66	49	14	2	0	0	0.0	6	7	2	9	1	.286	.327	8	2	OF-58
6 yrs.	334	348	86	13	2	4	1.1	51	31	16	51	8	.247	.330	53	12	OF-278, P-1

Dutch Mele

MELE, ALBERT ERNEST   BL TL 6'½"   195 lbs.
B. Jan. 11, 1915, New York, N. Y.   D. Feb. 12, 1975, Hollywood, Fla.

	G	AB	H	2B	3B	HR	HR%	R	RBI	BB	SO	SB	BA	SA	PH AB	PH H	G by POS
1937 CIN N	6	14	2	1	0	0	0.0	1	1	1	1	0	.143	.214	1	0	OF-5

Sam Mele

MELE, SABATH ANTHONY   BR TR 6'1"   183 lbs.
B. Jan. 21, 1923, Astoria, N. Y.
Manager 1961-67.

	G	AB	H	2B	3B	HR	HR%	R	RBI	BB	SO	SB	BA	SA	PH AB	PH H	G by POS
1947 BOS A	123	453	137	14	8	12	2.6	71	73	37	35	0	.302	.448	6	3	OF-115, 1B-1
1948	66	180	42	12	1	2	1.1	25	25	13	21	1	.233	.344	9	1	OF-55
1949 2 teams	BOS	A	(18G – .196)		WAS	A	(78G – .242)										
" total	96	310	73	13	3	3	1.0	22	32	24	48	4	.235	.326	15	2	OF-74, 1B-11
1950 WAS A	126	435	119	21	6	12	2.8	57	86	51	40	2	.274	.432	10	4	OF-99, 1B-16
1951	143	558	153	36	7	5	0.9	58	94	32	31	2	.274	.391	6	1	OF-124, 1B-15
1952 2 teams	WAS	A	(9G – .429)		CHI	A	(123G – .248)										
" total	132	451	117	21	2	16	3.5	48	69	49	42	1	.259	.421	12	2	OF-119, 1B-3
1953 CHI A	140	481	132	26	8	12	2.5	64	82	58	47	3	.274	.437	6	3	OF-138, 1B-2
1954 2 teams	BAL	A	(72G – .239)		BOS	A	(42G – .318)										
" total	114	362	97	15	4	12	3.3	39	55	30	38	1	.268	.431	19	7	OF-75, 1B-22
1955 2 teams	BOS	A	(14G – .129)		CIN	N	(35G – .210)										
" total	49	93	17	3	0	2	2.2	5	8	5	20	1	.183	.280	25	1	OF-20, 1B-1
1956 CLE A	57	114	29	7	0	4	3.5	17	20	12	20	0	.254	.421	28	8	OF-20, 1B-8
10 yrs.	1046	3437	916	168	39	80	2.3	406	544	311	342	15	.267	.408	136	32	OF-839, 1B-79

Francisco Melendez

MELENDEZ, FRANCISCO   BL TL 6'   170 lbs.
B. Jan. 25, 1964, Rio Piedras, Puerto Rico

	G	AB	H	2B	3B	HR	HR%	R	RBI	BB	SO	SB	BA	SA	PH AB	PH H	G by POS
1984 PHI N	21	23	3	0	0	0	0.0	2	1	5	0		.130	.130	13	1	1B-10

Luis Melendez

MELENDEZ, LUIS ANTONIO   BR TR 6'   165 lbs.
B. Aug. 11, 1949, Aibonito, Puerto Rico

	G	AB	H	2B	3B	HR	HR%	R	RBI	BB	SO	SB	BA	SA	PH AB	PH H	G by POS
1970 STL N	21	70	21	1	0	0	0.0	11	8	2	12	3	.300	.314	3	0	OF-18
1971	88	173	39	3	1	0	0.0	25	11	24	29	2	.225	.254	22	4	OF-66
1972	118	332	79	11	3	5	1.5	32	28	25	34	5	.238	.334	21	2	OF-105
1973	121	341	91	18	1	2	0.6	35	35	27	50	2	.267	.343	21	8	OF-95
1974	83	124	27	4	3	0	0.0	15	8	11	9	2	.218	.298	31	4	OF-46, SS-1
1975	110	291	77	8	5	2	0.7	33	27	16	25	3	.265	.347	35	6	OF-89
1976 2 teams	STL	N	(20G – .125)		SD	N	(72G – .244)										
" total	92	143	32	5	0	0	0.0	15	5	3	15	1	.224	.259	25	4	OF-68
1977 SD N	8	3	0	0	0	0	0.0	1	1	0	1	0	.000	.000	3	0	OF-2
8 yrs.	641	1477	366	50	13	9	0.6	167	122	109	175	18	.248	.318	161	30	OF-489, SS-1

Oscar Melillo

MELILLO, OSCAR DONALD (Ski, Spinach)   BR TR 5'8"   150 lbs.
B. Aug. 4, 1899, Chicago, Ill.   D. Nov. 14, 1963, Chicago, Ill.

	G	AB	H	2B	3B	HR	HR%	R	RBI	BB	SO	SB	BA	SA	PH AB	PH H	G by POS
1926 STL A	99	385	98	18	5	1	0.3	54	30	32	31	6	.255	.335	0	0	2B-88, 3B-11
1927	107	356	80	18	2	0	0.0	45	26	25	28	3	.225	.287	5	1	2B-101
1928	51	132	25	2	0	0	0.0	9	9	9	11	2	.189	.205	2	0	2B-28, 3B-19
1929	141	494	146	17	10	5	1.0	57	67	29	30	11	.296	.401	0	0	2B-141
1930	149	574	147	30	10	5	0.9	62	59	23	44	15	.256	.369	1	0	2B-148
1931	151	617	189	34	11	2	0.3	89	75	37	29	7	.306	.407	0	0	2B-151
1932	154	612	148	19	11	3	0.5	71	66	36	42	6	.242	.324	1	0	2B-153
1933	132	496	145	23	6	3	0.6	50	79	29	18	12	.292	.381	0	0	2B-130
1934	144	552	133	19	3	2	0.4	54	55	28	27	4	.241	.297	3	0	2B-141
1935 2 teams	STL	A	(19G – .206)		BOS	A	(106G – .261)										
" total	125	462	117	16	2	1	0.2	53	44	46	26	3	.253	.303	1	0	2B-123
1936 BOS A	98	327	74	12	4	0	0.0	39	32	28	16	0	.226	.287	4	2	2B-93
1937	26	56	14	2	0	0	0.0	8	6	5	4	0	.250	.286	2	1	2B-19, SS-2, 3B-2
12 yrs.	1377	5063	1316	210	64	22	0.4	591	548	327	306	69	.260	.340	19	4	2B-1316, 3B-32, SS-2

Joe Mellana

MELLANA, JOSEPH PETER   BR TR 5'10"   180 lbs.
B. Mar. 11, 1905, Oakland, Calif.   D. Nov. 1, 1969, Larkspur, Calif.

	G	AB	H	2B	3B	HR	HR%	R	RBI	BB	SO	SB	BA	SA	PH AB	PH H	G by POS
1927 PHI A	4	7	2	0	0	0	0.0	1	2	1	0		.286	.286	0	0	3B-2

Bill Mellor

MELLOR, WILLIAM HARPER   TR 6'
B. June 6, 1874, Camden, N. J.   D. Nov. 5, 1940, Bridgeton, R. I.

	G	AB	H	2B	3B	HR	HR%	R	RBI	BB	SO	SB	BA	SA	PH AB	PH H	G by POS
1902 BAL A	10	36	13	3	0	0	0.0	4	5	3		1	.361	.444	0	0	1B-10

Paul Meloan

MELOAN, PAUL (Molly)   BL TR 5'10½" 175 lbs.
B. Aug. 23, 1888, Paynesville, Mo.   D. Feb. 11, 1950, Taft, Calif.

	G	AB	H	2B	3B	HR	HR%	R	RBI	BB	SO	SB	BA	SA	PH AB	PH H	G by POS
1910 CHI A	65	222	54	6	6	0	0.0	23	23	17		4	.243	.324	0	0	OF-65
1911 2 teams	CHI	A	(1G – .333)		STL	A	(64G – .262)										
" total	65	209	55	11	2	3	1.4	30	15	15		7	.263	.378	9	0	OF-55
2 yrs.	130	431	109	17	8	3	0.7	53	38	32		11	.253	.350	9	0	OF-120

Bill Melton

MELTON, WILLIAM   BR TR 6'2"   200 lbs.
B. July 7, 1945, Gulfport, Miss.

	G	AB	H	2B	3B	HR	HR%	R	RBI	BB	SO	SB	BA	SA	PH AB	PH H	G by POS
1968 CHI A	34	109	29	8	0	2	1.8	5	16	10	32	1	.266	.394	1	0	3B-33
1969	157	556	142	26	2	23	4.1	67	87	56	106	1	.255	.433	4	1	3B-148, OF-11
1970	141	514	135	15	1	33	6.4	74	96	56	107	2	.263	.488	0	0	OF-71, 3B-70
1971	150	543	146	18	2	33	6.1	72	86	61	87	0	.269	.492	0	0	3B-148
1972	57	208	51	5	0	7	3.4	22	30	23	31	1	.245	.370	1	0	3B-56

	G	AB	H	2B	3B	HR	HR %	R	RBI	BB	SO	SB	BA	SA	Pinch Hit AB	Pinch Hit H	G by POS

Bill Melton continued

	G	AB	H	2B	3B	HR	HR %	R	RBI	BB	SO	SB	BA	SA	PH AB	PH H	G by POS
1973	152	560	155	29	1	20	3.6	83	87	75	66	4	.277	.439	0	0	3B-151, DH-1
1974	136	495	120	17	0	21	4.2	63	63	59	60	3	.242	.404	1	0	3B-123, DH-11
1975	149	512	123	16	0	15	2.9	62	70	78	106	5	.240	.359	0	0	3B-138, DH-11
1976 **CAL A**	118	341	71	17	3	6	1.8	31	42	44	53	2	.208	.328	26	7	DH-51, 1B-30, 3B-21
1977 **CLE A**	50	133	32	11	0	0	0.0	17	14	17	21	1	.241	.323	10	3	1B-15, DH-14, 3B-13
10 yrs.	1144	3971	1004	162	9	160	4.0	496	591	479	669	23	.253	.419	43	11	3B-901, DH-88, OF-82, 1B-45

Dave Melton

MELTON, DAVID OLIN
B. Oct. 3, 1928, Pampa, Tex.

BR TR 6'   185 lbs.

	G	AB	H	2B	3B	HR	HR %	R	RBI	BB	SO	SB	BA	SA	PH AB	PH H	G by POS
1956 **KC A**	3	3	1	0	0	0	0.0	0	0	0	0	0	.333	.333	0	0	OF-3
1958	9	6	0	0	0	0	0.0	0	0	0	5	0	.000	.000	6	0	OF-2
2 yrs.	12	9	1	0	0	0	0.0	0	0	0	5	0	.111	.111	6	0	OF-5

Mario Mendoza

MENDOZA, MARIO
Also known as Mario Alzpuru.
B. Dec. 26, 1950, Chihuahua, Mexico

BR TR 5'11"   170 lbs.

	G	AB	H	2B	3B	HR	HR %	R	RBI	BB	SO	SB	BA	SA	PH AB	PH H	G by POS
1974 **PIT N**	91	163	36	1	2	0	0.0	10	15	8	35	1	.221	.252	1	0	SS-87
1975	56	50	9	1	0	0	0.0	8	2	3	17	0	.180	.200	0	0	SS-53, 3B-1
1976	50	92	17	5	0	0	0.0	6	12	4	15	0	.185	.239	1	0	SS-45, 3B-2, 2B-1
1977	70	81	16	3	0	0	0.0	5	4	3	10	0	.198	.235	4	2	SS-45, 3B-19, P-1
1978	57	55	12	1	0	1	1.8	5	3	2	9	3	.218	.291	2	1	2B-21, 3B-18, SS-14
1979 **SEA A**	148	373	74	10	3	1	0.3	26	29	9	62	3	.198	.249	0	0	SS-148
1980	114	277	68	6	3	2	0.7	27	14	16	42	3	.245	.310	0	0	SS-114
1981 **TEX A**	88	229	53	6	1	0	0.0	18	22	7	25	2	.231	.266	0	0	SS-88
1982	12	17	2	0	0	0	0.0	1	0	0	4	0	.118	.118	0	0	SS-12
9 yrs.	686	1337	287	33	9	4	0.3	106	101	52	219	12	.215	.262	8	3	SS-606, 3B-40, 2B-22, P-1

LEAGUE CHAMPIONSHIP SERIES

	G	AB	H	2B	3B	HR	HR %	R	RBI	BB	SO	SB	BA	SA	PH AB	PH H	G by POS
1974 **PIT N**	3	5	1	0	0	0	0.0	0	1	1	0	0	.200	.200	0	0	SS-3

Mike Mendoza

MENDOZA, MICHAEL JOSEPH
B. Nov. 26, 1955, Inglewood, Calif.

BR TR 6'5"   215 lbs.

	G	AB	H	2B	3B	HR	HR %	R	RBI	BB	SO	SB	BA	SA	PH AB	PH H	G by POS
1979 **HOU N**	2	0	0	0	0	0	–	0	0	0	0	0	–	–	0	0	P-1

Minny Mendoza

MENDOZA, CHRISTOBAL RIGOBERTO
Also known as Christobal Rigoberto Aizpuru.
B. Nov. 16, 1933, Ceiba Del Agua, Cuba

BR TR 6'   180 lbs.

	G	AB	H	2B	3B	HR	HR %	R	RBI	BB	SO	SB	BA	SA	PH AB	PH H	G by POS
1970 **MIN A**	16	16	3	0	0	0	0.0	2	2	0	1	0	.188	.188	9	2	3B-5, 2B-4

Jock Menefee

MENEFEE, JOHN
B. Jan. 15, 1868, West Virginia   D. Mar. 11, 1953, Belle Vernon, Pa.

BR TR

	G	AB	H	2B	3B	HR	HR %	R	RBI	BB	SO	SB	BA	SA	PH AB	PH H	G by POS
1892 **PIT N**	2	3	0	0	0	0	0.0	0	0	0	0	0	.000	.000	0	0	OF-1, P-1
1893 **LOU N**	22	73	20	2	1	0	0.0	10	12	13	5	2	.274	.329	0	0	P-15, OF-7
1894 2 teams			LOU N (29G – .165)			PIT N (13G – .255)											
" total	42	126	25	2	2	0	0.0	13	11	11	10	4	.198	.246	0	0	P-41, 2B-1
1895 **PIT N**	2	0	0	0	0	0	–	0	0	0	0	0	–	–	0	0	P-2
1898 **NY N**	1	5	0	0	0	0	0.0	0	0	0		0	.000	.000	0	0	P-1
1900 **CHI N**	17	46	5	0	0	0	0.0	5	4	2		0	.109	.109	1	0	P-16
1901	48	152	39	5	3	0	0.0	19	13	8		4	.257	.329	1	0	OF-24, P-21, 1B-2, 2B-1
1902	65	216	50	4	1	0	0.0	24	15	15		4	.231	.259	0	0	OF-23, P-22, 1B-18, 3B-2, 2B-1
1903	22	64	13	3	0	0	0.0	3	2	3		0	.203	.250	0	0	P-20, 1B-2
9 yrs.	221	685	152	16	7	0	0.0	74	57	52	15	14	.222	.266	2	0	P-139, OF-55, 1B-22, 2B-3, 3B-2

Denis Menke

MENKE, DENIS JOHN
B. July 21, 1940, Algona, Iowa

BR TR 6'   185 lbs.

	G	AB	H	2B	3B	HR	HR %	R	RBI	BB	SO	SB	BA	SA	PH AB	PH H	G by POS
1962 **MIL N**	50	146	28	3	1	2	1.4	12	16	16	38	0	.192	.267	2	0	2B-20, 3B-15, SS-9, 1B-2, OF-1
1963	146	518	121	16	4	11	2.1	58	50	37	106	6	.234	.344	2	0	SS-82, 3B-51, 2B-22, OF-1, 1B-1
1964	151	505	143	29	5	20	4.0	79	65	68	77	4	.283	.479	2	1	SS-141, 2B-15, 3B-6
1965	71	181	44	13	1	4	2.2	16	18	18	28	1	.243	.392	12	2	SS-54, 1B-8, 3B-4
1966 **ATL N**	138	454	114	20	4	15	3.3	55	60	71	87	0	.251	.412	3	1	SS-106, 3B-39, 1B-7
1967	129	418	95	14	3	7	1.7	37	39	65	62	5	.227	.325	0	0	SS-124, 3B-3
1968 **HOU N**	150	542	135	23	6	6	1.1	56	56	64	81	5	.249	.347	1	0	2B-119, SS-35, 1B-5, 3B-4
1969	154	553	149	25	5	10	1.8	72	90	87	87	2	.269	.387	0	0	SS-131, 2B-23, 1B-9, 3B-1
1970	154	562	171	26	6	13	2.3	82	92	82	80	6	.304	.441	1	0	SS-133, 2B-21, 3B-5, 1B-5, OF-3
1971	146	475	117	26	3	1	0.2	57	43	59	68	4	.246	.320	9	1	1B-101, 3B-32, SS-17, 2B-5
1972 **CIN N**	140	447	104	19	2	9	2.0	41	50	58	76	0	.233	.345	3	1	3B-130, 1B-11
1973	139	241	46	10	0	3	1.2	38	26	69	53	1	.191	.270	8	2	3B-123, SS-7, 2B-5, 1B-1
1974 **HOU N**	30	29	3	1	0	0	0.0	2	1	4	10	0	.103	.138	8	2	1B-12, 3B-7, 2B-3, SS-2
13 yrs.	1598	5071	1270	225	40	101	2.0	605	606	698	853	34	.250	.370	51	9	SS-841, 3B-420, 2B-233, 1B-162, OF-5

LEAGUE CHAMPIONSHIP SERIES

	G	AB	H	2B	3B	HR	HR %	R	RBI	BB	SO	SB	BA	SA	PH AB	PH H	G by POS
1972 **CIN N**	5	16	4	1	0	0	0.0	1	1	4	3	0	.250	.313	0	0	3B-5
1973	3	9	2	0	0	1	11.1	1	1	1	2	0	.222	.556	1	0	3B-2
2 yrs.	8	25	6	1	0	1	4.0	2	2	5	5	0	.240	.400	1	0	3B-7

WORLD SERIES

	G	AB	H	2B	3B	HR	HR %	R	RBI	BB	SO	SB	BA	SA	PH AB	PH H	G by POS
1972 **CIN N**	7	24	2	0	0	1	4.2	1	2	2	6	0	.083	.208	0	0	3B-7

	G	AB	H	2B	3B	HR	HR %	R	RBI	BB	SO	SB	BA	SA	Pinch Hit AB	Pinch Hit H	G by POS

Mike Menosky

MENOSKY, MICHAEL WILLIAM (Leaping Mike)
B. Oct. 16, 1894, Glen Campbell, Pa. D. Apr. 11, 1983, Detroit, Mich. BL TR 5'10" 163 lbs.

	G	AB	H	2B	3B	HR	HR%	R	RBI	BB	SO	SB	BA	SA	AB	H	G by POS
1914 PIT F	68	140	37	4	1	2	1.4	26	9	16		5	.264	.350	17	6	OF-41
1915	17	21	2	0	0	0	0.0	3	1	2		2	.095	.095	5	0	OF-9
1916 WAS A	10	37	6	1	1	0	0.0	5	3	1	10	1	.162	.243	1	0	OF-9
1917	114	322	83	12	10	1	0.3	46	34	45	55	22	.258	.366	13	4	OF-94
1919	116	342	98	15	3	6	1.8	62	39	44	46	13	.287	.401	7	3	OF-103
1920 BOS A	141	532	158	24	9	3	0.6	80	64	65	52	23	.297	.393	0	0	OF-141
1921	133	477	143	18	5	3	0.6	77	43	60	45	12	.300	.377	0	0	OF-133
1922	126	406	115	16	5	3	0.7	61	32	40	33	9	.283	.369	21	7	OF-103
1923	84	188	43	8	4	0	0.0	22	25	22	19	3	.229	.314	23	6	OF-49
9 yrs.	809	2465	685	98	38	18	0.7	382	250	295	250	90	.278	.370	87	26	OF-682

Ed Mensor

MENSOR, EDWARD E. (The Midget)
B. Nov. 7, 1886, Woodville, Ont., Canada D. Apr. 20, 1970, Salem, Ore. BB TR 5'6" 145 lbs.

	G	AB	H	2B	3B	HR	HR%	R	RBI	BB	SO	SB	BA	SA	AB	H	G by POS
1912 PIT N	39	99	26	3	2	0	0.0	19	1	23	12	10	.263	.333	5	1	OF-32
1913	44	56	10	1	0	0	0.0	9	1	8	13	2	.179	.196	15	4	OF-18, SS-1, 2B-1
1914	44	89	18	2	1	1	1.1	15	6	22	13	2	.202	.281	6	0	OF-25
3 yrs.	127	244	54	6	3	1	0.4	43	8	53	38	14	.221	.283	26	5	OF-75, SS-1, 2B-1

Ted Menze

MENZE, THEODORE CHARLES
B. Nov. 4, 1897, St. Louis, Mo. D. Dec. 23, 1969, St. Louis, Mo. BR TR 5'9" 172 lbs.

	G	AB	H	2B	3B	HR	HR%	R	RBI	BB	SO	SB	BA	SA	AB	H	G by POS
1918 STL N	1	3	0	0	0	0	0.0	0	0	2	0	.000	.000	0	0	OF-1

Rudi Meoli

MEOLI, RUDOLPH BART
B. May 1, 1951, Troy, N. Y. BL TR 5'9" 165 lbs.

	G	AB	H	2B	3B	HR	HR%	R	RBI	BB	SO	SB	BA	SA	AB	H	G by POS
1971 CAL A	7	3	0	0	0	0	0.0	0	0	0	1	0	.000	.000	3	0	
1973	120	305	68	12	1	2	0.7	36	23	31	38	2	.223	.289	1	1	SS-95, 3B-13, 2B-8
1974	36	90	22	2	0	0	0.0	9	3	8	10	2	.244	.267	5	0	3B-20, SS-8, 2B-1, 1B-1
1975	70	126	27	2	1	0	0.0	12	6	15	20	3	.214	.246	8	1	SS-28, 3B-15, 2B-11, DH-3
1978 CHI N	47	29	3	0	1	0	0.0	10	2	6	4	1	.103	.172	19	2	2B-6, 3B-5
1979 PHI N	30	73	13	4	1	0	0.0	2	6	9	15	2	.178	.260	2	0	SS-16, 2B-15, 3B-1
6 yrs.	310	626	133	20	4	2	0.3	69	40	69	88	10	.212	.267	38	4	SS-147, 3B-54, 2B-41, DH-3, 1B-1

Orlando Mercado

MERCADO, ORLANDO
B. Nov. 7, 1961, Arecibo, Puerto Rico BR TR 6' 180 lbs.

	G	AB	H	2B	3B	HR	HR%	R	RBI	BB	SO	SB	BA	SA	AB	H	G by POS
1982 SEA A	9	17	2	0	0	1	5.9	1	6	0	5	0	.118	.294	0	0	C-8, DH-1
1983	66	178	35	11	2	1	0.6	10	16	14	27	2	.197	.298	2	0	C-65
1984	30	78	17	3	1	0	0.0	5	5	4	12	1	.218	.282	3	1	C-29
3 yrs.	105	273	54	14	3	2	0.7	16	27	18	44	3	.198	.293	5	1	C-102, DH-1

Win Mercer

MERCER, GEORGE BARCLAY
B. June 20, 1874, Chester, W. Va. D. Jan. 12, 1903, San Francisco, Calif. TR 5'7" 140 lbs.

	G	AB	H	2B	3B	HR	HR%	R	RBI	BB	SO	SB	BA	SA	AB	H	G by POS
1894 WAS N	52	162	46	5	2	2	1.2	27	29	9	20	9	.284	.377	0	0	P-49, OF-4
1895	63	196	50	9	1	1	0.5	26	26	12	32	7	.255	.327	5	2	P-43, SS-7, OF-5, 3B-3, 2B-1
1896	49	156	38	1	1	1	0.6	23	14	9	18	9	.244	.282	2	1	P-46, OF-1
1897	48	135	43	2	5	0	0.0	22	19	6		7	.319	.407	2	0	
1898	80	249	80	3	5	2	0.8	38	25	18		14	.321	.398	2	1	P-33, SS-23, OF-19, 3B-5, 2B-1
1899	108	375	112	6	7	1	0.3	73	35	32		16	.299	.360	6	0	3B-62, P-23, OF-16, SS-1, 1B-1
1900 NY N	75	248	73	4	0	0	0.0	32	27	26		15	.294	.310	1	0	P-32, 3B-19, OF-14, SS-7, 2B-3
1901 WAS A	51	140	42	7	2	0	0.0	26	16	23		10	.300	.379	4	0	P-24, OF-16, 1B-7, SS-1, 3B-1
1902 DET A	35	100	18	2	0	0	0.0	8	6	6		1	.180	.200	0	0	P-35
9 yrs.	561	1761	502	39	23	7	0.4	275	197	141	70	88	.285	.345	22	4	P-285, 3B-90, OF-75, SS-39, 1B-8, 2B-5

Andy Merchant

MERCHANT, JAMES ANDERSON
B. Aug. 30, 1950, Mobile, Ala. BL TR 5'11" 185 lbs.

	G	AB	H	2B	3B	HR	HR%	R	RBI	BB	SO	SB	BA	SA	AB	H	G by POS
1975 BOS A	1	4	2	0	0	0	0.0	1	0	1	0	0	.500	.500	0	0	C-1
1976	2	2	0	0	0	0	0.0	0	0	0	2	0	.000	.000	2	0	C-1
2 yrs.	3	6	2	0	0	0	0.0	1	0	1	2	0	.333	.333	2	0	C-2

Art Merewether

MEREWETHER, ARTHUR FRANCIS (Merry)
B. July 7, 1902, East Providence, R. I. BR TR 5'9½" 155 lbs.

	G	AB	H	2B	3B	HR	HR%	R	RBI	BB	SO	SB	BA	SA	AB	H	G by POS
1922 PIT N	1	1	0	0	0	0	0.0	0	0	0	0	0	.000	.000	1	0	

Fred Merkle

MERKLE, FREDERICK CHARLES
B. Dec. 20, 1888, Watertown, Wis. D. Mar. 2, 1956, Daytona Beach, Fla. BR TR 6'1" 190 lbs.

	G	AB	H	2B	3B	HR	HR%	R	RBI	BB	SO	SB	BA	SA	AB	H	G by POS
1907 NY N	15	47	12	1	0	0	0.0	0	5	1		0	.255	.277	0	0	1B-15
1908	38	41	11	2	1	1	2.4	6	7	4		0	.268	.439	16	2	1B-11, OF-5, 3B-1, 2B-1
1909	78	236	45	9	1	0	0.0	15	20	16		7	.191	.237	8	3	1B-69, 2B-1
1910	144	506	148	35	14	4	0.8	75	70	44	59	23	.292	.441	0	0	1B-144
1911	149	541	153	24	12	12	2.2	80	84	43	60	49	.283	.438	0	0	1B-148
1912	129	479	148	22	6	11	2.3	82	84	42	70	37	.309	.449	0	0	1B-129
1913	153	563	147	30	12	3	0.5	78	69	41	60	35	.261	.373	0	0	1B-153
1914	146	512	132	25	7	7	1.4	71	63	52	80	23	.258	.375	0	0	1B-146
1915	140	505	151	25	3	4	0.8	52	62	36	39	20	.299	.384	1	0	1B-111, OF-29
1916 2 teams		NY	N (112G –	.237)		BKN	N	(23G –	.232)								
" total	135	470	111	20	3	7	1.5	51	46	40	50	19	.236	.336	5	2	1B-127, OF-4
1917 2 teams		BKN	N (2G –	.125)		CHI	N	(146G –	.266)								
" total	148	557	147	31	9	3	0.5	66	57	42	61	13	.264	.368	1	0	1B-142, OF-6
1918 CHI N	129	482	143	25	5	3	0.6	55	65	35	36	21	.297	.388	0	0	1B-129

	G	AB	H	2B	3B	HR	HR %	R	RBI	BB	SO	SB	BA	SA	Pinch Hit AB	Pinch Hit H	G by POS

Fred Merkle continued

	G	AB	H	2B	3B	HR	HR %	R	RBI	BB	SO	SB	BA	SA	AB	H	G by POS
1919	133	498	133	20	6	3	0.6	52	62	33	35	20	.267	.349	0	0	1B-132
1920	92	330	94	20	4	3	0.9	33	38	24	32	3	.285	.397	6	0	1B-85, OF-1
1925 NY A	7	13	5	1	0	0	0.0	4	1	1	1	1	.385	.462	2	1	1B-5
1926	1	2	0	0	0	0	0.0	0	0	0	0	0	.000	.000	0	0	1B-1
16 yrs.	1637	5782	1580	290	83	61	1.1	720	733	454	583	271	.273	.384	39	8	1B-1547, OF-45, 2B-2, 3B-1

WORLD SERIES

	G	AB	H	2B	3B	HR	HR %	R	RBI	BB	SO	SB	BA	SA	AB	H	G by POS
1911 NY N	6	20	3	1	0	0	0.0	1	1	2	6	1	.150	.200	0	0	1B-6
1912	8	33	9	2	1	0	0.0	5	3	0	7	1	.273	.394	0	0	1B-8
1913	4	13	3	0	0	1	7.7	3	3	1	2	0	.231	.462	0	0	1B-4
1916 BKN N	3	4	1	0	0	0	0.0	0	0	2	0	0	.250	.250	1	0	1B-1
1918 CHI N	6	18	5	0	0	0	0.0	1	1	4	3	0	.278	.278	0	0	1B-6
5 yrs.	27	88	21	3	1	1	1.1	10	8	9	18	1	.239	.330	1	0	1B-25

Ed Merrill

              5'11"   176 lbs.

MERRILL, EDWARD S.
B. 1860, Chicago, Ill.   Deceased.

	G	AB	H	2B	3B	HR	HR %	R	RBI	BB	SO	SB	BA	SA	AB	H	G by POS
1882 WOR N	2	8	1	0	0	0	0.0	4		0	1		.125	.125	0	0	3B-2
1884 IND AA	55	196	35	3	1	0	0.0	14		6			.179	.204	0	0	2B-55
2 yrs.	57	204	36	3	1	0	0.0	14		6	1		.176	.201	0	0	2B-55, 3B-2

Lloyd Merriman

             BL TL 6'   190 lbs.

MERRIMAN, LLOYD ARCHER (Citation)
B. Aug. 2, 1924, Clovis, Calif.

	G	AB	H	2B	3B	HR	HR %	R	RBI	BB	SO	SB	BA	SA	AB	H	G by POS
1949 CIN N	103	287	66	12	5	4	1.4	35	26	21	36	2	.230	.348	11	1	OF-86
1950	92	298	77	15	3	2	0.7	44	31	30	23	6	.258	.349	4	1	OF-84
1951	114	359	87	23	2	5	1.4	34	36	31	34	8	.242	.359	14	4	OF-102
1954	73	112	30	8	1	0	0.0	12	16	23	10	3	.268	.357	38	11	OF-25
1955 2 teams	CHI A	(1G –	.000)					CHI N	(72G –	.214)							
" total	73	146	31	6	1	1	0.7	15	8	21	21	1	.212	.288	20	4	OF-49
5 yrs.	455	1202	291	64	12	12	1.0	140	117	126	124	20	.242	.345	87	21	OF-346

Bill Merritt

             BR TR 5'7"   160 lbs.

MERRITT, WILLIAM HENRY
B. July 30, 1870, Lowell, Mass.   D. Nov. 17, 1937, Lowell, Mass.

	G	AB	H	2B	3B	HR	HR %	R	RBI	BB	SO	SB	BA	SA	AB	H	G by POS
1891 CHI N	11	42	9	1	0	0	0.0	4	4	2	2	0	.214	.238	0	0	C-11, 1B-1
1892 LOU N	46	168	33	4	2	1	0.6	22	13	11	15	3	.196	.262	0	0	C-46
1893 BOS N	39	141	49	6	3	3	2.1	30	26	13	13	3	.348	.496	0	0	C-37, OF-2
1894 3 teams	BOS	N	(10G –	.231)		PIT	N	(36G –	.275)		CIN	N	(29G –	.327)			
" total	75	248	73	8	3	2	0.8	38	45	32	10	6	.294	.375	4	0	C-60, 1B-5, OF-4, 3B-3
1895 2 teams	CIN	N	(22G –	.177)		PIT	N	(67G –	.285)								
" total	89	318	82	7	1	0	0.0	41	39	24	21	4	.258	.286	1	0	C-83, 1B-2, 2B-1
1896 PIT N	77	282	82	8	2	1	0.4	26	42	18	10	3	.291	.344	3	1	C-62, 3B-5, 2B-3, 1B-3, SS-2
1897	62	209	55	6	1	1	0.5	21	26	9		2	.263	.316	2	0	C-53, 1B-7
1899 BOS N	1	2	0	0	0	0	0.0	0	0	0	0	0	.000	.000	0	0	C-1
8 yrs.	400	1410	383	40	12	8	0.6	182	195	109	71	21	.272	.334	10	1	C-353, 1B-18, 3B-8, OF-6, 2B-4, SS-2

George Merritt

                TR 6'   160 lbs.

MERRITT, GEORGE WASHINGTON
B. Apr. 14, 1880, Paterson, N.J.   D. Feb. 21, 1938, Memphis, Tenn.

	G	AB	H	2B	3B	HR	HR %	R	RBI	BB	SO	SB	BA	SA	AB	H	G by POS
1901 PIT N	4	11	3	1	0	0	0.0	2	0	0		0	.273	.455	1	0	P-3
1902	2	9	3	1	0	0	0.0	2	2	0		0	.333	.444	0	0	OF-2
1903	9	27	4	0	1	0	0.0	4	3	2		1	.148	.222	0	0	OF-7, P-1
3 yrs.	15	47	10	2	1	0	0.0	8	5	2		1	.213	.319	1	0	OF-9, P-4

Herm Merritt

                BR TR

MERRITT, HERMAN G.
B. Nov. 12, 1900, Independence, Kans.   D. May 26, 1957, Kansas City, Mo.

	G	AB	H	2B	3B	HR	HR %	R	RBI	BB	SO	SB	BA	SA	AB	H	G by POS
1921 DET A	20	46	17	1	2	0	0.0	3	6	1	5	1	.370	.478	1	0	SS-17

Howard Merritt

             BR TL 5'11"   170 lbs.

MERRITT, JOHN HOWARD (Lefty)
B. Oct. 6, 1894, Plantersville, Miss.   D. Nov. 3, 1955, Tupelo, Miss.

	G	AB	H	2B	3B	HR	HR %	R	RBI	BB	SO	SB	BA	SA	AB	H	G by POS
1913 NY N	1	0	0	0	0	0	–	0	0	0	0	0	–	–	0	0	OF-1

Jack Merson

             BR TR 5'11"   175 lbs.

MERSON, JOHN WARREN
B. Jan. 17, 1922, Elkridge, Md.

	G	AB	H	2B	3B	HR	HR %	R	RBI	BB	SO	SB	BA	SA	AB	H	G by POS
1951 PIT N	13	50	18	2	2	1	2.0	6	14	1	7	0	.360	.540	0	0	2B-13
1952	111	398	98	20	2	5	1.3	41	38	22	38	1	.246	.344	3	0	2B-81, 3B-27
1953 BOS A	1	4	0	0	0	0	0.0	0	0	0	0	0	.000	.000	0	0	2B-1
3 yrs.	125	452	116	22	4	6	1.3	47	52	23	45	1	.257	.363	3	0	2B-95, 3B-27

Sam Mertes

             BR TR 5'10"   185 lbs.

MERTES, SAMUEL BLAIR (Sandow)
B. Aug. 6, 1872, San Francisco, Calif.   D. Mar. 11, 1945, San Francisco, Calif.

	G	AB	H	2B	3B	HR	HR %	R	RBI	BB	SO	SB	BA	SA	AB	H	G by POS
1896 PHI N	37	143	34	4	4	0	0.0	20	14	8	10	19	.238	.322	1	0	OF-35, SS-1, 2B-1
1898 CHI N	83	269	80	4	8	1	0.4	45	47	34		27	.297	.383	5	0	OF-60, SS-14, 2B-4, 1B-2
1899	117	426	127	13	16	9	2.1	83	81	33		45	.298	.467	0	0	OF-108, 1B-3, SS-1
1900	127	481	142	25	4	7	1.5	72	60	42		38	.295	.407	0	0	OF-88, 1B-33, SS-7
1901 CHI A	137	545	151	16	17	5	0.9	94	98	52		46	.277	.396	0	0	2B-132, OF-5
1902	129	497	140	23	7	1	0.2	60	79	37		46	.282	.362	0	0	OF-120, SS-5, C-2, 3B-1, 2B-1, 1B-1, P-1
1903 NY N	138	517	145	32	14	7	1.4	100	104	61		45	.280	.437	0	0	OF-137, 1B-1, C-1
1904	148	532	147	28	11	4	0.8	83	78	54		47	.276	.393	0	0	OF-147, SS-1
1905	150	551	154	27	17	5	0.9	81	108	56		52	.279	.417	0	0	OF-150
1906 2 teams	NY	N	(71G –	.237)		STL	N	(53G –	.246)								
" total	124	444	107	16	10	1	0.2	57	52	45		31	.241	.329	0	0	OF-124
10 yrs.	1190	4405	1227	188	108	40	0.9	695	721	422	10	396	.279	.398	11	0	OF-974, 2B-138, 1B-40, SS-29, C-3, 3B-1, P-1

WORLD SERIES

	G	AB	H	2B	3B	HR	HR %	R	RBI	BB	SO	SB	BA	SA	AB	H	G by POS
1905 NY N	5	17	3	1	0	0	0.0	2	3	2	5	0	.176	.235	0	0	OF-5

	G	AB	H	2B	3B	HR	HR%	R	RBI	BB	SO	SB	BA	SA	Pinch Hit AB	Pinch Hit H	G by POS

Lennie Merullo

MERULLO, LEONARD RICHARD
B. May 5, 1917, Boston, Mass.   BR TR 5'11½" 166 lbs.

	G	AB	H	2B	3B	HR	HR%	R	RBI	BB	SO	SB	BA	SA	AB	H	G by POS
1941 CHI N	7	17	6	1	0	0	0.0	3	1	2	0	1	.353	.412	0	0	SS-7
1942	143	515	132	23	3	2	0.4	53	37	35	45	14	.256	.324	0	0	SS-143
1943	129	453	115	18	3	1	0.2	37	25	26	42	7	.254	.313	0	0	SS-125, 3B-2, 2B-1
1944	66	193	41	8	1	1	0.5	20	16	16	18	3	.212	.280	6	1	SS-56, 1B-1
1945	121	394	94	18	0	2	0.5	40	37	31	30	7	.239	.299	0	0	SS-118
1946	65	126	19	8	0	0	0.0	14	7	11	13	2	.151	.214	1	0	SS-44
1947	108	373	90	16	1	0	0.0	24	29	15	26	4	.241	.290	0	0	SS-108
7 yrs.	639	2071	497	92	8	6	0.3	191	152	136	174	38	.240	.301	7	1	SS-601, 3B-2, 2B-1, 1B-1
WORLD SERIES																	
1945 CHI N	3	2	0	0	0	0	0.0	0	0	0	1	0	.000	.000	0	0	SS-3

Steve Mesner

MESNER, STEPHEN MATHIAS
B. Jan. 13, 1918, Los Angeles, Calif.   D. Apr. 6, 1981, San Diego, Calif.   BR TR 5'9" 178 lbs.

	G	AB	H	2B	3B	HR	HR%	R	RBI	BB	SO	SB	BA	SA	AB	H	G by POS
1938 CHI N	2	4	1	0	0	0	0.0	2	0	1	1	0	.250	.250	1	0	SS-1
1939	17	43	12	4	0	0	0.0	7	6	3	4	0	.279	.372	3	0	SS-12, 3B-1, 2B-1
1941 STL N	24	69	10	1	0	0	0.0	8	10	5	6	0	.145	.159	1	0	3B-22
1943 CIN N	137	504	137	26	1	0	0.0	53	52	26	20	6	.272	.327	7	4	3B-130
1944	121	414	100	17	4	1	0.2	31	47	34	20	1	.242	.309	1	0	3B-120
1945	150	540	137	19	1	1	0.2	52	52	52	18	4	.254	.298	0	0	3B-148, 2B-3
6 yrs.	451	1574	397	67	6	2	0.1	153	167	121	69	11	.252	.306	13	4	3B-421, SS-13, 2B-4

Bobby Messenger

MESSENGER, CHARLES WALTER
B. Mar. 19, 1884, Bangor, Me.   D. July 10, 1951, Bath, Me.   BL TR 5'10½" 165 lbs.

	G	AB	H	2B	3B	HR	HR%	R	RBI	BB	SO	SB	BA	SA	AB	H	G by POS
1909 CHI A	31	112	19	1	1	0	0.0	18	0	13		7	.170	.196	0	0	OF-31
1910	9	26	6	0	1	0	0.0	7	4	4		3	.231	.308	1	0	OF-9
1911	13	17	2	0	1	0	0.0	4	0	3		0	.118	.235	9	2	OF-4
1914 STL A	1	2	0	0	0	0	0.0	0	0	0	0	0	.000	.000	0	0	OF-1
4 yrs.	54	157	27	1	3	0	0.0	29	4	20	0	10	.172	.217	10	2	OF-45

Tom Messitt

MESSITT, THOMAS JOHN
B. July 27, 1874, Philadelphia, Pa.   D. Sept. 22, 1934, Chicago, Ill.

	G	AB	H	2B	3B	HR	HR%	R	RBI	BB	SO	SB	BA	SA	AB	H	G by POS
1899 LOU N	3	11	1	0	0	0	0.0	0	0	0		0	.091	.091	0	0	C-3

Scat Metha

METHA, FRANK JOSEPH
B. Dec. 13, 1913, Los Angeles, Calif.   D. Mar. 2, 1975, Fountain Valley, Calif.   BR TR 5'11" 165 lbs.

	G	AB	H	2B	3B	HR	HR%	R	RBI	BB	SO	SB	BA	SA	AB	H	G by POS
1940 DET A	26	37	9	0	1	0	0.0	6	3	2	8	0	.243	.297	2	0	2B-10, 3B-6

Bud Metheny

METHENY, ARTHUR BEAUREGARD
B. June 1, 1915, St. Louis, Mo.   BL TL 5'11" 190 lbs.

	G	AB	H	2B	3B	HR	HR%	R	RBI	BB	SO	SB	BA	SA	AB	H	G by POS
1943 NY A	103	360	94	18	2	9	2.5	51	36	39	34	2	.261	.397	10	1	OF-91
1944	137	518	124	16	1	14	2.7	72	67	56	57	5	.239	.355	4	0	OF-132
1945	133	509	126	18	2	8	1.6	64	53	54	31	5	.248	.338	4	0	OF-128
1946	3	3	0	0	0	0	0.0	0	0	0	0	0	.000	.000	3	0	
4 yrs.	376	1390	344	52	5	31	2.2	187	156	149	122	12	.247	.359	21	1	OF-351
WORLD SERIES																	
1943 NY A	2	8	1	0	0	0	0.0	0	0	0	2	0	.125	.125	0	0	OF-2

Catfish Metkovich

METKOVICH, GEORGE MICHAEL
B. Oct. 8, 1921, Angel's Camp, Calif.   BL TL 6'1" 185 lbs.

	G	AB	H	2B	3B	HR	HR%	R	RBI	BB	SO	SB	BA	SA	AB	H	G by POS
1943 BOS A	78	321	79	14	4	5	1.6	34	27	19	38	1	.246	.361	0	0	OF-76, 1B-2
1944	134	549	152	28	8	9	1.6	94	59	31	57	13	.277	.406	2	1	OF-82, 1B-50
1945	138	539	140	26	3	5	0.9	65	62	51	70	19	.260	.347	3	0	1B-97, OF-42
1946	86	281	69	15	2	4	1.4	42	25	36	39	8	.246	.356	3	0	OF-81
1947 CLE A	126	473	120	22	7	5	1.1	68	40	32	51	5	.254	.362	6	2	OF-119, 1B-1
1949 CHI A	93	338	80	9	4	5	1.5	50	45	41	24	5	.237	.331	5	1	OF-87
1951 PIT N	120	423	124	21	3	3	0.7	51	40	28	23	3	.293	.378	13	6	OF-69, 1B-37
1952	125	373	101	18	3	7	1.9	41	41	32	29	5	.271	.391	20	4	1B-72, OF-33
1953 2 teams		PIT	N (26G –		.146)		CHI	N (61G –		.234)							
" total	87	165	35	9	1	3	1.8	24	19	22	13	2	.212	.333	33	8	OF-42, 1B-12
1954 MIL N	68	123	34	5	1	1	0.8	7	15	15	15	0	.276	.358	31	9	1B-18, OF-13
10 yrs.	1055	3585	934	167	36	47	1.3	476	373	307	359	61	.261	.367	116	31	OF-644, 1B-289
WORLD SERIES																	
1946 BOS A	2	2	1	1	0	0	0.0	1	0	0	0	0	.500	1.000	2	1	

Charlie Metro

METRO, CHARLES
Born Charles Moreskonich.
B. Apr. 28, 1919, Nanty-Glo, Pa.
Manager 1962, 1970.   BR TR 5'11½" 178 lbs.

	G	AB	H	2B	3B	HR	HR%	R	RBI	BB	SO	SB	BA	SA	AB	H	G by POS
1943 DET A	44	40	8	0	0	0	0.0	12	2	3	6	1	.200	.200	2	0	OF-14
1944 2 teams		DET	A (38G –		.192)		PHI	A (24G –		.100)							
" total	62	118	19	0	1	0	0.0	12	6	10	16	1	.161	.178	8	2	OF-31, 3B-5, 2B-2
1945 PHI A	65	200	42	10	1	3	1.5	18	15	23	33	1	.210	.315	9	3	OF-57
3 yrs.	171	358	69	10	2	3	0.8	42	23	36	55	3	.193	.257	19	5	OF-102, 3B-5, 2B-2

Lenny Metz

METZ, LEONARD RAYMOND
B. July 6, 1899, Louisville, Colo.   D. Feb. 24, 1953, Denver, Colo.   BR TR 5'11" 178 lbs.

	G	AB	H	2B	3B	HR	HR%	R	RBI	BB	SO	SB	BA	SA	AB	H	G by POS
1923 PHI N	12	37	8	0	0	0	0.0	4	3	4	3	0	.216	.216	0	0	SS-6, 2B-6
1924	7	7	2	0	0	0	0.0	1	1	1	0	0	.286	.286	0	0	SS-6
1925	11	14	0	0	0	0	0.0	1	0	0	2	0	.000	.000	0	0	SS-9, 2B-2
3 yrs.	30	58	10	0	0	0	0.0	6	4	5	5	0	.172	.172	0	0	SS-21, 2B-8

	G	AB	H	2B	3B	HR	HR %	R	RBI	BB	SO	SB	BA	SA	Pinch Hit AB	Pinch Hit H	G by POS

Roger Metzger

METZGER, ROGER HENRY
B. Oct. 10, 1947, Fredericksburg, Tex.
BB TR 6'   165 lbs.

	G	AB	H	2B	3B	HR	HR %	R	RBI	BB	SO	SB	BA	SA	PH AB	PH H	G by POS
1970 CHI N	1	2	0	0	0	0	0.0	0	0	0	0	0	.000	.000	0	0	SS-1
1971 HOU N	150	562	132	14	11	0	0.0	64	26	44	50	15	.235	.299	1	1	SS-148
1972	153	641	142	12	3	2	0.3	84	38	60	71	23	.222	.259	0	0	SS-153
1973	154	580	145	11	14	1	0.2	67	35	39	70	10	.250	.322	1	0	SS-149
1974	143	572	145	18	10	0	0.0	66	30	37	73	9	.253	.320	0	0	SS-143
1975	127	450	102	7	9	2	0.4	54	26	41	39	4	.227	.296	2	1	SS-126
1976	152	481	101	13	8	0	0.0	37	29	52	63	1	.210	.270	1	0	SS-150, 2B-2
1977	97	269	50	9	6	0	0.0	24	16	32	24	2	.186	.264	1	0	SS-96, 2B-1
1978 2 teams	HOU N (45G – .220)					SF N (75G – .260)											
" total	120	358	88	10	2	0	0.0	28	23	24	26	8	.246	.285	4	1	SS-116, 2B-1
1979 SF N	94	259	65	7	8	0	0.0	24	31	23	31	11	.251	.340	6	1	SS-78, 2B-10, 3B-1
1980	28	27	2	0	0	0	0.0	5	0	3	2	0	.074	.074	8	1	SS-13, 2B-1
11 yrs.	1219	4201	972	101	71	5	0.1	453	254	355	449	83	.231	.293	23	5	SS-1173, 2B-15, 3B-1

Bill Metzig

METZIG, WILLIAM ANDREW
B. Dec. 4, 1920, Fort Dodge, Iowa
BR TR 6'1"   180 lbs.

	G	AB	H	2B	3B	HR	HR %	R	RBI	BB	SO	SB	BA	SA	PH AB	PH H	G by POS
1944 CHI A	5	16	2	0	0	0	0.0	1	1	1	4	0	.125	.125	0	0	2B-5

Alex Metzler

METZLER, ALEXANDER
B. Jan. 4, 1903, Fresno, Calif.   D. Nov. 30, 1973, Fresno, Calif.
BL TR 5'9"   167 lbs.

	G	AB	H	2B	3B	HR	HR %	R	RBI	BB	SO	SB	BA	SA	PH AB	PH H	G by POS
1925 CHI N	9	38	7	2	0	0	0.0	2	2	3	7	0	.184	.237	0	0	OF-9
1926 PHI A	20	67	16	3	0	0	0.0	8	12	7	5	1	.239	.284	3	1	OF-17
1927 CHI A	134	543	173	29	11	3	0.6	87	61	61	39	15	.319	.429	0	0	OF-134
1928	139	464	141	18	14	3	0.6	71	55	77	30	16	.304	.422	6	2	OF-134
1929	146	568	156	23	13	2	0.4	80	49	80	45	11	.275	.371	4	0	OF-141
1930 2 teams	CHI A (56G – .184)					STL A (56G – .258)											
" total	112	285	68	10	3	1	0.4	42	28	32	18	5	.239	.305	24	4	OF-83
6 yrs.	560	1965	561	85	41	9	0.5	290	207	260	144	48	.285	.384	37	7	OF-518

Bob Meusel

MEUSEL, ROBERT WILLIAM (Long Bob)
Brother of Irish Meusel.
B. July 19, 1896, San Jose, Calif.   D. Nov. 28, 1977, Downey, Calif.
BR TR 6'3"   190 lbs.

	G	AB	H	2B	3B	HR	HR %	R	RBI	BB	SO	SB	BA	SA	PH AB	PH H	G by POS
1920 NY A	119	460	151	40	7	11	2.4	75	83	20	72	4	.328	.517	8	5	OF-64, 3B-45, 1B-2
1921	149	598	190	40	16	24	4.0	104	135	34	88	17	.318	.559	2	2	OF-147
1922	121	473	151	26	11	16	3.4	61	84	40	58	13	.319	.522	0	0	OF-121
1923	132	460	144	29	10	9	2.0	59	91	31	52	13	.313	.478	9	4	OF-121
1924	143	579	188	40	11	12	2.1	93	120	32	43	26	.325	.494	0	0	OF-143, 3B-2
1925	156	624	181	34	12	33	5.3	101	138	54	55	10	.290	.542	0	0	OF-131, 3B-27
1926	108	413	130	22	3	12	2.9	73	81	37	32	16	.315	.470	1	0	OF-107
1927	135	516	174	47	9	8	1.6	75	103	45	58	24	.337	.510	3	1	OF-131
1928	131	518	154	45	5	11	2.1	77	113	47	56	6	.297	.467	0	0	OF-96
1929	100	391	102	15	3	10	2.6	46	57	17	42	2	.261	.391	3	0	OF-112
1930 CIN N	113	443	128	30	8	10	2.3	62	62	26	63	9	.289	.460	1	0	OF-112
11 yrs.	1407	5475	1693	368	95	156	2.8	826	1067	375	619	140	.309	.497	27	12	OF-1304, 3B-74, 1B-2
WORLD SERIES																	
1921 NY A	8	30	6	2	0	0	0.0	3	3	2	5	1	.200	.267	0	0	OF-8
1922	5	20	6	1	0	0	0.0	2	2	1	3	1	.300	.350	0	0	OF-5
1923	6	26	7	1	2	0	0.0	1	8	0	3	0	.269	.462	0	0	OF-6
1926	7	21	5	1	1	0	0.0	3	0	1	6	1	.238	.381	0	0	OF-7
1927	4	17	2	0	0	0	0.0	1	1	1	7	1	.118	.118	0	0	OF-4
1928	4	15	3	1	0	1	6.7	5	3	2	5	2	.200	.467	0	0	OF-34
6 yrs.	34	129	29	6	3	1	0.8	15	17	12	24	5	.225	.341	0	0	OF-
				4th							8th						

Irish Meusel

MEUSEL, EMIL FREDERICK
Brother of Bob Meusel.
B. June 9, 1893, Oakland, Calif.   D. Mar. 1, 1963, Long Beach, Calif.
BR TR 5'11½"   178 lbs.

	G	AB	H	2B	3B	HR	HR %	R	RBI	BB	SO	SB	BA	SA	PH AB	PH H	G by POS
1914 WAS A	1	2	0	0	0	0	0.0	0	0	0	0	0	.000	.000	0	0	OF-1
1918 PHI N	124	473	132	25	6	4	0.8	48	62	30	21	18	.279	.383	0	0	OF-120, 2B-4
1919	135	521	159	26	7	5	1.0	65	59	15	13	24	.305	.411	5	1	OF-128
1920	138	518	160	27	8	14	2.7	75	69	32	27	17	.309	.473	7	1	OF-129, 1B-3
1921 2 teams	PHI N (89G – .353)					NY N (62G – .329)											
" total	151	586	201	33	13	14	2.4	96	87	33	29	13	.343	.515	0	0	OF-147
1922 NY N	154	617	204	28	17	16	2.6	100	132	35	33	12	.331	.509	0	0	OF-154
1923	146	595	177	22	14	19	3.2	102	125	38	16	8	.297	.477	1	0	OF-145
1924	139	549	170	26	9	6	1.1	75	102	33	18	11	.310	.423	1	1	OF-138
1925	135	516	169	35	8	21	4.1	82	111	26	19	5	.328	.548	8	2	OF-126
1926	129	449	131	25	10	6	1.3	51	65	16	18	5	.292	.432	15	2	OF-112
1927 BKN N	42	74	18	3	1	1	1.4	7	7	11	5	0	.243	.351	23	6	OF-17
11 yrs.	1294	4900	1521	250	93	106	2.2	701	819	269	199	113	.310	.464	60	13	OF-1217, 2B-4, 1B-3
WORLD SERIES																	
1921 NY N	8	29	10	2	1	1	3.4	4	7	2	3	1	.345	.586	0	0	OF-8
1922	5	20	5	0	0	1	5.0	3	7	0	1	0	.250	.400	0	0	OF-5
1923	6	25	7	1	1	1	4.0	3	2	0	2	0	.280	.520	0	0	OF-6
1924	4	13	2	0	0	0	0.0	0	1	2	0	0	.154	.154	1	0	OF-23
4 yrs.	23	87	24	3	2	3	3.4	10	17	4	6	1	.276	.460	1	0	OF-23

Benny Meyer

MEYER, BERNHARD (Earache)
Brother of Lee Meyer.
B. Jan. 1, 1888, Hematite, Mo.   D. Feb. 6, 1974, Festus, Mo.
BR TR 5'9"   170 lbs.

	G	AB	H	2B	3B	HR	HR %	R	RBI	BB	SO	SB	BA	SA	PH AB	PH H	G by POS
1913 BKN N	38	87	17	0	1	1	1.1	12	10	10	14	8	.195	.253	2	0	OF-27, C-1
1914 BAL F	143	500	152	18	10	5	1.0	76	40	71		23	.304	.410	5	1	OF-132, SS-4
1915 2 teams	BAL F (35G – .242)					BUF F (93G – .231)											
" total	128	453	106	10	6	1	0.2	57	34	77		15	.234	.289	7	2	OF-122
1925 PHI N	1	1	1	0	0	0	0.0	1	0	0	0	0	1.000	2.000	0	0	2B-1
4 yrs.	310	1041	276	29	17	7	0.7	146	84	158	14	46	.265	.346	14	3	OF-281, SS-4, 2B-1, C-1

	G	AB	H	2B	3B	HR	HR %	R	RBI	BB	SO	SB	BA	SA	Pinch Hit AB	Pinch Hit H	G by POS

Billy Meyer

MEYER, WILLIAM ADAM
B. Jan. 14, 1892, Knoxville, Tenn.   D. Mar. 31, 1957, Knoxville, Tenn.
Manager 1948-52.
BR TR 5'9½" 170 lbs.

	G	AB	H	2B	3B	HR	HR %	R	RBI	BB	SO	SB	BA	SA	PH AB	PH H	G by POS
1913 CHI A	1	1	1	0	0	0	0.0	0	0	0	0	0	1.000	1.000	0	0	C-1
1916 PHI A	50	138	32	2	2	1	0.7	6	12	8	11	3	.232	.297	2	0	C-48
1917	62	162	38	5	1	0	0.0	9	9	7	14	0	.235	.278	7	0	C-55
3 yrs.	113	301	71	7	3	1	0.3	15	21	15	25	3	.236	.289	9	0	C-104

Dan Meyer

MEYER, DANIEL THOMAS
B. Aug. 3, 1952, Hamilton, Ohio
BL TR 5'11" 180 lbs.

	G	AB	H	2B	3B	HR	HR %	R	RBI	BB	SO	SB	BA	SA	PH AB	PH H	G by POS
1974 DET A	13	50	10	1	1	3	6.0	5	7	1	1	1	.200	.440	1	0	OF-12
1975	122	470	111	17	3	8	1.7	56	47	26	25	8	.236	.336	2	1	OF-74, 1B-46
1976	105	294	74	8	4	2	0.7	37	16	17	22	10	.252	.327	36	8	OF-47, 1B-19
1977 SEA A	159	582	159	24	4	22	3.8	75	90	43	51	11	.273	.442	2	0	1B-159
1978	123	444	101	18	1	8	1.8	38	56	24	39	7	.227	.327	1	0	1B-121, OF-2
1979	144	525	146	21	7	20	3.8	72	74	29	35	11	.278	.459	7	2	3B-101, OF-31, 1B-15
1980	146	531	146	25	6	11	2.1	56	71	31	42	8	.275	.407	17	3	OF-123, DH-7, 3B-5, 1B-4
1981	83	252	66	10	1	3	1.2	26	22	10	16	4	.262	.345	19	3	3B-49, OF-14, DH-3, 1B-3
1982 OAK A	120	383	92	17	3	8	2.1	28	59	19	33	1	.240	.363	29	4	1B-58, DH-38, OF-11
1983	69	169	32	9	0	1	0.6	15	13	19	11	0	.189	.260	7	1	1B-41, DH-12, OF-11, 3B-1
1984	20	22	7	3	1	0	0.0	1	4	0	2	0	.318	.545	17	4	1B-3, DH-2
11 yrs.	1104	3722	944	153	31	86	2.3	409	459	219	277	61	.254	.381	138	26	1B-469, OF-325, 3B-156, DH-62

Dutch Meyer

MEYER, LAMBERT DANIEL
B. Oct. 6, 1915, Waco, Tex.
BR TR 5'10½" 181 lbs.

	G	AB	H	2B	3B	HR	HR %	R	RBI	BB	SO	SB	BA	SA	PH AB	PH H	G by POS
1937 CHI N	1	0	0	0	0	0	—	0	0	0	0	0	—	—	0	0	
1940 DET A	23	58	15	3	0	0	0.0	12	6	4	10	2	.259	.310	3	0	2B-21
1941	46	153	29	9	1	1	0.7	12	14	8	13	1	.190	.281	6	2	2B-40
1942	14	52	17	3	0	2	3.8	5	9	4	4	0	.327	.500	0	0	2B-14
1945 CLE A	130	524	153	29	8	7	1.3	71	48	40	32	2	.292	.418	0	0	2B-130
1946	72	207	48	5	3	0	0.0	13	16	26	16	0	.232	.285	7	1	2B-64
6 yrs.	286	994	262	49	12	10	1.0	113	93	82	75	5	.264	.367	16	3	2B-269

George Meyer

MEYER, GEORGE FRANCIS
B. Aug. 3, 1909, Chicago, Ill.
BR TR 5'9" 160 lbs.

	G	AB	H	2B	3B	HR	HR %	R	RBI	BB	SO	SB	BA	SA	PH AB	PH H	G by POS
1938 CHI A	24	81	24	2	2	0	0.0	10	9	11	17	3	.296	.370	0	0	2B-24

Lee Meyer

MEYER, LEE
Brother of Benny Meyer.
TR

	G	AB	H	2B	3B	HR	HR %	R	RBI	BB	SO	SB	BA	SA	PH AB	PH H	G by POS
1909 BKN N	7	23	3	0	0	0	0.0	1	0	2		0	.130	.130	0	0	SS-7

Scott Meyer

MEYER, SCOTT WILLIAM
B. Aug. 9, 1957, Midlothian, Ill.
BR TR 6'1" 195 lbs.

	G	AB	H	2B	3B	HR	HR %	R	RBI	BB	SO	SB	BA	SA	PH AB	PH H	G by POS
1978 OAK A	8	9	1	1	0	0	0.0	1	0	0	4	0	.111	.222	2	0	C-7, DH-1

Levi Meyerle

MEYERLE, LEVI SAMUEL (Long Levi)
B. 1849, Philadelphia, Pa.   D. Nov. 4, 1921, Philadelphia, Pa.
BR TR 6'1" 177 lbs.

	G	AB	H	2B	3B	HR	HR %	R	RBI	BB	SO	SB	BA	SA	PH AB	PH H	G by POS
1876 PHI N	55	256	87	12	8	0	0.0	46	34	3	2		.340	.449	0	0	3B-49, OF-3, 2B-3, P-2
1877 CIN N	27	107	35	7	2	0	0.0	11	15	0	4		.327	.430	0	0	SS-18, 2B-12, OF-1
1884 PHI U	3	11	1	1	0	0	0.0	0		0			.091	.182	0	0	1B-2, OF-1
3 yrs.	85	374	123	20	10	0	0.0	57	49	3	6		.329	.436	0	0	3B-49, SS-18, 2B-15, OF-5, 1B-2, P-2

Bert Meyers

MEYERS, JAMES ALBERT
B. Apr. 8, 1874, Frederick, Md.   D. Dec. 12, 1915, Washington, D. C.

	G	AB	H	2B	3B	HR	HR %	R	RBI	BB	SO	SB	BA	SA	PH AB	PH H	G by POS
1896 STL N	122	454	116	12	8	0	0.0	47	37	40		32	8	.256	.317	0	0	3B-121, SS-1
1898 WAS N	31	110	29	1	4	0	0.0	14	13	13			2	.264	.345	0	0	3B-31
1900 PHI N	7	28	5	1	0	0	0.0	5	2	3			1	.179	.214	0	0	3B-7
3 yrs.	160	592	150	14	12	0	0.0	66	52	56		32	11	.253	.318	0	0	3B-159, SS-1

Chief Meyers

MEYERS, JOHN TORTES
B. July 29, 1880, Riverside, Calif.   D. July 25, 1971, San Bernardino, Calif.
BR TR 5'11" 194 lbs.

	G	AB	H	2B	3B	HR	HR %	R	RBI	BB	SO	SB	BA	SA	PH AB	PH H	G by POS
1909 NY N	90	220	61	10	5	1	0.5	15	30	22		3	.277	.382	24	8	C-64
1910	127	365	104	18	0	1	0.3	25	62	40	18	5	.285	.342	9	1	C-117
1911	133	391	130	18	9	1	0.3	48	61	25	33	7	.332	.432	4	1	C-128
1912	126	371	133	16	5	6	1.6	60	54	47	20	8	.358	.477	2	1	C-122
1913	120	378	118	18	5	3	0.8	37	47	37	22	7	.312	.410	2	1	C-116
1914	134	381	109	13	5	1	0.3	33	55	34	25	4	.286	.354	1	1	C-126
1915	110	289	67	10	5	1	0.3	24	26	26	18	4	.232	.311	7	3	C-96
1916 BKN N	80	239	59	10	0	0	0.0	21	21	26	15	2	.247	.314	11	1	C-74
1917 2 teams	BKN	N	(47G —	.212)		BOS	N	(25G —	.250)								
" total	72	200	45	7	4	0	0.0	13	7	17	11	4	.225	.300	4	0	C-68
9 yrs.	992	2834	826	120	41	14	0.5	276	363	274	162	44	.291	.378	68	16	C-925

WORLD SERIES																	
1911 NY N	6	20	6	2	0	0	0.0	2	2	0	3	0	.300	.400	0	0	C-6
1912	8	28	10	0	1	0	0.0	2	3	2	3	1	.357	.429	0	0	C-8
1913	1	4	0	0	0	0	0.0	0	0	0	0	0	.000	.000	0	0	C-1
1916 BKN N	3	10	2	0	1	0	0.0	0	1	1	0	0	.200	.400	0	0	C-3
4 yrs.	18	62	18	2	2	0	0.0	4	6	3	6	1	.290	.387	0	0	C-18

Henry Meyers

MEYERS, HENRY L.
B. 1860, Philadelphia, Pa.   D. June 28, 1898, Harrisburg, Pa.

	G	AB	H	2B	3B	HR	HR %	R	RBI	BB	SO	SB	BA	SA	PH AB	PH H	G by POS
1890 PHI AA	5	19	3	0	0	0	0.0	2		1		2	.158	.158	0	0	3B-5

	G	AB	H	2B	3B	HR	HR %	R	RBI	BB	SO	SB	BA	SA	Pinch Hit AB	Pinch Hit H	G by POS

Lew Meyers

MEYERS, LOUIS HENRY
B. Dec. 9, 1859, Cincinnati, Ohio   D. Nov. 30, 1920, Cincinnati, Ohio

BR TR 5'11" 165 lbs.

	G	AB	H	2B	3B	HR	HR %	R	RBI	BB	SO	SB	BA	SA	PH AB	PH H	G by POS
1884 CIN U	2	3	0	0	0	0	0.0	1	1	1			.000	.000	0	0	C-2, OF-1

Bob Micelotta

MICELOTTA, ROBERT PETER (Mickey)
B. Oct. 20, 1928, Corona, N. Y.

BR TR 5'11" 185 lbs.

	G	AB	H	2B	3B	HR	HR %	R	RBI	BB	SO	SB	BA	SA	PH AB	PH H	G by POS
1954 PHI N	13	3	0	0	0	0	0.0	2	0	1	1	0	.000	.000	2	0	SS-1
1955	4	4	0	0	0	0	0.0	0	0	0	0	0	.000	.000	2	0	SS-2
2 yrs.	17	7	0	0	0	0	0.0	2	0	1	1	0	.000	.000	4	0	SS-3

Gene Michael

MICHAEL, GENE RICHARD (Stick)
B. June 2, 1938, Kent, Ohio
Manager 1981-82.

BB TR 6'2" 183 lbs.

	G	AB	H	2B	3B	HR	HR %	R	RBI	BB	SO	SB	BA	SA	PH AB	PH H	G by POS
1966 PIT N	30	33	5	2	1	0	0.0	9	2	0	7	0	.152	.273	10	3	SS-8, 2B-2, 3B-1
1967 LA N	98	223	45	3	1	0	0.0	20	7	11	30	1	.202	.224	2	0	SS-83
1968 NY A	61	116	23	3	0	1	0.9	8	8	2	23	3	.198	.250	0	0	SS-43, P-1
1969	119	412	112	24	4	2	0.5	41	31	43	56	7	.272	.364	1	0	SS-118
1970	134	435	93	10	1	2	0.5	42	38	50	93	3	.214	.255	6	4	SS-123, 3B-4, 2B-3
1971	139	456	102	15	6	3	0.7	36	35	48	64	3	.224	.276	6	2	SS-136
1972	126	391	91	7	4	1	0.3	29	32	32	45	4	.233	.279	5	2	SS-121
1973	129	418	94	11	1	3	0.7	30	47	26	51	1	.225	.278	2	0	SS-129
1974	81	177	46	9	0	0	0.0	19	13	14	24	0	.260	.311	1	1	2B-45, SS-39, 3B-2
1975 DET A	56	145	31	2	0	3	2.1	15	13	8	28	0	.214	.290	1	0	SS-44, 2B-7, 3B-4
10 yrs.	973	2806	642	86	12	15	0.5	249	226	234	421	22	.229	.284	32	13	SS-844, 2B-57, 3B-11, P-1

Cass Michaels

MICHAELS, CASIMIR EUGENE
Played as Cass Kwietniewski 1943, Part of 1944.   Also known as Casimir Eugene Kwietniewski
B. Mar. 4, 1926, Detroit, Mich.   D. Nov. 12, 1982, Grosse Pointe, Mich.

BR TR 5'11" 175 lbs.

	G	AB	H	2B	3B	HR	HR %	R	RBI	BB	SO	SB	BA	SA	PH AB	PH H	G by POS
1943 CHI A	2	7	0	0	0	0	0.0	0	0	0	0	0	.000	.000	0	0	SS-2
1944	27	68	12	4	1	0	0.0	4	5	2	5	0	.176	.265	1	0	SS-21, 3B-3
1945	129	445	109	8	5	2	0.4	47	54	37	28	8	.245	.299	2	0	2B-66, 3B-13, SS-6
1946	91	291	75	8	0	1	0.3	37	22	29	36	9	.258	.296	3	0	2B-60, 3B-44, SS-2
1947	110	355	97	15	4	3	0.8	31	34	39	28	10	.273	.363	3	0	SS-85, 2B-55, OF-1
1948	145	484	120	12	6	5	1.0	47	56	69	42	8	.248	.329	4	2	SS-154
1949	154	561	173	27	9	6	1.1	73	83	101	50	5	.308	.421	0	0	2B-154
1950 2 teams		CHI A (36G – .312)				WAS A (106G – .250)											
" total	142	526	140	14	7	8	1.5	69	66	68	47	2	.266	.365	3	2	2B-139
1951 WAS A	138	485	125	20	4	4	0.8	59	45	61	41	1	.258	.340	7	2	2B-128
1952 3 teams		WAS A (22G – .233)				STL A (55G – .265)				PHI A (55G – .250)							
" total	132	452	114	16	8	5	1.1	50	50	53	42	4	.252	.356	6	2	2B-85, 3B-42
1953 PHI A	117	411	103	10	1	12	2.9	53	42	51	56	7	.251	.363	6	2	2B-110
1954 CHI A	101	282	74	13	2	7	2.5	35	44	56	31	10	.262	.397	0	0	3B-91, 2B-2
12 yrs.	1288	4367	1142	147	46	53	1.2	508	501	566	406	64	.262	.353	42	10	2B-800, SS-240, 3B-195, OF-1

Ralph Michaels

MICHAELS, RALPH JOSEPH
B. May 3, 1902, Etna, Pa.

BR TR 5'10½" 178 lbs.

	G	AB	H	2B	3B	HR	HR %	R	RBI	BB	SO	SB	BA	SA	PH AB	PH H	G by POS
1924 CHI N	8	11	4	0	0	0	0.0	2	0	0	1	0	.364	.364	3	1	SS-4
1925	22	50	14	1	0	0	0.0	10	6	6	9	1	.280	.300	3	0	3B-15, SS-1, 2B-1, 1B-1
1926	2	0	0	0	0	0	–	1	0	0	0	0	–	–	0	0	
3 yrs.	32	61	18	1	0	0	0.0	11	8	6	10	1	.295	.311	6	1	3B-15, SS-5, 2B-1, 1B-1

Ed Mickelson

MICKELSON, EDWARD ALLEN
B. Sept. 9, 1926, Ottawa, Ill.

BR TR 6'3" 205 lbs.

	G	AB	H	2B	3B	HR	HR %	R	RBI	BB	SO	SB	BA	SA	PH AB	PH H	G by POS
1950 STL N	5	10	1	0	0	0	0.0	1	0	2	3	0	.100	.100	1	0	1B-4
1953 STL A	7	15	2	1	0	0	0.0	1	2	0	6	0	.133	.200	3	0	1B-3
1957 CHI N	6	12	0	0	0	0	0.0	0	1	0	4	0	.000	.000	4	0	1B-2
3 yrs.	18	37	3	1	0	0	0.0	2	3	4	13	0	.081	.108	8	0	1B-9

Ezra Midkiff

MIDKIFF, EZRA MILLINGTON (Salt Rock)
B. Nov. 13, 1882, Salt Rock, W. Va.   D. Mar. 20, 1957, Huntington, W. Va.

BL TR 5'10" 180 lbs.

	G	AB	H	2B	3B	HR	HR %	R	RBI	BB	SO	SB	BA	SA	PH AB	PH H	G by POS
1909 CIN N	1	2	0	0	0	0	0.0	0	0	0		0	.000	.000	0	0	3B-1
1912 NY A	21	86	21	1	0	0	0.0	9	9	7		4	.244	.256	0	0	3B-21
1913	83	284	56	9	1	0	0.0	22	14	12	33	9	.197	.236	1	0	3B-76, SS-4, 2B-2
3 yrs.	105	372	77	10	1	0	0.0	31	23	19	33	13	.207	.239	1	0	3B-98, SS-4, 2B-2

Ed Mierkowicz

MIERKOWICZ, EDWARD FRANK (Butch)
B. Mar. 6, 1924, Wyandotte, Mich.

BR TR 6'4" 205 lbs.

	G	AB	H	2B	3B	HR	HR %	R	RBI	BB	SO	SB	BA	SA	PH AB	PH H	G by POS
1945 DET A	10	15	2	2	0	0	0.0	4	2	1	3	0	.133	.267	3	1	OF-6
1947	21	42	8	1	0	1	2.4	6	1	1	12	1	.190	.286	9	1	OF-10
1948	3	5	1	0	0	0	0.0	0	1	2	2	0	.200	.200	2	0	OF-1
1950 STL N	1	1	0	0	0	0	0.0	0	0	0	1	0	.000	.000	1	0	
4 yrs.	35	63	11	3	0	1	1.6	6	4	4	18	1	.175	.270	15	2	OF-17
WORLD SERIES																	
1945 DET A	1	0	0	0	0	0	–	0	0	0	0	0	–	–	0	0	OF-1

Larry Miggins

MIGGINS, LAWRENCE EDWARD (Irish)
B. Aug. 20, 1925, Bronx, N. Y.

BR TR 6'4" 198 lbs.

	G	AB	H	2B	3B	HR	HR %	R	RBI	BB	SO	SB	BA	SA	PH AB	PH H	G by POS
1948 STL N	1	1	0	0	0	0	0.0	0	0	0	0	0	.000	.000	1	0	
1952	42	96	22	5	1	2	2.1	7	10	3	19	0	.229	.365	16	4	OF-25, 1B-1
2 yrs.	43	97	22	5	1	2	2.1	7	10	3	19	0	.227	.361	17	4	OF-25, 1B-1

John Mihalic

MIHALIC, JOHN MICHAEL
B. Nov. 13, 1911, Cleveland, Ohio

BR TR 5'11" 172 lbs.

	G	AB	H	2B	3B	HR	HR %	R	RBI	BB	SO	SB	BA	SA	PH AB	PH H	G by POS
1935 WAS A	6	22	5	3	0	0	0.0	4	6	2	3	1	.227	.364	0	0	SS-6
1936	25	88	21	2	1	0	0.0	15	8	14	14	2	.239	.284	0	0	2B-25

	G	AB	H	2B	3B	HR	HR %	R	RBI	BB	SO	SB	BA	SA	Pinch Hit AB	Pinch Hit H	G by POS

John Mihalic continued

	G	AB	H	2B	3B	HR	HR %	R	RBI	BB	SO	SB	BA	SA	AB	H	G by POS
1937	38	107	27	5	2	0	0.0	13	8	17	9	2	.252	.336	5	0	2B-28, SS-3
3 yrs.	69	217	53	10	3	0	0.0	32	22	33	26	5	.244	.318	5	0	2B-53, SS-9

Eddie Miksis

MIKSIS, EDWARD THOMAS
B. Sept. 11, 1926, Burlington, N. J.   BR TR 6'½"   185 lbs.

	G	AB	H	2B	3B	HR	HR %	R	RBI	BB	SO	SB	BA	SA	AB	H	G by POS
1944 BKN N	26	91	20	2	0	0	0.0	12	11	6	11	4	.220	.242	1	0	3B-15, SS-10
1946	23	48	7	0	0	0	0.0	3	5	3	3	0	.146	.146	3	0	3B-13, 2B-1
1947	45	86	23	1	0	4	4.7	18	10	9	8	0	.267	.419	12	1	2B-13, OF-11, 3B-5, SS-2
1948	86	221	47	7	1	2	0.9	28	16	19	27	5	.213	.281	3	1	2B-54, 3B-22, SS-5
1949	50	113	25	5	0	1	0.9	17	6	7	8	3	.221	.292	8	0	3B-29, SS-4, 2B-3, 1B-1
1950	51	76	19	2	1	2	2.6	13	10	5	10	3	.250	.382	4	1	SS-15, 2B-15, 3B-7
1951 2 teams	BKN	N	(19G –	.200)		CHI	N	(102G –	.266)								
" total	121	431	114	14	3	4	0.9	54	35	34	38	11	.265	.339	5	1	2B-103, 3B-6
1952 CHI N	93	383	89	20	1	2	0.5	44	19	20	32	4	.232	.305	1	0	2B-54, SS-40
1953	142	577	145	17	6	8	1.4	61	39	33	59	13	.251	.343	0	0	2B-92, SS-53
1954	38	99	20	3	0	2	2.0	9	3	3	9	1	.202	.293	10	0	2B-21, 3B-2, OF-1
1955	131	481	113	14	2	9	1.9	52	41	32	55	3	.235	.328	2	0	OF-111, 3B-18
1956	114	356	85	10	3	9	2.5	54	27	32	40	4	.239	.360	13	6	3B-48, OF-33, 2B-19, SS-2
1957 2 teams	STL	N	(49G –	.211)		BAL	A	(1G –	.000)								
" total	50	39	8	0	0	1	2.6	3	2	7	7	0	.205	.282	15	3	OF-31
1958 2 teams	BAL	A	(3G –	.000)		CIN	N	(69G –	.140)								
" total	72	52	7	0	0	0	0.0	15	4	5	6	1	.135	.135	5	0	OF-32, 3B-14, 2B-7, SS-6, 1B-1
14 yrs.	1042	3053	722	95	17	44	1.4	383	228	215	313	52	.236	.322	82	13	2B-382, OF-219, 3B-179, SS-137, 1B-2

WORLD SERIES

	G	AB	H	2B	3B	HR	HR %	R	RBI	BB	SO	SB	BA	SA	AB	H	G by POS
1947 BKN N	5	4	1	0	0	0	0.0	1	0	0	1	0	.250	.250	3	0	OF-2
1949	3	7	2	1	0	0	0.0	0	0	0	1	0	.286	.429	1	1	3B-2
2 yrs.	8	11	3	1	0	0	0.0	1	0	0	2	0	.273	.364	4	1	OF-2, 3B-2

Clyde Milan

MILAN, JESSE CLYDE (Deerfoot)
Brother of Horace Milan.
B. Mar. 25, 1887, Linden, Tenn.   D. Mar. 3, 1953, Orlando, Fla.
Manager 1922.   BL TR 5'9"   168 lbs.

	G	AB	H	2B	3B	HR	HR %	R	RBI	BB	SO	SB	BA	SA	AB	H	G by POS
1907 WAS A	48	183	51	5	2	0	0.0	22	9	8		8	.279	.328	1	0	OF-47
1908	130	485	116	10	12	1	0.0	55	32	38		29	.239	.315	8	1	OF-122
1909	130	400	80	12	4	1	0.3	36	15	31		10	.200	.258	9	3	OF-120
1910	142	531	148	17	6	0	0.0	89	16	71		44	.279	.333	1	0	OF-142
1911	154	616	194	24	8	3	0.5	109	35	74		58	.315	.394	0	0	OF-154
1912	154	601	184	19	11	1	0.2	105	79	63		88	.306	.379	0	0	OF-154
1913	154	579	174	18	9	3	0.5	92	54	58	25	75	.301	.378	0	0	OF-154
1914	115	437	129	19	11	1	0.2	63	39	32	26	38	.295	.396	2	0	OF-113
1915	153	573	165	13	7	2	0.3	83	66	53	32	40	.288	.346	1	0	OF-151
1916	150	565	154	14	3	1	0.2	58	45	56	31	34	.273	.313	0	0	OF-149
1917	155	579	170	15	4	0	0.0	60	48	58	26	20	.294	.333	2	0	OF-153
1918	128	503	146	18	5	0	0.0	56	56	36	14	26	.290	.346	4	1	OF-124
1919	88	321	92	12	6	0	0.0	43	37	40	16	11	.287	.361	2	1	OF-86
1920	126	506	163	22	5	3	0.6	70	41	28	12	10	.322	.403	3	0	OF-123
1921	112	406	117	19	11	1	0.2	55	40	37	13	4	.288	.397	12	4	OF-98
1922	42	74	17	5	0	0	0.0	8	5	2	2	0	.230	.297	29	4	OF-11
16 yrs.	1981	7359	2100	242	104	17	0.2	1004	617	685	197	495	.285	.353	74	14	OF-1901

Horace Milan

MILAN, HORACE ROBERT
Brother of Clyde Milan.
B. Apr. 7, 1894, Linden, Tenn.   D. June 29, 1955, Texarkana, Tex.   BR TR 5'9"   175 lbs.

	G	AB	H	2B	3B	HR	HR %	R	RBI	BB	SO	SB	BA	SA	AB	H	G by POS
1915 WAS A	11	27	11	1	1	0	0.0	6	7	8	7	2	.407	.519	0	0	OF-10
1917	31	73	21	3	1	0	0.0	8	9	4	9	4	.288	.356	8	2	OF-23
2 yrs.	42	100	32	4	2	0	0.0	14	16	12	16	6	.320	.400	8	2	OF-33

Larry Milbourne

MILBOURNE, LAWRENCE WILLIAM
B. Feb. 14, 1951, Port Morris, N. J.   BB TR 6'   161 lbs.

	G	AB	H	2B	3B	HR	HR %	R	RBI	BB	SO	SB	BA	SA	AB	H	G by POS
1974 HOU N	112	136	38	2	1	0	0.0	31	9	10	14	6	.279	.309	1	0	2B-87, SS-8, OF-4
1975	73	151	32	1	2	1	0.7	17	9	6	14	1	.212	.265	4	1	2B-43, SS-22
1976	59	145	36	4	0	0	0.0	22	7	14	10	6	.248	.276	18	3	2B-32
1977 SEA A	86	242	53	10	0	2	0.8	24	21	6	20	3	.219	.285	9	1	2B-41, SS-40, DH-1, 3B-1
1978	93	234	53	6	2	2	0.9	31	20	9	6	5	.226	.295	3	2	3B-32, SS-23, 2B-15, DH-10
1979	123	356	99	13	4	2	0.6	40	26	19	20	5	.278	.354	30	12	SS-65, 2B-49, 3B-11
1980	106	258	68	6	6	0	0.0	31	26	19	13	7	.264	.333	19	3	2B-38, SS-34, DH-8, 3B-6
1981 NY A	61	163	51	7	2	1	0.6	24	12	9	14	2	.313	.399	3	2	SS-39, 2B-14, DH-3, 3B-3
1982 3 teams	NY	A	(14G –	.148)		MIN	A	(29G –	.235)		CLE	A	(82G –	.275)			
" total	125	416	107	13	5	2	0.5	40	26	20	32	3	.257	.327	8	1	2B-92, SS-30, 3B-12, DH-1
1983 2 teams	PHI	N	(41G –	.242)		NY	A	(31G –	.200)								
" total	72	136	30	4	1	0	0.0	8	6	9	17	3	.221	.265	9	1	2B-46, SS-14, 3B-7
1984 SEA A	79	211	56	5	1	1	0.5	22	22	12	16	0	.265	.313	23	8	3B-40, 2B-14, DH-6, SS-5
11 yrs.	989	2448	623	71	24	11	0.4	290	184	133	176	41	.254	.317	127	34	2B-471, SS-280, 3B-112, DH-29, OF-4

DIVISIONAL PLAYOFF SERIES

	G	AB	H	2B	3B	HR	HR %	R	RBI	BB	SO	SB	BA	SA	AB	H	G by POS
1981 NY A	5	19	6	1	0	0	0.0	4	0	0	1	0	.316	.368	0	0	SS-5

LEAGUE CHAMPIONSHIP SERIES

	G	AB	H	2B	3B	HR	HR %	R	RBI	BB	SO	SB	BA	SA	AB	H	G by POS
1981 NY A	3	13	6	0	0	0	0.0	4	1	0	0	0	.462	.462	0	0	SS-3

WORLD SERIES

	G	AB	H	2B	3B	HR	HR %	R	RBI	BB	SO	SB	BA	SA	AB	H	G by POS
1981 NY A	6	20	5	2	0	0	0.0	2	3	4	0	0	.250	.350	0	0	SS-6

	G	AB	H	2B	3B	HR	HR %	R	RBI	BB	SO	SB	BA	SA	Pinch Hit AB	Pinch Hit H	G by POS

Dee Miles

MILES, WILSON DANIEL
B. Feb. 15, 1909, Kellerman, Ala.   D. Nov. 2, 1976, Birmingham, Ala.
BL TL 6'   175 lbs.

	G	AB	H	2B	3B	HR	HR %	R	RBI	BB	SO	SB	BA	SA	AB	H	G by POS
1935 WAS A	60	216	57	5	2	0	0.0	28	29	7	13	6	.264	.306	13	4	OF-45
1936	25	59	14	1	2	0	0.0	8	7	1	5	0	.237	.322	14	1	OF-10
1939 PHI A	106	320	96	17	6	1	0.3	49	37	15	17	3	.300	.400	29	7	OF-77
1940	88	236	71	9	6	1	0.4	26	23	8	18	1	.301	.403	33	8	OF-50
1941	80	170	53	7	1	0	0.0	14	15	4	8	0	.312	.365	45	15	OF-35
1942	99	346	94	12	5	0	0.0	41	22	12	10	5	.272	.335	10	3	OF-81
1943 BOS A	45	121	26	2	2	0	0.0	9	10	3	3	0	.215	.264	21	5	OF-25
7 yrs.	503	1468	411	53	24	2	0.1	175	143	50	74	15	.280	.353	165	43	OF-323

Don Miles

MILES, DONALD RAY
B. Mar. 13, 1936, Indianapolis, Ind.
BL TL 6'1"   210 lbs.

	G	AB	H	2B	3B	HR	HR %	R	RBI	BB	SO	SB	BA	SA	AB	H	G by POS
1958 LA N	8	22	4	0	0	0	0.0	2	0	0	6	0	.182	.182	3	0	OF-5

Mike Miley

MILEY, MICHAEL WILFRED
B. Mar. 30, 1953, Yazoo City, Miss.   D. Jan. 6, 1977, Baton Rouge, La.
BB TR 6'1"   185 lbs.

	G	AB	H	2B	3B	HR	HR %	R	RBI	BB	SO	SB	BA	SA	AB	H	G by POS
1975 CAL A	70	224	39	3	2	4	1.8	17	26	16	54	0	.174	.259	0	0	SS-70
1976	14	38	7	2	0	0	0.0	4	4	4	8	1	.184	.237	0	0	SS-14
2 yrs.	84	262	46	5	2	4	1.5	21	30	20	62	1	.176	.256	0	0	SS-84

Felix Millan

MILLAN, FELIX BERNARDO
B. Aug. 21, 1943, Yabucoa, Puerto Rico
BR TR 5'11"   172 lbs.

	G	AB	H	2B	3B	HR	HR %	R	RBI	BB	SO	SB	BA	SA	AB	H	G by POS
1966 ATL N	37	91	25	6	0	0	0.0	20	5	2	6	3	.275	.341	3	0	2B-25, SS-1, 3B-1
1967	41	136	32	3	3	2	1.5	13	6	4	10	0	.235	.346	0	0	2B-41
1968	149	570	165	22	2	1	0.2	49	33	22	26	6	.289	.340	0	0	2B-145
1969	162	652	174	23	5	6	0.9	98	57	34	35	14	.267	.345	0	0	2B-162
1970	142	590	183	25	5	2	0.3	100	37	35	23	16	.310	.380	0	0	2B-142
1971	143	577	167	20	8	2	0.3	65	45	37	22	11	.289	.362	1	1	2B-141
1972	125	498	128	19	3	1	0.2	46	38	23	28	6	.257	.313	5	1	2B-120
1973 NY N	153	638	185	23	4	3	0.5	82	37	35	22	2	.290	.353	0	0	2B-153
1974	136	518	139	15	2	1	0.2	50	33	31	14	5	.268	.311	1	1	2B-134
1975	162	676	191	37	2	1	0.1	81	56	36	28	1	.283	.348	0	0	2B-162
1976	139	531	150	25	2	1	0.2	55	35	41	19	2	.282	.343	4	1	2B-136
1977	91	314	78	11	2	2	0.6	40	21	18	9	1	.248	.315	0	0	2B-89
12 yrs.	1480	5791	1617	229	38	22	0.4	699	403	318	242	67	.279	.343	14	4	2B-1450, SS-1, 3B-1

LEAGUE CHAMPIONSHIP SERIES

	G	AB	H	2B	3B	HR	HR %	R	RBI	BB	SO	SB	BA	SA	AB	H	G by POS
1969 ATL N	3	12	4	1	0	0	0.0	2	0	3	0	0	.333	.417	0	0	2B-3
1973 NY N	5	19	6	0	0	0	0.0	5	2	3	1	0	.316	.316	0	0	2B-5
2 yrs.	8	31	10	1	0	0	0.0	7	2	6	1	0	.323	.355	0	0	2B-8

WORLD SERIES

	G	AB	H	2B	3B	HR	HR %	R	RBI	BB	SO	SB	BA	SA	AB	H	G by POS
1973 NY N	7	32	6	1	1	0	0.0	3	1	1	1	0	.188	.281	0	0	2B-7

Frank Millard

MILLARD, FRANK E.
B. July 4, 1865, E. St. Louis, Ill.   D. July 4, 1892, Galveston, Tex.

	G	AB	H	2B	3B	HR	HR %	R	RBI	BB	SO	SB	BA	SA	AB	H	G by POS
1890 STL AA	1	1	0	0	0	0	0.0	0		1		0	.000	.000	0	0	2B-1

Bert Miller

MILLER, BERT
Deceased.

	G	AB	H	2B	3B	HR	HR %	R	RBI	BB	SO	SB	BA	SA	AB	H	G by POS
1897 PHI N	3	11	2	0	0	0	0.0	2	1	2		0	.182	.182	0	0	2B-3

Bill Miller

MILLER, WILLIAM
B. Cleveland, Ohio

	G	AB	H	2B	3B	HR	HR %	R	RBI	BB	SO	SB	BA	SA	AB	H	G by POS
1902 PIT N	1	5	1	0	0	0	0.0	0	2	0		0	.200	.200	0	0	OF-1

Bing Miller

MILLER, EDMUND JOHN
Brother of Ralph Miller.
B. Aug. 30, 1894, Vinton, Iowa   D. May 7, 1966, Philadelphia, Pa.
BR TR 6'   185 lbs.

	G	AB	H	2B	3B	HR	HR %	R	RBI	BB	SO	SB	BA	SA	AB	H	G by POS
1921 WAS A	114	420	121	28	8	9	2.1	57	71	25	50	3	.288	.457	5	2	OF-109
1922 PHI A	143	535	180	29	12	21	3.9	90	90	24	42	10	.336	.553	4	1	OF-139
1923	123	458	137	25	4	12	2.6	68	64	27	34	9	.299	.450	3	0	OF-119
1924	113	398	136	22	4	6	1.5	62	62	12	24	11	.342	.462	9	3	OF-94, 1B-7
1925	124	474	151	29	10	10	2.1	78	81	19	14	11	.319	.485	3	0	OF-115, 1B-12
1926 2 teams		PHI	A (38G –	.291)		STL	A	(94G –	.331)								
" total	132	463	149	33	7	6	1.3	73	63	33	18	11	.322	.462	2	1	OF-128, 1B-1
1927 STL A	144	492	160	32	7	5	1.0	83	75	30	26	9	.325	.449	16	6	OF-126
1928 PHI A	139	510	168	34	7	8	1.6	76	85	27	24	10	.329	.471	5	0	OF-133
1929	147	556	186	32	16	8	1.4	84	93	40	25	24	.335	.492	1	0	OF-145
1930	154	585	177	38	7	9	1.5	89	100	47	22	13	.303	.438	0	0	OF-154
1931	137	534	150	43	5	8	1.5	76	77	36	16	5	.281	.425	0	0	OF-137
1932	95	305	90	17	3	8	2.6	40	58	20	11	7	.295	.449	8	2	OF-84
1933	67	120	33	7	1	2	1.7	22	17	12	7	4	.275	.400	30	7	OF-30, 1B-6
1934	81	177	43	10	2	1	0.6	22	22	16	14	1	.243	.339	33	10	OF-46
1935 BOS A	78	138	42	8	1	3	2.2	18	26	10	8	0	.304	.442	43	13	OF-29
1936	30	47	14	2	1	1	2.1	9	6	5	5	0	.298	.447	13	1	OF-13
16 yrs.	1821	6212	1937	389	95	117	1.9	947	990	383	340	128	.312	.462	175	46	OF-1601, 1B-26

WORLD SERIES

	G	AB	H	2B	3B	HR	HR %	R	RBI	BB	SO	SB	BA	SA	AB	H	G by POS
1929 PHI A	5	19	7	1	0	0	0.0	1	4	0	2	0	.368	.421	0	0	OF-5
1930	6	21	3	2	0	0	0.0	0	3	0	4	0	.143	.238	0	0	OF-7
1931	7	26	7	1	0	0	0.0	3	1	0	4	0	.269	.308	0	0	OF-7
3 yrs.	18	66	17	4	0	0	0.0	4	8	0	10	0	.258	.318	0	0	OF-18

	G	AB	H	2B	3B	HR	HR %	R	RBI	BB	SO	SB	BA	SA	Pinch Hit AB	Pinch Hit H	G by POS

Bruce Miller

MILLER, CHARLES BRUCE
B. Mar. 3, 1949, Ft. Wayne, Ind.
BR TR 6'1" 185 lbs.

	G	AB	H	2B	3B	HR	HR %	R	RBI	BB	SO	SB	BA	SA	AB	H	G by POS
1973 SF N	12	21	3	0	0	0	0.0	1	2	2	3	0	.143	.143	4	0	3B-4, 2B-3, SS-1
1974	73	198	55	7	1	0	0.0	19	16	11	15	1	.278	.323	10	3	3B-41, SS-13, 2B-9
1975	99	309	74	6	3	1	0.3	22	31	15	26	0	.239	.288	12	1	3B-68, 2B-21, SS-6
1976	12	25	4	1	0	0	0.0	1	2	2	5	0	.160	.200	2	0	2B-8, 3B-2
4 yrs.	196	553	136	14	4	1	0.2	43	51	30	49	1	.246	.291	28	4	3B-115, 2B-41, SS-20

Charlie Miller

MILLER, CHARLES ELMER
B. Jan. 4, 1892 D. Apr. 23, 1972, Warrensburg, Mo.
TR

	G	AB	H	2B	3B	HR	HR %	R	RBI	BB	SO	SB	BA	SA	AB	H	G by POS
1912 STL A	1	2	0	0	0	0	0.0	0	0	0		0	.000	.000	0	0	SS-1

Charlie Miller

MILLER, CHARLES HESS
B. Dec. 30, 1877, Conestoga Center, Pa. D. Jan. 13, 1951, Millersville, Pa.
BR TR 6' 190 lbs.

	G	AB	H	2B	3B	HR	HR %	R	RBI	BB	SO	SB	BA	SA	AB	H	G by POS
1915 BAL F	1	1	0	0	0	0	0.0	0	0	0		0	.000	.000	1	0	

Charlie Miller

MILLER, CHARLES MARION
B. Sept. 18, 1889, Woodville, Ohio D. June 16, 1961, Houston, Tex.
BL TL 5'8½" 155 lbs.

	G	AB	H	2B	3B	HR	HR %	R	RBI	BB	SO	SB	BA	SA	AB	H	G by POS
1913 STL N	4	12	2	0	0	0	0.0	0	1	0	2	0	.167	.167	1	0	OF-3
1914	36	36	7	1	0	0	0.0	4	2	3	9	2	.194	.222	11	2	OF-19
2 yrs.	40	48	9	1	0	0	0.0	4	3	3	11	2	.188	.208	12	2	OF-22

Dakin Miller

MILLER, DAKIN EVANS
B. Sept. 2, 1877, Malvern, Iowa D. Apr. 20, 1950, Stockton, Calif.
BL TR 5'10" 175 lbs.

	G	AB	H	2B	3B	HR	HR %	R	RBI	BB	SO	SB	BA	SA	AB	H	G by POS
1902 CHI N	51	187	46	4	1	0	0.0	17	13	7		10	.246	.278	0	0	OF-51

Darrell Miller

MILLER, DARRELL KEITH
B. Feb. 26, 1959, Washington, D. C.
BR TR 6'2" 200 lbs.

	G	AB	H	2B	3B	HR	HR %	R	RBI	BB	SO	SB	BA	SA	AB	H	G by POS
1984 CAL A	17	41	7	0	0	0	0.0	5	1	4	9	0	.171	.171	1	0	1B-16, OF-1

Doc Miller

MILLER, ROY OSCAR
B. 1883, Chatham, Ont., Canada D. July 31, 1938, Jersey City, N. J.
BL TL 5'10½" 170 lbs.

	G	AB	H	2B	3B	HR	HR %	R	RBI	BB	SO	SB	BA	SA	AB	H	G by POS
1910 2 teams		CHI N (1G – .000)						BOS N (130G – .286)									
" total	131	483	138	27	4	3	0.6	48	55	33	52	17	.286	.377	1	0	OF-130
1911 BOS N	146	577	192	36	3	7	1.2	69	91	43	43	32	.333	.442	0	0	OF-146
1912 2 teams		BOS N (51G – .234)						PHI N (67G – .288)									
" total	118	378	98	20	6	2	0.5	50	45	23	30	9	.259	.360	28	7	OF-90
1913 PHI N	69	87	30	6	0	0	0.0	9	11	6	6	2	.345	.414	56	20	OF-12
1914 CIN N	47	192	49	7	2	0	0.0	8	33	16	18	4	.255	.313	35	12	OF-47
5 yrs.	511	1717	507	96	15	12	0.7	184	235	121	149	64	.295	.390	120	39	OF-425

Doggie Miller

MILLER, GEORGE FREDERICK (Foghorn, Calliope)
B. Aug. 15, 1864, Brooklyn, N. Y. D. Apr. 6, 1909, Brooklyn, N. Y.
BR TR 5'6"

	G	AB	H	2B	3B	HR	HR %	R	RBI	BB	SO	SB	BA	SA	AB	H	G by POS
1884 PIT AA	89	347	78	10	2	0	0.0	46		13				.225	.265	0	0	OF-49, C-36, 3B-3, 2B-1
1885	42	166	27	3	1	0	0.0	19		4				.163	.193	0	0	C-33, OF-6, SS-2, 3B-2
1886	83	317	80	15	1	2	0.6	70		43				.252	.325	0	0	C-61, OF-23, 2B-1
1887 PIT N	87	342	83	17	4	1	0.3	58	34	35	13	33		.243	.325	0	0	C-73, OF-14, 3B-1
1888	103	404	112	17	5	0	0.0	50	36	18	16	27		.277	.344	0	0	C-68, OF-32, 3B-4
1889	104	422	113	25	3	6	1.4	77	56	31	11	16		.268	.384	0	0	C-76, OF-27, 3B-3
1890	138	549	150	24	3	4	0.7	85	66	68	11	32		.273	.350	0	0	3B-88, OF-25, SS-13, C-10, 2B-6
1891	135	548	156	19	6	4	0.7	80	57	59	26	35		.285	.363	0	0	C-41, SS-37, 3B-34, OF-24, 1B-1
1892	149	623	158	15	12	2	0.3	103	59	69	14	28		.254	.326	0	0	OF-76, C-63, SS-19, 3B-2
1893	41	154	28	6	1	0	0.0	23	17	17	8	3		.182	.234	1	0	C-40
1894 STL N	127	481	163	9	11	8	1.7	93	86	58	9	17		.339	.453	2	0	3B-52, C-41, 2B-18, 1B-12, OF-4, SS-1
1895	121	490	143	15	4	5	1.0	81	74	25	12	18		.292	.369	0	0	3B-46, C-46, OF-21, SS-9, 1B-6
1896 LOU N	98	324	89	17	4	1	0.3	54	33	27	9	16		.275	.361	9	6	C-48, 2B-25, OF-8, 3B-8, 1B-3, SS-2
13 yrs.	1317	5167	1380	192	57	33	0.6	839	517	467	129	225		.267	.345	12	6	C-636, OF-309, 3B-243, SS-83, 2B-51, 1B-22

Dots Miller

MILLER, JOHN BARNEY
B. Sept. 9, 1886, Kearny, N. J. D. Sept. 5, 1923, Saranac Lake, N. Y.
BR TR 5'11½" 170 lbs.

	G	AB	H	2B	3B	HR	HR %	R	RBI	BB	SO	SB	BA	SA	AB	H	G by POS
1909 PIT N	151	560	156	31	13	3	0.5	71	87	39		14	.279	.396	1	0	2B-150
1910	120	444	101	13	10	1	0.2	45	48	33	41	11	.227	.309	1	0	2B-117, SS-2
1911	137	470	126	17	8	6	1.3	82	78	51	48	17	.268	.377	5	1	2B-129
1912	148	567	156	33	12	4	0.7	74	87	37	45	18	.275	.397	1	0	1B-147
1913	154	580	158	24	20	7	1.2	75	90	37	52	20	.272	.419	0	0	1B-150, SS-3
1914 STL N	155	573	166	27	10	4	0.7	67	88	34	52	16	.290	.393	0	0	1B-98, SS-53, 2B-5
1915	150	553	146	17	10	2	0.4	73	72	43	48	27	.264	.342	0	0	1B-83, 2B-55, 3B-9, SS-3
1916	143	505	120	22	7	1	0.2	47	46	40	49	18	.238	.315	0	0	1B-93, 2B-38, SS-21, 3B-1
1917	148	544	135	15	9	2	0.4	61	45	33	52	14	.248	.320	0	0	2B-92, 1B-46, SS-11
1919	101	346	80	10	4	1	0.3	38	24	13	23	6	.231	.292	5	2	1B-68, 2B-28
1920 PHI N	98	343	87	12	2	1	0.3	41	27	16	17	13	.254	.309	2	0	2B-59, 3B-17, SS-12, 1B-9, OF-1
1921	84	320	95	11	3	0	0.0	37	23	15	27	3	.297	.350	1	0	3B-41, 1B-38, 2B-6
12 yrs.	1589	5805	1526	232	108	32	0.6	711	715	391	454	177	.263	.357	16	3	1B-732, 2B-679, SS-105, 3B-68, OF-1

WORLD SERIES

	G	AB	H	2B	3B	HR	HR %	R	RBI	BB	SO	SB	BA	SA	AB	H	G by POS
1909 PIT N	7	28	7	1	0	0	0.0	2	4	2	4	3	.250	.286	0	0	2B-7

	G	AB	H	2B	3B	HR	HR %	R	RBI	BB	SO	SB	BA	SA	Pinch Hit AB	Pinch Hit H	G by POS

Dusty Miller
MILLER, CHARLES BRADLEY
B. Sept. 10, 1868, Oil City, Pa.   D. Jan. 13, 1943, St. Martinsville, La.
BL TR 5'11½" 170 lbs.

	G	AB	H	2B	3B	HR	HR %	R	RBI	BB	SO	SB	BA	SA	AB	H	G by POS
1889 BAL AA	11	40	6	1	1	0	0.0	4	6	2	11	3	.150	.225	0	0	SS-8, OF-3
1890 STL AA	26	96	21	5	3	1	1.0	17		8		4	.219	.365	0	0	OF-24, SS-3
1895 CIN N	132	529	177	31	18	8	1.5	103	112	33	34	43	.335	.507	0	0	OF-132
1896	125	504	162	38	12	4	0.8	91	93	33	30	76	.321	.468	0	0	OF-125
1897	119	440	139	27	1	4	0.9	83	70	48		29	.316	.409	0	0	OF-119
1898	152	586	175	24	12	3	0.5	99	90	38		32	.299	.396	0	0	OF-152
1899 2 teams	CIN	N	(80G	–	.251)	STL	N	(10G	–	.205)							
" total	90	362	89	13	5	0	0.0	47	40	12		19	.246	.309	0	0	OF-90
7 yrs.	655	2557	769	139	52	20	0.8	444	411	174	75	206	.301	.419	0	0	OF-645, SS-11

Ed Miller
MILLER, EDWIN
B. Nov. 24, 1888, Annville, Pa.   D. Apr. 17, 1980, South Lebanon, Pa.
BR TR 6' 180 lbs.

	G	AB	H	2B	3B	HR	HR %	R	RBI	BB	SO	SB	BA	SA	AB	H	G by POS
1912 STL A	13	46	9	1	0	0	0.0	4	5	2		1	.196	.217	0	0	1B-8, SS-5
1914	34	58	8	0	1	0	0.0	8	4	4	13	1	.138	.172	8	0	1B-8, OF-5, 2B-5, 3B-2
1918 CLE A	32	96	22	4	3	0	0.0	9	3	12	10	2	.229	.333	2	0	1B-22, OF-4
3 yrs.	79	200	39	5	4	0	0.0	21	12	18	23	4	.195	.260	10	0	1B-38, OF-9, SS-5, 2B-5, 3B-2

Ed Miller
MILLER, L. EDWARD
B. Tecumseh, Mich.   Deceased.

	G	AB	H	2B	3B	HR	HR %	R	RBI	BB	SO	SB	BA	SA	AB	H	G by POS
1884 TOL AA	8	24	6	0	0	0	0.0	2		1			.250	.250	0	0	OF-8

Eddie Miller
MILLER, EDWARD LEE
B. June 29, 1957, San Pablo, Calif.
BB TR 5'9" 175 lbs.

	G	AB	H	2B	3B	HR	HR %	R	RBI	BB	SO	SB	BA	SA	AB	H	G by POS
1977 TEX A	17	6	2	0	0	0	0.0	7	1	1	1	3	.333	.333	0	0	DH-3, OF-2
1978 ATL N	6	21	3	1	0	0	0.0	5	2	2	4	3	.143	.190	0	0	OF-5
1979	27	113	35	1	0	0	0.0	12	5	5	24	15	.310	.319	0	0	OF-27
1980	11	19	3	0	0	0	0.0	3	0	0	5	1	.158	.158	0	0	OF-9
1981	50	134	31	3	1	0	0.0	29	7	7	29	23	.231	.269	6	2	OF-36
1982 DET A	14	25	1	0	0	0	0.0	3	0	4	4	0	.040	.040	1	0	OF-8, DH-1
1984 SD N	13	14	4	0	1	1	7.1	4	2	0	4	4	.286	.643	1	0	OF-8
7 yrs.	138	332	79	5	2	1	0.3	63	17	19	71	49	.238	.274	8	2	OF-95, DH-4

Eddie Miller
MILLER, EDWARD ROBERT (Eppie)
B. Nov. 26, 1916, Pittsburgh, Pa.
BR TR 5'9" 180 lbs.

	G	AB	H	2B	3B	HR	HR %	R	RBI	BB	SO	SB	BA	SA	AB	H	G by POS
1936 CIN N	5	10	1	0	0	0	0.0	0	0	1	1	0	.100	.100	2	0	SS-4, 2B-1
1937	36	60	9	3	1	0	0.0	3	5	3	8	0	.150	.233	2	0	SS-30, 3B-4
1939 BOS N	77	296	79	12	2	4	1.4	32	31	16	21	0	.267	.361	0	0	SS-77
1940	151	569	157	33	3	14	2.5	78	79	41	43	8	.276	.418	0	0	SS-151
1941	154	585	140	27	3	6	1.0	54	68	35	72	8	.239	.326	0	0	SS-154
1942	144	534	130	28	2	6	1.1	47	47	22	42	11	.243	.337	0	0	SS-144
1943 CIN N	154	576	129	26	4	2	0.3	49	71	33	43	8	.224	.293	0	0	SS-154
1944	155	536	112	21	5	4	0.7	48	55	41	41	9	.209	.289	0	0	SS-155
1945	115	421	100	27	4	13	3.1	46	49	18	38	4	.238	.404	0	0	SS-115
1946	91	299	58	10	0	6	2.0	30	36	25	34	5	.194	.288	3	1	SS-88
1947	151	545	146	38	4	19	3.5	69	87	49	40	5	.268	.457	0	0	SS-151
1948 PHI N	130	468	115	20	1	14	3.0	45	61	19	40	1	.246	.382	7	0	SS-122
1949	85	266	55	10	1	6	2.3	21	29	29	21	1	.207	.320	3	1	2B-82, SS-1
1950 STL N	64	172	39	8	0	3	1.7	17	22	19	21	0	.227	.326	11	1	SS-51, 2B-1
14 yrs.	1512	5337	1270	263	28	97	1.8	539	640	351	465	64	.238	.352	26	3	SS-1397, 2B-84, 3B-4

Elmer Miller
MILLER, ELMER
B. July 28, 1890, Sandusky, Ohio   D. Nov. 28, 1944, Beloit, Wis.
BR TR 6' 175 lbs.

	G	AB	H	2B	3B	HR	HR %	R	RBI	BB	SO	SB	BA	SA	AB	H	G by POS
1912 STL N	12	37	7	1	0	0	0.0	5	3	4	9	1	.189	.216	1	0	OF-11
1915 NY A	26	83	12	1	0	0	0.0	4	3	4	14	0	.145	.157	0	0	OF-26
1916	43	152	34	3	2	1	0.7	12	18	11	18	8	.224	.289	0	0	OF-42
1917	114	379	95	11	3	3	0.8	43	35	40	44	11	.251	.319	1	0	OF-112
1918	67	202	49	9	2	1	0.5	18	22	19	17	2	.243	.322	4	0	OF-62
1921	56	242	72	9	8	4	1.7	41	36	19	16	2	.298	.450	0	0	OF-56
1922 2 teams	NY	A	(51G	–	.267)	BOS	A	(44G	–	.190)							
" total	95	319	74	9	5	7	2.2	47	34	16	22	5	.232	.357	9	1	OF-83
7 yrs.	413	1414	343	43	20	16	1.1	170	151	113	140	29	.243	.335	15	1	OF-392

WORLD SERIES

	G	AB	H	2B	3B	HR	HR %	R	RBI	BB	SO	SB	BA	SA	AB	H	G by POS
1921 NY A	8	31	5	1	0	0	0.0	3	2	2	5	0	.161	.194	0	0	OF-8

Elmer Miller
MILLER, ELMER LeROY
B. Apr. 17, 1904, Detroit, Mich.
BL TL 5'11" 185 lbs.

	G	AB	H	2B	3B	HR	HR %	R	RBI	BB	SO	SB	BA	SA	AB	H	G by POS
1929 PHI N	31	38	9	1	0	1	2.6	4	1		5	0	.237	.342	17	2	P-8, OF-4

Fred Miller
MILLER, FREDERICK
B. Philadelphia, Pa.   Deceased.

	G	AB	H	2B	3B	HR	HR %	R	RBI	BB	SO	SB	BA	SA	AB	H	G by POS
1892 WAS N	1	3	0	0	0	0	0.0	0	0	0	1	0	.000	.000	0	0	SS-1

George Miller
MILLER, GEORGE C.
B. Feb. 19, 1853, Newport, Ky.   D. July 25, 1929, Cincinnati, Ohio
BR TR 5'5" 160 lbs.

	G	AB	H	2B	3B	HR	HR %	R	RBI	BB	SO	SB	BA	SA	AB	H	G by POS
1877 CIN N	11	37	6	1	0	0	0.0	4	3	5	2		.162	.189	0	0	C-11
1884 CIN AA	6	20	5	1	1	0	0.0	6		1			.250	.400	0	0	C-6
2 yrs.	17	57	11	2	1	0	0.0	10	3	6	2		.193	.263	0	0	C-17

Hack Miller
MILLER, JAMES ELDRIDGE
B. Feb. 13, 1911, Celeste, Tex.   D. Nov. 21, 1966, Dallas, Tex.
BR TR 5'11½" 215 lbs.

	G	AB	H	2B	3B	HR	HR %	R	RBI	BB	SO	SB	BA	SA	AB	H	G by POS
1944 DET A	5	5	1	0	0	1	20.0	1	3	1	1	0	.200	.800	0	0	C-5

	G	AB	H	2B	3B	HR	HR %	R	RBI	BB	SO	SB	BA	SA	Pinch Hit AB	Pinch Hit H	G by POS

Hack Miller continued

	G	AB	H	2B	3B	HR	HR%	R	RBI	BB	SO	SB	BA	SA	PH AB	PH H	G by POS
1945	2	4	3	0	0	0	0.0	0	1	0	0	0	.750	.750	0	0	C-2
2 yrs.	7	9	4	0	0	1	11.1	1	4	1	1	0	.444	.778	0	0	C-7

Hack Miller

MILLER, LAWRENCE H.
B. Jan. 1, 1894, Chicago, Ill.   D. Sept. 17, 1971, Oakland, Calif.   BR TR 5'9" 195 lbs.

	G	AB	H	2B	3B	HR	HR%	R	RBI	BB	SO	SB	BA	SA	PH AB	PH H	G by POS
1916 BKN N	3	3	1	0	1	0	0.0	0	1	1	1	0	.333	1.000	0	0	OF-3
1918 BOS A	12	29	8	2	0	0	0.0	2	4	0	4	0	.276	.345	2	0	OF-10
1922 CHI N	122	466	164	28	5	12	2.6	61	78	26	39	3	.352	.511	6	2	OF-116
1923	135	485	146	24	2	20	4.1	74	88	27	39	6	.301	.482	4	4	OF-129
1924	53	131	44	8	1	4	3.1	17	25	8	11	1	.336	.504	20	7	OF-32
1925	24	86	24	3	2	2	2.3	10	9	2	9	0	.279	.430	3	2	OF-21
6 yrs.	349	1200	387	65	11	38	3.2	164	205	64	103	10	.323	.490	35	15	OF-311
WORLD SERIES																	
1918 BOS A	1	1	0	0	0	0	0.0	0	0	0	0	0	.000	.000	1	0	

Hughie Miller

MILLER, HUGH STANLEY (Cotton)
B. Dec. 28, 1887, St. Louis, Mo.   D. Dec. 24, 1945, Jefferson Barracks, Mo.   BR TR 6'1½" 175 lbs.

	G	AB	H	2B	3B	HR	HR%	R	RBI	BB	SO	SB	BA	SA	PH AB	PH H	G by POS
1911 PHI N	1	0	0	0	0	0	–	0	0	0	0	0	–	–	0	0	
1914 STL F	132	490	109	20	5	0	0.0	51	46	27		4	.222	.284	2	1	1B-130
1915	7	6	3	1	0	0	0.0	0	3	0		0	.500	.667	1	0	1B-6
3 yrs.	140	496	112	21	5	0	0.0	51	49	27		4	.226	.288	3	1	1B-136

Jake Miller

MILLER, JACOB GEORGE
Born Jacob George Munzing.
B. Dec. 1, 1895, Baltimore, Md.   D. Aug. 24, 1974, Towson, Md.   BR TR 5'10" 170 lbs.

	G	AB	H	2B	3B	HR	HR%	R	RBI	BB	SO	SB	BA	SA	PH AB	PH H	G by POS
1922 PIT N	3	11	1	0	0	0	0.0	0	0	2	0	1	.091	.091	0	0	OF-3

Jim Miller

MILLER, JAMES McCURDY (Rabbit)
B. Oct. 2, 1880, Pittsburgh, Pa.   D. Feb. 7, 1937, Pittsburgh, Pa.   BR TR 5'8" 165 lbs.

	G	AB	H	2B	3B	HR	HR%	R	RBI	BB	SO	SB	BA	SA	PH AB	PH H	G by POS
1901 NY N	18	58	8	0	0	0	0.0	3	3	6		1	.138	.138	0	0	2B-18

Joe Miller

MILLER, JOSEPH A.
B. Feb. 17, 1861, Baltimore, Md.   D. Apr. 23, 1928, Wheeling, W. Va.   5'9½" 165 lbs.

	G	AB	H	2B	3B	HR	HR%	R	RBI	BB	SO	SB	BA	SA	PH AB	PH H	G by POS
1884 TOL AA	105	423	101	12	8	1	0.2	46		26			.239	.312	0	0	SS-105
1885 LOU AA	98	339	62	9	5	0	0.0	44		28			.183	.239	0	0	SS-79, 3B-11, 2B-8
2 yrs.	203	762	163	21	13	1	0.1	90		54			.214	.280	0	0	SS-184, 3B-11, 2B-8

John Miller

MILLER, JOHN ALLEN
B. Mar. 14, 1944, Alhambra, Calif.   BR TR 5'11" 195 lbs.

	G	AB	H	2B	3B	HR	HR%	R	RBI	BB	SO	SB	BA	SA	PH AB	PH H	G by POS
1966 NY A	6	23	2	0	0	1	4.3	1	2	0	9	0	.087	.217	0	0	OF-3, 1B-3
1969 LA N	26	38	8	1	0	1	2.6	3	1	2	9	0	.211	.316	15	3	OF-6, 1B-5, 3B-2, 2B-1
2 yrs.	32	61	10	1	0	2	3.3	4	3	2	18	0	.164	.279	15	3	OF-9, 1B-8, 3B-2, 2B-1

Lemmie Miller

MILLER, LEMMIE EARL
B. Dec. 12, 1956, Plata, Md.   BR TR 6'1" 190 lbs.

	G	AB	H	2B	3B	HR	HR%	R	RBI	BB	SO	SB	BA	SA	PH AB	PH H	G by POS
1984 LA N	8	12	2	0	0	0	0.0	1	0	1	2	0	.167	.167	5	1	OF-5

Norm Miller

MILLER, NORMAN CALVIN
B. Feb. 5, 1946, Los Angeles, Calif.   BL TR 5'10" 185 lbs.

	G	AB	H	2B	3B	HR	HR%	R	RBI	BB	SO	SB	BA	SA	PH AB	PH H	G by POS
1965 HOU N	11	15	3	0	0	0	0.0	2	1	1	7	0	.200	.333	7	1	OF-2
1966	11	34	5	0	0	1	2.9	1	3	2	8	0	.147	.235	2	0	OF-8, 3B-2
1967	64	190	39	9	3	1	0.5	15	14	19	42	2	.205	.300	13	2	OF-53
1968	79	257	61	18	2	6	2.3	35	28	22	48	6	.237	.393	6	2	OF-74
1969	119	409	108	21	4	4	1.0	58	50	47	77	4	.264	.364	2	0	OF-114
1970	90	226	54	9	0	4	1.8	29	29	41	33	3	.239	.332	19	5	OF-72, C-1
1971	45	74	19	5	0	2	2.7	5	10	5	13	0	.257	.405	28	9	OF-20, C-1
1972	67	107	26	4	0	4	3.7	18	13	13	23	1	.243	.393	31	10	OF-29
1973 2 teams	HOU N (3G – .000)				ATL N (9G – .375)												
" total	12	11	3	1	0	1	9.1	2	6	3	5	0	.273	.636	8	1	OF-2
1974 ATL N	42	41	7	1	0	1	2.4	1	5	7	9	1	.171	.268	31	6	OF-4
10 yrs.	540	1364	325	68	10	24	1.8	166	159	160	265	16	.238	.356	147	36	OF-378, 3B-2, C-2

Otto Miller

MILLER, LOWELL OTTO (Moonie)
B. June 1, 1889, Minden, Neb.   D. Mar. 29, 1962, Brooklyn, N. Y.   BR TR 6' 196 lbs.

	G	AB	H	2B	3B	HR	HR%	R	RBI	BB	SO	SB	BA	SA	PH AB	PH H	G by POS
1910 BKN N	31	66	11	3	0	0	0.0	5	2	2	19	1	.167	.212	3	0	C-28
1911	25	62	13	2	0	0	0.0	7	8	0	4	2	.210	.306	2	0	C-22
1912	98	316	88	18	1	1	0.3	35	31	18	50	11	.278	.351	2	2	C-94
1913	104	320	87	11	7	0	0.0	26	26	10	31	7	.272	.350	0	0	C-103, 1B-1
1914	54	169	39	6	1	0	0.0	17	9	7	20	0	.231	.278	3	1	C-50
1915	84	254	57	4	6	0	0.0	20	25	6	28	3	.224	.287	1	0	C-84
1916	73	216	55	9	2	1	0.5	16	17	7	29	6	.255	.329	4	2	C-69
1917	92	274	63	5	4	1	0.4	19	17	14	29	5	.230	.288	0	0	C-91
1918	75	228	44	6	1	0	0.0	8	8	9	20	1	.193	.228	11	1	C-62, 1B-1
1919	51	164	37	5	0	0	0.0	18	5	7	14	2	.226	.256	0	0	C-51
1920	90	301	87	9	2	0	0.0	16	33	9	18	0	.289	.332	1	0	C-89
1921	91	286	67	8	6	1	0.3	22	27	9	26	2	.234	.315	0	0	C-91
1922	59	180	47	11	1	1	0.6	20	23	6	13	0	.261	.350	2	1	C-57
13 yrs.	927	2836	695	97	33	5	0.2	229	231	104	301	40	.245	.308	29	7	C-891, 1B-2
WORLD SERIES																	
1916 BKN N	2	8	1	0	0	0	0.0	0	0	0	1	0	.125	.125	0	0	C-2
1920	6	14	2	0	0	0	0.0	0	0	1	2	0	.143	.143	0	0	C-6
2 yrs.	8	22	3	0	0	0	0.0	0	0	1	3	0	.136	.136	0	0	C-8

	G	AB	H	2B	3B	HR	HR %	R	RBI	BB	SO	SB	BA	SA	Pinch Hit AB	Pinch Hit H	G by POS

Otto Miller

MILLER, OTIS LOUIS
B. Feb. 2, 1901, Belleville, Ill. D. July 26, 1959, Belleville, Ill.
BR TR 5'10½" 168 lbs.

	G	AB	H	2B	3B	HR	HR %	R	RBI	BB	SO	SB	BA	SA	Pinch Hit AB	Pinch Hit H	G by POS
1927 STL A	51	76	17	5	0	0	0.0	8	8	8	5	0	.224	.289	5	0	SS-35, 3B-11
1930 BOS A	112	370	106	22	5	0	0.0	49	40	26	21	2	.286	.373	13	5	3B-83, 2B-15
1931	107	389	106	12	1	0	0.0	38	43	15	20	1	.272	.308	10	1	3B-75, 2B-25
1932	2	2	0	0	0	0	0.0	0	0	0	0	0	.000	.000	2	0	
4 yrs.	272	837	229	39	6	0	0.0	95	91	49	46	3	.274	.335	30	6	3B-169, 2B-40, SS-35

Ralph Miller

MILLER, RALPH JOSEPH
B. Feb. 29, 1896, Ft. Wayne, Ind. D. Mar. 18, 1939, Fort Wayne, Ind.
BR TR 6' 190 lbs.

	G	AB	H	2B	3B	HR	HR %	R	RBI	BB	SO	SB	BA	SA	Pinch Hit AB	Pinch Hit H	G by POS
1920 PHI N	97	338	74	14	1	0	0.0	28	28	11	32	3	.219	.266	0	0	3B-91, 1B-3, SS-2, OF-1
1921	57	204	62	10	0	3	1.5	19	26	6	10	3	.304	.397	2	1	SS-46, 3B-10
1924 WAS A	9	15	2	0	0	0	0.0	1	0	1	1	0	.133	.133	6	0	2B-3
3 yrs.	163	557	138	24	1	3	0.5	48	54	18	43	6	.248	.311	8	1	3B-101, SS-48, 2B-3, 1B-3, OF-1

WORLD SERIES
| 1924 WAS A | 4 | 11 | 2 | 0 | 0 | 0 | 0.0 | 0 | 2 | 1 | 0 | 0 | .182 | .182 | 0 | 0 | 3B-4 |

Ray Miller

MILLER, RAYMOND PETER
B. Apr. 9, 1888, Pittsburgh, Pa. D. Apr. 7, 1927, Pittsburgh, Pa.
BL TL 5'10" 168 lbs.

	G	AB	H	2B	3B	HR	HR %	R	RBI	BB	SO	SB	BA	SA	Pinch Hit AB	Pinch Hit H	G by POS
1917 2 teams	CLE A (19G – .190)			PIT N (6G – .148)													
" total	25	48	8	2	0	0	0.0	2	2	10	6	0	.167	.208	12	2	1B-10

Rick Miller

MILLER, RICHARD ALAN
B. Apr. 19, 1948, Grand Rapids, Mich.
BL TL 6' 175 lbs.

	G	AB	H	2B	3B	HR	HR %	R	RBI	BB	SO	SB	BA	SA	Pinch Hit AB	Pinch Hit H	G by POS
1971 BOS A	15	33	11	5	0	1	3.0	9	7	8	8	0	.333	.576	0	0	OF-14
1972	89	98	21	4	1	3	3.1	13	15	11	27	0	.214	.367	7	0	OF-75
1973	143	441	115	17	7	6	1.4	65	43	51	59	12	.261	.372	3	1	OF-137
1974	114	280	73	8	1	5	1.8	41	22	37	47	13	.261	.350	1	0	OF-105
1975	77	108	21	2	1	0	0.0	21	15	21	20	3	.194	.231	9	1	OF-65
1976	105	269	76	15	3	0	0.0	40	27	34	47	11	.283	.361	17	5	OF-82, DH-4
1977	86	189	48	9	3	0	0.0	34	24	22	30	11	.254	.333	6	2	OF-79, DH-1
1978 CAL A	132	475	125	25	4	1	0.2	66	37	54	70	5	.263	.339	5	1	OF-129
1979	120	427	125	15	5	2	0.5	60	28	50	69	5	.293	.365	1	0	OF-117, DH-2
1980	129	412	113	14	3	2	0.5	52	38	48	71	7	.274	.337	10	4	OF-118
1981 BOS A	97	316	92	17	2	2	0.6	38	33	28	36	3	.291	.377	3	1	OF-95
1982	135	409	104	13	2	4	1.0	50	38	40	41	5	.254	.325	8	2	OF-127
1983	104	262	75	10	2	2	0.8	41	21	28	30	3	.286	.363	35	16	OF-66, DH-2, 1B-2
1984	95	123	32	5	1	0	0.0	17	12	17	22	1	.260	.317	53	14	OF-31, 1B-8
14 yrs.	1441	3842	1031	159	35	28	0.7	547	360	449	577	77	.268	.350	158	47	OF-1240, 1B-10, DH-9

LEAGUE CHAMPIONSHIP SERIES
| 1979 CAL A | 4 | 16 | 4 | 0 | 0 | 0 | 0.0 | 2 | 0 | 0 | 1 | 0 | .250 | .250 | 0 | 0 | OF-4 |

WORLD SERIES
| 1975 BOS A | 3 | 2 | 0 | 0 | 0 | 0 | 0.0 | 0 | 0 | 0 | 0 | 0 | .000 | .000 | 0 | 0 | OF-2 |

Rod Miller

MILLER, RODNEY CARTER
B. Jan. 16, 1940, Portland, Ore.
BL TR 5'10" 160 lbs.

	G	AB	H	2B	3B	HR	HR %	R	RBI	BB	SO	SB	BA	SA	Pinch Hit AB	Pinch Hit H	G by POS
1957 BKN N	1	1	0	0	0	0	0.0	0	0	0	1	0	.000	.000	1	0	

Rudy Miller

MILLER, RUDEL CHARLES
B. July 12, 1900, Kalamazoo, Mich.
BR TR 6'1" 180 lbs.

	G	AB	H	2B	3B	HR	HR %	R	RBI	BB	SO	SB	BA	SA	Pinch Hit AB	Pinch Hit H	G by POS
1929 PHI A	2	4	1	0	0	0	0.0	1	1	3	0	0	.250	.250	0	0	3B-2

Tom Miller

MILLER, THOMAS ROYALL
B. July 5, 1897, Powhatan Ct. House, Va. D. Aug. 13, 1980, Richmond, Va.
BL TR 5'11" 180 lbs.

	G	AB	H	2B	3B	HR	HR %	R	RBI	BB	SO	SB	BA	SA	Pinch Hit AB	Pinch Hit H	G by POS
1918 BOS N	2	2	0	0	0	0	0.0	0	0	0	0	1	.000	.000	2	0	
1919	7	6	2	0	0	0	0.0	2	0	0	1	0	.333	.333	6	2	
2 yrs.	9	8	2	0	0	0	0.0	2	0	0	1	1	.250	.250	8	2	

Ward Miller

MILLER, WARD TAYLOR (Windy)
B. July 5, 1884, Mt. Carroll, Ill. D. Sept. 4, 1958, Dixon, Ill.
BL TR 5'11" 177 lbs.

	G	AB	H	2B	3B	HR	HR %	R	RBI	BB	SO	SB	BA	SA	Pinch Hit AB	Pinch Hit H	G by POS
1909 2 teams	PIT N (15G – .143)			CIN N (43G – .310)													
" total	58	169	43	3	2	0	0.0	19	8	10		11	.254	.296	13	1	OF-40
1910 CIN N	81	126	30	6	0	0	0.0	21	10	22	13	10	.238	.286	40	11	OF-26
1912 CHI N	86	241	74	11	4	0	0.0	45	22	26	18	11	.307	.386	15	6	OF-64
1913	80	203	48	5	7	1	0.5	23	16	34	33	13	.236	.345	13	8	OF-63
1914 STL F	121	402	118	17	7	4	1.0	49	50	59		18	.294	.400	8	3	OF-111
1915	154	536	164	19	9	1	0.2	80	63	79		33	.306	.381	0	0	OF-154
1916 STL A	146	485	129	17	5	1	0.2	72	50	72	76	25	.266	.328	9	3	OF-135, 2B-1
1917	43	82	17	1	1	1	1.2	13	2	16	15	7	.207	.280	12	4	OF-25
8 yrs.	769	2244	623	79	35	8	0.4	322	221	318	155	128	.278	.355	110	36	OF-618, 2B-1

Warren Miller

MILLER, WARREN LEMUEL
B. July 14, 1885, Philadelphia, Pa. D. Aug. 12, 1956, Philadelphia, Pa.
BL TL 5'10" 160 lbs.

	G	AB	H	2B	3B	HR	HR %	R	RBI	BB	SO	SB	BA	SA	Pinch Hit AB	Pinch Hit H	G by POS
1909 WAS A	26	51	11	0	0	0	0.0	5	1	4		0	.216	.216	0	0	OF-15
1911	21	34	5	0	0	0	0.0	3	0	0		0	.147	.147	11	1	OF-9
2 yrs.	47	85	16	0	0	0	0.0	8	1	4		0	.188	.188	11	1	OF-24

Wally Millies

MILLIES, WALTER LOUIS
B. Oct. 18, 1906, Chicago, Ill.
BR TR 5'10½" 170 lbs.

	G	AB	H	2B	3B	HR	HR %	R	RBI	BB	SO	SB	BA	SA	Pinch Hit AB	Pinch Hit H	G by POS
1934 BKN N	2	7	0	0	0	0	0.0	0	0	0	0	0	.000	.000	0	0	C-2
1936 WAS A	74	215	67	10	2	0	0.0	26	25	11	8	1	.312	.377	1	0	C-72
1937	59	179	40	7	1	0	0.0	21	28	9	15	1	.223	.274	4	1	C-56
1939 PHI N	84	205	48	3	0	0	0.0	12	12	9	5	0	.234	.249	0	0	C-84
1940	26	43	3	0	0	0	0.0	1	0	4	4	0	.070	.070	2	0	C-24

	G	AB	H	2B	3B	HR	HR %	R	RBI	BB	SO	SB	BA	SA	Pinch Hit AB	Pinch Hit H	G by POS

Wally Millies continued

	G	AB	H	2B	3B	HR	HR %	R	RBI	BB	SO	SB	BA	SA	PH AB	PH H	G by POS
1941	1	2	0	0	0	0	0.0	0	0	0	0	0	.000	.000	0	0	C-1
6 yrs.	246	651	158	20	3	0	0.0	60	65	33	32	2	.243	.283	7	1	C-239

Jocko Milligan

MILLIGAN, JOHN BR TR 6' 195 lbs.
B. Aug. 8, 1861, Philadelphia, Pa.   D. Aug. 30, 1923, Philadelphia, Pa.

	G	AB	H	2B	3B	HR	HR %	R	RBI	BB	SO	SB	BA	SA	PH AB	PH H	G by POS
1884 PHI AA	66	268	77	20	3	3	1.1	39		8			.287	.418	0	0	C-65, OF-1
1885	67	265	71	15	4	2	0.8	35		7			.268	.377	0	0	C-61, 1B-6, OF-2
1886	75	301	76	17	3	5	1.7	52		21			.252	.379	0	0	C-40, 1B-29, OF-5, 3B-2
1887	95	377	114	27	4	2	0.5	54		21		8	.302	.411	0	0	1B-50, C-47, OF-1
1888 STL AA	63	219	55	6	2	5	2.3	19	37	17		3	.251	.365	0	0	C-58, 1B-5
1889	72	273	100	30	2	12	4.4	53	76	16	19	2	.366	.623	0	0	C-66, 1B-9
1890 PHI P	62	234	69	9	3	3	1.3	38	57	19	19	2	.295	.397	0	0	C-59, 1B-3
1891 PHI AA	118	455	138	35	12	11	2.4	75	106	56	51	2	.303	.505	0	0	C-87, 1B-32
1892 WAS N	88	323	89	19	9	5	1.5	40	43	26	24	2	.276	.437	1	0	C-59, 1B-28
1893 2 teams	BAL	N	(24G –	.245)		NY	N	(42G –	.231)								
" total	66	249	59	10	8	2	0.8	35	44	19	20	4	.237	.365	1	0	C-43, 1B-22
10 yrs.	772	2964	848	188	50	50	1.7	440	362	210	133	23	.286	.434	2	0	C-585, 1B-184, OF-9, 3B-2

Bill Mills

MILLS, WILLIAM HENRY BR TR 5'10" 175 lbs.
B. Nov. 2, 1920, Boston, Mass.

	G	AB	H	2B	3B	HR	HR %	R	RBI	BB	SO	SB	BA	SA	PH AB	PH H	G by POS
1944 PHI A	5	4	1	0	0	0	0.0	0	0	1	1	0	.250	.250	3	1	C-1

Brad Mills

MILLS, JAMES BRADLEY BL TR 6' 195 lbs.
B. Jan. 19, 1957, Lemon Cove, Calif.

	G	AB	H	2B	3B	HR	HR %	R	RBI	BB	SO	SB	BA	SA	PH AB	PH H	G by POS
1980 MON N	21	60	18	1	0	0	0.0	1	8	5	6	0	.300	.317	4	2	3B-18
1981	17	21	5	1	0	0	0.0	3	1	2	1	0	.238	.286	9	3	3B-7, 2B-2
1982	54	67	15	3	0	1	1.5	6	2	5	11	0	.224	.313	40	10	3B-13
1983	14	20	5	0	0	0	0.0	1	1	2	3	0	.250	.250	9	2	3B-3, 1B-1
4 yrs.	106	168	43	5	0	1	0.6	11	12	14	21	0	.256	.304	62	17	3B-41, 2B-2, 1B-1

DIVISIONAL PLAYOFF SERIES

	G	AB	H	2B	3B	HR	HR %	R	RBI	BB	SO	SB	BA	SA	PH AB	PH H	G by POS
1981 MON N	1	0	0	0	0	0	–	0	0	1	0	0	–	–	0	0	

Buster Mills

MILLS, COLONEL BUSTER BR TR 5'11½" 195 lbs.
B. Sept. 16, 1908, Ranger, Tex.
Manager 1953.

	G	AB	H	2B	3B	HR	HR %	R	RBI	BB	SO	SB	BA	SA	PH AB	PH H	G by POS
1934 STL N	29	72	17	4	1	1	1.4	7	8	4	11	0	.236	.361	9	3	OF-18
1935 BKN N	17	56	12	2	1	1	1.8	12	7	5	11	1	.214	.339	0	0	OF-17
1937 BOS A	123	505	149	25	8	7	1.4	85	58	46	41	11	.295	.418	3	1	OF-120
1938 STL A	123	466	133	24	4	3	0.6	66	46	43	46	7	.285	.373	10	1	OF-113
1940 NY A	34	63	25	3	3	1	1.6	10	15	7	5	0	.397	.587	18	6	OF-14
1942 CLE A	80	195	54	4	2	1	0.5	19	26	23	18	5	.277	.333	24	4	OF-53
1946	9	22	6	0	0	0	0.0	1	3	3	5	0	.273	.273	3	0	OF-6
7 yrs.	415	1379	396	62	19	14	1.0	200	163	131	137	24	.287	.390	67	15	OF-341

Everett Mills

MILLS, EVERETT 6'1" 174 lbs.
B. 1845, Newark, N. J.   D. June 22, 1908, Newark, N. J.

	G	AB	H	2B	3B	HR	HR %	R	RBI	BB	SO	SB	BA	SA	PH AB	PH H	G by POS
1876 HAR N	63	254	66	8	1	0	0.0	28	23	1	3		.260	.299	0	0	1B-63

Frank Mills

MILLS, FRANK LeMOYNE BL TR 6' 180 lbs.
B. May 13, 1895, Knoxville, Ohio   D. Aug. 31, 1983

	G	AB	H	2B	3B	HR	HR %	R	RBI	BB	SO	SB	BA	SA	PH AB	PH H	G by POS
1914 CLE A	4	8	1	0	0	0	0.0	0	0	1	2	0	.125	.125	1	1	C-2

Jack Mills

MILLS, ABBOTT PAIGE BL TR 6' 165 lbs.
B. Oct. 23, 1889, S. Williamstown, Mass.   D. June 3, 1973, Washington, D. C.

	G	AB	H	2B	3B	HR	HR %	R	RBI	BB	SO	SB	BA	SA	PH AB	PH H	G by POS
1911 CLE A	13	17	5	0	0	0	0.0	5	1	1		1	.294	.294	0	0	3B-7

Rupert Mills

MILLS, RUPERT FRANK BR TR 6'2" 185 lbs.
B. Oct. 12, 1892, Newark, N. J.   D. July 20, 1929, Lake Hopatcong, N. J.

	G	AB	H	2B	3B	HR	HR %	R	RBI	BB	SO	SB	BA	SA	PH AB	PH H	G by POS
1915 NWK F	41	134	27	5	1	0	0.0	12	16	6		6	.201	.254	3	0	1B-37

Pete Milne

MILNE, WILLIAM JAMES BL TL 6'1" 180 lbs.
B. Apr. 10, 1925, Mobile, Ala.

	G	AB	H	2B	3B	HR	HR %	R	RBI	BB	SO	SB	BA	SA	PH AB	PH H	G by POS
1948 NY N	12	27	6	0	0	0	0.0	2	1	6	0		.222	.296	1	0	OF-9
1949	31	29	7	1	0	1	3.4	5	6	3	6	0	.241	.379	24	6	OF-1
1950	4	4	1	0	1	0	0.0	1	1	0	1	0	.250	.750	4	1	
3 yrs.	47	60	14	1	2	1	1.7	6	9	4	13	0	.233	.367	29	7	OF-10

Brian Milner

MILNER, BRIAN TATE BR TR 6'2" 200 lbs.
B. Nov. 17, 1959, Ft. Worth, Tex.

	G	AB	H	2B	3B	HR	HR %	R	RBI	BB	SO	SB	BA	SA	PH AB	PH H	G by POS
1978 TOR A	2	9	4	0	0	0	0.0	3	2	0	1	0	.444	.667	0	0	C-2

Eddie Milner

MILNER, EDDIE JAMES (Greyhound) BL TL 5'11" 173 lbs.
B. May 21, 1955, Columbus, Ohio

	G	AB	H	2B	3B	HR	HR %	R	RBI	BB	SO	SB	BA	SA	PH AB	PH H	G by POS
1980 CIN N	6	3	0	0	0	0	0.0	1	0	0	0	0	.000	.000	3	0	
1981	8	5	1	1	0	0	0.0	0	1	1	1	0	.200	.400	3	0	OF-4
1982	113	407	109	23	5	4	1.0	61	31	41	40	18	.268	.378	6	2	OF-107
1983	146	502	131	23	6	9	1.8	77	33	68	60	41	.261	.384	8	2	OF-139
1984	117	336	78	8	4	7	2.1	44	29	51	50	21	.232	.342	14	2	OF-108
5 yrs.	390	1253	319	55	15	20	1.6	183	94	161	151	80	.255	.370	34	6	OF-358

	G	AB	H	2B	3B	HR	HR %	R	RBI	BB	SO	SB	BA	SA	Pinch Hit AB	Pinch Hit H	G by POS

John Milner

MILNER, JOHN DAVID (Hammer)
B. Dec. 28, 1949, Atlanta, Ga.

BL TL 6' 185 lbs.

	G	AB	H	2B	3B	HR	HR %	R	RBI	BB	SO	SB	BA	SA	AB	H	G by POS
1971 NY N	9	18	3	1	0	0	0.0	1	1	0	3	0	.167	.222	6	0	OF-3
1972	117	362	86	12	2	17	4.7	52	38	51	74	2	.238	.423	12	3	OF-91, 1B-10
1973	129	451	108	12	3	23	5.1	69	72	62	84	1	.239	.432	4	0	1B-95, OF-29
1974	137	507	128	19	0	20	3.9	70	63	66	77	10	.252	.408	2	2	1B-133
1975	91	220	42	11	0	7	3.2	24	29	33	22	1	.191	.336	32	3	OF-31, 1B-29
1976	127	443	120	25	4	15	3.4	56	78	65	53	0	.271	.447	12	6	1B-112, OF-12
1977	131	388	99	20	3	12	3.1	43	57	61	55	6	.255	.415	21	2	1B-87, OF-22
1978 PIT N	108	295	80	17	0	6	2.0	39	38	34	25	5	.271	.390	15	4	OF-69, 1B-28
1979	128	326	90	9	4	16	4.9	52	60	53	37	3	.276	.475	26	7	OF-64, 1B-48
1980	114	238	58	6	0	8	3.4	31	34	52	29	2	.244	.370	33	8	1B-70, OF-11
1981 2 teams		PIT	N (34G –	.237)		MON	N	(31G –	.237)								
" total	65	135	32	6	0	5	3.7	12	18	17	9	0	.237	.393	26	9	1B-29, OF-8
1982 2 teams		MON	N (26G –	.107)		PIT	N	(33G –	.240)								
" total	59	53	9	2	0	2	3.8	6	10	10	5	1	.170	.321	43	7	1B-6
12 yrs.	1215	3436	855	140	16	131	3.8	455	498	504	473	31	.249	.413	232	51	1B-547, OF-440

DIVISIONAL PLAYOFF SERIES

| 1981 MON N | 2 | 2 | 1 | 0 | 0 | 0 | 0.0 | 0 | 1 | 0 | 0 | 0 | .500 | .500 | 2 | 1 | |

LEAGUE CHAMPIONSHIP SERIES

1973 NY N	5	17	3	0	0	0	0.0	2	1	5	3	0	.176	.176	0	0	1B-5
1979 PIT N	3	9	0	0	0	0	0.0	0	0	2	0	0	.000	.000	0	0	OF-3
1981 MON N	1	1	0	0	0	0	0.0	0	0	0	1	0	.000	.000	1	0	
3 yrs.	9	27	3	0	0	0	0.0	2	1	7	4	0	.111	.111	1	0	1B-5, OF-3

WORLD SERIES

1973 NY N	7	27	8	0	0	0	0.0	2	2	5	1	0	.296	.296	0	0	1B-7
1979 PIT N	3	9	3	1	0	0	0.0	2	1	2	0	0	.333	.444	0	0	OF-3
2 yrs.	10	36	11	1	0	0	0.0	4	3	7	1	0	.306	.333	0	0	1B-7, OF-3

Mike Milosevich

MILOSEVICH, MICHAEL (Mollie)
B. Jan. 13, 1915, Zeigler, Ill.   D. Feb. 3, 1966, E. Chicago, Ind.

BR TR 5'10½" 172 lbs.

	G	AB	H	2B	3B	HR	HR %	R	RBI	BB	SO	SB	BA	SA	AB	H	G by POS
1944 NY A	94	312	77	11	4	0	0.0	27	32	30	37	1	.247	.308	2	0	SS-91
1945	30	69	15	2	0	0	0.0	5	7	6	6	0	.217	.246	6	0	SS-22, 2B-1
2 yrs.	124	381	92	13	4	0	0.0	32	39	36	43	1	.241	.297	8	0	SS-113, 2B-1

Dan Minahan

MINAHAN, DANIEL JOSEPH
B. Nov. 28, 1865, Troy, N. Y.   D. Aug. 8, 1929, Troy, N. Y.

BR TR 5'10" 145 lbs.

	G	AB	H	2B	3B	HR	HR %	R	RBI	BB	SO	SB	BA	SA	AB	H	G by POS
1895 LOU N	8	34	13	0	0	0	0.0	6	6	1	1	0	.382	.382	0	0	3B-7, OF-2

Don Mincher

MINCHER, DONALD RAY
B. June 24, 1938, Huntsville, Ala.

BL TR 6'3" 205 lbs.

	G	AB	H	2B	3B	HR	HR %	R	RBI	BB	SO	SB	BA	SA	AB	H	G by POS
1960 WAS A	27	79	19	4	1	2	2.5	10	5	11	11	0	.241	.392	7	2	1B-20
1961 MIN A	35	101	19	5	1	5	5.0	18	11	22	11	0	.188	.406	8	0	1B-29
1962	86	121	29	1	1	9	7.4	20	29	34	24	0	.240	.488	45	9	1B-25
1963	82	225	58	8	0	17	7.6	41	42	30	51	0	.258	.520	14	0	1B-60
1964	120	287	68	12	4	23	8.0	45	56	27	51	0	.237	.547	41	7	1B-76
1965	128	346	87	17	3	22	6.4	43	65	49	73	1	.251	.509	29	6	1B-99, OF-1
1966	139	431	108	30	0	14	3.2	53	62	58	68	3	.251	.418	8	3	1B-130
1967 CAL A	147	487	133	23	3	25	5.1	81	76	69	69	0	.273	.487	6	1	1B-142, OF-1
1968	120	399	94	12	1	13	3.3	35	48	43	65	0	.236	.384	9	3	1B-113
1969 SEA A	140	427	105	14	0	25	5.9	53	78	78	69	10	.246	.454	9	2	1B-122
1970 OAK A	140	463	114	18	0	27	5.8	62	74	56	71	5	.246	.460	3	0	1B-137
1971 2 teams		OAK	A (28G –	.239)		WAS	A	(100G –	.291)								
" total	128	415	116	21	2	12	2.9	44	53	73	66	3	.280	.427	12	2	1B-115
1972 2 teams		TEX	A (61G –	.236)		OAK	A	(47G –	.148)								
" total	108	245	53	11	0	6	2.4	25	44	56	39	2	.216	.335	30	7	1B-70
13 yrs.	1400	4026	1003	176	16	200	5.0	530	643	606	668	24	.249	.450	221	42	1B-1138, OF-2

LEAGUE CHAMPIONSHIP SERIES

| 1972 OAK A | 1 | 1 | 0 | 0 | 0 | 0 | 0.0 | 0 | 0 | 0 | 1 | 0 | .000 | .000 | 1 | 0 | |

WORLD SERIES

1965 MIN A	7	23	3	0	0	1	4.3	3	1	2	7	0	.130	.261	0	0	1B-7
1972 OAK A	3	1	1	0	0	0	0.0	0	1	0	0	0	1.000	1.000	1	1	
2 yrs.	10	24	4	0	0	1	4.2	3	2	2	7	0	.167	.292	1	1	1B-7

Minnie Minoso

MINOSO, SATURNINO ORESTES ARRIETA ARMAS
B. Nov. 29, 1922, Havana, Cuba

BR TR 5'10" 175 lbs.

	G	AB	H	2B	3B	HR	HR %	R	RBI	BB	SO	SB	BA	SA	AB	H	G by POS
1949 CLE A	9	16	3	0	0	1	6.3	2	1	2	2	0	.188	.375	1	0	OF-7
1951 2 teams		CLE	A (8G –	.429)		CHI	A	(138G –	.324)								
" total	146	530	173	34	14	10	1.9	112	76	72	42	31	.326	.500	2	0	OF-82, 3B-68, 1B-7, SS-1
1952 CHI A	147	569	160	24	9	13	2.3	96	61	71	46	22	.281	.424	0	0	OF-143, 3B-9, SS-1
1953	157	556	174	24	8	15	2.7	104	104	74	43	25	.313	.466	0	0	OF-147, 3B-10
1954	153	568	182	29	18	19	3.3	119	116	77	46	18	.320	.535	0	0	OF-146, 3B-9
1955	139	517	149	26	7	10	1.9	79	70	76	43	19	.288	.424	1	0	OF-138, 3B-2
1956	151	545	172	29	11	21	3.9	106	88	86	40	12	.316	.525	3	1	OF-148, 3B-8, 1B-1
1957	153	568	176	36	5	12	2.1	96	103	79	54	18	.310	.454	0	0	OF-152, 3B-1
1958 CLE A	149	556	168	25	2	24	4.3	94	80	59	53	14	.302	.484	3	1	OF-147, 3B-1
1959	148	570	172	32	0	21	3.7	92	92	54	46	8	.302	.468	0	0	OF-148
1960 CHI A	154	591	184	32	4	20	3.4	89	105	52	63	17	.311	.481	0	0	OF-154
1961	152	540	151	28	3	14	2.6	91	82	67	46	9	.280	.420	1	1	OF-147
1962 STL N	39	97	19	5	0	1	1.0	14	10	7	17	4	.196	.278	6	0	OF-27
1963 WAS A	109	315	72	12	2	4	1.3	38	30	33	38	8	.229	.317	26	4	OF-74, 3B-8
1964 CHI A	30	31	7	0	0	1	3.2	4	5	5	3	0	.226	.323	22	4	OF-5
1976	3	8	1	0	0	0	0.0	0	0	0	2	0	.125	.125	0	0	DH-3
1980	2	2	0	0	0	0	0.0	0	0	0	0	0	.000	.000	2	0	
17 yrs.	1841	6579	1963	336	83	186	2.8	1136	1023	814	584	205	.298	.459	67	11	OF-1665, 3B-116, 1B-8, DH-3, SS-2

	G	AB	H	2B	3B	HR	HR %	R	RBI	BB	SO	SB	BA	SA	Pinch Hit AB	Pinch Hit H	G by POS

Willie Miranda

MIRANDA, GUILLERMO PEREZ
B. May 24, 1926, Velasco, Cuba

BB TR 5'9½" 150 lbs.

	G	AB	H	2B	3B	HR	HR %	R	RBI	BB	SO	SB	BA	SA	PH AB	PH H	G by POS
1951 WAS A	7	9	4	0	0	0	0.0	2	0	0	0	0	.444	.444	2	2	SS-2, 1B-1
1952 3 teams	CHI A (12G – .250)			STL A (7G – .091)				CHI A (58G – .218)									
" total	77	161	34	4	2	0	0.0	16	8	16	15	1	.211	.261	1	0	SS-61, 3B-5, 2B-2
1953 2 teams	STL A (17G – .167)			NY A (48G – .224)													
" total	65	64	14	0	0	1	1.6	14	5	6	11	2	.219	.266	0	0	SS-53, 3B-6
1954 NY A	92	116	29	4	2	1	0.9	12	12	10	10	0	.250	.345	1	0	SS-88, 2B-4, 3B-1
1955 BAL A	153	487	124	12	6	1	0.2	42	38	42	58	4	.255	.310	0	0	SS-153, 2B-1
1956	148	461	100	16	4	2	0.4	38	34	46	73	3	.217	.282	0	0	SS-147
1957	115	314	61	3	0	0	0.0	29	20	24	42	2	.194	.204	0	0	SS-115
1958	102	214	43	6	0	1	0.5	15	8	14	25	1	.201	.243	0	0	SS-102
1959	65	88	14	5	0	0	0.0	8	7	7	16	0	.159	.216	0	0	SS-47, 3B-11, 2B-5
9 yrs.	824	1914	423	50	14	6	0.3	176	132	165	250	13	.221	.271	4	2	SS-768, 3B-23, 2B-12, 1B-1

John Misse

MISSE, JOHN BEVERLEY
B. May 30, 1885, Highland, Kans. D. Mar. 18, 1970, St. Joseph, Mo.

BR TR 5'8" 150 lbs.

	G	AB	H	2B	3B	HR	HR %	R	RBI	BB	SO	SB	BA	SA	PH AB	PH H	G by POS
1914 STL F	99	306	60	8	1	0	0.0	28	22	36		3	.196	.229	0	0	2B-50, SS-48, 3B-2

Bobby Mitchell

MITCHELL, ROBERT VAN
B. Apr. 7, 1955, Salt Lake City, Utah

BL TL 5'10" 170 lbs.

	G	AB	H	2B	3B	HR	HR %	R	RBI	BB	SO	SB	BA	SA	PH AB	PH H	G by POS
1980 LA N	9	3	1	0	0	0	0.0	1	0	1	0	0	.333	.333	1	1	OF-8
1981	10	8	1	0	0	0	0.0	0	0	1	4	0	.125	.125	2	0	OF-7
1982 MIN A	124	454	113	11	6	2	0.4	48	28	54	53	8	.249	.313	3	1	OF-121
1983	59	152	35	4	2	1	0.7	26	15	28	21	1	.230	.303	13	3	OF-44
4 yrs.	202	617	150	15	8	3	0.5	75	43	84	78	9	.243	.308	19	5	OF-180

Bobby Mitchell

MITCHELL, ROBERT VANCE
B. Oct. 22, 1943, Norristown, Pa.

BR TR 6'3" 185 lbs.

	G	AB	H	2B	3B	HR	HR %	R	RBI	BB	SO	SB	BA	SA	PH AB	PH H	G by POS
1970 NY A	10	22	5	2	0	0	0.0	1	4	2	3	0	.227	.318	3	1	OF-7
1971 MIL A	35	55	10	1	1	2	3.6	7	6	6	18	0	.182	.345	12	2	OF-19
1973	47	130	29	6	0	5	3.8	12	20	5	32	4	.223	.385	7	2	OF-20, DH-19
1974	88	173	42	6	2	5	2.9	27	20	18	46	7	.243	.387	9	2	DH-53, OF-26
1975	93	229	57	14	3	9	3.9	39	41	25	69	3	.249	.454	13	2	OF-72, DH-11
5 yrs.	273	609	143	29	6	21	3.4	86	91	56	168	14	.235	.406	44	9	OF-144, DH-83

Clarence Mitchell

MITCHELL, CLARENCE ELMER
B. Feb. 22, 1891, Franklin, Neb. D. Nov. 6, 1963, Grand Island, Neb.

BL TL 5'11½" 190 lbs.

	G	AB	H	2B	3B	HR	HR %	R	RBI	BB	SO	SB	BA	SA	PH AB	PH H	G by POS
1911 DET A	5	4	2	0	0	0	0.0	2	0	1		0	.500	.500	0	0	P-5
1916 CIN N	56	117	28	2	1	0	0.0	11	11	4	6	1	.239	.274	14	4	P-29, 1B-9, OF-3
1917	47	90	25	3	0	0	0.0	13	5	5	5	0	.278	.311	1	0	P-32, 1B-6, OF-5
1918 BKN N	10	24	6	1	1	0	0.0	2	2	0	3	0	.250	.375	2	0	OF-6, 1B-2, P-1
1919	34	49	18	1	0	1	2.0	7	2	4	4	0	.367	.449	9	3	P-23
1920	55	107	25	2	2	0	0.0	9	11	8	9	1	.234	.290	18	6	P-19, 1B-11, OF-4
1921	46	91	24	5	0	0	0.0	11	12	5	7	3	.264	.319	3	0	P-37, 1B-4
1922	55	155	45	6	3	3	1.9	21	28	19	6	0	.290	.426	9	4	1B-42, P-5
1923 PHI N	53	78	21	3	2	1	1.3	10	9	4	11	0	.269	.397	24	6	P-29
1924	69	102	26	3	0	0	0.0	7	13	2	7	1	.255	.284	37	6	P-30
1925	52	92	18	2	0	0	0.0	7	13	5	9	2	.196	.217	17	1	P-32, 1B-2
1926	39	78	19	4	0	0	0.0	8	6	5	5	0	.244	.295	7	1	P-28, 1B-4
1927	18	42	10	2	0	1	2.4	5	6	2	1	0	.238	.357	3	0	P-13
1928 2 teams	PHI N (5G – .250)			STL N (19G – .125)													
" total	24	60	8	1	0	0	0.0	0	1	0	3	0	.133	.150	1	0	P-22
1929 STL N	26	66	18	3	1	0	0.0	9	9	4	6	1	.273	.348	0	0	P-25
1930 2 teams	STL N (1G – .500)			NY N (24G – .255)													
" total	25	49	13	1	0	0	0.0	9	1	5	0	0	.265	.286	0	0	P-25
1931 NY N	27	73	16	2	0	1	1.4	5	4	2	4	0	.219	.288	0	0	P-27
1932	8	10	2	0	0	0	0.0	2	0	1	1	0	.200	.200	0	0	P-8
18 yrs.	649	1287	324	41	10	7	0.5	138	133	72	92	9	.252	.315	145	31	P-390, 1B-80, OF-18
WORLD SERIES																	
1920 BKN N	2	3	1	0	0	0	0.0	0	0	0	0	0	.333	.333	1	1	P-1
1928 STL N	1	2	0	0	0	0	0.0	0	0	0	0	0	.000	.000	0	0	P-1
2 yrs.	3	5	1	0	0	0	0.0	0	0	0	0	0	.200	.200	1	1	P-2

Dale Mitchell

MITCHELL, LOREN DALE
B. Aug. 23, 1921, Colony, Okla.

BL TL 6'1" 195 lbs.

	G	AB	H	2B	3B	HR	HR %	R	RBI	BB	SO	SB	BA	SA	PH AB	PH H	G by POS
1946 CLE A	11	44	19	3	0	0	0.0	7	5	1	2	1	.432	.500	0	0	OF-11
1947	123	493	156	16	10	1	0.2	69	34	23	14	2	.316	.396	8	3	OF-115
1948	141	608	204	30	8	4	0.7	82	56	45	17	13	.336	.431	2	1	OF-140
1949	149	640	203	16	23	3	0.5	81	56	43	11	10	.317	.428	0	0	OF-149
1950	130	506	156	27	5	3	0.6	81	49	67	21	3	.308	.399	4	1	OF-127
1951	134	510	148	21	7	11	2.2	83	62	53	16	7	.290	.424	10	2	OF-124
1952	134	511	165	26	3	5	1.0	61	58	52	9	6	.323	.415	5	1	OF-128
1953	134	500	150	26	4	13	2.6	76	60	42	20	3	.300	.446	13	2	OF-125
1954	53	60	17	1	0	1	1.7	6	6	9	1	0	.283	.350	44	14	OF-6, 1B-1
1955	61	58	15	2	1	0	0.0	4	10	4	3	0	.259	.328	45	13	1B-8, OF-3
1956 2 teams	CLE A (38G – .133)			BKN N (19G – .292)													
" total	57	54	11	0	0	0	0.0	5	7	7	5	0	.204	.222	46	10	OF-3
11 yrs.	1127	3984	1244	169	61	41	1.0	555	403	346	119	45	.312	.416	177	47	OF-931, 1B-9
WORLD SERIES																	
1948 CLE A	6	23	4	1	0	1	4.3	4	1	2	0	0	.174	.348	0	0	OF-6
1954	3	2	0	0	0	0	0.0	0	0	1	0	0	.000	.000	2	0	
1956 BKN N	4	4	0	0	0	0	0.0	0	0	0	1	0	.000	.000	4	0	
3 yrs.	13	29	4	1	0	1	3.4	4	1	3	1	0	.138	.276	6	0	OF-6

	G	AB	H	2B	3B	HR	HR %	R	RBI	BB	SO	SB	BA	SA	Pinch Hit AB	Pinch Hit H	G by POS

Fred Mitchell

MITCHELL, FREDERICK FRANCIS
Born Frederick Francis Yapp.
B. June 5, 1878, Cambridge, Mass. D. Oct. 13, 1970, Newton, Mass.
Manager 1917-23.
BR TR 5'9½" 185 lbs.

	G	AB	H	2B	3B	HR	HR %	R	RBI	BB	SO	SB	BA	SA	Pinch Hit AB	Pinch Hit H	G by POS
1901 BOS A	20	44	7	0	2	0	0.0	5	4	2		0	.159	.250	0	0	P-17, 2B-2, SS-1
1902 2 teams	BOS	A (1G – .000)		PHI	A	(20G – .188)											
" total	21	49	9	1	0	0	0.0	7	3	1		1	.184	.245	1	0	P-19, OF-1
1903 PHI N	29	95	19	4	0	0	0.0	11	10	0		0	.200	.242	1	1	P-28
1904 2 teams	PHI	N (25G – .207)		BKN	N	(8G – .292)											
" total	33	106	24	4	2	0	0.0	12	9	6		1	.226	.302	0	0	P-21, 1B-9, 3B-2, OF-1
1905 BKN N	27	79	15	0	0	0	0.0	4	8	4		0	.190	.190	2	1	P-12, 1B-7, 3B-4, OF-1, SS-1
1910 NY A	68	196	45	7	2	0	0.0	16	18	9		6	.230	.286	6	2	C-68
1913 BOS N	4	3	1	0	0	0	0.0	0	0	0	2	0	.333	.333	3	1	
7 yrs.	202	572	120	16	7	0	0.0	55	52	22	2	8	.210	.262	13	5	P-97, C-68, 1B-16, 3B-6, OF-3, SS-2, 2B-2

Johnny Mitchell

MITCHELL, JOHN FRANKLIN
B. Aug. 9, 1894, Detroit, Mich. D. Nov. 4, 1965, Birmingham, Mich.
BB TR 5'8" 155 lbs.

	G	AB	H	2B	3B	HR	HR %	R	RBI	BB	SO	SB	BA	SA	Pinch Hit AB	Pinch Hit H	G by POS
1921 NY A	13	42	11	1	0	0	0.0	4	2	4	4	1	.262	.286	0	0	SS-7, 2B-5
1922 2 teams	NY	A (4G – .000)		BOS	A	(59G – .251)											
" total	63	207	51	4	1	0	0.5	21	8	16	18	1	.246	.290	1	0	SS-62
1923 BOS A	92	347	78	15	4	0	0.0	40	19	34	18	7	.225	.291	0	0	SS-87, 2B-5
1924 BKN N	64	243	64	10	0	1	0.4	42	16	37	22	3	.263	.317	0	0	SS-64
1925	97	336	84	8	3	0	0.0	45	18	28	19	2	.250	.292	1	0	SS-90
5 yrs.	329	1175	288	38	8	2	0.2	152	63	119	81	14	.245	.296	2	0	SS-310, 2B-10

Kevin Mitchell

MITCHELL, KEVIN DARNELL
B. Jan. 13, 1962, San Diego, Calif.
BR TR 5'10" 185 lbs.

	G	AB	H	2B	3B	HR	HR %	R	RBI	BB	SO	SB	BA	SA	Pinch Hit AB	Pinch Hit H	G by POS
1984 NY N	7	14	3	0	0	0	0.0	0	1	0	3	0	.214	.214	4	1	3B-5

Mike Mitchell

MITCHELL, MICHAEL FRANCIS
B. Dec. 12, 1879, Springfield, Ohio D. July 16, 1961, Phoenix, Ariz.
BR TR 6'1" 185 lbs.

	G	AB	H	2B	3B	HR	HR %	R	RBI	BB	SO	SB	BA	SA	Pinch Hit AB	Pinch Hit H	G by POS
1907 CIN N	148	558	163	17	12	3	0.5	64	47	37		17	.292	.382	0	0	OF-146, 1B-2
1908	119	406	90	9	6	1	0.2	41	37	46		18	.222	.281	0	0	OF-118, 1B-1
1909	145	523	162	17	17	4	0.8	83	86	57		37	.310	.430	0	0	OF-144, 1B-1
1910	156	583	167	16	18	5	0.9	79	88	59	56	35	.286	.401	0	0	OF-149, 1B-7
1911	142	529	154	22	22	2	0.4	74	84	44	34	35	.291	.427	2	0	OF-140
1912	157	552	156	14	13	4	0.7	60	78	41	43	23	.283	.377	2	1	OF-144
1913 2 teams	CHI	N (81G – .259)		PIT	N	(54G – .271)											
" total	135	477	126	19	8	5	1.0	62	51	46	48	23	.264	.369	0	0	OF-135
1914 2 teams	PIT	N (76G – .234)		WAS	N	(55G – .285)											
" total	131	466	119	16	8	3	0.6	51	43	38	35	14	.255	.343	2	0	OF-129
8 yrs.	1133	4094	1137	130	104	27	0.7	514	514	368	216	202	.278	.380	6	1	OF-1105, 1B-11

Ralph Mitterling

MITTERLING, RALPH (Sarge)
B. Apr. 19, 1890, Freeburg, Pa. D. Jan. 22, 1956, Pittsburgh, Pa.
BR TR 5'10" 165 lbs.

	G	AB	H	2B	3B	HR	HR %	R	RBI	BB	SO	SB	BA	SA	Pinch Hit AB	Pinch Hit H	G by POS
1916 PHI A	13	39	6	0	0	0	0.0	1	2	3	6	0	.154	.154	1	0	OF-12

George Mitterwald

MITTERWALD, GEORGE EUGENE
B. June 7, 1945, Berkeley, Calif.
BR TR 6'2" 195 lbs.

	G	AB	H	2B	3B	HR	HR %	R	RBI	BB	SO	SB	BA	SA	Pinch Hit AB	Pinch Hit H	G by POS
1966 MIN A	3	5	1	0	0	0	0.0	1	0	0	0	0	.200	.200	0	0	C-3
1968	11	34	7	1	0	0	0.0	1	1	3	8	0	.206	.235	1	0	C-10
1969	69	187	48	8	0	5	2.7	18	13	17	47	0	.257	.380	6	1	C-63, OF-1
1970	117	369	82	12	2	15	4.1	36	46	34	84	3	.222	.388	1	0	C-117
1971	125	388	97	13	1	13	3.4	38	44	39	104	3	.250	.389	7	2	C-120
1972	64	163	30	4	1	1	0.6	12	8	9	37	0	.184	.239	4	1	C-61
1973	125	432	112	15	0	16	3.7	50	64	39	111	3	.259	.405	3	0	C-122, DH-3
1974 CHI N	78	215	54	7	0	7	3.3	17	28	18	42	1	.251	.381	11	3	C-68
1975	84	200	44	4	3	5	2.5	19	26	19	42	0	.220	.345	15	3	C-59, 1B-10
1976	101	303	65	7	0	5	1.7	19	28	16	63	1	.215	.287	16	1	C-64, 1B-25
1977	110	349	83	22	0	9	2.6	40	43	28	69	3	.238	.378	2	0	C-109, 1B-1
11 yrs.	887	2645	623	93	7	76	2.9	251	301	222	607	14	.236	.362	66	11	C-796, 1B-36, DH-3, OF-1

LEAGUE CHAMPIONSHIP SERIES

	G	AB	H	2B	3B	HR	HR %	R	RBI	BB	SO	SB	BA	SA	Pinch Hit AB	Pinch Hit H	G by POS
1969 MIN A	2	7	1	0	0	0	0.0	0	0	1	3	0	.143	.143	0	0	C-2
1970	3	8	4	1	0	0	0.0	2	2	0	2	0	.500	.625	0	0	C-2
2 yrs.	5	15	5	1	0	0	0.0	2	2	1	5	0	.333	.400	0	0	C-4

Johnny Mize

MIZE, JOHN ROBERT (The Big Cat)
B. Jan. 7, 1913, Demorest, Ga.
Hall of Fame 1981.
BL TR 6'2" 215 lbs.

	G	AB	H	2B	3B	HR	HR %	R	RBI	BB	SO	SB	BA	SA	Pinch Hit AB	Pinch Hit H	G by POS
1936 STL N	126	414	136	30	8	19	4.6	76	93	50	32	1	.329	.577	15	7	1B-97, OF-8
1937	145	560	204	40	7	25	4.5	103	113	56	57	2	.364	.595	1	0	1B-144
1938	149	531	179	34	16	27	5.1	85	102	74	47	0	.337	.614	7	1	1B-140
1939	153	564	197	44	14	28	5.0	104	108	92	49	0	.349	.626	1	0	1B-152
1940	155	579	182	31	13	43	7.4	111	137	82	49	7	.314	.636	2	1	1B-153
1941	126	473	150	39	8	16	3.4	67	100	70	45	4	.317	.535	4	1	1B-122
1942 NY N	142	541	165	25	7	26	4.8	97	110	60	39	3	.305	.521	3	0	1B-138
1946	101	377	127	18	3	22	5.8	70	70	62	26	3	.337	.576	0	0	1B-101
1947	154	586	177	26	2	51	8.7	137	138	74	42	2	.302	.614	0	0	1B-154
1948	152	560	162	26	4	40	7.1	110	125	94	37	4	.289	.564	0	0	1B-152
1949 2 teams	NY	N (106G – .263)		NY	A	(13G – .261)											
" total	119	411	108	16	0	19	4.6	63	64	54	21	1	.263	.440	8	2	1B-107
1950 NY A	90	274	76	12	0	25	9.1	43	72	29	24	0	.277	.595	16	3	1B-72
1951	113	332	86	14	1	10	3.0	37	49	36	24	1	.259	.398	21	9	1B-93
1952	78	137	36	9	0	4	2.9	9	29	11	15	0	.263	.416	48	10	1B-27
1953	81	104	26	3	0	4	3.8	6	27	12	17	0	.250	.394	61	19	1B-15
15 yrs.	1884	6443	2011	367	83	359	5.6	1118	1337	856	524	28	.312	.562	187	53	1B-1667, OF-8
														8th			

	G	AB	H	2B	3B	HR	HR %	R	RBI	BB	SO	SB	BA	SA	Pinch Hit AB	H	G by POS

Johnny Mize continued

WORLD SERIES

	G	AB	H	2B	3B	HR	HR %	R	RBI	BB	SO	SB	BA	SA	PH AB	PH H	G by POS
1949 NY A	2	2	2	0	0	0	0.0	0	2	0	0	0	1.000	1.000	2	2	
1950	4	15	2	0	0	0	0.0	0	0	0	1	0	.133	.133	0	0	1B-4
1951	4	7	2	1	0	0	0.0	2	1	2	0	0	.286	.429	2	0	1B-2
1952	5	15	6	1	0	3	20.0	3	6	3	1	0	.400	1.067	1	1	1B-4
1953	3	3	0	0	0	0	0.0	0	0	0	1	0	.000	.000	3	0	
5 yrs.	18	42	12	2	0	3	7.1	5	9	5	3	0	.286	.548	8	3	1B-10
															3rd	1st	

John Mizerock

MIZEROCK, JOHN JOSEPH
B. Dec. 8, 1960, Punxsutawney, Pa.
BL TR 6' 180 lbs.

	G	AB	H	2B	3B	HR	HR %	R	RBI	BB	SO	SB	BA	SA	PH AB	PH H	G by POS
1983 HOU N	33	85	13	4	1	1	1.2	8	10	12	15	0	.153	.259	0	0	C-33

Bill Mizeur

MIZEUR, WILLIAM FRANCIS (Bad Bill)
B. June 22, 1897, Nokomis, Ill.   D. Aug. 27, 1976, Decatur, Ill.
BL TR 6' 180 lbs.

	G	AB	H	2B	3B	HR	HR %	R	RBI	BB	SO	SB	BA	SA	PH AB	PH H	G by POS
1923 STL A	1	1	0	0	0	0	0.0	0	0	0	0	0	.000	.000	1	0	
1924	1	1	0	0	0	0	0.0	0	0	0	0	0	.000	.000	1	0	
2 yrs.	2	2	0	0	0	0	0.0	0	0	0	0	0	.000	.000	2	0	

Dave Moates

MOATES, DAVID ALLAN
B. Jan. 30, 1948, Smyrna, Ga.
BL TL 5'9" 163 lbs.

	G	AB	H	2B	3B	HR	HR %	R	RBI	BB	SO	SB	BA	SA	PH AB	PH H	G by POS
1974 TEX A	1	0	0	0	0	0	–	0	0	0	0	0	–	–	0	0	
1975	54	175	48	9	0	3	1.7	21	14	13	15	9	.274	.377	0	0	OF-51, DH-1
1976	85	137	33	7	1	0	0.0	21	13	11	18	6	.241	.307	7	3	OF-66, DH-7
3 yrs.	140	312	81	16	1	3	1.0	42	27	24	33	15	.260	.346	7	3	OF-117, DH-8

Danny Moeller

MOELLER, DANIEL EDWARD
B. Mar. 23, 1885, DeWitt, Iowa   D. Apr. 14, 1951, Florence, Ala.
BB TR 5'11" 165 lbs.

	G	AB	H	2B	3B	HR	HR %	R	RBI	BB	SO	SB	BA	SA	PH AB	PH H	G by POS
1907 PIT N	11	42	12	1	1	0	0.0	4	3	4		2	.286	.357	0	0	OF-11
1908	36	109	21	3	1	0	0.0	14	9	9		4	.193	.239	7	0	OF-27
1912 WAS A	132	519	143	26	10	6	1.2	90	46	52		30	.276	.399	0	0	OF-132
1913	153	589	139	15	10	5	0.8	88	42	72	103	62	.236	.321	0	0	OF-153
1914	151	571	143	19	10	1	0.2	83	45	71	89	26	.250	.324	1	0	OF-150
1915	118	438	99	11	10	2	0.5	65	23	59	63	32	.226	.311	1	0	OF-116
1916 2 teams			WAS	A	(78G – .246)			CLE	A	(25G – .067)							
" total	103	270	61	8	1	1	0.4	35	24	35	41	15	.226	.274	21	4	OF-73, 2B-1
7 yrs.	704	2538	618	83	43	15	0.6	379	192	302	296	171	.243	.328	30	4	OF-662, 2B-1

Joe Moffett

MOFFETT, JOSEPH W.
Brother of Sam Moffett.
B. June, 1859, Wheeling, W. Va.

	G	AB	H	2B	3B	HR	HR %	R	RBI	BB	SO	SB	BA	SA	PH AB	PH H	G by POS
1884 TOL AA	56	204	41	5	3	0	0.0	17		2			.201	.255	0	0	1B-38, 3B-12, OF-3, 2B-3

Sam Moffett

MOFFETT, SAMUEL R.
Brother of Joe Moffett.
B. 1857, Wheeling, W. Va.   D. May 5, 1907, Butte, Mont.
TR

	G	AB	H	2B	3B	HR	HR %	R	RBI	BB	SO	SB	BA	SA	PH AB	PH H	G by POS
1884 CLE N	67	256	47	12	2	0	0.0	26	14	8	56		.184	.246	0	0	OF-42, P-24, 1B-2, 3B-1, 2B-1
1887 IND N	11	41	5	1	0	0	0.0	6	1	1	6	2	.122	.146	0	0	P-6, OF-5
1888	10	35	4	0	0	0	0.0	6	0	5	4	0	.114	.114	0	0	P-7, OF-3
3 yrs.	88	332	56	13	2	0	0.0	38	15	14	66	2	.169	.220	0	0	OF-50, P-37, 1B-2, 3B-1, 2B-1

John Mohardt

MOHARDT, JOHN HENRY
B. Jan. 23, 1898, Pittsburgh, Pa.   D. Nov. 24, 1961, La Jolla, Calif.
BR TR 5'10" 165 lbs.

	G	AB	H	2B	3B	HR	HR %	R	RBI	BB	SO	SB	BA	SA	PH AB	PH H	G by POS
1922 DET A	5	1	1	0	0	0	0.0	2	0	1	0	0	1.000	1.000	0	0	OF-3

Kid Mohler

MOHLER, ERNEST FOLLETTE
B. Dec. 13, 1874, Oneida, Ill.   D. Nov. 4, 1961, San Francisco, Calif.
BR TL 5'4½" 145 lbs.

	G	AB	H	2B	3B	HR	HR %	R	RBI	BB	SO	SB	BA	SA	PH AB	PH H	G by POS
1894 WAS N	3	9	1	0	0	0	0.0	0	2	4	0	0	.111	.111	0	0	2B-3

Johnny Mokan

MOKAN, JOHN LEO
B. Sept. 23, 1895, Buffalo, N. Y.
BR TR 5'7" 165 lbs.

	G	AB	H	2B	3B	HR	HR %	R	RBI	BB	SO	SB	BA	SA	PH AB	PH H	G by POS
1921 PIT N	19	52	14	3	2	0	0.0	7	9	5	3	0	.269	.404	3	0	OF-13
1922 2 teams			PIT	N	(31G – .258)			PHI	N	(47G – .252)							
" total	78	240	61	10	3	3	1.3	29	35	25	28	1	.254	.350	14	3	OF-54, 3B-2
1923 PHI N	113	400	125	23	3	10	2.5	76	48	53	31	6	.313	.460	6	1	OF-105, 3B-1
1924	96	366	95	15	7	7	1.9	50	44	30	27	7	.260	.363	2	1	OF-94
1925	75	209	69	11	2	6	2.9	30	42	27	9	3	.330	.488	6	1	OF-68
1926	127	456	138	23	5	6	1.3	68	62	41	31	4	.303	.414	2	1	OF-123
1927	74	213	61	13	2	0	0.0	22	33	25	21	5	.286	.366	9	2	OF-63
7 yrs.	582	1936	563	98	17	32	1.7	282	273	206	150	26	.291	.409	42	9	OF-520, 3B-3

Fenton Mole

MOLE, FENTON LeROY (Muscles)
B. June 14, 1925, San Leandro, Calif.
BL TL 6'1½" 200 lbs.

	G	AB	H	2B	3B	HR	HR %	R	RBI	BB	SO	SB	BA	SA	PH AB	PH H	G by POS
1949 NY A	10	27	5	2	1	0	0.0	2	4	2	5	0	.185	.333	2	1	1B-8

Bob Molinaro

MOLINARO, ROBERT JOSEPH (Molly)
B. May 21, 1950, Newark, N. J.
BL TR 6' 180 lbs.

	G	AB	H	2B	3B	HR	HR %	R	RBI	BB	SO	SB	BA	SA	PH AB	PH H	G by POS
1975 DET A	6	19	5	0	1	0	0.0	2	1	1	0	0	.263	.368	0	0	OF-6
1977 2 teams			DET	A	(4G – .250)			CHI	A	(1G – .500)							
" total	5	6	2	1	0	0	0.0	0	0	0	3	1	.333	.500	4	1	OF-1
1978 CHI A	105	286	75	5	5	6	2.1	39	27	19	12	4	.262	.378	12	4	OF-62, DH-32
1979 BAL A	8	6	0	0	0	0	0.0	0	0	1	3	1	.000	.000	1	0	OF-5
1980 CHI A	119	344	100	16	4	5	1.5	48	36	26	29	18	.291	.404	21	7	OF-49, DH-47

	G	AB	H	2B	3B	HR	HR %	R	RBI	BB	SO	SB	BA	SA	Pinch Hit AB	Pinch Hit H	G by POS

Bob Molinaro continued

	G	AB	H	2B	3B	HR	HR %	R	RBI	BB	SO	SB	BA	SA	PH AB	PH H	G by POS
1981	47	42	11	1	1	1	2.4	7	9	8	1	1	.262	.405	35	9	DH-4, OF-2
1982 2 teams		CHI	N (65G – .197)		PHI	N (19G – .286)											
" total	84	80	17	1	0	1	1.3	6	14	9	6	2	.213	.263	67	14	OF-4
1983 2 teams		PHI	N (19G – .111)		DET	A (8G – .000)											
" total	27	20	2	1	0	1	5.0	4	3	1	3	1	.100	.300	20	2	DH-1
8 yrs.	401	803	212	25	11	14	1.7	106	90	65	57	46	.264	.375	160	37	OF-129, DH-84

Paul Molitor

MOLITOR, PAUL LEO
B. Aug. 22, 1956, St. Paul, Minn.   BR TR 6'   185 lbs.

	G	AB	H	2B	3B	HR	HR %	R	RBI	BB	SO	SB	BA	SA	PH AB	PH H	G by POS
1978 MIL A	125	521	142	26	4	6	1.2	73	45	19	54	30	.273	.372	3	0	2B-91, SS-31, DH-2, 3B-1
1979	140	584	188	27	16	9	1.5	88	62	48	48	33	.322	.469	2	0	2B-122, SS-10, DH-8
1980	111	450	137	29	2	9	2.0	81	37	48	48	34	.304	.438	2	1	2B-91, SS-12, DH-7, 3B-1
1981	64	251	67	11	0	2	0.8	45	19	25	29	10	.267	.335	1	0	OF-46, DH-16
1982	160	666	201	26	8	19	2.9	136	71	69	93	41	.302	.450	0	0	3B-150, DH-6, SS-4
1983	152	608	164	28	6	15	2.5	95	47	59	74	41	.270	.410	2	0	3B-146, DH-2
1984	13	46	10	1	0	0	0.0	3	6	2	8	1	.217	.239	2	0	3B-7, DH-4
7 yrs.	765	3126	909	148	36	60	1.9	521	287	270	354	190	.291	.419	12	1	3B-305, 2B-304, SS-57, OF-46, DH-45

DIVISIONAL PLAYOFF SERIES

	G	AB	H	2B	3B	HR	HR %	R	RBI	BB	SO	SB	BA	SA	PH AB	PH H	G by POS
1981 MIL A	5	20	5	0	0	1	5.0	2	1	2	5	0	.250	.400	0	0	OF-5

LEAGUE CHAMPIONSHIP SERIES

	G	AB	H	2B	3B	HR	HR %	R	RBI	BB	SO	SB	BA	SA	PH AB	PH H	G by POS
1982 MIL A	5	19	6	1	0	2	10.5	4	5	2	3	1	.316	.684	0	0	3B-5

WORLD SERIES

	G	AB	H	2B	3B	HR	HR %	R	RBI	BB	SO	SB	BA	SA	PH AB	PH H	G by POS
1982 MIL A	7	31	11	0	0	0	0.0	5	2	2	4	1	.355	.355	0	0	3B-7

Fred Mollenkamp

MOLLENKAMP, FREDERICK HENRY
B. Mar. 15, 1890, Cincinnati, Ohio   D. Nov. 1, 1948, Cincinnati, Ohio

	G	AB	H	2B	3B	HR	HR %	R	RBI	BB	SO	SB	BA	SA	PH AB	PH H	G by POS
1914 PHI N	3	8	1	0	0	0	0.0	0	0	1			.125	.125	0	0	1B-3

Fritz Mollwitz

MOLLWITZ, FREDERICK AUGUST (Zip)
B. June 16, 1890, Kolberg, Germany   D. Oct. 3, 1967, Bradenton, Fla.   BR TR 6'2"   170 lbs.

	G	AB	H	2B	3B	HR	HR %	R	RBI	BB	SO	SB	BA	SA	PH AB	PH H	G by POS
1913 CHI N	2	7	3	0	0	0	0.0	1	0	0	0	0	.429	.429	0	0	1B-2
1914 2 teams		CHI	N (13G – .150)		CIN	N (32G – .162)											
" total	45	131	21	2	0	0	0.0	12	6	3	12	3	.160	.176	6	0	1B-36, OF-1
1915 CIN N	153	525	136	21	3	1	0.2	36	51	15	49	19	.259	.316	0	0	1B-153
1916 2 teams		CIN	N (65G – .224)		CHI	N (33G – .268)											
" total	98	254	60	6	4	0	0.0	13	27	12	18	10	.236	.291	20	5	1B-73, OF-6
1917 PIT N	36	140	36	4	1	0	0.0	15	12	8	8	4	.257	.300	0	0	1B-36, 2B-1
1918	119	432	116	12	7	0	0.0	43	45	23	24	23	.269	.329	0	0	1B-119
1919 2 teams		PIT	N (56G – .173)		STL	N (25G – .229)											
" total	81	251	48	5	4	0	0.0	18	17	22	21	11	.191	.243	2	1	1B-77, OF-2
7 yrs.	534	1740	420	50	19	1	0.1	138	158	83	132	70	.241	.294	28	6	1B-496, OF-9, 2B-1

Blas Monaco

MONACO, BLAS
B. Nov. 16, 1915, San Antonio, Tex.   BB TR 5'11"   170 lbs.

	G	AB	H	2B	3B	HR	HR %	R	RBI	BB	SO	SB	BA	SA	PH AB	PH H	G by POS
1937 CLE A	5	7	2	0	1	0	0.0	2	2	2	2	0	.286	.571	2	1	2B-3
1946	12	6	0	0	0	0	0.0	2	0	1	1	0	.000	.000	6	0	
2 yrs.	17	13	2	0	1	0	0.0	4	2	3	3	0	.154	.308	8	1	2B-3

Freddie Moncewicz

MONCEWICZ, FREDERICK ALFRED
B. Sept. 1, 1903, Brockton, Mass.   D. Apr. 23, 1969, Brockton, Mass.   BR TR 5'8½"   175 lbs.

	G	AB	H	2B	3B	HR	HR %	R	RBI	BB	SO	SB	BA	SA	PH AB	PH H	G by POS
1928 BOS A	3	1	0	0	0	0	0.0	0	0	0	1	0	.000	.000	0	0	SS-2

Al Monchak

MONCHAK, ALEX
B. Mar. 5, 1917, Bayonne, N. J.   BR TR 6'   180 lbs.

	G	AB	H	2B	3B	HR	HR %	R	RBI	BB	SO	SB	BA	SA	PH AB	PH H	G by POS
1940 PHI N	19	14	2	0	0	0	0.0	0	0	6	1	0	.143	.143	1	0	SS-9, 2B-1

Rick Monday

MONDAY, ROBERT JAMES
B. Nov. 20, 1945, Batesville, Ark.   BL TL 6'3"   195 lbs.

	G	AB	H	2B	3B	HR	HR %	R	RBI	BB	SO	SB	BA	SA	PH AB	PH H	G by POS
1966 KC A	17	41	4	1	1	0	0.0	4	2	6	16	1	.098	.171	1	0	OF-15
1967	124	406	102	14	6	14	3.4	52	58	42	107	3	.251	.419	13	2	OF-113
1968 OAK A	148	482	132	24	7	8	1.7	56	49	72	143	14	.274	.402	6	2	OF-144
1969	122	399	108	17	4	12	3.0	57	54	72	100	12	.271	.424	5	1	OF-119
1970	112	376	109	19	7	10	2.7	63	37	58	99	17	.290	.457	1	0	OF-109
1971	116	355	87	9	3	18	5.1	53	56	49	93	6	.245	.439	7	2	OF-111
1972 CHI N	138	434	108	22	5	11	2.5	68	42	78	102	12	.249	.399	3	0	OF-134
1973	149	554	148	24	5	26	4.7	93	56	92	124	5	.267	.469	3	1	OF-148
1974	142	538	158	19	7	20	3.7	84	58	70	94	7	.294	.467	4	0	OF-139
1975	136	491	131	29	4	17	3.5	89	60	83	95	8	.267	.446	4	1	OF-131
1976	137	534	145	20	5	32	6.0	107	77	60	125	5	.272	.507	4	1	OF-103, 1B-32
1977 LA N	118	392	90	13	1	15	3.8	47	48	60	109	1	.230	.383	6	0	OF-115, 1B-3
1978	119	342	87	14	1	19	5.6	54	57	49	100	2	.254	.468	16	2	OF-103, 1B-1
1979	12	33	10	0	0	1	3.0	2	2	5	6	0	.303	.303	1	1	OF-10
1980	96	194	52	7	1	10	5.2	35	25	28	49	2	.268	.469	36	8	OF-50
1981	66	130	41	1	2	11	8.5	24	25	24	42	1	.315	.608	23	8	OF-41
1982	104	210	54	6	4	11	5.2	37	42	39	51	2	.257	.481	35	4	OF-57, 1B-4
1983	99	178	44	7	1	6	3.4	21	20	29	42	0	.247	.399	42	8	OF-42, 1B-4
1984	31	47	9	2	0	1	2.1	4	7	8	16	0	.191	.298	17	3	1B-10, OF-2
19 yrs.	1986	6136	1619	248	64	241	3.9	950	775	924	1513	98	.264	.443	227	44	OF-1688, 1B-54

DIVISIONAL PLAYOFF SERIES

	G	AB	H	2B	3B	HR	HR %	R	RBI	BB	SO	SB	BA	SA	PH AB	PH H	G by POS
1981 LA N	5	14	3	0	0	0	0.0	1	1	2	4	0	.214	.214	0	0	OF-5

LEAGUE CHAMPIONSHIP SERIES

	G	AB	H	2B	3B	HR	HR %	R	RBI	BB	SO	SB	BA	SA	PH AB	PH H	G by POS
1971 OAK A	1	3	0	0	0	0	0.0	0	0	1	2	0	.000	.000	0	0	OF-1

	G	AB	H	2B	3B	HR	HR %	R	RBI	BB	SO	SB	BA	SA	Pinch Hit AB	Pinch Hit H	G by POS

Rick Monday continued

	G	AB	H	2B	3B	HR	HR %	R	RBI	BB	SO	SB	BA	SA	AB	H	G by POS
1977 **LA** **N**	3	7	2	1	0	0	0.0	1	0	2	1	0	.286	.429	1	0	OF-3
1978	3	10	2	0	1	0	0.0	2	0	1	5	0	.200	.400	1	0	OF-3
1981	3	9	3	0	0	1	11.1	2	1	0	4	0	.333	.667	1	0	OF-2
1983	1	0	0	0	0	0	—	0	0	0	0	0	—	—	1	0	
5 yrs.	11	29	7	1	1	1	3.4	5	1	4	12	0	.241	.448	3	0	OF-9
WORLD SERIES																	
1977 **LA** **N**	4	12	2	0	0	0	0.0	0	0	0	3	0	.167	.167	0	0	OF-4
1978	5	13	2	1	0	0	0.0	2	0	4	3	0	.154	.231	0	0	OF-4
1981	5	13	3	1	0	0	0.0	1	0	3	6	0	.231	.308	1	0	OF-4
3 yrs.	14	38	7	2	0	0	0.0	3	0	7	12	0	.184	.237	1	0	OF-12

Don Money

MONEY, DONALD WAYNE (Brooks)
B. June 7, 1947, Washington, D. C.   BR TR 6'1"   170 lbs.

	G	AB	H	2B	3B	HR	HR %	R	RBI	BB	SO	SB	BA	SA	AB	H	G by POS
1968 **PHI** **N**	4	13	3	2	0	0	0.0	1	2	2	4	0	.231	.385	0	0	SS-4
1969	127	450	103	22	2	6	1.3	41	42	43	83	1	.229	.327	1	0	SS-126
1970	120	447	132	25	4	14	3.1	66	66	43	68	4	.295	.463	0	0	3B-119, SS-2
1971	121	439	98	22	8	7	1.6	40	38	31	80	4	.223	.358	5	1	3B-68, OF-40, 2B-20
1972	152	536	119	16	2	15	2.8	54	52	41	92	5	.222	.343	1	0	3B-151, SS-2
1973 **MIL** **A**	145	556	158	28	2	11	2.0	75	61	53	53	22	.284	.401	2	0	3B-124, SS-21
1974	159	**629**	178	32	3	15	2.4	85	65	62	80	19	.283	.415	0	0	3B-157, DH-1, 2B-1
1975	109	405	112	16	1	15	3.7	58	43	31	51	7	.277	.432	5	1	3B-99, SS-7
1976	117	439	117	18	4	12	2.7	51	62	47	50	6	.267	.408	8	1	3B-103, DH-10, SS-1
1977	152	570	159	28	3	25	4.4	86	83	57	70	8	.279	.470	2	2	2B-116, OF-23, 3B-15, DH-7
1978	137	518	152	30	2	14	2.7	88	54	48	70	3	.293	.440	5	2	1B-61, 2B-36, 3B-25, DH-15, SS-2
1979	92	350	83	20	1	6	1.7	52	38	40	47	1	.237	.351	3	1	DH-33, 3B-26, 1B-19, 2B-16
1980	86	289	74	17	1	17	5.9	39	46	40	36	0	.256	.498	5	2	3B-55, DH-14, 1B-14, 2B-2
1981	60	185	40	7	0	2	1.1	17	14	19	27	0	.216	.286	3	1	3B-56, DH-2, 1B-1
1982	96	275	78	14	3	16	5.8	40	55	32	38	0	.284	.531	21	2	DH-66, 3B-16, 1B-11, 2B-1
1983	43	114	17	5	0	1	0.9	5	8	11	17	0	.149	.219	12	0	DH-28, 3B-11, 1B-2
16 yrs.	1720	6215	1623	302	36	176	2.8	798	729	600	866	80	.261	.406	73	14	3B-1025, 2B-192, DH-176, SS-165, 1B-108, OF-63
DIVISIONAL PLAYOFF SERIES																	
1981 **MIL** **A**	2	3	0	0	0	0	0.0	0	0	0	0	0	.000	.000	2	0	DH-1, 2B-1
LEAGUE CHAMPIONSHIP SERIES																	
1982 **MIL** **A**	4	11	2	1	0	0	0.0	2	1	3	3	0	.182	.182	0	0	DH-4
WORLD SERIES																	
1982 **MIL** **A**	5	13	3	1	0	0	0.0	4	1	2	3	0	.231	.308	1	0	DH-4

Frank Monroe

MONROE, FRANK W.
B. Hamilton, Ohio   Deceased.

	G	AB	H	2B	3B	HR	HR %	R	RBI	BB	SO	SB	BA	SA	AB	H	G by POS
1884 **IND** **AA**	2	8	0	0	0	0	0.0	1		0			.000	.000	0	0	OF-1, C-1

John Monroe

MONROE, JOHN ALLEN
B. Aug. 24, 1898, Farmersville, Tex.   D. June 19, 1956, Conroe, Tex.   BR TR 5'8"   160 lbs.

	G	AB	H	2B	3B	HR	HR %	R	RBI	BB	SO	SB	BA	SA	AB	H	G by POS
1921 **2 teams**		**NY** **N** (19G – .143)				**PHI** **N** (41G – .286)											
" total	60	154	41	4	2	2	1.3	17	11	14	15	2	.266	.357	5	1	2B-36, 3B-9, SS-1

Ed Montague

MONTAGUE, EDWARD FRANCIS
B. July 24, 1906, San Francisco, Calif.   BR TR 5'10"   165 lbs.

	G	AB	H	2B	3B	HR	HR %	R	RBI	BB	SO	SB	BA	SA	AB	H	G by POS
1928 **CLE** **A**	32	51	12	0	1	0	0.0	12	3	6	7	0	.235	.275	1	1	SS-15, 3B-9
1930	58	179	47	5	2	1	0.6	37	16	37	38	1	.263	.330	0	0	SS-46, 3B-13
1931	64	193	55	8	3	1	0.5	27	26	21	22	3	.285	.373	0	0	SS-64
1932	66	192	47	5	1	0	0.0	29	24	21	24	3	.245	.281	0	0	SS-57, 3B-11
4 yrs.	220	615	161	18	7	2	0.3	105	69	85	91	7	.262	.324	1	1	SS-182, 3B-33

Willie Montanez

MONTANEZ, GUILLERMO NARANJO
B. Apr. 1, 1948, Catano, Puerto Rico   BL TL 6'   170 lbs.

	G	AB	H	2B	3B	HR	HR %	R	RBI	BB	SO	SB	BA	SA	AB	H	G by POS
1966 **CAL** **A**	8	2	0	0	0	0	0.0	2	0	0	2	1	.000	.000	2	0	1B-2
1970 **PHI** **N**	18	25	6	0	0	0	0.0	3	3	1	4	0	.240	.240	6	3	OF-10, 1B-5
1971	158	599	153	27	6	30	5.0	78	99	67	105	4	.255	.471	1	1	OF-158, 1B-9
1972	147	531	131	**39**	3	13	2.4	60	64	58	108	1	.247	.405	5	4	OF-130, 1B-14
1973	146	552	145	16	5	11	2.0	69	65	46	80	2	.263	.370	6	3	1B-99, OF-51
1974	143	527	160	33	1	7	1.3	55	79	32	57	3	.304	.410	6	2	1B-137, OF-1
1975 **2 teams**		**PHI** **N** (21G – .286)				**SF** **N** (135G – .305)											
" total	156	602	182	34	2	10	1.7	61	101	49	62	6	.302	.415	2	1	1B-155
1976 **2 teams**		**SF** **N** (60G – .309)				**ATL** **N** (103G – .321)											
" total	163	650	206	29	2	11	1.7	74	84	36	47	2	.317	.418	2	1	1B-161
1977 **ATL** **N**	136	544	156	31	4	20	3.7	70	68	35	60	1	.287	.458	2	1	1B-134
1978 **NY** **N**	159	609	156	32	0	17	2.8	66	96	60	92	9	.256	.392	1	0	1B-158
1979 **2 teams**		**NY** **N** (109G – .234)				**TEX** **A** (38G – .319)											
" total	147	554	142	25	0	13	2.3	55	71	33	62	0	.256	.372	4	1	1B-127, DH-17
1980 **2 teams**		**SD** **N** (128G – .274)				**MON** **N** (14G – .211)											
" total	142	500	136	12	4	6	1.2	40	64	39	55	3	.272	.348	11	3	1B-128
1981 **2 teams**		**MON** **N** (26G – .177)				**PIT** **N** (29G – .263)											
" total	55	100	21	0	1	1	1.0	8	6	5	11	0	.210	.260	30	9	1B-27
1982 **2 teams**		**PIT** **N** (36G – .281)				**PHI** **N** (18G – .063)											
" total	54	48	10	1	0	0	0.0	4	2	4	6	0	.208	.229	43	9	1B-8, OF-2
14 yrs.	1632	5843	1604	279	25	139	2.4	645	802	465	751	32	.275	.402	121	38	1B-1164, OF-352, DH-17

	G	AB	H	2B	3B	HR	HR %	R	RBI	BB	SO	SB	BA	SA	Pinch Hit AB	Pinch Hit H	G by POS

Rene Monteagudo

MONTEAGUDO, RENE MIRANDA
Father of Aurelio Monteagudo.
B. Mar. 12, 1916, Santa Clara, Cuba   D. Sept. 14, 1973, Hialeah, Fla.   BL TL 5'7"   165 lbs.

	G	AB	H	2B	3B	HR	HR %	R	RBI	BB	SO	SB	BA	SA	PH AB	PH H	G by POS
1938 WAS A	5	6	3	0	0	0	0.0	0	1	0	0	0	.500	.500	0	0	P-5
1940	27	33	6	1	1	0	0.0	4	1	1	4	0	.182	.273	0	0	P-27
1944	10	38	11	2	0	0	0.0	2	4	0	1	0	.289	.342	1	1	OF-9
1945 PHI N	114	193	58	6	0	0	0.0	26	15	28	7	2	.301	.332	52	18	OF-35, P-14
4 yrs.	156	270	78	9	1	0	0.0	32	21	29	12	2	.289	.330	53	19	P-46, OF-44

Felipe Montemayor

MONTEMAYOR, FELIPE ANGEL (Monty)
B. Feb. 7, 1930, Monterrey, Mexico   BL TL 6'2"   185 lbs.

	G	AB	H	2B	3B	HR	HR %	R	RBI	BB	SO	SB	BA	SA	PH AB	PH H	G by POS
1953 PIT N	28	55	6	4	0	0	0.0	5	2	4	13	0	.109	.182	13	1	OF-12
1955	36	95	20	1	3	2	2.1	10	8	18	24	1	.211	.347	8	1	OF-28
2 yrs.	64	150	26	5	3	2	1.3	15	10	22	37	1	.173	.287	21	2	OF-40

Al Montgomery

MONTGOMERY, ALVIN ATLAS
B. July 3, 1920, Loving, N. M.   D. Apr. 26, 1942, Waverly, Va.   BR TR 5'10½" 185 lbs.

	G	AB	H	2B	3B	HR	HR %	R	RBI	BB	SO	SB	BA	SA	PH AB	PH H	G by POS
1941 BOS N	42	52	10	1	0	0	0.0	4	4	9	8	0	.192	.212	10	0	C-30

Bob Montgomery

MONTGOMERY, ROBERT EDWARD
B. Apr. 16, 1944, Nashville, Tenn.   BR TR 6'1"   195 lbs.

	G	AB	H	2B	3B	HR	HR %	R	RBI	BB	SO	SB	BA	SA	PH AB	PH H	G by POS
1970 BOS A	22	78	14	2	0	1	1.3	8	4	6	20	0	.179	.244	1	0	C-22
1971	67	205	49	11	2	2	1.0	19	24	16	43	1	.239	.341	2	0	C-66
1972	24	77	22	1	0	2	2.6	7	7	3	17	0	.286	.377	2	1	C-22
1973	34	128	41	6	2	7	5.5	18	25	7	36	0	.320	.563	1	0	C-33
1974	88	254	64	10	0	4	1.6	26	38	13	50	3	.252	.339	5	2	C-79, DH-5
1975	62	195	44	10	1	2	1.0	16	26	4	37	1	.226	.318	3	0	C-53, 1B-6, DH-3
1976	31	93	23	3	1	3	3.2	10	13	5	20	0	.247	.398	1	0	C-30, DH-1
1977	17	40	12	2	0	2	5.0	6	7	4	9	0	.300	.500	2	1	C-15
1978	10	29	7	1	1	0	0.0	2	5	2	12	0	.241	.345	0	0	C-10
1979	32	86	30	4	1	0	0.0	13	7	4	24	1	.349	.419	0	0	C-31
10 yrs.	387	1185	306	50	8	23	1.9	125	156	64	268	6	.258	.372	17	4	C-361, DH-9, 1B-6

WORLD SERIES

	G	AB	H	2B	3B	HR	HR %	R	RBI	BB	SO	SB	BA	SA	PH AB	PH H	G by POS
1975 BOS A	1	1	0	0	0	0	0.0	0	0	0	0	0	.000	.000	0	0	

Allan Montreuil

MONTREUIL, ALLAN ARTHUR
B. Aug. 23, 1943, New Orleans, La.   BR TR 5'5"   158 lbs.

	G	AB	H	2B	3B	HR	HR %	R	RBI	BB	SO	SB	BA	SA	PH AB	PH H	G by POS
1972 CHI N	5	11	1	0	0	0	0.0	0	0	1	4	0	.091	.091	0	0	2B-5

Danny Monzon

MONZON, DANIEL FRANCIS
B. May 17, 1946, New York, N. Y.   BR TR 5'10"   182 lbs.

	G	AB	H	2B	3B	HR	HR %	R	RBI	BB	SO	SB	BA	SA	PH AB	PH H	G by POS
1972 MIN A	55	55	15	1	0	0	0.0	13	5	8	12	1	.273	.291	13	1	2B-13, 3B-5, SS-3, OF-1
1973	39	76	17	1	1	0	0.0	10	4	11	9	1	.224	.263	3	0	2B-17, 3B-14, OF-1
2 yrs.	94	131	32	2	1	0	0.0	23	9	19	21	2	.244	.275	16	1	2B-30, 3B-19, SS-3, OF-2

Joe Moock

MOOCK, JOSEPH GEOFFREY
B. Mar. 12, 1944, Plaquemine, La.   BL TR 6'1"   180 lbs.

	G	AB	H	2B	3B	HR	HR %	R	RBI	BB	SO	SB	BA	SA	PH AB	PH H	G by POS
1967 NY N	13	40	9	2	0	0	0.0	5	0	7	7	0	.225	.275	1	0	3B-12

George Moolic

MOOLIC, GEORGE HENRY (Prunes)
B. 1865, Lawrence, Mass.   D. Feb. 19, 1915, Lawrence, Mass.   BR TR 5'7"   145 lbs.

	G	AB	H	2B	3B	HR	HR %	R	RBI	BB	SO	SB	BA	SA	PH AB	PH H	G by POS
1886 CHI N	16	56	8	3	0	0	0.0	9	2	2	17		.143	.196	0	0	C-15, OF-2

Wally Moon

MOON, WALLACE WADE
B. Apr. 3, 1930, Bay, Ark.   BL TR 6'   169 lbs.

	G	AB	H	2B	3B	HR	HR %	R	RBI	BB	SO	SB	BA	SA	PH AB	PH H	G by POS
1954 STL N	151	635	193	29	9	12	1.9	106	76	71	73	18	.304	.435	2	0	OF-148
1955	152	593	175	24	8	19	3.2	86	76	47	65	11	.295	.459	8	2	OF-100, 1B-51
1956	149	540	161	22	11	16	3.0	86	68	80	50	12	.298	.469	0	0	OF-97, 1B-52
1957	142	516	152	28	5	24	4.7	86	73	62	57	5	.295	.508	9	1	OF-133
1958	108	290	69	10	3	7	2.4	36	38	47	30	2	.238	.366	23	2	OF-82
1959 LA N	145	543	164	26	11	19	3.5	93	74	81	64	15	.302	.495	3	2	OF-143, 1B-1
1960	138	469	140	21	6	13	2.8	74	69	67	53	6	.299	.452	12	3	OF-127
1961	134	463	152	25	3	17	3.7	79	88	89	79	7	.328	.505	3	0	OF-133
1962	95	244	59	9	1	4	1.6	36	31	30	33	5	.242	.336	32	6	OF-36, 1B-32
1963	122	343	90	13	2	8	2.3	41	48	45	43	5	.262	.382	25	6	OF-96
1964	68	118	26	2	1	2	1.7	8	9	12	22	1	.220	.305	43	8	OF-23
1965	53	89	18	3	0	1	1.1	6	11	13	22	2	.202	.270	25	5	OF-23
12 yrs.	1457	4843	1399	212	60	142	2.9	737	661	644	591	89	.289	.445	185	35	OF-1141, 1B-136

WORLD SERIES

	G	AB	H	2B	3B	HR	HR %	R	RBI	BB	SO	SB	BA	SA	PH AB	PH H	G by POS
1959 LA N	6	23	6	0	0	1	4.3	3	2	2	2	1	.261	.391	0	0	OF-6
1965	2	2	0	0	0	0	0.0	0	0	0	0	0	.000	.000	2	0	
2 yrs.	8	25	6	0	0	1	4.0	3	2	2	2	1	.240	.360	2	0	OF-6

Al Moore

MOORE, ALBERT JAMES
B. Aug. 4, 1902, Brooklyn, N. Y.   D. Nov. 29, 1974, New York, N. Y.   BR TR 5'10"   174 lbs.

	G	AB	H	2B	3B	HR	HR %	R	RBI	BB	SO	SB	BA	SA	PH AB	PH H	G by POS
1925 NY N	2	8	1	0	0	0	0.0	0	0	1	2	0	.125	.125	0	0	OF-2
1926	28	81	18	4	0	0	0.0	12	10	5	7	2	.222	.272	4	0	OF-20
2 yrs.	30	89	19	4	0	0	0.0	12	10	6	9	2	.213	.258	4	0	OF-22

Anse Moore

MOORE, ANSELM WINN
B. Sept. 22, 1917, Delhi, La.   BL TR 6'1"   190 lbs.

	G	AB	H	2B	3B	HR	HR %	R	RBI	BB	SO	SB	BA	SA	PH AB	PH H	G by POS
1946 DET A	51	134	28	4	0	1	0.7	16	8	12	9	1	.209	.261	16	4	OF-32

	G	AB	H	2B	3B	HR	HR %	R	RBI	BB	SO	SB	BA	SA	Pinch Hit AB	Pinch Hit H	G by POS

Archie Moore

MOORE, ARCHIE FRANCIS
B. Aug. 30, 1941, Upper Darby, Pa.   BL TL 6'2"   190 lbs.

	G	AB	H	2B	3B	HR	HR %	R	RBI	BB	SO	SB	BA	SA	AB	H	G by POS
1964 NY A	31	23	4	2	0	0	0.0	4	1	2	9	0	.174	.261	13	3	OF-8, 1B-7
1965	9	17	7	2	0	1	5.9	1	4	4	4	0	.412	.706	4	1	OF-5
2 yrs.	40	40	11	4	0	1	2.5	5	5	6	13	0	.275	.450	17	4	OF-13, 1B-7

Bill Moore

MOORE, WILLIAM HENRY
B. Dec. 12, 1901, Kansas City, Mo.   D. May 24, 1972, Kansas City, Mo.   BL TR 6'   180 lbs.

	G	AB	H	2B	3B	HR	HR %	R	RBI	BB	SO	SB	BA	SA	AB	H	G by POS
1926 BOS A	5	18	3	0	0	0	0.0	2	0	0	4	0	.167	.167	0	0	C-5
1927	44	69	15	2	0	0	0.0	7	4	13	8	0	.217	.246	1	0	C-42
2 yrs.	49	87	18	2	0	0	0.0	9	4	13	12	0	.207	.230	1	0	C-47

Charley Moore

MOORE, CHARLES WESLEY
B. Dec. 1, 1884, Jackson County, Ind.   D. July 29, 1970, Portland, Ore.   BR TR 5'10"   160 lbs.

	G	AB	H	2B	3B	HR	HR %	R	RBI	BB	SO	SB	BA	SA	AB	H	G by POS
1912 CHI N	5	9	2	0	1	0	0.0	2	2	0	1	0	.222	.444	0	0	SS-2, 3B-1, 2B-1

Charlie Moore

MOORE, CHARLES WILLIAM JR.
B. June 21, 1953, Birmingham, Ala.   BR TR 5'11"   190 lbs.

	G	AB	H	2B	3B	HR	HR %	R	RBI	BB	SO	SB	BA	SA	AB	H	G by POS
1973 MIL A	8	27	5	0	1	0	0.0	0	3	2	4	0	.185	.259	0	0	C-8
1974	72	204	50	10	4	0	0.0	17	19	21	34	3	.245	.333	6	3	C-61, DH-6
1975	73	241	70	20	1	1	0.4	26	29	17	31	1	.290	.394	7	3	C-47, OF-22, DH-1
1976	87	241	46	7	4	3	1.2	33	16	43	45	1	.191	.290	2	0	C-49, OF-28, DH-2, 3B-1
1977	138	375	93	15	6	5	1.3	42	45	31	39	1	.248	.360	4	3	C-137
1978	96	268	72	7	1	5	1.9	30	31	12	24	4	.269	.358	1	0	C-95
1979	111	337	101	16	2	5	1.5	45	38	29	32	8	.300	.404	19	6	C-106, 2B-2
1980	111	320	93	13	2	2	0.6	42	30	24	28	10	.291	.363	27	8	C-105
1981	48	156	47	8	3	1	0.6	16	9	12	13	1	.301	.410	4	1	C-34, OF-8, DH-6
1982	133	456	116	22	4	6	1.3	53	45	29	49	2	.254	.360	10	3	OF-115, C-20, 2B-1
1983	151	529	150	27	6	2	0.4	65	49	55	42	11	.284	.369	0	0	OF-150, C-7, DH-1
1984	70	188	44	7	1	2	1.1	13	17	10	26	0	.234	.314	5	2	OF-61, C-7
12 yrs.	1098	3342	887	152	35	32	1.0	382	331	285	367	42	.265	.361	85	29	C-676, OF-384, DH-16, 2B-3, 3B-1

DIVISIONAL PLAYOFF SERIES

	G	AB	H	2B	3B	HR	HR %	R	RBI	BB	SO	SB	BA	SA	AB	H	G by POS
1981 MIL A	4	9	2	0	0	0	0.0	0	1	1	2	0	.222	.222	0	0	DH-2, OF-2

LEAGUE CHAMPIONSHIP SERIES

	G	AB	H	2B	3B	HR	HR %	R	RBI	BB	SO	SB	BA	SA	AB	H	G by POS
1982 MIL A	5	13	6	0	0	0	0.0	3	0	1	2	0	.462	.462	0	0	OF-5

WORLD SERIES

	G	AB	H	2B	3B	HR	HR %	R	RBI	BB	SO	SB	BA	SA	AB	H	G by POS
1982 MIL A	7	26	9	3	0	0	0.0	3	2	1	0	0	.346	.462	0	0	OF-7

Dee Moore

MOORE, D C
B. Apr. 6, 1914, Hedley, Tex.   BR TR 6'   200 lbs.

	G	AB	H	2B	3B	HR	HR %	R	RBI	BB	SO	SB	BA	SA	AB	H	G by POS
1936 CIN N	6	10	4	2	1	0	0.0	4	1	1	3	0	.400	.800	4	1	P-2, C-1
1937	7	13	1	0	0	0	0.0	2	0	1	2	0	.077	.077	1	0	C-6
1943 2 teams		BKN N (37G – .253)				PHI N (37G – .239)											
" total	74	192	47	7	1	1	0.5	21	20	26	16	1	.245	.307	13	1	C-36, 3B-14, OF-6, 1B-1
1946 PHI N	11	13	1	0	0	0	0.0	2	1	7	3	0	.077	.077	2	0	C-6, 1B-2
4 yrs.	98	228	53	9	2	1	0.4	29	22	34	24	1	.232	.303	20	2	C-49, 3B-14, OF-6, 1B-3, P-2

Eddie Moore

MOORE, GRAHAM EDWARD
B. Jan. 18, 1899, Barlow, Ky.   D. Feb. 10, 1976, Fort Myers, Fla.   BR TR 5'7"   165 lbs.

	G	AB	H	2B	3B	HR	HR %	R	RBI	BB	SO	SB	BA	SA	AB	H	G by POS
1923 PIT N	6	26	7	1	0	0	0.0	6	1	2	3	1	.269	.308	0	0	SS-6
1924	72	209	75	8	4	2	1.0	47	13	27	12	6	.359	.464	8	4	OF-35, 3B-14, 2B-4
1925	142	547	163	29	8	6	1.1	106	77	73	26	19	.298	.413	2	2	2B-122, OF-15, 3B-3
1926 2 teams		PIT N (43G – .227)				BOS N (54G – .266)											
" total	97	316	79	11	3	0	0.0	36	34	28	18	9	.250	.304	9	3	2B-62, SS-15, 3B-10
1927 BOS N	112	411	124	14	4	1	0.2	53	32	39	17	5	.302	.363	6	3	3B-52, 2B-39, OF-16, SS-1
1928	68	215	51	9	0	2	0.9	27	18	19	12	7	.237	.307	5	0	OF-54, 2B-1
1929 BKN N	111	402	119	18	6	0	0.0	48	48	44	16	3	.296	.371	1	1	2B-74, SS-36, OF-2, 3B-1
1930	76	196	55	13	1	1	0.5	24	20	21	7	1	.281	.372	9	5	OF-23, 2B-23, SS-17, 3B-1
1932 NY N	37	87	23	3	0	1	1.1	9	6	9	6	1	.264	.333	4	0	SS-21, 3B-6, 2B-5
1934 CLE A	27	65	10	2	0	0	0.0	4	8	10	4	0	.154	.185	3	0	2B-18, 3B-3, SS-2
10 yrs.	748	2474	706	108	26	13	0.5	360	257	272	121	52	.285	.366	47	18	2B-348, OF-145, SS-98, 3B-90

WORLD SERIES

	G	AB	H	2B	3B	HR	HR %	R	RBI	BB	SO	SB	BA	SA	AB	H	G by POS
1925 PIT N	7	26	6	1	0	1	3.8	7	2	5	2	0	.231	.385	0	0	2B-7

Ferdie Moore

MOORE, FERDINAND DePAGE
B. Feb. 21, 1896, Camden, N. J.   D. May 6, 1947, Atlantic City, N. J.

	G	AB	H	2B	3B	HR	HR %	R	RBI	BB	SO	SB	BA	SA	AB	H	G by POS
1914 PHI A	2	4	2	0	0	0	0.0	1	1	0	2	0	.500	.500	0	0	1B-2

Gary Moore

MOORE, GARY DOUGLAS
B. Feb. 24, 1945, Tulsa, Okla.   BR TL 5'10"   175 lbs.

	G	AB	H	2B	3B	HR	HR %	R	RBI	BB	SO	SB	BA	SA	AB	H	G by POS
1970 LA N	7	16	3	0	2	0	0.0	2	0	1	1	1	.188	.438	2	1	OF-5, 1B-1

Gene Moore

MOORE, EUGENE, JR. (Rowdy)
Son of Gene Moore.
B. Aug. 26, 1909, Lancaster, Tex.   BL TL 5'11"   175 lbs.

	G	AB	H	2B	3B	HR	HR %	R	RBI	BB	SO	SB	BA	SA	AB	H	G by POS
1931 CIN N	4	14	2	1	0	0	0.0	2	1	0	0	0	.143	.214	1	0	OF-3
1933 STL N	11	38	15	3	2	0	0.0	6	8	4	10	1	.395	.579	1	0	OF-10
1934	9	18	5	1	0	0	0.0	2	1	2	2	0	.278	.333	6	2	OF-3
1935	3	3	0	0	0	0	0.0	0	0	0	1	0	.000	.000	3	0	
1936 BOS N	151	637	185	38	12	13	2.0	91	67	40	80	6	.290	.449	0	0	OF-151
1937	148	561	159	29	10	16	2.9	88	70	61	73	11	.283	.456	0	0	OF-148

	G	AB	H	2B	3B	HR	HR %	R	RBI	BB	SO	SB	BA	SA	Pinch Hit AB	Pinch Hit H	G by POS

Gene Moore continued

	G	AB	H	2B	3B	HR	HR%	R	RBI	BB	SO	SB	BA	SA	PH AB	PH H	G by POS
1938	54	180	49	8	3	3	1.7	27	19	16	20	1	.272	.400	5	1	OF-47
1939 BKN N	107	306	69	13	6	3	1.0	45	39	40	50	4	.225	.337	18	3	OF-86, 1B-1
1940 2 teams		BKN N (10G – .269)				BOS N (103G – .292)											
" total	113	389	113	26	1	5	1.3	49	41	26	35	5	.290	.393	16	3	OF-100
1941 BOS N	129	397	108	17	8	5	1.3	42	43	45	37	5	.272	.393	16	3	OF-110
1942 WAS A	1	2	0	0	0	0	0.0	0	0	0	1	0	.000	.000	0	0	OF-1
1943	92	254	68	14	3	2	0.8	41	39	19	29	0	.268	.370	30	12	OF-57, 1B-1
1944 STL N	110	390	93	13	6	6	1.5	56	58	24	37	0	.238	.349	11	5	OF-98, 1B-1
1945	110	354	92	16	2	5	1.4	48	50	40	26	1	.260	.359	10	0	OF-100
14 yrs.	1042	3543	958	179	53	58	1.6	497	436	317	401	31	.270	.400	112	27	OF-914, 1B-3

WORLD SERIES

	G	AB	H	2B	3B	HR	HR%	R	RBI	BB	SO	SB	BA	SA	PH AB	PH H	G by POS
1944 STL A	6	22	4	0	0	0	0.0	4	0	3	6	0	.182	.182	0	0	OF-6

Harry Moore

MOORE, HENRY S.
Deceased.

	G	AB	H	2B	3B	HR	HR%	R	RBI	BB	SO	SB	BA	SA	PH AB	PH H	G by POS
1884 WAS U	111	461	155	23	5	1	0.2	77		19			.336	.414	0	0	OF-105, SS-8

Jackie Moore

MOORE, JACKIE SPENCER   BR TR 6'   180 lbs.
B. Feb. 19, 1939, Jay, Fla.
Manager 1984.

	G	AB	H	2B	3B	HR	HR%	R	RBI	BB	SO	SB	BA	SA	PH AB	PH H	G by POS
1965 DET A	21	53	5	0	0	0	0.0	2	2	6	12	0	.094	.094	1	0	C-20

Jerry Moore

MOORE, JEREMIAH S.
B. Detroit, Mich.   D. Sept. 26, 1908, Wayne, Mich.

	G	AB	H	2B	3B	HR	HR%	R	RBI	BB	SO	SB	BA	SA	PH AB	PH H	G by POS
1884 2 teams		ALT U (20G – .313)				CLE N (9G – .200)											
" total	29	110	31	3	1	1	0.9	11	10	0	5		.282	.355	0	0	C-21, OF-9
1885 DET N	6	23	4	1	0	0	0.0	2	0	1	3		.174	.217	0	0	C-6
2 yrs.	35	133	35	4	1	1	0.8	13	10	1	8		.263	.331	0	0	C-27, OF-9

Jim Moore

MOORE, JAMES WILLIAM   BR TR 6'½"   187 lbs.
B. Apr. 24, 1903, Paris, Tenn.

	G	AB	H	2B	3B	HR	HR%	R	RBI	BB	SO	SB	BA	SA	PH AB	PH H	G by POS
1930 2 teams		CHI A (16G – .205)				PHI A (15G – .380)											
" total	31	89	27	5	0	2	2.2	14	14	8	7	1	.303	.427	9	4	OF-22
1931 PHI A	49	143	32	5	1	2	1.4	18	21	11	13	0	.224	.315	11	0	OF-36
2 yrs.	80	232	59	10	1	4	1.7	32	35	19	20	1	.254	.358	20	4	OF-58

WORLD SERIES

	G	AB	H	2B	3B	HR	HR%	R	RBI	BB	SO	SB	BA	SA	PH AB	PH H	G by POS
1930 PHI A	3	3	1	0	0	0	0.0	0	0	1	1	0	.333	.333	1	1	OF-1
1931	2	3	1	0	0	0	0.0	0	0	0	1	0	.333	.333	1	0	OF-1
2 yrs.	5	6	2	0	0	0	0.0	0	0	1	2	0	.333	.333	2	1	OF-2

Joe Moore

MOORE, JOE GREGG (Jo-Jo, The Gause Ghost)   BL TR 5'11"   155 lbs.
B. Dec. 25, 1908, Gause, Tex.

	G	AB	H	2B	3B	HR	HR%	R	RBI	BB	SO	SB	BA	SA	PH AB	PH H	G by POS
1930 NY N	3	5	1	0	0	0	0.0	1	0	0	1	0	.200	.200	2	1	OF-1
1931	4	8	2	1	0	0	0.0	0	3	0	1	1	.250	.375	3	0	OF-1
1932	86	361	110	15	2	2	0.6	53	27	20	18	4	.305	.374	0	0	OF-86
1933	132	524	153	16	5	0	0.0	56	42	21	27	4	.292	.342	0	0	OF-132
1934	139	580	192	37	4	15	2.6	106	61	31	23	5	.331	.486	8	1	OF-131
1935	155	681	201	28	9	15	2.2	108	71	53	24	5	.295	.429	0	0	OF-155
1936	152	649	205	29	9	7	1.1	110	63	37	27	2	.316	.421	3	0	OF-149
1937	142	580	180	37	10	6	1.0	89	57	46	37	7	.310	.440	2	0	OF-140
1938	125	506	153	23	6	11	2.2	76	56	22	27	2	.302	.437	10	1	OF-114
1939	138	562	151	23	2	10	1.8	80	47	45	17	5	.269	.370	2	1	OF-136
1940	138	543	150	33	4	6	1.1	83	46	43	30	7	.276	.385	3	0	OF-133
1941	121	428	117	16	2	7	1.6	47	40	30	15	4	.273	.369	3	1	OF-116
12 yrs.	1335	5427	1615	258	53	79	1.5	809	513	348	247	46	.298	.408	36	5	OF-1294

WORLD SERIES

	G	AB	H	2B	3B	HR	HR%	R	RBI	BB	SO	SB	BA	SA	PH AB	PH H	G by POS
1933 NY N	5	22	5	1	0	0	0.0	1	1	1	3	0	.227	.273	0	0	OF-5
1936	6	28	6	2	0	1	3.6	4	1	1	4	0	.214	.393	0	0	OF-6
1937	5	23	9	1	0	0	0.0	1	1	0	1	0	.391	.435	0	0	OF-5
3 yrs.	16	73	20	4	0	1	1.4	6	3	2	8	0	.274	.370	0	0	OF-16

Johnny Moore

MOORE, JOHN FRANCIS   BL TR 5'10½"   175 lbs.
B. Mar. 23, 1902, Waterville, Conn.

	G	AB	H	2B	3B	HR	HR%	R	RBI	BB	SO	SB	BA	SA	PH AB	PH H	G by POS
1928 CHI N	4	4	0	0	0	0	0.0	0	0	0	0	0	.000	.000	4	0	
1929	37	63	18	1	0	2	3.2	13	8	4	6	0	.286	.397	15	5	OF-15
1931	39	104	25	3	1	2	1.9	19	16	7	5	1	.240	.346	15	3	OF-22
1932	119	443	135	24	5	13	2.9	59	64	22	38	4	.305	.470	10	4	OF-109
1933 CIN N	135	514	135	19	5	1	0.2	60	44	29	16	4	.263	.325	3	1	OF-132
1934 2 teams		CIN N (16G – .190)				PHI N (116G – .343)											
" total	132	500	165	35	7	11	2.2	73	98	43	20	7	.330	.494	6	1	OF-125
1935 PHI N	153	600	194	33	3	19	3.2	84	93	45	50	4	.323	.483	3	0	OF-150
1936	124	472	155	24	3	16	3.4	85	68	26	22	1	.328	.494	10	4	OF-112
1937	96	307	98	16	2	9	2.9	46	59	18	18	2	.319	.472	20	7	OF-72
1945 CHI N	7	6	1	0	0	0	0.0	0	2	1	1	0	.167	.167	6	1	
10 yrs.	846	3013	926	155	26	73	2.4	439	452	195	176	23	.307	.449	92	26	OF-737

WORLD SERIES

	G	AB	H	2B	3B	HR	HR%	R	RBI	BB	SO	SB	BA	SA	PH AB	PH H	G by POS
1932 CHI N	2	7	0	0	0	0	0.0	1	0	2	1	0	.000	.000	0	0	OF-2

	G	AB	H	2B	3B	HR	HR %	R	RBI	BB	SO	SB	BA	SA	Pinch Hit AB	Pinch Hit H	G by POS

Junior Moore

MOORE, ALVIN EARL
B. Jan. 25, 1953, Waskom, Tex.
BR TR 5'11" 195 lbs.

	G	AB	H	2B	3B	HR	HR %	R	RBI	BB	SO	SB	BA	SA	AB	H	G by POS
1976 ATL N	20	26	7	1	0	0	0.0	1	2	4	4	0	.269	.308	12	4	3B-6, OF-1, 2B-1
1977	112	361	94	9	3	5	1.4	41	34	33	29	4	.260	.343	10	3	3B-104, 2B-1
1978 CHI A	24	65	19	0	1	0	0.0	8	4	6	7	1	.292	.323	5	2	DH-12, 3B-6, OF-5
1979	88	201	53	6	2	1	0.5	24	23	12	20	0	.264	.328	25	6	OF-61, DH-10, 2B-2
1980	45	121	31	4	1	1	0.8	9	10	7	11	0	.256	.331	4	2	3B-34, OF-3, DH-2, 1B-1
5 yrs.	289	774	204	20	7	7	0.9	83	73	62	71	5	.264	.335	56	17	3B-150, OF-70, DH-24, 2B-4, 1B-1

Kelvin Moore

MOORE, KELVIN ORLANDO
B. Sept. 26, 1957, LeRoy, Ala.
BR TL 6'1" 195 lbs.

	G	AB	H	2B	3B	HR	HR %	R	RBI	BB	SO	SB	BA	SA	AB	H	G by POS
1981 OAK A	14	47	12	0	1	1	2.1	5	3	5	15	1	.255	.362	1	0	1B-13
1982	21	67	15	1	1	2	3.0	6	6	3	23	0	.224	.358	1	0	1B-20
1983	41	124	26	4	0	5	4.0	12	16	10	39	2	.210	.363	0	0	1B-40
3 yrs.	76	238	53	5	2	8	3.4	23	25	18	77	3	.223	.361	2	0	1B-73

DIVISIONAL PLAYOFF SERIES

	G	AB	H	2B	3B	HR	HR %	R	RBI	BB	SO	SB	BA	SA	AB	H	G by POS
1981 OAK A	2	8	0	0	0	0	0.0	0	0	0	2	0	.000	.000	0	0	1B-2

LEAGUE CHAMPIONSHIP SERIES

	G	AB	H	2B	3B	HR	HR %	R	RBI	BB	SO	SB	BA	SA	AB	H	G by POS
1981 OAK A	3	9	2	0	0	0	0.0	0	0	0	1	0	.222	.222	0	0	1B-3

Randy Moore

MOORE, RANDOLPH EDWARD
B. June 21, 1905, Naples, Tex.
BL TR 6' 185 lbs.

	G	AB	H	2B	3B	HR	HR %	R	RBI	BB	SO	SB	BA	SA	AB	H	G by POS
1927 CHI A	6	15	0	0	0	0	0.0	0	0	0	2	0	.000	.000	2	0	OF-4
1928	24	61	13	4	1	0	0.0	6	5	3	5	0	.213	.311	6	2	OF-16
1930 BOS N	83	191	55	9	0	2	1.0	24	34	10	13	3	.288	.366	30	6	OF-34, 3B-13
1931	83	192	50	8	1	3	1.6	19	34	13	3	1	.260	.359	32	6	OF-29, 3B-22, 2B-1
1932	107	351	103	21	2	3	0.9	41	43	15	11	1	.293	.390	14	4	OF-41, 3B-31, 1B-22, C-1
1933	135	497	150	23	7	8	1.6	64	70	40	16	3	.302	.425	6	1	OF-122, 1B-10
1934	123	422	120	21	2	7	1.7	55	64	40	16	2	.284	.393	13	5	OF-72, 1B-37
1935	125	407	112	20	4	4	1.0	42	42	26	16	1	.275	.373	23	5	OF-78, 1B-21
1936 BKN N	42	88	21	3	0	0	0.0	4	14	8	1	0	.239	.273	18	7	OF-21
1937 2 teams	BKN N (13G – .136)					STL N (8G – .000)											
" total	21	29	3	1	0	0	0.0	3	2	3	2	0	.103	.138	9	0	C-10, OF-1
10 yrs.	749	2253	627	110	17	27	1.2	258	308	158	85	11	.278	.378	153	36	OF-418, 1B-90, 3B-66, C-11, 2B-1

Scrappy Moore

MOORE, WILLIAM ALLEN
B. Dec. 16, 1892, St. Louis, Mo. D. Oct. 13, 1964, Little Rock, Ark.
BR TR 5'8" 153 lbs.

	G	AB	H	2B	3B	HR	HR %	R	RBI	BB	SO	SB	BA	SA	AB	H	G by POS
1917 STL A	4	8	1	0	0	0	0.0	1	0	1	0	0	.125	.125	2	1	3B-2

Terry Moore

MOORE, TERRY BLUFORD
B. May 27, 1912, Vernon, Ala.
Manager 1954.
BR TR 5'11" 195 lbs.

	G	AB	H	2B	3B	HR	HR %	R	RBI	BB	SO	SB	BA	SA	AB	H	G by POS
1935 STL N	119	456	131	34	3	6	1.3	63	53	15	40	13	.287	.414	0	0	OF-117
1936	143	590	156	39	4	5	0.8	85	47	37	52	9	.264	.369	7	2	OF-133
1937	115	461	123	17	3	5	1.1	76	43	32	41	13	.267	.349	8	1	OF-106
1938	94	312	85	21	3	4	1.3	49	21	46	19	9	.272	.397	9	1	OF-75, 3B-6
1939	130	417	123	25	2	17	4.1	65	77	43	38	6	.295	.487	7	2	OF-121, P-1
1940	136	537	163	33	4	17	3.2	92	64	42	44	18	.304	.475	3	0	OF-133
1941	122	493	145	26	4	6	1.2	86	68	52	31	3	.294	.400	1	0	OF-121
1942	130	489	141	26	3	6	1.2	80	49	56	26	10	.288	.391	4	2	OF-126, 3B-1
1946	91	278	73	14	1	3	1.1	32	28	18	26	0	.263	.353	25	6	OF-66
1947	127	460	130	17	1	7	1.5	61	45	38	39	1	.283	.370	6	1	OF-120
1948	91	207	48	11	0	4	1.9	30	18	27	12	0	.232	.343	17	4	OF-71
11 yrs.	1298	4700	1318	263	28	80	1.7	719	513	406	368	82	.280	.399	87	19	OF-1189, 3B-7, P-1

WORLD SERIES

	G	AB	H	2B	3B	HR	HR %	R	RBI	BB	SO	SB	BA	SA	AB	H	G by POS
1942 STL N	5	17	5	1	0	0	0.0	2	2	2	3	0	.294	.353	0	0	OF-5
1946	7	27	4	0	0	0	0.0	1	2	2	6	0	.148	.148	0	0	OF-7
2 yrs.	12	44	9	1	0	0	0.0	3	4	4	9	0	.205	.227	0	0	OF-12

Andres Mora

MORA, ANDRES
Also known as Andres Ibarra.
B. May 25, 1955, Saltillo, Mexico
BR TR 6' 180 lbs.

	G	AB	H	2B	3B	HR	HR %	R	RBI	BB	SO	SB	BA	SA	AB	H	G by POS
1976 BAL A	73	220	48	11	0	6	2.7	18	25	13	49	1	.218	.350	10	4	DH-34, OF-31
1977	77	233	57	8	2	13	5.6	32	44	5	53	0	.245	.464	16	7	OF-57, DH-5, 3B-1
1978	76	229	49	8	0	8	3.5	21	14	13	47	0	.214	.354	13	0	OF-69, DH-1
1980 CLE A	9	18	2	0	0	0	0.0	0	0	0	0	0	.111	.111	6	1	OF-3
4 yrs.	235	700	156	27	2	27	3.9	71	83	31	149	1	.223	.383	45	12	OF-160, DH-40, 3B-1

Jerry Morales

MORALES, JULIO RUBEN
B. Feb. 18, 1949, Yabucoa, Puerto Rico
BR TR 5'10" 155 lbs.

	G	AB	H	2B	3B	HR	HR %	R	RBI	BB	SO	SB	BA	SA	AB	H	G by POS
1969 SD N	19	41	8	2	0	1	2.4	5	6	5	7	0	.195	.317	0	0	OF-19
1970	28	58	9	0	1	1	1.7	6	4	3	11	0	.155	.241	2	0	OF-26
1971	12	17	2	0	0	0	0.0	1	1	2	2	1	.118	.118	2	0	OF-7
1972	115	347	83	15	2	4	1.2	38	18	35	54	4	.239	.357	19	3	OF-96, 3B-4
1973	122	388	109	23	2	9	2.3	47	34	27	55	6	.281	.420	22	9	OF-100
1974 CHI N	151	534	146	21	7	15	2.8	70	82	46	63	2	.273	.423	8	2	OF-143
1975	153	578	156	21	0	12	2.1	62	91	50	65	3	.270	.369	2	1	OF-151
1976	140	537	147	17	0	16	3.0	66	67	41	49	3	.274	.395	5	1	OF-136
1977	136	490	142	34	5	11	2.2	56	69	43	75	0	.290	.447	11	3	OF-128
1978 STL N	130	457	109	19	4	4	0.9	44	46	33	44	4	.239	.341	8	1	OF-126
1979 DET A	129	440	93	23	1	14	3.2	50	56	30	56	10	.211	.364	7	0	OF-119, DH-7
1980 NY N	94	193	49	7	1	3	1.6	19	30	13	31	2	.254	.347	30	7	OF-63
1981 CHI N	84	245	70	6	2	1	0.4	27	25	22	29	1	.286	.339	12	3	OF-72
1982	65	116	33	2	2	4	3.4	14	30	9	24	1	.284	.440	30	10	OF-41

	G	AB	H	2B	3B	HR	HR%	R	RBI	BB	SO	SB	BA	SA	Pinch Hit AB	Pinch Hit H	G by POS

Jerry Morales continued

	G	AB	H	2B	3B	HR	HR%	R	RBI	BB	SO	SB	BA	SA	AB	H	G by POS
1983	63	87	17	9	0	0	0.0	11	11	7	19	0	.195	.299	41	8	OF-29
15 yrs.	1441	4528	1173	199	36	95	2.1	516	570	366	567	37	.259	.382	199	49	OF-1256, DH-7, 3B-4

Jose Morales

MORALES, JOSE MANUEL   BR TR 5'11" 187 lbs.
B. Dec. 30, 1944, St. Croix, Virgin Islands

	G	AB	H	2B	3B	HR	HR%	R	RBI	BB	SO	SB	BA	SA	AB	H	G by POS
1973 2 teams	OAK	A	(6G –	.286)		MON	N	(5G –	.400)								
" total	11	19	6	1	0	0	0.0	0	1	1	5	0	.316	.368	7	3	DH-3
1974 MON N	25	26	7	4	0	1	3.8	3	5	1	7	0	.269	.538	22	5	C-2
1975	93	163	49	6	1	2	1.2	18	24	14	21	0	.301	.387	51	15	1B-27, OF-6, C-5
1976	104	158	50	11	0	4	2.5	12	37	3	20	0	.316	.462	78	25[1]	1B-21, C-12
1977	65	74	15	4	1	1	1.4	7	9	5	12	0	.203	.324	52	10	1B-8, C-8
1978 MIN A	101	242	76	13	1	2	0.8	22	38	20	35	0	.314	.401	46	14	DH-77, OF-1, 1B-1, C-1
1979	92	191	51	5	1	2	1.0	21	27	14	27	0	.267	.335	42	9	DH-77, 1B-1
1980	97	241	73	17	2	8	3.3	36	36	22	19	0	.303	.490	36	13	DH-86, 1B-2, C-2
1981 BAL A	38	86	21	3	0	2	2.3	6	14	3	13	0	.244	.349	19	5	DH-22, 1B-3
1982 2 teams	BAL	A	(3G –	.000)		LA	N	(35G –	.300)								
" total	38	33	9	1	0	1	3.0	1	8	4	10	0	.273	.394	33	9	
1983 LA N	47	53	15	3	0	3	5.7	4	8	1	11	0	.283	.509	40	12	1B-4
1984	22	19	3	0	0	0	0.0	0	0	1	2	0	.158	.158	19	3	
12 yrs.	733	1305	375	68	6	26	2.0	126	207	89	182	0	.287	.408	445 **4th**	123 **3rd**	DH-265, 1B-67, C-30, OF-7

LEAGUE CHAMPIONSHIP SERIES
| 1983 LA N | 2 | 2 | 0 | 0 | 0 | 0 | 0.0 | 0 | 0 | 0 | 1 | 0 | .000 | .000 | 2 | 0 | |

Rich Morales

MORALES, RICHARD ANGELO   BR TR 5'11" 170 lbs.
B. Sept. 20, 1943, San Francisco, Calif.

	G	AB	H	2B	3B	HR	HR%	R	RBI	BB	SO	SB	BA	SA	AB	H	G by POS
1967 CHI A	8	10	0	0	0	0	0.0	0	0	0	2	0	.000	.000	0	0	SS-7
1968	10	29	5	0	0	0	0.0	2	0	2	5	0	.172	.172	0	0	SS-7, 2B-5
1969	55	121	26	0	1	0	0.0	12	6	7	18	1	.215	.231	3	1	2B-38, SS-13, 3B-1
1970	62	112	18	2	0	1	0.9	6	2	9	16	1	.161	.205	9	1	SS-24, 3B-20, 2B-12
1971	84	185	45	8	0	2	1.1	19	14	22	26	2	.243	.319	12	3	SS-57, 3B-18, 2B-3, OF-1
1972	110	287	59	7	1	2	0.7	24	20	19	49	2	.206	.258	5	1	SS-86, 2B-16, 3B-14
1973 2 teams	CHI	A	(7G –	.000)		SD	N	(90G –	.164)								
" total	97	248	40	6	1	0	0.0	10	17	28	37	0	.161	.194	2	0	2B-81, SS-10, 3B-5
1974 SD N	54	61	12	3	0	1	1.6	8	5	8	6	1	.197	.295	2	1	SS-29, 2B-18, 3B-6, 1B-1
8 yrs.	480	1053	205	26	3	6	0.6	81	64	95	159	7	.195	.242	33	7	SS-233, 2B-173, 3B-64, OF-1, 1B-1

Al Moran

MORAN, RICHARD ALAN   BR TR 6'1½" 190 lbs.
B. Dec. 5, 1938, Detroit, Mich.

	G	AB	H	2B	3B	HR	HR%	R	RBI	BB	SO	SB	BA	SA	AB	H	G by POS
1963 NY N	119	331	64	5	2	1	0.3	26	23	36	60	3	.193	.230	1	0	SS-116, 3B-1
1964	16	22	5	0	0	0	0.0	2	4	2	2	0	.227	.227	0	0	SS-15, 3B-1
2 yrs.	135	353	69	5	2	1	0.3	28	27	38	62	3	.195	.229	1	0	SS-131, 3B-2

Bill Moran

MORAN, WILLIAM L.
B. Oct. 10, 1869, Joliet, Ill.   D. Apr. 8, 1916, Joliet, Ill.

	G	AB	H	2B	3B	HR	HR%	R	RBI	BB	SO	SB	BA	SA	AB	H	G by POS
1892 STL N	24	81	11	1	0	0	0.0	2	5	2	12	0	.136	.148	0	0	C-22
1895 CHI N	15	55	9	2	1	1	1.8	8	9	3	2	2	.164	.291	0	0	C-15
2 yrs.	39	136	20	3	1	1	0.7	10	14	5	14	2	.147	.206	0	0	C-37

Billy Moran

MORAN, WILLIAM NELSON   BR TR 5'11" 185 lbs.
B. Nov. 27, 1933, Montgomery, Ala.

	G	AB	H	2B	3B	HR	HR%	R	RBI	BB	SO	SB	BA	SA	AB	H	G by POS
1958 CLE A	115	257	58	11	0	1	0.4	26	18	13	23	3	.226	.280	4	0	2B-74, SS-38
1959	11	17	5	0	0	0	0.0	1	2	0	1	0	.294	.294	0	0	2B-6, SS-5
1961 LA A	54	173	45	7	1	2	1.2	17	22	17	16	0	.260	.347	0	0	2B-51, SS-2
1962	160	659	186	25	3	17	2.6	90	74	39	80	5	.282	.407	0	0	2B-160
1963	153	597	164	29	5	7	1.2	67	65	31	57	1	.275	.375	2	1	2B-151
1964 2 teams	LA	A	(50G –	.268)		CLE	A	(69G –	.205)								
" total	119	349	84	16	1	1	0.3	40	21	31	36	1	.241	.301	12	2	3B-89, 2B-18, 1B-2, SS-1
1965 CLE A	22	24	3	0	0	0	0.0	1	0	2	5	0	.125	.125	13	2	2B-7, SS-1
7 yrs.	634	2076	545	88	10	28	1.3	242	202	133	218	10	.263	.355	31	5	2B-467, 3B-89, SS-47, 1B-2

Charley Moran

MORAN, CHARLES BARTHELL (Uncle Charlie)   BR TR 5'8" 180 lbs.
B. Feb. 22, 1878, Nashville, Tenn.   D. June 13, 1949, Horse Cave, Ky.

	G	AB	H	2B	3B	HR	HR%	R	RBI	BB	SO	SB	BA	SA	AB	H	G by POS
1903 STL N	4	14	6	0	0	0	0.0	2	1	0		1	.429	.429	0	0	P-3, SS-1
1908	21	63	11	1	2	0	0.0	2	2	0		0	.175	.254	5	2	C-16
2 yrs.	25	77	17	1	2	0	0.0	4	3	0		1	.221	.286	5	2	C-16, P-3, SS-1

Charlie Moran

MORAN, CHARLES VINCENT   TR
B. Mar. 26, 1879, Washington, D. C.   D. Apr. 11, 1934, Washington, D. C.

	G	AB	H	2B	3B	HR	HR%	R	RBI	BB	SO	SB	BA	SA	AB	H	G by POS
1903 WAS A	98	373	84	14	5	1	0.3	41	24	33		8	.225	.298	0	0	SS-96, 2B-2
1904 2 teams	WAS	A	(62G –	.222)		STL	A	(82G –	.173)								
" total	144	515	101	13	1	0	0.0	42	21	48		9	.196	.225	0	0	3B-82, SS-61, OF-1
1905 STL A	28	82	16	1	0	0	0.0	6	5	10		3	.195	.207	2	1	2B-21, 3B-7
3 yrs.	270	970	201	28	6	1	0.1	89	50	91		20	.207	.252	2	1	SS-157, 3B-89, 2B-23, OF-1

Herbie Moran

MORAN, JOHN HERBERT   BL TR 5'5"
B. Feb. 16, 1884, Costello, Pa.   D. Sept. 21, 1954, Clarkson, N. Y.

	G	AB	H	2B	3B	HR	HR%	R	RBI	BB	SO	SB	BA	SA	AB	H	G by POS
1908 2 teams	PHI	A	(19G –	.153)		BOS	N	(8G –	.276)								
" total	27	88	17	0	0	0	0.0	7	6	8		2	.193	.193	0	0	OF-27
1909 BOS N	8	31	7	1	0	0	0.0	8	0	5		0	.226	.258	0	0	OF-8
1910	20	67	8	0	0	0	0.0	11	3	13	14	6	.119	.119	0	0	OF-20
1912 BKN N	130	508	140	18	10	3	0.6	77	40	69	38	28	.276	.356	0	0	OF-129

	G	AB	H	2B	3B	HR	HR %	R	RBI	BB	SO	SB	BA	SA	Pinch Hit AB	H	G by POS

Herbie Moran continued

	G	AB	H	2B	3B	HR	HR %	R	RBI	BB	SO	SB	BA	SA	AB	H	G by POS
1913	132	515	137	15	5	0	0.0	71	26	45	29	21	.266	.315	3	0	OF-129
1914 2 teams		CIN N (107G – .235)					BOS N (41G – .266)										
" total	148	549	134	13	6	1	0.2	67	39	58	40	30	.244	.295	0	0	OF-148
1915 BOS N	130	419	84	13	5	0	0.0	59	21	66	41	16	.200	.255	6	1	OF-123
7 yrs.	595	2177	527	60	26	2	0.1	300	135	264	162	103	.242	.296	9	1	OF-584

WORLD SERIES

	G	AB	H	2B	3B	HR	HR %	R	RBI	BB	SO	SB	BA	SA	AB	H	G by POS
1914 BOS N	3	13	1	1	0	0	0.0	2	0	1	1	1	.077	.154	0	0	OF-3

Pat Moran

MORAN, PATRICK JOSEPH
B. Feb. 7, 1876, Fitchburg, Mass.   D. Mar. 7, 1924, Orlando, Fla.
Manager 1915-23.

TR

	G	AB	H	2B	3B	HR	HR %	R	RBI	BB	SO	SB	BA	SA	AB	H	G by POS
1901 BOS N	53	180	38	5	1	2	1.1	12	18	3		3	.211	.283	0	0	C-28, 1B-13, 3B-4, OF-3, SS-3, 2B-1
1902	80	251	60	5	5	1	0.4	22	24	17		6	.239	.311	6	1	C-71, 1B-3, OF-1
1903	109	389	102	25	5	7	1.8	40	54	29		8	.262	.406	1	0	C-107, 1B-1
1904	113	398	90	11	3	4	1.0	26	34	18		10	.226	.299	2	0	C-72, 3B-39, 1B-2
1905	85	267	64	11	5	2	0.7	22	22	8		3	.240	.341	7	0	C-78
1906 CHI N	70	226	57	13	1	0	0.0	22	35	7		6	.252	.319	9	0	C-61
1907	65	198	45	5	1	1	0.5	8	19	10		5	.227	.278	6	2	C-59
1908	50	150	39	5	1	0	0.0	12	12	13		6	.260	.307	4	0	C-45
1909	77	246	54	11	1	1	0.4	18	23	16		2	.220	.285	2	1	C-74
1910 PHI N	68	199	47	7	1	0	0.0	13	11	17	16	6	.236	.281	11	1	C-56
1911	34	103	19	3	0	0	0.0	2	8	3	13	0	.184	.214	1	0	C-32
1912	13	26	3	1	0	0	0.0	1	1	1	7	0	.115	.154	4	1	C-13
1913	1	1	0	0	0	0	0.0	0	0	0	0	0	.000	.000	1	0	
1914	1	0	0	0	0	0	–	0	1	0	0	0	–	–	0	0	C-1
14 yrs.	819	2634	618	102	24	18	0.7	198	262	142	36	55	.235	.312	54	6	C-697, 3B-43, 1B-19, OF-4, SS-3, 2B-1

WORLD SERIES

	G	AB	H	2B	3B	HR	HR %	R	RBI	BB	SO	SB	BA	SA	AB	H	G by POS
1906 CHI N	2	2	0	0	0	0	0.0	0	0	0	0	0	.000	.000	2	0	
1907	1	0	0	0	0	0	–	0	0	0	0	0	–	–	0	0	
2 yrs.	3	2	0	0	0	0	0.0	0	0	0	0	0	.000	.000	2	0	

Roy Moran

MORAN, ROY ELLIS (Deedle)
B. Sept. 17, 1884, Iona, Ind.   D. July 18, 1966, Atlanta, Ga.

BR TR 5'8"   155 lbs.

	G	AB	H	2B	3B	HR	HR %	R	RBI	BB	SO	SB	BA	SA	AB	H	G by POS
1912 WAS A	5	13	2	0	0	0	0.0	1	0	0		3	.154	.154	0	0	OF-5

Ray Morehart

MOREHART, RAYMOND ANDERSON
B. Dec. 2, 1899, near Abner, Tex.

BL TR 5'9"   157 lbs.

	G	AB	H	2B	3B	HR	HR %	R	RBI	BB	SO	SB	BA	SA	AB	H	G by POS
1924 CHI A	31	100	20	4	2	0	0.0	10	8	17	7	3	.200	.280	2	0	SS-27, 2B-2
1926	73	192	61	10	3	0	0.0	27	21	11	15	3	.318	.401	17	6	2B-48
1927 NY A	73	195	50	7	2	1	0.5	45	20	29	18	4	.256	.328	14	2	2B-53
3 yrs.	177	487	131	21	7	1	0.2	82	49	57	40	10	.269	.347	33	8	2B-103, SS-27

Dan Morejon

MOREJON, DANIEL TERRES
B. July 21, 1930, Havana, Cuba

BR TR 6'1"   175 lbs.

	G	AB	H	2B	3B	HR	HR %	R	RBI	BB	SO	SB	BA	SA	AB	H	G by POS
1958 CIN N	12	26	5	0	0	0	0.0	4	1	9	2	1	.192	.192	1	0	OF-11

Keith Moreland

MORELAND, BOBBY KEITH
B. May 2, 1954, Dallas, Tex.

BR TR 6'   190 lbs.

	G	AB	H	2B	3B	HR	HR %	R	RBI	BB	SO	SB	BA	SA	AB	H	G by POS
1978 PHI N	1	2	0	0	0	0	0.0	0	0	0	0	0	.000	.000	0	0	C-1
1979	14	48	18	3	2	0	0.0	3	8	3	5	0	.375	.521	1	0	C-13
1980	62	159	50	8	0	4	2.5	13	29	8	14	3	.314	.440	17	7	C-39, 3B-4, OF-2
1981	61	196	50	7	0	6	3.1	16	37	15	13	1	.255	.383	5	1	C-50, 3B-7, OF-2, 1B-2
1982 CHI N	138	476	124	17	2	15	3.2	50	68	46	71	0	.261	.399	6	1	OF-86, C-44, 3B-2
1983	154	533	161	30	3	16	3.0	76	70	68	73	0	.302	.460	2	0	OF-151, C-3
1984	140	495	138	17	3	16	3.2	59	80	34	71	1	.279	.422	15	2	OF-103, 1B-29, 3B-8, C-3
7 yrs.	570	1909	541	82	10	57	3.0	217	292	174	247	5	.283	.426	46	11	OF-344, C-153, 1B-31, 3B-21

DIVISIONAL PLAYOFF SERIES

	G	AB	H	2B	3B	HR	HR %	R	RBI	BB	SO	SB	BA	SA	AB	H	G by POS
1981 PHI N	4	13	6	0	0	1	7.7	2	3	1	1	0	.462	.692	0	0	C-4

LEAGUE CHAMPIONSHIP SERIES

	G	AB	H	2B	3B	HR	HR %	R	RBI	BB	SO	SB	BA	SA	AB	H	G by POS
1980 PHI N	2	1	0	0	0	0	0.0	0	1	0	0	0	.000	.000	1	0	C-1
1984 CHI N	5	18	6	2	0	0	0.0	3	2	1	1	0	.333	.444	0	0	OF-5
2 yrs.	7	19	6	2	0	0	0.0	3	3	1	1	0	.316	.421	1	0	OF-5, C-1

WORLD SERIES

	G	AB	H	2B	3B	HR	HR %	R	RBI	BB	SO	SB	BA	SA	AB	H	G by POS
1980 PHI N	3	12	4	0	0	0	0.0	0	1	1	0	1	.333	.333	0	0	DH-3

Harry Morelock

MORELOCK, A. HARRY
B. Philadelphia, Pa.

	G	AB	H	2B	3B	HR	HR %	R	RBI	BB	SO	SB	BA	SA	AB	H	G by POS
1891 PHI N	4	14	1	0	0	0	0.0	0		3	3	0	.071	.071	0	0	SS-4
1892	1	3	0	0	0	0	0.0	0		1	0	0	.000	.000	0	0	3B-1
2 yrs.	5	17	1	0	0	0	0.0	0		4	3	0	.059	.059	0	0	SS-4, 3B-1

Jose Moreno

MORENO, JOSE
Also known as Jose Santos.
B. Nov. 2, 1957, Santo Domingo, Dominican Republic

BB TR 6'   175 lbs.

	G	AB	H	2B	3B	HR	HR %	R	RBI	BB	SO	SB	BA	SA	AB	H	G by POS
1980 NY N	37	46	9	2	1	2	4.3	6	9	3	12	1	.196	.413	26	4	3B-4, 2B-4
1981 SD N	34	48	11	2	0	0	0.0	5	6	1	8	4	.229	.271	23	6	OF-9, 2B-1
1982 CAL A	11	3	0	0	0	0	0.0	3	0	2	0	0	.000	.000	0	0	2B-2, DH-1
3 yrs.	82	97	20	4	1	2	2.1	14	15	6	20	5	.206	.330	49	10	OF-9, 2B-7, 3B-4, DH-1

	G	AB	H	2B	3B	HR	HR %	R	RBI	BB	SO	SB	BA	SA	Pinch Hit AB	Pinch Hit H	G by POS

Omar Moreno

MORENO, OMAR RENAN
B. Oct. 24, 1953, Chiriqui, Panama
BL TL 6'2" 180 lbs.

	G	AB	H	2B	3B	HR	HR %	R	RBI	BB	SO	SB	BA	SA	AB	H	G by POS
1975 PIT N	6	6	1	0	0	0	0.0	1	0	1	1	1	.167	.167	2	0	OF-1
1976	48	122	33	4	1	2	1.6	24	12	16	24	15	.270	.369	4	2	OF-42
1977	150	492	118	19	9	7	1.4	69	34	38	102	53	.240	.358	6	0	OF-147
1978	155	515	121	15	7	2	0.4	95	33	81	104	71	.235	.303	4	1	OF-152
1979	162	695	196	21	12	8	1.2	110	69	51	104	77	.282	.381	0	0	OF-162
1980	162	676	168	20	13	2	0.3	87	36	57	101	96	.249	.325	0	0	OF-162
1981	103	434	120	18	8	1	0.2	62	35	26	76	39	.276	.362	0	0	OF-103
1982	158	645	158	18	9	3	0.5	82	44	44	121	60	.245	.315	1	0	OF-157
1983 2 teams	HOU N	(97G –	.242)			NY A	(48G –	.250)									
" total	145	557	136	21	12	1	0.2	65	42	30	103	37	.244	.330	0	0	OF-145
1984 NY A	117	355	92	12	6	4	1.1	37	38	18	48	20	.259	.361	0	0	OF-108, DH-1
10 yrs.	1206	4497	1143	148	77	30	0.7	632	343	362	784	469	.254	.341	17	3	OF-1179, DH-1

LEAGUE CHAMPIONSHIP SERIES

	G	AB	H	2B	3B	HR	HR %	R	RBI	BB	SO	SB	BA	SA	AB	H	G by POS
1979 PIT N	3	12	3	0	1	0	0.0	3	0	2	2	1	.250	.417	0	0	OF-3

WORLD SERIES

	G	AB	H	2B	3B	HR	HR %	R	RBI	BB	SO	SB	BA	SA	AB	H	G by POS
1979 PIT N	7	33	11	2	0	0	0.0	4	3	1	7	0	.333	.394	0	0	OF-7

Bill Morgan

MORGAN, HENRY WILLIAM
B. Oct., 1857, Washington, D. C. Deceased.

	G	AB	H	2B	3B	HR	HR %	R	RBI	BB	SO	SB	BA	SA	AB	H	G by POS
1884 3 teams	WAS AA	(45G –	.173)			RIC AA	(11G –	.167)			BAL U	(2G –	.222)				
" total	58	207	36	1	2	0	0.0	11		11			.174	.198	0	0	OF-34, C-16, P-5, 2B-4, SS-2

Bobby Morgan

MORGAN, ROBERT MORRIS
B. June 29, 1926, Oklahoma City, Okla.
BR TR 5'9" 175 lbs.

	G	AB	H	2B	3B	HR	HR %	R	RBI	BB	SO	SB	BA	SA	AB	H	G by POS
1950 BKN N	67	199	45	10	3	7	3.5	38	21	32	43	0	.226	.412	5	1	3B-52, SS-10
1952	67	191	45	8	0	7	3.7	36	16	46	35	2	.236	.387	2	0	3B-60, 2B-5, SS-4
1953	69	196	51	6	2	7	3.6	35	33	33	47	2	.260	.418	9	0	3B-36, SS-21
1954 PHI N	135	455	119	25	2	14	3.1	58	50	70	68	3	.262	.418	0	0	SS-129, 3B-8, 2B-5
1955	136	483	112	20	2	10	2.1	61	49	73	72	6	.232	.344	6	1	2B-88, SS-41, 3B-6, 1B-1
1956 2 teams	PHI N	(8G –	.200)			STL N	(61G –	.195)									
" total	69	138	27	7	0	3	2.2	15	21	21	28	0	.196	.312	29	5	3B-16, 2B-16, SS-6
1957 2 teams	PHI N	(2G –	.000)			CHI N	(125G –	.207)									
" total	127	425	88	20	2	5	1.2	43	27	52	87	5	.207	.299	0	0	2B-118, 3B-12
1958 CHI N	1	1	0	0	0	0	0.0	0	0	0	1	0	.000	.000	0	0	
8 yrs.	671	2088	487	96	11	53	2.5	286	217	327	381	18	.233	.366	52	8	2B-232, SS-211, 3B-190, 1B-1

WORLD SERIES

	G	AB	H	2B	3B	HR	HR %	R	RBI	BB	SO	SB	BA	SA	AB	H	G by POS
1952 BKN N	2	1	0	0	0	0	0.0	0	0	0	0	0	.000	.000	1	0	3B-2
1953	1	1	0	0	0	0	0.0	0	0	0	0	0	.000	.000	1	0	
2 yrs.	3	2	0	0	0	0	0.0	0	0	0	0	0	.000	.000	2	0	3B-2

Charlie Morgan

MORGAN, CHARLES H.
Deceased.

	G	AB	H	2B	3B	HR	HR %	R	RBI	BB	SO	SB	BA	SA	AB	H	G by POS
1882 PIT AA	17	66	17	2	1	0	0.0	10		4			.258	.318	0	0	OF-11, C-7
1883	32	114	18	2	1	0	0.0	12		7			.158	.193	0	0	SS-21, OF-6, C-5, 2B-2
2 yrs.	49	180	35	4	2	0	0.0	22		11			.194	.239	0	0	SS-21, OF-17, C-12, 2B-2

Chet Morgan

MORGAN, CHESTER COLLINS (Chick)
B. June 6, 1910, Cleveland, Miss.
BL TR 5'9" 160 lbs.

	G	AB	H	2B	3B	HR	HR %	R	RBI	BB	SO	SB	BA	SA	AB	H	G by POS
1935 DET A	14	23	4	1	0	0	0.0	2	1	5	0	0	.174	.217	9	1	OF-4
1938	74	306	87	6	1	0	0.0	50	27	20	12	5	.284	.310	0	0	OF-74
2 yrs.	88	329	91	7	1	0	0.0	52	28	25	12	5	.277	.304	9	1	OF-78

Dan Morgan

MORGAN, DANIEL
B. 1855, Mo. Deceased.

	G	AB	H	2B	3B	HR	HR %	R	RBI	BB	SO	SB	BA	SA	AB	H	G by POS
1878 MIL N	14	56	11	0	0	0	0.0	2	5	3	9		.196	.196	0	0	OF-13, 3B-3, 2B-1

Ed Morgan

MORGAN, EDWARD CARRE
B. May 22, 1904, Cairo, Ill. D. Apr. 9, 1980, New Orleans, La.
BR TR 6'½" 180 lbs.

	G	AB	H	2B	3B	HR	HR %	R	RBI	BB	SO	SB	BA	SA	AB	H	G by POS
1928 CLE A	76	265	83	24	6	4	1.5	42	54	21	17	5	.313	.494	1	1	1B-36, OF-21, 3B-14
1929	93	318	101	19	10	3	0.9	60	37	37	23	4	.318	.469	12	4	OF-81
1930	150	584	204	47	11	26	4.5	122	136	62	66	8	.349	.601	2	0	1B-150, OF-19
1931	131	462	162	33	4	11	2.4	87	86	83	46	4	.351	.511	10	2	1B-117, 3B-3
1932	144	532	156	32	7	4	0.8	96	68	94	44	7	.293	.402	1	0	1B-142
1933	39	121	32	3	3	1	0.8	10	13	7	9	1	.264	.364	7	2	1B-32, OF-1
1934 BOS A	138	528	141	28	4	3	0.6	95	79	81	46	7	.267	.352	1	0	1B-137
7 yrs.	771	2810	879	186	45	52	1.9	512	473	385	251	36	.313	.467	34	9	1B-614, OF-122, 3B-17

Eddie Morgan

MORGAN, EDWIN WILLIS (Pepper)
B. Nov. 19, 1914, Brady Lake, Ohio D. June 27, 1982, Lakewood, Ohio
BL TL 5'10" 160 lbs.

	G	AB	H	2B	3B	HR	HR %	R	RBI	BB	SO	SB	BA	SA	AB	H	G by POS
1936 STL N	8	18	5	0	0	1	5.6	4	3	2	4	0	.278	.444	3	2	OF-4
1937 BKN N	31	48	9	3	0	0	0.0	4	5	9	7	0	.188	.250	8	1	OF-7, 1B-7
2 yrs.	39	66	14	3	0	1	1.5	8	8	11	11	0	.212	.303	11	3	OF-11, 1B-7

Joe Morgan

MORGAN, JOSEPH LEONARD
B. Sept. 19, 1943, Bonham, Tex.
BL TR 5'7" 150 lbs.

	G	AB	H	2B	3B	HR	HR %	R	RBI	BB	SO	SB	BA	SA	AB	H	G by POS
1963 HOU N	8	25	6	0	1	0	0.0	5	3	5	5	1	.240	.320	1	0	2B-7
1964	10	37	7	0	0	0	0.0	4	0	6	7	0	.189	.189	0	0	2B-10
1965	157	601	163	22	12	14	2.3	100	40	97	77	20	.271	.418	0	0	2B-157
1966	122	425	121	14	8	5	1.2	60	42	89	43	11	.285	.391	4	1	2B-117
1967	133	494	136	27	11	6	1.2	73	42	81	51	29	.275	.411	3	0	2B-130, OF-1
1968	10	20	5	0	1	0	0.0	6	0	7	4	3	.250	.350	3	0	2B-5, OF-1
1969	147	535	126	18	5	15	2.8	94	43	110	74	49	.236	.372	2	1	2B-132, OF-14

	G	AB	H	2B	3B	HR	HR %	R	RBI	BB	SO	SB	BA	SA	Pinch Hit AB	Pinch Hit H	G by POS

Joe Morgan continued

	G	AB	H	2B	3B	HR	HR%	R	RBI	BB	SO	SB	BA	SA	PH AB	PH H	G by POS
1970	144	548	147	28	9	8	1.5	102	52	102	55	42	.268	.396	2	1	2B-142
1971	160	583	149	27	11	13	2.2	87	56	88	52	40	.256	.407	4	1	2B-157
1972 CIN N	149	552	161	23	4	16	2.9	122	73	115	44	58	.292	.435	1	1	2B-149
1973	157	576	167	35	2	26	4.5	116	82	111	61	67	.290	.493	3	3	2B-154
1974	149	512	150	31	3	22	4.3	107	67	120	69	58	.293	.494	6	2	2B-142
1975	146	498	163	27	6	17	3.4	107	94	132	52	67	.327	.508	4	1	2B-142
1976	141	472	151	30	5	27	5.7	113	111	114	41	60	.320	.576	6	0	2B-133
1977	153	521	150	21	6	22	4.2	113	78	117	58	49	.288	.478	2	0	2B-151
1978	132	441	104	27	0	13	2.9	68	75	79	40	19	.236	.385	9	2	2B-124
1979	127	436	109	26	1	9	2.1	70	32	93	45	28	.250	.376	3	0	2B-121
1980 HOU N	141	461	112	17	5	11	2.4	66	49	93	47	24	.243	.373	21	4	2B-130
1981 SF N	90	308	74	16	1	8	2.6	47	31	66	37	14	.240	.377	3	1	2B-87
1982	134	463	134	19	4	14	3.0	68	61	85	60	24	.289	.438	12	4	2B-120, 3B-3
1983 PHI N	123	404	93	20	1	16	4.0	72	59	89	54	18	.230	.403	10	3	2B-117
1984 OAK A	117	369	90	21	0	6	1.6	50	43	66	39	8	.244	.350	12	2	2B-100
22 yrs.	2650	9281	2518	449	96	268	2.9	1651	1134	1865 3rd	1015	689 6th	.271	.427	111	27	2B-2527, OF-16, 3B-3

LEAGUE CHAMPIONSHIP SERIES

	G	AB	H	2B	3B	HR	HR%	R	RBI	BB	SO	SB	BA	SA	PH AB	PH H	G by POS
1972 CIN N	5	19	5	0	0	2	10.5	5	3	1	2	1	.263	.579	0	0	2B-5
1973	5	20	2	1	0	0	0.0	1	1	2	2	0	.100	.150	0	0	2B-5
1975	3	11	3	3	0	0	0.0	2	1	3	2	4	.273	.545	0	0	2B-3
1976	3	7	0	0	0	0	0.0	2	0	6	1	2	.000	.000	0	0	2B-3
1979	3	11	0	0	0	0	0.0	0	0	3	1	1	.000	.000	0	0	2B-3
1980 HOU N	4	13	2	1	1	0	0.0	1	0	6	1	0	.154	.385	0	0	2B-4
1983 PHI N	4	15	1	0	0	0	0.0	1	0	2	1	0	.067	.067	0	0	2B-4
7 yrs.	27	96	13	5	1	2	2.1	12	5	23	10	8	.135	.271	0	0	2B-27

WORLD SERIES

	G	AB	H	2B	3B	HR	HR%	R	RBI	BB	SO	SB	BA	SA	PH AB	PH H	G by POS
1972 CIN N	7	24	3	2	0	0	0.0	4	1	6	3	2	.125	.208	0	0	2B-7
1975	7	27	7	1	0	0	0.0	4	3	5	1	2	.259	.296	0	0	2B-7
1976	4	15	5	1	1	1	6.7	3	2	2	2	2	.333	.733	0	0	2B-4
1983 PHI N	5	19	5	0	1	2	10.5	3	2	2	3	1	.263	.684	0	0	2B-5
4 yrs.	23	85	20	4	2	3	3.5	14	8	15 9th	9	7	.235	.435	0	0	2B-23

Joe Morgan

MORGAN, JOSEPH MICHAEL
B. Nov. 19, 1930, Walpole, Mass.   BL TR 5'10" 170 lbs.

	G	AB	H	2B	3B	HR	HR%	R	RBI	BB	SO	SB	BA	SA	PH AB	PH H	G by POS
1959 2 teams		MIL	N (13G –	.217)		KC	A (20G –	.190)									
" total	33	44	9	1	1	0	0.0	4	4	5	11	0	.205	.273	22	5	2B-7, 3B-2
1960 2 teams		PHI	N (26G –	.133)		CLE	A (22G –	.298)									
" total	48	130	25	4	2	2	1.5	11	6	12	15	0	.192	.300	10	1	3B-36, OF-2
1961 CLE A	4	10	2	0	0	0	0.0	0	0	1	3	0	.200	.200	2	0	OF-2
1964 STL N	3	3	0	0	0	0	0.0	0	0	0	2	0	.000	.000	3	0	
4 yrs.	88	187	36	5	3	2	1.1	15	10	18	31	0	.193	.283	37	6	3B-38, 2B-7, OF-4

Ray Morgan

MORGAN, RAYMOND CARYLL
B. June 14, 1889, Baltimore, Md.   D. Feb. 15, 1940, Baltimore, Md.   BR TR 5'8½" 155 lbs.

	G	AB	H	2B	3B	HR	HR%	R	RBI	BB	SO	SB	BA	SA	PH AB	PH H	G by POS
1911 WAS A	25	89	19	2	0	0	0.0	11	5	4		2	.213	.236	0	0	3B-25
1912	80	273	65	10	7	1	0.4	40	30	29		11	.238	.337	0	0	2B-75, SS-4, 3B-1
1913	137	481	131	19	8	0	0.0	58	57	68	63	19	.272	.345	0	0	2B-133, SS-4
1914	147	491	126	22	8	1	0.2	50	49	62	34	24	.257	.340	1	0	2B-146
1915	62	193	45	5	4	0	0.0	21	21	30	15	6	.233	.301	1	0	2B-57, SS-2, 3B-2
1916	99	315	84	12	4	1	0.3	41	29	59	29	14	.267	.340	3	0	2B-82, SS-9, 1B-3, 3B-1
1917	101	338	90	9	1	1	0.3	32	33	40	29	7	.266	.308	2	0	2B-95, 3B-3
1918	88	300	70	11	1	0	0.0	25	30	28	14	4	.233	.277	4	1	2B-80, OF-2
8 yrs.	739	2480	630	90	33	4	0.2	278	254	320	184	87	.254	.322	11	1	2B-668, 3B-32, SS-19, 1B-3, OF-2

Red Morgan

MORGAN, JAMES EDWARD
B. Oct. 6, 1883, Council Bluffs, Iowa   TR

	G	AB	H	2B	3B	HR	HR%	R	RBI	BB	SO	SB	BA	SA	PH AB	PH H	G by POS
1906 BOS A	88	307	66	6	3	1	0.3	20	21	16		7	.215	.264	0	0	3B-88

Vern Morgan

MORGAN, VERNON THOMAS
B. Aug. 8, 1928, Emporia, Va.   D. Nov. 8, 1975, Minneapolis, Minn.   BL TR 6'1" 190 lbs.

	G	AB	H	2B	3B	HR	HR%	R	RBI	BB	SO	SB	BA	SA	PH AB	PH H	G by POS
1954 CHI N	24	64	15	2	0	0	0.0	3	2	1	10	0	.234	.266	7	1	3B-15
1955	7	7	1	0	0	0	0.0	1	1	3	4	0	.143	.143	3	0	3B-2
2 yrs.	31	71	16	2	0	0	0.0	4	3	4	14	0	.225	.254	10	1	3B-17

Moe Morhardt

MORHARDT, MEREDITH GOODWIN
B. Jan. 16, 1937, Manchester, Conn.   BL TL 6'1" 185 lbs.

	G	AB	H	2B	3B	HR	HR%	R	RBI	BB	SO	SB	BA	SA	PH AB	PH H	G by POS
1961 CHI N	7	18	5	0	0	0	0.0	1	3	5	5	0	.278	.278	0	0	1B-7
1962	18	16	2	0	0	0	0.0	1	2	2	8	0	.125	.125	16	2	
2 yrs.	25	34	7	0	0	0	0.0	2	5	7	13	0	.206	.206	16	2	1B-7

Gene Moriarity

MORIARITY, EUGENE JOHN
B. Holyoke, Mass.   Deceased.   BL 5'8" 190 lbs.

	G	AB	H	2B	3B	HR	HR%	R	RBI	BB	SO	SB	BA	SA	PH AB	PH H	G by POS
1884 2 teams		BOS	N (4G –	.063)		IND	AA (10G –	.216)									
" total	14	53	9	2	0	0	0.0	5		0	8		.170	.245	0	0	OF-11, P-2, 3B-1
1885 DET N	11	39	1	1	0	0	0.0	1	0	0	10		.026	.051	0	0	OF-6, 3B-4, SS-1, P-1
1892 STL N	47	177	31	4	1	3	1.7	20	19	4	37	7	.175	.260	0	0	OF-47
3 yrs.	72	269	41	5	3	3	1.1	26	18	4	55	7	.152	.227	0	0	OF-64, 3B-5, P-3, SS-1

Bill Moriarty

MORIARITY, WILLIAM JOSEPH
Brother of George Moriarity.
B. 1883, Chicago, Ill.   D. Dec. 25, 1916, Chicago, Ill.   BR TR 6'2" 180 lbs.

	G	AB	H	2B	3B	HR	HR%	R	RBI	BB	SO	SB	BA	SA	PH AB	PH H	G by POS
1909 CIN N	6	20	4	1	0	0	0.0	1		1		2	.200	.250	0	0	SS-6

	G	AB	H	2B	3B	HR	HR %	R	RBI	BB	SO	SB	BA	SA	Pinch Hit AB	Pinch Hit H	G by POS

Ed Moriarty

MORIARTY, EDWARD JEROME　　　　　　　　　BR TR 5'10½" 180 lbs.
B. Oct. 12, 1912, Holyoke, Mass.

	G	AB	H	2B	3B	HR	HR %	R	RBI	BB	SO	SB	BA	SA	PH AB	PH H	G by POS
1935 BOS N	8	34	11	2	1	1	2.9	4	1	0	6	0	.324	.529	0	0	2B-8
1936	6	6	1	0	0	0	0.0	0	0	0	1	0	.167	.167	6	1	
2 yrs.	14	40	12	2	1	1	2.5	4	1	0	7	0	.300	.475	6	1	2B-8

George Moriarty

MORIARTY, GEORGE JOSEPH　　　　　　　　　BR TR 6'　　185 lbs.
Brother of Bill Moriarty.
B. July 7, 1884, Chicago, Ill.　　D. Apr. 8, 1964, Miami, Fla.
Manager 1927-28.

	G	AB	H	2B	3B	HR	HR %	R	RBI	BB	SO	SB	BA	SA	PH AB	PH H	G by POS
1903 CHI N	1	5	0	0	0	0	0.0	1	0	0		0	.000	.000	0	0	3B-1
1904	4	13	0	0	0	0	0.0	0	0	1		0	.000	.000	0	0	OF-2, 3B-2
1906 NY A	65	197	46	7	7	0	0.0	22	23	17		8	.234	.340	4	1	3B-39, OF-15, 1B-5, 2B-1
1907	126	437	121	16	5	0	0.0	51	43	25		28	.277	.336	1	0	1B-91, 1B-22, OF-9, 2B-8, SS-1
1908	101	348	82	12	1	0	0.0	25	27	11		22	.236	.276	8	2	1B-52, 3B-28, OF-10, 2B-4
1909 DET A	133	473	129	20	4	1	0.2	43	39	24		34	.273	.338	3	1	3B-106, 1B-24
1910	136	490	123	24	3	2	0.4	53	60	33		33	.251	.324	1	0	3B-134
1911	130	478	116	20	4	1	0.2	51	60	27		28	.243	.308	0	0	3B-129, 1B-1
1912	105	375	93	23	1	0	0.0	38	54	26		27	.248	.315	1	1	1B-71, 3B-33
1913	102	347	83	5	2	0	0.0	29	30	24	25	33	.239	.265	0	0	3B-93, OF-7
1914	130	465	118	19	5	1	0.2	56	40	39	27	34	.254	.323	0	0	3B-126, 1B-3
1915	31	38	8	1	0	0	0.0	2	0	5	7	1	.211	.237	10	2	3B-12, OF-1, 2B-1, 1B-1
1916 CHI A	7	5	1	0	0	0	0.0	1	0	2	0	0	.200	.200	3	1	3B-1, 1B-1
13 yrs.	1071	3671	920	147	32	5	0.1	372	376	234	59	248	.251	.312	31	8	3B-795, 1B-180, OF-44, 2B-14, SS-1

WORLD SERIES

	G	AB	H	2B	3B	HR	HR %	R	RBI	BB	SO	SB	BA	SA	PH AB	PH H	G by POS
1909 DET A	7	22	6	1	0	0	0.0	4	1	3	1	0	.273	.318	0	0	3B-7

Bill Morley

MORLEY, WILLIAM　　　　　　　　　BR TR 5'11" 170 lbs.
Born William Morley Jennings.
B. Jan. 23, 1890, Holland, Mich.

	G	AB	H	2B	3B	HR	HR %	R	RBI	BB	SO	SB	BA	SA	PH AB	PH H	G by POS
1913 WAS A	2	3	0	0	0	0	0.0	0	0	0	0	0	.000	.000	0	0	2B-1

Jeff Moronko

MORONKO, JEFFREY ROBERT　　　　　　　　　BR TR 6'2" 190 lbs.
B. Aug. 17, 1959, Pasadena, Tex.

	G	AB	H	2B	3B	HR	HR %	R	RBI	BB	SO	SB	BA	SA	PH AB	PH H	G by POS
1984 CLE A	7	19	3	1	0	0	0.0	1	3	3	5	0	.158	.211	1	0	3B-6, DH-1

John Morrill

MORRILL, JOHN FRANCIS (Honest John)　　　　　　　　　BR TR 5'10½" 155 lbs.
B. Feb. 19, 1855, Boston, Mass.　　D. Apr. 2, 1932, Boston, Mass.
Manager 1882-89.

	G	AB	H	2B	3B	HR	HR %	R	RBI	BB	SO	SB	BA	SA	PH AB	PH H	G by POS
1876 BOS N	66	278	73	5	2	0	0.0	38	26	3	5		.263	.295	0	0	2B-37, C-23, OF-5, 1B-3
1877	61	242	73	5	1	0	0.0	47	28	6	15		.302	.331	0	0	3B-30, 1B-18, OF-11, 2B-3
1878	60	233	56	5	1	0	0.0	26	23	5	16		.240	.270	0	0	1B-59, OF-1, 3B-1
1879	84	348	98	18	5	0	0.0	56	49	14	32		.282	.362	0	0	3B-51, 1B-33
1880	86	342	81	16	8	2	0.6	51	44	11	37		.237	.348	0	0	1B-46, 3B-40, P-3
1881	81	311	90	19	3	1	0.3	47	39	12	30		.289	.379	0	0	1B-74, 2B-4, 3B-2, P-2
1882	83	349	101	19	11	2	0.6	73	54	18	29		.289	.424	0	0	1B-76, SS-3, 2B-2, OF-1, 3B-1, P-1
1883	97	404	129	33	16	6	1.5	83	68	15	68		.319	.525	0	0	1B-81, OF-7, 3B-6, SS-2, 2B-2, P-2
1884	111	438	114	19	7	3	0.7	80		30	87		.260	.356	0	0	1B-91, 2B-17, P-7, 3B-2, OF-1
1885	111	394	89	20	7	4	1.0	74	44	64	78		.226	.343	0	0	1B-92, 2B-17, 3B-2
1886	117	430	106	25	6	7	1.6	86	69	56	81		.247	.381	0	0	SS-55, 1B-42, 2B-20, P-1
1887	127	504	141	32	6	12	2.4	79	81	37	86	19	.280	.438	0	0	1B-127
1888	135	486	96	18	7	4	0.8	60	39	55	68	21	.198	.288	0	0	1B-133, 2B-2
1889 WAS N	44	146	27	5	0	2	1.4	20	16	30	23	12	.185	.260	0	0	1B-40, 3B-3, 2B-1, P-1
1890 BOS P	2	7	1	0	0	0	0.0	1	2	2	1	0	.143	.143	0	0	SS-1, 1B-1
15 yrs.	1265	4912	1275	239	80	43	0.9	821	582	358	656	52	.260	.367	0	0	1B-916, 3B-138, 2B-105, SS-61, OF-26, C-23, P-17

Bugs Morris

Playing record listed under Bugs Bennett

Doyt Morris

MORRIS, DOYT THEODORE　　　　　　　　　BR TR 6'3" 195 lbs.
B. July 15, 1916, Stanley, N. C.

	G	AB	H	2B	3B	HR	HR %	R	RBI	BB	SO	SB	BA	SA	PH AB	PH H	G by POS
1937 PHI A	6	13	2	0	0	0	0.0	0	0	0	3	0	.154	.154	3	1	OF-3

P. Morris

MORRIS, P.
B. Rockford, Ill.　　Deceased.

	G	AB	H	2B	3B	HR	HR %	R	RBI	BB	SO	SB	BA	SA	PH AB	PH H	G by POS
1884 WAS U	1	3	0	0	0	0	0.0	0		0			.000	.000	0	0	SS-1

Walter Morris

MORRIS, JOHN WALTER　　　　　　　　　TR
B. Jan. 31, 1881, Rockwall, Tex.　　D. Aug. 2, 1961, Dallas, Tex.

	G	AB	H	2B	3B	HR	HR %	R	RBI	BB	SO	SB	BA	SA	PH AB	PH H	G by POS
1908 STL N	23	73	13	1	1	0	0.0	1	2	0		1	.178	.219	1	0	SS-23

William Morris

Playing record listed under John Fluhrer

Jim Morrison

MORRISON, JAMES FORREST　　　　　　　　　BR TR 5'11" 175 lbs.
B. Sept. 23, 1952, Pensacola, Fla.

	G	AB	H	2B	3B	HR	HR %	R	RBI	BB	SO	SB	BA	SA	PH AB	PH H	G by POS
1977 PHI N	5	7	3	0	0	0	0.0	3	1	1	1	0	.429	.429	0	0	3B-5
1978	53	108	17	1	1	3	2.8	12	10	10	21	1	.157	.269	12	0	2B-31, 3B-3, OF-1
1979 CHI A	67	240	66	14	0	14	5.8	38	35	15	48	11	.275	.508	4	0	2B-48, 3B-29
1980	162	604	171	40	0	15	2.5	66	57	36	74	9	.283	.424	0	0	2B-161, DH-1, SS-1

	G	AB	H	2B	3B	HR	HR %	R	RBI	BB	SO	SB	BA	SA	Pinch Hit AB	H	G by POS

Jim Morrison continued

	G	AB	H	2B	3B	HR	HR%	R	RBI	BB	SO	SB	BA	SA	PH AB	PH H	G by POS
1981	90	290	68	8	1	10	3.4	27	34	10	29	3	.234	.372	2	0	3B-87, DH-1, 2B-1
1982 2 teams	CHI	A (51G – .223)				PIT	N (44G – .279)										
" total	95	252	61	11	4	11	4.4	27	34	18	29	2	.242	.448	16	3	3B-76, OF-2, DH-1, SS-1, 2B-1
1983 PIT N	66	158	48	7	2	6	3.8	16	25	9	25	2	.304	.487	15	4	2B-28, 3B-25, SS-7
1984	100	304	87	14	2	11	3.6	38	45	20	52	0	.286	.454	13	1	3B-61, 2B-26, SS-2, 1B-1
8 yrs.	638	1963	521	95	10	70	3.6	227	241	119	279	28	.265	.431	62	8	2B-296, 3B-286, SS-11, DH-3, OF-3, 1B-1

LEAGUE CHAMPIONSHIP SERIES

	G	AB	H	2B	3B	HR	HR%	R	RBI	BB	SO	SB	BA	SA	PH AB	PH H	G by POS
1978 PHI N	1	1	0	0	0	0	0.0	0	0	0	1	0	.000	.000	1	0	

Jon Morrison

MORRISON, JONATHAN W.
B. 1859, Port Huron, Mich.　Deceased.

	G	AB	H	2B	3B	HR	HR%	R	RBI	BB	SO	SB	BA	SA	PH AB	PH H	G by POS
1884 IND AA	44	182	48	6	8	1	0.5	26		7			.264	.401	0	0	OF-44
1887 NY AA	9	34	4	0	0	0	0.0	7		6		0	.118	.118	0	0	OF-9
2 yrs.	53	216	52	6	8	1	0.5	33		13		0	.241	.356	0	0	OF-53

Tom Morrison

MORRISON, THOMAS J.
B. 1861　Deceased.　　　　5'3"　145 lbs.

	G	AB	H	2B	3B	HR	HR%	R	RBI	BB	SO	SB	BA	SA	PH AB	PH H	G by POS
1895 LOU N	6	22	6	0	2	0	0.0	3	4	1	1	0	.273	.455	0	0	SS-3, 3B-3
1896	8	27	4	1	0	0	0.0	3	0	4	4	0	.148	.185	0	0	3B-5, OF-2, SS-1
2 yrs.	14	49	10	1	2	0	0.0	6	4	5	5	0	.204	.306	0	0	3B-8, SS-4, OF-2

Jack Morrissey

MORRISSEY, JOHN ALBERT (King)
B. May 2, 1876, Lansing, Mich.　D. Oct. 30, 1936, Lansing, Mich.　　BR TR 5'10"　160 lbs.

	G	AB	H	2B	3B	HR	HR%	R	RBI	BB	SO	SB	BA	SA	PH AB	PH H	G by POS
1902 CIN N	12	39	11	1	1	0	0.0	5	3	4		0	.282	.359	0	0	2B-11, OF-1
1903	29	89	22	1	0	0	0.0	14	9	14		3	.247	.258	2	0	2B-17, OF-8, SS-2
2 yrs.	41	128	33	2	1	0	0.0	19	12	18		3	.258	.289	2	0	2B-28, OF-9, SS-2

Jo-Jo Morrissey

MORRISSEY, JOSEPH ANSELM
B. Jan. 16, 1904, Warren, R. I.　D. May 2, 1950, Worcester, Mass.　　BR TR 6'1½"　178 lbs.

	G	AB	H	2B	3B	HR	HR%	R	RBI	BB	SO	SB	BA	SA	PH AB	PH H	G by POS
1932 CIN N	89	269	65	10	1	0	0.0	15	13	14	15	2	.242	.286	1	0	SS-45, 2B-42, 3B-12, OF-1
1933	148	534	123	20	0	0	0.0	43	26	20	22	5	.230	.268	1	1	2B-88, SS-63, 3B-15
1936 CHI A	17	38	7	1	0	0	0.0	3	6	2	3	0	.184	.211	4	2	3B-9, SS-4, 2B-1
3 yrs.	254	841	195	31	1	0	0.0	61	45	36	40	7	.232	.271	6	3	2B-131, SS-112, 3B-36, OF-1

John Morrissey

MORRISSEY, JOHN H.
Brother of Tom Morrissey.
B. Janesville, Wis.　D. Apr. 29, 1884, Janesville, Wis.

	G	AB	H	2B	3B	HR	HR%	R	RBI	BB	SO	SB	BA	SA	PH AB	PH H	G by POS
1881 BUF N	12	47	10	2	0	0	0.0	3	3	0	3		.213	.255	0	0	3B-12
1882 DET N	2	7	2	0	0	0	0.0	1	0	0	2		.286	.286	0	0	3B-2
2 yrs.	14	54	12	2	0	0	0.0	4	3	0	5		.222	.259	0	0	3B-14

Tom Morrissey

MORRISSEY, THOMAS J.
Brother of John Morrissey.
B. 1861, Janesville, Wis.　D. Sept. 23, 1941, Janeville, Wis.

	G	AB	H	2B	3B	HR	HR%	R	RBI	BB	SO	SB	BA	SA	PH AB	PH H	G by POS
1884 MIL U	12	47	8	2	0	0	0.0	3		0			.170	.213	0	0	3B-12

Bud Morse

MORSE, NEWELL OBEDIAH
B. Sept. 4, 1904, Berkeley, Calif.　　BL TR 5'9"　150 lbs.

	G	AB	H	2B	3B	HR	HR%	R	RBI	BB	SO	SB	BA	SA	PH AB	PH H	G by POS
1929 PHI A	8	27	2	0	0	0	0.0	1	0	2		0	.074	.074	0	0	2B-8

Hap Morse

MORSE, PETER RAYMOND
B. Dec. 6, 1886, St. Paul, Minn.　D. June 19, 1974, St. Paul, Minn.　　TR

	G	AB	H	2B	3B	HR	HR%	R	RBI	BB	SO	SB	BA	SA	PH AB	PH H	G by POS
1911 STL N	4	8	0	0	0	0	0.0	0	0	1	2	0	.000	.000	1	0	SS-2, OF-1

Bubba Morton

MORTON, WYCLIFFE NATHANIEL
B. Dec. 13, 1931, Washington, D. C.　　BR TR 5'10"　175 lbs.

	G	AB	H	2B	3B	HR	HR%	R	RBI	BB	SO	SB	BA	SA	PH AB	PH H	G by POS
1961 DET A	77	108	31	5	1	2	1.9	26	19	9	25	3	.287	.407	37	11	OF-30
1962	90	195	51	6	3	4	2.1	30	17	32	32	1	.262	.385	21	5	OF-62, 1B-3
1963 2 teams	DET	A (6G – .091)				MIL	N (15G – .179)										
" total	21	39	6	0	0	0	0.0	3	6	4	4	0	.154	.154	10	1	OF-12
1966 CAL A	15	50	11	1	0	0	0.0	4	4	2	6	1	.220	.240	0	0	OF-14
1967	80	201	63	9	3	0	0.0	23	32	22	29	0	.313	.388	25	8	OF-61
1968	81	163	44	6	0	1	0.6	13	18	14	18	2	.270	.325	33	10	OF-50, 3B-1
1969	87	172	42	10	1	7	4.1	18	32	28	29	0	.244	.436	34	10	OF-49, 1B-1
7 yrs.	451	928	248	37	8	14	1.5	117	128	111	143	7	.267	.370	160	45	OF-278, 1B-4, 3B-1

Charlie Morton

MORTON, CHARLES HAZEN
B. Oct. 12, 1854, Kingsville, Ohio　D. Dec. 13, 1921, Akron, Ohio
Manager 1884-85, 1890.

	G	AB	H	2B	3B	HR	HR%	R	RBI	BB	SO	SB	BA	SA	PH AB	PH H	G by POS
1882 2 teams	PIT	AA (25G – .282)				STL	AA (9G – .063)										
" total	34	135	31	0	4	0	0.0	14		7			.230	.289	0	0	OF-28, 2B-7, 3B-3, SS-1
1884 TOL AA	32	111	18	6	2	0	0.0	11		7			.162	.252	0	0	3B-16, OF-15, P-3, 2B-1
1885 DET N	22	79	14	1	2	0	0.0	9	3	5	10		.177	.241	0	0	3B-18, SS-4
3 yrs.	88	325	63	7	8	0	0.0	34	2	19	10		.194	.265	0	0	OF-43, 3B-37, 2B-8, SS-5, P-3

Guy Morton

MORTON, GUY, JR. (Moose)
Son of Guy Morton.
B. Nov. 4, 1930, Tuscaloosa, Ala.　　BR TR 6'2"　200 lbs.

	G	AB	H	2B	3B	HR	HR%	R	RBI	BB	SO	SB	BA	SA	PH AB	PH H	G by POS
1954 BOS A	1	1	0	0	0	0	0.0	0	0	0	1	0	.000	.000	1	0	

	G	AB	H	2B	3B	HR	HR %	R	RBI	BB	SO	SB	BA	SA	Pinch Hit AB	Pinch Hit H	G by POS

Walt Moryn

MORYN, WALTER JOSEPH (Moose)   BL TR 6'2"   205 lbs.
B. Apr. 12, 1926, St. Paul, Minn.

	G	AB	H	2B	3B	HR	HR %	R	RBI	BB	SO	SB	BA	SA	AB	H	G by POS
1954 BKN N	48	91	25	4	2	2	2.2	16	14	7	11	0	.275	.429	23	5	OF-21
1955	11	19	5	1	0	1	5.3	3	3	5	4	0	.263	.474	4	0	OF-7
1956 CHI N	147	529	151	27	3	23	4.3	69	67	50	67	4	.285	.478	6	0	OF-141
1957	149	568	164	33	0	19	3.3	76	88	50	90	0	.289	.447	4	1	OF-147
1958	143	512	135	26	7	26	5.1	77	77	62	83	1	.264	.494	6	4	OF-141
1959	117	381	89	14	1	14	3.7	41	48	44	66	0	.234	.386	13	5	OF-104
1960 2 teams	CHI	N (38G –	.294)		STL	N (75G –	.245)										
" total	113	309	81	8	3	13	4.2	36	46	30	57	2	.262	.434	22	3	OF-92
1961 2 teams	STL	N (17G –	.125)		PIT	N (40G –	.200)										
" total	57	97	17	3	0	3	3.1	6	11	3	15	0	.175	.299	36	6	OF-18
8 yrs.	785	2506	667	116	16	101	4.0	324	354	251	393	7	.266	.446	114	24	OF-671

Ross Moschitto

MOSCHITTO, ROSS ALLEN   BR TR 6'2"   175 lbs.
B. Feb. 15, 1945, Fresno, Calif.

	G	AB	H	2B	3B	HR	HR %	R	RBI	BB	SO	SB	BA	SA	AB	H	G by POS
1965 NY A	96	27	5	0	0	1	3.7	12	3	0	12	0	.185	.296	1	0	OF-89
1967	14	9	1	0	0	0	0.0	1	0	1	2	0	.111	.111	6	0	OF-8
2 yrs.	110	36	6	0	0	1	2.8	13	3	1	14	0	.167	.250	7	0	OF-97

Lloyd Moseby

MOSEBY, LLOYD ANTHONY   BL TR 6'3"   200 lbs.
B. Nov. 5, 1959, Portland, Ark.

	G	AB	H	2B	3B	HR	HR %	R	RBI	BB	SO	SB	BA	SA	AB	H	G by POS
1980 TOR A	114	389	89	24	1	9	2.3	44	46	25	85	4	.229	.365	2	0	OF-104, DH-6
1981	100	378	88	16	2	9	2.4	36	43	24	86	11	.233	.357	2	0	OF-100
1982	147	487	115	20	9	9	1.8	51	52	33	106	11	.236	.370	7	3	OF-145
1983	151	539	170	31	7	18	3.3	104	81	51	85	27	.315	.499	9	4	OF-147
1984	158	592	166	28	15	18	3.0	97	92	78	122	39	.280	.470	3	1	OF-156
5 yrs.	670	2385	628	119	34	63	2.6	332	314	211	484	92	.263	.421	23	8	OF-652, DH-6

Arnie Moser

MOSER, ARNOLD ROBERT   BR TR 5'11"   165 lbs.
B. Aug. 9, 1915, Houston, Tex.

	G	AB	H	2B	3B	HR	HR %	R	RBI	BB	SO	SB	BA	SA	AB	H	G by POS
1937 CIN N	5	5	0	0	0	0	0.0	0	0	0	2	0	.000	.000	5	0	

Gerry Moses

MOSES, GERALD BRAHEEN   BR TR 6'3"   210 lbs.
B. Aug. 9, 1946, Yazoo City, Miss.

	G	AB	H	2B	3B	HR	HR %	R	RBI	BB	SO	SB	BA	SA	AB	H	G by POS
1965 BOS A	4	4	1	0	0	1	25.0	1	1	0	2	0	.250	1.000	4	1	
1968	6	18	6	0	0	2	11.1	2	4	1	4	0	.333	.667	0	0	C-6
1969	53	135	41	9	1	4	3.0	13	17	5	23	0	.304	.474	17	2	C-36
1970	92	315	83	18	1	6	1.9	26	35	21	45	1	.263	.384	5	2	C-88, OF-1
1971 CAL A	69	181	41	8	2	4	2.2	12	15	10	34	0	.227	.359	8	0	C-63, OF-1
1972 CLE A	52	141	31	3	0	4	2.8	9	14	11	29	0	.220	.326	10	2	C-39, 1B-3
1973 NY A	21	59	15	2	0	0	0.0	5	3	2	6	0	.254	.288	3	1	C-17, DH-1
1974 DET A	74	198	47	6	3	4	2.0	19	19	11	38	0	.237	.359	1	0	C-74
1975 2 teams	CHI	A (2G –	.500)		SD	N (13G –	.158)										
" total	15	21	4	2	1	0	0.0	2	1	2	3	0	.190	.381	6	1	C-5, DH-1, 1B-1
9 yrs.	386	1072	269	48	8	25	2.3	89	109	63	184	1	.251	.381	54	9	C-328, 1B-4, DH-2, OF-2

John Moses

MOSES, JOHN WILLIAM   BB TL 5'10"   165 lbs.
B. Aug. 9, 1957, Los Angeles, Calif.

	G	AB	H	2B	3B	HR	HR %	R	RBI	BB	SO	SB	BA	SA	AB	H	G by POS
1982 SEA A	22	44	14	5	1	1	2.3	7	3	4	5	5	.318	.545	2	1	OF-19
1983	93	130	27	4	1	0	0.0	19	6	12	20	11	.208	.254	4	1	OF-71, DH-10
1984	19	35	12	1	1	0	0.0	3	2	2	5	1	.343	.429	0	0	OF-19, DH-1
3 yrs.	134	209	53	10	3	1	0.5	29	11	18	30	17	.254	.344	6	2	OF-109, DH-11

Wally Moses

MOSES, WALLACE   BL TL 5'10"   160 lbs.
B. Oct. 8, 1910, Uvalda, Ga.

	G	AB	H	2B	3B	HR	HR %	R	RBI	BB	SO	SB	BA	SA	AB	H	G by POS
1935 PHI A	85	345	112	21	3	5	1.4	60	35	25	18	3	.325	.446	6	4	OF-80
1936	146	585	202	35	11	7	1.2	98	66	62	32	12	.345	.479	2	0	OF-144
1937	154	649	208	48	13	25	3.9	113	86	54	38	9	.320	.550	0	0	OF-154
1938	142	589	181	29	8	8	1.4	86	49	58	31	15	.307	.424	3	1	OF-139
1939	115	437	134	28	7	3	0.7	68	33	44	23	7	.307	.423	11	2	OF-103
1940	142	537	166	41	9	9	1.7	91	50	75	44	6	.309	.469	8	1	OF-133
1941	116	438	132	31	4	4	0.9	78	35	62	27	3	.301	.418	6	1	OF-109
1942 CHI A	146	577	156	28	4	7	1.2	74	49	74	27	16	.270	.369	1	0	OF-145
1943	150	599	147	22	12	3	0.5	82	48	55	47	56	.245	.337	2	0	OF-148
1944	136	535	150	26	9	3	0.6	82	34	52	22	21	.280	.379	1	0	OF-134
1945	140	569	168	35	15	2	0.4	79	50	69	33	11	.295	.420	1	0	OF-139
1946 2 teams	CHI	A (56G –	.274)		BOS	A (48G –	.206)										
" total	104	343	82	20	4	6	1.7	33	33	31	35	4	.239	.373	24	4	OF-80
1947 BOS A	90	255	70	18	2	2	0.8	32	27	27	16	3	.275	.384	29	5	OF-58
1948	78	189	49	12	1	2	1.1	26	29	21	19	5	.259	.365	27	6	OF-45
1949 PHI A	110	308	85	19	3	1	0.3	49	25	51	19	1	.276	.367	17	5	OF-62
1950	88	265	70	16	5	2	0.8	47	21	40	17	0	.264	.385	21	4	OF-62
1951	70	136	26	6	0	0	0.0	17	9	21	9	2	.191	.235	34	4	OF-27
17 yrs.	2012	7356	2138	435	110	89	1.2	1114	679	821	457	174	.291	.416	193	37	OF-1792

WORLD SERIES

	G	AB	H	2B	3B	HR	HR %	R	RBI	BB	SO	SB	BA	SA	AB	H	G by POS
1946 BOS A	4	12	5	0	0	0	0.0	1	0	1	2	0	.417	.417	0	0	OF-4

Doc Moskiman

MOSKIMAN, WILLIAM BANKHEAD   BR TR 6'   170 lbs.
B. Dec. 20, 1879, Oakland, Calif.   D. Jan. 11, 1953, San Leandro, Calif.

	G	AB	H	2B	3B	HR	HR %	R	RBI	BB	SO	SB	BA	SA	AB	H	G by POS
1910 BOS A	5	9	1	0	0	0	0.0	0	1	1	2		.111	.111	0	0	1B-2, OF-1

Jim Mosolf

MOSOLF, JAMES FREDERICK   BL TR 5'10"   186 lbs.
B. Aug. 21, 1905, Puyallup, Wash.   D. Dec. 28, 1979, Dallas, Ore.

	G	AB	H	2B	3B	HR	HR %	R	RBI	BB	SO	SB	BA	SA	AB	H	G by POS
1929 PIT N	8	13	6	1	1	0	0.0	3	2	1	1	0	.462	.692	4	2	OF-3
1930	40	51	17	2	1	0	0.0	16	9	8	7	0	.333	.412	22	8	OF-12, P-1

	G	AB	H	2B	3B	HR	HR %	R	RBI	BB	SO	SB	BA	SA	Pinch Hit AB	Pinch Hit H	G by POS

Jim Mosolf continued

	G	AB	H	2B	3B	HR	HR%	R	RBI	BB	SO	SB	BA	SA	AB	H	G by POS
1931	39	44	11	1	0	1	2.3	7	8	8	5	0	.250	.341	30	6	OF-4
1933 CHI N	31	82	22	5	1	1	1.2	13	9	5	8	0	.268	.390	8	3	OF-22
4 yrs.	118	190	56	9	3	2	1.1	39	28	22	21	0	.295	.405	64	19	OF-41, P-1

Charlie Moss

MOSS, CHARLES CROSBY
B. Mar. 20, 1911, Meridian, Miss.

BR TR 5'10" 160 lbs.

	G	AB	H	2B	3B	HR	HR%	R	RBI	BB	SO	SB	BA	SA	AB	H	G by POS
1934 PHI A	10	10	2	0	0	0	0.0	3	1	0	0	0	.200	.200	4	1	C-6
1935	4	3	1	0	0	0	0.0	1	1	1	0	0	.333	.333	2	1	C-1
1936	33	44	11	1	1	0	0.0	2	10	6	5	1	.250	.318	14	2	C-19
3 yrs.	47	57	14	1	1	0	0.0	6	12	7	5	1	.246	.298	20	4	C-26

Howie Moss

MOSS, HOWARD GLENN
B. Oct. 17, 1918, Gastonia, N. C.

BR TR 5'11½" 185 lbs.

	G	AB	H	2B	3B	HR	HR%	R	RBI	BB	SO	SB	BA	SA	AB	H	G by POS
1942 NY N	7	14	0	0	0	0	0.0	0	0	0	4	0	.000	.000	4	0	OF-3
1946 2 teams	CIN N (7G – .192)			CLE A (8G – .063)													
" total	15	58	7	0	0	0	0.0	3	1	3	13	0	.121	.121	1	0	3B-8, OF-6
2 yrs.	22	72	7	0	0	0	0.0	3	1	3	17	0	.097	.097	5	0	OF-9, 3B-8

Les Moss

MOSS, JOHN LESTER
B. May 14, 1925, Tulsa, Okla.
Manager 1968, 1979.

BR TR 5'11" 205 lbs.

	G	AB	H	2B	3B	HR	HR%	R	RBI	BB	SO	SB	BA	SA	AB	H	G by POS
1946 STL A	12	35	13	3	0	0	0.0	4	5	3	5	1	.371	.457	0	0	C-12
1947	96	274	43	5	2	6	2.2	17	27	35	48	0	.157	.255	1	0	C-96
1948	107	335	86	12	1	14	4.2	35	46	39	50	0	.257	.424	5	0	C-103
1949	97	278	81	11	0	10	3.6	28	39	49	32	0	.291	.439	12	2	C-83
1950	84	222	59	6	0	8	3.6	24	34	26	32	0	.266	.401	19	5	C-60
1951 2 teams	STL A (16G – .170)			BOS A (71G – .198)													
" total	87	249	48	8	0	4	1.6	23	33	31	42	1	.193	.273	6	0	C-81
1952 STL A	52	118	29	3	0	3	2.5	11	12	15	13	0	.246	.347	13	4	C-39
1953	78	239	66	14	1	2	0.8	21	28	18	31	0	.276	.368	6	0	C-71
1954 BAL A	50	126	31	3	0	0	0.0	7	5	14	16	0	.246	.270	12	2	C-38
1955 2 teams	BAL A (29G – .339)			CHI A (32G – .254)													
" total	61	115	34	3	0	4	3.5	10	13	13	14	0	.296	.426	12	2	C-49
1956 CHI A	56	127	31	4	0	10	7.9	20	22	18	15	0	.244	.512	8	1	C-49
1957	42	115	31	3	0	2	1.7	10	12	20	18	0	.270	.348	4	2	C-39
1958	2	1	0	0	0	0	0.0	0	0	1	0	0	.000	.000	1	0	
13 yrs.	824	2234	552	75	4	63	2.8	210	276	282	316	2	.247	.369	99	18	C-720

Johnny Mostil

MOSTIL, JOHN ANTHONY
B. June 1, 1896, Chicago, Ill. D. Dec. 10, 1970, Midlothian, Ill.

BR TR 5'8½" 168 lbs.

	G	AB	H	2B	3B	HR	HR%	R	RBI	BB	SO	SB	BA	SA	AB	H	G by POS
1918 CHI A	10	33	9	2	2	0	0.0	4	4	1	6	1	.273	.455	0	0	2B-9
1921	100	326	98	21	7	3	0.9	43	42	28	35	10	.301	.436	5	2	OF-91, 2B-1
1922	132	458	139	28	14	7	1.5	74	70	38	39	14	.303	.472	9	4	OF-132
1923	153	546	159	37	15	3	0.5	91	64	62	51	41	.291	.430	4	0	OF-143, 3B-6, SS-1
1924	118	385	125	22	5	4	1.0	75	49	45	41	7	.325	.439	14	5	OF-102
1925	153	605	181	36	16	2	0.3	135	50	90	52	43	.299	.421	0	0	OF-153
1926	148	600	197	41	15	4	0.7	120	42	79	55	35	.328	.467	0	0	OF-147
1927	13	16	2	0	0	0	0.0	3	1	0	1	1	.125	.125	1	0	OF-6
1928	133	503	136	19	8	0	0.0	69	51	66	54	23	.270	.340	2	0	OF-131
1929	12	35	8	3	0	0	0.0	4	3	6	2	1	.229	.314	0	0	OF-11
10 yrs.	972	3507	1054	209	82	23	0.7	618	376	415	336	176	.301	.427	35	11	OF-916, 2B-10, 3B-6, SS-1

Manny Mota

MOTA, MANUEL RAFAEL GERONIMO
B. Feb. 18, 1938, Santo Domingo, Dominican Republic

BR TR 5'10" 160 lbs.

	G	AB	H	2B	3B	HR	HR%	R	RBI	BB	SO	SB	BA	SA	AB	H	G by POS
1962 SF N	47	74	13	1	0	0	0.0	9	9	7	8	3	.176	.189	15	1	OF-27, 3B-7, 2B-3
1963 PIT N	59	126	34	2	3	0	0.0	20	7	7	18	0	.270	.333	22	6	OF-37, 2B-1
1964	115	271	75	8	3	5	1.8	43	32	10	31	4	.277	.384	21	5	OF-93, 2B-1, C-1
1965	121	294	82	7	6	4	1.4	47	29	22	32	2	.279	.384	32	11	OF-95
1966	116	322	107	16	7	5	1.6	54	46	25	28	7	.332	.472	26	10	OF-96, 3B-4
1967	120	349	112	14	8	4	1.1	53	56	14	46	3	.321	.441	30	5	OF-99, 3B-2
1968	111	331	93	10	2	1	0.3	35	33	20	19	4	.281	.332	21	5	OF-92, 3B-1, 2B-1
1969 2 teams	MON N (31G – .315)			LA N (85G – .323)													
" total	116	383	123	7	5	3	0.8	41	30	32	36	6	.321	.389	16	2	OF-102
1970 LA N	124	417	127	12	6	3	0.7	63	37	47	37	11	.305	.384	16	6	OF-111, 3B-1
1971	91	269	84	13	5	0	0.0	24	34	20	20	4	.312	.398	15	5	OF-80
1972	118	371	120	16	5	5	1.3	57	48	27	15	4	.323	.434	25	10	OF-99
1973	89	293	92	11	2	0	0.0	33	23	25	12	1	.314	.365	14	5	OF-74
1974	66	57	16	2	0	0	0.0	5	16	5	4	0	.281	.316	53	15	OF-3
1975	52	49	13	1	0	0	0.0	3	10	5	1	0	.265	.286	40	10	OF-5
1976	50	52	15	3	0	0	0.0	1	13	7	5	0	.288	.346	40	12	OF-6
1977	49	38	15	1	0	1	2.6	5	4	10	0	1	.395	.500	36	14	OF-1
1978	37	33	10	1	0	0	0.0	2	6	3	4	0	.303	.333	33	10	
1979	47	42	15	0	0	0	0.0	1	3	3	4	0	.357	.357	42	15	OF-1
1980	7	7	3	0	0	0	0.0	0	2	0	0	0	.429	.429	7	3	
1982	1	1	0	0	0	0	0.0	0	0	0	0	0	.000	.000	1	0	
20 yrs.	1536	3779	1149	125	52	31	0.8	496	438	289	320	50	.304	.389	505	150	OF-1021, 3B-15, 2B-6, C-1
															2nd	**1st**	

LEAGUE CHAMPIONSHIP SERIES

	G	AB	H	2B	3B	HR	HR%	R	RBI	BB	SO	SB	BA	SA	AB	H	G by POS
1974 LA N	3	3	1	0	0	0	0.0	0	1	0	0	0	.333	.333	3	1	OF-1
1977	1	1	1	1	0	0	0.0	1	0	0	0	0	1.000	2.000	1	1	
1978	2	1	1	1	0	0	0.0	0	0	0	0	0	1.000	1.000	1	1	
3 yrs.	6	5	3	2	0	0	0.0	1	1	0	0	0	.600	1.000	5	3	OF-1

WORLD SERIES

	G	AB	H	2B	3B	HR	HR%	R	RBI	BB	SO	SB	BA	SA	AB	H	G by POS
1977 LA N	3	3	0	0	0	0	0.0	0	0	0	1	0	.000	.000	3	0	

	G	AB	H	2B	3B	HR	HR %	R	RBI	BB	SO	SB	BA	SA	Pinch Hit AB	Pinch Hit H	G by POS

Manny Mota continued

	G	AB	H	2B	3B	HR	HR%	R	RBI	BB	SO	SB	BA	SA	PH AB	PH H	G by POS
1978	1	0	0	0	0	0	–	0	0	1	0	0	–	–	0	0	
2 yrs.	4	3	0	0	0	0	0.0	0	0	1	1	0	.000	.000	3	0	

Darryl Motley

MOTLEY, DARRYL DeWAYNE
B. Jan. 21, 1960, Muskogee, Okla.   BR TR 5'9"   196 lbs.

	G	AB	H	2B	3B	HR	HR%	R	RBI	BB	SO	SB	BA	SA	PH AB	PH H	G by POS
1981 KC A	42	125	29	4	0	2	1.6	15	8	7	15	1	.232	.312	3	0	OF-39
1983	19	68	16	1	2	3	4.4	9	11	2	8	2	.235	.441	1	1	OF-18, DH-1
1984	146	522	148	24	6	15	2.9	64	70	28	73	10	.284	.439	9	1	OF-138
3 yrs.	207	715	193	29	8	20	2.8	88	89	37	96	13	.270	.417	13	2	OF-195, DH-1

LEAGUE CHAMPIONSHIP SERIES

	G	AB	H	2B	3B	HR	HR%	R	RBI	BB	SO	SB	BA	SA	PH AB	PH H	G by POS
1984 KC A	3	12	2	0	0	0	0.0	0	1	1	3	0	.167	.167	0	0	OF-3

Bitsy Mott

MOTT, ELISHA MATTHEW
B. June 12, 1918, Arcadia, Fla.   BR TR 5'8"   155 lbs.

	G	AB	H	2B	3B	HR	HR%	R	RBI	BB	SO	SB	BA	SA	PH AB	PH H	G by POS
1945 PHI N	90	289	64	8	0	0	0.0	21	22	27	25	2	.221	.249	0	0	SS-63, 2B-27, 3B-7

Curt Motton

MOTTON, CURTELL HOWARD
B. Sept. 24, 1940, Darnell, La.   BR TR 5'8"   164 lbs.

	G	AB	H	2B	3B	HR	HR%	R	RBI	BB	SO	SB	BA	SA	PH AB	PH H	G by POS
1967 BAL A	27	65	13	2	0	2	3.1	5	9	5	14	0	.200	.323	11	1	OF-18
1968	83	217	43	7	0	8	3.7	27	25	31	43	1	.198	.341	27	5	OF-54
1969	56	89	27	6	0	6	6.7	15	21	13	10	3	.303	.573	25	8	OF-20
1970	52	84	19	3	1	3	3.6	16	19	18	20	1	.226	.393	26	4	OF-20
1971	38	53	10	1	0	4	7.5	13	8	10	12	0	.189	.434	15	3	OF-16
1972 2 teams		MIL	A	(6G –	.167)		CAL	A	(42G –	.154)							
" total	48	45	7	1	0	1	2.2	7	3	6	14	0	.156	.244	18	1	OF-12
1973 BAL A	5	6	2	0	0	1	16.7	2	4	1	1	0	.333	.833	2	0	DH-1, OF-1
1974	7	8	0	0	0	0	0.0	0	0	2	2	0	.000	.000	3	0	OF-2, DH-1
8 yrs.	316	567	121	20	1	25	4.4	85	89	86	116	5	.213	.384	127	22	OF-143, DH-2

LEAGUE CHAMPIONSHIP SERIES

	G	AB	H	2B	3B	HR	HR%	R	RBI	BB	SO	SB	BA	SA	PH AB	PH H	G by POS
1969 BAL A	2	2	1	0	0	0	0.0	1	0	0	0	0	.500	.500	2	1	
1971	1	1	1	1	0	0	0.0	0	1	0	0	0	1.000	2.000	1	1	
1974	1	1	0	0	0	0	0.0	0	0	0	2	0	.000	.000	1	0	
3 yrs.	4	4	2	1	0	0	0.0	1	1	0	2	0	.500	.750	4	2	

WORLD SERIES

	G	AB	H	2B	3B	HR	HR%	R	RBI	BB	SO	SB	BA	SA	PH AB	PH H	G by POS
1969 BAL A	1	1	0	0	0	0	0.0	0	0	0	0	0	.000	.000	1	0	

Frank Motz

MOTZ, FRANK H.
B. Oct. 1, 1868, Freeburg, Pa.   D. Mar. 18, 1944, Akron, Ohio   6'2"   175 lbs.

	G	AB	H	2B	3B	HR	HR%	R	RBI	BB	SO	SB	BA	SA	PH AB	PH H	G by POS
1890 PHI N	1	2	0	0	0	0	0.0	1	3	1	1	1	.000	.000	0	0	1B-1
1893 CIN N	43	156	40	7	1	2	1.3	16	25	19	10	3	.256	.353	0	0	1B-43
1894	18	69	14	4	0	0	0.0	8	12	9	1	2	.203	.261	0	0	1B-18
3 yrs.	62	227	54	11	1	2	0.9	25	40	29	12	6	.238	.322	0	0	1B-62

Ollie Moulton

MOULTON, ALBERT THEODORE
B. Jan. 16, 1886, Medway, Mass.   D. July 10, 1968, Peabody, Mass.   BR TR 5'5½"   140 lbs.

	G	AB	H	2B	3B	HR	HR%	R	RBI	BB	SO	SB	BA	SA	PH AB	PH H	G by POS
1911 STL A	4	15	1	0	0	0	0.0	4	1	4		0	.067	.067	0	0	2B-4

Frank Mountain

MOUNTAIN, FRANK HENRY
B. May 17, 1860, Ft. Edward, N. Y.   D. Nov. 19, 1939, Schenectady, N. Y.

	G	AB	H	2B	3B	HR	HR%	R	RBI	BB	SO	SB	BA	SA	PH AB	PH H	G by POS
1880 TRO N	2	9	2	0	0	0	0.0	1		0	4		.222	.222	0	0	P-2
1881 DET N	1	25	4	1	0	0	0.0	0	4	2	8		.160	.280	0	0	P-7
1882 3 teams		WOR	N	(5G –	.063)		PHI	AA	(9G –	.333)		WOR	N	(20G –	.271)		
" total	34	122	32	5	2	2	1.6	14	6	5	23		.262	.385	0	0	P-26, OF-7, 1B-2, SS-1
1883 COL AA	70	276	60	14	5	3	1.1	36		9			.217	.337	0	0	P-59, OF-12
1884	58	210	50	7	3	4	1.9	26		9			.238	.357	0	0	P-42, OF-17
1885 PIT AA	5	20	2	0	1	0	0.0	1		1			.100	.200	0	0	P-5
1886	18	55	8	1	0	0	0.0	6			13		.145	.200	0	0	1B-16, P-2
7 yrs.	194	717	158	28	13	9	1.3	84	9	39	35		.220	.333	0	0	P-143, OF-36, 1B-18, SS-1

Ray Mowe

MOWE, RAYMOND BENJAMIN
B. July 12, 1889, Rochester, Ind.   D. Aug. 14, 1968, Sarasota, Fla.   BL TR 5'7½"   160 lbs.

	G	AB	H	2B	3B	HR	HR%	R	RBI	BB	SO	SB	BA	SA	PH AB	PH H	G by POS
1913 BKN N	5	9	1	0	0	0	0.0	0	0	0	1	0	.111	.111	1	0	SS-2

Mike Mowrey

MOWREY, HARRY HARLAN
B. Apr. 20, 1884, Brown's Mill, Pa.   D. Mar. 20, 1947, Chambersburg, Pa.   BR TR 5'8½"   160 lbs.

	G	AB	H	2B	3B	HR	HR%	R	RBI	BB	SO	SB	BA	SA	PH AB	PH H	G by POS
1905 CIN N	7	30	8	1	0	0	0.0	4	6	1		0	.267	.300	0	0	3B-7
1906	21	53	17	3	0	0	0.0	3	6	5		2	.321	.377	4	1	3B-15, SS-1, 2B-1
1907	138	448	113	16	6	1	0.2	43	44	35		10	.252	.321	0	0	3B-127, SS-11
1908	77	227	50	9	1	0	0.0	17	23	12		5	.220	.269	12	2	3B-56, OF-3, SS-3
1909 2 teams		CIN	N	(38G –	.191)		STL	N	(12G –	.241)							
" total	50	144	29	6	0	0	0.0	13	9	24		3	.201	.243	6	1	3B-24, SS-13, 2B-7
1910 STL N	143	489	138	24	6	2	0.4	69	70	67	38	21	.282	.368	0	0	3B-141
1911	137	471	126	29	7	0	0.0	59	61	59	46	15	.268	.359	1	0	3B-134, SS-1
1912	114	408	104	13	8	2	0.5	59	50	46	29	19	.255	.341	4	1	3B-108
1913	131	449	116	18	4	0	0.0	61	33	53	40	21	.258	.316	0	0	3B-130
1914 PIT N	79	284	72	7	5	1	0.4	24	25	22	20	8	.254	.324	0	0	3B-78
1915 PIT F	151	521	146	26	6	1	0.2	56	49	66		40	.280	.359	0	0	3B-151
1916 BKN N	144	495	121	22	8	0	0.0	57	60	50	60	16	.244	.313	0	0	3B-144
1917	83	271	58	9	5	0	0.0	20	25	29	25	7	.214	.284	1	0	3B-80, 2B-2
13 yrs.	1275	4290	1098	183	54	7	0.2	485	461	469	258	167	.256	.329	28	5	3B-1195, SS-29, 2B-10, OF-3

WORLD SERIES

	G	AB	H	2B	3B	HR	HR%	R	RBI	BB	SO	SB	BA	SA	PH AB	PH H	G by POS
1916 BKN N	5	17	3	0	0	0	0.0	2	1	3	2	0	.176	.176	0	0	3B-5

	G	AB	H	2B	3B	HR	HR %	R	RBI	BB	SO	SB	BA	SA	Pinch Hit AB	Pinch Hit H	G by POS

Joe Mowry

MOWRY, JOSEPH ALOYSIUS
B. Apr. 6, 1908, St. Louis, Mo.
BB TR 6' 198 lbs.

	G	AB	H	2B	3B	HR	HR %	R	RBI	BB	SO	SB	BA	SA	PH AB	PH H	G by POS
1933 BOS N	86	249	55	8	5	0	0.0	25	20	15	22	1	.221	.293	20	7	OF-64
1934	25	79	17	3	0	1	1.3	9	4	3	13	0	.215	.291	3	0	OF-20, 2B-1
1935	81	136	36	8	1	1	0.7	17	13	11	13	0	.265	.360	30	10	OF-45
3 yrs.	192	464	108	19	6	2	0.4	51	37	29	48	1	.233	.313	53	17	OF-129, 2B-1

Mike Moynahan

MOYNAHAN, MICHAEL
B. 1856, Chicago, Ill.   D. Apr. 9, 1899, Chicago, Ill.
BL

	G	AB	H	2B	3B	HR	HR %	R	RBI	BB	SO	SB	BA	SA	PH AB	PH H	G by POS
1880 BUF N	27	100	33	5	1	0	0.0	12	14	6	9		.330	.400	0	0	SS-27
1881 2 teams	CLE	N (33G – .230)			DET	N (1G – .250)											
" total	34	139	32	5	1	0	0.0	13	8	3	15		.230	.281	0	0	OF-32, 3B-2
1883 PHI AA	95	400	123	18	10	1	0.3	90		30			.308	.410	0	0	SS-95
1884 2 teams	PHI	AA (1G – .000)			CLE	N (12G – .289)											
" total	13	49	13	2	1	0	0.0	9	6	7	11		.265	.347	0	0	2B-6, OF-4, SS-3
4 yrs.	169	688	201	30	13	1	0.1	124	28	46	35		.292	.378	0	0	SS-125, OF-36, 2B-6, 3B-2

Bill Mueller

MUELLER, WILLIAM LAWRENCE (Hawk)
B. Nov. 9, 1920, Bay City, Mich.
BR TR 6'1½" 180 lbs.

	G	AB	H	2B	3B	HR	HR %	R	RBI	BB	SO	SB	BA	SA	PH AB	PH H	G by POS
1942 CHI A	26	85	14	1	0	0	0.0	5	5	12	9	2	.165	.176	1	0	OF-26
1945	13	9	0	0	0	0	0.0	3	0	2	1	1	.000	.000	1	0	OF-7
2 yrs.	39	94	14	1	0	0	0.0	8	5	14	10	3	.149	.160	2	0	OF-33

Don Mueller

MUELLER, DONALD FREDERICK (Mandrake the Magician)
Son of Walter Mueller.
B. Apr. 14, 1927, St. Louis, Mo.
BL TR 6' 185 lbs.

	G	AB	H	2B	3B	HR	HR %	R	RBI	BB	SO	SB	BA	SA	PH AB	PH H	G by POS
1948 NY N	36	81	29	4	1	1	1.2	12	9	0	3	0	.358	.469	14	6	OF-22
1949	51	56	13	4	0	0	0.0	5	1	5	6	0	.232	.304	42	7	OF-6
1950	132	525	153	15	6	7	1.3	60	84	10	26	1	.291	.383	6	2	OF-125
1951	122	469	130	10	7	16	3.4	58	69	19	13	1	.277	.431	7	1	OF-115
1952	126	456	128	14	7	12	2.6	61	49	34	24	2	.281	.421	4	0	OF-120
1953	131	480	160	12	2	6	1.3	56	60	19	13	2	.333	.404	8	4	OF-122
1954	153	619	212	35	8	4	0.6	90	71	22	17	2	.342	.444	1	1	OF-153
1955	147	605	185	21	4	8	1.3	67	83	19	12	1	.306	.393	1	1	OF-146
1956	138	453	122	12	1	5	1.1	38	41	15	7	0	.269	.333	21	6	OF-117
1957	135	450	116	7	1	6	1.3	45	37	13	16	2	.258	.318	23	6	OF-115
1958 CHI A	70	166	42	5	0	0	0.0	7	16	11	9	0	.253	.283	26	9	OF-43
1959	4	4	2	0	0	0	0.0	0	0	0	0	0	.500	.500	4	2	
12 yrs.	1245	4364	1292	139	37	65	1.5	499	520	167	146	11	.296	.390	157	44	OF-1084
WORLD SERIES																	
1954 NY N	4	18	7	0	0	0	0.0	4	1	0	1	0	.389	.389	0	0	OF-4

Emmett Mueller

MUELLER, EMMETT JEROME (Heinie)
B. July 20, 1912, St. Louis, Mo.
BB TR 5'6" 167 lbs.

	G	AB	H	2B	3B	HR	HR %	R	RBI	BB	SO	SB	BA	SA	PH AB	PH H	G by POS
1938 PHI N	136	444	111	12	4	4	0.9	53	34	64	43	2	.250	.322	7	1	2B-111, 3B-21
1939	115	341	95	19	4	9	2.6	46	43	33	34	4	.279	.437	26	8	2B-51, OF-17, 3B-17, SS-1
1940	97	263	65	13	2	3	1.1	24	28	37	23	2	.247	.346	18	4	2B-34, OF-31, 3B-13, 1B-2
1941	93	233	53	11	1	1	0.4	21	22	22	24	2	.227	.296	24	2	2B-29, OF-21, 3B-19
4 yrs.	441	1281	324	55	11	17	1.3	144	127	156	124	10	.253	.353	75	15	2B-225, 3B-70, OF-69, 1B-2, SS-1

Heinie Mueller

MUELLER, CLARENCE FRANCIS
Brother of Walter Mueller.
B. Sept. 16, 1899, Creve Coeur, Mo.   D. Jan. 23, 1974, Desoto, Mo.
BL TL 5'8" 158 lbs.

	G	AB	H	2B	3B	HR	HR %	R	RBI	BB	SO	SB	BA	SA	PH AB	PH H	G by POS
1920 STL N	4	22	7	1	0	0	0.0	0	0	2	4	1	.318	.364	0	0	OF-4
1921	55	176	62	10	6	1	0.6	25	34	11	22	2	.352	.494	1	0	OF-54
1922	61	159	43	7	2	3	1.9	20	26	14	18	2	.270	.396	17	5	OF-44
1923	78	265	91	16	9	5	1.9	39	41	18	16	4	.343	.528	4	3	OF-74
1924	92	296	78	12	6	2	0.7	39	37	19	16	8	.264	.365	10	1	OF-53, 1B-27
1925	78	243	76	16	4	1	0.4	33	26	17	11	0	.313	.424	5	2	OF-72
1926 2 teams	STL	N (52G – .267)			NY	N (85G – .249)											
" total	137	496	127	13	7	7	1.4	72	57	32	23	15	.256	.353	3	2	OF-133
1927 NY N	84	190	55	6	1	3	1.6	33	19	25	12	2	.289	.379	18	3	OF-56, 1B-1
1928 BOS N	42	151	34	3	1	0	0.0	25	19	17	9	1	.225	.258	1	1	OF-41
1929	46	93	19	2	1	0	0.0	10	11	12	12	2	.204	.247	16	4	OF-24
1935 STL A	16	27	5	1	0	0	0.0	0	1	1	4	0	.185	.222	11	3	1B-3, OF-2
11 yrs.	693	2118	597	87	37	22	1.0	296	272	168	147	37	.282	.389	86	24	OF-557, 1B-31

Ray Mueller

MUELLER, RAY COLEMAN (Iron Man)
B. Mar. 8, 1912, Pittsburg, Kans.
BR TR 5'9" 175 lbs.

	G	AB	H	2B	3B	HR	HR %	R	RBI	BB	SO	SB	BA	SA	PH AB	PH H	G by POS
1935 BOS N	42	97	22	5	0	3	3.1	10	11	3	11	0	.227	.371	2	0	C-40
1936	24	71	14	4	0	0	0.0	5	5	5	17	0	.197	.254	1	0	C-23
1937	64	187	47	9	2	4	2.1	21	26	18	36	1	.251	.353	6	0	C-57
1938	83	274	65	8	6	4	1.5	23	35	16	28	3	.237	.354	8	2	C-75
1939 PIT N	86	180	42	8	1	2	1.1	14	18	14	22	0	.233	.322	3	1	C-81
1940	4	3	1	0	0	0	0.0	1	1	2	0	0	.333	.333	0	0	C-4
1943 CIN N	141	427	111	19	4	8	1.9	50	52	56	42	1	.260	.379	1	0	C-140
1944	155	555	159	24	4	10	1.8	54	73	53	47	4	.286	.398	0	0	C-155
1946	111	378	96	18	4	8	2.1	35	48	27	37	0	.254	.386	14	0	C-100
1947	71	192	48	11	0	6	3.1	17	33	16	25	1	.250	.401	12	5	C-55
1948	14	34	7	1	0	0	0.0	1	2	2	2	0	.206	.235	4	1	C-10
1949 2 teams	CIN	N (32G – .274)			NY	N (56G – .224)											
" total	88	276	67	6	2	6	2.2	24	36	18	27	2	.243	.344	1	0	C-87

	G	AB	H	2B	3B	HR	HR %	R	RBI	BB	SO	SB	BA	SA	Pinch Hit AB	Pinch Hit H	G by POS

Ray Mueller continued

		G	AB	H	2B	3B	HR	HR %	R	RBI	BB	SO	SB	BA	SA	AB	H	G by POS
1950	2 teams	NY	N	(4G –	.091)		PIT	N	(67G –	.269)								
"	total	71	167	43	8	0	6	3.6	17	24	11	16	2	.257	.413	4	1	C-67
1951	BOS N	28	70	11	2	0	1	1.4	8	9	7	11	0	.157	.229	4	1	C-23
	14 yrs.	982	2911	733	123	23	56	1.9	281	373	250	322	14	.252	.368	60	11	C-917

Walter Mueller

MUELLER, WALTER JOHN BR TR 5'8" 160 lbs.
Father of Don Mueller. Brother of Heinie Mueller.
B. Dec. 6, 1894, Central, Mo.   D. Aug. 16, 1971, St. Louis, Mo.

		G	AB	H	2B	3B	HR	HR %	R	RBI	BB	SO	SB	BA	SA	AB	H	G by POS
1922	PIT N	32	122	33	5	1	2	1.6	21	18	5	7	1	.270	.377	0	0	OF-31
1923		40	111	34	4	4	0	0.0	11	20	4	6	2	.306	.414	14	6	OF-26
1924		30	50	13	1	1	0	0.0	6	8	4	4	1	.260	.320	14	2	OF-15
1926		19	62	15	0	1	0	0.0	8	3	0	2	0	.242	.274	4	0	OF-15
	4 yrs.	121	345	95	10	7	2	0.6	46	49	13	19	4	.275	.362	32	8	OF-87

Mike Muldoon

MULDOON, MICHAEL   5'11"
B. Hartford, Conn.   Deceased.

		G	AB	H	2B	3B	HR	HR %	R	RBI	BB	SO	SB	BA	SA	AB	H	G by POS
1882	CLE N	84	341	84	17	5	6	1.8	50	45	10	28		.246	.378	0	0	3B-61, OF-23
1883		98	378	86	22	3	0	0.0	54		10	39		.228	.302	0	0	3B-98, OF-2
1884		110	422	101	16	6	2	0.5	46	38	18	67		.239	.320	0	0	3B-109, OF-1, 2B-1
1885	BAL AA	102	410	103	20	6	2	0.5	47		20			.251	.344	0	0	3B-101, 2B-1
1886		101	381	76	13	8	0	0.0	57		34			.199	.276	0	0	2B-57, 3B-44
	5 yrs.	495	1932	450	88	28	10	0.5	254	83	92	134		.233	.323	0	0	3B-413, 2B-59, OF-26

Tony Mullane

MULLANE, ANTHONY JOHN (Count, The Apollo of the Box) BB TB 5'10½" 165 lbs.
B. Feb. 20, 1859, Cork, Ireland   BL 1882
D. Apr. 25, 1944, Chicago, Ill.

		G	AB	H	2B	3B	HR	HR %	R	RBI	BB	SO	SB	BA	SA	AB	H	G by POS
1881	DET N	5	19	5	0	0	0	0.0	0	1	0	0		.263	.263	0	0	P-5
1882	LOU AA	77	303	78	13	1	0	0.0	46		13			.257	.307	0	0	P-55, 1B-13, OF-12, 2B-2
1883	STL AA	83	307	69	11	6	0	0.0	38		13			.225	.300	0	0	P-53, OF-30, 2B-3, 1B-2
1884	TOL AA	95	352	97	19	3	3	0.9	49		33			.276	.372	0	0	P-68, OF-18, 1B-7, 3B-6, SS-1, 2B-1
1886	CIN AA	91	324	73	12	5	0	0.0	59		25			.225	.293	0	0	P-63, OF-27, 1B-4, 3B-2, SS-1, 2B-1
1887		56	199	44	6	3	3	1.5	35		16		20	.221	.327	0	0	P-48, OF-9
1888		51	175	44	4	4	1	0.6	27	16	8		4	.251	.337	0	0	P-44, 1B-4, OF-3, 2B-2
1889		63	196	58	16	4	0	0.0	53	29	27	21	24	.296	.418	0	0	P-33, 3B-18, OF-12, 1B-4
1890	CIN N	81	286	79	9	8	0	0.0	41	34	39	30	19	.276	.364	0	0	OF-28, P-25, 3B-21, SS-10, 1B-1
1891		64	209	31	1	2	0	0.0	16	10	18	33	4	.148	.172	0	0	P-51, OF-12, 3B-3
1892		39	118	20	3	1	0	0.0	14	9	9	8	4	.169	.212	0	0	P-37, 1B-2
1893	2 teams	CIN	N	(16G –	.288)		BAL	N	(38G –	.228)								
"	total	54	166	41	2	1	1	0.6	26	20	10	17	6	.247	.289	1	0	P-49, OF-2, 3B-1, 1B-1
1894	2 teams	BAL	N	(21G –	.396)		CLE	N	(4G –	.077)								
"	total	25	66	22	3	0	0	0.0	3	9	10	5	3	.333	.379	0	0	P-25
	13 yrs.	784	2720	661	99	38	8	0.3	407	128	221	114	92	.243	.316	1	0	P-556, OF-153, 3B-51, 1B-38, SS-12, 2B-9

Greg Mulleavy

MULLEAVY, GREGORY THOMAS (Moe) BR TR 5'9" 167 lbs.
B. Sept. 25, 1905, Detroit, Mich.   D. Feb. 1, 1980, Arcadia, Calif.

		G	AB	H	2B	3B	HR	HR %	R	RBI	BB	SO	SB	BA	SA	AB	H	G by POS
1930	CHI A	77	289	76	14	5	0	0.0	27	28	20	23	5	.263	.346	4	1	SS-73
1932		1	3	0	0	0	0	0.0	0	0	0	0	0	.000	.000	0	0	2B-1
1933	BOS A	1	0	0	0	0	0	–	1	0	0	0	0	–	–	0	0	
	3 yrs.	79	292	76	14	5	0	0.0	28	28	20	23	5	.260	.342	4	1	SS-73, 2B-1

Billy Mullen

MULLEN, WILLIAM JOHN BR TR 5'8" 160 lbs.
B. Jan. 23, 1896, St. Louis, Mo.   D. May 4, 1971, St. Louis, Mo.

		G	AB	H	2B	3B	HR	HR %	R	RBI	BB	SO	SB	BA	SA	AB	H	G by POS
1920	STL A	1	1	0	0	0	0	0.0	0	0	0	0	0	.000	.000	1	0	
1921		4	4	0	0	0	0	0.0	0	0	2	1	0	.000	.000	2	0	3B-2
1923	BKN N	4	11	3	0	0	0	0.0	1	0	0	0	0	.273	.273	0	0	3B-4
1926	DET A	11	13	1	0	0	0	0.0	2	0	5	1	1	.077	.077	2	0	3B-9
1928	STL A	15	18	7	1	0	0	0.0	2	2	3	4	0	.389	.444	8	3	3B-6
	5 yrs.	35	47	11	1	0	0	0.0	5	2	10	6	1	.234	.255	13	3	3B-21

Charlie Mullen

MULLEN, CHARLES GEORGE BR TR 5'10½" 155 lbs.
B. Mar. 15, 1889, Seattle, Wash.   D. June 6, 1963, Seattle, Wash.

		G	AB	H	2B	3B	HR	HR %	R	RBI	BB	SO	SB	BA	SA	AB	H	G by POS
1910	CHI A	41	123	24	2	1	0	0.0	15	13	4		1	.195	.228	1	1	1B-37, OF-2
1911		20	59	12	2	1	0	0.0	7	5	5		1	.203	.271	0	0	1B-20
1914	NY A	93	323	84	8	0	0	0.0	33	44	33	55	10	.260	.285	0	0	1B-93
1915		40	90	24	1	0	0	0.0	11	7	10	12	5	.267	.278	10	3	1B-27
1916		59	146	39	9	1	0	0.0	11	18	9	13	7	.267	.342	14	5	2B-20, 1B-17, OF-6
	5 yrs.	253	741	183	22	3	0	0.0	77	87	61	80	28	.247	.285	25	9	1B-194, 2B-20, OF-8

John Mullen

MULLEN, JOHN BL TL
B. Philadelphia, Pa.   Deceased.

		G	AB	H	2B	3B	HR	HR %	R	RBI	BB	SO	SB	BA	SA	AB	H	G by POS
1876	PHI N	1	3	0	0	0	0	0.0	0	0	0	0		.000	.000	0	0	C-1

Moon Mullen

MULLEN, FORD PARKER BL TR 5'9" 165 lbs.
B. Feb. 9, 1917, Olympia, Wash.

		G	AB	H	2B	3B	HR	HR %	R	RBI	BB	SO	SB	BA	SA	AB	H	G by POS
1944	PHI N	118	464	124	9	4	0	0.0	51	31	28	32	4	.267	.304	3	0	2B-114, 3B-1, C-1

Freddie Muller

MULLER, FREDERICK WILLIAM BR TR 5'10" 170 lbs.
B. Dec. 21, 1907, Newark, Calif.   D. Oct. 20, 1976, Davis, Calif.

		G	AB	H	2B	3B	HR	HR %	R	RBI	BB	SO	SB	BA	SA	AB	H	G by POS
1933	BOS A	15	48	9	1	1	0	0.0	6	3	5	5	1	.188	.250	1	0	2B-14
1934		2	1	0	0	0	0	0.0	1	0	1	0	0	.000	.000	0	0	3B-1, 2B-1
	2 yrs.	17	49	9	1	1	0	0.0	7	3	6	5	1	.184	.245	1	0	2B-15, 3B-1

	G	AB	H	2B	3B	HR	HR %	R	RBI	BB	SO	SB	BA	SA	Pinch Hit AB	Pinch Hit H	G by POS

Mulligan

MULLIGAN,
B. Philadelphia, Pa.   Deceased.

	G	AB	H	2B	3B	HR	HR%	R	RBI	BB	SO	SB	BA	SA	AB	H	G by POS
1884 WAS U	1	4	1	0	0	0	0.0	2		0			.250	.250	0	0	3B-1

Eddie Mulligan

MULLIGAN, EDWARD JOSEPH   BR TR 5'9"   152 lbs.
B. Aug. 27, 1894, St. Louis, Mo.   D. Mar. 15, 1982, San Rafael, Calif.

	G	AB	H	2B	3B	HR	HR%	R	RBI	BB	SO	SB	BA	SA	AB	H	G by POS
1915 CHI N	11	22	8	1	0	0	0.0	5	2	5	1	2	.364	.409	0	0	SS-10, 3B-1
1916	58	189	29	3	4	0	0.0	13	9	8	30	1	.153	.212	0	0	SS-58
1921 CHI A	152	609	153	21	12	1	0.2	82	45	32	53	13	.251	.330	0	0	3B-152, SS-1
1922	103	372	87	14	8	0	0.0	39	31	22	32	7	.234	.315	10	2	3B-86, SS-7
1928 PIT N	27	43	10	2	0	0	0.0	4	1	3	4	0	.233	.279	9	5	3B-6, 2B-4
5 yrs.	351	1235	287	41	24	1	0.1	143	88	70	120	23	.232	.307	19	7	3B-245, SS-76, 2B-4

George Mullin

MULLIN, GEORGE JOSEPH (Wabash George)   BR TR 5'11"   188 lbs.
B. July 4, 1880, Toledo, Ohio   D. Jan. 7, 1944, Wabash, Ind.

	G	AB	H	2B	3B	HR	HR%	R	RBI	BB	SO	SB	BA	SA	AB	H	G by POS
1902 DET A	40	120	39	4	3	0	0.0	20	11	8		1	.325	.408	2	0	P-35, OF-4
1903	46	126	35	9	1	1	0.8	11	12	2		1	.278	.389	4	1	P-41, OF-1
1904	53	151	45	11	2	0	0.0	14	8	10		1	.298	.397	6	2	P-45, OF-2
1905	47	135	35	4	0	0	0.0	15	12	12		4	.259	.289	2	0	P-44
1906	50	142	32	6	4	0	0.0	13	6	4		2	.225	.324	8	3	P-40
1907	70	157	34	5	3	0	0.0	16	13	12		2	.217	.287	20	5	P-46
1908	55	125	32	2	2	1	0.8	13	8	7		2	.256	.328	14	3	P-39
1909	53	126	27	7	0	0	0.0	13	17	13		2	.214	.270	10	1	P-40, OF-2
1910	50	129	33	6	2	1	0.8	15	11	8		1	.256	.357	9	0	P-38, OF-2
1911	40	98	28	7	2	0	0.0	4	5	10		1	.286	.398	8	2	P-30
1912	38	90	25	5	1	0	0.0	13	12	17		0	.278	.356	8	1	P-30
1913 2 teams		DET	A (12G –	.350)		WAS	A (12G –	.190)									
" total	24	41	11	0	0	0	0.0	5	1	6	6	1	.268	.268	3	1	P-19
1914 IND F	43	77	24	5	3	0	0.0	11	21	11		0	.312	.455	6	1	P-36
1915 NWK F	6	10	1	0	0	0	0.0	0	0			0	.100	.100	1	0	P-5
14 yrs.	615	1527	401	71	23	3	0.2	163	137	122	6	18	.263	.345	101	20	P-488, OF-11
WORLD SERIES																	
1907 DET A	2	6	0	0	0	0	0.0	0	0	0	1	0	.000	.000	0	0	P-2
1908	1	3	1	0	0	0	0.0	1	1	1	0	0	.333	.333	0	0	P-1
1909	6	16	3	1	0	0	0.0	1	0	1	3	0	.188	.250	2	0	P-4
3 yrs.	9	25	4	1	0	0	0.0	2	1	2	4	0	.160	.200	2	0	P-7

Henry Mullin

MULLIN, HENRY
B. Boston, Mass.   Deceased.

	G	AB	H	2B	3B	HR	HR%	R	RBI	BB	SO	SB	BA	SA	AB	H	G by POS
1884 2 teams		WAS	AA (34G –	.142)		BOS	U (2G –	.000)									
" total	36	128	17	3	1	0	0.0	14		8			.133	.172	0	0	OF-36, 3B-1

Jim Mullin

MULLIN, JAMES HENRY   TR 5'10"   173 lbs.
B. Oct. 16, 1883, New York, N. Y.   D. Jan. 24, 1925, Philadelphia, Pa.

	G	AB	H	2B	3B	HR	HR%	R	RBI	BB	SO	SB	BA	SA	AB	H	G by POS
1904 2 teams		PHI	A (41G –	.218)		WAS	A (27G –	.186)									
" total	68	212	43	3	2	1	0.5	19	13	9		7	.203	.250	6	0	2B-32, 1B-26, SS-2, OF-1
1905 WAS A	50	163	31	7	6	0	0.0	18	13	5		5	.190	.307	4	0	2B-39, 1B-7
2 yrs.	118	375	74	10	8	1	0.3	37	26	14		12	.197	.275	10	0	2B-71, 1B-33, SS-2, OF-1

Pat Mullin

MULLIN, PATRICK JOSEPH   BL TR 6'2"   190 lbs.
B. Nov. 1, 1917, Trotter, Pa.

	G	AB	H	2B	3B	HR	HR%	R	RBI	BB	SO	SB	BA	SA	AB	H	G by POS
1940 DET A	4	4	0	0	0	0	0.0	0	0	0	0	0	.000	.000	3	0	OF-1
1941	54	220	76	11	5	5	2.3	42	23	18	18	5	.345	.509	2	0	OF-51
1946	93	276	68	13	4	3	1.1	34	35	25	36	3	.246	.355	14	1	OF-75
1947	116	398	102	28	6	15	3.8	62	62	63	66	3	.256	.470	9	3	OF-106
1948	138	496	143	16	11	23	4.6	91	80	77	57	1	.288	.504	4	0	OF-131
1949	104	310	83	8	6	12	3.9	55	59	42	29	1	.268	.448	26	6	OF-79
1950	69	142	31	5	0	6	4.2	16	23	20	23	1	.218	.380	33	6	OF-32
1951	110	295	83	11	6	12	4.1	41	51	40	38	2	.281	.481	30	5	OF-83
1952	97	255	64	13	5	7	2.7	29	35	31	30	4	.251	.424	30	6	OF-65
1953	79	97	26	1	0	4	4.1	11	17	14	15	0	.268	.402	57	13	OF-14
10 yrs.	864	2493	676	106	43	87	3.5	381	385	330	312	20	.271	.453	208	40	OF-637

Rance Mulliniks

MULLINIKS, STEVEN RANCE   BL TR 5'11"   162 lbs.
B. Jan. 15, 1956, Tulare, Calif.

	G	AB	H	2B	3B	HR	HR%	R	RBI	BB	SO	SB	BA	SA	AB	H	G by POS
1977 CAL A	78	271	73	13	2	3	1.1	36	21	23	36	1	.269	.365	1	0	SS-77
1978	50	119	22	3	1	1	0.8	6	6	8	23	2	.185	.252	1	0	SS-47, DH-2
1979	22	68	10	0	0	1	1.5	7	8	4	14	0	.147	.191	0	0	SS-22
1980 KC A	36	54	14	3	0	0	0.0	8	6	7	10	0	.259	.315	0	0	SS-18, 2B-14
1981	24	44	10	3	0	0	0.0	6	5	2	7	0	.227	.295	0	0	2B-10, SS-7, 3B-5
1982 TOR A	112	311	76	25	0	4	1.3	32	35	37	49	3	.244	.363	22	3	3B-102, SS-16
1983	129	364	100	34	3	10	2.7	54	49	57	43	0	.275	.467	23	10	3B-116, SS-15, 2B-2
1984	125	343	111	21	5	3	0.9	41	42	33	44	2	.324	.440	18	6	3B-119, SS-3, 2B-1
8 yrs.	576	1574	416	102	11	22	1.4	190	172	171	226	8	.264	.385	65	19	3B-342, SS-205, 2B-27, DH-2

Fran Mullins

MULLINS, FRANCIS JOSEPH   BR TR 6'   180 lbs.
B. May 14, 1957, Oakland, Calif.

	G	AB	H	2B	3B	HR	HR%	R	RBI	BB	SO	SB	BA	SA	AB	H	G by POS
1980 CHI A	21	62	12	4	0	0	0.0	9	3	9	8	0	.194	.258	0	0	3B-21
1984 SF N	57	110	24	8	0	2	1.8	8	10	9	29	3	.218	.345	3	2	SS-28, 3B-28, 2B-4
2 yrs.	78	172	36	12	0	2	1.2	17	13	18	37	3	.209	.314	3	2	3B-49, SS-28, 2B-4

	G	AB	H	2B	3B	HR	HR %	R	RBI	BB	SO	SB	BA	SA	Pinch Hit AB	Pinch Hit H	G by POS

Joe Mulvey

MULVEY, JOSEPH H.
B. Oct. 27, 1858, Providence, R. I.   D. Aug. 21, 1928, Philadelphia, Pa.   BR TR

Year	Team	Lg	G	AB	H	2B	3B	HR	HR%	R	RBI	BB	SO	SB	BA	SA	PH AB	PH H	G by POS
1883	2 teams	PRO N (4G – .125)					PHI N (3G – .500)												
"	total		7	28	8	2	0	0	0.0	3		0	2		.286	.357	0	0	SS-4, 3B-3
1884	PHI	N	100	401	92	11	2	2	0.5	47		4	49		.229	.282	0	0	3B-100
1885			107	443	119	25	6	6	1.4	74		3	18		.269	.393	0	0	3B-107
1886			107	430	115	16	10	2	0.5	71	53	15	31		.267	.365	0	0	3B-107, OF-1
1887			111	474	136	21	6	2	0.4	93	78	21	14	43	.287	.369	0	0	3B-111
1888			100	398	86	12	3	0	0.0	37	39	9	33	18	.216	.261	0	0	3B-100
1889			129	544	157	21	9	6	1.1	77	77	23	25	23	.289	.393	0	0	3B-129
1890	PHI	P	120	519	149	26	15	6	1.2	96	87	27	36	20	.287	.430	0	0	3B-120
1891	PHI	AA	113	453	115	9	13	5	1.1	62	66	17	32	11	.254	.364	0	0	3B-113
1892	PHI	N	25	98	14	1	1	0	0.0	9	4	6	9	2	.143	.173	0	0	3B-25
1893	WAS	N	55	226	53	9	4	0	0.0	21	19	7	8	2	.235	.310	0	0	3B-55
1895	BKN	N	13	49	15	4	1	0	0.0	8	8	2	0	1	.306	.429	0	0	3B-13
12 yrs.			987	4063	1059	157	70	29	0.7	598	430	134	257	120	.261	.355	0	0	3B-983, SS-4, OF-1

Jerry Mumphrey

MUMPHREY, JERRY WAYNE
B. Sept. 9, 1952, Tyler, Tex.   BB TR 6'2"   185 lbs.

Year	Team	Lg	G	AB	H	2B	3B	HR	HR%	R	RBI	BB	SO	SB	BA	SA	PH AB	PH H	G by POS
1974	STL	N	5	2	0	0	0	0	0.0	2	0	0	0	0	.000	.000	0	0	OF-1
1975			11	16	6	2	0	0	0.0	2	1	4	3	0	.375	.500	4	2	OF-3
1976			112	384	99	15	5	1	0.3	51	26	37	53	22	.258	.331	10	3	OF-94
1977			145	463	133	20	10	2	0.4	73	38	47	70	22	.287	.387	16	3	OF-133
1978			125	367	96	13	4	2	0.5	41	37	30	40	14	.262	.335	16	5	OF-116
1979			124	339	100	10	3	3	0.9	53	32	26	39	8	.295	.369	16	5	OF-114
1980	SD	N	160	564	168	24	3	4	0.7	61	59	49	90	52	.298	.372	6	1	OF-153
1981	NY	A	80	319	98	11	5	6	1.9	44	32	24	27	14	.307	.429	0	0	OF-79
1982			123	477	143	24	10	9	1.9	76	68	50	66	11	.300	.449	0	0	OF-123
1983	2 teams	NY A (83G – .262)					HOU N (44G – .336)												
"	total		127	410	118	21	6	8	2.0	58	53	50	56	7	.288	.427	2	0	OF-126
1984	HOU	N	151	524	152	20	3	9	1.7	66	83	56	79	15	.290	.391	13	5	OF-137
11 yrs.			1163	3865	1113	160	49	44	1.1	527	429	373	523	165	.288	.389	83	24	OF-1079

DIVISIONAL PLAYOFF SERIES

1981	NY	A	5	21	2	0	0	0	0.0	2	0	0	1	1	.095	.095	0	0	OF-5

LEAGUE CHAMPIONSHIP SERIES

1981	NY	A	3	12	6	1	0	0	0.0	2	0	3	2	0	.500	.583	0	0	OF-3

WORLD SERIES

1981	NY	A	5	15	3	0	0	0	0.0	2	0	3	2	1	.200	.200	0	0	OF-5

John Munce

MUNCE, JOHN LEWIS
B. Nov. 18, 1857, Philadelphia, Pa.   D. Mar. 15, 1917, Philadelphia, Pa.   6'

1884	WIL	U	7	21	4	0	0	0	0.0	1		1			.190	.190	0	0	OF-7

Jake Munch

MUNCH, JACOB FERDINAND
B. Nov. 16, 1890, Morton, Pa.   D. June 8, 1966, Lansdowne, Pa.   BL TL 6'2½"   170 lbs.

1918	PHI	A	22	30	8	0	1	0	0.0	4		0	5	0	.267	.333	17	4	OF-2, 1B-2

George Mundinger

MUNDINGER, GEORGE (Mundy)
B. Nov. 20, 1854, New Orleans, La.   D. Oct. 12, 1910, Covington, La.   BR TR 6'2"   200 lbs.

1884	IND	AA	3	8	2	0	0	0	0.0	1		0			.250	.250	0	0	C-3

Bill Mundy

MUNDY, WILLIAM EDWARD
B. June 28, 1889, Salineville, Ohio   D. Sept. 23, 1958, Kalamazoo, Mich.   BL TL 5'10"   154 lbs.

1913	BOS	A	15	47	12	0	0	0	0.0	4	4	4	12	0	.255	.255	1	0	1B-14

Joe Munson

MUNSON, JOSEPH MARTIN NAPOLEON
Born Joseph Martin Napoleon Carlson.
B. Nov. 6, 1899, Renovo, Pa.   BL TR 5'9"   184 lbs.

1925	CHI	N	9	35	13	3	1	0	0.0	5	3	3	1	1	.371	.514	0	0	OF-9
1926			33	101	26	2	2	3	3.0	17	15	8	4	0	.257	.406	4	1	OF-28
2 yrs.			42	136	39	5	3	3	2.2	22	18	11	5	1	.287	.434	4	1	OF-37

Red Munson

MUNSON, CLARENCE HANFORD
B. July 31, 1883, Cincinnati, Ohio   D. Feb. 19, 1957, Mishawaka, Ind.   TR

1905	PHI	N	9	26	3	1	0	0	0.0	1		2		0	.115	.154	1	0	C-8

Thurman Munson

MUNSON, THURMAN LEE
B. June 7, 1947, Akron, Ohio   D. Aug. 2, 1979, Canton, Ohio   BR TR 5'11"   190 lbs.

1969	NY	A	26	86	22	1	2	1	1.2	6	9	10	10	0	.256	.349	1	0	C-25
1970			132	453	137	25	4	6	1.3	59	53	57	56	5	.302	.415	9	3	C-125
1971			125	451	113	15	4	10	2.2	71	42	52	65	6	.251	.368	10	3	C-117, OF-1
1972			140	511	143	16	3	7	1.4	54	46	47	58	6	.280	.364	8	2	C-132
1973			147	519	156	29	4	20	3.9	80	74	48	64	4	.301	.487	2	0	C-142
1974			144	517	135	19	2	13	2.5	64	60	44	66	2	.261	.381	2	0	C-137, DH-4
1975			157	597	190	24	3	12	2.0	83	102	45	52	3	.318	.429	1	0	C-130, DH-22, OF-2, 1B-2, 3B-1
1976			152	616	186	27	1	17	2.8	79	105	29	38	14	.302	.432	4	3	C-121, DH-21, OF-11
1977			149	595	183	28	5	18	3.0	85	100	39	55	5	.308	.462	2	0	C-136, DH-10
1978			154	617	183	27	1	6	1.0	73	71	35	70	2	.297	.373	1	1	C-125, DH-14, OF-13
1979			97	382	110	18	3	3	0.8	42	39	32	37	1	.288	.374	1	0	C-88, DH-5, 1B-3
11 yrs.			1423	5344	1558	229	32	113	2.1	696	701	438	571	48	.292	.410	41	12	C-1278, DH-76, OF-27, 1B-5, 3B-1

LEAGUE CHAMPIONSHIP SERIES

1976	NY	A	5	23	10	1	0	0	0.0	3	3	0	1	0	.435	.522	0	0	C-5
1977			5	21	6	1	0	1	4.8	3	5	0	2	0	.286	.476	0	0	C-5

	G	AB	H	2B	3B	HR	HR%	R	RBI	BB	SO	SB	BA	SA	Pinch Hit AB	Pinch Hit H	G by POS

Thurman Munson continued

	G	AB	H	2B	3B	HR	HR%	R	RBI	BB	SO	SB	BA	SA	PH AB	PH H	G by POS
1978	4	18	5	1	0	1	5.6	2	2	0	0	0	.278	.500	0	0	C-4
3 yrs.	14	62	21	4	0	2	3.2	8	10	0	3	0	.339	.500	0	0	C-14

WORLD SERIES

	G	AB	H	2B	3B	HR	HR%	R	RBI	BB	SO	SB	BA	SA	PH AB	PH H	G by POS
1976 NY A	4	17	9	0	0	0	0.0	2	2	0	1	0	.529	.529	0	0	C-4
1977	6	25	8	2	0	1	4.0	4	3	2	8	0	.320	.520	0	0	C-6
1978	6	25	8	0	0	0	0.0	5	7	3	7	1	.320	.440	0	0	C-6
3 yrs.	16	67	25	5	0	1	1.5	11	12	5	16	1	.373	.493	0	0	C-16
													3rd				

John Munyan

MUNYAN, JOHN B.
B. Nov. 14, 1860, Chester, Pa.   D. Feb. 18, 1945, Johnson City, N. Y.

	G	AB	H	2B	3B	HR	HR%	R	RBI	BB	SO	SB	BA	SA	PH AB	PH H	G by POS
1887 CLE AA	16	58	14	1	1	0	0.0	9		3		4	.241	.293	0	0	OF-12, C-3, 3B-2
1890 2 teams	COL AA (2G – .143)			STL AA (96G – .266)													
" total	98	349	92	15	7	4	1.1	62		32		11	.264	.381	0	0	C-83, OF-9, 2B-5, 3B-3, SS-1
1891 STL AA	62	182	42	4	3	0	0.0	44	20	43	39	13	.231	.286	0	0	C-45, OF-12, SS-5, 3B-3
3 yrs.	176	589	148	20	11	4	0.7	115	19	78	39	28	.251	.343	0	0	C-131, OF-33, 3B-8, SS-6, 2B-5

Bobby Murcer

MURCER, BOBBY RAY
B. May 20, 1946, Oklahoma City, Okla.   BL TR 5'11" 160 lbs.

	G	AB	H	2B	3B	HR	HR%	R	RBI	BB	SO	SB	BA	SA	PH AB	PH H	G by POS
1965 NY A	11	37	9	0	1	1	2.7	2	4	5	12	0	.243	.378	0	0	SS-11
1966	21	69	12	1	1	0	0.0	3	5	4	5	2	.174	.217	1	0	SS-18
1969	152	564	146	24	4	26	4.6	82	82	50	103	7	.259	.454	5	0	OF-118, 3B-31
1970	159	581	146	23	3	23	4.0	95	78	87	100	15	.251	.420	2	1	OF-155
1971	146	529	175	25	6	25	4.7	94	94	91	60	14	.331	.543	4	1	OF-143
1972	153	585	171	30	7	33	5.6	102	96	63	67	11	.292	.537	3	2	OF-151
1973	160	616	187	29	2	22	3.6	83	95	50	67	6	.304	.464	0	0	OF-160
1974	156	606	166	25	4	10	1.7	69	88	57	59	14	.274	.378	1	0	OF-156
1975 SF N	147	526	157	29	4	11	2.1	80	91	91	45	9	.298	.432	3	2	OF-144
1976	147	533	138	20	2	23	4.3	73	90	84	78	12	.259	.433	2	0	OF-146
1977 CHI N	154	554	147	18	3	27	4.9	90	89	80	77	16	.265	.455	5	2	OF-150, SS-1, 2B-1
1978	146	499	140	22	6	9	1.8	66	64	80	57	14	.281	.403	10	4	OF-138
1979 2 teams	CHI N (58G – .258)			NY A (74G – .273)													
" total	132	454	121	16	1	15	3.3	64	55	61	52	3	.267	.405	5	1	OF-124
1980 NY A	100	297	80	9	1	13	4.4	41	57	34	28	2	.269	.438	22	7	OF-59, DH-33
1981	50	117	31	6	0	6	5.1	14	24	12	15	0	.265	.470	22	6	DH-33
1982	65	141	32	6	0	7	5.0	12	30	12	15	2	.227	.418	30	6	DH-47
1983	9	22	4	2	0	1	4.5	2	1	1	1	0	.182	.409	4	0	DH-5
17 yrs.	1908	6730	1862	285	45	252	3.7	972	1043	862	841	127	.277	.445	119	32	OF-1644, DH-118, 3B-31, SS-30, 2B-1

DIVISIONAL PLAYOFF SERIES

	G	AB	H	2B	3B	HR	HR%	R	RBI	BB	SO	SB	BA	SA	PH AB	PH H	G by POS
1981 NY A	2	1	0	0	0	0	0.0	0	0	0	1	0	.000	.000	1	0	

LEAGUE CHAMPIONSHIP SERIES

	G	AB	H	2B	3B	HR	HR%	R	RBI	BB	SO	SB	BA	SA	PH AB	PH H	G by POS
1980 NY A	1	4	0	0	0	0	0.0	0	0	0	2	0	.000	.000	0	0	DH-1
1981	1	3	1	0	0	0	0.0	0	0	1	1	0	.333	.333	0	0	DH-1
2 yrs.	2	7	1	0	0	0	0.0	0	0	1	3	0	.143	.143	0	0	DH-2

WORLD SERIES

	G	AB	H	2B	3B	HR	HR%	R	RBI	BB	SO	SB	BA	SA	PH AB	PH H	G by POS
1981 NY A	4	3	0	0	0	0	0.0	0	0	0	0	0	.000	.000	3	0	

Simmy Murch

MURCH, SIMEON AUGUSTUS   TR 6'4" 220 lbs.
B. Nov. 21, 1880, Castine, Me.   D. June 6, 1939, Exeter, N. H.

	G	AB	H	2B	3B	HR	HR%	R	RBI	BB	SO	SB	BA	SA	PH AB	PH H	G by POS
1904 STL N	13	51	7	1	0	0	0.0	3	1	1		0	.137	.157	0	0	3B-6, 2B-6, SS-1
1905	3	9	1	0	0	0	0.0	0	0	0		0	.111	.111	1	0	2B-2, SS-1
1908 BKN N	6	11	2	1	0	0	0.0	1	0	1		0	.182	.273	4	0	1B-2
3 yrs.	22	71	10	2	0	0	0.0	4	1	2		0	.141	.169	5	0	2B-8, 3B-6, SS-2, 1B-2

Wilbur Murdock

MURDOCK, WILBUR EDWIN
B. Mar. 14, 1875, Avon, N. Y.   D. Oct. 29, 1941, Los Angeles, Calif.

	G	AB	H	2B	3B	HR	HR%	R	RBI	BB	SO	SB	BA	SA	PH AB	PH H	G by POS
1908 STL N	27	62	16	3	0	0	0.0	5	5	3		4	.258	.306	9	2	OF-16

Tim Murnane

MURNANE, TIMOTHY HAYES   BL TR 5'9½" 172 lbs.
B. June 4, 1852, Naugatuck, Conn.   D. Feb. 13, 1917, Boston, Mass.
Manager 1884.

	G	AB	H	2B	3B	HR	HR%	R	RBI	BB	SO	SB	BA	SA	PH AB	PH H	G by POS
1876 BOS N	69	308	87	4	3	2	0.6	60	34	8	12		.282	.334	0	0	1B-65, OF-3, 2B-1
1877	35	140	39	7	1	1	0.7	23	15	6	7		.279	.364	0	0	OF-30, 1B-5
1878 PRO N	49	188	45	6	1	0	0.0	35	14	8	12		.239	.282	0	0	1B-48, OF-1
1884 BOS U	76	311	73	5	2	0	0.0	55		22			.235	.264	0	0	1B-63, OF-16
4 yrs.	229	947	244	22	7	3	0.3	173	63	44	31		.258	.305	0	0	1B-181, OF-50, 2B-1

Billy Murphy

MURPHY, WILLIAM EUGENE   BR TR 6'1" 191 lbs.
B. May 7, 1944, Pineville, La.

	G	AB	H	2B	3B	HR	HR%	R	RBI	BB	SO	SB	BA	SA	PH AB	PH H	G by POS
1966 NY N	84	135	31	4	1	3	2.2	15	13	7	34	1	.230	.341	25	5	OF-57

Buzz Murphy

MURPHY, ROBERT R.   BL TL 5'8½" 155 lbs.
B. Apr. 26, 1895, Denver, Colo.   D. May 11, 1938, Denver, Colo.

	G	AB	H	2B	3B	HR	HR%	R	RBI	BB	SO	SB	BA	SA	PH AB	PH H	G by POS
1918 BOS N	9	32	12	2	3	1	3.1	6	9	3	5	0	.375	.719	0	0	OF-9
1919 WAS A	79	252	66	7	4	0	0.0	19	28	19	32	5	.262	.321	6	1	OF-73
2 yrs.	88	284	78	9	7	1	0.4	25	37	22	37	5	.275	.366	6	1	OF-82

Clarence Murphy

MURPHY, CLARENCE
Deceased.

	G	AB	H	2B	3B	HR	HR%	R	RBI	BB	SO	SB	BA	SA	PH AB	PH H	G by POS
1886 LOU AA	1	3	0	0	0	0	0.0	0		0			.000	.000	0	0	OF-1

	G	AB	H	2B	3B	HR	HR %	R	RBI	BB	SO	SB	BA	SA	Pinch Hit AB	Pinch Hit H	G by POS

Connie Murphy

MURPHY, CORNELIUS DAVID　　　　　　　　　　　　　　　BL TR 5'8"　155 lbs.
B. Nov. 1, 1870, Northfield, Mass.　　D. Dec. 14, 1945, New Bedford, Mass.

	G	AB	H	2B	3B	HR	HR %	R	RBI	BB	SO	SB	BA	SA	PH AB	PH H	G by POS
1893 CIN N	6	17	3	1	0	0	0.0	3	2	1	2	0	.176	.235	2	0	C-4
1894	1	4	0	0	0	0	0.0	0	0	1	1	0	.000	.000	0	0	C-1
2 yrs.	7	21	3	1	0	0	0.0	3	2	2	3	0	.143	.190	2	0	C-5

Dale Murphy

MURPHY, DALE BRYAN　　　　　　　　　　　　　　　　　BR TR 6'4"　210 lbs.
B. Mar. 12, 1956, Portland, Ore.

	G	AB	H	2B	3B	HR	HR %	R	RBI	BB	SO	SB	BA	SA	PH AB	PH H	G by POS
1976 ATL N	19	65	17	6	0	0	0.0	3	9	7	9	0	.262	.354	0	0	C-19
1977	18	76	24	8	1	2	2.6	5	14	0	8	0	.316	.526	0	0	C-18
1978	151	530	120	14	3	23	4.3	66	79	42	145	11	.226	.394	7	3	1B-129, C-21
1979	104	384	106	7	2	21	5.5	53	57	38	67	6	.276	.469	2	0	1B-76, C-27
1980	156	569	160	27	2	33	5.8	98	89	59	133	9	.281	.510	1	0	OF-154, 1B-1
1981	104	369	91	12	1	13	3.5	43	50	44	72	14	.247	.390	2	0	OF-103, 1B-3
1982	162	598	168	23	2	36	6.0	113	109	93	134	23	.281	.507	1	1	OF-162
1983	162	589	178	24	4	36	6.1	131	121	90	110	30	.302	.540	2	0	OF-160
1984	162	607	176	32	8	36	5.9	94	100	79	134	19	.290	.547	2	0	OF-160
9 yrs.	1038	3787	1040	153	23	200	5.3	606	628	452	812	112	.275	.486	17	4	OF-739, 1B-209, C-85

LEAGUE CHAMPIONSHIP SERIES

	G	AB	H	2B	3B	HR	HR %	R	RBI	BB	SO	SB	BA	SA	PH AB	PH H	G by POS
1982 ATL N	3	11	3	0	0	0	0.0	1	0	0	2	1	.273	.273	0	0	OF-3

Danny Murphy

MURPHY, DANIEL FRANCIS　　　　　　　　　　　　　　　BR TR 5'9"　175 lbs.
B. Aug. 11, 1876, Philadelphia, Pa.　　D. Nov. 22, 1955, Jersey City, N. J.

	G	AB	H	2B	3B	HR	HR %	R	RBI	BB	SO	SB	BA	SA	PH AB	PH H	G by POS
1900 NY N	22	74	20	1	0	0	0.0	11	6	8		4	.270	.284	0	0	2B-22
1901	28	102	19	3	0	0	0.0	6	6	4		1	.186	.216	0	0	2B-28
1902 PHI A	76	291	91	11	8	1	0.3	48	48	13		12	.313	.416	0	0	2B-76
1903	133	513	140	31	11	1	0.2	65	60	13		17	.273	.382	0	0	2B-133
1904	150	557	160	30	17	7	1.3	78	77	22		22	.287	.440	0	0	2B-150
1905	150	533	148	34	4	6	1.1	71	71	42		23	.278	.390	0	0	2B-150
1906	119	448	135	28	6	2	0.4	48	60	21		17	.301	.404	0	0	2B-119
1907	124	469	127	23	3	2	0.4	51	57	30		11	.271	.345	1	0	2B-122
1908	142	525	139	28	6	4	0.8	51	66	32		16	.265	.364	0	0	OF-84, 2B-56, 1B-2
1909	149	541	152	28	14	5	0.9	61	69	35		19	.281	.412	0	0	OF-149
1910	151	560	168	28	18	4	0.7	70	64	31		18	.300	.436	0	0	OF-151
1911	141	508	167	27	11	6	1.2	104	66	50		22	.329	.461	1	0	OF-136, 2B-4
1912	36	130	42	6	2	2	1.5	27	20	16		8	.323	.446	0	0	OF-36
1913	40	59	19	5	1	0	0.0	3	6	4	8	0	.322	.441	31	8	OF-9
1914 BKN F	52	161	49	9	0	4	2.5	16	32	17		4	.304	.435	6	0	OF-46
1915	5	6	1	0	0	0	0.0	0	0	0		0	.167	.167	3	1	OF-1, 2B-1
16 yrs.	1518	5477	1577	292	101	44	0.8	710	708	338	8	194	.288	.402	42	9	2B-861, OF-612, 1B-2

WORLD SERIES

	G	AB	H	2B	3B	HR	HR %	R	RBI	BB	SO	SB	BA	SA	PH AB	PH H	G by POS
1905 PHI A	5	16	3	1	0	0	0.0	0	0	0	2	0	.188	.250	0	0	2B-5
1910	5	20	7	3	0	1	5.0	6	8	1	0	1	.350	.650	0	0	OF-5
1911	6	23	7	3	0	0	0.0	4	2	0	3	0	.304	.435	0	0	OF-6
3 yrs.	16	59	17	7	0	1	1.7	10	10	1	5	1	.288	.458	0	0	OF-11, 2B-5
				8th													

Danny Murphy

MURPHY, DANIEL FRANCIS　　　　　　　　　　　　　　　BL TR 5'11"　185 lbs.
B. Aug. 23, 1942, Beverly, Mass.

	G	AB	H	2B	3B	HR	HR %	R	RBI	BB	SO	SB	BA	SA	PH AB	PH H	G by POS
1960 CHI N	31	75	9	2	0	1	1.3	7	6	4	13	0	.120	.187	7	0	OF-21
1961	4	13	5	0	0	2	15.4	3	3	1	5	0	.385	.846	0	0	OF-4
1962	14	35	7	3	1	0	0.0	5	3	2	9	0	.200	.343	6	0	OF-9
1969 CHI A	17	1	0	0	0	0	0.0	0	0	2	0	0	.000	.000	0	0	P-17
1970	51	6	2	0	0	1	16.7	3	1	2	2	0	.333	.833	0	0	P-51
5 yrs.	117	130	23	5	1	4	3.1	18	13	11	29	0	.177	.323	13	0	P-68, OF-34

Danny Murphy

MURPHY, DANIEL JOSEPH (Handsome Dan)
B. Sept. 10, 1864, Brooklyn, N. Y.　　D. Dec. 14, 1915, Brooklyn, N. Y.

	G	AB	H	2B	3B	HR	HR %	R	RBI	BB	SO	SB	BA	SA	PH AB	PH H	G by POS
1892 NY N	8	26	3	0	0	0	0.0	2	0	4		0	.115	.115	0	0	C-8

Dave Murphy

MURPHY, DAVID FRANCIS (Dirty Dave)　　　　　　　　　　　　　　　TR
B. May 4, 1876, N. Adams, Mass.　　D. Apr. 8, 1940, Adams, Mass.

	G	AB	H	2B	3B	HR	HR %	R	RBI	BB	SO	SB	BA	SA	PH AB	PH H	G by POS
1905 BOS N	3	11	2	0	0	0	0.0	0	1	0		0	.182	.182	0	0	SS-2, 3B-1

Dick Murphy

MURPHY, RICHARD LEE　　　　　　　　　　　　　　　　　BL TL 5'11"　170 lbs.
B. Oct. 25, 1931, Cincinnati, Ohio

	G	AB	H	2B	3B	HR	HR %	R	RBI	BB	SO	SB	BA	SA	PH AB	PH H	G by POS
1954 CIN N	6	1	0	0	0	0	0.0	1	0	1	0	0	.000	.000	1	0	

Dummy Murphy

MURPHY, HERBERT COURTLAND　　　　　　　　　　　　　BR TR 5'10"　165 lbs.
B. Dec. 18, 1886, Olney, Ill.　　D. Aug. 9, 1962, Tallahassee, Fla.

	G	AB	H	2B	3B	HR	HR %	R	RBI	BB	SO	SB	BA	SA	PH AB	PH H	G by POS
1914 PHI N	9	26	4	1	0	0	0.0	1	3	1	4	0	.154	.192	0	0	SS-9

Dwayne Murphy

MURPHY, DWAYNE KEITH　　　　　　　　　　　　　　　　BL TR 6'1"　180 lbs.
B. Mar. 18, 1955, Merced, Calif.

	G	AB	H	2B	3B	HR	HR %	R	RBI	BB	SO	SB	BA	SA	PH AB	PH H	G by POS
1978 OAK A	60	52	10	2	0	0	0.0	15	5	7	14	0	.192	.231	4	1	OF-45, DH-5
1979	121	388	99	10	4	11	2.8	57	40	84	80	15	.255	.387	2	1	OF-118
1980	159	573	157	18	2	13	2.3	86	68	102	96	26	.274	.380	0	0	OF-158
1981	107	390	98	10	3	15	3.8	58	60	73	91	10	.251	.408	0	0	OF-106, DH-1
1982	151	543	129	15	1	27	5.0	84	94	93	122	26	.238	.418	3	0	OF-147, DH-1, SS-1
1983	130	471	107	17	2	17	3.6	55	75	62	105	7	.227	.380	1	0	OF-124, DH-7
1984	153	559	143	18	2	33	5.9	93	88	74	111	4	.256	.472	0	0	OF-153
7 yrs.	881	2976	743	90	14	116	3.9	448	430	495	619	88	.250	.406	10	2	OF-851, DH-14, SS-1

DIVISIONAL PLAYOFF SERIES

	G	AB	H	2B	3B	HR	HR %	R	RBI	BB	SO	SB	BA	SA	PH AB	PH H	G by POS
1981 OAK A	3	11	6	1	0	1	9.1	4	2	1	1	0	.545	.909	0	0	OF-3

LEAGUE CHAMPIONSHIP SERIES

	G	AB	H	2B	3B	HR	HR %	R	RBI	BB	SO	SB	BA	SA	PH AB	PH H	G by POS
1981 OAK A	3	8	2	1	0	0	0.0	0	1	2	3	0	.250	.375	0	0	OF-3

	G	AB	H	2B	3B	HR	HR%	R	RBI	BB	SO	SB	BA	SA	Pinch Hit AB	H	G by POS

Ed Murphy

MURPHY, EDWARD JOSEPH
B. Aug. 23, 1918, Joliet, Ill.   BR TR 5'11"   190 lbs.

	G	AB	H	2B	3B	HR	HR%	R	RBI	BB	SO	SB	BA	SA	PH AB	H	G by POS
1942 PHI N	13	28	7	2	0	0	0.0	2	4	2	4	0	.250	.321	5	1	1B-8

Eddie Murphy

MURPHY, JOHN EDWARD (Honest Eddie)
B. Oct. 2, 1891, Hancock, N. Y.   D. Feb. 21, 1969, Dunmore, Pa.   BL TR 5'9"   155 lbs.

	G	AB	H	2B	3B	HR	HR%	R	RBI	BB	SO	SB	BA	SA	PH AB	H	G by POS
1912 PHI A	33	142	45	4	1	0	0.0	24	6	11			7	.317	.359	0	0	OF-33
1913	136	508	150	14	7	1	0.2	105	30	70	44	21	.295	.356	1	0	OF-135
1914	148	573	156	12	9	3	0.5	101	43	87	46	36	.272	.340	0	0	OF-148
1915 2 teams		PHI	A (68G – .231)		CHI	A (70G – .315)											
" total	138	533	146	14	9	0	0.0	88	43	68	27	33	.274	.334	4	0	OF-128, 3B-6
1916 CHI A	51	105	22	5	1	0	0.0	14	4	9	5	3	.210	.276	20	4	OF-24, 3B-1
1917	53	51	16	2	1	0	0.0	9	16	5	1	4	.314	.392	32	12	OF-9
1918	91	286	85	9	3	0	0.0	36	23	22	18	6	.297	.350	18	4	OF-63, 2B-8
1919	30	35	17	4	0	0	0.0	8	5	7	0	0	.486	.600	21	8	OF-6
1920	58	118	40	2	1	0	0.0	22	19	12	4	1	.339	.373	33	13	OF-19, 3B-3
1921	6	5	1	0	0	0	0.0	1	0	0	0	0	.200	.200	5	1	
1926 PIT N	16	17	2	0	0	0	0.0	3	6	3	0	0	.118	.118	11	1	OF-3
11 yrs.	760	2373	680	66	32	4	0.2	411	195	294	145	111	.287	.346	145	43	OF-568, 3B-10, 2B-8
WORLD SERIES																	
1913 PHI A	5	22	5	0	0	0	0.0	2	0	2	0	0	.227	.227	0	0	OF-5
1914	4	16	3	2	0	0	0.0	2	0	2	2	0	.188	.313	0	0	OF-4
1919 CHI A	3	2	0	0	0	0	0.0	0	0	0	1	0	.000	.000	2	0	
3 yrs.	12	40	8	2	0	0	0.0	4	0	4	3	0	.200	.250	2	0	OF-9

Frank Murphy

MURPHY, FRANK MORTON
B. 1880, Hackensack, N. J.   D. Nov. 2, 1912, New York, N. Y.

	G	AB	H	2B	3B	HR	HR%	R	RBI	BB	SO	SB	BA	SA	PH AB	H	G by POS
1901 2 teams		BOS	N (45G – .261)		NY	N (12G – .125)											
" total	57	224	52	5	3	1	0.4	17	20	7		7	.232	.295	0	0	OF-57

Howard Murphy

MURPHY, HOWARD
B. Jan. 1, 1882, Birmingham, Ala.   D. Oct. 5, 1926, Fort Worth, Tex.   BL TR 5'8½"   150 lbs.

	G	AB	H	2B	3B	HR	HR%	R	RBI	BB	SO	SB	BA	SA	PH AB	H	G by POS
1909 STL N	25	60	12	0	0	0	0.0	3	3	4		1	.200	.200	5	1	OF-19

Larry Murphy

MURPHY, LAWRENCE PATRICK
Deceased.   BL

	G	AB	H	2B	3B	HR	HR%	R	RBI	BB	SO	SB	BA	SA	PH AB	H	G by POS
1891 WAS AA	101	400	106	15	3	1	0.3	73	35	63	27	29	.265	.325	0	0	OF-101

Leo Murphy

MURPHY, LEO JOSEPH (Red)
B. Jan. 7, 1889, Terre Haute, Ind.   D. Aug. 12, 1960, Racine, Wis.   BR TR 6'1"   179 lbs.

	G	AB	H	2B	3B	HR	HR%	R	RBI	BB	SO	SB	BA	SA	PH AB	H	G by POS
1915 PIT N	34	41	4	0	0	0	0.0	4	4	4	12	0	.098	.098	9	1	C-34

Mike Murphy

MURPHY, MICHAEL JEROME
B. Aug. 19, 1888, Forestville, Pa.   D. Oct. 26, 1952, Johnson City, N. Y.   BR TR

	G	AB	H	2B	3B	HR	HR%	R	RBI	BB	SO	SB	BA	SA	PH AB	H	G by POS
1912 STL N	1	1	0	0	0	0	0.0	0	1	0	0	0	.000	.000	0	0	C-1
1916 PHI A	14	27	3	0	0	0	0.0	0	1	1	3	0	.111	.111	2	0	C-12
2 yrs.	15	28	3	0	0	0	0.0	0	2	1	3	0	.107	.107	2	0	C-13

Morg Murphy

MURPHY, MORGAN EDWARD
B. Feb. 12, 1867, E. Providence, R. I.   D. Oct. 3, 1938, Providence, R. I.   BR TR 5'8"   160 lbs.

	G	AB	H	2B	3B	HR	HR%	R	RBI	BB	SO	SB	BA	SA	PH AB	H	G by POS
1890 BOS P	68	246	56	10	2	2	0.8	38	32	24	31	16	.228	.309	0	0	C-67, SS-2, OF-1, 3B-1
1891 BOS AA	106	402	87	11	4	4	1.0	60	54	36	58	17	.216	.294	0	0	C-104, OF-4
1892 CIN N	74	234	46	8	2	2	0.9	29	24	25	57	4	.197	.274	0	0	C-74
1893	57	200	47	5	1	1	0.5	25	19	14	35	1	.235	.285	0	0	C-56, 1B-1
1894	75	255	70	9	0	1	0.4	42	37	26	34	6	.275	.322	0	0	C-74, SS-1, 3B-1
1895	25	82	22	2	0	0	0.0	15	16	11	8	6	.268	.293	0	0	C-25
1896 STL N	49	175	45	5	2	0	0.0	12	11	8	14	1	.257	.309	1	0	C-48
1897	62	207	35	2	0	0	0.0	13	12	6		1	.169	.179	0	0	C-53, 1B-8
1898 2 teams		PIT	N (5G – .125)		PHI	N (25G – .198)											
" total	30	102	19	3	0	0	0.0	6	13	7		0	.186	.216	0	0	C-30
1900 PHI N	11	36	10	0	1	0	0.0	2	3	0		0	.278	.333	0	0	C-11
1901 PHI N	9	28	6	1	0	0	0.0	5	6	0		1	.214	.250	0	0	C-8, 1B-1
11 yrs.	566	1967	443	56	12	10	0.5	247	227	157	237	53	.225	.281	1	0	C-550, 1B-10, OF-5, SS-3, 3B-2

Pat Murphy

MURPHY, PATRICK J.
B. Jan. 2, 1857, Auburn, Mass.   D. May 16, 1927, Worcester, Mass.   5'6"   165 lbs.

	G	AB	H	2B	3B	HR	HR%	R	RBI	BB	SO	SB	BA	SA	PH AB	H	G by POS
1887 NY N	17	56	12	2	0	0	0.0	4	4	2	4	1	.214	.250	0	0	C-17
1888	28	106	18	1	0	0	0.0	11	4	6	11	3	.170	.179	0	0	C-28
1889	9	28	10	1	1	1	3.6	5	4	2	0	0	.357	.571	0	0	C-9
1890	32	119	28	5	1	0	0.0	14	9	14	13	3	.235	.294	0	0	C-29, OF-3, SS-1
4 yrs.	86	309	68	9	2	1	0.3	34	21	24	28	7	.220	.272	0	0	C-83, OF-3, SS-1

Soldier Boy Murphy

MURPHY, JOHN P.
B. 1879, New Haven, Conn.   D. June 1, 1914, Baker, Ore.

	G	AB	H	2B	3B	HR	HR%	R	RBI	BB	SO	SB	BA	SA	PH AB	H	G by POS
1902 STL N	1	3	2	1	0	0	0.0	1	1	1		0	.667	1.000	0	0	3B-1
1903 DET A	5	22	4	1	0	0	0.0	1	1	0		0	.182	.227	0	0	SS-5
2 yrs.	6	25	6	2	0	0	0.0	2	2	1		0	.240	.320	0	0	SS-5, 3B-1

Tony Murphy

MURPHY, FRANK J.
B. Brooklyn, N. Y.   Deceased.

	G	AB	H	2B	3B	HR	HR%	R	RBI	BB	SO	SB	BA	SA	PH AB	H	G by POS
1884 NY AA	1	3	1	0	0	0	0.0	1		0			.333	.333	0	0	C-1

Column headers: **G | AB | H | 2B | 3B | HR | HR % | R | RBI | BB | SO | SB | BA | SA | Pinch Hit AB | Pinch Hit H | G by POS**

Willie Murphy

MURPHY, WILLIAM N. (Gentle Willie)
B. 1865, Boston, Mass. Deceased. — 5'11" 198 lbs.

Year/Team	G	AB	H	2B	3B	HR	HR%	R	RBI	BB	SO	SB	BA	SA	PH AB	PH H	G by POS
1884 3 teams	CLE N (42G – .226) WAS AA (5G – .476) BOS U (1G – .000)																
" total	48	192	48	3	3	1	0.5	21	9	3	23		.250	.313	0	0	OF-47, 3B-1, C-1

Yale Murphy

MURPHY, WILLIAM HENRY
B. Nov. 11, 1869, Southville, Mass. D. Feb. 14, 1906, Southville, Mass. — 5'3" 125 lbs.

Year/Team	G	AB	H	2B	3B	HR	HR%	R	RBI	BB	SO	SB	BA	SA	PH AB	PH H	G by POS
1894 NY N	74	280	76	6	2	0	0.0	64	28	51	23	28	.271	.307	0	0	SS-49, OF-20, 3B-3, 2B-1, 1B-1
1895	51	184	37	6	2	0	0.0	35	16	27	13	7	.201	.255	0	0	OF-33, SS-8, 3B-8, 2B-1
1897	5	8	0	0	0	0	0.0	1	1	2		0	.000	.000	0	0	SS-3, 2B-2
3 yrs.	130	472	113	12	4	0	0.0	100	45	80	36	35	.239	.282	0	0	SS-60, OF-53, 3B-11, 2B-4, 1B-1

Bill Murray

MURRAY, WILLIAM ALLENWOOD (Dasher)
B. Sept. 6, 1893, Vinalhaven, Me. D. Sept. 14, 1943, Boston, Mass. — BR TR 5'11" 165 lbs.

Year/Team	G	AB	H	2B	3B	HR	HR%	R	RBI	BB	SO	SB	BA	SA	PH AB	PH H	G by POS
1917 WAS A	8	21	3	0	1	0	0.0	2	4	2	2	1	.143	.238	0	0	2B-6, SS-1

Bobby Murray

MURRAY, ROBERT HAYES
B. July 4, 1894, St. Albans, Vt. D. Jan. 4, 1979, Nashua, N.H. — BL TR 5'8" 160 lbs.

Year/Team	G	AB	H	2B	3B	HR	HR%	R	RBI	BB	SO	SB	BA	SA	PH AB	PH H	G by POS
1923 WAS A	10	39	7	1	0	0	0.0	2	2	1	4	1	.179	.205	0	0	3B-10

Ed Murray

MURRAY, EDWARD FRANCIS
B. May 8, 1895, Mystic, Conn. D. Nov. 8, 1970, Cheyenne, Wyo. — BR TR 5'6" 145 lbs.

Year/Team	G	AB	H	2B	3B	HR	HR%	R	RBI	BB	SO	SB	BA	SA	PH AB	PH H	G by POS
1917 STL A	1	1	0	0	0	0	0.0	0	0	0	1	0	.000	.000	0	0	SS-1

Eddie Murray

MURRAY, EDDIE CLARENCE
Brother of Rich Murray.
B. Feb. 24, 1956, Los Angeles, Calif. — BB TR 6'2" 190 lbs.

Year/Team	G	AB	H	2B	3B	HR	HR%	R	RBI	BB	SO	SB	BA	SA	PH AB	PH H	G by POS
1977 BAL A	160	611	173	29	2	27	4.4	81	88	48	104	0	.283	.470	4	0	DH-111, 1B-42, OF-3
1978	161	610	174	32	3	27	4.4	85	95	70	97	6	.285	.480	0	0	1B-157, 3B-3, DH-1
1979	159	606	179	30	2	25	4.1	90	99	72	78	10	.295	.475	0	0	1B-157, DH-2
1980	158	621	186	36	2	32	5.2	100	116	54	71	7	.300	.519	3	1	1B-154, DH-1
1981	99	378	111	21	2	22	5.8	57	78	40	43	2	.294	.534	0	0	1B-99
1982	151	550	174	30	1	32	5.8	87	110	70	82	7	.316	.549	0	0	1B-149, DH-2
1983	156	582	178	30	3	33	5.7	115	111	86	90	5	.306	.538	2	0	1B-153, DH-3
1984	162	588	180	26	3	29	4.9	97	110	107	87	10	.306	.509	0	0	1B-159, DH-3
8 yrs.	1206	4546	1355	234	18	227	5.0	712	807	547	652	47	.298	.507	9	1	1B-1070, DH-122, OF-3, 3B-3

LEAGUE CHAMPIONSHIP SERIES

Year/Team	G	AB	H	2B	3B	HR	HR%	R	RBI	BB	SO	SB	BA	SA	PH AB	PH H	G by POS
1979 BAL A	4	12	5	0	0	1	8.3	3	5	5	2	0	.417	.667	0	0	1B-4
1983	4	15	4	0	0	1	6.7	5	3	3	3	1	.267	.467	0	0	1B-4
2 yrs.	8	27	9	0	0	2	7.4	8	8	8	5	1	.333	.556	0	0	1B-8

WORLD SERIES

Year/Team	G	AB	H	2B	3B	HR	HR%	R	RBI	BB	SO	SB	BA	SA	PH AB	PH H	G by POS
1979 BAL A	7	26	4	1	0	1	3.8	3	2	4	4	1	.154	.308	0	0	1B-7
1983	5	20	5	0	0	2	10.0	2	3	1	4	0	.250	.550	0	0	1B-5
2 yrs.	12	46	9	1	0	3	6.5	5	5	5	8	1	.196	.413	0	0	1B-12

Jim Murray

MURRAY, JAMES OSCAR
B. Jan. 16, 1878, Galveston, Tex. D. Apr. 25, 1945, Galveston, Tex. — BR TL

Year/Team	G	AB	H	2B	3B	HR	HR%	R	RBI	BB	SO	SB	BA	SA	PH AB	PH H	G by POS
1902 CHI N	12	47	8	0	0	0	0.0	3	1	2		0	.170	.170	0	0	OF-12
1911 STL A	31	102	19	5	0	3	2.9	8	11	5		0	.186	.324	6	1	OF-25
1914 BOS N	39	112	26	4	2	0	0.0	10	12	6	24	2	.232	.304	6	2	OF-32
3 yrs.	82	261	53	9	2	3	1.1	21	24	13	24	2	.203	.287	12	3	OF-69

Larry Murray

MURRAY, LARRY
B. Mar. 1, 1953, Chicago, Ill. — BB TR 5'11" 179 lbs.

Year/Team	G	AB	H	2B	3B	HR	HR%	R	RBI	BB	SO	SB	BA	SA	PH AB	PH H	G by POS
1974 NY A	6	1	0	0	0	0	0.0	1	0	0	0	0	.000	.000	0	0	OF-3
1975	6	1	0	0	0	0	0.0	1	0	0	1	0	.000	.000	0	0	OF-4
1976	8	10	1	0	0	0	0.0	2	2	1	2	2	.100	.100	0	0	OF-7
1977 OAK A	90	162	29	5	2	1	0.6	19	9	17	36	12	.179	.253	3	1	OF-78, DH-3, SS-1
1978	11	12	1	0	0	0	0.0	1	0	3	2	0	.083	.083	2	0	OF-6
1979	105	226	42	11	2	2	0.9	25	20	28	34	6	.186	.279	1	0	OF-90, 2B-3
6 yrs.	226	412	73	16	4	3	0.7	49	31	49	74	20	.177	.257	6	1	OF-188, DH-3, 2B-3, SS-1

Miah Murray

MURRAY, JEREMIAH J.
B. Jan. 1, 1865, Boston, Mass. D. Jan. 11, 1922, Boston, Mass. — BR 170 lbs.

Year/Team	G	AB	H	2B	3B	HR	HR%	R	RBI	BB	SO	SB	BA	SA	PH AB	PH H	G by POS
1884 PRO N	8	27	5	0	0	0	0.0	1		1	8		.185	.185	0	0	C-7, OF-1, 1B-1
1885 LOU AA	12	43	8	0	0	0	0.0	4		2			.186	.186	0	0	C-12, 1B-2
1888 WAS N	12	42	4	1	0	0	0.0	1	3	1	7	0	.095	.119	0	0	C-10, 1B-2
1891 WAS AA	2	8	0	0	0	0	0.0	0		0	1		.000	.000	0	0	C-2
4 yrs.	34	120	17	1	0	0	0.0	6	2	4	16	0	.142	.150	0	0	C-31, 1B-5, OF-1

Ray Murray

MURRAY, RAYMOND LEE (Deacon)
B. Oct. 12, 1917, Spring Hope, N.C. — BR TR 6'3" 204 lbs.

Year/Team	G	AB	H	2B	3B	HR	HR%	R	RBI	BB	SO	SB	BA	SA	PH AB	PH H	G by POS
1948 CLE A	4	4	0	0	0	0	0.0	0	0	0	3	0	.000	.000	4	0	
1950	55	139	38	8	2	1	0.7	16	13	12	13	1	.273	.381	8	2	C-45
1951 2 teams	CLE A (1G – 1.000) PHI A (40G – .213)																
" total	41	123	27	6	0	0	0.0	10	14	14	8	0	.220	.268	1	0	C-40
1952 PHI A	44	136	28	5	0	1	0.7	14	10	9	13	0	.206	.265	2	1	C-42
1953	84	268	76	14	3	6	2.2	25	41	18	25	0	.284	.425	6	2	C-78
1954 BAL A	22	61	15	4	1	0	0.0	4	2	2	5	0	.246	.344	2	0	C-21
6 yrs.	250	731	184	37	6	8	1.1	69	80	55	67	1	.252	.352	21	5	C-226

	G	AB	H	2B	3B	HR	HR %	R	RBI	BB	SO	SB	BA	SA	Pinch Hit AB	Pinch Hit H	G by POS

Red Murray

MURRAY, JOHN JOSEPH
B. Mar. 4, 1884, Arnot, Pa.   D. Dec. 4, 1958, Sayre, Pa.
BR TR 5'10½" 190 lbs.

	G	AB	H	2B	3B	HR	HR %	R	RBI	BB	SO	SB	BA	SA	AB	H	G by POS
1906 STL N	46	144	37	9	7	1	0.7	18	16	9		5	.257	.438	5	0	OF-34, C-7
1907	132	485	127	10	10	7	1.4	46	46	24		23	.262	.367	1	1	OF-131
1908	154	593	167	19	15	7	1.2	64	62	37		48	.282	.400	0	0	OF-154
1909 NY N	149	570	150	15	12	7	1.2	74	91	44		48	.263	.368	0	0	OF-148
1910	149	553	153	27	8	4	0.7	78	87	52	51	57	.277	.376	1	1	OF-148
1911	140	488	142	27	15	3	0.6	70	78	43	37	48	.291	.426	6	1	OF-131
1912	143	549	152	26	20	3	0.5	83	92	27	45	38	.277	.413	0	0	OF-143
1913	147	520	139	21	3	2	0.4	70	59	34	28	35	.267	.331	0	0	OF-147
1914	86	139	31	6	3	0	0.0	19	23	9	7	11	.223	.309	26	4	OF-49
1915 2 teams	NY N (45G – .220)					CHI N (51G – .299)											
" total	96	271	71	7	3	3	1.1	32	22	15	23	8	.262	.343	17	8	OF-73, 2B-1
1917 NY N	22	22	1	1	0	0	0.0	1	3	4	3	0	.045	.091	8	0	OF-11, C-1
11 yrs.	1264	4334	1170	168	96	37	0.9	555	579	298	194	321	.270	.379	64	15	OF-1169, C-8, 2B-1
WORLD SERIES																	
1911 NY N	6	21	0	0	0	0	0.0	0	0	2	5	0	.000	.000	0	0	OF-6
1912	8	31	10	4	1	0	0.0	5	5	2	2	0	.323	.516	0	0	OF-8
1913	5	16	4	0	0	0	0.0	2	1	2	2	2	.250	.250	0	0	OF-5
3 yrs.	19	68	14	4	1	0	0.0	7	6	6	9	2	.206	.294	0	0	OF-19

Rich Murray

MURRAY, RICHARD DALE
Brother of Eddie Murray.
B. July 6, 1957, Los Angeles, Calif.
BR TR 6'4"   195 lbs.

	G	AB	H	2B	3B	HR	HR %	R	RBI	BB	SO	SB	BA	SA	AB	H	G by POS
1980 SF N	53	194	42	8	2	4	2.1	19	24	11	48	2	.216	.340	0	0	1B-53
1983	4	10	2	0	0	0	0.0	0	1	0	3	0	.200	.200	1	0	1B-3
2 yrs.	57	204	44	8	2	4	2.0	19	25	11	51	2	.216	.333	1	0	1B-56

Tom Murray

MURRAY, THOMAS W.
B. 1866, Savannah, Ga.   Deceased.

	G	AB	H	2B	3B	HR	HR %	R	RBI	BB	SO	SB	BA	SA	AB	H	G by POS
1894 PHI N	1	2	0	0	0	0	0.0	0	0	0	2	0	.000	.000	0	0	SS-1

Tony Murray

MURRAY, ANTHONY JOSEPH
B. Apr. 30, 1904, Chicago, Ill.   D. Mar. 19, 1974, Chicago, Ill.
BR TR 5'10½" 154 lbs.

	G	AB	H	2B	3B	HR	HR %	R	RBI	BB	SO	SB	BA	SA	AB	H	G by POS
1923 CHI N	2	4	1	0	0	0	0.0	0	0	0	0	0	.250	.250	0	0	OF-2

Ivan Murrell

MURRELL, IVAN AUGUSTO
B. Apr. 24, 1945, Almirante, Panama
BR TR 6'2"   195 lbs.

	G	AB	H	2B	3B	HR	HR %	R	RBI	BB	SO	SB	BA	SA	AB	H	G by POS
1963 HOU N	2	5	1	0	0	0	0.0	1	0	0	2	0	.200	.200	0	0	OF-2
1964	10	14	2	1	0	0	0.0	1	1	0	6	0	.143	.214	3	0	OF-5
1967	10	29	9	0	0	0	0.0	2	1	1	9	1	.310	.310	4	0	OF-6
1968	32	59	6	1	0	0	0.0	3	3	1	17	0	.102	.153	12	2	OF-15
1969 SD N	111	247	63	10	6	3	1.2	19	25	11	65	3	.255	.381	36	5	OF-72, 1B-2
1970	125	347	85	9	3	12	3.5	43	35	17	93	9	.245	.392	24	4	OF-101, 1B-1
1971	103	255	60	6	3	7	2.7	23	24	7	60	5	.235	.365	33	3	OF-72
1972	5	7	1	0	0	0	0.0	0	1	0	3	0	.143	.143	3	0	OF-1
1973	93	210	48	13	1	9	4.3	23	21	2	52	2	.229	.429	35	2	OF-37, 1B-24
1974 ATL N	73	133	33	1	1	2	1.5	11	12	5	35	0	.248	.316	30	5	OF-32, 1B-13
10 yrs.	564	1306	308	41	15	33	2.5	126	123	44	342	20	.236	.366	180	21	OF-343, 1B-40

Danny Murtaugh

MURTAUGH, DANIEL EDWARD
B. Oct. 8, 1917, Chester, Pa.   D. Dec. 2, 1976, Chester, Pa.
Manager 1957-64, 1967, 1970-71, 1973-76.
BR TR 5'9"   165 lbs.

	G	AB	H	2B	3B	HR	HR %	R	RBI	BB	SO	SB	BA	SA	AB	H	G by POS
1941 PHI N	85	347	76	8	1	0	0.0	34	11	26	31	18	.219	.248	0	0	2B-85, SS-1
1942	144	506	122	16	4	0	0.0	48	27	49	39	13	.241	.289	2	0	SS-60, 3B-53, 2B-32
1943	113	451	123	17	4	1	0.2	65	35	57	27	15	.273	.335	0	0	2B-113
1946	6	19	4	1	0	1	5.3	1	3	2	2	0	.211	.421	0	0	2B-6
1947 BOS N	3	8	1	0	0	0	0.0	0	0	1	2	0	.125	.125	0	0	2B-2
1948 PIT N	146	514	149	21	5	1	0.2	56	71	60	40	10	.290	.356	0	0	2B-146
1949	75	236	48	7	2	2	0.8	16	24	29	17	2	.203	.275	1	1	2B-74
1950	118	367	108	20	5	2	0.5	34	37	47	42	3	.294	.392	4	2	2B-108
1951	77	151	30	7	0	1	0.7	9	11	16	19	0	.199	.265	13	3	2B-65, 3B-3
9 yrs.	767	2599	661	97	21	8	0.3	263	219	287	215	49	.254	.317	25	8	2B-631, SS-61, 3B-56

Tony Muser

MUSER, ANTHONY JOSEPH
B. Aug. 1, 1947, Van Nuys, Calif.
BL TL 6'2"   180 lbs.

	G	AB	H	2B	3B	HR	HR %	R	RBI	BB	SO	SB	BA	SA	AB	H	G by POS
1969 BOS A	2	9	1	0	0	0	0.0	0	1	1	1	0	.111	.111	0	0	1B-2
1971 CHI A	11	16	5	0	1	0	0.0	2	0	1	1	0	.313	.438	7	2	1B-4
1972	44	61	17	2	2	1	1.6	6	9	2	6	1	.279	.426	12	4	1B-29, OF-1
1973	109	309	88	14	3	4	1.3	38	30	33	36	6	.285	.388	9	4	1B-89, OF-2
1974	103	206	60	5	4	1	0.5	16	18	6	22	1	.291	.340	13	3	1B-80, DH-13
1975 2 teams	CHI A (43G – .243)					BAL A (80G – .317)											
" total	123	193	53	6	0	0	0.0	22	17	15	17	2	.275	.306	18	6	1B-103
1976 BAL A	136	326	74	7	1	1	0.3	25	30	21	34	1	.227	.264	16	4	1B-109, OF-12, DH-10
1977	120	118	27	6	0	0	0.0	14	7	13	16	1	.229	.280	31	6	1B-77, OF-11, DH-1
1978 MIL A	15	30	4	1	0	0	0.0	0	5	3	5	0	.133	.233	3	0	1B-12
9 yrs.	663	1268	329	41	9	7	0.6	123	117	95	138	14	.259	.323	109	29	1B-505, OF-26, DH-24

Stan Musial

MUSIAL, STANLEY FRANK (Stan the Man)
B. Nov. 21, 1920, Donora, Pa.
Hall of Fame 1969.
BL TL 6'   175 lbs.

	G	AB	H	2B	3B	HR	HR %	R	RBI	BB	SO	SB	BA	SA	AB	H	G by POS
1941 STL N	12	47	20	4	0	1	2.1	8	7	2	1	1	.426	.574	1	0	OF-11
1942	140	467	147	32	10	10	2.1	87	72	62	25	6	.315	.490	2	0	OF-135
1943	157	617	220	48	20	13	2.1	108	81	72	18	9	.357	.562	2	1	OF-155
1944	146	568	197	51	14	12	2.1	112	94	90	28	7	.347	.549	0	0	OF-146
1946	156	624	228	50	20	16	2.6	124	103	73	31	7	.365	.587	0	0	1B-114, OF-42
1947	149	587	183	30	13	19	3.2	113	95	80	24	4	.312	.504	0	0	1B-149

	G	AB	H	2B	3B	HR	HR %	R	RBI	BB	SO	SB	BA	SA	Pinch Hit AB	Pinch Hit H	G by POS

Stan Musial continued

	G	AB	H	2B	3B	HR	HR %	R	RBI	BB	SO	SB	BA	SA	AB	H	G by POS
1948	155	611	**230**	46	18	39	6.4	**135**	**131**	79	34	7	**.376**	**.702**	0	0	OF-155, 1B-2
1949	157	612	**207**	41	13	36	5.9	128	123	107	38	3	.338	.624	0	0	OF-156, 1B-1
1950	146	555	192	41	7	28	5.0	105	109	87	36	5	.346	.596	1	0	OF-77, 1B-69
1951	152	578	205	30	12	32	5.5	124	108	98	40	4	.355	.614	1	1	OF-91, 1B-60
1952	154	578	**194**	42	6	21	3.6	**105**	91	96	29	7	.336	.538	0	0	OF-135, 1B-25, P-1
1953	157	593	200	**53**	9	30	5.1	127	113	**105**	32	3	.337	.609	0	0	OF-157
1954	153	591	195	41	9	35	5.9	**120**	126	103	39	1	.330	.607	0	0	OF-152, 1B-10
1955	154	562	179	30	4	33	5.9	97	108	80	39	5	.319	.566	0	0	1B-110, OF-51
1956	156	594	184	33	6	27	4.5	87	**109**	75	39	2	.310	.522	0	0	1B-103, OF-53
1957	134	502	176	38	3	29	5.8	82	102	66	34	1	**.351**	.612	4	2	1B-130
1958	135	472	159	35	2	17	3.6	64	62	72	26	0	.337	.528	12	5	1B-124
1959	115	341	87	13	2	14	4.1	37	44	60	25	0	.255	.428	22	5	1B-90, OF-3
1960	116	331	91	17	1	17	5.1	49	63	41	34	1	.275	.486	28	4	OF-59, 1B-29
1961	123	372	107	22	4	15	4.0	46	70	52	35	0	.288	.489	19	5	OF-103
1962	135	433	143	18	1	19	4.4	57	82	64	46	3	.330	.508	13	8	OF-119
1963	124	337	86	10	2	12	3.6	34	58	35	43	2	.255	.404	21	4	OF-96
22 yrs.	3026	10972	3630	725	177	475	4.3	1949	1951	1599	696	78	.331	.559	126	35	OF-1896, 1B-1016, P-1
	5th	5th	4th	3rd				6th	5th	8th				9th			

WORLD SERIES																	
1942 STL N	5	18	4	1	0	0	0.0	2	2	4	0	0	.222	.278	0	0	OF-5
1943	5	18	5	0	0	0	0.0	2	0	2	2	0	.278	.278	0	0	OF-5
1944	6	23	7	2	0	1	4.3	2	2	2	0	0	.304	.522	0	0	OF-6
1946	7	27	6	4	1	0	0.0	3	4	4	2	1	.222	.444	0	0	1B-7
4 yrs.	23	86	22	7	1	1	1.2	9	8	12	4	1	.256	.395	0	0	OF-16, 1B-7
				8th													

Danny Musser

MUSSER, WILLIAM DANIEL   BL TR 5'9½" 160 lbs.
B. Sept. 5, 1905, Zion, Pa.

	G	AB	H	2B	3B	HR	HR %	R	RBI	BB	SO	SB	BA	SA	AB	H	G by POS
1932 WAS A	1	2	1	0	0	0	0.0	0	0	0	0	0	.500	.500	0	0	3B-1

George Myatt

MYATT, GEORGE EDWARD (Mercury, Stud, Foghorn)   BL TR 5'11" 167 lbs.
B. June 14, 1914, Denver, Colo.
Manager 1968-69.

	G	AB	H	2B	3B	HR	HR %	R	RBI	BB	SO	SB	BA	SA	AB	H	G by POS
1938 NY N	43	170	52	2	1	3	1.8	27	10	14	13	10	.306	.382	0	0	SS-24, 3B-19
1939	22	53	10	2	0	0	0.0	7	3	6	6	2	.189	.226	5	0	3B-14
1943 WAS A	42	53	13	3	0	0	0.0	11	3	13	7	3	.245	.302	12	1	2B-11, SS-2, 3B-2
1944	140	538	153	19	6	0	0.0	86	40	54	44	26	.284	.342	0	0	2B-121, SS-15, OF-3
1945	133	490	145	17	7	1	0.2	81	39	63	43	30	.296	.365	1	0	2B-94, OF-32, 3B-6, SS-1
1946	15	34	8	1	0	0	0.0	7	4	7	2	3	.235	.265	4	1	3B-7, 2B-2
1947	12	7	0	0	0	0	0.0	1	0	4	4	0	.000	.000	6	0	2B-1
7 yrs.	407	1345	381	44	14	4	0.3	220	99	156	120	72	.283	.346	28	2	2B-229, 3B-48, SS-42, OF-35

Glenn Myatt

MYATT, GLENN CALVIN   BL TR 5'11" 165 lbs.
B. July 9, 1897, Argenta, Ark.   D. Aug. 9, 1969, Houston, Tex.

	G	AB	H	2B	3B	HR	HR %	R	RBI	BB	SO	SB	BA	SA	AB	H	G by POS
1920 PHI A	70	196	49	8	3	0	0.0	14	18	12	22	1	.250	.321	8	1	OF-37, C-21
1921	44	69	14	2	0	0	0.0	6	5	6	7	0	.203	.232	7	1	C-27
1923 CLE A	92	220	63	7	6	3	1.4	36	40	16	18	0	.286	.414	18	6	C-69
1924	105	342	117	22	7	8	2.3	55	73	33	12	6	.342	.518	9	2	C-95
1925	106	358	97	15	9	11	3.1	51	54	29	24	2	.271	.455	5	1	C-98, OF-1
1926	56	117	29	5	2	0	0.0	14	13	13	13	1	.248	.325	18	3	C-35
1927	55	94	23	6	0	2	2.1	15	8	12	7	1	.245	.372	25	5	C-26
1928	58	125	36	7	2	1	0.8	9	15	13	13	0	.288	.400	26	8	C-30
1929	59	129	30	4	1	1	0.8	14	17	7	5	0	.233	.302	14	1	C-41
1930	86	265	78	23	2	2	0.8	30	37	18	17	2	.294	.419	13	3	C-71
1931	65	195	48	14	2	1	0.5	21	29	21	13	2	.246	.354	9	3	C-58
1932	82	252	62	12	1	8	3.2	45	46	28	21	2	.246	.397	16	3	C-65
1933	40	77	18	4	0	0	0.0	10	7	15	8	0	.234	.286	12	3	C-27
1934	36	107	34	6	1	0	0.0	18	12	13	5	1	.318	.393	0	0	C-34
1935 2 teams		CLE	A	(10G –	.083)			NY	N	(13G –	.222)						
" total	23	54	7	1	1	1	1.9	3	8	4	6	0	.130	.241	9	1	C-14
1936 DET A	27	78	17	1	0	0	0.0	5	9	4	4	0	.218	.231	1	1	C-27
16 yrs.	1004	2678	722	137	37	38	1.4	346	387	249	195	18	.270	.391	190	42	C-738, OF-38

Buddy Myer

MYER, CHARLES SOLOMON   BL TR 5'10½" 163 lbs.
B. Mar. 16, 1904, Ellisville, Miss.   D. Oct. 31, 1974, Baton Rouge, La.

	G	AB	H	2B	3B	HR	HR %	R	RBI	BB	SO	SB	BA	SA	AB	H	G by POS
1925 WAS A	4	8	2	0	0	0	0.0	1	0	0	1	0	.250	.250	0	0	SS-4
1926	132	434	132	18	6	1	0.2	66	62	45	19	10	.304	.380	3	2	SS-117, 3B-8
1927 2 teams		WAS	A	(15G –	.216)		BOS	A	(133G –	.288)							
" total	148	520	146	23	11	2	0.4	66	54	56	18	12	.281	.379	8	1	SS-116, 3B-14, OF-10, 2B-1
1928 BOS A	147	536	168	26	6	1	0.2	78	44	53	28	30	.313	.390	1	1	3B-144
1929 WAS A	141	563	169	29	10	3	0.5	80	82	63	33	18	.300	.403	1	1	2B-88, 3B-53
1930	138	541	164	18	8	2	0.4	97	61	58	31	14	.303	.377	0	0	2B-137
1931	139	591	173	33	11	4	0.7	114	56	58	42	11	.293	.406	0	0	2B-137
1932	143	577	161	38	16	5	0.9	120	52	69	33	12	.279	.426	3	1	2B-139
1933	131	530	160	29	15	4	0.8	95	61	60	29	6	.302	.436	1	0	2B-129
1934	139	524	160	33	8	3	0.6	103	57	102	32	6	.305	.416	4	1	2B-135
1935	151	616	215	36	11	5	0.8	115	100	96	40	7	**.349**	.468	0	0	2B-151
1936	51	156	42	5	2	0	0.0	31	15	42	11	7	.269	.327	7	1	2B-43
1937	125	430	126	16	10	1	0.2	54	65	78	41	2	.293	.384	5	1	2B-119, OF-1
1938	127	437	147	22	8	6	1.4	79	71	93	32	9	.336	.465	5	1	2B-121
1939	83	258	78	10	3	1	0.4	33	32	40	18	4	.302	.376	17	3	2B-65
1940	71	210	61	14	4	0	0.0	28	29	34	10	6	.290	.395	14	1	2B-54

	G	AB	H	2B	3B	HR	HR %	R	RBI	BB	SO	SB	BA	SA	Pinch Hit AB	Pinch Hit H	G by POS

Buddy Myer continued

	G	AB	H	2B	3B	HR	HR %	R	RBI	BB	SO	SB	BA	SA	AB	H	G by POS
1941	53	107	27	3	1	0	0.0	14	9	18	10	2	.252	.299	25	6	2B-24
17 yrs.	1923	7038	2131	353	130	38	0.5	1174	850	965	428	156	.303	.406	94	20	2B-1340, SS-237, 3B-219, OF-13

WORLD SERIES

	G	AB	H	2B	3B	HR	HR %	R	RBI	BB	SO	SB	BA	SA	AB	H	G by POS
1925 WAS A	3	8	2	0	0	0	0.0	0	0	1	2	0	.250	.250	0	0	3B-3
1933	5	20	6	1	0	0	0.0	2	2	2	3	0	.300	.350	0	0	2B-5
2 yrs.	8	28	8	1	0	0	0.0	2	2	3	5	0	.286	.321	0	0	2B-5, 3B-3

Al Myers

MYERS, ALBERT (Cod)   BR TR 5'10" 165 lbs.
B. Oct. 22, 1863, Danville, Ill.   D. Oct. 13, 1915, Washington, D. C.

	G	AB	H	2B	3B	HR	HR %	R	RBI	BB	SO	SB	BA	SA	AB	H	G by POS
1884 MIL U	12	46	15	6	0	0	0.0	6		0			.326	.457	0	0	2B-12
1885 PHI N	93	357	73	13	2	1	0.3	25		11	41		.204	.261	0	0	2B-93
1886 KC N	118	473	131	22	9	4	0.8	69	51	22	42		.277	.387	0	0	2B-118
1887 WAS N	105	362	84	9	5	2	0.6	45	36	40	26	18	.232	.301	0	0	2B-78, SS-27
1888	132	502	104	12	7	2	0.4	46	46	37	46	20	.207	.271	0	0	2B-132
1889 2 teams	WAS N	(46G –	.261)		PHI N	(75G –	.269)										
" total	121	481	128	17	2	0	0.0	76	48	58	16	18	.266	.310	0	0	2B-121
1890 PHI N	117	487	135	29	7	2	0.4	95	81	57	46	44	.277	.378	0	0	2B-117
1891	135	514	118	27	2	2	0.4	67	69	69	46	8	.230	.302	0	0	2B-135
8 yrs.	833	3222	788	135	34	13	0.4	429	330	294	263	108	.245	.320	0	0	2B-806, SS-27

Billy Myers

MYERS, WILLIAM HARRISON   BR TR 5'8" 168 lbs.
Brother of Lynn Myers.
B. Aug. 14, 1910, Enola, Pa.

	G	AB	H	2B	3B	HR	HR %	R	RBI	BB	SO	SB	BA	SA	AB	H	G by POS
1935 CIN N	117	445	119	15	10	5	1.1	60	36	29	81	10	.267	.380	0	0	SS-112
1936	98	323	87	9	6	6	1.9	45	27	28	56	6	.269	.390	0	0	SS-98
1937	124	335	84	13	3	7	2.1	35	43	44	57	0	.251	.391	0	0	SS-121, 2B-6
1938	134	442	112	18	6	12	2.7	57	47	41	80	2	.253	.403	0	0	SS-123, 2B-11
1939	151	509	143	18	6	9	1.8	79	56	71	90	4	.281	.393	0	0	SS-151
1940	90	282	57	14	2	5	1.8	33	30	30	56	0	.202	.319	0	0	SS-88
1941 CHI N	24	63	14	1	0	1	1.6	10	4	7	25	1	.222	.286	0	0	SS-19, 2B-1
7 yrs.	738	2399	616	88	33	45	1.9	319	243	250	445	23	.257	.377	0	0	SS-712, 2B-18

WORLD SERIES

	G	AB	H	2B	3B	HR	HR %	R	RBI	BB	SO	SB	BA	SA	AB	H	G by POS
1939 CIN N	4	12	4	0	1	0	0.0	2	0	2	3	0	.333	.500	0	0	SS-4
1940	7	23	3	0	0	0	0.0	0	2	2	5	0	.130	.130	0	0	SS-7
2 yrs.	11	35	7	0	1	0	0.0	2	2	4	8	0	.200	.257	0	0	SS-11

George Myers

MYERS, GEORGE D.   BR TR
B. Nov. 13, 1860, Buffalo, N. Y.   D. Dec. 14, 1926, Buffalo, N. Y.

	G	AB	H	2B	3B	HR	HR %	R	RBI	BB	SO	SB	BA	SA	AB	H	G by POS
1884 BUF N	78	325	59	9	2	2	0.6	34		13	33		.182	.240	0	0	C-49, OF-34
1885	89	326	67	7	2	0	0.0	40	19	23	40		.206	.239	0	0	C-69, OF-23
1886 STL N	79	295	56	7	3	0	0.0	26	27	18	42		.190	.234	0	0	C-72, OF-6, 3B-1
1887 IND N	69	235	51	8	1	1	0.4	25	20	22	7	26	.217	.272	0	0	C-50, OF-15, 1B-6, 3B-1
1888	66	248	59	9	0	2	0.8	36	16	16	14	28	.238	.298	0	0	C-47, 3B-14, OF-10, 1B-1
1889	43	149	29	3	0	0	0.0	22	12	17	13	12	.195	.215	0	0	OF-23, C-18, 1B-1
6 yrs.	424	1578	321	43	8	5	0.3	183	93	109	149	66	.203	.250	0	0	C-305, OF-111, 3B-16, 1B-8

Hap Myers

MYERS, RALPH EDWARD   BR TR 6'3" 175 lbs.
B. Apr. 8, 1888, San Francisco, Calif.   D. June 30, 1967, San Francisco, Calif.

	G	AB	H	2B	3B	HR	HR %	R	RBI	BB	SO	SB	BA	SA	AB	H	G by POS
1910 BOS A	3	6	2	0	0	0	0.0	0	0	0		0	.333	.333	1	0	OF-2
1911 2 teams	STL A	(11G –	.297)		BOS A	(13G –	.368)										
" total	24	75	25	3	0	0	0.0	7	1	5		4	.333	.373	0	0	1B-23
1913 BOS N	140	524	143	20	1	2	0.4	74	50	38	48	57	.273	.326	5	3	1B-135
1914 BKN F	92	305	67	10	5	1	0.3	61	29	44		43	.220	.295	0	0	1B-88
1915	118	341	98	9	1	1	0.3	61	36	32		28	.287	.328	7	1	1B-107
5 yrs.	377	1251	335	42	7	4	0.3	203	116	119	48	132	.268	.322	13	4	1B-353, OF-2

Henry Myers

MYERS, HENRY C.   BR TR 5'9" 159 lbs.
B. May, 1858, Philadelphia, Pa.   D. Apr. 18, 1895, Philadelphia, Pa.
Manager 1882.

	G	AB	H	2B	3B	HR	HR %	R	RBI	BB	SO	SB	BA	SA	AB	H	G by POS
1881 PRO N	1	4	0	0	0	0	0.0	0		0		2	.000	.000	0	0	SS-1
1882 BAL AA	69	294	53	3	0	0	0.0	43		12			.180	.190	0	0	SS-68, P-6
1884 WIL U	6	24	3	0	0	0	0.0	3		0			.125	.125	0	0	SS-5, 2B-1
3 yrs.	76	322	56	3	0	0	0.0	46		12		2	.174	.183	0	0	SS-74, P-6, 2B-1

Hy Myers

MYERS, HENRY HARRISON   BR TR 5'9½" 175 lbs.
B. Apr. 27, 1889, East Liverpool, Ohio   D. May 1, 1965, Minerva, Ohio

	G	AB	H	2B	3B	HR	HR %	R	RBI	BB	SO	SB	BA	SA	AB	H	G by POS
1909 BKN N	6	22	5	1	0	0	0.0	1	6	2		1	.227	.273	0	0	OF-6
1911	13	43	7	1	0	0	0.0	2	0	2	3	1	.163	.186	0	0	OF-13
1914	70	227	65	3	9	0	0.0	35	17	7	24	2	.286	.379	5	2	OF-60
1915	153	605	150	21	7	2	0.3	69	46	17	51	19	.248	.316	0	0	OF-153
1916	113	412	108	12	14	3	0.7	54	36	21	35	17	.262	.381	6	1	OF-106
1917	120	471	126	15	10	1	0.2	37	41	18	25	5	.268	.348	3	0	OF-66, 1B-22, 2B-19, 3B-15
1918	107	407	104	9	8	4	1.0	36	36	20	26	17	.256	.346	0	0	OF-107
1919	133	512	157	23	14	5	1.0	62	73	23	34	13	.307	.436	0	0	OF-131
1920	154	582	177	36	22	4	0.7	83	80	35	54	9	.304	.462	0	0	OF-152, 3B-2
1921	144	549	158	14	4	4	0.7	51	68	22	51	8	.288	.350	0	0	OF-124, 2B-21, 3B-1
1922	153	618	196	20	9	6	1.0	82	89	13	26	9	.317	.408	0	0	OF-153, 2B-1
1923 STL N	96	330	99	18	2	2	0.6	29	48	12	19	5	.300	.385	6	1	OF-87
1924	43	124	26	5	1	1	0.8	12	15	3	10	1	.210	.290	5	0	OF-22, 3B-12, 2B-3
1925 3 teams	STL N	(1G –	.000)		CIN N	(3G –	.167)		STL N	(1G –	1.000)						
" total	5	8	2	1	0	0	0.0	2	0	0	0	0	.250	.375	2	1	OF-3
14 yrs.	1310	4910	1380	179	100	32	0.7	555	559	195	358	107	.281	.378	27	5	OF-1183, 2B-44, 3B-30, 1B-22

	G	AB	H	2B	3B	HR	HR %	R	RBI	BB	SO	SB	BA	SA	Pinch Hit AB	Pinch Hit H	G by POS

Hy Myers continued

WORLD SERIES

	G	AB	H	2B	3B	HR	HR %	R	RBI	BB	SO	SB	BA	SA	AB	H	G by POS
1916 BKN N	5	22	4	0	0	1	4.5	2	3	0	3	0	.182	.318	0	0	OF-5
1920	7	26	6	0	0	0	0.0	0	1	0	1	0	.231	.231	0	0	OF-7
2 yrs.	12	48	10	0	0	1	2.1	2	4	0	4	0	.208	.271	0	0	OF-12

Lynn Myers

MYERS, LINWOOD LINCOLN
Brother of Billy Myers.
B. Feb. 23, 1914, Enola, Pa.

BR TR 5'6½" 145 lbs.

	G	AB	H	2B	3B	HR	HR %	R	RBI	BB	SO	SB	BA	SA	AB	H	G by POS
1938 STL N	70	227	55	10	2	1	0.4	18	19	9	25	9	.242	.317	0	0	SS-69
1939	74	117	28	6	1	0	0.0	24	10	12	23	1	.239	.308	5	3	SS-36, 2B-13, 3B-5
2 yrs.	144	344	83	16	3	1	0.3	42	29	21	48	10	.241	.314	5	3	SS-105, 2B-13, 3B-5

Richie Myers

MYERS, RICHARD
B. Apr. 7, 1930, Sacramento, Calif.

BR TR 5'6" 150 lbs.

	G	AB	H	2B	3B	HR	HR %	R	RBI	BB	SO	SB	BA	SA	AB	H	G by POS
1956 CHI N	4	1	0	0	0	0	0.0	1	0	0	0	0	.000	.000	1	0	

Bill Nagel

NAGEL, WILLIAM TAYLOR
B. Aug. 19, 1915, Memphis, Tenn.

BR TR 6' 190 lbs.

	G	AB	H	2B	3B	HR	HR %	R	RBI	BB	SO	SB	BA	SA	AB	H	G by POS
1939 PHI A	105	341	86	19	4	12	3.5	39	39	25	86	2	.252	.437	4	0	2B-56, 3B-43, P-1
1941 PHI A	17	56	8	1	1	0	0.0	2	6	3	14	0	.143	.196	2	0	2B-12, OF-2, 3B-1
1945 CHI A	67	220	46	10	3	3	1.4	21	27	15	41	3	.209	.323	9	0	1B-57, 3B-1
3 yrs.	189	617	140	30	8	15	2.4	62	72	43	141	5	.227	.374	15	0	2B-68, 1B-57, 3B-45, OF-2, P-1

Lou Nagelsen

NAGELSEN, LOUIS MARCELLUS
Born Louis Marcellus Nageleisen.
B. June 29, 1887, Piqua, Ohio   D. Oct. 22, 1965, Fort Wayne, Ind.

BR TR 6'2" 180 lbs.

	G	AB	H	2B	3B	HR	HR %	R	RBI	BB	SO	SB	BA	SA	AB	H	G by POS
1912 CLE A	2	3	0	0	0	0	0.0	0	0	0	0	0	.000	.000	0	0	C-2

Rusty Nagelson

NAGELSON, RUSSELL CHARLES
B. Sept. 19, 1944, Cincinnati, Ohio

BL TR 6' 205 lbs.

	G	AB	H	2B	3B	HR	HR %	R	RBI	BB	SO	SB	BA	SA	AB	H	G by POS
1968 CLE A	5	3	1	0	0	0	0.0	0	0	2	2	0	.333	.333	4	1	
1969	12	17	6	0	0	0	0.0	1	0	3	3	0	.353	.353	7	1	OF-3, 1B-1
1970 2 teams		DET A	(28G –	.188)		CLE A	(17G –	.125)									OF-8, 1B-1
" total	45	56	9	1	0	1	1.8	8	4	8	15	0	.161	.232	31	6	OF-11, 1B-2
3 yrs.	62	76	16	1	0	1	1.3	9	4	13	20	0	.211	.263	42	8	

Tom Nagle

NAGLE, THOMAS EDWARD
B. Oct. 30, 1865, Milwaukee, Wis.   D. Mar. 9, 1946, Milwaukee, Wis.

BR TR 5'10" 150 lbs.

	G	AB	H	2B	3B	HR	HR %	R	RBI	BB	SO	SB	BA	SA	AB	H	G by POS
1890 CHI N	38	144	39	5	1	1	0.7	21	11	7	24	4	.271	.340	0	0	C-33, OF-6
1891	8	25	3	0	0	0	0.0	3	1	1	3	0	.120	.120	0	0	C-7, OF-1
2 yrs.	46	169	42	5	1	1	0.6	24	12	8	27	4	.249	.308	0	0	C-40, OF-7

Bill Nahorodny

NAHORODNY, WILLIAM GERARD
B. Aug. 31, 1953, Hamtramck, Mich.

BR TR 6'2" 200 lbs.

	G	AB	H	2B	3B	HR	HR %	R	RBI	BB	SO	SB	BA	SA	AB	H	G by POS
1976 PHI N	3	5	1	1	0	0	0.0	0	0	0	0	0	.200	.400	2	0	C-2
1977 CHI A	7	23	6	1	0	1	4.3	3	4	2	3	0	.261	.435	0	0	C-7
1978	107	347	82	11	2	8	2.3	29	35	23	52	1	.236	.349	1	0	C-104, 1B-4, DH-1
1979	65	179	46	10	0	6	3.4	20	29	18	23	0	.257	.413	11	6	C-60, DH-3
1980 ATL N	59	157	38	12	0	5	3.2	14	18	8	21	0	.242	.414	6	1	C-54, 1B-1
1981	14	13	3	1	0	0	0.0	0	2	1	3	0	.231	.308	9	3	C-3, 1B-1
1982 CLE A	39	94	21	5	1	4	4.3	4	18	2	9	0	.223	.426	7	2	C-35
1983 DET A	2	1	0	0	0	0	0.0	0	0	1	0	0	.000	.000	1	0	
1984 SEA A	12	25	6	0	0	1	4.0	2	3	1	7	0	.240	.360	1	0	C-10, 1B-1
9 yrs.	308	844	203	41	3	25	3.0	74	109	56	118	1	.241	.385	38	12	C-275, 1B-7, DH-4

Frank Naleway

NALEWAY, FRANK (Chick)
B. July 4, 1901, Chicago, Ill.   D. Jan. 28, 1949, Chicago, Ill.

BR TR 5'9½" 165 lbs.

	G	AB	H	2B	3B	HR	HR %	R	RBI	BB	SO	SB	BA	SA	AB	H	G by POS
1924 CHI A	1	2	0	0	0	0	0.0	0	0	0	0	0	.000	.000	0	0	SS-1

Doc Nance

NANCE, WILLIAM G. (Kid)
Born William G. Cooper.
B. Aug. 2, 1877, Fort Worth, Tex.   D. May 28, 1958, Ft. Worth, Tex.

BR TR

	G	AB	H	2B	3B	HR	HR %	R	RBI	BB	SO	SB	BA	SA	AB	H	G by POS
1897 LOU N	35	120	29	5	3	3	2.5	25	17	20		3	.242	.408	0	0	OF-35
1898	22	76	24	5	0	1	1.3	13	16	12		2	.316	.421	0	0	OF-22
1901 DET A	132	461	129	24	5	3	0.7	72	66	51		9	.280	.373	0	0	OF-132
1904 STL A	1	3	1	0	0	0	0.0	0		0			.333	.333	0	0	OF-1
4 yrs.	190	660	183	34	8	7	1.1	110	99	83		14	.277	.385	0	0	OF-190

Al Naples

NAPLES, ALOYSIUS FRANCIS
B. Aug. 29, 1927, Staten Island, N. Y.

BR TR 5'9" 168 lbs.

	G	AB	H	2B	3B	HR	HR %	R	RBI	BB	SO	SB	BA	SA	AB	H	G by POS
1949 STL A	2	7	1	1	0	0	0.0	0	0	0	1	0	.143	.286	0	0	SS-2

Danny Napoleon

NAPOLEON, DANIEL
B. Jan. 11, 1942, Claysburg, Pa.

BR TR 5'11" 190 lbs.

	G	AB	H	2B	3B	HR	HR %	R	RBI	BB	SO	SB	BA	SA	AB	H	G by POS
1965 NY N	68	97	14	1	1	0	0.0	5	7	8	23	0	.144	.175	45	9	OF-15, 3B-7
1966	12	33	7	2	0	0	0.0	2	0	1	10	0	.212	.273	1	0	OF-10
2 yrs.	80	130	21	3	1	0	0.0	7	7	9	33	0	.162	.200	46	9	OF-25, 3B-7

Hal Naragon

NARAGON, HAROLD RICHARD
B. Oct. 1, 1928, Zanesville, Ohio

BL TR 6' 160 lbs.

	G	AB	H	2B	3B	HR	HR %	R	RBI	BB	SO	SB	BA	SA	AB	H	G by POS
1951 CLE A	3	8	2	0	0	0	0.0	1	0	1	0	0	.250	.250	1	1	C-2
1954	46	101	24	2	2	0	0.0	10	12	9	12	0	.238	.297	1	0	C-45
1955	57	127	41	9	2	1	0.8	12	14	15	8	1	.323	.449	13	1	C-52

	G	AB	H	2B	3B	HR	HR %	R	RBI	BB	SO	SB	BA	SA	Pinch Hit AB	Pinch Hit H	G by POS

Hal Naragon continued

	G	AB	H	2B	3B	HR	HR %	R	RBI	BB	SO	SB	BA	SA	AB	H	G by POS
1956	53	122	35	3	1	3	2.5	11	18	13	9	0	.287	.402	14	5	C-48
1957	57	121	31	1	1	0	0.0	12	8	12	9	0	.256	.281	24	4	C-39
1958	9	9	3	0	1	0	0.0	2	0	0	0	0	.333	.556	9	3	
1959 2 teams	CLE A (14G – .278)					WAS A (71G – .241)											
" total	85	231	57	7	3	0	0.0	18	16	11	11	0	.247	.303	24	3	C-64
1960 WAS A	33	92	19	2	0	0	0.0	7	5	8	4	0	.207	.228	4	0	C-29
1961 MIN A	57	139	42	2	1	2	1.4	10	11	4	8	0	.302	.374	20	3	C-36
1962	24	35	8	1	0	0	0.0	1	3	3	1	0	.229	.257	15	1	C-9
10 yrs.	424	985	262	27	11	6	0.6	83	87	76	62	1	.266	.334	125	23	C-324
WORLD SERIES																	
1954 CLE A	1	0	0	0	0	0	–	0	0	0	0	0	–	–	0	0	C-1

Bill Narleski

NARLESKI, WILLIAM EDWARD (Cap)
Father of Ray Narleski.
B. June 9, 1899, Perth Amboy, N. J.   D. July 22, 1964, Laurel Springs, N. J.

BR TR 5'9"   160 lbs.

	G	AB	H	2B	3B	HR	HR %	R	RBI	BB	SO	SB	BA	SA	AB	H	G by POS
1929 BOS A	96	260	72	16	1	0	0.0	31	25	21	22	4	.277	.346	3	1	SS-51, 2B-28, 3B-10
1930	39	98	23	9	0	0	0.0	11	7	7	5	0	.235	.327	0	0	SS-19, 3B-14, 2B-5
2 yrs.	135	358	95	25	1	0	0.0	42	32	28	27	4	.265	.341	3	1	SS-70, 2B-33, 3B-24

Jerry Narron

NARRON, JERRY AUSTIN
B. Jan. 15, 1956, Goldsboro, N. C.

BL TR 6'3"   205 lbs.

	G	AB	H	2B	3B	HR	HR %	R	RBI	BB	SO	SB	BA	SA	AB	H	G by POS
1979 NY A	61	123	21	3	1	4	3.3	17	18	9	26	0	.171	.309	4	0	C-56
1980 SEA A	48	107	21	3	0	4	3.7	7	18	13	18	0	.196	.336	14	3	C-39, DH-1
1981	76	203	45	5	0	3	1.5	13	17	16	35	0	.222	.291	15	3	C-65
1983 CAL A	10	22	3	0	0	1	4.5	1	4	1	3	0	.136	.273	6	0	C-6, DH-1
1984	69	150	37	5	0	3	2.0	9	17	8	12	0	.247	.340	29	7	C-46, 1B-7
5 yrs.	264	605	127	16	1	15	2.5	47	74	47	94	0	.210	.314	68	13	C-212, 1B-7, DH-2

Sam Narron

NARRON, SAMUEL
B. Aug. 25, 1913, Middlesex, N. C.

BR TR 5'10"   180 lbs.

	G	AB	H	2B	3B	HR	HR %	R	RBI	BB	SO	SB	BA	SA	AB	H	G by POS
1935 STL N	4	7	3	0	0	0	0.0	0	0	0	0	0	.429	.429	3	2	C-1
1942	10	10	4	0	0	0	0.0	0	1	0	2	0	.400	.400	8	3	C-2
1943	10	11	1	0	0	0	0.0	0	0	1	2	0	.091	.091	7	1	C-3
3 yrs.	24	28	8	0	0	0	0.0	0	1	1	4	0	.286	.286	18	6	C-6
WORLD SERIES																	
1943 STL N	1	1	0	0	0	0	0.0	0	0	0	0	0	.000	.000	1	0	

Billy Nash

NASH, WILLIAM MITCHELL
B. June 24, 1865, Richmond, Va.   D. Nov. 16, 1929, East Orange, N. J.
Manager 1896.

BR TR 5'8½"   167 lbs.

	G	AB	H	2B	3B	HR	HR %	R	RBI	BB	SO	SB	BA	SA	AB	H	G by POS
1884 RIC AA	45	166	33	8	8	1	0.6	31		12				.199	.361	0	0	3B-45
1885 BOS N	26	94	24	4	0	0	0.0	9	11	2	9		.255	.298	0	0	3B-19, 2B-8
1886	109	417	117	11	8	1	0.2	61	45	24	28		.281	.353	0	0	3B-90, SS-17
1887	121	475	140	24	12	7	1.5	100	94	60	40	43	.295	.440	0	0	3B-117, OF-5
1888	135	526	149	18	15	4	0.8	71	75	50	46	20	.283	.397	0	0	3B-105, 2B-31
1889	128	481	132	20	2	3	0.6	84	76	79	44	26	.274	.343	0	0	3B-128, P-1
1890 BOS P	129	488	130	28	6	5	1.0	103	90	88	43	26	.266	.379	0	0	3B-128, P-1
1891 BOS N	140	537	148	24	9	5	0.9	92	95	74	50	28	.276	.382	0	0	3B-140
1892	135	526	137	25	5	4	0.8	94	95	59	41	31	.260	.350	0	0	3B-135, OF-1
1893	128	485	141	27	6	10	2.1	115	123	85	29	30	.291	.433	0	0	3B-128
1894	132	512	148	23	6	8	1.6	132	87	91	23	20	.289	.404	0	0	3B-132
1895	132	508	147	23	6	10	2.0	97	108	74	19	18	.289	.417	0	0	3B-132
1896 PHI N	65	227	56	9	1	3	1.3	29	30	34	21	3	.247	.335	0	0	3B-65
1897	104	337	87	20	2	0	0.0	45	39	60		4	.258	.329	1	1	3B-79, SS-19, 2B-4
1898	20	70	17	2	1	0	0.0	9	9	11			.243	.300	0	0	3B-20
15 yrs.	1549	5849	1606	266	87	61	1.0	1072	976	803	383	249	.275	.381	1	1	3B-1464, 2B-43, SS-36, OF-6, P-2

Cotton Nash

NASH, CHARLES FRANCIS
B. July 24, 1942, Jersey City, N. J.

BR TR 6'6"   220 lbs.

	G	AB	H	2B	3B	HR	HR %	R	RBI	BB	SO	SB	BA	SA	AB	H	G by POS
1967 CHI A	3	3	0	0	0	0	0.0	1	0	1	0	0	.000	.000	0	0	1B-3
1969 MIN A	6	9	2	0	0	0	0.0	0	0	1	2	0	.222	.222	0	0	1B-6, OF-1
1970	4	4	1	0	0	0	0.0	1	2	1	1	0	.250	.250	2	0	1B-2
3 yrs.	13	16	3	0	0	0	0.0	2	2	3	3	0	.188	.188	2	0	1B-11, OF-1

Ken Nash

NASH, KENNETH LELAND
Also known as J. A. Costello.
B. July 14, 1888, S. Weymouth, Mass.   D. Feb. 16, 1977, Epsom, N. H.

BB TR 5'8"   140 lbs.

	G	AB	H	2B	3B	HR	HR %	R	RBI	BB	SO	SB	BA	SA	AB	H	G by POS
1912 CLE A	11	23	4	0	0	0	0.0	2	0	3		0	.174	.174	3	0	SS-8
1914 STL N	24	51	14	3	1	0	0.0	4	6	6	10	1	.275	.373	5	1	3B-10, 2B-6, SS-3
2 yrs.	35	74	18	3	1	0	0.0	6	6	9	10	1	.243	.311	8	1	SS-11, 3B-10, 2B-6

Pete Naton

NATON, PETER ALPHONSUS
B. Sept. 9, 1931, Flushing, N. Y.

BR TR 6'1"   200 lbs.

	G	AB	H	2B	3B	HR	HR %	R	RBI	BB	SO	SB	BA	SA	AB	H	G by POS
1953 PIT N	6	12	2	0	0	0	0.0	2	1	2	1	0	.167	.167	1	0	C-4

Sandy Nava

NAVA, VINCENT P.
B. Apr. 12, 1850, San Francisco, Calif.   D. June 15, 1906, Baltimore, Md.

5'6"   155 lbs.

	G	AB	H	2B	3B	HR	HR %	R	RBI	BB	SO	SB	BA	SA	AB	H	G by POS
1882 PRO N	28	97	20	2	0	0	0.0	15		1	13		.206	.227	0	0	C-27, OF-1
1883	29	100	24	4	2	0	0.0	18		3	17		.240	.320	0	0	C-27, OF-2
1884	34	116	11	0	0	0	0.0	10		11	35		.095	.095	0	0	C-27, SS-6, 2B-1
1885 BAL AA	8	27	5	1	0	0	0.0	2		1			.185	.222	0	0	C-8
1886	2	5	1	0	0	0	0.0	0					.200	.200	0	0	SS-1, C-1
5 yrs.	101	345	61	7	2	0	0.0	45		16	65		.177	.209	0	0	C-90, SS-7, OF-3, 2B-1

	G	AB	H	2B	3B	HR	HR %	R	RBI	BB	SO	SB	BA	SA	Pinch Hit AB	Pinch Hit H	G by POS

Earl Naylor

NAYLOR, EARL EUGENE
B. May 19, 1919, Kansas City, Mo.
BR TR 6' 190 lbs.

	G	AB	H	2B	3B	HR	HR %	R	RBI	BB	SO	SB	BA	SA	PH AB	PH H	G by POS
1942 PHI N	76	168	33	4	1	0	0.0	9	14	11	18	1	.196	.232	17	5	OF-34, P-20, 1B-1
1943	33	120	21	2	0	3	2.5	12	14	12	16	1	.175	.267	0	0	OF-33
1946 BKN N	3	2	0	0	0	0	0.0	1	0	0	1	0	.000	.000	2	0	
3 yrs.	112	290	54	6	1	3	1.0	22	28	23	35	2	.186	.245	19	5	OF-67, P-20, 1B-1

Jack Neagle

NEAGLE, JOHN HENRY
B. Jan. 2, 1858, Syracuse, N. Y.   D. Sept. 20, 1904, Syracuse, N. Y.
BR TR 5'6" 155 lbs.

	G	AB	H	2B	3B	HR	HR %	R	RBI	BB	SO	SB	BA	SA	PH AB	PH H	G by POS
1879 CIN N	3	12	2	0	0	0	0.0	2		0	0		.167	.167	0	0	OF-2, P-2
1883 3 teams			PHI	N (18G –	.164)		BAL	AA (9G –	.286)		PIT	AA (27G –	.188)				
" total	54	209	41	5	1	0	0.0	23		8	9		.196	.230	0	0	OF-32, P-30
1884 PIT AA	43	148	22	6	0	0	0.0	13		6			.149	.189	0	0	P-38, OF-6
3 yrs.	100	369	65	11	1	0	0.0	37	2	14	9		.176	.211	0	0	P-70, OF-40

Charlie Neal

NEAL, CHARLES LENARD
B. Jan. 30, 1931, Longview, Tex.
BR TR 5'10" 165 lbs.

	G	AB	H	2B	3B	HR	HR %	R	RBI	BB	SO	SB	BA	SA	PH AB	PH H	G by POS
1956 BKN N	62	136	39	5	1	2	1.5	22	14	14	19	2	.287	.382	8	3	2B-51, SS-1
1957	128	448	121	13	7	12	2.7	62	62	53	83	11	.270	.411	1	1	SS-100, 3B-23, 2B-3
1958 LA N	140	473	120	9	6	22	4.7	87	65	61	91	7	.254	.438	2	1	2B-132, 3B-9
1959	151	616	177	30	11	19	3.1	103	83	43	86	17	.287	.464	0	0	2B-151, SS-1
1960	139	477	122	23	2	8	1.7	60	40	48	75	5	.256	.363	2	0	2B-136, SS-3
1961	108	341	80	6	1	10	2.9	40	48	30	49	3	.235	.346	4	1	2B-104
1962 NY N	136	508	132	14	9	11	2.2	59	58	56	90	2	.260	.388	0	0	2B-85, SS-39, 3B-12
1963 2 teams			NY	N (72G –	.225)		CIN	N (34G –	.156)								
" total	106	317	67	13	1	3	0.9	28	21	32	64	1	.211	.287	15	3	3B-85, SS-9, 2B-1
8 yrs.	970	3316	858	113	38	87	2.6	461	391	337	557	48	.259	.394	32	9	2B-663, SS-153, 3B-129

WORLD SERIES																	
1956 BKN N	1	4	0	0	0	0	0.0	0	0	0	1	0	.000	.000	0	0	2B-1
1959 LA N	6	27	10	2	0	2	7.4	4	6	0	1	1	.370	.667	0	0	2B-6
2 yrs.	7	31	10	2	0	2	6.5	4	6	0	2	1	.323	.581	0	0	2B-7

Offa Neal

NEAL, THEOPHILUS FOUNTAIN
B. June 5, 1876, Logan, Ill.   D. Apr. 11, 1950, Mt. Vernon, Ill.
BL TR 6' 185 lbs.

	G	AB	H	2B	3B	HR	HR %	R	RBI	BB	SO	SB	BA	SA	PH AB	PH H	G by POS
1905 NY N	4	13	0	0	0	0	0.0	0		0		0	.000	.000	0	0	3B-3, 2B-1

Greasy Neale

NEALE, ALFRED EARLE
B. Nov. 5, 1891, Parkersburg, W. Va.   D. Nov. 2, 1973, Lake Worth, Fla.
BL TR 6' 170 lbs.

	G	AB	H	2B	3B	HR	HR %	R	RBI	BB	SO	SB	BA	SA	PH AB	PH H	G by POS
1916 CIN N	138	530	139	13	5	0	0.0	53	20	19	79	17	.262	.306	3	0	OF-133
1917	121	385	113	14	9	3	0.8	40	33	24	36	25	.294	.400	2	0	OF-119
1918	107	371	100	11	11	1	0.3	59	32	24	38	23	.270	.367	4	0	OF-102
1919	139	500	121	10	12	1	0.2	57	54	47	51	28	.242	.316	1	0	OF-138
1920	150	530	135	10	7	3	0.6	55	46	45	48	29	.255	.317	0	0	OF-150
1921 2 teams			PHI	N (22G –	.211)		CIN	N (63G –	.241)								
" total	85	298	70	11	5	0	0.0	46	13	36	25	12	.235	.305	3	0	OF-82
1922 CIN N	25	43	10	2	1	0	0.0	11	2	6	3	5	.233	.326	3	1	OF-10
1924	3	4	0	0	0	0	0.0	0	0	0	1	0	.000	.000	0	0	OF-2
8 yrs.	768	2661	688	71	50	8	0.3	321	200	201	281	139	.259	.332	16	1	OF-736

WORLD SERIES																	
1919 CIN N	8	28	10	1	1	0	0.0	3	4	2	5	1	.357	.464	0	0	OF-8

Jim Nealon

NEALON, JAMES JOSEPH
B. Dec. 13, 1884, Sacramento, Calif.   D. Apr. 2, 1910, San Francisco, Calif.

	G	AB	H	2B	3B	HR	HR %	R	RBI	BB	SO	SB	BA	SA	PH AB	PH H	G by POS
1906 PIT N	154	556	142	21	12	3	0.5	82	**83**	53		15	.255	.353	0	0	1B-154
1907	105	381	98	10	8	0	0.0	29	47	23		11	.257	.325	1	0	1B-104
2 yrs.	259	937	240	31	20	3	0.3	111	130	76		26	.256	.342	1	0	1B-258

Tom Needham

NEEDHAM, THOMAS J. (Deerfoot)
B. Apr. 7, 1879, Ireland   D. Dec. 13, 1926, Steubenville, Ohio
BR TR 5'10" 180 lbs.

	G	AB	H	2B	3B	HR	HR %	R	RBI	BB	SO	SB	BA	SA	PH AB	PH H	G by POS
1904 BOS N	84	269	70	12	3	4	1.5	18	19	11		3	.260	.372	6	0	C-77, OF-1
1905	83	271	59	6	1	2	0.7	21	17	24		3	.218	.269	1	0	C-77, OF-3, 1B-2
1906	83	285	54	8	2	1	0.4	11	12	13		3	.189	.242	2	0	C-76, 2B-5, 1B-2, OF-1, 3B-1
1907	86	260	51	6	2	1	0.4	19	19	18		4	.196	.246	5	0	C-78, 1B-1
1908 NY N	54	91	19	3	0	0	0.0	8	11	12		0	.209	.242	5	0	C-47
1909 CHI N	13	28	4	0	0	0	0.0	3	0	0		0	.143	.143	6	2	C-7
1910	31	76	14	3	1	0	0.0	9	10	10	10	1	.184	.250	3	0	C-27, 1B-1
1911	27	62	12	2	0	0	0.0	4	5	9	14	2	.194	.226	3	0	C-23
1912	33	90	16	5	0	0	0.0	12	10	7	13	3	.178	.233	1	0	C-32
1913	20	42	10	4	1	0	0.0	5	11	4	8	0	.238	.381	4	0	C-14, 1B-1
1914	9	17	2	1	0	0	0.0	3	3	1	4	1	.118	.176	2	0	C-7
11 yrs.	523	1491	311	50	8	8	0.5	113	117	109	49	20	.209	.272	38	2	C-465, 1B-7, OF-5, 2B-5, 3B-1

WORLD SERIES																	
1910 CHI N	1	1	0	0	0	0	0.0	0	0	0	0	0	.000	.000	1	0	

Cal Neeman

NEEMAN, CALVIN AMANDUS
B. Feb. 18, 1929, Valmeyer, Ill.
BR TR 6'1" 192 lbs.

	G	AB	H	2B	3B	HR	HR %	R	RBI	BB	SO	SB	BA	SA	PH AB	PH H	G by POS
1957 CHI N	122	415	107	17	1	10	2.4	37	39	22	87	0	.258	.376	4	0	C-118
1958	76	201	52	7	0	12	6.0	30	29	21	41	0	.259	.473	8	0	C-71
1959	44	105	17	2	0	3	2.9	7	9	11	23	0	.162	.267	5	0	C-38
1960 2 teams			CHI	N (9G –	.154)		PHI	N (59G –	.181)								
" total	68	173	31	7	2	4	2.3	13	13	16	47	0	.179	.312	4	0	C-61
1961 PHI N	19	31	7	1	0	0	0.0	0	2	4	8	1	.226	.258	0	0	C-19
1962 PIT N	24	50	9	1	1	1	2.0	5	5	3	10	0	.180	.300	0	0	C-24

	G	AB	H	2B	3B	HR	HR %	R	RBI	BB	SO	SB	BA	SA	Pinch Hit AB	Pinch Hit H	G by POS

Cal Neeman continued

	G	AB	H	2B	3B	HR	HR %	R	RBI	BB	SO	SB	BA	SA	PH AB	PH H	G by POS
1963 2 teams		CLE A (9G – .000)				WAS A (14G – .056)											
" total	23	27	1	0	0	0	0.0	1	0	2	5	0	.037	.037	2	0	C-21
7 yrs.	376	1002	224	35	4	30	3.0	93	97	79	221	1	.224	.356	23	0	C-352

Doug Neff

NEFF, DOUGLAS WILLIAMS
B. Oct. 8, 1891, Harrisonburg, Va. D. May 23, 1932, Cape Charles, Va. BR TR 5'9" 141 lbs.

	G	AB	H	2B	3B	HR	HR %	R	RBI	BB	SO	SB	BA	SA	PH AB	PH H	G by POS
1914 WAS A	3	2	0	0	0	0	0.0	0	0	0	0	0	.000	.000	0	0	SS-3
1915	30	60	10	1	0	0	0.0	1	4	4	6	1	.167	.183	0	0	3B-12, 2B-10, SS-7
2 yrs.	33	62	10	1	0	0	0.0	1	4	4	6	1	.161	.177	0	0	3B-12, SS-10, 2B-10

Bob Neighbors

NEIGHBORS, ROBERT OTIS
B. Nov. 9, 1917, Talahina, Okla. D. Aug. 8, 1952, North Korea BR TR 5'11" 165 lbs.

	G	AB	H	2B	3B	HR	HR %	R	RBI	BB	SO	SB	BA	SA	PH AB	PH H	G by POS
1939 STL A	7	11	2	0	0	1	9.1	3	1	0	1	0	.182	.455	0	0	SS-5

Cy Neighbors

NEIGHBORS, CECIL F.
B. Sept. 23, 1880, Mo. D. May 20, 1964, Tacoma, Wash. BR

	G	AB	H	2B	3B	HR	HR %	R	RBI	BB	SO	SB	BA	SA	PH AB	PH H	G by POS
1908 PIT N	1	0	0	0	0	0	–	0	0	0		0	–	–	0	0	OF-1

Tommy Neill

NEILL, THOMAS WHITE
B. Nov. 7, 1919, Hartselle, Ala. BL TR 6'2" 200 lbs.

	G	AB	H	2B	3B	HR	HR %	R	RBI	BB	SO	SB	BA	SA	PH AB	PH H	G by POS
1946 BOS N	13	45	12	2	0	0	0.0	8	7	2	1	0	.267	.311	0	0	OF-13
1947	7	10	2	0	1	0	0.0	1	0	1	2	0	.200	.400	4	2	OF-7
2 yrs.	20	55	14	2	1	0	0.0	9	7	3	3	0	.255	.327	4	2	OF-20

Bernie Neis

NEIS, BERNARD EDMUND
B. Sept. 26, 1895, Bloomington, Ill.
D. Nov. 29, 1972, Inverness, Fla. BB TR 5'7" 160 lbs.
BR 1920-21,1926

	G	AB	H	2B	3B	HR	HR %	R	RBI	BB	SO	SB	BA	SA	PH AB	PH H	G by POS
1920 BKN N	95	249	63	11	2	2	0.8	38	22	26	35	9	.253	.337	4	0	OF-83
1921	102	230	59	5	4	4	1.7	34	34	25	41	9	.257	.365	16	6	OF-77, 2B-1
1922	61	70	16	4	1	1	1.4	15	9	13	8	3	.229	.357	9	1	OF-27
1923	126	445	122	17	4	5	1.1	78	37	36	38	8	.274	.364	8	1	OF-111
1924	80	211	64	8	3	4	1.9	43	26	27	17	4	.303	.427	11	2	OF-62
1925 BOS N	106	355	101	20	2	5	1.4	47	45	38	19	8	.285	.394	6	0	OF-87
1926	30	93	20	5	2	0	0.0	16	8	8	10	4	.215	.312	2	0	OF-23
1927 2 teams		CLE A (32G – .302)				CHI A (45G – .289)											
" total	77	172	51	14	0	4	2.3	26	29	28	18	1	.297	.448	20	5	OF-50
8 yrs.	677	1825	496	84	18	25	1.4	297	210	201	186	46	.272	.379	84	21	OF-520, 2B-1

WORLD SERIES

	G	AB	H	2B	3B	HR	HR %	R	RBI	BB	SO	SB	BA	SA	PH AB	PH H	G by POS
1920 BKN N	4	5	0	0	0	0	0.0	0	0	1	0	0	.000	.000	1	0	OF-2

Ernie Neitzke

NEITZKE, ERNEST FREDRICH
B. Nov. 13, 1894, Toledo, Ohio D. Apr. 27, 1977, Sylvania, Ohio BR TR 5'10" 180 lbs.

	G	AB	H	2B	3B	HR	HR %	R	RBI	BB	SO	SB	BA	SA	PH AB	PH H	G by POS
1921 BOS A	11	25	6	0	0	0	0.0	3	1	4	4	0	.240	.240	0	0	OF-8, P-2

Bob Nelson

NELSON, ROBERT SIDNEY (Tex, Babe)
B. Aug. 7, 1936, Dallas, Tex. BL TL 6'3" 205 lbs.

	G	AB	H	2B	3B	HR	HR %	R	RBI	BB	SO	SB	BA	SA	PH AB	PH H	G by POS
1955 BAL A	25	31	6	0	0	0	0.0	4	1	7	13	0	.194	.194	16	3	OF-6, 1B-2
1956	39	68	14	2	0	0	0.0	5	5	7	22	0	.206	.235	15	4	OF-24
1957	15	23	5	0	2	0	0.0	2	5	1	5	0	.217	.391	6	3	OF-8
3 yrs.	79	122	25	2	2	0	0.0	11	11	15	40	0	.205	.254	37	10	OF-38, 1B-2

Candy Nelson

NELSON, JOHN W
B. Mar. 12, 1854, Portland, Me. D. Sept. 4, 1910, Brooklyn, N. Y. BL TR 5'6" 145 lbs.

	G	AB	H	2B	3B	HR	HR %	R	RBI	BB	SO	SB	BA	SA	PH AB	PH H	G by POS
1878 IND N	19	84	11	1	0	0	0.0	12	5	5	11		.131	.143	0	0	SS-19
1879 TRO N	28	106	28	7	1	0	0.0	17	10	8	4		.264	.349	0	0	SS-24, OF-4
1881 WOR N	24	103	29	1	0	1	1.0	13	15	5	6		.282	.320	0	0	SS-24
1883 NY AA	97	417	127	19	6	0	0.0	75		31			.305	.379	0	0	SS-97
1884	111	432	110	15	3	1	0.2	114		74			.255	.310	0	0	SS-110, 2B-1
1885	107	420	107	12	4	1	0.2	98		61			.255	.310	0	0	SS-107, 3B-1
1886	109	413	93	7	2	0	0.0	69		64			.225	.252	0	0	SS-73, OF-36
1887 2 teams		NY AA (68G – .245)				NY N (1G – .000)											
" total	69	259	63	5	1	0	0.0	61		48	1	29	.243	.270	0	0	OF-37, SS-32, 3B-1, 2B-1
1890 B-B AA	60	223	56	3	2	0	0.0	44		35		12	.251	.283	0	0	SS-57, OF-4
9 yrs.	624	2457	624	70	19	3	0.1	523	30	331	22	41	.254	.302	0	0	SS-543, OF-81, 3B-2, 2B-2

Dave Nelson

NELSON, DAVID EARL
B. June 20, 1944, Fort Sill, Okla. BB TR 5'10" 160 lbs.

	G	AB	H	2B	3B	HR	HR %	R	RBI	BB	SO	SB	BA	SA	PH AB	PH H	G by POS
1968 CLE A	88	189	44	4	5	0	0.0	26	19	17	35	23	.233	.307	2	0	2B-59, SS-14
1969	52	123	25	0	0	0	0.0	11	6	9	26	4	.203	.203	5	0	2B-33, OF-2
1970 WAS A	47	107	17	1	0	0	0.0	5	4	7	24	2	.159	.168	11	2	2B-33
1971	85	329	92	11	3	5	1.5	47	33	23	29	17	.280	.377	3	0	3B-84, 2B-1
1972 TEX A	145	499	113	16	3	2	0.4	68	28	67	81	51	.226	.283	6	0	3B-119, OF-15
1973	142	576	165	24	4	7	1.2	71	48	34	78	43	.286	.378	2	0	2B-140
1974	121	474	112	13	1	3	0.6	71	42	34	72	25	.236	.287	0	0	2B-120, DH-1
1975	28	80	17	1	0	2	2.5	9	10	8	11	6	.213	.300	2	1	2B-23, DH-1
1976 KC A	78	153	36	4	2	1	0.7	24	19	14	26	15	.235	.307	16	0	2B-46, DH-22, 1B-3
1977	27	48	9	3	0	0	0.0	8	4	7	11	1	.188	.292	5	2	2B-11, DH-7
10 yrs.	813	2578	630	77	19	20	0.8	340	211	220	392	187	.244	.312	52	7	2B-466, 3B-203, DH-31, OF-17, SS-14, 1B-3

LEAGUE CHAMPIONSHIP SERIES

	G	AB	H	2B	3B	HR	HR %	R	RBI	BB	SO	SB	BA	SA	PH AB	PH H	G by POS
1976 KC A	2	2	0	0	0	0	0.0	0	0	0	1	0	.000	.000	2	0	

	G	AB	H	2B	3B	HR	HR %	R	RBI	BB	SO	SB	BA	SA	Pinch Hit AB	Pinch Hit H	G by POS

Jamie Nelson

NELSON, JAMES VICTOR
B. Sept. 5, 1959, Clinton, Okla.
BR TR 5'11" 180 lbs.

	G	AB	H	2B	3B	HR	HR %	R	RBI	BB	SO	SB	BA	SA	PH AB	PH H	G by POS
1983 SEA A	40	96	21	3	0	1	1.0	9	5	13	12	4	.219	.281	1	0	C-39

Lynn Nelson

NELSON, LYNN BERNARD (Line Drive)
B. Feb. 24, 1905, Sheldon, N. D.   D. Feb. 15, 1955, Kansas City, Mo.
BL TR 5'10½" 170 lbs.

	G	AB	H	2B	3B	HR	HR %	R	RBI	BB	SO	SB	BA	SA	PH AB	PH H	G by POS
1930 CHI N	37	18	4	1	1	0	0.0	0	2	0	1	0	.222	.389	0	0	P-37
1933	29	21	5	1	1	0	0.0	5	1	1	3	0	.238	.381	0	0	P-24
1934	2	0	0	0	0	0	–	0	0	0	0	0	–	–	0	0	P-2
1937 PHI A	74	113	40	6	2	4	3.5	18	29	6	13	1	.354	.549	38	9	P-30, OF-6
1938	67	112	31	0	0	0	0.0	12	15	7	12	0	.277	.277	32	6	P-32
1939	40	80	15	2	0	0	0.0	3	5	2	13	0	.188	.213	5	1	P-35
1940 DET A	19	23	8	0	0	1	4.3	4	3	0	6	0	.348	.478	14	5	P-6
7 yrs.	268	367	103	10	4	5	1.4	42	55	16	48	1	.281	.371	89	21	P-166, OF-6

Ray Nelson

NELSON, RAYMOND
Also known as Raymond N. Kellogg.
B. Aug. 4, 1875, Holyoke, Mass.   D. Jan. 8, 1961, Mount Vernon, N. Y.
BR TR 5'9" 150 lbs.

	G	AB	H	2B	3B	HR	HR %	R	RBI	BB	SO	SB	BA	SA	PH AB	PH H	G by POS
1901 NY N	39	130	26	2	0	0	0.0	12	7	10		3	.200	.215	0	0	2B-39

Ricky Nelson

NELSON, RICKY LEE
B. May 8, 1959, Eloy, Ariz.
BL TR 6' 200 lbs.

	G	AB	H	2B	3B	HR	HR %	R	RBI	BB	SO	SB	BA	SA	PH AB	PH H	G by POS
1983 SEA A	98	291	74	13	3	5	1.7	32	36	17	50	7	.254	.371	12	5	OF-91, DH-1
1984	9	15	3	0	0	1	6.7	2	2	2	4	0	.200	.400	5	1	DH-3, OF-2
2 yrs.	107	306	77	13	3	6	2.0	34	38	19	54	7	.252	.373	17	6	OF-93, DH-4

Rocky Nelson

NELSON, GLENN RICHARD
B. Nov. 18, 1924, Portsmouth, Ohio
BL TL 5'10½" 175 lbs.

	G	AB	H	2B	3B	HR	HR %	R	RBI	BB	SO	SB	BA	SA	PH AB	PH H	G by POS
1949 STL N	82	244	54	8	4	4	1.6	28	32	11	12	1	.221	.336	8	2	1B-70
1950	76	235	58	10	4	1	0.4	27	20	26	9	4	.247	.336	4	1	1B-70
1951 3 teams		STL	N (9G –	.222)		PIT	N (71G –	.267)		CHI	A (6G –	.000)					
" total	86	218	56	8	4	1	0.5	32	15	12	7	0	.257	.344	31	6	1B-36, OF-13
1952 BKN N	37	39	10	1	0	0	0.0	6	3	7	4	0	.256	.282	27	7	1B-5
1954 CLE A	4	4	0	0	0	0	0.0	0	0	0	1	0	.000	.000	3	0	1B-2
1956 2 teams		BKN	N (31G –	.208)		STL	N (38G –	.232)									
" total	69	152	33	7	0	7	4.6	13	23	10	16	0	.217	.401	26	3	1B-39, OF-8
1959 PIT N	98	175	51	11	0	6	3.4	31	32	23	19	0	.291	.457	33	13	1B-56, OF-2
1960	93	200	60	11	1	7	3.5	34	35	24	15	1	.300	.470	18	4	1B-73
1961	75	127	25	5	1	5	3.9	15	13	17	11	0	.197	.370	37	5	1B-35
9 yrs.	620	1394	347	61	14	31	2.2	186	173	130	94	6	.249	.379	187	41	1B-386, OF-23
WORLD SERIES																	
1952 BKN N	4	3	0	0	0	0	0.0	0	0	1	2	0	.000	.000	3	0	1B-3
1960 PIT N	4	9	3	0	0	1	11.1	2	2	1	0	0	.333	.667	1	0	1B-3
2 yrs.	8	12	3	0	0	1	8.3	2	2	2	2	0	.250	.500	4	0	1B-6

Tom Nelson

NELSON, THOMAS COUSINEAU
B. May 1, 1917, Chicago, Ill.   D. Sept. 24, 1973, San Diego, Calif.
BR TR 6' 180 lbs.

	G	AB	H	2B	3B	HR	HR %	R	RBI	BB	SO	SB	BA	SA	PH AB	PH H	G by POS
1945 BOS N	40	121	20	2	0	0	0.0	6	6	4	13	1	.165	.182	8	1	3B-20, 2B-12

Dick Nen

NEN, RICHARD LeROY
B. Sept. 24, 1939, South Gate, Calif.
BL TL 6'2" 200 lbs.

	G	AB	H	2B	3B	HR	HR %	R	RBI	BB	SO	SB	BA	SA	PH AB	PH H	G by POS
1963 LA N	7	8	1	0	0	1	12.5	2	1	3	3	0	.125	.500	4	0	1B-5
1965 WAS A	69	246	64	7	1	6	2.4	18	31	19	47	1	.260	.370	5	1	1B-65
1966	94	235	50	8	0	6	2.6	20	30	28	46	0	.213	.323	20	3	1B-76
1967	110	238	52	7	1	6	2.5	21	29	21	39	0	.218	.332	40	6	1B-65, OF-1
1968 CHI N	81	94	17	1	1	2	2.1	8	16	6	17	0	.181	.277	28	4	1B-52
1970 WAS A	6	5	1	0	0	0	0.0	1	0	0	0	0	.200	.200	5	1	1B-1
6 yrs.	367	826	185	23	3	21	2.5	70	107	77	152	1	.224	.335	102	15	1B-264, OF-1

Jack Ness

NESS, JOHN CHARLES
B. Nov. 11, 1885, Chicago, Ill.   D. Dec. 3, 1957, DeLand, Fla.
BR TR 6'2" 165 lbs.

	G	AB	H	2B	3B	HR	HR %	R	RBI	BB	SO	SB	BA	SA	PH AB	PH H	G by POS
1911 DET A	12	39	6	0	0	0	0.0	6	2	2		4	.154	.154	0	0	1B-12
1916 CHI A	75	258	69	7	5	1	0.4	32	34	9	32	4	.267	.345	6	3	1B-69
2 yrs.	87	297	75	7	5	1	0.3	38	36	11	32	4	.253	.320	6	3	1B-81

Graig Nettles

NETTLES, GRAIG
Brother of Jim Nettles.
B. Aug. 20, 1944, San Diego, Calif.
BL TR 6' 180 lbs.

	G	AB	H	2B	3B	HR	HR %	R	RBI	BB	SO	SB	BA	SA	PH AB	PH H	G by POS
1967 MIN A	3	3	1	1	0	0	0.0	0	0	0	0	0	.333	.667	3	1	
1968	22	76	17	2	1	5	6.6	13	8	7	20	0	.224	.474	0	0	OF-16, 3B-5, 1B-3
1969	96	225	50	9	2	7	3.1	27	26	32	47	1	.222	.373	28	4	OF-54, 3B-21
1970 CLE A	157	549	129	13	1	26	4.7	81	62	81	77	3	.235	.404	5	1	3B-154, OF-3
1971	158	598	156	18	1	28	4.7	78	86	82	56	7	.261	.435	0	0	3B-158
1972	150	557	141	28	0	17	3.1	65	70	57	50	2	.253	.395	0	0	3B-150
1973 NY A	160	552	129	18	0	22	4.0	65	81	78	76	0	.234	.386	1	0	3B-157, DH-2
1974	155	566	139	21	1	22	3.9	74	75	59	75	1	.246	.403	1	0	3B-154, SS-1
1975	157	581	155	24	4	21	3.6	71	91	51	88	1	.267	.430	0	0	3B-157
1976	158	583	148	29	2	32	5.5	88	93	62	94	11	.254	.475	1	0	3B-158, SS-1
1977	158	589	150	23	4	37	6.3	99	107	68	79	2	.255	.496	0	0	3B-156, DH-1
1978	159	587	162	23	2	27	4.6	81	93	59	69	1	.276	.460	0	0	3B-144
1979	145	521	132	15	1	20	3.8	71	73	59	53	1	.253	.401	2	0	3B-88, SS-1
1980	89	324	79	14	0	16	4.9	52	45	42	42	0	.244	.435	3	1	3B-97, DH-4
1981	103	349	85	7	1	15	4.3	46	46	47	49	0	.244	.398	3	1	3B-113, DH-3
1982	122	405	94	11	2	18	4.4	47	55	51	49	1	.232	.402	10	1	3B-126, DH-1
1983	129	462	123	17	3	20	4.3	56	75	51	65	0	.266	.446	6	3	3B-126, DH-1

	G	AB	H	2B	3B	HR	HR %	R	RBI	BB	SO	SB	BA	SA	Pinch Hit AB	Pinch Hit H	G by POS

Graig Nettles continued

	G	AB	H	2B	3B	HR	HR %	R	RBI	BB	SO	SB	BA	SA	PH AB	PH H	G by POS
1984 SD N	124	395	90	11	1	20	5.1	56	65	58	55	0	.228	.413	13	3	3B-119
18 yrs.	2245	7922	1980	284	26	353	4.5	1070	1151	944	1044	31	.250	.426	76	15	3B-2116, OF-73, DH-11, SS-5, 1B-3

DIVISIONAL PLAYOFF SERIES
	G	AB	H	2B	3B	HR	HR %	R	RBI	BB	SO	SB	BA	SA	PH AB	PH H	G by POS
1981 NY A	5	17	1	0	0	0	0.0	1	1	3	1	0	.059	.059	0	0	3B-5

LEAGUE CHAMPIONSHIP SERIES
	G	AB	H	2B	3B	HR	HR %	R	RBI	BB	SO	SB	BA	SA	PH AB	PH H	G by POS
1969 MIN A	1	1	1	0	0	0	0.0	0	0	0	0	0	1.000	1.000	1	1	
1976 NY A	5	17	4	1	0	2	11.8	2	4	3	3	0	.235	.647	0	0	3B-5
1977	5	20	3	0	0	0	0.0	1	1	0	3	0	.150	.150	0	0	3B-5
1978	4	15	5	0	1	1	6.7	3	2	0	1	0	.333	.667	0	0	3B-4
1980	2	6	1	0	0	1	16.7	1	1	0	1	0	.167	.667	0	0	3B-4
1981	3	12	6	2	0	1	8.3	2	9	1	0	0	.500	.917	1	0	3B-3
1984 SD N	4	14	2	0	0	0	0.0	1	2	1	1	0	.143	.143	0	0	3B-4
7 yrs.	24	85	22	3	1	5	5.9	10	19	5	9	0	.259	.494	2	1	3B-23

WORLD SERIES
	G	AB	H	2B	3B	HR	HR %	R	RBI	BB	SO	SB	BA	SA	PH AB	PH H	G by POS
1976 NY A	4	12	3	0	0	0	0.0	0	2	3	1	0	.250	.250	0	0	3B-4
1977	6	21	4	1	0	0	0.0	1	2	2	3	0	.190	.238	0	0	3B-6
1978	6	25	4	0	0	0	0.0	2	1	0	6	0	.160	.160	0	0	3B-6
1981	3	10	4	1	0	0	0.0	1	0	1	1	0	.400	.500	0	0	3B-3
1984 SD N	5	12	3	0	0	0	0.0	2	2	5	0	0	.250	.250	0	0	3B-5
5 yrs.	24	80	18	2	0	0	0.0	6	7	11	11	0	.225	.250	0	0	3B-24

Jim Nettles

NETTLES, JAMES WILLIAM
Brother of Graig Nettles.
B. Mar. 2, 1947, San Diego, Calif.   BL TL 6'   186 lbs.

	G	AB	H	2B	3B	HR	HR %	R	RBI	BB	SO	SB	BA	SA	PH AB	PH H	G by POS
1970 MIN A	13	20	5	0	0	0	0.0	3	0	1	5	0	.250	.250	1	0	OF-11
1971	70	168	42	5	1	6	3.6	17	24	19	24	3	.250	.399	8	2	OF-62
1972	102	235	48	5	2	4	1.7	28	15	32	52	4	.204	.294	20	7	OF-78, 1B-1
1974 DET A	43	141	32	5	1	6	4.3	20	17	15	26	3	.227	.404	1	1	OF-41
1979 KC A	11	23	2	0	0	0	0.0	0	1	3	2	0	.087	.087	2	0	OF-8, 1B-1
1981 OAK A	1	0	0	0	0	0	–	0	0	0	0	0	–	–	0	0	OF-1
6 yrs.	240	587	129	15	4	16	2.7	68	57	70	109	10	.220	.341	32	10	OF-201, 1B-2

Morris Nettles

NETTLES, MORRIS JR.
B. Jan. 26, 1952, Los Angeles, Calif.   BL TL 6'1"   170 lbs.

	G	AB	H	2B	3B	HR	HR %	R	RBI	BB	SO	SB	BA	SA	PH AB	PH H	G by POS
1974 CAL A	56	175	48	4	0	0	0.0	27	8	17	38	20	.274	.297	2	1	OF-54
1975	112	294	68	11	0	0	0.0	50	23	26	57	22	.231	.269	6	2	OF-90, DH-9
2 yrs.	168	469	116	15	0	0	0.0	77	31	43	95	42	.247	.279	8	3	OF-144, DH-9

Milo Netzel

NETZEL, MILES A.
B. May 12, 1887, Olean, N. Y.   D. Mar. 18, 1938, Ventura, Calif.   TR

	G	AB	H	2B	3B	HR	HR %	R	RBI	BB	SO	SB	BA	SA	PH AB	PH H	G by POS
1909 CLE A	10	37	7	1	0	0	0.0	2	3	3		1	.189	.216	1	1	3B-6, OF-2

Otto Neu

NEU, OTTO ADAM (Ott)
B. Sept. 24, 1894, Springfield, Ohio   D. Sept. 19, 1932, Kenton, Ohio   BR TR 5'11"   170 lbs.

	G	AB	H	2B	3B	HR	HR %	R	RBI	BB	SO	SB	BA	SA	PH AB	PH H	G by POS
1917 STL A	1	0	0	0	0	0	–	0	0	0	0	0	–	–	0	0	SS-1

Johnny Neun

NEUN, JOHN HENRY
B. Oct. 28, 1900, Baltimore, Md.   BB TL 5'10½"   175 lbs.
Manager 1946-48.   BR 1928

	G	AB	H	2B	3B	HR	HR %	R	RBI	BB	SO	SB	BA	SA	PH AB	PH H	G by POS
1925 DET A	60	75	20	3	3	0	0.0	15	4	9	12	2	.267	.387	33	8	1B-13
1926	97	242	72	14	4	0	0.0	47	15	27	26	4	.298	.388	42	12	1B-49
1927	79	204	66	9	4	0	0.0	38	27	35	13	22	.324	.407	17	6	1B-53
1928	36	108	23	1	0	0	0.0	15	5	7	10	2	.213	.259	11	3	1B-25
1930 BOS N	81	212	69	12	2	2	0.9	39	23	21	18	9	.325	.429	23	8	1B-55
1931	79	104	23	1	3	0	0.0	17	11	11	14	2	.221	.288	34	4	1B-36
6 yrs.	432	945	273	42	17	2	0.2	171	85	110	93	41	.289	.376	160	41	1B-231

Don Newcombe

NEWCOMBE, DONALD (Newk)
B. June 14, 1926, Madison, N. J.   BR TR 6'4"   220 lbs.

	G	AB	H	2B	3B	HR	HR %	R	RBI	BB	SO	SB	BA	SA	PH AB	PH H	G by POS
1949 BKN N	39	96	22	4	0	0	0.0	8	10	5	16	0	.229	.271	1	0	P-38
1950	40	97	24	3	1	1	1.0	8	8	10	19	0	.247	.330	0	0	P-40
1951	40	103	23	3	1	0	0.0	11	8	8	9	0	.223	.272	0	0	P-40
1954	31	47	15	1	0	0	0.0	6	4	4	6	0	.319	.340	1	0	P-29
1955	57	117	42	9	1	7	6.0	18	23	6	18	1	.359	.632	21	8	P-34
1956	52	111	26	6	0	2	1.8	13	16	12	18	1	.234	.342	12	0	P-38
1957	34	74	17	2	1	1	1.4	8	7	11	11	0	.230	.297	3	0	P-28
1958 2 teams		LA	N (11G – .417)		CIN	N (39G – .350)											
" total	50	72	26	1	0	1	1.4	11	9	10	12	0	.361	.417	16	6	P-31
1959 CIN N	61	105	32	2	0	3	2.9	10	21	17	23	0	.305	.410	21	5	P-30
1960 2 teams		CIN	N (24G – .139)		CLE	A (24G – .300)											
" total	48	56	11	2	0	0	0.0	1	2	4	15	0	.196	.232	12	1	P-36
10 yrs.	452	878	238	33	3	15	1.7	94	108	87	147	2	.271	.367	87	20	P-344

WORLD SERIES
	G	AB	H	2B	3B	HR	HR %	R	RBI	BB	SO	SB	BA	SA	PH AB	PH H	G by POS
1949 BKN N	2	4	0	0	0	0	0.0	0	0	0	3	0	.000	.000	0	0	P-2
1955	1	3	0	0	0	0	0.0	0	0	0	0	0	.000	.000	0	0	P-1
1956	2	1	0	0	0	0	0.0	0	0	0	0	0	.000	.000	0	0	P-2
3 yrs.	5	8	0	0	0	0	0.0	0	0	0	3	0	.000	.000	0	0	P-5

John Newell

NEWELL, JOHN A.
B. Jan. 14, 1868, Wilmington, Del.   D. Jan. 28, 1919, Wilmington, Del.   BR TL

	G	AB	H	2B	3B	HR	HR %	R	RBI	BB	SO	SB	BA	SA	PH AB	PH H	G by POS
1891 PIT N	5	18	2	0	0	0	0.0	1	2	0		0	.111	.111	0	0	3B-5

	G	AB	H	2B	3B	HR	HR %	R	RBI	BB	SO	SB	BA	SA	Pinch Hit AB	Pinch Hit H	G by POS

T. E. Newell

NEWELL, T. E.
B. St. Louis, Mo.   Deceased.

	G	AB	H	2B	3B	HR	HR%	R	RBI	BB	SO	SB	BA	SA	AB	H	G by POS
1877 STL N	1	3	0	0	0	0	0.0	0	0	0	0		.000	.000	0	0	SS-1

Charlie Newman

NEWMAN, CHARLES DECKER   BR TR 5'11"   160 lbs.
B. Nov. 5, 1868, Juda, Wis.   D. Nov. 23, 1947, San Diego, Calif.

	G	AB	H	2B	3B	HR	HR%	R	RBI	BB	SO	SB	BA	SA	AB	H	G by POS
1892 2 teams	NY	N (3G – .333)			CHI	N (16G – .164)											
" total	19	73	14	0	0	0	0.0	5	3	3	6	5	.192	.192	0	0	OF-19

Jeff Newman

NEWMAN, JEFFREY LYNN   BR TR 6'2"   215 lbs.
B. Sept. 11, 1948, Ft. Worth, Tex.

	G	AB	H	2B	3B	HR	HR%	R	RBI	BB	SO	SB	BA	SA	AB	H	G by POS
1976 OAK A	43	77	15	4	0	0	0.0	5	4	4	12	0	.195	.247	0	0	C-43
1977	94	162	36	9	0	4	2.5	17	15	4	24	2	.222	.352	1	0	C-94, P-1
1978	105	268	64	7	1	9	3.4	25	32	18	40	0	.239	.373	24	6	C-61, 1B-36, DH-2
1979	143	516	119	17	2	22	4.3	53	71	27	88	2	.231	.399	2	0	C-81, 1B-46, DH-7, 3B-7
1980	127	438	102	19	1	15	3.4	37	56	25	81	3	.233	.384	12	5	1B-60, C-55, DH-9, 3B-2, 2B-1
1981	68	216	50	12	0	3	1.4	17	15	9	28	0	.231	.329	5	0	C-37, 1B-30
1982	72	251	50	11	0	6	2.4	19	30	14	49	0	.199	.315	1	1	C-67, 1B-3, DH-1, 3B-1
1983 BOS A	59	132	25	4	0	3	2.3	11	7	10	31	0	.189	.288	4	1	C-51, DH-6
1984	24	63	14	2	0	1	1.6	5	3	5	16	0	.222	.302	0	0	C-24
9 yrs.	735	2123	475	85	4	63	3.0	189	233	116	369	7	.224	.357	56	15	C-513, 1B-175, DH-25, 3B-10, 2B-1, P-1

DIVISIONAL PLAYOFF SERIES

	G	AB	H	2B	3B	HR	HR%	R	RBI	BB	SO	SB	BA	SA	AB	H	G by POS
1981 OAK A	1	3	0	0	0	0	0.0	0	0	0	1	0	.000	.000	0	0	C-1

LEAGUE CHAMPIONSHIP SERIES

	G	AB	H	2B	3B	HR	HR%	R	RBI	BB	SO	SB	BA	SA	AB	H	G by POS
1981 OAK A	2	5	0	0	0	0	0.0	0	0	0	2	0	.000	.000	0	0	C-2

Pat Newnam

NEWNAM, PATRICK HENRY   BR TR
B. Dec. 10, 1880, Hemstead, Tex.   D. June 20, 1938, San Antonio, Tex.

	G	AB	H	2B	3B	HR	HR%	R	RBI	BB	SO	SB	BA	SA	AB	H	G by POS
1910 STL A	103	384	83	3	8	2	0.5	45	26	29		16	.216	.281	0	0	1B-103
1911	20	62	12	4	0	0	0.0	11	5	12		4	.194	.258	0	0	1B-20
2 yrs.	123	446	95	7	8	2	0.4	56	31	41		20	.213	.278	0	0	1B-123

Skeeter Newsome

NEWSOME, LAMAR ASHBY   BR TR 5'9"   155 lbs.
B. Oct. 18, 1910, Phenix City, Ala.

	G	AB	H	2B	3B	HR	HR%	R	RBI	BB	SO	SB	BA	SA	AB	H	G by POS
1935 PHI A	59	145	30	7	1	1	0.7	18	10	5	9	2	.207	.290	7	0	SS-24, 2B-13, 3B-4, OF-1
1936	127	471	106	15	2	0	0.0	41	46	25	27	13	.225	.265	2	0	SS-123, 2B-2, OF-1, 3B-1
1937	122	438	111	22	1	1	0.2	53	30	37	22	11	.253	.315	0	0	SS-122
1938	17	48	13	4	0	0	0.0	7	7	1	4	1	.271	.354	0	0	SS-15
1939	99	248	55	9	1	0	0.0	22	17	19	12	5	.222	.266	1	0	SS-93, 2B-2
1941 BOS A	93	227	51	6	0	2	0.9	28	17	22	11	10	.225	.278	0	0	SS-69, 2B-23
1942	29	95	26	6	0	0	0.0	7	9	9	5	2	.274	.337	0	0	3B-12, 2B-10, SS-7
1943	114	449	119	21	2	1	0.2	48	22	21	21	5	.265	.327	0	0	SS-98, 3B-15
1944	136	472	114	26	3	0	0.0	41	41	33	21	4	.242	.309	0	0	SS-126, 2B-8, 3B-1
1945	125	438	127	30	1	1	0.2	45	48	20	15	6	.290	.370	1	0	2B-82, SS-33, 3B-11
1946 PHI N	112	375	87	10	2	1	0.3	35	23	30	23	4	.232	.277	3	0	SS-107, 2B-3, 3B-2
1947	95	310	71	8	2	2	0.6	36	22	24	24	4	.229	.287	1	1	SS-85, 2B-6, 3B-1
12 yrs.	1128	3716	910	164	15	9	0.2	381	292	246	194	67	.245	.304	15	1	SS-902, 2B-149, 3B-47, OF-2

Gus Niarhos

NIARHOS, CONSTANTINE GREGORY   BR TR 6'   160 lbs.
B. Dec. 6, 1920, Birmingham, Ala.

	G	AB	H	2B	3B	HR	HR%	R	RBI	BB	SO	SB	BA	SA	AB	H	G by POS
1946 NY A	37	40	9	1	1	0	0.0	11	2	11	2	1	.225	.300	2	0	C-29
1948	83	228	61	12	2	0	0.0	41	19	52	15	1	.268	.338	0	0	C-82
1949	32	43	12	2	1	0	0.0	7	6	13	8	0	.279	.372	2	1	C-30
1950 2 teams	NY	A (1G – .000)			CHI	A (41G – .324)											
" total	42	105	34	4	0	0	0.0	17	16	14	6	0	.324	.362	2	0	C-36
1951 CHI A	66	168	43	6	0	1	0.6	27	10	47	9	4	.256	.310	4	2	C-59
1952 BOS A	29	58	6	0	0	0	0.0	4	4	12	9	0	.103	.103	3	0	C-25
1953	16	35	7	1	1	0	0.0	6	2	4	4	0	.200	.286	0	0	C-16
1954 PHI N	3	5	1	0	0	0	0.0	0	0	0	0	0	.200	.200	0	0	C-3
1955	7	9	1	0	0	0	0.0	1	0	0	2	0	.111	.111	0	0	C-7
9 yrs.	315	691	174	26	5	1	0.1	114	59	153	56	6	.252	.308	13	3	C-287

WORLD SERIES

	G	AB	H	2B	3B	HR	HR%	R	RBI	BB	SO	SB	BA	SA	AB	H	G by POS
1949 NY A	1	0	0	0	0	0	–	0	0	0	0	0	–	–	0	0	C-1

Charlie Nice

NICE, CHARLES REIFF
B. July 1, 1870, Philadelphia, Pa.   D. May 9, 1908, Philadelphia, Pa.

	G	AB	H	2B	3B	HR	HR%	R	RBI	BB	SO	SB	BA	SA	AB	H	G by POS
1895 BOS N	9	35	8	5	0	2	5.7	7	9	4	2	0	.229	.543	0	0	SS-9

Sam Nichol

NICHOL, SAMUEL ANDERSON   5'9"   160 lbs.
B. Apr. 20, 1869, Ireland   D. Apr. 19, 1937, Steubenville, Ohio

	G	AB	H	2B	3B	HR	HR%	R	RBI	BB	SO	SB	BA	SA	AB	H	G by POS
1888 PIT N	8	22	1	0	0	0	0.0	3	0	2	2	0	.045	.045	0	0	OF-8
1890 COL AA	14	56	9	0	0	0	0.0	7		2		3	.161	.161	0	0	OF-14
2 yrs.	22	78	10	0	0	0	0.0	10		4	2	3	.128	.128	0	0	OF-22

Don Nicholas

NICHOLAS, DONALD LEIGH   BL TR 5'7"   150 lbs.
B. Oct. 30, 1930, Phoenix, Ariz.

	G	AB	H	2B	3B	HR	HR%	R	RBI	BB	SO	SB	BA	SA	AB	H	G by POS
1952 CHI A	3	2	0	0	0	0	0.0	0	0	0	0	0	.000	.000	2	0	OF-3
1954	7	0	0	0	0	0	–	3	0	1	0	0	–	–	0	0	OF-7
2 yrs.	10	2	0	0	0	0	0.0	3	0	1	0	0	.000	.000	2	0	OF-10

	G	AB	H	2B	3B	HR	HR %	R	RBI	BB	SO	SB	BA	SA	Pinch Hit AB	Pinch Hit H	G by POS

Simon Nicholls

NICHOLLS, SIMON BURDETTE
B. July 17, 1882, Germantown, Md.   D. Mar. 12, 1911, Baltimore, Md.   BL TR

	G	AB	H	2B	3B	HR	HR %	R	RBI	BB	SO	SB	BA	SA	AB	H	G by POS
1903 DET A	2	8	3	0	0	0	0.0	0	0	0		0	.375	.375	0	0	SS-2
1906 PHI A	12	44	8	1	0	0	0.0	1	1	3		0	.182	.205	0	0	SS-12
1907	126	460	139	12	2	0	0.0	75	23	24		13	.302	.337	2	0	SS-82, 2B-28, 3B-13
1908	150	550	119	17	3	4	0.7	58	31	35		14	.216	.280	0	0	SS-120, 2B-23, 3B-7
1909	21	71	15	2	1	0	0.0	10	3	3		0	.211	.268	1	0	SS-14, 3B-5, 1B-1
1910 CLE A	3	0	0	0	0	0	–	0	0	0		0			0	0	SS-3
6 yrs.	314	1133	284	32	6	4	0.4	144	58	65		27	.251	.300	3	0	SS-233, 2B-51, 3B-25, 1B-1

Al Nichols

NICHOLS, ALFRED H.
B. Brooklyn, N. Y.   Deceased.   5'11"   180 lbs.

	G	AB	H	2B	3B	HR	HR %	R	RBI	BB	SO	SB	BA	SA	AB	H	G by POS
1876 NY N	57	212	38	4	0	0	0.0	20	9	2	3		.179	.198	0	0	3B-57
1877 LOU N	6	19	4	0	1	0	0.0	1	0	0	2		.211	.316	0	0	2B-3, SS-1, 3B-1, 1B-1
2 yrs.	63	231	42	4	1	0	0.0	21	9	2	5		.182	.208	0	0	3B-58, 2B-3, SS-1, 1B-1

Art Nichols

NICHOLS, ARTHUR FRANCIS
Born Arthur Francis Meikle.
B. July 14, 1871, Manchester, N. H.   D. Aug. 9, 1945, Willimantic, Conn.   BR TR 5'10"   175 lbs.

	G	AB	H	2B	3B	HR	HR %	R	RBI	BB	SO	SB	BA	SA	AB	H	G by POS
1898 CHI N	14	42	12	1	0	0	0.0	7	6	4		6	.286	.310	0	0	C-14
1899	17	47	12	2	0	1	2.1	5	11	0		3	.255	.362	2	0	C-15
1900	8	25	5	0	0	0	0.0	1	0	3		1	.200	.200	1	0	C-7
1901 STL N	93	308	75	11	3	1	0.3	50	33	10		14	.244	.308	0	0	C-47, OF-40
1902	73	251	67	12	0	1	0.4	36	31	21		18	.267	.327	2	0	1B-56, C-11, OF-4
1903	36	120	23	2	0	0	0.0	13	9	12		9	.192	.208	1	0	1B-25, OF-7, C-2
6 yrs.	241	793	194	28	3	3	0.4	112	90	50		51	.245	.299	12	0	C-96, 1B-81, OF-51

Kid Nichols

NICHOLS, CHARLES AUGUSTUS
B. Sept. 14, 1869, Madison, Wis.   D. Apr. 11, 1953, Kansas City, Mo.   BR TR 5'10½"   175 lbs.
Manager 1904-05.
Hall of Fame 1949.

	G	AB	H	2B	3B	HR	HR %	R	RBI	BB	SO	SB	BA	SA	AB	H	G by POS
1890 BOS N	49	174	43	5	1	0	0.0	18	23	11	36	2	.247	.287	0	0	P-48, OF-2
1891	52	183	36	6	0	0	0.0	21	27	12	31	1	.197	.230	0	0	P-52
1892	57	197	39	6	2	2	1.0	21	21	16	51	3	.198	.279	0	0	P-53, OF-5
1893	53	177	39	3	2	2	1.1	25	26	15	22	4	.220	.294	0	0	P-52, OF-1
1894	51	170	50	11	2	0	0.0	39	34	16	24	1	.294	.382	0	0	P-50, OF-1
1895	49	157	37	3	2	0	0.0	23	18	14	28	0	.236	.280	0	0	P-48, OF-1
1896	51	147	28	3	3	1	0.7	27	24	12	18	2	.190	.272	0	0	P-49, OF-2
1897	46	147	39	5	0	3	2.0	20	28	7		4	.265	.361	0	0	P-46
1898	51	158	38	3	3	2	1.3	26	23	4		0	.241	.335	0	0	P-50, 1B-1
1899	42	136	26	3	0	1	0.7	13	12	6		1	.191	.235	0	0	P-42
1900	29	90	18	0	0	1	1.1	14	7	7		0	.200	.233	0	0	P-29
1901	55	163	46	8	7	4	2.5	16	28	8		0	.282	.491	4	2	P-38, OF-7, 1B-5
1904 STL N	36	109	17	1	2	0	0.0	7	5	7		0	.156	.202	0	0	P-36
1905 2 teams			STL N (8G – .227)			PHI N (17G – .189)											
" total	25	75	15	1	0	0	0.0	3	2	2		0	.200	.213	0	0	P-24, OF-1
1906 PHI N	4	3	0	0	0	0	0.0	0	0	0		0	.000	.000	0	0	P-4
15 yrs.	650	2086	471	58	24	16	0.8	273	278	137	210	19	.226	.300	4	2	P-621, OF-20, 1B-6

Reid Nichols

NICHOLS, THOMAS REID
B. Aug. 5, 1958, Ocala, Fla.   BR TR 5'11"   165 lbs.

	G	AB	H	2B	3B	HR	HR %	R	RBI	BB	SO	SB	BA	SA	AB	H	G by POS
1980 BOS A	12	36	8	0	1	0	0.0	5	3	3	8	0	.222	.278	0	0	OF-9, DH-1
1981	39	48	9	0	1	0	0.0	13	3	2	6	0	.188	.229	1	0	OF-27, DH-7, 3B-1
1982	92	245	74	16	1	7	2.9	35	33	14	28	5	.302	.461	6	0	OF-82, DH-4
1983	100	274	78	22	1	6	2.2	35	22	26	36	7	.285	.438	19	6	OF-72, DH-18, SS-1
1984	73	124	28	5	1	1	0.8	14	14	12	18	2	.226	.306	20	5	OF-48, DH-1
5 yrs.	316	727	197	43	5	14	1.9	102	75	57	96	14	.271	.402	46	11	OF-238, DH-31, SS-1, 3B-1

Roy Nichols

NICHOLS, ROY
B. Mar. 3, 1921, Little Rock, Ark.   BR TR 5'11"   155 lbs.

	G	AB	H	2B	3B	HR	HR %	R	RBI	BB	SO	SB	BA	SA	AB	H	G by POS
1944 NY N	11	9	2	1	0	0	0.0	3	0	2	2	0	.222	.333	1	0	3B-1, 2B-1

Tricky Nichols

NICHOLS, FREDERICK C.
B. 1856, Bridgeport, Conn.   D. Feb. 2, 1918, Bridgeport, Conn.   BR TR 5'7½"   150 lbs.

	G	AB	H	2B	3B	HR	HR %	R	RBI	BB	SO	SB	BA	SA	AB	H	G by POS
1876 BOS N	1	4	0	0	0	0	0.0	0	0	0	0		.000	.000	0	0	P-1
1877 STL N	51	186	31	4	2	0	0.0	22	9	3	15		.167	.210	0	0	P-42, OF-16
1878 PRO N	11	49	9	2	0	0	0.0	2	2	2	10		.184	.224	0	0	P-11
1880 WOR N	2	7	0	0	0	0	0.0	0		0	0		.000	.000	0	0	P-2
1882 BAL AA	26	95	15	1	0	0	0.0	4		7			.158	.168	0	0	P-16, OF-14
5 yrs.	91	341	55	7	2	0	0.0	28	11	12	25		.161	.194	0	0	P-72, OF-30

Bill Nicholson

NICHOLSON, WILLIAM BECK (Swish)
B. Dec. 11, 1914, Chestertown, Md.   BL TR 6'   205 lbs.

	G	AB	H	2B	3B	HR	HR %	R	RBI	BB	SO	SB	BA	SA	AB	H	G by POS
1936 PHI A	11	12	0	0	0	0	0.0	2	0	0	5	0	.000	.000	10	0	OF-1
1939 CHI N	58	220	65	12	5	5	2.3	37	38	20	29	0	.295	.464	0	0	OF-58
1940	135	491	146	27	7	25	5.1	78	98	50	67	2	.297	.534	9	2	OF-123
1941	147	532	135	26	1	26	4.9	74	98	82	91	1	.254	.453	4	0	OF-143
1942	152	588	173	22	11	21	3.6	83	78	76	80	8	.294	.476	1	0	OF-151
1943	154	608	188	30	9	29	4.8	95	128	71	78	4	.309	.531	0	0	OF-154
1944	156	582	167	35	8	33	5.7	116	122	93	71	4	.287	.545	0	0	OF-156
1945	151	559	136	28	4	13	2.3	82	88	92	73	4	.243	.377	0	0	OF-151
1946	105	296	65	13	2	8	2.7	36	41	44	44	1	.220	.358	18	6	OF-80
1947	148	487	119	28	1	26	5.3	69	75	87	83	1	.244	.466	7	0	OF-140
1948	143	494	129	24	5	19	3.8	68	67	81	60	2	.261	.445	4	3	OF-136
1949 PHI N	98	299	70	18	3	11	3.7	42	40	45	53	1	.234	.391	7	0	OF-91

	G	AB	H	2B	3B	HR	HR %	R	RBI	BB	SO	SB	BA	SA	Pinch Hit AB	Pinch Hit H	G by POS

Bill Nicholson continued

	G	AB	H	2B	3B	HR	HR %	R	RBI	BB	SO	SB	BA	SA	AB	H	G by POS
1950	41	58	13	2	1	3	5.2	3	10	8	16	0	.224	.448	24	5	OF-15
1951	85	170	41	9	2	8	4.7	23	30	25	24	0	.241	.459	36	11	OF-41
1952	55	88	24	3	0	6	6.8	17	19	14	26	0	.273	.511	31	8	OF-19
1953	38	62	13	5	1	2	3.2	12	16	12	20	0	.210	.419	23	2	OF-12
16 yrs.	1677	5546	1484	272	60	235	4.2	837	948	800	820	27	.268	.465	174	37	OF-1471

WORLD SERIES

	G	AB	H	2B	3B	HR	HR %	R	RBI	BB	SO	SB	BA	SA	AB	H	G by POS
1945 CHI N	7	28	6	1	1	0	0.0	1	8	2	5	0	.214	.321	0	0	OF-7

Dave Nicholson

BR TR 6'2" 215 lbs.

NICHOLSON, DAVID LAWRENCE
B. Aug. 29, 1939, St. Louis, Mo.

	G	AB	H	2B	3B	HR	HR %	R	RBI	BB	SO	SB	BA	SA	AB	H	G by POS
1960 BAL A	54	113	21	1	1	5	4.4	17	11	20	55	0	.186	.345	9	0	OF-44
1962	97	173	30	4	1	9	5.2	25	15	27	76	3	.173	.364	4	0	OF-80
1963 CHI A	126	449	103	11	4	22	4.9	53	70	63	175	2	.229	.419	3	1	OF-123
1964	97	294	60	6	1	13	4.4	40	39	52	126	0	.204	.364	7	1	OF-92
1965	54	85	13	2	1	2	2.4	11	12	9	40	0	.153	.271	12	0	OF-36
1966 HOU N	100	280	69	8	4	10	3.6	36	34	46	92	1	.246	.411	16	2	OF-90
1967 ATL N	10	25	5	0	0	0	0.0	2	1	2	9	0	.200	.200	1	0	OF-7
7 yrs.	538	1419	301	32	12	61	4.3	184	179	219	573	6	.212	.381	52	4	OF-472

Fred Nicholson

BR TR 5'10½" 173 lbs.

NICHOLSON, FREDERICK
B. Sept. 1, 1894, Honey Grove, Tex.

	G	AB	H	2B	3B	HR	HR %	R	RBI	BB	SO	SB	BA	SA	AB	H	G by POS
1917 DET A	13	14	4	1	0	0	0.0	4	1	1	2	0	.286	.357	4	1	OF-3
1919 PIT N	30	66	18	2	2	1	1.5	8	6	6	11	2	.273	.409	11	2	OF-17, 1B-1
1920	99	247	89	16	7	4	1.6	33	30	18	31	9	.360	.530	38	12	OF-58
1921 BOS N	83	245	80	11	7	5	2.0	36	41	17	29	5	.327	.490	15	3	OF-59, 1B-4, 2B-2
1922	78	222	56	4	5	2	0.9	31	29	23	24	5	.252	.342	12	3	OF-63
5 yrs.	303	794	247	34	21	12	1.5	112	107	65	97	21	.311	.452	80	21	OF-200, 1B-5, 2B-2

Ovid Nicholson

BL TR 5'9½" 155 lbs.

NICHOLSON, OVID EDWARD
B. Dec. 30, 1888, Salem, Ind.   D. Mar. 24, 1968, Salem, Ind.

	G	AB	H	2B	3B	HR	HR %	R	RBI	BB	SO	SB	BA	SA	AB	H	G by POS
1912 PIT N	6	11	5	0	0	0	0.0	2	3	1	2	0	.455	.455	0	0	OF-4

Parson Nicholson

6'6" 190 lbs.

NICHOLSON, THOMAS C. (Beacon)
B. Apr. 14, 1862, Pleasant Valley, Ohio   D. Feb. 28, 1917, Bellaire, Ohio

	G	AB	H	2B	3B	HR	HR %	R	RBI	BB	SO	SB	BA	SA	AB	H	G by POS
1888 DET N	24	85	22	2	3	1	1.2	11	9	2	7	6	.259	.388	0	0	2B-24
1890 TOL AA	134	523	140	16	11	4	0.8	78		42		46	.268	.363	0	0	2B-134, C-1
1895 WAS N	10	38	7	2	1	0	0.0	7	5	7	4	6	.184	.289	0	0	SS-10
3 yrs.	168	646	169	20	15	5	0.8	96	14	51	11	58	.262	.362	0	0	2B-158, SS-10, C-1

George Nicol

TL

NICOL, GEORGE EDWARD
B. Oct. 17, 1870, Barry, Ill.   D. Aug. 10, 1924, Milwaukee, Wis.

	G	AB	H	2B	3B	HR	HR %	R	RBI	BB	SO	SB	BA	SA	AB	H	G by POS
1890 STL AA	3	7	2	1	0	0	0.0	4		4		0	.286	.429	0	0	P-3
1891 CHI N	3	6	2	0	1	0	0.0	3		0	1	0	.333	.667	0	0	P-3
1894 2 teams		PIT	N	(8G –	.450)		LOU	N	(27G –	.352)							
" total	35	128	47	7	4	0	0.0	20	22	2	4	4	.367	.484	0	0	OF-26, P-9
3 yrs.	41	141	51	8	5	0	0.0	24	24	6	5	4	.362	.489	0	0	OF-26, P-15

Hugh Nicol

BR TR 5'4" 145 lbs.

NICOL, HUGH N.
B. Jan. 1, 1858, Campsie, Scotland   D. June 27, 1921, Lafayette, Ind.
Manager 1897.

	G	AB	H	2B	3B	HR	HR %	R	RBI	BB	SO	SB	BA	SA	AB	H	G by POS
1881 CHI N	26	108	22	2	0	0	0.0	13	7	4	12		.204	.222	0	0	OF-26, SS-1
1882	47	186	37	9	1	1	0.5	19	16	7	29		.199	.274	0	0	OF-47, SS-8
1883 STL AA	94	368	106	13	3	0	0.0	73		18			.288	.340	0	0	OF-84, 2B-11
1884	110	442	115	14	5	0	0.0	79		22			.260	.314	0	0	OF-87, 2B-23, SS-1, 3B-1
1885	112	425	88	11	1	0	0.0	59		34			.207	.238	0	0	OF-111, 3B-1
1886	67	253	52	6	3	0	0.0	44		26			.206	.253	0	0	OF-57, SS-8, 2B-4
1887 CIN AA	125	475	102	18	2	1	0.2	122		86		138	.215	.267	0	0	OF-125, 2B-12, SS-1
1888	135	548	131	10	2	1	0.2	112	35	67		103	.239	.270	0	0	OF-115, 2B-7, 3B-3
1889	122	474	121	7	8	2	0.4	82	58	54	35	80	.255	.316	0	0	OF-46, SS-3, 2B-1
1890 CIN N	50	186	39	1	4	0	0.0	28	19	19	12	24	.210	.258	0	0	OF-823, 2B-58, SS-22, 3B-5
10 yrs.	888	3465	813	91	29	5	0.1	631	135	337	88	345	.235	.282	0	0	

Steve Nicosia

BR TR 5'10" 185 lbs.

NICOSIA, STEVEN RICHARD
B. Aug. 6, 1955, Paterson, N. J.

	G	AB	H	2B	3B	HR	HR %	R	RBI	BB	SO	SB	BA	SA	AB	H	G by POS
1978 PIT N	3	5	0	0	0	0	0.0	0	0	1	0	0	.000	.000	1	0	C-1
1979	70	191	55	16	0	4	2.1	22	13	23	17	0	.288	.435	6	0	C-65
1980	60	176	38	8	0	1	0.6	16	22	19	16	0	.216	.278	2	0	C-58
1981	54	169	39	10	1	2	1.2	21	18	13	10	3	.231	.337	2	0	C-52
1982	39	100	28	3	0	1	1.0	6	7	11	13	0	.280	.340	2	1	C-35, OF-3
1983 2 teams		PIT	N	(21G –	.130)		SF	N	(15G –	.333)							
" total	36	79	17	2	0	1	1.3	8	7	4	9	0	.215	.278	9	3	C-24
1984 SF N	48	132	40	11	2	2	1.5	9	19	8	14	1	.303	.462	10	4	C-41
7 yrs.	310	852	217	50	3	11	1.3	82	86	79	79	4	.255	.359	32	8	C-276, OF-3

WORLD SERIES

	G	AB	H	2B	3B	HR	HR %	R	RBI	BB	SO	SB	BA	SA	AB	H	G by POS
1979 PIT N	4	16	1	0	0	0	0.0	1	0	0	2	0	.063	.063	0	0	C-4

Charlie Niebergall

BR TR 5'10" 160 lbs.

NIEBERGALL, CHARLES ARTHUR (Nig)
B. May 23, 1899, New York, N. Y.   D. Aug. 29, 1982, Holiday, Fla.

	G	AB	H	2B	3B	HR	HR %	R	RBI	BB	SO	SB	BA	SA	AB	H	G by POS
1921 STL N	5	6	1	0	0	0	0.0	1	0	0	0	0	.167	.167	2	1	C-3
1923	9	28	3	1	0	0	0.0	2	1	2	2	0	.107	.143	1	0	C-7
1924	40	58	17	6	0	0	0.0	6	7	3	9	0	.293	.397	6	2	C-34
3 yrs.	54	92	21	7	0	0	0.0	9	8	5	11	0	.228	.304	9	3	C-44

	G	AB	H	2B	3B	HR	HR %	R	RBI	BB	SO	SB	BA	SA	Pinch Hit AB	H	G by POS

Al Niehaus

NIEHAUS, ALBERT BERNARD   BR TR 5'11" 175 lbs.
B. June 1, 1901, Cincinnati, Ohio   D. Oct. 14, 1931, Cincinnati, Ohio

	G	AB	H	2B	3B	HR	HR %	R	RBI	BB	SO	SB	BA	SA	PH AB	PH H	G by POS
1925 2 teams		PIT	N	(17G – .219)				CIN	N	(51G – .299)							
" total	68	211	58	18	2	0	0.0	23	21	14	15	1	.275	.379	8	3	1B-60

Bert Niehoff

NIEHOFF, JOHN ALBERT   BR TR 5'10½" 170 lbs.
B. May 13, 1884, Louisville, Colo.   D. Dec. 8, 1974, Inglewood, Calif.

	G	AB	H	2B	3B	HR	HR %	R	RBI	BB	SO	SB	BA	SA	PH AB	PH H	G by POS
1913 CIN N	2	8	0	0	0	0	0.0	0	0	0	2	0	.000	.000	0	0	3B-2
1914	142	484	117	16	9	4	0.8	46	49	38	77	20	.242	.337	5	2	3B-134, 2B-3
1915 PHI N	148	529	126	27	2	2	0.4	61	49	30	63	21	.238	.308	0	0	2B-148
1916	146	548	133	42	4	4	0.7	65	61	37	57	20	.243	.356	0	0	2B-146, 3B-1
1917	114	361	92	17	4	2	0.6	30	42	23	29	8	.255	.341	7	0	2B-96, 1B-7, 3B-6
1918 2 teams		STL	N	(22G – .179)				NY	N	(7G – .261)							
" total	29	107	21	2	0	0	0.0	8	6	3	14	2	.196	.215	0	0	2B-29
6 yrs.	581	2037	489	104	19	12	0.6	210	207	131	242	71	.240	.327	12	2	2B-422, 3B-143, 1B-7
WORLD SERIES																	
1915 PHI N	5	16	1	0	0	0	0.0	0	1	0	5	0	.063	.063	0	0	2B-5

Milt Nielsen

NIELSEN, MILTON ROBERT   BL TL 5'11" 190 lbs.
B. Feb. 8, 1925, Tyler, Minn.

	G	AB	H	2B	3B	HR	HR %	R	RBI	BB	SO	SB	BA	SA	PH AB	PH H	G by POS
1949 CLE A	3	9	1	0	0	0	0.0	1	0	2	4	0	.111	.111	0	0	OF-3
1951	16	6	0	0	0	0	0.0	1	0	1	1	0	.000	.000	6	0	
2 yrs.	19	15	1	0	0	0	0.0	2	0	3	5	0	.067	.067	6	0	OF-3

Bob Nieman

NIEMAN, ROBERT CHARLES   BR TR 5'11" 195 lbs.
B. Jan. 26, 1927, Cincinnati, Ohio

	G	AB	H	2B	3B	HR	HR %	R	RBI	BB	SO	SB	BA	SA	PH AB	PH H	G by POS
1951 STL A	12	43	16	3	1	2	4.7	6	8	3	5	0	.372	.628	1	1	OF-11
1952	131	478	138	22	2	18	3.8	66	74	46	73	0	.289	.456	9	1	OF-125
1953 DET A	142	508	143	32	5	15	3.0	72	69	57	57	0	.281	.453	7	1	OF-135
1954	91	251	66	14	1	8	3.2	24	35	22	32	0	.263	.422	26	8	OF-62
1955 CHI A	99	272	77	11	2	11	4.0	36	53	36	37	1	.283	.460	24	7	OF-78
1956 2 teams		CHI	A	(14G – .300)				BAL	A	(114G – .322)							
" total	128	428	137	21	6	14	3.3	63	68	90	63	1	.320	.495	1	1	OF-124
1957 BAL A	129	445	123	17	6	13	2.9	61	70	63	86	4	.276	.429	9	0	OF-120
1958	105	366	119	20	2	16	4.4	56	60	44	57	2	.325	.522	6	1	OF-100
1959	118	360	105	18	2	21	5.8	49	60	42	55	1	.292	.528	17	4	OF-97
1960 STL N	81	188	54	13	5	4	2.1	19	31	24	31	0	.287	.473	26	4	OF-55
1961 2 teams		STL	N	(6G – .471)				CLE	A	(39G – .354)							
" total	45	82	31	7	0	2	2.4	2	12	7	6	1	.378	.537	27	9	OF-16
1962 2 teams		CLE	A	(2G – .000)				SF	N	(30G – .300)							
" total	32	31	9	2	0	1	3.2	1	4	1	10	0	.290	.452	30	8	OF-3
12 yrs.	1113	3452	1018	180	32	125	3.6	455	544	435	512	10	.295	.474	183	45	OF-926
WORLD SERIES																	
1962 SF N	1	0	0	0	0	0	–	0	0	1	0	0	–	–	0	0	

Butch Nieman

NIEMAN, ELMER LeROY   BL TL 6'2" 195 lbs.
B. Feb. 8, 1918, Herkimer, Kans.

	G	AB	H	2B	3B	HR	HR %	R	RBI	BB	SO	SB	BA	SA	PH AB	PH H	G by POS
1943 BOS N	101	335	84	15	8	7	2.1	39	46	39	39	4	.251	.406	2	0	OF-93
1944	134	468	124	16	6	16	3.4	65	65	47	47	5	.265	.427	9	2	OF-126
1945	97	247	61	15	0	14	5.7	43	56	43	33	11	.247	.478	36	11	OF-57
3 yrs.	332	1050	269	46	14	37	3.5	147	167	129	119	20	.256	.432	47	13	OF-276

Al Niemiec

NIEMIEC, ALFRED JOSEPH   BR TR 5'11" 158 lbs.
B. May 18, 1911, Meriden, Conn.

	G	AB	H	2B	3B	HR	HR %	R	RBI	BB	SO	SB	BA	SA	PH AB	PH H	G by POS
1934 BOS A	9	32	7	0	0	0	0.0	2	3	3	4	0	.219	.219	0	0	2B-9
1936 PHI A	69	203	40	3	2	1	0.5	22	20	26	16	2	.197	.246	10	1	2B-52, SS-5
2 yrs.	78	235	47	3	2	1	0.4	24	23	29	20	2	.200	.243	10	1	2B-61, SS-5

Tom Nieto

NIETO, THOMAS ANDREW   BR TR 6'1" 205 lbs.
B. Oct. 27, 1960, Downey, Calif.

	G	AB	H	2B	3B	HR	HR %	R	RBI	BB	SO	SB	BA	SA	PH AB	PH H	G by POS
1984 STL N	33	86	24	4	0	3	3.5	7	12	5	18	0	.279	.430	2	0	C-32

Tom Niland

NILAND, THOMAS JAMES (Honest Tom)   BR TR 5'11" 160 lbs.
B. Apr. 14, 1870, Brookfield, Mass.   D. Apr. 30, 1950, Lynn, Mass.

	G	AB	H	2B	3B	HR	HR %	R	RBI	BB	SO	SB	BA	SA	PH AB	PH H	G by POS
1896 STL N	18	68	12	0	1	0	0.0	3	3	5	4	0	.176	.206	0	0	OF-13, SS-5

Billy Niles

NILES, WILLIAM A.   BR TR
B. 1869, Covington, Ky.   D. June 1, 1937, Houston, Tex.

	G	AB	H	2B	3B	HR	HR %	R	RBI	BB	SO	SB	BA	SA	PH AB	PH H	G by POS
1895 PIT N	11	37	8	0	0	0	0.0	2	0	5	2	2	.216	.216	0	0	3B-10, 2B-1

Harry Niles

NILES, HARRY CLYDE   BR TR
B. Sept. 10, 1880, Buchanan, Mich.   D. Apr. 18, 1953, Sturgis, Mich.

	G	AB	H	2B	3B	HR	HR %	R	RBI	BB	SO	SB	BA	SA	PH AB	PH H	G by POS
1906 STL A	142	541	124	14	4	2	0.4	71	31	46		30	.229	.281	0	0	OF-108, 3B-34
1907	120	492	142	9	5	2	0.4	65	35	28		19	.289	.339	3	2	2B-116, OF-1
1908 2 teams		NY	A	(96G – .249)				BOS	A	(17G – .273)							
" total	113	394	99	14	6	5	1.3	47	27	31		21	.251	.355	5	0	2B-93, OF-7, SS-2
1909 BOS A	145	546	134	12	5	1	0.2	64	38	39		27	.245	.291	1	1	OF-117, 3B-13, SS-9, 2B-5
1910 2 teams		BOS	A	(18G – .211)				CLE	A	(70G – .213)							
" total	88	297	63	9	4	2	0.7	31	21	19		10	.212	.290	8	2	OF-71, SS-7, 3B-5
5 yrs.	608	2270	562	58	24	12	0.5	278	152	163		107	.248	.310	17	5	OF-304, 2B-214, 3B-52, SS-18

Rabbit Nill

NILL, GEORGE CHARLES   BR TR 5'7" 160 lbs.
B. July 14, 1881, Fort Wayne, Ind.   D. May 24, 1962, Fort Wayne, Ind.

	G	AB	H	2B	3B	HR	HR %	R	RBI	BB	SO	SB	BA	SA	PH AB	PH H	G by POS
1904 WAS A	15	48	8	0	1	0	0.0	4	3	5		0	.167	.208	0	0	2B-15
1905	103	319	58	7	3	3	0.9	46	31	33		12	.182	.251	10	3	3B-54, 2B-33, SS-6

	G	AB	H	2B	3B	HR	HR %	R	RBI	BB	SO	SB	BA	SA	Pinch Hit AB	Pinch Hit H	G by POS

Rabbit Nill continued

	G	AB	H	2B	3B	HR	HR %	R	RBI	BB	SO	SB	BA	SA	PH AB	PH H	G by POS
1906	89	315	74	8	2	0	0.0	37	15	47		16	.235	.273	2	0	SS-31, 2B-25, OF-15, 3B-15
1907 2 teams	WAS A (66G – .219)					CLE A (12G – .279)											
" total	78	258	59	8	3	0	0.0	26	27	18		8	.229	.283	8	2	2B-32, OF-25, 3B-10, SS-2
1908 CLE A	10	23	5	0	0	0	0.0	3	1	0		0	.217	.217	1	0	SS-6, OF-2, 2B-1
5 yrs.	295	963	204	23	9	3	0.3	116	77	103		36	.212	.264	21	5	2B-106, 3B-79, SS-45, OF-42

Al Nixon

NIXON, ALBERT RICHARD   BR TL 5'7½" 164 lbs.
B. Apr. 11, 1886, Atlantic City, N. J.   D. Nov. 9, 1960, Opelousas, La.

	G	AB	H	2B	3B	HR	HR %	R	RBI	BB	SO	SB	BA	SA	PH AB	PH H	G by POS
1915 BKN N	14	26	6	1	0	0	0.0	3	2	2	4	1	.231	.269	2	1	OF-14
1916	1	2	2	0	0	0	0.0	0	0	0	0	0	1.000	1.000	1	1	OF-1
1918	6	11	5	0	0	0	0.0	1	0	0	0	0	.455	.455	1	1	OF-4
1921 BOS N	55	138	33	6	3	1	0.7	25	9	7	11	3	.239	.348	6	1	OF-45
1922	86	318	84	14	4	2	0.6	35	22	9	19	6	.264	.352	6	2	OF-79
1923	88	321	88	12	4	0	0.0	53	19	24	14	2	.274	.336	1	0	OF-80
1926 PHI N	93	311	91	18	2	4	1.3	38	41	13	20	5	.293	.402	3	0	OF-88
1927	54	154	48	7	0	0	0.0	18	18	5	5	1	.312	.357	5	1	OF-44
1928	25	64	15	2	0	0	0.0	7	7	6	4	1	.234	.266	3	1	OF-20
9 yrs.	422	1345	372	60	13	7	0.5	180	118	66	77	19	.277	.356	27	7	OF-375

Otis Nixon

NIXON, OTIS JUNIOR   BB TR 6'2" 175 lbs.
B. Jan. 9, 1959, Columbus County, N. C.

	G	AB	H	2B	3B	HR	HR %	R	RBI	BB	SO	SB	BA	SA	PH AB	PH H	G by POS
1983 NY A	13	14	2	0	0	0	0.0	2	0	1	5	2	.143	.143	0	0	OF-9
1984 CLE A	49	91	14	0	0	0	0.0	16	1	8	11	12	.154	.154	0	0	OF-46
2 yrs.	62	105	16	0	0	0	0.0	18	1	9	16	14	.152	.152	0	0	OF-55

Russ Nixon

NIXON, RUSSELL EUGENE   BL TR 6'1" 195 lbs.
B. Feb. 19, 1935, Cleveland, Ohio
Manager 1982-83.

	G	AB	H	2B	3B	HR	HR %	R	RBI	BB	SO	SB	BA	SA	PH AB	PH H	G by POS
1957 CLE A	62	185	52	7	1	2	1.1	15	18	12	12	0	.281	.362	8	1	C-57
1958	113	376	113	17	4	9	2.4	42	46	13	38	0	.301	.439	18	4	C-101
1959	82	258	62	10	3	1	0.4	23	29	15	28	0	.240	.314	9	2	C-74
1960 2 teams	CLE A (25G – .244)					BOS A (80G – .298)											
" total	105	354	101	22	3	6	1.7	30	39	19	29	0	.285	.415	11	2	C-99
1961 BOS A	87	242	70	12	2	1	0.4	24	19	13	19	0	.289	.368	18	8	C-66
1962	65	151	42	7	2	1	0.7	11	19	8	14	0	.278	.371	28	10	C-38
1963	98	287	77	18	1	5	1.7	27	30	22	32	0	.268	.390	25	6	C-76
1964	81	163	38	7	0	1	0.6	10	20	14	29	0	.233	.294	34	9	C-45
1965	59	137	37	5	1	0	0.0	11	11	6	23	0	.270	.321	24	5	C-38
1966 MIN A	51	96	25	2	1	0	0.0	5	7	7	13	0	.260	.302	22	5	C-32
1967	74	170	40	6	1	1	0.6	16	22	18	29	0	.235	.300	19	4	C-69
1968 BOS A	29	85	13	2	0	0	0.0	1	6	7	13	0	.153	.176	2	1	C-27
12 yrs.	906	2504	670	115	19	27	1.1	215	266	154	279	0	.268	.361	218	59	C-722

Ray Noble

NOBLE, RAFAEL MIGUEL   BR TR 5'11½" 185 lbs.
B. Mar. 15, 1922, Central Hatillo, Cuba

	G	AB	H	2B	3B	HR	HR %	R	RBI	BB	SO	SB	BA	SA	PH AB	PH H	G by POS
1951 NY N	55	141	33	6	0	5	3.5	16	26	6	26	0	.234	.383	18	3	C-41
1952	6	5	0	0	0	0	0.0	0	0	0	1	0	.000	.000	1	0	C-5
1953	46	97	20	0	1	4	4.1	15	14	19	14	1	.206	.351	4	0	C-41
3 yrs.	107	243	53	6	1	9	3.7	31	40	25	41	1	.218	.362	23	3	C-87

WORLD SERIES

	G	AB	H	2B	3B	HR	HR %	R	RBI	BB	SO	SB	BA	SA	PH AB	PH H	G by POS
1951 NY N	2	2	0	0	0	0	0.0	0	0	0	1	0	.000	.000	2	0	C-2

Junior Noboa

NOBOA, MILICADES ARTURO   BR TR 5'10" 155 lbs.
B. Nov. 10, 1964, Azua, Dominican Republic

	G	AB	H	2B	3B	HR	HR %	R	RBI	BB	SO	SB	BA	SA	PH AB	PH H	G by POS
1984 CLE A	23	11	4	0	0	0	0.0	3	0	0	1	0	.364	.364	0	0	2B-19, DH-1

George Noftsker

NOFTSKER, GEORGE WASHINGTON   BR TR 5'8" 135 lbs.
B. Aug. 24, 1859, Shippensburg, Pa.   D. May 8, 1931, Shippensburg, Pa.

	G	AB	H	2B	3B	HR	HR %	R	RBI	BB	SO	SB	BA	SA	PH AB	PH H	G by POS
1884 ALT U	7	25	1	0	0	0	0.0						.040	.040	0	0	OF-5, C-3

Joe Nolan

NOLAN, JOSEPH WILLIAM JR.   BL TR 5'11" 175 lbs.
B. May 12, 1951, St. Louis, Mo.

	G	AB	H	2B	3B	HR	HR %	R	RBI	BB	SO	SB	BA	SA	PH AB	PH H	G by POS
1972 NY N	4	10	0	0	0	0	0.0	0	0	1	3	0	.000	.000	1	0	C-3
1975 ATL N	4	4	1	0	0	0	0.0	0	0	1	0	0	.250	.250	3	1	C-1
1977	62	82	23	3	0	3	3.7	13	9	13	12	1	.280	.427	39	14	C-19
1978	95	213	49	7	3	4	1.9	22	22	34	28	3	.230	.347	34	6	C-61
1979	89	230	57	9	3	4	1.7	28	21	27	28	1	.248	.365	14	1	C-74
1980 2 teams	ATL N (17G – .273)					CIN N (53G – .312)											
" total	70	176	54	8	0	3	1.7	16	26	15	12	0	.307	.403	15	3	C-57
1981 CIN N	81	236	73	18	1	1	0.4	25	26	24	19	1	.309	.407	9	3	C-81
1982 BAL A	77	219	51	7	1	6	2.7	24	35	16	35	1	.233	.356	12	2	C-72
1983	73	184	51	11	1	5	2.7	25	24	16	31	0	.277	.429	12	2	C-65
1984	35	62	18	1	1	1	1.6	2	9	12	10	0	.290	.387	15	4	DH-11, C-6
10 yrs.	590	1416	377	64	10	27	1.9	155	172	159	178	7	.266	.383	154	35	C-439, DH-11

LEAGUE CHAMPIONSHIP SERIES

	G	AB	H	2B	3B	HR	HR %	R	RBI	BB	SO	SB	BA	SA	PH AB	PH H	G by POS
1983 BAL A	1	0	0	0	0	0	–	0	1	0	0	0	–	–	0	0	

WORLD SERIES

	G	AB	H	2B	3B	HR	HR %	R	RBI	BB	SO	SB	BA	SA	PH AB	PH H	G by POS
1983 BAL A	2	2	0	0	0	0	0.0	0	0	1	0	0	.000	.000	1	0	C-2

	G	AB	H	2B	3B	HR	HR %	R	RBI	BB	SO	SB	BA	SA	Pinch Hit AB	Pinch Hit H	G by POS

The Only Nolan

NOLAN, EDWARD SYLVESTER
B. Nov. 7, 1857, Paterson, N. J.   D. May 18, 1913, Paterson, N. J.   BR TR 5'8"   171 lbs.

	G	AB	H	2B	3B	HR	HR %	R	RBI	BB	SO	SB	BA	SA	PH AB	PH H	G by POS
1878 IND N	38	152	37	8	0	0	0.0	11	16	2	10		.243	.296	0	0	P-38, OF-1
1881 CLE N	41	168	41	5	1	0	0.0	12	18	4	13		.244	.286	0	0	P-22, OF-14, 3B-6
1883 PIT AA	7	26	8	1	0	0	0.0	4		1			.308	.346	0	0	P-7, OF-1
1884 WIL U	9	33	9	2	1	0	0.0	5		2			.273	.394	0	0	P-5, OF-4
1885 PHI N	7	26	2	1	0	0	0.0	1		3	8		.077	.115	0	0	P-7, OF-1
5 yrs.	102	405	97	17	2	0	0.0	33	34	12	31		.240	.291	0	0	P-79, OF-21, 3B-6

Red Nonnenkamp

NONNENKAMP, LEO WILLIAM
B. July 7, 1911, St. Louis, Mo.   BL TL 5'11"   165 lbs.

	G	AB	H	2B	3B	HR	HR %	R	RBI	BB	SO	SB	BA	SA	PH AB	PH H	G by POS
1933 PIT N	1	1	0	0	0	0	0.0	0	0	0	1	0	.000	.000	1	0	
1938 BOS A	87	180	51	4	1	0	0.0	37	18	21	13	6	.283	.317	34	10	OF-39, 1B-5
1939	58	75	18	2	1	0	0.0	12	5	12	6	0	.240	.293	34	9	OF-15
1940	9	7	0	0	0	0	0.0	0	1	1	4	0	.000	.000	7	0	
4 yrs.	155	263	69	6	2	0	0.0	49	24	34	24	6	.262	.300	76	19	OF-54, 1B-5

Pete Noonan

NOONAN, PETER JOHN
B. Nov. 24, 1881, W. Stockbridge, Mass.   D. Jan. 11, 1965, Pittsfield, Mass.   BR TR 6'   180 lbs.

	G	AB	H	2B	3B	HR	HR %	R	RBI	BB	SO	SB	BA	SA	PH AB	PH H	G by POS
1904 PHI A	39	114	23	3	1	2	1.8	13	13	1		1	.202	.298	6	1	C-22, 1B-10
1906 2 teams		CHI N (5G – .333)				STL N (44G – .168)											
" total	49	128	22	1	3	1	0.8	8	9	11		1	.172	.250	8	2	C-23, 1B-17
1907 STL N	74	236	53	7	3	1	0.4	19	16	9		3	.225	.292	5	1	C-70
3 yrs.	162	478	98	11	7	4	0.8	40	38	21		5	.205	.282	19	4	C-115, 1B-27

Tim Nordbrook

NORDBROOK, TIMOTHY CHARLES
B. July 4, 1949, Baltimore, Md.   BR TR 6'1"   180 lbs.

	G	AB	H	2B	3B	HR	HR %	R	RBI	BB	SO	SB	BA	SA	PH AB	PH H	G by POS
1974 BAL A	6	15	4	0	0	0	0.0	4	1	2	2	1	.267	.267	0	0	SS-5, 2B-1
1975	40	34	4	1	0	0	0.0	6	0	7	7	0	.118	.147	0	0	SS-73
1976 2 teams		BAL A (27G – .227)				CAL A (5G – .000)											
" total	32	30	5	0	0	0	0.0	5	0	4	8	1	.167	.167	0	0	SS-16, 2B-15, DH-1
1977 2 teams		CHI A (15G – .000)				TOR A (24G – .175)											
" total	39	83	16	0	1	0	0.0	11	2	11	15	2	.193	.217	12	3	SS-35, DH-2, 3B-1
1978 2 teams		TOR A (7G – .000)				MIL A (2G – .000)											
" total	9	5	0	0	0	0	0.0	1	0	1	1	0	.000	.000	0	0	SS-9
1979 MIL A	2	2	1	0	0	0	0.0	0	0	0	0	0	.500	.500	0	0	SS-2
6 yrs.	128	169	30	1	1	0	0.0	27	3	25	33	4	.178	.195	12	3	SS-140, 2B-16, DH-3, 3B-1

Wayne Nordhagen

NORDHAGEN, WAYNE OREN
B. July 4, 1948, Thief River Falls, Minn.   BR TR 6'2"   205 lbs.

	G	AB	H	2B	3B	HR	HR %	R	RBI	BB	SO	SB	BA	SA	PH AB	PH H	G by POS
1976 CHI A	22	53	10	2	0	0	0.0	6	5	4	12	0	.189	.226	2	0	OF-10, DH-6, C-5
1977	52	124	39	7	3	4	3.2	16	22	2	12	1	.315	.516	7	2	OF-46, C-3, DH-2
1978	68	206	62	16	0	5	2.4	28	35	5	18	0	.301	.451	15	6	OF-36, DH-16, C-12
1979	78	193	54	15	0	7	3.6	20	25	13	22	0	.280	.466	21	7	DH-47, OF-12, C-5, P-2
1980	123	415	115	22	4	15	3.6	45	59	10	45	0	.277	.458	21	5	OF-74, DH-32
1981	65	208	64	8	1	6	2.9	19	33	10	25	0	.308	.442	7	1	OF-60
1982 2 teams		TOR A (72G – .270)				PIT N (1G – .500)											
" total	73	189	52	6	0	1	0.5	12	22	10	23	0	.275	.323	26	11	OF-60, 1B-10, OF-1
1983 CHI N	21	35	5	1	0	1	2.9	1	4	0	5	0	.143	.257	15	2	OF-7
8 yrs.	502	1423	401	77	8	39	2.7	147	205	54	162	1	.282	.429	114	34	OF-246, DH-163, C-25, 1B-10, P-2

Lou Nordyke

NORDYKE, LOUIS ELLIS
B. Aug. 7, 1876, Brighton, Iowa   D. Sept. 27, 1945, Los Angeles, Calif.   BR TR

	G	AB	H	2B	3B	HR	HR %	R	RBI	BB	SO	SB	BA	SA	PH AB	PH H	G by POS
1906 STL A	25	53	13	1	0	0	0.0	4	7	10		3	.245	.264	12	3	1B-12

Irv Noren

NOREN, IRVING ARNOLD
B. Nov. 29, 1924, Jamestown, N. Y.   BL TL 6'   190 lbs.

	G	AB	H	2B	3B	HR	HR %	R	RBI	BB	SO	SB	BA	SA	PH AB	PH H	G by POS
1950 WAS A	138	542	160	27	10	14	2.6	80	98	67	77	5	.295	.459	0	0	OF-121, 1B-17
1951	129	509	142	33	5	8	1.6	82	86	51	35	10	.279	.411	3	0	OF-126
1952 2 teams		WAS A (12G – .245)				NY A (93G – .235)											
" total	105	321	76	16	3	5	1.6	40	23	32	37	5	.237	.352	18	3	OF-72, 1B-19
1953 NY A	109	345	92	12	6	6	1.7	55	46	42	39	3	.267	.388	15	3	OF-96
1954	125	426	136	21	6	12	2.8	70	66	43	38	4	.319	.481	12	3	OF-116, 1B-1
1955	132	371	94	19	1	8	2.2	49	59	43	33	5	.253	.375	11	1	OF-126
1956	29	37	8	1	0	0	0.0	4	6	12	7	0	.216	.243	13	4	OF-10, 1B-1
1957 2 teams		KC A (81G – .213)				STL N (17G – .367)											
" total	98	190	45	12	1	3	1.6	11	26	15	25	0	.237	.358	54	13	1B-25, OF-14
1958 STL N	117	178	47	9	1	4	2.2	24	22	13	21	0	.264	.393	43	8	OF-77
1959 2 teams		STL N (8G – .125)				CHI N (65G – .321)											
" total	73	164	51	7	2	4	2.4	27	19	13	26	2	.311	.451	29	12	OF-42, 1B-2
1960 2 teams		CHI N (12G – .091)				LA N (26G – .200)											
" total	38	36	6	0	1	2	2.8	4	4	4	12	0	.167	.250	32	5	OF-1, 1B-1
11 yrs.	1093	3119	857	157	35	65	2.1	443	453	335	350	34	.275	.410	230	52	OF-801, 1B-66
WORLD SERIES																	
1952 NY A	4	10	3	0	0	0	0.0	0	1	1	3	0	.300	.300	1	1	OF-3
1953	2	1	0	0	0	0	0.0	0	0	1	0	0	.000	.000	1	0	
1955	5	16	1	0	0	0	0.0	0	1	1	1	0	.063	.063	0	0	OF-5
3 yrs.	11	27	4	0	0	0	0.0	0	2	3	4	0	.148	.148	2	1	OF-8

Bill Norman

NORMAN, HENRY WILLIS PATRICK
B. July 16, 1910, St. Louis, Mo.   D. Apr. 21, 1962, Milwaukee, Wis.   BR TR 6'2"   190 lbs.
Manager 1958-59.

	G	AB	H	2B	3B	HR	HR %	R	RBI	BB	SO	SB	BA	SA	PH AB	PH H	G by POS
1931 CHI A	24	55	10	2	0	0	0.0	7	6	4	10	0	.182	.218	4	0	OF-17
1932	13	48	11	3	1	0	0.0	6	2	2	3	0	.229	.333	0	0	OF-13
2 yrs.	37	103	21	5	1	0	0.0	13	8	6	13	0	.204	.272	4	0	OF-30

	G	AB	H	2B	3B	HR	HR %	R	RBI	BB	SO	SB	BA	SA	Pinch Hit AB	H	G by POS

Dan Norman

NORMAN, DANIEL EDMUND
B. Jan. 11, 1955, Los Angeles, Calif.

BR TR 6'2" 195 lbs.

	G	AB	H	2B	3B	HR	HR %	R	RBI	BB	SO	SB	BA	SA	AB	H	G by POS
1977 NY N	7	16	4	1	0	0	0.0	2	0	4	2	0	.250	.313	1	0	OF-6
1978	19	64	17	0	1	4	6.3	7	10	2	14	1	.266	.484	1	0	OF-18
1979	44	110	27	3	1	3	2.7	9	11	10	26	2	.245	.373	13	3	OF-33
1980	69	92	17	1	1	2	2.2	5	9	6	14	5	.185	.283	47	8	OF-31
1982 MON N	53	66	14	3	0	2	3.0	6	7	7	20	0	.212	.348	21	3	OF-107
5 yrs.	192	348	79	8	3	11	3.2	29	37	29	76	8	.227	.362	83	14	OF-107

Nelson Norman

NORMAN, NELSON AUGUSTO (Gus)
B. May 23, 1958, San Pedro de Macoris, Dominican Republic

BR TR 6'2" 160 lbs.

	G	AB	H	2B	3B	HR	HR %	R	RBI	BB	SO	SB	BA	SA	AB	H	G by POS
1978 TEX A	23	34	9	2	0	0	0.0	1	1	0	5	0	.265	.324	0	0	SS-18, 3B-6
1979	147	343	76	9	3	0	0.0	36	21	19	41	4	.222	.265	1	0	SS-142, 2B-1
1980	17	32	7	0	0	0	0.0	4	1	1	1	0	.219	.219	0	0	SS-17
1981	7	13	3	1	0	0	0.0	1	2	1	2	0	.231	.308	0	0	SS-5
1982 PIT N	3	3	0	0	0	0	0.0	0	0	0	0	0	.000	.000	0	0	2B-2, SS-1
5 yrs.	197	425	95	12	3	0	0.0	42	25	21	49	4	.224	.266	1	0	SS-183, 3B-6, 2B-3

Jim Norris

NORRIS, JAMES FRANCIS
B. Dec. 20, 1948, Brooklyn, N. Y.

BL TL 5'10" 175 lbs.

	G	AB	H	2B	3B	HR	HR %	R	RBI	BB	SO	SB	BA	SA	AB	H	G by POS
1977 CLE A	133	440	119	23	6	2	0.5	59	37	64	57	26	.270	.364	10	5	OF-124, 1B-3
1978	113	315	89	14	5	2	0.6	41	27	42	20	12	.283	.378	20	5	OF-78, DH-15, 1B-6
1979	124	353	87	15	6	3	0.8	50	30	44	35	15	.246	.348	18	4	OF-93, DH-13
1980 TEX A	119	174	43	5	0	0	0.0	23	16	23	16	6	.247	.276	31	9	OF-82, 1B-10, DH-1
4 yrs.	489	1282	338	57	17	7	0.5	173	110	173	128	59	.264	.351	79	23	OF-377, DH-29, 1B-19

Leo Norris

NORRIS, LEO JOHN
B. May 17, 1908, Bay St. Louis, Miss.

BR TR 5'11" 165 lbs.

	G	AB	H	2B	3B	HR	HR %	R	RBI	BB	SO	SB	BA	SA	AB	H	G by POS
1936 PHI N	154	581	154	27	4	11	1.9	64	76	39	79	4	.265	.382	0	0	SS-121, 2B-38
1937	116	381	98	24	3	9	2.4	45	36	21	53	3	.257	.407	5	0	2B-74, 3B-24, SS-20
2 yrs.	270	962	252	51	7	20	2.1	109	112	60	132	7	.262	.392	5	0	SS-141, 2B-112, 3B-24

Billy North

NORTH, WILLIAM ALEX
B. May 15, 1948, Seattle, Wash.

BB TR 5'11" 185 lbs.

	G	AB	H	2B	3B	HR	HR %	R	RBI	BB	SO	SB	BA	SA	AB	H	G by POS
1971 CHI N	8	16	6	0	0	0	0.0	3	0	4	6	1	.375	.375	0	0	OF-6
1972	66	127	23	2	3	0	0.0	22	4	13	33	6	.181	.244	13	3	OF-48
1973 OAK A	146	554	158	10	5	5	0.9	98	34	78	89	53	.285	.348	2	0	OF-138, DH-6
1974	149	543	141	20	5	4	0.7	79	33	69	86	54	.260	.337	1	1	OF-138, DH-8
1975	140	524	143	17	5	1	0.2	74	43	81	80	30	.273	.330	1	1	OF-138, DH-1
1976	154	590	163	20	5	2	0.3	91	31	73	95	75	.276	.337	1	0	OF-144, DH-8
1977	56	184	48	3	3	1	0.5	32	9	32	25	17	.261	.326	4	0	OF-52, DH-1
1978 2 teams		OAK A (24G – .212)				LA N (110G – .234)											
" total	134	356	82	14	0	0	0.0	59	15	74	61	30	.230	.270	9	4	OF-120
1979 SF N	142	460	119	15	4	5	1.1	87	30	96	84	58	.259	.341	11	1	OF-130
1980	128	415	104	12	1	1	0.2	73	19	81	78	45	.251	.292	19	5	OF-115
1981	46	131	29	7	0	1	0.8	22	12	26	28	26	.221	.298	7	1	OF-37
11 yrs.	1169	3900	1016	120	31	20	0.5	640	230	627	665	395	.261	.323	68	16	OF-1066, DH-24
LEAGUE CHAMPIONSHIP SERIES																	
1974 OAK A	4	16	1	1	0	0	0.0	3	0	2	1	1	.063	.125	0	0	OF-4
1975	3	10	0	0	0	0	0.0	0	1	2	0	0	.000	.000	0	0	OF-3
1978 LA N	4	8	0	0	0	0	0.0	0	0	0	1	0	.000	.000	0	0	OF-4
3 yrs.	11	34	1	1	0	0	0.0	3	1	4	2	1	.029	.059	0	0	OF-11
WORLD SERIES																	
1974 OAK A	5	17	1	0	0	0	0.0	3	0	2	5	1	.059	.059	0	0	OF-5
1978 LA N	4	8	1	1	0	0	0.0	2	2	1	0	1	.125	.250	1	1	
2 yrs.	9	25	2	1	0	0	0.0	5	2	3	5	2	.080	.120	1	1	OF-5

Hub Northen

NORTHEN, HUBBARD ELWIN
B. Aug. 16, 1885, Atlanta, Tex.   D. Oct. 1, 1947, Shreveport, La.

BL TL 5'8" 175 lbs.

	G	AB	H	2B	3B	HR	HR %	R	RBI	BB	SO	SB	BA	SA	AB	H	G by POS
1910 STL A	26	96	19	1	0	0	0.0	6	16	5		2	.198	.208	0	0	OF-26
1911 2 teams		CIN N (1G – .000)				BKN N (19G – .316)											
" total	20	76	24	2	2	0	0.0	16	1	14	9	4	.316	.395	0	0	OF-19
1912 BKN N	118	412	116	26	6	2	0.5	54	46	41	46	8	.282	.388	15	4	OF-102
3 yrs.	164	584	159	29	8	2	0.3	76	63	60	55	14	.272	.360	15	4	OF-147

Ron Northey

NORTHEY, RONALD JAMES (The Round Man)
Father of Scott Northey.
B. Apr. 26, 1920, Mahanoy City, Pa.   D. Apr. 16, 1971, Pittsburgh, Pa.

BL TR 5'10" 195 lbs.

	G	AB	H	2B	3B	HR	HR %	R	RBI	BB	SO	SB	BA	SA	AB	H	G by POS
1942 PHI N	127	402	101	13	2	5	1.2	31	31	28	33	2	.251	.331	17	4	OF-109
1943	147	586	163	31	5	16	2.7	72	68	51	52	2	.278	.430	2	0	OF-145
1944	152	570	164	35	9	22	3.9	72	104	67	51	1	.288	.496	1	0	OF-151
1946	128	438	109	24	6	16	3.7	55	62	39	59	1	.249	.441	14	5	OF-111
1947 2 teams		PHI N (13G – .255)				STL N (110G – .293)											
" total	123	358	103	22	3	15	4.2	59	66	54	32	1	.288	.492	13	3	OF-107, 3B-2
1948 STL N	96	246	79	10	1	13	5.3	40	64	38	25	0	.321	.528	25	11	OF-67
1949	90	265	69	18	2	7	2.6	28	50	31	15	0	.260	.423	12	0	OF-73
1950 2 teams		CIN N (27G – .260)				CHI N (53G – .281)											
" total	80	191	52	14	0	9	4.7	22	29	25	15	0	.272	.487	27	5	OF-51
1952 CHI N	1	1	0	0	0	0	0.0	0	0	0	0	0	.000	.000	1	0	
1955 CHI A	14	14	5	2	0	1	7.1	1	4	3	3	0	.357	.714	10	4	OF-2
1956	53	48	17	2	0	3	6.3	4	23	8	1	0	.354	.583	39	15	OF-4
1957 2 teams		CHI A (40G – .185)				PHI N (33G – .269)											
" total	73	53	12	1	0	1	1.9	1	12	17	11	0	.226	.302	53	12	
12 yrs.	1084	3172	874	172	28	108	3.4	385	513	361	297	7	.276	.450	214	59	OF-820, 3B-2

	G	AB	H	2B	3B	HR	HR %	R	RBI	BB	SO	SB	BA	SA	Pinch Hit AB	H	G by POS

Scott Northey

NORTHEY, SCOTT RICHARD
Son of Ron Northey.
B. Oct. 15, 1946, Philadelphia, Pa.　　BR TR 6'　175 lbs.

	G	AB	H	2B	3B	HR	HR%	R	RBI	BB	SO	SB	BA	SA	AB	H	G by POS
1969 KC A	20	61	16	2	2	1	1.6	11	7	7	19	6	.262	.410	0	0	OF-18

Jim Northrup

NORTHRUP, JAMES THOMAS
B. Nov. 24, 1939, Breckenridge, Mich.　　BL TR 6'3"　190 lbs.

	G	AB	H	2B	3B	HR	HR%	R	RBI	BB	SO	SB	BA	SA	AB	H	G by POS
1964 DET A	5	12	1	1	0	0	0.0	1	0	0	3	1	.083	.167	3	0	OF-2
1965	80	219	45	12	3	2	0.9	20	16	12	50	1	.205	.315	24	3	OF-54
1966	123	419	111	24	6	16	3.8	53	58	33	52	4	.265	.465	10	2	OF-113
1967	144	495	134	18	6	10	2.0	63	61	43	83	7	.271	.392	5	1	OF-143
1968	154	580	153	29	7	21	3.6	76	90	50	87	4	.264	.447	4	0	OF-151
1969	148	543	160	31	5	25	4.6	79	66	52	83	4	.295	.508	5	0	OF-143
1970	139	504	132	21	3	24	4.8	71	80	58	68	3	.262	.458	3	1	OF-136
1971	136	459	124	27	2	16	3.5	72	71	60	43	7	.270	.442	14	5	OF-108, 1B-32
1972	134	426	111	15	2	8	1.9	40	42	38	47	4	.261	.362	14	2	OF-127, 1B-2
1973	119	404	124	14	7	12	3.0	55	44	38	41	4	.307	.465	8	2	OF-116
1974 3 teams	DET A (97G – .237)					MON N (21G – .241)				BAL A	(8G – .571)						
" total	126	437	106	13	1	14	3.2	46	53	43	56	0	.243	.373	10	2	OF-116
1975 BAL A	84	194	53	13	0	5	2.6	27	29	22	22	0	.273	.418	22	8	OF-58, DH-3
12 yrs.	1392	4692	1254	218	42	153	3.3	603	610	449	635	39	.267	.429	122	28	OF-1267, 1B-34, DH-3

LEAGUE CHAMPIONSHIP SERIES

	G	AB	H	2B	3B	HR	HR%	R	RBI	BB	SO	SB	BA	SA	AB	H	G by POS
1972 DET A	5	14	5	0	0	0	0.0	0	1	2	3	0	.357	.357	0	0	OF-5

WORLD SERIES

	G	AB	H	2B	3B	HR	HR%	R	RBI	BB	SO	SB	BA	SA	AB	H	G by POS
1968 DET A	7	28	7	0	1	2	7.1	4	8	1	5	0	.250	.536	0	0	OF-7

Willie Norwood

NORWOOD, WILLIE
B. Nov. 7, 1950, Green County, Ala.　　BR TR 6'　185 lbs.

	G	AB	H	2B	3B	HR	HR%	R	RBI	BB	SO	SB	BA	SA	AB	H	G by POS
1977 MIN A	39	83	19	3	0	3	3.6	15	9	6	17	6	.229	.373	7	1	OF-28, DH-5
1978	125	428	109	22	3	8	1.9	56	46	28	64	25	.255	.376	8	2	OF-115, DH-12
1979	96	270	67	13	3	6	2.2	32	30	20	51	9	.248	.385	14	5	OF-71, DH-14
1980	34	73	12	2	0	1	1.4	6	8	3	13	1	.164	.233	7	2	OF-17, DH-9
4 yrs.	294	854	207	40	6	18	2.1	109	93	57	145	41	.242	.367	36	10	OF-231, DH-40

Joe Nossek

NOSSEK, JOSEPH RUDOLPH
B. Nov. 8, 1940, Cleveland, Ohio　　BR TR 6'　178 lbs.

	G	AB	H	2B	3B	HR	HR%	R	RBI	BB	SO	SB	BA	SA	AB	H	G by POS
1964 MIN A	7	1	0	0	0	0	0.0	0	0	0	0	0	.000	.000	1	0	OF-2
1965	87	170	37	9	0	2	1.2	19	16	7	22	2	.218	.306	28	7	OF-48, 3B-9
1966 2 teams	MIN A (4G – .000)					KC A (87G – .261)											
" total	91	230	60	10	3	1	0.4	13	27	8	21	4	.261	.343	17	8	OF-80, 3B-1
1967 KC A	87	166	34	1	0	0	0.0	12	10	4	26	2	.205	.253	28	1	OF-63
1969 2 teams	OAK A (13G – .000)					STL N (9G – .200)											
" total	22	11	1	0	0	0	0.0	2	0	0	3	0	.091	.091	4	1	OF-13
1970 STL N	1	1	0	0	0	0	0.0	0	0	0	0	0	.000	.000	1	0	
6 yrs.	295	579	132	25	4	3	0.5	47	53	19	72	8	.228	.301	79	17	OF-206, 3B-10

WORLD SERIES

	G	AB	H	2B	3B	HR	HR%	R	RBI	BB	SO	SB	BA	SA	AB	H	G by POS
1965 MIN A	6	20	4	0	0	0	0.0	0	0	0	1	0	.200	.200	1	1	OF-5

Lou Novikoff

NOVIKOFF, LOUIE ALEXANDER (The Mad Russian)
B. Oct. 12, 1915, Glendale, Ariz.　D. Sept. 30, 1970, South Gate, Calif.　BR TR 5'10"　185 lbs.

	G	AB	H	2B	3B	HR	HR%	R	RBI	BB	SO	SB	BA	SA	AB	H	G by POS
1941 CHI N	62	203	49	8	0	5	2.5	22	24	11	15	0	.241	.355	8	3	OF-54
1942	128	483	145	25	5	7	1.4	48	64	24	28	3	.300	.416	8	2	OF-120
1943	78	233	65	7	3	0	0.0	22	28	18	15	0	.279	.335	15	6	OF-61
1944	71	139	39	4	2	3	2.2	15	19	10	11	1	.281	.403	39	12	OF-29
1946 PHI N	17	23	7	1	0	0	0.0	0	3	1	2	0	.304	.348	14	6	OF-3
5 yrs.	356	1081	305	45	10	15	1.4	107	138	64	71	4	.282	.384	84	29	OF-267

Rube Novotney

NOVOTNEY, RALPH JOSEPH
B. Aug. 5, 1924, Streator, Ill.　　BR TR 6'　187 lbs.

	G	AB	H	2B	3B	HR	HR%	R	RBI	BB	SO	SB	BA	SA	AB	H	G by POS
1949 CHI N	22	67	18	2	1	0	0.0	4	6	3	11	0	.269	.328	2	1	C-20

Les Nunamaker

NUNAMAKER, LESLIE GRANT
B. Aug. 25, 1889, Aurora, Neb.　D. Nov. 14, 1938, Hastings, Neb.　BR TR 6'2"　190 lbs.

	G	AB	H	2B	3B	HR	HR%	R	RBI	BB	SO	SB	BA	SA	AB	H	G by POS
1911 BOS A	62	183	47	4	3	0	0.0	18	19	12		1	.257	.311	3	0	C-59
1912	35	103	26	5	2	0	0.0	15	6	6		1	.252	.340	0	0	C-35
1913	29	65	14	5	2	0	0.0	9	9	8	8	2	.215	.354	1	0	C-27
1914 2 teams	BOS A (4G – .200)					NY A (87G – .265)											
" total	91	262	69	10	3	2	0.8	19	29	23	34	11	.263	.347	10	3	C-72, 1B-6
1915 NY A	87	249	56	6	3	0	0.0	24	17	23	24	3	.225	.273	6	2	C-77, 1B-2
1916	91	260	77	14	7	0	0.0	25	28	34	21	4	.296	.404	11	6	C-79
1917	104	310	81	9	2	0	0.0	22	33	21	25	5	.261	.303	13	7	C-91
1918 STL A	85	274	71	9	2	0	0.0	22	22	28	16	6	.259	.307	3	3	C-81, OF-1, 1B-1
1919 CLE A	26	56	14	1	1	0	0.0	6	7	2	6	0	.250	.304	10	3	C-16
1920	34	54	18	3	3	0	0.0	10	14	4	5	1	.333	.500	10	1	C-17, 1B-6
1921	46	131	47	7	2	0	0.0	16	24	11	8	1	.359	.443	0	0	C-41
1922	25	43	13	2	0	0	0.0	8	7	4	3	0	.302	.349	11	3	C-15
12 yrs.	715	1990	533	75	30	2	0.1	194	215	176	150	36	.268	.339	78	28	C-615, 1B-15, OF-1

WORLD SERIES

	G	AB	H	2B	3B	HR	HR%	R	RBI	BB	SO	SB	BA	SA	AB	H	G by POS
1920 CLE A	2	2	1	0	0	0	0.0	0	0	0	0	0	.500	.500	2	1	C-1

Emory Nusz

NUSZ, EMORY MOBERLY
B. Apr. 2, 1866, Frederick, Md.　D. Aug. 3, 1893, Point of Rocks, Md.

	G	AB	H	2B	3B	HR	HR%	R	RBI	BB	SO	SB	BA	SA	AB	H	G by POS
1884 WAS U	1	4	0	0	0	0	0.0	1		0			.000	.000	0	0	OF-1

	G	AB	H	2B	3B	HR	HR %	R	RBI	BB	SO	SB	BA	SA	Pinch Hit AB	Pinch Hit H	G by POS

Dizzy Nutter

NUTTER, EVERETT CLARENCE
B. Aug. 27, 1893, Roseville, Ohio   D. July 25, 1958, Battle Creek, Mich.

BL TR 5'9"   160 lbs.

	G	AB	H	2B	3B	HR	HR %	R	RBI	BB	SO	SB	BA	SA	AB	H	G by POS
1919 BOS N	18	52	11	0	0	0	0.0	4	3	4	5	1	.212	.212	5	0	OF-12

Chris Nyman

NYMAN, CHRISTOPHER CURTIS
Brother of Nyls Nyman.
B. June 6, 1955, Pomona, Calif.

BR TR 6'4"   200 lbs.

	G	AB	H	2B	3B	HR	HR %	R	RBI	BB	SO	SB	BA	SA	AB	H	G by POS
1982 CHI A	28	65	16	1	0	0	0.0	6	2	3	9	3	.246	.262	5	0	1B-24, OF-2
1983	21	28	8	0	0	2	7.1	12	4	4	7	2	.286	.500	0	0	DH-10, 1B-10
2 yrs.	49	93	24	1	0	2	2.2	18	6	7	16	5	.258	.333	5	0	1B-34, DH-10, OF-2

Nyls Nyman

NYMAN, NYLS WALLACE
Also known as Rex Nyman.   Brother of Chris Nyman.
B. Mar. 7, 1954, Detroit, Mich.

BL TL 6'   170 lbs.

	G	AB	H	2B	3B	HR	HR %	R	RBI	BB	SO	SB	BA	SA	AB	H	G by POS
1974 CHI A	5	14	9	2	1	0	0.0	5	4	0	1	1	.643	.929	1	1	OF-3
1975	106	327	74	6	3	2	0.6	36	28	11	34	10	.226	.281	3	1	OF-94, DH-4
1976	8	15	2	1	0	0	0.0	2	1	0	3	1	.133	.200	0	0	OF-7
1977	1	1	0	0	0	0	0.0	0	0	0	0	0	.000	.000	0	0	
4 yrs.	120	357	85	9	4	2	0.6	43	33	11	38	12	.238	.303	4	2	OF-104, DH-4

Rebel Oakes

OAKES, ENNIS TELFLAIR
B. Dec. 17, 1886, Homer, La.   D. Feb. 29, 1948, Shreveport, La.
Manager 1914-15.

BL TR 5'8"   170 lbs.

	G	AB	H	2B	3B	HR	HR %	R	RBI	BB	SO	SB	BA	SA	AB	H	G by POS
1909 CIN N	120	415	112	10	5	3	0.7	55	31	40		23	.270	.340	7	2	OF-113
1910 STL N	131	468	118	14	6	0	0.0	50	43	38	38	18	.252	.308	3	1	OF-127
1911	154	551	145	13	6	2	0.4	69	59	41	35	25	.263	.319	2	1	OF-151
1912	136	495	139	19	5	3	0.6	57	58	31	24	26	.281	.358	1	1	OF-136
1913	146	537	156	14	5	0	0.0	59	49	43	32	22	.291	.335	2	1	OF-144
1914 PIT F	145	571	178	18	10	7	1.2	82	75	35		28	.312	.415	0	0	OF-145
1915	153	580	161	24	5	0	0.0	55	82	37		21	.278	.336	0	0	OF-153
7 yrs.	985	3617	1009	112	42	15	0.4	427	397	265	129	163	.279	.346	15	6	OF-969

Prince Oana

OANA, HENRY KAUHANE
B. Jan. 22, 1908, Waipahu, Hawaii   D. June 19, 1976, Austin, Tex.

BR TR 6'2"   193 lbs.

	G	AB	H	2B	3B	HR	HR %	R	RBI	BB	SO	SB	BA	SA	AB	H	G by POS
1934 PHI N	6	21	5	1	0	0	0.0	3	3	0	1	0	.238	.286	2	1	OF-4
1943 DET A	20	26	10	2	1	1	3.8	5	7	1	2	0	.385	.654	9	3	P-10
1945	4	5	1	0	0	0	0.0	0	0	0	0	0	.200	.200	1	0	P-3
3 yrs.	30	52	16	3	1	1	1.9	8	10	1	3	0	.308	.462	12	4	P-13, OF-4

Johnny Oates

OATES, JOHNNY LANE
B. Jan. 21, 1946, Sylva, N. C.

BL TR 5'11"   188 lbs.

	G	AB	H	2B	3B	HR	HR %	R	RBI	BB	SO	SB	BA	SA	AB	H	G by POS
1970 BAL A	5	18	5	1	0	0	0.0	2	2	2	0	0	.278	.389	1	1	C-4
1972	85	253	66	12	1	4	1.6	20	21	28	31	5	.261	.364	10	1	C-82
1973 ATL N	93	322	80	6	0	4	1.2	27	27	22	31	1	.248	.304	6	2	C-86
1974	100	291	65	10	0	1	0.3	22	21	23	24	2	.223	.268	15	4	C-91
1975 2 teams		ATL N (8G – .222)			PHI N (90G – .286)												
" total	98	287	81	15	0	1	0.3	28	25	34	33	1	.282	.345	13	2	C-88
1976 PHI N	37	99	25	2	0	0	0.0	10	8	8	12	0	.253	.273	8	2	C-33
1977 LA N	60	156	42	4	0	3	1.9	18	11	11	11	1	.269	.353	6	0	C-56
1978	40	75	23	1	0	0	0.0	5	6	5	3	0	.307	.320	14	3	C-24
1979	26	46	6	2	0	0	0.0	4	2	4	1	0	.130	.174	6	1	C-20
1980 NY A	39	64	12	3	0	1	1.6	6	3	2	3	1	.188	.281	0	0	C-39
1981	10	26	5	1	0	0	0.0	4	0	2	0	0	.192	.231	0	0	C-10
11 yrs.	593	1637	410	56	2	14	0.9	146	126	141	149	11	.250	.313	79	16	C-533
LEAGUE CHAMPIONSHIP SERIES																	
1976 PHI N	1	1	0	0	0	0	0.0	0	0	0	0	0	.000	.000	0	0	C-1
WORLD SERIES																	
1977 LA N	1	1	0	0	0	0	0.0	0	0	0	0	0	.000	.000	1	0	C-1
1978	1	1	1	0	0	0	0.0	0	0	0	1	0	1.000	1.000	0	0	C-1
2 yrs.	2	2	1	0	0	0	0.0	0	0	0	1	0	.500	.500	1	0	C-2

Henry Oberbeck

OBERBECK, HENRY A.
B. May 17, 1858, Missouri   D. Aug. 26, 1921, St. Louis, Mo.

	G	AB	H	2B	3B	HR	HR %	R	RBI	BB	SO	SB	BA	SA	AB	H	G by POS
1883 2 teams		PIT AA (2G – .222)			STL AA (4G – .000)												
" total	6	23	2	1	0	0	0.0	1		0			.087	.130	0	0	OF-4, 1B-2
1884 2 teams		BAL U (33G – .184)			KC U (27G – .189)												
" total	60	215	40	7	0	0	0.0	26		10			.186	.219	0	0	OF-35, 3B-23, P-8, 1B-3
2 yrs.	66	238	42	8	0	0	0.0	27		10			.176	.210	0	0	OF-39, 3B-23, P-8, 1B-5

Ken Oberkfell

OBERKFELL, KENNETH RAY
B. May 4, 1956, Maryville, Ill.

BL TR 6'   175 lbs.

	G	AB	H	2B	3B	HR	HR %	R	RBI	BB	SO	SB	BA	SA	AB	H	G by POS
1977 STL N	9	9	1	0	0	0	0.0	0	1	0	3	0	.111	.111	3	0	2B-6
1978	24	50	6	1	0	0	0.0	7	0	3	1	0	.120	.140	3	0	2B-17, 3B-4
1979	135	369	111	19	5	1	0.3	53	35	57	35	4	.301	.388	13	3	2B-117, 3B-17, SS-2
1980	116	422	128	27	6	3	0.7	58	46	51	23	4	.303	.417	1	0	2B-101, 3B-16
1981	102	376	110	12	6	2	0.5	43	45	37	28	13	.293	.372	1	0	3B-102, SS-1
1982	137	470	136	22	5	2	0.4	55	34	40	31	11	.289	.370	3	1	3B-135, 2B-1
1983	151	488	143	26	5	3	0.6	62	38	61	27	12	.293	.385	8	3	3B-127, 2B-32, SS-1
1984 2 teams		STL N (50G – .309)			ATL N (50G – .233)												
" total	100	324	87	19	2	1	0.3	38	21	31	27	2	.269	.349	6	1	3B-91, 2B-6, SS-1
8 yrs.	774	2508	722	126	29	12	0.5	316	220	280	175	46	.288	.376	38	8	3B-492, 2B-280, SS-5
LEAGUE CHAMPIONSHIP SERIES																	
1982 STL N	3	15	3	1	0	0	0.0	1	2	1	0	0	.200	.200	0	0	3B-3
WORLD SERIES																	
1982 STL N	7	24	7	1	0	0	0.0	4	1	2	1	2	.292	.333	0	0	3B-7

	G	AB	H	2B	3B	HR	HR %	R	RBI	BB	SO	SB	BA	SA	Pinch Hit AB	Pinch Hit H	G by POS

Mike O'Berry

O'BERRY, PRESTON MICHAEL
B. Apr. 20, 1954, Birmingham, Ala.　　　BR TR 6'2"　190 lbs.

	G	AB	H	2B	3B	HR	HR %	R	RBI	BB	SO	SB	BA	SA	AB	H	G by POS
1979 BOS A	43	59	10	1	0	1	1.7	8	4	5	16	0	.169	.237	0	0	C-43
1980 CHI N	19	48	10	1	0	0	0.0	7	5	5	13	0	.208	.229	0	0	C-19
1981 CIN N	55	111	20	3	1	1	0.9	6	5	14	19	0	.180	.252	0	0	C-55
1982	21	45	10	2	0	0	0.0	5	3	10	13	0	.222	.267	0	0	C-21
1983 CAL A	26	60	10	1	0	1	1.7	7	5	3	11	0	.167	.233	1	0	C-26
1984 NY A	13	32	8	2	0	0	0.0	3	5	2	2	0	.250	.313	1	0	C-12, 3B-1
6 yrs.	177	355	68	10	1	3	0.8	36	27	39	74	0	.192	.251	2	0	C-176, 3B-1

Jim O'Bradovich

O'BRADOVICH, JAMES THOMAS
B. Sept. 13, 1949, Ft. Campbell, Ky.　　　BL TL 6'2"　200 lbs.

	G	AB	H	2B	3B	HR	HR %	R	RBI	BB	SO	SB	BA	SA	AB	H	G by POS
1978 HOU N	10	17	3	0	1	0	0.0	3	2	1	3	0	.176	.294	6	0	1B-3

Billy O'Brien

O'BRIEN, WILLIAM SMITH
B. Apr. 16, 1860, Albany, N. Y.　　D. May 27, 1911, Kansas City, Mo.　　BR　6'　185 lbs.

	G	AB	H	2B	3B	HR	HR %	R	RBI	BB	SO	SB	BA	SA	AB	H	G by POS
1884 2 teams		STP U (8G – .233)			KC U (4G – .235)												
" total	12	47	11	3	0	0	0.0	3		0			.234	.298	0	0	3B-11, P-2, 1B-1
1887 WAS N	113	453	126	16	12	19	4.2	71	73	21	17	11	.278	.492	0	0	1B-104, OF-4, 3B-4, 2B-2
1888	133	528	119	15	2	9	1.7	42	66	9	70	10	.225	.313	0	0	1B-132, 3B-1
1889	2	8	0	0	0	0	0.0	1	0	1	1	0	.000	.000	0	0	1B-2
1890 B-B AA	96	388	108	25	8	4	1.0	47		28		5	.278	.415	0	0	1B-96
5 yrs.	356	1424	364	59	22	32	2.2	164	138	59	88	26	.256	.395	0	0	1B-335, 3B-16, OF-4, 2B-2, P-2

Darby O'Brien

O'BRIEN, WILLIAM D.
B. Sept. 1, 1863, Peoria, Ill.　　D. June 15, 1893, Peoria, Ill.　　BR TR 5'11½" 185 lbs.

	G	AB	H	2B	3B	HR	HR %	R	RBI	BB	SO	SB	BA	SA	AB	H	G by POS
1887 NY AA	127	522	157	30	13	5	1.0	97		40		49	.301	.437	0		OF-121, 1B-10, SS-2, 3B-1, P-1
1888 BKN AA	136	532	149	27	6	2	0.4	105	65	30		55	.280	.365	0	0	OF-136
1889	136	567	170	30	11	5	0.9	146	80	61	76	91	.300	.418	0	0	OF-136
1890 BKN N	85	350	110	28	6	2	0.6	78	63	32	43	38	.314	.446	0	0	OF-85
1891	103	395	100	18	6	5	1.3	79	57	39	53	31	.253	.367	0	0	OF-103
1892	122	490	119	14	5	1	0.2	72	56	29	52	57	.243	.298	0	0	OF-122
6 yrs.	709	2856	805	147	47	20	0.7	577	320	231	224	321	.282	.387	0	0	OF-703, 1B-10, SS-2, 3B-1, P-1

Eddie O'Brien

O'BRIEN, EDWARD JOSEPH
Brother of Johnny O'Brien.
B. Dec. 11, 1930, South Amboy, N. J.　　　BR TR 5'9"　165 lbs.

	G	AB	H	2B	3B	HR	HR %	R	RBI	BB	SO	SB	BA	SA	AB	H	G by POS
1953 PIT N	89	261	62	5	3	0	0.0	21	14	17	30	6	.238	.280	4	0	SS-81
1955	75	236	55	3	1	0	0.0	26	8	18	13	4	.233	.254	3	1	OF-56, 3B-7, SS-4
1956	63	53	14	2	0	0	0.0	17	3	2	2	1	.264	.302	1	0	SS-23, OF-6, 3B-4, 2B-2, P-1
1957	3	4	0	0	0	0	0.0	0	0	0	0	0	.000	.000	0	0	P-3
1958	1	0	0	0	0	0		0	0	0	0	0	–	–	0	0	P-1
5 yrs.	231	554	131	10	4	0	0.0	64	25	37	45	11	.236	.269	8	1	SS-108, OF-62, 3B-11, P-5, 2B-2

George O'Brien

O'BRIEN, GEORGE JOSEPH
B. Nov. 4, 1889, Cleveland, Ohio　　D. Mar. 24, 1966, Columbus, Ohio　　BR TR

	G	AB	H	2B	3B	HR	HR %	R	RBI	BB	SO	SB	BA	SA	AB	H	G by POS
1915 STL A	3	9	2	0	0	0	0.0	1	0	1	2	0	.222	.222	0	0	C-3

Jack O'Brien

O'BRIEN, JOHN JOSEPH
B. Feb. 5, 1873, Watervliet, N. Y.　　D. June 11, 1933, Watervliet, N. Y.　　5'8"　185 lbs.

	G	AB	H	2B	3B	HR	HR %	R	RBI	BB	SO	SB	BA	SA	AB	H	G by POS
1899 WAS N	127	468	132	11	5	6	1.3	68	51	31		17	.282	.365	1	0	OF-121, 3B-4
1901 2 teams		WAS A (11G – .178)			CLE A (92G – .283)												
" total	103	420	114	14	5	0	0.0	59	44	25		15	.271	.329	0	0	OF-103, 3B-1
1903 BOS A	96	338	71	14	4	3	0.9	44	38	21		10	.210	.302	9	2	OF-71, 3B-11, 2B-4, SS-1
3 yrs.	326	1226	317	39	14	9	0.7	171	133	77		42	.259	.335	10	2	OF-295, 3B-16, 2B-4, SS-1
WORLD SERIES																	
1903 BOS A	2	2	0	0	0	0	0.0	0	0	0	1	0	.000	.000	2	0	

Jack O'Brien

O'BRIEN, JOHN K.
Born John K. Byrne.
B. June 12, 1860, Philadelphia, Pa.　　D. Nov. 2, 1910, Philadelphia, Pa.　　BR TR 5'10" 186 lbs.

	G	AB	H	2B	3B	HR	HR %	R	RBI	BB	SO	SB	BA	SA	AB	H	G by POS
1882 PHI AA	62	241	73	13	3	3	1.2	44		13			.303	.419	0	0	C-45, OF-18, 3B-1, 1B-1
1883	94	390	113	14	10	0	0.0	74		25			.290	.377	0	0	C-58, OF-25, 3B-19, SS-1
1884	36	138	39	6	1	1	0.7	25		9			.283	.362	0	0	C-30, OF-5, 1B-1
1885	62	225	60	9	1	2	0.9	35		20			.267	.342	0	0	C-43, SS-9, 1B-7, OF-3, 3B-2
1886	105	423	107	25	7	0	0.0	65		38			.253	.345	0	0	C-36, 3B-27, 1B-24, SS-10, OF-3, OF-3
1887 BKN AA	30	123	28	4	1	1	0.8	18		6		8	.228	.301	0	0	C-25, OF-4, 2B-1
1888 BAL AA	57	196	44	11	5	0	0.0	25	18	17		14	.224	.332	0	0	C-37, OF-13, 1B-7
1890 PHI AA	109	433	113	24	14	4	0.9	80		52		31	.261	.409	0	0	1B-109, OF-1, C-1
8 yrs.	555	2169	577	106	42	11	0.5	366	17	180		53	.266	.369	0	0	C-275, 1B-149, OF-72, 3B-49, SS-20, 2B-8

Jerry O'Brien

O'BRIEN, JEREMIAH
B. Feb. 2, 1864, New York　　D. July 5, 1911, Susquehanna River, Pa.

	G	AB	H	2B	3B	HR	HR %	R	RBI	BB	SO	SB	BA	SA	AB	H	G by POS
1887 WAS N	1	4	0	0	0	0	0.0	0	0	0	2	0	.000	.000	0	0	2B-1

John O'Brien

O'BRIEN, JOHN E.
B. Oct. 22, 1851, Columbus, Ohio　　D. Dec. 31, 1914, Fall River, Mass.　　5'9"　187 lbs.

	G	AB	H	2B	3B	HR	HR %	R	RBI	BB	SO	SB	BA	SA	AB	H	G by POS
1884 BAL U	18	77	19	1	1	0	0.0	7		2			.247	.286	0	0	OF-18

John O'Brien

O'BRIEN, JOHN J. (Chewing Gum)
B. July 14, 1870, St. John, N. B., Canada   D. May 13, 1913, Lewiston, Me.   BL TR

	G	AB	H	2B	3B	HR	HR%	R	RBI	BB	SO	SB	BA	SA	PH AB	PH H	G by POS
1891 BKN N	43	167	41	4	2	0	0.0	22	26	12	17	4	.246	.293	0	0	2B-43
1893 CHI N	4	14	5	0	1	0	0.0	3	1	2	2	0	.357	.500	0	0	2B-4
1895 LOU N	128	539	138	10	4	1	0.2	82	50	45	20	15	.256	.295	0	0	2B-125, 1B-3
1896 2 teams								LOU N (49G – .339)		WAS N (73G – .267)							
" total	122	456	135	15	4	6	1.3	62	57	40	19	8	.296	.386	0	0	2B-122
1897 WAS N	86	320	78	12	2	3	0.9	37	45	19		6	.244	.322	0	0	2B-86
1899 2 teams								BAL N (39G – .193)		PIT N (79G – .226)							
" total	118	414	89	6	4	2	0.5	40	50	36		12	.215	.263	0	0	2B-118
6 yrs.	501	1910	486	47	17	12	0.6	246	229	154	58	45	.254	.316	0	0	2B-498, 1B-3

Johnny O'Brien

O'BRIEN, JOHN THOMAS
Brother of Eddie O'Brien.
B. Dec. 11, 1930, South Amboy, N. J.   BR TR 5'9" 170 lbs.

	G	AB	H	2B	3B	HR	HR%	R	RBI	BB	SO	SB	BA	SA	PH AB	PH H	G by POS
1953 PIT N	89	279	69	13	2	2	0.7	28	22	21	36	1	.247	.330	5	0	2B-77, SS-1
1955	84	278	83	15	2	1	0.4	22	25	20	19	1	.299	.378	5	0	2B-78
1956	73	104	18	1	0	0	0.0	13	3	5	7	0	.173	.183	8	1	2B-53, P-8, SS-1
1957	34	35	11	2	1	0	0.0	7	1	1	4	0	.314	.429	3	1	P-16, SS-8, 2B-2
1958 2 teams								PIT N (3G – .000)		STL N (12G – .000)							
" total	15	3	0	0	0	0	0.0	4	0	1	1	0	.000	.000	2	0	SS-5, 2B-1, P-1
1959 MIL N	44	116	23	4	0	1	0.9	16	8	11	15	0	.198	.259	0	0	2B-37
6 yrs.	339	815	204	35	5	4	0.5	90	59	59	82	2	.250	.320	23	2	2B-248, P-25, SS-15

Mickey O'Brien

O'BRIEN, FRANK ALOYSIUS
B. Sept. 13, 1894, San Francisco, Calif.   D. Nov. 4, 1971, Monterrey Park, Calif.   BR TR 5'8" 160 lbs.

	G	AB	H	2B	3B	HR	HR%	R	RBI	BB	SO	SB	BA	SA	PH AB	PH H	G by POS
1923 PHI N	15	21	7	2	0	0	0.0	3	0	2	1	0	.333	.429	6	2	C-9

Pete O'Brien

O'BRIEN, PETER F.
B. June 16, 1868, Chicago, Ill.   Deceased.

	G	AB	H	2B	3B	HR	HR%	R	RBI	BB	SO	SB	BA	SA	PH AB	PH H	G by POS
1890 CHI N	27	106	30	7	0	3	2.8	15	16	5	10	4	.283	.434	0	0	2B-27

Pete O'Brien

O'BRIEN, PETER JAMES
B. June 16, 1867, Chicago, Ill.   D. June 30, 1937, York Township, Ill.   BL TR 5'9½" 165 lbs.

	G	AB	H	2B	3B	HR	HR%	R	RBI	BB	SO	SB	BA	SA	PH AB	PH H	G by POS
1901 CIN N	16	54	11	1	0	1	1.9	1	3	2		0	.204	.278	1	0	2B-15
1906 STL A	151	524	122	9	4	2	0.4	44	57	42		25	.233	.277	0	0	2B-120, 3B-20, SS-11
1907 2 teams								CLE A (43G – .228)		WAS A (39G – .187)							
" total	82	279	58	8	3	0	0.0	15	18	19		5	.208	.258	4	1	3B-40, SS-22, 2B-18
3 yrs.	249	857	191	18	7	3	0.4	60	78	63		30	.223	.271	5	1	2B-153, 3B-60, SS-33

Pete O'Brien

O'BRIEN, PETER MICHAEL
B. Feb. 9, 1958, Santa Monica, Calif.   BL TL 6' 180 lbs.

	G	AB	H	2B	3B	HR	HR%	R	RBI	BB	SO	SB	BA	SA	PH AB	PH H	G by POS
1982 TEX A	20	67	16	4	1	4	6.0	13	13	6	8	1	.239	.507	0	0	OF-11, DH-4, 1B-3
1983	154	524	124	24	5	8	1.5	53	53	58	62	5	.237	.347	6	2	1B-133, OF-27, DH-1
1984	142	520	149	26	2	18	3.5	57	80	53	50	3	.287	.448	2	1	1B-141, OF-1
3 yrs.	316	1111	289	54	8	30	2.7	123	146	117	120	9	.260	.404	8	3	1B-277, OF-39, DH-5

Ray O'Brien

O'BRIEN, RAYMOND JOSEPH
B. Oct. 31, 1892, St. Louis, Mo.   D. Mar. 31, 1942, St. Louis, Mo.   BL TL 5'9" 175 lbs.

	G	AB	H	2B	3B	HR	HR%	R	RBI	BB	SO	SB	BA	SA	PH AB	PH H	G by POS
1916 PIT N	16	57	12	3	2	0	0.0	5	3	1	14	0	.211	.333	1	0	OF-14

Syd O'Brien

O'BRIEN, SYDNEY LLOYD
B. Dec. 18, 1944, Compton, Calif.   BR TR 6'1" 185 lbs.

	G	AB	H	2B	3B	HR	HR%	R	RBI	BB	SO	SB	BA	SA	PH AB	PH H	G by POS
1969 BOS A	100	263	64	10	5	9	3.4	47	29	15	37	2	.243	.422	18	5	3B-53, SS-15, 2B-12
1970 CHI A	121	441	109	13	2	8	1.8	48	44	22	62	3	.247	.340	8	2	3B-68, 2B-43, SS-5
1971 CAL A	90	251	50	8	1	5	2.0	25	21	15	33	0	.199	.299	20	6	SS-52, 2B-7, 3B-6, OF-1, 1B-1
1972 2 teams								CAL A (36G – .179)		MIL A (31G – .207)							
" total	67	97	19	4	0	2	2.1	15	6	8	23	0	.196	.299	22	4	3B-17, 2B-10, SS-4, 1B-1
4 yrs.	378	1052	242	35	8	24	2.3	135	100	60	155	5	.230	.347	68	17	3B-144, SS-76, 2B-72, 1B-2, OF-1

Tom O'Brien

O'BRIEN, THOMAS H.
B. Salem, Mass.   D. Apr. 21, 1921, Worcester, Mass.   BR TR

	G	AB	H	2B	3B	HR	HR%	R	RBI	BB	SO	SB	BA	SA	PH AB	PH H	G by POS
1882 WOR N	22	89	18	1	1	0	0.0	9	7	1	10		.202	.236	0	0	OF-20, 2B-2, 3B-1
1883 BAL AA	33	138	37	6	4	0	0.0	16		5			.268	.370	0	0	2B-29, OF-4
1884 BOS U	103	449	118	31	8	4	0.9	80		12			.263	.394	0	0	2B-99, OF-3, 1B-2, C-1
1885 BAL AA	8	33	7	3	0	0	0.0	4		2			.212	.303	0	0	1B-6, 2B-2
1887 NY AA	31	129	25	3	2	0	0.0	13		2		10	.194	.248	0	0	1B-20, OF-8, 3B-2, 2B-2, P-1
1890 ROC AA	73	273	52	6	5	0	0.0	36		30		6	.190	.249	0	0	1B-68, 2B-8
6 yrs.	270	1111	257	50	20	4	0.4	158	7	52	10	16	.231	.323	0	0	2B-142, 1B-96, OF-35, 3B-3, C-1, P-1

Tom O'Brien

O'BRIEN, THOMAS J.
B. Feb. 20, 1873, Verona, Pa.   D. Feb. 4, 1901, Phoenix, Ariz.

	G	AB	H	2B	3B	HR	HR%	R	RBI	BB	SO	SB	BA	SA	PH AB	PH H	G by POS
1897 BAL N	50	147	37	6	0	0	0.0	25	32	20		7	.252	.293	2	1	1B-25, OF-24
1898 2 teams								BAL N (18G – .217)		PIT N (107G – .259)							
" total	125	473	120	10	8	1	0.2	62	59	35		13	.254	.315	2	0	OF-85, 1B-21, 3B-8, 2B-7, SS-4
1899 NY N	150	573	170	21	10	6	1.0	100	7	44		23	.297	.400	0	0	OF-127, 3B-21, SS-2, 2B-1, 1B-1
1900 PIT N	102	376	109	22	6	3	0.8	61	61	21		12	.290	.404	5	1	1B-65, OF-25, 2B-4, SS-2
4 yrs.	427	1569	436	59	24	10	0.6	248	229	120		55	.278	.365	9	2	OF-261, 1B-112, 3B-29, 2B-12, SS-8

	G	AB	H	2B	3B	HR	HR %	R	RBI	BB	SO	SB	BA	SA	Pinch Hit AB	Pinch Hit H	G by POS

Tommy O'Brien

O'BRIEN, THOMAS EDWARD (Obie)　BR TR 5'11" 195 lbs.
B. Dec. 19, 1918, Anniston, Ala.　D. Nov. 5, 1978, Anniston, Ala.

	G	AB	H	2B	3B	HR	HR %	R	RBI	BB	SO	SB	BA	SA	PH AB	PH H	G by POS
1943 PIT N	89	232	72	12	7	2	0.9	35	26	15	24	0	.310	.448	27	7	OF-48, 3B-9
1944	85	156	39	6	2	3	1.9	27	20	21	12	1	.250	.372	33	5	OF-48
1945	58	161	54	6	5	0	0.0	23	18	9	13	0	.335	.435	12	3	OF-45
1949 BOS A	49	125	28	5	0	3	2.4	24	10	21	12	1	.224	.336	12	1	OF-32
1950 2 teams			BOS	A	(9G –	.129)		WAS	A	(3G –	.111)						
" total	12	40	5	1	0	0	0.0	1	4	4	5	0	.125	.150	0	0	OF-12
5 yrs.	293	714	198	30	14	8	1.1	110	78	70	66	2	.277	.392	84	16	OF-185, 3B-9

Whitey Ock

OCK, HAROLD DAVID　BR TR 5'11" 180 lbs.
B. Mar. 17, 1912, Brooklyn, N. Y.　D. Mar. 18, 1975, Mount Kisco, N. Y.

	G	AB	H	2B	3B	HR	HR %	R	RBI	BB	SO	SB	BA	SA	PH AB	PH H	G by POS
1935 BKN N	1	3	0	0	0	0	0.0	0	1	0	2	0	.000	.000	0	0	C-1

Danny O'Connell

O'CONNELL, DANIEL FRANCIS　BR TR 5'11" 168 lbs.
B. Jan. 21, 1927, Paterson, N. J.　D. Oct. 2, 1969, Clifton, N. J.

	G	AB	H	2B	3B	HR	HR %	R	RBI	BB	SO	SB	BA	SA	PH AB	PH H	G by POS
1950 PIT N	79	315	92	16	1	8	2.5	39	32	24	33	7	.292	.425	2	0	SS-65, 3B-12
1953	149	588	173	26	8	7	1.2	88	55	57	42	3	.294	.401	0	0	3B-104, 2B-47
1954 MIL N	146	541	151	28	4	2	0.4	61	37	38	46	2	.279	.357	0	0	2B-103, 3B-35, 1B-8, SS-1
1955	124	453	102	15	4	6	1.3	47	40	28	43	2	.225	.316	6	1	2B-114, 3B-7, SS-1
1956	139	498	119	17	9	2	0.4	71	42	76	42	3	.239	.321	1	0	2B-138, 3B-4, SS-1
1957 2 teams			MIL	N	(48G –	.235)		NY	N	(95G –	.266)						
" total	143	547	140	27	4	8	1.5	86	36	52	50	9	.256	.364	1	0	2B-130, 3B-30
1958 SF N	107	306	71	12	2	3	1.0	44	23	51	35	2	.232	.314	0	0	2B-104, 3B-3
1959	34	58	11	3	0	0	0.0	6	0	5	15	0	.190	.241	0	0	3B-26, 2B-8
1961 WAS A	138	493	128	30	1	1	0.2	61	37	77	62	15	.260	.331	5	4	3B-73, 2B-61
1962	84	236	62	7	2	2	0.8	24	18	23	28	5	.263	.335	20	8	3B-41, 2B-22
10 yrs.	1143	4035	1049	181	35	39	1.0	527	320	431	396	48	.260	.351	39	16	2B-713, 3B-335, SS-68, 1B-8

Jimmy O'Connell

O'CONNELL, JAMES JOSEPH　BL TR 5'10½" 175 lbs.
B. Feb. 11, 1901, Sacramento, Calif.　D. Nov. 11, 1976, Bakersfield, Calif.

	G	AB	H	2B	3B	HR	HR %	R	RBI	BB	SO	SB	BA	SA	PH AB	PH H	G by POS
1923 NY N	87	252	63	9	2	6	2.4	42	39	34	32	7	.250	.373	10	0	OF-64, 1B-8
1924	52	104	33	4	2	2	1.9	24	18	11	16	2	.317	.452	15	4	OF-29, 2B-1
2 yrs.	139	356	96	13	4	8	2.2	66	57	45	48	9	.270	.396	25	4	OF-93, 1B-8, 2B-1

WORLD SERIES

	G	AB	H	2B	3B	HR	HR %	R	RBI	BB	SO	SB	BA	SA	PH AB	PH H	G by POS
1923 NY N	2	1	0	0	0	0	0.0	0	0	0	1	0	.000	.000	1	0	

John O'Connell

O'CONNELL, JOHN CHARLES　BR TR 6' 170 lbs.
B. June 13, 1905, Pittsburgh, Pa.

	G	AB	H	2B	3B	HR	HR %	R	RBI	BB	SO	SB	BA	SA	PH AB	PH H	G by POS
1928 PIT N	1	1	0	0	0	0	0.0	0	0	0	0	0	.000	.000	0	0	C-1
1929	2	7	1	1	0	0	0.0	1	0	1	1	0	.143	.286	0	0	C-2
2 yrs.	3	8	1	1	0	0	0.0	1	0	1	1	0	.125	.250	0	0	C-3

John O'Connell

O'CONNELL, JOHN JOSEPH
B. May 16, 1872, Lawrence, Mass.　D. May 14, 1908, Derry, N. H.

	G	AB	H	2B	3B	HR	HR %	R	RBI	BB	SO	SB	BA	SA	PH AB	PH H	G by POS
1891 BAL AA	8	29	5	1	0	0	0.0	2	7	3	6	2	.172	.207	0	0	SS-3, 2B-3, OF-2
1902 DET A	8	22	4	0	0	0	0.0	1	0	3		0	.182	.182	0	0	2B-6, 1B-2
2 yrs.	16	51	9	1	0	0	0.0	3	7	6	6	2	.176	.196	0	0	2B-9, SS-3, OF-2, 1B-2

Pat O'Connell

O'CONNELL, PATRICK　5'10" 175 lbs.
B. 1862, Lewiston, Me.　D. May 5, 1892

	G	AB	H	2B	3B	HR	HR %	R	RBI	BB	SO	SB	BA	SA	PH AB	PH H	G by POS
1890 B-B AA	11	40	9	2	1	0	0.0	7		7		3	.225	.325	0	0	3B-10, 1B-1

Pat O'Connell

O'CONNELL, PATRICK H.　BL TR 5'11"
B. June 10, 1861, Bangor, Me.　D. Jan. 24, 1943, Lewiston, Me.

	G	AB	H	2B	3B	HR	HR %	R	RBI	BB	SO	SB	BA	SA	PH AB	PH H	G by POS
1886 BAL AA	42	166	30	3	2	0	0.0	20		1			.181	.223	0	0	OF-41, 1B-1, P-1

Dan O'Connor

O'CONNOR, DANIEL CORNELIUS　BL TR 6'2" 185 lbs.
B. Aug., 1868, Guelph, Ont., Canada　D. Mar. 3, 1942, Guelph, Ont., Canada

	G	AB	H	2B	3B	HR	HR %	R	RBI	BB	SO	SB	BA	SA	PH AB	PH H	G by POS
1890 LOU AA	6	26	12	1	1	0	0.0	3		1		5	.462	.577	0	0	1B-6

Jack O'Connor

O'CONNOR, JOHN JOSEPH (Peach Pie)　BR TR 5'10" 170 lbs.
B. Mar. 3, 1867, St. Louis, Mo.　D. Nov. 14, 1937, St. Louis, Mo.
Manager 1910.

	G	AB	H	2B	3B	HR	HR %	R	RBI	BB	SO	SB	BA	SA	PH AB	PH H	G by POS
1887 CIN AA	12	40	4	0	0	0	0.0	4		2		3	.100	.100	0	0	OF-7, C-5
1888	36	137	28	3	1	1	0.7	14	17	6		12	.204	.263	0	0	OF-34, C-2
1889 COL AA	107	398	107	17	7	4	1.0	69	60	33	37	26	.269	.377	0	0	C-84, OF-19, 2B-4, 1B-3
1890	121	457	148	14	10	2	0.4	89		38		29	.324	.411	0	0	C-106, OF-9, SS-8, 2B-2, 3B-1
1891	56	229	61	12	3	0	0.0	28	37	11	14	10	.266	.345	0	0	OF-40, C-21
1892 CLE N	140	572	142	22	5	1	0.2	71	58	25	48	17	.248	.309	1	0	OF-106, C-34
1893	96	384	110	23	1	3	0.8	72	75	29	12	29	.286	.375	0	0	C-56, OF-44
1894	86	330	104	23	7	2	0.6	67	51	15	7	15	.315	.445	1	0	C-45, OF-33, 1B-7
1895	89	340	99	14	10	0	0.0	51	58	30	22	11	.291	.391	0	0	C-47, 1B-41, 3B-1
1896	68	256	76	11	1	1	0.4	41	43	15	12	15	.297	.359	3	2	C-37, 1B-17, OF-12
1897	103	397	115	21	4	2	0.5	49	69	26		20	.290	.378	4	3	OF-52, 1B-36, C-13
1898	131	478	119	17	4	1	0.2	50	56	26		8	.249	.308	1	0	1B-69, C-48, OF-15
1899 STL N	84	289	73	5	6	0	0.0	33	43	15		7	.253	.311	2	0	C-57, 1B-26
1900 2 teams			STL	N	(10G –	.219)		PIT	N	(43G –	.238)						
" total	53	179	42	4	1	0	0.0	19	25	5		5	.235	.268	1	0	C-50, 1B-2
1901 PIT N	61	202	39	7	3	0	0.0	16	22	10		2	.193	.257	2	0	C-59
1902	49	170	50	1	2	1	0.6	13	28	3		2	.294	.341	0	0	C-42, 1B-6, OF-1
1903 NY A	64	212	43	4	1	0	0.0	13	12	6		4	.203	.231	0	0	C-63, 1B-1
1904 STL A	14	47	10	1	0	0	0.0	4	2	1		0	.213	.234	0	0	C-14
1906	58	174	33	0	0	0	0.0	8	11	2		4	.190	.190	4	0	C-54
1907	25	89	14	2	0	0	0.0	2	4	0		0	.157	.180	0	0	C-25

	G	AB	H	2B	3B	HR	HR %	R	RBI	BB	SO	SB	BA	SA	Pinch Hit AB	Pinch Hit H	G by POS

Jack O'Connor continued

	G	AB	H	2B	3B	HR	HR %	R	RBI	BB	SO	SB	BA	SA	PH AB	PH H	G by POS
1910	1	0	0	0	0	0	–	0	0	0		0	–	–	0	0	C-1
21 yrs.	1454	5380	1417	201	66	18	0.3	713	670	301	152	219	.263	.335	19	5	C-863, OF-372, 1B-208, SS-8, 2B-6, 3B-2

John O'Connor

O'CONNOR, JOHN J.
B. Unknown.

TR

	G	AB	H	2B	3B	HR	HR %	R	RBI	BB	SO	SB	BA	SA	PH AB	PH H	G by POS
1916 CHI N	1	0	0	0	0	0	–	0	0	0	0	0	–	–	0	0	

Paddy O'Connor

O'CONNOR, PATRICK FRANCIS
B. Aug. 4, 1879, Windsor Locks, Conn.   D. Aug. 17, 1950, Springfield, Mass.

BR TR 5'8"   168 lbs.

	G	AB	H	2B	3B	HR	HR %	R	RBI	BB	SO	SB	BA	SA	PH AB	PH H	G by POS
1908 PIT N	12	16	3	0	0	0	0.0	1	2	0		0	.188	.188	7	2	C-4
1909	9	16	5	1	0	0	0.0	1	3	0		0	.313	.375	5	0	C-3, 3B-1
1910	6	4	1	0	0	0	0.0	0	0	1	1	0	.250	.250	4	1	C-1
1914 STL N	10	9	0	0	0	0	0.0	0	0	2	2	0	.000	.000	2	0	C-7
1915 PIT F	70	219	50	10	1	0	0.0	15	16	14		4	.228	.283	4	1	C-66
1918 NY A	1	3	1	0	0	0	0.0	0	0	0		1	.333	.333	0	0	C-1
6 yrs.	108	267	60	11	1	0	0.0	17	21	17	4	4	.225	.273	22	4	C-82, 3B-1

WORLD SERIES

	G	AB	H	2B	3B	HR	HR %	R	RBI	BB	SO	SB	BA	SA	PH AB	PH H	G by POS
1909 PIT N	1	1	0	0	0	0	0.0	0	0	0	1	0	.000	.000	1	0	

Hank O'Day

O'DAY, HENRY FRANCIS
B. July 8, 1863, Chicago, Ill.   D. July 2, 1935, Chicago, Ill.
Manager 1912, 1914.

TR

	G	AB	H	2B	3B	HR	HR %	R	RBI	BB	SO	SB	BA	SA	PH AB	PH H	G by POS
1884 TOL AA	64	242	51	9	1	0	0.0	23		10			.211	.256	0	0	P-39, OF-24, 3B-3, 1B-3
1885 PIT AA	13	49	12	2	1	0	0.0	7		1			.245	.327	0	0	P-12, OF-3
1886 WAS N	6	19	1	0	0	0	0.0	0	0	0	9		.053	.053	0	0	P-6
1887	36	116	23	3	0	0	0.0	10	7	7	15	1	.198	.224	0	0	P-30, SS-6, OF-2
1888	47	166	23	2	0	0	0.0	6	6	4	41	3	.139	.151	0	0	P-46, SS-2
1889 2 teams		WAS	N	(13G –	.182)		NY	N	(10G –	.097)							
" total	23	75	11	1	0	0	0.0	6	7	7	17	2	.147	.160	0	0	P-23
1890 NY P	43	150	34	2	1	0	0.7	24	23	10	27	1	.227	.273	0	0	P-43
7 yrs.	232	817	155	19	3	1	0.1	76	42	39	109	7	.190	.224	0	0	P-199, OF-29, SS-8, 3B-3, 1B-3

Ken O'Dea

O'DEA, JAMES KENNETH
B. Mar. 16, 1913, Lima, N. Y.

BL TR 6'   180 lbs.

	G	AB	H	2B	3B	HR	HR %	R	RBI	BB	SO	SB	BA	SA	PH AB	PH H	G by POS
1935 CHI N	76	202	52	13	2	6	3.0	30	38	26	18	0	.257	.431	9	1	C-63
1936	80	189	58	10	3	2	1.1	36	38	38	18	0	.307	.423	22	7	C-55
1937	83	219	66	7	5	4	1.8	31	32	24	26	1	.301	.434	13	3	C-64
1938	86	247	65	12	1	3	1.2	22	33	12	18	1	.263	.356	13	2	C-71
1939 NY N	52	97	17	1	0	3	3.1	7	11	10	16	0	.175	.278	26	3	C-30
1940	48	96	23	4	1	0	0.0	9	12	16	15	0	.240	.302	14	2	C-31
1941	59	89	19	5	1	3	3.4	13	17	8	20	0	.213	.393	42	9	C-14
1942 STL N	58	192	45	7	1	5	2.6	22	32	17	23	0	.234	.359	9	1	C-49
1943	71	203	57	11	2	3	1.5	15	25	19	25	0	.281	.399	14	4	C-56
1944	85	265	66	11	2	6	2.3	35	37	37	29	1	.249	.374	14	4	C-69
1945	100	307	78	18	2	4	1.3	36	43	50	31	0	.254	.365	8	0	C-91
1946 2 teams		STL	N	(22G –	.123)		BOS	N	(12G –	.219)							
" total	34	89	14	2	0	1	1.1	6	5	16	12	0	.157	.213	0	0	C-34
12 yrs.	832	2195	560	101	20	40	1.8	262	323	273	251	3	.255	.374	184	36	C-627

WORLD SERIES

	G	AB	H	2B	3B	HR	HR %	R	RBI	BB	SO	SB	BA	SA	PH AB	PH H	G by POS
1935 CHI N	1	1	1	0	0	0	0.0	0	1	0	0	0	1.000	1.000	1	1	
1938	3	5	1	0	0	1	20.0	1	2	1	0	0	.200	.800	2	0	C-1
1942 STL N	1	1	1	0	0	0	0.0	0	1	0	0	0	1.000	1.000	1	1	
1943	2	3	2	0	0	0	0.0	0	0	0	0	0	.667	.667	1	0	C-1
1944	3	3	1	0	0	0	0.0	0	2	0	0	0	.333	.333	3	1	
5 yrs.	10	13	6	0	0	1	7.7	1	6	1	0	0	.462	.692	8	3	C-2
															3rd	1st	

Paul O'Dea

O'DEA, PAUL (Lefty)
B. July 3, 1920, Cleveland, Ohio   D. Dec. 11, 1978, Cleveland, Ohio

BL TL 6'   200 lbs.

	G	AB	H	2B	3B	HR	HR %	R	RBI	BB	SO	SB	BA	SA	PH AB	PH H	G by POS
1944 CLE A	76	173	55	9	0	0	0.0	25	13	23	21	2	.318	.370	25	5	OF-41, 1B-3, P-3
1945	87	221	52	2	2	1	0.5	21	21	20	26	3	.235	.276	30	7	OF-53, P-1
2 yrs.	163	394	107	11	2	1	0.3	46	34	43	47	5	.272	.317	55	12	OF-94, P-4, 1B-3

Heinie Odom

ODOM, HERMAN BOYD
B. Oct. 13, 1900, Rusk, Tex.   D. Aug. 31, 1970, Rusk, Tex.

BB TR 6'   170 lbs.

	G	AB	H	2B	3B	HR	HR %	R	RBI	BB	SO	SB	BA	SA	PH AB	PH H	G by POS
1925 NY A	1	1	1	0	0	0	0.0	0	0	0	0	0	1.000	1.000	0	0	3B-1

O'Donnell

O'DONNELL,
B. Littlestown, Pa.   Deceased.

	G	AB	H	2B	3B	HR	HR %	R	RBI	BB	SO	SB	BA	SA	PH AB	PH H	G by POS
1884 PHI U	1	4	1	0	0	0	0.0		0		0		.250	.250	0	0	C-1

Harry O'Donnell

O'DONNELL, HARRY HERMAN
B. Apr. 2, 1894, Philadelphia, Pa.   D. Jan. 31, 1958, Philadelphia, Pa.

BR TR 5'10"   180 lbs.

	G	AB	H	2B	3B	HR	HR %	R	RBI	BB	SO	SB	BA	SA	PH AB	PH H	G by POS
1927 PHI N	16	16	1	0	0	0	0.0	2	2	2	0	.063	.063	4	0	C-12

Lefty O'Doul

O'DOUL, FRANCIS JOSEPH
B. Mar. 4, 1897, San Francisco, Calif.   D. Dec. 7, 1969, San Francisco, Calif.

BL TL 6'   180 lbs.

	G	AB	H	2B	3B	HR	HR %	R	RBI	BB	SO	SB	BA	SA	PH AB	PH H	G by POS
1919 NY A	19	16	4	0	0	0	0.0	2	1	1	2	1	.250	.250	14	4	P-3, OF-1
1920	13	12	2	1	0	0	0.0	2	1	1	1	0	.167	.250	9	1	P-2, OF-1
1922	8	9	3	1	0	0	0.0	0	4	0	2	0	.333	.444	2	1	P-6
1923 BOS A	36	35	5	0	0	0	0.0	4	2	3	0	.143	.143	12	2	P-23
1928 NY N	114	354	113	19	4	8	2.3	67	46	30	8	9	.319	.463	8	4	OF-94

	G	AB	H	2B	3B	HR	HR %	R	RBI	BB	SO	SB	BA	SA	Pinch Hit AB	Pinch Hit H	G by POS

Lefty O'Doul continued

	G	AB	H	2B	3B	HR	HR %	R	RBI	BB	SO	SB	BA	SA	AB	H	G by POS
1929 PHI N	154	638	**254**	35	6	32	5.0	152	122	76	19	2	**.398**	.622	0	0	OF-154
1930	140	528	202	37	7	22	4.2	122	97	63	21	3	.383	.604	8	3	OF-131
1931 BKN N	134	512	172	32	11	7	1.4	85	75	48	16	5	.336	.482	2	2	OF-132
1932	148	595	219	32	8	21	3.5	120	90	50	20	11	**.368**	.555	0	0	OF-148
1933 2 teams			BKN	N	(43G –	.252)		NY	N	(78G –	.306)						
" total	121	388	110	14	2	14	3.6	45	56	44	23	3	.284	.438	14	5	OF-104
1934 NY N	83	177	56	4	3	9	5.1	27	46	18	7	2	.316	.525	37	10	OF-38
11 yrs.	970	3264	1140	175	41	113	3.5	624	542	333	122	36	.349	.532	106	32	OF-803, P-34

WORLD SERIES

	G	AB	H	2B	3B	HR	HR %	R	RBI	BB	SO	SB	BA	SA	AB	H	G by POS
1933 NY N	1	1	1	0	0	0	0.0	1	2	0	0	0	1.000	1.000	1	1	

John O'Dowd

O'DOWD, JOHN LEO   TR
B. Jan. 3, 1891, S. Weymouth, Mass.   D. Jan. 31, 1981, Fort Lauderdale, Fla.

	G	AB	H	2B	3B	HR	HR %	R	RBI	BB	SO	SB	BA	SA	AB	H	G by POS
1912 NY A	10	31	6	1	0	0	0.0	1	0	6		0	.194	.226	0	0	SS-10

Fred Odwell

ODWELL, FREDERICK WILLIAM (Fritz)   BR TR 5'9½" 160 lbs.
B. Sept. 25, 1872, Downsville, N. Y.   D. Aug. 19, 1948, Downsville, N. Y.

	G	AB	H	2B	3B	HR	HR %	R	RBI	BB	SO	SB	BA	SA	AB	H	G by POS
1904 CIN N	129	468	133	22	10	1	0.2	75	58	26		30	.284	.380	2	1	OF-126, 2B-1
1905	130	468	113	10	9	9	1.9	79	65	26		21	.241	.359	4	3	OF-126
1906	58	202	45	5	4	0	0.0	20	21	15		11	.223	.287	1	0	OF-57
1907	94	274	74	5	7	0	0.0	24	24	22		10	.270	.339	5	0	OF-84, 2B-1
4 yrs.	411	1412	365	42	30	10	0.7	198	168	89		72	.258	.352	12	4	OF-393, 2B-2

Chuck Oertel

OERTEL, CHARLES FRANK (Ducky, Snuffy)   BL TR 5'8" 165 lbs.
B. Mar. 12, 1931, Coffeyville, Kans.

	G	AB	H	2B	3B	HR	HR %	R	RBI	BB	SO	SB	BA	SA	AB	H	G by POS
1958 BAL A	14	12	2	0	0	1	8.3	4	1	1	1	0	.167	.417	8	0	OF-2

Ron Oester

OESTER, RONALD JOHN   BB TR 6'2" 185 lbs.
B. May 5, 1956, Cincinnati, Ohio

	G	AB	H	2B	3B	HR	HR %	R	RBI	BB	SO	SB	BA	SA	AB	H	G by POS
1978 CIN N	6	8	3	0	0	0	0.0	1	1	0	2	0	.375	.375	0	0	SS-6
1979	6	3	0	0	0	0	0.0	0	0	0	1	0	.000	.000	1	0	SS-2
1980	100	303	84	16	2	2	0.7	40	20	26	44	6	.277	.363	10	3	2B-79, SS-17, 3B-3
1981	105	354	96	16	7	5	1.4	45	42	42	49	2	.271	.398	0	0	2B-103, SS-9
1982	151	549	143	19	4	9	1.6	63	47	35	82	5	.260	.359	6	1	2B-118, SS-29, 3B-13
1983	157	549	145	23	5	11	2.0	63	58	49	106	2	.264	.384	5	2	2B-154
1984	150	553	134	26	3	3	0.5	54	38	41	97	7	.242	.316	6	2	2B-147, SS-1
7 yrs.	675	2319	605	100	21	30	1.3	266	206	193	381	22	.261	.361	28	8	2B-601, SS-64, 3B-16

Bob O'Farrell

O'FARRELL, ROBERT ARTHUR   BR TR 5'9½" 180 lbs.
B. Oct. 19, 1896, Waukegan, Ill.
Manager 1927, 1934.

	G	AB	H	2B	3B	HR	HR %	R	RBI	BB	SO	SB	BA	SA	AB	H	G by POS
1915 CHI N	2	3	1	0	0	0	0.0	0	0	0	0	0	.333	.333	0	0	C-2
1916	1	0	0	0	0	0	0.0	0	0	0	0	0	—	—	0	0	C-1
1917	3	8	3	2	0	0	0.0	1	1	1	0	1	.375	.625	0	0	C-3
1918	52	113	32	7	3	1	0.9	9	14	10	15	0	.283	.425	7	2	C-45
1919	49	125	27	4	2	0	0.0	11	9	7	10	2	.216	.280	9	1	C-38
1920	94	270	67	11	4	3	1.1	29	19	34	23	1	.248	.352	8	0	C-86
1921	96	260	65	12	7	4	1.5	32	32	18	14	2	.250	.396	6	1	C-90
1922	128	392	127	18	8	4	1.0	68	60	79	34	5	.324	.441	2	1	C-125
1923	131	452	144	25	4	12	2.7	73	84	67	38	10	.319	.471	6	3	C-124
1924	71	183	44	6	2	3	1.6	25	28	30	13	2	.240	.344	10	3	C-57
1925 2 teams			CHI	N	(17G –	.182)		STL	N	(94G –	.278)						
" total	111	339	92	13	3	3	0.9	39	35	48	31	0	.271	.354	14	4	C-95
1926 STL N	147	492	144	30	9	7	1.4	63	68	61	44	1	.293	.433	1	1	C-146
1927	61	178	47	10	1	0	0.0	19	18	23	22	3	.264	.331	6	2	C-53
1928 2 teams			STL	N	(16G –	.212)		NY	N	(75G –	.195)						
" total	91	185	37	7	0	2	1.1	29	24	47	25	4	.200	.270	9	1	C-77
1929 NY N	91	248	76	14	3	4	1.6	35	42	28	30	3	.306	.435	4	2	C-84
1930	94	249	75	16	4	4	1.6	37	54	31	21	1	.301	.446	23	6	C-69
1931	85	174	39	8	3	1	0.6	11	19	21	23	0	.224	.322	5	0	C-80
1932	50	67	16	3	0	0	0.0	7	8	11	10	0	.239	.284	5	1	C-41
1933 STL N	55	163	39	4	2	2	1.2	16	20	15	25	0	.239	.325	4	1	C-50
1934 2 teams			CIN	N	(44G –	.244)		CHI	N	(22G –	.224)						
" total	66	190	45	11	3	1	0.5	13	14	14	30	0	.237	.342	2	0	C-64
1935 STL N	14	10	0	0	0	0	0.0	0	0	2	0	0	.000	.000	4	0	C-8
21 yrs.	1492	4101	1120	201	58	51	1.2	517	549	547	408	35	.273	.388	125	29	C-1338

WORLD SERIES

	G	AB	H	2B	3B	HR	HR %	R	RBI	BB	SO	SB	BA	SA	AB	H	G by POS
1918 CHI N	3	3	0	0	0	0	0.0	0	0	0	0	0	.000	.000	3	0	C-1
1926 STL N	7	23	7	1	0	0	0.0	2	2	2	2	0	.304	.348	0	0	C-7
2 yrs.	10	26	7	1	0	0	0.0	2	2	2	2	0	.269	.308	3	0	C-8

Rowland Office

OFFICE, ROWLAND JOHNIE   BL TL 6' 170 lbs.
B. Oct. 25, 1952, Sacramento, Calif.

	G	AB	H	2B	3B	HR	HR %	R	RBI	BB	SO	SB	BA	SA	AB	H	G by POS
1972 ATL N	2	5	2	0	0	0	0.0	1	0	1	2	0	.400	.400	1	0	OF-1
1974	131	248	61	16	1	3	1.2	20	31	16	30	5	.246	.355	11	4	OF-119
1975	126	355	103	14	1	3	0.8	30	30	23	41	2	.290	.361	20	7	OF-107
1976	99	359	101	17	1	4	1.1	51	34	37	49	2	.281	.368	5	2	OF-92
1977	124	428	103	13	1	5	1.2	42	39	23	58	2	.241	.311	20	5	OF-104, 1B-1
1978	146	404	101	13	1	9	2.2	40	40	22	52	8	.250	.354	18	0	OF-136
1979	124	277	69	14	2	2	0.7	35	37	27	33	5	.249	.336	21	5	OF-97
1980 MON N	116	292	78	13	4	6	2.1	36	30	36	39	2	.267	.401	17	6	OF-97
1981	26	40	7	0	0	0	0.0	4	6	0	6	0	.175	.175	13	3	OF-1
1982	3	3	1	1	0	0	0.0	0	0	0	1	0	.333	.667	2	0	OF-1
1983 NY A	2	2	0	0	0	0	0.0	0	0	0	0	0	.000	.000	1	0	OF-2
11 yrs.	899	2413	626	101	11	32	1.3	259	242	189	311	27	.259	.350	129	35	OF-771, 1B-1

	G	AB	H	2B	3B	HR	HR %	R	RBI	BB	SO	SB	BA	SA	Pinch Hit AB	Pinch Hit H	G by POS

Jim Oglesby

OGLESBY, JAMES DORN
B. Aug. 10, 1905, Schofield, Mo.   D. Sept. 1, 1955, Tulsa, Okla.   BL TL 6'   190 lbs.

	G	AB	H	2B	3B	HR	HR %	R	RBI	BB	SO	SB	BA	SA	AB	H	G by POS
1936 PHI A	3	11	2	0	0	0	0.0	0	2	2	0	0	.182	.182	0	0	1B-3

Ben Oglivie

OGLIVIE, BENJAMIN AMBROSIO
B. Feb. 11, 1949, Colon, Panama   BL TL 6'2"   160 lbs.

	G	AB	H	2B	3B	HR	HR %	R	RBI	BB	SO	SB	BA	SA	AB	H	G by POS
1971 BOS A	14	38	10	3	0	0	0.0	2	4	0	5	0	.263	.342	5	0	OF-11
1972	94	253	61	10	2	8	3.2	27	30	18	61	1	.241	.391	24	9	OF-65
1973	58	147	32	9	1	2	1.4	16	9	9	32	1	.218	.333	10	2	OF-32, DH-13
1974 DET A	92	252	68	11	3	4	1.6	28	29	34	38	12	.270	.385	19	5	OF-63, 1B-10, DH-4
1975	100	332	95	14	1	9	2.7	45	36	16	62	11	.286	.416	3	0	OF-86, 1B-5, DH-2
1976	115	305	87	12	3	15	4.9	36	47	11	44	9	.285	.492	38	9	OF-64, 1B-9, DH-1
1977	132	450	118	24	2	21	4.7	63	61	40	80	9	.262	.464	12	4	OF-118, DH-2
1978 MIL A	128	469	142	29	4	18	3.8	71	72	52	69	11	.303	.497	6	1	OF-89, DH-27, 1B-11
1979	139	514	145	30	4	29	5.6	88	81	48	56	12	.282	.525	6	3	OF-120, DH-13, 1B-9
1980	156	592	180	26	2	41	6.9	94	118	54	71	11	.304	.563	0	0	OF-152, DH-4
1981	107	400	97	15	2	14	3.5	53	72	37	49	2	.243	.395	1	1	OF-101, DH-6
1982	159	602	147	22	1	34	5.6	92	102	70	81	3	.244	.453	1	0	OF-159
1983	125	411	115	19	3	13	3.2	49	66	60	64	4	.280	.436	10	3	OF-113, DH-8
1984	131	461	121	16	2	12	2.6	49	60	44	56	0	.262	.384	10	3	OF-125, DH-1
14 yrs.	1550	5226	1418	240	30	220	4.2	713	787	493	768	86	.271	.455	145	40	OF-1298, DH-81, 1B-44

DIVISIONAL PLAYOFF SERIES

	G	AB	H	2B	3B	HR	HR %	R	RBI	BB	SO	SB	BA	SA	AB	H	G by POS
1981 MIL A	5	18	3	1	0	0	0.0	0	1	0	7	0	.167	.222	0	0	OF-5

LEAGUE CHAMPIONSHIP SERIES

	G	AB	H	2B	3B	HR	HR %	R	RBI	BB	SO	SB	BA	SA	AB	H	G by POS
1982 MIL A	4	15	2	0	0	1	6.7	1	1	0	3	0	.133	.333	0	0	OF-4

WORLD SERIES

	G	AB	H	2B	3B	HR	HR %	R	RBI	BB	SO	SB	BA	SA	AB	H	G by POS
1982 MIL A	7	27	6	0	1	1	3.7	4	1	2	4	0	.222	.407	0	0	OF-7

Brusie Ogrodowski

OGRODOWSKI, AMBROSE FRANCIS
B. Feb. 17, 1912, Hoytville, Pa.   D. Mar. 5, 1956, San Francisco, Calif.   BR TR 5'11"   175 lbs.

	G	AB	H	2B	3B	HR	HR %	R	RBI	BB	SO	SB	BA	SA	AB	H	G by POS
1936 STL N	94	237	54	15	1	1	0.4	28	20	10	20	0	.228	.312	9	1	C-85
1937	90	279	65	10	3	3	1.1	37	31	11	17	2	.233	.323	3	2	C-87
2 yrs.	184	516	119	25	4	4	0.8	65	51	21	37	2	.231	.318	12	3	C-172

Hal O'Hagan

O'HAGAN, HAROLD P.
B. Sept. 30, 1873, Washington, D. C.   D. Jan. 14, 1913, Newark, N. J.   6'   173 lbs.

	G	AB	H	2B	3B	HR	HR %	R	RBI	BB	SO	SB	BA	SA	AB	H	G by POS
1892 WAS N	1	4	1	0	0	0	0.0	0		0		2	.250	.250	0	0	C-1
1902 3 teams	CHI	N (31G –	.194)		NY	N (26G –	.143)		CLE	A (3G –	.385)						
" total	60	205	38	5	4	0	0.0	17	19	13		13	.185	.249	0	0	1B-52, OF-8
2 yrs.	61	209	39	5	4	0	0.0	18	19	13	2	13	.187	.249	0	0	1B-52, OF-8, C-1

Bill O'Hara

O'HARA, WILLIAM ALEXANDER
B. Aug. 14, 1883, Toronto, Ont., Canada   D. June 15, 1931, Jersey City, N. J.   BL TR

	G	AB	H	2B	3B	HR	HR %	R	RBI	BB	SO	SB	BA	SA	AB	H	G by POS
1909 NY N	115	360	85	9	3	1	0.3	48	30	41		31	.236	.286	0	0	OF-115
1910 STL N	9	20	3	0	0	0	0.0	1	2	1		3	.150	.150	0	0	OF-4, 1B-1
2 yrs.	124	380	88	9	3	1	0.3	49	32	42	3	31	.232	.279	0	0	OF-119, 1B-1

Kid O'Hara

O'HARA, JAMES FRANCIS
B. Dec. 19, 1875, Wilkes-Barre, Pa.   D. Dec. 1, 1954, Canton, Ohio   BB TR 5'7½"   152 lbs.

	G	AB	H	2B	3B	HR	HR %	R	RBI	BB	SO	SB	BA	SA	AB	H	G by POS
1904 BOS N	8	29	6	0	0	0	0.0	3	0	4		1	.207	.207	0	0	OF-8

Tom O'Hara

O'HARA, THOMAS F.
B. July 13, 1885, Waverly, N. Y.   D. June 8, 1954, Denver, Colo.

	G	AB	H	2B	3B	HR	HR %	R	RBI	BB	SO	SB	BA	SA	AB	H	G by POS
1906 STL N	14	53	16	1	0	0	0.0	8	0	3		3	.302	.321	0	0	OF-14
1907	48	173	41	2	1	0	0.0	11	5	12		1	.237	.260	1	0	OF-47
2 yrs.	62	226	57	3	1	0	0.0	19	5	15		4	.252	.274	1	0	OF-61

Len Okrie

OKRIE, LEONARD JOSEPH
Son of Frank Okrie.
B. July 16, 1923, Detroit, Mich.   BR TR 6'1"   185 lbs.

	G	AB	H	2B	3B	HR	HR %	R	RBI	BB	SO	SB	BA	SA	AB	H	G by POS
1948 WAS A	19	42	10	0	1	0	0.0	1	1	1	7	0	.238	.286	2	0	C-17
1950	17	27	6	0	0	0	0.0	1	2	6	7	0	.222	.222	0	0	C-17
1951	5	8	1	1	0	0	0.0	1	0	2	1	0	.125	.250	0	0	C-5
1952 BOS A	1	1	0	0	0	0	0.0	0	0	0	1	0	.000	.000	0	0	C-1
4 yrs.	42	78	17	1	1	0	0.0	3	3	9	16	0	.218	.256	2	0	C-40

David Oldfield

OLDFIELD, DAVID
B. Nov. 18, 1864, Kensington, Pa.   D. Aug. 28, 1939, Philadelphia, Pa.   BB TL 5'7"   175 lbs.

	G	AB	H	2B	3B	HR	HR %	R	RBI	BB	SO	SB	BA	SA	AB	H	G by POS
1883 BAL AA	1	4	0	0	0	0	0.0	0		0		0	.000	.000	0	0	C-1
1885 BKN AA	10	25	8	1	0	0	0.0	2		3		0	.320	.360	0	0	C-9, OF-2
1886 2 teams	BKN	AA (14G –	.236)		WAS	N (21G –	.141)										
" total	35	126	23	3	0	0	0.0	9	2	7	15		.183	.206	0	0	C-25, OF-10, SS-1
3 yrs.	46	155	31	4	0	0	0.0	11	1	10	15		.200	.226	0	0	C-35, OF-12, SS-1

John Oldham

OLDHAM, JOHN HARDIN
B. Nov. 6, 1932, Salinas, Calif.   BR TL 6'3"   198 lbs.

	G	AB	H	2B	3B	HR	HR %	R	RBI	BB	SO	SB	BA	SA	AB	H	G by POS
1956 CIN N	1	0	0	0	0	0	0.0	0	0	0	0	0	–	–	0	0	

Bob Oldis

OLDIS, ROBERT CARL
B. Jan. 5, 1928, Preston, Iowa   BR TR 6'1"   185 lbs.

	G	AB	H	2B	3B	HR	HR %	R	RBI	BB	SO	SB	BA	SA	AB	H	G by POS
1953 WAS A	7	16	4	0	0	0	0.0	0	3	1	2	0	.250	.250	0	0	C-7
1954	11	24	8	1	0	0	0.0	1	0	1	3	0	.333	.375	1	0	C-8, 3B-2
1955	6	6	0	0	0	0	0.0	1	0	1	0	0	.000	.000	0	0	C-6
1960 PIT N	22	20	4	1	0	0	0.0	1	1	1	2	0	.200	.250	0	0	C-22
1961	4	5	0	0	0	0	0.0	0	0	0	0	0	.000	.000	0	0	C-4

	G	AB	H	2B	3B	HR	HR %	R	RBI	BB	SO	SB	BA	SA	Pinch Hit AB	Pinch Hit H	G by POS

Bob Oldis continued

	G	AB	H	2B	3B	HR	HR%	R	RBI	BB	SO	SB	BA	SA	AB	H	G by POS
1962 PHI N	38	80	21	1	0	1	1.3	9	10	13	10	0	.263	.313	7	2	C-30
1963	47	85	19	3	0	0	0.0	8	8	3	5	0	.224	.259	11	3	C-43
7 yrs.	135	236	56	6	0	1	0.4	20	22	20	22	0	.237	.275	19	5	C-120, 3B-2

WORLD SERIES

	G	AB	H	2B	3B	HR		R	RBI	BB	SO	SB	BA	SA	AB	H	G by POS
1960 PIT N	2	0	0	0	0	0	−	0	0	0	0	0	−	−	0	0	C-2

Rube Oldring

OLDRING, REUBEN HENRY
B. May 30, 1884, New York, N. Y.   D. Sept. 9, 1961, Bridgeton, N. J.   BR TR 5'10" 186 lbs.

	G	AB	H	2B	3B	HR	HR%	R	RBI	BB	SO	SB	BA	SA	AB	H	G by POS
1905 NY A	8	30	9	0	1	1	3.3	2	6	2		4	.300	.467	0	0	SS-8
1906 PHI A	59	174	42	10	1	0	0.0	15	19	2		7	.241	.310	2	0	3B-49, SS-3, 2B-2, 1B-1
1907	117	441	126	27	9	1	0.2	48	40	7		29	.286	.395	0	0	OF-117
1908	116	434	96	14	2	1	0.2	38	39	18		13	.221	.270	0	0	OF-116
1909	90	326	75	13	8	1	0.3	39	28	20		17	.230	.328	0	0	OF-89, 1B-1
1910	134	546	168	27	14	4	0.7	79	57	23		17	.308	.430	0	0	OF-134
1911	121	495	147	11	14	3	0.6	84	59	21		21	.297	.394	1	0	OF-119
1912	98	395	119	14	5	1	0.3	61	24	10		17	.301	.370	1	0	OF-97
1913	136	538	152	27	9	5	0.9	101	71	34	37	40	.283	.394	0	0	OF-136, SS-5
1914	119	466	129	21	7	3	0.6	68	49	18	35	14	.277	.371	2	0	OF-117
1915	107	408	101	23	3	6	1.5	49	42	22	21	11	.248	.363	3	2	OF-96, 3B-8
1916 2 teams		PHI	A (40G −	.247)		NY	A	(43G −	.234)								
" total	83	304	73	16	3	1	0.3	27	26	21	22	7	.240	.322	0	0	OF-83
1918 PHI A	49	133	31	2	1	0	0.0	5	11	8	10	0	.233	.263	15	4	OF-30, 3B-2, 2B-2
13 yrs.	1237	4690	1268	205	77	27	0.6	616	471	206	125	197	.270	.364	24	6	OF-1134, 3B-59, SS-16, 2B-4, 1B-2

WORLD SERIES

	G	AB	H	2B	3B	HR	HR%	R	RBI	BB	SO	SB	BA	SA	AB	H	G by POS
1911 PHI A	6	25	5	2	0	1	4.0	2	3	0	6	0	.200	.400	0	0	OF-6
1913	5	22	6	0	1	0	0.0	5	0	0	5	0	.273	.364	0	0	OF-5
1914	4	15	1	0	0	0	0.0	0	0	0	1	0	.067	.067	0	0	OF-4
3 yrs.	15	62	12	2	1	1	1.6	7	3	0	12	1	.194	.306	0	0	OF-15

Charley O'Leary

O'LEARY, CHARLES TIMOTHY
B. Oct. 15, 1882, Chicago, Ill.   D. Jan. 6, 1941, Chicago, Ill.   BR TR 5'7" 165 lbs.

	G	AB	H	2B	3B	HR	HR%	R	RBI	BB	SO	SB	BA	SA	AB	H	G by POS
1904 DET A	135	456	97	10	3	1	0.2	39	16	21		9	.213	.254	0	0	SS-135
1905	148	512	109	13	1	1	0.2	47	33	29		13	.213	.248	0	0	SS-148
1906	128	443	97	13	2	2	0.5	34	34	17		8	.219	.271	1	1	SS-127
1907	139	465	112	19	1	0	0.0	61	34	32		11	.241	.286	1	0	SS-138
1908	65	211	53	9	3	0	0.0	21	17	9		4	.251	.322	0	0	SS-64, 2B-1
1909	76	261	53	10	0	0	0.0	29	13	6		9	.203	.241	0	0	3B-54, 2B-15, SS-4, OF-2
1910	65	211	51	7	1	0	0.0	23	9	9		7	.242	.284	0	0	2B-38, SS-16, 3B-6
1911	74	256	68	8	2	0	0.0	29	25	21		10	.266	.313	0	0	2B-67, 3B-6
1912	3	10	2	0	0	0	0.0	1	1	0		0	.200	.200	0	0	2B-3
1913 STL N	120	404	88	15	5	0	0.0	32	31	20	34	3	.218	.280	1	0	SS-102, 2B-15
1934 STL A	1	1	1	0	0	0	0.0	1	0	0	0	0	1.000	1.000	1	1	
11 yrs.	954	3230	731	104	18	4	0.1	317	213	164	34	74	.226	.273	6	2	SS-734, 2B-139, 3B-66, OF-2

WORLD SERIES

	G	AB	H	2B	3B	HR	HR%	R	RBI	BB	SO	SB	BA	SA	AB	H	G by POS
1907 DET A	5	17	1	0	0	0	0.0	0	0	1	3	0	.059	.059	0	0	SS-5
1908	5	19	3	0	0	0	0.0	2	0	0	3	0	.158	.158	0	0	SS-5
1909	1	3	0	0	0	0	0.0	0	0	0	0	0	.000	.000	0	0	3B-1
3 yrs.	11	39	4	0	0	0	0.0	2	0	1	6	0	.103	.103	0	0	SS-10, 3B-1

Dan O'Leary

O'LEARY, DANIEL (Hustling Dan)
B. Oct. 22, 1856, Detroit, Mich.   D. June 24, 1922, Chicago, Ill.   BL
Manager 1884.

	G	AB	H	2B	3B	HR	HR%	R	RBI	BB	SO	SB	BA	SA	AB	H	G by POS
1879 PRO N	2	7	3	0	0	0	0.0	1	2	0	0		.429	.429	0	0	OF-2
1880 BOS N	3	12	3	2	0	0	0.0	1	1	0	3		.250	.417	0	0	OF-3
1881 DET N	2	8	0	0	0	0	0.0	0	0	0	2		.000	.000	0	0	OF-2
1882 WOR N	6	22	4	1	0	0	0.0	2	2	5	5		.182	.227	0	0	OF-6
1884 CIN U	32	132	34	0	2	1	0.8	14		5			.258	.311	0	0	OF-32
5 yrs.	45	181	44	3	2	1	0.6	18	5	10	10		.243	.298	0	0	OF-45

Frank Olin

OLIN, FRANKLIN WALTER
B. Jan. 9, 1860, Woodford, Vt.   D. May 21, 1951, St. Louis, Mo.   BL

	G	AB	H	2B	3B	HR	HR%	R	RBI	BB	SO	SB	BA	SA	AB	H	G by POS
1884 3 teams		WAS	AA (21G −	.386)		WAS	U (1G −	.000)		TOL	AA (26G −	.256)					
" total	48	173	54	4	2	1	0.6	28		13			.312	.376	0	0	OF-38, 2B-12
1885 DET N	1	4	2	0	0	0	0.0	1	0	0	0		.500	.500	0	0	3B-1
2 yrs.	49	177	56	4	2	1	0.6	29		13	0		.316	.379	0	0	OF-38, 2B-12, 3B-1

Tony Oliva

OLIVA, ANTONIO PEDRO
B. July 20, 1940, Pinar del Rio, Cuba   BL TR 6'1" 175 lbs.

	G	AB	H	2B	3B	HR	HR%	R	RBI	BB	SO	SB	BA	SA	AB	H	G by POS
1962 MIN A	9	9	4	1	0	0	0.0	3	3	3	2	0	.444	.556	5	2	OF-2
1963	7	7	3	0	0	0	0.0	0	1	0	2	0	.429	.429	7	3	
1964	161	672	217	43	9	32	4.8	109	94	34	68	12	.323	.557	2	1	OF-159
1965	149	576	185	40	5	16	2.8	107	98	55	64	19	.321	.491	1	0	OF-147
1966	159	622	191	32	7	25	4.0	99	87	42	72	13	.307	.502	1	1	OF-159
1967	146	557	161	34	6	17	3.1	76	83	44	61	11	.289	.463	1	1	OF-146
1968	128	470	136	24	5	18	3.8	54	68	45	61	10	.289	.477	2	0	OF-126
1969	153	637	197	39	4	24	3.8	97	101	45	66	10	.309	.496	1	0	OF-152
1970	157	628	204	36	7	23	3.7	96	107	38	67	5	.325	.514	1	1	OF-157
1971	126	487	164	30	3	22	4.5	73	81	25	44	4	.337	.546	5	0	OF-121
1972	10	28	9	1	0	0	0.0	1	1	2	5	0	.321	.357	1	0	OF-9
1973	146	571	166	20	0	16	2.8	63	92	45	44	2	.291	.410	4	2	DH-142
1974	127	459	131	16	2	13	2.8	43	57	27	31	0	.285	.414	13	4	DH-112
1975	131	455	123	10	0	13	2.9	46	58	41	45	0	.270	.378	10	5	DH-120

	G	AB	H	2B	3B	HR	HR %	R	RBI	BB	SO	SB	BA	SA	Pinch Hit AB	Pinch Hit H	G by POS

Tony Oliva continued

	G	AB	H	2B	3B	HR	HR %	R	RBI	BB	SO	SB	BA	SA	PH AB	PH H	G by POS
1976	67	123	26	3	0	1	0.8	3	16	2	13	0	.211	.260	32	7	DH-32
15 yrs.	1676	6301	1917	329	48	220	3.5	870	947	448	645	86	.304	.476	86	30	OF-1178, DH-406

LEAGUE CHAMPIONSHIP SERIES

	G	AB	H	2B	3B	HR	HR %	R	RBI	BB	SO	SB	BA	SA	PH AB	PH H	G by POS
1969 MIN A	3	13	5	2	0	1	7.7	3	2	1	3	1	.385	.769	0	0	OF-3
1970	3	12	6	2	0	1	8.3	2	1	0	1	0	.500	.917	0	0	OF-3
2 yrs.	6	25	11	4	0	2	8.0	5	3	1	4	1	.440	.840	0	0	OF-6

WORLD SERIES

	G	AB	H	2B	3B	HR	HR %	R	RBI	BB	SO	SB	BA	SA	PH AB	PH H	G by POS
1965 MIN A	7	26	5	1	0	1	3.8	2	2	1	6	0	.192	.346	0	0	OF-7

Ed Olivares
OLIVARES, EDWARD BALZAC — BR TR 5'11" 180 lbs.
B. Nov. 5, 1938, Mayaguez, Puerto Rico

	G	AB	H	2B	3B	HR	HR %	R	RBI	BB	SO	SB	BA	SA	PH AB	PH H	G by POS
1960 STL N	3	5	0	0	0	0	0.0	2	0	0	3	0	.000	.000	2	0	2B-1
1961	21	30	5	0	0	0	0.0	2	1	0	4	1	.167	.167	11	1	OF-10
2 yrs.	24	35	5	0	0	0	0.0	4	1	0	7	1	.143	.143	13	1	OF-10, 2B-1

Al Oliver
OLIVER, ALBERT (Mr. Scoop) — BL TL 6' 195 lbs.
B. Oct. 14, 1946, Portsmouth, Ohio

	G	AB	H	2B	3B	HR	HR %	R	RBI	BB	SO	SB	BA	SA	PH AB	PH H	G by POS
1968 PIT N	4	8	1	0	0	0	0.0	1	0	0	4	0	.125	.125	3	0	OF-1
1969	129	463	132	19	2	17	3.7	55	70	21	38	8	.285	.445	7	0	1B-106, OF-21
1970	151	551	149	33	5	12	2.2	63	83	35	35	1	.270	.414	4	2	OF-80, 1B-77
1971	143	529	149	31	7	14	2.6	69	64	27	72	4	.282	.446	6	0	OF-116, 1B-25
1972	140	565	176	27	4	12	2.1	88	89	34	44	2	.312	.437	1	0	OF-138, 1B-3
1973	158	654	191	38	7	20	3.1	90	99	22	52	6	.292	.463	2	0	OF-109, 1B-50
1974	147	617	198	38	12	11	1.8	96	85	33	58	10	.321	.475	2	1	OF-98, 1B-49
1975	155	628	176	39	8	18	2.9	90	84	25	73	4	.280	.454	1	0	OF-153, 1B-4
1976	121	443	143	22	5	12	2.7	62	61	26	29	6	.323	.476	11	3	OF-106, 1B-3
1977	154	568	175	29	6	19	3.3	75	82	40	38	13	.308	.481	6	3	OF-148
1978 TEX A	133	525	170	35	5	14	2.7	65	89	31	41	8	.324	.490	0	0	OF-107, DH-26
1979	136	492	159	28	4	12	2.4	69	76	34	34	4	.323	.470	13	5	OF-119, DH-10
1980	163	656	209	43	3	19	2.9	96	117	39	47	5	.319	.480	2	1	OF-157, DH-4, 1B-1
1981	102	421	130	29	1	4	1.0	53	55	24	28	3	.309	.411	1	1	DH-101, 1B-1
1982 MON N	160	617	204	43	2	22	3.6	90	109	61	59	5	.331	.514	1	1	1B-159
1983	157	614	184	38	3	8	1.3	70	84	44	44	1	.300	.410	4	2	1B-153, OF-1
1984 2 teams	SF N (91G – .298)						PHI N (28G – .312)										
" total	119	432	130	26	2	0	0.0	36	48	27	36	3	.301	.370	16	4	1B-101, OF-5
17 yrs.	2272	8783	2676	518	76	214	2.4	1168	1296	523	732	83	.305	.454	80	23	OF-1359, 1B-732, DH-141

LEAGUE CHAMPIONSHIP SERIES

	G	AB	H	2B	3B	HR	HR %	R	RBI	BB	SO	SB	BA	SA	PH AB	PH H	G by POS
1970 PIT N	2	8	2	0	0	0	0.0	0	1	1	0	0	.250	.250	0	0	1B-2
1971	4	12	3	0	0	1	8.3	2	5	1	3	0	.250	.500	0	0	OF-4
1972	5	20	5	2	1	1	5.0	3	3	0	4	0	.250	.600	0	0	OF-5
1974	4	14	2	0	0	0	0.0	1	1	2	2	0	.143	.143	0	0	OF-3
1975	3	11	2	0	0	1	9.1	1	2	2	0	0	.182	.455	0	0	OF-3
5 yrs.	18	65	14	2	1	3	4.6	7	12	6	9	0	.215	.415	0	0	OF-16, 1B-2

WORLD SERIES

	G	AB	H	2B	3B	HR	HR %	R	RBI	BB	SO	SB	BA	SA	PH AB	PH H	G by POS
1971 PIT N	5	19	4	2	0	0	0.0	1	2	2	5	0	.211	.316	1	0	OF-4

Bob Oliver
OLIVER, ROBERT LEE — BR TR 6'3" 205 lbs.
B. Feb. 28, 1943, Shreveport, La.

	G	AB	H	2B	3B	HR	HR %	R	RBI	BB	SO	SB	BA	SA	PH AB	PH H	G by POS
1965 PIT N	3	2	0	0	0	0	0.0	1	0	0	0	0	.000	.000	0	0	OF-3
1969 KC A	118	394	100	8	4	13	3.3	43	43	21	74	5	.254	.393	7	2	OF-98, 1B-12, 3B-8
1970	160	612	159	24	6	27	4.4	83	99	42	126	3	.260	.451	2	0	1B-115, 3B-46
1971	128	373	91	12	2	8	2.1	35	52	14	88	0	.244	.351	22	5	1B-68, OF-48, 3B-2
1972 2 teams	CAL A (134G – .269)						KC A (16G – .270)										
" total	150	572	154	22	5	20	3.5	54	76	29	109	5	.269	.430	1	0	1B-127, OF-24
1973 CAL A	151	544	144	24	1	18	3.3	51	89	33	100	1	.265	.412	12	2	3B-49, OF-47, 1B-32, DH-12
1974 2 teams	CAL A (110G – .248)						BAL A (9G – .150)										
" total	119	379	92	11	1	8	2.1	23	59	16	56	3	.243	.340	24	4	1B-61, 3B-46, OF-4, DH-2
1975 NY A	18	38	5	1	0	0	0.0	3	1	1	9	0	.132	.158	6	1	1B-8, DH-3, 3B-1
8 yrs.	847	2914	745	102	19	94	3.2	293	419	156	562	17	.256	.400	74	14	1B-423, OF-224, 3B-152, DH-17

Dave Oliver
OLIVER, DAVID JACOB — BL TR 5'11" 175 lbs.
B. Apr. 7, 1951, Stockton, Calif.

	G	AB	H	2B	3B	HR	HR %	R	RBI	BB	SO	SB	BA	SA	PH AB	PH H	G by POS
1977 CLE A	7	22	7	0	1	0	0.0	2	3	4	0	0	.318	.409	1	0	2B-7

Dick Oliver
Playing record listed under Dick Barrett

Gene Oliver
OLIVER, EUGENE GEORGE — BR TR 6'2" 225 lbs.
B. Mar. 22, 1936, Moline, Ill.

	G	AB	H	2B	3B	HR	HR %	R	RBI	BB	SO	SB	BA	SA	PH AB	PH H	G by POS
1959 STL N	68	172	42	9	0	6	3.5	14	28	7	41	3	.244	.401	18	4	OF-42, C-9, 1B-5
1961	22	52	14	2	0	4	7.7	8	9	6	10	0	.269	.538	5	1	C-15, OF-1
1962	122	345	89	19	1	14	4.1	42	45	50	59	5	.258	.441	19	6	C-98, OF-8, 1B-3
1963 2 teams	STL N (39G – .225)						MIL N (95G – .250)										
" total	134	398	97	16	2	17	4.3	44	65	40	78	4	.244	.422	16	2	1B-55, C-37, OF-35
1964 MIL N	93	279	77	15	1	13	4.7	45	49	17	41	3	.276	.477	23	3	1B-76, C-1
1965	122	392	106	20	0	21	5.4	56	58	36	61	5	.270	.482	12	3	C-64, 1B-52, OF-1
1966 ATL N	76	191	37	9	1	8	4.2	19	24	16	43	2	.194	.377	24	5	C-48, 1B-5, OF-2
1967 2 teams	ATL N (17G – .196)						PHI N (85G – .224)										
" total	102	314	69	18	0	10	3.2	37	40	35	64	2	.220	.373	11	0	C-93, 1B-2
1968 2 teams	BOS A (16G – .143)						CHI N (8G – .364)										
" total	24	46	9	0	0	0	0.0	3	2	7	14	0	.196	.196	10	3	C-11, OF-2, 1B-2

	G	AB	H	2B	3B	HR	HR %	R	RBI	BB	SO	SB	BA	SA	Pinch Hit AB	Pinch Hit H	G by POS

Gene Oliver continued

	G	AB	H	2B	3B	HR	HR%	R	RBI	BB	SO	SB	BA	SA	PH AB	PH H	G by POS
1969 CHI N	23	27	6	3	0	0	0.0	0	0	1	9	0	.222	.333	14	4	C-6
10 yrs.	786	2216	546	111	5	93	4.2	268	320	215	420	24	.246	.427	152	31	C-382, 1B-200, OF-91

Nate Oliver

OLIVER, NATHANIEL (Pee Wee)
B. Dec. 13, 1940, St. Petersburg, Fla.
BR TR 5'10" 160 lbs.

	G	AB	H	2B	3B	HR	HR%	R	RBI	BB	SO	SB	BA	SA	PH AB	PH H	G by POS
1963 LA N	65	163	39	2	3	1	0.6	23	9	13	25	3	.239	.307	6	0	2B-57, SS-2
1964	99	321	78	9	0	0	0.0	28	21	31	57	7	.243	.271	1	0	2B-98, SS-1
1965	8	1	1	0	0	0	0.0	3	0	0	0	1	1.000	1.000	0	0	2B-2
1966	80	119	23	2	0	0	0.0	17	3	13	17	3	.193	.210	3	1	2B-68, SS-2, 3B-1
1967	77	232	55	6	2	0	0.0	18	7	13	50	3	.237	.280	12	3	2B-39, SS-32, OF-1
1968 SF N	36	73	13	2	0	0	0.0	3	1	1	13	0	.178	.205	3	0	2B-14, SS-13, 3B-1
1969 2 teams	NY	A	(1G – .000)		CHI	N	(44G – .159)										
" total	45	45	7	3	0	1	2.2	15	4	1	10	0	.156	.289	4	0	2B-13
7 yrs.	410	954	216	24	5	2	0.2	107	45	72	172	17	.226	.268	29	4	2B-291, SS-50, 3B-2, OF-1

WORLD SERIES

	G	AB	H	2B	3B	HR	HR%	R	RBI	BB	SO	SB	BA	SA	PH AB	PH H	G by POS
1966 LA N	1	0	0	0	0	0	–	0	0	0	0	0	–	–	0	0	

Tom Oliver

OLIVER, THOMAS NOBLE (Rebel)
B. Jan. 15, 1903, Montgomery, Ala.
BR TR 6' 168 lbs.

	G	AB	H	2B	3B	HR	HR%	R	RBI	BB	SO	SB	BA	SA	PH AB	PH H	G by POS
1930 BOS A	154	646	189	34	2	0	0.0	86	46	42	25	6	.293	.351	0	0	OF-154
1931	148	586	162	35	5	0	0.0	52	70	25	17	4	.276	.353	0	0	OF-148
1932	122	455	120	23	3	0	0.0	39	37	25	12	1	.264	.327	5	1	OF-116
1933	90	244	63	9	1	0	0.0	25	23	13	7	1	.258	.303	2	1	OF-86
4 yrs.	514	1931	534	101	11	0	0.0	202	176	105	61	12	.277	.340	7	2	OF-504

Luis Olmo

OLMO, LUIS FRANCISCO RODRIGUEZ (Jibaro)
B. Aug. 11, 1919, Arecibo, Puerto Rico
BR TR 5'11½" 185 lbs.

	G	AB	H	2B	3B	HR	HR%	R	RBI	BB	SO	SB	BA	SA	PH AB	PH H	G by POS
1943 BKN N	57	238	72	6	4	4	1.7	39	37	8	20	3	.303	.412	0	0	OF-57
1944	136	520	134	20	5	9	1.7	65	85	17	37	10	.258	.367	6	3	OF-64, 2B-42, 3B-31
1945	141	556	174	27	13	10	1.8	62	110	36	33	15	.313	.462	3	0	OF-106, 3B-31, 2B-1
1949	38	105	32	4	1	1	1.0	15	14	5	11	2	.305	.390	4	2	OF-34
1950 BOS N	69	154	35	7	1	5	3.2	23	22	18	23	3	.227	.383	12	0	OF-55, 3B-1
1951	21	56	11	1	1	0	0.0	4	4	4	4	0	.196	.250	3	0	OF-16
6 yrs.	462	1629	458	65	25	29	1.8	208	272	88	128	33	.281	.405	28	5	OF-332, 3B-63, 2B-43

WORLD SERIES

	G	AB	H	2B	3B	HR	HR%	R	RBI	BB	SO	SB	BA	SA	PH AB	PH H	G by POS
1949 BKN N	4	11	3	0	0	1	9.1	2	2	0	2	0	.273	.545	0	0	OF-4

Al Olsen

OLSEN, ALBERT WILLIAM (Ole)
B. Mar. 30, 1921, San Diego, Calif.
BL TL 6' 165 lbs.

	G	AB	H	2B	3B	HR	HR%	R	RBI	BB	SO	SB	BA	SA	PH AB	PH H	G by POS
1943 BOS A	1	0	0	0	0	0	–	0	0	1	0	1	–	–	0	0	

Barney Olsen

OLSEN, BERNARD CHARLES
B. Sept. 11, 1919, Everett, Mass. D. Mar. 30, 1977, Everett, Mass.
BR TR 5'11" 179 lbs.

	G	AB	H	2B	3B	HR	HR%	R	RBI	BB	SO	SB	BA	SA	PH AB	PH H	G by POS
1941 CHI N	24	73	21	6	1	1	1.4	13	4	4	11	0	.288	.438	1	1	OF-23

Ivy Olson

OLSON, IVAN MASSIE
B. Oct. 14, 1885, Kansas City, Mo. D. Sept. 1, 1965, Inglewood, Calif.
BR TR 5'10½" 175 lbs.

	G	AB	H	2B	3B	HR	HR%	R	RBI	BB	SO	SB	BA	SA	PH AB	PH H	G by POS
1911 CLE A	140	545	142	20	8	1	0.2	89	50	34		20		.261	.332	0	0	SS-139, 3B-1
1912	123	467	118	13	1	0	0.0	68	33	21		16		.253	.285	8	1	SS-56, 3B-35, 2B-21, OF-3
1913	104	370	92	13	3	0	0.0	47	32	22	28	7	.249	.300	7	2	3B-73, 1B-22, 2B-1
1914	89	310	75	6	2	1	0.3	22	20	13	24	15	.242	.284	6	0	SS-31, 2B-23, 3B-19, OF-6, 1B-3
1915 2 teams	CIN	N	(63G – .232)		BKN	N	(18G – .077)										
" total	81	233	50	5	5	0	0.0	20	17	13	13	10	.215	.279	8	0	2B-47, 3B-16, SS-7, 1B-7, OF-1
1916 BKN N	108	351	89	13	4	1	0.3	29	38	21	27	14	.254	.322	2	0	SS-103, 2B-3, 1B-1
1917	139	580	156	18	5	2	0.3	64	38	14	34	6	.269	.328	0	0	SS-133, 3B-6
1918	126	506	121	16	4	1	0.2	63	17	27	18	21	.239	.292	0	0	SS-126
1919	140	590	164	14	9	1	0.2	73	38	30	12	26	.278	.337	0	0	SS-140
1920	143	637	162	13	11	1	0.2	71	46	20	19	4	.254	.314	0	0	SS-125, 2B-21
1921	151	652	174	22	10	3	0.5	88	35	28	26	4	.267	.345	0	0	SS-133, 2B-20
1922	136	551	150	26	6	1	0.2	63	47	25	10	8	.272	.347	0	0	SS-85, 2B-51
1923	82	292	76	11	1	1	0.3	33	35	14	10	5	.260	.315	2	2	2B-72, 3B-3, SS-2, 1B-1
1924	10	27	6	1	0	0	0.0	0	0	3	1	0	.222	.259	0	0	SS-8, 2B-2
14 yrs.	1572	6111	1575	191	69	13	0.2	730	446	285	222	156	.258	.318	33	5	SS-1054, 2B-295, 3B-153, 1B-34, OF-10

WORLD SERIES

	G	AB	H	2B	3B	HR	HR%	R	RBI	BB	SO	SB	BA	SA	PH AB	PH H	G by POS
1916 BKN N	5	16	4	0	1	0	0.0	1	2	2	2	0	.250	.375	0	0	SS-5
1920	7	25	8	1	0	0	0.0	2	0	3	1	0	.320	.360	0	0	SS-7
2 yrs.	12	41	12	1	1	0	0.0	3	2	5	3	0	.293	.366	0	0	SS-12

Karl Olson

OLSON, KARL ARTHUR (Ole)
B. July 6, 1930, Ross, Calif.
BR TR 6'3" 205 lbs.

	G	AB	H	2B	3B	HR	HR%	R	RBI	BB	SO	SB	BA	SA	PH AB	PH H	G by POS
1951 BOS A	5	10	1	0	0	0	0.0	0	0	0	3	0	.100	.100	0	0	OF-5
1953	25	57	7	2	0	1	1.8	5	6	1	9	0	.123	.211	1	0	OF-24
1954	101	227	59	12	2	1	0.4	25	20	12	23	2	.260	.344	21	3	OF-78
1955	26	48	12	1	2	0	0.0	7	1	1	10	0	.250	.354	3	2	OF-21
1956 WAS A	106	313	77	10	2	4	1.3	34	22	28	41	1	.246	.329	10	2	OF-101
1957 2 teams	WAS	A	(8G – .167)		DET	A	(8G – .143)										
" total	16	26	4	0	0	0	0.0	3	1	1	8	0	.154	.154	5	0	OF-11
6 yrs.	279	681	160	25	6	6	0.9	74	50	43	94	3	.235	.316	40	7	OF-240

	G	AB	H	2B	3B	HR	HR %	R	RBI	BB	SO	SB	BA	SA	Pinch Hit AB	Pinch Hit H	G by POS

Marv Olson

OLSON, MARVIN CLEMENT (Sparky)
B. May 28, 1907, Gaysville, S. D.
BR TR 5'7" 160 lbs.

	G	AB	H	2B	3B	HR	HR %	R	RBI	BB	SO	SB	BA	SA	AB	H	G by POS
1931 BOS A	15	53	10	1	0	0	0.0	8	5	9	3	0	.189	.208	0	0	2B-15
1932	115	403	100	14	6	0	0.0	58	25	61	26	1	.248	.313	7	2	2B-106, 3B-1
1933	3	1	0	0	0	0	0.0	1	0	0	1	0	.000	.000	0	0	2B-1
3 yrs.	133	457	110	15	6	0	0.0	67	30	70	30	1	.241	.300	7	2	2B-122, 3B-1

Tom O'Malley

O'MALLEY, THOMAS PATRICK
B. Dec. 25, 1960, Orange, N. J.
BL TR 6' 170 lbs.

	G	AB	H	2B	3B	HR	HR %	R	RBI	BB	SO	SB	BA	SA	AB	H	G by POS
1982 SF N	92	291	80	12	4	2	0.7	26	27	33	39	0	.275	.364	9	3	3B-83, SS-1, 2B-1
1983	135	410	106	16	1	5	1.2	40	45	52	47	2	.259	.339	17	5	3B-117
1984 2 teams	SF	N (13G – .120)		CHI	A (12G – .125)												
" total	25	41	5	0	0	0	0.0	2	3	2	7	0	.122	.122	13	2	3B-13
3 yrs.	252	742	191	28	5	7	0.9	68	75	87	93	2	.257	.337	39	10	3B-213, SS-1, 2B-1

Ollie O'Mara

O'MARA, OLIVER EDWARD
B. Mar. 8, 1891, St. Louis, Mo.
BR TR 5'8" 140 lbs.

	G	AB	H	2B	3B	HR	HR %	R	RBI	BB	SO	SB	BA	SA	AB	H	G by POS
1912 DET A	1	4	0	0	0	0	0.0	0	0	0		0	.000	.000	0	0	SS-1
1914 BKN N	67	247	65	10	2	1	0.4	41	7	16	26	14	.263	.332	0	0	SS-63
1915	149	577	141	26	3	0	0.0	77	31	51	40	11	.244	.300	0	0	SS-149
1916	72	193	39	5	2	0	0.0	18	15	12	20	10	.202	.249	11	1	SS-51
1918	121	450	96	8	1	1	0.2	29	24	7	18	11	.213	.242	0	0	3B-121
1919	2	7	0	0	0	0	0.0	1	0	0	0	0	.000	.000	0	0	3B-2
6 yrs.	412	1478	341	49	8	2	0.1	166	77	86	104	46	.231	.279	11	1	SS-264, 3B-123

WORLD SERIES
| 1916 BKN N | 1 | 1 | 0 | 0 | 0 | 0 | 0.0 | 0 | 0 | 0 | 1 | 0 | .000 | .000 | 1 | 0 | |

Tom O'Meara

O'MEARA, THOMAS EDWARD
B. Dec. 12, 1872, Chicago, Ill. D. Feb. 16, 1902, Ft. Wayne, Ind.

	G	AB	H	2B	3B	HR	HR %	R	RBI	BB	SO	SB	BA	SA	AB	H	G by POS
1895 CLE N	1	1	0	0	0	0	0.0	1	0	1	0	0	.000	.000	0	0	C-1
1896	12	33	5	0	0	0	0.0	5	0	5	7	0	.152	.152	2	0	C-9, 1B-1
2 yrs.	13	34	5	0	0	0	0.0	6	0	6	7	0	.147	.147	2	0	C-10, 1B-1

Dennie O'Neil

O'NEIL, DANIEL J.
B. Apr. 10, 1860, Tralee, Ireland D. May 18, 1926, Holyoke, Mass.
TL 6'2½" 200 lbs.

	G	AB	H	2B	3B	HR	HR %	R	RBI	BB	SO	SB	BA	SA	AB	H	G by POS
1893 STL N	7	25	3	0	0	0	0.0	2	4	0	3	0	.120	.120	0	0	1B-7

John O'Neil

O'NEIL, JOHN FRANCIS
B. Apr. 19, 1920, Shelbiana, Ky.
BR TR 5'9" 155 lbs.

	G	AB	H	2B	3B	HR	HR %	R	RBI	BB	SO	SB	BA	SA	AB	H	G by POS
1946 PHI N	46	94	25	3	0	0	0.0	12	9	5	12	0	.266	.298	3	0	SS-32

Mickey O'Neil

O'NEIL, GEORGE MICHAEL
B. Apr. 12, 1900, St. Louis, Mo. D. Apr. 8, 1964, St. Louis, Mo.
BR TR 5'10" 185 lbs.

	G	AB	H	2B	3B	HR	HR %	R	RBI	BB	SO	SB	BA	SA	AB	H	G by POS
1919 BOS N	11	28	6	0	0	0	0.0	3	1	1	7	0	.214	.214	0	0	C-11
1920	112	304	86	5	4	0	0.0	19	28	21	20	4	.283	.326	0	3	C-105, 2B-1
1921	98	277	69	9	4	2	0.7	26	29	23	21	2	.249	.332	3	0	C-95
1922	83	251	56	5	2	0	0.0	18	26	14	11	1	.223	.259	3	0	C-79
1923	96	306	65	7	4	0	0.0	29	20	17	14	3	.212	.261	1	0	C-95
1924	106	362	89	4	1	0	0.0	32	22	14	27	4	.246	.262	0	0	C-106
1925	70	222	57	6	5	2	0.9	29	30	21	16	1	.257	.356	1	0	C-69
1926 BKN N	75	201	42	5	3	0	0.0	19	20	23	8	3	.209	.264	1	0	C-74
1927 2 teams	WAS	A (5G – .000)		NY	N (16G – .132)												
" total	21	44	5	0	0	0	0.0	2	3	5	3	0	.114	.114	1	0	C-20
9 yrs.	672	1995	475	41	23	4	0.2	177	179	139	127	18	.238	.288	17	3	C-654, 2B-1

Bill O'Neill

O'NEILL, WILLIAM JOHN
B. Jan. 22, 1880, St. John, N. B., Canada D. July 27, 1920, St. John, N. B., Canada
BB 5'11"

	G	AB	H	2B	3B	HR	HR %	R	RBI	BB	SO	SB	BA	SA	AB	H	G by POS
1904 2 teams	BOS	A (17G – .196)		WAS	A (95G – .244)												
" total	112	416	99	11	1	1	0.2	40	21	24		22	.238	.276	6	2	OF-102, 2B-3, SS-2
1906 CHI A	94	330	82	4	1	1	0.3	37	21	22		19	.248	.276	1	0	OF-93
2 yrs.	206	746	181	15	2	2	0.3	77	42	46		41	.243	.276	7	2	OF-195, 2B-3, SS-2

WORLD SERIES
| 1906 CHI A | 1 | 1 | 0 | 0 | 0 | 0 | 0.0 | 1 | 0 | 0 | 0 | 0 | .000 | .000 | 0 | 0 | OF-1 |

Fred O'Neill

O'NEILL, FREDERICK JAMES
B. 1865, London, Ont., Canada D. Mar. 7, 1892, London, Ont., Canada

	G	AB	H	2B	3B	HR	HR %	R	RBI	BB	SO	SB	BA	SA	AB	H	G by POS
1887 NY AA	6	26	8	1	1	0	0.0	4		1		3	.308	.423	0	0	OF-6

Harry O'Neill

O'NEILL, HARRY MINK
B. May 8, 1917, Philadelphia, Pa. D. Mar. 6, 1945, Iwo Jima, Marianas Is.
BR TR 6'3" 205 lbs.

	G	AB	H	2B	3B	HR	HR %	R	RBI	BB	SO	SB	BA	SA	AB	H	G by POS
1939 PHI A	1	0	0	0	0	0	–	0	0	0	0	0	–	–	0	0	C-1

Jack O'Neill

O'NEILL, JOHN JOSEPH
Brother of Jim O'Neill. Brother of Steve O'Neill.
Brother of Mike O'Neill.
B. Jan. 10, 1873, Maam, Ireland D. June 29, 1935, Scranton, Pa.
BR TR 5'10" 165 lbs.

	G	AB	H	2B	3B	HR	HR %	R	RBI	BB	SO	SB	BA	SA	AB	H	G by POS
1902 STL N	63	192	27	1	1	0	0.0	13	12	13		2	.141	.156	4	0	C-59
1903	75	246	58	9	1	0	0.0	23	27	13		11	.236	.280	1	0	C-74
1904 CHI N	51	168	36	5	0	1	0.6	8	19	6		1	.214	.262	2	0	C-49
1905	53	172	34	4	2	0	0.0	16	12	8		6	.198	.244	3	0	C-50
1906 BOS N	61	167	30	5	1	0	0.0	14	4	12		0	.180	.222	7	2	C-48, 1B-2, OF-1
5 yrs.	303	945	185	24	5	1	0.1	74	74	52		20	.196	.235	17	2	C-280, 1B-2, OF-1

	G	AB	H	2B	3B	HR	HR %	R	RBI	BB	SO	SB	BA	SA	Pinch Hit AB	Pinch Hit H	G by POS

Jim O'Neill

O'NEILL, JAMES LEO
Brother of Steve O'Neill. Brother of Mike O'Neill.
Brother of Jack O'Neill.
B. Feb. 23, 1893, Minooka, Pa.   D. Sept. 5, 1976, Chambersburg, Pa.

BR TR 5'10½" 165 lbs.

	G	AB	H	2B	3B	HR	HR %	R	RBI	BB	SO	SB	BA	SA	AB	H	G by POS
1920 WAS A	86	294	85	17	7	1	0.3	27	40	13	30	7	.289	.405	2	0	SS-80, 2B-2
1923	23	33	9	1	0	0	0.0	6	3	1	3	0	.273	.303	2	0	2B-8, 3B-6, OF-1
2 yrs.	109	327	94	18	7	1	0.3	33	43	14	33	7	.287	.394	4	0	SS-80, 2B-10, 3B-6, OF-1

John O'Neill

O'NEILL, JOHN J.
B. New York, N. Y.

TR

	G	AB	H	2B	3B	HR	HR %	R	RBI	BB	SO	SB	BA	SA	AB	H	G by POS
1899 NY N	2	7	0	0	0	0	0.0	0	0	0		0	.000	.000	0	0	C-2
1902	2	8	0	0	0	0	0.0	0	0	0		0	.000	.000	0	0	C-2
2 yrs.	4	15	0	0	0	0	0.0	0	0	0		0	.000	.000	0	0	C-4

Mike O'Neill

O'NEILL, MICHAEL JOYCE
Played as Mike Joyce 1901.   Brother of Jim O'Neill.
Brother of Jack O'Neill.   Brother of Steve O'Neill.
B. Sept. 7, 1877, Galway, Ireland   D. Aug. 12, 1959, Scranton, Pa.

BL TL 5'11"   185 lbs.

	G	AB	H	2B	3B	HR	HR %	R	RBI	BB	SO	SB	BA	SA	AB	H	G by POS
1901 STL N	6	15	6	0	0	0	0.0	3	2	3		0	.400	.400	1	1	P-5
1902	51	135	43	5	3	2	1.5	21	15	2		0	.319	.444	12	1	P-36, OF-3
1903	41	110	25	2	2	0	0.0	12	6	8		3	.227	.282	7	3	P-19, OF-13
1904	30	91	21	7	2	0	0.0	9	16	5		0	.231	.352	2	1	P-25, OF-3
1907 CIN N	9	29	2	0	2	0	0.0	5	2	2		1	.069	.207	0	0	OF-9
5 yrs.	137	380	97	14	9	2	0.5	50	41	20		4	.255	.355	22	6	P-85, OF-28

Peaches O'Neill

O'NEILL, PHILIP BERNARD
B. Aug. 30, 1879, Anderson, Ind.   D. Aug. 2, 1955, Anderson, Ind.

BR TR 5'11"   165 lbs.

	G	AB	H	2B	3B	HR	HR %	R	RBI	BB	SO	SB	BA	SA	AB	H	G by POS
1904 CIN N	8	15	4	0	0	0	0.0	0	1	1		0	.267	.267	2	0	C-5, 1B-1

Steve O'Neill

O'NEILL, STEPHEN FRANCIS
Brother of Jim O'Neill.   Brother of Jack O'Neill.
Brother of Mike O'Neill.
B. July 6, 1891, Minooka, Pa.   D. Jan. 26, 1962, Cleveland, Ohio
Manager 1935-37, 1943-48, 1950-54.

BR TR 5'10"   165 lbs.

	G	AB	H	2B	3B	HR	HR %	R	RBI	BB	SO	SB	BA	SA	AB	H	G by POS
1911 CLE A	9	27	4	1	0	0	0.0	1	1	4		2	.148	.185	0	0	C-9
1912	68	215	49	4	0	0	0.0	17	14	12		2	.228	.247	1	0	C-67
1913	78	234	69	13	3	0	0.0	19	29	10	24	5	.295	.376	0	0	C-78
1914	86	269	68	12	2	0	0.0	28	20	15	35	1	.253	.312	4	1	C-81, 1B-1
1915	121	386	91	14	2	2	0.5	32	34	26	41	2	.236	.298	6	1	C-115
1916	130	378	89	23	0	0	0.0	30	29	24	33	2	.235	.296	2	1	C-128
1917	129	370	68	10	2	0	0.0	21	29	41	55	2	.184	.222	2	0	C-127
1918	114	359	87	8	7	1	0.3	34	35	48	22	5	.242	.312	1	0	C-113
1919	125	398	115	35	7	2	0.5	46	47	48	21	4	.289	.427	2	0	C-123
1920	149	489	157	39	5	3	0.6	63	55	69	39	3	.321	.440	1	0	C-148
1921	106	335	108	22	1	1	0.3	39	50	57	22	0	.322	.403	1	0	C-105
1922	133	392	122	27	4	2	0.5	33	65	73	25	2	.311	.416	2	0	C-130
1923	113	330	82	12	0	0	0.0	31	50	64	34	0	.248	.285	2	0	C-111
1924 BOS A	106	307	73	15	1	0	0.0	29	38	63	23	0	.238	.293	14	2	C-92
1925 NY A	35	91	26	5	0	1	1.1	7	13	10	3	0	.286	.374	3	0	C-31
1927 STL A	74	191	44	7	0	1	0.5	14	22	20	6	0	.230	.283	13	5	C-60
1928	10	24	7	1	0	0	0.0	4	6	8	0	0	.292	.333	0	0	C-10
17 yrs.	1586	4795	1259	248	34	13	0.3	448	537	592	383	30	.263	.337	54	10	C-1528, 1B-1

WORLD SERIES
	G	AB	H	2B	3B	HR	HR %	R	RBI	BB	SO	SB	BA	SA	AB	H	G by POS
1920 CLE A	7	21	7	3	0	0	0.0	1	2	4	3	0	.333	.476	0	0	C-7

Tip O'Neill

O'NEILL, JAMES EDWARD
B. May 25, 1858, Woodstock, Ont., Canada   D. Dec. 31, 1915, Woodstock, Ont., Canada

BR TR 6'½"   167 lbs.

	G	AB	H	2B	3B	HR	HR %	R	RBI	BB	SO	SB	BA	SA	AB	H	G by POS
1883 NY N	23	76	15	3	0	0	0.0	8		3	15		.197	.237	0	0	P-19, OF-7
1884 STL AA	78	297	82	14	11	3	1.0	49		12			.276	.428	0	0	OF-64, P-17, 1B-1
1885	52	206	72	6	5	3	1.5	44		13			.350	.471	0	0	OF-52
1886	138	579	190	28	15	3	0.5	106		47			.328	.444	0	0	OF-138
1887	124	517	225	52	19	14	2.7	167		50		30	.435	.691	0	0	OF-124
1888	130	529	177	24	10	5	0.9	96	98	44		26	.335	.446	0	0	OF-130
1889	134	534	179	33	8	9	1.7	123	110	72	37	28	.335	.478	0	0	OF-134
1890 CHI P	137	577	174	20	16	3	0.5	112	75	65	36	29	.302	.407	0	0	OF-137
1891 STL AA	129	521	167	28	4	10	1.9	112	95	62	33	25	.321	.447	0	0	OF-129
1892 CIN N	109	419	105	14	6	2	0.5	63	52	53	25	14	.251	.327	0	0	OF-109
10 yrs.	1054	4255	1386	222	94	52	1.2	880	429	421	146	152	.326	.459	0	0	OF-1024, P-36, 1B-1

Curly Onis

ONIS, MANUEL DOMINGUEZ (Ralph)
B. Oct. 24, 1908, Tampa, Fla.

BR TR 5'9"   180 lbs.

	G	AB	H	2B	3B	HR	HR %	R	RBI	BB	SO	SB	BA	SA	AB	H	G by POS
1935 BKN N	1	1	1	0	0	0	0.0	0	0	0	0	0	1.000	1.000	0	0	C-1

Eddie Onslow

ONSLOW, EDWARD JOSEPH
Brother of Jack Onslow.
B. Feb. 17, 1893, Meadville, Pa.   D. May 8, 1981, Dennison, Ohio

BL TL 6'   170 lbs.

	G	AB	H	2B	3B	HR	HR %	R	RBI	BB	SO	SB	BA	SA	AB	H	G by POS
1912 DET A	35	128	29	1	2	1	0.8	11	13	3		3	.227	.289	0	0	1B-35
1913	17	55	14	1	0	0	0.0	7	8	5	9	1	.255	.273	0	0	1B-17
1918 CLE A	2	6	1	0	0	0	0.0	0	0	0	1	0	.167	.167	1	0	OF-1
1927 WAS A	9	18	4	1	0	0	0.0	1	1	1	0	0	.222	.278	3	0	1B-5
4 yrs.	63	207	48	3	2	1	0.5	19	22	9	10	4	.232	.280	4	0	1B-57, OF-1

	G	AB	H	2B	3B	HR	HR %	R	RBI	BB	SO	SB	BA	SA	Pinch Hit AB	Pinch Hit H	G by POS

Jack Onslow

ONSLOW, JOHN JAMES
Brother of Eddie Onslow.
B. Oct. 13, 1888, Scottdale, Pa.   D. Dec. 22, 1960, Concord, Mass.
Manager 1949-50.
BR TR 5'11"   180 lbs.

	G	AB	H	2B	3B	HR	HR %	R	RBI	BB	SO	SB	BA	SA	PH AB	PH H	G by POS
1912 DET A	31	69	11	1	0	0	0.0	7	4	10		1	.159	.174	0	0	C-31
1917 NY N	9	8	2	1	0	0	0.0	1	0	0	1	0	.250	.375	0	0	C-9
2 yrs.	40	77	13	2	0	0	0.0	8	4	10	1	1	.169	.195	0	0	C-40

Steve Ontiveros

ONTIVEROS, STEVEN ROBERT
B. Oct. 26, 1951, Bakersfield, Calif.
BB TR 6'   185 lbs.

	G	AB	H	2B	3B	HR	HR %	R	RBI	BB	SO	SB	BA	SA	PH AB	PH H	G by POS
1973 SF N	24	33	8	0	0	1	3.0	3	5	4	7	0	.242	.333	17	5	1B-5, OF-1
1974	120	343	91	15	1	4	1.2	45	33	57	41	0	.265	.350	23	4	3B-75, 1B-19, OF-2
1975	108	325	94	16	0	3	0.9	21	31	55	44	2	.289	.366	11	2	3B-89, OF-8, 1B-4
1976	59	74	13	3	0	0	0.0	8	5	6	11	0	.176	.216	44	8	OF-7, 3B-7, 1B-4
1977 CHI N	156	546	163	32	3	10	1.8	54	68	81	69	3	.299	.423	3	1	3B-155
1978	82	276	67	14	4	1	0.4	34	22	34	33	0	.243	.333	4	2	3B-77, 1B-1
1979	152	519	148	28	2	4	0.8	58	57	58	68	0	.285	.370	9	3	3B-142, 1B-1
1980	31	77	16	3	0	1	1.3	7	3	14	17	0	.208	.286	6	0	3B-24
8 yrs.	732	2193	600	111	10	24	1.1	230	224	309	290	5	.274	.366	117	25	3B-569, 1B-34, OF-18

Jose Oquendo

OQUENDO, JOSE MANUEL
B. July 4, 1963, Rio Peidras, Puerto Rico
BR TR 5'10"   145 lbs.

	G	AB	H	2B	3B	HR	HR %	R	RBI	BB	SO	SB	BA	SA	PH AB	PH H	G by POS
1983 NY N	120	328	70	7	0	1	0.3	29	17	19	60	8	.213	.244	1	0	SS-116
1984	81	189	42	5	0	0	0.0	23	10	15	26	10	.222	.249	3	2	SS-67
2 yrs.	201	517	112	12	0	1	0.2	52	27	34	86	18	.217	.246	4	2	SS-183

Ernie Oravetz

ORAVETZ, ERNEST EUGENE
B. Jan. 24, 1932, Johnstown, Pa.
BB TL 5'4"   145 lbs.

	G	AB	H	2B	3B	HR	HR %	R	RBI	BB	SO	SB	BA	SA	PH AB	PH H	G by POS
1955 WAS A	100	263	71	5	1	0	0.0	24	25	26	19	1	.270	.297	35	6	OF-57
1956	88	137	34	3	2	0	0.0	20	11	27	20	1	.248	.299	49	11	OF-31
2 yrs.	188	400	105	8	3	0	0.0	44	36	53	39	2	.263	.298	84	17	OF-88

Tony Ordenana

ORDENANA, ANTONIO RODRIGUEZ
B. Oct. 30, 1918, Guanabacoa, Havana, Cuba
BR TR 5'10"   150 lbs.

	G	AB	H	2B	3B	HR	HR %	R	RBI	BB	SO	SB	BA	SA	PH AB	PH H	G by POS
1943 PIT N	1	4	2	0	0	0	0.0	0	3	0	0	0	.500	.500	0	0	SS-1

Joe Orengo

ORENGO, JOSEPH CHARLES
B. Nov. 29, 1914, San Francisco, Calif.
BR TR 6'   185 lbs.

	G	AB	H	2B	3B	HR	HR %	R	RBI	BB	SO	SB	BA	SA	PH AB	PH H	G by POS
1939 STL N	7	3	0	0	0	0	0.0	0	0	0	1	0	.000	.000	0	0	SS-7
1940	129	415	119	23	4	7	1.7	58	56	65	90	9	.287	.412	0	0	2B-77, 3B-34, SS-19
1941 NY N	77	252	54	11	2	4	1.6	23	25	28	49	1	.214	.321	3	1	3B-59, SS-9, 2B-6
1943 2 teams	NY	N (83G – .218)		BKN	N (7G – .200)												
" total	90	281	61	10	2	6	2.1	29	30	40	48	1	.217	.331	2	2	1B-82, 3B-6
1944 DET A	46	154	31	10	0	0	0.0	14	10	20	29	1	.201	.266	1	0	SS-29, 3B-11, 1B-5, 2B-2
1945 CHI A	17	15	1	0	0	0	0.0	5	1	3	2	0	.067	.067	5	0	3B-7, 1B-1
6 yrs.	366	1120	266	54	8	17	1.5	129	122	156	219	12	.238	.346	11	3	3B-117, 1B-87, 2B-86, SS-64

George Orme

ORME, GEORGE WILLIAM
B. Sept. 16, 1891, Lebanon, Ind.   D. Mar. 16, 1962, Indianapolis, Ind.
BR TR 5'10"   160 lbs.

	G	AB	H	2B	3B	HR	HR %	R	RBI	BB	SO	SB	BA	SA	PH AB	PH H	G by POS
1920 BOS A	4	6	2	0	0	0	0.0	4	1	3	0	0	.333	.333	0	0	OF-3

Jess Orndorff

ORNDORFF, JESSE WALWORTH THAYER
B. Jan. 15, 1881, Chicago, Ill.   D. Sept. 28, 1960, Cardiff-By-The-Sea, Calif.
BB TR 6'   168 lbs.

	G	AB	H	2B	3B	HR	HR %	R	RBI	BB	SO	SB	BA	SA	PH AB	PH H	G by POS
1907 BOS N	5	17	2	0	0	0	0.0	0	0	0		0	.118	.118	0	0	C-5

Charlie O'Rourke

O'ROURKE, JAMES PATRICK
B. June 22, 1937, Walla Walla, Wash.
BR TR 6'2"   195 lbs.

	G	AB	H	2B	3B	HR	HR %	R	RBI	BB	SO	SB	BA	SA	PH AB	PH H	G by POS
1959 STL N	2	2	0	0	0	0	0.0	0	0	0	0	0	.000	.000	2	0	

Frank O'Rourke

O'ROURKE, FRANCIS JAMES (Blackie)
B. Nov. 28, 1891, Hamilton, Ont., Canada
BR TR 5'10½"   165 lbs.

	G	AB	H	2B	3B	HR	HR %	R	RBI	BB	SO	SB	BA	SA	PH AB	PH H	G by POS
1912 BOS N	61	196	24	3	1	0	0.0	11	16	11	50	1	.122	.148	0	0	SS-59
1917 BKN N	64	198	47	7	1	0	0.0	18	15	14	25	11	.237	.283	4	0	3B-58
1918	4	12	2	0	0	0	0.0	0	2	1	3	0	.167	.167	1	1	2B-2, OF-1
1920 WAS A	14	54	16	1	0	0	0.0	8	5	2	5	2	.296	.315	0	0	SS-13, 3B-1
1921	123	444	104	17	8	3	0.7	51	54	26	56	6	.234	.329	0	0	SS-122
1922 BOS A	67	216	57	14	3	1	0.5	28	17	20	28	6	.264	.370	0	0	SS-48, 3B-19
1924 DET A	47	181	50	11	2	0	0.0	28	19	12	19	7	.276	.359	0	0	2B-40, SS-7
1925	124	482	141	40	7	5	1.0	88	57	32	37	5	.293	.436	0	0	2B-118, 3B-6
1926	111	363	88	16	1	1	0.3	43	41	35	33	8	.242	.300	3	0	3B-58, 2B-41, SS-10
1927 STL A	140	538	144	25	3	1	0.2	85	39	64	43	19	.268	.331	2	0	3B-120, 2B-16, 1B-3
1928	99	391	103	24	3	1	0.3	54	62	21	19	10	.263	.348	3	0	3B-96, SS-2
1929	154	585	147	23	9	2	0.3	81	62	41	28	7	.251	.332	0	0	3B-151, 2B-3, SS-2
1930	115	400	107	15	4	1	0.3	52	41	35	30	11	.268	.333	4	1	3B-84, SS-23, 1B-3
1931	8	9	2	0	0	0	0.0	0	0	0	1	1	.222	.222	3	0	SS-2, 1B-1
14 yrs.	1131	4069	1032	196	42	15	0.4	547	430	314	377	101	.254	.333	20	2	3B-593, SS-288, 2B-220, 1B-7, OF-1

Jim O'Rourke

O'ROURKE, JAMES HENRY (Orator Jim)
Father of Queenie O'Rourke.
B. Aug. 24, 1852, Bridgeport, Conn.   D. Jan. 8, 1919, Bridgeport, Conn.
Manager 1881-84, 1893.
Hall of Fame 1945.
BR TR 5'8"   185 lbs.

	G	AB	H	2B	3B	HR	HR %	R	RBI	BB	SO	SB	BA	SA	PH AB	PH H	G by POS
1876 BOS N	70	312	102	17	3	2	0.6	61	43	15	17		.327	.420	0	0	OF-68, 1B-2, C-1
1877	61	265	96	14	4	0	0.0	68	23	20	9		.362	.445	0	0	OF-60, 1B-1
1878	60	255	71	17	7	1	0.4	44	29	5	21		.278	.412	0	0	OF-57, 1B-2, C-2
1879 PRO N	81	362	126	19	9	1	0.3	69	46	13	10		.348	.459	0	0	OF-56, 1B-20, C-5, 3B-3

	G	AB	H	2B	3B	HR	HR %	R	RBI	BB	SO	SB	BA	SA	Pinch Hit AB	Pinch Hit H	G by POS

Jim O'Rourke continued

	G	AB	H	2B	3B	HR	HR %	R	RBI	BB	SO	SB	BA	SA	AB	H	G by POS
1880 BOS N	86	363	100	20	11	6	1.7	71	45	21	8		.275	.441	0	0	OF-37, 1B-19, SS-17, 3B-10, C-9
1881 BUF N	83	348	105	21	7	0	0.0	71	30	27	18		.302	.402	0	0	3B-56, OF-18, C-8, SS-3, 1B-1
1882	84	370	104	15	6	2	0.5	62		13	13		.281	.370	0	0	OF-81, SS-2, C-2, 3B-1
1883	94	436	143	29	8	1	0.2	102		15	13		.328	.438	0	0	OF-61, C-33, 3B-8, SS-3, P-2
1884	108	467	**162**	33	7	5	1.1	119		35	17		.347	.480	0	0	OF-86, 1B-18, C-10, P-4, 3B-1
1885 NY N	112	477	143	21	**16**	5	1.0	119		40	21		.300	.442	0	0	OF-112, C-8
1886	105	440	136	26	6	1	0.2	106	34	39	21		.309	.402	0	0	OF-63, C-47, 1B-2
1887	103	397	113	15	13	3	0.8	73	88	36	11	46	.285	.411	0	0	C-40, 3B-38, OF-28, 2B-2
1888	107	409	112	16	6	4	1.0	50	50	24	30	25	.274	.372	0	0	OF-87, C-15, 1B-4, 3B-2
1889	128	502	161	36	7	3	0.6	89	81	40	34	33	.321	.438	0	0	OF-128, C-1
1890 NY P	111	478	172	37	5	9	1.9	112	115	33	20	23	.360	.515	0	0	OF-111
1891 NY N	136	555	164	28	7	5	0.9	92	95	26	29	19	.295	.398	0	0	OF-126, C-14
1892	115	448	136	28	5	0	0.0	62	56	30	30	16	.304	.388	0	0	OF-111, C-4, 1B-1
1893 WAS N	129	547	157	22	5	3	0.5	75	95	49	26	15	.287	.362	0	0	OF-87, 1B-33, C-9
1904 NY N	1	4	1	0	0	0	0.0	1	0	0		0	.250	.250	0	0	C-1
19 yrs.	1774	7435	2304	414	132	51	0.7	1446	830	481	348	177	.310	.422	0	0	OF-1377, C-209, 3B-119, 1B-103, SS-25, P-6, 2B-2

Joe O'Rourke

O'ROURKE, JOSEPH LEO, JR.
Son of Patsy O'Rourke.
B. Oct. 28, 1904, Philadelphia, Pa.
BL TR 5'7" 145 lbs.

	G	AB	H	2B	3B	HR	HR %	R	RBI	BB	SO	SB	BA	SA	AB	H	G by POS
1929 PHI N	3	3	0	0	0	0	0.0	0	0	0	1	0	.000	.000	3	0	

John O'Rourke

O'ROURKE, JOHN
Brother of Jim O'Rourke.
B. 1853, Bridgeport, Conn.   D. June 23, 1911, Boston, Mass.
BL TL 6' 190 lbs.

	G	AB	H	2B	3B	HR	HR %	R	RBI	BB	SO	SB	BA	SA	AB	H	G by POS
1879 BOS N	72	317	108	17	11	6	1.9	69	**62**	8	32		.341	**.521**	0	0	OF-71
1880	81	313	86	22	8	3	1.0	30	36	18	32		.275	.425	0	0	OF-81
1883 NY AA	77	315	85	19	5	2	0.6	49		21			.270	.381	0	0	OF-76, 1B-1
3 yrs.	230	945	279	58	24	11	1.2	148	98	47	64		.295	.442	0	0	OF-228, 1B-1

Patsy O'Rourke

O'ROURKE, JOSEPH LEO, SR.
Father of Joe O'Rourke.
B. Apr. 13, 1881, Philadelphia, Pa.   D. Apr. 18, 1956, Philadelphia, Pa.
BR TR 5'7" 160 lbs.

	G	AB	H	2B	3B	HR	HR %	R	RBI	BB	SO	SB	BA	SA	AB	H	G by POS
1908 STL N	53	164	32	4	2	0	0.0	8	16	14		2	.195	.244	0	0	SS-53

Queenie O'Rourke

O'ROURKE, JAMES STEPHEN
Son of Jim O'Rourke.
B. Dec. 26, 1889, Bridgeport, Conn.   D. Dec. 22, 1955, Sparrows Point, Md.
BR TR 5'7" 150 lbs.

	G	AB	H	2B	3B	HR	HR %	R	RBI	BB	SO	SB	BA	SA	AB	H	G by POS
1908 NY A	34	108	25	1	0	0	0.0	9	5	3		4	.231	.241	2	0	OF-14, SS-11, 2B-4, 3B-3

Tim O'Rourke

O'ROURKE, TIMOTHY PATRICK (Voiceless Tim)
B. May 18, 1864, Chicago, Ill.   D. Apr. 20, 1938, Seattle, Wash.
TR 5'10" 170 lbs.

	G	AB	H	2B	3B	HR	HR %	R	RBI	BB	SO	SB	BA	SA	AB	H	G by POS
1890 SYR AA	87	332	94	13	6	1	0.3	48		36		22	.283	.367	0	0	3B-87
1891 COL AA	34	136	38	1	3	0	0.0	22	12	15	7	9	.279	.331	0	0	3B-34
1892 BAL N	63	239	74	8	4	0	0.0	40	35	24	19	12	.310	.377	0	0	SS-58, OF-4, 3B-1
1893 2 teams	BAL N (31G – .363)							LOU N (92G – .281)									
" total	123	487	148	12	5	0	0.0	102	72	89	19	27	.304	.349	0	0	SS-61, OF-51, 3B-11
1894 3 teams	LOU N (55G – .277)							STL N (18G – .282)			WAS N (7G – .200)						
" total	80	316	86	9	5	0	0.0	60	39	33	13	11	.272	.332	0	0	1B-30, 3B-21, OF-18, SS-6, 2B-5
5 yrs.	387	1510	440	43	23	1	0.1	272	157	197	58	81	.291	.352	0	0	3B-154, SS-125, OF-73, 1B-30, 2B-5

Tom O'Rourke

O'ROURKE, THOMAS JOSEPH
B. 1862, New York, N. Y.   D. July 19, 1929, New York, N. Y.
5'9" 158 lbs.

	G	AB	H	2B	3B	HR	HR %	R	RBI	BB	SO	SB	BA	SA	AB	H	G by POS
1887 BOS N	22	78	12	3	0	0	0.0	12	10	7	6	4	.154	.192	0	0	C-21, OF-1, 3B-1
1888	20	74	13	0	0	0	0.0	3	4	1	9	2	.176	.176	0	0	C-20, OF-1
1890 2 teams	NY N (2G – .000)				SYR AA (41G – .216)												
" total	43	160	33	8	0	0	0.0	17		13		2	.206	.256	0	0	C-42, 1B-1
3 yrs.	85	312	58	11	0	0	0.0	32	14	21	15	8	.186	.221	0	0	C-83, OF-2, 3B-1, 1B-1

Bill Orr

ORR, WILLIAM JOHN
B. Apr. 22, 1891, San Francisco, Calif.   D. Mar. 10, 1967, St. Helena, Calif.
BR TR 5'11" 168 lbs.

	G	AB	H	2B	3B	HR	HR %	R	RBI	BB	SO	SB	BA	SA	AB	H	G by POS
1913 PHI A	27	67	13	1	1	0	0.0	6	7	4	10	1	.194	.239	1	0	SS-16, 1B-3, 3B-2, 2B-2
1914	10	24	4	1	1	0	0.0	3	1	2	5	1	.167	.292	3	1	SS-6, 3B-1
2 yrs.	37	91	17	2	2	0	0.0	9	8	6	15	2	.187	.253	4	1	SS-22, 3B-3, 1B-3, 2B-2

Dave Orr

ORR, DAVID L.
B. Sept. 29, 1859, New York, N. Y.   D. June 3, 1915, Brooklyn, N. Y.
Manager 1887.
BR TR

	G	AB	H	2B	3B	HR	HR %	R	RBI	BB	SO	SB	BA	SA	AB	H	G by POS
1883 2 teams	NY AA (13G – .320)				NY N (1G – .000)												
" total	14	53	16	4	3	2	3.8	6		0	1		.302	.604	0	0	1B-13, OF-1
1884 NY AA	110	458	162	32	13	9	2.0	82		5			.354	.539	0	0	1B-110, OF-3
1885	107	444	152	29	**21**	6	1.4	76		8			.342	**.543**	0	0	1B-107, P-3
1886	136	571	**193**	25	**31**	7	1.2	93		17			.338	**.527**	0	0	1B-136
1887	84	345	127	25	10	2	0.6	63		22		17	.368	.516	0	0	1B-81, OF-3
1888 BKN AA	99	394	120	20	5	1	0.3	57	59	7		11	.305	.388	0	0	1B-99
1889 COL AA	134	560	183	31	12	4	0.7	70	87	9	38	12	.327	.446	0	0	1B-134
1890 BKN P	107	464	173	32	13	6	1.3	89	124	30	11	10	.373	.537	0	0	1B-107
8 yrs.	791	3289	1126	198	108	37	1.1	536	269	98	50	50	.342	.502	0	0	1B-787, OF-7, P-3

	G	AB	H	2B	3B	HR	HR %	R	RBI	BB	SO	SB	BA	SA	Pinch Hit AB	Pinch Hit H	G by POS

Ernie Orsatti

ORSATTI, ERNESTO RALPH
B. Sept. 8, 1903, Los Angeles, Calif.   D. Sept. 4, 1968, Canoga Park, Calif.
BL TL 5'7½"   154 lbs.

	G	AB	H	2B	3B	HR	HR %	R	RBI	BB	SO	SB	BA	SA	PH AB	PH H	G by POS
1927 STL N	27	92	29	7	3	0	0.0	15	12	11	12	2	.315	.457	1	0	OF-26
1928	27	69	21	6	0	3	4.3	10	15	10	11	0	.304	.522	3	0	OF-17, 1B-5
1929	113	346	115	21	7	3	0.9	64	39	33	43	7	.332	.460	17	6	OF-77, 1B-10
1930	48	131	42	8	4	1	0.8	24	15	12	18	1	.321	.466	12	3	1B-22, OF-11
1931	78	158	46	16	6	0	0.0	27	19	14	16	1	.291	.468	15	2	OF-45, 1B-1
1932	101	375	126	27	6	2	0.5	44	44	18	29	5	.336	.456	3	2	OF-96, 1B-1
1933	120	436	130	21	6	0	0.0	55	38	33	33	14	.298	.374	9	3	OF-101, 1B-3
1934	105	337	101	14	4	0	0.0	39	31	27	31	6	.300	.365	10	2	OF-90
1935	90	221	53	9	3	1	0.5	28	24	18	25	10	.240	.321	23	5	OF-60
9 yrs.	709	2165	663	129	39	10	0.5	306	237	176	218	46	.306	.416	93	23	OF-523, 1B-42
WORLD SERIES																	
1928 STL N	4	7	2	1	0	0	0.0	1	0	1	3	0	.286	.429	2	0	OF-1
1930	1	1	0	0	0	0	0.0	0	0	0	0	0	.000	.000	1	0	
1931	1	3	0	0	0	0	0.0	0	0	0	3	0	.000	.000	0	0	OF-1
1934	7	22	7	0	1	0	0.0	3	2	3	1	0	.318	.409	1	0	OF-6
4 yrs.	13	33	9	1	1	0	0.0	4	2	4	7	0	.273	.364	4	0	OF-8

John Orsino

ORSINO, JOHN JOSEPH (Horse)
B. Apr. 22, 1938, Teaneck, N. J.
BR TR 6'3"   215 lbs.

	G	AB	H	2B	3B	HR	HR %	R	RBI	BB	SO	SB	BA	SA	PH AB	PH H	G by POS
1961 SF N	25	83	23	3	2	4	4.8	5	12	3	13	0	.277	.506	3	2	C-25
1962	18	48	13	2	0	0	0.0	4	4	5	11	0	.271	.313	3	1	C-16
1963 BAL A	116	379	103	18	1	19	5.0	53	56	38	53	2	.272	.475	5	2	C-109, 1B-3
1964	81	248	55	10	0	8	3.2	21	23	23	55	0	.222	.359	12	3	C-66, 1B-5
1965	77	232	54	10	2	9	3.9	30	28	23	51	1	.233	.409	14	4	C-62, 1B-5
1966 WAS A	14	23	4	1	0	0	0.0	1	0	0	7	0	.174	.217	7	1	1B-5, C-2
1967	1	1	0	0	0	0	0.0	0	0	0	1	0	.000	.000	1	0	
7 yrs.	332	1014	252	44	5	40	3.9	114	123	92	191	3	.249	.420	45	13	C-280, 1B-18
WORLD SERIES																	
1962 SF N	1	1	0	0	0	0	0.0	0	0	0	0	0	.000	.000	0	0	C-1

Joe Orsulak

ORSULAK, JOSEPH MICHAEL
B. May 31, 1962, Parsippany, N. J.
BL TL 6'1"   185 lbs.

	G	AB	H	2B	3B	HR	HR %	R	RBI	BB	SO	SB	BA	SA	PH AB	PH H	G by POS
1983 PIT N	7	11	2	0	0	0	0.0	0	1	0	2	0	.182	.182	3	0	OF-4
1984	32	67	17	1	2	0	0.0	12	3	1	7	3	.254	.328	6	1	OF-25
2 yrs.	39	78	19	1	2	0	0.0	12	4	1	9	3	.244	.308	9	1	OF-29

Jorge Orta

ORTA, JORGE NUNEZ
B. Nov. 26, 1950, Mazatlan, Mexico
BL TR 5'10"   170 lbs.

	G	AB	H	2B	3B	HR	HR %	R	RBI	BB	SO	SB	BA	SA	PH AB	PH H	G by POS
1972 CHI A	51	124	25	3	1	3	2.4	20	11	6	37	3	.202	.315	11	1	SS-18, 2B-14, 3B-9
1973	128	425	113	9	10	6	1.4	46	40	37	87	8	.266	.376	5	2	2B-122, SS-1
1974	139	525	166	31	2	10	1.9	73	67	40	88	9	.316	.440	7	1	2B-123, DH-10, SS-3
1975	140	542	165	26	10	11	2.0	64	83	48	67	16	.304	.450	3	2	2B-135, DH-2
1976	158	636	174	29	8	14	2.2	74	72	38	77	24	.274	.410	3	0	OF-77, 3B-49, DH-31
1977	144	564	159	27	8	11	2.0	71	84	46	49	4	.282	.417	7	1	2B-139
1978	117	420	115	19	2	13	3.1	45	53	42	39	1	.274	.421	3	1	2B-114, DH-2
1979	113	325	85	18	3	11	3.4	49	46	44	33	1	.262	.437	22	4	DH-62, 2B-41
1980 CLE A	129	481	140	18	3	10	2.1	78	64	71	44	6	.291	.403	2	0	OF-120, DH-7
1981	88	338	92	14	3	5	1.5	50	34	21	43	4	.272	.376	5	2	OF-86
1982 LA N	86	115	25	5	0	2	1.7	13	8	12	13	0	.217	.313	60	9	OF-17
1983 TOR A	103	245	58	6	3	10	4.1	30	38	19	29	1	.237	.408	26	5	DH-69, OF-17
1984 KC A	122	403	120	23	7	9	2.2	50	50	28	39	0	.298	.457	13	4	DH-83, OF-26, 2B-1
13 yrs.	1518	5143	1437	228	60	115	2.2	663	650	452	645	77	.279	.414	167	32	2B-689, OF-343, DH-266, 3B-58, SS-22
LEAGUE CHAMPIONSHIP SERIES																	
1984 KC A	3	10	1	0	1	0	0.0	1	1	0	2	0	.100	.300	0	0	DH-3

Frank Ortenzio

ORTENZIO, FRANK JOSEPH JR.
B. Feb. 24, 1951, Fresno, Calif.
BR TR 6'2"   215 lbs.

	G	AB	H	2B	3B	HR	HR %	R	RBI	BB	SO	SB	BA	SA	PH AB	PH H	G by POS
1973 KC A	9	25	7	2	0	1	4.0	1	6	2	6	0	.280	.480	1	0	1B-7, DH-1

Al Orth

ORTH, ALBERT LEWIS (The Curveless Wonder)
B. Sept. 5, 1872, Danville, Ind.   D. Oct. 8, 1948, Lynchburg, Va.
BL TR 6'   200 lbs.

	G	AB	H	2B	3B	HR	HR %	R	RBI	BB	SO	SB	BA	SA	PH AB	PH H	G by POS
1895 PHI N	11	45	16	4	0	1	2.2	8	13	1	6	0	.356	.511	0	0	P-11
1896	25	82	21	3	3	1	1.2	12	13	3	11	2	.256	.402	0	0	P-25
1897	53	152	50	7	4	1	0.7	26	17	3		5	.329	.447	11	1	P-36, OF-6
1898	39	123	36	6	4	1	0.8	17	14	3		1	.293	.431	6	2	P-32, OF-1
1899	22	62	13	3	1	1	1.6	5	5	1		2	.210	.339	0	0	P-21, OF-1
1900	39	129	40	4	1	1	0.8	6	21	2		2	.310	.380	3	0	P-33, OF-3
1901	41	128	36	6	0	1	0.8	14	15	3		3	.281	.352	2	1	P-35, OF-4
1902 WAS A	56	175	38	3	2	2	1.1	20	10	9		2	.217	.291	3	1	P-38, OF-13, SS-1, 1B-1
1903	55	162	49	9	7	0	0.0	19	11	4		3	.302	.444	6	0	P-36, SS-7, OF-4, 1B-2
1904 2 teams		WAS A (31G – .216)					NY A (26G – .297)										
" total	57	166	41	4	2	0	0.0	13	18	1		4	.247	.295	4	1	P-30, OF-20
1905 NY A	54	131	24	3	1	1	0.8	13	8	4		2	.183	.244	11	2	P-40, OF-1, 1B-1
1906	47	135	37	2	2	1	0.7	12	17	6		2	.274	.341	1	0	P-45, OF-1
1907	44	105	34	6	0	1	1.0	11	13	4		1	.324	.410	5	0	P-36, OF-1
1908	38	69	20	1	2	0	0.0	4	4	2		0	.290	.362	13	4	P-21
1909	22	34	9	0	1	0	0.0	0	0	5		1	.265	.324	13	3	2B-6, P-1
15 yrs.	603	1698	464	61	30	12	0.7	183	184	51	17	30	.273	.366	78	17	P-440, OF-55, SS-8, 2B-6, 1B-4

	G	AB	H	2B	3B	HR	HR %	R	RBI	BB	SO	SB	BA	SA	Pinch Hit AB	Pinch Hit H	G by POS

Jose Ortiz

ORTIZ, JOSE LUIS
B. June 25, 1947, Ponce, Puerto Rico
BR TR 5'9½" 155 lbs.

	G	AB	H	2B	3B	HR	HR %	R	RBI	BB	SO	SB	BA	SA	PH AB	PH H	G by POS
1969 CHI A	16	11	3	1	0	0	0.0	0	2	1	0	0	.273	.364	1	0	OF-8
1970	15	24	8	1	0	0	0.0	4	1	2	2	1	.333	.375	1	0	OF-8
1971 CHI N	36	88	26	7	1	0	0.0	10	3	4	10	2	.295	.398	1	0	OF-20
3 yrs.	67	123	37	9	1	0	0.0	14	6	7	12	3	.301	.390	3	0	OF-36

Junior Ortiz

ORTIZ, ADALBERTO JR.
Also known as Adalberto Jr. Colon.
B. Oct. 24, 1959, Humacao, Puerto Rico
BR TR 5'11" 174 lbs.

	G	AB	H	2B	3B	HR	HR %	R	RBI	BB	SO	SB	BA	SA	PH AB	PH H	G by POS
1982 PIT N	7	15	3	1	0	0	0.0	1	0	1	3	0	.200	.267	0	0	C-7
1983 2 teams		PIT	N	(5G –	.125)		NY	N	(68G –	.254)							
" total	73	193	48	5	0	0	0.0	11	12	4	34	1	.249	.275	5	2	C-71
1984 NY N	40	91	18	3	0	0	0.0	6	11	5	15	1	.198	.231	10	1	C-32
3 yrs.	120	299	69	9	0	0	0.0	18	23	10	52	2	.231	.261	15	3	C-110

Roberto Ortiz

ORTIZ, ROBERTO GONZALEZ NUNEZ
Brother of Baby Ortiz.
B. June 30, 1915, Camaguey, Cuba   D. Sept. 15, 1971, Miami, Fla.
BR TR 6'4" 200 lbs.

	G	AB	H	2B	3B	HR	HR %	R	RBI	BB	SO	SB	BA	SA	PH AB	PH H	G by POS
1941 WAS A	22	79	26	1	2	1	1.3	10	17	3	10	0	.329	.430	1	0	OF-21
1942	20	42	7	1	3	1	2.4	4	4	5	11	0	.167	.405	7	0	OF-9
1943	1	4	1	0	0	0	0.0	0	0	0	0	0	.250	.250	0	0	OF-1
1944	85	316	80	11	4	5	1.6	36	35	19	47	4	.253	.361	5	1	OF-80
1949	40	129	36	3	0	1	0.8	12	11	9	12	0	.279	.326	8	4	OF-32
1950 2 teams		WAS	A	(39G –	.227)		PHI	A	(6G –	.071)							
" total	45	89	18	2	1	0	0.0	5	11	7	15	0	.202	.247	21	2	OF-22
6 yrs.	213	659	168	18	10	8	1.2	67	78	43	95	4	.255	.349	42	7	OF-165

Ossie Orwoll

ORWOLL, OSWALD CHRISTIAN
B. Nov. 17, 1900, Portland, Ore.   D. May 8, 1967, Decorah, Iowa
BL TL 6' 174 lbs.

	G	AB	H	2B	3B	HR	HR %	R	RBI	BB	SO	SB	BA	SA	PH AB	PH H	G by POS
1928 PHI A	64	170	52	13	2	0	0.0	28	22	16	24	3	.306	.406	1	1	1B-34, P-27
1929	30	51	13	2	1	0	0.0	6	6	2	11	0	.255	.333	8	2	P-12, OF-9
2 yrs.	94	221	65	15	3	0	0.0	34	28	18	35	3	.294	.389	9	3	P-39, 1B-34, OF-9

Fred Osborn

OSBORN, WILFRED PEARL
B. Nov. 28, 1883, Sycamore, Ohio   D. Sept. 2, 1954, Upper Sandusky, Ohio
BL TR 5'9" 178 lbs.

	G	AB	H	2B	3B	HR	HR %	R	RBI	BB	SO	SB	BA	SA	PH AB	PH H	G by POS
1907 PHI N	56	163	45	2	3	0	0.0	22	9	3		4	.276	.325	19	7	OF-36, 1B-1
1908	152	555	148	19	12	2	0.4	62	44	30		16	.267	.355	0	0	OF-152
1909	58	189	35	4	1	0	0.0	14	19	12		6	.185	.217	6	1	OF-54
3 yrs.	266	907	228	25	16	2	0.2	98	72	45		26	.251	.321	25	8	OF-242, 1B-1

Bobo Osborne

OSBORNE, LAWRENCE SIDNEY
Son of Tiny Osborne.
B. Oct. 12, 1935, Chattahoochee, Ga.
BL TR 6'1" 205 lbs.

	G	AB	H	2B	3B	HR	HR %	R	RBI	BB	SO	SB	BA	SA	PH AB	PH H	G by POS
1957 DET A	11	27	4	1	0	0	0.0	4	1	3	7	0	.148	.185	2	0	OF-5, 1B-4
1958	2	2	0	0	0	0	0.0	0	0	0	0	0	.000	.000	2	0	
1959	86	209	40	7	1	3	1.4	27	21	16	41	1	.191	.278	23	0	1B-56, OF-1
1961	71	93	20	7	0	2	2.2	8	13	20	15	1	.215	.355	41	10	1B-11, 3B-8
1962	64	74	17	1	0	0	0.0	12	7	16	25	0	.230	.243	29	6	3B-13, 1B-7, C-1
1963 WAS A	125	358	76	14	1	12	3.4	42	44	49	83	0	.212	.358	22	5	1B-81, 3B-16
6 yrs.	359	763	157	30	2	17	2.2	93	86	104	171	2	.206	.317	119	21	1B-159, 3B-37, OF-6, C-1

Fred Osborne

OSBORNE, FREDERICK W.
B. Nevada, Ohio   Deceased.

	G	AB	H	2B	3B	HR	HR %	R	RBI	BB	SO	SB	BA	SA	PH AB	PH H	G by POS
1890 PIT N	41	168	40	8	3	1	0.6	24	14	6	18	0	.238	.339	0	0	OF-35, P-8

Harry Ostdiek

OSTDIEK, HENRY GIRARD
B. Apr. 12, 1881, Ottumwa, Iowa   D. May 6, 1956, Minneapolis, Minn.
BR TR 5'11" 185 lbs.

	G	AB	H	2B	3B	HR	HR %	R	RBI	BB	SO	SB	BA	SA	PH AB	PH H	G by POS
1904 CLE A	7	18	3	0	1	0	0.0	1	3	3		1	.167	.278	0	0	C-7
1908 BOS A	1	3	0	0	0	0	0.0	0	0	0		0	.000	.000	0	0	C-1
2 yrs.	8	21	3	0	1	0	0.0	1	3	3		1	.143	.238	0	0	C-8

Champ Osteen

OSTEEN, JAMES CHAMPLIN
B. Feb. 24, 1877, Hendersonville, N. C.   D. Dec. 14, 1962, Greenville, S. C.
BL TR 5'8" 150 lbs.

	G	AB	H	2B	3B	HR	HR %	R	RBI	BB	SO	SB	BA	SA	PH AB	PH H	G by POS
1903 WAS A	10	40	8	0	2	0	0.0	4	4	2		0	.200	.300	0	0	SS-10
1904 NY A	28	107	21	1	4	2	1.9	15	9	1		0	.196	.336	0	0	3B-11, SS-8, 1B-4
1908 STL N	29	112	22	4	0	0	0.0	2	11	0		0	.196	.232	0	0	SS-17, 3B-12
1909	16	45	9	1	0	0	0.0	6	7	7		1	.200	.222	0	0	SS-16
4 yrs.	83	304	60	6	6	2	0.7	27	31	10		1	.197	.276	0	0	SS-51, 3B-29, 1B-4

Red Ostergard

OSTERGARD, ROY LUND
B. May 16, 1896, Denmark, Wis.   D. Jan. 13, 1977, Hemet, Calif.
BR TR 5'10½" 175 lbs.

	G	AB	H	2B	3B	HR	HR %	R	RBI	BB	SO	SB	BA	SA	PH AB	PH H	G by POS
1921 CHI A	12	11	4	0	0	0	0.0	2	0	0	2	0	.364	.364	11	4	

Charlie Osterhout

OSTERHOUT, CHARLES H.
B. 1857, Syracuse, N. Y.   D. May 21, 1933, Syracuse, N. Y.

	G	AB	H	2B	3B	HR	HR %	R	RBI	BB	SO	SB	BA	SA	PH AB	PH H	G by POS
1879 SYR N	2	8	0	0	0	0	0.0	0		0			.000	.000	0	0	OF-1, C-1

Brian Ostrosser

OSTROSSER, BRIAN LEONARD
B. June 17, 1949, Stoney Creek, Ont., Canada
BL TR 6' 175 lbs.

	G	AB	H	2B	3B	HR	HR %	R	RBI	BB	SO	SB	BA	SA	PH AB	PH H	G by POS
1973 NY N	4	5	0	0	0	0	0.0	0	0	0	2	0	.000	.000	0	0	SS-4

John Ostrowski

OSTROWSKI, JOHN THADDEUS
B. Oct. 17, 1917, Chicago, Ill.
BR TR 5'10½" 170 lbs.

	G	AB	H	2B	3B	HR	HR %	R	RBI	BB	SO	SB	BA	SA	PH AB	PH H	G by POS
1943 CHI N	10	29	6	0	1	0	0.0	2	3	3	8	0	.207	.276	0	0	OF-5, 3B-4
1944	8	13	2	1	0	0	0.0	2	2	1	4	0	.154	.231	5	2	OF-2
1945	7	10	3	2	0	0	0.0	4	1	0	0	0	.300	.500	2	0	3B-4

	G	AB	H	2B	3B	HR	HR %	R	RBI	BB	SO	SB	BA	SA	Pinch Hit AB	Pinch Hit H	G by POS

John Ostrowski continued

	G	AB	H	2B	3B	HR	HR %	R	RBI	BB	SO	SB	BA	SA	PH AB	PH H	G by POS
1946	64	160	34	4	2	3	1.9	20	12	20	31	1	.213	.319	10	0	3B-50, 2B-1
1948 BOS A	1	1	0	0	0	0	0.0	0	0	0	1	0	.000	.000	1	0	
1949 CHI A	49	158	42	9	4	5	3.2	19	31	15	41	4	.266	.468	6	1	OF-41, 3B-8
1950 2 teams	CHI	A (22G –	.245)		WAS	A	(55G –	.227)									
" total	77	190	44	4	2	6	3.2	26	25	29	40	2	.232	.368	16	0	OF-61
7 yrs.	216	561	131	20	9	14	2.5	73	74	68	125	7	.234	.376	40	3	OF-109, 3B-66, 2B-1

Reggie Otero

OTERO, REGINO JOSEPH GOMEZ
B. Sept. 7, 1915, Havana, Cuba

BL TR 5'11" 160 lbs.

	G	AB	H	2B	3B	HR	HR %	R	RBI	BB	SO	SB	BA	SA	PH AB	PH H	G by POS
1945 CHI N	14	23	9	0	0	0	0.0	1	5	2	2	0	.391	.391	6	0	1B-8

Amos Otis

OTIS, AMOS JOSEPH
B. Apr. 26, 1947, Mobile, Ala.

BR TR 5'11½" 165 lbs.

	G	AB	H	2B	3B	HR	HR %	R	RBI	BB	SO	SB	BA	SA	PH AB	PH H	G by POS
1967 NY N	19	59	13	2	0	0	0.0	6	1	5	13	0	.220	.254	0	0	OF-16, 3B-1
1969	48	93	14	3	1	0	0.0	6	4	6	27	1	.151	.204	10	1	OF-35, 3B-3
1970 KC A	159	620	176	36	9	11	1.8	91	58	68	67	33	.284	.424	1	1	OF-159
1971	147	555	167	26	4	15	2.7	80	79	40	74	52	.301	.443	4	0	OF-144
1972	143	540	158	28	2	11	2.0	75	54	50	59	28	.293	.413	5	1	OF-137
1973	148	583	175	21	4	26	4.5	89	93	63	47	13	.300	.484	1	0	OF-135, DH-14
1974	146	552	157	31	9	12	2.2	87	73	58	67	18	.284	.438	3	1	OF-143, DH-2
1975	132	470	116	26	6	9	1.9	87	46	66	48	39	.247	.385	4	0	OF-130
1976	153	592	165	40	2	18	3.0	93	86	55	100	26	.279	.444	0	0	OF-152
1977	142	478	120	20	8	17	3.6	85	78	71	88	23	.251	.433	3	1	OF-140
1978	141	486	145	30	7	22	4.5	74	96	66	54	32	.298	.525	3	0	OF-136, DH-1
1979	151	577	170	28	2	18	3.1	100	90	68	92	30	.295	.444	1	1	OF-146, DH-4
1980	107	394	99	16	3	10	2.5	56	53	39	70	16	.251	.383	2	1	OF-105
1981	99	372	100	22	3	9	2.4	49	57	31	59	16	.269	.417	2	1	OF-97, DH-1
1982	125	475	136	25	3	11	2.3	73	88	37	65	9	.286	.421	1	0	OF-125
1983	96	356	93	16	3	4	1.1	35	41	27	63	5	.261	.357	2	1	OF-96, DH-1
1984 PIT N	40	97	16	4	0	0	0.0	6	10	7	15	0	.165	.206	7	2	OF-32
17 yrs.	1996	7299	2020	374	66	193	2.6	1092	1007	757	1008	341	.277	.425	48	11	OF-1928, DH-23, 3B-4

DIVISIONAL PLAYOFF SERIES
	G	AB	H	2B	3B	HR	HR %	R	RBI	BB	SO	SB	BA	SA	PH AB	PH H	G by POS
1981 KC A	3	12	0	0	0	0	0.0	0	1	0	4	0	.000	.000	0	0	OF-3

LEAGUE CHAMPIONSHIP SERIES
	G	AB	H	2B	3B	HR	HR %	R	RBI	BB	SO	SB	BA	SA	PH AB	PH H	G by POS
1976 KC A	1	1	0	0	0	0	0.0	0	0	0	0	0	.000	.000	1	0	OF-5
1977	5	16	2	1	0	0	0.0	1	2	2	3	2	.125	.188	0	0	OF-4
1978	4	14	6	2	0	0	0.0	2	1	3	5	4	.429	.571	0	0	OF-3
1980	3	12	4	1	0	0	0.0	2	0	0	3	2	.333	.417	0	0	OF-3
4 yrs.	13	43	12	4	0	0	0.0	5	3	5	11	8	.279	.372	1	1	OF-13

WORLD SERIES
	G	AB	H	2B	3B	HR	HR %	R	RBI	BB	SO	SB	BA	SA	PH AB	PH H	G by POS
1980 KC A	6	23	11	2	0	3	13.0	4	7	3	3	0	.478	.957	0	0	OF-6

Bill Otis

OTIS, PAUL FRANKLIN
B. Dec. 24, 1889, Scituate, Mass.

BL TR 5'10½" 150 lbs.

	G	AB	H	2B	3B	HR	HR %	R	RBI	BB	SO	SB	BA	SA	PH AB	PH H	G by POS
1912 NY A	4	20	1	0	0	0	0.0	1	2	3		0	.050	.050	0	0	OF-4

Billy Ott

OTT, WILLIAM JOSEPH
B. Nov. 23, 1940, New York, N. Y.

BB TR 6'1" 180 lbs.

	G	AB	H	2B	3B	HR	HR %	R	RBI	BB	SO	SB	BA	SA	PH AB	PH H	G by POS
1962 CHI N	12	28	4	0	0	1	3.6	3	2	2	10	0	.143	.250	5	1	OF-7
1964	20	39	7	3	0	0	0.0	4	1	3	10	0	.179	.256	10	2	OF-10
2 yrs.	32	67	11	3	0	1	1.5	7	3	5	20	0	.164	.254	15	3	OF-17

Ed Ott

OTT, NATHAN EDWARD
B. July 11, 1951, Muncy, Pa.

BL TR 5'10" 190 lbs.

	G	AB	H	2B	3B	HR	HR %	R	RBI	BB	SO	SB	BA	SA	PH AB	PH H	G by POS
1974 PIT N	7	5	0	0	0	0	0.0	0	0	0	1	0	.000	.000	5	0	OF-2
1975	5	5	1	0	0	0	0.0	0	0	0	0	0	.200	.200	3	0	C-2
1976	27	39	12	2	0	0	0.0	2	5	3	5	0	.308	.359	17	6	C-8
1977	104	311	82	14	3	7	2.3	40	38	32	41	7	.264	.395	18	3	C-90
1978	112	379	102	18	4	9	2.4	49	38	27	56	4	.269	.409	15	5	C-97, OF-4
1979	117	403	110	20	2	7	1.7	49	51	26	62	0	.273	.385	3	1	C-116
1980	120	392	102	14	0	8	2.0	35	41	33	47	1	.260	.357	7	1	C-117, OF-3
1981 CAL A	75	258	56	8	1	2	0.8	20	22	17	42	2	.217	.279	5	0	C-72
8 yrs.	567	1792	465	76	10	33	1.8	196	195	138	254	14	.259	.368	73	16	C-502, OF-9

LEAGUE CHAMPIONSHIP SERIES
	G	AB	H	2B	3B	HR	HR %	R	RBI	BB	SO	SB	BA	SA	PH AB	PH H	G by POS
1979 PIT N	3	13	3	0	0	0	0.0	0	0	0	2	0	.231	.231	0	0	C-3

WORLD SERIES
	G	AB	H	2B	3B	HR	HR %	R	RBI	BB	SO	SB	BA	SA	PH AB	PH H	G by POS
1979 PIT N	3	12	4	1	0	0	0.0	2	3	0	2	0	.333	.417	0	0	C-3

Mel Ott

OTT, MELVIN THOMAS (Master Melvin)
B. Mar. 2, 1909, Gretna, La. D. Nov. 21, 1958, New Orleans, La.
Manager 1942-48.
Hall of Fame 1951.

BL TR 5'9" 170 lbs.

	G	AB	H	2B	3B	HR	HR %	R	RBI	BB	SO	SB	BA	SA	PH AB	PH H	G by POS
1926 NY N	35	60	23	2	0	0	0.0	7	4	1	9	1	.383	.417	24	9	OF-10
1927	82	163	46	7	3	1	0.6	23	19	13	9	2	.282	.380	46	11	OF-32
1928	124	435	140	26	4	18	4.1	69	77	52	36	3	.322	.524	3	0	OF-115, 2B-5, 3B-1
1929	150	545	179	37	2	42	7.7	138	151	113	38	6	.328	.635	0	0	OF-149, 2B-1
1930	148	521	182	34	5	25	4.8	122	119	103	35	9	.349	.578	1	0	OF-146
1931	138	497	145	23	8	29	5.8	104	115	80	44	10	.292	.545	1	1	OF-137
1932	154	566	180	30	8	38	6.7	119	123	100	39	6	.318	.601	0	0	OF-154
1933	152	580	164	36	1	23	4.0	98	103	75	48	1	.283	.467	0	0	OF-152
1934	153	582	190	29	10	35	6.0	119	135	85	43	0	.326	.591	0	0	OF-153
1935	152	593	191	33	6	31	5.2	113	114	82	58	7	.322	.555	0	0	OF-137, 3B-15
1936	150	534	175	28	6	33	6.2	120	135	111	41	6	.328	.588	1	1	OF-148

	G	AB	H	2B	3B	HR	HR %	R	RBI	BB	SO	SB	BA	SA	Pinch Hit AB	Pinch Hit H	G by POS

Mel Ott continued

	G	AB	H	2B	3B	HR	HR%	R	RBI	BB	SO	SB	BA	SA	AB	H	G by POS
1937	151	545	160	28	2	**31**	5.7	99	95	**102**	69	7	.294	.523	1	0	OF-91, 3B-60
1938	152	527	164	23	6	**36**	6.8	116	116	118	47	2	.311	.583	1	0	3B-113, OF-37
1939	125	396	122	23	2	27	6.8	85	80	100	50	2	.308	.581	9	2	OF-96, 3B-20
1940	151	536	155	27	3	19	3.5	89	79	100	50	6	.289	.457	0	0	OF-111, 3B-42
1941	148	525	150	29	0	27	5.1	89	90	100	68	5	.286	.495	2	0	OF-145
1942	152	549	162	21	0	**30**	5.5	118	93	**109**	61	6	.295	.497	0	0	OF-152
1943	125	380	89	12	2	18	4.7	65	47	95	48	7	.234	.418	6	1	OF-111, 3B-1
1944	120	399	115	16	4	26	6.5	91	82	90	47	2	.288	.544	10	2	OF-103, 3B-4
1945	135	451	139	23	0	21	4.7	73	79	71	41	1	.308	.499	15	4	OF-118
1946	31	68	5	1	0	1	1.5	2	4	8	15	0	.074	.132	13	1	OF-16
1947	4	4	0	0	0	0	0.0	0	0	0	0	0	.000	.000	4	0	
22 yrs.	2732	9456	2876	488	72	511	5.4	1859 9th	1860 8th	1708 6th	896	89	.304	.533	137	32	OF-2313, 3B-256, 2B-6

WORLD SERIES

	G	AB	H	2B	3B	HR	HR%	R	RBI	BB	SO	SB	BA	SA	AB	H	G by POS
1933 NY N	5	18	7	0	0	2	11.1	3	4	4	4	0	.389	.722	0	0	OF-5
1936	6	23	7	2	0	1	4.3	4	3	3	1	0	.304	.522	0	0	OF-6
1937	5	20	4	0	0	1	5.0	1	3	1	4	0	.200	.350	0	0	3B-5
3 yrs.	16	61	18	2	0	4	6.6	8	10	8	9	0	.295	.525	0	0	OF-11, 3B-5

Joe Otten

OTTEN, JOSEPH G.
B. Murphysboro, Ill. Deceased.

	G	AB	H	2B	3B	HR	HR%	R	RBI	BB	SO	SB	BA	SA	AB	H	G by POS
1895 STL N	26	87	21	0	0	0	0.0	8	8	5	8	2	.241	.241	0	0	C-24, OF-2

Billy Otterson

OTTERSON, WILLIAM JOHN BR TR 5'7" 135 lbs.
B. May 4, 1862, Pittsburgh, Pa. D. Sept. 21, 1940, Pittsburgh, Pa.

	G	AB	H	2B	3B	HR	HR%	R	RBI	BB	SO	SB	BA	SA	AB	H	G by POS
1887 BKN AA	30	100	20	4	1	2	2.0	16		8		8	2	.200	.320	0	0	SS-30

Johnny Oulliber

OULLIBER, JOHN ANDREW BR TR 5'11" 165 lbs.
B. Feb. 24, 1911, New Orleans, La. D. Dec. 26, 1980, New Orleans, La.

	G	AB	H	2B	3B	HR	HR%	R	RBI	BB	SO	SB	BA	SA	AB	H	G by POS
1933 CLE A	22	75	20	1	0	0	0.0	9	3	4	5	0	.267	.280	4	0	OF-18

Chick Outen

OUTEN, WILLIAM AUSTIN BL TR 6' 200 lbs.
B. June 17, 1905, Mt. Holly, N. C. D. Sept. 11, 1961, Durham, N. C.

	G	AB	H	2B	3B	HR	HR%	R	RBI	BB	SO	SB	BA	SA	AB	H	G by POS
1933 BKN N	93	153	38	10	0	4	2.6	20	17	20	15	1	.248	.392	31	1	C-56

Jimmy Outlaw

OUTLAW, JAMES PAULUS BR TR 5'8" 165 lbs.
B. Jan. 20, 1913, Orme, Tenn.

	G	AB	H	2B	3B	HR	HR%	R	RBI	BB	SO	SB	BA	SA	AB	H	G by POS
1937 CIN N	49	165	45	7	3	0	0.0	18	11	3	31	2	.273	.352	4	0	3B-41
1938	4	0	0	0	0	0	—	1	0	0	0	0	—	—	0	0	
1939 BOS N	65	133	35	2	0	0	0.0	15	5	10	14	1	.263	.278	16	4	OF-39, 3B-2
1943 DET A	20	67	18	1	0	1	1.5	8	6	8	4	0	.269	.328	4	1	OF-16
1944	139	535	146	20	6	3	0.6	69	57	41	40	7	.273	.350	3	0	OF-137
1945	132	446	121	16	5	0	0.0	56	34	45	33	6	.271	.330	7	0	OF-105, 3B-21
1946	92	299	78	14	2	2	0.7	36	31	29	24	5	.261	.341	5	1	OF-43, 3B-38
1947	70	127	29	7	1	0	0.0	20	15	21	14	3	.228	.299	3	0	OF-37, 3B-9
1948	74	198	56	12	0	0	0.0	33	25	31	15	0	.283	.343	11	4	3B-47, OF-13
1949	5	4	1	0	0	0	0.0	1	0	0	1	0	.250	.250	4	1	
10 yrs.	650	1974	529	79	17	6	0.3	257	184	188	176	24	.268	.334	57	11	OF-390, 3B-158

WORLD SERIES

	G	AB	H	2B	3B	HR	HR%	R	RBI	BB	SO	SB	BA	SA	AB	H	G by POS
1945 DET A	7	28	5	0	0	0	0.0	1	3	2	1	1	.179	.179	0	0	3B-7

Dave Owen

OWEN, DAVE BB TR 6'1" 175 lbs.
Brother of Spike Owen.
B. Apr. 25, 1958, Cleburne, Tex.

	G	AB	H	2B	3B	HR	HR%	R	RBI	BB	SO	SB	BA	SA	AB	H	G by POS
1983 CHI N	16	22	2	0	1	0	0.0	1	2	2	7	1	.091	.182	0	0	SS-14, 3B-3
1984	47	93	18	2	2	1	1.1	8	10	8	15	1	.194	.290	3	2	SS-35, 3B-6, 2B-4
2 yrs.	63	115	20	2	3	1	0.9	9	12	10	22	2	.174	.270	3	2	SS-49, 3B-9, 2B-4

Larry Owen

OWEN, LAWRENCE THOMAS BR TR 5'11" 185 lbs.
B. May 31, 1955, Cleveland, Ohio

	G	AB	H	2B	3B	HR	HR%	R	RBI	BB	SO	SB	BA	SA	AB	H	G by POS
1981 ATL N	13	16	0	0	0	0	0.0	0	0	1	4	0	.000	.000	4	0	C-10
1982	2	3	1	1	0	0	0.0	1	0	0	1	0	.333	.667	0	0	C-2
1983	17	17	2	0	0	0	0.0	0	1	0	2	0	.118	.118	1	0	C-16
3 yrs.	32	36	3	1	0	0	0.0	1	1	1	7	0	.083	.111	5	0	C-28

Marv Owen

OWEN, MARVIN JAMES BR TR 6'1" 175 lbs.
B. Mar. 22, 1906, Agnew, Calif.

	G	AB	H	2B	3B	HR	HR%	R	RBI	BB	SO	SB	BA	SA	AB	H	G by POS
1931 DET A	105	377	84	11	6	3	0.8	35	39	29	38	2	.223	.308	3	1	SS-37, 3B-37, 1B-27, 2B-4
1933	138	550	144	24	9	2	0.4	77	65	44	56	2	.262	.349	1	0	3B-136
1934	154	565	179	34	9	8	1.4	79	96	59	37	3	.317	.451	0	0	3B-154
1935	134	483	127	24	5	2	0.4	52	71	43	37	1	.263	.346	2	1	3B-131
1936	154	583	172	20	4	9	1.5	72	105	53	41	9	.295	.389	0	0	3B-153, 1B-2
1937	107	396	114	22	5	1	0.3	48	45	41	24	3	.288	.376	1	0	3B-106
1938 CHI A	141	577	162	23	6	6	1.0	84	55	45	31	6	.281	.373	1	0	3B-140
1939	58	194	46	9	0	0	0.0	22	15	16	15	0	.237	.284	2	0	3B-55
1940 BOS A	20	57	12	0	0	0	0.0	4	6	8	4	0	.211	.211	3	0	3B-9, 1B-8
9 yrs.	1011	3782	1040	167	44	31	0.8	473	497	338	283	30	.275	.367	13	2	3B-921, SS-37, 1B-37, 2B-4

WORLD SERIES

	G	AB	H	2B	3B	HR	HR%	R	RBI	BB	SO	SB	BA	SA	AB	H	G by POS
1934 DET A	7	29	2	0	0	0	0.0	0	1	0	5	1	.069	.069	0	0	3B-7
1935	6	20	1	0	0	0	0.0	2	1	2	3	0	.050	.050	0	0	3B-2
2 yrs.	13	49	3	0	0	0	0.0	2	2	2	8	1	.061	.061	0	0	3B-9

	G	AB	H	2B	3B	HR	HR %	R	RBI	BB	SO	SB	BA	SA	Pinch Hit AB	Pinch Hit H	G by POS

Mickey Owen

OWEN, ARNOLD MALCOLM
B. Apr. 4, 1916, Nixa, Mo.   BR TR 5'10" 190 lbs.

	G	AB	H	2B	3B	HR	HR %	R	RBI	BB	SO	SB	BA	SA	PH AB	PH H	G by POS
1937 STL N	80	234	54	4	2	0	0.0	17	20	15	13	1	.231	.265	2	0	C-78
1938	122	397	106	25	2	4	1.0	45	36	32	14	2	.267	.370	5	1	C-116
1939	131	344	89	18	2	3	0.9	32	35	43	28	6	.259	.349	5	0	C-126
1940	117	307	81	16	2	0	0.0	27	27	34	13	4	.264	.329	4	2	C-113
1941 BKN N	128	386	89	15	2	1	0.3	32	44	34	14	1	.231	.288	0	0	C-128
1942	133	421	109	16	3	0	0.0	53	44	44	17	10	.259	.311	0	0	C-133
1943	106	365	95	11	2	0	0.0	31	54	25	15	4	.260	.301	5	1	C-100, 3B-3, SS-1
1944	130	461	126	20	3	1	0.2	43	42	36	17	4	.273	.336	4	1	C-125, 2B-1
1945	24	84	24	9	0	0	0.0	5	11	10	2	0	.286	.393	0	0	C-24
1949 CHI N	62	198	54	9	3	2	1.0	15	18	12	13	1	.273	.379	3	1	C-59
1950	86	259	63	11	0	2	0.8	22	21	13	16	2	.243	.309	1	0	C-86
1951	58	125	23	6	0	0	0.0	10	15	19	13	1	.184	.232	1	0	C-57
1954 BOS A	32	68	16	3	0	1	1.5	6	11	9	6	0	.235	.324	1	1	C-30
13 yrs.	1209	3649	929	163	21	14	0.4	338	378	326	181	36	.255	.322	31	7	C-1175, 3B-3, SS-1, 2B-1

WORLD SERIES

	G	AB	H	2B	3B	HR	HR %	R	RBI	BB	SO	SB	BA	SA	PH AB	PH H	G by POS
1941 BKN N	5	12	2	0	1	0	0.0	1	2	3	0	0	.167	.333	0	0	C-5

Spike Owen

OWEN, SPIKE D.
Brother of Dave Owen.
B. Apr. 19, 1961, Cleburne, Tex.   BB TR 5'9" 160 lbs.

	G	AB	H	2B	3B	HR	HR %	R	RBI	BB	SO	SB	BA	SA	PH AB	PH H	G by POS
1983 SEA A	80	306	60	11	3	2	0.7	36	21	24	44	10	.196	.271	1	0	SS-80
1984	152	530	130	18	8	3	0.6	67	43	46	63	16	.245	.326	1	1	SS-151
2 yrs.	232	836	190	29	11	5	0.6	103	64	70	107	26	.227	.306	2	1	SS-231

Frank Owens

OWENS, FRANK WALTER
B. Jan. 26, 1886, Toronto, Ont., Canada   D. July 2, 1958, Minneapolis, Minn.   BR TR 6' 170 lbs.

	G	AB	H	2B	3B	HR	HR %	R	RBI	BB	SO	SB	BA	SA	PH AB	PH H	G by POS
1905 BOS A	1	2	0	0	0	0	0.0	0	0	0		0	.000	.000	0	0	C-1
1909 CHI A	64	174	35	4	1	0	0.0	12	17	8		3	.201	.236	6	1	C-57
1914 BKN F	58	184	51	7	3	2	1.1	15	20	9		2	.277	.380	0	0	C-58
1915 BAL F	99	334	84	14	7	3	0.9	32	28	17		4	.251	.362	0	0	C-99
4 yrs.	222	694	170	25	11	5	0.7	59	65	34		9	.245	.334	6	1	C-215

Jack Owens

OWENS, FURMAN LEE
B. June 6, 1910, Converse, S. C.   D. Nov. 14, 1958, Greenville, S. C.   BR TR 6'1" 186 lbs.

	G	AB	H	2B	3B	HR	HR %	R	RBI	BB	SO	SB	BA	SA	PH AB	PH H	G by POS
1935 PHI A	2	8	2	0	0	0	0.0	0	1	0	1	0	.250	.250	0	0	C-2

Red Owens

OWENS, THOMAS LLEWELLYN
B. Nov. 1, 1874, Pottsville, Pa.   D. Aug. 21, 1952, Harrisburg, Pa.   BR TR

	G	AB	H	2B	3B	HR	HR %	R	RBI	BB	SO	SB	BA	SA	PH AB	PH H	G by POS
1899 PHI N	8	21	1	0	0	0	0.0	0	1	2		0	.048	.048	0	0	2B-8
1905 BKN N	43	168	36	6	2	1	0.6	14	20	6		1	.214	.292	0	0	2B-43
2 yrs.	51	189	37	6	2	1	0.5	14	21	8		1	.196	.265	0	0	2B-51

Henry Oxley

OXLEY, HENRY HAVELOCK
B. Jan. 4, 1858, Covehead, P. E. I., Canada   D. Oct. 12, 1945, Somerville, Mass.

	G	AB	H	2B	3B	HR	HR %	R	RBI	BB	SO	SB	BA	SA	PH AB	PH H	G by POS
1884 2 teams	NY N (3G – .000)				NY AA (1G – .000)												
" total	4	7	0	0	0	0	0.0		1	2			.000	.000	0	0	C-3

Andy Oyler

OYLER, ANDREW PAUL (Pepper)
B. May 5, 1880, Newville, Pa.   D. Oct. 24, 1970, Cumberland County, Pa.   BR TR 5'6½" 138 lbs.

	G	AB	H	2B	3B	HR	HR %	R	RBI	BB	SO	SB	BA	SA	PH AB	PH H	G by POS
1902 BAL A	27	77	17	1	0	1	1.3	9	6	8		3	.221	.273	2	0	3B-20, OF-3, SS-2, 2B-1

Ray Oyler

OYLER, RAYMOND FRANCIS
B. Aug. 4, 1938, Indianapolis, Ind.   D. Jan. 26, 1981, Seattle, Wash.   BR TR 5'11" 165 lbs.

	G	AB	H	2B	3B	HR	HR %	R	RBI	BB	SO	SB	BA	SA	PH AB	PH H	G by POS
1965 DET A	82	194	36	6	0	5	2.6	22	13	21	61	1	.186	.294	11	3	SS-57, 2B-11, 3B-1, 1B-1
1966	71	210	36	8	3	1	0.5	16	9	23	62	0	.171	.252	1	0	SS-69
1967	148	367	76	14	2	1	0.3	33	29	37	91	0	.207	.264	0	0	SS-146
1968	111	215	29	6	1	1	0.5	13	12	20	59	0	.135	.186	0	0	SS-111
1969 SEA A	106	255	42	5	0	7	2.7	24	22	31	80	1	.165	.267	0	0	SS-106
1970 CAL A	24	24	2	0	0	0	0.0	2	1	3	6	0	.083	.083	7	0	SS-13, 3B-2
6 yrs.	542	1265	221	39	6	15	1.2	110	86	135	359	2	.175	.251	19	3	SS-502, 2B-11, 3B-3, 1B-1

WORLD SERIES

	G	AB	H	2B	3B	HR	HR %	R	RBI	BB	SO	SB	BA	SA	PH AB	PH H	G by POS
1968 DET A	4	0	0	0	0	0	–	0	0	0	0	0	–	–	0	0	SS-4

Ed Pabst

PABST, EDWARD D. A.
B. 1868, St. Louis, Mo.   D. June 19, 1940, St. Louis, Mo.   5'11" 170 lbs.

	G	AB	H	2B	3B	HR	HR %	R	RBI	BB	SO	SB	BA	SA	PH AB	PH H	G by POS
1890 2 teams	PHI AA (8G – .400)				STL AA (4G – .143)												
" total	12	39	12	2	1	0	0.0	8		5		3	.308	.410	0	0	OF-12

John Paciorek

PACIOREK, JOHN FRANCIS
Brother of Tom Paciorek.
B. Feb. 11, 1945, Detroit, Mich.   BR TR 6'2" 200 lbs.

	G	AB	H	2B	3B	HR	HR %	R	RBI	BB	SO	SB	BA	SA	PH AB	PH H	G by POS
1963 HOU N	1	3	3	0	0	0	0.0	4	3	2	0	0	1.000	1.000	0	0	OF-1

Tom Paciorek

PACIOREK, THOMAS MARIAN
Brother of John Paciorek.
B. Nov. 2, 1946, Detroit, Mich.   BR TR 6'4" 215 lbs.

	G	AB	H	2B	3B	HR	HR %	R	RBI	BB	SO	SB	BA	SA	PH AB	PH H	G by POS
1970 LA N	8	9	2	1	0	0	0.0	2	0	0	3	0	.222	.333	5	1	OF-3
1971	2	2	1	0	0	0	0.0	0	1	0	0	0	.500	.500	2	1	OF-1
1972	11	47	12	4	0	1	2.1	4	6	1	7	1	.255	.404	0	0	OF-6, 1B-6
1973	96	195	51	8	0	5	2.6	26	18	11	35	1	.262	.379	17	4	OF-77, 1B-4
1974	85	175	42	8	1	1	0.6	23	24	10	32	1	.240	.371	18	6	OF-77, 1B-1
1975	62	145	28	8	0	1	0.7	14	5	11	29	4	.193	.269	10	2	OF-54
1976 ATL N	111	324	94	10	4	4	1.2	39	36	19	57	2	.290	.383	20	8	OF-84, 1B-12, 3B-3

	G	AB	H	2B	3B	HR	HR %	R	RBI	BB	SO	SB	BA	SA	Pinch Hit AB	Pinch Hit H	G by POS

Tom Paciorek continued

Year	Team	G	AB	H	2B	3B	HR	HR%	R	RBI	BB	SO	SB	BA	SA	PH AB	PH H	G by POS
1977		72	155	37	8	0	3	1.9	20	15	6	46	1	.239	.348	32	6	1B-32, OF-9, 3B-1
1978 2 teams	ATL N (5G – .333)							SEA A (70G – .299)										
" total	75	260	78	20	3	4	1.5	34	30	15	40	2	.300	.446	7	2	OF-54, DH-12, 1B-5
1979 SEA A	103	310	89	23	4	6	1.9	38	42	28	62	6	.287	.445	17	4	OF-75, 1B-15
1980	126	418	114	19	1	15	3.6	44	59	17	67	3	.273	.431	14	6	OF-60, 1B-36, DH-23
1981	104	405	132	28	2	14	3.5	50	66	35	50	13	.326	.509	1	1	OF-103
1982 CHI A	104	382	119	27	4	11	2.9	49	55	24	53	3	.312	.490	0	0	1B-102, OF-6
1983	115	420	129	32	3	9	2.1	65	63	25	58	6	.307	.462	9	3	1B-67, OF-55, DH-2
1984	111	363	93	21	2	4	1.1	35	29	25	69	6	.256	.358	18	7	1B-67, OF-41
15 yrs.	1185	3610	1021	217	29	78	2.2	443	449	227	608	51	.283	.424	170	47	OF-705, 1B-347, DH-37, 3B-2

LEAGUE CHAMPIONSHIP SERIES

Year	Team	G	AB	H	2B	3B	HR	HR%	R	RBI	BB	SO	SB	BA	SA	PH AB	PH H	G by POS
1974 LA N	1	1	1	0	0	0	0.0	0	0	0	0	0	1.000	1.000	1	1	OF-1
1983 CHI A	4	16	4	0	0	0	0.0	1	1	1	2	0	.250	.250	0	0	1B-3
2 yrs.	5	17	5	0	0	0	0.0	1	1	1	2	0	.294	.294	1	1	1B-3, OF-1

WORLD SERIES

Year	Team	G	AB	H	2B	3B	HR	HR%	R	RBI	BB	SO	SB	BA	SA	PH AB	PH H	G by POS
1974 LA N	3	2	1	1	0	0	0.0	1	0	0	0	0	.500	1.000	2	1	

Frankie Pack

PACK, FRANKIE   BL TR 6'   190 lbs.
B. Apr. 10, 1928, Morristown, Tenn.

Year	Team	G	AB	H	2B	3B	HR	HR%	R	RBI	BB	SO	SB	BA	SA	PH AB	PH H	G by POS
1949 STL A	1	1	0	0	0	0	0.0	0	0	0	1	0	.000	.000	1	0	

Dick Padden

PADDEN, RICHARD JOSEPH (Brains)   BR TR 5'10½" 165 lbs.
B. Sept. 17, 1870, Martins Ferry, Ohio   D. Oct. 31, 1922, Martins Ferry, Ohio

Year	Team	G	AB	H	2B	3B	HR	HR%	R	RBI	BB	SO	SB	BA	SA	PH AB	PH H	G by POS
1896 PIT N	61	219	53	4	8	2	0.9	33	24	14		9	8	.242	.361	0	0	2B-61
1897	134	517	146	16	10	2	0.4	84	58	38			18	.282	.364	0	0	2B-134
1898	128	463	119	7	6	2	0.4	61	43	35			11	.257	.311	0	0	2B-128
1899 WAS N	134	451	125	20	7	2	0.4	66	61	24			27	.277	.366	1	1	SS-85, 2B-48
1901 STL N	123	488	125	17	7	2	0.4	71	62	31			26	.256	.332	0	0	2B-115, SS-8
1902 STL A	117	413	109	26	3	1	0.2	54	40	30			11	.264	.349	0	0	2B-117
1903	29	94	19	3	0	0	0.0	7	6	9			5	.202	.234	0	0	2B-29
1904	132	453	108	19	4	0	0.0	42	36	40			23	.238	.298	0	0	2B-132
1905	16	58	10	1	1	0	0.0	5	4	3			3	.172	.224	0	0	2B-16
9 yrs.	874	3156	814	113	46	11	0.3	423	334	224	9	132	.258	.333	1	1	2B-780, SS-93

Tom Padden

PADDEN, THOMAS FRANCIS   BR TR 5'11½" 170 lbs.
B. Oct. 6, 1908, Manchester, N. H.   D. June 11, 1973, Manchester, N. H.

Year	Team	G	AB	H	2B	3B	HR	HR%	R	RBI	BB	SO	SB	BA	SA	PH AB	PH H	G by POS
1932 PIT N	47	118	31	6	1	0	0.0	13	10	9	7	0	.263	.331	3	1	C-43
1933	30	90	19	2	0	0	0.0	5	8	2	6	0	.211	.233	3	0	C-27
1934	82	237	76	12	2	0	0.0	27	22	30	23	3	.321	.388	4	1	C-76
1935	97	302	82	9	1	1	0.3	35	30	48	26	1	.272	.318	3	1	C-94
1936	88	281	70	9	2	1	0.4	22	31	22	41	0	.249	.306	1	0	C-87
1937	35	98	28	2	0	0	0.0	14	8	13	11	1	.286	.306	1	0	C-34
1943 2 teams	PHI N (17G – .293)							WAS A (3G – .000)										
" total	20	44	12	0	0	0	0.0	6	1	3	7	0	.273	.273	2	0	C-18
7 yrs.	399	1170	318	40	6	2	0.2	122	110	127	121	5	.272	.321	17	3	C-379

Del Paddock

PADDOCK, DELMAR HAROLD   BL TR 5'9"   165 lbs.
B. June 8, 1887, Volga, S. D.   D. Feb. 6, 1952, Remer, Minn.

Year	Team	G	AB	H	2B	3B	HR	HR%	R	RBI	BB	SO	SB	BA	SA	PH AB	PH H	G by POS
1912 2 teams	CHI A (1G – .000)							NY A (45G – .288)										
" total	46	157	45	5	3	1	0.6	26	14	23		9	.287	.376	2	0	3B-41, 2B-2, OF-1

Don Padgett

PADGETT, DON WILSON (Red)   BL TR 6'   190 lbs.
B. Dec. 5, 1911, Caroleen, N. C.   D. Dec. 9, 1980, High Point, N. C.

Year	Team	G	AB	H	2B	3B	HR	HR%	R	RBI	BB	SO	SB	BA	SA	PH AB	PH H	G by POS
1937 STL N	123	446	140	22	6	10	2.2	62	74	30	43	4	.314	.457	13	4	OF-109
1938	110	388	105	26	5	8	2.1	59	65	18	28	0	.271	.425	18	6	OF-71, 1B-16, C-6
1939	92	233	93	15	3	5	2.1	38	53	18	11	0	.399	.554	21	9	C-61, 1B-6
1940	93	240	58	15	1	6	2.5	24	41	26	14	1	.242	.388	16	3	C-72, 1B-3
1941	107	324	80	18	0	5	1.5	39	44	21	16	0	.247	.349	22	3	OF-62, C-18, 1B-2
1946 2 teams	BKN N (19G – .167)							BOS N (44G – .255)										
" total	63	128	30	4	0	3	2.3	8	30	9	11	0	.234	.336	27	4	C-36
1947 PHI N	75	158	50	8	1	0	0.0	14	24	16	5	0	.316	.380	31	8	C-39
1948	36	74	17	3	0	0	0.0	3	7	3	2	0	.230	.270	13	2	C-19
8 yrs.	699	1991	573	111	16	37	1.9	247	338	141	130	6	.288	.415	161	34	C-251, OF-242, 1B-26

Ernie Padgett

PADGETT, ERNEST KITCHEN (Red)   BR TR 5'8"   155 lbs.
B. Mar. 1, 1899, Philadelphia, Pa.   D. Apr. 15, 1957, East Orange, N. J.

Year	Team	G	AB	H	2B	3B	HR	HR%	R	RBI	BB	SO	SB	BA	SA	PH AB	PH H	G by POS
1923 BOS N	4	11	2	0	0	0	0.0	3	0	2	0	0	.182	.182	1	0	SS-2, 2B-1
1924	138	502	128	25	9	1	0.2	42	46	37	56	4	.255	.347	0	0	3B-113, 2B-29
1925	86	256	78	9	7	0	0.0	31	29	14	14	3	.305	.395	15	4	2B-47, SS-18, 3B-7
1926 CLE A	36	62	13	0	1	0	0.0	7	6	8	3	1	.210	.242	3	0	2B-29, SS-2
1927	7	7	2	0	0	0	0.0	1	0	0	2	0	.286	.286	3	1	2B-4
5 yrs.	271	838	223	34	17	1	0.1	84	81	61	75	8	.266	.351	22	5	3B-149, 2B-81, SS-22

Dennis Paepke

PAEPKE, DENNIS RAE   BR TR 6'   202 lbs.
B. Apr. 17, 1945, Long Beach, Calif.

Year	Team	G	AB	H	2B	3B	HR	HR%	R	RBI	BB	SO	SB	BA	SA	PH AB	PH H	G by POS
1969 KC A	12	27	3	1	0	0	0.0	2	0	2	3	0	.111	.148	4	0	C-8
1971	60	152	31	6	0	2	1.3	11	14	8	29	0	.204	.283	16	3	C-32, OF-17
1972	2	6	0	0	0	0	0.0	0	0	1	2	0	.000	.000	0	0	C-2
1974	6	12	2	0	0	0	0.0	0	0	1	2	0	.167	.167	1	0	C-4, OF-1
4 yrs.	80	197	36	7	0	2	1.0	13	14	12	36	0	.183	.249	21	3	C-46, OF-18

	G	AB	H	2B	3B	HR	HR %	R	RBI	BB	SO	SB	BA	SA	Pinch Hit AB	H	G by POS

Andy Pafko

PAFKO, ANDREW (Pruschka, Handy Andy)
B. Feb. 25, 1921, Boyceville, Wis.   BR TR 6'   190 lbs.

	G	AB	H	2B	3B	HR	HR %	R	RBI	BB	SO	SB	BA	SA	PH AB	PH H	G by POS
1943 CHI N	13	58	22	3	0	0	0.0	7	10	2	5	1	.379	.431	0	0	OF-13
1944	128	469	126	16	2	6	1.3	47	62	28	23	2	.269	.350	5	1	OF-123
1945	144	534	159	24	12	12	2.2	64	110	45	36	5	.298	.455	4	1	OF-140
1946	65	234	66	6	4	3	1.3	18	39	27	15	4	.282	.380	1	0	OF-64
1947	129	513	155	25	7	13	2.5	68	66	31	39	4	.302	.454	2	0	OF-127
1948	142	548	171	30	2	26	4.7	82	101	50	50	3	.312	.516	2	1	3B-139
1949	144	519	146	29	2	18	3.5	79	69	63	33	4	.281	.449	1	1	OF-98, 3B-49
1950	146	514	156	24	8	36	7.0	95	92	69	32	4	.304	.591	2	1	OF-144
1951 2 teams	CHI	N	(49G –	.264)		BKN	N	(84G –	.249)								
" total	133	455	116	16	3	30	6.6	68	93	52	37	2	.255	.501	6	1	OF-126
1952 BKN N	150	551	158	17	5	19	3.4	76	85	64	48	4	.287	.439	4	1	OF-139, 3B-13
1953 MIL N	140	516	153	23	4	17	3.3	70	72	37	33	2	.297	.455	1	0	OF-139
1954	138	510	146	22	4	14	2.7	61	69	37	36	1	.286	.427	0	0	OF-138
1955	86	252	67	3	5	5	2.0	29	34	7	23	1	.266	.377	22	3	OF-58, 3B-12
1956	45	93	24	5	0	2	2.2	15	9	10	13	0	.258	.376	12	3	OF-37
1957	83	220	61	6	1	8	3.6	31	27	10	22	1	.277	.423	22	3	OF-69
1958	95	164	39	7	1	3	1.8	17	23	15	17	0	.238	.348	13	3	OF-93
1959	71	142	31	8	2	1	0.7	17	15	14	15	0	.218	.324	13	2	OF-64
17 yrs.	1852	6292	1796	264	62	213	3.4	844	976	561	477	38	.285	.449	110	20	OF-1572, 3B-213

WORLD SERIES

	G	AB	H	2B	3B	HR	HR %	R	RBI	BB	SO	SB	BA	SA	PH AB	PH H	G by POS
1945 CHI N	7	28	6	2	1	0	0.0	5	2	2	5	0	.214	.357	0	0	OF-7
1952 BKN N	7	21	4	0	0	0	0.0	0	2	0	4	0	.190	.190	2	0	OF-5
1957 MIL N	6	14	3	0	0	0	0.0	1	0	0	1	0	.214	.214	1	0	OF-5
1958	4	9	3	1	0	0	0.0	0	1	0	0	0	.333	.444	0	0	OF-4
4 yrs.	24	72	16	3	1	0	0.0	6	5	2	10	0	.222	.292	3	0	OF-21

Jose Pagan

PAGAN, JOSE ANTONIO
B. May 5, 1935, Barceloneta, Puerto Rico   BR TR 5'9"   160 lbs.

	G	AB	H	2B	3B	HR	HR %	R	RBI	BB	SO	SB	BA	SA	PH AB	PH H	G by POS
1959 SF N	31	46	8	1	0	0	0.0	7	1	2	8	1	.174	.196	4	0	3B-18, SS-5, 2B-3
1960	18	49	14	2	0	0	0.0	8	2	1	6	2	.286	.408	6	0	SS-11, 3B-1
1961	134	434	110	15	2	5	1.2	38	46	31	45	8	.253	.332	1	1	SS-132, OF-4
1962	164	580	150	25	6	7	1.2	73	57	47	77	13	.259	.359	0	0	SS-164
1963	148	483	113	12	1	6	1.2	46	39	26	67	10	.234	.300	4	1	SS-143, OF-1, 2B-1
1964	134	367	82	10	1	1	0.3	33	28	35	66	5	.223	.264	0	0	SS-132, OF-8
1965 2 teams	SF	N	(26G –	.205)		PIT	N	(42G –	.237)								
" total	68	121	26	5	0	0	0.0	16	6	9	16	2	.215	.256	7	1	3B-83, SS-18, OF-3, 2B-3
1966 PIT N	109	368	97	15	6	4	1.1	44	54	13	38	0	.264	.370	10	2	3B-25, OF-23, SS-16, 2B-2, C-1
1967	81	211	61	6	2	1	0.5	17	19	10	28	1	.289	.351	13	4	3B-30, OF-19, SS-8, 2B-2, 1B-1
1968	80	163	36	7	1	4	2.5	24	21	11	32	2	.221	.350	22	5	3B-44, OF-23, 2B-1
1969	108	274	78	11	4	9	3.3	29	42	17	46	1	.285	.453	42	19	3B-53, OF-4, 2B-1, 1B-1
1970	95	230	61	14	1	7	3.0	21	29	20	24	1	.265	.426	35	9	3B-41, OF-3, 1B-2
1971	57	158	38	1	0	5	3.2	16	15	16	25	0	.241	.342	12	2	3B-32, OF-2
1972	53	127	32	9	0	3	2.4	11	8	5	17	0	.252	.394	22	6	3B-16, 1B-5, OF-2, 2B-1
1973 PHI N	46	78	16	5	0	0	0.0	4	5	1	15	0	.205	.269	29	6	1B-5
15 yrs.	1326	3689	922	138	26	52	1.4	387	372	244	510	46	.250	.344	207	56	SS-662, 3B-358, OF-92, 2B-14, 1B-9, C-1

LEAGUE CHAMPIONSHIP SERIES

	G	AB	H	2B	3B	HR	HR %	R	RBI	BB	SO	SB	BA	SA	PH AB	PH H	G by POS
1970 PIT N	1	3	1	0	0	0	0.0	0	0	1	1	0	.333	.333	0	0	3B-1
1971	1	1	0	0	0	0	0.0	0	0	0	0	0	.000	.000	0	0	3B-1
2 yrs.	2	4	1	0	0	0	0.0	0	0	1	1	0	.250	.250	0	0	3B-2

WORLD SERIES

	G	AB	H	2B	3B	HR	HR %	R	RBI	BB	SO	SB	BA	SA	PH AB	PH H	G by POS
1962 SF N	7	19	7	0	0	1	5.3	2	2	0	1	0	.368	.526	0	0	SS-7
1971 PIT N	4	15	4	2	0	0	0.0	0	2	0	1	0	.267	.400	0	0	3B-4
2 yrs.	11	34	11	2	0	1	2.9	2	4	0	2	0	.324	.471	0	0	SS-7, 3B-4

Mike Page

PAGE, MICHAEL RANDY
B. July 12, 1940, Woodruff, S. C.   BL TR 6'2½"   210 lbs.

	G	AB	H	2B	3B	HR	HR %	R	RBI	BB	SO	SB	BA	SA	PH AB	PH H	G by POS
1968 ATL N	20	28	5	0	0	0	0.0	1	1	1	9	0	.179	.179	13	1	OF-6

Mitchell Page

PAGE, MITCHELL OTIS
B. Oct. 15, 1951, Los Angeles, Calif.   BL TR 6'2"   205 lbs.

	G	AB	H	2B	3B	HR	HR %	R	RBI	BB	SO	SB	BA	SA	PH AB	PH H	G by POS
1977 OAK A	145	501	154	28	8	21	4.2	85	75	78	95	42	.307	.521	6	2	OF-133, DH-8
1978	147	516	147	25	7	17	3.3	62	70	53	95	23	.285	.459	1	0	OF-114, DH-33
1979	133	478	118	11	2	9	1.9	51	42	52	93	17	.247	.335	1	0	OF-126, OF-4
1980	110	348	85	10	4	17	4.9	58	51	35	87	14	.244	.443	19	2	DH-101
1981	34	92	13	1	0	4	4.3	9	13	7	29	2	.141	.283	4	1	DH-29
1982	31	78	20	5	0	4	5.1	14	7	7	24	3	.256	.474	3	0	DH-24
1983	57	79	19	3	0	0	0.0	16	1	10	22	3	.241	.278	12	3	DH-34, OF-10
1984 PIT N	16	12	4	1	0	0	0.0	2	0	3	4	0	.333	.417	12	4	
8 yrs.	673	2104	560	84	21	72	3.4	297	259	245	449	104	.266	.429	58	12	DH-355, OF-261

Karl Pagel

PAGEL, KARL DOUGLAS
B. Mar. 29, 1955, Madison, Wis.   BL TL 6'2"   188 lbs.

	G	AB	H	2B	3B	HR	HR %	R	RBI	BB	SO	SB	BA	SA	PH AB	PH H	G by POS
1978 CHI N	2	2	0	0	0	0	0.0	0	0	0	2	0	.000	.000	2	0	
1979	1	1	0	0	0	0	0.0	0	0	0	1	0	.000	.000	1	0	
1981 CLE A	14	15	4	0	2	1	6.7	3	4	4	1	0	.267	.733	5	1	1B-6, DH-1
1982	23	18	3	0	0	0	0.0	3	2	7	11	0	.167	.167	8	2	1B-10, DH-1
1983	8	20	6	0	0	0	0.0	1	1	0	5	0	.300	.300	3	1	DH-5, OF-1
5 yrs.	48	56	13	0	2	1	1.8	7	7	11	20	0	.232	.357	19	4	1B-16, DH-7, OF-1

	G	AB	H	2B	3B	HR	HR %	R	RBI	BB	SO	SB	BA	SA	Pinch Hit AB	Pinch Hit H	G by POS

Jim Pagliaroni

PAGLIARONI, JAMES VINCENT (Pag)
B. Dec. 8, 1937, Dearborn, Mich. BR TR 6'4" 210 lbs.

	G	AB	H	2B	3B	HR	HR %	R	RBI	BB	SO	SB	BA	SA	AB	H	G by POS
1955 BOS A	1	0	0	0	0	0	–	0	1	0	0	0	–	–	0	0	C-1
1960	28	62	19	5	2	2	3.2	7	9	13	11	0	.306	.548	7	1	C-18
1961	120	376	91	17	0	16	4.3	50	58	55	74	1	.242	.415	14	3	C-108
1962	90	260	67	14	0	11	4.2	39	37	36	55	2	.258	.438	13	2	C-73
1963 PIT N	92	252	58	5	0	11	4.4	27	26	36	57	0	.230	.381	9	3	C-85
1964	97	302	89	12	3	10	3.3	33	36	41	56	1	.295	.454	1	0	C-96
1965	134	403	108	15	0	17	4.2	42	65	41	84	0	.268	.432	4	1	C-131
1966	123	374	88	20	0	11	2.9	37	49	50	71	0	.235	.377	7	1	C-118
1967	44	100	20	1	1	0	0.0	4	9	16	26	0	.200	.230	7	0	C-38
1968 OAK A	66	199	49	4	0	6	3.0	19	20	24	42	0	.246	.357	3	1	C-63
1969 2 teams		OAK A (14G – .148)			SEA A (40G – .264)												
" total	54	137	33	5	1	6	4.4	11	16	18	18	0	.241	.423	16	6	C-36, 1B-2, OF-1
11 yrs.	849	2465	622	98	7	90	3.7	269	326	330	494	4	.252	.407	81	18	C-767, 1B-2, OF-1

Mike Pagliarulo

PAGLIARULO, MICHAEL TIMOTHY
B. Mar. 15, 1960, Medford, Mass. BB TR 6'2" 195 lbs.

	G	AB	H	2B	3B	HR	HR %	R	RBI	BB	SO	SB	BA	SA	AB	H	G by POS
1984 NY A	67	201	48	15	3	7	3.5	24	34	15	46	0	.239	.448	0	0	3B-67

Eddie Palmer

PALMER, EDWIN HENRY (Baldy)
B. June 1, 1893, Petty, Tex. D. Jan. 9, 1983, Marlow, Okla. BR TR 5'9½" 175 lbs.

	G	AB	H	2B	3B	HR	HR %	R	RBI	BB	SO	SB	BA	SA	AB	H	G by POS
1917 PHI A	16	52	11	1	0	0	0.0	7	5	7	7	1	.212	.231	2	0	3B-13, SS-1

Joe Palmisano

PALMISANO, JOSEPH
B. Nov. 19, 1902, West Point, Ga. D. Nov. 5, 1971, Albuquerque, N. M. BR TR 5'8" 160 lbs.

	G	AB	H	2B	3B	HR	HR %	R	RBI	BB	SO	SB	BA	SA	AB	H	G by POS
1931 PHI A	19	44	10	2	0	0	0.0	5	4	6	3	0	.227	.273	2	0	C-16, 2B-1

Stan Palys

PALYS, STANLEY FRANCIS
B. May 1, 1930, Blakely, Pa. BR TR 6'2" 190 lbs.

	G	AB	H	2B	3B	HR	HR %	R	RBI	BB	SO	SB	BA	SA	AB	H	G by POS
1953 PHI N	2	2	0	0	0	0	0.0	0	0	1	0	0	.000	.000	0	0	OF-1
1954	2	4	1	0	0	0	0.0	0	0	1	1	0	.250	.250	1	0	OF-1
1955 2 teams		PHI N (15G – .288)			CIN N (79G – .230)												
" total	94	274	66	17	0	8	2.9	37	38	18	40	2	.241	.391	22	4	OF-70, 1B-1
1956 CIN N	40	53	12	0	0	2	3.8	5	5	6	13	0	.226	.340	24	6	OF-10
4 yrs.	138	333	79	17	0	10	3.0	42	43	26	54	2	.237	.378	47	10	OF-82, 1B-1

Jim Pankovits

PANKOVITS, JAMES FRANKLIN
B. Aug. 6, 1955, Pennington Gap, Va. BR TR 5'10" 174 lbs.

	G	AB	H	2B	3B	HR	HR %	R	RBI	BB	SO	SB	BA	SA	AB	H	G by POS
1984 HOU N	53	81	23	7	0	1	1.2	6	14	2	20	2	.284	.407	40	9	2B-15, SS-4, OF-3

Ken Pape

PAPE, KENNETH WAYNE
B. Oct. 1, 1951, San Antonio, Tex. BR TR 5'11" 195 lbs.

	G	AB	H	2B	3B	HR	HR %	R	RBI	BB	SO	SB	BA	SA	AB	H	G by POS
1976 TEX A	21	23	5	1	0	1	4.3	7	4	3	2	0	.217	.391	1	0	SS-6, 3B-4, DH-3, 2B-1

Stan Papi

PAPI, STANLEY GERARD
B. Feb. 4, 1951, Fresno, Calif. BR TR 6' 170 lbs.

	G	AB	H	2B	3B	HR	HR %	R	RBI	BB	SO	SB	BA	SA	AB	H	G by POS
1974 STL N	8	4	1	0	0	0	0.0	0	1	0	0	0	.250	.250	1	0	SS-7, 2B-1
1977 MON N	13	43	10	2	1	0	0.0	5	4	1	9	1	.233	.326	0	0	3B-10, SS-2, 2B-1
1978	67	152	35	11	0	0	0.0	15	11	10	28	0	.230	.303	24	3	SS-22, 3B-15, 2B-5
1979 BOS A	50	117	22	8	0	1	0.9	9	6	5	20	0	.188	.282	3	0	2B-26, SS-21, DH-1
1980 2 teams		BOS A (1G – .000)			DET A (46G – .237)												
" total	47	114	27	3	4	3	2.6	12	17	5	24	0	.237	.412	4	1	2B-31, 3B-12, SS-5, 1B-1
1981 DET A	40	93	19	2	1	3	3.2	8	12	3	18	1	.204	.344	4	1	3B-32, DH-3, 2B-1, 1B-1
6 yrs.	225	523	114	26	6	7	1.3	49	51	24	99	2	.218	.331	36	5	3B-69, 2B-65, SS-57, DH-4, 1B-2, OF-1

Freddy Parent

PARENT, FREDERICK ALFRED
B. Nov. 25, 1875, Biddeford, Me. D. Nov. 2, 1972, Sanford, Me. BR TR 5'5½" 148 lbs.

	G	AB	H	2B	3B	HR	HR %	R	RBI	BB	SO	SB	BA	SA	AB	H	G by POS
1899 STL N	2	8	1	0	0	0	0.0	0	1	0		0	.125	.125	0	0	2B-2
1901 BOS A	138	517	158	23	9	4	0.8	87	59	41		16	.306	.408	0	0	SS-138
1902	138	567	156	31	8	3	0.5	91	62	24		16	.275	.374	0	0	SS-138
1903	139	560	170	31	17	4	0.7	83	80	13		24	.304	.441	0	0	SS-139
1904	155	591	172	22	9	6	1.0	85	77	28		20	.291	.389	0	0	SS-155
1905	153	602	141	16	5	0	0.0	55	53	47		25	.234	.277	0	0	SS-153
1906	149	600	141	14	10	1	0.2	67	49	31		16	.235	.297	0	0	SS-143, 2B-6
1907	114	409	113	19	5	1	0.2	51	26	22		12	.276	.355	3B-7, 2B-5
1908 CHI A	119	391	81	7	5	0	0.0	28	35	50		9	.207	.251	0	0	SS-118
1909	136	472	123	10	5	0	0.0	61	30	46		32	.261	.303	0	0	SS-98, OF-37, 2B-1
1910	81	258	46	6	1	1	0.4	23	16	29		14	.178	.221	0	0	OF-62, 2B-11, SS-4, 3B-1
1911	3	9	4	1	0	0	0.0	2	3	2		0	.444	.556	0	0	2B-3
12 yrs.	1327	4984	1306	180	74	20	0.4	633	471	333		184	.262	.340	12	2	SS-1129, OF-146, 2B-28, 3B-8

WORLD SERIES

	G	AB	H	2B	3B	HR	HR %	R	RBI	BB	SO	SB	BA	SA	AB	H	G by POS
1903 BOS A	8	32	9	0	3	0	0.0	8	3	1	1	0	.281	.469	0	0	SS-8
					4th												

Kelly Paris

PARIS, KELLY JAY
B. Oct. 17, 1957, Encino, Calif. BB TR 6' 175 lbs.

	G	AB	H	2B	3B	HR	HR %	R	RBI	BB	SO	SB	BA	SA	AB	H	G by POS
1982 STL N	12	29	3	0	0	0	0.0	1	1	0	7	0	.103	.103	3	1	3B-5, SS-4
1983 CIN N	56	120	30	6	0	0	0.0	13	7	15	22	8	.250	.300	11	1	3B-16, 2B-10, SS-7, 1B-3
2 yrs.	68	149	33	6	0	0	0.0	14	8	15	29	8	.221	.262	14	2	3B-21, SS-11, 2B-10, 1B-3

	G	AB	H	2B	3B	HR	HR%	R	RBI	BB	SO	SB	BA	SA	Pinch Hit AB	Pinch Hit H	G by POS

Tony Parisse

PARISSE, LOUIS PETER
B. June 25, 1911, Philadelphia, Pa.　　D. June 2, 1956, Philadelphia, Pa.
BR TR 5'10"　165 lbs.

	G	AB	H	2B	3B	HR	HR%	R	RBI	BB	SO	SB	BA	SA	AB	H	G by POS
1943 PHI A	6	17	3	0	0	0	0.0	0	1	2	2	0	.176	.176	1	0	C-5
1944	4	4	0	0	0	0	0.0	0	0	0	1	0	.000	.000	2	0	C-2
2 yrs.	10	21	3	0	0	0	0.0	0	1	2	3	0	.143	.143	3	0	C-7

Ace Parker

PARKER, CLARENCE McKAY
B. May 17, 1912, Portsmouth, Va.
BR TR 6'　180 lbs.

	G	AB	H	2B	3B	HR	HR%	R	RBI	BB	SO	SB	BA	SA	AB	H	G by POS
1937 PHI A	38	94	11	0	1	2	2.1	8	13	4	17	0	.117	.202	3	2	SS-19, 2B-9, OF-5
1938	56	113	26	5	0	0	0.0	12	12	10	16	1	.230	.274	4	1	SS-26, 3B-9, 2B-9
2 yrs.	94	207	37	5	1	2	1.0	20	25	14	33	1	.179	.242	7	3	SS-45, 2B-18, 3B-9, OF-5

Billy Parker

PARKER, WILLIAM DAVID
B. Jan. 14, 1947, Hayneville, Ala.
BR TR 5'8"　168 lbs.

	G	AB	H	2B	3B	HR	HR%	R	RBI	BB	SO	SB	BA	SA	AB	H	G by POS
1971 CAL A	20	70	16	0	1	1	1.4	4	6	2	20	1	.229	.300	0	0	2B-20
1972	36	80	17	2	0	2	2.5	11	8	9	17	0	.213	.313	1	0	3B-21, 2B-9, OF-5, SS-1
1973	38	102	23	2	1	0	0.0	14	7	8	23	0	.225	.265	1	0	2B-32, SS-3
3 yrs.	94	252	56	4	2	3	1.2	29	21	19	60	1	.222	.290	2	0	2B-61, 3B-21, OF-5, SS-4

Dave Parker

PARKER, DAVID GENE (The Cobra)
B. June 9, 1951, Cincinnati, Ohio
BL TR 6'5"　230 lbs.

	G	AB	H	2B	3B	HR	HR%	R	RBI	BB	SO	SB	BA	SA	AB	H	G by POS
1973 PIT N	54	139	40	9	1	4	2.9	17	14	2	27	1	.288	.453	15	4	OF-39
1974	73	220	62	10	3	4	1.8	27	29	10	53	3	.282	.409	21	4	OF-49, 1B-6
1975	148	558	172	35	10	25	4.5	75	101	38	89	8	.308	.541	7	4	OF-141
1976	138	537	168	28	10	13	2.4	82	90	30	80	19	.313	.475	4	2	OF-134
1977	159	637	215	44	8	21	3.3	107	88	58	107	17	.338	.531	0	0	OF-158, 2B-1
1978	148	581	194	32	12	30	5.2	102	117	57	92	20	.334	.585	0	0	OF-147
1979	158	622	193	45	7	25	4.0	109	94	67	101	20	.310	.526	0	0	OF-158
1980	139	518	153	31	1	17	3.3	71	79	25	69	10	.295	.458	7	2	OF-130
1981	67	240	62	14	3	9	3.8	29	48	9	25	6	.258	.454	6	3	OF-60
1982	73	244	66	19	3	6	2.5	41	29	22	45	7	.270	.447	7	2	OF-63
1983	144	552	154	29	4	12	2.2	68	69	28	89	12	.279	.411	2	0	OF-142
1984 CIN N	156	607	173	28	0	16	2.6	73	94	41	89	11	.285	.410	6	0	OF-151
12 yrs.	1457	5455	1652	324	62	182	3.3	801	852	387	866	134	.303	.485	75	21	OF-1372, 1B-6, 2B-1

LEAGUE CHAMPIONSHIP SERIES

	G	AB	H	2B	3B	HR	HR%	R	RBI	BB	SO	SB	BA	SA	AB	H	G by POS
1974 PIT N	3	8	1	0	0	0	0.0	0	0	0	1	0	.125	.125	1	0	OF-2
1975	3	10	0	0	0	0	0.0	2	0	1	3	0	.000	.000	0	0	OF-3
1979	3	12	4	0	0	0	0.0	2	2	2	3	1	.333	.333	0	0	OF-3
3 yrs.	9	30	5	0	0	0	0.0	4	2	3	7	1	.167	.167	1	0	OF-8

WORLD SERIES

	G	AB	H	2B	3B	HR	HR%	R	RBI	BB	SO	SB	BA	SA	AB	H	G by POS
1979 PIT N	7	29	10	3	0	0	0.0	2	4	2	7	0	.345	.448	0	0	OF-7

Dixie Parker

PARKER, DOUGLAS WOOLEY
B. Apr. 24, 1895, Forest Home, Ala.　　D. May 15, 1972, Tuscaloosa, Ala.
BL TR 5'11"　160 lbs.

	G	AB	H	2B	3B	HR	HR%	R	RBI	BB	SO	SB	BA	SA	AB	H	G by POS
1923 PHI N	4	5	1	0	0	0	0.0	0	1	0	1	0	.200	.200	0	0	C-2

Pat Parker

PARKER, CLARENCE PERKINS
B. May 22, 1893, Somerville, Mass.　　D. Mar. 21, 1967, Claremont, N. H.
BR TR 5'7"　160 lbs.

	G	AB	H	2B	3B	HR	HR%	R	RBI	BB	SO	SB	BA	SA	AB	H	G by POS
1915 STL A	3	6	1	0	0	0	0.0	0	1	0	3	0	.167	.167	1	0	OF-2

Salty Parker

PARKER, FRANCIS JAMES
B. July 8, 1913, East St. Louis, Ill.
Manager 1967, 1972.
BR TR 6'　173 lbs.

	G	AB	H	2B	3B	HR	HR%	R	RBI	BB	SO	SB	BA	SA	AB	H	G by POS
1936 DET A	11	25	7	2	0	0	0.0	6	4	2	3	0	.280	.360	0	0	SS-7, 1B-2

Wes Parker

PARKER, MAURICE WESLEY
B. Nov. 13, 1939, Evanston, Ill.
BB TL 6'1"　180 lbs.

	G	AB	H	2B	3B	HR	HR%	R	RBI	BB	SO	SB	BA	SA	AB	H	G by POS
1964 LA N	124	214	55	7	1	3	1.4	29	10	14	45	5	.257	.341	30	6	OF-69, 1B-31
1965	154	542	129	24	7	8	1.5	80	51	75	95	13	.238	.352	1	1	1B-154, OF-1
1966	156	475	120	17	5	12	2.5	67	51	69	83	7	.253	.385	7	1	1B-140, OF-14
1967	139	413	102	16	5	5	1.2	56	31	65	83	10	.247	.346	13	5	1B-112, OF-18
1968	135	468	112	22	2	3	0.6	42	27	49	87	4	.239	.314	6	0	1B-114, OF-28
1969	132	471	131	23	4	13	2.8	76	68	56	46	4	.278	.427	5	3	1B-128, OF-2
1970	161	614	196	47	4	10	1.6	84	111	79	70	8	.319	.458	0	0	1B-161
1971	157	533	146	24	1	6	1.1	69	62	63	63	6	.274	.356	1	1	1B-148, OF-18
1972	130	427	119	14	3	4	0.9	45	59	62	43	3	.279	.354	8	2	1B-120, OF-5
9 yrs.	1288	4157	1110	194	32	64	1.5	548	470	532	615	60	.267	.375	71	19	1B-1108, OF-155

WORLD SERIES

	G	AB	H	2B	3B	HR	HR%	R	RBI	BB	SO	SB	BA	SA	AB	H	G by POS
1965 LA N	7	23	7	0	1	1	4.3	3	2	3	3	2	.304	.522	0	0	1B-7
1966	4	13	3	2	0	0	0.0	0	0	1	3	0	.231	.385	0	0	1B-4
2 yrs.	11	36	10	2	1	1	2.8	3	2	4	6	2	.278	.472	0	0	1B-11

Frank Parkinson

PARKINSON, FRANK JOSEPH
B. Mar. 23, 1895, Dickson City, Pa.　　D. July 4, 1960, Trenton, N. J.
BR TR 5'11"　175 lbs.

	G	AB	H	2B	3B	HR	HR%	R	RBI	BB	SO	SB	BA	SA	AB	H	G by POS
1921 PHI N	108	391	99	20	2	5	1.3	36	32	13	81	3	.253	.353	1	0	SS-105, 3B-1
1922	141	545	150	18	6	15	2.8	86	70	55	93	1	.275	.413	2	0	2B-139
1923	67	219	53	12	0	3	1.4	21	28	13	31	0	.242	.338	5	1	2B-37, SS-15, 3B-11
1924	62	156	33	7	0	1	0.6	14	19	14	28	3	.212	.276	5	1	3B-28, SS-21, 2B-10
4 yrs.	378	1311	335	57	8	24	1.8	157	149	95	233	9	.256	.366	13	2	2B-186, SS-141, 3B-40

Art Parks

PARKS, ARTIE WILLIAM
B. Nov. 1, 1911, Paris, Ark.
BL TR 5'9"　170 lbs.

	G	AB	H	2B	3B	HR	HR%	R	RBI	BB	SO	SB	BA	SA	AB	H	G by POS
1937 BKN N	7	16	5	2	0	0	0.0	2	0	2	2	0	.313	.438	3	0	OF-4
1939	71	239	65	13	2	1	0.4	27	19	28	14	2	.272	.356	4	2	OF-65
2 yrs.	78	255	70	15	2	1	0.4	29	19	30	16	2	.275	.361	7	2	OF-69

	G	AB	H	2B	3B	HR	HR %	R	RBI	BB	SO	SB	BA	SA	Pinch Hit AB	Pinch Hit H	G by POS

Bill Parks

PARKS, WILLIAM ROBERT
B. June 4, 1849, Easton, Pa.   D. Oct. 10, 1911, Easton, Pa.
Manager 1875.
BR TR 5'8"   150 lbs.

	G	AB	H	2B	3B	HR	HR %	R	RBI	BB	SO	SB	BA	SA	Pinch Hit AB	Pinch Hit H	G by POS
1876 BOS N	1	4	0	0	0	0	0.0	0	0	0	0		.000	.000	0	0	OF-1

Sam Parrilla

PARRILLA, SAMUEL
B. June 12, 1943, Santurce, Puerto Rico
BR TR 5'11"   185 lbs.

	G	AB	H	2B	3B	HR	HR %	R	RBI	BB	SO	SB	BA	SA	Pinch Hit AB	Pinch Hit H	G by POS
1970 PHI N	11	16	2	1	0	0	0.0	1	0	1	4	0	.125	.188	7	1	OF-3

Lance Parrish

PARRISH, LANCE MICHAEL
B. June 15, 1956, McKeesport, Pa.
BR TR 6'3"   210 lbs.

	G	AB	H	2B	3B	HR	HR %	R	RBI	BB	SO	SB	BA	SA	Pinch Hit AB	Pinch Hit H	G by POS
1977 DET A	12	46	9	2	0	3	6.5	10	7	5	12	0	.196	.435	0	0	C-12
1978	85	288	63	11	3	14	4.9	37	41	21	71	0	.219	.424	6	1	C-79
1979	143	493	136	26	3	19	3.9	65	65	49	105	6	.276	.456	3	1	C-142
1980	144	553	158	34	6	24	4.3	79	82	31	109	6	.286	.499	4	1	C-121, DH-16, OF-5, 1B-5
1981	96	348	85	18	2	10	2.9	39	46	34	52	2	.244	.394	0	0	C-90, DH-5
1982	133	486	138	19	2	32	6.6	75	87	40	99	3	.284	.529	2	1	C-132, OF-1
1983	155	605	163	42	3	27	4.5	80	114	44	106	1	.269	.483	2	0	C-131, DH-27
1984	147	578	137	16	2	33	5.7	75	98	41	120	2	.237	.443	3	1	C-127, DH-22
8 yrs.	915	3397	889	168	21	162	4.8	460	540	255	674	20	.262	.467	20	5	C-834, DH-70, OF-6, 1B-5

LEAGUE CHAMPIONSHIP SERIES

	G	AB	H	2B	3B	HR	HR %	R	RBI	BB	SO	SB	BA	SA	Pinch Hit AB	Pinch Hit H	G by POS
1984 DET A	3	12	3	1	0	1	8.3	1	3	0	3	0	.250	.583	0	0	C-3

WORLD SERIES

	G	AB	H	2B	3B	HR	HR %	R	RBI	BB	SO	SB	BA	SA	Pinch Hit AB	Pinch Hit H	G by POS
1984 DET A	5	18	5	1	0	1	5.6	3	2	3	2	1	.278	.500	0	0	C-5

Larry Parrish

PARRISH, LARRY ALTON
B. Nov. 10, 1953, Winter Haven, Fla.
BR TR 6'3"   190 lbs.

	G	AB	H	2B	3B	HR	HR %	R	RBI	BB	SO	SB	BA	SA	Pinch Hit AB	Pinch Hit H	G by POS
1974 MON N	25	69	14	5	0	0	0.0	9	4	6	19	0	.203	.275	1	0	3B-24
1975	145	532	146	32	5	10	1.9	50	65	28	74	4	.274	.410	5	1	3B-143, SS-1, 2B-1
1976	154	543	126	28	5	11	2.0	65	61	41	91	2	.232	.363	1	0	3B-153
1977	123	402	99	19	2	11	2.7	50	46	37	71	2	.246	.386	14	4	3B-115
1978	144	520	144	39	4	15	2.9	68	70	32	103	2	.277	.454	5	3	3B-139
1979	153	544	167	39	2	30	5.5	83	82	41	101	5	.307	.551	0	0	3B-153
1980	126	452	115	27	3	15	3.3	55	72	36	80	2	.254	.427	1	0	3B-124
1981	97	349	85	19	3	8	2.3	41	44	28	73	0	.244	.384	1	0	3B-95
1982 TEX A	128	440	116	15	2	17	3.9	59	62	30	84	5	.264	.414	5	2	OF-124, 3B-3, DH-2
1983	145	555	151	26	4	26	4.7	76	88	46	91	0	.272	.474	1	0	OF-132, DH-13
1984	156	613	175	42	1	22	3.6	73	101	42	116	2	.285	.465	1	0	OF-81, DH-63, 3B-12
11 yrs.	1396	5019	1338	291	29	165	3.3	629	695	367	903	24	.267	.435	34	10	3B-961, OF-337, DH-78, SS-1, 2B-1

DIVISIONAL PLAYOFF SERIES

	G	AB	H	2B	3B	HR	HR %	R	RBI	BB	SO	SB	BA	SA	Pinch Hit AB	Pinch Hit H	G by POS
1981 MON N	5	20	3	1	0	0	0.0	3	1	1	3	0	.150	.200	0	0	3B-5

LEAGUE CHAMPIONSHIP SERIES

	G	AB	H	2B	3B	HR	HR %	R	RBI	BB	SO	SB	BA	SA	Pinch Hit AB	Pinch Hit H	G by POS
1981 MON N	5	19	5	2	0	0	0.0	2	2	1	1	0	.263	.368	0	0	3B-5

Jiggs Parrott

PARROTT, WALTER E.
Brother of Tom Parrott.
B. July 14, 1871, Portland, Ore.   D. Apr. 16, 1898, Phoenix, Ariz.
5'11"   160 lbs.

	G	AB	H	2B	3B	HR	HR %	R	RBI	BB	SO	SB	BA	SA	Pinch Hit AB	Pinch Hit H	G by POS
1892 CHI N	78	335	72	9	5	2	0.6	40	22	8	30	7	.215	.290	0	0	3B-78
1893	110	455	111	10	9	1	0.2	54	46	13	25	25	.244	.312	0	0	3B-99, 2B-7, OF-4
1894	127	532	139	17	9	3	0.6	83	64	16	35	30	.261	.344	0	0	2B-123, 3B-1
1895	3	4	1	0	0	0	0.0	0	0	0	0	0	.250	.250	0	0	OF-1, SS-1, 1B-1
4 yrs.	318	1326	323	36	23	6	0.5	177	151	37	90	62	.244	.319	0	0	3B-178, 2B-130, OF-5, SS-1, 1B-1

Tom Parrott

PARROTT, THOMAS WILLIAM (Tacky Tom)
Brother of Jiggs Parrott.
B. Apr. 10, 1868, Portland, Ore.   D. Jan. 1, 1932, Dundee, Ore.
BR TR 6'2"   170 lbs.

	G	AB	H	2B	3B	HR	HR %	R	RBI	BB	SO	SB	BA	SA	Pinch Hit AB	Pinch Hit H	G by POS
1893 2 teams		CHI	N	(7G –	.259)			CIN	N	(24G –	.191)						
" total	31	95	20	2	1	1	1.1	9	12	2	11	0	.211	.284	1	0	P-26, 3B-2, OF-1, 2B-1
1894 CIN N	68	229	74	12	6	4	1.7	51	40	17	10	4	.323	.480	3	2	P-41, OF-13, 1B-12, SS-1, 3B-1, 2B-1
1895	64	201	69	13	7	3	1.5	35	41	11	8	10	.343	.522	0	0	P-41, 1B-14, OF-9
1896 STL N	118	474	138	13	12	7	1.5	62	70	11	24	12	.291	.414	0	0	OF-108, P-7, 1B-6
4 yrs.	281	999	301	40	26	15	1.5	157	163	41	53	26	.301	.438	4	2	OF-131, P-115, 1B-32, 3B-3, 2B-2, SS-1

Casey Parsons

PARSONS, CASEY ROBERT
B. Apr. 14, 1954, Wenatchee, Wash.
BL TR 6'1"   180 lbs.

	G	AB	H	2B	3B	HR	HR %	R	RBI	BB	SO	SB	BA	SA	Pinch Hit AB	Pinch Hit H	G by POS
1981 SEA A	36	22	5	1	0	1	4.5	6	5	1	4	0	.227	.409	8	1	OF-24, 1B-1
1983 CHI A	8	5	1	0	0	0	0.0	1	0	2	1	0	.200	.200	4	0	OF-3, DH-2
1984	1	1	0	0	0	0	0.0	0	0	0	1	0	.000	.000	1	0	
3 yrs.	45	28	6	1	0	1	3.6	7	5	3	6	0	.214	.357	13	1	OF-27, DH-2, 1B-1

Dixie Parsons

PARSONS, EDWARD DIXON
B. May 12, 1916, Talladega, Ala.
BR TR 6'2"   180 lbs.

	G	AB	H	2B	3B	HR	HR %	R	RBI	BB	SO	SB	BA	SA	Pinch Hit AB	Pinch Hit H	G by POS
1939 DET A	5	1	0	0	0	0	0.0	0	0	1	1	0	.000	.000	1	0	C-4
1942	63	188	37	4	0	2	1.1	8	11	13	22	1	.197	.250	0	0	C-62
1943	40	106	15	3	0	0	0.0	2	4	6	16	0	.142	.170	1	0	C-40
3 yrs.	108	295	52	7	0	2	0.7	10	15	20	39	1	.176	.220	2	0	C-106

John Parsons

PARSONS, JOHN S.
B. Napoleon, Ohio   Deceased.

	G	AB	H	2B	3B	HR	HR %	R	RBI	BB	SO	SB	BA	SA	Pinch Hit AB	Pinch Hit H	G by POS
1884 CIN AA	1	3	0	0	0	0	0.0	0		0			.000	.000	0	0	OF-1

	G	AB	H	2B	3B	HR	HR %	R	RBI	BB	SO	SB	BA	SA	Pinch Hit AB	Pinch Hit H	G by POS

Roy Partee

PARTEE, ROY ROBERT   BR TR 5'10" 180 lbs.
B. Sept. 7, 1917, Los Angeles, Calif.

	G	AB	H	2B	3B	HR	HR %	R	RBI	BB	SO	SB	BA	SA	PH AB	PH H	G by POS
1943 BOS A	96	299	84	14	2	0	0.0	30	31	39	33	0	.281	.341	5	2	C-91
1944	89	280	68	12	0	2	0.7	18	41	37	29	0	.243	.307	5	1	C-85
1946	40	111	35	5	2	0	0.0	13	9	13	14	0	.315	.396	1	1	C-38
1947	60	169	39	2	0	0	0.0	14	16	18	23	0	.231	.243	6	0	C-54
1948 STL A	82	231	47	8	1	0	0.0	14	17	25	21	2	.203	.247	6	0	C-76
5 yrs.	367	1090	273	41	5	2	0.2	89	114	132	120	2	.250	.303	23	4	C-344

WORLD SERIES
| 1946 BOS A | 5 | 10 | 1 | 0 | 0 | 0 | 0.0 | 1 | 1 | 1 | 2 | 0 | .100 | .100 | 1 | 0 | C-5 |

Steve Partenheimer

PARTENHEIMER, HAROLD PHILIP   BR TR 5'8½" 145 lbs.
Father of Stan Partenheimer.
B. Aug. 30, 1891, Greenfield, Mass.   D. June 16, 1971, Mansfield, Ohio

	G	AB	H	2B	3B	HR	HR %	R	RBI	BB	SO	SB	BA	SA	PH AB	PH H	G by POS
1913 DET A	1	2	0	0	0	0	0.0	0	0	0	0	0	.000	.000	0	0	3B-1

Jay Partridge

PARTRIDGE, JAMES BAGG   BL TR 5'11" 160 lbs.
B. Nov. 15, 1902, Mountville, Ga.   D. Jan. 4, 1974, Nashville, Tenn.

	G	AB	H	2B	3B	HR	HR %	R	RBI	BB	SO	SB	BA	SA	PH AB	PH H	G by POS
1927 BKN N	146	572	149	17	6	7	1.2	72	40	20	36	9	.260	.348	6	1	2B-140
1928	37	73	18	0	1	0	0.0	18	12	13	6	2	.247	.274	11	4	2B-18, 3B-2
2 yrs.	183	645	167	17	7	7	1.1	90	52	33	42	11	.259	.340	17	5	2B-158, 3B-2

Ben Paschal

PASCHAL, BENJAMIN EDWIN   BR TR 5'11" 185 lbs.
B. Oct. 13, 1895, Enterprise, Ala.   D. Nov. 10, 1974, Charlotte, N. C.

	G	AB	H	2B	3B	HR	HR %	R	RBI	BB	SO	SB	BA	SA	PH AB	PH H	G by POS
1915 CLE A	9	9	1	0	0	0	0.0	0	0	0	3	0	.111	.111	9	1	OF-7
1920 BOS A	9	28	10	0	0	0	0.0	5	5	5	2	1	.357	.357	2	1	OF-4
1924 NY A	4	12	3	1	0	0	0.0	2	3	1	0	0	.250	.333	1	0	OF-4
1925	89	247	89	16	5	12	4.9	49	56	22	29	14	.360	.611	21	5	OF-66
1926	96	258	74	12	3	7	2.7	46	33	26	35	7	.287	.438	18	6	OF-74
1927	50	82	26	9	2	2	2.4	16	16	4	10	0	.317	.549	22	5	OF-27
1928	65	79	25	6	1	1	1.3	12	15	8	11	1	.316	.456	35	8	OF-25
1929	42	72	15	3	0	2	2.8	13	11	6	3	1	.208	.333	20	3	OF-20
8 yrs.	364	787	243	47	11	24	3.0	143	139	72	93	24	.309	.488	128	29	OF-223

WORLD SERIES
1926 NY A	5	4	1	0	0	0	0.0	0	1	1	2	0	.250	.250	4	1	
1928	3	10	2	0	0	0	0.0	0	1	1	0	0	.200	.200	1	1	OF-3
2 yrs.	8	14	3	0	0	0	0.0	0	2	2	2	0	.214	.214	5	2	OF-3

Johnny Pasek

PASEK, JOHN PAUL   BR TR 5'10" 175 lbs.
B. June 25, 1905, Niagara Falls, N. Y.   D. Mar. 13, 1976, St. Petersburg, Fla.

	G	AB	H	2B	3B	HR	HR %	R	RBI	BB	SO	SB	BA	SA	PH AB	PH H	G by POS
1933 DET A	28	61	15	4	0	0	0.0	6	4	7	7	2	.246	.311	0	0	C-28
1934 CHI A	4	9	3	0	0	0	0.0	1	0	1	1	0	.333	.333	0	0	C-4
2 yrs.	32	70	18	4	0	0	0.0	7	4	8	8	2	.257	.314	0	0	C-32

Dode Paskert

PASKERT, GEORGE HENRY   BR TR 5'11" 165 lbs.
B. Aug. 28, 1881, Cleveland, Ohio   D. Feb. 12, 1959, Cleveland, Ohio

	G	AB	H	2B	3B	HR	HR %	R	RBI	BB	SO	SB	BA	SA	PH AB	PH H	G by POS
1907 CIN N	16	50	14	4	0	1	2.0	10	8	2		2	.280	.420	0	0	OF-16
1908	118	395	96	14	4	1	0.3	40	36	27		25	.243	.306	3	1	OF-116
1909	104	322	81	7	4	0	0.0	49	33	34		23	.252	.298	16	3	OF-82, 1B-6
1910	144	506	152	21	5	2	0.4	63	46	70	60	51	.300	.374	2	0	OF-139, 1B-2
1911 PHI N	153	560	153	18	5	4	0.7	96	47	70	70	28	.273	.345	0	0	OF-153
1912	145	540	170	37	5	2	0.4	102	43	91	67	36	.315	.413	0	0	OF-141, 2B-2, 3B-1
1913	124	454	119	21	9	4	0.9	83	29	65	69	12	.262	.374	4	0	OF-120
1914	132	451	119	25	6	3	0.7	59	44	56	68	23	.264	.366	3	0	OF-128, SS-4
1915	109	328	80	17	4	3	0.9	51	39	35	38	9	.244	.348	10	3	OF-104, 1B-5
1916	149	555	155	30	7	8	1.4	82	46	54	76	22	.279	.402	2	1	OF-146, SS-1
1917	141	546	137	27	11	4	0.7	78	43	62	63	19	.251	.363	1	1	OF-138
1918 CHI N	127	461	132	24	3	3	0.7	69	59	53	49	20	.286	.371	0	0	OF-121, 3B-6
1919	87	270	53	11	3	2	0.7	21	29	28	33	7	.196	.281	8	1	OF-80
1920	139	487	136	22	10	5	1.0	57	71	64	58	16	.279	.396	1	0	OF-137
1921 CIN N	27	92	16	1	1	0	0.0	8	4	4	8	0	.174	.207	1	0	OF-24
15 yrs.	1715	6017	1613	279	77	42	0.7	868	577	715	659	293	.268	.361	51	10	OF-1645, 1B-13, 3B-7, SS-5, 2B-2

WORLD SERIES
1915 PHI N	5	19	3	0	0	0	0.0	2	0	1	2	0	.158	.158	0	0	OF-5
1918 CHI N	6	21	4	1	0	0	0.0	0	2	2	2	0	.190	.238	0	0	OF-6
2 yrs.	11	40	7	1	0	0	0.0	2	2	3	4	0	.175	.200	0	0	OF-11

Kevin Pasley

PASLEY, KEVIN PATRICK   BR TR 6' 185 lbs.
B. July 22, 1953, New York, N. Y.

	G	AB	H	2B	3B	HR	HR %	R	RBI	BB	SO	SB	BA	SA	PH AB	PH H	G by POS
1974 LA N	1	0	0	0	0	0	–	0	0	0	0	0	–	–	0	0	C-1
1976	23	52	12	2	0	0	0.0	4	2	3	7	0	.231	.269	0	0	C-23
1977 2 teams	LA	N (2G – .333)		SEA	A	(4G –	.385)										
" total	6	16	6	0	0	0	0.0	1	2	1	2	0	.375	.375	0	0	C-6
1978 SEA A	25	54	13	5	0	1	1.9	3	5	2	4	0	.241	.389	0	0	C-25
4 yrs.	55	122	31	7	0	1	0.8	8	9	6	13	0	.254	.336	0	0	C-55

Mike Pasquariello

PASQUARIELLO, MICHAEL JOHN (Toney)   BR TR 6'2" 190 lbs.
B. Nov. 7, 1898, Philadelphia, Pa.   D. Apr. 5, 1965, Bridgeport, Conn.

	G	AB	H	2B	3B	HR	HR %	R	RBI	BB	SO	SB	BA	SA	PH AB	PH H	G by POS
1919 2 teams	PHI	N (1G – 1.000)		STL	N	(1G –	.000)										
" total	2	2	1	0	0	0	0.0	1	0	0	1	0	.500	.500	1	0	1B-1

Cliff Pasternicky

PASTERNICKY, CLIFFORD SCOT   BR TR 6' 180 lbs.
B. Nov. 18, 1958, Seattle, Wash.

	G	AB	H	2B	3B	HR	HR %	R	RBI	BB	SO	SB	BA	SA	PH AB	PH H	G by POS
1983 KC A	10	32	4	0	0	2	6.3	4	5	0	3	0	.125	.313	0	0	3B-10

	G	AB	H	2B	3B	HR	HR %	R	RBI	BB	SO	SB	BA	SA	Pinch Hit AB	Pinch Hit H	G by POS

Bob Pate

PATE, ROBERT WAYNE
B. Dec. 3, 1953, Los Angeles, Calif.
BR TR 6'3" 200 lbs.

	G	AB	H	2B	3B	HR	HR %	R	RBI	BB	SO	SB	BA	SA	AB	H	G by POS
1980 **MON N**	23	39	10	2	0	0	0.0	3	5	3	6	0	.256	.308	5	1	OF-18
1981	8	6	2	0	0	0	0.0	0	0	1	0	0	.333	.333	2	0	OF-5
2 yrs.	31	45	12	2	0	0	0.0	3	5	4	6	0	.267	.311	7	1	OF-23

Freddie Patek

PATEK, FREDDIE JOE (The Flea, Moochie)
B. Oct. 9, 1944, Sequin, Tex.
BR TR 5'5" 148 lbs.

	G	AB	H	2B	3B	HR	HR %	R	RBI	BB	SO	SB	BA	SA	AB	H	G by POS
1968 **PIT N**	61	208	53	4	2	2	1.0	31	18	12	37	18	.255	.322	1	0	SS-52, OF-5, 3B-1
1969	147	460	110	9	1	5	1.1	48	32	53	86	15	.239	.296	0	0	SS-146
1970	84	237	58	10	5	1	0.4	42	19	29	46	8	.245	.342	11	3	SS-65
1971 **KC A**	147	591	158	21	11	6	1.0	86	36	44	80	49	.267	.371	1	0	SS-147
1972	136	518	110	25	4	0	0.0	59	32	47	64	33	.212	.276	0	0	SS-136
1973	135	501	117	19	5	5	1.0	82	45	54	63	36	.234	.321	0	0	SS-135
1974	149	537	121	18	6	3	0.6	72	38	77	69	33	.225	.298	0	0	SS-149
1975	136	483	110	14	5	5	1.0	58	45	42	65	32	.228	.308	1	0	SS-136, DH-1
1976	144	432	104	19	3	1	0.2	58	43	50	63	51	.241	.306	0	0	SS-143, DH-1
1977	154	497	130	26	6	5	1.0	72	60	41	84	53	.262	.368	0	0	SS-154
1978	138	440	109	23	1	2	0.5	54	46	42	56	38	.248	.318	1	1	SS-137
1979	106	306	77	17	0	1	0.3	30	37	16	42	11	.252	.317	0	0	SS-104
1980 **CAL A**	86	273	72	10	5	5	1.8	41	34	15	26	7	.264	.392	4	0	SS-81
1981	27	47	11	1	1	0	0.0	3	5	1	6	1	.234	.298	1	0	2B-16, 3B-7, SS-3
14 yrs.	1650	5530	1340	216	55	41	0.7	736	490	523	787	385	.242	.324	20	5	SS-1588, 2B-16, 3B-8, OF-5, DH-2

LEAGUE CHAMPIONSHIP SERIES

	G	AB	H	2B	3B	HR	HR %	R	RBI	BB	SO	SB	BA	SA	AB	H	G by POS
1970 **PIT N**	1	3	0	0	0	0	0.0	0	0	1	2	0	.000	.000	0	0	SS-1
1976 **KC A**	5	18	7	2	0	0	0.0	2	4	0	1	0	.389	.500	0	0	SS-5
1977	5	18	7	3	1	0	0.0	4	5	1	2	0	.389	.667	0	0	SS-5
1978	4	13	1	0	0	1	7.7	2	2	1	4	0	.077	.308	0	0	SS-4
4 yrs.	15	52	15	5	1	1	1.9	8	11	3	9	0	.288	.481	0	0	SS-15

Bob Patrick

PATRICK, ROBERT LEE
B. Oct. 27, 1917, Fort Smith, Ark.
BR TR 6'2" 190 lbs.

	G	AB	H	2B	3B	HR	HR %	R	RBI	BB	SO	SB	BA	SA	AB	H	G by POS
1941 **DET A**	5	7	2	0	0	0	0.0	2	0	0	1	0	.286	.286	2	1	OF-3
1942	4	8	2	1	0	1	12.5	1	3	1	0	0	.250	.750	1	0	OF-3
2 yrs.	9	15	4	1	0	1	6.7	3	3	1	1	0	.267	.533	3	1	OF-6

Harry Pattee

PATTEE, HARRY ERNEST
B. Jan. 17, 1882, Charlestown, Mass. D. July 17, 1971, Lynchburg, Va.
BL TR 5'8" 149 lbs.

	G	AB	H	2B	3B	HR	HR %	R	RBI	BB	SO	SB	BA	SA	AB	H	G by POS
1908 **BKN N**	80	264	57	5	2	0	0.0	19	9	25		24	.216	.250	6	1	2B-74

Claire Patterson

PATTERSON, LORENZO CLAIRE
B. Oct. 5, 1887, Arkansas City, Kans. D. Mar. 28, 1913, Mohava, Calif.
BL TR 6' 180 lbs.

	G	AB	H	2B	3B	HR	HR %	R	RBI	BB	SO	SB	BA	SA	AB	H	G by POS
1909 **CIN N**	4	8	1	0	0	0	0.0	0	1	0		0	.125	.125	2	0	OF-2

Ham Patterson

PATTERSON, HAMILTON
Brother of Pat Patterson.
B. Oct. 13, 1877, Belleville, Ill. D. Nov. 25, 1945, E. St. Louis, Ill.
TR

	G	AB	H	2B	3B	HR	HR %	R	RBI	BB	SO	SB	BA	SA	AB	H	G by POS
1909 2 teams				STL A (17G – .204)			CHI A (1G – .000)										
" total	18	52	10	1	0	0	0.0	4	5	1		1	.192	.212	5	0	1B-7, OF-6

Hank Patterson

PATTERSON, HENRY JOSEPH
B. July 17, 1907, San Francisco, Calif. D. Sept. 30, 1970, Panorama City, Calif.
BR TR 5'11½" 170 lbs.

	G	AB	H	2B	3B	HR	HR %	R	RBI	BB	SO	SB	BA	SA	AB	H	G by POS
1932 **BOS A**	1	1	0	0	0	0	0.0	0	0	0	0	0	.000	.000	0	0	C-1

Mike Patterson

PATTERSON, MICHAEL LEE
B. Jan. 26, 1958, Los Angeles, Calif.
BR TR 5'10" 170 lbs.

	G	AB	H	2B	3B	HR	HR %	R	RBI	BB	SO	SB	BA	SA	AB	H	G by POS
1981 2 teams				OAK A (12G – .348)			NY A (4G – .222)										
" total	16	32	10	1	3	0	0.0	6	1	2	5	0	.313	.531	5	2	OF-9, DH-2
1982 **NY A**	11	16	3	1	0	1	6.3	3	1	2	6	1	.188	.438	0	0	OF-9, DH-1
2 yrs.	27	48	13	2	3	1	2.1	9	2	4	11	1	.271	.500	5	2	OF-18, DH-3

Pat Patterson

PATTERSON, WILLIAM JENNINGS
Brother of Ham Patterson.
B. Jan. 29, 1897, Belleville, Ill. D. Oct. 1, 1977, St. Louis, Mo.
BR TR 6' 175 lbs.

	G	AB	H	2B	3B	HR	HR %	R	RBI	BB	SO	SB	BA	SA	AB	H	G by POS
1921 **NY N**	23	35	14	0	0	1	2.9	5	5	2	5	0	.400	.486	2	0	3B-14, SS-7

George Pattison

PATTISON, GEORGE
Deceased.

	G	AB	H	2B	3B	HR	HR %	R	RBI	BB	SO	SB	BA	SA	AB	H	G by POS
1884 **PHI U**	2	7	1	0	0	0	0.0	0		0			.143	.143	0	0	OF-2

Bill Patton

PATTON, GEORGE WILLIAM
B. Oct. 7, 1912, Cornwall, Pa.
BR TR 6'2" 180 lbs.

	G	AB	H	2B	3B	HR	HR %	R	RBI	BB	SO	SB	BA	SA	AB	H	G by POS
1935 **PHI A**	9	10	3	1	0	0	0.0	1	2	2	3	0	.300	.400	4	1	C-3

Gene Patton

PATTON, GENE TUNNEY
B. July 8, 1926, Coatesville, Pa.
BL TR 5'10" 165 lbs.

	G	AB	H	2B	3B	HR	HR %	R	RBI	BB	SO	SB	BA	SA	AB	H	G by POS
1944 **BOS N**	1	0	0	0	0	0	–	0	0	0	0	0	–	–	0	0	

Tom Patton

PATTON, THOMAS ALLEN
B. Sept. 5, 1935, Honey Brook, Pa.
BR TR 5'9½" 185 lbs.

	G	AB	H	2B	3B	HR	HR %	R	RBI	BB	SO	SB	BA	SA	AB	H	G by POS
1957 **BAL A**	1	2	0	0	0	0	0.0	0	0	0	2	0	.000	.000	0	0	C-1

	G	AB	H	2B	3B	HR	HR %	R	RBI	BB	SO	SB	BA	SA	Pinch Hit AB	Pinch Hit H	G by POS

Lou Paul

PAUL, LOUIS
B. Unknown.   BR TR

	G	AB	H	2B	3B	HR	HR %	R	RBI	BB	SO	SB	BA	SA	AB	H	G by POS
1876 PHI N	3	12	2	1	0	0	0.0	2	0	0	0		.167	.250	0	0	C-3

Carlos Paula

PAULA, CARLOS CONILL   BR TR 6'3" 195 lbs.
B. Nov. 28, 1927, Havana, Cuba   D. Apr. 25, 1983, Miami, Fla.

	G	AB	H	2B	3B	HR	HR %	R	RBI	BB	SO	SB	BA	SA	AB	H	G by POS
1954 WAS A	9	24	4	1	0	0	0.0	2	2	2	4	0	.167	.208	3	0	OF-6
1955	115	351	105	20	7	6	1.7	34	45	17	43	2	.299	.447	28	8	OF-85
1956	33	82	15	2	1	3	3.7	8	13	8	15	0	.183	.341	11	3	OF-20
3 yrs.	157	457	124	23	8	9	2.0	44	60	27	62	2	.271	.416	42	11	OF-111

Gene Paulette

PAULETTE, EUGENE EDWARD   BR TR 6' 150 lbs.
B. May 26, 1891, Centralia, Ill.   D. Feb. 8, 1966, Little Rock, Ark.

	G	AB	H	2B	3B	HR	HR %	R	RBI	BB	SO	SB	BA	SA	AB	H	G by POS
1911 NY N	10	12	2	0	0	0	0.0	1	1	0	1	0	.167	.167	0	0	1B-7, SS-1, 3B-1
1916 STL A	5	4	2	0	0	0	0.0	1	0	1	1	0	.500	.500	4	2	1B-1
1917 2 teams	STL	A (12G –	.182)		STL	N (95G –	.265)										
" total	107	354	92	21	7	0	0.0	35	34	19	19	9	.260	.359	6	1	1B-98, 2B-3, 3B-1
1918 STL N	125	461	126	15	3	0	0.0	33	52	27	16	11	.273	.319	3	0	1B-97, SS-12, 2B-7, OF-6, 3B-2, P-1
1919 2 teams	STL	N (43G –	.215)		PHI	N (67G –	.259)										
" total	110	387	94	14	3	1	0.3	31	42	28	16	14	.243	.302	3		2B-53, 1B-36, OF-10, SS-3
1920 PHI N	143	562	162	16	6	1	0.2	59	36	33	16	9	.288	.343	2	1	1B-139, SS-2
6 yrs.	500	1780	478	66	19	2	0.1	160	165	108	69	43	.269	.330	18	4	1B-377, 2B-63, SS-18, OF-16, 3B-4, P-1

Si Pauxtis

PAUXTIS, SIMON FRANCIS   BR TR 6' 175 lbs.
B. July 20, 1885, Pittston, Pa.   D. Mar. 13, 1961, Philadelphia, Pa.

	G	AB	H	2B	3B	HR	HR %	R	RBI	BB	SO	SB	BA	SA	AB	H	G by POS
1909 CIN N	4	8	1	0	0	0	0.0	2	0	0		0	.125	.125	0	0	C-4

Don Pavletich

PAVLETICH, DONALD STEPHEN   BR TR 5'11" 190 lbs.
B. July 13, 1938, Milwaukee, Wis.

	G	AB	H	2B	3B	HR	HR %	R	RBI	BB	SO	SB	BA	SA	AB	H	G by POS
1957 CIN N	1	1	0	0	0	0	0.0	0	0	0	0	0	.000	.000	1	0	
1959	1	0	0	0	0	0	–	1	0	0	0	0	–	–	0	0	
1962	34	63	14	3	0	1	1.6	7	7	8	18	0	.222	.317	11	3	1B-25, C-2
1963	71	183	38	11	0	5	2.7	18	18	17	12	0	.208	.350	16	0	1B-57, C-13
1964	34	91	22	4	0	5	5.5	12	11	10	17	0	.242	.451	7	1	C-27, 1B-1
1965	68	191	61	11	1	8	4.2	25	32	23	27	1	.319	.513	11	4	C-54, 1B-9
1966	83	235	69	13	2	12	5.1	29	38	18	37	1	.294	.519	23	6	C-55, 1B-10
1967	74	231	55	14	3	6	2.6	25	34	21	38	2	.238	.403	8	1	C-66, 1B-6, 3B-1
1968	46	98	28	3	1	2	2.0	11	11	8	23	0	.286	.398	20	4	1B-22, C-5
1969 CHI A	78	188	46	12	0	6	3.2	26	33	28	45	0	.245	.404	19	4	C-51, 1B-13
1970 BOS A	32	65	9	1	1	0	0.0	4	6	10	15	1	.138	.185	7	1	1B-16, C-10
1971	14	27	7	1	0	1	3.7	5	3	5	5	0	.259	.407	5	1	C-8
12 yrs.	536	1373	349	73	8	46	3.4	163	193	148	237	5	.254	.420	128	25	C-291, 1B-159, 3B-1

Ted Pawelek

PAWELEK, THEODORE JOHN (Porky)   BL TR 5'10½" 202 lbs.
B. Aug. 15, 1919, Chicago Heights, Ill.   D. Feb. 12, 1964, Chicago Heights, Ill.

	G	AB	H	2B	3B	HR	HR %	R	RBI	BB	SO	SB	BA	SA	AB	H	G by POS
1946 CHI N	4	4	1	1	0	0	0.0	0	0	0	0	0	.250	.500	3	1	C-1

Stan Pawloski

PAWLOSKI, STANLEY WALTER   BR TR 6'1" 175 lbs.
B. Sept. 6, 1931, Wanamie, Pa.

	G	AB	H	2B	3B	HR	HR %	R	RBI	BB	SO	SB	BA	SA	AB	H	G by POS
1955 CLE A	2	8	1	0	0	0	0.0	0	0	0	2	0	.125	.125	0	0	2B-2

Fred Payne

PAYNE, FREDERICK THOMAS   BR TR
B. Sept. 2, 1880, Camden, N. Y.   D. Jan. 16, 1954, Camden, N. Y.

	G	AB	H	2B	3B	HR	HR %	R	RBI	BB	SO	SB	BA	SA	AB	H	G by POS
1906 DET A	72	222	60	5	5	0	0.0	23	20	13		4	.270	.338	7	3	C-47, OF-17
1907	53	169	28	2	2	0	0.0	17	14	7		4	.166	.201	1	0	C-46, OF-5
1908	20	45	3	0	0	0	0.0	3	2	3		1	.067	.067	2	0	C-16, OF-2
1909 CHI A	32	82	20	2	0	0	0.0	8	12	5		0	.244	.268	2	1	C-27, OF-3
1910	91	257	56	5	4	0	0.0	17	19	11		6	.218	.268	9	2	C-78, OF-2
1911	66	133	27	2	1	1	0.8	14	19	8		6	.203	.256	9	3	C-56
6 yrs.	334	908	194	16	12	1	0.1	82	86	47		21	.214	.261	30	9	C-270, OF-29
WORLD SERIES																	
1907 DET A	2	4	1	0	0	0	0.0	0	1	0		0	.250	.250	0	0	C-1

George Paynter

PAYNTER, GEORGE WASHINGTON   BR TR 5'9" 125 lbs.
Born George Washington Paner.
B. July 6, 1871, Cincinnati, Ohio   D. Oct. 1, 1950, Cincinnati, Ohio

	G	AB	H	2B	3B	HR	HR %	R	RBI	BB	SO	SB	BA	SA	AB	H	G by POS
1894 STL N	1	4	0	0	0	0	0.0	0	0	1	0	1	.000	.000	0	0	OF-1

Johnny Peacock

PEACOCK, JOHN GASTON   BL TR 5'11" 165 lbs.
B. Jan. 10, 1910, Fremont, N. C.   D. Oct. 17, 1981, Wilson, N. C.

	G	AB	H	2B	3B	HR	HR %	R	RBI	BB	SO	SB	BA	SA	AB	H	G by POS
1937 BOS A	9	32	10	2	1	0	0.0	3	6	1	0	0	.313	.438	0	0	C-9
1938	72	195	59	7	1	1	0.5	29	39	17	4	4	.303	.364	15	4	C-57, OF-1, 1B-1
1939	92	274	76	11	4	0	0.0	33	36	29	11	1	.277	.347	10	3	C-84
1940	63	131	37	4	1	0	0.0	20	13	23	10	1	.282	.328	12	3	C-48
1941	79	261	74	20	1	0	0.0	28	27	21	3	2	.284	.368	9	3	C-70
1942	88	286	76	7	3	0	0.0	17	25	21	11	1	.266	.311	8	1	C-82
1943	48	114	23	1	0	0	0.0	7	7	10	9	1	.202	.246	14	2	C-32
1944 2 teams	BOS	A (4G –	.000)		PHI	N (83G –	.225)										
" total	87	257	57	9	3	0	0.0	21	21	31	5	1	.222	.280	12	4	C-75, 2B-1
1945 2 teams	PHI	N (33G –	.203)		BKN	N (48G –	.255)										
" total	81	184	43	11	1	0	0.0	17	20	30	10	3	.234	.304	19	4	C-61
9 yrs.	619	1734	455	74	16	1	0.1	175	194	183	63	14	.262	.325	99	24	C-518, OF-1, 2B-1, 1B-1

	G	AB	H	2B	3B	HR	HR%	R	RBI	BB	SO	SB	BA	SA	Pinch Hit AB	H	G by POS

Elias Peak

PEAK, ELIAS
B. May 23, 1859, Philadelphia, Pa.   D. Dec. 17, 1916, Philadelphia, Pa.

1884 2 teams	BOS U (1G – .667)			PHI U (54G – .195)													
" total	55	218	44	6	4	0	0.0	37		8			.202	.266	0	0	2B-47, OF-6, SS-2

Dickey Pearce

PEARCE, RICHARD J.   5'3½" 161 lbs.
B. Jan. 2, 1836, Brooklyn, N. Y.   D. Oct. 12, 1908, Wareham, Mass.
Manager 1872, 1875.

1876 STL N	25	102	21	1	0	0	0.0	12	10	3	5		.206	.216	0	0	SS-23, OF-1, 2B-1
1877	8	29	5	0	0	0	0.0	1	4	1	4		.172	.172	0	0	SS-8
2 yrs.	33	131	26	1	0	0	0.0	13	14	4	9		.198	.206	0	0	SS-31, OF-1, 2B-1

Ducky Pearce

PEARCE, WILLIAM C.   BR TR 6'1" 185 lbs.
B. Mar. 17, 1885, Corning, Ohio   D. May 22, 1933, Brownstown, Ind.

1908 CIN N	2	2	0	0	0	0	0.0	0	0	0		0	.000	.000	0	0	C-2
1909	2	2	0	0	0	0	0.0	0	0	0		0	.000	.000	0	0	C-2
2 yrs.	4	4	0	0	0	0	0.0	0	0	0		0	.000	.000	0	0	C-4

Harry Pearce

PEARCE, HARRY JAMES   BR TR 5'9" 158 lbs.
B. July 12, 1889, Philadelphia, Pa.   D. Jan. 8, 1942, Philadelphia, Pa.

1917 PHI N	7	16	4	3	0	0	0.0	2	2	0	4	0	.250	.438	0	0	SS-4
1918	60	164	40	3	2	0	0.0	16	18	9	31	5	.244	.287	2	0	2B-46, SS-2, 3B-1, 1B-1
1919	68	244	44	3	3	0	0.0	24	9	8	27	6	.180	.217	0	0	2B-43, SS-23, 3B-2
3 yrs.	135	424	88	9	5	0	0.0	42	29	17	62	11	.208	.252	2	0	2B-89, SS-29, 3B-3, 1B-1

Albie Pearson

PEARSON, ALBERT GREGORY   BL TL 5'5" 140 lbs.
B. Sept. 12, 1934, Alhambra, Calif.

1958 WAS A	146	530	146	25	5	3	0.6	63	33	64	31	7	.275	.358	4	2	OF-141
1959 2 teams	WAS A (25G – .188)			BAL A (80G – .232)													
" total	105	218	47	5	2	0	0.0	31	8	27	8	5	.216	.257	29	6	OF-71
1960 BAL A	48	82	20	2	0	1	1.2	17	6	17	3	4	.244	.305	13	4	OF-32
1961 LA A	144	427	123	21	3	7	1.6	92	41	96	40	11	.288	.400	23	9	OF-113
1962	160	614	160	29	6	5	0.8	115	42	95	36	15	.261	.352	0	0	OF-160
1963	154	578	176	26	5	6	1.0	92	47	92	37	17	.304	.398	4	0	OF-148
1964	107	265	59	5	1	2	0.8	34	16	35	22	6	.223	.272	31	7	OF-66
1965 CAL A	122	360	100	17	2	4	1.1	41	21	51	17	12	.278	.369	27	6	OF-101
1966	2	3	0	0	0	0	0.0	0	0	1	1	0	.000	.000	2	0	OF-1
9 yrs.	988	3077	831	130	24	28	0.9	485	214	477	195	77	.270	.355	133	34	OF-833

Dave Pearson

PEARSON, DAVID P.   BR TR 5'7" 142 lbs.
Born David P. Pierson.   Brother of Dick Pierson.
B. Aug. 20, 1855, Wilkes-Barre, Pa.   D. Nov. 11, 1922, Trenton, N. J.

1876 CIN N	57	233	55	4	1	0	0.0	33	13	1	9		.236	.262	0	0	C-31, OF-30, SS-1, 3B-1, 2B-1, P-1

Charlie Pechous

PECHOUS, CHARLES EDWARD   BR TR 6' 170 lbs.
B. Oct. 5, 1896, Chicago, Ill.   D. Sept. 13, 1980, Kenosha, Wis.

1915 CHI F	18	51	9	3	0	0	0.0	4	4	4		1	.176	.235	0	0	3B-18
1916 CHI N	22	69	10	1	1	0	0.0	5	4	3	21	1	.145	.188	0	0	3B-22
1917	13	41	10	0	0	0	0.0	2	1	2	9	1	.244	.244	0	0	3B-7, SS-5
3 yrs.	53	161	29	4	1	0	0.0	11	9	9	30	3	.180	.217	0	0	3B-47, SS-5

Hal Peck

PECK, HAROLD ARTHUR   BL TL 5'11" 175 lbs.
B. Apr. 20, 1917, Big Bend, Wis.

1943 BKN N	1	1	0	0	0	0	0.0	0	0	0	0	0	.000	.000	1	0	
1944 PHI A	2	8	2	0	0	0	0.0	0	1	0	2	0	.250	.250	0	0	OF-2
1945	112	449	124	22	9	5	1.1	51	39	37	28	5	.276	.399	2	0	OF-110
1946	48	150	37	8	2	2	1.3	14	11	16	14	1	.247	.367	12	3	OF-35
1947 CLE A	114	392	115	18	2	8	2.0	58	44	27	31	3	.293	.411	11	4	OF-97
1948	45	63	18	3	0	0	0.0	12	8	4	8	1	.286	.333	30	8	OF-9
1949	33	29	9	1	0	0	0.0	1	9	3	3	0	.310	.345	28	8	OF-2
7 yrs.	355	1092	305	52	13	15	1.4	136	112	87	86	10	.279	.392	84	23	OF-255

WORLD SERIES

1948 CLE A	1	0	0	0	0	0	–	0	0	0	0	0	–	–	0	0	OF-1

Roger Peckinpaugh

PECKINPAUGH, ROGER THORPE   BR TR 5'10½" 165 lbs.
B. Feb. 5, 1891, Wooster, Ohio   D. Nov. 17, 1977, Cleveland, Ohio
Manager 1914, 1928-33, 1941.

1910 CLE A	15	45	9	0	0	0	0.0	1	6	1		3	.200	.200	1	0	SS-14
1912	69	236	50	4	1	1	0.4	18	22	16		11	.212	.250	2	0	SS-67
1913 2 teams	CLE A (1G – .000)			NY A (95G – .268)													
" total	96	340	91	10	7	1	0.3	36	32	24	47	19	.268	.347	1	0	SS-94
1914 NY A	157	570	127	14	6	3	0.5	55	51	51	73	38	.223	.284	1	0	SS-157
1915	142	540	119	18	7	5	0.9	67	44	49	72	19	.220	.307	0	0	SS-142
1916	146	552	141	22	8	4	0.7	65	58	62	50	18	.255	.346	0	0	SS-146
1917	148	543	141	24	7	0	0.0	63	41	64	46	17	.260	.330	0	0	SS-148
1918	122	446	103	15	3	0	0.0	59	43	43	41	12	.231	.278	0	0	SS-122
1919	122	453	138	20	2	7	1.5	89	33	59	37	10	.305	.404	1	0	SS-121
1920	139	534	144	26	6	8	1.5	109	54	72	47	8	.270	.386	1	0	SS-137
1921	149	577	166	25	7	8	1.4	128	71	84	44	2	.288	.397	0	0	SS-149
1922 WAS A	147	520	132	14	4	2	0.4	62	48	55	32	11	.254	.308	0	0	SS-147
1923	154	568	150	18	4	2	0.4	73	62	64	30	10	.264	.320	0	0	SS-154
1924	155	523	142	20	5	2	0.4	72	73	72	45	11	.272	.340	0	0	SS-155
1925	126	422	124	16	4	4	0.9	67	64	49	23	13	.294	.379	0	0	SS-155
1926	57	147	35	4	1	1	0.7	19	14	28	12	3	.238	.299	9	2	SS-46, 1B-1

	G	AB	H	2B	3B	HR	HR %	R	RBI	BB	SO	SB	BA	SA	Pinch Hit AB	Pinch Hit H	G by POS

Roger Peckinpaugh continued

	G	AB	H	2B	3B	HR	HR %	R	RBI	BB	SO	SB	BA	SA	AB	H	G by POS
1927 CHI A	68	217	64	6	3	0	0.0	23	23	21	6	2	.295	.350	7	2	SS-60
17 yrs.	2012	7233	1876	256	75	48	0.7	1006	739	814	609	207	.259	.335	22	4	SS-1983, 1B-2

WORLD SERIES

	G	AB	H	2B	3B	HR	HR %	R	RBI	BB	SO	SB	BA	SA	AB	H	G by POS
1921 NY A	8	28	5	1	0	0	0.0	2	0	4	3	0	.179	.214	0	0	SS-8
1924 WAS A	4	12	5	2	0	0	0.0	1	2	1	0	1	.417	.583	0	0	SS-4
1925	7	24	6	1	0	1	4.2	1	2	1	2	1	.250	.417	0	0	SS-7
3 yrs.	19	64	16	4	0	1	1.6	4	4	6	5	2	.250	.359	0	0	SS-19

Les Peden

PEDEN, LESLIE EARL
B. Sept. 17, 1923, Azle, Tex.   BR TR 6'1½" 212 lbs.

	G	AB	H	2B	3B	HR	HR %	R	RBI	BB	SO	SB	BA	SA	AB	H	G by POS
1953 WAS A	9	28	7	1	0	1	3.6	4	1	4	3	0	.250	.393	1	1	C-8

Chick Pedroes

PEDROES, CHARLES P.
B. Oct. 27, 1869, Chicago, Ill.   D. Aug. 6, 1927, Chicago, Ill.

	G	AB	H	2B	3B	HR	HR %	R	RBI	BB	SO	SB	BA	SA	AB	H	G by POS
1902 CHI N	2	6	0	0	0	0	0.0	0	0	0		0	.000	.000	0	0	OF-2

Homer Peel

PEEL, HOMER HEFNER
B. Oct. 10, 1902, Port Sullivan, Tex.   BR TR 5'9½" 170 lbs.

	G	AB	H	2B	3B	HR	HR %	R	RBI	BB	SO	SB	BA	SA	AB	H	G by POS
1927 STL N	2	2	0	0	0	0	0.0	0	0	0	1	0	.000	.000	1	0	OF-1
1929 PHI N	53	156	42	12	1	0	0.0	16	19	12	7	1	.269	.359	13	1	OF-39, 1B-1
1930 STL N	26	73	12	2	0	0	0.0	9	10	3	4	0	.164	.192	4	1	OF-21
1933 NY N	84	148	38	1	1	1	0.7	16	12	14	10	0	.257	.297	35	9	OF-45
1934	21	41	8	0	0	1	2.4	7	3	1	2	0	.195	.268	10	2	OF-10
5 yrs.	186	420	100	15	2	2	0.5	48	44	30	24	1	.238	.298	63	13	OF-116, 1B-1

WORLD SERIES

	G	AB	H	2B	3B	HR	HR %	R	RBI	BB	SO	SB	BA	SA	AB	H	G by POS
1933 NY N	2	2	1	0	0	0	0.0	0	0	0	0	0	.500	.500	1	1	OF-1

Jack Peerson

PEERSON, JACK CHILES
B. Aug. 28, 1910, Brunswick, Ga.   D. Oct. 23, 1966, Fort Walton Beach, Fla.   BR TR 5'11" 175 lbs.

	G	AB	H	2B	3B	HR	HR %	R	RBI	BB	SO	SB	BA	SA	AB	H	G by POS
1935 PHI A	10	19	6	1	0	0	0.0	3	1	1	1	0	.316	.368	4	1	SS-4
1936	8	34	11	1	1	0	0.0	7	5	0	3	0	.324	.412	0	0	SS-7, 2B-1
2 yrs.	18	53	17	2	1	0	0.0	10	6	1	4	0	.321	.396	4	1	SS-11, 2B-1

Charlie Peete

PEETE, CHARLES (Mule)
B. Feb. 22, 1931, Franklin, Va.   D. Nov. 27, 1956, Caracas, Venezuela   BL TR 5'9½" 190 lbs.

	G	AB	H	2B	3B	HR	HR %	R	RBI	BB	SO	SB	BA	SA	AB	H	G by POS
1956 STL N	23	52	10	2	2	0	0.0	3	6	6	10	0	.192	.308	4	1	OF-21

Heinie Peitz

PEITZ, HENRY CLEMENT
Brother of Joe Peitz.
B. Nov. 28, 1870, St. Louis, Mo.   D. Oct. 23, 1943, Cincinnati, Ohio   BR TR 5'11" 165 lbs.

	G	AB	H	2B	3B	HR	HR %	R	RBI	BB	SO	SB	BA	SA	AB	H	G by POS
1892 STL N	1	3	0	0	0	0	0.0	0	0	0	0	0	.000	.000	0	0	C-1
1893	96	362	92	12	9	1	0.3	53	45	54	20	12	.254	.345	0	0	C-74, SS-11, OF-10, 1B-5
1894	99	338	89	19	9	3	0.9	52	49	43	21	14	.263	.399	0	0	3B-47, C-39, 1B-14, P-1
1895	90	334	95	14	12	2	0.6	44	65	29	20	9	.284	.416	0	0	C-71, 1B-11, 3B-10
1896 CIN N	68	211	63	12	5	2	0.9	33	34	30	15	7	.299	.431	1	0	C-67
1897	77	266	78	11	7	1	0.4	35	44	18		3	.293	.398	4	0	C-71, P-2
1898	105	330	90	15	5	1	0.3	49	43	35		9	.273	.358	3	1	C-101
1899	93	290	79	13	2	1	0.3	45	43	45		11	.272	.341	2	0	C-91, P-1
1900	91	294	75	14	1	2	0.7	34	34	20		5	.255	.330	4	0	C-80, 1B-8
1901	82	269	82	13	5	1	0.4	24	24	23		3	.305	.401	6	2	C-49, 2B-21, 3B-6, 1B-2
1902	112	387	122	22	5	1	0.3	54	60	24		7	.315	.406	5	1	2B-48, C-47, 3B-6, 1B-6
1903	105	358	93	15	3	0	0.0	45	42	37		7	.260	.318	2	1	C-78, 1B-11, 3B-9, 2B-4
1904	84	272	66	13	2	1	0.4	32	30	14		1	.243	.316	2	1	C-64, 1B-18, 3B-1
1905 PIT N	88	278	62	10	0	0	0.0	18	27	24		2	.223	.259	2	0	C-87, 2B-1
1906	40	125	30	8	0	0	0.0	13	20	13		2	.240	.304	2	0	C-38
1913 STL N	3	4	1	0	1	0	0.0	1	0	0	0	0	.250	.750	0	0	C-2, OF-1
16 yrs.	1234	4121	1117	191	66	16	0.4	532	560	409	76	91	.271	.361	33	6	C-960, 3B-79, 1B-75, 2B-74, OF-11, SS-11, P-4

Joe Peitz

PEITZ, JOSEPH
Brother of Heinie Peitz.
B. Nov. 8, 1869, St. Louis, Mo.   D. Dec. 4, 1919, St. Louis, Mo.

	G	AB	H	2B	3B	HR	HR %	R	RBI	BB	SO	SB	BA	SA	AB	H	G by POS
1894 STL N	7	26	11	2	3	0	0.0	10	3	6	1	2	.423	.731	0	0	OF-7

Eddie Pellagrini

PELLAGRINI, EDWARD CHARLES
B. Mar. 13, 1918, Boston, Mass.   BR TR 5'9" 160 lbs.

	G	AB	H	2B	3B	HR	HR %	R	RBI	BB	SO	SB	BA	SA	AB	H	G by POS
1946 BOS A	22	71	15	3	1	2	2.8	7	4	3	18	1	.211	.366	0	0	3B-14, SS-9
1947	74	231	47	8	1	4	1.7	29	19	23	35	2	.203	.299	3	0	3B-42, C-39, 1B-6
1948 STL A	105	290	69	8	3	2	0.7	31	27	34	40	1	.238	.307	2	1	SS-98
1949	79	235	56	8	1	2	0.9	26	15	14	24	2	.238	.306	1	0	SS-76
1951 PHI N	86	197	46	4	5	5	2.5	31	30	23	25	5	.234	.381	12	2	2B-53, SS-8, 3B-6
1952 CIN N	46	100	17	2	0	1	1.0	15	3	8	18	1	.170	.220	6	1	2B-22, 1B-8, SS-1, 3B-1
1953 PIT N	78	174	44	3	2	4	2.3	16	19	14	20	1	.253	.362	32	8	2B-31, 3B-12, SS-3
1954	73	125	27	6	0	0	0.0	12	16	9	21	0	.216	.264	34	7	3B-31, 2B-7, SS-1
8 yrs.	563	1423	321	42	13	20	1.4	167	133	128	201	13	.226	.316	90	19	SS-222, 2B-113, 3B-106, 1B-8

William Pelouze

PELOUZE, WILLIAM NELSON
B. Sept. 12, 1865, Washington, D. C.   D. June 20, 1943, Lake Geneva, Wis.   TR 5'8" 170 lbs.

	G	AB	H	2B	3B	HR	HR %	R	RBI	BB	SO	SB	BA	SA	AB	H	G by POS
1886 STL N	1	3	0	0	0	0	0.0	0	0	0		2	.000	.000	0	0	OF-1

	G	AB	H	2B	3B	HR	HR %	R	RBI	BB	SO	SB	BA	SA	Pinch Hit AB	Pinch Hit H	G by POS

John Peltz

PELTZ, JOHN
B. Apr. 23, 1861, New Orleans, La.   D. Feb. 27, 1906, New Orleans, La.

	G	AB	H	2B	3B	HR	HR%	R	RBI	BB	SO	SB	BA	SA	AB	H	G by POS
1884 IND AA	106	393	86	13	17	3	0.8	40		7			.219	.361	0	0	OF-106
1888 BAL AA	1	4	1	0	0	0	0.0	1	0	0		1	.250	.250	0	0	OF-1
1890 3 teams	B-B	AA (98G – .227)				SYR	AA (5G – .176)			TOL	AA (20G – .247)						
" total	123	474	108	12	9	1	0.2	65		38		17	.228	.297	0	0	OF-123
3 yrs.	230	871	195	25	26	4	0.5	106		45		18	.224	.326	0	0	OF-230

Brock Pemberton

PEMBERTON, BROCK
B. Nov. 5, 1953, Tulsa, Okla.   BB TL 6'3" 190 lbs.

	G	AB	H	2B	3B	HR	HR%	R	RBI	BB	SO	SB	BA	SA	AB	H	G by POS
1974 NY N	11	22	4	0	0	0	0.0	0	1	0	3	0	.182	.182	7	3	1B-4
1975	2	2	0	0	0	0	0.0	0	0	0	1	0	.000	.000	2	0	
2 yrs.	13	24	4	0	0	0	0.0	0	1	0	4	0	.167	.167	9	3	1B-4

Bert Pena

PENA, ADALBERTO
Also known as Adalberto Rivera.
B. July 11, 1959, Santurce, Puerto Rico   BR TR 5'11" 165 lbs.

	G	AB	H	2B	3B	HR	HR%	R	RBI	BB	SO	SB	BA	SA	AB	H	G by POS
1981 HOU N	4	2	1	0	0	0	0.0	0	0	0	0	0	.500	.500	2	1	SS-3
1983	4	8	1	0	0	0	0.0	0	0	2	2	0	.125	.125	0	0	SS-4
1984	24	39	8	1	0	1	2.6	3	4	3	8	0	.205	.308	2	0	SS-21
3 yrs.	32	49	10	1	0	1	2.0	3	4	5	10	0	.204	.286	4	1	SS-28

Roberto Pena

PENA, RAMIREZ ROBERTO
B. Apr. 17, 1940, Santo Domingo, Dominican Republic   BR TR 5'8" 175 lbs.

	G	AB	H	2B	3B	HR	HR%	R	RBI	BB	SO	SB	BA	SA	AB	H	G by POS
1965 CHI N	51	170	37	5	1	2	1.2	17	12	16	19	1	.218	.294	1	0	SS-50
1966	6	17	3	2	0	0	0.0	0	1	0	4	0	.176	.294	2	0	SS-5
1968 PHI N	138	500	130	13	2	1	0.2	56	38	34	63	3	.260	.300	1	1	SS-133
1969 SD N	139	472	118	16	3	4	0.8	44	30	21	63	0	.250	.322	18	5	SS-65, 2B-33, 3B-27, 1B-12
1970 2 teams	OAK	A (19G – .259)				MIL	A (121G – .238)										
" total	140	474	114	20	1	3	0.6	40	45	28	49	4	.241	.306	11	2	SS-111, 2B-15, 1B-7, 3B-5
1971 MIL A	113	274	65	9	3	3	1.1	17	28	15	37	2	.237	.325	29	5	1B-50, 3B-37, SS-23, 2B-1
6 yrs.	587	1907	467	65	10	13	0.7	174	154	114	235	10	.245	.310	62	13	SS-387, 3B-69, 1B-69, 2B-49

Tony Pena

PENA, ANTONIO FRANCESCO
Also known as Antonio Francesco Padilla.
B. June 4, 1957, Monte Cristi, Dominican Republic   BR TR 6' 175 lbs.

	G	AB	H	2B	3B	HR	HR%	R	RBI	BB	SO	SB	BA	SA	AB	H	G by POS
1980 PIT N	8	21	9	1	1	0	0.0	1	1	0	4	0	.429	.571	2	1	C-6
1981	66	210	63	9	1	2	1.0	16	17	8	23	1	.300	.381	2	1	C-64
1982	138	497	147	28	4	11	2.2	53	63	17	57	2	.296	.435	2	0	C-137
1983	151	542	163	22	3	15	2.8	51	70	31	73	6	.301	.435	2	1	C-149
1984	147	546	156	27	2	15	2.7	77	78	36	79	12	.286	.425	1	1	C-146
5 yrs.	510	1816	538	87	11	43	2.4	198	229	92	236	21	.296	.427	7	4	C-502

Elmer Pence

PENCE, ELMER CLAIR
B. Aug. 17, 1900, Valley Springs, Calif.   D. Sept. 17, 1968, San Francisco, Calif.   BR TR 6' 185 lbs.

	G	AB	H	2B	3B	HR	HR%	R	RBI	BB	SO	SB	BA	SA	AB	H	G by POS
1922 CHI A	1	0	0	0	0	0	–	0	0	0	0	0	–	–	0	0	OF-1

Jim Pendleton

PENDLETON, JAMES EDWARD
B. Jan. 7, 1924, St. Charles, Mo.   BR TR 6' 185 lbs.

	G	AB	H	2B	3B	HR	HR%	R	RBI	BB	SO	SB	BA	SA	AB	H	G by POS
1953 MIL N	120	251	75	12	4	7	2.8	48	27	7	36	6	.299	.462	5	0	OF-105, SS-7
1954	71	173	38	3	1	1	0.6	20	16	4	21	2	.220	.266	16	3	OF-50
1955	8	10	0	0	0	0	0.0	0	0	0	2	0	.000	.000	5	0	OF-1, SS-1, 3B-1
1956	14	11	0	0	0	0	0.0	0	0	1	3	0	.000	.000	9	0	SS-3, 3B-2, 2B-1, 1B-1
1957 PIT N	46	59	18	1	1	0	0.0	9	9	9	14	0	.305	.356	24	6	OF-9, 3B-2, SS-1
1958	3	3	1	0	0	0	0.0	0	0	0	0	0	.333	.333	3	1	
1959 CIN N	65	113	29	2	0	3	2.7	13	9	8	18	3	.257	.354	19	6	OF-24, 3B-16, SS-3
1962 HOU N	117	321	79	12	2	8	2.5	30	36	14	57	0	.246	.371	23	7	OF-90, 1B-8, 3B-3, SS-2
8 yrs.	444	941	240	30	8	19	2.0	120	97	43	151	11	.255	.365	104	23	OF-279, 3B-24, SS-17, 1B-9, 2B-1

Terry Pendleton

PENDLETON, TERRY LEE
B. July 16, 1960, Port Hueneme, Calif.   BB TR 5'9" 180 lbs.

	G	AB	H	2B	3B	HR	HR%	R	RBI	BB	SO	SB	BA	SA	AB	H	G by POS
1984 STL N	67	262	85	16	3	1	0.4	37	33	16	32	20	.324	.420	1	0	3B-66

Jimmy Peoples

PEOPLES, JAMES ELSWORTH
B. Oct. 8, 1863, Big Beaver, Mich.   D. Aug. 29, 1920, Detroit, Mich.   TR 165 lbs.

	G	AB	H	2B	3B	HR	HR%	R	RBI	BB	SO	SB	BA	SA	AB	H	G by POS
1884 CIN AA	69	267	45	2	3	0	0.0	28		6			.169	.199	0	0	SS-47, C-14, OF-10, 3B-1, 1B-1
1885 2 teams	CIN	AA (7G – .182)				BKN	AA (41G – .199)										
" total	48	173	34	4	1	1	0.6	22		6			.197	.249	0	0	C-42, OF-2, SS-2, P-2, 3B-1, 1B-1
1886 BKN AA	93	340	74	7	3	3	0.9	43		20			.218	.282	0	0	C-76, SS-14, OF-8, 3B-1
1887	73	268	68	14	2	1	0.4	36		16		22	.254	.332	0	0	C-57, OF-8, SS-4, 1B-4, 2B-1
1888	32	103	20	5	3	0	0.0	15	17	8		10	.194	.301	0	0	C-25, SS-5, OF-2
1889 COL AA	29	100	23	6	2	1	1.0	13	16	6	8	3	.230	.360	0	0	C-22, OF-5, 2B-2, SS-1
6 yrs.	344	1251	264	38	14	6	0.5	157	32	62	8	35	.211	.278	0	0	C-236, SS-73, OF-35, 1B-6, 3B-3, 2B-3, P-2

Joe Pepitone

PEPITONE, JOSEPH ANTHONY (Pepi)
B. Oct. 9, 1940, Brooklyn, N.Y.   BL TL 6'2" 185 lbs.

	G	AB	H	2B	3B	HR	HR%	R	RBI	BB	SO	SB	BA	SA	AB	H	G by POS
1962 NY A	63	138	33	3	2	7	5.1	14	17	3	21	1	.239	.442	19	5	OF-32, 1B-16
1963	157	580	157	16	3	27	4.7	79	89	23	63	3	.271	.448	9	1	1B-143, OF-16
1964	160	613	154	12	3	28	4.6	71	100	24	63	2	.251	.418	3	1	1B-155, OF-30
1965	143	531	131	18	3	18	3.4	51	62	43	59	4	.247	.394	2	0	1B-115, OF-41
1966	152	585	149	21	4	31	5.3	85	83	29	58	4	.255	.463	1	0	1B-119, OF-55

	G	AB	H	2B	3B	HR	HR %	R	RBI	BB	SO	SB	BA	SA	Pinch Hit AB	Pinch Hit H	G by POS

Joe Pepitone continued

	G	AB	H	2B	3B	HR	HR %	R	RBI	BB	SO	SB	BA	SA	AB	H	G by POS
1967	133	501	126	18	3	13	2.6	45	64	34	62	1	.251	.377	4	1	OF-123, 1B-6
1968	108	380	93	9	3	15	3.9	41	56	37	45	8	.245	.403	4	0	OF-92, 1B-12
1969	135	513	124	16	3	27	5.3	49	70	30	42	8	.242	.442	4	2	1B-132
1970 2 teams		HOU	N	(75G –	.251)		CHI	N	(56G –	.268)							
" total	131	492	127	18	7	26	5.3	82	79	33	43	5	.258	.482	2	0	OF-84, 1B-63
1971 CHI N	115	427	131	19	4	16	3.7	50	61	24	41	1	.307	.482	2	1	1B-95, OF-23
1972	66	214	56	5	0	8	3.7	23	21	13	22	1	.262	.397	5	1	1B-66
1973 2 teams		CHI	N	(31G –	.268)		ATL	N	(3G –	.364)							
" total	34	123	34	3	0	3	2.4	16	19	9	7	3	.276	.374	3	1	1B-31
12 yrs.	1397	5097	1315	158	35	219	4.3	606	721	302	526	41	.258	.432	58	13	1B-953, OF-496

WORLD SERIES																	
1963 NY A	4	13	2	0	0	0	0.0	0	0	1	3	0	.154	.154	0	0	1B-4
1964	7	26	4	1	0	1	3.8	1	5	2	3	0	.154	.308	0	0	1B-7
2 yrs.	11	39	6	1	0	1	2.6	1	5	3	6	0	.154	.256	0	0	1B-11

Henry Peploski

PEPLOSKI, HENRY STEPHEN (Pep)
Brother of Pepper Peploski.
B. Sept. 15, 1905, Garlin, Poland   D. Jan. 28, 1982, Dover, N. J.

BL TR 5'9"   155 lbs.

	G	AB	H	2B	3B	HR	HR %	R	RBI	BB	SO	SB	BA	SA	AB	H	G by POS
1929 BOS N	6	10	2	0	0	0	0.0	1	1	1	3	0	.200	.200	4	1	3B-2

Pepper Peploski

PEPLOSKI, JOSEPH ANTHONY
Brother of Henry Peploski.
B. Sept. 12, 1891, Brooklyn, N. Y.

BR TR 5'8"   155 lbs.

	G	AB	H	2B	3B	HR	HR %	R	RBI	BB	SO	SB	BA	SA	AB	H	G by POS
1913 DET A	2	4	2	0	0	0	0.0	1	0	0	0	0	.500	.500	0	0	3B-2

Don Pepper

PEPPER, DONALD HOYTE
B. Oct. 8, 1943, Saratoga Springs, N. Y.

BL TL 6'4½"   215 lbs.

	G	AB	H	2B	3B	HR	HR %	R	RBI	BB	SO	SB	BA	SA	AB	H	G by POS
1966 DET A	4	3	0	0	0	0	0.0	0	0	0	1	0	.000	.000	3	0	1B-1

Ray Pepper

PEPPER, RAYMOND WATSON
B. Aug. 5, 1905, Decatur, Ala.

BR TR 6'2"   195 lbs.

	G	AB	H	2B	3B	HR	HR %	R	RBI	BB	SO	SB	BA	SA	AB	H	G by POS
1932 STL N	21	57	14	2	1	0	0.0	3	7	5	13	1	.246	.316	4	0	OF-17
1933	3	9	2	0	0	1	11.1	2	2	0	1	0	.222	.556	1	0	OF-2
1934 STL A	148	564	168	24	6	7	1.2	71	101	29	67	1	.298	.399	12	2	OF-136
1935	92	261	66	15	3	4	1.5	20	37	20	32	0	.253	.379	34	7	OF-57
1936	75	124	35	5	0	2	1.6	13	23	5	23	0	.282	.371	54	18	OF-18
5 yrs.	339	1015	285	46	10	14	1.4	109	170	59	136	2	.281	.387	105	27	OF-230

Jack Perconte

PERCONTE, JOHN PATRICK
B. Aug. 31, 1954, Joliet, Ill.

BL TR 5'10"   160 lbs.

	G	AB	H	2B	3B	HR	HR %	R	RBI	BB	SO	SB	BA	SA	AB	H	G by POS
1980 LA N	14	17	4	0	0	0	0.0	2	2	2	1	3	.235	.235	3	0	2B-9
1981	8	9	2	0	1	0	0.0	2	1	2	2	1	.222	.444	5	2	2B-2
1982 CLE A	93	219	52	4	0	0	0.0	27	15	22	25	9	.237	.292	7	1	2B-82, DH-2
1983	14	26	7	1	0	0	0.0	1	0	5	2	3	.269	.308	2	1	2B-13
1984 SEA A	155	612	180	24	4	0	0.0	93	31	57	47	29	.294	.346	4	1	2B-256, DH-2
5 yrs.	284	883	245	29	9	0	0.0	125	49	88	77	45	.277	.331	21	5	2B-362

Marty Perez

PEREZ, MARTIN ROMAN
B. Feb. 28, 1948, Visalia, Calif.

BR TR 5'11"   160 lbs.

	G	AB	H	2B	3B	HR	HR %	R	RBI	BB	SO	SB	BA	SA	AB	H	G by POS
1969 CAL A	13	13	3	0	0	0	0.0	3	0	2	1	0	.231	.231	0	0	SS-7, 3B-2, 2B-2
1970	3	3	0	0	0	0	0.0	0	1	0	0	0	.000	.000	0	0	SS-2
1971 ATL N	130	410	93	15	3	4	1.0	28	32	25	44	1	.227	.307	2	0	SS-126, 2B-1
1972	141	479	109	13	1	1	0.2	33	28	30	55	0	.228	.265	1	0	SS-141
1973	141	501	125	15	3	8	1.6	66	57	49	66	2	.250	.347	5	2	SS-139
1974	127	447	116	20	5	2	0.4	51	34	35	51	2	.260	.340	8	1	2B-102, SS-14, 3B-6
1975	120	461	127	14	2	2	0.4	50	34	37	44	2	.275	.328	0	0	2B-116, SS-7
1976 2 teams		ATL	N	(31G –	.250)		SF	N	(93G –	.259)							
" total	124	428	110	17	3	0	0.7	49	32	38	37	3	.257	.322	5	1	2B-107, SS-22, 3B-2
1977 2 teams		NY	A	(1G –	.500)		OAK	A	(115G –	.231)							
" total	116	377	88	14	5	2	0.5	32	23	29	66	0	.233	.313	3	1	2B-105, 3B-13, SS-4
1978 OAK A	16	12	0	0	0	0	0.0	1	0	0	5	0	.000	.000	0	0	3B-11, SS-3, 2B-1
10 yrs.	931	3131	771	108	22	22	0.7	313	241	245	369	11	.246	.316	24	5	SS-465, 2B-434, 3B-34

Tony Perez

PEREZ, ATANASIO RIGAL
B. May 14, 1942, Camaguey, Cuba

BR TR 6'2"   175 lbs.

	G	AB	H	2B	3B	HR	HR %	R	RBI	BB	SO	SB	BA	SA	AB	H	G by POS
1964 CIN N	12	25	2	1	0	0	0.0	1	1	3	9	0	.080	.120	6	0	1B-6
1965	104	281	73	14	4	12	4.3	40	47	21	67	0	.260	.466	25	6	1B-93
1966	99	257	68	10	4	4	1.6	25	39	14	44	1	.265	.381	28	5	1B-75
1967	156	600	174	28	7	26	4.3	78	102	33	102	0	.290	.490	0	0	3B-139, 1B-18, 2B-1
1968	160	625	176	25	7	18	2.9	93	92	51	92	3	.282	.430	0	0	3B-160
1969	160	629	185	31	2	37	5.9	103	122	63	131	4	.294	.526	0	0	3B-160
1970	158	587	186	28	6	40	6.8	107	129	83	134	8	.317	.589	1	0	3B-153, 1B-8
1971	158	609	164	22	3	25	4.1	72	91	51	120	4	.269	.438	1	0	3B-148, 1B-44
1972	136	515	146	33	7	21	4.1	64	90	55	121	4	.283	.497	2	0	1B-136
1973	151	564	177	33	3	27	4.8	73	101	74	117	3	.314	.527	1	0	1B-151
1974	158	596	158	28	2	28	4.7	81	101	61	112	1	.265	.460	1	0	1B-157
1975	137	511	144	28	3	20	3.9	74	109	54	101	1	.282	.466	4	0	1B-132
1976	139	527	137	32	6	19	3.6	77	91	50	88	10	.260	.452	8	3	1B-136
1977 MON N	154	559	158	32	6	19	3.4	71	91	63	111	4	.283	.463	6	1	1B-148
1978	148	544	158	38	3	14	2.6	63	78	38	104	2	.290	.449	0	0	1B-145
1979	132	489	132	29	4	13	2.7	58	73	38	82	2	.270	.425	3	1	1B-129
1980 BOS A	151	585	161	31	3	25	4.3	73	105	41	93	1	.275	.467	1	0	1B-137, DH-13
1981	84	306	77	11	3	9	2.9	35	39	27	66	0	.252	.395	5	2	1B-56, DH-23
1982	69	196	51	14	2	6	3.1	18	31	19	48	0	.260	.444	21	5	DH-46, 1B-2
1983 PHI N	91	253	61	11	2	6	2.4	18	43	28	57	1	.241	.372	19	4	1B-69

	G	AB	H	2B	3B	HR	HR %	R	RBI	BB	SO	SB	BA	SA	Pinch Hit AB	Pinch Hit H	G by POS

Tony Perez continued

	G	AB	H	2B	3B	HR	HR %	R	RBI	BB	SO	SB	BA	SA	AB	H	G by POS
1984 CIN N	71	137	33	6	1	2	1.5	9	15	11	21	0	.241	.343	38	11	1B-31
21 yrs.	2628	9395	2621	485	78	371	3.9	1233	1590	878	1820 3rd	49	.279	.466	172	38	1B-1673, 3B-760, DH-82, 2B-1

LEAGUE CHAMPIONSHIP SERIES

	G	AB	H	2B	3B	HR	HR %	R	RBI	BB	SO	SB	BA	SA	AB	H	G by POS
1970 CIN N	3	12	4	2	0	1	8.3	1	2	1	1	0	.333	.750	0	0	3B-3
1972	5	20	4	1	0	0	0.0	0	2	0	7	0	.200	.250	0	0	1B-5
1973	5	22	2	0	0	1	4.5	1	2	0	4	0	.091	.227	0	0	1B-5
1975	3	12	5	0	0	1	8.3	3	4	1	2	0	.417	.667	0	0	1B-3
1976	3	10	2	0	0	0	0.0	1	3	1	2	0	.200	.200	0	0	1B-3
1983 PHI N	1	1	1	0	0	0	0.0	0	0	0	0	0	1.000	1.000	1	1	
6 yrs.	20	77	18	3	0	3	3.9	6	13	3	16	0	.234	.390	1	1	1B-16, 3B-3

WORLD SERIES

	G	AB	H	2B	3B	HR	HR %	R	RBI	BB	SO	SB	BA	SA	AB	H	G by POS
1970 CIN N	5	18	1	0	0	0	0.0	2	0	3	4	0	.056	.056	0	0	3B-5
1972	7	23	10	2	0	0	0.0	3	2	4	4	0	.435	.522	0	0	1B-7
1975	7	28	5	0	0	3	10.7	4	7	3	9	1	.179	.500	0	0	1B-7
1976	4	16	5	1	0	0	0.0	1	2	1	2	0	.313	.375	0	0	1B-4
1983 PHI N	4	10	2	0	0	0	0.0	0	0	0	2	0	.200	.200	2	1	1B-2
5 yrs.	27	95	23	3	0	3	3.2	10	11	11	21	1	.242	.368	2	1	1B-20, 3B-5

Broderick Perkins

PERKINS, BRODERICK PHILLIP
B. Nov. 23, 1954, Pittsburg, Calif.   BL TL 5'10" 180 lbs.

	G	AB	H	2B	3B	HR	HR %	R	RBI	BB	SO	SB	BA	SA	AB	H	G by POS
1978 SD N	62	217	52	14	1	2	0.9	14	33	5	29	4	.240	.341	5	0	1B-59
1979	57	87	23	0	0	0	0.0	8	8	8	12	0	.264	.264	26	4	1B-28
1980	43	100	37	9	0	2	2.0	18	14	11	10	2	.370	.520	12	4	1B-20, OF-10
1981	92	254	71	18	3	2	0.8	27	40	14	16	0	.280	.398	14	4	1B-80, OF-3
1982	125	347	94	10	4	2	0.6	32	34	26	20	2	.271	.340	29	11	1B-98, OF-11
1983 CLE A	79	184	50	10	0	0	0.0	23	24	9	19	1	.272	.326	28	5	1B-19, OF-17, DH-16
1984	58	66	13	1	0	0	0.0	5	4	7	10	0	.197	.212	41	6	DH-10, 1B-2
7 yrs.	516	1255	340	62	8	8	0.6	127	157	80	116	9	.271	.352	155	34	1B-306, OF-41, DH-26

Cy Perkins

PERKINS, RALPH FOSTER
B. Feb. 27, 1896, Gloucester, Mass.   D. Oct. 2, 1963, Philadelphia, Pa.   BR TR 5'10½" 158 lbs.

	G	AB	H	2B	3B	HR	HR %	R	RBI	BB	SO	SB	BA	SA	AB	H	G by POS
1915 PHI A	7	20	4	1	0	0	0.0	2	0	3	3	0	.200	.250	1	0	C-6
1917	6	18	3	0	0	0	0.0	1	2	2	1	0	.167	.167	0	0	C-6
1918	68	218	41	4	1	0	0.5	9	14	8	15	1	.188	.229	7	1	C-60
1919	101	305	77	12	7	2	0.7	22	29	27	22	2	.252	.357	6	1	C-87, SS-8
1920	148	493	128	24	6	5	1.0	40	52	28	35	5	.260	.363	1	0	C-146, 2B-1
1921	141	538	155	31	4	12	2.2	58	73	32	32	5	.288	.428	0	0	C-141
1922	148	505	135	20	6	6	1.2	58	69	40	30	1	.267	.366	7	1	C-141
1923	143	500	135	34	5	2	0.4	53	65	65	30	1	.270	.370	4	1	C-137
1924	128	392	95	19	4	0	0.0	31	32	31	20	3	.242	.311	0	0	C-128
1925	65	140	43	10	0	1	0.7	21	18	26	6	0	.307	.400	4	1	C-58, 3B-1
1926	63	148	43	6	0	0	0.0	14	19	18	7	0	.291	.331	7	4	C-55
1927	59	137	35	7	2	1	0.7	11	15	12	8	0	.255	.358	2	0	C-54, 1B-1
1928	19	29	5	0	0	0	0.0	1	1	1	1	0	.172	.172	0	0	C-19
1929	38	76	16	4	0	0	0.0	4	9	5	4	0	.211	.263	0	0	C-38
1930	20	38	6	2	0	0	0.0	1	4	2	3	0	.158	.211	0	0	C-19, 1B-1
1931 NY A	16	47	12	1	0	0	0.0	3	7	1	4	0	.255	.277	0	0	C-16
1934 DET A	1	1	0	0	0	0	0.0	0	0	0	0	0	.000	.000	1	0	
17 yrs.	1171	3605	933	175	35	30	0.8	329	409	301	221	18	.259	.352	40	9	C-1111, SS-8, 1B-2, 3B-1, 2B-1

Sam Perlozzo

PERLOZZO, SAMUEL BENEDICT
B. Mar. 4, 1951, Cumberland, Md.   BR TR 5'9" 170 lbs.

	G	AB	H	2B	3B	HR	HR %	R	RBI	BB	SO	SB	BA	SA	AB	H	G by POS
1977 MIN A	10	24	7	0	2	0	0.0	6	0	2	3	0	.292	.458	2	0	2B-10, 3B-1
1979 SD N	2	2	0	0	0	0	0.0	0	0	1	0	0	.000	.000	0	0	2B-2
2 yrs.	12	26	7	0	2	0	0.0	6	0	3	3	0	.269	.423	2	0	2B-12, 3B-1

Jack Perrin

PERRIN, JOHN STEPHENSON
B. Feb. 4, 1893, Escanaba, Mich.   D. June 24, 1969, Detroit, Mich.   BL TR 5'9" 160 lbs.

	G	AB	H	2B	3B	HR	HR %	R	RBI	BB	SO	SB	BA	SA	AB	H	G by POS
1921 BOS A	4	13	3	0	0	0	0.0	3	1	0	3	0	.231	.231	0	0	OF-4

Nig Perrine

PERRINE, JOHN GROVER
B. Jan. 14, 1885, Clinton, Wis.   D. Aug. 13, 1948, Kansas City, Mo.   TR

	G	AB	H	2B	3B	HR	HR %	R	RBI	BB	SO	SB	BA	SA	AB	H	G by POS
1907 WAS A	44	146	25	4	1	0	0.0	13	15	13		10	.171	.212	0	0	2B-24, SS-18, 3B-2

George Perring

PERRING, GEORGE WILSON
B. Aug. 13, 1884, Sharon, Wis.   D. Aug. 20, 1960, Beloit, Wis.   BR TR 6' 190 lbs.

	G	AB	H	2B	3B	HR	HR %	R	RBI	BB	SO	SB	BA	SA	AB	H	G by POS
1908 CLE A	89	310	67	8	5	0	0.0	23	19	16		0	.216	.274	0	0	SS-48, 3B-41
1909	88	283	63	10	9	0	0.0	26	20	19		6	.223	.322	0	0	3B-66, SS-11, 2B-8
1910	39	122	27	6	3	0	0.0	14	8	3		3	.221	.320	2	0	3B-33, 1B-4
1914 KC F	144	496	138	28	10	2	0.4	68	69	59		7	.278	.387	6	3	3B-101, 1B-41, SS-1, P-1
1915	153	553	143	23	7	6	1.1	67	67	55		10	.259	.358	0	0	3B-102, 2B-31, 1B-31, SS-1
5 yrs.	513	1764	438	75	34	8	0.5	198	183	152		26	.248	.343	8	3	3B-343, 1B-76, SS-61, 2B-39, P-1

Bob Perry

PERRY, MELVIN GRAY
B. Sept. 14, 1934, New Bern, N. C.   BR TR 6'2" 180 lbs.

	G	AB	H	2B	3B	HR	HR %	R	RBI	BB	SO	SB	BA	SA	AB	H	G by POS
1963 LA A	61	166	42	9	0	3	1.8	16	14	9	31	1	.253	.361	4	2	OF-55
1964	70	221	61	8	1	3	1.4	19	16	14	52	1	.276	.362	7	0	OF-62
2 yrs.	131	387	103	17	1	6	1.6	35	30	23	83	2	.266	.362	11	2	OF-117

Boyd Perry

PERRY, BOYD GLENN
B. Mar. 21, 1914, Snow Camp, N. C.
BR TR 5'10" 158 lbs.

	G	AB	H	2B	3B	HR	HR%	R	RBI	BB	SO	SB	BA	SA	PH AB	PH H	G by POS
1941 DET A	36	83	15	5	0	0	0.0	9	11	10	9	1	.181	.241	0	0	SS-25, 2B-11

Clay Perry

PERRY, CLAYTON SHIELDS
B. Dec. 18, 1881, Rice Lake, Wis.　D. Jan. 16, 1954, Rice Lake, Wis.
BR TR 5'10½" 175 lbs.

	G	AB	H	2B	3B	HR	HR%	R	RBI	BB	SO	SB	BA	SA	PH AB	PH H	G by POS
1908 DET A	5	11	2	0	0	0	0.0	0	0	0		0	.182	.182	0	0	3B-5

Gerald Perry

PERRY, GERALD JUNE
B. Oct. 30, 1960, Savannah, Ga.
BL TR 5'11" 172 lbs.

	G	AB	H	2B	3B	HR	HR%	R	RBI	BB	SO	SB	BA	SA	PH AB	PH H	G by POS
1983 ATL N	27	39	14	2	0	1	2.6	5	6	5	4	0	.359	.487	16	7	1B-7, OF-1
1984	122	347	92	12	2	7	2.0	52	47	61	38	15	.265	.372	16	8	1B-64, OF-53
2 yrs.	149	386	106	14	2	8	2.1	57	53	66	42	15	.275	.383	32	15	1B-71, OF-54

Hank Perry

PERRY, WILLIAM HENRY (Socks)
B. July 28, 1886, Howell, Mich.　D. July 18, 1956, Pontiac, Mich.
BL TR 5'11" 190 lbs.

	G	AB	H	2B	3B	HR	HR%	R	RBI	BB	SO	SB	BA	SA	PH AB	PH H	G by POS
1912 DET A	13	36	6	1	0	0	0.0	3	0	3		0	.167	.194	6	3	OF-7

Johnny Pesky

PESKY, JOHN MICHAEL
Born John Michael Paveskovich.
B. Sept. 27, 1919, Portland, Ore.
Manager 1963-64, 1980.
BL TR 5'9" 168 lbs.

	G	AB	H	2B	3B	HR	HR%	R	RBI	BB	SO	SB	BA	SA	PH AB	PH H	G by POS
1942 BOS A	147	620	205	29	9	2	0.3	105	51	42	36	12	.331	.416	0	0	SS-147
1946	153	621	208	43	4	2	0.3	115	55	65	29	9	.335	.427	0	0	SS-153
1947	155	638	207	27	8	0	0.0	106	39	72	22	12	.324	.392	0	0	SS-133, 3B-22
1948	143	565	159	26	6	3	0.5	124	55	99	32	3	.281	.365	2	1	3B-141
1949	148	604	185	27	7	2	0.3	111	69	100	19	8	.306	.384	0	0	3B-148
1950	127	490	153	22	6	1	0.2	112	49	104	31	2	.312	.388	2	0	3B-116, SS-8
1951	131	480	150	20	6	3	0.6	93	41	84	15	2	.313	.398	9	3	SS-106, 3B-11, 2B-5
1952 2 teams	BOS A (25G – .149)				DET A (69G – .254)												
" total	94	244	55	6	0	1	0.4	36	11	57	16	1	.225	.262	14	1	SS-43, 3B-22, 2B-22
1953 DET A	103	308	90	22	1	2	0.6	43	24	27	10	3	.292	.390	30	12	2B-73
1954 2 teams	DET A (20G – .176)				WAS A (49G – .253)												
" total	69	175	43	4	3	1	0.6	22	10	13	8	1	.246	.320	29	4	2B-37, SS-1
10 yrs.	1270	4745	1455	226	50	17	0.4	867	404	663	218	53	.307	.386	86	21	SS-591, 3B-460, 2B-137

WORLD SERIES

	G	AB	H	2B	3B	HR	HR%	R	RBI	BB	SO	SB	BA	SA	PH AB	PH H	G by POS
1946 BOS A	7	30	7	0	0	0	0.0	2	0	1	3	1	.233	.233	0	0	SS-7

Bill Peterman

PETERMAN, WILLIAM DAVID
B. Apr. 20, 1921, Philadelphia, Pa.
BR TR 6'2" 185 lbs.

	G	AB	H	2B	3B	HR	HR%	R	RBI	BB	SO	SB	BA	SA	PH AB	PH H	G by POS
1942 PHI N	1	1	1	0	0	0	0.0	0	0	0	0	0	1.000	1.000	0	0	C-1

Gary Peters

PETERS, GARY CHARLES
B. Apr. 21, 1937, Grove City, Pa.
BL TL 6'2" 200 lbs.

	G	AB	H	2B	3B	HR	HR%	R	RBI	BB	SO	SB	BA	SA	PH AB	PH H	G by POS
1959 CHI A	2	0	0	0	0	0	–	0	0	0	0	0	–	–	0	0	P-2
1960	2	0	0	0	0	0	–	0	0	0	0	0	–	–	0	0	P-2
1961	3	3	1	0	0	0	0.0	1	0	0	1	0	.333	.333	0	0	P-3
1962	5	0	0	0	0	0	–	0	0	0	0	0	–	–	0	0	P-5
1963	50	81	21	4	1	3	3.7	9	12	3	19	0	.259	.444	1	0	P-41
1964	54	120	25	7	0	4	3.3	9	19	2	29	0	.208	.367	15	4	P-37
1965	42	72	13	1	0	1	1.4	2	6	2	15	0	.181	.236	7	3	P-33
1966	38	81	19	3	2	1	1.2	12	9	0	19	0	.235	.358	5	1	P-30
1967	48	99	21	0	2	2	2.0	10	13	2	23	0	.212	.313	6	1	P-38
1968	46	72	15	3	1	2	2.8	10	8	6	13	0	.208	.361	14	2	P-31
1969	37	71	12	4	0	2	2.8	9	4	2	15	0	.169	.310	0	0	P-36
1970 BOS A	37	82	20	3	1	1	1.2	12	11	8	11	0	.244	.341	0	0	P-34
1971	53	96	26	4	0	3	3.1	7	19	3	20	0	.271	.406	18	5	P-34
1972	33	30	6	2	0	0	0.0	2	1	1	7	0	.200	.267	0	0	P-33
14 yrs.	450	807	179	31	7	19	2.4	86	102	29	172	0	.222	.348	66	16	P-359

John Peters

PETERS, JOHN WILLIAM (Shotgun)
B. July 14, 1893, Kansas City, Kans.　D. Feb. 21, 1932, Kansas City, Mo.
BR TR 6' 192 lbs.

	G	AB	H	2B	3B	HR	HR%	R	RBI	BB	SO	SB	BA	SA	PH AB	PH H	G by POS
1915 DET A	1	3	0	0	0	0	0.0	0	0	0	1	0	.000	.000	0	0	C-1
1918 CLE A	1	1	0	0	0	0	0.0	0	0	1	1	0	.000	.000	0	0	C-1
1921 PHI N	55	155	45	4	0	3	1.9	7	23	6	13	1	.290	.374	10	5	C-44
1922	55	143	35	9	1	4	2.8	15	24	9	18	0	.245	.406	15	3	C-39
4 yrs.	112	302	80	13	1	7	2.3	22	47	16	33	1	.265	.384	25	8	C-85

Johnny Peters

PETERS, JOHN PAUL
B. Apr. 8, 1850, Louisiana, Mo.　D. Jan. 4, 1924, St. Louis, Mo.
BR TR 180 lbs.

	G	AB	H	2B	3B	HR	HR%	R	RBI	BB	SO	SB	BA	SA	PH AB	PH H	G by POS
1876 CHI N	66	316	111	14	2	1	0.3	70	47	3	2		.351	.418	0	0	SS-66, P-1
1877	60	265	84	10	3	0	0.0	45	41	1	7		.317	.377	0	0	SS-60
1878 MIL N	55	246	76	6	1	0	0.0	33	22	5	8		.309	.341	0	0	2B-34, SS-22
1879 CHI N	83	379	93	13	2	1	0.3	45	31	1	19		.245	.298	0	0	SS-83
1880 PRO N	86	359	82	5	0	0	0.0	30	24	5	15		.228	.242	0	0	SS-86
1881 BUF N	54	229	49	8	1	0	0.0	21	25	3	12		.214	.258	0	0	SS-53, 2B-1
1882 PIT AA	78	333	96	10	1	0	0.0	46		4			.288	.324	0	0	SS-77, 2B-1
1883	8	28	3	0	0	0	0.0	3		0			.107	.107	0	0	SS-8
1884	1	4	0	0	0	0	0.0	0		0			.000	.000	0	0	SS-1
9 yrs.	491	2159	594	66	10	2	0.1	293	190	22	63		.275	.318	0	0	SS-456, 2B-35, OF-1, P-1

Ricky Peters

PETERS, RICHARD DEVIN
B. Nov. 21, 1955, Lynwood, Calif.
BB TR 5'9" 170 lbs.

	G	AB	H	2B	3B	HR	HR%	R	RBI	BB	SO	SB	BA	SA	PH AB	PH H	G by POS
1979 DET A	12	19	5	0	0	0	0.0	3	2	5	3	0	.263	.263	1	0	DH-3, 3B-3, 2B-2, OF-1
1980	133	477	139	19	7	2	0.4	79	42	54	48	13	.291	.373	13	3	OF-109, DH-11
1981	63	207	53	7	3	0	0.0	26	15	29	28	1	.256	.319	5	1	OF-38, DH-19

	G	AB	H	2B	3B	HR	HR %	R	RBI	BB	SO	SB	BA	SA	Pinch Hit AB	Pinch Hit H	G by POS

Ricky Peters continued

	G	AB	H	2B	3B	HR	HR%	R	RBI	BB	SO	SB	BA	SA	AB	H	G by POS
1983 OAK A	55	178	51	7	0	0	0.0	20	20	12	21	4	.287	.326	2	1	OF-47, DH-8
4 yrs.	263	881	248	33	10	2	0.2	128	79	100	100	18	.281	.348	21	5	OF-195, DH-41, 3B-3, 2B-2

Rusty Peters

PETERS, RUSSELL DIXON
B. Dec. 14, 1914, Roanoke, Va.

BR TR 5'11" 170 lbs.

	G	AB	H	2B	3B	HR	HR%	R	RBI	BB	SO	SB	BA	SA	AB	H	G by POS
1936 PHI A	45	119	26	3	2	3	2.5	12	16	4	28	1	.218	.353	7	0	SS-25, 3B-10, OF-2, 2B-1
1937	116	339	88	17	6	3	0.9	39	43	41	59	4	.260	.372	6	3	2B-70, 3B-31, SS-13
1938	2	7	0	0	0	0	0.0	0	0	0	1	0	.000	.000	0	0	SS-2
1940 CLE A	30	71	17	3	2	0	0.0	5	7	4	14	1	.239	.338	9	3	2B-9, SS-6, 3B-6, 1B-1
1941	29	63	13	2	0	0	0.0	6	2	7	10	0	.206	.238	1	0	SS-11, 3B-9, 2B-3
1942	34	58	13	5	1	0	0.0	6	2	2	14	0	.224	.345	5	1	SS-24, 3B-1, 2B-1
1943	79	215	47	6	2	1	0.5	22	19	18	29	1	.219	.279	11	2	3B-46, SS-14, 2B-6, OF-2
1944	88	282	63	13	3	1	0.4	23	24	15	35	2	.223	.301	5	1	2B-63, SS-13, 3B-8
1946	9	21	6	0	0	0	0.0	0	2	1	1	0	.286	.286	2	1	SS-7
1947 STL A	39	47	16	4	0	0	0.0	10	2	6	8	0	.340	.426	11	6	2B-13, SS-2
10 yrs.	471	1222	289	53	16	8	0.7	123	117	98	199	9	.236	.326	57	17	2B-166, SS-117, 3B-111, OF-4, 1B-1

Bob Peterson

PETERSON, ROBERT A.
B. July 16, 1884, Philadelphia, Pa.   D. Nov. 27, 1962, Evesham Township, N. J.

TR

	G	AB	H	2B	3B	HR	HR%	R	RBI	BB	SO	SB	BA	SA	AB	H	G by POS
1906 BOS A	39	118	24	1	1	1	0.8	10	9	11		1	.203	.254	2	0	C-30, 2B-3, 1B-2, OF-1
1907	4	13	1	0	0	0	0.0	1	0	0		0	.077	.077	0	0	C-4
2 yrs.	43	131	25	1	1	1	0.8	11	9	11		1	.191	.237	2	0	C-34, 2B-3, 1B-2, OF-1

Buddy Peterson

PETERSON, CARL FRANCIS
B. Apr. 23, 1925, Portland, Ore.

BR TR 5'9½" 170 lbs.

	G	AB	H	2B	3B	HR	HR%	R	RBI	BB	SO	SB	BA	SA	AB	H	G by POS
1955 CHI A	6	21	6	1	0	0	0.0	7	3	2	2	0	.286	.333	1	1	SS-6
1957 BAL A	7	17	3	2	0	0	0.0	1	0	2	2	0	.176	.294	1	0	SS-7
2 yrs.	13	38	9	3	0	0	0.0	8	3	4	4	0	.237	.316	2	1	SS-13

Cap Peterson

PETERSON, CHARLES ANDREW
B. Aug. 15, 1942, Tacoma, Wash.   D. May 17, 1980, Tacoma, Wash.

BR TR 6'2" 195 lbs.

	G	AB	H	2B	3B	HR	HR%	R	RBI	BB	SO	SB	BA	SA	AB	H	G by POS
1962 SF N	4	6	1	0	0	0	0.0	1	0	1	4	0	.167	.167	3	0	SS-2
1963	22	54	14	2	0	1	1.9	7	2	2	13	0	.259	.352	8	1	2B-8, 3B-5, OF-3, SS-1
1964	66	74	15	1	1	1	1.4	8	8	3	20	0	.203	.284	55	12	OF-10, 1B-2, 3B-1, 2B-1
1965	63	105	26	7	0	3	2.9	14	15	10	16	0	.248	.400	38	5	OF-27
1966	89	190	45	6	1	2	1.1	13	19	11	32	2	.237	.311	37	5	OF-51, 1B-2
1967 WAS A	122	405	97	17	2	8	2.0	35	46	32	61	0	.240	.351	21	3	OF-101
1968	94	226	46	8	1	3	1.3	20	18	18	31	2	.204	.288	39	11	OF-52
1969 CLE A	76	110	25	3	0	1	0.9	8	14	24	18	0	.227	.282	39	9	OF-30, 3B-4
8 yrs.	536	1170	269	44	5	19	1.6	106	122	101	195	4	.230	.325	240	46	OF-274, 3B-10, 2B-9, 1B-4, SS-3

Hardy Peterson

PETERSON, HARDING WILLIAM
B. Oct. 17, 1929, Perth Amboy, N. J.

BR TR 6' 205 lbs.

	G	AB	H	2B	3B	HR	HR%	R	RBI	BB	SO	SB	BA	SA	AB	H	G by POS
1955 PIT N	32	81	20	6	0	1	1.2	7	10	7	7	0	.247	.358	2	0	C-31
1957	30	73	22	2	1	2	2.7	10	11	9	10	0	.301	.438	0	0	C-30
1958	2	6	2	0	0	0	0.0	0	0	1	0	0	.333	.333	0	0	C-2
1959	2	1	0	0	0	0	0.0	0	0	0	0	0	.000	.000	0	0	C-2
4 yrs.	66	161	44	8	1	3	1.9	17	21	17	17	0	.273	.391	2	0	C-65

Ted Petosky

PETOSKY, FRED LEE
B. Jan. 5, 1911, St. Charles, Mich.

BR TR 5'11½" 183 lbs.

	G	AB	H	2B	3B	HR	HR%	R	RBI	BB	SO	SB	BA	SA	AB	H	G by POS
1934 CIN N	6	7	0	0	0	0	0.0	0	1	0	5	0	.000	.000	4	0	OF-2
1935	4	5	2	0	0	0	0.0	0	0	0	1	1	.400	.400	1	1	OF-2
2 yrs.	10	12	2	0	0	0	0.0	0	1	0	6	1	.167	.167	5	1	OF-4

Gene Petralli

PETRALLI, EUGENE JAMES
B. Sept. 25, 1959, Sacramento, Calif.

BB TR 6'1" 180 lbs.

	G	AB	H	2B	3B	HR	HR%	R	RBI	BB	SO	SB	BA	SA	AB	H	G by POS
1982 TOR A	16	44	16	2	0	0	0.0	3	1	4	6	0	.364	.409	3	1	C-12, 3B-3
1983	6	4	0	0	0	0	0.0	0	0	1	1	1	.000	.000	1	0	C-5, DH-1
1984	3	3	0	0	0	0	0.0	0	0	0	0	0	.000	.000	2	0	DH-1, C-1
3 yrs.	25	51	16	2	0	0	0.0	3	1	5	7	1	.314	.353	6	1	C-18, 3B-3, DH-2

Rico Petrocelli

PETROCELLI, AMERICO PETER
B. June 27, 1943, Brooklyn, N. Y.

BR TR 6' 175 lbs.

	G	AB	H	2B	3B	HR	HR%	R	RBI	BB	SO	SB	BA	SA	AB	H	G by POS
1963 BOS A	1	4	1	1	0	0	0.0	0	1	0	1	0	.250	.500	0	0	SS-1
1965	103	323	75	15	2	13	4.0	38	33	36	71	0	.232	.412	8	0	SS-93
1966	139	522	124	20	1	18	3.4	58	59	41	99	1	.238	.383	6	0	SS-127, 3B-5
1967	142	491	127	24	2	17	3.5	53	66	49	93	2	.259	.420	1	0	SS-141
1968	123	406	95	17	2	12	3.0	41	46	31	73	0	.234	.374	4	1	SS-117, 1B-1
1969	154	535	159	32	2	40	7.5	92	97	98	68	3	.297	.589	0	0	SS-153, 3B-1
1970	157	583	152	31	3	29	5.0	82	103	67	82	1	.261	.473	1	0	SS-141, 3B-18
1971	158	553	139	24	4	28	5.1	82	89	91	108	2	.251	.461	2	1	3B-156
1972	147	521	125	15	2	15	2.9	62	75	78	91	0	.240	.363	1	1	3B-146
1973	100	356	87	13	1	13	3.7	44	45	47	64	0	.244	.396	1	0	3B-99
1974	129	454	121	23	1	15	3.3	53	76	48	74	1	.267	.421	5	1	3B-116, DH-9
1975	115	402	96	15	1	7	1.7	31	59	41	66	0	.239	.333	1	0	3B-112, DH-1
1976	85	240	51	7	1	3	1.3	17	24	34	36	0	.213	.288	2	0	3B-73, 2B-5, DH-4, SS-1, 1B-1
13 yrs.	1553	5390	1352	237	22	210	3.9	653	773	661	926	10	.251	.420	32	4	SS-774, 3B-726, DH-14, 2B-5, 1B-2

LEAGUE CHAMPIONSHIP SERIES

	G	AB	H	2B	3B	HR	HR%	R	RBI	BB	SO	SB	BA	SA	AB	H	G by POS
1975 BOS A	3	12	2	0	0	1	8.3	1	2	1	3	0	.167	.417	0	0	3B-3

	G	AB	H	2B	3B	HR	HR %	R	RBI	BB	SO	SB	BA	SA	Pinch Hit AB	Pinch Hit H	G by POS

Rico Petrocelli continued

	G	AB	H	2B	3B	HR	HR %	R	RBI	BB	SO	SB	BA	SA	AB	H	G by POS
WORLD SERIES																	
1967 BOS A	7	20	4	1	0	2	10.0	3	3	3	8	0	.200	.550	0	0	SS-7
1975	7	26	8	1	0	0	0.0	3	4	3	6	0	.308	.346	0	0	3B-7
2 yrs.	14	46	12	2	0	2	4.3	6	7	6	14	0	.261	.435	0	0	SS-7, 3B-7

Pat Pettee

PETTEE, PATRICK E.
B. Jan. 10, 1863, Natick, Mass. D. Oct. 9, 1934, Natick, Mass.
BR TR 5'10" 170 lbs.

	G	AB	H	2B	3B	HR	HR %	R	RBI	BB	SO	SB	BA	SA	AB	H	G by POS
1891 LOU AA	2	5	0	0	0	0	0.0	1	0	3	1	1	.000	.000	0	0	2B-2

Ned Pettigrew

PETTIGREW, JIM NED
B. Aug. 25, 1881, Honey Grove, Tex. D. Aug. 20, 1952, Duncan, Okla.
BR TR 5'11" 175 lbs.

	G	AB	H	2B	3B	HR	HR %	R	RBI	BB	SO	SB	BA	SA	AB	H	G by POS
1914 BUF F	2	2	0	0	0	0	0.0	0	0	0		0	.000	.000	2	0	

Joe Pettini

PETTINI, JOSEPH PAUL
B. Jan. 26, 1955, Windsor Heights, W. Va.
BR TR 5'9" 165 lbs.

	G	AB	H	2B	3B	HR	HR %	R	RBI	BB	SO	SB	BA	SA	AB	H	G by POS
1980 SF N	63	190	44	3	1	1	0.5	19	9	17	33	5	.232	.274	2	1	SS-42, 3B-18, 2B-8
1981	35	29	2	1	0	0	0.0	3	2	4	5	1	.069	.103	1	0	SS-12, 2B-12, 3B-9
1982	29	39	8	1	0	0	0.0	5	2	3	4	0	.205	.231	2	0	SS-26, 3B-1
1983	61	86	16	0	1	0	0.0	11	7	9	11	4	.186	.209	3	0	SS-26, 2B-14, 3B-12
4 yrs.	188	344	70	5	2	1	0.3	38	20	33	53	10	.203	.238	8	1	SS-106, 3B-40, 2B-34

Gary Pettis

PETTIS, GARY GEORGE
B. Apr. 3, 1958, Oakland, Calif.
BB TR 6'1" 165 lbs.

	G	AB	H	2B	3B	HR	HR %	R	RBI	BB	SO	SB	BA	SA	AB	H	G by POS
1982 CAL A	10	5	1	0	0	1	20.0	5	1	0	2	0	.200	.800	0	0	OF-8
1983	22	85	25	2	3	3	3.5	19	6	7	15	8	.294	.494	0	0	OF-21
1984	140	397	90	11	6	2	0.5	63	29	60	115	48	.227	.300	2	0	OF-134
3 yrs.	172	487	116	13	9	6	1.2	87	36	67	132	56	.238	.339	2	0	OF-163

Bob Pettit

PETTIT, ROBERT HENRY
B. July 19, 1861, Williamstown, Mass. D. Nov. 1, 1910, Derby, Conn.
BL 5'9" 160 lbs.

	G	AB	H	2B	3B	HR	HR %	R	RBI	BB	SO	SB	BA	SA	AB	H	G by POS
1887 CHI N	32	138	36	3	3	2	1.4	29	12	8	15	16	.261	.370	0	0	OF-32, C-1, P-1
1888	43	169	43	1	4	4	2.4	23	23	7	9	7	.254	.379	0	0	OF-43
1891 C-M AA	21	80	14	4	0	1	1.3	10	5	7	7	2	.175	.263	0	0	2B-9, OF-7, 3B-6
3 yrs.	96	387	93	8	7	7	1.8	62	40	22	31	25	.240	.351	0	0	OF-82, 2B-9, 3B-6, C-1, P-1

Larry Pezold

PEZOLD, LORENZ JOHANNES
B. June 22, 1893, New Orleans, La. D. Oct. 22, 1957, Baton Rouge, La.
BR TR 5'9½" 175 lbs.

	G	AB	H	2B	3B	HR	HR %	R	RBI	BB	SO	SB	BA	SA	AB	H	G by POS
1914 CLE A	23	71	16	0	1	0	0.0	4	5	9	6	2	.225	.254	2	0	3B-20, OF-1

Big Jeff Pfeffer

PFEFFER, FRANCIS XAVIER
Brother of Jeff Pfeffer.
B. Mar. 31, 1882, Champaign, Ill. D. Dec. 19, 1954, Kankakee, Ill.
BR TR

	G	AB	H	2B	3B	HR	HR %	R	RBI	BB	SO	SB	BA	SA	AB	H	G by POS
1905 CHI N	15	40	8	3	0	0	0.0	4	3	0		2	.200	.275	0	0	P-15
1906 BOS N	60	158	31	3	3	1	0.6	10	11	5		2	.196	.272	8	0	P-35, OF-14
1907	21	60	15	3	0	0	0.0	1	6	2		0	.250	.300	2	0	P-19
1908	4	2	0	0	0	0	0.0	0	0	0		0	.000	.000	0	0	P-4
1910 CHI N	14	17	3	1	1	0	0.0	1	2	1		0	.176	.353	0	0	P-13, OF-1
1911 BOS N	33	46	9	2	0	1	2.2	4	6	5	7	0	.196	.304	3	0	P-26, OF-3, 1B-1
6 yrs.	147	323	66	12	4	2	0.6	20	28	13	8	4	.204	.285	13	0	P-112, OF-18, 1B-1

Fred Pfeffer

PFEFFER, NATHANIEL FREDERICK (Dandelion)
B. Mar. 17, 1860, Louisville, Ky. D. Apr. 10, 1932, Chicago, Ill.
Manager 1892.
BR TR 5'10½" 168 lbs.

	G	AB	H	2B	3B	HR	HR %	R	RBI	BB	SO	SB	BA	SA	AB	H	G by POS
1882 TRO N	85	330	72	7	4	1	0.3	26	31	1	24		.218	.273	0	0	SS-83, 2B-2
1883 CHI N	96	371	87	22	7	1	0.3	41		8	50		.235	.340	0	0	2B-79, SS-18, 3B-1, 1B-1
1884	112	467	135	10	10	25	5.4	105		25	47		.289	.514	0	0	2B-112
1885	112	469	113	12	6	6	1.3	90	71	26	47		.241	.330	0	0	2B-109, P-5, OF-1
1886	118	474	125	17	8	7	1.5	88	95	36	46		.264	.378	0	0	2B-118, 1B-1
1887	123	479	133	21	6	16	3.3	95	89	34	20	57	.278	.447	0	0	2B-123, OF-2
1888	135	517	129	22	10	8	1.5	90	57	32	38	64	.250	.377	0	0	2B-135
1889	134	531	121	15	7	7	1.3	85	77	53	51	45	.228	.322	0	0	2B-134
1890 CHI P	124	499	128	21	8	5	1.0	86	80	44	23	27	.257	.361	0	0	2B-124
1891 CHI N	137	498	123	12	9	7	1.4	93	77	79	60	40	.247	.349	0	0	2B-116, 1B-10, OF-1, P-1
1892 LOU N	124	470	121	14	9	2	0.4	78	76	67	36	27	.257	.338	0	0	2B-125
1893	125	508	129	29	12	3	0.6	85	75	51	18	32	.254	.376	0	0	2B-90, SS-15, P-1
1894	104	409	126	12	14	5	1.2	69	59	30	14	31	.308	.443	0	0	SS-5, 2B-3, 1B-3
1895	11	45	13	1	0	0	0.0	8	5	5	3	2	.289	.311	0	0	2B-11
1896 2 teams	NY N (4G – .143)			CHI N (94G – .244)													
" total	98	374	90	16	7	2	0.5	46	56	24	21	22	.241	.337	0	0	2B-98
1897 CHI N	32	114	26	0	1	0	0.0	10	11	12		5	.228	.246	0	0	2B-32
16 yrs.	1670	6555	1671	231	118	95	1.4	1094	859	527	498	352	.255	.370	0	0	2B-1537, SS-121, 1B-15, P-7, OF-4, 3B-1

Monte Pfeiffer

PFEIFFER, MONTAGUE
B. 1891, New York, N. Y. D. Sept. 27, 1941
BR TR 5'4½" 147 lbs.

	G	AB	H	2B	3B	HR	HR %	R	RBI	BB	SO	SB	BA	SA	AB	H	G by POS
1913 PHI A	1	3	0	0	0	0	0.0	0	0	1	0	0	.000	.000	1	0	SS-1

Bobby Pfeil

PFEIL, ROBERT RAYMOND
B. Nov. 13, 1943, Passaic, N. J.
BR TR 6'1" 180 lbs.

	G	AB	H	2B	3B	HR	HR %	R	RBI	BB	SO	SB	BA	SA	AB	H	G by POS
1969 NY N	62	211	49	9	0	0	0.0	20	10	7	27	0	.232	.275	9	5	3B-49, 2B-11, OF-2
1971 PHI N	44	70	19	3	0	2	2.9	5	9	6	9	1	.271	.400	17	3	3B-15, C-4, OF-3, SS-1, 2B-1, 1B-1
2 yrs.	106	281	68	12	0	2	0.7	25	19	13	36	1	.242	.306	26	8	3B-64, 2B-12, OF-5, C-4, SS-1, 1B-1

	G	AB	H	2B	3B	HR	HR%	R	RBI	BB	SO	SB	BA	SA	Pinch Hit AB	H	G by POS

George Pfister

PFISTER, GEORGE EDWARD
B. Sept. 4, 1918, Bound Brook, N. J.　　　　BR TR 6'　200 lbs.

	G	AB	H	2B	3B	HR	HR%	R	RBI	BB	SO	SB	BA	SA	PH AB	PH H	G by POS
1941 BKN N	1	2	0	0	0	0	0.0	0	0	0	0	0	.000	.000	0	0	C-1

Monte Pfyl

PFYL, MEINHARD CHARLES
B. May 11, 1884, St. Louis, Mo.　D. Oct. 18, 1945, San Francisco, Calif.　　BL TL 6'3"　190 lbs.

	G	AB	H	2B	3B	HR	HR%	R	RBI	BB	SO	SB	BA	SA	PH AB	PH H	G by POS
1907 NY N	1	0	0	0	0	0	–	0	0	0		0	–	–	0	0	1B-1

Art Phelan

PHELAN, ARTHUR THOMAS (Dugan)
B. Aug. 14, 1887, Niantic, Ill.　D. Dec. 27, 1964, Fort Worth, Tex.　　BR TR 5'8"　160 lbs.

	G	AB	H	2B	3B	HR	HR%	R	RBI	BB	SO	SB	BA	SA	PH AB	PH H	G by POS
1910 CIN N	23	42	9	0	0	0	0.0	7	4	7	6	5	.214	.214	2	0	3B-8, 2B-5, OF-3, SS-1
1912	130	461	112	9	11	3	0.7	56	54	46	37	25	.243	.330	0	0	3B-127, 2B-3
1913 CHI N	90	259	65	11	6	2	0.8	41	35	29	25	8	.251	.363	7	3	2B-46, 3B-38, SS-1
1914	25	46	13	2	1	0	0.0	5	3	4	3	0	.283	.370	13	6	3B-7, 2B-3, SS-2
1915	133	448	98	16	7	3	0.7	41	35	55	42	12	.219	.306	0	0	3B-110, 2B-24
5 yrs.	401	1256	297	38	25	8	0.6	150	131	141	113	50	.236	.326	22	9	3B-290, 2B-81, SS-4, OF-3

Dan Phelan

PHELAN, DANIEL B.
B. Waterbury, Conn.　Deceased.

	G	AB	H	2B	3B	HR	HR%	R	RBI	BB	SO	SB	BA	SA	PH AB	PH H	G by POS
1890 LOU AA	8	32	8	1	1	0	0.0	4		0		1	.250	.344	0	0	1B-8

Dick Phelan

PHELAN, JAMES D.
B. Dec. 10, 1854, Towanda, Pa.　D. Feb. 13, 1931, San Antonio, Tex.

	G	AB	H	2B	3B	HR	HR%	R	RBI	BB	SO	SB	BA	SA	PH AB	PH H	G by POS
1884 BAL U	101	402	99	13	3	3	0.7	63		12			.246	.316	0	0	2B-100, 3B-5, OF-1
1885 2 teams		BUF N (4G – .125)				STL N (2G – .250)											
" total	6	20	3	1	0	1	5.0	3	4	0		5	.150	.350	0	0	2B-4, 3B-2
2 yrs.	107	422	102	14	3	4	0.9	66	3	12		5	.242	.318	0	0	2B-104, 3B-7, OF-1

Babe Phelps

PHELPS, ERNEST GORDON (Blimp)
B. Apr. 19, 1908, Odenton, Md.　　BL TR 6'2"　225 lbs.

	G	AB	H	2B	3B	HR	HR%	R	RBI	BB	SO	SB	BA	SA	PH AB	PH H	G by POS
1931 WAS A	3	3	1	0	0	0	0.0	0	0	0	0	0	.333	.333	3	1	
1933 CHI N	3	7	2	0	0	0	0.0	0	2	0	1	0	.286	.286	1	0	C-2
1934	44	70	20	5	2	2	2.9	7	12	1	8	0	.286	.500	26	9	C-18
1935 BKN N	47	121	44	7	2	5	4.1	17	22	9	10	0	.364	.579	12	6	C-34
1936	115	319	117	23	2	5	1.6	36	57	27	18	1	.367	.498	15	5	C-98, OF-1
1937	121	409	128	37	3	7	1.7	42	58	25	28	2	.313	.469	8	1	C-111
1938	66	208	64	12	2	5	2.4	33	46	23	15	2	.308	.457	9	1	C-55
1939	98	323	92	21	2	6	1.9	33	42	24	24	0	.285	.418	6	1	C-92
1940	118	370	109	24	5	13	3.5	47	61	30	27	2	.295	.492	16	2	C-99, 1B-1
1941	16	30	7	3	0	2	6.7	3	4	1	2	0	.233	.533	5	1	C-11
1942 PIT N	95	257	73	11	1	9	3.5	21	41	20	21	2	.284	.440	22	7	C-72
11 yrs.	726	2117	657	143	19	54	2.6	239	345	160	154	9	.310	.472	123	34	C-592, OF-1, 1B-1

Ed Phelps

PHELPS, EDWARD JOSEPH
B. Mar. 3, 1879, Albany, N. Y.　D. Jan. 31, 1942, East Greenbush, N. Y.　　BR TR 5'10"　185 lbs.

	G	AB	H	2B	3B	HR	HR%	R	RBI	BB	SO	SB	BA	SA	PH AB	PH H	G by POS
1902 PIT N	18	61	13	1	0	0	0.0	5	6	4		2	.213	.230	0	0	C-13, 1B-5
1903	81	273	77	7	3	2	0.7	32	31	17		2	.282	.352	1	0	C-76, 1B-3
1904	94	302	73	5	3	0	0.0	29	28	15		2	.242	.278	1	0	C-91, 1B-1
1905 CIN N	44	156	36	5	3	0	0.0	18	18	12		4	.231	.301	0	0	C-44
1906 2 teams	55	CIN N (12G – .275)				PIT N (43G – .237)											
" total	55	158	39	3	3	1	0.6	12	17	12		3	.247	.323	2	0	C-52
1907 PIT N	43	113	24	1	0	0	0.0	11	12	9		1	.212	.221	6	0	C-35, 1B-1
1908	34	64	15	2	0	0	0.0	3	11	2		0	.234	.328	12	7	C-20
1909 STL N	100	306	76	13	1	0	0.0	43	22	39		7	.248	.297	19	3	C-82
1910	93	270	71	4	2	0	0.0	25	37	36	29	9	.263	.293	13	3	C-80
1912 BKN N	52	111	32	4	3	0	0.0	8	23	16	15	1	.288	.378	20	4	C-32
1913	15	18	4	0	0	0	0.0	0	2	1	2	0	.222	.222	10	2	C-4
11 yrs.	629	1832	460	45	20	3	0.2	186	205	163	46	31	.251	.302	84	19	C-529, 1B-10
WORLD SERIES																	
1903 PIT N	8	26	6	2	0	0	0.0	1	2	1	6	0	.231	.308	1	0	C-7

Ken Phelps

PHELPS, KENNETH ALLEN
B. Aug. 6, 1954, Seattle, Wash.　　BL TL 6'1"　209 lbs.

	G	AB	H	2B	3B	HR	HR%	R	RBI	BB	SO	SB	BA	SA	PH AB	PH H	G by POS
1980 KC A	3	4	0	0	0	0	0.0	0	0	0	2	0	.000	.000	1	0	1B-2
1981	21	22	3	0	1	0	0.0	1	1	1	13	0	.136	.227	15	2	DH-4, 1B-2
1982 MON N	10	8	2	0	0	0	0.0	0	0	0	3	0	.250	.250	8	2	
1983 SEA A	50	127	30	4	1	7	5.5	10	16	13	25	0	.236	.449	11	3	1B-22, DH-19
1984	101	290	70	9	0	24	8.3	52	51	61	73	3	.241	.521	15	2	DH-84, 1B-9
5 yrs.	185	451	105	13	2	31	6.9	63	68	75	116	3	.233	.477	50	9	DH-107, 1B-35

Neal Phelps

PHELPS, CORNELIUS CARMAN
B. Nov. 19, 1840, New York, N. Y.　D. Feb. 12, 1885, New York, N. Y.

	G	AB	H	2B	3B	HR	HR%	R	RBI	BB	SO	SB	BA	SA	PH AB	PH H	G by POS
1876 2 teams		NY N (1G – .000)				PHI N (1G – .000)											
" total	2	7	0	0	0	0	0.0	0	0	0	1	0	.000	.000	0	0	OF-1, C-1

Dave Philley

PHILLEY, DAVID EARL
B. May 16, 1920, Paris, Tex.　　BB TR 6'　188 lbs.

	G	AB	H	2B	3B	HR	HR%	R	RBI	BB	SO	SB	BA	SA	PH AB	PH H	G by POS
1941 CHI A	7	9	2	1	0	0	0.0	4	0	3	3	0	.222	.333	4	0	OF-2
1946	17	68	24	2	3	0	0.0	10	17	4	4	5	.353	.471	0	0	OF-17
1947	143	551	142	25	11	2	0.4	55	45	35	39	21	.258	.354	6	2	OF-133, 3B-4
1948	137	488	140	28	3	5	1.0	51	42	50	33	8	.287	.387	8	1	OF-128
1949	146	598	171	20	8	0	0.0	84	44	54	51	13	.286	.346	1	0	OF-145
1950	156	619	150	21	5	14	2.3	69	80	52	57	6	.242	.360	1	0	OF-154

	G	AB	H	2B	3B	HR	HR %	R	RBI	BB	SO	SB	BA	SA	Pinch Hit AB	Pinch Hit H	G by POS

Dave Philley *continued*

		G	AB	H	2B	3B	HR	HR %	R	RBI	BB	SO	SB	BA	SA	PH AB	PH H	G by POS
1951 2 teams	CHI A (7G – .240)							PHI A (125G – .263)										
" total	132	493	129	20	7	7	1.4	71	61	65	41	10	.262	.373	5	1	OF-126
1952 PHI A	151	586	154	25	4	7	1.2	80	71	59	35	11	.263	.355	0	0	OF-149, 3B-2
1953	157	620	188	30	9	9	1.5	80	59	51	35	13	.303	.424	1	0	OF-157, 3B-1
1954 CLE A	133	452	102	13	3	12	2.7	48	60	57	48	2	.226	.347	4	1	OF-129
1955 2 teams	CLE A (43G – .298)							BAL A (83G – .299)										
" total	126	415	124	17	5	8	1.9	65	50	46	48	1	.299	.422	10	4	OF-116, 3B-2
1956 2 teams	BAL A (32G – .205)							CHI A (86G – .265)										
" total	118	396	98	18	4	5	1.3	57	64	48	40	4	.247	.351	12	0	OF-61, 1B-51, 3B-5
1957 2 teams	CHI A (22G – .324)							DET A (65G – .283)										
" total	87	244	72	12	1	2	0.8	24	25	11	26	4	.295	.377	29	12	OF-29, 1B-29, 3B-1
1958 PHI N	91	207	64	11	4	3	1.4	30	31	15	20	1	.309	.444	44	18	OF-24, 1B-18
1959	99	254	74	18	2	7	2.8	32	37	18	27	0	.291	.461	38	15	OF-34, 1B-24
1960 3 teams	PHI N (14G – .333)							SF N (39G – .164)				BAL A (14G – .265)						
" total	67	110	24	4	1	2	1.8	13	16	13	21	1	.218	.327	48	11	OF-21, 3B-4, 1B-2
1961 BAL A	99	144	36	9	2	1	0.7	13	23	10	20	2	.250	.361	72	24	OF-25, 1B-1
1962 BOS A	38	42	6	2	0	0	0.0	3	4	5	3	0	.143	.190	28	4	OF-4
18 yrs.	1904	6296	1700	276	72	84	1.3	789	729	596	551	102	.270	.377	311	93	OF-1454, 1B-125, 3B-19

WORLD SERIES

	G	AB	H	2B	3B	HR	HR %	R	RBI	BB	SO	SB	BA	SA	PH AB	PH H	G by POS
1954 CLE A	4	8	1	0	0	0	0.0	0	0	1	3	0	.125	.125	2	0	OF-2

Adolfo Phillips

PHILLIPS, ADOLFO EMILIO
B. Dec. 16, 1941, Bethania, Panama

BR TR 6'1" 175 lbs.

		G	AB	H	2B	3B	HR	HR %	R	RBI	BB	SO	SB	BA	SA	PH AB	PH H	G by POS
1964 PHI N		13	13	3	0	0	0	0.0	4	0	3	3	0	.231	.231	6	2	OF-4
1965		41	87	20	4	0	3	3.4	14	5	5	34	3	.230	.379	6	1	OF-32
1966 2 teams	PHI N (2G – .000)							CHI N (116G – .262)										
" total	118	419	109	29	1	16	3.8	69	36	43	135	32	.260	.449	4	1	OF-112
1967 CHI N	144	448	120	20	7	17	3.8	66	70	80	93	24	.268	.458	2	0	OF-141
1968	143	439	106	20	5	13	3.0	49	33	47	90	9	.241	.399	2	0	OF-141
1969 2 teams	CHI N (28G – .224)							MON N (58G – .216)										
" total	86	248	54	7	5	4	1.6	30	8	35	77	7	.218	.335	4	0	OF-78
1970 MON N	92	214	51	6	3	6	2.8	36	21	36	51	7	.238	.379	18	3	OF-75
1972 CLE A	12	7	0	0	0	0	0.0	2	0	2	2	0	.000	.000	3	0	OF-10
8 yrs.	649	1875	463	86	21	59	3.1	270	173	251	485	82	.247	.410	45	7	OF-593

Bill Phillips

PHILLIPS, WILLIAM B.
B. 1857, St. John, N. B., Canada   D. Oct. 6, 1900, Chicago, Ill.

BR TR 202 lbs.

	G	AB	H	2B	3B	HR	HR %	R	RBI	BB	SO	SB	BA	SA	PH AB	PH H	G by POS
1879 CLE N	81	365	99	15	4	0	0.0	58	29	2	20		.271	.334	0	0	1B-75, C-11, OF-2
1880	85	334	85	14	10	1	0.3	41		6	29		.254	.365	0	0	1B-85
1881	85	357	97	18	10	1	0.3	51	44	5	19		.272	.387	0	0	1B-85
1882	78	335	87	17	7	4	1.2	40	47	7	18		.260	.388	0	0	1B-78, C-1
1883	97	382	94	29	8	2	0.5	42		8	49		.246	.380	0	0	1B-97
1884	111	464	128	25	12	3	0.6	58	46	18	80		.276	.401	0	0	1B-111
1885 BKN AA	99	391	118	16	11	3	0.8	65		27			.302	.422	0	0	1B-99
1886	141	585	160	26	15	0	0.0	68		33			.274	.369	0	0	1B-141
1887	132	533	142	34	11	2	0.4	82		45		16	.266	.383	0	0	1B-132
1888 KC AA	129	509	120	20	10	1	0.2	57	56	27		10	.236	.320	0	0	1B-129
10 yrs.	1038	4255	1130	214	98	17	0.4	562	222	178	215	26	.266	.374	0	0	1B-1032, C-12, OF-2

Bubba Phillips

PHILLIPS, JOHN MELVIN
B. Feb. 24, 1930, West Point, Miss.

BR TR 5'9" 180 lbs.

	G	AB	H	2B	3B	HR	HR %	R	RBI	BB	SO	SB	BA	SA	PH AB	PH H	G by POS
1955 DET A	95	184	43	4	0	3	1.6	18	23	14	20	2	.234	.304	17	1	OF-65, 3B-4
1956 CHI A	67	99	27	6	0	2	2.0	16	11	6	12	1	.273	.394	13	4	OF-35, 3B-2
1957	121	393	106	13	3	7	1.8	38	42	28	32	5	.270	.372	3	0	3B-97, OF-20
1958	84	260	71	10	0	5	1.9	26	30	15	14	3	.273	.369	4	0	3B-47, OF-37
1959	117	379	100	27	1	5	1.3	43	40	27	28	1	.264	.380	1	0	3B-100, OF-23
1960 CLE A	113	304	63	14	1	4	1.3	34	33	14	37	1	.207	.299	5	0	3B-85, OF-25, SS-1
1961	143	546	144	23	1	18	3.3	64	72	29	61	1	.264	.408	0	0	3B-143
1962	148	562	145	26	0	10	1.8	53	54	20	55	4	.258	.358	1	0	3B-145, OF-3, 2B-1
1963 DET A	128	464	114	11	2	5	1.1	42	45	19	42	6	.246	.310	6	2	3B-117, OF-5
1964	46	87	22	1	0	3	3.4	14	6	10	13	1	.253	.368	17	4	3B-22, OF-1
10 yrs.	1062	3278	835	135	8	62	1.9	348	356	182	314	25	.255	.358	67	11	3B-762, OF-214, SS-1, 2B-1

WORLD SERIES

	G	AB	H	2B	3B	HR	HR %	R	RBI	BB	SO	SB	BA	SA	PH AB	PH H	G by POS
1959 CHI A	3	10	3	1	0	0	0.0	0	0	0	0	0	.300	.400	0	0	3B-3

Damon Phillips

PHILLIPS, DAMON ROSWELL (Dee)
B. June 8, 1919, Corsicanna, Tex.

BR TR 6' 176 lbs.

	G	AB	H	2B	3B	HR	HR %	R	RBI	BB	SO	SB	BA	SA	PH AB	PH H	G by POS
1942 CIN N	28	84	17	2	0	0	0.0	4	6	7	5	0	.202	.226	1	0	SS-27
1944 BOS N	140	489	126	30	1	1	0.2	35	53	28	34	1	.258	.329	0	0	3B-90, SS-60
1946	2	2	1	0	0	0	0.0	0	0	0	0	0	.500	.500	2	1	
3 yrs.	170	575	144	32	1	1	0.2	39	59	35	39	1	.250	.315	3	1	3B-90, SS-87

Dick Phillips

PHILLIPS, RICHARD EUGENE
B. Nov. 24, 1931, Racine, Wis.

BL TR 6' 180 lbs.

	G	AB	H	2B	3B	HR	HR %	R	RBI	BB	SO	SB	BA	SA	PH AB	PH H	G by POS
1962 SF N	5	3	0	0	0	0	0.0	0	1	1	1	0	.000	.000	3	0	1B-1
1963 WAS A	124	321	76	8	0	10	3.1	33	32	29	35	1	.237	.355	39	8	1B-48, 2B-5, 3B-4
1964	109	234	54	6	1	2	0.9	17	23	27	22	1	.231	.291	39	5	1B-61, 3B-4
1966	25	37	6	0	0	0	0.0	3	4	2	5	0	.162	.162	18	2	1B-5
4 yrs.	263	595	136	14	1	12	2.0	54	60	59	63	2	.229	.316	99	15	1B-135, 3B-8, 2B-5

Ed Phillips

PHILLIPS, HOWARD EDWARD
B. July 8, 1931, St. Louis, Mo.

BB TR 6'1" 180 lbs.

	G	AB	H	2B	3B	HR	HR %	R	RBI	BB	SO	SB	BA	SA	PH AB	PH H	G by POS
1953 STL N	9	0	0	0	0	0	–	4	0	0	0	0	–	–	0	0	

	G	AB	H	2B	3B	HR	HR %	R	RBI	BB	SO	SB	BA	SA	Pinch Hit AB	Pinch Hit H	G by POS

Eddie Phillips

PHILLIPS, EDWARD DAVID
B. Feb. 17, 1901, Worcester, Mass.   D. Jan. 26, 1968, Buffalo, N. Y.
BR TR 6'   178 lbs.

	G	AB	H	2B	3B	HR	HR %	R	RBI	BB	SO	SB	BA	SA	PH AB	PH H	G by POS
1924 BOS N	3	3	0	0	0	0	0.0	0	0	0	2	0	.000	.000	2	0	C-1
1929 DET A	68	221	52	13	1	2	0.9	24	21	20	16	0	.235	.330	4	1	C-63
1931 PIT N	106	353	82	18	3	7	2.0	30	44	41	49	1	.232	.360	1	0	C-103
1932 NY A	9	31	9	1	0	2	6.5	4	4	2	3	1	.290	.516	0	0	C-9
1934 WAS A	56	169	33	6	1	2	1.2	6	16	26	24	1	.195	.278	3	0	C-53
1935 CLE A	70	220	60	16	1	1	0.5	18	41	15	21	0	.273	.368	1	0	C-69
6 yrs.	312	997	236	54	6	14	1.4	82	126	104	115	3	.237	.345	11	1	C-298

Jack Phillips

PHILLIPS, JACK DORN (Stretch)
B. Sept. 6, 1921, Clarence, N. Y.
BR TR 6'4"   193 lbs.

	G	AB	H	2B	3B	HR	HR %	R	RBI	BB	SO	SB	BA	SA	PH AB	PH H	G by POS
1947 NY A	16	36	10	0	1	1	2.8	5	2	3	5	0	.278	.417	4	0	1B-10
1948 "	1	2	0	0	0	0	0.0	0	0	0	1	0	.000	.000	0	0	1B-1
1949 2 teams			NY	A (45G – .308)		PIT	N (18G – .232)										
" total	63	147	41	7	2	1	0.7	22	13	16	15	2	.279	.374	7	2	1B-54, 3B-1
1950 PIT N	69	208	61	7	6	5	2.4	25	34	20	17	1	.293	.457	11	3	1B-54, 3B-3, P-1
1951	70	156	37	7	3	0	0.0	12	12	15	17	1	.237	.321	12	2	1B-53, 3B-4
1952	1	1	0	0	0	0	0.0	0	0	0	0	0	.000	.000	0	0	1B-1
1955 DET A	55	117	37	8	2	1	0.9	15	20	10	12	0	.316	.444	17	8	1B-35, 3B-3
1956	67	224	66	13	2	1	0.4	31	20	21	19	1	.295	.384	9	5	1B-56, OF-1, 2B-1
1957	1	1	0	0	0	0	0.0	1	0	0	0	0	.000	.000	1	0	
9 yrs.	343	892	252	42	16	9	1.0	111	101	85	86	5	.283	.396	61	18	1B-264, 3B-11, OF-1, 2B-1, P-1

WORLD SERIES

	G	AB	H	2B	3B	HR	HR %	R	RBI	BB	SO	SB	BA	SA	PH AB	PH H	G by POS
1947 NY A	2	2	0	0	0	0	0.0	0	0	0	0	0	.000	.000	1	0	1B-1

John Phillips

PHILLIPS, JOHN STEPHEN
B. May 24, 1921, St. Louis, Mo.   D. June 9, 1958, St. Louis, Mo.
BR TR 6'1"   185 lbs.

	G	AB	H	2B	3B	HR	HR %	R	RBI	BB	SO	SB	BA	SA	PH AB	PH H	G by POS
1945 NY N	2	2	1	0	0	0	0.0	1	0	0	0	0	.500	.500	0	0	P-1

Marr Phillips

PHILLIPS, MARR B.
B. June 16, 1862, Pittsburgh, Pa.   D. Apr. 2, 1928, Pittsburgh, Pa.

	G	AB	H	2B	3B	HR	HR %	R	RBI	BB	SO	SB	BA	SA	PH AB	PH H	G by POS
1884 IND AA	97	413	111	18	8	0	0.0	41		5				.269	.351	0	0	SS-97
1885 2 teams			DET	N (33G – .209)		PIT	AA (4G – .267)										
" total	37	154	33	5	0	0	0.0	14	17	2	13		.214	.247	0	0	SS-37
1890 ROC AA	64	257	53	8	0	0	0.0	18		16		10	.206	.237	0	0	SS-64
3 yrs.	198	824	197	31	8	0	0.0	73	16	23	13	10	.239	.296	0	0	SS-198

Mike Phillips

PHILLIPS, MICHAEL DWAINE
B. Aug. 19, 1950, Beaumont, Tex.
BL TR 6'   170 lbs.

	G	AB	H	2B	3B	HR	HR %	R	RBI	BB	SO	SB	BA	SA	PH AB	PH H	G by POS
1973 SF N	63	104	25	3	4	1	1.0	18	9	6	17	0	.240	.375	5	1	3B-28, SS-20, 2B-7
1974	100	283	62	6	1	2	0.7	19	20	14	37	4	.219	.269	13	2	3B-34, 2B-30, SS-23
1975 2 teams			SF	N (10G – .194)		NY	N (116G – .256)										
" total	126	414	104	10	2	1	0.2	34	29	31	51	4	.251	.316	3	0	SS-115, 2B-7, 3B-6
1976 NY N	87	262	67	4	0	4	1.5	30	29	25	29	2	.256	.363	13	3	SS-53, 2B-19, 3B-10
1977 2 teams			NY	N (38G – .209)		STL	N (48G – .241)										
" total	86	173	39	5	3	1	0.6	22	12	20	36	1	.225	.306	24	0	2B-35, SS-29, 3B-14
1978 STL N	76	164	44	8	1	1	0.6	14	28	13	25	0	.268	.348	19	1	2B-55, SS-10, 3B-1
1979	44	97	22	3	1	1	1.0	10	6	10	9	0	.227	.309	1	0	SS-25, 2B-16, 3B-1
1980	63	128	30	5	0	0	0.0	13	7	9	17	0	.234	.273	9	2	SS-37, 2B-9, 3B-8
1981 2 teams			SD	N (14G – .207)		MON	N (34G – .218)										
" total	48	84	18	2	1	0	0.0	6	4	5	18	1	.214	.262	5	1	SS-27, 2B-15
1982 MON N	14	8	1	0	0	0	0.0	0	1	1	3	0	.125	.125	1	0	2B-10, SS-2
1983	5	2	0	0	0	0	0.0	0	0	0	0	0	.000	.000	0	0	SS-3, 3B-2
11 yrs.	712	1719	412	46	24	11	0.6	166	145	133	242	12	.240	.314	93	10	SS-344, 2B-203, 3B-104

DIVISIONAL PLAYOFF SERIES

	G	AB	H	2B	3B	HR	HR %	R	RBI	BB	SO	SB	BA	SA	PH AB	PH H	G by POS
1981 MON N	1	1	0	0	0	0	0.0	0	0	0	0	0	.000	.000	0	0	2B-1

Tony Phillips

PHILLIPS, KEITH ANTHONY
B. Apr. 25, 1959, Atlanta, Ga.
BB TR 5'10"   160 lbs.

	G	AB	H	2B	3B	HR	HR %	R	RBI	BB	SO	SB	BA	SA	PH AB	PH H	G by POS
1982 OAK A	40	81	17	2	2	0	0.0	11	8	12	26	2	.210	.284	0	0	SS-39
1983	148	412	102	12	3	4	1.0	54	35	48	70	16	.248	.320	1	1	SS-101, 2B-63, 3B-4, DH-1
1984	154	451	120	24	3	4	0.9	62	37	42	86	10	.266	.359	2	0	SS-91, 2B-90, OF-1
3 yrs.	342	944	239	38	8	8	0.8	127	80	102	182	28	.253	.336	3	1	SS-231, 2B-153, 3B-4, DH-1, OF-1

Rob Picciolo

PICCIOLO, ROBERT MICHAEL
B. Feb. 4, 1953, Santa Monica, Calif.
BR TR 6'2"   185 lbs.

	G	AB	H	2B	3B	HR	HR %	R	RBI	BB	SO	SB	BA	SA	PH AB	PH H	G by POS
1977 OAK A	148	419	84	12	3	2	0.5	35	22	9	55	1	.200	.258	0	0	SS-148
1978	78	93	21	1	0	2	2.2	16	7	2	13	1	.226	.301	0	0	SS-41, 2B-19, 3B-13
1979	115	348	88	16	2	2	0.6	37	27	3	45	2	.253	.328	1	1	SS-105, 2B-6, 3B-4, OF-1
1980	95	271	65	9	2	5	1.8	32	18	2	63	1	.240	.343	1	0	SS-49, 2B-47, OF-1
1981	82	179	48	5	3	2	2.2	23	13	5	22	0	.268	.397	0	0	SS-82
1982 2 teams			OAK	A (18G – .224)		MIL	A (22G – .286)										
" total	40	70	17	2	0	0	0.0	10	4	2	14	1	.243	.271	5	2	SS-24, 2B-11, DH-1
1983 MIL A	14	27	6	3	0	0	0.0	1	0	1	4	0	.222	.333	3	0	SS-7, 3B-2, 2B-2, DH-1, 1B-1
1984 CAL A	87	119	24	6	0	1	0.8	18	9	0	21	0	.202	.277	1	0	SS-66, 3B-13, 2B-9, OF-1
8 yrs.	659	1526	353	54	10	16	1.0	173	101	23	237	6	.231	.311	11	3	SS-522, 2B-94, 3B-32, OF-3, DH-2, 1B-1

DIVISIONAL PLAYOFF SERIES

	G	AB	H	2B	3B	HR	HR %	R	RBI	BB	SO	SB	BA	SA	PH AB	PH H	G by POS
1981 OAK A	1	3	1	0	0	0	0.0	0	0	0	0	0	.333	.333	0	0	SS-1

LEAGUE CHAMPIONSHIP SERIES

	G	AB	H	2B	3B	HR	HR %	R	RBI	BB	SO	SB	BA	SA	PH AB	PH H	G by POS
1981 OAK A	2	5	1	0	0	0	0.0	1	0	0	2	0	.200	.200	0	0	SS-2

	G	AB	H	2B	3B	HR	HR %	R	RBI	BB	SO	SB	BA	SA	Pinch Hit AB	Pinch Hit H	G by POS

Nick Picciuto

PICCIUTO, NICHOLAS THOMAS　　　　　　　　　　　BR TR 5'8½" 165 lbs.
B. Aug. 27, 1921, Newark, N. J.

	G	AB	H	2B	3B	HR	HR%	R	RBI	BB	SO	SB	BA	SA	PH AB	PH H	G by POS
1945 PHI N	36	89	12	6	0	0	0.0	7	6	6	17	0	.135	.202	2	0	3B-30, 2B-4

Val Picinich

PICINICH, VALENTINE JOHN　　　　　　　　　　　BR TR 5'9" 165 lbs.
B. Sept. 8, 1896, New York, N. Y.　　D. Dec. 5, 1942, Nobleboro, Me.

	G	AB	H	2B	3B	HR	HR%	R	RBI	BB	SO	SB	BA	SA	PH AB	PH H	G by POS
1916 PHI A	40	118	23	3	1	0	0.0	8	5	6	33	1	.195	.237	3	2	C-37
1917	2	6	2	0	0	0	0.0	0	0	1	2	0	.333	.333	0	0	C-2
1918 WAS A	47	148	34	3	2	1	0.7	13	12	9	25	0	.230	.297	1	0	C-46
1919	80	212	58	12	3	3	1.4	18	22	17	43	6	.274	.401	11	2	C-69
1920	48	133	27	6	2	3	2.3	14	14	9	33	0	.203	.346	2	0	C-45
1921	45	141	39	9	0	0	0.0	10	12	16	21	1	.277	.340	0	0	C-45
1922	76	210	48	12	2	0	0.0	16	19	23	33	1	.229	.305	0	0	C-76
1923 BOS A	87	268	74	21	1	2	0.7	33	31	46	32	3	.276	.384	6	0	C-81
1924	68	158	42	5	3	1	0.6	24	24	28	19	5	.266	.354	16	3	C-51
1925	90	251	64	21	0	1	0.4	31	25	33	21	2	.255	.351	11	3	C-74, 1B-2
1926 CIN N	89	240	63	16	1	2	0.8	33	31	29	22	4	.263	.363	2	2	C-86
1927	65	173	44	8	3	0	0.0	16	12	24	15	3	.254	.335	4	0	C-61
1928	96	324	98	15	1	7	2.2	29	35	20	25	1	.302	.420	2	0	C-93
1929 BKN N	93	273	71	16	6	4	1.5	28	31	34	24	3	.260	.407	6	1	C-85
1930	35	46	10	3	0	0	0.0	4	3	5	6	1	.217	.283	1	0	C-22
1931	24	45	12	4	0	1	2.2	5	4	4	9	1	.267	.422	5	2	C-24
1932	41	70	18	6	0	1	1.4	8	11	4	8	0	.257	.386	16	3	C-24
1933 2 teams		BKN	N (6G – .167)			PIT	N	(16G – .250)									
" total	22	58	14	5	0	1	1.7	7	7	5	11	0	.241	.379	0	0	C-22
18 yrs.	1048	2874	741	165	25	27	0.9	297	298	313	382	31	.258	.361	86	18	C-943, 1B-2

Charlie Pick

PICK, CHARLES THOMAS　　　　　　　　　　　BL TR 5'10" 160 lbs.
B. Apr. 10, 1888, Brookneal, Va.　　D. June 26, 1954, Lynchburg, Va.

	G	AB	H	2B	3B	HR	HR%	R	RBI	BB	SO	SB	BA	SA	PH AB	PH H	G by POS
1914 WAS A	10	23	9	0	0	0	0.0	0	1	4	4	1	.391	.391	2	1	OF-7
1915	3	2	0	0	0	0	0.0	0	0	0	0	0	.000	.000	2	0	
1916 PHI A	121	398	96	10	3	0	0.0	29	20	40	24	25	.241	.281	5	1	3B-108, OF-8
1918 CHI N	29	89	29	4	1	0	0.0	13	12	14	4	7	.326	.393	0	0	2B-20, 3B-8
1919 2 teams		CHI	N (75G – .242)			BOS	N	(34G – .254)									
" total	109	383	94	9	7	1	0.3	39	25	21	17	21	.245	.313	3	1	2B-92, 3B-8, OF-3, 1B-2
1920 BOS N	95	383	105	16	6	2	0.5	34	28	23	11	10	.274	.363	1	1	2B-94
6 yrs.	367	1278	333	39	17	3	0.2	115	86	102	60	64	.261	.325	13	4	2B-206, 3B-124, OF-18, 1B-2

WORLD SERIES

	G	AB	H	2B	3B	HR	HR%	R	RBI	BB	SO	SB	BA	SA	PH AB	PH H	G by POS
1918 CHI N	6	18	7	1	0	0	0.0	2	0	1	1	0	.389	.444	0	0	2B-6

Eddie Pick

PICK, EDGAR EVERETT　　　　　　　　　　　BB TR 6' 185 lbs.
B. May 7, 1899, Attleboro, Mass.　　D. May 13, 1967, Santa Monica, Calif.

	G	AB	H	2B	3B	HR	HR%	R	RBI	BB	SO	SB	BA	SA	PH AB	PH H	G by POS
1923 CIN N	9	8	3	0	0	0	0.0	2	2	3	3	0	.375	.375	2	0	OF-4
1924	3	2	0	0	0	0	0.0	0	0	0	1	0	.000	.000	1	0	OF-1
1927 CHI N	54	181	31	5	2	2	1.1	23	15	20	26	0	.171	.254	0	0	3B-49, OF-1, 2B-1
3 yrs.	66	191	34	5	2	2	1.0	25	17	23	30	0	.178	.257	3	0	3B-49, OF-6, 2B-1

Ollie Pickering

PICKERING, OLIVER DANIEL　　　　　　　　　　　BL TR 5'11" 170 lbs.
B. Apr. 9, 1870, Olney, Ill.　　D. Jan. 20, 1952, Vincennes, Ind.

	G	AB	H	2B	3B	HR	HR%	R	RBI	BB	SO	SB	BA	SA	PH AB	PH H	G by POS
1896 LOU N	45	165	50	6	4	1	0.6	28	22	12		11	13	.303	.406	0	0	OF-45
1897 2 teams		LOU	N (63G – .252)			CLE	N	(46G – .352)									
" total	109	428	126	10	4	2	0.5	67	43	36		38	.294	.350	1	0	OF-108, 2B-1
1901 CLE A	137	547	169	25	6	0	0.0	102	40	58		36	.309	.377	0	0	OF-137
1902	69	293	75	5	2	3	1.0	46	26	19		22	.256	.317	2	2	OF-64, 1B-2
1903 PHI A	137	512	144	18	6	1	0.2	93	36	53		40	.281	.346	2	0	OF-135
1904	124	455	103	10	3	0	0.0	56	30	45		17	.226	.262	2	0	OF-121
1907 STL A	151	576	159	15	10	0	0.0	63	60	35		15	.276	.337	1	0	OF-151
1908 WAS A	113	373	84	7	4	2	0.5	45	30	28		13	.225	.282	14	3	OF-98
8 yrs.	885	3349	910	96	39	9	0.3	500	287	286	11	194	.272	.332	22	5	OF-859, 1B-2, 2B-1

Urbane Pickering

PICKERING, URBANE HENRY (Dick)　　　　　　　　　　　BR TR 5'10" 180 lbs.
B. June 3, 1899, Hoxie, Kans.　　D. May 13, 1970, Modesto, Calif.

	G	AB	H	2B	3B	HR	HR%	R	RBI	BB	SO	SB	BA	SA	PH AB	PH H	G by POS
1931 BOS A	103	341	86	13	4	9	2.6	48	52	33	53	3	.252	.393	12	3	3B-74, 2B-16
1932	132	457	119	28	5	2	0.4	47	40	39	71	3	.260	.357	5	2	3B-126, C-1
2 yrs.	235	798	205	41	9	11	1.4	95	92	72	124	6	.257	.372	17	5	3B-200, 2B-16, C-1

Dave Pickett

PICKETT, DAVID T.　　　　　　　　　　　5'7½" 170 lbs.
B. May 26, 1874, Brookline, Mass.　　D. Apr. 22, 1950, Easton, Mass.

	G	AB	H	2B	3B	HR	HR%	R	RBI	BB	SO	SB	BA	SA	PH AB	PH H	G by POS
1898 BOS N	14	43	12	1	0	0	0.0	3	3	6		2	.279	.302	0	0	OF-14

John Pickett

PICKETT, JOHN THOMAS　　　　　　　　　　　BR TR
B. Feb. 20, 1866, Chicago, Ill.　　D. July 4, 1922, Chicago, Ill.

	G	AB	H	2B	3B	HR	HR%	R	RBI	BB	SO	SB	BA	SA	PH AB	PH H	G by POS
1889 KC AA	53	201	45	7	0	0	0.0	20	29	12	11	21	7	.224	.259	0	0	OF-28, 3B-14, 2B-11
1890 PHI P	100	407	114	7	9	4	1.0	82	64	40	17	12	.280	.371	0	0	2B-100
1892 BAL N	36	141	30	2	3	1	0.7	13	12	7	10	2	.213	.291	0	0	2B-36
3 yrs.	189	749	189	16	12	5	0.7	115	88	58	48	21	.252	.326	0	0	2B-147, OF-28, 3B-14

Ty Pickup

PICKUP, CLARENCE WILLIAM　　　　　　　　　　　BR TR 6' 180 lbs.
B. Oct. 29, 1897, Philadelphia, Pa.　　D. Aug. 2, 1974, Philadelphia, Pa.

	G	AB	H	2B	3B	HR	HR%	R	RBI	BB	SO	SB	BA	SA	PH AB	PH H	G by POS
1918 PHI N	1	1	1	0	0	0	0.0	0	0	0	0	0	1.000	1.000	0	0	OF-1

	G	AB	H	2B	3B	HR	HR %	R	RBI	BB	SO	SB	BA	SA	Pinch Hit AB	Pinch Hit H	G by POS

Gracie Pierce

PIERCE, GRAYSON S.
B. New York, N. Y.   D. Aug. 28, 1894, New York, N. Y.   BL TR 5'11"   176 lbs.

	G	AB	H	2B	3B	HR	HR %	R	RBI	BB	SO	SB	BA	SA	PH AB	PH H	G by POS
1882 2 teams		LOU	AA (9G – .303)			BAL	AA (41G – .199)										
" total	50	184	40	3	1	0	0.0	11		4			.217	.245	0	0	2B-47, OF-3, SS-1
1883 2 teams		COL	AA (11G – .171)			NY	N (18G – .081)										
" total	29	103	12	0	1	0	0.0	8		1	9		.117	.136	0	0	OF-23, 2B-7
1884 NY AA	5	20	5	1	0	0	0.0	2		0			.250	.300	0	0	OF-3, 2B-3
3 yrs.	84	307	57	4	2	0	0.0	21		5	9		.186	.212	0	0	2B-57, OF-29, SS-1

Jack Pierce

PIERCE, LAVERN JACK
B. June 2, 1948, Laurel, Miss.   BB TR 6'   210 lbs.

	G	AB	H	2B	3B	HR	HR %	R	RBI	BB	SO	SB	BA	SA	PH AB	PH H	G by POS
1973 ATL N	11	20	1	0	0	0	0.0	0	0	1	8	0	.050	.050	5	0	1B-6
1974	6	9	1	0	0	0	0.0	1	0	1	0	0	.111	.111	3	1	1B-2
1975 DET A	53	170	40	6	1	8	4.7	19	22	20	40	0	.235	.424	4	0	1B-49
3 yrs.	70	199	42	6	1	8	4.0	20	22	22	48	0	.211	.372	12	1	1B-57

Maury Pierce

PIERCE, MAURICE
B. Baltimore, Md.   Deceased.

	G	AB	H	2B	3B	HR	HR %	R	RBI	BB	SO	SB	BA	SA	PH AB	PH H	G by POS
1884 WAS U	2	7	1	0	0	0	0.0	0		0			.143	.143	0	0	3B-2

Andy Piercy

PIERCY, ANDREW J.
B. Aug., 1856, San Jose, Calif.   D. Dec. 27, 1932, San Jose, Calif.   TR

	G	AB	H	2B	3B	HR	HR %	R	RBI	BB	SO	SB	BA	SA	PH AB	PH H	G by POS
1881 CHI N	2	8	2	0	0	0	0.0	1	0	0	1		.250	.250	0	0	3B-1, 2B-1

Dick Pierre

PIERRE, RICHARD J.
B. Grand Haven, Mich.   Deceased.

	G	AB	H	2B	3B	HR	HR %	R	RBI	BB	SO	SB	BA	SA	PH AB	PH H	G by POS
1883 PHI N	5	19	3	0	0	0	0.0	1		0	2		.158	.158	0	0	SS-5

Jimmy Piersall

PIERSALL, JAMES ANTHONY
B. Nov. 14, 1929, Waterbury, Conn.   BR TR 6'   175 lbs.

	G	AB	H	2B	3B	HR	HR %	R	RBI	BB	SO	SB	BA	SA	PH AB	PH H	G by POS
1950 BOS A	6	7	2	0	0	0	0.0	4	0	4	0	0	.286	.286	1	1	OF-2
1952	56	161	43	8	0	1	0.6	28	16	28	26	3	.267	.335	0	0	SS-30, OF-22, 3B-1
1953	151	585	159	21	9	3	0.5	76	52	41	52	11	.272	.354	0	0	OF-151
1954	133	474	135	24	2	8	1.7	77	38	36	42	5	.285	.395	6	0	OF-126
1955	149	515	146	25	5	13	2.5	68	62	67	52	6	.283	.427	2	1	OF-147
1956	155	601	176	40	6	14	2.3	91	87	58	48	7	.293	.449	0	0	OF-155
1957	151	609	159	27	5	19	3.1	103	63	62	54	14	.261	.415	0	0	OF-151
1958	130	417	99	13	5	8	1.9	55	48	42	43	12	.237	.350	5	1	OF-125
1959 CLE A	100	317	78	13	2	4	1.3	42	30	24	31	6	.246	.338	6	1	OF-91, 3B-1
1960	138	486	137	12	4	18	3.7	70	66	24	38	18	.282	.434	7	1	OF-134
1961	121	484	156	26	7	6	1.2	81	40	43	46	8	.322	.442	1	1	OF-120
1962 WAS A	135	471	115	20	4	4	0.8	38	31	39	53	12	.244	.329	5	1	OF-132
1963 3 teams		WAS	A (29G – .245)			NY	N (40G – .194)			LA	A (20G – .308)						
" total	89	270	63	6	1	2	0.7	26	19	21	30	5	.233	.285	7	2	OF-77
1964 LA A	87	255	80	11	0	2	0.8	28	13	16	32	5	.314	.380	13	2	OF-72
1965 CAL A	53	112	30	5	2	2	1.8	10	12	5	15	2	.268	.402	14	3	OF-41
1966	75	123	26	5	0	0	0.0	14	14	13	19	1	.211	.252	15	4	OF-63
1967	5	3	0	0	0	0	0.0	0	0	0	2	0	.000	.000	3	0	OF-1
17 yrs.	1734	5890	1604	256	52	104	1.8	811	591	523	583	115	.272	.386	85	18	OF-1610, SS-30, 3B-2

Dick Pierson

PIERSON, EDMUND DANA
Brother of Dave Pearson.
B. 1858, Newark, N. J.   D. July 20, 1922, Newark, N. J.   TR

	G	AB	H	2B	3B	HR	HR %	R	RBI	BB	SO	SB	BA	SA	PH AB	PH H	G by POS
1885 NY AA	3	9	1	0	0	0	0.0	1		2			.111	.111	0	0	2B-3

Tony Piet

PIET, ANTHONY FRANCIS
Also known as Anthony Francis Pietruszka.
B. Dec. 7, 1906, Berwick, Pa.   D. Dec. 1, 1981, Hinsdale, Ill.   BR TR 6'   175 lbs.

	G	AB	H	2B	3B	HR	HR %	R	RBI	BB	SO	SB	BA	SA	PH AB	PH H	G by POS
1931 PIT N	44	167	50	12	4	0	0.0	22	24	13	24	10	.299	.419	0	0	2B-44, SS-1
1932	154	574	162	25	8	7	1.2	66	85	46	56	19	.282	.390	0	0	2B-154
1933	107	362	117	21	5	1	0.3	45	42	19	28	12	.323	.417	0	0	2B-97
1934 CIN N	106	421	109	20	5	1	0.2	58	38	23	44	6	.259	.337	9	2	3B-51, 2B-49
1935 2 teams		CIN	N (6G – .200)			CHI	A (77G – .298)										
" total	83	297	88	18	5	3	1.0	49	29	33	27	2	.296	.421	1	0	2B-59, 3B-17, OF-1
1936 CHI A	109	352	96	15	2	7	2.0	69	42	66	48	15	.273	.386	7	1	2B-68, 3B-32
1937	100	332	78	15	1	4	1.2	34	38	32	36	14	.235	.322	1	1	3B-86, 2B-13
1938 DET A	41	80	17	6	0	0	0.0	9	14	15	11	2	.213	.288	17	5	3B-18, 2B-1
8 yrs.	744	2585	717	132	30	23	0.9	352	312	247	274	80	.277	.378	39	11	2B-485, 3B-204, OF-1, SS-1

Sandy Piez

PIEZ, CHARLES WILLIAM
B. Oct. 13, 1888, New York, N. Y.   D. Dec. 29, 1930, Atlantic City, N. J.   BR TR 5'10"   170 lbs.

	G	AB	H	2B	3B	HR	HR %	R	RBI	BB	SO	SB	BA	SA	PH AB	PH H	G by POS
1914 NY N	35	8	3	0	1	0	0.0	9	3	1	4		.375	.625	0	0	OF-4

Joe Pignatano

PIGNATANO, JOSEPH BENJAMIN
B. Aug. 4, 1929, Brooklyn, N. Y.   BR TR 5'10"   180 lbs.

	G	AB	H	2B	3B	HR	HR %	R	RBI	BB	SO	SB	BA	SA	PH AB	PH H	G by POS
1957 BKN N	8	14	3	1	0	0	0.0	0	1	0	5	0	.214	.286	0	0	C-6
1958 LA N	63	142	31	4	0	9	6.3	18	17	16	26	4	.218	.437	3	0	C-57
1959	52	139	33	4	1	1	0.7	17	11	21	15	1	.237	.302	0	0	C-49
1960	58	90	21	4	0	2	2.2	11	9	15	17	1	.233	.344	5	3	C-40
1961 KC A	92	243	59	10	3	4	1.6	31	22	36	42	2	.243	.358	7	1	C-83, 3B-2
1962 2 teams		SF	N (7G – .200)			NY	N (27G – .232)										
" total	34	61	14	2	0	0	0.0	4	2	6	11	0	.230	.262	5	0	C-32
6 yrs.	307	689	161	25	4	16	2.3	81	62	94	116	8	.234	.351	20	4	C-267, 3B-2
WORLD SERIES																	
1959 LA N	1	0	0	0	0	0	–	0	0	0	0	0	–	–	0	0	C-1

	G	AB	H	2B	3B	HR	HR%	R	RBI	BB	SO	SB	BA	SA	Pinch Hit AB	Pinch Hit H	G by POS

Jay Pike

PIKE, JACOB EMANUEL
Brother of Lip Pike.
B. Brooklyn, N. Y.   Deceased.

	G	AB	H	2B	3B	HR	HR%	R	RBI	BB	SO	SB	BA	SA	PH AB	PH H	G by POS
1877 HAR N	1	4	1	0	0	0	0.0	0	0	0	0		.250	.250	0	0	OF-1

Jess Pike

BL TL 6'3"   175 lbs.

PIKE, JESS WILLARD
B. July 31, 1915, Dustin, Okla.   D. Mar. 28, 1984, San Diego, Calif.

	G	AB	H	2B	3B	HR	HR%	R	RBI	BB	SO	SB	BA	SA	PH AB	PH H	G by POS
1946 NY N	16	41	7	1	1	1	2.4	4	6	6	9	0	.171	.317	4	0	OF-10

Lip Pike

BL TL 5'8"   158 lbs.

PIKE, LIPMAN EMANUEL
Brother of Jay Pike.
B. May 25, 1845, New York, N. Y.   D. Oct. 10, 1893, Brooklyn, N. Y.
Manager 1871, 1874, 1877.

	G	AB	H	2B	3B	HR	HR%	R	RBI	BB	SO	SB	BA	SA	PH AB	PH H	G by POS
1876 STL N	63	282	91	19	10	1	0.4	55	50	8	9		.323	.472	0	0	OF-62, 2B-2
1877 CIN N	58	262	78	12	4	4	1.5	45	23	9	7		.298	.420	0	0	OF-38, 2B-22, SS-2
1878 2 teams	CIN	N (31G –	.324)		PRO	N	(5G –	.227)									
" total	36	167	52	5	2	0	0.0	32	15	5	10		.311	.365	0	0	OF-31, 2B-5
1881 WOR N	5	18	2	0	0	0	0.0	1	0	4	3		.111	.111	0	0	OF-5
1887 NY AA	1	4	0	0	0	0	0.0	0		0		0	.000	.000	0	0	OF-1
5 yrs.	163	733	223	36	16	5	0.7	133	88	26	29	0	.304	.417	0	0	OF-137, 2B-29, SS-2

Al Pilarcik

BL TL 5'10"   180 lbs.

PILARCIK, ALFRED JAMES
B. July 3, 1930, Whiting, Ind.

	G	AB	H	2B	3B	HR	HR%	R	RBI	BB	SO	SB	BA	SA	PH AB	PH H	G by POS
1956 KC A	69	239	60	10	1	4	1.7	28	22	30	32	9	.251	.351	4	1	OF-67
1957 BAL A	142	407	113	16	3	9	2.2	52	49	53	28	14	.278	.398	15	3	OF-126
1958	141	379	92	21	0	1	0.3	40	24	42	37	7	.243	.306	24	7	OF-118
1959	130	273	77	12	1	3	1.1	37	16	30	25	9	.282	.366	21	7	OF-106
1960	104	194	48	5	1	4	2.1	30	17	15	16	0	.247	.345	23	6	OF-75
1961 2 teams	KC	A (35G –	.200)		CHI	A	(47G –	.177)									
" total	82	122	23	2	1	1	0.8	18	15	15	12	2	.189	.246	28	6	OF-38
6 yrs.	668	1614	413	66	7	22	1.4	205	143	185	150	41	.256	.346	115	30	OF-530

Andy Pilney

BR TR 5'11"   174 lbs.

PILNEY, ANTONE JAMES
B. Jan. 19, 1913, Frontenac, Kans.

	G	AB	H	2B	3B	HR	HR%	R	RBI	BB	SO	SB	BA	SA	PH AB	PH H	G by POS
1936 BOS N	3	2	0	0	0	0	0.0	0	0	0	1	0	.000	.000	2	0	

George Pinckney

BR TR

PINCKNEY, GEORGE BURTON
B. Jan. 11, 1862, Peoria, Ill.   D. Nov. 9, 1926, Peoria, Ill.

	G	AB	H	2B	3B	HR	HR%	R	RBI	BB	SO	SB	BA	SA	PH AB	PH H	G by POS
1884 CLE N	36	144	45	9	0	0	0.0	18	16	10	7		.313	.375	0	0	2B-25, SS-11
1885 BKN AA	110	447	124	16	5	0	0.0	77		27			.277	.336	0	0	2B-57, 3B-51, SS-3
1886	141	597	156	22	7	0	0.0	119		70			.261	.322	0	0	3B-141, P-1
1887	138	580	155	26	6	3	0.5	133		61		59	.267	.348	0	0	3B-136, SS-2
1888	143	575	156	18	8	4	0.7	134	52	66		51	.271	.351	0	0	3B-143
1889	138	545	134	25	7	4	0.7	103	82	59	43	47	.246	.339	0	0	3B-138
1890 BKN N	126	485	150	20	9	7	1.4	115	83	80	19	47	.309	.431	0	0	3B-126
1891	135	501	137	19	6	2	0.4	80	71	66	32	44	.273	.347	0	0	3B-130, SS-5
1892 STL N	78	290	50	3	2	0	0.0	31	25	36	26	4	.172	.197	0	0	3B-78
1893 LOU N	118	446	105	12	6	1	0.2	64	62	50	8	12	.235	.296	0	0	3B-118
10 yrs.	1163	4610	1212	170	56	21	0.5	874	391	525	135	264	.263	.338	0	0	3B-1061, 2B-82, SS-21, P-1

Babe Pinelli

BR TR 5'9"   165 lbs.

PINELLI, RALPH ARTHUR
Born Rinaldo Angelo Paolinelli.
B. Oct. 18, 1895, San Francisco, Calif.   D. Oct. 22, 1984, Daly City, Calif.

	G	AB	H	2B	3B	HR	HR%	R	RBI	BB	SO	SB	BA	SA	PH AB	PH H	G by POS
1918 CHI A	24	78	18	1	1	1	1.3	7	7	7	8	3	.231	.308	0	0	3B-24
1920 DET A	102	284	65	9	3	0	0.0	33	21	25	16	6	.229	.282	4	0	3B-74, SS-18, 2B-1
1922 CIN N	156	547	167	19	7	1	0.2	77	72	48	37	17	.305	.371	0	0	3B-156
1923	117	423	117	14	5	0	0.0	44	51	27	29	10	.277	.333	0	0	3B-116
1924	144	510	156	16	7	0	0.0	61	70	32	32	23	.306	.365	1	1	3B-143
1925	130	492	139	33	6	2	0.4	68	49	22	28	8	.283	.386	2	3	3B-109, SS-17
1926	71	207	46	7	4	0	0.0	26	24	15	5	2	.222	.295	3	1	3B-40, SS-27, 2B-3
1927	30	76	15	2	0	1	1.3	11	4	6	7	2	.197	.263	0	0	3B-15, DH-9, 2B-5
8 yrs.	774	2617	723	101	33	5	0.2	327	298	182	162	71	.276	.346	14	4	3B-677, SS-71, 2B-9

Lou Piniella

BR TR 6'   182 lbs.

PINIELLA, LOUIS VICTOR
B. Aug. 28, 1943, Tampa, Fla.

	G	AB	H	2B	3B	HR	HR%	R	RBI	BB	SO	SB	BA	SA	PH AB	PH H	G by POS
1964 BAL A	4	1	0	0	0	0	0.0	0	0	0	0	0	.000	.000	1	0	
1968 CLE A	6	5	0	0	0	0	0.0	1	1	0	0	0	.000	.000	2	0	OF-2
1969 KC A	135	493	139	21	6	11	2.2	43	68	33	56	2	.282	.416	9	3	OF-129
1970	144	542	163	24	5	11	2.0	54	88	35	42	3	.301	.424	4	1	OF-139, 1B-1
1971	126	448	125	21	5	3	0.7	43	51	21	43	5	.279	.368	13	3	OF-115
1972	151	574	179	33	4	11	1.9	65	72	34	59	7	.312	.441	1	0	OF-150
1973	144	513	128	28	1	9	1.8	53	69	30	65	5	.250	.361	7	1	OF-128, DH-9
1974 NY A	140	518	158	26	0	9	1.7	71	70	32	58	1	.305	.407	2	0	OF-130, DH-6, 1B-1
1975	74	199	39	4	1	0	0.0	7	22	16	22	0	.196	.226	19	4	OF-46, DH-38
1976	100	327	92	16	6	3	0.9	36	38	18	34	0	.281	.394	14	4	OF-49, DH-38
1977	103	339	112	19	3	12	3.5	47	45	20	31	2	.330	.510	11	2	OF-51, DH-43, 1B-1
1978	130	472	148	34	5	6	1.3	67	69	34	36	3	.314	.445	9	4	OF-103, DH-23
1979	130	461	137	22	2	11	2.4	49	69	17	31	3	.297	.425	12	6	OF-112, DH-16
1980	116	321	92	18	0	2	0.6	39	27	29	20	0	.287	.361	24	7	OF-104, DH-7
1981	60	159	44	9	0	5	3.1	16	18	13	9	0	.277	.428	9	1	OF-36, DH-19
1982	102	261	80	17	1	6	2.3	33	37	18	18	0	.307	.448	25	9	DH-55, OF-40
1983	53	148	43	9	1	2	1.4	19	16	11	12	1	.291	.405	10	3	OF-43, DH-1
1984	29	86	26	4	1	1	1.2	8	6	7	5	0	.302	.407	3	0	OF-24, DH-2
18 yrs.	1747	5867	1705	305	41	102	1.7	651	766	368	541	32	.291	.409	175	46	OF-1401, DH-231, 1B-3

DIVISIONAL PLAYOFF SERIES

	G	AB	H	2B	3B	HR	HR%	R	RBI	BB	SO	SB	BA	SA	PH AB	PH H	G by POS
1981 NY A	4	10	2	1	0	1	10.0	1	3	0	0	0	.200	.600	2	1	DH-4

	G	AB	H	2B	3B	HR	HR %	R	RBI	BB	SO	SB	BA	SA	Pinch Hit AB	Pinch Hit H	G by POS

Lou Piniella continued

LEAGUE CHAMPIONSHIP SERIES

	G	AB	H	2B	3B	HR	HR%	R	RBI	BB	SO	SB	BA	SA	AB	H	G by POS
1976 NY A	4	11	3	1	0	0	0.0	1	0	0	1	0	.273	.364	1	0	DH-3
1977	5	21	7	3	0	0	0.0	1	2	0	1	0	.333	.476	0	0	OF-4
1978	4	17	4	0	0	0	0.0	2	0	0	3	0	.235	.235	0	0	OF-4
1980	2	5	1	0	0	1	20.0	1	1	2	1	0	.200	.800	0	0	OF-2
1981	3	5	3	0	0	1	20.0	2	3	0	0	0	.600	1.200	2	1	OF-1
5 yrs.	18	59	18	4	0	2	3.4	7	6	2	6	0	.305	.475	3	2	OF-11, DH-3

WORLD SERIES

	G	AB	H	2B	3B	HR	HR%	R	RBI	BB	SO	SB	BA	SA	AB	H	G by POS
1976 NY A	4	9	3	1	0	0	0.0	1	0	0	0	0	.333	.444	2	0	OF-2
1977	6	22	6	0	0	0	0.0	1	3	0	3	0	.273	.273	0	0	OF-6
1978	6	25	7	0	0	0	0.0	3	4	0	0	1	.280	.280	0	0	OF-6
1981	6	16	7	1	0	0	0.0	2	3	0	1	1	.438	.500	3	2	OF-3
4 yrs.	22	72	23	2	0	0	0.0	7	10	0	4	2	.319	.347	5	2	OF-17

Vada Pinson

PINSON, VADA EDWARD
B. Aug. 8, 1938, Memphis, Tenn.　　　　BL TL 5'11"　170 lbs.

	G	AB	H	2B	3B	HR	HR%	R	RBI	BB	SO	SB	BA	SA	AB	H	G by POS
1958 CIN N	27	96	26	7	0	1	1.0	20	8	11	18	2	.271	.375	0	0	OF-27
1959	154	648	205	47	9	20	3.1	131	84	55	98	21	.316	.509	0	0	OF-154
1960	154	652	187	37	12	20	3.1	107	61	47	96	32	.287	.472	0	0	OF-154
1961	154	607	208	34	8	16	2.6	101	87	39	63	23	.343	.504	1	1	OF-153
1962	155	619	181	31	7	23	3.7	107	100	45	68	26	.292	.477	3	1	OF-152
1963	162	652	204	37	14	22	3.4	96	106	36	80	27	.313	.514	0	0	OF-162
1964	156	625	166	23	11	23	3.7	99	84	42	99	8	.266	.448	1	0	OF-156
1965	159	669	204	34	10	22	3.3	97	94	43	81	21	.305	.484	0	0	OF-159
1966	156	618	178	35	6	16	2.6	70	76	33	83	18	.288	.442	3	2	OF-154
1967	158	650	187	28	13	18	2.8	90	66	26	86	26	.288	.454	2	0	OF-157
1968	130	499	135	29	6	5	1.0	60	48	32	59	17	.271	.383	10	2	OF-123
1969 STL N	132	495	126	22	6	10	2.0	58	70	35	63	4	.255	.384	8	1	OF-124
1970 CLE A	148	574	164	28	6	24	4.2	74	82	28	69	7	.286	.481	8	1	OF-141, 1B-7
1971	146	566	149	23	4	11	1.9	60	35	21	58	25	.263	.376	7	2	OF-141, 1B-3
1972 CAL A	136	484	133	24	2	7	1.4	56	49	30	54	17	.275	.376	7	1	OF-134, 1B-1
1973	124	466	121	14	6	8	1.7	56	57	20	55	5	.260	.367	4	1	OF-120
1974 KC A	115	406	112	18	2	6	1.5	46	41	21	45	21	.276	.374	9	3	OF-110, DH-2, 1B-1
1975	103	319	71	14	5	4	1.3	38	22	10	21	5	.223	.335	17	2	OF-82, DH-5, 1B-4
18 yrs.	2469	9645	2757	485	127	256	2.7	1366	1170	574	1196	305	.286	.442	80	17	OF-2403, 1B-16, DH-7

WORLD SERIES

	G	AB	H	2B	3B	HR	HR%	R	RBI	BB	SO	SB	BA	SA	AB	H	G by POS
1961 CIN N	5	22	2	1	0	0	0.0	0	0	0	1	0	.091	.136	0	0	OF-5

Wally Pipp

PIPP, WALTER CLEMENT
B. Feb. 17, 1893, Chicago, Ill.　　D. Jan. 11, 1965, Grand Rapids, Mich.　　BL TL 6'1"　180 lbs.

	G	AB	H	2B	3B	HR	HR%	R	RBI	BB	SO	SB	BA	SA	AB	H	G by POS
1913 DET A	12	31	5	0	3	0	0.0	3	5	2	6	0	.161	.355	2	0	1B-10
1915 NY A	136	479	118	20	13	4	0.8	59	60	66	81	18	.246	.367	2	2	1B-134
1916	151	545	143	20	14	12	2.2	70	93	54	82	16	.262	.417	1	1	1B-148
1917	155	587	143	29	12	9	1.5	82	70	60	66	11	.244	.380	0	0	1B-155
1918	91	349	106	15	9	2	0.6	48	44	22	34	11	.304	.415	0	0	1B-91
1919	138	523	144	23	10	7	1.3	74	50	39	42	9	.275	.398	0	0	1B-138
1920	153	610	171	30	14	11	1.8	109	76	48	54	4	.280	.430	0	0	1B-153
1921	153	588	174	35	9	8	1.4	96	97	45	28	17	.296	.427	0	0	1B-153
1922	152	577	190	32	10	9	1.6	96	90	56	32	7	.329	.466	0	0	1B-152
1923	144	569	173	19	8	6	1.1	79	108	36	28	6	.304	.397	0	0	1B-144
1924	153	589	174	30	19	9	1.5	88	113	51	36	12	.295	.457	0	0	1B-153
1925	62	178	41	6	3	3	1.7	19	24	13	12	3	.230	.348	9	0	1B-47
1926 CIN N	155	574	167	22	15	6	1.0	72	99	49	26	8	.291	.413	0	0	1B-155
1927	122	443	115	19	6	2	0.5	49	41	32	11	7	.260	.343	3	1	1B-114
1928	95	272	77	11	3	2	0.7	30	26	23	13	1	.283	.368	20	6	1B-72
15 yrs.	1872	6914	1941	311	148	90	1.3	974	996	596	551	125	.281	.408	41	12	1B-1819

WORLD SERIES

	G	AB	H	2B	3B	HR	HR%	R	RBI	BB	SO	SB	BA	SA	AB	H	G by POS
1921 NY A	8	26	4	1	0	0	0.0	1	2	2	3	1	.154	.192	0	0	1B-8
1922	5	21	6	1	0	0	0.0	0	3	0	2	1	.286	.333	0	0	1B-5
1923	6	20	5	0	0	0	0.0	2	2	4	1	0	.250	.250	0	0	1B-6
3 yrs.	19	67	15	2	0	0	0.0	3	7	6	6	2	.224	.254	0	0	1B-19

Jim Pisoni

PISONI, JAMES PETE
B. Aug. 14, 1929, St. Louis, Mo.　　　BR TR 5'10"　169 lbs.

	G	AB	H	2B	3B	HR	HR%	R	RBI	BB	SO	SB	BA	SA	AB	H	G by POS
1953 STL A	3	12	1	0	0	1	8.3	1	1	1	5	0	.083	.333	0	0	OF-3
1956 KC A	10	30	8	0	0	2	6.7	4	5	2	8	0	.267	.467	1	0	OF-9
1957	44	97	23	2	2	3	3.1	14	12	10	17	0	.237	.392	0	0	OF-44
1959 2 teams	MIL	N (9G –	.167)		NY	A	(17G –	.176)									
" total	26	41	7	1	1	0	0.0	6	1	3	15	0	.171	.244	1	0	OF-24
1960 NY A	20	9	1	0	0	0	0.0	1	1	1	2	0	.111	.111	0	0	OF-18
5 yrs.	103	189	40	3	3	6	3.2	26	20	16	47	0	.212	.354	2	0	OF-98

Alex Pitko

PITKO, ALEXANDER (Spunk)
B. Nov. 22, 1914, Burlington, N. J.　　　BR TR 5'10"　180 lbs.

	G	AB	H	2B	3B	HR	HR%	R	RBI	BB	SO	SB	BA	SA	AB	H	G by POS
1938 PHI N	7	19	6	1	0	0	0.0	2	2	3	3	1	.316	.368	0	0	OF-7
1939 WAS A	4	8	1	0	0	0	0.0	0	1	1	3	0	.125	.125	1	0	OF-3
2 yrs.	11	27	7	1	0	0	0.0	2	3	4	6	1	.259	.296	1	0	OF-10

Jake Pitler

PITLER, JACOB ALBERT
B. Apr. 22, 1894, New York, N. Y.　　D. Feb. 3, 1968, Binghamton, N. Y.　　BR TR 5'8"　150 lbs.

	G	AB	H	2B	3B	HR	HR%	R	RBI	BB	SO	SB	BA	SA	AB	H	G by POS
1917 PIT N	109	382	89	8	5	0	0.0	39	23	30	24	6	.233	.280	0	0	2B-106, OF-3
1918	2	1	0	0	0	0	0.0	1	0	1	0	2	.000	.000	0	0	2B-1
2 yrs.	111	383	89	8	5	0	0.0	40	23	31	24	8	.232	.279	0	0	2B-107, OF-3

	G	AB	H	2B	3B	HR	HR %	R	RBI	BB	SO	SB	BA	SA	Pinch Hit AB	Pinch Hit H	G by POS

Pinky Pittenger

PITTENGER, CLARKE ALONZO — BR TR 5'10" 160 lbs.
B. Feb. 24, 1899, Hudson, Mich.   D. Nov. 4, 1977, Ft. Lauderdale, Fla.

	G	AB	H	2B	3B	HR	HR %	R	RBI	BB	SO	SB	BA	SA	AB	H	G by POS
1921 BOS A	40	91	18	1	0	0	0.0	6	5	4	13	3	.198	.209	6	1	OF-27, 3B-3, SS-2, 2B-1
1922	66	186	48	3	0	0	0.0	16	7	9	10	2	.258	.274	1	0	3B-31, SS-29
1923	60	177	38	5	0	0	0.0	15	15	5	10	3	.215	.243	2	0	2B-42, SS-10, 3B-3
1925 CHI N	59	173	54	7	2	0	0.0	21	15	12	7	5	.312	.376	6	1	SS-24, 3B-24
1927 CIN N	31	84	23	5	0	1	1.2	17	10	2	5	4	.274	.369	0	0	2B-20, SS-9, 3B-2
1928	40	38	9	0	1	0	0.0	12	4	0	1	2	.237	.289	3	0	SS-12, 3B-4, 2B-4
1929	77	210	62	11	0	0	0.0	31	27	5	4	8	.295	.348	0	0	SS-50, 3B-8, 2B-4
7 yrs.	373	959	252	32	3	1	0.1	118	83	37	50	27	.263	.306	18	2	SS-136, 3B-75, 2B-71, OF-27

Joe Pittman

PITTMAN, JOSEPH WAYNE — BR TR 6'1" 180 lbs.
B. Jan., 1954, Houston, Tex.

	G	AB	H	2B	3B	HR	HR %	R	RBI	BB	SO	SB	BA	SA	AB	H	G by POS
1981 HOU N	52	135	38	4	2	0	0.0	11	7	11	16	4	.281	.341	16	4	2B-35, 3B-4
1982 2 teams		HOU N (15G – .200)				SD N (55G – .254)											
" total	70	128	32	3	0	0	0.0	16	7	9	15	8	.250	.273	15	2	2B-30, SS-13, 3B-3, OF-1
1984 SF N	17	22	5	0	0	0	0.0	2	2	0	6	1	.227	.227	3	0	SS-6, 2B-5, 3B-2
3 yrs.	139	285	75	7	2	0	0.0	29	16	20	37	13	.263	.302	34	6	2B-70, SS-19, 3B-9, OF-1
DIVISIONAL PLAYOFF SERIES																	
1981 HOU N	2	2	0	0	0	0	0.0	0	0	0	0	0	.000	.000	2	0	

Gaylen Pitts

PITTS, GAYLEN RICHARD — BR TR 6'1" 175 lbs.
B. June 6, 1946, Wichita, Kans.

	G	AB	H	2B	3B	HR	HR %	R	RBI	BB	SO	SB	BA	SA	AB	H	G by POS
1974 OAK A	18	41	10	3	0	0	0.0	4	3	5	4	0	.244	.317	1	1	3B-11, 2B-6, 1B-1
1975	10	3	1	1	0	0	0.0	1	1	0	0	0	.333	.667	0	0	3B-6, SS-2, 2B-1
2 yrs.	28	44	11	4	0	0	0.0	5	4	5	4	0	.250	.341	1	1	3B-17, 2B-7, SS-2, 1B-1

Herman Pitz

PITZ, HERMAN
B. July 18, 1865, Brooklyn, N. Y.   D. Sept. 3, 1924, Far Rockaway, N. Y.

	G	AB	H	2B	3B	HR	HR %	R	RBI	BB	SO	SB	BA	SA	AB	H	G by POS
1890 2 teams		B-B AA (61G – .138)				SYR AA (29G – .221)											
" total	90	284	47	0	0	0	0.0	43			58		39	.165	.165	0	0	C-61, 3B-16, OF-10, SS-3, 2B-1

Don Plarski

PLARSKI, DONALD JOSEPH — BR TR 5'6" 160 lbs.
B. Nov. 9, 1929, Chicago, Ill.   D. Dec. 29, 1981, St. Louis, Mo.

	G	AB	H	2B	3B	HR	HR %	R	RBI	BB	SO	SB	BA	SA	AB	H	G by POS
1955 KC A	8	11	1	0	0	0	0.0	0	0	0	2	1	.091	.091	1	0	OF-6

Elmo Plaskett

PLASKETT, ELMO ALEXANDER — BR TR 5'10" 195 lbs.
B. June 27, 1938, Frederiksted, Virgin Islands

	G	AB	H	2B	3B	HR	HR %	R	RBI	BB	SO	SB	BA	SA	AB	H	G by POS
1962 PIT N	7	14	4	0	0	1	7.1	2	3	1	3	0	.286	.500	4	0	C-4
1963	10	21	3	0	0	0	0.0	1	2	0	5	0	.143	.143	5	1	C-5, 3B-1
2 yrs.	17	35	7	0	0	1	2.9	3	5	1	8	0	.200	.286	9	1	C-9, 3B-1

Whitey Platt

PLATT, MIZELL GEORGE — BR TR 6'1½" 190 lbs.
B. Aug. 21, 1920, West Palm Beach, Fla.   D. July 27, 1970, West Palm Beach, Fla.

	G	AB	H	2B	3B	HR	HR %	R	RBI	BB	SO	SB	BA	SA	AB	H	G by POS
1942 CHI N	4	16	1	0	0	0	0.0	1	2	0	3	0	.063	.063	0	0	OF-4
1943	20	41	7	3	0	0	0.0	2	2	1	7	0	.171	.244	4	1	OF-14
1946 CHI A	84	247	62	8	5	3	1.2	28	32	17	34	1	.251	.360	24	6	OF-61
1948 STL A	123	454	123	22	10	7	1.5	57	82	39	51	1	.271	.410	8	2	OF-114
1949	102	244	63	8	2	3	1.2	29	29	24	27	0	.258	.344	34	7	OF-59, 1B-2
5 yrs.	333	1002	256	41	17	13	1.3	117	147	81	122	2	.255	.369	70	16	OF-252, 1B-2

Al Platte

PLATTE, ALFRED JOSEPH — BL TL 5'11" 165 lbs.
B. Apr. 13, 1890, Grand Rapids, Mich.   D. Aug. 29, 1976, Grand Rapids, Mich.

	G	AB	H	2B	3B	HR	HR %	R	RBI	BB	SO	SB	BA	SA	AB	H	G by POS
1913 DET A	7	18	2	1	0	0	0.0	1	0	1	1	0	.111	.167	2	0	OF-5

Rance Pless

PLESS, RANCE — BR TR 6' 195 lbs.
B. Dec. 6, 1925, Greeneville, Tenn.

	G	AB	H	2B	3B	HR	HR %	R	RBI	BB	SO	SB	BA	SA	AB	H	G by POS
1956 KC A	48	85	23	3	1	0	0.0	4	9	10	13	0	.271	.329	26	7	1B-15, 3B-5

Herb Plews

PLEWS, HERBERT EUGENE — BL TR 5'11" 160 lbs.
B. June 14, 1928, Helena, Mont.

	G	AB	H	2B	3B	HR	HR %	R	RBI	BB	SO	SB	BA	SA	AB	H	G by POS
1956 WAS A	91	256	69	10	7	1	0.4	24	25	26	40	1	.270	.375	24	4	2B-66, SS-5, 3B-2
1957	104	329	89	19	4	1	0.3	51	26	28	39	0	.271	.362	25	5	2B-79, 3B-11, SS-4
1958	111	380	98	12	6	2	0.5	46	29	17	45	2	.258	.337	22	4	2B-64, 3B-36
1959 2 teams		WAS A (27G – .225)				BOS A (13G – .083)											
" total	40	52	10	1	0	0	0.0	4	2	3	9	0	.192	.212	32	7	2B-8
4 yrs.	346	1017	266	42	17	4	0.4	125	82	74	133	3	.262	.348	103	20	2B-217, 3B-49, SS-9

Walter Plock

PLOCK, WALTER S. — 6'3"
B. July 2, 1869, Philadelphia, Pa.   D. Apr. 28, 1900, Richmond, Va.

	G	AB	H	2B	3B	HR	HR %	R	RBI	BB	SO	SB	BA	SA	AB	H	G by POS
1891 PHI N	2	5	2	0	0	0	0.0	2	0	0	1	0	.400	.400	0	0	OF-2

Bill Plummer

PLUMMER, WILLIAM FRANCIS — BR TR 6'1" 190 lbs.
B. Mar. 21, 1947, Anderson, Calif.

	G	AB	H	2B	3B	HR	HR %	R	RBI	BB	SO	SB	BA	SA	AB	H	G by POS
1968 CHI N	2	2	0	0	0	0	0.0	0	0	0	1	0	.000	.000	1	0	C-1
1970 CIN N	4	8	1	0	0	0	0.0	0	0	0	2	0	.125	.125	0	0	C-4
1971	10	19	0	0	0	0	0.0	0	0	0	4	0	.000	.000	3	0	C-4, 3B-2
1972	38	102	19	4	0	2	2.0	8	9	4	20	0	.186	.284	0	0	C-35, 3B-1, 1B-1
1973	50	119	18	2	0	2	1.7	8	11	18	26	1	.151	.227	2	0	C-42, 1B-5
1974	50	120	27	7	0	1	1.7	7	10	6	21	1	.225	.333	1	0	C-49, 3B-1
1975	65	159	29	7	0	1	0.6	17	19	24	28	1	.182	.245	4	1	C-63
1976	56	153	38	6	1	4	2.6	16	19	14	36	0	.248	.379	3	2	C-54
1977	51	117	16	5	0	1	0.9	10	7	17	34	1	.137	.205	2	0	C-50

	G	AB	H	2B	3B	HR	HR %	R	RBI	BB	SO	SB	BA	SA	Pinch Hit AB	Pinch Hit H	G by POS

Bill Plummer continued

	G	AB	H	2B	3B	HR	HR%	R	RBI	BB	SO	SB	BA	SA	PH AB	PH H	G by POS
1978 SEA A	41	93	20	5	0	2	2.2	6	7	12	19	0	.215	.333	1	0	C-40
10 yrs.	367	892	168	37	1	14	1.6	72	82	95	191	4	.188	.279	17	3	C-342, 3B-9, 1B-1

Biff Pocoroba

POCOROBA, BIFF BENEDICT   BB TR 5'10"   175 lbs.
B. July 25, 1953, Burbank, Calif.

	G	AB	H	2B	3B	HR	HR%	R	RBI	BB	SO	SB	BA	SA	PH AB	PH H	G by POS
1975 ATL N	67	188	48	7	1	1	0.5	15	22	20	11	0	.255	.319	8	3	C-62
1976	54	174	42	7	0	0	0.0	16	14	19	12	1	.241	.282	2	0	C-54
1977	113	321	93	24	1	8	2.5	46	44	57	27	3	.290	.445	20	3	C-100
1978	92	289	70	8	0	6	2.1	21	34	29	14	0	.242	.332	13	2	C-79
1979	28	38	12	4	0	0	0.0	6	4	7	0	1	.316	.421	16	6	C-7
1980	70	83	22	4	0	2	2.4	7	8	11	11	1	.265	.386	53	15	C-10
1981	57	122	22	4	0	0	0.0	4	8	12	15	0	.180	.213	26	4	3B-21, C-9
1982	56	120	33	7	0	2	1.7	5	22	13	12	0	.275	.383	17	4	C-36, 3B-2
1983	55	120	32	6	0	2	1.7	11	16	12	7	0	.267	.367	20	1	C-34
1984	4	2	0	0	0	0	0.0	1	0	2	0	0	.000	.000	2	0	
10 yrs.	596	1457	374	71	2	21	1.4	132	172	182	109	6	.257	.351	177	38	C-391, 3B-23

LEAGUE CHAMPIONSHIP SERIES

	G	AB	H	2B	3B	HR	HR%	R	RBI	BB	SO	SB	BA	SA	PH AB	PH H	G by POS
1982 ATL N	1	1	0	0	0	0	0.0	0	0	0	0	0	.000	.000	1	0	

Mike Poepping

POEPPING, MICHAEL HAROLD   BR TR 6'6"   230 lbs.
B. Aug. 7, 1950, Little Falls, Minn.

	G	AB	H	2B	3B	HR	HR%	R	RBI	BB	SO	SB	BA	SA	PH AB	PH H	G by POS
1975 MIN A	14	37	5	1	0	0	0.0	0	1	5	7	0	.135	.162	1	0	OF-13

Jimmy Pofahl

POFAHL, JAMES WILLARD   BR TR 5'11"   173 lbs.
B. June 18, 1917, Faribault, Minn.

	G	AB	H	2B	3B	HR	HR%	R	RBI	BB	SO	SB	BA	SA	PH AB	PH H	G by POS
1940 WAS A	119	406	95	23	5	2	0.5	34	36	37	55	2	.234	.330	2	0	SS-112, 2B-4
1941	22	75	14	3	2	0	0.0	9	6	10	11	1	.187	.280	0	0	SS-21
1942	84	283	59	7	2	0	0.0	22	28	29	30	4	.208	.247	6	2	SS-49, 2B-15, 3B-1a
3 yrs.	225	764	168	33	9	2	0.3	65	70	76	96	7	.220	.295	8	2	SS-182, 2B-19, 3B-14

John Poff

POFF, JOHN WILLIAM   BL TL 6'2"   190 lbs.
B. Oct. 23, 1952, Chillicothe, Ohio

	G	AB	H	2B	3B	HR	HR%	R	RBI	BB	SO	SB	BA	SA	PH AB	PH H	G by POS
1979 PHI N	12	19	2	1	0	0	0.0	2	1	1	4	0	.105	.158	6	0	OF-4, 1B-1
1980 MIL A	19	68	17	1	2	1	1.5	7	7	3	7	0	.250	.368	2	1	DH-7, OF-7, 1B-3
2 yrs.	31	87	19	2	2	1	1.1	9	8	4	11	0	.218	.322	8	1	OF-11, DH-7, 1B-4

Aaron Pointer

POINTER, AARON ELTON (Hawk)   BR TR 6'2"   185 lbs.
B. Apr. 19, 1942, Little Rock, Ark.

	G	AB	H	2B	3B	HR	HR%	R	RBI	BB	SO	SB	BA	SA	PH AB	PH H	G by POS
1963 HOU N	2	5	1	0	0	0	0.0	0	0	0	1	0	.200	.200	0	0	OF-1
1966	11	26	9	1	0	1	3.8	5	5	5	6	1	.346	.500	1	0	OF-11
1967	27	70	11	4	0	1	1.4	6	10	13	26	1	.157	.257	3	0	OF-22
3 yrs.	40	101	21	5	0	2	2.0	11	15	18	33	2	.208	.317	4	0	OF-34

Hugh Poland

POLAND, HUGH REID   BL TR 5'11½" 185 lbs.
B. Jan. 19, 1913, Tompkinsville, Ky.   D. Mar. 30, 1984, Guthrie, Ky.

	G	AB	H	2B	3B	HR	HR%	R	RBI	BB	SO	SB	BA	SA	PH AB	PH H	G by POS
1943 2 teams	NY N (4G – .083)							BOS N (44G – .191)									
" total	48	153	28	7	1	0	0.0	5	5	5	11	0	.183	.242	5	1	C-42
1944 BOS N	8	23	3	1	0	0	0.0	1	2	0	1	0	.130	.174	2	0	C-6
1946	4	6	1	1	0	0	0.0	0	0	0	0	0	.167	.333	2	1	C-2
1947 2 teams	PHI N (4G – .000)							CIN N (16G – .333)									
" total	20	26	6	1	0	0	0.0	1	2	1	4	0	.231	.269	14	4	C-5
1948 CIN N	3	3	1	0	0	0	0.0	0	0	0	0	0	.333	.333	3	1	
5 yrs.	83	211	39	10	1	0	0.0	7	19	6	16	0	.185	.242	26	7	C-55

Mark Polhemus

POLHEMUS, MARK L. (Humpty Dumpty)   5'6½"   185 lbs.
B. Oct. 4, 1864, Brooklyn, N. Y.   D. Nov. 12, 1923, Lynn, Mass.

	G	AB	H	2B	3B	HR	HR%	R	RBI	BB	SO	SB	BA	SA	PH AB	PH H	G by POS
1887 IND N	20	75	18	1	0	0	0.0	6	8	2	9	4	.240	.253	0	0	OF-20

Nick Polly

POLLY, NICHOLAS JOSEPH   BR TR 5'11"   190 lbs.
Born Nicholas Joseph Polachanin.
B. Apr. 18, 1917, Chicago, Ill.

	G	AB	H	2B	3B	HR	HR%	R	RBI	BB	SO	SB	BA	SA	PH AB	PH H	G by POS
1937 BKN N	10	18	4	0	0	0	0.0	2	2	0	1	0	.222	.222	3	1	3B-7
1945 BOS A	4	7	1	0	0	0	0.0	0	1	0	1	0	.143	.143	2	0	3B-2
2 yrs.	14	25	5	0	0	0	0.0	2	3	0	2	0	.200	.200	5	1	3B-9

Ralph Pond

POND, RALPH BENJAMIN
B. May 4, 1888, Eau Claire, Wis.   D. Sept. 8, 1947, Cleveland, Ohio

	G	AB	H	2B	3B	HR	HR%	R	RBI	BB	SO	SB	BA	SA	PH AB	PH H	G by POS
1910 BOS A	1	4	1	0	0	0	0.0	0	0	0		1	.250	.250	0	0	OF-1

Harlin Pool

POOL, HARLIN WELTY (Samson)   BL TR 5'10"   195 lbs.
B. Mar. 12, 1908, Lakeport, Calif.   D. Feb. 15, 1963, Rodeo, Calif.

	G	AB	H	2B	3B	HR	HR%	R	RBI	BB	SO	SB	BA	SA	PH AB	PH H	G by POS
1934 CIN N	99	358	117	22	5	2	0.6	38	50	17	18	3	.327	.433	6	3	OF-94
1935	28	68	12	6	2	0	0.0	8	11	2	2	0	.176	.324	9	1	OF-18
2 yrs.	127	426	129	28	7	2	0.5	46	61	19	20	3	.303	.415	15	4	OF-112

Jim Poole

POOLE, JAMES RALPH (Easy)   BL TR 6'   175 lbs.
B. May 12, 1895, Taylorsville, N. C.   D. Jan. 2, 1975, Hickory, N. C.

	G	AB	H	2B	3B	HR	HR%	R	RBI	BB	SO	SB	BA	SA	PH AB	PH H	G by POS
1925 PHI A	133	480	143	29	8	5	1.0	65	67	27	37	5	.298	.423	6	2	1B-123
1926	112	361	106	23	5	8	2.2	49	63	23	25	4	.294	.452	9	2	1B-101, OF-1
1927	38	99	22	2	0	0	0.0	4	10	9	6	0	.222	.242	8	0	1B-31
3 yrs.	283	940	271	54	13	13	1.4	118	140	59	68	9	.288	.415	23	4	1B-255, OF-1

	G	AB	H	2B	3B	HR	HR%	R	RBI	BB	SO	SB	BA	SA	Pinch Hit AB	Pinch Hit H	G by POS

Ray Poole

POOLE, RAYMOND HERMAN
B. Jan. 16, 1920, Salisbury, N. C.
BL TR 6' 180 lbs.

	G	AB	H	2B	3B	HR	HR%	R	RBI	BB	SO	SB	BA	SA	PH AB	PH H	G by POS
1941 PHI A	2	2	0	0	0	0	0.0	0	0	0	1	0	.000	.000	2	0	
1947	13	13	3	0	0	0	0.0	1	1	1	4	0	.231	.231	13	3	
2 yrs.	15	15	3	0	0	0	0.0	1	1	1	5	0	.200	.200	15	3	

Tom Poorman

POORMAN, THOMAS IVERSON
B. Oct. 14, 1857, Lock Haven, Pa.   D. Feb. 18, 1905, Lock Haven, Pa.
BL TR 5'10½" 170 lbs.

	G	AB	H	2B	3B	HR	HR%	R	RBI	BB	SO	SB	BA	SA	PH AB	PH H	G by POS
1880 2 teams	BUF	N	(19G –	.157)	CHI	N	(7G –	.200)									
" total	26	95	16	2	2	0	0.0	8	1	0	15		.168	.232	0	0	OF-17, P-13
1884 TOL AA	94	382	89	8	7	0	0.0	56		10			.233	.291	0	0	OF-93, P-1
1885 BOS N	56	227	54	5	3	3	1.3	44	25	7	32		.238	.326	0	0	OF-56
1886	96	371	97	16	6	3	0.8	72	41	19	52		.261	.361	0	0	OF-96
1887 PHI AA	135	585	155	18	19	4	0.7	140		35		88	.265	.381	0	0	OF-135, 2B-2, P-1
1888	97	383	87	16	6	2	0.5	76	44	31		46	.227	.316	0	0	OF-97
6 yrs.	504	2043	498	65	43	12	0.6	396	111	102	99	134	.244	.335	0	0	OF-494, P-15, 2B-2

Dave Pope

POPE, DAVID
B. June 17, 1925, Talladega, Ala.
BL TR 5'10½" 170 lbs.

	G	AB	H	2B	3B	HR	HR%	R	RBI	BB	SO	SB	BA	SA	PH AB	PH H	G by POS
1952 CLE A	12	34	10	1	1	1	2.9	9	4	1	7	0	.294	.471	3	0	OF-10
1954	60	102	30	2	1	4	3.9	21	13	10	22	2	.294	.451	19	5	OF-29
1955 2 teams	CLE	A	(35G –	.298)	BAL	A	(86G –	.248)									
" total	121	326	86	13	4	7	2.1	38	52	28	65	5	.264	.393	31	12	OF-104
1956 2 teams	BAL	A	(12G –	.158)	CLE	A	(25G –	.243)									
" total	37	89	20	3	1	0	0.0	7	4	1	19	0	.225	.281	13	2	OF-22
4 yrs.	230	551	146	19	7	12	2.2	75	73	40	113	7	.265	.390	66	19	OF-165

WORLD SERIES

	G	AB	H	2B	3B	HR	HR%	R	RBI	BB	SO	SB	BA	SA	PH AB	PH H	G by POS
1954 CLE A	3	3	0	0	0	0	0.0	0	0	1	1	0	.000	.000	3	0	OF-2

Paul Popovich

POPOVICH, PAUL EDWARD
B. Aug. 18, 1940, Flemington, W. Va.
BR TR 6' 175 lbs.
BB 1968

	G	AB	H	2B	3B	HR	HR%	R	RBI	BB	SO	SB	BA	SA	PH AB	PH H	G by POS
1964 CHI N	1	1	1	0	0	0	0.0	0	0	0	0	0	1.000	1.000	1	1	
1966	2	6	0	0	0	0	0.0	0	0	0	2	0	.000	.000	0	0	2B-2
1967	49	159	34	4	0	0	0.0	18	2	9	12	0	.214	.239	5	0	SS-31, 2B-17, 3B-2
1968 LA N	134	418	97	8	1	2	0.5	35	25	29	37	1	.232	.270	4	0	2B-89, SS-45, 3B-7
1969 2 teams	LA	N	(28G –	.200)	CHI	N	(60G –	.312)									
" total	88	204	58	6	0	1	0.5	31	18	19	18	0	.284	.328	25	8	2B-48, SS-10, 3B-6, OF-1
1970 CHI N	78	186	47	5	1	4	2.2	22	20	18	18	0	.253	.355	26	2	2B-22, SS-17, 3B-16
1971	89	226	49	7	1	4	1.8	24	28	14	17	0	.217	.310	30	2	2B-40, 3B-16, SS-1
1972	58	129	25	3	2	1	0.8	8	11	12	8	0	.194	.271	12	2	2B-36, SS-8, 3B-1
1973	99	280	66	6	3	2	0.7	24	24	18	27	3	.236	.300	9	1	2B-84, SS-9, 3B-1
1974 PIT N	59	83	18	2	1	0	0.0	9	5	5	10	0	.217	.265	38	9	2B-12, SS-10
1975	25	40	8	1	0	0	0.0	5	1	3	2	0	.200	.225	15	3	SS-8, 2B-8
11 yrs.	682	1732	403	42	9	14	0.8	176	134	127	151	4	.233	.292	165	28	2B-358, SS-139, 3B-49, OF-1

LEAGUE CHAMPIONSHIP SERIES

	G	AB	H	2B	3B	HR	HR%	R	RBI	BB	SO	SB	BA	SA	PH AB	PH H	G by POS
1974 PIT N	3	5	3	0	0	0	0.0	1	0	0	0	0	.600	.600	3	3	SS-3

Tom Poquette

POQUETTE, THOMAS ARTHUR
B. Oct. 30, 1951, Eau Claire, Wis.
BL TR 5'10" 175 lbs.

	G	AB	H	2B	3B	HR	HR%	R	RBI	BB	SO	SB	BA	SA	PH AB	PH H	G by POS
1973 KC A	21	28	6	1	0	0	0.0	4	3	1	4	1	.214	.250	0	0	OF-20
1976	104	344	104	18	10	2	0.6	43	34	29	31	6	.302	.430	7	1	OF-98, DH-2
1977	106	342	100	23	6	2	0.6	43	33	19	21	1	.292	.412	12	1	OF-96
1978	80	204	44	9	2	4	2.0	16	30	14	9	2	.216	.338	21	6	OF-63, DH-1
1979 2 teams	KC	A	(21G –	.192)	BOS	A	(63G –	.331)									
" total	84	180	56	9	0	2	1.1	15	26	9	11	2	.311	.394	28	4	OF-53, DH-4
1981 2 teams	BOS	A	(3G –	.000)	TEX	A	(30G –	.156)									
" total	33	66	10	1	0	0	0.0	2	7	5	1	0	.152	.167	12	3	OF-20
1982 KC A	24	62	9	1	0	0	0.0	4	3	4	5	1	.145	.161	3	0	OF-23
7 yrs.	452	1226	329	62	18	10	0.8	127	136	81	82	13	.268	.373	83	15	OF-373, DH-7

LEAGUE CHAMPIONSHIP SERIES

	G	AB	H	2B	3B	HR	HR%	R	RBI	BB	SO	SB	BA	SA	PH AB	PH H	G by POS
1976 KC A	5	16	3	2	0	0	0.0	1	4	2	3	0	.188	.313	0	0	OF-5
1977	2	6	1	0	0	0	0.0	0	0	0	0	0	.167	.167	0	0	OF-2
1978	1	1	0	0	0	0	0.0	0	0	0	0	0	.000	.000	1	0	OF-7
3 yrs.	8	23	4	2	0	0	0.0	1	4	2	3	0	.174	.261	1	0	OF-7

Bob Porter

PORTER, ROBERT LEE, JR.
B. July 22, 1959, Yuma, Ariz.
BL TL 5'10" 180 lbs.

	G	AB	H	2B	3B	HR	HR%	R	RBI	BB	SO	SB	BA	SA	PH AB	PH H	G by POS
1981 ATL N	17	14	4	1	0	0	0.0	2	4	2	1	0	.286	.357	14	4	OF-4, 1B-1
1982	24	27	3	0	0	0	0.0	1	0	1	9	0	.111	.111	16	1	OF-4, 1B-1
2 yrs.	41	41	7	1	0	0	0.0	3	4	3	10	0	.171	.195	30	5	OF-8, 1B-2

Dan Porter

PORTER, DANIEL EDWARD
B. Oct. 17, 1931, Decatur, Ill.
BL TL 6' 164 lbs.

	G	AB	H	2B	3B	HR	HR%	R	RBI	BB	SO	SB	BA	SA	PH AB	PH H	G by POS
1951 WAS A	13	19	4	0	0	0	0.0	2	0	2	4	0	.211	.211	9	2	OF-3

Darrell Porter

PORTER, DARRELL RAY
B. Jan. 17, 1952, Joplin, Mo.
BL TR 6' 193 lbs.

	G	AB	H	2B	3B	HR	HR%	R	RBI	BB	SO	SB	BA	SA	PH AB	PH H	G by POS
1971 MIL A	22	70	15	2	0	2	2.9	4	9	9	20	2	.214	.329	1	0	C-22
1972	18	56	7	1	0	1	1.8	2	2	5	21	0	.125	.196	0	0	C-18
1973	117	350	89	19	2	16	4.6	50	67	57	85	5	.254	.457	9	4	C-90, DH-19
1974	131	432	104	15	4	12	2.8	59	56	50	88	8	.241	.377	5	1	C-124, DH-2
1975	130	409	95	12	5	18	4.4	66	60	89	77	2	.232	.418	2	0	C-111, DH-2
1976	119	389	81	14	1	5	1.3	43	32	51	61	5	.208	.288	7	1	C-125, DH-1
1977 KC A	130	425	117	21	3	16	3.8	61	60	53	70	1	.275	.452	5	2	C-145, DH-4
1978	150	520	138	27	6	18	3.5	77	78	75	75	0	.265	.444	5	2	C-141, DH-15
1979	157	533	155	23	10	20	3.8	101	112	121	65	3	.291	.484	0	0	C-141, DH-15

	G	AB	H	2B	3B	HR	HR%	R	RBI	BB	SO	SB	BA	SA	Pinch Hit AB	Pinch Hit H	G by POS

Darrell Porter continued

	G	AB	H	2B	3B	HR	HR%	R	RBI	BB	SO	SB	BA	SA	AB	H	G by POS
1980	118	418	104	14	2	7	1.7	51	51	69	50	1	.249	.342	4	0	C-81, DH-34
1981 STL N	61	174	39	10	2	6	3.4	22	31	39	32	1	.224	.408	6	0	C-52
1982	120	373	86	18	5	12	3.2	46	48	66	66	1	.231	.402	8	1	C-111
1983	145	443	116	24	3	15	3.4	57	66	68	94	1	.262	.431	19	6	C-133
1984	127	422	98	16	3	11	2.6	56	68	60	79	5	.232	.363	11	2	C-122
14 yrs.	1545	5014	1244	216	46	159	3.2	695	740	812	883	32	.248	.405	82	19	C-1392, DH-86

LEAGUE CHAMPIONSHIP SERIES

	G	AB	H	2B	3B	HR	HR%	R	RBI	BB	SO	SB	BA	SA	AB	H	G by POS
1977 KC A	5	15	5	0	0	0	0.0	3	0	3	0	0	.333	.333	0	0	C-5
1978	4	14	5	1	0	0	0.0	1	3	2	0	0	.357	.429	0	0	C-4
1980	3	10	1	0	0	0	0.0	2	0	1	0	0	.100	.100	0	0	C-3
1982 STL N	3	9	5	3	0	0	0.0	3	1	5	2	0	.556	.889	0	0	C-3
4 yrs.	15	48	16	4	0	0	0.0	9	4	11	2	0	.333	.417	0	0	C-15

WORLD SERIES

	G	AB	H	2B	3B	HR	HR%	R	RBI	BB	SO	SB	BA	SA	AB	H	G by POS
1980 KC A	5	14	2	0	0	0	0.0	1	0	3	4	0	.143	.143	1	0	C-4
1982 STL N	7	28	8	2	0	1	3.6	1	5	1	0	0	.286	.464	0	0	C-7
2 yrs.	12	42	10	2	0	1	2.4	2	5	4	8	0	.238	.357	1	0	C-11

Dick Porter

PORTER, RICHARD TWILLEY (Twitchy)   BL TR 5'10"   170 lbs.
B. Dec. 30, 1901, Princess Ann, Md.   D. Sept. 24, 1974, Philadelphia, Pa.

	G	AB	H	2B	3B	HR	HR%	R	RBI	BB	SO	SB	BA	SA	AB	H	G by POS
1929 CLE A	71	192	63	16	5	1	0.5	26	24	17	14	3	.328	.479	20	9	OF-30, 2B-22
1930	119	480	168	43	8	4	0.8	100	57	55	31	3	.350	.498	1	1	OF-118
1931	114	414	129	24	3	1	0.2	82	38	56	36	6	.312	.391	4	1	OF-109, 2B-1
1932	146	621	191	42	8	4	0.6	106	62	64	43	2	.308	.420	1	0	OF-145
1933	132	499	133	19	6	0	0.0	73	41	51	42	4	.267	.329	6	2	OF-124
1934 2 teams		CLE	A	(13G –	.227)			BOS	A	(80G –	.302)						
" total	93	309	90	15	7	1	0.3	40	62	25	20	5	.291	.395	16	2	OF-85
6 yrs.	675	2515	774	159	37	11	0.4	427	284	268	186	23	.308	.414	48	15	OF-611, 2B-23

Irv Porter

PORTER, IRVING MARBLE   BB TR 5'9"   155 lbs.
B. May 17, 1888, Lynn, Mass.   D. Feb. 20, 1971, Lynn, Mass.

	G	AB	H	2B	3B	HR	HR%	R	RBI	BB	SO	SB	BA	SA	AB	H	G by POS
1914 CHI A	1	4	1	0	0	0	0.0	1	0	0	1	0	.250	.250	0	0	OF-1

J. W. Porter

PORTER, J. W. (Jay)   BR TR 6'2"   180 lbs.
B. Jan. 17, 1933, Shawnee, Okla.

	G	AB	H	2B	3B	HR	HR%	R	RBI	BB	SO	SB	BA	SA	AB	H	G by POS
1952 STL A	33	104	26	4	1	0	0.0	12	7	10	10	4	.250	.308	1	0	OF-29, 3B-2
1955 DET A	24	55	13	2	0	0	0.0	6	3	8	15	0	.236	.273	8	2	1B-6, OF-4, C-4
1956	14	21	2	0	0	0	0.0	3	0	0	8	0	.095	.095	10	0	OF-2, C-2
1957	58	140	35	8	0	2	1.4	14	18	14	20	0	.250	.350	17	4	OF-27, C-12, 1B-3
1958 CLE A	40	85	17	1	0	4	4.7	13	19	9	23	0	.200	.353	17	3	C-20, 1B-4, 3B-1
1959 2 teams		WAS	A	(37G –	.226)			STL	N	(23G –	.212)						
" total	60	139	31	7	0	2	1.4	13	12	12	20	0	.223	.317	6	2	C-53, 1B-3
6 yrs.	229	544	124	22	1	8	1.5	58	62	53	96	4	.228	.316	59	11	C-91, OF-62, 1B-16, 3B-3

Leo Posada

POSADA, LEOPOLDO JESUS (Popy)   BR TR 5'11"   175 lbs.
B. Apr. 15, 1936, Havana, Cuba

	G	AB	H	2B	3B	HR	HR%	R	RBI	BB	SO	SB	BA	SA	AB	H	G by POS
1960 KC A	10	36	13	0	2	1	2.8	8	2	3	7	1	.361	.556	1	0	OF-9
1961	116	344	87	10	4	7	2.0	37	53	36	66	1	.253	.366	12	5	OF-102
1962	29	46	9	1	0	0	0.0	6	3	7	14	0	.196	.261	16	3	OF-11
3 yrs.	155	426	109	11	7	8	1.9	51	58	46	105	1	.256	.371	29	8	OF-122

Lew Post

POST, LEWIS G.
B. Apr. 12, 1875, Hastings, Mich.   D. Aug. 21, 1944, Chicago, Ill.

	G	AB	H	2B	3B	HR	HR%	R	RBI	BB	SO	SB	BA	SA	AB	H	G by POS
1902 DET A	3	12	1	0	0	0	0.0	2	2	0		0	.083	.083	0	0	OF-3

Sam Post

POST, SAMUEL GILBERT   BL TL 6'1½"   170 lbs.
B. Nov. 17, 1896, Richmond, Va.   D. Mar. 31, 1971, Portsmouth, Va.

	G	AB	H	2B	3B	HR	HR%	R	RBI	BB	SO	SB	BA	SA	AB	H	G by POS
1922 BKN N	9	25	7	0	0	0	0.0	3	4	1	4	1	.280	.280	1	1	2B-8

Wally Post

POST, WALTER CHARLES   BR TR 6'1"   190 lbs.
B. July 9, 1929, St. Wendelin, Ohio   D. Jan. 5, 1982, St. Henry, Ohio

	G	AB	H	2B	3B	HR	HR%	R	RBI	BB	SO	SB	BA	SA	AB	H	G by POS
1949 CIN N	6	8	2	0	0	0	0.0	1	1	0	3	0	.250	.250	2	2	OF-3
1951	15	41	9	3	0	1	2.4	6	7	3	4	0	.220	.366	2	1	OF-9
1952	19	58	9	1	0	2	3.4	5	7	4	20	0	.155	.276	3	0	OF-16
1953	11	33	8	1	0	1	3.0	3	4	4	6	1	.242	.364	0	0	OF-11
1954	130	451	115	21	3	18	4.0	46	83	26	70	2	.255	.435	13	3	OF-116
1955	154	601	186	33	3	40	6.7	116	109	60	102	7	.309	.574	0	0	OF-154
1956	143	539	134	25	3	36	6.7	94	83	37	124	6	.249	.506	0	0	OF-136
1957	134	467	114	26	2	20	4.3	68	74	33	84	2	.244	.437	10	2	OF-124
1958 PHI N	110	379	107	21	3	12	3.2	51	62	32	74	0	.282	.449	20	5	OF-91
1959	132	468	119	17	6	22	4.7	62	94	36	101	0	.254	.457	12	3	OF-120
1960 2 teams		PHI	N	(34G –	.286)			CIN	N	(77G –	.281)						
" total	111	333	94	20	1	19	5.7	47	50	37	75	0	.282	.520	24	2	OF-89
1961 CIN N	99	282	83	16	3	20	7.1	44	57	22	61	0	.294	.585	25	7	OF-81
1962	109	285	75	10	3	17	6.0	43	62	32	67	1	.263	.498	27	9	OF-90
1963 2 teams		CIN	N	(5G –	.000)			MIN	A	(21G –	.191)						
" total	26	54	9	0	1	2	3.7	7	6	2	18	0	.167	.315	12	0	OF-13
1964 CLE A	5	8	0	0	0	0	0.0	1	0	3	4	0	.000	.000	3	0	OF-2
15 yrs.	1204	4007	1064	194	28	210	5.2	594	699	331	813	19	.266	.485	159	34	OF-1055

WORLD SERIES

	G	AB	H	2B	3B	HR	HR%	R	RBI	BB	SO	SB	BA	SA	AB	H	G by POS
1961 CIN N	5	18	6	1	0	1	5.6	3	2	1	1	0	.333	.556	0	0	OF-5

Mike Potter

POTTER, MICHAEL GARY   BR TR 6'1"   195 lbs.
B. May 16, 1951, Montebello, Calif.

	G	AB	H	2B	3B	HR	HR%	R	RBI	BB	SO	SB	BA	SA	AB	H	G by POS
1976 STL N	9	16	0	0	0	0	0.0	0	0	1	6	0	.000	.000	5	0	OF-4

	G	AB	H	2B	3B	HR	HR %	R	RBI	BB	SO	SB	BA	SA	Pinch Hit AB	Pinch Hit H	G by POS

Mike Potter continued

	G	AB	H	2B	3B	HR	HR %	R	RBI	BB	SO	SB	BA	SA	PH AB	PH H	G by POS
1977	5	7	0	0	0	0	0.0	0	0	0	2	0	.000	.000	5	0	OF-1
2 yrs.	14	23	0	0	0	0	0.0	0	0	1	8	0	.000	.000	10	0	OF-5

Dan Potts

POTTS, DANIEL
B. Kent, Ohio   Deceased.

	G	AB	H	2B	3B	HR	HR %	R	RBI	BB	SO	SB	BA	SA	PH AB	PH H	G by POS
1892 WAS N	1	4	1	0	0	0	0.0	0	0	0	1	0	.250	.250	0	0	C-1

John Potts

POTTS, JOHN FREDERICK (Fred)   BL TR 5'7"   165 lbs.
B. Feb. 6, 1887, Tipp City, Ohio   D. Sept. 5, 1962, Cleveland, Ohio

	G	AB	H	2B	3B	HR	HR %	R	RBI	BB	SO	SB	BA	SA	PH AB	PH H	G by POS
1914 KC F	41	102	27	4	0	1	1.0	14	9	25		7	.265	.333	8	1	OF-31

Ken Poulsen

POULSEN, KEN STERLING   BL TR 6'1"   190 lbs.
B. Aug. 4, 1947, Van Nuys, Calif.

	G	AB	H	2B	3B	HR	HR %	R	RBI	BB	SO	SB	BA	SA	PH AB	PH H	G by POS
1967 BOS A	5	5	1	1	0	0	0.0	0	0	0	2	0	.200	.400	2	0	3B-2, SS-1

Abner Powell

POWELL, CHARLES ABNER   BR TR 5'7"   160 lbs.
B. Dec. 15, 1860, Shenandoah, Pa.   D. Aug. 7, 1953, New Orleans, La.

	G	AB	H	2B	3B	HR	HR %	R	RBI	BB	SO	SB	BA	SA	PH AB	PH H	G by POS
1884 WAS U	48	191	54	10	5	0	0.0	36		3			.283	.387	0	0	OF-30, P-18, 3B-2, SS-1, 2B-1
1886 2 teams		BAL AA (11G –		.179)		CIN AA (19G –		.230)									
" total	30	113	24	3	2	0	0.0	17		5	8		.212	.274	0	0	OF-17, P-11, SS-6
2 yrs.	78	304	78	13	7	0	0.0	53					.257	.345	0	0	OF-47, P-29, SS-7, 3B-2, 2B-1

Bob Powell

POWELL, ROBERT LEROY   BR TR 6'1"   190 lbs.
B. Oct. 17, 1933, Flint, Mich.

	G	AB	H	2B	3B	HR	HR %	R	RBI	BB	SO	SB	BA	SA	PH AB	PH H	G by POS
1955 CHI A	1	0	0	0	0	0	–	0	0	0	0	0	–	–	0	0	
1957	1	0	0	0	0	0	–	1	0	0	0	0	–	–	0	0	
2 yrs.	2	0	0	0	0	0	–	1	0	0	0	0	–	–	0	0	

Boog Powell

POWELL, JOHN WESLEY   BL TR 6'4½"   230 lbs.
B. Aug. 17, 1941, Lakeland, Fla.

	G	AB	H	2B	3B	HR	HR %	R	RBI	BB	SO	SB	BA	SA	PH AB	PH H	G by POS
1961 BAL A	4	13	1	0	0	0	0.0	0	1	0	2	0	.077	.077	1	0	OF-3
1962	124	400	97	13	2	15	3.8	44	53	38	79	1	.243	.398	10	2	OF-112, 1B-1
1963	140	491	130	22	2	25	5.1	67	82	49	87	1	.265	.470	3	1	OF-121, 1B-23
1964	134	424	123	17	0	39	9.2	74	99	76	91	0	.290	.606	12	2	OF-124, 1B-5
1965	144	472	117	20	2	17	3.6	54	72	71	93	1	.248	.407	8	1	1B-78, OF-71
1966	140	491	141	18	0	34	6.9	78	109	67	125	0	.287	.532	4	2	1B-136
1967	125	415	97	14	1	13	3.1	53	55	55	94	1	.234	.366	13	4	1B-114
1968	154	550	137	21	1	22	4.0	60	85	73	97	7	.249	.411	4	1	1B-149
1969	152	533	162	25	0	37	6.9	83	121	72	76	1	.304	.559	7	1	1B-144
1970	154	526	156	28	0	35	6.7	82	114	104	80	1	.297	.549	8	2	1B-145
1971	128	418	107	19	0	22	5.3	59	92	82	64	1	.256	.459	4	1	1B-124
1972	140	465	117	20	1	21	4.5	53	81	65	92	4	.252	.434	7	1	1B-133
1973	114	370	98	13	1	11	3.0	52	54	85	64	0	.265	.395	6	3	1B-111
1974	110	344	91	13	1	12	3.5	37	45	52	58	0	.265	.413	8	1	1B-102, DH-5
1975 CLE A	134	435	129	18	0	27	6.2	64	86	59	72	1	.297	.524	11	4	1B-121, DH-5
1976	95	293	63	9	0	9	3.1	29	33	41	43	1	.215	.338	10	3	1B-89
1977 LA N	50	41	10	0	0	0	0.0	0	5	12	9	0	.244	.244	36	8	1B-4
17 yrs.	2042	6681	1776	270	11	339	5.1	889	1187	1001	1226	20	.266	.462	152	37	1B-1479, OF-431, DH-6
LEAGUE CHAMPIONSHIP SERIES																	
1969 BAL A	3	13	5	0	0	1	7.7	2	1	2	0	0	.385	.615	0	0	1B-3
1970	3	14	6	2	0	1	7.1	2	6	3	3	0	.429	.786	0	0	1B-3
1971	3	10	3	0	0	2	20.0	4	3	3	1	0	.300	.900	0	0	1B-3
1973	1	4	0	0	0	0	0.0	1	0	0	0	0	.000	.000	0	0	1B-1
1974	2	8	1	0	0	0	0.0	0	1	0	3	0	.125	.125	0	0	1B-2
5 yrs.	12	49	15	2	0	4	8.2	9	11	5	7	0	.306	.592	0	0	1B-12
WORLD SERIES																	
1966 BAL A	4	14	5	1	0	0	0.0	1	1	0	1	0	.357	.429	0	0	1B-4
1969	5	19	5	0	0	0	0.0	0	0	1	4	0	.263	.263	0	0	1B-5
1970	5	17	5	1	0	2	11.8	6	5	5	2	0	.294	.706	0	0	1B-5
1971	7	27	3	0	0	0	0.0	1	1	1	3	0	.111	.111	0	0	1B-7
4 yrs.	21	77	18	2	0	2	2.6	8	7	7	10	0	.234	.338	0	0	1B-21

Hosken Powell

POWELL, HOSKEN   BL TL 6'1"   175 lbs.
B. May 14, 1955, Salem, Ala.

	G	AB	H	2B	3B	HR	HR %	R	RBI	BB	SO	SB	BA	SA	PH AB	PH H	G by POS
1978 MIN A	121	381	94	20	2	3	0.8	55	31	45	31	11	.247	.333	7	2	OF-117
1979	104	338	99	17	3	2	0.6	49	36	33	25	5	.293	.379	15	2	OF-93, DH-5
1980	137	485	127	17	5	6	1.2	58	35	32	46	14	.262	.355	14	2	OF-129
1981	80	264	63	11	3	2	0.8	30	25	17	31	7	.239	.326	11	3	OF-64, DH-8
1982 TOR A	112	265	73	13	4	3	1.1	43	26	12	23	4	.275	.389	30	10	OF-75, DH-19
1983	40	83	14	0	0	1	1.2	6	7	5	8	2	.169	.205	12	2	OF-33, DH-1, 1B-1
6 yrs.	594	1816	470	78	17	17	0.9	241	160	144	164	43	.259	.349	89	21	OF-511, DH-33, 1B-1

Jake Powell

POWELL, ALVIN JACOB   BR TR 5'11½" 180 lbs.
B. July 15, 1908, Silver Spring, Md.   D. Nov. 4, 1948, Washington, D. C.

	G	AB	H	2B	3B	HR	HR %	R	RBI	BB	SO	SB	BA	SA	PH AB	PH H	G by POS
1930 WAS A	3	4	0	0	0	0	0.0	1	0	0	1	0	.000	.000	1	0	OF-2
1934	9	35	10	2	0	0	0.0	6	1	4	2	1	.286	.343	0	0	OF-9
1935	139	551	172	26	10	6	1.1	88	98	37	37	15	.312	.428	2	0	OF-136, 2B-2
1936 2 teams		WAS A (53G –		.290)		NY A (87G –		.306)									
" total	140	538	161	24	8	8	1.5	102	78	52	51	26	.299	.418	4	3	OF-137
1937 NY A	97	365	96	22	3	3	0.8	54	45	25	36	7	.263	.364	3	0	OF-94
1938	45	164	42	12	1	2	1.2	27	20	15	20	3	.256	.378	1	0	OF-43
1939	31	86	21	4	1	1	1.2	12	9	3	8	1	.244	.349	4	1	OF-23

	G	AB	H	2B	3B	HR	HR %	R	RBI	BB	SO	SB	BA	SA	Pinch Hit AB	Pinch Hit H	G by POS

Jake Powell continued

	G	AB	H	2B	3B	HR	HR%	R	RBI	BB	SO	SB	BA	SA	AB	H	G by POS
1940	12	27	5	0	0	0	0.0	3	2	1	4	0	.185	.185	2	0	OF-7
1943 WAS A	37	132	35	10	2	0	0.0	14	20	5	13	3	.265	.371	3	1	OF-33
1944	96	367	88	9	1	1	0.3	29	37	16	26	7	.240	.278	5	0	OF-90, 3B-1
1945 2 teams	WAS	A (31G – .194)				PHI	N	(48G – .231)									
" total	79	271	59	7	0	1	0.4	17	17	16	21	2	.218	.255	4	1	OF-71
11 yrs.	688	2540	689	116	26	22	0.9	353	327	174	219	65	.271	.363	29	6	OF-645, 2B-2, 3B-1
WORLD SERIES																	
1936 NY A	6	22	10	1	0	1	4.5	8	5	4	4	1	.455	.636	0	0	OF-6
1937	1	1	0	0	0	0	0.0	0	0	0	1	0	.000	.000	1	0	
1938	1	0	0	0	0	0	–	0	0	0	0	0	–	–	0	0	P-1
3 yrs.	8	23	10	1	0	1	4.3	8	5	4	5	1	.435	.609	1	0	OF-6, P-1

Jim Powell

POWELL, JAMES E.
B. 1859, Richmond, Va.   Deceased.   5'10"   170 lbs.

	G	AB	H	2B	3B	HR	HR%	R	RBI	BB	SO	SB	BA	SA	AB	H	G by POS
1884 RIC AA	41	151	37	8	4	0	0.0	23		7			.245	.351	0	0	1B-41

Martin Powell

POWELL, MARTIN J.
B. Mar. 25, 1856, Fitchburg, Mass.   D. Feb. 5, 1888, Fitchburg, Mass.   BL   6'½"

	G	AB	H	2B	3B	HR	HR%	R	RBI	BB	SO	SB	BA	SA	AB	H	G by POS
1881 DET N	55	219	74	9	4	1	0.5	47	38	15	9		.338	.429	0	0	1B-55, C-1
1882	80	338	81	13	6	1	0.3	44	29	19	27		.240	.287	0	0	1B-80
1883	101	421	115	17	5	1	0.2	76		28	23		.273	.344	0	0	1B-101
1884 CIN U	43	185	59	4	2	1	0.5	46		13			.319	.378	0	0	1B-43
1885 PHI AA	19	75	12	0	3	0	0.0	5		1			.160	.240	0	0	1B-19
5 yrs.	298	1238	341	43	14	4	0.3	218	67	76	59		.275	.342	0	0	1B-298, C-1

Paul Powell

POWELL, PAUL RAY
B. Mar. 19, 1948, San Angelo, Tex.   BR   TR   5'11"   185 lbs.

	G	AB	H	2B	3B	HR	HR%	R	RBI	BB	SO	SB	BA	SA	AB	H	G by POS
1971 MIN A	20	31	5	0	0	1	3.2	7	2	3	12	0	.161	.258	2	0	OF-15
1973 LA N	2	1	0	0	0	0	0.0	0	0	0	1	0	.000	.000	1	0	OF-1
1975	8	10	2	1	0	0	0.0	2	0	1	2	0	.200	.300	0	0	C-7, OF-1
3 yrs.	30	42	7	1	0	1	2.4	9	2	4	15	0	.167	.262	3	0	OF-17, C-7

Ray Powell

POWELL, RAYMOND REATH (Rabbit)
B. Nov. 20, 1888, Siloam Springs, Ark.   D. Oct. 16, 1962, Chillicothe, Mo.   BL   TR   5'9"   160 lbs.

	G	AB	H	2B	3B	HR	HR%	R	RBI	BB	SO	SB	BA	SA	AB	H	G by POS
1913 DET A	2	0	0	0	0	0	–	0	0	0	0	0	–	–	0	0	OF-1
1917 BOS N	88	357	97	10	4	4	1.1	42	30	24	54	12	.272	.356	0	0	OF-88
1918	53	188	40	7	5	0	0.0	31	20	29	30	2	.213	.303	0	0	OF-53
1919	123	470	111	12	12	2	0.4	51	33	41	79	16	.236	.326	1	0	OF-122
1920	147	609	137	12	12	6	1.0	69	29	44	83	10	.225	.314	0	0	OF-147
1921	149	624	191	25	18	12	1.9	114	74	58	85	6	.306	.462	0	0	OF-149
1922	142	550	163	22	11	6	1.1	82	37	59	66	3	.296	.409	5	0	OF-136
1923	97	338	102	20	4	4	1.2	57	38	45	36	1	.302	.420	8	3	OF-84
1924	74	188	49	9	1	1	0.5	21	15	21	28	1	.261	.335	23	6	OF-46
9 yrs.	875	3324	890	117	67	35	1.1	467	276	321	461	51	.268	.375	37	9	OF-826

Tom Power

POWER, THOMAS E.
B. San Francisco, Calif.   D. Feb. 25, 1898, San Francisco, Calif.

	G	AB	H	2B	3B	HR	HR%	R	RBI	BB	SO	SB	BA	SA	AB	H	G by POS
1890 B-B AA	38	125	26	3	1	0	0.0	11		13		6	.208	.248	0	0	1B-26, 2B-12

Vic Power

POWER, VICTOR PELLOT
B. Nov. 1, 1931, Arecibo, Puerto Rico   BR   TR   6'   186 lbs.

	G	AB	H	2B	3B	HR	HR%	R	RBI	BB	SO	SB	BA	SA	AB	H	G by POS
1954 PHI A	127	462	118	17	5	8	1.7	36	38	19	19	2	.255	.366	7	3	OF-101, 1B-21, SS-1, 3B-1
1955 KC A	147	596	190	34	10	19	3.2	91	76	35	27	0	.319	.505	3	1	1B-144
1956	127	530	164	21	5	14	2.6	77	63	24	16	2	.309	.447	4	2	1B-76, 2B-47, OF-7
1957	129	467	121	15	1	14	3.0	48	42	19	21	3	.259	.385	10	2	1B-113, OF-6, 2B-4
1958 2 teams	KC	A (52G – .302)				CLE	A	(93G – .317)									
" total	145	590	184	37	10	16	2.7	98	80	20	14	3	.312	.490	3	0	1B-91, 3B-42, 2B-28, SS-2, OF-4
1959 CLE A	147	595	172	31	6	10	1.7	102	60	40	22	9	.289	.412	0	0	1B-121, 2B-21, 3B-7
1960	147	580	167	26	3	10	1.7	69	84	24	20	9	.288	.395	0	0	1B-147, SS-5, 3B-4
1961	147	563	151	34	4	5	0.9	64	63	38	16	4	.268	.369	0	0	1B-141, 2B-7
1962 MIN A	144	611	177	28	2	16	2.6	80	63	22	35	7	.290	.421	3	2	1B-142, 2B-2
1963	138	541	146	28	2	10	1.8	65	52	22	24	3	.270	.384	7	2	1B-124, 2B-18, 3B-5
1964 3 teams	MIN	A (19G – .222)				LA	A	(68G – .249)			PHI	N	(18G – .208)				
" total	105	314	75	12	0	3	1.0	24	17	11	20	1	.239	.306	14	2	1B-77, 3B-28, 2B-6
1965 CAL A	124	197	51	7	1	1	0.5	11	20	5	13	2	.259	.320	15	1	1B-107, 2B-6, 3B-2
12 yrs.	1627	6046	1716	290	49	126	2.1	765	658	279	247	45	.284	.411	66	16	1B-1304, 2B-139, OF-115, 3B-89, SS-8

Johnny Powers

POWERS, JOHN CALVIN
B. July 8, 1929, Birmingham, Ala.   BL   TR   6'1"   185 lbs.

	G	AB	H	2B	3B	HR	HR%	R	RBI	BB	SO	SB	BA	SA	AB	H	G by POS
1955 PIT N	2	4	1	0	0	0	0.0	0	0	0	0	0	.250	.250	0	0	OF-2
1956	11	21	1	0	0	0	0.0	0	0	1	4	0	.048	.048	6	0	OF-5
1957	20	35	10	3	0	2	5.7	7	8	5	9	0	.286	.543	6	3	OF-8, 2B-1
1958	57	82	15	1	0	2	2.4	6	2	8	19	0	.183	.268	38	8	OF-14
1959 CIN N	43	43	11	2	1	2	4.7	8	4	3	13	0	.256	.488	36	8	OF-9
1960 2 teams	BAL	A (10G – .111)				CLE	A	(8G – .167)									
" total	18	30	4	1	1	0	0.0	5	0	5	3	0	.133	.233	9	0	OF-9
6 yrs.	151	215	42	7	2	6	2.8	26	14	22	48	0	.195	.330	98	19	OF-43, 2B-1

Les Powers

POWERS, LESLIE EDWIN
B. Nov. 5, 1912, Seattle, Wash.   BL   TL   6'   175 lbs.

	G	AB	H	2B	3B	HR	HR%	R	RBI	BB	SO	SB	BA	SA	AB	H	G by POS
1938 NY N	3	3	0	0	0	0	0.0	0	0	0	1	0	.000	.000	3	0	
1939 PHI N	19	52	18	1	1	0	0.0	7	2	4	6	0	.346	.404	4	1	1B-13
2 yrs.	22	55	18	1	1	0	0.0	7	2	4	7	0	.327	.382	7	1	1B-13

	G	AB	H	2B	3B	HR	HR %	R	RBI	BB	SO	SB	BA	SA	Pinch Hit AB	H	G by POS

Mike Powers

POWERS, ELLIS FOREE
B. Mar. 2, 1906, Crestwood, Ky.   D. Dec. 2, 1983, Louisville, Ky.
BL TL 6'1"   185 lbs.

	G	AB	H	2B	3B	HR	HR %	R	RBI	BB	SO	SB	BA	SA	AB	H	G by POS
1932 CLE A	14	33	6	4	0	0	0.0	4	5	2	2	0	.182	.303	5	0	OF-8
1933	24	47	13	2	1	0	0.0	6	2	6	6	2	.277	.362	11	3	OF-11
2 yrs.	38	80	19	6	1	0	0.0	10	7	8	8	2	.238	.338	16	3	OF-19

Mike Powers

POWERS, MICHAEL RILEY
B. Sept. 22, 1870, Pittsfield, Mass.   D. Apr. 26, 1909, Philadelphia, Pa.
BR TR 5'7"   166 lbs.

	G	AB	H	2B	3B	HR	HR %	R	RBI	BB	SO	SB	BA	SA	AB	H	G by POS
1898 LOU N	34	99	27	4	3	1	1.0	13	19	5		1	.273	.404	5	0	C-22, 1B-6, OF-1
1899 2 teams		LOU N (49G – .207)					WAS N (14G – .263)										
" total	63	207	45	10	2	0	0.0	18	25	7		1	.217	.285	5	0	C-50, 1B-8
1901 PHI A	116	431	108	26	5	1	0.2	53	47	18		10	.251	.341	2	1	C-111, 1B-3
1902	71	246	65	7	1	2	0.8	35	39	14		3	.264	.325	1	0	C-68, 1B-3
1903	75	247	56	11	1	0	0.0	19	23	9		5	.227	.279	2	0	C-66, 1B-7
1904	57	184	35	3	0	0	0.0	11	11	6		3	.190	.207	0	0	C-56, OF-1
1905 3 teams		PHI A (19G – .131)					NY A (11G – .182)			PHI A (21G – .183)							
" total	51	154	25	1	0	0	0.0	11	12	4	0	1	.162	.169	0	0	C-44, 1B-7
1906 PHI A	58	185	29	1	0	0	0.0	5	7	1		2	.157	.162	0	0	C-57, 1B-1
1907	59	159	29	3	0	0	0.0	9	9	7		1	.182	.201	0	0	C-59
1908	62	172	31	6	1	0	0.0	8	7	5		1	.180	.227	0	0	C-60, 1B-2
1909	1	4	1	0	0	0	0.0	1	0	0		0	.250	.250	0	0	C-1
11 yrs.	647	2088	451	72	13	4	0.2	183	199	72		27	.216	.269	15	1	C-594, 1B-37, OF-2
WORLD SERIES																	
1905 PHI A	3	7	1	1	0	0	0.0	0	0	0	0	0	.143	.286	0	0	C-3

Phil Powers

POWERS, PHILIP J. (Grandmother)
B. July 26, 1854, New York, N. Y.   D. Dec. 22, 1914, New York, N. Y.
BR TR

	G	AB	H	2B	3B	HR	HR %	R	RBI	BB	SO	SB	BA	SA	AB	H	G by POS
1878 CHI N	8	31	5	1	0	0	0.0	2	2	1	5		.161	.258	0	0	C-8
1880 BOS N	37	126	18	5	0	0	0.0	11	10	5	15		.143	.183	0	0	C-37, OF-2
1881 CLE N	5	15	1	0	0	0	0.0	1	0	1	2		.067	.067	0	0	C-4, 3B-1
1882 CIN AA	16	60	13	1	1	0	0.0	4		3			.217	.267	0	0	C-10, 1B-5, OF-1
1883	30	114	28	1	4	0	0.0	16		3			.246	.325	0	0	C-17, OF-13
1884	34	130	18	1	0	0	0.0	10		5			.138	.146	0	0	C-31, OF-2, 1B-2
1885 2 teams		CIN AA (15G – .267)					BAL AA (9G – .118)										
" total	24	94	20	3	0	0	0.0	12					.213	.245	0	0	C-23, OF-1
7 yrs.	154	570	103	12	6	0	0.0	56	12	19	22		.181	.223	0	0	C-130, OF-19, 1B-7, 3B-1

Carl Powis

POWIS, CARL EDGAR (Jug)
B. Jan. 11, 1928, Philadelphia, Pa.
BR TR 6'   185 lbs.

	G	AB	H	2B	3B	HR	HR %	R	RBI	BB	SO	SB	BA	SA	AB	H	G by POS
1957 BAL A	15	41	8	3	1	0	0.0	4	2	7	9	2	.195	.317	2	0	OF-13

Johnny Pramesa

PRAMESA, JOHN STEVEN
B. Aug. 28, 1925, Barton, Ohio
BR TR 6'2"   210 lbs.

	G	AB	H	2B	3B	HR	HR %	R	RBI	BB	SO	SB	BA	SA	AB	H	G by POS
1949 CIN N	17	25	6	1	0	1	4.0	2	2	3	5	0	.240	.400	4	1	C-13
1950	74	228	70	10	1	5	2.2	14	30	19	15	0	.307	.425	1	0	C-73
1951	72	227	52	5	2	6	2.6	12	22	5	17	0	.229	.348	9	2	C-63
1952 CHI N	22	46	13	1	0	1	2.2	1	5	4	4	0	.283	.370	5	2	C-17
4 yrs.	185	526	141	17	3	13	2.5	29	59	31	41	0	.268	.386	19	5	C-166

Del Pratt

PRATT, DERRILL BURNHAM
B. Jan. 10, 1888, Walhalla, S. C.   D. Sept. 30, 1977, Texas City, Tex.
BR TR 5'11"   175 lbs.

	G	AB	H	2B	3B	HR	HR %	R	RBI	BB	SO	SB	BA	SA	AB	H	G by POS
1912 STL A	151	570	172	26	15	5	0.9	76	69	36		24	.302	.426	0	0	2B-121, SS-21, OF-8, 3B-1
1913	155	592	175	31	13	2	0.3	60	87	40	57	37	.296	.402	0	0	2B-146, 1B-9
1914	158	584	165	34	13	5	0.9	85	65	50	45	37	.283	.411	0	0	2B-152, OF-5, SS-1
1915	159	602	175	31	11	3	0.5	61	78	26	43	32	.291	.394	0	0	2B-158
1916	158	596	159	35	12	5	0.8	64	103	54	56	26	.267	.391	0	0	2B-158
1917	123	450	111	22	8	1	0.2	40	53	33	36	18	.247	.338	0	0	2B-119, 1B-4
1918 NY A	126	477	131	19	7	2	0.4	65	55	35	26	12	.275	.356	0	0	2B-126
1919	140	527	154	27	7	4	0.8	69	56	36	24	22	.292	.393	0	0	2B-140
1920	154	574	180	37	8	4	0.7	84	97	50	24	12	.314	.427	0	0	2B-154
1921 BOS A	135	521	169	36	10	5	1.0	80	100	44	10	8	.324	.461	1	0	2B-134
1922	154	607	183	44	7	6	1.0	73	86	53	20	7	.301	.427	0	0	2B-154
1923 DET A	101	297	92	18	3	0	0.0	43	40	25	9	5	.310	.391	8	4	2B-60, 1B-17, 3B-12
1924	121	429	130	32	3	1	0.2	56	77	31	10	6	.303	.399	1	0	2B-63, 1B-51, 3B-4
13 yrs.	1835	6826	1996	392	117	43	0.6	856	966	513	360	246	.292	.403	10	4	2B-1685, 1B-81, SS-22, 3B-17, OF-13

Frank Pratt

PRATT, FRANCIS BRUCE (Truckhorse)
B. Aug. 24, 1897, Blocton, Ala.   D. Apr. 8, 1974, Centreville, Ala.
BL TR 5'9½"   155 lbs.

	G	AB	H	2B	3B	HR	HR %	R	RBI	BB	SO	SB	BA	SA	AB	H	G by POS
1921 CHI A	1	1	0	0	0	0	0.0	0	0	0	0	0	.000	.000	1	0	

Larry Pratt

PRATT, LESTER JOHN
B. Oct. 8, 1887, Gibson City, Ill.   D. Jan. 8, 1969, Peoria, Ill.
BR TR 6'   183 lbs.

	G	AB	H	2B	3B	HR	HR %	R	RBI	BB	SO	SB	BA	SA	AB	H	G by POS
1914 BOS A	5	4	0	0	0	0	0.0	0	0	0	4	0	.000	.000	4	0	C-5
1915 2 teams		BKN F (20G – .184)					NWK F (5G – .500)										
" total	25	49	11	3	0	1	1.9	7	2	5		4	.208	.321	4	0	C-20
2 yrs.	30	57	11	3	0	1	1.8	7	2	5	4	4	.193	.298	4	0	C-25

Mel Preibisch

PREIBISCH, MELVIN ADOLPHUS (Primo)
B. Nov. 23, 1914, Sealy, Tex.   D. Apr. 12, 1980, Sealy, Tex.
BR TR 5'11"   185 lbs.

	G	AB	H	2B	3B	HR	HR %	R	RBI	BB	SO	SB	BA	SA	AB	H	G by POS
1940 BOS N	11	40	9	2	0	0	0.0	3	5	2	4	0	.225	.275	0	0	OF-11
1941	5	4	0	0	0	0	0.0	0	0	1	2	0	.000	.000	2	0	OF-2
2 yrs.	16	44	9	2	0	0	0.0	3	5	3	6	0	.205	.250	2	0	OF-13

Bobby Prescott

PRESCOTT, GEORGE BERTRAND
B. Mar. 27, 1931, Colon, Panama
BR TR 5'11" 180 lbs.

	G	AB	H	2B	3B	HR	HR %	R	RBI	BB	SO	SB	BA	SA	Pinch Hit AB	Pinch Hit H	G by POS
1961 KC A	10	12	1	0	0	0	0.0	0	0	2	5	0	.083	.083	7	1	OF-2

Jim Presley

PRESLEY, JAMES ARTHUR
B. Oct. 23, 1961, Pensacola, Fla.
BR TR 6'1" 176 lbs.

	G	AB	H	2B	3B	HR	HR %	R	RBI	BB	SO	SB	BA	SA	Pinch Hit AB	Pinch Hit H	G by POS
1984 SEA A	70	251	57	12	1	10	4.0	27	36	6	63	1	.227	.402	1	0	3B-69, DH-1

Walt Preston

PRESTON, WALTER B.
B. 1870, Richmond, Va. Deceased.
6' 180 lbs.

	G	AB	H	2B	3B	HR	HR %	R	RBI	BB	SO	SB	BA	SA	Pinch Hit AB	Pinch Hit H	G by POS
1895 LOU N	50	197	55	6	4	1	0.5	42	24	17	17	11	.279	.365	0	0	OF-26, 3B-25

Jackie Price

PRICE, JOHN THOMAS REID
B. Nov. 13, 1912, Winborn, Miss. D. Oct. 2, 1967, San Francisco, Calif.
BL TR 5'10½" 150 lbs.

	G	AB	H	2B	3B	HR	HR %	R	RBI	BB	SO	SB	BA	SA	Pinch Hit AB	Pinch Hit H	G by POS
1946 CLE A	7	13	3	0	0	0	0.0	1	0	0	0	0	.231	.231	2	1	SS-4

Jim Price

PRICE, JIMMIE WILLIAM
B. Oct. 13, 1941, Harrisburg, Pa.
BR TR 6' 192 lbs.

	G	AB	H	2B	3B	HR	HR %	R	RBI	BB	SO	SB	BA	SA	Pinch Hit AB	Pinch Hit H	G by POS
1967 DET A	44	92	24	4	0	0	0.0	9	8	4	10	0	.261	.304	20	5	C-24
1968	64	132	23	4	0	3	2.3	12	13	13	14	0	.174	.273	22	5	C-42
1969	72	192	45	8	0	9	4.7	21	28	18	20	0	.234	.417	21	2	C-51
1970	52	132	24	4	0	5	3.8	12	15	21	23	0	.182	.326	12	1	C-38
1971	29	54	13	2	0	1	1.9	4	7	6	3	0	.241	.333	2	0	C-25
5 yrs.	261	602	129	22	0	18	3.0	58	71	62	70	0	.214	.341	77	13	C-180

WORLD SERIES

	G	AB	H	2B	3B	HR	HR %	R	RBI	BB	SO	SB	BA	SA	Pinch Hit AB	Pinch Hit H	G by POS
1968 DET A	2	2	0	0	0	0	0.0	0	0	0	1	0	.000	.000	2	0	

Joe Price

PRICE, JOSEPH PRESTON (Lumber)
B. Apr. 10, 1897, Milligan College, Tenn. D. Jan. 15, 1961, Washington, D.C.
BR TR 6'1½" 187 lbs.

	G	AB	H	2B	3B	HR	HR %	R	RBI	BB	SO	SB	BA	SA	Pinch Hit AB	Pinch Hit H	G by POS
1928 NY N	1	1	0	0	0	0	0.0	0	0	0	1	0	.000	.000	0	0	OF-1

Bob Prichard

PRICHARD, ROBERT ALEXANDER
B. Oct. 21, 1917, Paris, Tex.
BL TL 6'1" 195 lbs.

	G	AB	H	2B	3B	HR	HR %	R	RBI	BB	SO	SB	BA	SA	Pinch Hit AB	Pinch Hit H	G by POS
1939 WAS A	26	85	20	5	0	0	0.0	8	8	19	16	0	.235	.294	0	0	1B-26

Gerry Priddy

PRIDDY, GERALD EDWARD
B. Nov. 9, 1919, Los Angeles, Calif. D. Mar. 3, 1980, North Hollywood, Calif.
BR TR 5'11½" 180 lbs.

	G	AB	H	2B	3B	HR	HR %	R	RBI	BB	SO	SB	BA	SA	Pinch Hit AB	Pinch Hit H	G by POS
1941 NY A	56	174	37	7	0	1	0.6	18	26	18	16	4	.213	.270	2	1	2B-31, 3B-14, 1B-10
1942	59	189	53	9	2	2	1.1	23	28	31	27	0	.280	.381	3	1	3B-35, 1B-11, 2B-8, SS-3
1943 WAS A	149	560	152	31	3	4	0.7	68	62	67	76	5	.271	.359	0	0	2B-134, SS-15, 3B-1
1946	138	511	130	22	8	6	1.2	54	58	57	73	9	.254	.364	0	0	2B-138
1947	147	505	108	20	3	3	0.6	42	49	62	79	7	.214	.283	1	0	2B-146
1948 STL A	151	560	166	40	9	8	1.4	96	79	86	71	6	.296	.443	3	0	2B-146
1949	145	544	158	26	4	11	2.0	83	63	80	81	5	.290	.414	0	0	2B-145
1950 DET A	157	618	171	26	6	13	2.1	104	75	95	95	2	.277	.401	0	0	2B-157
1951	154	584	152	22	6	8	1.4	73	57	69	73	4	.260	.360	0	0	2B-154, SS-1
1952	75	279	79	23	3	4	1.4	37	20	42	29	1	.283	.430	0	0	2B-75
1953	65	196	46	6	2	1	0.5	14	24	17	19	1	.235	.301	9	2	2B-45, 1B-11, 3B-2
11 yrs.	1296	4720	1252	232	46	61	1.3	612	541	624	639	44	.265	.373	18	4	2B-1179, 3B-52, 1B-32, SS-19

WORLD SERIES

	G	AB	H	2B	3B	HR	HR %	R	RBI	BB	SO	SB	BA	SA	Pinch Hit AB	Pinch Hit H	G by POS
1942 NY A	3	10	1	1	0	0	0.0	0	1	1	0	0	.100	.200	0	0	1B-3

Johnnie Priest

PRIEST, JOHN GOODING
B. June 23, 1886, St. Joseph, Mo. D. Nov. 4, 1979, Washington, D.C.
BR TR 5'11" 170 lbs.

	G	AB	H	2B	3B	HR	HR %	R	RBI	BB	SO	SB	BA	SA	Pinch Hit AB	Pinch Hit H	G by POS
1911 NY A	7	21	3	0	0	0	0.0	2	2	2		3	.143	.143	0	0	2B-5, 3B-2
1912	2	2	1	0	0	0	0.0	1	1	0		0	.500	.500	2	1	
2 yrs.	9	23	4	0	0	0	0.0	3	3	2		3	.174	.174	2	1	2B-5, 3B-2

Walter Prince

PRINCE, WALTER FARR
B. May 9, 1861, Amherst, N.H. D. Mar. 2, 1938, Bristol, N.H.
BL TR 5'10" 175 lbs.

	G	AB	H	2B	3B	HR	HR %	R	RBI	BB	SO	SB	BA	SA	Pinch Hit AB	Pinch Hit H	G by POS
1883 LOU AA	4	11	2	0	0	0	0.0	1		0			.182	.182	0	0	OF-2, 1B-2, SS-1
1884 3 teams	DET N (7G – .143)			WAS AA (43G – .217)			WAS U (1G – .250)										
" total	51	191	40	3	2	0	0.0	22		16	4		.209	.246	0	0	1B-44, OF-7
2 yrs.	55	202	42	3	2	0	0.0	23		16	4		.208	.243	0	0	1B-46, OF-9, SS-1

Buddy Pritchard

PRITCHARD, HAROLD WILLIAM
B. Jan. 25, 1936, South Gate, Calif.
BR TR 6' 165 lbs.

	G	AB	H	2B	3B	HR	HR %	R	RBI	BB	SO	SB	BA	SA	Pinch Hit AB	Pinch Hit H	G by POS
1957 PIT N	23	11	1	1	0	0	0.0	1	0	0	4	0	.091	.091	5	0	SS-10, 2B-3

Lou Proctor

PROCTOR, LOU
B. Unknown.

	G	AB	H	2B	3B	HR	HR %	R	RBI	BB	SO	SB	BA	SA	Pinch Hit AB	Pinch Hit H	G by POS
1912 STL A	1	0	0	0	0	0	–	0	0	1		0	–	–	0	0	

George Proeser

PROESER, GEORGE (Yats)
B. May 30, 1864, Cincinnati, Ohio D. Oct. 14, 1941, New Burlington, Ohio
5'10" 190 lbs.

	G	AB	H	2B	3B	HR	HR %	R	RBI	BB	SO	SB	BA	SA	Pinch Hit AB	Pinch Hit H	G by POS
1888 CLE AA	7	23	7	2	0	0	0.0	5	1			0	.304	.391	0	0	P-7
1890 SYR AA	13	53	13	1	1	1	1.9	11			10	1	.245	.358	0	0	OF-13
2 yrs.	20	76	20	3	1	1	1.3	16	1		11	1	.263	.368	0	0	OF-13, P-7

Jake Propst

PROPST, WILLIAM JACOB
B. Mar. 10, 1895, Kennedy, Ala. D. Feb. 24, 1967, Columbus, Miss.
BL TR 5'10" 165 lbs.

	G	AB	H	2B	3B	HR	HR %	R	RBI	BB	SO	SB	BA	SA	Pinch Hit AB	Pinch Hit H	G by POS
1923 WAS A	1	1	0	0	0	0	0.0	0	0	0	0	0	.000	.000	1	0	

	G	AB	H	2B	3B	HR	HR %	R	RBI	BB	SO	SB	BA	SA	Pinch Hit AB	Pinch Hit H	G by POS

Doc Prothro

PROTHRO, JAMES THOMPSON
B. July 16, 1893, Memphis, Tenn.   D. Oct. 14, 1971, Memphis, Tenn.
Manager 1939-41.
BR TR 5'10½" 170 lbs.

	G	AB	H	2B	3B	HR	HR %	R	RBI	BB	SO	SB	BA	SA	PH AB	PH H	G by POS
1920 WAS A	6	13	5	0	0	0	0.0	2	2	0	4	0	.385	.385	2	1	SS-2, 3B-2
1923	6	8	2	0	1	0	0.0	2	3	1	3	0	.250	.500	0	0	3B-6
1924	46	159	53	11	5	0	0.0	17	24	15	11	4	.333	.465	0	0	3B-45
1925 BOS A	119	415	130	23	3	0	0.0	44	51	52	21	9	.313	.383	7	1	3B-108, SS-3
1926 CIN N	3	5	1	0	1	0	0.0	1	1	1	1	0	.200	.600	1	0	3B-2
5 yrs.	180	600	191	34	10	0	0.0	66	81	69	40	13	.318	.408	10	1	3B-163, SS-5

Gibby Pruess

PRUESS, EARL HENRY
B. Apr. 2, 1895, Chicago, Ill.   D. Aug. 28, 1979, Chicago, Ill.
BR TR 5'10½" 170 lbs.

	G	AB	H	2B	3B	HR	HR %	R	RBI	BB	SO	SB	BA	SA	PH AB	PH H	G by POS
1920 STL A	1	0	0	0	0	0	-	1	0	1	0	1	-	-	0	0	OF-1

Jim Pruett

PRUETT, JAMES CALVIN
B. Dec. 16, 1917, Nashville, Tenn.
BR TR 5'10" 178 lbs.

	G	AB	H	2B	3B	HR	HR %	R	RBI	BB	SO	SB	BA	SA	PH AB	PH H	G by POS
1944 PHI A	3	4	1	0	0	0	0.0	1	1	1	0	0	.250	.250	1	0	C-2
1945	6	9	2	0	0	0	0.0	1	0	1	2	0	.222	.222	2	0	C-4
2 yrs.	9	13	3	0	0	0	0.0	2	1	2	2	0	.231	.231	3	0	C-6

Ron Pruitt

PRUITT, RONALD RALPH (Do-It)
B. Oct. 21, 1951, Flint, Mich.
BR TR 6' 185 lbs.

	G	AB	H	2B	3B	HR	HR %	R	RBI	BB	SO	SB	BA	SA	PH AB	PH H	G by POS
1975 TEX A	14	17	3	0	0	0	0.0	2	0	1	3	0	.176	.176	0	0	C-13, OF-1
1976 CLE A	47	86	23	1	1	0	0.0	7	5	16	8	2	.267	.302	7	3	OF-26, 3B-6, C-6, DH-4, 1B-1
1977	78	219	63	10	2	2	0.9	29	32	28	22	2	.288	.379	8	1	OF-69, DH-4, C-4, 3B-1
1978	71	187	44	6	1	6	3.2	17	17	16	20	2	.235	.374	10	3	C-48, OF-16, DH-5, 3B-2
1979	64	166	47	7	0	2	1.2	23	21	19	21	2	.283	.361	18	6	OF-29, DH-14, C-11, 3B-3
1980 2 teams	CLE A (23G – .306)			CHI A		(33G –	.300)										OF-17, DH-9, 3B-5, C-5,
" total	56	106	32	3	0	2	1.9	9	15	12	13	0	.302	.387	20	5	1B-1
1981 CLE A	5	9	0	0	0	0	0.0	0	0	1	2	0	.000	.000	2	0	OF-3, DH-1, C-1
1982 SF N	5	4	2	1	0	0	0.0	1	2	1	1	0	.500	.750	2	1	OF-1, C-1
1983	1	1	0	0	0	0	0.0	0	0	0	0	0	.000	.000	1	0	
9 yrs.	341	795	214	28	4	12	1.5	88	92	94	90	8	.269	.360	68	19	OF-162, C-89, DH-37, 3B-17, 1B-2

Greg Pryor

PRYOR, GREGORY RUSSELL
B. Oct. 2, 1949, Marietta, Ohio
BR TR 6' 180 lbs.

	G	AB	H	2B	3B	HR	HR %	R	RBI	BB	SO	SB	BA	SA	PH AB	PH H	G by POS
1976 TEX A	5	8	3	0	0	0	0.0	2	1	0	1	0	.375	.375	0	0	2B-3, SS-1, 3B-1
1978 CHI A	82	222	58	11	0	2	0.9	27	15	11	18	3	.261	.338	0	0	2B-35, SS-28, 3B-20
1979	143	476	131	23	3	3	0.6	60	34	35	41	3	.275	.355	1	0	SS-119, 2B-25, 3B-22
1980	122	338	81	18	4	1	0.3	32	29	12	35	2	.240	.325	5	1	SS-76, 3B-41, 2B-5, DH-1
1981	47	76	17	1	0	0	0.0	4	6	6	8	0	.224	.237	1	0	3B-27, SS-13, 2B-5
1982 KC A	73	152	41	10	1	2	1.3	23	12	10	20	2	.270	.388	3	0	3B-40, 2B-15, 1B-14, SS-7
1983	68	115	25	4	0	1	0.9	9	14	7	8	0	.217	.278	1	0	3B-60, 1B-6, 2B-3
1984	123	270	71	11	1	4	1.5	32	25	12	28	0	.263	.356	3	1	3B-105, 2B-22, SS-2, DH-1, 1B-1
8 yrs.	663	1657	427	78	9	13	0.8	189	136	93	159	10	.258	.339	14	2	3B-316, SS-246, 2B-113, 1B-21, DH-2

LEAGUE CHAMPIONSHIP SERIES

	G	AB	H	2B	3B	HR	HR %	R	RBI	BB	SO	SB	BA	SA	PH AB	PH H	G by POS
1984 KC A	1	0	0	0	0	0	-	0	0	0	0	0	-	-	0	0	3B-1

George Puccinelli

PUCCINELLI, GEORGE LAWRENCE (Count)
B. June 22, 1906, San Francisco, Calif.   D. Apr. 16, 1956, San Francisco, Calif.
BR TR 6'½" 190 lbs.

	G	AB	H	2B	3B	HR	HR %	R	RBI	BB	SO	SB	BA	SA	PH AB	PH H	G by POS
1930 STL N	11	16	9	1	0	3	18.8	5	8	0	1	0	.563	1.188	8	4	OF-3
1932	31	108	30	8	0	3	2.8	17	11	12	13	1	.278	.435	1	0	OF-30
1934 STL A	10	26	6	1	0	2	7.7	4	5	1	8	0	.231	.500	4	0	OF-6
1936 PHI A	135	457	127	30	3	11	2.4	83	78	65	70	2	.278	.429	17	3	OF-117
4 yrs.	187	607	172	40	3	19	3.1	109	102	78	92	3	.283	.453	30	7	OF-156

WORLD SERIES

	G	AB	H	2B	3B	HR	HR %	R	RBI	BB	SO	SB	BA	SA	PH AB	PH H	G by POS
1930 STL N	1	1	0	0	0	0	0.0	0	0	0	0	0	.000	.000	1	0	

Kirby Puckett

PUCKETT, KIRBY
B. Mar. 14, 1961, Chicago, Ill.
BR TR 5'8" 178 lbs.

	G	AB	H	2B	3B	HR	HR %	R	RBI	BB	SO	SB	BA	SA	PH AB	PH H	G by POS
1984 MIN A	128	557	165	12	5	0	0.0	63	31	16	69	14	.296	.336	0	0	OF-128

John Puhl

PUHL, JOHN
B. 1875, Bayonne, N.J.   D. Aug. 24, 1900, Bayonne, N.J.

	G	AB	H	2B	3B	HR	HR %	R	RBI	BB	SO	SB	BA	SA	PH AB	PH H	G by POS
1898 NY N	2	9	2	0	0	0	0.0	1	1	0		0	.222	.222	0	0	3B-2
1899	1	2	0	0	0	0	0.0	0	0	0		0	.000	.000	0	0	3B-1
2 yrs.	3	11	2	0	0	0	0.0	1	1	0		0	.182	.182	0	0	3B-3

Terry Puhl

PUHL, TERRY STEPHEN
B. July 8, 1956, Melville, Sask., Canada
BL TR 6'2" 195 lbs.

	G	AB	H	2B	3B	HR	HR %	R	RBI	BB	SO	SB	BA	SA	PH AB	PH H	G by POS
1977 HOU N	60	229	69	13	5	0	0.0	40	10	30	31	10	.301	.402	0	0	OF-59
1978	149	585	169	25	6	3	0.5	87	35	48	46	32	.289	.368	1	1	OF-148
1979	157	600	172	22	4	8	1.3	87	49	58	46	30	.287	.377	5	1	OF-152
1980	141	535	151	24	5	13	2.4	75	55	60	52	27	.282	.419	6	0	OF-135
1981	96	350	88	19	4	3	0.9	43	28	31	49	22	.251	.354	8	1	OF-88
1982	145	507	133	17	9	8	1.6	64	50	64	51	49	.262	.379	7	3	OF-138
1983	137	465	136	25	7	8	1.7	66	44	36	48	24	.292	.428	15	4	OF-124
1984	132	449	135	19	7	9	2.0	66	55	59	45	13	.301	.434	5	2	OF-126
8 yrs.	1017	3720	1053	164	47	52	1.4	528	326	373	366	175	.283	.394	47	12	OF-970

DIVISIONAL PLAYOFF SERIES

	G	AB	H	2B	3B	HR	HR %	R	RBI	BB	SO	SB	BA	SA	PH AB	PH H	G by POS
1981 HOU N	5	21	4	1	0	0	0.0	2	0	0	1	1	.190	.238	0	0	OF-5

	G	AB	H	2B	3B	HR	HR %	R	RBI	BB	SO	SB	BA	SA	Pinch Hit AB	Pinch Hit H	G by POS

Terry Puhl continued

LEAGUE CHAMPIONSHIP SERIES
| 1980 HOU N | 5 | 19 | 10 | 2 | 0 | 0 | 0.0 | 4 | 3 | 3 | 2 | 2 | .526 | .632 | 1 | 0 | OF-4 |

Rich Puig

PUIG, RICHARD GERALD
B. Mar. 16, 1953, Tampa, Fla. BL TR 5'10" 165 lbs.

| 1974 NY N | 4 | 10 | 0 | 0 | 0 | 0 | 0.0 | 0 | 0 | 1 | 2 | 0 | .000 | .000 | 0 | 0 | 2B-3, 3B-1 |

Luis Pujols

PUJOLS, LUIS BIENVENIDO
Also known as Luis Bienvenido Toribia.
B. Nov. 18, 1955, Santiago Rodriguez, Dominican Republic BR TR 6'2" 175 lbs.

1977 HOU N	6	15	1	0	0	0	0.0	0	0	0	5	0	.067	.067	0	0	C-6
1978	56	153	20	8	1	1	0.7	11	11	12	45	0	.131	.216	0	0	C-55, 1B-1
1979	26	75	17	2	1	0	0.0	7	8	2	14	0	.227	.280	0	0	C-26
1980	78	221	44	6	1	0	0.0	15	20	13	29	0	.199	.235	0	0	C-75, 3B-1
1981	40	117	28	3	1	1	0.9	5	14	10	17	1	.239	.308	7	0	C-39
1982	65	176	35	6	2	4	2.3	8	15	10	40	0	.199	.324	1	0	C-64
1983	40	87	17	2	0	0	0.0	4	12	5	14	0	.195	.218	0	0	C-39
1984 KC A	4	5	1	0	0	0	0.0	0	1	0	0	0	.200	.200	1	0	C-4
8 yrs.	315	849	163	27	6	6	0.7	50	81	52	164	1	.192	.259	12	1	C-308, 3B-1, 1B-1

DIVISIONAL PLAYOFF SERIES
| 1981 HOU N | 2 | 6 | 0 | 0 | 0 | 0 | 0.0 | 0 | 0 | 0 | 1 | 0 | .000 | .000 | 0 | 0 | C-2 |

LEAGUE CHAMPIONSHIP SERIES
| 1980 HOU N | 4 | 10 | 1 | 0 | 1 | 0 | 0.0 | 1 | 0 | 3 | 0 | 0 | .100 | .300 | 0 | 0 | C-4 |

Blondie Purcell

PURCELL, WILLIAM ALOYSIUS
B. Mar. 16, 1854, Paterson, N. J. Deceased.
Manager 1883. BR TR 5'9½" 159 lbs.

1879 2 teams	SYR N	(63G –	.260)		CIN N	(12G –	.220)										
" total	75	327	83	3	0	0	0.0	42	29	3	16		.254	.291	0	0	OF-57, P-24, C-1
1880 CIN N	77	325	95	13	6	1	0.3	48	24	5	13		.292	.378	0	0	OF-55, P-25, SS-1
1881 2 teams	CLE N	(20G –	.175)		BUF N	(30G –	.292)										
" total	50	193	47	9	3	0	0.0	18	21	14	16		.244	.321	0	0	OF-45, P-9
1882 BUF N	84	380	105	18	6	2	0.5	79		14	27		.276	.371	0	0	OF-82, P-6
1883 PHI N	97	425	114	20	5	1	0.2	70		13	26		.268	.346	0	0	3B-46, OF-44, P-11
1884	103	428	108	11	4	1	0.2	67		29	30		.252	.318	0	0	OF-103, P-1
1885 2 teams	PHI	AA (66G –	.296)		BOS N	(21G –	.218)										
" total	87	391	109	16	6	0	0.0	80	3	19	15		.279	.350	0	0	OF-87, P-1
1886 BAL AA	26	85	19	0	1	0	0.0	17		17			.224	.247	0	0	OF-26, SS-1, P-1
1887	140	567	142	25	8	4	0.7	101		46		88	.250	.344	0	0	OF-140, P-1
1888 2 teams	BAL	AA (101G –	.236)		PHI	AA (18G –	.167)										
" total	119	472	107	12	5	2	0.4	63	45	32		26	.227	.286	0	0	OF-117, SS-2, 3B-1, 1B-1
1889 PHI AA	129	507	160	19	7	2	0.4	72	85	50	27	22	.316	.381	0	0	OF-129
1890	110	463	128	28	3	2	0.4	110		43		48	.276	.363	0	0	OF-110
12 yrs.	1097	4563	1217	177	60	13	0.3	767	207	285	170	184	.267	.340	0	0	OF-995, P-79, 3B-47, SS-4, 1B-1, C-1

Pid Purdy

PURDY, EVERETT VIRGIL
B. June 15, 1904, Beatrice, Neb. D. Jan. 16, 1951, Beatrice, Neb. BL TR 5'6" 150 lbs.

1926 CHI A	11	33	6	2	1	0	0.0	5	6	2	1	0	.182	.303	2	0	OF-9
1927 CIN N	18	62	22	2	4	1	1.6	15	12	4	3	0	.355	.565	2	1	OF-16
1928	70	223	69	11	1	0	0.0	32	25	23	13	1	.309	.368	8	6	OF-61
1929	82	181	49	7	5	1	0.6	22	16	19	8	2	.271	.381	33	8	OF-42
4 yrs.	181	499	146	22	11	2	0.4	74	59	48	25	3	.293	.393	45	15	OF-128

Jesse Purnell

PURNELL, JESSE RHOADES (Scrappy)
B. May 11, 1879, Glenside, Pa. D. July 4, 1966, Philadelphia, Pa. BL TR 5'5½" 140 lbs.

| 1904 PHI N | 7 | 19 | 2 | 0 | 0 | 0 | 0.0 | 2 | 1 | 4 | | 1 | .105 | .105 | 0 | 0 | 3B-7 |

Billy Purtell

PURTELL, WILLIAM PATRICK
B. Jan. 6, 1886, Columbus, Ohio D. Mar. 17, 1962, Bradenton, Fla. BR TR 5'9" 170 lbs.

1908 CHI A	26	69	9	2	0	0	0.0	3	3	2		2	.130	.159	1	0	3B-25
1909	103	361	93	9	3	0	0.0	34	40	19		14	.258	.299	0	0	3B-71, 2B-32
1910 2 teams	CHI	A (102G –	.234)		BOS	A (49G –	.208)										
" total	151	536	121	6	5	2	0.4	36	51	39		7	.226	.267	0	0	3B-143, SS-8
1911 BOS A	27	82	23	5	2	0	0.0	5	7	1		1	.280	.415	5	1	3B-16, SS-3, 2B-3, OF-1
1914 DET A	26	76	13	4	0	0	0.0	4	3	2	7	0	.171	.224	8	1	3B-16, SS-1, 1B-1
5 yrs.	333	1124	259	26	11	2	0.2	82	104	63	7	24	.230	.278	14	2	3B-271, 2B-36, SS-12, OF-1

Ed Putman

PUTMAN, EDDIE WILLIAM
B. Sept. 25, 1953, Los Angeles, Calif. BR TR 6'1" 190 lbs.

1976 CHI N	5	7	3	0	0	0	0.0	0	0	0	0	0	.429	.429	2	1	C-3, 1B-1
1978	17	25	5	0	0	0	0.0	2	3	4	6	0	.200	.200	5	2	3B-8, 1B-3, C-2
1979 DET A	21	39	9	3	0	2	5.1	4	4	4	12	0	.231	.462	3	0	C-16, 1B-5
3 yrs.	43	71	17	3	0	2	2.8	6	7	8	18	0	.239	.366	10	3	C-21, 1B-9, 3B-8

Pat Putnam

PUTNAM, PATRICK EDWARD
B. Dec. 3, 1953, Bethel, Vt. BL TR 6' 205 lbs.

1977 TEX A	11	26	8	4	0	0	0.0	0	0	1	4	0	.308	.462	2	1	1B-7, DH-3
1978	20	46	7	1	0	1	2.2	4	2	2	5	0	.152	.239	5	1	DH-12, 1B-4
1979	139	426	118	19	2	18	4.2	57	64	23	50	1	.277	.458	21	8	1B-96, DH-32
1980	147	410	108	16	2	13	3.2	42	55	36	49	0	.263	.407	18	8	1B-137, DH-1, 3B-1
1981	95	297	79	17	2	8	2.7	33	35	17	38	4	.266	.418	2	0	1B-94, OF-3
1982	43	122	28	8	0	2	1.6	14	9	10	18	0	.230	.344	6	1	1B-39, OF-1, 3B-1
1983 SEA A	144	469	126	23	2	19	4.1	58	67	39	57	2	.269	.448	12	4	1B-125, DH-11

	G	AB	H	2B	3B	HR	HR%	R	RBI	BB	SO	SB	BA	SA	PH AB	PH H	G by POS

Pat Putnam *continued*

Year/Team	G	AB	H	2B	3B	HR	HR%	R	RBI	BB	SO	SB	BA	SA	PH AB	PH H	G by POS
1984 2 teams SEA A (64G – .200) MIN A (14G – .079)										16	39	3	.176	.244	25	4	DH-14, OF-13, 1B-6
" total	78	193	34	7	0	2	1.0	12	20	16	39	3	.176	.244	25	4	
8 yrs.	677	1989	508	95	8	63	3.2	223	255	144	260	10	.255	.406	91	27	1B-508, DH-73, OF-17, 3B-2

Jim Pyburn

PYBURN, JAMES EDWARD
B. Nov. 1, 1932, Fairfield, Ala.
BR TR 6' 190 lbs.

Year/Team	G	AB	H	2B	3B	HR	HR%	R	RBI	BB	SO	SB	BA	SA	PH AB	PH H	G by POS
1955 BAL A	39	98	20	2	2	0	0.0	5	7	8	24	1	.204	.265	6	1	3B-33, OF-1
1956	84	156	27	3	3	2	1.3	23	11	17	26	4	.173	.269	7	2	OF-77
1957	35	40	9	0	0	1	2.5	8	2	9	6	1	.225	.300	5	1	OF-28, C-1
3 yrs.	158	294	56	5	5	3	1.0	36	20	34	56	6	.190	.272	18	4	OF-106, 3B-33, C-1

Frankie Pytlak

PYTLAK, FRANK ANTHONY
B. July 30, 1908, Buffalo, N. Y.   D. May 8, 1977, Buffalo, N. Y.
BR TR 5'7½" 160 lbs.

Year/Team	G	AB	H	2B	3B	HR	HR%	R	RBI	BB	SO	SB	BA	SA	PH AB	PH H	G by POS
1932 CLE A	12	29	7	1	1	0	0.0	5	4	3	2	0	.241	.345	0	0	C-12
1933	80	248	77	10	6	2	0.8	36	33	17	10	3	.310	.423	6	3	C-69
1934	91	289	75	12	4	0	0.0	46	35	36	11	11	.260	.329	3	1	C-88
1935	55	149	44	6	1	1	0.7	14	12	11	4	3	.295	.369	7	3	C-48
1936	75	224	72	15	4	0	0.0	35	31	24	11	5	.321	.424	15	3	C-58
1937	125	397	125	15	6	1	0.3	60	44	52	15	16	.315	.390	9	4	C-115
1938	113	364	112	14	7	1	0.3	46	43	36	15	9	.308	.393	15	2	C-99
1939	63	183	49	2	5	0	0.0	20	14	20	5	1	.268	.333	5	3	C-51
1940	62	149	21	2	1	0	0.0	16	16	17	5	0	.141	.168	3	1	C-58, OF-1
1941 BOS A	106	336	91	23	1	2	0.6	36	39	28	19	5	.271	.363	11	4	C-91
1945	9	17	2	0	0	0	0.0	1	0	3	0	0	.118	.118	2	0	C-6
1946	4	14	2	0	0	0	0.0	1	1	9	0	0	.143	.143	0	0	C-4
12 yrs.	795	2399	677	100	36	7	0.3	316	272	247	97	56	.282	.363	76	24	C-699, OF-1

Jim Qualls

QUALLS, JAMES ROBERT
B. Oct. 9, 1946, Exeter, Calif.
BB TR 5'10" 158 lbs.

Year/Team	G	AB	H	2B	3B	HR	HR%	R	RBI	BB	SO	SB	BA	SA	PH AB	PH H	G by POS
1969 CHI N	43	120	30	5	3	0	0.0	12	9	2	14	2	.250	.342	4	2	OF-35, 2B-4
1970 MON N	9	9	1	0	0	0	0.0	1	1	0	0	0	.111	.111	5	1	OF-2, 2B-2
1972 CHI A	11	10	0	0	0	0	0.0	0	0	0	2	0	.000	.000	7	0	OF-1
3 yrs.	63	139	31	5	3	0	0.0	13	10	2	16	2	.223	.302	16	3	OF-38, 2B-6

Billy Queen

QUEEN, BILLY EDDLEMAN (Doc)
B. Nov. 28, 1928, Gastonia, N. C.
BR TR 6'1" 185 lbs.

Year/Team	G	AB	H	2B	3B	HR	HR%	R	RBI	BB	SO	SB	BA	SA	PH AB	PH H	G by POS
1954 MIL N	3	2	0	0	0	0	0.0	0	0	0	2	0	.000	.000	2	0	OF-1

Mel Queen

QUEEN, MELVIN DOUGLAS
Son of Mel Queen.
B. Mar. 26, 1942, Johnson City, N. Y.
BL TR 6'1" 189 lbs.

Year/Team	G	AB	H	2B	3B	HR	HR%	R	RBI	BB	SO	SB	BA	SA	PH AB	PH H	G by POS
1964 CIN N	48	95	19	2	0	2	2.1	7	12	4	19	0	.200	.284	26	5	OF-20
1965	5	3	0	0	0	0	0.0	0	0	0	1	0	.000	.000	3	0	OF-1
1966	56	55	7	1	0	0	0.0	4	5	10	12	0	.127	.145	17	3	OF-32, P-7
1967	49	81	17	4	0	0	0.0	6	5	4	10	2	.210	.259	13	1	P-31
1968	10	8	1	0	0	0	0.0	2	0	1	3	0	.125	.125	3	0	P-5
1969	2	6	1	0	0	0	0.0	0	1	0	2	0	.167	.167	2	0	P-2
1970 CAL A	37	16	4	0	0	0	0.0	1	1	0	2	0	.250	.250	4	3	P-34
1971	45	8	0	0	0	0	0.0	1	1	1	0	0	.000	.000	2	0	P-44
1972	17	2	0	0	0	0	0.0	0	0	1	1	0	.000	.000	0	0	P-17
9 yrs.	269	274	49	7	0	2	0.7	20	25	21	50	2	.179	.226	68	12	P-140, OF-53

George Quellich

QUELLICH, GEORGE WILLIAM
B. Feb. 10, 1906, Johnsville, Calif.   D. Aug. 31, 1958, Johnsville, Calif.
BR TR 6'1" 180 lbs.

Year/Team	G	AB	H	2B	3B	HR	HR%	R	RBI	BB	SO	SB	BA	SA	PH AB	PH H	G by POS
1931 DET A	13	54	12	5	0	1	1.9	6	11	3	4	1	.222	.370	0	0	OF-13

Joe Quest

QUEST, JOSEPH L.
B. 1852, New Castle, Pa.   Deceased.
BR TR 5'6" 150 lbs.

Year/Team	G	AB	H	2B	3B	HR	HR%	R	RBI	BB	SO	SB	BA	SA	PH AB	PH H	G by POS
1878 IND N	62	278	57	3	2	0	0.0	45	13	12	24		.205	.230	0	0	2B-62
1879 CHI N	83	334	69	16	1	0	0.0	38	22	9	33		.207	.260	0	0	2B-83
1880	82	300	71	12	1	0	0.0	37	27	8	16		.237	.283	0	0	2B-80, SS-2, 3B-1
1881	78	293	72	6	0	1	0.3	35	26	2	29		.246	.276	0	0	2B-77, SS-1
1882	42	159	32	5	2	0	0.0	24	15	8	16		.201	.258	0	0	2B-41, SS-1
1883 2 teams DET N (37G – .234) STL AA (19G – .256)										11	18		.242	.321	0	0	2B-56
" total	56	215	52	11	3	0	0.0	34		11	18		.242	.321	0	0	
1884 2 teams STL AA (81G – .206) PIT AA (12G – .209)										19			.207	.269	0	0	2B-87, SS-5, OF-1
" total	93	353	73	12	5	0	0.0	48		19			.207	.269	0	0	2B-39, SS-15, OF-1
1885 DET N	55	200	39	8	2	0	0.0	24	21	14	25		.195	.255	0	0	SS-41, 2B-2
1886 PHI AA	42	150	31	4	1	0	0.0	14		20			.207	.247	0	0	2B-2
9 yrs.	593	2282	496	77	17	2	0.0	299	124	103	161		.217	.267	0	0	2B-527, SS-65, OF-2, 3B-1

Jim Quick

QUICK, JAMES HAROLD
B. Oct. 4, 1919, Rome, Ga.
BR TR 5'10½" 163 lbs.

Year/Team	G	AB	H	2B	3B	HR	HR%	R	RBI	BB	SO	SB	BA	SA	PH AB	PH H	G by POS
1939 WAS A	12	41	10	1	1	0	0.0	3	2	1	1	1	.244	.268	1	0	SS-10

Frank Quilici

QUILICI, FRANK RALPH (Guido)
B. May 11, 1939, Chicago, Ill.
Manager 1972-75.
BR TR 6'1" 170 lbs.

Year/Team	G	AB	H	2B	3B	HR	HR%	R	RBI	BB	SO	SB	BA	SA	PH AB	PH H	G by POS
1965 MIN A	56	149	31	5	1	0	0.0	16	7	15	33	1	.208	.255	2	0	2B-52, SS-4
1967	23	19	2	1	0	0	0.0	2	0	3	4	0	.105	.158	2	0	2B-13, 3B-8, SS-1
1968	97	229	56	11	4	1	0.4	22	22	21	45	0	.245	.341	6	1	2B-48, 3B-40, SS-6, 1B-1
1969	118	144	25	3	1	2	1.4	19	12	12	22	2	.174	.250	7	2	3B-84, 2B-36, SS-1

	G	AB	H	2B	3B	HR	HR %	R	RBI	BB	SO	SB	BA	SA	Pinch Hit AB	Pinch Hit H	G by POS

Frank Quilici continued

	G	AB	H	2B	3B	HR	HR %	R	RBI	BB	SO	SB	BA	SA	AB	H	G by POS
1970	111	141	32	3	0	2	1.4	19	12	15	16	0	.227	.291	3	1	2B-73, 3B-27, SS-1
5 yrs.	405	682	146	23	6	5	0.7	78	53	66	120	3	.214	.287	20	4	2B-222, 3B-159, SS-13, 1B-1

LEAGUE CHAMPIONSHIP SERIES
| 1970 MIN A | 3 | 2 | 0 | 0 | 0 | 0 | 0.0 | 0 | | 0 | 1 | 0 | .000 | .000 | 1 | 0 | 2B-2 |

WORLD SERIES
| 1965 MIN A | 7 | 20 | 4 | 2 | 0 | 0 | 0.0 | 2 | 1 | 4 | 3 | 0 | .200 | .300 | 0 | 0 | 2B-7 |

Lee Quillin

QUILLIN, LEON ABNER
B. May 5, 1882, North Branch, Minn.   D. Mar. 14, 1965, St. Paul, Minn.   TR

	G	AB	H	2B	3B	HR	HR %	R	RBI	BB	SO	SB	BA	SA	AB	H	G by POS
1906 CHI A	4	9	3	0	0	0	0.0	1	0	0		1	.333	.333	1	0	SS-3
1907	49	151	29	5	0	0	0.0	17	14	10		8	.192	.225	0	0	3B-48
2 yrs.	53	160	32	5	0	0	0.0	18	14	10		9	.200	.231	1	0	3B-48, SS-3

Finners Quinlan

QUINLAN, THOMAS ALOYSIUS   BL TL 5'8"   154 lbs.
B. Oct. 21, 1887, Scranton, Pa.   D. Feb. 17, 1966, Scranton, Pa.

	G	AB	H	2B	3B	HR	HR %	R	RBI	BB	SO	SB	BA	SA	AB	H	G by POS
1913 STL N	13	50	8	0	0	0	0.0	1	1	1	9	0	.160	.160	1	0	OF-12
1915 CHI A	42	114	22	3	0	0	0.0	11	7	4	11	3	.193	.219	4	0	OF-32
2 yrs.	55	164	30	3	0	0	0.0	12	8	5	20	3	.183	.201	5	0	OF-44

Larry Quinlan

QUINLAN, LAWRENCE A.
B. Marlboro, Mass.

	G	AB	H	2B	3B	HR	HR %	R	RBI	BB	SO	SB	BA	SA	AB	H	G by POS
1891 BOS AA	2	5	0	0	0	0	0.0	0	0	0	2	0	.000	.000	0	0	OF-1, C-1

Frank Quinn

QUINN, FRANK J.
B. Grand Rapids, Mich.   D. Feb. 17, 1920, Camden, Ind.

	G	AB	H	2B	3B	HR	HR %	R	RBI	BB	SO	SB	BA	SA	AB	H	G by POS
1899 CHI N	12	34	6	0	1	0	0.0	6	1	6		1	.176	.235	1	0	OF-10, 2B-1

Joe Quinn

QUINN, JOSEPH C.   5'8½"   148 lbs.
B. 1851, Chicago, Ill.   D. Jan. 2, 1909, Chicago, Ill.

	G	AB	H	2B	3B	HR	HR %	R	RBI	BB	SO	SB	BA	SA	AB	H	G by POS
1877 CHI N	4	14	1	0	0	0	0.0	1	0	1	0		.071	.071	0	0	OF-4

Joe Quinn

QUINN, JOSEPH J.   BR TR 5'7"   158 lbs.
B. Dec. 25, 1864, Sydney, Australia   D. Nov. 12, 1940, St. Louis, Mo.
Manager 1895, 1899.

	G	AB	H	2B	3B	HR	HR %	R	RBI	BB	SO	SB	BA	SA	AB	H	G by POS
1884 STL U	103	429	116	21	1	0	0.0	74		9			.270	.324	0	0	1B-100, OF-3, SS-1
1885 STL N	97	343	73	8	2	0	0.0	27	15	9	38		.213	.248	0	0	OF-57, 3B-31, 1B-11
1886	75	271	63	11	3	1	0.4	33	21	8	31		.232	.306	0	0	OF-48, 2B-15, 1B-7, 3B-4, SS-2
1888 BOS N	38	156	47	8	3	4	2.6	19	29	2	5	12	.301	.468	0	0	2B-38
1889	112	444	116	13	5	2	0.5	57	69	25	21	24	.261	.327	0	0	SS-63, 2B-47, 3B-2
1890 BOS P	130	509	153	19	8	7	1.4	87	82	44	24	29	.301	.411	0	0	2B-130
1891 BOS N	124	508	122	8	10	3	0.6	70	63	28	28	24	.240	.313	0	0	2B-124
1892	143	532	116	14	1	1	0.2	63	59	35	40	17	.218	.254	0	0	2B-143
1893 STL N	135	547	126	18	6	0	0.0	68	71	33	7	24	.230	.285	0	0	2B-135
1894	106	405	116	18	1	4	1.0	59	61	24	8	25	.286	.365	0	0	2B-106
1895	134	543	169	19	9	2	0.4	84	74	36	6	22	.311	.390	0	0	2B-134
1896 2 teams		STL	N	(48G –	.209)			BAL	N	(24G –	.329)						
" total	72	273	67	7	2	1	0.4	41	22	15	6	14	.245	.297	2	0	2B-56, OF-8, 3B-5, SS-1
1897 BAL N	75	285	74	11	4	1	0.4	33	45	13		12	.260	.337	2	0	3B-37, SS-21, 2B-11, OF-6, 1B-2
1898 2 teams		BAL	N	(12G –	.250)			STL	N	(103G –	.251)						
" total	115	407	102	11	5	0	0.0	40	41	25		13	.251	.302	0	0	2B-63, SS-41, 3B-8, OF-2
1899 CLE N	147	615	176	24	6	0	0.0	73	72	21		22	.286	.345	0	0	2B-147
1900 2 teams		STL	N	(22G –	.263)			CIN	N	(74G –	.274)						
" total	96	346	94	7	2	1	0.3	30	36	26		11	.272	.312	1	0	2B-88, SS-6, 3B-1
1901 WAS A	66	266	67	11	2	3	1.1	33	36	11		7	.252	.342	0	0	2B-66
17 yrs.	1768	6879	1797	228	70	30	0.4	891	795	364	214	256	.261	.328	6	0	2B-1303, SS-135, OF-124, 1B-120, 3B-88

John Quinn

QUINN, JOHN EDWARD PICK (Pit)   BR TR 6'2"   185 lbs.
B. Sept. 12, 1885, Framingham, Mass.   D. Apr. 9, 1956, Marlboro, Mass.

	G	AB	H	2B	3B	HR	HR %	R	RBI	BB	SO	SB	BA	SA	AB	H	G by POS
1911 PHI N	1	2	0	0	0	0	0.0	0	0	0	0	0	.000	.000	0	0	C-1

Paddy Quinn

QUINN, PATRICK
B. Boston, Mass.   D. Mar., 1893

	G	AB	H	2B	3B	HR	HR %	R	RBI	BB	SO	SB	BA	SA	AB	H	G by POS
1881 2 teams		BOS	N	(1G –	.000)			WOR	N	(2G –	.143)						
" total	3	11	1	0	0	0	0.0	0	1	1	2		.091	.091	0	0	C-2, 1B-1

Tom Quinn

QUINN, THOMAS G.   BR TR 5'8"   180 lbs.
B. Apr. 25, 1864, Pittsburgh, Pa.   D. July 24, 1932, Swissvale, Pa.

	G	AB	H	2B	3B	HR	HR %	R	RBI	BB	SO	SB	BA	SA	AB	H	G by POS
1886 PIT AA	3	11	0	0	0	0	0.0	1		0			.000	.000	0	0	C-3
1889 BAL AA	55	194	34	1	1	1	0.5	18	15	19	22	6	.175	.211	0	0	C-55
1890 PIT P	55	207	44	4	3	1	0.5	23	15	17	8	1	.213	.275	0	0	C-55
3 yrs.	113	412	78	6	4	2	0.5	42	29	36	30	7	.189	.238	0	0	C-113

Luis Quinones

QUINONES, LUIS RAUL   BB TR 5'10"   150 lbs.
B. Apr. 28, 1962, Ponce, Puerto Rico

	G	AB	H	2B	3B	HR	HR %	R	RBI	BB	SO	SB	BA	SA	AB	H	G by POS
1983 OAK A	19	42	8	2	1	0	0.0	5	4	1	4	1	.190	.286	1	1	2B-6, DH-4, OF-4, 3B-4, SS-3

	G	AB	H	2B	3B	HR	HR %	R	RBI	BB	SO	SB	BA	SA	Pinch Hit AB	H	G by POS

Marshall Quinton

QUINTON, MARSHALL J.
B. Philadelphia, Pa. Deceased.

5'11"   190 lbs.

	G	AB	H	2B	3B	HR	HR %	R	RBI	BB	SO	SB	BA	SA	AB	H	G by POS
1884 RIC AA	26	94	22	5	0	0	0.0	12		0			.234	.287	0	0	C-14, OF-10, SS-2
1885 PHI AA	7	29	6	1	0	0	0.0	6		1			.207	.241	0	0	C-7
2 yrs.	33	123	28	6	0	0	0.0	18		1			.228	.276	0	0	C-21, OF-10, SS-2

Jamie Quirk

QUIRK, JAMES PATRICK
B. Oct. 22, 1954, Whittier, Calif.

BL TR 6'4"   190 lbs.

	G	AB	H	2B	3B	HR	HR %	R	RBI	BB	SO	SB	BA	SA	AB	H	G by POS
1975 KC A	14	39	10	0	0	1	2.6	2	5	2	7	0	.256	.333	1	1	OF-10, 3B-2, DH-1
1976	64	114	28	6	0	1	0.9	11	15	2	22	0	.246	.325	32	7	DH-19, SS-12, 3B-11, 1B-2
1977 MIL A	93	221	48	14	1	3	1.4	16	13	8	47	0	.217	.330	29	5	DH-53, OF-10, 3B-8
1978 KC A	17	29	6	2	0	0	0.0	3	2	5	4	0	.207	.276	4	2	3B-10, SS-2, DH-1
1979	51	79	24	6	1	1	1.3	8	11	5	13	0	.304	.443	30	8	DH-9, C-9, SS-5, 3B-3
1980	62	163	45	5	0	5	3.1	13	21	7	24	3	.276	.399	12	1	3B-28, C-15, OF-7, 1B-1
1981	46	100	25	7	0	0	0.0	8	10	6	17	0	.250	.320	18	4	C-22, 3B-8, DH-1, 2B-1
1982	36	78	18	3	0	1	1.3	8	5	3	15	0	.231	.308	7	1	C-29, 1B-6, OF-1, 3B-1
1983 STL N	48	86	18	2	1	2	2.3	3	11	6	27	0	.209	.326	17	1	C-22, 3B-7, SS-1
1984 2 teams	CHI	A (3G – .000)							CLE	A	(1G – 1.000)						
" total	4	3	1	0	0	1	33.3	1	2	0	2	0	.333	1.333	2	0	3B-1, C-1
10 yrs.	435	912	223	45	3	15	1.6	73	95	44	178	3	.245	.350	152	30	C-98, DH-84, 3B-79, OF-28, SS-20, 1B-9, 2B-1

LEAGUE CHAMPIONSHIP SERIES

	G	AB	H	2B	3B	HR	HR %	R	RBI	BB	SO	SB	BA	SA	AB	H	G by POS
1976 KC A	4	7	1	0	1	0	0.0	1	2	0	2	0	.143	.429	1	0	DH-2

Johnny Rabb

RABB, JOHN ANDREW
B. June 23, 1960, Los Angeles, Calif.

BR TR 6'1"   179 lbs.

	G	AB	H	2B	3B	HR	HR %	R	RBI	BB	SO	SB	BA	SA	AB	H	G by POS
1982 SF N	2	2	1	0	0	0	0.0	0	0	0	1	0	.500	1.500	1	0	OF-1
1983	40	104	24	9	0	1	1.0	10	14	9	17	1	.231	.346	6	2	C-31, OF-2
1984	54	82	16	1	0	3	3.7	10	9	10	33	1	.195	.317	28	2	1B-13, OF-8, C-6
3 yrs.	96	188	41	10	0	4	2.1	20	23	19	51	2	.218	.346	35	4	C-37, 1B-13, OF-11

Joe Rabbitt

RABBITT, JOSEPH PATRICK
B. Jan. 15, 1901, Frontenac, Kans.   D. Dec. 5, 1969, Norwalk, Conn.

BL TR 5'10"   165 lbs.

	G	AB	H	2B	3B	HR	HR %	R	RBI	BB	SO	SB	BA	SA	AB	H	G by POS
1922 CLE A	2	3	1	0	0	0	0.0	1	0	0	0	0	.333	.333	0	0	OF-1

Marv Rackley

RACKLEY, MARVIN EUGENE
B. July 25, 1921, Seneca, S. C.

BL TL 5'10"   170 lbs.

	G	AB	H	2B	3B	HR	HR %	R	RBI	BB	SO	SB	BA	SA	AB	H	G by POS
1947 BKN N	18	9	2	0	0	0	0.0	2	1	1	0	0	.222	.222	5	1	OF-2
1948	88	281	92	13	5	0	0.0	55	15	19	25	8	.327	.409	11	3	OF-74
1949 3 teams	BKN	N (11G – .444)				PIT	N	(11G – .314)			BKN	N	(54G – .291)				
" total	74	185	56	7	1	1	0.5	30	17	16	11	2	.303	.368	17	6	OF-55
1950 CIN N	5	2	1	0	0	0	0.0	0	1	0	0	0	.500	.500	2	1	
4 yrs.	185	477	151	20	6	1	0.2	87	35	36	36	10	.317	.390	35	11	OF-131

WORLD SERIES

	G	AB	H	2B	3B	HR	HR %	R	RBI	BB	SO	SB	BA	SA	AB	H	G by POS
1949 BKN N	2	5	0	0	0	0	0.0	0	0	0	2	0	.000	.000	0	0	OF-2

Old Hoss Radbourn

RADBOURN, CHARLES GARDNER
Brother of George Radbourn.
B. Dec. 11, 1854, Rochester, N. Y.   D. Feb. 5, 1897, Bloomington, Ill.
Hall of Fame 1939.

BR TR 5'9"   168 lbs.

	G	AB	H	2B	3B	HR	HR %	R	RBI	BB	SO	SB	BA	SA	AB	H	G by POS
1880 BUF N	6	21	3	0	0	0	0.0	1	1	0	1		.143	.143	0	0	OF-3, 2B-3
1881 PRO N	72	270	59	9	0	0	0.0	27	28	10	15		.219	.252	0	0	P-40, OF-25, SS-13
1882	83	326	78	11	0	1	0.3	30		12	22		.239	.282	0	0	P-55, OF-31, SS-1
1883	89	381	108	11	3	3	0.8	59		14	16		.283	.352	0	0	P-76, OF-20, 1B-2
1884	87	361	83	7	1	1	0.3	48		26	42		.230	.263	0	0	P-75, OF-7, 1B-5, SS-2, 2B-1
1885	66	249	58	9	2	0	0.0	34	22	36	35		.233	.285	0	0	P-49, OF-16, 2B-2
1886 BOS N	66	253	60	5	1	2	0.8	30	22	17	36		.237	.289	0	0	P-58
1887	51	175	40	2	2	1	0.6	25	24	18	21	6	.229	.280	0	0	P-50, OF-2
1888	24	79	17	1	0	0	0.0	6	6	3	14	4	.215	.228	0	0	P-24
1889	35	122	23	1	0	1	0.8	17	13	9	19	3	.189	.221	0	0	P-33, OF-2, 3B-1
1890 BOS P	45	154	39	6	0	0	0.0	20	16	9	20	7	.253	.292	0	0	P-41, OF-4, 1B-1
1891 CIN N	29	96	17	2	2	0	0.0	11	10	4	11	0	.177	.240	0	0	P-26, OF-2, 3B-1
12 yrs.	653	2487	585	64	11	9	0.4	308	142	158	244	21	.235	.281	0	0	P-527, OF-112, SS-16, 1B-8, 2B-6, 3B-2

Rip Radcliff

RADCLIFF, RAYMOND ALLEN
B. Jan. 19, 1906, Kiowa, Okla.   D. May 23, 1962, Enid, Okla.

BL TL 5'10"   170 lbs.

	G	AB	H	2B	3B	HR	HR %	R	RBI	BB	SO	SB	BA	SA	AB	H	G by POS
1934 CHI A	14	56	15	2	1	0	0.0	7	5	0	2	1	.268	.339	0	0	OF-14
1935	146	623	178	28	8	10	1.6	95	68	53	21	4	.286	.404	2	0	OF-142
1936	138	618	207	31	7	8	1.3	120	82	44	12	6	.335	.447	6	3	OF-132
1937	144	584	190	38	10	4	0.7	105	79	53	25	6	.325	.445	5	3	OF-139
1938	129	503	166	23	6	5	1.0	64	81	36	17	5	.330	.429	7	2	OF-99, 1B-23
1939	113	397	105	25	2	2	0.5	49	53	26	21	1	.264	.353	13	1	OF-78, 1B-20
1940 STL A	150	584	**200**	33	9	7	1.2	83	81	47	20	6	.342	.466	5	1	OF-139, 1B-4
1941 2 teams	STL	A (19G – .282)				DET	N	(96G – .317)									
" total	115	450	140	16	7	5	1.1	59	58	29	14	5	.311	.411	8	0	OF-101, 1B-3
1942 DET A	62	144	36	5	0	1	0.7	13	20	9	6	0	.250	.306	29	3	OF-24, 1B-4
1943	70	115	30	4	0	0	0.0	3	10	13	3	1	.261	.296	44	11	OF-19, 1B-1
10 yrs.	1081	4074	1267	205	50	42	1.0	598	532	310	141	40	.311	.417	119	24	OF-887, 1B-55

Dave Rader

RADER, DAVID MARTIN
B. Dec. 26, 1948, Claremore, Okla.

BL TR 5'11"   165 lbs.

	G	AB	H	2B	3B	HR	HR %	R	RBI	BB	SO	SB	BA	SA	AB	H	G by POS
1971 SF N	3	4	0	0	0	0	0.0	0	0	0	0	0	.000	.000	3	0	C-1
1972	133	459	119	14	1	6	1.3	44	41	29	31	1	.259	.333	9	2	C-127
1973	148	462	106	15	4	9	1.9	59	41	63	22	0	.229	.338	4	3	C-148

	G	AB	H	2B	3B	HR	HR %	R	RBI	BB	SO	SB	BA	SA	Pinch Hit AB	Pinch Hit H	G by POS

Dave Rader continued

	G	AB	H	2B	3B	HR	HR %	R	RBI	BB	SO	SB	BA	SA	PH AB	PH H	G by POS
1974	113	323	94	16	2	1	0.3	26	26	31	21	1	.291	.362	13	4	C-109
1975	98	292	85	15	0	5	1.7	39	31	32	30	1	.291	.394	7	1	C-94
1976	88	255	67	15	0	1	0.4	25	22	27	21	2	.263	.333	12	2	C-81
1977 STL N	66	114	30	7	1	1	0.9	15	16	9	10	3	.263	.368	28	9	C-38
1978 CHI N	116	305	62	13	3	3	1.0	29	36	34	26	1	.203	.295	13	4	C-114
1979 PHI N	31	54	11	1	1	1	1.9	3	5	6	7	0	.204	.315	7	1	C-25
1980 BOS A	50	137	45	11	0	3	2.2	14	17	14	12	1	.328	.474	9	2	C-34, DH-9
10 yrs.	846	2405	619	107	12	30	1.2	254	235	245	180	10	.257	.349	105	28	C-771, DH-9

Don Rader

RADER, DONALD RUSSELL   BL TR 5'10" 164 lbs.
B. Sept. 5, 1893, Wolcott, Ind.   D. June 28, 1983, Walla Walla, Wash.

	G	AB	H	2B	3B	HR	HR %	R	RBI	BB	SO	SB	BA	SA	PH AB	PH H	G by POS
1913 CHI A	2	3	1	1	0	0	0.0	1	0	0	0	0	.333	.667	0	0	OF-1, 3B-1
1921 PHI N	9	32	9	2	0	0	0.0	4	3	3	5	0	.281	.344	0	0	SS-9
2 yrs.	11	35	10	3	0	0	0.0	5	3	3	5	0	.286	.371	0	0	SS-9, OF-1, 3B-1

Doug Rader

RADER, DOUGLAS LEE (Rojo, The Red Rooster)   BR TR 6'2" 208 lbs.
B. July 30, 1944, Chicago, Ill.
Manager 1983-84.

	G	AB	H	2B	3B	HR	HR %	R	RBI	BB	SO	SB	BA	SA	PH AB	PH H	G by POS
1967 HOU N	47	162	54	10	4	2	1.2	24	26	7	31	0	.333	.481	6	1	1B-36, 3B-7
1968	98	333	89	16	4	6	1.8	42	43	31	51	2	.267	.393	7	3	3B-86, 1B-5
1969	155	569	140	25	3	11	1.9	62	83	62	103	1	.246	.359	0	0	3B-154, 1B-4
1970	156	576	145	25	3	25	4.3	90	87	57	102	3	.252	.452	1	0	3B-154, 1B-1
1971	135	484	118	21	4	12	2.5	51	56	40	112	5	.244	.378	1	0	3B-135
1972	152	553	131	24	7	22	4.0	70	90	57	120	5	.237	.425	0	0	3B-152
1973	154	574	146	26	0	21	3.7	79	89	46	97	4	.254	.409	2	0	3B-152
1974	152	533	137	27	3	17	3.2	61	78	60	131	7	.257	.415	0	0	3B-152
1975	129	448	100	23	2	12	2.7	41	48	42	101	5	.223	.364	4	2	3B-124, SS-2
1976 SD N	139	471	121	22	4	9	1.9	45	55	55	102	3	.257	.378	2	0	3B-137
1977 2 teams		SD N (52G – .271)				TOR A		(96G – .240)									
" total	148	483	121	26	5	18	3.7	66	67	71	107	2	.251	.437	11	1	3B-96, DH-34, 1B-7, OF-1
11 yrs.	1465	5186	1302	245	39	155	3.0	631	722	528	1057	37	.251	.403	34	7	3B-1349, 1B-53, DH-34, SS-2, OF-1

Paul Radford

RADFORD, PAUL REVERE   BR TR 5'6" 148 lbs.
B. Oct. 14, 1861, Roxbury, Mass.   D. Feb. 21, 1945, Boston, Mass.

	G	AB	H	2B	3B	HR	HR %	R	RBI	BB	SO	SB	BA	SA	PH AB	PH H	G by POS
1883 BOS N	72	258	53	6	3	0	0.0	46	14	9	26		.205	.252	0	0	OF-72
1884 PRO N	97	355	70	11	2	1	0.3	56		25	43		.197	.248	0	0	OF-96, P-2
1885	105	371	90	12	5	0	0.0	55	32	33	43		.243	.302	0	0	OF-88, SS-16, P-3, 2B-1
1886 KC N	122	493	113	17	5	0	0.0	78	20	58	48		.229	.284	0	0	OF-92, SS-30, 2B-1
1887 NY AA	122	486	129	15	5	4	0.8	127		106		73	.265	.342	0	0	SS-76, OF-37, 2B-18, P-2
1888 BKN AA	90	308	67	9	3	2	0.6	48	29	35		33	.218	.286	0	0	OF-88, 2B-2
1889 CLE N	136	487	116	21	5	1	0.2	94	46	91	37	30	.238	.308	0	0	OF-136, 3B-1
1890 CLE P	122	466	136	24	12	2	0.4	98	62	82	28	25	.292	.408	0	0	OF-80, SS-36, 3B-7, 2B-4, P-1
1891 BOS N	133	456	118	11	5	0	0.0	102	65	96	36	55	.259	.305	0	0	SS-131, OF-4, P-1
1892 WAS N	137	510	130	19	4	1	0.2	93	37	86	47	35	.255	.314	0	0	OF-62, 3B-54, SS-20, 2B-2
1893	124	464	106	18	3	2	0.4	87	34	105	42	32	.228	.293	0	0	OF-123, 2B-1, P-1
1894	95	325	78	13	5	0	0.0	61	49	65	23	24	.240	.311	0	0	SS-47, 2B-25, OF-24
12 yrs.	1361	4979	1206	176	57	13	0.3	945	388	791	373	307	.242	.308	0	0	OF-902, SS-356, 3B-62, 2B-54, P-10

Jack Radtke

RADTKE, JACK WILLIAM   BB TR 5'8" 155 lbs.
B. Apr. 14, 1913, Denver, Colo.

	G	AB	H	2B	3B	HR	HR %	R	RBI	BB	SO	SB	BA	SA	PH AB	PH H	G by POS
1936 BKN N	33	31	3	0	0	0	0.0	8	2	4	9	3	.097	.097	1	0	2B-14, 3B-5, SS-4

Jack Rafter

RAFTER, JOHN CORNELIUS   BR TR 5'8" 165 lbs.
B. Feb. 20, 1875, Troy, N. Y.   D. Jan. 5, 1943, Troy, N. Y.

	G	AB	H	2B	3B	HR	HR %	R	RBI	BB	SO	SB	BA	SA	PH AB	PH H	G by POS
1904 PIT N	1	3	0	0	0	0	0.0	0	0	0		0	.000	.000	0	0	C-1

Tom Raftery

RAFTERY, THOMAS FRANCIS   BR TR 6'
B. Oct. 5, 1881, Haverhill, Mass.   D. Dec. 31, 1954, Boston, Mass.

	G	AB	H	2B	3B	HR	HR %	R	RBI	BB	SO	SB	BA	SA	PH AB	PH H	G by POS
1909 CLE A	8	32	7	2	1	0	0.0	6	0	4		1	.219	.344	0	0	OF-8

Tom Ragland

RAGLAND, THOMAS   BR TR 5'10" 155 lbs.
B. June 16, 1946, Talladega, Ala.

	G	AB	H	2B	3B	HR	HR %	R	RBI	BB	SO	SB	BA	SA	PH AB	PH H	G by POS
1971 WAS A	10	23	4	0	0	0	0.0	1	0	0	5	0	.174	.174	0	0	2B-10
1972 TEX A	25	58	10	2	0	0	0.0	3	2	5	11	0	.172	.207	4	0	2B-13, 3B-5, SS-3
1973 CLE A	67	183	47	7	1	0	0.0	16	12	8	31	2	.257	.306	2	0	2B-65, SS-2
3 yrs.	102	264	61	9	1	0	0.0	20	14	13	47	2	.231	.273	6	0	2B-88, SS-5, 3B-5

Larry Raines

RAINES, LAWRENCE GLENN HOPE   BR TR 5'10" 165 lbs.
B. Mar. 9, 1930, St. Albans, W. Va.   D. Jan. 28, 1978, Lansing, Mich.

	G	AB	H	2B	3B	HR	HR %	R	RBI	BB	SO	SB	BA	SA	PH AB	PH H	G by POS
1957 CLE A	96	244	64	14	0	2	0.8	39	16	19	40	5	.262	.344	21	5	3B-27, SS-25, 2B-10, OF-8
1958	7	9	0	0	0	0	0.0	0	0	0	5	0	.000	.000	2	0	2B-2
2 yrs.	103	253	64	14	0	2	0.8	39	16	19	45	5	.253	.332	23	5	3B-27, SS-25, 2B-12, OF-8

Tim Raines

RAINES, TIMOTHY   BB TR 5'8" 160 lbs.
B. Sept. 16, 1959, Sanford, Fla.

	G	AB	H	2B	3B	HR	HR %	R	RBI	BB	SO	SB	BA	SA	PH AB	PH H	G by POS
1979 MON N	6	0	0	0	0	0	–	3	0	0	0	2	–	–	0	0	
1980	15	20	1	0	0	0	0.0	5	0	6	3	5	.050	.050	0	0	2B-7, OF-1
1981	88	313	95	13	7	5	1.6	61	37	45	31	71	.304	.438	0	0	OF-81, 2B-1
1982	156	647	179	32	8	4	0.6	90	43	75	83	78	.277	.369	0	0	OF-120, 2B-36

	G	AB	H	2B	3B	HR	HR %	R	RBI	BB	SO	SB	BA	SA	Pinch Hit AB	Pinch Hit H	G by POS

Tim Raines continued

	G	AB	H	2B	3B	HR	HR %	R	RBI	BB	SO	SB	BA	SA	PH AB	PH H	G by POS
1983	156	615	183	32	8	11	1.8	133	71	97	70	90	.298	.429	1	1	OF-154, 2B-7
1984	160	622	192	38	9	8	1.3	106	60	87	69	75	.309	.437	0	0	OF-160, 2B-2
6 yrs.	581	2217	650	115	32	28	1.3	398	211	310	256	321	.293	.412	1	1	OF-516, 2B-53

LEAGUE CHAMPIONSHIP SERIES

	G	AB	H	2B	3B	HR	HR %	R	RBI	BB	SO	SB	BA	SA	PH AB	PH H	G by POS
1981 MON N	5	21	5	2	0	0	0.0	1	1	0	3	0	.238	.333	0	0	OF-5

John Rainey

RAINEY, JOHN PAUL
B. July 26, 1864, Birmingham, Mich.   D. Nov. 11, 1912, Detroit, Mich.

BL TR 6'1½"   164 lbs.

	G	AB	H	2B	3B	HR	HR %	R	RBI	BB	SO	SB	BA	SA	PH AB	PH H	G by POS
1887 NY N	17	58	17	3	0	0	0.0	6	12	5	6	0	.293	.345	0	0	3B-17
1890 BUF P	42	166	39	5	1	1	0.6	29	20	24	15	12	.235	.295	0	0	OF-28, SS-7, 3B-6, 2B-2
2 yrs.	59	224	56	8	1	1	0.4	35	32	29	21	12	.250	.308	0	0	OF-28, 3B-23, SS-7, 2B-2

Gary Rajsich

RAJSICH, GARY LOUIS
Brother of Dave Rajsich.
B. Oct. 28, 1954, Youngstown, Ohio

BL TL 6'2"   190 lbs.

	G	AB	H	2B	3B	HR	HR %	R	RBI	BB	SO	SB	BA	SA	PH AB	PH H	G by POS
1982 NY N	80	162	42	8	3	2	1.2	17	17	12	40	1	.259	.383	35	2	OF-35, 1B-2
1983	11	36	12	3	0	1	2.8	5	3	3	1	0	.333	.500	1	0	OF-10
1984 STL N	7	7	1	0	0	0	0.0	1	2	2	1	0	.143	.143	4	1	1B-3
3 yrs.	98	205	55	11	3	3	1.5	23	17	22	42	1	.268	.395	40	3	OF-45, 1B-5

Doc Ralston

RALSTON, SAMUEL BERYL
B. Aug. 3, 1885, Pierpont, Ohio   D. Aug. 29, 1950, Lancaster, Pa.

BR TR 6'   185 lbs.

	G	AB	H	2B	3B	HR	HR %	R	RBI	BB	SO	SB	BA	SA	PH AB	PH H	G by POS
1910 WAS A	22	73	15	1	0	0	0.0	4	3	3		2	.205	.219	0	0	OF-22

Bob Ramazzotti

RAMAZZOTTI, ROBERT LOUIS
B. Jan. 16, 1917, Elanora, Pa.

BR TR 5'8½"   175 lbs.

	G	AB	H	2B	3B	HR	HR %	R	RBI	BB	SO	SB	BA	SA	PH AB	PH H	G by POS
1946 BKN N	62	120	25	4	0	0	0.0	10	7	9	13	0	.208	.242	15	1	3B-30, 2B-16
1948	4	3	0	0	0	0	0.0	0	0	0	1	0	.000	.000	2	0	3B-2, 2B-1
1949 2 teams		BKN	N	(5G –	.154)			CHI	N	(65G –	.179)						
" total	70	203	36	3	1	1	0.5	15	9	5	36	9	.177	.217	11	2	3B-39, SS-12, 2B-4
1950 CHI N	61	145	38	3	3	1	0.7	19	6	4	16	3	.262	.345	6	2	2B-31, 3B-10, SS-3
1951	73	158	39	5	2	1	0.6	13	15	10	23	0	.247	.323	9	2	SS-51, 2B-6, 3B-1
1952	50	183	52	5	3	1	0.5	26	12	14	14	3	.284	.361	0	0	2B-50
1953	26	39	6	2	0	0	0.0	3	4	3	4	0	.154	.205	3	0	2B-18
7 yrs.	346	851	196	22	9	4	0.5	86	53	45	107	15	.230	.291	46	7	2B-126, 3B-82, SS-66

Mario Ramirez

RAMIREZ, MARIO
Also known as Mario Torres.
B. Sept. 12, 1957, Yauco, Puerto Rico

BR TR 5'9"   155 lbs.

	G	AB	H	2B	3B	HR	HR %	R	RBI	BB	SO	SB	BA	SA	PH AB	PH H	G by POS
1980 NY N	18	24	5	0	0	0	0.0	2	0	1	7	0	.208	.208	0	0	SS-7, 2B-4, 3B-3
1981 SD N	13	13	1	0	0	0	0.0	1	1	2	5	0	.077	.077	3	1	SS-2, 3B-2
1982	13	23	4	1	0	0	0.0	1	1	2	4	0	.174	.217	5	1	SS-8, 3B-1, 2B-1
1983	55	107	21	6	3	0	0.0	11	12	20	23	0	.196	.308	15	0	SS-38, 3B-1
1984	48	59	7	1	0	2	3.4	12	9	13	14	0	.119	.237	3	0	SS-33, 3B-6, 2B-2
5 yrs.	147	226	38	8	3	2	0.9	27	23	38	53	0	.168	.257	26	2	SS-88, 3B-13, 2B-7

LEAGUE CHAMPIONSHIP SERIES

	G	AB	H	2B	3B	HR	HR %	R	RBI	BB	SO	SB	BA	SA	PH AB	PH H	G by POS
1984 SD N	2	2	0	0	0	0	0.0	0	0	0		0	.000	.000	2	0	

Milt Ramirez

RAMIREZ, MILTON
B. Apr. 2, 1950, Mayaguez, Puerto Rico

BR TR 5'9"   150 lbs.

	G	AB	H	2B	3B	HR	HR %	R	RBI	BB	SO	SB	BA	SA	PH AB	PH H	G by POS
1970 STL N	62	79	15	2	1	0	0.0	8	3	8	9	0	.190	.241	1	0	SS-59, 3B-1
1971	4	11	3	0	0	0	0.0	2	0	2	1	0	.273	.273	0	0	SS-4
1979 OAK A	28	62	10	1	1	0	0.0	4	3	3	8	0	.161	.210	0	0	3B-12, 2B-11, SS-8
3 yrs.	94	152	28	3	2	0	0.0	14	6	13	18	0	.184	.230	1	0	SS-71, 3B-13, 2B-11

Orlando Ramirez

RAMIREZ, ORLANDO
Also known as Orlando Leal.
B. Feb. 28, 1950, Cartagena, Colombia

BR TR 5'10"   175 lbs.

	G	AB	H	2B	3B	HR	HR %	R	RBI	BB	SO	SB	BA	SA	PH AB	PH H	G by POS
1974 CAL A	31	86	14	0	0	0	0.0	4	7	6	23	2	.163	.163	0	0	SS-31
1975	44	100	24	4	1	0	0.0	10	4	11	22	9	.240	.300	1	0	SS-40
1976	30	70	14	1	0	0	0.0	3	5	6	11	3	.200	.214	0	0	SS-30
1977	25	13	1	0	0	0	0.0	6	0	0	3	1	.077	.077	0	0	2B-5, SS-3, DH-1
1979	13	12	0	0	0	0	0.0	1	0	1	6	1	.000	.000	0	0	SS-10, DH-1
5 yrs.	143	281	53	5	1	0	0.0	24	16	24	65	16	.189	.214	1	0	SS-114, 2B-5, DH-2

Rafael Ramirez

RAMIREZ, RAFAEL EMILIO
B. Feb. 18, 1959, San Pedro de Macoris, Dominican Republic

BR TR 6'   170 lbs.

	G	AB	H	2B	3B	HR	HR %	R	RBI	BB	SO	SB	BA	SA	PH AB	PH H	G by POS
1980 ATL N	50	165	44	6	1	2	1.2	17	11	2	33	2	.267	.352	0	0	SS-46
1981	95	307	67	16	2	2	0.7	30	20	24	47	7	.218	.303	0	0	SS-95
1982	157	609	169	24	4	10	1.6	74	52	36	49	27	.278	.379	0	0	SS-157
1983	152	622	185	13	5	7	1.1	82	58	36	48	16	.297	.368	1	0	SS-152
1984	145	591	157	22	4	2	0.3	51	48	26	70	14	.266	.327	0	0	SS-145
5 yrs.	599	2294	622	81	16	23	1.0	254	189	124	247	66	.271	.350	1	0	SS-595

LEAGUE CHAMPIONSHIP SERIES

	G	AB	H	2B	3B	HR	HR %	R	RBI	BB	SO	SB	BA	SA	PH AB	PH H	G by POS
1982 ATL N	3	11	2	0	0	0	0.0	1	1	1	1	0	.182	.182	0	0	SS-3

Bobby Ramos

RAMOS, ROBERTO
B. Nov. 5, 1955, Havana, Cuba

BR TR 5'11"   190 lbs.

	G	AB	H	2B	3B	HR	HR %	R	RBI	BB	SO	SB	BA	SA	PH AB	PH H	G by POS
1978 MON N	2	4	0	0	0	0	0.0	0	0	0	1	0	.000	.000	1	0	C-1
1980	13	32	5	2	0	0	0.0	5	2	5	5	0	.156	.219	1	0	C-12
1981	26	41	8	1	0	1	2.4	4	3	3	5	0	.195	.293	3	2	C-23
1982 NY A	4	11	1	0	0	1	9.1	1	2	0	3	0	.091	.364	0	0	C-4
1983 MON N	27	61	14	3	1	0	0.0	2	5	8	11	0	.230	.311	0	0	C-25

	G	AB	H	2B	3B	HR	HR %	R	RBI	BB	SO	SB	BA	SA	Pinch Hit AB	Pinch Hit H	G by POS

Bobby Ramos continued

	G	AB	H	2B	3B	HR	HR %	R	RBI	BB	SO	SB	BA	SA	AB	H	G by POS
1984	31	83	16	1	0	2	2.4	8	5	6	13	0	.193	.277	0	0	C-31
6 yrs.	103	232	44	7	1	4	1.7	20	17	22	38	0	.190	.280	5	3	C-96

Chucho Ramos

RAMOS, JESUS MANUEL GARCIA
B. Apr. 12, 1918, Maturin, Venezuela

BR TL 5'10½" 167 lbs.

	G	AB	H	2B	3B	HR	HR %	R	RBI	BB	SO	SB	BA	SA	AB	H	G by POS
1944 CIN N	4	10	5	1	0	0	0.0	1	0	0	0	0	.500	.600	0	0	OF-3

Domingo Ramos

RAMOS, DOMINGO ANTONIO
B. Mar. 29, 1958, Santiago, Dominican Republic

BR TR 5'10" 154 lbs.

	G	AB	H	2B	3B	HR	HR %	R	RBI	BB	SO	SB	BA	SA	AB	H	G by POS
1978 NY A	1	0	0	0	0	0	—	0	0	0	0	0	—	—	0	0	SS-1
1980 TOR A	5	16	2	0	0	0	0.0	0	0	2	5	0	.125	.125	0	0	SS-2, 2B-2
1982 SEA A	8	26	4	2	0	0	0.0	3	1	3	2	0	.154	.231	0	0	SS-8
1983	53	127	36	4	0	2	1.6	14	10	7	12	3	.283	.362	9	1	SS-28, 3B-8, 2B-8, DH-2
1984	59	81	15	2	0	0	0.0	6	2	5	12	2	.185	.210	2	0	3B-38, SS-13, 1B-5, 2B-3
5 yrs.	126	250	57	8	0	2	0.8	23	13	17	31	5	.228	.284	11	1	SS-52, 3B-46, 2B-13, 1B-5, DH-2

Bill Ramsey

RAMSEY, WILLIAM THRACE (Square Jaw)
B. Feb. 20, 1921, Osceola, Ark.

BR TR 6'1" 190 lbs.

	G	AB	H	2B	3B	HR	HR %	R	RBI	BB	SO	SB	BA	SA	AB	H	G by POS
1945 BOS N	78	137	40	8	0	1	0.7	16	12	4	22	1	.292	.372	29	5	OF-43

Mike Ramsey

RAMSEY, MICHAEL JEFFREY
B. May 29, 1954, Roanoke, Va.

BB TR 6'1" 170 lbs.

	G	AB	H	2B	3B	HR	HR %	R	RBI	BB	SO	SB	BA	SA	AB	H	G by POS
1978 STL N	12	5	1	0	0	0	0.0	4	0	0	1	0	.200	.200	1	0	SS-4
1980	59	126	33	8	1	0	0.0	11	8	3	17	0	.262	.341	18	6	2B-24, SS-20, 3B-8
1981	47	124	32	3	0	0	0.0	19	9	8	16	4	.258	.282	7	1	SS-35, 3B-5, OF-1, 2B-1
1982	112	256	59	8	2	1	0.4	18	21	22	34	6	.230	.289	16	4	2B-43, 3B-28, SS-22, OF-2
1983	97	175	46	4	3	1	0.6	25	16	12	23	4	.263	.337	6	1	2B-66, SS-20, 3B-8, OF-1
1984 2 teams		STL N (21G – .067)				MON N (37G – .214)											
" total	58	85	16	2	0	0	0.0	3	3	1	16	0	.188	.212	2	0	SS-33, 2B-19, 3B-1
6 yrs.	385	771	187	25	6	2	0.3	80	57	46	107	14	.243	.298	50	12	2B-153, SS-134, 3B-50, OF-4

WORLD SERIES

	G	AB	H	2B	3B	HR	HR %	R	RBI	BB	SO	SB	BA	SA	AB	H	G by POS
1982 STL N	3	1	0	0	0	0	0.0	1	0	0	1	0	.000	.000	0	0	3B-2

Dick Rand

RAND, RICHARD HILTON
B. Mar. 7, 1931, South Gate, Calif.

BR TR 6'2" 185 lbs.

	G	AB	H	2B	3B	HR	HR %	R	RBI	BB	SO	SB	BA	SA	AB	H	G by POS
1953 STL N	9	31	9	1	0	0	0.0	3	1	2	6	0	.290	.323	0	0	C-9
1955	3	10	3	0	0	1	10.0	1	3	1	1	0	.300	.600	0	0	C-3
1957 PIT N	60	105	23	2	1	1	1.0	7	9	11	24	0	.219	.286	3	1	C-57
3 yrs.	72	146	35	3	1	2	1.4	11	13	14	31	0	.240	.315	3	1	C-69

Bob Randall

RANDALL, ROBERT LEE
B. June 10, 1949, Norton, Kans.

BR TR 6'2" 175 lbs.

	G	AB	H	2B	3B	HR	HR %	R	RBI	BB	SO	SB	BA	SA	AB	H	G by POS
1976 MIN A	153	475	127	18	4	1	0.2	55	34	28	38	3	.267	.328	0	0	2B-153
1977	103	306	73	13	2	0	0.0	36	22	15	25	1	.239	.294	5	1	2B-101, DH-4, 3B-1, 1B-1
1978	119	330	89	11	3	0	0.0	36	21	24	22	5	.270	.321	11	2	2B-116, 3B-2, DH-1
1979	80	199	49	7	0	0	0.0	25	14	15	17	2	.246	.281	13	2	2B-71, 3B-7, OF-1, SS-1
1980	5	15	3	1	0	0	0.0	2	0	1	0	0	.200	.267	1	0	3B-4, 2B-1
5 yrs.	460	1325	341	50	9	1	0.1	154	91	83	102	11	.257	.311	30	5	2B-442, 3B-14, DH-5, OF-1, SS-1, 1B-1

Newt Randall

RANDALL, NEWTON J.
B. Feb. 3, 1880, New Lowell, Ont., Canada   D. May 3, 1955, Duluth, Minn.

BR TR 5'10"

	G	AB	H	2B	3B	HR	HR %	R	RBI	BB	SO	SB	BA	SA	AB	H	G by POS
1907 2 teams		CHI N (22G – .205)				BOS N (75G – .213)											
" total	97	336	71	10	5	0	0.0	22	19	27		6	.211	.271	3	0	OF-94

Lenny Randle

RANDLE, LEONARD SHENOFF
B. Feb. 12, 1949, Long Beach, Calif.

BR TR 5'10" 169 lbs.

	G	AB	H	2B	3B	HR	HR %	R	RBI	BB	SO	SB	BA	SA	AB	H	G by POS
1971 WAS A	75	215	47	11	0	2	0.9	27	13	24	56	1	.219	.298	6	0	2B-66
1972 TEX A	74	249	48	13	0	2	0.8	23	21	13	51	4	.193	.269	4	0	2B-65, SS-4, OF-2
1973	10	29	6	1	1	1	3.4	3	1	0	2	0	.207	.414	0	0	2B-5, OF-2
1974	151	520	157	17	4	1	0.2	65	49	29	43	26	.302	.356	2	2	3B-89, 2B-40, OF-21, DH-2, SS-1
1975	156	601	166	24	7	4	0.7	85	57	57	80	16	.276	.359	4	1	2B-79, OF-66, 3B-17, DH-3, C-1
1976	142	539	121	11	6	1	0.2	53	51	46	63	30	.224	.273	2	0	2B-113, OF-30, 3B-2, DH-1
1977 NY N	136	513	156	22	7	5	1.0	78	27	65	70	33	.304	.404	5	0	3B-110, 2B-20, OF-6, SS-1
1978	132	437	102	16	8	2	0.5	53	35	64	57	14	.233	.320	15	5	3B-124, 2B-5
1979 NY A	20	39	7	0	0	0	0.0	2	3	3	2	0	.179	.179	5	1	OF-11, DH-2
1980 CHI N	130	489	135	19	6	5	1.0	67	39	50	55	19	.276	.370	8	4	3B-111, 2B-17, OF-6
1981 SEA A	82	273	63	9	1	4	1.5	22	25	17	22	11	.231	.315	5	0	3B-59, 2B-21, OF-5, SS-3
1982	30	46	8	2	0	0	0.0	10	1	4	4	2	.174	.217	1	1	DH-13, 3B-9, 2B-6
12 yrs.	1138	3950	1016	145	40	27	0.7	488	322	372	505	156	.257	.335	57	14	3B-521, 2B-437, OF-149, DH-21, SS-10, C-1

Willie Randolph

RANDOLPH, WILLIAM LARRY
B. July 6, 1954, Holly Hill, S. C.

BR TR 5'11" 165 lbs.

	G	AB	H	2B	3B	HR	HR %	R	RBI	BB	SO	SB	BA	SA	AB	H	G by POS
1975 PIT N	30	61	10	1	0	0	0.0	9	3	7	6	1	.164	.180	8	2	2B-14, 3B-1
1976 NY A	125	430	115	15	4	1	0.2	59	40	58	39	37	.267	.328	1	0	2B-124
1977	147	551	151	28	11	4	0.7	91	40	64	53	13	.274	.387	0	0	2B-147
1978	134	499	139	18	6	3	0.6	87	42	82	51	36	.279	.357	0	0	2B-134
1979	153	574	155	15	13	5	0.9	98	61	95	39	33	.270	.368	0	0	2B-153

	G	AB	H	2B	3B	HR	HR %	R	RBI	BB	SO	SB	BA	SA	Pinch Hit AB	Pinch Hit H	G by POS

Willie Randolph continued

	G	AB	H	2B	3B	HR	HR %	R	RBI	BB	SO	SB	BA	SA	AB	H	G by POS
1980	138	513	151	23	7	7	1.4	99	46	119	45	30	.294	.407	0	0	2B-138
1981	93	357	83	14	3	2	0.6	59	24	57	24	14	.232	.305	0	0	2B-93
1982	144	553	155	21	4	3	0.5	85	36	75	35	16	.280	.349	0	0	2B-142, DH-1
1983	104	420	117	21	1	2	0.5	73	38	53	32	12	.279	.348	0	0	2B-104
1984	142	564	162	24	2	2	0.4	86	31	86	42	10	.287	.348	0	0	2B-142
10 yrs.	1210	4522	1238	180	51	29	0.6	746	361	696	366	202	.274	.355	9	2	2B-1191, DH-1, 3B-1

DIVISIONAL PLAYOFF SERIES

	G	AB	H	2B	3B	HR	HR %	R	RBI	BB	SO	SB	BA	SA	AB	H	G by POS
1981 NY A	5	20	4	0	0	0	0.0	0	1	1	4	0	.200	.200	0	0	2B-5

LEAGUE CHAMPIONSHIP SERIES

	G	AB	H	2B	3B	HR	HR %	R	RBI	BB	SO	SB	BA	SA	AB	H	G by POS
1975 PIT N	2	2	0	0	0	0	0.0	1	0	0	1	0	.000	.000	1	0	2B-1
1976 NY A	5	17	2	0	0	0	0.0	0	1	3	1	1	.118	.118	0	0	2B-5
1977	5	18	5	1	0	0	0.0	4	2	1	0	0	.278	.333	0	0	2B-5
1980	3	13	5	2	0	0	0.0	0	1	1	3	0	.385	.538	0	0	2B-3
1981	3	12	4	0	0	1	8.3	2	2	0	1	0	.333	.583	0	0	2B-3
5 yrs.	18	62	16	3	0	1	1.6	7	6	5	6	1	.258	.355	1	0	2B-17

WORLD SERIES

	G	AB	H	2B	3B	HR	HR %	R	RBI	BB	SO	SB	BA	SA	AB	H	G by POS
1976 NY A	4	14	1	0	0	0	0.0	1	0	1	3	0	.071	.071	0	0	2B-4
1977	6	25	4	2	0	1	4.0	5	1	2	2	0	.160	.360	0	0	2B-6
1981	6	18	4	1	1	2	11.1	5	3	9	0	1	.222	.722	0	0	2B-6
3 yrs.	16	57	9	3	1	3	5.3	11	4	12	5	1	.158	.404	0	0	2B-16

Merritt Ranew

RANEW, MERRITT THOMAS
B. May 10, 1938, Albany, Ga.   BL TR 5'11" 170 lbs.

	G	AB	H	2B	3B	HR	HR %	R	RBI	BB	SO	SB	BA	SA	AB	H	G by POS
1962 HOU N	71	218	51	6	8	4	1.8	26	24	14	43	2	.234	.390	15	1	C-58
1963 CHI N	78	154	52	8	1	3	1.9	18	15	9	32	1	.338	.461	41	17	C-37, 1B-7
1964 2 teams			CHI	N	(16G –	.091)		MIL	N	(9G –	.118)						
" total	25	50	5	0	0	0	0.0	1	1	2	9	0	.100	.100	11	2	C-12
1965 CAL A	41	91	19	4	0	1	1.1	12	10	7	22	0	.209	.286	17	2	C-24
1969 SEA A	54	81	20	2	0	0	0.0	11	4	10	14	0	.247	.272	31	6	C-13, OF-3, 3B-1
5 yrs.	269	594	147	20	9	8	1.3	68	54	42	120	3	.247	.352	115	28	C-144, 1B-7, OF-3, 3B-1

Jeff Ransom

RANSOM, JEFFREY DEAN
B. Nov. 11, 1960, Fresno, Calif.   BB TR 5'11" 185 lbs.

	G	AB	H	2B	3B	HR	HR %	R	RBI	BB	SO	SB	BA	SA	AB	H	G by POS
1981 SF N	5	15	4	1	0	0	0.0	2	0	1	1	0	.267	.333	0	0	C-5
1982	15	44	7	0	0	0	0.0	5	3	6	7	0	.159	.159	1	0	C-14
1983	6	20	4	0	0	1	5.0	3	3	4	7	0	.200	.350	0	0	C-6
3 yrs.	26	79	15	1	0	1	1.3	10	6	11	15	0	.190	.241	1	0	C-25

Earl Rapp

RAPP, EARL WELLINGTON
B. May 20, 1921, Corunna, Mich.   BL TR 6'2" 185 lbs.

	G	AB	H	2B	3B	HR	HR %	R	RBI	BB	SO	SB	BA	SA	AB	H	G by POS
1949 2 teams			DET	A	(1G –	.000)		CHI	A	(19G –	.259)						
" total	20	54	14	1	0	0	0.0	3	11	6	6	1	.259	.315	5	1	OF-13
1951 2 teams			NY	N	(13G –	.091)		STL	A	(26G –	.327)						
" total	39	109	33	5	3	2	1.8	14	15	13	14	1	.303	.459	12	1	OF-25
1952 2 teams			STL	A	(30G –	.143)		WAS	A	(46G –	.284)						
" total	76	116	26	10	0	0	0.0	10	13	6	21	0	.224	.310	54	10	OF-17
3 yrs.	135	279	73	16	4	2	0.7	27	39	25	41	2	.262	.369	71	12	OF-55

Goldie Rapp

RAPP, JOSEPH ALOYSIUS
B. Feb. 6, 1892, Cincinnati, Ohio   D. July 1, 1966, La Mesa, Calif.   BB TR 5'10" 165 lbs.

	G	AB	H	2B	3B	HR	HR %	R	RBI	BB	SO	SB	BA	SA	AB	H	G by POS
1921 2 teams			NY	N	(58G –	.215)		PHI	N	(52G –	.277)						
" total	110	383	95	16	2	1	0.3	49	25	29	21	9	.248	.308	1	0	3B-106, 2B-1
1922 PHI N	119	502	127	26	3	0	0.0	58	38	32	29	6	.253	.317	0	0	3B-117, SS-2
1923	47	179	47	5	0	1	0.6	27	10	14	14	1	.263	.307	2	1	3B-45
3 yrs.	276	1064	269	47	5	2	0.2	134	73	75	64	16	.253	.312	3	1	3B-268, SS-2, 2B-1

Bill Rariden

RARIDEN, WILLIAM ANGEL (Bedford Bill)
B. Feb. 5, 1888, Bedford, Ind.   D. Aug. 28, 1942, Bedford, Ind.   BR TR 5'10" 168 lbs.

	G	AB	H	2B	3B	HR	HR %	R	RBI	BB	SO	SB	BA	SA	AB	H	G by POS
1909 BOS N	13	42	6	1	0	0	0.0	1	1	4		1	.143	.167	0	0	C-13
1910	49	137	31	5	1	1	0.7	15	14	12	22	1	.226	.299	0	0	C-49
1911	70	246	56	9	0	0	0.0	22	21	21	18	3	.228	.264	1	0	C-65, 3B-3, 2B-1
1912	79	247	55	3	1	1	0.4	27	14	18	35	3	.223	.255	6	2	C-73
1913	95	246	58	9	2	3	1.2	31	30	30	21	5	.236	.325	5	1	C-87
1914 IND F	131	396	93	15	5	0	0.0	44	47	61		12	.235	.298	1	0	C-130
1915 NWK F	142	444	120	30	7	0	0.0	49	40	60		4	.270	.369	0	0	C-142
1916 NY N	120	351	78	9	3	1	0.3	23	29	55	32	4	.222	.274	1	1	C-119
1917	104	266	72	10	1	0	0.0	20	25	42	17	3	.271	.316	0	0	C-100
1918	69	183	41	5	1	0	0.0	15	17	15	15	1	.224	.262	4	0	C-63
1919 CIN N	75	218	47	6	3	0	0.0	16	24	17	19	4	.216	.284	4	2	C-70
1920	39	101	25	3	0	0	0.0	9	10	5	0	2	.248	.277	2	0	C-37
12 yrs.	986	2877	682	105	24	7	0.2	272	272	340	179	47	.237	.298	24	6	C-948, 3B-3, 2B-1

WORLD SERIES

	G	AB	H	2B	3B	HR	HR %	R	RBI	BB	SO	SB	BA	SA	AB	H	G by POS
1917 NY N	5	13	5	0	0	0	0.0	2	2	2	1	0	.385	.385	0	0	C-5
1919 CIN N	5	19	4	0	0	0	0.0	0	2	0	0	1	.211	.211	0	0	C-5
2 yrs.	10	32	9	0	0	0	0.0	2	4	2	1	1	.281	.281	0	0	C-10

Morrie Rath

RATH, MAURICE CHARLES
B. Dec. 25, 1887, Mobeetie, Tex.   D. Nov. 18, 1945, Upper Darby, Pa.   BL TR 5'8½" 160 lbs.

	G	AB	H	2B	3B	HR	HR %	R	RBI	BB	SO	SB	BA	SA	AB	H	G by POS
1909 PHI A	7	26	7	1	0	0	0.0	4	3	2		1	.269	.308	0	0	SS-4, 3B-2
1910 2 teams			PHI	A	(18G –	.154)		CLE	A	(24G –	.194)						
" total	42	93	17	3	0	0	0.0	8	1	15		2	.183	.215	3	0	3B-33, 2B-3, SS-1
1912 CHI A	157	591	161	10	2	1	0.2	104	19	95		30	.272	.301	0	0	2B-157
1913	90	295	59	2	0	0	0.0	37	12	46	22	22	.200	.207	2	1	2B-86
1919 CIN N	138	537	142	13	1	1	0.2	77	29	64	24	17	.264	.298	0	0	2B-138

	G	AB	H	2B	3B	HR	HR %	R	RBI	BB	SO	SB	BA	SA	Pinch Hit AB	Pinch Hit H	G by POS

Morrie Rath continued

	G	AB	H	2B	3B	HR	HR%	R	RBI	BB	SO	SB	BA	SA	AB	H	G by POS
1920	129	506	135	7	4	2	0.4	61	28	36	24	10	.267	.308	1	0	2B-126, OF-1, 3B-1
6 yrs.	563	2048	521	36	7	4	0.2	291	92	258	70	82	.254	.285	6	1	2B-510, 3B-36, SS-5, OF-1

WORLD SERIES
| 1919 CIN N | 8 | 31 | 7 | 1 | 0 | 0 | 0.0 | 5 | 2 | 4 | 1 | 2 | .226 | .258 | 0 | 0 | 2B-8 |

Gene Ratliff

RATLIFF, KELLY EUGENE
B. Sept. 28, 1945, Macon, Ga.   BR TR 6'5" 185 lbs.

| 1965 HOU N | 4 | 4 | 0 | 0 | 0 | 0 | 0.0 | 0 | 0 | 0 | 4 | 0 | .000 | .000 | 4 | 0 | |

Paul Ratliff

RATLIFF, PAUL HAWTHORNE
B. Jan. 23, 1944, San Diego, Calif.   BL TR 6'2" 190 lbs.

1963 MIN A	10	21	4	1	0	1	4.8	2	3	2	7	0	.190	.381	4	2	C-7
1970	69	149	40	7	2	5	3.4	19	22	15	51	0	.268	.443	22	4	C-53
1971 2 teams	MIN	A (21G – .159)			MIL	A	(23G – .171)										
" total	44	85	14	2	0	5	5.9	6	13	9	38	0	.165	.365	16	1	C-28
1972 MIL A	22	42	3	0	0	1	2.4	1	4	2	23	0	.071	.143	10	0	C-13
4 yrs.	145	297	61	10	2	12	4.0	28	42	28	119	0	.205	.374	52	7	C-101

LEAGUE CHAMPIONSHIP SERIES
| 1970 MIN A | 1 | 4 | 1 | 0 | 0 | 0 | 0.0 | 0 | 0 | 0 | 1 | 0 | .250 | .250 | 0 | 0 | C-1 |

Tommy Raub

RAUB, THOMAS JEFFERSON
B. Dec. 1, 1870, Raubsville, Pa.   D. Feb. 16, 1949, Phillipsburg, N. J.   BR TR 5'10" 155 lbs.

1903 CHI N	36	84	19	3	2	0	0.0	6	7	5		3	.226	.310	8	3	C-12, 1B-6, OF-5, 3B-4
1906 STL N	24	78	22	2	4	0	0.0	9	2	4		2	.282	.410	0	0	C-22
2 yrs.	60	162	41	5	6	0	0.0	15	9	9		5	.253	.358	8	3	C-34, 1B-6, OF-5, 3B-4

Bob Raudman

RAUDMAN, ROBERT JOYCE (Shorty)
B. Mar. 14, 1942, Erie, Pa.   BL TL 5'9½" 185 lbs.

1966 CHI N	8	29	7	2	0	0	0.0	2	1	1	4	0	.241	.310	0	0	OF-8
1967	8	26	4	0	0	0	0.0	0	1	1	4	0	.154	.154	0	0	OF-8
2 yrs.	16	55	11	2	0	0	0.0	1	3	2	8	0	.200	.236	0	0	OF-16

Johnny Rawlings

RAWLINGS, JOHN WILLIAM
B. Aug. 17, 1892, Bloomfield, Iowa   D. Oct. 16, 1972, Los Angeles, Calif.   BR TR 5'8" 158 lbs.

1914 2 teams	CIN	N (33G – .217)			KC	F	(61G – .212)										
" total	94	253	54	4	0	0	0.0	28	23	28	8	7	.213	.229	7	1	SS-66, 3B-10, 2B-7
1915 KC F	120	399	86	9	2	2	0.5	40	24	27		17	.216	.263	0	0	SS-120
1917 BOS N	122	371	95	9	4	2	0.5	37	31	38	32	12	.256	.318	5	1	2B-96, SS-17, OF-1, 3B-1
1918	111	410	85	7	3	0	0.0	32	21	30	31	10	.207	.239	1	0	SS-91, 2B-20, OF-18
1919	77	275	70	8	2	1	0.4	30	16	16	20	10	.255	.309	3	0	2B-58, OF-12, SS-5
1920 2 teams	BOS	N (5G – .000)			PHI	N	(98G – .234)										
" total	103	387	90	19	2	3	0.8	39	32	22	26	9	.233	.315	2	0	2B-98
1921 2 teams	PHI	N (60G – .291)			NY	N	(86G – .267)										
" total	146	561	156	22	3	2	0.4	60	46	26	31	8	.278	.339	0	0	2B-146, SS-1
1922 NY N	88	308	87	13	8	1	0.3	46	30	23	15	7	.282	.386	5	1	2B-77, 3B-5
1923 PIT N	119	461	131	18	4	1	0.2	53	45	25	29	9	.284	.347	0	0	2B-119
1924	3	3	1	0	0	0	0.0	0	2	0	0	0	.333	.333	3	1	
1925	36	110	31	7	0	2	1.8	17	13	8	8	0	.282	.400	3	0	2B-29
1926	61	181	42	6	0	0	0.0	27	20	14	10	3	.232	.265	2	1	2B-59
12 yrs.	1080	3719	928	122	28	14	0.4	409	303	257	210	92	.250	.309	31	5	2B-709, SS-280, OF-31, 3B-16

WORLD SERIES
| 1921 NY N | 8 | 30 | 10 | 3 | 0 | 0 | 0.0 | 4 | 0 | 3 | | 0 | .333 | .433 | 0 | 0 | 2B-8 |

Irv Ray

RAY, IRVING BURTON (Stubby)
B. Jan. 22, 1864, Harrington, Me.   D. Feb. 21, 1948, Harrington, Me.   TL 5'6"

1888 BOS N	50	206	51	2	3	2	1.0	26	26	6	11	7	.248	.316	0	0	SS-48, 2B-3
1889 2 teams	BOS	N (9G – .303)			BAL	AA	(26G – .340)										
" total	35	139	46	1	0	0	0.0	28	19	11	6	13	.331	.381	0	0	SS-25, OF-6, 3B-4
1890 B-B AA	38	139	50	6	2	1	0.7	28		15		11	.360	.453	0	0	SS-38
1891 BAL AA	103	418	116	17	5	0	0.0	72	58	54	18	28	.278	.342	0	0	OF-64, SS-40
4 yrs.	226	902	263	30	11	3	0.3	154	103	86	35	59	.292	.359	0	0	SS-151, OF-70, 3B-4, 2B-3

Johnny Ray

RAY, JOHNNY CORNELIUS
B. Mar. 1, 1957, Chouteau, Okla.   BB TR 5'11" 170 lbs.

1981 PIT N	31	102	25	11	0	0	0.0	10	6	6	9	0	.245	.353	2	1	2B-31
1982	162	647	182	30	7	7	1.1	79	63	36	34	16	.281	.382	0	0	2B-162
1983	151	576	163	38	7	5	0.9	68	53	35	26	18	.283	.399	5	1	2B-151, 3B-1
1984	155	555	173	38	6	6	1.1	75	67	37	31	11	.312	.434	9	3	2B-149
4 yrs.	499	1880	543	117	20	18	1.0	232	189	114	100	45	.289	.401	16	5	2B-493, 3B-1

Larry Ray

RAY, LARRY DALE
B. Mar. 11, 1958, Madison, Ind.   BL TR 6' 190 lbs.

| 1982 HOU N | 5 | 6 | 1 | 0 | 0 | 0 | 0.0 | 0 | 1 | 0 | 4 | 0 | .167 | .167 | 4 | 1 | OF-1 |

Floyd Rayford

RAYFORD, FLOYD KINNARD
B. July 27, 1957, Memphis, Tenn.   BR TR 5'10" 190 lbs.

1980 BAL A	8	18	4	0	0	0	0.0	1	1	0	5	0	.222	.222	2	1	3B-4, DH-1, 2B-1
1982	34	53	7	0	0	3	5.7	7	5	6	14	0	.132	.302	1	1	3B-27, DH-2, C-2
1983 STL N	56	104	22	4	0	3	2.9	5	14	10	27	1	.212	.337	26	5	3B-33
1984 BAL A	86	250	64	14	0	4	1.6	24	27	12	51	0	.256	.360	4	1	C-66, 3B-22, 1B-1
4 yrs.	184	425	97	18	0	10	2.4	37	47	28	97	1	.228	.341	33	8	3B-86, C-68, DH-3, 2B-1, 1B-1

	G	AB	H	2B	3B	HR	HR %	R	RBI	BB	SO	SB	BA	SA	Pinch Hit AB	Pinch Hit H	G by POS

Jimmy Reese *continued*

	G	AB	H	2B	3B	HR	HR %	R	RBI	BB	SO	SB	BA	SA	AB	H	G by POS
1932 STL N	90	309	82	15	0	2	0.6	38	26	20	19	4	.265	.333	10	4	2B-77
3 yrs.	232	742	206	39	4	8	1.1	123	70	48	37	7	.278	.373	33	15	2B-186, 3B-5

Pee Wee Reese

REESE, HAROLD HENRY (The Little Colonel)
B. July 23, 1918, Ekron, Ky.
Hall of Fame 1984.
BR TR 5'10" 160 lbs.

	G	AB	H	2B	3B	HR	HR %	R	RBI	BB	SO	SB	BA	SA	AB	H	G by POS
1940 BKN N	84	312	85	8	4	5	1.6	58	28	45	42	15	.272	.372	0	0	SS-83
1941	152	595	136	23	5	2	0.3	76	46	68	56	10	.229	.294	1	0	SS-151
1942	151	564	144	24	5	3	0.5	87	53	82	55	15	.255	.332	0	0	SS-151
1946	152	542	154	16	10	5	0.9	79	60	87	71	10	.284	.378	0	0	SS-152
1947	142	476	135	24	4	12	2.5	81	73	104	67	7	.284	.426	0	0	SS-142
1948	151	566	155	31	4	9	1.6	96	75	79	63	25	.274	.390	2	0	SS-149
1949	155	617	172	27	3	16	2.6	132	73	116	59	26	.279	.410	0	0	SS-155
1950	141	531	138	21	5	11	2.1	97	52	91	62	17	.260	.380	0	0	SS-134, 3B-7
1951	154	616	176	20	8	10	1.6	94	84	81	57	20	.286	.393	0	0	SS-154
1952	149	559	152	18	8	6	1.1	94	58	86	59	30	.272	.365	4	1	SS-145
1953	140	524	142	25	7	13	2.5	108	61	82	61	22	.271	.420	3	0	SS-135
1954	141	554	171	35	8	10	1.8	98	69	90	62	8	.309	.455	1	1	SS-140
1955	145	553	156	29	4	10	1.8	99	61	78	60	8	.282	.403	3	0	SS-142
1956	147	572	147	19	2	9	1.6	85	46	56	69	13	.257	.344	1	0	SS-136, 3B-12
1957	103	330	74	3	1	1	0.3	33	29	39	32	5	.224	.248	4	1	3B-75, SS-23
1958 LA N	59	147	33	7	2	4	2.7	21	17	26	15	1	.224	.381	15	1	SS-22, 3B-21
16 yrs.	2166	8058	2170	330	80	126	1.6	1338	885	1210	890	232	.269	.377	34	4	SS-2014, 3B-115

WORLD SERIES

	G	AB	H	2B	3B	HR	HR %	R	RBI	BB	SO	SB	BA	SA	AB	H	G by POS
1941 BKN N	5	20	4	0	0	0	0.0	1	2	0	0	0	.200	.200	0	0	SS-5
1947	7	23	7	1	0	0	0.0	5	4	6	3	3	.304	.348	0	0	SS-7
1949	5	19	6	1	0	1	5.3	2	2	1	0	1	.316	.526	0	0	SS-5
1952	7	29	10	0	0	1	3.4	4	4	2	2	1	.345	.448	0	0	SS-7
1953	6	24	5	0	1	0	0.0	0	0	4	1	0	.208	.292	0	0	SS-6
1955	7	27	8	1	0	0	0.0	5	2	3	5	0	.296	.333	0	0	SS-7
1956	7	27	6	0	1	0	0.0	3	2	2	6	0	.222	.296	0	0	SS-7
7 yrs.	44	169	46	3	2	2	1.2	20	16	18	17	5	.272	.349	0	0	SS-44
	9th	9th	5th														

Rich Reese

REESE, RICHARD BENJAMIN
B. Sept. 29, 1941, Leipsic, Ohio
BL TL 6'3" 185 lbs.

	G	AB	H	2B	3B	HR	HR %	R	RBI	BB	SO	SB	BA	SA	AB	H	G by POS
1964 MIN A	10	7	0	0	0	0	0.0	0	0	0	1	0	.000	.000	7	0	1B-1
1965	14	7	2	1	0	0	0.0	0	0	2	2	0	.286	.429	4	1	1B-6, OF-1
1966	3	2	0	0	0	0	0.0	0	0	1	2	0	.000	.000	2	0	1B-1
1967	95	101	25	5	0	4	4.0	13	20	8	17	0	.248	.416	41	13	1B-36, OF-10
1968	126	332	86	15	2	4	1.2	40	28	18	36	3	.259	.352	30	6	1B-87, OF-15
1969	132	419	135	24	4	16	3.8	52	69	23	57	1	.322	.513	17	4	1B-117, OF-5
1970	153	501	131	15	5	10	2.0	63	56	48	70	5	.261	.371	12	4	1B-146
1971	120	329	72	8	3	10	3.0	40	39	20	35	7	.219	.353	20	6	1B-95, OF-9
1972	132	197	43	3	2	5	2.5	23	26	25	27	0	.218	.330	26	7	1B-98, OF-13
1973 2 teams	MIN	A	(22G –	.174)		DET	A	(59G –	.137)								
" total	81	125	18	2	1	3	2.4	17	7	13	23	0	.144	.248	15	3	1B-54, OF-21
10 yrs.	866	2020	512	73	17	52	2.6	248	245	158	270	16	.253	.384	174	44	1B-640, OF-74

LEAGUE CHAMPIONSHIP SERIES

	G	AB	H	2B	3B	HR	HR %	R	RBI	BB	SO	SB	BA	SA	AB	H	G by POS
1969 MIN A	3	12	2	0	0	0	0.0	0	2	1	1	0	.167	.167	0	0	1B-3
1970	2	7	1	0	0	0	0.0	0	0	1	1	0	.143	.143	0	0	1B-2
2 yrs.	5	19	3	0	0	0	0.0	0	2	2	2	0	.158	.158	0	0	1B-5

Bobby Reeves

REEVES, ROBERT EDWIN (Gunner)
B. June 24, 1904, Hill City, Tenn.
BR TR 5'11" 170 lbs.

	G	AB	H	2B	3B	HR	HR %	R	RBI	BB	SO	SB	BA	SA	AB	H	G by POS
1926 WAS A	20	49	11	0	1	0	0.0	4	7	6	9	1	.224	.265	1	0	3B-16, SS-1, 2B-1
1927	112	380	97	11	5	1	0.3	37	39	21	53	3	.255	.318	0	0	SS-96, 3B-12, 2B-2
1928	102	353	107	16	8	3	0.8	44	42	24	47	4	.303	.419	2	1	SS-66, 2B-22, 3B-8, OF-1
1929 BOS A	140	460	114	19	2	2	0.4	66	28	60	57	7	.248	.311	1	0	3B-132, 2B-2, SS-1
1930	92	272	59	7	4	2	0.7	41	18	50	36	6	.217	.294	4	1	3B-62, SS-15, 2B-11
1931	36	84	14	2	2	0	0.0	11	1	14	16	0	.167	.238	2	0	2B-29, P-1
6 yrs.	502	1598	402	55	22	8	0.5	203	135	175	218	21	.252	.329	10	2	SS-230, 3B-178, 2B-67, OF-1, 1B-1, P-1

Rudy Regalado

REGALADO, RUDOLPH VALENTINO
B. May 21, 1930, Los Angeles, Calif.
BR TR 6'1" 185 lbs.

	G	AB	H	2B	3B	HR	HR %	R	RBI	BB	SO	SB	BA	SA	AB	H	G by POS
1954 CLE A	65	180	45	5	0	2	1.1	21	24	19	16	0	.250	.311	8	1	3B-50, 2B-2
1955	10	26	7	2	0	0	0.0	2	5	2	4	0	.269	.346	1	0	3B-8, 2B-1
1956	16	47	11	1	0	0	0.0	4	2	4	1	0	.234	.255	1	0	3B-14, 1B-1
3 yrs.	91	253	63	8	0	2	0.8	27	31	25	21	0	.249	.304	10	1	3B-72, 2B-3, 1B-1

WORLD SERIES

	G	AB	H	2B	3B	HR	HR %	R	RBI	BB	SO	SB	BA	SA	AB	H	G by POS
1954 CLE A	4	3	1	0	0	0	0.0	0	1	0	0	0	.333	.333	2	1	3B-1

Bill Regan

REGAN, WILLIAM WRIGHT
B. Jan. 23, 1899, Pittsburgh, Pa. D. June 11, 1968, Pittsburgh, Pa.
BR TR 5'10" 155 lbs.

	G	AB	H	2B	3B	HR	HR %	R	RBI	BB	SO	SB	BA	SA	AB	H	G by POS
1926 BOS A	108	403	106	21	3	4	1.0	40	34	23	37	6	.263	.360	2	0	2B-106
1927	129	468	128	37	10	2	0.4	43	66	26	51	10	.274	.408	7	1	2B-121
1928	138	511	135	30	6	7	1.4	53	75	21	40	9	.264	.387	2	0	2B-137, OF-1
1929	104	371	107	27	7	1	0.3	38	54	22	38	7	.288	.407	2	1	2B-91, 3B-10, 1B-1
1930	134	507	135	35	10	3	0.6	54	53	25	60	4	.266	.393	5	2	2B-127, 3B-2
1931 PIT N	28	104	21	8	0	1	1.0	8	10	5	19	2	.202	.308	0	0	2B-28
6 yrs.	641	2364	632	158	36	18	0.8	236	292	122	245	38	.267	.387	16	4	2B-610, 3B-12, OF-1, 1B-1

	G	AB	H	2B	3B	HR	HR %	R	RBI	BB	SO	SB	BA	SA	Pinch Hit AB	H	G by POS

Tony Rego
REGO, ANTONE Born Antone DoRego. BR TR 5'5½" 140 lbs.
B. Oct. 31, 1897, Wailuku, Hawaii   D. Jan. 6, 1978, Tulsa, Okla.

	G	AB	H	2B	3B	HR	HR%	R	RBI	BB	SO	SB	BA	SA	AB	H	G by POS
1924 STL A	23	58	13	1	0	0	0.0	5	5	1	3	0	.224	.241	1	1	C-22
1925	20	32	13	2	1	0	0.0	5	3	3	2	0	.406	.531	1	0	C-19
2 yrs.	43	90	26	3	1	0	0.0	10	8	4	5	0	.289	.344	2	1	C-41

Wally Rehg
REHG, WALTER PHILLIP BR TR 5'8" 160 lbs.
B. Aug. 31, 1888, Summerfield, Ill.   D. Apr. 5, 1946, Burbank, Calif.

	G	AB	H	2B	3B	HR	HR%	R	RBI	BB	SO	SB	BA	SA	AB	H	G by POS
1912 PIT N	8	9	0	0	0	0	0.0	1	0	2	1	0	.000	.000	4	0	OF-2
1913 BOS A	30	101	28	3	2	0	0.0	14	9	2	7	4	.277	.347	2	1	OF-27
1914	84	151	33	4	2	0	0.0	14	11	18	11	5	.219	.272	36	10	OF-42
1915	5	5	1	0	0	0	0.0	2	0	0	1	1	.200	.200	3	1	OF-1
1917 BOS N	86	341	92	12	6	1	0.3	48	31	24	32	13	.270	.349	0	0	OF-86
1918	40	133	32	5	1	1	0.8	6	12	5	14	3	.241	.316	2	0	OF-38
1919 CIN N	5	12	2	0	0	0	0.0	1	3	1	0	0	.167	.167	0	0	OF-5
7 yrs.	258	752	188	24	11	2	0.3	86	66	52	66	26	.250	.319	47	12	OF-201

Frank Reiber
REIBER, FRANK BERNARD (Tubby) BR TR 5'8½" 169 lbs.
B. Sept. 19, 1909, Huntington, W. Va.

	G	AB	H	2B	3B	HR	HR%	R	RBI	BB	SO	SB	BA	SA	AB	H	G by POS
1933 DET A	13	18	5	0	1	1	5.6	3	3	2	3	0	.278	.556	6	1	C-6
1934	3	1	0	0	0	0	0.0	0	0	2	0	0	.000	.000	1	0	
1935	8	11	3	0	0	0	0.0	3	1	3	3	0	.273	.273	2	0	C-5
1936	20	55	15	2	0	1	1.8	7	5	5	7	0	.273	.364	2	0	C-17, OF-1
4 yrs.	44	85	23	2	1	2	2.4	13	9	12	13	0	.271	.388	11	1	C-28, OF-1

Herm Reich
REICH, HERMAN CHARLES BR TL 6'2" 200 lbs.
B. Nov. 23, 1917, Bell, Calif.

	G	AB	H	2B	3B	HR	HR%	R	RBI	BB	SO	SB	BA	SA	AB	H	G by POS
1949 3 teams	WAS A (2G – .000)			CLE A (1G – .500)			CHI N (108G – .280)										
" total	111	390	109	18	2	3	0.8	43	34	14	33	4	.279	.359	10	1	1B-85, OF-17

Rick Reichardt
REICHARDT, FREDERIC CARL BR TR 6'3" 210 lbs.
B. Mar. 16, 1943, Madison, Wis.

	G	AB	H	2B	3B	HR	HR%	R	RBI	BB	SO	SB	BA	SA	AB	H	G by POS
1964 LA A	11	37	6	0	0	0	0.0	0	0	1	12	1	.162	.162	0	0	OF-11
1965 CAL A	20	75	20	4	0	1	1.3	8	6	5	12	4	.267	.360	4	0	OF-20
1966	89	319	92	5	4	16	5.0	48	44	27	61	8	.288	.480	2	1	OF-87
1967	146	498	132	14	2	17	3.4	56	69	35	90	5	.265	.404	9	2	OF-138
1968	151	534	136	20	3	21	3.9	62	73	42	118	8	.255	.421	5	1	OF-148
1969	137	493	125	11	4	13	2.6	60	68	43	100	3	.254	.371	0	0	OF-136, 1B-3
1970 2 teams	CAL A (9G – .167)			WAS A (107G – .253)													
" total	116	283	71	14	2	15	5.3	43	47	26	69	2	.251	.473	41	8	OF-80, 3B-1
1971 CHI A	138	496	138	14	2	19	3.8	53	62	37	90	5	.278	.429	7	2	OF-128, 1B-9
1972	101	291	73	14	4	8	2.7	31	43	28	63	2	.251	.409	10	1	OF-90
1973 2 teams	CHI A (46G – .275)			KC A (41G – .220)													
" total	87	280	70	13	3	6	2.1	30	33	19	57	2	.250	.382	9	3	OF-44, DH-37
1974 KC A	1	1	1	0	0	0	0.0	0	0	0	0	0	1.000	1.000	1	1	
11 yrs.	997	3307	864	109	24	116	3.5	391	445	263	672	40	.261	.414	84	19	OF-882, DH-37, 1B-12, 3B-1

Dick Reichle
REICHLE, RICHARD WENDELL BL TR 6' 185 lbs.
B. Nov. 23, 1896, Lincoln, Ill.   D. June 13, 1967, St. Louis, Mo.

	G	AB	H	2B	3B	HR	HR%	R	RBI	BB	SO	SB	BA	SA	AB	H	G by POS
1922 BOS A	6	24	6	1	0	0	0.0	3	0	0	2	0	.250	.292	0	0	OF-6
1923	122	361	93	17	3	1	0.3	40	39	22	34	3	.258	.330	19	5	OF-93
2 yrs.	128	385	99	18	3	1	0.3	43	39	22	36	3	.257	.327	19	5	OF-99

Billy Reid
REID, WILLIAM ALEXANDER BR TR 6' 170 lbs.
B. May 17, 1857, London, Ont., Canada   D. June 26, 1940, London, Ont., Canada

	G	AB	H	2B	3B	HR	HR%	R	RBI	BB	SO	SB	BA	SA	AB	H	G by POS
1883 BAL AA	24	97	27	3	0	0	0.0	14		4				.278	.309	0	0	2B-23, SS-1
1884 PIT AA	19	70	17	2	0	0	0.0	11		4				.243	.271	0	0	OF-17, 3B-1, 2B-1, 1B-1
2 yrs.	43	167	44	5	0	0	0.0	25		8				.263	.293	0	0	2B-24, OF-17, SS-1, 3B-1, 1B-1

Scott Reid
REID, SCOTT DONALD BL TR 6'1" 195 lbs.
B. Jan. 7, 1947, Chicago, Ill.

	G	AB	H	2B	3B	HR	HR%	R	RBI	BB	SO	SB	BA	SA	AB	H	G by POS
1969 PHI N	13	19	4	0	0	0	0.0	5	0	7	5	0	.211	.211	5	1	OF-5
1970	25	49	6	1	0	0	0.0	5	1	11	22	0	.122	.143	4	0	OF-18
2 yrs.	38	68	10	1	0	0	0.0	10	1	18	27	0	.147	.162	9	1	OF-23

Charlie Reilley
REILLEY, CHARLES E. BR TR 5'10" 165 lbs.
B. 1856, Hartford, Conn.   D. 1888

	G	AB	H	2B	3B	HR	HR%	R	RBI	BB	SO	SB	BA	SA	AB	H	G by POS
1879 TRO N	62	236	54	5	1	0	0.0	17	19	1	20		.229	.258	0	0	C-49, 1B-11, OF-2
1880 CIN N	30	103	21	1	0	0	0.0	8	9	0	5		.204	.214	0	0	OF-16, C-13, 3B-4
1881 2 teams	DET N (19G – .171)			WOR N (2G – .375)													
" total	21	78	15	2	0	0	0.0	10	4	0	11		.192	.218	0	0	C-12, OF-4, SS-3, 3B-3, 1B-1
1882 PRO N	3	11	2	0	0	0	0.0	0		1	2		.182	.182	0	0	C-3
4 yrs.	116	428	92	8	1	0	0.0	35	32	2	38		.215	.238	0	0	C-77, OF-22, 1B-12, 3B-7, SS-3

Duke Reilley
REILLEY, ALEXANDER ALOYSIUS (Midget) BB TR 5'4½" 148 lbs.
B. Aug. 25, 1884, Chicago, Ill.   D. Mar. 4, 1968, Indianapolis, Ind.

	G	AB	H	2B	3B	HR	HR%	R	RBI	BB	SO	SB	BA	SA	AB	H	G by POS
1909 CLE A	20	62	13	0	0	0	0.0	10	0	4		5	.210	.210	0	0	OF-18

Arch Reilly
REILLY, ARCHER EDWIN BR TR 5'10" 163 lbs.
B. Aug. 17, 1891, Alton, Ill.   D. Nov. 29, 1963, Columbus, Ohio

	G	AB	H	2B	3B	HR	HR%	R	RBI	BB	SO	SB	BA	SA	AB	H	G by POS
1917 PIT N	1	0	0	0	0	0	–	0	0	0	0	0	–	–	0	0	3B-1

Barney Reilly

REILLY, BERNARD EUGENE   BR TR 6' 175 lbs.
B. Feb. 7, 1885, Brockton, Mass.   D. Nov. 15, 1934, St. Joseph, Mo.

	G	AB	H	2B	3B	HR	HR%	R	RBI	BB	SO	SB	BA	SA	Pinch Hit AB	Pinch Hit H	G by POS
1909 CHI A	12	25	5	0	0	0	0.0	3	3	3		2	.200	.200	0	0	2B-11, OF-1

Charlie Reilly

REILLY, CHARLES THOMAS (Princeton Charlie)   BB TR 5'11" 190 lbs.
B. June 24, 1855, New Brunswick, N. J.   D. Dec. 16, 1937, Los Angeles, Calif.

	G	AB	H	2B	3B	HR	HR%	R	RBI	BB	SO	SB	BA	SA	Pinch Hit AB	Pinch Hit H	G by POS
1889 COL AA	6	23	11	1	0	3	13.0	5	6	2	2	9	.478	.913	0	0	3B-6
1890	137	530	141	23	4	4	0.8	75		35		43	.266	.343	0	0	3B-136, 2B-1
1891 PIT N	114	415	91	8	5	3	0.7	43	44	29	58	20	.219	.284	0	0	3B-99, SS-11, OF-4
1892 PHI N	91	331	65	7	3	1	0.3	42	24	18	43	13	.196	.245	2	1	3B-70, OF-15, 2B-4
1893	104	416	102	16	7	4	1.0	64	56	33	36	13	.245	.346	0	0	3B-104
1894	39	135	40	1	2	0	0.0	21	19	16	10	9	.296	.333	0	0	3B-28, OF-5, 2B-4, SS-1, 1B-1
1895	49	179	48	6	1	0	0.0	28	25	13	12	7	.268	.313	0	0	SS-34, 3B-11, 2B-3, OF-1
1897 WAS N	101	351	97	18	3	2	0.6	64	60	34		18	.276	.362	0	0	3B-101
8 yrs.	641	2380	595	80	24	17	0.7	342	234	180	161	132	.250	.325	2	1	3B-555, SS-46, OF-25, 2B-12, 1B-1

Hal Reilly

REILLY, HAROLD J.
B. Unknown.

	G	AB	H	2B	3B	HR	HR%	R	RBI	BB	SO	SB	BA	SA	Pinch Hit AB	Pinch Hit H	G by POS
1919 CHI N	1	3	0	0	0	0	0.0	0	0	0	1	0	.000	.000	0	0	OF-1

Joe Reilly

REILLY, JOSEPH J.
B. New York, N. Y.   Deceased.

	G	AB	H	2B	3B	HR	HR%	R	RBI	BB	SO	SB	BA	SA	Pinch Hit AB	Pinch Hit H	G by POS
1884 BOS U	3	11	0	0	0	0	0.0	1		1			.000	.000	0	0	OF-2, 3B-1
1885 NY AA	10	40	7	3	0	0	0.0	6		2			.175	.250	0	0	2B-8, 3B-2
2 yrs.	13	51	7	3	0	0	0.0	7		3			.137	.196	0	0	2B-8, 3B-3, OF-2

Josh Reilly

REILLY, CHARLES
B. 1868, San Francisco, Calif.   D. June 13, 1938, San Francisco, Calif.

	G	AB	H	2B	3B	HR	HR%	R	RBI	BB	SO	SB	BA	SA	Pinch Hit AB	Pinch Hit H	G by POS
1896 CHI N	9	42	9	1	0	0	0.0	6	2	1	1	2	.214	.238	0	0	2B-8, SS-1

Long John Reilly

REILLY, JOHN GOOD   BR TR 6'3" 178 lbs.
B. Oct. 5, 1858, Cincinnati, Ohio   D. May 31, 1937, Cincinnati, Ohio

	G	AB	H	2B	3B	HR	HR%	R	RBI	BB	SO	SB	BA	SA	Pinch Hit AB	Pinch Hit H	G by POS
1880 CIN N	73	272	56	8	4	0	0.0	21	16	3	36		.206	.265	0		1B-72, OF-3
1883 CIN AA	98	437	136	21	14	9	2.1	103		9			.311	.485	0		1B-98, OF-1
1884	105	448	152	24	19	11	2.5	114		5			.339	.551	0		1B-103, OF-3, SS-1
1885	111	482	143	18	11	5	1.0	92		11			.297	.411	0		1B-107, OF-7
1886	115	441	117	12	11	4	0.9	92		31			.265	.370	0		1B-110, OF-6
1887	134	551	170	35	14	10	1.8	106		22		50	.309	.477	0		1B-127, OF-9
1888	127	527	169	28	14	13	2.5	112	103	17		82	.321	.501	0		1B-117, OF-10
1889	111	427	111	24	13	5	1.2	84	66	34	37	43	.260	.412	0		1B-109, OF-2
1890 CIN N	133	553	166	25	26	6	1.1	114	86	16	41	29	.300	.472	0		1B-132, OF-1
1891	135	546	132	20	13	4	0.7	60	64	9	42	22	.242	.348	0		1B-100, OF-36
10 yrs.	1142	4684	1352	215	139	67	1.4	898	335	157	156	226	.289	.437	0		1B-1075, OF-78, SS-1

Tom Reilly

REILLY, THOMAS HENRY   BR TR 5'10"
B. Aug. 3, 1884, St. Louis, Mo.   D. Oct. 19, 1918, New Orleans, La.

	G	AB	H	2B	3B	HR	HR%	R	RBI	BB	SO	SB	BA	SA	Pinch Hit AB	Pinch Hit H	G by POS
1908 STL N	29	81	14	1	0	1	1.2	5	3	2		4	.173	.222	0	0	SS-29
1909	5	7	2	0	1	0	0.0	0	2	0		0	.286	.571	0	0	SS-5
1914 CLE A	1	1	0	0	0	0	0.0	0	0	0	0	0	.000	.000	1	0	
3 yrs.	35	89	16	1	1	1	1.1	5	5	2	0	4	.180	.247	1	0	SS-34

Mike Reinbach

REINBACH, MICHAEL WAYNE   BL TR 6'2" 195 lbs.
B. Aug. 6, 1949, San Diego, Calif.

	G	AB	H	2B	3B	HR	HR%	R	RBI	BB	SO	SB	BA	SA	Pinch Hit AB	Pinch Hit H	G by POS
1974 BAL A	12	20	5	1	0	0	0.0	2	2	2	5	0	.250	.300	7	1	DH-3, OF-3

Art Reinholz

REINHOLZ, ARTHUR AUGUST   BR TR 5'10½" 175 lbs.
B. Jan. 27, 1903, Detroit, Mich.   D. Dec. 29, 1980, New Port Richey, Fla.

	G	AB	H	2B	3B	HR	HR%	R	RBI	BB	SO	SB	BA	SA	Pinch Hit AB	Pinch Hit H	G by POS
1928 CLE A	2	3	1	0	0	0	0.0	0	0		1	0	.333	.333	0	0	3B-2

Wally Reinicker

REINICKER, WALTER JOSEPH   BR TR 5'6" 150 lbs.
Also known as Walter Joseph Smith.
B. Apr. 21, 1890, Pittsburgh, Pa.   D. Apr. 18, 1957, Pittsburgh, Pa.

	G	AB	H	2B	3B	HR	HR%	R	RBI	BB	SO	SB	BA	SA	Pinch Hit AB	Pinch Hit H	G by POS
1915 BAL F	3	8	1	0	0	0	0.0	0	0	0		0	.125	.125	0	0	3B-3

Charlie Reipschlager

REIPSCHLAGER, CHARLES W.   5'8" 176 lbs.
Born Fred W. Strothkamp.
B. June 11, 1864, New York, N. Y.   D. Sept. 19, 1960, St. Petersburg, Fla.

	G	AB	H	2B	3B	HR	HR%	R	RBI	BB	SO	SB	BA	SA	Pinch Hit AB	Pinch Hit H	G by POS
1883 NY AA	37	145	27	4	2	0	0.0	8		4			.186	.241	0	0	C-29, OF-8
1884	59	233	56	13	2	0	0.0	21		1			.240	.313	0	0	C-51, OF-8
1885	72	268	65	11	1	0	0.0	29		9			.243	.291	0	0	C-59, OF-6, 3B-6, SS-1, 2B-1
1886	65	232	49	4	6	0	0.0	21		9			.211	.280	0	0	C-57, OF-9
1887 CLE AA	63	231	49	8	3	0	0.0	20		11		7	.212	.273	0	0	C-48, 1B-16
5 yrs.	296	1109	246	40	14	0	0.0	99		34		7	.222	.283	0	0	C-244, OF-31, 1B-16, 3B-6, SS-1, 2B-1

Bobby Reis

REIS, ROBERT JOSEPH THOMAS   BR TR 6'1" 175 lbs.
B. Jan. 2, 1909, Woodside, N. Y.   D. May 1, 1973, St. Paul, Minn.

	G	AB	H	2B	3B	HR	HR%	R	RBI	BB	SO	SB	BA	SA	Pinch Hit AB	Pinch Hit H	G by POS
1931 BKN N	6	17	5	0	0	0	0.0	3	2	2	0	0	.294	.294	0	0	3B-6
1932	1	4	1	0	0	0	0.0	0	0	0	1	0	.250	.250	0	0	3B-1
1935	52	85	21	3	2	0	0.0	10	4	6	13	2	.247	.329	9	3	OF-21, P-14, 2B-4, 3B-1, 1B-1
1936 BOS N	37	60	13	2	0	0	0.0	3	5	3	6	0	.217	.250	0	0	P-35, OF-2
1937	45	86	21	5	0	0	0.0	10	6	13	12	2	.244	.302	13	4	OF-18, 1B-4, P-4

	G	AB	H	2B	3B	HR	HR %	R	RBI	BB	SO	SB	BA	SA	Pinch Hit AB	Pinch Hit H	G by POS

Bobby Reis continued

	G	AB	H	2B	3B	HR	HR %	R	RBI	BB	SO	SB	BA	SA	AB	H	G by POS
1938	34	49	9	0	0	0	0.0	6	4	1	3	1	.184	.184	2	0	P-16, OF-10, SS-3, 2B-1, C-1
6 yrs.	175	301	70	10	2	0	0.0	32	21	25	35	5	.233	.279	24	7	P-69, OF-51, 3B-8, 2B-5, 1B-5, SS-3, C-1

Pete Reiser

REISER, HAROLD PATRICK (Pistol Pete)
B. Mar. 17, 1919, St. Louis, Mo.
D. Oct. 25, 1981, Palm Springs, Calif.

BL TR 5'11" 185 lbs.
BB 1948-51

	G	AB	H	2B	3B	HR	HR %	R	RBI	BB	SO	SB	BA	SA	AB	H	G by POS
1940 BKN N	58	225	66	11	4	3	1.3	34	20	15	33	2	.293	.418	6	0	3B-30, OF-17, SS-5
1941	137	536	184	39	17	14	2.6	117	76	46	71	4	.343	.558	1	0	OF-133
1942	125	480	149	33	5	10	2.1	89	64	48	45	20	.310	.463	0	0	OF-125
1946	122	423	117	21	5	11	2.6	75	73	55	58	34	.277	.428	10	3	OF-97, 3B-15
1947	110	388	120	23	2	5	1.3	68	46	68	41	14	.309	.418	2	0	OF-108
1948	64	127	30	8	2	1	0.8	17	19	29	21	4	.236	.354	21	10	OF-30, 3B-4
1949 BOS N	84	221	60	8	3	8	3.6	32	40	33	42	3	.271	.443	10	4	OF-63, 3B-4
1950	53	78	16	2	0	1	1.3	12	10	18	22	1	.205	.269	24	3	OF-24, 3B-1
1951 PIT N	74	140	38	9	3	2	1.4	22	13	27	20	4	.271	.421	33	11	OF-27, 3B-5
1952 CLE A	34	44	6	1	0	3	6.8	7	7	4	16	1	.136	.364	15	1	OF-10
10 yrs.	861	2662	786	155	41	58	2.2	473	368	343	369	87	.295	.450	122	32	OF-634, 3B-59, SS-5

WORLD SERIES																	
1941 BKN N	5	20	4	1	1	1	5.0	1	3	1	6	0	.200	.500	0	0	OF-5
1947	5	8	2	0	0	0	0.0	1	0	3	1	0	.250	.250	0	0	OF-3
2 yrs.	10	28	6	1	1	1	3.6	2	3	4	7	0	.214	.429	0	0	OF-8

Charlie Reising

REISING, CHARLES (Pop)
D. July 26, 1915, Louisville, Ky.

	G	AB	H	2B	3B	HR	HR %	R	RBI	BB	SO	SB	BA	SA	AB	H	G by POS
1884 IND AA	2	8	0	0	0	0	0.0	0		1			.000	.000	0	0	OF-2

Al Reiss

REISS, ALBERT ALLEN
B. Jan. 8, 1909, Elizabeth, N. J.

BB TR 5'10½" 165 lbs.

	G	AB	H	2B	3B	HR	HR %	R	RBI	BB	SO	SB	BA	SA	AB	H	G by POS
1932 PHI A	9	5	1	0	0	0	0.0	0	1	1	1	0	.200	.200	2	0	SS-6

Heinie Reitz

REITZ, HENRY P.
B. June 29, 1867, Chicago, Ill.   D. Nov. 10, 1914, San Francisco, Calif.

TR 5'7½" 160 lbs.

	G	AB	H	2B	3B	HR	HR %	R	RBI	BB	SO	SB	BA	SA	AB	H	G by POS
1893 BAL N	130	490	140	17	13	1	0.2	90	76	65	32	24	.286	.380	0	0	2B-130
1894	108	446	135	22	31	2	0.4	86	105	42	24	18	.303	.504	0	0	2B-97, 3B-12
1895	71	245	72	15	5	0	0.0	45	29	18	11	15	.294	.396	3	0	2B-48, 3B-18, SS-1
1896	120	464	133	15	6	4	0.9	76	106	49	32	28	.287	.371	0	0	2B-118, SS-3
1897	128	477	138	15	6	2	0.4	76	84	50		23	.289	.358	0	0	2B-128
1898 WAS N	132	489	148	20	2	2	0.4	62	47	32		11	.303	.364	0	0	2B-132
1899 PIT N	34	130	34	4	2	0	0.0	11	15	10		3	.262	.323	0	0	2B-34
7 yrs.	723	2741	800	108	65	11	0.4	446	462	266	99	122	.292	.391	3	0	2B-687, 3B-30, SS-4

Ken Reitz

REITZ, KENNETH JOHN
B. June 24, 1951, San Francisco, Calif.

BR TR 6' 180 lbs.

	G	AB	H	2B	3B	HR	HR %	R	RBI	BB	SO	SB	BA	SA	AB	H	G by POS
1972 STL N	21	78	28	4	0	0	0.0	5	10	2	4	0	.359	.410	1	0	3B-20
1973	147	426	100	20	2	6	1.4	40	42	9	25	0	.235	.333	12	2	3B-135, SS-1
1974	154	579	157	28	2	7	1.2	48	54	23	63	0	.271	.363	3	1	3B-151, SS-2
1975	161	592	159	25	1	5	0.8	43	63	22	54	1	.269	.340	1	0	3B-160
1976 SF N	155	577	154	21	1	5	0.9	40	66	24	48	5	.267	.333	1	0	3B-155, SS-1
1977 STL N	157	587	153	36	1	17	2.9	58	79	19	74	2	.261	.412	0	0	3B-157
1978	150	540	133	26	2	10	1.9	41	75	23	61	1	.246	.357	4	4	3B-150
1979	159	605	162	41	2	8	1.3	42	73	25	85	1	.268	.382	2	0	3B-158
1980	151	523	141	33	0	8	1.5	39	58	22	44	0	.270	.379	1	0	3B-150
1981 CHI N	82	260	56	9	1	2	0.8	10	28	15	56	0	.215	.281	1	0	3B-81
1982 PIT N	7	10	0	0	0	0	0.0	0	0	0	4	0	.000	.000	3	0	3B-4
11 yrs.	1344	4777	1243	243	12	68	1.4	366	548	184	518	10	.260	.359	28	7	3B-1321, SS-4

Butch Rementer

REMENTER, WILLIS J H
B. Mar. 14, 1878, Philadelphia, Pa.   D. Sept. 23, 1922, Philadelphia, Pa.

TR

	G	AB	H	2B	3B	HR	HR %	R	RBI	BB	SO	SB	BA	SA	AB	H	G by POS
1904 PHI N	1	2	0	0	0	0	0.0	0	0		0	0	.000	.000	0	0	C-1

Jack Remsen

REMSEN, JOHN J.
B. 1851, Brooklyn, N. Y.   Deceased.

BR TR 5'11½" 170 lbs.

	G	AB	H	2B	3B	HR	HR %	R	RBI	BB	SO	SB	BA	SA	AB	H	G by POS
1876 HAR N	69	324	89	12	5	1	0.3	62	30	1	15		.275	.352	0	0	OF-69
1877 STL N	33	123	32	3	4	0	0.0	14	13	4	3		.260	.350	0	0	OF-33
1878 CHI N	56	224	52	11	1	1	0.4	32	19	17	33		.232	.304	0	0	OF-56
1879	42	152	33	4	2	0	0.0	14	8	2	23		.217	.270	0	0	OF-31, 1B-11
1881 CLE N	48	172	30	4	3	0	0.0	14	13	9	31		.174	.233	0	0	OF-48
1884 2 teams				PHI	N (12G –	.209)			BKN	AA (81G –	.223)						
" total	93	344	76	8	6	3	0.9	54		29	9		.221	.305	0	0	OF-93
6 yrs.	341	1339	312	42	21	5	0.4	190	83	62	114		.233	.307	0	0	OF-330, 1B-11

Jerry Remy

REMY, GERALD PETER
B. Nov. 8, 1952, Fall River, Mass.

BL TR 5'9" 165 lbs.

	G	AB	H	2B	3B	HR	HR %	R	RBI	BB	SO	SB	BA	SA	AB	H	G by POS
1975 CAL A	147	569	147	17	5	1	0.2	82	46	45	55	34	.258	.311	0	0	2B-147
1976	143	502	132	14	3	0	0.0	64	28	38	43	35	.263	.303	1	1	2B-133, DH-5
1977	154	575	145	19	10	4	0.7	74	44	59	59	41	.252	.341	1	0	2B-152, 3B-1
1978 BOS A	148	583	162	24	6	2	0.3	87	44	40	55	30	.278	.350	0	0	2B-140, DH-4, SS-1
1979	80	306	91	11	2	0	0.0	49	29	26	25	14	.297	.346	1	0	2B-76
1980	63	230	72	7	2	0	0.0	24	9	10	14	14	.313	.361	4	1	2B-60, OF-1
1981	88	358	110	9	1	0	0.0	55	31	36	30	9	.307	.338	1	0	2B-87
1982	155	636	178	22	3	0	0.0	89	47	55	77	16	.280	.324	1	0	2B-154
1983	146	592	163	16	5	0	0.0	73	43	40	35	11	.275	.319	2	0	2B-144

	G	AB	H	2B	3B	HR	HR %	R	RBI	BB	SO	SB	BA	SA	Pinch Hit AB	Pinch Hit H	G by POS

Jerry Remy continued

	G	AB	H	2B	3B	HR	HR%	R	RBI	BB	SO	SB	BA	SA	AB	H	G by POS
1984	30	104	26	1	1	0	0.0	8	8	7	11	4	.250	.279	5	0	2B-24
10 yrs.	1154	4455	1226	140	38	7	0.2	605	329	356	404	208	.275	.328	16	2	2B-1117, DH-9, OF-1, SS-1, 3B-1

Rick Renick

RENICK, WARREN RICHARD
B. Mar. 16, 1944, London, Ohio   BR TR 6'   188 lbs.

	G	AB	H	2B	3B	HR	HR%	R	RBI	BB	SO	SB	BA	SA	AB	H	G by POS
1968 MIN A	42	97	21	5	2	3	3.1	16	13	9	42	0	.216	.402	1	0	SS-40
1969	71	139	34	3	0	5	3.6	21	17	12	32	0	.245	.374	25	8	3B-30, OF-10, SS-6
1970	81	179	41	8	0	7	3.9	20	25	22	29	0	.229	.391	26	7	3B-30, OF-25, SS-1
1971	27	45	10	2	0	1	2.2	4	8	5	14	0	.222	.333	13	1	OF-7, 3B-7
1972	55	93	16	2	0	4	4.3	10	8	15	25	0	.172	.323	24	2	OF-21, 1B-6, 3B-4, SS-1
5 yrs.	276	553	122	20	2	20	3.6	71	71	63	142	0	.221	.373	89	18	3B-71, OF-63, SS-48, 1B-6

LEAGUE CHAMPIONSHIP SERIES

	G	AB	H	2B	3B	HR	HR%	R	RBI	BB	SO	SB	BA	SA	AB	H	G by POS
1969 MIN A	1	1	0	0	0	0	0.0	0	0	0	0	0	.000	.000	1	0	
1970	2	5	1	0	0	0	0.0	0	0	0	1	0	.200	.200	1	0	3B-1
2 yrs.	3	6	1	0	0	0	0.0	0	0	0	1	0	.167	.167	2	0	3B-1

Bill Renna

RENNA, WILLIAM BENEDITTO (Big Bill)
B. Oct. 14, 1924, Hanford, Calif.   BR TR 6'3"   218 lbs.

	G	AB	H	2B	3B	HR	HR%	R	RBI	BB	SO	SB	BA	SA	AB	H	G by POS
1953 NY A	61	121	38	6	3	2	1.7	19	13	13	31	0	.314	.463	17	5	OF-40
1954 PHI A	123	422	98	15	4	13	3.1	52	53	41	60	1	.232	.379	9	3	OF-115
1955 KC A	100	249	53	7	3	7	2.8	33	28	31	42	0	.213	.349	23	4	OF-79
1956	33	48	13	3	0	2	4.2	12	5	3	10	1	.271	.458	9	2	OF-25
1958 BOS A	39	56	15	5	0	4	7.1	5	18	6	14	0	.268	.571	25	7	OF-11
1959	14	22	2	0	0	0	0.0	2	2	5	9	0	.091	.091	8	1	OF-7
6 yrs.	370	918	219	36	10	28	3.1	123	119	99	166	2	.239	.391	91	22	OF-277

Tony Rensa

RENSA, TONY GEORGE (Pug)
B. Sept. 29, 1901, Parsons, Pa.   BR TR 5'10"   180 lbs.

	G	AB	H	2B	3B	HR	HR%	R	RBI	BB	SO	SB	BA	SA	AB	H	G by POS
1930 2 teams			DET A (20G – .270)				PHI N (54G – .285)										
" total	74	209	59	13	3	4	1.9	37	34	16	25	1	.282	.431	6	1	C-67
1931 PHI N	19	29	3	1	0	0	0.0	2	2	6	2	0	.103	.138	2	0	C-17
1933 NY A	8	29	9	2	1	0	0.0	4	3	1	3	0	.310	.448	0	0	C-8
1937 CHI A	26	57	17	5	1	0	0.0	10	5	8	6	3	.298	.421	2	1	C-23
1938	59	165	41	5	0	3	1.8	15	19	25	16	1	.248	.333	2	0	C-57
1939	14	25	5	0	0	0	0.0	3	2	1	2	0	.200	.200	1	1	C-13
6 yrs.	200	514	134	26	5	7	1.4	71	65	57	54	5	.261	.372	13	3	C-185

Bob Repass

REPASS, ROBERT WILLIS
B. Nov. 6, 1917, West Pittston, Pa.   BR TR 6'1"   185 lbs.

	G	AB	H	2B	3B	HR	HR%	R	RBI	BB	SO	SB	BA	SA	AB	H	G by POS
1939 STL N	3	6	2	1	0	0	0.0	0	1	0	2	0	.333	.500	1	1	2B-2
1942 WAS A	81	259	62	11	1	2	0.8	30	23	33	30	6	.239	.313	6	1	2B-33, 3B-29, SS-11
2 yrs.	84	265	64	12	1	2	0.8	30	24	33	32	6	.242	.317	7	2	2B-35, 3B-29, SS-11

Roger Repoz

REPOZ, ROGER ALLEN
B. Aug. 3, 1940, Bellingham, Wash.   BL TL 6'3"   190 lbs.

	G	AB	H	2B	3B	HR	HR%	R	RBI	BB	SO	SB	BA	SA	AB	H	G by POS
1964 NY A	11	1	0	0	0	0	0.0	1	0	1	1	0	.000	.000	1	0	OF-9
1965	79	218	48	7	4	12	5.5	34	28	25	57	1	.220	.454	11	0	OF-69
1966 2 teams			NY A (37G – .349)				KC A (101G – .216)										
" total	138	362	84	14	4	11	3.0	44	43	48	88	3	.232	.384	16	2	OF-82, 1B-45
1967 2 teams			KC A (40G – .241)				CAL A (74G – .250)										
" total	114	263	65	15	2	7	2.7	34	28	31	57	6	.247	.399	23	4	OF-94
1968 CAL A	133	375	90	8	1	13	3.5	30	54	38	83	8	.240	.371	25	6	OF-114
1969	103	219	36	1	1	8	3.7	25	19	32	52	1	.164	.288	24	2	OF-48, 1B-31
1970	137	407	97	17	6	18	4.4	50	47	45	90	4	.238	.442	20	3	OF-110, 1B-18
1971	113	297	59	11	1	13	4.4	39	42	60	69	3	.199	.374	8	1	OF-97, 1B-13
1972	3	3	1	0	0	0	0.0	0	0	0	2	0	.333	.333	3	1	
9 yrs.	831	2145	480	73	19	82	3.8	257	261	280	499	26	.224	.390	131	19	OF-623, 1B-107

Rip Repulski

REPULSKI, ELDON JOHN
B. Oct. 4, 1927, Sauk Rapids, Minn.   BR TR 6'   195 lbs.

	G	AB	H	2B	3B	HR	HR%	R	RBI	BB	SO	SB	BA	SA	AB	H	G by POS
1953 STL N	153	567	156	25	4	15	2.6	75	66	33	71	3	.275	.413	0	0	OF-153
1954	152	619	175	39	5	19	3.1	99	79	43	75	8	.283	.454	0	0	OF-152
1955	147	512	138	28	2	23	4.5	64	73	49	66	5	.270	.467	10	3	OF-141
1956	112	376	104	18	3	11	2.9	44	55	24	46	2	.277	.428	17	7	OF-100
1957 PHI N	134	516	134	23	4	20	3.9	65	68	19	74	7	.260	.436	3	0	OF-130
1958	85	238	58	9	4	13	5.5	33	40	15	47	0	.244	.479	30	8	OF-56
1959 LA N	53	94	24	4	0	2	2.1	11	14	13	23	0	.255	.362	25	8	OF-31
1960 2 teams			LA N (4G – .200)				BOS A (73G – .243)										
" total	77	141	34	6	1	3	2.1	14	20	10	26	0	.241	.362	39	9	OF-35
1961 BOS A	15	25	7	1	0	0	0.0	2	1	1	5	0	.280	.320	10	3	OF-4
9 yrs.	928	3088	830	153	23	106	3.4	407	416	207	433	25	.269	.436	134	38	OF-802

WORLD SERIES

	G	AB	H	2B	3B	HR	HR%	R	RBI	BB	SO	SB	BA	SA	AB	H	G by POS
1959 LA N	1	0	0	0	0	0	–	0	0	1	0	0	–	–	0	0	OF-1

Dino Restelli

RESTELLI, DINO PAUL (Dingo)
B. Sept. 23, 1924, St. Louis, Mo.   BR TR 6'1½"   191 lbs.

	G	AB	H	2B	3B	HR	HR%	R	RBI	BB	SO	SB	BA	SA	AB	H	G by POS
1949 PIT N	72	232	58	11	0	12	5.2	41	40	35	26	3	.250	.453	8	2	OF-61, 1B-1
1951	21	38	7	1	0	1	2.6	1	3	2	4	0	.184	.289	8	1	OF-11
2 yrs.	93	270	65	12	0	13	4.8	42	43	37	30	3	.241	.430	16	3	OF-72, 1B-1

	G	AB	H	2B	3B	HR	HR %	R	RBI	BB	SO	SB	BA	SA	Pinch Hit AB	Pinch Hit H	G by POS

Merv Rettenmund

RETTENMUND, MERVIN WELDON
B. June 6, 1943, Flint, Mich.   BR TR 5'10" 190 lbs.

	G	AB	H	2B	3B	HR	HR %	R	RBI	BB	SO	SB	BA	SA	PH AB	PH H	G by POS
1968 **BAL A**	31	64	19	5	0	2	3.1	10	7	18	20	1	.297	.469	6	3	OF-23
1969	95	190	47	10	3	4	2.1	27	25	28	28	6	.247	.395	17	2	OF-78
1970	106	338	109	17	2	18	5.3	60	58	38	59	13	.322	.544	17	5	OF-93
1971	141	491	156	23	4	11	2.2	81	75	87	60	15	.318	.448	3	0	OF-134
1972	102	301	70	10	2	6	2.0	40	21	41	37	6	.233	.339	10	3	OF-98
1973	95	321	84	17	2	9	2.8	59	44	57	38	11	.262	.411	11	5	OF-90
1974 **CIN N**	80	208	45	6	0	6	2.9	30	28	37	39	5	.216	.332	14	3	OF-69
1975	93	188	45	6	1	2	1.1	24	19	35	22	5	.239	.314	30	6	OF-61, 3B-1
1976 **SD N**	86	140	32	7	0	2	1.4	16	11	29	23	4	.229	.321	40	12	OF-43
1977	107	126	36	6	1	4	3.2	23	17	33	28	1	.286	.444	67	21	OF-27, 3B-1
1978 **CAL A**	50	108	29	5	1	0	0.9	16	14	30	13	0	.269	.361	15	2	OF-22, DH-18
1979	35	76	20	2	0	1	1.3	7	10	11	14	1	.263	.329	10	4	DH-17, OF-9
1980	2	4	1	0	0	0	0.0	0	0	1	1	0	.250	.250	1	0	DH-1
13 yrs.	1023	2555	693	114	16	66	2.6	393	329	445	382	68	.271	.406	241	66	OF-747, DH-36, 3B-2
LEAGUE CHAMPIONSHIP SERIES																	
1969 **BAL A**	1	0	0	0	0	0	–	0	0	0	0	0	–	–	0	0	
1970	1	3	1	0	0	0	0.0	1	1	2	1	1	.333	.333	0	0	OF-1
1971	3	8	2	1	0	0	0.0	0	1	0	3	0	.250	.375	0	0	OF-3
1973	3	11	1	0	0	0	0.0	1	0	3	2	0	.091	.091	0	0	OF-3
1975 **CIN N**	2	1	0	0	0	0	0.0	0	0	1	0	0	.000	.000	1	0	
1979 **CAL A**	2	2	0	0	0	0	0.0	0	0	2	1	0	.000	.000	0	0	DH-2
6 yrs.	12	25	4	1	0	0	0.0	2	2	8	7	1	.160	.200	1	0	OF-7, DH-2
WORLD SERIES																	
1969 **BAL A**	1	0	0	0	0	0	–	0	0	0	0	0	–	–	0	0	
1970	2	5	2	0	0	1	20.0	2	2	1	0	0	.400	1.000	1	0	OF-1
1971	7	27	5	0	0	1	3.7	3	4	0	4	0	.185	.296	1	0	OF-6
1975 **CIN N**	3	3	0	0	0	0	0.0	0	0	0	1	0	.000	.000	3	0	
4 yrs.	13	35	7	0	0	2	5.7	5	6	1	5	0	.200	.371	5	0	OF-7

Ken Retzer

RETZER, KENNETH LEO
B. Apr. 30, 1934, Wood River, Ill.   BL TR 6' 185 lbs.

	G	AB	H	2B	3B	HR	HR %	R	RBI	BB	SO	SB	BA	SA	PH AB	PH H	G by POS
1961 **WAS A**	16	53	18	4	0	1	1.9	7	3	4	5	1	.340	.472	0	0	C-16
1962	109	340	97	11	2	8	2.4	36	37	26	21	2	.285	.400	11	2	C-99
1963	95	265	64	10	0	5	1.9	21	31	17	20	2	.242	.336	15	2	C-81
1964	17	32	3	0	0	0	0.0	1	1	5	4	0	.094	.094	4	2	C-13
4 yrs.	237	690	182	25	2	14	2.0	65	72	52	50	5	.264	.367	30	6	C-209

Dave Revering

REVERING, DAVID ALVIN
B. Feb. 12, 1953, Roseville, Calif.   BL TR 6'4" 210 lbs.

	G	AB	H	2B	3B	HR	HR %	R	RBI	BB	SO	SB	BA	SA	PH AB	PH H	G by POS
1978 **OAK A**	152	521	141	21	3	16	3.1	49	46	26	55	0	.271	.415	12	3	1B-138, DH-3
1979	125	472	136	25	5	19	4.0	63	77	34	65	1	.288	.483	3	2	1B-104, DH-18
1980	106	376	109	21	5	15	4.0	48	62	32	37	1	.290	.492	11	4	1B-95, DH-5
1981 **2 teams**		OAK	A (31G – .230)			NY	A (45G – .235)										
" total	76	206	48	5	2	4	1.9	20	17	22	32	0	.233	.335	11	1	1B-73, DH-2
1982 **3 teams**		NY	A (14G – .150)			TOR	A (55G – .215)			SEA	A (29G – .207)						
" total	98	257	52	11	1	8	3.1	25	32	34	51	0	.202	.346	20	2	DH-50, 1B-44
5 yrs.	557	1832	486	83	16	62	3.4	205	234	148	240	2	.265	.430	57	12	1B-454, DH-78
DIVISIONAL PLAYOFF SERIES																	
1981 **NY A**	2	0	0	0	0	0	–	0	0	0	0	0	–	–	0	0	1B-2
LEAGUE CHAMPIONSHIP SERIES																	
1981 **NY A**	2	2	1	0	0	0	0.0	0	0	0	0	0	.500	.500	0	0	1B-2

Gil Reyes

REYES, GILBERTO R.
Also known as Gilberto R. Polanco.
B. Dec. 10, 1963, Santo Domingo, Dominican Republic   BR TR 6'3" 195 lbs.

	G	AB	H	2B	3B	HR	HR %	R	RBI	BB	SO	SB	BA	SA	PH AB	PH H	G by POS
1983 **LA N**	19	31	5	2	0	0	0.0	1	0	0	5	0	.161	.226	0	0	C-19
1984	4	5	0	0	0	0	0.0	0	0	0	3	0	.000	.000	2	0	C-2
2 yrs.	23	36	5	2	0	0	0.0	1	0	0	8	0	.139	.194	2	0	C-21

Nap Reyes

REYES, NAPOLEON AGUILERA
B. Nov. 24, 1919, San Luis, Cuba   BR TR 6'1" 205 lbs.

	G	AB	H	2B	3B	HR	HR %	R	RBI	BB	SO	SB	BA	SA	PH AB	PH H	G by POS
1943 **NY N**	40	125	32	4	2	0	0.0	13	13	4	12	2	.256	.320	1	0	1B-38, 3B-1
1944	116	374	108	16	5	8	2.1	38	53	15	24	2	.289	.422	11	4	1B-63, 3B-37, OF-3
1945	122	431	124	15	4	5	1.2	39	44	25	26	1	.288	.376	3	0	3B-115, 1B-5
1950	1	1	0	0	0	0	0.0	0	0	0	0	0	.000	.000	0	0	1B-1
4 yrs.	279	931	264	35	11	13	1.4	90	110	44	62	5	.284	.387	15	4	3B-153, 1B-107, OF-3

Bill Reynolds

REYNOLDS, WILLIAM DEE
B. Aug. 14, 1884, Eastland, Tex.   D. June 5, 1924, Carnegie, Okla.   BR TR 6' 185 lbs.

	G	AB	H	2B	3B	HR	HR %	R	RBI	BB	SO	SB	BA	SA	PH AB	PH H	G by POS
1913 **NY A**	5	5	0	0	0	0	0.0	0	0	0	1	0	.000	.000	0	0	C-5
1914	4	5	2	0	0	0	0.0	0	0	0	3	0	.400	.400	3	1	C-1
2 yrs.	9	10	2	0	0	0	0.0	0	0	0	4	0	.200	.200	3	1	C-6

Carl Reynolds

REYNOLDS, CARL NETTLES
B. Feb. 1, 1903, LaRue, Tex.   D. May 29, 1978, Houston, Tex.   BR TR 6' 194 lbs.

	G	AB	H	2B	3B	HR	HR %	R	RBI	BB	SO	SB	BA	SA	PH AB	PH H	G by POS
1927 **CHI A**	14	42	9	3	0	1	2.4	5	7	5	7	1	.214	.357	0	0	OF-13
1928	84	291	94	21	11	2	0.7	51	36	17	13	15	.323	.491	10	6	OF-74
1929	131	517	164	24	12	11	2.1	81	67	20	37	19	.317	.474	0	0	OF-131
1930	138	563	202	25	18	22	3.9	103	100	20	39	16	.359	.584	5	0	OF-132
1931	118	462	134	24	14	6	1.3	71	77	24	26	17	.290	.442	9	3	OF-109
1932 **WAS A**	102	406	124	28	7	9	2.2	53	63	14	19	8	.305	.475	5	1	OF-95
1933 **STL A**	135	475	136	26	14	8	1.7	81	71	50	25	5	.286	.451	13	3	OF-124
1934 **BOS A**	113	413	125	26	9	4	1.0	61	86	27	28	5	.303	.438	14	3	OF-100
1935	78	244	66	13	4	6	2.5	33	35	24	20	4	.270	.430	11	2	OF-64

	G	AB	H	2B	3B	HR	HR %	R	RBI	BB	SO	SB	BA	SA	Pinch Hit AB	H	G by POS

Carl Reynolds continued

	G	AB	H	2B	3B	HR	HR %	R	RBI	BB	SO	SB	BA	SA	PH AB	PH H	G by POS
1936 WAS A	89	293	81	18	2	4	1.4	41	41	21	22	8	.276	.392	15	3	OF-72
1937 CHI N	7	11	3	1	0	0	0.0	0	1	2	2	0	.273	.364	4	1	OF-2
1938	125	497	150	28	10	3	0.6	59	67	22	32	9	.302	.416	0	0	OF-125
1939	88	281	69	10	6	4	1.4	33	44	16	38	5	.246	.367	14	3	OF-72
13 yrs.	1222	4495	1357	247	107	80	1.8	672	695	262	308	112	.302	.458	100	25	OF-1113

WORLD SERIES

	G	AB	H	2B	3B	HR	HR %	R	RBI	BB	SO	SB	BA	SA	PH AB	PH H	G by POS
1938 CHI N	4	12	0	0	0	0	0.0	0	0	1	3	0	.000	.000	1	0	OF-3

Charlie Reynolds

REYNOLDS, CHARLES LAWRENCE
B. May 1, 1865, Williamsburgh, Ind.   D. July 3, 1944, Denver, Colo.

	G	AB	H	2B	3B	HR	HR %	R	RBI	BB	SO	SB	BA	SA	PH AB	PH H	G by POS
1889 2 teams	KC	AA (1G –	.250)		BKN	AA (12G –	.214)										
" total	13	46	10	1	1	0	0.0	6	4	1	7	2	.217	.283	0	0	C-13

Craig Reynolds

REYNOLDS, GORDON CRAIG   BL TR 6'1"   175 lbs.
B. Dec. 27, 1952, Houston, Tex.

	G	AB	H	2B	3B	HR	HR %	R	RBI	BB	SO	SB	BA	SA	PH AB	PH H	G by POS
1975 PIT N	31	76	17	3	0	0	0.0	8	4	3	5	0	.224	.263	1	1	SS-30
1976	7	4	1	0	0	1	25.0	1	1	0	0	0	.250	1.000	0	0	SS-4, 2B-1
1977 SEA A	135	420	104	12	3	4	1.0	41	28	15	23	6	.248	.319	2	1	SS-134
1978	148	548	160	16	7	5	0.9	57	44	36	41	9	.292	.374	1	0	SS-146
1979 HOU N	146	555	147	20	9	0	0.0	63	39	21	49	12	.265	.333	5	1	SS-143
1980	137	381	86	9	6	3	0.8	34	28	20	39	2	.226	.304	2	1	SS-135
1981	87	323	84	10	12	4	1.2	43	31	12	31	3	.260	.402	2	0	SS-85
1982	54	118	30	2	3	1	0.8	16	7	11	9	3	.254	.347	5	0	SS-35, 3B-3
1983	65	98	21	3	0	1	1.0	10	6	6	10	0	.214	.276	12	2	2B-26, 3B-15, SS-8, OF-1
1984	146	527	137	15	11	6	1.1	61	60	22	53	7	.260	.364	4	2	SS-143, 3B-1
10 yrs.	956	3050	787	90	51	25	0.8	334	248	146	260	42	.258	.346	34	8	SS-863, 2B-27, 3B-23, OF-1

DIVISIONAL PLAYOFF SERIES

	G	AB	H	2B	3B	HR	HR %	R	RBI	BB	SO	SB	BA	SA	PH AB	PH H	G by POS
1981 HOU N	2	3	1	0	0	0	0.0	1	0	0	1	0	.333	.333	1	1	SS-1

LEAGUE CHAMPIONSHIP SERIES

	G	AB	H	2B	3B	HR	HR %	R	RBI	BB	SO	SB	BA	SA	PH AB	PH H	G by POS
1975 PIT N	2	1	0	0	0	0	0.0	0	0	0	0	0	.000	.000	0	0	SS-1
1980 HOU N	4	13	2	1	0	0	0.0	2	0	3	1	0	.154	.231	0	0	SS-4
2 yrs.	6	14	2	1	0	0	0.0	2	0	3	1	0	.143	.214	0	0	SS-5

Danny Reynolds

REYNOLDS, DANIEL VANCE (Squirrel)   BR TR 5'11"   158 lbs.
B. Nov. 27, 1919, Stony Point, N. C.

	G	AB	H	2B	3B	HR	HR %	R	RBI	BB	SO	SB	BA	SA	PH AB	PH H	G by POS
1945 CHI A	29	72	12	2	1	0	0.0	6	4	3	8	1	.167	.222	4	0	SS-14, 2B-11

Don Reynolds

REYNOLDS, DONALD EDWARD   BR TR 5'8"   178 lbs.
Brother of Hal Reynolds.
B. Apr. 16, 1953, Arkadelphia, Ark.

	G	AB	H	2B	3B	HR	HR %	R	RBI	BB	SO	SB	BA	SA	PH AB	PH H	G by POS
1978 SD N	57	87	22	2	0	0	0.0	8	10	15	14	1	.253	.276	30	7	OF-25
1979	30	45	10	1	2	0	0.0	6	6	7	6	0	.222	.333	12	0	OF-14
2 yrs.	87	132	32	3	2	0	0.0	14	16	22	20	1	.242	.295	42	7	OF-39

Hal Reynolds

REYNOLDS, HAROLD CRAIG   BB TR 5'11"   165 lbs.
Brother of Don Reynolds.
B. Nov. 26, 1960, Eugene, Ore.

	G	AB	H	2B	3B	HR	HR %	R	RBI	BB	SO	SB	BA	SA	PH AB	PH H	G by POS
1983 SEA A	20	59	12	4	1	0	0.0	8	1	2	9	0	.203	.305	0	0	2B-18
1984	10	10	3	0	0	0	0.0	3	0	0	1	1	.300	.300	0	0	2B-6
2 yrs.	30	69	15	4	1	0	0.0	11	1	2	10	1	.217	.304	0	0	2B-24

R. J. Reynolds

REYNOLDS, ROBERT JAMES   BB TR 6'   180 lbs.
B. Apr. 19, 1959, Sacramento, Calif.

	G	AB	H	2B	3B	HR	HR %	R	RBI	BB	SO	SB	BA	SA	PH AB	PH H	G by POS
1983 LA N	24	55	13	0	0	2	3.6	5	11	3	11	5	.236	.345	7	2	OF-18
1984	73	240	62	12	2	2	0.8	23	24	14	38	7	.258	.350	13	5	OF-63
2 yrs.	97	295	75	12	2	4	1.4	28	35	17	49	12	.254	.349	20	7	OF-81

Ronn Reynolds

REYNOLDS, RONN DWAYNE   BR TR 6'   200 lbs.
B. Sept. 29, 1958, Wichita, Kans.

	G	AB	H	2B	3B	HR	HR %	R	RBI	BB	SO	SB	BA	SA	PH AB	PH H	G by POS
1982 NY N	2	4	0	0	0	0	0.0	0	0	1	1	0	.000	.000	0	0	C-2
1983	24	66	13	1	0	0	0.0	4	2	8	12	0	.197	.212	0	0	C-24
2 yrs.	26	70	13	1	0	0	0.0	4	2	9	13	0	.186	.200	0	0	C-26

Tommie Reynolds

REYNOLDS, THOMAS D.   BR TR 6'2"   190 lbs.
B. Aug. 15, 1941, Arizona, La.   BB 1967

	G	AB	H	2B	3B	HR	HR %	R	RBI	BB	SO	SB	BA	SA	PH AB	PH H	G by POS
1963 KC A	8	19	1	1	0	0	0.0	1	0	1	7	0	.053	.105	3	0	OF-5
1964	31	94	19	1	0	2	2.1	11	9	10	22	0	.202	.277	5	2	OF-25, 3B-3
1965	90	270	64	11	3	1	0.4	34	22	36	41	9	.237	.311	7	1	OF-83, 3B-1
1967 NY N	101	136	28	1	0	2	1.5	16	9	11	26	1	.206	.257	22	5	OF-72, 3B-5, C-1
1969 OAK A	107	315	81	10	0	2	0.6	51	20	34	29	1	.257	.308	20	6	OF-89
1970 CAL A	59	120	30	3	1	1	0.8	11	6	6	10	1	.250	.317	24	4	OF-32, 3B-1
1971	45	86	16	3	0	2	2.3	4	8	9	6	0	.186	.291	21	4	OF-26, 3B-1
1972 MIL A	72	130	26	5	1	2	1.5	13	13	10	25	0	.200	.300	32	7	OF-41, 3B-1, 1B-1
8 yrs.	513	1170	265	35	5	12	1.0	141	87	117	166	12	.226	.296	134	29	OF-373, 3B-12, 1B-1, C-1

Bobby Rhawn

RHAWN, ROBERT JOHN (Rocky)   BR TR 5'8"   180 lbs.
B. Feb. 13, 1919, Catawissa, Pa.   D. 1984, Danville, Pa.

	G	AB	H	2B	3B	HR	HR %	R	RBI	BB	SO	SB	BA	SA	PH AB	PH H	G by POS
1947 NY N	13	45	14	3	0	1	2.2	7	3	8	1	0	.311	.444	0	0	2B-8, 3B-5
1948	36	44	12	2	1	1	2.3	11	8	6	3	3	.273	.432	4	2	SS-14, 3B-7
1949 3 teams	NY	N (14G –	.172)		PIT	N (3G –	.143)		CHI	A (24G –	.205)						
" total	41	109	21	4	1	0	0.0	20	7	19	10	1	.193	.248	3	1	3B-21, 2B-8, SS-3
3 yrs.	90	198	47	9	2	2	1.0	38	18	35	17	4	.237	.333	7	3	3B-33, SS-17, 2B-16

	G	AB	H	2B	3B	HR	HR %	R	RBI	BB	SO	SB	BA	SA	Pinch Hit AB	Pinch Hit H	G by POS

Cy Rheam

RHEAM, KENNETH JOHNSTON
B. Sept. 28, 1893, Pittsburgh, Pa.   D. Oct. 23, 1947, Pittsburgh, Pa.
BR TR 6' 175 lbs.

	G	AB	H	2B	3B	HR	HR%	R	RBI	BB	SO	SB	BA	SA	PH AB	PH H	G by POS
1914 PIT F	73	214	45	5	3	0	0.0	15	20	9		6	.210	.262	5	1	1B-43, 3B-13, 2B-11, OF-1
1915	34	69	12	0	0	1	1.4	10	5	1		4	.174	.217	4	1	OF-22, 1B-1
2 yrs.	107	283	57	5	3	1	0.4	25	25	10		10	.201	.251	9	2	1B-44, OF-23, 3B-13, 2B-11

Billy Rhiel

RHIEL, WILLIAM JOSEPH
B. Aug. 16, 1900, Youngstown, Ohio   D. Aug. 16, 1946, Youngstown, Ohio
BR TR 5'11" 175 lbs.

	G	AB	H	2B	3B	HR	HR%	R	RBI	BB	SO	SB	BA	SA	PH AB	PH H	G by POS
1929 BKN N	76	205	57	9	4	4	2.0	27	25	19	25	0	.278	.420	14	2	2B-47, 3B-7, SS-2
1930 BOS N	20	47	8	4	0	0	0.0	3	4	2	5	0	.170	.255	3	0	3B-13, 2B-2
1932 DET A	84	250	70	13	3	3	1.2	30	38	17	23	2	.280	.392	27	13	3B-36, 1B-12, OF-8, 2B-1
1933	19	17	3	0	1	0	0.0	1	1	5	4	0	.176	.294	13	3	OF-1
4 yrs.	199	519	138	26	8	7	1.3	61	68	43	57	2	.266	.387	57	18	3B-56, 2B-50, 1B-12, OF-9, SS-2

Dusty Rhodes

RHODES, JAMES LAMAR
B. May 13, 1927, Mathews, Ala.
BL TR 6' 178 lbs.

	G	AB	H	2B	3B	HR	HR%	R	RBI	BB	SO	SB	BA	SA	PH AB	PH H	G by POS
1952 NY N	67	176	44	8	1	10	5.7	34	36	23	33	1	.250	.477	9	1	OF-56
1953	76	163	38	7	0	11	6.7	18	30	10	28	0	.233	.479	29	5	OF-47
1954	82	164	56	7	3	15	9.1	31	50	18	25	1	.341	.695	45	15	OF-37
1955	94	187	57	5	2	6	3.2	22	32	27	26	1	.305	.449	44	11	OF-45
1956	111	244	53	10	3	8	3.3	20	33	30	41	0	.217	.381	39	7	OF-68
1957	92	190	39	5	1	4	2.1	20	19	18	34	0	.205	.305	46	7	OF-44
1959 SF N	54	48	9	2	0	0	0.0	1	7	5	9	0	.188	.229	48	9	
7 yrs.	576	1172	296	44	10	54	4.6	146	207	131	196	3	.253	.445	260	55	OF-297

WORLD SERIES

	G	AB	H	2B	3B	HR	HR%	R	RBI	BB	SO	SB	BA	SA	PH AB	PH H	G by POS
1954 NY N	3	6	4	0	0	2	33.3	2	7	1	2	0	.667	1.667	3	3	OF-2
															1st		

Keith Rhomberg

RHOMBERG, KEVIN JAY
B. Nov. 22, 1955, Dubuque, Iowa
BR TR 6' 175 lbs.

	G	AB	H	2B	3B	HR	HR%	R	RBI	BB	SO	SB	BA	SA	PH AB	PH H	G by POS
1982 CLE A	16	18	6	0	0	1	5.6	3	1	2	4	0	.333	.500	2	0	OF-7, DH-4, 3B-1
1983	12	21	10	0	0	0	0.0	2	2	2	4	1	.476	.476	1	0	OF-9, DH-1
1984	13	8	2	0	0	0	0.0	0	0	0	3	0	.250	.250	3	0	OF-7, DH-1, 2B-1, 1B-1
3 yrs.	41	47	18	0	0	1	2.1	5	3	4	11	1	.383	.447	6	0	OF-23, DH-6, 3B-1, 2B-1, 1B-1

Hal Rhyne

RHYNE, HAROLD J.
B. Mar. 30, 1899, Paso Robles, Calif.   D. Jan. 7, 1971, Orangevale, Calif.
BR TR 5'8½" 163 lbs.

	G	AB	H	2B	3B	HR	HR%	R	RBI	BB	SO	SB	BA	SA	PH AB	PH H	G by POS
1926 PIT N	109	366	92	14	3	2	0.5	46	39	35	21	1	.251	.322	0	0	2B-66, SS-44, 3B-1
1927	62	168	46	5	0	0	0.0	21	17	14	9	0	.274	.304	1	0	2B-45, 3B-10, SS-7
1929 BOS A	120	346	87	24	5	0	0.0	41	38	25	14	4	.251	.350	1	0	SS-114, OF-1, 3B-1
1930	107	296	60	8	5	0	0.0	34	23	25	19	1	.203	.264	0	0	SS-107
1931	147	565	154	34	3	0	0.0	75	51	57	41	3	.273	.343	0	0	SS-147
1932	71	207	47	12	5	0	0.0	26	14	23	14	3	.227	.333	10	3	SS-55, 3B-4, 2B-1
1933 CHI A	39	83	22	1	1	0	0.0	9	10	5	9	1	.265	.301	6	1	2B-19, 3B-13, SS-2
7 yrs.	655	2031	508	98	22	2	0.1	252	192	184	127	13	.250	.323	18	4	SS-476, 2B-131, 3B-29, OF-1

WORLD SERIES

	G	AB	H	2B	3B	HR	HR%	R	RBI	BB	SO	SB	BA	SA	PH AB	PH H	G by POS
1927 PIT N	1	4	0	0	0	0	0.0	0	0	0	0	0	.000	.000	0	0	2B-1

Bob Rice

RICE, ROBERT TURNBULL
B. May 28, 1899, Philadelphia, Pa.
BR TR 5'10" 170 lbs.

	G	AB	H	2B	3B	HR	HR%	R	RBI	BB	SO	SB	BA	SA	PH AB	PH H	G by POS
1926 PHI N	19	54	8	0	1	0	0.0	3	10	3	4	0	.148	.185	0	0	3B-15, SS-2, 2B-2

Del Rice

RICE, DELBERT W.
B. Oct. 27, 1922, Portsmouth, Ohio   D. Jan. 26, 1983, Buena Park, Calif.
Manager 1972.
BR TR 6'2" 190 lbs.

	G	AB	H	2B	3B	HR	HR%	R	RBI	BB	SO	SB	BA	SA	PH AB	PH H	G by POS
1945 STL N	83	253	66	17	3	1	0.4	27	28	16	33	0	.261	.364	6	1	C-77
1946	55	139	38	8	1	1	0.7	10	12	8	16	0	.273	.367	2	0	C-53
1947	97	261	57	7	3	12	4.6	28	44	36	40	1	.218	.406	3	0	C-94
1948	100	290	57	10	1	4	1.4	24	34	37	46	1	.197	.279	0	0	C-99
1949	92	284	67	16	1	4	1.4	25	29	30	40	0	.236	.342	0	0	C-92
1950	130	414	101	20	3	9	2.2	39	54	43	65	0	.244	.372	0	0	C-130
1951	122	374	94	13	1	9	2.4	34	47	34	26	0	.251	.364	3	0	C-120
1952	147	495	128	27	2	11	2.2	43	65	33	38	0	.259	.388	1	0	C-147
1953	135	419	99	22	1	6	1.4	32	37	48	49	0	.236	.337	0	0	C-135
1954	56	147	37	10	1	2	1.4	13	16	16	21	0	.252	.374	4	2	C-52
1955 2 teams	STL N (20G – .203)				MIL N (27G – .197)												
" total	47	130	26	3	1	3	2.3	11	14	13	18	0	.200	.308	7	0	C-40
1956 MIL N	71	188	40	9	1	3	1.6	15	17	18	34	0	.213	.319	5	1	C-65
1957	54	144	33	1	1	9	6.3	15	20	17	37	0	.229	.438	6	1	C-48
1958	43	121	27	7	0	1	0.8	10	8	8	30	0	.223	.306	6	2	C-38
1959	13	29	6	0	0	0	0.0	3	1	2	2	0	.207	.207	4	1	C-9
1960 3 teams	CHI N (18G – .231)				STL N (1G – .000)				BAL A (1G – .000)								
" total	20	55	12	3	0	0	0.0	4	3	4	7	0	.218	.273	0	0	C-20
1961 LA A	44	83	20	4	0	4	4.8	11	11	20	19	0	.241	.434	15	4	C-22
17 yrs.	1309	3826	908	177	20	79	2.1	342	441	382	522	2	.237	.356	62	12	C-1249

WORLD SERIES

	G	AB	H	2B	3B	HR	HR%	R	RBI	BB	SO	SB	BA	SA	PH AB	PH H	G by POS
1946 STL N	3	6	3	1	0	0	0.0	2	0	2	0	0	.500	.667	0	0	C-3
1957 MIL N	2	6	1	0	0	0	0.0	0	0	1	2	0	.167	.167	0	0	C-2
2 yrs.	5	12	4	1	0	0	0.0	2	0	3	2	0	.333	.417	0	0	C-5

	G	AB	H	2B	3B	HR	HR %	R	RBI	BB	SO	SB	BA	SA	Pinch Hit AB	Pinch Hit H	G by POS

Hal Rice

RICE, HAROLD HOUSTEN (Hoot)
B. Feb. 11, 1924, Morganette, W. Va.   BL TR 6'1"   195 lbs.

	G	AB	H	2B	3B	HR	HR %	R	RBI	BB	SO	SB	BA	SA	PH AB	PH H	G by POS
1948 STL N	8	31	10	1	2	0	0.0	3	3	2	4	0	.323	.484	0	0	OF-8
1949	40	46	9	2	1	1	2.2	3	9	3	7	0	.196	.348	27	6	OF-10
1950	44	128	27	3	1	2	1.6	12	11	10	10	0	.211	.297	6	1	OF-37
1951	69	236	60	12	1	4	1.7	20	38	24	22	0	.254	.364	5	1	OF-63
1952	98	295	85	14	5	7	2.4	37	45	16	26	1	.288	.441	19	3	OF-81
1953 2 teams	STL	N (8G –	.250)		PIT	N	(78G –	.311)									
" total	86	294	91	16	1	4	1.4	39	42	17	25	0	.310	.412	17	3	OF-70
1954 2 teams	PIT	N (28G –	.173)		CHI	N	(51G –	.153)									
" total	79	153	25	4	1	1	0.7	15	14	22	39	0	.163	.222	29	2	OF-48
7 yrs.	424	1183	307	52	12	19	1.6	129	162	94	133	1	.260	.372	103	16	OF-317

Harry Rice

RICE, HARRY FRANCIS
B. Nov. 22, 1901, Ware Station, Ill.   D. Jan. 1, 1971, Portland, Ore.   BL TR 5'9"   185 lbs.

	G	AB	H	2B	3B	HR	HR %	R	RBI	BB	SO	SB	BA	SA	PH AB	PH H	G by POS
1923 STL A	4	3	0	0	0	0	0.0	0	0	0	0	0	.000	.000	3	0	
1924	43	92	26	7	0	0	0.0	19	15	7	5	1	.283	.359	22	7	3B-15, 2B-4, OF-2, SS-2, 1B-2
1925	103	354	127	25	8	11	3.1	87	47	54	15	8	.359	.568	14	6	OF-85, 1B-3, 3B-1, 2B-1, C-1
1926	148	578	181	27	10	9	1.6	86	59	63	40	10	.313	.441	4	2	OF-133, 3B-7, 2B-4, SS-2
1927	137	520	149	26	9	7	1.3	90	68	50	21	6	.287	.412	0	0	OF-130, 3B-7
1928 DET A	131	510	154	21	12	6	1.2	87	81	44	27	20	.302	.425	2	0	OF-129, 3B-2
1929	130	536	163	33	7	6	1.1	97	69	61	23	6	.304	.425	1	0	OF-127, 3B-3
1930 2 teams	DET	A (37G –	.305)		NY	A	(100G –	.298)									
" total	137	474	142	23	5	9	1.9	78	98	50	29	3	.300	.426	8	1	OF-122, 1B-6, 3B-1
1931 WAS A	47	162	43	5	6	0	0.0	32	15	12	10	2	.265	.370	5	3	OF-42
1933 CIN N	143	510	133	19	6	0	0.0	44	54	35	24	4	.261	.322	1	0	OF-141, 3B-1
10 yrs.	1023	3739	1118	186	63	48	1.3	620	506	376	194	60	.299	.421	60	19	OF-911, 3B-37, 1B-11, 2B-9, SS-4, C-1

Jim Rice

RICE, JAMES EDWARD
B. Mar. 8, 1953, Anderson, S. C.   BR TR 6'2"   200 lbs.

	G	AB	H	2B	3B	HR	HR %	R	RBI	BB	SO	SB	BA	SA	PH AB	PH H	G by POS
1974 BOS A	24	67	18	2	1	1	1.5	6	13	4	12	0	.269	.373	6	0	DH-16, OF-3
1975	144	564	174	29	4	22	3.9	92	102	36	122	10	.309	.491	0	0	OF-90, DH-54
1976	153	581	164	25	8	25	4.3	75	85	28	123	3	.282	.482	3	1	OF-98, DH-54
1977	160	644	206	29	15	39	6.1	104	114	53	120	5	.320	.593	0	0	DH-116, OF-44
1978	163	677	213	25	15	46	6.8	121	139	58	126	7	.315	.600	0	0	OF-114, DH-49
1979	158	619	201	39	6	39	6.3	117	130	57	97	9	.325	.596	1	0	OF-125, DH-33
1980	124	504	148	22	6	24	4.8	81	86	30	87	8	.294	.504	0	0	OF-109, DH-15
1981	108	451	128	18	1	17	3.8	51	62	34	76	2	.284	.441	0	0	OF-108
1982	145	573	177	24	5	24	4.2	86	97	55	98	0	.309	.494	0	0	OF-145
1983	155	626	191	34	1	39	6.2	90	126	52	102	0	.305	.550	0	0	OF-151, DH-4
1984	159	657	184	25	7	28	4.3	98	122	44	102	4	.280	.467	0	0	OF-157, DH-2
11 yrs.	1493	5963	1804	272	69	304	5.1	921	1076	451	1065	53	.303	.524	10	1	OF-1144, DH-343

Len Rice

RICE, LEONARD OLIVER
B. Sept. 2, 1918, Lead, S. D.   BR TR 6'   175 lbs.

	G	AB	H	2B	3B	HR	HR %	R	RBI	BB	SO	SB	BA	SA	PH AB	PH H	G by POS
1944 CIN N	10	4	0	0	0	0	0.0	1	0	0	0	0	.000	.000	1	0	C-5
1945 CHI N	32	99	23	3	0	0	0.0	10	7	5	8	2	.232	.263	2	0	C-29
2 yrs.	42	103	23	3	0	0	0.0	11	7	5	8	2	.223	.252	3	0	C-34

Sam Rice

RICE, EDGAR CHARLES
B. Feb. 20, 1890, Morocco, Ind.   D. Oct. 13, 1974, Rossmor, Md.   BL TR 5'9"   150 lbs.
Hall of Fame 1963.

	G	AB	H	2B	3B	HR	HR %	R	RBI	BB	SO	SB	BA	SA	PH AB	PH H	G by POS
1915 WAS A	4	8	3	0	0	0	0.0	1	0	0	1	0	.375	.375	0	0	P-4
1916	58	197	59	8	3	1	0.5	26	17	15	13	4	.299	.386	6	2	OF-46, P-5
1917	155	586	177	25	7	0	0.0	77	69	50	41	35	.302	.369	0	0	OF-155
1918	7	23	8	1	0	0	0.0	3	3	2	0	1	.348	.391	1	0	OF-6
1919	141	557	179	23	9	3	0.5	80	71	42	26	26	.321	.411	0	0	OF-141
1920	153	624	211	29	9	3	0.5	83	80	39	23	63	.338	.428	0	0	OF-153
1921	143	561	185	39	4	0	0.7	83	79	38	10	25	.330	.467	1	0	OF-141
1922	154	633	187	37	13	6	0.9	91	69	48	13	20	.295	.423	0	0	OF-154
1923	148	595	188	35	18	3	0.5	117	75	57	12	20	.316	.450	1	0	OF-147
1924	154	646	216	38	14	1	0.2	106	76	46	24	24	.334	.441	0	0	OF-154
1925	152	649	227	31	13	1	0.2	111	87	37	10	26	.350	.442	0	0	OF-152
1926	152	641	216	32	14	3	0.5	98	76	42	20	25	.337	.445	0	0	OF-152
1927	142	603	179	33	14	2	0.3	98	65	36	11	19	.297	.408	3	0	OF-139
1928	148	616	202	32	15	2	0.3	95	55	49	15	16	.328	.438	0	0	OF-147
1929	150	616	199	39	10	1	0.2	119	62	55	9	16	.323	.424	2	0	OF-147
1930	147	593	207	35	13	1	0.2	121	73	55	14	13	.349	.457	0	0	OF-145
1931	120	413	128	21	8	0	0.0	81	42	35	11	6	.310	.400	7	1	OF-105
1932	106	288	93	16	7	1	0.3	58	34	32	6	7	.323	.438	33	5	OF-69
1933	73	85	25	4	3	1	1.2	19	12	3	7	0	.294	.447	28	7	OF-39
1934 CLE A	97	335	98	19	1	1	0.3	48	33	28	9	5	.293	.364	23	1	OF-78
20 yrs.	2404	9269	2987	497	184	34	0.4	1515	79	709	275	351	.322	.427	105	20	OF-2270, P-9

WORLD SERIES																	
1924 WAS A	7	29	6	0	0	0	0.0	2	1	3	2	2	.207	.207	0	0	OF-7
1925	7	33	12	0	0	0	0.0	5	3	0	1	0	.364	.364	0	0	OF-7
1933	1	1	1	0	0	0	0.0	0	0	0	0	0	1.000	1.000	1	1	
3 yrs.	15	63	19	0	0	0	0.0	7	4	3	3	2	.302	.302	1	1	OF-14

Lee Richard

RICHARD, LEE EDWARD (Bee Bee)
B. Sept. 18, 1948, Lafayette, La.   BR TR 5'11"   165 lbs.

	G	AB	H	2B	3B	HR	HR %	R	RBI	BB	SO	SB	BA	SA	PH AB	PH H	G by POS
1971 CHI A	87	260	60	7	3	2	0.8	38	17	20	46	8	.231	.304	6	0	SS-68, OF-16
1972	11	29	7	0	0	0	0.0	5	1	0	7	1	.241	.241	1	0	OF-6, SS-1
1974	32	67	11	1	0	0	0.0	5	1	5	8	0	.164	.179	0	0	3B-12, SS-6, DH-5, 2B-3, OF-1

	G	AB	H	2B	3B	HR	HR %	R	RBI	BB	SO	SB	BA	SA	Pinch Hit AB	Pinch Hit H	G by POS

Lee Richard continued

	G	AB	H	2B	3B	HR	HR %	R	RBI	BB	SO	SB	BA	SA	PH AB	PH H	G by POS
1975	43	45	9	0	1	0	0.0	11	5	4	7	2	.200	.244	0	0	3B-12, SS-9, DH-5, 2B-5
1976 STL N	66	91	16	4	2	0	0.0	12	5	4	9	1	.176	.264	3	0	2B-26, SS-12, 3B-1
5 yrs.	239	492	103	12	6	2	0.4	71	29	33	77	12	.209	.270	10	1	SS-96, 2B-34, 3B-25, OF-23, DH-10

Fred Richards

RICHARDS, FRED CHARLES (Fuzzy)
B. Nov. 3, 1927, Warren, Ohio
BL TL 6'1½" 185 lbs.

	G	AB	H	2B	3B	HR	HR %	R	RBI	BB	SO	SB	BA	SA	PH AB	PH H	G by POS
1951 CHI N	10	27	8	2	0	0	0.0	1	4	2	3	0	.296	.370	1	0	1B-9

Gene Richards

RICHARDS, EUGENE
B. Sept. 29, 1953, Monticello, S. C.
BL TL 6' 175 lbs.

	G	AB	H	2B	3B	HR	HR %	R	RBI	BB	SO	SB	BA	SA	PH AB	PH H	G by POS
1977 SD N	146	525	152	16	11	5	1.0	79	32	60	80	56	.290	.390	14	4	OF-109, 1B-32
1978	154	555	171	26	12	4	0.7	90	45	64	80	37	.308	.420	9	1	OF-124, 1B-26
1979	150	545	152	17	9	4	0.7	77	41	47	62	24	.279	.365	20	3	OF-132
1980	158	642	193	26	8	4	0.6	91	41	61	73	61	.301	.385	2	1	OF-156
1981	104	393	113	14	12	3	0.8	47	42	53	44	20	.288	.407	2	1	OF-102
1982	132	521	149	13	8	3	0.6	63	28	36	52	30	.286	.359	3	0	OF-103, 1B-25
1983	95	233	64	11	3	3	1.3	37	22	17	17	14	.275	.386	36	6	OF-54
1984 SF N	87	135	34	4	0	0	0.0	18	4	18	28	5	.252	.281	48	10	OF-26
8 yrs.	1026	3549	1028	127	63	26	0.7	502	255	356	436	247	.290	.383	134	26	OF-806, 1B-83

Paul Richards

RICHARDS, PAUL RAPIER
B. Nov. 21, 1908, Waxahachie, Tex.
Manager 1951-61, 1976.
BR TR 6'1½" 180 lbs.

	G	AB	H	2B	3B	HR	HR %	R	RBI	BB	SO	SB	BA	SA	PH AB	PH H	G by POS
1932 BKN N	3	8	0	0	0	0	0.0	0	0	0	2	0	.000	.000	0	0	C-3
1933 NY N	51	87	17	3	0	0	0.0	4	10	3	12	0	.195	.230	14	2	C-36
1934	42	75	12	1	0	0	0.0	10	3	13	8	0	.160	.173	3	2	C-37
1935 2 teams	NY N (7G – .250)		PHI A (85G – .245)														
" total	92	261	64	10	1	4	1.5	31	29	26	13	0	.245	.337	6	2	C-83
1943 DET A	100	313	69	7	1	5	1.6	32	33	38	35	1	.220	.297	0	0	C-100
1944	95	300	71	13	0	3	1.0	24	37	35	30	8	.237	.310	3	0	C-90
1945	83	234	60	12	1	3	1.3	26	32	19	31	4	.256	.355	0	0	C-83
1946	57	139	28	5	2	0	0.0	13	11	23	18	2	.201	.266	3	2	C-54
8 yrs.	523	1417	321	51	5	15	1.1	140	155	157	149	15	.227	.301	29	8	C-486

WORLD SERIES

	G	AB	H	2B	3B	HR	HR %	R	RBI	BB	SO	SB	BA	SA	PH AB	PH H	G by POS
1945 DET A	7	19	4	2	0	0	0.0	0	6	4	3	0	.211	.316	0	0	C-7

Nolen Richardsen

RICHARDSEN, CLIFFORD NOLEN
B. Jan. 18, 1903, Chattanooga, Tenn.   D. Sept. 25, 1951, Athens, Ga.
BR TR 6'1½" 170 lbs.

	G	AB	H	2B	3B	HR	HR %	R	RBI	BB	SO	SB	BA	SA	PH AB	PH H	G by POS
1929 DET A	13	21	4	0	0	0	0.0	2	2	2	1	1	.190	.190	0	0	SS-13
1931	38	148	40	9	2	0	0.0	13	16	6	3	2	.270	.358	0	0	3B-38
1932	69	155	34	5	2	0	0.0	13	12	9	13	5	.219	.277	0	0	3B-65, SS-4
1935 NY N	12	46	10	1	1	0	0.0	3	5	3	1	0	.217	.283	0	0	SS-12
1938 CIN N	35	100	29	4	0	0	0.0	8	10	3	4	0	.290	.330	0	0	SS-35
1939	1	3	0	0	0	0	0.0	0	0	0	0	0	.000	.000	0	0	SS-1
6 yrs.	168	473	117	19	5	0	0.0	39	45	23	22	8	.247	.309	0	0	3B-103, SS-65

Richardson

RICHARDSON,
B. Boston, Mass.   Deceased.

	G	AB	H	2B	3B	HR	HR %	R	RBI	BB	SO	SB	BA	SA	PH AB	PH H	G by POS
1884 C-P U	1	4	0	0	0	0	0.0	0		0			.000	.000	0	0	2B-1

Bill Richardson

RICHARDSON, WILLIAM HEZEKIAH
B. Oct. 8, 1877, Decatur County, Ind.   D. Apr. 11, 1954, Batesville, Ind.

	G	AB	H	2B	3B	HR	HR %	R	RBI	BB	SO	SB	BA	SA	PH AB	PH H	G by POS
1901 STL N	15	52	11	2	0	2	3.8	7	7	6		1	.212	.365	0	0	1B-15

Bobby Richardson

RICHARDSON, ROBERT CLINTON
B. Aug. 19, 1935, Sumter, S. C.
BR TR 5'9" 170 lbs.

	G	AB	H	2B	3B	HR	HR %	R	RBI	BB	SO	SB	BA	SA	PH AB	PH H	G by POS
1955 NY A	11	26	4	0	0	0	0.0	2	3	2	0	1	.154	.154	0	0	2B-6, SS-4
1956	5	7	1	0	0	0	0.0	1	0	0	1	0	.143	.143	0	0	2B-5
1957	97	305	78	11	1	0	0.0	36	19	9	26	1	.256	.298	1	0	2B-93
1958	73	182	45	6	2	0	0.0	18	14	8	5	1	.247	.302	0	0	2B-51, 3B-13, SS-2
1959	134	469	141	18	6	2	0.4	53	33	26	20	5	.301	.377	0	0	2B-109, SS-14, 3B-12
1960	150	460	116	12	3	1	0.2	45	26	35	19	6	.252	.298	1	0	2B-141, 3B-11
1961	162	662	173	17	5	3	0.5	80	49	30	23	9	.261	.316	1	0	2B-161
1962	161	692	209	38	5	8	1.2	99	59	37	24	11	.302	.406	0	0	2B-161
1963	151	630	167	20	6	3	0.5	72	48	25	22	15	.265	.330	1	0	2B-150
1964	159	679	181	25	4	4	0.6	90	50	28	36	11	.267	.333	2	1	2B-157, SS-1
1965	160	664	164	28	2	6	0.9	76	47	37	39	7	.247	.322	3	0	2B-158
1966	149	610	153	21	3	7	1.1	71	42	25	28	6	.251	.330	2	0	2B-147, 3B-2
12 yrs.	1412	5386	1432	196	37	34	0.6	643	390	262	243	73	.266	.335	11	1	2B-1339, 3B-38, SS-21

WORLD SERIES

	G	AB	H	2B	3B	HR	HR %	R	RBI	BB	SO	SB	BA	SA	PH AB	PH H	G by POS
1957 NY A	2	0	0	0	0	0	–	0	0	0	0	0	–	–	0	0	2B-1
1958	4	5	0	0	0	0	0.0	0	0	0	0	0	.000	.000	0	0	3B-4
1960	7	30	11	2	2	1	3.3	8	12	1	0	0	.367	.667	0	0	2B-7
1961	5	23	9	1	0	0	0.0	2	0	0	0	1	.391	.435	0	0	2B-5
1962	7	27	4	0	0	0	0.0	3	0	1	1	0	.148	.148	0	0	2B-7
1963	4	14	3	1	0	0	0.0	0	0	1	3	0	.214	.286	0	0	2B-4
1964	7	32	13	2	0	0	0.0	3	3	0	2	1	.406	.469	0	0	2B-7
7 yrs.	36	131	40	6	2	1	0.8	16	15	5	7	2	.305	.405	0	0	2B-31, 3B-4

Danny Richardson

RICHARDSON, DANIEL
B. Jan. 25, 1863, Elmira, N. Y.   D. Sept. 12, 1926, New York, N. Y.
Manager 1892.
BR TR 5'8" 165 lbs.

	G	AB	H	2B	3B	HR	HR %	R	RBI	BB	SO	SB	BA	SA	PH AB	PH H	G by POS
1884 NY N	74	277	70	8	1	1	0.4	36		16	17		.253	.300	0	0	OF-55, SS-19

	G	AB	H	2B	3B	HR	HR %	R	RBI	BB	SO	SB	BA	SA	Pinch Hit AB	H	G by POS

Danny Richardson continued

	G	AB	H	2B	3B	HR	HR%	R	RBI	BB	SO	SB	BA	SA	PH AB	PH H	G by POS
1885	49	198	52	9	3	0	0.0	26		10	14		.263	.338	0	0	OF-22, 3B-21, P-9
1886	68	237	55	9	1	1	0.4	43	27	17	21		.232	.291	0	0	OF-64, P-5, SS-1, 3B-1, 2B-1
1887	122	450	125	19	10	3	0.7	79	62	36	25		.278	.384	0	0	2B-108, 3B-14
1888	135	561	127	16	7	8	1.4	82	61	15	35	35	.226	.323	0	0	2B-135
1889	125	497	139	22	8	7	1.4	88	100	46	37	32	.280	.398	0	0	2B-125
1890 NY P	123	528	135	12	9	4	0.8	102	80	37	19	37	.256	.335	0	0	SS-68, 2B-56
1891 NY N	123	516	139	18	5	5	1.0	85	51	33	27	28	.269	.353	0	0	2B-114, SS-9
1892 WAS N	142	551	132	13	4	3	0.5	48	58	25	45	25	.240	.294	0	0	SS-93, 2B-49, 3B-1
1893 BKN N	54	206	46	6	2	0	0.0	36	27	13	18	7	.223	.272	0	0	2B-46, 3B-5, SS-3
1894 LOU N	116	430	109	17	2	1	0.2	51	40	35	31	8	.253	.309	0	0	SS-107, 2B-10
11 yrs.	1131	4451	1129	149	52	33	0.7	676	505	283	289	213	.254	.333	0	0	2B-644, SS-300, OF-141, 3B-42, P-14

Hardy Richardson

RICHARDSON, ABRAM HARDING (Old True Blue)   BR TR 5'9½" 170 lbs.
B. Apr. 21, 1855, Clarksboro, N. J.   D. Jan. 14, 1931, Utica, N. Y.

	G	AB	H	2B	3B	HR	HR%	R	RBI	BB	SO	SB	BA	SA	PH AB	PH H	G by POS
1879 BUF N	79	336	95	18	10	0	0.0	54	37	16	30		.283	.396	0	0	3B-78, C-1
1880	83	343	89	18	8	0	0.0	48	17	14	37		.259	.359	0	0	3B-81, C-5
1881	83	344	100	18	9	2	0.6	62	53	12	27		.291	.413	0	0	OF-79, 2B-5, SS-1, 3B-1
1882	83	354	96	20	8	2	0.6	61		11	33		.271	.390	0	0	2B-83
1883	92	399	124	34	7	1	0.3	73		22	20		.311	.439	0	0	2B-92
1884	102	439	132	27	9	6	1.4	85		22	41		.301	.444	0	0	2B-71, OF-24, 3B-5, 1B-3
1885	96	426	136	19	11	6	1.4	90	44	20	22		.319	.458	0	0	2B-50, OF-48, SS-1, P-1
1886 DET N	125	**538**	189	27	11	**11**	2.0	125	61	46	27		.351	.504	0	0	OF-80, 2B-42, P-4, SS-3, 3B-2
1887	120	543	178	25	18	11	2.0	131	94	31	40	29	.328	.501	0	0	2B-64, OF-59
1888	58	266	77	18	1	7	2.6	60	32	17	23	13	.289	.444	0	0	2B-58
1889 BOS N	132	536	163	33	9	7	1.3	122	79	48	44	47	.304	.438	0	0	2B-86, OF-46
1890 BOS P	130	555	181	26	14	11	2.0	126	**143**	52	46	42	.326	.483	0	0	OF-124, SS-6, 1B-1
1891 BOS AA	74	278	71	9	4	7	2.5	45	51	40	26	16	.255	.392	0	0	OF-60, 3B-9, SS-4, 1B-3
1892 2 teams	WAS	N	(10G –	.108)		NY	N	(64G –	.214)								
" total	74	285	57	11	5	2	0.7	38	34	26	29	16	.200	.295	0	0	2B-34, OF-19, SS-6, 3B-2
14 yrs.	1331	5642	1688	303	124	73	1.3	1120	645	377	445	163	.299	.436	0	0	2B-585, OF-544, 3B-178, SS-21, 1B-16, C-6, P-5

Ken Richardson

RICHARDSON, KENNETH FRANKLIN   BR TR 5'10½" 187 lbs.
B. May 2, 1915, Orleans, Ind.

	G	AB	H	2B	3B	HR	HR%	R	RBI	BB	SO	SB	BA	SA	PH AB	PH H	G by POS
1942 PHI A	6	15	1	0	0	0	0.0	1	0	2	0	0	.067	.067	1	0	OF-3, 3B-1, 1B-1
1946 PHI N	6	20	3	1	0	0	0.0	1	2	0	2	0	.150	.200	0	0	2B-6
2 yrs.	12	35	4	1	0	0	0.0	2	2	2	2	0	.114	.143	1	0	2B-6, OF-3, 3B-1, 1B-1

Tom Richardson

RICHARDSON, THOMAS MITCHELL   6' 190 lbs.
B. Aug. 7, 1883, Louisville, Ill.   D. Nov. 15, 1939, Onawa, Iowa

	G	AB	H	2B	3B	HR	HR%	R	RBI	BB	SO	SB	BA	SA	PH AB	PH H	G by POS
1917 STL A	1	1	0	0	0	0	0.0	0	0	0	0	0	.000	.000	1	0	

Mike Richardt

RICHARDT, MICHAEL ANTHONY   BR TR 6' 170 lbs.
B. May 24, 1958, Los Angeles, Calif.

	G	AB	H	2B	3B	HR	HR%	R	RBI	BB	SO	SB	BA	SA	PH AB	PH H	G by POS
1980 TEX A	22	71	16	2	0	0	0.0	2	8	1	7	0	.225	.254	0	0	2B-20, DH-1
1982	119	402	97	10	0	3	0.7	34	43	23	42	9	.241	.289	1	0	2B-98, DH-15, OF-6
1983	22	83	13	2	1	1	1.2	9	7	2	11	2	.157	.241	2	0	2B-20
1984 2 teams	TEX	A	(7G –	.111)		HOU	N	(16G –	.267)								
" total	23	24	5	1	0	0	0.0	1	2	1	2	0	.208	.250	17	4	2B-4
4 yrs.	186	580	131	15	1	4	0.7	46	60	27	62	11	.226	.276	20	4	2B-142, DH-16, OF-6

Lance Richbourg

RICHBOURG, LANCE CLAYTON   BL TR 5'10½" 160 lbs.
B. Dec. 18, 1897, DeFuniak Springs, Fla.   D. Sept. 10, 1975, Crestview, Fla.

	G	AB	H	2B	3B	HR	HR%	R	RBI	BB	SO	SB	BA	SA	PH AB	PH H	G by POS
1921 PHI N	10	5	1	1	0	0	0.0	2	0	3		1	.200	.400	2	0	2B-4
1924 WAS A	15	32	9	2	1	0	0.0	3	1	2	6	0	.281	.406	6	4	OF-7
1927 BOS N	115	450	139	12	9	2	0.4	57	34	22	30	24	.309	.389	4	1	OF-110
1928	148	612	206	26	12	2	0.3	105	52	62	39	11	.337	.428	0	0	OF-148
1929	139	557	170	24	13	3	0.5	76	56	42	26	7	.305	.411	3	0	OF-134
1930	130	529	161	23	8	3	0.6	81	54	19	31	13	.304	.395	2	1	OF-128
1931	97	286	82	11	6	2	0.7	32	29	19	14	9	.287	.388	22	5	OF-71
1932 CHI N	44	148	38	2	2	1	0.7	22	21	8	4	0	.257	.318	10	3	OF-33
8 yrs.	698	2619	806	101	51	13	0.5	378	247	174	153	65	.308	.400	49	14	OF-631, 2B-4

Don Richmond

RICHMOND, DONALD LESTER   BL TR 6'1" 175 lbs.
B. Oct. 27, 1919, Gillett, Pa.   D. May 24, 1981, Elmira, N. Y.

	G	AB	H	2B	3B	HR	HR%	R	RBI	BB	SO	SB	BA	SA	PH AB	PH H	G by POS
1941 PHI A	9	35	7	1	1	0	0.0	3	5	0	1	0	.200	.286	0	0	3B-9
1946	16	62	18	3	0	1	1.6	3	9	0	10	1	.290	.387	0	0	3B-16
1947	19	21	4	1	1	0	0.0	2	4	3	3	0	.190	.333	11	2	3B-4, 2B-1
1951 STL N	12	34	3	1	0	1	2.9	3	4	3	3	0	.088	.206	0	0	3B-11
4 yrs.	56	152	32	6	2	2	1.3	11	22	6	17	1	.211	.316	11	2	3B-40, 2B-1

John Richmond

RICHMOND, JOHN H.   TR
B. 1854, Pennsylvania   Deceased.

	G	AB	H	2B	3B	HR	HR%	R	RBI	BB	SO	SB	BA	SA	PH AB	PH H	G by POS
1879 SYR N	62	254	54	8	4	1	0.4	31	23	4	24		.213	.287	0	0	OF-35, SS-28, C-2
1880 BOS N	32	129	32	3	1	0	0.0	12	9	2	18		.248	.287	0	0	SS-31, OF-1
1881	27	98	27	2	2	1	1.0	13	12	6	7		.276	.367	0	0	OF-25, SS-2
1882 2 teams	CLE	N	(41G –	.171)		PHI	AA	(18G –	.185)								
" total	59	205	36	8	4	0	0.0	20	11	22	27		.176	.254	0	0	OF-59
1883 COL AA	92	385	109	7	8	0	0.0	63		25			.283	.343	0	0	SS-91, OF-2
1884	105	398	100	13	7	3	0.8	57		35			.251	.342	0	0	SS-105
1885 PIT AA	34	131	27	2	2	0	0.0	14		8			.206	.252	0	0	SS-23, OF-11
7 yrs.	411	1600	385	43	28	5	0.3	210	55	102	76		.241	.312	0	0	SS-280, OF-133, C-2

	G	AB	H	2B	3B	HR	HR %	R	RBI	BB	SO	SB	BA	SA	Pinch Hit AB	Pinch Hit H	G by POS

Lee Richmond

RICHMOND, J. LEE   TL 5'10" 142 lbs.
B. May 5, 1857, Sheffield, Ohio   D. Sept. 30, 1929, Toledo, Ohio

	G	AB	H	2B	3B	HR	HR %	R	RBI	BB	SO	SB	BA	SA	AB	H	G by POS
1879 BOS N	1	6	2	0	0	0	0.0	0	1	0	1		.333	.333	0	0	P-1
1880 WOR N	77	309	70	8	4	0	0.0	44		9	32		.227	.278	0	0	P-74, OF-20
1881	61	252	63	5	1	0	0.0	31	28	10	10		.250	.278	0	0	P-53, OF-11
1882	55	228	64	8	9	2	0.9	50	28	9	11		.281	.421	0	0	P-48, OF-11
1883 PRO N	49	194	55	8	6	1	0.5	41		15	19		.284	.402	0	0	OF-41, P-12
1886 CIN AA	8	29	8	0	0	0	0.0	3		3			.276	.276	0	0	OF-7, P-3
6 yrs.	251	1018	262	29	20	3	0.3	169	57	46	73		.257	.334	0	0	P-191, OF-90

Al Richter

RICHTER, ALLEN GORDON   BR TR 6' 175 lbs.
B. Feb. 7, 1927, Norfolk, Va.

	G	AB	H	2B	3B	HR	HR %	R	RBI	BB	SO	SB	BA	SA	AB	H	G by POS
1951 BOS A	5	11	1	0	0	0	0.0	1	0	3	0	0	.091	.091	2	0	SS-3
1953	1	0	0	0	0	0	–	0	0	0	0	0	–	–	0	0	SS-1
2 yrs.	6	11	1	0	0	0	0.0	1	0	3	0	0	.091	.091	2	0	SS-4

John Richter

RICHTER, JOHN M.
B. Feb. 8, 1873, Louisville, Ky.   D. Oct. 4, 1927, Louisville, Ky.

	G	AB	H	2B	3B	HR	HR %	R	RBI	BB	SO	SB	BA	SA	AB	H	G by POS
1898 LOU N	3	13	2	0	0	0	0.0	1	0	0		0	.154	.154	0	0	3B-3

Joe Rickert

RICKERT, JOSEPH FRANCIS (Diamond Joe)   BR TR 5'10½" 165 lbs.
B. Dec. 12, 1876, London, Ohio   D. Oct. 15, 1943, Springfield, Ohio

	G	AB	H	2B	3B	HR	HR %	R	RBI	BB	SO	SB	BA	SA	AB	H	G by POS
1898 PIT N	2	6	1	0	0	0	0.0	0	0	0		0	.167	.167	0	0	OF-2
1901 BOS N	13	60	10	1	2	0	0.0	6	1	3		1	.167	.250	0	0	OF-13
2 yrs.	15	66	11	1	2	0	0.0	6	1	3		1	.167	.242	0	0	OF-15

Marv Rickert

RICKERT, MARVIN AUGUST (Twitch)   BL TR 6'2" 195 lbs.
B. Jan. 8, 1921, Long Branch, Wash.   D. June 3, 1978, Oakville, Wash.

	G	AB	H	2B	3B	HR	HR %	R	RBI	BB	SO	SB	BA	SA	AB	H	G by POS
1942 CHI N	8	26	7	0	0	0	0.0	5	1	1	5	0	.269	.269	1	0	OF-6
1946	111	392	103	18	3	7	1.8	44	47	28	54	3	.263	.378	6	0	OF-104
1947	71	137	20	0	2	2	1.5	7	15	15	17	0	.146	.190	27	6	OF-30, 1B-7
1948 2 teams	CIN	N (8G – .167)				BOS	N (3G – .231)										
" total	11	19	4	0	1	0	0.0	1	2	0	1	0	.211	.316	6	1	OF-3
1949 BOS N	100	277	81	18	3	6	2.2	44	49	23	38	1	.292	.444	12	3	OF-75, 1B-12
1950 2 teams	PIT	N (17G – .150)				CHI	A (84G – .237)										
" total	101	298	69	9	2	4	1.3	38	31	21	46	0	.232	.315	20	1	OF-81, 1B-1
6 yrs.	402	1149	284	45	9	19	1.7	139	145	88	161	4	.247	.352	72	11	OF-299, 1B-20

WORLD SERIES

	G	AB	H	2B	3B	HR	HR %	R	RBI	BB	SO	SB	BA	SA	AB	H	G by POS
1948 BOS N	5	19	4	0	0	1	5.3	2	2	0	4	0	.211	.368	0	0	OF-5

Dave Ricketts

RICKETTS, DAVID WILLIAM   BB TR 6' 190 lbs.
Brother of Dick Ricketts.
B. July 12, 1935, Pottstown, Pa.

	G	AB	H	2B	3B	HR	HR %	R	RBI	BB	SO	SB	BA	SA	AB	H	G by POS
1963 STL N	3	8	2	0	0	0	0.0	0	0	0	2	0	.250	.250	0	0	C-3
1965	11	29	7	0	0	0	0.0	1	0	1	3	0	.241	.241	1	0	C-11
1967	52	99	27	8	0	1	1.0	11	14	4	7	0	.273	.384	32	7	C-21
1968	20	22	3	0	0	0	0.0	1	1	0	3	0	.136	.136	19	2	C-1
1969	30	44	12	1	0	0	0.0	2	5	4	5	0	.273	.295	18	5	C-8
1970 PIT N	14	11	2	0	0	0	0.0	0	0	1	3	0	.182	.182	7	1	C-7
6 yrs.	130	213	53	9	0	1	0.5	15	20	10	23	0	.249	.305	77	15	C-51

WORLD SERIES

	G	AB	H	2B	3B	HR	HR %	R	RBI	BB	SO	SB	BA	SA	AB	H	G by POS
1967 STL N	3	3	0	0	0	0	0.0	0	0	0	0	0	.000	.000	3	0	
1968	1	1	1	0	0	0	0.0	0	0	0	0	0	1.000	1.000	1	1	
2 yrs.	4	4	1	0	0	0	0.0	0	0	0	0	0	.250	.250	4	1	

Branch Rickey

RICKEY, WESLEY BRANCH (The Mahatma)   BL TR 5'9" 175 lbs.
B. Dec. 20, 1881, Stockdale, Ohio   D. Dec. 9, 1965, Columbia, Mo.
Manager 1913-15, 1919-25.
Hall of Fame 1967.

	G	AB	H	2B	3B	HR	HR %	R	RBI	BB	SO	SB	BA	SA	AB	H	G by POS
1905 STL A	1	3	0	0	0	0	0.0	0	0	0		0	.000	.000	0	0	C-1
1906	64	201	57	7	3	3	1.5	22	24	16		4	.284	.393	7	2	C-54, OF-1
1907 NY A	52	137	25	2	3	0	0.0	16	15	11		4	.182	.241	12	1	OF-22, C-11, 1B-9
1914 STL A	2	2	0	0	0	0	0.0	0	0	0	1	0	.000	.000	2	0	
4 yrs.	119	343	82	9	6	3	0.9	38	39	27	1	8	.239	.327	21	3	C-66, OF-23, 1B-9

Chris Rickley

RICKLEY, CHRISTIAN   5'8" 160 lbs.
B. Oct. 7, 1859, Philadelphia, Pa.   D. Oct. 25, 1911, Philadelphia, Pa.

	G	AB	H	2B	3B	HR	HR %	R	RBI	BB	SO	SB	BA	SA	AB	H	G by POS
1884 PHI U	6	25	5	2	0	0	0.0	5		2			.200	.280	0	0	SS-6

John Ricks

RICKS, JOHN
Deceased.

	G	AB	H	2B	3B	HR	HR %	R	RBI	BB	SO	SB	BA	SA	AB	H	G by POS
1891 STL AA	5	18	3	0	0	0	0.0	3	0	0	2	0	.167	.167	0	0	3B-5
1894 STL N	1	1	0	0	0	0	0.0	0	0	0	0	0	.000	.000	0	0	3B-1
2 yrs.	6	19	3	0	0	0	0.0	3	0	0	2	0	.158	.158	0	0	3B-6

Art Rico

RICO, ARTHUR RAYMOND   BR TR 5'9½" 185 lbs.
B. July 23, 1896, Roxbury, Mass.   D. Jan. 3, 1919, Boston, Mass.

	G	AB	H	2B	3B	HR	HR %	R	RBI	BB	SO	SB	BA	SA	AB	H	G by POS
1916 BOS N	4	4	0	0	0	0	0.0	0	0	0	0	0	.000	.000	0	0	C-4
1917	13	14	4	1	0	0	0.0	1	2	0	2	0	.286	.357	0	0	C-11, OF-2
2 yrs.	17	18	4	1	0	0	0.0	1	2	0	2	0	.222	.278	0	0	C-15, OF-2

Fred Rico

RICO, ALFREDO CRUZ   BR TR 5'10" 180 lbs.
B. July 4, 1944, Jerome, Ariz.

	G	AB	H	2B	3B	HR	HR %	R	RBI	BB	SO	SB	BA	SA	AB	H	G by POS
1969 KC A	12	26	6	2	0	0	0.0	2	2	9	10	0	.231	.308	1	0	OF-9, 3B-1

	G	AB	H	2B	3B	HR	HR %	R	RBI	BB	SO	SB	BA	SA	Pinch Hit AB	Pinch Hit H	G by POS

Harry Riconda

RICONDA, HENRY PAUL
B. Mar. 17, 1897, New York, N. Y.   D. Nov. 15, 1958, Mahopac, N. Y.
BR TR 5'10"   175 lbs.

	G	AB	H	2B	3B	HR	HR %	R	RBI	BB	SO	SB	BA	SA	AB	H	G by POS
1923 PHI A	55	175	46	11	4	0	0.0	23	12	12	18	4	.263	.371	4	0	3B-47, SS-2
1924	83	281	71	16	3	1	0.4	34	21	27	43	3	.253	.342	4	0	3B-73, SS-2, C-1
1926 BOS N	4	12	2	0	0	0	0.0	1	0	2	2	0	.167	.167	0	0	3B-4
1928 BKN N	92	281	63	15	4	3	1.1	22	35	20	28	6	.224	.338	1	0	2B-53, 3B-21, SS-16
1929 PIT N	8	15	7	2	0	0	0.0	3	2	0	0	0	.467	.600	3	1	SS-4
1930 CIN N	1	1	0	0	0	0	0.0	0	0	0	0	0	.000	.000	1	0	
6 yrs.	243	765	189	44	11	4	0.5	83	70	61	91	13	.247	.349	13	1	3B-145, 2B-53, SS-24, C-1

John Riddle

RIDDLE, JOHN H.
B. Philadelphia, Pa.   Deceased.

	G	AB	H	2B	3B	HR	HR %	R	RBI	BB	SO	SB	BA	SA	AB	H	G by POS
1889 WAS N	11	37	8	3	0	0	0.0	3	3	2	8	0	.216	.297	0	0	C-9, OF-2
1890 PHI AA	27	85	7	0	1	0	0.0	7		17		4	.082	.106	0	0	C-13, OF-12, 2B-2, 3B-1
2 yrs.	38	122	15	3	1	0	0.0	10	3	19	8	4	.123	.164	0	0	C-22, OF-14, 2B-2, 3B-1

Johnny Riddle

RIDDLE, JOHN LUDY (Mutt)
Brother of Elmer Riddle.
B. Oct. 3, 1905, Clinton, S. C.
BR TR 5'11"   190 lbs.

	G	AB	H	2B	3B	HR	HR %	R	RBI	BB	SO	SB	BA	SA	AB	H	G by POS
1930 CHI A	25	58	14	3	1	0	0.0	7	4	3	6	0	.241	.328	0	0	C-25
1937 2 teams			WAS A	(8G –	.269)		BOS N	(2G –	.000)								
" total	10	29	7	0	0	0	0.0	2	3	1	2	0	.241	.241	0	0	C-10
1938 BOS N	19	57	16	1	0	0	0.0	6	2	4	2	0	.281	.298	0	0	C-19
1941 CIN N	10	10	3	0	0	0	0.0	2	0	0	1	0	.300	.300	0	0	C-10
1944	1	0	0	0	0	0	–	0	0	0	0	0	–	–	0	0	C-1
1945	23	45	8	0	0	0	0.0	0	2	4	6	0	.178	.178	1	0	C-23
1948 PIT N	10	15	3	0	0	0	0.0	1	0	1	2	0	.200	.200	0	0	C-10
7 yrs.	98	214	51	4	1	0	0.0	18	11	13	19	0	.238	.266	1	0	C-98

Hank Riebe

RIEBE, HARVEY DONALD
B. Oct. 10, 1921, Cleveland, Ohio
BR TR 5'9½"   175 lbs.

	G	AB	H	2B	3B	HR	HR %	R	RBI	BB	SO	SB	BA	SA	AB	H	G by POS
1942 DET A	11	35	11	2	0	0	0.0	1	2	0	6	0	.314	.371	0	0	C-11
1947	8	7	0	0	0	0	0.0	0	2	0	2	0	.000	.000	5	0	C-3
1948	25	62	12	0	0	0	0.0	0	5	3	5	0	.194	.194	1	0	C-24
1949	17	33	6	2	0	0	0.0	1	2	0	5	1	.182	.242	6	1	C-11
4 yrs.	61	137	29	4	0	0	0.0	2	11	3	18	1	.212	.241	12	1	C-49

Joe Riggert

RIGGERT, JOSEPH ALOYSIUS
B. Dec. 11, 1886, Janesville, Wis.   D. Dec. 10, 1973, Kansas City, Mo.
BR TR 5'9½"   170 lbs.

	G	AB	H	2B	3B	HR	HR %	R	RBI	BB	SO	SB	BA	SA	AB	H	G by POS
1911 BOS A	50	146	31	4	4	2	1.4	19	13	12		5	.212	.336	8	3	OF-38
1914 2 teams			BKN N	(27G –	.193)		STL N	(34G –	.213)								
" total	61	172	35	6	5	2	1.2	15	14	9	34	6	.203	.331	8	0	OF-50
1919 BOS N	63	240	68	8	5	4	1.7	34	17	25	30	9	.283	.408	0	0	OF-61
3 yrs.	174	558	134	18	14	8	1.4	68	44	46	64	20	.240	.366	16	3	OF-149

Lew Riggs

RIGGS, LEWIS SIDNEY
B. Apr. 22, 1910, Mebane, N. C.   D. Aug. 12, 1975, Durham, N. C.
BL TR 6'   175 lbs.

	G	AB	H	2B	3B	HR	HR %	R	RBI	BB	SO	SB	BA	SA	AB	H	G by POS
1934 STL N	2	1	0	0	0	0	0.0	0	0	0	1	0	.000	.000	1	0	
1935 CIN N	142	532	148	26	8	5	0.9	73	46	43	32	8	.278	.385	2	0	3B-135
1936	141	538	138	20	12	6	1.1	69	57	38	33	5	.257	.372	1	1	3B-140
1937	122	384	93	17	5	6	1.6	43	45	24	17	4	.242	.359	17	4	3B-100, 2B-4, SS-1
1938	142	531	134	21	13	2	0.4	53	55	40	28	3	.252	.352	2	0	3B-142
1939	22	38	6	1	0	0	0.0	5	1	5	4	1	.158	.184	6	1	3B-11
1940	41	72	21	7	1	1	1.4	8	9	2	4	0	.292	.458	27	8	3B-11
1941 BKN N	77	197	60	13	4	5	2.5	27	36	16	12	1	.305	.487	29	10	3B-43, 2B-1, 1B-1
1942	70	180	50	5	0	3	1.7	20	22	13	9	0	.278	.356	21	8	3B-46, 1B-1
1946	1	4	0	0	0	0	0.0	0	0	0	0	0	.000	.000	0	0	3B-1
10 yrs.	760	2477	650	110	43	28	1.1	298	271	181	140	22	.262	.375	106	32	3B-629, 2B-5, 1B-2, SS-1

WORLD SERIES

	G	AB	H	2B	3B	HR	HR %	R	RBI	BB	SO	SB	BA	SA	AB	H	G by POS
1940 CIN N	3	3	0	0	0	0	0.0	1	0	0	2	0	.000	.000	3	0	
1941 BKN N	3	8	2	0	0	0	0.0	0	1	1	1	0	.250	.250	1	1	3B-2
2 yrs.	6	11	2	0	0	0	0.0	1	1	1	3	0	.182	.182	4	1	3B-2

Billy Rigney

RIGNEY, WILLIAM JOSEPH (Specs, The Cricket)
B. Jan. 29, 1918, Alameda, Calif.
Manager 1956-72, 1976.
BR TR 6'1"   178 lbs.

	G	AB	H	2B	3B	HR	HR %	R	RBI	BB	SO	SB	BA	SA	AB	H	G by POS
1946 NY N	110	360	85	9	1	3	0.8	38	31	36	29	9	.236	.292	3	0	3B-73, SS-33
1947	130	531	142	24	3	17	3.2	84	59	51	54	7	.267	.420	1	1	2B-72, 3B-41, SS-24
1948	113	424	112	17	3	10	2.4	72	43	47	54	4	.264	.389	2	0	2B-105, SS-7
1949	122	389	108	19	6	6	1.5	53	47	47	38	3	.278	.404	4	0	SS-81, 2B-26, 3B-14
1950	56	83	15	2	0	0	0.0	8	8	8	13	0	.181	.205	20	3	2B-23, 3B-11
1951	44	69	16	2	0	4	5.8	9	9	8	7	0	.232	.435	16	4	3B-12, 2B-9
1952	60	90	27	5	1	1	1.1	15	14	11	6	2	.300	.411	31	10	3B-10, 2B-9, SS-4, 1B-1
1953	19	20	5	0	0	0	0.0	2	1	0	5	0	.250	.250	15	3	3B-2, 2B-1
8 yrs.	654	1966	510	78	14	41	2.1	281	212	208	206	25	.259	.376	92	21	2B-245, 3B-163, SS-149, 1B-1

WORLD SERIES

	G	AB	H	2B	3B	HR	HR %	R	RBI	BB	SO	SB	BA	SA	AB	H	G by POS
1951 NY N	4	4	1	0	0	0	0.0	0	1	0	1	0	.250	.250	4	1	

Topper Rigney

RIGNEY, EMORY ELMO
B. Jan. 7, 1897, Groveton, Tex.   D. June 6, 1972, San Antonio, Tex.
BR TR 5'9"   150 lbs.

	G	AB	H	2B	3B	HR	HR %	R	RBI	BB	SO	SB	BA	SA	AB	H	G by POS
1922 DET A	155	536	161	17	7	2	0.4	68	63	68	44	17	.300	.369	0	0	SS-155
1923	129	470	148	24	11	1	0.2	63	74	55	35	7	.315	.419	0	0	SS-129
1924	147	499	144	29	9	4	0.8	81	93	102	39	11	.289	.407	1	0	SS-146
1925	62	146	36	5	2	2	1.4	21	18	21	15	2	.247	.349	6	0	SS-51, 3B-4
1926 BOS A	148	525	142	32	6	4	0.8	71	53	108	31	6	.270	.377	2	0	SS-146

	G	AB	H	2B	3B	HR	HR %	R	RBI	BB	SO	SB	BA	SA	Pinch Hit AB	Pinch Hit H	G by POS

Topper Rigney continued

	G	AB	H	2B	3B	HR	HR %	R	RBI	BB	SO	SB	BA	SA	PH AB	PH H	G by POS
1927 2 teams	BOS A (8G – .111)				WAS A (45G – .273)												
" total	53	150	38	6	4	0	0.0	20	13	23	12	1	.253	.347	10	4	SS-33, 3B-10
6 yrs.	694	2326	669	113	39	13	0.6	324	314	377	176	44	.288	.387	19	4	SS-660, 3B-14

Culley Rikard

RIKARD, CULLEY
B. May 9, 1914, Oxford, Miss.   BL TR 6'   183 lbs.

	G	AB	H	2B	3B	HR	HR %	R	RBI	BB	SO	SB	BA	SA	PH AB	PH H	G by POS
1941 PIT N	6	20	4	1	0	0	0.0	1	0	1	1	0	.200	.250	1	0	OF-5
1942	38	52	10	2	1	0	0.0	6	5	7	8	0	.192	.269	15	4	OF-16
1947	109	324	93	16	4	4	1.2	57	32	50	39	1	.287	.398	29	6	OF-79
3 yrs.	153	396	107	19	5	4	1.0	64	37	58	48	1	.270	.374	45	10	OF-100

Billy Riley

RILEY, WILLIAM JAMES (Pigtail Billy)
B. Nov., 1853, Philadelphia, Pa.   D. Nov. 9, 1887, Cincinnati, Ohio   BR TR 5'10"   160 lbs.

	G	AB	H	2B	3B	HR	HR %	R	RBI	BB	SO	SB	BA	SA	PH AB	PH H	G by POS
1879 CLE N	44	165	24	2	0	0	0.0	14	9	2	26		.145	.158	0	0	OF-43, 1B-1, C-1

Jim Riley

RILEY, JAMES NORMAN
B. May 25, 1895, Bayfield, N. B., Canada   D. May 25, 1969, Seguin, Tex.   BL TR 5'10½" 185 lbs.

	G	AB	H	2B	3B	HR	HR %	R	RBI	BB	SO	SB	BA	SA	PH AB	PH H	G by POS
1921 STL A	4	11	0	0	0	0	0.0	0	0	1	3	0	.000	.000	0	0	2B-4
1923 WAS A	2	3	0	0	0	0	0.0	1	0	2	0	0	.000	.000	0	0	1B-2
2 yrs.	6	14	0	0	0	0	0.0	1	0	3	3	0	.000	.000	0	0	2B-4, 1B-2

Jimmy Riley

RILEY, JAMES JOSEPH
B. Nov. 10, 1886, Buffalo, N. Y.   D. Mar. 25, 1949, Buffalo, N. Y.   BR TR 6'   165 lbs.

	G	AB	H	2B	3B	HR	HR %	R	RBI	BB	SO	SB	BA	SA	PH AB	PH H	G by POS
1910 BOS N	1	1	0	0	0	0	0.0	0	1	0	1	0	.000	.000	0	0	OF-1

Lee Riley

RILEY, LEON FRANCIS
B. Aug. 20, 1906, Princeton, Neb.   D. Sept. 13, 1970, Schenectady, N. Y.   BL TR 6'1"   185 lbs.

	G	AB	H	2B	3B	HR	HR %	R	RBI	BB	SO	SB	BA	SA	PH AB	PH H	G by POS
1944 PHI N	4	12	1	1	0	0	0.0	1	0	0	0	0	.083	.167	1	0	OF-3

Frank Ringo

RINGO, FRANK C.
B. Oct. 12, 1860, Parksville, Mo.   D. Apr. 12, 1889, Kansas City, Mo.   5'11"   175 lbs.

	G	AB	H	2B	3B	HR	HR %	R	RBI	BB	SO	SB	BA	SA	PH AB	PH H	G by POS
1883 PHI N	60	221	42	10	1	0	0.0	24		6	34		.190	.244	0	0	C-39, OF-11, SS-6, 3B-5, 2B-2
1884 2 teams	PHI N (26G – .132)				PHI AA (2G – .000)												
" total	28	97	12	2	0	0	0.0	4		3	19		.124	.144	0	0	C-28
1885 2 teams	DET N (17G – .246)				PIT AA (3G – .182)												
" total	20	76	18	3	0	0	0.0	12	2	0	7		.237	.276	0	0	C-11, 3B-8, OF-1
1886 2 teams	PIT AA (15G – .214)				KC N (16G – .232)												
" total	31	112	25	9	2	0	0.0	9	7	6	10		.223	.339	0	0	C-19, 1B-9, OF-2, 3B-1
4 yrs.	139	506	97	24	3	0	0.0	49	8	15	70		.192	.251	0	0	C-97, OF-14, 3B-14, 1B-9, SS-6, 2B-2

Bob Rinker

RINKER, ROBERT JOHN
B. Apr. 21, 1921, Audenried, Pa.   BR TR 6'   190 lbs.

	G	AB	H	2B	3B	HR	HR %	R	RBI	BB	SO	SB	BA	SA	PH AB	PH H	G by POS
1950 PHI A	3	3	1	0	0	0	0.0	0	0	0	0	0	.333	.333	2	1	C-1

Juan Rios

RIOS, JUAN O. VELEZ
B. July 14, 1945, Mayaguez, Puerto Rico   BR TR 6'3"   185 lbs.

	G	AB	H	2B	3B	HR	HR %	R	RBI	BB	SO	SB	BA	SA	PH AB	PH H	G by POS
1969 KC A	87	196	44	5	1	1	0.5	20	5	7	19	1	.224	.276	12	3	2B-46, SS-32, 3B-4

Cal Ripken

RIPKEN, CALVIN EDWIN JR.
B. Aug. 24, 1960, Havre de Grace, Md.   BR TR 6'4"   200 lbs.

	G	AB	H	2B	3B	HR	HR %	R	RBI	BB	SO	SB	BA	SA	PH AB	PH H	G by POS
1981 BAL A	23	39	5	0	0	0	0.0	1	0	1	8	0	.128	.128	4	0	SS-12, 3B-6
1982	160	598	158	32	5	28	4.7	90	93	46	95	3	.264	.475	0	0	SS-94, 3B-71
1983	162	663	211	47	2	27	4.1	121	102	58	97	0	.318	.517	0	0	SS-162
1984	162	641	195	37	7	27	4.2	103	86	71	89	2	.304	.510	0	0	SS-162
4 yrs.	507	1941	569	116	14	82	4.2	315	281	176	289	5	.293	.494	4	0	SS-430, 3B-77

LEAGUE CHAMPIONSHIP SERIES

	G	AB	H	2B	3B	HR	HR %	R	RBI	BB	SO	SB	BA	SA	PH AB	PH H	G by POS
1983 BAL A	4	15	6	2	0	0	0.0	5	1	2	3	0	.400	.533	0	0	SS-4

WORLD SERIES

	G	AB	H	2B	3B	HR	HR %	R	RBI	BB	SO	SB	BA	SA	PH AB	PH H	G by POS
1983 BAL A	5	18	3	0	0	0	0.0	2	1	3	4	0	.167	.167	0	0	SS-5

Jimmy Ripple

RIPPLE, JAMES ALBERT
B. Oct. 14, 1909, Export, Pa.   D. July 16, 1959, Greensburg, Pa.   BL TR 5'10"   170 lbs.   BB 1936

	G	AB	H	2B	3B	HR	HR %	R	RBI	BB	SO	SB	BA	SA	PH AB	PH H	G by POS
1936 NY N	96	311	95	17	2	7	2.3	42	47	28	15	1	.305	.441	19	9	OF-76
1937	121	426	135	23	3	5	1.2	70	66	29	20	3	.317	.420	11	4	OF-111
1938	134	501	131	21	3	10	2.0	68	60	49	21	2	.261	.375	3	0	OF-131
1939 2 teams	NY N (66G – .228)				BKN N (28G – .330)												
" total	94	229	63	12	4	1	0.4	28	40	19	15	0	.275	.376	38	9	OF-51
1940 2 teams	BKN N (7G – .231)				CIN N (32G – .307)												
" total	39	114	34	10	0	4	3.5	16	20	15	7	1	.298	.491	5	1	OF-33
1941 CIN N	38	102	22	6	1	1	1.0	10	9	9	4	0	.216	.324	11	2	OF-25
1943 PHI N	32	126	30	3	1	0	0.0	8	15	7	7	0	.238	.278	1	0	OF-31
7 yrs.	554	1809	510	92	14	28	1.5	241	257	156	89	7	.282	.395	88	25	OF-458

WORLD SERIES

	G	AB	H	2B	3B	HR	HR %	R	RBI	BB	SO	SB	BA	SA	PH AB	PH H	G by POS
1936 NY N	5	12	4	0	0	1	8.3	2	3	3	3	0	.333	.583	0	0	OF-5
1937	5	17	5	0	0	0	0.0	2	0	3	1	0	.294	.294	0	0	OF-5
1940 CIN N	7	21	7	2	0	1	4.8	3	6	4	2	0	.333	.571	0	0	OF-7
3 yrs.	17	50	16	2	0	2	4.0	7	9	10	6	0	.320	.480	0	0	OF-17

	G	AB	H	2B	3B	HR	HR %	R	RBI	BB	SO	SB	BA	SA	Pinch Hit AB	Pinch Hit H	G by POS

Swede Risberg

RISBERG, CHARLES AUGUST   BR TR 6'   165 lbs.
B. Oct. 13, 1894, San Francisco, Calif.   D. Oct. 13, 1975, Red Bluff, Calif.

	G	AB	H	2B	3B	HR	HR %	R	RBI	BB	SO	SB	BA	SA	AB	H	G by POS
1917 CHI A	149	474	96	20	8	1	0.2	59	45	59	65	16	.203	.285	2	1	SS-146
1918	82	273	70	12	3	1	0.4	36	27	23	32	5	.256	.333	4	1	SS-30, 3B-24, 2B-12, 1B-7, OF-3
1919	119	414	106	19	6	2	0.5	48	38	35	38	19	.256	.345	0	0	SS-97, 1B-22
1920	126	458	122	21	10	2	0.4	53	65	31	45	12	.266	.369	2	0	SS-124
4 yrs.	476	1619	394	72	27	6	0.4	196	175	148	180	52	.243	.332	8	2	SS-397, 1B-29, 3B-24, 2B-12, OF-3

WORLD SERIES

	G	AB	H	2B	3B	HR	HR %	R	RBI	BB	SO	SB	BA	SA	AB	H	G by POS
1917 CHI A	2	2	1	0	0	0	0.0	0	1	0	0	0	.500	.500	2	1	
1919	8	25	2	0	1	0	0.0	3	0	5	3	1	.080	.160	0	0	SS-8
2 yrs.	10	27	3	0	1	0	0.0	3	1	5	3	1	.111	.185	2	1	SS-8

Pop Rising

RISING, PERCIVAL SUMNER
B. Jan., 1877, Pennsylvania   D. Jan. 28, 1938, Rochester, Pa.

	G	AB	H	2B	3B	HR	HR %	R	RBI	BB	SO	SB	BA	SA	AB	H	G by POS
1905 BOS A	8	18	2	1	1	0	0.0	2	2	2		0	.111	.278	4	0	OF-3, 3B-1

Claude Ritchey

RITCHEY, CLAUDE CASSIUS (Little All Right)   BB TR 5'6½"   167 lbs.
B. Oct. 5, 1873, Emlenton, Pa.   D. Nov. 8, 1951, Emlenton, Pa.

	G	AB	H	2B	3B	HR	HR %	R	RBI	BB	SO	SB	BA	SA	AB	H	G by POS
1897 CIN N	101	337	95	12	4	0	0.0	58	41	42		11	.282	.341	0	0	SS-70, OF-22, 2B-8
1898 LOU N	152	558	145	10	4	5	0.9	66	51	46		19	.260	.319	0	0	SS-80, 2B-71
1899	147	540	167	15	7	4	0.7	67	71	49		21	.309	.385	0	0	2B-137, SS-11
1900 PIT N	123	476	139	17	8	1	0.2	62	67	29		18	.292	.368	0	0	2B-123
1901	140	540	160	20	4	1	0.2	66	74	47		15	.296	.354	0	0	2B-139, SS-1
1902	115	405	112	13	1	2	0.5	54	55	53		10	.277	.328	0	0	2B-114, OF-1
1903	138	506	145	28	10	4	0.8	66	59	55		15	.287	.381	0	0	2B-137
1904	156	544	143	22	12	0	0.0	79	51	59		12	.263	.347	0	0	2B-156, SS-2
1905	153	533	136	29	6	0	0.0	54	52	51		12	.255	.332	0	0	2B-153, SS-2
1906	152	484	130	21	5	1	0.2	46	62	68		6	.269	.339	1	1	2B-151
1907 BOS N	144	499	127	17	4	2	0.4	45	51	50		8	.255	.317	0	0	2B-144
1908	121	421	115	10	3	2	0.5	44	36	50		7	.273	.325	1	0	2B-120
1909	30	87	15	1	0	0	0.0	4	3	8		1	.172	.184	4	1	2B-25
13 yrs.	1672	5930	1629	215	68	18	0.3	711	673	607		155	.275	.343	6	2	2B-1478, SS-166, OF-23

WORLD SERIES

	G	AB	H	2B	3B	HR	HR %	R	RBI	BB	SO	SB	BA	SA	AB	H	G by POS
1903 PIT N	8	27	3	1	0	0	0.0	2	2	4	7	1	.111	.148	0	0	2B-8

Ritter

RITTER,
Deceased.

	G	AB	H	2B	3B	HR	HR %	R	RBI	BB	SO	SB	BA	SA	AB	H	G by POS
1885 BUF N	2	6	1	0	0	0	0.0	0	0	0	2		.167	.167	0	0	2B-2

Floyd Ritter

RITTER, FLOYD ALEXANDER   BR TR 5'8"   155 lbs.
B. June 1, 1870, Dorset, Ohio   D. Feb. 7, 1943, Stevenson, Wash.

	G	AB	H	2B	3B	HR	HR %	R	RBI	BB	SO	SB	BA	SA	AB	H	G by POS
1890 TOL AA	1	3	0	0	0	0	0.0	0		0		0	.000	.000	0	0	C-1

Lou Ritter

RITTER, LOUIS ELMER (Old Dog)   TR 5'9"   150 lbs.
B. Sept. 7, 1875, Liverpool, Pa.   D. May 27, 1952, Harrisburg, Pa.

	G	AB	H	2B	3B	HR	HR %	R	RBI	BB	SO	SB	BA	SA	AB	H	G by POS
1902 BKN N	16	57	12	2	0	0	0.0	5	2	1		2	.211	.246	0	0	C-16
1903	78	259	61	9	6	0	0.0	26	37	19		9	.236	.317	2	1	C-74, OF-2
1904	72	214	53	4	1	0	0.0	23	19	20		17	.248	.276	7	2	C-57, 2B-5, 3B-1
1905	92	311	68	10	5	1	0.3	32	28	15		16	.219	.293	2	0	C-84, OF-4, 3B-2
1906	73	226	47	1	3	0	0.0	22	15	16		6	.208	.239	6	1	C-53, OF-9, 1B-3, 3B-2
1907	93	271	55	6	1	0	0.0	15	17	18		5	.203	.232	3	0	C-89
1908	38	99	19	2	1	0	0.0	6	2	7		0	.192	.232	1	0	C-37
7 yrs.	462	1437	315	34	17	1	0.1	129	120	96		55	.219	.269	21	4	C-410, OF-15, 3B-5, 2B-5, 1B-3

Ed Ritterson

RITTERSON, EDWARD W.   BR TR 5'8"
B. Apr. 26, 1855, Pennsylvania   D. July 28, 1917, East Rockhill, Pa.

	G	AB	H	2B	3B	HR	HR %	R	RBI	BB	SO	SB	BA	SA	AB	H	G by POS
1876 PHI N	16	52	13	3	0	0	0.0	8	4	0	2		.250	.308	0	0	C-14, OF-4, 3B-1

Jim Ritz

RITZ, JAMES L.
B. 1874, Pittsburgh, Pa.   D. Nov. 10, 1896, Pittsburgh, Pa.

	G	AB	H	2B	3B	HR	HR %	R	RBI	BB	SO	SB	BA	SA	AB	H	G by POS
1894 PIT N	1	4	0	0	0	0	0.0	1	0	0	0	1	.000	.000	0	0	3B-1

Bombo Rivera

RIVERA, JESUS TORRES   BR TR 5'10"   187 lbs.
B. Aug. 2, 1952, Ponce, Puerto Rico

	G	AB	H	2B	3B	HR	HR %	R	RBI	BB	SO	SB	BA	SA	AB	H	G by POS
1975 MON N	5	9	1	0	0	0	0.0	0	2	3	0	.111	.111	1	0	OF-5
1976	68	185	51	11	4	2	1.1	22	19	13	32	1	.276	.411	15	5	OF-56
1978 MIN A	101	251	68	8	2	3	1.2	35	23	35	47	5	.271	.355	19	4	OF-94, DH-1
1979	112	263	74	13	5	2	0.8	37	31	17	40	5	.281	.392	26	6	OF-105, DH-2
1980	44	113	25	7	0	3	2.7	13	10	4	20	0	.221	.363	6	1	OF-37, DH-1
1982 KC A	5	10	1	0	0	0	0.0	1	0	0	2	0	.100	.100	1	0	OF-3
6 yrs.	335	831	220	39	11	10	1.2	109	83	71	144	11	.265	.374	68	16	OF-300, DH-4

German Rivera

RIVERA, GERMAN   BR TR 6'2"   170 lbs.
Also known as German Diaz.
B. July 6, 1960, Santurce, Puerto Rico

	G	AB	H	2B	3B	HR	HR %	R	RBI	BB	SO	SB	BA	SA	AB	H	G by POS
1983 LA N	13	17	6	1	0	0	0.0	1	0	2	2	0	.353	.412	5	1	3B-8
1984	94	227	59	12	2	2	0.9	20	17	21	30	1	.260	.357	5	1	3B-90
2 yrs.	107	244	65	13	2	2	0.8	21	17	23	32	1	.266	.361	10	2	3B-98

	G	AB	H	2B	3B	HR	HR %	R	RBI	BB	SO	SB	BA	SA	Pinch Hit AB	H	G by POS

Jim Rivera

RIVERA, MANUEL JOSEPH (Jungle Jim)
B. July 22, 1922, New York, N. Y.   BL TL 6'   196 lbs.

	G	AB	H	2B	3B	HR	HR %	R	RBI	BB	SO	SB	BA	SA	PH AB	H	G by POS
1952 2 teams		STL A	(97G –	.256)		CHI A	(53G –	.249)									
" total	150	537	136	20	9	7	1.3	72	48	50	86	21	.253	.363	6	2	OF-141
1953 CHI A	156	567	147	26	16	11	1.9	79	78	53	70	22	.259	.420	0	0	OF-156
1954	145	490	140	16	8	13	2.7	62	61	49	68	18	.286	.431	3	0	OF-143
1955	147	454	120	24	4	10	2.2	71	52	62	59	25	.264	.401	7	2	OF-143
1956	139	491	125	23	5	12	2.4	76	66	49	75	20	.255	.395	9	2	OF-134
1957	125	402	103	21	6	14	3.5	51	52	40	80	18	.256	.443	11	3	OF-82, 1B-31
1958	116	276	62	8	4	9	3.3	37	35	24	49	21	.225	.380	9	0	OF-99
1959	80	177	39	9	4	4	2.3	18	19	11	19	5	.220	.384	4	0	OF-69
1960	48	17	5	0	0	1	5.9	17	1	3	3	4	.294	.471	2	0	OF-24
1961 2 teams	CHI	A	(1G –	.000)		KC	A	(64G –	.241)								
" total	65	141	34	8	0	2	1.4	20	10	24	14	6	.241	.340	23	4	OF-43
10 yrs.	1171	3552	911	155	56	83	2.3	503	422	365	523	160	.256	.402	74	13	OF-1034, 1B-31

WORLD SERIES
| 1959 CHI A | 5 | 11 | 0 | 0 | 0 | 0 | 0.0 | 1 | 0 | 3 | 1 | 0 | .000 | .000 | 0 | 1 | OF-5 |

Mickey Rivers

RIVERS, JOHN MILTON
B. Oct. 31, 1948, Miami, Fla.   BL TL 5'10"   165 lbs.

	G	AB	H	2B	3B	HR	HR %	R	RBI	BB	SO	SB	BA	SA	PH AB	H	G by POS
1970 CAL A	17	25	8	2	0	0	0.0	6	3	3	5	1	.320	.400	9	1	OF-5
1971	78	268	71	12	2	1	0.4	31	12	19	38	13	.265	.336	7	2	OF-75
1972	58	159	34	6	2	0	0.0	18	7	8	26	4	.214	.277	7	2	OF-48
1973	30	129	45	6	4	0	0.0	26	16	8	11	8	.349	.457	0	0	OF-29
1974	118	466	133	19	11	3	0.6	69	31	39	47	30	.285	.393	1	0	OF-116
1975	155	616	175	17	13	1	0.2	70	53	43	42	70	.284	.359	2	0	OF-152, DH-1
1976 NY A	137	590	184	31	8	8	1.4	95	67	13	51	43	.312	.432	1	1	OF-136
1977	138	565	184	18	5	12	2.1	79	69	18	45	22	.326	.439	4	0	OF-136, DH-1
1978	141	559	148	25	8	11	2.0	78	48	29	51	25	.265	.397	3	2	OF-138
1979 2 teams	NY	A	(74G –	.287)		TEX	A	(58G –	.300)								
" total	132	533	156	27	8	9	1.7	72	50	22	39	10	.293	.424	6	2	OF-126, DH-1
1980 TEX A	147	630	210	32	6	7	1.1	96	60	20	34	18	.333	.437	4	1	OF-141, DH-4
1981	99	399	114	21	2	3	0.8	62	26	24	31	9	.286	.371	5	0	OF-97
1982	19	68	16	1	1	1	1.5	6	4	0	7	0	.235	.324	3	1	DH-16
1983	96	309	88	17	0	1	0.3	37	20	11	21	9	.285	.350	20	8	DH-53, OF-23
1984	102	313	94	13	1	4	1.3	40	33	9	23	5	.300	.387	31	8	DH-48, OF-30
15 yrs.	1467	5629	1660	247	71	61	1.1	785	499	266	471	267	.295	.397	103	28	OF-1252, DH-124

LEAGUE CHAMPIONSHIP SERIES
1976 NY A	5	23	8	0	1	0	0.0	5	0	1	1	0	.348	.435	0	0	OF-5
1977	5	23	9	2	0	0	0.0	5	2	0	2	1	.391	.478	0	0	OF-5
1978	4	11	5	0	0	0	0.0	0	0	2	0	0	.455	.455	0	0	OF-4
3 yrs.	14	57	22	2	1	0	0.0	10	2	3	3	1	.386	.456	0	0	OF-14

WORLD SERIES
1976 NY A	4	18	3	0	0	0	0.0	1	0	1	2	1	.167	.167	0	0	OF-4
1977	6	27	6	2	0	0	0.0	1	1	0	2	1	.222	.296	0	0	OF-6
1978	5	18	6	0	0	0	0.0	2	1	0	2	1	.333	.333	1	0	OF-4
3 yrs.	15	63	15	2	0	0	0.0	4	2	1	6	3	.238	.270	1	0	OF-14

Johnny Rizzo

RIZZO, JOHN COSTA
B. July 30, 1912, Houston, Tex.   D. Dec. 4, 1977, Houston, Tex.   BR TR 6'   190 lbs.

	G	AB	H	2B	3B	HR	HR %	R	RBI	BB	SO	SB	BA	SA	PH AB	H	G by POS
1938 PIT N	143	555	167	31	9	23	4.1	97	111	54	61	1	.301	.514	1	0	OF-140
1939	94	330	86	23	3	6	1.8	49	55	42	27	0	.261	.403	5	1	OF-86
1940 3 teams	PIT	N	(9G –	.179)		CIN	N	(31G –	.282)		PHI	N	(103G –	.292)			
" total	143	505	143	19	2	24	4.8	71	72	56	50	3	.283	.471	6	1	OF-128, 3B-7
1941 PHI N	99	235	51	9	2	4	1.7	20	24	24	34	1	.217	.323	30	5	OF-62, 3B-2
1942 BKN N	78	217	50	8	0	4	1.8	31	27	24	25	2	.230	.323	6	0	OF-70
5 yrs.	557	1842	497	90	16	61	3.3	268	289	200	197	7	.270	.435	48	7	OF-486, 3B-9

Phil Rizzuto

RIZZUTO, PHILIP FRANCIS (Scooter)
B. Sept. 25, 1918, New York, N. Y.   BR TR 5'6"   150 lbs.

	G	AB	H	2B	3B	HR	HR %	R	RBI	BB	SO	SB	BA	SA	PH AB	H	G by POS
1941 NY A	133	515	158	20	9	3	0.6	65	46	27	36	14	.307	.398	3	0	SS-128
1942	144	553	157	24	7	4	0.7	79	68	44	40	22	.284	.374	0	0	SS-144
1946	126	471	121	17	1	2	0.4	53	38	34	39	14	.257	.310	0	0	SS-125
1947	153	549	150	26	9	2	0.4	78	60	57	31	11	.273	.364	1	1	SS-151
1948	128	464	117	13	2	6	1.3	65	50	60	24	6	.252	.328	0	0	SS-128
1949	153	614	169	22	7	5	0.8	110	64	72	34	18	.275	.358	0	0	SS-152
1950	155	617	200	36	7	7	1.1	125	66	91	38	12	.324	.439	0	0	SS-155
1951	144	540	148	21	6	2	0.4	87	43	58	27	18	.274	.346	0	0	SS-144
1952	152	578	147	24	10	2	0.3	89	43	67	42	17	.254	.341	0	0	SS-152
1953	134	413	112	21	3	2	0.5	54	54	71	39	4	.271	.351	0	0	SS-133
1954	127	307	60	11	0	2	0.7	47	15	41	23	3	.195	.251	1	1	SS-126, 2B-1
1955	81	143	37	4	1	1	0.7	19	9	22	18	7	.259	.322	0	0	SS-79, 2B-1
1956	31	52	12	0	0	0	0.0	6	6	6	6	3	.231	.231	0	0	SS-30
13 yrs.	1661	5816	1588	239	62	38	0.7	877	562	650	397	149	.273	.355	5	2	SS-1647, 2B-2

WORLD SERIES
1941 NY A	5	18	2	0	0	0	0.0	0	0	3	1	1	.111	.111	0	0	SS-5
1942	5	21	8	0	0	1	4.8	2	1	2	1	2	.381	.524	0	0	SS-5
1947	7	26	8	1	0	0	0.0	3	2	4	0	2	.308	.346	0	0	SS-7
1949	5	18	3	0	0	0	0.0	2	1	3	1	1	.167	.167	0	0	SS-5
1950	4	14	2	0	0	0	0.0	1	0	3	0	0	.143	.143	0	0	SS-4
1951	6	25	8	0	0	1	4.0	5	3	2	3	0	.320	.440	0	0	SS-6
1952	7	27	4	1	0	0	0.0	2	0	5	2	0	.148	.185	0	0	SS-7
1953	6	19	6	1	0	0	0.0	4	0	3	2	1	.316	.368	0	0	SS-6
1955	7	15	4	0	0	0	0.0	2	1	5	1	2	.267	.267	0	0	SS-7
9 yrs.	52	183	45	3	0	2	1.1	21	8	30	11	10	.246	.295	0	0	SS-52
	6th	7th	7th					10th		4th		3rd					

	G	AB	H	2B	3B	HR	HR %	R	RBI	BB	SO	SB	BA	SA	Pinch Hit AB	Pinch Hit H	G by POS

Mel Roach

ROACH, MELVIN EARL
B. Jan. 25, 1933, Richmond, Va.   BR TR 6'1" 190 lbs.

	G	AB	H	2B	3B	HR	HR %	R	RBI	BB	SO	SB	BA	SA	AB	H	G by POS
1953 MIL N	5	2	0	0	0	0	0.0	1	0	0	1	0	.000	.000	1	0	2B-1
1954	3	4	0	0	0	0	0.0	0	0	0	1	0	.000	.000	2	0	1B-1
1957	7	6	1	0	0	0	0.0	1	0	0	3	0	.167	.167	3	0	2B-5
1958	44	136	42	7	0	3	2.2	14	10	6	15	0	.309	.426	12	3	2B-27, OF-7, 1B-1
1959	19	31	3	0	0	0	0.0	1	0	2	4	0	.097	.097	5	0	2B-8, OF-4, 3B-1
1960	48	140	42	12	0	3	2.1	12	18	6	19	0	.300	.450	10	3	OF-21, 2B-20, 3B-1, 1B-1
1961 2 teams	MIL	N (13G –	.167)		CHI	N	(23G –	.128)									
" total	36	75	11	2	0	1	1.3	4	7	5	13	1	.147	.213	13	3	OF-9, 1B-9, 2B-7
1962 PHI N	65	105	20	4	0	0	0.0	9	8	5	19	0	.190	.229	28	4	3B-26, 2B-9, 1B-4, OF-3
8 yrs.	227	499	119	25	0	7	1.4	42	43	24	75	1	.238	.331	74	13	2B-77, OF-44, 3B-28, 1B-16

Mike Roach

ROACH, JAMES MICHAEL
B. 1876, New York, N. Y.   D. Nov. 12, 1916, Binghamton, N. Y.

	G	AB	H	2B	3B	HR	HR %	R	RBI	BB	SO	SB	BA	SA	AB	H	G by POS
1899 WAS N	24	78	17	1	0	0	0.0	7	7	3		3	.218	.231	2	1	C-20, 1B-3

Roxy Roach

ROACH, WILBUR CHARLES   BR TR
B. Nov. 28, 1884, Morrisdale Mines, Pa.   D. Dec. 25, 1947, Bay City, Mich.

	G	AB	H	2B	3B	HR	HR %	R	RBI	BB	SO	SB	BA	SA	AB	H	G by POS
1910 NY A	70	220	47	9	2	0	0.0	27	20	29		15	.214	.273	3	0	SS-58, OF-9
1911	13	40	10	2	1	0	0.0	4	2	6		0	.250	.350	0	0	SS-8, 2B-5
1912 WAS A	2	2	1	0	0	1	50.0	1	1	0		0	.500	2.000	0	0	SS-2
1915 BUF F	92	346	93	20	3	2	0.6	35	31	17		11	.269	.361	0	0	SS-92
4 yrs.	177	608	151	31	6	3	0.5	67	54	52		26	.248	.334	3	0	SS-160, OF-9, 2B-5

Mike Roarke

ROARKE, MICHAEL THOMAS   BR TR 6'2" 195 lbs.
B. Nov. 8, 1930, West Warwick, R. I.

	G	AB	H	2B	3B	HR	HR %	R	RBI	BB	SO	SB	BA	SA	AB	H	G by POS
1961 DET A	86	229	51	6	1	2	0.9	21	22	20	31	0	.223	.284	1	0	C-85
1962	56	136	29	4	1	4	2.9	11	14	13	17	0	.213	.346	3	1	C-53
1963	23	44	14	0	0	0	0.0	5	1	2	3	0	.318	.318	7	1	C-16
1964	29	82	19	1	0	0	0.0	4	7	10	10	0	.232	.244	2	1	C-27
4 yrs.	194	491	113	11	2	6	1.2	41	44	45	61	0	.230	.297	13	3	C-181

Fred Roat

ROAT, FREDERICK
B. Feb. 10, 1868, Oregon, Ill.   D. Sept. 24, 1918, Oregon, Ill.

	G	AB	H	2B	3B	HR	HR %	R	RBI	BB	SO	SB	BA	SA	AB	H	G by POS
1890 PIT N	57	215	48	2	2	2	0.9	18	17	16	22	7	.223	.260	0	0	3B-44, 1B-9, OF-4
1892 CHI N	8	31	6	0	1	0	0.0	4	2	2	3	2	.194	.258	0	0	2B-8
2 yrs.	65	246	54	2	1	2	0.8	22	19	18	25	9	.220	.260	0	0	3B-44, 1B-9, 2B-8, OF-4

Tommy Robello

ROBELLO, THOMAS VARDASCO (Tony)   BR TR 5'10½" 175 lbs.
B. Feb. 9, 1913, San Leandro, Calif.

	G	AB	H	2B	3B	HR	HR %	R	RBI	BB	SO	SB	BA	SA	AB	H	G by POS
1933 CIN N	14	30	7	3	0	0	0.0	1	3	1	5	0	.233	.333	1	0	2B-11, 3B-2
1934	2	2	0	0	0	0	0.0	0	0	0	1	0	.000	.000	2	0	
2 yrs.	16	32	7	3	0	0	0.0	1	3	1	6	0	.219	.313	3	0	2B-11, 3B-2

Skippy Roberge

ROBERGE, JOSEPH ALBERT ARMAND   BR TR 5'11" 185 lbs.
B. May 19, 1917, Lowell, Mass.

	G	AB	H	2B	3B	HR	HR %	R	RBI	BB	SO	SB	BA	SA	AB	H	G by POS
1941 BOS N	55	167	36	6	0	0	0.0	12	15	9	18	0	.216	.251	2	1	2B-46, 3B-5, SS-2
1942	74	172	37	7	0	1	0.6	10	12	9	19	1	.215	.273	2	0	2B-29, 3B-27, SS-6
1946	48	169	39	6	2	2	1.2	13	20	7	12	1	.231	.325	0	0	3B-48
3 yrs.	177	508	112	19	2	3	0.6	35	47	25	49	2	.220	.283	4	1	3B-80, 2B-75, SS-8

Curt Roberts

ROBERTS, CURTIS BENJAMIN   BR TR 5'8" 165 lbs.
B. Aug. 16, 1929, Pineland, Tex.   D. Nov. 14, 1969, Oakland, Calif.

	G	AB	H	2B	3B	HR	HR %	R	RBI	BB	SO	SB	BA	SA	AB	H	G by POS
1954 PIT N	134	496	115	18	7	1	0.2	47	36	55	49	6	.232	.302	2	1	2B-131
1955	6	17	2	1	0	0	0.0	1	0	2	1	0	.118	.176	0	0	2B-6
1956	31	62	11	5	2	0	0.0	6	4	5	12	1	.177	.323	4	1	2B-27
3 yrs.	171	575	128	24	9	1	0.2	54	40	62	62	7	.223	.301	6	2	2B-164

Dave Roberts

ROBERTS, DAVID LEONARD   BL TL 6' 172 lbs.
B. June 30, 1933, Panama City, Panama

	G	AB	H	2B	3B	HR	HR %	R	RBI	BB	SO	SB	BA	SA	AB	H	G by POS
1962 HOU N	16	53	13	3	0	1	1.9	3	10	8	8	0	.245	.358	4	1	OF-12, 1B-6
1964	61	125	23	4	1	1	0.8	9	7	14	28	0	.184	.256	22	4	1B-34, OF-4
1966 PIT N	14	16	2	1	0	0	0.0	3	0	0	7	0	.125	.188	9	2	1B-2
3 yrs.	91	194	38	8	1	2	1.0	15	17	22	43	0	.196	.278	35	7	1B-42, OF-16

Dave Roberts

ROBERTS, DAVID WAYNE   BR TR 6'3" 215 lbs.
B. Feb. 17, 1951, Lebanon, Ore.

	G	AB	H	2B	3B	HR	HR %	R	RBI	BB	SO	SB	BA	SA	AB	H	G by POS
1972 SD N	100	418	102	17	0	5	1.2	38	33	18	64	7	.244	.321	0	0	3B-84, 2B-20, SS-3, C-1
1973	127	479	137	20	3	21	4.4	56	64	17	83	11	.286	.472	8	1	3B-111, 2B-12
1974	113	318	53	10	1	5	1.6	26	18	32	69	2	.167	.252	4	1	3B-103, SS-3, OF-1
1975	33	113	32	2	0	2	1.8	7	12	13	19	3	.283	.354	0	0	3B-30, OF-1
1977	82	186	41	14	1	1	0.5	15	23	11	32	2	.220	.323	16	3	C-63, 3B-2, 2B-2, SS-1
1978	54	97	21	4	1	1	1.0	7	7	12	25	0	.216	.309	4	0	C-41, 1B-8, OF-2
1979 TEX A	44	84	22	2	1	3	3.6	12	14	7	17	1	.262	.417	4	2	C-14, OF-11, 2B-8, 1B-6, DH-4, 3B-1
1980	101	235	56	4	0	10	4.3	27	30	13	38	0	.238	.383	13	4	3B-37, SS-33, C-22, OF-5, 2B-4, 1B-4
1981 HOU N	27	54	13	3	0	1	1.9	4	5	3	6	1	.241	.352	11	2	1B-10, 3B-7, 2B-3, C-1
1982 PHI N	28	33	6	1	0	0	0.0	2	2	2	8	0	.182	.212	2	0	3B-11, C-10, 2B-7
10 yrs.	709	2017	483	77	7	49	2.4	194	208	128	361	27	.239	.357	62	13	3B-386, C-152, 2B-61, SS-40, 1B-28, OF-19, DH-4

DIVISIONAL PLAYOFF SERIES

	G	AB	H	2B	3B	HR	HR %	R	RBI	BB	SO	SB	BA	SA	AB	H	G by POS
1981 HOU N	1	1	0	0	0	0	0.0	0	0	0	1	0	.000	.000	1	0	

	G	AB	H	2B	3B	HR	HR %	R	RBI	BB	SO	SB	BA	SA	Pinch Hit AB	Pinch Hit H	G by POS

Leon Roberts

ROBERTS, LEON KAUFFMAN BR TR 6'3" 200 lbs.
B. Jan. 22, 1951, Vicksburg, Mich.

	G	AB	H	2B	3B	HR	HR %	R	RBI	BB	SO	SB	BA	SA	PH AB	PH H	G by POS
1974 DET A	17	63	17	3	2	0	0.0	5	7	3	10	0	.270	.381	1	0	OF-17
1975	129	447	115	17	5	10	2.2	51	38	36	94	3	.257	.385	3	1	OF-127, DH-1
1976 HOU N	87	235	68	11	2	7	3.0	31	33	19	43	1	.289	.443	27	7	OF-60
1977	19	27	2	0	0	0	0.0	1	2	1	8	0	.074	.074	10	2	OF-9
1978 SEA A	134	472	142	21	7	22	4.7	78	92	41	52	6	.301	.515	8	4	OF-128, DH-2
1979	140	450	122	24	6	15	3.3	61	54	56	64	3	.271	.451	12	4	OF-136, DH-1
1980	119	374	94	18	3	10	2.7	48	33	43	59	8	.251	.396	12	2	OF-104, DH-4
1981 TEX A	72	233	65	17	2	4	1.7	26	31	25	38	3	.279	.421	4	0	OF-71
1982 2 teams		TEX A	(31G –	.233)		TOR A	(40G –	.229)									
" total	71	178	41	7	0	2	1.1	13	11	11	30	1	.230	.303	16	4	OF-44, DH-22
1983 KC A	84	213	55	7	0	8	3.8	24	24	17	27	1	.258	.404	13	4	OF-76, DH-1
1984	29	45	10	1	1	0	0.0	4	3	4	3	0	.222	.289	13	3	OF-16, DH-3, P-1
11 yrs.	901	2737	731	126	28	78	2.8	342	328	256	428	26	.267	.419	119	31	OF-788, DH-34, P-1

Red Roberts

ROBERTS, CHARLES EMORY BR TR 6' 170 lbs.
B. Aug. 8, 1918, Carrollton, Ga.

	G	AB	H	2B	3B	HR	HR %	R	RBI	BB	SO	SB	BA	SA	PH AB	PH H	G by POS
1943 WAS A	9	23	6	1	0	1	4.3	1	3	4	2	0	.261	.435	1	0	SS-6, 3B-1

Skipper Roberts

ROBERTS, CLARENCE ASHLEY BL TR 5'10½" 175 lbs.
B. Jan. 11, 1888, Wardner, Ida.   D. Dec. 24, 1963, Long Beach, Calif.

	G	AB	H	2B	3B	HR	HR %	R	RBI	BB	SO	SB	BA	SA	PH AB	PH H	G by POS
1913 STL N	26	41	6	2	0	0	0.0	4	3	3	13	1	.146	.195	7	0	C-16
1914 2 teams		PIT F	(52G –	.234)		CHI F	(4G –	.333)									
" total	56	97	23	4	2	1	1.0	12	9	3		3	.237	.351	29	8	C-23, OF-1
2 yrs.	82	138	29	6	2	1	0.7	16	12	6	13	4	.210	.304	36	8	C-39, OF-1

Andre Robertson

ROBERTSON, ANDRE LEVETT BR TR 5'10" 155 lbs.
B. Oct. 2, 1957, Orange, Tex.

	G	AB	H	2B	3B	HR	HR %	R	RBI	BB	SO	SB	BA	SA	PH AB	PH H	G by POS
1981 NY A	10	19	5	0	0	0	0.0	1	0	0	3	1	.263	.316	0	0	SS-8, 2B-3
1982	44	118	26	5	0	2	1.7	16	9	8	19	0	.220	.314	3	0	SS-27, 2B-15, 3B-2
1983	98	322	80	16	3	1	0.3	37	22	8	54	2	.248	.326	0	0	SS-78, 2B-29
1984	52	140	30	5	1	0	0.0	10	6	4	20	0	.214	.264	0	0	SS-49, 2B-6
4 yrs.	204	599	141	27	4	3	0.5	64	37	20	96	3	.235	.309	3	0	SS-162, 2B-53, 3B-2

LEAGUE CHAMPIONSHIP SERIES

	G	AB	H	2B	3B	HR	HR %	R	RBI	BB	SO	SB	BA	SA	PH AB	PH H	G by POS
1981 NY A	1	1	0	0	0	0	0.0	0	0	0	0	0	.000	.000	0	0	SS-1

WORLD SERIES

	G	AB	H	2B	3B	HR	HR %	R	RBI	BB	SO	SB	BA	SA	PH AB	PH H	G by POS
1981 NY A	1	0	0	0	0	0	–	0	0	0	0	0	–	–	0	0	

Bob Robertson

ROBERTSON, ROBERT EUGENE BR TR 6'1" 195 lbs.
B. Oct. 2, 1946, Frostburg, Md.

	G	AB	H	2B	3B	HR	HR %	R	RBI	BB	SO	SB	BA	SA	PH AB	PH H	G by POS
1967 PIT N	9	35	6	0	0	2	5.7	4	4	3	12	0	.171	.343	0	0	1B-9
1969	32	96	20	4	1	1	1.0	7	9	8	30	1	.208	.302	5	2	1B-26
1970	117	390	112	19	4	27	6.9	69	82	51	98	4	.287	.564	8	2	1B-99, 3B-5, OF-3
1971	131	469	127	18	2	26	5.5	65	72	60	101	1	.271	.484	5	0	1B-126
1972	115	306	59	11	0	12	3.9	25	41	41	84	1	.193	.346	4	0	1B-89, OF-23, 3B-11
1973	119	397	95	16	0	14	3.5	43	40	55	77	0	.239	.385	10	1	1B-107
1974	91	236	54	11	0	16	6.8	25	48	33	48	0	.229	.479	28	8	1B-63
1975	75	124	34	4	0	6	4.8	17	18	23	25	0	.274	.452	40	6	1B-27
1976	61	129	28	5	1	2	1.6	10	25	16	23	0	.217	.318	25	3	1B-29
1978 SEA A	64	174	40	5	2	8	4.6	17	28	24	39	0	.230	.420	16	4	DH-29, 1B-18
1979 TOR A	15	29	3	0	0	1	3.4	1	1	3	9	0	.103	.207	3	0	1B-9, DH-4
11 yrs.	829	2385	578	93	10	115	4.8	283	368	317	546	7	.242	.434	144	26	1B-602, DH-33, OF-26, 3B-16

LEAGUE CHAMPIONSHIP SERIES

	G	AB	H	2B	3B	HR	HR %	R	RBI	BB	SO	SB	BA	SA	PH AB	PH H	G by POS
1970 PIT N	2	5	1	1	0	0	0.0	0	0	0	0	0	.200	.400	1	0	1B-1
1971	4	16	7	1	0	4	25.0	5	6	0	2	0	.438	1.250	0	0	1B-4
1972	4	0	0	0	0	0	–	0	0	1	0	0	–	–	0	0	1B-4
1974	1	5	0	0	0	0	0.0	1	0	0	0	0	.000	.000	0	0	1B-1
1975	3	2	1	0	0	0	0.0	0	1	1	0	0	.500	.500	2	1	1B-1
5 yrs.	14	28	9	2	0	4	14.3	6	7	2	2	0	.321	.821	3	1	1B-11

WORLD SERIES

	G	AB	H	2B	3B	HR	HR %	R	RBI	BB	SO	SB	BA	SA	PH AB	PH H	G by POS
1971 PIT N	7	25	6	0	0	2	8.0	4	5	4	8	0	.240	.480	0	0	1B-7

Daryl Robertson

ROBERTSON, DARYL BERDINE BR TR 6' 184 lbs.
B. Jan. 5, 1936, Cripple Creek, Colo.

	G	AB	H	2B	3B	HR	HR %	R	RBI	BB	SO	SB	BA	SA	PH AB	PH H	G by POS
1962 CHI N	9	19	2	0	0	0	0.0	0	2	2	10	0	.105	.105	2	0	SS-6, 3B-1

Dave Robertson

ROBERTSON, DAVIS AYDELOTTE BL TL 6' 186 lbs.
B. Sept. 25, 1889, Portsmouth, Va.   D. Nov. 5, 1970, Virginia Beach, Va.

	G	AB	H	2B	3B	HR	HR %	R	RBI	BB	SO	SB	BA	SA	PH AB	PH H	G by POS
1912 NY N	3	2	1	0	0	0	0.0	0	1	0	1	1	.500	.500	0	0	1B-1
1914	82	256	68	12	3	2	0.8	25	32	10	26	9	.266	.359	10	0	OF-71
1915	138	544	160	17	10	3	0.6	72	58	22	52	22	.294	.379	3	0	OF-138
1916	150	587	180	18	8	12	2.0	88	69	14	56	21	.307	.426	5	2	OF-144
1917	142	532	138	16	9	12	2.3	64	54	10	47	17	.259	.391	1	1	OF-140
1919 2 teams		NY	N (1G –	.000)		CHI	N (27G –	.208)									
" total	28	96	20	2	0	1	1.0	8	10	1	10	3	.208	.260	2	0	OF-25
1920 CHI N	134	500	150	29	11	10	2.0	68	75	40	44	17	.300	.462	0	0	OF-134
1921 2 teams		CHI	N (22G –	.222)		PIT	N (60G –	.322)									
" total	82	266	82	21	3	6	2.3	36	62	13	19	4	.308	.477	15	4	OF-65
1922 NY N	42	47	13	2	0	1	2.1	5	3	3	7	0	.277	.383	30	7	OF-8
9 yrs.	801	2830	812	117	44	47	1.7	366	364	113	262	94	.287	.409	66	14	OF-725, 1B-1

WORLD SERIES

	G	AB	H	2B	3B	HR	HR %	R	RBI	BB	SO	SB	BA	SA	PH AB	PH H	G by POS
1917 NY N	6	22	11	1	1	0	0.0	3	1	0	0	2	.500	.636	0	0	OF-6

	G	AB	H	2B	3B	HR	HR%	R	RBI	BB	SO	SB	BA	SA	Pinch Hit AB	Pinch Hit H	G by POS

Don Robertson

ROBERTSON, DONALD ALEXANDER
B. Oct. 15, 1930, Harvey, Ill.   BL TL 5'10" 180 lbs.

	G	AB	H	2B	3B	HR	HR%	R	RBI	BB	SO	SB	BA	SA	AB	H	G by POS
1954 CHI N	14	6	0	0	0	0	0.0	2	0	0	2	0	.000	.000	4	0	OF-6

Gene Robertson

ROBERTSON, EUGENE EDWARD
B. Dec. 25, 1899, St. Louis, Mo.   D. Oct. 21, 1981, Fallon, Nev.   BL TR 5'7" 152 lbs.

	G	AB	H	2B	3B	HR	HR%	R	RBI	BB	SO	SB	BA	SA	AB	H	G by POS
1919 STL A	5	7	1	0	0	0	0.0	1	0	1	2	0	.143	.143	2	0	SS-2
1922	18	27	8	2	1	0	0.0	2	1	0	1	1	.296	.444	3	2	3B-7, SS-6, 2B-1
1923	78	251	62	10	1	0	0.0	36	17	21	7	4	.247	.295	0	0	3B-74, 2B-1
1924	121	439	140	25	4	4	0.9	70	52	35	14	3	.319	.421	5	2	3B-110, 2B-2
1925	154	582	158	26	5	14	2.4	97	76	81	30	10	.271	.405	0	0	3B-154, SS-1
1926	78	247	62	12	6	1	0.4	23	19	17	10	5	.251	.360	10	4	3B-55, SS-10, 2B-3
1928 NY A	83	251	73	9	4	1	0.4	29	36	14	6	2	.291	.339	9	0	3B-70, 2B-3
1929 2 teams		NY	A	(90G –	.298)			BOS	N	(8G –	.286)						
" total	98	337	100	15	6	0	0.0	46	41	29	6	4	.297	.377	12	2	3B-83, SS-1
1930 BOS N	21	59	11	1	0	0	0.0	7	7	5	3	0	.186	.203	2	0	3B-17
9 yrs.	656	2200	615	100	23	20	0.9	311	249	203	79	29	.280	.373	43	10	3B-570, SS-20, 2B-10
WORLD SERIES																	
1928 NY A	3	8	1	0	0	0	0.0	1	2	1	0	0	.125	.125	1	0	3B-3

Jim Robertson

ROBERTSON, ALFRED JAMES
B. Jan. 29, 1928, Chicago, Ill.   BR TR 5'9" 183 lbs.

	G	AB	H	2B	3B	HR	HR%	R	RBI	BB	SO	SB	BA	SA	AB	H	G by POS
1954 PHI A	63	147	27	8	0	0	0.0	9	8	23	25	0	.184	.238	9	1	C-50
1955 KC A	6	8	2	0	0	0	0.0	1	0	1	2	0	.250	.250	2	0	C-4
2 yrs.	69	155	29	8	0	0	0.0	10	8	24	27	0	.187	.239	11	1	C-54

Sherry Robertson

ROBERTSON, SHERRARD ALEXANDER
B. Jan. 1, 1919, Montreal, Que., Canada   D. Oct. 23, 1970, Houghton, S. D.   BL TR 6' 180 lbs.

	G	AB	H	2B	3B	HR	HR%	R	RBI	BB	SO	SB	BA	SA	AB	H	G by POS
1940 WAS A	10	33	7	0	1	0	0.0	4	0	5	6	0	.212	.273	0	0	SS-10
1941	1	3	0	0	0	0	0.0	0	0	0	3	0	.000	.000	0	0	3B-1
1943	59	120	26	4	1	3	2.5	22	14	17	19	0	.217	.342	26	5	3B-27, SS-1
1946	74	230	46	4	3	6	2.6	30	19	30	42	6	.200	.330	13	0	3B-38, 2B-14, SS-12, OF-1
1947	95	266	62	9	3	1	0.4	25	23	32	52	4	.233	.301	23	3	OF-55, 3B-10, 2B-4
1948	71	187	46	11	3	2	1.1	19	22	24	26	8	.246	.369	17	7	OF-51
1949	110	374	94	17	3	11	2.9	59	42	42	35	10	.251	.401	9	2	2B-71, 3B-19, OF-13
1950	71	123	32	3	3	2	1.6	19	16	22	18	1	.260	.382	32	7	OF-14, 2B-12, 3B-1
1951	62	111	21	2	1	2	1.8	9	14	10	9	2	.189	.252	34	6	OF-22
1952 2 teams		WAS	A	(1G –	.000)			PHI	A	(43G –	.200)						
" total	44	60	12	3	0	0	0.0	8	5	21	15	1	.200	.250	19	6	2B-8, OF-7, 3B-2
10 yrs.	597	1507	346	55	18	26	1.7	200	151	202	238	32	.230	.342	173	35	OF-163, 2B-109, 3B-98, SS-23

Aaron Robinson

ROBINSON, AARON ANDREW
B. June 23, 1915, Lancaster, S. C.   D. Mar. 9, 1966, Lancaster, S. C.   BL TR 6'2" 205 lbs.

	G	AB	H	2B	3B	HR	HR%	R	RBI	BB	SO	SB	BA	SA	AB	H	G by POS
1943 NY A	1	1	0	0	0	0	0.0	0	0	0	1	0	.000	.000	1	0	
1945	50	160	45	6	1	8	5.0	19	24	21	23	0	.281	.481	4	3	C-45
1946	100	330	98	17	2	16	4.8	32	64	48	39	0	.297	.506	4	1	C-95
1947	82	252	68	11	5	5	2.0	23	36	40	26	0	.270	.413	7	1	C-74
1948 CHI A	98	326	82	14	2	8	2.5	47	39	46	30	0	.252	.380	6	1	C-92
1949 DET A	110	331	89	12	0	13	3.9	38	56	73	21	0	.269	.423	2	0	C-108
1950	107	283	64	7	0	9	3.2	37	37	75	35	0	.226	.346	3	3	C-103
1951 2 teams		DET	A	(36G –	.207)			BOS	A	(26G –	.203)						
" total	62	156	32	7	1	2	1.3	12	16	34	19	0	.205	.301	2	1	C-60
8 yrs.	610	1839	478	74	11	61	3.3	208	272	337	194	0	.260	.412	29	10	C-577
WORLD SERIES																	
1947 NY A	3	10	2	0	0	0	0.0	2	1	2	1	0	.200	.200	0	0	C-3

Bill Robinson

ROBINSON, WILLIAM HENRY
B. June 26, 1943, McKeesport, Pa.   BR TR 6'2" 189 lbs.

	G	AB	H	2B	3B	HR	HR%	R	RBI	BB	SO	SB	BA	SA	AB	H	G by POS
1966 ATL N	6	11	3	0	1	0	0.0	1	3	0	1	0	.273	.455	1	0	OF-5
1967 NY A	116	342	67	6	1	7	2.0	31	29	28	56	2	.196	.281	15	0	OF-102
1968	107	342	82	16	7	6	1.8	34	40	26	54	7	.240	.380	9	1	OF-98
1969	87	222	38	11	2	3	1.4	23	21	16	39	3	.171	.279	29	4	OF-62, 1B-1
1972 PHI N	82	188	45	9	1	8	4.3	19	21	5	30	2	.239	.426	9	1	OF-72
1973	124	452	130	32	1	25	5.5	62	65	27	91	5	.288	.529	12	4	OF-113, 3B-14
1974	100	280	66	14	1	5	1.8	32	29	17	61	5	.236	.346	19	5	OF-87
1975 PIT N	92	200	56	12	2	6	3.0	26	33	11	36	3	.280	.450	33	5	OF-57
1976	122	393	119	22	3	21	5.3	55	64	16	73	2	.303	.534	11	5	OF-78, 3B-37, 1B-3
1977	137	507	154	32	1	26	5.1	74	104	25	92	12	.304	.525	8	0	1B-86, OF-43, 3B-17
1978	136	499	123	36	2	14	2.8	70	80	35	105	14	.246	.411	12	4	OF-127, 3B-29, 1B-3
1979	148	421	111	17	6	24	5.7	59	75	24	81	13	.264	.504	12	3	OF-125, 1B-28, 3B-3
1980	100	272	78	10	1	12	4.4	28	36	15	45	1	.287	.463	16	5	1B-49, OF-41
1981	39	88	19	3	0	2	2.3	8	8	5	18	1	.216	.318	15	1	1B-23, OF-7, 3B-1
1982 2 teams		PIT	N	(31G –	.239)			PHI	N	(35G –	.261)						
" total	66	140	35	9	0	7	5.0	14	31	12	34	1	.250	.464	26	5	OF-41, 1B-5
1983 PHI N	10	7	1	0	0	0	0.0	0	2	1	4	0	.143	.143	7	1	1B-3, 3B-2, OF-1
16 yrs.	1472	4364	1127	229	29	166	3.8	536	641	263	820	71	.258	.438	222	40	OF-1059, 1B-201, 3B-103
LEAGUE CHAMPIONSHIP SERIES																	
1975 PIT N	2	2	0	0	0	0	0.0	0	0	0	1	0	.000	.000	2	0	
1979	3	3	0	0	0	0	0.0	0	0	0	0	0	.000	.000	2	0	OF-3
2 yrs.	5	5	0	0	0	0	0.0	0	0	0	1	0	.000	.000	2	0	OF-3
WORLD SERIES																	
1979 PIT N	7	19	5	1	0	0	0.0	2	2	0	4	0	.263	.316	1	1	OF-6

	G	AB	H	2B	3B	HR	HR %	R	RBI	BB	SO	SB	BA	SA	Pinch Hit AB	Pinch Hit H	G by POS

Brooks Robinson

ROBINSON, BROOKS CALBERT
B. May 18, 1937, Little Rock, Ark.
Hall of Fame 1983.
BR TR 6'1" 180 lbs.

	G	AB	H	2B	3B	HR	HR %	R	RBI	BB	SO	SB	BA	SA	AB	H	G by POS
1955 **BAL A**	6	22	2	0	0	0	0.0	0	1	0	10	0	.091	.091	0	0	3B-6
1956	15	44	10	4	0	1	2.3	5	1	1	5	0	.227	.386	1	0	3B-14, 2B-1
1957	50	117	28	6	1	2	1.7	13	14	7	10	1	.239	.359	5	0	3B-47
1958	145	463	110	16	3	3	0.6	31	32	31	51	1	.238	.305	4	1	3B-140, 2B-16
1959	88	313	89	15	2	4	1.3	29	24	17	37	2	.284	.383	1	1	3B-87, 2B-1
1960	152	595	175	27	9	14	2.4	74	88	35	49	2	.294	.440	0	0	3B-152, 2B-3
1961	163	**668**	192	38	7	7	1.0	89	61	47	57	1	.287	.397	0	0	3B-163, 2B-2, SS-1
1962	162	634	192	29	9	23	3.6	77	86	42	70	3	.303	.486	0	0	3B-162, SS-3, 2B-2
1963	161	589	148	26	4	11	1.9	67	67	46	84	2	.251	.365	1	0	3B-160, SS-1
1964	163	612	194	35	3	28	4.6	82	118	51	64	1	.317	.521	0	0	3B-163
1965	144	559	166	25	2	18	3.2	81	80	47	47	3	.297	.445	1	1	3B-143
1966	157	620	167	35	2	23	3.7	91	100	56	36	2	.269	.444	0	0	3B-157
1967	158	610	164	25	5	22	3.6	88	77	54	54	1	.269	.434	0	0	3B-158
1968	162	608	154	36	6	17	2.8	65	75	44	55	1	.253	.416	0	0	3B-162
1969	156	598	140	21	3	23	3.8	73	84	56	55	2	.234	.395	0	0	3B-156
1970	158	608	168	31	4	18	3.0	84	94	53	53	1	.276	.429	2	0	3B-156
1971	156	589	160	21	1	20	3.4	67	92	63	50	0	.272	.413	0	0	3B-156
1972	153	556	139	23	2	8	1.4	48	64	43	45	1	.250	.342	3	0	3B-152
1973	155	549	141	17	2	9	1.6	53	72	55	50	2	.257	.344	1	0	3B-154
1974	153	553	159	27	0	7	1.3	46	59	56	47	2	.288	.374	0	0	3B-153
1975	144	482	97	15	1	6	1.2	50	53	44	33	0	.201	.274	2	0	3B-143
1976	71	218	46	8	2	3	1.4	16	11	8	24	0	.211	.307	2	0	3B-71
1977	24	47	7	2	0	1	2.1	3	4	4	4	0	.149	.255	8	1	3B-15
23 yrs.	2896	10654	2848	482	68	268	2.5	1232	1357	860	990	28	.267	.401	31	4	3B-2870, 2B-25, SS-5
		8th		7th													

LEAGUE CHAMPIONSHIP SERIES
	G	AB	H	2B	3B	HR	HR %	R	RBI	BB	SO	SB	BA	SA	AB	H	G by POS
1969 **BAL A**	3	14	7	1	0	0	0.0	1	0	0	0	0	.500	.571	0	0	3B-3
1970	3	12	7	2	0	0	0.0	4	1	0	1	0	.583	.750	0	0	3B-3
1971	3	11	4	1	0	1	9.1	2	3	0	1	0	.364	.727	0	0	3B-3
1973	5	20	5	2	0	0	0.0	1	2	1	1	0	.250	.350	0	0	3B-5
1974	4	12	1	0	0	1	8.3	1	1	1	0	0	.083	.333	0	0	3B-4
5 yrs.	18	69	24	6	0	2	2.9	9	7	2	3	0	.348	.522	0	0	3B-18

WORLD SERIES
	G	AB	H	2B	3B	HR	HR %	R	RBI	BB	SO	SB	BA	SA	AB	H	G by POS
1966 **BAL A**	4	14	3	0	0	1	7.1	2	1	1	0	0	.214	.429	0	0	3B-4
1969	5	19	1	0	0	0	0.0	0	2	0	3	0	.053	.053	0	0	3B-5
1970	5	21	9	2	0	2	9.5	5	6	0	2	0	.429	.810	0	0	3B-5
1971	7	22	7	0	0	0	0.0	2	5	3	1	0	.318	.318	0	0	3B-7
4 yrs.	21	76	20	2	0	3	3.9	9	14	4	6	0	.263	.408	0	0	3B-21

Bruce Robinson

ROBINSON, BRUCE PHILIP
Brother of Dave Robinson.
B. Apr. 16, 1954, LaJolla, Calif.
BL TR 6'1" 185 lbs.

	G	AB	H	2B	3B	HR	HR %	R	RBI	BB	SO	SB	BA	SA	AB	H	G by POS
1978 **OAK A**	28	84	21	3	1	0	0.0	5	8	3	8	0	.250	.310	1	0	C-28
1979 **NY A**	6	12	2	0	0	0	0.0	0	2	1	0	0	.167	.167	0	0	C-6
1980	4	5	0	0	0	0	0.0	0	0	0	4	0	.000	.000	1	0	C-3
3 yrs.	38	101	23	3	1	0	0.0	5	10	4	12	0	.228	.277	2	0	C-37

Charlie Robinson

ROBINSON, CHARLES HENRY
B. July 27, 1856, Westerly, R. I.   D. May 18, 1913, Providence, R. I.
BL TR

	G	AB	H	2B	3B	HR	HR %	R	RBI	BB	SO	SB	BA	SA	AB	H	G by POS
1884 **IND AA**	20	80	23	2	0	0	0.0	11		3				.288	.313	0	0	C-17, SS-3, OF-1
1885 **BKN AA**	11	40	6	2	1	0	0.0	5		3				.150	.250	0	0	C-11
2 yrs.	31	120	29	4	1	0	0.0	16		6				.242	.292	0	0	C-28, SS-3, OF-1

Craig Robinson

ROBINSON, CRAIG GEORGE
B. Aug. 21, 1948, Abington, Pa.
BR TR 5'10" 165 lbs.

	G	AB	H	2B	3B	HR	HR %	R	RBI	BB	SO	SB	BA	SA	AB	H	G by POS
1972 **PHI N**	5	15	3	1	0	0	0.0	0	0	1	2	0	.200	.267	0	0	SS-4
1973	46	146	33	7	0	0	0.0	11	7	0	25	1	.226	.274	2	0	SS-42, 2B-4
1974 **ATL N**	145	452	104	4	4	0	0.0	52	29	30	57	11	.230	.265	1	1	SS-142
1975 2 teams		**ATL N** (11G – .059)				**SF N** (29G – .069)											
" total	40	46	3	1	0	0	0.0	5	0	2	11	0	.065	.087	2	0	SS-19, 2B-9
1976 2 teams		**SF N** (15G – .308)				**ATL N** (15G – .235)											
" total	30	30	8	1	0	0	0.0	8	5	8	6	0	.267	.300	3	2	2B-12, SS-3, 3B-3
1977 **ATL N**	27	29	6	1	0	0	0.0	4	1	1	6	0	.207	.241	4	0	SS-23
6 yrs.	293	718	157	15	6	0	0.0	80	42	42	107	12	.219	.256	12	3	SS-233, 2B-25, 3B-3

Dave Robinson

ROBINSON, DAVID TANNER
Brother of Bruce Robinson.
B. May 22, 1946, Minneapolis, Minn.
BB TL 6'1" 186 lbs.

	G	AB	H	2B	3B	HR	HR %	R	RBI	BB	SO	SB	BA	SA	AB	H	G by POS
1970 **SD N**	15	38	12	2	0	2	5.3	5	6	5	4	2	.316	.526	2	0	OF-13
1971	7	6	0	0	0	0	0.0	0	0	1	3	0	.000	.000	6	0	
2 yrs.	22	44	12	2	0	2	4.5	5	6	6	7	2	.273	.455	8	0	OF-13

Earl Robinson

ROBINSON, EARL JOHN
B. Nov. 3, 1936, New Orleans, La.
BR TR 6'1" 190 lbs.

	G	AB	H	2B	3B	HR	HR %	R	RBI	BB	SO	SB	BA	SA	AB	H	G by POS
1958 **LA N**	8	15	3	0	0	0	0.0	3	0	1	4	0	.200	.200	0	0	3B-6
1961 **BAL A**	96	222	59	12	3	8	3.6	37	30	31	54	4	.266	.455	20	5	OF-82
1962	29	63	18	3	1	1	1.6	12	4	8	10	2	.286	.413	6	1	OF-17
1964	37	121	33	5	1	3	2.5	11	10	7	24	1	.273	.405	2	1	OF-34
4 yrs.	170	421	113	20	5	12	2.9	63	44	47	92	7	.268	.425	28	9	OF-133, 3B-6

Eddie Robinson

ROBINSON, WILLIAM EDWARD
B. Dec. 15, 1920, Paris, Tex.
BL TR 6'2½" 210 lbs.

	G	AB	H	2B	3B	HR	HR %	R	RBI	BB	SO	SB	BA	SA	AB	H	G by POS
1942 **CLE A**	8	8	1	0	0	0	0.0	1	2	1	0	0	.125	.125	6	1	1B-1
1946	7	27	11	0	0	3	11.1	5	4	1	4	0	.407	.741	0	0	1B-7

	G	AB	H	2B	3B	HR	HR %	R	RBI	BB	SO	SB	BA	SA	Pinch Hit AB	Pinch Hit H	G by POS

Eddie Robinson continued

	G	AB	H	2B	3B	HR	HR %	R	RBI	BB	SO	SB	BA	SA	PH AB	PH H	G by POS
1947	95	318	78	10	1	14	4.4	52	52	30	18	1	.245	.415	5	1	1B-87
1948	134	493	125	18	5	16	3.2	53	83	36	42	1	.254	.408	4	1	1B-131
1949 WAS A	143	527	155	27	3	18	3.4	66	78	67	30	3	.294	.459	0	0	1B-143
1950 2 teams		WAS	A (36G – .240)			CHI	A (119G – .311)										
" total	155	553	163	15	4	21	3.8	83	86	85	32	0	.295	.450	0	0	1B-155
1951 CHI A	151	564	159	23	5	29	5.1	85	117	77	54	2	.282	.495	2	0	1B-147
1952	155	594	176	33	1	22	3.7	79	104	70	49	2	.296	.466	0	0	1B-155
1953 PHI A	156	615	152	28	4	22	3.6	64	102	63	56	1	.247	.413	1	0	1B-155
1954 NY A	85	142	37	9	0	3	2.1	11	27	19	21	0	.261	.387	49	15	1B-29
1955	88	173	36	1	0	16	9.2	25	42	36	26	0	.208	.491	34	5	1B-46
1956 2 teams		NY	A (26G – .222)			KC	A (75G – .198)										
" total	101	226	46	6	1	7	3.1	20	23	31	23	0	.204	.332	34	6	1B-61
1957 3 teams		DET	A (13G – .000)			CLE	A (19G – .222)		BAL	A (4G – .000)							
" total	36	39	6	1	0	1	2.6	1	3	4	4	0	.154	.256	21	1	1B-8
13 yrs.	1314	4279	1145	171	24	172	4.0	545	723	520	359	10	.268	.439	156	30	1B-1125
WORLD SERIES																	
1948 CLE A	6	20	6	0	0	0	0.0	0	1	1	0	0	.300	.300	0	0	1B-6
1955 NY A	4	3	2	0	0	0	0.0	0	1	2	1	0	.667	.667	1	1	1B-1
2 yrs.	10	23	8	0	0	0	0.0	0	2	3	1	0	.348	.348	1	1	1B-7

Floyd Robinson

ROBINSON, FLOYD ANDREW
B. May 9, 1936, Prescott, Ark.
BL TR 5'9"   175 lbs.

	G	AB	H	2B	3B	HR	HR %	R	RBI	BB	SO	SB	BA	SA	PH AB	PH H	G by POS
1960 CHI A	22	46	13	0	0	0	0.0	7	1	11	8	2	.283	.283	4	0	OF-17
1961	132	432	134	20	7	11	2.5	69	59	52	32	7	.310	.465	23	6	OF-106
1962	156	600	187	45	10	11	1.8	89	109	72	47	4	.312	.475	1	0	OF-155
1963	146	527	149	21	6	13	2.5	71	71	62	43	4	.283	.419	9	2	OF-137
1964	141	525	158	17	3	11	2.1	83	59	70	41	9	.301	.408	6	2	OF-138
1965	156	577	153	15	6	14	2.4	70	66	76	51	4	.265	.385	9	2	OF-153
1966	127	342	81	11	2	5	1.5	44	35	44	32	8	.237	.325	17	0	OF-113
1967 CIN N	55	130	31	6	2	1	0.8	19	10	14	14	3	.238	.338	15	2	OF-39
1968 2 teams		OAK	A (53G – .247)			BOS	A (24G – .125)										
" total	77	105	23	5	0	1	1.0	6	16	7	14	1	.219	.295	42	9	OF-29
9 yrs.	1012	3284	929	140	36	67	2.0	458	426	408	282	42	.283	.409	126	23	OF-887

Frank Robinson

ROBINSON, FRANK
B. Aug. 31, 1935, Beaumont, Tex.
Manager 1975-77, 1981-84.
Hall of Fame 1982.
BR TR 6'1"   183 lbs.

	G	AB	H	2B	3B	HR	HR %	R	RBI	BB	SO	SB	BA	SA	PH AB	PH H	G by POS
1956 CIN N	152	572	166	27	6	38	6.6	**122**	83	64	95	8	.290	.558	0	0	OF-152
1957	150	611	197	29	5	29	4.7	97	75	44	92	10	.322	.529	0	0	OF-136, 1B-24
1958	148	554	149	25	6	31	5.6	90	83	62	80	10	.269	.504	5	0	OF-138, 3B-11
1959	146	540	168	31	4	36	6.7	106	125	69	93	18	.311	.583	0	0	1B-125, OF-40
1960	139	464	138	33	6	31	6.7	86	83	82	67	13	.297	**.595**	10	5	1B-78, OF-51, 3B-1
1961	153	545	176	32	7	37	6.8	117	124	71	64	22	.323	**.611**	4	2	OF-150, 3B-1
1962	162	609	208	**51**	2	39	6.4	**134**	136	76	62	18	.342	**.624**	0	0	OF-161
1963	140	482	125	19	3	21	4.4	79	91	81	69	26	.259	.442	2	2	OF-139, 1B-1
1964	156	568	174	38	6	29	5.1	103	96	79	67	23	.306	.548	0	0	OF-156
1965	156	582	172	33	5	33	5.7	109	113	70	100	13	.296	.540	1	1	OF-155
1966 BAL A	155	576	182	34	2	49	8.5	**122**	**122**	87	90	8	**.316**	**.637**	1	1	OF-151, 1B-3
1967	129	479	149	23	7	30	6.3	83	94	71	84	2	.311	.576	0	0	OF-126, 1B-2
1968	130	421	113	27	1	15	3.6	69	52	73	84	11	.268	.444	12	4	OF-117, 1B-3
1969	148	539	166	19	5	32	5.9	111	100	88	62	9	.308	.540	3	2	OF-134, 1B-19
1970	132	471	144	24	1	25	5.3	88	78	69	70	2	.306	.520	6	3	OF-120, 1B-7
1971	133	455	128	16	2	28	6.2	82	99	72	62	3	.281	.510	8	0	OF-92, 1B-37
1972 LA N	103	342	86	6	1	19	5.6	41	59	55	76	2	.251	.442	5	0	OF-95
1973 CAL A	147	534	142	29	0	30	5.6	85	97	82	93	1	.266	.489	2	1	DH-127, OF-17
1974 2 teams		CAL	A (129G – .251)			CLE	A (15G – .200)										
" total	144	477	117	27	3	22	4.6	81	68	85	95	5	.245	.453	6	0	DH-134, 1B-4, OF-1
1975 CLE A	49	118	28	5	0	9	7.6	19	24	29	15	0	.237	.508	6	2	DH-42
1976	36	67	15	0	0	3	4.5	5	10	11	12	0	.224	.358	16	5	DH-18, 1B-2, OF-1
21 yrs.	2808	10006	2943	528	72	586	5.9	1829	1812	1420	1532	204	.294	.537	87	28	OF-2132, DH-321, 1B-305, 3B-13
								4th	10th								

LEAGUE CHAMPIONSHIP SERIES																	
1969 BAL A	3	12	4	2	0	1	8.3	1	2	3	3	0	.333	.750	0	0	OF-3
1970	3	10	2	0	0	1	10.0	3	2	5	2	0	.200	.500	0	0	OF-3
1971	3	12	1	1	0	0	0.0	2	1	1	4	0	.083	.167	0	0	OF-3
3 yrs.	9	34	7	3	0	2	5.9	6	5	9	9	0	.206	.471	0	0	OF-9

WORLD SERIES																	
1961 CIN N	5	15	3	2	0	1	6.7	3	4	3	4	0	.200	.533	0	0	OF-5
1966 BAL A	4	14	4	0	1	2	14.3	4	3	2	3	0	.286	.857	0	0	OF-4
1969	5	16	3	0	0	1	6.3	2	1	4	3	0	.188	.375	0	0	OF-5
1970	5	22	6	0	0	2	9.1	5	4	0	5	0	.273	.545	0	0	OF-5
1971	7	25	7	0	0	2	8.0	5	2	2	8	0	.280	.520	0	0	OF-7
5 yrs.	26	92	23	2	1	8	8.7	19	14	11	23	0	.250	.554	0	0	OF-26
								7th	3rd		10th						

Fred Robinson

ROBINSON, FREDERIC HENRY
Brother of Wilbert Robinson.
B. July 6, 1856, South Acton, Mass.   D. Dec. 18, 1933, Hudson, Mass.
BR TR

	G	AB	H	2B	3B	HR	HR %	R	RBI	BB	SO	SB	BA	SA	PH AB	PH H	G by POS
1884 CIN U	3	13	3	0	0	0	0.0	1					.231	.231	0	0	2B-3

Jackie Robinson

ROBINSON, JACK ROOSEVELT
B. Jan. 31, 1919, Cairo, Ga.   D. Oct. 24, 1972, Stamford, Conn.
Hall of Fame 1962.
BR TR 5'11½" 195 lbs.

	G	AB	H	2B	3B	HR	HR %	R	RBI	BB	SO	SB	BA	SA	PH AB	PH H	G by POS
1947 BKN N	151	590	175	31	5	12	2.0	125	48	74	36	**29**	.297	.427	0	0	1B-151

	G	AB	H	2B	3B	HR	HR %	R	RBI	BB	SO	SB	BA	SA	Pinch Hit AB	Pinch Hit H	G by POS

Jackie Robinson continued

	G	AB	H	2B	3B	HR	HR %	R	RBI	BB	SO	SB	BA	SA	AB	H	G by POS
1948	147	574	170	38	8	12	2.1	108	85	57	37	22	.296	.453	2	1	2B-116, 1B-30, 3B-6
1949	156	593	203	38	12	16	2.7	122	124	86	27	37	.342	.528	0	0	2B-156
1950	144	518	170	39	4	14	2.7	99	81	80	24	12	.328	.500	2	1	2B-144
1951	153	548	185	33	7	19	3.5	106	88	79	27	25	.338	.527	3	1	2B-153
1952	149	510	157	17	3	19	3.7	104	75	106	40	24	.308	.465	2	0	2B-146
1953	136	484	159	34	7	12	2.5	109	95	74	30	17	.329	.502	5	1	OF-76, 3B-44, 2B-9, 1B-6, SS-1
1954	124	386	120	22	4	15	3.9	62	59	63	20	7	.311	.505	7	1	OF-64, 3B-50, 2B-4
1955	105	317	81	6	2	8	2.5	51	36	61	18	12	.256	.363	9	1	3B-84, OF-10, 2B-1, 1B-1
1956	117	357	98	15	2	10	2.8	61	43	60	32	12	.275	.412	10	1	3B-72, 2B-22, 1B-9, OF-2
10 yrs.	1382	4877	1518	273	54	137	2.8	947	734	740	291	197	.311	.474	40	7	2B-751, 3B-256, 1B-197, OF-152, SS-1

WORLD SERIES

	G	AB	H	2B	3B	HR	HR %	R	RBI	BB	SO	SB	BA	SA	AB	H	G by POS
1947 BKN N	7	27	7	2	0	0	0.0	3	3	2	4	2	.259	.333	0	0	1B-7
1949	5	16	3	1	0	0	0.0	2	2	4	2	0	.188	.250	0	0	2B-5
1952	7	23	4	0	0	1	4.3	4	2	7	5	2	.174	.304	0	0	2B-7
1953	6	25	8	2	0	0	0.0	3	2	1	0	1	.320	.400	0	0	OF-6
1955	6	22	4	1	0	0	0.0	5	1	2	1	1	.182	.318	0	0	3B-6
1956	7	24	6	1	0	1	4.2	5	2	5	2	0	.250	.417	0	0	3B-7
6 yrs.	38	137	32	7	1	2	1.5	22	12	21	14	6	.234	.343	0	0	3B-13, 2B-12, 1B-7, OF-6
				8th				9th		8th							

John Robinson

ROBINSON, JOHN
B. E. Greenwich, Conn. TR

	G	AB	H	2B	3B	HR	HR %	R	RBI	BB	SO	SB	BA	SA	AB	H	G by POS
1902 NY N	4	9	0	0	0	0	0.0	0	0	0		0	.000	.000	1	0	C-3

Rabbit Robinson

ROBINSON, CLYDE WILLIAM (Tug) BR TR 5'5" 148 lbs.
B. Mar. 5, 1882, Wellsburg, W. Va. D. Apr. 9, 1915, Waterbury, Conn.

	G	AB	H	2B	3B	HR	HR %	R	RBI	BB	SO	SB	BA	SA	AB	H	G by POS
1903 WAS A	103	373	79	10	8	1	0.3	41	20	33		16	.212	.290	0	0	2B-45, OF-30, SS-24, 3B-5
1904 DET A	101	320	77	13	6	0	0.0	30	37	29		14	.241	.319	5	1	SS-30, 3B-26, OF-20, 2B-19
1910 CIN N	2	7	0	0	0	0	0.0	0	1	1	0	0	.000	.000	0	0	3B-2
3 yrs.	206	700	156	23	14	1	0.1	71	58	63	0	30	.223	.300	5	1	2B-64, SS-54, OF-50, 3B-33

Wilbert Robinson

ROBINSON, WILBERT (Uncle Robbie) BR TR 5'8½" 215 lbs.
Brother of Fred Robinson.
B. June 2, 1863, Bolton, Mass. D. Aug. 8, 1934, Atlanta, Ga.
Manager 1902, 1914-31.
Hall of Fame 1945.

	G	AB	H	2B	3B	HR	HR %	R	RBI	BB	SO	SB	BA	SA	AB	H	G by POS
1886 PHI AA	87	342	69	11	3	1	0.3	57		21			.202	.260	0	0	C-61, 1B-22, OF-5
1887	68	264	60	6	2	1	0.4	28		14		15	.227	.277	0	0	C-67, 1B-3, OF-1
1888	66	254	62	7	2	1	0.4	32	31	9		11	.244	.299	0	0	C-65, 1B-1
1889	69	264	61	13	2	0	0.0	31	28	6	34	9	.231	.295	0	0	C-69
1890 2 teams	96				PHI	AA (82G – .237)		B-B	AA (14G – .271)								
" total	96	377	91	14	4	4	1.1	39		19		21	.241	.332	0	0	C-93, 1B-3
1891 BAL AA	93	334	72	8	5	2	0.6	25	46	16	37	18	.216	.287	0	0	C-92, OF-1
1892 BAL N	90	330	88	14	4	2	0.6	36	57	15	35	5	.267	.352	0	0	C-87, 1B-2, OF-1
1893	95	359	120	21	3	3	0.8	49	57	26	22	17	.334	.435	1	0	C-93, 1B-1
1894	109	414	146	21	4	1	0.2	69	98	46	18	12	.353	.430	0	0	C-109
1895	77	282	74	19	1	0	0.0	38	48	12	19	11	.262	.337	2	1	C-75
1896	67	245	85	9	6	2	0.8	43	38	14	13	9	.347	.457	0	0	C-67
1897	48	181	57	9	0	0	0.0	25	23	8		0	.315	.365	0	0	C-48
1898	79	289	80	12	2	0	0.0	29	38	16		3	.277	.332	1	1	C-77
1899	108	356	101	15	2	0	0.0	40	47	31		5	.284	.337	3	2	C-105
1900 STL N	60	210	52	5	1	0	0.0	26	28	11		7	.248	.281	5	1	C-54
1901 BAL A	71	241	72	12	3	0	0.0	34	26	10		9	.299	.373	1	0	C-67
1902	91	335	98	16	7	1	0.3	39	57	12		11	.293	.391	4	2	C-87
17 yrs.	1374	5077	1388	212	51	18	0.4	640	621	286	178	163	.273	.346	17	7	C-1316, 1B-32, OF-8

Yank Robinson

ROBINSON, WILLIAM H. BL TR 5'6½" 170 lbs.
B. Sept. 19, 1859, Philadelphia, Pa. D. Aug. 25, 1894, St. Louis, Mo.

	G	AB	H	2B	3B	HR	HR %	R	RBI	BB	SO	SB	BA	SA	AB	H	G by POS
1882 DET N	11	39	7	1	0	0	0.0	1	2	1	13		.179	.205	0	0	SS-10, OF-1, P-1
1884 BAL U	102	415	111	24	4	2	0.5	101		37			.267	.359	0	0	3B-71, SS-14, C-11, P-11, 2B-3
1885 STL AA	78	287	75	8	8	0	0.0	63		29			.261	.345	0	0	OF-52, 2B-19, C-5, 3B-2, 1B-1
1886	133	481	132	26	9	3	0.6	89		64			.274	.385	0	0	2B-125, 3B-6, OF-1, SS-1, P-1
1887	125	430	131	32	4	1	0.2	102		92		75	.305	.405	0	0	2B-117, 3B-6, OF-2, SS-2, C-1, P-1
1888	134	455	105	17	6	3	0.7	111	53	116		56	.231	.314	0	0	2B-102, SS-34
1889	132	452	94	17	3	5	1.1	97	70	118	55	39	.208	.292	0	0	2B-132
1890 PIT P	98	306	70	10	3	0	0.0	59	38	101	33	17	.229	.284	0	0	2B-98
1891 2 teams	98				C-M	AA (97G – .178)		STL	AA (1G – .000)								
" total	98	345	61	9	4	1	0.3	48	37	68	51	23	.177	.235	0	0	2B-98
1892 WAS N	67	218	39	4	3	0	0.0	26	19	38	28	11	.179	.225	0	0	3B-58, SS-5, 2B-4
10 yrs.	978	3428	825	148	44	15	0.4	697	219	664	180	221	.241	.323	0	0	2B-698, 3B-143, SS-66, OF-56, P-14, 1B-1

Rafael Robles

ROBLES, RAFAEL ORLANDO BR TR 6' 170 lbs.
B. Oct. 20, 1947, San Pedro de Macoris, Dominican Republic

	G	AB	H	2B	3B	HR	HR %	R	RBI	BB	SO	SB	BA	SA	AB	H	G by POS
1969 SD N	6	20	2	0	0	0	0.0	1	0	1	3	1	.100	.100	0	0	SS-6
1970	23	89	19	1	0	0	0.0	5	3	5	11	3	.213	.225	0	0	SS-23

	G	AB	H	2B	3B	HR	HR %	R	RBI	BB	SO	SB	BA	SA	Pinch Hit AB	Pinch Hit H	G by POS

Rafael Robles continued

	G	AB	H	2B	3B	HR	HR %	R	RBI	BB	SO	SB	BA	SA	AB	H	G by POS
1972	18	24	4	0	0	0	0.0	1	0	0	3	0	.167	.167	8	1	SS-15, 3B-1
3 yrs.	47	133	25	1	0	0	0.0	7	3	6	17	4	.188	.195	8	1	SS-44, 3B-1

Sergio Robles

ROBLES, SERGIO VALENZUELA
B. Apr. 16, 1946, Magdalena, Mexico

BR TR 6'2" 190 lbs.

	G	AB	H	2B	3B	HR	HR %	R	RBI	BB	SO	SB	BA	SA	AB	H	G by POS
1972 BAL A	2	5	1	0	0	0	0.0	0	0	0	0	0	.200	.200	1	1	C-1
1973	8	13	1	0	0	0	0.0	0	0	3	1	0	.077	.077	0	0	C-8
1976 LA N	6	3	0	0	0	0	0.0	0	0	0	2	0	.000	.000	0	0	C-6
3 yrs.	16	21	2	0	0	0	0.0	0	0	3	3	0	.095	.095	1	1	C-15

Tom Robson

ROBSON, THOMAS JAMES
B. Jan. 15, 1946, Rochester, N. Y.

BR TR 6'3" 215 lbs.

	G	AB	H	2B	3B	HR	HR %	R	RBI	BB	SO	SB	BA	SA	AB	H	G by POS
1974 TEX A	6	13	3	1	0	0	0.0	2	2	4	3	0	.231	.308	0	0	DH-5, 1B-1
1975	17	35	7	0	0	0	0.0	3	2	1	3	0	.200	.200	8	2	1B-5, DH-4
2 yrs.	23	48	10	1	0	0	0.0	5	4	5	6	0	.208	.229	8	2	DH-9, 1B-6

Mickey Rocco

ROCCO, MICHAEL DOMINICK
B. Mar. 2, 1916, St. Paul, Minn.

BL TL 5'11" 188 lbs.

	G	AB	H	2B	3B	HR	HR %	R	RBI	BB	SO	SB	BA	SA	AB	H	G by POS
1943 CLE A	108	405	97	14	4	5	1.2	43	46	51	40	1	.240	.331	0	0	1B-108
1944	155	653	174	29	7	13	2.0	87	70	56	51	4	.266	.392	0	0	1B-155
1945	143	565	149	28	6	10	1.8	81	56	52	40	0	.264	.388	2	0	1B-141
1946	34	98	24	2	0	2	2.0	8	14	15	15	1	.245	.327	6	1	1B-27
4 yrs.	440	1721	444	73	17	30	1.7	219	186	174	146	6	.258	.372	8	1	1B-431

Jack Roche

ROCHE, JOHN JOSEPH (Red)
B. Nov. 22, 1890, Los Angeles, Calif.

BR TR 6'1" 178 lbs.

	G	AB	H	2B	3B	HR	HR %	R	RBI	BB	SO	SB	BA	SA	AB	H	G by POS
1914 STL N	12	9	6	2	1	0	0.0	1	3	0	1	1	.667	1.111	6	5	C-9
1915	46	39	8	0	1	0	0.0	2	6	4	8	1	.205	.256	37	8	C-4
1917	1	1	0	0	0	0	0.0	0	0	0	0	0	.000	.000	0	0	C-1
3 yrs.	59	49	14	2	2	0	0.0	3	9	4	9	2	.286	.408	43	13	C-14

Ben Rochefort

ROCHEFORT, BENNETT HAROLD
Also known as Bennett Harold Rochefort Gilbert.
B. Aug. 15, 1896, Camden, N. J.   D. Apr. 2, 1981, Red Bank, N. J.

BL TR 6'2" 185 lbs.

	G	AB	H	2B	3B	HR	HR %	R	RBI	BB	SO	SB	BA	SA	AB	H	G by POS
1914 PHI A	1	2	1	0	0	0	0.0	0	0	0	1	0	.500	.500	0	0	1B-1

Lou Rochelli

ROCHELLI, LOUIS JOSEPH
B. Jan. 11, 1919, Williamson, Ill.

BR TR 6'1" 175 lbs.

	G	AB	H	2B	3B	HR	HR %	R	RBI	BB	SO	SB	BA	SA	AB	H	G by POS
1944 BKN N	5	17	3	0	1	0	0.0	0	2	2	6	0	.176	.294	0	0	SS-5

Les Rock

ROCK, LESTER HENRY
Born Lester Henry Schwarzrock.
B. Aug. 19, 1912, Springfield, Minn.

BL TR 6'2" 184 lbs.

	G	AB	H	2B	3B	HR	HR %	R	RBI	BB	SO	SB	BA	SA	AB	H	G by POS
1936 CHI A	2	1	0	0	0	0	0.0	0	0	0	0	0	.000	.000	0	0	1B-2

Ike Rockenfeld

ROCKENFELD, ISAAC B.
B. Nov. 3, 1876, Omaha, Neb.   D. Feb. 21, 1927, San Diego, Calif.

BR TR

	G	AB	H	2B	3B	HR	HR %	R	RBI	BB	SO	SB	BA	SA	AB	H	G by POS
1905 STL A	95	322	70	12	0	0	0.0	40	16	46		11	.217	.255	0	0	2B-95
1906	27	89	21	4	0	0	0.0	3	8	1		0	.236	.281	1	1	2B-26
2 yrs.	122	411	91	16	0	0	0.0	43	24	47		11	.221	.260	1	1	2B-121

Pat Rockett

ROCKETT, PATRICK EDWARD
B. Jan. 9, 1955, San Antonio, Tex.

BR TR 5'11" 170 lbs.

	G	AB	H	2B	3B	HR	HR %	R	RBI	BB	SO	SB	BA	SA	AB	H	G by POS
1976 ATL N	4	5	1	0	0	0	0.0	0	0	0	1	0	.200	.200	3	0	SS-2
1977	93	264	67	10	0	1	0.4	27	24	27	32	1	.254	.303	4	2	SS-84
1978	55	142	20	2	0	0	0.0	6	4	13	12	1	.141	.155	1	0	SS-51
3 yrs.	152	411	88	12	0	1	0.2	33	28	40	45	2	.214	.251	8	2	SS-137

Andre Rodgers

RODGERS, KENNETH ANDRE IAN (Andy)
B. Dec. 2, 1934, Nassau, Bahamas

BR TR 6'3" 200 lbs.

	G	AB	H	2B	3B	HR	HR %	R	RBI	BB	SO	SB	BA	SA	AB	H	G by POS
1957 NY N	32	86	21	2	1	3	3.5	8	9	9	21	0	.244	.395	2	0	SS-20, 3B-8
1958 SF N	22	63	13	3	1	2	3.2	7	11	4	14	0	.206	.381	4	1	SS-18
1959	71	228	57	12	1	6	2.6	32	24	32	50	2	.250	.390	2	1	SS-66
1960	81	217	53	8	5	2	0.9	22	22	24	44	1	.244	.355	16	7	SS-41, 3B-21, 1B-6, OF-2
1961 CHI N	73	214	57	17	0	6	2.8	27	23	25	54	1	.266	.430	7	1	1B-42, SS-24, OF-2, 2B-1
1962	138	461	128	20	8	5	1.1	40	44	44	93	5	.278	.388	6	0	SS-133, 1B-1
1963	150	516	118	17	4	5	1.0	51	33	65	90	5	.229	.306	0	0	SS-150
1964	129	448	107	17	3	12	2.7	50	46	53	88	5	.239	.371	3	0	SS-126
1965 PIT N	75	178	51	12	0	2	1.1	17	25	18	28	2	.287	.388	26	8	SS-33, 3B-15, 1B-6, 2B-1
1966	36	49	9	1	0	0	0.0	6	4	8	7	0	.184	.204	23	6	3B-5, OF-3, 3B-3, 1B-2
1967	47	61	14	3	0	2	3.3	8	4	8	18	1	.230	.377	22	4	1B-9, 3B-5, SS-3, 2B-2
11 yrs.	854	2521	628	112	23	45	1.8	268	245	290	507	22	.249	.365	111	28	SS-619, 1B-66, 3B-52, OF-7, 2B-4

Bill Rodgers

RODGERS, WILBUR KINCAID (Raw Meat Bill)
B. Apr. 18, 1887, Amberly Village, Ohio   D. Dec. 24, 1978, Goliad, Tex.

BL TR 5'8½" 170 lbs.

	G	AB	H	2B	3B	HR	HR %	R	RBI	BB	SO	SB	BA	SA	AB	H	G by POS
1915 3 teams	CLE A (16G – .311)			BOS A (11G – .000)			CIN N (72G – .239)										
" total	99	264	65	15	4	0	0.0	30	19	22	38	11	.246	.333	8	2	2B-75, SS-6, OF-1, 3B-1
1916 CIN N	3	4	0	0	0	0	0.0	0	0	0	2	0	.000	.000	1	0	SS-1
2 yrs.	102	268	65	15	4	0	0.0	30	19	22	40	11	.243	.328	9	2	2B-75, SS-7, OF-1, 3B-1

	G	AB	H	2B	3B	HR	HR %	R	RBI	BB	SO	SB	BA	SA	Pinch Hit AB	Pinch Hit H	G by POS

Bill Rodgers

RODGERS, WILLIAM SHERMAN
B. Dec. 5, 1922, Harrisburg, Pa.

BL TL 6' 162 lbs.

	G	AB	H	2B	3B	HR	HR %	R	RBI	BB	SO	SB	BA	SA	PH AB	PH H	G by POS
1944 PIT N	2	4	1	0	0	0	0.0	1	0	0	1	0	.250	.250	0	0	OF-1
1945	1	1	1	0	0	0	0.0	0	0	0	0	0	1.000	1.000	1	1	
2 yrs.	3	5	2	0	0	0	0.0	1	0	0	1	0	.400	.400	1	1	OF-1

Buck Rodgers

RODGERS, ROBERT LEROY
B. Aug. 16, 1938, Delaware, Ohio
Manager 1980-82.

BB TR 6'2" 190 lbs.

BR 1968

	G	AB	H	2B	3B	HR	HR %	R	RBI	BB	SO	SB	BA	SA	PH AB	PH H	G by POS
1961 LA A	16	56	18	2	0	2	3.6	8	13	1	6	0	.321	.464	3	2	C-14
1962	155	565	146	34	6	6	1.1	65	61	45	68	1	.258	.372	11	1	C-150
1963	100	300	70	6	0	4	1.3	24	23	29	35	2	.233	.293	15	5	C-85
1964	148	514	125	18	3	4	0.8	38	54	40	71	4	.243	.313	5	2	C-146
1965 CAL A	132	411	86	14	3	1	0.2	33	32	35	61	4	.209	.265	8	2	C-128
1966	133	454	107	20	3	7	1.5	45	48	29	57	3	.236	.339	7	3	C-133
1967	139	429	94	13	3	6	1.4	29	41	34	55	1	.219	.305	6	0	C-134, OF-1
1968	91	258	49	6	0	1	0.4	13	14	16	48	2	.190	.225	7	0	C-87
1969	18	46	9	1	0	0	0.0	4	2	5	8	0	.196	.217	0	0	C-18
9 yrs.	932	3033	704	114	18	31	1.0	259	288	234	409	17	.232	.312	62	15	C-895, OF-1

Eric Rodin

RODIN, ERIC CHAPMAN
B. Feb. 5, 1930, Orange, N. J.

BR TR 6'2" 215 lbs.

	G	AB	H	2B	3B	HR	HR %	R	RBI	BB	SO	SB	BA	SA	PH AB	PH H	G by POS
1954 NY N	5	6	0	0	0	0	0.0	0	0	0	2	0	.000	.000	3	0	OF-3

Aurelio Rodriguez

RODRIGUEZ, AURELIO ITUARTE (Leo)
B. Dec. 28, 1947, Cananea Sonora, Mexico

BR TR 5'10" 180 lbs.

	G	AB	H	2B	3B	HR	HR %	R	RBI	BB	SO	SB	BA	SA	PH AB	PH H	G by POS
1967 CAL A	29	130	31	3	1	1	0.8	14	8	2	21	1	.238	.300	0	0	3B-29
1968	76	223	54	10	1	1	0.4	14	16	17	35	0	.242	.309	3	2	3B-70, 2B-2
1969	159	561	130	17	2	7	1.2	47	49	32	88	5	.232	.307	0	0	3B-159
1970 2 teams	CAL A (17G – .270)							WAS	A (142G – .247)								
" total	159	610	152	33	7	19	3.1	70	83	40	87	15	.249	.420	0	0	3B-153, SS-7
1971 DET A	154	604	153	30	7	15	2.5	68	39	27	93	4	.253	.401	3	1	3B-153, SS-1
1972	153	601	142	23	5	13	2.2	65	56	28	104	2	.236	.356	1	0	3B-153, SS-2
1973	160	555	123	27	3	9	1.6	46	58	31	85	3	.222	.330	0	0	3B-160, SS-1
1974	159	571	127	23	5	5	0.9	54	49	26	70	2	.222	.306	0	0	3B-159
1975	151	507	124	20	6	13	2.6	47	60	30	63	1	.245	.385	0	0	3B-151
1976	128	480	115	13	2	8	1.7	40	50	19	61	0	.240	.325	0	0	3B-128
1977	96	306	67	14	1	10	3.3	30	32	16	36	1	.219	.369	10	1	3B-95, SS-1
1978	134	385	102	25	2	7	1.8	40	43	19	37	0	.265	.395	20	7	3B-131
1979	106	343	87	18	0	5	1.5	27	36	11	40	0	.254	.350	3	0	3B-106, 1B-1
1980 2 teams	SD	N (89G – .200)						NY	A (52G – .220)								
" total	141	339	71	13	3	5	1.5	21	27	13	61	1	.209	.310	6	0	3B-137, 2B-6, SS-2
1981 NY A	27	52	18	2	0	2	3.8	4	8	2	10	0	.346	.500	1	1	3B-20, 2B-3, DH-2, 1B-1
1982 CHI A	118	257	62	15	1	3	1.2	24	31	11	35	0	.241	.342	1	0	3B-112, 2B-3, SS-2
1983 2 teams	BAL	A (45G – .119)						CHI	A (22G – .200)								
" total	67	87	12	1	0	1	1.1	3	9	0	16	0	.138	.184	0	0	3B-67
17 yrs.	2017	6611	1570	287	46	124	1.9	612	648	324	942	35	.237	.351	48	12	3B-1983, SS-16, 2B-14, DH-2, 1B-2

LEAGUE CHAMPIONSHIP SERIES

	G	AB	H	2B	3B	HR	HR %	R	RBI	BB	SO	SB	BA	SA	PH AB	PH H	G by POS
1972 DET A	5	16	0	0	0	0	0.0	0	0	2	0	0	.000	.000	0	0	3B-5
1980 NY A	2	6	2	1	0	0	0.0	0	0	0	0	0	.333	.500	0	0	3B-1
1981	1	0	0	0	0	0	–	0	0	0	0	0	–	–	0	0	3B-1
1983 CHI A	2	0	0	0	0	0	–	0	0	0	0	0	–	–	0	0	3B-2
4 yrs.	10	22	2	1	0	0	0.0	0	0	2	2	0	.091	.136	0	0	3B-10

WORLD SERIES

	G	AB	H	2B	3B	HR	HR %	R	RBI	BB	SO	SB	BA	SA	PH AB	PH H	G by POS
1981 NY A	4	12	5	0	0	0	0.0	1	0	1	2	0	.417	.417	0	0	3B-3

Eduardo Rodriguez

RODRIGUEZ, EDWIN
Also known as Edwin Morales.
B. Aug. 14, 1960, Ponce, Puerto Rico

BR TR 5'11" 172 lbs.

	G	AB	H	2B	3B	HR	HR %	R	RBI	BB	SO	SB	BA	SA	PH AB	PH H	G by POS
1982 NY A	3	9	3	0	0	0	0.0	2	1	1	1	0	.333	.333	0	0	2B-3
1983 SD N	7	12	2	1	0	0	0.0	1	0	1	3	0	.167	.250	0	0	2B-5, SS-2, 3B-1
2 yrs.	10	21	5	1	0	0	0.0	3	1	2	4	0	.238	.286	0	0	2B-8, SS-2, 3B-1

Ellie Rodriguez

RODRIGUEZ, ELISIO
B. May 24, 1946, Fajardo, Puerto Rico

BR TR 5'11" 185 lbs.

	G	AB	H	2B	3B	HR	HR %	R	RBI	BB	SO	SB	BA	SA	PH AB	PH H	G by POS
1968 NY A	9	24	5	0	0	0	0.0	1	1	3	3	0	.208	.208	0	0	C-9
1969 KC A	95	267	63	10	2	2	0.7	27	20	31	26	3	.236	.296	6	1	C-90
1970	80	231	52	8	2	1	0.4	25	15	27	35	2	.225	.290	5	2	C-75
1971 MIL A	115	319	67	10	1	1	0.3	28	30	41	51	1	.210	.257	6	1	C-114
1972	116	355	101	14	2	2	0.6	31	35	52	43	1	.285	.352	3	1	C-114
1973	94	290	78	8	1	0	0.0	30	30	41	28	4	.269	.303	6	1	C-75, DH-14
1974 CAL A	140	395	100	20	0	7	1.8	48	36	69	56	4	.253	.357	4	3	C-137, DH-1
1975	90	226	53	6	0	3	1.3	20	27	49	37	2	.235	.301	0	0	C-90
1976 LA N	36	66	14	0	0	0	0.0	10	9	19	12	0	.212	.212	1	1	C-33
9 yrs.	775	2173	533	76	6	16	0.7	220	203	332	291	17	.245	.308	31	10	C-737, DH-15

Hec Rodriguez

RODRIGUEZ, ANTONIO HECTOR
B. June 13, 1920, Villa Alquizar, Cuba

BR TR 5'8" 165 lbs.

	G	AB	H	2B	3B	HR	HR %	R	RBI	BB	SO	SB	BA	SA	PH AB	PH H	G by POS
1952 CHI A	124	407	108	14	0	1	0.2	55	40	47	22	7	.265	.307	8	2	3B-113

Jose Rodriguez

RODRIGUEZ, JOSE
B. Feb. 23, 1894, Havana, Cuba   D. Mar. 23, 1948, Havana, Cuba

BR TR 6' 170 lbs.

	G	AB	H	2B	3B	HR	HR %	R	RBI	BB	SO	SB	BA	SA	PH AB	PH H	G by POS
1916 NY N	1	0	0	0	0	0	–	0	0	0	0	0	–	–	0	0	
1917	7	20	4	0	1	0	0.0	2	2	2	1	2	.200	.300	0	0	1B-7
1918	50	125	20	0	2	0	0.0	15	15	12	3	6	.160	.192	2	0	2B-40, 1B-8, 3B-2
3 yrs.	58	145	24	0	3	0	0.0	17	17	14	4	8	.166	.207	2	0	2B-40, 1B-15, 3B-2

	G	AB	H	2B	3B	HR	HR %	R	RBI	BB	SO	SB	BA	SA	Pinch Hit AB	Pinch Hit H	G by POS

Vic Rodriguez

RODRIGUEZ, VICTOR M.
Also known as Victor M. Rivera.
B. July 14, 1961, New York, N. Y.

BR TR 5'11" 160 lbs.

	G	AB	H	2B	3B	HR	HR%	R	RBI	BB	SO	SB	BA	SA	PH AB	PH H	G by POS
1984 BAL A	11	17	7	3	0	0	0.0	4	2	0	2	0	.412	.588	0	0	2B-7, DH-3

Gary Roenicke

ROENICKE, GARY STEVEN
Brother of Ron Roenicke.
B. Dec. 5, 1954, Covina, Calif.

BR TR 6'3" 205 lbs.

	G	AB	H	2B	3B	HR	HR%	R	RBI	BB	SO	SB	BA	SA	PH AB	PH H	G by POS
1976 MON N	29	90	20	3	1	2	2.2	9	5	4	18	0	.222	.344	4	1	OF-25
1978 BAL A	27	58	15	3	0	3	5.2	5	15	8	3	0	.259	.466	6	1	OF-20
1979	133	376	98	16	1	25	6.6	60	64	61	74	1	.261	.508	2	0	OF-130, DH-2
1980	118	297	71	13	0	10	3.4	40	28	41	49	2	.239	.384	12	6	OF-113
1981	85	219	59	16	0	3	1.4	31	20	23	29	1	.269	.384	16	3	OF-83
1982	137	393	106	25	1	21	5.3	58	74	70	73	6	.270	.499	18	5	OF-125, 1B-10
1983	115	323	84	13	0	19	5.9	45	64	30	35	2	.260	.477	38	8	OF-100, 1B-7, DH-2, 3B-2
1984	121	326	73	19	1	10	3.1	36	44	58	43	1	.224	.380	21	5	OF-117
8 yrs.	765	2082	526	108	4	93	4.5	284	314	295	324	13	.253	.442	117	29	OF-713, 1B-17, DH-4, 3B-2

LEAGUE CHAMPIONSHIP SERIES

	G	AB	H	2B	3B	HR	HR%	R	RBI	BB	SO	SB	BA	SA	PH AB	PH H	G by POS
1979 BAL A	2	5	1	0	0	0	0.0	1	1	0	0	0	.200	.200	1	0	OF-2
1983	3	4	3	1	0	1	25.0	4	4	5	0	0	.750	1.750	0	0	OF-3
2 yrs.	5	9	4	1	0	1	11.1	5	5	5	0	0	.444	.889	1	0	OF-5

WORLD SERIES

	G	AB	H	2B	3B	HR	HR%	R	RBI	BB	SO	SB	BA	SA	PH AB	PH H	G by POS
1979 BAL A	6	16	2	1	0	0	0.0	1	0	0	6	0	.125	.188	1	0	OF-5
1983	3	7	0	0	0	0	0.0	0	0	0	2	0	.000	.000	2	0	OF-2
2 yrs.	9	23	2	1	0	0	0.0	1	0	0	8	0	.087	.130	3	0	OF-7

Ron Roenicke

ROENICKE, RONALD JON
Brother of Gary Roenicke.
B. Aug. 19, 1956, Covina, Calif.

BB TL 6' 180 lbs.

	G	AB	H	2B	3B	HR	HR%	R	RBI	BB	SO	SB	BA	SA	PH AB	PH H	G by POS
1981 LA N	22	47	11	0	0	0	0.0	6	0	6	8	1	.234	.234	4	0	OF-20
1982	109	143	37	8	0	1	0.7	18	12	21	32	5	.259	.336	44	13	OF-72
1983 2 teams					LA	N (81G –	.221)		SEA	A (59G –	.253)						
" total	140	343	82	16	0	6	1.7	35	35	47	48	9	.239	.338	24	5	OF-116, 1B-6, DH-1
1984 SD N	12	20	6	1	0	1	5.0	4	2	2	5	0	.300	.500	2	0	OF-10
4 yrs.	283	553	136	25	0	8	1.4	63	49	76	93	15	.246	.335	74	18	OF-218, 1B-6, DH-1

WORLD SERIES

	G	AB	H	2B	3B	HR	HR%	R	RBI	BB	SO	SB	BA	SA	PH AB	PH H	G by POS
1984 SD N	2	0	0	0	0	0	–	0	0	0	0	0	–	–	0	0	OF-1

Oscar Roettger

ROETTGER, OSCAR FREDERICK LOUIS
Brother of Wally Roettger.
B. Feb. 19, 1900, St. Louis, Mo.

BR TR 6' 170 lbs.

	G	AB	H	2B	3B	HR	HR%	R	RBI	BB	SO	SB	BA	SA	PH AB	PH H	G by POS
1923 NY A	5	2	0	0	0	0	0.0	0	0	0	0	0	.000	.000	0	0	P-5
1924	1	0	0	0	0	0	–	0	0	0	0	0	–	–	0	0	P-1
1927 BKN N	5	4	0	0	0	0	0.0	0	0	1	1	0	.000	.000	2	0	OF-1
1932 PHI A	26	60	14	1	0	0	0.0	7	6	5	4	0	.233	.250	10	0	1B-15
4 yrs.	37	66	14	1	0	0	0.0	7	6	6	5	0	.212	.227	12	0	1B-15, P-6, OF-1

Wally Roettger

ROETTGER, WALTER HENRY
Brother of Oscar Roettger.
B. Aug. 28, 1902, St. Louis, Mo.   D. Sept. 14, 1951, Champaign, Ill.

BR TR 6'1½" 190 lbs.

	G	AB	H	2B	3B	HR	HR%	R	RBI	BB	SO	SB	BA	SA	PH AB	PH H	G by POS
1927 STL N	5	1	0	0	0	0	0.0	0	0	1	0	0	.000	.000	0	0	OF-3
1928	68	261	89	17	4	6	2.3	27	44	10	22	2	.341	.506	2	0	OF-66
1929	79	269	68	11	3	3	1.1	27	42	13	27	0	.253	.349	10	1	OF-69
1930 NY A	121	420	119	15	5	5	1.2	51	51	25	29	1	.283	.379	7	3	OF-114
1931 2 teams					CIN	N (44G –	.351)		STL	N (45G –	.285)						
" total	89	336	108	23	6	1	0.3	41	37	16	23	1	.321	.435	3	1	OF-86
1932 CIN N	106	347	96	18	3	3	0.9	26	43	23	24	0	.277	.372	10	3	OF-94
1933	84	209	50	7	1	1	0.5	13	17	8	10	0	.239	.297	28	8	OF-55
1934 PIT N	47	106	26	5	1	0	0.0	7	11	3	8	0	.245	.311	23	7	OF-23
8 yrs.	599	1949	556	96	23	19	1.0	192	245	99	143	4	.285	.387	83	23	OF-510

WORLD SERIES

	G	AB	H	2B	3B	HR	HR%	R	RBI	BB	SO	SB	BA	SA	PH AB	PH H	G by POS
1931 STL N	3	14	4	1	0	0	0.0	1	0	0	3	0	.286	.357	0	0	OF-3

Ed Roetz

ROETZ, EDWARD BERNARD
B. Aug. 6, 1905, Philadelphia, Pa.   D. Mar. 16, 1965, Philadelphia, Pa.

BR TR 5'10" 160 lbs.

	G	AB	H	2B	3B	HR	HR%	R	RBI	BB	SO	SB	BA	SA	PH AB	PH H	G by POS
1929 STL A	16	45	11	4	1	0	0.0	7	5	4	6	0	.244	.378	0	0	SS-8, 1B-5, 2B-2, 3B-1

Billy Rogell

ROGELL, WILLIAM GEORGE
B. Nov. 24, 1904, Springfield, Ill.

BB TR 5'10½" 163 lbs.

	G	AB	H	2B	3B	HR	HR%	R	RBI	BB	SO	SB	BA	SA	PH AB	PH H	G by POS
1925 BOS A	58	169	33	5	1	0	0.0	12	17	11	17	0	.195	.237	2	0	2B-49, SS-6
1927	82	207	55	14	6	2	1.0	35	28	24	28	3	.266	.420	15	3	3B-53, OF-2, 2B-2
1928	102	296	69	10	4	0	0.0	33	29	22	47	2	.233	.294	7	1	SS-67, 2B-22, OF-6, 3B-3
1930 DET A	54	144	24	4	2	0	0.0	20	9	15	23	1	.167	.222	2	0	SS-33, 3B-13, OF-1
1931	48	185	56	12	3	2	1.1	21	24	24	17	8	.303	.432	0	0	SS-48
1932	143	554	150	29	6	9	1.6	88	61	50	38	14	.271	.394	0	0	SS-139, 3B-4
1933	155	587	173	42	11	0	0.0	67	57	79	33	6	.295	.404	0	0	SS-155
1934	154	592	175	32	8	3	0.5	114	100	74	36	13	.296	.392	0	0	SS-154
1935	150	560	154	23	11	6	1.1	88	71	80	29	3	.275	.388	0	0	SS-150
1936	146	585	160	27	5	6	1.0	85	68	73	41	14	.274	.368	1	0	SS-146, 3B-1
1937	146	536	148	30	7	8	1.5	85	64	83	48	5	.276	.403	0	0	SS-146
1938	136	501	130	22	8	3	0.6	76	55	86	37	9	.259	.353	2	0	SS-134
1939	74	174	40	6	3	2	1.1	24	23	26	14	3	.230	.333	3	0	SS-43, 3B-21, 2B-2
1940 CHI N	33	59	8	0	0	1	1.7	7	3	2	8	1	.136	.186	6	1	SS-14, 3B-9, 2B-3
14 yrs.	1481	5149	1375	256	75	42	0.8	755	609	649	416	82	.267	.370	38	5	SS-1235, 3B-104, 2B-78, OF-9

	G	AB	H	2B	3B	HR	HR %	R	RBI	BB	SO	SB	BA	SA	Pinch Hit AB	Pinch Hit H	G by POS

Billy Rogell continued

WORLD SERIES

	G	AB	H	2B	3B	HR	HR %	R	RBI	BB	SO	SB	BA	SA	PH AB	PH H	G by POS
1934 DET A	7	29	8	1	0	0	0.0	3	4	1	4	0	.276	.310	0	0	SS-7
1935	6	24	7	2	0	0	0.0	1	1	2	5	0	.292	.375	0	0	SS-6
2 yrs.	13	53	15	3	0	0	0.0	4	5	3	9	0	.283	.340	0	0	SS-13

Emmett Rogers

ROGERS, EMMETT
B. 1865, Rome, N. Y.   Deceased.

5'10"   165 lbs.

	G	AB	H	2B	3B	HR	HR %	R	RBI	BB	SO	SB	BA	SA	PH AB	PH H	G by POS
1890 TOL AA	35	110	19	3	3	0	0.0	18		14		2	.173	.255	0	0	C-34, OF-1

Jay Rogers

ROGERS, JAY LOUIS
B. Aug. 3, 1888, Sandusky, N. Y.   D. July 1, 1964, Carlisle, Pa.

BR TR 5'11½" 178 lbs.

	G	AB	H	2B	3B	HR	HR %	R	RBI	BB	SO	SB	BA	SA	PH AB	PH H	G by POS
1914 NY A	5	8	0	0	0	0	0.0	0	0	0	4	0	.000	.000	1	0	C-4

Jim Rogers

ROGERS, JAMES F.
B. Apr. 9, 1872, Hartford, Conn.   D. Jan. 21, 1900, Bridgeport, Conn.
Manager 1897.

5'7½"   180 lbs.

	G	AB	H	2B	3B	HR	HR %	R	RBI	BB	SO	SB	BA	SA	PH AB	PH H	G by POS
1896 2 teams	WAS N (38G – .279)					LOU N (72G – .259)											
" total	110	444	118	14	10	1	0.2	60	68	25	23	16	.266	.349	0	0	1B-60, 3B-32, SS-12, 2B-6, OF-1
1897 LOU N	41	150	22	3	2	2	1.3	22	22	22		4	.147	.233	0	0	2B-39, 1B-3
2 yrs.	151	594	140	17	12	3	0.5	82	90	47	23	20	.236	.320	0	0	1B-63, 2B-45, 3B-32, SS-12, OF-1

Packy Rogers

ROGERS, STANLEY FRANK
Born Stanley Frank Hazinski.
B. Apr. 26, 1913, Swoyersville, Pa.

BR TR 5'8"   175 lbs.

	G	AB	H	2B	3B	HR	HR %	R	RBI	BB	SO	SB	BA	SA	PH AB	PH H	G by POS
1938 BKN N	23	37	7	1	1	0	0.0	3	5	6	6	0	.189	.270	2	0	SS-9, 3B-8, 2B-3, OF-1

Mike Rogodzinski

ROGODZINSKI, MICHAEL GEORGE
B. Feb. 22, 1948, Evanston, Ill.

BL TR 6'   185 lbs.

	G	AB	H	2B	3B	HR	HR %	R	RBI	BB	SO	SB	BA	SA	PH AB	PH H	G by POS
1973 PHI N	66	80	19	3	0	2	2.5	13	7	12	19	0	.238	.350	47	16	OF-16
1974	17	15	1	0	0	0	0.0	1	1	2	3	0	.067	.067	15	1	OF-1
1975	16	19	5	1	0	0	0.0	3	4	3	2	0	.263	.316	11	4	OF-2
3 yrs.	99	114	25	4	0	2	1.8	17	12	17	24	0	.219	.307	73	21	OF-19

George Rohe

ROHE, GEORGE ANTHONY
B. Sept. 15, 1875, Cincinnati, Ohio   D. June 10, 1957, Cincinnati, Ohio

BR TR 5'9"   165 lbs.

	G	AB	H	2B	3B	HR	HR %	R	RBI	BB	SO	SB	BA	SA	PH AB	PH H	G by POS
1901 BAL A	14	36	10	2	0	0	0.0	7	4	5		1	.278	.333	1	0	1B-8, 3B-6
1905 CHI A	34	113	24	1	0	1	0.9	14	12	12		2	.212	.248	1	0	3B-17, 2B-16
1906	75	225	58	5	1	0	0.0	14	25	16		8	.258	.289	12	2	3B-57, 2B-5, OF-1
1907	144	494	105	11	2	2	0.4	46	51	39		16	.213	.255	2	0	3B-76, 2B-39, SS-30
4 yrs.	267	868	197	19	3	3	0.3	81	92	72		27	.227	.266	16	2	3B-156, 2B-60, SS-30, 1B-8, OF-1

WORLD SERIES

	G	AB	H	2B	3B	HR	HR %	R	RBI	BB	SO	SB	BA	SA	PH AB	PH H	G by POS
1906 CHI A	6	21	7	1	2	0	0.0	2	4	3	1	2	.333	.571	0	0	3B-6

Dan Rohn

ROHN, DANIEL JAY
B. Jan. 10, 1956, Alpena, Miss.

BL TR 5'8"   165 lbs.

	G	AB	H	2B	3B	HR	HR %	R	RBI	BB	SO	SB	BA	SA	PH AB	PH H	G by POS
1983 CHI N	23	31	12	3	0	0	0.0	3	6	2	2	1	.387	.613	17	6	2B-6, SS-1
1984	25	31	4	0	0	1	3.2	1	3	1	6	0	.129	.226	13	2	3B-7, SS-5, 2B-5
2 yrs.	48	62	16	3	0	1	1.6	4	9	3	8	1	.258	.419	30	8	2B-11, 3B-7, SS-6

Ray Rohwer

ROHWER, RAY
B. June 5, 1895, Dixon, Calif.

BL TL 5'10"   155 lbs.

	G	AB	H	2B	3B	HR	HR %	R	RBI	BB	SO	SB	BA	SA	PH AB	PH H	G by POS
1921 PIT N	30	40	10	3	2	0	0.0	6	6	4	8	0	.250	.425	18	2	OF-10
1922	53	129	38	6	3	3	2.3	19	22	10	17	1	.295	.457	19	5	OF-30
2 yrs.	83	169	48	9	5	3	1.8	25	28	14	25	1	.284	.450	37	7	OF-40

Tony Roig

ROIG, ANTON AMBROSE
B. Dec. 23, 1928, New Orleans, La.

BR TR 6'2"   188 lbs.

	G	AB	H	2B	3B	HR	HR %	R	RBI	BB	SO	SB	BA	SA	PH AB	PH H	G by POS
1953 WAS A	3	8	1	1	0	0	0.0	0	0	0	1	0	.125	.250	1	1	2B-2
1955	29	57	13	1	1	0	0.0	3	4	2	15	0	.228	.281	3	1	SS-21, 3B-8, 2B-1
1956	44	119	25	5	2	0	0.0	11	7	20	29	2	.210	.286	3	1	2B-30, SS-19
3 yrs.	76	184	39	7	3	0	0.0	14	11	22	45	2	.212	.283	7	3	SS-40, 2B-30, 3B-8

Cookie Rojas

ROJAS, OCTAVIO RIVAS
B. Mar. 6, 1939, Havana, Cuba

BR TR 5'10"   160 lbs.

	G	AB	H	2B	3B	HR	HR %	R	RBI	BB	SO	SB	BA	SA	PH AB	PH H	G by POS
1962 CIN N	39	86	19	2	0	0	0.0	9	6	9	4	1	.221	.244	2	0	2B-30, 3B-1
1963 PHI N	64	77	17	0	1	1	1.3	18	2	3	8	4	.221	.286	8	3	2B-25, OF-1
1964	109	340	99	19	5	2	0.6	58	31	22	17	1	.291	.394	16	1	OF-70, 2B-20, SS-18, 3B-1, C-1
1965	142	521	158	25	3	3	0.6	78	42	42	33	5	.303	.380	11	2	2B-84, OF-55, SS-11, C-2, 1B-1
1966	156	626	168	18	1	6	1.0	77	55	35	46	4	.268	.329	1	0	2B-106, OF-56, SS-2
1967	147	528	137	21	2	4	0.8	60	45	30	58	8	.259	.330	5	2	2B-137, OF-9, C-3, SS-2, 3B-1, P-1
1968	152	621	144	19	0	9	1.4	53	48	16	55	4	.232	.306	2	0	2B-150, C-1
1969	110	391	89	11	1	4	1.0	35	30	23	28	1	.228	.292	11	1	2B-95, OF-2
1970 2 teams	STL N (23G – .106)					KC A (98G – .260)											
" total	121	431	105	13	2	5	1.2	38	30	23	33	3	.244	.302	12	2	2B-107, OF-6, SS-2
1971 KC A	115	414	124	22	2	6	1.4	56	59	39	35	8	.300	.406	2	0	2B-111, SS-2, OF-1
1972	137	487	127	25	0	3	0.6	49	53	41	35	2	.261	.331	2	0	2B-133, 3B-6, SS-2
1973	139	551	152	29	3	6	1.1	78	69	37	38	18	.276	.372	3	2	2B-137
1974	144	542	147	17	1	6	1.1	52	60	30	43	8	.271	.339	8	1	2B-141
1975	120	406	103	18	2	2	0.5	34	37	30	24	4	.254	.323	8	3	2B-117, DH-1

	G	AB	H	2B	3B	HR	HR %	R	RBI	BB	SO	SB	BA	SA	Pinch Hit AB	Pinch Hit H	G by POS

Cookie Rojas continued

	G	AB	H	2B	3B	HR	HR%	R	RBI	BB	SO	SB	BA	SA	AB	H	G by POS
1976	63	132	32	6	0	0	0.0	11	16	8	15	2	.242	.288	28	7	2B-40, DH-9, 3B-6, 1B-1
1977	64	156	39	9	1	0	0.0	8	10	8	17	1	.250	.321	17	3	3B-31, 2B-16, DH-6
16 yrs.	1822	6309	1660	254	25	54	0.9	714	593	396	489	74	.263	.337	136	27	2B-1449, OF-200, 3B-46, SS-39, DH-16, C-7, 1B-2, P-1

LEAGUE CHAMPIONSHIP SERIES

	G	AB	H	2B	3B	HR	HR%	R	RBI	BB	SO	SB	BA	SA	AB	H	G by POS
1976 KC A	4	9	3	0	0	0	0.0	2	1	0	0	1	.333	.333	2	0	2B-4
1977	1	4	1	0	0	0	0.0	0	0	0	1	1	.250	.250	0	0	DH-1
2 yrs.	5	13	4	0	0	0	0.0	2	1	0	1	2	.308	.308	2	0	2B-4, DH-1

Stan Rojek

ROJEK, STANLEY ANDREW   BR TR 5'10" 170 lbs.
B. Apr. 21, 1919, North Tonawanda, N. Y.

	G	AB	H	2B	3B	HR	HR%	R	RBI	BB	SO	SB	BA	SA	AB	H	G by POS
1942 BKN N	1	0	0	0	0	0	—	0	1	0	0	0	—	—	0	0	SS-15, 2B-6, 3B-4
1946	45	47	13	2	1	0	0.0	11	2	4	1	1	.277	.362	10	3	SS-15, 2B-6, 3B-4
1947	32	80	21	0	1	0	0.0	7	7	7	3	1	.263	.288	1	0	SS-17, 3B-9, 2B-7
1948 PIT N	156	641	186	27	5	4	0.6	85	51	61	41	24	.290	.367	0	0	SS-156
1949	144	557	136	19	2	0	0.0	72	31	50	31	4	.244	.285	0	0	SS-144
1950	76	230	59	12	1	0	0.0	28	17	18	13	2	.257	.317	4	0	SS-68, 2B-3
1951 2 teams	PIT	N (8G – .188)		STL	N	(51G –	.274)										
" total	59	202	54	7	3	0	0.0	21	14	10	11	0	.267	.332	0	0	SS-59
1952 STL A	9	7	1	0	0	0	0.0	0	0	2	0	0	.143	.143	2	0	SS-4, 2B-1
8 yrs.	522	1764	470	67	13	4	0.2	225	122	152	100	32	.266	.326	17	3	SS-463, 2B-17, 3B-13

Red Rolfe

ROLFE, ROBERT ABIAL   BL TR 5'11½" 170 lbs.
B. Oct. 17, 1908, Penacook, N. H.   D. July 8, 1969, Gilford, N. H.
Manager 1949-52.

	G	AB	H	2B	3B	HR	HR%	R	RBI	BB	SO	SB	BA	SA	AB	H	G by POS
1931 NY A	1	0	0	0	0	0	—	0	0	0	0	0	—	—	0	0	SS-1
1934	89	279	80	13	2	0	0.0	54	18	26	16	2	.287	.348	15	5	SS-46, 3B-26
1935	149	639	192	33	9	5	0.8	108	67	57	39	7	.300	.404	0	0	3B-136, SS-17
1936	135	568	181	39	15	10	1.8	116	70	68	38	3	.319	.493	0	0	3B-133
1937	154	648	179	34	10	4	0.6	143	62	90	53	4	.276	.378	0	0	3B-154
1938	151	631	196	36	8	10	1.6	132	80	74	44	13	.311	.441	0	0	3B-151
1939	152	648	213	46	10	14	2.2	139	80	81	41	7	.329	.495	0	0	3B-152
1940	139	588	147	26	6	10	1.7	102	53	50	48	4	.250	.366	1	0	3B-138
1941	136	561	148	22	5	8	1.4	106	42	57	38	3	.264	.364	2	0	3B-134
1942	69	265	58	8	2	8	3.0	42	25	23	18	1	.219	.355	8	1	3B-60
10 yrs.	1175	4827	1394	257	67	69	1.4	942	497	526	335	44	.289	.413	26	6	3B-1084, SS-64

WORLD SERIES

	G	AB	H	2B	3B	HR	HR%	R	RBI	BB	SO	SB	BA	SA	AB	H	G by POS
1936 NY A	6	25	10	0	0	0	0.0	5	4	3	1	0	.400	.400	0	0	3B-6
1937	5	20	6	2	1	0	0.0	3	1	3	2	0	.300	.500	0	0	3B-5
1938	4	18	3	0	0	0	0.0	0	1	0	3	1	.167	.167	0	0	3B-4
1939	4	16	2	0	0	0	0.0	2	0	0	0	0	.125	.125	0	0	3B-4
1941	5	20	6	0	0	0	0.0	2	0	2	1	0	.300	.300	0	0	3B-5
1942	4	17	6	2	0	0	0.0	5	0	1	2	0	.353	.471	0	0	3B-4
6 yrs.	28	116	33	4	1	0	0.0	17	6	9	9	1	.284	.336	0	0	3B-28

Ray Rolling

ROLLING, RAYMOND COPELAND   BR TR 5'10½" 160 lbs.
B. Sept. 8, 1886, Martinsburg, Mo.   D. Aug. 25, 1966, St. Paul, Minn.

	G	AB	H	2B	3B	HR	HR%	R	RBI	BB	SO	SB	BA	SA	AB	H	G by POS
1912 STL N	5	15	3	0	0	0	0.0	0	0	0	5	0	.200	.200	0	0	2B-4

Red Rollings

ROLLINGS, WILLIAM RUSSELL   BL TR 5'11" 167 lbs.
B. Mar. 31, 1904, Mobile, Ala.   D. Dec. 31, 1964, Mobile, Ala.

	G	AB	H	2B	3B	HR	HR%	R	RBI	BB	SO	SB	BA	SA	AB	H	G by POS
1927 BOS A	82	184	49	4	1	0	0.0	19	9	12	10	3	.266	.299	14	6	3B-44, 1B-10, 2B-2
1928	50	48	11	3	1	0	0.0	7	9	6	8	0	.229	.333	29	7	1B-5, OF-4, 2B-4, 3B-1
1930 BOS N	52	123	29	6	0	0	0.0	10	10	9	5	2	.236	.285	12	4	3B-28, 2B-10
3 yrs.	184	355	89	13	2	0	0.0	36	28	27	23	5	.251	.299	55	17	3B-73, 2B-16, 1B-15, OF-4

Rich Rollins

ROLLINS, RICHARD JOHN (Red)   BR TR 5'10" 185 lbs.
B. Apr. 16, 1938, Mt. Pleasant, Pa.

	G	AB	H	2B	3B	HR	HR%	R	RBI	BB	SO	SB	BA	SA	AB	H	G by POS
1961 MIN A	13	17	5	1	0	0	0.0	3	3	2	2	0	.294	.353	3	2	2B-5, 3B-4
1962	159	624	186	23	5	16	2.6	96	96	75	62	3	.298	.428	0	0	3B-159, SS-1
1963	136	531	163	23	1	16	3.0	75	61	36	59	2	.307	.444	4	0	3B-132, 2B-1
1964	148	596	161	25	10	12	2.0	87	68	53	80	2	.270	.406	1	0	3B-146
1965	140	469	117	22	1	5	1.1	59	32	37	54	4	.249	.333	13	2	3B-112, 2B-16
1966	90	269	66	7	1	10	3.7	30	40	13	34	0	.245	.390	21	8	3B-65, 2B-2, OF-1
1967	109	339	83	11	2	6	1.8	31	39	27	58	1	.245	.342	14	4	3B-97
1968	93	203	49	5	0	6	3.0	14	30	10	34	3	.241	.355	41	8	3B-56
1969 SEA A	58	187	42	7	0	4	2.1	15	21	7	19	2	.225	.326	14	4	3B-47, SS-1
1970 2 teams	MIL	A (14G – .200)		CLE	A	(42G –	.233)										
" total	56	68	15	1	0	2	2.9	9	9	6	9	0	.221	.324	42	8	3B-12
10 yrs.	1002	3303	887	125	20	77	2.3	419	399	266	411	17	.269	.388	153	36	3B-830, 2B-24, SS-2, OF-1

WORLD SERIES

	G	AB	H	2B	3B	HR	HR%	R	RBI	BB	SO	SB	BA	SA	AB	H	G by POS
1965 MIN A	3	2	0	0	0	0	0.0	0	0	1	0	0	.000	.000	2	0	

Rollinson

ROLLINSON,
Deceased.

	G	AB	H	2B	3B	HR	HR%	R	RBI	BB	SO	SB	BA	SA	AB	H	G by POS
1884 WAS U	1	3	0	0	0	0	0.0	0		0			.000	.000	0	0	C-1

Bill Roman

ROMAN, WILLIAM ANTHONY   BL TL 6'4" 190 lbs.
B. Oct. 11, 1938, Detroit, Mich.

	G	AB	H	2B	3B	HR	HR%	R	RBI	BB	SO	SB	BA	SA	AB	H	G by POS
1964 DET A	3	8	3	0	0	1	12.5	2	1	0	2	0	.375	.750	2	1	1B-2
1965	21	27	2	0	0	0	0.0	0	0	2	7	0	.074	.074	13	2	1B-6
2 yrs.	24	35	5	0	0	1	2.9	2	1	2	9	0	.143	.229	15	3	1B-8

	G	AB	H	2B	3B	HR	HR %	R	RBI	BB	SO	SB	BA	SA	Pinch Hit AB	Pinch Hit H	G by POS

Johnny Romano

ROMANO, JOHN ANTHONY (Honey)
B. Aug. 23, 1934, Hoboken, N. J.   BR TR 5'11"   205 lbs.

	G	AB	H	2B	3B	HR	HR %	R	RBI	BB	SO	SB	BA	SA	AB	H	G by POS
1958 CHI A	4	7	2	0	0	0	0.0	1	1	1	0	0	.286	.286	2	0	C-2
1959	53	126	37	5	1	5	4.0	20	25	23	18	0	.294	.468	13	8	C-38
1960 CLE A	108	316	86	12	2	16	5.1	40	52	37	50	0	.272	.475	11	0	C-99
1961	142	509	152	29	1	21	4.1	76	80	61	60	0	.299	.483	2	0	C-141
1962	135	459	120	19	3	25	5.4	71	81	73	64	0	.261	.479	4	3	C-130
1963	89	255	55	5	2	10	3.9	28	34	38	49	4	.216	.369	16	4	C-71, OF-4
1964	106	352	85	18	1	19	5.4	46	47	51	83	2	.241	.460	10	2	C-96, 1B-1
1965 CHI A	122	356	86	11	0	18	5.1	39	48	59	74	0	.242	.424	8	1	C-111, OF-4, 1B-2
1966	122	329	76	12	0	15	4.6	33	47	58	72	0	.231	.404	16	4	C-102
1967 STL N	24	58	7	1	0	0	0.0	1	2	13	15	1	.121	.138	4	0	C-20
10 yrs.	905	2767	706	112	10	129	4.7	355	417	414	485	7	.255	.443	86	22	C-810, OF-8, 1B-3
WORLD SERIES																	
1959 CHI A	2	1	0	0	0	0	0.0	0	0	0	0	0	.000	.000	1	0	

Ed Romero

ROMERO, EDGARDO
B. Dec. 9, 1957, Santurce, Puerto Rico   BR TR 5'11"   160 lbs.

	G	AB	H	2B	3B	HR	HR %	R	RBI	BB	SO	SB	BA	SA	AB	H	G by POS
1977 MIL A	10	25	7	1	0	0	0.0	4	2	4	3	0	.280	.320	0	0	SS-10
1980	42	104	27	7	0	1	1.0	20	10	9	11	2	.260	.356	1	0	SS-22, 2B-15, 3B-3
1981	44	91	18	3	0	1	1.1	6	10	4	9	0	.198	.264	0	0	SS-22, 2B-18, 3B-3
1982	52	144	36	8	0	1	0.7	18	7	8	16	0	.250	.326	2	1	2B-39, SS-10, 3B-2, OF-1
1983	59	145	46	7	0	1	0.7	17	18	8	8	1	.317	.386	14	6	SS-22, OF-15, DH-5, 3B-5, 2B-3
1984	116	357	90	12	0	1	0.3	36	31	29	25	3	.252	.294	1	0	3B-59, SS-39, 2B-11, 1B-4, DH-2, OF-1
6 yrs.	323	866	224	38	0	5	0.6	101	78	62	72	6	.259	.320	18	7	SS-125, 2B-86, 3B-72, OF-17, DH-7, 1B-4
DIVISIONAL PLAYOFF SERIES																	
1981 MIL A	1	2	1	0	0	0	0.0	1	0	0	1	0	.500	.500	0	0	2B-1

Henri Rondeau

RONDEAU, HENRI JOSEPH
B. May 5, 1887, Danielson, Conn.   D. May 28, 1943, Woonsocket, R. I.   BR TR 5'10½" 175 lbs.

	G	AB	H	2B	3B	HR	HR %	R	RBI	BB	SO	SB	BA	SA	AB	H	G by POS
1913 DET A	35	70	13	2	0	0	0.0	5	5	14	16	1	.186	.214	13	2	C-14, 1B-6
1915 WAS A	14	40	7	0	0	0	0.0	3	4	4	3	1	.175	.175	3	0	OF-11
1916	50	162	36	5	3	1	0.6	20	28	18	18	7	.222	.309	0	0	OF-48
3 yrs.	99	272	56	7	3	1	0.4	28	37	36	37	9	.206	.265	16	2	OF-59, C-14, 1B-6

Gene Roof

ROOF, EUGENE LAWRENCE
Brother of Phil Roof.
B. Jan. 13, 1958, Mayfield, Ky.   BB TR 6'2"   180 lbs.

	G	AB	H	2B	3B	HR	HR %	R	RBI	BB	SO	SB	BA	SA	AB	H	G by POS
1981 STL N	23	60	18	6	0	0	0.0	11	3	12	16	5	.300	.400	2	0	OF-20
1982	11	15	4	0	0	0	0.0	3	2	1	4	2	.267	.267	7	2	OF-5
1983 2 teams	STL	N (6G –	.000)		MON	N	(8G –	.167)									
" total	14	15	2	2	0	0	0.0	3	1	1	3	0	.133	.267	7	1	OF-6
3 yrs.	48	90	24	8	0	0	0.0	17	6	14	23	7	.267	.356	16	3	OF-31

Phil Roof

ROOF, PHILLIP ANTHONY
Brother of Gene Roof.
B. Mar. 5, 1941, Paducah, Ky.   BR TR 6'2"   190 lbs.

	G	AB	H	2B	3B	HR	HR %	R	RBI	BB	SO	SB	BA	SA	AB	H	G by POS
1961 MIL N	1	0	0	0	0	0	–	0	0	0	0	0	–	–	0	0	C-1
1964	1	2	0	0	0	0	0.0	0	0	0	1	0	.000	.000	0	0	C-1
1965 2 teams	CAL	A (9G –	.136)		CLE	A	(43G –	.173)									
" total	52	74	12	1	0	0	0.0	4	3	5	19	0	.162	.176	4	0	C-50
1966 KC A	127	369	77	14	3	7	1.9	33	44	37	95	0	.209	.320	4	0	C-123, 1B-2
1967	114	327	67	14	5	6	1.8	23	24	23	85	4	.205	.333	1	0	C-113
1968 OAK A	34	64	12	0	0	1	1.6	5	2	2	15	1	.188	.234	2	0	C-32
1969	106	247	58	6	1	2	0.8	19	19	33	55	1	.235	.291	1	0	C-106
1970 MIL A	110	321	73	7	1	13	4.0	39	37	32	72	3	.227	.377	3	1	C-107, 1B-1
1971 2 teams	MIL	A (41G –	.193)		MIN	A	(31G –	.241)									
" total	72	201	43	6	1	5	0.5	12	16	16	46	0	.214	.269	5	0	C-68
1972 MIN A	61	146	30	11	1	3	2.1	16	12	6	27	0	.205	.356	5	0	C-61
1973	47	117	23	4	1	1	0.9	10	15	13	27	0	.197	.274	0	0	C-47
1974	44	97	19	1	0	2	2.1	10	13	6	24	0	.196	.268	0	0	C-44
1975	63	126	38	2	0	7	5.6	18	21	9	28	0	.302	.484	0	0	C-63
1976 2 teams	MIN	A (18G –	.217)		CHI	A	(4G –	.111)									
" total	22	55	11	3	0	0	0.0	1	4	2	9	0	.200	.255	5	1	C-16, DH-1
1977 TOR A	3	5	0	0	0	0	0.0	0	0	0	1	0	.000	.000	0	0	C-3
15 yrs.	857	2151	463	69	13	43	2.0	190	210	184	504	11	.215	.319	25	2	C-835, 1B-3, DH-1

George Rooks

ROOKS, GEORGE BRINTON McCLELLAN
Born George Brinton McClellan Ruckser.
B. Oct. 21, 1863, Chicago, Ill.   D. Mar. 11, 1935, Chicago, Ill.   BR TR 5'11"   170 lbs.

	G	AB	H	2B	3B	HR	HR %	R	RBI	BB	SO	SB	BA	SA	AB	H	G by POS
1891 BOS N	5	16	2	0	0	0	0.0	0	4	1	0	0	.125	.125	0	0	OF-5

Frank Rooney

ROONEY, FRANK L.
B. Oct. 12, 1884, Podebrady, Poland   D. Apr. 6, 1977, Bessemer, Mich.

	G	AB	H	2B	3B	HR	HR %	R	RBI	BB	SO	SB	BA	SA	AB	H	G by POS
1914 IND F	12	35	7	0	1	1	2.9	1	8	1	2		.200	.343	3	0	1B-9

Pat Rooney

ROONEY, PATRICK EUGENE
B. Nov. 28, 1957, Chicago, Ill.   BR TR 6'1"   190 lbs.

	G	AB	H	2B	3B	HR	HR %	R	RBI	BB	SO	SB	BA	SA	AB	H	G by POS
1981 MON N	4	5	0	0	0	0	0.0	0	0	0	3	0	.000	.000	2	0	OF-2

Jorge Roque

ROQUE, JORGE
B. Apr. 28, 1950, Ponce, Puerto Rico   BR TR 5'10"   158 lbs.

	G	AB	H	2B	3B	HR	HR %	R	RBI	BB	SO	SB	BA	SA	AB	H	G by POS
1970 STL N	5	1	0	0	0	0	0.0	2	0	0	1	0	.000	.000	1	0	OF-1
1971	3	10	3	0	0	0	0.0	2	1	0	3	1	.300	.300	0	0	OF-3

	G	AB	H	2B	3B	HR	HR %	R	RBI	BB	SO	SB	BA	SA	Pinch Hit AB	Pinch Hit H	G by POS

Jorge Roque continued

	G	AB	H	2B	3B	HR	HR%	R	RBI	BB	SO	SB	BA	SA	AB	H	G by POS
1972	32	67	7	2	1	1	1.5	3	5	6	19	1	.104	.209	6	1	OF-24
1973 MON N	25	61	9	2	0	1	1.6	7	6	4	17	2	.148	.230	0	0	OF-24
4 yrs.	65	139	19	4	1	2	1.4	14	12	10	40	4	.137	.223	7	1	OF-52

Luis Rosado

ROSADO, LUIS (Papo)
Also known as Luis Robles.
B. Dec. 6, 1955, Santurce, Puerto Rico

BR TR 6'   180 lbs.

	G	AB	H	2B	3B	HR	HR%	R	RBI	BB	SO	SB	BA	SA	AB	H	G by POS
1977 NY N	9	24	5	1	0	0	0.0	1	3	1	3	0	.208	.250	1	0	1B-7, C-1
1980	2	4	0	0	0	0	0.0	0	0	0	1	0	.000	.000	1	0	1B-1
2 yrs.	11	28	5	1	0	0	0.0	1	3	1	4	0	.179	.214	2	0	1B-8, C-1

Buddy Rosar

ROSAR, WARREN VINCENT
B. July 3, 1914, Buffalo, N. Y.   D. May 6, 1979

BR TR 5'9"   190 lbs.

	G	AB	H	2B	3B	HR	HR%	R	RBI	BB	SO	SB	BA	SA	AB	H	G by POS
1939 NY A	43	105	29	5	1	0	0.0	18	12	13	10	4	.276	.343	4	3	C-35
1940	73	228	68	11	3	4	1.8	34	37	19	11	7	.298	.425	10	4	C-63
1941	67	209	60	17	2	1	0.5	25	36	22	10	0	.287	.402	6	0	C-60
1942	69	209	48	10	0	2	1.0	18	34	17	20	1	.230	.306	12	3	C-58
1943 CLE A	115	382	108	17	1	1	0.3	53	41	33	12	0	.283	.340	6	1	C-114
1944	99	331	87	9	3	0	0.0	29	30	34	17	1	.263	.308	1	0	C-98
1945 PHI A	92	300	63	12	1	1	0.3	23	25	20	16	2	.210	.267	5	1	C-85
1946	121	424	120	22	2	2	0.5	34	47	36	17	1	.283	.358	4	1	C-117
1947	102	359	93	20	2	1	0.3	40	33	40	13	1	.259	.334	1	0	C-102
1948	90	302	77	13	0	4	1.3	30	41	39	12	0	.255	.338	0	0	C-90
1949	32	95	19	2	0	0	0.0	7	6	16	5	0	.200	.221	1	0	C-31
1950 BOS A	27	84	25	2	0	1	1.2	13	12	7	4	0	.298	.357	2	1	C-25
1951	58	170	39	7	0	1	0.6	11	13	19	14	0	.229	.288	2	0	C-56
13 yrs.	988	3198	836	147	15	18	0.6	335	367	315	161	17	.261	.334	54	14	C-934

WORLD SERIES

	G	AB	H	2B	3B	HR	HR%	R	RBI	BB	SO	SB	BA	SA	AB	H	G by POS
1941 NY A	1	0	0	0	0	0	–	0	0	0	0	0	–	–	0	0	C-1
1942	1	1	1	0	0	0	0.0	0	0	0	0	0	1.000	1.000	1	1	
2 yrs.	2	1	1	0	0	0	0.0	0	0	0	0	0	1.000	1.000	1	1	C-1

Jimmy Rosario

ROSARIO, ANGEL RAMON
B. May 5, 1945, Bayamon, Puerto Rico

BB TR 5'11"   170 lbs.

	G	AB	H	2B	3B	HR	HR%	R	RBI	BB	SO	SB	BA	SA	AB	H	G by POS
1971 SF N	92	192	43	6	1	0	0.0	26	13	33	35	7	.224	.266	11	1	OF-67
1972	7	2	0	0	0	0	0.0	1	0	0	0	0	.000	.000	2	0	OF-1
1976 MIL A	15	37	7	0	0	1	2.7	4	5	3	8	1	.189	.270	1	0	OF-12, DH-2
3 yrs.	114	231	50	6	1	1	0.4	31	18	36	43	8	.216	.264	14	1	OF-80, DH-2

LEAGUE CHAMPIONSHIP SERIES

	G	AB	H	2B	3B	HR	HR%	R	RBI	BB	SO	SB	BA	SA	AB	H	G by POS
1971 SF N	1	0	0	0	0	0	–	0	0	0	0	0	–	–	0	0	

Santiago Rosario

ROSARIO, SANTIAGO
B. July 25, 1939, Guayanilla, Puerto Rico

BL TL 5'11"   165 lbs.

	G	AB	H	2B	3B	HR	HR%	R	RBI	BB	SO	SB	BA	SA	AB	H	G by POS
1965 KC A	81	85	20	3	0	2	2.4	8	8	6	16	0	.235	.341	46	11	1B-31, OF-3

Pete Rose

ROSE, PETER EDWARD (Charlie Hustle)
B. Apr. 14, 1941, Cincinnati, Ohio
Manager 1984.

BB TR 5'11"   192 lbs.

	G	AB	H	2B	3B	HR	HR%	R	RBI	BB	SO	SB	BA	SA	AB	H	G by POS
1963 CIN N	157	623	170	25	9	6	1.0	101	41	55	72	13	.273	.371	0	0	2B-157, OF-1
1964	136	516	139	13	2	4	0.8	64	34	36	51	4	.269	.326	11	2	2B-128
1965	162	670	209	35	11	11	1.6	117	81	69	76	8	.312	.446	0	0	2B-162
1966	156	654	205	38	5	16	2.4	97	70	37	61	4	.313	.460	0	0	2B-140, 3B-16
1967	148	585	176	32	8	12	2.1	86	76	56	66	11	.301	.444	0	0	OF-123, 2B-35
1968	149	626	210	42	6	10	1.6	94	49	56	76	3	.335	.470	0	0	OF-148, 2B-3, 1B-1
1969	156	627	218	33	11	16	2.6	120	82	88	65	7	.348	.512	0	0	OF-156, 2B-2
1970	159	649	205	37	9	15	2.3	120	52	73	64	12	.316	.470	1	0	OF-159
1971	160	632	192	27	4	13	2.1	86	44	68	50	13	.304	.421	2	0	OF-158
1972	154	645	198	31	11	6	0.9	107	57	73	46	10	.307	.417	0	0	OF-154
1973	160	680	230	36	8	5	0.7	115	64	65	42	10	.338	.437	0	0	OF-159
1974	163	652	185	45	7	3	0.5	110	51	106	54	2	.284	.388	0	0	OF-163
1975	162	662	210	47	4	7	1.1	112	74	89	50	0	.317	.432	0	0	3B-137, OF-35
1976	162	665	215	42	6	10	1.5	130	63	86	54	9	.323	.450	3	2	3B-159, OF-1
1977	162	655	204	38	7	9	1.4	95	64	66	42	16	.311	.432	1	0	3B-161
1978	159	655	198	51	3	7	1.1	103	52	62	30	13	.302	.421	0	0	3B-156, OF-7, 1B-2
1979 PHI N	163	628	208	40	5	4	0.6	90	59	95	32	20	.331	.430	0	0	1B-159, 3B-5, 2B-1
1980	162	655	185	42	1	1	0.2	95	64	66	33	12	.282	.354	1	0	1B-162
1981	107	431	140	18	5	0	0.0	73	33	46	26	4	.325	.390	0	0	1B-107
1982	162	634	172	25	4	3	0.5	80	54	66	32	8	.271	.338	0	0	1B-162
1983	151	493	121	14	3	0	0.0	52	45	52	28	7	.245	.286	22	8	1B-112, OF-35
1984 2 teams		MON N	(95G –	.259)		CIN N	(26G –	.365)									
" total	121	374	107	15	2	0	0.0	43	34	40	27	1	.286	.337	27	7	1B-63, OF-28
22 yrs.	3371	13411	4097	726	131	158	1.2	2090	1243	1450	1077	187	.305	.415	68	19	OF-1327, 1B-768, 3B-634, 2B-628
	1st	1st	2nd	2nd				4th									

DIVISIONAL PLAYOFF SERIES

	G	AB	H	2B	3B	HR	HR%	R	RBI	BB	SO	SB	BA	SA	AB	H	G by POS
1981 PHI N	5	20	6	1	0	0	0.0	1	2	2	0	0	.300	.350	0	0	1B-5

LEAGUE CHAMPIONSHIP SERIES

	G	AB	H	2B	3B	HR	HR%	R	RBI	BB	SO	SB	BA	SA	AB	H	G by POS
1970 CIN N	3	13	3	0	0	0	0.0	1	1	0	0	0	.231	.231	0	0	OF-3
1972	5	20	9	4	0	0	0.0	1	2	1	2	0	.450	.650	0	0	OF-5
1973	5	21	8	1	0	2	9.5	3	2	2	2	0	.381	.714	0	0	OF-5
1975	3	14	5	0	0	1	7.1	3	2	0	2	0	.357	.571	0	0	3B-3
1976	3	14	6	2	1	0	0.0	3	2	1	0	0	.429	.714	0	0	3B-3
1980 PHI N	5	20	8	0	0	0	0.0	3	2	5	3	0	.400	.400	0	0	1B-5

	G	AB	H	2B	3B	HR	HR %	R	RBI	BB	SO	SB	BA	SA	Pinch Hit AB	H	G by POS

Pete Rose continued

	G	AB	H	2B	3B	HR	HR%	R	RBI	BB	SO	SB	BA	SA	PH AB	PH H	G by POS
1983	4	16	6	0	0	0	0.0	3	0	1	1	1	.375	.375	0	0	1B-4
7 yrs.	28	118	45	7	1	3	2.5	17	11	10	10	1	.381	.534	0	0	OF-13, 1B-9, 3B-6

WORLD SERIES

	G	AB	H	2B	3B	HR	HR%	R	RBI	BB	SO	SB	BA	SA	PH AB	PH H	G by POS
1970 CIN N	5	20	5	1	0	1	5.0	2	2	2	0	0	.250	.450	0	0	OF-5
1972	7	28	6	0	0	1	3.6	3	2	4	4	1	.214	.321	0	0	OF-7
1975	7	27	10	1	1	0	0.0	3	2	5	1	0	.370	.481	0	0	3B-7
1976	4	16	3	1	0	0	0.0	1	1	2	1	0	.188	.250	0	0	3B-4
1980 PHI N	6	23	6	1	0	0	0.0	2	1	2	2	0	.261	.304	0	0	1B-6
1983	5	16	5	1	0	0	0.0	1	1	1	3	0	.313	.375	1	0	1B-3
6 yrs.	34	130	35	5	2	1.5		12	9	16	12	1	.269	.369	1	0	OF-12, 3B-11, 1B-9

Johnny Roseboro

ROSEBORO, JOHN JUNIOR
B. May 13, 1933, Ashland, Ohio

BL TR 5'11½" 190 lbs.

	G	AB	H	2B	3B	HR	HR%	R	RBI	BB	SO	SB	BA	SA	PH AB	PH H	G by POS
1957 BKN N	35	69	10	2	0	2	2.9	6	6	10	20	0	.145	.261	3	0	C-19, 1B-5
1958 LA N	114	384	104	11	9	14	3.6	52	43	36	56	11	.271	.456	7	1	C-104, OF-5
1959	118	397	92	14	7	10	2.5	39	38	52	69	7	.232	.378	2	0	C-117
1960	103	287	61	15	3	8	2.8	22	42	44	53	7	.213	.369	14	4	C-87, 3B-1, 1B-1
1961	128	394	99	16	6	18	4.6	59	59	56	62	6	.251	.459	7	3	C-125
1962	128	389	97	16	7	7	1.8	45	55	50	60	12	.249	.380	4	0	C-128
1963	135	470	111	13	7	9	1.9	50	49	36	50	7	.236	.351	3	1	C-134
1964	134	414	119	24	4	3	0.7	42	45	44	61	3	.287	.372	12	4	C-128
1965	136	437	102	10	0	8	1.8	42	57	34	51	1	.233	.311	9	4	C-131, 3B-1
1966	142	445	123	23	2	9	2.0	47	53	44	51	3	.276	.398	8	1	C-138
1967	116	334	91	18	2	4	1.2	37	24	38	33	2	.272	.374	17	5	C-107
1968 MIN A	135	380	82	12	0	8	2.1	31	39	46	57	2	.216	.311	22	3	C-117
1969	115	361	95	12	0	3	0.8	33	32	39	44	5	.263	.321	3	0	C-111
1970 WAS A	46	86	20	4	0	1	1.2	7	6	18	10	1	.233	.314	17	3	C-30
14 yrs.	1585	4847	1206	190	44	104	2.1	512	548	547	677	67	.249	.371	128	29	C-1476, 1B-6, OF-5, 3B-2

LEAGUE CHAMPIONSHIP SERIES

	G	AB	H	2B	3B	HR	HR%	R	RBI	BB	SO	SB	BA	SA	PH AB	PH H	G by POS
1969 MIN A	2	5	1	0	0	0	0.0	0	0	0	0	0	.200	.200	0	0	C-2

WORLD SERIES

	G	AB	H	2B	3B	HR	HR%	R	RBI	BB	SO	SB	BA	SA	PH AB	PH H	G by POS
1959 LA N	6	21	2	0	0	0	0.0	0	1	0	2	0	.095	.095	0	0	C-6
1963	4	14	2	0	0	1	7.1	1	3	0	4	0	.143	.357	0	0	C-4
1965	7	21	6	1	0	0	0.0	1	3	5	3	1	.286	.333	0	0	C-7
1966	4	14	1	0	0	0	0.0	0	0	0	3	0	.071	.071	0	0	C-4
4 yrs.	21	70	11	1	0	1	1.4	2	7	5	12	1	.157	.214	0	0	C-21

Bob Roselli

ROSELLI, ROBERT EDWARD
B. Dec. 10, 1931, San Francisco, Calif.

BR TR 5'11" 185 lbs.

	G	AB	H	2B	3B	HR	HR%	R	RBI	BB	SO	SB	BA	SA	PH AB	PH H	G by POS
1955 MIL N	6	9	2	1	0	0	0.0	1	0	1	4	0	.222	.333	3	1	C-2
1956	4	2	1	0	0	1	50.0	1	1	0	1	0	.500	2.000	1	1	C-3
1958	1	1	0	0	0	0	0.0	0	0	0	0	0	.000	.000	1	0	
1961 CHI A	22	38	10	3	0	0	0.0	2	4	0	11	0	.263	.342	12	4	C-10
1962	35	64	12	3	1	1	1.6	4	5	11	15	1	.188	.313	15	2	C-20
5 yrs.	68	114	25	7	1	2	1.8	8	10	12	31	1	.219	.351	32	7	C-35

Dave Rosello

ROSELLO, DAVID RODRIGUEZ
B. June 25, 1950, Mayaguez, Puerto Rico

BR TR 5'11" 160 lbs.

	G	AB	H	2B	3B	HR	HR%	R	RBI	BB	SO	SB	BA	SA	PH AB	PH H	G by POS
1972 CHI N	5	12	3	0	0	1	8.3	2	3	3	2	0	.250	.500	0	0	SS-5
1973	16	38	10	2	0	0	0.0	4	2	2	4	2	.263	.316	1	0	2B-13, SS-1
1974	62	148	30	7	0	0	0.0	9	10	10	28	1	.203	.250	2	1	2B-49, SS-12
1975	19	58	15	2	0	1	1.7	7	8	9	8	0	.259	.345	0	0	SS-19
1976	91	227	55	5	1	1	0.4	27	11	41	33	1	.242	.286	1	0	SS-86, 2B-1
1977	56	82	18	2	1	1	1.2	18	9	12	12	0	.220	.305	22	7	3B-21, SS-10, 2B-3
1979 CLE A	59	107	26	6	1	3	2.8	20	14	15	27	1	.243	.402	3	1	2B-33, 3B-14, SS-11
1980	71	117	29	3	0	2	1.7	16	12	9	19	0	.248	.325	1	0	2B-43, 3B-22, SS-3, DH-1
1981	43	84	20	4	0	1	1.2	11	7	7	12	0	.238	.321	10	1	2B-26, 3B-8, DH-4, SS-4
9 yrs.	422	873	206	31	4	10	1.1	114	76	108	145	5	.236	.313	40	10	2B-168, SS-151, 3B-65, DH-5

Chief Roseman

ROSEMAN, JAMES JOHN
B. 1856, New York, N. Y.   D. July 4, 1938, Brooklyn, N. Y.
Manager 1890.

BR TR 5'10" 167 lbs.

	G	AB	H	2B	3B	HR	HR%	R	RBI	BB	SO	SB	BA	SA	PH AB	PH H	G by POS
1882 TRO N	82	331	78	21	6	1	0.3	41	43	3	41		.236	.344	0	0	OF-82
1883 NY AA	93	398	100	13	6	0	0.0	48		11			.251	.314	0	0	OF-91, 1B-2
1884	107	436	130	16	11	4	0.9	97		21			.298	.413	0	0	OF-107
1885	101	410	114	13	15	3	0.7	72		25			.278	.405	0	0	OF-101, P-1
1886	134	559	127	19	10	5	0.9	90		24			.227	.324	0	0	OF-134, P-1
1887 3 teams	PHI	AA (21G – .219)			NY	AA (60G – .228)			BKN	AA (1G – .333)							
" total	82	317	72	12	2	0	0.0	48		19	6		.227	.278	0	0	OF-80, 1B-3, P-2
1890 2 teams	STL	AA (80G – .341)			LOU	AA (2G – .250)											
" total	82	310	105	26	0	2	0.6	47		30		7	.339	.442	0	0	OF-58, 1B-24
7 yrs.	681	2761	726	120	50	15	0.5	443	43	133	41	13	.263	.359	0	0	OF-654, 1B-29, P-4

Al Rosen

ROSEN, ALBERT LEONARD (Flip)
B. Feb. 29, 1924, Spartanburg, S. C.

BR TR 5'10½" 180 lbs.

	G	AB	H	2B	3B	HR	HR%	R	RBI	BB	SO	SB	BA	SA	PH AB	PH H	G by POS
1947 CLE A	7	9	1	0	0	0	0.0	1	0	0	3	0	.111	.111	4	1	3B-2, OF-1
1948	5	5	1	0	0	0	0.0	0	0	0	2	0	.200	.200	3	1	3B-2
1949	23	44	7	0	0	0	0.0	3	5	7	4	0	.159	.205	13	2	3B-10
1950	155	554	159	23	4	37	6.7	100	116	100	72	5	.287	.543	1	0	3B-154
1951	154	573	152	30	1	24	4.2	82	102	85	71	7	.265	.447	0	0	3B-154
1952	148	567	171	32	5	28	4.9	101	105	75	54	8	.302	.524	0	0	3B-147, 1B-4, SS-3
1953	155	599	201	27	5	43	7.2	115	145	85	48	8	.336	.613	4	1	3B-154
1954	137	466	140	20	2	24	5.2	76	102	85	43	6	.300	.506	5	2	3B-87, 1B-46, SS-1, 2B-1
1955	139	492	120	13	1	21	4.3	61	81	92	44	4	.244	.402	2	0	3B-106, 1B-41

	G	AB	H	2B	3B	HR	HR %	R	RBI	BB	SO	SB	BA	SA	Pinch Hit AB	H	G by POS

Al Rosen continued

	G	AB	H	2B	3B	HR	HR %	R	RBI	BB	SO	SB	BA	SA	AB	H	G by POS
1956	121	416	111	18	2	15	3.6	64	61	58	44	1	.267	.428	4	0	3B-116
10 yrs.	1044	3725	1063	165	20	192	5.2	603	717	587	385	39	.285	.495	33	6	3B-932, 1B-92, SS-5, OF-1, 2B-1

WORLD SERIES

	G	AB	H	2B	3B	HR	HR %	R	RBI	BB	SO	SB	BA	SA	AB	H	G by POS
1948 CLE A	1	1	0	0	0	0	0.0	0	0	0	0	0	.000	.000	1	0	
1954	3	12	3	0	0	0	0.0	0	0	1	0	0	.250	.250	0	0	3B-3
2 yrs.	4	13	3	0	0	0	0.0	0	0	1	0	0	.231	.231	1	0	3B-3

Goody Rosen

ROSEN, GOODWIN GEORGE   BL TL 5'10"   155 lbs.
B. Aug. 28, 1912, Toronto, Ont., Canada

	G	AB	H	2B	3B	HR	HR %	R	RBI	BB	SO	SB	BA	SA	AB	H	G by POS
1937 BKN N	22	77	24	5	1	0	0.0	10	6	6	6	2	.312	.403	0	0	OF-21
1938	138	473	133	17	11	4	0.8	75	51	65	43	0	.281	.389	19	2	OF-113
1939	54	183	46	6	4	1	0.5	22	12	23	21	4	.251	.344	4	0	OF-47
1944	89	264	69	8	3	0	0.0	38	23	26	27	0	.261	.314	21	5	OF-65
1945	145	606	197	24	11	12	2.0	126	75	50	36	4	.325	.460	3	0	OF-141
1946 2 teams		BKN	N	(3G –	.333)		NY	N	(100G –	.281)							
" total	103	313	88	11	4	5	1.6	39	30	48	33	2	.281	.390	15	3	OF-85
6 yrs.	551	1916	557	71	34	22	1.1	310	197	218	166	12	.291	.398	62	10	OF-472

Harry Rosenberg

ROSENBERG, HARRY   BR TR 5'10"   180 lbs.
Brother of Lou Rosenberg.
B. June 22, 1909, San Francisco, Calif.

	G	AB	H	2B	3B	HR	HR %	R	RBI	BB	SO	SB	BA	SA	AB	H	G by POS
1930 NY N	9	5	0	0	0	0	0.0	1	0	1	4	0	.000	.000	4	0	OF-3

Lou Rosenberg

ROSENBERG, LOUIS C.   BR TR 5'7"   155 lbs.
Brother of Harry Rosenberg.
B. Mar. 5, 1903, San Francisco, Calif.

	G	AB	H	2B	3B	HR	HR %	R	RBI	BB	SO	SB	BA	SA	AB	H	G by POS
1923 CHI A	3	4	1	0	0	0	0.0	0	0	0	1	0	.250	.250	1	0	2B-2

Max Rosenfeld

ROSENFELD, MAX   BR TR 5'8"   175 lbs.
B. Dec. 23, 1902, New York, N. Y.   D. Mar. 10, 1969, Miami, Fla.

	G	AB	H	2B	3B	HR	HR %	R	RBI	BB	SO	SB	BA	SA	AB	H	G by POS
1931 BKN N	3	9	2	1	0	0	0.0	0	0	1	1	0	.222	.333	0	0	OF-3
1932	34	39	14	3	0	2	5.1	8	7	0	10	2	.359	.590	3	0	OF-30
1933	5	9	1	0	0	0	0.0	0	0	1	1	0	.111	.111	1	0	OF-2
3 yrs.	42	57	17	4	0	2	3.5	8	7	2	12	2	.298	.474	4	0	OF-35

Larry Rosenthal

ROSENTHAL, LAWRENCE JOHN   BL TL 6'½"   190 lbs.
B. May 21, 1912, St. Paul, Minn.

	G	AB	H	2B	3B	HR	HR %	R	RBI	BB	SO	SB	BA	SA	AB	H	G by POS
1936 CHI A	85	317	89	15	8	3	0.9	71	46	59	37	2	.281	.407	4	3	OF-80
1937	58	97	28	5	3	0	0.0	20	9	9	20	1	.289	.402	29	9	OF-25
1938	61	105	30	5	1	1	1.0	14	12	12	13	0	.286	.381	30	6	OF-22
1939	107	324	86	21	5	10	3.1	50	51	53	46	6	.265	.454	12	1	OF-93
1940	107	276	83	14	5	6	2.2	46	42	64	32	2	.301	.453	11	2	OF-91
1941 2 teams		CHI	A	(20G –	.237)		CLE	A	(45G –	.187)							
" total	65	134	28	7	1	1	0.7	19	9	21	15	1	.209	.299	30	6	OF-32, 1B-1
1944 2 teams		NY	A	(36G –	.198)		PHI	A	(32G –	.204)							
" total	68	155	31	5	0	1	0.6	14	15	24	24	1	.200	.252	19	4	OF-45
1945 PHI A	28	75	15	3	2	0	0.0	6	5	9	8	0	.200	.293	4	0	OF-21
8 yrs.	579	1483	390	75	25	22	1.5	240	189	251	195	13	.263	.392	139	31	OF-409, 1B-1

Si Rosenthal

ROSENTHAL, SIMON   BL TL 5'9"   165 lbs.
B. Nov. 13, 1903, Boston, Mass.   D. Apr. 7, 1969, Boston, Mass.

	G	AB	H	2B	3B	HR	HR %	R	RBI	BB	SO	SB	BA	SA	AB	H	G by POS
1925 BOS A	19	72	19	5	2	0	0.0	6	8	7	3	1	.264	.389	2	0	OF-17
1926	104	285	76	12	3	4	1.4	34	34	19	18	4	.267	.372	35	9	OF-67
2 yrs.	123	357	95	17	5	4	1.1	40	42	26	21	5	.266	.375	37	9	OF-84

Jack Roser

ROSER, JOHN JOSEPH (Bunny)   BL TL 5'11"   175 lbs.
B. Nov. 15, 1901, St. Louis, Mo.   D. May 6, 1976, Rocky Hill, Conn.

	G	AB	H	2B	3B	HR	HR %	R	RBI	BB	SO	SB	BA	SA	AB	H	G by POS
1922 BOS N	32	113	27	3	4	0	0.0	13	16	10	19	2	.239	.336	0	0	OF-32

Chet Ross

ROSS, CHESTER JAMES   BR TR 6'1"   195 lbs.
B. Apr. 1, 1917, Buffalo, N. Y.   D. Apr. 24, 1982, Mayfield, Ky.

	G	AB	H	2B	3B	HR	HR %	R	RBI	BB	SO	SB	BA	SA	AB	H	G by POS
1939 BOS N	11	31	10	1	1	0	0.0	4	0	2	10	0	.323	.419	3	0	OF-8
1940	149	569	160	23	14	17	3.0	84	89	59	127	4	.281	.460	0	0	OF-149
1941	29	50	6	1	0	0	0.0	1	4	9	17	0	.120	.140	17	2	OF-12
1942	76	220	43	7	2	5	2.3	20	19	16	37	0	.195	.314	18	4	OF-57
1943	94	285	62	12	2	7	2.5	27	32	26	67	1	.218	.347	19	5	OF-78
1944	54	154	35	9	2	5	3.2	20	26	12	23	1	.227	.409	15	2	OF-38
6 yrs.	413	1309	316	53	21	34	2.6	156	170	124	281	6	.241	.392	72	13	OF-342

Don Ross

ROSS, DONALD RAYMOND   BR TR 6'1"   185 lbs.
B. July 16, 1914, Pasadena, Calif.

	G	AB	H	2B	3B	HR	HR %	R	RBI	BB	SO	SB	BA	SA	AB	H	G by POS
1938 DET A	77	265	69	7	1	1	0.4	22	30	28	11	1	.260	.306	2	0	3B-75
1940 BKN N	10	38	11	2	0	1	2.6	4	8	3	3	1	.289	.421	0	0	3B-10
1942 DET A	87	226	62	10	2	3	1.3	29	30	36	16	2	.274	.376	22	8	OF-38, 3B-20
1943	89	247	66	13	0	0	0.0	19	18	20	3	2	.267	.320	24	5	OF-38, SS-18, 2B-7, 3B-1
1944	66	167	35	5	0	2	1.2	14	15	14	9	2	.210	.275	24	8	OF-37, SS-2, 1B-1
1945 2 teams		DET	A	(8G –	.379)		CLE	A	(106G –	.262)							
" total	114	392	106	19	2	0.5		29	47	47	16	2	.270	.339	1	1	3B-114
1946 CLE A	55	153	41	7	0	3	2.0	12	14	17	12	0	.268	.373	12	1	3B-41, OF-2
7 yrs.	498	1488	390	63	4	12	0.8	129	162	165	70	10	.262	.334	85	23	3B-261, OF-115, SS-20, 2B-7, 1B-1

	G	AB	H	2B	3B	HR	HR %	R	RBI	BB	SO	SB	BA	SA	Pinch Hit AB	Pinch Hit H	G by POS

Joe Rossi

ROSSI, JOSEPH ANTHONY
B. Mar. 13, 1923, Oakland, Calif.

BR TR 6'1" 205 lbs.

	G	AB	H	2B	3B	HR	HR %	R	RBI	BB	SO	SB	BA	SA	PH AB	PH H	G by POS
1952 CIN N	55	145	32	0	1	1	0.7	14	6	20	20	1	.221	.255	8	2	C-46

Claude Rossman

ROSSMAN, CLAUDE R.
B. June 17, 1881, Philmont, N. Y.   D. Jan. 18, 1928, Poughkeepsie, N. Y.

BL TL 6'

	G	AB	H	2B	3B	HR	HR %	R	RBI	BB	SO	SB	BA	SA	PH AB	PH H	G by POS
1904 CLE A	18	62	13	5	0	0	0.0	5	6	0		0	.210	.290	1	1	OF-17
1906	118	396	122	13	2	1	0.3	49	53	17		11	.308	.359	11	4	1B-105, OF-1
1907 DET A	153	571	158	21	8	0	0.0	60	69	33		20	.277	.342	0	0	1B-153
1908	138	524	154	33	13	2	0.4	45	71	27		8	.294	.418	0	0	1B-138
1909 2 teams			DET	A (82G –	.261)			STL	A (2G –	.125)							
" total	84	295	76	8	3	0	0.0	16	39	13		10	.258	.305	5	0	1B-75, OF-2
5 yrs.	511	1848	523	80	26	3	0.2	175	238	90		49	.283	.359	17	5	1B-471, OF-20
WORLD SERIES																	
1907 DET A	5	20	8	0	1	0	0.0	1	2	1	0	2	.400	.500	0	0	1B-5
1908	5	19	4	0	0	0	0.0	3	3	1	4	0	.211	.211	0	0	1B-5
2 yrs.	10	39	12	0	1	0	0.0	4	5	2	4	2	.308	.359	0	0	1B-10

Braggo Roth

ROTH, ROBERT FRANK
Brother of Frank Roth.
B. Aug. 28, 1892, Burlington, Wis.   D. Sept. 11, 1936, Chicago, Ill.

BR TR 5'7½" 170 lbs.

	G	AB	H	2B	3B	HR	HR %	R	RBI	BB	SO	SB	BA	SA	PH AB	PH H	G by POS
1914 CHI A	34	126	37	4	6	1	0.8	14	10	8	25	3	.294	.444	0	0	OF-34
1915 2 teams		CHI	A (70G –	.250)			CLE	A (39G –	.299)								
" total	109	384	103	10	17	7	1.8	67	55	51	72	26	.268	.438	4	0	OF-69, 3B-35
1916 CLE A	125	409	117	19	7	4	1.0	50	72	38	48	29	.286	.396	12	6	OF-112
1917	145	495	141	30	9	1	0.2	69	72	52	73	51	.285	.388	10	3	OF-135
1918	106	375	106	21	12	1	0.3	53	59	53	41	35	.283	.411	0	0	OF-106
1919 2 teams		PHI	A (48G –	.323)			BOS	A (63G –	.256)								
" total	111	422	121	22	12	5	1.2	65	52	39	53	20	.287	.431	5	1	OF-103
1920 WAS A	138	468	136	23	8	9	1.9	80	92	75	57	24	.291	.432	8	3	OF-128
1921 NY A	43	152	43	9	2	2	1.3	29	10	19	20	1	.283	.408	6	2	OF-37
8 yrs.	811	2831	804	138	73	30	1.1	427	422	335	389	189	.284	.416	45	15	OF-724, 3B-35

Frank Roth

ROTH, FRANCIS CHARLES
Brother of Braggo Roth.
B. Oct. 11, 1878, Chicago, Ill.   D. Mar. 27, 1955, Burlington, Wis.

BR TR 5'10" 160 lbs.

	G	AB	H	2B	3B	HR	HR %	R	RBI	BB	SO	SB	BA	SA	PH AB	PH H	G by POS
1903 PHI N	68	220	60	11	4	0	0.0	27	22	9		3	.273	.359	7	3	C-60, 3B-1
1904	81	229	59	8	1	1	0.4	28	20	12		8	.258	.314	12	4	C-67, 2B-1, 1B-1
1905 STL A	35	107	25	3	0	0	0.0	9	7	6		1	.234	.262	5	0	C-29
1906 CHI A	16	51	10	1	1	0	0.0	4	7	3		1	.196	.255	1	0	C-15
1909 CIN N	56	147	35	7	2	0	0.0	12	16	6		5	.238	.313	2	0	C-54
1910	26	29	7	2	0	0	0.0	3	3	0		2	.241	.310	19	4	C-4, OF-1
6 yrs.	282	783	196	32	8	1	0.1	83	75	36		19	.250	.315	46	11	C-229, OF-1, 3B-1, 2B-1, 1B-1

Bob Rothel

ROTHEL, ROBERT BURTON
B. Sept. 17, 1923, Columbia Station, Ohio

BR TR 5'10½" 170 lbs.

	G	AB	H	2B	3B	HR	HR %	R	RBI	BB	SO	SB	BA	SA	PH AB	PH H	G by POS
1945 CLE A	4	10	2	0	0	0	0.0	0	0	3	1	0	.200	.200	0	0	3B-4

Bobby Rothermel

ROTHERMEL, EDWARD HILL
B. Dec. 18, 1870, Fleetwood, Pa.   D. Feb. 11, 1927, Detroit, Mich.

	G	AB	H	2B	3B	HR	HR %	R	RBI	BB	SO	SB	BA	SA	PH AB	PH H	G by POS
1899 BAL N	10	21	2	0	0	0	0.0	1	3	1		0	.095	.095	2	1	2B-5, 3B-2, SS-1

Jack Rothfuss

ROTHFUSS, JOHN ALBERT
B. Apr. 18, 1872, Newark, N. J.   D. Apr. 20, 1947, Basking Ridge, N. J.

BR TR 5'11½" 195 lbs.

	G	AB	H	2B	3B	HR	HR %	R	RBI	BB	SO	SB	BA	SA	PH AB	PH H	G by POS
1897 PIT N	35	115	36	3	1	2	1.7	20	18	5		3	.313	.409	2	0	1B-32

Claude Rothgeb

ROTHGEB, CLAUDE JAMES
B. Jan. 1, 1880, Milford, Ill.   D. July 6, 1944, Manitowoc, Wis.

6'½" 200 lbs.

	G	AB	H	2B	3B	HR	HR %	R	RBI	BB	SO	SB	BA	SA	PH AB	PH H	G by POS
1905 WAS A	6	13	2	0	0	0	0.0	2	0	0		1	.154	.154	3	0	OF-3

Jack Rothrock

ROTHROCK, JOHN HOUSTON
B. Mar. 14, 1905, Long Beach, Calif.
D. Feb. 2, 1980, San Bernardino, Calif.

BB TR 5'11½" 165 lbs.
BR 1925-27

	G	AB	H	2B	3B	HR	HR %	R	RBI	BB	SO	SB	BA	SA	PH AB	PH H	G by POS
1925 BOS A	22	55	19	3	3	0	0.0	6	7	3	7	0	.345	.509	0	0	SS-22
1926	15	17	5	1	0	0	0.0	3	2	3	1	0	.294	.353	10	4	SS-2
1927	117	428	111	24	8	1	0.2	61	36	24	46	5	.259	.360	6	1	SS-40, 2B-36, 3B-20, 1B-13
1928	117	344	92	9	4	3	0.9	52	22	33	40	12	.267	.343	9	2	OF-53, 3B-17, 1B-16, SS-13, 2B-2, C-1, P-1
1929	143	473	142	19	7	6	1.3	70	59	43	47	23	.300	.408	10	2	OF-128
1930	45	65	18	3	1	0	0.0	4	4	2	9	0	.277	.354	32	9	OF-9, 3B-1
1931	133	475	132	32	3	4	0.8	81	42	47	48	13	.278	.383	20	9	OF-79, 2B-23, 1B-8, 3B-2, SS-1
1932 2 teams		BOS	A (12G –	.208)			CHI	A (39G –	.188)								
" total	51	112	22	3	1	0	0.0	11	6	10	14	4	.196	.241	7	1	OF-31, 3B-8, 1B-1
1934 STL N	154	647	184	35	3	11	1.7	106	72	49	56	10	.284	.399	0	0	OF-154, 2B-1
1935	129	502	137	18	5	3	0.6	76	56	57	29	7	.273	.347	1	0	OF-127
1937 PHI A	88	232	62	15	0	0	0.0	28	21	28	15	1	.267	.332	29	8	OF-58, 2B-1
11 yrs.	1014	3350	924	162	35	28	0.8	498	327	299	312	75	.276	.370	124	36	OF-639, SS-78, 2B-63, 3B-48, 1B-38, C-1, P-1
WORLD SERIES																	
1934 STL N	7	30	7	3	1	0	0.0	3	6	1	2	0	.233	.400	0	0	OF-7

	G	AB	H	2B	3B	HR	HR %	R	RBI	BB	SO	SB	BA	SA	Pinch Hit AB	Pinch Hit H	G by POS

Edd Roush

ROUSH, EDD J (Eddie)
B. May 8, 1893, Oakland City, Ind.
Hall of Fame 1962.
BL TL 5'11" 170 lbs.

	G	AB	H	2B	3B	HR	HR %	R	RBI	BB	SO	SB	BA	SA	PH AB	PH H	G by POS
1913 CHI A	9	10	1	0	0	0	0.0	2	0	0	2	0	.100	.100	4	1	OF-2
1914 IND F	74	166	54	8	4	1	0.6	26	30	6		12	.325	.440	27	7	OF-43, 1B-2
1915 NWK F	145	551	164	20	11	3	0.5	73	60	38		28	.298	.390	1	1	OF-144
1916 2 teams	NY	N (39G – .188)			CIN	N	(69G – .287)										
" total	108	341	91	7	15	0	0.0	38	20	14	23	19	.267	.375	23	2	OF-84
1917 CIN N	136	522	178	19	14	4	0.8	82	67	27	24	21	.341	.454	1	0	OF-134
1918	113	435	145	18	10	5	1.1	61	62	22	10	24	.333	.455	0	0	OF-113
1919	133	504	162	19	12	4	0.8	73	71	42	19	20	.321	.431	0	0	OF-133
1920	149	579	196	22	16	4	0.7	81	90	42	22	36	.339	.453	0	0	OF-139, 1B-11, 2B-1
1921	112	418	147	27	12	4	1.0	68	71	31	8	19	.352	.502	2	1	OF-108
1922	49	165	58	7	4	1	0.6	29	24	19	5	5	.352	.461	6	1	OF-43
1923	138	527	185	41	18	6	1.1	88	88	46	16	10	.351	.531	1	0	OF-137
1924	121	483	168	23	21	6	1.2	67	72	22	11	17	.348	.501	2	2	OF-119
1925	134	540	183	28	16	8	1.5	91	83	35	14	22	.339	.494	0	0	OF-134
1926	144	563	182	37	10	7	1.2	95	79	38	17	8	.323	.462	0	0	OF-144, 1B-1
1927 NY N	140	570	173	27	4	7	1.2	83	58	26	15	18	.304	.402	2	0	OF-138
1928	46	163	41	5	3	2	1.2	20	13	14	8	1	.252	.356	6	3	OF-39
1929	115	450	146	19	7	8	1.8	76	52	45	16	6	.324	.451	6	3	OF-107
1931 CIN N	101	376	102	12	5	1	0.3	46	41	17	5	2	.271	.338	13	3	OF-88
18 yrs.	1967	7363	2376	339	182	68	0.9	1099	981	484	215	268	.323	.446	94	24	OF-1849, 1B-14, 2B-1
WORLD SERIES																	
1919 CIN N	8	28	6	2	1	0	0.0	6	7	3	0	2	.214	.357	0	0	OF-8

Phil Routcliffe

ROUTCLIFFE, PHILIP JOHN
B. Oct. 24, 1870, Oswego, N. Y.   D. Oct. 4, 1918, Oswego, N. Y.
BR TR 6' 175 lbs.

	G	AB	H	2B	3B	HR	HR %	R	RBI	BB	SO	SB	BA	SA	PH AB	PH H	G by POS
1890 PIT N	1	4	1	0	0	0	0.0	1	1	0		1	.250	.250	0	0	OF-1

Dave Rowan

ROWAN, DAVID
Also known as David Drohan.
B. Dec. 6, 1882, Eananoque, Ont., Canada   D. July 30, 1955, Toronto, Ont., Canada

	G	AB	H	2B	3B	HR	HR %	R	RBI	BB	SO	SB	BA	SA	PH AB	PH H	G by POS
1911 STL A	18	65	25	1	1	0	0.0	7	11	4		0	.385	.431	0	0	1B-18

Wade Rowdon

ROWDON, WADE
B. Sept. 7, 1960, Riverhead, N. Y.
BR TR 6'2" 170 lbs.

	G	AB	H	2B	3B	HR	HR %	R	RBI	BB	SO	SB	BA	SA	PH AB	PH H	G by POS
1984 CIN N	4	7	2	0	0	0	0.0	0	0	0	1	0	.286	.286	0	0	SS-1, 3B-1

Dave Rowe

ROWE, DAVID ELI
Brother of Jack Rowe.
B. Feb., 1856, Jacksonville, Ill.   D. Oct. 12, 1918
Manager 1886, 1888.
BR TR 5'9" 180 lbs.

	G	AB	H	2B	3B	HR	HR %	R	RBI	BB	SO	SB	BA	SA	PH AB	PH H	G by POS
1877 CHI N	2	7	2	0	0	0	0.0	0	0	0	3		.286	.286	0	0	OF-2, P-1
1882 CLE N	24	97	25	4	3	1	1.0	13	17	4	9		.258	.392	0	0	OF-23, P-1
1883 BAL AA	59	256	80	11	6	0	0.0	40		2			.313	.402	0	0	OF-50, SS-7, 1B-3, P-1
1884 STL U	109	485	142	32	11	3	0.6	95		10			.293	.423	0	0	OF-92, SS-14, 2B-2, 1B-2, P-1
1885 STL N	16	62	10	3	0	0	0.0	8	3	5	8		.161	.210	0	0	OF-16
1886 KC N	105	429	103	24	8	3	0.7	53	57	15	43		.240	.354	0	0	OF-90, SS-11, 2B-4
1888 KC AA	32	122	21	3	4	0	0.0	14	13	6		2	.172	.262	0	0	OF-32
7 yrs.	347	1458	383	77	32	7	0.5	223	90	42	63	2	.263	.374	0	0	OF-305, SS-32, 2B-6, 1B-5, P-4

Harland Rowe

ROWE, HARLAND STIMSON (Hypie)
B. Apr. 20, 1896, Springvale, Me.   D. May 26, 1969, Springvale, Me.
BL TR 6'1" 170 lbs.

	G	AB	H	2B	3B	HR	HR %	R	RBI	BB	SO	SB	BA	SA	PH AB	PH H	G by POS
1916 PHI A	17	36	5	1	0	0	0.0	2	3	2	8	0	.139	.167	6	1	3B-7, OF-1

Jack Rowe

ROWE, JOHN CHARLES
Brother of Dave Rowe.
B. Dec. 18, 1856, Harrisburg, Pa.   D. Apr. 25, 1911, St. Louis, Mo.
Manager 1890.
BL TR 5'8" 170 lbs.

	G	AB	H	2B	3B	HR	HR %	R	RBI	BB	SO	SB	BA	SA	PH AB	PH H	G by POS
1879 BUF N	8	34	12	1	0	0	0.0	8	8	0	1		.353	.382	0	0	C-6, OF-2
1880	79	326	82	10	6	1	0.3	43	36	6	17		.252	.328	0	0	C-60, OF-25, 3B-3
1881	64	246	82	11	11	1	0.4	30	43	1	12		.333	.480	0	0	C-46, SS-7, 3B-7, OF-5
1882	75	308	82	14	5	1	0.3	43		12	0		.266	.354	0	0	C-46, SS-22, 3B-7, OF-1
1883	87	374	104	18	7	1	0.3	65		15	14		.278	.372	0	0	C-49, OF-28, SS-18, 3B-3
1884	93	400	126	14	14	4	1.0	85		23	14		.315	.450	0	0	C-65, OF-30, SS-6
1885	98	421	122	28	8	2	0.5	62	51	13	19		.290	.409	0	0	SS-65, C-23, OF-12
1886 DET N	111	468	142	21	9	6	1.3	97	87	26	27		.303	.425	0	0	SS-110, C-3
1887	124	537	171	30	10	6	1.1	135	96	39	11	22	.318	.445	0	0	SS-124
1888	105	451	125	19	8	2	0.4	62	74	19	28	10	.277	.368	0	0	SS-105
1889 PIT N	75	317	82	14	3	2	0.6	57	32	22	16	5	.259	.341	0	0	SS-75
1890 BUF P	125	504	126	22	7	2	0.4	77	76	48	18	10	.250	.333	0	0	SS-125
12 yrs.	1044	4386	1256	202	88	28	0.6	764	503	224	177	47	.286	.392	0	0	SS-657, C-298, OF-103, 3B-20

Schoolboy Rowe

ROWE, LYNWOOD THOMAS
B. Jan. 11, 1910, Waco, Tex.   D. Jan. 8, 1961, El Dorado, Ark.
BR TR 6'4½" 210 lbs.

	G	AB	H	2B	3B	HR	HR %	R	RBI	BB	SO	SB	BA	SA	PH AB	PH H	G by POS
1933 DET A	21	50	11	1	0	0	0.0	6	6	1	4	0	.220	.240	1	0	P-19
1934	51	109	33	8	1	2	1.8	15	22	6	20	0	.303	.450	6	1	P-45
1935	45	109	34	3	2	3	2.8	19	28	12	12	0	.312	.459	3	1	P-42
1936	45	90	23	2	1	1	1.1	16	12	13	15	0	.256	.333	4	2	P-41
1937	10	10	2	0	0	0	0.0	2	1	1	4	0	.200	.200	0	0	P-10
1938	4	6	1	1	0	0	0.0	1	0	0	1	0	.167	.333	0	0	P-4
1939	31	61	15	0	1	1	1.6	7	12	5	7	1	.246	.328	3	1	P-28

	G	AB	H	2B	3B	HR	HR %	R	RBI	BB	SO	SB	BA	SA	Pinch Hit AB	Pinch Hit H	G by POS

Schoolboy Rowe continued

	G	AB	H	2B	3B	HR	HR%	R	RBI	BB	SO	SB	BA	SA	AB	H	G by POS
1940	27	67	18	6	1	1	1.5	7	18	5	13	1	.269	.433	0	0	P-27
1941	32	55	15	0	3	1	1.8	10	12	5	8	0	.273	.436	5	3	P-27
1942 2 teams	DET	A (2G – .000)			BKN	N	(14G – .211)										
" total	16	23	4	0	0	0	0.0	2	2	1	4	0	.174	.174	5	1	P-11
1943 PHI N	82	120	36	7	0	4	3.3	14	18	15	21	0	.300	.458	49	15	P-27
1946	30	61	11	5	0	1	1.6	4	6	3	16	0	.180	.311	12	2	P-17
1947	43	79	22	2	0	2	2.5	9	11	13	18	0	.278	.380	12	2	P-31
1948	31	52	10	0	0	1	1.9	3	4	4	10	1	.192	.250	1	0	P-30
1949	23	17	4	1	0	1	5.9	1	1	2	4	0	.235	.471	0	0	P-23
15 yrs.	491	909	239	36	9	18	2.0	116	153	86	157	3	.263	.382	101	28	P-382
WORLD SERIES																	
1934 DET A	3	7	0	0	0	0	0.0	0	0	0	5	0	.000	.000	0	0	P-3
1935	3	8	2	1	0	0	0.0	0	0	0	1	0	.250	.375	0	0	P-3
1940	2	1	0	0	0	0	0.0	0	0	0	1	0	.000	.000	0	0	P-2
3 yrs.	8	16	2	1	0	0	0.0	0	0	0	7	0	.125	.188	0	0	P-8

Bama Rowell

ROWELL, CARVEL WILLIAM
B. Jan. 13, 1916, Citronelle, Ala. BL TR 5'11" 185 lbs.

	G	AB	H	2B	3B	HR	HR%	R	RBI	BB	SO	SB	BA	SA	AB	H	G by POS
1939 BOS N	21	59	11	2	0	0	0.0	5	6	1	4	0	.186	.288	5	0	OF-16
1940	130	486	148	19	8	3	0.6	46	58	18	22	12	.305	.395	8	2	2B-115, OF-7
1941	138	483	129	23	6	7	1.4	49	60	39	36	11	.267	.383	6	1	2B-112, OF-14, 3B-2
1946	95	293	82	12	6	3	1.0	37	31	29	15	5	.280	.392	9	4	OF-85
1947	113	384	106	23	2	5	1.3	48	40	18	14	7	.276	.385	4	1	OF-100, 2B-7, 3B-4
1948 PHI N	77	196	47	16	2	1	0.5	15	22	8	14	2	.240	.357	28	7	3B-18, OF-17, 2B-12
6 yrs.	574	1901	523	95	26	19	1.0	200	217	113	105	37	.275	.382	60	15	2B-246, OF-239, 3B-24

Ed Rowen

ROWEN, W. EDWARD
B. Oct. 22, 1857, Bridgeport, Conn. D. Feb. 22, 1892, Bridgeport, Conn. 6'1" 170 lbs.

	G	AB	H	2B	3B	HR	HR%	R	RBI	BB	SO	SB	BA	SA	AB	H	G by POS
1882 BOS N	83	327	81	7	4	1	0.3	36	43	19	18		.248	.303	0	0	OF-48, C-34, SS-6, 3B-1
1883 PHI AA	49	196	43	10	1	0	0.0	28		10			.219	.281	0	0	C-44, OF-8, 3B-1, 2B-1
1884	4	15	6	1	0	0	0.0	4		1			.400	.467	0	0	C-4
3 yrs.	136	538	130	18	5	1	0.2	68	43	30	18		.242	.299	0	0	C-82, OF-56, SS-6, 3B-2, 2B-1

Chuck Rowland

ROWLAND, CHARLIE LELAND
B. July 23, 1899, Warrenton, N. C. BR TR 6'1" 185 lbs.

	G	AB	H	2B	3B	HR	HR%	R	RBI	BB	SO	SB	BA	SA	AB	H	G by POS
1923 PHI A	5	6	0	0	0	0	0.0	0	0	0	2	0	.000	.000	1	0	C-4

Jim Roxburgh

ROXBURGH, JAMES A.
B. Jan. 17, 1858, San Francisco, Calif. D. Feb. 21, 1934, San Francisco, Calif. BR TR

	G	AB	H	2B	3B	HR	HR%	R	RBI	BB	SO	SB	BA	SA	AB	H	G by POS
1884 BAL AA	2	4	2	0	0	0	0.0	1		1			.500	.500	0	0	C-2
1887 PHI AA	2	8	1	0	0	0	0.0	0		0			.125	.125	0	0	C-2, 2B-1
2 yrs.	4	12	3	0	0	0	0.0	1		1		0	.250	.250	0	0	C-4, 2B-1

Jerry Royster

ROYSTER, JERON KENNIS
B. Oct. 18, 1952, Sacramento, Calif. BR TR 6' 165 lbs.

	G	AB	H	2B	3B	HR	HR%	R	RBI	BB	SO	SB	BA	SA	AB	H	G by POS
1973 LA N	10	19	4	0	0	0	0.0	1	2	0	5	1	.211	.211	0	0	3B-6, 2B-1
1974	6	0	0	0	0	0	–	2	0	0	0	0	–	–	0	0	OF-1, 3B-1, 2B-1
1975	13	36	9	2	1	0	0.0	2	1	1	3	1	.250	.361	2	0	OF-7, 2B-4, 3B-3, SS-1
1976 ATL N	149	533	132	13	1	5	0.9	65	45	52	53	24	.248	.304	1	0	3B-148, SS-2
1977	140	445	96	10	2	6	1.3	64	28	38	67	28	.216	.288	4	0	3B-56, SS-51, 2B-38
1978	140	529	137	17	8	2	0.4	67	35	56	49	27	.259	.333	4	2	2B-75, SS-60, 3B-1
1979	154	601	164	25	6	3	0.5	103	51	62	59	35	.273	.349	3	0	3B-80, 2B-77
1980	123	392	95	17	5	1	0.3	42	20	37	48	22	.242	.319	4	1	2B-49, 3B-48, OF-41
1981	64	93	19	4	1	0	0.0	13	9	7	14	7	.204	.269	17	4	3B-24, 2B-13
1982	108	261	77	13	2	2	0.8	43	25	22	36	14	.295	.383	6	1	3B-62, OF-25, 2B-16, SS-10
1983	91	268	63	10	3	3	1.1	32	30	28	35	11	.235	.328	4	1	3B-47, 2B-26, OF-18, SS-13
1984	81	227	47	13	2	1	0.4	22	21	15	41	6	.207	.295	15	1	2B-29, 3B-17, SS-16, OF-11
12 yrs.	1079	3404	843	124	31	23	0.7	456	267	318	410	176	.248	.323	60	10	3B-493, 2B-329, SS-153, OF-103
LEAGUE CHAMPIONSHIP SERIES																	
1982 ATL N	3	11	2	0	0	0	0.0	0	0	0	2	0	.182	.182	0	0	OF-3

Willie Royster

ROYSTER, WILLIE ARTHUR
B. Apr. 11, 1954, Clarksville, Va. BR TR 5'11" 180 lbs.

	G	AB	H	2B	3B	HR	HR%	R	RBI	BB	SO	SB	BA	SA	AB	H	G by POS
1981 BAL A	4	4	0	0	0	0	0.0	0	0	0	2	0	.000	.000	1	0	C-4

Vic Roznovsky

ROZNOVSKY, VICTOR JOSEPH
B. Oct. 19, 1938, Shiner, Tex. BL TR 6' 170 lbs.

	G	AB	H	2B	3B	HR	HR%	R	RBI	BB	SO	SB	BA	SA	AB	H	G by POS
1964 CHI N	35	76	15	1	0	0	0.0	2	5	5	18	0	.197	.211	16	1	C-26
1965	71	172	38	4	1	3	1.7	9	15	16	30	1	.221	.308	11	4	C-63
1966 BAL A	41	97	23	5	0	1	1.0	4	10	9	11	0	.237	.320	5	2	C-34
1967	45	97	20	5	0	0	0.0	7	10	1	20	0	.206	.258	20	6	C-23
1969 PHI N	13	13	3	0	0	0	0.0	0	0	1	4	0	.231	.231	12	3	C-2
5 yrs.	205	455	99	15	1	4	0.9	22	38	32	83	1	.218	.281	64	16	C-148

Al Rubeling

RUBELING, ALBERT WILLIAM
B. May 10, 1913, Baltimore, Md. BR TR 6' 185 lbs.

	G	AB	H	2B	3B	HR	HR%	R	RBI	BB	SO	SB	BA	SA	AB	H	G by POS
1940 PHI A	108	376	92	16	6	4	1.1	49	38	48	58	4	.245	.351	0	0	3B-98, 2B-10
1941	6	19	5	0	0	0	0.0	0	2	2	1	0	.263	.263	0	0	3B-6
1943 PIT N	47	168	44	8	4	0	0.0	23	9	8	17	0	.262	.357	2	1	2B-44, 3B-1

	G	AB	H	2B	3B	HR	HR %	R	RBI	BB	SO	SB	BA	SA	Pinch Hit AB	Pinch Hit H	G by POS

Al Rubeling *continued*

	G	AB	H	2B	3B	HR	HR %	R	RBI	BB	SO	SB	BA	SA	AB	H	G by POS
1944	92	184	45	7	2	4	2.2	22	30	19	19	4	.245	.370	41	9	OF-18, 2B-17, 3B-16
4 yrs.	253	747	186	31	12	8	1.1	94	79	77	95	8	.249	.355	43	10	3B-121, 2B-71, OF-18

John Ruberto

RUBERTO, JOHN EDWARD (Sonny)
B. Jan. 2, 1946, Staten Island, N. Y.

BR TR 5'11" 175 lbs.

		G	AB	H	2B	3B	HR	HR %	R	RBI	BB	SO	SB	BA	SA	AB	H	G by POS
1969 SD	N	19	21	3	0	0	0	0.0	3	0	1	7	0	.143	.143	1	0	C-15
1972 CIN	N	2	3	0	0	0	0	0.0	0	0	0	1	0	.000	.000	0	0	C-2
2 yrs.		21	24	3	0	0	0	0.0	3	0	1	8	0	.125	.125	1	0	C-17

Art Ruble

RUBLE, WILLIAM ARTHUR (Speedy)
B. Mar. 11, 1903, Knoxville, Tenn.   D. Nov. 1, 1983, Maryville, Tenn.

BL TR 5'10½" 168 lbs.

		G	AB	H	2B	3B	HR	HR %	R	RBI	BB	SO	SB	BA	SA	AB	H	G by POS
1927 DET	A	56	91	15	4	2	0	0.0	16	11	14	15	2	.165	.253	2	0	OF-43
1934 PHI	N	19	54	15	4	0	0	0.0	7	8	7	3	0	.278	.352	4	0	OF-14
2 yrs.		75	145	30	8	2	0	0.0	23	19	21	18	2	.207	.290	7	0	OF-57

Johnny Rucker

RUCKER, JOHN JOEL (The Crabapple Comet)
B. Jan. 15, 1917, Crabapple, Ga.

BL TR 6'2" 175 lbs.

		G	AB	H	2B	3B	HR	HR %	R	RBI	BB	SO	SB	BA	SA	AB	H	G by POS
1940 NY	N	86	277	82	7	5	4	1.4	38	23	7	32	4	.296	.401	20	8	OF-57
1941		143	622	179	38	9	1	0.2	95	42	29	61	8	.288	.383	1	1	OF-142
1943		132	505	138	19	4	2	0.4	56	46	22	44	4	.273	.339	13	3	OF-117
1944		144	587	143	14	8	6	1.0	79	39	24	48	8	.244	.325	2	0	OF-139
1945		105	429	117	19	11	7	1.6	58	51	20	36	7	.273	.417	4	1	OF-98
1946		95	197	52	8	2	1	0.5	28	13	7	27	4	.264	.340	12	3	OF-54
6 yrs.		705	2617	711	105	39	21	0.8	354	214	109	248	35	.272	.366	52	16	OF-607

John Rudderham

RUDDERHAM, JOHN EDMUND
B. Aug. 30, 1863, Quincy, Mass.   D. Apr. 3, 1942, Randolph, Mass.

BR TR 5'7" 145 lbs.

		G	AB	H	2B	3B	HR	HR %	R	RBI	BB	SO	SB	BA	SA	AB	H	G by POS
1884 BOS	U	1	4	1	0	0	0	0.0	0		0			.250	.250	0	0	OF-1

Joe Rudi

RUDI, JOSEPH ODEN
B. Sept. 7, 1946, Modesto, Calif.

BR TR 6'2" 200 lbs.

		G	AB	H	2B	3B	HR	HR %	R	RBI	BB	SO	SB	BA	SA	AB	H	G by POS
1967 KC	A	19	43	8	2	0	0	0.0	4	1	3	7	0	.186	.233	4	0	1B-9, OF-6
1968 OAK	A	68	181	32	5	1	1	0.6	10	12	12	32	1	.177	.232	17	2	OF-56
1969		35	122	23	3	1	2	1.6	10	6	5	16	1	.189	.279	5	1	OF-18, 1B-11
1970		106	350	108	23	2	11	3.1	40	42	16	61	3	.309	.480	18	2	OF-63, 1B-28
1971		127	513	137	23	4	10	1.9	62	52	28	62	3	.267	.386	3	0	OF-121, 1B-5
1972		147	593	181	32	9	19	3.2	94	75	37	62	3	.305	.486	0	0	OF-147, 3B-1
1973		120	437	118	25	1	12	2.7	53	66	30	72	0	.270	.414	2	0	OF-117, DH-1, 1B-1
1974		158	593	174	39	4	22	3.7	73	99	34	92	2	.293	.484	1	0	OF-140, 1B-27, DH-2
1975		126	468	130	26	6	21	4.5	66	75	40	56	2	.278	.484	2	1	1B-91, OF-44, DH-2
1976		130	500	135	32	3	13	2.6	54	94	41	71	6	.270	.424	2	1	OF-126, DH-2, 1B-2
1977 CAL	A	64	242	64	13	2	13	5.4	48	53	22	48	1	.264	.496	0	0	OF-61, DH-3
1978		133	497	127	27	1	17	3.4	58	79	28	82	2	.256	.416	4	1	OF-111, DH-11, 1B-10
1979		90	330	80	11	3	11	3.3	35	61	24	61	0	.242	.394	4	2	OF-80, 1B-5, DH-3
1980		104	372	88	17	1	16	4.3	42	53	17	84	1	.237	.417	7	2	OF-86, DH-3
1981 BOS	A	49	122	22	3	0	6	4.9	14	24	8	29	0	.180	.352	22	5	DH-21, 1B-5, OF-1
1982 OAK	A	71	193	41	6	1	5	2.6	21	18	24	35	0	.212	.332	10	0	1B-49, OF-14, DH-3
16 yrs.		1547	5556	1468	287	39	179	3.2	684	810	369	870	25	.264	.427	101	17	OF-1195, 1B-249, DH-51, 3B-1

LEAGUE CHAMPIONSHIP SERIES

		G	AB	H	2B	3B	HR	HR %	R	RBI	BB	SO	SB	BA	SA	AB	H	G by POS
1971 OAK	A	2	7	1	1	0	0	0.0	0	0	1	0	0	.143	.286	0	0	OF-2
1972		5	20	5	1	0	0	0.0	1	2	1	4	0	.250	.300	0	0	OF-5
1973		5	18	4	0	0	1	5.6	1	3	3	1	0	.222	.389	0	0	OF-5
1974		4	13	2	0	1	0	0.0	0	1	3	2	0	.154	.308	0	0	OF-4
1975		3	12	3	2	0	0	0.0	1	0	0	1	0	.250	.417	0	0	1B-2
5 yrs.		19	70	15	4	1	1	1.4	3	6	8	8	0	.214	.343	0	0	OF-16, 1B-2

WORLD SERIES

		G	AB	H	2B	3B	HR	HR %	R	RBI	BB	SO	SB	BA	SA	AB	H	G by POS
1972 OAK	A	7	25	6	0	0	1	4.0	1	1	2	5	0	.240	.360	0	0	OF-7
1973		7	27	9	2	0	0	0.0	3	4	3	4	0	.333	.407	0	0	OF-7
1974		5	18	6	0	0	1	5.6	1	4	0	3	0	.333	.500	0	0	1B-2
3 yrs.		19	70	21	2	0	2	2.9	5	9	5	12	0	.300	.414	0	0	OF-14, 1B-2

Dutch Rudolph

RUDOLPH, JOHN HERMAN
B. July 10, 1882, Natrona, Pa.   D. Apr. 17, 1967, Natrona, Pa.

BL TL 5'10" 160 lbs.

		G	AB	H	2B	3B	HR	HR %	R	RBI	BB	SO	SB	BA	SA	AB	H	G by POS
1903 PHI	N	1	1	0	0	0	0	0.0	0		0		0	.000	.000	1	0	
1904 CHI	N	2	3	1	0	0	0	0.0	0		0		0	.333	.333	0	0	OF-2
2 yrs.		3	4	1	0	0	0	0.0	0		0		0	.250	.250	1	0	OF-2

Ken Rudolph

RUDOLPH, KENNETH VICTOR
B. Dec. 29, 1946, Rockford, Ill.

BR TR 6'1" 180 lbs.

		G	AB	H	2B	3B	HR	HR %	R	RBI	BB	SO	SB	BA	SA	AB	H	G by POS
1969 CHI	N	27	34	7	1	0	1	2.9	7	6	6	11	0	.206	.324	10	3	C-11, OF-3
1970		20	40	4	1	0	0	0.0	1	2	1	12	0	.100	.125	3	0	C-16
1971		25	76	15	3	0	0	0.0	5	7	6	20	0	.197	.237	0	0	C-25
1972		42	106	25	1	1	2	1.9	10	9	6	14	1	.236	.321	1	0	C-41
1973		64	170	35	8	1	2	1.2	12	17	7	25	1	.206	.300	0	0	C-64
1974 SF	N	57	158	41	3	0	0	0.0	11	10	21	19	0	.259	.278	0	0	C-56
1975 STL	N	44	80	16	2	0	1	1.3	5	6	3	10	0	.200	.263	14	1	C-31
1976		27	50	8	3	0	0	0.0	5	5	1	7	0	.160	.220	13	4	C-14
1977 2 teams		SF	N (11G –	.200)		BAL	A (11G –	.286)										
" total		22	29	7	1	0	0	0.0	3	2	1	7	0	.241	.276	5	0	C-22
9 yrs.		328	743	158	23	2	6	0.8	55	64	52	121	2	.213	.273	46	8	C-280, OF-3

	G	AB	H	2B	3B	HR	HR %	R	RBI	BB	SO	SB	BA	SA	Pinch Hit AB	H	G by POS

Muddy Ruel

RUEL, HEROLD DOMINIC
B. Feb. 20, 1896, St. Louis, Mo. D. Nov. 13, 1963, Palo Alto, Calif.
Manager 1947.
BR TR 5'9" 150 lbs.

	G	AB	H	2B	3B	HR	HR %	R	RBI	BB	SO	SB	BA	SA	AB	H	G by POS
1915 STL A	10	14	0	0	0	0	0.0	0	1	5	5	0	.000	.000	2	0	C-6
1917 NY A	6	17	2	0	0	0	0.0	1	1	2	2	1	.118	.118	2	0	C-6
1918	3	6	2	0	0	0	0.0	0	0	2	1	1	.333	.333	0	0	C-2
1919	81	233	56	6	0	0	0.0	18	31	34	26	4	.240	.266	0	0	C-81
1920	82	261	70	14	1	1	0.4	30	15	15	18	4	.268	.341	1	0	C-80
1921 BOS A	113	358	99	21	1	1	0.3	41	43	41	15	2	.277	.349	2	0	C-109
1922	116	361	92	15	1	0	0.0	34	28	41	26	4	.255	.302	4	1	C-112
1923 WAS A	136	449	142	24	3	0	0.0	63	54	55	21	4	.316	.383	3	2	C-133
1924	149	501	142	20	2	0	0.0	50	57	62	20	7	.283	.331	2	1	C-147
1925	127	393	122	9	2	0	0.0	55	54	63	16	4	.310	.344	0	0	C-126, 1B-1
1926	117	368	110	22	4	1	0.3	42	53	61	14	7	.299	.389	0	0	C-117
1927	131	428	132	16	5	1	0.2	61	52	63	18	9	.308	.376	2	0	C-128
1928	108	350	90	18	2	0	0.0	31	55	44	14	12	.257	.320	4	2	C-101, 1B-2
1929	69	188	46	4	2	0	0.0	16	20	31	7	0	.245	.287	6	0	C-63
1930	66	198	50	3	4	0	0.0	18	26	24	13	1	.253	.308	4	2	C-60
1931 2 teams			BOS A (33G – .301)						DET A (14G – .120)								
" total	47	133	31	6	0	0	0.0	7	9	14	7	0	.233	.278	2	0	C-44
1932 DET A	50	136	32	4	2	0	0.0	10	18	17	6	1	.235	.294	3	1	C-49
1933 STL A	28	63	12	2	0	0	0.0	13	8	24	4	0	.190	.222	5	0	C-28
1934 CHI A	22	57	12	3	0	0	0.0	4	7	8	5	0	.211	.263	1	0	C-21
19 yrs.	1461	4514	1242	187	29	4	0.1	494	532	606	238	61	.275	.332	41	9	C-1413, 1B-3
WORLD SERIES																	
1924 WAS A	7	21	2	1	0	0	0.0	2	0	6	1	0	.095	.143	0	0	C-7
1925	7	19	6	1	0	0	0.0	0	1	3	2	0	.316	.368	0	0	C-7
2 yrs.	14	40	8	2	0	0	0.0	2	1	9	3	0	.200	.250	0	0	C-14

Dutch Ruether

RUETHER, WALTER HENRY
B. Sept. 13, 1893, Alameda, Calif. D. May 16, 1970, Phoenix, Ariz.
BL TL 6'1½" 180 lbs.

	G	AB	H	2B	3B	HR	HR %	R	RBI	BB	SO	SB	BA	SA	AB	H	G by POS
1917 2 teams			CHI N (31G – .273)						CIN N (19G – .208)								
" total	50	68	17	3	3	0	0.0	4	12	11	17	1	.250	.382	22	6	P-17, 1B-5
1918 CIN N	2	3	0	0	0	0	0.0	0	0	0	2	0	.000	.000	0	0	P-2
1919	42	92	24	2	3	0	0.0	8	6	4	18	1	.261	.348	7	2	P-33
1920	45	104	20	4	0	0	0.0	3	10	5	24	0	.192	.231	7	0	P-37, 1B-1
1921 BKN N	49	97	34	5	2	2	2.1	12	13	4	9	1	.351	.505	11	3	P-36
1922	67	125	26	6	1	2	1.6	12	20	12	11	0	.208	.320	27	6	P-35
1923	49	117	32	1	0	0	0.0	6	10	12	12	0	.274	.282	12	3	P-34, 1B-1
1924	32	62	15	1	1	0	0.0	4	5	2	2	0	.242	.290	4	0	P-30
1925 WAS A	55	108	36	3	2	1	0.9	18	15	10	8	0	.333	.426	19	6	P-30, 1B-1
1926 2 teams			WAS A (47G – .250)						NY A (13G – .095)								
" total	60	113	25	2	0	1	0.9	8	11	6	11	0	.221	.265	30	6	P-28
1927 NY A	35	80	21	3	0	1	1.3	7	10	8	15	0	.263	.338	6	2	P-27
11 yrs.	488	969	250	30	12	7	0.7	83	111	77	129	3	.258	.335	145	34	P-309, 1B-8
WORLD SERIES																	
1919 CIN N	3	6	4	1	2	0	0.0	2	4	1	0	0	.667	1.500	1	0	P-2
1925 WAS A	1	1	0	0	0	0	0.0	0	0	0	0	0	.000	.000	1	0	
1926 NY A	3	4	0	0	0	0	0.0	0	0	0	0	0	.000	.000	2	0	P-1
3 yrs.	7	11	4	1	2	0	0.0	2	4	1	0	0	.364	.818	4	0	P-3

Rudy Rufer

RUFER, RUDOLPH JOSEPH
B. Oct. 28, 1926, Ridgewood, N. Y.
BR TR 6'½" 165 lbs.

	G	AB	H	2B	3B	HR	HR %	R	RBI	BB	SO	SB	BA	SA	AB	H	G by POS
1949 NY N	7	15	1	0	0	0	0.0	1	2	2	0	0	.067	.067	0	0	SS-7
1950	15	11	1	0	0	0	0.0	1	0	0	1	1	.091	.091	3	0	SS-8
2 yrs.	22	26	2	0	0	0	0.0	2	2	2	1	1	.077	.077	3	0	SS-15

Red Ruffing

RUFFING, CHARLES HERBERT
B. May 3, 1904, Granville, Ill.
Hall of Fame 1967.
BR TR 6'1½" 205 lbs.

	G	AB	H	2B	3B	HR	HR %	R	RBI	BB	SO	SB	BA	SA	AB	H	G by POS
1924 BOS A	8	7	1	0	1	0	0.0	0	0	0	1	0	.143	.429	0	0	P-8
1925	37	79	17	4	2	0	0.0	6	11	1	22	0	.215	.316	0	0	P-37
1926	37	51	10	1	0	1	2.0	8	5	2	12	0	.196	.275	0	0	P-37
1927	29	55	14	3	1	0	0.0	5	4	0	6	0	.255	.345	2	0	P-26
1928	60	121	38	13	1	2	1.7	12	19	3	12	0	.314	.488	17	5	P-42
1929	60	114	35	9	0	2	1.8	9	17	2	13	0	.307	.439	22	6	P-35, OF-2
1930 2 teams			BOS A (6G – .273)						NY A (52G – .374)								
" total	58	110	40	8	2	4	3.6	17	22	7	8	0	.364	.582	17	6	P-38
1931 NY A	48	109	36	8	1	3	2.8	14	12	11	13	0	.330	.505	10	3	P-37, OF-1
1932	55	124	38	6	1	3	2.4	20	19	6	10	0	.306	.444	18	4	P-35
1933	55	115	29	3	1	2	1.7	10	13	7	15	0	.252	.348	19	2	P-35
1934	45	113	28	3	0	2	1.8	11	13	3	17	0	.248	.327	8	0	P-36
1935	50	109	37	10	0	2	1.8	13	18	3	9	0	.339	.486	18	8	P-30
1936	53	127	37	5	0	5	3.9	14	22	11	12	0	.291	.449	17	6	P-33
1937	54	129	26	3	0	1	0.8	11	10	13	24	0	.202	.248	21	6	P-31
1938	45	107	24	4	1	3	2.8	12	17	17	21	0	.224	.364	12	2	P-31
1939	44	114	35	1	0	1	0.9	12	20	7	18	1	.307	.342	11	1	P-28
1940	33	89	11	4	0	1	1.1	8	7	3	9	0	.124	.202	1	0	P-30
1941	38	89	27	8	1	2	2.2	10	22	4	12	0	.303	.483	15	6	P-23
1942	30	80	20	4	0	1	1.3	8	13	5	13	0	.250	.338	6	1	P-24
1945	21	46	10	0	1	1	2.2	4	5	0	8	0	.217	.326	10	1	P-11
1946	8	25	3	1	0	0	0.0	1	1	1	8	0	.120	.160	0	0	P-8
1947 CHI A	14	24	5	0	0	0	0.0	2	3	1	3	0	.208	.208	4	1	P-9
22 yrs.	882	1937	521	98	13	36	1.9	207	273	97	266	1	.269	.389	228	58	P-624, OF-3
WORLD SERIES																	
1932 NY A	2	4	0	0	0	0	0.0	0	0	1	1	0	.000	.000	0	0	P-1
1936	3	5	0	0	0	0	0.0	0	0	0	2	0	.000	.000	1	0	P-2

	G	AB	H	2B	3B	HR	HR %	R	RBI	BB	SO	SB	BA	SA	Pinch Hit AB	Pinch Hit H	G by POS

Red Ruffing continued

	G	AB	H	2B	3B	HR	HR%	R	RBI	BB	SO	SB	BA	SA	AB	H	G by POS
1937	1	4	2	1	0	0	0.0	0	3	0	0	0	.500	.750	0	0	P-1
1938	2	6	1	0	0	0	0.0	1	1	1	0	0	.167	.167	0	0	P-2
1939	1	3	1	0	0	0	0.0	0	0	0	1	0	.333	.333	0	0	P-1
1941	1	3	0	0	0	0	0.0	0	0	0	0	0	.000	.000	0	0	P-1
1942	4	9	2	0	0	0	0.0	0	0	0	2	0	.222	.222	2	0	P-2
7 yrs.	14	34	6	1	0	0	0.0	1	4	3	6	0	.176	.206	3	0	P-10

Chico Ruiz

RUIZ, HIRALDO SABLON　　　　　　　　　　BB　TR　6'　　169 lbs.
B. Dec. 12, 1938, Santo Domingo, Cuba　　D. Feb. 9, 1972, San Diego, Calif.

	G	AB	H	2B	3B	HR	HR%	R	RBI	BB	SO	SB	BA	SA	AB	H	G by POS
1964 CIN N	77	311	76	13	2	2	0.6	33	16	7	41	11	.244	.318	3	0	3B-49, 2B-30
1965	29	18	2	1	0	0	0.0	7	1	0	5	1	.111	.167	7	2	3B-4, SS-3
1966	82	110	28	2	1	0	0.0	13	5	5	14	1	.255	.291	35	13	3B-27, OF-8, SS-6
1967	105	250	55	12	4	0	0.0	32	13	11	35	9	.220	.300	17	3	2B-56, 3B-13, SS-11, OF-5
1968	85	139	36	2	1	0	0.0	15	9	12	18	4	.259	.288	31	7	2B-34, 1B-16, 3B-5, SS-3
1969	88	196	48	4	1	0	0.0	19	13	14	28	4	.245	.276	11	2	2B-39, SS-29, 3B-7, 1B-2, OF-1
1970 CAL A	68	107	26	3	1	0	0.0	10	12	7	16	3	.243	.290	30	3	3B-27, SS-3, 2B-3, 1B-2, C-1
1971	31	19	5	0	0	0	0.0	4	0	2	7	1	.263	.263	11	3	3B-3, 2B-2
8 yrs.	565	1150	276	37	10	2	0.2	133	69	58	164	34	.240	.295	145	33	2B-164, 3B-135, SS-55, 1B-20, OF-14, C-1

Chico Ruiz

RUIZ, MANUEL (Manny)　　　　　　　　　　BR　TR　5'11½"　170 lbs.
B. Nov. 1, 1951, Santurce, Puerto Rico

	G	AB	H	2B	3B	HR	HR%	R	RBI	BB	SO	SB	BA	SA	AB	H	G by POS
1978 ATL N	18	46	13	3	0	0	0.0	3	2	2	4	0	.283	.348	1	0	2B-14, 3B-1
1980	25	26	8	2	1	0	0.0	3	2	3	7	0	.308	.462	5	1	3B-16, SS-4, 2B-2
2 yrs.	43	72	21	5	1	0	0.0	6	4	5	11	0	.292	.389	6	1	3B-17, 2B-16, SS-4

Joe Rullo

RULLO, JOSEPH VINCENT　　　　　　　　　BR　TR　5'11"　168 lbs.
B. June 16, 1916, New York, N. Y.　　D. Oct. 28, 1969, Philadelphia, Pa.

	G	AB	H	2B	3B	HR	HR%	R	RBI	BB	SO	SB	BA	SA	AB	H	G by POS
1943 PHI A	16	55	16	3	0	0	0.0	2	6	8	7	0	.291	.345	0	0	2B-16
1944	35	96	16	0	0	0	0.0	5	5	6	19	1	.167	.167	0	0	2B-33, 1B-1
2 yrs.	51	151	32	3	0	0	0.0	7	11	14	26	1	.212	.232	0	0	2B-49, 1B-1

Bill Rumler

RUMLER, WILLIAM GEORGE　　　　　　　　BR　TR　6'1"　190 lbs.
B. Mar. 27, 1891, Milford, Neb.　　D. May 26, 1966, Lincoln, Neb.

	G	AB	H	2B	3B	HR	HR%	R	RBI	BB	SO	SB	BA	SA	AB	H	G by POS
1914 STL A	33	46	8	1	0	0	0.0	2	6	3	12	2	.174	.196	13	2	C-9, OF-6
1916	27	37	12	3	0	0	0.0	6	10	3	7	0	.324	.405	15	6	C-9
1917	78	88	23	3	4	1	1.1	7	16	8	9	2	.261	.420	71	16	OF-9
3 yrs.	138	171	43	7	4	1	0.6	15	32	14	28	4	.251	.357	99	24	C-18, OF-15

Paul Runge

RUNGE, PAUL WILLIAM　　　　　　　　　　BR　TR　6'　　165 lbs.
B. May 21, 1958, Kingston, N. Y.

	G	AB	H	2B	3B	HR	HR%	R	RBI	BB	SO	SB	BA	SA	AB	H	G by POS
1981 ATL N	10	27	7	1	0	0	0.0	2	4	4	4	0	.259	.296	0	0	SS-10
1982	4	2	0	0	0	0	0.0	0	0	0	0	0	.000	.000	2	0	
1983	5	8	2	0	0	0	0.0	0	1	1	4	0	.250	.250	1	0	2B-2
1984	28	90	24	3	1	0	0.0	5	3	10	14	5	.267	.322	0	0	2B-22, SS-7, 3B-3
4 yrs.	47	127	33	4	1	0	0.0	7	6	15	22	5	.260	.307	3	0	2B-24, SS-17, 3B-3

Pete Runnels

RUNNELS, JAMES EDWARD　　　　　　　　BL　TR　6'　　170 lbs.
B. Jan. 28, 1928, Lufkin, Tex.
Manager 1966.

	G	AB	H	2B	3B	HR	HR%	R	RBI	BB	SO	SB	BA	SA	AB	H	G by POS
1951 WAS A	78	273	76	12	2	0	0.0	31	25	31	24	0	.278	.337	5	0	SS-73
1952	152	555	158	18	3	1	0.2	70	64	72	55	0	.285	.333	4	1	SS-147, 2B-1
1953	137	486	125	15	5	2	0.4	64	50	64	36	3	.257	.321	8	3	SS-121, 2B-11
1954	139	488	131	17	15	2	0.4	75	56	78	60	2	.268	.383	5	2	SS-107, 2B-27, OF-1
1955	134	503	143	17	4	2	0.4	66	49	55	51	3	.284	.346	4	0	2B-132, SS-2
1956	147	578	179	29	9	8	1.4	72	76	58	64	5	.310	.433	2	1	1B-81, 2B-69, SS-3
1957	134	473	109	18	4	2	0.4	53	35	55	51	2	.230	.298	12	2	1B-72, 3B-32, 2B-23
1958 BOS A	147	568	183	32	5	8	1.4	103	59	87	49	1	.322	.438	0	0	2B-106, 1B-42
1959	147	560	176	33	6	6	1.1	95	57	95	48	6	.314	.427	2	1	2B-101, 1B-57, 3B-3
1960	143	528	169	29	2	2	0.4	80	35	71	51	5	.320	.394	2	1	2B-129, 1B-57, 3B-3
1961	143	360	114	20	3	3	0.8	49	38	46	32	5	.317	.414	23	5	1B-113, 3B-11, 2B-7, SS-1
1962	152	562	183	33	5	10	1.8	80	60	79	57	3	.326	.456	1	0	1B-151
1963 HOU N	124	388	98	9	1	2	0.5	35	23	45	42	2	.253	.296	16	4	1B-70, 2B-36, 3B-3
1964	22	51	10	1	0	0	0.0	3	3	8	7	0	.196	.216	6	0	1B-14
14 yrs.	1799	6373	1854	283	64	49	0.8	876	630	844	627	37	.291	.378	90	20	1B-644, 2B-642, SS-463, 3B-49, OF-1

Amos Rusie

RUSIE, AMOS WILSON (The Hoosier Thunderbolt)　　　BR　TR　6'1"　200 lbs.
B. May 30, 1871, Mooresville, Ind.　　D. Dec. 6, 1942, Seattle, Wash.
Hall of Fame 1977.

	G	AB	H	2B	3B	HR	HR%	R	RBI	BB	SO	SB	BA	SA	AB	H	G by POS
1889 IND N	33	103	18	3	1	0	0.0	15	4	2	19	3	.175	.223	0	0	P-33
1890 NY N	73	284	79	13	6	0	0.0	31	28	7	26	6	.278	.366	0	0	P-67, OF-14
1891	62	220	54	5	2	0	0.0	30	15	3	25	2	.245	.286	1	0	P-61, OF-1
1892	69	252	53	6	4	1	0.4	18	26	3	29	4	.210	.278	1	0	P-64, OF-4
1893	56	212	57	3	4	3	1.4	32	27	3	19	0	.269	.363	0	0	P-56
1894	56	186	52	5	4	3	1.6	20	26	5	24	5	.280	.398	2	1	P-54
1895	53	179	44	3	1	0	0.6	14	19	0	28	2	.246	.291	3	0	P-49, OF-1
1897	40	144	40	1	3	0	0.0	25	22	3		1	.278	.326	2	0	P-38
1898	41	138	29	2	4	0	0.0	23	8	1		2	.210	.283	2	1	P-37, OF-1, 1B-1
1901 CIN N	3	8	1	0	0	0	0.0	0	1	0		0	.125	.125	0	0	P-3
10 yrs.	486	1726	427	41	29	8	0.5	208	176	27	170	25	.247	.319	11	2	P-462, OF-21, 1B-1

	G	AB	H	2B	3B	HR	HR %	R	RBI	BB	SO	SB	BA	SA	Pinch Hit AB	Pinch Hit H	G by POS

Bill Russell

RUSSELL, WILLIAM ELLIS
B. Oct. 21, 1948, Pittsburg, Kans.

BR TR 6'   175 lbs.

	G	AB	H	2B	3B	HR	HR %	R	RBI	BB	SO	SB	BA	SA	AB	H	G by POS
1969 LA N	98	212	48	6	2	5	2.4	35	15	22	45	4	.226	.344	22	6	OF-86
1970	81	278	72	11	9	0	0.0	30	28	16	28	9	.259	.363	7	1	OF-79, SS-1
1971	91	211	48	7	4	2	0.9	29	15	11	39	6	.227	.327	3	0	2B-41, OF-40, SS-6
1972	129	434	118	19	5	4	0.9	47	34	34	64	14	.272	.366	5	2	SS-121, OF-6
1973	162	615	163	26	3	4	0.7	55	56	34	63	15	.265	.337	0	0	SS-162
1974	160	553	149	18	6	5	0.9	61	65	53	53	14	.269	.351	1	0	SS-160, OF-1
1975	84	252	52	9	2	0	0.0	24	14	23	28	5	.206	.258	0	0	SS-83
1976	149	554	152	17	3	5	0.9	53	65	21	46	15	.274	.343	0	0	SS-149
1977	153	634	176	28	6	4	0.6	84	51	24	43	16	.278	.360	0	0	SS-153
1978	155	625	179	32	4	3	0.5	72	46	30	34	10	.286	.365	1	0	SS-155
1979	153	627	170	26	4	7	1.1	72	56	24	43	6	.271	.359	3	1	SS-150
1980	130	466	123	23	2	3	0.6	38	34	18	44	13	.264	.341	1	0	SS-129
1981	82	262	61	9	2	0	0.0	20	22	19	20	2	.233	.282	0	0	SS-80
1982	153	497	136	20	2	3	0.6	44	46	63	30	10	.274	.340	2	2	SS-150
1983	131	451	111	13	1	1	0.2	47	30	33	31	13	.246	.286	5	0	SS-127
1984	89	262	70	12	1	0	0.0	25	19	25	24	4	.267	.321	6	1	SS-65, OF-18, 2B-5
16 yrs.	2000	6933	1828	276	56	46	0.7	756	596	450	635	156	.264	.340	56	13	SS-1691, OF-230, 2B-46
DIVISIONAL PLAYOFF SERIES																	
1981 LA N	5	16	4	1	0	0	0.0	1	2	3	1	0	.250	.313	0	0	SS-5
LEAGUE CHAMPIONSHIP SERIES																	
1974 LA N	4	18	7	0	0	0	0.0	1	3	1	0	0	.389	.389	0	0	SS-4
1977	4	18	5	1	0	0	0.0	3	2	0	0	0	.278	.333	0	0	SS-4
1978	4	17	7	1	0	0	0.0	1	2	1	1	0	.412	.471	0	0	SS-4
1981	5	16	5	0	1	0	0.0	2	1	1	1	0	.313	.438	0	0	SS-5
1983	4	14	4	0	0	0	0.0	1	0	2	4	1	.286	.286	0	0	SS-4
5 yrs.	21	83	28	2	1	0	0.0	8	8	5	6	1	.337	.386	0	0	SS-21
WORLD SERIES																	
1974 LA N	5	18	4	0	1	0	0.0	0	2	0	2	0	.222	.333	0	0	SS-5
1977	6	26	4	0	1	0	0.0	3	2	1	3	0	.154	.231	0	0	SS-6
1978	6	26	11	2	0	0	0.0	1	2	2	2	1	.423	.500	0	0	SS-6
1981	6	25	6	0	0	0	0.0	1	2	0	1	1	.240	.240	0	0	SS-6
4 yrs.	23	95	25	2	2	0	0.0	5	8	3	8	2	.263	.326	0	0	SS-23

Harvey Russell

RUSSELL, HARVEY HOLMES
B. Jan. 10, 1887, Marshall, Va.   D. Jan. 8, 1980, Alexandria, Va.

BL TR 5'9½" 163 lbs.

	G	AB	H	2B	3B	HR	HR %	R	RBI	BB	SO	SB	BA	SA	AB	H	G by POS
1914 BAL F	81	168	39	3	2	0	0.0	18	13	18		2	.232	.274	29	7	C-47, OF-1, SS-1
1915	53	73	19	1	2	0	0.0	5	11	14		1	.260	.329	24	5	C-21
2 yrs.	134	241	58	4	4	0	0.0	23	24	32		3	.241	.290	53	12	C-68, OF-1, SS-1

Jim Russell

RUSSELL, JAMES WILLIAM
B. Oct. 1, 1918, Fayette City, Pa.

BB TR 6'1"   181 lbs.

	G	AB	H	2B	3B	HR	HR %	R	RBI	BB	SO	SB	BA	SA	AB	H	G by POS
1942 PIT N	3	14	1	0	0	0	0.0	2	0	1	4	0	.071	.071	1	0	OF-3
1943	146	533	138	19	11	4	0.8	79	44	77	67	12	.259	.358	7	2	OF-134, 1B-6
1944	152	580	181	34	14	8	1.4	109	66	79	63	6	.312	.460	2	0	OF-149
1945	146	510	145	24	8	12	2.4	88	77	71	40	15	.284	.433	6	0	OF-140
1946	146	516	143	29	6	8	1.6	68	50	67	54	11	.277	.403	5	1	OF-134, 1B-5
1947	128	478	121	21	8	8	1.7	68	51	63	58	7	.253	.381	9	3	OF-119
1948 BOS N	89	322	85	18	1	9	2.8	44	54	46	31	4	.264	.410	4	0	OF-84
1949	130	415	96	22	1	8	1.9	57	54	64	68	3	.231	.347	6	0	OF-120
1950 BKN N	78	214	49	8	2	10	4.7	37	32	31	36	1	.229	.425	18	3	OF-55
1951	16	13	0	0	0	0	0.0	2	0	4	6	0	.000	.000	10	0	OF-4
10 yrs.	1034	3595	959	175	51	67	1.9	554	428	503	427	59	.267	.400	68	9	OF-942, 1B-11

John Russell

RUSSELL, JOHN WILLIAM
B. Jan. 5, 1961, Oklahoma City, Okla.

BR TR 6'   195 lbs.

	G	AB	H	2B	3B	HR	HR %	R	RBI	BB	SO	SB	BA	SA	AB	H	G by POS
1984 PHI N	39	99	28	8	1	2	2.0	11	11	12	33	0	.283	.444	9	4	OF-29, C-2

Lloyd Russell

RUSSELL, LLOYD OPAL (Tex)
B. Apr. 10, 1913, Atoka, Okla.   D. May 24, 1968, Waco, Tex.

BR TR 5'11" 166 lbs.

	G	AB	H	2B	3B	HR	HR %	R	RBI	BB	SO	SB	BA	SA	AB	H	G by POS
1938 CLE A	2	0	0	0	0	0	–	0	0	0	0	0	–	–	0	0	

Paul Russell

RUSSELL, BENJAMIN PAUL
B. 1870, Reading, Pa.   D. Pottstown, Pa.

	G	AB	H	2B	3B	HR	HR %	R	RBI	BB	SO	SB	BA	SA	AB	H	G by POS
1894 STL N	3	10	1	0	0	0	0.0	1	0	0	2	0	.100	.100	0	0	OF-1, 3B-1, 2B-1

Reb Russell

RUSSELL, EWELL ALBERT
B. Apr. 12, 1889, Jackson, Miss.   D. Sept. 30, 1973, Indianapolis, Ind.

BL TL 5'11" 185 lbs.

	G	AB	H	2B	3B	HR	HR %	R	RBI	BB	SO	SB	BA	SA	AB	H	G by POS
1913 CHI A	52	106	20	5	3	0	0.0	9	7	1	29	0	.189	.292	1	1	P-51
1914	43	64	17	1	1	0	0.0	6	7	1	14	0	.266	.313	5	2	P-38
1915	45	86	21	2	3	0	0.0	11	7	4	14	1	.244	.337	3	0	P-41
1916	56	91	13	2	0	0	0.0	9	6	0	18	1	.143	.165	0	0	P-56
1917	39	68	19	3	3	0	0.0	5	9	2	10	0	.279	.412	3	1	P-35, OF-1
1918	27	50	7	3	0	0	0.0	2	3	0	6	0	.140	.200	6	1	P-19, OF-1
1919	1	0	0	0	0	0	–	0	0	0	0	0	–	–	0	0	P-1
1922 PIT N	60	220	81	14	8	12	5.5	51	75	14	18	4	.368	.668	0	0	OF-60
1923	94	291	84	18	7	9	3.1	49	58	20	21	3	.289	.491	17	5	OF-76
9 yrs.	417	976	262	48	25	21	2.2	142	172	42	130	9	.268	.433	35	8	P-241, OF-138
WORLD SERIES																	
1917 CHI A	1	0	0	0	0	0	–	0	0	0	0	0	–	–	0	0	P-1

	G	AB	H	2B	3B	HR	HR %	R	RBI	BB	SO	SB	BA	SA	Pinch Hit AB	Pinch Hit H	G by POS

Rip Russell

RUSSELL, GLEN DAVID   BR TR 6'1"   180 lbs.
B. Jan. 26, 1915, Los Angeles, Calif.   D. Sept. 26, 1976, Los Alamitos, Calif.

	G	AB	H	2B	3B	HR	HR %	R	RBI	BB	SO	SB	BA	SA	PH AB	PH H	G by POS
1939 CHI N	143	542	148	24	5	9	1.7	55	79	36	56	2	.273	.386	0	0	1B-143
1940	68	215	53	7	2	5	2.3	15	33	8	23	1	.247	.367	15	5	1B-51, 3B-3
1941	6	17	5	1	0	0	0.0	1	1	1	5	0	.294	.353	0	0	1B-5
1942	102	302	73	9	0	8	2.6	32	41	17	21	0	.242	.351	31	5	1B-35, 2B-24, 3B-10, OF-3
1946 BOS A	80	274	57	10	1	6	2.2	22	35	13	30	1	.208	.318	9	2	3B-70, 2B-3
1947	26	52	8	1	0	1	1.9	8	3	8	7	0	.154	.231	12	1	3B-13
6 yrs.	425	1402	344	52	8	29	2.1	133	192	83	142	4	.245	.356	67	13	1B-234, 3B-96, 2B-27, OF-3

WORLD SERIES																	
1946 BOS A	2	2	2	0	0	0	0.0	1	0	0	0	0	1.000	1.000	2	2	3B-1

Hank Ruszkowski

RUSZKOWSKI, HENRY ALEXANDER   BR TR 6'   190 lbs.
B. Nov. 10, 1925, Cleveland, Ohio

	G	AB	H	2B	3B	HR	HR %	R	RBI	BB	SO	SB	BA	SA	PH AB	PH H	G by POS
1944 CLE A	3	8	3	0	0	0	0.0	1	0	1	1	0	.375	.375	1	0	C-2
1945	14	49	10	0	0	0	0.0	2	5	4	9	0	.204	.204	0	0	C-14
1947	23	27	7	2	0	3	11.1	5	4	2	6	0	.259	.667	7	2	C-16
3 yrs.	40	84	20	2	0	3	3.6	8	10	6	16	0	.238	.369	8	2	C-32

Babe Ruth

RUTH, GEORGE HERMAN (The Sultan of Swat, The Bambino)   BL TL 6'2"   215 lbs.
B. Feb. 6, 1895, Baltimore, Md.   D. Aug. 16, 1948, New York, N. Y.
Hall of Fame 1936.

	G	AB	H	2B	3B	HR	HR %	R	RBI	BB	SO	SB	BA	SA	PH AB	PH H	G by POS
1914 BOS A	5	10	2	1	0	0	0.0	1	0	0	4	0	.200	.300	1	0	P-4
1915	42	92	29	10	1	4	4.3	16	21	9	23	0	.315	.576	10	1	P-32
1916	67	136	37	5	3	3	2.2	18	16	10	23	0	.272	.419	19	4	P-44
1917	52	123	40	6	3	2	1.6	14	12	12	18	0	.325	.472	7	1	P-41
1918	95	317	95	26	11	11	3.5	50	66	57	58	6	.300	.555	3	1	OF-59, P-20, 1B-13
1919	130	432	139	34	12	29	6.7	103	114	101	58	7	.322	.657	1	0	OF-111, P-17, 1B-4
1920 NY A	142	458	172	36	9	54	11.8[1]	158	137	148	80	14	.376	.847[1]	1	0	OF-139, 1B-2, P-1
1921	152	540	204	44	16	59	10.9	177	171	144	81	17	.378	.846	0	0	OF-152, 1B-2, P-2
1922	110	406	128	24	8	35	8.6	94	99	84	80	2	.315	.672	0	0	OF-110, 1B-1
1923	152	522	205	45	13	41	7.9	151	131	170[1]	93	17	.393	.764	0	0	OF-148, 1B-4
1924	153	529	200	39	7	46	8.7	143	121	142	81	9	.378	.739	1	1	OF-152
1925	98	359	104	12	2	25	7.0	61	66	59	68	2	.290	.543	0	0	OF-98
1926	152	495	184	30	5	47	9.5	139	145	144	76	11	.372	.737	3	0	OF-149, 1B-2
1927	151	540	192	29	8	60	11.1	158	164	138	89	7	.356	.772	0	0	OF-151
1928	154	536	173	29	8	54	10.1	163	142	135	87	4	.323	.709	0	0	OF-154
1929	135	499	172	26	6	46	9.2	121	154	72	60	5	.345	.697	2	1	OF-133
1930	145	518	186	28	9	49	9.5	150	153	136	61	10	.359	.732	0	0	OF-144, P-1
1931	145	534	199	31	3	46	8.6	149	163	128	51	5	.373	.700	2	0	OF-142, 1B-1
1932	133	457	156	13	5	41	9.0	120	137	130	62	2	.341	.661	1	1	OF-127, 1B-1
1933	137	459	138	21	3	34	7.4	97	103	114	90	4	.301	.582	4	1	OF-132, 1B-1, P-1
1934	125	365	105	17	4	22	6.0	78	84	103	63	1	.288	.537	11	2	OF-111
1935 BOS N	28	72	13	0	0	6	8.3	13	12	20	24	0	.181	.431	1	0	OF-26
22 yrs.	2503	8399	2873	506	136	714	8.5	2174	2211	2056	1330	123	.342	.690	67	13	OF-2238, P-163, 1B-31
							2nd	1st	2nd	2nd	1st			1st			

WORLD SERIES																	
1915 BOS A	1	1	0	0	0	0	0.0	0	0	0	0	0	.000	.000	1	0	
1916	1	5	0	0	0	0	0.0	0	1	0	2	0	.000	.000	0	0	P-1
1918	3	5	1	0	1	0	0.0	0	2	0	2	0	.200	.600	0	0	OF-2
1921 NY A	6	16	5	0	0	1	6.3	3	4	5	8	2	.313	.500	1	0	OF-5
1922	5	17	2	1	0	0	0.0	1	1	2	3	0	.118	.176	0	0	OF-5
1923	6	19	7	1	1	3	15.8	8	3	8	6	0	.368	1.000	0	0	1B-1
1926	7	20	6	0	0	4	20.0	6	5	11	2	1	.300	.900	0	0	OF-7
1927	4	15	6	0	0	2	13.3	4	7	2	2	1	.400	.800	0	0	OF-4
1928	4	16	10	3	0	3	18.8	9	4	1	8	0	.625	1.375	0	0	OF-4
1932	4	15	5	0	0	2	13.3	6	6	4	3	0	.333	.733	0	0	OF-4
10 yrs.	41	129	42	5	2	15	11.6	37	33	33	30	4	.326	.744	2	0	OF-31, 1B-1, P-1
	10th		10th				2nd	1st	3rd	4th	2nd	4th			2nd		

Jim Rutherford

RUTHERFORD, JAMES HOLLIS   BL TR 6'1"   180 lbs.
B. Sept. 26, 1886, Stillwater, Minn.   D. Sept. 18, 1956, Cleveland, Ohio

	G	AB	H	2B	3B	HR	HR %	R	RBI	BB	SO	SB	BA	SA	PH AB	PH H	G by POS
1910 CLE A	1	2	1	0	0	0	0.0	0	0	0		0	.500	.500	0	0	OF-1

Mickey Rutner

RUTNER, MILTON   BR TR 5'11½" 185 lbs.
B. Mar. 18, 1920, Hempstead, N. Y.

	G	AB	H	2B	3B	HR	HR %	R	RBI	BB	SO	SB	BA	SA	PH AB	PH H	G by POS
1947 PHI A	12	48	12	1	0	1	2.1	4	4	3	2	0	.250	.333	1	0	3B-11

Mark Ryal

RYAL, MARK DWAYNE   BL TL 6'1"   180 lbs.
B. Apr. 28, 1960, Henryetta, Okla.

	G	AB	H	2B	3B	HR	HR %	R	RBI	BB	SO	SB	BA	SA	PH AB	PH H	G by POS
1982 KC A	6	13	1	0	0	0	0.0	0	0	1	3	0	.077	.077	1	0	OF-5

Blondy Ryan

RYAN, JOHN COLLINS   BR TR 6'1"   178 lbs.
B. Jan. 4, 1906, Lynn, Mass.   D. Nov. 28, 1959, Swampscott, Mass.

	G	AB	H	2B	3B	HR	HR %	R	RBI	BB	SO	SB	BA	SA	PH AB	PH H	G by POS
1930 CHI A	28	87	18	0	4	1	1.1	9	10	6	13	2	.207	.333	0	0	3B-23, SS-2, 2B-1
1933 NY N	146	525	125	10	5	3	0.6	47	48	15	62	0	.238	.293	0	0	SS-146
1934	110	385	93	19	0	2	0.5	35	41	19	68	3	.242	.306	1	0	3B-65, SS-30, 2B-25
1935 2 teams	PHI N (39G — .264)				NY A (30G — .238)												
" total	69	234	59	4	3	1	0.4	25	21	10	30	1	.252	.308	2	1	SS-65, 3B-1, 2B-1
1937 NY N	21	75	18	3	1	1	1.3	10	13	6	8	0	.240	.347	1	0	SS-19, 3B-1, 2B-1
1938	12	24	5	0	0	0	0.0	1	0	1	3	0	.208	.208	2	1	2B-5, 3B-3, SS-2
6 yrs.	386	1330	318	36	13	8	0.6	127	133	57	184	6	.239	.304	6	3	SS-264, 3B-93, 2B-33

WORLD SERIES																	
1933 NY N	5	18	5	0	0	0	0.0	0	1	1	5	0	.278	.278	0	0	SS-5

	G	AB	H	2B	3B	HR	HR %	R	RBI	BB	SO	SB	BA	SA	Pinch Hit AB	Pinch Hit H	G by POS

Blondy Ryan continued

	G	AB	H	2B	3B	HR	HR%	R	RBI	BB	SO	SB	BA	SA	AB	H	G by POS
1937	1	1	0	0	0	0	0.0	0	0	0	1	0	.000	.000	1	0	
2 yrs.	6	19	5	0	0	0	0.0	0	1	1	6	0	.263	.263	1	0	SS-5

Bud Ryan

RYAN, JOHN BUDD   BL TR 5'9½" 172 lbs.
B. Oct. 6, 1885, Denver, Colo.   D. July 9, 1956, Sacramento, Calif.

	G	AB	H	2B	3B	HR	HR%	R	RBI	BB	SO	SB	BA	SA	AB	H	G by POS
1912 CLE A	93	328	89	12	9	1	0.3	53	31	30		12	.271	.372	3	1	OF-90
1913	73	243	72	6	1	0	0.0	26	32	11	13	9	.296	.329	4	2	OF-67, 1B-1
2 yrs.	166	571	161	18	10	1	0.2	79	63	41	13	21	.282	.354	7	3	OF-157, 1B-1

Connie Ryan

RYAN, CORNELIUS JOSEPH   BR TR 5'11" 175 lbs.
B. Feb. 27, 1920, New Orleans, La.
Manager 1975, 1977.

	G	AB	H	2B	3B	HR	HR%	R	RBI	BB	SO	SB	BA	SA	AB	H	G by POS
1942 NY N	11	27	5	0	0	0	0.0	2	4	3	1	.185	.185	0	0	2B-11
1943 BOS N	132	457	97	10	2	1	0.2	52	24	58	56	7	.212	.249	1	0	2B-100, 3B-30
1944	88	332	98	18	5	4	1.2	56	25	36	40	13	.295	.416	0	0	2B-80, 3B-14
1946	143	502	121	28	8	1	0.2	55	48	55	63	7	.241	.335	1	0	2B-120, 3B-24
1947	150	544	144	33	5	5	0.9	60	69	71	60	5	.265	.371	0	0	2B-150, SS-1
1948	51	122	26	3	0	0	0.0	14	10	21	16	0	.213	.238	7	1	2B-40, 3B-4
1949	85	208	52	13	1	6	2.9	28	20	21	30	1	.250	.409	23	5	3B-25, 2B-18, 2B-16, 1B-3
1950 2 teams		BOS	N (20G –	.194)		CIN	N (106G –	.259)									
" total	126	439	109	20	5	6	1.4	57	49	64	55	4	.248	.358	1	0	2B-123
1951 CIN N	136	473	112	17	4	16	3.4	75	53	79	72	11	.237	.391	7	3	2B-121, 3B-3, 1B-2, OF-1
1952 PHI N	154	577	139	24	6	12	2.1	81	49	69	72	13	.241	.366	0	0	2B-154
1953 2 teams		PHI	N (90G –	.296)		CHI	A (17G –	.222)									
" total	107	301	85	15	6	5	1.7	53	32	39	47	7	.282	.422	22	8	2B-65, 3B-16, 1B-2
1954 CIN N	1	0	0	0	0	0	–	0	0	1	0	0	–	–	0	0	
12 yrs.	1184	3982	988	181	42	56	1.4	535	381	518	514	69	.248	.357	62	17	2B-980, 3B-116, SS-19, 1B-7, OF-1

WORLD SERIES

	G	AB	H	2B	3B	HR	HR%	R	RBI	BB	SO	SB	BA	SA	AB	H	G by POS
1948 BOS N	2	1	0	0	0	0	0.0	0	0	0	1	0	.000	.000	1	0	

Cyclone Ryan

RYAN, DANIEL R.   6'
B. 1866, Capperwhite, Ireland   D. Jan. 30, 1917, Medfield, Mass.

	G	AB	H	2B	3B	HR	HR%	R	RBI	BB	SO	SB	BA	SA	AB	H	G by POS
1887 NY AA	8	32	7	1	0	0	0.0	4		3		1	.219	.250	0	0	1B-8, P-2
1891 BOS N	1	1	0	0	0	0	0.0	0	0	0	0	0	.000	.000	0	0	P-1
2 yrs.	9	33	7	1	0	0	0.0	4		3	0	1	.212	.242	0	0	1B-8, P-3

J. Ryan

RYAN, J.
Deceased.

	G	AB	H	2B	3B	HR	HR%	R	RBI	BB	SO	SB	BA	SA	AB	H	G by POS
1895 STL N	2	2	0	0	0	0	0.0	0	0	0	0	0	.000	.000	0	0	3B-2

Jack Ryan

RYAN, JOHN FRANCIS   BR TR 6' 185 lbs.
B. May 5, 1905, Mineral, Kans.   D. Sept. 2, 1967, Rochester, Minn.

	G	AB	H	2B	3B	HR	HR%	R	RBI	BB	SO	SB	BA	SA	AB	H	G by POS
1929 BOS A	2	3	0	0	0	0	0.0	0	0	0	0	0	.000	.000	0	0	OF-2

Jimmy Ryan

RYAN, JAMES E.   BR TL 5'9" 162 lbs.
B. Feb. 11, 1863, Clinton, Mass.   D. Oct. 26, 1923, Chicago, Ill.

	G	AB	H	2B	3B	HR	HR%	R	RBI	BB	SO	SB	BA	SA	AB	H	G by POS
1885 CHI N	3	13	6	1	0	0	0.0	2	2	1	1		.462	.538	0	0	SS-2, OF-1
1886	84	327	100	17	6	4	1.2	58	53	12	28		.306	.431	0	0	OF-70, SS-6, 3B-6, 2B-5, P-5
1887	126	508	145	23	10	11	2.2	117	74	53	19	50	.285	.435	0	0	OF-122, P-8, 2B-3
1888	129	549	182	33	10	16	2.9	115	64	35	50	60	.332	.515	0	0	OF-128, P-8
1889	135	576	187	31	14	17	3.0	140	72	70	62	45	.325	.516	0	0	OF-106, SS-29
1890 CHI P	118	486	165	32	5	6	1.2	99	89	60	36	30	.340	.463	0	0	OF-118
1891 CHI N	118	505	145	22	15	9	1.8	110	66	53	38	27	.287	.444	0	0	OF-117, SS-2, P-2
1892	128	505	148	21	11	10	2.0	105	65	61	41	27	.293	.438	0	0	OF-120, SS-9
1893	83	341	102	21	7	3	0.9	82	30	59	25	8	.299	.428	0	0	OF-73, SS-10, P-1
1894	108	481	173	37	7	3	0.6	133	62	50	23	11	.360	.484	0	0	OF-108
1895	108	443	143	22	8	6	1.4	83	49	48	22	18	.323	.449	0	0	OF-108
1896	128	490	153	24	10	3	0.6	83	86	46	16	29	.312	.420	0	0	OF-128
1897	136	520	160	33	17	5	1.0	103	85	50		27	.308	.465	0	0	OF-136
1898	144	572	185	32	13	4	0.7	122	79	73		29	.323	.446	0	0	OF-144
1899	125	525	158	20	10	3	0.6	91	68	43		9	.301	.394	0	0	OF-125
1900	105	415	115	25	4	5	1.2	66	59	29		19	.277	.393	0	0	OF-105
1902 WAS A	120	484	155	32	6	6	1.2	92	44	43		10	.320	.448	0	0	OF-120
1903	114	437	107	25	4	7	1.6	42	46	17		9	.245	.368	0	0	OF-114
18 yrs.	2012	8177	2529	451	157	118	1.4	1643	1093	803	361	408	.309	.446	0	0	OF-1943, SS-58, P-24, 2B-8, 3B-6

John Ryan

RYAN, JOHN A.
Born Daniel Sheehan.
B. Birmingham, Mich.   Deceased.

	G	AB	H	2B	3B	HR	HR%	R	RBI	BB	SO	SB	BA	SA	AB	H	G by POS
1884 2 teams		WAS	U (7G –	.143)		WIL	U (2G –	.167)									
" total	9	34	5	0	1	0	0.0	2		2			.147	.206	0	0	OF-9, 3B-1

John Ryan

RYAN, JOHN BERNARD (Jack)   BR TR 5'10½" 165 lbs.
B. Nov. 12, 1869, Haverhill, Mass.   D. Aug. 21, 1952, Boston, Mass.

	G	AB	H	2B	3B	HR	HR%	R	RBI	BB	SO	SB	BA	SA	AB	H	G by POS
1889 LOU AA	21	79	14	1	0	0	0.0	8	2	3	17	2	.177	.190	0	0	C-15, OF-4, 3B-2
1890	93	337	73	16	4	0	0.0	43		12		6	.217	.288	0	0	C-89, OF-3, SS-1, 1B-1
1891	75	253	57	5	4	2	0.8	24	25	15	40	3	.225	.300	0	0	C-56, 1B-11, 3B-6, OF-4, 2B-3
1894 BOS N	53	201	54	12	7	1	0.5	39	29	13	16	3	.269	.413	0	0	C-51, 1B-2
1895	49	189	55	7	0	0	0.0	22	18	6	6	3	.291	.328	0	0	C-43, 2B-5, OF-1
1896	8	32	3	1	0	0	0.0	2	0	0	1	0	.094	.125	0	0	C-8
1898 BKN N	87	301	57	11	4	0	0.0	39	24	15		5	.189	.252	0	0	C-84, 3B-4, 1B-1

	G	AB	H	2B	3B	HR	HR %	R	RBI	BB	SO	SB	BA	SA	Pinch Hit AB	Pinch Hit H	G by POS

John Ryan continued

	G	AB	H	2B	3B	HR	HR %	R	RBI	BB	SO	SB	BA	SA	AB	H	G by POS
1899 BAL N	2	4	2	1	0	0	0.0	0	1	0		1	.500	.750	0	0	C-2
1901 STL N	83	300	59	6	5	0	0.0	27	31	7		5	.197	.250	1	0	C-65, 2B-9, 1B-5, OF-3
1902	76	267	48	4	4	0	0.0	23	14	4		2	.180	.225	0	0	C-66, 3B-4, 1B-4, 2B-2, SS-1, P-1
1903	67	227	54	5	1	1	0.4	18	10	10		2	.238	.282	0	0	C-47, 1B-18, SS-2
1912 WAS A	1	1	0	0	0	0	0.0	0	0	0		0	.000	.000	0	0	3B-1
1913	1	1	0	0	0	0	0.0	0	0	0	0	0	.000	.000	0	0	C-1
13 yrs.	616	2192	476	69	29	4	0.2	245	154	85	80	32	.217	.281	1	0	C-527, 1B-42, 2B-19, 3B-17, OF-15, SS-4, P-1

Johnny Ryan

RYAN, JOHN JOSEPH
B. Philadelphia, Pa.   D. Mar. 22, 1902, Philadelphia, Pa.

5'7½"   150 lbs.

	G	AB	H	2B	3B	HR	HR %	R	RBI	BB	SO	SB	BA	SA	AB	H	G by POS
1876 LOU N	64	241	61	5	1	1	0.4	32	18	6	23		.253	.295	0	0	OF-64, P-1
1877 CIN N	6	26	4	0	1	0	0.0	2	2	1	5		.154	.231	0	0	OF-6
2 yrs.	70	267	65	5	2	1	0.4	34	20	7	28		.243	.288	0	0	OF-70, P-1

Lew Ryan

Playing record listed under Lew Malone

Mike Ryan

RYAN, MICHAEL JAMES
B. Nov. 25, 1941, Haverhill, Mass.

BR TR 6'2"   205 lbs.

	G	AB	H	2B	3B	HR	HR %	R	RBI	BB	SO	SB	BA	SA	AB	H	G by POS
1964 BOS A	1	3	1	0	0	0	0.0	0	2	1	0	0	.333	.333	0	0	C-1
1965	33	107	17	0	1	3	2.8	9	9	5	19	0	.159	.262	0	0	C-33
1966	116	369	79	15	3	2	0.5	27	32	29	68	1	.214	.287	3	1	C-114
1967	79	226	45	4	2	2	0.9	21	27	26	42	2	.199	.261	0	0	C-79
1968 PHI N	96	296	53	6	1	1	0.3	12	15	15	59	0	.179	.216	1	0	C-96
1969	133	446	91	17	2	12	2.7	41	44	30	66	1	.204	.332	1	0	C-132
1970	46	134	24	8	0	2	1.5	14	11	16	24	0	.179	.284	0	0	C-46
1971	43	134	22	5	1	3	2.2	9	6	10	32	0	.164	.284	0	0	C-46
1972	46	106	19	4	0	2	1.9	6	10	10	25	0	.179	.274	0	0	C-27
1973	28	69	16	1	2	1	1.4	7	5	6	19	0	.232	.348	1	0	C-15
1974 PIT N	15	30	3	0	0	0	0.0	2	0	4	16	0	.100	.100	0	0	C-15
11 yrs.	636	1920	370	60	12	28	1.5	146	161	152	370	4	.193	.280	6	1	C-632

WORLD SERIES

	G	AB	H	2B	3B	HR	HR %	R	RBI	BB	SO	SB	BA	SA	AB	H	G by POS
1967 BOS A	1	2	0	0	0	0	0.0	0	0	0	1	0	.000	.000	0	0	C-1

Tom Ryder

RYDER, THOMAS
Deceased.

	G	AB	H	2B	3B	HR	HR %	R	RBI	BB	SO	SB	BA	SA	AB	H	G by POS
1884 STL U	8	28	7	1	0	0	0.0	4		2			.250	.286	0	0	OF-8

Gene Rye

RYE, EUGENE RUDOLPH (Half-Pint)
Born Eugene Rudolph Mercantelli.
B. Nov. 15, 1906, Chicago, Ill.   D. Jan. 21, 1980, Park Ridge, Ill.

BL TR 5'6"   165 lbs.

	G	AB	H	2B	3B	HR	HR %	R	RBI	BB	SO	SB	BA	SA	AB	H	G by POS
1931 BOS A	17	39	7	0	0	0	0.0	3	1	2	5	0	.179	.179	7	1	OF-10

Alex Sabo

SABO, ALEXANDER (Giz)
Born Alexander Szabo.
B. Feb. 14, 1910, New Brunswick, N. J.

BR TR 6'   192 lbs.

	G	AB	H	2B	3B	HR	HR %	R	RBI	BB	SO	SB	BA	SA	AB	H	G by POS
1936 WAS A	4	8	3	0	0	0	0.0	1	1	0	2	0	.375	.375	1	1	C-4
1937	1	0	0	0	0	0	–	0	0	0	0	0	–	–	0	0	C-1
2 yrs.	5	8	3	0	0	0	0.0	1	1	0	2	0	.375	.375	1	1	C-5

Frank Sacka

SACKA, FRANK
B. Aug. 30, 1924, Romulus, Mich.

BR TR 6'   195 lbs.

	G	AB	H	2B	3B	HR	HR %	R	RBI	BB	SO	SB	BA	SA	AB	H	G by POS
1951 WAS A	7	16	4	0	0	0	0.0	1	3	0	5	0	.250	.250	1	0	C-6
1953	7	18	5	0	0	0	0.0	2	3	3	1	0	.278	.278	1	0	C-6
2 yrs.	14	34	9	0	0	0	0.0	3	6	3	6	0	.265	.265	2	0	C-12

Mike Sadek

SADEK, MICHAEL GEORGE
B. May 30, 1946, Minneapolis, Minn.

BR TR 5'9"   165 lbs.

	G	AB	H	2B	3B	HR	HR %	R	RBI	BB	SO	SB	BA	SA	AB	H	G by POS
1973 SF N	39	66	11	1	0	0	0.0	6	4	11	8	1	.167	.212	0	0	C-35
1975	42	106	25	5	2	0	0.0	14	9	14	14	1	.236	.321	4	3	C-38
1976	55	93	19	2	0	0	0.0	8	7	11	10	0	.204	.226	2	1	C-51
1977	61	126	29	7	0	1	0.8	12	15	12	5	2	.230	.310	4	2	C-57
1978	40	109	26	3	0	2	1.8	15	9	10	11	1	.239	.321	0	0	C-37
1979	63	126	30	5	0	1	0.8	14	11	15	24	1	.238	.302	3	0	C-60, OF-1
1980	64	151	38	4	1	1	0.7	14	16	27	18	0	.252	.311	3	0	C-59
1981	19	36	6	3	0	0	0.0	5	3	8	7	0	.167	.250	0	0	C-19
8 yrs.	383	813	184	30	4	5	0.6	88	74	108	97	6	.226	.292	16	6	C-356, OF-1

Bob Sadowski

SADOWSKI, ROBERT FRANK (Sid)
B. Jan. 15, 1937, St. Louis, Mo.

BL TR 6'   175 lbs.

	G	AB	H	2B	3B	HR	HR %	R	RBI	BB	SO	SB	BA	SA	AB	H	G by POS
1960 STL N	1	1	0	0	0	0	0.0	0	0	1	0	0	.000	.000	0	0	2B-1
1961 PHI N	16	54	7	0	0	0	0.0	4	0	4	7	1	.130	.130	3	0	3B-14
1962 CHI A	79	130	30	3	3	6	4.6	22	24	13	22	0	.231	.438	44	10	3B-16, 2B-12
1963 LA A	88	144	36	6	0	1	0.7	12	22	15	34	2	.250	.313	50	12	OF-25, 3B-6, 2B-4
4 yrs.	184	329	73	9	3	7	2.1	38	46	33	63	3	.222	.331	97	22	3B-36, OF-25, 2B-17

Eddie Sadowski

SADOWSKI, EDWARD ROMAN
Brother of Ted Sadowski.   Brother of Bob Sadowski.
B. Jan. 19, 1932, Pittsburgh, Pa.

BR TR 5'11"   175 lbs.

	G	AB	H	2B	3B	HR	HR %	R	RBI	BB	SO	SB	BA	SA	AB	H	G by POS
1960 BOS A	38	93	20	2	0	3	3.2	10	8	8	13	0	.215	.333	0	0	C-36
1961 LA A	69	164	38	13	0	4	2.4	16	12	11	33	2	.232	.384	9	1	C-56
1962	27	55	11	4	0	1	1.8	4	3	2	14	1	.200	.327	7	1	C-18

	G	AB	H	2B	3B	HR	HR %	R	RBI	BB	SO	SB	BA	SA	Pinch Hit AB	Pinch Hit H	G by POS

Eddie Sadowski continued

	G	AB	H	2B	3B	HR	HR%	R	RBI	BB	SO	SB	BA	SA	PH AB	PH H	G by POS
1963	80	174	30	1	1	4	2.3	24	15	17	33	2	.172	.259	6	1	C-68
1966 ATL N	3	9	1	0	0	0	0.0	1	1	1	1	0	.111	.111	0	0	C-3
5 yrs.	217	495	100	20	1	12	2.4	55	39	39	94	5	.202	.319	22	3	C-181

Tom Saffell

SAFFELL, THOMAS JUDSON
B. July 26, 1921, Etowah, Tenn.   BL TR 5'11" 170 lbs.

	G	AB	H	2B	3B	HR	HR%	R	RBI	BB	SO	SB	BA	SA	PH AB	PH H	G by POS
1949 PIT N	73	205	66	7	1	2	1.0	36	25	21	27	5	.322	.395	18	6	OF-53
1950	67	182	37	7	0	2	1.1	18	6	14	34	1	.203	.275	21	4	OF-43
1951	49	65	13	0	0	1	1.5	11	5	5	18	1	.200	.246	24	3	OF-17
1955 2 teams		PIT	N (73G – .168)		KC	A	(9G –	.216)									
" total	82	150	27	1	0	1	0.7	26	4	19	29	2	.180	.207	17	4	OF-56
4 yrs.	271	602	143	15	1	6	1.0	91	40	59	108	9	.238	.296	80	17	OF-169

Harry Sage

SAGE, HARRY (Doc)
B. Mar. 16, 1864, Rock Island, Ill.   D. May 27, 1947, Rock Island, Ill.   BR TR 5'10" 185 lbs.

	G	AB	H	2B	3B	HR	HR%	R	RBI	BB	SO	SB	BA	SA	PH AB	PH H	G by POS
1890 TOL AA	81	275	41	8	4	2	0.7	40		29		10	.149	.229	0	0	C-80, OF-1

Vic Saier

SAIER, VICTOR SYLVESTER
B. May 4, 1891, Lansing, Mich.   D. May 14, 1967, East Lansing, Mich.   BL TR 5'11" 185 lbs.

	G	AB	H	2B	3B	HR	HR%	R	RBI	BB	SO	SB	BA	SA	PH AB	PH H	G by POS
1911 CHI N	86	259	67	15	1	1	0.4	42	37	25	37	11	.259	.336	12	4	1B-73
1912	122	451	130	25	14	2	0.4	74	61	34	65	11	.288	.419	1	0	1B-120
1913	148	518	149	14	21	14	2.7	93	92	62	62	26	.288	.477	1	0	1B-148
1914	153	537	129	24	8	18	3.4	87	72	94	61	19	.240	.415	0	0	1B-153
1915	144	497	131	35	11	11	2.2	74	64	64	62	29	.264	.445	4	1	1B-139
1916	147	498	126	25	3	7	1.4	60	50	79	68	20	.253	.357	0	0	1B-147
1917	6	21	5	1	0	0	0.0	5	2	2	1	0	.238	.286	0	0	1B-6
1919 PIT N	58	166	37	3	3	2	1.2	19	17	18	13	5	.223	.313	7	3	1B-51
8 yrs.	864	2947	774	142	61	55	1.9	454	395	378	369	121	.263	.408	25	8	1B-837

Ebba St. Claire

ST. CLAIRE, EDWARD JOSEPH
Father of Randy St. Claire.   BB TR 6'1" 219 lbs.
B. Aug. 5, 1921, Whitehall, N. Y.   D. Aug. 22, 1982, Whitehall, N. Y.

	G	AB	H	2B	3B	HR	HR%	R	RBI	BB	SO	SB	BA	SA	PH AB	PH H	G by POS
1951 BOS N	72	220	62	17	2	1	0.5	22	25	12	24	0	.282	.391	10	3	C-62
1952	39	108	23	2	0	2	1.9	5	4	8	12	0	.213	.287	5	1	C-34
1953 MIL N	33	80	16	3	0	2	2.5	7	5	3	9	0	.200	.313	7	1	C-27
1954 NY N	20	42	11	1	0	2	4.8	5	6	12	7	0	.262	.429	4	1	C-16
4 yrs.	164	450	112	23	2	7	1.6	39	40	35	52	0	.249	.356	26	6	C-139

Lenn Sakata

SAKATA, LENN HARUKI
B. June 8, 1954, Honolulu, Hawaii   BR TR 5'9" 160 lbs.

	G	AB	H	2B	3B	HR	HR%	R	RBI	BB	SO	SB	BA	SA	PH AB	PH H	G by POS
1977 MIL A	53	154	25	2	0	2	1.3	13	12	9	22	1	.162	.214	0	0	2B-53
1978	30	78	15	4	0	0	0.0	8	3	8	11	1	.192	.244	0	0	2B-29
1979	4	14	7	2	0	0	0.0	1	1	0	1	0	.500	.643	0	0	2B-4
1980 BAL A	43	83	16	3	2	1	1.2	12	9	6	10	2	.193	.313	5	4	2B-34, SS-4, DH-1
1981	61	150	34	4	0	5	3.3	19	15	11	18	4	.227	.353	1	0	SS-42, 2B-20
1982	136	343	89	18	1	6	1.7	40	31	30	39	7	.259	.370	9	3	2B-83, SS-56
1983	66	134	34	7	0	3	2.2	23	12	16	17	8	.254	.373	3	0	2B-60, DH-1, C-1
1984	81	157	30	1	0	3	1.9	23	11	6	15	4	.191	.255	5	1	2B-76, OF-1
8 yrs.	474	1113	250	41	3	20	1.8	139	94	86	133	27	.225	.321	23	8	2B-359, SS-102, DH-2, OF-1, C-1

WORLD SERIES

	G	AB	H	2B	3B	HR	HR%	R	RBI	BB	SO	SB	BA	SA	PH AB	PH H	G by POS
1983 BAL A	1	1	0	0	0	0	0.0	0	0	0	0	0	.000	.000	0	0	2B-1

Mark Salas

SALAS, MARK B
B. Mar. 8, 1961, Montebello, Calif.   BL TR 6' 180 lbs.

	G	AB	H	2B	3B	HR	HR%	R	RBI	BB	SO	SB	BA	SA	PH AB	PH H	G by POS
1984 STL N	14	20	2	1	0	0	0.0	1	1	0	3	0	.100	.150	8	1	C-4, OF-3

Argenis Salazar

SALAZAR, ARGENIS ANTONIO
B. Nov. 11, 1961, El Tigre, Venezuela   BR TR 5'11" 170 lbs.

	G	AB	H	2B	3B	HR	HR%	R	RBI	BB	SO	SB	BA	SA	PH AB	PH H	G by POS
1983 MON N	36	37	8	1	1	0	0.0	5	1	1	8	0	.216	.297	2	0	SS-34
1984	80	174	27	4	2	0	0.0	12	12	4	38	1	.155	.201	0	0	SS-80
2 yrs.	116	211	35	5	3	0	0.0	17	13	5	46	1	.166	.218	2	0	SS-114

Luis Salazar

SALAZAR, LUIS ERNESTO
B. May 19, 1956, Barcelona, Venezuela   BR TR 6' 185 lbs.

	G	AB	H	2B	3B	HR	HR%	R	RBI	BB	SO	SB	BA	SA	PH AB	PH H	G by POS
1980 SD N	44	169	57	4	7	1	0.6	28	25	9	25	11	.337	.462	0	0	3B-42, OF-4
1981	109	400	121	19	6	3	0.8	37	38	16	72	11	.303	.403	2	0	3B-94, OF-23
1982	145	524	127	15	5	8	1.5	55	62	23	80	32	.242	.336	2	0	3B-129, SS-18, OF-1
1983	134	481	124	16	2	14	2.9	52	45	17	80	24	.258	.387	6	2	3B-118, SS-19
1984	93	228	55	7	2	3	1.3	20	17	6	38	11	.241	.329	14	4	3B-58, OF-24, SS-4
5 yrs.	525	1802	484	61	22	29	1.6	192	187	71	295	89	.269	.375	24	6	3B-441, OF-52, SS-41

LEAGUE CHAMPIONSHIP SERIES

	G	AB	H	2B	3B	HR	HR%	R	RBI	BB	SO	SB	BA	SA	PH AB	PH H	G by POS
1984 SD N	3	5	1	0	1	0	0.0	0	0	0	1	0	.200	.600	1	0	3B-1

WORLD SERIES

	G	AB	H	2B	3B	HR	HR%	R	RBI	BB	SO	SB	BA	SA	PH AB	PH H	G by POS
1984 SD N	4	3	1	0	0	0	0.0	0	0	0	0	0	.333	.333	1	1	3B-1

Ed Sales

SALES, EDWARD A.
B. 1861, Harrisburg, Pa.   D. Aug. 10, 1912, New Haven, Conn.   TR

	G	AB	H	2B	3B	HR	HR%	R	RBI	BB	SO	SB	BA	SA	PH AB	PH H	G by POS
1890 PIT N	51	189	43	7	3	1	0.5	19	23	16	15	3	.228	.312	0	0	SS-51

	G	AB	H	2B	3B	HR	HR %	R	RBI	BB	SO	SB	BA	SA	Pinch Hit AB	Pinch Hit H	G by POS

Bill Salkeld

SALKELD, WILLIAM FRANKLIN
B. Mar. 8, 1917, Pocatello, Ida.   D. Apr. 22, 1967, Los Angeles, Calif.
BL TR 5'10"   190 lbs.

	G	AB	H	2B	3B	HR	HR %	R	RBI	BB	SO	SB	BA	SA	PH AB	PH H	G by POS
1945 PIT N	95	267	83	16	1	15	5.6	45	52	50	16	2	.311	.547	8	2	C-86
1946	69	160	47	8	0	3	1.9	18	19	39	16	2	.294	.400	17	3	C-51
1947	47	61	13	2	0	0	0.0	5	8	6	8	0	.213	.246	29	9	C-15
1948 BOS N	78	198	48	8	1	8	4.0	26	28	42	37	1	.242	.414	12	1	C-59
1949	66	161	41	5	0	5	3.1	17	25	44	24	1	.255	.379	4	0	C-63
1950 CHI A	1	3	0	0	0	0	0.0	0	0	1	0	0	.000	.000	0	0	C-1
6 yrs.	356	850	232	39	2	31	3.6	111	132	182	101	6	.273	.433	70	15	C-275

WORLD SERIES
| 1948 BOS N | 5 | 9 | 2 | 0 | 0 | 1 | 11.1 | 2 | 1 | 5 | 1 | 0 | .222 | .556 | 1 | 0 | C-5 |

Chico Salmon

SALMON, RUTHERFORD EDUARDO
B. Dec. 3, 1940, Colon, Panama
BR TR 5'10"   160 lbs.

	G	AB	H	2B	3B	HR	HR %	R	RBI	BB	SO	SB	BA	SA	PH AB	PH H	G by POS
1964 CLE A	86	283	87	17	2	4	1.4	43	25	13	37	10	.307	.424	6	2	OF-53, 2B-32, 1B-13
1965	79	120	29	8	0	3	2.5	20	12	5	19	7	.242	.383	19	5	1B-28, OF-17, 3B-5, 2B-5
1966	126	422	108	13	2	7	1.7	46	40	21	41	10	.256	.346	10	2	SS-61, 2B-28, 1B-24, OF-10, 3B-6
1967	90	203	46	13	1	2	1.0	19	19	17	29	10	.227	.330	5	3	OF-28, 2B-24, 1B-24, SS-14, 3B-4
1968	103	276	59	8	1	3	1.1	24	12	12	30	7	.214	.283	9	0	2B-45, 3B-18, SS-15, OF-13, 1B-11
1969 BAL A	52	91	27	5	0	3	3.3	18	12	10	22	0	.297	.451	14	3	1B-17, SS-9, 2B-9, 3B-3, OF-1
1970	63	172	43	4	0	7	4.1	19	22	8	30	2	.250	.395	13	2	SS-33, 2B-12, 3B-11, 1B-2
1971	42	84	15	1	0	2	2.4	11	7	3	21	0	.179	.262	19	3	2B-9, 1B-9, 3B-6, SS-5
1972	17	16	1	1	0	0	0.0	2	0	1	4	0	.063	.125	14	1	1B-2, 3B-1
9 yrs.	658	1667	415	70	6	31	1.9	202	149	89	233	46	.249	.354	109	21	2B-164, SS-137, 1B-130, OF-122, 3B-54

LEAGUE CHAMPIONSHIP SERIES
| 1969 BAL A | 1 | 1 | 0 | 0 | 0 | 0 | 0.0 | 0 | 0 | 0 | 0 | 0 | .000 | .000 | 1 | 0 | |

WORLD SERIES
1969 BAL A	2	0	0	0	0	0	–	0	0	0	0	0	–	–	0	0	
1970	1	1	1	0	0	0	0.0	1	0	0	0	0	1.000	1.000	1	1	
2 yrs.	3	1	1	0	0	0	0.0	1	0	0	0	0	1.000	1.000	1	1	

Jack Saltzgaver

SALTZGAVER, OTTO HAMLIN
B. Jan. 23, 1905, Croton, Iowa   D. Feb. 2, 1978, Keokuk, Iowa
BL TR 5'11"   165 lbs.

	G	AB	H	2B	3B	HR	HR %	R	RBI	BB	SO	SB	BA	SA	PH AB	PH H	G by POS
1932 NY A	20	47	6	2	1	0	0.0	10	5	10	10	1	.128	.213	2	0	2B-16
1934	94	350	95	8	1	6	1.7	64	36	48	28	8	.271	.351	6	2	3B-84, 1B-4
1935	61	149	39	6	0	3	2.0	17	18	23	12	0	.262	.362	12	2	2B-25, 3B-18, 1B-6
1936	34	90	19	5	0	1	1.1	14	13	13	18	0	.211	.300	2	1	3B-16, 2B-6, 1B-4
1937	17	11	2	0	0	0	0.0	6	0	3	4	0	.182	.182	2	1	1B-4
1945 PIT N	52	117	38	5	3	0	0.0	20	10	8	8	0	.325	.419	20	3	2B-31, 3B-1
6 yrs.	278	764	199	26	5	10	1.3	131	82	105	80	9	.260	.347	44	8	3B-119, 2B-78, 1B-18

Ed Samcoff

SAMCOFF, EDWARD WILLIAM
B. Sept. 1, 1924, Sacramento, Calif.
BR TR 5'10"   165 lbs.

	G	AB	H	2B	3B	HR	HR %	R	RBI	BB	SO	SB	BA	SA	PH AB	PH H	G by POS
1951 PHI A	4	11	0	0	0	0	0.0	0	0	1	2	0	.000	.000	1	0	2B-3

Ron Samford

SAMFORD, RONALD EDWARD
B. Feb. 28, 1930, Dallas, Tex.
BR TR 5'11"   156 lbs.

	G	AB	H	2B	3B	HR	HR %	R	RBI	BB	SO	SB	BA	SA	PH AB	PH H	G by POS
1954 NY N	12	5	0	0	0	0	0.0	2	0	0	1	0	.000	.000	1	0	2B-3
1955 DET A	1	1	0	0	0	0	0.0	0	0	0	1	0	.000	.000	0	0	SS-1
1957	54	91	20	1	2	0	0.0	6	5	6	15	1	.220	.275	0	0	SS-35, 2B-11, 3B-4
1959 WAS A	91	237	53	13	0	5	2.1	23	22	11	29	1	.224	.342	3	0	SS-64, 2B-23
4 yrs.	158	334	73	14	2	5	1.5	31	27	17	46	2	.219	.317	4	0	SS-100, 2B-37, 3B-4

Billy Sample

SAMPLE, WILLIAM AMOS
B. Apr. 2, 1955, Roanoke, Va.
BR TR 5'9"   175 lbs.

	G	AB	H	2B	3B	HR	HR %	R	RBI	BB	SO	SB	BA	SA	PH AB	PH H	G by POS
1978 TEX A	8	15	7	2	0	0	0.0	2	3	0	3	0	.467	.600	2	1	DH-3, OF-2
1979	128	325	95	21	2	5	1.5	60	35	37	28	8	.292	.415	18	5	OF-103, DH-9
1980	99	204	53	10	0	4	2.0	29	19	18	15	8	.260	.368	23	5	OF-72, DH-4
1981	66	230	65	16	0	3	1.3	36	25	17	21	4	.283	.391	3	0	OF-64
1982	97	360	94	14	2	10	2.8	56	29	27	35	10	.261	.394	1	0	OF-91, DH-1
1983	147	554	152	28	3	12	2.2	80	57	44	46	44	.274	.401	2	0	OF-146
1984	130	489	121	20	2	5	1.0	67	33	29	46	18	.247	.327	11	4	OF-122, DH-2
7 yrs.	675	2177	587	111	9	39	1.8	330	201	172	194	92	.270	.383	60	15	OF-600, DH-19

Amado Samuel

SAMUEL, AMADO RUPERTO
B. Dec. 6, 1938, San Pedro de Macoris, Dominican Republic
BR TR 6'1"   170 lbs.

	G	AB	H	2B	3B	HR	HR %	R	RBI	BB	SO	SB	BA	SA	PH AB	PH H	G by POS
1962 MIL N	76	209	43	10	0	3	1.4	16	20	12	54	0	.206	.297	5	1	SS-36, 2B-28, 3B-3
1963	15	17	3	1	0	0	0.0	0	0	0	4	0	.176	.235	0	0	SS-7, 2B-5
1964 NY N	53	142	33	7	0	0	0.0	7	5	4	24	0	.232	.282	2	1	SS-34, 3B-17, 2B-3
3 yrs.	144	368	79	18	0	3	0.8	23	25	16	82	0	.215	.288	7	2	SS-77, 2B-35, 3B-20

Juan Samuel

SAMUEL, JUAN MILTON
B. Dec. 9, 1961, San Pedro de Macoris, Dominican Republic
BR TR 5'11"   165 lbs.

	G	AB	H	2B	3B	HR	HR %	R	RBI	BB	SO	SB	BA	SA	PH AB	PH H	G by POS
1983 PHI N	18	65	18	1	2	2	3.1	14	5	4	16	3	.277	.446	0	0	2B-18
1984	160	701	191	36	19	15	2.1	105	69	28	168	72	.272	.442	2	1	2B-160
2 yrs.	178	766	209	37	21	17	2.2	119	74	32	184	75	.273	.443	2	1	2B-178

LEAGUE CHAMPIONSHIP SERIES
| 1983 PHI N | 1 | 0 | 0 | 0 | 0 | 0 | – | 0 | 0 | 0 | 0 | 0 | – | – | 0 | 0 | |

WORLD SERIES
| 1983 PHI N | 3 | 1 | 0 | 0 | 0 | 0 | 0.0 | 0 | 0 | 0 | 0 | 0 | .000 | .000 | 1 | 0 | |

	G	AB	H	2B	3B	HR	HR %	R	RBI	BB	SO	SB	BA	SA	Pinch Hit AB	Pinch Hit H	G by POS

Ike Samuls

SAMULS, SAMUEL EARL
B. Feb. 20, 1876, Chicago, Ill.   D. Jan. 1, 1942, Los Angeles, Calif.
BR TR

	G	AB	H	2B	3B	HR	HR%	R	RBI	BB	SO	SB	BA	SA	PH AB	PH H	G by POS
1895 STL N	24	74	17	2	0	0	0.0	5	5	5	7	5	.230	.257	0	0	3B-21, SS-3

Gus Sanberg

SANBERG, GUSTAVE E.
B. Feb. 23, 1896, Long Island City, N. Y.   D. Feb. 3, 1930, Los Angeles, Calif.
BR TR 6'1" 189 lbs.

	G	AB	H	2B	3B	HR	HR%	R	RBI	BB	SO	SB	BA	SA	PH AB	PH H	G by POS
1923 CIN N	7	17	3	1	0	0	0.0	1	1	1	1	0	.176	.235	2	1	C-5
1924	24	52	9	0	0	0	0.0	1	3	2	7	0	.173	.173	0	0	C-24
2 yrs.	31	69	12	1	0	0	0.0	2	4	3	8	0	.174	.188	2	1	C-29

Alejandro Sanchez

SANCHEZ, ALEJANDRO
Also known as Alejandro Pimentel.
B. Feb. 26, 1959, San Pedro, Dominican Republic
BR TR 6' 175 lbs.

	G	AB	H	2B	3B	HR	HR%	R	RBI	BB	SO	SB	BA	SA	PH AB	PH H	G by POS
1982 PHI N	7	14	4	1	0	2	14.3	3	4	0	4	0	.286	.786	1	1	OF-4
1983	8	7	2	0	0	0	0.0	2	2	0	2	0	.286	.286	4	2	OF-2
1984 SF N	13	41	8	0	1	0	0.0	3	2	0	12	2	.195	.244	2	0	OF-11
3 yrs.	28	62	14	1	1	2	3.2	8	8	0	18	2	.226	.371	7	3	OF-17

Celerino Sanchez

SANCHEZ, CELERINO
B. Feb. 3, 1944, Veracruz, Mexico
BR TR 5'11" 160 lbs.

	G	AB	H	2B	3B	HR	HR%	R	RBI	BB	SO	SB	BA	SA	PH AB	PH H	G by POS
1972 NY A	71	250	62	8	3	0	0.0	18	22	12	30	0	.248	.304	1	0	3B-68
1973	34	64	14	3	0	1	1.6	12	9	2	12	1	.219	.313	7	0	DH-11, 3B-11, OF-2, SS-2
2 yrs.	105	314	76	11	3	1	0.3	30	31	14	42	1	.242	.306	8	0	3B-79, DH-11, OF-2, SS-2

Orlando Sanchez

SANCHEZ, ORLANDO
B. Sept. 7, 1956, Canovanas, Puerto Rico
BL TR 6' 185 lbs.

	G	AB	H	2B	3B	HR	HR%	R	RBI	BB	SO	SB	BA	SA	PH AB	PH H	G by POS
1981 STL N	27	49	14	2	1	0	0.0	5	6	2	6	1	.286	.367	11	3	C-18
1982	26	37	7	0	1	0	0.0	6	3	5	5	0	.189	.243	9	2	C-15
1983	6	6	0	0	0	0	0.0	0	0	0	4	0	.000	.000	5	0	C-1
1984 2 teams	KC A (10G – .100)			BAL A	(4G – .250)												
" total	14	18	3	1	0	0	0.0	0	3	0	4	0	.167	.222	10	2	C-5
4 yrs.	73	110	24	3	2	0	0.0	11	12	7	19	1	.218	.282	35	7	C-39

Heinie Sand

SAND, JOHN HENRY
B. July 3, 1897, San Francisco, Calif.   D. Nov. 3, 1958, San Francisco, Calif.
BR TR 5'8" 160 lbs.

	G	AB	H	2B	3B	HR	HR%	R	RBI	BB	SO	SB	BA	SA	PH AB	PH H	G by POS
1923 PHI N	132	470	107	16	5	4	0.9	85	32	82	56	7	.228	.309	1	0	SS-120, 3B-11
1924	137	539	132	21	6	6	1.1	79	40	52	57	5	.245	.340	0	0	SS-137
1925	148	496	138	30	7	3	0.6	69	55	64	65	1	.278	.385	4	0	SS-143
1926	149	567	154	30	5	4	0.7	99	37	66	56	2	.272	.363	0	0	SS-149
1927	141	535	160	22	8	1	0.2	87	49	58	59	5	.299	.376	2	1	SS-86, 3B-58
1928	141	426	90	26	1	0	0.0	38	38	60	47	1	.211	.277	4	1	SS-137
6 yrs.	848	3033	781	145	32	18	0.6	457	251	382	340	21	.258	.344	11	2	SS-772, 3B-69

Ryne Sandberg

SANDBERG, RYNE DEE
B. Sept. 18, 1959, Spokane, Wash.
BR TR 6'1" 175 lbs.

	G	AB	H	2B	3B	HR	HR%	R	RBI	BB	SO	SB	BA	SA	PH AB	PH H	G by POS
1981 PHI N	13	6	1	0	0	0	0.0	2	0	0	1	0	.167	.167	0	0	SS-5, 2B-1
1982 CHI N	156	635	172	33	5	7	1.1	103	54	36	90	32	.271	.372	1	0	3B-133, 2B-24
1983	158	633	165	25	4	8	1.3	94	48	51	79	37	.261	.351	4	2	2B-157, SS-1
1984	156	636	200	36	19	19	3.0	114	84	52	101	32	.314	.520	0	0	2B-156
4 yrs.	483	1910	538	94	28	34	1.8	313	186	139	271	101	.282	.414	5	2	2B-338, 3B-133, SS-6
LEAGUE CHAMPIONSHIP SERIES																	
1984 CHI N	5	19	7	2	0	0	0.0	3	2	3	2	3	.368	.474	0	0	2B-5

Ben Sanders

SANDERS, ALEXANDER BENNETT
B. Feb. 16, 1865, Catharpin, Va.   D. Aug. 29, 1930, Memphis, Tenn.
BR TR 6' 210 lbs.

	G	AB	H	2B	3B	HR	HR%	R	RBI	BB	SO	SB	BA	SA	PH AB	PH H	G by POS
1888 PHI N	57	236	58	11	2	1	0.4	26	25	8	12	13	.246	.322	0	0	P-31, OF-25, 3B-1
1889	44	169	47	8	2	0	0.0	21	21	6	11	4	.278	.349	0	0	P-44, OF-3
1890 PHI P	52	189	59	6	6	0	0.0	31	30	10	10	2	.312	.407	0	0	P-43, OF-10
1891 PHI AA	40	156	39	6	4	1	0.6	24	19	7	12	2	.250	.359	1	0	OF-22, P-19
1892 LOU N	54	198	54	12	2	3	1.5	30	18	16	17	6	.273	.399	0	0	P-31, 1B-15, OF-9
5 yrs.	247	948	257	43	16	5	0.5	132	113	47	62	27	.271	.366	1	0	P-168, OF-69, 1B-15, 3B-1

John Sanders

SANDERS, JOHN FRANK
B. Nov. 20, 1945, Grand Island, Neb.
BR TR 6'2" 200 lbs.

	G	AB	H	2B	3B	HR	HR%	R	RBI	BB	SO	SB	BA	SA	PH AB	PH H	G by POS
1965 KC A	1	0	0	0	0	0	–	0	0	0	0	0	–	–	0	0	

Ray Sanders

SANDERS, RAYMOND FLOYD
B. Dec. 4, 1916, Bonne Terre, Mo.   D. Oct. 28, 1983, Washington, Mo.
BL TR 6'2" 185 lbs.

	G	AB	H	2B	3B	HR	HR%	R	RBI	BB	SO	SB	BA	SA	PH AB	PH H	G by POS
1942 STL N	95	282	71	17	2	5	1.8	37	39	42	31	2	.252	.379	15	2	1B-77
1943	144	478	134	21	5	11	2.3	69	73	77	33	1	.280	.414	3	0	1B-141
1944	154	601	177	34	9	12	2.0	87	102	71	50	2	.295	.441	3	1	1B-152
1945	143	537	148	29	3	8	1.5	85	78	83	55	3	.276	.385	1	0	1B-142
1946 BOS N	80	259	63	12	0	6	2.3	43	35	50	38	0	.243	.359	2	1	1B-77
1948	5	4	1	0	0	0	0.0	0	2	1	0	0	.250	.250	4	1	
1949	9	21	3	1	0	0	0.0	0	0	4	9	0	.143	.190	1	0	1B-7
7 yrs.	630	2182	597	114	19	42	1.9	321	329	328	216	8	.274	.401	29	5	1B-596
WORLD SERIES																	
1942 STL N	2	1	0	0	0	0	0.0	1	0	1	0	0	.000	.000	1	0	
1943	5	17	5	0	0	1	5.9	3	2	3	4	0	.294	.471	0	0	1B-5
1944	6	21	6	0	0	1	4.8	5	1	5	8	0	.286	.429	0	0	1B-6
1948 BOS N	1	1	0	0	0	0	0.0	0	0	0	0	0	.000	.000	1	0	
4 yrs.	14	40	11	0	0	2	5.0	9	3	9	12	0	.275	.425	2	0	1B-11

	G	AB	H	2B	3B	HR	HR %	R	RBI	BB	SO	SB	BA	SA	Pinch Hit AB	Pinch Hit H	G by POS

Reggie Sanders

SANDERS, REGINALD JEROME
B. Sept. 9, 1949, Birmingham, Ala.
BR TR 6'2" 205 lbs.

	G	AB	H	2B	3B	HR	HR%	R	RBI	BB	SO	SB	BA	SA	PH AB	PH H	G by POS
1974 DET A	26	99	27	7	0	3	3.0	12	10	5	20	1	.273	.434	0	0	1B-25, DH-1

Mike Sandlock

SANDLOCK, MICHAEL JOSEPH
B. Oct. 17, 1915, Old Greenwich, Conn.
BB TR 6'1" 180 lbs.
BL 1944

	G	AB	H	2B	3B	HR	HR%	R	RBI	BB	SO	SB	BA	SA	PH AB	PH H	G by POS
1942 BOS N	2	1	1	0	0	0	0.0	1	0	0	0	0	1.000	1.000	0	0	SS-2
1944	30	30	3	0	0	0	0.0	1	2	5	3	0	.100	.100	0	0	3B-22, SS-7
1945 BKN N	80	195	55	14	2	2	1.0	21	17	18	19	2	.282	.405	4	2	C-47, SS-22, 2B-4, 3B-2
1946	19	34	5	0	0	0	0.0	1	0	3	4	0	.147	.147	1	1	C-17, 3B-1
1953 PIT N	64	186	43	5	0	0	0.0	10	12	12	19	0	.231	.258	0	0	C-64
5 yrs.	195	446	107	19	2	2	0.4	34	31	38	45	2	.240	.305	5	3	C-128, SS-31, 3B-25, 2B-4

Charlie Sands

SANDS, CHARLES DUANE
B. Dec. 17, 1947, Newport News, Va.
BL TR 6'2" 200 lbs.

	G	AB	H	2B	3B	HR	HR%	R	RBI	BB	SO	SB	BA	SA	PH AB	PH H	G by POS
1967 NY A	1	1	0	0	0	0	0.0	0	0	0	1	0	.000	.000	1	0	
1971 PIT N	28	25	5	2	0	1	4.0	4	5	7	6	0	.200	.400	18	5	C-3
1972	1	1	0	0	0	0	0.0	0	0	0	0	0	.000	.000	1	0	
1973 CAL A	17	33	9	2	1	1	3.0	5	5	5	10	0	.273	.485	6	0	C-10
1974	43	83	16	2	0	4	4.8	6	13	23	17	0	.193	.361	12	1	DH-21, C-5
1975 OAK A	3	2	1	0	0	0	0.0	0	0	1	1	0	.500	.500	2	1	DH-1
6 yrs.	93	145	31	6	1	6	4.1	15	23	36	35	0	.214	.393	40	7	DH-22, C-18

WORLD SERIES																	
1971 PIT N	1	1	0	0	0	0	0.0	0	0	0	1	0	.000	.000	1	0	

Tom Sandt

SANDT, THOMAS JAMES
B. Dec. 22, 1950, Brooklyn, N. Y.
BR TR 5'11" 175 lbs.

	G	AB	H	2B	3B	HR	HR%	R	RBI	BB	SO	SB	BA	SA	PH AB	PH H	G by POS
1975 OAK A	1	0	0	0	0	0	–	0	0	0	0	0	–	–	0	0	2B-1
1976	41	67	14	1	0	0	0.0	6	3	7	9	0	.209	.224	2	0	SS-29, 2B-9, 3B-2
2 yrs.	42	67	14	1	0	0	0.0	6	3	7	9	0	.209	.224	2	0	SS-29, 2B-10, 3B-2

Jack Sanford

SANFORD, JOHN DOWARD
B. June 23, 1917, Chatham, Va.
BR TR 6'3" 195 lbs.

	G	AB	H	2B	3B	HR	HR%	R	RBI	BB	SO	SB	BA	SA	PH AB	PH H	G by POS
1940 WAS A	34	122	24	4	2	0	0.0	5	10	6	17	0	.197	.262	0	0	1B-34
1941	3	5	2	0	1	0	0.0	1	1	1	1	0	.400	.800	1	1	1B-1
1946	10	26	6	0	1	0	0.0	7	1	2	6	0	.231	.308	4	0	1B-6
3 yrs.	47	153	32	4	4	0	0.0	13	11	9	24	0	.209	.288	5	1	1B-41

Manny Sanguillen

SANGUILLEN, MANUEL DeJESUS
B. Mar. 21, 1944, Colon, Panama
BR TR 6' 193 lbs.

	G	AB	H	2B	3B	HR	HR%	R	RBI	BB	SO	SB	BA	SA	PH AB	PH H	G by POS
1967 PIT N	30	96	26	4	0	0	0.0	6	8	4	12	0	.271	.313	1	0	C-28
1969	129	459	139	21	6	5	1.1	62	57	12	48	8	.303	.407	18	7	C-113
1970	128	486	158	19	9	7	1.4	63	61	17	45	2	.325	.444	3	1	C-125
1971	138	533	170	26	5	7	1.3	60	81	19	32	6	.319	.426	4	2	C-135
1972	136	520	155	18	8	7	1.3	55	71	21	38	1	.298	.404	10	4	C-127, OF-2
1973	149	589	166	26	7	12	2.0	64	65	17	29	2	.282	.411	4	1	C-89, OF-59
1974	151	596	171	21	4	7	1.2	77	68	21	27	2	.287	.371	4	1	C-151
1975	133	481	158	24	4	9	1.9	60	58	48	31	5	.328	.451	2	0	C-132
1976	114	389	113	16	6	2	0.5	52	36	28	18	2	.290	.378	5	2	C-111
1977 OAK A	152	571	157	17	5	6	1.1	42	58	22	35	2	.275	.354	3	2	C-77, DH-58, OF-9, 1B-7
1978 PIT N	85	220	58	5	1	3	1.4	15	16	9	10	2	.264	.336	27	5	1B-40, C-18
1979	56	74	17	5	2	0	0.0	8	4	2	5	0	.230	.351	42	9	C-8, 1B-5
1980	47	48	12	3	0	0	0.0	2	2	3	1	3	.250	.313	37	12	1B-5
13 yrs.	1448	5062	1500	205	57	65	1.3	566	585	223	331	35	.296	.398	160	46	C-1114, OF-70, DH-58, 1B-57

LEAGUE CHAMPIONSHIP SERIES																	
1970 PIT N	3	12	2	0	0	0	0.0	0	0	0	1	0	.167	.167	0	0	C-3
1971	4	15	4	0	0	0	0.0	1	1	1	1	1	.267	.267	0	0	C-4
1972	5	16	5	1	0	1	6.3	4	2	0	0	0	.313	.563	1	1	C-5
1974	4	16	4	1	0	0	0.0	0	0	0	0	0	.250	.313	0	0	C-4
1975	3	12	2	0	0	0	0.0	0	0	0	0	0	.167	.167	0	0	C-3
5 yrs.	19	71	17	2	0	1	1.4	5	3	1	2	1	.239	.310	1	1	C-19

WORLD SERIES																	
1971 PIT N	7	29	11	1	0	0	0.0	3	0	0	3	2	.379	.414	0	0	C-7
1979	3	3	1	0	0	0	0.0	0	1	0	0	0	.333	.333	3	1	
2 yrs.	10	32	12	1	0	0	0.0	3	1	0	3	2	.375	.406	3	1	C-7

Ed Sanicki

SANICKI, EDWARD ROBERT (Butch)
B. July 7, 1924, Wallington, N. J.
BR TR 5'9½" 175 lbs.

	G	AB	H	2B	3B	HR	HR%	R	RBI	BB	SO	SB	BA	SA	PH AB	PH H	G by POS
1949 PHI N	7	13	3	0	0	3	23.1	4	7	1	4	0	.231	.923	1	0	OF-6
1951	13	4	2	1	0	0	0.0	1	1	1	1	1	.500	.750	1	0	OF-10
2 yrs.	20	17	5	1	0	3	17.6	5	8	2	5	1	.294	.882	2	0	OF-16

Ben Sankey

SANKEY, BENJAMIN TURNER
B. Sept. 2, 1907, Nauvoo, Ala.
BR TR 5'10" 155 lbs.

	G	AB	H	2B	3B	HR	HR%	R	RBI	BB	SO	SB	BA	SA	PH AB	PH H	G by POS
1929 PIT N	2	7	1	0	0	0	0.0	1	0	0	1	0	.143	.143	0	0	SS-2
1930	13	30	5	0	0	0	0.0	6	0	2	3	0	.167	.167	0	0	SS-6, 2B-4
1931	57	132	30	2	5	0	0.0	14	14	14	10	0	.227	.318	4	0	SS-49, 3B-2, 2B-2
3 yrs.	72	169	36	2	5	0	0.0	21	14	16	14	0	.213	.284	4	0	SS-57, 2B-6, 3B-2

Rafael Santana

SANTANA, RAFAEL FRANCISCO
Also known as Rafael Francisco DeLaCruz.
B. Jan. 31, 1958, La Romana, Dominican Republic
BR TR 6'1" 156 lbs.

	G	AB	H	2B	3B	HR	HR%	R	RBI	BB	SO	SB	BA	SA	PH AB	PH H	G by POS
1983 STL N	30	14	3	0	0	0	0.0	1	2	2	2	0	.214	.214	4	0	2B-9, SS-6, 3B-4
1984 NY N	51	152	42	11	1	1	0.7	14	12	9	17	0	.276	.382	1	0	SS-50
2 yrs.	81	166	45	11	1	1	0.6	15	14	11	19	0	.271	.367	5	0	SS-56, 2B-9, 3B-4

	G	AB	H	2B	3B	HR	HR %	R	RBI	BB	SO	SB	BA	SA	Pinch Hit AB	Pinch Hit H	G by POS

Ron Santo

SANTO, RONALD EDWARD
B. Feb. 25, 1940, Seattle, Wash.

BR TR 6' 190 lbs.

	G	AB	H	2B	3B	HR	HR %	R	RBI	BB	SO	SB	BA	SA	AB	H	G by POS
1960 CHI N	95	347	87	24	2	9	2.6	44	44	31	44	0	.251	.409	1	0	3B-94
1961	154	578	164	32	6	23	4.0	84	83	73	77	2	.284	.479	1	1	3B-153
1962	162	604	137	20	4	17	2.8	44	83	65	94	4	.227	.358	2	0	3B-157, SS-8
1963	162	630	187	29	6	25	4.0	79	99	42	92	6	.297	.481	0	0	3B-162
1964	161	592	185	33	13	30	5.1	94	114	86	96	3	.313	.564	0	0	3B-161
1965	164	608	173	30	4	33	5.4	88	101	88	109	3	.285	.510	0	0	3B-164
1966	155	561	175	21	8	30	5.3	93	94	95	78	4	.312	.538	0	0	3B-152, SS-8
1967	161	586	176	23	4	31	5.3	107	98	96	103	1	.300	.512	0	0	3B-161
1968	162	577	142	17	3	26	4.5	86	98	96	106	3	.246	.421	0	0	3B-162
1969	160	575	166	18	4	29	5.0	97	123	96	97	1	.289	.485	1	0	3B-160
1970	154	555	148	30	4	26	4.7	83	114	92	108	2	.267	.476	2	1	3B-152, OF-1
1971	154	555	148	22	1	21	3.8	77	88	79	95	4	.267	.423	1	0	3B-149, OF-6
1972	133	464	140	25	5	17	3.7	68	74	69	75	1	.302	.487	1	1	3B-129, 2B-3, OF-1, SS-1
1973	149	536	143	29	2	20	3.7	65	77	63	97	1	.267	.440	2	0	3B-146
1974 CHI A	117	375	83	12	1	5	1.3	29	41	37	72	0	.221	.299	5	3	DH-47, 2B-39, 3B-28, 1B-3, SS-1
15 yrs.	2243	8143	2254	365	67	342	4.2	1138	1331	1108	1343	35	.277	.464	16	6	3B-2130, DH-47, 2B-42, SS-18, OF-8, 1B-3

Rafael Santo Domingo

SANTO DOMINGO, RAFAEL
Also known as Rafael Molina.
B. Nov. 24, 1955, Orocovis, Puerto Rico

BB TR 6' 160 lbs.

	G	AB	H	2B	3B	HR	HR %	R	RBI	BB	SO	SB	BA	SA	AB	H	G by POS
1979 CIN N	7	6	1	0	0	0	0.0	0	0	1	3	0	.167	.167	6	1	

Ed Santry

SANTRY, EDWARD
B. Chicago, Ill.   D. Mar. 6, 1899, Chicago, Ill.

	G	AB	H	2B	3B	HR	HR %	R	RBI	BB	SO	SB	BA	SA	AB	H	G by POS
1884 DET N	6	22	4	0	0	0	0.0	1		1	2		.182	.182	0	0	SS-5, 2B-1

Joe Sargent

SARGENT, JOSEPH ALEXANDER (Horse Belly)
B. Sept. 24, 1893, Rochester, N. Y.   D. July 5, 1950, Rochester, N. Y.

BR TR 5'10" 165 lbs.

	G	AB	H	2B	3B	HR	HR %	R	RBI	BB	SO	SB	BA	SA	AB	H	G by POS
1921 DET A	66	178	45	8	5	2	1.1	21	22	24	26	2	.253	.388	1	0	2B-24, 3B-23, SS-19

Bill Sarni

SARNI, WILLIAM FLORINE
B. Sept. 19, 1927, Los Angeles, Calif.   D. Apr. 15, 1983, Creve Coeur, Mo.

BR TR 5'11" 180 lbs.

	G	AB	H	2B	3B	HR	HR %	R	RBI	BB	SO	SB	BA	SA	AB	H	G by POS
1951 STL N	36	86	15	1	0	0	0.0	7	2	9	13	1	.174	.186	1	0	C-35
1952	3	5	1	0	0	0	0.0	0	0	0	1	0	.200	.200	0	0	C-3
1954	123	380	114	18	4	9	2.4	40	70	25	42	3	.300	.439	6	3	C-118
1955	107	325	83	15	2	3	0.9	32	34	27	33	1	.255	.342	11	3	C-99
1956 2 teams		STL	N	(43G –	.291)		NY	N	(78G –	.231)								
" total	121	386	98	16	5	10	2.6	28	45	28	46	1	.254	.399	6	1	C-116
5 yrs.	390	1182	311	50	11	22	1.9	107	151	89	135	6	.263	.380	24	7	C-371

Tom Satriano

SATRIANO, THOMAS VICTOR (Satch)
B. Aug. 28, 1940, Pittsburgh, Pa.

BL TR 6'1" 185 lbs.

	G	AB	H	2B	3B	HR	HR %	R	RBI	BB	SO	SB	BA	SA	AB	H	G by POS
1961 LA A	35	96	19	5	1	1	1.0	15	8	12	16	2	.198	.302	3	0	3B-23, 2B-10, SS-1
1962	10	19	8	2	0	2	10.5	4	6	0	1	0	.421	.842	7	3	3B-5
1963	23	50	9	1	0	0	0.0	1	2	9	10	0	.180	.200	9	0	3B-13, C-2, 1B-1
1964	108	255	51	9	0	1	0.4	18	17	30	37	0	.200	.247	19	4	3B-38, 1B-32, C-25, SS-2, 2B-1
1965 CAL A	47	79	13	2	0	1	1.3	8	4	10	10	1	.165	.228	11	1	3B-15, 2B-12, C-12, 1B-3
1966	103	226	54	5	3	0	0.0	16	24	27	32	3	.239	.288	8	1	C-43, 1B-36, 3B-25, 2B-4
1967	90	201	45	7	0	4	2.0	13	21	28	25	1	.224	.318	22	4	3B-38, C-23, 2B-15, 1B-5
1968	111	297	75	9	0	8	2.7	20	35	37	44	0	.253	.364	17	4	C-85, 2B-14, 3B-11, 1B-1
1969 2 teams		CAL	A	(41G –	.259)		BOS	A	(47G –	.189)								
" total	88	235	52	4	0	1	0.4	14	27	40	27	0	.221	.251	9	3	C-80, 1B-5, 2B-2
1970 BOS A	59	165	39	9	1	3	1.8	21	13	21	23	0	.236	.358	7	1	C-51
10 yrs.	674	1623	365	53	5	21	1.3	130	157	214	225	7	.225	.303	112	21	C-321, 3B-168, 1B-83, 2B-58, SS-3

Frank Saucier

SAUCIER, FRANCIS FIELD
B. May 28, 1926, Leslie, Mo.

BL TR 6'1" 180 lbs.

	G	AB	H	2B	3B	HR	HR %	R	RBI	BB	SO	SB	BA	SA	AB	H	G by POS
1951 STL A	18	14	1	1	0	0	0.0	4	1	3	4	0	.071	.143	7	1	OF-3

Ed Sauer

SAUER, EDWARD (Horn)
Brother of Hank Sauer.
B. Jan. 3, 1920, Pittsburgh, Pa.

BR TR 6'1" 188 lbs.

	G	AB	H	2B	3B	HR	HR %	R	RBI	BB	SO	SB	BA	SA	AB	H	G by POS
1943 CHI N	14	55	15	3	0	0	0.0	3	9	3	6	1	.273	.327	0	0	OF-13, 3B-1
1944	23	50	11	4	0	0	0.0	3	5	2	6	0	.220	.300	9	2	OF-12
1945	49	93	24	4	1	2	2.2	8	11	8	23	2	.258	.387	15	3	OF-26
1949 2 teams		STL	N	(24G –	.222)		BOS	N	(79G –	.266)								
" total	103	259	67	14	1	3	1.2	31	32	20	42	0	.259	.355	19	4	OF-81, 3B-2
4 yrs.	189	457	117	25	2	5	1.1	45	57	33	77	3	.256	.352	43	9	OF-132, 3B-3
WORLD SERIES																	
1945 CHI N	2	2	0	0	0	0	0.0	0	0	0	2	0	.000	.000	2	0	

Hank Sauer

SAUER, HENRY JOHN
Brother of Ed Sauer.
B. Mar. 17, 1919, Pittsburgh, Pa.

BR TR 6'2" 198 lbs.

	G	AB	H	2B	3B	HR	HR %	R	RBI	BB	SO	SB	BA	SA	AB	H	G by POS
1941 CIN N	9	33	10	4	0	0	0.0	4	5	1	4	0	.303	.424	1	1	OF-8
1942	7	20	5	0	0	2	10.0	4	4	2	2	0	.250	.550	3	1	1B-4
1945	31	116	34	1	0	5	4.3	18	20	6	16	2	.293	.431	1	0	OF-28, 1B-3
1948	145	530	138	22	1	35	6.6	78	97	60	85	2	.260	.504	2	0	OF-132, 1B-12
1949 2 teams		CIN	N	(42G –	.237)		CHI	N	(96G –	.291)								
" total	138	509	140	23	1	31	6.1	81	99	55	66	0	.275	.507	3	0	OF-135, 1B-1
1950 CHI N	145	540	148	32	2	32	5.9	85	103	60	67	1	.274	.519	3	2	OF-125, 1B-18

	G	AB	H	2B	3B	HR	HR %	R	RBI	BB	SO	SB	BA	SA	Pinch Hit AB	Pinch Hit H	G by POS

Hank Sauer continued

	G	AB	H	2B	3B	HR	HR %	R	RBI	BB	SO	SB	BA	SA	AB	H	G by POS
1951	141	525	138	19	4	30	5.7	77	89	45	77	2	.263	.486	8	1	OF-132
1952	151	567	153	31	3	37	6.5	89	121	77	92	1	.270	.531	0	0	OF-151
1953	108	395	104	16	5	19	4.8	61	60	50	56	0	.263	.473	5	1	OF-105
1954	142	520	150	18	1	41	7.9	98	103	70	68	2	.288	.563	1	0	OF-141
1955	79	261	55	8	1	12	4.6	29	28	26	47	0	.211	.387	10	4	OF-68
1956 STL N	75	151	45	4	0	5	3.3	11	24	25	31	0	.298	.424	31	6	OF-37
1957 NY N	127	378	98	14	1	26	6.9	46	76	49	59	1	.259	.508	24	7	OF-98
1958 SF N	88	236	59	8	0	12	5.1	27	46	35	37	0	.250	.436	19	2	OF-67
1959	13	15	1	0	0	1	6.7	1	1	0	7	0	.067	.267	12	1	OF-1
15 yrs.	1399	4796	1278	200	19	288	6.0	709	876	561	714	11	.266	.496	123	22	OF-1228, 1B-38

Rusty Saunders

SAUNDERS, RUSSELL COLLIER
B. Mar. 12, 1906, Trenton, N. J.   D. Nov. 24, 1967, Ocean County, N. J.
BR TR 6'2"   205 lbs.

	G	AB	H	2B	3B	HR	HR %	R	RBI	BB	SO	SB	BA	SA	AB	H	G by POS
1927 PHI A	5	15	2	1	0	0	0.0	2	2	3	2	0	.133	.200	1	0	OF-4

Al Sauters

SAUTERS, AL
B. Philadelphia, Pa.   Deceased.

	G	AB	H	2B	3B	HR	HR %	R	RBI	BB	SO	SB	BA	SA	AB	H	G by POS
1890 PHI AA	14	41	4	0	0	0	0.0	1		11		0	.098	.098	0	0	3B-11, OF-2, 2B-2

Don Savage

SAVAGE, DONALD ANTHONY
B. Mar. 5, 1919, Bloomfield, N. J.   D. Dec. 25, 1961, Montclair, N. J.
BR TR 6'   180 lbs.

	G	AB	H	2B	3B	HR	HR %	R	RBI	BB	SO	SB	BA	SA	AB	H	G by POS
1944 NY A	71	239	63	7	5	4	1.7	31	24	20	41	1	.264	.385	10	1	3B-60
1945	34	58	13	1	0	0	0.0	5	3	3	14	1	.224	.241	9	2	3B-14, OF-2
2 yrs.	105	297	76	8	5	4	1.3	36	27	23	55	2	.256	.357	19	3	3B-74, OF-2

Hal Savage

SAVAGE, HAROLD JAMES
B. Aug. 29, 1883, Southington, Conn.   D. June 26, 1940, Newcastle, Pa.
BL TR 5'5"   150 lbs.

	G	AB	H	2B	3B	HR	HR %	R	RBI	BB	SO	SB	BA	SA	AB	H	G by POS
1912 PHI N	2	3	0	0	0	0	0.0	1	0	1	0	0	.000	.000	0	0	2B-1
1914 PIT F	132	479	136	9	9	1	0.2	81	26	67		17	.284	.347	3	0	OF-93, 3B-29, SS-11, 2B-3
1915	14	21	3	0	0	0	0.0	0	0	1		0	.143	.143	7	2	OF-3, 3B-1
3 yrs.	148	503	139	9	9	1	0.2	82	26	69		17	.276	.336	10	2	OF-96, 3B-30, SS-11, 2B-4

Ted Savage

SAVAGE, THEODORE EDMUND
B. Feb. 21, 1937, Venice, Ill.
BR TR 6'1"   185 lbs.

	G	AB	H	2B	3B	HR	HR %	R	RBI	BB	SO	SB	BA	SA	AB	H	G by POS
1962 PHI N	127	335	89	11	2	7	2.1	54	39	40	66	16	.266	.373	21	3	OF-109
1963 PIT N	85	149	29	2	1	5	3.4	22	14	14	31	4	.195	.322	33	5	OF-47
1965 STL N	30	63	10	3	0	1	1.6	7	4	6	9	1	.159	.254	7	2	OF-20
1966	16	29	5	2	1	0	0.0	4	3	4	7	4	.172	.310	9	2	OF-7
1967 2 teams		STL	N	(9G –	.125)		CHI	N	(96G –	.218)							
" total	105	233	50	10	1	5	2.1	41	33	41	57	7	.215	.330	17	4	OF-86, 3B-1
1968 2 teams		CHI	N	(3G –	.250)		LA	N	(61G –	.206)							
" total	64	134	28	6	1	2	1.5	7	7	10	21	1	.209	.313	21	3	OF-41
1969 CIN N	68	110	25	7	0	2	1.8	20	11	20	27	3	.227	.345	27	5	OF-17, 2B-1
1970 MIL A	114	276	77	10	5	12	4.3	43	50	57	44	10	.279	.482	31	6	OF-82, 1B-1
1971 2 teams		MIL	A	(14G –	.176)		KC	A	(19G –	.172)							
" total	33	46	8	0	0	0	0.0	4	2	8	10	3	.174	.174	18	2	OF-15
9 yrs.	642	1375	321	51	11	34	2.5	202	163	200	272	49	.233	.361	184	32	OF-424, 3B-1, 2B-1, 1B-1

Bob Saverine

SAVERINE, ROBERT PAUL (Rabbit)
B. June 2, 1941, Norwalk, Conn.
BB TR 5'10"   160 lbs.

	G	AB	H	2B	3B	HR	HR %	R	RBI	BB	SO	SB	BA	SA	AB	H	G by POS
1959 BAL A	1	0	0	0	0	0	–	1	0	0	0	0	–	–	0	0	
1962	8	21	5	2	0	0	0.0	2	3	1	3	0	.238	.333	1	0	2B-7
1963	115	167	39	1	2	1	0.6	21	12	25	44	8	.234	.281	16	6	OF-59, 2B-19, SS-13
1964	46	34	5	1	0	0	0.0	14	0	3	6	3	.147	.176	3	0	SS-15, OF-9
1966 WAS A	120	406	102	10	4	5	1.2	54	24	27	62	4	.251	.333	19	5	2B-70, 3B-26, SS-11, OF-9
1967	89	233	55	13	0	0	0.0	22	8	17	34	8	.236	.292	25	4	2B-48, SS-10, 3B-8, OF-2
6 yrs.	379	861	206	27	6	6	0.7	114	47	73	149	23	.239	.305	64	15	2B-144, OF-72, SS-49, 3B-34

Carl Sawatski

SAWATSKI, CARL ERNEST (Swats)
B. Nov. 4, 1927, Shickshinny, Pa.
BL TR 5'10"   210 lbs.

	G	AB	H	2B	3B	HR	HR %	R	RBI	BB	SO	SB	BA	SA	AB	H	G by POS
1948 CHI N	2	2	0	0	0	0	0.0	0	0	0	0	0	.000	.000	2	0	C-32
1950	38	103	18	1	0	1	1.0	4	7	11	19	0	.175	.214	7	0	C-32
1953	43	59	13	3	0	1	1.7	5	5	7	7	0	.220	.322	29	6	C-15
1954 CHI A	43	109	20	3	3	1	0.9	6	12	15	20	0	.183	.294	8	1	C-33
1957 MIL N	58	105	25	4	0	6	5.7	13	17	10	15	0	.238	.448	31	6	C-28
1958 2 teams		MIL	N	(10G –	.100)		PHI	N	(60G –	.230)							
" total	70	193	43	4	1	5	2.6	13	13	18	47	0	.223	.332	13	4	C-56
1959 PHI N	74	198	58	10	0	9	4.5	15	43	32	36	0	.293	.480	7	1	C-69
1960 STL N	78	179	41	4	0	6	3.4	16	27	22	24	0	.229	.352	27	7	C-67
1961	86	174	52	8	0	10	5.7	23	33	25	17	0	.299	.517	39	10	C-60, OF-1
1962	85	222	56	9	1	13	5.9	26	42	36	38	0	.252	.477	15	2	C-70
1963	56	105	25	0	0	6	5.7	12	14	15	28	2	.238	.410	31	4	C-27
11 yrs.	633	1449	351	46	5	58	4.0	133	213	191	251	2	.242	.401	209	41	C-457, OF-1

WORLD SERIES

	G	AB	H	2B	3B	HR	HR %	R	RBI	BB	SO	SB	BA	SA	AB	H	G by POS
1957 MIL N	2	2	0	0	0	0	0.0	0	0	0	0	2	.000	.000	2	0	

Carl Sawyer

SAWYER, CARL EVERETT (Huck)
B. Oct. 19, 1890, Seattle, Wash.   D. Jan. 17, 1957, Los Angeles, Calif.
BR TR 5'11"   160 lbs.

	G	AB	H	2B	3B	HR	HR %	R	RBI	BB	SO	SB	BA	SA	AB	H	G by POS
1915 WAS A	10	32	8	1	0	0	0.0	8	3	4	5	2	.250	.281	0	0	2B-6, SS-4
1916	16	31	6	1	0	0	0.0	3	2	4	4	3	.194	.226	0	0	2B-6, SS-5, 3B-1
2 yrs.	26	63	14	2	0	0	0.0	11	5	8	9	5	.222	.254	0	0	2B-12, SS-9, 3B-1

	G	AB	H	2B	3B	HR	HR %	R	RBI	BB	SO	SB	BA	SA	Pinch Hit AB	Pinch Hit H	G by POS

Dave Sax

SAX, DAVID JOHN
Brother of Steve Sax.
B. Sept. 22, 1958, West Sacramento, Calif.
BR TR 6' 175 lbs.

	G	AB	H	2B	3B	HR	HR%	R	RBI	BB	SO	SB	BA	SA	PH AB	PH H	G by POS
1982 LA N	2	2	0	0	0	0	0.0	0	0	0	0	0	.000	.000	1	0	OF-1
1983	7	8	0	0	0	0	0.0	0	1	0	0	0	.000	.000	4	0	C-4
2 yrs.	9	10	0	0	0	0	0.0	0	1	0	0	0	.000	.000	5	0	C-4, OF-1

Ollie Sax

SAX, ERIK OLIVER
B. Nov. 5, 1904, Branford, Conn. D. Mar. 21, 1982, Newark, N. J.
BR TR 5'8" 164 lbs.

	G	AB	H	2B	3B	HR	HR%	R	RBI	BB	SO	SB	BA	SA	PH AB	PH H	G by POS
1928 STL A	16	17	3	0	0	0	0.0	4	0	5	3	0	.176	.176	1	0	3B-9

Steve Sax

SAX, STEPHEN LOUIS
Brother of Dave Sax.
B. Jan. 20, 1960, Sacramento, Calif.
BR TR 5'11" 185 lbs.

	G	AB	H	2B	3B	HR	HR%	R	RBI	BB	SO	SB	BA	SA	PH AB	PH H	G by POS
1981 LA N	31	119	33	2	0	2	1.7	15	9	7	14	5	.277	.345	2	1	2B-29
1982	150	638	180	23	7	4	0.6	88	47	49	53	49	.282	.359	1	1	2B-149
1983	155	623	175	18	5	5	0.8	94	41	58	73	56	.281	.350	4	1	2B-152
1984	145	569	138	24	4	1	0.2	70	35	47	53	34	.243	.304	3	0	2B-141
4 yrs.	481	1949	526	67	16	12	0.6	267	132	161	193	144	.270	.339	10	3	2B-471

DIVISIONAL PLAYOFF SERIES

	G	AB	H	2B	3B	HR	HR%	R	RBI	BB	SO	SB	BA	SA	PH AB	PH H	G by POS
1981 LA N	1	0	0	0	0	0	–	0	0	0	0	0	–	–	0	0	2B-1

LEAGUE CHAMPIONSHIP SERIES

	G	AB	H	2B	3B	HR	HR%	R	RBI	BB	SO	SB	BA	SA	PH AB	PH H	G by POS
1981 LA N	1	0	0	0	0	0	–	0	0	0	0	0	–	–	0	0	2B-1
1983	4	16	4	0	0	0	0.0	0	0	1	0	1	.250	.250	0	0	2B-4
2 yrs.	5	16	4	0	0	0	0.0	0	0	1	0	1	.250	.250	0	0	2B-5

WORLD SERIES

	G	AB	H	2B	3B	HR	HR%	R	RBI	BB	SO	SB	BA	SA	PH AB	PH H	G by POS
1981 LA N	2	1	0	0	0	0	0.0	0	0	0	0	0	.000	.000	1	0	2B-1

Jimmy Say

SAY, JAMES I.
Brother of Lew Say.
B. 1862, Baltimore, Md. D. June 23, 1894, Baltimore, Md.

	G	AB	H	2B	3B	HR	HR%	R	RBI	BB	SO	SB	BA	SA	PH AB	PH H	G by POS
1882 2 teams		LOU	AA (1G – .250)			PHI	AA	(22G – .207)									
" total	23	86	18	2	0	0	0.0	13		1			.209	.233	0	0	SS-22, 3B-1
1884 2 teams		WIL	U (16G – .220)			KC	U	(2G – .250)									
" total	18	67	15	1	2	0	0.0	3		1			.224	.299	0	0	3B-18
1887 CLE AA	16	64	24	5	3	0	0.0	9		1		0	.375	.547	0	0	3B-16
3 yrs.	57	217	57	8	5	0	0.0	25		3		0	.263	.346	0	0	3B-35, SS-22

Lew Say

SAY, LOUIS I
Brother of Jimmy Say.
B. Feb. 4, 1854, Baltimore, Md. D. June 5, 1930, Fallston, Md.
BR TR 5'7" 145 lbs.

	G	AB	H	2B	3B	HR	HR%	R	RBI	BB	SO	SB	BA	SA	PH AB	PH H	G by POS
1880 CIN N	48	191	38	8	0	0	0.0	14	15	4	31		.199	.251	0	0	SS-48
1882 PHI AA	49	199	45	4	3	1	0.5	35		8			.226	.291	0	0	SS-49
1883 BAL AA	74	324	83	13	2	1	0.3	52		10			.256	.318	0	0	SS-74
1884 2 teams		BAL	U (78G – .239)			KC	U	(17G – .200)									
" total	95	409	95	16	2	3	0.7	71		13			.232	.303	0	0	SS-94, 2B-1
4 yrs.	266	1123	261	41	8	5	0.4	172	15	35	31		.232	.297	0	0	SS-265, 2B-1

Jerry Scala

SCALA, GERARD MICHAEL
B. Sept. 27, 1926, Bayonne, N. J.
BL TR 5'11" 178 lbs.

	G	AB	H	2B	3B	HR	HR%	R	RBI	BB	SO	SB	BA	SA	PH AB	PH H	G by POS
1948 CHI A	3	6	0	0	0	0	0.0	1	0	0	3	0	.000	.000	0	0	OF-2
1949	37	120	30	7	1	1	0.8	17	13	17	19	3	.250	.350	5	1	OF-37
1950	40	67	13	2	1	0	0.0	8	6	10	10	0	.194	.254	5	3	OF-23
3 yrs.	80	193	43	9	2	1	0.5	26	19	27	32	3	.223	.306	10	4	OF-62

Frank Scalzi

SCALZI, FRANK JOSEPH
B. June 16, 1913, Lafferty, Ohio D. Aug. 25, 1984, Pittsburgh, Pa.
BR TR 5'6" 160 lbs.

	G	AB	H	2B	3B	HR	HR%	R	RBI	BB	SO	SB	BA	SA	PH AB	PH H	G by POS
1939 NY N	11	18	6	0	0	0	0.0	3	0	3	2	1	.333	.333	2	0	SS-5, 3B-1

Johnny Scalzi

SCALZI, JOHN ANTHONY
B. Mar. 22, 1907, Stamford, Conn. D. Sept. 27, 1962, Port Chester, N. Y.
BR TR 5'7" 170 lbs.

	G	AB	H	2B	3B	HR	HR%	R	RBI	BB	SO	SB	BA	SA	PH AB	PH H	G by POS
1931 BOS N	2	1	0	0	0	0	0.0	0	0	0	1	0	.000	.000	1	0	

Mort Scanlan

SCANLAN, MORTIMER J.
B. Mar. 18, 1861, Chicago, Ill. D. Dec. 29, 1928, Chicago, Ill.

	G	AB	H	2B	3B	HR	HR%	R	RBI	BB	SO	SB	BA	SA	PH AB	PH H	G by POS
1890 NY N	3	10	0	0	0	0	0.0	0	0	2	5	1	.000	.000	0	0	1B-3

Pat Scanlon

SCANLON, JAMES PATRICK
B. Sept. 23, 1952, Minneapolis, Minn.
BL TR 6' 180 lbs.

	G	AB	H	2B	3B	HR	HR%	R	RBI	BB	SO	SB	BA	SA	PH AB	PH H	G by POS
1974 MON N	2	4	1	0	0	0	0.0	1	0	1	0	0	.250	.250	1	0	3B-1
1975	60	109	20	3	1	2	1.8	5	15	17	25	0	.183	.284	26	3	3B-28, 1B-1
1976	11	27	5	1	0	1	3.7	2	2	2	5	0	.185	.333	4	1	3B-7, 1B-1
1977 SD N	47	79	15	3	0	1	1.3	9	11	12	20	0	.190	.266	21	2	2B-15, 3B-11, OF-1
4 yrs.	120	219	41	7	1	4	1.8	17	28	31	51	0	.187	.283	52	6	3B-47, 2B-15, 1B-2, OF-1

John Scannell

SCANNELL, JOHN J.
Born Patrick Scanlon.
Deceased.

	G	AB	H	2B	3B	HR	HR%	R	RBI	BB	SO	SB	BA	SA	PH AB	PH H	G by POS
1884 BOS U	6	24	7	1	0	0	0.0	2		0			.292	.333	0	0	OF-6

Russ Scarritt

SCARRITT, RUSSELL MALLORY
B. Jan. 14, 1903, Pensacola, Fla.
BL TR 5'10½" 165 lbs.

	G	AB	H	2B	3B	HR	HR%	R	RBI	BB	SO	SB	BA	SA	PH AB	PH H	G by POS
1929 BOS A	151	540	159	26	17	1	0.2	69	71	34	38	13	.294	.411	4	1	OF-145
1930	113	447	129	17	8	2	0.4	48	48	12	49	4	.289	.376	3	0	OF-110
1931	10	39	6	1	0	0	0.0	2	1	2	2	0	.154	.179	1	0	OF-9

	G	AB	H	2B	3B	HR	HR %	R	RBI	BB	SO	SB	BA	SA	Pinch Hit AB	Pinch Hit H	G by POS

Russ Scarritt continued

	G	AB	H	2B	3B	HR	HR %	R	RBI	BB	SO	SB	BA	SA	AB	H	G by POS
1932 PHI N	11	11	2	0	0	0	0.0	0	0	1	2	0	.182	.182	6	1	OF-1
4 yrs.	285	1037	296	44	25	3	0.3	119	120	49	91	17	.285	.385	14	2	OF-265

Les Scarsella

SCARSELLA, LESLIE GEORGE
B. Nov. 23, 1913, Santa Cruz, Calif.   D. Dec. 17, 1958, San Francisco, Calif.
BL TL 5'11"   185 lbs.

	G	AB	H	2B	3B	HR	HR %	R	RBI	BB	SO	SB	BA	SA	AB	H	G by POS
1935 CIN N	6	10	2	1	0	0	0.0	4	0	3	1	0	.200	.300	2	0	1B-2
1936	115	485	152	21	9	3	0.6	63	65	14	36	6	.313	.412	0	0	1B-115
1937	110	329	81	11	4	3	0.9	35	34	17	26	5	.246	.331	27	9	1B-65, OF-14
1939	16	14	2	0	0	0	0.0	0	2	0	2	0	.143	.143	14	2	1B-12
1940 BOS N	15	60	18	1	3	0	0.0	7	8	3	5	2	.300	.417	3	1	1B-12
5 yrs.	262	898	255	34	16	6	0.7	109	109	37	70	13	.284	.378	46	12	1B-194, OF-14

Paul Schaal

SCHAAL, PAUL
B. Mar. 3, 1943, Pittsburgh, Pa.
BR TR 5'11"   165 lbs.

	G	AB	H	2B	3B	HR	HR %	R	RBI	BB	SO	SB	BA	SA	AB	H	G by POS
1964 LA A	17	32	4	0	0	0	0.0	3	0	2	5	0	.125	.125	0	0	3B-9, 2B-9
1965 CAL A	155	483	108	12	2	9	1.9	48	45	61	88	6	.224	.313	1	1	3B-153, 2B-1
1966	138	386	94	15	7	6	1.6	59	24	68	56	6	.244	.365	4	0	3B-131
1967	99	272	51	9	1	6	2.2	31	20	38	39	2	.188	.294	7	0	3B-88, SS-2, 2B-1
1968	60	219	46	7	1	2	0.9	22	16	16	29	5	.210	.279	2	0	3B-58
1969 KC A	61	205	54	6	0	1	0.5	22	13	25	27	2	.263	.307	3	0	3B-49, SS-6, 2B-6
1970	124	380	102	12	3	5	1.3	50	35	43	39	7	.268	.355	17	3	3B-97, SS-10, 2B-6
1971	161	548	150	31	6	11	2.0	80	63	103	51	7	.274	.412	0	0	3B-161
1972	127	435	99	19	3	6	1.4	47	41	61	59	1	.228	.326	3	1	3B-123, SS-1
1973	121	396	114	14	3	8	2.0	61	42	63	45	5	.288	.399	1	0	3B-121
1974 2 teams	KC	A (12G –	.176)		CAL	A (53G –	.248)										
" total	65	199	47	7	0	3	1.5	13	24	23	32	2	.236	.317	3	0	3B-63
11 yrs.	1128	3555	869	132	26	57	1.6	436	323	516	466	43	.244	.344	41	5	3B-1053, 2B-23, SS-19

Germany Schaefer

SCHAEFER, HERMAN A.
B. Feb. 4, 1878, Chicago, Ill.   D. May 16, 1919, Saranac Lake, N. Y.
BR TR

	G	AB	H	2B	3B	HR	HR %	R	RBI	BB	SO	SB	BA	SA	AB	H	G by POS
1901 CHI N	2	5	3	1	0	0	0.0	0	0	2		0	.600	.800	0	0	3B-1, 2B-1
1902	81	291	57	2	3	0	0.0	32	14	19		12	.196	.223	0	0	3B-75, 1B-3, OF-2, SS-1
1905 DET A	153	554	135	17	9	2	0.4	64	47	45		19	.244	.318	0	0	2B-151, SS-3
1906	124	446	106	14	3	2	0.4	48	42	32		31	.238	.296	2	1	2B-114, SS-7
1907	109	372	96	12	3	1	0.3	45	32	30		21	.258	.315	2	0	2B-74, SS-18, 3B-14, OF-1
1908	153	584	151	20	10	3	0.5	96	52	37		40	.259	.342	0	0	SS-68, 2B-58, 3B-29
1909 2 teams	DET	A (87G –	.250)		WAS	A (37G –	.242)										
" total	124	408	101	17	1	1	0.2	39	26	20		14	.248	.301	4	0	2B-118, OF-1, 3B-1
1910 WAS A	74	229	63	6	5	0	0.0	27	14	25		17	.275	.345	10	2	2B-35, OF-26, 3B-2
1911	125	440	147	14	7	0	0.0	74	45	57		22	.334	.398	9	3	1B-108, OF-7
1912	60	166	41	7	3	0	0.0	21	19	23		11	.247	.325	11	2	OF-19, 2B-15, 1B-15, P-1
1913	52	100	32	1	1	0	0.0	17	7	15	12	6	.320	.350	21	11	2B-17, 1B-5, 3B-2, OF-1, P-1
1914	25	29	7	1	0	0	0.0	6	2	3	5	4	.241	.276	14	3	OF-3, 2B-3
1915 NWK F	59	154	33	5	3	0	0.0	26	8	25		3	.214	.286	5	2	OF-17, 1B-13, 3B-9, 2B-2
1916 NY A	1	0	0	0	0	0	–	0	0	0	0	0	–	–	0	0	OF-1
1918 CLE A	1	5	0	0	0	0	0.0	2	0	0	0	1	.000	.000	0	0	2B-1
15 yrs.	1143	3783	972	117	48	9	0.2	497	308	333	17	201	.257	.320	88	24	2B-589, 1B-144, 3B-133, SS-97, OF-78, P-2

WORLD SERIES																	
1907 DET A	5	21	3	0	0	0	0.0	1	0	0	3	1	.143	.143	0	0	2B-5
1908	5	16	2	0	0	0	0.0	0	0	1	4	0	.125	.125	0	0	3B-2
2 yrs.	10	37	5	0	0	0	0.0	1	0	1	7	1	.135	.135	0	0	2B-5, 3B-2

Harry Schafer

SCHAFER, HARRY C. (Silk Stocking)
B. Aug. 14, 1846, Philadelphia, Pa.   D. Feb. 28, 1935, Philadelphia, Pa.
BR TR 5'9½"   143 lbs.

	G	AB	H	2B	3B	HR	HR %	R	RBI	BB	SO	SB	BA	SA	AB	H	G by POS
1876 BOS N	70	286	72	11	0	0	0.0	47	35	4	11		.252	.290	0	0	3B-70
1877	33	141	39	5	2	0	0.0	20	13	0	7		.277	.340	0	0	OF-23, 3B-9, SS-1
1878	2	8	1	0	0	0	0.0	0	0	0	1		.125	.125	0	0	OF-2
3 yrs.	105	435	112	16	2	0	0.0	67	48	4	19		.257	.303	0	0	3B-79, OF-25, SS-1

Jimmie Schaffer

SCHAFFER, JIMMIE RONALD
B. Apr. 5, 1936, Limeport, Pa.
BR TR 5'9"   170 lbs.

	G	AB	H	2B	3B	HR	HR %	R	RBI	BB	SO	SB	BA	SA	AB	H	G by POS
1961 STL N	68	153	39	7	0	1	0.7	15	16	9	29	0	.255	.320	1	1	C-68
1962	70	66	16	2	1	0	0.0	7	6	6	16	1	.242	.303	1	0	C-69
1963 CHI N	57	142	34	7	0	7	4.9	17	19	11	35	0	.239	.437	4	0	C-54
1964	54	122	25	6	1	2	1.6	9	9	17	17	2	.205	.320	9	3	C-43
1965 2 teams	CHI	A (17G –	.194)		NY	N (24G –	.135)										
" total	41	68	11	5	1	0	0.0	2	1	4	19	0	.162	.265	7	0	C-35
1966 PHI N	18	15	2	1	0	1	6.7	2	4	1	7	0	.133	.400	2	0	C-6
1967	2	2	0	0	0	0	0.0	1	0	1	1	0	.000	.000	1	0	C-1
1968 CIN N	4	6	1	0	0	0	0.0	0	1	0	3	0	.167	.167	2	0	C-2
8 yrs.	314	574	128	28	3	11	1.9	53	56	49	127	3	.223	.340	23	4	C-278

Johnny Schaive

SCHAIVE, JOHN EDWARD
B. Feb. 25, 1934, Springfield, Ill.
BR TR 5'8"   175 lbs.

	G	AB	H	2B	3B	HR	HR %	R	RBI	BB	SO	SB	BA	SA	AB	H	G by POS
1958 WAS A	7	24	6	0	0	0	0.0	1	1	1	4	0	.250	.250	1	0	2B-16
1959	16	59	9	2	0	0	0.0	3	2	0	7	0	.153	.186	0	0	2B-4
1960	6	12	3	1	0	0	0.0	1	0	0	3	0	.250	.333	3	1	2B-6
1962	82	225	57	15	1	6	2.7	20	29	6	25	0	.253	.409	27	5	3B-49, 2B-6
1963	3	3	0	0	0	0	0.0	0	0	0	1	0	.000	.000	3	0	
5 yrs.	114	323	75	18	1	6	1.9	25	32	7	40	0	.232	.350	34	6	3B-49, 2B-26

	G	AB	H	2B	3B	HR	HR %	R	RBI	BB	SO	SB	BA	SA	Pinch Hit AB	Pinch Hit H	G by POS

Ray Schalk

SCHALK, RAYMOND WILLIAM (Cracker)
B. Aug. 12, 1892, Harvel, Ill.   D. May 19, 1970, Chicago, Ill.
Manager 1927-28.
Hall of Fame 1955.

BR TR 5'9"   165 lbs.

Year/Team	G	AB	H	2B	3B	HR	HR %	R	RBI	BB	SO	SB	BA	SA	AB	H	G by POS
1912 CHI A	23	63	18	2	0	0	0.0	7	8	3		2	.286	.317	0	0	C-23
1913	128	401	98	15	5	1	0.2	38	38	27	36	14	.244	.314	3	0	C-125
1914	135	392	106	13	2	0	0.0	30	36	38	24	24	.270	.314	9	3	C-124
1915	135	413	110	14	4	1	0.2	46	54	62	21	15	.266	.327	1	1	C-134
1916	129	410	95	12	9	0	0.0	36	41	41	31	30	.232	.305	3	0	C-124
1917	140	424	96	12	4	3	0.7	48	51	59	27	19	.226	.295	1	0	C-139
1918	108	333	73	6	3	0	0.0	35	22	36	22	12	.219	.255	2	1	C-106
1919	131	394	111	9	3	0	0.0	57	34	51	25	11	.282	.320	0	0	C-129
1920	151	485	131	25	5	1	0.2	64	61	68	19	10	.270	.348	0	0	C-151
1921	128	416	105	24	4	0	0.0	32	47	40	36	3	.252	.329	2	0	C-126
1922	142	442	124	22	3	4	0.9	57	60	67	36	12	.281	.371	0	0	C-142
1923	123	382	87	12	2	1	0.3	42	44	39	28	6	.228	.277	2	0	C-121
1924	57	153	30	4	2	1	0.7	15	11	21	10	1	.196	.268	1	0	C-56
1925	125	343	94	18	1	0	0.0	44	52	57	27	11	.274	.332	0	0	C-125
1926	82	226	60	9	1	0	0.0	26	32	27	11	5	.265	.314	1	0	C-80
1927	16	26	6	2	0	0	0.0	2	2	2	1	0	.231	.308	1	0	C-15
1928	2	1	1	0	0	0	0.0	0	1	0	0	1	1.000	1.000	0	0	C-1
1929 NY N	5	2	0	0	0	0	0.0	0	0	0	1	0	.000	.000	0	0	C-5
18 yrs.	1760	5306	1345	199	48	12	0.2	579	594	638	355	176	.253	.316	28	5	C-1726

WORLD SERIES

	G	AB	H	2B	3B	HR	HR %	R	RBI	BB	SO	SB	BA	SA	AB	H	G by POS
1917 CHI A	6	19	5	0	0	0	0.0	1	0	2	1	1	.263	.263	0	0	C-6
1919	8	23	7	0	0	0	0.0	1	2	4	2	1	.304	.304	0	0	C-8
2 yrs.	14	42	12	0	0	0	0.0	2	2	6	3	2	.286	.286	0	0	C-14

Roy Schalk

SCHALK, LeROY JOHN
B. Nov. 9, 1908, Chicago, Ill.

BR TR 5'10"   168 lbs.

	G	AB	H	2B	3B	HR	HR %	R	RBI	BB	SO	SB	BA	SA	AB	H	G by POS
1932 NY A	3	12	3	1	0	0	0.0	3	0	2	2	0	.250	.333	0	0	2B-3
1944 CHI A	146	587	129	14	4	1	0.2	47	44	45	52	5	.220	.262	0	0	2B-142, SS-5
1945	133	513	127	23	1	1	0.2	50	65	32	41	3	.248	.302	0	0	2B-133
3 yrs.	282	1112	259	38	5	2	0.2	100	109	79	95	8	.233	.281	0	0	2B-278, SS-5

Biff Schaller

SCHALLER, WALTER
B. Sept. 23, 1889, Chicago, Ill.   D. Oct. 9, 1939, Emeryville, Calif.

BL TR

	G	AB	H	2B	3B	HR	HR %	R	RBI	BB	SO	SB	BA	SA	AB	H	G by POS
1911 DET A	40	60	8	0	1	1	1.7	8	7	4		1	.133	.217	17	6	OF-16, 1B-1
1913 CHI A	34	96	21	3	0	0	0.0	12	4	20	16	5	.219	.250	2	0	OF-32
2 yrs.	74	156	29	3	1	1	0.6	20	11	24	16	6	.186	.237	19	6	OF-48, 1B-1

Bobby Schang

SCHANG, ROBERT MARTIN
Brother of Wally Schang.
B. Dec. 7, 1886, Wales Center, N. Y.   D. Aug. 29, 1966, Sacramento, Calif.

BR TR 5'7"   165 lbs.

	G	AB	H	2B	3B	HR	HR %	R	RBI	BB	SO	SB	BA	SA	AB	H	G by POS
1914 PIT N	11	35	8	1	1	0	0.0	0	1	0	10	0	.229	.314	1	0	C-10
1915 2 teams		PIT	N (56G – .184)			NY	N	(12G – .143)									
" total	68	146	26	6	3	0	0.0	14	5	18	37	3	.178	.260	9	0	C-50
1927 STL N	3	5	1	0	0	0	0.0	0	0	0	0	0	.200	.200	0	0	C-3
3 yrs.	82	186	35	7	4	0	0.0	14	6	18	47	3	.188	.269	10	0	C-63

Wally Schang

SCHANG, WALTER HENRY
Brother of Bobby Schang.
B. Aug. 22, 1889, South Wales, N. Y.   D. Mar. 6, 1965, St. Louis, Mo.

BB TR 5'10"   180 lbs.
BR 1927-28

	G	AB	H	2B	3B	HR	HR %	R	RBI	BB	SO	SB	BA	SA	AB	H	G by POS
1913 PHI A	77	207	55	16	3	3	1.4	32	30	34	44	4	.266	.415	4	1	C-71
1914	107	307	88	11	8	3	1.0	44	45	32	33	7	.287	.404	5	1	C-100
1915	116	359	89	9	11	1	0.3	64	44	66	47	18	.248	.343	5	1	3B-43, OF-41, C-26
1916	110	338	90	15	8	7	2.1	41	38	38	44	14	.266	.420	11	0	OF-61, C-36
1917	118	316	90	14	9	3	0.9	41	36	29	24	6	.285	.415	18	2	C-79, 3B-12, OF-7
1918 BOS A	88	225	55	7	1	0	0.0	36	20	46	35	4	.244	.284	8	3	C-57, OF-16, 3B-5, SS-1
1919	113	330	101	16	3	0	0.0	43	55	71	42	15	.306	.373	5	0	C-103
1920	122	387	118	30	7	4	1.0	58	51	64	37	7	.305	.450	8	1	C-73, OF-40
1921 NY A	134	424	134	30	5	6	1.4	77	55	78	35	7	.316	.453	2	0	C-132
1922	124	408	130	21	7	1	0.2	46	53	53	36	12	.319	.412	5	1	C-124
1923	84	272	75	8	2	2	0.7	39	29	27	17	5	.276	.342	2	0	C-81
1924	114	356	104	19	7	5	1.4	46	52	48	43	2	.292	.427	4	0	C-109
1925	73	167	40	8	1	2	1.2	17	24	17	9	3	.240	.335	11	2	C-58
1926 STL A	103	285	94	19	5	8	2.8	36	50	32	20	5	.330	.516	17	7	C-82, OF-3
1927	97	263	84	15	2	5	1.9	40	42	41	33	3	.319	.449	18	6	C-75
1928	91	245	70	10	5	3	1.2	41	39	68	26	8	.286	.404	7	3	C-82
1929	94	249	59	10	5	5	2.0	43	36	74	22	1	.237	.378	7	1	C-85
1930 PHI A	45	92	16	4	1	1	1.1	16	9	17	15	0	.174	.272	6	1	C-36
1931 DET A	30	76	14	2	0	0	0.0	9	2	14	11	1	.184	.211	0	0	C-30
19 yrs.	1840	5306	1506	264	90	59	1.1	769	710	849	573	122	.284	.401	143	30	C-1439, OF-168, 3B-60, SS-1

WORLD SERIES

	G	AB	H	2B	3B	HR	HR %	R	RBI	BB	SO	SB	BA	SA	AB	H	G by POS
1913 PHI A	4	14	5	0	1	1	7.1	2	6	2	4	0	.357	.714	0	0	C-4
1914	4	12	2	1	0	0	0.0	1	0	1	4	0	.167	.250	0	0	C-4
1918 BOS A	5	9	4	0	0	0	0.0	1	1	2	3	1	.444	.444	2	1	C-5
1921 NY A	8	21	6	1	1	0	0.0	1	1	5	4	0	.286	.429	0	0	C-8
1922	5	16	3	1	0	0	0.0	0	0	0	3	0	.188	.250	0	0	C-5
1923	6	22	7	1	0	0	0.0	3	0	1	2	0	.318	.364	0	0	C-6
6 yrs.	32	94	27	4	2	1	1.1	8	8	11	20	1	.287	.404	2	1	C-32

	G	AB	H	2B	3B	HR	HR%	R	RBI	BB	SO	SB	BA	SA	PH AB	PH H	G by POS

Art Scharein

SCHAREIN, ARTHUR OTTO (Scoop)   BR TR 6'   175 lbs.
Brother of George Scharein.
B. June 30, 1905, Decatur, Ill.   D. July 2, 1969, San Antonio, Tex.

	G	AB	H	2B	3B	HR	HR%	R	RBI	BB	SO	SB	BA	SA	PH AB	PH H	G by POS
1932 STL A	81	303	92	19	2	0	0.0	43	42	25	10	4	.304	.380	0	0	3B-77, SS-3, 2B-2
1933	123	471	96	13	3	0	0.0	49	26	41	21	7	.204	.244	2	0	3B-95, SS-24, 2B-7
1934	1	2	1	0	0	0	0.0	0	2	0	0	0	.500	.500	2	1	
3 yrs.	205	776	189	32	5	0	0.0	92	70	66	31	11	.244	.298	4	1	3B-172, SS-27, 2B-9

George Scharein

SCHAREIN, GEORGE ALBERT (Tom)   BR TR 6'1"   174 lbs.
Brother of Art Scharein.
B. Nov. 21, 1914, Decatur, Ill.   D. Dec. 23, 1981, Decatur, Ill.

	G	AB	H	2B	3B	HR	HR%	R	RBI	BB	SO	SB	BA	SA	PH AB	PH H	G by POS
1937 PHI N	146	511	123	20	1	0	0.0	44	57	36	47	13	.241	.284	0	0	SS-146
1938	117	390	93	16	4	1	0.3	47	29	16	33	11	.238	.308	1	0	SS-77, 2B-39, 3B-1
1939	118	399	95	17	1	1	0.3	35	33	13	40	4	.238	.293	0	0	SS-117
1940	7	17	5	0	0	0	0.0	0	0	0	3	0	.294	.294	0	0	SS-7
4 yrs.	388	1317	316	53	6	2	0.2	126	119	65	123	28	.240	.294	1	0	SS-347, 2B-39, 3B-1

Nick Scharf

SCHARF, EDWARD T.
B. 1859, Baltimore, Md.   D. May 12, 1937, Baltimore, Md.

	G	AB	H	2B	3B	HR	HR%	R	RBI	BB	SO	SB	BA	SA	PH AB	PH H	G by POS
1882 BAL AA	10	39	8	1	1	1	2.6	4		0			.205	.359	0	0	OF-9, 3B-1
1883	3	13	2	1	0	0	0.0	1		1			.154	.231	0	0	SS-3
2 yrs.	13	52	10	2	1	1	1.9	5		1			.192	.327	0	0	OF-9, SS-3, 3B-1

Al Scheer

SCHEER, ALLEN G.   BL TR 5'9"   165 lbs.
B. Oct. 21, 1888, Dayton, Ohio   D. May 6, 1959, Logansport, Ind.

	G	AB	H	2B	3B	HR	HR%	R	RBI	BB	SO	SB	BA	SA	PH AB	PH H	G by POS
1913 BKN N	6	22	5	0	0	0	0.0	3	0	2	4	1	.227	.227	0	0	OF-6
1914 IND F	120	363	111	23	6	3	0.8	63	45	49		9	.306	.427	13	5	OF-102, 2B-4, SS-1
1915 NWK F	155	546	146	25	14	2	0.4	75	60	65		31	.267	.375	0	0	OF-155
3 yrs.	281	931	262	48	20	5	0.5	141	105	116	4	41	.281	.392	13	5	OF-263, 2B-4, SS-1

Heinie Scheer

SCHEER, HENRY WILLIAM   BR TR 5'8"   146 lbs.
B. July 31, 1900, New York, N. Y.   D. Mar. 21, 1976, New Haven, Conn.

	G	AB	H	2B	3B	HR	HR%	R	RBI	BB	SO	SB	BA	SA	PH AB	PH H	G by POS
1922 PHI A	51	135	23	3	0	4	3.0	10	12	3	25	1	.170	.281	10	2	2B-29, 3B-10
1923	69	210	50	8	1	2	1.0	26	21	17	41	3	.238	.314	4	0	2B-61
2 yrs.	120	345	73	11	1	6	1.7	36	33	20	66	4	.212	.301	14	2	2B-90, 3B-10

Fritz Scheeren

SCHEEREN, FREDERICK (Dutch)   BR TR 6'   180 lbs.
B. July 1, 1891, Kokomo, Ind.   D. June 17, 1973, Oil City, Pa.

	G	AB	H	2B	3B	HR	HR%	R	RBI	BB	SO	SB	BA	SA	PH AB	PH H	G by POS
1914 PIT N	11	31	9	0	1	1	3.2	4	2	1	6	1	.290	.452	1	0	OF-10
1915	4	3	0	0	0	0	0.0	0	0	0	0	0	.000	.000	3	0	OF-1
2 yrs.	15	34	9	0	1	1	2.9	4	2	1	6	1	.265	.412	4	0	OF-11

Bob Scheffing

SCHEFFING, ROBERT BODEN   BR TR 6'2"   180 lbs.
B. Aug. 11, 1915, Overland, Mo.
Manager 1957-59, 1961-63.

	G	AB	H	2B	3B	HR	HR%	R	RBI	BB	SO	SB	BA	SA	PH AB	PH H	G by POS
1941 CHI N	51	132	32	8	0	1	0.8	9	20	5	19	2	.242	.326	17	3	C-34
1942	44	102	20	3	0	2	2.0	7	12	7	11	2	.196	.284	12	1	C-32
1946	63	115	32	4	1	0	0.0	8	18	12	18	0	.278	.330	19	7	C-43
1947	110	363	96	11	5	5	1.4	33	50	25	25	2	.264	.364	13	5	C-97
1948	102	293	88	18	2	5	1.7	23	45	22	27	0	.300	.427	23	6	C-78
1949	55	149	40	6	1	3	2.0	12	19	9	9	0	.268	.383	14	3	C-40
1950 2 teams							CHI N (12G – .188)			CIN N (21G – .277)							
" total	33	63	16	1	0	2	3.2	4	7	4	4	0	.254	.365	19	5	C-14
1951 2 teams							CIN N (47G – .254)			STL N (12G – .111)							
" total	59	140	33	2	0	2	1.4	9	16	19	14	0	.236	.293	7	2	C-52
8 yrs.	517	1357	357	53	9	20	1.5	105	187	103	127	6	.263	.360	124	33	C-390

Ted Scheffler

SCHEFFLER, THEODORE J.   BR TR 5'10"   160 lbs.
B. Apr. 5, 1864, New York, N. Y.   D. Feb. 24, 1949, Jamaica, N. Y.

	G	AB	H	2B	3B	HR	HR%	R	RBI	BB	SO	SB	BA	SA	PH AB	PH H	G by POS
1888 DET N	27	94	19	3	1	0	0.0	17	4	9	9	4	.202	.255	0	0	OF-27
1890 ROC AA	119	445	109	12	6	3	0.6	111		78	77	77	.245	.319	0	0	OF-119, C-1
2 yrs.	146	539	128	15	7	3	0.6	128	4	87	9	81	.237	.308	0	0	OF-146, C-1

Carl Scheib

SCHEIB, CARL ALVIN   BR TR 6'1"   192 lbs.
B. Jan. 1, 1927, Gratz, Pa.

	G	AB	H	2B	3B	HR	HR%	R	RBI	BB	SO	SB	BA	SA	PH AB	PH H	G by POS
1943 PHI A	6	5	0	0	0	0	0.0	0	0	0	3	0	.000	.000	0	0	P-6
1944	15	10	3	2	0	0	0.0	1	0	0	2	0	.300	.500	0	0	P-15
1945	4	2	0	0	0	0	0.0	0	0	0	0	0	.000	.000	0	0	P-4
1947	22	45	6	0	0	0	0.0	4	3	1	3	0	.133	.133	1	0	P-21
1948	52	104	31	8	3	2	1.9	14	21	8	17	0	.298	.490	16	7	P-32, OF-2
1949	47	72	17	2	0	0	0.0	9	10	8	10	0	.236	.264	9	2	P-38
1950	50	52	13	0	1	1	1.9	6	6	1	9	0	.250	.346	7	1	P-43
1951	48	53	21	2	2	2	3.8	9	8	1	5	0	.396	.623	2	1	P-46
1952	44	82	18	0	0	0	0.0	4	7	0	9	1	.220	.220	14	2	P-30
1953	35	41	8	0	0	0	0.0	4	4	2	1	0	.195	.195	8	2	P-28
1954 2 teams							PHI A (1G – .000)			STL N (3G – .000)							
" total	4	2	0	0	0	0	0.0	0	0	0	0	0	.000	.000	0	0	P-4
11 yrs.	327	468	117	14	6	5	1.1	51	59	21	59	1	.250	.338	57	15	P-267, OF-2

Frank Scheibeck

SCHEIBECK, FRANK S.   BR TR 5'7"   145 lbs.
B. June 28, 1865, Detroit, Mich.   D. Oct. 22, 1956, Detroit, Mich.

	G	AB	H	2B	3B	HR	HR%	R	RBI	BB	SO	SB	BA	SA	PH AB	PH H	G by POS
1887 CLE AA	3	9	2	0	0	0	0.0	2		2		0	.222	.222	0	0	SS-1, 3B-1, P-1
1888 DET N	1	4	0	0	0	0	0.0	0		0	0	0	.000	.000	0	0	SS-1
1890 TOL AA	134	485	117	13	5	1	0.2	72		76		57	.241	.295	0	0	SS-134
1894 2 teams							PIT N (28G – .353)			WAS N (52G – .230)							
" total	80	298	81	4	7	1	0.3	69	27	56	33	18	.272	.342	4	1	SS-63, OF-9, 3B-3, 2B-2
1895 WAS N	48	167	31	5	2	0	0.0	17	25	17	21	5	.186	.240	0	0	SS-44, 3B-2, 2B-2

	G	AB	H	2B	3B	HR	HR %	R	RBI	BB	SO	SB	BA	SA	Pinch Hit AB	Pinch Hit H	G by POS

Frank Scheibeck continued

	G	AB	H	2B	3B	HR	HR%	R	RBI	BB	SO	SB	BA	SA	PH AB	PH H	G by POS
1899	27	94	27	4	1	0	0.0	19	9	11		5	.287	.351	0	0	SS-27
1901 CLE A	93	329	70	11	3	0	0.0	33	38	18		3	.213	.264	1	0	SS-92
1906 DET A	3	10	1	0	0	0	0.0	1	0	2		0	.100	.100	0	0	2B-3
8 yrs.	389	1396	329	37	18	2	0.1	213	98	182	54	88	.236	.292	5	1	SS-362, OF-9, 2B-7, 3B-6, P-1

Richie Scheinblum

SCHEINBLUM, RICHARD ALAN
B. Nov. 5, 1942, New York, N. Y.   BB TR 6'1"   180 lbs.

	G	AB	H	2B	3B	HR	HR%	R	RBI	BB	SO	SB	BA	SA	PH AB	PH H	G by POS
1965 CLE A	4	1	0	0	0	0	0.0	1	0	0	0	0	.000	.000	1	0	
1967	18	66	21	4	2	0	0.0	8	6	5	10	0	.318	.439	0	0	OF-18
1968	19	55	12	5	0	0	0.0	3	5	5	8	0	.218	.309	2	0	OF-16
1969	102	199	37	5	1	1	0.5	13	13	19	30	0	.186	.236	54	14	OF-50
1971 WAS A	27	49	7	3	0	0	0.0	5	4	8	5	0	.143	.204	13	3	OF-13
1972 KC A	134	450	135	21	4	8	1.8	60	66	58	40	0	.300	.418	16	7	OF-119
1973 2 teams	CIN N (29G – .222)			CAL A (77G – .328)													
" total	106	283	87	12	2	4	1.4	33	29	45	31	0	.307	.406	21	6	OF-73, DH-7
1974 3 teams	CAL A (10G – .154)			KC A (36G – .181)			STL N (6G – .333)										
" total	52	115	21	2	0	0	0.0	8	4	9	11	0	.183	.200	27	5	DH-18, OF-10
8 yrs.	462	1218	320	52	9	13	1.1	131	127	149	135	0	.263	.352	134	35	OF-299, DH-25

Danny Schell

SCHELL, CLYDE DANIEL
B. Dec. 26, 1927, Fostoria, Mich.   D. May 11, 1972, Mayville, Mich.   BR TR 6'1"   195 lbs.

	G	AB	H	2B	3B	HR	HR%	R	RBI	BB	SO	SB	BA	SA	PH AB	PH H	G by POS
1954 PHI N	92	272	77	14	3	7	2.6	25	33	17	31	0	.283	.434	24	5	OF-69
1955	2	2	0	0	0	0	0.0	0	0	0	1	0	.000	.000	2	0	
2 yrs.	94	274	77	14	3	7	2.6	25	33	17	32	0	.281	.431	26	5	OF-69

Al Schellhase

SCHELLHASE, ALBERT HERMAN (Schelley)
B. Sept. 13, 1864, Evansville, Ind.   D. Jan. 3, 1919, Evansville, Ind.   TR

	G	AB	H	2B	3B	HR	HR%	R	RBI	BB	SO	SB	BA	SA	PH AB	PH H	G by POS
1890 BOS N	9	29	4	0	0	0	0.0	1	1	1	10	0	.138	.138	0	0	OF-5, C-2, SS-1, 3B-1
1891 LOU AA	7	20	3	0	0	0	0.0	4	1	1	2	3	.150	.150	0	0	C-7
2 yrs.	16	49	7	0	0	0	0.0	5	2	2	12	3	.143	.143	0	0	C-9, OF-5, SS-1, 3B-1

Fred Schemanske

SCHEMANSKE, FREDERICK GEORGE (Buck)
B. Apr. 28, 1903, Detroit, Mich.   D. Feb. 18, 1960, Detroit, Mich.   BR TR 6'2"   190 lbs.

	G	AB	H	2B	3B	HR	HR%	R	RBI	BB	SO	SB	BA	SA	PH AB	PH H	G by POS
1923 WAS A	2	2	2	0	0	0	0.0	0	2	1	0	0	1.000	1.000	2	2	P-1

Mike Schemer

SCHEMER, MICHAEL
B. Nov. 20, 1917, Baltimore, Md.   D. Apr. 22, 1983, Miami, Fla.   BL TL 6'   180 lbs.

	G	AB	H	2B	3B	HR	HR%	R	RBI	BB	SO	SB	BA	SA	PH AB	PH H	G by POS
1945 NY N	31	108	36	3	1	1	0.9	10	10	6	1	2	.333	.407	4	0	1B-27
1946	1	1	0	0	0	0	0.0	0	0	0	0	0	.000	.000	1	0	
2 yrs.	32	109	36	3	1	1	0.9	10	10	6	1	2	.330	.404	5	0	1B-27

Bill Schenck

SCHENCK, WILLIAM G.
B. Brooklyn, N. Y.   Deceased.   5'7"   171 lbs.

	G	AB	H	2B	3B	HR	HR%	R	RBI	BB	SO	SB	BA	SA	PH AB	PH H	G by POS
1882 LOU AA	60	231	60	11	3	0	0.0	37		8			.260	.333	0	0	3B-58, SS-2, P-2
1884 RIC AA	42	151	31	4	0	3	2.0	14		1			.205	.291	0	0	SS-40, 2B-2
1885 BKN AA	1	4	0	0	0	0	0.0	0		0			.000	.000	0	0	3B-1
3 yrs.	103	386	91	15	3	3	0.8	51		9			.236	.313	0	0	3B-59, SS-42, 2B-2, P-2

Hank Schenz

SCHENZ, HENRY LEONARD
B. Apr. 11, 1919, New Richmond, Ohio   BR TR 5'9½"   175 lbs.

	G	AB	H	2B	3B	HR	HR%	R	RBI	BB	SO	SB	BA	SA	PH AB	PH H	G by POS
1946 CHI N	6	11	2	0	0	0	0.0	1	1	0	0	1	.182	.182	0	0	3B-5
1947	7	14	1	0	0	0	0.0	2	0	2	1	0	.071	.071	0	0	3B-5
1948	96	337	88	17	1	1	0.3	43	14	18	15	3	.261	.326	10	1	2B-78, 3B-5
1949	7	14	6	0	0	0	0.0	2	1	1	0	2	.429	.429	0	0	3B-5
1950 PIT N	58	101	23	4	2	1	1.0	17	5	6	7	0	.228	.337	14	5	2B-21, 3B-12, SS-4
1951 2 teams	PIT N (25G – .213)			NY N (8G – .000)													
" total	33	61	13	1	0	0	0.0	6	3	0	2	0	.213	.230	1	0	2B-19, 3B-2
6 yrs.	207	538	133	22	3	2	0.4	70	24	27	25	6	.247	.310	25	6	2B-118, 3B-34, SS-4
WORLD SERIES																	
1951 NY N	1	0	0	0	0	0	–	0	0	0	0	0	–	–	0	0	

Joe Schepner

SCHEPNER, JOSEPH MAURICE
B. Aug. 10, 1895, Aliquippa, Pa.   D. July 25, 1959, Mobile, Ala.   BR TR 5'10"   160 lbs.

	G	AB	H	2B	3B	HR	HR%	R	RBI	BB	SO	SB	BA	SA	PH AB	PH H	G by POS
1919 STL A	14	48	10	4	0	0	0.0	2	6	1	5	0	.208	.292	1	0	3B-13

Bob Scherbarth

SCHERBARTH, ROBERT ELMER
B. Jan. 18, 1926, Milwaukee, Wis.   BR TR 6'   180 lbs.

	G	AB	H	2B	3B	HR	HR%	R	RBI	BB	SO	SB	BA	SA	PH AB	PH H	G by POS
1950 BOS A	1	0	0	0	0	0	0.0	0	0	0	0	0	–	–	0	0	C-1

Harry Scherer

SCHERER, HARRY
Deceased.

	G	AB	H	2B	3B	HR	HR%	R	RBI	BB	SO	SB	BA	SA	PH AB	PH H	G by POS
1889 LOU AA	1	3	1	0	0	0	0.0	0	0	0	0	0	.333	.333	0	0	OF-1

Lou Schiappacasse

SCHIAPPACASSE, LOUIS JOSEPH
B. Mar. 29, 1881, Ann Arbor, Mich.   D. Sept. 20, 1910, Ann Arbor, Mich.   BR TR

	G	AB	H	2B	3B	HR	HR%	R	RBI	BB	SO	SB	BA	SA	PH AB	PH H	G by POS
1902 DET A	2	5	0	0	0	0	0.0	0	1	1		0	.000	.000	0	0	OF-2

Morrie Schick

SCHICK, MAURICE FRANCIS
B. Apr. 17, 1892, Chicago, Ill.   D. Oct. 25, 1979, Hazel Crest, Ill.   BR TR 5'11"   170 lbs.

	G	AB	H	2B	3B	HR	HR%	R	RBI	BB	SO	SB	BA	SA	PH AB	PH H	G by POS
1917 CHI N	14	34	5	0	0	0	0.0	3	3	3	10	0	.147	.147	0	0	OF-12

	G	AB	H	2B	3B	HR	HR %	R	RBI	BB	SO	SB	BA	SA	Pinch Hit AB	Pinch Hit H	G by POS

Chuck Schilling

SCHILLING, CHARLES THOMAS
B. Oct. 25, 1937, Brooklyn, N. Y.   BR TR 5'10" 160 lbs.

	G	AB	H	2B	3B	HR	HR %	R	RBI	BB	SO	SB	BA	SA	AB	H	G by POS
1961 **BOS A**	158	646	167	25	2	5	0.8	87	62	78	77	7	.259	.327	1	0	2B-158
1962	119	413	95	17	1	7	1.7	48	35	29	48	1	.230	.327	0	0	2B-118
1963	146	576	135	25	0	8	1.4	63	33	41	72	3	.234	.319	4	0	2B-143
1964	47	163	32	6	0	0	0.0	18	7	15	22	0	.196	.233	5	3	2B-42
1965	71	171	41	3	2	3	1.8	14	9	13	17	0	.240	.333	28	6	2B-41
5 yrs.	541	1969	470	76	5	23	1.2	230	146	176	236	11	.239	.317	38	9	2B-502

Bill Schindler

SCHINDLER, WILLIAM GIBBON
B. July 10, 1896, Perryville, Mo.   D. Feb. 6, 1979, Perryville, Mo.   BR TR 5'11" 160 lbs.

	G	AB	H	2B	3B	HR	HR %	R	RBI	BB	SO	SB	BA	SA	AB	H	G by POS
1920 **STL N**	1	2	0	0	0	0	0.0	0	0	0	1	0	.000	.000	0	0	C-1

Dutch Schirick

SCHIRICK, HARRY ERNEST
B. June 15, 1890, Ruby, N. Y.   D. Nov. 12, 1968, Kingston, N. Y.   BR TR 5'8" 160 lbs.

	G	AB	H	2B	3B	HR	HR %	R	RBI	BB	SO	SB	BA	SA	AB	H	G by POS
1914 **STL A**	1	0	0	0	0	0	–	0	0	1	0	2	–	–	0	0	

Larry Schlafly

SCHLAFLY, HARRY LAWRENCE
B. Sept. 20, 1878, Port Washington, Ohio   D. June 27, 1919, Beach City, Ohio   BR TR
Manager 1914-15.

	G	AB	H	2B	3B	HR	HR %	R	RBI	BB	SO	SB	BA	SA	AB	H	G by POS
1902 **CHI N**	10	31	10	0	3	0	0.0	5	5	6		2	.323	.516	0	0	OF-5, 2B-4, 3B-2
1906 **WAS A**	123	426	105	13	8	2	0.5	60	30	50		29	.246	.329	0	0	2B-123
1907	24	74	10	0	0	2	2.7	10	4	22		7	.135	.216	0	0	2B-24
1914 **BUF F**	51	127	33	7	1	2	1.6	16	19	12		3	.260	.378	14	5	2B-23, 1B-7, OF-1, 3B-1, C-1
4 yrs.	208	658	158	20	12	6	0.9	91	58	90		41	.240	.334	14	5	2B-174, 1B-7, OF-6, 3B-3, C-1

Admiral Schlei

SCHLEI, GEORGE HENRY
B. Jan. 12, 1878, Cincinnati, Ohio   D. Jan. 24, 1958, Huntington, W. Va.   BR TR 5'8½" 179 lbs.

	G	AB	H	2B	3B	HR	HR %	R	RBI	BB	SO	SB	BA	SA	AB	H	G by POS
1904 **CIN N**	97	291	69	8	3	0	0.0	25	32	17		7	.237	.285	7	1	C-88
1905	99	314	71	8	3	1	0.3	32	36	22		9	.226	.280	4	2	C-89, 1B-6
1906	116	388	95	13	8	4	1.0	44	54	29		7	.245	.351	4	1	C-91, 1B-21
1907	84	246	67	3	2	0	0.0	28	27	28		5	.272	.301	11	3	C-67, 1B-3, OF-2
1908	92	300	66	6	4	1	0.3	31	22	22		2	.220	.277	4	1	C-88
1909 **NY N**	92	279	68	12	0	0	0.0	25	30	40		4	.244	.287	3	0	C-89
1910	55	99	19	2	1	0	0.0	10	8	14	10	4	.192	.232	6	1	C-49
1911	1	1	0	0	0	0	0.0	0	0	0		1	.000	.000	1	0	
8 yrs.	636	1918	455	52	21	6	0.3	195	209	172	11	38	.237	.296	40	9	C-561, 1B-30, OF-2

Rudy Schlesinger

SCHLESINGER, WILLIAM CORDES
B. Nov. 5, 1942, Cincinnati, Ohio   BR TR 6'2" 175 lbs.

	G	AB	H	2B	3B	HR	HR %	R	RBI	BB	SO	SB	BA	SA	AB	H	G by POS
1965 **BOS A**	1	1	0	0	0	0	0.0	0	0	0	0	0	.000	.000	1	0	

Dutch Schliebner

SCHLIEBNER, FREDERICK PAUL
B. May 19, 1891, Charlottenburg, Germany   D. Apr. 15, 1975, Toledo, Ohio   BR TR 5'10" 180 lbs.

	G	AB	H	2B	3B	HR	HR %	R	RBI	BB	SO	SB	BA	SA	AB	H	G by POS
1923 **2 teams**			**BKN**	**N**	(19G –	.250)		**STL**	**A**	(127G –	.275)						
" total	146	520	141	23	6	4	0.8	61	56	44	67	4	.271	.362	0	0	1B-146

Jay Schlueter

SCHLUETER, JAY D.
B. July 31, 1949, Phoenix, Ariz.   BR TR 6' 182 lbs.

	G	AB	H	2B	3B	HR	HR %	R	RBI	BB	SO	SB	BA	SA	AB	H	G by POS
1971 **HOU N**	7	3	1	0	0	0	0.0	0	0	1	0	0	.333	.333	2	1	OF-2

Norm Schlueter

SCHLUETER, NORMAN JOHN
B. Sept. 25, 1916, Belleville, Ill.   BR TR 5'10" 175 lbs.

	G	AB	H	2B	3B	HR	HR %	R	RBI	BB	SO	SB	BA	SA	AB	H	G by POS
1938 **CHI A**	35	118	27	5	1	0	0.0	11	7	4	15	1	.229	.288	1	0	C-34
1939	34	56	13	2	1	0	0.0	5	8	1	11	2	.232	.304	2	0	C-32
1944 **CLE A**	49	122	15	4	0	0	0.0	2	11	12	22	0	.123	.156	6	0	C-109
3 yrs.	118	296	55	11	2	0	0.0	18	26	17	48	3	.186	.236	9	0	C-109

Ray Schmandt

SCHMANDT, RAYMOND HENRY
B. Jan. 25, 1896, St. Louis, Mo.   D. Feb. 1, 1969, St. Louis, Mo.   BR TR 6'1" 175 lbs.

	G	AB	H	2B	3B	HR	HR %	R	RBI	BB	SO	SB	BA	SA	AB	H	G by POS
1915 **STL A**	3	4	0	0	0	0	0.0	0	0	0	1	0	.000	.000	2	0	1B-1
1918 **BKN N**	34	114	35	5	4	0	0.0	11	18	7	7	1	.307	.421	0	0	2B-34
1919	47	127	21	4	0	0	0.0	8	10	4	13	0	.165	.197	10	2	2B-18, 1B-12, 3B-6
1920	28	63	15	2	1	0	0.0	7	7	3	4	1	.238	.302	6	3	1B-20
1921	95	350	107	8	5	1	0.3	42	43	11	22	3	.306	.366	2	0	1B-92
1922	110	396	106	17	3	2	0.5	54	44	21	28	6	.268	.341	0	0	1B-110
6 yrs.	317	1054	284	36	13	3	0.3	122	122	46	75	11	.269	.337	20	5	1B-235, 2B-52, 3B-6

WORLD SERIES

	G	AB	H	2B	3B	HR	HR %	R	RBI	BB	SO	SB	BA	SA	AB	H	G by POS
1920 **BKN N**	1	1	0	0	0	0	0.0	0	0	0	0	0	.000	.000	1	0	

George Schmees

SCHMEES, GEORGE EDWARD (Rocky)
B. Sept. 6, 1924, Cincinnati, Ohio   BL TL 6' 190 lbs.

	G	AB	H	2B	3B	HR	HR %	R	RBI	BB	SO	SB	BA	SA	AB	H	G by POS
1952 **2 teams**			**STL**	**A**	(34G –	.131)		**BOS**	**A**	(42G –	.203)						
" total	76	125	21	4	1	0	0.0	17	6	12	29	0	.168	.216	12	0	OF-48, 1B-4, P-2

Bob Schmidt

SCHMIDT, ROBERT BENJAMIN
B. Apr. 22, 1933, St. Louis, Mo.   BR TR 6'2" 205 lbs.

	G	AB	H	2B	3B	HR	HR %	R	RBI	BB	SO	SB	BA	SA	AB	H	G by POS
1958 **SF N**	127	393	96	20	2	14	3.6	46	54	33	59	0	.244	.412	6	2	C-123
1959	71	181	44	7	1	5	2.8	17	20	13	24	0	.243	.376	3	0	C-70
1960	110	344	92	12	1	8	2.3	31	37	26	51	0	.267	.378	3	0	C-108
1961 **2 teams**			**SF**	**N**	(2G –	.167)		**CIN**	**N**	(27G –	.129)						
" total	29	76	10	0	1	1	1.3	4	5	8	15	0	.132	.171	0	0	C-29
1962 **WAS A**	88	256	62	14	0	10	3.9	28	31	14	37	0	.242	.414	4	1	C-88
1963	9	15	3	1	0	0	0.0	3	0	3	5	0	.200	.267	5	0	C-6

	G	AB	H	2B	3B	HR	HR %	R	RBI	BB	SO	SB	BA	SA	Pinch Hit AB	Pinch Hit H	G by POS

Bob Schmidt continued

	G	AB	H	2B	3B	HR	HR %	R	RBI	BB	SO	SB	BA	SA	AB	H	G by POS
1965 NY A	20	40	10	1	0	1	2.5	4	3	3	8	0	.250	.350	0	0	C-20
7 yrs.	454	1305	317	55	4	39	3.0	133	150	100	199	0	.243	.381	21	3	C-444

Boss Schmidt

SCHMIDT, CHARLES
Brother of Walter Schmidt.
B. Sept. 12, 1880, Coal Hill, Ark.   D. Nov. 14, 1932, Clarksville, Ark.   BB TR 5'11"   200 lbs.

	G	AB	H	2B	3B	HR	HR %	R	RBI	BB	SO	SB	BA	SA	AB	H	G by POS
1906 DET A	68	216	47	4	3	0	0.0	13	10	6		1	.218	.264	1	0	C-67
1907	104	349	85	6	6	0	0.0	32	23	5		8	.244	.295	1	0	C-104
1908	122	419	111	14	3	1	0.2	45	38	16		5	.265	.320	1	1	C-121
1909	84	253	53	8	2	1	0.4	21	28	7		7	.209	.269	2	1	C-81, OF-1
1910	71	197	51	7	7	1	0.5	22	23	2		2	.259	.381	5	2	C-66
1911	28	46	13	2	1	0	0.0	4	2	0		0	.283	.370	17	6	C-9, OF-1
6 yrs.	477	1480	360	41	22	3	0.2	137	124	36		23	.243	.307	27	10	C-448, OF-2

WORLD SERIES

	G	AB	H	2B	3B	HR	HR %	R	RBI	BB	SO	SB	BA	SA	AB	H	G by POS
1907 DET A	4	12	2	0	0	0	0.0	0	0	2	1	0	.167	.167	1	0	C-3
1908	4	14	1	0	0	0	0.0	0	1	0	2	0	.071	.071	0	0	C-4
1909	6	18	4	2	0	0	0.0	0	4	2	0	0	.222	.333	0	0	C-6
3 yrs.	14	44	7	2	0	0	0.0	0	5	4	3	0	.159	.205	1	0	C-13

Butch Schmidt

SCHMIDT, CHARLES JOHN
B. July 19, 1887, Baltimore, Md.   D. Sept. 4, 1952, Baltimore, Md.   BL TL 6'1½"   200 lbs.

	G	AB	H	2B	3B	HR	HR %	R	RBI	BB	SO	SB	BA	SA	AB	H	G by POS
1909 NY A	1	2	0	0	0	0	0.0	0	0	0		0	.000	.000	0	0	P-1
1913 BOS N	22	78	24	2	2	1	1.3	6	14	2	5	1	.308	.423	0	0	1B-22
1914	147	537	153	17	9	1	0.2	67	71	43	55	14	.285	.356	0	0	1B-147
1915	127	458	115	26	7	2	0.4	46	60	36	59	3	.251	.352	0	0	1B-127
4 yrs.	297	1075	292	45	18	4	0.4	119	145	81	119	18	.272	.358	0	0	1B-296, P-1

WORLD SERIES

	G	AB	H	2B	3B	HR	HR %	R	RBI	BB	SO	SB	BA	SA	AB	H	G by POS
1914 BOS N	4	17	5	0	0	0	0.0	2	2	0	2	1	.294	.294	0	0	1B-4

Dave Schmidt

SCHMIDT, DAVID FREDERICK
B. Dec. 22, 1956, Mesa, Ariz.   BR TR 6'1"   190 lbs.

	G	AB	H	2B	3B	HR	HR %	R	RBI	BB	SO	SB	BA	SA	AB	H	G by POS
1981 BOS A	15	42	10	1	0	2	4.8	6	3	7	17	0	.238	.405	1	1	C-15

Mike Schmidt

SCHMIDT, MICHAEL JACK
B. Sept. 27, 1949, Dayton, Ohio   BR TR 6'2"   195 lbs.

	G	AB	H	2B	3B	HR	HR %	R	RBI	BB	SO	SB	BA	SA	AB	H	G by POS
1972 PHI N	13	34	7	0	0	1	2.9	2	3	5	15	0	.206	.294	1	0	3B-11, 2B-1
1973	132	367	72	11	0	18	4.9	43	52	62	136	8	.196	.373	9	2	3B-125, 2B-4, SS-2, 1B-2
1974	162	568	160	28	7	36	6.3	108	116	106	138	23	.282	.546	0	0	3B-162
1975	158	562	140	34	3	38	6.8	93	95	101	180	29	.249	.523	1	0	3B-151, SS-10
1976	160	584	153	31	4	38	6.5	112	107	100	149	14	.262	.524	0	0	3B-160
1977	154	544	149	27	11	38	7.0	114	101	104	122	15	.274	.574	2	0	3B-149, SS-2, 2B-1
1978	145	513	129	27	2	21	4.1	93	78	91	103	19	.251	.435	4	1	3B-140, SS-1
1979	160	541	137	25	4	45	8.3	109	114	120	115	9	.253	.564	2	0	3B-157, SS-2
1980	150	548	157	25	8	48	8.8	104	121	89	119	12	.286	.624	1	0	3B-149
1981	102	354	112	19	2	31	8.8	78	91	73	71	12	.316	.644	1	1	3B-101
1982	148	514	144	26	3	35	6.8	108	87	107	131	14	.280	.547	0	0	3B-148
1983	154	534	136	16	4	40	7.5	104	109	128	148	7	.255	.524	0	0	3B-153, SS-2
1984	151	528	146	23	3	36	6.8	93	106	92	116	5	.277	.536	4	3	3B-145, 1B-2, SS-1
13 yrs.	1789	6191	1642	292	51	425	6.9 4th	1161	1180	1178	1543	167	.265	.535	25	7	3B-1751, SS-20, 2B-6, 1B-4

DIVISIONAL PLAYOFF SERIES

	G	AB	H	2B	3B	HR	HR %	R	RBI	BB	SO	SB	BA	SA	AB	H	G by POS
1981 PHI N	5	16	4	1	0	1	6.3	3	2	4	2	0	.250	.500	0	0	3B-5

LEAGUE CHAMPIONSHIP SERIES

	G	AB	H	2B	3B	HR	HR %	R	RBI	BB	SO	SB	BA	SA	AB	H	G by POS
1976 PHI N	3	13	4	2	0	0	0.0	1	2	0	1	0	.308	.462	0	0	3B-3
1977	4	16	1	0	0	0	0.0	2	1	2	3	0	.063	.063	0	0	3B-4
1978	4	15	3	2	0	0	0.0	1	1	2	2	0	.200	.333	0	0	3B-4
1980	5	24	5	1	0	0	0.0	1	1	1	6	1	.208	.250	0	0	3B-5
1983	4	15	7	2	0	1	6.7	5	2	2	3	0	.467	.800	0	0	3B-4
5 yrs.	20	83	20	7	0	2	1.2	10	7	7	15	1	.241	.361	0	0	3B-20

WORLD SERIES

	G	AB	H	2B	3B	HR	HR %	R	RBI	BB	SO	SB	BA	SA	AB	H	G by POS
1980 PHI N	6	21	8	1	0	2	9.5	6	7	4	3	0	.381	.714	0	0	3B-6
1983	5	20	1	0	0	0	0.0	0	0	0	6	0	.050	.050	0	0	3B-5
2 yrs.	11	41	9	1	0	2	4.9	6	7	4	9	0	.220	.390	0	0	3B-11

Walter Schmidt

SCHMIDT, WALTER JOSEPH
Brother of Boss Schmidt.
B. Mar. 20, 1887, Coal Hill, Ark.   D. July 4, 1973, Modesto, Calif.   BR TR 5'9"   159 lbs.

	G	AB	H	2B	3B	HR	HR %	R	RBI	BB	SO	SB	BA	SA	AB	H	G by POS
1916 PIT N	64	184	35	1	2	2	1.1	16	15	10	13	3	.190	.250	3	1	C-57
1917	75	183	45	7	0	0	0.0	9	17	11	11	4	.246	.284	7	1	C-61
1918	105	323	77	6	3	0	0.0	31	27	17	19	7	.238	.276	1	1	C-104
1919	85	267	67	9	2	0	0.0	23	29	23	9	5	.251	.300	0	0	C-85
1920	94	310	86	8	4	0	0.0	22	20	24	15	9	.277	.329	1	0	C-92
1921	114	393	111	9	3	0	0.0	30	38	12	13	10	.282	.321	3	0	C-111
1922	40	152	50	11	1	0	0.0	21	22	1	5	2	.329	.414	0	0	C-40
1923	97	335	83	7	2	0	0.0	39	37	22	12	10	.248	.281	0	0	C-96
1924	58	177	43	3	2	1	0.6	16	20	13	5	6	.243	.299	0	1	C-57
1925 STL N	37	87	22	2	1	0	0.0	9	9	4	3	1	.253	.299	4	1	C-31
10 yrs.	769	2411	619	63	20	3	0.1	216	234	137	105	57	.257	.303	20	5	C-734

Hank Schmulbach

SCHMULBACH, HENRY ALRIVES
B. Jan. 17, 1925, East St. Louis, Ill.   BL TR 5'11"   165 lbs.

	G	AB	H	2B	3B	HR	HR %	R	RBI	BB	SO	SB	BA	SA	AB	H	G by POS
1943 STL A	1	0	0	0	0	0	–	1	0	0	0	0	–	–	0	0	

	G	AB	H	2B	3B	HR	HR %	R	RBI	BB	SO	SB	BA	SA	Pinch Hit AB	Pinch Hit H	G by POS

Dave Schneck

SCHNECK, DAVID LEE
B. June 18, 1949, Allentown, Pa.

BL TL 5'10" 200 lbs.

	G	AB	H	2B	3B	HR	HR %	R	RBI	BB	SO	SB	BA	SA	PH AB	PH H	G by POS
1972 NY N	37	123	23	3	2	3	2.4	7	10	10	26	0	.187	.317	4	0	OF-33
1973	13	36	7	0	1	0	0.0	2	0	1	4	0	.194	.250	1	0	OF-12
1974	93	254	52	11	1	5	2.0	23	25	16	43	4	.205	.315	6	1	OF-84
3 yrs.	143	413	82	14	4	8	1.9	32	35	27	73	4	.199	.310	11	1	OF-129

Red Schoendienst

SCHOENDIENST, ALBERT FRED
B. Feb. 2, 1923, Germantown, Ill.
Manager 1965-76, 1980.

BB TR 6' 170 lbs.

	G	AB	H	2B	3B	HR	HR %	R	RBI	BB	SO	SB	BA	SA	PH AB	PH H	G by POS
1945 STL N	137	565	157	22	6	1	0.2	89	47	21	17	26	.278	.343	7	2	OF-118, SS-10, 2B-1
1946	142	606	170	28	5	0	0.0	94	34	37	27	12	.281	.343	1	0	2B-128, 3B-12, SS-4
1947	151	659	167	25	9	3	0.5	91	48	48	27	6	.253	.332	3	1	2B-142, 3B-5, OF-1
1948	119	408	111	21	4	4	1.0	64	36	28	16	1	.272	.373	17	4	2B-96
1949	151	640	190	25	2	3	0.5	102	54	51	18	8	.297	.356	1	1	2B-138, SS-14, 3B-6, OF-2
1950	153	642	177	43	9	7	1.1	81	63	33	32	3	.276	.403	0	0	2B-143, SS-10, 3B-1
1951	135	553	160	32	7	6	1.1	88	54	35	23	0	.289	.405	1	1	2B-124, SS-8
1952	152	620	188	40	7	7	1.1	91	67	42	30	9	.303	.424	0	0	2B-142, 3B-11, SS-3
1953	146	564	193	35	5	15	2.7	107	79	60	23	3	.342	.502	6	4	2B-140
1954	148	610	192	38	8	5	0.8	98	79	54	22	4	.315	.428	4	1	2B-144
1955	145	553	148	21	8	11	2.0	68	51	54	28	7	.268	.376	2	0	2B-142
1956 2 teams	STL	N	(40G –	.314)		NY	N	(92G –	.296)								
" total	132	487	147	21	3	2	0.4	61	29	41	15	1	.302	.370	10	4	2B-121
1957 2 teams	NY	N	(57G –	.307)		MIL	N	(93G –	.310)								
" total	150	648	200	31	8	15	2.3	91	65	33	15	4	.309	.451	1	0	2B-149, OF-2
1958 MIL N	106	427	112	23	1	1	0.2	47	24	31	21	3	.262	.328	2	0	2B-105
1959	5	3	0	0	0	0	0.0	0	0	0	0	0	.000	.000	1	0	2B-4
1960	68	226	58	9	1	1	0.4	21	19	17	13	1	.257	.319	4	0	2B-62
1961 STL N	72	120	36	9	0	1	0.8	9	12	12	6	1	.300	.400	48	16	2B-32
1962	98	143	43	4	0	2	1.4	21	12	9	12	0	.301	.371	72	22	2B-21, 3B-4
1963	6	5	0	0	0	0	0.0	0	0	0	1	0	.000	.000	5	0	
19 yrs.	2216	8479	2449	427	78	84	1.0	1223	773	606	346	89	.289	.387	185	56	2B-1834, OF-123, SS-49, 3B-39

WORLD SERIES

	G	AB	H	2B	3B	HR	HR %	R	RBI	BB	SO	SB	BA	SA	PH AB	PH H	G by POS
1946 STL N	7	30	7	1	0	0	0.0	3	1	0	2	1	.233	.267	0	0	2B-7
1957 MIL N	5	18	5	1	0	0	0.0	0	2	0	1	0	.278	.333	0	0	2B-5
1958	7	30	9	3	1	0	0.0	5	0	2	1	0	.300	.467	0	0	2B-7
3 yrs.	19	78	21	5	1	0	0.0	8	3	2	4	1	.269	.359	0	0	2B-19

Jumbo Schoeneck

SCHOENECK, LEWIS N.
B. Mar. 3, 1862, Chicago, Ill.   D. Jan. 20, 1930, Chicago, Ill.

BR TR 235 lbs.

	G	AB	H	2B	3B	HR	HR %	R	RBI	BB	SO	SB	BA	SA	PH AB	PH H	G by POS
1884 2 teams	C-P	U	(90G –	.317)		BAL	U	(16G –	.250)								
" total	106	426	131	24	2	2	0.5	61		8			.308	.387	0	0	1B-105, SS-1
1888 IND N	48	169	40	4	0	0	0.0	15	20	9	24	11	.237	.260	0	0	1B-48, P-2
1889	16	62	15	2	2	0	0.0	3	8	3	3	1	.242	.339	0	0	1B-16
3 yrs.	170	657	186	30	4	2	0.3	79	27	20	27	12	.283	.350	0	0	1B-169, P-2, SS-1

Dick Schofield

SCHOFIELD, JOHN RICHARD (Ducky)
Father of Dick Schofield.
B. Jan. 7, 1935, Springfield, Ill.

BB TR 5'9" 163 lbs.

	G	AB	H	2B	3B	HR	HR %	R	RBI	BB	SO	SB	BA	SA	PH AB	PH H	G by POS
1953 STL N	33	39	7	0	0	2	5.1	9	4	2	11	0	.179	.333	1	0	SS-15
1954	43	7	1	0	1	0	0.0	17	1	0	3	1	.143	.429	3	1	SS-11
1955	12	4	0	0	0	0	0.0	3	0	0	1	0	.000	.000	2	0	SS-3
1956	16	30	3	2	0	0	0.0	3	1	0	6	0	.100	.167	4	0	SS-9
1957	65	56	9	0	0	0	0.0	10	1	7	13	1	.161	.161	11	1	SS-23
1958 2 teams	STL	N	(39G –	.213)		PIT	N	(26G –	.148)								
" total	65	135	27	4	1	1	0.7	20	10	26	21	0	.200	.267	14	3	SS-32, 3B-2
1959 PIT N	81	145	34	10	1	1	0.7	21	9	16	22	1	.234	.338	14	3	2B-28, SS-8, OF-3
1960	65	102	34	4	0	0	0.0	9	10	16	20	0	.333	.392	19	5	SS-23, 2B-10, 3B-1
1961	60	78	15	2	1	0	0.0	16	2	10	19	0	.192	.244	18	3	3B-11, SS-9, 2B-5, OF-3
1962	54	104	30	3	0	2	1.9	19	10	17	22	0	.288	.375	26	8	3B-20, 2B-2, SS-1
1963	138	541	133	18	2	3	0.6	54	32	69	83	2	.246	.303	0	0	SS-117, 2B-20, 3B-1
1964	121	398	98	22	5	3	0.8	50	36	54	60	1	.246	.349	10	0	SS-111
1965 2 teams	PIT	N	(31G –	.229)		SF	N	(101G –	.203)								
" total	132	488	102	15	1	2	0.4	52	25	48	69	3	.209	.256	11	1	SS-121
1966 3 teams	SF	N	(11G –	.063)		NY	A	(25G –	.155)		LA	N	(20G –	.257)			
" total	56	144	28	2	0	0	0.0	19	6	19	18	1	.194	.208	4	1	SS-30, 3B-19
1967 LA N	84	232	50	10	1	2	0.9	23	15	31	40	1	.216	.293	6	0	SS-69, 2B-4, 3B-2
1968 STL N	69	127	28	7	1	1	0.8	14	8	13	31	1	.220	.315	11	0	SS-43, 2B-23
1969 BOS A	94	226	58	9	3	2	0.9	30	20	29	44	0	.257	.350	33	11	2B-37, SS-11, 3B-9, OF-5
1970	76	139	26	1	2	1	0.7	16	14	21	26	0	.187	.245	43	7	3B-15, 2B-15, SS-3
1971 2 teams	STL	N	(34G –	.217)		MIL	A	(23G –	.107)								
" total	57	88	16	4	0	1	1.1	9	7	12	17	0	.182	.261	17	5	SS-21, 3B-15, 2B-15
19 yrs.	1321	3083	699	113	20	21	0.7	394	211	390	526	12	.227	.297	247	49	SS-660, 2B-159, 3B-95, OF-11

WORLD SERIES

	G	AB	H	2B	3B	HR	HR %	R	RBI	BB	SO	SB	BA	SA	PH AB	PH H	G by POS
1960 PIT N	3	3	1	0	0	0	0.0	0	0	1	0	0	.333	.333	3	1	SS-2
1968 STL N	2	0	0	0	0	0	–	0	0	0	0	0	–	–	0	0	
2 yrs.	5	3	1	0	0	0	0.0	0	0	1	0	0	.333	.333	3	1	SS-2

Dick Schofield

SCHOFIELD, RICHARD CRAIG
Son of Dick Schofield.
B. Nov. 21, 1962, Springfield, Ill.

BR TR 5'10" 175 lbs.

	G	AB	H	2B	3B	HR	HR %	R	RBI	BB	SO	SB	BA	SA	PH AB	PH H	G by POS
1983 CAL A	21	54	11	2	0	3	5.6	4	4	6	8	0	.204	.407	0	0	SS-21
1984	140	400	77	10	3	4	1.0	39	21	33	79	4	.193	.263	0	0	SS-140
2 yrs.	161	454	88	12	3	7	1.5	43	25	39	87	4	.194	.280	0	0	SS-161

	G	AB	H	2B	3B	HR	HR %	R	RBI	BB	SO	SB	BA	SA	Pinch Hit AB	Pinch Hit H	G by POS

Otto Schomberg

SCHOMBERG, OTTO H.
Born Otto H. Shambrick.
B. Nov. 14, 1864, Milwaukee, Wis.   D. May 3, 1927, Ottawa, Kans.

BL TL

	G	AB	H	2B	3B	HR	HR %	R	RBI	BB	SO	SB	BA	SA	PH AB	PH H	G by POS
1886 PIT AA	72	246	67	6	6	1	0.4	53		57			.272	.358	0	0	1B-72
1887 IND N	112	419	129	18	16	5	1.2	91	83	56	32	21	.308	.463	0	0	1B-112, OF-1
1888	30	112	24	5	1	1	0.9	11	10	10	12	6	.214	.304	0	0	OF-15, 1B-15
3 yrs.	214	777	220	29	23	7	0.9	155	92	123	44	27	.283	.407	0	0	1B-199, OF-16

Jerry Schoonmaker

SCHOONMAKER, JERALD LEE
B. Dec. 14, 1933, Seymour, Mo.

BR TR 5'11" 190 lbs.

	G	AB	H	2B	3B	HR	HR %	R	RBI	BB	SO	SB	BA	SA	PH AB	PH H	G by POS
1955 WAS A	20	46	7	0	1	1	2.2	5	4	5	11	1	.152	.261	3	0	OF-15
1957	30	23	2	1	0	0	0.0	5	0	2	11	0	.087	.130	7	0	OF-13
2 yrs.	50	69	9	1	1	1	1.4	10	4	7	22	1	.130	.217	10	0	OF-28

Paul Schramka

SCHRAMKA, PAUL EDWARD
B. Mar. 22, 1928, Milwaukee, Wis.

BL TL 6' 185 lbs.

	G	AB	H	2B	3B	HR	HR %	R	RBI	BB	SO	SB	BA	SA	PH AB	PH H	G by POS
1953 CHI N	2	0	0	0	0	0	–	0	0	0	0	0	–	–	0	0	OF-1

Ossee Schreckengost

SCHRECKENGOST, OSSEE FREEMAN
Also appeared in box score as Schreck
B. Apr. 11, 1875, New Bethlehem, Pa.   D. July 9, 1914, Philadelphia, Pa.

BR TR 5'10" 180 lbs.

	G	AB	H	2B	3B	HR	HR %	R	RBI	BB	SO	SB	BA	SA	PH AB	PH H	G by POS
1897 LOU N	1	3	0	0	0	0	0.0	0	0	0		0	.000	.000	0	0	C-1
1898 CLE N	10	35	11	2	3	0	0.0	5	10	0		1	.314	.543	0	0	C-9
1899 2 teams	STL	N (72G – .278)			CLE	N	(43G – .313)										
" total	115	427	124	20	5	2	0.5	57	47	21		18	.290	.375	6	0	C-64, 1B-43, OF-2, SS-1, 2B-1
1901 BOS A	86	280	85	13	5	0	0.0	37	38	19		6	.304	.386	9	3	C-72, 1B-4
1902 2 teams	CLE	A (18G – .338)			PHI	A	(79G – .324)										
" total	97	358	117	17	2	2	0.6	50	52	9		5	.327	.402	2	0	C-71, 1B-24, OF-1
1903 PHI A	92	306	78	13	4	3	1.0	26	30	11		0	.255	.353	5	1	C-77, 1B-10
1904	95	311	58	9	1	1	0.3	23	21	5		3	.186	.232	3	1	C-84, 1B-9
1905	121	416	113	19	6	0	0.0	30	45	3		9	.272	.346	7	1	C-112, 1B-2
1906	98	338	96	20	1	1	0.3	29	41	10		5	.284	.358	5	0	C-89, 1B-4
1907	101	356	97	16	3	0	0.0	30	38	17		4	.272	.334	2	0	C-99, 1B-2
1908 2 teams	PHI	A (71G – .222)			CHI	N	(6G – .188)										
" total	77	223	49	7	1	0	0.0	17	16	7		1	.220	.260	5	3	C-72, 1B-1
11 yrs.	893	3053	828	136	31	9	0.3	304	338	102		52	.271	.345	45	9	C-750, 1B-99, OF-3, SS-1, 2B-1

WORLD SERIES

	G	AB	H	2B	3B	HR	HR %	R	RBI	BB	SO	SB	BA	SA	PH AB	PH H	G by POS
1905 PHI A	3	9	2	1	0	0	0.0	2	0	0	0	0	.222	.333	0	0	C-3

Hank Schreiber

SCHREIBER, HENRY WALTER
B. July 12, 1891, Cleveland, Ohio   D. Feb. 21, 1968, Indianapolis, Ind.

BR TR 5'11" 165 lbs.

	G	AB	H	2B	3B	HR	HR %	R	RBI	BB	SO	SB	BA	SA	PH AB	PH H	G by POS
1914 CHI A	1	2	0	0	0	0	0.0	0		0		0	.000	.000	0	0	OF-1
1917 BOS N	2	7	2	0	0	0	0.0	1	0	0	1	0	.286	.286	0	0	SS-1, 3B-1
1919 CIN N	19	58	13	4	0	0	0.0	5	4	0	12	0	.224	.293	0	0	3B-17, SS-2
1921 NY N	4	6	2	0	0	0	0.0	2	2	1	1	0	.333	.333	0	0	SS-2, 2B-2, 3B-1
1926 CHI N	10	18	1	1	0	0	0.0	2	0	0	1	0	.056	.111	0	0	SS-3, 3B-3, 2B-1
5 yrs.	36	91	18	5	0	0	0.0	10	6	1	16	0	.198	.253	0	0	3B-22, SS-8, 2B-3, OF-1

Ted Schreiber

SCHREIBER, THEODORE HENRY
B. July 11, 1938, Brooklyn, N. Y.

BR TR 5'11" 175 lbs.

	G	AB	H	2B	3B	HR	HR %	R	RBI	BB	SO	SB	BA	SA	PH AB	PH H	G by POS
1963 NY N	39	50	8	0	0	0	0.0	1	2	4	14	0	.160	.160	10	0	3B-17, SS-9, 2B-3

Pop Schriver

SCHRIVER, WILLIAM FREDERICK
B. June 11, 1866, Brooklyn, N. Y.   D. Dec. 27, 1932, Brooklyn, N. Y.

BR TR 5'10" 185 lbs.

	G	AB	H	2B	3B	HR	HR %	R	RBI	BB	SO	SB	BA	SA	PH AB	PH H	G by POS
1886 BKN AA	8	21	1	0	0	0	0.0	2		2			.048	.048	0	0	OF-5, C-3
1888 PHI N	40	134	26	5	2	1	0.7	15	23	7	21	2	.194	.284	0	0	C-27, SS-6, 3B-6, OF-1
1889	55	211	56	10	0	1	0.5	24	19	16	8	5	.265	.327	0	0	C-48, 2B-6, 3B-1
1890	57	223	61	9	6	0	0.0	37	35	22	15	9	.274	.368	0	0	C-34, 1B-10, 3B-8, 2B-3, OF-2
1891 CHI N	27	90	30	1	4	1	1.1	15	21	10	9	1	.333	.467	0	0	C-27, 1B-2
1892	92	326	73	10	6	1	0.3	40	34	27	25	4	.224	.301	0	0	C-82, OF-10
1893	64	229	65	8	3	4	1.7	49	34	14	9	4	.284	.397	0	0	C-56, OF-5
1894	96	349	96	12	3	3	0.9	55	47	29	21	9	.275	.352	1	0	C-88, SS-3, 3B-3, 1B-2
1895 NY N	24	92	29	2	1	1	1.1	16	16	9	10	3	.315	.391	0	0	C-18, 1B-6
1897 CIN N	61	178	54	12	4	1	0.6	29	30	19		3	.303	.433	5	1	C-53
1898 PIT N	95	315	72	15	3	0	0.0	25	32	23		3	.229	.295	2	0	C-92, 1B-1
1899	91	301	85	19	5	1	0.3	31	49	23		4	.282	.389	5	1	C-78, 1B-8
1900	37	92	27	7	0	1	1.1	12	12	10		0	.293	.402	9	3	C-24, 1B-1
1901 STL N	53	166	45	7	3	1	0.6	17	23	12		2	.271	.367	9	3	C-24, 1B-19
14 yrs.	800	2727	720	117	40	16	0.6	367	374	223	118	46	.264	.354	34	8	C-654, 1B-49, OF-23, 3B-18, SS-9, 2B-9

Bob Schroder

SCHRODER, ROBERT JAMES
B. Dec. 30, 1944, Ridgefield, N. J.

BL TR 6' 175 lbs.

	G	AB	H	2B	3B	HR	HR %	R	RBI	BB	SO	SB	BA	SA	PH AB	PH H	G by POS
1965 SF N	31	9	2	0	0	0	0.0	4	1	1	1	0	.222	.222	6	2	2B-4, 3B-1
1966	10	33	8	0	0	0	0.0	0	2	0	2	0	.242	.242	1	0	SS-9
1967	62	135	31	4	0	0	0.0	20	7	15	15	1	.230	.259	17	3	2B-45, 3B-4
1968	35	44	7	1	1	0	0.0	5	2	7	3	0	.159	.227	11	1	2B-12, SS-4, 3B-2
4 yrs.	138	221	48	5	1	0	0.0	29	12	23	21	1	.217	.249	35	6	2B-61, SS-13, 3B-7

Bill Schroeder

SCHROEDER, ALFRED WILLIAM III
B. Sept. 7, 1958, Baltimore, Md.

BR TR 6'2" 210 lbs.

	G	AB	H	2B	3B	HR	HR %	R	RBI	BB	SO	SB	BA	SA	PH AB	PH H	G by POS
1983 MIL A	23	73	13	2	1	3	4.1	7	7	3	23	0	.178	.356	0	0	C-23
1984	61	210	54	6	0	14	6.7	29	25	8	54	0	.257	.486	1	0	C-58, DH-3, 1B-1
2 yrs.	84	283	67	8	1	17	6.0	36	32	11	77	0	.237	.452	1	0	C-81, DH-3, 1B-1

	G	AB	H	2B	3B	HR	HR %	R	RBI	BB	SO	SB	BA	SA	Pinch Hit AB	Pinch Hit H	G by POS

Rick Schu

SCHU, RICK SPENCER
B. Jan. 26, 1962, Philadelphia, Pa.
BR TR 6' 170 lbs.

	G	AB	H	2B	3B	HR	HR %	R	RBI	BB	SO	SB	BA	SA	AB	H	G by POS
1984 PHI N	17	29	8	2	1	2	6.9	12	5	6	6	0	.276	.621	2	0	3B-15

Heinie Schuble

SCHUBLE, HENRY GEORGE
B. Nov. 1, 1906, Houston, Tex.
BR TR 5'9" 152 lbs.

	G	AB	H	2B	3B	HR	HR %	R	RBI	BB	SO	SB	BA	SA	AB	H	G by POS
1927 STL N	65	218	56	6	2	4	1.8	29	28	7	27	0	.257	.358	0	0	SS-65
1929 DET A	92	258	60	11	7	2	0.8	35	28	19	23	3	.233	.353	1	0	SS-86, 3B-2
1932	101	340	92	20	6	5	1.5	57	52	24	37	14	.271	.409	2	0	3B-76, SS-15
1933	49	96	21	4	1	0	0.0	12	6	5	17	2	.219	.281	9	4	3B-23, SS-2, 2B-1
1934	11	15	4	2	0	0	0.0	2	2	1	4	0	.267	.400	4	0	SS-3, 3B-2, 2B-1
1935	11	8	2	0	0	0	0.0	3	0	1	0	0	.250	.250	2	1	3B-2, 2B-1
1936 STL N	2	0	0	0	0	0	–	0	0	0	0	0	–	–	0	0	3B-1
7 yrs.	331	935	235	43	16	11	1.2	138	116	57	108	19	.251	.367	18	5	SS-171, 3B-106, 2B-3

Wes Schulmerich

SCHULMERICH, EDWARD WESLEY
B. Aug. 21, 1901, Hillsboro, Ore.
BR TR 5'11" 210 lbs.

	G	AB	H	2B	3B	HR	HR %	R	RBI	BB	SO	SB	BA	SA	AB	H	G by POS
1931 BOS N	95	327	101	17	7	2	0.6	36	43	28	30	0	.309	.422	6	3	OF-87
1932	119	404	105	22	5	11	2.7	47	57	27	61	5	.260	.421	18	4	OF-101
1933 2 teams		BOS N (29G – .247)						PHI N (97G – .334)									
" total	126	450	143	25	5	9	2.0	63	72	37	55	1	.318	.456	7	2	OF-118
1934 2 teams		PHI N (15G – .250)						CIN N (74G – .263)									
" total	89	261	68	9	3	5	1.9	23	20	26	51	1	.261	.375	19	8	OF-69
4 yrs.	429	1442	417	73	20	27	1.9	169	192	118	197	7	.289	.424	50	17	OF-375

Art Schult

SCHULT, ARTHUR WILLIAM (Dutch)
B. June 20, 1928, Brooklyn, N. Y.
BR TR 6'3" 210 lbs.

	G	AB	H	2B	3B	HR	HR %	R	RBI	BB	SO	SB	BA	SA	AB	H	G by POS
1953 NY A	7	0	0	0	0	0	–	3	0	0	0	0	–	–	0	0	
1956 CIN N	5	7	3	0	0	0	0.0	3	2	1	1	0	.429	.429	3	2	OF-1
1957 2 teams		CIN N (21G – .265)						WAS A (77G – .263)									
" total	98	281	74	16	0	4	1.4	34	39	14	32	0	.263	.363	26	5	OF-36, 1B-35
1959 CHI N	42	118	32	7	0	2	1.7	17	14	7	14	0	.271	.381	9	2	1B-23, OF-15
1960	12	15	2	1	0	0	0.0	1	1	1	3	0	.133	.200	7	1	OF-4, 1B-1
5 yrs.	164	421	111	24	0	6	1.4	58	56	23	50	0	.264	.363	45	10	1B-59, OF-56

Fred Schulte

SCHULTE, FRED WILLIAM (Fritz)
Also known as Fred William Schult.
B. Jan. 13, 1901, Belvidere, Ill.   D. May 20, 1983, Belvidere, Ill.
BR TR 6'1" 183 lbs.

	G	AB	H	2B	3B	HR	HR %	R	RBI	BB	SO	SB	BA	SA	AB	H	G by POS
1927 STL A	60	189	60	16	5	3	1.6	32	34	20	14	5	.317	.503	8	4	OF-49
1928	146	556	159	44	6	7	1.3	90	85	51	60	6	.286	.424	1	1	OF-143
1929	121	446	137	24	5	3	0.7	63	71	59	44	8	.307	.404	3	1	OF-116
1930	113	392	109	23	5	5	1.3	59	62	41	44	12	.278	.401	7	1	OF-98, 1B-5
1931	134	553	168	32	7	9	1.6	100	65	56	49	6	.304	.436	0	0	OF-134
1932	146	565	166	35	6	9	1.6	106	73	71	44	5	.294	.425	8	5	OF-129, 1B-5
1933 WAS A	144	550	162	30	7	5	0.9	98	87	61	27	10	.295	.402	1	0	OF-142
1934	136	524	156	32	6	3	0.6	72	73	53	34	3	.298	.399	2	1	OF-134
1935	75	224	60	6	4	2	0.9	33	23	26	22	0	.268	.357	22	5	OF-55
1936 PIT N	74	238	62	7	3	1	0.4	28	17	20	20	1	.261	.328	17	7	OF-55
1937	29	20	2	0	0	0	0.0	5	3	4	3	0	.100	.100	12	1	OF-4
11 yrs.	1178	4257	1241	249	54	47	1.1	686	593	462	361	56	.292	.409	83	26	OF-1059, 1B-10
WORLD SERIES																	
1933 WAS A	5	21	7	1	0	1	4.8	1	4	1	1	0	.333	.524	0	0	OF-5

Ham Schulte

SCHULTE, HERMAN JOSEPH
Born Herman Joseph Schultehenrich. Brother of Len Schulte.
B. Sept. 1, 1912, St. Charles, Mo.
BR TR 5'8½" 158 lbs.

	G	AB	H	2B	3B	HR	HR %	R	RBI	BB	SO	SB	BA	SA	AB	H	G by POS
1940 PHI N	120	436	103	18	2	1	0.2	44	21	32	30	3	.236	.294	1	0	2B-119, SS-1

Jack Schulte

SCHULTE, JOHN HERMAN
Also known as Frank Schulte.
B. Nov. 15, 1881, Cincinnati, Ohio   D. Aug. 17, 1975, Roseville, Mich.
BR TR 5'9" 180 lbs.

	G	AB	H	2B	3B	HR	HR %	R	RBI	BB	SO	SB	BA	SA	AB	H	G by POS
1906 BOS N	2	7	0	0	0	0	0.0	0		0		0	.000	.000	0	0	SS-2

Johnny Schulte

SCHULTE, JOHN CLEMENT
B. Sept. 8, 1896, Fredericktown, Mo.   D. June 28, 1978, St. Louis, Mo.
BL TR 5'11" 190 lbs.

	G	AB	H	2B	3B	HR	HR %	R	RBI	BB	SO	SB	BA	SA	AB	H	G by POS
1923 STL A	7	3	0	0	0	0	0.0	1	1	4	0	0	.000	.000	2	0	1B-1, C-1
1927 STL N	64	156	45	8	2	9	5.8	35	32	47	19	1	.288	.538	3	1	C-59
1928 PHI N	65	113	28	2	2	4	3.5	14	17	15	12	0	.248	.407	26	6	C-34
1929 CHI N	31	69	18	3	0	0	0.0	6	9	7	11	0	.261	.304	1	1	C-30
1932 2 teams		STL A (15G – .208)						BOS N (10G – .222)									
" total	25	33	7	2	0	1	3.0	3	5	3	7	0	.212	.364	8	1	C-16
5 yrs.	192	374	98	15	4	14	3.7	59	64	76	49	1	.262	.436	40	9	C-140, 1B-1

Len Schulte

SCHULTE, LEONARD WILLIAM
Born Leonard William Schultehenrich. Brother of Ham Schulte.
B. Dec. 5, 1916, St. Charles, Mo.
BR TR 5'10" 160 lbs.

	G	AB	H	2B	3B	HR	HR %	R	RBI	BB	SO	SB	BA	SA	AB	H	G by POS
1944 STL A	1	0	0	0	0	0	–	0	0	1	0	0	–	–	0	0	
1945	119	430	106	16	1	0	0.0	37	36	24	35	0	.247	.288	3	0	3B-71, 2B-37, SS-14
1946	4	5	2	0	0	0	0.0	1	2	0	0	0	.400	.400	3	1	3B-1, 2B-1
3 yrs.	124	435	108	16	1	0	0.0	38	38	25	35	0	.248	.290	6	1	3B-72, 2B-38, SS-14

Wildfire Schulte

SCHULTE, FRANK
B. Sept. 17, 1882, Cohocton, N. Y.   D. Aug. 17, 1975, Roseville, Mich.
BL TR 5'11" 170 lbs.

	G	AB	H	2B	3B	HR	HR %	R	RBI	BB	SO	SB	BA	SA	AB	H	G by POS
1904 CHI N	20	84	24	4	3	2	2.4	16	13	2		1	.286	.476	0	0	OF-20
1905	123	493	135	15	14	1	0.2	67	47	32		16	.274	.367	0	0	OF-123
1906	146	563	158	18	13	7	1.2	77	60	31		25	.281	.396	0	0	OF-146
1907	97	342	98	14	7	2	0.6	44	32	22		7	.287	.386	5	1	OF-91

	G	AB	H	2B	3B	HR	HR %	R	RBI	BB	SO	SB	BA	SA	Pinch Hit AB	Pinch Hit H	G by POS

Wildfire Schulte continued

	G	AB	H	2B	3B	HR	HR %	R	RBI	BB	SO	SB	BA	SA	AB	H	G by POS
1908	102	386	91	20	2	1	0.3	42	43	29		15	.236	.306	0	0	OF-102
1909	140	538	142	16	11	4	0.7	57	60	24		23	.264	.357	0	0	OF-140
1910	151	559	168	29	15	10	1.8	93	68	39	57	22	.301	.460	1	0	OF-150
1911	154	577	173	30	21	21	3.6	105	121	76	68	23	.300	.534	0	0	OF-154
1912	139	553	146	27	11	13	2.4	90	70	53	70	17	.264	.423	0	0	OF-139
1913	132	495	138	28	6	9	1.8	85	72	39	68	21	.279	.414	2	1	OF-129
1914	137	465	112	22	7	5	1.1	54	61	39	55	16	.241	.351	3	1	OF-134
1915	151	550	137	20	6	12	2.2	66	69	49	68	19	.249	.373	3	1	OF-147
1916 2 teams	CHI	N (72G – .296)			PIT	N	(55G – .254)										
" total	127	407	113	16	4	5	1.2	43	41	37	54	14	.278	.373	9	1	OF-113
1917 2 teams	PIT	N (30G – .214)			PHI	N	(64G – .215)										
" total	94	252	54	15	1	1	0.4	32	22	26	36	9	.214	.294	21	5	OF-70
1918 WAS A	93	267	77	14	3	0	0.0	35	44	47	36	5	.288	.363	16	5	OF-75
15 yrs.	1806	6531	1766	288	124	93	1.4	906	823	545	512	233	.270	.395	60	15	OF-1733

WORLD SERIES

	G	AB	H	2B	3B	HR	HR %	R	RBI	BB	SO	SB	BA	SA	AB	H	G by POS
1906 CHI N	6	26	7	3	0	0	0.0	1	3	1	3	0	.269	.385	0	0	OF-6
1907	5	20	5	0	0	0	0.0	3	2	1	2	1	.250	.250	0	0	OF-5
1908	5	18	7	0	1	0	0.0	4	2	2	1	2	.389	.500	0	0	OF-5
1910	5	17	6	3	0	0	0.0	3	2	2	3	0	.353	.529	0	0	OF-5
4 yrs.	21	81	25	6	1	0	0.0	11	9	6	9	3	.309	.407	0	0	OF-21

Howie Schultz

SCHULTZ, HOWARD HENRY (Steeple, Stretch)
B. July 3, 1922, St. Paul, Minn. BR TR 6'6" 200 lbs.

	G	AB	H	2B	3B	HR	HR %	R	RBI	BB	SO	SB	BA	SA	AB	H	G by POS
1943 BKN N	45	182	49	12	0	1	0.5	20	34	6	24	3	.269	.352	0	0	1B-45
1944	138	526	134	32	3	11	2.1	59	83	24	67	6	.255	.390	6	5	1B-136
1945	39	142	34	8	2	1	0.7	18	19	10	14	2	.239	.345	1	0	1B-38
1946	90	249	63	14	1	3	1.2	27	27	16	34	2	.253	.353	3	0	1B-87
1947 2 teams	BKN	N (2G – .000)			PHI	N	(114G – .223)										
" total	116	404	90	19	1	6	1.5	30	35	21	70	0	.223	.319	1	0	1B-115
1948 2 teams	PHI	N (6G – .077)			CIN	N	(36G – .167)										
" total	42	85	13	0	0	2	2.4	9	10	5	9	2	.153	.224	10	2	1B-29
6 yrs.	470	1588	383	85	7	24	1.5	163	208	82	218	15	.241	.349	21	7	1B-450

Joe Schultz

SCHULTZ, JOSEPH CHARLES (Germany)
Father of Joe Schultz.
B. July 24, 1893, Pittsburgh, Pa. D. Apr. 13, 1941, Columbia, S. C. BR TR 5'11½" 172 lbs.

	G	AB	H	2B	3B	HR	HR %	R	RBI	BB	SO	SB	BA	SA	AB	H	G by POS
1912 BOS N	4	12	3	1	0	0	0.0	1	4	0	2	0	.250	.333	0	0	2B-4
1913	9	18	4	0	0	0	0.0	2	1	2	7	0	.222	.222	1	0	OF-5, 2B-1
1915 2 teams	BKN	N (56G – .292)			CHI	N	(7G – .250)										
" total	63	128	37	3	2	0	0.0	14	7	10	20	3	.289	.344	29	8	3B-55, 2B-2, SS-1
1916 PIT N	77	204	53	8	2	0	0.0	18	22	7	14	6	.260	.319	20	5	3B-24, 2B-24, OF-6, SS-1
1919 STL N	88	229	58	9	1	2	0.9	24	21	11	7	4	.253	.328	31	8	OF-49, 2B-5
1920	99	320	84	5	5	0	0.0	38	32	21	11	5	.263	.309	14	2	OF-80
1921	92	275	85	20	3	6	2.2	37	45	15	11	4	.309	.469	18	6	OF-67, 3B-3, 1B-2
1922	112	344	108	13	4	2	0.6	50	64	19	10	3	.314	.392	22	8	OF-89
1923	2	7	2	0	0	0	0.0	0	1	1	0	0	.286	.286	0	0	OF-2
1924 2 teams	STL	N (12G – .167)			PHI	N	(88G – .282)										
" total	100	296	82	15	1	5	1.7	35	31	23	18	6	.277	.385	17	6	OF-78
1925 2 teams	PHI	N (24G – .344)			CIN	N	(33G – .323)										
" total	57	126	42	9	1	0	0.0	16	21	7	2	4	.333	.421	18	3	OF-35, 2B-1
11 yrs.	703	1959	558	83	19	15	0.8	235	249	116	102	35	.285	.370	170	46	OF-411, 3B-82, 2B-37, SS-2, 1B-2

Joe Schultz

SCHULTZ, JOSEPH CHARLES, JR. (Dode)
Son of Joe Schultz.
B. Aug. 29, 1918, Chicago, Ill.
Manager 1969, 1973. BL TR 5'11" 180 lbs.

	G	AB	H	2B	3B	HR	HR %	R	RBI	BB	SO	SB	BA	SA	AB	H	G by POS
1939 PIT N	4	14	4	2	0	0	0.0	3	2	2	0	0	.286	.429	0	0	C-4
1940	16	36	7	0	1	0	0.0	2	4	2	1	0	.194	.250	3	2	C-13
1941	2	2	1	0	0	0	0.0	1	0	0	0	0	.500	.500	0	0	
1943 STL A	46	92	22	5	0	0	0.0	6	8	9	8	0	.239	.293	23	6	C-19
1944	3	8	2	0	0	0	0.0	1	0	1	0	0	.250	.250	1	0	C-3
1945	41	44	13	2	0	0	0.0	1	8	3	1	0	.295	.341	35	11	C-4
1946	42	57	22	4	0	0	0.0	1	14	11	2	0	.386	.456	23	10	C-17
1947	43	38	7	0	0	1	2.6	3	1	4	5	0	.184	.263	38	7	
1948	43	37	7	0	0	0	0.0	0	9	6	3	0	.189	.189	37	7	
9 yrs.	240	328	85	13	1	1	0.3	18	46	37	21	0	.259	.314	160	43	C-67

John Schultz

SCHULTZ, JOHN
B. St. Louis, Mo. Deceased.

	G	AB	H	2B	3B	HR	HR %	R	RBI	BB	SO	SB	BA	SA	AB	H	G by POS
1891 STL AA	1	2	0	0	0	0	0.0	0	0	0	0	0	.000	.000	0	0	C-1

Bill Schuster

SCHUSTER, WILLIAM CHARLES (Broadway)
B. Aug. 4, 1914, Buffalo, N. Y. BR TR 5'9" 164 lbs.

	G	AB	H	2B	3B	HR	HR %	R	RBI	BB	SO	SB	BA	SA	AB	H	G by POS
1937 PIT N	3	6	3	0	0	0	0.0	2	1	1	0	0	.500	.500	0	0	SS-2
1939 BOS N	2	3	0	0	0	0	0.0	0	0	1	0	0	.000	.000	0	0	SS-1, 3B-1
1943 CHI N	13	51	15	2	1	0	0.0	3	0	3	2	0	.294	.373	0	0	SS-13
1944	60	154	34	7	1	1	0.6	14	14	12	16	4	.221	.299	11	3	2B-66, SS-38
1945	45	47	9	2	1	0	0.0	8	2	7	4	2	.191	.277	2	0	SS-22, 2B-3, 3B-1
5 yrs.	123	261	61	11	3	1	0.4	27	17	23	23	6	.234	.310	13	3	SS-76, 2B-69, 3B-2

WORLD SERIES

	G	AB	H	2B	3B	HR	HR %	R	RBI	BB	SO	SB	BA	SA	AB	H	G by POS
1945 CHI N	2	1	0	0	0	0	0.0	1	0	0	0	0	.000	.000	0	0	SS-1

	G	AB	H	2B	3B	HR	HR %	R	RBI	BB	SO	SB	BA	SA	Pinch Hit AB	Pinch Hit H	G by POS

Bill Schwartz

SCHWARTZ, WILLIAM CHARLES (Blab)   BR TR 6'2" 185 lbs.
B. Apr. 22, 1884, Cleveland, Ohio   D. Aug. 29, 1961, Nashville, Tenn.

	G	AB	H	2B	3B	HR	HR %	R	RBI	BB	SO	SB	BA	SA	PH AB	PH H	G by POS
1904 CLE A	24	86	13	2	0	0	0.0	5	0	0		4	.151	.174	1	0	1B-22, 3B-1

Pop Schwartz

SCHWARTZ, WILLIAM AUGUST   BR TR
B. Apr. 3, 1864, Jamestown, Ky.   D. Dec. 22, 1940, Newport, Ky.

	G	AB	H	2B	3B	HR	HR %	R	RBI	BB	SO	SB	BA	SA	PH AB	PH H	G by POS
1883 COL AA	2	4	1	0	0	0	0.0	0		0			.250	.250	0	0	1B-1, C-1
1884 CIN U	29	106	25	4	0	1	0.9	14		3			.236	.302	0	0	C-25, OF-3, 3B-1
2 yrs.	31	110	26	4	0	1	0.9	14		3			.236	.300	0	0	C-26, OF-3, 3B-1, 1B-1

Randy Schwartz

SCHWARTZ, DOUGLAS RANDALL   BL TL 6'3" 230 lbs.
B. Feb. 9, 1944, Los Angeles, Calif.

	G	AB	H	2B	3B	HR	HR %	R	RBI	BB	SO	SB	BA	SA	PH AB	PH H	G by POS
1965 KC A	6	7	2	0	0	0	0.0	0	1	0	4	0	.286	.286	3	1	1B-2
1966	10	11	1	0	0	0	0.0	0	1	1	3	0	.091	.091	9	1	1B-2
2 yrs.	16	18	3	0	0	0	0.0	0	2	1	7	0	.167	.167	12	2	1B-4

Bill Schwarz

SCHWARZ, WILLIAM DeWITT   TR
B. Jan. 30, 1891, Birmingham, Ala.   D. June 24, 1949, Jacksonville, Fla.

	G	AB	H	2B	3B	HR	HR %	R	RBI	BB	SO	SB	BA	SA	PH AB	PH H	G by POS
1914 NY A	1	1	0	0	0	0	0.0	0	0	0	1	0	.000	.000	0	0	C-1

Al Schweitzer

SCHWEITZER, ALBERT CASPER (Cheese)   BR TR 5'7½" 170 lbs.
B. Dec. 23, 1882, Cleveland, Ohio   D. Jan. 27, 1969, Newark, Ohio

	G	AB	H	2B	3B	HR	HR %	R	RBI	BB	SO	SB	BA	SA	PH AB	PH H	G by POS
1908 STL A	64	182	53	4	2	1	0.5	22	14	20		6	.291	.352	9	1	OF-55
1909	27	76	17	2	0	0	0.0	7	2	5		3	.224	.250	5	0	OF-22
1910	113	379	87	11	2	2	0.5	37	37	36		26	.230	.285	3	1	OF-109
1911	76	237	51	11	4	0	0.0	31	34	43		12	.215	.295	8	0	OF-68
4 yrs.	280	874	208	28	8	3	0.3	97	87	104		47	.238	.299	25	2	OF-254

Pius Schwert

SCHWERT, PIUS LOUIS   BR TR 5'10½" 160 lbs.
B. Nov. 22, 1892, Angola, N. Y.   D. Mar. 11, 1941, Washington, D. C.

	G	AB	H	2B	3B	HR	HR %	R	RBI	BB	SO	SB	BA	SA	PH AB	PH H	G by POS
1914 NY A	2	5	0	0	0	0	0.0	0	2	2	2	0	.000	.000	0	0	C-2
1915	9	18	5	3	0	0	0.0	6	6	1	6	0	.278	.444	0	0	C-9
2 yrs.	11	23	5	3	0	0	0.0	6	8	3	8	0	.217	.348	0	0	C-11

Art Schwind

SCHWIND, ARTHUR EDWIN   BB TR 5'8" 150 lbs.
B. Nov. 4, 1889, Fort Wayne, Ind.   D. Jan. 13, 1968, Sullivan, Ill.

	G	AB	H	2B	3B	HR	HR %	R	RBI	BB	SO	SB	BA	SA	PH AB	PH H	G by POS
1912 BOS N	1	2	1	0	0	0	0.0	0	0	0	0	0	.500	.500	0	0	3B-1

Jerry Schypinski

SCHYPINSKI, GERALD ALBERT   BL TR 5'10" 170 lbs.
B. Sept. 16, 1931, Detroit, Mich.

	G	AB	H	2B	3B	HR	HR %	R	RBI	BB	SO	SB	BA	SA	PH AB	PH H	G by POS
1955 KC A	22	69	15	2	0	0	0.0	7	5	1	6	0	.217	.246	0	0	SS-21, 2B-2

Mike Scioscia

SCIOSCIA, MICHAEL LORRI   BL TR 6'2" 200 lbs.
B. Nov. 27, 1958, Darby, Pa.

	G	AB	H	2B	3B	HR	HR %	R	RBI	BB	SO	SB	BA	SA	PH AB	PH H	G by POS
1980 LA N	54	134	34	5	1	1	0.7	8	8	12	9	1	.254	.328	1	0	C-54
1981	93	290	80	10	0	2	0.7	27	29	36	18	0	.276	.331	2	1	C-91
1982	129	365	80	11	1	5	1.4	31	38	44	31	2	.219	.296	8	0	C-123
1983	12	35	11	3	0	1	2.9	3	7	5	2	0	.314	.486	1	0	C-11
1984	114	341	93	18	0	5	1.5	29	38	52	26	2	.273	.370	7	0	C-112
5 yrs.	402	1165	298	47	2	14	1.2	98	120	149	86	5	.256	.336	19	1	C-391

DIVISIONAL PLAYOFF SERIES

	G	AB	H	2B	3B	HR	HR %	R	RBI	BB	SO	SB	BA	SA	PH AB	PH H	G by POS
1981 LA N	4	13	2	0	0	0	0.0	0	1	1	2	0	.154	.154	0	0	C-4

LEAGUE CHAMPIONSHIP SERIES

	G	AB	H	2B	3B	HR	HR %	R	RBI	BB	SO	SB	BA	SA	PH AB	PH H	G by POS
1981 LA N	5	15	2	0	0	1	6.7	1	1	2	1	0	.133	.333	0	0	C-5

WORLD SERIES

	G	AB	H	2B	3B	HR	HR %	R	RBI	BB	SO	SB	BA	SA	PH AB	PH H	G by POS
1981 LA N	3	4	1	0	0	0	0.0	1	0	1	0	0	.250	.250	1	0	C-3

Lou Scoffic

SCOFFIC, LOUIS (Weaser)   BR TR 5'10" 182 lbs.
B. May 20, 1913, Herrin, Ill.

	G	AB	H	2B	3B	HR	HR %	R	RBI	BB	SO	SB	BA	SA	PH AB	PH H	G by POS
1936 STL N	4	7	3	0	0	0	0.0	2	2	1	2	0	.429	.429	0	0	OF-3

Daryl Sconiers

SCONIERS, DARYL ANTHONY   BL TL 6'2" 185 lbs.
B. Oct. 3, 1958, San Bernardino, Calif.

	G	AB	H	2B	3B	HR	HR %	R	RBI	BB	SO	SB	BA	SA	PH AB	PH H	G by POS
1981 CAL A	15	52	14	1	1	1	1.9	6	7	1	10	0	.269	.385	1	0	1B-12, DH-3
1982	12	13	2	0	0	0	0.0	0	2	2	1	0	.154	.154	7	1	1B-3, DH-1
1983	106	314	86	19	3	8	2.5	49	46	17	41	4	.274	.430	28	8	1B-57, DH-27, OF-1
1984	57	160	39	4	0	4	2.5	14	17	13	16	1	.244	.344	10	6	1B-41, DH-1
4 yrs.	190	539	141	24	4	13	2.4	69	72	33	68	5	.262	.393	46	15	1B-113, DH-32, OF-1

Scott

SCOTT,
Deceased.

	G	AB	H	2B	3B	HR	HR %	R	RBI	BB	SO	SB	BA	SA	PH AB	PH H	G by POS
1884 BAL U	13	53	12	1	1	1	1.9	10		2			.226	.340	0	0	OF-13, 3B-1

Don Scott

SCOTT, DONALD MALCOLM   BB TR 5'11" 185 lbs.
B. Aug. 16, 1961, Dunedin, Fla.

	G	AB	H	2B	3B	HR	HR %	R	RBI	BB	SO	SB	BA	SA	PH AB	PH H	G by POS
1983 TEX A	2	4	0	0	0	0	0.0	0	0	0	0	0	.000	.000	0	0	C-2
1984	81	235	52	9	0	3	1.3	16	20	20	44	0	.221	.298	0	0	C-80
2 yrs.	83	239	52	9	0	3	1.3	16	20	20	44	0	.218	.293	0	0	C-82

Everett Scott

SCOTT, LEWIS EVERETT (Deacon)   BR TR 5'8" 148 lbs.
B. Nov. 19, 1892, Bluffton, Ind.   D. Nov. 2, 1960, Fort Wayne, Ind.

	G	AB	H	2B	3B	HR	HR %	R	RBI	BB	SO	SB	BA	SA	PH AB	PH H	G by POS
1914 BOS A	144	539	129	15	6	2	0.4	66	37	32	43	9	.239	.301	1	1	SS-143
1915	100	359	72	11	0	0	0.0	25	28	17	21	4	.201	.231	0	0	SS-100
1916	123	366	85	19	2	0	0.0	37	27	23	24	8	.232	.295	0	0	SS-121, 3B-1, 2B-1
1917	157	528	127	24	7	0	0.0	40	50	20	46	12	.241	.313	0	0	SS-157

	G	AB	H	2B	3B	HR	HR %	R	RBI	BB	SO	SB	BA	SA	Pinch Hit AB	Pinch Hit H	G by POS

Everett Scott continued

	G	AB	H	2B	3B	HR	HR%	R	RBI	BB	SO	SB	BA	SA	PH AB	PH H	G by POS
1918	126	443	98	11	5	0	0.0	40	43	12	16	11	.221	.269	0	0	SS-126
1919	138	507	141	19	0	0	0.0	41	38	19	26	8	.278	.316	0	0	SS-138
1920	154	569	153	21	12	4	0.7	41	61	21	15	4	.269	.369	0	0	SS-154
1921	154	576	151	21	9	1	0.2	65	60	27	21	5	.262	.335	0	0	SS-154
1922 NY A	154	557	150	23	5	3	0.5	64	45	23	22	2	.269	.345	0	0	SS-154
1923	152	533	131	16	4	6	1.1	48	60	13	19	1	.246	.325	0	0	SS-152
1924	153	548	137	12	4	4	0.7	56	64	21	15	3	.250	.316	0	0	SS-153
1925 2 teams	55	NY A (22G – .217)				WAS A (33G – .272)											
" total	55	163	41	6	1	0	0.0	13	22	6	6	1	.252	.301	4	2	SS-48, 3B-2
1926 2 teams	44	CHI A (40G – .252)				CIN N (4G – .667)											
" total	44	149	40	10	1	0	0.0	16	14	9	8	1	.268	.349	1	0	SS-43
13 yrs.	1654	5837	1455	208	58	20	0.3	552	549	243	282	69	.249	.315	6	3	SS-1643, 3B-3, 2B-1

WORLD SERIES

	G	AB	H	2B	3B	HR	HR%	R	RBI	BB	SO	SB	BA	SA	PH AB	PH H	G by POS
1915 BOS A	5	18	1	0	0	0	0.0	0	0	0	3	0	.056	.056	0	0	SS-5
1916	5	16	2	0	1	0	0.0	1	1	1	1	0	.125	.250	0	0	SS-5
1918	6	20	2	0	0	0	0.0	0	0	1	1	0	.100	.100	0	0	SS-6
1922 NY A	5	14	2	0	0	0	0.0	0	1	1	0	0	.143	.143	0	0	SS-5
1923	6	22	7	0	0	0	0.0	2	3	0	1	0	.318	.318	0	0	SS-6
5 yrs.	27	90	14	0	1	0	0.0	3	5	3	6	0	.156	.178	0	0	SS-27

George Scott

SCOTT, GEORGE CHARLES, JR. (Boomer)
B. Mar. 23, 1944, Greenville, Miss.   BR TR 6'2" 200 lbs.

	G	AB	H	2B	3B	HR	HR%	R	RBI	BB	SO	SB	BA	SA	PH AB	PH H	G by POS
1966 BOS A	162	601	147	18	7	27	4.5	73	90	65	152	4	.245	.433	1	1	1B-158, 3B-5
1967	159	565	171	21	7	19	3.4	74	82	63	119	10	.303	.465	5	3	1B-152, 3B-2
1968	124	350	60	14	0	3	0.9	23	25	26	88	3	.171	.237	4	0	1B-112, 3B-6
1969	152	549	139	14	5	16	2.9	63	52	61	74	4	.253	.384	0	0	3B-109, 1B-53
1970	127	480	142	24	5	16	3.3	50	63	44	95	4	.296	.467	0	0	3B-68, 1B-59
1971	146	537	141	16	4	24	4.5	72	78	41	102	0	.263	.441	3	1	1B-143
1972 MIL A	152	578	154	24	4	20	3.5	71	88	43	130	16	.266	.426	3	1	1B-139, 3B-23
1973	158	604	185	30	4	24	4.0	98	107	61	94	9	.306	.488	1	1	1B-157, DH-1
1974	158	604	170	36	2	17	2.8	74	82	59	90	9	.281	.432	1	0	1B-148, DH-9
1975	158	617	176	26	4	36	5.8	86	109	51	97	6	.285	.515	1	0	1B-144, DH-12, 3B-5
1976	156	606	166	21	5	18	3.0	73	77	53	118	0	.274	.414	1	0	1B-155
1977 BOS A	157	584	157	26	5	33	5.7	103	95	57	112	1	.269	.500	2	0	1B-157
1978	120	412	96	16	4	12	2.9	51	54	44	86	1	.233	.379	2	0	1B-113, DH-7
1979 3 teams	105	BOS A (45G – .224)				KC A (44G – .267)				NY A (16G – .318)							
" total	105	346	88	20	4	6	1.7	46	49	31	61	2	.254	.387	10	2	1B-83, DH-17, 3B-1
14 yrs.	2034	7433	1992	306	60	271	3.6	957	1051	699	1418	69	.268	.435	40	10	1B-1773, 3B-219, DH-46

WORLD SERIES

	G	AB	H	2B	3B	HR	HR%	R	RBI	BB	SO	SB	BA	SA	PH AB	PH H	G by POS
1967 BOS A	7	26	6	1	1	0	0.0	3	0	3	6	0	.231	.346	0	0	1B-7

Jack Scott

SCOTT, JOHN WILLIAM
B. Apr. 18, 1892, Ridgeway, N. C.   D. Nov. 30, 1959, Durham, N. C.   BL TR 6'2½" 199 lbs.

	G	AB	H	2B	3B	HR	HR%	R	RBI	BB	SO	SB	BA	SA	PH AB	PH H	G by POS
1916 PIT N	3	2	0	0	0	0	0.0	0	0	1	1	0	.000	.000	1	0	P-1
1917 BOS N	7	16	2	0	0	0	0.0	0	0	4	4	0	.125	.125	0	0	P-7
1919	24	40	7	1	0	0	0.0	4	4	1	8	0	.175	.200	3	0	P-19, OF-1
1920	44	99	21	3	0	0	0.0	5	4	5	16	0	.212	.242	0	0	P-44
1921	51	88	30	5	1	1	1.1	14	12	5	7	0	.341	.455	3	0	P-47
1922 2 teams	18	CIN N (1G – .000)				NY N (17G – .267)											
" total	18	31	8	0	0	0	0.0	2	4	1	3	0	.258	.258	0	0	P-18
1923 NY N	40	79	25	4	0	1	1.3	12	10	3	5	1	.316	.405	0	0	P-40
1925	41	87	21	4	1	1	1.1	7	6	8	15	0	.241	.345	5	1	P-36
1926	51	83	28	4	2	1	1.2	8	13	3	6	0	.337	.470	1	0	P-50
1927 PHI N	83	114	33	6	0	1	0.9	6	17	9	9	0	.289	.368	28	7	P-48
1928 NY N	16	15	4	1	0	0	0.0	3	2	1	2	0	.267	.333	0	0	P-16
1929	30	26	8	3	0	0	0.0	6	1	2	0	0	.308	.423	0	0	P-30
12 yrs.	408	680	187	31	4	5	0.7	67	73	39	76	1	.275	.354	41	8	P-356, OF-1

WORLD SERIES

	G	AB	H	2B	3B	HR	HR%	R	RBI	BB	SO	SB	BA	SA	PH AB	PH H	G by POS
1922 NY N	1	4	1	0	0	0	0.0	0	0	0	1	0	.250	.250	0	0	P-1
1923	2	1	0	0	0	0	0.0	0	0	0	0	0	.000	.000	0	0	P-1
2 yrs.	3	5	1	0	0	0	0.0	0	0	0	1	0	.200	.200	0	0	P-2

Jim Scott

SCOTT, JAMES WALTER
B. Sept. 22, 1888, Shenandoah, Pa.   D. May 12, 1972, So. Pasadena, Fla.   BR TR 5'9½" 165 lbs.

	G	AB	H	2B	3B	HR	HR%	R	RBI	BB	SO	SB	BA	SA	PH AB	PH H	G by POS
1914 PIT F	8	24	6	1	0	0	0.0	2	1	5		1	.250	.292	0	0	SS-8

John Scott

SCOTT, JOHN HENRY
B. Jan. 24, 1952, Jackson, Miss.   BR TR 6'2" 165 lbs.

	G	AB	H	2B	3B	HR	HR%	R	RBI	BB	SO	SB	BA	SA	PH AB	PH H	G by POS
1974 SD N	14	15	1	0	0	0	0.0	3	0	0	4	1	.067	.067	0	0	OF-8
1975	25	9	0	0	0	0	0.0	6	0	0	2	2	.000	.000	9	0	OF-1
1977 TOR A	79	233	56	9	0	2	0.9	26	15	8	39	10	.240	.305	4	0	OF-67, DH-2
3 yrs.	118	257	57	9	0	2	0.8	35	15	8	45	13	.222	.280	13	0	OF-76, DH-2

LeGrant Scott

SCOTT, LeGRANT EDWARD
B. July 25, 1910, Cleveland, Ohio   BL TL 5'8½" 170 lbs.

	G	AB	H	2B	3B	HR	HR%	R	RBI	BB	SO	SB	BA	SA	PH AB	PH H	G by POS
1939 PHI N	76	232	65	15	1	1	0.4	31	26	22	14	5	.280	.366	18	5	OF-55

Milt Scott

SCOTT, MILTON PARKER (Mikado Milt)
B. Jan. 17, 1866, Chicago, Ill.   D. Nov. 3, 1938, Baltimore, Md.   5'9" 160 lbs.

	G	AB	H	2B	3B	HR	HR%	R	RBI	BB	SO	SB	BA	SA	PH AB	PH H	G by POS
1882 CHI N	1	5	2	0	0	0	0.0	1	0	0	0		.400	.400	0	0	1B-1
1884 DET N	110	438	108	17	5	3	0.7	29		9	62		.247	.329	0	0	1B-110
1885 2 teams	93	DET N (38G – .264)				PIT AA (55G – .248)											
" total	93	358	91	14	1	0	0.0	29	12	9	16		.254	.299	0	0	1B-93

	G	AB	H	2B	3B	HR	HR %	R	RBI	BB	SO	SB	BA	SA	Pinch Hit AB	Pinch Hit H	G by POS

Milt Scott continued

	G	AB	H	2B	3B	HR	HR %	R	RBI	BB	SO	SB	BA	SA	AB	H	G by POS
1886 BAL AA	137	484	92	11	4	2	0.4	48		22			.190	.242	0	0	1B-137, P-1
4 yrs.	341	1285	293	42	10	5	0.4	107	11	40	78		.228	.288	0	0	1B-341, P-1

Pete Scott

SCOTT, FLOYD JOHN
B. Dec. 21, 1898, Woodland, Calif.   D. May 3, 1953, Daly City, Calif.

BR TR 5'11½" 175 lbs.

	G	AB	H	2B	3B	HR	HR %	R	RBI	BB	SO	SB	BA	SA	AB	H	G by POS
1926 CHI N	77	189	54	13	1	3	1.6	34	34	22	31	3	.286	.413	4	1	OF-59, 3B-1
1927	71	156	49	18	1	0	0.0	28	21	19	18	1	.314	.442	31	7	OF-36
1928 PIT N	60	177	55	10	4	5	2.8	33	33	18	14	1	.311	.497	6	2	OF-42, 1B-8
3 yrs.	208	522	158	41	6	8	1.5	95	88	59	63	5	.303	.450	41	10	OF-137, 1B-8, 3B-1

Rodney Scott

SCOTT, RODNEY DARRELL
B. Oct. 16, 1953, Indianapolis, Ind.

BR TR 6'   160 lbs.

	G	AB	H	2B	3B	HR	HR %	R	RBI	BB	SO	SB	BA	SA	AB	H	G by POS
1975 KC A	48	15	1	0	0	0	0.0	13	0	1	3	4	.067	.067	1	0	DH-22, 2B-9, SS-8
1976 MON N	7	10	4	0	0	0	0.0	3	0	1	1	2	.400	.400	0	0	2B-6, SS-3
1977 OAK A	133	364	95	4	4	0	0.0	56	20	43	50	33	.261	.294	8	3	2B-71, SS-70, 3B-5, DH-1, OF-1
1978 CHI N	78	227	64	5	1	0	0.0	41	15	43	41	27	.282	.313	3	0	3B-60, OF-10, SS-6, 2B-6
1979 MON N	151	562	134	12	5	3	0.5	69	42	66	82	39	.238	.294	1	1	2B-113, SS-39
1980	154	567	127	13	13	0	0.0	84	46	70	75	63	.224	.293	3	2	2B-129, SS-21
1981	95	336	69	9	3	0	0.0	43	26	50	35	30	.205	.250	0	0	2B-93
1982 2 teams		MON	N	(14G –	.200)			NY	A	(10G –	.192)						
" total	24	51	10	0	0	0	0.0	7	1	7	4	7	.196	.196	2	0	2B-16, SS-6
8 yrs.	690	2132	504	43	26	3	0.1	316	150	281	291	205	.236	.285	18	6	2B-443, SS-153, 3B-65, DH-23, OF-11

LEAGUE CHAMPIONSHIP SERIES

	G	AB	H	2B	3B	HR	HR %	R	RBI	BB	SO	SB	BA	SA	AB	H	G by POS
1981 MON N	5	18	3	0	0	0	0.0	0	0	1	3	1	.167	.167	0	0	2B-5

Tony Scott

SCOTT, ANTHONY
B. Sept. 18, 1951, Cincinnati, Ohio

BB TR 6'   164 lbs.

	G	AB	H	2B	3B	HR	HR %	R	RBI	BB	SO	SB	BA	SA	AB	H	G by POS
1973 MON N	11	1	0	0	0	0	0.0	2	0	1	1	0	.000	.000	1	0	OF-3
1974	19	7	2	0	0	0	0.0	2	1	1	3	1	.286	.286	1	1	OF-16
1975	92	143	26	4	2	0	0.0	19	11	12	38	5	.182	.238	8	1	OF-71
1977 STL N	95	292	85	16	3	3	1.0	38	41	33	48	13	.291	.397	10	1	OF-89
1978	96	219	50	5	2	1	0.5	28	14	14	41	5	.228	.283	30	6	OF-77
1979	153	587	152	22	10	6	1.0	69	68	34	92	37	.259	.361	3	1	OF-151
1980	143	415	104	19	3	0	0.0	51	28	35	68	22	.251	.311	8	2	OF-134
1981 2 teams		STL	N	(45G –	.227)			HOU	N	(55G –	.293)						
" total	100	401	106	18	4	4	1.0	49	39	20	54	18	.264	.359	0	0	OF-99
1982 HOU N	132	460	110	16	3	1	0.2	43	29	15	56	18	.239	.293	10	2	OF-129
1983	80	186	42	6	1	2	1.1	20	17	11	39	5	.226	.301	27	5	OF-61
1984 2 teams		HOU	N	(25G –	.190)			MON	N	(45G –	.254)						
" total	70	92	22	5	0	0	0.0	10	5	11	24	1	.239	.293	38	10	OF-23
11 yrs.	991	2803	699	111	28	17	0.6	331	253	186	464	125	.249	.327	136	29	OF-853

DIVISIONAL PLAYOFF SERIES

	G	AB	H	2B	3B	HR	HR %	R	RBI	BB	SO	SB	BA	SA	AB	H	G by POS
1981 HOU N	5	20	3	0	0	0	0.0	0	2	1	6	0	.150	.150	0	0	OF-5

Jim Scranton

SCRANTON, JAMES DEAN
B. Apr. 5, 1960, Torrence, Calif.

BR TR 6'   180 lbs.

	G	AB	H	2B	3B	HR	HR %	R	RBI	BB	SO	SB	BA	SA	AB	H	G by POS
1984 KC A	2	2	0	0	0	0	0.0	0	0	0	0	0	.000	.000	1	0	SS-1, 3B-1

Chuck Scrivener

SCRIVENER, WAYNE ALLISON
B. Oct. 3, 1947, Alexandria, Va.

BR TR 5'9"   170 lbs.

	G	AB	H	2B	3B	HR	HR %	R	RBI	BB	SO	SB	BA	SA	AB	H	G by POS
1975 DET A	4	16	4	1	0	0	0.0	0	0	0	1	1	.250	.313	0	0	3B-3, SS-2
1976	80	222	49	7	1	2	0.9	28	16	19	34	1	.221	.288	2	0	2B-43, SS-37, 3B-5
1977	61	72	6	0	0	0	0.0	10	2	5	9	0	.083	.083	0	0	SS-50, 2B-8, 3B-3
3 yrs.	145	310	59	8	1	2	0.6	38	18	24	44	2	.190	.242	2	0	SS-89, 2B-51, 3B-11

Ken Sears

SEARS, KENNETH EUGENE (Ziggy)
B. July 6, 1917, Streator, Ill.   D. July 17, 1968, Bridgeport, Tex.

BL TR 6'1"   200 lbs.

	G	AB	H	2B	3B	HR	HR %	R	RBI	BB	SO	SB	BA	SA	AB	H	G by POS
1943 NY A	60	187	52	7	0	2	1.1	22	22	11	18	1	.278	.348	10	3	C-50
1946 STL A	7	15	5	0	0	0	0.0	1	1	3	0	0	.333	.333	3	1	C-4
2 yrs.	67	202	57	7	0	2	1.0	23	23	14	18	1	.282	.347	13	4	C-54

Jimmy Sebring

SEBRING, JAMES DENNISON
B. Mar. 25, 1882, Liberty, Pa.   D. Dec. 22, 1909, Williamsport, Pa.

BL TL 6'   180 lbs.

	G	AB	H	2B	3B	HR	HR %	R	RBI	BB	SO	SB	BA	SA	AB	H	G by POS
1902 PIT N	19	80	26	4	4	0	0.0	15	15	5		2	.325	.475	0	0	OF-19
1903	124	506	140	16	13	4	0.8	71	64	32		20	.277	.383	0	0	OF-124
1904 2 teams		PIT	N	(80G –	.269)			CIN	N	(56G –	.225)						
" total	136	527	132	20	9	0	0.0	50	56	31		16	.250	.323	0	0	OF-136
1905 CIN N	58	217	62	10	5	2	0.9	31	28	14		11	.286	.406	2	0	OF-56
1909 2 teams		BKN	N	(25G –	.099)			WAS	A	(1G –	.000)						
" total	26	81	8	1	0	0	0.0	11	5	11		3	.099	.136	0	0	OF-26
5 yrs.	363	1411	368	51	32	6	0.4	178	168	93		52	.261	.355	2	0	OF-361

WORLD SERIES

	G	AB	H	2B	3B	HR	HR %	R	RBI	BB	SO	SB	BA	SA	AB	H	G by POS
1903 PIT N	8	30	11	0	1	1	3.3	3	5	1	4	0	.367	.533	0	0	OF-8

Frank Secory

SECORY, FRANK EDWARD
B. Aug. 24, 1912, Mason City, Iowa

BR TR 6'1"   200 lbs.

	G	AB	H	2B	3B	HR	HR %	R	RBI	BB	SO	SB	BA	SA	AB	H	G by POS
1940 DET A	1	1	0	0	0	0	0.0	0	0	0	1	0	.000	.000	1	0	
1942 CIN N	2	5	0	0	0	0	0.0	1	1	3	2	0	.000	.000	0	0	OF-2
1944 CHI N	22	56	18	1	0	4	7.1	10	17	6	8	1	.321	.554	4	0	OF-17
1945	35	57	9	0	0	0	0.0	4	6	2	7	0	.158	.175	21	2	OF-12
1946	33	43	10	3	0	3	7.0	6	12	6	6	0	.233	.512	22	4	OF-9
5 yrs.	93	162	37	5	0	7	4.3	21	36	17	24	1	.228	.389	48	6	OF-40

WORLD SERIES

	G	AB	H	2B	3B	HR	HR %	R	RBI	BB	SO	SB	BA	SA	AB	H	G by POS
1945 CHI N	5	5	2	0	0	0	0.0	0	0	0	2	0	.400	.400	5	2	

	G	AB	H	2B	3B	HR	HR %	R	RBI	BB	SO	SB	BA	SA	Pinch Hit AB	Pinch Hit H	G by POS

Charlie See

SEE, CHARLES HENRY (Chad)
B. Oct. 13, 1896, Pleasantville, N. Y.   D. July 19, 1948, Bridgeport, Conn.
BL TR 5'10½" 175 lbs.

	G	AB	H	2B	3B	HR	HR %	R	RBI	BB	SO	SB	BA	SA	AB	H	G by POS
1919 CIN N	8	14	4	0	0	0	0.0	1	1	1	0	0	.286	.286	2	0	OF-4
1920	47	82	25	4	0	0	0.0	9	15	1	7	2	.305	.354	24	8	OF-17, P-1
1921	37	106	26	5	1	1	0.9	11	7	7	5	3	.245	.340	7	2	OF-29
3 yrs.	92	202	55	9	1	1	0.5	21	23	9	12	5	.272	.342	33	10	OF-50, P-1

Bob Seeds

SEEDS, ROBERT IRA (Suitcase Bob)
B. Feb. 24, 1907, Ringgold, Tex.
BR TR 6' 180 lbs.

	G	AB	H	2B	3B	HR	HR %	R	RBI	BB	SO	SB	BA	SA	AB	H	G by POS
1930 CLE A	85	277	79	11	3	3	1.1	37	32	12	22	1	.285	.379	15	4	OF-70
1931	48	134	41	4	1	1	0.7	26	10	11	11	1	.306	.373	9	1	OF-33, 1B-2
1932 2 teams	CLE	A (2G –	.000)		CHI	A	(116G –	.290)									
" total	118	438	126	18	6	2	0.5	53	45	31	37	5	.288	.370	4	0	OF-113
1933 BOS A	82	230	56	13	4	0	0.0	26	23	21	20	1	.243	.335	7	2	1B-41, OF-32
1934 2 teams	BOS	A (8G –	.167)		CLE	A	(61G –	.247)									
" total	69	192	47	8	1	0	0.0	28	19	21	14	2	.245	.297	15	3	OF-49
1936 NY A	13	42	11	1	0	4	9.5	12	10	5	3	3	.262	.571	1	0	OF-9, 3B-3
1938 NY N	81	296	86	12	3	9	3.0	35	52	20	33	0	.291	.443	2	0	OF-76
1939	63	173	46	5	1	5	2.9	33	26	22	31	1	.266	.393	12	2	OF-50
1940	56	155	45	5	2	4	2.6	18	16	17	19	0	.290	.426	15	4	OF-40
9 yrs.	615	1937	537	77	21	28	1.4	268	233	160	190	14	.277	.382	80	16	OF-472, 1B-43, 3B-3
WORLD SERIES																	
1936 NY A	1	0	0	0	0	0	–	0	0	0	0	0	–	–	0	0	

Pat Seerey

SEEREY, JAMES PATRICK
B. Mar. 17, 1923, Wilburton, Okla.
BR TR 5'10" 200 lbs.

	G	AB	H	2B	3B	HR	HR %	R	RBI	BB	SO	SB	BA	SA	AB	H	G by POS
1943 CLE A	26	72	16	3	0	1	1.4	8	5	4	19	0	.222	.306	9	2	OF-16
1944	101	342	80	16	0	15	4.4	39	39	19	99	0	.234	.412	18	3	OF-86
1945	126	414	98	22	2	14	3.4	56	56	66	97	1	.237	.401	8	0	OF-117
1946	117	404	91	17	2	26	6.4	57	62	65	101	2	.225	.470	2	0	OF-115
1947	82	216	37	4	1	11	5.1	24	29	34	66	0	.171	.352	12	1	OF-68
1948 2 teams	CLE	A (10G –	.261)		CHI	A	(95G –	.229)									
" total	105	363	84	11	0	19	5.2	51	70	90	102	0	.231	.419	3	0	OF-100
1949 CHI A	4	4	0	0	0	0	0.0	1	0	3	1	0	.000	.000	2	0	OF-2
7 yrs.	561	1815	406	73	5	86	4.7	236	261	281	485	3	.224	.412	54	6	OF-504

Emmett Seery

SEERY, JOHN EMMETT
B. Feb. 13, 1861, Princeville, Ill.   Deceased.
BL TR

	G	AB	H	2B	3B	HR	HR %	R	RBI	BB	SO	SB	BA	SA	AB	H	G by POS
1884 2 teams	BAL	U (105G –	.311)		KC	U	(1G –	.500)									
" total	106	467	146	26	7	2	0.4	115		21				.313	.411	0	0	OF-105, C-3, 3B-2
1885 STL N	59	216	35	7	0	1	0.5	20	14	16	37		.162	.208	0	0	OF-59, 3B-1
1886	126	453	108	22	6	2	0.4	73	48	57	82		.238	.327	0	0	OF-126, P-2
1887 IND N	122	465	104	18	15	4	0.9	104	28	71	68	48	.224	.353	0	0	OF-122, SS-1
1888	133	500	110	20	10	5	1.0	87	50	64	73	80	.220	.330	0	0	OF-133, SS-1
1889	127	526	165	26	12	8	1.5	123	59	67	59	19	.314	.454	0	0	OF-127
1890 BKN P	104	394	88	12	7	1	0.3	78	50	70	36	44	.223	.297	0	0	OF-104
1891 C-M AA	97	372	106	15	10	4	1.1	77	36	81	52	19	.285	.411	0	0	OF-97
1892 LOU N	42	154	31	6	1	0	0.0	18	15	24	19	6	.201	.253	0	0	OF-42
9 yrs.	916	3547	893	152	68	27	0.8	695	299	471	426	216	.252	.356	0	0	OF-915, 3B-3, C-3, SS-2, P-2

Kal Segrist

SEGRIST, KAL HILL
B. Apr. 14, 1931, Greenville, Tex.
BR TR 6' 180 lbs.

	G	AB	H	2B	3B	HR	HR %	R	RBI	BB	SO	SB	BA	SA	AB	H	G by POS
1952 NY A	13	23	1	0	0	0	0.0	3	1	3	1	0	.043	.043	1	0	2B-11, 3B-1
1955 BAL A	7	9	3	0	0	0	0.0	1	0	2	0	0	.333	.333	2	1	3B-3, 2B-1, 1B-1
2 yrs.	20	32	4	0	0	0	0.0	4	1	5	1	0	.125	.125	3	1	2B-12, 3B-4, 1B-1

Kurt Seibert

SEIBERT, KURT ELLIOTT
B. Oct. 16, 1955, Cheverly, Md.
BB TR 6' 165 lbs.

	G	AB	H	2B	3B	HR	HR %	R	RBI	BB	SO	SB	BA	SA	AB	H	G by POS
1979 CHI N	7	2	0	0	0	0	0.0	2	0	0	1	0	.000	.000	1	0	3B-1

Rick Seilheimer

SEILHEIMER, RICKY ALLEN
B. Aug. 30, 1960, Brenham, Tex.
BL TR 5'11" 185 lbs.

	G	AB	H	2B	3B	HR	HR %	R	RBI	BB	SO	SB	BA	SA	AB	H	G by POS
1980 CHI A	21	52	11	3	1	1	1.9	4	3	4	15	1	.212	.365	0	0	C-21

Kip Selbach

SELBACH, ALBERT KARL
B. Mar. 24, 1872, Columbus, Ohio   D. Feb. 17, 1956, Columbus, Ohio
BR TR 5'7" 190 lbs.

	G	AB	H	2B	3B	HR	HR %	R	RBI	BB	SO	SB	BA	SA	AB	H	G by POS
1894 WAS N	97	372	114	21	17	7	1.9	69	71	51	20	21	.306	.511	0	0	OF-80, SS-19
1895	129	516	166	21	22	6	1.2	115	55	69	28	31	.322	.483	0	0	OF-118, SS-6, 2B-5
1896	127	487	148	17	13	5	1.0	100	100	76	28	49	.304	.423	2	2	OF-126
1897	124	486	152	25	16	5	1.0	113	59	80		46	.313	.461	0	0	OF-124
1898	132	515	156	28	11	3	0.6	88	60	64		25	.303	.417	0	0	OF-131, SS-1
1899 CIN N	140	521	154	27	11	3	0.6	104	87	70		38	.296	.407	0	0	OF-140
1900 NY N	141	523	176	29	12	4	0.8	98	68	72		36	.336	.461	0	0	OF-141
1901	125	502	145	29	6	1	0.2	89	56	45		8	.289	.376	0	0	OF-125
1902 BAL A	128	503	161	27	9	3	0.6	86	60	58		22	.320	.427	1	1	OF-127
1903 WAS A	141	536	134	23	12	3	0.6	68	49	41		20	.250	.354	0	0	OF-140, 3B-1
1904 2 teams	WAS	A (48G –	.275)		BOS	A	(98G –	.258)									
" total	146	554	146	27	12	0	0.0	65	44	72		19	.264	.356	0	0	OF-146
1905 BOS A	124	418	103	16	6	4	1.0	54	47	67		12	.246	.342	5	1	OF-116
1906	60	228	48	9	2	0	0.0	15	23	18		7	.211	.268	2	0	OF-58
13 yrs.	1614	6161	1803	299	149	44	0.7	1064	779	783	76	334	.293	.411	10	4	OF-1572, SS-26, 2B-5, 3B-1

	G	AB	H	2B	3B	HR	HR %	R	RBI	BB	SO	SB	BA	SA	Pinch Hit AB	Pinch Hit H	G by POS

George Selkirk

SELKIRK, GEORGE ALEXANDER (Twinkletoes)
B. Jan. 4, 1908, Huntsville, Ont., Canada
BL TR 6'1" 182 lbs.

	G	AB	H	2B	3B	HR	HR %	R	RBI	BB	SO	SB	BA	SA	PH AB	PH H	G by POS
1934 NY A	46	176	55	7	1	5	2.8	23	38	15	17	1	.313	.449	0	0	OF-46
1935	128	491	153	29	12	11	2.2	64	94	44	36	2	.312	.487	2	1	OF-127
1936	137	493	152	28	9	18	3.7	93	107	94	60	13	.308	.511	0	0	OF-135
1937	78	256	84	13	5	18	7.0	49	68	34	24	8	.328	.629	5	1	OF-69
1938	99	335	85	12	5	10	3.0	58	62	68	52	9	.254	.409	2	0	OF-95
1939	128	418	128	17	4	21	5.0	103	101	103	49	12	.306	.517	5	0	OF-124
1940	118	379	102	17	5	19	5.0	68	71	84	43	3	.269	.491	7	2	OF-111
1941	70	164	36	5	0	6	3.7	30	25	28	30	1	.220	.360	19	4	OF-47
1942	42	78	15	3	0	0	0.0	15	10	16	8	0	.192	.231	19	4	OF-19
9 yrs.	846	2790	810	131	41	108	3.9	503	576	486	319	49	.290	.483	59	12	OF-773

WORLD SERIES

	G	AB	H	2B	3B	HR	HR %	R	RBI	BB	SO	SB	BA	SA	PH AB	PH H	G by POS
1936 NY A	6	24	8	0	1	2	8.3	6	3	4	4	0	.333	.667	0	0	OF-6
1937	5	19	5	1	0	0	0.0	5	6	2	0	0	.263	.316	0	0	OF-5
1938	3	10	2	0	0	0	0.0	0	1	2	1	0	.200	.200	0	0	OF-3
1939	4	12	2	1	0	0	0.0	0	0	3	2	0	.167	.250	0	0	OF-4
1941	2	2	1	0	0	0	0.0	0	0	0	0	0	.500	.500	2	1	
1942	1	1	0	0	0	0	0.0	0	0	0	0	0	.000	.000	1	0	
6 yrs.	21	68	18	2	1	2	2.9	11	10	11	7	0	.265	.412	3	1	OF-18

Rube Sellers

SELLERS, OLIVER
B. Mar. 7, 1881, Duquesne, Pa.   D. Jan. 14, 1952, Pittsburgh, Pa.
BR TR 5'10" 180 lbs.

	G	AB	H	2B	3B	HR	HR %	R	RBI	BB	SO	SB	BA	SA	PH AB	PH H	G by POS
1910 BOS N	12	32	5	0	0	0	0.0	3	2	6	5	1	.156	.156	3	0	OF-9

Carey Selph

SELPH, CAREY ISUM
B. Dec. 5, 1901, Donaldson, Ark.   D. Feb. 24, 1976, Houston, Tex.
BR TR 5'9½" 175 lbs.

	G	AB	H	2B	3B	HR	HR %	R	RBI	BB	SO	SB	BA	SA	PH AB	PH H	G by POS
1929 STL N	25	51	12	1	1	0	0.0	8	7	6	4	1	.235	.294	5	1	2B-16
1932 CHI A	116	396	112	19	8	0	0.0	50	51	31	9	7	.283	.371	18	2	3B-71, 2B-26
2 yrs.	141	447	124	20	9	0	0.0	58	58	37	13	8	.277	.362	23	3	3B-71, 2B-42

Mike Sember

SEMBER, MICHAEL DAVID
B. Feb. 24, 1953, Hammond, Ind.
BR TR 6' 185 lbs.

	G	AB	H	2B	3B	HR	HR %	R	RBI	BB	SO	SB	BA	SA	PH AB	PH H	G by POS
1977 CHI N	3	4	1	0	0	0	0.0	0	0	0	2	0	.250	.250	2	0	2B-1
1978	9	3	1	0	0	0	0.0	2	0	1	1	0	.333	.333	2	1	3B-7, SS-1
2 yrs.	12	7	2	0	0	0	0.0	2	0	1	3	0	.286	.286	4	1	3B-7, SS-1, 2B-1

Andy Seminick

SEMINICK, ANDREW WASIL
B. Sept. 12, 1920, Pierce, W. Va.
BR TR 5'11" 187 lbs.

	G	AB	H	2B	3B	HR	HR %	R	RBI	BB	SO	SB	BA	SA	PH AB	PH H	G by POS
1943 PHI N	22	72	13	2	0	2	2.8	9	5	7	22	0	.181	.292	0	0	C-22, OF-1
1944	22	63	14	2	1	0	0.0	9	4	6	17	2	.222	.286	4	0	C-11, OF-7
1945	80	188	45	7	2	6	3.2	18	26	18	38	3	.239	.394	6	0	C-70, 3B-4, OF-1
1946	124	406	107	15	5	12	3.0	55	52	39	86	2	.264	.414	6	0	C-118
1947	111	337	85	16	2	13	3.9	48	50	58	69	4	.252	.427	3	0	C-107
1948	125	391	88	11	3	13	3.3	49	44	58	68	4	.225	.368	1	0	C-124
1949	109	334	81	11	2	24	7.2	52	68	69	74	0	.243	.503	8	1	C-98
1950	130	393	113	15	3	24	6.1	55	68	68	50	0	.288	.524	7	2	C-124
1951	101	291	66	8	1	11	3.8	42	37	63	67	1	.227	.375	9	0	C-91
1952 CIN N	108	336	86	16	1	14	4.2	38	50	35	65	1	.256	.435	9	0	C-99
1953	119	387	91	12	0	19	4.9	46	64	49	82	2	.235	.413	7	1	C-112
1954	86	247	58	9	4	7	2.8	25	30	48	39	0	.235	.389	5	3	C-82
1955 2 teams					CIN	N (6G – .133)		PHI	N (93G – .246)								
" total	99	304	73	12	1	12	3.9	33	35	32	62	1	.240	.405	6	0	C-93
1956 PHI N	60	161	32	3	1	7	4.3	16	23	31	38	3	.199	.360	6	0	C-54
1957	8	11	1	0	0	0	0.0	0	0	1	3	0	.091	.091	0	0	C-8
15 yrs.	1304	3921	953	139	26	164	4.2	495	556	582	780	23	.243	.417	77	8	C-1213, OF-9, 3B-4

WORLD SERIES

	G	AB	H	2B	3B	HR	HR %	R	RBI	BB	SO	SB	BA	SA	PH AB	PH H	G by POS
1950 PHI N	4	11	2	0	0	0	0.0	0	1	3	0	.182	.182	0	0	C-4

Sonny Senerchia

SENERCHIA, EMANUEL ROBERT
B. Apr. 6, 1931, Newark, N. J.
BR TR 6'1" 195 lbs.

	G	AB	H	2B	3B	HR	HR %	R	RBI	BB	SO	SB	BA	SA	PH AB	PH H	G by POS
1952 PIT N	29	100	22	5	0	3	3.0	5	11	4	21	0	.220	.360	1	0	3B-28

Paul Sentelle

SENTELLE, LEOPOLD THEODORE
B. Aug. 27, 1879, New Orleans, La.   D. Apr. 27, 1923, Cincinnati, Ohio
TR 5'9" 176 lbs.

	G	AB	H	2B	3B	HR	HR %	R	RBI	BB	SO	SB	BA	SA	PH AB	PH H	G by POS
1906 PHI N	63	192	44	5	1	1	0.5	19	14	14		15	.229	.281	8	0	3B-33, 2B-19, OF-2, SS-1
1907	3	3	0	0	0	0	0.0	0	0	1		0	.000	.000	0	0	SS-2, OF-1
2 yrs.	66	195	44	5	1	1	0.5	19	14	15		15	.226	.277	8	0	3B-33, 2B-19, OF-3, SS-3

Ted Sepkowski

SEPKOWSKI, THEODORE WALTER
Born Theodore Walter Sczepkowski.
B. Nov. 9, 1923, Baltimore, Md.
BL TR 5'11" 190 lbs.

	G	AB	H	2B	3B	HR	HR %	R	RBI	BB	SO	SB	BA	SA	PH AB	PH H	G by POS
1942 CLE A	5	10	1	0	0	0	0.0	0	0	0	3	0	.100	.100	2	0	2B-2
1946	2	8	4	1	0	0	0.0	2	1	0	0	0	.500	.625	0	0	3B-2
1947 2 teams					CLE	A (10G – .125)		NY	A (2G – .000)								
" total	12	8	1	1	0	0	0.0	1	0	1	1	0	.125	.250	8	1	OF-1
3 yrs.	19	26	6	2	0	0	0.0	3	1	1	4	0	.231	.308	10	1	3B-2, 2B-2, OF-1

Bill Serena

SERENA, WILLIAM ROBERT
B. Oct. 2, 1924, Alameda, Calif.
BR TR 5'9½" 175 lbs.

	G	AB	H	2B	3B	HR	HR %	R	RBI	BB	SO	SB	BA	SA	PH AB	PH H	G by POS
1949 CHI N	12	37	8	3	0	1	2.7	3	7	7	9	0	.216	.378	1	0	3B-11
1950	127	435	104	20	4	17	3.9	56	61	65	75	1	.239	.421	2	1	3B-125
1951	13	39	13	3	1	1	2.6	8	4	11	4	0	.333	.538	0	0	3B-12
1952	122	390	107	21	5	15	3.8	49	61	39	83	1	.274	.469	14	4	3B-58, 2B-49
1953	93	275	69	10	5	10	3.6	30	52	41	46	0	.251	.433	13	4	2B-49, 3B-28

	G	AB	H	2B	3B	HR	HR %	R	RBI	BB	SO	SB	BA	SA	Pinch Hit AB	H	G by POS

Bill Serena continued

	G	AB	H	2B	3B	HR	HR %	R	RBI	BB	SO	SB	BA	SA	AB	H	G by POS
1954	41	63	10	0	1	4	6.3	8	13	14	18	0	.159	.381	22	4	3B-12, 2B-2
6 yrs.	408	1239	311	57	16	48	3.9	154	198	177	235	2	.251	.439	52	13	3B-246, 2B-100

Paul Serna

SERNA, PAUL DAVID
B. Nov. 16, 1958, El Centro, Calif.

BR TR 5'8" 170 lbs.

	G	AB	H	2B	3B	HR	HR %	R	RBI	BB	SO	SB	BA	SA	AB	H	G by POS
1981 SEA A	30	94	24	2	0	4	4.3	11	9	3	11	2	.255	.404	0	0	SS-23, 2B-7
1982	65	169	38	3	0	3	1.8	15	8	4	13	0	.225	.296	3	0	SS-31, 2B-18, 3B-15, DH-2
2 yrs.	95	263	62	5	0	7	2.7	26	17	7	24	2	.236	.335	3	0	SS-54, 2B-25, 3B-15, DH-2

Walter Sessi

SESSI, WALTER ANTHONY (Watsie)
B. July 23, 1918, Finleyville, Pa.

BL TL 6'3" 225 lbs.

	G	AB	H	2B	3B	HR	HR %	R	RBI	BB	SO	SB	BA	SA	AB	H	G by POS
1941 STL N	5	13	0	0	0	0	0.0	2	0	1	2	0	.000	.000	2	0	OF-3
1946	15	14	2	0	0	1	7.1	2	2	1	4	0	.143	.357	14	2	
2 yrs.	20	27	2	0	0	1	3.7	4	2	2	6	0	.074	.185	16	2	OF-3

John Sevcik

SEVCIK, JOHN JOSEPH
B. July 11, 1942, Oak Park, Ill.

BR TR 6'2" 205 lbs.

	G	AB	H	2B	3B	HR	HR %	R	RBI	BB	SO	SB	BA	SA	AB	H	G by POS
1965 MIN A	12	16	1	1	0	0	0.0	1	0	1	5	0	.063	.125	2	0	C-11

Hank Severeid

SEVEREID, HENRY LEVAI
B. June 1, 1891, Story City, Iowa   D. Dec. 17, 1968, San Antonio, Tex.

BR TR 6' 175 lbs.

	G	AB	H	2B	3B	HR	HR %	R	RBI	BB	SO	SB	BA	SA	AB	H	G by POS
1911 CIN N	37	56	17	6	1	0	0.0	5	10	3	6	0	.304	.446	17	4	C-22
1912	50	114	27	0	3	0	0.0	10	13	8	11	0	.237	.289	15	3	C-20, 1B-7, OF-6
1913	8	6	0	0	0	0	0.0	0	0	1	1	0	.000	.000	5	0	C-2, OF-1
1915 STL A	80	203	45	6	1	1	0.5	12	22	16	25	2	.222	.276	15	1	C-64
1916	100	293	80	8	2	0	0.0	23	34	26	17	3	.273	.314	8	1	C-89, 3B-1, 1B-1
1917	143	501	133	23	4	1	0.2	45	57	28	20	6	.265	.333	2	0	C-139, 1B-1
1918	51	133	34	4	0	0	0.0	8	11	18	4	4	.256	.286	7	3	C-42
1919	112	351	87	12	2	0	0.0	16	36	21	13	2	.248	.293	9	1	C-103
1920	123	422	117	14	5	2	0.5	46	49	33	11	5	.277	.348	6	1	C-117
1921	143	472	153	23	7	2	0.4	66	78	42	9	7	.324	.415	14	2	C-126
1922	137	517	166	32	7	3	0.6	49	78	28	12	1	.321	.427	3	0	C-134
1923	122	432	133	27	6	3	0.7	50	51	31	11	3	.308	.433	6	4	C-116
1924	137	432	133	23	4	0	0.9	37	48	36	15	1	.308	.398	6	1	C-129
1925 2 teams		STL	A (34G – .367)			WAS	A (50G – .355)										
" total	84	219	79	17	1	1	0.5	26	35	22	8	0	.361	.461	14	4	C-66
1926 2 teams		WAS	A (22G – .206)			NY	A (41G – .268)										
" total	63	161	41	9	1	0	0.0	15	17	16	6	1	.255	.323	6	1	C-56
15 yrs.	1390	4312	1245	204	42	17	0.4	408	539	329	169	35	.289	.367	133	25	C-1225, 1B-9, OF-7, 3B-1

WORLD SERIES

	G	AB	H	2B	3B	HR	HR %	R	RBI	BB	SO	SB	BA	SA	AB	H	G by POS
1925 WAS A	1	3	1	0	0	0	0.0	0	0	0	0	0	.333	.333	0	0	C-1
1926 NY A	7	22	6	1	0	0	0.0	1	1	1	2	0	.273	.318	0	0	C-7
2 yrs.	8	25	7	1	0	0	0.0	1	1	1	2	0	.280	.320	0	0	C-8

Rich Severson

SEVERSON, RICHARD ALLEN
B. Jan. 18, 1945, Artesia, Calif.

BR TR 6' 174 lbs.

	G	AB	H	2B	3B	HR	HR %	R	RBI	BB	SO	SB	BA	SA	AB	H	G by POS
1970 KC A	77	240	60	11	1	1	0.4	22	22	16	33	0	.250	.317	6	1	SS-50, 2B-25
1971	16	30	9	0	2	0	0.0	4	1	3	5	0	.300	.433	3	1	SS-6, 2B-6, 3B-1
2 yrs.	93	270	69	11	3	1	0.4	26	23	19	38	0	.256	.330	9	2	SS-56, 2B-31, 3B-1

Ed Seward

SEWARD, EDWARD WILLIAM
Born Edward William Sourhardt.
B. June 29, 1867, Cleveland, Ohio   D. July 30, 1947, Cleveland, Ohio

TR 5'7" 175 lbs.

	G	AB	H	2B	3B	HR	HR %	R	RBI	BB	SO	SB	BA	SA	AB	H	G by POS
1885 PRO N	1	3	0	0	0	0	0.0	0	0	0	2		.000	.000	0	0	P-1
1887 PHI AA	74	266	50	10	0	5	1.9	31		16		14	.188	.282	0	0	P-55, OF-21
1888	64	225	32	3	3	2	0.9	27	14	18		12	.142	.209	0	0	P-57, OF-7
1889	46	143	31	5	3	2	1.4	22	17	22	19	6	.217	.336	0	0	P-39, OF-8, 2B-1
1890	26	72	10	4	0	0	0.0	7		8		3	.139	.194	0	0	P-21, OF-6
1891 CLE N	7	19	4	2	0	0	0.0	2	1	3	4	0	.211	.316	0	0	OF-3, P-3, 1B-1
6 yrs.	218	728	127	24	6	9	1.2	89	31	67	25	35	.174	.261	0	0	P-176, OF-45, 2B-1, 1B-1

George Seward

SEWARD, GEORGE E.
B. St. Louis, Mo.   Deceased.

5'7½" 145 lbs.

	G	AB	H	2B	3B	HR	HR %	R	RBI	BB	SO	SB	BA	SA	AB	H	G by POS
1876 NY N	1	3	0	0	0	0	0.0	0	0	0	0		.000	.000	0	0	2B-1
1882 STL AA	38	144	31	1	1	0	0.0	23		12			.215	.236	0	0	OF-35, C-5
2 yrs.	39	147	31	1	1	0	0.0	23		12			.211	.231	0	0	OF-35, C-5, 2B-1

Joe Sewell

SEWELL, JOSEPH WHEELER
Brother of Luke Sewell.   Brother of Tommy Sewell.
B. Oct. 9, 1898, Titus, Ala.
Hall of Fame 1977.

BL TR 5'6½" 155 lbs.

	G	AB	H	2B	3B	HR	HR %	R	RBI	BB	SO	SB	BA	SA	AB	H	G by POS
1920 CLE A	22	70	23	4	1	0	0.0	14	12	9	4	1	.329	.414	0	0	SS-22
1921	154	572	182	36	12	4	0.7	101	91	80	17	7	.318	.444	0	0	SS-154
1922	153	558	167	28	7	2	0.4	80	83	73	20	10	.299	.385	1	0	SS-139, 2B-12
1923	153	553	195	41	10	3	0.5	98	109	98	12	9	.353	.479	2	0	SS-151
1924	153	594	188	45	5	4	0.7	99	104	67	13	3	.316	.429	0		SS-153
1925	155	608	204	37	7	1	0.2	78	98	64	4	7	.336	.424	0	0	SS-155, 2B-3
1926	154	578	187	41	5	4	0.7	91	85	65	6	17	.324	.433	0	0	SS-154
1927	153	569	180	48	5	1	0.2	83	92	51	7	3	.316	.424	0	0	SS-153
1928	155	588	190	40	2	4	0.7	79	70	58	9	7	.323	.418	0	0	SS-137, 3B-19
1929	152	578	182	38	3	7	1.2	90	73	48	4	6	.315	.427	0	0	3B-152
1930	109	353	102	17	6	0	0.0	44	48	42	3	1	.289	.371	8	1	3B-97

	G	AB	H	2B	3B	HR	HR %	R	RBI	BB	SO	SB	BA	SA	Pinch Hit AB	H	G by POS

Joe Sewell continued

	G	AB	H	2B	3B	HR	HR %	R	RBI	BB	SO	SB	BA	SA	AB	H	G by POS
1931 NY A	130	484	146	22	1	6	1.2	102	64	62	8	1	.302	.388	8	1	3B-121, 2B-1
1932	124	503	137	21	3	11	2.2	95	68	56	3	0	.272	.392	1	0	3B-122
1933	135	524	143	18	1	2	0.4	87	54	71	4	2	.273	.323	5	3	3B-131
14 yrs.	1902	7132	2226	436	68	49	0.7	1141	1051	844	114	74	.312	.413	25	5	SS-1216, 3B-642, 2B-16

WORLD SERIES

	G	AB	H	2B	3B	HR	HR %	R	RBI	BB	SO	SB	BA	SA	AB	H	G by POS
1920 CLE A	7	23	4	0	0	0	0.0	0	0	2	1	0	.174	.174	0	0	SS-7
1932 NY A	4	15	5	1	0	0	0.0	4	3	4	0	0	.333	.400	0	0	3B-4
2 yrs.	11	38	9	1	0	0	0.0	4	3	6	1	0	.237	.263	0	0	SS-7, 3B-4

Luke Sewell

SEWELL, JAMES LUTHER   BR TR 5'9"   160 lbs.
Brother of Tommy Sewell.   Brother of Joe Sewell.
B. Jan. 5, 1901, Titus, Ala.
Manager 1941-46, 1949-52.

	G	AB	H	2B	3B	HR	HR %	R	RBI	BB	SO	SB	BA	SA	AB	H	G by POS
1921 CLE A	3	6	0	0	0	0	0.0	0	1	0	3	0	.000	.000	0	0	C-3
1922	41	87	23	5	0	0	0.0	14	10	5	8	1	.264	.322	1	0	C-38
1923	10	10	2	0	1	0	0.0	2	1	1	0	0	.200	.400	2	0	C-7
1924	63	165	48	9	1	0	0.0	27	17	22	13	1	.291	.358	3	1	C-56
1925	74	220	51	10	2	0	0.0	30	18	33	18	6	.232	.295	4	1	C-66, OF-2
1926	126	433	103	16	4	0	0.0	41	46	36	27	9	.238	.293	1	0	C-125
1927	128	470	138	27	6	0	0.0	52	53	20	23	4	.294	.377	2	0	C-126
1928	122	411	111	16	9	3	0.7	52	52	26	27	3	.270	.375	4	1	C-118
1929	124	406	96	17	3	1	0.2	41	39	29	26	6	.236	.300	0	0	C-124
1930	76	292	75	21	2	1	0.3	40	43	14	9	5	.257	.353	0	0	C-76
1931	108	375	103	30	4	1	0.3	45	53	36	17	1	.275	.384	3	1	C-105
1932	87	300	76	20	2	2	0.7	36	52	38	24	4	.253	.353	2	0	C-84
1933 WAS A	141	474	125	30	4	2	0.4	65	61	48	24	7	.264	.357	0	0	C-141
1934	72	207	49	7	3	2	1.0	21	21	22	10	0	.237	.329	7	2	C-50, OF-7, 1B-6, 3B-1, 2B-1
1935 CHI A	118	421	120	19	3	2	0.5	52	67	32	18	3	.285	.359	5	0	C-112
1936	128	451	113	20	5	5	1.1	59	73	54	16	11	.251	.350	2	0	C-126
1937	122	412	111	21	6	1	0.2	51	61	46	18	4	.269	.357	3	2	C-118
1938	65	211	45	4	1	0	0.0	23	27	20	20	0	.213	.242	0	0	C-65
1939 CLE A	16	20	3	1	0	0	0.0	1	1	3	1	0	.150	.200	0	0	C-15, 1B-1
1942 STL A	6	12	1	0	0	0	0.0	1	0	1	5	0	.083	.083	0	0	C-6
20 yrs.	1630	5383	1393	273	56	20	0.4	653	696	486	307	65	.259	.341	39	8	C-1561, OF-9, 1B-7, 3B-1, 2B-1

WORLD SERIES

	G	AB	H	2B	3B	HR	HR %	R	RBI	BB	SO	SB	BA	SA	AB	H	G by POS
1933 WAS A	5	17	3	0	0	0	0.0	1	1	2	0	1	.176	.176	0	0	C-5

Tommy Sewell

SEWELL, THOMAS WESLEY   BL TR 5'7½"   155 lbs.
Brother of Joe Sewell.   Brother of Luke Sewell.
B. Apr. 16, 1906, Titus, Ala.   D. July 30, 1956, Montgomery, Ala.

	G	AB	H	2B	3B	HR	HR %	R	RBI	BB	SO	SB	BA	SA	AB	H	G by POS
1927 CHI N	1	1	0	0	0	0	0.0	0	0	0	0	0	.000	.000	1	0	

Jimmy Sexton

SEXTON, JIMMY DALE   BR TR 5'10"   175 lbs.
B. Oct. 15, 1951, Mobile, Ala.

	G	AB	H	2B	3B	HR	HR %	R	RBI	BB	SO	SB	BA	SA	AB	H	G by POS
1977 SEA A	14	37	8	1	1	1	2.7	5	3	2	6	1	.216	.378	0	0	SS-12
1978 HOU N	88	141	29	3	2	2	1.4	17	6	13	28	16	.206	.298	6	1	SS-58, 3B-8, 2B-3
1979	52	43	9	0	0	0	0.0	8	1	7	7	1	.209	.209	17	3	SS-11, 3B-4, 2B-2
1981 OAK A	7	3	0	0	0	0	0.0	3	0	0	2	2	.000	.000	0	0	DH-1, 3B-1
1982	69	139	34	4	0	2	1.4	19	14	9	24	16	.245	.317	0	0	SS-47, 3B-8, DH-5
1983 STL N	6	9	1	1	0	0	0.0	1	0	1	4	0	.111	.222	1	0	SS-4, 3B-2
6 yrs.	236	372	81	9	3	5	1.3	53	24	32	71	36	.218	.298	24	4	SS-132, 3B-23, DH-6, 2B-5

Tom Sexton

SEXTON, THOMAS W.
B. Mar. 14, 1865, Milwaukee, Wis.   D. Feb. 8, 1934, Rock Island, Ill.

	G	AB	H	2B	3B	HR	HR %	R	RBI	BB	SO	SB	BA	SA	AB	H	G by POS
1884 MIL U	12	47	11	2	0	0	0.0	9		4			.234	.277	0	0	SS-12

Socks Seybold

SEYBOLD, RALPH ORLANDO   BR TR 5'11"   175 lbs.
B. Nov. 23, 1870, Washingtonville, Ohio   D. Dec. 22, 1921, Greensburg, Pa.

	G	AB	H	2B	3B	HR	HR %	R	RBI	BB	SO	SB	BA	SA	AB	H	G by POS
1899 CIN N	22	85	19	5	1	0	0.0	13	8	6		2	.224	.306	0	0	OF-22
1901 PHI A	114	457	152	24	14	8	1.8	74	90	40		15	.333	.499	0	0	OF-100, 1B-14
1902	137	522	165	27	12	16	3.1	91	97	43		6	.316	.506	0	0	OF-136
1903	137	522	156	45	8	8	1.5	78	84	38		5	.299	.462	0	0	OF-120, 1B-18
1904	143	510	149	26	9	3	0.6	56	64	42		12	.292	.396	3	0	OF-129, 1B-13
1905	132	488	132	37	4	6	1.2	64	59	42		5	.270	.400	0	0	OF-132
1906	116	411	130	23	2	5	1.2	41	59	30		9	.316	.418	2	0	OF-114
1907	147	564	153	28	4	5	0.9	58	92	40		10	.271	.362	0	0	OF-147
1908	48	130	28	2	0	0	0.0	5	3	12		2	.215	.231	12	2	OF-34
9 yrs.	996	3689	1084	217	54	51	1.4	480	556	293		66	.294	.423	17	2	OF-934, 1B-45

WORLD SERIES

	G	AB	H	2B	3B	HR	HR %	R	RBI	BB	SO	SB	BA	SA	AB	H	G by POS
1905 PHI A	5	16	2	0	0	0	0.0	0	0	2	3	0	.125	.125	0	0	OF-5

Cy Seymour

SEYMOUR, JAMES BENTLEY   BL TL 6'   200 lbs.
B. Dec. 9, 1872, Albany, N. Y.   D. Sept. 20, 1919, New York, N. Y.

	G	AB	H	2B	3B	HR	HR %	R	RBI	BB	SO	SB	BA	SA	AB	H	G by POS
1896 NY N	12	32	7	0	0	0	0.0	2	0	0	7	0	.219	.219	1	0	P-11, OF-1
1897	44	137	33	5	1	2	1.5	13	14	4		3	.241	.336	0	0	P-38, OF-6
1898	80	297	82	5	2	4	1.3	41	23	9		8	.276	.347	0	0	P-45, OF-35, 2B-1
1899	50	159	52	3	2	2	1.3	25	27	4		2	.327	.409	6	1	P-32, OF-8, 1B-3, 3B-1
1900	23	40	12	0	0	0	0.0	9	2	3		0	.300	.300	6	1	P-13, OF-3, 1B-1
1901 BAL A	137	552	167	19	8	1	0.2	85	77	28		38	.303	.371	0	0	OF-133, 1B-1

	G	AB	H	2B	3B	HR	HR %	R	RBI	BB	SO	SB	BA	SA	Pinch Hit AB	H	G by POS

Cy Seymour continued

1902 2 teams	BAL	A	(72G – .268)		CIN	N	(62G – .349)										
" total	134	515	157	16	10	5	1.0	66	78	30		20	.305	.404	0	0	OF-133, 3B-1, P-1
1903 CIN N	135	558	191	25	7	1.3		85	72	33		25	.342	.478	0	0	OF-135
1904	131	531	166	26	13	5	0.9	71	58	29		11	.313	.439	1	1	OF-130
1905	149	581	219	40	21	8	1.4	95	121	51		21	.377	.559	0	0	OF-149
1906 2 teams	CIN	N	(79G – .257)		NY	N	(72G – .320)										
" total	151	576	165	19	5	8	1.4	70	80	42		29	.286	.378	0	0	OF-151
1907 NY N	131	473	139	25	8	3	0.6	46	75	36		21	.294	.400	5	0	OF-126
1908	156	587	157	23	2	5	0.9	60	92	30		18	.267	.339	1	0	OF-155
1909	80	280	87	12	5	1	0.4	37	30	25		14	.311	.400	6	1	OF-74
1910	79	287	76	9	4	1	0.3	32	40	23	18	10	.265	.334	2	0	OF-76
1913 BOS N	39	73	13	2	0	0	0.0	2	10	7	7	2	.178	.205	15	3	OF-18
16 yrs.	1531	5678	1723	229	96	52	0.9	739	799	354	32	222	.303	.405	43	7	OF-1333, P-140, 1B-5, 3B-2, 2B-1

Ralph Shafer

SHAFER, RALPH NEWTON   5'11"
B. Mar. 17, 1894, Cincinnati, Ohio   D. Feb. 5, 1950, Akron, Ohio

	G	AB	H	2B	3B	HR	HR%	R	RBI	BB	SO	SB	BA	SA	AB	H	G by POS
1914 PIT N	1	0	0	0	0	0	–	0	0	0	0	0	–	–	0	0	

Tillie Shafer

SHAFER, ARTHUR JOSEPH   BB TR 5'10"   165 lbs.
B. Mar. 22, 1889, Los Angeles, Calif.   D. Jan. 10, 1962, Los Angeles, Calif.

	G	AB	H	2B	3B	HR	HR%	R	RBI	BB	SO	SB	BA	SA	AB	H	G by POS
1909 NY N	38	84	15	2	1	0	0.0	11	7	14		6	.179	.226	5	0	3B-16, 2B-13, OF-2
1910	29	21	4	1	0	0	0.0	5	1	0	6	0	.190	.238	6	1	3B-8, SS-2, 2B-2
1912	78	163	47	4	1	0	0.0	48	23	30	19	22	.288	.325	7	1	SS-31, 2B-20, 3B-7
1913	138	508	146	17	12	5	1.0	74	52	61	55	32	.287	.398	1	0	3B-79, 2B-25, SS-17, OF-15
4 yrs.	283	776	212	24	14	5	0.6	138	83	105	80	60	.273	.360	19	2	3B-110, 2B-60, SS-50, OF-17

WORLD SERIES

	G	AB	H	2B	3B	HR	HR%	R	RBI	BB	SO	SB	BA	SA	AB	H	G by POS
1912 NY N	3	0	0	0	0	0	–	0	0	0	0	0	–	–	0	0	SS-3
1913	5	19	3	1	1	0	0.0	2	1	2	3	0	.158	.316	0	0	3B-1
2 yrs.	8	19	3	1	1	0	0.0	2	1	2	3	0	.158	.316	0	0	SS-3, 3B-1

Frank Shaffer

SHAFFER, FRANK
Deceased.

1884 3 teams	ALT	U	(19G – .284)		KC	U	(44G – .171)		BAL	U	(3G – .077)						
" total	66	251	50	5	2	0	0.0	30		18			.199	.235	0	0	OF-62, C-4, 3B-2, SS-1, 2B-1

Orator Shaffer

SHAFFER, GEORGE   BL TR 5'9"   165 lbs.
Brother of Taylor Shaffer.
B. 1852, Philadelphia, Pa.   Deceased.

	G	AB	H	2B	3B	HR	HR%	R	RBI	BB	SO	SB	BA	SA	AB	H	G by POS
1877 LOU N	61	260	74	9	5	3	1.2	38	34	9	17		.285	.392	0	0	OF-60, 1B-1
1878 IND N	63	266	90	19	6	0	0.0	48	30	13	20		.338	.455	0	0	OF-63
1879 CHI N	73	316	96	13	0	0	0.0	53	35	6	28		.304	.345	0	0	OF-72, 3B-1
1880 CLE N	83	338	90	14	9	0	0.0	62		17	36		.266	.361	0	0	OF-83
1881	85	343	88	13	6	1	0.3	48	34	23	20		.257	.338	0	0	OF-85
1882	84	313	67	14	2	3	1.0	37	28	27	27		.214	.300	0	0	OF-84
1883 BUF N	95	401	117	11	3	0	0.0	67		27	39		.292	.334	0	0	OF-95
1884 STL U	106	467	168	40	10	2	0.4	130		30			.360	.501	0	0	OF-100, 2B-7, 1B-1
1885 2 teams	STL	N	(69G – .195)		PHI	AA	(2G – .222)										
" total	71	266	52	11	3	0	0.0	31	18	20	31		.195	.259	0	0	OF-71
1886 PHI AA	21	82	22	3	3	0	0.0	15	8				.268	.378	0	0	OF-22
1890	100	390	110	15	5	1	0.3	55		47		29	.282	.354	0	0	OF-98, 1B-3
11 yrs.	842	3442	974	162	52	10	0.3	584	179	227	218	29	.283	.369	0	0	OF-833, 2B-7, 1B-5, 3B-1

Taylor Shaffer

SHAFFER, TAYLOR
Brother of Orator Shaffer.
B. July, 1870, Philadelphia, Pa.   Deceased.

	G	AB	H	2B	3B	HR	HR%	R	RBI	BB	SO	SB	BA	SA	AB	H	G by POS
1890 PHI AA	69	261	45	3	4	0	0.0	28		28		19	.172	.215	0	0	2B-69

Art Shamsky

SHAMSKY, ARTHUR LEWIS   BL TL 6'1"   168 lbs.
B. Oct. 14, 1941, St. Louis, Mo.

	G	AB	H	2B	3B	HR	HR%	R	RBI	BB	SO	SB	BA	SA	AB	H	G by POS
1965 CIN N	64	96	25	4	3	2	2.1	13	10	10	29	1	.260	.427	45	13	OF-18, 1B-1
1966	96	234	54	5	0	21	9.0	41	47	32	45	0	.231	.521	24	5	OF-74
1967	76	147	29	3	1	3	2.0	6	13	15	34	0	.197	.293	34	10	OF-40
1968 NY N	116	345	82	14	4	12	3.5	30	48	21	58	1	.238	.406	23	1	OF-82, 1B-17
1969	100	303	91	9	3	14	4.6	42	47	36	32	1	.300	.488	13	5	OF-78, 1B-9
1970	122	403	118	19	2	11	2.7	48	49	49	33	1	.293	.432	11	2	OF-58, 1B-56
1971	68	135	25	6	2	5	3.7	13	18	21	18	1	.185	.370	24	3	OF-38, 1B-1
1972 2 teams	CHI	N	(15G – .125)		OAK	A	(8G – .000)										
" total	23	23	2	0	0	0	0.0	1	1	4	5	0	.087	.087	15	2	1B-4
8 yrs.	665	1686	426	60	15	68	4.0	194	233	188	254	5	.253	.427	189	41	OF-388, 1B-88

LEAGUE CHAMPIONSHIP SERIES

	G	AB	H	2B	3B	HR	HR%	R	RBI	BB	SO	SB	BA	SA	AB	H	G by POS
1969 NY N	3	13	7	0	0	0	0.0	3	3	1	0	0	.538	.538	0	0	OF-3

WORLD SERIES

	G	AB	H	2B	3B	HR	HR%	R	RBI	BB	SO	SB	BA	SA	AB	H	G by POS
1969 NY N	3	6	0	0	0	0	0.0	0	0	0	0	0	.000	.000	2	0	OF-1

Warren Shanabrook

SHANABROOK, WARREN H.
B. Nov. 30, 1885, Massillon, Ohio   D. Mar. 10, 1964, North Canton, Ohio

	G	AB	H	2B	3B	HR	HR%	R	RBI	BB	SO	SB	BA	SA	AB	H	G by POS
1906 WAS A	1	2	0	0	0	0	0.0	0	0	0		0	.000	.000	0	0	3B-1

	G	AB	H	2B	3B	HR	HR %	R	RBI	BB	SO	SB	BA	SA	Pinch Hit AB	Pinch Hit H	G by POS

Wally Shaner

SHANER, WALTER DEDAKER (Skinny)   BR TR 6'2"   195 lbs.
B. May 24, 1900, Lynchburg, Va.

	G	AB	H	2B	3B	HR	HR %	R	RBI	BB	SO	SB	BA	SA	AB	H	G by POS
1923 CLE A	3	4	1	0	0	0	0.0	1	0	1	1	0	.250	.250	0	0	OF-2, 3B-1
1926 BOS A	69	191	54	12	2	0	0.0	20	21	17	13	1	.283	.366	18	2	OF-48
1927	122	406	111	33	6	3	0.7	54	49	21	35	11	.273	.406	11	1	OF-108, 1B-1
1929 CIN N	13	28	9	0	0	1	3.6	5	4	4	5	1	.321	.429	2	1	1B-8, OF-2
4 yrs.	207	629	175	45	8	4	0.6	80	74	43	54	13	.278	.394	31	4	OF-160, 1B-9, 3B-1

Howard Shanks

SHANKS, HOWARD SAMUEL (Hank)   BR TR 5'11"   170 lbs.
B. July 21, 1890, Chicago, Ill.   D. July 30, 1941, Monaca, Pa.

	G	AB	H	2B	3B	HR	HR %	R	RBI	BB	SO	SB	BA	SA	AB	H	G by POS
1912 WAS A	115	399	92	14	7	1	0.3	52	47	40		21	.231	.308	2	0	OF-113
1913	109	390	99	11	5	1	0.3	38	37	15	40	24	.254	.315	0	0	OF-109
1914	143	500	112	22	10	4	0.8	44	64	29	51	18	.224	.332	3	0	OF-139
1915	141	492	123	19	8	0	0.0	52	47	30	42	12	.250	.321	2	1	OF-80, 3B-49, 2B-10
1916	140	471	119	15	7	1	0.2	51	48	41	34	23	.253	.321	4	2	OF-88, 3B-31, SS-8, 1B-7
1917	126	430	87	15	5	0	0.0	45	28	33	37	15	.202	.260	6	0	SS-90, OF-26, 1B-2
1918	120	436	112	19	4	1	0.2	42	56	31	21	23	.257	.326	6	2	OF-64, 2B-47, 3B-3
1919	135	491	122	8	7	1	0.2	33	54	25	48	13	.248	.299	1	1	SS-94, 2B-34, OF-6
1920	128	444	119	16	7	4	0.9	56	37	29	43	11	.268	.363	6	0	3B-63, OF-35, 1B-14, 2B-5, SS-1
1921	154	562	170	25	19	7	1.2	81	69	57	38	11	.302	.452	0	0	3B-154
1922	84	272	77	10	9	1	0.4	35	32	25	25	6	.283	.397	3	0	3B-54, OF-27
1923 BOS A	131	464	118	19	5	3	0.6	38	57	19	37	6	.254	.336	5	0	3B-85, 2B-36, OF-6, SS-2
1924	72	193	50	16	3	0	0.0	22	25	20	11	1	.259	.373	5	0	SS-37, 3B-22, OF-4, 2B-2, 1B-2
1925 NY A	66	155	40	3	1	1	0.6	15	18	20	15	1	.258	.310	13	4	3B-26, 2B-21, OF-4
14 yrs.	1664	5699	1440	212	97	25	0.4	604	619	414	442	185	.253	.337	56	10	OF-701, 3B-487, SS-232, 2B-155, 1B-25

Doc Shanley

SHANLEY, HARRY ROOT   BR TR 5'11"   174 lbs.
B. Jan. 30, 1889, Granbury, Tex.   D. Dec. 13, 1934, St. Petersburg, Fla.

	G	AB	H	2B	3B	HR	HR %	R	RBI	BB	SO	SB	BA	SA	AB	H	G by POS
1912 STL A	5	8	0	0	0	0	0.0	1	1	2		0	.000	.000	0	0	SS-4

Jim Shanley

SHANLEY, JAMES H.
B. New York, N. Y.   D. Nov. 4, 1904, Brooklyn, N. Y.

	G	AB	H	2B	3B	HR	HR %	R	RBI	BB	SO	SB	BA	SA	AB	H	G by POS
1876 NY N	2	8	1	0	0	0	0.0	0	0	0	0		.125	.125	0	0	OF-2

Dan Shannon

SHANNON, DANIEL W.   175 lbs.
B. Mar. 23, 1865, Bridgeport, Conn.   D. Oct. 25, 1913, Bridgeport, Conn.
Manager 1889, 1891.

	G	AB	H	2B	3B	HR	HR %	R	RBI	BB	SO	SB	BA	SA	AB	H	G by POS
1889 LOU AA	121	498	128	22	12	4	0.8	90	48	42	52	26	.257	.373	0	0	2B-121
1890 2 teams	PHI	P (19G – .240)			NY	P (83G – .216)											
" total	102	399	88	12	9	4	1.0	74	60	29	46	25	.221	.326	0	0	2B-96, SS-6
1891 WAS AA	19	67	9	2	0	0	0.0	7	3	6	9	3	.134	.164	0	0	SS-14, 2B-5
3 yrs.	242	964	225	36	21	8	0.8	171	111	77	107	54	.233	.339	0	0	2B-222, SS-20

Frank Shannon

SHANNON, FRANK E. (Tod)   5'2"   155 lbs.
B. Dec. 3, 1873, San Francisco, Calif.   Deceased.

	G	AB	H	2B	3B	HR	HR %	R	RBI	BB	SO	SB	BA	SA	AB	H	G by POS
1892 WAS N	1	4	1	0	0	0	0.0	0	2	0	2	0	.250	.250	0	0	SS-1
1896 LOU N	31	115	18	1	1	1	0.9	14	15	13	15	3	.157	.209	0	0	SS-28, 3B-3
2 yrs.	32	119	19	1	1	1	0.8	14	17	13	17	3	.160	.210	0	0	SS-29, 3B-3

Joe Shannon

SHANNON, JOSEPH ALOYSIUS   BR TR 5'11"   170 lbs.
Brother of Red Shannon.
B. Feb. 11, 1895, Jersey City, N. J.   D. July 28, 1955, Jersey City, N. J.

	G	AB	H	2B	3B	HR	HR %	R	RBI	BB	SO	SB	BA	SA	AB	H	G by POS
1915 BOS N	5	10	2	0	0	0	0.0	3	1	0	3	0	.200	.200	2	1	OF-4, 2B-1

Mike Shannon

SHANNON, THOMAS MICHAEL (Moonman)   BR TR 6'3"   195 lbs.
B. July 15, 1939, St. Louis, Mo.

	G	AB	H	2B	3B	HR	HR %	R	RBI	BB	SO	SB	BA	SA	AB	H	G by POS
1962 STL N	10	15	2	0	0	0	0.0	3	0	1	3	0	.133	.133	0	0	OF-7
1963	32	26	8	0	0	1	3.8	3	2	0	6	0	.308	.423	4	1	OF-26
1964	88	253	66	8	2	9	3.6	30	43	19	54	4	.261	.415	2	0	OF-88
1965	124	244	54	17	3	3	1.2	32	25	28	46	2	.221	.352	19	2	OF-101, C-4
1966	137	459	132	20	6	16	3.5	61	64	37	106	8	.288	.462	2	1	OF-129, C-1
1967	130	482	118	18	3	12	2.5	53	77	37	89	2	.245	.369	2	1	3B-122, OF-6
1968	156	576	153	29	2	15	2.6	62	79	37	114	1	.266	.401	0	0	3B-156
1969	150	551	140	15	5	12	2.2	51	55	49	87	1	.254	.365	2	1	3B-149
1970	52	174	37	9	2	0	0.0	18	22	16	20	1	.213	.287	5	1	3B-51
9 yrs.	879	2780	710	116	23	68	2.4	313	367	224	525	19	.255	.387	43	8	3B-478, OF-357, C-5
WORLD SERIES																	
1964 STL N	7	28	6	0	0	1	3.6	6	2	0	9	1	.214	.321	0	0	OF-7
1967	7	24	5	1	0	1	4.2	3	2	1	4	0	.208	.375	0	0	3B-7
1968	7	29	8	1	0	1	3.4	3	4	1	5	0	.276	.414	0	0	3B-7
3 yrs.	21	81	19	2	0	3	3.7	12	8	2	18	1	.235	.370	0	0	3B-14, OF-7

Owen Shannon

SHANNON, OWEN DENNIS IGNATIUS   BR TR
B. Dec. 22, 1885, Omaha, Neb.   D. Apr. 10, 1918, Omaha, Neb.

	G	AB	H	2B	3B	HR	HR %	R	RBI	BB	SO	SB	BA	SA	AB	H	G by POS
1903 STL A	9	28	6	2	0	0	0.0	1	3	1		0	.214	.286	0	0	C-8, 1B-1
1907 WAS A	4	7	1	0	0	0	0.0	0	0	0		0	.143	.143	0	0	C-4
2 yrs.	13	35	7	2	0	0	0.0	1	3	1		0	.200	.257	0	0	C-12, 1B-1

Red Shannon

SHANNON, MAURICE JOSEPH   BB TR 5'11"   170 lbs.
Brother of Joe Shannon.
B. Feb. 11, 1895, Jersey City, N. J.   D. Apr. 12, 1970, Jersey City, N. J.

	G	AB	H	2B	3B	HR	HR %	R	RBI	BB	SO	SB	BA	SA	AB	H	G by POS
1915 BOS N	1	3	0	0	0	0	0.0	0	0	0	0	0	.000	.000	0	0	2B-1
1917 PHI A	11	35	10	0	0	0	0.0	8	7	6	9	2	.286	.286	1	0	SS-10
1918	72	225	54	6	5	0	0.0	23	16	42	52	5	.240	.311	0	0	SS-45, 2B-26

	G	AB	H	2B	3B	HR	HR %	R	RBI	BB	SO	SB	BA	SA	Pinch Hit AB	H	G by POS

Red Shannon continued

1919 2 teams	PHI A (39G – .271)				BOS A (80G – .259)												
" total	119	445	117	18	9	0	0.0	50	31	29	70	11	.263	.344	3	1	2B-116
1920 2 teams	WAS A (62G – .288)				PHI A (25G – .170)												
" total	87	310	79	9	8	0	0.0	34	33	26	44	3	.255	.335	1	0	SS-55, 2B-16, 3B-15
1921 PHI A	1	1	0	0	0	0	0.0	0	0	0	0	0	.000	.000	1	0	
1926 CHI N	19	51	17	5	0	0	0.0	9	4	6	3	0	.333	.431	5	2	SS-13
7 yrs.	310	1070	277	38	22	0	0.0	124	91	109	178	21	.259	.336	11	3	2B-159, SS-123, 3B-15

Spike Shannon

SHANNON, WILLIAM PORTER   BB TR 5'11"   180 lbs.
B. Feb. 7, 1878, Pittsburgh, Pa.   D. May 16, 1940, Minneapolis, Minn.

1904 STL N	134	500	140	10	3	1	0.2	84	26	50		34	.280	.318	1	0	OF-133
1905	140	544	146	16	3	0	0.0	73	41	47		27	.268	.309	0	0	OF-140
1906 2 teams	STL N (80G – .258)				NY N (76G – .254)												
" total	156	589	151	9	1	0	0.0	78	50	70		33	.256	.275	0	0	OF-156
1907 NY N	155	585	155	12	5	1	0.2	104	33	82		33	.265	.308	0	0	OF-155
1908 2 teams	NY N (77G – .224)				PIT N (32G – .197)												
" total	109	395	85	2	3	1	0.3	44	33	37		18	.215	.243	2	0	OF-106
5 yrs.	694	2613	677	49	15	3	0.1	383	183	286		145	.259	.293	3	0	OF-690

Wally Shannon

SHANNON, WALTER CHARLES   BL TR 6'   178 lbs.
B. Jan. 23, 1934, Cleveland, Ohio

1959 STL N	47	95	27	5	0	0	0.0	5	5	0	12	0	.284	.337	28	9	SS-21, 2B-10
1960	18	23	4	0	0	0	0.0	2	1	3	6	0	.174	.174	9	1	2B-15, SS-1
2 yrs.	65	118	31	5	0	0	0.0	7	6	3	18	0	.263	.305	37	10	2B-25, SS-22

Billy Shantz

SHANTZ, WILMER EBERT   BR TR 6'1"   160 lbs.
Brother of Bobby Shantz.
B. July 31, 1927, Pottstown, Pa.

1954 PHI A	51	164	42	9	3	1	0.6	13	17	17	23	0	.256	.366	0	0	C-51
1955 KC A	79	217	56	4	1	1	0.5	18	12	11	14	0	.258	.300	1	0	C-78
1960 NY A	1	0	0	0	0	0	–	0	0	0	0	0	–	–	0	0	C-1
3 yrs.	131	381	98	13	4	2	0.5	31	29	28	37	0	.257	.328	1	0	C-130

Ralph Sharman

SHARMAN, RALPH EDWARD (Bally)   BR TR 5'11"   176 lbs.
B. Apr. 11, 1895, South Norwood, Ohio   D. May 24, 1918, Camp Sheridan, Ala.

1917 PHI A	13	37	11	2	1	0	0.0	2	3	2	1	1	.297	.405	2	0	OF-10

Dick Sharon

SHARON, RICHARD LOUIS   BR TR 6'2"   195 lbs.
B. Apr. 15, 1950, San Mateo, Calif.

1973 DET A	91	178	43	9	0	7	3.9	20	16	10	31	2	.242	.410	3	1	OF-91
1974	60	129	28	4	0	2	1.6	12	10	14	29	4	.217	.295	5	0	OF-56
1975 SD N	91	160	31	7	0	4	2.5	14	20	26	35	0	.194	.313	33	8	OF-57
3 yrs.	242	467	102	20	0	13	2.8	46	46	50	95	6	.218	.345	41	9	OF-204

Bill Sharp

SHARP, WILLIAM HOWARD   BL TL 5'10"   178 lbs.
B. Jan. 18, 1950, Lima, Ohio

1973 CHI A	77	196	54	8	3	4	2.0	23	22	19	28	2	.276	.408	5	2	OF-70, DH-1
1974	100	320	81	13	2	4	1.3	45	24	25	37	0	.253	.344	3	1	OF-99
1975 2 teams	CHI A (18G – .200)				MIL A (125G – .255)												
" total	143	408	102	27	3	1	0.2	38	38	21	29	0	.250	.338	10	1	OF-138
1976 MIL A	78	180	44	4	0	0	0.0	16	11	10	15	1	.244	.267	17	5	OF-56, DH-7
4 yrs.	398	1104	281	52	8	9	0.8	122	95	75	109	3	.255	.341	35	9	OF-363, DH-8

Bud Sharpe

SHARPE, BAYARD HESTON   BL TR
B. Aug. 6, 1881, West Chester, Pa.   D. May 31, 1916, Haddock, Ga.

1905 BOS N	46	170	31	3	2	0	0.0	8	11	7		0	.182	.224	1	0	OF-42, C-3, 1B-1
1910 2 teams	BOS N (115G – .239)				PIT N (4G – .188)												
" total	119	455	108	14	4	0	0.0	32	30	14	33	4	.237	.286	2	1	1B-117
2 yrs.	165	625	139	17	6	0	0.0	40	41	21	33	4	.222	.269	3	1	1B-118, OF-42, C-3

John Sharrott

SHARROTT, JOHN HENRY   BL TL 5'9"   165 lbs.
B. Aug. 13, 1869, Bangor, Me.   D. Dec. 31, 1927, Los Angeles, Calif.

1890 NY N	32	109	22	3	2	0	0.0	16	14	0	14	6	.202	.266	0	0	P-25, OF-9
1891	10	30	10	2	0	1	3.3	5	7	1	2	3	.333	.500	0	0	P-10
1892	4	8	1	0	0	0	0.0	1	0	0	1	0	.125	.125	0	0	OF-3, P-1
1893 PHI N	50	152	38	4	3	1	0.7	25	22	8	14	6	.250	.336	4	2	OF-33, P-12
4 yrs.	96	299	71	9	5	2	0.7	47	43	9	31	15	.237	.321	4	2	P-48, OF-45

Shag Shaughnessy

SHAUGHNESSY, FRANCIS JOSEPH   BR TR 6'1½"   185 lbs.
B. Apr. 8, 1883, Montreal, Que., Canada   D. May 15, 1969, Montreal, Que., Canada

1905 WAS A	1	3	0	0	0	0	0.0	0	0	0		0	.000	.000	0	0	OF-1
1908 PHI A	8	29	9	0	0	0	0.0	2	1	2		3	.310	.310	0	0	OF-8
2 yrs.	9	32	9	0	0	0	0.0	2	1	2		3	.281	.281	0	0	OF-9

Al Shaw

SHAW, ALBERT SIMPSON   BL TR 5'8½"   165 lbs.
B. Mar. 1, 1881, Toledo, Ill.   D. Dec. 30, 1974, Danville, Ill.

1907 STL N	8	23	7	0	0	0	0.0	2	1	3		1	.304	.304	0	0	OF-8
1908	107	367	97	13	4	1	0.3	40	19	25		9	.264	.330	10	5	OF-91, SS-4, 3B-1
1909	114	331	82	12	7	2	0.6	45	34	55		15	.248	.344	15	3	OF-92
1914 BKN F	112	376	122	27	7	5	1.3	81	49	44		24	.324	.473	7	5	OF-102
1915 KC F	132	448	126	22	10	6	1.3	67	67	46		15	.281	.415	6	1	OF-124
5 yrs.	473	1545	434	74	28	14	0.9	235	170	173		64	.281	.392	38	14	OF-417, SS-4, 3B-1

	G	AB	H	2B	3B	HR	HR %	R	RBI	BB	SO	SB	BA	SA	Pinch Hit AB	Pinch Hit H	G by POS

Al Shaw

SHAW, ALFRED   BR TR 5'8"   170 lbs.
B. Oct. 3, 1874, Burslem, England   D. Mar. 25, 1958, Uhrichsville, Ohio

	G	AB	H	2B	3B	HR	HR %	R	RBI	BB	SO	SB	BA	SA	AB	H	G by POS
1901 DET A	55	171	46	7	0	1	0.6	20	23	10		2	.269	.327	4	0	C-42, 1B-9, 3B-2, SS-1
1907 BOS A	76	198	38	1	3	0	0.0	10	7	18		4	.192	.227	1	0	C-73, 1B-1
1908 CHI A	32	49	4	1	0	0	0.0	0	2	2		0	.082	.102	3	0	C-29
1909 BOS N	17	41	4	0	0	0	0.0	1	0	5		0	.098	.098	2	0	C-13
4 yrs.	180	459	92	9	3	1	0.2	31	32	35		6	.200	.240	10	0	C-157, 1B-10, 3B-2, SS-1

Ben Shaw

SHAW, BENJAMIN NATHANIEL   BR TR 5'11½" 190 lbs.
B. June 18, 1893, La Center, Ky.   D. Mar. 16, 1959, Aurora, Ohio

	G	AB	H	2B	3B	HR	HR %	R	RBI	BB	SO	SB	BA	SA	AB	H	G by POS
1917 PIT N	2	2	0	0	0	0	0.0	0	0	0	0	0	.000	.000	2	0	
1918	21	36	7	1	0	0	0.0	5	2	2	2	0	.194	.222	1	0	1B-9, C-5
2 yrs.	23	38	7	1	0	0	0.0	5	2	2	2	0	.184	.211	3	0	1B-9, C-5

Dupee Shaw

SHAW, FREDERICK LANDER   TL
B. May 31, 1859, Charlestown, Mass.   D. June 11, 1938, Everett, Mass.

	G	AB	H	2B	3B	HR	HR %	R	RBI	BB	SO	SB	BA	SA	AB	H	G by POS
1883 DET N	38	141	29	3	0	0	0.0	13		3	36		.206	.227	0	0	P-26, OF-15
1884 2 teams	DET	N (36G –	.191)		BOS	U (44G –	.242)										
" total	80	289	63	12	1	1	0.3	29		9	21		.218	.277	0	0	P-67, OF-19
1885 PRO N	49	165	22	2	0	0	0.0	17	9	4	38		.133	.145	0	0	P-49, OF-2
1886 WAS N	45	148	13	2	0	0	0.0	13	6	14	44		.088	.101	0	0	P-45, OF-1
1887	21	70	13	2	0	0	0.0	7	3	8	14	1	.186	.214	0	0	P-21
1888	3	10	0	0	0	0	0.0	0	0	0	3	0	.000	.000	0	0	P-3
6 yrs.	236	823	140	21	1	1	0.1	79	17	38	156	1	.170	.202	0	0	P-211, OF-37

Royal Shaw

SHAW, ROYAL N.   BL TR 5'8"   165 lbs.
B. Sept. 29, 1884, Yakima, Wash.   D. July 3, 1969, Yakima, Wash.

	G	AB	H	2B	3B	HR	HR %	R	RBI	BB	SO	SB	BA	SA	AB	H	G by POS
1908 PIT N	1	1	0	0	0	0	0.0	0		0		0	.000	.000	1	0	

Danny Shay

SHAY, DANIEL C.   TR 5'10"
B. Nov. 8, 1876, Kansas City, Mo.   D. Dec. 1, 1927, Kansas City, Mo.

	G	AB	H	2B	3B	HR	HR %	R	RBI	BB	SO	SB	BA	SA	AB	H	G by POS
1901 CLE A	19	75	17	2	2	0	0.0	4	10	2		0	.227	.307	0	0	SS-19
1904 STL N	99	340	87	11	1	1	0.3	45	18	39		36	.256	.303	1	0	SS-97, 2B-2
1905	78	281	67	12	1	0	0.0	30	28	35		11	.238	.288	0	0	SS-39, 2B-39
1907 NY N	35	79	15	1	1	1	1.3	10	6	12		5	.190	.266	11	2	2B-13, SS-9, OF-2
4 yrs.	231	775	186	26	5	2	0.3	89	62	88		52	.240	.294	12	2	SS-164, 2B-54, OF-2

Marty Shay

SHAY, ARTHUR JOSEPH   BR TR 5'7½" 148 lbs.
B. Apr. 25, 1896, Boston, Mass.   D. Feb. 20, 1951, Worcester, Mass.

	G	AB	H	2B	3B	HR	HR %	R	RBI	BB	SO	SB	BA	SA	AB	H	G by POS
1916 CHI N	2	7	2	0	0	0	0.0	0	0	0	1	0	.286	.286	0	0	SS-2
1924 BOS N	19	68	16	3	1	0	0.0	4	2	5	5	2	.235	.309	0	0	2B-19, SS-1
2 yrs.	21	75	18	3	1	0	0.0	4	2	5	6	2	.240	.307	0	0	2B-19, SS-3

Gerry Shea

SHEA, GERALD J.   TR 5'7"   160 lbs.
B. July 26, 1881, St. Louis, Mo.   D. May 3, 1964, Berkeley, Mo.

	G	AB	H	2B	3B	HR	HR %	R	RBI	BB	SO	SB	BA	SA	AB	H	G by POS
1905 STL N	2	6	2	0	0	0	0.0	0	0	0		0	.333	.333	0	0	C-2

Merv Shea

SHEA, MERVIN DAVID JOHN   BR TR 5'11" 175 lbs.
B. Sept. 5, 1900, San Francisco, Calif.   D. Jan. 27, 1953, Sacramento, Calif.

	G	AB	H	2B	3B	HR	HR %	R	RBI	BB	SO	SB	BA	SA	AB	H	G by POS
1927 DET A	34	85	15	6	3	0	0.0	5	9	7	15	0	.176	.318	3	0	C-31
1928	39	85	20	2	3	0	0.0	8	9	9	11	2	.235	.329	7	0	C-30
1929	50	162	47	6	0	3	1.9	23	24	19	18	2	.290	.383	3	0	C-50
1933 2 teams	BOS	A (16G –	.143)		STL	A (94G –	.262)										
" total	110	335	81	14	1	1	0.3	27	35	47	33	2	.242	.299	8	2	C-101
1934 CHI A	62	176	28	3	0	0	0.0	8	5	24	19	0	.159	.176	2	0	C-60
1935	46	122	28	2	0	0	0.0	8	13	30	9	0	.230	.246	2	0	C-43
1936	14	24	3	0	0	0	0.0	3	2	6	5	0	.125	.125	0	0	C-14
1937	25	71	15	1	0	0	0.0	7	5	15	10	1	.211	.225	0	0	C-25
1938 BKN N	48	120	22	5	0	0	0.0	14	12	28	20	1	.183	.225	0	0	C-47
1939 DET A	4	2	0	0	0	0	0.0	0	0	0	1	0	.000	.000	0	0	C-4
1944 PHI N	7	15	4	0	0	1	6.7	2	1	4	4	0	.267	.467	1	0	C-6
11 yrs.	439	1197	263	39	7	5	0.4	105	115	189	145	8	.220	.277	26	2	C-411

Nap Shea

SHEA, JOHN EDWARD   BR TR 5'5"   155 lbs.
B. May 23, 1874, Ware, Mass.   D. July 8, 1968, Bloomfield Hills, Mich.

	G	AB	H	2B	3B	HR	HR %	R	RBI	BB	SO	SB	BA	SA	AB	H	G by POS
1902 PHI N	3	8	1	0	0	0	0.0	1	0	1		0	.125	.125	0	0	C-3

Dave Shean

SHEAN, DAVID WILLIAM   BR TR 5'11" 175 lbs.
B. May 23, 1878, Ware, Mass.   D. May 22, 1963, Boston, Mass.

	G	AB	H	2B	3B	HR	HR %	R	RBI	BB	SO	SB	BA	SA	AB	H	G by POS
1906 PHI N	22	75	16	3	2	0	0.0	7	3	5		6	.213	.307	0	0	2B-22
1908 PHI N	14	48	7	2	0	0	0.0	4	2	1		1	.146	.188	0	0	SS-14
1909 2 teams	PHI	N (36G –	.232)		BOS	N (75G –	.247)										
" total	111	379	92	13	6	1	0.3	46	33	31		17	.243	.317	10	3	2B-86, 1B-11, OF-3, SS-1
1910 BOS N	150	543	130	12	7	3	0.6	52	36	42	45	16	.239	.304	2	1	2B-148
1911 CHI N	54	145	28	4	0	0	0.0	17	15	8	15	4	.193	.221	9	1	2B-23, SS-19, 3B-1
1912 BOS N	4	10	3	0	0	0	0.0	1	0	1	2	0	.300	.300	1	0	SS-4
1917 CIN N	131	442	93	9	5	2	0.5	36	35	22	39	10	.210	.267	0	0	2B-131
1918 BOS A	115	425	112	16	3	0	0.0	58	34	40	25	11	.264	.315	0	0	2B-115
1919	29	100	14	0	0	0	0.0	4	8	5	7	1	.140	.140	0	0	2B-29
9 yrs.	630	2167	495	59	23	6	0.3	225	166	155	133	66	.228	.285	22	5	2B-554, SS-38, 1B-11, OF-3, 3B-1

WORLD SERIES																	
1918 BOS A	6	19	4	1	0	0	0.0	2	0	4	3	1	.211	.263	0	0	2B-6

	G	AB	H	2B	3B	HR	HR %	R	RBI	BB	SO	SB	BA	SA	Pinch Hit AB	Pinch Hit H	G by POS

Ray Shearer

SHEARER, RAY SOLOMON
B. Sept. 19, 1929, Jacobus, Pa.   D. Feb. 22, 1982, York, Pa.
BR TR 6'   200 lbs.

	G	AB	H	2B	3B	HR	HR%	R	RBI	BB	SO	SB	BA	SA	PH AB	PH H	G by POS
1957 MIL N	2	2	1	0	0	0	0.0	1	0	1	1	0	.500	.500	1	1	OF-1

John Shearon

SHEARON, JOHN M.
B. 1870, Pittsburgh, Pa.   D. Feb. 1, 1923, Bradford, Pa.

	G	AB	H	2B	3B	HR	HR%	R	RBI	BB	SO	SB	BA	SA	PH AB	PH H	G by POS
1891 CLE N	30	124	30	1	1	0	0.0	10	13	1	15	6	.242	.266	0	0	OF-28, P-6
1896	16	64	11	0	1	0	0.0	6	3	4	6	3	.172	.203	0	0	OF-16
2 yrs.	46	188	41	1	2	0	0.0	16	16	5	21	9	.218	.245	0	0	OF-44, P-6

Jimmy Sheckard

SHECKARD, SAMUEL JAMES TILDEN
B. Nov. 23, 1878, Upper Chanceford, Pa.   D. Jan. 15, 1947, Lancaster, Pa.
BL TR 5'9"   175 lbs.

	G	AB	H	2B	3B	HR	HR%	R	RBI	BB	SO	SB	BA	SA	PH AB	PH H	G by POS
1897 BKN N	13	49	16	3	3	3	6.1	12	14	6		5	.327	.653	0	0	SS-11, OF-2
1898	105	409	119	17	9	4	1.0	51	64	37		8	.291	.406	0	0	OF-105, 3B-1
1899 BAL N	147	536	158	18	10	3	0.6	104	75	56		77	.295	.382	0	0	OF-146, 1B-1
1900 BKN N	85	273	82	19	10	1	0.4	74	39	42		30	.300	.454	6	1	OF-78
1901	133	558	197	31	19	11	2.0	116	104	47		35	.353	**.536**	0	0	OF-121, 3B-12
1902 2 teams		BAL A (4G – .267)						BKN N	(123G – .270)								
" total	127	501	135	21	10	4	0.8	89	37	58		25	.269	.375	0	0	OF-127
1903 BKN N	139	515	171	29	9	9	1.7	99	75	75		67	.332	.476	0	0	OF-139
1904	143	507	121	23	6	1	0.2	70	46	56		21	.239	.314	0	0	OF-141, 2B-2
1905	130	480	140	20	11	3	0.6	58	41	61		23	.292	.398	0	0	OF-129
1906 CHI N	149	549	144	27	10	1	0.2	90	45	67		30	.262	.353	0	0	OF-149
1907	142	484	129	23	1	1	0.2	76	36	76		31	.267	.324	1	0	OF-142
1908	115	403	93	18	3	2	0.5	54	22	62		18	.231	.305	0	0	OF-115
1909	148	525	134	29	5	1	0.2	81	43	72		15	.255	.335	0	0	OF-148
1910	144	507	130	27	6	5	1.0	82	51	83	53	22	.256	.363	1	1	OF-143
1911	156	539	149	26	11	4	0.7	121	50	147	58	32	.276	.388	0	0	OF-156
1912	146	523	128	22	10	3	0.6	85	47	122	81	15	.245	.342	0	0	OF-146
1913 2 teams		STL N (52G – .199)						CIN N	(47G – .190)								
" total	99	252	49	3	4	0	0.0	34	24	68	41	11	.194	.238	12	2	OF-84
17 yrs.	2121	7610	2095	356	136	56	0.7	1296	813	1135	233	465	.275	.380	20	4	OF-2071, 3B-13, SS-11, 2B-2, 1B-1

WORLD SERIES

	G	AB	H	2B	3B	HR	HR%	R	RBI	BB	SO	SB	BA	SA	PH AB	PH H	G by POS
1906 CHI N	6	21	0	0	0	0	0.0	0	1	2	4	1	.000	.000	0	0	OF-6
1907	5	21	5	2	0	0	0.0	0	2	0	1	1	.238	.333	0	0	OF-5
1908	5	21	5	2	0	0	0.0	2	1	2	3	1	.238	.333	0	0	OF-5
1910	5	14	4	2	0	0	0.0	5	1	7	2	1	.286	.429	0	0	OF-5
4 yrs.	21	77	14	6	0	0	0.0	7	5	11	10	4	.182	.260	0	0	OF-21

Biff Sheehan

SHEEHAN, TIMOTHY JAMES
B. Feb. 13, 1868, Hartford, Conn.   D. Oct. 21, 1923, Hartford, Conn.
TR 5'9"   165 lbs.

	G	AB	H	2B	3B	HR	HR%	R	RBI	BB	SO	SB	BA	SA	PH AB	PH H	G by POS
1895 STL N	52	180	57	3	6	1	0.6	24	18	20	6	7	.317	.417	0	0	OF-41, 1B-11
1896	6	19	3	0	0	0	0.0	0	1	4	0	0	.158	.158	0	0	OF-6
2 yrs.	58	199	60	3	6	1	0.5	24	19	24	6	7	.302	.392	0	0	OF-47, 1B-11

Dan Sheehan

SHEEHAN, DANIEL
B. Dec. 18, 1872, Cleveland, Ohio
5'6"   142 lbs.

	G	AB	H	2B	3B	HR	HR%	R	RBI	BB	SO	SB	BA	SA	PH AB	PH H	G by POS
1900 NY N	1	2	0	0	0	0	0.0	0	0	0		0	.000	.000	0	0	SS-1

Jack Sheehan

SHEEHAN, JOHN THOMAS
B. Apr. 15, 1893, Chicago, Ill.
BL TR 5'8½"   165 lbs.

	G	AB	H	2B	3B	HR	HR%	R	RBI	BB	SO	SB	BA	SA	PH AB	PH H	G by POS
1920 BKN N	3	5	2	1	0	0	0.0	0	0	1	0	0	.400	.600	0	0	SS-2, 3B-1
1921	5	12	0	0	0	0	0.0	2	0	0	1	0	.000	.000	0	0	2B-2, SS-1, 3B-1
2 yrs.	8	17	2	1	0	0	0.0	2	0	1	1	0	.118	.176	0	0	SS-3, 3B-2, 2B-2

WORLD SERIES

	G	AB	H	2B	3B	HR	HR%	R	RBI	BB	SO	SB	BA	SA	PH AB	PH H	G by POS
1920 BKN N	3	11	2	0	0	0	0.0	0	0	0	1	0	.182	.182	0	0	3B-3

Jim Sheehan

SHEEHAN, JAMES THOMAS (Big Jim)
B. June 3, 1913, New Haven, Conn.
BR TR 6'2"   196 lbs.

	G	AB	H	2B	3B	HR	HR%	R	RBI	BB	SO	SB	BA	SA	PH AB	PH H	G by POS
1936 NY N	1	4	0	0	0	0	0.0	0	0	0	2	0	.000	.000	0	0	C-1

Tommy Sheehan

SHEEHAN, THOMAS H.
B. Nov. 6, 1877, Sacramento, Calif.   D. May 22, 1959, Canal Zone, Panama
TR

	G	AB	H	2B	3B	HR	HR%	R	RBI	BB	SO	SB	BA	SA	PH AB	PH H	G by POS
1906 PIT N	95	315	76	6	3	1	0.3	28	34	18		13	.241	.289	5	1	3B-90
1907	75	226	62	2	3	0	0.0	23	25	23		10	.274	.310	6	2	3B-57, SS-10
1908 BKN N	146	468	100	18	2	0	0.0	45	29	53		9	.214	.261	1	1	3B-145
3 yrs.	316	1009	238	26	8	1	0.1	96	88	94		32	.236	.280	12	4	3B-292, SS-10

Bud Sheely

SHEELY, HOLLIS KIMBALL
Son of Earl Sheely.
B. Nov. 26, 1920, Spokane, Wash.
BL TR 6'1"   200 lbs.

	G	AB	H	2B	3B	HR	HR%	R	RBI	BB	SO	SB	BA	SA	PH AB	PH H	G by POS
1951 CHI A	34	89	16	2	0	0	0.0	2	7	6	7	0	.180	.202	1	0	C-33
1952	36	75	18	2	0	0	0.0	1	3	12	7	0	.240	.267	6	2	C-31
1953	31	46	10	1	0	0	0.0	4	2	9	8	0	.217	.239	10	4	C-17
3 yrs.	101	210	44	5	0	0	0.0	7	12	27	22	0	.210	.233	17	6	C-81

Earl Sheely

SHEELY, EARL HOMER (Whitey)
Father of Bud Sheely.
B. Feb. 12, 1893, Bushnell, Ill.   D. Sept. 16, 1952, Seattle, Wash.
BR TR 6'3½"   195 lbs.

	G	AB	H	2B	3B	HR	HR%	R	RBI	BB	SO	SB	BA	SA	PH AB	PH H	G by POS
1921 CHI A	154	563	171	25	6	11	2.0	68	95	57	34	4	.304	.428	0	0	1B-154
1922	149	526	167	37	4	6	1.1	72	80	60	27	4	.317	.437	0	0	1B-149
1923	156	570	169	25	3	4	0.7	74	88	79	30	5	.296	.372	0	0	1B-156
1924	146	535	171	34	3	3	0.6	84	103	95	28	7	.320	.411	0	0	1B-146
1925	153	600	189	43	3	9	1.5	93	111	68	23	3	.315	.442	0	0	1B-153
1926	145	525	157	40	2	6	1.1	77	89	75	13	3	.299	.417	0	0	1B-144

	G	AB	H	2B	3B	HR	HR%	R	RBI	BB	SO	SB	BA	SA	Pinch Hit AB	Pinch Hit H	G by POS

Earl Sheely continued

	G	AB	H	2B	3B	HR	HR%	R	RBI	BB	SO	SB	BA	SA	PH AB	PH H	G by POS
1927	45	129	27	3	0	2	1.6	11	16	20	5	1	.209	.279	8	1	1B-36
1929 PIT N	139	485	142	22	4	6	1.2	63	88	75	24	6	.293	.392	0	0	1B-139
1931 BOS N	147	538	147	15	2	1	0.2	30	77	34	21	0	.273	.314	3	0	1B-143
9 yrs.	1234	4471	1340	244	27	48	1.1	572	747	563	205	33	.300	.399	11	1	1B-1220

Charlie Sheerin

SHEERIN, CHARLES JOSEPH
B. Apr. 17, 1911, Brooklyn, N. Y.
BR TR 5'11½" 198 lbs.

	G	AB	H	2B	3B	HR	HR%	R	RBI	BB	SO	SB	BA	SA	PH AB	PH H	G by POS
1936 PHI N	39	72	19	4	0	0	0.0	4	4	7	18	0	.264	.319	2	1	2B-17, 3B-13, SS-5

Larry Sheets

SHEETS, LARRY KENT
B. Dec. 6, 1959, Staunton, Va.
BL TR 6'4" 210 lbs.

	G	AB	H	2B	3B	HR	HR%	R	RBI	BB	SO	SB	BA	SA	PH AB	PH H	G by POS
1984 BAL A	8	16	7	1	0	1	6.3	3	2	1	3	0	.438	.688	1	0	OF-7

John Shelby

SHELBY, JOHN T.
B. Feb. 23, 1958, Lexington, Ky.
BB TR 6'1" 175 lbs.

	G	AB	H	2B	3B	HR	HR%	R	RBI	BB	SO	SB	BA	SA	PH AB	PH H	G by POS
1981 BAL A	7	2	0	0	0	0	0.0	2	0	0	1	2	.000	.000	0	0	OF-4
1982	26	35	11	3	0	1	2.9	8	2	0	5	0	.314	.486	3	1	OF-24
1983	126	325	84	15	2	5	1.5	52	27	18	64	15	.258	.363	27	7	OF-115, DH-1
1984	128	383	80	12	5	6	1.6	44	30	20	71	12	.209	.313	12	4	OF-124
4 yrs.	287	745	175	30	7	12	1.6	106	59	38	141	29	.235	.342	42	12	OF-267, DH-1

LEAGUE CHAMPIONSHIP SERIES

	G	AB	H	2B	3B	HR	HR%	R	RBI	BB	SO	SB	BA	SA	PH AB	PH H	G by POS
1983 BAL A	3	9	2	0	0	0	0.0	1	0	1	3	1	.222	.222	0	0	OF-2

WORLD SERIES

	G	AB	H	2B	3B	HR	HR%	R	RBI	BB	SO	SB	BA	SA	PH AB	PH H	G by POS
1983 BAL A	5	9	4	0	0	0	0.0	1	1	0	4	0	.444	.444	3	0	OF-5

Bob Sheldon

SHELDON, BOB MITCHELL
B. Nov. 27, 1950, Montebello, Calif.
BL TR 6' 170 lbs.

	G	AB	H	2B	3B	HR	HR%	R	RBI	BB	SO	SB	BA	SA	PH AB	PH H	G by POS
1974 MIL A	10	17	2	1	1	0	0.0	4	0	4	2	0	.118	.294	1	0	DH-4, 2B-3
1975	53	181	52	3	3	0	0.0	17	14	13	14	0	.287	.337	6	3	2B-44, DH-6
1977	31	64	13	4	1	0	0.0	9	3	6	9	0	.203	.297	8	2	DH-17, 2B-5
3 yrs.	94	262	67	8	5	0	0.0	30	17	23	25	0	.256	.324	15	5	2B-52, DH-27

Hugh Shelley

SHELLEY, HUBERT LENEIRRE
B. Oct. 26, 1910, Rogers, Tex.   D. June 16, 1978, Beaumont, Tex.
BR TR 6' 170 lbs.

	G	AB	H	2B	3B	HR	HR%	R	RBI	BB	SO	SB	BA	SA	PH AB	PH H	G by POS
1935 DET A	7	8	2	0	0	0	0.0	1	1	2	1	0	.250	.250	2	1	OF-5

Skeeter Shelton

SHELTON, ANDREW KEMPER
B. June 29, 1888, Huntington, W. Va.   D. Jan. 9, 1954, Huntington, W. Va.
BR TR

	G	AB	H	2B	3B	HR	HR%	R	RBI	BB	SO	SB	BA	SA	PH AB	PH H	G by POS
1915 NY A	10	40	1	0	0	0	0.0	1	0	2	10	0	.025	.025	0	0	OF-10

Stan Shemo

SHEMO, STEPHEN MICHAEL
B. Apr. 9, 1915, Swoyersville, Pa.
BR TR 5'11" 175 lbs.

	G	AB	H	2B	3B	HR	HR%	R	RBI	BB	SO	SB	BA	SA	PH AB	PH H	G by POS
1944 BOS N	18	31	9	2	0	0	0.0	3	1	1	3	0	.290	.355	0	0	2B-16, 3B-2
1945	17	46	11	1	0	0	0.0	4	7	1	3	0	.239	.261	0	0	2B-12, 3B-3, SS-1
2 yrs.	35	77	20	3	0	0	0.0	7	8	2	6	0	.260	.299	0	0	2B-28, 3B-5, SS-1

Jack Shepard

SHEPARD, JACK LEROY
B. May 13, 1932, Clovis, Calif.
BR TR 6'2" 195 lbs.

	G	AB	H	2B	3B	HR	HR%	R	RBI	BB	SO	SB	BA	SA	PH AB	PH H	G by POS
1953 PIT N	2	4	1	0	0	0	0.0	0	0	0	2	0	.250	.250	0	0	C-2
1954	82	227	69	8	2	3	1.3	24	22	26	33	0	.304	.396	14	4	C-67
1955	94	264	63	10	2	2	0.8	24	23	33	25	1	.239	.314	18	5	C-77
1956	100	256	62	11	2	7	2.7	24	30	25	37	1	.242	.383	15	4	C-86, 1B-2
4 yrs.	278	751	195	29	6	12	1.6	72	75	84	97	2	.260	.362	47	13	C-232, 1B-2

Ron Shepherd

SHEPHERD, RONALD WAYNE
B. Oct. 27, 1960, Longview, Tex.
BR TR 6'4" 180 lbs.

	G	AB	H	2B	3B	HR	HR%	R	RBI	BB	SO	SB	BA	SA	PH AB	PH H	G by POS
1984 TOR A	12	4	0	0	0	0	0.0	0	0	0	3	0	.000	.000	0	0	OF-5, DH-4

Ray Shepherdson

SHEPHERDSON, RAYMOND FRANCIS
B. May 3, 1897, Little Falls, N. Y.   D. Nov. 8, 1975, Little Falls, N. Y.
BR TR 5'11½" 170 lbs.

	G	AB	H	2B	3B	HR	HR%	R	RBI	BB	SO	SB	BA	SA	PH AB	PH H	G by POS
1924 STL N	3	6	0	0	0	0	0.0	1	0	0	3	0	.000	.000	0	0	C-3

Neill Sheridan

SHERIDAN, NEILL RAWLINS (Wild Horse)
B. Nov. 20, 1921, Sacramento, Calif.
BR TR 6'1½" 195 lbs.

	G	AB	H	2B	3B	HR	HR%	R	RBI	BB	SO	SB	BA	SA	PH AB	PH H	G by POS
1948 BOS A	2	1	0	0	0	0	0.0	0	0	0	1	0	.000	.000	1	0	

Pat Sheridan

SHERIDAN, PATRICK ARTHUR
B. Dec. 4, 1957, Ann Arbor, Mich.
BL TR 6'3" 175 lbs.

	G	AB	H	2B	3B	HR	HR%	R	RBI	BB	SO	SB	BA	SA	PH AB	PH H	G by POS
1981 KC A	3	1	0	0	0	0	0.0	0	0	0	1	0	.000	.000	0	0	OF-3
1983	109	333	90	12	2	7	2.1	43	36	20	64	19	.270	.381	19	5	OF-100
1984	138	481	136	24	4	8	1.7	64	53	41	91	19	.283	.399	8	4	OF-134
3 yrs.	250	815	226	36	6	15	1.8	107	89	61	156	31	.277	.391	27	9	OF-237

LEAGUE CHAMPIONSHIP SERIES

	G	AB	H	2B	3B	HR	HR%	R	RBI	BB	SO	SB	BA	SA	PH AB	PH H	G by POS
1984 KC A	3	6	0	0	0	0	0.0	1	0	3	3	0	.000	.000	0	0	OF-3

Red Sheridan

SHERIDAN, EUGENE ANTHONY (Gene)
B. Nov. 14, 1896, Brooklyn, N. Y.   D. Nov. 25, 1975, Queens, N. Y.
BR TR 5'10½" 160 lbs.

	G	AB	H	2B	3B	HR	HR%	R	RBI	BB	SO	SB	BA	SA	PH AB	PH H	G by POS
1918 BKN N	2	4	1	0	0	0	0.0	0	0	1	0	1	.250	.250	0	0	2B-2
1920	3	2	0	0	0	0	0.0	0	0	0	1	0	.000	.000	0	0	SS-3
2 yrs.	5	6	1	0	0	0	0.0	0	0	1	1	1	.167	.167	0	0	SS-3, 2B-2

	G	AB	H	2B	3B	HR	HR %	R	RBI	BB	SO	SB	BA	SA	Pinch Hit AB	Pinch Hit H	G by POS

Ed Sherling

SHERLING, EDWARD CREECH (Shine)
B. July 18, 1897, Coalburg, Ala.   D. Nov. 16, 1965, Enterprise, Ala.
BR TR 6'1" 185 lbs.

	G	AB	H	2B	3B	HR	HR %	R	RBI	BB	SO	SB	BA	SA	AB	H	G by POS
1924 PHI A	4	2	1	1	0	0	0.0	2	0	0	0	0	.500	1.000	2	1	

Monk Sherlock

SHERLOCK, JOHN CLINTON
Brother of Vince Sherlock.
B. Oct. 26, 1904, Buffalo, N. Y.
BR TR 5'10" 175 lbs.

	G	AB	H	2B	3B	HR	HR %	R	RBI	BB	SO	SB	BA	SA	AB	H	G by POS
1930 PHI N	92	299	97	18	2	0	0.0	51	38	27	28	0	.324	.398	15	6	1B-70, 2B-5, OF-1

Vince Sherlock

SHERLOCK, VINCENT THOMAS
Brother of Monk Sherlock.
B. Mar. 27, 1909, Buffalo, N. Y.
BR TR 6' 180 lbs.

	G	AB	H	2B	3B	HR	HR %	R	RBI	BB	SO	SB	BA	SA	AB	H	G by POS
1935 BKN N	9	26	12	1	0	0	0.0	4	6	1	2	1	.462	.500	0	0	2B-8

Dennis Sherrill

SHERRILL, DENNIS LEE
B. Mar. 3, 1956, Miami, Fla.
BR TR 6' 165 lbs.

	G	AB	H	2B	3B	HR	HR %	R	RBI	BB	SO	SB	BA	SA	AB	H	G by POS
1978 NY A	2	1	0	0	0	0	0.0	1	0	0	1	0	.000	.000	0	0	DH-1, 3B-1
1980	3	4	1	0	0	0	0.0	0	0	0	1	0	.250	.250	0	0	SS-2, 2B-1
2 yrs.	5	5	1	0	0	0	0.0	1	0	0	2	0	.200	.200	0	0	SS-2, DH-1, 3B-1, 2B-1

Norm Sherry

SHERRY, NORMAN BURT
Brother of Larry Sherry.
B. July 16, 1931, New York, N. Y.
Manager 1976-77.
BR TR 5'11" 180 lbs.

	G	AB	H	2B	3B	HR	HR %	R	RBI	BB	SO	SB	BA	SA	AB	H	G by POS
1959 LA N	2	3	1	0	0	0	0.0	0	2	0	0	0	.333	.333	0	0	C-2
1960	47	138	39	4	1	8	5.8	22	19	12	29	0	.283	.500	5	1	C-44
1961	47	121	31	2	0	5	4.1	10	21	9	30	0	.256	.397	10	1	C-45
1962	35	88	16	2	0	3	3.4	7	16	6	17	0	.182	.307	1	1	C-34
1963 NY N	63	147	20	1	0	2	1.4	6	11	10	26	1	.136	.184	2	1	C-61
5 yrs.	194	497	107	9	1	18	3.6	45	69	37	102	1	.215	.346	18	4	C-186

Barry Shetrone

SHETRONE, BARRY STEVAN
B. July 6, 1938, Baltimore, Md.
BL TR 6'2" 190 lbs.

	G	AB	H	2B	3B	HR	HR %	R	RBI	BB	SO	SB	BA	SA	AB	H	G by POS
1959 BAL A	33	79	16	1	1	0	0.0	8	5	5	9	3	.203	.241	6	0	OF-23
1960	1	0	0	0	0	0	–	1	0	0	0	0	–	–	0	0	
1961	3	7	1	0	0	0	0.0	0	1	0	2	0	.143	.143	1	0	OF-2
1962	21	24	6	1	0	1	4.2	3	1	0	5	0	.250	.417	12	4	OF-6
1963 WAS A	2	2	0	0	0	0	0.0	0	0	0	0	0	.000	.000	2	0	
5 yrs.	60	112	23	2	1	1	0.9	12	7	5	16	3	.205	.268	21	4	OF-31

John Shetzline

SHETZLINE, JOHN HENRY
B. 1850, Philadelphia, Pa.   D. Dec. 15, 1892, Philadelphia, Pa.
5'11½" 190 lbs.

	G	AB	H	2B	3B	HR	HR %	R	RBI	BB	SO	SB	BA	SA	AB	H	G by POS
1882 BAL AA	73	282	62	8	3	0	0.0	23		5			.220	.270	0	0	3B-52, 2B-20, OF-1, SS-1

Jimmy Shevlin

SHEVLIN, JAMES CORNELIUS
B. July 9, 1909, Cincinnati, Ohio   D. Oct. 30, 1974, Ft. Lauderdale, Fla.
BL TL 5'10½" 155 lbs.

	G	AB	H	2B	3B	HR	HR %	R	RBI	BB	SO	SB	BA	SA	AB	H	G by POS
1930 DET A	28	14	2	0	0	0	0.0	4	2	2	3	0	.143	.143	2	0	1B-25
1932 CIN N	7	24	5	2	0	0	0.0	3	4	4	0	4	.208	.292	0	0	1B-7
1934	18	39	12	2	0	0	0.0	6	6	6	5	0	.308	.359	8	3	1B-10
3 yrs.	53	77	19	4	0	0	0.0	13	12	12	8	4	.247	.299	10	3	1B-42

Pete Shields

SHIELDS, FRANCIS LeROY
B. Sept. 21, 1891, Swiftwater, Miss.   D. Feb. 11, 1961, Jackson, Miss.
BR TR 6' 175 lbs.

	G	AB	H	2B	3B	HR	HR %	R	RBI	BB	SO	SB	BA	SA	AB	H	G by POS
1915 CLE A	23	72	15	6	0	0	0.0	4	6	4	14	3	.208	.292	0	0	1B-23

Jim Shilling

SHILLING, JAMES ROBERT
B. May 14, 1915, Tulsa, Okla.
BR TR 5'11" 175 lbs.

	G	AB	H	2B	3B	HR	HR %	R	RBI	BB	SO	SB	BA	SA	AB	H	G by POS
1939 2 teams		CLE A (31G – .276)			PHI N (11G – .303)												
" total	42	131	37	8	5	0	0.0	11	16	8	13	1	.282	.420	1	0	2B-32, SS-6, 3B-3, OF-1

Ginger Shinault

SHINAULT, ENOCH ERSKINE
B. Sept. 6, 1892, Memphis, Tenn.   D. Dec. 29, 1930, Denver, Colo.
BR TR 5'11" 170 lbs.

	G	AB	H	2B	3B	HR	HR %	R	RBI	BB	SO	SB	BA	SA	AB	H	G by POS
1921 CLE A	22	29	11	1	0	0	0.0	5	3	6	5	1	.379	.414	1	0	C-22
1922	13	15	2	1	0	0	0.0	1	0	0	2	0	.133	.200	2	0	C-11
2 yrs.	35	44	13	2	0	0	0.0	6	3	6	7	1	.295	.341	3	0	C-33

Bill Shindle

SHINDLE, WILLIAM
B. 1860, Gloucester City, N. J.   D. June 3, 1936, Lakeland, N. Y.
BR TR 6' 155 lbs.

	G	AB	H	2B	3B	HR	HR %	R	RBI	BB	SO	SB	BA	SA	AB	H	G by POS
1886 DET N	7	26	7	0	0	0	0.0	4	4	0	5		.269	.269	0	0	SS-7
1887	22	84	24	3	2	0	0.0	17	12	7	10	13	.286	.369	0	0	3B-21, OF-1
1888 BAL AA	135	514	107	14	8	1	0.2	61	53	20	52		.208	.272	0	0	3B-135
1889	138	567	178	24	7	3	0.5	122	64	42	37	56	.314	.397	0	0	3B-138
1890 PHI P	132	584	188	21	21	10	1.7	127	90	40	30	51	.322	.481	0	0	SS-130, 3B-2
1891 PHI N	103	415	87	13	1	0	0.0	68	38	33	39	17	.210	.246	0	0	3B-100, SS-3
1892 BAL N	143	619	156	20	18	3	0.5	100	50	35	34	24	.252	.357	0	0	3B-134, SS-9
1893	125	521	136	22	11	1	0.2	100	75	66	17	17	.261	.351	0	0	3B-125
1894 BKN N	116	476	141	22	9	4	0.8	94	96	29	20	19	.296	.405	0	0	3B-116
1895	118	486	135	22	3	3	0.6	92	69	47	28	17	.278	.354	0	0	3B-116
1896	131	516	144	24	9	1	0.2	75	61	24	20	24	.279	.366	0	0	3B-131
1897	134	542	154	32	6	3	0.6	83	105	35		23	.284	.382	0	0	3B-134
1898	120	466	105	10	3	1	0.2	50	41	10		3	.225	.266	0	0	3B-120
13 yrs.	1424	5816	1562	227	98	30	0.5	993	758	388	240	316	.269	.357	0	0	3B-1272, SS-149, OF-1

	G	AB	H	2B	3B	HR	HR %	R	RBI	BB	SO	SB	BA	SA	Pinch Hit AB	Pinch Hit H	G by POS

Razor Shines

SHINES, RAYMOND ANTHONY   BB TR 6'1"   210 lbs.
B. July 18, 1956, Durham, N. C.

	G	AB	H	2B	3B	HR	HR %	R	RBI	BB	SO	SB	BA	SA	AB	H	G by POS
1983 MON N	3	2	1	0	0	0	0.0	0	0	0	0	0	.500	.500	1	1	OF-1
1984	12	20	6	1	0	0	0.0	0	2	0	3	0	.300	.350	9	2	1B-3, 3B-1
2 yrs.	15	22	7	1	0	0	0.0	0	2	0	3	0	.318	.364	10	3	1B-3, OF-1, 3B-1

Ralph Shinners

SHINNERS, RALPH PETER   BR TR 6'   180 lbs.
B. Oct. 4, 1895, Monches, Wis.   D. July 23, 1962, Milwaukee, Wis.

	G	AB	H	2B	3B	HR	HR %	R	RBI	BB	SO	SB	BA	SA	AB	H	G by POS
1922 NY N	56	135	34	4	2	0	0.0	16	15	5	22	3	.252	.311	12	2	OF-37
1923	13	13	2	1	0	0	0.0	5	0	2	1	0	.154	.231	9	1	OF-6
1925 STL N	74	251	74	9	2	7	2.8	39	36	12	19	8	.295	.430	7	3	OF-66
3 yrs.	163	399	110	14	4	7	1.8	60	51	19	42	11	.276	.383	28	6	OF-109

Tim Shinnick

SHINNICK, TIMOTHY JAMES (Good Eye)   BB TR 6'   150 lbs.
B. Nov. 6, 1867, Exeter, N. H.   D. May 18, 1944, Exeter, N. H.

	G	AB	H	2B	3B	HR	HR %	R	RBI	BB	SO	SB	BA	SA	AB	H	G by POS
1890 LOU AA	133	493	126	16	11	1	0.2	87		62		62	.256	.339	0	0	2B-130, 3B-3
1891	128	443	98	10	11	1	0.2	79	54	54	47	36	.221	.300	0	0	2B-120, 3B-7, SS-1
2 yrs.	261	936	224	26	22	2	0.2	166	53	116	47	98	.239	.321	0	0	2B-250, 3B-10, SS-1

Bill Shipke

SHIPKE, WILLIAM M. (Muskrat Bill)   TR
Born William M. Shipkrethaver.
B. Nov. 18, 1882, St. Louis, Mo.   D. Sept. 10, 1940, Omaha, Neb.

	G	AB	H	2B	3B	HR	HR %	R	RBI	BB	SO	SB	BA	SA	AB	H	G by POS
1906 CLE A	2	6	0	0	0	0	0.0	0	0	0		0	.000	.000	0	0	2B-2
1907 WAS A	64	189	37	3	2	1	0.5	17	9	15		6	.196	.249	1	0	3B-63
1908	111	341	71	7	8	0	0.0	40	20	38		15	.208	.276	0	0	3B-110, 2B-1
1909	9	16	2	1	0	0	0.0	2	0	2		0	.125	.188	0	0	3B-5, SS-1
4 yrs.	186	552	110	11	10	1	0.2	59	29	55		21	.199	.261	1	0	3B-178, 2B-3, SS-1

Art Shires

SHIRES, CHARLES ARTHUR (Art the Great)   BL TR 6'1"   195 lbs.
B. Aug. 13, 1907, Milford, Tex.   D. July 13, 1967, Italy, Tex.

	G	AB	H	2B	3B	HR	HR %	R	RBI	BB	SO	SB	BA	SA	AB	H	G by POS
1928 CHI A	33	123	42	6	1	1	0.8	20	11	13	10	0	.341	.431	1	1	1B-32
1929	100	353	110	20	7	3	0.8	41	41	32		4	.312	.433	9	1	1B-88, 2B-2
1930 2 teams		CHI	A (37G –	.258)		WAS	A (38G –	.369)									
" total	75	212	64	10	1	2	0.9	25	37	11	11	3	.302	.387	19	6	1B-54
1932 BOS N	82	298	71	9	3	5	1.7	32	30	25	21	1	.238	.339	2	0	1B-82
4 yrs.	290	986	287	45	12	11	1.1	118	119	81	62	8	.291	.395	31	8	1B-256, 2B-2

Bart Shirley

SHIRLEY, BARTON ARVIN   BR TR 5'10"   183 lbs.
B. Jan. 4, 1940, Corpus Christi, Tex.

	G	AB	H	2B	3B	HR	HR %	R	RBI	BB	SO	SB	BA	SA	AB	H	G by POS
1964 LA N	18	62	17	1	1	0	0.0	6	7	4	8	0	.274	.323	0	0	3B-10, SS-8
1966	12	5	1	0	0	0	0.0	2	0	0	2	0	.200	.200	4	1	SS-5
1967 NY N	6	12	0	0	0	0	0.0	1	0	0	5	0	.000	.000	2	0	2B-3
1968 LA N	39	83	15	3	0	0	0.0	6	4	10	13	0	.181	.217	1	0	SS-21, 2B-18
4 yrs.	75	162	33	4	1	0	0.0	15	11	14	28	0	.204	.241	7	1	SS-34, 2B-21, 3B-10

Mule Shirley

SHIRLEY, ERNEST RAEFORD   BL TL 5'11"   180 lbs.
B. May 24, 1901, Snow Hill, N. C.   D. Aug. 4, 1955, Goldsboro, N. C.

	G	AB	H	2B	3B	HR	HR %	R	RBI	BB	SO	SB	BA	SA	AB	H	G by POS
1924 WAS A	30	77	18	2	2	0	0.0	12	16	3	7	0	.234	.312	4	2	1B-25, C-1
1925	14	23	3	1	0	0	0.0	2	2	1	7	0	.130	.174	5	1	1B-9
2 yrs.	44	100	21	3	2	0	0.0	14	18	4	14	0	.210	.280	9	3	1B-34, C-1

WORLD SERIES																	
1924 WAS A	3	2	1	0	0	0	0.0	1	1	0	0	0	.500	.500	2	1	

Ivey Shiver

SHIVER, IVEY MERWIN (Chick)   BR TR 6'1½"   190 lbs.
B. Jan. 22, 1906, Sylvester, Ga.   D. Aug. 31, 1972, Savannah, Ga.

	G	AB	H	2B	3B	HR	HR %	R	RBI	BB	SO	SB	BA	SA	AB	H	G by POS
1931 DET A	2	9	1	0	0	0	0.0	2	0	0	3	0	.111	.111	0	0	OF-2
1934 CIN N	19	59	12	1	0	2	3.4	6	6	3	15	1	.203	.322	4	1	OF-15
2 yrs.	21	68	13	1	0	2	2.9	8	6	3	18	1	.191	.294	4	1	OF-17

George Shoch

SHOCH, GEORGE QUINTUS   BR TR
B. Jan. 6, 1859, Philadelphia, Pa.   D. Sept. 30, 1937, Philadelphia, Pa.

	G	AB	H	2B	3B	HR	HR %	R	RBI	BB	SO	SB	BA	SA	AB	H	G by POS
1886 WAS N	26	95	28	2	1	1	1.1	11	18	2	13		.295	.368	0	0	OF-25, SS-1
1887	70	264	63	9	1	1	0.4	47	18	21	16	29	.239	.292	0	0	OF-63, SS-6, 2B-1
1888	90	317	58	6	3	2	0.6	46	24	25	22	23	.183	.240	0	0	SS-52, OF-35, 2B-1, P-1
1889	30	109	26	2	0	0	0.0	12	11	20	5	9	.239	.257	0	0	OF-29, SS-1
1891 C-M AA	34	127	40	7	1	1	0.8	29	16	18	5	12	.315	.409	0	0	SS-25, 3B-9
1892 BAL N	76	308	85	15	3	1	0.3	42	50	24	19	14	.276	.354	0	0	SS-57, OF-12, 3B-7
1893 BKN N	94	327	86	17	1	2	0.6	53	54	48	13	9	.263	.339	0	0	OF-46, 3B-37, SS-11, 2B-3
1894	64	239	77	6	5	1	0.4	47	37	26	6	16	.322	.402	0	0	OF-35, 3B-14, 2B-9, SS-6
1895	61	216	56	9	7	0	0.0	49	29	32	6	7	.259	.366	0	0	OF-39, 2B-13, SS-6, 3B-3
1896	76	250	73	7	4	1	0.4	36	28	33	10	11	.292	.364	1	0	2B-62, OF-10, 3B-3, SS-1
1897	85	284	79	9	2	0	0.0	42	38	49		6	.278	.324	0	0	2B-68, SS-13, OF-4
11 yrs.	706	2536	671	89	28	10	0.4	414	323	298	115	136	.265	.334	1	0	OF-298, SS-179, 2B-157, 3B-73, P-1

Costen Shockley

SHOCKLEY, JOHN COSTEN   BL TL 6'2"   200 lbs.
B. Feb. 8, 1942, Georgetown, Del.

	G	AB	H	2B	3B	HR	HR %	R	RBI	BB	SO	SB	BA	SA	AB	H	G by POS
1964 PHI N	11	35	8	0	0	1	2.9	4	2	2	8	0	.229	.314	2	0	1B-9
1965 CAL A	40	107	20	2	0	2	1.9	5	17	9	16	0	.187	.262	6	1	1B-31, OF-1
2 yrs.	51	142	28	2	0	3	2.1	9	19	11	24	0	.197	.275	8	1	1B-40, OF-1

Charlie Shoemaker

SHOEMAKER, CHARLES LANDIS   BL TR 5'10"   155 lbs.
B. Aug. 10, 1939, Los Angeles, Calif.

	G	AB	H	2B	3B	HR	HR %	R	RBI	BB	SO	SB	BA	SA	AB	H	G by POS
1961 KC A	7	26	10	2	0	0	0.0	5	1	2	2	0	.385	.462	1	0	2B-6
1962	5	11	2	0	0	0	0.0	1	0	0	2	0	.182	.182	1	0	2B-4

	G	AB	H	2B	3B	HR	HR %	R	RBI	BB	SO	SB	BA	SA	Pinch Hit AB	Pinch Hit H	G by POS

Charlie Shoemaker continued

	G	AB	H	2B	3B	HR	HR %	R	RBI	BB	SO	SB	BA	SA	AB	H	G by POS
1964	16	52	11	2	2	0	0.0	6	3	0	9	0	.212	.327	1	0	2B-14
3 yrs.	28	89	23	4	2	0	0.0	12	4	2	13	0	.258	.348	3	0	2B-24

Strick Shofner

SHOFNER, FRANK STRICKLAND
B. July 23, 1920, Crawford, Tex.   BL TR 5'10½" 187 lbs.

	G	AB	H	2B	3B	HR	HR %	R	RBI	BB	SO	SB	BA	SA	AB	H	G by POS
1947 BOS A	5	13	2	0	1	0	0.0	1	0	0	3	0	.154	.308	1	0	3B-4

Eddie Shokes

SHOKES, EDWARD CHRISTOPHER
B. Jan. 27, 1920, Charleston, S. C.   BL TL 6' 170 lbs.

	G	AB	H	2B	3B	HR	HR %	R	RBI	BB	SO	SB	BA	SA	AB	H	G by POS
1941 CIN N	1	1	0	0	0	0	0.0	0	0	0	1	0	.000	.000	1	0	
1946	31	83	10	1	0	0	0.0	3	5	18	21	1	.120	.133	1	0	1B-29
2 yrs.	32	84	10	1	0	0	0.0	3	5	18	22	1	.119	.131	2	0	1B-29

Ray Shook

SHOOK, RAYMOND CURTIS
B. Nov. 18, 1890, Perry, Ohio   D. Sept. 16, 1970, South Bend, Ind.   BR TR 5'7½" 155 lbs.

	G	AB	H	2B	3B	HR	HR %	R	RBI	BB	SO	SB	BA	SA	AB	H	G by POS
1916 CHI A	1	0	0	0	0	0	–	0	0	0	0	0	–	–	0	0	

Ron Shoop

SHOOP, RONALD LEE
B. Sept. 19, 1931, Rural Valley, Pa.   BR TR 5'11" 180 lbs.

	G	AB	H	2B	3B	HR	HR %	R	RBI	BB	SO	SB	BA	SA	AB	H	G by POS
1959 DET A	3	7	1	0	0	0	0.0	1	1	0	1	0	.143	.143	0	0	C-3

Tom Shopay

SHOPAY, THOMAS MICHAEL
B. Feb. 21, 1945, Bristol, Conn.   BL TR 5'9½" 160 lbs.

	G	AB	H	2B	3B	HR	HR %	R	RBI	BB	SO	SB	BA	SA	AB	H	G by POS
1967 NY A	8	27	8	1	0	2	7.4	2	6	1	5	2	.296	.556	1	0	OF-7
1969	28	48	4	0	1	0	0.0	2	0	2	10	0	.083	.125	13	2	OF-11
1971 BAL A	47	74	19	2	0	0	0.0	10	5	3	7	2	.257	.284	30	8	OF-13
1972	49	40	9	0	0	0	0.0	3	2	5	12	0	.225	.225	32	7	OF-3
1975	40	31	5	1	0	0	0.0	4	2	4	7	3	.161	.194	11	2	OF-13, DH-3, C-1
1976	14	20	4	0	0	0	0.0	4	1	3	3	1	.200	.200	4	1	OF-11, C-1
1977	67	69	13	3	0	1	1.4	15	4	8	7	3	.188	.275	10	2	OF-52, DH-2
7 yrs.	253	309	62	7	1	3	1.0	40	20	26	51	11	.201	.259	101	22	OF-110, DH-5, C-2
WORLD SERIES																	
1971 BAL A	5	4	0	0	0	0	0.0	0	0	0	0	0	.000	.000	4	0	

Dave Short

SHORT, DAVID ORVIS
B. May 11, 1917, Magnolia, Ark.   D. Nov. 22, 1983, Shreveport, La.   BL TR 5'11½" 162 lbs.

	G	AB	H	2B	3B	HR	HR %	R	RBI	BB	SO	SB	BA	SA	AB	H	G by POS
1940 CHI A	4	3	1	0	0	0	0.0	1	0	1	2	0	.333	.333	3	1	
1941	3	8	0	0	0	0	0.0	0	0	2	1	0	.000	.000	1	0	OF-2
2 yrs.	7	11	1	0	0	0	0.0	1	0	3	3	0	.091	.091	4	1	OF-2

Chick Shorten

SHORTEN, CHARLES HENRY
B. Apr. 19, 1892, Scranton, Pa.   D. Oct. 23, 1965, Scranton, Pa.   BL TL 6' 175 lbs.

	G	AB	H	2B	3B	HR	HR %	R	RBI	BB	SO	SB	BA	SA	AB	H	G by POS
1915 BOS A	6	14	3	1	0	0	0.0	1	0	0	2	0	.214	.286	1	0	OF-5
1916	53	112	33	2	1	0	0.0	14	11	10	8	1	.295	.330	17	3	OF-33
1917	69	168	30	4	2	0	0.0	12	16	10	10	2	.179	.226	24	5	OF-43
1919 DET A	95	270	85	9	3	0	0.0	37	22	22	13	5	.315	.370	19	5	OF-75
1920	116	364	105	9	6	1	0.3	35	40	28	14	5	.288	.354	15	5	OF-99
1921	92	217	59	11	3	0	0.0	33	23	20	11	2	.272	.350	37	9	OF-52, C-1
1922 STL A	55	131	36	12	5	2	1.5	22	16	16	8	0	.275	.489	20	5	OF-32
1924 CIN N	41	69	19	3	0	0	0.0	7	6	4	2	0	.275	.319	21	6	OF-15
8 yrs.	527	1345	370	51	20	3	0.2	161	134	110	68	12	.275	.349	154	38	OF-354, C-1
WORLD SERIES																	
1916 BOS A	2	7	4	0	0	0	0.0	0	2	0	1	0	.571	.571	0	0	OF-2

Burt Shotton

SHOTTON, BURTON EDWIN (Barney)
B. Oct. 18, 1884, Brownhelm, Ohio   D. July 29, 1962, Lake Wales, Fla.   BL TR 5'11" 175 lbs.
Manager 1928-34, 1947-50.

	G	AB	H	2B	3B	HR	HR %	R	RBI	BB	SO	SB	BA	SA	AB	H	G by POS
1909 STL A	17	61	16	0	1	0	0.0	5		5			3	.262	.295	0	0	OF-17
1911	139	572	146	11	8	0	0.0	85	36	51		26	.255	.302	0	0	OF-139
1912	154	580	168	15	8	2	0.3	87	40	86		35	.290	.353	0	0	OF-154
1913	147	549	163	23	8	1	0.2	105	28	99	63	43	.297	.373	1	0	OF-146
1914	154	579	156	19	9	0	0.0	82	38	64	66	40	.269	.333	2	0	OF-152
1915	156	559	158	18	11	1	0.2	93	30	118	62	43	.283	.360	2	0	OF-154
1916	157	618	174	23	6	1	0.2	97	36	111	67	41	.282	.343	0	0	OF-157
1917	118	398	89	9	1	1	0.3	47	20	62	47	16	.224	.259	5	0	OF-107
1918 WAS A	126	505	132	16	7	0	0.0	68	21	67	28	25	.261	.321	3	1	OF-122
1919 STL N	85	270	77	13	5	1	0.4	35	20	22	25	17	.285	.381	14	1	OF-67
1920	62	180	41	5	0	1	0.6	28	12	18	14	5	.228	.272	7	1	OF-51
1921	38	48	12	1	1	1	2.1	9	7	7	4	0	.250	.375	22	7	OF-11
1922	34	30	6	1	0	0	0.0	5	2	4	6	0	.200	.233	26	5	OF-3
1923	1	0	0	0	0	0	–	1	0	0		0	–	–	0	0	
14 yrs.	1388	4949	1338	154	65	9	0.2	747	290	714	382	294	.270	.333	82	15	OF-1280

John Shoupe

SHOUPE, JOHN F.
B. Sept. 30, 1851, Cincinnati, Ohio   D. Feb. 13, 1920, Cincinnati, Ohio   BL TR 5'7" 140 lbs.

	G	AB	H	2B	3B	HR	HR %	R	RBI	BB	SO	SB	BA	SA	AB	H	G by POS
1879 TRO N	11	44	4	0	0	0	0.0	5	1	0	3		.091	.091	0	0	SS-10, 2B-1
1882 STL AA	2	7	0	0	0	0	0.0	1		0			.000	.000	0	0	2B-2
1884 WAS U	1	4	3	0	0	0	0.0	1		0			.750	.750	0	0	OF-1
3 yrs.	14	55	7	0	0	0	0.0	7	1	0	3		.127	.127	0	0	SS-10, 2B-3, OF-1

	G	AB	H	2B	3B	HR	HR %	R	RBI	BB	SO	SB	BA	SA	Pinch Hit AB	Pinch Hit H	G by POS

John Shovlin

SHOVLIN, JOHN JOSEPH (Brode)   BR TR 5'7"   163 lbs.
B. Jan. 14, 1891, Drifton, Pa.   D. Feb. 16, 1976, Bethesda, Md.

	G	AB	H	2B	3B	HR	HR %	R	RBI	BB	SO	SB	BA	SA	PH AB	PH H	G by POS
1911 PIT N	2	1	0	0	0	0	0.0	1	0	0	1	0	.000	.000	1	0	
1919 STL A	9	35	7	0	0	0	0.0	4	1	5	2	0	.200	.200	0	0	2B-9
1920	7	7	2	0	0	0	0.0	2	2	0	0	0	.286	.286	2	0	SS-5
3 yrs.	18	43	9	0	0	0	0.0	7	3	5	3	0	.209	.209	3	0	2B-9, SS-5

George Shuba

SHUBA, GEORGE THOMAS (Shotgun)   BL TR 5'11"   180 lbs.
B. Dec. 13, 1924, Youngstown, Ohio

	G	AB	H	2B	3B	HR	HR %	R	RBI	BB	SO	SB	BA	SA	PH AB	PH H	G by POS
1948 BKN N	63	161	43	6	0	4	2.5	21	32	34	31	1	.267	.379	6	2	OF-56
1949	1	1	0	0	0	0	0.0	0	0	0	0	0	.000	.000	1	0	
1950	34	111	23	8	2	3	2.7	15	12	13	22	2	.207	.396	5	1	OF-27
1952	94	256	78	12	1	9	3.5	40	40	38	29	1	.305	.465	25	8	OF-67
1953	74	169	43	12	1	5	3.0	19	23	17	20	1	.254	.426	29	7	OF-44
1954	45	65	10	5	0	2	3.1	3	10	7	10	0	.154	.323	30	4	OF-13
1955	44	51	14	2	0	1	2.0	8	8	11	10	0	.275	.373	29	11	OF-9
7 yrs.	355	814	211	45	4	24	2.9	106	125	120	122	5	.259	.413	125	33	OF-216

WORLD SERIES

	G	AB	H	2B	3B	HR	HR %	R	RBI	BB	SO	SB	BA	SA	PH AB	PH H	G by POS
1952 BKN N	4	10	3	1	0	0	0.0	0	0	0	4	0	.300	.400	1	0	OF-3
1953	2	1	1	0	0	1	0.0	1	2	0	0	0	1.000	4.000	1	1	
1955	1	1	0	0	0	0	0.0	0	0	0	0	0	.000	.000	1	0	
3 yrs.	7	12	4	1	0	1	8.3	1	2	0	4	0	.333	.667	3	1	OF-3

Frank Shugart

SHUGART, FRANK H.   BR TR 5'8"   170 lbs.
Born Frank H. Shugarts.
B. Dec. 10, 1866, Luthersburg, Pa.   D. Sept. 9, 1944, Clearfield, Pa.

	G	AB	H	2B	3B	HR	HR %	R	RBI	BB	SO	SB	BA	SA	PH AB	PH H	G by POS
1890 CHI P	29	106	20	5	5	0	0.0	8	15	5	13	5	.189	.330	0	0	SS-25, OF-5
1891 PIT N	75	320	88	19	8	2	0.6	57	33	20	26	21	.275	.403	0	0	SS-75
1892	137	554	148	19	14	0	0.0	94	62	47	48	28	.267	.352	0	0	SS-134, C-2, OF-1
1893 2 teams		PIT	N	(52G –	.262)		STL	N	(59G –	.280)							
" total	111	456	124	17	7	1	0.2	78	60	41	25	25	.272	.346	0	0	SS-74, OF-29, 3B-9
1894 STL N	133	527	154	19	18	7	1.3	103	72	38	37	21	.292	.436	0	0	OF-122, SS-7, 3B-7
1895 LOU N	113	473	125	14	13	4	0.8	61	70	31	25	14	.264	.374	0	0	SS-88, OF-27
1897 PHI N	40	163	41	8	2	5	3.1	20	25	8		5	.252	.417	0	0	SS-40
1901 CHI A	107	415	104	9	12	2	0.5	62	47	28		12	.251	.345	0	0	SS-107
8 yrs.	745	3014	804	110	79	21	0.7	483	384	218	174	131	.267	.377	0	0	SS-550, OF-184, 3B-16, C-2

Vince Shupe

SHUPE, VINCENT WILLIAM   BL TL 5'11"   180 lbs.
B. Sept. 5, 1921, East Canton, Ohio   D. Apr. 5, 1962, Canton, Ohio

	G	AB	H	2B	3B	HR	HR %	R	RBI	BB	SO	SB	BA	SA	PH AB	PH H	G by POS
1945 BOS N	78	283	76	8	0	0	0.0	22	15	17	16	3	.269	.297	1	1	1B-77

Eddie Sicking

SICKING, EDWARD JOSEPH   BB TR 5'9½"   165 lbs.
B. Mar. 30, 1897, St. Bernard, Ohio   D. Aug. 30, 1978, Cincinnati, Ohio

	G	AB	H	2B	3B	HR	HR %	R	RBI	BB	SO	SB	BA	SA	PH AB	PH H	G by POS
1916 CHI N	1	1	0	0	0	0	0.0	0	0	0	0	0	.000	.000	1	0	
1918 NY N	46	132	33	4	0	0	0.0	9	12	6	11	2	.250	.280	3	0	3B-24, 2B-18, SS-2
1919 2 teams		NY	N	(6G –	.333)		PHI	N	(61G –	.216)							
" total	67	200	45	2	1	0	0.0	18	18	9	17	4	.225	.245	3	0	SS-41, 2B-21
1920 2 teams		NY	N	(46G –	.172)		CIN	N	(37G –	.268)							
" total	83	257	56	6	4	0	0.0	23	26	23	15	8	.218	.249	1	0	2B-40, 3B-30, SS-12
1927 PIT N	6	7	1	1	0	0	0.0	1	3	1	0	0	.143	.286	0	0	2B-5
5 yrs.	203	597	135	13	2	0	0.0	51	59	39	43	14	.226	.255	8	0	2B-84, SS-55, 3B-54

Norm Siebern

SIEBERN, NORMAN LEROY   BL TR 6'2"   200 lbs.
B. July 26, 1933, St. Louis, Mo.

	G	AB	H	2B	3B	HR	HR %	R	RBI	BB	SO	SB	BA	SA	PH AB	PH H	G by POS
1956 NY A	54	162	33	1	4	4	2.5	27	21	19	38	1	.204	.333	6	0	OF-51
1958	136	460	138	19	5	14	3.0	79	55	66	87	5	.300	.454	2	1	OF-133
1959	120	380	103	17	0	11	2.9	52	53	41	71	3	.271	.403	20	9	OF-93, 1B-2
1960 KC A	144	520	145	31	6	19	3.7	69	69	72	68	0	.279	.471	4	1	OF-75, 1B-69
1961	153	560	166	36	5	18	3.2	68	98	82	92	2	.296	.475	2	0	1B-109, OF-47
1962	162	600	185	25	6	25	4.2	114	117	110	88	3	.308	.495	0	0	1B-162
1963	152	556	151	25	2	16	2.9	80	83	79	82	1	.272	.410	5	2	1B-131, OF-16
1964 BAL A	150	478	117	24	2	12	2.5	92	56	106	87	2	.245	.379	6	0	1B-149
1965	106	297	76	13	4	8	2.7	44	32	50	49	1	.256	.407	28	2	1B-76
1966 CAL A	125	336	83	14	1	5	1.5	29	41	63	61	0	.247	.339	23	6	1B-99
1967 2 teams		SF	N	(46G –	.155)		BOS	A	(33G –	.205)							
" total	79	102	18	1	3	0	0.0	8	11	20	21	0	.176	.245	45	7	1B-28, OF-3
1968 BOS A	27	30	2	0	0	0	0.0	0	0	0	5	0	.067	.067	24	1	OF-2, 1B-2
12 yrs.	1408	4481	1217	206	38	132	2.9	662	636	708	749	18	.272	.423	165	29	1B-827, OF-420

WORLD SERIES

	G	AB	H	2B	3B	HR	HR %	R	RBI	BB	SO	SB	BA	SA	PH AB	PH H	G by POS
1956 NY A	1	1	0	0	0	0	0.0	0	0	0	0	0	.000	.000	1	0	
1958	3	8	1	0	0	0	0.0	1	0	3	2	0	.125	.125	0	0	OF-3
1967 BOS A	3	3	1	0	0	0	0.0	0	1	0	0	0	.333	.333	2	0	OF-1
3 yrs.	7	12	2	0	0	0	0.0	1	1	3	2	0	.167	.167	3	0	OF-4

Dick Siebert

SIEBERT, RICHARD WALTHER   BL TL 6'   170 lbs.
Father of Paul Siebert.
B. Feb. 19, 1912, Fall River, Mass.   D. Nov. 9, 1978, Minneapolis, Minn.

	G	AB	H	2B	3B	HR	HR %	R	RBI	BB	SO	SB	BA	SA	PH AB	PH H	G by POS
1932 BKN N	6	7	2	0	0	0	0.0	1	0	2	2	0	.286	.286	3	1	1B-6
1936	2	0	0	0	0	0	0.0	0	0	0	0	0	.000	.000	1	0	OF-1
1937 STL N	22	38	7	2	0	0	0.0	3	2	4	8	1	.184	.237	13	3	1B-7
1938 2 teams		STL	N	(1G –	1.000)		PHI	A	(48G –	.284)							
" total	49	195	56	8	3	0	0.0	24	28	10	9	2	.287	.359	3	2	1B-46
1939 PHI A	101	402	118	28	3	6	1.5	58	47	21	22	4	.294	.423	2	0	1B-99
1940	154	595	170	31	6	5	0.8	69	77	33	34	8	.286	.383	0	0	1B-154
1941	123	467	156	28	8	5	1.1	63	79	37	22	1	.334	.460	0	0	1B-123
1942	153	612	159	25	7	2	0.3	57	74	24	17	4	.260	.333	0	0	1B-152
1943	146	558	140	26	7	1	0.2	50	72	33	21	6	.251	.328	1	0	1B-145

	G	AB	H	2B	3B	HR	HR %	R	RBI	BB	SO	SB	BA	SA	Pinch Hit AB	Pinch Hit H	G by POS

Dick Siebert continued

	G	AB	H	2B	3B	HR	HR%	R	RBI	BB	SO	SB	BA	SA	AB	H	G by POS
1944	132	468	143	27	5	6	1.3	52	52	62	17	2	.306	.423	0	0	1B-74, OF-58
1945	147	573	153	29	1	7	1.2	62	51	50	33	2	.267	.358	0	0	1B-147
11 yrs.	1035	3917	1104	204	40	32	0.8	439	482	276	185	30	.282	.379	23	6	1B-953, OF-59

Fred Siefke

SIEFKE, FREDERICK EDWIN
B. Mar. 27, 1870, New York, N. Y.   D. Apr. 18, 1893, New York, N. Y.

	G	AB	H	2B	3B	HR	HR%	R	RBI	BB	SO	SB	BA	SA	AB	H	G by POS
1890 B-B AA	16	58	8	2	0	0	0.0	1		5		2	.138	.172	0	0	3B-16

John Siegel

SIEGEL, JOHN
B. York, Pa.   Deceased.

	G	AB	H	2B	3B	HR	HR%	R	RBI	BB	SO	SB	BA	SA	AB	H	G by POS
1884 PHI U	8	31	7	2	0	0	0.0	4		1			.226	.290	0	0	3B-8

Johnny Siegle

SIEGLE, JOHN HERBERT   BR TR 5'10"   165 lbs.
B. July 8, 1874, Columbus, Ohio   D. Feb. 12, 1968, Urbana, Ohio

	G	AB	H	2B	3B	HR	HR%	R	RBI	BB	SO	SB	BA	SA	AB	H	G by POS
1905 CIN N	17	56	17	1	2	1	1.8	9	8	7		0	.304	.446	1	1	OF-16
1906	22	68	8	2	2	0	0.0	4	7	3		0	.118	.206	1	0	OF-21
2 yrs.	39	124	25	3	4	1	0.8	13	15	10		0	.202	.315	2	1	OF-37

Oscar Siemer

SIEMER, OSCAR SYLVESTER (Cotton)   BR TR 5'9"   162 lbs.
B. Aug. 14, 1901, St. Louis, Mo.   D. Dec. 5, 1959, St. Louis, Mo.

	G	AB	H	2B	3B	HR	HR%	R	RBI	BB	SO	SB	BA	SA	AB	H	G by POS
1925 BOS N	16	46	14	0	1	1	2.2	5	6	1	0	0	.304	.413	0	0	C-16
1926	31	73	15	1	0	0	0.0	3	5	2	7	0	.205	.219	1	0	C-30
2 yrs.	47	119	29	1	1	1	0.8	8	11	3	7	0	.244	.294	1	0	C-46

Roy Sievers

SIEVERS, ROY EDWARD (Squirrel)   BR TR 6'1"   195 lbs.
B. Nov. 18, 1926, St. Louis, Mo.

	G	AB	H	2B	3B	HR	HR%	R	RBI	BB	SO	SB	BA	SA	AB	H	G by POS
1949 STL A	140	471	144	28	4	16	3.4	84	91	70	75	1	.306	.471	7	2	OF-125, 3B-7
1950	113	370	88	20	4	10	2.7	46	57	34	42	1	.238	.395	15	2	OF-78, 3B-21
1951	31	89	20	2	1	1	1.1	10	11	9	21	0	.225	.303	8	1	OF-25
1952	11	30	6	3	0	0	0.0	3	5	1	4	0	.200	.300	5	0	1B-7
1953	92	285	77	15	0	8	2.8	37	35	32	47	0	.270	.407	17	3	1B-76
1954 WAS A	145	514	119	26	6	24	4.7	75	102	80	77	2	.232	.446	5	0	OF-133, 1B-8
1955	144	509	138	20	8	25	4.9	74	106	73	66	1	.271	.489	2	0	OF-129, 1B-17, 3B-2
1956	152	550	139	27	2	29	5.3	92	95	100	88	0	.253	.467	0	0	OF-78, 1B-76
1957	152	572	172	23	5	42	7.3	99	114	76	55	1	.301	.579	2	2	OF-130, 1B-21
1958	148	550	162	18	1	39	7.1	85	108	53	63	3	.295	.544	4	1	OF-114, 1B-33
1959	115	385	93	19	0	21	5.5	55	49	53	62	1	.242	.455	7	1	1B-93, OF-13
1960 CHI A	127	444	131	22	0	28	6.3	87	93	74	69	1	.295	.534	9	1	1B-114, OF-6
1961	141	492	145	26	6	27	5.5	76	92	61	62	1	.295	.537	10	4	1B-132
1962 PHI N	144	477	125	19	5	21	4.4	61	80	56	80	2	.262	.455	12	1	1B-130, OF-7
1963	138	450	108	19	2	19	4.2	46	82	43	72	0	.240	.418	18	6	1B-126
1964 2 teams	PHI	N (49G –	.183)			WAS	A	(33G –	.172)								
" total	82	178	32	4	1	8	4.5	12	27	22	34	0	.180	.348	29	6	1B-48
1965 WAS A	12	21	4	1	0	0	0.0	3	0	4	3	0	.190	.238	4	1	1B-7
17 yrs.	1887	6387	1703	292	42	318	5.0	945	1147	841	920	14	.267	.475	154	31	1B-888, OF-838, 3B-30

Frank Siffel

SIFFEL, FRANK
B. 1860, Germany   D. Oct. 26, 1909, Philadelphia, Pa.

	G	AB	H	2B	3B	HR	HR%	R	RBI	BB	SO	SB	BA	SA	AB	H	G by POS
1884 PHI AA	7	17	3	1	0	0	0.0	3		0			.176	.235	0	0	C-7
1885	3	10	1	0	0	0	0.0	0		0			.100	.100	0	0	C-2, OF-1
2 yrs.	10	27	4	1	0	0	0.0	3		0			.148	.185	0	0	C-9, OF-1

Frank Sigafoos

SIGAFOOS, FRANCIS LEONARD   BR TR 5'9"   170 lbs.
B. Mar. 21, 1904, Easton, Pa.   D. Apr. 12, 1968, Indianapolis, Ind.

	G	AB	H	2B	3B	HR	HR%	R	RBI	BB	SO	SB	BA	SA	AB	H	G by POS
1926 PHI A	13	43	11	0	0	0	0.0	4	2	0	3	0	.256	.256	1	0	SS-12
1929 2 teams	DET	A	(14G –	.174)			CHI	A	(7G –	.333)							
" total	21	26	5	1	0	0	0.0	4	3	7	5	0	.192	.231	1	0	3B-6, 2B-6, SS-5
1931 CIN N	21	65	11	2	0	0	0.0	6	8	0	6	0	.169	.200	4	1	3B-15, SS-2
3 yrs.	55	134	27	3	0	0	0.0	14	13	7	14	0	.201	.224	6	1	3B-21, SS-19, 2B-6

Paddy Siglin

SIGLIN, WESLEY PETER   BR TR 5'10"   160 lbs.
B. Sept. 24, 1891, Aurelia, Iowa   D. Aug. 5, 1956, Oakland, Calif.

	G	AB	H	2B	3B	HR	HR%	R	RBI	BB	SO	SB	BA	SA	AB	H	G by POS
1914 PIT N	14	39	6	0	0	0	0.0	4	2	4	6	1	.154	.154	3	1	2B-11
1915	6	7	2	0	0	0	0.0	1	0	1	2	1	.286	.286	3	0	2B-1
1916	3	4	1	0	0	0	0.0	0	0	0	2	0	.250	.250	0	0	2B-3
3 yrs.	23	50	9	0	0	0	0.0	5	2	5	10	2	.180	.180	6	1	2B-15

Tripp Sigman

SIGMAN, WESLEY TRIPLETT   BL TR 6'   180 lbs.
B. Jan. 17, 1899, Mooresville, N. C.   D. Mar. 8, 1971, Augusta, Ga.

	G	AB	H	2B	3B	HR	HR%	R	RBI	BB	SO	SB	BA	SA	AB	H	G by POS
1929 PHI N	10	29	15	1	0	2	6.9	8	9	3	1	0	.517	.759	0	0	OF-10
1930	52	100	27	4	1	4	4.0	15	6	6	9	1	.270	.450	32	8	OF-19
2 yrs.	62	129	42	5	1	6	4.7	23	15	9	10	1	.326	.519	32	8	OF-29

Eddie Silber

SILBER, EDWARD JAMES   BR TR 5'11"   170 lbs.
B. June 6, 1914, Philadelphia, Pa.   D. Oct. 26, 1976, Dunedin, Fla.

	G	AB	H	2B	3B	HR	HR%	R	RBI	BB	SO	SB	BA	SA	AB	H	G by POS
1937 STL A	22	83	26	2	0	0	0.0	10	4	5	13	0	.313	.337	1	1	OF-21
1939	1	1	0	0	0	0	0.0	0	0	0	1	0	.000	.000	1	0	
2 yrs.	23	84	26	2	0	0	0.0	10	4	5	14	0	.310	.333	2	1	OF-21

Ed Silch

SILCH, EDWARD (Baldy)   TR
B. Feb. 22, 1865, St. Louis, Mo.   D. Jan. 15, 1895, St. Louis, Mo.

	G	AB	H	2B	3B	HR	HR%	R	RBI	BB	SO	SB	BA	SA	AB	H	G by POS
1888 BKN AA	14	48	13	4	0	0	0.0	5	3	4		4	.271	.354	0	0	OF-14

	G	AB	H	2B	3B	HR	HR%	R	RBI	BB	SO	SB	BA	SA	Pinch Hit AB	H	G by POS

Danny Silva

SILVA, DANIEL JAMES BR TR 6' 170 lbs.
B. Oct. 5, 1896, Everett, Mass.   D. Apr. 4, 1974, Hyannis, Mass.

	G	AB	H	2B	3B	HR	HR%	R	RBI	BB	SO	SB	BA	SA	AB	H	G by POS
1919 WAS A	1	4	1	0	0	0	0.0	0	0	0	0	0	.250	.250	0	0	3B-1

Al Silvera

SILVERA, AARON ALBERT BR TR 6' 180 lbs.
B. Aug. 26, 1935, San Diego, Calif.

	G	AB	H	2B	3B	HR	HR%	R	RBI	BB	SO	SB	BA	SA	AB	H	G by POS
1955 CIN N	13	7	1	0	0	0	0.0	3	2	0	1	0	.143	.143	6	1	OF-1
1956	1	0	0	0	0	0	–	0	0	0	0	0	–	–	0	0	
2 yrs.	14	7	1	0	0	0	0.0	3	2	0	1	0	.143	.143	6	1	OF-1

Charlie Silvera

SILVERA, CHARLES ANTHONY RYAN (Swede) BR TR 5'10" 175 lbs.
B. Oct. 13, 1924, San Francisco, Calif.

	G	AB	H	2B	3B	HR	HR%	R	RBI	BB	SO	SB	BA	SA	AB	H	G by POS
1948 NY A	4	14	8	0	0	0	0.0	1	1	0	1	0	.571	.714	0	0	C-4
1949	58	130	41	2	0	0	0.0	8	13	18	5	2	.315	.331	6	3	C-51
1950	18	25	4	0	0	0	0.0	2	1	1	2	0	.160	.160	3	1	C-15
1951	18	51	14	3	0	1	2.0	5	7	5	3	0	.275	.392	0	0	C-18
1952	20	55	18	3	0	0	0.0	4	11	5	2	0	.327	.382	0	0	C-20
1953	42	82	23	3	1	0	0.0	11	12	9	5	0	.280	.341	2	1	C-39, 3B-1
1954	20	37	10	1	0	0	0.0	1	4	3	2	0	.270	.297	2	0	C-18
1955	14	26	5	0	0	0	0.0	1	1	6	4	0	.192	.192	2	0	C-11
1956	7	9	2	0	0	0	0.0	0	0	2	3	0	.222	.222	0	0	C-7
1957 CHI N	26	53	11	3	0	0	0.0	1	2	4	5	0	.208	.264	0	0	C-26
10 yrs.	227	482	136	15	2	1	0.2	34	52	53	32	2	.282	.328	15	5	C-209, 3B-1

WORLD SERIES
| 1949 NY A | 1 | 2 | 0 | 0 | 0 | 0 | 0.0 | 0 | 0 | 0 | 0 | 0 | .000 | .000 | 0 | 0 | C-1 |

Luis Silverio

SILVERIO, LUIS PASCUAL BR TR 5'11" 165 lbs.
B. Dec. 23, 1956, Santiago, Dominican Republic

	G	AB	H	2B	3B	HR	HR%	R	RBI	BB	SO	SB	BA	SA	AB	H	G by POS
1978 KC A	8	11	6	2	1	0	0.0	7	3	2	3	1	.545	.909	0	0	OF-6, DH-2

Tom Silverio

SILVERIO, TOMAS ROBERTO BL TL 5'10" 170 lbs.
B. Oct. 14, 1945, Santiago, Dominican Republic

	G	AB	H	2B	3B	HR	HR%	R	RBI	BB	SO	SB	BA	SA	AB	H	G by POS
1970 CAL A	15	15	0	0	0	0	0.0	1	0	2	4	0	.000	.000	10	0	OF-5, 1B-1
1971	3	3	1	0	0	0	0.0	0	0	0	0	0	.333	.333	3	1	OF-1
1972	13	12	2	0	0	0	0.0	1	0	0	5	0	.167	.167	7	1	OF-4
3 yrs.	31	30	3	0	0	0	0.0	2	0	2	9	0	.100	.100	20	2	OF-10, 1B-1

Ken Silvestri

SILVESTRI, KENNETH JOSEPH (Hawk) BB TR 6'1" 200 lbs.
B. May 3, 1916, Chicago, Ill.
Manager 1967.

	G	AB	H	2B	3B	HR	HR%	R	RBI	BB	SO	SB	BA	SA	AB	H	G by POS
1939 CHI A	22	75	13	3	0	2	2.7	6	5	6	13	0	.173	.293	2	1	C-20
1940	28	24	6	2	0	2	8.3	5	10	4	7	0	.250	.583	24	6	C-1
1941 NY A	17	40	10	5	0	1	2.5	6	4	7	6	0	.250	.450	3	0	C-13
1946	13	21	6	1	0	0	0.0	4	1	3	7	0	.286	.333	1	0	C-12
1947	3	10	2	0	0	0	0.0	0	0	2	2	0	.200	.200	0	0	C-3
1949 PHI N	4	4	0	0	0	0	0.0	1	0	2	1	0	.000	.000	2	0	SS-1, 2B-1, C-1
1950	11	20	5	0	1	0	0.0	2	4	4	3	0	.250	.350	2	1	C-9
1951	4	9	2	0	0	0	0.0	2	1	3	2	0	.222	.222	0	0	C-3
8 yrs.	102	203	44	11	1	5	2.5	26	25	31	41	0	.217	.355	34	8	C-62, SS-1, 2B-1

WORLD SERIES
| 1950 PHI N | 1 | 0 | 0 | 0 | 0 | 0 | – | 0 | 0 | 0 | 0 | 0 | – | – | 0 | 0 | C-1 |

Al Simmons

SIMMONS, ALOYSIUS HARRY (Bucketfoot Al) BR TR 5'11" 190 lbs.
Born Alois Szymanski.
B. May 22, 1902, Milwaukee, Wis.   D. May 26, 1956, Milwaukee, Wis.
Hall of Fame 1953.

	G	AB	H	2B	3B	HR	HR%	R	RBI	BB	SO	SB	BA	SA	AB	H	G by POS
1924 PHI A	152	594	183	31	9	8	1.3	69	102	30	60	16	.308	.431	0	0	OF-152
1925	153	658	253	43	12	24	3.6	122	129	35	41	7	.384	.596	0	0	OF-153
1926	147	581	199	53	10	19	3.3	90	109	48	49	10	.343	.566	0	0	OF-147
1927	106	406	159	36	11	15	3.7	86	108	31	30	10	.392	.645	0	0	OF-105
1928	119	464	163	33	9	15	3.2	78	107	31	30	1	.351	.558	3	2	OF-114
1929	143	581	212	41	9	34	5.9	114	157	31	38	4	.365	.642	0	0	OF-142
1930	138	554	211	41	16	36	6.5	152	165	39	34	9	.381	.708	2	1	OF-136
1931	128	513	200	37	13	22	4.3	105	128	47	45	3	.390	.641	0	0	OF-128
1932	154	670	216	28	9	35	5.2	144	151	47	76	4	.322	.548	0	0	OF-154
1933 CHI A	146	605	200	29	10	14	2.3	85	119	39	49	5	.331	.481	1	0	OF-145
1934	138	558	192	36	7	18	3.2	102	104	53	58	3	.344	.530	0	0	OF-138
1935	128	525	140	22	7	16	3.0	68	79	33	43	4	.267	.427	3	0	OF-126
1936 DET A	143	568	186	38	6	13	2.3	96	112	49	35	6	.327	.484	4	1	OF-138, 1B-1
1937 WAS A	103	419	117	21	10	8	1.9	60	84	27	35	3	.279	.434	1	0	OF-102
1938	125	470	142	23	6	21	4.5	79	95	38	40	2	.302	.511	9	2	OF-117
1939 2 teams		BOS N (93G – .282)						CIN N (9G – .143)									
" total	102	351	96	17	5	7	2.0	39	44	24	43	0	.274	.410	14	2	OF-87
1940 PHI A	37	81	25	4	0	1	1.2	7	19	4	8	0	.309	.395	16	8	OF-18
1941	9	24	3	1	0	0	0.0	1	1	1	2	0	.125	.167	4	0	OF-5
1943 BOS A	40	133	27	5	0	1	0.8	9	12	8	21	0	.203	.263	7	0	OF-33
1944 PHI A	4	6	3	0	0	0	0.0	1	2	0	0	0	.500	.500	2	1	OF-2
20 yrs.	2215	8761	2927	539	149	307	3.5	1507	1827	615	737	87	.334	.535	66	17	OF-2142, 1B-1

WORLD SERIES
1929 PHI A	5	20	6	1	0	2	10.0	6	5	1	4	0	.300	.650	0	0	OF-5
1930	6	22	8	2	0	2	9.1	4	4	2	2	0	.364	.727	0	0	OF-6
1931	7	27	9	2	0	2	7.4	4	8	3	3	0	.333	.630	0	0	OF-7
1939 CIN N	1	4	1	1	0	0	0.0	1	0	0	0	0	.250	.500	0	0	OF-1
4 yrs.	19	73	24	6	0	6	8.2	15	17	6	9	0	.329	.658	0	0	OF-19
							6th							4th			

	G	AB	H	2B	3B	HR	HR %	R	RBI	BB	SO	SB	BA	SA	Pinch Hit AB	Pinch Hit H	G by POS

Hack Simmons

SIMMONS, GEORGE WASHINGTON   BR TR 5'8"   179 lbs.
B. Jan. 29, 1885, Brooklyn, N. Y.   D. Apr. 26, 1942, Arverne, N. Y.

	G	AB	H	2B	3B	HR	HR %	R	RBI	BB	SO	SB	BA	SA	AB	H	G by POS
1910 DET A	42	110	25	3	1	0	0.0	12	9	10		1	.227	.273	10	3	1B-22, 3B-7, OF-2
1912 NY A	110	401	96	17	2	0	0.0	45	41	33		19	.239	.292	4	0	2B-88, 1B-13, SS-4
1914 BAL F	114	352	95	16	5	1	0.3	50	38	32		7	.270	.352	13	7	OF-73, 2B-26, 1B-4, SS-2, 3B-1
1915	39	88	18	7	1	1	1.1	8	14	10		1	.205	.341	13	5	OF-13, 2B-13
4 yrs.	305	951	234	43	9	2	0.2	115	102	85		28	.246	.317	40	15	2B-127, OF-88, 1B-39, 3B-8, SS-6

John Simmons

SIMMONS, JOHN EARL   BR TR 6'1½"   192 lbs.
B. July 7, 1924, Birmingham, Ala.

	G	AB	H	2B	3B	HR	HR %	R	RBI	BB	SO	SB	BA	SA	AB	H	G by POS
1949 WAS A	62	93	20	0	0	0	0.0	12	5	11	6	0	.215	.215	23	5	OF-26

Nelson Simmons

SIMMONS, NELSON BERNARD III   BB TR 6'1"   195 lbs.
B. June 27, 1963, Washington, D. C.

	G	AB	H	2B	3B	HR	HR %	R	RBI	BB	SO	SB	BA	SA	AB	H	G by POS
1984 DET A	9	30	13	2	0	0	0.0	4	3	2	5	1	.433	.500	1	0	OF-5, DH-4

Ted Simmons

SIMMONS, TED LYLE   BB TR 5'11"   193 lbs.
B. Aug. 9, 1949, Highland Park, Mich.

	G	AB	H	2B	3B	HR	HR %	R	RBI	BB	SO	SB	BA	SA	AB	H	G by POS
1968 STL N	2	3	1	0	0	0	0.0	0	0	1	1	0	.333	.333	0	0	C-2
1969	5	14	3	0	1	0	0.0	3	3	1	1	0	.214	.357	1	0	C-4
1970	82	284	69	8	2	3	1.1	29	24	37	37	2	.243	.317	4	1	C-79
1971	133	510	155	32	4	7	1.4	64	77	36	50	1	.304	.424	6	1	C-130
1972	152	594	180	36	6	16	2.7	70	96	29	57	1	.303	.465	2	0	C-135, 1B-15
1973	161	619	192	36	2	13	2.1	62	91	61	47	2	.310	.438	1	0	C-153, 1B-6, OF-2
1974	152	599	163	33	6	20	3.3	66	103	47	35	0	.272	.447	2	1	C-141, 1B-12
1975	157	581	193	32	3	18	3.1	80	100	63	35	1	.332	.491	5	1	C-154, OF-2, 1B-2
1976	150	546	159	35	4	5	0.9	60	75	73	35	0	.291	.394	7	4	C-113, 1B-30, OF-7, 3B-2
1977	150	516	164	25	3	21	4.1	82	95	79	37	2	.318	.500	17	2	C-144, OF-1
1978	152	516	148	40	5	22	4.3	71	80	77	39	1	.287	.512	10	3	C-134, OF-23
1979	123	448	127	22	0	26	5.8	68	87	61	34	0	.283	.507	4	0	C-122
1980	145	495	150	33	2	21	4.2	84	98	59	45	1	.303	.505	15	3	C-129, OF-5
1981 MIL A	100	380	82	13	2	14	3.7	45	61	23	32	0	.216	.376	3	1	C-75, DH-22, 1B-4
1982	137	539	145	29	0	23	4.3	73	97	32	40	0	.269	.451	2	1	C-121, DH-15
1983	153	600	185	39	3	13	2.2	76	108	41	51	4	.308	.448	4	0	C-86, DH-66
1984	132	497	110	23	2	4	0.8	44	52	30	40	3	.221	.300	6	1	DH-77, 1B-37, 3B-14
17 yrs.	2086	7741	2226	436	45	226	2.9	974	1247	750	616	18	.288	.443	89	19	C-1722, DH-180, 1B-106, OF-40, 3B-16

DIVISIONAL PLAYOFF SERIES

	G	AB	H	2B	3B	HR	HR %	R	RBI	BB	SO	SB	BA	SA	AB	H	G by POS
1981 MIL A	5	19	4	1	0	1	5.3	1	4	2	2	0	.211	.421	0	0	C-5

LEAGUE CHAMPIONSHIP SERIES

	G	AB	H	2B	3B	HR	HR %	R	RBI	BB	SO	SB	BA	SA	AB	H	G by POS
1982 MIL A	5	18	3	0	0	0	0.0	3	1	1	4	0	.167	.167	0	0	C-5

WORLD SERIES

	G	AB	H	2B	3B	HR	HR %	R	RBI	BB	SO	SB	BA	SA	AB	H	G by POS
1982 MIL A	7	23	4	0	2	2	8.7	2	3	5	3	0	.174	.435	0	0	C-7

Henry Simon

SIMON, HENRY J.
B. Aug. 25, 1862, Utica, N. Y.   D. Jan. 2, 1925, Albany, N. Y.

	G	AB	H	2B	3B	HR	HR %	R	RBI	BB	SO	SB	BA	SA	AB	H	G by POS
1887 CLE AA	3	10	1	0	0	0	0.0	1		0		0	.100	.100	0	0	OF-3
1890 2 teams		B-B	AA (89G – .257)		SYR	AA (38G – .301)											
" total	127	529	143	22	14	2	0.4	99		51		35	.270	.376	0	0	OF-127
2 yrs.	130	539	144	22	14	2	0.4	100		51		35	.267	.371	0	0	OF-130

Mike Simon

SIMON, MICHAEL EDWARD   BR TR 5'11"   188 lbs.
B. Apr. 13, 1883, Hayden, Ind.   D. June 10, 1963, Los Angeles, Calif.

	G	AB	H	2B	3B	HR	HR %	R	RBI	BB	SO	SB	BA	SA	AB	H	G by POS
1909 PIT N	11	18	3	0	0	0	0.0	2	2	1		0	.167	.167	1	1	C-9
1910	22	50	10	0	1	0	0.0	3	5	1	2	1	.200	.240	7	0	C-14
1911	71	215	49	4	3	0	0.0	19	22	10	14	1	.228	.274	3	0	C-68
1912	42	113	34	7	0	0	0.0	10	11	5	9	1	.301	.336	2	0	C-40
1913	92	255	63	6	2	1	0.4	23	17	10	15	3	.247	.298	0	0	C-92
1914 STL F	93	276	57	11	2	0	0.0	21	21	18		2	.207	.261	13	2	C-78
1915 BKN F	47	142	25	5	1	0	0.0	7	12	9		1	.176	.225	2	0	C-45
7 yrs.	378	1069	241	28	10	1	0.1	85	90	54	40	9	.225	.273	28	3	C-346

Syl Simon

SIMON, SYLVESTER ADAM   BR TR 5'10½"   170 lbs.
B. Dec. 14, 1897, Evansville, Ind.   D. Feb. 28, 1973, Evansville, Ind.

	G	AB	H	2B	3B	HR	HR %	R	RBI	BB	SO	SB	BA	SA	AB	H	G by POS
1923 STL A	1	1	0	0	0	0	0.0	0	0	0	0	0	.000	.000	1	0	
1924	22	32	8	1	1	0	0.0	5	6	2	5	0	.250	.344	10	2	3B-6, SS-5
2 yrs.	23	33	8	1	1	0	0.0	5	6	2	5	0	.242	.333	11	2	3B-6, SS-5

Mel Simons

SIMONS, MELBERN ELLIS (Butch)   BL TR 5'10"   175 lbs.
B. July 1, 1900, Carlyle, Ill.   D. Nov. 10, 1974, Paducah, Ky.

	G	AB	H	2B	3B	HR	HR %	R	RBI	BB	SO	SB	BA	SA	AB	H	G by POS
1931 CHI A	68	189	52	9	0	0	0.0	24	12	12	17	1	.275	.323	6	1	OF-59
1932	7	5	0	0	0	0	0.0	0	0	0	1	0	.000	.000	1	0	OF-6
2 yrs.	75	194	52	9	0	0	0.0	24	12	12	18	1	.268	.314	7	1	OF-65

Dick Simpson

SIMPSON, RICHARD CHARLES   BR TR 6'4"   176 lbs.
B. July 28, 1943, Washington, D. C.

	G	AB	H	2B	3B	HR	HR %	R	RBI	BB	SO	SB	BA	SA	AB	H	G by POS
1962 LA A	6	8	2	1	0	0	0.0	1		2	3	0	.250	.375	2	0	OF-4
1964	21	50	7	1	0	2	4.0	11	4	8	15	2	.140	.280	0	0	OF-16
1965 CAL A	8	27	6	1	0	0	0.0	2	3	2	8	1	.222	.259	0	0	OF-8
1966 CIN N	92	84	20	2	0	4	4.8	26	14	10	32	0	.238	.405	18	2	OF-64
1967	44	54	14	3	0	1	1.9	8	6	7	11	0	.259	.370	9	4	OF-26

	G	AB	H	2B	3B	HR	HR %	R	RBI	BB	SO	SB	BA	SA	Pinch Hit AB	Pinch Hit H	G by POS

Dick Simpson continued

	G	AB	H	2B	3B	HR	HR %	R	RBI	BB	SO	SB	BA	SA	AB	H	G by POS
1968 2 teams	STL N (26G – .232)			HOU N (59G – .186)													
" total	85	233	46	7	2	6	2.6	36	19	28	82	4	.197	.322	3	0	OF-71
1969 2 teams	NY A (6G – .273)			SEA A (26G – .176)													
" total	32	62	12	4	0	2	3.2	10	9	7	23	3	.194	.355	8	0	OF-22
7 yrs.	288	518	107	19	2	15	2.9	94	56	64	174	10	.207	.338	40	6	OF-211

Harry Simpson

SIMPSON, HARRY LEON (Suitcase)
B. Dec. 3, 1925, Atlanta, Ga.　D. Apr. 3, 1979, Akron, Ohio
BL TR 6'1"　180 lbs.

	G	AB	H	2B	3B	HR	HR %	R	RBI	BB	SO	SB	BA	SA	AB	H	G by POS
1951 CLE A	122	332	76	7	0	7	2.1	51	24	45	48	6	.229	.313	10	2	OF-68, 1B-50
1952	146	545	145	21	10	10	1.8	66	65	56	82	5	.266	.396	1	1	OF-127, 1B-28
1953	82	242	55	3	1	7	2.9	25	22	18	27	0	.227	.335	10	1	OF-69, 1B-2
1955 2 teams	CLE A (3G – .000)			KC A (112G – .301)													
" total	115	397	119	16	7	5	1.3	43	52	36	61	3	.300	.413	11	4	OF-100, 1B-3
1956 KC A	141	543	159	22	11	21	3.9	76	105	47	82	2	.293	.490	3	0	OF-111, 1B-32
1957 2 teams	KC A (50G – .296)			NY A (75G – .250)													
" total	125	403	109	16	9	13	3.2	51	63	31	64	1	.270	.452	20	4	OF-63, 1B-48
1958 2 teams	NY A (24G – .216)			KC A (78G – .264)													
" total	102	263	67	9	2	7	2.7	22	33	32	45	0	.255	.384	30	5	1B-43, OF-26
1959 3 teams	KC A (8G – .286)			CHI A (38G – .187)			PIT N (9G – .267)										
" total	55	104	22	1	1	3	2.9	9	17	6	20	0	.212	.385	34	6	OF-15, 1B-5
8 yrs.	888	2829	752	101	41	73	2.6	343	381	271	429	17	.266	.408	119	23	OF-579, 1B-211

WORLD SERIES
	G	AB	H	2B	3B	HR	HR %	R	RBI	BB	SO	SB	BA	SA	AB	H	G by POS
1957 NY A	5	12	1	0	0	0	0.0	0	1	0	4	0	.083	.083	1	0	1B-4

Joe Simpson

SIMPSON, JOSEPH ALLEN
B. Dec. 31, 1951, Purcell, Okla.
BL TL 6'3"　175 lbs.

	G	AB	H	2B	3B	HR	HR %	R	RBI	BB	SO	SB	BA	SA	AB	H	G by POS
1975 LA N	9	6	2	0	0	0	0.0	3	0	0	2	0	.333	.333	1	0	OF-6
1976	23	30	4	1	0	0	0.0	2	0	1	6	0	.133	.167	4	0	OF-20
1977	29	23	4	0	0	0	0.0	2	1	2	6	1	.174	.174	0	0	OF-28, 1B-1
1978	10	5	2	0	0	0	0.0	1	1	0	2	0	.400	.400	0	0	OF-10
1979 SEA A	120	265	75	11	0	2	0.8	29	27	11	21	6	.283	.347	9	2	OF-105, DH-3
1980	129	365	91	15	3	3	0.8	42	34	28	43	17	.249	.332	11	1	OF-119, 1B-3
1981	91	288	64	11	3	2	0.7	32	30	15	41	12	.222	.302	7	1	OF-88
1982	105	296	76	14	4	2	0.7	39	23	22	48	8	.257	.351	7	3	OF-97
1983 KC A	91	119	20	2	2	0	0.0	16	8	11	21	1	.168	.218	2	0	1B-54, OF-38, DH-2, P-2
9 yrs.	607	1397	338	54	12	9	0.6	166	124	90	190	45	.242	.317	37	7	OF-511, 1B-58, DH-5, P-2

Duke Sims

SIMS, DUANE B
B. June 5, 1941, Salt Lake City, Utah
BL TR 6'2"　197 lbs.

	G	AB	H	2B	3B	HR	HR %	R	RBI	BB	SO	SB	BA	SA	AB	H	G by POS
1964 CLE A	2	6	0	0	0	0	0.0	0	0	0	2	0	.000	.000	1	0	C-1
1965	48	118	21	0	0	6	5.1	9	15	15	33	0	.178	.331	12	2	C-40
1966	52	133	35	2	2	6	4.5	12	19	11	31	0	.263	.444	9	0	C-48
1967	88	272	55	8	2	12	4.4	25	37	30	64	3	.202	.379	5	2	C-85
1968	122	361	90	21	0	11	3.0	48	44	62	68	1	.249	.399	9	2	C-84, 1B-31, OF-4
1969	114	326	77	8	0	18	5.5	40	45	66	80	1	.236	.426	13	1	C-102, OF-3, 1B-1
1970	110	345	91	12	0	23	6.7	46	56	46	59	0	.264	.499	9	1	C-39, OF-36, 1B-29
1971 LA N	90	230	63	7	2	6	2.6	23	25	30	39	0	.274	.400	18	2	C-74
1972 2 teams	LA N (51G – .192)			DET A (38G – .316)													
" total	89	249	60	11	0	6	2.4	18	30	36	41	0	.241	.357	12	3	C-73, OF-4
1973 2 teams	DET A (80G – .242)			NY A (4G – .333)													
" total	84	261	64	10	0	9	3.4	34	31	33	37	1	.245	.387	9	1	C-69, OF-6, DH-2
1974 2 teams	NY A (5G – .133)			TEX A (39G – .208)													
" total	44	121	24	1	0	3	2.5	8	8	9	29	0	.198	.281	7	3	C-31, DH-5, OF-1
11 yrs.	843	2422	580	80	6	100	4.1	263	310	338	483	6	.239	.401	104	17	C-646, 1B-61, OF-54, DH-7

LEAGUE CHAMPIONSHIP SERIES
	G	AB	H	2B	3B	HR	HR %	R	RBI	BB	SO	SB	BA	SA	AB	H	G by POS
1972 DET A	4	14	3	2	1	0	0.0	0	0	1	2	0	.214	.500	0	0	C-2

Greg Sims

SIMS, GREGORY EMMETT
B. June 28, 1946, San Francisco, Calif.
BB TR 6'　190 lbs.

	G	AB	H	2B	3B	HR	HR %	R	RBI	BB	SO	SB	BA	SA	AB	H	G by POS
1966 HOU N	7	6	1	0	0	0	0.0	1	0	1	3	0	.167	.167	5	1	OF-1

Matt Sinatro

SINATRO, MATTHEW STEPHEN
B. Mar. 22, 1960, Hartford, Conn.
BR TR 5'9"　174 lbs.

	G	AB	H	2B	3B	HR	HR %	R	RBI	BB	SO	SB	BA	SA	AB	H	G by POS
1981 ATL N	12	32	9	1	1	0	0.0	4	4	5	4	1	.281	.375	0	0	C-12
1982	37	81	11	2	0	1	1.2	10	4	4	9	0	.136	.198	0	0	C-35
1983	7	12	2	0	0	0	0.0	0	2	2	1	0	.167	.167	0	0	C-7
1984	2	4	0	0	0	0	0.0	0	0	0	0	0	.000	.000	0	0	C-2
4 yrs.	58	129	22	3	1	1	0.8	14	10	11	14	1	.171	.233	0	0	C-56

Hosea Siner

SINER, HOSEA JOHN
B. Mar. 20, 1885, Shelburn, Ind.　D. June 10, 1948, Sullivan, Ind.
BR TR 5'10½"	185 lbs.

	G	AB	H	2B	3B	HR	HR %	R	RBI	BB	SO	SB	BA	SA	AB	H	G by POS
1909 BOS N	10	23	3	0	0	0	0.0	1	1	2		0	.130	.130	2	0	3B-5, SS-1, 2B-1

Ken Singleton

SINGLETON, KENNETH WAYNE
B. June 10, 1947, New York, N. Y.
BB TR 6'4"　210 lbs.

	G	AB	H	2B	3B	HR	HR %	R	RBI	BB	SO	SB	BA	SA	AB	H	G by POS
1970 NY N	69	198	52	8	0	5	2.5	22	26	30	48	1	.263	.379	18	4	OF-51
1971	115	298	73	5	0	13	4.4	34	46	61	64	0	.245	.393	23	6	OF-96
1972 MON N	142	507	139	23	2	14	2.8	77	50	70	99	5	.274	.410	5	1	OF-137
1973	162	560	169	26	2	23	4.1	100	103	123	91	2	.302	.479	3	0	OF-161
1974	148	511	141	20	2	9	1.8	68	74	93	84	5	.276	.376	5	1	OF-143
1975 BAL A	155	586	176	37	4	15	2.6	88	55	118	82	3	.300	.454	1	0	OF-155
1976	154	544	151	25	2	13	2.4	62	70	79	76	2	.278	.403	1	0	OF-134, DH-19
1977	152	536	176	24	0	24	4.5	90	99	107	101	0	.328	.507	0	0	OF-150, DH-1
1978	149	502	147	21	2	20	4.0	67	81	98	94	0	.293	.462	3	0	OF-140, DH-5

	G	AB	H	2B	3B	HR	HR %	R	RBI	BB	SO	SB	BA	SA	Pinch Hit AB	Pinch Hit H	G by POS

Ken Singleton continued

	G	AB	H	2B	3B	HR	HR %	R	RBI	BB	SO	SB	BA	SA	PH AB	PH H	G by POS
1979	159	570	168	29	1	35	6.1	93	111	109	118	3	.295	.533	0	0	OF-143, DH-16
1980	156	583	177	28	3	24	4.1	85	104	92	94	0	.304	.485	0	0	OF-151, DH-5
1981	103	363	101	16	1	13	3.6	48	49	61	59	0	.278	.435	1	0	OF-72, DH-30
1982	156	561	141	27	2	14	2.5	71	77	86	93	0	.251	.381	4	1	DH-148, OF-5
1983	151	507	140	21	3	18	3.6	52	84	99	83	0	.276	.436	6	4	DH-150
1984	111	363	78	7	1	6	1.7	28	36	37	60	0	.215	.289	17	2	DH-103
15 yrs.	2082	7189	2029	317	25	246	3.4	985	1065	1263	1246	21	.282	.436	87	19	OF-1538, DH-477

LEAGUE CHAMPIONSHIP SERIES

	G	AB	H	2B	3B	HR	HR %	R	RBI	BB	SO	SB	BA	SA	PH AB	PH H	G by POS
1979 BAL A	4	16	6	2	0	0	0.0	4	2	1	2	0	.375	.500	0	0	OF-4
1983	4	12	3	2	0	0	0.0	0	1	2	2	0	.250	.417	0	0	DH-4
2 yrs.	8	28	9	4	0	0	0.0	4	3	3	4	0	.321	.464	0	0	DH-4, OF-4

WORLD SERIES

	G	AB	H	2B	3B	HR	HR %	R	RBI	BB	SO	SB	BA	SA	PH AB	PH H	G by POS
1979 BAL A	7	28	10	1	0	0	0.0	1	2	2	5	0	.357	.393	0	0	OF-7
1983	2	1	0	0	0	0	0.0	0	1	1	1	0	.000	.000	1	0	
2 yrs.	9	29	10	1	0	0	0.0	1	3	3	6	0	.345	.379	1	0	OF-7

Fred Sington

SINGTON, FREDERICK WILLIAM
B. Feb. 24, 1910, Birmingham, Ala. BR TR 6'2" 215 lbs.

	G	AB	H	2B	3B	HR	HR %	R	RBI	BB	SO	SB	BA	SA	PH AB	PH H	G by POS
1934 WAS A	9	35	10	2	0	0	0.0	2	6	4	3	0	.286	.343	0	0	OF-9
1935	20	22	4	0	0	0	0.0	1	3	5	1	0	.182	.182	11	2	OF-4
1936	25	94	30	8	0	1	1.1	13	28	15	9	0	.319	.436	0	0	OF-25
1937	78	228	54	15	4	3	1.3	27	36	37	33	1	.237	.377	14	0	OF-64
1938 BKN N	17	53	19	6	1	2	3.8	10	5	13	5	1	.358	.623	0	0	OF-17
1939	32	84	23	5	0	1	1.2	13	7	15	15	0	.274	.369	6	2	OF-22
6 yrs.	181	516	140	36	5	7	1.4	66	85	89	66	2	.271	.401	31	4	OF-141

Dick Sipek

SIPEK, RICHARD FRANCIS
B. Jan. 16, 1923, Chicago, Ill. BL TR 5'9" 170 lbs.

	G	AB	H	2B	3B	HR	HR %	R	RBI	BB	SO	SB	BA	SA	PH AB	PH H	G by POS
1945 CIN N	82	156	38	6	2	0	0.0	14	13	9	15	0	.244	.308	45	10	OF-31

John Sipin

SIPIN, JOHN WHITE
B. Aug. 29, 1946, Watsonville, Calif. BR TR 6'1½" 175 lbs.

	G	AB	H	2B	3B	HR	HR %	R	RBI	BB	SO	SB	BA	SA	PH AB	PH H	G by POS
1969 SD N	68	229	51	12	2	2	0.9	22	9	8	44	2	.223	.319	5	2	2B-60

Dick Sisler

SISLER, RICHARD ALLAN
Son of George Sisler. Brother of Dave Sisler.
B. Nov. 2, 1920, St. Louis, Mo.
Manager 1964-65. BL TR 6'2" 205 lbs.

	G	AB	H	2B	3B	HR	HR %	R	RBI	BB	SO	SB	BA	SA	PH AB	PH H	G by POS
1946 STL N	83	235	61	11	2	3	1.3	17	42	14	28	0	.260	.362	13	4	1B-37, OF-29
1947	46	74	15	2	1	0	0.0	4	9	3	8	0	.203	.257	30	4	1B-10, OF-5
1948 PHI N	121	446	122	21	3	11	2.5	60	56	47	46	1	.274	.408	2	0	1B-120
1949	121	412	119	19	6	7	1.7	42	50	25	38	0	.289	.415	23	6	1B-96
1950	141	523	155	29	4	13	2.5	79	83	64	50	1	.296	.442	2	1	OF-137
1951	125	428	123	20	5	8	1.9	46	52	40	39	1	.287	.414	11	4	OF-111
1952 2 teams	130	445	114	15	6	13	2.9	51	64	32	40	3	.256	.404	6	1	1B-114, OF-7
" total CIN N (11G – .185) STL N (119G – .261)																	
1953 STL N	32	43	11	1	0	0	0.0	3	4	1	4	0	.256	.326	22	5	1B-10
8 yrs.	799	2606	720	118	28	55	2.1	302	360	226	253	6	.276	.406	109	25	1B-387, OF-289

WORLD SERIES

	G	AB	H	2B	3B	HR	HR %	R	RBI	BB	SO	SB	BA	SA	PH AB	PH H	G by POS
1946 STL N	2	2	0	0	0	0	0.0	0	0	0	0	0	.000	.000	2	0	
1950 PHI N	4	17	1	0	0	0	0.0	0	1	0	5	0	.059	.059	0	0	OF-4
2 yrs.	6	19	1	0	0	0	0.0	0	1	0	5	0	.053	.053	2	0	OF-4

George Sisler

SISLER, GEORGE HAROLD (Gorgeous George)
Father of Dick Sisler. Father of Dave Sisler.
B. Mar. 24, 1893, Manchester, Ohio D. Mar. 26, 1973, St. Louis, Mo.
Manager 1924-26.
Hall of Fame 1939. BL TL 5'11" 170 lbs.

	G	AB	H	2B	3B	HR	HR %	R	RBI	BB	SO	SB	BA	SA	PH AB	PH H	G by POS
1915 STL A	81	274	78	10	2	3	1.1	28	29	7	27	10	.285	.369	0	0	1B-37, OF-29, P-15
1916	151	580	177	21	11	4	0.7	83	76	40	37	34	.305	.400	2	0	1B-139, OF-3, P-3, 3B-2
1917	135	539	190	30	9	2	0.4	60	52	30	19	37	.353	.453	0	0	1B-133, 2B-2
1918	114	452	154	21	9	2	0.4	69	41	40	17	45	.341	.440	0	0	1B-114, P-2
1919	132	511	180	31	15	10	2.0	96	83	27	20	28	.352	.530	1	1	1B-131
1920	154	631	257¹	49	18	19	3.0	137	122	46	19	42	.407	.632	0	0	1B-154
1921	138	582	216	38	18	11	1.9	125	104	34	27	35	.371	.555	0	0	1B-138
1922	142	586	246	42	18	8	1.4	134	105	49	14	51	.420	.594	1	0	1B-141
1924	151	636	194	27	10	9	1.4	94	74	31	29	19	.305	.421	0	0	1B-151
1925	150	649	224	21	15	12	1.8	100	105	27	24	11	.345	.479	0	0	1B-150, P-1
1926	150	613	178	21	12	7	1.1	78	71	30	30	12	.290	.398	0	0	1B-149, P-1
1927	149	614	201	32	8	5	0.8	87	97	24	15	27	.327	.430	0	0	1B-149
1928 2 teams	138	540	179	27	4	4	0.7	72	70	31	17	11	.331	.419	10	3	1B-123, OF-5, P-1
" total WAS A (20G – .245) BOS N (118G – .340)																	
1929 BOS N	154	629	205	40	9	1	0.2	67	79	33	17	6	.326	.423	0	0	1B-154
1930	116	431	133	15	7	3	0.7	54	67	23	15	7	.309	.397	8	2	1B-107
15 yrs.	2055	8267	2812	425	165	100	1.2	1284	1175	472	327	375	.340	.468	22	6	1B-1970, OF-37, P-23, 3B-2, 2B-2

Sibby Sisti

SISTI, SEBASTIAN DANIEL
B. July 26, 1920, Buffalo, N. Y. BR TR 5'11" 175 lbs.

	G	AB	H	2B	3B	HR	HR %	R	RBI	BB	SO	SB	BA	SA	PH AB	PH H	G by POS
1939 BOS N	63	215	49	7	1	1	0.5	19	11	12	38	4	.228	.284	1	0	2B-34, 3B-17, SS-10
1940	123	459	115	19	5	6	1.3	73	34	36	64	4	.251	.353	2	0	3B-102, 2B-16
1941	140	541	140	24	3	1	0.2	72	45	38	76	7	.259	.320	1	0	3B-137, SS-2, 2B-2
1942	129	407	86	11	4	4	1.0	50	35	45	55	5	.211	.287	2	0	2B-124, OF-1
1946	1	0	0	0	0	0		0	0	0	0	0			0	0	3B-1
1947	56	153	43	8	0	2	1.3	22	15	20	17	2	.281	.373	3	1	SS-51, 2B-1

	G	AB	H	2B	3B	HR	HR %	R	RBI	BB	SO	SB	BA	SA	Pinch Hit AB	Pinch Hit H	G by POS

Sibby Sisti continued

	G	AB	H	2B	3B	HR	HR %	R	RBI	BB	SO	SB	BA	SA	AB	H	G by POS
1948	83	221	54	6	2	0	0.0	30	21	31	34	0	.244	.290	2	1	2B-44, SS-26
1949	101	268	69	12	0	5	1.9	39	22	34	42	1	.257	.358	6	3	OF-48, 2B-21, SS-18, 3B-1
1950	69	105	18	3	1	2	1.9	21	11	16	19	1	.171	.276	7	3	SS-23, 2B-19, 3B-13, OF-1, 1B-1
1951	114	362	101	20	2	2	0.6	46	38	32	50	4	.279	.362	4	2	2B-52, SS-25, 3B-6, OF-1, 1B-1
1952	90	245	52	10	1	4	1.6	19	24	14	43	2	.212	.310	13	1	2B-33, OF-23, SS-18, 3B-9
1953 **MIL N**	38	23	5	1	0	0	0.0	8	4	5	2	0	.217	.261	1	0	2B-13, SS-6, 3B-4
1954	9	0	0	0	0	0	–	2	0	0	0	0	–	–	0	0	
13 yrs.	1016	2999	732	121	19	27	0.9	401	260	283	440	30	.244	.324	42	11	2B-359, 3B-290, SS-179, OF-74, 1B-2

WORLD SERIES
	G	AB	H	2B	3B	HR	HR %	R	RBI	BB	SO	SB	BA	SA	AB	H	G by POS
1948 **BOS N**	2	1	0	0	0	0	0.0	0	0	0	0	0	.000	.000	1	0	2B-2

Ed Sixsmith

SIXSMITH, EDWARD
B. Feb. 26, 1863, Philadelphia, Pa.   D. Dec. 12, 1926, Philadelphia, Pa.

	G	AB	H	2B	3B	HR	HR %	R	RBI	BB	SO	SB	BA	SA	AB	H	G by POS
1884 **PHI N**	1	2	0	0	0	0	0.0	0		0	0		.000	.000	0	0	C-1

Ted Sizemore

SIZEMORE, TED CRAWFORD
B. Apr. 15, 1946, Gadsden, Ala.   BR TR 5'10" 165 lbs.

	G	AB	H	2B	3B	HR	HR %	R	RBI	BB	SO	SB	BA	SA	AB	H	G by POS
1969 **LA N**	159	590	160	20	5	4	0.7	69	46	45	40	5	.271	.342	0	0	2B-118, SS-46, OF-1
1970	96	340	104	10	1	1	0.3	40	34	34	19	5	.306	.350	3	2	2B-86, OF-9, SS-2
1971 **STL N**	135	478	126	14	5	3	0.6	53	42	42	26	4	.264	.333	6	3	2B-93, SS-39, OF-15, 3B-1
1972	120	439	116	17	4	2	0.5	53	38	37	36	8	.264	.335	13	1	2B-111
1973	142	521	147	22	1	1	0.2	69	54	68	34	6	.282	.334	1	0	2B-139, 3B-3
1974	129	504	126	17	0	2	0.4	68	47	70	37	8	.250	.296	2	0	2B-128, OF-1, SS-1
1975	153	562	135	23	1	3	0.5	56	49	45	37	1	.240	.301	1	1	2B-153
1976 **LA N**	84	266	64	8	1	0	0.0	18	18	15	22	2	.241	.278	13	5	2B-71, 3B-3, C-2
1977 **PHI N**	152	519	146	20	3	4	0.8	64	47	52	40	8	.281	.355	1	0	2B-152
1978	108	351	77	12	0	0	0.0	38	25	25	29	8	.219	.254	1	0	2B-107
1979 **2 teams**		**CHI**	N (98G –	.248)		**BOS**	A (26G –	.261)									
" total	124	418	105	24	0	3	0.7	48	30	36	30	4	.251	.330	3	0	2B-122, C-2
1980 **BOS A**	9	23	5	1	0	0	0.0	1	0	0	0	0	.217	.261	1	0	2B-8
12 yrs.	1411	5011	1311	188	21	23	0.5	577	430	469	350	59	.262	.321	45	12	2B-1288, SS-88, OF-26, 3B-7, C-4

LEAGUE CHAMPIONSHIP SERIES
	G	AB	H	2B	3B	HR	HR %	R	RBI	BB	SO	SB	BA	SA	AB	H	G by POS
1977 **PHI N**	4	13	3	0	0	0	0.0	1	0	2	0	0	.231	.231	0	0	2B-4
1978	4	13	5	0	1	0	0.0	3	1	1	0	0	.385	.538	0	0	2B-4
2 yrs.	8	26	8	0	1	0	0.0	4	1	3	0	0	.308	.385	0	0	2B-8

Frank Skaff

SKAFF, FRANCIS MICHAEL
B. Sept. 30, 1913, LaCrosse, Wis.   BR TR 5'10" 185 lbs.
Manager 1966.

	G	AB	H	2B	3B	HR	HR %	R	RBI	BB	SO	SB	BA	SA	AB	H	G by POS
1935 **BKN N**	6	11	6	1	1	0	0.0	4	3	0	2	0	.545	.818	3	1	3B-3
1943 **PHI A**	32	64	18	2	1	1	1.6	8	8	6	11	0	.281	.391	7	1	1B-18, 3B-3, SS-1
2 yrs.	38	75	24	3	2	1	1.3	12	11	6	13	0	.320	.453	10	2	1B-18, 3B-6, SS-1

Dave Skaggs

SKAGGS, DAVID LINDSEY
B. June 12, 1951, Santa Monica, Calif.   BR TR 6'2" 200 lbs.

	G	AB	H	2B	3B	HR	HR %	R	RBI	BB	SO	SB	BA	SA	AB	H	G by POS
1977 **BAL A**	80	216	62	9	1	1	0.5	22	24	20	34	0	.287	.352	0	0	C-80
1978	36	86	13	1	1	0	0.0	6	2	9	14	0	.151	.186	1	0	C-35
1979	63	137	34	8	0	1	0.7	9	14	13	14	0	.248	.328	0	0	C-63
1980 **2 teams**		**BAL**	A (2G –	.200)		**CAL**	A (24G –	.197)									
" total	26	71	14	0	0	1	1.4	7	9	9	14	0	.197	.239	0	0	C-26
4 yrs.	205	510	123	18	2	3	0.6	44	49	51	76	0	.241	.302	1	0	C-204

LEAGUE CHAMPIONSHIP SERIES
	G	AB	H	2B	3B	HR	HR %	R	RBI	BB	SO	SB	BA	SA	AB	H	G by POS
1979 **BAL A**	1	4	0	0	0	0	0.0	0	0	0	0	0	.000	.000	0	0	C-1

WORLD SERIES
	G	AB	H	2B	3B	HR	HR %	R	RBI	BB	SO	SB	BA	SA	AB	H	G by POS
1979 **BAL A**	1	3	1	0	0	0	0.0	1	0	0	0	0	.333	.333	0	0	C-1

Bud Sketchley

SKETCHLEY, HARRY CLEMENT
B. Mar. 30, 1919, Virden, Man., Canada   D. Dec. 19, 1979, Los Angeles, Calif.   BL TL 5'10½" 180 lbs.

	G	AB	H	2B	3B	HR	HR %	R	RBI	BB	SO	SB	BA	SA	AB	H	G by POS
1942 **CHI A**	13	36	7	1	0	0	0.0	1	3	7	4	0	.194	.222	1	0	OF-12

Roe Skidmore

SKIDMORE, ROBERT ROE
B. Oct. 30, 1945, Decatur, Ill.   BR TL 6'3" 188 lbs.

	G	AB	H	2B	3B	HR	HR %	R	RBI	BB	SO	SB	BA	SA	AB	H	G by POS
1970 **CHI N**	1	1	1	0	0	0	0.0	0	0	0	0	0	1.000	1.000	1	1	

Bill Skiff

SKIFF, WILLIAM FRANKLIN
B. Oct. 16, 1895, New Rochelle, N.Y.   D. Dec. 25, 1976, Bronxville, N.Y.   BR TR 5'10" 170 lbs.

	G	AB	H	2B	3B	HR	HR %	R	RBI	BB	SO	SB	BA	SA	AB	H	G by POS
1921 **PIT N**	16	45	13	2	0	0	0.0	7	11	0	4	1	.289	.333	2	1	C-13
1926 **NY A**	6	11	1	0	0	0	0.0	0	0	0	1	0	.091	.091	0	0	C-6
2 yrs.	22	56	14	2	0	0	0.0	7	11	0	5	1	.250	.286	2	1	C-19

Skinner

SKINNER,
Deceased.

	G	AB	H	2B	3B	HR	HR %	R	RBI	BB	SO	SB	BA	SA	AB	H	G by POS
1884 **2 teams**		**BAL**	U (1G –	.333)		**C-P**	U (1G –	.333)									
" total	2	6	2	0	0	0	0.0	1		0			.333	.333	0	0	OF-2

	G	AB	H	2B	3B	HR	HR %	R	RBI	BB	SO	SB	BA	SA	Pinch Hit AB	Pinch Hit H	G by POS

Bob Skinner

SKINNER, ROBERT RALPH
Father of Joel Skinner.
B. Oct. 3, 1931, La Jolla, Calif.
Manager 1968-69, 1977.

BL TR 6'4" 190 lbs.

	G	AB	H	2B	3B	HR	HR %	R	RBI	BB	SO	SB	BA	SA	AB	H	G by POS
1954 PIT N	132	470	117	15	9	8	1.7	67	46	47	59	4	.249	.370	11	6	1B-118, OF-2
1956	113	233	47	8	3	5	2.1	29	29	26	50	1	.202	.326	54	9	OF-36, 1B-24, 3B-1
1957	126	387	118	12	6	13	3.4	58	45	38	50	10	.305	.468	27	8	OF-93, 1B-9, 3B-1
1958	144	529	170	33	9	13	2.5	93	70	58	55	12	.321	.491	3	1	OF-141
1959	143	547	153	18	4	13	2.4	78	61	67	65	10	.280	.399	1	0	OF-142, 1B-1
1960	145	571	156	33	6	15	2.6	83	86	59	86	11	.273	.431	5	2	OF-141
1961	119	381	102	20	3	3	0.8	61	42	51	49	3	.268	.360	18	4	OF-97
1962	144	510	154	29	7	20	3.9	87	75	76	89	10	.302	.504	4	3	OF-139
1963 2 teams	PIT	N	(34G –	.270)		CIN	N	(72G –	.253)								
" total	106	316	82	15	7	3	0.9	43	25	34	64	5	.259	.380	22	6	OF-83
1964 2 teams	CIN	N	(25G –	.220)		STL	N	(55G –	.271)								
" total	80	177	45	8	0	4	2.3	16	21	15	32	0	.254	.367	37	8	OF-43
1965 STL N	80	152	47	5	4	5	3.3	25	26	12	30	1	.309	.493	47	15	OF-33
1966	49	45	7	1	0	1	2.2	2	5	2	17	0	.156	.244	45	7	
12 yrs.	1381	4318	1198	197	58	103	2.4	642	531	485	646	67	.277	.421	274	69	OF-950, 1B-152, 3B-2

WORLD SERIES

	G	AB	H	2B	3B	HR	HR %	R	RBI	BB	SO	SB	BA	SA	AB	H	G by POS
1960 PIT N	2	5	1	0	0	0	0.0	2	1	1	0	1	.200	.200	0	0	OF-2
1964 STL N	4	3	2	1	0	0	0.0	0	1	1	0	0	.667	1.000	3	2	
2 yrs.	6	8	3	1	0	0	0.0	2	2	2	0	1	.375	.500	3	2	OF-2

Camp Skinner

SKINNER, ELISHA HARRISON
B. June 25, 1897, Douglasville, Ga.   D. Aug. 4, 1944, Douglasville, Ga.

BL TR 5'11" 165 lbs.

	G	AB	H	2B	3B	HR	HR %	R	RBI	BB	SO	SB	BA	SA	AB	H	G by POS
1922 NY A	27	33	6	0	0	0	0.0	1	2	0	4	1	.182	.182	24	4	OF-4
1923 BOS A	7	13	3	2	0	0	0.0	1	1	0	0	0	.231	.385	5	2	OF-2
2 yrs.	34	46	9	2	0	0	0.0	2	3	0	4	1	.196	.239	29	6	OF-6

Joel Skinner

SKINNER, JOEL PATRICK
Son of Bob Skinner.
B. Feb. 27, 1961, San Diego, Calif.

BR TR 6'4" 195 lbs.

	G	AB	H	2B	3B	HR	HR %	R	RBI	BB	SO	SB	BA	SA	AB	H	G by POS
1983 CHI A	6	11	3	0	0	0	0.0	2	1	0	1	0	.273	.273	0	0	C-6
1984	43	80	17	2	0	0	0.0	4	3	7	19	1	.213	.238	0	0	C-43
2 yrs.	49	91	20	2	0	0	0.0	6	4	7	20	1	.220	.242	0	0	C-49

Lou Skizas

SKIZAS, LOUIS PETER (The Nervous Greek)
B. June 2, 1932, Chicago, Ill.

BR TR 5'11" 175 lbs.

	G	AB	H	2B	3B	HR	HR %	R	RBI	BB	SO	SB	BA	SA	AB	H	G by POS
1956 2 teams	NY	A	(6G –	.167)		KC	A	(83G –	.316)								
" total	89	303	95	11	3	11	3.6	39	40	15	19	3	.314	.479	15	3	OF-74
1957 KC A	119	376	92	14	1	18	4.8	34	44	27	15	5	.245	.431	24	2	OF-76, 3B-32
1958 DET A	23	33	8	2	0	1	3.0	4	2	5	1	0	.242	.394	13	2	OF-5, 3B-4
1959 CHI A	8	13	1	0	0	0	0.0	3	0	3	2	0	.077	.077	2	0	OF-6
4 yrs.	239	725	196	27	4	30	4.1	80	86	50	37	8	.270	.443	54	7	OF-161, 3B-36

Bill Skowron

SKOWRON, WILLIAM JOSEPH (Moose)
B. Dec. 18, 1930, Chicago, Ill.

BR TR 5'11" 195 lbs.

	G	AB	H	2B	3B	HR	HR %	R	RBI	BB	SO	SB	BA	SA	AB	H	G by POS
1954 NY A	87	215	73	12	9	7	3.3	37	41	19	18	2	.340	.577	22	7	1B-61, 3B-5, 2B-2
1955	108	288	92	17	3	12	4.2	46	61	21	32	1	.319	.524	35	6	1B-74, 3B-3
1956	134	464	143	21	6	23	5.0	78	90	50	60	4	.308	.528	12	2	1B-120, 3B-2
1957	122	457	139	15	5	17	3.7	54	88	31	60	3	.304	.470	9	3	1B-115
1958	126	465	127	22	3	14	3.0	61	73	28	69	1	.273	.424	7	3	1B-118, 3B-2
1959	74	282	84	13	5	15	5.3	39	59	20	47	1	.298	.539	3	1	1B-72
1960	146	538	166	34	3	26	4.8	63	91	38	95	2	.309	.528	6	1	1B-142
1961	150	561	150	23	4	28	5.0	76	89	35	108	0	.267	.472	1	0	1B-149
1962	140	478	129	16	6	23	4.8	63	80	36	99	0	.270	.473	12	4	1B-135
1963 LA N	89	237	48	8	0	4	1.7	19	19	13	49	0	.203	.287	24	6	1B-66, 3B-1
1964 2 teams	WAS	A	(73G –	.271)		CHI	A	(73G –	.293)								
" total	146	535	151	21	3	17	3.2	47	79	30	92	0	.282	.428	13	3	1B-136
1965 CHI A	146	559	153	24	3	18	3.2	63	78	32	77	1	.274	.424	1	1	1B-145
1966	120	337	84	15	2	6	1.8	27	29	26	45	1	.249	.359	23	3	1B-98
1967 2 teams	CHI	A	(8G –	.000)		CAL	A	(62G –	.220)								
" total	70	131	27	2	1	1	0.8	8	11	4	19	0	.206	.260	37	7	1B-32
14 yrs.	1658	5547	1566	243	53	211	3.8	681	888	383	870	16	.282	.459	205	47	1B-1463, 3B-13, 2B-2

WORLD SERIES

	G	AB	H	2B	3B	HR	HR %	R	RBI	BB	SO	SB	BA	SA	AB	H	G by POS
1955 NY A	5	12	4	2	0	1	8.3	2	3	0	1	0	.333	.750	2	0	1B-3
1956	3	10	1	0	0	1	10.0	1	4	0	3	0	.100	.400	1	0	1B-2
1957	2	4	0	0	0	0	0.0	0	0	0	0	0	.000	.000	1	0	1B-2
1958	7	27	7	0	0	2	7.4	3	7	1	4	0	.259	.481	0	0	1B-7
1960	7	32	12	2	0	2	6.3	7	6	0	6	0	.375	.625	0	0	1B-7
1961	5	17	6	0	0	1	5.9	3	5	3	4	0	.353	.529	0	0	1B-5
1962	6	18	4	0	1	0	0.0	1	1	1	5	0	.222	.333	0	0	1B-6
1963 LA N	4	13	5	0	0	1	7.7	2	3	1	3	0	.385	.615	0	0	1B-4
8 yrs.	39	133	39	4	1	8	6.0	19	29	6	26	0	.293	.519	4	0	1B-36
				7th					6th			6th					

Bob Skube

SKUBE, ROBERT JACOB
B. Oct. 8, 1957, Northridge, Calif.

BL TL 6' 182 lbs.

	G	AB	H	2B	3B	HR	HR %	R	RBI	BB	SO	SB	BA	SA	AB	H	G by POS
1982 MIL A	4	3	2	0	0	0	0.0	0	0	0	0	0	.667	.667	3	2	DH-1, OF-1
1983	12	25	5	1	1	0	0.0	2	9	4	7	0	.200	.320	2	0	OF-8, DH-2, 1B-1
2 yrs.	16	28	7	1	1	0	0.0	2	9	4	7	0	.250	.357	5	2	OF-9, DH-3, 1B-1

Gordon Slade

SLADE, GORDON (Oskie)
B. Oct. 9, 1904, Salt Lake City, Utah   D. Jan. 2, 1974, Long Beach, Calif.

BR TR 5'10½" 160 lbs.

	G	AB	H	2B	3B	HR	HR %	R	RBI	BB	SO	SB	BA	SA	AB	H	G by POS
1930 BKN N	25	37	8	2	0	1	2.7	8	2	3	5	0	.216	.351	0	0	SS-21
1931	85	272	65	13	2	1	0.4	27	29	23	28	2	.239	.313	0	0	SS-82, 3B-2

	G	AB	H	2B	3B	HR	HR %	R	RBI	BB	SO	SB	BA	SA	Pinch Hit AB	Pinch Hit H	G by POS

Gordon Slade continued

	G	AB	H	2B	3B	HR	HR %	R	RBI	BB	SO	SB	BA	SA	AB	H	G by POS
1932	79	250	60	15	1	1	0.4	23	23	11	26	3	.240	.320	1	1	SS-55, 3B-23
1933 STL N	39	62	7	1	0	0	0.0	6	3	6	7	1	.113	.129	3	0	SS-31, 2B-1
1934 CIN N	138	555	158	19	8	4	0.7	61	52	25	34	6	.285	.369	1	0	SS-97, 2B-39
1935	71	196	55	10	0	1	0.5	22	14	16	16	0	.281	.347	7	2	SS-30, 2B-19, OF-8, 3B-7
6 yrs.	437	1372	353	60	11	8	0.6	147	123	84	116	12	.257	.335	12	3	SS-316, 2B-59, 3B-32, OF-8

Art Sladen

SLADEN, ARTHUR W.
B. Oct. 28, 1860, Dracut, Mass.   D. Feb. 28, 1914, Dracut, Mass.

	G	AB	H	2B	3B	HR	HR %	R	RBI	BB	SO	SB	BA	SA	AB	H	G by POS
1884 BOS U	2	7	0	0	0	0	0.0	0		0			.000	.000	0	0	OF-2

Jimmy Slagle

SLAGLE, JAMES FRANKLIN (Rabbit, Shorty, The Human Mosquito)
BL TR 5'7"
B. July 11, 1873, Worthville, Pa.   D. May 10, 1956, Chicago, Ill.

	G	AB	H	2B	3B	HR	HR %	R	RBI	BB	SO	SB	BA	SA	AB	H	G by POS
1899 WAS N	147	599	163	15	8	0	0.0	92	41	55		22	.272	.324	1	0	OF-146
1900 PHI N	141	574	165	16	9	0	0.0	115	45	60		34	.287	.347	0	0	OF-141
1901 2 teams			PHI	N	(48G –	.202)		BOS	N	(66G –	.271)						
" total	114	438	106	13	2	1	0.2	55	27	50		19	.242	.288	0	0	OF-114
1902 CHI N	115	454	143	11	4	0	0.0	64	28	53		40	.315	.357	2	1	OF-113
1903	139	543	162	20	6	0	0.0	104	44	81		33	.298	.357	0	0	OF-139
1904	120	481	125	12	10	1	0.2	73	31	41		28	.260	.333	0	0	OF-120
1905	155	568	153	19	4	0	0.0	96	37	97		27	.269	.317	0	0	OF-155
1906	127	498	119	8	6	0	0.0	71	33	63		25	.239	.279	0	0	OF-127
1907	136	489	126	6	6	0	0.0	71	32	76		28	.258	.294	0	0	OF-135
1908	104	352	78	4	1	0	0.0	38	26	43		17	.222	.239	2	0	OF-101
10 yrs.	1298	4996	1340	124	56	2	0.0	779	344	619		273	.268	.317	5	1	OF-1291

WORLD SERIES

	G	AB	H	2B	3B	HR	HR %	R	RBI	BB	SO	SB	BA	SA	AB	H	G by POS
1907 CHI N	5	22	6	0	0	0	0.0	3	4	2	5	6	.273	.273	0	0	OF-5

Jack Slattery

SLATTERY, JOHN TERRENCE
BR TR 6'2"   191 lbs.
B. Jan. 6, 1877, Boston, Mass.   D. July 17, 1949, Boston, Mass.
Manager 1928.

	G	AB	H	2B	3B	HR	HR %	R	RBI	BB	SO	SB	BA	SA	AB	H	G by POS
1901 BOS A	1	3	1	0	0	0	0.0	1	1	1		0	.333	.333	0	0	C-1
1903 2 teams			CLE	A	(4G –	.000)		CHI	A	(63G –	.218)						
" total	67	222	46	3	2	0	0.0	9	20	2		2	.207	.239	4	0	C-56, 1B-7
1906 STL N	3	7	2	0	0	0	0.0	0	0	1		0	.286	.286	1	0	C-2
1909 WAS A	32	56	12	2	0	0	0.0	4	6	2		1	.214	.250	15	4	1B-11, C-5
4 yrs.	103	288	61	5	2	0	0.0	14	27	6		3	.212	.243	20	4	C-64, 1B-18

Mike Slattery

SLATTERY, MICHAEL J.
BL TL 6'2"   210 lbs.
B. Oct. 28, 1865, Boston, Mass.   D. Oct. 16, 1904, Boston, Mass.

	G	AB	H	2B	3B	HR	HR %	R	RBI	BB	SO	SB	BA	SA	AB	H	G by POS
1884 BOS U	106	413	86	6	2	0	0.0	60		4			.208	.232	0	0	OF-96, 1B-11
1888 NY N	103	391	96	12	6	1	0.3	50	35	13	28	26	.246	.315	0	0	OF-103
1889	12	48	14	2	0	1	2.1	7	12	4	3	2	.292	.396	0	0	OF-12
1890 NY P	97	411	126	20	11	5	1.2	80	67	27	25	18	.307	.445	0	0	OF-97
1891 2 teams			CIN	N	(41G –	.209)		WAS	AA	(15G –	.283)						
" total	56	218	50	4	2	1	0.5	32	21	14	15	7	.229	.280	0	0	OF-56
5 yrs.	374	1481	372	44	21	8	0.5	229	134	62	71	53	.251	.325	0	0	OF-364, 1B-11

Don Slaught

SLAUGHT, DONALD MARTIN
BR TR 6'   185 lbs.
B. Sept. 11, 1959, Long Beach, Calif.

	G	AB	H	2B	3B	HR	HR %	R	RBI	BB	SO	SB	BA	SA	AB	H	G by POS
1982 KC A	43	115	32	6	0	3	2.6	14	8	9	12	0	.278	.409	0	0	C-43
1983	83	276	86	13	4	0	0.0	21	28	11	27	3	.312	.388	5	2	C-79, DH-1
1984	124	409	108	27	4	4	1.0	48	42	20	55	0	.264	.379	5	2	C-123, DH-1
3 yrs.	250	800	226	46	8	7	0.9	83	78	40	94	3	.283	.386	10	4	C-245, DH-2

LEAGUE CHAMPIONSHIP SERIES

	G	AB	H	2B	3B	HR	HR %	R	RBI	BB	SO	SB	BA	SA	AB	H	G by POS
1984 KC A	3	11	4	0	0	0	0.0	0	0	0	0	0	.364	.364	0	0	C-3

Enos Slaughter

SLAUGHTER, ENOS BRADSHER (Country)
BL TR 5'9½"   180 lbs.
B. Apr. 27, 1916, Roxboro, N. C.

	G	AB	H	2B	3B	HR	HR %	R	RBI	BB	SO	SB	BA	SA	AB	H	G by POS
1938 STL N	112	395	109	20	10	8	2.0	59	58	32	38	1	.276	.438	20	2	OF-92
1939	149	604	193	52	5	12	2.0	95	86	44	53	2	.320	.482	0	0	OF-149
1940	140	516	158	25	13	17	3.3	96	73	50	35	8	.306	.504	7	2	OF-132
1941	113	425	132	22	9	13	3.1	71	76	53	28	4	.311	.496	2	0	OF-108
1942	152	591	188	31	17	13	2.2	100	98	88	30	9	.318	.494	1	0	OF-151
1946	156	609	183	30	8	18	3.0	100	130	69	41	9	.300	.465	0	0	OF-156
1947	147	551	162	31	13	10	1.8	100	86	59	27	4	.294	.452	4	0	OF-142
1948	146	549	176	27	11	11	2.0	91	90	81	29	4	.321	.470	1	0	OF-146
1949	151	568	191	34	13	13	2.3	92	96	79	37	3	.336	.511	1	0	OF-150
1950	148	556	161	26	7	10	1.8	82	101	66	33	3	.290	.415	3	2	OF-145
1951	123	409	115	17	8	4	1.0	48	64	68	25	7	.281	.391	11	2	OF-106
1952	140	510	153	17	12	11	2.2	73	101	70	25	6	.300	.445	3	1	OF-137
1953	143	492	143	34	9	6	1.2	64	89	80	28	4	.291	.433	7	2	OF-137
1954 NY A	69	125	31	4	2	1	0.8	19	19	28	8	0	.248	.336	31	11	OF-30
1955 2 teams			NY	A	(10G –	.111)		KC	A	(108G –	.322)						
" total	118	276	87	12	4	5	1.8	50	35	41	18	2	.315	.442	42	16	OF-77
1956 2 teams			KC	A	(91G –	.278)		NY	A	(24G –	.289)						
" total	115	306	86	18	5	2	0.7	52	27	34	26	2	.281	.392	45	11	OF-76
1957 NY A	96	209	53	7	1	5	2.4	24	34	40	19	0	.254	.368	33	8	OF-64
1958	77	138	42	4	1	4	2.9	21	19	21	16	2	.304	.493	48	13	OF-35
1959 2 teams			NY	A	(74G –	.172)		MIL	N	(11G –	.167)						
" total	85	117	20	2	0	6	5.1	10	22	16	22	1	.171	.342	48	7	OF-32
19 yrs.	2380	7946	2383	413	148	169	2.1	1247	1304	1019	538	71	.300	.453	306	77	OF-2065

WORLD SERIES

	G	AB	H	2B	3B	HR	HR %	R	RBI	BB	SO	SB	BA	SA	AB	H	G by POS
1942 STL N	5	19	5	1	0	1	5.3	3	2	3	2	0	.263	.474	0	0	OF-5

	G	AB	H	2B	3B	HR	HR %	R	RBI	BB	SO	SB	BA	SA	Pinch Hit AB	Pinch Hit H	G by POS

Enos Slaughter continued

1946	7	25	8	1	1	1	4.0	5	2	4	3	1	.320	.560	0	0	OF-7
1956 NY A	6	20	7	0	0	1	5.0	6	4	4	0	0	.350	.500	0	0	OF-6
1957	5	12	3	1	0	0	0.0	2	0	3	2	0	.250	.333	0	0	OF-5
1958	4	3	0	0	0	0	0.0	1	0	1	1	0	.000	.000	3	0	
5 yrs.	27	79	23	3	1	3	3.8	17	8	15	8	1	.291	.468	3	0	OF-23

Scottie Slayback

SLAYBACK, ELBERT
B. Oct. 5, 1901, Paducah, Ky.   D. Nov. 30, 1979, Cincinnati, Ohio   BR TR 5'8"   165 lbs.

	G	AB	H	2B	3B	HR	HR %	R	RBI	BB	SO	SB	BA	SA	AB	H	G by POS
1926 NY N	2	8	0	0	0	0	0.0	0	0	0	0	0	.000	.000	0	0	2B-2

Bruce Sloan

SLOAN, ADAM BRUCE (Fatso)
B. Oct. 4, 1914, McAlester, Okla.   D. Sept. 24, 1973, Oklahoma City, Okla.   BL TL 5'9"   195 lbs.

	G	AB	H	2B	3B	HR	HR %	R	RBI	BB	SO	SB	BA	SA	AB	H	G by POS
1944 NY N	59	104	28	4	1	1	1.0	7	9	13	8	0	.269	.356	34	8	OF-21

Tod Sloan

SLOAN, YALE YEASTMAN
B. Dec. 24, 1890, Madisonville, Tenn.   D. Sept. 12, 1956, Akron, Ohio   BL TR 6'   175 lbs.

	G	AB	H	2B	3B	HR	HR %	R	RBI	BB	SO	SB	BA	SA	AB	H	G by POS
1913 STL A	7	26	7	1	0	0	0.0	2	2	1	9	1	.269	.308	0	0	OF-7
1917	109	313	72	6	2	2	0.6	32	25	28	34	8	.230	.281	27	5	OF-77
1919	27	63	15	1	3	0	0.0	9	6	12	3	0	.238	.349	4	2	OF-20
3 yrs.	143	402	94	8	5	2	0.5	43	33	41	46	9	.234	.294	31	7	OF-104

Ron Slocum

SLOCUM, RONALD REECE
B. July 2, 1945, Modesto, Calif.   BR TR 6'2"   185 lbs.

	G	AB	H	2B	3B	HR	HR %	R	RBI	BB	SO	SB	BA	SA	AB	H	G by POS
1969 SD N	13	24	7	1	0	1	4.2	6	5	0	5	0	.292	.458	1	0	3B-4, 2B-4, SS-1
1970	60	71	10	2	2	1	1.4	8	11	8	24	0	.141	.268	0	0	C-19, SS-17, 3B-11, 2B-9
1971	7	18	0	0	0	0	0.0	1	0	0	8	0	.000	.000	0	0	3B-6
3 yrs.	80	113	17	3	2	2	1.8	15	16	8	37	0	.150	.265	1	0	3B-21, C-19, SS-18, 2B-13

Charlie Small

SMALL, CHARLES ALBERT
B. Oct. 24, 1905, Auburn, Me.   D. Jan. 14, 1953, Auburn, Me.   BL TR 5'11"   186 lbs.

	G	AB	H	2B	3B	HR	HR %	R	RBI	BB	SO	SB	BA	SA	AB	H	G by POS
1930 BOS A	25	18	3	1	0	0	0.0	1	0	2	5	1	.167	.222	17	3	OF-1

Hank Small

SMALL, GEORGE HENRY
B. July 3, 1953, Atlanta, Ga.   BR TR 6'3"   205 lbs.

	G	AB	H	2B	3B	HR	HR %	R	RBI	BB	SO	SB	BA	SA	AB	H	G by POS
1978 ATL N	1	4	0	0	0	0	0.0	0	0	0	0	0	.000	.000	0	0	1B-1

Jim Small

SMALL, JAMES ARTHUR
B. Mar. 8, 1937, Portland, Ore.   BL TL 6'½"   180 lbs.

	G	AB	H	2B	3B	HR	HR %	R	RBI	BB	SO	SB	BA	SA	AB	H	G by POS
1955 DET A	12	4	0	0	0	0	0.0	2	0	1	1	0	.000	.000	2	0	OF-4
1956	58	91	29	4	2	0	0.0	13	10	6	10	0	.319	.407	15	7	OF-26
1957	36	42	9	2	0	0	0.0	7	0	2	11	0	.214	.262	13	2	OF-14
1958 KC A	2	4	0	0	0	0	0.0	0	0	1	0	0	.000	.000	1	0	OF-1
4 yrs.	108	141	38	6	2	0	0.0	22	10	10	22	0	.270	.340	31	9	OF-45

Roy Smalley

SMALLEY, ROY FREDERICK
Father of Roy Smalley.
B. June 9, 1926, Springfield, Mo.   BR TR 6'3"   190 lbs.

	G	AB	H	2B	3B	HR	HR %	R	RBI	BB	SO	SB	BA	SA	AB	H	G by POS
1948 CHI N	124	361	78	11	4	4	1.1	25	36	23	76	0	.216	.302	0	0	SS-124
1949	135	477	117	21	10	8	1.7	57	35	36	77	2	.245	.382	3	1	SS-132
1950	154	557	128	21	9	21	3.8	58	85	49	114	2	.230	.413	0	0	SS-154
1951	79	238	55	7	4	8	3.4	24	31	25	53	0	.231	.395	4	2	SS-74
1952	87	261	58	14	1	5	1.9	36	30	29	58	0	.222	.341	5	1	SS-82
1953	82	253	63	9	0	6	2.4	20	25	28	57	0	.249	.356	5	1	SS-77
1954 MIL N	25	36	8	0	0	1	2.8	5	7	4	9	0	.222	.306	8	2	SS-9, 2B-7, 1B-2
1955 PHI N	92	260	51	11	1	7	2.7	33	39	39	58	0	.196	.327	3	1	SS-87, 3B-1, 2B-1
1956	65	168	38	9	3	0	0.0	14	16	23	29	0	.226	.315	4	0	SS-60
1957	28	31	5	0	1	1	3.2	5	1	1	9	0	.161	.323	6	0	SS-20
1958	1	2	0	0	0	0	0.0	0	0	0	1	0	.000	.000	0	0	SS-1
11 yrs.	872	2644	601	103	33	61	2.3	277	305	257	541	4	.227	.360	38	8	SS-820, 2B-8, 1B-2, 3B-1

Roy Smalley

SMALLEY, ROY FREDERICK
Son of Roy Smalley.
B. Oct. 25, 1952, Los Angeles, Calif.   BB TR 6'1"   185 lbs.

	G	AB	H	2B	3B	HR	HR %	R	RBI	BB	SO	SB	BA	SA	AB	H	G by POS
1975 TEX A	78	250	57	8	0	3	1.2	22	33	30	42	4	.228	.296	2	1	SS-59, 2B-19, C-1
1976 2 teams	TEX A (41G – .225)				MIN A (103G – .271)												
" total	144	513	133	18	3	6	1.2	61	64	76	106	2	.259	.324	0	0	SS-108, 2B-38
1977 MIN A	150	584	135	21	5	6	1.0	93	56	74	89	5	.231	.315	1	0	SS-150
1978	158	586	160	31	3	19	3.2	80	77	85	70	2	.273	.433	1	1	SS-157
1979	162	621	168	28	3	24	3.9	94	95	80	80	2	.271	.441	0	0	SS-161, 1B-1
1980	133	486	135	24	1	12	2.5	64	63	65	63	3	.278	.405	4	1	SS-125, DH-3, 1B-3
1981	56	167	44	7	1	7	4.2	24	22	31	24	0	.263	.443	5	1	SS-37, DH-15, 1B-1
1982 2 teams	MIN A (4G – .154)				NY A (142G – .257)												
" total	146	499	127	15	2	20	4.0	57	67	71	104	0	.255	.413	7	0	SS-93, 3B-53, DH-4, 2B-1
1983 NY A	130	451	124	24	1	18	4.0	70	62	58	68	3	.275	.452	4	1	SS-91, 3B-26, 1B-22
1984 2 teams	NY A (67G – .239)				CHI A (47G – .170)												
" total	114	344	73	12	1	11	3.2	32	39	37	65	1	.212	.349	21	6	3B-73, SS-16, DH-7, 1B-6
10 yrs.	1271	4501	1156	188	20	123	2.7	597	558	607	711	24	.257	.389	45	11	SS-997, 3B-152, 2B-58, 1B-33, DH-29, C-1

Will Smalley

SMALLEY, WILLIAM DARWIN
B. June 27, 1871, Oakland, Calif.   D. Oct. 11, 1891, Bay City, Mich.   BR TR

	G	AB	H	2B	3B	HR	HR %	R	RBI	BB	SO	SB	BA	SA	AB	H	G by POS
1890 CLE N	136	502	107	11	1	0	0.0	62	42	60	44	10	.213	.239	0	0	3B-136
1891 WAS AA	11	38	6	0	1	0	0.0	5	3	5	2	0	.158	.211	0	0	3B-9, 2B-2
2 yrs.	147	540	113	11	2	0	0.0	67	45	65	46	10	.209	.237	0	0	3B-145, 2B-2

	G	AB	H	2B	3B	HR	HR %	R	RBI	BB	SO	SB	BA	SA	Pinch Hit AB	Pinch Hit H	G by POS

Joe Smaza

SMAZA, JOSEPH PAUL BL TL 5'11" 175 lbs.
B. July 7, 1923, Detroit, Mich. D. Apr. 30, 1979, Royal Oak, Mich.

	G	AB	H	2B	3B	HR	HR %	R	RBI	BB	SO	SB	BA	SA	Pinch Hit AB	Pinch Hit H	G by POS
1946 CHI A	2	5	1	0	0	0	0.0	2	0	0	0	0	.200	.200	0	0	OF-1

Bill Smiley

SMILEY, WILLIAM B.
B. 1856, Baltimore, Md. D. July 11, 1884, Baltimore, Md.

	G	AB	H	2B	3B	HR	HR %	R	RBI	BB	SO	SB	BA	SA	Pinch Hit AB	Pinch Hit H	G by POS
1882 2 teams		STL	AA (59G – .213)					**BAL**	AA (16G – .148)								
" total	75	301	60	4	2	0	0.0	33		6			.199	.226	0	0	2B-73, OF-2, SS-2

Al Smith

SMITH, ALPHONSE EUGENE (Fuzzy) BR TR 6'½" 189 lbs.
B. Feb. 7, 1928, Kirkwood, Mo.

	G	AB	H	2B	3B	HR	HR %	R	RBI	BB	SO	SB	BA	SA	Pinch Hit AB	Pinch Hit H	G by POS
1953 CLE A	47	150	36	9	0	3	2.0	28	14	20	25	2	.240	.360	2	1	OF-39, 3B-2
1954	131	481	135	29	6	11	2.3	101	50	88	65	2	.281	.435	2	0	OF-109, 3B-21, SS-4
1955	154	607	186	27	4	22	3.6	123	77	93	77	11	.306	.473	0	0	OF-120, 3B-45, SS-5, 2B-1
1956	141	526	144	26	5	16	3.0	87	71	84	72	6	.274	.433	1	0	OF-122, 3B-28, 2B-1
1957	135	507	125	23	5	11	2.2	78	49	79	70	12	.247	.377	1	0	3B-84, OF-50
1958 CHI A	139	480	121	23	5	12	2.5	61	58	48	77	3	.252	.396	3	1	OF-138, 3B-1
1959	129	472	112	16	4	17	3.6	65	55	46	74	7	.237	.396	1	0	OF-128, 3B-1
1960	142	536	169	31	3	12	2.2	80	72	50	65	8	.315	.451	1	0	OF-141
1961	147	532	148	29	4	28	5.3	88	93	56	67	4	.278	.506	5	2	3B-80, OF-71
1962	142	511	149	23	8	16	3.1	62	82	57	60	3	.292	.462	4	2	3B-105, OF-39
1963 BAL A	120	368	100	17	1	10	2.7	45	39	32	74	9	.272	.405	21	5	OF-97
1964 2 teams		CLE	A (61G – .162)					**BOS**	A (29G – .216)								
" total	90	187	33	5	1	6	3.2	25	16	21	42	0	.176	.310	30	4	OF-56, 3B-12
12 yrs.	1517	5357	1458	258	46	164	3.1	843	676	674	768	67	.272	.429	71	15	OF-1110, 3B-379, SS-9, 2B-2

WORLD SERIES

	G	AB	H	2B	3B	HR	HR %	R	RBI	BB	SO	SB	BA	SA	Pinch Hit AB	Pinch Hit H	G by POS
1954 CLE A	4	14	3	0	0	1	7.1	2	2	2	2	0	.214	.429	0	0	OF-4
1959 CHI A	6	20	5	3	0	0	0.0	1	1	4	4	0	.250	.400	0	0	OF-6
2 yrs.	10	34	8	3	0	1	2.9	3	3	6	6	0	.235	.412	0	0	OF-10

Bernie Smith

SMITH, CALVIN BERNARD BR TR 5'9" 164 lbs.
B. Sept. 4, 1941, Lutcher, La.

	G	AB	H	2B	3B	HR	HR %	R	RBI	BB	SO	SB	BA	SA	Pinch Hit AB	Pinch Hit H	G by POS
1970 MIL A	44	76	21	3	1	1	1.3	8	6	11	12	1	.276	.382	17	5	OF-39
1971	15	36	5	1	0	1	2.8	1	3	0	5	0	.139	.250	5	0	OF-12
2 yrs.	59	112	26	4	1	2	1.8	9	9	11	17	1	.232	.339	22	5	OF-51

Bill Smith

SMITH, WILLIAM E.
B. East Liverpool, Ohio Deceased.

	G	AB	H	2B	3B	HR	HR %	R	RBI	BB	SO	SB	BA	SA	Pinch Hit AB	Pinch Hit H	G by POS
1884 CLE N	1	3	0	0	0	0	0.0	0	0	0	2		.000	.000	0	0	OF-1

Billy Smith

SMITH, BILLY EDWARD BB TR 6'2½" 185 lbs.
B. July 14, 1953, Jonesboro Hodge, La.

	G	AB	H	2B	3B	HR	HR %	R	RBI	BB	SO	SB	BA	SA	Pinch Hit AB	Pinch Hit H	G by POS
1975 CAL A	59	143	29	5	1	0	0.0	10	14	12	27	1	.203	.252	0	0	SS-50, 1B-6, DH-4, 3B-2
1976	13	8	3	0	0	0	0.0	0	0	0	2	0	.375	.375	3	1	SS-10, DH-1
1977 BAL A	109	367	79	12	2	5	1.4	44	29	33	71	3	.215	.300	4	1	2B-104, SS-5, 1B-2, 3B-1
1978	85	250	65	12	2	5	2.0	29	30	27	40	3	.260	.384	3	0	2B-83, SS-2
1979	68	189	47	9	4	6	3.2	18	33	15	33	1	.249	.434	3	0	2B-63, SS-5
1981 SF N	36	61	11	0	0	1	1.6	6	5	9	16	0	.180	.230	12	4	SS-21, 2B-5, 3B-3
6 yrs.	370	1018	234	38	9	17	1.7	107	111	96	189	8	.230	.335	25	6	2B-255, SS-93, 1B-8, 3B-6, DH-5

LEAGUE CHAMPIONSHIP SERIES

	G	AB	H	2B	3B	HR	HR %	R	RBI	BB	SO	SB	BA	SA	Pinch Hit AB	Pinch Hit H	G by POS
1979 BAL A	1	4	0	0	0	0	0.0	0	0	0	1	0	.000	.000	0	0	2B-1

WORLD SERIES

	G	AB	H	2B	3B	HR	HR %	R	RBI	BB	SO	SB	BA	SA	Pinch Hit AB	Pinch Hit H	G by POS
1979 BAL A	4	7	2	0	0	0	0.0	1	0	2	0	0	.286	.286	1	1	2B-2

Bob Smith

SMITH, ROBERT ELDRIDGE BR TR 5'10" 175 lbs.
B. Apr. 22, 1898, Rogersville, Tenn.

	G	AB	H	2B	3B	HR	HR %	R	RBI	BB	SO	SB	BA	SA	Pinch Hit AB	Pinch Hit H	G by POS
1923 BOS N	115	375	94	16	3	0	0.0	30	40	17	35	4	.251	.309	3	1	SS-101, 2B-8
1924	106	347	79	12	3	2	0.6	32	38	15	26	5	.228	.297	2	0	SS-80, 3B-23
1925	58	174	49	9	4	0	0.0	17	23	5	6	2	.282	.379	8	0	SS-21, 2B-15, P-13, OF-1
1926	40	84	25	6	2	0	0.0	10	13	2	4	0	.298	.417	7	4	P-33
1927	54	109	27	3	1	1	0.9	10	10	2	4	0	.248	.321	13	2	P-41
1928	39	92	23	2	0	1	1.1	11	8	1	6	2	.250	.304	1	0	P-38
1929	39	99	17	4	2	1	1.0	12	8	2	8	1	.172	.283	0	0	P-34, SS-5
1930	39	81	19	2	0	0	0.0	7	4	0	5	0	.235	.259	1	0	P-38
1931 CHI N	36	87	19	2	0	0	0.0	7	4	5	2	0	.218	.241	0	0	P-36
1932	36	42	10	4	1	0	0.0	5	4	0	2	1	.238	.381	0	0	P-34, 2B-2
1933 2 teams		CIN	N (23G – .200)					**BOS**	N (14G – .200)								
" total	37	45	9	1	0	0	0.0	3	3	1	1	1	.200	.267	1	1	P-30, SS-1
1934 BOS N	42	36	9	1	0	0	0.0	5	3	0	1	0	.250	.278	0	0	P-39
1935	47	63	17	0	0	0	0.0	3	4	1	5	0	.270	.270	1	1	P-46
1936	35	45	10	2	0	0	0.0	1	4	0	4	0	.222	.267	0	0	P-35
1937	19	10	2	0	0	0	0.0	1	0	1	1	0	.200	.200	0	0	P-18
15 yrs.	742	1689	409	64	17	5	0.3	154	166	52	110	16	.242	.309	37	9	P-435, SS-208, 2B-25, 3B-23, OF-1

WORLD SERIES

	G	AB	H	2B	3B	HR	HR %	R	RBI	BB	SO	SB	BA	SA	Pinch Hit AB	Pinch Hit H	G by POS
1932 CHI N	1	0	0	0	0	0	–	0	0	0	0	0	–	–	0	0	P-1

Bobby Gene Smith

SMITH, BOBBY GENE BR TR 5'11" 180 lbs.
B. May 28, 1934, Hood River, Ore.

	G	AB	H	2B	3B	HR	HR %	R	RBI	BB	SO	SB	BA	SA	Pinch Hit AB	Pinch Hit H	G by POS
1957 STL N	93	185	39	7	1	3	1.6	24	18	13	35	1	.211	.308	11	1	OF-79
1958	28	88	25	3	0	2	2.3	8	5	2	18	1	.284	.386	1	0	OF-27
1959	43	60	13	1	1	1	1.7	11	7	1	9	0	.217	.317	7	2	OF-32
1960 PHI N	98	217	62	5	2	4	1.8	24	27	10	28	2	.286	.382	35	11	OF-70, 3B-1

	G	AB	H	2B	3B	HR	HR %	R	RBI	BB	SO	SB	BA	SA	Pinch Hit AB	Pinch Hit H	G by POS

Bobby Gene Smith continued

	G	AB	H	2B	3B	HR	HR%	R	RBI	BB	SO	SB	BA	SA	PH AB	PH H	G by POS
1961	79	174	44	7	0	2	1.1	16	18	15	32	0	.253	.328	31	6	OF-47
1962 3 teams		NY	N (8G – .136)		CHI	N (13G – .172)		STL	N (91G – .231)								
" total	112	181	38	9	1	1	0.6	17	16	12	22	1	.210	.287	18	2	OF-93
1965 CAL A	23	57	13	3	0	0	0.0	1	5	2	10	0	.228	.281	7	2	OF-15
7 yrs.	476	962	234	35	5	13	1.4	101	96	55	154	5	.243	.331	110	24	OF-363, 3B-1

Broadway Aleck Smith

SMITH, ALEXANDER BENJAMIN   TR
B. 1871, New York, N. Y.   D. July 9, 1919, New York, N. Y.

	G	AB	H	2B	3B	HR	HR%	R	RBI	BB	SO	SB	BA	SA	PH AB	PH H	G by POS
1897 BKN N	66	237	71	13	1	1	0.4	36	39	4		12	.300	.376	0	0	C-43, OF-18, 1B-6
1898	52	199	52	6	5	0	0.0	25	23	3		7	.261	.342	2	0	OF-26, C-20, 3B-2, 2B-2, 1B-1
1899 2 teams		BKN	N (17G – .180)		BAL	N (41G – .383)											
" total	58	181	57	6	5	0	0.0	23	31	6		7	.315	.403	1	0	C-53, OF-2, 1B-1
1900 BKN N	7	25	6	0	0	0	0.0	2	3	1		2	.240	.240	0	0	3B-6, C-1
1901 NY N	26	78	11	0	1	0	0.0	5	6	0		3	.141	.167	1	0	C-25
1902 BAL A	41	145	34	3	0	0	0.0	10	21	8		5	.234	.255	0	0	C-27, 1B-7, OF-4, 2B-3, 3B-1
1903 BOS A	11	33	10	1	0	0	0.0	4	4	0		0	.303	.333	1	0	C-10
1904 CHI N	10	29	6	1	0	0	0.0	2	1	3		1	.207	.241	2	0	OF-6, 3B-1, C-1
1906 NY N	16	28	5	0	0	0	0.0	0	2	1		1	.179	.179	4	1	C-8, 1B-3, OF-1
9 yrs.	287	955	252	30	12	1	0.1	107	130	26		38	.264	.324	11	1	C-188, OF-57, 1B-18, 3B-10, 2B-5

Bull Smith

SMITH, LEWIS OSCAR   TR 6'   180 lbs.
B. Aug. 20, 1880, Plum, W. Va.   D. May 1, 1928, Charlestown, W. Va.

	G	AB	H	2B	3B	HR	HR%	R	RBI	BB	SO	SB	BA	SA	PH AB	PH H	G by POS
1904 PIT N	13	42	6	0	1	0	0.0	2	0	1		0	.143	.190	0	0	OF-13
1906 CHI N	1	1	0	0	0	0	0.0	0	0	0		0	.000	.000	1	0	
1911 WAS A	1	0	0	0	0	0	–	0	0	0		0	–	–	0	0	
3 yrs.	15	43	6	0	1	0	0.0	2	0	1		0	.140	.186	1	0	OF-13

Carr Smith

SMITH, CARR E.   BR TR 6'   175 lbs.
B. Apr. 8, 1901, Kernersville, N. C.

	G	AB	H	2B	3B	HR	HR%	R	RBI	BB	SO	SB	BA	SA	PH AB	PH H	G by POS
1923 WAS A	5	9	1	1	0	0	0.0	0	1	0	0	0	.111	.222	1	0	OF-4
1924	5	10	2	0	0	0	0.0	1	0	0	3	0	.200	.200	1	0	OF-4
2 yrs.	10	19	3	1	0	0	0.0	1	1	0	3	0	.158	.211	2	0	OF-8

Charley Smith

SMITH, CHARLES WILLIAM   BR TR 6'1"   170 lbs.
B. Sept. 15, 1937, Charleston, S. C.

	G	AB	H	2B	3B	HR	HR%	R	RBI	BB	SO	SB	BA	SA	PH AB	PH H	G by POS
1960 LA N	18	60	10	1	0	0	0.0	2	5	1	15	0	.167	.217	0	0	3B-18
1961 2 teams		LA	N (9G – .250)		PHI	N (112G – .248)											
" total	121	435	108	14	4	11	2.5	47	50	24	82	3	.248	.375	5	1	3B-98, SS-17
1962 CHI N	65	145	30	4	0	2	1.4	11	17	9	32	0	.207	.276	13	2	3B-54
1963	4	7	2	1	0	0	0.0	0	1	0	2	0	.286	.571	3	1	SS-1
1964 2 teams		CHI	N (2G – .143)		NY	N (127G – .239)											
" total	129	450	107	12	1	20	4.4	45	58	20	102	2	.238	.402	7	2	3B-87, SS-36, OF-13
1965 NY N	135	499	122	20	3	16	3.2	49	62	17	123	2	.244	.393	3	0	3B-131, SS-6, 2B-1
1966 STL N	116	391	104	13	4	10	2.6	34	43	22	81	0	.266	.396	8	3	3B-107, SS-1
1967 NY N	135	425	95	15	3	9	2.1	38	38	32	110	0	.224	.336	20	6	3B-115
1968	46	70	16	4	1	1	1.4	2	7	5	18	0	.229	.357	31	10	3B-13
1969 CHI N	2	2	0	0	0	0	0.0	0	0	0	0	0	.000	.000	2	0	
10 yrs.	771	2484	594	83	18	69	2.8	228	281	130	565	7	.239	.370	92	25	3B-623, SS-61, OF-13, 2B-1

Chris Smith

SMITH, CHRISTOPHER WILLIAM   BB TR 6'   185 lbs.
B. July 18, 1957, Torrance, Calif.

	G	AB	H	2B	3B	HR	HR%	R	RBI	BB	SO	SB	BA	SA	PH AB	PH H	G by POS
1981 MON N	7	7	0	0	0	0	0.0	0	0	0	2	0	.000	.000	7	0	2B-1
1982	2	2	0	0	0	0	0.0	0	0	0	1	0	.000	.000	2	0	
1983 SF N	22	67	22	6	1	1	1.5	13	11	7	12	0	.328	.493	3	3	1B-15, OF-4, 3B-1
3 yrs.	31	76	22	6	1	1	1.3	13	11	7	15	0	.289	.434	12	3	1B-15, OF-4, 3B-1, 2B-1

Dick Smith

SMITH, RICHARD ARTHUR   BR TR 6'2"   205 lbs.
B. May 17, 1939, Lebanon, Ore.

	G	AB	H	2B	3B	HR	HR%	R	RBI	BB	SO	SB	BA	SA	PH AB	PH H	G by POS
1963 NY N	20	42	10	0	1	0	0.0	4	3	5	10	3	.238	.286	5	1	OF-10, 1B-2
1964	46	94	21	6	1	0	0.0	14	3	1	29	6	.223	.309	8	1	1B-18, OF-13
1965 LA N	10	6	0	0	0	0	0.0	0	1	0	3	0	.000	.000	0	0	OF-9
3 yrs.	76	142	31	6	2	0	0.0	18	7	6	42	9	.218	.289	13	2	OF-32, 1B-20

Dick Smith

SMITH, RICHARD HARRISON   BR TR 5'8"   160 lbs.
B. July 21, 1927, Blandsburg, Pa.

	G	AB	H	2B	3B	HR	HR%	R	RBI	BB	SO	SB	BA	SA	PH AB	PH H	G by POS
1951 PIT N	12	46	8	0	0	0	0.0	2	4	8	8	0	.174	.174	0	0	3B-12
1952	29	66	7	1	0	0	0.0	8	5	9	3	0	.106	.121	2	0	3B-16, SS-4, 2B-4
1953	13	43	7	0	1	0	0.0	4	2	6	6	0	.163	.209	2	0	SS-13
1954	12	31	3	1	1	0	0.0	2	0	6	5	0	.097	.194	3	0	3B-9
1955	4	0	0	0	0	0	–	1	0	1	0	0	–	–	0	0	SS-1
5 yrs.	70	186	25	2	2	0	0.0	17	11	30	22	0	.134	.167	5	0	3B-37, SS-18, 2B-4

Dick Smith

SMITH, RICHARD KELLY   BR TR 6'5"   200 lbs.
B. Aug. 25, 1944, Lincolnton, N. C.

	G	AB	H	2B	3B	HR	HR%	R	RBI	BB	SO	SB	BA	SA	PH AB	PH H	G by POS
1969 WAS A	21	28	3	0	0	0	0.0	2	0	4	7	0	.107	.107	8	0	OF-9

Earl Smith

SMITH, EARL CALVIN   BR TR 6'   185 lbs.
B. Mar. 14, 1928, Sunnyside, Wash.

	G	AB	H	2B	3B	HR	HR%	R	RBI	BB	SO	SB	BA	SA	PH AB	PH H	G by POS
1955 PIT N	5	16	1	0	0	0	0.0	1	0	4	2	0	.063	.063	0	0	OF-5

	G	AB	H	2B	3B	HR	HR%	R	RBI	BB	SO	SB	BA	SA	Pinch Hit AB	Pinch Hit H	G by POS

Earl Smith

SMITH, EARL LEONARD
B. Jan. 20, 1891, Oak Hill, Ohio.   D. Mar. 14, 1943, Portsmouth, Ohio.   BL TR 5'11" 170 lbs.

	G	AB	H	2B	3B	HR	HR%	R	RBI	BB	SO	SB	BA	SA	AB	H	G by POS
1916 CHI N	14	27	7	1	1	0	0.0	2	4	2	5	1	.259	.370	7	1	OF-7
1917 STL A	52	199	56	7	7	0	0.0	31	10	15	21	5	.281	.387	1	1	OF-51
1918	89	286	77	10	5	0	0.0	28	32	13	16	13	.269	.339	8	4	OF-81
1919	88	252	63	12	5	1	0.4	21	36	18	27	1	.250	.349	14	5	OF-68
1920	103	353	108	21	8	3	0.8	45	55	13	18	11	.306	.436	16	2	3B-70, OF-15
1921 2 teams		STL	A (25G –	.333)		WAS	A	(59G –	.217)								
" total	84	258	65	9	4	4	1.6	27	26	13	23	1	.252	.364	20	6	OF-47, 3B-14
1922 WAS A	65	205	53	12	2	1	0.5	22	23	8	17	4	.259	.351	10	2	OF-49, 3B-1
7 yrs.	495	1580	429	72	32	9	0.6	176	186	82	127	36	.272	.375	76	21	OF-318, 3B-85

Earl Smith

SMITH, EARL SUTTON (Oil)
B. Feb. 14, 1897, Sheridan, Ark.   D. June 9, 1963, Little Rock, Ark.   BL TR 5'10½" 180 lbs.

	G	AB	H	2B	3B	HR	HR%	R	RBI	BB	SO	SB	BA	SA	AB	H	G by POS
1919 NY N	21	36	9	2	1	0	0.0	5	8	3	3	1	.250	.361	6	0	C-14, 2B-1
1920	91	262	77	7	1	1	0.4	20	30	18	16	5	.294	.340	8	4	C-82
1921	89	229	77	8	4	10	4.4	35	51	27	8	4	.336	.537	8	3	C-78
1922	90	234	65	11	4	9	3.8	29	39	37	12	1	.278	.474	12	3	C-75
1923 2 teams		NY	N (24G –	.206)		BOS	N	(72G –	.288)								
" total	96	225	62	16	2	4	1.8	24	23	26	11	0	.276	.418	35	6	C-46
1924 2 teams		BOS	N (33G –	.271)		PIT	N	(39G –	.369)								
" total	72	170	57	13	1	4	2.4	13	29	19	7	2	.335	.494	21	10	C-48
1925 PIT N	109	329	103	22	3	8	2.4	34	64	31	13	4	.313	.471	12	5	C-96
1926	105	292	101	17	2	2	0.7	29	46	28	7	1	.346	.438	7	5	C-98
1927	66	189	51	3	1	5	2.6	16	25	21	11	0	.270	.376	5	3	C-61
1928 2 teams		PIT	N (32G –	.247)		STL	N	(24G –	.224)								
" total	56	143	34	8	0	2	1.4	11	18	16	11	0	.238	.336	8	0	C-46
1929 STL N	57	145	50	8	0	1	0.7	9	22	18	6	0	.345	.421	7	2	C-50
1930	8	10	0	0	0	0	0.0	0	0	3	1	0	.000	.000	0	0	C-6
12 yrs.	860	2264	686	115	19	46	2.0	225	355	247	106	18	.303	.432	129	41	C-700, 2B-1
WORLD SERIES																	
1921 NY N	3	7	0	0	0	0	0.0	0	0	1	0	0	.000	.000	1	0	C-2
1922	4	7	1	0	0	0	0.0	0	0	0	2	0	.143	.143	3	0	C-1
1925 PIT N	6	20	7	1	0	0	0.0	0	1	1	2	0	.350	.400	0	0	C-6
1927	3	8	0	0	0	0	0.0	0	0	0	0	0	.000	.000	1	0	C-2
1928 STL N	1	4	3	0	0	0	0.0	0	0	0	0	0	.750	.750	0	0	C-1
5 yrs.	17	46	11	1	0	0	0.0	0	0	2	4	0	.239	.261	5	0	C-12

Edgar Smith

SMITH, ALBERT EDGAR
B. Oct. 15, 1860, North Haven, Conn.   Deceased.

	G	AB	H	2B	3B	HR	HR%	R	RBI	BB	SO	SB	BA	SA	AB	H	G by POS
1883 BOS N	30	115	25	5	3	0	0.0	16	5	11			.217	.313	0	0	OF-30, C-1

Edgar Smith

SMITH, EDGAR EUGENE
B. June 12, 1862, Providence, R. I.   D. Nov. 3, 1892, Providence, R. I.   BR TR 5'10" 160 lbs.

	G	AB	H	2B	3B	HR	HR%	R	RBI	BB	SO	SB	BA	SA	AB	H	G by POS
1883 2 teams		PRO	N (2G –	.222)		PHI	N	(1G –	.750)								
" total	3	13	5	1	0	0	0.0	3		0	2		.385	.462	0	0	OF-3, 1B-2, P-1
1884 WAS AA	14	57	5	0	1	0	0.0	5		1			.088	.123	0	0	OF-12, P-3
1885 PRO N	1	4	1	0	0	0	0.0	0	0	0			.250	.250	0	0	P-1
1890 CLE N	8	24	7	0	1	0	0.0	2	4	4	1	0	.292	.375	0	0	P-6, OF-2
4 yrs.	26	98	18	1	2	0	0.0	10	3	5	3	0	.184	.235	0	0	OF-17, P-11, 1B-2

Elmer Smith

SMITH, ELMER ELLSWORTH
B. Mar. 23, 1868, Pittsburgh, Pa.   D. Nov. 3, 1945, Pittsburgh, Pa.   BL TL 5'11" 178 lbs.

	G	AB	H	2B	3B	HR	HR%	R	RBI	BB	SO	SB	BA	SA	AB	H	G by POS
1886 CIN AA	10	32	9	1	0	0	0.0	9		9			.281	.375	0	0	P-10, OF-1
1887	52	186	47	10	6	0	0.0	26		11		5	.253	.371	0	0	P-52, OF-2
1888	40	129	29	4	1	0	0.0	15	9	20		2	.225	.271	0	0	P-40, OF-2
1889	29	83	23	3	1	2	2.4	12	17	7	18	1	.277	.410	0	0	P-29
1892 PIT N	138	511	140	18	14	4	0.8	86	63	82	43	22	.274	.387	0	0	OF-124, P-17
1893	128	518	179	26	23	7	1.4	121	103	77	23	26	.346	.525	0	0	OF-128
1894	125	489	174	33	19	6	1.2	128	72	65	12	33	.356	.538	0	0	OF-125, P-1
1895	124	492	146	16	13	1	0.2	109	81	55	25	35	.297	.388	1	0	OF-123
1896	122	484	175	22	14	6	1.2	121	94	74	18	33	.362	.502	0	0	OF-122
1897	123	467	145	19	17	6	1.3	99	54	70		25	.310	.463	0	0	OF-123
1898 CIN N	123	486	166	21	10	1	0.2	79	66	69		20	.342	.432	0	0	OF-123, P-1
1899	87	339	101	13	6	1	0.3	65	24	47		10	.298	.381	0	0	OF-87
1900 2 teams		CIN	N (29G –	.279)		NY	N	(87G –	.277)								
" total	116	425	118	13	11	3	0.7	61	52	42		20	.278	.381	4	0	OF-110
1901 2 teams		PIT	N (4G –	.000)		BOS	N	(18G –	.175)								
" total	22	63	10	2	1	0	0.0	5	3	8		2	.159	.222	4	0	OF-16
14 yrs.	1239	4704	1462	201	137	37	0.8	934	637	636	139	234	.311	.435	9	0	OF-1086, P-150

Elmer Smith

SMITH, ELMER JOHN
B. Sept. 21, 1892, Sandusky, Ohio.   D. Aug. 3, 1984, Columbia, Ky.   BL TR 5'10" 165 lbs.

	G	AB	H	2B	3B	HR	HR%	R	RBI	BB	SO	SB	BA	SA	AB	H	G by POS
1914 CLE A	13	53	17	3	0	0	0.0	5	8	2	11	1	.321	.377	0	0	OF-13
1915	144	476	118	23	12	3	0.6	37	67	36	75	10	.248	.366	19	6	OF-123
1916 2 teams		CLE	A (79G –	.277)		WAS	A	(45G –	.214)								
" total	124	381	95	25	6	5	1.3	37	67	36	63	7	.249	.386	18	7	OF-102
1917 2 teams		WAS	A (35G –	.222)		CLE	A	(64G –	.261)								
" total	99	278	68	9	4	3	1.1	29	39	18	32	7	.245	.338	26	4	OF-69
1919 CLE A	114	395	110	24	6	9	2.3	60	54	41	30	15	.278	.438	3	0	OF-111
1920	129	456	144	37	10	12	2.6	82	103	53	35	5	.316	.520	0	0	OF-129
1921	129	431	125	28	9	16	3.7	98	84	56	46	0	.290	.508	2	0	OF-127
1922 2 teams		BOS	A (73G –	.286)		NY	A	(21G –	.185)								
" total	94	258	71	13	6	7	2.7	44	37	28	26	0	.275	.453	21	6	OF-69
1923 NY A	70	183	56	6	2	7	3.8	30	35	21	21	3	.306	.475	21	11	OF-47
1925 CIN N	96	284	77	13	7	8	2.8	47	46	28	20	6	.271	.451	13	5	OF-80
10 yrs.	1012	3195	881	181	62	70	2.2	469	540	319	359	54	.276	.437	123	39	OF-870
WORLD SERIES																	
1920 CLE A	5	13	4	0	1	1	7.7	1	6	1	1	0	.308	.692	1	0	OF-5

	G	AB	H	2B	3B	HR	HR %	R	RBI	BB	SO	SB	BA	SA	Pinch Hit AB	Pinch Hit H	G by POS

Elmer Smith continued

	G	AB	H	2B	3B	HR	HR%	R	RBI	BB	SO	SB	BA	SA	AB	H	G by POS
1922 NY A	2	2	0	0	0	0	0.0	0	0	0	2	0	.000	.000	2	0	
2 yrs.	7	15	4	0	1	1	6.7	1	6	1	3	0	.267	.600	3	0	OF-5

Ernie Smith

SMITH, ERNEST HENRY   BR TR 5'8"   155 lbs.
B. Oct. 11, 1901, Paterson, N. J.   D. Apr. 6, 1973, Brooklyn, N. Y.

	G	AB	H	2B	3B	HR	HR%	R	RBI	BB	SO	SB	BA	SA	AB	H	G by POS
1930 CHI A	24	79	19	3	0	0	0.0	5	3	5	6	2	.241	.278	3	1	SS-21

Frank Smith

SMITH, FRANK L.
B. Nov. 24, 1857, Canada   D. Oct. 11, 1928, Canandaigua, N. Y.

	G	AB	H	2B	3B	HR	HR%	R	RBI	BB	SO	SB	BA	SA	AB	H	G by POS
1884 PIT AA	10	36	9	0	1	0	0.0	3		0			.250	.306	0	0	C-7, OF-3

Fred Smith

SMITH, FRED VINCENT   BR TR 5'11½" 185 lbs.
Brother of Charlie Smith.
B. July 29, 1886, Cleveland, Ohio   D. May 28, 1961, Cleveland, Ohio

	G	AB	H	2B	3B	HR	HR%	R	RBI	BB	SO	SB	BA	SA	AB	H	G by POS
1913 BOS N	92	285	65	9	3	0	0.0	35	27	29	55	7	.228	.281	2	1	3B-59, 2B-14, SS-11, OF-4
1914 BUF F	145	473	104	12	10	2	0.4	48	45	49		24	.220	.300	0	0	3B-127, SS-19, 1B-1
1915 2 teams		BUF	F (35G –	.237)		BKN	F	(110G –	.247)								
" total	145	499	122	18	10	5	1.0	49	69	38		23	.244	.351	2	0	3B-126, SS-16
1917 STL N	56	165	30	0	2	1	0.6	11	17	17	22	4	.182	.224	1	0	3B-51, 2B-2, SS-1
4 yrs.	438	1422	321	39	25	8	0.6	143	158	133	77	58	.226	.305	5	1	3B-253, SS-157, 2B-16, OF-4, 1B-1

George Smith

SMITH, GEORGE CORNELIUS   BR TR 5'10"   170 lbs.
B. July 7, 1938, St. Petersburg, Fla.

	G	AB	H	2B	3B	HR	HR%	R	RBI	BB	SO	SB	BA	SA	AB	H	G by POS
1963 DET A	52	171	37	8	2	0	0.0	16	17	18	34	4	.216	.287	0	0	2B-52
1964	5	7	2	0	0	0	0.0	1	2	1	4	1	.286	.286	1	1	2B-3
1965	32	53	5	0	0	1	1.9	6	1	3	18	0	.094	.151	5	0	2B-22, SS-3, 3B-3
1966 BOS A	128	403	86	19	4	8	2.0	41	37	37	86	4	.213	.340	4	0	2B-109, SS-19
4 yrs.	217	634	130	27	6	9	1.4	64	57	59	142	9	.205	.309	10	1	2B-186, SS-22, 3B-3

Germany Smith

SMITH, GEORGE J.   BR TR 6'   175 lbs.
B. Apr. 21, 1863, Pittsburgh, Pa.   D. Dec. 1, 1927, Altoona, Pa.

	G	AB	H	2B	3B	HR	HR%	R	RBI	BB	SO	SB	BA	SA	AB	H	G by POS
1884 2 teams		ALT	U (25G –	.315)		CLE	N	(72G –	.254)								
" total	97	399	108	22	5	4	1.0	40	26	3	45		.271	.381	0	0	SS-55, 2B-42, P-1
1885 BKN AA	108	419	108	17	11	4	1.0	63		10			.258	.379	0	0	SS-108
1886	105	426	105	17	6	2	0.5	66		19			.246	.329	0	0	SS-105, OF-1, C-1
1887	103	435	128	19	16	4	0.9	79		13		26	.294	.439	0	0	SS-101, 3B-2
1888	103	402	86	10	7	3	0.7	47	61	22		27	.214	.296	0	0	SS-103, 2B-1
1889	121	446	103	22	3	3	0.7	89	53	40	42	35	.231	.314	0	0	SS-105, OF-1
1890 BKN N	129	481	92	6	5	1	0.2	76	47	42	23	24	.191	.231	0	0	SS-129
1891 CIN N	138	512	103	11	5	3	0.6	50	53	38	32	16	.201	.260	0	0	SS-138
1892	139	506	121	13	6	8	1.6	58	63	42	52	19	.239	.336	0	0	SS-139
1893	130	500	118	18	6	3	0.6	63	56	38	20	14	.236	.314	0	0	SS-130
1894	127	482	127	33	5	3	0.6	73	76	41	28	15	.263	.371	0	0	SS-127
1895	127	503	151	23	6	4	0.8	75	74	34	24	13	.300	.394	0	0	SS-127
1896	120	456	131	22	9	2	0.4	65	71	28	22	22	.287	.388	0	0	SS-120
1897 BKN N	112	428	86	17	3	0	0.0	47	29	14		1	.201	.255	0	0	SS-112
1898 STL N	51	157	25	2	1	1	0.6	16	9	24		1	.159	.204	0	0	SS-51
15 yrs.	1710	6552	1592	252	94	45	0.7	907	618	408	288	213	.243	.331	0	0	SS-1665, 2B-43, OF-2, 3B-2, C-1, P-1

Hal Smith

SMITH, HAROLD RAYMOND (Cura)   BR TR 5'10½" 186 lbs.
B. June 1, 1931, Barling, Ark.

	G	AB	H	2B	3B	HR	HR%	R	RBI	BB	SO	SB	BA	SA	AB	H	G by POS
1956 STL N	75	227	64	12	0	5	2.2	27	23	15	22	1	.282	.401	9	3	C-66
1957	100	333	93	12	3	2	0.6	25	37	18	18	2	.279	.351	4	2	C-97
1958	77	220	50	4	1	1	0.5	13	24	14	14	0	.227	.268	5	0	C-71
1959	142	452	122	15	3	13	2.9	35	50	15	28	2	.270	.403	1	0	C-141
1960	127	337	77	16	0	2	0.6	20	28	29	33	1	.228	.294	5	1	C-124
1961	45	125	31	4	1	0	0.0	6	10	11	12	0	.248	.296	1	0	C-45
1965 PIT N	4	3	0	0	0	0	0.0	0	0	0	1	0	.000	.000	0	0	C-4
7 yrs.	570	1697	437	63	8	23	1.4	126	172	102	128	6	.258	.345	25	6	C-548

Hal Smith

SMITH, HAROLD WAYNE   BR TR 6'   195 lbs.
B. Dec. 7, 1930, West Frankfort, Ill.

	G	AB	H	2B	3B	HR	HR%	R	RBI	BB	SO	SB	BA	SA	AB	H	G by POS
1955 BAL A	135	424	115	23	4	4	0.9	41	52	30	21	1	.271	.373	11	4	C-125
1956 2 teams		BAL	A (78G –	.262)		KC	A	(36G –	.275)								
" total	114	371	99	23	2	5	1.3	31	42	20	34	2	.267	.380	8	0	C-107
1957 KC A	107	360	109	26	0	13	3.6	41	41	14	44	2	.303	.483	8	1	C-103
1958	99	315	86	19	2	5	1.6	32	46	25	47	0	.273	.394	10	5	3B-43, C-31, 1B-14
1959	108	292	84	12	0	5	1.7	36	31	34	39	0	.288	.380	12	4	3B-77, C-22
1960 PIT N	77	258	76	18	2	11	4.3	37	45	22	48	1	.295	.508	6	2	C-71
1961	67	193	43	10	0	3	1.6	12	26	11	38	0	.223	.321	2	1	C-65
1962 HOU N	109	345	81	14	0	12	3.5	32	35	24	55	0	.235	.380	14	3	C-92, 3B-6, 1B-2
1963	31	58	14	2	0	0	0.0	1	2	4	15	0	.241	.276	19	3	C-11
1964 CIN N	32	66	8	1	0	0	0.0	6	3	12	20	1	.121	.136	12	2	C-20
10 yrs.	879	2682	715	148	10	58	2.2	269	323	196	361	7	.267	.394	102	25	C-647, 3B-126, 1B-16
WORLD SERIES																	
1960 PIT N	3	8	3	0	0	1	12.5	1	3	1	0	0	.375	.750	0	0	C-3

Hap Smith

SMITH, HENRY JOSEPH   BL TR 6'   185 lbs.
B. July 14, 1883, Coquille, Ore.   D. Feb. 26, 1961, San Jose, Calif.

	G	AB	H	2B	3B	HR	HR%	R	RBI	BB	SO	SB	BA	SA	AB	H	G by POS
1910 BKN N	35	76	18	2	0	0	0.0	6	5	4	14	4	.237	.263	17	3	OF-16

	G	AB	H	2B	3B	HR	HR %	R	RBI	BB	SO	SB	BA	SA	Pinch Hit AB	Pinch Hit H	G by POS

Harry Smith

SMITH, HARRY THOMAS   BR TR
B. Oct. 31, 1874, Yorkshire, England   D. Feb. 17, 1933, Salem, N. J.
Manager 1909.

	G	AB	H	2B	3B	HR	HR %	R	RBI	BB	SO	SB	BA	SA	PH AB	PH H	G by POS
1901 PHI A	11	34	11	1	0	0	0.0	3	3	2			1	.324	.353	1	1	C-9, OF-1
1902 PIT N	50	185	35	4	1	0	0.0	14	12	4			4	.189	.222	0	0	C-50
1903	61	212	37	3	2	0	0.0	15	19	12			2	.175	.208	0	0	C-60, OF-1
1904	47	141	35	3	1	0	0.0	17	18	16			5	.248	.284	0	0	C-44, OF-3
1905	1	3	0	0	0	0	0.0	0	1	0			1	.000	.000	0	0	C-1
1906	1	1	0	0	0	0	0.0	0	0	0			0	.000	.000	0	0	C-1
1907	18	38	10	1	0	0	0.0	4	1	4			0	.263	.289	0	0	C-18
1908 BOS N	41	130	32	2	2	1	0.8	13	16	7			2	.246	.315	3	0	C-38
1909	43	113	19	4	1	0	0.0	9	4	5			3	.168	.221	12	2	C-31
1910	70	147	35	4	0	1	0.7	8	15	5	14	5	.238	.286	32	6	C-38
10 yrs.	343	1004	214	22	7	2	0.2	83	89	55	14	23	.213	.255	48	9	C-290, OF-5
WORLD SERIES																	
1903 PIT N	1	3	0	0	0	0	0.0	0	0	0	0	0	.000	.000	0	0	C-1

Harry Smith

SMITH, HARRY W.   BR TR 6' 175 lbs.
B. Feb. 5, 1856, N. Vernon, Ind.   D. June 4, 1898, N. Vernon, Ind.

	G	AB	H	2B	3B	HR	HR %	R	RBI	BB	SO	SB	BA	SA	PH AB	PH H	G by POS
1877 2 teams	CHI N (24G – .202)					CIN N (10G – .250)											
" total	34	130	28	3	1	0	0.0	11	6	5	11		.215	.254	0	0	2B-17, OF-13, C-8
1889 LOU AA	1	2	1	0	0	0	0.0	0	1	0	1	0	.500	.500	0	0	OF-1, C-1
2 yrs.	35	132	29	3	1	0	0.0	11	7	5	12	0	.220	.258	0	0	2B-17, OF-14, C-9

Harry Smith

SMITH, JAMES HARRY   BR TR 5'10" 180 lbs.
B. May 15, 1890, Baltimore, Md.   D. Apr. 1, 1922, Charlotte, N. C.

	G	AB	H	2B	3B	HR	HR %	R	RBI	BB	SO	SB	BA	SA	PH AB	PH H	G by POS
1914 NY N	5	7	3	0	0	0	0.0	0	2	3	1	1	.429	.429	1	0	C-4
1915 2 teams	NY N (21G – .125)					BKN F (28G – .200)											
" total	49	97	17	0	1	1	1.0	6	7	13	12	2	.175	.227	7	2	C-37, OF-1
1917 CIN N	8	17	2	0	0	0	0.0	0	1	2	7	0	.118	.118	1	0	C-7
1918	13	27	5	1	2	0	0.0	4	4	3	6	1	.185	.370	5	1	C-6, OF-1
4 yrs.	75	148	27	1	3	1	0.7	10	14	21	26	4	.182	.250	14	3	C-54, OF-2

Harvey Smith

SMITH, HARVEY FETTERHOFF   BR TR 5'8" 160 lbs.
B. July 24, 1871, Union Deposit, Pa.   D. Nov. 12, 1962, Harrisburg, Pa.

	G	AB	H	2B	3B	HR	HR %	R	RBI	BB	SO	SB	BA	SA	PH AB	PH H	G by POS
1896 WAS N	36	131	36	7	2	0	0.0	21	17	12	7	9	.275	.359	0	0	3B-36

Heinie Smith

SMITH, GEORGE HENRY   BR TR 5'9½" 160 lbs.
B. Oct. 24, 1871, Pittsburgh, Pa.   D. June 25, 1939, Buffalo, N. Y.
Manager 1902.

	G	AB	H	2B	3B	HR	HR %	R	RBI	BB	SO	SB	BA	SA	PH AB	PH H	G by POS
1897 LOU N	21	76	20	3	0	1	1.3	7	7	3			1	.263	.342	0	0	2B-21
1898	35	121	23	4	0	0	0.0	14	13	6			6	.190	.223	2	1	2B-33
1899 PIT N	15	53	15	3	1	0	0.0	9	12	5			2	.283	.377	0	0	2B-15, SS-1
1901 NY N	9	29	6	2	1	1	3.4	5	4	1			1	.207	.448	0	0	2B-7, P-2
1902	138	511	129	19	2	0	0.0	46	33	17			32	.252	.297	0	0	2B-138
1903 DET A	93	336	75	11	3	1	0.3	36	22	19			12	.223	.283	0	0	2B-93
6 yrs.	311	1126	268	42	7	3	0.3	117	91	51		54	.238	.296	2	1	2B-307, P-2, SS-1

Jack Smith

SMITH, JOHN JOSEPH   TR
Also known as John Joseph Coffey.
B. Aug. 8, 1893, Oswaya, Pa.   D. Dec. 4, 1962, New York, N. Y.

	G	AB	H	2B	3B	HR	HR %	R	RBI	BB	SO	SB	BA	SA	PH AB	PH H	G by POS
1912 DET A	1	0	0	0	0	0	–	0	0	0	0	0	–	–	0	0	3B-1

Jack Smith

SMITH, JOHN W.   BL TL 5'8" 165 lbs.
Born Jan Smadt.
B. June 23, 1895, Chicago, Ill.   D. May 2, 1972, Westchester, Ill.

	G	AB	H	2B	3B	HR	HR %	R	RBI	BB	SO	SB	BA	SA	PH AB	PH H	G by POS
1915 STL N	4	16	3	0	1	0	0.0	2	0	1	5	0	.188	.313	0	0	OF-4
1916	130	357	87	6	5	6	1.7	43	34	20	50	24	.244	.339	7	1	OF-120
1917	137	462	137	16	11	3	0.6	64	34	38	65	25	.297	.398	8	4	OF-128
1918	42	166	35	2	1	0	0.0	24	4	7	21	5	.211	.235	0	0	OF-42
1919	119	408	91	16	3	0	0.0	47	15	26	29	30	.223	.277	0	0	OF-111
1920	91	313	104	22	5	0	0.3	53	28	25	23	14	.332	.444	4	1	OF-83
1921	116	411	135	22	9	7	1.7	86	33	21	24	11	.328	.477	4	0	OF-103
1922	143	510	158	23	12	8	1.6	117	46	50	30	18	.310	.449	4	1	OF-136
1923	124	407	126	16	6	5	1.2	98	41	27	20	32	.310	.415	3	0	OF-107
1924	124	459	130	18	6	2	0.4	91	33	33	27	24	.283	.362	6	1	OF-114
1925	80	243	61	11	4	4	1.6	53	31	19	13	20	.251	.379	10	4	OF-64
1926 2 teams	STL N (1G – .000)					BOS N (96G – .311)											
" total	97	323	100	15	2	2	0.6	46	25	28	11	11	.310	.387	9	0	OF-83
1927 BOS N	84	183	58	6	4	1	0.5	27	24	16	12	8	.317	.410	30	8	OF-48
1928	96	254	71	9	2	1	0.4	30	32	21	14	6	.280	.343	25	9	OF-65
1929	19	20	5	0	0	0	0.0	2	2	2	2	0	.250	.250	3	0	OF-9
15 yrs.	1406	4532	1301	182	71	40	0.9	783	382	334	348	228	.287	.385	113	29	OF-1217

Jimmy Smith

SMITH, JAMES LAWRENCE   BR TR 5'10" 158 lbs.
B. May 15, 1895, Pittsburgh, Pa.   D. Jan. 1, 1974, Pittsburgh, Pa.

	G	AB	H	2B	3B	HR	HR %	R	RBI	BB	SO	SB	BA	SA	PH AB	PH H	G by POS
1914 CHI F	3	6	3	1	0	0	0.0	1	1	0			0	.500	.667	0	0	SS-3
1915 2 teams	CHI F (95G – .217)					BAL F (33G – .176)											
" total	128	426	88	12	5	5	1.2	41	41	25		7	.207	.293	0	0	SS-125, 2B-1
1916 PIT N	36	96	18	1	1	0	0.0	4	5	6	22	0	.188	.219	0	0	SS-27, 3B-6
1917 NY N	36	96	22	5	1	0	0.0	12	2	9	18	6	.229	.302	0	0	2B-29, SS-7
1918 BOS N	34	102	23	3	4	1	1.0	8	14	3	13	1	.225	.363	0	0	SS-9, 2B-7, OF-6, 3B-5
1919 CIN N	28	40	11	1	3	1	2.5	9	10	4	8	1	.275	.525	0	0	3B-6, SS-5, OF-4, 2B-4
1921 PHI N	67	247	57	8	1	4	1.6	31	22	11	28	2	.231	.320	0	0	2B-66
1922	38	114	25	1	0	1	0.9	13	6	5	9	1	.219	.254	2	0	SS-23, 2B-13, 3B-1
8 yrs.	370	1127	247	32	15	12	1.1	119	101	63	98	18	.219	.306	2	0	SS-199, 2B-120, 3B-18, OF-10

	G	AB	H	2B	3B	HR	HR%	R	RBI	BB	SO	SB	BA	SA	Pinch Hit AB	Pinch Hit H	G by POS

Jimmy Smith continued

WORLD SERIES

	G	AB	H	2B	3B	HR	HR%	R	RBI	BB	SO	SB	BA	SA	AB	H	G by POS
1919 CIN N	1	0	0	0	0	0	–	0	0	0	0	0	–	–	0	0	

Jimmy Smith

SMITH, JAMES LORNE
B. Sept. 8, 1954, Santa Monica, Calif. BR TR 6'3" 180 lbs.

	G	AB	H	2B	3B	HR	HR%	R	RBI	BB	SO	SB	BA	SA	AB	H	G by POS
1982 PIT N	42	42	10	2	1	0	0.0	5	4	5	7	0	.238	.333	1	0	SS-29, 2B-3, 3B-1

Joe Smith

SMITH, SALVATORE GIUSEPPE
Also known as Salvatore Giuseppe Persico.
B. Dec. 29, 1893, New York, N. Y. D. Sept. 23, 1962, Teaneck, N. J. BR TR 5'8" 190 lbs.

	G	AB	H	2B	3B	HR	HR%	R	RBI	BB	SO	SB	BA	SA	AB	H	G by POS
1913 NY A	13	32	5	0	0	0	0.0	1	2	1	14	1	.156	.156	0	0	C-13

John Smith

SMITH, JOHN J.
B. Apr. 6, 1858, Ireland D. Jan. 6, 1899, San Francisco, Calif.

	G	AB	H	2B	3B	HR	HR%	R	RBI	BB	SO	SB	BA	SA	AB	H	G by POS
1882 2 teams			TRO N (35G – .242)					WOR N (19G – .243)									
" total	54	219	53	7	5	0	0.0	37	19	8	34		.242	.320	0	0	1B-54

John Smith

SMITH, JOHN MARSHALL
B. Sept. 27, 1906, Washington, D. C. BB TR 6'1" 165 lbs.

	G	AB	H	2B	3B	HR	HR%	R	RBI	BB	SO	SB	BA	SA	AB	H	G by POS
1931 BOS A	4	15	2	0	0	0	0.0	2	1	2	1	1	.133	.133	0	0	1B-4

Jud Smith

SMITH, JUDSON GRANT
B. Jan. 13, 1869, Green Oak, Mich. D. Dec. 7, 1947, Los Angeles, Calif. BR TR

	G	AB	H	2B	3B	HR	HR%	R	RBI	BB	SO	SB	BA	SA	AB	H	G by POS
1893 2 teams			CIN N (17G – .233)					STL N (4G – .077)									
" total	21	56	11	1	0	1	1.8	8	5	10	7	1	.196	.268	0	0	3B-10, OF-9, SS-1
1896 PIT N	10	35	12	2	1	0	0.0	6	4	2	2	3	.343	.457	0	0	3B-10
1898 WAS N	66	234	71	7	5	3	1.3	33	28	22		11	.303	.415	0	0	3B-47, SS-10, 1B-7, 2B-1
1901 PIT N	6	21	3	1	0	0	0.0	1	0	3		0	.143	.190	0	0	3B-6
4 yrs.	103	346	97	11	6	4	1.2	48	37	37	9	15	.280	.382	0	0	3B-73, SS-11, OF-9, 1B-7, 2B-1

Keith Smith

SMITH, KEITH LAVARNE
B. May 3, 1953, Palmetto, Fla. BR TR 5'9" 178 lbs.

	G	AB	H	2B	3B	HR	HR%	R	RBI	BB	SO	SB	BA	SA	AB	H	G by POS
1977 TEX A	23	67	16	4	0	2	3.0	13	6	4	7	2	.239	.388	3	1	OF-22
1979 STL N	6	13	3	0	0	0	0.0	1	0	0	1	0	.231	.231	0	0	OF-5
1980	24	31	4	1	0	0	0.0	3	2	2	2	0	.129	.161	17	3	OF-7
3 yrs.	53	111	23	5	0	2	1.8	17	8	6	10	2	.207	.306	20	4	OF-34

Keith Smith

SMITH, PATRICK KEITH
B. Oct. 20, 1961, Los Angeles, Calif. BR TR 6'1" 175 lbs.

	G	AB	H	2B	3B	HR	HR%	R	RBI	BB	SO	SB	BA	SA	AB	H	G by POS
1984 NY A	2	4	0	0	0	0	0.0	0	0	0	2	0	.000	.000	0	0	SS-2

Ken Smith

SMITH, KENNETH EARL
B. Feb. 12, 1958, Youngstown, Ohio BL TR 6'1" 195 lbs.

	G	AB	H	2B	3B	HR	HR%	R	RBI	BB	SO	SB	BA	SA	AB	H	G by POS
1981 ATL N	5	3	1	1	0	0	0.0	0	0	0	1	0	.333	.667	0	0	1B-4
1982	48	41	12	1	0	0	0.0	6	3	6	13	0	.293	.317	35	8	1B-6, OF-3
1983	30	12	2	0	0	1	8.3	2	2	1	5	1	.167	.417	8	1	1B-13
3 yrs.	83	56	15	2	0	1	1.8	8	5	7	19	1	.268	.357	43	9	1B-23, OF-3

Klondike Smith

SMITH, ARMSTRONG FREDERICK
B. Jan. 4, 1887, London, England D. Nov. 15, 1959, Springfield, Mass. BL TL 5'9" 160 lbs.

	G	AB	H	2B	3B	HR	HR%	R	RBI	BB	SO	SB	BA	SA	AB	H	G by POS
1912 NY A	7	27	5	1	0	0	0.0	0	0	0		1	.185	.222	0	0	OF-7

Leo Smith

SMITH, LIONEL H
B. May 13, 1859, Brooklyn, N. Y. D. Aug. 30, 1935, Brooklyn, N. Y. 5'6" 142 lbs.

	G	AB	H	2B	3B	HR	HR%	R	RBI	BB	SO	SB	BA	SA	AB	H	G by POS
1890 ROC AA	35	112	21	1	3	0	0.0	11		14		1	.188	.250	0	0	SS-35

Lonnie Smith

SMITH, LONNIE
B. Dec. 22, 1955, Chicago, Ill. BR TR 5'9" 170 lbs.

	G	AB	H	2B	3B	HR	HR%	R	RBI	BB	SO	SB	BA	SA	AB	H	G by POS
1978 PHI N	17	4	0	0	0	0	0.0	6	0	4	3	4	.000	.000	1	0	OF-11
1979	17	30	5	2	0	0	0.0	4	3	1	7	2	.167	.233	4	0	OF-11
1980	100	298	101	14	4	3	1.0	69	20	26	48	33	.339	.443	8	2	OF-82
1981	62	176	57	14	3	2	1.1	40	11	18	14	21	.324	.472	5	3	OF-51
1982 STL N	156	592	182	35	8	8	1.4	120	69	64	74	68	.307	.434	9	1	OF-149
1983	130	492	158	31	5	8	1.6	83	45	41	55	43	.321	.453	5	1	OF-126
1984	145	504	126	20	4	6	1.2	77	49	70	90	50	.250	.341	3	1	OF-140
7 yrs.	627	2096	629	116	24	27	1.3	399	197	224	291	221	.300	.417	35	8	OF-570

DIVISIONAL PLAYOFF SERIES

	G	AB	H	2B	3B	HR	HR%	R	RBI	BB	SO	SB	BA	SA	AB	H	G by POS
1981 PHI N	5	19	5	1	0	0	0.0	1	0	0	4	0	.263	.316	0	0	OF-5

LEAGUE CHAMPIONSHIP SERIES

	G	AB	H	2B	3B	HR	HR%	R	RBI	BB	SO	SB	BA	SA	AB	H	G by POS
1980 PHI N	3	5	3	0	0	0	0.0	2	0	0	0	1	.600	.600	0	0	OF-2
1982 STL N	3	11	3	0	0	0	0.0	1	1	0	1	0	.273	.273	0	0	OF-3
2 yrs.	6	16	6	0	0	0	0.0	3	1	0	1	1	.375	.375	0	0	OF-5

WORLD SERIES

	G	AB	H	2B	3B	HR	HR%	R	RBI	BB	SO	SB	BA	SA	AB	H	G by POS
1980 PHI N	6	19	5	1	0	0	0.0	2	1	1	1	0	.263	.316	0	0	OF-4
1982 STL N	7	28	9	4	1	0	0.0	6	1	1	5	2	.321	.536	0	0	OF-6
2 yrs.	13	47	14	5	1	0	0.0	8	2	2	6	2	.298	.447	0	0	OF-10

Mayo Smith

SMITH, EDWARD MAYO
B. Jan. 17, 1915, New London, Mo. D. Nov. 24, 1977, Boynton Beach, Fla. BL TR 6' 183 lbs.
Manager 1955-59, 1967-70.

	G	AB	H	2B	3B	HR	HR%	R	RBI	BB	SO	SB	BA	SA	AB	H	G by POS
1945 PHI A	73	203	43	5	0	0	0.0	18	11	36	13	0	.212	.236	6	4	OF-65

	G	AB	H	2B	3B	HR	HR %	R	RBI	BB	SO	SB	BA	SA	Pinch Hit AB	Pinch Hit H	G by POS

Mike Smith

SMITH, ELWOOD HOPE   BL TR 5'11½" 170 lbs.
B. Nov. 16, 1904, Norfolk, Va.   D. May 31, 1981, Chesapeake, Va.

	G	AB	H	2B	3B	HR	HR%	R	RBI	BB	SO	SB	BA	SA	PH AB	PH H	G by POS
1926 NY N	4	7	1	0	0	0	0.0	0	0	0	2	0	.143	.143	3	0	OF-1

Milt Smith

SMITH, MILTON   BR TR 5'10" 165 lbs.
B. Mar. 27, 1929, Columbus, Ga.

	G	AB	H	2B	3B	HR	HR%	R	RBI	BB	SO	SB	BA	SA	PH AB	PH H	G by POS
1955 CIN N	36	102	20	3	1	3	2.9	15	8	13	24	2	.196	.333	2	1	3B-28, 2B-5

Nate Smith

SMITH, NATHANIEL BEVERLY   BR TR 5'11" 170 lbs.
B. Apr. 26, 1935, Chicago, Ill.

	G	AB	H	2B	3B	HR	HR%	R	RBI	BB	SO	SB	BA	SA	PH AB	PH H	G by POS
1962 BAL A	5	9	2	1	0	0	0.0	3	0	1	4	0	.222	.333	2	1	C-3

Ollie Smith

SMITH, OLIVER H.
B. 1868, Mt. Vernon, Ohio   Deceased.

	G	AB	H	2B	3B	HR	HR%	R	RBI	BB	SO	SB	BA	SA	PH AB	PH H	G by POS
1894 LOU N	38	134	40	6	1	3	2.2	26	20	27	15	13	.299	.425	0	0	OF-38

Ozzie Smith

SMITH, OSBORNE EARL   BB TR 5'11" 150 lbs.
B. Dec. 26, 1954, Mobile, Ala.

	G	AB	H	2B	3B	HR	HR%	R	RBI	BB	SO	SB	BA	SA	PH AB	PH H	G by POS
1978 SD N	159	590	152	17	6	1	0.2	69	46	47	43	40	.258	.312	1	0	SS-159
1979	156	587	124	18	6	0	0.0	77	27	37	37	28	.211	.262	0	0	SS-155
1980	158	609	140	18	5	0	0.0	67	35	71	49	57	.230	.276	0	0	SS-158
1981	110	450	100	11	2	0	0.0	53	21	41	37	22	.222	.256	0	0	SS-110
1982 STL N	140	488	121	24	1	2	0.4	58	43	68	32	25	.248	.314	1	0	SS-139
1983	159	552	134	30	6	3	0.5	69	50	64	36	34	.243	.335	2	0	SS-158
1984	124	412	106	20	5	1	0.2	53	44	56	17	35	.257	.337	0	0	SS-124
7 yrs.	1006	3688	877	138	31	7	0.2	446	266	384	251	241	.238	.298	4	0	SS-1003

LEAGUE CHAMPIONSHIP SERIES

	G	AB	H	2B	3B	HR	HR%	R	RBI	BB	SO	SB	BA	SA	PH AB	PH H	G by POS
1982 STL N	3	9	5	0	0	0	0.0	0	3	3	0	1	.556	.556	0	0	SS-3

WORLD SERIES

	G	AB	H	2B	3B	HR	HR%	R	RBI	BB	SO	SB	BA	SA	PH AB	PH H	G by POS
1982 STL N	7	24	5	0	0	0	0.0	3	1	3	0	1	.208	.208	0	0	SS-7

Paddy Smith

SMITH, LAWRENCE PATRICK   BL TR 6' 195 lbs.
B. May 16, 1894, Pelham, N. Y.

	G	AB	H	2B	3B	HR	HR%	R	RBI	BB	SO	SB	BA	SA	PH AB	PH H	G by POS
1920 BOS A	2	2	0	0	0	0	0.0	0	0	0	1	0	.000	.000	1	0	C-1

Paul Smith

SMITH, PAUL LESLIE   BL TL 5'8" 165 lbs.
B. Mar. 19, 1931, New Castle, Pa.

	G	AB	H	2B	3B	HR	HR%	R	RBI	BB	SO	SB	BA	SA	PH AB	PH H	G by POS
1953 PIT N	118	389	110	12	7	4	1.0	41	44	24	23	3	.283	.380	23	8	1B-74, OF-19
1957	81	150	38	4	0	3	2.0	12	11	12	17	0	.253	.340	45	9	OF-33, 1B-1
1958 2 teams		PIT N (6G – .333)					CHI N (18G – .150)										
" total	24	23	4	0	0	0	0.0	1	1	6	4	0	.174	.174	13	3	1B-4
3 yrs.	223	562	152	16	7	7	1.2	54	56	42	44	3	.270	.361	81	20	1B-79, OF-52

Paul Smith

SMITH, PAUL STONER   BL TR 6'1" 190 lbs.
B. May 7, 1888, Mt. Zion, Ill.   D. July 3, 1958, Decatur, Ill.

	G	AB	H	2B	3B	HR	HR%	R	RBI	BB	SO	SB	BA	SA	PH AB	PH H	G by POS
1916 CIN N	10	44	10	0	1	0	0.0	5	1	1	8	3	.227	.273	0	0	OF-10

Pop Smith

SMITH, CHARLES MARVIN   BR TR 5'11" 170 lbs.
B. Oct. 12, 1856, Digby, N. S., Canada   D. Apr. 18, 1927, Boston, Mass.

	G	AB	H	2B	3B	HR	HR%	R	RBI	BB	SO	SB	BA	SA	PH AB	PH H	G by POS
1880 CIN N	83	334	69	10	9	0	0.0	35	27	6	36		.207	.290	0	0	2B-83
1881 3 teams		CLE N (10G – .118)					WOR N (11G – .073)				BUF N (3G – .000)						
" total	24	86	7	0	0	0	0.0	5	6	6	18		.081	.081	0	0	3B-10, OF-8, 2B-6
1882 2 teams		BAL AA (1G – .000)					LOU AA (3G – .182)										
" total	4	14	2	0	0	0	0.0	1		0			.143	.143	0	0	SS-3, OF-1
1883 COL AA	97	405	106	14	17	4	1.0	82		22			.262	.410	0	0	2B-73, 3B-24, P-3
1884	108	445	106	18	10	6	1.3	78		20			.238	.364	0	0	2B-108
1885 PIT AA	106	453	113	11	13	0	0.0	85		25			.249	.331	0	0	2B-106
1886	126	483	105	20	9	2	0.4	75		42			.217	.308	0	0	SS-98, 2B-28, C-1
1887 PIT N	122	456	98	12	7	2	0.4	69	54	30	48	30	.215	.285	0	0	2B-89, SS-33
1888	131	481	99	15	8	2	0.4	61	52	22	78	37	.206	.270	0	0	SS-75, 2B-56
1889 2 teams		PIT N (72G – .209)					BOS N (59G – .260)										
" total	131	466	108	23	6	5	1.1	47	59	47	68	23	.232	.339	0	0	SS-117, 2B-9, OF-3, 3B-3
1890 BOS N	134	463	106	16	12	1	0.2	82	53	80	81	54	.229	.322	0	0	2B-134, SS-1
1891 WAS AA	27	90	16	2	2	0	0.0	13	13	13	16	2	.178	.244	0	0	2B-19, SS-5, 3B-4
12 yrs.	1093	4176	935	141	87	24	0.6	633	264	313	345	131	.224	.317	0	0	2B-711, SS-332, 3B-41, OF-12, P-3, C-1

Ray Smith

SMITH, RAYMOND EDWARD   BR TR 6'1" 185 lbs.
B. Sept. 18, 1955, Glendale, Calif.

	G	AB	H	2B	3B	HR	HR%	R	RBI	BB	SO	SB	BA	SA	PH AB	PH H	G by POS
1981 MIN A	15	40	8	1	0	1	2.5	4	1	0	3	0	.200	.300	0	0	C-15
1982	9	23	5	0	1	0	0.0	1	1	1	3	0	.217	.304	0	0	C-9
1983	59	152	34	5	0	0	0.0	11	8	10	12	1	.224	.257	0	0	C-59
3 yrs.	83	215	47	6	1	1	0.5	16	10	11	18	1	.219	.270	0	0	C-83

Red Smith

SMITH, JAMES CARLISLE   BR TR 5'11" 165 lbs.
B. Apr. 6, 1890, Greenville, S. C.   D. Oct. 10, 1966, Atlanta, Ga.

	G	AB	H	2B	3B	HR	HR%	R	RBI	BB	SO	SB	BA	SA	PH AB	PH H	G by POS
1911 BKN N	28	111	29	6	1	0	0.0	10	19	5	13	5	.261	.333	0	0	3B-28
1912	128	486	139	28	6	4	0.8	75	57	54	51	22	.286	.393	3	1	3B-125
1913	151	540	160	40	10	6	1.1	70	76	45	67	22	.296	.441	0	0	3B-151
1914 2 teams		BKN N (90G – .245)					BOS N (60G – .314)										
" total	150	537	146	27	9	7	1.3	69	85	58	50	15	.272	.395	0	0	3B-150
1915 BOS N	157	549	145	34	4	2	0.4	66	65	67	49	10	.264	.352	0	0	3B-157
1916	150	509	132	16	10	3	0.6	48	60	53	55	13	.259	.348	0	0	3B-150
1917	147	505	149	31	6	2	0.4	60	62	53	61	16	.295	.392	1	0	3B-147
1918	119	429	128	20	3	2	0.5	55	65	45	47	8	.298	.373	0	0	3B-119

	G	AB	H	2B	3B	HR	HR%	R	RBI	BB	SO	SB	BA	SA	Pinch Hit AB	H	G by POS

Red Smith continued

	G	AB	H	2B	3B	HR	HR%	R	RBI	BB	SO	SB	BA	SA	AB	H	G by POS
1919	87	241	59	6	0	1	0.4	24	25	40	22	6	.245	.282	15	4	OF-48, 3B-23
9 yrs.	1117	3907	1087	208	49	27	0.7	477	514	420	415	117	.278	.377	19	5	3B-1050, OF-48

Red Smith

SMITH, MARVIN HAROLD   BL TR 5'7"   165 lbs.
B. July 17, 1900, Ashley, Ill.   D. Feb. 19, 1961, Los Angeles, Calif.

	G	AB	H	2B	3B	HR	HR%	R	RBI	BB	SO	SB	BA	SA	AB	H	G by POS
1925 PHI A	20	14	4	0	0	0	0.0	1	1	2	5	0	.286	.286	0	0	SS-16, 3B-2

Red Smith

SMITH, RICHARD PAUL   BR TR 5'10"   185 lbs.
B. May 18, 1904, Brokaw, Wis.   D. Mar. 8, 1978, Toledo, Ohio

	G	AB	H	2B	3B	HR	HR%	R	RBI	BB	SO	SB	BA	SA	AB	H	G by POS
1927 NY N	1	0	0	0	0	0	–	0	0	0	0	0	–	–	0	0	C-1

Red Smith

SMITH, WILLARD JEHU   BR TR 5'8"   165 lbs.
B. Apr. 11, 1892, Logansport, Ind.   D. July 17, 1972, Noblesville, Ind.

	G	AB	H	2B	3B	HR	HR%	R	RBI	BB	SO	SB	BA	SA	AB	H	G by POS
1917 PIT N	11	21	3	1	0	0	0.0	1	2	3	4	1	.143	.190	4	1	C-6
1918	15	24	4	1	0	0	0.0	1	3	3	0	0	.167	.208	4	0	C-10
2 yrs.	26	45	7	2	0	0	0.0	2	5	6	4	1	.156	.200	8	1	C-16

Reggie Smith

SMITH, CARL REGINALD   BB TR 6'   180 lbs.
B. Apr. 2, 1945, Shreveport, La.

	G	AB	H	2B	3B	HR	HR%	R	RBI	BB	SO	SB	BA	SA	AB	H	G by POS
1966 BOS A	6	26	4	1	0	0	0.0	1	0	0	5	0	.154	.192	0	0	OF-6
1967	158	565	139	24	6	15	2.7	78	61	57	95	16	.246	.389	10	1	OF-144, 2B-6
1968	155	558	148	37	5	15	2.7	78	69	64	77	22	.265	.430	0	0	OF-155
1969	143	543	168	29	7	25	4.6	87	93	54	67	7	.309	.527	4	1	OF-139
1970	147	580	176	32	7	22	3.8	109	74	51	60	10	.303	.497	2	0	OF-145
1971	159	618	175	33	2	30	4.9	85	96	63	82	11	.283	.489	0	0	OF-159
1972	131	467	126	25	4	21	4.5	75	74	68	63	15	.270	.475	2	0	OF-129
1973	115	423	128	23	2	21	5.0	79	69	68	49	3	.303	.515	1	0	OF-104, DH-8, 1B-1
1974 STL N	143	517	160	26	9	23	4.4	79	100	71	70	4	.309	.528	10	4	OF-132, 1B-1
1975	135	477	144	26	3	19	4.0	67	76	63	59	9	.302	.488	7	3	OF-69, 1B-66, 3B-1
1976 2 teams		STL	N	(47G –	.218)		LA	N	(65G –	.280)							
" total	112	395	100	15	5	18	4.6	55	49	32	70	3	.253	.453	8	4	OF-74, 1B-17, 3B-14
1977 LA N	148	488	150	27	4	32	6.6	104	87	104	76	7	.307	.576	6	1	OF-140
1978	128	447	132	27	2	29	6.5	82	93	70	90	12	.295	.559	2	0	OF-126
1979	68	234	64	13	1	10	4.3	41	32	31	50	6	.274	.466	5	2	OF-62
1980	92	311	100	13	0	15	4.8	47	55	41	63	5	.322	.508	6	3	OF-84
1981	41	35	7	1	0	1	2.9	5	8	7	8	0	.200	.314	31	6	1B-2
1982 SF N	106	349	99	11	0	18	5.2	51	56	46	46	7	.284	.470	6	1	1B-99
17 yrs.	1987	7033	2020	363	57	314	4.5	1123	1092	890	1030	137	.287	.489	100	26	OF-1668, 1B-186, 3B-15, DH-8, 2B-6

DIVISIONAL PLAYOFF SERIES

	G	AB	H	2B	3B	HR	HR%	R	RBI	BB	SO	SB	BA	SA	AB	H	G by POS
1981 LA N	2	1	0	0	0	0	0.0	0	1	0	1	0	.000	.000	1	0	

LEAGUE CHAMPIONSHIP SERIES

	G	AB	H	2B	3B	HR	HR%	R	RBI	BB	SO	SB	BA	SA	AB	H	G by POS
1977 LA N	4	16	3	0	1	0	0.0	2	1	2	5	1	.188	.313	0	0	OF-4
1978	4	16	3	1	0	0	0.0	2	1	0	2	0	.188	.250	0	0	OF-4
1981	1	1	1	0	0	0	0.0	0	1	0	0	0	1.000	1.000	1	1	
3 yrs.	9	33	7	1	1	0	0.0	4	3	2	7	1	.212	.303	1	1	OF-8

WORLD SERIES

	G	AB	H	2B	3B	HR	HR%	R	RBI	BB	SO	SB	BA	SA	AB	H	G by POS
1967 BOS A	7	24	6	1	0	2	8.3	3	3	2	2	0	.250	.542	0	0	OF-7
1977 LA N	6	22	6	1	0	3	13.6	7	5	4	3	0	.273	.727	0	0	OF-6
1978	6	25	5	0	0	1	4.0	3	5	2	6	0	.200	.320	0	0	OF-6
1981	2	2	1	0	0	0	0.0	0	0	0	1	0	.500	.500	2	1	
4 yrs.	21	73	18	2	0	6	8.2 6th	13	13	8	12	0	.247	.521	2	1	OF-19

Skyrocket Smith

SMITH, SAMUEL J.   BR
B. Mar. 19, 1868, St. Louis, Mo.   D. Apr. 26, 1916, St. Louis, Mo.

	G	AB	H	2B	3B	HR	HR%	R	RBI	BB	SO	SB	BA	SA	AB	H	G by POS
1888 LOU AA	58	206	49	9	4	1	0.5	27	31	24		5	.238	.335	0	0	1B-58

Stub Smith

SMITH, JAMES A.
B. Nov. 26, 1876, Elmwood, Ill.   Deceased.

	G	AB	H	2B	3B	HR	HR%	R	RBI	BB	SO	SB	BA	SA	AB	H	G by POS
1898 BOS N	3	10	1	0	0	0	0.0	1	0	0		0	.100	.100	0	0	SS-3

Syd Smith

SMITH, SYDNEY   BR TR 5'10"   190 lbs.
B. Aug. 31, 1883, Smithville, S. C.   D. June 5, 1961, Orangeburg, S. C.

	G	AB	H	2B	3B	HR	HR%	R	RBI	BB	SO	SB	BA	SA	AB	H	G by POS
1908 2 teams		PHI	A	(46G –	.203)		STL	A	(27G –	.184)							
" total	73	204	40	12	4	1	0.5	14	15	8		2	.196	.309	10	1	C-61, 1B-6, OF-2
1910 CLE A	9	27	9	1	0	0	0.0	1	3	3		0	.333	.370	0	0	C-9
1911	58	154	46	8	1	1	0.6	8	21	11		0	.299	.383	7	3	C-48, 3B-1, 1B-1
1914 PIT N	5	11	3	0	0	0	0.0	1	1	0	1	0	.273	.273	2	0	C-3
1915	1	1	0	0	0	0	0.0	0	0	0	0	0	.000	.000	1	0	
5 yrs.	146	397	98	21	5	2	0.5	24	40	22	1	2	.247	.340	20	4	C-121, 1B-7, OF-2, 3B-1

Tom Smith

SMITH, THOMAS N.
B. Baltimore, Md.   Deceased.

	G	AB	H	2B	3B	HR	HR%	R	RBI	BB	SO	SB	BA	SA	AB	H	G by POS
1882 PHI AA	20	65	6	0	0	0	0.0	0		12			.092	.092	0	0	3B-11, SS-4, OF-3, 2B-2

Tommy Smith

SMITH, TOMMY ALEXANDER   BL TR 6'4"   210 lbs.
B. Aug. 18, 1948, Albemarle, N. C.

	G	AB	H	2B	3B	HR	HR%	R	RBI	BB	SO	SB	BA	SA	AB	H	G by POS
1973 CLE A	14	41	10	2	0	2	4.9	6	3	1	2	1	.244	.439	0	0	OF-13
1974	23	31	3	1	0	0	0.0	4	0	2	7	0	.097	.129	2	0	OF-17, DH-1
1975	8	8	1	0	0	0	0.0	0	2	0	1	0	.125	.125	1	0	DH-3, OF-3
1976	55	164	42	3	1	2	1.2	17	12	8	8	8	.256	.323	2	0	OF-50, DH-2
1977 SEA A	21	27	7	1	1	0	0.0	1	4	0	6	0	.259	.370	8	2	OF-14
5 yrs.	121	271	63	7	2	4	1.5	28	21	11	24	9	.232	.317	13	2	OF-97, DH-6

	G	AB	H	2B	3B	HR	HR%	R	RBI	BB	SO	SB	BA	SA	Pinch Hit AB	Pinch Hit H	G by POS

Tony Smith

SMITH, ANTHONY   BR TR 5'9" 150 lbs.
B. May 14, 1884, Chicago, Ill.   D. Feb. 27, 1964, Galveston, Tex.

	G	AB	H	2B	3B	HR	HR%	R	RBI	BB	SO	SB	BA	SA	PH AB	PH H	G by POS
1907 WAS A	51	139	26	1	1	0	0.0	12	8	18		3	.187	.209	0	0	SS-51
1910 BKN N	106	321	58	10	1	1	0.3	31	16	69	53	9	.181	.227	0	0	SS-101, 3B-6
1911	13	40	6	1	0	0	0.0	3	2	8	7	1	.150	.175	0	0	SS-10, 2B-3
3 yrs.	170	500	90	12	2	1	0.2	46	26	95	60	13	.180	.218	0	0	SS-162, 3B-6, 2B-3

Vinnie Smith

SMITH, VINCENT AMBROSE   BR TR 6'1" 176 lbs.
B. Dec. 7, 1915, Richmond, Va.   D. Dec. 14, 1979, Virginia Beach, Va.

	G	AB	H	2B	3B	HR	HR%	R	RBI	BB	SO	SB	BA	SA	PH AB	PH H	G by POS
1941 PIT N	9	33	10	1	0	0	0.0	3	5	1	5	0	.303	.333	0	0	C-9
1946	7	21	4	0	0	0	0.0	2	0	1	5	0	.190	.190	0	0	C-7
2 yrs.	16	54	14	1	0	0	0.0	5	5	2	10	0	.259	.278	0	0	C-16

Wally Smith

SMITH, WALLACE H.   BR TR 5'11½" 180 lbs.
B. Mar. 13, 1889, Philadelphia, Pa.   D. June 10, 1930, Florence, Ariz.

	G	AB	H	2B	3B	HR	HR%	R	RBI	BB	SO	SB	BA	SA	PH AB	PH H	G by POS
1911 STL N	81	194	42	6	5	2	1.0	23	19	21	33	5	.216	.330	16	2	3B-26, SS-25, 2B-8, OF-1
1912	75	219	56	5	5	0	0.0	22	26	29	27	4	.256	.324	12	0	3B-32, SS-22, 1B-6
1914 WAS A	45	97	19	4	1	0	0.0	11	8	3	12	3	.196	.258	11	1	2B-12, SS-7, 1B-7, 3B-5, OF-1
3 yrs.	201	510	117	15	11	2	0.4	56	53	53	72	12	.229	.314	39	3	3B-63, SS-54, 2B-20, 1B-13, OF-2

Wib Smith

SMITH, WILBUR FLOYD   BL TR 5'10½" 165 lbs.
B. Aug. 30, 1886, Evart, Mich.   D. Nov. 18, 1959, Fargo, N. D.

	G	AB	H	2B	3B	HR	HR%	R	RBI	BB	SO	SB	BA	SA	PH AB	PH H	G by POS
1909 STL A	17	42	8	0	0	0	0.0	3	2		0	0	.190	.190	3	1	C-13, 1B-1

Willie Smith

SMITH, WILLIE (Wonderful Willie)   BL TL 6' 182 lbs.
B. Feb. 11, 1939, Anniston, Ala.

	G	AB	H	2B	3B	HR	HR%	R	RBI	BB	SO	SB	BA	SA	PH AB	PH H	G by POS
1963 DET A	17	8	1	0	0	0	0.0	2	0	0	1	0	.125	.125	2	0	P-11
1964 LA N	118	359	108	14	6	11	3.1	46	51	8	39	7	.301	.465	23	10	OF-87, P-15
1965 CAL A	136	459	120	14	9	14	3.1	52	57	32	60	9	.261	.423	21	4	OF-123, 1B-2
1966	90	195	36	3	2	1	0.5	18	20	12	37	1	.185	.236	41	5	OF-52
1967 CLE A	21	32	7	2	0	0	0.0	0	2	1	10	0	.219	.281	16	4	OF-4, 1B-3
1968 2 teams	CLE	A	(33G –	.143)	CHI	N	(55G –	.275)									
" total	88	184	45	10	2	5	2.7	14	28	15	47	0	.245	.402	36	10	OF-39, 1B-11, P-3
1969 CHI N	103	195	48	9	1	9	4.6	21	25	25	49	1	.246	.441	40	12	OF-33, 1B-24
1970	87	167	36	9	1	5	3.0	15	24	11	32	2	.216	.371	40	9	1B-43, OF-1
1971 CIN N	31	55	9	2	0	1	1.8	3	4	3	9	0	.164	.255	20	0	1B-10
9 yrs.	691	1654	410	63	21	46	2.8	171	211	107	284	20	.248	.395	239	54	OF-339, 1B-93, P-29

Homer Smoot

SMOOT, HOMER VERNON   BL TR 6' 190 lbs.
B. Mar. 26, 1878, Galestown, Md.   D. Mar. 25, 1928, Salisbury, Md.

	G	AB	H	2B	3B	HR	HR%	R	RBI	BB	SO	SB	BA	SA	PH AB	PH H	G by POS
1902 STL N	129	518	161	19	4	3	0.6	58	48	23		20	.311	.380	0	0	OF-129
1903	129	500	148	22	8	4	0.8	67	49	32		17	.296	.396	0	0	OF-129
1904	137	520	146	23	6	3	0.6	58	66	37		23	.281	.365	0	0	OF-137
1905	139	534	166	21	16	4	0.7	73	58	33		21	.311	.433	1	0	OF-138
1906 2 teams	STL	N	(86G –	.248)	CIN	N	(60G –	.259)									
" total	146	563	142	17	11	1	0.2	52	48	24		3	.252	.327	1	0	OF-145
5 yrs.	680	2635	763	102	45	15	0.6	308	269	149		84	.290	.380	2	0	OF-678

Henry Smoyer

SMOYER, HENRY NEITZ (Hennie)   BR TR 5'6"
Also known as Henry Neitz Smowrey.
B. Apr. 24, 1890, Fredericksburg, Pa.   D. Feb. 28, 1958, Dubois, Pa.

	G	AB	H	2B	3B	HR	HR%	R	RBI	BB	SO	SB	BA	SA	PH AB	PH H	G by POS
1912 STL A	6	14	3	0	0	0	0.0	1	0	2		0	.214	.214	0	0	SS-4, 3B-2

Frank Smykal

SMYKAL, FRANK JOHN   BR TR 5'7" 150 lbs.
Born Frank John Smejkal.
B. Oct. 13, 1889, Chicago, Ill.   D. Aug. 11, 1950, Chicago, Ill.

	G	AB	H	2B	3B	HR	HR%	R	RBI	BB	SO	SB	BA	SA	PH AB	PH H	G by POS
1916 PIT N	6	10	3	0	0	0	0.0	1	2	3		1	1	.300	.300	0	0	SS-5, 3B-1

Clancy Smyres

SMYRES, CLARENCE MELVIN   BB TL 5'11½" 175 lbs.
B. May 24, 1922, Culver City, Calif.

	G	AB	H	2B	3B	HR	HR%	R	RBI	BB	SO	SB	BA	SA	PH AB	PH H	G by POS
1944 BKN N	5	2	0	0	0	0	0.0	1	0	0	0	0	.000	.000	2	0	

Red Smyth

SMYTH, JAMES DANIEL   BL TR 5'9" 152 lbs.
B. Jan. 30, 1893, Holly Springs, Miss.   D. Apr. 14, 1958, Inglewood, Calif.

	G	AB	H	2B	3B	HR	HR%	R	RBI	BB	SO	SB	BA	SA	PH AB	PH H	G by POS
1915 BKN N	19	22	3	1	0	0	0.0	3	3	4	2	1	.136	.182	4	0	OF-9
1916	2	5	0	0	0	0	0.0	0	0	0	3	0	.000	.000	1	0	2B-2
1917 2 teams	BKN	N	(29G –	.125)	STL	N	(28G –	.208)									
" total	57	96	18	0	2	0	0.0	10	5	8	15	3	.188	.229	24	5	OF-25, 3B-4
1918 STL N	40	113	24	1	2	0	0.0	19	4	16	11	3	.212	.257	1	0	OF-25, 2B-11
4 yrs.	118	236	45	2	4	0	0.0	32	12	28	31	7	.191	.233	30	5	OF-59, 2B-13, 3B-4

John Sneed

SNEED, JOHN L.
B. Columbus, Ohio   D. Jan. 4, 1899, Memphis, Tenn.

	G	AB	H	2B	3B	HR	HR%	R	RBI	BB	SO	SB	BA	SA	PH AB	PH H	G by POS
1884 IND AA	27	102	22	4	0	1	1.0	14		6			.216	.284	0	0	OF-27
1890 2 teams	TOL	AA	(9G –	.200)	COL	AA	(128G –	.291)									
" total	137	514	147	13	15	2	0.4	117		71		44	.286	.381	0	0	OF-135, SS-2
1891 COL AA	99	366	94	9	6	1	0.3	66	61	55	29	24	.257	.322	0	0	OF-99
3 yrs.	263	982	263	26	21	4	0.4	197	60	132	29	68	.268	.349	0	0	OF-261, SS-2

Charlie Snell

SNELL, CHARLES ANTHONY   BR TR 5'11" 160 lbs.
B. Nov. 29, 1892, Reading, Pa.

	G	AB	H	2B	3B	HR	HR%	R	RBI	BB	SO	SB	BA	SA	PH AB	PH H	G by POS
1912 STL A	8	19	4	1	0	0	0.0	0	0	3		0	.211	.263	0	0	C-8

	G	AB	H	2B	3B	HR	HR %	R	RBI	BB	SO	SB	BA	SA	Pinch Hit AB	H	G by POS

Wally Snell

SNELL, WALTER HENRY (Doc)
B. Apr. 19, 1889, West Bridgewater, Mass.   D. July 23, 1980, Providence, R. I.
BR TR 5'10" 170 lbs.

	G	AB	H	2B	3B	HR	HR%	R	RBI	BB	SO	SB	BA	SA	PH AB	PH H	G by POS
1913 BOS A	5	8	3	0	0	0	0.0	1	0	0	0	1	.375	.375	4	2	C-1

Bernie Snider

SNIDER, BERNARD AUSTIN
B. Aug. 25, 1913, Philadelphia, Pa.
BR TR 6' 175 lbs.

	G	AB	H	2B	3B	HR	HR%	R	RBI	BB	SO	SB	BA	SA	PH AB	PH H	G by POS
1935 PHI A	10	32	11	1	0	0	0.0	5	3	1	2	0	.344	.375	2	0	2B-5, SS-4

Duke Snider

SNIDER, EDWIN DONALD (The Silver Fox)
B. Sept. 19, 1926, Los Angeles, Calif.
Hall of Fame 1980.
BL TR 6' 179 lbs.

	G	AB	H	2B	3B	HR	HR%	R	RBI	BB	SO	SB	BA	SA	PH AB	PH H	G by POS
1947 BKN N	40	83	20	3	1	0	0.0	6	5	3	24	2	.241	.301	15	4	OF-25
1948	53	160	39	6	6	5	3.1	22	21	12	27	4	.244	.450	6	2	OF-47
1949	146	552	161	28	7	23	4.2	100	92	56	92	12	.292	.493	1	1	OF-145
1950	152	620	199	31	10	31	5.0	109	107	58	79	16	.321	.553	1	1	OF-151
1951	150	606	168	26	6	29	4.8	96	101	62	97	14	.277	.483	0	0	OF-150
1952	144	534	162	25	7	21	3.9	80	92	55	77	7	.303	.494	2	1	OF-141
1953	153	590	198	38	4	42	7.1	132	126	82	90	16	.336	.627	4	3	OF-151
1954	149	584	199	39	10	40	6.8	120	130	84	96	6	.341	.647	1	1	OF-148
1955	148	538	166	34	6	42	7.8	126	136	104	87	9	.309	.628	1	0	OF-146
1956	151	542	158	33	2	43	7.9	112	101	99	101	3	.292	.598	1	1	OF-150
1957	139	508	139	25	7	40	7.9	91	92	77	104	5	.274	.587	3	2	OF-136
1958 LA N	106	327	102	12	3	15	4.6	45	58	32	49	2	.312	.505	15	4	OF-92
1959	126	370	114	11	2	23	6.2	59	88	58	71	1	.308	.535	21	7	OF-107
1960	101	235	57	13	5	14	6.0	38	36	46	54	1	.243	.519	25	6	OF-75
1961	85	233	69	8	3	16	6.9	35	56	29	43	1	.296	.562	18	4	OF-66
1962	80	158	44	11	3	5	3.2	28	30	36	32	2	.278	.481	33	6	OF-39
1963 NY N	129	354	86	8	3	14	4.0	44	45	56	74	0	.243	.401	29	6	OF-106
1964 SF N	91	167	35	7	0	4	2.4	16	17	22	40	0	.210	.323	47	10	OF-43
18 yrs.	2143	7161	2116	358	85	407	5.7	1259	1333	971	1237	99	.295	.540	223	59	OF-1918

WORLD SERIES																	
1949 BKN N	5	21	3	1	0	0	0.0	2	0	0	8	0	.143	.190	0	0	OF-5
1952	7	29	10	2	0	4	13.8	5	8	1	5	1	.345	.828	0	0	OF-7
1953	6	25	8	3	0	1	4.0	3	5	2	6	0	.320	.560	0	0	OF-6
1955	7	25	8	1	0	4	16.0	5	7	2	6	0	.320	.840	0	0	OF-7
1956	7	23	7	1	0	1	4.3	5	4	6	8	0	.304	.478	0	0	OF-7
1959 LA N	4	10	2	0	0	1	10.0	1	2	2	0	0	.200	.500	1	0	OF-3
6 yrs.	36	133	38	8	0	11	8.3	21	26	13	33	1	.286	.594	1	0	OF-35
				6th		4th	5th	10th	7th		3rd						

Roxy Snipes

SNIPES, WYATT EURE (Rock)
B. Oct. 28, 1896, Marion, S. C.   D. May 1, 1941, Fayetteville, N. C.
BL TR 6' 185 lbs.

	G	AB	H	2B	3B	HR	HR%	R	RBI	BB	SO	SB	BA	SA	PH AB	PH H	G by POS
1923 CHI A	1	1	0	0	0	0	0.0	0	0	0	0	0	.000	.000	1	0	

Chappie Snodgrass

SNODGRASS, AMZIE BEAL
B. Mar. 18, 1870, Springfield, Ohio   D. Sept. 7, 1951, New York, N. Y.
BR TR 6'1" 160 lbs.

	G	AB	H	2B	3B	HR	HR%	R	RBI	BB	SO	SB	BA	SA	PH AB	PH H	G by POS
1901 BAL A	3	10	1	0	0	0	0.0	1	0	1		0	.100	.100	0	0	OF-2

Fred Snodgrass

SNODGRASS, FRED CARLISLE (Snow)
B. Oct. 19, 1887, Ventura, Calif.   D. Apr. 5, 1974, Ventura, Calif.
BR TR 5'11½" 175 lbs.

	G	AB	H	2B	3B	HR	HR%	R	RBI	BB	SO	SB	BA	SA	PH AB	PH H	G by POS
1908 NY N	6	4	1	0	0	0	0.0	2	1	0		1	.250	.250	1	0	C-3
1909	28	70	21	5	0	1	1.4	10	6	7		10	.300	.414	6	1	OF-19, C-2, 1B-1
1910	123	396	127	22	8	2	0.5	69	44	71	52	33	.321	.432	10	3	OF-101, 1B-9, 3B-1, C-1
1911	151	534	157	27	10	1	0.2	83	77	72	59	51	.294	.388	0	0	OF-149, 2B-1, 1B-1
1912	146	535	144	24	9	3	0.6	91	69	70	65	43	.269	.364	2	0	OF-116, 1B-28, 2B-1
1913	141	457	133	21	6	3	0.7	65	49	53	44	27	.291	.383	3	0	OF-133, 1B-3, 2B-1
1914	113	392	103	20	4	0	0.0	54	44	37	43	25	.263	.334	6	1	OF-96, 1B-14, 3B-1, 2B-1
1915 2 teams	NY	N (103G – .194)			BOS	N	(23G – .278)										
" total	126	331	71	11	0	0	0.0	46	29	42	42	11	.215	.248	4	1	OF-121, 1B-5
1916 BOS N	112	382	95	13	5	1	0.3	33	32	34	54	14	.249	.317	1	0	OF-110
9 yrs.	946	3101	852	143	42	11	0.4	453	351	386	359	215	.275	.359	33	6	OF-845, 1B-61, C-6, 2B-4, 3B-2

WORLD SERIES																	
1911 NY N	6	19	2	0	0	0	0.0	1	1	2	7	0	.105	.105	0	0	OF-6
1912	8	33	7	2	0	0	0.0	2	2	2	5	1	.212	.273	0	0	OF-8
1913	2	3	1	0	0	0	0.0	0	0	0	0	0	.333	.333	0	0	1B-1
3 yrs.	16	55	10	2	0	0	0.0	3	3	4	12	1	.182	.218	0	0	OF-14, 1B-1

Charlie Snyder

SNYDER, CHARLES
B. Camden, N. J.   D. Mar. 10, 1901, Philadelphia, Pa.

	G	AB	H	2B	3B	HR	HR%	R	RBI	BB	SO	SB	BA	SA	PH AB	PH H	G by POS
1890 PHI AA	9	33	9	1	0	0	0.0	5		2		0	.273	.303	0	0	OF-5, C-5

Cooney Snyder

SNYDER, FRANK C.
B. Toronto, Ont., Canada   D. May 9, 1917, Toronto, Ont., Canada

	G	AB	H	2B	3B	HR	HR%	R	RBI	BB	SO	SB	BA	SA	PH AB	PH H	G by POS
1898 LOU N	17	61	10	0	0	0	0.0	4	6	3		0	.164	.164	0	0	C-17

Frank Snyder

SNYDER, FRANK ELTON (Pancho)
B. May 27, 1893, San Antonio, Tex.   D. Jan. 5, 1962, San Antonio, Tex.
BR TR 6'2" 185 lbs.

	G	AB	H	2B	3B	HR	HR%	R	RBI	BB	SO	SB	BA	SA	PH AB	PH H	G by POS
1912 STL N	11	18	2	0	0	0	0.0	2	0	2	7	1	.111	.111	0	0	C-11
1913	7	21	4	0	0	0	0.0	1	2	0	4	0	.190	.286	0	0	C-7
1914	100	326	75	15	4	1	0.3	19	25	13	28	1	.230	.310	2	0	C-98
1915	144	473	141	22	7	2	0.4	41	55	39	49	3	.298	.387	1	0	C-144
1916	132	406	105	12	4	0	0.0	23	39	18	31	5	.259	.308	13	5	C-72, 1B-46, SS-1
1917	115	313	74	9	2	1	0.3	18	33	27	43	4	.236	.288	18	6	C-94
1918	39	112	28	7	1	0	0.0	5	10	6	13	4	.250	.330	9	2	C-27, 1B-3

	G	AB	H	2B	3B	HR	HR %	R	RBI	BB	SO	SB	BA	SA	Pinch Hit AB	Pinch Hit H	G by POS

Frank Snyder continued

	G	AB	H	2B	3B	HR	HR%	R	RBI	BB	SO	SB	BA	SA	AB	H	G by POS
1919 2 teams		STL	N	(50G –	.182)		NY	N	(32G –	.228)							
" total	82	246	49	10	2	0	0.0	14	25	13	22	3	.199	.256	2	1	C-79, 1B-1
1920 NY N	87	264	66	13	4	3	1.1	26	27	17	18	2	.250	.364	3	0	C-84
1921	108	309	99	13	2	8	2.6	36	45	27	24	3	.320	.453	5	2	C-101
1922	104	318	109	21	5	5	1.6	34	51	23	25	1	.343	.487	5	2	C-97
1923	120	402	103	13	6	5	1.2	37	63	24	29	5	.256	.356	8	5	C-112
1924	118	354	107	18	3	5	1.4	37	53	30	43	3	.302	.412	8	3	C-110
1925	107	325	78	9	1	11	3.4	21	51	20	49	0	.240	.375	11	5	C-96
1926	55	148	32	3	2	5	3.4	10	16	13	13	0	.216	.365	0	0	C-55
1927 STL N	63	194	50	5	0	1	0.5	7	30	9	18	0	.258	.299	1	1	C-62
16 yrs.	1392	4229	1122	170	44	47	1.1	331	525	281	416	37	.265	.360	86	32	C-1249, 1B-50, SS-1
WORLD SERIES																	
1921 NY N	7	22	8	1	0	1	4.5	4	3	0	2	0	.364	.545	1	0	C-6
1922	4	15	5	0	0	0	0.0	1	0	0	1	0	.333	.333	0	0	C-4
1923	5	17	2	0	0	1	5.9	1	2	0	2	0	.118	.294	0	0	C-5
1924	1	1	0	0	0	0	0.0	0	0	0	0	0	.000	.000	1	0	
4 yrs.	17	55	15	1	0	2	3.6	6	5	0	5	0	.273	.400	2	0	C-15

Jack Snyder

SNYDER, JOHN WILLIAM   BR TR 5'9''   168 lbs.
B. Oct. 6, 1886, Lincoln Township, Pa.   D. Dec. 13, 1981, Brownsville, Pa.

	G	AB	H	2B	3B	HR	HR%	R	RBI	BB	SO	SB	BA	SA	AB	H	G by POS
1914 BUF F	1	0	0	0	0	0	–	0	0	1		0	–	–	0	0	C-1
1917 BKN N	7	11	3	0	0	0	0.0	1	1	0	2	0	.273	.273	1	0	C-5
2 yrs.	8	11	3	0	0	0	0.0	1	1	1	2	0	.273	.273	1	0	C-6

Jerry Snyder

SNYDER, GERALD GEORGE   BR TR 6'   170 lbs.
B. July 21, 1929, Jenks, Okla.

	G	AB	H	2B	3B	HR	HR%	R	RBI	BB	SO	SB	BA	SA	AB	H	G by POS
1952 WAS A	36	57	9	2	0	0	0.0	5	2	5	8	1	.158	.193	7	0	2B-19, SS-4
1953	29	62	21	4	0	0	0.0	10	4	5	8	1	.339	.403	0	0	SS-17, 2B-4
1954	64	154	36	3	1	0	0.0	17	17	15	18	3	.234	.266	1	0	SS-48, 2B-3
1955	46	107	24	5	0	0	0.0	7	5	6	6	1	.224	.271	6	1	2B-22, SS-20
1956	43	148	40	3	1	2	1.4	14	14	10	9	1	.270	.345	1	0	SS-35, 2B-7
1957	42	93	14	1	0	1	1.1	6	4	4	9	0	.151	.194	12	3	SS-15, 2B-13, 3B-1
1958	6	9	1	0	0	0	0.0	1	1	1	1	0	.111	.111	2	0	2B-2, SS-1
7 yrs.	266	630	145	18	2	3	0.5	60	47	46	59	7	.230	.279	29	4	SS-140, 2B-70, 3B-1

Jim Snyder

SNYDER, JAMES C A   BR TR 6'1''   185 lbs.
B. Aug. 13, 1932, Dearborn, Mich.

	G	AB	H	2B	3B	HR	HR%	R	RBI	BB	SO	SB	BA	SA	AB	H	G by POS
1961 MIN A	3	5	0	0	0	0	0.0	0	0	0	1	0	.000	.000	0	0	2B-3
1962	12	10	1	0	0	0	0.0	1	0	0	0	0	.100	.100	0	0	2B-5, 1B-1
1964	26	71	11	2	0	1	1.4	3	9	4	11	0	.155	.225	0	0	2B-25
3 yrs.	41	86	12	2	0	1	1.2	4	9	4	12	0	.140	.198	0	0	2B-33, 1B-1

Pop Snyder

SNYDER, CHARLES N.   BR TR 5'11½'' 184 lbs.
B. Oct. 6, 1854, Washington, D. C.   D. Oct. 29, 1924, Washington, D. C.
Manager 1882-84, 1891.

	G	AB	H	2B	3B	HR	HR%	R	RBI	BB	SO	SB	BA	SA	AB	H	G by POS
1876 LOU N	56	224	44	4	1	0	0.4	21	9	2	7		.196	.237	0	0	C-55, OF-4
1877	61	248	64	7	2	2	0.8	23	28	3	14		.258	.327	0	0	C-61, OF-1, SS-1
1878 BOS N	60	226	48	5	0	0	0.0	21	14	1	19		.212	.235	0	0	C-58, OF-2
1879	81	329	78	16	3	2	0.6	42	35	5	31		.237	.322	0	0	C-80, OF-1
1881	62	219	50	8	0	0	0.0	14	16	3	23		.228	.265	0	0	C-60, OF-1, SS-1, 2B-1
1882 CIN AA	72	309	90	12	2	1	0.3	49		9			.291	.353	0	0	C-70, 1B-2, OF-1
1883	58	250	64	14	6	0	0.0	38		8			.256	.360	0	0	C-57, SS-2
1884	67	268	69	9	9	0	0.0	32		7			.257	.358	0	0	C-65, 1B-2, OF-1
1885	39	152	36	4	3	1	0.7	13		6			.237	.322	0	0	C-38, 1B-1
1886	60	220	41	8	3	0	0.0	33		13			.186	.250	0	0	C-41, 1B-19, OF-1
1887 CLE AA	74	282	72	12	6	0	0.0	33		9		5	.255	.340	0	0	C-63, 1B-13
1888	64	237	51	7	3	0	0.0	22	14	6		9	.215	.270	0	0	C-58, 1B-4, OF-3
1889 CLE N	22	83	16	3	0	0	0.0	5	12	2	12	4	.193	.229	0	0	C-22
1890 CLE P	13	48	9	1	0	0	0.0	5	12	1	9	1	.188	.208	0	0	C-13
1891 WAS AA	8	27	5	0	1	0	0.0	4	2	0	3	0	.185	.259	0	0	1B-4, C-3, OF-1
15 yrs.	797	3122	737	110	39	7	0.2	355	142	75	118	19	.236	.303	0	0	C-744, 1B-45, OF-17, SS-4, 2B-1

Redleg Snyder

SNYDER, EMANUEL SEBASTIAN   BR TR 5'10''   175 lbs.
Born Emanuel Sebastian Schneider.
B. Dec. 12, 1854, Camden, N. J.   D. Nov. 24, 1932, Camden, N. J.

	G	AB	H	2B	3B	HR	HR%	R	RBI	BB	SO	SB	BA	SA	AB	H	G by POS
1876 CIN N	55	205	31	3	1	0	0.0	10	12	1	19		.151	.176	0	0	OF-55
1884 WIL U	17	52	10	0	0	0	0.0	4		1			.192	.192	0	0	1B-16, OF-1
2 yrs.	72	257	41	3	1	0	0.0	14	12	2	19		.160	.179	0	0	OF-56, 1B-16

Russ Snyder

SNYDER, RUSSELL HENRY   BL TR 6'1''   190 lbs.
B. June 22, 1934, Oak, Neb.

	G	AB	H	2B	3B	HR	HR%	R	RBI	BB	SO	SB	BA	SA	AB	H	G by POS
1959 KC A	73	243	76	13	2	3	1.2	41	21	19	29	6	.313	.420	8	2	OF-64
1960	125	304	79	10	5	4	1.3	45	26	20	28	7	.260	.365	32	5	OF-91
1961 BAL A	115	312	91	13	5	1	0.3	46	13	20	32	5	.292	.375	8	0	OF-108
1962	139	416	127	19	4	9	2.2	47	40	17	46	7	.305	.435	21	6	OF-121
1963	148	429	110	21	2	7	1.6	51	36	40	48	18	.256	.364	22	4	OF-130
1964	56	93	27	3	0	1	1.1	11	7	11	22	0	.290	.355	18	3	OF-40
1965	132	345	93	11	2	1	0.3	49	29	27	38	3	.270	.322	23	4	OF-106
1966	117	373	114	21	5	3	0.8	66	41	38	37	2	.306	.413	15	2	OF-104
1967	108	275	65	8	2	4	1.5	40	23	32	48	5	.236	.324	33	4	OF-69
1968 2 teams		CHI	A	(38G –	.134)		CLE	A	(68G –	.281)							
" total	106	299	72	10	2	3	1.0	32	28	29	37	1	.241	.318	29	6	OF-76, 1B-1
1969 CLE A	122	266	66	10	0	2	0.8	26	24	25	33	3	.248	.308	41	7	OF-84

	G	AB	H	2B	3B	HR	HR %	R	RBI	BB	SO	SB	BA	SA	Pinch Hit AB	Pinch Hit H	G by POS

Russ Snyder continued

	G	AB	H	2B	3B	HR	HR %	R	RBI	BB	SO	SB	BA	SA	AB	H	G by POS
1970 MIL A	124	276	64	11	0	4	1.4	34	31	16	40	1	.232	.315	28	6	OF-106
12 yrs.	1365	3631	984	150	29	42	1.2	488	319	294	438	58	.271	.363	278	49	OF-1099, 1B-1

WORLD SERIES

	G	AB	H	2B	3B	HR	HR %	R	RBI	BB	SO	SB	BA	SA	AB	H	G by POS
1966 BAL A	3	6	1	0	0	0	0.0	1	1	2	0	0	.167	.167	0	0	OF-3

Louis Sockalexis

SOCKALEXIS, LOUIS FRANCIS (Chief) BL TR
B. Oct. 24, 1871, Old Town, Me.   D. Dec. 24, 1913, Burlington, Me.

	G	AB	H	2B	3B	HR	HR %	R	RBI	BB	SO	SB	BA	SA	AB	H	G by POS
1897 CLE N	66	278	94	9	8	3	1.1	43	42	18		16	.338	.460	0	0	OF-66
1898	21	67	15	2	0	0	0.0	11	10	1		0	.224	.254	4	1	OF-16
1899	7	22	6	1	0	0	0.0	0	3	1		0	.273	.318	2	0	OF-5
3 yrs.	94	367	115	12	8	3	0.8	54	55	20		16	.313	.414	6	1	OF-87

Bill Sodd

SODD, WILLIAM   BR TR 6'2"   210 lbs.
B. Sept. 18, 1914, Fort Worth, Tex.

	G	AB	H	2B	3B	HR	HR %	R	RBI	BB	SO	SB	BA	SA	AB	H	G by POS
1937 CLE A	1	1	0	0	0	0	0.0	0	0	0	1	0	.000	.000	1	0	

Eric Soderholm

SODERHOLM, ERIC THANE   BR TR 5'11"   187 lbs.
B. Sept. 24, 1948, Cortland, N. Y.

	G	AB	H	2B	3B	HR	HR %	R	RBI	BB	SO	SB	BA	SA	AB	H	G by POS
1971 MIN A	21	64	10	4	0	1	1.6	9	4	10	17	0	.156	.266	0	0	3B-20
1972	93	287	54	10	0	13	4.5	28	39	19	48	3	.188	.359	11	3	3B-79
1973	35	111	33	7	2	1	0.9	22	9	21	16	1	.297	.423	3	1	3B-33, SS-1
1974	141	464	128	18	3	10	2.2	63	51	48	68	7	.276	.392	6	0	3B-130, SS-1
1975	117	419	120	17	2	11	2.6	62	58	53	66	3	.286	.415	1	0	3B-113, DH-3
1977 CHI A	130	460	129	20	3	25	5.4	77	67	47	47	2	.280	.500	0	0	3B-126, DH-3
1978	143	457	118	17	1	20	4.4	57	67	39	44	2	.258	.431	7	4	3B-128, DH-11, 2B-1
1979 2 teams		CHI A	(56G –	.252)		TEX A	(63G –	.272)									
" total	119	357	93	14	2	10	2.8	46	53	31	28	0	.261	.395	14	3	3B-93, DH-14, 1B-2
1980 NY A	95	275	79	13	1	11	4.0	38	35	27	25	0	.287	.462	11	3	DH-51, 3B-37
9 yrs.	894	2894	764	120	14	102	3.5	402	383	295	359	18	.264	.421	53	14	3B-759, DH-82, SS-2, 1B-2, 2B-1

LEAGUE CHAMPIONSHIP SERIES

	G	AB	H	2B	3B	HR	HR %	R	RBI	BB	SO	SB	BA	SA	AB	H	G by POS
1980 NY A	2	6	1	0	0	0	0.0	0	0	0	0	0	.167	.167	0	0	DH-2

Rick Sofield

SOFIELD, RICHARD MICHAEL   BL TR 6'1"   195 lbs.
B. Dec. 16, 1956, Cheyenne, Wyo.

	G	AB	H	2B	3B	HR	HR %	R	RBI	BB	SO	SB	BA	SA	AB	H	G by POS
1979 MIN A	35	93	28	5	0	0	0.0	8	12	12	27	2	.301	.355	3	1	OF-35
1980	131	417	103	18	4	9	2.2	52	49	24	92	4	.247	.374	13	4	OF-126, DH-2
1981	41	102	18	2	0	0	0.0	9	5	8	22	3	.176	.196	7	1	OF-34
3 yrs.	207	612	149	25	4	9	1.5	69	66	44	141	9	.243	.342	23	6	OF-195, DH-2

Tony Solaita

SOLAITA, TOLIA   BL TL 6'   210 lbs.
B. Jan. 15, 1947, Nuuyli, American Samoa

	G	AB	H	2B	3B	HR	HR %	R	RBI	BB	SO	SB	BA	SA	AB	H	G by POS
1968 NY A	1	1	0	0	0	0	0.0	0	0	0	1	0	.000	.000	0	0	1B-1
1974 KC A	96	239	64	12	0	7	2.9	31	30	35	70	0	.268	.406	13	4	1B-65, DH-14, OF-1
1975	93	231	60	11	0	16	6.9	35	44	39	79	0	.260	.515	15	3	DH-37, 1B-35
1976 2 teams		KC A	(31G –	.235)		CAL A	(63G –	.270)									
" total	94	283	74	13	0	9	3.2	29	42	40	61	1	.261	.403	13	4	1B-59, DH-21
1977 CAL A	116	324	78	15	0	14	4.3	40	53	56	77	1	.241	.417	23	8	1B-91, DH-6
1978	60	94	21	3	0	1	1.1	10	14	16	25	0	.223	.287	34	9	DH-18, 1B-11
1979 2 teams		MON N	(29G –	.286)		TOR A	(36G –	.265)									
" total	65	144	39	12	1	3	2.1	19	20	28	32	0	.271	.431	14	2	DH-26, 1B-19
7 yrs.	525	1316	336	66	1	50	3.8	164	203	214	345	2	.255	.421	112	30	1B-281, DH-122, OF-1

Moe Solomon

SOLOMON, MOSES H. (The Rabbi of Swat)   BL TL 5'9½"   180 lbs.
B. Dec. 8, 1900, New York, N. Y.   D. June 25, 1966, Miami, Fla.

	G	AB	H	2B	3B	HR	HR %	R	RBI	BB	SO	SB	BA	SA	AB	H	G by POS
1923 NY N	2	8	3	1	0	0	0.0	0	1	0	1	0	.375	.500	0	0	OF-2

Moose Solters

SOLTERS, JULIUS JOSEPH   BR TR 6'   190 lbs.
Born Julius Joseph Soltesz.
B. Mar. 22, 1906, Pittsburgh, Pa.   D. Sept. 28, 1975, Pittsburgh, Pa.

	G	AB	H	2B	3B	HR	HR %	R	RBI	BB	SO	SB	BA	SA	AB	H	G by POS
1934 BOS A	101	365	109	25	4	7	1.9	61	58	18	50	9	.299	.447	13	4	OF-89
1935 2 teams		BOS A	(24G –	.241)		STL A	(127G –	.330)									
" total	151	631	201	45	7	18	2.9	94	112	36	42	11	.319	.498	3	1	OF-148
1936 STL A	152	628	183	45	7	17	2.7	100	134	41	76	3	.291	.467	3	0	OF-147
1937 CLE A	152	589	190	42	11	20	3.4	90	109	42	56	6	.323	.533	3	0	OF-149
1938	67	199	40	6	3	2	1.0	30	22	13	28	4	.201	.291	23	4	OF-46
1939 2 teams		CLE A	(41G –	.275)		STL A	(40G –	.206)									
" total	81	233	55	13	3	2	0.9	33	33	19	35	3	.236	.343	27	7	OF-55
1940 CHI A	116	428	132	28	3	12	2.8	65	80	27	54	3	.308	.472	9	1	OF-107
1941	76	251	65	9	4	4	1.6	24	43	18	31	3	.259	.375	12	3	OF-63
1943	42	97	15	0	0	1	1.0	6	8	7	5	0	.155	.186	19	2	OF-21
9 yrs.	938	3421	990	213	42	83	2.4	503	599	221	377	42	.289	.449	112	22	OF-825

Jock Somerlott

SOMERLOTT, JOHN WESLEY   BR TR 6'   160 lbs.
B. Oct. 26, 1882, Flint, Ind.   D. Apr. 21, 1965, Butler, Ind.

	G	AB	H	2B	3B	HR	HR %	R	RBI	BB	SO	SB	BA	SA	AB	H	G by POS
1910 WAS A	16	63	14	0	0	0	0.0	6	2	3		2	.222	.222	0	0	1B-16
1911	13	40	7	0	0	0	0.0	2	2	0		2	.175	.175	1	1	1B-12
2 yrs.	29	103	21	0	0	0	0.0	8	4	3		4	.204	.204	1	1	1B-28

Kid Somers

SOMERS, WILLIAM
B. Toronto, Ont., Canada   D. Oct. 16, 1895, Toronto, Ont., Canada

	G	AB	H	2B	3B	HR	HR %	R	RBI	BB	SO	SB	BA	SA	AB	H	G by POS
1893 STL N	2	1	0	0	0	0	0.0	1	0	0		0	.000	.000	0	0	OF-1, C-1

	G	AB	H	2B	3B	HR	HR%	R	RBI	BB	SO	SB	BA	SA	Pinch Hit AB	H	G by POS

Ed Somerville

SOMERVILLE, EDWARD
B. Philadelphia, Pa. D. Sept. 30, 1877, Hamilton, Ont., Canada

	G	AB	H	2B	3B	HR	HR%	R	RBI	BB	SO	SB	BA	SA	PH AB	PH H	G by POS
1876 LOU N	64	256	48	5	1	0	0.0	29	14	1	6		.188	.215	0	0	2B-64

Joe Sommer

SOMMER, JOSEPH JOHN   BR TR
B. Nov. 20, 1858, Covington, Ky. D. Jan. 16, 1938, Cincinnati, Ohio

	G	AB	H	2B	3B	HR	HR%	R	RBI	BB	SO	SB	BA	SA	PH AB	PH H	G by POS
1880 CIN N	24	88	16	1	0	0	0.0	10	6	0		2	.182	.193	0	0	OF-22, SS-1, 3B-1, C-1
1882 CIN AA	80	354	102	12	6	1	0.3	82		24			.288	.364	0	0	OF-80
1883	97	413	115	5	7	3	0.7	79		20			.278	.346	0	0	OF-94, 3B-3, P-1
1884 BAL AA	107	479	129	11	10	4	0.8	96		8			.269	.359	0	0	3B-97, OF-9, 2B-1
1885	110	471	118	23	6	1	0.2	84		24			.251	.331	0	0	OF-107, SS-2, 3B-2, P-2, 1B-1
1886	139	560	117	18	4	1	0.2	79		24			.209	.261	0	0	OF-95, 2B-32, 3B-11, SS-3, P-1
1887	131	463	123	11	5	0	0.0	88		63		29	.266	.311	0	0	OF-110, 2B-13, 3B-10, SS-2, P-1
1888	79	297	65	10	0	0	0.0	31	35	18		13	.219	.253	0	0	OF-44, SS-34, 2B-2, 1B-1
1889	106	386	85	13	2	1	0.3	51	36	42	49	18	.220	.272	0	0	OF-105, SS-1
1890 2 teams			CLE N (9G – .229)					B-B AA (38G – .256)									
" total	47	164	41	5	2	0	0.0	17		15	3	10	.250	.305	0	0	OF-47, P-1
10 yrs.	920	3675	911	109	42	11	0.3	617	77	238	54	70	.248	.309	0	0	OF-713, 3B-124, 2B-48, SS-43, P-6, 1B-2, C-1

Bill Sommers

SOMMERS, WILLIAM DUNN   BR TR 6'   170 lbs.
B. Feb. 17, 1923, Brooklyn, N. Y.

	G	AB	H	2B	3B	HR	HR%	R	RBI	BB	SO	SB	BA	SA	PH AB	PH H	G by POS
1950 STL A	65	137	35	5	1	0	0.0	24	14	25	14	0	.255	.307	11	1	3B-37, 2B-21

Pete Sommers

SOMMERS, JOSEPH ANDREWS   BR
B. Oct. 26, 1866, Cleveland, Ohio D. July 22, 1908, Cleveland, Ohio

	G	AB	H	2B	3B	HR	HR%	R	RBI	BB	SO	SB	BA	SA	PH AB	PH H	G by POS
1887 NY AA	33	116	21	3	0	1	0.9	9		7		6	.181	.233	0	0	C-31, OF-1, 1B-1
1888 BOS N	4	13	3	1	0	0	0.0	1	0	0	3	0	.231	.308	0	0	C-4
1889 2 teams			CHI N (12G – .222)					IND N (23G – .250)									
" total	35	129	31	7	2	2	1.6	17	22	3	24	2	.240	.372	0	0	C-32, OF-3
1890 2 teams			NY N (17G – .106)					CLE N (9G – .206)									
" total	26	81	12	2	2	0	0.0	8	2	6	15	0	.148	.222	0	0	C-19, 1B-5, OF-3
4 yrs.	98	339	67	13	4	3	0.9	35	23	16	42	8	.198	.286	0	0	C-86, OF-7, 1B-6

Bill Sorrell

SORRELL, WILLIAM   BL TR 6'   190 lbs.
B. Oct. 14, 1940, Morehead, Ky.

	G	AB	H	2B	3B	HR	HR%	R	RBI	BB	SO	SB	BA	SA	PH AB	PH H	G by POS
1965 PHI N	10	13	5	0	0	1	7.7	2	2	2	1	0	.385	.615	7	3	3B-1
1967 SF N	18	17	3	1	0	0	0.0	1	1	3	2	0	.176	.235	10	2	OF-5
1970 KC A	57	135	36	2	0	4	3.0	12	14	10	13	1	.267	.370	23	6	3B-29, OF-4, 1B-3
3 yrs.	85	165	44	3	0	5	3.0	15	17	15	16	1	.267	.376	40	11	3B-30, OF-9, 1B-3

Chick Sorrells

SORRELLS, RAYMOND EDWIN (Red)   BR TR 5'9"   155 lbs.
B. July 31, 1896, Stringtown, Okla.

	G	AB	H	2B	3B	HR	HR%	R	RBI	BB	SO	SB	BA	SA	PH AB	PH H	G by POS
1922 CLE A	2	1	0	0	0	0	0.0	0	0	0	0	0	.000	.000	0	0	SS-1

Denny Sothern

SOTHERN, DENNIS ELWOOD   BR TR 5'11"   175 lbs.
B. Jan. 20, 1904, Washington, D. C. D. Dec. 7, 1977, Durham, N. C.

	G	AB	H	2B	3B	HR	HR%	R	RBI	BB	SO	SB	BA	SA	PH AB	PH H	G by POS
1926 PHI N	14	53	13	1	0	3	5.7	5	10	4	10	0	.245	.434	1	1	OF-13
1928	141	579	165	27	5	5	0.9	82	38	34	53	17	.285	.375	2	2	OF-136
1929	76	294	90	21	3	5	1.7	52	27	16	24	13	.306	.449	1	0	OF-71
1930 2 teams			PHI N (90G – .280)					PIT N (17G – .176)									
" total	107	398	106	30	1	6	1.5	70	40	25	41	8	.266	.392	8	4	OF-97
1931 BKN N	19	31	5	1	0	0	0.0	10	0	4	8	0	.161	.194	3	1	OF-10
5 yrs.	357	1355	379	80	9	19	1.4	219	115	83	136	38	.280	.394	15	8	OF-327

Steve Souchock

SOUCHOCK, STEPHEN (Bud)   BR TR 6'2½"   203 lbs.
B. Mar. 3, 1919, Yatesboro, Pa.

	G	AB	H	2B	3B	HR	HR%	R	RBI	BB	SO	SB	BA	SA	PH AB	PH H	G by POS
1946 NY A	47	86	26	3	3	2	2.3	15	10	7	13	0	.302	.477	17	5	1B-20
1948	44	118	24	3	1	3	2.5	11	11	7	13	0	.203	.322	11	2	1B-32
1949 CHI A	84	252	59	13	5	7	2.8	29	37	25	38	5	.234	.409	17	4	OF-39, 1B-30
1951 DET A	91	188	46	10	4	11	5.9	33	28	18	27	0	.245	.505	34	7	OF-59, 2B-1, 1B-1
1952	92	265	66	16	4	13	4.9	40	45	21	28	1	.249	.487	17	4	OF-56, 3B-13, 1B-9
1953	89	278	84	13	3	11	4.0	29	46	8	35	5	.302	.489	10	3	OF-80, 1B-1
1954	25	39	7	0	1	3	7.7	6	8	2	10	1	.179	.462	14	2	OF-9, 3B-2
1955	1	1	1	0	0	0	0.0	0	1	0	0	0	1.000	1.000	1	1	
8 yrs.	473	1227	313	58	20	50	4.1	163	186	88	164	15	.255	.457	121	28	OF-243, 1B-93, 3B-15, 2B-1

Clyde Southwick

SOUTHWICK, CLYDE AUBRA   BL TR 6'   180 lbs.
B. Nov. 3, 1886, Maxwell, Iowa D. Oct. 14, 1961, Freeport, Ill.

	G	AB	H	2B	3B	HR	HR%	R	RBI	BB	SO	SB	BA	SA	PH AB	PH H	G by POS
1911 STL A	4	12	3	0	0	0	0.0	3	0	1		0	.250	.250	0	0	C-4

Bill Southworth

SOUTHWORTH, WILLIAM FREDERICK   BR TR 6'2"   205 lbs.
B. Nov. 10, 1945, Madison, Wis.

	G	AB	H	2B	3B	HR	HR%	R	RBI	BB	SO	SB	BA	SA	PH AB	PH H	G by POS
1964 MIL N	3	7	2	0	0	1	14.3	2	2	0	3	0	.286	.714	1	0	3B-2

Billy Southworth

SOUTHWORTH, WILLIAM HARRISON   BL TR 5'9"   170 lbs.
B. Mar. 9, 1893, Harvard, Neb. D. Nov. 15, 1969, Columbus, Ohio
Manager 1929, 1940-51.

	G	AB	H	2B	3B	HR	HR%	R	RBI	BB	SO	SB	BA	SA	PH AB	PH H	G by POS
1913 CLE A	1	0	0	0	0	0	–	0	0	0	0	0	–	–	0	0	OF-1
1915	60	177	39	2	5	0	0.0	25	8	36	12	2	.220	.288	8	0	OF-44
1918 PIT N	64	246	84	5	7	2	0.8	37	43	26	9	19	.341	.443	0	0	OF-64
1919	121	453	127	14	14	4	0.9	56	61	32	22	23	.280	.400	0	0	OF-121
1920	146	546	155	17	13	2	0.4	64	53	52	20	23	.284	.374	2	0	OF-142

	G	AB	H	2B	3B	HR	HR %	R	RBI	BB	SO	SB	BA	SA	Pinch Hit AB	Pinch Hit H	G by POS

Billy Southworth continued

	G	AB	H	2B	3B	HR	HR %	R	RBI	BB	SO	SB	BA	SA	AB	H	G by POS
1921 BOS N	141	569	175	25	15	7	1.2	86	79	36	13	22	.308	.441	0	0	OF-141
1922	43	158	51	4	4	4	2.5	27	18	18	1	4	.323	.475	2	0	OF-41
1923	153	611	195	29	16	6	1.0	95	78	61	23	14	.319	.448	0	0	OF-151, 2B-2
1924 NY N	94	281	72	13	0	3	1.1	40	36	32	16	1	.256	.335	16	2	OF-75
1925	123	473	138	19	5	6	1.3	79	44	51	11	6	.292	.391	4	0	OF-120
1926 2 teams	NY	N	(36G –	.328)		STL	N	(99G –	.317)								
" total	135	507	162	28	7	16	3.2	99	99	33	10	14	.320	.497	5	4	OF-127
1927 STL N	92	306	92	15	5	2	0.7	52	39	23	7	10	.301	.402	9	2	OF-83
1929	19	32	6	2	0	0	0.0	1	3	2	4	0	.188	.250	13	1	OF-5
13 yrs.	1192	4359	1296	173	91	52	1.2	661	561	402	148	138	.297	.415	56	9	OF-1115, 2B-2

WORLD SERIES																	
1924 NY N	5	1	0	0	0	0	0.0	1	0	0	0	0	.000	.000	1	0	OF-2
1926 STL N	7	29	10	1	1	1	3.4	6	4	0	0	1	.345	.552	0	0	OF-7
2 yrs.	12	30	10	1	1	1	3.3	7	4	0	0	1	.333	.533	1	0	OF-9

Len Sowders

SOWDERS, LEONARD
Brother of John Sowders.   Brother of Bill Sowders.
B. June 29, 1861, Louisville, Ky.   D. Nov. 19, 1888, Indianapolis, Ind.

	G	AB	H	2B	3B	HR	HR %	R	RBI	BB	SO	SB	BA	SA	AB	H	G by POS
1886 BAL AA	23	76	20	3	1	0	0.0	10		12			.263	.329	0	0	OF-23, 1B-1

Al Spalding

SPALDING, ALBERT GOODWILL   BR TR 6'1"   170 lbs.
B. Sept. 2, 1850, Byron, Ill.   D. Sept. 9, 1915, Point Loma, Calif.
Manager 1876-77.
Hall of Fame 1939.

	G	AB	H	2B	3B	HR	HR %	R	RBI	BB	SO	SB	BA	SA	AB	H	G by POS
1876 CHI N	66	292	91	14	2	0	0.0	54	44	6	3		.312	.373	0	0	P-61, OF-10, 1B-3
1877	60	254	65	7	6	0	0.0	29	35	3	16		.256	.331	0	0	1B-45, 2B-13, P-4, 3B-2
1878	1	4	2	0	0	0	0.0	0	0	0	0		.500	.500	0	0	2B-1
3 yrs.	127	550	158	21	8	0	0.0	83	79	9	19		.287	.355	0	0	P-65, 1B-48, 2B-14, OF-10, 3B-2

Dick Spalding

SPALDING, CHARLES HARRY   BL TL 5'11"   185 lbs.
B. Oct. 13, 1893, Philadelphia, Pa.   D. Feb. 3, 1950, Philadelphia, Pa.

	G	AB	H	2B	3B	HR	HR %	R	RBI	BB	SO	SB	BA	SA	AB	H	G by POS
1927 PHI N	115	442	131	16	3	0	0.0	68	25	38	40	5	.296	.346	1	0	OF-113
1928 WAS A	16	23	8	0	0	0	0.0	1	0	0	4	0	.348	.348	2	0	OF-11
2 yrs.	131	465	139	16	3	0	0.0	69	25	38	44	5	.299	.346	3	0	OF-124

Al Spangler

SPANGLER, ALBERT DONALD   BL TL 6'   175 lbs.
B. July 8, 1933, Philadelphia, Pa.

	G	AB	H	2B	3B	HR	HR %	R	RBI	BB	SO	SB	BA	SA	AB	H	G by POS
1959 MIL N	6	12	5	0	1	0	0.0	3	0	1	1	1	.417	.583	1	1	OF-4
1960	101	105	28	5	2	0	0.0	26	6	14	17	6	.267	.352	4	0	OF-92
1961	68	97	26	2	0	0	0.0	23	6	28	9	4	.268	.289	16	3	OF-44
1962 HOU N	129	418	119	10	9	5	1.2	51	35	70	46	7	.285	.388	8	1	OF-121
1963	120	430	121	25	4	4	0.9	52	27	50	38	5	.281	.386	7	3	OF-113
1964	135	449	110	18	5	4	0.9	51	38	41	43	7	.245	.334	10	2	OF-127
1965 2 teams	HOU	N	(38G –	.214)		CAL	A	(51G –	.260)								
" total	89	208	49	2	1	1	0.5	35	8	22	17	5	.236	.269	26	4	OF-57
1966 CAL A	6	9	6	0	0	0	0.0	2	0	2	2	0	.667	.667	3	3	OF-3
1967 CHI N	62	130	33	7	0	0	0.0	18	13	23	17	2	.254	.308	23	4	OF-41
1968	88	177	48	9	3	2	1.1	21	18	20	24	0	.271	.390	41	10	OF-48
1969	82	213	45	8	1	4	1.9	23	23	21	16	0	.211	.315	26	1	OF-58
1970	21	14	2	1	0	1	7.1	2	1	3	3	0	.143	.429	11	2	OF-6
1971	5	5	2	0	0	0	0.0	0	0	0	1	0	.400	.400	5	2	
13 yrs.	912	2267	594	87	26	21	0.9	307	175	295	234	37	.262	.351	181	36	OF-714

Bob Speake

SPEAKE, ROBERT CHARLES (Spook)   BL TL 6'1"   178 lbs.
B. Aug. 22, 1930, Springfield, Mo.

	G	AB	H	2B	3B	HR	HR %	R	RBI	BB	SO	SB	BA	SA	AB	H	G by POS
1955 CHI N	95	261	57	9	5	12	4.6	36	43	28	71	3	.218	.429	24	5	OF-55, 1B-8
1957	129	418	97	14	5	16	3.8	65	50	38	68	5	.232	.404	23	9	OF-60, 1B-39
1958 SF N	66	71	15	3	0	3	4.2	9	10	13	15	0	.211	.380	41	7	OF-10, 1B-1
1959	15	11	1	0	0	0	0.0	0	1	1	4	0	.091	.091	11	1	
4 yrs.	305	761	170	26	10	31	4.1	110	104	80	158	8	.223	.406	99	22	OF-125, 1B-47

Tris Speaker

SPEAKER, TRISTRAM E (The Grey Eagle, Spoke)   BL TL 5'11½"   193 lbs.
B. Apr. 4, 1888, Hubbard, Tex.   D. Dec. 8, 1958, Lake Whitney, Tex.
Manager 1919-26.
Hall of Fame 1937.

	G	AB	H	2B	3B	HR	HR %	R	RBI	BB	SO	SB	BA	SA	AB	H	G by POS
1907 BOS A	7	19	3	0	0	0	0.0	0	1	1		0	.158	.158	3	0	OF-4
1908	31	118	26	2	3	0	0.0	12	9	4		2	.220	.288	0	0	OF-31
1909	143	544	168	26	13	7	1.3	73	77	38		35	.309	.443	1	0	OF-142
1910	141	538	183	20	14	7	1.3	92	65	52		35	.340	.468	0	0	OF-140
1911	141	510	167	34	13	8	1.6	88	80	59		25	.327	.492	3	2	OF-138
1912	153	580	222	53	12	10	1.7	136	98	82		52	.383	.567	0	0	OF-153
1913	141	520	190	35	22	3	0.6	94	81	65	22	46	.365	.535	2	0	OF-139
1914	158	571	193	46	18	4	0.7	100	90	77	25	42	.338	.503	1	0	OF-156, 1B-1, P-1
1915	150	547	176	25	12	0	0.0	108	69	81	14	29	.322	.411	0	0	OF-150
1916 CLE A	151	546	211	41	8	2	0.4	102	83	82	20	35	.386	.502	0	0	OF-151
1917	142	523	184	42	11	2	0.4	90	60	67	14	30	.352	.486	0	0	OF-142
1918	127	471	150	33	11	0	0.0	73	61	64	9	27	.318	.435	0	0	OF-127
1919	134	494	146	38	12	2	0.4	83	63	73	12	15	.296	.433	0	0	OF-134
1920	150	552	214	50	11	8	1.4	137	107	97	13	10	.388	.562	1	0	OF-149
1921	132	506	183	52	14	3	0.6	107	74	68	12	2	.362	.538	4	2	OF-128
1922	131	426	161	48	8	11	2.6	85	71	77	11	8	.378	.606	17	9	OF-110
1923	150	574	218	59	11	17	3.0	133	130	93	15	10	.380	.610	0	0	OF-150
1924	135	486	167	36	9	9	1.9	94	65	72	13	5	.344	.510	7	3	OF-128
1925	117	429	167	35	5	12	2.8	79	87	70	12	5	.389	.578	4	1	OF-109

	G	AB	H	2B	3B	HR	HR %	R	RBI	BB	SO	SB	BA	SA	Pinch Hit AB	Pinch Hit H	G by POS

Tris Speaker continued

	G	AB	H	2B	3B	HR	HR %	R	RBI	BB	SO	SB	BA	SA	AB	H	G by POS
1926	150	540	164	52	8	7	1.3	96	86	94	15	6	.304	.469	1	0	OF-149
1927 WAS A	141	523	171	43	6	2	0.4	71	73	55	8	9	.327	.444	4	0	OF-120, 1B-17
1928 PHI A	64	191	51	23	2	3	1.6	28	29	10	5	5	.267	.455	12	3	OF-50
22 yrs.	2789	10208	3515	793	223	117	1.1	1881	1559	1381	220	433	.344	.500	60	20	OF-2700, 1B-18, P-1
			5th	1st	6th			8th		7th							

WORLD SERIES

	G	AB	H	2B	3B	HR	HR %	R	RBI	BB	SO	SB	BA	SA	AB	H	G by POS
1912 BOS A	8	30	9	1	2	0	0.0	4	2	4	2	1	.300	.467	0	0	OF-8
1915	5	17	5	0	1	0	0.0	2	0	4	1	0	.294	.412	0	0	OF-5
1920 CLE A	7	25	8	2	1	0	0.0	6	1	3	1	0	.320	.480	0	0	OF-7
3 yrs.	20	72	22	3	4	0	0.0	12	3	11	4	1	.306	.458	0	0	OF-20
					1st												

Horace Speed

SPEED, HORACE ARTHUR
B. Oct. 4, 1951, Los Angeles, Calif.

BR TR 6'1" 180 lbs.

	G	AB	H	2B	3B	HR	HR %	R	RBI	BB	SO	SB	BA	SA	AB	H	G by POS
1975 SF N	17	15	2	1	0	0	0.0	2	1	1	8	0	.133	.200	1	0	OF-9
1978 CLE A	70	106	24	4	1	0	0.0	13	4	14	31	2	.226	.283	4	0	OF-61, DH-3
1979	26	14	2	0	0	0	0.0	6	1	5	7	2	.143	.143	0	0	OF-16, DH-4
3 yrs.	113	135	28	5	1	0	0.0	21	6	20	46	4	.207	.259	5	0	OF-86, DH-7

Chris Speier

SPEIER, CHRIS EDWARD
B. June 28, 1950, Alameda, Calif.

BR TR 6'1" 175 lbs.

	G	AB	H	2B	3B	HR	HR %	R	RBI	BB	SO	SB	BA	SA	AB	H	G by POS
1971 SF N	157	601	141	17	6	8	1.3	74	46	56	90	4	.235	.323	2	1	SS-156
1972	150	562	151	25	2	15	2.7	74	71	82	92	9	.269	.400	0	0	SS-150
1973	153	542	135	17	4	11	2.0	58	71	66	69	4	.249	.356	3	2	SS-150, 2B-1
1974	141	501	125	19	5	9	1.8	55	53	62	64	3	.250	.361	4	2	SS-135, 2B-4
1975	141	487	132	30	5	10	2.1	60	69	70	50	4	.271	.415	4	0	SS-136, 3B-1
1976	145	495	112	18	4	3	0.6	51	40	60	52	2	.226	.297	5	1	SS-135, 2B-7, 3B-5, 1B-1
1977 2 teams		SF	N	(6G – .176)		MON	N	(139G – .235)									
" total	145	548	128	31	6	5	0.9	59	38	67	81	1	.234	.339	2	0	SS-143
1978 MON N	150	501	126	18	3	5	1.0	47	51	60	75	1	.251	.329	2	0	SS-148
1979	113	344	78	13	1	7	2.0	31	26	43	45	0	.227	.331	0	0	SS-112
1980	128	388	103	14	4	1	0.3	35	32	52	38	0	.265	.330	0	0	SS-127, 2B-1
1981	96	307	69	10	2	2	0.7	33	25	38	29	1	.225	.290	0	0	SS-96
1982	156	530	136	26	4	7	1.3	41	60	47	67	1	.257	.360	1	0	SS-155
1983	88	261	67	12	2	2	0.8	31	22	29	37	2	.257	.341	5	1	SS-74, 3B-12, 2B-2
1984 3 teams		MON	N	(25G – .150)		STL	N	(38G – .178)		MIN	A	(12G – .212)					
" total	75	191	34	7	1	3	1.6	12	10	13	34	0	.178	.272	16	3	SS-59, 3B-6
14 yrs.	1838	6258	1537	257	49	88	1.4	661	614	745	823	32	.246	.345	44	10	SS-1776, 3B-24, 2B-15, 1B-1

DIVISIONAL PLAYOFF SERIES

	G	AB	H	2B	3B	HR	HR %	R	RBI	BB	SO	SB	BA	SA	AB	H	G by POS
1981 MON N	5	15	6	2	0	0	0.0	4	3	4	2	0	.400	.533	0	0	SS-5

LEAGUE CHAMPIONSHIP SERIES

	G	AB	H	2B	3B	HR	HR %	R	RBI	BB	SO	SB	BA	SA	AB	H	G by POS
1971 SF N	4	14	5	1	0	1	7.1	4	1	1	0	0	.357	.643	0	0	SS-4
1981 MON N	5	16	3	0	0	0	0.0	0	0	2	0	0	.188	.188	0	0	SS-5
2 yrs.	9	30	8	1	0	1	3.3	4	1	3	0	0	.267	.400	0	0	SS-9

Bob Spence

SPENCE, JOHN ROBERT
B. Feb. 10, 1946, San Diego, Calif.

BL TR 6'4" 215 lbs.

	G	AB	H	2B	3B	HR	HR %	R	RBI	BB	SO	SB	BA	SA	AB	H	G by POS
1969 CHI A	12	26	4	1	0	0	0.0	0	3	0	9	0	.154	.192	7	0	1B-6
1970	46	130	29	4	1	4	3.1	11	15	11	32	0	.223	.362	9	1	1B-37
1971	14	27	4	0	0	0	0.0	2	1	5	6	0	.148	.148	5	0	1B-7
3 yrs.	72	183	37	5	1	4	2.2	13	19	16	47	0	.202	.306	21	1	1B-50

Stan Spence

SPENCE, STANLEY ORVIL
B. Mar. 20, 1915, South Portsmouth, Ky. D. Jan. 9, 1983, Kinston, N. C.

BL TL 5'10½" 180 lbs.

	G	AB	H	2B	3B	HR	HR %	R	RBI	BB	SO	SB	BA	SA	AB	H	G by POS
1940 BOS A	51	68	19	2	1	2	2.9	5	13	4	9	0	.279	.426	33	11	OF-15
1941	86	203	47	10	3	2	1.0	22	28	18	14	1	.232	.340	33	6	OF-52, 1B-1
1942 WAS A	149	629	203	27	15	4	0.6	94	79	62	16	5	.323	.432	0	0	OF-149
1943	149	570	152	23	10	12	2.1	72	88	84	39	8	.267	.405	1	0	OF-148
1944	153	592	187	31	8	18	3.0	83	100	69	28	3	.316	.486	0	0	OF-150, 1B-3
1946	152	578	169	50	10	16	2.8	83	87	62	31	1	.292	.497	1	0	OF-150
1947	147	506	141	22	6	16	3.2	62	73	81	41	2	.279	.441	5	0	OF-142
1948 BOS A	114	391	92	17	4	12	3.1	71	61	82	33	0	.235	.391	9	3	OF-92, 1B-14
1949 2 teams		BOS	A	(7G – .150)		STL	A	(104G – .245)									
" total	111	334	80	14	3	13	3.9	49	46	58	37	1	.240	.416	16	2	OF-90, 1B-1
9 yrs.	1112	3871	1090	196	60	95	2.5	541	575	520	248	21	.282	.437	98	22	OF-988, 1B-19

Ben Spencer

SPENCER, LLOYD BENJAMIN
B. May 15, 1890, Patapsco, Md. D. Sept. 1, 1970, Finksburg, Md.

BL TL 5'8" 160 lbs.

	G	AB	H	2B	3B	HR	HR %	R	RBI	BB	SO	SB	BA	SA	AB	H	G by POS
1913 WAS A	8	21	6	1	1	0	0.0	2	2	4		0	.286	.429	0	0	OF-8

Chet Spencer

SPENCER, CHESTER ARTHUR
B. Mar. 4, 1883, South Webster, Ohio D. Nov. 10, 1938, Portsmouth, Ohio

BL TR 6' 180 lbs.

	G	AB	H	2B	3B	HR	HR %	R	RBI	BB	SO	SB	BA	SA	AB	H	G by POS
1906 BOS N	8	27	4	1	0	0	0.0	1	0	0		0	.148	.185	0	0	OF-8

Daryl Spencer

SPENCER, DARYL DEAN (Big Dee)
B. July 13, 1929, Wichita, Kans.

BR TR 6'2½" 185 lbs.

	G	AB	H	2B	3B	HR	HR %	R	RBI	BB	SO	SB	BA	SA	AB	H	G by POS
1952 NY N	7	17	5	0	1	0	0.0	0	3	1	4	0	.294	.412	1	0	SS-3, 3B-3
1953	118	408	85	18	5	20	4.9	55	56	42	74	0	.208	.424	3	0	SS-53, 3B-36, 2B-32
1956	146	489	108	13	2	14	2.9	46	42	35	65	1	.221	.342	2	0	2B-70, SS-66, 3B-12
1957	148	534	133	31	2	11	2.1	65	50	50	50	3	.249	.376	2	0	SS-110, 2B-36, 3B-6
1958 SF N	148	539	138	20	5	17	3.2	71	74	73	60	1	.256	.406	0	0	SS-134, 2B-17
1959	152	555	147	20	1	12	2.2	59	62	58	67	5	.265	.369	1	0	2B-151, SS-4
1960 STL N	148	507	131	20	3	16	3.2	70	58	81	74	1	.258	.404	2	1	SS-138, 2B-16

	G	AB	H	2B	3B	HR	HR %	R	RBI	BB	SO	SB	BA	SA	Pinch Hit AB	Pinch Hit H	G by POS

Daryl Spencer continued

	G	AB	H	2B	3B	HR	HR %	R	RBI	BB	SO	SB	BA	SA	AB	H	G by POS
1961 2 teams	STL	N (37G – .254)			LA	N	(60G – .243)										
" total	97	319	79	11	0	12	3.8	46	48	43	52	1	.248	.395	1	0	3B-57, SS-40
1962 LA N	77	157	37	5	1	2	1.3	24	12	32	31	0	.236	.318	13	1	3B-57, SS-10
1963 2 teams	LA	N (7G – .111)			CIN	N	(50G – .239)										
" total	57	164	38	7	0	1	0.6	21	23	34	39	1	.232	.293	7	0	3B-51
10 yrs.	1098	3689	901	145	20	105	2.8	457	428	449	516	13	.244	.380	32	2	SS-558, 2B-322, 3B-222

Jim Spencer

SPENCER, JAMES LLOYD
B. July 30, 1947, Hanover, Pa. BL TL 6'2" 195 lbs.

	G	AB	H	2B	3B	HR	HR %	R	RBI	BB	SO	SB	BA	SA	AB	H	G by POS
1968 CAL A	19	68	13	1	0	0	0.0	2	5	3	10	0	.191	.206	0	0	1B-19
1969	113	386	98	14	3	10	2.6	39	31	26	53	1	.254	.383	8	2	1B-107
1970	146	511	140	20	4	12	2.3	61	68	28	61	0	.274	.399	6	2	1B-142
1971	148	510	121	21	2	18	3.5	50	59	48	63	0	.237	.392	7	1	1B-145
1972	82	212	47	5	0	1	0.5	13	14	12	25	0	.222	.259	22	4	1B-35, OF-24
1973 2 teams	CAL	A (29G – .241)			TEX	A	(102G – .267)										
" total	131	439	115	16	5	6	1.4	45	54	43	50	0	.262	.362	8	0	1B-125, DH-3
1974 TEX A	118	352	98	11	4	7	2.0	36	44	22	27	1	.278	.392	8	3	1B-60, DH-54
1975	132	403	107	18	1	11	2.7	50	47	35	43	0	.266	.397	8	3	1B-99, DH-25
1976 CHI A	150	518	131	13	2	14	2.7	53	70	49	52	6	.253	.367	4	0	1B-143, DH-2
1977	128	470	116	16	1	18	3.8	56	69	36	50	1	.247	.400	2	1	1B-125
1978 NY A	71	150	34	9	1	7	4.7	12	24	15	32	0	.227	.440	24	7	DH-35, 1B-15
1979	106	295	85	15	3	23	7.8	60	53	38	25	0	.288	.593	16	3	DH-71, 1B-26
1980	97	259	61	9	0	13	5.0	38	43	30	44	1	.236	.421	22	8	1B-75, DH-15
1981 2 teams	NY	A (25G – .143)			OAK	A	(54G – .205)										
" total	79	234	44	8	0	4	1.7	20	13	19	27	1	.188	.274	13	4	1B-73
1982 OAK A	33	101	17	3	1	2	2.0	6	5	3	20	0	.168	.277	3	2	1B-32
15 yrs.	1553	4908	1227	179	27	146	3.0	541	599	407	582	11	.250	.387	151	40	1B-1221, DH-205, OF-24

DIVISIONAL PLAYOFF SERIES

	G	AB	H	2B	3B	HR	HR %	R	RBI	BB	SO	SB	BA	SA	AB	H	G by POS
1981 OAK A	1	4	1	1	0	0	0.0	0	0	0	0	0	.250	.500	0	0	1B-1

LEAGUE CHAMPIONSHIP SERIES

	G	AB	H	2B	3B	HR	HR %	R	RBI	BB	SO	SB	BA	SA	AB	H	G by POS
1980 NY A	1	1	0	0	0	0	0.0	0	0	0	0	0	.000	.000	1	0	
1981 OAK A	2	2	0	0	0	0	0.0	0	0	0	0	0	.000	.000	2	0	1B-2
2 yrs.	3	3	0	0	0	0	0.0	0	0	0	0	0	.000	.000	3	0	1B-2

WORLD SERIES

	G	AB	H	2B	3B	HR	HR %	R	RBI	BB	SO	SB	BA	SA	AB	H	G by POS
1978 NY A	4	12	2	0	0	0	0.0	3	0	2	4	0	.167	.167	1	0	1B-3

Roy Spencer

SPENCER, ROY HAMPTON
B. Feb. 22, 1900, Scranton, N. C.   D. Feb. 8, 1973, Port Charlotte, Fla. BR TR 5'10" 168 lbs.

	G	AB	H	2B	3B	HR	HR %	R	RBI	BB	SO	SB	BA	SA	AB	H	G by POS
1925 PIT N	14	28	6	1	0	0	0.0	1	2	1	3	1	.214	.250	3	0	C-11
1926	28	43	17	3	0	0	0.0	5	4	1	0	0	.395	.465	10	6	C-16
1927	38	92	26	3	1	0	0.0	9	13	3	3	0	.283	.337	4	2	C-34
1929 WAS A	50	116	18	4	0	1	0.9	18	9	8	15	0	.155	.216	5	1	C-41
1930	93	321	82	11	4	0	0.0	32	36	18	27	3	.255	.315	0	0	C-93
1931	145	483	133	16	3	1	0.2	48	60	35	21	0	.275	.327	0	0	C-145
1932	102	317	78	9	0	1	0.3	28	41	24	17	0	.246	.284	3	1	C-98
1933 CLE A	75	227	46	5	2	0	0.0	26	23	23	17	0	.203	.242	3	1	C-72
1934	5	7	1	1	0	0	0.0	0	0	1	0	1	.143	.286	1	1	C-4
1936 NY N	19	18	5	1	0	0	0.0	3	3	2	3	0	.278	.333	2	1	C-14
1937 BKN N	51	117	24	2	2	0	0.0	5	4	8	17	0	.205	.256	5	0	C-45
1938	16	45	12	1	1	0	0.0	2	6	5	6	0	.267	.333	0	0	C-16
12 yrs.	636	1814	448	57	13	3	0.2	177	203	128	130	4	.247	.298	36	13	C-589

WORLD SERIES

	G	AB	H	2B	3B	HR	HR %	R	RBI	BB	SO	SB	BA	SA	AB	H	G by POS
1927 PIT N	1	1	0	0	0	0	0.0	0	0	0	0	0	.000	.000	0	0	C-1

Tom Spencer

SPENCER, HUBERT THOMAS
B. Feb. 28, 1951, Gallipolis, Ohio BR TR 6' 170 lbs.

	G	AB	H	2B	3B	HR	HR %	R	RBI	BB	SO	SB	BA	SA	AB	H	G by POS
1978 CHI A	29	65	12	1	0	0	0.0	3	4	2	9	0	.185	.200	7	0	OF-27, DH-2

Tubby Spencer

SPENCER, EDWARD RUSSELL
B. Jan. 26, 1884, Oil City, Pa.   D. Feb. 1, 1945, San Francisco, Calif. BR TR

	G	AB	H	2B	3B	HR	HR %	R	RBI	BB	SO	SB	BA	SA	AB	H	G by POS
1905 STL A	35	115	27	1	2	0	0.0	6	11	7		2	.235	.278	1	1	C-34
1906	58	188	33	6	1	0	0.0	15	17	7		4	.176	.218	3	0	C-54
1907	71	230	61	11	1	0	0.0	27	24	7		1	.265	.322	8	2	C-63
1908	91	286	60	6	1	0	0.0	19	28	17		1	.210	.238	2	1	C-89
1909 BOS N	28	74	12	1	0	0	0.0	6	9	6		2	.162	.176	2	0	C-26
1911 PHI N	11	32	5	1	0	1	3.1	2	3	3	7	0	.156	.281	0	0	C-11
1916 DET A	19	54	20	1	1	1	1.9	7	10	6	6	2	.370	.481	0	0	C-19
1917	70	192	46	8	3	0	0.0	13	22	15	15	0	.240	.313	8	0	C-62
1918	66	155	34	8	1	0	0.0	11	8	19	18	1	.219	.284	17	3	C-48, 1B-1
9 yrs.	449	1326	298	43	10	2	0.2	106	132	87	46	13	.225	.277	41	7	C-406, 1B-1

Vern Spencer

SPENCER, VERNON MURRAY
B. Feb. 24, 1896, Wixom, Mich.   D. June 3, 1971, Wixom, Mich. BL TR 5'7" 165 lbs.

	G	AB	H	2B	3B	HR	HR %	R	RBI	BB	SO	SB	BA	SA	AB	H	G by POS
1920 NY N	45	140	28	2	3	0	0.0	15	19	11	17	4	.200	.257	3	0	OF-40

Paul Speraw

SPERAW, PAUL BACHMAN (Polly, Birdie)
B. Oct. 5, 1893, Annville, Pa.   D. Feb. 22, 1962, Cedar Rapids, Iowa BR TR 5'8½" 145 lbs.

	G	AB	H	2B	3B	HR	HR %	R	RBI	BB	SO	SB	BA	SA	AB	H	G by POS
1920 STL A	1	2	0	0	0	0	0.0	0	0	0	0	0	.000	.000	0	0	3B-1

Ed Sperber

SPERBER, EDWIN GEORGE
B. Jan. 21, 1895, Cincinnati, Ohio   D. Jan. 5, 1976, Cincinnati, Ohio BL TL 5'11" 175 lbs.

	G	AB	H	2B	3B	HR	HR %	R	RBI	BB	SO	SB	BA	SA	AB	H	G by POS
1924 BOS N	24	59	17	2	0	1	1.7	8	12	10	9	3	.288	.373	2	0	OF-17

	G	AB	H	2B	3B	HR	HR %	R	RBI	BB	SO	SB	BA	SA	Pinch Hit AB	Pinch Hit H	G by POS

Ed Sperber continued

	G	AB	H	2B	3B	HR	HR %	R	RBI	BB	SO	SB	BA	SA	AB	H	G by POS
1925	2	2	0	0	0	0	0.0	0	0	0	0	0	.000	.000	2	0	
2 yrs.	26	61	17	2	0	1	1.6	8	12	10	9	3	.279	.361	4	0	OF-17

Rob Sperring

SPERRING, ROBERT WALTER
B. Oct. 10, 1949, San Francisco, Calif.
BR TR 6'1" 185 lbs.

	G	AB	H	2B	3B	HR	HR %	R	RBI	BB	SO	SB	BA	SA	AB	H	G by POS
1974 CHI N	42	107	22	3	0	1	0.9	9	5	9	28	1	.206	.262	1	0	2B-35, SS-8
1975	65	144	30	4	1	1	0.7	25	9	16	31	0	.208	.271	1	0	3B-22, 2B-17, SS-16, OF-8
1976	43	93	24	3	0	0	0.0	8	7	9	25	0	.258	.290	1	0	3B-20, SS-15, 2B-4, OF-3
1977 HOU N	58	129	24	3	0	1	0.8	6	9	12	23	0	.186	.233	10	3	SS-22, 2B-20, 3B-11
4 yrs.	208	473	100	13	1	3	0.6	48	30	46	107	1	.211	.262	13	3	2B-76, SS-61, 3B-53, OF-11

Stan Sperry

SPERRY, STANLEY KENNETH
B. Feb. 19, 1914, Evansville, Wis. D. Sept. 27, 1962, Evansville, Wis.
BL TR 5'10½" 164 lbs.

	G	AB	H	2B	3B	HR	HR %	R	RBI	BB	SO	SB	BA	SA	AB	H	G by POS
1936 PHI N	20	37	5	3	0	0	0.0	2	4	3	5	0	.135	.216	3	1	2B-15
1938 PHI A	60	253	69	6	3	0	0.0	28	27	15	9	1	.273	.320	0	0	2B-60
2 yrs.	80	290	74	9	3	0	0.0	30	31	18	14	1	.255	.307	3	1	2B-75

Harry Spies

SPIES, HENRY
B. June 12, 1866, New Orleans, La. D. July 8, 1942, Los Angeles, Calif.
BR TR 5'11½" 170 lbs.

	G	AB	H	2B	3B	HR	HR %	R	RBI	BB	SO	SB	BA	SA	AB	H	G by POS
1895 2 teams		CIN N (14G – .220)				LOU N (72G – .268)											
" total	86	326	85	14	8	2	0.6	44	40	14	21	4	.261	.371	0	0	1B-49, C-38, SS-1

Ed Spiezio

SPIEZIO, EDWARD WAYNE
B. Oct. 31, 1941, Joliet, Ill.
BR TR 5'11" 180 lbs.

	G	AB	H	2B	3B	HR	HR %	R	RBI	BB	SO	SB	BA	SA	AB	H	G by POS
1964 STL N	12	12	4	0	0	0	0.0	0	0	0	1	0	.333	.333	12	4	
1965	10	18	3	0	0	0	0.0	0	5	1	4	0	.167	.167	7	2	3B-3
1966	26	73	16	5	1	2	2.7	4	10	5	11	1	.219	.397	6	0	3B-19
1967	55	105	22	2	0	3	2.9	9	10	7	18	2	.210	.314	27	8	3B-19, OF-7
1968	29	51	8	0	0	0	0.0	1	2	5	6	1	.157	.157	14	4	OF-11, 3B-2
1969 SD N	121	355	83	9	0	13	3.7	29	43	38	64	1	.234	.369	23	5	3B-98, OF-1
1970	110	316	90	18	1	12	3.8	45	42	43	42	4	.285	.462	21	7	3B-93
1971	97	308	71	10	1	7	2.3	16	36	22	50	6	.231	.338	7	2	3B-91, OF-1
1972 2 teams	94	SD N (20G – .138)				CHI A (74G – .238)											
" total	94	306	70	12	1	2	0.7	22	26	14	49	1	.229	.294	17	1	3B-79
9 yrs.	554	1544	367	56	4	39	2.5	126	174	135	245	16	.238	.355	134	33	3B-404, OF-20

WORLD SERIES																	
1967 STL N	1	1	0	0	0	0	0.0	0	0	0	0	0	.000	.000	1	0	
1968	1	1	1	0	0	0	0.0	0	0	0	0	0	1.000	1.000	1	1	
2 yrs.	2	2	1	0	0	0	0.0	0	0	0	0	0	.500	.500	2	1	

Charlie Spikes

SPIKES, LESLIE CHARLES
B. Jan. 23, 1951, Bogalusa, La.
BR TR 6'3" 215 lbs.

	G	AB	H	2B	3B	HR	HR %	R	RBI	BB	SO	SB	BA	SA	AB	H	G by POS
1972 NY A	14	34	5	1	0	0	0.0	2	3	1	13	0	.147	.176	5	0	OF-9
1973 CLE A	140	506	120	12	3	23	4.5	68	73	45	103	5	.237	.409	2	1	OF-111, DH-26
1974	155	568	154	23	1	22	3.9	63	80	34	100	10	.271	.431	1	0	OF-154
1975	111	345	79	13	3	11	3.2	41	33	30	51	7	.229	.380	17	7	OF-103, DH-2
1976	101	334	79	11	5	3	0.9	34	31	23	50	5	.237	.326	8	0	OF-98, DH-2
1977	32	95	22	2	0	3	3.2	13	11	11	17	0	.232	.347	7	1	OF-27, DH-2
1978 DET A	10	28	7	1	0	0	0.0	1	2	2	6	0	.250	.286	0	0	OF-9
1979 ATL N	66	93	26	8	0	3	3.2	12	21	5	30	0	.280	.462	47	16	OF-15
1980	41	36	10	1	0	0	0.0	6	2	3	18	0	.278	.306	31	10	OF-7
9 yrs.	670	2039	502	72	12	65	3.2	240	256	154	388	27	.246	.389	118	35	OF-533, DH-32

Harry Spilman

SPILMAN, HARRY WILLIAM
B. July 18, 1954, Albany, Ga.
BL TR 6'1" 180 lbs.

	G	AB	H	2B	3B	HR	HR %	R	RBI	BB	SO	SB	BA	SA	AB	H	G by POS
1978 CIN N	4	4	1	0	0	0	0.0	1	0	0	1	0	.250	.250	4	1	1B-12, 3B-4
1979	43	56	12	3	0	0	0.0	7	5	7	5	0	.214	.268	22	5	1B-18, OF-2, 3B-1, C-1
1980	65	101	27	4	0	4	4.0	14	19	9	19	0	.267	.426	41	12	1B-15, 3B-3
1981 2 teams	51	CIN N (23G – .167)				HOU N (28G – .294)											
" total	51	58	14	1	0	0	0.0	9	4	5	10	0	.241	.259	29	9	1B-11
1982 HOU N	38	61	17	2	0	3	4.9	7	11	5	10	0	.279	.459	26	6	1B-19, C-6
1983	42	78	13	3	0	1	1.3	7	9	5	12	0	.167	.244	20	1	1B-8, C-8
1984	32	72	19	2	0	2	2.8	14	15	12	10	0	.264	.375	10	1	1B-93, C-15, 3B-8, OF-2
7 yrs.	275	430	103	15	0	10	2.3	59	63	43	67	0	.240	.344	152	35	1B-93, C-15, 3B-8, OF-2

DIVISIONAL PLAYOFF SERIES																	
1981 HOU N	1	1	0	0	0	0	0.0	0	0	0	0	0	.000	.000	1	0	

LEAGUE CHAMPIONSHIP SERIES																	
1979 CIN N	2	2	0	0	0	0	0.0	0	0	0	0	0	.000	.000	2	0	

Hal Spindel

SPINDEL, HAROLD STEWART
B. May 27, 1913, Chandler, Okla.
BR TR 6' 185 lbs.

	G	AB	H	2B	3B	HR	HR %	R	RBI	BB	SO	SB	BA	SA	AB	H	G by POS
1939 STL A	48	119	32	3	1	0	0.0	13	11	8	7	0	.269	.311	15	6	C-32
1945 PHI N	36	87	20	3	0	0	0.0	7	8	6	7	0	.230	.264	4	0	C-31
1946	1	3	1	0	0	0	0.0	0	1	0	0	0	.333	.333	0	0	C-1
3 yrs.	85	209	53	6	1	0	0.0	20	20	14	14	0	.254	.292	19	6	C-64

Andy Spognardi

SPOGNARDI, ANDREA ETTORE
B. Oct. 18, 1908, Boston, Mass.
BL TR 5'9½" 160 lbs.

	G	AB	H	2B	3B	HR	HR %	R	RBI	BB	SO	SB	BA	SA	AB	H	G by POS
1932 BOS A	17	34	10	1	0	0	0.0	9	1	6	6	0	.294	.324	1	1	2B-9, SS-3, 3B-2

	G	AB	H	2B	3B	HR	HR %	R	RBI	BB	SO	SB	BA	SA	Pinch Hit AB	Pinch Hit H	G by POS

Al Spohrer

SPOHRER, ALFRED RAY
B. Dec. 3, 1902, Philadelphia, Pa.   D. July 17, 1972, Plymouth, N. H.
BR TR 5'10½" 175 lbs.

	G	AB	H	2B	3B	HR	HR %	R	RBI	BB	SO	SB	BA	SA	Pinch Hit AB	Pinch Hit H	G by POS
1928 2 teams		NY	N (3G – .000)			BOS	N (48G – .218)										
" total	51	126	27	3	0	0	0.0	15	9	5	11	1	.214	.238	3	1	C-51
1929 BOS N	114	342	93	21	8	2	0.6	42	48	26	35	1	.272	.398	4	1	C-109
1930	112	356	113	22	8	2	0.6	44	37	22	24	3	.317	.441	3	1	C-108
1931	114	350	84	17	5	0	0.0	23	27	22	27	2	.240	.317	3	0	C-111
1932	104	335	90	12	2	0	0.0	31	33	15	26	2	.269	.316	3	0	C-100
1933	67	184	46	6	1	1	0.5	11	12	11	13	3	.250	.310	2	0	C-65
1934	100	265	59	15	0	0	0.0	25	17	14	18	1	.223	.279	0	0	C-98
1935	92	260	63	7	1	1	0.4	22	16	9	12	0	.242	.288	2	0	C-90
8 yrs.	754	2218	575	103	25	6	0.3	213	199	124	166	13	.259	.336	20	3	C-732

Jim Spotts

SPOTTS, JAMES RUSSELL
B. Apr. 10, 1909, Honeybrook, Pa.   D. June 15, 1964, Medford, N. J.
BR TR 5'10½" 175 lbs.

	G	AB	H	2B	3B	HR	HR %	R	RBI	BB	SO	SB	BA	SA	Pinch Hit AB	Pinch Hit H	G by POS
1930 PHI N	3	2	0	0	0	0	0.0	1	0	1	1	0	.000	.000	1	0	C-2

Charlie Sprague

SPRAGUE, CHARLES WELLINGTON
B. Oct. 10, 1864, Cleveland, Ohio   D. Dec. 31, 1912, Des Moines, Iowa
BL TL 5'11" 150 lbs.

	G	AB	H	2B	3B	HR	HR %	R	RBI	BB	SO	SB	BA	SA	Pinch Hit AB	Pinch Hit H	G by POS
1887 CHI N	3	13	2	0	0	0	0.0	0	0	0	2	0	.154	.154	0	0	P-3, OF-1
1889 CLE N	2	7	1	0	0	0	0.0	2	1	1	0	1	.143	.143	0	0	P-2
1890 TOL AA	55	199	47	5	6	1	0.5	25		16		10	.236	.337	0	0	OF-40, P-19
3 yrs.	60	219	50	5	6	1	0.5	27	1	17	2	11	.228	.320	0	0	OF-41, P-24

Harry Spratt

SPRATT, HENRY LEE
B. July 10, 1887, Broadford, Va.   D. July 3, 1969, Washington, Pa.
BL TR 5'8½" 175 lbs.

	G	AB	H	2B	3B	HR	HR %	R	RBI	BB	SO	SB	BA	SA	Pinch Hit AB	Pinch Hit H	G by POS
1911 BOS N	62	154	37	4	4	2	1.3	22	13	13	25	1	.240	.357	19	5	SS-26, 2B-5, OF-4, 3B-4
1912	27	89	23	3	2	3	3.4	6	15	7	11	2	.258	.438	4	0	SS-23
2 yrs.	89	243	60	7	6	5	2.1	28	28	20	36	3	.247	.387	23	5	SS-49, 2B-5, OF-4, 3B-4

George Spriggs

SPRIGGS, GEORGE HERMAN
B. May 22, 1941, Newell, Md.
BL TR 5'11" 175 lbs.

	G	AB	H	2B	3B	HR	HR %	R	RBI	BB	SO	SB	BA	SA	Pinch Hit AB	Pinch Hit H	G by POS
1965 PIT N	9	2	1	0	0	0	0.0	5	0	0	0	2	.500	.500	1	0	OF-1
1966	9	7	1	0	0	0	0.0	0	0	0	3	0	.143	.143	7	1	
1967	38	57	10	1	1	0	0.0	14	5	6	20	3	.175	.228	21	3	OF-13
1969 KC A	23	29	4	2	1	0	0.0	4	0	3	8	0	.138	.276	14	1	OF-6
1970	51	130	27	2	3	1	0.8	12	7	14	32	4	.208	.292	10	2	OF-36
5 yrs.	130	225	43	5	5	1	0.4	35	12	23	63	9	.191	.271	53	7	OF-56

Joe Sprinz

SPRINZ, JOSEPH CONRAD (Mule)
B. Aug. 3, 1902, St. Louis, Mo.
BR TR 5'11" 185 lbs.

	G	AB	H	2B	3B	HR	HR %	R	RBI	BB	SO	SB	BA	SA	Pinch Hit AB	Pinch Hit H	G by POS
1930 CLE A	17	45	8	1	0	0	0.0	5	2	4	4	0	.178	.200	0	0	C-17
1931	1	3	0	0	0	0	0.0	0	0	0	0	0	.000	.000	0	0	C-1
1933 STL N	3	5	1	0	0	0	0.0	1	0	1	1	0	.200	.200	0	0	C-3
3 yrs.	21	53	9	1	0	0	0.0	6	2	5	5	0	.170	.189	0	0	C-21

Freddy Spurgeon

SPURGEON, FRED
B. Oct. 9, 1901, Wabash, Ind.   D. Nov. 5, 1970, Kalamazoo, Mich.
BR TR 5'11½" 160 lbs.

	G	AB	H	2B	3B	HR	HR %	R	RBI	BB	SO	SB	BA	SA	Pinch Hit AB	Pinch Hit H	G by POS
1924 CLE A	3	8	1	1	0	0	0.0	4	0	0	0	0	.125	.250	0	0	2B-3
1925	107	376	108	9	3	0	0.0	50	32	15	21	8	.287	.327	2	0	3B-56, 2B-46, SS-3
1926	149	614	181	31	8	0	0.0	101	49	27	36	7	.295	.355	0	0	2B-149
1927	57	179	45	6	1	1	0.6	30	19	18	14	8	.251	.313	1	1	2B-52
4 yrs.	316	1177	335	47	7	1	0.1	181	100	60	71	23	.285	.339	3	1	2B-250, 3B-56, SS-3

Ed Spurney

SPURNEY, EDWARD FREDERICK
B. Jan. 19, 1872, Cleveland, Ohio   D. Oct. 12, 1932, Cleveland, Ohio

	G	AB	H	2B	3B	HR	HR %	R	RBI	BB	SO	SB	BA	SA	Pinch Hit AB	Pinch Hit H	G by POS
1891 PIT N	3	7	2	1	0	0	0.0	2	0	2	1	0	.286	.429	0	0	SS-3

Mike Squires

SQUIRES, MICHAEL LYNN
B. Mar. 5, 1952, Kalamazoo, Mich.
BL TL 5'11" 185 lbs.

	G	AB	H	2B	3B	HR	HR %	R	RBI	BB	SO	SB	BA	SA	Pinch Hit AB	Pinch Hit H	G by POS
1975 CHI A	20	65	15	0	0	0	0.0	5	4	8	5	3	.231	.231	0	0	1B-20
1977	3	3	0	0	0	0	0.0	0	0	0	1	0	.000	.000	2	0	1B-1
1978	46	150	42	9	2	0	0.0	25	19	16	21	4	.280	.367	1	0	1B-45
1979	122	295	78	10	1	2	0.7	44	22	22	9	15	.264	.325	6	1	1B-110, OF-1
1980	131	343	97	11	3	2	0.6	38	33	33	24	8	.283	.350	14	4	1B-114, C-2
1981	92	294	78	9	0	0	0.0	35	25	22	17	7	.265	.296	6	2	1B-88, OF-1
1982	116	195	52	9	3	1	0.5	33	21	14	13	3	.267	.359	14	3	1B-109
1983	143	153	34	4	1	1	0.7	21	11	22	11	3	.222	.281	23	4	1B-124, DH-5, 3B-1
1984	104	82	15	1	0	0	0.0	9	6	6	7	2	.183	.195	22	3	1B-77, 3B-13, OF-3, P-1
9 yrs.	777	1580	411	53	10	6	0.4	210	141	143	108	45	.260	.318	88	18	1B-688, 3B-14, DH-5, OF-5, C-2, P-1

LEAGUE CHAMPIONSHIP SERIES

	G	AB	H	2B	3B	HR	HR %	R	RBI	BB	SO	SB	BA	SA	Pinch Hit AB	Pinch Hit H	G by POS
1983 CHI A	4	4	0	0	0	0	0.0	0	0	0	0	0	.000	.000	2	0	1B-3

Marv Staehle

STAEHLE, MARVIN GUSTAVE
B. Mar. 13, 1942, Oak Park, Ill.
BL TR 5'10" 165 lbs.

	G	AB	H	2B	3B	HR	HR %	R	RBI	BB	SO	SB	BA	SA	Pinch Hit AB	Pinch Hit H	G by POS
1964 CHI A	6	5	2	0	0	0	0.0	0	2	0	0	1	.400	.400	5	2	
1965	7	7	3	0	0	0	0.0	0	2	0	0	0	.429	.429	7	3	
1966	8	15	2	0	0	0	0.0	2	0	4	2	1	.133	.133	2	0	2B-6
1967	32	54	6	1	0	0	0.0	1	1	4	8	1	.111	.130	8	0	2B-17, SS-5
1969 MON N	6	17	7	2	0	1	5.9	4	1	2	0	0	.412	.706	2	1	2B-4
1970	104	321	70	9	1	0	0.0	41	26	39	21	1	.218	.252	13	2	2B-91, SS-1
1971 ATL N	22	36	4	0	0	0	0.0	5	1	5	4	0	.111	.111	11	0	2B-7, 3B-1
7 yrs.	185	455	94	12	1	1	0.2	53	33	54	35	4	.207	.244	48	8	2B-125, SS-6, 3B-1

	G	AB	H	2B	3B	HR	HR %	R	RBI	BB	SO	SB	BA	SA	Pinch Hit AB	Pinch Hit H	G by POS

Bob Stafford

STAFFORD, ROBERT LEE
Deceased.

	G	AB	H	2B	3B	HR	HR%	R	RBI	BB	SO	SB	BA	SA	AB	H	G by POS
1890 BUF P	15	49	7	1	0	0	0.0	11	3	7	8	2	.143	.163	0	0	P-12, OF-4
1893 NY N	67	281	79	7	4	5	1.8	58	27	25	31	19	.281	.388	0	0	OF-67
1894	14	46	10	1	1	0	0.0	10	4	10	7	2	.217	.283	1	0	3B-6, OF-5, 2B-1, 1B-1
1895	124	463	129	12	5	3	0.6	79	73	40	32	42	.279	.346	0	0	2B-110, OF-12, 3B-2
1896	59	230	66	9	1	0	0.0	28	40	13	18	15	.287	.335	0	0	OF-53, SS-6
1897 2 teams	NY	N (7G – .087)				LOU	N (111G – .278)										
" total	118	455	122	16	5	7	1.5	68	56	34		14	.268	.371	1	0	SS-105, OF-12, 3B-1
1898 2 teams	LOU	N (49G – .298)				BOS	N (37G – .260)										
" total	86	304	86	5	0	2	0.7	47	33	23		10	.283	.319	1	0	OF-57, 2B-28, 3B-1, 1B-1
1899 2 teams	BOS	N (55G – .302)				WAS	N (31G – .246)										
" total	86	300	84	9	3	4	1.3	40	54	12		13	.280	.370	5	1	OF-41, 2B-28, SS-18, 3B-2
8 yrs.	569	2128	583	60	19	21	1.0	341	290	164	96	117	.274	.350	8	1	OF-251, 2B-161, SS-129, 3B-12, P-12, 1B-2

General Stafford

STAFFORD, JAMES JOSEPH   5'9"   185 lbs.
Brother of John Stafford.
B. July 9, 1868, Webster, Mass.   D. Sept. 11, 1923, Worcester, Mass.

	G	AB	H	2B	3B	HR	HR%	R	RBI	BB	SO	SB	BA	SA	AB	H	G by POS
1890 PHI AA	1	2	0	0	0	0	0.0	0		0		0	.000	.000	0	0	OF-1

Heinie Stafford

STAFFORD, HENRY ALEXANDER   BR TR 5'7"   160 lbs.
B. Nov. 1, 1891, Orleans, Vt.   D. Jan. 29, 1972, Lake Worth, Fla.

	G	AB	H	2B	3B	HR	HR%	R	RBI	BB	SO	SB	BA	SA	AB	H	G by POS
1916 NY N	1	1	0	0	0	0	0.0	0	0	0	0	0	.000	.000	1	0	

Steve Staggs

STAGGS, STEPHEN ROBERT   BR TR 5'9"   150 lbs.
B. May 6, 1951, Anchorage, Alaska

	G	AB	H	2B	3B	HR	HR%	R	RBI	BB	SO	SB	BA	SA	AB	H	G by POS
1977 TOR A	72	291	75	11	6	2	0.7	37	28	36	38	5	.258	.357	1	0	2B-72
1978 OAK A	47	78	19	2	2	0	0.0	10	0	19	17	2	.244	.321	4	2	2B-40, DH-2, SS-2, 3B-2
2 yrs.	119	369	94	13	8	2	0.5	47	28	55	55	7	.255	.350	5	2	2B-112, DH-2, SS-2, 3B-2

Chick Stahl

STAHL, CHARLES SYLVESTER   BL TL 5'10"   160 lbs.
Brother of Jake Stahl.
B. Jan. 10, 1873, Fort Wayne, Ind.   D. Mar. 28, 1907, West Baden, Ind.
Manager 1906.

	G	AB	H	2B	3B	HR	HR%	R	RBI	BB	SO	SB	BA	SA	AB	H	G by POS
1897 BOS N	114	469	168	30	13	4	0.9	111	97	38		18	.358	.503	1	0	OF-111
1898	125	469	146	21	8	3	0.6	69	52	46		6	.311	.409	0	0	OF-125
1899	148	576	202	23	18	8	1.4	122	53	72		33	.351	.495	0	0	OF-148, P-1
1900	136	553	163	23	16	5	0.9	88	82	34		27	.295	.421	1	1	OF-135
1901 BOS A	131	515	159	20	16	6	1.2	106	72	54		29	.309	.445	0	0	OF-131
1902	127	508	164	22	11	2	0.4	92	58	37		24	.323	.421	2	2	OF-125
1903	77	299	82	12	6	2	0.7	60	44	28		10	.274	.375	3	0	OF-74
1904	157	587	173	27	19	3	0.5	84	67	64		11	.295	.421	0	0	OF-157
1905	134	500	129	17	4	0	0.0	61	47	50		18	.258	.308	0	0	OF-134
1906	155	595	170	24	6	4	0.7	62	51	47		13	.286	.366	0	0	OF-155
10 yrs.	1304	5071	1556	219	117	37	0.7	855	623	470		189	.307	.418	7	3	OF-1295, P-1

WORLD SERIES

	G	AB	H	2B	3B	HR	HR%	R	RBI	BB	SO	SB	BA	SA	AB	H	G by POS
1903 BOS A	8	33	10	1	3 (4th)	0	0.0	6	3	1	2	2	.303	.515	0	0	OF-8

Jake Stahl

STAHL, GARLAND   BR TR
Brother of Chick Stahl.
B. Apr. 13, 1879, Elkhart, Ind.   D. Sept. 18, 1922, Los Angeles, Calif.
Manager 1905-06, 1912-13.

	G	AB	H	2B	3B	HR	HR%	R	RBI	BB	SO	SB	BA	SA	AB	H	G by POS
1903 BOS A	40	92	22	3	5	2	2.2	14	8	4		1	.239	.446	11	5	C-28, OF-1
1904 WAS A	142	520	136	29	12	3	0.6	54	50	21		25	.262	.381	0	0	1B-119, OF-23
1905	141	501	122	22	12	5	1.0	66	66	28		41	.244	.365	1	0	1B-140
1906	137	482	107	9	8	0	0.0	38	51	21		30	.222	.274	1	0	1B-136
1908 2 teams	NY	A (74G – .255)				BOS	A (79G – .248)										
" total	153	532	134	27	16	2	0.4	63	65	31		30	.252	.374	1	0	1B-85, OF-67
1909 BOS A	127	435	128	19	12	6	1.4	62	60	43		16	.294	.434	1	0	1B-126
1910	144	531	144	19	16	10	1.9	68	77	42		22	.271	.424	2	0	1B-142
1912	95	326	98	21	6	3	0.9	40	60	31		13	.301	.429	3	1	1B-92
1913	2	2	0	0	0	0	0.0	0	0	0		1	.000	.000	2	0	
9 yrs.	981	3421	891	149	87	31	0.9	405	437	221	1	178	.260	.382	22	6	1B-840, OF-91, C-28

WORLD SERIES

	G	AB	H	2B	3B	HR	HR%	R	RBI	BB	SO	SB	BA	SA	AB	H	G by POS
1912 BOS A	8	32	9	2	0	0	0.0	3	2	0	6	2	.281	.344	0	0	1B-8

Larry Stahl

STAHL, LARRY FLOYD   BL TL 6'   175 lbs.
B. June 29, 1941, Belleville, Ill.

	G	AB	H	2B	3B	HR	HR%	R	RBI	BB	SO	SB	BA	SA	AB	H	G by POS
1964 KC A	15	46	12	1	0	3	6.5	7	6	1	10	0	.261	.478	5	1	OF-10
1965	28	81	16	2	1	4	4.9	9	14	5	16	1	.198	.395	7	1	OF-21
1966	119	312	78	11	5	5	1.6	37	34	17	63	5	.250	.365	31	7	OF-94
1967 NY N	71	155	37	5	0	1	0.6	9	18	8	25	2	.239	.290	30	5	OF-43
1968	53	183	43	7	2	3	1.6	15	10	21	38	3	.235	.344	3	1	OF-47, 1B-9
1969 SD N	95	162	32	6	2	3	1.9	10	10	17	31	3	.198	.315	44	6	OF-31, 1B-13
1970	52	66	12	2	0	0	0.0	5	3	2	14	2	.182	.212	33	7	OF-20
1971	114	308	78	13	4	8	2.6	27	36	26	59	4	.253	.399	26	8	OF-75, 1B-7
1972	107	297	67	9	3	7	2.4	31	20	31	67	1	.226	.347	28	5	OF-76, 1B-1
1973 CIN N	76	111	25	2	2	2	1.8	17	12	14	34	1	.225	.333	45	11	OF-29, 1B-2
10 yrs.	730	1721	400	58	19	36	2.1	167	163	142	357	22	.232	.351	252	52	OF-452, 1B-32

LEAGUE CHAMPIONSHIP SERIES

	G	AB	H	2B	3B	HR	HR%	R	RBI	BB	SO	SB	BA	SA	AB	H	G by POS
1973 CIN N	4	4	2	0	0	0	0.0	1	0	0	1	0	.500	.500	4	2	

	G	AB	H	2B	3B	HR	HR %	R	RBI	BB	SO	SB	BA	SA	Pinch Hit AB	Pinch Hit H	G by POS

Roy Staiger

STAIGER, ROY JOSEPH (Linus)
B. Jan. 6, 1950, Tulsa, Okla.
BR TR 6' 200 lbs.

	G	AB	H	2B	3B	HR	HR %	R	RBI	BB	SO	SB	BA	SA	PH AB	PH H	G by POS
1975 NY N	13	19	3	1	0	0	0.0	2	0	0	4	0	.158	.211	0	0	3B-13
1976	95	304	67	8	1	2	0.7	23	26	25	35	3	.220	.273	1	0	3B-93, SS-1
1977	40	123	31	9	0	2	1.6	16	11	4	20	1	.252	.374	0	0	3B-36, SS-1
1979 NY A	4	11	3	1	0	0	0.0	1	1	1	0	0	.273	.364	0	0	3B-4
4 yrs.	152	457	104	19	1	4	0.9	42	38	30	59	4	.228	.300	1	0	3B-146, SS-2

Tuck Stainback

STAINBACK, GEORGE TUCKER
B. Aug. 4, 1910, Los Angeles, Calif.
BR TR 5'11½" 175 lbs.

	G	AB	H	2B	3B	HR	HR %	R	RBI	BB	SO	SB	BA	SA	PH AB	PH H	G by POS
1934 CHI N	104	359	110	14	3	2	0.6	47	46	8	42	7	.306	.379	8	3	OF-96, 3B-1
1935	47	94	24	4	0	3	3.2	16	11	0	13	1	.255	.394	10	3	OF-28
1936	44	75	13	3	0	1	1.3	13	5	6	14	1	.173	.253	9	1	OF-26
1937	72	160	37	7	1	0	0.0	18	14	7	16	3	.231	.288	10	2	OF-49
1938 3 teams	STL N (6G – .000)			PHI N (30G – .259)				BKN N (35G – .327)									
" total	71	195	55	9	3	1	0.5	26	31	5	10	2	.282	.374	17	4	OF-50
1939 BKN N	168	201	54	7	0	3	1.5	22	19	4	23	0	.269	.348	10	2	OF-55
1940 DET A	15	40	9	2	0	0	0.0	4	1	1	9	0	.225	.275	5	1	OF-9
1941	94	200	49	8	1	2	1.0	19	10	3	21	6	.245	.325	8	1	OF-80
1942 NY A	15	10	2	0	0	0	0.0	0	0	0	2	0	.200	.200	1	0	OF-3
1943	71	231	60	11	2	0	0.0	31	10	7	16	3	.260	.325	5	3	OF-61
1944	30	78	17	3	0	0	0.0	13	5	3	7	1	.218	.256	5	1	OF-24
1945	95	327	84	12	2	5	1.5	40	32	13	20	0	.257	.352	9	2	OF-83
1946 PHI A	97	291	71	10	2	0	0.0	35	20	7	20	3	.244	.292	23	5	OF-66
13 yrs.	917	2261	585	90	14	17	0.8	284	204	64	213	27	.259	.333	120	28	OF-630, 3B-1

WORLD SERIES

	G	AB	H	2B	3B	HR	HR %	R	RBI	BB	SO	SB	BA	SA	PH AB	PH H	G by POS
1942 NY A	2	0	0	0	0	0	–	0	0	0	0	0	–	–	0	0	
1943	5	17	3	0	0	0	0.0	0	0	0	2	0	.176	.176	0	0	OF-5
2 yrs.	7	17	3	0	0	0	0.0	0	0	0	2	0	.176	.176	0	0	OF-5

Gale Staley

STALEY, GEORGE GAYLORD
B. May 2, 1899, De Pere, Wis.
BL TR 5'8½" 167 lbs.

	G	AB	H	2B	3B	HR	HR %	R	RBI	BB	SO	SB	BA	SA	PH AB	PH H	G by POS
1925 CHI N	7	26	11	2	0	0	0.0	2	3	2	1	0	.423	.500	0	0	2B-7

Virgil Stallcup

STALLCUP, THOMAS VIRGIL (Red)
B. Jan. 3, 1922, Ravensford, N. C.
BR TR 6'3" 185 lbs.

	G	AB	H	2B	3B	HR	HR %	R	RBI	BB	SO	SB	BA	SA	PH AB	PH H	G by POS
1947 CIN N	8	1	0	0	0	0	0.0	1	0	0	1	0	.000	.000	0	0	SS-1
1948	149	539	123	30	4	3	0.6	40	65	18	52	2	.228	.315	1	1	SS-148
1949	141	575	146	28	5	3	0.5	49	45	9	44	1	.254	.336	0	0	SS-141
1950	136	483	121	23	2	8	1.7	44	54	17	39	4	.251	.356	0	0	SS-136
1951	121	428	103	17	2	8	1.9	33	49	6	40	2	.241	.346	4	0	SS-117
1952 2 teams	CIN N (2G – .000)			STL N (29G – .129)													
" total	31	32	4	1	0	0	0.0	4	1	1	5	0	.125	.156	14	3	SS-13
1953 STL N	1	1	0	0	0	0	0.0	0	0	0	0	0	.000	.000	0	0	
7 yrs.	587	2059	497	99	13	22	1.1	171	214	51	181	9	.241	.334	20	4	SS-556

George Staller

STALLER, GEORGE WALBORN (Stopper)
B. Apr. 1, 1916, Rutherford Heights, Pa.
BL TL 5'11" 190 lbs.

	G	AB	H	2B	3B	HR	HR %	R	RBI	BB	SO	SB	BA	SA	PH AB	PH H	G by POS
1943 PHI A	21	85	23	1	3	3	3.5	14	12	5	6	1	.271	.459	0	0	OF-20

George Stallings

STALLINGS, GEORGE TWEEDY (The Miracle Man)
B. Nov. 17, 1867, Augusta, Ga. D. May 13, 1929, Haddock, Ga.
Manager 1897-98, 1901, 1909-10, 1913-20.
BR TR

	G	AB	H	2B	3B	HR	HR %	R	RBI	BB	SO	SB	BA	SA	PH AB	PH H	G by POS
1890 BKN N	4	11	0	0	0	0	0.0	1	0	1		3	.000	.000	0	0	C-4
1897 PHI N	2	9	2	1	0	0	0.0	1	0	0		0	.222	.333	0	0	OF-1, 1B-1
1898	1	0	0	0	0	0	–	0	0	0		0	–	–	0	0	
3 yrs.	7	20	2	1	0	0	0.0	3	0	1		3	.100	.150	0	0	C-4, OF-1, 1B-1

Oscar Stanage

STANAGE, OSCAR HARLAND
B. Mar. 17, 1883, Tulare, Calif. D. Nov. 11, 1964, Detroit, Mich.
BR TR 5'11" 190 lbs.

	G	AB	H	2B	3B	HR	HR %	R	RBI	BB	SO	SB	BA	SA	PH AB	PH H	G by POS
1906 CIN N	1	1	0	0	0	0	0.0	0	0	0		0	.000	.000	0	0	C-1
1909 DET A	77	252	66	8	6	0	0.0	17	21	11		2	.262	.341	0	0	C-77
1910	88	275	57	7	4	2	0.7	24	25	20		1	.207	.284	4	0	C-84
1911	141	503	133	13	7	3	0.6	45	51	20		3	.264	.336	0	0	C-141
1912	119	394	103	9	4	0	0.0	35	41	34		3	.261	.305	0	0	C-119
1913	80	241	54	13	2	0	0.0	19	21	21	35	2	.224	.295	2	2	C-77
1914	122	400	77	8	4	0	0.0	16	25	24	58	2	.193	.233	0	0	C-122
1915	100	300	67	9	2	1	0.3	27	31	20	41	5	.223	.277	0	0	C-100
1916	94	291	69	17	3	0	0.0	16	30	17	48	3	.237	.316	0	0	C-94
1917	99	297	61	14	1	0	0.0	19	30	20	35	3	.205	.259	4	1	C-95
1918	54	186	47	4	0	1	0.5	9	14	11	18	2	.253	.290	2	0	C-47, 1B-5
1919	38	120	29	4	1	0	0.8	9	15	7	12	1	.242	.317	1	0	C-36, 1B-1
1920	78	238	55	17	0	0	0.0	12	17	14	21	0	.231	.303	1	0	C-78
1925	3	5	1	0	0	0	0.0	0	0	0	0	0	.200	.200	0	0	C-3
14 yrs.	1094	3503	819	123	34	8	0.2	248	321	219	268	30	.234	.295	14	3	C-1074, 1B-6

WORLD SERIES

	G	AB	H	2B	3B	HR	HR %	R	RBI	BB	SO	SB	BA	SA	PH AB	PH H	G by POS
1909 DET A	2	5	1	0	0	0	0.0	0	2	0	2	0	.200	.200	0	0	C-2

Jerry Standaert

STANDAERT, JEROME JOHN
B. Nov. 2, 1901, Chicago, Ill. D. Aug. 4, 1964, Chicago, Ill.
BR TR 5'10" 168 lbs.

	G	AB	H	2B	3B	HR	HR %	R	RBI	BB	SO	SB	BA	SA	PH AB	PH H	G by POS
1925 BKN N	1	1	0	0	0	0	0.0	0	0	0	1	0	.000	.000	1	0	
1926	66	113	39	8	2	0	0.0	13	14	5	7	0	.345	.451	22	6	2B-21, 3B-14, SS-6
1929 BOS A	19	18	3	2	0	0	0.0	1	4	3	2	0	.167	.278	8	1	1B-10
3 yrs.	86	132	42	10	2	0	0.0	14	18	8	10	0	.318	.424	31	7	2B-21, 3B-14, 1B-10, SS-6

	G	AB	H	2B	3B	HR	HR %	R	RBI	BB	SO	SB	BA	SA	Pinch Hit AB	Pinch Hit H	G by POS

Tom Stankard

STANKARD, THOMAS FRANCIS   BR TR 6'1"   190 lbs.
B. Mar. 20, 1882, Waltham, Mass.   D. June 13, 1958, Waltham, Mass.

	G	AB	H	2B	3B	HR	HR %	R	RBI	BB	SO	SB	BA	SA	PH AB	PH H	G by POS
1904 PIT N	2	2	0	0	0	0	0.0	0	0	0		0	.000	.000	0	0	SS-1, 3B-1

Eddie Stanky

STANKY, EDWARD RAYMOND (The Brat, Muggsy)   BR TR 5'8"   170 lbs.
B. Sept. 3, 1916, Philadelphia, Pa.
Manager 1952-55, 1966-68, 1977.

	G	AB	H	2B	3B	HR	HR %	R	RBI	BB	SO	SB	BA	SA	PH AB	PH H	G by POS
1943 CHI N	142	510	125	15	1	0	0.0	92	47	92	42	4	.245	.278	0	0	2B-131, SS-12, 3B-2
1944 2 teams		CHI N (13G – .240)			BKN N (89G – .276)												
" total	102	286	78	9	3	0	0.0	36	16	46	15	4	.273	.325	5	0	2B-61, SS-38, 3B-4
1945 BKN N	153	555	143	29	5	1	0.2	128	39	148	42	6	.258	.333	0	0	2B-153, SS-1
1946	144	483	132	24	7	0	0.0	98	36	137	56	8	.273	.352	2	0	2B-141
1947	146	559	141	24	5	3	0.5	97	53	103	39	3	.252	.329	0	0	2B-146
1948 BOS N	67	247	79	14	2	2	0.8	49	29	61	13	3	.320	.417	1	1	2B-66
1949	138	506	144	24	5	1	0.2	90	42	113	41	3	.285	.358	3	0	2B-135
1950 NY N	152	527	158	25	5	8	1.5	115	51	144	50	9	.300	.412	0	0	2B-151
1951	145	515	127	17	2	14	2.7	88	43	127	63	8	.247	.369	4	0	2B-140
1952 STL N	53	83	19	4	0	0	0.0	13	7	19	9	0	.229	.277	26	9	2B-20
1953	17	30	8	0	0	0	0.0	5	1	6	4	0	.267	.267	5	0	2B-8
11 yrs.	1259	4301	1154	185	35	29	0.7	811	364	996	374	48	.268	.348	46	10	2B-1152, SS-51, 3B-6

WORLD SERIES

	G	AB	H	2B	3B	HR	HR %	R	RBI	BB	SO	SB	BA	SA	PH AB	PH H	G by POS
1947 BKN N	7	25	6	1	0	0	0.0	4	2	3	2	0	.240	.280	0	0	2B-7
1948 BOS N	6	14	4	1	0	0	0.0	0	1	7	1	0	.286	.357	0	0	2B-6
1951 NY N	6	22	3	0	0	0	0.0	3	1	3	2	0	.136	.136	0	0	2B-6
3 yrs.	19	61	13	2	0	0	0.0	7	4	13	5	0	.213	.246	0	0	2B-19

Fred Stanley

STANLEY, FREDRICK BLAIR (Chicken)   BR TR 5'10"   165 lbs.
B. Aug. 13, 1947, Farnhamville, Iowa

	G	AB	H	2B	3B	HR	HR %	R	RBI	BB	SO	SB	BA	SA	PH AB	PH H	G by POS
1969 SEA A	17	43	12	2	1	0	0.0	2	4	3	8	1	.279	.372	1	0	SS-15, 2B-1
1970 MIL A	6	0	0	0	0	0	–	1	0	0	0	0	–	–	0	0	2B-2
1971 CLE A	60	129	29	4	0	2	1.6	14	12	27	25	1	.225	.302	0	0	SS-55, 2B-3
1972 2 teams		CLE A (6G – .167)			SD N (39G – .200)												
" total	45	97	19	3	0	0	0.0	16	2	14	22	1	.196	.227	4	1	SS-22, 2B-22, 3B-4
1973 NY A	26	66	14	0	1	1	1.5	6	5	7	16	0	.212	.288	0	0	SS-21, 2B-3
1974	33	38	7	0	0	0	0.0	2	3	3	2	1	.184	.184	1	0	SS-19, 2B-15
1975	117	252	56	5	1	0	0.0	34	15	21	27	3	.222	.250	0	0	SS-83, 2B-33, 3B-1
1976	110	260	62	2	2	1	0.4	32	20	34	29	1	.238	.273	1	0	SS-110, 2B-3
1977	48	46	12	0	0	1	2.2	6	7	8	6	1	.261	.326	0	0	SS-42, 2B-3, 2B-2
1978	81	160	35	7	0	1	0.6	14	9	25	31	0	.219	.281	0	0	SS-71, 2B-11, 3B-4
1979	57	100	20	1	0	2	2.0	9	14	5	17	0	.200	.270	0	0	SS-31, 3B-16, 2B-8, 1B-1
1980	49	86	18	3	0	0	0.0	13	5	5	5	0	.209	.244	0	0	SS-19, 3B-17, 3B-12
1981 OAK A	66	145	28	4	0	0	0.0	15	7	15	23	2	.193	.221	0	0	SS-62, 2B-6
1982	101	228	44	7	0	2	0.9	33	17	29	32	0	.193	.250	0	0	SS-98, 3B-2
14 yrs.	816	1650	356	38	5	10	0.6	197	120	196	243	11	.216	.263	7	1	SS-648, 2B-128, 3B-40, 1B-1

DIVISIONAL PLAYOFF SERIES

	G	AB	H	2B	3B	HR	HR %	R	RBI	BB	SO	SB	BA	SA	PH AB	PH H	G by POS
1981 OAK A	3	6	0	0	0	0	0.0	0	0	1	1	0	.000	.000	0	0	SS-3

LEAGUE CHAMPIONSHIP SERIES

	G	AB	H	2B	3B	HR	HR %	R	RBI	BB	SO	SB	BA	SA	PH AB	PH H	G by POS
1976 NY A	5	15	5	2	0	0	0.0	1	0	2	0	0	.333	.467	0	0	SS-5
1977	2	0	0	0	0	0	–	0	0	0	0	0	–	–	0	0	SS-2
1978	2	5	1	0	0	0	0.0	0	0	0	2	0	.200	.200	0	0	2B-2
1981 OAK A	2	3	1	0	0	0	0.0	0	1	0	1	0	.333	.333	0	0	SS-2
4 yrs.	11	23	7	2	0	0	0.0	1	1	2	3	0	.304	.391	0	0	SS-9, 2B-2

WORLD SERIES

	G	AB	H	2B	3B	HR	HR %	R	RBI	BB	SO	SB	BA	SA	PH AB	PH H	G by POS
1976 NY A	4	6	1	1	0	0	0.0	1	1	3	1	0	.167	.333	0	0	SS-4
1977	1	0	0	0	0	0	–	0	0	0	0	0	–	–	0	0	SS-1
1978	3	5	1	1	0	0	0.0	0	0	1	0	0	.200	.400	0	0	2B-3
3 yrs.	8	11	2	2	0	0	0.0	1	1	4	1	0	.182	.364	0	0	SS-5, 2B-3

Jim Stanley

STANLEY, JAMES F.   BB TR 5'6"   148 lbs.
B. 1889

	G	AB	H	2B	3B	HR	HR %	R	RBI	BB	SO	SB	BA	SA	PH AB	PH H	G by POS
1914 CHI F	54	98	19	3	0	0	0.0	13	4	19		2	.194	.224	6	0	SS-40, 3B-3, OF-1, 2B-1

Joe Stanley

STANLEY, JOSEPH
B. N. J.   Deceased.

	G	AB	H	2B	3B	HR	HR %	R	RBI	BB	SO	SB	BA	SA	PH AB	PH H	G by POS
1884 BAL U	6	21	5	1	0	0	0.0	3		0			.238	.286	0	0	OF-6

Joe Stanley

STANLEY, JOSEPH BERNARD   BB TR 5'9½"   150 lbs.
Brother of Buck Stanley.
B. Apr. 2, 1881, Washington, D. C.   D. Sept. 13, 1967, Detroit, Mich.

	G	AB	H	2B	3B	HR	HR %	R	RBI	BB	SO	SB	BA	SA	PH AB	PH H	G by POS
1897 WAS N	1	1	0	0	0	0	0.0	0	0	0		0	.000	.000	0	0	P-1
1902 WAS A	3	12	4	0	0	0	0.0	2	1	0		0	.333	.333	0	0	OF-3
1903 BOS N	86	308	77	12	5	1	0.3	40	47	18		10	.250	.331	5	0	OF-77, SS-1, P-1
1904	3	8	0	0	0	0	0.0	0	0	0		0	.000	.000	0	0	OF-3
1905 WAS A	28	92	24	2	1	1	1.1	13	17	7		4	.261	.337	1	0	OF-27
1906	73	221	36	0	4	0	0.0	18	9	20		6	.163	.199	10	0	OF-64, P-1
1909 CHI N	22	52	7	1	0	0	0.0	4	2	6		0	.135	.154	6	0	OF-16
7 yrs.	216	694	148	15	10	2	0.3	77	76	51		20	.213	.272	22	1	OF-190, P-3, SS-1

Mickey Stanley

STANLEY, MITCHELL JACK   BR TR 6'1"   185 lbs.
B. July 20, 1942, Grand Rapids, Mich.

	G	AB	H	2B	3B	HR	HR %	R	RBI	BB	SO	SB	BA	SA	PH AB	PH H	G by POS
1964 DET A	4	11	3	0	0	0	0.0	3	1	0	1	0	.273	.273	0	0	OF-4
1965	30	117	28	6	0	3	2.6	14	13	3	12	1	.239	.368	0	0	OF-29
1966	92	235	68	15	4	3	1.3	28	19	17	20	2	.289	.426	9	0	OF-82
1967	145	333	70	7	3	7	2.1	38	24	29	46	9	.210	.312	13	1	OF-128, 1B-8
1968	153	583	151	16	6	11	1.9	88	60	42	57	6	.259	.364	6	0	OF-130, 1B-15, SS-9, 2B-1

	G	AB	H	2B	3B	HR	HR %	R	RBI	BB	SO	SB	BA	SA	Pinch Hit AB	Pinch Hit H	G by POS

Mickey Stanley continued

	G	AB	H	2B	3B	HR	HR %	R	RBI	BB	SO	SB	BA	SA	AB	H	G by POS
1969	149	592	139	28	1	16	2.7	73	70	52	56	8	.235	.367	7	2	OF-101, SS-59, 1B-4
1970	142	568	143	21	11	13	2.3	83	47	45	56	10	.252	.396	5	2	OF-132, 1B-9
1971	139	401	117	14	5	7	1.7	43	41	24	44	1	.292	.404	6	3	OF-139
1972	142	435	102	16	6	14	3.2	45	55	29	49	1	.234	.395	5	3	OF-139
1973	157	602	147	23	5	17	2.8	81	57	48	65	0	.244	.384	0	0	OF-157
1974	99	394	87	13	2	8	2.0	40	34	26	63	5	.221	.325	1	0	OF-91, 1B-12, 2B-1
1975	52	164	42	7	3	3	1.8	26	19	15	27	1	.256	.390	3	2	OF-28, 1B-14, 3B-7, DH-1
1976	84	214	55	17	1	4	1.9	34	29	14	19	2	.257	.402	19	6	OF-38, 1B-17, 3B-11, SS-3, 2B-3
1977	75	222	51	9	1	8	3.6	30	23	18	30	0	.230	.387	13	3	OF-57, SS-3, 1B-3, DH-2
1978	53	151	40	9	0	3	2.0	15	8	9	19	0	.265	.384	12	2	OF-34, 1B-12
15 yrs.	1516	5022	1243	201	48	117	2.3	641	500	371	564	44	.248	.377	99	27	OF-1289, 1B-94, SS-74, 3B-18, 2B-4, DH-3

LEAGUE CHAMPIONSHIP SERIES

	G	AB	H	2B	3B	HR	HR %	R	RBI	BB	SO	SB	BA	SA	AB	H	G by POS
1972 DET A	4	6	2	0	0	0	0.0	0	0	0	0	0	.333	.333	1	0	OF-3

WORLD SERIES

	G	AB	H	2B	3B	HR	HR %	R	RBI	BB	SO	SB	BA	SA	AB	H	G by POS
1968 DET A	7	28	6	0	1	0	0.0	4	0	2	4	0	.214	.286	0	0	SS-7

John Stansbury

STANSBURY, JOHN JAMES
B. Dec. 6, 1886, Phillipsburg, N. J.   D. Dec. 26, 1970, Easton, Pa.   BR TR

	G	AB	H	2B	3B	HR	HR %	R	RBI	BB	SO	SB	BA	SA	AB	H	G by POS
1918 BOS A	20	47	6	1	0	0	0.0	3	2	6	3	0	.128	.149	0	0	3B-18, OF-2

Buck Stanton

STANTON, GEORGE WASHINGTON
B. June 19, 1906, Stantonsburg, N. C.   BL TL 5'10"   150 lbs.

	G	AB	H	2B	3B	HR	HR %	R	RBI	BB	SO	SB	BA	SA	AB	H	G by POS
1931 STL A	13	15	3	2	0	0	0.0	3	0	0	6	0	.200	.333	10	1	OF-1

Harry Stanton

STANTON, HARRY ANDREW
Deceased.   TR

	G	AB	H	2B	3B	HR	HR %	R	RBI	BB	SO	SB	BA	SA	AB	H	G by POS
1900 STL N	1	0	0	0	0	0	–	0	0	0		0	–	–	0	0	C-1

Leroy Stanton

STANTON, LEROY BOBBY (Lee)
B. Apr. 10, 1946, Latta, S. C.   BR TR 6'1"   195 lbs.

	G	AB	H	2B	3B	HR	HR %	R	RBI	BB	SO	SB	BA	SA	AB	H	G by POS
1970 NY N	4	4	1	0	1	0	0.0	0	0	0	0	0	.250	.750	3	0	OF-1
1971	5	21	4	1	0	0	0.0	2	2	2	4	0	.190	.238	0	0	OF-5
1972 CAL A	127	402	101	15	3	12	3.0	44	39	22	100	2	.251	.393	7	1	OF-124
1973	119	306	72	9	2	8	2.6	41	34	27	88	3	.235	.356	11	5	OF-107
1974	118	415	111	21	2	11	2.7	48	62	33	107	10	.267	.407	7	1	OF-114
1975	137	440	115	20	3	14	3.2	67	82	52	85	18	.261	.416	10	0	OF-131, DH-1
1976	93	231	44	13	1	2	0.9	12	25	24	57	2	.190	.281	15	3	OF-79, DH-4
1977 SEA A	133	454	125	24	1	27	5.9	56	90	42	115	0	.275	.511	11	4	OF-91, DH-33
1978	93	302	55	11	0	3	1.0	24	24	34	80	1	.182	.248	5	0	DH-59, OF-30
9 yrs.	829	2575	628	114	13	77	3.0	294	358	236	636	36	.244	.388	69	14	OF-682, DH-97

Tom Stanton

STANTON, THOMAS P.
B. Oct. 25, 1874, St. Louis, Mo.   D. Jan. 17, 1957, St. Louis, Mo.

	G	AB	H	2B	3B	HR	HR %	R	RBI	BB	SO	SB	BA	SA	AB	H	G by POS
1904 CHI N	1	3	0	0	0	0	0.0	0	0	0		0	.000	.000	0	0	C-1

Joe Staples

STAPLES, JOSEPH F.
B. Buffalo, N. Y.   Deceased.

	G	AB	H	2B	3B	HR	HR %	R	RBI	BB	SO	SB	BA	SA	AB	H	G by POS
1885 BUF N	7	22	1	0	0	0	0.0	0	0	0	9		.045	.045	0	0	OF-6, 2B-1

Dave Stapleton

STAPLETON, DAVID LESLIE
B. Jan. 16, 1954, Fairhope, Ala.   BR TR 6'1"   178 lbs.

	G	AB	H	2B	3B	HR	HR %	R	RBI	BB	SO	SB	BA	SA	AB	H	G by POS
1980 BOS A	106	449	144	33	5	7	1.6	61	45	13	32	3	.321	.463	4	1	2B-94, 1B-8, OF-6, DH-3, 3B-2
1981	93	355	101	17	1	10	2.8	45	42	21	22	0	.285	.423	4	0	SS-33, 3B-25, 2B-23, 1B-12
1982	150	538	142	28	1	14	2.6	66	65	31	40	2	.264	.398	5	0	1B-106, SS-27, 2B-9, 3B-5, DH-4, OF-1
1983	151	542	134	31	1	10	1.8	54	66	40	44	1	.247	.363	1	0	1B-145, 2B-5
1984	13	39	9	2	0	0	0.0	4	1	3	3	0	.231	.282	2	1	1B-10, DH-1
5 yrs.	513	1923	530	111	8	41	2.1	230	219	108	141	6	.276	.406	16	2	1B-281, 2B-131, SS-60, 3B-32, DH-8, OF-7

Willie Stargell

STARGELL, WILVER DORNEL
B. Mar. 6, 1940, Earlsboro, Okla.   BL TL 6'2"   188 lbs.

	G	AB	H	2B	3B	HR	HR %	R	RBI	BB	SO	SB	BA	SA	AB	H	G by POS
1962 PIT N	10	31	9	3	1	0	0.0	1	4	3	10	0	.290	.452	2	0	OF-9
1963	108	304	74	11	6	11	3.6	34	47	19	85	0	.243	.428	25	2	OF-65, 1B-16
1964	117	421	115	19	7	21	5.0	53	78	17	92	1	.273	.501	12	2	OF-59, 1B-50
1965	144	533	145	25	8	27	5.1	68	107	39	127	1	.272	.501	5	1	OF-137, 1B-7
1966	140	485	153	30	0	33	6.8	84	102	48	109	2	.315	.581	9	3	OF-127, 1B-15
1967	134	462	125	18	6	20	4.3	54	73	67	103	1	.271	.465	6	1	OF-98, 1B-37
1968	128	435	103	15	1	24	5.5	57	67	47	105	5	.237	.441	5	0	OF-113, 1B-13
1969	145	522	160	31	6	29	5.6	89	92	61	120	1	.307	.556	8	1	OF-116, 1B-23
1970	136	474	125	18	3	31	6.5	70	85	44	119	0	.264	.511	9	4	OF-125, 1B-1
1971	141	511	151	26	0	48	9.4	104	125	83	154	0	.295	.628	3	1	OF-135
1972	138	495	145	28	2	33	6.7	75	112	65	129	1	.293	.558	5	0	1B-101, OF-32
1973	148	522	156	43	3	44	8.4	106	119	80	129	0	.299	.646	7	2	OF-142
1974	140	508	153	37	4	25	4.9	90	96	87	106	0	.301	.537	3	0	OF-135, 1B-1
1975	124	461	136	32	2	22	4.8	71	90	58	109	0	.295	.516	2	1	1B-122
1976	117	428	110	20	3	20	4.7	54	65	50	101	2	.257	.458	7	0	1B-111
1977	63	186	51	12	0	13	7.0	29	35	31	55	0	.274	.548	10	2	1B-55
1978	122	390	115	18	2	28	7.2	60	97	50	93	3	.295	.567	10	3	1B-112

	G	AB	H	2B	3B	HR	HR%	R	RBI	BB	SO	SB	BA	SA	Pinch Hit AB	Pinch Hit H	G by POS

Willie Stargell continued

1979	126	424	119	19	0	32	7.5	60	82	47	105	0	.281	.552	15	7	1B-113
1980	67	202	53	10	1	11	5.4	28	38	26	52	0	.262	.485	11	3	1B-54
1981	38	60	17	4	0	0	0.0	2	9	5	9	0	.283	.350	26	8	1B-9
1982	74	73	17	4	0	3	4.1	6	17	10	24	0	.233	.411	56	14	1B-8
21 yrs.	2360	7927	2232	423	55	475	6.0	1195	1540	937	1936	17	.282	.529	236	55	OF-1293, 1B-848
												2nd					

LEAGUE CHAMPIONSHIP SERIES
1970 PIT N	3	12	6	1	0	0	0.0	0	1	1	1	0	.500	.583	0	0	OF-3
1971	4	14	0	0	0	0	0.0	1	0	2	6	0	.000	.000	0	0	OF-4
1972	5	16	1	1	0	0	0.0	1	1	2	5	0	.063	.125	0	0	1B-5
1974	4	15	6	0	0	2	13.3	3	4	1	2	0	.400	.800	0	0	OF-4
1975	3	11	2	1	0	0	0.0	1	0	1	3	0	.182	.273	0	0	1B-3
1979	3	11	5	2	0	2	18.2	2	6	3	2	0	.455	1.182	0	0	1B-3
6 yrs.	22	79	20	5	0	4	5.1	8	12	10	19	0	.253	.468	0	0	OF-11, 1B-11

WORLD SERIES
1971 PIT N	7	24	5	1	0	0	0.0	3	1	7	9	0	.208	.250	0	0	OF-7
1979	7	30	12	4	0	3	10.0	7	7	0	6	0	.400	.833	0	0	1B-7
2 yrs.	14	54	17	5	0	3	5.6	10	8	7	15	0	.315	.574	0	0	OF-7, 1B-7

Dolly Stark

STARK, MONROE RANDOLPH   BR TR
B. Jan. 19, 1885, Ripley, Miss.   D. Dec. 1, 1924, Memphis, Tenn.

1909 CLE A	19	60	12	0	0	0	0.0	4	1	6		4	.200	.200	0	0	SS-19
1910 BKN N	30	103	17	3	0	0	0.0	7	8	7	19	2	.165	.194	0	0	SS-30
1911	70	193	57	4	1	0	0.0	25	19	20	24	6	.295	.326	11	3	SS-34, 2B-18, 3B-3
1912	8	22	4	0	0	0	0.0	2	2	1	3	2	.182	.182	1	0	SS-7
4 yrs.	127	378	90	7	1	0	0.0	38	30	34	46	14	.238	.262	12	3	SS-90, 2B-18, 3B-3

George Starnagle

STARNAGLE, GEORGE HENRY   BR TR
Born George Henry Steurnagel.
B. Oct. 6, 1873, Belleville, Ill.   D. Feb. 15, 1946, Belleville, Ill.

| 1902 CLE A | 1 | 3 | 0 | 0 | 0 | 0 | 0.0 | 0 | 0 | 0 | | 0 | .000 | .000 | 0 | 0 | C-1 |

Charlie Starr

STARR, CHARLES WATKIN   TR
B. Aug. 30, 1878, Pike County, Ohio   D. Oct. 18, 1937, Pasadena, Calif.

1905 STL A	24	97	20	0	0	0	0.0	9	6	7		0	.206	.206	2	0	2B-16, 3B-6
1908 PIT N	20	59	11	2	0	0	0.0	8	8	13		6	.186	.220	1	0	2B-12, SS-5, 3B-2
1909 2 teams		BOS	N (61G –	.222)		PHI	N (3G –	.000)									
" total	64	219	48	2	3	0	0.0	16	6	31		7	.219	.256	3	0	2B-54, SS-6, 3B-3
3 yrs.	108	375	79	4	3	0	0.0	33	20	51		13	.211	.237	6	0	2B-82, SS-11, 3B-11

Chick Starr

STARR, WILLIAM   BR TR 6'1" 175 lbs.
B. Feb. 26, 1911, Brooklyn, N. Y.

1935 WAS A	12	24	5	0	0	0	0.0	1	1	0	1	0	.208	.208	0	0	C-12
1936	1	0	0	0	0	0	–	0	0	0	0	0	–	–	0	0	C-1
2 yrs.	13	24	5	0	0	0	0.0	1	1	0	1	0	.208	.208	0	0	C-13

Joe Start

START, JOSEPH (Old Reliable)   BL TL 5'9" 165 lbs.
B. Oct. 14, 1842, New York, N. Y.   D. Mar. 27, 1927, Providence, R. I.

1876 NY N	56	264	73	6	0	0	0.0	40	21	1	2		.277	.299	0	0	1B-56
1877 HAR N	60	271	90	3	6	1	0.4	55	21	6	2		.332	.399	0	0	1B-60
1878 CHI N	61	285	100	12	5	1	0.4	58	27	2	3		.351	.439	0	0	1B-61
1879 PRO N	66	317	101	11	5	2	0.6	70	37	7	4		.319	.404	0	0	1B-65, OF-1
1880	82	345	96	14	6	0	0.0	53	27	13	20		.278	.354	0	0	1B-82
1881	79	348	114	12	6	0	0.0	56	29	9	7		.328	.397	0	0	1B-79
1882	82	356	117	8	10	0	0.0	58		11	7		.329	.407	0	0	1B-82
1883	87	370	105	16	7	1	0.3	63		22	16		.284	.373	0	0	1B-87
1884	93	381	105	10	5	2	0.5	80		35	25		.276	.344	0	0	1B-93
1885	101	374	103	11	4	0	0.0	47	41	39	10		.275	.326	0	0	1B-101
1886 WAS N	31	122	27	4	1	0	0.0	10	17	5	13		.221	.270	0	0	1B-31
11 yrs.	798	3433	1031	107	55	7	0.2	590	220	150	109		.300	.370	0	0	1B-797, OF-1

Joe Staton

STATON, JOSEPH (Slim)   BL TL 6'3" 175 lbs.
B. Mar. 8, 1948, Seattle, Wash.

1972 DET A	6	2	0	0	0	0	0.0	1	0	1	1	0	.000	.000	0	0	1B-2
1973	9	17	4	0	0	0	0.0	2	3	0	3	1	.235	.235	2	0	1B-5
2 yrs.	15	19	4	0	0	0	0.0	3	3	0	4	1	.211	.211	2	0	1B-7

Jigger Statz

STATZ, ARNOLD JOHN   BR TR 5'7½" 150 lbs.
B. Oct. 20, 1897, Waukegan, Ill.   BB 1922

1919 NY N	21	60	18	2	1	0	0.0	7	6	3	8	2	.300	.367	0	0	OF-18, 2B-5
1920 2 teams		NY	N (16G –	.133)		BOS	A (2G –	.000)									
" total	18	33	4	0	1	0	0.0	0	5	2	9	0	.121	.182	3	0	OF-14
1922 CHI N	110	462	137	19	5	1	0.2	77	34	41	31	16	.297	.366	0	0	OF-110
1923	154	655	209	33	8	10	1.5	110	70	56	42	29	.319	.440	0	0	OF-154
1924	135	549	152	22	5	3	0.5	69	49	37	50	13	.277	.352	2	1	OF-131, 2B-1
1925	38	148	38	6	3	2	1.4	21	14	11	16	4	.257	.378	1	0	OF-37
1927 BKN N	130	507	139	24	7	1	0.2	64	21	26	43	10	.274	.355	4	0	OF-122, 2B-1
1928	77	171	40	8	1	0	0.0	28	16	18	12	3	.234	.292	5	2	OF-77, 2B-1
8 yrs.	683	2585	737	114	31	17	0.7	376	215	194	211	77	.285	.373	15	3	OF-663, 2B-8

Rusty Staub

STAUB, DANIEL JOSEPH   BL TR 6'2" 190 lbs.
B. Apr. 1, 1944, New Orleans, La.

1963 HOU N	150	513	115	17	4	6	1.2	43	45	59	58	0	.224	.308	5	0	1B-109, OF-49
1964	89	292	63	10	2	8	2.7	26	35	21	31	1	.216	.346	8	3	1B-49, OF-38
1965	131	410	105	20	1	14	3.4	43	63	52	57	3	.256	.412	16	5	OF-112, 1B-1

	G	AB	H	2B	3B	HR	HR %	R	RBI	BB	SO	SB	BA	SA	Pinch Hit AB	H	G by POS

Rusty Staub continued

	G	AB	H	2B	3B	HR	HR%	R	RBI	BB	SO	SB	BA	SA	PH AB	PH H	G by POS
1966	153	554	155	28	3	13	2.3	60	81	58	61	2	.280	.412	6	3	OF-148, 1B-1
1967	149	546	182	44	1	10	1.8	71	74	60	47	0	.333	.473	5	1	OF-144
1968	161	591	172	37	1	6	1.0	54	72	73	57	2	.291	.387	0	0	1B-147, OF-15
1969 MON N	158	549	166	26	5	29	5.3	89	79	110	61	3	.302	.526	2	1	OF-156
1970	160	569	156	23	7	30	5.3	98	94	112	93	12	.274	.497	3	2	OF-160
1971	162	599	186	34	6	19	3.2	94	97	74	42	9	.311	.482	5	1	OF-162
1972 NY N	66	239	70	11	0	9	3.8	32	38	31	13	0	.293	.452	1	0	OF-65
1973	152	585	163	36	1	15	2.6	77	76	74	52	1	.279	.421	0	0	OF-152
1974	151	561	145	22	2	19	3.4	65	78	77	39	2	.258	.406	4	2	OF-147
1975	155	574	162	30	4	19	3.3	93	105	77	55	2	.282	.448	2	1	OF-153
1976 DET A	161	589	176	28	3	15	2.5	73	96	83	49	3	.299	.433	0	0	OF-126, DH-36
1977	158	623	173	34	3	22	3.5	84	101	59	47	1	.278	.448	2	0	DH-156
1978	162	642	175	30	1	24	3.7	75	121	76	35	3	.273	.435	0	0	DH-162
1979 2 teams	DET A (68G – .236)					MON N	(38G – .267)										
" total	106	332	81	15	1	12	3.6	41	54	46	28	1	.244	.404	14	2	DH-66, 1B-22, OF-1
1980 TEX A	109	340	102	23	2	9	2.6	42	55	39	18	1	.300	.459	15	5	DH-57, 1B-30, OF-14
1981 NY N	70	161	51	9	0	5	3.1	9	21	22	12	1	.317	.466	24	9	1B-41
1982	112	219	53	9	0	3	1.4	11	27	24	10	0	.242	.324	57	12	OF-27, 1B-18
1983	104	115	34	6	0	3	2.6	5	28	14	10	0	.296	.426	81[1]	24	OF-5, 1B-5
1984	78	72	19	4	0	1	1.4	2	18	4	9	0	.264	.361	66	18	1B-3
22 yrs.	2897	9675	2704	496	47	291	3.0	1187	1458	1245	884	47	.279	.431	316	89	OF-1674, DH-477, 1B-426
	7th																

LEAGUE CHAMPIONSHIP SERIES

	G	AB	H	2B	3B	HR	HR%	R	RBI	BB	SO	SB	BA	SA	PH AB	PH H	G by POS
1973 NY N	4	15	3	0	0	3	20.0	4	5	3	2	0	.200	.800	0	0	OF-4

WORLD SERIES

	G	AB	H	2B	3B	HR	HR%	R	RBI	BB	SO	SB	BA	SA	PH AB	PH H	G by POS
1973 NY N	7	26	11	2	0	1	3.8	1	6	2	2	0	.423	.615	0	0	OF-6

Dan Stearns

STEARNS, DANIEL ECKFORD BR TR 6'1" 185 lbs.
B. Oct. 17, 1861, Buffalo, N. Y. D. June 28, 1944, Glendale, Calif.

	G	AB	H	2B	3B	HR	HR%	R	RBI	BB	SO	SB	BA	SA	PH AB	PH H	G by POS
1880 BUF N	28	104	19	6	1	0	0.0	8	13	3	23		.183	.260	0	0	OF-20, C-8, 3B-5, SS-1
1881 DET N	3	11	1	1	0	0	0.0	1	0	0	2		.091	.182	0	0	SS-3
1882 CIN AA	49	214	55	10	2	0	0.0	28		6			.257	.322	0	0	1B-35, OF-12, 2B-2, SS-1
1883 BAL AA	93	382	94	10	9	1	0.3	54		34			.246	.327	0	0	1B-92, OF-1
1884	100	396	94	12	3	3	0.8	61		28			.237	.306	0	0	1B-100, 2B-1
1885 2 teams	BAL AA (67G – .186)					BUF N	(30G – .200)										
" total	97	358	68	9	9	1	0.3	47	9	46	23		.190	.274	0	0	1B-75, SS-19, C-4, OF-3
1889 KC AA	139	560	160	24	13	2	0.4	96	87	56	69	67	.286	.386	0	0	1B-135, 3B-4
7 yrs.	509	2025	491	72	37	7	0.3	295	109	173	117	67	.242	.325	0	0	1B-437, OF-36, SS-24, C-12, 3B-9, 2B-3

John Stearns

STEARNS, JOHN HARDIN BR TR 6' 185 lbs.
B. Aug. 21, 1951, Denver, Colo.

	G	AB	H	2B	3B	HR	HR%	R	RBI	BB	SO	SB	BA	SA	PH AB	PH H	G by POS
1974 PHI N	1	2	1	0	0	0	0.0	0	0	0	0	0	.500	.500	1	1	C-1
1975 NY N	59	169	32	5	1	3	1.8	25	10	17	15	4	.189	.284	8	1	C-54
1976	32	103	27	6	0	2	1.9	13	10	16	11	1	.262	.379	3	0	C-30
1977	139	431	108	25	1	12	2.8	52	55	77	76	9	.251	.397	9	1	C-127, 1B-6
1978	143	477	126	24	1	15	3.1	65	73	70	57	25	.264	.413	4	2	C-141, 3B-1
1979	155	538	131	29	2	9	1.7	58	66	52	57	15	.243	.355	12	1	C-121, 1B-16, 3B-11, OF-6
1980	91	319	91	25	1	0	0.0	42	45	33	24	7	.285	.370	5	2	C-74, 1B-16, 3B-1
1981	80	273	74	12	1	1	0.4	25	24	24	17	12	.271	.333	6	1	C-66, 1B-9, 3B-4
1982	98	352	103	25	3	4	1.1	46	28	30	35	17	.293	.415	6	2	C-81, 3B-12
1983	4	0	0	0	0	0	–	2	0	0	0	0	–	–	0	0	
1984	8	17	3	1	0	0	0.0	6	1	4	2	1	.176	.235	2	1	C-4, 1B-2
11 yrs.	810	2681	696	152	10	46	1.7	334	312	323	294	91	.260	.375	56	12	C-699, 1B-49, 3B-29, OF-6

Stedronske

STEDRONSKE,
B. Troy, N. Y. Deceased.

	G	AB	H	2B	3B	HR	HR%	R	RBI	BB	SO	SB	BA	SA	PH AB	PH H	G by POS
1879 CHI N	4	12	1	0	0	0	0.0	0	0	0	3		.083	.083	0	0	3B-4

Farmer Steelman

STEELMAN, MORRIS JAMES TR
B. June 29, 1875, Millville, N. J. D. Sept. 16, 1944, Merchantville, N. J.

	G	AB	H	2B	3B	HR	HR%	R	RBI	BB	SO	SB	BA	SA	PH AB	PH H	G by POS
1899 LOU N	4	15	1	0	1	0	0.0	2	2	2		0	.067	.200	0	0	C-4
1900 BKN N	1	4	0	0	0	0	0.0	0	0	0		0	.000	.000	0	0	C-1
1901 2 teams	BKN N (1G – .333)					PHI A	(27G – .261)										
" total	28	91	24	2	0	0	0.0	5	7	10		4	.264	.286	0	0	C-15, OF-12
1902 PHI A	10	32	6	1	0	0	0.0	1	6	2		2	.188	.219	0	0	OF-5, C-5
4 yrs.	43	142	31	3	1	0	0.0	8	15	14		6	.218	.254	0	0	C-25, OF-17

Fred Steere

STEERE, FREDERICK EUGENE
B. Aug. 16, 1872, S. Scituate, R. I. D. Mar. 13, 1942

	G	AB	H	2B	3B	HR	HR%	R	RBI	BB	SO	SB	BA	SA	PH AB	PH H	G by POS
1894 PIT N	10	39	8	0	0	0	0.0	3	4	2	1	2	.205	.205	0	0	SS-10

John Stefero

STEFERO, JOHN ROBERT BL TR 5'8" 185 lbs.
B. Sept. 22, 1959, Sumter, S. C.

	G	AB	H	2B	3B	HR	HR%	R	RBI	BB	SO	SB	BA	SA	PH AB	PH H	G by POS
1983 BAL A	9	11	5	1	0	0	0.0	2	4	3	2	0	.455	.545	2	0	C-9

Dave Stegman

STEGMAN, DAVID WILLIAM BR TR 5'11" 190 lbs.
B. Jan. 30, 1954, Inglewood, Calif.

	G	AB	H	2B	3B	HR	HR%	R	RBI	BB	SO	SB	BA	SA	PH AB	PH H	G by POS
1978 DET A	8	14	4	2	0	1	7.1	3	3	1	2	0	.286	.643	0	0	OF-7
1979	12	31	6	0	0	3	9.7	6	5	2	3	1	.194	.484	1	0	OF-12
1980	65	130	23	5	0	2	1.5	12	9	14	23	1	.177	.262	6	1	OF-57, DH-2
1982 NY A	2	0	0	0	0	0	–	0	0	0	0	0	–	–	0	0	
1983 CHI A	30	53	9	2	0	0	0.0	5	4	10	9	0	.170	.208	0	0	OF-29

	G	AB	H	2B	3B	HR	HR %	R	RBI	BB	SO	SB	BA	SA	Pinch Hit AB	Pinch Hit H	G by POS

Al Stokes

STOKES, ALBERT JOHN
Born Albert John Stacek.
B. Jan. 1, 1900, Chicago, Ill.
BR TR 5'10" 170 lbs.

	G	AB	H	2B	3B	HR	HR %	R	RBI	BB	SO	SB	BA	SA	AB	H	G by POS
1925 **BOS A**	17	52	11	0	1	0	0.0	7	1	4	8	0	.212	.250	0	0	C-17
1926	30	86	14	3	3	0	0.0	7	6	8	28	0	.163	.267	1	0	C-29
2 yrs.	47	138	25	3	4	0	0.0	14	7	12	36	0	.181	.261	1	0	C-46

Gene Stone

STONE, EUGENE DANIEL
B. Jan. 16, 1944, Pacoima, Calif.
BL TL 5'11" 190 lbs.

	G	AB	H	2B	3B	HR	HR %	R	RBI	BB	SO	SB	BA	SA	AB	H	G by POS
1969 **PHI N**	18	28	6	0	1	0	0.0	4	0	4	9	0	.214	.286	10	2	1B-5

George Stone

STONE, GEORGE ROBERT
B. Sept. 7, 1877, Lost Nation, Iowa   D. Jan. 3, 1945, Clinton, Iowa
BL TL 5'7" 175 lbs.

	G	AB	H	2B	3B	HR	HR %	R	RBI	BB	SO	SB	BA	SA	AB	H	G by POS
1903 **BOS A**	2	2	0	0	0	0	0.0	0	0	0		0	.000	.000	2	0	
1905 **STL A**	154	632	187	25	13	7	1.1	76	52	44		26	.296	.410	0	0	OF-154
1906	154	581	208	25	20	6	1.0	91	71	52		35	.358	.501	0	0	OF-154
1907	155	596	191	13	11	4	0.7	77	59	59		23	.320	.399	0	0	OF-155
1908	148	588	165	21	8	5	0.9	89	31	55		20	.281	.369	0	0	OF-148
1909	83	310	89	5	4	1	0.3	33	15	24		8	.287	.339	2	0	OF-81
1910	152	562	144	17	12	0	0.0	60	40	48		20	.256	.329	5	1	OF-147
7 yrs.	848	3271	984	106	68	23	0.7	426	268	282		132	.301	.396	9	1	OF-839

Jeff Stone

STONE, JEFFREY GLEN
B. Dec. 26, 1960, Kennett, Mo.
BL TR 6' 175 lbs.

	G	AB	H	2B	3B	HR	HR %	R	RBI	BB	SO	SB	BA	SA	AB	H	G by POS
1983 **PHI N**	9	4	3	0	2	0	0.0	2	3	0	1	4	.750	1.750	1	1	OF-1
1984	51	185	67	4	6	1	0.5	27	15	9	26	27	.362	.465	5	0	OF-46
2 yrs.	60	189	70	4	8	1	0.5	29	18	9	27	31	.370	.492	6	1	OF-47

John Stone

STONE, JONATHON THOMAS (Rocky)
B. Oct. 10, 1905, Lynchburg, Tenn.   D. Nov. 11, 1955, Shelbyville, Tenn.
BL TR 6'1" 178 lbs.

	G	AB	H	2B	3B	HR	HR %	R	RBI	BB	SO	SB	BA	SA	AB	H	G by POS
1928 **DET A**	26	113	40	10	3	2	1.8	20	21	5	8	1	.354	.549	0	0	OF-26
1929	51	150	39	11	2	2	1.3	23	15	11	13	1	.260	.400	15	4	OF-36
1930	126	422	132	29	11	3	0.7	60	56	32	49	6	.313	.455	18	4	OF-108
1931	147	584	191	28	11	10	1.7	86	76	56	48	13	.327	.464	0	0	OF-147
1932	144	582	173	35	12	17	2.9	106	108	58	64	2	.297	.486	3	0	OF-141
1933	148	574	161	33	11	11	1.9	86	80	54	37	1	.280	.434	5	3	OF-141
1934 **WAS A**	113	419	132	28	7	7	1.7	77	67	52	26	1	.315	.465	4	2	OF-112
1935	125	454	143	27	18	1	0.2	78	78	39	29	4	.315	.460	14	2	OF-114
1936	123	437	149	22	11	15	3.4	95	90	60	26	8	.341	.545	6	2	OF-114
1937	139	542	179	33	15	6	1.1	84	88	66	36	6	.330	.480	1	0	OF-137
1938	56	213	52	12	4	3	1.4	24	28	30	16	2	.244	.380	1	0	OF-53
11 yrs.	1198	4490	1391	268	105	77	1.7	739	707	463	352	45	.310	.468	67	17	OF-1129

Ron Stone

STONE, HARRY RONALD
B. Sept. 9, 1942, Corning, Calif.
BL TL 6'2" 185 lbs.

	G	AB	H	2B	3B	HR	HR %	R	RBI	BB	SO	SB	BA	SA	AB	H	G by POS
1966 **KC A**	26	22	6	1	0	0	0.0	2	0	0	2	1	.273	.318	15	4	OF-4, 1B-3
1969 **PHI N**	103	222	53	7	1	1	0.5	22	24	29	28	3	.239	.293	28	2	OF-69
1970	123	321	84	12	5	3	0.9	30	39	38	45	5	.262	.358	23	4	OF-99, 1B-6
1971	95	185	42	8	1	2	1.1	16	23	25	36	2	.227	.314	43	7	OF-51, 1B-3
1972	41	54	9	0	1	0	0.0	3	3	9	11	0	.167	.204	22	3	OF-15
5 yrs.	388	804	194	28	8	6	0.7	73	89	101	122	11	.241	.318	131	20	OF-238, 1B-12

Tige Stone

STONE, WILLIAM ARTHUR
B. Sept. 18, 1906, Macon, Ga.   D. Jan. 1, 1960, Jacksonville, Fla.
BR TR 5'8" 145 lbs.

	G	AB	H	2B	3B	HR	HR %	R	RBI	BB	SO	SB	BA	SA	AB	H	G by POS
1923 **STL N**	5	1	1	0	0	0	0.0	0	2	0		2	1.000	1.000	0	0	OF-4, P-1

John Stoneham

STONEHAM, JOHN ANDREW
B. Nov. 8, 1908, Wood River, Ill.
BL TR 5'9½" 168 lbs.

	G	AB	H	2B	3B	HR	HR %	R	RBI	BB	SO	SB	BA	SA	AB	H	G by POS
1933 **CHI A**	10	25	3	0	0	1	4.0	4	3	2	2	0	.120	.240	0	0	OF-9

Howie Storie

STORIE, HOWARD EDWARD
B. May 15, 1911, Pittsfield, Mass.   D. July 27, 1968, Pittsfield, Mass.
BR TR 5'10" 175 lbs.

	G	AB	H	2B	3B	HR	HR %	R	RBI	BB	SO	SB	BA	SA	AB	H	G by POS
1931 **BOS A**	6	17	2	0	0	0	0.0	2	0	3	2	0	.118	.118	0	0	C-6
1932	6	8	3	0	0	0	0.0	0	0	0	0	0	.375	.375	1	0	C-5
2 yrs.	12	25	5	0	0	0	0.0	2	0	3	2	0	.200	.200	1	0	C-11

Alan Storke

STORKE, ALAN MARSHALL
B. Sept. 27, 1884, Auburn, N.Y.   D. Mar. 18, 1910, Newton, Mass.
TR

	G	AB	H	2B	3B	HR	HR %	R	RBI	BB	SO	SB	BA	SA	AB	H	G by POS
1906 **PIT N**	5	12	3	1	0	0	0.0	1	1	1		1	.250	.333	2	1	3B-2, SS-1
1907	112	357	92	6	6	1	0.3	24	39	16		6	.258	.317	10	3	3B-67, 1B-23, 2B-7, SS-5
1908	64	202	51	5	3	1	0.5	20	12	9		4	.252	.322	8	0	1B-49, 3B-6, 2B-1
1909 **2 teams**		PIT	N (37G – .254)				STL	N (48G – .282)									
" total	85	292	79	10	2	0	0.0	23	22	19		6	.271	.318	4	1	SS-44, 1B-19, 3B-14, 2B-4
4 yrs.	266	863	225	22	11	2	0.2	68	74	45		17	.261	.319	24	5	1B-91, 3B-89, SS-50, 2B-12

Lin Storti

STORTI, LINDO IVAN
B. Dec. 5, 1906, Santa Monica, Calif.
D. July 24, 1982, Ontario, Calif.
BB TR 5'11" 165 lbs.
BR 1930

	G	AB	H	2B	3B	HR	HR %	R	RBI	BB	SO	SB	BA	SA	AB	H	G by POS
1930 **STL A**	7	28	9	1	1	0	0.0	6	2	2	6	0	.321	.429	1	0	2B-6
1931	86	273	60	15	4	3	1.1	32	26	15	50	0	.220	.337	9	2	3B-67, 2B-7
1932	53	193	50	11	2	3	1.6	19	26	5	20	1	.259	.383	2	0	3B-51
1933	70	210	41	7	4	3	1.4	26	21	25	31	2	.195	.310	13	3	3B-32, 2B-24
4 yrs.	216	704	160	34	11	9	1.3	83	75	47	107	3	.227	.345	25	5	3B-150, 2B-37

	G	AB	H	2B	3B	HR	HR %	R	RBI	BB	SO	SB	BA	SA	Pinch Hit AB	Pinch Hit H	G by POS

Tom Stouch

STOUCH, THOMAS CARL
B. Dec. 2, 1870, Perryville, Ohio   D. Oct. 7, 1956, Lancaster, Pa.

	G	AB	H	2B	3B	HR	HR %	R	RBI	BB	SO	SB	BA	SA	AB	H	G by POS
1898 LOU N	4	16	5	1	0	0	0.0	4	6	1		0	.313	.375	0	0	2B-4

George Stovall

STOVALL, GEORGE THOMAS (Firebrand)   BR TR 6'2" 180 lbs.
Brother of Jesse Stovall.
B. Nov. 23, 1878, Independence, Mo.   D. Nov. 5, 1951, Burlington, Iowa
Manager 1911-15.

	G	AB	H	2B	3B	HR	HR %	R	RBI	BB	SO	SB	BA	SA	AB	H	G by POS
1904 CLE A	52	182	54	10	1	1	0.5	18	31	2		4	.297	.379	1	0	1B-38, 2B-9, OF-3, 3B-1
1905	111	419	114	31	3	1	0.2	41	47	13		13	.272	.368	3	0	1B-59, 2B-46, OF-4
1906	116	443	121	19	5	0	0.0	54	37	8		15	.273	.339	9	3	1B-55, 3B-30, 2B-19
1907	124	466	110	17	6	1	0.2	38	36	18		13	.236	.305	0	0	1B-122, 3B-2
1908	138	534	156	29	6	2	0.4	71	45	17		14	.292	.380	0	0	1B-132, OF-5, SS-1
1909	145	565	139	17	10	2	0.4	60	49	6		25	.246	.322	0	0	1B-145
1910	142	521	136	19	4	0	0.0	47	52	14		16	.261	.313	7	2	1B-132, 2B-2
1911	126	458	124	17	7	0	0.0	48	79	21		11	.271	.338	5	1	1B-118, 2B-2
1912 STL A	115	398	101	17	5	0	0.0	35	45	14		11	.254	.322	21	4	1B-94
1913	89	303	87	14	3	1	0.3	34	24	7	23	7	.287	.363	13	2	1B-76
1914 KC F	124	450	128	20	5	7	1.6	51	75	23		6	.284	.398	8	2	1B-116, 3B-1
1915	130	480	111	21	3	0	0.0	48	44	31		8	.231	.288	1	0	1B-129
12 yrs.	1412	5219	1381	231	58	15	0.3	545	564	174	23	143	.265	.340	68	14	1B-1216, 2B-78, 3B-34, OF-12, SS-1

Harry Stovey

STOVEY, HARRY DUFFIELD   BR TR 5'11½" 180 lbs.
Born Harry Duffield Stow.
B. Dec. 20, 1856, Philadelphia, Pa.   D. Sept. 20, 1937, New Bedford, Mass.

	G	AB	H	2B	3B	HR	HR %	R	RBI	BB	SO	SB	BA	SA	AB	H	G by POS
1880 WOR N	83	355	94	21	14	6	1.7	76		12	46		.265	.454	0	0	OF-46, 1B-37, P-2
1881	75	341	92	25	7	2	0.6	57	30	12	23		.270	.402	0	0	1B-57, OF-18
1882	84	360	104	13	10	5	1.4	90	26	22	34		.289	.422	0	0	1B-43, OF-41
1883 PHI AA	94	421	148	32	8	14	3.3	110		26			.352	.565	0	0	1B-93, OF-3, P-1
1884	106	443	179	25	25	11	2.5	126		26			.404	.648	0	0	1B-104
1885	112	486	164	27	11	13	2.7	130		39			.337	.519	0	0	1B-82, OF-30
1886	123	489	154	28	11	7	1.4	115		64			.315	.460	0	0	OF-63, 1B-62, P-1
1887	124	497	142	31	12	4	0.8	125		56		74	.286	.421	0	0	OF-80, 1B-46
1888	130	530	152	25	20	9	1.7	127	65	62		87	.287	.460	0	0	OF-118, 1B-13
1889	137	556	171	37	14	19	3.4	152	119	77	68	63	.308	.527	0	0	OF-137, 1B-1
1890 BOS P	118	481	143	25	12	11	2.3	142	83	81	38	97	.297	.468	0	0	OF-117, 1B-1
1891 BOS N	134	544	152	31	20	16	2.9	118	95	78	69	57	.279	.498	0	0	OF-135, 1B-1
1892 2 teams		BOS	N (38G –	.164)			BAL	N (74G –	.272)								
" total	112	429	101	20	15	2	0.5	79	67	54	51	40	.235	.366	0	0	OF-102, 1B-10
1893 2 teams		BAL	N (8G –	.154)			BKN	N (48G –	.251)								
" total	56	201	48	8	6	1	0.5	47	34	52	14	23	.239	.353	1	0	OF-55
14 yrs.	1488	6133	1844	348	185	120	2.0	1494	518	661	343	441	.301	.476	1	0	OF-945, 1B-550, P-4

Ray Stoviak

STOVIAK, RAYMOND THOMAS   BL TL 6'1" 195 lbs.
B. June 6, 1915, Scottdale, Pa.

	G	AB	H	2B	3B	HR	HR %	R	RBI	BB	SO	SB	BA	SA	AB	H	G by POS
1938 PHI N	10	10	0	0	0	0	0.0	1	0	0	3	0	.000	.000	3	0	OF-4

Joe Strain

STRAIN, JOSEPH ALLAN, JR.   BR TR 5'10" 169 lbs.
B. Apr. 30, 1954, Denver, Colo.

	G	AB	H	2B	3B	HR	HR %	R	RBI	BB	SO	SB	BA	SA	AB	H	G by POS
1979 SF N	67	257	62	8	1	1	0.4	27	12	13	21	8	.241	.292	0	0	2B-67, 3B-1
1980	77	189	54	6	0	0	0.0	26	16	10	10	1	.286	.317	30	4	2B-42, 3B-6, SS-1
1981 CHI N	25	74	14	1	0	0	0.0	7	1	5	7	0	.189	.203	3	2	2B-20
3 yrs.	169	520	130	15	1	1	0.2	60	29	28	38	9	.250	.288	33	10	2B-129, 3B-7, SS-1

Paul Strand

STRAND, PAUL EDWARD   BR TL 6'½" 190 lbs.
B. Dec. 19, 1893, Carbonado, Wash.   D. July 2, 1974, Salt Lake City, Utah

	G	AB	H	2B	3B	HR	HR %	R	RBI	BB	SO	SB	BA	SA	AB	H	G by POS
1913 BOS N	7	6	1	0	0	0	0.0	0	0	0	0	0	.167	.167	0	0	P-7
1914	16	19	2	2	0	0	0.0	2	3	1	5	0	.105	.211	1	0	P-16
1915	45	22	2	0	0	0	0.0	3	2	0	4	0	.091	.091	9	2	P-6, OF-5
1924 PHI A	47	167	38	9	4	0	0.0	15	13	8	9	3	.228	.329	3	0	OF-44
4 yrs.	115	214	43	11	4	0	0.0	20	18	9	18	3	.201	.290	13	2	OF-49, P-29

Johnny Strands

STRANDS, JOHN LAWRENCE   BR TR 5'10½" 165 lbs.
B. Dec. 5, 1885, Chicago, Ill.   D. Jan. 19, 1957, Forest Park, Ill.

	G	AB	H	2B	3B	HR	HR %	R	RBI	BB	SO	SB	BA	SA	AB	H	G by POS
1915 NWK F	35	75	14	3	1	1	1.3	7	11	6		1	.187	.293	12	2	3B-12, 2B-9, OF-2

Sammy Strang

STRANG, SAMUEL NICKLIN (The Dixie Thrush)   BB TR 5'8" 160 lbs.
Also known as Samuel Strang Nicklin.
B. Dec. 16, 1876, Chattanooga, Tenn.   D. Mar. 13, 1932, Chattanooga, Tenn.

	G	AB	H	2B	3B	HR	HR %	R	RBI	BB	SO	SB	BA	SA	AB	H	G by POS
1896 LOU N	14	46	12	0	0	0	0.0	6	7	6	6	4	.261	.261	0	0	SS-14
1900 CHI N	27	102	29	3	0	0	0.0	15	9	8		1	.284	.314	0	0	3B-16, SS-9, 2B-2
1901 NY N	135	493	139	14	6	1	0.2	55	34	59		40	.282	.341	0	0	3B-91, 2B-37, OF-5, SS-4
1902 2 teams		CHI	A (137G –	.295)			CHI	N (3G –	.364)								
" total	140	547	162	18	5	3	0.5	109	46	76		39	.296	.364	0	0	3B-139, 2B-2
1903 BKN N	135	508	138	21	5	0	0.0	101	38	75		46	.272	.333	0	0	3B-124, OF-8, 2B-3
1904	77	271	52	11	0	1	0.4	28	9	45		16	.192	.244	0	0	2B-63, 3B-12, SS-1
1905 NY N	111	294	76	9	4	3	1.0	51	29	58		23	.259	.347	14	8	2B-47, OF-38, SS-9, 3B-1, 1B-1
1906	113	313	100	16	4	4	1.3	50	49	54		21	.319	.435	9	1	2B-57, OF-39, SS-4, 3B-3, 1B-1
1907	123	306	77	20	4	4	1.3	56	30	60		21	.252	.382	19	4	OF-70, 2B-13, 3B-7, 1B-5, SS-1
1908	28	53	5	0	0	0	0.0	8	2	23		5	.094	.094	4	2	1B-14, OF-5, SS-3
10 yrs.	903	2933	790	112	28	16	0.5	479	253	464	6	216	.269	.343	46	15	3B-393, 2B-238, OF-165, SS-45, 1B-7

WORLD SERIES

	G	AB	H	2B	3B	HR	HR %	R	RBI	BB	SO	SB	BA	SA	AB	H	G by POS
1905 NY N	1	1	0	0	0	0	0.0	0	0	0	1	0	.000	.000	1	0	

	G	AB	H	2B	3B	HR	HR%	R	RBI	BB	SO	SB	BA	SA	Pinch Hit AB	Pinch Hit H	G by POS

Alan Strange

STRANGE, ALAN COCHRANE (Inky)   BR TR 5'9" 162 lbs.
B. Nov. 7, 1909, Philadelphia, Pa.

	G	AB	H	2B	3B	HR	HR%	R	RBI	BB	SO	SB	BA	SA	PH AB	PH H	G by POS
1934 STL A	127	430	100	17	2	1	0.2	39	45	48	28	3	.233	.288	2	0	SS-125
1935 2 teams	STL A (49G – .231)				WAS A (20G – .185)												
" total	69	201	44	8	2	0	0.0	11	22	21	8	0	.219	.279	2	0	SS-65
1940 STL A	54	167	31	8	3	0	0.0	26	6	22	12	2	.186	.269	13	3	SS-35, 2B-4
1941	45	112	26	4	0	0	0.0	14	11	15	5	1	.232	.268	7	1	SS-32, 1B-2, 3B-1
1942	19	37	10	2	0	0	0.0	3	5	3	0	0	.270	.324	3	0	3B-10, SS-3, 2B-1
5 yrs.	314	947	211	39	7	1	0.1	93	89	109	53	6	.223	.282	27	4	SS-260, 3B-11, 2B-5, 1B-2

Asa Stratton

STRATTON, ASA EVANS
B. Feb. 10, 1853, Grafton, Mass.   D. Aug. 14, 1925, Fitchburg, Mass.

	G	AB	H	2B	3B	HR	HR%	R	RBI	BB	SO	SB	BA	SA	PH AB	PH H	G by POS
1881 WOR N	1	4	1	0	0	0	0.0	0	0	0	2		.250	.250	0	0	SS-1

Scott Stratton

STRATTON, C. SCOTT   TR 6' 180 lbs.
B. Oct. 2, 1869, Campbellsburg, Ky.   D. Mar. 8, 1939, Louisville, Ky.

	G	AB	H	2B	3B	HR	HR%	R	RBI	BB	SO	SB	BA	SA	PH AB	PH H	G by POS
1888 LOU AA	67	249	64	8	1	1	0.4	35	29	12		10	.257	.309	0	0	OF-38, P-33
1889	62	229	66	7	5	4	1.7	30	34	13	36	10	.288	.415	0	0	OF-29, P-19, 1B-17
1890	55	189	61	3	5	0	0.0	29		16		8	.323	.392	0	0	P-50, OF-5
1891 2 teams	PIT N (2G – .125)				LOU AA (34G – .235)												
" total	36	123	28	2	0	0	0.0	10	8	11	16	8	.228	.244	0	0	P-22, 1B-8, OF-6
1892 LOU N	63	219	56	2	9	0	0.0	22	23	17	21	9	.256	.347	0	0	P-42, OF-17, 1B-6
1893	61	221	50	8	5	0	0.0	34	16	25	15	6	.226	.308	0	0	P-38, OF-23, 1B-1
1894 2 teams	LOU N (13G – .324)				CHI N (23G – .375)												
" total	36	133	48	6	6	3	2.3	38	27	10	3	4	.361	.564	2	0	P-22, OF-10, 1B-2
1895 CHI N	10	24	7	1	1	0	0.0	3	2	4	2	1	.292	.417	1	0	P-5, OF-4
8 yrs.	390	1387	380	37	32	8	0.6	201	139	108	93	56	.274	.364	3	0	P-231, OF-132, 1B-34

Joe Straub

STRAUB, JOSEPH
B. Jan. 19, 1858, Milwaukee, Wis.   D. Feb. 13, 1929, Pueblo, Fla.

	G	AB	H	2B	3B	HR	HR%	R	RBI	BB	SO	SB	BA	SA	PH AB	PH H	G by POS
1880 TRO N	3	12	3	0	0	0	0.0	1		1	3		.250	.250	0	0	C-3
1882 PHI AA	8	32	6	2	0	0	0.0	2		1			.188	.250	0	0	C-7, OF-1
1883 COL AA	27	100	13	0	0	0	0.0	4		4			.130	.130	0	0	C-14, 1B-12, OF-1
3 yrs.	38	144	22	2	0	0	0.0	7		6	3		.153	.167	0	0	C-24, 1B-12, OF-2

Joe Strauss

STRAUSS, JOSEPH (The Socker)   BR TR
B. Mar. 17, 1844, Gecse, Hungary   D. June 25, 1906, Cincinnati, Ohio

	G	AB	H	2B	3B	HR	HR%	R	RBI	BB	SO	SB	BA	SA	PH AB	PH H	G by POS
1884 KC U	16	60	12	3	0	0	0.0	4		1			.200	.250	0	0	OF-10, C-3, 2B-2, 3B-1
1885 LOU AA	2	6	1	0	0	0	0.0	0		0			.167	.167	0	0	OF-1, C-1
1886 2 teams	LOU AA (74G – .215)				BKN AA (9G – .250)												
" total	83	333	73	6	7	1	0.3	42		9			.219	.288	0	0	OF-80, C-3, P-2
3 yrs.	101	399	86	9	7	1	0.3	46		10			.216	.281	0	0	OF-91, C-7, 2B-2, P-2, 3B-1

Darryl Strawberry

STRAWBERRY, DARRYL EUGENE   BL TL 6'6" 190 lbs.
B. Mar. 12, 1962, Los Angeles, Calif.

	G	AB	H	2B	3B	HR	HR%	R	RBI	BB	SO	SB	BA	SA	PH AB	PH H	G by POS
1983 NY N	122	420	108	15	7	26	6.2	63	74	47	128	19	.257	.512	4	0	OF-117
1984	147	522	131	27	4	26	5.0	75	97	75	131	27	.251	.467	4	2	OF-146
2 yrs.	269	942	239	42	11	52	5.5	138	171	122	259	46	.254	.487	8	2	OF-263

Gabby Street

STREET, CHARLES EVARD (Old Sarge)   BR TR 5'11" 180 lbs.
B. Sept. 30, 1882, Huntsville, Ala.   D. Feb. 6, 1951, Joplin, Mo.
Manager 1929-33, 1938.

	G	AB	H	2B	3B	HR	HR%	R	RBI	BB	SO	SB	BA	SA	PH AB	PH H	G by POS
1904 CIN N	11	33	4	1	0	0	0.0	1	0	1		2	.121	.152	0	0	C-11
1905 3 teams	CIN N (2G – .000)			BOS N (3G – .167)				CIN N (29G – .253)									
" total	34	105	25	5	0	0	0.0	8	8	8			.238	.305	3	0	C-30
1908 WAS A	131	394	81	12	7	1	0.3	31	32	40		5	.206	.279	3	2	C-128
1909	137	407	86	12	1	0	0.0	25	29	26		2	.211	.246	0	0	C-137
1910	89	257	52	6	0	1	0.4	13	16	23		1	.202	.237	3	1	C-86
1911	72	216	48	7	1	0	0.0	16	14	14		4	.222	.264	1	0	C-71
1912 NY A	28	88	16	1	1	0	0.0	4	6	7		1	.182	.216	0	0	C-28
1931 STL N	1	1	0	0	0	0	0.0	0	0	0	0	0	.000	.000	0	0	C-1
8 yrs.	503	1501	312	44	11	2	0.1	98	105	119	0	17	.208	.256	10	3	C-492

Walt Streuli

STREULI, WALTER HERBERT   BR TR 6'2" 195 lbs.
B. Sept. 26, 1935, Memphis, Tenn.

	G	AB	H	2B	3B	HR	HR%	R	RBI	BB	SO	SB	BA	SA	PH AB	PH H	G by POS
1954 DET A	1	0	0	0	0	0	–	0	0	1	0	0	–	–	0	0	C-1
1955	2	4	1	1	0	0	0.0	1	1	0	0	0	.250	.500	0	0	C-2
1956	3	8	2	1	0	0	0.0	0	1	1	2	0	.250	.375	0	0	C-3
3 yrs.	6	12	3	2	0	0	0.0	1	2	2	2	0	.250	.417	0	0	C-6

Cub Stricker

STRICKER, JOHN A.   BR TR 5'4½" 145 lbs.
Also known as John A. Streaker.
B. Feb. 15, 1860, Philadelphia, Pa.   D. Nov. 19, 1937, Philadelphia, Pa.

	G	AB	H	2B	3B	HR	HR%	R	RBI	BB	SO	SB	BA	SA	PH AB	PH H	G by POS
1882 PHI AA	72	272	59	6	1	0	0.0	34		15			.217	.246	0	0	2B-72, P-2, OF-1
1883	89	330	90	8	0	1	0.3	67		19			.273	.306	0	0	2B-88, C-2
1884	107	399	92	16	11	1	0.3	59		19			.231	.333	0	0	2B-107, OF-1, C-1, P-1
1885	106	398	93	9	3	1	0.3	71		21			.234	.279	0	0	2B-106
1887 CLE AA	131	534	141	19	4	2	0.4	122		53		86	.264	.326	0	0	2B-126, SS-6, P-3
1888	127	493	115	13	6	1	0.2	80	33	50		60	.233	.290	0	0	2B-122, OF-6, P-2
1889 CLE N	136	566	142	10	4	1	0.2	83	47	58	18	32	.251	.288	0	0	2B-135, SS-1
1890 CLE P	127	544	133	19	8	2	0.4	93	65	54	16	24	.244	.320	0	0	2B-109, SS-20
1891 BOS AA	139	514	111	15	4	0	0.0	96	46	63	34	54	.216	.261	0	0	2B-139
1892 2 teams	STL N (28G – .204)				BAL N (75G – .264)												
" total	103	367	91	6	5	3	0.8	57	48	42	25	18	.248	.316	0	0	2B-75
1893 WAS N	59	218	40	7	0	0	0.0	28	20	20	12	4	.183	.225	0	0	2B-39, OF-12, SS-4, 3B-4
11 yrs.	1196	4635	1107	128	47	12	0.3	790	258	414	105	278	.239	.294	0	0	2B-1118, SS-31, OF-20, P-8, 3B-4, C-3

	G	AB	H	2B	3B	HR	HR %	R	RBI	BB	SO	SB	BA	SA	Pinch Hit AB	Pinch Hit H	G by POS

George Strickland

STRICKLAND, GEORGE BEVAN (Bo)
B. Jan. 10, 1926, New Orleans, La.
Manager 1966.

BR TR 6'1" 175 lbs.

	G	AB	H	2B	3B	HR	HR %	R	RBI	BB	SO	SB	BA	SA	PH AB	PH H	G by POS
1950 PIT N	23	27	3	0	0	0	0.0	0	2	3	8	0	.111	.111	1	1	SS-19, 3B-1
1951	138	454	98	12	7	9	2.0	59	47	65	83	4	.216	.333	0	0	SS-125, 2B-13
1952 2 teams		PIT	N (76G –	.177)		CLE	A (31G –	.216)									
" total	107	320	60	10	2	6	1.9	25	30	35	60	4	.188	.288	1	0	SS-58, 2B-46, 3B-1, 1B-1
1953 CLE A	123	419	119	17	4	5	1.2	43	47	51	52	0	.284	.379	0	0	SS-122, 1B-1
1954	112	361	77	12	3	6	1.7	42	37	55	62	2	.213	.313	0	0	SS-112
1955	130	388	81	9	5	2	0.5	34	34	49	60	1	.209	.273	1	0	SS-128
1956	85	171	36	1	2	3	1.8	22	17	22	27	0	.211	.292	2	0	SS-28, 2B-28, 3B-26
1957	89	201	47	8	2	1	0.5	21	19	26	29	0	.234	.308	2	0	2B-48, SS-23, 3B-19
1959	132	441	105	15	2	3	0.7	55	48	52	64	1	.238	.302	1	0	3B-80, SS-50, 2B-4
1960	32	42	7	0	0	1	2.4	4	3	4	8	0	.167	.238	3	0	SS-14, 3B-12, 2B-2
10 yrs.	971	2824	633	84	27	36	1.3	305	284	362	453	12	.224	.311	11	1	SS-679, 2B-141, 3B-139, 1B-2

WORLD SERIES

	G	AB	H	2B	3B	HR	HR %	R	RBI	BB	SO	SB	BA	SA	PH AB	PH H	G by POS
1954 CLE A	3	9	0	0	0	0	0.0	0	0	0	2	0	.000	.000	0	0	SS-3

George Strief

STRIEF, GEORGE ANDREW
B. Oct. 16, 1856, Cincinnati, Ohio   D. Apr. 1, 1946, Cleveland, Ohio

BR TR 5'7" 172 lbs.

	G	AB	H	2B	3B	HR	HR %	R	RBI	BB	SO	SB	BA	SA	PH AB	PH H	G by POS
1879 CLE N	71	264	46	7	1	0	0.0	24	15	10	23		.174	.208	0	0	OF-55, 2B-16
1882 PIT AA	79	297	58	9	6	2	0.7	45		13			.195	.286	0	0	2B-78, SS-1
1883 STL AA	82	302	68	9	0	1	0.3	22		12			.225	.265	0	0	2B-67, OF-15
1884 4 teams		STL	AA (48G –	.201)		KC	U (15G –	.107)		C-P	U (15G –	.208)		CLE	N (8G –	.241)	
" total	86	322	61	17	2	2	0.6	35		20	5		.189	.273	0	0	OF-49, 2B-34, 3B-2, 1B-1
1885 PHI AA	44	175	48	8	5	0	0.0	19		9			.274	.377	0	0	3B-19, SS-10, OF-8, 2B-7
5 yrs.	362	1360	281	50	14	5	0.4	145	15	64	28		.207	.275	0	0	2B-202, OF-127, 3B-21, SS-11, 1B-1

John Strike

STRIKE, JOHN
B. 1865, Pennsylvania   Deceased.

	G	AB	H	2B	3B	HR	HR %	R	RBI	BB	SO	SB	BA	SA	PH AB	PH H	G by POS
1882 LOU AA	32	110	18	6	1	0	0.0	17		9			.164	.236	0	0	C-21, OF-6, 2B-6, SS-1, 1B-1
1886 PHI N	2	7	0	0	0	0	0.0	0		0	4		.000	.000	0	0	P-2, OF-1
2 yrs.	34	117	18	6	1	0	0.0	17		9	4		.154	.222	0	0	C-21, OF-7, 2B-6, P-2, SS-1, 1B-1

Lou Stringer

STRINGER, LOUIS BERNARD
B. May 13, 1917, Grand Rapids, Mich.

BR TR 5'11" 173 lbs.

	G	AB	H	2B	3B	HR	HR %	R	RBI	BB	SO	SB	BA	SA	PH AB	PH H	G by POS
1941 CHI N	145	512	126	31	4	5	1.0	59	53	59	86	3	.246	.352	0	0	2B-137, SS-7
1942	121	406	96	10	5	9	2.2	45	44	31	55	3	.236	.352	7	3	2B-113, 3B-1
1946	80	209	51	3	1	3	1.4	26	19	26	34	0	.244	.311	5	0	2B-62, SS-1, 3B-1
1948 BOS A	4	11	1	0	0	1	9.1	1	1	0	3	0	.091	.364	2	0	2B-2
1949	35	41	11	4	0	1	2.4	10	6	5	10	0	.268	.439	9	1	2B-9
1950	24	17	5	1	0	0	0.0	7	2	0	4	1	.294	.353	9	2	3B-3, SS-1, 2B-1
6 yrs.	409	1196	290	49	10	19	1.6	148	122	121	192	7	.242	.348	32	6	2B-324, SS-9, 3B-5

Joe Stripp

STRIPP, JOSEPH VALENTINE (Jersey Joe)
B. Feb. 3, 1903, Harrison, N. J.

BR TR 5'11½" 175 lbs.

	G	AB	H	2B	3B	HR	HR %	R	RBI	BB	SO	SB	BA	SA	PH AB	PH H	G by POS
1928 CIN N	42	139	40	7	3	1	0.7	18	17	8	8	0	.288	.403	2	1	OF-21, 3B-17, SS-1
1929	64	187	40	3	2	3	1.6	24	20	24	15	2	.214	.299	7	2	3B-55, 2B-2
1930	130	464	142	37	6	3	0.6	74	64	51	37	15	.306	.431	6	0	1B-75, 3B-48
1931	105	426	138	26	2	3	0.7	71	42	21	31	5	.324	.415	1	1	3B-96, 1B-9
1932 BKN N	138	534	162	36	9	6	1.1	94	64	36	30	14	.303	.438	0	0	3B-93, 1B-43
1933	141	537	149	20	7	1	0.2	69	51	26	23	5	.277	.346	1	1	3B-140
1934	104	384	121	19	6	1	0.3	50	40	22	20	2	.315	.404	1	0	3B-96, 1B-7, SS-1
1935	109	373	114	13	5	3	0.8	44	43	22	15	2	.306	.391	4	2	3B-88, 1B-15, OF-1
1936	110	439	139	31	1	1	0.2	51	60	22	12	2	.317	.399	3	1	3B-106
1937	90	300	73	10	2	1	0.3	37	26	20	18	1	.243	.300	9	3	3B-66, 1B-14, SS-3
1938 2 teams		STL	N (54G –	.286)		BOS	N (59G –	.275)									
" total	113	428	120	17	0	1	0.2	43	37	28	17	2	.280	.327	4	2	3B-109
11 yrs.	1146	4211	1238	219	43	24	0.6	575	464	280	226	50	.294	.384	38	13	3B-914, 1B-163, OF-22, SS-5, 2B-2

Allie Strobel

STROBEL, ALBERT IRVING
B. June 11, 1884, Boston, Mass.   D. Feb. 10, 1955, Hollywood, Calif.

BR TR 6' 160 lbs.

	G	AB	H	2B	3B	HR	HR %	R	RBI	BB	SO	SB	BA	SA	PH AB	PH H	G by POS
1905 BOS N	5	19	2	0	0	0	0.0	1	2	0		0	.105	.105	0	0	3B-4, OF-1
1906	100	317	64	10	3	1	0.3	28	24	29		2	.202	.262	1	0	2B-93, SS-6, OF-1
2 yrs.	105	336	66	10	3	1	0.3	29	26	29		2	.196	.253	1	0	2B-93, SS-6, 3B-4, OF-2

Jim Stroner

STRONER, JAMES M.
B. May 29, 1904, Chicago, Ill.   D. Nov. 16, 1971, Chicago, Ill.

BR TR 5'10" 175 lbs.

	G	AB	H	2B	3B	HR	HR %	R	RBI	BB	SO	SB	BA	SA	PH AB	PH H	G by POS
1929 PIT N	6	8	3	1	0	0	0.0	0	0	1	0	0	.375	.500	3	2	3B-2

Ed Stroud

STROUD, EDWIN MARVIN (The Creeper)
B. Oct. 31, 1939, Lapine, Ala.

BL TR 5'11" 180 lbs.

	G	AB	H	2B	3B	HR	HR %	R	RBI	BB	SO	SB	BA	SA	PH AB	PH H	G by POS
1966 CHI A	12	36	6	2	0	0	0.0	3	1	2	8	3	.167	.222	0	0	OF-11
1967 2 teams		CHI	A (20G –	.296)		WAS	A (87G –	.201)									
" total	107	231	49	5	4	1	0.4	42	13	26	34	15	.212	.281	6	0	OF-91
1968 WAS A	105	306	73	10	10	4	1.3	41	23	20	50	9	.239	.376	22	2	OF-84
1969	123	206	52	5	6	4	1.9	35	29	30	33	12	.252	.393	44	14	OF-85
1970	129	433	115	11	5	5	1.2	69	32	40	79	29	.266	.349	19	6	OF-118
1971 CHI A	53	141	25	4	3	0	0.0	19	2	11	20	4	.177	.248	14	2	OF-44
6 yrs.	529	1353	320	37	28	14	1.0	209	100	129	224	72	.237	.336	105	24	OF-433

	G	AB	H	2B	3B	HR	HR %	R	RBI	BB	SO	SB	BA	SA	Pinch Hit AB	H	G by POS

Denny Sullivan

SULLIVAN, DENNIS J.
B. June 26, 1858, Boston, Mass.   D. Dec. 31, 1925, Boston, Mass.

	G	AB	H	2B	3B	HR	HR%	R	RBI	BB	SO	SB	BA	SA	AB	H	G by POS
1879 PRO N	5	19	5	2	0	0	0.0	5	2	1		1	.263	.368	0	0	3B-4, OF-1
1880 BOS N	1	4	1	0	0	0	0.0	1	1	0		1	.250	.250	0	0	C-1
2 yrs.	6	23	6	2	0	0	0.0	6	3	1		2	.261	.348	0	0	3B-4, OF-1, C-1

Denny Sullivan

SULLIVAN, DENNIS WILLIAM   BL TR
B. Sept. 28, 1882, Hillsboro, Wis.   D. June 2, 1956, Los Angeles, Calif.

	G	AB	H	2B	3B	HR	HR%	R	RBI	BB	SO	SB	BA	SA	AB	H	G by POS
1905 WAS A	3	11	0	0	0	0	0.0	0	0	1		0	.000	.000	0	0	OF-3
1907 BOS A	144	551	135	18	6	1	0.2	73	26	44		16	.245	.283	0	0	OF-144
1908 2 teams		BOS	A	(101G –	.241)			CLE	A	(3G –	.000)						
" total	104	359	85	7	7	0	0.0	33	25	14		15	.237	.295	4	0	OF-101
1909 CLE A	3	2	1	0	0	0	0.0	0	0	0		0	.500	.500	1	1	OF-2
4 yrs.	254	923	221	25	7	1	0.1	106	51	59		31	.239	.285	5	1	OF-250

Eddie Sullivan

Playing record listed under Eddie Collins

Haywood Sullivan

SULLIVAN, HAYWOOD COOPER   BR TR 6'4"   210 lbs.
Father of Marc Sullivan.
B. Dec. 15, 1930, Donalsonville, Ga.
Manager 1965.

	G	AB	H	2B	3B	HR	HR%	R	RBI	BB	SO	SB	BA	SA	AB	H	G by POS
1955 BOS A	2	6	0	0	0	0	0.0	1	0	0	1	0	.000	.000	0	0	C-2
1957	2	1	0	0	0	0	0.0	0	0	0	0	0	.000	.000	1	0	C-1
1959	4	2	0	0	0	0	0.0	0	0	1	1	0	.000	.000	1	0	C-50
1960	52	124	20	1	0	3	2.4	9	10	16	24	0	.161	.242	2	0	C-88, 1B-16, OF-5
1961 KC A	117	331	80	16	2	6	1.8	42	40	46	45	1	.242	.356	12	4	C-88, 1B-16, OF-5
1962	95	274	68	7	2	4	1.5	33	29	31	54	1	.248	.332	2	1	C-94, 1B-1
1963	40	113	24	6	1	0	0.0	9	8	15	15	0	.212	.283	5	0	C-37
7 yrs.	312	851	192	30	5	13	1.5	94	87	109	140	2	.226	.318	23	5	C-274, 1B-17, OF-5

Jack Sullivan

SULLIVAN, CARL MANUEL   BR TR 5'11"   185 lbs.
B. Feb. 22, 1918, Princeton, Tex.

	G	AB	H	2B	3B	HR	HR%	R	RBI	BB	SO	SB	BA	SA	AB	H	G by POS
1944 DET A	1	1	0	0	0	0	0.0	0	0	0	0	0	.000	.000	0	0	2B-1

Joe Sullivan

SULLIVAN, JOSEPH DANIEL
B. Jan. 6, 1870, Charlestown, Mass.   D. Nov. 2, 1897, Charlestown, Mass.

	G	AB	H	2B	3B	HR	HR%	R	RBI	BB	SO	SB	BA	SA	AB	H	G by POS
1893 WAS N	128	508	135	16	13	2	0.4	72	64	36	24	7	.266	.360	0	0	SS-128
1894 2 teams		WAS	N	(17G –	.250)			PHI	N	(75G –	.352)						
" total	92	364	122	13	8	3	0.8	70	68	29	12	13	.335	.440	1	0	SS-81, 2B-8, OF-1, 3B-1
1895 PHI N	94	373	126	7	3	2	0.5	75	50	24	20	15	.338	.389	0	0	SS-89, OF-6
1896 2 teams		PHI	N	(48G –	.251)			STL	N	(51G –	.292)						
" total	99	403	110	9	5	4	1.0	70	45	27	24	14	.273	.350	0	0	OF-90, 2B-7, SS-2, 3B-2
4 yrs.	413	1648	493	45	29	11	0.7	287	227	116	80	49	.299	.382	1	0	SS-300, OF-97, 2B-15, 3B-3

John Sullivan

SULLIVAN, JOHN EUGENE   TR
B. Feb. 16, 1873, Ill.   D. June 5, 1924, St. Paul, Minn.

	G	AB	H	2B	3B	HR	HR%	R	RBI	BB	SO	SB	BA	SA	AB	H	G by POS
1905 DET A	12	31	5	0	0	0	0.0	4	4	4		0	.161	.161	0	0	C-12
1908 PIT N	1	1	0	0	0	0	0.0	0	0	0		0	.000	.000	0	0	C-1
2 yrs.	13	32	5	0	0	0	0.0	4	4	4		0	.156	.156	0	0	C-13

John Sullivan

SULLIVAN, JOHN LAWRENCE   BR TR 5'11"   180 lbs.
B. Mar. 21, 1890, Williamsport, Pa.   D. Apr. 1, 1966, Milton, Pa.

	G	AB	H	2B	3B	HR	HR%	R	RBI	BB	SO	SB	BA	SA	AB	H	G by POS
1920 BOS N	82	250	74	14	4	1	0.4	36	28	29	29	3	.296	.396	6	3	OF-66, 1B-6
1921 2 teams		BOS	N	(5G –	.000)			CHI	N	(76G –	.329)						
" total	81	245	79	14	4	4	1.6	28	41	19	26	3	.322	.461	14	3	OF-65
2 yrs.	163	495	153	28	8	5	1.0	64	69	48	55	6	.309	.428	20	6	OF-131, 1B-6

John Sullivan

SULLIVAN, JOHN PATRICK   BR TR 5'10"   170 lbs.
B. Nov. 2, 1920, Chicago, Ill.

	G	AB	H	2B	3B	HR	HR%	R	RBI	BB	SO	SB	BA	SA	AB	H	G by POS
1942 WAS A	94	357	84	16	1	0	0.0	38	42	25	30	2	.235	.286	1	0	SS-92
1943	134	456	95	12	2	1	0.2	49	55	57	59	6	.208	.250	0	0	SS-133
1944	138	471	118	12	1	0	0.0	49	30	52	43	3	.251	.280	0	0	SS-138
1947	49	133	34	0	1	0	0.0	13	5	22	14	0	.256	.271	1	0	SS-40, 2B-1
1948	85	173	36	4	1	0	0.0	25	12	22	25	2	.208	.243	9	0	SS-57, 2B-4
1949 STL N	105	243	55	8	3	0	0.0	29	18	38	35	5	.226	.284	3	0	SS-71, 3B-23, 2B-6
6 yrs.	605	1833	422	52	9	1	0.1	203	162	216	206	18	.230	.270	14	0	SS-531, 3B-23, 2B-11

John Sullivan

SULLIVAN, JOHN PETER   BL TR 6'   195 lbs.
B. Jan. 3, 1941, Somerville, N. J.

	G	AB	H	2B	3B	HR	HR%	R	RBI	BB	SO	SB	BA	SA	AB	H	G by POS
1963 DET A	3	5	0	0	0	0	0.0	0	0	2	1	0	.000	.000	0	0	C-2
1964	2	3	0	0	0	0	0.0	0	0	0	1	0	.000	.000	0	0	C-2
1965	34	86	23	0	0	2	2.3	5	11	9	13	0	.267	.337	4	1	C-29
1967 NY N	65	147	32	5	0	0	0.0	4	6	6	26	0	.218	.252	26	4	C-57
1968 PHI N	12	18	4	0	0	0	0.0	0	1	2	4	0	.222	.222	7	1	C-8
5 yrs.	116	259	59	5	0	2	0.8	9	18	19	45	0	.228	.270	37	6	C-98

Marc Sullivan

SULLIVAN, MARC COOPER   BR TR 6'4"   198 lbs.
Son of Haywood Sullivan.
B. July 25, 1958, Quincy, Mass.

	G	AB	H	2B	3B	HR	HR%	R	RBI	BB	SO	SB	BA	SA	AB	H	G by POS
1982 BOS A	2	6	2	0	0	0	0.0	0	0	0	2	0	.333	.333	0	0	C-2
1984	2	6	3	0	0	0	0.0	1	1	1	0	0	.500	.500	0	0	C-2
2 yrs.	4	12	5	0	0	0	0.0	1	1	1	2	0	.417	.417	0	0	C-4

	G	AB	H	2B	3B	HR	HR %	R	RBI	BB	SO	SB	BA	SA	Pinch Hit AB	H	G by POS

Marty Sullivan

SULLIVAN, MARTIN C.
B. Oct. 20, 1862, Lowell, Mass.   D. Jan. 6, 1894, Lowell, Mass.   BR TR

	G	AB	H	2B	3B	HR	HR %	R	RBI	BB	SO	SB	BA	SA	AB	H	G by POS
1887 CHI N	115	472	134	13	16	7	1.5	98	77	36	53	35	.284	.424	0	0	OF-115, P-1
1888	75	314	74	12	6	7	2.2	40	39	15	32	9	.236	.379	0	0	OF-75
1889 IND N	69	256	73	11	3	4	1.6	45	35	50	31	15	.285	.398	0	0	OF-64, 1B-5
1890 BOS N	121	505	144	19	7	6	1.2	82	61	56	48	33	.285	.386	0	0	OF-120, 3B-1
1891 2 teams	BOS	N	(17G –	.224)		CLE	N	(1G –	.250)								
" total	18	71	16	1	0	2	2.8	15	8	5	4	7	.225	.324	0	0	OF-18
5 yrs.	398	1618	441	56	32	26	1.6	280	220	162	168	99	.273	.395	0	0	OF-392, 1B-5, 3B-1, P-1

Mike Sullivan

SULLIVAN, MICHAEL J.
B. June 10, 1860, Philadelphia, Pa.   D. Mar. 21, 1929, Webster, Mass.

	G	AB	H	2B	3B	HR	HR %	R	RBI	BB	SO	SB	BA	SA	AB	H	G by POS
1888 PHI AA	28	112	31	5	6	1	0.9	20	19	3		10	.277	.455	0	0	OF-18, 3B-10

Pat Sullivan

SULLIVAN, PATRICK B.
B. Dec. 22, 1862, Milwaukee, Wis.   D. Mar. 29, 1886   TR 5'11" 165 lbs.

	G	AB	H	2B	3B	HR	HR %	R	RBI	BB	SO	SB	BA	SA	AB	H	G by POS
1884 KC U	31	114	22	2	1	1	0.9	15		4			.193	.254	0	0	3B-21, OF-9, C-1, P-1

Russ Sullivan

SULLIVAN, RUSSELL GUY
B. Feb. 19, 1923, Fredericksburg, Va.   BL TR 6' 196 lbs.

	G	AB	H	2B	3B	HR	HR %	R	RBI	BB	SO	SB	BA	SA	AB	H	G by POS
1951 DET A	7	26	5	1	0	1	3.8	2	1	2	1	0	.192	.346	0	0	OF-7
1952	15	52	17	2	1	3	5.8	7	5	3	5	1	.327	.577	1	1	OF-14
1953	23	72	18	5	1	1	1.4	7	6	13	5	0	.250	.389	3	0	OF-20
3 yrs.	45	150	40	8	2	5	3.3	16	12	18	11	1	.267	.447	4	1	OF-41

Sleeper Sullivan

SULLIVAN, THOMAS JEFFERSON
B. St. Louis, Mo.   D. Sept. 25, 1899, Camden, N. J.   BR 175 lbs.

	G	AB	H	2B	3B	HR	HR %	R	RBI	BB	SO	SB	BA	SA	AB	H	G by POS
1881 BUF N	35	121	23	4	0	0	0.0	13	15	1	21		.190	.223	0	0	C-31, OF-5
1882 STL AA	51	188	34	3	3	0	0.0	24		3			.181	.229	0	0	C-50, P-1
1883	8	27	6	0	1	0	0.0	2		0			.222	.296	0	0	C-6, OF-2
1884 STL U	2	9	1	0	0	0	0.0	0		0			.111	.111	0	0	OF-1, C-1, P-1
4 yrs.	96	345	64	7	4	0	0.0	39	15	4	21		.186	.229	0	0	C-88, OF-8, P-2

Suter Sullivan

SULLIVAN, SUTER G.
B. Oct. 14, 1872, Baltimore, Md.   D. Apr. 19, 1925, Baltimore, Md.

	G	AB	H	2B	3B	HR	HR %	R	RBI	BB	SO	SB	BA	SA	AB	H	G by POS
1898 STL N	42	144	32	3	0	0	0.0	10	12	13		1	.222	.243	2	0	SS-23, OF-10, 2B-6, 1B-1, P-1
1899 CLE N	127	473	116	16	3	0	0.0	37	55	25		16	.245	.292	0	0	3B-101, OF-20, SS-3, 1B-3, 2B-2
2 yrs.	169	617	148	19	3	0	0.0	47	67	38		17	.240	.280	2	0	3B-101, OF-30, SS-26, 2B-8, 1B-4, P-1

Ted Sullivan

SULLIVAN, THEODORE PAUL
B. 1852, County Clare, Ireland   D. July 5, 1929, Washington, D. C.
Manager 1883-84, 1888.

	G	AB	H	2B	3B	HR	HR %	R	RBI	BB	SO	SB	BA	SA	AB	H	G by POS
1884 KC U	3	9	3	0	0	0	0.0	0		1			.333	.333	0	0	OF-2, SS-1

Tom Sullivan

SULLIVAN, THOMAS BRANDON
B. Dec. 19, 1906, Nome, Alaska   D. Aug. 16, 1944, Seattle, Wash.   BR TR 6' 190 lbs.

	G	AB	H	2B	3B	HR	HR %	R	RBI	BB	SO	SB	BA	SA	AB	H	G by POS
1925 CIN N	1	1	0	0	0	0	0.0	0	0	0	0	0	.000	.000	0	0	C-1

Homer Summa

SUMMA, HOMER WAYNE
B. Nov. 3, 1898, Gentry, Mo.   D. Jan. 29, 1966, Los Angeles, Calif.   BL TR 5'10½" 170 lbs.

	G	AB	H	2B	3B	HR	HR %	R	RBI	BB	SO	SB	BA	SA	AB	H	G by POS
1920 PIT N	10	22	7	1	1	0	0.0	1	1	3	1	1	.318	.455	4	1	OF-6
1922 CLE A	12	46	16	3	3	1	2.2	9	6	1	1	1	.348	.609	0	0	OF-12
1923	137	525	172	27	6	3	0.6	92	69	33	20	9	.328	.419	1	1	OF-136
1924	111	390	113	21	6	2	0.5	55	38	11	16	4	.290	.390	14	2	OF-95
1925	75	224	74	10	1	0	0.0	28	25	13	6	3	.330	.384	17	2	OF-54, 3B-2
1926	154	581	179	31	6	4	0.7	74	76	47	9	15	.308	.403	0	0	OF-154
1927	145	574	164	41	7	4	0.7	72	74	32	18	6	.286	.402	0	0	OF-145
1928	134	504	143	26	3	3	0.6	60	57	20	15	4	.284	.365	2	0	OF-132
1929 PHI A	37	81	22	4	0	0	0.0	12	10	2	1	1	.272	.321	12	2	OF-24
1930	25	54	15	2	1	1	1.9	10	5	4	1	0	.278	.407	7	2	OF-15
10 yrs.	840	3001	905	166	34	18	0.6	413	361	166	88	44	.302	.398	57	10	OF-773, 3B-2

WORLD SERIES

	G	AB	H	2B	3B	HR	HR %	R	RBI	BB	SO	SB	BA	SA	AB	H	G by POS
1929 PHI A	1	1	0	0	0	0	0.0	0	0	0	1	0	.000	.000	1	0	

Champ Summers

SUMMERS, JOHN JUNIOR II
B. June 15, 1946, Bremerton, Wash.   BL TR 6'2" 205 lbs.

	G	AB	H	2B	3B	HR	HR %	R	RBI	BB	SO	SB	BA	SA	AB	H	G by POS
1974 OAK A	20	24	3	1	0	0	0.0	2	3	1	5	0	.125	.167	7	1	OF-12, DH-2
1975 CHI N	76	91	21	5	1	1	1.1	14	16	10	13	0	.231	.341	46	14	OF-18
1976	83	126	26	2	0	3	2.4	11	13	13	31	1	.206	.294	47	12	OF-26, 1B-10, C-1
1977 CIN N	59	76	13	4	0	3	3.9	11	6	6	16	0	.171	.342	38	6	OF-16, 3B-1
1978	13	35	9	2	0	1	2.9	4	3	7	4	2	.257	.400	0	0	OF-12
1979 2 teams	CIN	N	(27G –	.200)		DET	A	(90G –	.313)								
" total	117	306	89	14	2	21	6.9	57	62	53	48	7	.291	.556	23	5	OF-82, DH-10, 1B-10
1980 DET A	120	347	103	19	1	17	4.9	61	60	52	52	4	.297	.504	26	7	DH-64, OF-47, 1B-1
1981	64	165	42	8	0	3	1.8	16	21	19	35	1	.255	.358	14	3	DH-37, OF-18
1982 SF N	70	125	31	5	0	4	3.2	15	19	16	17	0	.248	.384	31	10	OF-31, 1B-3
1983	29	22	3	0	0	0	0.0	3	3	7	8	0	.136	.136	20	3	OF-1
1984 SD N	47	54	10	3	0	1	1.9	5	12	4	15	0	.185	.296	36	7	1B-8
11 yrs.	698	1371	350	63	4	54	3.9	199	218	188	244	15	.255	.425	288	68	OF-263, DH-113, 1B-32, 3B-1, C-1

LEAGUE CHAMPIONSHIP SERIES

	G	AB	H	2B	3B	HR	HR %	R	RBI	BB	SO	SB	BA	SA	AB	H	G by POS
1984 SD N	2	2	0	0	0	0	0.0	0		0	1	0	.000	.000	0	0	

WORLD SERIES

	G	AB	H	2B	3B	HR	HR %	R	RBI	BB	SO	SB	BA	SA	AB	H	G by POS
1984 SD N	1	1	0	0	0	0	0.0	0	0	0	1	0	.000	.000	1	0	

	G	AB	H	2B	3B	HR	HR%	R	RBI	BB	SO	SB	BA	SA	Pinch Hit AB	Pinch Hit H	G by POS

Carl Sumner

SUMNER, CARL RINGDAHL (Lefty)
B. Sept. 28, 1908, Cambridge, Mass.
BL TL 5'8" 160 lbs.

	G	AB	H	2B	3B	HR	HR%	R	RBI	BB	SO	SB	BA	SA	AB	H	G by POS
1928 BOS A	16	29	8	1	1	0	0.0	6	3	5	6	0	.276	.379	3	1	OF-10

Art Sunday

SUNDAY, ARTHUR
Also known as August Wacher.
B. Jan. 21, 1862, Springfield, Ohio   Deceased.
5'9" 193 lbs.

	G	AB	H	2B	3B	HR	HR%	R	RBI	BB	SO	SB	BA	SA	AB	H	G by POS
1890 BKN P	24	83	22	5	1	0	0.0	26	13	15	9	0	.265	.349	0	0	OF-25

Billy Sunday

SUNDAY, WILLIAM ASHLEY (The Evangelist)
B. Nov. 19, 1862, Ames, Iowa   D. Nov. 6, 1935, Chicago, Ill.
BL TR 5'10" 160 lbs.

	G	AB	H	2B	3B	HR	HR%	R	RBI	BB	SO	SB	BA	SA	AB	H	G by POS
1883 CHI N	14	54	13	4	0	0	0.0	6		1	18		.241	.315	0	0	OF-14
1884	43	176	39	4	1	4	2.3	25		4	36		.222	.324	0	0	OF-43
1885	46	172	44	3	3	2	1.2	36	20	12	33		.256	.343	0	0	OF-46
1886	28	103	25	2	2	0	0.0	16	6	7	26		.243	.301	0	0	OF-28
1887	50	199	58	6	6	3	1.5	41	32	21	20	34	.291	.427	0	0	OF-50
1888 PIT N	120	505	119	14	3	0	0.0	69	15	12	36	71	.236	.275	0	0	OF-120
1889	81	321	77	10	6	2	0.6	62	25	27	33	47	.240	.327	0	0	OF-81
1890 2 teams		PIT	N	(86G –	.257)		PHI	N	(31G –	.261)							
" total	117	477	123	12	3	1	0.2	84	39	50	27	84	.258	.302	0	0	OF-117, P-1
8 yrs.	499	2007	498	55	24	12	0.6	339	136	134	229	236	.248	.317	0	0	OF-499, P-1

Jim Sundberg

SUNDBERG, JAMES HOWARD
B. May 18, 1951, Galesburg, Ill.
BR TR 6' 190 lbs.

	G	AB	H	2B	3B	HR	HR%	R	RBI	BB	SO	SB	BA	SA	AB	H	G by POS
1974 TEX A	132	368	91	13	3	3	0.8	45	36	62	61	2	.247	.323	1	0	C-132
1975	155	472	94	9	0	6	1.3	45	36	51	77	3	.199	.256	0	0	C-155
1976	140	448	102	24	2	3	0.7	33	34	37	61	0	.228	.310	1	1	C-140
1977	149	453	132	20	3	6	1.3	61	65	53	77	2	.291	.389	1	1	C-149
1978	149	518	144	23	6	6	1.2	54	58	64	70	2	.278	.380	1	0	C-148, DH-1
1979	150	495	136	23	4	5	1.0	50	64	51	51	3	.275	.368	1	0	C-150
1980	151	505	138	24	1	10	2.0	59	63	64	67	2	.273	.384	3	2	C-151
1981	102	339	94	17	2	3	0.9	42	28	50	48	2	.277	.366	2	1	C-98, OF-2
1982	139	470	118	22	5	10	2.1	37	47	49	57	2	.251	.383	1	0	C-132, OF-1
1983	131	378	76	14	0	2	0.5	30	28	35	64	0	.201	.254	1	0	C-131
1984 MIL A	110	348	91	19	4	7	2.0	43	43	38	63	1	.261	.399	3	0	C-109
11 yrs.	1508	4794	1216	208	30	61	1.3	499	502	554	696	19	.254	.348	21	6	C-1495, OF-3, DH-1

George Susce

SUSCE, GEORGE CYRIL METHODIUS (Good Kid)
Father of George Susce.
B. Aug. 13, 1908, Pittsburgh, Pa.
BR TR 5'11½" 200 lbs.

	G	AB	H	2B	3B	HR	HR%	R	RBI	BB	SO	SB	BA	SA	AB	H	G by POS
1929 PHI N	17	17	5	3	0	1	5.9	5	1	1	2	0	.294	.647	5	0	C-11
1932 DET A	2	0	0	0	0	0	–	0	0	0	0	0	–	–	0	0	C-2
1939 PIT N	31	75	17	3	1	1	1.3	8	4	12	5	0	.227	.333	0	0	1B-31
1940 STL A	61	113	24	4	0	0	0.0	6	13	9	9	1	.212	.248	0	0	C-61
1941 CLE A	1	0	0	0	0	0	–	0	0	0	0	0	–	–	0	0	C-1
1942	2	1	1	0	0	0	0.0	1	0	1	0	0	1.000	1.000	0	0	C-2
1943	3	1	0	0	0	0	0.0	0	0	0	0	0	.000	.000	0	0	C-3
1944	29	61	14	1	0	0	0.0	3	4	2	5	0	.230	.246	0	0	C-29
8 yrs.	146	268	61	11	1	2	0.7	23	22	25	21	1	.228	.299	5	0	C-109, 1B-31

Pete Susko

SUSKO, PETER JONATHAN
B. July 2, 1904, Laura, Ohio   D. May 22, 1978, Jacksonville, Fla.
BL TL 5'11" 172 lbs.

	G	AB	H	2B	3B	HR	HR%	R	RBI	BB	SO	SB	BA	SA	AB	H	G by POS
1934 WAS A	58	224	64	5	3	2	0.9	25	25	18	10	3	.286	.362	0	0	1B-58

Butch Sutcliffe

SUTCLIFFE, CHARLES INIGO
B. July 22, 1915, Fall River, Mass.
BR TR 5'8½" 165 lbs.

	G	AB	H	2B	3B	HR	HR%	R	RBI	BB	SO	SB	BA	SA	AB	H	G by POS
1938 BOS N	4	4	1	0	0	0	0.0	1	2	2	1	0	.250	.250	0	0	C-3

Sy Sutcliffe

SUTCLIFFE, EDWARD ELMER
B. Apr. 15, 1863, Wheaton, Ill.   D. Feb. 13, 1893, Wheaton, Ill.
BL 6'2" 170 lbs.

	G	AB	H	2B	3B	HR	HR%	R	RBI	BB	SO	SB	BA	SA	AB	H	G by POS
1884 CHI N	4	15	3	1	0	0	0.0	4		2	4		.200	.267	0	0	C-4
1885 2 teams		CHI	N	(11G –	.186)		STL	N	(16G –	.122)							
" total	27	92	14	2	1	0	0.0	7	8	7	15		.152	.196	0	0	C-25, OF-3
1888 DET N	49	191	49	5	3	0	0.0	17	23	5	14	6	.257	.314	0	0	SS-24, C-14, 1B-5, OF-4, 2B-2
1889 CLE N	46	161	40	3	2	1	0.6	17	21	14	6	5	.248	.311	0	0	C-37, 1B-8, OF-1
1890 CLE P	99	386	127	14	8	2	0.5	62	60	33	16	10	.329	.422	0	0	OF-35, C-22, SS-3, 3B-1
1891 WAS AA	53	201	71	8	3	2	1.0	29	33	17	17	8	.353	.453	0	0	SS-25, C-22, SS-3, 3B-1
1892 BAL N	66	276	77	10	7	1	0.4	41	27	14	15	12	.279	.377	0	0	1B-66
7 yrs.	344	1322	381	43	24	6	0.5	177	171	92	87	41	.288	.371	0	0	C-186, 1B-79, OF-58, SS-31, 3B-3, 2B-2

Gary Sutherland

SUTHERLAND, GARY LYNN
Brother of Darrell Sutherland.
B. Sept. 27, 1944, Glendale, Calif.
BR TR 6' 185 lbs.

	G	AB	H	2B	3B	HR	HR%	R	RBI	BB	SO	SB	BA	SA	AB	H	G by POS
1966 PHI N	3	3	0	0	0	0	0.0	0	0	0	0	0	.000	.000	2	0	SS-1
1967	103	231	57	12	1	1	0.4	23	19	17	22	0	.247	.320	22	4	SS-66, OF-25
1968	67	138	38	7	0	0	0.0	16	15	8	15	0	.275	.326	31	9	2B-17, SS-10, 3B-10, OF-7
1969 MON N	141	544	130	26	1	3	0.6	63	35	37	31	5	.239	.307	1	0	2B-139, SS-15, OF-1
1970	116	359	74	10	0	3	0.8	37	26	31	22	2	.206	.259	23	4	2B-97, SS-15, 3B-1
1971	111	304	78	7	2	4	1.3	25	26	18	12	3	.257	.332	19	3	2B-56, SS-46, OF-4, 3B-2
1972 HOU N	5	8	1	0	0	0	0.0	0	1	0	1	0	.125	.125	4	0	3B-1, 2B-1
1973	16	54	14	5	0	0	0.0	8	3	3	5	0	.259	.352	2	1	2B-14, SS-1
1974 DET A	149	619	157	20	1	5	0.8	60	49	26	37	1	.254	.313	2	1	2B-147, SS-10, 3B-4
1975	129	503	130	12	3	6	1.2	51	39	45	41	0	.258	.330	1	0	2B-128

	G	AB	H	2B	3B	HR	HR %	R	RBI	BB	SO	SB	BA	SA	Pinch Hit AB	H	G by POS

Gary Sutherland continued

	G	AB	H	2B	3B	HR	HR%	R	RBI	BB	SO	SB	BA	SA	PH AB	PH H	G by POS
1976 2 teams	DET A (42G – .205)				MIL A (59G – .217)												
" total	101	232	49	7	2	1	0.4	19	15	15	19	0	.211	.272	12	2	2B-87, DH-8, 1B-2
1977 SD N	80	103	25	3	0	1	1.0	9	11	7	15	0	.243	.301	38	12	2B-30, 3B-21, 1B-4
1978 STL N	10	6	1	0	0	0	0.0	1	0	0	0	0	.167	.167	6	1	2B-1
13 yrs.	1031	3104	754	109	10	24	0.8	308	239	207	219	11	.243	.308	163	37	2B-717, SS-164, 3B-39, OF-37, DH-8, 1B-6

Leo Sutherland

SUTHERLAND, LEONARDO CANTIN
B. Apr. 6, 1958, Santiago, Cuba
BL TL 5'10" 165 lbs.

	G	AB	H	2B	3B	HR	HR%	R	RBI	BB	SO	SB	BA	SA	PH AB	PH H	G by POS
1980 CHI A	34	89	23	3	0	0	0.0	9	5	1	11	4	.258	.292	10	4	OF-23
1981	11	12	2	0	0	0	0.0	6	0	3	1	2	.167	.167	1	0	OF-7
2 yrs.	45	101	25	3	0	0	0.0	15	5	4	12	6	.248	.277	11	4	OF-30

Ezra Sutton

SUTTON, EZRA BALLOU
B. Sept. 17, 1850, Palmyra, N. Y.   D. June 20, 1907, Braintree, Mass.
BR TR 5'8½" 153 lbs.

	G	AB	H	2B	3B	HR	HR%	R	RBI	BB	SO	SB	BA	SA	PH AB	PH H	G by POS
1876 PHI N	54	236	70	12	7	1	0.4	45	31	3	2		.297	.419	0	0	1B-29, 2B-15, 3B-8, OF-4
1877 BOS N	58	253	74	10	6	0	0.0	43	39	4	10		.292	.379	0	0	SS-36, 3B-22
1878	60	239	54	9	3	1	0.4	31	29	2	14		.226	.301	0	0	3B-59, SS-1
1879	84	339	84	13	4	0	0.0	54	34	2	18		.248	.310	0	0	SS-51, 3B-33
1880	76	288	72	9	2	0	0.0	41	25	7	7		.250	.295	0	0	SS-39, 3B-37
1881	83	333	97	12	4	0	0.0	43	31	13	9		.291	.351	0	0	3B-81, SS-2
1882	81	319	80	8	1	2	0.6	44	38	24	25		.251	.301	0	0	3B-77, SS-4
1883	94	414	134	28	15	3	0.7	101	73	17	12		.324	.486	0	0	3B-93, OF-1, SS-1
1884	110	468	162	28	7	3	0.6	102		29	22		.346	.455	0	0	3B-110
1885	110	457	143	23	8	4	0.9	78	47	17	25		.313	.425	0	0	3B-91, SS-16, 2B-2, 1B-1
1886	116	499	138	21	6	3	0.6	83	48	26	21		.277	.361	0	0	OF-43, SS-28, 3B-28, 2B-18
1887	77	326	99	14	9	3	0.9	58	46	13	6	17	.304	.429	0	0	SS-37, OF-18, 2B-13, 3B-11
1888	28	110	24	3	1	1	0.9	16	16	7	3	10	.218	.291	0	0	3B-27, SS-1
13 yrs.	1031	4281	1231	190	73	21	0.5	739	457	164	174	27	.288	.381	0	0	3B-677, SS-216, OF-66, 2B-48, 1B-30

Harry Swacina

SWACINA, HARRY JOSEPH (Swats)
B. Aug. 22, 1881, St. Louis, Mo.   D. June 21, 1944, Birmingham, Ala.
BR TR 6'2" 190 lbs.

	G	AB	H	2B	3B	HR	HR%	R	RBI	BB	SO	SB	BA	SA	PH AB	PH H	G by POS
1907 PIT N	26	95	19	1	1	0	0.0	9	10	4		1	.200	.232	0	0	1B-26
1908	53	176	38	6	1	0	0.0	7	13	5		4	.216	.261	2	1	1B-50
1914 BAL F	158	617	173	26	8	0	0.0	70	90	14		15	.280	.348	0	0	1B-158
1915	85	301	74	13	1	1	0.3	24	38	9		9	.246	.306	8	1	1B-75, 2B-1
4 yrs.	322	1189	304	46	11	1	0.1	110	151	32		29	.256	.315	10	2	1B-309, 2B-1

Andy Swan

SWAN, ANDREW J.
Deceased.

	G	AB	H	2B	3B	HR	HR%	R	RBI	BB	SO	SB	BA	SA	PH AB	PH H	G by POS
1884 2 teams	WAS AA (5G – .143)				RIC AA (3G – .500)												
" total	8	31	8	1	0	0		5		0			.258	.290	0	0	1B-6, 3B-2

Pinky Swander

SWANDER, EDWARD O.
B. July 4, 1880, Portsmouth, Ohio   D. Oct. 24, 1944, Springfield, Mass.

	G	AB	H	2B	3B	HR	HR%	R	RBI	BB	SO	SB	BA	SA	PH AB	PH H	G by POS
1903 STL A	14	51	14	2	2	0	0.0	9	6	10		0	.275	.392	0	0	OF-14
1904	1	1	0	0	0	0	0.0	0	0	0		0	.000	.000	1	0	
2 yrs.	15	52	14	2	2	0	0.0	9	6	10		0	.269	.385	1	0	OF-14

Bill Swanson

SWANSON, WILLIAM ANDREW
B. Oct. 12, 1888, New York, N. Y.   D. Oct. 16, 1954, New York, N. Y.
BB TR 5'7" 140 lbs.

	G	AB	H	2B	3B	HR	HR%	R	RBI	BB	SO	SB	BA	SA	PH AB	PH H	G by POS
1914 BOS A	11	20	4	2	0	0	0.0	1	3	4		0	.200	.300	1	0	2B-6, 3B-3, SS-1

Evar Swanson

SWANSON, ERNEST EVAR
B. Oct. 15, 1902, DeKalb, Ill.   D. July 17, 1973, Galesburg, Ill.
BR TR 5'9" 170 lbs.

	G	AB	H	2B	3B	HR	HR%	R	RBI	BB	SO	SB	BA	SA	PH AB	PH H	G by POS
1929 CIN N	145	574	172	35	12	4	0.7	100	43	41	47	33	.300	.423	2	1	OF-142
1930	95	301	93	15	3	2	0.7	43	22	11	17	4	.309	.399	15	1	OF-71
1932 CHI A	14	52	16	3	1	0	0.0	9	8	8	3	0	.308	.404	0	0	OF-14
1933	144	539	165	25	7	1	0.2	102	63	93	35	19	.306	.384	6	2	OF-139
1934	117	426	127	9	5	0	0.0	71	34	59	31	10	.298	.343	9	2	OF-105
5 yrs.	515	1892	573	87	28	7	0.4	325	170	212	133	69	.303	.390	32	6	OF-471

Karl Swanson

SWANSON, KARL EDWARD
B. Dec. 17, 1903, North Henderson, Ill.
BL TR 5'10" 155 lbs.

	G	AB	H	2B	3B	HR	HR%	R	RBI	BB	SO	SB	BA	SA	PH AB	PH H	G by POS
1928 CHI A	22	64	9	1	0	0	0.0	2	6	4	7	3	.141	.156	1	0	2B-21
1929	2	1	0	0	0	0	0.0	0	0	0	0	0	.000	.000	1	0	
2 yrs.	24	65	9	1	0	0	0.0	2	6	4	7	3	.138	.154	1	0	2B-21

Stan Swanson

SWANSON, STANLEY LAWRENCE
B. May 19, 1944, Yuba City, Calif.
BR TR 5'11" 168 lbs.

	G	AB	H	2B	3B	HR	HR%	R	RBI	BB	SO	SB	BA	SA	PH AB	PH H	G by POS
1971 MON N	49	106	26	3	0	2	1.9	14	11	10	13	1	.245	.330	10	3	OF-38

Ed Swartwood

SWARTWOOD, CYRUS EDWARD
B. Jan. 12, 1859, Rockford, Ill.   D. May 10, 1924, Pittsburgh, Pa.
BL TR 198 lbs.

	G	AB	H	2B	3B	HR	HR%	R	RBI	BB	SO	SB	BA	SA	PH AB	PH H	G by POS
1881 BUF N	1	3	1	0	0	0	0.0	0	0		1	0	.333	.333	0	0	OF-1
1882 PIT AA	76	325	107	18	11	5	1.5	86		21			.329	.498	0	0	OF-73, 1B-4
1883	94	413	147	24	8	3	0.7	86		24			.356	.475	0	0	1B-60, OF-37, C-3
1884	102	399	115	19	6	0	0.0	74		33			.288	.366	0	0	OF-79, 1B-22, 3B-1, P-1
1885 BKN AA	99	399	106	8	9	0	0.0	80		36			.266	.331	0	0	OF-95, 1B-4, SS-1, C-1
1886	122	471	132	13	10	3	0.6	95		70			.280	.369	0	0	OF-122, C-1
1887	91	363	92	14	8	1	0.3	72		46		29	.253	.344	0	0	OF-91

	G	AB	H	2B	3B	HR	HR %	R	RBI	BB	SO	SB	BA	SA	Pinch Hit AB	Pinch Hit H	G by POS

Ed Swartwood continued

	G	AB	H	2B	3B	HR	HR %	R	RBI	BB	SO	SB	BA	SA	AB	H	G by POS
1890 TOL AA	126	462	151	23	11	3	0.6	106		80		53	.327	.444	0	0	OF-126, P-1
1892 PIT N	13	42	10	1	0	0	0.0	8	4	13	11	1	.238	.262	0	0	OF-13
9 yrs.	724	2877	861	120	63	15	0.5	607	3	324	11	83	.299	.400	0	0	OF-637, 1B-90, C-5, P-2, SS-1, 3B-1

Charlie Sweasy

SWEASY, CHARLES JAMES   BR TR 5'9"   172 lbs.
Born Charles James Swasey.
B. Nov. 2, 1847, Newark, N. J.   D. Mar. 30, 1908, Newark, N. J.
Manager 1875.

	G	AB	H	2B	3B	HR	HR %	R	RBI	BB	SO	SB	BA	SA	AB	H	G by POS
1876 CIN N	56	225	46	5	2	0	0.0	18	10	2	5		.204	.244	0	0	2B-55, OF-1
1878 PRO N	55	212	37	3	0	0	0.0	23	8	7	23		.175	.189	0	0	2B-55
2 yrs.	111	437	83	8	2	0	0.0	41	18	9	28		.190	.217	0	0	2B-110, OF-1

Bill Sweeney

SWEENEY, WILLIAM JOHN   BR TR 5'11"   175 lbs.
B. Mar. 6, 1886, Covington, Ky.   D. May 26, 1948, Cambridge, Mass.

	G	AB	H	2B	3B	HR	HR %	R	RBI	BB	SO	SB	BA	SA	AB	H	G by POS
1907 2 teams	CHI N (3G – .100)				BOS N	(58G – .262)											
" total	61	201	51	2	0	0	0.0	25	19	16		9	.254	.264	2	0	3B-23, SS-18, OF-11, 2B-5, 1B-1
1908 BOS N	127	418	102	15	3	0	0.0	44	40	45		17	.244	.294	3	2	3B-123, SS-2, 2B-1
1909	138	493	120	19	3	1	0.2	45	36	37		25	.243	.300	0	0	3B-112, SS-26
1910	150	499	133	22	4	5	1.0	43	46	61	28	25	.267	.357	4	3	SS-110, 3B-21, 1B-17
1911	137	523	164	33	6	3	0.6	92	63	77	26	33	.314	.417	1	1	2B-136
1912	153	593	204	31	13	1	0.2	84	100	68	34	27	.344	.445	0	0	2B-153
1913	139	502	129	17	6	0	0.0	65	47	66	50	18	.257	.315	2	1	2B-137
1914 CHI N	134	463	101	14	5	1	0.2	45	38	53	15	18	.218	.276	0	0	2B-134
8 yrs.	1039	3692	1004	153	40	11	0.3	443	389	423	153	172	.272	.344	12	7	2B-566, 3B-279, SS-156, 1B-18, OF-11

Bill Sweeney

SWEENEY, WILLIAM JOSEPH   BR TR 5'11"   180 lbs.
B. Dec. 29, 1904, Cleveland, Ohio   D. Apr. 18, 1957, San Diego, Calif.

	G	AB	H	2B	3B	HR	HR %	R	RBI	BB	SO	SB	BA	SA	AB	H	G by POS
1928 DET A	89	309	78	15	5	0	0.0	47	19	15	28	12	.252	.333	8	1	1B-75, OF-3
1930 BOS A	88	243	75	13	0	4	1.6	32	30	9	15	5	.309	.412	25	4	1B-56, 3B-1
1931	131	498	147	30	3	1	0.2	48	58	20	30	5	.295	.373	6	4	1B-124
3 yrs.	308	1050	300	58	8	5	0.5	127	107	44	73	22	.286	.370	39	9	1B-255, OF-3, 3B-1

Charlie Sweeney

SWEENEY, CHARLES FRANCIS (Buck)
B. Apr. 15, 1890, Philadelphia, Pa.   D. Mar. 15, 1955, Pittsburgh, Pa.

	G	AB	H	2B	3B	HR	HR %	R	RBI	BB	SO	SB	BA	SA	AB	H	G by POS
1914 PHI A	1	1	0	0	0	0	0.0	0	0	0	1	0	.000	.000	0	0	OF-1

Charlie Sweeney

SWEENEY, CHARLES J.   TR 5'10½" 181 lbs.
B. Apr. 13, 1863, San Francisco, Calif.   D. Apr. 4, 1902, San Francisco, Calif.

	G	AB	H	2B	3B	HR	HR %	R	RBI	BB	SO	SB	BA	SA	AB	H	G by POS
1882 PRO N	1	4	0	0	0	0	0.0	0		0	1		.000	.000	0	0	OF-1
1883	22	87	19	3	0	0	0.0	9		2	10		.218	.253	0	0	P-20, OF-7
1884 2 teams	PRO N (41G – .298)				STL U	(45G – .316)											
" total	86	339	104	23	2	2	0.6	55		21	17		.307	.404	0	0	P-60, OF-30, 1B-2
1885 STL N	71	267	55	7	1	0	0.0	27	24	12	33		.206	.240	0	0	OF-39, P-35
1886	17	64	16	2	0	0	0.0	4	7	3	10		.250	.281	0	0	P-11, OF-4, SS-2
1887 CLE AA	36	133	30	4	4	0	0.0	22		21		11	.226	.316	0	0	1B-20, OF-10, P-3, SS-2, 3B-2
6 yrs.	233	894	224	39	7	2	0.2	117	30	59	71	11	.251	.317	0	0	P-129, OF-91, 1B-22, SS-4, 3B-2

Dan Sweeney

SWEENEY, DANIEL J.   5'5"   135 lbs.
B. Jan. 28, 1868, Philadelphia, Pa.   D. July 13, 1913, Louisville, Ky.

	G	AB	H	2B	3B	HR	HR %	R	RBI	BB	SO	SB	BA	SA	AB	H	G by POS
1895 LOU N	22	90	24	5	0	1	1.1	18	16	17	2	2	.267	.356	0	0	OF-22

Hank Sweeney

SWEENEY, HENRY LEON   BL TL 6'   185 lbs.
B. Dec. 28, 1915, Franklin, Tenn.   D. May 6, 1980, Columbia, Tenn.

	G	AB	H	2B	3B	HR	HR %	R	RBI	BB	SO	SB	BA	SA	AB	H	G by POS
1944 PIT N	1	2	0	0	0	0	0.0	0	0	0	1	0	.000	.000	0	0	1B-1

Jeff Sweeney

SWEENEY, EDWARD FRANCIS   BR TR
B. July 19, 1888, Chicago, Ill.   D. July 4, 1947, Chicago, Ill.

	G	AB	H	2B	3B	HR	HR %	R	RBI	BB	SO	SB	BA	SA	AB	H	G by POS
1908 NY A	32	82	12	2	0	0	0.0	4	2	5		0	.146	.171	5	0	C-25, OF-1, 1B-1
1909	67	176	47	3	0	0	0.0	19	21	16		3	.267	.284	2	0	C-62, 1B-3
1910	78	215	43	4	0	0	0.0	25	15	17		12	.200	.256	1	0	C-78
1911	83	229	53	6	5	0	0.0	17	18	14		8	.231	.301	0	0	C-83
1912	110	351	94	12	1	0	0.0	37	30	27		6	.268	.308	2	1	C-108
1913	117	351	93	10	2	2	0.6	35	40	37	41	11	.265	.322	3	1	C-112, 1B-1
1914	87	258	55	8	1	1	0.4	25	22	35	30	19	.213	.264	8	2	C-78
1915	53	137	26	2	0	0	0.0	12	5	25	12	3	.190	.204	0	0	C-53
1919 PIT N	17	42	4	1	0	0	0.0	0	0	5	6	1	.095	.119	2	1	C-15
9 yrs.	644	1841	427	48	13	3	0.2	174	151	181	89	63	.232	.277	23	5	C-614, 1B-5, OF-1

Jerry Sweeney

SWEENEY, JEREMIAH H.   5'9½"   157 lbs.
B. 1860, Boston, Mass.   D. Aug. 25, 1891, Boston, Mass.

	G	AB	H	2B	3B	HR	HR %	R	RBI	BB	SO	SB	BA	SA	AB	H	G by POS
1884 KC U	31	129	34	3	0	0	0.0	16		4			.264	.287	0	0	1B-31

Pete Sweeney

SWEENEY, PETER JAY   BR TR
B. Dec. 31, 1863, Calif.   D. Aug. 22, 1901, San Francisco, Calif.

	G	AB	H	2B	3B	HR	HR %	R	RBI	BB	SO	SB	BA	SA	AB	H	G by POS
1888 WAS N	11	44	8	0	1	0	0.0	3	5	0	4	0	.182	.227	0	0	3B-8, OF-3
1889 2 teams	WAS N (49G – .228)				STL AA	(9G – .368)											
" total	58	231	58	9	3	1	0.4	21	31	12	31	10	.251	.329	0	0	3B-55, OF-2, 2B-1
1890 3 teams	STL AA (49G – .179)				LOU AA (2G – .143)			PHI AA (14G – .163)									
" total	65	246	43	5	3	0	0.0	29		25		9	.175	.220	0	0	2B-32, 3B-23, OF-6, 1B-3, SS-2
3 yrs.	134	521	109	14	7	1	0.2	53	36	37	35	19	.209	.269	0	0	3B-86, 2B-33, OF-11, 1B-3, SS-2

	G	AB	H	2B	3B	HR	HR %	R	RBI	BB	SO	SB	BA	SA	Pinch Hit AB	H	G by POS

Rooney Sweeney

SWEENEY, JOHN J.
B. 1860   D. June 1, 1889, New York, N. Y.   5'8"   155 lbs.

	G	AB	H	2B	3B	HR	HR %	R	RBI	BB	SO	SB	BA	SA	PH AB	PH H	G by POS
1883 BAL AA	25	101	21	5	2	0	0.0	13		4			.208	.297	0	0	C-23, OF-3
1884 BAL U	48	186	42	7	1	0	0.0	37		15			.226	.274	0	0	C-33, OF-16, 3B-1
1885 STL N	3	11	1	0	0	0	0.0	1	0	0		4	.091	.091	0	0	OF-2, C-1
3 yrs.	76	298	64	12	3	0	0.0	51		19		4	.215	.275	0	0	C-57, OF-21, 3B-1

Rick Sweet

SWEET, RICHARD JOE
B. Sept. 7, 1952, Longview, Wash.   BB   TR   6'1"   200 lbs.

	G	AB	H	2B	3B	HR	HR %	R	RBI	BB	SO	SB	BA	SA	PH AB	PH H	G by POS
1978 SD N	88	226	50	8	0	1	0.4	15	11	27	22	1	.221	.270	12	0	C-76
1982 2 teams	NY	N (3G – .333)			SEA	A	(88G – .256)										
" total	91	261	67	6	1	4	1.5	29	24	20	25	3	.257	.333	21	2	C-83
1983 SEA A	93	249	55	9	0	1	0.4	18	22	13	26	2	.221	.269	20	8	C-85
3 yrs.	272	736	172	23	1	6	0.8	62	57	60	73	6	.234	.292	53	10	C-244

Sweigert

SWEIGERT,
Deceased.

	G	AB	H	2B	3B	HR	HR %	R	RBI	BB	SO	SB	BA	SA	PH AB	PH H	G by POS
1890 PHI AA	1	1	0	0	0	0	0.0	0		1		1	.000	.000	0	0	OF-1

Augie Swentor

SWENTOR, AUGUST WILLIAM
B. Nov. 21, 1899, Seymour, Conn.   D. Nov. 10, 1969, Waterbury, Conn.   BR   TR   6'   185 lbs.

	G	AB	H	2B	3B	HR	HR %	R	RBI	BB	SO	SB	BA	SA	PH AB	PH H	G by POS
1922 CHI A	1	1	0	0	0	0	0.0	0	0	0	1	0	.000	.000	0	0	C-1

Pop Swett

SWETT, WILLIAM E.
B. Apr. 16, 1870, San Francisco, Calif.   D. Nov. 22, 1934, San Francisco, Calif.

	G	AB	H	2B	3B	HR	HR %	R	RBI	BB	SO	SB	BA	SA	PH AB	PH H	G by POS
1890 BOS P	37	94	18	4	3	1	1.1	16	12	16	26	4	.191	.330	0	0	C-34, OF-3

Bob Swift

SWIFT, ROBERT VIRGIL
B. Mar. 6, 1915, Salina, Kans.   D. Oct. 17, 1966, Detroit, Mich.   BR   TR   5'11½"   180 lbs.
Manager 1966.

	G	AB	H	2B	3B	HR	HR %	R	RBI	BB	SO	SB	BA	SA	PH AB	PH H	G by POS
1940 STL A	130	398	97	20	1	0	0.0	37	39	28	39	1	.244	.299	2	0	C-128
1941	63	170	44	7	0	0	0.0	13	21	22	11	2	.259	.300	5	1	C-58
1942 2 teams	STL	A (29G – .197)			PHI	A	(60G – .229)										
" total	89	268	59	7	0	1	0.4	12	23	16	22	1	.220	.257	1	0	C-88
1943 PHI A	77	224	43	5	1	1	0.4	16	11	35	16	0	.192	.237	0	0	C-77
1944 DET A	80	247	63	11	1	1	0.4	15	19	27	27	2	.255	.320	4	1	C-76
1945	95	279	65	5	0	0	0.0	19	24	25	22	1	.233	.251	1	0	C-94
1946	42	107	25	2	0	2	1.9	13	10	14	7	0	.234	.308	0	0	C-42
1947	97	279	70	11	0	1	0.4	23	21	33	16	2	.251	.301	1	0	C-97
1948	113	292	65	6	0	4	1.4	23	33	51	29	1	.223	.284	1	0	C-112
1949	74	189	45	6	0	2	1.1	16	18	26	20	0	.238	.302	6	1	C-69
1950	67	132	30	4	0	2	1.5	14	9	25	6	0	.227	.303	1	0	C-66
1951	44	104	20	0	0	0	0.0	8	5	12	10	0	.192	.192	1	0	C-43
1952	28	58	8	1	0	0	0.0	3	4	7	7	0	.138	.155	1	0	C-28
1953	2	3	1	1	0	0	0.0	0	1	2	1	0	.333	.667	1	0	C-2
14 yrs.	1001	2750	635	86	3	14	0.5	212	238	323	233	10	.231	.280	23	3	C-980

WORLD SERIES

	G	AB	H	2B	3B	HR	HR %	R	RBI	BB	SO	SB	BA	SA	PH AB	PH H	G by POS
1945 DET A	3	4	1	0	0	0	0.0	1	0	2	0	0	.250	.250	0	0	C-3

Charlie Swindell

SWINDELL, CHARLES J.
B. Oct. 26, 1878, Rockford, Ill.   D. July 22, 1940, Portland, Ore.   TR   5'11½"   180 lbs.

	G	AB	H	2B	3B	HR	HR %	R	RBI	BB	SO	SB	BA	SA	PH AB	PH H	G by POS
1904 STL N	3	8	1	0	0	0	0.0	0		0		0	.125	.125	0	0	C-3

Steve Swisher

SWISHER, STEVEN EUGENE
B. Aug. 9, 1951, Parkersburg, W. Va.   BR   TR   6'2"   205 lbs.

	G	AB	H	2B	3B	HR	HR %	R	RBI	BB	SO	SB	BA	SA	PH AB	PH H	G by POS
1974 CHI N	90	280	60	5	0	5	1.8	21	27	37	63	0	.214	.286	0	0	C-90
1975	93	254	54	16	2	1	0.4	20	22	30	57	1	.213	.303	0	0	C-93
1976	109	377	89	13	5	5	1.3	25	42	20	82	2	.236	.326	4	1	C-107
1977	74	205	39	7	0	5	2.4	21	15	9	47	0	.190	.298	4	1	C-72
1978 STL N	45	115	32	5	1	1	0.9	11	10	8	14	1	.278	.365	3	1	C-42
1979	38	73	11	1	1	1	1.4	4	3	6	17	0	.151	.233	5	0	C-33
1980	18	24	6	1	0	0	0.0	2	2	1	7	0	.250	.292	9	2	C-8
1981 SD N	16	28	4	0	0	0	0.0	2	0	2	11	0	.143	.143	7	1	C-10
1982	26	58	10	1	0	2	3.4	2	3	5	24	0	.172	.293	0	0	C-26
9 yrs.	509	1414	305	49	7	20	1.4	108	124	118	322	4	.216	.303	32	6	C-481

Ron Swoboda

SWOBODA, RONALD ALAN (Rocky)
B. June 30, 1944, Baltimore, Md.   BR   TR   6'2"   195 lbs.

	G	AB	H	2B	3B	HR	HR %	R	RBI	BB	SO	SB	BA	SA	PH AB	PH H	G by POS
1965 NY N	135	399	91	15	3	19	4.8	52	50	33	102	2	.228	.424	26	7	OF-112
1966	112	342	76	9	4	8	2.3	34	50	31	76	4	.222	.342	19	8	OF-97
1967	134	449	126	17	3	13	2.9	47	53	41	96	3	.281	.419	9	2	OF-108, 1B-20
1968	132	450	109	14	6	11	2.4	46	59	52	113	8	.242	.373	9	4	OF-125
1969	109	327	77	10	2	9	2.8	38	52	43	90	1	.235	.361	9	2	OF-97
1970	115	245	57	8	4	9	3.7	29	40	40	72	2	.233	.392	20	5	OF-100
1971 2 teams	MON	N (39G – .253)			NY	A	(54G – .261)										
" total	93	213	55	6	4	2	0.9	24	26	38	51	0	.258	.352	29	4	OF-73
1972 NY A	63	113	28	8	0	1	0.9	9	12	17	29	0	.248	.345	26	4	OF-35, 1B-2
1973	35	43	5	0	0	1	2.3	6	2	4	18	0	.116	.186	1	1	OF-20, DH-4
9 yrs.	928	2581	624	87	24	73	2.8	285	344	299	647	20	.242	.379	148	37	OF-767, 1B-22, DH-4

WORLD SERIES

	G	AB	H	2B	3B	HR	HR %	R	RBI	BB	SO	SB	BA	SA	PH AB	PH H	G by POS
1969 NY N	4	15	6	1	0	0	0.0	1	1	1	3	0	.400	.467	0	0	OF-4

	G	AB	H	2B	3B	HR	HR %	R	RBI	BB	SO	SB	BA	SA	Pinch Hit AB	Pinch Hit H	G by POS

Jose Tartabull continued

	G	AB	H	2B	3B	HR	HR %	R	RBI	BB	SO	SB	BA	SA	AB	H	G by POS
1963	79	242	58	8	5	1	0.4	27	19	17	17	16	.240	.326	6	1	OF-71
1964	104	100	20	2	0	0	0.0	9	3	5	12	4	.200	.220	41	5	OF-59
1965	68	218	68	11	4	1	0.5	28	19	18	20	11	.312	.413	13	7	OF-54
1966 2 teams	KC	A	(37G –	.236)		BOS	A	(68G –	.277)								
" total	105	322	84	9	7	0	0.0	41	15	17	24	19	.261	.332	24	3	OF-79
1967 BOS A	115	247	55	1	2	0	0.0	36	10	23	26	6	.223	.243	32	9	OF-83
1968	72	139	39	6	0	0	0.0	24	6	6	5	2	.281	.324	30	8	OF-43
1969 OAK A	75	266	71	11	1	0	0.0	28	11	9	11	3	.267	.316	11	2	OF-63
1970	24	13	3	2	0	0	0.0	5	2	0	2	1	.231	.385	7	0	OF-6
9 yrs.	749	1857	484	56	24	2	0.1	247	107	115	136	81	.261	.320	183	40	OF-543

WORLD SERIES

	G	AB	H	2B	3B	HR	HR %	R	RBI	BB	SO	SB	BA	SA	AB	H	G by POS
1967 BOS A	7	13	2	0	0	0	0.0	1	0	1	2	0	.154	.154	1	0	OF-6

Willie Tasby

TASBY, WILLIE — BR TR 5'11" 170 lbs.
B. Jan. 8, 1933, Shreveport, La.

	G	AB	H	2B	3B	HR	HR %	R	RBI	BB	SO	SB	BA	SA	AB	H	G by POS
1958 BAL A	18	50	10	3	0	1	2.0	6	1	7	15	1	.200	.320†	1	0	OF-16
1959	142	505	126	16	5	13	2.6	69	48	34	80	3	.250	.378	4	1	OF-137
1960 2 teams	BAL	A	(39G –	.212)		BOS	A	(105G –	.281)								
" total	144	470	126	19	2	7	1.5	77	40	60	66	4	.268	.362	7	3	OF-138
1961 WAS A	141	494	124	13	2	17	3.4	54	63	58	94	4	.251	.389	0	0	OF-139
1962 2 teams	WAS	A	(11G –	.206)		CLE	A	(75G –	.241)								
" total	86	233	55	7	0	4	1.7	29	17	27	47	0	.236	.318	16	1	OF-76, 3B-1
1963 CLE A	52	116	26	3	1	4	3.4	11	5	15	25	0	.224	.371	14	0	OF-37, 2B-1
6 yrs.	583	1868	467	61	10	46	2.5	246	174	201	327	12	.250	.367	42	5	OF-543, 3B-1, 2B-1

Bennie Tate

TATE, HENRY BENNETT — BL TR 5'8" 165 lbs.
B. Dec. 3, 1901, Whitwell, Tenn.   D. Oct. 27, 1973, W. Frankfort, Ill.

	G	AB	H	2B	3B	HR	HR %	R	RBI	BB	SO	SB	BA	SA	AB	H	G by POS
1924 WAS A	21	43	13	2	0	0	0.0	2	7	1	2	0	.302	.349	6	3	C-14
1925	16	27	13	3	0	0	0.0	0	7	2	2	0	.481	.593	2	1	C-14
1926	59	142	38	5	2	1	0.7	17	13	15	1	0	.268	.352	9	2	C-45
1927	61	131	41	5	1	1	0.8	12	24	8	4	0	.313	.389	16	5	C-39
1928	57	122	30	6	0	0	0.0	10	15	10	4	0	.246	.295	25	9	C-30
1929	81	265	78	12	3	0	0.0	26	30	16	8	2	.294	.362	6	3	C-74
1930 2 teams	WAS	A	(14G –	.250)		CHI	A	(72G –	.317)								
" total	86	250	78	11	2	0	0.0	27	29	18	11	2	.312	.372	5	2	C-79
1931 CHI A	89	273	73	12	3	0	0.0	27	22	26	10	1	.267	.333	4	1	C-85
1932 2 teams	CHI	A	(4G –	.100)		BOS	A	(81G –	.245)								
" total	85	283	68	12	5	2	0.7	22	26	21	6	0	.240	.339	5	3	C-80
1934 CHI N	11	24	3	0	0	0	0.0	1	0	1	3	0	.125	.125	3	0	C-8
10 yrs.	566	1560	435	68	16	4	0.3	144	173	118	51	5	.279	.351	81	29	C-468

WORLD SERIES

	G	AB	H	2B	3B	HR	HR %	R	RBI	BB	SO	SB	BA	SA	AB	H	G by POS
1924 WAS A	3	0	0	0	0	0	–	0	1	3	0	0	–	–	0	0	

Hugh Tate

TATE, HUGH HENRY — BR TR 5'11" 190 lbs.
B. May 19, 1880, Everett, Pa.   D. Aug. 7, 1956, Greenville, Pa.

	G	AB	H	2B	3B	HR	HR %	R	RBI	BB	SO	SB	BA	SA	AB	H	G by POS
1905 WAS A	4	10	3	0	1	0	0.0	1	2	0		1	.300	.500	1	0	OF-3

Lee Tate

TATE, LEE WILLIE (Skeeter) — BR TR 5'10" 165 lbs.
B. Mar. 18, 1932, Black Rock, Ark.

	G	AB	H	2B	3B	HR	HR %	R	RBI	BB	SO	SB	BA	SA	AB	H	G by POS
1958 STL N	10	35	7	2	0	0	0.0	4	1	4	3	0	.200	.257	1	1	SS-9
1959	41	50	7	1	1	1	2.0	5	4	5	7	0	.140	.260	0	0	SS-39, 3B-2, 2B-2
2 yrs.	51	85	14	3	1	1	1.2	9	5	9	10	0	.165	.259	1	1	SS-48, 3B-2, 2B-2

Pop Tate

TATE, EDWARD CHRISTOPHER (Dimples) — BR TL
B. Dec. 22, 1861, Richmond, Va.   D. June 25, 1932, Richmond, Va.

	G	AB	H	2B	3B	HR	HR %	R	RBI	BB	SO	SB	BA	SA	AB	H	G by POS
1885 BOS N	4	13	2	0	0	0	0.0	1	2	1	3		.154	.154	0	0	C-4
1886	31	106	24	3	1	0	0.0	13	3	7	17		.226	.274	0	0	C-31
1887	60	231	60	5	3	0	0.0	34	27	8	9	7	.260	.307	0	0	C-53, OF-8
1888	41	148	34	7	1	1	0.7	18	6	8	7	3	.230	.311	0	0	C-41, OF-1
1889 BAL AA	72	253	46	6	3	1	0.4	28	27	13	37	4	.182	.241	0	0	C-62, 1B-10
1890 B-B AA	19	71	13	1	1	0	0.0	7		4		3	.183	.225	0	0	C-11, 1B-8
6 yrs.	227	822	179	22	9	2	0.2	101	65	41	73	17	.218	.274	0	0	C-202, 1B-18, OF-9

Jarvis Tatum

TATUM, JARVIS — BR TR 6' 185 lbs.
B. Oct. 11, 1946, Fresno, Calif.

	G	AB	H	2B	3B	HR	HR %	R	RBI	BB	SO	SB	BA	SA	AB	H	G by POS
1968 CAL A	17	51	9	1	0	0	0.0	7	2	0	9	0	.176	.196	3	0	OF-11
1969	10	22	7	0	0	0	0.0	2	0	0	6	0	.318	.318	4	0	OF-5
1970	75	181	43	7	0	0	0.0	28	6	17	35	1	.238	.276	13	1	OF-58
3 yrs.	102	254	59	8	0	0	0.0	37	8	17	50	1	.232	.264	20	1	OF-74

Tommy Tatum

TATUM, V. T. — BR TR 6' 185 lbs.
B. July 16, 1919, Boyd, Tex.

	G	AB	H	2B	3B	HR	HR %	R	RBI	BB	SO	SB	BA	SA	AB	H	G by POS
1941 BKN N	8	12	2	1	0	0	0.0	1	1	1	3	0	.167	.250	4	0	OF-4
1947 2 teams	BKN	N	(4G –	.000)		CIN	N	(69G –	.273)								
" total	73	182	48	5	2	1	0.5	19	16	16	17	7	.264	.330	7	0	OF-52, 2B-1
2 yrs.	81	194	50	6	2	1	0.5	20	17	17	20	7	.258	.325	11	0	OF-56, 2B-1

Fred Tauby

TAUBY, FRED JOSEPH — BR TR 5'9½" 168 lbs.
Born Fred Joseph Taubensee.
B. Mar. 27, 1906, Canton, Ohio   D. Nov. 23, 1955, Concordia, Calif.

	G	AB	H	2B	3B	HR	HR %	R	RBI	BB	SO	SB	BA	SA	AB	H	G by POS
1935 CHI A	13	32	4	1	0	0	0.0	5	2	2	3	0	.125	.156	4	0	OF-7
1937 PHI N	11	20	0	0	0	0	0.0	2	3	0	5	1	.000	.000	3	0	OF-7
2 yrs.	24	52	4	1	0	0	0.0	7	5	2	8	1	.077	.096	7	0	OF-14

	G	AB	H	2B	3B	HR	HR %	R	RBI	BB	SO	SB	BA	SA	Pinch Hit AB	Pinch Hit H	G by POS

Don Taussig

TAUSSIG, DONALD FRANKLIN
B. Feb. 19, 1932, New York, N. Y.
BR TR 6' 190 lbs.

	G	AB	H	2B	3B	HR	HR %	R	RBI	BB	SO	SB	BA	SA	AB	H	G by POS
1958 SF N	39	50	10	0	0	1	2.0	10	4	3	8	0	.200	.260	3	1	OF-36
1961 STL N	98	188	54	14	5	2	1.1	27	25	16	34	2	.287	.447	8	2	OF-87
1962 HOU N	16	25	5	0	0	1	4.0	1	1	2	11	0	.200	.320	11	3	OF-4
3 yrs.	153	263	69	14	5	4	1.5	38	30	21	53	2	.262	.399	22	6	OF-127

Jackie Tavener

TAVENER, JOHN ADAM
B. Dec. 27, 1897, Celina, Ohio   D. Sept. 14, 1969, Fort Worth, Tex.
BL TR 5'5" 138 lbs.

	G	AB	H	2B	3B	HR	HR %	R	RBI	BB	SO	SB	BA	SA	AB	H	G by POS
1921 DET A	2	4	0	0	0	0	0.0	0	0	0	1	0	.000	.000	0	0	SS-2
1925	134	453	111	11	11	0	0.0	45	47	39	60	5	.245	.318	0	0	SS-134
1926	156	532	141	22	14	1	0.2	65	58	52	53	8	.265	.365	0	0	SS-156
1927	116	419	115	22	9	5	1.2	60	59	36	38	20	.274	.406	1	0	SS-114
1928	132	473	123	24	15	5	1.1	59	52	33	51	13	.260	.406	0	0	SS-131
1929 CLE A	92	250	53	9	4	2	0.8	25	27	26	28	1	.212	.304	0	0	SS-89
6 yrs.	632	2131	543	88	53	13	0.6	254	243	186	231	47	.255	.364	1	0	SS-626

Alex Taveras

TAVERAS, ALEJANDRO
Also known as Alejandro Betances.
B. Oct. 9, 1955, Santiago, Dominican Republic
BR TR 5'10" 155 lbs.

	G	AB	H	2B	3B	HR	HR %	R	RBI	BB	SO	SB	BA	SA	AB	H	G by POS
1976 HOU N	14	46	10	0	0	0	0.0	3	2	2	1	1	.217	.217	0	0	SS-7, 2B-7
1982 LA N	11	3	1	1	0	0	0.0	1	2	0	1	0	.333	.667	0	0	3B-4, 2B-4, SS-2
1983	10	4	0	0	0	0	0.0	0	0	0	1	0	.000	.000	0	0	SS-3, 2B-2, 3B-1
3 yrs.	35	53	11	1	0	0	0.0	4	4	2	3	1	.208	.226	0	0	SS-12, 2B-13, 3B-5

Frank Taveras

TAVERAS, FRANKLIN FABIAN
B. Dec. 24, 1950, Villa Vasquez, Dominican Republic
BR TR 6' 155 lbs.

	G	AB	H	2B	3B	HR	HR %	R	RBI	BB	SO	SB	BA	SA	AB	H	G by POS
1971 PIT N	1	0	0	0	0	0	–	0	0	0	0	0	–	–	0	0	SS-4
1972	4	3	0	0	0	0	0.0	0	0	1	1	0	.000	.000	0	0	SS-124
1974	126	333	82	4	2	0	0.0	33	26	25	41	13	.246	.270	0	0	SS-124
1975	134	378	80	9	4	0	0.0	44	23	37	42	17	.212	.257	0	0	SS-132
1976	144	519	134	8	6	0	0.0	76	24	44	79	58	.258	.297	1	0	SS-141
1977	147	544	137	20	10	1	0.2	72	29	38	71	70	.252	.331	0	0	SS-146
1978	157	654	182	31	9	0	0.0	81	38	29	60	46	.278	.353	0	0	SS-157
1979 2 teams	PIT N (1G – .244)					NY N (153G – .263)											
" total	164	680	178	29	9	1	0.1	93	34	33	74	44	.262	.335	1	1	SS-164
1980 NY N	141	562	157	27	0	0	0.0	65	25	23	64	32	.279	.327	5	0	SS-140
1981	84	283	65	11	3	0	0.0	30	11	12	36	16	.230	.290	4	1	SS-79
1982 MON N	48	87	14	5	1	0	0.0	9	4	7	6	4	.161	.241	2	1	SS-26, 2B-19
11 yrs.	1150	4043	1029	144	44	2	0.0	503	214	249	474	300	.255	.313	13	3	SS-1113, 2B-19

LEAGUE CHAMPIONSHIP SERIES

	G	AB	H	2B	3B	HR	HR %	R	RBI	BB	SO	SB	BA	SA	AB	H	G by POS
1974 PIT N	2	2	0	0	0	0	0.0	0	0	0	0	1	.000	.000	0	0	SS-2
1975	3	7	1	0	0	0	0.0	0	1	1	2	0	.143	.143	0	0	SS-3
2 yrs.	5	9	1	0	0	0	0.0	0	1	1	2	1	.111	.111	0	0	SS-5

Bennie Taylor

TAYLOR, BENJAMIN EUGENE
B. Sept. 30, 1927, Metropolis, Ill.
BL TL 6' 195 lbs.

	G	AB	H	2B	3B	HR	HR %	R	RBI	BB	SO	SB	BA	SA	AB	H	G by POS
1951 STL A	33	93	24	2	1	3	3.2	14	6	9	22	1	.258	.398	7	2	1B-25
1952 DET A	7	18	3	0	0	0	0.0	0	0	0	5	0	.167	.167	3	0	1B-4
1955 MIL N	12	10	1	0	0	0	0.0	2	0	2	4	0	.100	.100	9	1	1B-1
3 yrs.	52	121	28	2	1	3	2.5	16	6	11	31	1	.231	.339	19	3	1B-30

Bill Taylor

TAYLOR, JOSEPH CEPHUS (Cash)
B. Mar. 2, 1926, Chapman, Ala.
BL TL 6'1" 185 lbs.

	G	AB	H	2B	3B	HR	HR %	R	RBI	BB	SO	SB	BA	SA	AB	H	G by POS
1954 NY N	55	65	12	1	0	2	3.1	4	10	3	15	0	.185	.292	42	9	OF-9
1955	65	64	17	4	0	4	6.3	9	12	1	16	0	.266	.516	60	15	OF-2
1956	1	4	1	1	0	0	0.0	0	0	0	1	0	.250	.500	0	0	OF-1
1957 2 teams	NY N (11G – .000)					DET A (9G – .348)											
" total	20	32	8	2	0	1	3.1	4	3	1	5	0	.250	.406	13	2	OF-5
1958 DET A	8	8	3	0	0	0	0.0	0	1	0	2	0	.375	.375	6	3	OF-1
5 yrs.	149	173	41	8	0	7	4.0	17	26	5	39	0	.237	.405	121	29	OF-18

Billy Taylor

TAYLOR, WILLIAM HENRY (Bollicky)
B. 1855, Washington, D. C.   D. May 14, 1900, Jacksonville, Fla.
BR TR 5'11½" 204 lbs.

	G	AB	H	2B	3B	HR	HR %	R	RBI	BB	SO	SB	BA	SA	AB	H	G by POS
1881 3 teams	WOR N (6G – .107)					DET N (1G – .500)			CLE N (24G – .243)								
" total	31	135	30	4	0	0	0.0	9	15	0	10		.222	.252	0	0	OF-28, 3B-2, P-2
1882 PIT AA	70	299	84	16	12	4	1.3	40		7			.281	.455	0	0	C-27, 1B-23, 3B-14, OF-8, P-1
1883	83	369	96	13	7	2	0.5	43		9			.260	.350	0	0	OF-37, C-33, P-19, 1B-9
1884 2 teams	STL U (43G – .366)					PHI AA (30G – .252)											
" total	73	297	96	29	3	3	1.0	52		9			.323	.471	0	0	P-63, 1B-10, OF-4
1885 PHI AA	6	21	4	0	0	0	0.0	0		0			.190	.190	0	0	P-6
1886 BAL AA	10	39	12	0	1	0	0.0	4		1			.308	.359	0	0	P-8, 1B-1, C-1
1887 PHI AA	1	4	1	0	0	0	0.0	0		0		0	.250	.250	0	0	P-1
7 yrs.	274	1164	323	62	23	9	0.8	148	15	26		10	0	.277	.393	0	0	P-100, OF-77, C-61, 1B-43, 3B-16

Bob Taylor

TAYLOR, ROBERT LEE
B. Mar. 20, 1944, Leland, Miss.
BL TR 5'9" 170 lbs.

	G	AB	H	2B	3B	HR	HR %	R	RBI	BB	SO	SB	BA	SA	AB	H	G by POS
1970 SF N	63	84	16	0	0	2	2.4	12	10	12	13	0	.190	.262	28	6	OF-26, C-1

	G	AB	H	2B	3B	HR	HR %	R	RBI	BB	SO	SB	BA	SA	Pinch Hit AB	Pinch Hit H	G by POS

Zack Taylor continued

	G	AB	H	2B	3B	HR	HR %	R	RBI	BB	SO	SB	BA	SA	PH AB	PH H	G by POS
1923	96	337	97	11	6	0	0.0	29	46	9	13	2	.288	.356	11	4	C-84
1924	99	345	100	9	4	1	0.3	36	39	14	14	0	.290	.348	6	2	C-93
1925	109	352	109	16	4	3	0.9	33	44	17	19	0	.310	.403	12	2	C-96
1926 BOS N	125	432	110	22	3	0	0.0	36	42	28	27	1	.255	.319	1	0	C-123
1927 2 teams	BOS	N	(30G –	.240)		NY	N	(83G –	.233)								
" total	113	354	83	9	4	1	0.3	26	35	25	25	2	.234	.291	5	1	C-108
1928 BOS N	125	399	100	15	1	2	0.5	36	30	33	29	2	.251	.308	1	0	C-124
1929 2 teams	BOS	N	(34G –	.248)		CHI	N	(64G –	.274)								
" total	98	316	84	23	3	1	0.3	37	41	26	27	0	.266	.367	3	0	C-95
1930 CHI N	32	95	22	2	1	1	1.1	12	11	2	12	0	.232	.305	2	0	C-28
1931	8	4	1	0	0	0	0.0	0	0	2	1	0	.250	.250	1	0	C-5
1932	21	30	6	1	0	0	0.0	0	3	1	4	0	.200	.233	7	1	C-14
1933	16	11	0	0	0	0	0.0	0	0	0	1	0	.000	.000	4	0	C-12
1934 NY A	4	7	1	0	0	0	0.0	0	0	0	1	0	.143	.143	1	0	C-3
1935 BKN N	26	54	7	3	0	0	0.0	6	5	2	8	0	.130	.185	0	0	C-26
16 yrs.	918	2865	748	113	28	9	0.3	258	311	161	192	9	.261	.329	55	10	C-857

WORLD SERIES

	G	AB	H	2B	3B	HR	HR %	R	RBI	BB	SO	SB	BA	SA	PH AB	PH H	G by POS
1929 CHI N	5	17	3	0	0	0	0.0	0	3	0	3	0	.176	.176	0	0	C-5

Birdie Tebbetts

TEBBETTS, GEORGE ROBERT   BR TR 5'11½" 170 lbs.
B. Nov. 10, 1912, Burlington, Vt.
Manager 1954-58, 1961-66.

	G	AB	H	2B	3B	HR	HR %	R	RBI	BB	SO	SB	BA	SA	PH AB	PH H	G by POS
1936 DET A	10	33	10	1	2	1	3.0	7	4	5	3	0	.303	.545	0	0	C-10
1937	50	162	31	4	3	2	1.2	15	16	10	13	0	.191	.290	2	0	C-48
1938	53	143	42	6	2	1	0.7	16	25	12	13	1	.294	.385	9	3	C-53
1939	106	341	89	22	2	4	1.2	37	53	25	20	2	.261	.372	6	1	C-100
1940	111	379	112	24	4	4	1.1	46	46	35	14	4	.296	.412	2	0	C-107
1941	110	359	102	19	4	2	0.6	28	47	38	29	1	.284	.376	12	3	C-98
1942	99	308	76	11	0	1	0.3	24	27	39	17	4	.247	.292	2	2	C-97
1946	87	280	68	11	2	1	0.4	20	34	28	23	1	.243	.307	0	0	C-87
1947 2 teams	DET	A	(20G –	.094)		BOS	A	(90G –	.299)								
" total	110	344	92	11	0	1	0.3	23	30	24	33	2	.267	.308	1	0	C-109
1948 BOS A	128	446	125	26	2	5	1.1	54	68	62	32	5	.280	.381	1	0	C-126
1949	122	404	109	14	0	5	1.2	42	48	62	22	8	.270	.342	4	1	C-118
1950	79	268	83	10	1	8	3.0	33	45	29	26	1	.310	.444	3	1	C-74
1951 CLE A	55	137	36	6	0	2	1.5	8	18	8	7	0	.263	.350	11	5	C-44
1952	42	101	25	4	0	1	1.0	4	8	12	9	0	.248	.317	5	2	C-37
14 yrs.	1162	3705	1000	169	22	38	1.0	357	469	389	261	29	.270	.358	58	18	C-1108

WORLD SERIES

	G	AB	H	2B	3B	HR	HR %	R	RBI	BB	SO	SB	BA	SA	PH AB	PH H	G by POS
1940 DET A	4	11	0	0	0	0	0.0	0	0	0	0	0	.000	.000	1	0	C-3

Patsy Tebeau

TEBEAU, OLIVER WENDELL   BR TR
Brother of White Wings Tebeau.
B. Dec. 5, 1864, St. Louis, Mo.   D. May 15, 1918, St. Louis, Mo.
Manager 1890-1900.

	G	AB	H	2B	3B	HR	HR %	R	RBI	BB	SO	SB	BA	SA	PH AB	PH H	G by POS
1887 CHI N	20	68	11	3	0	0	0.0	8	10	4	4	8	.162	.206	0	0	3B-20
1889 CLE N	136	521	147	20	6	8	1.5	72	76	37	41	26	.282	.390	0	0	3B-136
1890 CLE P	110	450	135	26	6	5	1.1	86	74	34	20	14	.300	.418	0	0	3B-110
1891 CLE N	61	249	65	8	3	1	0.4	38	41	16	13	12	.261	.329	0	0	3B-61, OF-1
1892	86	340	83	13	3	2	0.6	47	49	23	34	6	.244	.318	0	0	3B-74, 2B-5, 1B-4, SS-3
1893	116	486	160	32	8	2	0.4	90	102	32	11	19	.329	.440	0	0	1B-57, 3B-56, 2B-3
1894	125	523	158	23	7	3	0.6	82	89	35	35	30	.302	.390	0	0	1B-115, 2B-10, 3B-2, SS-1
1895	63	264	84	13	2	2	0.8	50	52	16	18	8	.318	.405	0	0	1B-49, 2B-9, 3B-6
1896	132	543	146	22	6	2	0.4	56	94	21	22	20	.269	.343	0	0	1B-122, 3B-7, 2B-5, SS-1, P-1
1897	109	412	110	15	9	0	0.0	62	59	30		11	.267	.347	0	0	1B-18, 3B-2, SS-1
1898	131	477	123	11	4	1	0.2	53	63	53		5	.258	.304	0	0	1B-91, 2B-34, SS-7, 3B-3
1899 STL N	77	281	69	10	3	1	0.4	27	26	18		5	.246	.313	0	0	1B-65, SS-11, 3B-1, 2B-1
1900	1	4	0	0	0	0	0.0	0	0	0		0	.000	.000	0	0	SS-1
13 yrs.	1167	4618	1291	196	57	27	0.6	671	735	319	198	164	.280	.364	0	0	1B-595, 3B-478, 2B-85, SS-25, OF-1, P-1

Pussy Tebeau

TEBEAU, CHARLES ALSTON   5'10" 175 lbs.
B. Feb. 22, 1870, Worcester, Mass.   D. Mar. 25, 1950, Pittsfield, Mass.

	G	AB	H	2B	3B	HR	HR %	R	RBI	BB	SO	SB	BA	SA	PH AB	PH H	G by POS
1895 CLE N	2	6	3	0	0	0	0.0	3	1	2	1	1	.500	.500	0	0	OF-2

White Wings Tebeau

TEBEAU, GEORGE E. (Hard Call)   BR TR 5'9" 175 lbs.
Brother of Patsy Tebeau.
B. Dec. 26, 1862, St. Louis, Mo.   D. Feb. 4, 1923, Denver, Colo.

	G	AB	H	2B	3B	HR	HR %	R	RBI	BB	SO	SB	BA	SA	PH AB	PH H	G by POS
1887 CIN AA	85	318	94	12	5	4	1.3	57		31		37	.296	.403	0	0	OF-84, P-1
1888	121	411	94	12	12	3	0.7	72	51	61		37	.229	.338	0	0	OF-121
1889	135	496	125	21	11	7	1.4	110	70	69	62	61	.252	.381	0	0	OF-134, 1B-1
1890 TOL AA	94	381	102	16	10	1	0.3	71		51		55	.268	.370	0	0	OF-94, P-1
1894 2 teams	WAS	N	(61G –	.225)		CLE	N	(40G –	.313)								
" total	101	372	97	19	10	0	0.0	73	53	62	38	26	.261	.366	0	0	OF-88, 1B-12, 3B-1
1895 CLE N	91	337	110	16	6	0	0.0	57	68	50	28	12	.326	.409	0	0	OF-49, 1B-42
6 yrs.	627	2315	622	96	54	15	0.6	440	241	324	128	228	.269	.376	0	0	OF-570, 1B-55, P-2, 3B-1

Dick Teed

TEED, RICHARD LEROY   BB TR 5'11" 180 lbs.
B. Mar. 8, 1926, Springfield, Mass.

	G	AB	H	2B	3B	HR	HR %	R	RBI	BB	SO	SB	BA	SA	PH AB	PH H	G by POS
1953 BKN N	1	1	0	0	0	0	0.0	0	0	0	1	0	.000	.000	1	0	

	G	AB	H	2B	3B	HR	HR %	R	RBI	BB	SO	SB	BA	SA	Pinch Hit AB	Pinch Hit H	G by POS

Johnny Temple

TEMPLE, JOHN ELLIS
B. Aug. 8, 1928, Lexington, N. C.

BR TR 5'11" 175 lbs.

	G	AB	H	2B	3B	HR	HR %	R	RBI	BB	SO	SB	BA	SA	PH AB	PH H	G by POS
1952 CIN N	30	97	19	3	0	1	1.0	8	5	5	1	2	.196	.258	6	2	2B-22
1953	63	110	29	4	0	1	0.9	14	9	7	12	1	.264	.327	8	5	2B-44
1954	146	505	155	14	8	0	0.0	60	44	62	24	21	.307	.366	0	0	2B-144
1955	150	588	165	20	3	0	0.0	94	50	80	32	19	.281	.325	1	1	2B-149, SS-1
1956	154	632	180	18	3	2	0.3	88	41	58	40	14	.285	.332	0	0	2B-154, OF-1
1957	145	557	158	24	4	0	0.0	85	37	94	34	19	.284	.341	1	0	2B-145
1958	141	542	166	31	6	3	0.6	82	47	91	41	15	.306	.402	0	0	2B-141, 1B-1
1959	149	598	186	35	6	8	1.3	102	67	72	40	14	.311	.430	0	0	2B-149
1960 CLE A	98	381	102	13	1	2	0.5	50	19	32	20	11	.268	.323	4	3	2B-77, 3B-17
1961	129	518	143	22	3	3	0.6	73	30	61	36	9	.276	.347	0	0	2B-129
1962 2 teams	BAL A (78G – .263)					HOU N (31G – .263)											
" total	109	365	96	12	1	1	0.3	42	29	43	33	8	.263	.310	12	1	2B-97, 3B-1
1963 HOU N	100	322	85	12	1	1	0.3	22	17	41	24	7	.264	.317	9	2	2B-61, 3B-29
1964 CIN N	6	3	0	0	0	0	0.0	0	0	2	1	0	.000	.000	3	0	
13 yrs.	1420	5218	1484	208	36	22	0.4	720	395	648	338	140	.284	.351	44	14	2B-1312, 3B-47, OF-1, SS-1, 1B-1

Garry Templeton

TEMPLETON, GARRY LEWIS (Jump Steady)
B. Mar. 24, 1956, Lockey, Tex.

BB TR 5'11" 175 lbs.

	G	AB	H	2B	3B	HR	HR %	R	RBI	BB	SO	SB	BA	SA	PH AB	PH H	G by POS
1976 STL N	53	213	62	8	2	1	0.5	32	17	7	33	11	.291	.362	1	0	SS-53
1977	153	621	200	19	18	8	1.3	94	79	15	70	28	.322	.449	2	0	SS-151
1978	155	647	181	31	13	2	0.3	82	47	22	87	34	.280	.377	2	0	SS-155
1979	154	672	211	32	19	9	1.3	105	62	18	91	26	.314	.458	1	0	SS-150
1980	118	504	161	19	9	4	0.8	83	43	18	43	31	.319	.417	2	0	SS-115
1981	80	333	96	16	8	1	0.3	47	33	14	55	8	.288	.393	4	0	SS-76
1982 SD N	141	563	139	25	8	6	1.1	76	64	26	82	27	.247	.352	6	1	SS-136
1983	126	460	121	20	2	3	0.7	39	40	21	57	16	.263	.335	3	0	SS-123
1984	148	493	127	19	3	2	0.4	40	35	39	81	8	.258	.320	2	0	SS-146
9 yrs.	1128	4506	1298	189	82	36	0.8	598	420	180	599	189	.288	.390	23	1	SS-1105

LEAGUE CHAMPIONSHIP SERIES

	G	AB	H	2B	3B	HR	HR %	R	RBI	BB	SO	SB	BA	SA	PH AB	PH H	G by POS
1984 SD N	5	15	5	1	0	0	0.0	2	2	2	0	1	.333	.400	0	0	SS-5

WORLD SERIES

	G	AB	H	2B	3B	HR	HR %	R	RBI	BB	SO	SB	BA	SA	PH AB	PH H	G by POS
1984 SD N	5	19	6	1	0	0	0.0	1	0	0	3	0	.316	.368	0	0	SS-5

Gene Tenace

TENACE, FURY GENE
B. Oct. 10, 1946, Russellton, Pa.

BR TR 6' 190 lbs.

	G	AB	H	2B	3B	HR	HR %	R	RBI	BB	SO	SB	BA	SA	PH AB	PH H	G by POS
1969 OAK A	16	38	6	0	0	1	2.6	1	2	1	15	0	.158	.237	5	0	C-13
1970	38	105	32	6	0	7	6.7	19	20	23	30	0	.305	.562	7	2	C-30
1971	65	179	49	7	0	7	3.9	26	25	29	34	2	.274	.430	13	4	C-52, OF-1
1972	82	227	51	5	3	5	2.2	22	32	24	42	0	.225	.339	17	7	C-49, OF-9, 1B-7, 3B-2, 2B-2
1973	160	510	132	18	2	24	4.7	83	84	101	94	2	.259	.443	2	0	1B-134, C-33, DH-3, 2B-1
1974	158	484	102	17	1	26	5.4	71	73	110	105	2	.211	.411	0	0	1B-106, C-79, 2B-3
1975	158	498	127	17	0	29	5.8	83	87	106	127	7	.255	.464	0	0	C-125, 1B-68, DH-1
1976	128	417	104	19	1	22	5.3	64	66	81	91	5	.249	.458	3	0	1B-70, C-65, DH-2
1977 SD N	147	437	102	24	4	15	3.4	66	61	125	119	5	.233	.410	5	0	C-99, 1B-36, 3B-14
1978	142	401	90	18	4	16	4.0	60	61	101	98	6	.224	.409	7	1	1B-80, C-71, 3B-1
1979	151	463	122	16	4	20	4.3	61	67	105	106	2	.263	.445	7	2	C-94, 1B-72
1980	133	316	70	11	1	17	5.4	46	50	92	63	4	.222	.424	16	2	C-104, 1B-19
1981 STL N	58	129	30	7	0	5	3.9	26	22	38	26	0	.233	.403	12	3	C-38, 1B-7
1982	66	124	32	9	0	7	5.6	18	18	36	31	1	.258	.500	12	3	C-37, 1B-7
1983 PIT N	53	62	11	5	0	0	0.0	7	6	12	17	0	.177	.258	29	3	1B-19, C-3, OF-1
15 yrs.	1555	4390	1060	179	20	201	4.6	653	674	984	998	36	.241	.429	135	27	C-892, 1B-625, 3B-17, OF-11, DH-6, 2B-6

LEAGUE CHAMPIONSHIP SERIES

	G	AB	H	2B	3B	HR	HR %	R	RBI	BB	SO	SB	BA	SA	PH AB	PH H	G by POS
1971 OAK A	1	3	0	0	0	0	0.0	0	0	1	1	0	.000	.000	0	0	C-1
1972	5	17	1	0	0	0	0.0	1	1	3	5	0	.059	.059	0	0	C-5
1973	5	17	4	1	0	0	0.0	3	0	2	4	1	.235	.294	0	0	1B-5
1974	4	11	0	0	0	0	0.0	1	1	4	4	1	.000	.000	0	0	1B-4
1975	3	9	0	0	0	0	0.0	0	0	3	2	0	.000	.000	0	0	C-3
5 yrs.	18	57	5	1	0	0	0.0	5	2	13	16	2	.088	.105	0	0	1B-9, C-9

WORLD SERIES

	G	AB	H	2B	3B	HR	HR %	R	RBI	BB	SO	SB	BA	SA	PH AB	PH H	G by POS
1972 OAK A	7	23	8	1	0	4	17.4	5	9	2	4	0	.348	.913	0	0	C-6
1973	7	19	3	1	0	0	0.0	0	3	11	7	0	.158	.211	0	0	C-3
1974	5	9	2	0	0	0	0.0	0	0	3	4	0	.222	.222	0	0	1B-5
1982 STL N	5	6	0	0	0	0	0.0	0	0	1	2	0	.000	.000	4	0	DH-1
4 yrs.	24	57	13	2	0	4	7.0 9th	5	12	17	17	0	.228	.474	4	0	C-9, 1B-5, DH-1

Tom Tennant

TENNANT, THOMAS FRANCIS
B. July 3, 1882, Monroe, Wis. D. Feb. 15, 1955, San Carlos, Calif.

BL TL 5'11" 165 lbs.

	G	AB	H	2B	3B	HR	HR %	R	RBI	BB	SO	SB	BA	SA	PH AB	PH H	G by POS
1912 STL A	2	2	0	0	0	0	0.0	0	0		0		.000	.000	2	0	

Fred Tenney

TENNEY, FREDERICK CLAY
B. July 9, 1854, Marlboro, N. H. D. June 15, 1919, Fall River, Mass.

	G	AB	H	2B	3B	HR	HR %	R	RBI	BB	SO	SB	BA	SA	PH AB	PH H	G by POS
1884 3 teams	WAS U (32G – .235)					BOS U (4G – .118)				WIL U (1G – .000)							
" total	37	139	30	3	1	0	0.0	18	0	6	0	0	.216	.252	0	0	OF-27, 1B-6, P-5

Fred Tenney

TENNEY, FREDERICK CLAY
B. June 9, 1859, Georgetown, Mass. D. July 3, 1952, Boston, Mass.
Manager 1905-07, 1911.

BL TL 5'9" 155 lbs.

	G	AB	H	2B	3B	HR	HR %	R	RBI	BB	SO	SB	BA	SA	PH AB	PH H	G by POS
1894 BOS N	27	86	34	7	1	2	2.3	23	21	12	9	6	.395	.570	0	0	C-20, OF-6, 1B-1
1895	49	174	48	9	1	1	0.6	35	21	24	5	6	.276	.356	0	0	OF-28, C-21
1896	88	348	117	14	3	2	0.6	64	49	36	12	18	.336	.411	1	0	OF-60, C-27
1897	132	566	184	24	3	1	0.2	125	85	49		34	.325	.383	0	0	1B-128, OF-4

	G	AB	H	2B	3B	HR	HR %	R	RBI	BB	SO	SB	BA	SA	Pinch Hit AB	H	G by POS

Fred Tenney continued

	G	AB	H	2B	3B	HR	HR %	R	RBI	BB	SO	SB	BA	SA	AB	H	G by POS
1898	117	488	163	25	5	0	0.0	106	62	33		23	.334	.406	0	0	1B-117, C-1
1899	150	603	209	19	17	1	0.2	115	67	63		28	.347	.439	0	0	1B-150
1900	112	437	122	13	5	1	0.2	77	56	39		17	.279	.339	1	0	1B-111
1901	115	457	127	13	1	1	0.2	66	22	37		15	.278	.317	0	0	1B-113, C-2
1902	134	489	154	18	3	2	0.4	88	30	73		21	.315	.376	0	0	1B-134
1903	122	447	140	22	3	3	0.7	79	41	70		21	.313	.396	0	0	1B-122
1904	147	533	144	17	9	1	0.2	76	37	57		17	.270	.341	0	0	1B-144, OF-4
1905	149	549	158	18	3	0	0.0	84	28	67		17	.288	.332	1	0	1B-148, P-1
1906	143	544	154	12	8	1	0.2	61	28	58		17	.283	.340	0	0	1B-143
1907	150	554	151	18	8	0	0.0	83	26	82		15	.273	.334	1	0	1B-149
1908 **NY N**	156	583	149	20	1	2	0.3	101	49	72		17	.256	.304	0	0	1B-156
1909	101	375	88	8	2	3	0.8	43	30	52		8	.235	.291	1	0	1B-98
1911 **BOS N**	102	369	97	13	4	1	0.3	52	36	50	17	5	.263	.328	4	1	1B-93, OF-2
17 yrs.	1994	7602	2239	270	77	22	0.3	1278	688	874	43	285	.295	.359	9	1	1B-1807, OF-104, C-71, P-1

Frank Tepedino

TEPEDINO, FRANK RONALD
B. Nov. 23, 1947, Brooklyn, N. Y.　　　　　　BL TL 5'11" 185 lbs.

	G	AB	H	2B	3B	HR	HR %	R	RBI	BB	SO	SB	BA	SA	AB	H	G by POS
1967 **NY A**	9	5	2	0	0	0	0.0	0	0	1	1	0	.400	.400	5	2	1B-1
1969	13	39	9	0	0	0	0.0	6	4	4	4	1	.231	.231	1	0	OF-1, 1B-1
1970	16	19	6	2	0	0	0.0	2	2	1	2	0	.316	.421	11	4	OF-1, 1B-1
1971 **2 teams**		**NY A**	(6G –	.000)		**MIL A**	(53G –	.198)									
"　total	59	112	21	1	0	2	1.8	11	7	4	17	2	.188	.250	28	3	1B-28, OF-1
1972 **NY A**	8	8	0	0	0	0	0.0	0	0	0	1	0	.000	.000	8	0	
1973 **ATL N**	74	148	45	5	0	4	2.7	20	29	13	21	0	.304	.419	24	9	1B-58
1974	78	169	39	5	1	0	0.0	11	16	9	13	1	.231	.272	33	8	1B-46
1975	8	7	0	0	0	0	0.0	0	0	1	2	0	.000	.000	7	0	
8 yrs.	265	507	122	13	1	6	1.2	50	58	33	61	4	.241	.306	117	26	1B-134, OF-15

Joe Tepsic

TEPSIC, JOSEPH JOHN
B. Sept. 18, 1923, Slovan, Pa.　　　　　　BR TR 5'9" 170 lbs.

	G	AB	H	2B	3B	HR	HR %	R	RBI	BB	SO	SB	BA	SA	AB	H	G by POS
1946 **BKN N**	15	5	0	0	0	0	0.0	2	0	1	1	0	.000	.000	3	0	OF-1

Jerry Terrell

TERRELL, JERRY WAYNE
B. July 13, 1946, Waseca, Minn.　　　　　　BR TR 5'11" 165 lbs.

	G	AB	H	2B	3B	HR	HR %	R	RBI	BB	SO	SB	BA	SA	AB	H	G by POS
1973 **MIN A**	124	438	116	15	2	1	0.2	43	32	21	56	13	.265	.315	3	1	SS-81, DH-30, 3B-30, 2B-14, OF-1
1974	116	229	56	4	6	0	0.0	43	19	11	27	3	.245	.314	7	1	SS-34, 2B-26, 3B-21, DH-12, OF-3, 1B-2
1975	108	385	110	16	2	1	0.3	48	36	19	27	4	.286	.345	4	1	SS-41, 2B-39, 1B-15, 3B-12, OF-6, DH-2
1976	89	171	42	3	1	0	0.0	29	8	9	15	11	.246	.275	5	1	2B-31, 3B-26, SS-16, DH-12, OF-6
1977	93	214	48	6	0	1	0.5	32	20	11	21	10	.224	.266	13	3	3B-59, 2B-14, DH-9, SS-7, OF-1, 1B-1
1978 **KC A**	73	133	27	1	0	0	0.0	14	8	4	13	8	.203	.211	3	1	2B-31, 3B-25, SS-11, 1B-5
1979	31	40	12	3	0	1	2.5	5	2	1	1	1	.300	.450	5	0	3B-19, 2B-7, DH-2, SS-1, P-1
1980	23	16	1	0	0	0	0.0	4	0	0	0	0	.063	.063	1	1	OF-7, 2B-3, 1B-3, DH-1, P-1
8 yrs.	657	1626	412	48	11	4	0.2	218	125	76	160	50	.253	.304	41	10	3B-192, SS-191, 2B-165, DH-68, 1B-26, OF-24, P-2

Tom Terrell

TERRELL, THOMAS
B. Louisville, Ky.　　D. July 9, 1893, Louisville, Ky.

	G	AB	H	2B	3B	HR	HR %	R	RBI	BB	SO	SB	BA	SA	AB	H	G by POS
1886 **LOU AA**	1	4	1	0	0	0	0.0	0		0			.250	.250	0	0	OF-1, C-1

Adonis Terry

TERRY, WILLIAM H
B. Aug. 7, 1864, Westfield, Mass.　　D. Feb. 24, 1915, Milwaukee, Wis.　　BR TR 168 lbs.

	G	AB	H	2B	3B	HR	HR %	R	RBI	BB	SO	SB	BA	SA	AB	H	G by POS
1884 **BKN AA**	68	240	56	10	3	0	0.0	16		8			.233	.300	0	0	P-57, OF-13
1885	71	264	45	1	3	1	0.4	23		10			.170	.208	0	0	OF-47, P-25, 3B-1
1886	75	299	71	8	9	2	0.0	34		10			.237	.344	0	0	P-34, OF-32, SS-13
1887	86	352	103	6	10	3	0.9	56		16		27	.293	.392	0	0	OF-49, P-40, SS-2
1888	30	115	29	6	4	0	0.0	13	8	5		7	.252	.304	0	0	P-23, OF-7, 1B-2
1889	49	160	48	6	6	2	1.3	29	26	14	14	8	.300	.400	0	0	P-41, 1B-10
1890 **BKN N**	99	363	101	17	9	4	1.1	63	59	40	34	32	.278	.408	0	0	OF-54, P-46, 1B-1
1891	30	91	19	7	1	0	0.0	10	6	9	26	4	.209	.308	0	0	P-25, OF-5
1892 **2 teams**		**BAL N**	(1G –	.000)		**PIT N**	(31G –	.160)									
"　total	32	104	16	0	4	2	1.9	10	11	10	12	2	.154	.288	0	0	P-31, OF-1
1893 **PIT N**	26	71	18	4	3	0	0.0	9	11	3	11	1	.254	.394	0	0	P-26
1894 **2 teams**		**PIT N**	(1G –	.000)		**CHI N**	(30G –	.347)									
"　total	31	95	33	4	2	0	0.0	19	17	11	12	3	.347	.432	0	0	P-24, OF-7, 1B-2
1895 **CHI N**	40	137	30	3	2	1	0.7	18	10	2	17	1	.219	.292	0	0	P-38, OF-1, SS-1
1896	30	99	26	4	2	0	0.0	14	15	8	12	4	.263	.343	0	0	P-30
1897	1	3	0	0	0	0	0.0	1	0	0		0	.000	.000	0	0	P-1
14 yrs.	668	2393	595	76	54	15	0.6	315	162	146	138	89	.249	.344	0	0	P-441, OF-216, SS-16, 1B-15, 3B-1

Bill Terry

TERRY, WILLIAM HAROLD (Memphis Bill)
B. Oct. 30, 1898, Atlanta, Ga.　　　　　　BL TL 6'1" 200 lbs.
Manager 1932-41.
Hall of Fame 1954.

	G	AB	H	2B	3B	HR	HR %	R	RBI	BB	SO	SB	BA	SA	AB	H	G by POS
1923 **NY N**	3	7	1	0	0	0	0.0	1	0	2	2	0	.143	.143	1	0	1B-2
1924	77	163	39	7	2	5	3.1	26	24	17	18	1	.239	.399	38	9	1B-42
1925	133	489	156	31	6	11	2.2	75	70	42	52	4	.319	.474	6	2	1B-126
1926	98	225	65	12	5	5	2.2	26	43	22	17	3	.289	.453	38	12	1B-38, OF-14

	G	AB	H	2B	3B	HR	HR %	R	RBI	BB	SO	SB	BA	SA	Pinch Hit AB	Pinch Hit H	G by POS

Bill Terry continued

	G	AB	H	2B	3B	HR	HR %	R	RBI	BB	SO	SB	BA	SA	AB	H	G by POS
1927	150	580	189	32	13	20	3.4	101	121	46	53	1	.326	.529	0	0	1B-150
1928	149	568	185	36	11	17	3.0	100	101	64	36	7	.326	.518	0	0	1B-149
1929	150	607	226	39	5	14	2.3	103	117	48	35	10	.372	.522	0	0	1B-149, OF-1
1930	154	633	254	39	15	23	3.6	139	129	57	33	8	**.401**	.619	0	0	1B-154
1931	153	611	213	43	**20**	9	1.5	121	112	47	36	8	.349	.529	0	0	1B-153
1932	154	643	225	42	11	28	4.4	124	117	32	23	4	.350	.580	0	0	1B-154
1933	123	475	153	20	5	6	1.3	68	58	40	23	3	.322	.423	6	4	1B-117
1934	153	602	213	30	6	8	1.3	109	83	60	47	0	.354	.463	0	0	1B-153
1935	145	596	203	32	8	6	1.0	91	64	41	55	7	.341	.451	2	1	1B-143
1936	79	229	71	10	5	2	0.9	36	39	19	19	0	.310	.424	22	6	1B-56
14 yrs.	1721	6428	2193	373	112	154	2.4	1120	1078	537	449	56	.341	.506	113	34	1B-1586, OF-15
WORLD SERIES																	
1924 NY N	5	14	6	0	1	1	7.1	3	1	3	1	0	.429	.786	1	0	1B-4
1933	5	22	6	1	0	1	4.5	3	1	0	0	0	.273	.455	0	0	1B-5
1936	6	25	6	0	0	0	0.0	1	5	1	4	0	.240	.240	0	0	1B-6
3 yrs.	16	61	18	1	1	2	3.3	7	7	4	5	0	.295	.443	1	0	1B-15

Zeb Terry

TERRY, ZEBULON ALEXANDER
B. June 17, 1891, Denison, Tex.　　　　BR TR 5'8" 129 lbs.

	G	AB	H	2B	3B	HR	HR %	R	RBI	BB	SO	SB	BA	SA	AB	H	G by POS
1916 CHI A	94	269	51	8	4	0	0.0	20	17	33	36	4	.190	.249	1	1	SS-93
1917	2	1	0	0	0	0	0.0	0	0	2	0	0	.000	.000	0	0	SS-1
1918 BOS N	28	105	32	2	2	0	0.0	17	8	8	14	1	.305	.362	0	0	SS-27
1919 PIT N	129	472	107	12	6	0	0.0	46	27	31	26	12	.227	.278	2	1	SS-127
1920 CHI N	133	496	139	26	9	0	0.0	56	52	44	22	12	.280	.369	0	0	SS-70, 2B-63
1921	123	488	134	18	1	2	0.4	59	45	27	19	1	.275	.328	1	0	2B-123
1922	131	496	142	24	2	0	0.0	56	67	34	16	2	.286	.343	0	0	2B-125, SS-4, 3B-3
7 yrs.	640	2327	605	90	24	2	0.1	254	216	179	133	32	.260	.322	4	2	SS-322, 2B-311, 3B-3

Wayne Terwilliger

TERWILLIGER, WILLARD WAYNE (Twig)
B. June 27, 1925, Clare, Mich.　　　　BR TR 5'11" 165 lbs.

	G	AB	H	2B	3B	HR	HR %	R	RBI	BB	SO	SB	BA	SA	AB	H	G by POS
1949 CHI N	36	112	25	2	1	2	1.8	11	10	16	22	0	.223	.313	1	0	2B-34
1950	133	480	116	22	3	10	2.1	63	32	43	63	13	.242	.363	4	1	2B-126, OF-1, 3B-1, 1B-1
1951 2 teams	87	242	55	7	0	0	0.0	37	14	37	28	4	.227	.256	7	3	2B-73, 3B-1
" total		CHI N (50G – .214)				BKN N (37G – .280)											
1953 WAS A	134	464	117	24	4	4	0.9	62	46	64	65	7	.252	.347	1	1	2B-133
1954	106	337	70	10	1	3	0.9	42	24	32	40	3	.208	.270	1	0	2B-90, 3B-10, SS-3
1955 NY N	80	257	66	16	1	1	0.4	29	18	36	42	2	.257	.339	0	0	2B-78, SS-1, 3B-1
1956	14	18	4	1	0	0	0.0	0	0	0	5	0	.222	.278	4	0	2B-6
1959 KC A	74	180	48	11	0	2	1.1	27	18	19	31	2	.267	.361	6	0	2B-63, SS-2, 3B-1
1960	2	1	0	0	0	0	0.0	0	0	0	0	0	.000	.000	0	0	2B-2
9 yrs.	666	2091	501	93	10	22	1.1	271	162	247	296	31	.240	.325	24	5	2B-605, 3B-14, SS-6, OF-1, 1B-1

Al Tesch

TESCH, ALBERT JOHN JR. (Tiny)
B. Jan. 27, 1891, Jersey City, N. J.　　D. Aug. 3, 1947, Jersey City, N. J.　　BB TR 5'10" 155 lbs.

	G	AB	H	2B	3B	HR	HR %	R	RBI	BB	SO	SB	BA	SA	AB	H	G by POS
1915 BKN F	8	7	2	1	0	0	0.0	2	2	0		0	.286	.429	1	0	2B-3

Nick Testa

TESTA, NICHOLAS
B. June 29, 1928, New York, N. Y.　　　　BR TR 5'8" 180 lbs.

	G	AB	H	2B	3B	HR	HR %	R	RBI	BB	SO	SB	BA	SA	AB	H	G by POS
1958 SF N	1	0	0	0	0	0	–	0	0	0	0	0	–	–	0	0	C-1

Dick Tettelbach

TETTELBACH, RICHARD MORLEY (Tut)
B. June 26, 1929, New Haven, Conn.　　　　BR TR 6' 195 lbs.

	G	AB	H	2B	3B	HR	HR %	R	RBI	BB	SO	SB	BA	SA	AB	H	G by POS
1955 NY A	2	5	0	0	0	0	0.0	0	0	0	0	0	.000	.000	0	0	OF-2
1956 WAS A	18	64	10	1	2	1	1.6	10	9	14	15	0	.156	.281	0	0	OF-18
1957	9	11	2	0	0	0	0.0	2	1	4	2	0	.182	.182	3	1	OF-3
3 yrs.	29	80	12	1	2	1	1.3	12	10	18	17	0	.150	.250	3	1	OF-23

Mickey Tettleton

TETTLETON, MICKEY LEE
B. Sept. 16, 1960, Oklahoma City, Okla.　　　　BB TR 6'1" 190 lbs.

	G	AB	H	2B	3B	HR	HR %	R	RBI	BB	SO	SB	BA	SA	AB	H	G by POS
1984 OAK A	33	76	20	2	1	1	1.3	10	5	11	21	0	.263	.355	3	0	C-32

Tim Teufel

TEUFEL, TIMOTHY SHAWN
B. July 7, 1958, Greenwich, Conn.　　　　BR TR 6' 175 lbs.

	G	AB	H	2B	3B	HR	HR %	R	RBI	BB	SO	SB	BA	SA	AB	H	G by POS
1983 MIN A	21	78	24	7	1	3	3.8	11	6	2	8	0	.308	.538	2	0	2B-18, DH-1, SS-1
1984	157	568	149	30	3	14	2.5	76	61	76	73	1	.262	.400	0	0	2B-157
2 yrs.	178	646	173	37	4	17	2.6	87	67	78	81	1	.268	.416	2	0	2B-175, DH-1, SS-1

George Textor

TEXTOR, GEORGE BERNHARDT (Tex)
B. Dec. 27, 1888, Newport, Ky.　　D. Mar. 10, 1954, Massillon, Ohio　　BB TR 5'10½" 174 lbs.

	G	AB	H	2B	3B	HR	HR %	R	RBI	BB	SO	SB	BA	SA	AB	H	G by POS
1914 IND F	22	57	10	0	0	0	0.0	2	4	2		0	.175	.175	1	0	C-21
1915 NWK F	3	6	2	0	0	0	0.0	1	0	0		0	.333	.333	0	0	C-3
2 yrs.	25	63	12	0	0	0	0.0	3	4	2		0	.190	.190	1	0	C-24

Moe Thacker

THACKER, MORRIS BENTON
B. May 21, 1934, Louisville, Ky.　　　　BR TR 6'3" 205 lbs.

	G	AB	H	2B	3B	HR	HR %	R	RBI	BB	SO	SB	BA	SA	AB	H	G by POS
1958 CHI N	11	24	6	1	0	2	8.3	4	3	1	7	0	.250	.542	2	1	C-9
1960	54	90	14	1	0	0	0.0	5	6	14	20	1	.156	.167	4	1	C-50
1961	25	35	6	0	0	0	0.0	3	2	11	11	0	.171	.171	0	0	C-25
1962	65	107	20	5	0	0	0.0	8	9	14	40	0	.187	.234	1	0	C-65
1963 STL N	3	4	0	0	0	0	0.0	0	0	0	3	0	.000	.000	0	0	C-3
5 yrs.	158	260	46	7	0	2	0.8	20	20	40	81	1	.177	.227	7	2	C-152

	G	AB	H	2B	3B	HR	HR %	R	RBI	BB	SO	SB	BA	SA	Pinch Hit AB	Pinch Hit H	G by POS

Ed Thayer

THAYER, EDWARD L.
B. Mechanic Falls, Me.   Deceased.

	G	AB	H	2B	3B	HR	HR %	R	RBI	BB	SO	SB	BA	SA	AB	H	G by POS
1876 NY N	1	4	0	0	0	0	0.0	0	0	0	0		.000	.000	0	0	2B-1

Ron Theobald

THEOBALD, RONALD MERRILL
B. July 28, 1944, Oakland, Calif.   BR TR 5'8"   165 lbs.

	G	AB	H	2B	3B	HR	HR %	R	RBI	BB	SO	SB	BA	SA	AB	H	G by POS
1971 MIL A	126	388	107	12	2	1	0.3	50	23	38	39	11	.276	.325	12	5	2B-111, SS-1, 3B-1
1972	125	391	86	11	0	1	0.3	45	19	68	38	0	.220	.256	14	4	2B-113
2 yrs.	251	779	193	23	2	2	0.3	95	42	106	77	11	.248	.290	26	9	2B-224, SS-1, 3B-1

George Theodore

THEODORE, GEORGE BASIL (The Stork)
B. Nov. 13, 1947, Salt Lake City, Utah   BR TR 6'4"   190 lbs.

	G	AB	H	2B	3B	HR	HR %	R	RBI	BB	SO	SB	BA	SA	AB	H	G by POS
1973 NY N	45	116	30	4	0	1	0.9	14	15	10	13	1	.259	.319	11	2	OF-33, 1B-4
1974	60	76	12	1	0	1	1.3	7	1	8	14	0	.158	.211	30	5	1B-14, OF-12
2 yrs.	105	192	42	5	0	2	1.0	21	16	18	27	1	.219	.276	41	7	OF-45, 1B-18
WORLD SERIES																	
1973 NY N	2	2	0	0	0	0	0.0	0	0	0	0	0	.000	.000	1	0	OF-1

Tommy Thevenow

THEVENOW, THOMAS JOSEPH
B. Sept. 6, 1903, Madison, Ind.   D. July 29, 1957, Madison, Ind.   BR TR 5'10"   155 lbs.

	G	AB	H	2B	3B	HR	HR %	R	RBI	BB	SO	SB	BA	SA	AB	H	G by POS
1924 STL N	23	89	18	4	1	0	0.0	4	7	1	6	1	.202	.270	0	0	SS-23
1925	50	175	47	7	2	0	0.0	17	17	7	12	3	.269	.331	0	0	SS-50
1926	156	563	144	15	5	2	0.4	64	63	27	26	8	.256	.311	0	0	SS-156
1927	59	191	37	6	1	0	0.0	23	4	14	8	2	.194	.236	0	0	SS-59
1928	69	171	35	8	3	0	0.0	11	13	20	12	0	.205	.287	0	0	SS-64, 3B-3, 1B-1
1929 PHI N	90	317	72	11	0	0	0.0	30	35	25	25	3	.227	.262	0	0	SS-90
1930	156	573	164	21	1	0	0.0	57	78	23	26	1	.286	.326	0	0	SS-156
1931 PIT N	120	404	86	12	1	0	0.0	35	38	28	22	0	.213	.248	0	0	SS-120
1932	59	194	46	3	3	0	0.0	12	26	7	12	0	.237	.284	6	0	SS-29, 3B-22
1933	73	253	79	5	1	0	0.0	20	34	3	5	2	.312	.340	9	1	2B-61, SS-3, 3B-1
1934	122	446	121	16	2	0	0.0	37	54	20	20	0	.271	.316	6	2	2B-75, 3B-44, SS-1
1935	110	408	97	9	9	0	0.0	38	47	12	23	1	.238	.304	7	1	3B-82, SS-13, 2B-8
1936 CIN N	106	321	75	7	2	0	0.0	25	36	15	23	2	.234	.268	1	0	SS-68, 2B-33, 3B-12
1937 BOS N	21	34	4	0	1	0	0.0	5	2	4	2	0	.118	.176	1	0	SS-12, 3B-6, 2B-2
1938 PIT N	15	25	5	0	0	0	0.0	2	2	4	0	0	.200	.200	1	0	2B-9, SS-4, 3B-1
15 yrs.	1229	4164	1030	124	32	2	0.0	380	456	210	222	23	.247	.294	31	4	SS-848, 2B-188, 3B-171, 1B-1
WORLD SERIES																	
1926 STL N	7	24	10	1	0	1	4.2	5	4	0	1	0	.417	.583	0	0	SS-7
1928	1	0	0	0	0	0	–	0	0	0	0	0	–	–	0	0	SS-1
2 yrs.	8	24	10	1	0	1	4.2	5	4	0	1	0	.417	.583	0	0	SS-8

Jake Thies

THIES, VERNON ARTHUR
B. Apr. 1, 1926, St. Louis, Mo.   BR TR 5'11"   170 lbs.

	G	AB	H	2B	3B	HR	HR %	R	RBI	BB	SO	SB	BA	SA	AB	H	G by POS
1954 PIT N	33	33	1	0	0	0	0.0	2	2	5	11	0	.030	.030	0	0	OF-33
1955	1	0	0	0	0	0	–	0	0	1	0	0	–	–	0	0	P-1
2 yrs.	34	33	1	0	0	0	0.0	2	2	6	11	0	.030	.030	0	0	OF-33, P-1

Bill Thomas

THOMAS, WILLIAM MISKEY
Brother of Roy Thomas.
B. Dec. 8, 1877, Norristown, Pa.   D. Jan. 14, 1950, Evansburg, Pa.   BR TR 5'10"   190 lbs.

	G	AB	H	2B	3B	HR	HR %	R	RBI	BB	SO	SB	BA	SA	AB	H	G by POS
1902 PHI N	6	17	2	0	0	0	0.0	1	0	1		0	.118	.118	1	0	OF-3, 2B-1, 1B-1

Bud Thomas

THOMAS, JOHN TILLMAN
B. Mar. 10, 1929, Sedalia, Mo.   BR TR 6'   160 lbs.

	G	AB	H	2B	3B	HR	HR %	R	RBI	BB	SO	SB	BA	SA	AB	H	G by POS
1951 STL A	14	20	7	0	0	1	5.0	3	1	0	3	2	.350	.500	0	0	SS-14

Danny Thomas

THOMAS, DANNY LEE
B. May 9, 1951, Birmingham, Ala.   D. June 12, 1980, Mobile, Ala.   BR TR 6'2"   190 lbs.

	G	AB	H	2B	3B	HR	HR %	R	RBI	BB	SO	SB	BA	SA	AB	H	G by POS
1976 MIL A	32	105	29	5	1	4	3.8	13	15	14	28	1	.276	.457	0	0	OF-32
1977	22	70	19	3	2	2	2.9	11	11	8	11	0	.271	.457	3	1	DH-9, OF-9
2 yrs.	54	175	48	8	3	6	3.4	24	26	22	39	1	.274	.457	3	1	OF-41, DH-9

Derrel Thomas

THOMAS, DERREL OSBON
B. Jan. 14, 1951, Los Angeles, Calif.   BB TR 6'   160 lbs.

	G	AB	H	2B	3B	HR	HR %	R	RBI	BB	SO	SB	BA	SA	AB	H	G by POS
1971 HOU N	5	5	0	0	0	0	0.0	0	0	0	2	0	.000	.000	0	0	2B-1
1972 SD N	130	500	115	15	5	5	1.0	48	36	41	73	9	.230	.310	2	0	2B-83, SS-49, OF-3
1973	113	404	96	7	1	0	0.0	41	22	34	52	15	.238	.260	6	2	SS-74, 2B-47
1974	141	523	129	24	6	3	0.6	48	41	51	58	7	.247	.333	5	3	2B-104, 3B-22, OF-20, SS-5
1975 SF N	144	540	149	21	9	6	1.1	99	48	57	56	28	.276	.381	2	1	2B-141, OF-1
1976	81	272	63	5	4	2	0.7	38	19	29	26	10	.232	.301	11	2	2B-69, OF-2, SS-1, 3B-1
1977	148	506	135	13	10	8	1.6	75	44	46	70	15	.267	.379	19	5	OF-78, 2B-27, SS-26, 3B-6, 1B-3
1978 SD N	128	352	80	10	2	3	0.9	36	26	35	37	11	.227	.293	7	1	OF-77, 2B-40, 3B-26, 1B-14
1979 LA N	141	406	104	15	4	5	1.2	47	44	41	49	18	.256	.350	11	0	OF-119, 3B-18, 2B-5, SS-3, 1B-1
1980	117	297	79	18	3	1	0.3	32	22	26	48	7	.266	.357	8	3	OF-52, SS-49, 2B-18, C-5, 3B-4
1981	80	218	54	4	0	4	1.8	25	24	25	23	7	.248	.321	3	0	2B-30, SS-26, OF-18, 3B-10
1982	66	98	26	2	1	0	0.0	13	2	10	12	2	.265	.306	5	0	OF-28, 2B-18, 3B-14, SS-6
1983	118	192	48	6	6	2	1.0	38	8	27	36	9	.250	.375	16	3	OF-82, SS-13, 2B-9, 3B-7

	G	AB	H	2B	3B	HR	HR%	R	RBI	BB	SO	SB	BA	SA	Pinch Hit AB	Pinch Hit H	G by POS

Derrel Thomas continued

	G	AB	H	2B	3B	HR	HR%	R	RBI	BB	SO	SB	BA	SA	AB	H	G by POS
1984 2 teams		MON N (108G – .255)			CAL A (14G – .138)												
" total	122	272	66	12	3	0	0.0	29	22	23	37	0	.243	.309	14	0	SS-66, OF-55, 2B-15, 3B-7, 1B-1
14 yrs.	1534	4585	1144	152	54	39	0.9	569	358	445	579	138	.250	.332	109	21	2B-607, OF-535, SS-318, 3B-115, 1B-19, C-5

DIVISIONAL PLAYOFF SERIES

	G	AB	H	2B	3B	HR	HR%	R	RBI	BB	SO	SB	BA	SA	AB	H	G by POS
1981 LA N	4	2	0	0	0	0	0.0	1	0	0	1	0	.000	.000	1	0	OF-4

LEAGUE CHAMPIONSHIP SERIES

	G	AB	H	2B	3B	HR	HR%	R	RBI	BB	SO	SB	BA	SA	AB	H	G by POS
1981 LA N	2	1	1	0	0	0	0.0	2	0	0	0	0	1.000	1.000	1	1	3B-1
1983	4	9	4	1	0	0	0.0	0	0	0	3	1	.444	.556	1	0	OF-4
2 yrs.	6	10	5	1	0	0	0.0	2	0	0	3	1	.500	.600	2	1	OF-4, 3B-1

WORLD SERIES

	G	AB	H	2B	3B	HR	HR%	R	RBI	BB	SO	SB	BA	SA	AB	H	G by POS
1981 LA N	5	7	0	0	0	0	0.0	2	1	1	2	0	.000	.000	2	0	SS-1

Frank Thomas

THOMAS, FRANK JOSEPH
B. June 11, 1929, Pittsburgh, Pa.
BR TR 6'3" 200 lbs.

	G	AB	H	2B	3B	HR	HR%	R	RBI	BB	SO	SB	BA	SA	AB	H	G by POS
1951 PIT N	39	148	39	9	2	2	1.4	21	16	9	15	0	.264	.392	3	1	OF-37
1952	6	21	2	0	0	0	0.0	1	0	1	1	0	.095	.095	0	0	OF-5
1953	128	455	116	22	1	30	6.6	68	102	50	93	1	.255	.505	9	1	OF-118
1954	153	577	172	32	7	23	4.0	81	94	51	74	3	.298	.497	1	1	OF-153
1955	142	510	125	16	2	25	4.9	72	72	60	76	2	.245	.431	3	1	OF-139
1956	157	588	166	24	3	25	4.3	69	80	36	61	0	.282	.461	2	0	3B-111, OF-56, 2B-4
1957	151	594	172	30	1	23	3.9	72	89	44	66	3	.290	.460	0	0	1B-71, OF-59, 3B-31
1958	149	562	158	26	4	35	6.2	89	109	42	79	0	.281	.528	1	0	3B-139, OF-8, 1B-2
1959 CIN N	108	374	84	18	2	12	3.2	41	47	27	56	0	.225	.380	8	1	3B-64, OF-33, 1B-14
1960 CHI N	135	479	114	12	1	21	4.4	54	64	28	74	1	.238	.399	11	4	1B-50, OF-49, 3B-33
1961 2 teams		CHI N (15G – .260)			MIL N (124G – .284)												
" total	139	473	133	15	3	27	5.7	65	73	31	78	2	.281	.497	11	1	OF-119, 1B-17
1962 NY N	156	571	152	23	3	34	6.0	69	94	48	95	2	.266	.496	11	4	OF-126, 1B-11, 3B-10
1963	126	420	109	9	1	15	3.6	34	60	33	48	0	.260	.393	15	4	OF-96, 1B-15, 3B-1
1964 2 teams		NY N (60G – .254)			PHI N (39G – .294)												
" total	99	340	92	17	1	10	2.9	39	45	15	41	1	.271	.415	14	4	1B-58, OF-31, 3B-2
1965 3 teams		PHI N (35G – .260)			HOU N (23G – .172)			MIL N (15G – .212)									
" total	73	168	37	9	0	4	2.4	17	17	9	36	0	.220	.345	29	3	1B-33, OF-16, 3B-3
1966 CHI N	5	5	0	0	0	0	0.0	0	0	0	1	0	.000	.000	5	0	
16 yrs.	1766	6285	1671	262	31	286	4.6	792	962	484	894	15	.266	.454	123	25	OF-1045, 3B-394, 1B-271, 2B-4

Fred Thomas

THOMAS, FREDERICK HARVEY
B. Dec. 19, 1892, Milwaukee, Wis.
BR TR 5'10" 160 lbs.

	G	AB	H	2B	3B	HR	HR%	R	RBI	BB	SO	SB	BA	SA	AB	H	G by POS
1918 BOS A	44	144	37	2	1	1	0.7	19	11	15	20	4	.257	.306	1	0	3B-41, SS-1
1919 PHI A	124	453	96	11	10	2	0.4	42	23	43	52	12	.212	.294	0	0	3B-124
1920 2 teams		PHI A (76G – .231)			WAS A (3G – .143)												
" total	79	262	60	6	3	1	0.4	27	11	26	18	8	.229	.286	1	0	3B-63, SS-12
3 yrs.	247	859	193	19	14	4	0.5	88	45	84	90	24	.225	.293	2	0	3B-228, SS-13

WORLD SERIES

	G	AB	H	2B	3B	HR	HR%	R	RBI	BB	SO	SB	BA	SA	AB	H	G by POS
1918 BOS A	6	17	2	0	0	0	0.0	0	1	1	2	0	.118	.118	0	0	3B-6

George Thomas

THOMAS, GEORGE EDWARD
B. Nov. 29, 1937, Minneapolis, Minn.
BR TR 6'3½" 190 lbs.

	G	AB	H	2B	3B	HR	HR%	R	RBI	BB	SO	SB	BA	SA	AB	H	G by POS
1957 DET A	1	1	0	0	0	0	0.0	0	0	0	1	0	.000	.000	1	0	3B-1
1958	1	0	0	0	0	0	–	0	0	0	0	0	–	–	0	0	OF-1
1961 2 teams		DET A (17G – .000)			LA A (79G – .280)												
" total	96	288	79	12	1	13	4.5	41	59	21	70	3	.274	.458	5	0	OF-47, 3B-38, SS-1
1962 LA A	56	181	43	10	2	4	2.2	13	12	21	37	0	.238	.381	5	1	OF-51
1963 2 teams		LA A (53G – .210)			DET A (44G – .239)												
" total	97	276	61	11	2	5	1.8	27	26	20	54	2	.221	.330	11	0	OF-79, 3B-10, 1B-4, 2B-1
1964 DET A	105	308	88	15	2	12	3.9	39	44	18	53	4	.286	.464	18	6	OF-90, 3B-1
1965	79	169	36	5	1	3	1.8	19	10	12	39	2	.213	.308	17	2	OF-59, 2B-1
1966 BOS A	69	173	41	4	0	5	2.9	25	20	23	33	1	.237	.347	13	3	OF-48, 3B-6, 1B-2, C-2
1967	65	89	19	2	0	1	1.1	10	6	3	23	0	.213	.270	18	2	OF-43, 1B-3, C-1
1968	12	10	2	0	0	1	10.0	3	1	1	3	1	.200	.500	1	0	OF-9
1969	29	51	18	3	1	0	0.0	9	8	3	11	0	.353	.451	6	1	OF-12, 1B-10, 3B-1, C-1
1970	38	99	34	8	0	2	2.0	13	13	11	12	0	.343	.485	6	3	OF-26, 3B-6
1971 2 teams		BOS A (9G – .077)			MIN A (23G – .267)												
" total	32	43	9	1	0	0	0.0	4	3	5	7	0	.209	.233	18	5	OF-16, 3B-1, 1B-1
13 yrs.	680	1688	430	71	9	46	2.7	203	202	138	343	13	.255	.389	119	23	OF-481, 3B-64, 1B-20, C-4, 2B-2, SS-1

WORLD SERIES

	G	AB	H	2B	3B	HR	HR%	R	RBI	BB	SO	SB	BA	SA	AB	H	G by POS
1967 BOS A	2	2	0	0	0	0	0.0	0	0	0	1	0	.000	.000	1	0	OF-1

Gorman Thomas

THOMAS, JAMES GORMAN
B. Dec. 12, 1950, Charleston, S. C.
BR TR 6'2" 210 lbs.

	G	AB	H	2B	3B	HR	HR%	R	RBI	BB	SO	SB	BA	SA	AB	H	G by POS
1973 MIL A	59	155	29	7	1	2	1.3	16	11	14	61	5	.187	.284	4	1	OF-50, DH-3, 3B-1
1974	17	46	12	4	0	2	4.3	10	11	8	15	4	.261	.478	3	1	OF-13, DH-2
1975	121	240	43	12	2	10	4.2	34	28	31	84	4	.179	.371	2	0	OF-113, DH-6
1976	99	227	45	9	2	8	3.5	27	36	31	67	2	.198	.361	12	1	OF-94, DH-1, 3B-1
1977	137	452	111	24	1	32	7.1	70	86	73	133	3	.246	.515	0	0	OF-137
1979	156	557	136	29	0	45	8.1	97	123	98	175	1	.244	.539	0	0	OF-152, DH-4
1980	162	628	150	26	3	38	6.1	78	105	58	170	8	.239	.471	0	0	OF-160, DH-2
1981	103	363	94	22	0	21	5.8	54	65	50	85	4	.259	.493	0	0	OF-97, DH-6
1982	158	567	139	29	1	39	6.9	96	112	84	143	3	.245	.506	0	0	OF-157
1983 2 teams		MIL A (46G – .183)			CLE A (106G – .221)												
" total	152	535	112	23	2	22	4.1	72	69	80	148	10	.209	.379	0	0	OF-152

	G	AB	H	2B	3B	HR	HR %	R	RBI	BB	SO	SB	BA	SA	Pinch Hit AB	Pinch Hit H	G by POS

Gorman Thomas continued

1984 SEA A	35	108	17	3	0	1	0.9	6	13	28	27	0	.157	.213	0	0	OF-34, DH-1
11 yrs.	1199	3878	888	188	11	220	5.7	560	659	555	1108	44	.229	.453	22	4	OF-1159, DH-25, 3B-2

DIVISIONAL PLAYOFF SERIES
| 1981 MIL A | 5 | 17 | 2 | 0 | 0 | 1 | 5.9 | 2 | 1 | 1 | 9 | 0 | .118 | .294 | 0 | 0 | OF-3, DH-2 |

LEAGUE CHAMPIONSHIP SERIES
| 1982 MIL A | 5 | 15 | 1 | 0 | 0 | 1 | 6.7 | 1 | 3 | 2 | 7 | 0 | .067 | .267 | 0 | 0 | OF-5 |

WORLD SERIES
| 1982 MIL A | 7 | 26 | 3 | 0 | 0 | 0 | 0.0 | 0 | 3 | 2 | 7 | 0 | .115 | .115 | 0 | 0 | OF-7 |

Herb Thomas

THOMAS, HERBERT MARK
B. May 26, 1902, Sampson City, Fla.
BR TR 5'4½" 157 lbs.

	G	AB	H	2B	3B	HR	HR %	R	RBI	BB	SO	SB	BA	SA	AB	H	G by POS
1924 BOS N	32	127	28	4	1	1	0.8	12	8	9	8	5	.220	.291	0	0	OF-32
1925	5	17	4	0	1	0	0.0	2	0	2	0	0	.235	.353	0	0	2B-5
1927 2 teams	BOS	N	(24G –	.230)		NY	N	(13G –	.176)								
" total	37	91	20	7	2	0	0.0	13	7	4	10	2	.220	.341	8	0	2B-17, OF-3, SS-3
3 yrs.	74	235	52	11	4	1	0.4	27	15	15	18	7	.221	.315	8	0	OF-35, 2B-22, SS-3

Ira Thomas

THOMAS, IRA FELIX
B. Jan. 22, 1881, Ballston Spa, N. Y.   D. Oct. 11, 1958, Philadelphia, Pa.
BR TR 6'2" 200 lbs.

	G	AB	H	2B	3B	HR	HR %	R	RBI	BB	SO	SB	BA	SA	AB	H	G by POS
1906 NY A	44	115	23	1	2	0	0.0	12	15	8		2	.200	.243	2	0	C-42
1907	80	208	40	5	4	1	0.5	20	24	10		5	.192	.269	16	2	C-66, 1B-2
1908 DET A	40	101	31	1	0	0	0.0	6	8	5		0	.307	.317	11	4	C-29
1909 PHI A	84	256	57	9	3	0	0.0	22	31	18		4	.223	.281	0	0	C-84
1910	60	180	50	8	2	1	0.6	14	19	6		2	.278	.361	0	0	C-60
1911	103	297	81	14	3	0	0.0	33	39	23		4	.273	.340	0	0	C-103
1912	46	139	30	4	2	1	0.7	14	13	8		3	.216	.295	0	0	C-46
1913	21	53	15	4	1	0	0.0	3	6	4	8	0	.283	.396	0	0	C-21
1914	2	3	0	0	0	0	0.0	0	0	0	0	0	.000	.000	1	0	C-1
1915	1	0	0	0	0	0	–	0	0	0	0	0	–	–	0	0	C-1
10 yrs.	481	1352	327	46	17	3	0.2	124	155	82	8	20	.242	.308	30	6	C-453, 1B-2

WORLD SERIES
1908 DET A	2	4	2	1	0	0	0.0	0	0	1		0	.500	.750	1	1	C-1
1910 PHI A	4	12	3	0	0	0	0.0	2	1	4	1	0	.250	.250	0	0	C-4
1911	4	12	1	0	0	0	0.0	1	1	1	2	0	.083	.083	0	0	C-4
3 yrs.	10	28	6	1	0	0	0.0	3	3	6	3	0	.214	.250	1	1	C-9

Kite Thomas

THOMAS, KEITH MARSHALL
B. Apr. 27, 1924, Kansas City, Kans.
BR TR 6'1½" 195 lbs.

	G	AB	H	2B	3B	HR	HR %	R	RBI	BB	SO	SB	BA	SA	AB	H	G by POS
1952 PHI A	75	116	29	6	1	6	5.2	24	18	20	27	0	.250	.474	35	8	OF-29
1953 2 teams	PHI	A	(24G –	.122)		WAS	A	(38G –	.293)								
" total	62	107	23	3	2	1	0.9	11	14	14	13	0	.215	.308	30	7	OF-23, C-1
2 yrs.	137	223	52	9	3	7	3.1	35	32	34	40	0	.233	.395	65	15	OF-52, C-1

Lee Thomas

THOMAS, JAMES LEROY
B. Feb. 5, 1936, Peoria, Ill.
BL TL 6'2" 195 lbs.

	G	AB	H	2B	3B	HR	HR %	R	RBI	BB	SO	SB	BA	SA	AB	H	G by POS
1961 2 teams	NY	A	(2G –	.500)		LA	A	(130G –	.284)								
" total	132	452	129	11	5	24	5.3	77	70	47	74	0	.285	.491	18	5	OF-86, 1B-34
1962 LA A	160	583	169	21	2	26	4.5	88	104	55	74	6	.290	.467	3	0	1B-90, OF-74
1963	149	528	116	12	6	9	1.7	52	55	53	82	6	.220	.316	6	2	1B-104, OF-43
1964 2 teams	LA	A	(47G –	.273)		BOS	A	(107G –	.257)								
" total	154	573	150	27	3	15	2.6	58	66	52	51	3	.262	.398	1	0	OF-154, 1B-2
1965 BOS A	151	521	141	27	4	22	4.2	74	75	72	42	6	.271	.464	9	1	1B-127, OF-20
1966 2 teams	ATL	N	(39G –	.198)		CHI	N	(75G –	.242)								
" total	114	275	61	5	1	7	2.5	26	24	24	30	1	.222	.324	33	9	1B-56, OF-17
1967 CHI N	77	191	42	4	1	2	1.0	16	23	14	22	1	.220	.283	22	4	OF-43, 1B-10
1968 HOU N	90	201	39	4	0	1	0.5	14	11	14	22	2	.194	.229	39	7	OF-48, 1B-2
8 yrs.	1027	3324	847	111	22	106	3.2	405	428	332	397	25	.255	.397	131	28	OF-485, 1B-425

Leo Thomas

THOMAS, LEO RAYMOND (Tommy)
B. Aug. 26, 1923, Turlock, Calif.
BR TR 5'11" 175 lbs.

	G	AB	H	2B	3B	HR	HR %	R	RBI	BB	SO	SB	BA	SA	AB	H	G by POS
1950 STL A	35	121	24	6	0	1	0.8	19	9	20	14	0	.198	.273	0	0	3B-35
1952 2 teams	STL	A	(41G –	.234)		CHI	A	(19G –	.167)								
" total	60	148	33	5	1	0	0.0	13	18	23	11	2	.223	.270	6	1	3B-46, SS-3, 2B-1
2 yrs.	95	269	57	11	1	1	0.4	32	27	43	25	2	.212	.271	6	1	3B-81, SS-3, 2B-1

Pinch Thomas

THOMAS, CHESTER DAVID
B. Jan. 24, 1888, Camp Point, Ill.   D. Dec. 24, 1953, Modesto, Calif.
BL TR 5'9½" 173 lbs.

	G	AB	H	2B	3B	HR	HR %	R	RBI	BB	SO	SB	BA	SA	AB	H	G by POS
1912 BOS A	12	30	6	0	0	0	0.0	0	5	2		1	.200	.200	0	0	C-12
1913	37	91	26	1	2	1	1.1	6	15	2	11	1	.286	.374	7	2	C-30
1914	63	130	25	1	0	0	0.0	9	5	18	17	1	.192	.200	1	0	C-61, 1B-1
1915	86	203	48	4	4	0	0.0	21	21	13	20	3	.236	.296	3	2	C-82
1916	99	216	57	10	1	1	0.5	21	21	33	13	4	.264	.333	6	2	C-90
1917	83	202	48	7	0	0	0.0	24	24	27	9	2	.238	.272	6	3	C-77
1918 CLE A	32	73	18	0	1	0	0.0	2	5	6	6	0	.247	.274	8	4	C-24
1919	34	46	5	0	0	0	0.0	2	2	4	3	0	.109	.109	13	0	C-21
1920	9	9	3	1	0	0	0.0	2	0	3	1	0	.333	.444	1	0	C-7
1921	21	35	9	3	0	0	0.0	1	4	10	2	0	.257	.343	2	0	C-19
10 yrs.	476	1035	245	27	8	2	0.2	88	102	118	82	12	.237	.284	47	13	C-423, 1B-1

WORLD SERIES
1915 BOS A	2	5	1	0	0	0	0.0	0	0	0		0	.200	.200	0	0	C-2
1916	3	7	1	0	1	0	0.0	0	0	0	1	0	.143	.429	0	0	C-3
1920 CLE A	1	0	0	0	0	0	–	0	0	0		0	–	–	0	0	C-1
3 yrs.	6	12	2	0	1	0	0.0	0	0	0	1	0	.167	.333	0	0	C-6

	G	AB	H	2B	3B	HR	HR %	R	RBI	BB	SO	SB	BA	SA	Pinch Hit AB	H	G by POS

Ray Thomas

THOMAS, RAYMOND JOSEPH
B. July 9, 1910, Dover, N. H.
BR TR 5'11" 175 lbs.

	G	AB	H	2B	3B	HR	HR %	R	RBI	BB	SO	SB	BA	SA	AB	H	G by POS
1938 BKN N	1	3	1	0	0	0	0.0	1	0	0	0	0	.333	.333	0	0	C-1

Red Thomas

THOMAS, ROBERT WILLIAM
B. Apr. 25, 1898, Hargrove, Ala.   D. Mar. 29, 1962, Fremont, Ohio
BR TR 5'11" 165 lbs.

	G	AB	H	2B	3B	HR	HR %	R	RBI	BB	SO	SB	BA	SA	AB	H	G by POS
1921 CHI N	8	30	8	3	0	1	3.3	5	5	4	5	0	.267	.467	0	0	OF-8

Roy Thomas

THOMAS, ROY ALLEN
Brother of Bill Thomas.
B. Mar. 24, 1874, Norristown, Pa.   D. Nov. 20, 1959, Norristown, Pa.
BL TL 5'11" 150 lbs.

	G	AB	H	2B	3B	HR	HR %	R	RBI	BB	SO	SB	BA	SA	AB	H	G by POS
1899 PHI N	150	547	178	12	4	0	0.0	137	47	115		42	.325	.362	1	0	OF-135, 1B-14
1900	140	531	168	4	3	0	0.0	134	33	115		37	.316	.335	1	0	OF-139, P-1
1901	129	479	148	5	2	1	0.2	102	28	100		27	.309	.334	0	0	OF-129
1902	138	500	143	4	7	0	0.0	89	24	107		17	.286	.322	0	0	OF-138
1903	130	477	156	11	2	1	0.2	88	27	107		17	.327	.365	0	0	OF-130
1904	139	496	144	6	6	3	0.6	92	29	102		28	.290	.345	0	0	OF-139
1905	147	562	178	11	6	0	0.0	118	31	93		23	.317	.358	0	0	OF-147
1906	142	493	125	10	7	0	0.0	81	16	107		22	.254	.302	0	0	OF-142
1907	121	419	102	15	3	1	0.2	70	23	83		11	.243	.301	0	0	OF-121
1908 2 teams		PHI	N	(6G – .167)		PIT	N	(102G – .256)									
" total	108	410	103	11	10	1	0.2	54	24	51		11	.251	.334	0	0	OF-107
1909 BOS N	83	281	74	9	1	0	0.0	36	11	47		5	.263	.302	5	2	OF-71
1910 PHI N	23	71	13	0	2	0	0.0	7	4	7	5	4	.183	.239	1	0	OF-20
1911	21	30	5	2	0	0	0.0	5	2	8	6	0	.167	.233	7	1	OF-11
13 yrs.	1471	5296	1537	100	53	7	0.1	1013	299	1042	11	244	.290	.333	17	3	OF-1429, 1B-14, P-1

Valmy Thomas

THOMAS, VALMY
B. Oct. 21, 1930, St. Thomas, Virgin Islands
BR TR 5'9" 165 lbs.

	G	AB	H	2B	3B	HR	HR %	R	RBI	BB	SO	SB	BA	SA	AB	H	G by POS
1957 NY N	88	241	60	10	3	6	2.5	30	31	16	29	0	.249	.390	1	0	C-88
1958 SF N	63	143	37	5	0	3	2.1	14	16	13	24	1	.259	.357	2	0	C-61
1959 PHI N	66	140	28	2	0	1	0.7	5	7	9	19	1	.200	.236	0	0	C-65, 3B-1
1960 BAL A	8	16	1	0	0	0	0.0	0	0	1	0	0	.063	.063	0	0	C-8
1961 CLE A	27	86	18	3	0	2	2.3	7	6	6	7	0	.209	.314	0	0	C-27
5 yrs.	252	626	144	20	3	12	1.9	56	60	45	79	2	.230	.329	3	0	C-249, 3B-1

Walt Thomas

THOMAS, WILLIAM WALTER
B. Apr. 28, 1884, Foot Of Ten, Pa.   D. June 4, 1950, Altoona, Pa.
BR TR 5'8"

	G	AB	H	2B	3B	HR	HR %	R	RBI	BB	SO	SB	BA	SA	AB	H	G by POS
1908 BOS N	5	13	2	0	0	0	0.0	2	1	3		2	.154	.154	0	0	SS-5

Art Thomason

THOMASON, ARTHUR WILSON (Sillie)
B. Feb. 12, 1889, Liberty, Mo.   D. May 2, 1944, Kansas City, Mo.
BL TL 5'8" 150 lbs.

	G	AB	H	2B	3B	HR	HR %	R	RBI	BB	SO	SB	BA	SA	AB	H	G by POS
1910 CLE A	17	57	9	0	1	0	0.0	3	2	5		3	.158	.193	0	0	OF-17

Gary Thomasson

THOMASSON, GARY LEAH
B. July 29, 1951, San Diego, Calif.
BL TL 6'1" 180 lbs.

	G	AB	H	2B	3B	HR	HR %	R	RBI	BB	SO	SB	BA	SA	AB	H	G by POS
1972 SF N	10	27	9	1	1	0	0.0	5	1	1	7	0	.333	.444	2	1	1B-7, OF-2
1973	112	235	67	10	4	4	1.7	35	30	22	43	2	.285	.413	18	4	1B-47, OF-43
1974	120	315	77	14	3	2	0.6	41	29	38	56	7	.244	.327	30	6	OF-76, 1B-15
1975	114	326	74	12	3	7	2.1	44	32	37	48	9	.227	.347	17	4	OF-74, 1B-17
1976	103	328	85	20	5	8	2.4	45	38	30	45	8	.259	.424	16	4	OF-54, 1B-39
1977	145	446	114	24	6	17	3.8	63	71	75	102	16	.256	.451	16	5	OF-113, 1B-31
1978 2 teams		OAK	A	(47G – .201)		NY	A	(55G – .276)									
" total	102	270	63	8	2	8	3.0	37	36	28	66	4	.233	.367	7	2	OF-94, 1B-5, DH-1
1979 LA N	115	315	78	11	1	14	4.4	39	45	43	70	4	.248	.422	18	2	OF-100, 1B-1
1980	80	111	24	3	0	1	0.9	6	12	17	26	0	.216	.270	45	11	OF-31, 1B-1
9 yrs.	901	2373	591	103	25	61	2.6	315	294	291	463	50	.249	.391	169	39	OF-587, 1B-163, DH-1

LEAGUE CHAMPIONSHIP SERIES

	G	AB	H	2B	3B	HR	HR %	R	RBI	BB	SO	SB	BA	SA	AB	H	G by POS
1978 NY A	3	1	0	0	0	0	0.0	0	0	0	0	0	.000	.000	1	0	OF-3

WORLD SERIES

	G	AB	H	2B	3B	HR	HR %	R	RBI	BB	SO	SB	BA	SA	AB	H	G by POS
1978 NY A	3	4	1	0	0	0	0.0	0	0	0	1	0	.250	.250	0	0	OF-3

Bobby Thompson

THOMPSON, BOBBY LaRUE
B. Nov. 3, 1953, Charlotte, N. C.
BB TR 5'11" 175 lbs.

	G	AB	H	2B	3B	HR	HR %	R	RBI	BB	SO	SB	BA	SA	AB	H	G by POS
1978 TEX A	64	120	27	3	3	2	1.7	23	12	9	26	7	.225	.350	0	0	OF-52, DH-3

Danny Thompson

THOMPSON, DANNY LEON
B. Feb. 1, 1947, Wichita, Kans.   D. Dec. 10, 1976, Rochester, Minn.
BR TR 6' 183 lbs.

	G	AB	H	2B	3B	HR	HR %	R	RBI	BB	SO	SB	BA	SA	AB	H	G by POS
1970 MIN A	96	302	66	9	0	0	0.0	25	22	7	39	0	.219	.248	3	1	2B-81, 3B-37, SS-6
1971	48	57	15	2	0	0	0.0	10	7	7	12	0	.263	.298	20	5	3B-17, 2B-3, SS-1
1972	144	573	158	22	6	4	0.7	54	48	34	57	3	.276	.356	0	0	SS-144
1973	99	347	78	13	2	1	0.3	29	36	16	41	1	.225	.282	2	0	SS-95, 3B-1
1974	97	264	66	6	1	4	1.5	25	25	22	29	1	.250	.326	6	0	SS-88, 3B-5, DH-1
1975	112	355	96	11	2	5	1.4	25	37	18	30	0	.270	.355	6	2	SS-100, 3B-7, DH-3, 2B-1
1976 2 teams		MIN	A	(34G – .234)		TEX	A	(64G – .214)									
" total	98	320	71	7	0	1	0.3	21	19	16	27	3	.222	.253	8	2	SS-44, 3B-39, 2B-14, DH-1
7 yrs.	694	2218	550	70	11	15	0.7	189	194	120	235	8	.248	.310	45	10	SS-478, 3B-106, 2B-99, DH-5

LEAGUE CHAMPIONSHIP SERIES

	G	AB	H	2B	3B	HR	HR %	R	RBI	BB	SO	SB	BA	SA	AB	H	G by POS
1970 MIN A	3	8	1	1	0	0	0.0	0	0	1	0	0	.125	.250	0	0	2B-3

	G	AB	H	2B	3B	HR	HR %	R	RBI	BB	SO	SB	BA	SA	Pinch Hit AB	Pinch Hit H	G by POS

Don Thompson

THOMPSON, DONALD NEWLIN   BL TL 6'   185 lbs.
B. Dec. 28, 1923, Swepsonville, N. C.

	G	AB	H	2B	3B	HR	HR %	R	RBI	BB	SO	SB	BA	SA	AB	H	G by POS
1949 BOS N	7	11	2	0	0	0	0.0	0	0	0	2	0	.182	.182	5	0	OF-2
1951 BKN N	80	118	27	3	0	0	0.0	25	6	12	12	2	.229	.254	11	3	OF-61
1953	96	153	37	5	0	1	0.7	25	12	14	13	2	.242	.294	13	0	OF-81
1954	34	25	1	0	0	0	0.0	2	1	5	5	0	.040	.040	5	0	OF-29
4 yrs.	217	307	67	8	0	1	0.3	52	19	31	32	4	.218	.254	34	3	OF-173

WORLD SERIES

	G	AB	H	2B	3B	HR	HR %	R	RBI	BB	SO	SB	BA	SA	AB	H	G by POS
1953 BKN N	2	0	0	0	0	0	—	0	0	0	0	0	—	—	0	0	OF-2

Frank Thompson

THOMPSON, FRANK E   BR TR 5'8"   155 lbs.
B. July 2, 1895, Springfield, Mo.   D. June 27, 1940, Mineral Township, Mo.

	G	AB	H	2B	3B	HR	HR %	R	RBI	BB	SO	SB	BA	SA	AB	H	G by POS
1920 STL A	22	53	9	0	0	0	0.0	7	5	13	10	1	.170	.170	2	0	3B-14, 2B-2

Fresco Thompson

THOMPSON, LAFAYETTE FRESCO (Tommy)   BR TR 5'8"   150 lbs.
B. June 6, 1902, Centreville, Ala.   D. Nov. 20, 1968, Fullerton, Calif.

	G	AB	H	2B	3B	HR	HR %	R	RBI	BB	SO	SB	BA	SA	AB	H	G by POS
1925 PIT N	14	37	9	2	1	0	0.0	4	8	4	1	2	.243	.351	2	0	2B-12
1926 NY N	2	8	5	0	0	0	0.0	1	1	2	0	1	.625	.625	0	0	2B-2
1927 PHI N	153	597	181	32	14	1	0.2	78	70	34	36	19	.303	.409	0	0	2B-153
1928	152	634	182	34	11	3	0.5	99	50	42	27	19	.287	.390	0	0	2B-152
1929	148	623	202	41	3	4	0.6	115	53	75	34	16	.324	.419	0	0	2B-148
1930	122	478	135	34	4	4	0.8	77	46	35	29	7	.282	.395	8	3	2B-112
1931 BKN N	74	181	48	6	1	1	0.6	26	21	23	16	5	.265	.326	4	1	2B-43, SS-10, 3B-5
1932	3	1	0	0	0	0	0.0	0	0	0	0	0	.000	.000	1	0	
1934 NY N	1	1	0	0	0	0	0.0	0	0	0	0	0	.000	.000	1	0	
9 yrs.	669	2560	762	149	34	13	0.5	400	249	215	143	69	.298	.398	16	4	2B-622, SS-10, 3B-5

Hank Thompson

THOMPSON, HENRY CURTIS   BL TR 5'9"   174 lbs.
B. Dec. 8, 1925, Oklahoma City, Okla.   D. Sept. 30, 1969, Fresno, Calif.

	G	AB	H	2B	3B	HR	HR %	R	RBI	BB	SO	SB	BA	SA	AB	H	G by POS
1947 STL A	27	78	20	1	1	0	0.0	10	5	10	7	2	.256	.295	8	3	2B-19
1949 NY N	75	275	77	10	4	9	3.3	51	34	42	30	5	.280	.444	4	1	2B-69, 3B-1
1950	148	512	148	17	6	20	3.9	82	91	83	60	8	.289	.463	1	0	3B-138, OF-10
1951	87	264	62	8	4	8	3.0	37	33	43	23	1	.235	.386	14	1	3B-71
1952	128	423	110	13	9	17	4.0	67	67	50	38	4	.260	.454	9	3	OF-72, 3B-46, 2B-4
1953	114	388	117	15	8	24	6.2	80	74	60	39	6	.302	.567	4	1	3B-101, OF-9, 2B-1
1954	136	448	118	18	1	26	5.8	76	86	90	58	5	.263	.482	5	0	3B-130, 2B-2, OF-1
1955	135	432	106	13	1	17	3.9	65	63	84	56	2	.245	.398	9	1	3B-124, 2B-7, SS-1
1956	83	183	43	9	0	8	4.4	24	29	31	26	2	.235	.415	24	8	3B-44, OF-10, SS-1
9 yrs.	933	3003	801	104	34	129	4.3	492	482	493	337	33	.267	.453	78	18	3B-655, OF-102, 2B-102, SS-2

WORLD SERIES

	G	AB	H	2B	3B	HR	HR %	R	RBI	BB	SO	SB	BA	SA	AB	H	G by POS
1951 NY N	5	14	2	0	0	0	0.0	2	0	5	2	0	.143	.143	0	0	OF-5
1954	4	11	4	1	0	0	0.0	6	2	7	1	0	.364	.455	0	0	3B-4
2 yrs.	9	25	6	1	0	0	0.0	8	2	12	3	0	.240	.280	0	0	OF-5, 3B-4

Homer Thompson

THOMPSON, THOMAS HOMER   BR TR 5'9"   160 lbs.
Brother of Tommy Thompson.
B. June 1, 1892, Spring City, Tenn.   D. Sept. 12, 1957, Atlanta, Ga.

	G	AB	H	2B	3B	HR	HR %	R	RBI	BB	SO	SB	BA	SA	AB	H	G by POS
1912 NY A	1	0	0	0	0	0	—	0	0		0		—	—	0	0	C-1

Jason Thompson

THOMPSON, JASON DOLPH   BL TL 6'4"   200 lbs.
B. July 6, 1954, Hollywood, Calif.

	G	AB	H	2B	3B	HR	HR %	R	RBI	BB	SO	SB	BA	SA	AB	H	G by POS
1976 DET A	123	412	90	12	1	17	4.1	45	54	68	72	2	.218	.376	3	0	1B-117
1977	158	585	158	24	5	31	5.3	87	105	73	91	0	.270	.487	0	0	1B-158
1978	153	589	169	25	3	26	4.4	79	96	74	96	0	.287	.472	1	0	1B-151
1979	145	492	121	16	1	20	4.1	58	79	70	90	2	.246	.404	8	2	1B-140, DH-2
1980 2 teams	DET A (36G – .214)					CAL A (102G – .317)											
" total	138	438	126	19	0	21	4.8	69	90	83	86	2	.288	.475	14	4	1B-83, DH-45
1981 PIT N	86	223	54	13	0	15	6.7	36	42	59	49	0	.242	.502	13	4	1B-78
1982	156	550	156	32	0	31	5.6	87	101	101	107	1	.284	.511	0	0	1B-155
1983	152	517	134	20	1	18	3.5	70	76	99	128	1	.259	.406	2	0	1B-151
1984	154	543	138	22	0	17	3.1	61	74	87	73	0	.254	.389	3	0	1B-152
9 yrs.	1265	4349	1146	183	11	196	4.5	592	717	714	792	8	.264	.446	44	11	1B-1185, DH-47

Milton Thompson

THOMPSON, MILTON BERNARD   BL TR 5'11"   160 lbs.
B. Jan. 5, 1959, Washington, D.C.

	G	AB	H	2B	3B	HR	HR %	R	RBI	BB	SO	SB	BA	SA	AB	H	G by POS
1984 ATL N	25	99	30	1	1	2	2.0	16	4	11	11	14	.303	.374	2	2	OF-25

Sam Thompson

THOMPSON, SAMUEL L. (Big Sam)   BL   6'2"   207 lbs.
B. Mar. 5, 1860, Danville, Ind.   D. Nov. 7, 1922, Detroit, Mich.
Hall of Fame 1974.

	G	AB	H	2B	3B	HR	HR %	R	RBI	BB	SO	SB	BA	SA	AB	H	G by POS
1885 DET N	63	254	77	11	9	7	2.8	58	44	16	22		.303	.500	0	0	OF-62, 3B-1
1886	122	503	156	18	13	8	1.6	101	89	35	31		.310	.445	0	0	OF-122
1887	127	545	203	29	23	11	2.0	118	166	32	19	22	.372	.571	0	0	OF-127
1888	56	238	67	10	8	6	2.5	51	40	23	10	5	.282	.466	0	0	OF-56
1889 PHI N	128	533	158	36	4	20	3.8	103	111	36	22	24	.296	.492	0	0	OF-128
1890	132	549	172	41	9	4	0.7	116	102	42	29	25	.313	.443	0	0	OF-132
1891	133	554	163	23	10	8	1.4	108	90	52	20	29	.294	.415	0	0	OF-133
1892	153	609	186	28	11	9	1.5	109	104	59	19	28	.305	.432	0	0	OF-153
1893	131	600	222	37	13	11	1.8	130	126	50	17	18	.370	.530	0	0	OF-131, 1B-1
1894	102	458	185	29	27	13	2.8	115	141	40	13	29	.404	.670	0	0	OF-102
1895	119	538	211	45	21	18	3.3	131	165	31	11	27	.392	.654	1	1	OF-118
1896	119	517	154	28	7	12	2.3	103	100	28	13	12	.298	.449	0	0	OF-119
1897	3	13	3	0	1	0	0.0	2	3	1		0	.231	.385	0	0	OF-3
1898	14	63	22	5	3	1	1.6	14	15	4		2	.349	.571	0	0	OF-14

	G	AB	H	2B	3B	HR	HR %	R	RBI	BB	SO	SB	BA	SA	Pinch Hit AB	Pinch Hit H	G by POS

Sam Thompson continued

	G	AB	H	2B	3B	HR	HR %	R	RBI	BB	SO	SB	BA	SA	AB	H	G by POS
1906 DET A	8	31	7	0	1	0	0.0	4	3	1		0	.226	.290	0	0	OF-8
15 yrs.	1410	6005	1986	340	160	128	2.1	1263	1299	450	226	221	.331	.505	1	1	OF-1408, 3B-1, 1B-1

Scot Thompson

THOMPSON, VERNON SCOT
B. Dec. 7, 1955, Grove City, Pa.   BL TL 6'3"   195 lbs.

	G	AB	H	2B	3B	HR	HR %	R	RBI	BB	SO	SB	BA	SA	AB	H	G by POS
1978 CHI N	19	36	15	3	0	0	0.0	7	2	2	4	0	.417	.500	12	6	OF-5, 1B-2
1979	128	346	100	13	5	2	0.6	36	29	17	37	4	.289	.373	33	12	OF-100
1980	102	226	48	10	1	2	0.9	26	13	28	31	6	.212	.292	21	6	OF-66, 1B-12
1981	57	115	19	5	0	0	0.0	8	8	7	8	2	.165	.209	22	2	OF-30, 1B-3
1982	49	74	27	5	1	0	0.0	11	7	5	4	0	.365	.459	27	7	OF-23, 1B-4
1983	53	88	17	3	1	0	0.0	4	10	3	14	0	.193	.250	28	6	OF-29, 1B-1
1984 SF N	120	245	75	7	1	1	0.4	30	31	30	26	5	.306	.355	31	5	1B-87, OF-6
7 yrs.	528	1130	301	46	9	5	0.4	122	100	92	124	17	.266	.336	174	44	OF-259, 1B-109

Shag Thompson

THOMPSON, JAMES ALFRED
B. Apr. 29, 1893, Haw River, N. C.   BL TR 5'8½"   165 lbs.

	G	AB	H	2B	3B	HR	HR %	R	RBI	BB	SO	SB	BA	SA	AB	H	G by POS
1914 PHI A	16	29	5	0	1	0	0.0	3	2	7	8	1	.172	.241	5	1	OF-8
1915	17	33	11	2	0	0	0.0	5	2	4	6	0	.333	.394	7	2	OF-7
1916	15	17	0	0	0	0	0.0	4	0	7	6	1	.000	.000	3	0	OF-7
3 yrs.	48	79	16	2	1	0	0.0	12	4	18	20	2	.203	.253	15	3	OF-22

Tim Thompson

THOMPSON, CHARLES LEMOINE
B. Mar. 1, 1924, Coalport, Pa.   BL TR 5'11"   190 lbs.

	G	AB	H	2B	3B	HR	HR %	R	RBI	BB	SO	SB	BA	SA	AB	H	G by POS
1954 BKN N	10	13	2	1	0	0	0.0	2	1	1	1	0	.154	.231	5	1	C-2, OF-1
1956 KC A	92	268	73	13	2	1	0.4	21	27	17	23	2	.272	.347	23	4	C-68
1957	81	230	47	10	0	7	3.0	25	19	18	26	0	.204	.339	19	1	C-62
1958 DET A	4	6	1	0	0	0	0.0	1	0	3	2	0	.167	.167	1	0	C-4
4 yrs.	187	517	123	24	2	8	1.5	49	47	39	52	2	.238	.338	48	6	C-136, OF-1

Tommy Thompson

THOMPSON, RUPERT LUCKHART
B. May 19, 1910, Elkhart, Ill. D. May 24, 1971, Auburn, Calif.   BL TR 5'9½"   155 lbs.

	G	AB	H	2B	3B	HR	HR %	R	RBI	BB	SO	SB	BA	SA	AB	H	G by POS
1933 BOS N	24	97	18	1	0	0	0.0	6	6	4	6	0	.186	.196	0	0	OF-24
1934	105	343	91	12	3	0	0.0	40	37	13	19	2	.265	.318	23	8	OF-82
1935	112	297	81	7	1	4	1.3	34	30	36	17	2	.273	.343	24	3	OF-85
1936	106	266	76	9	0	4	1.5	37	36	31	12	3	.286	.365	37	10	OF-39, 1B-25
1938 CHI A	19	18	2	0	0	0	0.0	2	2	1	2	0	.111	.111	17	2	1B-1
1939 2 teams						CHI A (1G – .000)			STL A (30G – .302)								
" total	31	86	26	5	0	1	1.2	23	8	23	7	0	.302	.395	5	1	OF-23
6 yrs.	397	1107	294	34	4	9	0.8	142	119	108	63	7	.266	.328	106	24	OF-253, 1B-26

Tug Thompson

THOMPSON, JOHN P. F.
B. Indianapolis, Ind. D. July, 1895, Wilmington, Del.   160 lbs.

	G	AB	H	2B	3B	HR	HR %	R	RBI	BB	SO	SB	BA	SA	AB	H	G by POS
1882 CIN AA	1	5	1	0	0	0	0.0	0		0			.200	.200	0	0	OF-1
1884 IND AA	24	97	20	3	0	0	0.0	10		2			.206	.237	0	0	OF-12, C-12
2 yrs.	25	102	21	3	0	0	0.0	10		2			.206	.235	0	0	OF-13, C-12

Bobby Thomson

THOMSON, ROBERT BROWN (The Staten Island Scot)
B. Oct. 25, 1923, Glasgow, Scotland   BR TR 6'2"   180 lbs.

	G	AB	H	2B	3B	HR	HR %	R	RBI	BB	SO	SB	BA	SA	AB	H	G by POS
1946 NY N	18	54	17	4	1	2	3.7	8	9	4	5	0	.315	.537	2	0	3B-16
1947	138	545	154	26	5	29	5.3	105	85	40	78	1	.283	.508	3	0	OF-127, 2B-9
1948	138	471	117	20	2	16	3.4	75	63	30	77	2	.248	.401	9	3	OF-125
1949	156	641	198	35	9	27	4.2	99	109	44	45	10	.309	.518	0	0	OF-156
1950	149	563	142	22	7	25	4.4	79	85	55	45	3	.252	.449	0	0	OF-149
1951	148	518	152	27	8	32	6.2	89	101	73	57	5	.293	.562	2	0	OF-77, 3B-69
1952	153	608	164	29	14	24	3.9	89	108	52	74	5	.270	.482	0	0	3B-91, OF-63
1953	154	608	175	22	6	26	4.3	80	106	43	57	4	.288	.472	0	0	OF-154
1954 MIL N	43	99	23	3	0	2	2.0	7	15	12	29	0	.232	.343	14	5	OF-26
1955	101	343	88	12	3	12	3.5	40	56	34	52	2	.257	.414	13	2	OF-91
1956	142	451	106	10	4	20	4.4	59	74	43	75	2	.235	.408	5	0	OF-136, 3B-3
1957 2 teams						MIL N (41G – .236)			NY N (81G – .242)								
" total	122	363	87	12	7	12	3.3	39	61	27	66	3	.240	.410	13	2	OF-109, 3B-1
1958 CHI N	152	547	155	27	5	21	3.8	67	82	56	76	0	.283	.466	1	1	OF-148, 3B-4
1959	122	374	97	15	2	11	2.9	55	52	35	50	1	.259	.398	9	4	OF-116
1960 2 teams						BOS A (40G – .263)			BAL A (3G – .000)								
" total	43	120	30	3	1	5	4.2	12	20	11	18	0	.250	.417	13	3	OF-29, 1B-1
15 yrs.	1779	6305	1705	267	74	264	4.2	903	1026	559	804	38	.270	.462	84	20	OF-1506, 3B-184, 2B-9, 1B-1

WORLD SERIES

	G	AB	H	2B	3B	HR	HR %	R	RBI	BB	SO	SB	BA	SA	AB	H	G by POS
1951 NY N	6	21	5	1	0	0	0.0	1	2	5	0	0	.238	.286	0	0	3B-6

Dickie Thon

THON, RICHARD WILLIAM
B. June 20, 1958, South Bend, Ind.   BR TR 5'11"   160 lbs.

	G	AB	H	2B	3B	HR	HR %	R	RBI	BB	SO	SB	BA	SA	AB	H	G by POS
1979 CAL A	35	56	19	3	0	0	0.0	6	8	5	10	0	.339	.393	0	0	2B-24, SS-8, DH-1, 3B-1
1980	80	267	68	12	2	0	0.0	32	15	10	28	7	.255	.315	13	2	SS-22, 2B-21, DH-15, 3B-10, 1B-1
1981 HOU N	49	95	26	6	0	0	0.0	13	3	9	13	6	.274	.337	2	0	2B-28, SS-13, 3B-5
1982	136	496	137	31	10	3	0.6	73	36	37	48	37	.276	.397	9	4	SS-119, 3B-8, 2B-1
1983	154	619	177	28	9	20	3.2	81	79	54	73	34	.286	.457	0	0	SS-154
1984	5	17	6	0	1	0	0.0	3	1	0	4	0	.353	.471	0	0	SS-5
6 yrs.	459	1550	433	80	22	23	1.5	208	142	115	176	84	.279	.404	24	6	SS-321, 2B-74, 3B-24, DH-16, 1B-1

DIVISIONAL PLAYOFF SERIES

	G	AB	H	2B	3B	HR	HR %	R	RBI	BB	SO	SB	BA	SA	AB	H	G by POS
1981 HOU N	4	11	2	0	0	0	0.0	0	0	1	0	0	.182	.182	1	0	SS-4

LEAGUE CHAMPIONSHIP SERIES

	G	AB	H	2B	3B	HR	HR %	R	RBI	BB	SO	SB	BA	SA	AB	H	G by POS
1979 CAL A	1	0	0	0	0	0	–	1	0	0	0	0	–	–	0	0	SS-1

	G	AB	H	2B	3B	HR	HR %	R	RBI	BB	SO	SB	BA	SA	Pinch Hit AB	Pinch Hit H	G by POS

Jack Thoney

THONEY, JOHN (Bullet Jack)
Born John Thoeny.
B. Dec. 8, 1880, Ft. Thomas, Ky.   D. Oct. 24, 1948, Covington, Ky.
BR TR

	G	AB	H	2B	3B	HR	HR %	R	RBI	BB	SO	SB	BA	SA	PH AB	PH H	G by POS
1902 2 teams	CLE	A	(28G –	.286)	BAL	A	(3G –	.000)									
" total	31	116	30	7	1	0	0.0	15	11	10		5	.259	.336	1	0	2B-14, SS-11, 3B-3, OF-2
1903 CLE A	32	122	25	3	0	1	0.8	10	9	2		7	.205	.254	2	0	OF-24, 2B-5, 3B-2
1904 2 teams	WAS	A	(17G –	.300)	NY	A	(36G –	.188)									
" total	53	198	45	7	2	0	0.0	23	18	9		11	.227	.283	1	0	OF-27, 3B-26
1908 BOS A	109	416	106	5	9	2	0.5	58	30	13		16	.255	.325	8	3	OF-101
1909	13	40	5	1	0	0	0.0	1	3	2		2	.125	.150	3	0	OF-10
1911	26	20	5	0	0	0	0.0	5	2	0		1	.250	.250	20	5	
6 yrs.	264	912	216	23	12	3	0.3	112	73	36		42	.237	.298	35	8	OF-164, 3B-31, 2B-19, SS-11

Andre Thornton

THORNTON, ANDRE
B. Aug. 13, 1949, Tuskegee, Ala.
BR TR 6'3"   200 lbs.

	G	AB	H	2B	3B	HR	HR %	R	RBI	BB	SO	SB	BA	SA	PH AB	PH H	G by POS
1973 CHI N	17	35	7	3	0	0	0.0	3	2	7	9	0	.200	.286	9	3	1B-9
1974	107	303	79	16	4	10	3.3	41	46	48	50	2	.261	.439	19	6	1B-90, 3B-1
1975	120	372	109	21	4	18	4.8	70	60	88	63	3	.293	.516	9	1	1B-113, 3B-2
1976 2 teams	CHI	N	(27G –	.200)	MON	N	(69G –	.191)									
" total	96	268	52	11	2	11	4.1	28	38	48	46	4	.194	.373	21	4	1B-68, OF-11
1977 CLE A	131	433	114	20	5	28	6.5	77	70	70	82	3	.263	.527	7	1	1B-117, DH-9
1978	145	508	133	22	4	33	6.5	97	105	93	72	4	.262	.516	1	1	1B-145
1979	143	515	120	31	1	26	5.0	89	93	90	93	5	.233	.449	0	0	1B-130, DH-13
1981	69	226	54	12	0	6	2.7	22	30	23	37	3	.239	.372	6	3	DH-53, 1B-11
1982	161	589	161	26	1	32	5.4	90	116	109	81	6	.273	.484	0	0	DH-152, 1B-8
1983	141	508	143	27	1	17	3.3	78	77	87	72	4	.281	.439	2	1	DH-114, 1B-27
1984	155	587	159	26	0	33	5.6	91	99	91	79	6	.271	.484	0	0	DH-144, 1B-11
11 yrs.	1285	4344	1131	215	22	214	4.9	686	736	754	684	40	.260	.468	74	20	1B-729, DH-485, OF-11, 3B-3

Otis Thornton

THORNTON, OTIS BENJAMIN
B. June 30, 1946, Docena, Ala.
BR TR 6'1"   186 lbs.

	G	AB	H	2B	3B	HR	HR %	R	RBI	BB	SO	SB	BA	SA	PH AB	PH H	G by POS
1973 HOU N	2	3	0	0	0	0	0.0	0	1	0	2	0	.000	.000	1	0	C-2

Walter Thornton

THORNTON, WALTER MILLER
B. Feb. 18, 1875, Lewiston, Me.   D. July 14, 1960, Los Angeles, Calif.
TL 6'1"   180 lbs.

	G	AB	H	2B	3B	HR	HR %	R	RBI	BB	SO	SB	BA	SA	PH AB	PH H	G by POS
1895 CHI N	8	22	7	1	0	1	4.5	4	7	3		1	.318	.500	0	0	P-7, 1B-1
1896	9	22	8	0	1	0	0.0	6	1	5		2	.364	.455	1	0	P-5, OF-3
1897	75	265	85	9	6	0	0.0	39	55	30		13	.321	.400	1	0	OF-59, P-16
1898	62	210	62	5	2	0	0.0	34	14	22		8	.295	.338	2	0	OF-34, P-28
4 yrs.	154	519	162	15	9	1	0.2	83	77	60		3	23	.312	.382	4	0	OF-96, P-56, 1B-1

Bob Thorpe

THORPE, BENJAMIN ROBERT
B. Nov. 19, 1926, Caryville, Fla.
BR TR 6'1½"   190 lbs.

	G	AB	H	2B	3B	HR	HR %	R	RBI	BB	SO	SB	BA	SA	PH AB	PH H	G by POS
1951 BOS N	2	2	1	0	1	0	0.0	1	1	0	0	0	.500	1.500	2	1	
1952	81	292	76	8	2	3	1.0	20	26	5	42	3	.260	.332	9	4	OF-72
1953 MIL N	27	37	6	1	0	0	0.0	1	5	1	6	0	.162	.189	9	1	OF-18
3 yrs.	110	331	83	9	3	3	0.9	22	32	6	48	3	.251	.323	20	6	OF-90

Jim Thorpe

THORPE, JAMES FRANCIS
B. May 28, 1888, Prague, Okla.   D. Mar. 28, 1953, Los Angeles, Calif.
BR TR 6'   200 lbs.

	G	AB	H	2B	3B	HR	HR %	R	RBI	BB	SO	SB	BA	SA	PH AB	PH H	G by POS
1913 NY N	19	35	5	0	0	1	2.9	6	2	1	9	2	.143	.229	6	2	OF-9
1914	30	31	6	1	0	0	0.0	5	2	0	4	1	.194	.226	22	5	OF-4
1915	17	52	12	3	1	0	0.0	8	1	2	16	4	.231	.327	1	0	OF-15
1917 2 teams	CIN	N	(77G –	.247)	NY	N	(26G –	.193)									
" total	103	308	73	5	10	4	1.3	41	40	14	45	12	.237	.357	14	3	OF-87
1918 NY N	58	113	28	4	4	1	0.9	15	11	4	18	3	.248	.381	11	3	OF-44
1919 2 teams	NY	N	(2G –	.333)	BOS	N	(60G –	.327)									
" total	62	159	52	7	3	1	0.6	16	26	6	30	7	.327	.428	11	1	OF-40, 1B-2
6 yrs.	289	698	176	20	18	7	1.0	91	82	27	122	29	.252	.362	65	14	OF-199, 1B-2
WORLD SERIES																	
1917 NY N	1	0	0	0	0	0	–	0	0	0	0	0	–	–	0	0	OF-1

Buck Thrasher

THRASHER, FRANK EDWARD
B. Aug. 6, 1889, Watkinsville, Ga.   D. June 12, 1938, Cleveland, Tenn.
BL TR 5'11"   182 lbs.

	G	AB	H	2B	3B	HR	HR %	R	RBI	BB	SO	SB	BA	SA	PH AB	PH H	G by POS
1916 PHI A	7	29	9	2	1	0	0.0	4	4	2	1	0	.310	.448	0	0	OF-7
1917	23	77	18	2	1	0	0.0	5	2	3	12	0	.234	.286	1	0	OF-22
2 yrs.	30	106	27	4	2	0	0.0	9	6	5	13	0	.255	.330	1	0	OF-29

Faye Throneberry

THRONEBERRY, MAYNARD FAYE
Brother of Marv Throneberry.
B. June 22, 1931, Memphis, Tenn.
BL TR 5'11"   185 lbs.

	G	AB	H	2B	3B	HR	HR %	R	RBI	BB	SO	SB	BA	SA	PH AB	PH H	G by POS
1952 BOS A	98	310	80	11	3	5	1.6	38	23	33	67	16	.258	.361	12	1	OF-86
1955	60	144	37	7	3	6	4.2	20	27	14	31	0	.257	.472	24	5	OF-34
1956	24	50	11	2	0	1	2.0	6	3	3	16	0	.220	.320	11	2	OF-13
1957 2 teams	BOS	A	(1G –	.000)	WAS	A	(68G –	.185)									
" total	69	196	36	8	2	2	1.0	21	12	17	38	0	.184	.276	7	0	OF-58
1958 WAS A	44	87	16	1	1	4	4.6	12	7	4	28	0	.184	.356	17	5	OF-26
1959	117	327	82	11	2	10	3.1	36	42	33	61	6	.251	.388	28	3	OF-86
1960	85	157	39	7	1	1	0.6	18	23	18	33	1	.248	.325	40	12	OF-34
1961 LA A	24	31	6	1	0	0	0.0	1	0	5	10	0	.194	.226	16	3	OF-5
8 yrs.	521	1302	307	48	12	29	2.2	152	137	127	284	23	.236	.358	155	31	OF-342

Marv Throneberry

THRONEBERRY, MARVIN EUGENE (Marvelous Marv)
Brother of Faye Throneberry.
B. Sept. 2, 1933, Collierville, Tenn.
BL TL 6'1"   190 lbs.

	G	AB	H	2B	3B	HR	HR %	R	RBI	BB	SO	SB	BA	SA	PH AB	PH H	G by POS
1955 NY A	1	2	2	1	0	0	0.0	1	3	0	0	1	1.000	1.500	0	0	1B-1

	G	AB	H	2B	3B	HR	HR %	R	RBI	BB	SO	SB	BA	SA	Pinch Hit AB	Pinch Hit H	G by POS

Marv Throneberry continued

	G	AB	H	2B	3B	HR	HR %	R	RBI	BB	SO	SB	BA	SA	AB	H	G by POS
1958	60	150	34	5	2	7	4.7	30	19	19	40	1	.227	.427	12	0	1B-40, OF-5
1959	80	192	46	5	0	8	4.2	27	22	18	51	0	.240	.391	15	1	1B-54, OF-13
1960 KC A	104	236	59	9	2	11	4.7	29	41	23	60	0	.250	.445	33	8	1B-71
1961 2 teams	KC	A	(40G –	.238)		BAL	A	(56G –	.208)								
" total	96	226	51	5	1	11	4.9	26	35	31	50	0	.226	.403	26	7	1B-41, OF-25
1962 2 teams	BAL	A	(9G –	.000)		NY	N	(116G –	.244)								
" total	125	366	87	11	3	16	4.4	30	49	38	89	1	.238	.415	26	5	1B-97, OF-2
1963 NY N	14	14	2	1	0	0	0.0	0	1	1	5	0	.143	.214	10	2	1B-3
7 yrs.	480	1186	281	37	8	53	4.5	143	170	130	295	3	.237	.416	122	23	1B-307, OF-45
WORLD SERIES																	
1958 NY A	1	1	0	0	0	0	0.0	0	0	0	1	0	.000	.000	1	0	

Bob Thurman

THURMAN, ROBERT BURNS   BL TL 6'1"   205 lbs.
B. May 14, 1921, Wichita, Kans.

	G	AB	H	2B	3B	HR	HR %	R	RBI	BB	SO	SB	BA	SA	AB	H	G by POS
1955 CIN N	82	152	33	2	3	7	4.6	19	22	17	26	0	.217	.408	44	9	OF-36
1956	80	139	41	5	2	8	5.8	25	22	10	14	0	.295	.532	48	9	OF-29
1957	74	190	47	4	2	16	8.4	38	40	15	33	0	.247	.542	34	9	OF-44
1958	94	178	41	7	4	4	2.2	23	20	20	38	1	.230	.382	48	11	OF-41
1959	4	4	1	0	0	0	0.0	1	2	0	1	0	.250	.250	4	1	
5 yrs.	334	663	163	18	11	35	5.3	106	106	62	112	1	.246	.465	178	39	OF-150

Sloppy Thurston

THURSTON, HOLLIS JOHN   BR TR 5'11"   165 lbs.
B. June 2, 1899, Fremont, Neb.   D. Sept. 14, 1973, Los Angeles, Calif.

	G	AB	H	2B	3B	HR	HR %	R	RBI	BB	SO	SB	BA	SA	AB	H	G by POS
1923 2 teams	STL	A	(2G –	.000)		CHI	A	(45G –	.316)								
" total	47	79	25	5	1	0	0.0	10	4	2	6	0	.316	.405	1	0	P-46
1924 CHI A	51	122	31	6	3	1	0.8	15	9	5	14	0	.254	.377	10	3	P-38, OF-1
1925	44	84	24	7	2	0	0.0	2	13	5	13	0	.286	.417	6	2	P-36
1926	38	61	19	4	0	0	0.0	5	5	3	6	0	.311	.377	5	0	P-31
1927 WAS A	42	92	29	4	2	2	2.2	11	17	5	10	1	.315	.467	9	1	P-29
1930 BKN N	36	50	10	3	0	1	2.0	3	11	0	16	0	.200	.320	10	2	P-24
1931	24	60	13	2	1	1	1.7	8	8	2	10	0	.217	.333	0	0	P-24
1932	29	56	17	5	1	0	0.0	7	5	2	9	0	.304	.429	1	0	P-28
1933	32	44	7	2	0	0	0.0	4	7	0	7	0	.159	.205	0	0	P-32
9 yrs.	343	648	175	38	10	5	0.8	65	79	24	91	1	.270	.383	42	8	P-288, OF-1

Eddie Tiemeyer

TIEMEYER, EDWARD CARL   BR TR 5'11½" 185 lbs.
B. May 9, 1885, Cincinnati, Ohio   D. Sept. 27, 1946, Cincinnati, Ohio

	G	AB	H	2B	3B	HR	HR %	R	RBI	BB	SO	SB	BA	SA	AB	H	G by POS
1906 CIN N	5	11	2	0	0	0	0.0	3	0	1		0	.182	.182	1	0	3B-3, P-1
1907	1	0	0	0	0	0	–	1	0	1		0	–	–	0	0	
1909 NY A	3	8	3	1	0	0	0.0	1	0	1		0	.375	.500	0	0	1B-3
3 yrs.	9	19	5	1	0	0	0.0	5	0	3		0	.263	.316	1	0	3B-3, 1B-3, P-1

Mike Tiernan

TIERNAN, MICHAEL JOSEPH (Silent Mike)   BL TL 5'11" 165 lbs.
B. Jan. 21, 1867, Trenton, N. J.   D. Nov. 9, 1918, New York, N. Y.

	G	AB	H	2B	3B	HR	HR %	R	RBI	BB	SO	SB	BA	SA	AB	H	G by POS
1887 NY N	103	407	117	13	12	10	2.5	82	62	32	31	28	.287	.452	0	0	OF-103, P-5
1888	113	443	130	16	8	9	2.0	75	52	42	42	52	.293	.427	0	0	OF-113
1889	122	499	167	22	14	11	2.2	147	73	96	32	33	.335	.501	0	0	OF-122
1890	133	553	168	25	21	13	2.4	132	59	68	53	56	.304	.495	0	0	OF-133
1891	134	542	166	30	12	17	3.1	111	73	69	32	53	.306	.500	0	0	OF-134
1892	116	450	129	16	10	5	1.1	79	66	57	46	20	.287	.400	0	0	OF-116
1893	125	511	158	19	12	15	2.9	114	102	72	24	26	.309	.481	0	0	OF-125
1894	112	424	117	19	13	5	1.2	84	77	54	21	28	.276	.417	1	0	OF-111
1895	120	476	165	23	21	7	1.5	127	70	66	19	36	.347	.527	0	0	OF-119
1896	133	521	192	24	16	7	1.3	132	89	77	18	35	.369	.516	0	0	OF-133
1897	127	528	174	29	10	5	0.9	123	72	61		40	.330	.451	0	0	OF-127
1898	103	415	116	15	11	4	1.0	90	49	43		19	.280	.398	0	0	OF-103
1899	35	137	35	4	2	0	0.0	17	7	10		2	.255	.314	0	0	OF-35
13 yrs.	1476	5906	1834	255	162	108	1.8	1313	851	747	318	428	.311	.463	1	0	OF-1474, P-5

Bill Tierney

TIERNEY, WILLIAM J.
B. May 14, 1858, Boston, Mass.   D. Sept. 21, 1898, Boston, Mass.

	G	AB	H	2B	3B	HR	HR %	R	RBI	BB	SO	SB	BA	SA	AB	H	G by POS
1882 CIN AA	1	5	0	0	0	0	0.0	1		0			.000	.000	0	0	1B-1
1884 BAL U	1	3	1	0	0	0	0.0	0		1			.333	.333	0	0	OF-1
2 yrs.	2	8	1	0	0	0	0.0	1		1			.125	.125	0	0	OF-1, 1B-1

Cotton Tierney

TIERNEY, JAMES ARTHUR   BR TR 5'8"   175 lbs.
B. Feb. 10, 1894, Kansas City, Kans.   D. Apr. 18, 1953, Kansas City, Mo.

	G	AB	H	2B	3B	HR	HR %	R	RBI	BB	SO	SB	BA	SA	AB	H	G by POS
1920 PIT N	12	46	11	5	0	0	0.0	4	8	3	4	1	.239	.348	0	0	2B-10, SS-2
1921	117	442	132	22	8	3	0.7	49	52	24	31	4	.299	.405	3	0	2B-72, 3B-37, OF-4, SS-3
1922	122	441	152	26	14	7	1.6	58	86	22	40	7	.345	.515	13	3	2B-105, OF-2, SS-1, 3B-1
1923 2 teams	PIT	N	(29G –	.292)		PHI	N	(121G –	.317)								
" total	150	600	187	36	3	13	2.2	90	88	26	52	5	.312	.447	0	0	2B-143, OF-5, 3B-2
1924 BOS N	136	505	131	16	1	6	1.2	38	58	22	37	11	.259	.331	2	1	2B-115, 3B-22
1925 BKN N	93	265	68	14	4	2	0.8	27	39	12	23	0	.257	.362	28	7	3B-61, 2B-1, 1B-1
6 yrs.	630	2299	681	119	30	31	1.3	266	331	109	187	28	.296	.415	46	11	2B-446, 3B-123, OF-11, SS-6, 1B-1

John Tilley

TILLEY, JOHN C.
B. 1856, New York, N. Y.   Deceased.

	G	AB	H	2B	3B	HR	HR %	R	RBI	BB	SO	SB	BA	SA	AB	H	G by POS
1882 CLE N	15	56	5	1	1	0	0.0	2	4	2	11		.089	.143	0	0	OF-15
1884 2 teams	TOL	AA	(17G –	.179)		STP	U	(9G –	.154)								
" total	26	82	14	3	0	0	0.0	7		7			.171	.207	0	0	OF-26
2 yrs.	41	138	19	4	1	0	0.0	9	4	9	11		.138	.181	0	0	OF-41

	G	AB	H	2B	3B	HR	HR %	R	RBI	BB	SO	SB	BA	SA	Pinch Hit AB	Pinch Hit H	G by POS

Phil Todt continued

	G	AB	H	2B	3B	HR	HR %	R	RBI	BB	SO	SB	BA	SA	AB	H	G by POS
1928	144	539	136	31	8	12	2.2	61	73	26	47	6	.252	.406	1	0	1B-144
1929	153	534	140	37	10	4	0.7	49	64	31	28	6	.262	.391	0	0	1B-153
1930	111	383	103	22	5	11	2.9	49	62	24	33	4	.269	.439	6	1	1B-104
1931 PHI A	62	197	48	14	2	5	2.5	23	44	8	22	1	.244	.411	8	2	1B-52
8 yrs.	957	3415	880	182	58	57	1.7	372	453	207	229	29	.258	.395	47	7	1B-904, OF-4

WORLD SERIES
| 1931 PHI A | 1 | 0 | 0 | 0 | 0 | 0 | – | 0 | 0 | 1 | 0 | 0 | – | – | 0 | 0 | |

Bobby Tolan

TOLAN, ROBERT
B. Nov. 19, 1945, Los Angeles, Calif.   BL TL 5'11"   170 lbs.

	G	AB	H	2B	3B	HR	HR %	R	RBI	BB	SO	SB	BA	SA	AB	H	G by POS
1965 STL N	17	69	13	2	0	0	0.0	8	6	0	4	2	.188	.217	0	0	OF-17
1966	43	93	16	5	1	1	1.1	10	6	6	15	1	.172	.280	12	3	OF-26, 1B-1
1967	110	265	67	7	3	6	2.3	35	32	19	43	12	.253	.370	33	10	OF-80, 1B-13
1968	92	278	64	12	1	5	1.8	28	17	13	42	9	.230	.335	23	2	OF-67, 1B-9
1969 CIN N	152	637	194	25	10	21	3.3	104	93	27	92	26	.305	.474	2	0	OF-150
1970	152	589	186	34	6	16	2.7	112	80	62	94	57	.316	.475	5	1	OF-150
1972	149	604	171	28	5	8	1.3	88	82	44	88	42	.283	.386	1	0	OF-149
1973	129	457	94	14	2	9	2.0	42	51	27	68	15	.206	.304	12	3	OF-120
1974 SD N	95	357	95	16	1	8	2.2	45	40	20	41	7	.266	.384	4	0	OF-88
1975	147	506	129	19	4	5	1.0	58	43	28	45	11	.255	.338	14	2	OF-120, 1B-27
1976 PHI N	110	272	71	7	0	5	1.8	32	35	7	39	10	.261	.342	33	4	1B-50, OF-35
1977 2 teams		PHI N	(15G –	.125)		PIT N	(49G –	.203)									
" total	64	90	17	4	0	2	2.2	8	10	5	14	1	.189	.300	40	8	1B-25, OF-2
1979 SD N	22	21	4	0	1	0	0.0	2	2	2	2	0	.190	.286	13	3	1B-5, OF-1
13 yrs.	1282	4238	1121	173	34	86	2.0	572	497	258	587	193	.265	.382	192	36	OF-1005, 1B-130

LEAGUE CHAMPIONSHIP SERIES
1970 CIN N	3	12	5	0	0	1	8.3	3	2	1	1	1	.417	.667	0	0	OF-3
1972	5	21	5	1	1	0	0.0	3	4	0	4	0	.238	.381	0	0	OF-5
1976 PHI N	3	2	0	0	0	0	0.0	0	0	1	0	0	.000	.000	2	0	OF-1
3 yrs.	11	35	10	1	1	1	2.9	6	6	2	5	1	.286	.457	2	0	OF-9

WORLD SERIES
1967 STL N	3	2	0	0	0	0	0.0	1	0	1	1	0	.000	.000	2	0	
1968	1	1	0	0	0	0	0.0	0	0	0	1	0	.000	.000	1	0	
1970 CIN N	5	19	4	1	0	1	5.3	5	5	3	2	1	.211	.421	0	0	OF-5
1972	7	26	7	1	0	0	0.0	2	6	1	4	5	.269	.308	0	0	OF-7
4 yrs.	16	48	11	2	0	1	2.1	8	7	5	8	6	.229	.333	3	0	OF-12

Wayne Tolleson

TOLLESON, JIMMY WAYNE
B. Nov. 22, 1959, Spartanburg, S. C.   BB TR 5'9"   160 lbs.

	G	AB	H	2B	3B	HR	HR %	R	RBI	BB	SO	SB	BA	SA	AB	H	G by POS
1981 TEX A	14	24	4	0	0	0	0.0	6	1	1	5	2	.167	.167	1	0	3B-6, SS-2
1982	38	70	8	1	0	0	0.0	6	2	5	14	1	.114	.129	0	0	SS-26, 3B-4, 2B-1
1983	134	470	122	13	2	3	0.6	64	20	40	68	33	.260	.315	0	0	2B-112, SS-26, DH-1
1984	118	338	72	9	2	0	0.0	35	9	27	47	22	.213	.251	0	0	2B-109, SS-7, 3B-5, DH-1, OF-1
4 yrs.	304	902	206	23	4	3	0.3	111	32	73	134	58	.228	.273	1	0	2B-222, SS-61, 3B-15, DH-2, OF-1

Tim Tolman

TOLMAN, TIMOTHY LEE
B. Apr. 20, 1956, Santa Monica, Calif.   BR TR 6'   190 lbs.

	G	AB	H	2B	3B	HR	HR %	R	RBI	BB	SO	SB	BA	SA	AB	H	G by POS
1981 HOU N	4	8	1	0	0	0	0.0	0	0	0	0	0	.125	.125	2	0	OF-3
1982	15	26	5	2	0	1	3.8	4	3	4	3	0	.192	.385	7	1	OF-5, 1B-1
1983	43	56	11	4	0	2	3.6	4	10	6	9	0	.196	.375	30	4	1B-7, OF-3
1984	14	17	3	1	0	0	0.0	2	0	0	3	0	.176	.235	10	1	OF-3, 1B-1
4 yrs.	76	107	20	7	0	3	2.8	10	13	10	15	0	.187	.336	49	6	OF-14, 1B-9

Chick Tolson

TOLSON, CHARLES JULIUS (Slug)
B. Nov. 6, 1898, Washington, D. C.   D. Apr. 16, 1965, Washington, D. C.   BR TR 6'   185 lbs.

	G	AB	H	2B	3B	HR	HR %	R	RBI	BB	SO	SB	BA	SA	AB	H	G by POS
1925 CLE A	3	12	3	0	0	0	0.0	0	0	2	1	0	.250	.250	0	0	1B-3
1926 CHI N	57	80	25	6	1	1	1.3	4	8	5	8	0	.313	.450	40	14	1B-13
1927	39	54	16	4	0	2	3.7	6	17	4	9	0	.296	.481	27	7	1B-8
1929	32	109	28	5	0	1	0.9	13	19	9	16	0	.257	.330	0	0	1B-32
1930	13	20	6	1	0	0	0.0	0	1	6	5	1	.300	.350	7	2	1B-5
5 yrs.	144	275	78	16	1	4	1.5	23	45	26	39	1	.284	.393	74	23	1B-61

WORLD SERIES
| 1929 CHI N | 1 | 1 | 0 | 0 | 0 | 0 | 0.0 | 0 | 0 | 0 | 1 | 0 | .000 | .000 | 1 | 0 | |

George Tomer

TOMER, GEORGE CLARENCE
B. Nov. 26, 1895, Perry, Iowa   BR TR 6'   180 lbs.

	G	AB	H	2B	3B	HR	HR %	R	RBI	BB	SO	SB	BA	SA	AB	H	G by POS
1913 STL A	1	1	0	0	0	0	0.0	0	0	0	1	0	.000	.000	1	0	

Phil Tomney

TOMNEY, PHILIP H.
B. July 17, 1863, Reading, Pa.   D. Mar. 18, 1892, Reading, Pa.   BR TR 5'7"   155 lbs.

	G	AB	H	2B	3B	HR	HR %	R	RBI	BB	SO	SB	BA	SA	AB	H	G by POS
1888 LOU AA	34	120	18	3	0	0	0.0	15	4	7		11	.150	.175	0	0	SS-34
1889	112	376	80	8	5	4	1.1	61	38	46	47	26	.213	.293	0	0	SS-112
1890	108	386	107	21	7	1	0.3	72		43		27	.277	.376	0	0	SS-108
3 yrs.	254	882	205	32	12	5	0.6	148	42	96	47	64	.232	.313	0	0	SS-254

Tony Tonneman

TONNEMAN, CHARLES RICHARD
B. Sept. 10, 1881, Chicago, Ill.   D. Aug. 7, 1951, Prescott, Ariz.   BR TR 5'10½" 175 lbs.

	G	AB	H	2B	3B	HR	HR %	R	RBI	BB	SO	SB	BA	SA	AB	H	G by POS
1911 BOS A	2	5	1	1	0	0	0.0	0	3	1		0	.200	.400	0	0	C-2

	G	AB	H	2B	3B	HR	HR %	R	RBI	BB	SO	SB	BA	SA	Pinch Hit AB	Pinch Hit H	G by POS

Bert Tooley

TOOLEY, ALBERT   BR TR 5'10" 155 lbs.
B. Aug. 30, 1886, Howell, Mich.   D. Aug. 17, 1976, Marshall, Mich.

	G	AB	H	2B	3B	HR	HR %	R	RBI	BB	SO	SB	BA	SA	AB	H	G by POS
1911 BKN N	119	433	89	11	3	1	0.2	55	29	53	63	18	.206	.252	3	1	SS-114
1912	77	265	62	6	5	2	0.8	34	37	19	21	12	.234	.317	0	0	SS-76
2 yrs.	196	698	151	17	8	3	0.4	89	66	72	84	30	.216	.277	3	1	SS-190

Specs Toporcer

TOPORCER, GEORGE   BL TR 5'10½" 165 lbs.
B. Feb. 9, 1899, New York, N. Y.

	G	AB	H	2B	3B	HR	HR %	R	RBI	BB	SO	SB	BA	SA	AB	H	G by POS
1921 STL N	22	53	14	1	0	0	0.0	4	2	3	4	1	.264	.283	6	1	2B-12, SS-2
1922	116	352	114	25	6	3	0.9	56	36	24	18	2	.324	.455	15	6	SS-91, 3B-6, OF-1, 2B-1
1923	97	303	77	11	3	3	1.0	45	35	41	14	4	.254	.340	8	3	2B-52, SS-33, 3B-1, 1B-1
1924	70	198	62	10	3	1	0.5	30	24	11	14	2	.313	.409	10	1	3B-33, SS-25, 2B-3
1925	83	268	76	13	4	2	0.7	38	26	36	15	7	.284	.384	8	2	SS-66, 2B-7
1926	64	88	22	3	2	0	0.0	13	9	8	9	1	.250	.330	23	9	2B-27, SS-5, 3B-1
1927	86	290	72	13	4	0	0.0	37	19	27	16	5	.248	.321	8	3	3B-54, SS-27, 2B-2, 1B-1
1928	8	14	0	0	0	0	0.0	0	0	0	3	0	.000	.000	6	0	2B-1, 1B-1
8 yrs.	546	1566	437	76	22	9	0.6	223	151	150	93	22	.279	.373	84	25	SS-249, 2B-105, 3B-95, 1B-3, OF-1

WORLD SERIES

	G	AB	H	2B	3B	HR	HR %	R	RBI	BB	SO	SB	BA	SA	AB	H	G by POS
1926 STL N	1	0	0	0	0	0	–	0	1	0	0	0	–	–	0	0	

Jeff Torborg

TORBORG, JEFFREY ALLEN   BR TR 6'½" 195 lbs.
B. Nov. 26, 1941, Plainfield, N. J.
Manager 1977-79.

	G	AB	H	2B	3B	HR	HR %	R	RBI	BB	SO	SB	BA	SA	AB	H	G by POS
1964 LA N	28	43	10	1	1	0	0.0	4	4	3	8	0	.233	.302	1	0	C-27
1965	56	150	36	5	1	3	2.0	8	13	10	26	0	.240	.347	6	1	C-53
1966	46	120	27	3	0	1	0.8	4	13	10	23	0	.225	.275	2	0	C-45
1967	76	196	42	4	1	2	1.0	11	12	13	31	1	.214	.276	1	1	C-75
1968	37	93	15	2	0	0	0.0	2	4	6	10	0	.161	.183	0	0	C-37
1969	51	124	23	4	0	0	0.0	7	7	9	17	1	.185	.218	1	0	C-50
1970	64	134	31	8	0	1	0.7	11	17	14	15	1	.231	.313	2	1	C-63
1971 CAL A	55	123	25	5	0	0	0.0	6	5	3	6	0	.203	.244	6	0	C-49
1972	59	153	32	3	0	0	0.0	5	8	14	21	0	.209	.229	1	0	C-58
1973	102	255	56	7	0	1	0.4	20	18	21	32	0	.220	.259	0	0	C-102
10 yrs.	574	1391	297	42	3	8	0.6	78	101	103	189	3	.214	.265	20	3	C-559

Earl Torgeson

TORGESON, CLIFFORD EARL (The Earl of Snohomish)   BL TL 6'3" 180 lbs.
B. Jan. 1, 1924, Snohomish, Wash.

	G	AB	H	2B	3B	HR	HR %	R	RBI	BB	SO	SB	BA	SA	AB	H	G by POS
1947 BOS N	128	399	112	20	6	16	4.0	73	78	82	59	11	.281	.481	11	1	1B-117
1948	134	438	111	23	5	10	2.3	70	67	81	54	19	.253	.397	4	2	1B-129
1949	25	100	26	5	1	4	4.0	17	19	13	4	4	.260	.450	0	0	1B-25
1950	156	576	167	30	3	23	4.0	120	87	119	69	15	.290	.472	0	0	1B-156
1951	155	581	153	21	4	24	4.1	99	92	102	70	20	.263	.437	0	0	1B-155
1952	122	382	88	17	0	5	1.3	49	34	81	38	11	.230	.314	12	2	1B-105, OF-5
1953 PHI N	111	379	104	25	8	11	2.9	58	64	53	57	7	.274	.470	6	1	1B-105
1954	135	490	133	22	6	5	1.0	63	54	75	52	7	.271	.371	1	0	1B-133
1955 2 teams		PHI	N	(47G –	.267)		DET	A	(89G –	.283)							
" total	136	450	125	15	4	10	2.2	87	67	93	49	11	.278	.396	9	3	1B-126
1956 DET A	117	318	84	9	3	12	3.8	61	42	78	47	6	.264	.425	27	10	1B-83
1957 2 teams		DET	A	(30G –	.240)		CHI	A	(86G –	.295)							
" total	116	301	86	13	3	8	2.7	58	51	61	54	7	.286	.429	28	8	1B-87, OF-1
1958 CHI A	96	188	50	8	0	10	5.3	37	30	48	29	7	.266	.468	24	9	1B-73
1959	127	277	61	5	3	9	3.2	40	45	62	55	7	.220	.357	24	5	1B-103
1960	68	57	15	2	0	2	3.5	12	9	21	8	1	.263	.404	41	12	1B-10
1961 2 teams		CHI	A	(20G –	.067)		NY	A	(22G –	.111)							
"	42	33	3	0	0	0	0.0	4	1	11	8	0	.091	.091	23	2	1B-9
15 yrs.	1668	4969	1318	215	46	149	3.0	848	740	980	653	133	.265	.417	210	55	1B-1416, OF-6

WORLD SERIES

	G	AB	H	2B	3B	HR	HR %	R	RBI	BB	SO	SB	BA	SA	AB	H	G by POS
1948 BOS N	5	18	7	3	0	0	0.0	2	1	2	1	1	.389	.556	0	0	1B-5
1959 CHI A	3	1	0	0	0	0	0.0	1	0	1	0	0	.000	.000	1	0	1B-1
2 yrs.	8	19	7	3	0	0	0.0	3	1	3	1	1	.368	.526	1	0	1B-6

Red Torphy

TORPHY, WALTER ANTHONY   BR TR 5'11" 169 lbs.
B. Nov. 6, 1891, Fall River, Mass.   D. Feb. 11, 1980, Fall River, Mass.

	G	AB	H	2B	3B	HR	HR %	R	RBI	BB	SO	SB	BA	SA	AB	H	G by POS
1920 BOS N	3	15	3	2	0	0	0.0	1	2	0	1	0	.200	.333	0	0	1B-3

Frank Torre

TORRE, FRANK JOSEPH   BL TL 6'4" 200 lbs.
Brother of Joe Torre.
B. Dec. 30, 1931, Brooklyn, N. Y.

	G	AB	H	2B	3B	HR	HR %	R	RBI	BB	SO	SB	BA	SA	AB	H	G by POS
1956 MIL N	111	159	41	6	0	0	0.0	17	16	11	4	1	.258	.296	23	5	1B-89
1957	129	364	99	19	5	5	1.4	46	40	29	19	0	.272	.393	15	5	1B-117
1958	138	372	115	22	5	6	1.6	41	55	42	14	2	.309	.444	17	6	1B-122
1959	115	263	60	15	1	1	0.4	23	33	35	12	0	.228	.304	28	7	1B-87
1960	21	44	9	1	0	0	0.0	2	5	3	2	0	.205	.227	3	1	1B-17
1962 PHI N	108	168	52	8	2	0	0.0	13	20	24	6	1	.310	.381	33	4	1B-76
1963	92	112	28	7	2	1	0.9	8	10	11	7	0	.250	.375	32	8	1B-56
7 yrs.	714	1482	404	78	15	13	0.9	150	179	155	64	4	.273	.372	151	36	1B-564

WORLD SERIES

	G	AB	H	2B	3B	HR	HR %	R	RBI	BB	SO	SB	BA	SA	AB	H	G by POS
1957 MIL N	7	10	3	0	0	2	20.0	2	3	2	0	0	.300	.900	1	0	1B-7
1958	7	17	3	0	0	0	0.0	0	1	2	0	0	.176	.176	3	0	1B-7
2 yrs.	14	27	6	0	0	2	7.4	2	4	4	0	0	.222	.444	4	0	1B-14

	G	AB	H	2B	3B	HR	HR %	R	RBI	BB	SO	SB	BA	SA	Pinch Hit AB	Pinch Hit H	G by POS

Joe Torre

TORRE, JOSEPH PAUL
Brother of Frank Torre.
B. July 18, 1940, Brooklyn, N. Y.
Manager 1977-84.
BR TR 6'2" 212 lbs.

	G	AB	H	2B	3B	HR	HR %	R	RBI	BB	SO	SB	BA	SA	PH AB	PH H	G by POS
1960 MIL N	2	2	1	0	0	0	0.0	0	0	0	1	0	.500	.500	2	1	
1961	113	406	113	21	4	10	2.5	40	42	28	60	3	.278	.424	3	2	C-112
1962	80	220	62	8	1	5	2.3	23	26	24	24	1	.282	.395	16	6	C-63
1963	142	501	147	19	4	14	2.8	57	71	42	79	1	.293	.431	7	1	C-105, 1B-37, OF-2
1964	154	601	193	36	5	20	3.3	87	109	36	67	2	.321	.498	2	1	C-96, 1B-70
1965	148	523	152	21	1	27	5.2	68	80	61	79	0	.291	.489	5	2	C-100, 1B-49
1966 ATL N	148	546	172	20	3	36	6.6	83	101	60	61	0	.315	.560	3	1	C-114, 1B-36
1967	135	477	132	18	1	20	4.2	67	68	49	75	2	.277	.444	6	1	C-114, 1B-23
1968	115	424	115	11	2	10	2.4	45	55	34	72	1	.271	.377	1	0	C-92, 1B-29
1969 STL N	159	602	174	29	6	18	3.0	72	101	66	85	0	.289	.447	1	0	1B-144, C-17
1970	161	624	203	27	9	21	3.4	89	100	70	91	2	.325	.498	0	0	C-90, 3B-73, 1B-1
1971	161	634	230	34	8	24	3.8	97	137	63	70	4	.363	.555	0	0	3B-161
1972	149	544	157	26	6	11	2.0	71	81	54	64	3	.289	.419	6	4	3B-117, 1B-27
1973	141	519	149	17	2	13	2.5	67	69	65	78	2	.287	.403	0	0	1B-114, 3B-58
1974	147	529	149	28	1	11	2.1	59	70	69	88	1	.282	.401	4	2	1B-139, 3B-18
1975 NY N	114	361	89	16	3	6	1.7	33	35	35	55	0	.247	.357	22	5	3B-83, 1B-24
1976	114	310	95	10	3	5	1.6	36	31	21	35	1	.306	.406	35	8	1B-78, 3B-4
1977	26	51	9	3	0	1	2.0	2	9	2	10	0	.176	.294	11	2	1B-16, 3B-1
18 yrs.	2209	7874	2342	344	59	252	3.2	996	1185	779	1094	23	.297	.452	124	36	C-903, 1B-787, 3B-515, OF-2

Felix Torres

TORRES, FELIX SANCHEZ
B. May 1, 1932, Ponce, Puerto Rico
BR TR 5'11" 165 lbs.

	G	AB	H	2B	3B	HR	HR %	R	RBI	BB	SO	SB	BA	SA	PH AB	PH H	G by POS
1962 LA A	127	451	117	19	4	11	2.4	44	74	28	73	0	.259	.392	6	1	3B-123
1963	138	463	121	32	1	4	0.9	40	51	30	73	1	.261	.361	12	3	3B-122, 1B-2
1964	100	277	64	10	0	12	4.3	25	28	13	56	1	.231	.397	23	3	3B-72, 1B-3
3 yrs.	365	1191	302	61	5	27	2.3	109	153	71	202	2	.254	.381	41	7	3B-317, 1B-5

Gil Torres

TORRES, DON GILBERTO NUNEZ
Son of Ricardo Torres.
B. Aug. 23, 1915, Regla, Cuba   D. Jan. 11, 1983, Regla, Cuba
BR TR 6' 155 lbs.

	G	AB	H	2B	3B	HR	HR %	R	RBI	BB	SO	SB	BA	SA	PH AB	PH H	G by POS
1940 WAS A	2	0	0	0	0	0	–	0	0	0	0	0	–	–	0	0	P-2
1944	134	524	140	20	6	0	0.0	42	58	21	24	10	.267	.328	0	0	3B-123, 2B-10, 1B-4
1945	147	562	133	12	5	0	0.0	39	48	21	29	7	.237	.276	0	0	SS-145, 3B-2
1946	63	185	47	8	0	0	0.0	18	13	11	12	3	.254	.297	5	0	SS-31, 3B-18, 2B-7, P-3
4 yrs.	346	1271	320	40	11	0	0.0	99	119	53	65	20	.252	.301	5	0	SS-176, 3B-143, 2B-17, P-5, 1B-4

Hector Torres

TORRES, HECTOR EPITACIO
B. Sept. 16, 1945, Monterrey, Mexico
BR TR 6' 175 lbs.

	G	AB	H	2B	3B	HR	HR %	R	RBI	BB	SO	SB	BA	SA	PH AB	PH H	G by POS
1968 HOU N	128	466	104	11	1	1	0.2	44	24	18	64	2	.223	.258	1	0	SS-127, 2B-1
1969	34	69	11	1	0	1	1.4	5	8	2	12	0	.159	.217	14	3	SS-22
1970	31	65	16	1	2	0	0.0	6	5	6	8	0	.246	.323	4	1	SS-22, 2B-6
1971 CHI N	31	58	13	3	0	0	0.0	4	2	4	10	0	.224	.276	4	1	SS-18, 2B-4
1972 MON N	83	181	28	4	1	2	1.1	14	7	13	26	0	.155	.221	7	1	2B-60, SS-16, OF-2, 3B-1, P-1
1973 HOU N	38	66	6	1	0	0	0.0	3	2	7	13	0	.091	.106	3	0	SS-22, 2B-13
1975 SD N	112	352	91	12	0	5	1.4	31	26	22	32	2	.259	.335	0	0	SS-75, 3B-42, 2B-16
1976	74	215	42	6	0	4	1.9	8	15	16	31	2	.195	.279	8	0	SS-63, 3B-4, 2B-3
1977 TOR A	91	266	64	7	3	5	1.9	33	26	16	33	1	.241	.346	2	1	SS-68, 2B-23, 3B-2
9 yrs.	622	1738	375	46	7	18	1.0	148	115	104	229	7	.216	.281	43	7	SS-433, 2B-126, 3B-49, OF-2, P-1

Ricardo Torres

TORRES, RICARDO J.
Father of Gil Torres.
B. 1894, Cuba   D. Havana, Cuba
BR TR 5'11" 160 lbs.

	G	AB	H	2B	3B	HR	HR %	R	RBI	BB	SO	SB	BA	SA	PH AB	PH H	G by POS
1920 WAS A	16	30	10	1	0	0	0.0	8	3	1	4	0	.333	.367	2	1	1B-7, C-5
1921	2	3	1	0	0	0	0.0	1	0	1	1	0	.333	.333	0	0	C-2
1922	4	4	0	0	0	0	0.0	0	0	0	1	0	.000	.000	1	0	C-3
3 yrs.	22	37	11	1	0	0	0.0	9	3	2	6	0	.297	.324	3	1	C-10, 1B-7

Rusty Torres

TORRES, ROSENDO JR.
B. Sept. 30, 1948, Aguadilla, Puerto Rico
BB TR 5'10" 175 lbs.

	G	AB	H	2B	3B	HR	HR %	R	RBI	BB	SO	SB	BA	SA	PH AB	PH H	G by POS
1971 NY A	9	26	10	3	0	2	7.7	5	3	0	8	0	.385	.731	4	0	OF-5
1972	80	199	42	7	0	3	1.5	15	13	18	44	0	.211	.291	22	7	OF-62
1973 CLE A	122	312	64	8	1	7	2.2	31	28	50	62	6	.205	.304	7	3	OF-114
1974	108	150	28	2	0	3	2.0	19	12	13	24	2	.187	.260	12	1	OF-94, DH-1
1976 CAL A	120	264	54	16	3	6	2.3	37	27	36	39	4	.205	.356	3	0	OF-105, DH-6, 3B-1
1977	58	77	12	1	1	3	3.9	9	10	10	18	0	.156	.312	2	1	OF-54
1978 CHI A	16	44	14	3	0	3	6.8	7	6	6	7	0	.318	.591	1	0	OF-14
1979	90	170	43	5	0	8	4.7	26	24	23	37	0	.253	.424	12	0	OF-85
1980 KC A	51	72	12	0	0	0	0.0	10	3	8	7	1	.167	.167	1	0	OF-40, DH-1
9 yrs.	654	1314	279	45	5	35	2.7	159	126	164	246	13	.212	.334	64	14	OF-573, DH-8, 3B-1

Cesar Tovar

TOVAR, CESAR LEONARDO (Pepito)
B. July 3, 1940, Caracas, Venezuela
BR TR 5'9" 155 lbs.

	G	AB	H	2B	3B	HR	HR %	R	RBI	BB	SO	SB	BA	SA	PH AB	PH H	G by POS
1965 MIN A	18	25	5	1	0	0	0.0	3	2	3	2	2	.200	.240	4	0	2B-4, OF-2, 3B-2, SS-1
1966	134	465	121	19	5	2	0.4	57	41	44	50	16	.260	.335	2	0	OF-76, SS-31, OF-24
1967	164	649	173	32	7	6	0.9	98	47	46	51	19	.267	.365	0	0	OF-74, 3B-70, 2B-36, SS-9
1968	157	613	167	31	6	6	1.0	89	47	34	41	35	.272	.372	3	0	OF-78, 3B-75, SS-35, 2B-18, 1B-1, C-1, P-1
1969	158	535	154	25	5	11	2.1	99	52	37	37	45	.288	.415	12	3	OF-113, 2B-41, 3B-20
1970	161	650	195	36	13	10	1.5	120	54	52	47	30	.300	.442	3	0	OF-151, 2B-8, 3B-4
1971	157	657	204	29	3	1	0.2	94	45	45	39	18	.311	.368	1	0	OF-154, 3B-7, 2B-2
1972	141	548	145	20	6	2	0.4	86	31	39	39	21	.265	.334	3	0	OF-139

	G	AB	H	2B	3B	HR	HR %	R	RBI	BB	SO	SB	BA	SA	Pinch Hit AB	Pinch Hit H	G by POS

Cesar Tovar continued

	G	AB	H	2B	3B	HR	HR%	R	RBI	BB	SO	SB	BA	SA	AB	H	G by POS
1973 PHI N	97	328	88	18	4	1	0.3	49	21	29	35	6	.268	.357	14	4	3B-46, OF-24, 2B-22
1974 TEX A	138	562	164	24	6	4	0.7	78	58	47	33	13	.292	.377	1	0	OF-135, DH-3
1975 2 teams	121	TEX A (102G – .258)		OAK A (19G – .231)													
" total	121	453	116	17	0	3	0.7	58	31	30	28	20	.256	.313	12	1	DH-73, OF-31, 2B-5, 3B-3, SS-1
1976 2 teams		OAK A (29G – .178)		NY A (13G – .154)													
" total	42	84	14	1	0	0	0.0	3	6	8	7	1	.167	.179	12	2	OF-20, DH-14, 2B-3
12 yrs.	1488	5569	1546	253	55	46	0.8	834	435	413	410	226	.278	.368	67	10	OF-945, 3B-227, 2B-215, DH-90, SS-77, 1B-1, C-1, P-1

LEAGUE CHAMPIONSHIP SERIES

	G	AB	H	2B	3B	HR	HR%	R	RBI	BB	SO	SB	BA	SA	AB	H	G by POS
1969 MIN A	3	13	1	0	0	0	0.0	0	0	1	2	0	.077	.077	0	0	OF-3
1970	3	13	5	0	1	0	0.0	2	1	0	0	0	.385	.538	0	0	OF-3
1975 OAK A	2	2	1	0	0	0	0.0	2	0	1	0	0	.500	.500	1	0	2B-1
3 yrs.	8	28	7	0	1	0	0.0	4	1	2	2	0	.250	.321	1	0	OF-6, 2B-1

Babe Towne

TOWNE, JAY KING   BL TR 5'10"
B. Mar. 12, 1880, Coon Rapids, Iowa   D. Oct. 29, 1938, Des Moines, Iowa

	G	AB	H	2B	3B	HR	HR%	R	RBI	BB	SO	SB	BA	SA	AB	H	G by POS
1906 CHI A	13	36	10	0	0	0	0.0	3	6	7		0	.278	.278	1	0	C-12

WORLD SERIES

	G	AB	H	2B	3B	HR	HR%	R	RBI	BB	SO	SB	BA	SA	AB	H	G by POS
1906 CHI A	1	1	0	0	0	0	0.0	0	0	0	0	0	.000	.000	1	0	

George Townsend

TOWNSEND, GEORGE HODGSON   BR TR 5'7½" 180 lbs.
B. June 4, 1867, Hartsdale, N.Y.   D. Mar. 15, 1930, New Haven, Conn.

	G	AB	H	2B	3B	HR	HR%	R	RBI	BB	SO	SB	BA	SA	AB	H	G by POS
1887 PHI AA	31	109	21	3	0	0	0.0	12		3		8	.193	.220	0	0	C-28, OF-3
1888	42	161	25	6	0	0	0.0	13	12	4		2	.155	.193	0	0	C-42
1890 B-B AA	18	67	16	4	1	0	0.0	6		4		3	.239	.328	0	0	C-18
1891 BAL AA	61	204	39	5	4	0	0.0	29	18	20	21	3	.191	.255	0	0	C-58, OF-3
4 yrs.	152	541	101	18	5	0	0.0	60	29	31	21	16	.187	.238	0	0	C-146, OF-6

Jim Toy

TOY, JAMES MADISON   BR TR 5'6" 160 lbs.
B. Feb. 20, 1858, Beaver Falls, Pa.   D. Mar. 13, 1919, Beaver Falls, Pa.

	G	AB	H	2B	3B	HR	HR%	R	RBI	BB	SO	SB	BA	SA	AB	H	G by POS
1887 CLE AA	109	423	94	20	5	1	0.2	56		17		8	.222	.300	0	0	1B-82, OF-11, C-10, 3B-8, SS-3
1890 B-B AA	44	160	29	3	0	0	0.0	11		11		2	.181	.200	0	0	C-44
2 yrs.	153	583	123	23	5	1	0.2	67		28		10	.211	.273	0	0	1B-82, C-54, OF-11, 3B-8, SS-3

Jim Traber

TRABER, JAMES JOSEPH   BL TL 6' 194 lbs.
B. Dec. 26, 1961, Columbus, Ohio

	G	AB	H	2B	3B	HR	HR%	R	RBI	BB	SO	SB	BA	SA	AB	H	G by POS
1984 BAL A	10	21	5	0	0	0	0.0	3	2	2	4	0	.238	.238	3	1	DH-9

Dick Tracewski

TRACEWSKI, RICHARD JOSEPH   BR TR 5'11" 160 lbs.
B. Feb. 3, 1935, Eynon, Pa.

	G	AB	H	2B	3B	HR	HR%	R	RBI	BB	SO	SB	BA	SA	AB	H	G by POS
1962 LA N	15	2	0	0	0	0	0.0	3	0	2	0	0	.000	.000	1	0	SS-4
1963	104	217	49	2	1	1	0.5	23	10	19	39	2	.226	.258	0	0	SS-81, 2B-23
1964	106	304	75	13	4	1	0.3	31	26	31	61	3	.247	.326	4	2	2B-56, 3B-30, SS-19
1965	78	186	40	6	0	1	0.5	17	20	25	30	2	.215	.263	8	1	3B-53, 2B-14, SS-7
1966 DET A	81	124	24	1	1	0	0.0	15	7	10	32	1	.194	.218	7	0	2B-70, SS-3
1967	74	107	30	4	2	1	0.9	19	9	8	20	1	.280	.383	9	3	SS-44, 2B-12, 3B-10
1968	90	212	33	3	1	4	1.9	30	15	24	51	3	.156	.236	9	1	SS-51, 3B-16, 2B-14
1969	66	79	11	2	0	0	0.0	10	4	15	20	3	.139	.165	3	1	SS-41, 2B-13, 3B-6
8 yrs.	614	1231	262	31	9	8	0.6	148	91	134	253	15	.213	.272	41	8	SS-250, 2B-202, 3B-115

WORLD SERIES

	G	AB	H	2B	3B	HR	HR%	R	RBI	BB	SO	SB	BA	SA	AB	H	G by POS
1963 LA N	4	13	2	0	0	0	0.0	1	0	1	2	0	.154	.154	0	0	2B-4
1965	6	17	2	0	0	0	0.0	0	0	1	5	0	.118	.118	1	0	2B-6
1968 DET A	2	0	0	0	0	0	–	1	0	0	0	0	–	–	0	0	3B-1
3 yrs.	12	30	4	0	0	0	0.0	2	0	2	7	0	.133	.133	1	0	2B-10, 3B-1

Jim Tracy

TRACY, JAMES EDWIN   BL TR 6' 185 lbs.
B. Dec. 31, 1955, Hamilton, Ohio

	G	AB	H	2B	3B	HR	HR%	R	RBI	BB	SO	SB	BA	SA	AB	H	G by POS
1980 CHI N	42	122	31	3	3	3	2.5	12	9	13	37	2	.254	.402	12	2	OF-31, 1B-1
1981	45	63	15	2	1	0	0.0	6	5	12	14	1	.238	.302	29	5	OF-11
2 yrs.	87	185	46	5	4	3	1.6	18	14	25	51	3	.249	.368	41	7	OF-42, 1B-1

Bill Traffley

TRAFFLEY, WILLIAM F.   BR TR 5'11½" 185 lbs.
Brother of John Traffley.
B. Dec. 21, 1859, Staten Island, N.Y.   D. June 24, 1908, Denver, Colo.

	G	AB	H	2B	3B	HR	HR%	R	RBI	BB	SO	SB	BA	SA	AB	H	G by POS
1878 CHI N	2	9	1	0	0	0	0.0	1	1	0	1		.111	.111	0	0	C-2
1883 CIN AA	30	105	21	5	0	0	0.0	17		4			.200	.248	0	0	C-29, SS-2
1884 BAL AA	53	210	37	4	6	0	0.0	25		3			.176	.252	0	0	C-47, OF-6, 1B-1
1885	69	254	39	4	5	1	0.4	27	17				.154	.220	0	0	C-61, OF-10, 2B-3
1886	25	85	18	0	1	0	0.0	15	10				.212	.235	0	0	C-25
5 yrs.	179	663	116	13	12	1	0.2	85	1	34	1		.175	.235	0	0	C-164, OF-16, 2B-3, SS-2, 1B-1

John Traffley

TRAFFLEY, JOHN   5'9" 180 lbs.
Brother of Bill Traffley.
B. 1862, Chicago, Ill.   D. July 13, 1900, Baltimore, Md.

	G	AB	H	2B	3B	HR	HR%	R	RBI	BB	SO	SB	BA	SA	AB	H	G by POS
1889 LOU AA	1	2	1	0	0	0	0.0	0	0	0	0	0	.500	.500	0	0	OF-1

	G	AB	H	2B	3B	HR	HR%	R	RBI	BB	SO	SB	BA	SA	Pinch Hit AB	Pinch Hit H	G by POS

Walt Tragesser

TRAGESSER, WALTER JOSEPH
B. June 14, 1887, Lafayette, Ind.   D. Dec. 14, 1970, Lafayette, Ind.   BR TR 6'   175 lbs.

Year Team	G	AB	H	2B	3B	HR	HR%	R	RBI	BB	SO	SB	BA	SA	PH AB	PH H	G by POS
1913 BOS N	2	0	0	0	0	0	–	0	0	0	0	0	–	–	0	0	C-2
1915	7	7	0	0	0	0	0.0	1	0	0	2	0	.000	.000	0	0	C-7
1916	41	54	11	1	0	0	0.0	3	4	5	10	0	.204	.222	11	1	C-29
1917	98	297	66	10	2	0	0.0	23	25	15	36	5	.222	.269	4	2	C-98
1918	7	1	0	0	0	0	0.0	0	0	0	0	0	.000	.000	0	0	C-7
1919 2 teams	BOS	N	(20G –	.175)		PHI	N	(35G –	.237)								
" total	55	154	34	9	0	0	0.0	10	11	11	41	5	.221	.279	6	2	C-48
1920 PHI N	62	176	37	11	1	6	3.4	17	26	4	36	4	.210	.386	8	2	C-52
7 yrs.	272	689	148	31	3	6	0.9	54	66	35	125	14	.215	.295	29	7	C-243

Red Tramback

TRAMBACK, STEPHEN JOSEPH
B. Nov. 1, 1915, Iselin, Pa.   D. Dec. 28, 1979, Buffalo, N. Y.   BL TL 6'   175 lbs.

Year Team	G	AB	H	2B	3B	HR	HR%	R	RBI	BB	SO	SB	BA	SA	PH AB	PH H	G by POS
1940 NY N	2	4	1	0	0	0	0.0	0	0	1	1	1	.250	.250	1	0	OF-1

Alan Trammell

TRAMMELL, ALAN STUART
B. Feb. 21, 1958, Garden Grove, Calif.   BR TR 6'   165 lbs.

Year Team	G	AB	H	2B	3B	HR	HR%	R	RBI	BB	SO	SB	BA	SA	PH AB	PH H	G by POS
1977 DET A	19	43	8	0	0	0	0.0	6	0	4	12	0	.186	.186	0	0	SS-19
1978	139	448	120	14	6	2	0.4	49	34	45	56	3	.268	.339	0	0	SS-139
1979	142	460	127	11	4	6	1.3	68	50	43	55	17	.276	.357	0	0	SS-142
1980	146	560	168	21	5	9	1.6	107	65	69	63	12	.300	.404	2	0	SS-144
1981	105	392	101	15	3	2	0.5	52	31	49	31	10	.258	.327	1	1	SS-105
1982	157	489	126	34	3	9	1.8	66	57	52	47	19	.258	.395	0	0	SS-157
1983	142	505	161	31	2	14	2.8	83	66	57	64	30	.319	.471	0	0	SS-140
1984	139	555	174	34	5	14	2.5	85	69	60	63	19	.314	.468	3	1	SS-114, DH-22
8 yrs.	989	3452	985	160	28	56	1.6	516	372	379	391	110	.285	.397	6	2	SS-960, DH-22
LEAGUE CHAMPIONSHIP SERIES																	
1984 DET A	3	11	4	0	1	1	9.1	2	3	3	1	0	.364	.818	0	0	SS-3
WORLD SERIES																	
1984 DET A	5	20	9	1	0	2	10.0	5	6	2	2	1	.450	.800	0	0	SS-5

Fred Traux

TRAUX, FREDERICK W.
D. Dec. 18, 1899, Omaha, Neb.

Year Team	G	AB	H	2B	3B	HR	HR%	R	RBI	BB	SO	SB	BA	SA	PH AB	PH H	G by POS
1890 PIT N	1	3	1	0	0	0	0.0	1	1	1	1	0	.333	.333	0	0	OF-1

Cecil Travis

TRAVIS, CECIL HOWELL
B. Aug. 8, 1913, Riverdale, Ga.   BL TR 6'1½"   185 lbs.

Year Team	G	AB	H	2B	3B	HR	HR%	R	RBI	BB	SO	SB	BA	SA	PH AB	PH H	G by POS
1933 WAS A	18	43	13	1	0	0	0.0	7	2	2	5	0	.302	.326	3	0	3B-15
1934	109	392	125	22	4	1	0.3	48	53	24	37	1	.319	.403	10	1	3B-99
1935	138	534	170	28	7	0	0.0	85	61	41	28	4	.318	.397	7	2	3B-114, OF-16
1936	138	517	164	34	10	2	0.4	77	92	39	21	4	.317	.433	10	4	SS-71, OF-53, 2B-4, 3B-2
1937	135	526	181	27	7	3	0.6	72	66	39	34	3	.344	.439	5	3	SS-129
1938	146	567	190	30	5	5	0.9	96	67	58	22	6	.335	.432	2	0	SS-143
1939	130	476	139	20	9	5	1.1	55	63	34	25	0	.292	.403	10	3	SS-118
1940	136	528	170	37	11	2	0.4	60	76	48	23	0	.322	.445	0	0	3B-113, SS-23
1941	152	608	218	39	19	7	1.2	106	101	52	25	2	.359	.520	0	0	SS-136, 3B-16
1945	15	54	13	2	1	0	0.0	4	10	4	5	0	.241	.315	1	0	3B-14
1946	137	465	117	22	3	1	0.2	45	56	45	47	2	.252	.318	6	1	SS-75, 3B-56
1947	74	204	44	4	1	1	0.5	10	10	16	19	1	.216	.260	24	3	3B-39, SS-15
12 yrs.	1328	4914	1544	266	77	27	0.5	665	657	402	291	23	.314	.416	78	17	SS-710, 3B-468, OF-69, 2B-4

Jim Tray

TRAY, JAMES
B. Feb. 14, 1860, Jackson, Mich.   D. July 28, 1905, Jackson, Mich.   5'8"   144 lbs.

Year Team	G	AB	H	2B	3B	HR	HR%	R	RBI	BB	SO	SB	BA	SA	PH AB	PH H	G by POS
1884 IND AA	6	21	6	0	0	0	0.0	2		2			.286	.286	0	0	C-4, 1B-2

Pie Traynor

TRAYNOR, HAROLD JOSEPH
B. Nov. 11, 1899, Framingham, Mass.   D. Mar. 16, 1972, Pittsburgh, Pa.   BR TR 6'   170 lbs.
Manager 1934-39.
Hall of Fame 1948.

Year Team	G	AB	H	2B	3B	HR	HR%	R	RBI	BB	SO	SB	BA	SA	PH AB	PH H	G by POS
1920 PIT N	17	52	11	3	0	0	0.0	6	2	3	6	1	.212	.308	0	0	SS-17
1921	7	19	5	0	0	0	0.0	0	2	1	2	0	.263	.263	2	1	3B-3, SS-1
1922	142	571	161	17	12	4	0.7	89	81	27	28	17	.282	.375	1	0	3B-124, SS-18
1923	153	616	208	19	19	12	1.9	108	101	34	19	28	.338	.489	0	0	3B-153
1924	142	545	160	26	13	5	0.9	86	82	37	26	24	.294	.417	1	0	3B-141
1925	150	591	189	39	14	6	1.0	114	106	52	19	15	.320	.464	0	0	3B-150, SS-1
1926	152	574	182	25	17	3	0.5	83	92	38	14	8	.317	.436	1	0	3B-148, SS-3
1927	149	573	196	32	9	5	0.9	93	106	22	11	11	.342	.455	0	0	3B-143, SS-9
1928	144	569	192	38	12	3	0.5	91	124	28	10	12	.337	.462	0	0	3B-144
1929	130	540	192	27	12	4	0.7	94	108	30	7	13	.356	.472	0	0	3B-130
1930	130	497	182	22	11	9	1.8	90	119	48	19	7	.366	.509	0	0	3B-130
1931	155	615	183	37	15	2	0.3	81	103	54	28	6	.298	.416	0	0	3B-155
1932	135	513	169	27	10	2	0.4	74	68	32	20	6	.329	.433	7	2	3B-127
1933	154	624	190	27	6	1	0.2	85	82	35	24	5	.304	.372	0	0	3B-154
1934	119	444	137	22	10	1	0.2	62	61	21	27	3	.309	.410	7	4	3B-110
1935	57	204	57	10	3	1	0.5	24	36	10	17	2	.279	.373	5	0	3B-49, 1B-1
1937	5	12	2	0	0	0	0.0	3	0	0	1	0	.167	.167	0	0	3B-3
17 yrs.	1941	7559	2416	371	164	58	0.8	1183	1273	472	278	158	.320	.435	24	7	3B-1864, SS-49, 1B-1
WORLD SERIES																	
1925 PIT N	7	26	9	0	2	1	3.8	2	4	3	1	1	.346	.615	0	0	3B-7
1927	4	15	3	1	0	0	0.0	1	0	0	1	0	.200	.267	0	0	3B-4
2 yrs.	11	41	12	1	2	1	2.4	3	4	3	2	1	.293	.488	0	0	3B-11

	G	AB	H	2B	3B	HR	HR %	R	RBI	BB	SO	SB	BA	SA	Pinch Hit AB	Pinch Hit H	G by POS

Fred Treacey

TREACEY, FREDERICK S.
Brother of Pete Treacey.
B. 1847, Brooklyn, N. Y.   Deceased.

TR 5'9½" 145 lbs.

	G	AB	H	2B	3B	HR	HR%	R	RBI	BB	SO	SB	BA	SA	PH AB	PH H	G by POS
1876 NY N	57	256	54	5	1	0	0.0	47	18	1	5		.211	.238	0	0	OF-57

Pete Treacey

TREACEY, PETER
Brother of Fred Treacey.
B. 1852, Brooklyn, N. Y.   Deceased.

	G	AB	H	2B	3B	HR	HR%	R	RBI	BB	SO	SB	BA	SA	PH AB	PH H	G by POS
1876 NY N	2	5	0	0	0	0	0.0	1	0	1	0		.000	.000	0	0	SS-2

George Treadway

TREADWAY, GEORGE B.
B. Nov. 11, 1866, Greenup County, Ky.   D. Nov. 17, 1928, Riverside, Calif.

BL

	G	AB	H	2B	3B	HR	HR%	R	RBI	BB	SO	SB	BA	SA	PH AB	PH H	G by POS
1893 BAL N	115	458	119	16	17	1	0.2	78	67	57	50	24	.260	.376	0	0	OF-115
1894 BKN N	123	479	157	27	26	4	0.8	124	102	72	43	27	.328	.518	1	0	OF-122, 1B-1
1895	86	339	87	14	3	7	2.1	54	54	33	22	9	.257	.378	0	0	OF-86
1896 LOU N	2	7	1	0	0	0	0.0	0	1	1	0	0	.143	.143	0	0	OF-1, 1B-1
4 yrs.	326	1283	364	57	46	12	0.9	256	224	163	115	60	.284	.428	1	0	OF-324, 1B-2

Ray Treadway

TREADWAY, EDGAR RAYMOND
B. Oct. 31, 1907, Ragland, Ala.   D. Oct. 12, 1935, Chattanooga, Tenn.

BL TR 5'6" 165 lbs.

	G	AB	H	2B	3B	HR	HR%	R	RBI	BB	SO	SB	BA	SA	PH AB	PH H	G by POS
1930 WAS A	6	19	4	2	0	0	0.0	1	1	0	3	0	.211	.316	2	1	3B-4

Red Treadway

TREADWAY, THADFORD LEON
B. Apr. 28, 1920, Athalone, N. C.

BL TL 5'10" 175 lbs.

	G	AB	H	2B	3B	HR	HR%	R	RBI	BB	SO	SB	BA	SA	PH AB	PH H	G by POS
1944 NY N	50	170	51	5	2	0	0.0	23	5	13	11	2	.300	.353	10	4	OF-38
1945	88	224	54	4	2	4	1.8	31	23	20	13	3	.241	.330	25	5	OF-60
2 yrs.	138	394	105	9	4	4	1.0	54	28	33	24	5	.266	.340	35	9	OF-98

Frank Trechock

TRECHOCK, FRANK ADAM
B. Dec. 24, 1915, Windber, Pa.

BR TR 5'10" 175 lbs.

	G	AB	H	2B	3B	HR	HR%	R	RBI	BB	SO	SB	BA	SA	PH AB	PH H	G by POS
1937 WAS A	1	4	2	0	0	0	0.0	0	0	0	1	0	.500	.500	0	0	SS-1

Nick Tremark

TREMARK, NICHOLAS JOSEPH
B. Oct. 15, 1912, Yonkers, N. Y.

BL TL 5'5" 150 lbs.

	G	AB	H	2B	3B	HR	HR%	R	RBI	BB	SO	SB	BA	SA	PH AB	PH H	G by POS
1934 BKN N	17	28	7	1	0	0	0.0	3	6	2	2	0	.250	.286	7	1	OF-9
1935	10	13	3	1	0	0	0.0	1	3	1	1	0	.231	.308	5	2	OF-4
1936	8	32	8	2	0	0	0.0	6	1	3	2	0	.250	.313	0	0	OF-8
3 yrs.	35	73	18	4	0	0	0.0	10	10	6	5	0	.247	.301	12	3	OF-21

Overton Tremper

TREMPER, CARLTON OVERTON
B. Mar. 22, 1906, Brooklyn, N. Y.

BR TR 5'10" 163 lbs.

	G	AB	H	2B	3B	HR	HR%	R	RBI	BB	SO	SB	BA	SA	PH AB	PH H	G by POS
1927 BKN N	36	60	14	0	0	0	0.0	4	4	0	2	0	.233	.233	8	1	OF-18
1928	10	31	6	2	1	0	0.0	1	1	0	1	0	.194	.323	1	1	OF-10
2 yrs.	46	91	20	2	1	0	0.0	5	5	0	3	0	.220	.264	9	2	OF-28

Mike Tresh

TRESH, MICHAEL
Father of Tom Tresh.
B. Feb. 23, 1914, Hazleton, Pa.   D. Oct. 4, 1966, Detroit, Mich.

BR TR 5'11" 170 lbs.

	G	AB	H	2B	3B	HR	HR%	R	RBI	BB	SO	SB	BA	SA	PH AB	PH H	G by POS
1938 CHI A	10	29	7	2	0	0	0.0	3	2	8	4	0	.241	.310	0	0	C-10
1939	119	352	91	5	2	0	0.0	49	38	64	30	3	.259	.284	0	0	C-119
1940	135	480	135	15	5	1	0.2	62	64	49	40	3	.281	.340	0	0	C-135
1941	115	390	98	10	1	0	0.0	38	33	38	27	1	.251	.282	0	0	C-115
1942	72	233	54	8	1	0	0.0	21	15	28	24	2	.232	.275	0	0	C-72
1943	86	279	60	3	0	0	0.0	20	20	37	20	2	.215	.226	1	0	C-85
1944	93	312	81	8	1	0	0.0	22	25	37	15	0	.260	.292	0	0	C-93
1945	150	458	114	11	0	0	0.0	50	47	65	37	6	.249	.273	0	0	C-150
1946	80	217	47	5	2	0	0.0	28	21	36	24	0	.217	.258	1	0	C-79
1947	90	274	66	6	2	0	0.0	19	20	26	26	2	.241	.277	1	0	C-89
1948	39	108	27	1	0	1	0.9	10	11	9	9	0	.250	.287	5	2	C-34
1949 CLE A	38	37	8	0	0	0	0.0	4	5	7	7	0	.216	.216	0	0	C-38
12 yrs.	1027	3169	788	74	14	2	0.1	326	297	402	263	19	.249	.283	7	2	C-1019

Tom Tresh

TRESH, THOMAS MICHAEL
Son of Mike Tresh.
B. Sept. 20, 1937, Detroit, Mich.

BB TR 6'1" 180 lbs.

	G	AB	H	2B	3B	HR	HR%	R	RBI	BB	SO	SB	BA	SA	PH AB	PH H	G by POS
1961 NY A	9	8	2	0	0	0	0.0	0	0	1	1	0	.250	.250	3	1	SS-3
1962	157	622	178	26	5	20	3.2	94	93	67	74	4	.286	.441	2	0	SS-111, OF-43
1963	145	520	140	28	5	25	4.8	91	71	83	79	3	.269	.487	1	0	OF-144
1964	153	533	131	25	5	16	3.0	75	73	73	110	13	.246	.402	7	1	OF-146
1965	156	602	168	29	6	26	4.3	94	74	59	92	5	.279	.477	2	0	OF-154
1966	151	537	125	12	4	27	5.0	76	68	86	89	5	.233	.421	3	1	OF-84, 3B-64
1967	130	448	98	23	3	14	3.1	45	53	50	86	1	.219	.377	10	1	OF-118
1968	152	507	99	18	3	11	2.2	60	52	76	97	10	.195	.308	6	1	SS-119, OF-27
1969 2 teams	NY	A (45G –	.182)		DET	A	(94G –	.224)									
" total	139	474	100	18	3	14	3.0	59	46	56	70	4	.211	.350	10	1	SS-118, OF-11, 3B-1
9 yrs.	1192	4251	1041	179	34	153	3.6	595	530	550	698	45	.245	.411	44	6	OF-727, SS-351, 3B-65
WORLD SERIES																	
1962 NY A	7	28	9	1	0	1	3.6	5	4	1	4	2	.321	.464	0	0	OF-7
1963	4	15	3	0	0	1	6.7	1	2	1	6	0	.200	.400	0	0	OF-4
1964	7	22	6	2	0	2	9.1	4	7	6	7	0	.273	.636	0	0	OF-7
3 yrs.	18	65	18	3	0	4	6.2	10	13	8	17	2	.277	.508	0	0	OF-18

Alex Trevino

TREVINO, ALEJANDRO
Also known as Alejandro Castro.   Brother of Bobby Trevino.
B. Aug. 26, 1957, Monterrey, Mexico

BR TR 5'10" 165 lbs.

	G	AB	H	2B	3B	HR	HR%	R	RBI	BB	SO	SB	BA	SA	PH AB	PH H	G by POS
1978 NY N	6	12	3	0	0	0	0.0	3	0	1	2	0	.250	.250	1	0	C-5, 3B-1

	G	AB	H	2B	3B	HR	HR %	R	RBI	BB	SO	SB	BA	SA	Pinch Hit AB	H	G by POS

Alex Trevino continued

	G	AB	H	2B	3B	HR	HR %	R	RBI	BB	SO	SB	BA	SA	AB	H	G by POS
1979	79	207	56	11	1	0	0.0	24	20	20	27	2	.271	.333	16	5	C-36, 3B-27, 2B-8
1980	106	355	91	11	2	0	0.0	26	37	13	41	0	.256	.299	12	3	C-86, 3B-14, 2B-1
1981	56	149	39	2	0	0	0.0	17	10	13	19	3	.262	.275	10	3	C-45, 2B-4, OF-2, 3B-1
1982 CIN N	120	355	89	10	3	1	0.3	24	33	34	34	3	.251	.304	7	1	C-116, 3B-2
1983	74	167	36	8	1	1	0.6	14	13	17	20	0	.216	.293	7	2	C-63, 3B-4, 2B-1
1984 2 teams	CIN	N (6G –	.167)		ATL	N (79G –	.244)										
" total	85	272	66	16	0	3	1.1	36	28	16	29	5	.243	.335	7	1	C-83
7 yrs.	526	1517	380	58	7	5	0.3	144	141	114	172	13	.250	.308	60	15	C-434, 3B-49, 2B-14, OF-2

Bobby Trevino

TREVINO, CARLOS CASTRO   BR TR 6'2"   185 lbs.
Brother of Alex Trevino.
B. Aug. 15, 1945, Monterrey, Mexico

	G	AB	H	2B	3B	HR	HR %	R	RBI	BB	SO	SB	BA	SA	AB	H	G by POS
1968 CAL A	17	40	9	1	0	0	0.0	1	2	9	0	.225	.250	6	0	OF-11

Gus Triandos

TRIANDOS, GUS CONSTANTIN   BR TR 6'3"   205 lbs.
B. July 30, 1930, San Francisco, Calif.

	G	AB	H	2B	3B	HR	HR %	R	RBI	BB	SO	SB	BA	SA	AB	H	G by POS
1953 NY A	18	51	8	2	0	1	2.0	5	6	3	9	0	.157	.255	3	1	1B-12, C-5
1954	2	1	0	0	0	0	0.0	0	0	0	1	0	.000	.000	1	0	C-1
1955 BAL A	140	481	133	17	3	12	2.5	47	65	40	55	0	.277	.399	14	2	1B-103, C-36, 3B-1
1956	131	452	126	18	1	21	4.6	47	88	48	73	0	.279	.462	5	1	C-89, 1B-52
1957	129	418	106	21	1	19	4.5	44	72	38	73	0	.254	.445	17	1	C-120
1958	137	474	116	10	0	30	6.3	59	79	60	65	1	.245	.456	8	2	C-132
1959	126	393	85	7	1	25	6.4	43	73	65	56	0	.216	.430	3	0	C-125
1960	109	364	98	18	0	12	3.3	36	54	41	62	0	.269	.418	4	0	C-105
1961	115	397	97	21	0	17	4.3	35	63	44	60	0	.244	.426	4	0	C-114
1962	66	207	33	7	0	6	2.9	20	23	29	43	0	.159	.280	4	1	C-63
1963 DET A	106	327	78	13	0	14	4.3	28	41	32	67	0	.239	.407	13	3	C-90
1964 PHI N	73	188	47	9	0	8	4.3	17	33	26	41	0	.250	.426	16	4	C-64, 1B-1
1965 2 teams	PHI	N (30G –	.171)		HOU	N (24G –	.181)										
" total	54	154	27	4	0	2	1.3	8	11	14	31	0	.175	.240	8	3	C-48
13 yrs.	1206	3907	954	147	6	167	4.3	389	608	440	636	1	.244	.413	100	18	C-992, 1B-168, 3B-1

Manny Trillo

TRILLO, JESUS MANUEL (Indio)   BR TR 6'1"   150 lbs.
Also known as Jesus Manuel Marcano.
B. Dec. 25, 1950, Edo Monagas, Venezuela

	G	AB	H	2B	3B	HR	HR %	R	RBI	BB	SO	SB	BA	SA	AB	H	G by POS
1973 OAK A	17	12	3	2	0	0	0.0	0	3	0	4	0	.250	.417	0	0	2B-16
1974	21	33	5	0	0	0	0.0	3	2	2	8	0	.152	.152	0	0	2B-21
1975 CHI N	154	545	135	12	2	7	1.3	55	70	45	78	1	.248	.316	1	0	2B-153, SS-1
1976	158	582	139	24	3	4	0.7	42	59	53	70	17	.239	.311	1	0	2B-156, SS-1
1977	152	504	141	18	5	7	1.4	51	57	44	58	3	.280	.377	5	0	2B-149
1978	152	552	144	17	5	4	0.7	53	55	50	67	0	.261	.332	2	2	2B-149
1979 PHI N	118	431	112	22	1	6	1.4	40	42	20	59	4	.260	.357	0	0	2B-118
1980	141	531	155	25	9	7	1.3	68	43	32	46	8	.292	.412	0	0	2B-140
1981	94	349	100	14	3	6	1.7	37	36	26	37	10	.287	.395	0	0	2B-94
1982	149	549	149	24	1	0	0.0	52	39	33	53	8	.271	.319	0	0	2B-149
1983 2 teams	CLE	A (88G –	.272)		MON	N (31G –	.264)										
" total	119	441	119	21	1	3	0.7	49	45	31	64	1	.270	.342	0	0	2B-118
1984 SF N	98	401	102	21	1	4	1.0	45	36	25	55	0	.254	.342	1	0	2B-96, 3B-4
12 yrs.	1373	4930	1304	200	31	48	1.0	495	487	361	599	52	.265	.347	10	2	2B-1359, 3B-4, SS-2

DIVISIONAL PLAYOFF SERIES

	G	AB	H	2B	3B	HR	HR %	R	RBI	BB	SO	SB	BA	SA	AB	H	G by POS
1981 PHI N	5	16	3	0	0	0	0.0	1	1	4	0	0	.188	.188	0	0	2B-5

LEAGUE CHAMPIONSHIP SERIES

	G	AB	H	2B	3B	HR	HR %	R	RBI	BB	SO	SB	BA	SA	AB	H	G by POS
1974 OAK A	1	0	0	0	0	0	–	1	0	0	0	0	–	–	0	0	
1980 PHI N	5	21	8	2	1	0	0.0	1	4	0	2	0	.381	.571	0	0	2B-5
2 yrs.	6	21	8	2	1	0	0.0	2	4	0	2	0	.381	.571	0	0	2B-5

WORLD SERIES

	G	AB	H	2B	3B	HR	HR %	R	RBI	BB	SO	SB	BA	SA	AB	H	G by POS
1980 PHI N	6	23	5	2	0	0	0.0	4	2	0	0	0	.217	.304	0	0	2B-6

Coaker Triplett

TRIPLETT, HERMAN COAKER   BR TR 5'11"   185 lbs.
B. Dec. 18, 1911, Boone, N. C.

	G	AB	H	2B	3B	HR	HR %	R	RBI	BB	SO	SB	BA	SA	AB	H	G by POS
1938 CHI N	12	36	9	2	1	0	0.0	4	2	0	1	0	.250	.361	3	0	OF-9
1941 STL N	76	185	53	6	3	3	1.6	29	21	18	27	0	.286	.400	25	5	OF-46
1942	64	154	42	7	4	1	0.6	18	23	17	15	1	.273	.390	16	2	OF-46
1943 2 teams	STL	N (9G –	.080)		PHI	N (105G –	.272)										
" total	114	385	100	16	4	15	3.9	46	56	29	34	2	.260	.439	16	4	OF-96
1944 PHI N	84	184	43	5	1	1	0.5	15	25	19	10	1	.234	.288	36	8	OF-44
1945	120	363	87	11	1	7	1.9	36	46	40	27	6	.240	.333	28	5	OF-92
6 yrs.	470	1307	334	47	14	27	2.1	148	173	123	114	10	.256	.375	124	24	OF-333

Hal Trosky

TROSKY, HAROLD ARTHUR, SR.   BL TR 6'2"   207 lbs.
Born Harold Arthur Troyavesky.   Father of Hal Trosky.   BB 1946
B. Nov. 11, 1912, Norway, Iowa   D. June 18, 1979, Cedar Rapids, Iowa

	G	AB	H	2B	3B	HR	HR %	R	RBI	BB	SO	SB	BA	SA	AB	H	G by POS
1933 CLE A	11	44	13	1	2	1	2.3	6	8	2	12	0	.295	.477	0	0	1B-11
1934	154	625	206	45	9	35	5.6	117	142	58	49	2	.330	.598	0	0	1B-154
1935	154	632	171	33	7	26	4.1	84	113	46	60	1	.271	.468	1	1	1B-153
1936	151	629	216	45	9	42	6.7	124	162	36	58	6	.343	.644	0	0	1B-151, 2B-1
1937	153	601	179	36	9	32	5.3	104	128	65	60	3	.298	.547	1	0	1B-152
1938	150	554	185	40	9	19	3.4	106	110	67	40	5	.334	.542	1	1	1B-148
1939	122	448	150	31	4	25	5.6	89	104	52	28	2	.335	.589	4	0	1B-118
1940	140	522	154	39	4	25	4.8	85	93	79	45	1	.295	.529	0	0	1B-139
1941	89	310	91	17	0	11	3.5	43	51	44	21	1	.294	.455	4	2	1B-85
1944 CHI A	135	497	120	32	2	10	2.0	55	70	62	30	3	.241	.374	4	1	1B-130
1946	88	299	76	12	3	2	0.7	22	31	34	37	4	.254	.334	6	1	1B-80
11 yrs.	1347	5161	1561	331	58	228	4.4	835	1012	545	440	28	.302	.522	21	6	1B-1321, 2B-1

	G	AB	H	2B	3B	HR	HR %	R	RBI	BB	SO	SB	BA	SA	Pinch Hit AB	H	G by POS

Mike Trost

TROST, MICHAEL J.
B. 1866, Philadelphia, Pa.   D. Mar. 24, 1901, Philadelphia, Pa.   6'½"   180 lbs.

	G	AB	H	2B	3B	HR	HR %	R	RBI	BB	SO	SB	BA	SA	PH AB	H	G by POS
1890 STL AA	17	51	13	2	0	1	2.0	10		6		4	.255	.353	0	0	C-13, OF-4
1895 LOU N	3	12	1	0	0	0	0.0	1	1	0	1	1	.083	.083	0	0	1B-3
2 yrs.	20	63	14	2	0	1	1.6	11	0	6	1	5	.222	.302	0	0	C-13, OF-4, 1B-3

Sam Trott

TROTT, SAMUEL W.
B. 1858, Washington, D. C.   D. June 5, 1925, Cantonsville, Md.   BL TR 5'9"   190 lbs.
Manager 1891.

	G	AB	H	2B	3B	HR	HR %	R	RBI	BB	SO	SB	BA	SA	PH AB	H	G by POS
1880 BOS N	39	125	26	4	1	0	0.0	14	9	3	5		.208	.256	0	0	C-36, OF-4
1881 DET N	6	25	5	2	1	0	0.0	3	2	1	3		.200	.360	0	0	C-6
1882	32	129	31	7	1	0	0.0	11	12	0	13		.240	.310	0	0	C-23, SS-3, 2B-3, 1B-3, OF-2, 3B-1
1883	75	295	72	14	1	0	0.0	27		10	23		.244	.298	0	0	2B-42, C-34, OF-6, 1B-1
1884 BAL AA	71	284	73	17	9	2	0.7	36		4			.257	.401	0	0	C-60, 2B-6, OF-5
1885	21	88	24	2	2	0	0.0	12		5			.273	.341	0	0	C-17, OF-4, 2B-2, SS-1
1887	85	300	77	16	3	0	0.0	44		27		8	.257	.330	0	0	C-69, 2B-11, OF-3, 1B-2, SS-1
1888	31	108	30	11	4	0	0.0	19	22	4		1	.278	.454	0	0	C-27, OF-3, 2B-1, 1B-1
8 yrs.	360	1354	338	73	22	2	0.1	166	45	54	44	9	.250	.340	0	0	C-272, 2B-65, OF-27, 1B-7, SS-5, 3B-1

Quincy Trouppe

TROUPPE, QUINCY THOMAS
B. Dec. 25, 1912, Dublin, Ga.   BB TR 6'2½"   225 lbs.

	G	AB	H	2B	3B	HR	HR %	R	RBI	BB	SO	SB	BA	SA	PH AB	H	G by POS
1952 CLE A	6	10	1	0	0	0	0.0	1	0	1	3	0	.100	.100	0	0	C-6

Dasher Troy

TROY, JOHN JOSEPH
B. May 8, 1856, New York, N. Y.   D. Mar. 30, 1938, Ozone Park, N. Y.   BR TR

	G	AB	H	2B	3B	HR	HR %	R	RBI	BB	SO	SB	BA	SA	PH AB	H	G by POS
1881 DET N	11	44	15	3	0	0	0.0	2	4	3	8		.341	.409	0	0	3B-7, 2B-4
1882 2 teams		DET	N	(40G –	.243)		PRO	N	(4G –	.235)							
" total	44	169	41	7	2	0	0.0	23	14	5	11		.243	.308	0	0	2B-31, SS-15
1883 NY N	85	316	68	7	5	0	0.0	37		9	33		.215	.269	0	0	2B-73, SS-12
1884 NY AA	107	421	111	22	10	2	0.5	80		19			.264	.378	0	0	2B-107
1885	45	177	39	3	3	2	1.1	24		5			.220	.305	0	0	2B-42, OF-2, SS-1
5 yrs.	292	1127	274	42	20	4	0.4	166	18	41	52		.243	.327	0	0	2B-257, SS-28, 3B-7, OF-2

Harry Truby

TRUBY, HARRY GARVIN (Bird Eye)
B. May 12, 1870, Ironton, Ohio   D. Mar. 21, 1953, Ironton, Ohio   TR 5'11"   185 lbs.

	G	AB	H	2B	3B	HR	HR %	R	RBI	BB	SO	SB	BA	SA	PH AB	H	G by POS
1895 CHI N	33	119	40	3	0	0	0.0	17	16	10	7	7	.336	.361	0	0	2B-33
1896 2 teams	37	CHI	N	(29G –	.257)		PIT	N	(8G –	.156)							
" total	37	141	33	2	2	2	1.4	14	34	8	9	5	.234	.319	0	0	2B-36
2 yrs.	70	260	73	5	2	2	0.8	31	50	18	16	12	.281	.338	0	0	2B-69

Frank Truesdale

TRUESDALE, FRANK DAY
B. Mar. 31, 1884, St. Louis, Mo.   D. Aug. 27, 1943, Albuquerque, N. M.   BB TR

	G	AB	H	2B	3B	HR	HR %	R	RBI	BB	SO	SB	BA	SA	PH AB	H	G by POS
1910 STL A	123	415	91	7	2	1	0.2	39	25	48		29	.219	.253	1	0	2B-123
1911	1	0	0	0	0	0	–	1	0	0			–	–	0	0	
1914 NY A	77	217	46	4	0	0	0.0	23	13	39	35	11	.212	.230	3	1	2B-67, 3B-4
1918 BOS A	15	36	10	1	0	0	0.0	6	2	4	5	1	.278	.306	4	1	2B-10
4 yrs.	216	668	147	12	2	1	0.1	69	40	91	40	41	.220	.249	8	2	2B-200, 3B-4

Ed Trumbull

TRUMBULL, EDWARD J.
Born Edward J. Trembly.
B. Nov. 3, 1860, Chicopee Falls, Mass.   Deceased.

	G	AB	H	2B	3B	HR	HR %	R	RBI	BB	SO	SB	BA	SA	PH AB	H	G by POS
1884 WAS AA	25	86	10	2	0	0	0.0	2		2			.116	.140	0	0	OF-15, P-10

Ollie Tucker

TUCKER, OLIVER DINWIDDIE
B. Jan. 27, 1902, Radiant, Va.   D. July 13, 1940, Radiant, Va.   BL TR 5'10"   180 lbs.

	G	AB	H	2B	3B	HR	HR %	R	RBI	BB	SO	SB	BA	SA	PH AB	H	G by POS
1927 WAS A	20	24	5	2	0	0	0.0	1	8	4	2	0	.208	.292	10	1	OF-5
1928 CLE A	14	47	6	0	0	1	2.1	5	2	7	3	0	.128	.191	0	0	OF-14
2 yrs.	34	71	11	2	0	1	1.4	6	10	11	5	0	.155	.225	10	1	OF-19

Thurman Tucker

TUCKER, THURMAN LOWELL (Joe E.)
B. Sept. 26, 1917, Gordon, Tex.   BL TR 5'10½" 165 lbs.

	G	AB	H	2B	3B	HR	HR %	R	RBI	BB	SO	SB	BA	SA	PH AB	H	G by POS
1942 CHI A	7	24	3	0	0	0	0.0	2	1	0	4	0	.125	.208	2	0	OF-5
1943	139	528	124	15	6	3	0.6	81	39	79	72	29	.235	.303	6	1	OF-132
1944	124	446	128	15	6	2	0.4	59	46	57	40	13	.287	.361	1	0	OF-120
1946	121	438	126	20	3	1	0.2	62	36	54	45	9	.288	.354	8	3	OF-110
1947	89	254	60	9	4	1	0.4	28	17	38	25	10	.236	.315	19	4	OF-65
1948 CLE A	83	242	63	13	4	1	0.4	52	19	31	17	11	.260	.343	10	3	OF-66
1949	80	197	48	5	2	0	0.0	28	14	18	19	4	.244	.289	22	2	OF-52
1950	57	101	18	2	0	1	1.0	13	7	14	14	1	.178	.228	18	3	OF-34
1951	1	1	0	0	0	0	0.0	0	0	0	1	0	.000	.000	1	0	
9 yrs.	701	2231	570	79	24	9	0.4	325	179	291	237	77	.255	.325	87	16	OF-584

WORLD SERIES

	G	AB	H	2B	3B	HR	HR %	R	RBI	BB	SO	SB	BA	SA	PH AB	H	G by POS
1948 CLE A	1	3	1	0	0	0	0.0	1	0	1	0	0	.333	.333	0	0	OF-1

Tommy Tucker

TUCKER, THOMAS JOSEPH
B. Oct. 28, 1863, Holyoke, Mass.   D. Oct. 22, 1935, Montague, Mass.   BB TR 5'11"   165 lbs.

	G	AB	H	2B	3B	HR	HR %	R	RBI	BB	SO	SB	BA	SA	PH AB	H	G by POS
1887 BAL AA	136	524	144	15	9	6	1.1	114		29		85	.275	.372	0	0	1B-136
1888	136	520	149	17	12	6	1.2	74	61	16		43	.287	.400	0	0	1B-129, OF-7, P-1
1889	134	527	196	22	11	5	0.9	103	99	42	26	63	.372	.484	0	0	1B-123, OF-12
1890 BOS N	132	539	159	17	8	1	0.2	104	62	56	22	43	.295	.362	0	0	1B-132
1891	140	548	148	16	5	2	0.4	103	69	37	30	26	.270	.328	0	0	1B-140, P-1
1892	149	542	153	13	5	1	0.2	85	62	45	35	22	.282	.341	0	0	1B-149
1893	121	486	138	13	2	7	1.4	83	91	27	31	8	.284	.362	0	0	1B-121

	G	AB	H	2B	3B	HR	HR %	R	RBI	BB	SO	SB	BA	SA	Pinch Hit AB	Pinch Hit H	G by POS

Tommy Tucker continued

	G	AB	H	2B	3B	HR	HR%	R	RBI	BB	SO	SB	BA	SA	AB	H	G by POS
1894	123	500	165	24	6	3	0.6	112	100	53	21	18	.330	.420	0	0	1B-123, OF-1
1895	125	462	115	19	6	3	0.6	87	73	61	29	15	.249	.335	0	0	1B-125
1896	122	474	144	27	5	2	0.4	74	72	30	29	6	.304	.395	0	0	1B-122
1897 2 teams		BOS	N	(4G –	.214)		WAS	N	(93G –	.338)							
" total	97	366	122	20	5	5	1.4	52	65	29		18	.333	.456	0	0	1B-97
1898 2 teams		BKN	N	(73G –	.279)		STL	N	(72G –	.238)							
" total	145	535	139	16	6	1	0.2	53	54	30		2	.260	.318	0	0	1B-145
1899 CLE N	127	456	110	19	3	0	0.0	40	40	24		3	.241	.296	0	0	1B-127
13 yrs.	1687	6479	1882	240	85	42	0.6	1084	847	479	223	352	.290	.373	0	0	1B-1669, OF-20, P-2

Jerry Turbidy

TURBIDY, JEREMIAH   BR TR 5'8"   165 lbs.
B. July 4, 1852, Dudley, Mass.   D. Sept. 5, 1920, Webster, Mass.

	G	AB	H	2B	3B	HR	HR%	R	RBI	BB	SO	SB	BA	SA	AB	H	G by POS
1884 KC U	13	49	11	4	0	0	0.0	5		3			.224	.306	0	0	SS-13

Eddie Turchin

TURCHIN, EDWARD LAWRENCE (Smiley)   BR TR 5'10"   165 lbs.
B. Feb. 10, 1917, New York, N.Y.   D. Feb. 8, 1982, Brookhaven, N.Y.

	G	AB	H	2B	3B	HR	HR%	R	RBI	BB	SO	SB	BA	SA	AB	H	G by POS
1943 CLE A	11	13	3	0	0	0	0.0	4	1	3	1	0	.231	.231	0	0	3B-4, SS-2

Pete Turgeon

TURGEON, EUGENE JOSEPH   BR TR 5'6"   145 lbs.
B. Jan. 3, 1897, Minneapolis, Minn.   D. Jan. 24, 1977, Wichita Falls, Tex.

	G	AB	H	2B	3B	HR	HR%	R	RBI	BB	SO	SB	BA	SA	AB	H	G by POS
1923 CHI N	3	6	1	0	0	0	0.0	1	0	0	0	0	.167	.167	0	0	SS-2

Earl Turner

TURNER, EARL EDWIN   BR TR 5'9"   170 lbs.
B. May 6, 1923, Pittsfield, Mass.

	G	AB	H	2B	3B	HR	HR%	R	RBI	BB	SO	SB	BA	SA	AB	H	G by POS
1948 PIT N	2	1	0	0	0	0	0.0	0	0	0	0	0	.000	.000	1	0	C-1
1950	40	74	18	0	0	3	4.1	10	5	4	13	1	.243	.365	6	1	C-34
2 yrs.	42	75	18	0	0	3	4.0	10	5	4	13	1	.240	.360	7	1	C-35

Jerry Turner

TURNER, JOHN WEBBER   BL TL 5'9"   180 lbs.
B. Jan. 17, 1954, Texarkana, Ark.

	G	AB	H	2B	3B	HR	HR%	R	RBI	BB	SO	SB	BA	SA	AB	H	G by POS
1974 SD N	17	48	14	1	0	0	0.0	4	2	3	5	2	.292	.313	6	3	OF-13
1975	11	22	6	0	0	0	0.0	1	0	2	1	0	.273	.273	6	3	OF-4
1976	105	281	75	16	5	5	1.8	41	37	32	38	12	.267	.413	25	5	OF-74
1977	118	289	71	16	1	10	3.5	43	48	31	43	12	.246	.412	45	12	OF-69
1978	106	225	63	9	1	8	3.6	28	37	21	32	6	.280	.436	49	20	OF-58
1979	138	448	111	23	2	9	2.0	55	61	34	58	4	.248	.368	28	5	OF-115
1980	85	153	44	5	0	3	2.0	22	18	10	18	8	.288	.379	47	13	OF-34
1981 2 teams		SD	N	(33G –	.226)		CHI	A	(10G –	.167)							
" total	43	43	9	0	0	2	4.7	6	8	5	5	0	.209	.349	29	5	OF-5
1982 DET A	85	210	52	3	0	8	3.8	21	27	20	37	1	.248	.376	24	4	DH-50, OF-13
1983 SD N	25	23	3	0	0	0	0.0	1	0	1	8	0	.130	.130	23	3	OF-1
10 yrs.	733	1742	448	73	9	45	2.6	222	238	159	245	45	.257	.387	282	73	OF-386, DH-50

Terry Turner

TURNER, TERRENCE LAMONT (Cotton)   BR TR 5'8"   149 lbs.
B. Feb. 28, 1881, Sandy Lake, Pa.   D. July 18, 1960, Cleveland, Ohio

	G	AB	H	2B	3B	HR	HR%	R	RBI	BB	SO	SB	BA	SA	AB	H	G by POS
1901 PIT N	2	7	3	0	0	0	0.0	0	1	0		0	.429	.429	0	0	3B-2
1904 CLE A	111	404	95	9	6	1	0.2	41	45	11		5	.235	.295	0	0	SS-111
1905	154	582	153	16	14	4	0.7	48	72	14		17	.263	.359	0	0	SS-154
1906	147	584	170	27	7	2	0.3	85	62	35		27	.291	.372	0	0	SS-147
1907	148	524	127	20	7	0	0.0	57	46	19		27	.242	.307	1	0	SS-145
1908	60	201	48	11	1	0	0.0	21	19	15		18	.239	.303	7	1	OF-36, SS-17
1909	53	208	52	7	4	0	0.0	25	16	14		14	.250	.322	1	0	SS-26, 2B-26
1910	150	574	132	14	6	0	0.0	71	33	53		31	.230	.275	1	0	SS-94, 3B-46, 2B-9
1911	117	417	105	16	9	0	0.0	59	28	34		29	.252	.333	0	0	3B-94, 2B-14, SS-10
1912	103	370	114	14	4	0	0.0	54	33	31		19	.308	.368	0	0	3B-103
1913	120	388	96	13	4	0	0.0	61	44	55	35	13	.247	.302	3	1	3B-71, 2B-25, SS-21
1914	120	428	105	14	9	1	0.2	43	33	44	36	17	.245	.327	0	0	3B-103, 2B-17
1915	95	262	66	14	1	0	0.0	35	14	29	13	12	.252	.313	3	0	2B-51, 3B-20
1916	124	428	112	15	3	0	0.0	52	38	40	29	15	.262	.311	5	1	3B-77, 2B-42
1917	69	180	37	7	0	0	0.0	16	15	14	19	4	.206	.244	5	0	3B-40, 2B-23, SS-1
1918	74	233	58	7	2	0	0.0	24	23	22	15	6	.249	.296	1	1	3B-46, 2B-26, SS-1
1919 PHI A	38	127	24	3	0	0	0.0	7	6	5	9	2	.189	.213	1	0	SS-19, 2B-17, 3B-1
17 yrs.	1685	5917	1497	207	77	8	0.1	699	528	435	156	256	.253	.318	28	4	SS-746, 3B-603, 2B-250, OF-36

Tom Turner

TURNER, THOMAS RICHARD   BR TR 6'½"   215 lbs.
B. Sept. 8, 1916, Custer County, Okla.

	G	AB	H	2B	3B	HR	HR%	R	RBI	BB	SO	SB	BA	SA	AB	H	G by POS
1940 CHI A	37	96	20	1	2	0	0.0	11	6	3	12	1	.208	.260	7	1	C-29
1941	38	126	30	5	0	0	0.0	7	8	9	15	2	.238	.278	3	1	C-35
1942	56	182	44	9	1	3	1.6	18	21	19	15	0	.242	.352	2	1	C-54
1943	51	154	37	7	1	2	1.3	16	11	13	21	1	.240	.338	2	0	C-49
1944 2 teams		CHI	A	(36G –	.230)		STL	A	(15G –	.320)							
" total	51	138	34	7	0	2	1.4	11	17	7	21	0	.246	.341	4	0	C-47
5 yrs.	233	696	165	29	4	7	1.0	63	63	51	84	4	.237	.320	18	3	C-214
WORLD SERIES																	
1944 STL A	1	1	0	0	0	0	0.0	0	0	0	0	0	.000	.000	1	0	

Tuck Turner

TURNER, GEORGE A.   BL
B. Feb. 13, 1873, Brighton, N.Y.   D. July 16, 1945, Staten Island, N.Y.

	G	AB	H	2B	3B	HR	HR%	R	RBI	BB	SO	SB	BA	SA	AB	H	G by POS
1893 PHI N	36	155	50	4	3	1	0.6	32	13	9	19	7	.323	.406	0	0	OF-36
1894	80	339	141	21	9	1	0.3	91	82	23	13	11	.416	.540	1	0	OF-78, P-1
1895	59	210	81	8	6	2	1.0	51	43	25	11	14	.386	.510	4	2	OF-55

	G	AB	H	2B	3B	HR	HR %	R	RBI	BB	SO	SB	BA	SA	Pinch Hit AB	Pinch Hit H	G by POS

Tuck Turner continued

	G	AB	H	2B	3B	HR	HR %	R	RBI	BB	SO	SB	BA	SA	AB	H	G by POS
1896 2 teams		PHI N (13G – .219)			STL N (51G – .246)												
" total	64	235	57	9	8	1	0.4	42	27	22	26	12	.243	.362	4	0	OF-59
1897 STL N	103	416	121	17	12	2	0.5	58	41	35		8	.291	.404	1	0	OF-102
1898	35	141	28	8	0	0	0.0	20	7	14		1	.199	.255	1	0	OF-34
6 yrs.	377	1496	478	67	38	7	0.5	294	213	128	69	53	.320	.429	11	2	OF-364, P-1

Bill Tuttle

TUTTLE, WILLIAM ROBERT
B. July 4, 1929, Elwood, Ill.   BR TR 6'   190 lbs.

	G	AB	H	2B	3B	HR	HR %	R	RBI	BB	SO	SB	BA	SA	AB	H	G by POS
1952 DET A	7	25	6	0	0	0	0.0	2	2	0	1	0	.240	.240	1	0	OF-6
1954	147	530	141	20	11	7	1.3	64	58	62	60	5	.266	.385	3	1	OF-145
1955	154	603	168	23	4	14	2.3	102	78	76	54	6	.279	.400	1	0	OF-154
1956	140	546	138	22	4	9	1.6	61	65	38	48	5	.253	.357	4	2	OF-137
1957	133	451	113	12	4	5	1.1	49	47	44	41	2	.251	.328	3	1	OF-128
1958 KC A	148	511	118	14	9	11	2.2	77	51	74	58	7	.231	.358	10	1	OF-145
1959	126	463	139	19	6	7	1.5	74	43	48	38	10	.300	.413	4	2	OF-121
1960	151	559	143	21	3	8	1.4	75	40	66	52	1	.256	.347	5	2	OF-148
1961 2 teams		KC A (25G – .262)			MIN A (113G – .246)												
" total	138	454	113	14	5	5	1.1	53	46	52	50	1	.249	.335	3	0	OF-89, 3B-85, 2B-2
1962 MIN A	110	123	26	4	1	1	0.8	21	13	19	14	1	.211	.285	6	1	OF-104
1963	16	3	0	0	0	0	0.0	0	0	1	0	0	.000	.000	2	0	OF-14
11 yrs.	1270	4268	1105	149	47	67	1.6	578	443	480	416	38	.259	.363	42	10	OF-1191, 3B-85, 2B-2

Guy Tutwiler

TUTWILER, GUY ISBELL (King Tut)
B. July 17, 1889, Coalburg, Ala.   D. Aug. 15, 1930, Birmingham, Ala.   BL TR 6'   175 lbs.

	G	AB	H	2B	3B	HR	HR %	R	RBI	BB	SO	SB	BA	SA	AB	H	G by POS
1911 DET A	13	32	6	2	0	0	0.0	3	3	2		0	.188	.250	3	0	2B-6, OF-3
1913	14	47	10	0	1	0	0.0	4	7	4	12	2	.213	.255	0	0	1B-14
2 yrs.	27	79	16	2	1	0	0.0	7	10	6	12	2	.203	.253	3	0	1B-14, 2B-6, OF-3

Old Hoss Twineham

TWINEHAM, ARTHUR W.
B. Nov. 26, 1866, Galesburg, Ill.   Deceased.   BL TR 6'1½"   190 lbs.

	G	AB	H	2B	3B	HR	HR %	R	RBI	BB	SO	SB	BA	SA	AB	H	G by POS
1893 STL N	14	48	15	2	0	0	0.0	8	11	1	2	0	.313	.354	0	0	C-14
1894	38	127	40	4	1	1	0.8	22	16	9	11	2	.315	.386	0	0	C-38
2 yrs.	52	175	55	6	1	1	0.6	30	27	10	13	2	.314	.377	0	0	C-52

Larry Twitchell

TWITCHELL, LAWRENCE GRANT
B. Feb. 18, 1864, Cleveland, Ohio   D. Aug. 23, 1930, Cleveland, Ohio   BR TR 6'   185 lbs.

	G	AB	H	2B	3B	HR	HR %	R	RBI	BB	SO	SB	BA	SA	AB	H	G by POS
1886 DET N	4	16	1	0	0	0	0.0	0	0	0	2		.063	.063	0	0	P-4, OF-2
1887	65	264	88	14	6	0	0.0	44	51	8	19	12	.333	.432	0	0	OF-53, P-15
1888	131	524	128	19	4	5	1.0	71	67	28	45	14	.244	.324	0	0	OF-131, P-2
1889 CLE N	134	549	151	16	11	4	0.7	73	95	29	37	17	.275	.366	0	0	OF-134, P-1
1890 2 teams		CLE P (56G – .223)			BUF P (44G – .221)												
" total	100	405	90	9	4	4	1.0	57	53	40	29	8	.222	.294	0	0	OF-88, P-13, 1B-3
1891 COL AA	57	224	62	9	4	2	0.9	32	35	20	28	10	.277	.379	0	0	OF-56, P-6
1892 WAS N	51	192	42	9	5	0	0.0	20	20	11	31	8	.219	.318	0	0	OF-48, SS-3, 3B-1
1893 LOU N	45	187	58	12	3	1	0.5	37	31	17	20	7	.310	.422	0	0	OF-45
1894	52	210	56	16	3	2	1.0	28	32	15	20	8	.267	.400	0	0	OF-51, P-1
9 yrs.	639	2571	676	104	40	18	0.7	362	384	168	231	84	.263	.356	0	0	OF-608, P-42, SS-3, 1B-3, 3B-1

Babe Twombly

TWOMBLY, CLARENCE EDWARD
Brother of George Twombly.
B. Jan. 18, 1896, Jamaica Plain, Mass.   D. Nov. 23, 1974, San Clemente, Calif.   BL TR 5'10"   165 lbs.

	G	AB	H	2B	3B	HR	HR %	R	RBI	BB	SO	SB	BA	SA	AB	H	G by POS
1920 CHI N	78	183	43	1	1	2	1.1	25	14	17	20	5	.235	.284	22	4	OF-45, 2B-2
1921	87	175	66	8	1	1	0.6	22	18	11	10	4	.377	.451	38	15	OF-45
2 yrs.	165	358	109	9	2	3	0.8	47	32	28	30	9	.304	.366	60	19	OF-90, 2B-2

George Twombly

TWOMBLY, GEORGE FREDERICK (Silent George)
Brother of Babe Twombly.
B. June 4, 1892, Boston, Mass.   D. Feb. 17, 1975, Lexington, Mass.   BR TR 5'9"   165 lbs.

	G	AB	H	2B	3B	HR	HR %	R	RBI	BB	SO	SB	BA	SA	AB	H	G by POS
1914 CIN N	68	240	56	0	5	0	0.0	22	19	14	27	12	.233	.275	0	0	OF-68
1915	46	66	13	0	1	0	0.0	5	5	8	8	5	.197	.227	14	4	OF-46
1916	3	5	0	0	0	0	0.0	0	0	1	1	0	.000	.000	2	0	OF-1
1917 BOS N	32	102	19	1	1	0	0.0	8	9	18	5	4	.186	.216	1	0	OF-29, 1B-1
1919 WAS A	1	4	0	0	0	0	0.0	0	0	0	0	0	.000	.000	0	0	OF-1
5 yrs.	150	417	88	1	7	0	0.0	35	33	41	41	21	.211	.247	17	4	OF-145, 1B-1

Jim Tyack

TYACK, JAMES FRED
B. Jan. 9, 1911, Florence, Mont.   BL TR 6'2"   195 lbs.

	G	AB	H	2B	3B	HR	HR %	R	RBI	BB	SO	SB	BA	SA	AB	H	G by POS
1943 PHI A	54	155	40	8	1	0	0.0	11	23	14	9	1	.258	.323	12	2	OF-38

Fred Tyler

TYLER, FREDERICK FRANKLIN
Brother of Lefty Tyler.
B. Dec. 16, 1891, Derry, N. H.   D. Oct. 14, 1945, Derry, N. H.   BR TR 5'10½" 180 lbs.

	G	AB	H	2B	3B	HR	HR %	R	RBI	BB	SO	SB	BA	SA	AB	H	G by POS
1914 BOS N	18	24	8	0	0	0	0.0	2	2	0	2	0	.333	.333	0	0	C-6

Johnnie Tyler

TYLER, JOHN ANTHONY (Ty Ty)
B. July 30, 1906, Mt. Pleasant, Pa.   BL TR 6'   175 lbs.
D. July 11, 1972, Mount Pleasant, Pa.   BB 1934

	G	AB	H	2B	3B	HR	HR %	R	RBI	BB	SO	SB	BA	SA	AB	H	G by POS
1934 BOS N	3	6	1	0	0	0	0.0	1	0	0	3	0	.167	.167	2	0	OF-1
1935	13	47	16	2	1	2	4.3	7	11	4	3	0	.340	.553	1	0	OF-11
2 yrs.	16	53	17	2	1	2	3.8	7	12	4	6	0	.321	.509	3	0	OF-12

	G	AB	H	2B	3B	HR	HR %	R	RBI	BB	SO	SB	BA	SA	Pinch Hit AB	Pinch Hit H	G by POS

Lefty Tyler

TYLER, GEORGE ALBERT
Brother of Fred Tyler.
B. Dec. 14, 1889, Derry, N. H.   D. Sept. 29, 1953, Lowell, Mass.
BL TL 6'   175 lbs.

	G	AB	H	2B	3B	HR	HR %	R	RBI	BB	SO	SB	BA	SA	PH AB	PH H	G by POS
1910 BOS N	2	4	2	0	0	0	0.0	0	0	1	0	0	.500	.500	0	0	P-2
1911	28	61	10	2	0	0	0.0	10	2	8	9	0	.164	.197	0	0	P-28
1912	42	96	19	3	0	0	0.0	8	5	4	16	0	.198	.229	0	0	P-42
1913	43	102	21	7	0	0	0.0	13	10	11	16	0	.206	.275	3	1	P-39
1914	38	94	19	1	0	0	0.0	6	4	4	20	0	.202	.213	0	0	P-38
1915	45	88	23	7	0	1	1.1	11	6	4	19	0	.261	.375	10	1	P-32
1916	39	93	19	3	1	3	3.2	10	20	9	15	0	.204	.355	3	0	P-34
1917	55	134	31	4	0	0	0.0	8	11	17	19	0	.231	.261	12	3	P-32, 1B-11
1918 CHI N	38	100	21	1	0	0	0.0	9	8	9	15	0	.210	.220	2	0	P-33
1919	6	7	1	0	0	0	0.0	0	1	3	2	0	.143	.143	0	0	P-6
1920	29	65	17	3	1	0	0.0	6	6	9	7	0	.262	.338	2	2	P-27
1921	19	26	6	2	0	0	0.0	4	2	1	5	0	.231	.308	7	2	P-10
12 yrs.	384	870	189	33	2	4	0.5	85	75	80	143	0	.217	.274	39	9	P-323, 1B-11
WORLD SERIES																	
1914 BOS N	1	3	0	0	0	0	0.0	0	0	0	1	0	.000	.000	0	0	P-1
1918 CHI N	3	5	1	0	0	0	0.0	0	2	2	0	0	.200	.200	0	0	P-3
2 yrs.	4	8	1	0	0	0	0.0	0	2	2	1	0	.125	.125	0	0	P-4

Earl Tyree

TYREE, EARL CARLTON
B. Mar. 4, 1890, Huntsville, Ill.   D. May 17, 1954, Rushville, Ill.
BR TR 5'8''   160 lbs.

	G	AB	H	2B	3B	HR	HR %	R	RBI	BB	SO	SB	BA	SA	PH AB	PH H	G by POS
1914 CHI N	1	4	0	0	0	0	0.0	1	0	0	0	0	.000	.000	0	0	C-1

Jim Tyrone

TYRONE, JAMES VERNON
Brother of Wayne Tyrone.
B. Jan. 29, 1949, Alice, Tex.
BR TR 6'1''   185 lbs.

	G	AB	H	2B	3B	HR	HR %	R	RBI	BB	SO	SB	BA	SA	PH AB	PH H	G by POS
1972 CHI N	13	8	0	0	0	0	0.0	1	0	0	3	1	.000	.000	3	0	OF-4
1974	57	81	15	0	1	3	3.7	19	3	6	8	1	.185	.321	28	7	OF-32, 3B-1
1975	11	22	5	0	1	0	0.0	0	3	1	4	1	.227	.318	5	1	OF-8
1977 OAK A	96	294	72	11	1	5	1.7	32	26	25	62	3	.245	.340	11	5	OF-81, DH-4, SS-1, 1B-1
4 yrs.	177	405	92	11	3	8	2.0	52	32	32	77	6	.227	.328	47	13	OF-125, DH-4, SS-1, 3B-1, 1B-1

Wayne Tyrone

TYRONE, OSCAR WAYNE
Brother of Jim Tyrone.
B. Aug. 1, 1950, Alice, Tex.
BR TR 6'1''   185 lbs.

	G	AB	H	2B	3B	HR	HR %	R	RBI	BB	SO	SB	BA	SA	PH AB	PH H	G by POS
1976 CHI N	30	57	13	1	0	1	1.8	3	8	3	21	0	.228	.298	14	4	OF-7, 3B-5, 1B-5

Mike Tyson

TYSON, MICHAEL RAY
B. Jan. 13, 1950, Rocky Mount, N. C.
BR TR 5'9''   170 lbs.

	G	AB	H	2B	3B	HR	HR %	R	RBI	BB	SO	SB	BA	SA	PH AB	PH H	G by POS
1972 STL N	13	37	7	1	0	0	0.0	1	0	1	9	0	.189	.216	0	0	2B-11, SS-2
1973	144	469	114	15	4	1	0.2	48	33	23	66	2	.243	.299	0	0	SS-128, 2B-16
1974	151	422	94	14	5	1	0.2	35	37	22	70	4	.223	.287	0	0	SS-143, 2B-12
1975	122	368	98	16	3	2	0.5	45	37	24	39	5	.266	.342	2	0	SS-95, 2B-24, 3B-5
1976	76	245	70	12	9	3	1.2	26	28	16	34	3	.286	.445	1	0	2B-74
1977	138	418	103	15	2	7	1.7	42	57	30	48	3	.246	.342	2	0	2B-135
1978	125	377	88	16	0	3	0.8	26	26	24	41	2	.233	.300	4	1	2B-124
1979	75	190	42	8	2	5	2.6	18	20	13	28	2	.221	.363	9	2	2B-71
1980 CHI N	123	341	81	19	3	3	0.9	34	23	15	61	1	.238	.337	6	2	2B-117
1981	50	92	17	2	0	2	2.2	6	8	7	15	1	.185	.272	13	4	2B-36, SS-1
10 yrs.	1017	2959	714	118	28	27	0.9	281	269	175	411	23	.241	.327	37	9	2B-620, SS-369, 3B-5

Turkey Tyson

TYSON, CECIL WASHINGTON
B. Dec. 6, 1914, Elm City, N. C.
BL TR 6'5½''   225 lbs.

	G	AB	H	2B	3B	HR	HR %	R	RBI	BB	SO	SB	BA	SA	PH AB	PH H	G by POS
1944 PHI N	1	0	0	0	0	0	–	0	0	0	0	0	–	–	1	0	

Ty Tyson

TYSON, ALBERT THOMAS
B. June 1, 1892, Wilkes-Barre, Pa.   D. Aug. 16, 1953, Buffalo, N. Y.
BR TR 5'11''   169 lbs.

	G	AB	H	2B	3B	HR	HR %	R	RBI	BB	SO	SB	BA	SA	PH AB	PH H	G by POS
1926 NY N	97	335	98	16	1	3	0.9	40	35	15	28	6	.293	.373	4	1	OF-92
1927	43	159	42	7	2	1	0.6	24	17	10	19	5	.264	.352	1	1	OF-41
1928 BKN N	59	210	57	11	1	1	0.5	25	21	10	14	3	.271	.348	1	0	OF-55
3 yrs.	199	704	197	34	4	5	0.7	89	73	35	61	14	.280	.361	6	2	OF-188

Bob Uecker

UECKER, ROBERT GEORGE
B. Jan. 26, 1935, Milwaukee, Wis.
BR TR 6'1''   190 lbs.

	G	AB	H	2B	3B	HR	HR %	R	RBI	BB	SO	SB	BA	SA	PH AB	PH H	G by POS
1962 MIL N	33	64	16	2	0	1	1.6	5	8	7	15	0	.250	.328	7	2	C-24
1963	13	16	4	2	0	0	0.0	3	0	2	5	0	.250	.375	7	2	C-6
1964 STL N	40	106	21	1	0	1	0.9	8	6	17	24	0	.198	.236	0	0	C-40
1965	53	145	33	7	0	2	1.4	17	10	24	27	0	.228	.317	5	0	C-49
1966 PHI N	78	207	43	6	0	7	3.4	15	30	22	36	0	.208	.338	4	0	C-76
1967 2 teams	PHI	N (18G – .171)				ATL	N (62G – .146)										
'' total	80	193	29	4	0	3	1.6	17	20	24	60	0	.150	.218	6	1	C-76
6 yrs.	297	731	146	22	0	14	1.9	65	74	96	167	0	.200	.287	29	5	C-271

Frenchy Uhalt

UHALT, BERNARD BARTHOLOMEW
B. Apr. 27, 1910, Bakersville, Calif.
BL TR 5'10''   180 lbs.

	G	AB	H	2B	3B	HR	HR %	R	RBI	BB	SO	SB	BA	SA	PH AB	PH H	G by POS
1934 CHI A	57	165	40	5	1	0	0.0	28	16	29	12	6	.242	.285	13	4	OF-40

Ted Uhlaender

UHLAENDER, THEODORE OTTO
B. Oct. 21, 1940, Chicago Heights, Ill.
BL TR 6'2''   190 lbs.

	G	AB	H	2B	3B	HR	HR %	R	RBI	BB	SO	SB	BA	SA	PH AB	PH H	G by POS
1965 MIN A	13	22	4	0	0	0	0.0	1	1	0	2	1	.182	.182	8	2	OF-4
1966	105	367	83	12	2	2	0.5	39	22	27	33	10	.226	.286	3	0	OF-100
1967	133	415	107	19	7	6	1.4	41	49	13	45	4	.258	.381	11	2	OF-118
1968	140	488	138	21	5	7	1.4	52	52	28	46	16	.283	.389	2	0	OF-129

	G	AB	H	2B	3B	HR	HR %	R	RBI	BB	SO	SB	BA	SA	Pinch Hit AB	Pinch Hit H	G by POS

Ted Uhlaender continued

	G	AB	H	2B	3B	HR	HR %	R	RBI	BB	SO	SB	BA	SA	PH AB	PH H	G by POS
1969	152	554	151	18	2	8	1.4	93	62	44	52	15	.273	.356	5	3	OF-150
1970 CLE A	141	473	127	21	2	11	2.3	56	46	39	44	3	.268	.391	11	5	OF-134
1971	141	500	144	20	3	2	0.4	52	47	38	44	3	.288	.352	11	2	OF-131
1972 CIN N	73	113	18	3	0	0	0.0	9	6	13	11	0	.159	.186	41	3	OF-27
8 yrs.	898	2932	772	114	21	36	1.2	343	285	202	277	52	.263	.353	92	17	OF-793
LEAGUE CHAMPIONSHIP SERIES																	
1969 MIN A	2	6	1	0	0	0	0.0	0	0	0	0	0	.167	.167	0	0	OF-2
1972 CIN N	2	2	1	0	0	0	0.0	0	0	0	0	0	.500	.500	2	1	
2 yrs.	4	8	2	0	0	0	0.0	0	0	0	0	0	.250	.250	2	1	OF-2
WORLD SERIES																	
1972 CIN N	4	4	1	1	0	0	0.0	0	0	0	1	0	.250	.500	4	1	

George Uhle

UHLE, GEORGE ERNEST (The Bull)
B. Sept. 18, 1898, Cleveland, Ohio
BR TR 6' 190 lbs.

	G	AB	H	2B	3B	HR	HR %	R	RBI	BB	SO	SB	BA	SA	PH AB	PH H	G by POS
1919 CLE A	26	43	13	2	1	0	0.0	7	6	1	5	0	.302	.395	0	0	P-26
1920	27	32	11	0	0	0	0.0	4	2	2	2	1	.344	.344	0	0	P-27
1921	48	94	23	2	3	1	1.1	21	18	6	9	0	.245	.362	0	0	P-41, C-1
1922	56	109	29	8	2	0	0.0	21	14	13	6	1	.266	.376	2	2	P-50
1923	58	144	52	10	3	0	0.0	23	22	7	10	2	.361	.472	3	0	P-54
1924	59	107	33	6	1	1	0.9	10	19	4	8	0	.308	.411	26	11	P-28
1925	56	104	29	3	3	0	0.0	10	13	7	7	0	.279	.365	22	5	P-29
1926	50	132	30	3	0	1	0.8	16	11	10	12	2	.227	.273	8	1	P-39
1927	43	79	21	7	1	0	0.0	4	14	5	12	0	.266	.380	18	5	P-25
1928	55	98	28	3	2	1	1.0	9	17	8	4	0	.286	.388	20	4	P-31
1929 DET A	40	108	37	1	1	0	0.0	18	13	6	6	0	.343	.370	7	1	P-32
1930	59	117	36	4	2	2	1.7	15	21	8	13	0	.308	.427	21	5	P-33
1931	53	90	22	6	0	2	2.2	8	7	8	8	0	.244	.378	21	3	P-29
1932	38	55	10	3	1	0	0.0	2	4	6	5	0	.182	.273	5	1	P-33
1933 3 teams	DET A (1G – .000)			NY N (8G – .000)			NY A (12G – .400)										
" total	21	25	8	1	0	0	0.0	2	1	5	5	0	.320	.360	2	0	P-19
1934 NY A	10	5	3	0	1	0	0.0	1	1	0	0	0	.600	1.000	0	0	P-10
1936 CLE A	24	21	8	1	0	1	4.8	1	4	2	0	0	.381	.571	14	6	P-7
17 yrs.	723	1363	393	60	21	9	0.7	172	187	98	112	6	.288	.383	169	44	P-513, C-1
WORLD SERIES																	
1920 CLE A	2	0	0	0	0	0	–	0	0	0	0	0	–	–	0	0	P-1

Maury Uhler

UHLER, MAURICE W.
B. Dec. 14, 1886, Pikesville, Md.   D. May 4, 1918, Baltimore, Md.
BR TR 5'11" 165 lbs.

	G	AB	H	2B	3B	HR	HR %	R	RBI	BB	SO	SB	BA	SA	PH AB	PH H	G by POS
1914 CIN N	46	56	12	2	0	0	0.0	12	3	5	11	4	.214	.250	3	0	OF-36

Charlie Uhlir

UHLIR, CHARLES
B. July 30, 1912, Chicago, Ill.
BL TL 5'7½" 150 lbs.

	G	AB	H	2B	3B	HR	HR %	R	RBI	BB	SO	SB	BA	SA	PH AB	PH H	G by POS
1934 CHI A	14	27	4	0	0	0	0.0	3	3	2	6	0	.148	.148	5	1	OF-6

Mike Ulisney

ULISNEY, MICHAEL EDWARD (Slugs)
B. Sept. 28, 1917, Greenwald, Pa.
BR TR 5'9" 165 lbs.

	G	AB	H	2B	3B	HR	HR %	R	RBI	BB	SO	SB	BA	SA	PH AB	PH H	G by POS
1945 BOS N	11	18	7	1	0	1	5.6	4	4	1	0	0	.389	.611	5	2	C-4

Scott Ullger

ULLGER, SCOTT MATTHEW
B. June 10, 1956, New York, N. Y.
BR TR 6'3" 196 lbs.

	G	AB	H	2B	3B	HR	HR %	R	RBI	BB	SO	SB	BA	SA	PH AB	PH H	G by POS
1983 MIN A	35	79	15	4	0	0	0.0	8	5	5	21	0	.190	.241	3	0	1B-30, 3B-3, DH-1

George Ulrich

ULRICH, GEORGE F.
B. Philadelphia, Pa.   D. Feb. 11, 1929

	G	AB	H	2B	3B	HR	HR %	R	RBI	BB	SO	SB	BA	SA	PH AB	PH H	G by POS
1892 WAS N	6	24	7	1	0	0	0.0	1	0	0	4	2	.292	.333	0	0	3B-3, SS-2, C-2
1893 CIN N	1	3	0	0	0	0	0.0	0	0	0	0	1	.000	.000	0	0	OF-1
1896 NY N	14	45	8	1	0	0	0.0	4	1	1	1	0	.178	.200	0	0	OF-11, 3B-3
3 yrs.	21	72	15	2	0	0	0.0	5	1	1	5	3	.208	.236	0	0	OF-12, 3B-6, SS-2, C-2

Tommy Umphlett

UMPHLETT, THOMAS MULLEN
B. May 12, 1930, Scotland Neck, N. C.
BR TR 6'2" 180 lbs.

	G	AB	H	2B	3B	HR	HR %	R	RBI	BB	SO	SB	BA	SA	PH AB	PH H	G by POS
1953 BOS A	137	495	140	27	5	3	0.6	53	59	34	30	4	.283	.376	1	0	OF-136
1954 WAS A	114	342	75	8	3	1	0.3	21	33	17	42	1	.219	.269	15	0	OF-101
1955	110	323	70	10	0	2	0.6	34	19	24	35	2	.217	.266	8	1	OF-103
3 yrs.	361	1160	285	45	8	6	0.5	108	111	75	107	7	.246	.314	24	1	OF-340

Bob Unglaub

UNGLAUB, ROBERT ALEXANDER
B. July 31, 1881, Baltimore, Md.   D. Nov. 29, 1916, Baltimore, Md.
Manager 1907.
BR TR

	G	AB	H	2B	3B	HR	HR %	R	RBI	BB	SO	SB	BA	SA	PH AB	PH H	G by POS
1904 2 teams	NY A (6G – .211)			BOS A (9G – .154)													
" total	15	32	6	1	0	0	0.0	3	4	1		0	.188	.219	4	0	3B-6, 2B-3, SS-2
1905 BOS A	43	121	27	5	1	0	0.0	18	11	6		2	.223	.281	12	2	3B-21, 2B-8, 1B-2
1907	139	544	138	17	13	1	0.2	49	62	23		14	.254	.338	0	0	1B-139
1908 2 teams	BOS A (72G – .263)			WAS A (72G – .308)													
" total	144	542	155	21	8	1	0.2	46	54	15		14	.286	.360	1	0	1B-76, 3B-39, 2B-27
1909 WAS A	130	480	127	14	9	3	0.6	43	41	22		15	.265	.350	1	0	1B-57, OF-43, 2B-25, 3B-4
1910	124	431	101	9	4	0	0.0	29	44	21		21	.234	.274	1	0	1B-124
6 yrs.	595	2150	554	67	35	5	0.2	188	216	88		66	.258	.328	19	2	1B-398, 3B-70, 2B-63, OF-43, SS-2

Al Unser

UNSER, ALBERT BERNARD
Father of Del Unser.
B. Oct. 12, 1912, Morrisonville, Ill.
BR TR 6'1" 175 lbs.

	G	AB	H	2B	3B	HR	HR %	R	RBI	BB	SO	SB	BA	SA	PH AB	PH H	G by POS
1942 DET A	4	8	3	0	0	0	0.0	2	0	0	2	0	.375	.375	0	0	C-4

	G	AB	H	2B	3B	HR	HR %	R	RBI	BB	SO	SB	BA	SA	Pinch Hit AB	Pinch Hit H	G by POS

Al Unser continued

	G	AB	H	2B	3B	HR	HR %	R	RBI	BB	SO	SB	BA	SA	AB	H	G by POS
1943	38	101	25	5	0	0	0.0	14	4	15	15	0	.248	.297	0	0	C-37
1944	11	25	3	0	1	1	4.0	2	5	3	2	0	.120	.320	5	2	2B-5, C-1
1945 CIN N	67	204	54	10	3	3	1.5	23	21	14	24	0	.265	.387	5	2	C-61
4 yrs.	120	338	85	15	4	4	1.2	41	30	32	43	0	.251	.355	10	4	C-103, 2B-5

Del Unser

UNSER, DELBERT BERNARD
Son of Al Unser.
B. Dec. 9, 1944, Decatur, Ill.

BL TL 6'1"   180 lbs.

	G	AB	H	2B	3B	HR	HR %	R	RBI	BB	SO	SB	BA	SA	AB	H	G by POS
1968 WAS A	156	635	146	13	7	1	0.2	66	30	46	66	11	.230	.277	1	1	OF-156, 1B-1
1969	153	581	166	19	8	7	1.2	69	57	58	54	8	.286	.382	11	3	OF-149
1970	119	322	83	5	1	5	1.6	37	30	30	29	1	.258	.326	21	6	OF-103
1971	153	581	148	19	6	9	1.5	63	41	59	68	11	.255	.355	2	0	OF-151
1972 CLE A	132	383	91	12	0	1	0.3	29	17	28	46	5	.238	.277	15	4	OF-119
1973 PHI N	136	440	127	20	4	11	2.5	64	52	47	55	5	.289	.427	12	2	OF-132
1974	142	454	120	18	5	11	2.4	72	61	50	62	6	.264	.399	13	2	OF-135
1975 NY N	147	531	156	18	2	10	1.9	65	53	37	76	4	.294	.392	3	1	OF-144
1976 2 teams	NY	N	(77G –	.228)		MON	N	(69G –	.227)								
" total	146	496	113	19	4	12	2.4	57	40	29	84	7	.228	.355	7	1	OF-142
1977 MON N	113	289	79	14	1	12	4.2	33	40	33	41	2	.273	.453	21	4	OF-72, 1B-27
1978	130	179	35	5	0	2	1.1	16	15	24	29	2	.196	.257	37	3	1B-64, OF-33
1979 PHI N	95	141	42	8	0	6	4.3	26	29	14	33	2	.298	.482	46	14	OF-30, 1B-22
1980	96	110	29	6	4	0	0.0	15	10	10	21	0	.264	.391	38	12	1B-31, OF-23
1981	62	59	9	3	0	0	0.0	5	6	13	9	0	.153	.203	26	5	1B-18, OF-16
1982	19	14	0	0	0	0	0.0	0	0	3	2	0	.000	.000	11	0	1B-5, OF-2
15 yrs.	1799	5215	1344	179	42	87	1.7	617	481	481	675	64	.258	.358	264	54	OF-1407, 1B-168
LEAGUE CHAMPIONSHIP SERIES																	
1980 PHI N	5	5	2	1	0	0	0.0	2	1	0	2	0	.400	.600	3	1	OF-2
WORLD SERIES																	
1980 PHI N	3	6	3	2	0	0	0.0	2	2	0	1	0	.500	.833	2	2	OF-3

John Upham

UPHAM, JOHN LESLIE
B. Dec. 29, 1941, Windsor, Ont., Canada

BL TL 6'   180 lbs.

	G	AB	H	2B	3B	HR	HR %	R	RBI	BB	SO	SB	BA	SA	AB	H	G by POS
1967 CHI N	8	3	2	0	0	0	0.0	1	0	0	0	0	.667	.667	3	2	P-5
1968	13	10	2	0	0	0	0.0	0	0	0	3	0	.200	.200	6	1	OF-2, P-2
2 yrs.	21	13	4	0	0	0	0.0	1	0	0	3	0	.308	.308	9	3	P-7, OF-2

Dixie Upright

UPRIGHT, ROY T.
B. May 30, 1926, Kannapolis, N. C.

BL TL 6'   175 lbs.

	G	AB	H	2B	3B	HR	HR %	R	RBI	BB	SO	SB	BA	SA	AB	H	G by POS
1953 STL A	9	8	2	0	0	1	12.5	3	1	1	3	0	.250	.625	8	2	

Willie Upshaw

UPSHAW, WILLIE CLAY
B. Apr. 27, 1957, Blanco, Tex.

BL TL 6'   185 lbs.

	G	AB	H	2B	3B	HR	HR %	R	RBI	BB	SO	SB	BA	SA	AB	H	G by POS
1978 TOR A	95	224	53	8	2	1	0.4	26	17	21	35	4	.237	.304	12	1	OF-52, DH-18, 1B-10
1980	34	61	13	3	1	1	1.6	10	5	6	14	1	.213	.344	9	2	1B-14, DH-12, OF-1
1981	61	111	19	3	1	4	3.6	15	10	11	16	2	.171	.324	17	4	DH-15, OF-14, 1B-14
1982	160	580	155	25	7	21	3.6	77	75	52	91	8	.267	.443	2	0	1B-155, DH-5
1983	160	579	177	26	7	27	4.7	99	104	61	98	10	.306	.515	4	1	1B-159, DH-1
1984	152	569	158	31	9	19	3.3	79	84	55	86	10	.278	.464	0	0	1B-151, DH-1
6 yrs.	662	2124	575	96	27	73	3.4	306	295	206	340	35	.271	.444	44	8	1B-503, OF-67, DH-52

Tom Upton

UPTON, THOMAS HERBERT (Muscles)
B. Dec. 29, 1926, Esther, Mo.

BR TR 6'   160 lbs.

	G	AB	H	2B	3B	HR	HR %	R	RBI	BB	SO	SB	BA	SA	AB	H	G by POS
1950 STL A	124	389	92	5	6	2	0.5	50	30	52	45	7	.237	.296	5	0	SS-115, 2B-2, 3B-1
1951	52	131	26	4	3	0	0.0	9	12	12	22	1	.198	.275	0	0	SS-47
1952 WAS A	5	5	0	0	0	0	0.0	1	0	1	0	0	.000	.000	0	0	SS-3
3 yrs.	181	525	118	9	9	2	0.4	60	42	65	67	8	.225	.288	5	0	SS-165, 2B-2, 3B-1

Luke Urban

URBAN, JOHN LOUIS
B. Mar. 22, 1898, Fall River, Mass.   D. Dec. 7, 1980, Somerset, Mass.

BR TR 5'8"   168 lbs.

	G	AB	H	2B	3B	HR	HR %	R	RBI	BB	SO	SB	BA	SA	AB	H	G by POS
1927 BOS N	35	111	32	5	0	0	0.0	11	10	3	6	1	.288	.333	1	1	C-34
1928	15	17	3	0	0	0	0.0	0	2	0	1	0	.176	.176	5	1	C-5
2 yrs.	50	128	35	5	0	0	0.0	11	12	3	7	1	.273	.313	6	2	C-39

Billy Urbanski

URBANSKI, WILLIAM MICHAEL
B. June 5, 1903, Staten Island, N. Y.   D. July 12, 1973, Perth Amboy, N. J.

BR TR 5'8"   165 lbs.

	G	AB	H	2B	3B	HR	HR %	R	RBI	BB	SO	SB	BA	SA	AB	H	G by POS
1931 BOS N	82	303	72	13	4	0	0.0	22	17	10	32	1	.238	.307	0	0	3B-68, SS-19
1932	136	563	153	25	8	8	1.4	80	46	28	60	8	.272	.387	0	0	SS-136
1933	144	566	142	21	4	0	0.0	65	35	33	48	4	.251	.302	1	0	SS-143
1934	146	605	177	30	6	7	1.2	104	53	56	37	4	.293	.397	1	0	SS-145
1935	132	514	118	17	0	4	0.8	53	30	40	32	3	.230	.286	0	0	SS-129
1936	122	494	129	17	5	0	0.0	55	26	31	42	2	.261	.316	3	1	SS-80, 3B-38
1937	1	1	0	0	0	0	0.0	0	0	0	1	0	.000	.000	0	0	
7 yrs.	763	3046	791	123	27	19	0.6	379	207	198	252	24	.260	.337	6	1	SS-652, 3B-106

Lou Ury

URY, LOUIS NEWTON
B. 1877, Fort Scott, Kans.   D. Mar. 4, 1918, Kansas City, Mo.

TR 6'

	G	AB	H	2B	3B	HR	HR %	R	RBI	BB	SO	SB	BA	SA	AB	H	G by POS
1903 STL N	2	7	1	0	0	0	0.0	0	0	0		0	.143	.143	0	0	1B-2

Bob Usher

USHER, ROBERT ROYCE
B. Mar. 1, 1925, San Diego, Calif.

BR TR 6'1½"   180 lbs.

	G	AB	H	2B	3B	HR	HR %	R	RBI	BB	SO	SB	BA	SA	AB	H	G by POS
1946 CIN N	92	152	31	5	1	1	0.7	16	14	13	27	2	.204	.270	1	0	OF-80, 3B-1
1947	9	22	4	0	1	1	4.5	2	1	2	2	0	.182	.318	0	0	OF-8
1950	106	321	83	17	0	6	1.9	51	35	27	38	3	.259	.368	10	2	OF-95
1951	114	303	63	12	2	5	1.7	27	25	19	36	4	.208	.310	13	2	OF-98

	G	AB	H	2B	3B	HR	HR%	R	RBI	BB	SO	SB	BA	SA	Pinch Hit AB	Pinch Hit H	G by POS

Bob Usher continued

	G	AB	H	2B	3B	HR	HR%	R	RBI	BB	SO	SB	BA	SA	PH AB	PH H	G by POS
1952 CHI N	1	0	0	0	0	0	–	0	0	1	0	0	–	–	0	0	
1957 2 teams		CLE A (10G – .125)				WAS A (96G – .261)											
" total	106	303	78	7	1	5	1.7	37	27	28	33	0	.257	.337	4	0	OF-99, 3B-1
6 yrs.	428	1101	259	41	4	18	1.6	133	102	90	136	9	.235	.329	28	4	OF-380, 3B-2

Dutch Ussat

USSAT, WILLIAM AUGUST   BR TR 6'1" 170 lbs.
B. Apr. 11, 1904, Dayton, Ohio D. May 29, 1959, Dayton, Ohio

	G	AB	H	2B	3B	HR	HR%	R	RBI	BB	SO	SB	BA	SA	PH AB	PH H	G by POS
1925 CLE A	1	1	0	0	0	0	0.0	0	0	0	0	0	.000	.000	0	0	2B-1
1927	4	16	3	0	1	0	0.0	4	2	2	1	0	.188	.313	0	0	3B-4
2 yrs.	5	17	3	0	1	0	0.0	4	2	2	1	0	.176	.294	0	0	3B-4, 2B-1

Tex Vache

VACHE, ERNEST LEWIS   BR TR 6'1" 195 lbs.
B. Nov. 17, 1895, Santa Monica, Calif. D. June 11, 1953, Los Angeles, Calif.

	G	AB	H	2B	3B	HR	HR%	R	RBI	BB	SO	SB	BA	SA	PH AB	PH H	G by POS
1925 BOS A	110	252	79	15	7	3	1.2	41	48	21	33	2	.313	.464	49	10	OF-53

Gene Vadeboncoeur

VADEBONCOEUR, EUGENE F.   5'6" 150 lbs.
B. Syracuse, N. Y. D. Oct. 16, 1935, Haverhill, Mass.

	G	AB	H	2B	3B	HR	HR%	R	RBI	BB	SO	SB	BA	SA	PH AB	PH H	G by POS
1884 PHI N	4	14	3	0	0	0	0.0	1		1	2		.214	.214	0	0	C-4

Howard Vahrenhorst

VAHRENHORST, HARRY HENRY   6'1" 175 lbs.
B. Feb. 13, 1885, St. Louis, Mo. D. Oct. 10, 1943, St. Louis, Mo.

	G	AB	H	2B	3B	HR	HR%	R	RBI	BB	SO	SB	BA	SA	PH AB	PH H	G by POS
1904 STL A	1	1	0	0	0	0	0.0	0	0		0	0	.000	.000	1	0	

Mike Vail

VAIL, MICHAEL LEWIS   BR TR 6'1" 180 lbs.
B. Nov. 10, 1951, San Francisco, Calif.

	G	AB	H	2B	3B	HR	HR%	R	RBI	BB	SO	SB	BA	SA	PH AB	PH H	G by POS
1975 NY N	38	162	49	8	1	3	1.9	17	17	9	37	0	.302	.420	1	1	OF-36
1976	53	143	31	5	1	0	0.0	8	9	6	19	0	.217	.266	17	4	OF-35
1977	108	279	73	12	1	8	2.9	29	35	19	58	0	.262	.398	30	4	OF-85
1978 2 teams		CLE A (14G – .235)				CHI N (74G – .333)											
" total	88	214	68	8	3	4	1.9	17	35	4	33	1	.318	.439	35	13	OF-54, DH-1, 3B-2
1979 CHI N	87	179	60	8	2	7	3.9	28	35	14	27	0	.335	.520	44	12	OF-39, 3B-2
1980	114	312	93	17	2	6	1.9	30	47	14	77	2	.298	.423	45	8	OF-77
1981 CIN N	31	31	5	0	0	0	0.0	1	3	0	9	0	.161	.161	28	5	OF-3
1982	78	189	48	10	1	4	2.1	9	29	6	33	0	.254	.381	29	8	OF-52
1983 2 teams		SF N (18G – .154)				MON N (34G – .283)											
" total	52	79	19	3	0	2	2.5	6	7	8	17	0	.241	.354	25	5	OF-17, 1B-5, 3B-1
1984 LA N	16	16	1	0	0	0	0.0	1	2	1	7	0	.063	.063	13	1	OF-1
10 yrs.	665	1604	447	71	11	34	2.1	146	219	81	317	3	.279	.400	267	61	OF-399, 1B-5, 3B-4, DH-1

Armando Valdes

VALDES, ARMANDO VIERA   BR TR 6' 175 lbs.
B. May 2, 1922, Cardenas, Cuba

	G	AB	H	2B	3B	HR	HR%	R	RBI	BB	SO	SB	BA	SA	PH AB	PH H	G by POS
1944 WAS A	1	1	0	0	0	0	0.0	0	0	0	0	0	.000	.000	1	0	

Sandy Valdespino

VALDESPINO, HILARIO BORROTO   BL TL 5'8" 170 lbs.
B. Jan. 14, 1939, San Jose de las Lajas, Cuba

	G	AB	H	2B	3B	HR	HR%	R	RBI	BB	SO	SB	BA	SA	PH AB	PH H	G by POS
1965 MIN A	108	245	64	8	2	1	0.4	38	22	20	28	7	.261	.322	47	10	OF-57
1966	52	108	19	1	1	2	1.9	11	9	4	24	2	.176	.259	27	2	OF-23
1967	99	97	16	2	0	1	1.0	9	3	5	22	3	.165	.216	33	7	OF-65
1968 ATL N	36	86	20	1	0	1	1.2	8	4	10	20	0	.233	.279	15	1	OF-20
1969 2 teams		HOU N (41G – .244)				SEA A (20G – .211)											
" total	61	157	37	5	0	0	0.0	20	14	16	26	2	.236	.268	22	3	OF-36
1970 MIL A	8	9	0	0	0	0	0.0	0	0	0	4	0	.000	.000	7	0	OF-1
1971 KC A	18	63	20	6	0	2	3.2	10	15	2	5	0	.317	.508	4	2	OF-15
7 yrs.	382	765	176	23	3	7	0.9	96	67	57	129	14	.230	.295	155	25	OF-217
WORLD SERIES																	
1965 MIN A	5	11	3	1	0	0	0.0	1	0	0	1	0	.273	.364	3	1	OF-2

Julio Valdez

VALDEZ, JULIO JULIAN   BB TR 6'2" 160 lbs.
B. July 3, 1956, Nizao De Peravia, Dominican Republic

	G	AB	H	2B	3B	HR	HR%	R	RBI	BB	SO	SB	BA	SA	PH AB	PH H	G by POS
1980 BOS A	8	19	5	1	0	1	5.3	4	4	0	5	2	.263	.474	0	0	SS-8
1981	17	23	5	0	0	0	0.0	1	3	0	2	0	.217	.217	0	0	SS-17
1982	28	20	5	1	0	0	0.0	3	1	0	7	1	.250	.300	2	1	SS-22, DH-3
1983	12	25	3	0	0	0	0.0	3	0	1	4	0	.120	.120	0	0	2B-9, SS-2, DH-1
4 yrs.	65	87	18	2	0	1	1.1	11	8	1	18	3	.207	.264	2	1	SS-49, 2B-9, DH-4

Jose Valdivielso

VALDIVIELSO, JOSE LOPEZ   BR TR 6'1" 175 lbs.
B. May 22, 1934, Matanzas, Cuba

	G	AB	H	2B	3B	HR	HR%	R	RBI	BB	SO	SB	BA	SA	PH AB	PH H	G by POS
1955 WAS A	94	294	65	12	5	2	0.7	32	28	21	38	1	.221	.316	0	0	SS-94
1956	90	246	58	8	2	4	1.6	18	29	29	36	3	.236	.333	1	0	SS-90
1959	24	14	4	0	0	0	0.0	1	0	1	3	0	.286	.286	1	1	SS-21
1960	117	268	57	1	1	2	0.7	23	19	20	36	1	.213	.246	0	0	SS-115, 3B-1
1961 MIN A	76	149	29	5	0	1	0.7	15	9	8	19	1	.195	.248	0	0	SS-43, 2B-15, 3B-14
5 yrs.	401	971	213	26	8	9	0.9	89	85	79	132	6	.219	.290	2	1	SS-363, 3B-15, 2B-15

Bob Valentine

VALENTINE, ROBERT
Deceased.

	G	AB	H	2B	3B	HR	HR%	R	RBI	BB	SO	SB	BA	SA	PH AB	PH H	G by POS
1876 NY N	1	3	0	0	0	0	0.0	0		0	0		.000	.000	0	0	C-1

Bobby Valentine

VALENTINE, ROBERT JOHN   BR TR 5'10" 189 lbs.
B. May 13, 1950, Stamford, Conn.

	G	AB	H	2B	3B	HR	HR%	R	RBI	BB	SO	SB	BA	SA	PH AB	PH H	G by POS
1969 LA N	5	0	0	0	0	0	–	3	0	0	0	0	–	–	0	0	
1971	101	281	70	10	2	1	0.4	32	25	15	20	5	.249	.310	14	5	SS-37, 3B-23, 2B-21, OF-11
1972	119	391	107	11	2	3	0.8	42	32	27	33	5	.274	.335	10	1	2B-49, 3B-39, OF-16, SS-10

	G	AB	H	2B	3B	HR	HR %	R	RBI	BB	SO	SB	BA	SA	Pinch Hit AB	Pinch Hit H	G by POS

Vince Ventura

VENTURA, VINCENT
B. Apr. 18, 1917, New York, N. Y.

BR TR 6'1½" 190 lbs.

	G	AB	H	2B	3B	HR	HR %	R	RBI	BB	SO	SB	BA	SA	PH AB	PH H	G by POS
1945 WAS A	18	58	12	0	0	0	0.0	4	2	4	4	0	.207	.207	3	1	OF-15

Emil Verban

VERBAN, EMIL MATTHEW (Dutch, The Antelope)
B. Aug. 27, 1915, Lincoln, Ill.

BR TR 5'11" 165 lbs.

	G	AB	H	2B	3B	HR	HR %	R	RBI	BB	SO	SB	BA	SA	PH AB	PH H	G by POS
1944 STL N	146	498	128	14	2	0	0.0	51	43	19	14	0	.257	.293	0	0	2B-146
1945	155	597	166	22	8	0	0.0	59	72	19	15	4	.278	.342	0	0	2B-155
1946 2 teams	STL N (1G – .000)			PHI N (138G – .275)													
" total	139	474	130	17	5	0	0.0	44	34	21	18	5	.274	.331	1	0	2B-138
1947 PHI N	155	540	154	14	8	0	0.0	50	42	23	8	5	.285	.341	0	0	2B-155
1948 2 teams	PHI N (55G – .231)			CHI N (56G – .294)													
" total	111	417	112	20	2	1	0.2	51	27	15	12	4	.269	.333	1	0	2B-110
1949 CHI N	98	343	99	11	1	0	0.0	38	22	8	2	3	.289	.327	7	1	2B-88
1950 2 teams	CHI N (45G – .108)			BOS N (4G – .000)													
" total	49	42	4	1	0	0	0.0	8	1	3	5	0	.095	.119	13	1	2B-10, SS-3, OF-1, 3B-1
7 yrs.	853	2911	793	99	26	1	0.0	301	241	108	74	21	.272	.325	22	2	2B-802, SS-3, OF-1, 3B-1

WORLD SERIES

	G	AB	H	2B	3B	HR	HR %	R	RBI	BB	SO	SB	BA	SA	PH AB	PH H	G by POS
1944 STL N	6	17	7	0	0	0	0.0	1	2	2	0	0	.412	.412	0	0	2B-6

Gene Verble

VERBLE, GENE KERMIT (Satchel)
B. June 29, 1928, Concord, N. C.

BR TR 5'10" 163 lbs.

	G	AB	H	2B	3B	HR	HR %	R	RBI	BB	SO	SB	BA	SA	PH AB	PH H	G by POS
1951 WAS A	68	177	36	3	2	0	0.0	16	15	18	10	1	.203	.243	16	2	SS-28, 2B-19, 3B-1
1953	13	21	4	0	0	0	0.0	4	2	2	1	0	.190	.190	1	0	SS-8
2 yrs.	81	198	40	3	2	0	0.0	20	17	20	11	1	.202	.237	17	2	SS-36, 2B-19, 3B-1

Frank Verdi

VERDI, FRANK MICHAEL
B. June 2, 1926, Brooklyn, N. Y.

BR TR 5'10½" 170 lbs.

	G	AB	H	2B	3B	HR	HR %	R	RBI	BB	SO	SB	BA	SA	PH AB	PH H	G by POS
1953 NY A	1	0	0	0	0	0	–	0	0	0	0	0	–	–	0	0	SS-1

Johnny Vergez

VERGEZ, JOHN LEWIS
B. July 9, 1906, Oakland, Calif.

BR TR 5'8" 165 lbs.

	G	AB	H	2B	3B	HR	HR %	R	RBI	BB	SO	SB	BA	SA	PH AB	PH H	G by POS
1931 NY N	152	565	157	24	2	13	2.3	67	81	29	65	11	.278	.396	0	0	3B-152
1932	118	376	98	21	3	6	1.6	42	43	25	36	1	.261	.380	3	1	3B-111, SS-1
1933	123	458	124	21	6	16	3.5	57	72	39	66	1	.271	.448	0	0	3B-123
1934	108	320	64	18	1	7	2.2	31	27	28	55	1	.200	.328	3	0	3B-104
1935 PHI N	148	546	136	27	4	9	1.6	56	63	46	67	8	.249	.363	0	0	3B-148, SS-2
1936 2 teams	PHI N (15G – .275)			STL N (8G – .167)													
" total	23	58	14	3	0	1	1.7	5	6	4	14	0	.241	.345	2	0	3B-20
6 yrs.	672	2323	593	114	16	52	2.2	258	292	171	303	22	.255	.385	8	1	3B-658, SS-3

Mickey Vernon

VERNON, JAMES BARTON
B. Apr. 22, 1918, Marcus Hook, Pa.
Manager 1961-63.

BL TL 6'2" 170 lbs.

	G	AB	H	2B	3B	HR	HR %	R	RBI	BB	SO	SB	BA	SA	PH AB	PH H	G by POS
1939 WAS A	76	276	71	15	4	1	0.4	23	30	24	28	1	.257	.351	0	0	1B-75
1940	5	19	3	0	0	0	0.0	0	0	0	3	0	.158	.158	1	0	1B-4
1941	138	531	159	27	11	9	1.7	73	93	43	51	9	.299	.443	6	2	1B-132
1942	151	621	168	34	6	9	1.4	76	86	39	63	25	.271	.388	0	0	1B-151
1943	145	553	148	29	8	7	1.3	89	70	66	55	24	.268	.387	1	1	1B-143
1946	148	587	207	51	8	8	1.4	88	85	49	64	14	.353	.508	1	1	1B-147
1947	154	600	159	29	12	7	1.2	77	85	49	42	12	.265	.388	0	0	1B-154
1948	150	558	135	27	7	3	0.5	78	48	54	43	15	.242	.332	1	0	1B-150
1949 CLE A	153	584	170	27	4	18	3.1	72	83	58	51	9	.291	.443	0	0	1B-153
1950 2 teams	CLE A (28G – .189)			WAS A (90G – .306)													
" total	118	417	117	17	3	9	2.2	55	75	62	39	8	.281	.400	8	1	1B-110
1951 WAS A	141	546	160	30	7	9	1.6	69	87	53	45	7	.293	.423	3	3	1B-137
1952	154	569	143	33	9	10	1.8	71	80	89	66	7	.251	.394	0	0	1B-153
1953	152	608	205	43	11	15	2.5	101	115	63	57	4	.337	.518	0	0	1B-152
1954	151	597	173	33	14	20	3.4	90	97	61	61	1	.290	.492	3	2	1B-148
1955	150	538	162	23	8	14	2.6	74	85	74	50	0	.301	.452	7	2	1B-144
1956 BOS A	119	403	125	28	4	15	3.7	67	84	57	40	1	.310	.511	10	4	1B-108
1957	102	270	65	18	1	7	2.6	36	38	41	35	0	.241	.393	22	6	1B-70
1958 CLE A	119	355	104	22	3	8	2.3	49	55	44	56	0	.293	.439	24	7	1B-96
1959 MIL N	74	91	20	4	0	3	3.3	8	14	7	20	0	.220	.363	59	13	1B-10, OF-4
1960 PIT N	9	8	1	0	0	0	0.0	0	1	1	0	0	.125	.125	8	1	
20 yrs.	2409	8731	2495	490	120	172	2.0	1196	1311	934	869	137	.286	.428	154	43	1B-2237, OF-4

Zoilo Versalles

VERSALLES, ZOILO CASANOVA (Zorro)
B. Dec. 18, 1939, Vedado, Cuba

BR TR 5'10" 146 lbs.

	G	AB	H	2B	3B	HR	HR %	R	RBI	BB	SO	SB	BA	SA	PH AB	PH H	G by POS
1959 WAS A	29	59	9	0	0	1	1.7	4	1	4	15	1	.153	.203	0	0	SS-29
1960	15	45	6	2	2	0	0.0	2	4	2	5	0	.133	.267	0	0	SS-15
1961 MIN A	129	510	143	25	5	7	1.4	65	53	25	61	16	.280	.390	0	0	SS-129
1962	160	568	137	18	3	17	3.0	69	67	37	71	5	.241	.373	0	0	SS-160
1963	159	621	162	31	13	10	1.6	74	54	33	66	7	.261	.401	0	0	SS-159
1964	160	659	171	33	10	20	3.0	94	64	42	88	14	.259	.431	1	1	SS-160
1965	160	666	182	45	12	19	2.9	126	77	41	122	27	.273	.462	0	0	SS-160
1966	137	543	135	20	6	7	1.3	73	36	40	85	10	.249	.346	2	0	SS-135
1967	160	581	116	16	7	6	1.0	63	50	33	113	5	.200	.282	0	0	SS-160
1968 LA N	122	403	79	16	3	2	0.5	29	24	26	84	6	.196	.266	2	1	SS-119
1969 2 teams	CLE A (72G – .226)			WAS A (31G – .267)													
" total	103	292	69	13	2	3	1.0	30	19	24	60	4	.236	.305	13	4	2B-52, 3B-35, SS-16
1971 ATL N	66	194	37	11	0	5	2.6	21	22	11	40	2	.191	.325	9	1	3B-30, SS-24, 2B-1
12 yrs.	1400	5141	1246	230	63	95	1.8	650	471	318	810	97	.242	.367	27	7	SS-1265, 3B-65, 2B-53

WORLD SERIES

	G	AB	H	2B	3B	HR	HR %	R	RBI	BB	SO	SB	BA	SA	PH AB	PH H	G by POS
1965 MIN A	7	28	8	1	1	1	3.6	3	4	2	7	1	.286	.500	0	0	SS-7

	G	AB	H	2B	3B	HR	HR %	R	RBI	BB	SO	SB	BA	SA	Pinch Hit AB	Pinch Hit H	G by POS

Tom Veryzer

VERYZER, THOMAS MARTIN
B. Feb. 11, 1953, Islip, N. Y.
BR TR 6'1½" 175 lbs.

	G	AB	H	2B	3B	HR	HR %	R	RBI	BB	SO	SB	BA	SA	PH AB	PH H	G by POS
1973 DET A	18	20	6	0	1	0	0.0	1	2	2	4	0	.300	.400	0	0	SS-18
1974	22	55	13	2	0	2	3.6	4	9	5	8	1	.236	.382	1	0	SS-20
1975	128	404	102	13	1	5	1.2	37	48	23	76	2	.252	.327	0	0	SS-128
1976	97	354	83	8	2	1	0.3	31	25	21	44	1	.234	.277	0	0	SS-97
1977	125	350	69	12	1	2	0.6	31	28	16	44	0	.197	.254	0	0	SS-124
1978 CLE A	130	421	114	18	4	1	0.2	48	32	13	36	1	.271	.340	0	0	SS-129
1979	149	449	99	9	3	0	0.0	41	34	34	54	2	.220	.254	0	0	SS-148
1980	109	358	97	12	0	2	0.6	28	28	10	25	0	.271	.321	0	0	SS-108
1981	75	221	54	4	0	0	0.0	13	14	10	10	1	.244	.262	0	0	SS-75
1982 NY N	40	54	18	2	0	0	0.0	6	4	3	4	1	.333	.370	0	0	2B-26, SS-16
1983 CHI N	59	88	18	3	0	1	1.1	5	3	3	13	0	.205	.273	11	3	SS-28, 3B-17
1984	44	74	14	1	0	0	0.0	5	4	3	11	0	.189	.203	0	0	SS-36, 3B-5, 2B-4
12 yrs.	996	2848	687	84	12	14	0.5	250	231	143	329	9	.241	.294	12	3	SS-927, 2B-30, 3B-22
LEAGUE CHAMPIONSHIP SERIES																	
1984 CHI N	3	1	0	0	0	0	0.0	0	0	0	0	0	.000	.000	0	0	3B-1

Ernie Vick

VICK, HENRY ARTHUR
B. July 2, 1900, Toledo, Ohio   D. July 16, 1980, Ann Arbor, Mich.
BR TR 5'9½" 185 lbs.

	G	AB	H	2B	3B	HR	HR %	R	RBI	BB	SO	SB	BA	SA	PH AB	PH H	G by POS
1922 STL N	3	6	2	2	0	0	0.0	1	0	0	0	0	.333	.667	0	0	C-3
1924	16	23	8	1	0	0	0.0	2	0	3	3	0	.348	.391	0	0	C-16
1925	14	32	6	2	1	0	0.0	3	3	3	1	0	.188	.313	5	0	C-9
1926	24	51	10	2	0	0	0.0	6	4	3	4	0	.196	.235	1	0	C-23
4 yrs.	57	112	26	7	1	0	0.0	12	7	9	8	0	.232	.313	6	0	C-51

Sammy Vick

VICK, SAMUEL BRUCE
B. Apr. 12, 1895, Batesville, Miss.
BR TR 5'10½" 163 lbs.

	G	AB	H	2B	3B	HR	HR %	R	RBI	BB	SO	SB	BA	SA	PH AB	PH H	G by POS
1917 NY A	10	36	10	3	0	0	0.0	4	2	1	6	2	.278	.361	0	0	OF-10
1918	2	3	2	0	0	0	0.0	1	1	0	0	0	.667	.667	1	0	OF-1
1919	106	407	101	15	9	2	0.5	59	27	35	55	9	.248	.344	5	1	OF-100
1920	51	118	26	7	1	0	0.0	21	11	14	20	1	.220	.297	17	6	OF-33
1921 BOS A	44	77	20	3	1	0	0.0	5	9	1	10	0	.260	.325	28	8	OF-14, C-1
5 yrs.	213	641	159	28	11	2	0.3	90	50	51	91	12	.248	.335	51	15	OF-158, C-1

George Vico

VICO, GEORGE STEVE (Sam)
B. Aug. 9, 1923, San Fernando, Calif.
BL TR 6'4" 200 lbs.

	G	AB	H	2B	3B	HR	HR %	R	RBI	BB	SO	SB	BA	SA	PH AB	PH H	G by POS
1948 DET A	144	521	139	23	9	8	1.5	50	58	39	39	2	.267	.392	2	0	1B-142
1949	67	142	27	5	2	4	2.8	15	18	21	17	0	.190	.338	13	2	1B-53
2 yrs.	211	663	166	28	11	12	1.8	65	76	60	56	2	.250	.380	15	2	1B-195

Jose Vidal

VIDAL, JOSE NICOLAS (Papito)
B. Apr. 3, 1940, Batey Lechugas, Dominican Republic
BR TR 6' 190 lbs.

	G	AB	H	2B	3B	HR	HR %	R	RBI	BB	SO	SB	BA	SA	PH AB	PH H	G by POS
1966 CLE A	17	32	6	1	1	0	0.0	4	3	5	11	0	.188	.281	4	0	OF-11
1967	16	34	4	0	0	0	0.0	4	0	7	12	0	.118	.118	4	1	OF-10
1968	37	54	9	0	0	2	3.7	5	5	2	15	3	.167	.278	11	1	OF-26, 1B-1
1969 SEA A	18	26	5	0	1	1	3.8	7	2	4	8	1	.192	.385	5	0	OF-6
4 yrs.	88	146	24	1	2	3	2.1	20	10	18	46	4	.164	.260	24	2	OF-53, 1B-1

Charlie Vinson

VINSON, CHARLES ANTHONY
B. Jan. 5, 1945, Washington, D. C.
BL TL 6'3" 207 lbs.

	G	AB	H	2B	3B	HR	HR %	R	RBI	BB	SO	SB	BA	SA	PH AB	PH H	G by POS
1966 CAL A	13	22	4	2	0	1	4.5	3	6	5	9	0	.182	.409	0	0	1B-11

Rube Vinson

VINSON, ERNEST AUGUSTUS
B. Mar. 20, 1879, Dover, Del.   D. Oct. 12, 1951, Chester, Pa.
5'9" 168 lbs.

	G	AB	H	2B	3B	HR	HR %	R	RBI	BB	SO	SB	BA	SA	PH AB	PH H	G by POS
1904 CLE A	15	49	15	1	0	0	0.0	12	2	10		2	.306	.327	0	0	OF-15
1905	38	133	26	3	1	0	0.0	12	9	7		4	.195	.233	2	0	OF-36
1906 CHI A	7	24	6	0	0	0	0.0	2	3	2		1	.250	.250	1	1	OF-4
3 yrs.	60	206	47	4	1	0	0.0	26	14	19		7	.228	.257	3	1	OF-55

Jim Viox

VIOX, JAMES HENRY
B. Dec. 30, 1890, Lockland, Ohio   D. Jan. 6, 1969, Erlanger, Ky.
BR TR 5'7" 150 lbs.

	G	AB	H	2B	3B	HR	HR %	R	RBI	BB	SO	SB	BA	SA	PH AB	PH H	G by POS
1912 PIT N	33	70	13	2	3	1	1.4	8	7	3	5	2	.186	.343	8	0	3B-10, SS-8, OF-3, 2B-1
1913	137	492	156	32	8	2	0.4	86	65	64	28	14	.317	.427	2	1	2B-124, SS-10
1914	143	506	134	18	5	1	0.2	52	57	63	33	9	.265	.326	1	0	2B-138, OF-2, SS-2
1915	150	503	129	17	8	2	0.4	56	45	75	31	12	.256	.334	2	1	2B-135, 3B-13, OF-2
1916	43	132	33	7	0	1	0.8	12	17	17	11	2	.250	.326	6	1	2B-25, 3B-11
5 yrs.	506	1703	465	76	24	7	0.4	214	191	222	108	39	.273	.358	19	3	2B-423, 3B-34, SS-20, OF-7

Bill Virdon

VIRDON, WILLIAM CHARLES
B. June 9, 1931, Hazel Park, Mich.
Manager 1972-84.
BL TR 6' 175 lbs.

	G	AB	H	2B	3B	HR	HR %	R	RBI	BB	SO	SB	BA	SA	PH AB	PH H	G by POS
1955 STL N	144	534	150	18	6	17	3.2	58	68	36	64	2	.281	.433	9	1	OF-142
1956 2 teams	STL N (24G – .211)							PIT N (133G – .334)									
" total	157	580	185	23	10	10	1.7	77	46	38	71	6	.319	.445	6	0	OF-154
1957 PIT N	144	561	141	28	11	8	1.4	59	50	33	69	3	.251	.383	5	1	OF-141
1958	144	604	161	24	11	9	1.5	75	46	52	70	5	.267	.387	1	0	OF-143
1959	144	519	132	24	2	8	1.5	67	41	55	65	7	.254	.355	0	0	OF-144
1960	120	409	108	16	9	8	2.0	60	40	40	44	8	.264	.406	9	3	OF-109
1961	146	599	156	22	8	9	1.5	81	58	49	45	5	.260	.369	1	0	OF-145
1962	156	663	164	27	10	6	0.9	82	47	36	65	5	.247	.345	0	0	OF-156
1963	142	554	149	22	6	8	1.4	58	53	43	55	1	.269	.374	0	0	OF-142
1964	145	473	115	11	3	3	0.6	59	27	30	48	1	.243	.298	10	2	OF-134
1965	135	481	134	22	5	4	0.8	58	24	30	49	4	.279	.370	11	1	OF-128
1968	6	3	1	0	0	1	33.3	1	2	0	2	0	.333	1.333	2	1	OF-4
12 yrs.	1583	5980	1596	237	81	91	1.5	735	502	442	647	47	.267	.379	54	9	OF-1542

	G	AB	H	2B	3B	HR	HR %	R	RBI	BB	SO	SB	BA	SA	Pinch Hit AB	Pinch Hit H	G by POS

Bill Virdon continued

WORLD SERIES

	G	AB	H	2B	3B	HR	HR %	R	RBI	BB	SO	SB	BA	SA	AB	H	G by POS
1960 PIT N	7	29	7	3	0	0	0.0	2	5	1	3	1	.241	.345	0	0	OF-7

Ozzie Virgil

VIRGIL, OSVALDO JOSE
Father of Ozzie Virgil.
B. May 17, 1933, Montecristi, Dominican Republic

BR TR 6'1" 174 lbs.

	G	AB	H	2B	3B	HR	HR %	R	RBI	BB	SO	SB	BA	SA	AB	H	G by POS
1956 NY N	3	12	5	1	1	0	0.0	2	2	0	0	1	.417	.667	0	0	3B-3
1957	96	226	53	0	2	4	1.8	26	24	14	27	2	.235	.305	8	2	3B-62, OF-24, SS-1
1958 DET A	49	193	47	10	2	3	1.6	19	19	8	20	1	.244	.363	1	0	3B-49
1960	62	132	30	4	2	3	2.3	16	13	4	14	1	.227	.356	8	2	3B-42, 2B-8, SS-5, C-1
1961 2 teams	DET	A	(20G –	.133)		KC	A	(11G –	.143)								
" total	31	51	7	0	0	1	2.0	2	1	1	8	0	.137	.196	12	3	3B-13, C-6, SS-1, 2B-1
1962 BAL A	1	0	0	0	0	0	–	0	0	1	0	0	–	–	0	0	
1965 PIT N	39	49	13	2	0	1	2.0	3	5	2	10	0	.265	.367	18	6	C-15, 3B-7, 2B-5
1966 SF N	42	89	19	2	0	2	2.2	7	9	4	12	1	.213	.303	12	1	3B-13, C-13, 1B-5, OF-2, 2B-2
1969	1	1	0	0	0	0	0.0	0	0	0	0	0	.000	.000	1	0	
9 yrs.	324	753	174	19	7	14	1.9	75	73	34	91	6	.231	.331	60	14	3B-189, C-35, OF-26, 2B-16, SS-7, 1B-5

Ozzie Virgil

VIRGIL, OSVALDO JOSE
Son of Ozzie Virgil.
B. Dec. 7, 1956, Mayaguez, Puerto Rico

BR TR 6'1" 180 lbs.

	G	AB	H	2B	3B	HR	HR %	R	RBI	BB	SO	SB	BA	SA	AB	H	G by POS
1980 PHI N	1	5	1	1	0	0	0.0	1	0	0	1	0	.200	.400	0	0	C-1
1981	6	6	0	0	0	0	0.0	0	0	0	2	0	.000	.000	5	0	C-1
1982	49	101	24	6	0	3	3.0	11	8	10	26	0	.238	.386	14	3	C-35
1983	55	140	30	7	0	6	4.3	11	23	8	34	0	.214	.393	8	2	C-51
1984	141	456	119	21	2	18	3.9	61	68	45	91	1	.261	.434	8	2	C-137
5 yrs.	252	708	174	35	2	27	3.8	84	99	63	154	1	.246	.415	35	7	C-225

LEAGUE CHAMPIONSHIP SERIES

	G	AB	H	2B	3B	HR	HR %	R	RBI	BB	SO	SB	BA	SA	AB	H	G by POS
1983 PHI N	1	1	0	0	0	0	0.0	0	0	0	1	0	.000	.000	1	0	

WORLD SERIES

	G	AB	H	2B	3B	HR	HR %	R	RBI	BB	SO	SB	BA	SA	AB	H	G by POS
1983 PHI N	3	2	1	0	0	0	0.0	0	1	0	0	0	.500	.500	2	1	C-1

Jake Virtue

VIRTUE, JACOB KITCHLINE
B. Mar. 2, 1865, Philadelphia, Pa.   D. Feb. 3, 1943, Camden, N. J.

BL

	G	AB	H	2B	3B	HR	HR %	R	RBI	BB	SO	SB	BA	SA	AB	H	G by POS
1890 CLE N	62	223	68	6	5	2	0.9	39	25	49	15	9	.305	.404	0	0	1B-62
1891	139	517	135	19	14	2	0.4	82	72	75	40	15	.261	.364	0	0	1B-139
1892	147	557	157	15	20	2	0.4	98	89	84	68	14	.282	.391	0	0	1B-147
1893	97	378	100	16	10	1	0.3	87	60	54	14	11	.265	.368	0	0	1B-73, OF-13, SS-5, 3B-5, P-1
1894	29	89	23	4	1	0	0.0	15	10	13	3	1	.258	.326	4	0	OF-21, 2B-3, 1B-2, P-1
5 yrs.	474	1764	483	60	50	7	0.4	321	256	275	140	50	.274	.376	4	0	1B-423, OF-34, SS-5, 3B-5, 2B-3, P-2

Joe Visner

VISNER, JOSEPH P.
B. Sept. 27, 1862, Minneapolis, Minn.   Deceased.

	G	AB	H	2B	3B	HR	HR %	R	RBI	BB	SO	SB	BA	SA	AB	H	G by POS
1885 BAL AA	4	13	3	0	0	0	0.0	2		2			.231	.231	0	0	OF-4
1889 BKN AA	80	295	76	12	10	8	2.7	56	68	36	36	13	.258	.447	0	0	C-53, OF-29
1890 PIT N	127	521	138	15	22	3	0.6	110	71	76	44	18	.265	.395	0	0	OF-127
1891 2 teams	WAS	AA	(18G –	.279)		STL	AA	(6G –	.148)								
" total	24	95	23	2	4	1	1.1	15	8	8	10	2	.242	.379	0	0	OF-23, 3B-1, C-1
4 yrs.	235	924	240	29	36	12	1.3	183	146	122	90	33	.260	.408	0	0	OF-183, C-54, 3B-1

Ossie Vitt

VITT, OSCAR JOSEPH
B. Jan. 4, 1890, San Francisco, Calif.   D. Jan. 31, 1963, Oakland, Calif.
Manager 1938-40.

BR TR 5'10" 150 lbs.

	G	AB	H	2B	3B	HR	HR %	R	RBI	BB	SO	SB	BA	SA	AB	H	G by POS
1912 DET A	73	273	67	4	4	0	0.0	39	19	18		17	.245	.289	7	1	OF-27, 3B-24, 2B-15
1913	99	359	86	11	3	2	0.6	45	33	31	18	5	.240	.304	2	0	2B-78, 3B-17, OF-2
1914	66	195	49	7	0	0	0.0	35	8	31	8	10	.251	.287	8	0	2B-36, 3B-16, OF-2, SS-1
1915	152	560	140	18	13	1	0.2	116	48	80	22	26	.250	.334	0	0	3B-151, 2B-2
1916	153	597	135	17	12	0	0.0	88	42	75	28	18	.226	.295	0	0	3B-151, SS-2
1917	140	512	130	13	6	0	0.0	65	47	56	15	18	.254	.303	0	0	3B-140
1918	81	267	64	5	2	0	0.0	29	17	32	6	5	.240	.273	3	0	3B-66, 2B-9, OF-3
1919 BOS A	133	469	114	10	3	0	0.0	64	40	44	11	9	.243	.277	0	0	3B-133
1920	87	296	65	10	4	1	0.3	50	28	43	10	5	.220	.291	1	0	3B-64, 2B-21
1921	78	232	44	11	0	0	0.0	29	12	45	13	1	.190	.246	2	1	3B-71, OF-3, 1B-2
10 yrs.	1062	3760	894	106	48	4	0.1	560	294	455	131	114	.238	.295	23	2	3B-833, 2B-161, OF-37, SS-3, 1B-2

Otto Vogel

VOGEL, OTTO HENRY
B. Oct. 26, 1899, Mendota, Ill.   D. July 19, 1969, Iowa City, Iowa

BR TR 6' 195 lbs.

	G	AB	H	2B	3B	HR	HR %	R	RBI	BB	SO	SB	BA	SA	AB	H	G by POS
1923 CHI N	41	81	17	0	1	1	1.2	10	6	7	11	2	.210	.272	6	1	OF-24, 3B-1
1924	70	172	46	11	2	1	0.6	28	24	10	26	4	.267	.372	9	2	OF-53, 3B-2
2 yrs.	111	253	63	11	3	2	0.8	38	30	17	37	6	.249	.340	15	3	OF-77, 3B-3

Clyde Vollmer

VOLLMER, CLYDE FREDERICK
B. Sept. 24, 1921, Cincinnati, Ohio

BR TR 6'1" 185 lbs.

	G	AB	H	2B	3B	HR	HR %	R	RBI	BB	SO	SB	BA	SA	AB	H	G by POS
1942 CIN N	12	43	4	0	0	1	2.3	2	4	1	5	0	.093	.163	1	0	OF-11
1946	9	22	4	0	0	0	0.0	1	1	1	3	2	.182	.182	1	0	OF-7
1947	78	155	34	10	0	1	0.6	19	13	9	18	0	.219	.303	11	3	OF-66
1948 2 teams	CIN	N	(7G –	.111)		WAS	A	(1G –	.400)								
" total	8	14	3	0	0	0	0.0	1	0	1	2	0	.214	.214	5	1	OF-3
1949 WAS A	129	443	112	17	1	14	3.2	58	59	53	62	1	.253	.391	13	5	OF-114

	G	AB	H	2B	3B	HR	HR %	R	RBI	BB	SO	SB	BA	SA	Pinch Hit AB	Pinch Hit H	G by POS

Clyde Vollmer continued

1950 2 teams		**WAS A** (6G – .286)			**BOS A** (57G – .284)												
" total	63	183	52	10	0	7	3.8	39	38	23	40	2	.284	.454	19	4	OF-42
1951 BOS A	115	386	97	9	2	22	5.7	66	85	55	66	0	.251	.456	6	1	OF-106
1952	90	250	66	12	4	11	4.4	35	50	39	47	2	.264	.476	20	5	OF-70
1953 2 teams		**BOS A** (1G – .000)			**WAS A** (118G – .260)												
" total	119	408	106	15	3	11	2.7	54	74	49	59	0	.260	.392	12	4	OF-106
1954 WAS A	62	117	30	4	0	2	1.7	8	15	12	28	0	.256	.342	31	6	OF-26
10 yrs.	685	2021	508	77	10	69	3.4	283	339	243	330	7	.251	.402	119	29	OF-551

Fritz Von Kolnitz

VON KOLNITZ, ALFRED HOLMES
B. May 20, 1893, Charleston, S. C.   D. Mar. 18, 1948, Mount Pleasant, S. C.   BR TR 5'10½" 175 lbs.

	G	AB	H	2B	3B	HR	HR %	R	RBI	BB	SO	SB	BA	SA	Pinch Hit AB	Pinch Hit H	G by POS
1914 CIN N	41	104	23	2	0	0	0.0	8	6	6	16	4	.221	.240	7	0	3B-20, OF-11, C-2, 1B-1
1915	50	78	15	4	1	0	0.0	6	6	7	11	1	.192	.269	20	6	3B-18, SS-6, 1B-3, C-2, OF-1
1916 CHI A	24	44	10	3	0	0	0.0	1	7	2	6	0	.227	.295	10	3	3B-13
3 yrs.	115	226	48	9	1	0	0.0	15	19	15	33	5	.212	.261	37	9	3B-51, OF-12, SS-6, 1B-4, C-4

Joe Vosmik

VOSMIK, JOSEPH FRANKLIN
B. Apr. 4, 1910, Cleveland, Ohio   D. Jan. 27, 1962, Cleveland, Ohio   BR TR 6' 185 lbs.

	G	AB	H	2B	3B	HR	HR %	R	RBI	BB	SO	SB	BA	SA	Pinch Hit AB	Pinch Hit H	G by POS
1930 CLE A	9	26	6	2	0	0	0.0	1	4	1	1	0	.231	.308	2	0	OF-5
1931	149	591	189	36	14	7	1.2	80	117	38	30	7	.320	.464	2	1	OF-147
1932	153	621	194	39	12	10	1.6	106	97	58	42	2	.312	.462	0	0	OF-153
1933	119	438	115	20	10	4	0.9	53	56	42	13	0	.263	.381	5	1	OF-113
1934	104	405	138	33	2	6	1.5	71	78	35	10	1	.341	.477	1	1	OF-104
1935	152	620	**216**	**47**	**20**	10	1.6	93	110	59	30	2	.348	.537	2	1	OF-150
1936	138	506	145	29	7	7	1.4	76	94	79	21	5	.287	.413	2	2	OF-136
1937 STL A	144	594	193	47	9	4	0.7	81	93	49	38	2	.325	.455	1	1	OF-143
1938 BOS A	146	621	**201**	37	6	9	1.4	121	86	59	26	0	.324	.446	0	0	OF-146
1939	145	554	153	29	6	7	1.3	89	84	66	33	4	.276	.388	0	0	OF-144
1940 BKN N	116	404	114	14	6	1	0.2	45	42	22	21	0	.282	.354	17	5	OF-99
1941	25	56	11	0	0	0	0.0	0	4	4	4	0	.196	.196	7	1	OF-18
1944 WAS A	14	36	7	2	0	0	0.0	2	9	2	3	0	.194	.250	2	0	OF-12
13 yrs.	1414	5472	1682	335	92	65	1.2	818	874	514	272	23	.307	.438	41	15	OF-1370

Alex Voss

VOSS, ALEXANDER
B. 1855, Roswell, Ga.   D. Aug. 31, 1906, Cincinnati, Ohio   BR TR 6'1" 180 lbs.

	G	AB	H	2B	3B	HR	HR %	R	RBI	BB	SO	SB	BA	SA	Pinch Hit AB	Pinch Hit H	G by POS
1884 2 teams		**WAS U** (63G – .192)			**KC U** (14G – .089)												
" total	77	290	51	9	0	0	0.0	34		5			.176	.207	0	0	P-34, OF-21, 3B-16, 1B-15, SS-1

Bill Voss

VOSS, WILLIAM EDWARD
B. Oct. 31, 1945, Glendale, Calif.   BL TL 6'2" 160 lbs.

	G	AB	H	2B	3B	HR	HR %	R	RBI	BB	SO	SB	BA	SA	Pinch Hit AB	Pinch Hit H	G by POS
1965 CHI A	11	33	6	0	1	1	3.0	4	3	3	5	0	.182	.333	0	0	OF-10
1966	2	2	0	0	0	0	0.0	0	0	0	2	0	.000	.000	1	0	OF-1
1967	13	22	2	0	0	0	0.0	4	0	0	1	0	.091	.091	0	0	OF-11
1968	61	167	26	2	1	2	1.2	14	15	16	34	5	.156	.216	7	2	OF-55
1969 CAL A	133	349	91	11	4	2	0.6	33	40	35	40	5	.261	.332	16	6	OF-111, 1B-2
1970	80	181	44	4	3	3	1.7	21	30	23	18	2	.243	.348	26	6	OF-55
1971 MIL A	97	275	69	4	0	10	3.6	31	30	24	45	2	.251	.375	20	5	OF-79
1972 3 teams		**MIL A** (27G – .083)			**OAK A** (40G – .227)			**STL N** (11G – .267)									
" total	78	148	29	8	1	1	0.7	12	9	16	22	0	.196	.284	30	5	OF-47
8 yrs.	475	1177	267	29	10	19	1.6	119	127	117	167	15	.227	.317	100	24	OF-369, 1B-2

Phil Voyles

VOYLES, PHILIP VANCE
B. May 12, 1900, Murphy, N. C.   D. Nov. 3, 1972, Marlboro, Mass.   BL TR 5'11½" 175 lbs.

	G	AB	H	2B	3B	HR	HR %	R	RBI	BB	SO	SB	BA	SA	Pinch Hit AB	Pinch Hit H	G by POS
1929 BOS N	20	68	16	0	2	0	0.0	9	14	6	8	0	.235	.294	0	0	OF-20

George Vukovich

VUKOVICH, GEORGE STEPHEN
B. June 24, 1956, Chicago, Ill.   BL TR 6' 198 lbs.

	G	AB	H	2B	3B	HR	HR %	R	RBI	BB	SO	SB	BA	SA	Pinch Hit AB	Pinch Hit H	G by POS
1980 PHI N	78	58	13	1	1	0	0.0	6	8	6	9	0	.224	.276	45	11	OF-28
1981	20	26	10	0	0	1	3.8	5	4	1	0	1	.385	.500	11	5	OF-9
1982	123	335	91	18	2	6	1.8	41	42	32	47	2	.272	.391	23	5	OF-102
1983 CLE A	124	312	77	13	2	3	1.0	31	44	24	37	3	.247	.330	10	3	OF-122
1984	134	437	133	22	5	9	2.1	38	60	34	61	1	.304	.439	13	2	OF-130
5 yrs.	479	1168	324	54	10	19	1.6	121	158	97	154	7	.277	.390	102	26	OF-391

DIVISIONAL PLAYOFF SERIES

	G	AB	H	2B	3B	HR	HR %	R	RBI	BB	SO	SB	BA	SA	Pinch Hit AB	Pinch Hit H	G by POS
1981 PHI N	5	9	4	0	0	1	11.1	1	2	0	3	0	.444	.778	4	3	OF-3

LEAGUE CHAMPIONSHIP SERIES

	G	AB	H	2B	3B	HR	HR %	R	RBI	BB	SO	SB	BA	SA	Pinch Hit AB	Pinch Hit H	G by POS
1980 PHI N	4	3	0	0	0	0	0.0	0	0	0	0	0	.000	.000	3	0	OF-1

John Vukovich

VUKOVICH, JOHN CHRISTOPHER
B. July 31, 1947, Sacramento, Calif.   BR TR 6'1" 187 lbs.

	G	AB	H	2B	3B	HR	HR %	R	RBI	BB	SO	SB	BA	SA	Pinch Hit AB	Pinch Hit H	G by POS
1970 PHI N	3	8	1	0	0	0	0.0	0	1	0	1	0	.125	.125	0	0	SS-2, 3B-1
1971	74	217	36	5	0	0	0.0	11	14	12	34	2	.166	.189	0	0	3B-74
1973 MIL A	55	128	16	3	0	2	1.6	10	9	9	40	0	.125	.195	1	0	3B-40, 1B-13, SS-1
1974	38	80	15	1	0	3	3.8	5	11	1	16	0	.188	.313	1	0	SS-12, 3B-12, 2B-11, 1B-4
1975 CIN N	31	38	8	3	0	0	0.0	4	2	4	5	0	.211	.289	0	0	3B-31
1976 PHI N	4	8	1	0	0	1	12.5	2	2	0	2	0	.125	.500	0	0	3B-4, 1B-1
1977	2	2	0	0	0	0	0.0	0	0	0	1	0	.000	.000	2	0	
1979	10	15	3	1	0	0	0.0	0	1	0	3	0	.200	.267	0	0	3B-7, 2B-3
1980	49	62	10	1	1	0	0.0	4	5	2	7	0	.161	.210	4	1	3B-34, 2B-9, SS-5, 1B-1
1981	11	1	0	0	0	0	0.0	1	0	0	0	0	.000	.000	0	0	3B-9, 2B-1, 1B-1
10 yrs.	277	559	90	14	1	6	1.1	37	44	29	109	4	.161	.222	8	2	3B-212, 2B-24, SS-20, 1B-20

	G	AB	H	2B	3B	HR	HR %	R	RBI	BB	SO	SB	BA	SA	Pinch Hit AB	Pinch Hit H	G by POS

Frank Waddey

WADDEY, FRANK ORUM
B. Aug. 21, 1905, Memphis, Tenn.
BL TL 5'10½" 185 lbs.

	G	AB	H	2B	3B	HR	HR %	R	RBI	BB	SO	SB	BA	SA	PH AB	PH H	G by POS
1931 STL A	14	22	6	1	0	0	0.0	3	2	2	3	0	.273	.318	7	2	OF-7

Gale Wade

WADE, GALEARD LEE
B. Jan. 20, 1929, Hollister, Mo.
BL TR 6'1½" 185 lbs.

	G	AB	H	2B	3B	HR	HR %	R	RBI	BB	SO	SB	BA	SA	PH AB	PH H	G by POS
1955 CHI N	9	33	6	1	0	1	3.0	5	1	4	3	0	.182	.303	0	0	OF-9
1956	10	12	0	0	0	0	0.0	0	0	1	0	0	.000	.000	3	0	OF-3
2 yrs.	19	45	6	1	0	1	2.2	5	1	5	3	0	.133	.222	3	0	OF-12

Ham Wade

WADE, ABRAHAM LINCOLN
B. Dec. 20, 1880, Spring City, Pa.   D. July 21, 1968, Riverside Township, N. J.
BR TR 5'8" 155 lbs.

	G	AB	H	2B	3B	HR	HR %	R	RBI	BB	SO	SB	BA	SA	PH AB	PH H	G by POS
1907 NY N	1	0	0	0	0	0		0		0		0	–	–	0	0	OF-1

Rip Wade

WADE, RICHARD FRANK
B. Jan. 12, 1898, Duluth, Minn.   D. June 15, 1957, Sandstone, Minn.
BL TR 5'11" 174 lbs.

	G	AB	H	2B	3B	HR	HR %	R	RBI	BB	SO	SB	BA	SA	PH AB	PH H	G by POS
1923 WAS A	33	69	16	2	2	2	2.9	8	14	5	10	0	.232	.406	8	1	OF-19

Woodie Wagenhurst

WAGENHURST, ELWOOD OTTO
B. June 3, 1863, Kutztown, Pa.   D. Feb. 12, 1946

	G	AB	H	2B	3B	HR	HR %	R	RBI	BB	SO	SB	BA	SA	PH AB	PH H	G by POS
1888 PHI N	2	8	1	0	0	0	0.0	0		0	1	0	.125	.125	0	0	3B-2

Bill Wagner

WAGNER, WILLIAM JOSEPH
B. Jan. 2, 1894, Jessup, Iowa   D. Jan. 11, 1951, Waterloo, Iowa
BR TR 6' 187 lbs.

	G	AB	H	2B	3B	HR	HR %	R	RBI	BB	SO	SB	BA	SA	PH AB	PH H	G by POS
1914 PIT N	3	1	0	0	0	0	0.0	0		0	0	0	.000	.000	0	0	C-3
1915	5	5	0	0	0	0	0.0	0	1	0	2	0	.000	.000	1	0	C-3
1916	19	38	9	0	2	0	0.0	2	2	5	8	0	.237	.342	4	1	C-15
1917	53	151	31	7	2	0	0.0	15	9	11	22	1	.205	.278	6	2	C-37, 1B-12
1918 BOS N	13	47	10	0	0	1	2.1	2	7	4	5	0	.213	.277	0	0	C-13
5 yrs.	93	242	50	7	4	1	0.4	19	18	21	37	1	.207	.281	11	3	C-71, 1B-12

Butts Wagner

WAGNER, ALBERT
Brother of Honus Wagner.
B. Sept. 17, 1869, Carnegie, Pa.   D. Nov. 26, 1928, Pittsburgh, Pa.
BR TR 5'10" 170 lbs.

	G	AB	H	2B	3B	HR	HR %	R	RBI	BB	SO	SB	BA	SA	PH AB	PH H	G by POS
1898 2 teams		WAS N (63G – .224)				BKN N (11G – .237)											
" total	74	261	59	12	3	1	0.4	22	34	16		4	.226	.307	1	0	3B-50, OF-10, SS-8, 2B-5

Hal Wagner

WAGNER, HAROLD EDWARD
B. July 2, 1915, East Riverton, N. J.   D. Aug. 4, 1979, Riverside, N. J.
BL TR 6' 165 lbs.

	G	AB	H	2B	3B	HR	HR %	R	RBI	BB	SO	SB	BA	SA	PH AB	PH H	G by POS
1937 PHI A	1	0	0	0	0	0		0	0	0	0	0	–	–	0	0	C-1
1938	33	88	20	2	1	0	0.0	10	8	8	9	0	.227	.273	3	1	C-30
1939	5	8	1	0	0	0	0.0	0	0	0	3	0	.125	.125	0	0	C-5
1940	34	75	19	5	1	0	0.0	9	10	11	6	0	.253	.347	5	2	C-28
1941	46	131	29	8	2	1	0.8	18	15	19	9	1	.221	.336	4	0	C-42
1942	104	288	68	17	1	1	0.3	26	30	24	29	1	.236	.313	12	2	C-94
1943	111	289	69	17	1	1	0.3	22	26	36	17	3	.239	.315	14	3	C-99
1944 2 teams		PHI A (5G – .250)				BOS A (66G – .332)											
" total	71	227	75	13	4	1	0.4	21	38	29	14	1	.330	.436	7	2	C-65
1946 BOS A	117	370	85	12	2	6	1.6	39	52	69	32	3	.230	.322	0	0	C-116
1947 2 teams		BOS A (21G – .231)				DET A (71G – .288)											
" total	92	256	70	13	0	5	2.0	24	39	37	21	0	.273	.383	1	1	C-92
1948 2 teams		DET A (54G – .202)				PHI N (3G – .000)											
" total	57	113	22	3	0	0	0.0	10	10	20	11	1	.195	.221	2	0	C-53
1949 PHI N	1	4	0	0	0	0	0.0	0	0	0	0	0	.000	.000	0	0	C-1
12 yrs.	672	1849	458	90	12	15	0.8	179	228	253	152	10	.248	.334	48	11	C-626

WORLD SERIES

	G	AB	H	2B	3B	HR	HR %	R	RBI	BB	SO	SB	BA	SA	PH AB	PH H	G by POS
1946 BOS A	5	13	0	0	0	0	0.0	0	0	0	1	0	.000	.000	0	0	C-5

Heinie Wagner

WAGNER, CHARLES F.
B. Sept. 23, 1881, New York, N. Y.   D. Mar. 20, 1943, New Rochelle, N. Y.
Manager 1930.
BR TR

	G	AB	H	2B	3B	HR	HR %	R	RBI	BB	SO	SB	BA	SA	PH AB	PH H	G by POS
1902 NY N	17	56	12	1	0	0	0.0	4	2	0		3	.214	.232	0	0	SS-17
1906 BOS A	9	32	9	0	0	0	0.0	1	4	1		2	.281	.281	0	0	2B-9
1907	111	385	82	10	4	2	0.5	29	21	31		20	.213	.273	0	0	SS-109, 3B-1, 2B-1
1908	153	526	130	11	5	1	0.2	62	46	27		20	.247	.293	0	0	SS-153
1909	124	430	110	16	7	1	0.2	51	49	35		18	.256	.333	0	0	SS-123, 2B-1
1910	142	491	134	26	7	1	0.2	61	52	44		26	.273	.360	2	0	SS-140
1911	80	261	67	13	8	1	0.4	34	38	29		15	.257	.379	8	2	2B-40, SS-32
1912	144	504	138	25	6	2	0.4	75	68	62		21	.274	.359	0	0	SS-144
1913	110	365	83	14	8	2	0.5	43	34	40	29	9	.227	.326	1	0	SS-105, 2B-4
1915	84	267	64	11	2	0	0.0	38	29	37	34	8	.240	.296	3	0	2B-79, OF-1, 3B-1
1916	6	8	4	1	0	0	0.0	2	0	3	0	2	.500	.625	0	0	3B-4, SS-1, 2B-1
1918	3	8	1	0	0	0	0.0	0	0	1	0	0	.125	.125	0	0	2B-2, 3B-1
12 yrs.	983	3333	834	128	47	10	0.3	400	343	310	63	144	.250	.326	14	2	SS-824, 2B-137, 3B-7, OF-1

WORLD SERIES

	G	AB	H	2B	3B	HR	HR %	R	RBI	BB	SO	SB	BA	SA	PH AB	PH H	G by POS
1912 BOS A	8	30	5	1	0	0	0.0	1	1	0	3	6	1	.167	.200	0	0	SS-8

Honus Wagner

WAGNER, JOHN PETER (The Flying Dutchman)
Brother of Butts Wagner.
B. Feb. 24, 1874, Carnegie, Pa.   D. Dec. 6, 1955, Carnegie, Pa.
Manager 1917.
Hall of Fame 1936.
BR TR 5'11" 200 lbs.

	G	AB	H	2B	3B	HR	HR %	R	RBI	BB	SO	SB	BA	SA	PH AB	PH H	G by POS
1897 LOU N	61	241	83	17	4	2	0.8	38	39	15		19	.344	.473	0	0	OF-52, 2B-9
1898	151	591	180	31	4	10	1.7	80	105	31		27	.305	.421	2	1	1B-75, 3B-65, 2B-10
1899	144	549	197	47	13	7	1.3	102	113	40		37	.359	.530	1	0	3B-75, OF-61, 2B-7, 1B-4

	G	AB	H	2B	3B	HR	HR %	R	RBI	BB	SO	SB	BA	SA	Pinch Hit AB	Pinch Hit H	G by POS

Honus Wagner continued

	G	AB	H	2B	3B	HR	HR%	R	RBI	BB	SO	SB	BA	SA	PH AB	PH H	G by POS
1900 **PIT N**	135	528	201	**45**	**22**	4	0.8	107	100	41		38	**.381**	**.572**	1	0	OF-118, 3B-9, 2B-7, 1B-3, P-1
1901	141	556	196	**39**	10	6	1.1	100	**126**	53		49	.353	.491	0	0	SS-62, OF-54, 3B-24, 2B-1
1902	137	538	177	**33**	16	3	0.6	**105**	91	43		42	.329	**.467**	0	0	OF-61, SS-44, 1B-32, 2B-1, P-1
1903	129	512	182	30	**19**	5	1.0	97	101	44		46	**.355**	.518	0	0	SS-111, OF-12, 1B-6
1904	132	490	171	**44**	14	4	0.8	97	75	59		53	**.349**	**.520**	1	0	SS-121, OF-8, 1B-3, 2B-2
1905	147	548	199	32	14	6	1.1	114	101	54		57	.363	.505	0	0	SS-145, OF-2
1906	142	516	175	**38**	9	2	0.4	**103**	71	58		53	**.339**	.459	1	0	SS-137, OF-2, 3B-1
1907	142	515	180	**38**	14	6	1.2	98	82	46		**61**	.350	**.513**	0	0	SS-138, 1B-4
1908	151	568	201	**39**	19	10	1.8	100	**109**	54		**53**	**.354**	**.542**	0	0	SS-151
1909	137	495	168	**39**	10	5	1.0	92	**100**	66		35	**.339**	**.489**	0	0	SS-136, OF-1
1910	150	556	**178**	34	8	4	0.7	90	81	59	47	24	.320	.432	0	0	SS-138, 1B-11, 2B-2
1911	130	473	158	23	16	9	1.9	87	89	67	34	20	**.334**	.507	0	0	SS-101, 1B-28, OF-1
1912	145	558	181	35	20	7	1.3	91	102	59	38	26	.324	.496	0	0	SS-143
1913	114	413	124	18	4	3	0.7	51	56	26	40	21	.300	.385	7	1	SS-105
1914	150	552	139	15	9	1	0.2	60	50	51	51	23	.252	.317	1	0	SS-132, 3B-17, 1B-1
1915	151	566	155	32	17	6	1.1	68	78	39	64	22	.274	.422	4	1	SS-131, 2B-12, 1B-10
1916	123	432	124	15	9	1	0.2	45	39	34	36	11	.287	.370	6	1	SS-92, 1B-24, 2B-4
1917	74	230	61	7	1	0	0.0	15	24	24	17	5	.265	.304	7	1	1B-47, 3B-18, 2B-2, SS-1
21 yrs.	2786	10427	3430	651	252	101	1.0	1740	1732	963	327	722	.329	.469	31	5	SS-1888, OF-372, 1B-248, 3B-209, 2B-57, P-2
		8th	6th	5th	3rd							5th					

WORLD SERIES

	G	AB	H	2B	3B	HR	HR%	R	RBI	BB	SO	SB	BA	SA	PH AB	PH H	G by POS
1903 **PIT N**	8	27	6	1	0	0	0.0	2	3	3	4	3	.222	.259	0	0	SS-8
1909	7	24	8	2	1	0	0.0	4	6	4	2	6	.333	.500	0	0	SS-7
2 yrs.	15	51	14	3	1	0	0.0	6	9	7	6	9	.275	.373	0	0	SS-15
												6th					

Joe Wagner

WAGNER, JOSEPH BERNARD
B. Apr. 24, 1889, New York, N. Y. D. Nov. 15, 1948, Bronx, N. Y.
BR TR 5'11" 165 lbs.

	G	AB	H	2B	3B	HR	HR%	R	RBI	BB	SO	SB	BA	SA	PH AB	PH H	G by POS
1915 **CIN N**	75	197	35	5	2	0	0.0	17	13	8	35	4	.178	.223	7	2	2B-46, SS-12, 3B-2

Leon Wagner

WAGNER, LEON LAMAR (Daddy Wags)
B. May 13, 1934, Chattanooga, Tenn.
BL TR 6'1" 195 lbs.

	G	AB	H	2B	3B	HR	HR%	R	RBI	BB	SO	SB	BA	SA	PH AB	PH H	G by POS
1958 **SF N**	74	221	70	9	0	13	5.9	31	35	18	34	1	.317	.534	18	4	OF-57
1959	87	129	29	4	3	5	3.9	20	22	25	24	0	.225	.419	52	10	OF-28
1960 **STL N**	39	98	21	2	0	4	4.1	12	11	17	17	0	.214	.357	7	1	OF-32
1961 **LA A**	133	453	127	19	2	28	6.2	74	79	48	65	5	.280	.517	16	3	OF-116
1962	160	612	164	21	5	37	6.0	96	107	50	87	7	.268	.500	3	1	OF-156
1963	149	550	160	11	1	26	4.7	73	90	49	73	5	.291	.456	9	2	OF-141
1964 **CLE A**	163	641	162	19	2	31	4.8	94	100	56	121	14	.253	.434	2	1	OF-163
1965	144	517	152	18	1	28	5.4	91	79	60	52	12	.294	.495	11	3	OF-134
1966	150	549	153	20	0	23	4.2	70	66	46	69	5	.279	.441	10	3	OF-139
1967	135	433	105	15	1	15	3.5	56	54	37	76	3	.242	.386	15	4	OF-117
1968 2 teams					CLE A (38G – .184)			CHI A (69G – .284)									
" total	107	211	55	12	0	1	0.5	19	24	27	37	2	.261	.332	46	11	OF-56
1969 **SF N**	11	12	4	0	0	0	0.0	0	2	2	1	0	.333	.333	7	3	OF-1
12 yrs.	1352	4426	1202	150	15	211	4.8	669	669	435	656	54	.272	.455	196	46	OF-1140

Mark Wagner

WAGNER, MARK DUANE
B. Mar. 4, 1954, Conneaut, Ohio
BR TR 6' 165 lbs.

	G	AB	H	2B	3B	HR	HR%	R	RBI	BB	SO	SB	BA	SA	PH AB	PH H	G by POS
1976 **DET A**	39	115	30	2	3	0	0.0	9	12	6	18	0	.261	.330	0	0	SS-39
1977	22	48	7	0	1	1	2.1	4	3	4	12	0	.146	.250	0	0	SS-21, 2B-1
1978	39	109	26	1	2	0	0.0	10	6	3	11	1	.239	.284	1	1	SS-35, 2B-4
1979	75	146	40	3	0	1	0.7	16	13	16	25	3	.274	.315	1	1	SS-41, 2B-29, 3B-2, DH-1
1980	45	72	17	1	0	0	0.0	5	3	7	11	0	.236	.250	2	0	SS-28, 3B-9, 2B-6
1981 **TEX A**	50	85	22	4	1	1	1.2	15	14	8	13	1	.259	.365	2	0	SS-43, 2B-4, 3B-2
1982	92	179	43	4	1	0	0.0	14	8	10	28	1	.240	.274	0	0	SS-60
1983	2	2	0	0	0	0	0.0	0	0	0	1	0	.000	.000	0	0	SS-2
1984 **OAK A**	82	86	20	5	1	0	0.0	8	12	7	11	2	.233	.314	1	0	SS-58, 3B-15, 2B-8, DH-3, P-1
9 yrs.	414	842	205	20	9	3	0.4	81	71	61	130	8	.243	.299	7	2	SS-327, 2B-52, 3B-28, DH-4, P-1

Kermit Wahl

WAHL, KERMIT EMERSON
B. Nov. 18, 1922, Columbia, S. D.
BR TR 5'11" 170 lbs.

	G	AB	H	2B	3B	HR	HR%	R	RBI	BB	SO	SB	BA	SA	PH AB	PH H	G by POS
1944 **CIN N**	4	1	0	0	0	0	0.0	0	0	0	0	0	.000	.000	0	0	3B-1
1945	71	194	39	8	2	0	0.0	18	10	23	22	2	.201	.263	0	0	2B-32, SS-31, 3B-7
1947	39	81	14	0	0	1	1.2	8	4	6	12	0	.173	.210	5	1	3B-20, SS-9, 2B-2
1950 **PHI A**	89	280	72	12	3	2	0.7	26	27	30	30	1	.257	.343	7	2	3B-61, SS-18, 2B-2
1951 2 teams					PHI A (20G – .186)			STL A (8G – .333)									
" total	28	86	20	3	1	0	0.0	6	9	9	8	0	.233	.291	4	0	3B-24
5 yrs.	231	642	145	23	6	3	0.5	58	50	68	72	3	.226	.294	16	3	3B-113, SS-58, 2B-36

Eddie Waitkus

WAITKUS, EDWARD STEPHEN
B. Sept. 4, 1919, Cambridge, Mass. D. Sept. 15, 1972, Boston, Mass.
BL TL 6' 170 lbs.

	G	AB	H	2B	3B	HR	HR%	R	RBI	BB	SO	SB	BA	SA	PH AB	PH H	G by POS
1941 **CHI N**	12	28	5	0	0	0	0.0	1	0	0	3	0	.179	.179	3	1	1B-9
1946	113	441	134	24	5	4	0.9	50	55	23	14	3	.304	.408	5	2	1B-106
1947	130	514	150	28	6	2	0.4	60	35	32	17	3	.292	.381	2	1	1B-126
1948	139	562	166	27	10	7	1.2	87	44	43	19	11	.295	.416	2	0	1B-116, OF-20
1949 **PHI N**	54	209	64	16	3	1	0.5	41	28	33	12	3	.306	.426	0	0	1B-54
1950	154	641	182	32	5	2	0.3	102	44	55	29	0	.284	.359	1	1	1B-154
1951	145	610	157	27	4	1	0.2	65	46	53	22	0	.257	.320	2	0	1B-144
1952	146	499	144	29	4	2	0.4	51	49	64	23	2	.289	.375	3	0	1B-143

	G	AB	H	2B	3B	HR	HR %	R	RBI	BB	SO	SB	BA	SA	Pinch Hit AB	Pinch Hit H	G by POS

Eddie Waitkus continued

	G	AB	H	2B	3B	HR	HR %	R	RBI	BB	SO	SB	BA	SA	AB	H	G by POS
1953	81	247	72	9	2	1	0.4	24	16	13	23	1	.291	.356	20	7	1B-59
1954 BAL A	95	311	88	17	4	2	0.6	35	33	28	25	0	.283	.383	15	4	1B-78
1955 2 teams	BAL A (38G – .259)			PHI N (33G – .280)													
" total	71	192	52	6	1	2	1.0	12	23	28	17	2	.271	.344	11	4	1B-57
11 yrs.	1140	4254	1214	215	44	24	0.6	528	373	372	204	28	.285	.374	64	19	1B-1046, OF-20
WORLD SERIES																	
1950 PHI N	4	15	4	1	0	0	0.0	0	0	2	0	0	.267	.333	0	0	1B-4

Charlie Waitt

WAITT, CHARLES C.
B. Oct. 14, 1853, Hallowell, Me.   Deceased.   5'11"   165 lbs.

	G	AB	H	2B	3B	HR	HR %	R	RBI	BB	SO	SB	BA	SA	AB	H	G by POS
1877 CHI N	10	41	4	0	0	0	0.0	2	2	0		3	.098	.098	0	0	OF-10
1882 BAL AA	72	250	39	4	0	0	0.0	19		13			.156	.172	0	0	OF-72
1883 PHI N	1	3	1	0	0	0	0.0	0		0		1	.333	.333	0	0	OF-1
3 yrs.	83	294	44	4	0	0	0.0	21	2	13		4	.150	.163	0	0	OF-83

Dick Wakefield

WAKEFIELD, RICHARD CUMMINGS
Son of Howard Wakefield.
B. May 6, 1921, Chicago, Ill.   BL TR 6'4"   210 lbs.

	G	AB	H	2B	3B	HR	HR %	R	RBI	BB	SO	SB	BA	SA	AB	H	G by POS
1941 DET A	7	7	1	0	0	0	0.0	0	0	0	1	0	.143	.143	6	1	OF-1
1943	155	633	200	38	8	7	1.1	91	79	62	60	4	.316	.434	0	0	OF-155
1944	78	276	98	15	5	12	4.3	53	53	55	29	2	.355	.576	0	0	OF-78
1946	111	396	106	11	5	12	3.0	64	59	59	55	3	.268	.412	4	0	OF-104
1947	112	368	104	15	5	8	2.2	59	51	80	44	1	.283	.416	10	4	OF-101
1948	110	322	89	20	5	11	3.4	50	53	70	55	0	.276	.472	22	7	OF-86
1949	59	126	26	3	1	6	4.8	17	19	32	24	0	.206	.389	18	3	OF-32
1950 NY A	3	2	1	0	0	0	0.0	0	1	1	1	0	.500	.500	2	1	
1952 NY N	3	2	0	0	0	0	0.0	0	0	1	0	0	.000	.000	2	0	
9 yrs.	638	2132	625	102	29	56	2.6	334	315	360	269	10	.293	.447	64	16	OF-557

Howard Wakefield

WAKEFIELD, HOWARD JOHN
Father of Dick Wakefield.
B. Apr. 2, 1884, Bucyrus, Ohio   D. Apr. 16, 1941, Chicago, Ill.   BR TR 6'1"   205 lbs.

	G	AB	H	2B	3B	HR	HR %	R	RBI	BB	SO	SB	BA	SA	AB	H	G by POS
1905 CLE A	9	25	4	0	0	0	0.0	3	1	0		0	.160	.160	1	0	C-8
1906 WAS A	77	211	59	9	2	1	0.5	17	21	7		6	.280	.355	16	9	C-60
1907 CLE A	26	37	5	2	0	0	0.0	4	3	3		0	.135	.189	15	2	C-11
3 yrs.	112	273	68	11	2	1	0.4	24	25	10		6	.249	.315	32	11	C-79

Ed Walczak

WALCZAK, EDWIN JOSEPH (Husky)
B. Sept. 21, 1915, Arctic, R. I.   BR TR 5'11"   180 lbs.

	G	AB	H	2B	3B	HR	HR %	R	RBI	BB	SO	SB	BA	SA	AB	H	G by POS
1945 PHI N	20	57	12	3	0	0	0.0	6	2	6	9	0	.211	.263	0	0	2B-17, SS-2

Fred Walden

WALDEN, FREDERICK THOMAS
B. June 25, 1890, Fayette, Mo.   D. Sept. 27, 1955, Jefferson Barracks, Mo.   BR TR

	G	AB	H	2B	3B	HR	HR %	R	RBI	BB	SO	SB	BA	SA	AB	H	G by POS
1912 STL A	1	0	0	0	0	0	0	–	0	0		0	–	–	0	0	C-1

Irv Waldron

WALDRON, IRVING
B. Jan. 21, 1876, Hillside, N. Y.   D. July 22, 1944, Worcester, Mass.   BR TR

	G	AB	H	2B	3B	HR	HR %	R	RBI	BB	SO	SB	BA	SA	AB	H	G by POS
1901 2 teams	MIL A (62G – .297)			WAS A (79G – .322)													
" total	141	598	186	22	9	0	0.0	102	51	38		20	.311	.378	1	1	OF-140

Chico Walker

WALKER, CLEOTHA
B. Nov. 25, 1957, Jackson, Miss.   BB TR 5'9"   170 lbs.

	G	AB	H	2B	3B	HR	HR %	R	RBI	BB	SO	SB	BA	SA	AB	H	G by POS
1980 BOS A	19	57	12	0	0	1	1.8	3	5	6	10	3	.211	.263	1	1	2B-11, DH-7
1981	6	17	6	0	0	0	0.0	3	2	1	2	0	.353	.353	1	0	2B-5
1983	4	5	2	2	0	0	0.0	2	1	0	0	0	.400	1.200	1	0	OF-3
1984	3	2	0	0	0	0	0.0	0	1	0	1	0	.000	.000	2	0	2B-1
4 yrs.	32	81	20	0	2	1	1.2	8	9	7	13	3	.247	.333	5	1	2B-17, DH-7, OF-3

Curt Walker

WALKER, WILLIAM CURTIS
B. July 3, 1896, Beeville, Tex.   D. Dec. 9, 1955, Beeville, Tex.   BL TR 5'9½"   170 lbs.

	G	AB	H	2B	3B	HR	HR %	R	RBI	BB	SO	SB	BA	SA	AB	H	G by POS
1919 NY A	1	1	0	0	0	0	0.0	0	0	0	0	0	.000	.000	1	0	
1920 NY N	8	14	1	0	0	0	0.0	0	0	1	3	0	.071	.071	4	0	OF-4
1921 2 teams	NY N (64G – .286)			PHI N (21G – .338)													
" total	85	269	81	15	6	3	1.1	41	43	20	13	4	.301	.435	1	1	OF-79
1922 PHI N	148	581	196	36	11	12	2.1	102	89	56	46	11	.337	.499	1	1	OF-147
1923	140	527	148	26	5	5	0.9	66	66	45	31	12	.281	.378	2	1	OF-140, 1B-1
1924 2 teams	PHI N (24G – .296)			CIN N (109G – .300)													
" total	133	468	140	27	11	5	1.1	66	54	51	19	7	.299	.436	4	1	OF-129
1925 CIN N	145	509	162	22	16	6	1.2	86	71	57	31	14	.318	.460	3	0	OF-141
1926	155	571	175	24	20	6	1.1	83	78	60	31	3	.306	.450	4	0	OF-152
1927	146	527	154	16	10	6	1.1	60	80	47	19	5	.292	.395	4	0	OF-141
1928	123	427	119	15	12	6	1.4	64	73	40	14	19	.279	.412	1	1	OF-122
1929	141	492	154	28	15	7	1.4	76	83	85	17	17	.313	.474	2	1	OF-138
1930	134	472	145	26	11	8	1.7	74	51	64	30	4	.307	.460	11	6	OF-120
12 yrs.	1359	4858	1475	235	117	64	1.3	718	688	535	254	96	.304	.440	37	12	OF-1313, 1B-1

Dixie Walker

WALKER, FRED (The People's Cherce)
Son of Dixie Walker.   Brother of Harry Walker.
B. Sept. 24, 1910, Villa Rica, Ga.   D. May 17, 1982, Birmingham, Ala.   BL TR 6'1"   175 lbs.

	G	AB	H	2B	3B	HR	HR %	R	RBI	BB	SO	SB	BA	SA	AB	H	G by POS
1931 NY A	2	10	3	2	0	0	0.0	1	1	0	4	0	.300	.500	0	0	OF-2
1933	98	328	90	15	7	15	4.6	68	51	26	28	2	.274	.500	18	4	OF-77
1934	17	17	2	0	0	0	0.0	2	0	1	3	0	.118	.118	12	2	OF-1
1935	8	13	2	1	0	0	0.0	1	1	0	1	0	.154	.231	5	1	OF-2

	G	AB	H	2B	3B	HR	HR %	R	RBI	BB	SO	SB	BA	SA	Pinch Hit AB	Pinch Hit H	G by POS

Dixie Walker continued

	G	AB	H	2B	3B	HR	HR %	R	RBI	BB	SO	SB	BA	SA	AB	H	G by POS
1936 2 teams	NY	A (6G – .350)			CHI	A	(26G – .271)										
" total	32	90	26	2	2	1	1.1	15	16	15	9	2	.289	.389	10	2	OF-22
1937 CHI A	154	593	179	28	16	9	1.5	105	95	78	26	1	.302	.449	0	0	OF-154
1938 DET A	127	454	140	27	6	6	1.3	84	43	65	32	5	.308	.434	10	3	OF-114
1939 2 teams	DET	A (43G – .305)			BKN	N	(61G – .280)										
" total	104	379	110	10	9	6	1.6	57	57	35	18	5	.290	.412	6	2	OF-96
1940 BKN N	143	556	171	37	8	6	1.1	75	66	42	21	3	.308	.435	6	4	OF-136
1941	148	531	165	32	8	9	1.7	88	71	70	18	4	.311	.452	2	0	OF-146
1942	118	393	114	28	1	6	1.5	57	54	47	15	1	.290	.412	6	2	OF-110
1943	138	540	163	32	6	5	0.9	83	71	49	24	3	.302	.411	2	1	OF-136
1944	147	535	191	37	8	13	2.4	77	91	72	27	6	.357	.529	7	2	OF-140
1945	154	607	182	42	9	8	1.3	102	124	75	16	6	.300	.438	1	0	OF-153
1946	150	576	184	29	9	9	1.6	80	116	67	28	14	.319	.448	1	0	OF-149
1947	148	529	162	31	3	9	1.7	77	94	97	26	6	.306	.427	1	0	OF-147
1948 PIT N	129	408	129	19	3	2	0.5	39	54	52	18	1	.316	.392	16	3	OF-112
1949	88	181	51	4	1	1	0.6	26	18	26	11	0	.282	.331	40	13	OF-39, 1B-3
18 yrs.	1905	6740	2064	376	96	105	1.6	1037	1023	817	325	59	.306	.437	143	39	OF-1736, 1B-3

WORLD SERIES

	G	AB	H	2B	3B	HR	HR %	R	RBI	BB	SO	SB	BA	SA	AB	H	G by POS
1941 BKN N	5	18	4	2	0	0	0.0	3	0	2	1	0	.222	.333	0	0	OF-5
1947	7	27	6	1	0	1	3.7	1	4	3	1	1	.222	.370	0	0	OF-7
2 yrs.	12	45	10	3	0	1	2.2	4	4	5	2	1	.222	.356	0	0	OF-12

Duane Walker

WALKER, DUANE ALLEN
B. Mar. 13, 1957, Pasadena, Tex.   BL TL 6'   180 lbs.

	G	AB	H	2B	3B	HR	HR %	R	RBI	BB	SO	SB	BA	SA	AB	H	G by POS
1982 CIN N	86	239	52	10	0	5	2.1	26	22	27	58	9	.218	.322	14	2	OF-69
1983	109	225	53	12	1	2	0.9	14	29	20	43	6	.236	.324	48	16	OF-60
1984	83	195	57	10	3	10	5.1	35	28	33	35	7	.292	.528	14	4	OF-68
3 yrs.	278	659	162	32	4	17	2.6	75	79	80	136	22	.246	.384	76	22	OF-197

Ernie Walker

WALKER, ERNEST ROBERT
Brother of Dixie Walker.
B. Sept. 17, 1890, Blossburg, Ala.   D. Apr. 1, 1965, Pell City, Ala.   BL TR 6'   165 lbs.

	G	AB	H	2B	3B	HR	HR %	R	RBI	BB	SO	SB	BA	SA	AB	H	G by POS
1913 STL A	7	14	3	0	0	0	0.0	0	2	0	5	0	.214	.214	5	2	OF-2
1914	71	131	39	5	3	1	0.8	19	14	13	26	6	.298	.405	29	10	OF-36
1915	50	109	23	4	2	0	0.0	15	9	23	32	5	.211	.284	14	3	OF-33
3 yrs.	128	254	65	9	5	1	0.4	34	25	36	63	11	.256	.343	48	15	OF-71

Fleet Walker

WALKER, MOSES FLEETWOOD
Brother of Welday Walker.
B. Oct. 7, 1857, Mt. Pleasant, Ohio   D. May 11, 1924, Steubenville, Ohio   BR TR

	G	AB	H	2B	3B	HR	HR %	R	RBI	BB	SO	SB	BA	SA	AB	H	G by POS
1884 TOL AA	42	152	40	2	3	0	0.0	23		8				.263	.316	0	0	C-41, OF-1

Frank Walker

WALKER, CHARLES FRANKLIN
B. Sept. 22, 1894, Enoree, S. C.   D. Sept. 16, 1974, Bristol, Tenn.   BR TR 5'11"   165 lbs.

	G	AB	H	2B	3B	HR	HR %	R	RBI	BB	SO	SB	BA	SA	AB	H	G by POS
1917 DET A	2	2	0	0	0	0	0.0	0	0	0	1	0	.000	.000	0	0	
1918	55	167	33	10	3	1	0.6	10	20	7	29	3	.198	.311	7	1	OF-45
1920 PHI A	24	91	21	2	2	0	0.0	10	10	5	14	0	.231	.297	0	0	OF-24
1921	19	66	15	3	0	1	1.5	6	6	8	11	1	.227	.318	0	0	OF-19
1925 NY N	39	81	18	1	0	1	1.2	12	5	9	11	1	.222	.272	7	1	OF-21
5 yrs.	139	407	87	16	5	3	0.7	38	41	29	66	5	.214	.300	14	2	OF-109

Gee Walker

WALKER, GERALD HOLMES
Brother of Hub Walker.
B. Mar. 19, 1908, Gulfport, Miss.   D. Mar. 20, 1981, Whitfield, Miss.   BR TR 5'11"   188 lbs.

	G	AB	H	2B	3B	HR	HR %	R	RBI	BB	SO	SB	BA	SA	AB	H	G by POS
1931 DET A	59	189	56	17	2	1	0.5	20	28	14	21	10	.296	.423	9	4	OF-44
1932	126	480	155	32	6	8	1.7	71	78	13	38	30	.323	.465	8	1	OF-116
1933	127	483	135	29	7	9	1.9	68	64	15	49	26	.280	.424	12	2	OF-113
1934	98	347	104	19	2	6	1.7	54	39	19	20	20	.300	.418	17	5	OF-80
1935	98	362	109	22	6	7	1.9	52	53	15	21	6	.301	.453	14	7	OF-85
1936	134	550	194	55	5	12	2.2	105	93	23	30	17	.353	.536	9	1	OF-125
1937	151	635	213	42	4	18	2.8	105	113	41	74	23	.335	.499	0	0	OF-151
1938 CHI A	120	442	135	23	6	16	3.6	69	87	38	32	9	.305	.493	12	4	OF-107
1939	149	598	174	30	11	13	2.2	95	111	28	43	17	.291	.443	2	0	OF-147
1940 WAS A	140	595	175	29	7	13	2.2	87	96	24	58	21	.294	.432	0	0	OF-140
1941 CLE A	121	445	126	26	11	6	1.3	56	48	18	46	12	.283	.431	13	5	OF-105
1942 CIN N	119	422	97	20	2	5	1.2	40	50	31	44	11	.230	.322	8	1	OF-110
1943	114	429	105	23	2	3	0.7	48	54	12	38	6	.245	.329	6	1	OF-106
1944	121	478	133	21	3	5	1.0	56	62	23	48	7	.278	.366	3	1	OF-117
1945	106	316	80	11	2	2	0.6	28	21	16	38	8	.253	.320	35	9	OF-67, 3B-3
15 yrs.	1783	6771	1991	399	76	124	1.8	954	997	330	600	223	.294	.430	148	41	OF-1613, 3B-3

WORLD SERIES

	G	AB	H	2B	3B	HR	HR %	R	RBI	BB	SO	SB	BA	SA	AB	H	G by POS
1934 DET A	3	3	1	0	0	0	0.0	0	1	0	1	0	.333	.333	3	1	
1935	3	4	1	0	0	0	0.0	1	0	1	0	0	.250	.250	2	0	OF-1
2 yrs.	6	7	2	0	0	0	0.0	1	1	1	1	0	.286	.286	5	1	OF-1

Greg Walker

WALKER, GREGORY LEE
B. Oct. 6, 1959, Douglas, Ga.   BL TR 6'3"   205 lbs.

	G	AB	H	2B	3B	HR	HR %	R	RBI	BB	SO	SB	BA	SA	AB	H	G by POS
1982 CHI A	11	17	7	2	1	2	11.8	2	7	2	3	0	.412	1.000	4	2	DH-4
1983	118	307	83	16	3	10	3.3	32	55	28	57	2	.270	.440	35	13	1B-59, DH-21
1984	136	442	130	29	2	24	5.4	62	75	35	66	8	.294	.532	16	3	1B-101, DH-21
3 yrs.	265	766	220	47	6	36	4.7	97	137	65	126	10	.287	.505	55	18	1B-160, DH-46

LEAGUE CHAMPIONSHIP SERIES

	G	AB	H	2B	3B	HR	HR %	R	RBI	BB	SO	SB	BA	SA	AB	H	G by POS
1983 CHI A	2	3	1	0	0	0	0.0	0	0	1	2	0	.333	.333	1	0	1B-1

	G	AB	H	2B	3B	HR	HR %	R	RBI	BB	SO	SB	BA	SA	Pinch Hit AB	Pinch Hit H	G by POS

Bucky Walters continued

	G	AB	H	2B	3B	HR	HR %	R	RBI	BB	SO	SB	BA	SA	AB	H	G by POS
1942	40	99	24	6	1	2	2.0	13	13	3	13	0	.242	.384	3	0	P-34, OF-1
1943	37	90	24	7	1	1	1.1	11	12	6	15	1	.267	.400	3	0	P-34
1944	37	107	30	4	0	0	0.0	9	13	8	18	0	.280	.318	3	1	P-34
1945	24	61	14	3	0	3	4.9	11	8	3	14	2	.230	.426	2	0	P-22
1946	24	55	7	2	0	0	0.0	6	5	4	12	2	.127	.164	1	0	P-22
1947	20	45	12	2	0	0	0.0	3	4	2	13	0	.267	.311	0	0	P-20
1948	7	15	4	0	0	0	0.0	0	2	0	2	0	.267	.267	0	0	P-7
1950 BOS N	1	2	0	0	0	0	0.0	0	0	0	0	0	.000	.000	0	0	P-1
19 yrs.	715	1966	477	99	16	23	1.2	227	234	114	303	12	.243	.344	64	14	P-428, 3B-184, 2B-16, OF-6

WORLD SERIES

	G	AB	H	2B	3B	HR	HR %	R	RBI	BB	SO	SB	BA	SA	AB	H	G by POS
1939 CIN N	2	3	0	0	0	0	0.0	0	0	0	0	0	.000	.000	0	0	P-2
1940	2	7	2	1	0	1	14.3	2	2	0	1	0	.286	.857	0	0	P-2
2 yrs.	4	10	2	1	0	1	10.0	2	2	0	1	0	.200	.600	0	0	P-4

Fred Walters

WALTERS, JAMES FRED (Whale)
B. Sept. 4, 1912, Laurel, Miss.   D. Feb. 1, 1980, Laurel, Miss.
BR TR 6'1"   210 lbs.

	G	AB	H	2B	3B	HR	HR %	R	RBI	BB	SO	SB	BA	SA	AB	H	G by POS
1945 BOS A	40	93	16	2	0	0	0.0	2	5	10	9	1	.172	.194	2	1	C-38

Ken Walters

WALTERS, KENNETH ROGERS
B. Nov. 11, 1933, Fresno, Calif.
BR TR 6'1"   180 lbs.

	G	AB	H	2B	3B	HR	HR %	R	RBI	BB	SO	SB	BA	SA	AB	H	G by POS
1960 PHI N	124	426	102	10	0	8	1.9	42	37	16	50	4	.239	.319	13	1	OF-119
1961	86	180	41	8	2	2	1.1	23	14	5	25	2	.228	.328	19	5	OF-56, 1B-5, 3B-1
1963 CIN N	49	75	14	2	0	1	1.3	6	7	4	14	0	.187	.253	29	5	OF-21, 1B-1
3 yrs.	259	681	157	20	2	11	1.6	71	58	25	89	6	.231	.314	61	11	OF-196, 1B-6, 3B-1

Roxy Walters

WALTERS, ALFRED JOHN
B. Nov. 5, 1892, San Francisco, Calif.   D. June 3, 1956, Alameda, Calif.
BR TR 5'8½"   160 lbs.

	G	AB	H	2B	3B	HR	HR %	R	RBI	BB	SO	SB	BA	SA	AB	H	G by POS
1915 NY A	2	3	1	0	0	0	0.0	0	0	0	0	0	.333	.333	0	0	C-2
1916	66	203	54	9	3	0	0.0	13	23	14	42	2	.266	.340	1	0	C-65
1917	61	171	45	2	0	0	0.0	16	14	9	22	2	.263	.275	4	1	C-57
1918	64	191	38	5	1	0	0.0	18	12	9	18	3	.199	.236	4	1	C-50, OF-9
1919 BOS A	48	135	26	2	0	0	0.0	7	9	7	15	1	.193	.207	1	1	C-47
1920	88	258	51	11	4	0	0.0	25	28	30	21	2	.198	.248	0	0	C-85, 1B-2
1921	54	169	34	4	1	0	0.0	17	13	10	11	3	.201	.237	0	0	C-54
1922	38	98	19	2	0	0	0.0	4	6	6	8	0	.194	.214	1	1	C-36
1923	40	104	26	4	0	0	0.0	9	5	2	6	0	.250	.288	1	1	C-36, 2B-1
1924 CLE A	32	74	19	2	0	0	0.0	10	5	10	6	0	.257	.284	0	0	C-25, 2B-7
1925	5	20	4	0	0	0	0.0	0	0	0	2	0	.200	.200	0	0	C-5
11 yrs.	498	1426	317	41	6	0	0.0	119	115	97	151	13	.222	.259	12	5	C-462, OF-9, 2B-8, 1B-2

Danny Walton

WALTON, DANIEL JAMES (Mickey)
B. July 14, 1947, Los Angeles, Calif.
BR TR 6'   195 lbs.

	G	AB	H	2B	3B	HR	HR %	R	RBI	BB	SO	SB	BA	SA	AB	H	G by POS
1968 HOU N	2	2	0	0	0	0	0.0	0	0	0	1	0	.000	.000	2	0	
1969 SEA A	23	92	20	1	2	3	3.3	12	10	5	26	2	.217	.370	0	0	OF-23
1970 MIL A	117	397	102	20	1	17	4.3	32	66	51	126	2	.257	.441	6	2	OF-114, 3B-1
1971 2 teams	MIL A (30G – .203)			NY A (5G – .143)													
" total	35	83	16	3	0	3	3.6	6	11	7	29	0	.193	.337	10	2	OF-23, 3B-1
1973 MIN A	37	96	17	1	1	4	4.2	13	8	17	28	0	.177	.333	5	0	OF-18, DH-11, 3B-1
1975	42	63	11	2	0	1	1.6	4	8	4	18	0	.175	.254	32	7	1B-7, DH-6, C-2
1976 LA N	18	15	2	0	0	0	0.0	0	2	1	2	0	.133	.133	15	2	
1977 HOU N	13	21	4	0	0	0	0.0	0	1	0	5	0	.190	.190	8	2	1B-5
1980 TEX A	10	10	2	0	0	0	0.0	2	1	3	5	0	.200	.200	7	2	DH-1
9 yrs.	297	779	174	27	4	28	3.6	69	107	88	240	4	.223	.376	85	17	OF-178, DH-18, 1B-12, 3B-3, C-2

Reggie Walton

WALTON, REGINALD SHERARD
B. Oct. 24, 1952, Kansas City, Mo.
BR TR 6'3"   205 lbs.

	G	AB	H	2B	3B	HR	HR %	R	RBI	BB	SO	SB	BA	SA	AB	H	G by POS
1980 SEA A	31	83	23	6	0	2	2.4	8	9	3	10	2	.277	.422	5	2	OF-17, DH-11
1981	12	6	0	0	0	0	0.0	1	0	1	2	0	.000	.000	4	0	OF-4, DH-1
1982 PIT N	13	15	3	1	0	0	0.0	1	0	1	1	0	.200	.267	10	0	OF-2
3 yrs.	56	104	26	7	0	2	1.9	10	9	5	13	2	.250	.375	19	2	OF-23, DH-12

Zach Walton

Playing record listed under Tom Zachary

Bill Wambsganss

WAMBSGANSS, WILLIAM ADOLPH
Also appeared in box score as Wamby
B. Mar. 19, 1894, Garfield Heights, Ohio
BR TR 5'11"   175 lbs.

	G	AB	H	2B	3B	HR	HR %	R	RBI	BB	SO	SB	BA	SA	AB	H	G by POS
1914 CLE A	43	143	31	6	2	0	0.0	12	12	8	24	2	.217	.287	0		SS-36, 2B-4
1915	121	375	73	4	4	0	0.0	30	21	36	50	8	.195	.227	6	0	2B-78, 3B-35
1916	136	475	117	14	4	0	0.0	57	45	41	40	13	.246	.293	1	0	SS-106, 2B-24, 3B-5
1917	141	499	127	17	6	0	0.0	52	43	37	42	16	.255	.313	1	0	2B-138, 1B-2
1918	87	315	93	15	2	0	0.0	34	40	21	21	16	.295	.356	0	0	2B-87
1919	139	526	146	17	6	2	0.4	60	60	32	24	18	.278	.344	0	0	2B-139
1920	153	565	138	16	11	1	0.2	83	55	54	26	9	.244	.317	0	0	2B-153
1921	107	410	117	28	5	2	0.5	80	46	44	27	13	.285	.393	0	0	2B-103, 3B-2
1922	143	538	141	22	6	0	0.0	89	47	60	26	17	.262	.325	1	0	2B-125, SS-16, C-1
1923	101	345	100	20	4	1	0.3	59	59	43	15	12	.290	.380	3	0	2B-84, 3B-4, SS-2
1924 BOS A	156	636	174	41	5	0	0.0	93	49	54	32	14	.274	.354	0	0	2B-155
1925	111	360	83	12	4	1	0.3	50	41	52	21	3	.231	.294	1	0	2B-103, 1B-6
1926 PHI A	54	54	19	3	0	0	0.0	11	1	8	8	1	.352	.407	20	4	SS-15, 2B-8
13 yrs.	1492	5241	1359	215	59	7	0.1	710	519	490	356	142	.259	.327	33	4	2B-1205, SS-175, 3B-46, 1B-8, C-1

WORLD SERIES

	G	AB	H	2B	3B	HR	HR %	R	RBI	BB	SO	SB	BA	SA	AB	H	G by POS
1920 CLE A	7	26	4	0	0	0	0.0	3	1	2	1	0	.154	.154	0	0	2B-7

	G	AB	H	2B	3B	HR	HR %	R	RBI	BB	SO	SB	BA	SA	Pinch Hit AB	Pinch Hit H	G by POS

Lloyd Waner

WANER, LLOYD JAMES (Little Poison)
Brother of Paul Waner.
B. Mar. 16, 1906, Harrah, Okla.   D. July 22, 1982, Oklahoma City, Okla.
Hall of Fame 1967.
BL TR 5'9"   150 lbs.

	G	AB	H	2B	3B	HR	HR %	R	RBI	BB	SO	SB	BA	SA	AB	H	G by POS
1927 PIT N	150	629	223	17	6	2	0.3	**133**	27	37	23	14	.355	.410	0	0	OF-150, 2B-1
1928	152	**659**	221	22	14	5	0.8	121	61	40	13	8	.335	.434	0	0	OF-152
1929	151	**662**	234	28	**20**	5	0.8	134	74	37	20	6	.353	.479	0	0	OF-151
1930	68	260	94	8	3	1	0.4	32	36	5	5	3	.362	.427	2	1	OF-65
1931	154	**681**	**214**	25	13	4	0.6	90	57	39	16	7	.314	.407	0	0	OF-153, 2B-1
1932	134	565	188	27	11	3	0.5	90	38	31	11	6	.333	.435	2	1	OF-131
1933	121	500	138	14	5	0	0.0	59	26	22	8	3	.276	.324	6	4	OF-114
1934	140	611	173	27	6	1	0.2	95	48	38	12	6	.283	.352	1	0	OF-139
1935	122	537	166	22	14	0	0.0	83	46	22	10	1	.309	.402	1	1	OF-121
1936	106	414	133	13	8	1	0.2	67	31	31	5	1	.321	.399	11	1	OF-92
1937	129	537	177	23	4	1	0.2	80	45	34	12	3	.330	.393	5	2	OF-123
1938	147	619	194	25	7	5	0.8	79	57	28	11	5	.313	.401	3	0	OF-144
1939	112	379	108	15	3	0	0.0	49	24	17	13	0	.285	.340	17	3	OF-92, 3B-1
1940	72	166	43	3	0	0	0.0	30	3	5	5	2	.259	.277	18	6	OF-42
1941 3 teams	PIT N (3G – .250)				BOS N (19G – .412)				CIN N (55G – .256)								
" total	77	219	64	5	1	0	0.0	26	11	12	0	1	.292	.324	11	4	OF-60
1942 PHI N	100	287	75	7	3	0	0.0	23	10	16	6	1	.261	.307	22	4	OF-75
1944 2 teams	BKN N (15G – .286)				PIT N (19G – .357)												
" total	34	28	9	0	0	0	0.0	5	3	5	0	0	.321	.321	18	7	OF-11
1945 PIT N	23	19	5	0	0	0	0.0	5	1	1	3	0	.263	.263	17	5	OF-3
18 yrs.	1992	7772	2459	281	118	28	0.4	1201	598	420	173	67	.316	.394	134	39	OF-1818, 2B-2, 3B-1

WORLD SERIES

	G	AB	H	2B	3B	HR	HR %	R	RBI	BB	SO	SB	BA	SA	AB	H	G by POS
1927 PIT N	4	15	6	1	1	0	0.0	5	0	1	0	0	.400	.600	0	0	OF-4

Paul Waner

WANER, PAUL GLEE (Big Poison)
Brother of Lloyd Waner.
B. Apr. 16, 1903, Harrah, Okla.   D. Aug. 29, 1965, Sarasota, Fla.
Hall of Fame 1952.
BL TL 5'8½"   153 lbs.

	G	AB	H	2B	3B	HR	HR %	R	RBI	BB	SO	SB	BA	SA	AB	H	G by POS
1926 PIT N	144	536	180	35	**22**	8	1.5	101	79	66	19	11	.336	.528	3	0	OF-139
1927	155	623	**237**	40	17	9	1.4	113	**131**	60	14	5	**.380**	.543	0	0	OF-143, 1B-14
1928	152	602	223	**50**	19	6	1.0	**142**	86	77	16	6	.370	.547	0	0	OF-131, 1B-24
1929	151	596	200	43	15	15	2.5	131	100	89	24	15	.336	.534	1	0	OF-143, 1B-7
1930	145	589	217	32	18	8	1.4	117	77	57	18	18	.368	.525	2	0	OF-143
1931	150	559	180	35	10	6	1.1	88	70	73	21	6	.322	.453	2	0	OF-138, 1B-10
1932	154	630	215	62	10	7	1.1	107	82	56	24	13	.341	.505	0	0	OF-154
1933	154	618	191	38	16	7	1.1	101	70	60	20	3	.309	.456	0	0	OF-154
1934	146	599	**217**	32	16	14	2.3	**122**	90	68	24	8	**.362**	.539	1	1	OF-145
1935	139	549	176	29	12	11	2.0	98	78	61	22	2	.321	.477	3	1	OF-136
1936	148	585	218	53	9	5	0.9	107	94	74	29	7	**.373**	.520	3	1	OF-145
1937	154	619	219	30	9	2	0.3	94	74	63	34	4	.354	.441	2	0	OF-150, 1B-3
1938	148	625	175	31	6	6	1.0	77	69	47	28	2	.280	.378	1	0	OF-147
1939	125	461	151	30	6	3	0.7	62	45	35	18	0	.328	.438	11	3	OF-106
1940	89	238	69	16	1	1	0.4	32	32	23	14	0	.290	.378	34	6	OF-45, 1B-8
1941 2 teams	BKN N (11G – .171)				BOS N (95G – .279)												
" total	106	329	88	10	2	2	0.6	45	50	55	14	1	.267	.322	18	3	OF-86, 1B-1
1942 BOS N	114	333	86	17	1	1	0.3	43	39	62	20	2	.258	.324	17	2	OF-94
1943 BKN N	82	225	70	16	0	1	0.4	29	26	35	9	0	.311	.396	21	10	OF-57
1944 2 teams	BKN N (83G – .287)				NY A (9G – .143)												
" total	92	143	40	4	1	0	0.0	17	17	29	8	1	.280	.322	45	13	OF-32
1945 NY A	1	0	0	0	0	0	–	0	0	1	0	0	–	–	0	0	
20 yrs.	2549	9459	3152	603	190	112	1.2	1626	1309	1091	376	104	.333	.473	164	40	OF-2288, 1B-67
				9th	10th												

WORLD SERIES

	G	AB	H	2B	3B	HR	HR %	R	RBI	BB	SO	SB	BA	SA	AB	H	G by POS
1927 PIT N	4	15	5	1	0	0	0.0	0	3	0	1	0	.333	.400	0	0	OF-4

Jack Wanner

WANNER, CLARENCE CURTIS
B. Nov. 29, 1885, Geneso, Ill.   D. May 28, 1919, Genesco, Ill.
BR TR 5'11½"   190 lbs.

	G	AB	H	2B	3B	HR	HR %	R	RBI	BB	SO	SB	BA	SA	AB	H	G by POS
1909 NY A	3	8	1	0	0	0	0.0	0	0	2		1	.125	.125	1	0	SS-2

Pee Wee Wanninger

WANNINGER, PAUL LOUIS
B. Dec. 12, 1902, Birmingham, Ala.   D. May 7, 1981, North Augusta, S. C.
BL TR 5'7"   150 lbs.

	G	AB	H	2B	3B	HR	HR %	R	RBI	BB	SO	SB	BA	SA	AB	H	G by POS
1925 NY A	117	403	95	13	6	1	0.2	35	22	11	34	3	.236	.305	1	1	SS-111, 3B-3, 2B-1
1927 2 teams	BOS A (18G – .200)				CIN N (28G – .247)												
" total	46	153	35	2	2	0	0.0	18	9	12	9	2	.229	.268	2	0	SS-43
2 yrs.	163	556	130	15	8	1	0.2	53	31	23	43	5	.234	.295	3	1	SS-154, 3B-3, 2B-1

Aaron Ward

WARD, AARON LEE
B. Aug. 28, 1896, Booneville, Ark.   D. Jan. 30, 1961, New Orleans, La.
BR TR 5'10½"   160 lbs.

	G	AB	H	2B	3B	HR	HR %	R	RBI	BB	SO	SB	BA	SA	AB	H	G by POS
1917 NY A	8	26	3	0	0	0	0.0	0	1	1	5	0	.115	.115	1	0	SS-7
1918	20	32	4	1	0	0	0.0	2	1	2	7	1	.125	.156	1	0	SS-11, OF-4, 2B-4
1919	27	34	7	2	0	0	0.0	5	2	5	6	0	.206	.265	14	4	1B-5, SS-2, 2B-1
1920	127	496	127	18	7	11	2.2	62	54	33	**84**	7	.256	.387	1	0	3B-114, SS-12
1921	153	556	170	30	10	5	0.9	77	75	42	68	6	.306	.423	0	0	2B-123, 3B-33
1922	154	558	149	19	5	7	1.3	69	68	45	64	7	.267	.357	0	0	2B-152, 3B-2
1923	152	567	161	26	11	10	1.8	79	82	56	65	8	.284	.422	0	0	2B-152
1924	120	400	101	13	10	8	2.0	42	66	40	45	1	.253	.395	0	0	2B-120, SS-1
1925	125	439	108	22	3	4	0.9	41	38	49	49	1	.246	.337	2	0	2B-120, 3B-10
1926	22	31	10	2	0	0	0.0	5	3	2	6	0	.323	.387	15	5	2B-4, 3B-1
1927 CHI A	145	463	125	25	8	5	1.1	75	56	63	56	6	.270	.391	1	0	2B-138, 3B-6
1928 CLE A	6	9	1	0	0	0	0.0	0	1	2	0	0	.111	.111	0	0	3B-3, SS-2, 2B-1
12 yrs.	1059	3611	966	158	54	50	1.4	457	446	339	457	37	.268	.383	35	9	2B-808, 3B-172, SS-35, 1B-5, OF-4

WORLD SERIES

	G	AB	H	2B	3B	HR	HR %	R	RBI	BB	SO	SB	BA	SA	AB	H	G by POS
1921 NY A	8	26	6	0	0	0	0.0	1	4	2	6	0	.231	.231	0	0	2B-8

	G	AB	H	2B	3B	HR	HR %	R	RBI	BB	SO	SB	BA	SA	Pinch Hit AB	Pinch Hit H	G by POS

Jack Warner continued

		G	AB	H	2B	3B	HR	HR%	R	RBI	BB	SO	SB	BA	SA	AB	H	G by POS
1906 2 teams	DET A (50G – .242)					WAS A (32G – .204)												
" total	82	256	58	8	3	1	0.4	20	19	14		7	.227	.293	1	0	C-81
1907 WAS A	72	207	53	5	0	0	0.0	11	17	12		3	.256	.280	8	1	C-64
1908	51	116	28	2	1	0	0.0	8	8	8		7	.241	.276	8	1	C-41, 1B-1
14 yrs.	1073	3494	870	81	35	6	0.2	348	303	181	33	83	.249	.297	29	4	C-1032, 1B-8, OF-1, 2B-1

Jack Warner

WARNER, JOHN RALPH　　　　　　　　　　　BR TR 5'9½" 165 lbs.
B. Aug. 29, 1903, Evansville, Ind.

	G	AB	H	2B	3B	HR	HR%	R	RBI	BB	SO	SB	BA	SA	AB	H	G by POS
1925 DET A	10	39	13	0	0	0	0.0	7	2	3	6	0	.333	.333	0	0	3B-10
1926	100	311	78	8	6	0	0.0	41	34	38	24	8	.251	.315	2	0	3B-95, SS-3
1927	139	559	149	22	9	1	0.2	78	45	47	45	15	.267	.343	1	0	3B-138
1928	75	206	44	4	4	0	0.0	33	13	16	15	4	.214	.272	1	0	3B-52, SS-7
1929 BKN N	17	62	17	2	0	0	0.0	3	4	7	6	3	.274	.306	0	0	SS-17
1930	21	25	8	1	0	0	0.0	4	0	2	7	1	.320	.360	3	1	3B-21
1931	9	4	2	0	0	0	0.0	2	0	1	1	0	.500	.500	0	0	SS-2, 3B-1
1933 PHI N	107	340	76	15	1	0	0.0	31	22	28	33	1	.224	.274	5	1	2B-71, 3B-30, SS-1
8 yrs.	478	1546	387	52	20	1	0.1	199	120	142	137	32	.250	.312	12	2	3B-347, 2B-71, SS-30

Jackie Warner

WARNER, JOHN JOSEPH　　　　　　　　　　　BR TR 6' 180 lbs.
B. Aug. 1, 1943, Monrovia, Calif.

	G	AB	H	2B	3B	HR	HR%	R	RBI	BB	SO	SB	BA	SA	AB	H	G by POS
1966 CAL A	45	123	26	4	1	7	5.7	22	16	9	55	0	.211	.431	4	0	OF-37

Hal Warnock

WARNOCK, HAROLD CHARLES　　　　　　　　BL TR 6'2" 180 lbs.
B. Jan. 6, 1912, New York, N. Y.

	G	AB	H	2B	3B	HR	HR%	R	RBI	BB	SO	SB	BA	SA	AB	H	G by POS
1935 STL A	6	7	2	2	0	0	0.0	1	0	0	3	0	.286	.571	6	1	OF-2

Bennie Warren

WARREN, BENNIE LOUIS　　　　　　　　　　BR TR 6'1" 184 lbs.
B. Mar. 2, 1912, Elk City, Okla.

	G	AB	H	2B	3B	HR	HR%	R	RBI	BB	SO	SB	BA	SA	AB	H	G by POS
1939 PHI N	18	56	13	0	0	1	1.8	4	7	7	7	0	.232	.286	1	1	C-17
1940	106	289	71	6	1	12	4.2	33	34	40	46	1	.246	.398	7	4	C-97, 1B-1
1941	121	345	74	13	2	9	2.6	34	35	44	66	0	.214	.342	11	4	C-110
1942	90	225	47	6	3	7	3.1	19	20	24	36	0	.209	.356	9	0	C-78, 1B-1
1946 NY N	39	69	11	1	1	4	5.8	7	8	14	21	0	.159	.377	7	0	C-30
1947	3	5	1	0	0	0	0.0	0	0	0	1	0	.200	.200	0	0	C-3
6 yrs.	377	989	217	26	7	33	3.3	97	104	129	177	1	.219	.360	35	9	C-335, 1B-2

Bill Warren

WARREN, WILLIAM HACKNEY (Hack)　　　　　BL TR 5'8" 165 lbs.
B. Feb. 11, 1883, Missouri　　D. Jan. 28, 1960, Whiteville, Tenn.

	G	AB	H	2B	3B	HR	HR%	R	RBI	BB	SO	SB	BA	SA	AB	H	G by POS
1914 IND F	26	50	12	2	0	0	0.0	5	5	5		2	.240	.280	3	0	C-23
1915 NWK F	5	3	1	0	0	0	0.0	0	1	0		0	.333	.333	3	1	1B-1, C-1
2 yrs.	31	53	13	2	0	0	0.0	5	6	5		2	.245	.283	6	1	C-24, 1B-1

Rabbit Warstler

WARSTLER, HAROLD BURTON　　　　　　　　BR TR 5'7½" 150 lbs.
B. Sept. 13, 1903, North Canton, Ohio　　D. May 31, 1964, North Canton, Ohio

		G	AB	H	2B	3B	HR	HR%	R	RBI	BB	SO	SB	BA	SA	AB	H	G by POS
1930 BOS A		55	162	30	2	3	1	0.6	16	13	20	21	0	.185	.253	0	0	SS-54
1931		66	181	44	5	3	0	0.0	20	10	15	27	2	.243	.304	5	0	2B-47, SS-19
1932		115	388	82	15	5	0	0.0	26	34	22	43	9	.211	.276	3	0	SS-107
1933		92	322	70	13	1	1	0.3	44	17	42	36	2	.217	.273	1	0	SS-87
1934 PHI A		117	419	99	19	3	1	0.2	56	36	51	30	9	.236	.303	4	0	2B-107, SS-2
1935		138	496	124	20	7	3	0.6	62	59	56	53	8	.250	.337	0	0	2B-136, 3B-2
1936 2 teams	PHI A (66G – .250)						BOS N (74G – .211)											
" total		140	540	123	14	6	1	0.2	54	41	58	49	2	.228	.281	0	0	SS-74, 2B-66
1937 BOS N		149	555	124	20	0	3	0.5	57	36	51	62	4	.223	.276	0	0	SS-149
1938		142	467	108	10	4	0	0.0	37	40	48	38	3	.231	.270	0	0	SS-135, 2B-7
1939		114	342	83	11	3	0	0.0	34	24	24	31	2	.243	.292	1	0	SS-49, 2B-43, 3B-21
1940 2 teams	BOS N (33G – .211)						CHI N (45G – .226)											
" total		78	216	48	4	1	1	0.5	25	22	18	24	1	.222	.264	6	1	2B-41, SS-29, 3B-2
11 yrs.		1206	4088	935	133	36	11	0.3	431	332	405	414	42	.229	.287	20	0	SS-705, 2B-442, 3B-25

Bill Warwick

WARWICK, FIRMAN NEWTON　　　　　　　　BR TR 6'½" 180 lbs.
B. Nov. 26, 1897, Philadelphia, Pa.

	G	AB	H	2B	3B	HR	HR%	R	RBI	BB	SO	SB	BA	SA	AB	H	G by POS
1921 PIT N	1	1	0	0	0	0	0.0	0	0	0	0	0	.000	.000	0	0	C-1
1925 STL N	13	41	12	1	2	1	2.4	8	6	5	5	0	.293	.488	0	0	C-13
1926	9	14	5	0	0	0	0.0	0	2	0	2	0	.357	.357	0	0	C-9
3 yrs.	23	56	17	1	2	1	1.8	8	8	5	7	0	.304	.446	0	0	C-23

Carl Warwick

WARWICK, CARL WAYNE　　　　　　　　　BR TL 5'10" 170 lbs.
B. Feb. 27, 1937, Dallas, Tex.

		G	AB	H	2B	3B	HR	HR%	R	RBI	BB	SO	SB	BA	SA	AB	H	G by POS
1961 2 teams	LA N (19G – .091)					STL N (55G – .250)											
" total		74	163	39	6	2	4	2.5	29	17	20	36	3	.239	.374	13	4	OF-60
1962 2 teams	STL N (13G – .348)					HOU N (130G – .260)											
" total		143	500	132	17	1	17	3.4	67	64	40	79	4	.264	.404	13	4	OF-138
1963 HOU N		150	528	134	19	5	7	1.3	49	47	49	70	3	.254	.348	10	2	OF-141, 1B-2
1964 STL N		88	158	41	7	1	3	1.9	14	15	11	30	2	.259	.373	43	11	OF-49
1965 2 teams	STL N (50G – .156)					BAL A (9G – .000)											
" total		59	91	12	2	1	0	0.0	6	6	7	20	1	.132	.176	36	4	OF-24, 1B-4
1966 CHI N		16	22	5	0	0	0	0.0	3	0	0	6	0	.227	.227	7	2	OF-10
6 yrs.		530	1462	363	51	10	31	2.1	168	149	127	241	13	.248	.360	122	27	OF-422, 1B-6

WORLD SERIES

	G	AB	H	2B	3B	HR	HR%	R	RBI	BB	SO	SB	BA	SA	AB	H	G by POS
1964 STL N	5	4	3	0	0	0	0.0	2	1	1	0	0	.750	.750	4	3 (1st)	

	G	AB	H	2B	3B	HR	HR %	R	RBI	BB	SO	SB	BA	SA	Pinch Hit AB	Pinch Hit H	G by POS

Jimmy Wasdell

WASDELL, JAMES CHARLES
B. May 15, 1914, Cleveland, Ohio   D. Aug. 6, 1983, New Port Ritchey, Fla.   BL TL 5'11" 185 lbs.

	G	AB	H	2B	3B	HR	HR %	R	RBI	BB	SO	SB	BA	SA	PH AB	PH H	G by POS
1937 WAS A	32	110	28	4	4	2	1.8	13	12	7	13	0	.255	.418	4	1	1B-21, OF-7
1938	53	140	33	2	1	2	1.4	19	16	12	12	5	.236	.307	18	4	1B-26, OF-6
1939	29	109	33	5	1	0	0.0	12	13	9	16	3	.303	.367	1	0	1B-28
1940 2 teams		WAS A (10G – .086)				BKN N (77G – .278)											
" total	87	265	67	15	4	3	1.1	38	37	20	31	4	.253	.374	14	5	OF-42, 1B-25
1941 BKN N	94	265	79	14	3	4	1.5	39	48	16	15	2	.298	.419	23	4	OF-54, 1B-15
1942 PIT N	122	409	106	11	2	3	0.7	44	38	47	22	1	.259	.318	16	1	OF-97, 1B-7
1943 2 teams		PIT N (4G – .500)				PHI N (141G – .261)											
" total	145	524	137	19	6	4	0.8	54	68	48	22	6	.261	.344	5	4	1B-82, OF-56
1944 PHI N	133	451	125	20	3	3	0.7	47	40	45	17	0	.277	.355	9	2	OF-121, 1B-4
1945	134	500	150	19	8	7	1.4	65	60	32	11	7	.300	.412	8	5	OF-65, 1B-63
1946 2 teams		PHI N (26G – .255)				CLE A (32G – .268)											
" total	58	92	24	0	2	1	1.1	8	9	7	6	1	.261	.337	36	10	OF-14, 1B-6
1947 CLE A	1	0	0	0	0	0	0.0	0	0	0	0	0	.000	.000	1	0	
11 yrs.	888	2866	782	109	34	29	1.0	339	341	243	165	29	.273	.365	135	36	OF-462, 1B-277

WORLD SERIES

	G	AB	H	2B	3B	HR	HR %	R	RBI	BB	SO	SB	BA	SA	PH AB	PH H	G by POS
1941 BKN N	3	5	1	1	0	0	0.0	0	2	0	0	0	.200	.400	3	1	OF-1

Link Wasem

WASEM, LINCOLN WILLIAM
B. Jan. 30, 1911, Birmingham, Ohio   D. Mar. 6, 1979, Laguna Beach, Calif.   BR TR 5'9½" 180 lbs.

	G	AB	H	2B	3B	HR	HR %	R	RBI	BB	SO	SB	BA	SA	PH AB	PH H	G by POS
1937 BOS N	2	1	0	0	0	0	0.0	0	0	0	0	0	.000	.000	0	0	C-2

Libe Washburn

WASHBURN, LIBE
B. June 16, 1874, Lyme, N. H.   D. Mar. 22, 1940, Malone, N. Y.   BB TL

	G	AB	H	2B	3B	HR	HR %	R	RBI	BB	SO	SB	BA	SA	PH AB	PH H	G by POS
1902 NY N	6	9	4	0	0	0	0.0	1	0	2		1	.444	.444	3	1	OF-3
1903 PHI N	8	18	3	0	0	0	0.0	1	1	1		0	.167	.167	2	0	P-4, OF-2
2 yrs.	14	27	7	0	0	0	0.0	2	1	3		1	.259	.259	5	1	OF-5, P-4

Claudell Washington

WASHINGTON, CLAUDELL
B. Aug. 31, 1954, Los Angeles, Calif.   BL TL 6' 190 lbs.

	G	AB	H	2B	3B	HR	HR %	R	RBI	BB	SO	SB	BA	SA	PH AB	PH H	G by POS
1974 OAK A	73	221	63	10	5	0	0.0	16	19	13	44	7	.285	.376	8	3	DH-38, OF-32
1975	148	590	182	24	7	10	1.7	86	77	32	80	40	.308	.424	2	1	OF-148
1976	134	490	126	20	6	5	1.0	65	53	30	90	37	.257	.353	3	2	OF-126, DH-6
1977 TEX A	129	521	148	31	2	12	2.3	63	68	25	112	21	.284	.420	2	0	OF-127
1978 2 teams		TEX A (12G – .167)				CHI A (86G – .264)											
" total	98	356	90	16	5	4	1.7	34	33	13	69	5	.253	.376	6	2	OF-89, DH-5
1979 CHI A	131	471	132	33	5	13	2.8	79	66	28	93	19	.280	.454	13	4	OF-122, DH-3
1980 2 teams		CHI A (32G – .289)				NY N (79G – .275)											
" total	111	374	104	20	6	11	2.9	53	54	25	82	21	.278	.452	17	1	OF-93, DH-2
1981 ATL N	85	320	93	22	3	5	1.6	37	37	15	47	12	.291	.425	5	3	OF-79
1982	150	563	150	24	6	16	2.8	94	80	50	107	33	.266	.416	7	0	OF-139
1983	134	496	138	24	8	9	1.8	75	44	35	103	31	.278	.413	7	2	OF-128
1984	120	416	119	21	2	17	4.1	62	61	59	77	21	.286	.469	12	2	OF-107
11 yrs.	1313	4818	1345	245	55	104	2.2	664	592	325	904	247	.279	.418	82	20	OF-1190, DH-54

LEAGUE CHAMPIONSHIP SERIES

	G	AB	H	2B	3B	HR	HR %	R	RBI	BB	SO	SB	BA	SA	PH AB	PH H	G by POS
1974 OAK A	4	11	3	1	0	0	0.0	1	0	0	0	0	.273	.364	1	1	OF-3
1975	3	12	3	1	0	0	0.0	1	1	0	2	0	.250	.333	0	0	OF-2
1982 ATL N	3	9	3	0	0	0	0.0	0	0	2	2	0	.333	.333	0	0	OF-3
3 yrs.	10	32	9	2	0	0	0.0	2	1	2	4	0	.281	.344	1	1	OF-8

WORLD SERIES

	G	AB	H	2B	3B	HR	HR %	R	RBI	BB	SO	SB	BA	SA	PH AB	PH H	G by POS
1974 OAK A	5	7	4	0	0	0	0.0	1	0	1	1	0	.571	.571	1	1	OF-5

George Washington

WASHINGTON, SLOANE VERNON
B. June 7, 1907, Linden, Tex.   BL TR 5'11½" 190 lbs.

	G	AB	H	2B	3B	HR	HR %	R	RBI	BB	SO	SB	BA	SA	PH AB	PH H	G by POS
1935 CHI A	108	339	96	22	3	8	2.4	40	47	10	18	1	.283	.437	29	9	OF-79
1936	20	49	8	2	0	1	2.0	6	5	1	4	0	.163	.265	6	1	OF-12
2 yrs.	128	388	104	24	3	9	2.3	46	52	11	22	1	.268	.415	35	10	OF-91

Herb Washington

WASHINGTON, HERBERT
B. Nov. 16, 1950, Flint, Mich.   BR TR 6' 170 lbs.

	G	AB	H	2B	3B	HR	HR %	R	RBI	BB	SO	SB	BA	SA	PH AB	PH H	G by POS
1974 OAK A	91	0	0	0	0	0	–	29	0	0	0	28	–	–	0	0	
1975	13	0	0	0	0	0	–	4	0	0	0	2	–	–	0	0	
2 yrs.	104	0	0	0	0	0	–	33	0	0	0	30	–	–	0	0	

LEAGUE CHAMPIONSHIP SERIES

	G	AB	H	2B	3B	HR	HR %	R	RBI	BB	SO	SB	BA	SA	PH AB	PH H	G by POS
1974 OAK A	2	0	0	0	0	0	–	0	0	0	0	0	–	–	0	0	

WORLD SERIES

	G	AB	H	2B	3B	HR	HR %	R	RBI	BB	SO	SB	BA	SA	PH AB	PH H	G by POS
1974 OAK A	3	0	0	0	0	0	–	0	0	0	0	0	–	–	0	0	

LaRue Washington

WASHINGTON, LaRue
B. Sept. 7, 1953, Long Beach, Calif.   BR TR 6' 170 lbs.

	G	AB	H	2B	3B	HR	HR %	R	RBI	BB	SO	SB	BA	SA	PH AB	PH H	G by POS
1978 TEX A	3	3	0	0	0	0	0.0	0	0	0	1	0	.000	.000	0	0	2B-2, DH-1
1979	25	18	5	0	0	0	0.0	5	2	4	0	2	.278	.278	0	0	OF-13, DH-1, 3B-1
2 yrs.	28	21	5	0	0	0	0.0	5	2	4	1	2	.238	.238	0	0	OF-13, DH-2, 2B-2, 3B-1

Ron Washington

WASHINGTON, RONALD
B. Apr. 29, 1952, New Orleans, La.   BR TR 5'11" 156 lbs.

	G	AB	H	2B	3B	HR	HR %	R	RBI	BB	SO	SB	BA	SA	PH AB	PH H	G by POS
1977 LA N	10	19	7	0	0	0	0.0	4	1	0	2	1	.368	.368	0	0	SS-10
1981 MIN A	28	84	19	3	1	0	0.0	8	5	4	14	4	.226	.286	0	0	SS-26, OF-2
1982	119	451	122	17	6	5	1.1	48	39	14	79	3	.271	.368	2	0	SS-91, 2B-37, 3B-1
1983	99	317	78	7	3	4	1.3	28	26	22	50	10	.246	.325	4	1	SS-81, 2B-14, DH-1, 3B-1
1984	88	197	58	11	5	3	1.5	25	23	4	31	1	.294	.447	12	2	SS-71, 2B-9, DH-4, 3B-2
5 yrs.	344	1068	284	38	15	12	1.1	113	94	44	176	19	.266	.363	18	3	SS-279, 2B-60, DH-5, 3B-4, OF-2

U. L. Washington

WASHINGTON, U. L.
B. Oct. 27, 1953, Atoka, Okla.   BB   TR   5'11"   175 lbs.

		G	AB	H	2B	3B	HR	HR %	R	RBI	BB	SO	SB	BA	SA	Pinch Hit AB	Pinch Hit H	G by POS
1977	KC A	10	20	4	1	1	0	0.0	0	1	5	4	1	.200	.350	0	0	SS-9, DH-1
1978		69	129	34	2	1	0	0.0	10	9	10	20	12	.264	.295	1	1	SS-49, 2B-19
1979		101	268	68	12	5	2	0.7	32	25	20	44	10	.254	.358	3	0	SS-50, 2B-46, DH-3, 3B-1
1980		153	549	150	16	11	6	1.1	79	53	53	78	20	.273	.375	2	1	SS-152
1981		98	339	77	19	1	2	0.6	40	29	41	43	10	.227	.307	0	0	SS-98
1982		119	437	125	19	3	10	2.3	64	60	38	48	23	.286	.412	2	0	SS-117, DH-1
1983		144	547	129	19	6	5	0.9	76	41	48	78	40	.236	.320	3	0	SS-140, DH-1
1984		63	170	38	6	0	1	0.6	18	10	14	31	4	.224	.276	0	0	SS-61
8 yrs.		757	2459	625	94	28	26	1.1	319	228	229	346	120	.254	.347	11	2	SS-676, 2B-65, DH-6, 3B-1

DIVISIONAL PLAYOFF SERIES
		G	AB	H	2B	3B	HR	HR %	R	RBI	BB	SO	SB	BA	SA	Pinch Hit AB	Pinch Hit H	G by POS
1981	KC A	3	9	2	0	0	0	0.0	0	0	0	1	0	.222	.222	0	0	SS-3

LEAGUE CHAMPIONSHIP SERIES
		G	AB	H	2B	3B	HR	HR %	R	RBI	BB	SO	SB	BA	SA	Pinch Hit AB	Pinch Hit H	G by POS
1980	KC A	3	11	4	1	0	0	0.0	1	1	2	3	0	.364	.455	0	0	SS-3
1984		2	1	0	0	0	0	0.0	0	0	0	1	0	.000	.000	1	0	
2 yrs.		5	12	4	1	0	0	0.0	1	1	2	4	0	.333	.417	1	0	SS-3

WORLD SERIES
		G	AB	H	2B	3B	HR	HR %	R	RBI	BB	SO	SB	BA	SA	Pinch Hit AB	Pinch Hit H	G by POS
1980	KC A	6	22	6	0	0	0	0.0	1	2	0	6	0	.273	.273	0	0	SS-6

John Wathan

WATHAN, JOHN DAVID (Duke)
B. Oct. 4, 1949, Cedar Rapids, Iowa   BR   TR   6'2"   205 lbs.

		G	AB	H	2B	3B	HR	HR %	R	RBI	BB	SO	SB	BA	SA	Pinch Hit AB	Pinch Hit H	G by POS
1976	KC A	27	42	12	1	0	0	0.0	5	5	2	5	0	.286	.310	2	1	C-23, 1B-3
1977		55	119	39	5	3	2	1.7	18	21	5	8	2	.328	.471	18	6	C-35, 1B-5
1978		67	190	57	10	1	2	1.1	19	28	3	12	2	.300	.395	13	6	1B-47, C-21
1979		90	199	41	7	3	2	1.0	26	28	7	24	2	.206	.302	31	5	1B-49, C-23, DH-11, OF-3
1980		126	453	138	14	7	6	1.3	57	58	50	42	17	.305	.406	10	3	C-77, OF-35, 1B-12
1981		89	301	76	9	3	1	0.3	24	19	19	23	11	.252	.312	4	0	C-73, OF-16, 1B-1
1982		121	448	121	11	3	3	0.7	79	51	48	46	36	.270	.328	2	0	C-120, 1B-3
1983		128	437	107	18	3	2	0.5	49	32	27	56	28	.245	.314	5	2	C-92, 1B-37, OF-9
1984		97	171	31	7	1	2	1.2	17	10	21	34	6	.181	.269	4	1	C-59, 1B-33, DH-4, OF-1
9 yrs.		800	2360	622	82	24	20	0.8	294	252	182	250	104	.264	.344	89	24	C-523, 1B-190, OF-64, DH-15

DIVISIONAL PLAYOFF SERIES
		G	AB	H	2B	3B	HR	HR %	R	RBI	BB	SO	SB	BA	SA	Pinch Hit AB	Pinch Hit H	G by POS
1981	KC A	3	10	3	0	0	0	0.0	1	1	1	1	0	.300	.300	0	0	C-3

LEAGUE CHAMPIONSHIP SERIES
		G	AB	H	2B	3B	HR	HR %	R	RBI	BB	SO	SB	BA	SA	Pinch Hit AB	Pinch Hit H	G by POS
1976	KC A	1	0	0	0	0	0	0.0	0	0	0	0	0	–	–	0	0	C-1
1977		4	6	0	0	0	0	0.0	0	0	0	3	0	.000	.000	2	0	1B-2
1978		1	3	0	0	0	0	0.0	0	0	0	0	0	.000	.000	0	0	1B-1
1980		3	6	0	0	0	0	0.0	1	0	3	1	0	.000	.000	1	0	OF-3
1984		1	1	0	0	0	0	0.0	0	0	0	0	0	.000		1	0	
5 yrs.		10	16	0	0	0	0	0.0	1	0	3	4	0	.000	.000	4	0	OF-3, 1B-3, C-1

WORLD SERIES
		G	AB	H	2B	3B	HR	HR %	R	RBI	BB	SO	SB	BA	SA	Pinch Hit AB	Pinch Hit H	G by POS
1980	KC A	3	7	2	0	0	0	0.0	1	1	1	0	0	.286	.286	1	0	C-2

Bill Watkins

WATKINS, WILLIAM HENRY
B. May 5, 1859, Brantford, Ont., Canada   D. June 9, 1937, Port Huron, Mich.   5'10"   156 lbs.
Manager 1884-89, 1893, 1898-99.

		G	AB	H	2B	3B	HR	HR %	R	RBI	BB	SO	SB	BA	SA	Pinch Hit AB	Pinch Hit H	G by POS
1884	IND AA	34	127	26	4	0	0	0.0	16		5			.205	.236	0	0	3B-23, 2B-9, SS-2

Dave Watkins

WATKINS, DAVID ROGER
B. Mar. 15, 1944, Owensboro, Ky.   BR   TR   5'10"   185 lbs.

		G	AB	H	2B	3B	HR	HR %	R	RBI	BB	SO	SB	BA	SA	Pinch Hit AB	Pinch Hit H	G by POS
1969	PHI N	69	148	26	2	1	4	2.7	17	12	22	53	2	.176	.284	11	1	C-54, OF-5, 3B-1

Ed Watkins

WATKINS, JAMES EDWARD
B. June 21, 1877, Philadelphia, Pa.   D. Mar. 29, 1933, Kelvin, Ariz.

		G	AB	H	2B	3B	HR	HR %	R	RBI	BB	SO	SB	BA	SA	Pinch Hit AB	Pinch Hit H	G by POS
1902	PHI N	1	3	0	0	0	0	0.0	0	0	0		0	.000	.000	0	0	OF-1

George Watkins

WATKINS, GEORGE ARCHIBALD
B. June 4, 1902, Palestine, Tex.   D. June 1, 1970, Houston, Tex.   BL   TR   6'   175 lbs.

		G	AB	H	2B	3B	HR	HR %	R	RBI	BB	SO	SB	BA	SA	Pinch Hit AB	Pinch Hit H	G by POS
1930	STL N	119	391	146	32	7	17	4.3	85	87	24	49	5	.373	.621	15	5	OF-89, 1B-13, 2B-1
1931		131	503	145	30	13	13	2.6	93	51	31	66	15	.288	.477	2	0	OF-129
1932		137	458	143	35	3	9	2.0	67	63	45	46	18	.312	.461	6	2	OF-120
1933		138	525	146	24	5	5	1.0	66	62	39	62	11	.278	.371	3	0	OF-135
1934	NY N	105	296	73	18	3	6	2.0	38	33	24	34	2	.247	.389	16	3	OF-81
1935	PHI N	150	600	162	25	5	17	2.8	80	76	40	78	3	.270	.413	2	1	OF-148
1936	2 teams		PHI N (19G – .243)					BKN N (105G – .255)										
"	total	124	434	110	28	6	6	1.4	61	48	43	47	7	.253	.387	8	2	OF-115
7 yrs.		904	3207	925	192	42	73	2.3	490	420	246	382	61	.288	.443	52	13	OF-817, 1B-13, 2B-1

WORLD SERIES
		G	AB	H	2B	3B	HR	HR %	R	RBI	BB	SO	SB	BA	SA	Pinch Hit AB	Pinch Hit H	G by POS
1930	STL N	4	12	2	0	0	1	8.3	2	1	1	3	0	.167	.417	0	0	OF-4
1931		5	14	4	1	0	1	7.1	4	2	2	1	1	.286	.571	0	0	OF-5
2 yrs.		9	26	6	1	0	2	7.7	6	3	3	4	1	.231	.500	0	0	OF-9

Neal Watlington

WATLINGTON, JULIUS NEAL
B. Dec. 25, 1922, Yanceyville, N. C.   BL   TR   6'   195 lbs.

		G	AB	H	2B	3B	HR	HR %	R	RBI	BB	SO	SB	BA	SA	Pinch Hit AB	Pinch Hit H	G by POS
1953	PHI A	21	44	7	1	0	0	0.0	3	3	3	8	0	.159	.182	12	2	C-9

Art Watson

WATSON, ARTHUR STANHOPE (Watty)
B. Jan. 11, 1884, Jeffersonville, Ind.   D. May 9, 1950, Buffalo, N. Y.   BL   TR   5'11"   170 lbs.

		G	AB	H	2B	3B	HR	HR %	R	RBI	BB	SO	SB	BA	SA	Pinch Hit AB	Pinch Hit H	G by POS
1914	BKN F	22	46	13	4	1	1	2.2	7	3	1		0	.283	.478	2	1	C-18

	G	AB	H	2B	3B	HR	HR %	R	RBI	BB	SO	SB	BA	SA	Pinch Hit AB	Pinch Hit H	G by POS

Art Watson continued

1915 **2 teams**	**BKN**	F (9G –	.263)	**BUF**	F	(22G –	.467)										
" total	31	49	19	1	3	1	2.0	10	14	3		0	.388	.592	16	6	C-13, OF-1
2 yrs.	53	95	32	5	4	2	2.1	17	17	4		0	.337	.537	18	7	C-31, OF-1

Bob Watson

WATSON, ALBERT BAILEY   BR TR 5'8"   154 lbs.
Brother of Frank Watt.
B. Dec. 12, 1899, Philadelphia, Pa.   D. Mar. 15, 1968, Norfolk, Va.

	G	AB	H	2B	3B	HR	HR %	R	RBI	BB	SO	SB	BA	SA	AB	H	G by POS
1920 **WAS A**	1	1	1	1	0	0	0.0	0	1	0	0	0	1.000	2.000	0	0	2B-1

Bob Watson

WATSON, ROBERT JOSE (Bull)   BR TR 6'1½"   201 lbs.
B. Apr. 10, 1946, Los Angeles, Calif.

	G	AB	H	2B	3B	HR	HR %	R	RBI	BB	SO	SB	BA	SA	AB	H	G by POS
1966 **HOU N**	1	1	0	0	0	0	0.0	0	0	0	0	0	.000	.000	1	0	
1967	6	14	3	0	0	1	7.1	1	2	0	3	0	.214	.429	3	0	1B-3
1968	45	140	32	7	0	2	1.4	13	8	13	32	1	.229	.321	5	0	OF-40
1969	20	40	11	3	0	0	0.0	3	3	6	5	0	.275	.350	5	3	OF-6, 1B-5, C-1
1970	97	327	89	19	2	11	3.4	48	61	24	59	1	.272	.443	13	5	1B-83, C-6, OF-1
1971	129	468	135	17	3	9	1.9	49	67	41	56	0	.288	.395	3	1	OF-87, 1B-45
1972	147	548	171	27	4	16	2.9	74	86	53	83	1	.312	.464	2	0	OF-143, 1B-2
1973	158	573	179	24	3	16	2.8	97	94	85	73	1	.312	.449	2	0	OF-142, 1B-26, C-3
1974	150	524	156	19	4	11	2.1	69	67	60	61	3	.298	.424	8	2	OF-140, 1B-35
1975	132	485	157	27	1	18	3.7	67	85	40	50	3	.324	.495	8	2	1B-118, OF-9
1976	157	585	183	31	3	16	2.7	76	102	62	64	3	.313	.458	3	0	1B-155
1977	151	554	160	38	6	22	4.0	77	110	57	69	5	.289	.498	5	3	1B-146
1978	139	461	133	25	4	14	3.0	51	79	51	57	3	.289	.451	9	0	1B-128
1979 **2 teams**	**HOU**	N (49G –	.239)	**BOS**	A	(84G –	.337)										
" total	133	475	144	23	4	16	3.4	63	71	45	56	3	.303	.469	6	0	1B-102, DH-26
1980 **NY A**	130	469	144	25	3	13	2.8	62	68	48	56	2	.307	.456	11	3	1B-104, DH-21
1981	59	156	33	3	3	6	3.8	15	12	24	17	0	.212	.385	13	3	1B-50, DH-6
1982 **2 teams**	**NY**	A (7G –	.235)	**ATL**	N	(57G –	.246)										
" total	64	131	32	6	1	5	3.8	19	25	17	20	1	.244	.420	25	6	1B-33, OF-2, DH-1
1983 **ATL N**	65	149	46	9	0	6	4.0	14	37	18	23	0	.309	.490	27	11	1B-34
1984	49	85	18	4	0	2	2.4	4	12	9	12	0	.212	.329	29	6	1B-19
19 yrs.	1832	6185	1826	307	41	184	3.0	802	989	653	796	27	.295	.447	178	45	1B-1088, OF-570, DH-54, C-10

DIVISIONAL PLAYOFF SERIES

	G	AB	H	2B	3B	HR	HR %	R	RBI	BB	SO	SB	BA	SA	AB	H	G by POS
1981 **NY A**	5	16	7	0	0	0	0.0	2	1	1	1	0	.438	.438	0	0	1B-5

LEAGUE CHAMPIONSHIP SERIES

	G	AB	H	2B	3B	HR	HR %	R	RBI	BB	SO	SB	BA	SA	AB	H	G by POS
1980 **NY A**	3	12	6	3	1	0	0.0	0	0	0	0	0	.500	.917	0	0	1B-3
1981	3	12	3	0	0	0	0.0	0	1	0	1	0	.250	.250	0	0	1B-3
2 yrs.	6	24	9	3	1	0	0.0	0	1	0	1	0	.375	.583	0	0	1B-6

WORLD SERIES

	G	AB	H	2B	3B	HR	HR %	R	RBI	BB	SO	SB	BA	SA	AB	H	G by POS
1981 **NY A**	6	22	7	1	0	2	9.1	2	7	3	0	0	.318	.636	0	0	1B-6

Johnny Watson

WATSON, JOHN THOMAS   BL TR 6'   175 lbs.
B. Jan. 16, 1908, Tazewell, Va.   D. Apr. 29, 1965, Huntington, W. Va.

	G	AB	H	2B	3B	HR	HR %	R	RBI	BB	SO	SB	BA	SA	AB	H	G by POS
1930 **DET A**	4	12	3	2	0	0	0.0	1	3	1	2	0	.250	.417	0	0	SS-4

Cliff Watwood

WATWOOD, JOHN CLIFFORD (Lefty)   BL TL 6'1"   186 lbs.
B. Aug. 17, 1905, Alexander City, Ala.   D. Mar. 1, 1980, Goodwater, Ala.

	G	AB	H	2B	3B	HR	HR %	R	RBI	BB	SO	SB	BA	SA	AB	H	G by POS
1929 **CHI A**	85	278	84	12	6	2	0.7	33	18	22	21	6	.302	.410	7	2	OF-77
1930	133	427	129	25	4	2	0.5	75	51	52	35	5	.302	.393	19	4	1B-62, OF-43
1931	128	367	104	16	6	1	0.3	51	47	56	30	9	.283	.368	17	5	OF-102, 1B-4
1932 **2 teams**	**CHI**	A (13G –	.306)	**BOS**	A	(95G –	.248)										
" total	108	315	81	13	0	0	0.0	31	30	21	14	7	.257	.298	27	9	OF-59, 1B-18
1933 **BOS A**	13	30	4	0	0	0	0.0	2	2	3	3	0	.133	.133	3	0	OF-9
1939 **PHI N**	2	6	1	0	0	0	0.0	0	0	0	0	0	.167	.167	0	0	1B-2
6 yrs.	469	1423	403	66	16	5	0.4	192	148	154	103	27	.283	.363	73	20	OF-290, 1B-86

Bob Way

WAY, ROBERT CLINTON   BR TR 5'10½" 168 lbs.
B. Apr. 2, 1906, Emlenton, Pa.   D. June 20, 1974, Pittsburgh, Pa.

	G	AB	H	2B	3B	HR	HR %	R	RBI	BB	SO	SB	BA	SA	AB	H	G by POS
1927 **CHI A**	5	3	1	0	0	0	0.0	3	1	0	1	0	.333	.333	3	1	2B-1

Roy Weatherly

WEATHERLY, CYRIL ROY (Stormy)   BL TR 5'6½" 170 lbs.
B. Feb. 25, 1915, Warren, Tex.

	G	AB	H	2B	3B	HR	HR %	R	RBI	BB	SO	SB	BA	SA	AB	H	G by POS
1936 **CLE A**	84	349	117	28	6	8	2.3	64	53	16	29	3	.335	.519	0	0	OF-84
1937	53	134	27	4	0	5	3.7	19	13	6	14	1	.201	.343	13	1	OF-38, 3B-1
1938	83	210	55	14	3	2	1.0	32	18	14	14	8	.262	.386	25	5	OF-55
1939	95	323	100	16	6	1	0.3	43	32	19	23	7	.310	.406	17	4	OF-76
1940	135	578	175	35	11	12	2.1	90	59	27	26	9	.303	.464	0	0	OF-135
1941	102	363	105	21	5	3	0.8	59	37	32	20	2	.289	.399	14	5	OF-88
1942	128	473	122	23	7	5	1.1	61	39	35	25	8	.258	.368	13	5	OF-117
1943 **NY A**	77	280	74	8	3	7	2.5	37	28	18	9	4	.264	.389	8	2	OF-68
1946	2	2	1	0	0	0	0.0	0	0	0	0	0	.500	.500	2	1	
1950 **NY N**	52	69	18	3	3	0	0.0	10	11	13	10	0	.261	.391	32	9	OF-15
10 yrs.	811	2781	794	152	44	43	1.5	415	290	180	170	42	.286	.418	124	32	OF-676, 3B-1

WORLD SERIES

	G	AB	H	2B	3B	HR	HR %	R	RBI	BB	SO	SB	BA	SA	AB	H	G by POS
1943 **NY A**	1	1	0	0	0	0	0.0	0	0	0	0	0	.000	.000	1	0	

Art Weaver

WEAVER, ARTHUR COGGSHALL   TR 6'1"
B. Apr. 7, 1879, Wichita, Kans.   D. Mar. 23, 1917, Denver, Colo.

	G	AB	H	2B	3B	HR	HR %	R	RBI	BB	SO	SB	BA	SA	AB	H	G by POS
1902 **STL N**	11	33	6	2	0	0	0.0	2	3	1		0	.182	.242	0	0	C-11
1903 **2 teams**	**STL**	N (16G –	.245)	**PIT**	N	(16G –	.229)										
" total	32	97	23	0	1	0	0.0	12	8	6		1	.237	.258	0	0	C-27, 1B-5
1905 **STL A**	28	92	11	2	1	0	0.0	5	3	1		0	.120	.163	0	0	C-28

	G	AB	H	2B	3B	HR	HR %	R	RBI	BB	SO	SB	BA	SA	Pinch Hit AB	Pinch Hit H	G by POS

Art Weaver continued

	G	AB	H	2B	3B	HR	HR%	R	RBI	BB	SO	SB	BA	SA	AB	H	G by POS
1908 CHI A	15	35	7	1	0	0	0.0	1	1	1		0	.200	.229	0	0	C-15
4 yrs.	86	257	47	5	2	0	0.0	20	15	9		1	.183	.218	0	0	C-81, 1B-5

Buck Weaver

WEAVER, GEORGE DANIEL   BB TR 5'11"   170 lbs.
B. Aug. 18, 1890, Pottstown, Pa.   D. Jan. 31, 1956, Chicago, Ill.

	G	AB	H	2B	3B	HR	HR%	R	RBI	BB	SO	SB	BA	SA	AB	H	G by POS
1912 CHI A	147	523	117	21	8	1	0.2	55	43	9		12	.224	.300	0	0	SS-147
1913	151	533	145	17	8	4	0.8	51	52	15	60	20	.272	.356	0	0	SS-151
1914	136	541	133	20	9	2	0.4	64	28	20	40	14	.246	.327	2	0	SS-134
1915	148	563	151	18	11	3	0.5	83	49	32	58	24	.268	.355	0	0	SS-148
1916	151	582	132	27	6	3	0.5	78	38	30	48	22	.227	.309	0	0	3B-85, SS-66
1917	118	447	127	16	5	3	0.7	64	32	27	29	19	.284	.362	1	0	3B-107, SS-10
1918	112	420	126	12	5	0	0.0	37	29	11	24	20	.300	.352	2	1	SS-98, 3B-11, 2B-1
1919	140	571	169	33	9	3	0.5	89	75	11	21	22	.296	.401	0	0	3B-97, SS-43
1920	151	630	210	35	8	2	0.3	104	75	28	23	19	.333	.424	0	0	3B-126, SS-25
9 yrs.	1254	4810	1310	199	69	21	0.4	625	421	183	303	172	.272	.356	5	1	SS-822, 3B-426, 2B-1
WORLD SERIES																	
1917 CHI A	6	21	7	1	0	0	0.0	3	1	0	2	0	.333	.381	0	0	SS-6
1919	8	34	11	4	1	0	0.0	4	0	0	2	0	.324	.500	0	0	3B-8
2 yrs.	14	55	18	5	1	0	0.0	7	1	0	4	0	.327	.455	0	0	3B-8, SS-6

Farmer Weaver

WEAVER, WILLIAM B.
B. Mar. 23, 1865, Parkersburg, W. Va.   D. Jan. 23, 1943, Akron, Ohio

	G	AB	H	2B	3B	HR	HR%	R	RBI	BB	SO	SB	BA	SA	AB	H	G by POS
1888 LOU AA	26	112	28	1	1	0	0.0	12	8	3		12	.250	.277	0	0	OF-26
1889	124	499	145	17	6	0	0.0	62	60	40	22	21	.291	.349	0	0	OF-123, C-2, 3B-1, 2B-1
1890	130	557	161	27	9	3	0.5	101		29		45	.289	.386	0	0	OF-127, SS-2, 3B-1
1891	135	565	160	25	7	1	0.2	76	55	33	23	30	.283	.358	0	0	OF-132, C-4
1892 LOU N	138	551	140	15	4	0	0.0	58	57	40	17	30	.254	.296	0	0	OF-122, C-15, 1B-10
1893	106	439	128	17	7	2	0.5	79	49	27	12	17	.292	.376	0	0	OF-85, C-21
1894 2 teams	LOU	N (64G –	.221)		PIT	N	(30G –	.348)									
" total	94	359	94	12	4	3	0.8	35	48	13	12	7	.262	.343	1	0	OF-36, C-31, SS-12, 1B-10, 3B-5, 2B-1
7 yrs.	753	3082	856	114	38	9	0.3	423	277	185	86	162	.278	.348	1	0	OF-651, C-73, 1B-20, SS-14, 3B-7, 2B-2

Billy Webb

WEBB, WILLIAM JOSEPH   BR TR 5'10"   161 lbs.
B. June 25, 1895, Chicago, Ill.   D. Jan. 12, 1943, Chicago, Ill.

	G	AB	H	2B	3B	HR	HR%	R	RBI	BB	SO	SB	BA	SA	AB	H	G by POS
1917 PIT N	5	15	3	0	0	0	0.0	1	0	2	3	0	.200	.200	1	0	2B-4, SS-1

Earl Webb

WEBB, WILLIAM EARL   BL TR 6'1"   185 lbs.
B. Sept. 17, 1898, Bon Air, Tenn.   D. May 23, 1965, Jamestown, Tenn.

	G	AB	H	2B	3B	HR	HR%	R	RBI	BB	SO	SB	BA	SA	AB	H	G by POS
1925 NY N	4	3	0	0	0	0	0.0	0	0	1	1	0	.000	.000	2	0	OF-86
1927 CHI N	102	332	100	18	4	14	4.2	58	52	48	31	3	.301	.506	15	3	OF-86
1928	62	140	35	7	3	3	2.1	22	23	14	17	0	.250	.407	24	8	OF-31
1930 BOS A	127	449	145	30	6	16	3.6	61	66	44	56	2	.323	.523	2	0	OF-116
1931	151	589	196	67	3	14	2.4	96	103	70	51	2	.333	.528	0	0	OF-151
1932 2 teams	BOS	A (52G –	.281)		DET	A	(87G –	.287)									
" total	139	530	151	28	9	8	1.5	72	78	64	33	1	.285	.417	1	0	OF-134, 1B-2
1933 2 teams	DET	A (6G –	.273)		CHI	A	(58G –	.290)									
" total	64	118	34	5	0	1	0.8	17	11	19	13	0	.288	.356	30	8	OF-18, 1B-10
7 yrs.	649	2161	661	155	25	56	2.6	326	333	260	202	8	.306	.478	81	21	OF-536, 1B-12

Skeeter Webb

WEBB, JAMES LAVERNE   BR TR 5'9½"   150 lbs.
B. Nov. 4, 1909, Meridian, Miss.

	G	AB	H	2B	3B	HR	HR%	R	RBI	BB	SO	SB	BA	SA	AB	H	G by POS
1932 STL N	1	0	0	0	0	0	–	0	0	0	0	0	–	–	0	0	SS-1
1938 CLE A	20	58	16	2	0	0	0.0	11	2	8	7	1	.276	.310	0	0	SS-13, 3B-3, 2B-2
1939	81	269	71	14	1	2	0.7	28	26	15	24	1	.264	.346	0	0	SS-81
1940 CHI A	84	334	79	11	2	1	0.3	33	29	30	33	3	.237	.290	2	0	2B-74, SS-7, 3B-1
1941	29	84	16	2	0	0	0.0	7	6	3	9	1	.190	.214	3	1	2B-18, SS-5, 3B-3
1942	32	94	16	2	1	0	0.0	5	4	4	13	1	.170	.213	0	0	2B-29
1943	58	213	50	5	2	0	0.0	15	22	6	19	5	.235	.277	3	0	2B-54
1944	139	513	108	19	6	0	0.0	44	30	20	39	7	.211	.271	0	0	SS-135, 2B-5
1945 DET A	118	407	81	12	2	0	0.0	43	21	30	35	8	.199	.238	0	0	SS-104, 2B-11
1946	64	169	37	1	1	0	0.0	12	17	9	18	3	.219	.237	1	0	2B-50, SS-8
1947	50	79	16	3	0	0	0.0	13	6	7	9	3	.203	.241	2	0	2B-30, SS-6
1948 PHI A	23	54	8	2	0	0	0.0	5	3	6	9	0	.148	.185	4	0	2B-9, SS-8
12 yrs.	699	2274	498	73	15	3	0.1	216	166	132	215	33	.219	.268	11	1	SS-368, 2B-282, 3B-7
WORLD SERIES																	
1945 DET A	7	27	5	0	0	0	0.0	4	1	3	1	0	.185	.185	0	0	SS-7

Joe Webber

WEBBER, JOSEPH
B. Hamilton, Ont., Canada   D. Dec. 15, 1921, Hamilton, Ont., Canada

	G	AB	H	2B	3B	HR	HR%	R	RBI	BB	SO	SB	BA	SA	AB	H	G by POS
1884 IND AA	3	8	0	0	0	0	0.0	0		0			.000	.000	0	0	C-3

Harry Weber

WEBER, HARRY
B. Indianapolis, Ind.   Deceased.

	G	AB	H	2B	3B	HR	HR%	R	RBI	BB	SO	SB	BA	SA	AB	H	G by POS
1884 DET N	2	8	0	0	0	0	0.0	0		0	2		.000	.000	0	0	OF-2

Mitch Webster

WEBSTER, MITCHELL DEAN   BB TL 6'1"   170 lbs.
B. May 16, 1959, Larned, Kans.

	G	AB	H	2B	3B	HR	HR%	R	RBI	BB	SO	SB	BA	SA	AB	H	G by POS
1983 TOR A	11	11	2	0	0	0	0.0	2	0	1	1	0	.182	.182	1	0	OF-7, DH-2
1984	26	22	5	2	1	0	0.0	9	4	1	7	0	.227	.409	7	1	OF-10, DH-9, 1B-1
2 yrs.	37	33	7	2	1	0	0.0	11	4	2	8	0	.212	.333	8	1	OF-17, DH-11, 1B-1

	G	AB	H	2B	3B	HR	HR %	R	RBI	BB	SO	SB	BA	SA	Pinch Hit AB	Pinch Hit H	G by POS

Ramon Webster

WEBSTER, RAMON ALBERTO
B. Aug. 31, 1942, Colon, Panama
BL TL 6'　185 lbs.

	G	AB	H	2B	3B	HR	HR %	R	RBI	BB	SO	SB	BA	SA	AB	H	G by POS
1967 KC A	122	360	92	15	4	11	3.1	41	51	32	44	5	.256	.411	26	5	1B-83, OF-15
1968 OAK A	66	196	42	11	1	3	1.5	17	23	12	24	3	.214	.327	11	6	1B-55
1969	64	77	20	0	1	1	1.3	5	13	12	8	0	.260	.325	39	10	1B-13
1970 SD N	95	116	30	3	0	2	1.7	12	11	11	12	1	.259	.336	70	17	1B-15, OF-1
1971 3 teams	SD	N	(10G –	.125)		CHI	N	(16G –	.313)		OAK	A	(7G –	.000)			
" total	33	29	6	2	0	0	0.0	1	0	3	6	0	.207	.276	27	4	1B-2
5 yrs.	380	778	190	31	6	17	2.2	76	98	70	94	9	.244	.365	173	42	1B-168, OF-16

Ray Webster

WEBSTER, RAYMOND GEORGE
B. Nov. 15, 1937, Grass Valley, Calif.
BR TR 6'　175 lbs.

	G	AB	H	2B	3B	HR	HR %	R	RBI	BB	SO	SB	BA	SA	AB	H	G by POS
1959 CLE A	40	74	15	2	1	2	2.7	10	10	5	7	1	.203	.338	8	1	2B-24, 3B-4
1960 BOS A	7	3	0	0	0	0	0.0	1	1	1	0	0	.000	.000	3	0	2B-1
2 yrs.	47	77	15	2	1	2	2.6	11	11	6	7	1	.195	.325	11	1	2B-25, 3B-4

Pete Weckbecker

WECKBECKER, PETER
B. Aug. 30, 1864, Butler, Pa.　D. May 16, 1935, Hampton, Va.
5'7"　150 lbs.

	G	AB	H	2B	3B	HR	HR %	R	RBI	BB	SO	SB	BA	SA	AB	H	G by POS
1889 IND N	1	1	0	0	0	0	0.0	0	2	0	0	0	.000	.000	0	0	C-1
1890 LOU AA	32	101	24	1	0	0	0.0	17		8		7	.238	.248	0	0	C-32
2 yrs.	33	102	24	1	0	0	0.0	17	2	8		7	.235	.245	0	0	C-33

Charlie Weeden

WEEDEN, CHARLES ALBERT
B. Dec. 21, 1882, Northwood, N. H.　D. Jan. 7, 1939, Northwood, N. H.
TR

	G	AB	H	2B	3B	HR	HR %	R	RBI	BB	SO	SB	BA	SA	AB	H	G by POS
1911 BOS N	1	1	0	0	0	0	0.0	0	0	0	0	0	.000	.000	1	0	

Johnny Weekly

WEEKLY, JOHN
B. June 14, 1937, Waterproof, La.　D. Nov. 24, 1974, Walnut Creek, Calif.
BR TR 6'　200 lbs.

	G	AB	H	2B	3B	HR	HR %	R	RBI	BB	SO	SB	BA	SA	AB	H	G by POS
1962 HOU N	13	26	5	1	0	2	7.7	3	2	7	4	0	.192	.462	6	1	OF-7
1963	34	80	18	3	0	3	3.8	4	14	7	14	0	.225	.375	12	3	OF-23
1964	6	15	2	0	0	0	0.0	0	3	1	3	0	.133	.133	1	0	OF-5
3 yrs.	53	121	25	4	0	5	4.1	7	19	15	21	0	.207	.364	19	4	OF-35

Stump Weidman

WEIDMAN, GEORGE E.
B. Feb. 17, 1861, Rochester, N. Y.　D. Mar. 2, 1905, New York, N. Y.
BR TR

	G	AB	H	2B	3B	HR	HR %	R	RBI	BB	SO	SB	BA	SA	AB	H	G by POS
1880 BUF N	23	78	8	1	0	0	0.0	8	3	2	11		.103	.115	0	0	P-17, OF-13
1881 DET N	13	47	12	1	0	0	0.0	8	5	2	2		.255	.277	0	0	P-13
1882	50	193	42	7	1	0	0.0	20	20	2	19		.218	.264	0	0	P-46, OF-6, SS-1
1883	79	313	58	6	1	1	0.3	34		4	38		.185	.220	0	0	P-52, OF-35, 2B-4
1884	81	300	49	6	0	0	0.0	24		13	41		.163	.183	0	0	OF-53, P-26, SS-1, 2B-1
1885	44	153	24	2	1	1	0.7	7	14	8	32		.157	.203	0	0	OF-38, P-37, 2B-1
1886 KC N	51	179	30	2	0	0	0.0	13	7	5	46		.168	.179	0	0	P-51, OF-3
1887 3 teams	DET	N	(21G –	.207)		NY	AA	(14G –	.152)		NY	N	(1G –	.333)			
" total	36	131	25	3	1	0	0.0	17	11	7	3	8	.191	.229	0	0	P-34, OF-5
1888 NY N	2	7	0	0	0	0	0.0	1	1	2	1	0	.000	.000	0	0	P-2
9 yrs.	379	1401	248	28	4	2	0.1	132	61	45	193	8	.177	.207	0	0	P-278, OF-153, 2B-6, SS-2

Ralph Weigel

WEIGEL, RALPH RICHARD (Wig)
B. Oct. 2, 1921, Coldwater, Ohio
BR TR 6'1"　180 lbs.

	G	AB	H	2B	3B	HR	HR %	R	RBI	BB	SO	SB	BA	SA	AB	H	G by POS
1946 CLE A	6	12	2	0	0	0	0.0	0	0	0	2	1	.167	.167	0	0	C-6
1948 CHI A	66	163	38	7	3	0	0.0	8	26	13	18	1	.233	.313	24	6	C-39, OF-2
1949 WAS A	34	60	14	2	0	0	0.0	4	4	8	6	0	.233	.267	12	2	C-21
3 yrs.	106	235	54	9	3	0	0.0	12	30	21	26	2	.230	.294	36	8	C-66, OF-2

Podgie Weihe

WEIHE, JOHN GARIBALDI
B. Nov. 13, 1862, Cincinnati, Ohio　D. Apr. 15, 1914, Cincinnati, Ohio
BR TR 5'11"　175 lbs.

	G	AB	H	2B	3B	HR	HR %	R	RBI	BB	SO	SB	BA	SA	AB	H	G by POS
1883 CIN AA	1	4	1	0	0	0	0.0	1		0			.250	.250	0	0	OF-1
1884 IND AA	63	256	65	13	2	4	1.6	29		9			.254	.367	0	0	OF-58, 2B-4, 1B-3
2 yrs.	64	260	66	13	2	4	1.5	30		9			.254	.365	0	0	OF-59, 2B-4, 1B-3

Elmer Weingartner

WEINGARTNER, ELMER WILLIAM (Dutch)
B. Aug. 13, 1918, Cleveland, Ohio
BR TR 5'11"　178 lbs.

	G	AB	H	2B	3B	HR	HR %	R	RBI	BB	SO	SB	BA	SA	AB	H	G by POS
1945 CLE A	20	39	9	1	0	0	0.0	5	1	4	11	0	.231	.256	0	0	SS-20

Phil Weintraub

WEINTRAUB, PHILIP
B. Oct. 12, 1907, Chicago, Ill.
BL TL 6'1"　195 lbs.

	G	AB	H	2B	3B	HR	HR %	R	RBI	BB	SO	SB	BA	SA	AB	H	G by POS
1933 NY N	8	15	3	0	0	1	6.7	3	1	3	2	0	.200	.400	1	1	OF-6
1934	31	74	26	2	0	0	0.0	13	15	15	10	0	.351	.378	10	1	OF-20
1935	64	112	27	3	3	1	0.9	18	6	17	13	0	.241	.348	29	5	1B-19, OF-7
1937 2 teams	CIN	N	(49G –	.271)		NY	N	(6G –	.333)								
" total	55	186	51	12	4	3	1.6	30	21	20	26	1	.274	.430	6	1	OF-48
1938 PHI N	100	351	109	23	2	4	1.1	51	45	64	43	1	.311	.422	2	0	1B-98
1944 NY N	104	361	114	18	9	13	3.6	55	77	59	59	0	.316	.524	5	2	1B-99
1945	82	283	77	9	1	10	3.5	45	42	54	29	2	.272	.417	4	1	1B-77
7 yrs.	444	1382	407	67	19	32	2.3	215	207	232	182	4	.295	.440	57	11	1B-293, OF-81

Al Weis

WEIS, ALBERT JOHN
B. Apr. 2, 1938, Franklin Square, N. Y.
BB TR 6'　160 lbs.
BR 1969

	G	AB	H	2B	3B	HR	HR %	R	RBI	BB	SO	SB	BA	SA	AB	H	G by POS
1962 CHI A	7	12	1	0	0	0	0.0	2	0	2	3	1	.083	.083	0	0	SS-4, 3B-1, 2B-1
1963	99	210	57	9	0	0	0.0	41	18	18	37	15	.271	.314	9	2	2B-48, SS-27, 3B-1
1964	133	328	81	4	4	2	0.6	36	23	22	41	22	.247	.302	6	1	2B-116, SS-9, OF-2
1965	103	135	40	4	3	1	0.7	29	12	12	22	4	.296	.393	6	2	2B-74, SS-7, OF-2, 3B-2
1966	129	187	29	4	1	0	0.0	20	9	17	50	3	.155	.176	0	0	2B-96, SS-18
1967	50	53	13	2	0	0	0.0	9	4	1	7	3	.245	.283	0	0	2B-32, SS-13
1968 NY N	90	274	47	6	0	1	0.4	15	14	21	63	3	.172	.204	3	0	SS-59, 2B-29, 3B-2
1969	103	247	53	9	2	2	0.8	20	23	15	51	3	.215	.291	3	0	SS-52, 2B-43, 3B-1

	G	AB	H	2B	3B	HR	HR %	R	RBI	BB	SO	SB	BA	SA	Pinch Hit AB	Pinch Hit H	G by POS

Al Weis continued

	G	AB	H	2B	3B	HR	HR%	R	RBI	BB	SO	SB	BA	SA	AB	H	G by POS
1970	75	121	25	7	1	1	0.8	20	11	7	21	1	.207	.306	2	0	2B-44, SS-15
1971	11	11	0	0	0	0	0.0	3	1	2	4	0	.000	.000	4	0	2B-5, 3B-2
10 yrs.	800	1578	346	45	11	7	0.4	195	115	117	299	55	.219	.275	33	5	2B-488, SS-204, 3B-9, OF-4

LEAGUE CHAMPIONSHIP SERIES

| 1969 NY N | 3 | 1 | 0 | 0 | 0 | 0 | 0.0 | 0 | 0 | 0 | 0 | 0 | .000 | .000 | 0 | 0 | 2B-3 |

WORLD SERIES

| 1969 NY N | 5 | 11 | 5 | 0 | 0 | 1 | 9.1 | 1 | 3 | 4 | 2 | 0 | .455 | .727 | 0 | 0 | 2B-5 |

Butch Weis

WEIS, ARTHUR JOHN   BL TL 5'11"   180 lbs.
B. Mar. 2, 1903, St. Louis, Mo.

	G	AB	H	2B	3B	HR	HR%	R	RBI	BB	SO	SB	BA	SA	AB	H	G by POS
1922 CHI N	2	2	1	0	0	0	0.0	2	0	0	0	0	.500	.500	2	1	
1923	22	26	6	1	0	0	0.0	2	2	5	8	0	.231	.269	13	3	OF-6
1924	39	133	37	8	1	0	0.0	19	23	15	14	4	.278	.353	1	1	OF-36
1925	67	180	48	5	3	2	1.1	16	25	23	22	2	.267	.361	20	3	OF-46
4 yrs.	130	341	92	14	4	2	0.6	39	50	43	44	6	.270	.352	36	8	OF-88

Bud Weiser

WEISER, HARRY BUDSON   BR TR 5'11"   165 lbs.
B. Jan. 8, 1891, Shamokin, Pa.   D. July 31, 1961, Shamokin, Pa.

	G	AB	H	2B	3B	HR	HR%	R	RBI	BB	SO	SB	BA	SA	AB	H	G by POS
1915 PHI N	37	64	9	2	0	0	0.0	6	8	7	12	1	.141	.172	8	3	OF-20
1916	4	10	3	1	0	0	0.0	1	1	0	3	1	.300	.400	0	0	OF-4
2 yrs.	41	74	12	3	0	0	0.0	7	9	7	15	2	.162	.203	8	3	OF-24

Gary Weiss

WEISS, GARY LEE   BL TR 5'10"   170 lbs.
B. Dec. 27, 1955, Brenham, Tex.

	G	AB	H	2B	3B	HR	HR%	R	RBI	BB	SO	SB	BA	SA	AB	H	G by POS
1980 LA N	8	0	0	0	0	0	–	2	0	0	0	0	–	–	0	0	
1981	14	19	2	0	0	0	0.0	2	1	1	4	0	.105	.105	1	0	SS-13
2 yrs.	22	19	2	0	0	0	0.0	4	1	1	4	0	.105	.105	1	0	SS-13

Joe Weiss

WEISS, JOSEPH HAROLD   BR TR 6'   165 lbs.
B. Jan. 27, 1894, Chicago, Ill.   D. July 7, 1967, Cedar Rapids, Iowa

	G	AB	H	2B	3B	HR	HR%	R	RBI	BB	SO	SB	BA	SA	AB	H	G by POS
1915 CHI F	29	85	19	1	2	0	0.0	6	11	3		0	.224	.282	0	0	1B-29

Johnny Welaj

WELAJ, JOHN LUDWIG   BR TR 6'   164 lbs.
B. May 27, 1914, Moss Creek, Pa.

	G	AB	H	2B	3B	HR	HR%	R	RBI	BB	SO	SB	BA	SA	AB	H	G by POS
1939 WAS A	63	201	55	11	2	1	0.5	23	33	13	20	13	.274	.363	7	2	OF-55
1940	88	215	55	9	0	3	1.4	31	21	19	20	8	.256	.340	20	7	OF-53
1941	49	96	20	4	0	0	0.0	16	5	6	16	3	.208	.250	22	7	OF-19
1943 PHI A	93	281	68	16	1	0	0.0	45	15	15	17	12	.242	.306	10	1	OF-72
4 yrs.	293	793	198	40	3	4	0.5	115	74	53	73	36	.250	.323	59	17	OF-199

Curt Welch

WELCH, CURTIS BENTON   BR TR 5'10"   175 lbs.
B. Feb. 11, 1862, East Liverpool, Ohio   D. Aug. 29, 1896, East Liverpool, Ohio

	G	AB	H	2B	3B	HR	HR%	R	RBI	BB	SO	SB	BA	SA	AB	H	G by POS
1884 TOL AA	109	425	95	24	5	0	0.0	61		10			.224	.304	0	0	OF-106, 2B-2, C-2, 1B-1, P-1
1885 STL AA	112	432	117	18	8	2	0.5	84		23			.271	.363	0	0	OF-112
1886	138	563	158	31	13	2	0.4	114		29			.281	.393	0	0	OF-138, 2B-2
1887	131	544	151	32	7	3	0.6	98		25		89	.278	.379	0	0	OF-123, 2B-8, 1B-1
1888 PHI AA	136	549	155	22	8	1	0.2	125	61	33		95	.282	.357	0	0	OF-135, 2B-3
1889	125	516	140	39	6	0	0.0	134	39	67	30	66	.271	.370	0	0	OF-125
1890 2 teams	PHI	AA (103G – .268)		B-B	AA (19G – .132)												
" total	122	464	115	25	4	2	0.4	116		58		72	.248	.332	0	0	OF-120, 1B-2, P-1
1891 BAL AA	132	514	138	22	10	3	0.6	122	55	77	42	50	.268	.368	0	0	OF-113, 2B-21, SS-2
1892 2 teams	BAL	N (63G – .236)		CIN	N (25G – .202)												
" total	88	331	75	1	5	2	0.6	56	29	43	17	21	.227	.278	0	0	OF-88
1893 LOU N	14	47	8	1	0	0	0.0	5	2	16	4	1	.170	.191	0	0	OF-14
10 yrs.	1107	4385	1152	215	66	15	0.3	915	185	381	93	394	.263	.352	0	0	OF-1074, 2B-36, 1B-4, SS-2, C-2, P-2

Frank Welch

WELCH, FRANK TIGUER (Bugger)   BR TR 5'9"   175 lbs.
B. Aug. 10, 1897, Birmingham, Ala.   D. July 25, 1957, Birmingham, Ala.

	G	AB	H	2B	3B	HR	HR%	R	RBI	BB	SO	SB	BA	SA	AB	H	G by POS
1919 PHI A	15	54	9	1	1	2	3.7	5	7	7	10	0	.167	.333	0	0	OF-15
1920	100	360	93	17	5	4	1.1	43	40	26	41	2	.258	.367	3	0	OF-97
1921	115	403	115	18	6	7	1.7	48	45	34	43	6	.285	.412	10	4	OF-104
1922	114	375	97	17	3	11	2.9	43	49	40	40	3	.259	.408	9	4	OF-104
1923	125	421	125	19	9	4	1.0	56	55	48	40	1	.297	.413	7	0	OF-117
1924	94	293	85	13	2	5	1.7	47	31	35	27	2	.290	.399	20	7	OF-74
1925	85	202	56	5	4	4	2.0	40	41	29	14	2	.277	.401	24	4	OF-57
1926	75	174	49	8	1	4	2.3	26	23	26	9	2	.282	.408	19	3	OF-49
1927 BOS A	15	28	5	2	0	0	0.0	2	4	5	1	0	.179	.250	8	2	OF-6
9 yrs.	738	2310	634	100	31	41	1.8	310	295	250	225	18	.274	.398	100	24	OF-623

Herb Welch

WELCH, HERBERT M. (Dutch)   BL TR 5'6"   154 lbs.
B. Oct. 19, 1898, RoEllen, Tenn.   D. Apr. 13, 1967, Memphis, Tenn.

	G	AB	H	2B	3B	HR	HR%	R	RBI	BB	SO	SB	BA	SA	AB	H	G by POS
1925 BOS A	13	38	11	0	1	0	0.0	2	2	2	6	0	.289	.342	0	0	SS-13

Mickey Welch

WELCH, MICHAEL FRANCIS (Smiling Mickey)   BR TR 5'8"   160 lbs.
B. July 4, 1859, Brooklyn, N. Y.   D. July 30, 1941, Nashua, N. H.
Hall of Fame 1973.

	G	AB	H	2B	3B	HR	HR%	R	RBI	BB	SO	SB	BA	SA	AB	H	G by POS
1880 TRO N	66	251	72	20	3	0	0.0	25		5	24		.287	.390	0	0	P-65, OF-2
1881	40	148	30	10	0	0	0.0	12	11	1	16		.203	.270	0	0	P-40
1882	38	151	37	6	0	1	0.7	26	17	5	16		.245	.305	0	0	P-33, OF-8
1883 NY N	84	320	75	12	5	3	0.9	42		10	38		.234	.331	0	0	P-54, OF-38
1884	71	249	60	14	3	3	1.2	47		16	49		.241	.357	0	0	P-65, OF-7
1885	56	199	41	8	0	2	1.0	28		14	39		.206	.276	0	0	P-56

	G	AB	H	2B	3B	HR	HR %	R	RBI	BB	SO	SB	BA	SA	Pinch Hit AB	Pinch Hit H	G by POS

Mickey Welch continued

	G	AB	H	2B	3B	HR	HR %	R	RBI	BB	SO	SB	BA	SA	AB	H	G by POS
1886	59	213	46	4	2	0	0.0	17	18	7	47		.216	.254	0	0	P-59, OF-3
1887	40	148	36	4	2	2	1.4	16	15	6	1	2	.243	.338	0	0	P-40, OF-1
1888	47	169	32	5	0	2	1.2	16	10	1	33	4	.189	.254	0	0	P-47
1889	45	156	30	5	1	0	0.0	20	12	5	27	0	.192	.237	0	0	P-45
1890	37	123	22	4	0	0	0.0	15	10	9	25	1	.179	.211	0	0	P-37
1891	22	71	10	0	0	0	0.0	4	4	3	13	0	.141	.141	0	0	P-22
1892	1	3	1	0	0	0	0.0	0	0	0	1	0	.333	.333	0	0	P-1
13 yrs.	606	2201	492	92	16	13	0.6	268	96	82	329	7	.224	.298	0	0	P-564, OF-59

Milt Welch

WELCH, MILTON EDWARD B. July 26, 1924, Farmersville, Ill. BR TR 5'10" 175 lbs.

	G	AB	H	2B	3B	HR	HR %	R	RBI	BB	SO	SB	BA	SA	AB	H	G by POS
1945 DET A	1	2	0	0	0	0	0.0	0	0	0	1	0	.000	.000	0	0	C-1

Harry Welchonce

WELCHONCE, HARRY MONROE B. Nov. 20, 1883, North Point, Pa. D. Feb. 26, 1977, Arcadia, Calif. BL TR 6' 170 lbs.

	G	AB	H	2B	3B	HR	HR %	R	RBI	BB	SO	SB	BA	SA	AB	H	G by POS
1911 PHI N	26	66	14	4	0	0	0.0	9	6	7	8	0	.212	.273	9	3	OF-17

Mike Welday

WELDAY, LYNDON EARL B. Dec. 19, 1879, Conway, Iowa D. May 28, 1942, Leavenworth, Kans. BL TL

	G	AB	H	2B	3B	HR	HR %	R	RBI	BB	SO	SB	BA	SA	AB	H	G by POS
1907 CHI A	24	35	8	1	1	0	0.0	2	0	6		0	.229	.314	6	1	OF-15
1909	29	74	14	0	0	0	0.0	3	5	4		2	.189	.189	8	2	OF-20
2 yrs.	53	109	22	1	1	0	0.0	5	5	10		2	.202	.229	14	3	OF-35

Ollie Welf

WELF, OLIVER HENRY B. Jan. 17, 1889, Cleveland, Ohio D. June 15, 1967, Cleveland, Ohio BR TL 5'9" 160 lbs.

	G	AB	H	2B	3B	HR	HR %	R	RBI	BB	SO	SB	BA	SA	AB	H	G by POS
1916 CLE A	1	0	0	0	0	0	–	0	0	0	0	0	–	–	0	0	

Bob Wellman

WELLMAN, ROBERT JOSEPH B. July 15, 1925, Cincinnati, Ohio BR TR 6'4" 210 lbs.

	G	AB	H	2B	3B	HR	HR %	R	RBI	BB	SO	SB	BA	SA	AB	H	G by POS
1948 PHI A	4	10	2	0	1	0	0.0	1	0	3	2	0	.200	.400	1	0	1B-2, OF-1
1950	11	15	5	0	0	1	6.7	1	1	0	3	0	.333	.533	8	2	OF-2
2 yrs.	15	25	7	0	1	1	4.0	2	1	3	5	0	.280	.480	9	2	OF-3, 1B-2

Brad Wellman

WELLMAN, BRAD EUGENE B. Aug. 17, 1959, Lodi, Calif. BR TR 6' 165 lbs.

	G	AB	H	2B	3B	HR	HR %	R	RBI	BB	SO	SB	BA	SA	AB	H	G by POS
1982 SF N	6	4	1	0	0	0	0.0	1	0	0	1	0	.250	.250	2	0	2B-2
1983	82	182	39	3	0	1	0.5	15	16	22	39	5	.214	.247	4	0	2B-74, SS-2
1984	93	265	60	9	1	2	0.8	23	25	19	41	10	.226	.291	6	3	2B-54, SS-33, 3B-10
3 yrs.	181	451	100	12	1	3	0.7	39	41	41	81	15	.222	.273	12	3	2B-130, SS-35, 3B-10

Greg Wells

WELLS, GREGORY DeWAYNE B. Apr. 25, 1954, Washington County, Ala. BR TR 6'5" 218 lbs.

	G	AB	H	2B	3B	HR	HR %	R	RBI	BB	SO	SB	BA	SA	AB	H	G by POS
1981 TOR A	32	73	18	5	0	0	0.0	7	5	5	12	0	.247	.315	8	3	1B-22, DH-3
1982 MIN A	15	54	11	1	2	0	0.0	5	3	1	8	0	.204	.296	1	1	1B-10, DH-5
2 yrs.	47	127	29	6	2	0	0.0	12	8	6	20	0	.228	.307	9	4	1B-32, DH-8

Jake Wells

WELLS, JACOB B. Aug. 9, 1863, Memphis, Tenn. D. Mar. 16, 1927, Hendersonville, N. C. BR TR

	G	AB	H	2B	3B	HR	HR %	R	RBI	BB	SO	SB	BA	SA	AB	H	G by POS
1888 DET N	16	57	9	1	0	0	0.0	5	2	0	5	0	.158	.175	0	0	C-16
1890 STL AA	30	105	25	3	0	0	0.0	17		10		1	.238	.267	0	0	C-28, OF-3
2 yrs.	46	162	34	4	0	0	0.0	22	2	10	5	1	.210	.235	0	0	C-44, OF-3

Leo Wells

WELLS, LEO DONALD B. July 18, 1917, Kansas City, Kans. BR TR 5'9" 170 lbs.

	G	AB	H	2B	3B	HR	HR %	R	RBI	BB	SO	SB	BA	SA	AB	H	G by POS
1942 CHI A	35	62	12	2	0	1	1.6	8	4	4	5	1	.194	.274	13	5	SS-12, 3B-6
1946	45	127	24	4	1	1	0.8	11	11	12	34	3	.189	.260	2	0	3B-38, SS-2
2 yrs.	80	189	36	6	1	2	1.1	19	15	16	39	4	.190	.265	15	5	3B-44, SS-14

Jimmy Welsh

WELSH, JAMES DANIEL B. Oct. 9, 1902, Oakland, Calif. D. Oct. 20, 1970, Oakdale, Calif. BL TR 6'1" 174 lbs.

	G	AB	H	2B	3B	HR	HR %	R	RBI	BB	SO	SB	BA	SA	AB	H	G by POS
1925 BOS N	122	484	151	25	8	7	1.4	69	63	20	24	7	.312	.440	3	0	OF-116, 2B-3
1926	134	490	136	18	11	3	0.6	69	57	33	28	6	.278	.378	4	0	OF-129
1927	131	497	143	26	7	9	1.8	72	54	23	27	11	.288	.423	1	0	OF-129, 1B-1
1928 NY N	124	476	146	22	5	9	1.9	77	54	29	30	4	.307	.431	3	1	OF-117
1929 2 teams	NY	N (38G – .248)						BOS	N (53G – .290)								
" total	91	315	86	15	7	4	1.3	49	24	22	12	4	.273	.403	3	0	OF-86
1930 BOS N	113	422	116	21	9	3	0.7	51	36	29	23	5	.275	.389	2	1	OF-110
6 yrs.	715	2684	778	127	47	35	1.3	387	288	156	144	37	.290	.411	16	2	OF-687, 2B-3, 1B-1

Tub Welsh

WELSH, JAMES J. B. July 3, 1866, St. Louis, Mo. Deceased.

	G	AB	H	2B	3B	HR	HR %	R	RBI	BB	SO	SB	BA	SA	AB	H	G by POS
1890 TOL AA	35	108	31	3	1	1	0.9	15		8		7	.287	.361	0	0	C-25, 1B-10
1895 LOU N	47	153	37	4	1	1	0.7	18	8	13	7	2	.242	.301	0	0	C-28, 1B-20
2 yrs.	82	261	68	7	2	2	0.8	33	7	21	7	9	.261	.326	0	0	C-53, 1B-30

Lew Wendell

WENDELL, LEWIS CHARLES B. Mar. 22, 1892, New York, N. Y. D. July 11, 1953, Bronx, N. Y. BR TR 5'11" 178 lbs.

	G	AB	H	2B	3B	HR	HR %	R	RBI	BB	SO	SB	BA	SA	AB	H	G by POS
1915 NY N	20	36	8	1	1	0	0.0	0	5	2	7	0	.222	.306	3	0	C-20
1916	2	2	0	0	0	0	0.0	0	0	0	2	0	.000	.000	2	0	
1924 PHI N	21	32	8	1	0	0	0.0	3	2	3	5	0	.250	.281	3	1	C-17
1925	18	26	2	0	0	0	0.0	0	3	1	3	0	.077	.077	8	0	C-9
1926	1	4	0	0	0	0	0.0	0	0	0	0	0	.000	.000	0	0	C-1
5 yrs.	62	100	18	2	1	0	0.0	3	10	6	17	0	.180	.220	16	1	C-47

	G	AB	H	2B	3B	HR	HR %	R	RBI	BB	SO	SB	BA	SA	Pinch Hit AB	H	G by POS

Jack Wentz

WENTZ, JOHN GEORGE
Born John George Wernz.
B. Mar. 4, 1863, Louisville, Ky.   D. Sept. 14, 1907, Louisville, Ky.
BR TR 5'10½" 175 lbs.

	G	AB	H	2B	3B	HR	HR %	R	RBI	BB	SO	SB	BA	SA	PH AB	H	G by POS
1891 LOU AA	1	4	1	0	0	0	0.0	0	0	0	0	0	.250	.250	0	0	2B-1

Stan Wentzel

WENTZEL, STANLEY AARON
B. Jan. 13, 1917, Lorane, Pa.
BR TR 6'1" 200 lbs.

1945 BOS N	4	19	4	0	1	0	0.0	1	0	0	3	1	.211	.316	0	0	OF-4

Julie Wera

WERA, JULIAN VALENTINE
B. Feb. 9, 1902, Winona, Minn.   D. Dec. 12, 1975, Rochester, Minn.
BR TR 5'8" 164 lbs.

1927 NY A	38	42	10	3	0	1	2.4	7	8	1	5	0	.238	.381	4	0	3B-19
1929	5	12	5	0	0	0	0.0	1	2	1	1	0	.417	.417	1	0	3B-4
2 yrs.	43	54	15	3	0	1	1.9	8	10	2	6	0	.278	.389	5	0	3B-23

Bill Werber

WERBER, WILLIAM MURRAY
B. June 20, 1908, Berwyn, Md.
BR TR 5'10" 170 lbs.

1930 NY A	4	14	4	0	0	0	0.0	5	2	3	1	0	.286	.286	0	0	SS-3, 3B-1
1933 2 teams		NY	A (3G – .000)		BOS	A (108G – .259)											
" total	111	427	110	30	6	3	0.7	64	39	33	39	15	.258	.377	4	1	SS-71, 3B-39, 2B-2
1934 BOS A	152	623	200	41	10	11	1.8	129	67	77	37	40	.321	.472	0	0	3B-130, SS-22
1935	124	462	118	30	3	14	3.0	84	61	69	41	29	.255	.424	1	0	3B-123
1936	145	535	147	29	6	10	1.9	89	67	89	37	23	.275	.407	0	0	3B-101, OF-45, 2B-1
1937 PHI A	128	493	144	31	4	7	1.4	85	70	74	39	35	.292	.414	2	0	3B-125, OF-3
1938	134	499	129	22	7	11	2.2	92	69	93	37	19	.259	.397	0	0	3B-134
1939 CIN N	147	599	173	35	5	5	0.8	115	57	91	46	15	.289	.389	0	0	3B-147
1940	143	584	162	35	5	12	2.1	105	48	68	40	16	.277	.416	0	0	3B-143
1941	109	418	100	9	2	4	1.0	56	46	53	24	14	.239	.299	1	0	3B-107
1942 NY N	98	370	76	9	2	1	0.3	51	13	51	22	9	.205	.249	3	1	3B-93
11 yrs.	1295	5024	1363	271	50	78	1.6	875	539	701	363	215	.271	.392	11	2	3B-1143, SS-96, OF-48, 2B-3

WORLD SERIES

1939 CIN N	4	16	4	0	0	0	0.0	1	2	2	0	0	.250	.250	0	0	3B-4
1940	7	27	10	4	0	0	0.0	5	2	4	2	0	.370	.519	0	0	3B-7
2 yrs.	11	43	14	4	0	0	0.0	6	4	6	2	0	.326	.419	0	0	3B-11

Perry Werden

WERDEN, PERCIVAL WHERRITT (Moose)
B. July 21, 1865, St. Louis, Mo.   D. Jan. 9, 1934, Minneapolis, Minn.
BR TR 6'2" 220 lbs.

1884 STL U	18	76	18	2	0	0	0.0	7		2		0	.237	.263	0	0	P-16, OF-6
1888 WAS N	3	10	3	0	0	0	0.0	0	2	1	4	0	.300	.300	0	0	OF-3
1890 TOL AA	128	498	147	22	20	6	1.2	113		78		59	.295	.456	0	0	1B-124, OF-5
1891 BAL AA	139	552	160	20	18	6	1.1	102	104	52	59	46	.290	.424	0	0	1B-139
1892 STL N	149	598	154	22	6	8	1.3	73	84	59	52	20	.258	.355	0	0	1B-149
1893	125	500	138	22	33	1	0.2	73	94	49	25	11	.276	.458	0	0	1B-124, OF-1
1897 LOU N	131	506	153	21	14	5	1.0	76	83	40		15	.302	.429	0	0	1B-131
7 yrs.	693	2740	773	109	91	26	0.9	444	366	281	140	150	.282	.417	0	0	1B-667, P-16, OF-15

Johnny Werhas

WERHAS, JOHN CHARLES (Peaches)
B. Feb. 7, 1938, Highland Park, Mich.
BR TR 6'2" 200 lbs.

1964 LA N	29	83	16	2	1	0	0.0	6	8	13	12	0	.193	.241	1	0	3B-28
1965	4	3	0	0	0	0	0.0	1	0	1	2	0	.000	.000	2	0	1B-1
1967 2 teams		LA	N (7G – .143)		CAL	A (49G – .160)											
" total	56	82	13	1	1	2	2.4	8	6	10	25	0	.159	.268	23	3	3B-30, 1B-4, OF-1
3 yrs.	89	168	29	3	2	2	1.2	15	14	24	39	0	.173	.250	26	3	3B-58, 1B-5, OF-1

Don Werner

WERNER, DONALD PAUL
B. Mar. 8, 1953, Appleton, Wis.
BR TR 6'1" 180 lbs.

1975 CIN N	7	8	1	0	0	0	0.0	0	0	0	0	0	.125	.125	0	0	C-7
1976	3	4	2	1	0	0	0.0	0	1	1	1	0	.500	.750	0	0	C-3
1977	10	23	4	0	0	2	8.7	3	4	2	3	0	.174	.435	0	0	C-10
1978	50	113	17	2	1	0	0.0	7	11	14	30	1	.150	.186	1	1	C-49
1980	24	64	11	2	0	0	0.0	2	5	7	10	1	.172	.203	1	1	C-24
1981 TEX A	2	8	2	0	0	0	0.0	1	0	0	2	0	.250	.250	0	0	DH-2
1982	22	59	12	2	0	0	0.0	4	3	3	7	0	.203	.237	0	0	C-22
7 yrs.	118	279	49	7	1	2	0.7	17	24	27	53	2	.176	.229	2	2	C-115, DH-2

Joe Werrick

WERRICK, JOSEPH ABRAHAM
B. Oct. 25, 1858, St. Paul, Minn.   D. May 10, 1943, St. Peter, Minn.
TR 5'9" 151 lbs.

1884 STP U	9	27	2	0	0	0	0.0	3		1			.074	.074	0	0	SS-9
1886 LOU AA	136	561	140	20	14	3	0.5	75		33			.250	.351	0	0	3B-136
1887	136	533	152	21	13	7	1.3	90		38		49	.285	.413	0	0	3B-136
1888	111	413	89	12	7	0	0.0	49	51	30		15	.215	.278	0	0	3B-89, SS-11, 2B-8, OF-3
4 yrs.	392	1534	383	53	34	10	0.7	217	50	102		64	.250	.348	0	0	3B-361, SS-20, 2B-8, OF-3

Don Wert

WERT, DONALD RALPH
B. July 29, 1938, Strasburg, Pa.
BR TR 5'10" 162 lbs.

1963 DET A	78	251	65	6	2	7	2.8	31	25	24	51	3	.259	.382	4	0	3B-47, 2B-21, SS-8
1964	148	525	135	18	5	9	1.7	63	55	50	74	3	.257	.362	3	0	3B-142, SS-4
1965	162	609	159	22	2	12	2.0	81	54	73	71	5	.261	.363	0	0	3B-161, SS-3, 2B-1
1966	150	559	150	20	2	11	2.0	56	70	64	69	6	.268	.370	0	0	3B-150
1967	142	534	137	23	2	6	1.1	60	40	44	59	1	.257	.341	2	0	3B-140, SS-1
1968	150	536	107	15	1	12	2.2	44	37	37	79	0	.200	.299	1	1	3B-150, SS-2
1969	132	423	95	11	1	14	3.3	46	50	49	60	3	.225	.355	2	0	3B-129
1970	128	363	79	13	0	6	1.7	34	33	44	56	1	.218	.303	15	2	3B-117, 2B-2

	G	AB	H	2B	3B	HR	HR %	R	RBI	BB	SO	SB	BA	SA	Pinch Hit AB	Pinch Hit H	G by POS

Don Wert continued

	G	AB	H	2B	3B	HR	HR%	R	RBI	BB	SO	SB	BA	SA	AB	H	G by POS
1971 WAS A	20	40	2	1	0	0	0.0	2	2	4	10	0	.050	.075	7	0	SS-7, 3B-7, 2B-1
9 yrs.	1110	3840	929	129	15	77	2.0	417	366	389	529	22	.242	.343	34	3	3B-1043, SS-25, 2B-25
WORLD SERIES																	
1968 DET A	6	17	2	0	0	0	0.0	1	2	6	5	0	.118	.118	0	0	3B-6

Dennis Werth

WERTH, DENNIS DEAN BR TR 6'1" 200 lbs.
B. Dec. 29, 1952, Lincoln, Ill.

	G	AB	H	2B	3B	HR	HR%	R	RBI	BB	SO	SB	BA	SA	AB	H	G by POS
1979 NY A	3	4	1	0	0	0	0.0	1	0	0	0	0	.250	.250	2	0	1B-1
1980	39	65	20	3	0	3	4.6	15	12	12	19	0	.308	.492	9	1	1B-12, DH-8, OF-8, 3B-1, C-1
1981	34	55	6	1	0	0	0.0	7	1	12	12	1	.109	.127	5	0	1B-19, OF-8, DH-4, C-3
1982 KC A	41	15	2	0	0	0	0.0	5	2	4	2	0	.133	.133	1	0	1B-35, C-2
4 yrs.	117	139	29	4	0	3	2.2	28	15	28	33	1	.209	.302	17	1	1B-67, OF-16, DH-12, C-6, 3B-1

Del Wertz

WERTZ, DWIGHT LEWIS BR TR 5'6½" 155 lbs.
B. 1887, Ohio

	G	AB	H	2B	3B	HR	HR%	R	RBI	BB	SO	SB	BA	SA	AB	H	G by POS
1914 BUF F	3	0	0	0	0	0	–	1	0	0		0	–	–	0	0	SS-1

Vic Wertz

WERTZ, VICTOR WOODROW BL TR 6' 186 lbs.
B. Feb. 9, 1925, York, Pa.   D. July 7, 1983, Detroit, Mich.

	G	AB	H	2B	3B	HR	HR%	R	RBI	BB	SO	SB	BA	SA	AB	H	G by POS
1947 DET A	102	333	96	22	4	6	1.8	60	44	47	66	2	.288	.432	18	5	OF-82
1948	119	391	97	19	9	7	1.8	49	67	48	70	0	.248	.396	19	4	OF-98
1949	155	608	185	26	6	20	3.3	96	133	80	61	2	.304	.465	0	0	OF-155
1950	149	559	172	37	4	27	4.8	99	123	91	55	0	.308	.533	4	2	OF-145
1951	138	501	143	24	4	27	5.4	86	94	78	61	0	.285	.511	6	0	OF-131
1952 2 teams		**DET**	**A**	(85G –	.246)			**STL**	**A**	(37G –	.346)						
" total	122	415	115	20	3	23	5.5	68	70	69	64	1	.277	.506	8	2	OF-115
1953 STL A	128	440	118	18	6	19	4.3	61	70	72	44	1	.268	.466	8	2	OF-121
1954 2 teams		**BAL**	**A**	(29G –	.202)			**CLE**	**A**	(94G –	.275)						
" total	123	389	100	15	2	15	3.9	38	61	45	57	0	.257	.422	7	1	1B-83, OF-32
1955 CLE A	74	257	65	11	2	14	5.4	30	55	32	33	1	.253	.475	5	2	1B-63, OF-9
1956	136	481	127	22	0	32	6.7	65	106	75	87	0	.264	.509	1	0	1B-133
1957	144	515	145	21	0	28	5.4	84	105	78	87	2	.282	.485	4	0	1B-139
1958	25	43	12	1	0	3	7.0	5	12	5	7	0	.279	.512	16	3	1B-8
1959 BOS A	94	247	68	13	0	7	2.8	38	49	22	32	0	.275	.413	33	7	1B-64
1960	131	443	125	22	0	19	4.3	45	103	37	54	0	.282	.460	18	10	1B-117
1961 2 teams		**BOS**	**A**	(99G –	.262)			**DET**	**A**	(8G –	.167)						
" total	107	323	84	16	2	11	3.4	33	61	38	44	0	.260	.424	18	3	1B-86
1962 DET A	74	105	34	2	0	5	4.8	7	18	5	13	0	.324	.486	53	17	1B-16
1963 2 teams		**DET**	**A**	(6G –	.000)			**MIN**	**A**	(35G –	.136)						
" total	41	49	6	0	0	3	6.1	3	7	6	6	0	.122	.306	30	4	1B-6
17 yrs.	1862	6099	1692	289	42	266	4.4	867	1178	828	841	9	.277	.469	248	62	OF-888, 1B-715
WORLD SERIES																	
1954 CLE A	4	16	8	2	1	1	6.3	2	3	2	2	0	.500	.938	0	0	1B-4

Jim Wessinger

WESSINGER, JAMES MICHAEL BR TR 5'11" 170 lbs.
B. Sept. 25, 1955, Utica, N. Y.

	G	AB	H	2B	3B	HR	HR%	R	RBI	BB	SO	SB	BA	SA	AB	H	G by POS
1979 ATL N	10	7	0	0	0	0	0.0	2	0	1	4	0	.000	.000	2	0	2B-2

Al West

Playing record listed under Al Hubbard

Billy West

WEST, WILLIAM NELSON BR TR
B. Aug. 21, 1840, Philadelphia, Pa.   D. Aug. 18, 1891, Philadelphia, Pa.

	G	AB	H	2B	3B	HR	HR%	R	RBI	BB	SO	SB	BA	SA	AB	H	G by POS
1876 NY N	1	4	0	0	0	0	0.0	0		0	0		.000	.000	0	0	2B-1

Buck West

WEST, MILTON DOUGLAS BR TR 5'10" 200 lbs.
B. Aug. 29, 1860, Spring Mill, Ohio   D. Jan. 12, 1929, Mansfield, Ohio

	G	AB	H	2B	3B	HR	HR%	R	RBI	BB	SO	SB	BA	SA	AB	H	G by POS
1884 CIN AA	33	131	32	2	9	0	0.0	20		2				.244	.397	0	0	OF-33
1890 CLE N	37	151	37	6	1	2	1.3	20	29	7	11	4	.245	.338	0	0	OF-37
2 yrs.	70	282	69	8	10	2	0.7	40	28	9	11	4	.245	.365	0	0	OF-70

Dick West

WEST, RICHARD THOMAS BR TR 6'2" 180 lbs.
B. Nov. 24, 1915, Louisville, Ky.

	G	AB	H	2B	3B	HR	HR%	R	RBI	BB	SO	SB	BA	SA	AB	H	G by POS
1938 CIN N	1	1	0	0	0	0	0.0	0	0	0	0	0	.000	.000	1	0	
1939	6	19	4	0	0	0	0.0	1	4	1	4	0	.211	.211	1	1	OF-5, C-1
1940	7	28	11	2	0	1	3.6	4	6	0	2	1	.393	.571	0	0	C-7
1941	67	172	37	5	2	1	0.6	15	17	6	23	4	.215	.285	1	0	C-64
1942	33	79	14	3	0	1	1.3	9	8	5	13	1	.177	.253	6	0	C-17, OF-6
1943	3	0	0	0	0	0	–	1	0	0	0	0	–	–	0	0	
6 yrs.	117	299	66	10	2	3	1.0	30	35	12	42	6	.221	.298	9	1	C-89, OF-11

Max West

WEST, MAX EDWARD BL TR 6'1½" 182 lbs.
B. Nov. 28, 1916, Dexter, Mo.

	G	AB	H	2B	3B	HR	HR%	R	RBI	BB	SO	SB	BA	SA	AB	H	G by POS
1938 BOS N	123	418	98	16	5	10	2.4	47	63	38	38	5	.234	.368	3	0	OF-109, 1B-7
1939	130	449	128	26	6	19	4.2	67	82	51	55	1	.285	.497	5	3	OF-124
1940	141	524	137	27	5	7	1.3	72	72	65	54	0	.261	.372	3	1	OF-102, 1B-36
1941	138	484	134	28	4	12	2.5	63	68	72	68	5	.277	.426	6	3	OF-132
1942	134	452	115	22	4	16	3.5	54	56	68	59	4	.254	.409	3	2	1B-85, OF-50
1946 2 teams		**BOS**	**N**	(1G –	.000)			**CIN**	**N**	(72G –	.213)						
" total	73	203	43	13	0	5	2.5	16	18	32	37	1	.212	.350	12	1	OF-58, 1B-1
1948 PIT N	87	146	26	4	0	8	5.5	19	21	27	29	1	.178	.370	32	5	1B-32, OF-16
7 yrs.	826	2676	681	136	20	77	2.9	338	380	353	340	19	.254	.407	64	15	OF-591, 1B-161

	G	AB	H	2B	3B	HR	HR %	R	RBI	BB	SO	SB	BA	SA	Pinch Hit AB	Pinch Hit H	G by POS

Max West

WEST, WALTER MAXWELL
B. July 14, 1904, Sunset, Tex.   D. Apr. 25, 1971, Houston, Tex.
BR TR 5'11"   165 lbs.

	G	AB	H	2B	3B	HR	HR %	R	RBI	BB	SO	SB	BA	SA	PH AB	PH H	G by POS
1928 BKN N	7	21	6	1	1	0	0.0	4	1	4	1	0	.286	.429	1	0	OF-7
1929	5	8	2	1	0	0	0.0	1	1	1	0	0	.250	.375	2	1	OF-2
2 yrs.	12	29	8	2	1	0	0.0	5	2	5	1	0	.276	.414	3	1	OF-9

Sammy West

WEST, SAMUEL FILMORE
B. Oct. 5, 1904, Longview, Tex.
BL TL 5'11"   165 lbs.

	G	AB	H	2B	3B	HR	HR %	R	RBI	BB	SO	SB	BA	SA	PH AB	PH H	G by POS
1927 WAS A	38	67	16	4	1	0	0.0	9	6	8	8	1	.239	.328	19	4	OF-18
1928	125	378	114	30	7	3	0.8	59	40	20	23	5	.302	.442	7	0	OF-116
1929	142	510	136	16	8	3	0.6	60	75	45	41	9	.267	.347	3	1	OF-139
1930	120	411	135	22	10	6	1.5	75	67	37	34	5	.328	.474	0	0	OF-118
1931	132	526	175	43	13	3	0.6	77	91	30	37	6	.333	.481	0	0	OF-127
1932	146	554	159	27	12	6	1.1	88	83	48	57	4	.287	.412	3	0	OF-143
1933 STL A	133	517	155	25	12	11	2.1	93	48	59	49	10	.300	.458	6	1	OF-127
1934	122	482	157	22	10	9	1.9	90	55	62	55	3	.326	.469	2	0	OF-120
1935	138	527	158	37	4	10	1.9	93	70	75	46	1	.300	.442	3	3	OF-135
1936	152	533	148	26	4	7	1.3	78	70	94	70	2	.278	.381	3	0	OF-148
1937	122	457	150	37	4	7	1.5	68	58	46	28	1	.328	.473	14	3	OF-105
1938 2 teams	STL A (44G – .309)			WAS A (92G – .302)													
" total	136	509	155	27	7	6	1.2	68	74	47	30	2	.305	.420	9	2	OF-126
1939 WAS A	115	390	110	20	8	3	0.8	52	52	67	29	1	.282	.397	6	0	OF-89, 1B-17
1940	57	99	25	6	1	1	1.0	7	18	16	13	0	.253	.364	26	8	1B-12, OF-9
1941	26	37	10	0	0	0	0.0	3	6	11	2	1	.270	.270	12	4	OF-8
1942 CHI A	49	151	35	5	0	0	0.0	14	25	31	18	2	.232	.265	2	0	OF-45
16 yrs.	1753	6148	1838	347	101	75	1.2	934	838	696	540	53	.299	.425	115	26	OF-1573, 1B-29

Oscar Westerberg

WESTERBERG, OSCAR WILLIAM
B. July 8, 1882   D. Apr. 17, 1909, Alameda, Calif.
TR

	G	AB	H	2B	3B	HR	HR %	R	RBI	BB	SO	SB	BA	SA	PH AB	PH H	G by POS
1907 BOS N	2	6	2	0	0	0	0.0	0	1	1		0	.333	.333	0	0	SS-2

Jim Westlake

WESTLAKE, JAMES PATRICK
Brother of Wally Westlake.
B. July 3, 1930, Sacramento, Calif.
BL TL 6'1"   190 lbs.

	G	AB	H	2B	3B	HR	HR %	R	RBI	BB	SO	SB	BA	SA	PH AB	PH H	G by POS
1955 PHI N	1	1	0	0	0	0	0.0	0	0	0	1	0	.000	.000	1	0	

Wally Westlake

WESTLAKE, WALDON THOMAS
Brother of Jim Westlake.
B. Nov. 8, 1920, Gridley, Calif.
BR TR 6'   186 lbs.

	G	AB	H	2B	3B	HR	HR %	R	RBI	BB	SO	SB	BA	SA	PH AB	PH H	G by POS
1947 PIT N	112	407	111	17	4	17	4.2	59	69	27	63	5	.273	.459	2	0	OF-109
1948	132	428	122	10	6	17	4.0	78	65	46	40	2	.285	.456	8	2	OF-125
1949	147	525	148	24	8	23	4.4	77	104	45	69	6	.282	.490	4	0	OF-143
1950	139	477	136	15	6	24	5.0	69	95	48	78	1	.285	.493	15	3	OF-123
1951 2 teams	PIT N (50G – .282)			STL N (73G – .255)													
" total	123	448	119	12	5	22	4.9	64	84	33	68	1	.266	.462	9	1	OF-79, 3B-34
1952 3 teams	STL N (21G – .216)			CIN N (59G – .202)			CLE A (29G – .232)										
" total	109	326	69	11	4	12	4.7	47	33	47	56	2	.212	.288	6	0	OF-104
1953 CLE A	82	218	72	7	1	9	4.1	42	46	35	29	2	.330	.495	7	0	OF-72
1954	85	240	63	9	2	11	4.6	36	42	26	37	0	.263	.454	11	2	OF-70
1955 2 teams	CLE A (16G – .250)			BAL A (8G – .125)													
" total	24	44	8	2	0	0	0.0	2	1	9	10	0	.182	.227	5	1	OF-14
1956 PHI N	5	4	0	0	0	0	0.0	0	0	1	3	0	.000	.000	4	0	
10 yrs.	958	3117	848	107	33	127	4.1	474	539	317	453	19	.272	.450	71	9	OF-839, 3B-34

WORLD SERIES
	G	AB	H	2B	3B	HR	HR %	R	RBI	BB	SO	SB	BA	SA	PH AB	PH H	G by POS
1954 CLE A	2	7	1	0	0	0	0.0	0	0	1	3	0	.143	.143	0	0	OF-2

Al Weston

WESTON, ALFRED JOHN
B. Dec. 11, 1905, Lynn, Mass.
BR TR 6'   195 lbs.

	G	AB	H	2B	3B	HR	HR %	R	RBI	BB	SO	SB	BA	SA	PH AB	PH H	G by POS
1929 BOS N	3	3	0	0	0	0	0.0	0	0	0	2	0	.000	.000	3	0	

Wes Westrum

WESTRUM, WESLEY NOREEN
B. Nov. 28, 1922, Clearbrook, Minn.
Manager 1965-67, 1974-75.
BR TR 5'11"   185 lbs.

	G	AB	H	2B	3B	HR	HR %	R	RBI	BB	SO	SB	BA	SA	PH AB	PH H	G by POS
1947 NY N	6	12	5	1	0	0	0.0	1	2	0	2	0	.417	.500	4	1	C-2
1948	66	125	20	3	1	4	3.2	14	16	20	36	3	.160	.296	2	0	C-63
1949	64	169	41	4	1	7	4.1	23	28	37	39	1	.243	.402	2	0	C-62
1950	140	437	103	13	3	23	5.3	68	71	92	73	2	.236	.437	0	0	C-139
1951	124	361	79	12	0	20	5.5	59	70	104	93	1	.219	.418	2	0	C-122
1952	114	322	71	11	0	14	4.3	47	43	76	68	1	.220	.385	2	0	C-112
1953	107	290	65	5	0	12	4.1	40	30	56	73	2	.224	.366	1	0	C-106, 3B-1
1954	98	246	46	3	1	8	3.3	25	27	45	60	0	.187	.305	0	0	C-98
1955	69	137	29	1	0	4	2.9	11	18	24	18	0	.212	.307	1	0	C-68
1956	68	132	29	5	2	3	2.3	10	8	25	28	0	.220	.356	1	1	C-67
1957	63	91	15	1	0	1	1.1	4	2	10	24	0	.165	.209	0	0	C-63
11 yrs.	919	2322	503	59	8	96	4.1	302	315	489	514	10	.217	.373	15	2	C-902, 3B-1

WORLD SERIES
	G	AB	H	2B	3B	HR	HR %	R	RBI	BB	SO	SB	BA	SA	PH AB	PH H	G by POS
1951 NY N	6	17	4	1	0	0	0.0	1	0	5	3	0	.235	.294	0	0	C-6
1954	4	11	3	0	0	0	0.0	0	3	1	3	0	.273	.273	0	0	C-4
2 yrs.	10	28	7	1	0	0	0.0	1	3	6	6	0	.250	.286	0	0	C-10

Buzz Wetzel

WETZEL, FRANKLIN BURTON
B. July 7, 1893, Columbus, Ind.   D. Mar. 5, 1942, Hollywood, Calif.
BR TR 5'9½"   177 lbs.

	G	AB	H	2B	3B	HR	HR %	R	RBI	BB	SO	SB	BA	SA	PH AB	PH H	G by POS
1920 STL A	6	19	9	1	1	0	0.0	5	5	4	1	0	.474	.632	1	1	OF-5
1921	61	119	25	2	0	2	1.7	16	10	9	20	0	.210	.277	32	5	OF-27
2 yrs.	67	138	34	3	1	2	1.4	21	15	13	21	0	.246	.326	33	6	OF-32

	G	AB	H	2B	3B	HR	HR %	R	RBI	BB	SO	SB	BA	SA	Pinch Hit AB	H	G by POS

Bill Whaley

WHALEY, WILLIAM CARL
B. Feb. 10, 1899, Indianapolis, Ind.   D. Mar. 3, 1943, Indianapolis, Ind.
BR TR 5'11"   178 lbs.

	G	AB	H	2B	3B	HR	HR%	R	RBI	BB	SO	SB	BA	SA	AB	H	G by POS
1923 STL A	23	50	12	2	1	0	0.0	5	1	4	2	0	.240	.320	8	1	OF-13

Bert Whaling

WHALING, ALBERT JAMES
B. June 22, 1888, Los Angeles, Calif.   D. Jan. 21, 1965, Sawtelle, Calif.
BR TR 6'   185 lbs.

	G	AB	H	2B	3B	HR	HR%	R	RBI	BB	SO	SB	BA	SA	AB	H	G by POS
1913 BOS N	79	211	51	8	2	0	0.0	22	25	10	32	3	.242	.299	2	1	C-77
1914	60	172	36	7	0	0	0.0	18	12	21	28	2	.209	.250	0	0	C-59
1915	72	190	42	6	2	0	0.0	10	13	8	38	0	.221	.274	2	0	C-72
3 yrs.	211	573	129	21	4	0	0.0	50	50	39	98	5	.225	.276	4	1	C-208

Mack Wheat

WHEAT, McKINLEY DAVIS
Brother of Zack Wheat.
B. June 9, 1893, Polo, Mo.   D. Aug. 14, 1979, Los Banos, Calif.
BR TR 5'11½"   167 lbs.

	G	AB	H	2B	3B	HR	HR%	R	RBI	BB	SO	SB	BA	SA	AB	H	G by POS
1915 BKN N	8	14	1	0	0	0	0.0	0	0	0	5	0	.071	.071	0	0	C-8
1916	2	2	0	0	0	0	0.0	0	0	0	1	0	.000	.000	0	0	C-2
1917	29	60	8	1	0	0	0.0	2	0	1	12	1	.133	.150	0	0	C-18, OF-9
1918	57	157	34	7	1	1	0.6	11	3	8	24	2	.217	.293	8	2	C-38, OF-7
1919	47	112	23	3	0	0	0.0	5	8	2	22	1	.205	.232	1	0	C-38
1920 PHI N	78	230	52	10	3	3	1.3	15	20	8	35	3	.226	.335	2	0	C-74
1921	10	27	5	2	1	0	0.0	1	4	0	3	0	.185	.333	1	1	C-9
7 yrs.	231	602	123	23	5	4	0.7	34	35	19	102	7	.204	.279	12	3	C-187, OF-16

Zack Wheat

WHEAT, ZACHARIAH DAVIS (Buck)
Brother of Mack Wheat.
B. May 23, 1888, Hamilton, Mo.   D. Mar. 11, 1972, Sedalia, Mo.
Hall of Fame 1959.
BL TR 5'10"   170 lbs.

	G	AB	H	2B	3B	HR	HR%	R	RBI	BB	SO	SB	BA	SA	AB	H	G by POS
1909 BKN N	26	102	31	7	3	0	0.0	15	4	6		1	.304	.431	0	0	OF-26
1910	156	606	172	36	15	2	0.3	78	55	47	80	16	.284	.403	0	0	OF-156
1911	140	534	153	26	13	5	0.9	55	76	29	58	21	.287	.412	4	2	OF-136
1912	123	453	138	28	7	8	1.8	70	65	39	40	16	.305	.450	3	0	OF-122
1913	138	535	161	28	10	7	1.3	64	71	25	45	19	.301	.430	2	0	OF-135
1914	145	533	170	26	9	9	1.7	66	89	47	50	20	.319	.452	1	0	OF-144
1915	146	528	136	15	12	5	0.9	64	66	52	42	21	.258	.360	2	1	OF-144
1916	149	568	177	32	13	9	1.6	76	73	43	49	19	.312	.461	0	0	OF-149
1917	109	362	113	15	11	1	0.3	38	41	20	18	5	.312	.423	10	2	OF-109
1918	105	409	137	15	3	0	0.0	39	51	16	17	9	.335	.386	0	0	OF-105
1919	137	536	159	23	11	5	0.9	70	62	33	27	15	.297	.409	0	0	OF-137
1920	148	583	191	26	13	9	1.5	89	73	48	21	8	.328	.463	0	0	OF-148
1921	148	568	182	31	10	14	2.5	91	85	44	19	11	.320	.484	0	0	OF-148
1922	152	600	201	29	12	16	2.7	92	112	45	22	9	.335	.503	0	0	OF-152
1923	98	349	131	13	5	8	2.3	63	65	23	12	3	.375	.510	11	4	OF-87
1924	141	566	212	41	8	14	2.5	92	97	49	18	3	.375	.549	1	0	OF-139
1925	150	616	221	42	14	14	2.3	125	103	45	22	3	.359	.541	1	0	OF-149
1926	111	411	119	31	2	5	1.2	68	35	21	14	4	.290	.411	9	2	OF-102
1927 PHI A	88	247	80	12	1	1	0.4	34	38	18	5	2	.324	.393	24	6	OF-62
19 yrs.	2410	9106	2884	476	172	132	1.4	1289	1261	650	559	205	.317	.450	68	17	OF-2350
WORLD SERIES																	
1916 BKN N	5	19	4	0	1	0	0.0	2	1	2	2	1	.211	.316	0	0	OF-5
1920	7	27	9	2	0	0	0.0	2	2	1	2	0	.333	.407	0	0	OF-7
2 yrs.	12	46	13	2	1	0	0.0	4	3	3	4	1	.283	.370	0	0	OF-12

Woody Wheaton

WHEATON, ELWOOD PIERCE
B. Oct. 3, 1914, Philadelphia, Pa.
BL TL 5'8½"   160 lbs.

	G	AB	H	2B	3B	HR	HR%	R	RBI	BB	SO	SB	BA	SA	AB	H	G by POS
1943 PHI A	7	30	6	2	0	0	0.0	2	2	3	2	0	.200	.267	0	0	OF-7
1944	30	59	11	2	0	0	0.0	1	5	5	3	1	.186	.220	11	2	P-11, OF-8
2 yrs.	37	89	17	4	0	0	0.0	3	7	8	5	1	.191	.236	11	2	OF-15, P-11

Dick Wheeler

WHEELER, RICHARD
Born Richard Wheeler Maynard.
B. Jan. 14, 1898, Keene, N. H.   D. Feb. 12, 1962, Lexington, Mass.
BR TR 5'11"   185 lbs.

	G	AB	H	2B	3B	HR	HR%	R	RBI	BB	SO	SB	BA	SA	AB	H	G by POS
1918 STL N	3	6	0	0	0	0	0.0	0	0	0	3	0	.000	.000	1	0	OF-2

Don Wheeler

WHEELER, DONALD WESLEY (Scotty)
B. Sept. 29, 1922, Minneapolis, Minn.
BR TR 5'10"   175 lbs.

	G	AB	H	2B	3B	HR	HR%	R	RBI	BB	SO	SB	BA	SA	AB	H	G by POS
1949 CHI A	67	192	46	9	2	1	0.5	17	22	27	19	2	.240	.323	8	1	C-58

Ed Wheeler

WHEELER, EDWARD L.
B. June 15, 1879, Sherman, Mich.   D. Aug. 15, 1960, Ft. Worth, Tex.
BB TR 5'10"   160 lbs.

	G	AB	H	2B	3B	HR	HR%	R	RBI	BB	SO	SB	BA	SA	AB	H	G by POS
1902 BKN N	30	96	12	0	0	0	0.0	4	5	3		1	.125	.125	3	0	3B-11, 2B-10, SS-5

Ed Wheeler

WHEELER, EDWARD RAYMOND
B. May 24, 1917, Los Angeles, Calif.   D. Aug. 15, 1960, Ft. Worth, Tex.
BR TR 5'9"   160 lbs.

	G	AB	H	2B	3B	HR	HR%	R	RBI	BB	SO	SB	BA	SA	AB	H	G by POS
1945 CLE A	46	72	14	2	0	0	0.0	12	2	8	13	1	.194	.222	7	3	3B-14, SS-11, 2B-3

George Wheeler

WHEELER, GEORGE HARRISON (Heavy)
B. Nov. 10, 1881, Shelburn, Ind.   D. June 14, 1918, Clinton, Ind.
BR TR 5'9½"   180 lbs.

	G	AB	H	2B	3B	HR	HR%	R	RBI	BB	SO	SB	BA	SA	AB	H	G by POS
1910 CIN N	3	3	0	0	0	0	0.0	0	0	0	2	0	.000	.000	3	0	

Harry Wheeler

WHEELER, HARRY EUGENE
B. Mar. 3, 1858, Versailles, Ind.   D. Oct. 9, 1900, Cincinnati, Ohio
BR TR 5'11"   165 lbs.

	G	AB	H	2B	3B	HR	HR%	R	RBI	BB	SO	SB	BA	SA	AB	H	G by POS
1878 PRO N	7	27	4	0	0	0	0.0	7	1	2	15		.148	.148	0	0	P-7
1879 CIN N	1	3	0	0	0	0	0.0	0	0	0	2		.000	.000	0	0	OF-1, P-1

	G	AB	H	2B	3B	HR	HR %	R	RBI	BB	SO	SB	BA	SA	Pinch Hit AB	Pinch Hit H	G by POS

Harry Wheeler continued

1880 2 teams	CLE	N	(1G –	.250)	CIN	N	(17G –	.092)									
" total	18	69	7	2	0	0	0.0	1	2	0	15		.101	.130	0	0	OF-18
1882 CIN AA	76	344	86	11	11	1	0.3	59		7			.250	.355	0	0	OF-64, 1B-12, P-4
1883 COL AA	82	371	84	6	6	1	0.3	42		6			.226	.283	0	0	OF-82, 2B-1, P-1
1884 4 teams	STL	AA	(5G –	.263)	KC	U	(14G –	.258)	C-P	U	(37G –	.228)		BAL	U	(17G –	.261)
" total	73	308	75	10	3	1	0.3	43		8			.244	.305	0	0	OF-72, P-1
6 yrs.	257	1122	256	29	20	3	0.3	152	3	23	32		.228	.298	0	0	OF-237, P-14, 1B-12, 2B-1

Bobby Wheelock

WHEELOCK, WARREN H.　　　　　　　　　　　BR TR　　150 lbs.
B. Aug. 6, 1864, Charlestown, Mass.　D. Mar. 13, 1928, Boston, Mass.

1887 BOS N	48	166	42	4	2	2	1.2	32	15	15	15	20	.253	.337	0	0	OF-28, SS-20, 2B-4
1890 COL AA	52	190	45	6	1	1	0.5	24		25		34	.237	.295	0	0	SS-52
1891	136	498	114	15	1	0	0.0	82	39	78	55	52	.229	.263	0	0	SS-136
3 yrs.	236	854	201	25	4	3	0.4	138	54	118	70	106	.235	.285	0	0	SS-208, OF-28, 2B-4

Jim Whelan

WHELAN, JAMES FRANCIS　　　　　　　　　　BR TR 5'8½" 165 lbs.
B. May 11, 1890, Kansas City, Mo.　D. Nov. 29, 1929, Dayton, Ohio

1913 STL N	1	1	0	0	0	0	0.0	0	0	0	0	0	.000	.000	1	0	

Tom Whelan

WHELAN, THOMAS JOSEPH　　　　　　　　　　BR TR 5'10" 180 lbs.
B. Jan. 3, 1894, Lynn, Mass.　D. June 26, 1957, Boston, Mass.

1920 BOS N	1	1	0	0	0	0	0.0	0	0	1	0	0	.000	.000	0	0	1B-1

Pete Whisenant

WHISENANT, THOMAS PETER　　　　　　　　　BR TR 6'2" 190 lbs.
B. Dec. 14, 1929, Asheville, N. C.

1952 BOS N	24	52	10	2	0	0	0.0	3	7	4	13	1	.192	.231	9	1	OF-14
1955 STL N	58	115	22	5	1	2	1.7	10	9	5	29	2	.191	.304	20	5	OF-40
1956 CHI N	103	314	75	16	3	11	3.5	37	46	24	53	8	.239	.414	8	2	OF-93
1957 CIN N	67	90	19	3	2	5	5.6	18	11	5	24	0	.211	.456	20	8	OF-43
1958	85	203	48	9	2	11	5.4	33	40	18	37	3	.236	.463	25	6	OF-66, 2B-1
1959	36	71	17	2	0	5	7.0	13	11	8	18	0	.239	.479	14	1	OF-21
1960 3 teams	CIN	N	(1G –	.000)	CLE	A	(7G –	.167)	WAS	A	(58G –	.226)					
" total	66	122	27	9	0	3	2.5	19	9	19	16	2	.221	.369	15	2	OF-49
1961 2 teams	MIN	A	(10G –	.000)	CIN	N	(26G –	.200)									
" total	36	21	3	0	0	0	0.0	7	1	3	6	1	.143	.143	13	1	OF-17, 3B-1, C-1
8 yrs.	475	988	221	46	8	37	3.7	140	134	86	196	17	.224	.399	124	26	OF-343, 3B-1, 2B-1, C-1

Larry Whisenton

WHISENTON, LARRY　　　　　　　　　　　　BL TL 6'1" 190 lbs.
B. July 3, 1956, St. Louis, Mo.

1977 ATL N	4	4	1	0	0	0	0.0	1	1	0	3	0	.250	.250	4	1	
1978	6	16	3	1	0	0	0.0	1	2	1	2	0	.188	.250	1	0	OF-4
1979	13	37	9	2	1	0	0.0	3	1	3	3	1	.243	.351	0	0	OF-13
1981	9	5	1	0	0	0	0.0	1	0	2	1	0	.200	.200	5	1	OF-2
1982	84	143	34	7	2	4	2.8	21	17	23	33	2	.238	.399	45	8	OF-34
5 yrs.	116	205	48	10	3	4	2.0	27	21	29	42	3	.234	.371	55	10	OF-53

LEAGUE CHAMPIONSHIP SERIES

1982 ATL N	2	2	0	0	0	0	0.0	0	0	0	1	0	.000	.000	2	0	

Lew Whistler

WHISTLER, LEWIS
Born Lewis Wissler.
B. Mar. 10, 1868, St. Louis, Mo.　D. Dec. 30, 1959, St. Louis, Mo.

1890 NY N	45	170	49	9	7	2	1.2	27	29	20	37	8	.288	.459	0	0	1B-45
1891	72	265	65	8	7	4	1.5	39	38	24	45	4	.245	.374	0	0	SS-33, OF-22, 1B-7, 2B-6, 3B-5
1892 2 teams	BAL	N	(52G –	.225)	LOU	N	(80G –	.235)									
" total	132	494	114	10	13	7	1.4	74	55	48	67	26	.231	.346	0	0	1B-123, 2B-10, OF-1
1893 2 teams	LOU	N	(13G –	.213)	STL	N	(10G –	.237)									
" total	23	85	19	2	1	0	0.0	10	11	8	7	1	.224	.271	0	0	1B-14, OF-9
4 yrs.	272	1014	247	29	28	13	1.3	150	133	100	156	39	.244	.366	0	0	1B-189, SS-33, OF-32, 2B-16, 3B-5

Lou Whitaker

WHITAKER, LOUIS RODMAN (Sweet Lou)　　　BL TR 5'11" 160 lbs.
B. May 12, 1957, Brooklyn, N. Y.

1977 DET A	11	32	8	1	0	0	0.0	5	2	4	6	2	.250	.281	0	0	2B-9
1978	139	484	138	12	7	3	0.6	71	58	61	65	7	.285	.357	6	3	2B-136, DH-2
1979	127	423	121	14	8	3	0.7	75	42	78	66	20	.286	.378	5	0	2B-126
1980	145	477	111	19	1	1	0.2	68	45	73	79	8	.233	.283	8	2	2B-143
1981	109	335	88	14	4	5	1.5	48	36	40	42	5	.263	.373	2	1	2B-108
1982	152	560	160	22	8	15	2.7	76	65	48	58	11	.286	.434	4	1	2B-149, DH-1
1983	161	643	206	40	6	12	1.9	94	72	67	70	17	.320	.457	7	3	2B-160
1984	143	558	161	25	1	13	2.3	90	56	62	63	6	.289	.407	6	1	2B-142
8 yrs.	987	3512	993	147	35	52	1.5	527	376	433	449	76	.283	.389	38	11	2B-973, DH-3

LEAGUE CHAMPIONSHIP SERIES

1984 DET A	3	14	2	0	0	0	0.0	3	0	0	3	0	.143	.143	0	0	2B-3

WORLD SERIES

1984 DET A	5	18	5	2	0	0	0.0	6	0	4	4	0	.278	.389	0	0	2B-5

Steve Whitaker

WHITAKER, STEVE EDWARD　　　　　　　　　BL TR 6' 180 lbs.
B. May 7, 1943, Tacoma, Wash.

1966 NY A	31	114	28	3	2	7	6.1	15	15	9	24	0	.246	.491	0	0	OF-31
1967	122	441	107	12	3	11	2.5	37	50	23	89	2	.243	.358	10	4	OF-114
1968	28	60	7	2	0	0	0.0	3	3	8	18	0	.117	.150	13	2	OF-14
1969 SEA A	69	116	29	2	1	6	5.2	15	13	12	29	2	.250	.440	25	5	OF-39

	G	AB	H	2B	3B	HR	HR %	R	RBI	BB	SO	SB	BA	SA	Pinch Hit AB	Pinch Hit H	G by POS

Steve Whitaker *continued*

	G	AB	H	2B	3B	HR	HR %	R	RBI	BB	SO	SB	BA	SA	AB	H	G by POS
1970 SF N	16	27	3	1	0	0	0.0	3	4	2	14	0	.111	.148	6	2	OF-9
5 yrs.	266	758	174	20	6	24	3.2	73	85	54	174	4	.230	.367	54	13	OF-207

Bill White

WHITE, WILLIAM BARNEY
B. June 25, 1924, Paris, Tex.

BR TR 5'10½" 190 lbs.

	G	AB	H	2B	3B	HR	HR %	R	RBI	BB	SO	SB	BA	SA	AB	H	G by POS
1945 BKN N	4	1	0	0	0	0	0.0	0	0	1	1	0	.000	.000	0	0	SS-1

Bill White

WHITE, WILLIAM DeKOVA
B. Jan. 28, 1934, Lakewood, Fla.

BL TL 6' 185 lbs.

	G	AB	H	2B	3B	HR	HR %	R	RBI	BB	SO	SB	BA	SA	AB	H	G by POS
1956 NY N	138	508	130	23	7	22	4.3	63	59	47	72	15	.256	.459	0	0	1B-138, OF-2
1958 SF N	26	29	7	1	0	1	3.4	5	4	7	5	1	.241	.379	16	4	1B-3, OF-2
1959 STL N	138	517	156	33	9	12	2.3	77	72	34	61	15	.302	.470	5	1	OF-92, 1B-71
1960	144	554	157	27	10	16	2.9	81	79	42	83	12	.283	.455	3	0	1B-123, OF-29
1961	153	591	169	28	11	20	3.4	89	90	64	84	8	.286	.472	3	0	1B-151
1962	159	614	199	31	3	20	3.3	93	102	58	69	9	.324	.482	1	0	1B-146, OF-27
1963	162	658	200	26	8	27	4.1	106	109	59	100	10	.304	.491	0	0	1B-162
1964	160	631	191	37	4	21	3.3	92	102	52	103	7	.303	.474	0	0	1B-160
1965	148	543	157	26	3	24	4.4	82	73	63	86	3	.289	.481	4	1	1B-144
1966 PHI N	159	577	159	23	6	22	3.8	85	103	68	109	16	.276	.451	4	0	1B-158
1967	110	308	77	6	2	8	2.6	29	33	52	61	6	.250	.360	14	0	1B-95
1968	127	385	92	16	2	9	2.3	34	40	39	79	0	.239	.361	20	5	1B-111
1969 STL N	49	57	12	1	0	0	0.0	7	4	11	15	1	.211	.228	31	5	1B-15
13 yrs.	1673	5972	1706	278	65	202	3.4	843	870	596	927	103	.286	.455	101	16	1B-1477, OF-152

WORLD SERIES

	G	AB	H	2B	3B	HR	HR %	R	RBI	BB	SO	SB	BA	SA	AB	H	G by POS
1964 STL N	7	27	3	1	0	0	0.0	2	2	2	6	1	.111	.148	0	0	1B-7

Bill White

WHITE, WILLIAM DIGHTON
B. May 1, 1860, Bellaire, Ohio   D. Dec. 31, 1924, Bellaire, Ohio

	G	AB	H	2B	3B	HR	HR %	R	RBI	BB	SO	SB	BA	SA	AB	H	G by POS
1884 PIT AA	74	291	66	7	10	0	0.0	25		13			.227	.320	0	0	SS-60, 3B-10, OF-4
1886 LOU AA	135	557	143	17	10	1	0.2	96		37			.257	.329	0	0	SS-135, P-1
1887	132	512	129	7	9	2	0.4	85		47		41	.252	.313	0	0	SS-132
1888 2 teams		LOU	AA (49G –	.278)			STL	AA	(76G –	.175)							
" total	125	473	103	8	8	3	0.6	66	60	28		21	.218	.288	0	0	SS-112, 3B-11, 2B-2
4 yrs.	466	1833	441	39	37	6	0.3	272	59	125		62	.241	.312	0	0	SS-439, 3B-21, OF-4, 2B-2, P-1

Bill White

WHITE, WILLIAM EDWARD
B. Milner, Ga.   Deceased.

	G	AB	H	2B	3B	HR	HR %	R	RBI	BB	SO	SB	BA	SA	AB	H	G by POS
1879 PRO N	1	4	1	0	0	0	0.0	1	0	0		1	.250	.250	0	0	1B-1

C. B. White

WHITE, C. B.
B. Wakeman, Ohio   Deceased.

	G	AB	H	2B	3B	HR	HR %	R	RBI	BB	SO	SB	BA	SA	AB	H	G by POS
1883 PHI N	1	1	0	0	0	0	0.0	0		0	0		.000	.000	0	0	SS-1, 3B-1

Charlie White

WHITE, CHARLES
B. Aug. 12, 1928, Kinston, N. C.

BL TR 5'11" 192 lbs.

	G	AB	H	2B	3B	HR	HR %	R	RBI	BB	SO	SB	BA	SA	AB	H	G by POS
1954 MIL N	50	93	22	4	0	1	1.1	14	8	9	8	0	.237	.312	24	4	C-28
1955	12	30	7	1	0	0	0.0	3	4	5	7	0	.233	.267	1	0	C-10
2 yrs.	62	123	29	5	0	1	0.8	17	12	14	15	0	.236	.301	25	4	C-38

Deacon White

WHITE, JAMES LAURIE
Brother of Will White.
B. Dec. 7, 1847, Caton, N. Y.   D. July 7, 1939, Aurora, Ill.
Manager 1879.

BL TR 5'11" 175 lbs.

	G	AB	H	2B	3B	HR	HR %	R	RBI	BB	SO	SB	BA	SA	AB	H	G by POS
1876 CHI N	66	303	104	18	1	1	0.3	66	60	7	3		.343	.419	0	0	C-63, OF-3, 1B-3, 3B-1, P-1
1877 BOS N	59	266	103	14	11	2	0.8	51	49	8	3		.387	.545	0	0	1B-35, OF-19, C-7
1878 CIN N	61	258	81	4	1	0	0.0	41	29	10	5		.314	.337	0	0	C-48, OF-16, 3B-1
1879	78	333	110	16	6	1	0.3	55	52	6	9		.330	.423	0	0	C-59, OF-21, 1B-2
1880	35	141	42	4	2	0	0.0	21	7	9	7		.298	.355	0	0	OF-33, 1B-3, 2B-1
1881 BUF N	78	319	99	24	4	0	0.0	58	53	9	8		.310	.411	0	0	1B-26, 2B-25, OF-17, 3B-7, C-4
1882	83	337	95	17	0	1	0.3	51		15	16		.282	.341	0	0	3B-63, C-20
1883	94	391	114	14	5	0	0.0	62		23	18		.292	.353	0	0	3B-77, C-22
1884	110	452	147	16	11	5	1.1	82		32	13		.325	.442	0	0	3B-108, C-3
1885	98	404	118	6	6	0	0.0	54	57	12	11		.292	.337	0	0	3B-98
1886 DET N	124	491	142	19	5	1	0.2	65	76	31	35		.289	.354	0	0	3B-124
1887	111	449	136	20	11	3	0.7	71	75	26	15	20	.303	.416	0	0	3B-106, OF-3, 1B-2
1888	125	527	157	22	5	4	0.8	75	71	21	24	12	.298	.381	0	0	3B-125
1889 PIT N	55	225	57	10	1	0	0.0	35	26	16	18	2	.253	.307	0	0	3B-52, 1B-3
1890 BUF P	122	439	114	13	4	0	0.0	62	47	67	30	3	.260	.308	0	0	3B-64, 1B-57, SS-1, C-1
15 yrs.	1299	5335	1619	217	73	18	0.3	849	602	292	215	37	.303	.382	0	0	3B-826, C-226, 1B-131, OF-112, 2B-26, P-2, SS-1

Doc White

WHITE, GUY HARRIS
B. Apr. 9, 1879, Washington, D. C.   D. Feb. 19, 1969, Silver Springs, Md.

BL TL 6'1" 150 lbs.

	G	AB	H	2B	3B	HR	HR %	R	RBI	BB	SO	SB	BA	SA	AB	H	G by POS
1901 PHI N	31	95	26	3	1	1	1.1	15	10	2		1	.274	.358	0	0	P-31, OF-1
1902	61	179	47	3	1	0	0.6	17	15	11		5	.263	.307	5	1	P-36, OF-19
1903 CHI A	38	99	20	3	0	0	0.0	10	5	19		1	.202	.232	0	0	P-37, OF-1
1904	33	76	12	2	0	0	0.0	7	2	10		3	.158	.184	0	0	P-30, OF-2
1905	37	86	14	4	1	0	0.0	7	7	4		3	.163	.233	0	0	P-36, OF-1
1906	28	65	12	1	1	0	0.0	11	3	13		3	.185	.231	0	0	P-28, OF-1
1907	48	90	20	1	0	0	0.0	12	2	12		2	.222	.233	0	0	P-46, OF-2
1908	51	109	25	1	0	0	0.0	12	10	12		4	.229	.239	6	1	P-41, OF-3

	G	AB	H	2B	3B	HR	HR %	R	RBI	BB	SO	SB	BA	SA	Pinch Hit AB	Pinch Hit H	G by POS

Doc White continued

	G	AB	H	2B	3B	HR	HR %	R	RBI	BB	SO	SB	BA	SA	PH AB	PH H	G by POS
1909	72	192	45	1	5	0	0.0	24	7	33		7	.234	.292	8	1	OF-40, P-24
1910	56	126	25	1	2	0	0.0	14	8	14		2	.198	.238	8	0	P-33, OF-14
1911	39	78	20	1	1	0	0.0	12	6	7		1	.256	.295	0	0	P-34, 1B-2, OF-1
1912	33	56	7	1	1	0	0.0	5	0	7		0	.125	.179	1	0	P-32
1913	20	25	3	0	0	0	0.0	1	0	3	1	0	.120	.120	0	0	P-19, 1B-1
13 yrs.	547	1276	276	22	13	2	0.2	147	75	147	1	32	.216	.259	28	3	P-427, OF-85, 1B-3

WORLD SERIES

	G	AB	H	2B	3B	HR	HR %	R	RBI	BB	SO	SB	BA	SA	PH AB	PH H	G by POS
1906 CHI A	3	3	0	0	0	0	0.0	0	0	1	0	0	.000	.000	0	0	P-3

Don White
WHITE, DONALD WILLIAM   BR TR 6'1"   195 lbs.
B. Jan. 8, 1919, Everett, Wash.

	G	AB	H	2B	3B	HR	HR %	R	RBI	BB	SO	SB	BA	SA	PH AB	PH H	G by POS
1948 PHI A	86	253	62	14	2	1	0.4	29	28	19	16	0	.245	.328	13	2	OF-54, 3B-17
1949	57	169	36	6	0	0	0.0	12	10	14	12	2	.213	.249	8	3	OF-47, 3B-4
2 yrs.	143	422	98	20	2	1	0.2	41	38	33	28	2	.232	.296	21	5	OF-101, 3B-21

Ed White
WHITE, EDWARD PERRY   BR TR 6'2"   200 lbs.
B. Apr. 6, 1926, Anniston, Ala.

	G	AB	H	2B	3B	HR	HR %	R	RBI	BB	SO	SB	BA	SA	PH AB	PH H	G by POS
1955 CHI A	3	4	2	0	0	0	0.0	0	0	1	1	0	.500	.500	1	0	OF-2

Elder White
WHITE, ELDER LAFAYETTE   BR TR 5'11"   165 lbs.
B. Dec. 23, 1934, Colerain, N. C.

	G	AB	H	2B	3B	HR	HR %	R	RBI	BB	SO	SB	BA	SA	PH AB	PH H	G by POS
1962 CHI N	23	53	8	2	0	0	0.0	4	1	8	11	3	.151	.189	6	1	SS-15, 2B-1

Frank White
WHITE, FRANK JR.   BR TR 5'11"   165 lbs.
B. Sept. 4, 1950, Greenville, Miss.

	G	AB	H	2B	3B	HR	HR %	R	RBI	BB	SO	SB	BA	SA	PH AB	PH H	G by POS
1973 KC A	51	139	31	6	1	0	0.0	20	5	8	23	3	.223	.281	1	0	SS-37, 2B-11
1974	99	204	45	6	3	1	0.5	19	18	5	33	3	.221	.294	3	0	2B-50, SS-29, 3B-16, DH-3
1975	111	304	76	10	2	7	2.3	43	36	20	39	11	.250	.365	0	0	2B-67, SS-42, 3B-4, DH-2
1976	152	446	102	17	6	2	0.4	39	46	19	42	20	.229	.307	0	0	2B-130, SS-37
1977	152	474	116	21	5	5	1.1	59	50	25	67	23	.245	.342	0	0	2B-152, SS-4
1978	143	461	127	24	6	7	1.5	66	50	26	59	13	.275	.399	3	0	2B-140
1979	127	467	124	26	4	10	2.1	73	48	25	54	28	.266	.403	1	0	2B-125
1980	154	560	148	23	4	7	1.3	70	60	19	69	19	.264	.357	3	0	2B-153
1981	94	364	91	17	1	9	2.5	35	38	19	50	4	.250	.376	1	1	2B-93
1982	145	524	156	45	6	11	2.1	71	56	16	65	10	.298	.469	1	0	2B-144
1983	146	549	143	35	6	11	2.0	52	77	20	51	13	.260	.406	3	2	2B-145
1984	129	479	130	22	5	17	3.5	58	56	27	72	5	.271	.445	1	0	2B-129
12 yrs.	1503	4971	1289	252	49	87	1.8	605	540	229	624	152	.259	.382	17	3	2B-1339, SS-149, 3B-20, DH-5

DIVISIONAL PLAYOFF SERIES

	G	AB	H	2B	3B	HR	HR %	R	RBI	BB	SO	SB	BA	SA	PH AB	PH H	G by POS
1981 KC A	3	11	2	0	0	0	0.0	1	0	1	1	0	.182	.182	0	0	2B-3

LEAGUE CHAMPIONSHIP SERIES

	G	AB	H	2B	3B	HR	HR %	R	RBI	BB	SO	SB	BA	SA	PH AB	PH H	G by POS
1976 KC A	4	8	1	0	0	0	0.0	2	0	0	1	0	.125	.125	0	0	2B-4
1977	5	18	5	1	0	0	0.0	1	2	0	4	1	.278	.333	0	0	2B-5
1978	4	13	3	0	0	0	0.0	1	2	0	0	0	.231	.231	0	0	2B-4
1980	3	11	6	1	0	1	9.1	3	3	0	0	1	.545	.909	0	0	2B-3
1984	3	12	1	0	0	0	0.0	1	0	0	3	0	.083	.083	0	0	2B-3
5 yrs.	19	62	16	2	0	1	1.6	8	7	0	8	2	.258	.339	0	0	2B-19

WORLD SERIES

	G	AB	H	2B	3B	HR	HR %	R	RBI	BB	SO	SB	BA	SA	PH AB	PH H	G by POS
1980 KC A	6	25	2	0	0	0	0.0	0	0	1	5	1	.080	.080	0	0	2B-6

Fuzz White
WHITE, ALBERT EUGENE   BL TR 6'   175 lbs.
B. June 27, 1918, Springfield, Mo.

	G	AB	H	2B	3B	HR	HR %	R	RBI	BB	SO	SB	BA	SA	PH AB	PH H	G by POS
1940 STL A	2	2	0	0	0	0	0.0	0	0	0	0	0	.000	.000	2	0	
1947 NY N	7	13	3	0	0	0	0.0	3	0	0	0	0	.231	.231	1	0	OF-5
2 yrs.	9	15	3	0	0	0	0.0	3	0	0	0	0	.200	.200	3	0	OF-5

Jack White
WHITE, JOHN PETER   BB TR 5'7½"   150 lbs.
B. Aug. 31, 1905, New York, N. Y.   D. June 19, 1971, Flushing, N. Y.

	G	AB	H	2B	3B	HR	HR %	R	RBI	BB	SO	SB	BA	SA	PH AB	PH H	G by POS
1927 CIN N	5	4	0	0	0	0	0.0	1	0	0	0	0	.000	.000	0	0	2B-3, SS-2
1928	1	3	0	0	0	0	0.0	0	0	0	1	0	.000	.000	0	0	2B-1
2 yrs.	6	7	0	0	0	0	0.0	1	0	0	1	0	.000	.000	0	0	2B-4, SS-2

Jerry White
WHITE, JEROME CARDELL   BB TR 5'10"   164 lbs.
B. Aug. 23, 1952, Shirley, Mass.

	G	AB	H	2B	3B	HR	HR %	R	RBI	BB	SO	SB	BA	SA	PH AB	PH H	G by POS
1974 MON N	9	10	4	1	1	0	0.0	0	2	0	0	3	.400	.700	0	0	OF-7
1975	39	97	29	4	1	2	2.1	14	7	10	7	5	.299	.423	3	0	OF-30
1976	114	278	68	11	1	2	0.7	32	21	27	31	15	.245	.313	17	2	OF-92
1977	16	21	4	0	0	0	0.0	4	1	1	3	1	.190	.190	10	2	OF-8
1978 2 teams	MON N (18G – .200)						CHI N (59G – .272)										
" total	77	146	39	6	0	1	0.7	24	10	24	19	5	.267	.329	12	3	OF-57
1979 MON N	88	138	41	7	1	3	2.2	30	18	21	23	8	.297	.428	38	12	OF-43
1980	110	214	56	9	3	7	3.3	22	23	30	37	8	.262	.430	29	6	OF-84
1981	59	119	26	5	1	3	2.5	11	11	13	17	5	.218	.353	18	5	OF-39
1982	69	115	28	6	1	2	1.7	13	13	8	26	3	.243	.365	39	10	OF-30
1983	40	34	5	1	0	0	0.0	4	0	12	8	4	.147	.176	23	2	OF-13
10 yrs.	621	1172	300	50	9	20	1.7	154	106	146	171	57	.256	.365	189	42	OF-403

DIVISIONAL PLAYOFF SERIES

	G	AB	H	2B	3B	HR	HR %	R	RBI	BB	SO	SB	BA	SA	PH AB	PH H	G by POS
1981 MON N	5	18	3	1	0	0	0.0	3	1	2	2	3	.167	.222	0	0	OF-5

LEAGUE CHAMPIONSHIP SERIES

	G	AB	H	2B	3B	HR	HR %	R	RBI	BB	SO	SB	BA	SA	PH AB	PH H	G by POS
1981 MON N	5	16	5	1	0	1	6.3	2	3	3	1	1	.313	.563	0	0	OF-5

	G	AB	H	2B	3B	HR	HR %	R	RBI	BB	SO	SB	BA	SA	Pinch Hit AB	Pinch Hit H	G by POS

Jo-Jo White

WHITE, JOYNER CLIFFORD
Father of Mike White.
B. June 1, 1909, Red Oak, Ga.
Manager 1960.

BL TR 5'11" 165 lbs.

	G	AB	H	2B	3B	HR	HR %	R	RBI	BB	SO	SB	BA	SA	AB	H	G by POS
1932 DET A	79	208	54	6	3	2	1.0	25	21	22	19	6	.260	.346	25	9	OF-47
1933	91	234	59	9	5	2	0.9	43	34	27	26	5	.252	.359	26	10	OF-54
1934	115	384	120	18	5	0	0.0	97	44	69	39	28	.313	.385	12	2	OF-100
1935	114	412	99	13	12	2	0.5	82	32	68	42	19	.240	.345	13	4	OF-98
1936	58	51	14	3	0	0	0.0	11	6	9	10	2	.275	.333	30	10	OF-18
1937	94	305	75	5	7	0	0.0	50	21	50	40	12	.246	.308	5	2	OF-82
1938	78	206	54	6	1	0	0.0	40	15	28	15	3	.262	.301	18	3	OF-55
1943 PHI A	139	500	124	17	7	1	0.2	69	30	61	51	12	.248	.316	5	1	OF-133
1944 2 teams		PHI	A (85G –	.221)		CIN	N (24G –	.235)									
" total	109	352	79	6	2	1	0.3	39	26	50	34	5	.224	.261	7	1	OF-97, SS-1
9 yrs.	877	2652	678	83	42	8	0.3	456	229	384	276	92	.256	.328	141	42	OF-684, SS-1
WORLD SERIES																	
1934 DET A	7	23	3	0	0	0	0.0	6	0	8	4	1	.130	.130	0	0	OF-7
1935	5	19	5	0	0	0	0.0	3	1	5	7	0	.263	.263	0	0	OF-5
2 yrs.	12	42	8	0	0	0	0.0	9	1	13	11	1	.190	.190	0	0	OF-12

John White

WHITE, JOHN WALLACE
B. Jan. 19, 1878, Indianapolis, Ind.   D. Sept. 30, 1963, Indianapolis, Ind.

BL TL

	G	AB	H	2B	3B	HR	HR %	R	RBI	BB	SO	SB	BA	SA	AB	H	G by POS
1904 BOS N	1	5	0	0	0	0	0.0	1	0	0		0	.000	.000	0	0	OF-1

Mike White

WHITE, JOYNER MICHAEL
Son of Jo-Jo White.
B. Dec. 18, 1938, Detroit, Mich.

BR TR 5'8" 160 lbs.

	G	AB	H	2B	3B	HR	HR %	R	RBI	BB	SO	SB	BA	SA	AB	H	G by POS
1963 HOU N	3	7	2	0	0	0	0.0	0	0	0	0	0	.286	.286	1	0	2B-2
1964	89	280	76	11	3	0	0.0	30	27	20	47	1	.271	.332	13	2	OF-72, 2B-10, 3B-3
1965	8	9	0	0	0	0	0.0	0	0	1	2	0	.000	.000	7	0	3B-1
3 yrs.	100	296	78	11	3	0	0.0	30	27	21	49	1	.264	.321	21	2	OF-72, 2B-12, 3B-4

Myron White

WHITE, MYRON ALAN
B. Aug. 1, 1957, Long Beach, Calif.

BL TL 5'11" 180 lbs.

	G	AB	H	2B	3B	HR	HR %	R	RBI	BB	SO	SB	BA	SA	AB	H	G by POS
1978 LA N	7	4	2	0	0	0	0.0	1	1	0	1	0	.500	.500	0	0	OF-4

Roy White

WHITE, ROY HILTON
B. Dec. 27, 1943, Los Angeles, Calif.

BB TR 5'10" 160 lbs.
BR 1965

	G	AB	H	2B	3B	HR	HR %	R	RBI	BB	SO	SB	BA	SA	AB	H	G by POS
1965 NY A	14	42	14	2	0	0	0.0	7	3	4	7	2	.333	.381	2	0	OF-10, 2B-1
1966	115	316	71	13	2	7	2.2	39	20	37	43	14	.225	.345	22	7	OF-82, 2B-2
1967	70	214	48	8	0	2	0.9	22	18	19	25	10	.224	.290	16	1	OF-36, 3B-17
1968	159	577	154	20	7	17	2.9	89	62	73	50	20	.267	.414	4	1	OF-154
1969	130	448	130	30	5	7	1.6	55	74	81	51	18	.290	.426	5	0	OF-126
1970	162	609	180	30	6	22	3.6	109	94	95	66	24	.296	.473	1	0	OF-161
1971	147	524	153	22	7	19	3.6	86	84	86	66	14	.292	.469	2	0	OF-145
1972	155	556	150	29	0	10	1.8	76	54	99	59	23	.270	.376	0	0	OF-155
1973	162	639	157	22	3	18	2.8	88	60	78	81	16	.246	.374	0	0	OF-162
1974	136	473	130	19	8	7	1.5	68	43	67	44	15	.275	.393	18	3	OF-67, DH-53
1975	148	556	161	32	5	12	2.2	81	59	72	50	16	.290	.430	4	1	OF-135, 1B-7, DH-2
1976	156	626	179	29	3	14	2.2	104	65	83	52	31	.286	.409	0	0	OF-156
1977	143	519	139	25	2	14	2.7	72	52	75	58	18	.268	.405	4	0	OF-135, DH-4
1978	103	346	93	13	3	8	2.3	44	43	42	35	10	.269	.393	9	0	OF-74, DH-23
1979	81	205	44	6	0	3	1.5	24	27	23	21	2	.215	.288	19	5	DH-29, OF-27
15 yrs.	1881	6650	1803	300	51	160	2.4	964	758	934	708	233	.271	.404	106	20	OF-1625, DH-111, 3B-17, 1B-7, 2B-3
LEAGUE CHAMPIONSHIP SERIES																	
1976 NY A	5	17	5	3	0	0	0.0	4	3	5	1	1	.294	.471	0	0	OF-5
1977	5	5	2	2	0	0	0.0	2	0	1	0	0	.400	.800	1	0	OF-1
1978	4	16	5	1	0	1	6.3	5	1	1	2	0	.313	.563	0	0	OF-3
3 yrs.	14	38	12	6	0	1	2.6	11	4	7	3	1	.316	.553	1	0	OF-9
WORLD SERIES																	
1976 NY A	4	15	2	0	0	0	0.0	0	0	3	0	0	.133	.133	0	0	OF-4
1977	2	2	0	0	0	0	0.0	0	0	0	0	0	.000	.000	2	0	
1978	6	24	8	0	0	1	4.2	9	4	4	5	2	.333	.458	0	0	OF-6
3 yrs.	12	41	10	0	0	1	2.4	9	4	7	5	2	.244	.317	2	0	OF-10

Sam White

WHITE, SAMUEL LAMBETH
B. Aug. 23, 1892, Greater Preston, England   D. Nov. 11, 1929, Philadelphia, Pa.

BL TR 6' 185 lbs.

	G	AB	H	2B	3B	HR	HR %	R	RBI	BB	SO	SB	BA	SA	AB	H	G by POS
1919 BOS N	1	1	0	0	0	0	0.0	0	0	0	0	0	.000	.000	0	0	C-1

Sammy White

WHITE, SAMUEL CHARLES
B. July 7, 1928, Wenatchee, Wash.

BR TR 6'3" 195 lbs.

	G	AB	H	2B	3B	HR	HR %	R	RBI	BB	SO	SB	BA	SA	AB	H	G by POS
1951 BOS A	4	11	2	0	0	0	0.0	0	0	0	3	0	.182	.182	0	0	C-4
1952	115	381	107	20	2	10	2.6	35	49	16	43	2	.281	.423	5	0	C-110
1953	136	476	130	34	2	13	2.7	59	64	29	48	3	.273	.435	7	2	C-131
1954	137	493	139	25	2	14	2.8	46	75	21	50	1	.282	.426	4	0	C-133
1955	143	544	142	30	4	11	2.0	65	64	44	58	1	.261	.392	0	0	C-143
1956	114	392	96	15	2	5	1.3	28	44	35	40	2	.245	.332	0	0	C-114
1957	111	340	73	10	1	3	0.9	24	31	25	38	0	.215	.276	0	0	C-111
1958	102	328	85	15	3	6	1.8	25	35	21	37	1	.259	.378	0	0	C-102
1959	119	377	107	13	4	1	0.3	34	42	23	39	4	.284	.347	1	0	C-119
1961 MIL N	21	63	14	1	0	1	1.6	1	5	2	9	0	.222	.286	0	0	C-20
1962 PHI N	41	97	21	4	0	2	2.1	7	12	2	16	0	.216	.320	2	0	C-40
11 yrs.	1043	3502	916	167	20	66	1.9	324	421	218	381	14	.262	.377	19	2	C-1027

	G	AB	H	2B	3B	HR	HR %	R	RBI	BB	SO	SB	BA	SA	Pinch Hit AB	Pinch Hit H	G by POS

Ted Williams continued

1960	113	310	98	15	0	29	9.4	56	72	75	41	1	.316	.645	19	1	OF-87
19 yrs.	2292	7706	2654	525	71	521	6.8	1798	1839	2019	709	24	.344	.634	111	33	OF-2151, P-1
						8th	6th		10th	2nd			6th	2nd			

WORLD SERIES

1946 BOS A	7	25	5	0	0	0	0.0	2	1	5	5	0	.200	.200	0	0	OF-7

Walt Williams

WILLIAMS, WALTER ALLEN (No-Neck)   BR TR 5'6" 165 lbs.
B. Dec. 19, 1943, Brownwood, Tex.

1964 HOU N	10	9	0	0	0	0	0.0	1	0	0	2	1	.000	.000	2	0	OF-5
1967 CHI A	104	275	66	16	3	3	1.1	35	15	17	20	3	.240	.353	30	4	OF-73
1968	63	133	32	6	0	1	0.8	6	8	4	17	0	.241	.308	28	5	OF-34
1969	135	471	143	22	1	3	0.6	59	32	26	33	6	.304	.374	24	7	OF-111
1970	110	315	79	18	1	3	1.0	43	15	19	30	3	.251	.343	29	8	OF-79
1971	114	361	106	17	3	8	2.2	43	35	24	27	5	.294	.424	27	9	OF-90, 3B-1
1972	77	221	55	7	1	2	0.9	22	11	13	20	6	.249	.317	23	4	OF-57, 3B-1
1973 CLE A	104	350	101	15	1	8	2.3	43	38	14	29	9	.289	.406	17	4	OF-61, DH-26
1974 NY A	43	53	6	0	0	0	0.0	5	3	1	10	1	.113	.113	15	1	OF-24, DH-3
1975	82	185	52	5	1	5	2.7	27	16	8	23	0	.281	.400	31	10	OF-31, DH-17, 2B-6
10 yrs.	842	2373	640	106	11	33	1.4	284	173	126	211	34	.270	.365	226	52	OF-565, DH-46, 2B-6, 3B-2

Wash Williams

WILLIAMS, WASHINGTON J.   5'11" 180 lbs.
B. Philadelphia, Pa.   D. Jan., 1890, Philadelphia, Pa.

1884 RIC AA	2	8	2	0	0	0	0.0	0		0			.250	.250	0	0	OF-2
1885 CHI N	1	4	1	0	0	0	0.0	0	0	0	0		.250	.250	0	0	OF-1, P-1
2 yrs.	3	12	3	0	0	0	0.0	0		0	0		.250	.250	0	0	OF-3, P-1

Woody Williams

WILLIAMS, WOODROW WILSON   BR TR 5'11" 175 lbs.
B. Aug. 22, 1912, Pamplin, Va.

1938 BKN N	20	51	17	1	1	0	0.0	6	6	4	1	1	.333	.392	0	0	SS-18, 3B-1
1943 CIN N	30	69	26	2	1	0	0.0	8	11	1	3	0	.377	.435	5	1	2B-12, 3B-7, SS-5
1944	155	653	157	23	3	1	0.2	73	35	44	24	7	.240	.289	0	0	2B-155
1945	133	482	114	14	0	0	0.0	46	27	39	24	6	.237	.266	0	0	2B-133
4 yrs.	338	1255	314	40	5	1	0.1	133	79	88	52	14	.250	.292	5	1	2B-300, SS-23, 3B-8

Howie Williamson

WILLIAMSON, NATHANIEL HOWARD   BL TL 6' 170 lbs.
B. Dec. 23, 1904, Little Rock, Ark.

1928 STL N	10	9	2	0	0	0	0.0	0	1	4	0	.222	.222	9	2		

Ned Williamson

WILLIAMSON, EDWARD NAGLE   BR TR 5'11" 170 lbs.
B. Oct. 24, 1857, Philadelphia, Pa.   D. Mar. 3, 1894, Hot Springs, Ark.

1878 IND N	63	250	58	10	2	1	0.4	31	19	5	15		.232	.300	0	0	3B-63
1879 CHI N	80	320	94	20	13	1	0.3	66	36	24	31		.294	.447	0	0	3B-70, 1B-6, C-4
1880	75	311	78	20	2	0	0.0	65	31	15	26		.251	.328	0	0	3B-63, C-11, 2B-3
1881	82	343	92	12	6	1	0.3	56	48	19	19		.268	.347	0	0	3B-76, 2B-4, P-3, SS-2, C-1
1882	83	348	98	27	4	3	0.9	66	60	27	21		.282	.408	0	0	3B-83, P-1
1883	98	402	111	49	5	2	0.5	83		22	48		.276	.438	0	0	3B-97, C-3, P-1
1884	107	417	116	18	8	27	6.5	84		42	56		.278	.554	0	0	3B-99, C-10, P-2
1885	113	407	97	16	5	3	0.7	87	64	75	60		.238	.324	0	0	3B-113, P-2, C-1
1886	121	430	93	17	8	6	1.4	69	58	80	71		.216	.335	0	0	SS-121, C-4, P-2
1887	127	439	117	20	14	9	2.1	77	78	73	57	45	.267	.437	0	0	SS-127, P-1
1888	132	452	113	9	14	8	1.8	75	73	65	71	25	.250	.385	0	0	SS-132
1889	47	173	41	3	1	1	0.6	16	30	23	22	2	.237	.283	0	0	SS-47
1890 CHI P	73	261	51	7	4	1	0.4	34	26	36	35	3	.195	.264	0	0	3B-52, SS-21
13 yrs.	1201	4553	1159	228	86	63	1.4	809	523	506	532	75	.255	.384	0	0	3B-716, SS-450, C-34, P-12, 2B-7, 1B-6

Julius Willigrod

WILLIGROD, JULIUS
D. Nov. 27, 1906, San Francisco, Calif.

1882 2 teams		DET N (1G – .333)				CLE N (9G – .139)											
" total	10	39	6	1	1	0	0.0	5	2	3	8		.154	.231	0	0	OF-9, SS-1

Hugh Willingham

WILLINGHAM, THOMAS HUGH   BR TR 6' 180 lbs.
B. May 30, 1908, Dalhart, Tex.

1930 CHI A	3	4	1	0	0	0	0.0	2	0	2	1	0	.250	.250	2	1	2B-1
1931 PHI N	23	35	9	2	1	1	2.9	5	3	2	9	0	.257	.457	5	1	SS-8, 3B-2, OF-1
1932	4	2	0	0	0	0	0.0	0	0	0	0	0	.000	.000	2	0	
1933	1	1	0	0	0	0	0.0	0	0	0	0	0	.000	.000	1	0	
4 yrs.	31	42	10	2	1	1	2.4	7	3	4	10	0	.238	.405	10	2	SS-8, 3B-2, OF-1, 2B-1

Wills

WILLS,
Deceased.

1884 2 teams		WAS AA (4G – .133)				KC U (5G – .143)											
" total	9	36	5	3	0	0		3		0			.139	.222	0	0	OF-9

Bump Wills

WILLS, ELLIOTT TAYLOR   BB TR 5'9" 172 lbs.
Son of Maury Wills.
B. July 27, 1952, Washington, D. C.

1977 TEX A	152	541	155	28	6	9	1.7	87	62	65	96	28	.287	.410	1	0	2B-150, SS-2, DH-1, 1B-1
1978	157	539	135	17	4	9	1.7	78	57	63	91	52	.250	.347	3	0	2B-156
1979	146	543	148	21	3	5	0.9	90	46	53	58	35	.273	.350	2	1	2B-146
1980	146	578	152	31	5	5	0.9	102	58	51	71	34	.263	.360	0	0	2B-144
1981	102	410	103	13	2	2	0.5	51	41	32	49	12	.251	.307	0	0	2B-101, DH-1

	G	AB	H	2B	3B	HR	HR %	R	RBI	BB	SO	SB	BA	SA	Pinch Hit AB	Pinch Hit H	G by POS

Bump Wills continued

	G	AB	H	2B	3B	HR	HR %	R	RBI	BB	SO	SB	BA	SA	AB	H	G by POS
1982 CHI N	128	419	114	18	4	6	1.4	64	38	46	76	35	.272	.377	21	6	2B-103
6 yrs.	831	3030	807	128	24	36	1.2	472	302	310	441	196	.266	.360	27	7	2B-800, DH-2, SS-2, 1B-1

Dave Wills

WILLS, DAVIS BOWLES
B. Jan. 26, 1877, Charlottesville, Va.　　D. Oct. 12, 1959, Washington, D. C.

	G	AB	H	2B	3B	HR	HR %	R	RBI	BB	SO	SB	BA	SA	AB	H	G by POS
1899 LOU N	24	94	21	3	1	0	0.0	15	12	2		1	.223	.277	0	0	1B-24

Maury Wills

WILLS, MAURICE MORNING
Father of Bump Wills.
B. Oct. 2, 1932, Washington, D. C.
Manager 1980-81.　　　　　　　　　　　　　　　　　　　BB TR 5'11" 170 lbs.

	G	AB	H	2B	3B	HR	HR %	R	RBI	BB	SO	SB	BA	SA	AB	H	G by POS
1959 LA N	83	242	63	5	2	0	0.0	27	7	13	27	7	.260	.298	0	0	SS-82
1960	148	516	152	15	2	0	0.0	75	27	35	47	50	.295	.331	0	0	SS-145
1961	148	613	173	12	10	1	0.2	105	31	59	50	35	.282	.339	1	0	SS-148
1962	165	695	208	13	10	6	0.9	130	48	51	57	104	.299	.373	0	0	SS-165
1963	134	527	159	19	3	0	0.0	83	34	44	48	40	.302	.349	0	0	SS-109, 3B-33
1964	158	630	173	15	5	2	0.3	81	34	41	73	53	.275	.324	4	0	SS-149, 3B-6
1965	158	650	186	14	7	0	0.0	92	33	40	64	94	.286	.329	2	0	SS-155
1966	143	594	162	14	2	1	0.2	60	39	34	60	38	.273	.308	1	0	SS-139, 3B-4
1967 PIT N	149	616	186	12	9	3	0.5	92	45	31	44	29	.302	.365	3	1	3B-144, SS-2
1968	153	627	174	12	6	0	0.0	76	31	45	57	52	.278	.316	3	0	3B-141, SS-10
1969 2 teams			MON	N	(47G –	.222)		LA	N	(104G –	.297)						
" total	151	623	171	10	8	4	0.6	80	47	59	61	40	.274	.335	1	1	SS-150, 2B-1
1970 LA N	132	522	141	19	3	0	0.0	77	34	50	34	28	.270	.318	5	1	SS-126, 3B-4
1971	149	601	169	14	3	3	0.5	73	44	40	44	15	.281	.329	6	1	SS-144, 3B-4
1972	71	132	17	3	1	0	0.0	16	4	10	18	1	.129	.167	5	1	SS-31, 3B-26
14 yrs.	1942	7588	2134	177	71	20	0.3	1067	458	552	684	586 8th	.281	.331	31	5	SS-1555, 3B-362, 2B-1

WORLD SERIES

	G	AB	H	2B	3B	HR	HR %	R	RBI	BB	SO	SB	BA	SA	AB	H	G by POS
1959 LA N	6	20	5	0	0	0	0.0	2	1	0	3	1	.250	.250	0	0	SS-6
1963	4	15	2	0	0	0	0.0	1	0	1	3	1	.133	.133	0	0	SS-4
1965	7	30	11	3	0	0	0.0	3	3	1	3	3	.367	.467	0	0	SS-7
1966	4	13	1	0	0	0	0.0	0	0	0	3	1	.077	.077	0	0	SS-4
4 yrs.	21	78	19	3	0	0	0.0	6	4	5	12	6	.244	.282	0	0	SS-21

Kid Willson

WILLSON, FRANK HOXIE
B. Nov. 3, 1895, Bloomington, Neb.　　D. Apr. 17, 1964, Union Gap, Wash.　　BL TR 6'1" 190 lbs.

	G	AB	H	2B	3B	HR	HR %	R	RBI	BB	SO	SB	BA	SA	AB	H	G by POS
1918 CHI A	4	1	0	0	0	0	0.0	2	0	1	1	0	.000	.000	1	0	
1927	7	10	1	0	0	0	0.0	1	1	0	2	0	.100	.100	4	0	OF-2
2 yrs.	11	11	1	0	0	0	0.0	3	1	1	3	0	.091	.091	5	0	OF-2

Walt Wilmot

WILMOT, WALTER R.
B. Oct. 18, 1863, Plover, Wis.　　D. Feb. 1, 1929, Chicago, Ill.　　BB TL

	G	AB	H	2B	3B	HR	HR %	R	RBI	BB	SO	SB	BA	SA	AB	H	G by POS
1888 WAS N	119	473	106	16	9	4	0.8	61	43	23	55	46	.224	.321	0	0	OF-119
1889	108	432	125	19	19	9	2.1	88	57	51	32	40	.289	.484	0	0	OF-108
1890 CHI N	139	571	159	15	12	14	2.5	114	99	64	44	76	.278	.420	0	0	OF-139
1891	121	498	139	14	10	11	2.2	102	71	55	21	42	.279	.414	0	0	OF-121
1892	92	380	82	7	7	2	0.5	47	35	40	20	31	.216	.287	0	0	OF-92
1893	94	392	118	14	14	3	0.8	69	61	40	8	39	.301	.431	1	0	OF-93
1894	133	597	197	45	12	5	0.8	134	130	35	23	74	.330	.471	0	0	OF-133
1895	108	466	132	16	6	8	1.7	86	72	30	19	28	.283	.395	0	0	OF-108
1897 NY N	11	34	9	2	0	1	2.9	8	4	2		1	.265	.412	1	0	OF-9
1898	35	138	33	4	2	2	1.4	16	22	9		4	.239	.341	1	0	OF-34
10 yrs.	960	3981	1100	152	91	59	1.5	725	594	349	222	381	.276	.405	3	0	OF-956

Archie Wilson

WILSON, ARCHIE CLIFTON
B. Nov. 25, 1923, Los Angeles, Calif.　　　　　　　　　　BR TR 5'11" 175 lbs.

	G	AB	H	2B	3B	HR	HR %	R	RBI	BB	SO	SB	BA	SA	AB	H	G by POS
1951 NY A	4	4	0	0	0	0	0.0	0	0	0	0	0	.000	.000	2	0	OF-2
1952 3 teams			NY	A	(3G –	.500)		WAS	A	(26G –	.208)		BOS	A	(18G –	.263)	
" total	47	136	31	5	3	0	0.0	9	17	7	14	0	.228	.309	9	3	OF-37
2 yrs.	51	140	31	5	3	0	0.0	9	17	7	14	0	.221	.300	11	3	OF-39

Art Wilson

WILSON, ARTHUR EARL (Dutch)
B. Dec. 11, 1885, Macon, Ill.　　D. June 12, 1960, Chicago, Ill.　　BR TR 5'8" 170 lbs.

	G	AB	H	2B	3B	HR	HR %	R	RBI	BB	SO	SB	BA	SA	AB	H	G by POS
1908 NY N	1	0	0	0	0	0	–	0	0	0		0	–	–	0	0	
1909	19	42	10	2	1	0	0.0	4	5	4		0	.238	.333	1	0	C-18
1910	26	52	14	4	1	0	0.0	10	5	9	6	2	.269	.385	0	0	C-25, 1B-1
1911	66	109	33	9	1	1	0.9	17	17	19	12	6	.303	.431	2	0	C-64
1912	65	121	35	6	0	3	2.5	17	19	13	14	2	.289	.413	3	1	C-61
1913	54	79	15	0	1	0	0.0	5	8	11	11	1	.190	.215	2	1	C-49, 1B-2
1914 CHI F	137	440	128	31	8	10	2.3	78	64	70		13	.291	.466	4	2	C-132
1915	96	269	82	11	2	7	2.6	44	31	65		4	.305	.439	7	2	C-87
1916 2 teams		PIT	N	(53G –	.258)		CHI	N	(36G –	.193)							
" total	89	242	55	8	3	1	0.4	16	17	19	41	5	.227	.298	14	2	C-73
1917 CHI N	81	211	45	9	2	2	0.9	17	25	32	36	6	.213	.303	4	2	C-75
1918 BOS N	89	280	69	8	2	0	0.0	15	19	24	31	5	.246	.289	2	0	C-85
1919	71	191	49	8	1	0	0.0	14	16	25	19	2	.257	.309	5	1	C-64, 1B-1
1920	16	19	1	0	0	0	0.0	0	0	1	1	0	.053	.053	7	0	3B-6, C-2
1921 CLE A	2	1	0	0	0	0	0.0	0	0	0	0	0	.000	.000	0	0	C-2
14 yrs.	812	2056	536	96	22	24	1.2	237	226	292	171	50	.261	.364	51	11	C-737, 3B-6, 1B-4

WORLD SERIES

	G	AB	H	2B	3B	HR	HR %	R	RBI	BB	SO	SB	BA	SA	AB	H	G by POS
1911 NY N	1	1	0	0	0	0	0.0	0	0	0	0	0	.000	.000	0	0	C-1
1912	2	1	1	0	0	0	0.0	0	0	0	0	0	1.000	1.000	0	0	C-2
1913	3	3	0	0	0	0	0.0	0	0	0	2	0	.000	.000	0	0	C-3
3 yrs.	6	5	1	0	0	0	0.0	0	0	0	2	0	.200	.200	0	0	C-6

	G	AB	H	2B	3B	HR	HR %	R	RBI	BB	SO	SB	BA	SA	Pinch Hit AB	Pinch Hit H	G by POS

Ivy Wingo continued

	G	AB	H	2B	3B	HR	HR %	R	RBI	BB	SO	SB	BA	SA	AB	H	G by POS
1914	80	237	71	8	5	4	1.7	24	26	18	17	15	.300	.426	4	2	C-70
1915 CIN N	119	339	75	11	6	3	0.9	26	29	13	33	10	.221	.316	17	2	C-97, OF-1
1916	119	347	85	8	11	2	0.6	30	40	25	27	4	.245	.349	10	5	C-107
1917	121	399	106	16	11	2	0.5	37	39	25	13	9	.266	.376	1	0	C-120
1918	100	323	82	15	6	0	0.0	36	31	19	18	6	.254	.337	2	1	C-93, OF-5
1919	76	245	67	12	6	0	0.0	30	27	23	19	4	.273	.371	1	0	C-75
1920	108	364	96	11	5	2	0.5	32	38	19	13	6	.264	.338	0	0	C-107, 2B-2
1921	97	295	79	7	6	3	1.0	20	38	21	14	3	.268	.363	4	1	C-92, OF-1
1922	80	260	74	13	3	1	1.2	24	45	23	11	1	.285	.392	2	0	C-78
1923	61	171	45	9	2	1	0.6	10	24	9	11	1	.263	.357	4	1	C-57
1924	66	192	55	5	4	1	0.5	21	23	14	8	1	.286	.370	1	0	C-65, 1B-1
1925	55	146	30	7	0	0	0.0	6	12	11	8	1	.205	.253	0	0	C-55
1926	7	10	2	0	0	0	0.0	0	1	1	0	0	.200	.200	0	0	C-7
1929	1	1	0	0	0	0	0.0	0	0	0	0	0	.000	.000	0	0	C-1
17 yrs.	1326	4001	1039	147	81	25	0.6	363	455	264	285	87	.260	.356	71	17	C-1231, OF-8, 1B-6, 2B-2
WORLD SERIES																	
1919 CIN N	3	7	4	0	0	0	0.0	1	1	3	1	0	.571	.571	0	0	C-3

George Winkelman

WINKELMAN, GEORGE EDWARD
B. Feb. 18, 1865, Washington, D. C.   D. May 19, 1960, Washington, D. C.

	G	AB	H	2B	3B	HR	HR %	R	RBI	BB	SO	SB	BA	SA	AB	H	G by POS
1883 LOU AA	4	13	0	0	0	0	0.0	2		1			.000	.000	0	0	OF-4

Herm Winningham

BL TR 6'   165 lbs.

WINNINGHAM, HERMAN S.
B. Dec. 1, 1961, Orangeburg, S. C.

	G	AB	H	2B	3B	HR	HR %	R	RBI	BB	SO	SB	BA	SA	AB	H	G by POS
1984 NY N	14	27	11	1	1	0	0.0	5	5	1	7	2	.407	.519	4	1	OF-10

Tom Winsett

BL TR 6'2"   190 lbs.

WINSETT, JOHN THOMAS (Long Tom)
B. Nov. 24, 1909, McKenzie, Tenn.

	G	AB	H	2B	3B	HR	HR %	R	RBI	BB	SO	SB	BA	SA	AB	H	G by POS
1930 BOS A	1	1	0	0	0	0	0.0	0	0	0	1	0	.000	.000	0	0	
1931	64	76	15	1	0	1	1.3	6	7	4	21	0	.197	.250	52	11	OF-8
1933	6	12	1	0	0	0	0.0	1	0	1	6	0	.083	.083	2	0	OF-4
1935 STL N	7	12	6	1	0	0	0.0	2	2	2	3	0	.500	.583	5	2	OF-2
1936 BKN N	22	85	20	7	0	1	1.2	13	18	11	14	0	.235	.353	1	1	OF-21
1937	118	350	83	15	5	5	1.4	32	42	45	64	3	.237	.351	15	5	OF-101, P-1
1938	12	30	9	1	0	1	3.3	6	7	6	4	0	.300	.433	2	0	OF-9
7 yrs.	230	566	134	25	5	8	1.4	60	76	69	113	3	.237	.341	77	19	OF-145, P-1

Kettle Wirtz

BR TR 5'11"   170 lbs.

WIRTZ, ELWOOD VERNON
B. Oct. 30, 1897, Edge Hill, Pa.   D. July 12, 1968, Sacramento, Calif.

	G	AB	H	2B	3B	HR	HR %	R	RBI	BB	SO	SB	BA	SA	AB	H	G by POS
1921 CHI N	7	11	2	0	0	0	0.0	0	1	0	3	0	.182	.182	2	2	C-5
1922	31	58	10	2	0	1	1.7	7	6	12	15	0	.172	.259	3	0	C-27
1923	5	5	1	0	0	0	0.0	2	1	2	0	0	.200	.200	0	0	C-3
1924 CHI A	6	12	1	0	0	0	0.0	0	0	2	2	1	.083	.083	0	0	C-5
4 yrs.	49	86	14	2	0	1	1.2	9	8	16	20	1	.163	.221	5	2	C-40

Bill Wise

WISE, WILLIAM E.
B. Mar. 15, 1861, Washington, D. C.   D. May 5, 1940, Washington, D. C.

	G	AB	H	2B	3B	HR	HR %	R	RBI	BB	SO	SB	BA	SA	AB	H	G by POS
1882 BAL AA	5	20	2	1	0	0	0.0	2		0			.100	.150	0	0	P-3, OF-2
1884 WAS U	85	339	79	17	1	2	0.6	51		12			.233	.307	0	0	P-50, OF-43, 3B-8, SS-2, 1B-1
1886 WAS N	1	3	0	0	0	0	0.0	0	0	0	0	1	.000	.000	0	0	
3 yrs.	91	362	81	18	1	2	0.6	53		12		1	.224	.296	0	0	P-53, OF-45, 3B-8, SS-2, 1B-1

Casey Wise

BB TR 6'   170 lbs.

WISE, KENDALL COLE
B. Sept. 8, 1932, Lafayette, Ind.

	G	AB	H	2B	3B	HR	HR %	R	RBI	BB	SO	SB	BA	SA	AB	H	G by POS
1957 CHI N	43	106	19	3	1	0	0.0	12	7	11	14	0	.179	.226	4	0	2B-31, SS-5
1958 MIL N	31	71	14	1	0	0	0.0	8	0	4	8	1	.197	.211	8	0	2B-10, SS-7, 3B-1
1959	22	76	13	2	0	1	1.3	11	5	10	5	0	.171	.237	1	0	2B-20, SS-5
1960 DET A	30	68	10	0	2	2	2.9	6	5	4	9	1	.147	.294	3	0	2B-17, SS-10, 3B-1
4 yrs.	126	321	56	6	3	3	0.9	37	17	29	36	2	.174	.240	16	0	2B-78, SS-27, 3B-2
WORLD SERIES																	
1958 MIL N	2	1	0	0	0	0	0.0	0	0	0	1	0	.000	.000	1	0	

Hughie Wise

BB TR 6'   178 lbs.

WISE, HUGH EDWARD
B. Mar. 9, 1906, Campbellsville, Ky.

	G	AB	H	2B	3B	HR	HR %	R	RBI	BB	SO	SB	BA	SA	AB	H	G by POS
1930 DET A	2	6	2	0	0	0	0.0	0	0	0	0	0	.333	.333	0	0	C-2

Nick Wise

BR TR 5'11"   194 lbs.

WISE, NICHOLAS JOSEPH
B. June 15, 1866, Boston, Mass.   D. Jan. 15, 1923, Boston, Mass.

	G	AB	H	2B	3B	HR	HR %	R	RBI	BB	SO	SB	BA	SA	AB	H	G by POS
1888 BOS N	1	3	0	0	0	0	0.0	0	0	0	0	0	.000	.000	0	0	OF-1, C-1

Sam Wise

BL TR 5'10½"   170 lbs.

WISE, SAMUEL WASHINGTON
B. Aug. 18, 1857, Akron, Ohio   D. Jan. 23, 1910, Akron, Ohio

	G	AB	H	2B	3B	HR	HR %	R	RBI	BB	SO	SB	BA	SA	AB	H	G by POS
1881 DET N	1	4	2	0	0	0	0.0	0	0	0	2		.500	.500	0	0	3B-1
1882 BOS N	78	298	66	11	4	4	1.3	44	34	5	45		.221	.326	0	0	SS-72, 3B-6
1883	96	406	110	25	7	4	1.0	73	58	13	74		.271	.397	0	0	SS-96
1884	114	426	91	15	9	4	0.9	60		25	104		.214	.319	0	0	SS-107, 2B-7
1885	107	424	120	20	10	4	0.9	71	46	25	61		.283	.406	0	0	SS-79, 2B-22, OF-6
1886	96	387	112	19	12	4	1.0	71	72	33	61		.289	.432	0	0	1B-57, 2B-20, SS-18
1887	113	467	156	27	17	9	1.9	103	92	36	44	43	.334	.522	0	0	SS-72, OF-27, 2B-16
1888	105	417	100	19	12	4	1.0	66	40	34	66	33	.240	.372	0	0	SS-89, 3B-6, 1B-5, OF-4, 2B-2

	G	AB	H	2B	3B	HR	HR %	R	RBI	BB	SO	SB	BA	SA	Pinch Hit AB	Pinch Hit H	G by POS

Sam Wise continued

	G	AB	H	2B	3B	HR	HR%	R	RBI	BB	SO	SB	BA	SA	AB	H	G by POS
1889 WAS N	121	472	118	15	8	4	0.8	79	62	61	62	24	.250	.341	0	0	2B-72, SS-26, 3B-13, OF-10
1890 BUF P	119	505	148	29	11	6	1.2	95	102	46	45	19	.293	.430	0	0	2B-119
1891 BAL AA	103	388	96	14	5	1	0.3	70	48	62	52	33	.247	.317	0	0	2B-99, SS-4
1893 WAS N	122	521	162	27	17	5	1.0	102	77	49	27	20	.311	.457	0	0	2B-91, 3B-31
12 yrs.	1175	4715	1281	221	112	49	1.0	834	631	389	643	172	.272	.397	0	0	SS-563, 2B-448, 1B-62, 3B-57, OF-47

Phil Wisner

WISNER, PHILIP N.
B. July, 1869, Washington, D. C.   Deceased.

TR

	G	AB	H	2B	3B	HR	HR%	R	RBI	BB	SO	SB	BA	SA	AB	H	G by POS
1895 WAS N	1	0	0	0	0	0	–	0	0	0	0	0	–	–	0	0	SS-1

Dave Wissman

WISSMAN, DAVID ALVIN
B. Feb. 17, 1941, Greenfield, Mass.

BL   TR   6'2"   178 lbs.

	G	AB	H	2B	3B	HR	HR%	R	RBI	BB	SO	SB	BA	SA	AB	H	G by POS
1964 PIT N	16	27	4	0	0	0	0.0	2	0	1	9	0	.148	.148	6	2	OF-10

Tex Wisterzil

WISTERZIL, GEORGE JOHN
B. Mar. 7, 1891, Detroit, Mich.   D. June 27, 1964, San Antonio, Tex.

BR   TR   5'9½"   150 lbs.

	G	AB	H	2B	3B	HR	HR%	R	RBI	BB	SO	SB	BA	SA	AB	H	G by POS
1914 BKN F	149	534	137	18	10	0	0.0	54	66	34		17	.257	.328	0	0	3B-149, 2B-1
1915 3 teams		BKN F (36G – .311)			CHI F (49G – .244)			STL F (8G – .208)									
" total	93	294	78	8	4	0	0.0	29	39	31		12	.265	.320	5	0	3B-87
2 yrs.	242	828	215	26	14	0	0.0	83	105	65		29	.260	.325	5	0	3B-236, 2B-1

Mickey Witek

WITEK, NICHOLAS JOSEPH
B. Dec. 19, 1915, Luzerne, Pa.

BR   TR   5'10"   170 lbs.

	G	AB	H	2B	3B	HR	HR%	R	RBI	BB	SO	SB	BA	SA	AB	H	G by POS
1940 NY N	119	433	111	7	0	3	0.7	34	31	24	17	2	.256	.293	1	1	SS-89, 2B-32
1941	26	94	34	5	0	1	1.1	11	16	4	2	0	.362	.447	0	0	2B-23
1942	148	553	144	19	6	5	0.9	72	48	36	20	2	.260	.344	1	0	2B-147
1943	153	622	195	17	0	6	1.0	68	55	41	23	1	.314	.370	0	0	2B-153
1946	82	284	75	13	2	4	1.4	32	29	28	10	1	.264	.366	7	2	2B-42, 3B-35
1947	51	160	35	4	1	3	1.9	22	17	15	12	1	.219	.313	8	0	2B-40, 3B-3
1949 NY A	1	1	1	0	0	0	0.0	0	0	0	0	0	1.000	1.000	1	1	
7 yrs.	580	2147	595	65	9	22	1.0	239	196	148	84	7	.277	.347	18	4	2B-437, SS-89, 3B-38

Corky Withrow

WITHROW, RAYMOND WALLACE
B. Nov. 28, 1937, High Coal, W. Va.

BR   TR   6'3½"   197 lbs.

	G	AB	H	2B	3B	HR	HR%	R	RBI	BB	SO	SB	BA	SA	AB	H	G by POS
1963 STL N	6	9	0	0	0	0	0.0	0	0	0	2	0	.000	.000	4	0	OF-2

Frank Withrow

WITHROW, FRANK BLAINE (Kid)
B. June 14, 1891, Greenwood, Mo.   D. Sept. 5, 1966, Omaha, Neb.

BR   TR   5'11½" 187 lbs.

	G	AB	H	2B	3B	HR	HR%	R	RBI	BB	SO	SB	BA	SA	AB	H	G by POS
1920 PHI N	48	132	24	4	1	0	0.0	8	12	8	26	0	.182	.227	0	0	C-48
1922	10	21	7	2	0	0	0.0	3	3	3	5	0	.333	.429	2	0	C-8
2 yrs.	58	153	31	6	1	0	0.0	11	15	11	31	0	.203	.255	2	0	C-56

Whitey Witt

WITT, LAWTON WALTER
Born Ladislaw Waldemar Wittkowski.
B. Sept. 28, 1895, Orange, Mass.

BL   TR   5'7"   150 lbs.

	G	AB	H	2B	3B	HR	HR%	R	RBI	BB	SO	SB	BA	SA	AB	H	G by POS
1916 PHI A	143	563	138	16	15	2	0.4	64	36	55	71	19	.245	.337	1	0	SS-142
1917	128	452	114	13	4	0	0.0	62	28	65	45	12	.252	.299	4	0	SS-111, OF-7, 3B-6
1919	122	460	123	15	6	0	0.0	56	33	46	26	11	.267	.326	4	1	OF-59, 2B-56, 3B-2
1920	65	218	70	11	3	1	0.5	29	25	27	16	2	.321	.413	2	0	OF-49, 2B-11, SS-2
1921	154	629	198	31	11	4	0.6	100	45	77	52	16	.315	.418	0	0	OF-154
1922 NY A	140	528	157	11	6	4	0.8	98	40	89	29	5	.297	.364	1	1	OF-139
1923	146	596	187	18	10	6	1.0	113	56	67	42	2	.314	.408	2	0	OF-144
1924	147	600	178	26	5	1	0.2	88	36	45	20	9	.297	.362	3	0	OF-143
1925	31	40	8	2	1	0	0.0	9	0	6	2	1	.200	.300	9	3	OF-10
1926 BKN N	63	85	22	1	1	0	0.0	13	3	12	6	1	.259	.294	28	6	OF-22
10 yrs.	1139	4171	1195	144	62	18	0.4	632	302	489	309	78	.287	.364	54	11	OF-727, SS-255, 2B-67, 3B-8

WORLD SERIES

	G	AB	H	2B	3B	HR	HR%	R	RBI	BB	SO	SB	BA	SA	AB	H	G by POS
1922 NY A	5	18	4	1	1	0	0.0	1	0	1	2	0	.222	.389	0	0	OF-5
1923	6	25	6	2	0	0	0.0	1	4	1	1	0	.240	.320	0	0	OF-6
2 yrs.	11	43	10	3	1	0	0.0	2	4	2	3	0	.233	.349	0	0	OF-11

Jerry Witte

WITTE, JEROME CHARLES
B. July 30, 1915, St. Louis, Mo.

BR   TR   6'1"   190 lbs.

	G	AB	H	2B	3B	HR	HR%	R	RBI	BB	SO	SB	BA	SA	AB	H	G by POS
1946 STL A	18	73	14	2	0	2	2.7	7	4	0	18	0	.192	.301	0	0	1B-18
1947	34	99	14	2	1	2	2.0	4	12	11	22	0	.141	.242	8	0	1B-27
2 yrs.	52	172	28	4	1	4	2.3	11	16	11	40	0	.163	.267	8	0	1B-45

John Wockenfuss

WOCKENFUSS, JOHNNY BILTON
B. Feb. 27, 1949, Welch, W. Va.

BR   TR   6'   190 lbs.

	G	AB	H	2B	3B	HR	HR%	R	RBI	BB	SO	SB	BA	SA	AB	H	G by POS
1974 DET A	13	29	4	1	0	0	0.0	1	2	3	2	0	.138	.172	0	0	C-13
1975	35	118	27	6	3	4	3.4	15	13	10	15	0	.229	.432	1	0	C-34
1976	60	144	32	7	2	3	2.1	18	10	17	14	0	.222	.361	1	0	C-59
1977	53	164	45	8	1	9	5.5	26	25	14	18	0	.274	.500	9	2	C-37, OF-9, DH-3
1978	71	187	53	5	0	7	3.7	23	22	21	14	0	.283	.422	17	6	OF-60, DH-2
1979	87	231	61	9	1	15	6.5	27	46	18	40	2	.264	.506	20	5	1B-31, C-20, DH-18, OF-6
1980	126	372	102	13	2	16	4.3	56	65	68	64	1	.274	.449	17	4	1B-52, DH-28, C-25, OF-23
1981	70	172	37	4	0	9	5.2	20	25	28	22	0	.215	.395	13	1	DH-39, 1B-25, C-5, OF-1
1982	70	193	58	9	0	8	4.1	28	32	29	21	0	.301	.472	11	4	C-24, DH-17, 1B-17, OF-10, 3B-1
1983	92	245	66	8	1	9	3.7	32	44	31	37	1	.269	.420	24	7	DH-39, C-29, 1B-13, OF-1, 3B-1

	G	AB	H	2B	3B	HR	HR %	R	RBI	BB	SO	SB	BA	SA	Pinch Hit AB	Pinch Hit H	G by POS

John Wockenfuss continued

	G	AB	H	2B	3B	HR	HR%	R	RBI	BB	SO	SB	BA	SA	AB	H	G by POS
1984 PHI N	86	180	52	3	1	6	3.3	20	24	30	24	1	.289	.417	27	6	1B-39, C-21, 3B-2
11 yrs.	763	2035	537	73	11	86	4.2	266	308	269	271	5	.264	.437	140	35	C-267, 1B-177, DH-146, OF-110, 3B-4

Andy Woehr

WOEHR, ANDREW EMIL
B. Feb. 4, 1896, Fort Wayne, Ind.   BR TR 5'11" 165 lbs.

	G	AB	H	2B	3B	HR	HR%	R	RBI	BB	SO	SB	BA	SA	AB	H	G by POS
1923 PHI N	13	41	14	2	0	0	0.0	3	3	1	1	0	.341	.390	0	0	3B-13
1924	50	152	33	4	5	0	0.0	11	17	5	8	2	.217	.309	3	0	3B-44, 2B-1
2 yrs.	63	193	47	6	5	0	0.0	14	20	6	9	2	.244	.326	3	0	3B-57, 2B-1

Joe Woerlin

WOERLIN, JOSEPH
B. Oct. 9, 1864, France   D. June 22, 1919, St. Louis, Mo.

	G	AB	H	2B	3B	HR	HR%	R	RBI	BB	SO	SB	BA	SA	AB	H	G by POS
1895 WAS N	1	3	1	0	0	0	0.0	0		0		0	.333	.333	0	0	SS-1

Jim Wohlford

WOHLFORD, JAMES EUGENE (Wolfie)
B. Feb. 28, 1951, Visalia, Calif.   BR TR 5'11" 175 lbs.

	G	AB	H	2B	3B	HR	HR%	R	RBI	BB	SO	SB	BA	SA	AB	H	G by POS
1972 KC A	15	25	6	1	0	0	0.0	3	0	2	6	0	.240	.280	4	0	2B-8
1973	45	109	29	1	3	2	1.8	21	10	11	12	1	.266	.385	5	1	DH-19, OF-13
1974	143	501	136	16	7	2	0.4	55	44	39	74	16	.271	.343	9	2	OF-138, DH-1
1975	116	353	90	10	5	0	0.0	45	30	34	37	12	.255	.312	14	2	OF-102, DH-4
1976	107	293	73	10	2	1	0.3	47	24	29	24	22	.249	.307	16	2	OF-93, DH-3, 2B-1
1977 MIL A	129	391	97	16	3	2	0.5	41	36	21	49	17	.248	.320	4	1	OF-125, 2B-1
1978	46	118	35	7	2	1	0.8	16	19	6	10	3	.297	.415	8	2	OF-35, DH-4
1979	63	175	46	13	1	1	0.6	19	17	8	28	6	.263	.366	2	1	OF-55, DH-5
1980 SF N	91	193	54	6	4	1	0.5	17	24	13	23	1	.280	.368	48	12	OF-49, 3B-1
1981	50	68	11	3	0	1	1.5	4	7	4	9	0	.162	.250	40	5	OF-10
1982	97	250	64	12	1	2	0.8	37	25	30	36	8	.256	.336	27	5	OF-72
1983 MON N	83	141	39	8	0	1	0.7	7	14	5	14	0	.277	.355	31	11	OF-61
1984	95	213	64	13	2	5	2.3	20	29	14	19	3	.300	.451	39	8	OF-59, 3B-2
13 yrs.	1080	2830	744	116	30	19	0.7	332	279	216	341	89	.263	.345	247	52	OF-812, DH-36, 2B-10, 3B-3

LEAGUE CHAMPIONSHIP SERIES

	G	AB	H	2B	3B	HR	HR%	R	RBI	BB	SO	SB	BA	SA	AB	H	G by POS
1976 KC A	5	11	2	0	0	0	0.0	3	0	3	1	2	.182	.182	1	1	OF-5

John Wojcik

WOJCIK, JOHN JOSEPH
B. Apr. 6, 1942, Olean, N. Y.   BL TR 6' 175 lbs.

	G	AB	H	2B	3B	HR	HR%	R	RBI	BB	SO	SB	BA	SA	AB	H	G by POS
1962 KC A	16	43	13	4	0	0	0.0	8	9	13	4	3	.302	.395	4	2	OF-12
1963	19	59	11	0	0	0	0.0	7	2	8	8	2	.186	.186	2	0	OF-17
1964	6	22	3	0	0	0	0.0	1	0	2	8	0	.136	.136	0	0	OF-6
3 yrs.	41	124	27	4	0	0	0.0	16	11	23	20	5	.218	.250	6	2	OF-35

Chicken Wolf

WOLF, WILLIAM VAN WINKLE
B. May 12, 1862, Louisville, Ky.   D. May 16, 1903, Louisville, Ky.
Manager 1889.   BR TR 5'9" 190 lbs.

	G	AB	H	2B	3B	HR	HR%	R	RBI	BB	SO	SB	BA	SA	AB	H	G by POS
1882 LOU AA	78	318	95	11	8	0	0.0	46		9			.299	.384	0	0	OF-70, SS-9, 1B-1, P-1
1883	98	389	102	17	9	1	0.3	59		5			.262	.360	0	0	OF-78, C-20, SS-5, 2B-1
1884	110	486	146	24	11	3	0.6	79		4			.300	.414	0	0	OF-101, C-11, SS-1, 3B-1, 1B-1
1885	112	483	141	23	17	1	0.2	79		11			.292	.416	0	0	OF-111, C-2, 3B-1, P-1
1886	130	545	148	17	12	3	0.6	93		27			.272	.363	0	0	OF-122, 1B-8, C-3, 2B-1, P-1
1887	137	569	160	28	13	1	0.2	103		34		45	.281	.381	0	0	OF-128, 1B-11
1888	128	538	154	28	11	0	0.0	80	67	25		41	.286	.379	0	0	OF-85, SS-39, 3B-4, C-3, 1B-1
1889	130	546	159	20	9	3	0.5	72	57	29	34	18	.291	.377	0	0	OF-88, 1B-16, 2B-13, SS-10, 3B-7
1890	134	543	197	29	11	4	0.7	100		43		46	.363	.479	0	0	OF-123, 3B-12
1891	138	537	136	17	8	1	0.2	67	82	42	36	13	.253	.320	0	0	OF-133, 1B-5, 3B-1
1892 STL N	3	14	2	0	0	0	0.0	1	1	0	1	0	.143	.143	0	0	OF-3
11 yrs.	1198	4968	1440	214	109	17	0.3	779	206	229	71	163	.290	.387	0	0	OF-1042, SS-64, 1B-43, C-39, 3B-26, 2B-15, P-3

Ray Wolf

WOLF, RAYMOND BERNARD
B. July 15, 1904, Chicago, Ill.   D. Oct. 6, 1979, Fort Worth, Tex.   BR TR 5'11" 175 lbs.

	G	AB	H	2B	3B	HR	HR%	R	RBI	BB	SO	SB	BA	SA	AB	H	G by POS
1927 CIN N	1	1	0	0	0	0	0.0	0	0	0	0	0	.000	.000	0	0	1B-1

Harry Wolfe

WOLFE, HAROLD
B. Nov. 24, 1888, Worcester, Mass.   D. July 28, 1971   BR TR 5'8" 160 lbs.

	G	AB	H	2B	3B	HR	HR%	R	RBI	BB	SO	SB	BA	SA	AB	H	G by POS
1917 2 teams		CHI N (9G – .400)			PIT N (3G – .000)												
" total	12	10	2	0	0	0	0.0	1	2	5		0	.200	.200	3	0	OF-2, SS-2, 2B-1

Larry Wolfe

WOLFE, LAURENCE MARCY
B. Mar. 2, 1953, Melbourne, Fla.   BR TR 5'11" 170 lbs.

	G	AB	H	2B	3B	HR	HR%	R	RBI	BB	SO	SB	BA	SA	AB	H	G by POS
1977 MIN A	8	25	6	1	0	0	0.0	3	6	1	0	0	.240	.280	3	2	3B-8
1978	88	235	55	10	1	3	1.3	25	25	36	27	0	.234	.323	7	2	3B-81, SS-7
1979 BOS A	47	78	19	4	0	3	3.8	12	15	17	21	0	.244	.410	8	4	2B-27, 3B-9, SS-2, DH-1, 1B-1, C-1
1980	18	23	3	1	0	1	4.3	3	4	0	5	0	.130	.304	3	1	3B-14, DH-4
4 yrs.	161	361	83	16	1	7	1.9	43	50	54	53	0	.230	.338	21	9	3B-112, 2B-27, SS-9, DH-5, 1B-1, C-1

Polly Wolfe

WOLFE, ROY CHAMBERLAIN
B. Sept. 1, 1888, Knoxville, Ill.   D. Nov. 21, 1938, Morris, Ill.   BL TR 5'10" 170 lbs.

	G	AB	H	2B	3B	HR	HR%	R	RBI	BB	SO	SB	BA	SA	AB	H	G by POS
1912 CHI A	1	1	0	0	0	0	0.0	0	0	0		0	.000	.000	1	0	

	G	AB	H	2B	3B	HR	HR %	R	RBI	BB	SO	SB	BA	SA	Pinch Hit AB	Pinch Hit H	G by POS

Polly Wolfe continued

	G	AB	H	2B	3B	HR	HR%	R	RBI	BB	SO	SB	BA	SA	AB	H	G by POS
1914	9	28	6	0	0	0	0.0	0	0	3	6	1	.214	.214	1	0	OF-8
2 yrs.	10	29	6	0	0	0	0.0	0	0	3	6	1	.207	.207	2	0	OF-8

Abraham Wolstenholme

WOLSTENHOLME, ABRAHAM LINCOLN
B. Mar. 4, 1861, Philadelphia, Pa.   D. Mar. 4, 1916, Philadelphia, Pa.

	G	AB	H	2B	3B	HR	HR%	R	RBI	BB	SO	SB	BA	SA	AB	H	G by POS
1883 PHI N	3	11	1	1	0	0	0.0		0	0			.091	.182	0	0	C-2, OF-1

Harry Wolter

WOLTER, HARRY MEIGS   BL TL 5'10" 175 lbs.
B. July 11, 1884, Monterey, Calif.   D. July 7, 1970, Palo Alto, Calif.

	G	AB	H	2B	3B	HR	HR%	R	RBI	BB	SO	SB	BA	SA	AB	H	G by POS
1907 3 teams		CIN N (4G – .133)			PIT N (1G – .000)			STL N (16G – .340)									
" total	21	63	18	0	0	0	0.0	5	7	3		1	.286	.286	4	0	OF-13, P-4
1909 BOS A	54	119	29	2	4	2	1.7	14	10	9		2	.244	.378	13	1	1B-17, P-10, OF-9
1910 NY A	135	479	128	15	9	4	0.8	84	42	66		39	.267	.361	2	0	OF-130
1911	122	434	132	17	15	4	0.9	78	36	62		28	.304	.440	3	2	OF-113, 1B-2
1912	12	32	11	2	1	0	0.0	8	1	10		5	.344	.469	3	0	OF-9
1913	126	425	108	18	6	2	0.5	53	43	80	50	13	.254	.339	3	1	OF-121
1917 CHI N	117	353	88	15	7	0	0.0	44	28	38	40	7	.249	.331	16	7	OF-97, 1B-1
7 yrs.	587	1905	514	69	42	12	0.6	286	167	268	90	95	.270	.369	44	11	OF-492, 1B-20, P-14

Harry Wolverton

WOLVERTON, HARRY STERLING   BL TR
B. Dec. 6, 1873, Mt. Vernon, Ohio   D. Feb. 4, 1937, Oakland, Calif.
Manager 1912.

	G	AB	H	2B	3B	HR	HR%	R	RBI	BB	SO	SB	BA	SA	AB	H	G by POS
1898 CHI N	13	49	16	1	0	0	0.0	4	2	1		1	.327	.347	0	0	3B-13
1899	99	389	111	14	11	1	0.3	50	49	30		14	.285	.386	0	0	3B-98, SS-1
1900 2 teams		CHI N (3G – .182)			PHI N (101G – .282)												
" total	104	394	110	10	8	3	0.8	44	58	22		5	.279	.368	0	0	3B-104
1901 PHI N	93	379	117	15	4	0	0.0	42	43	22		13	.309	.369	0	0	3B-93
1902 2 teams		WAS A (59G – .249)			PHI N (34G – .294)												
" total	93	385	102	11	5	1	0.3	47	39	22		11	.265	.327	0	0	3B-93
1903 PHI N	123	494	152	13	12	0	0.0	72	53	18		10	.308	.383	0	0	3B-123
1904	102	398	106	15	5	0	0.0	43	49	26		18	.266	.329	0	0	3B-102
1905 BOS N	122	463	104	15	7	2	0.4	38	55	23		10	.225	.300	0	0	3B-122
1912 NY A	33	50	15	1	1	0	0.0	6	4	2		1	.300	.360	26	10	3B-7
9 yrs.	782	3001	833	95	53	7	0.2	346	352	166		83	.278	.352	26	10	3B-755, SS-1

Sid Womack

WOMACK, SIDNEY KIRK (Tex)   BR TR 5'10½" 185 lbs.
B. Oct. 2, 1896, Greensburg, La.   D. Aug. 8, 1958, Jackson, Miss.

	G	AB	H	2B	3B	HR	HR%	R	RBI	BB	SO	SB	BA	SA	AB	H	G by POS
1926 BOS N	1	3	0	0	0	0	0.0	0		1	0	0	.000	.000	0	0	C-1

Bob Wood

WOOD, ROBERT LYNN   BR TR
B. July 28, 1865, Thorn Hill, Ohio   D. May 22, 1943, Youngstown, Ohio

	G	AB	H	2B	3B	HR	HR%	R	RBI	BB	SO	SB	BA	SA	AB	H	G by POS
1898 CIN N	39	109	30	.6	0	0	0.0	14	16	9		1	.275	.330	8	3	C-29, OF-1, 1B-1
1899	62	194	61	11	7	0	0.0	34	24	25		3	.314	.443	2	1	C-53, OF-2, 3B-2, 1B-1
1900	45	139	37	8	1	0	0.0	17	22	10		3	.266	.338	11	4	C-18, 3B-15, OF-1
1901 CLE A	98	346	101	23	3	1	0.3	45	49	12		6	.292	.384	4	1	C-84, 3B-4, OF-3, SS-1, 2B-1, 1B-1
1902	81	258	76	18	2	0	0.0	23	40	27		1	.295	.380	9	2	C-52, 1B-16, OF-2, 3B-1, 2B-1
1904 DET A	49	175	43	6	2	1	0.6	15	17	5		1	.246	.320	2	0	C-47
1905	8	24	2	1	0	0	0.0	1	0	1		0	.083	.125	1	0	C-7
7 yrs.	382	1245	350	73	15	2	0.2	149	168	89		15	.281	.369	37	8	C-290, 3B-22, 1B-19, OF-9, 2B-2, SS-1

Doc Wood

WOOD, CHARLES SPENCER   BR TR 5'11" 145 lbs.
B. Feb. 28, 1900, Batesville, Miss.   D. Nov. 3, 1974, New Orleans, La.

	G	AB	H	2B	3B	HR	HR%	R	RBI	BB	SO	SB	BA	SA	AB	H	G by POS
1923 PHI A	3	3	1	0	0	0	0.0	0	0	0	0	0	.333	.333	0	0	SS-3

Fred Wood

WOOD, FRED S.   5'5" 160 lbs.
Brother of Pete Wood.
B. 1863, Hamilton, Ont., Canada   D. Aug. 28, 1933, New York, N. Y.

	G	AB	H	2B	3B	HR	HR%	R	RBI	BB	SO	SB	BA	SA	AB	H	G by POS
1884 DET N	12	42	2	0	0	0	0.0	4		3	18		.048	.048	0	0	C-7, OF-6, SS-1
1885 BUF N	1	4	1	0	0	0	0.0	0		0	0		.250	.250	0	0	C-1
2 yrs.	13	46	3	0	0	0	0.0	4		3	18		.065	.065	0	0	C-8, OF-6, SS-1

George Wood

WOOD, GEORGE A. (Dandy)   BL TR 5'10½" 175 lbs.
B. Nov. 9, 1858, Boston, Mass.   D. Apr. 4, 1924, Harrisburg, Pa.
Manager 1891.

	G	AB	H	2B	3B	HR	HR%	R	RBI	BB	SO	SB	BA	SA	AB	H	G by POS
1880 WOR N	81	327	80	16	5	0	0.0	37		10	37		.245	.324	0	0	OF-80, 3B-2, 1B-1
1881 DET N	80	337	100	18	9	2	0.6	54	32	19	32		.297	.421	0	0	OF-80
1882	84	375	101	12	12	7	1.9	69	29	14	30		.269	.421	0	0	OF-84
1883	99	441	133	26	11	5	1.1	81		25	37		.302	.444	0	0	OF-99, P-1
1884	114	473	119	16	10	8	1.7	79		39	75		.252	.378	0	0	OF-114, 3B-1
1885	82	362	105	19	8	5	1.4	62	28	13	19		.290	.428	0	0	OF-70, 3B-12, SS-1, P-1
1886 PHI N	106	450	123	18	15	4	0.9	81	50	23	75		.273	.407	0	0	OF-97, SS-6, 3B-2
1887	113	491	142	22	19	14	2.9	118	66	40	51	19	.289	.497	0	0	OF-104, SS-3, 3B-3, 2B-3
1888	106	433	99	19	6	6	1.4	67	15	39	44	20	.229	.342	0	0	OF-104, 3B-2, P-2
1889 2 teams		PHI N (97G – .251)			BAL AA (3G – .200)												
" total	100	432	108	21	4	5	1.2	78	54	53	35	18	.250	.352	0	0	OF-95, SS-6, P-1
1890 PHI N	132	539	156	20	14	9	1.7	115	102	51	35	20	.289	.429	0	0	OF-132, 3B-1
1891 PHI AA	132	528	163	18	14	3	0.6	105	61	72	52	22	.309	.413	0	0	OF-122, 3B-6, SS-5
1892 2 teams		BAL N (21G – .224)			CIN N (30G – .196)												
" total	51	183	38	3	5	0	0.0	19	24	20	25	5	.208	.279	0	0	OF-51
13 yrs.	1280	5371	1467	228	132	68	1.3	965	460	418	547	104	.273	.403	0	0	OF-1232, 3B-30, SS-21, P-5, 2B-3, 1B-1

	G	AB	H	2B	3B	HR	HR %	R	RBI	BB	SO	SB	BA	SA	Pinch Hit AB	Pinch Hit H	G by POS

Harry Wood

WOOD, HAROLD AUSTIN
B. Baltimore, Md.   D. May 18, 1935, Bethesda, Md.
BL TR 5'10"   155 lbs.

	G	AB	H	2B	3B	HR	HR%	R	RBI	BB	SO	SB	BA	SA	PH AB	PH H	G by POS
1903 **CIN N**	2	3	0	0	0	0	0.0	0	0	1		0	.000	.000	1	0	OF-2

Jake Wood

WOOD, JACOB
B. June 22, 1937, Elizabeth, N. J.
BR TR 6'1"   163 lbs.

	G	AB	H	2B	3B	HR	HR%	R	RBI	BB	SO	SB	BA	SA	PH AB	PH H	G by POS
1961 **DET A**	162	663	171	17	14	11	1.7	96	69	58	141	30	.258	.376	1	0	2B-162
1962	111	367	83	10	5	8	2.2	68	30	33	59	24	.226	.346	11	2	2B-90
1963	85	351	95	11	2	11	3.1	50	27	24	61	18	.271	.407	1	0	2B-81, 3B-1
1964	64	125	29	2	2	1	0.8	11	7	4	24	0	.232	.304	29	7	1B-11, 2B-10, 3B-6, OF-1
1965	58	104	30	3	0	2	1.9	12	7	10	19	3	.288	.375	25	9	2B-20, SS-1, 3B-1, 1B-1
1966	98	230	58	9	3	2	0.9	39	27	28	48	4	.252	.343	40	6	2B-52, 3B-4, 1B-2
1967 2 teams			**DET**	A	(14G –	.050)		**CIN**	N	(16G –	.118)						
" total	30	37	3	1	0	0	0.0	3	1	2	10	0	.081	.108	19	2	OF-2, 2B-2, 1B-2
7 yrs.	608	1877	469	53	26	35	1.9	279	168	159	362	79	.250	.362	126	26	2B-417, 1B-16, 3B-12, OF-3, SS-1

Joe Wood

WOOD, JOE (Smoky Joe)
Father of Joe Wood.
B. Oct. 25, 1889, Kansas City, Mo.
BR TR 5'11"   180 lbs.

	G	AB	H	2B	3B	HR	HR%	R	RBI	BB	SO	SB	BA	SA	PH AB	PH H	G by POS
1908 **BOS A**	6	7	0	0	0	0	0.0	1	0	0		0	.000	.000	0	0	P-6
1909	24	55	9	0	1	0	0.0	4	3	2		0	.164	.200	0	0	P-24
1910	35	69	18	2	1	1	1.4	9	5	5		0	.261	.362	0	0	P-35
1911	44	88	23	4	2	2	2.3	15	11	10		1	.261	.420	0	0	P-44
1912	43	124	36	13	1	1	0.8	17	13	11		0	.290	.435	0	0	P-43
1913	24	56	15	5	0	0	0.0	10	10	4	7	1	.268	.357	1	0	P-23
1914	20	43	6	1	0	0	0.0	2	1	3	14	1	.140	.163	2	0	P-18
1915	29	54	14	1	1	1	1.9	6	7	5	10	1	.259	.370	1	0	P-25
1917 **CLE A**	10	6	0	0	0	0	0.0	1	0	0	3	0	.000	.000	2	0	P-5
1918	119	422	125	22	4	5	1.2	41	66	36	38	8	.296	.403	1	0	OF-95, 2B-19, 1B-4
1919	72	192	49	10	5	1	0.5	30	27	32	21	3	.255	.375	6	0	OF-64, P-1
1920	61	137	37	11	2	1	0.7	25	30	25	16	1	.270	.401	0	0	OF-54, P-10
1921	66	194	71	16	5	4	2.1	32	60	25	17	2	.366	.562	0	0	OF-64
1922	142	505	150	33	8	8	1.6	74	92	50	63	5	.297	.442	1	0	OF-140, 1B-1
14 yrs.	695	1952	553	118	30	24	1.2	267	325	208	189	23	.283	.411	13	0	OF-417, P-234, 2B-19, 1B-5

WORLD SERIES	G	AB	H	2B	3B	HR	HR%	R	RBI	BB	SO	SB	BA	SA	PH AB	PH H	G by POS
1912 **BOS A**	4	7	2	0	0	0	0.0	1	1	1	0	0	.286	.286	0	0	P-4
1920 **CLE A**	4	10	2	1	0	0	0.0	2	0	1	2	0	.200	.300	1	0	OF-4
2 yrs.	8	17	4	1	0	0	0.0	3	1	2	2	0	.235	.294	1	0	OF-4, P-4

Joe Wood

WOOD, JOSEPH PERRY
B. Oct. 3, 1919, Houston, Tex.
BR TR 5'9½"   160 lbs.

	G	AB	H	2B	3B	HR	HR%	R	RBI	BB	SO	SB	BA	SA	PH AB	PH H	G by POS
1943 **DET A**	60	164	53	4	4	1	0.6	22	17	6	13	2	.323	.415	10	3	2B-22, 3B-18

Ken Wood

WOOD, KENNETH LANIER
B. July 1, 1924, Lincolnton, N. C.
BR TR 6'   200 lbs.

	G	AB	H	2B	3B	HR	HR%	R	RBI	BB	SO	SB	BA	SA	PH AB	PH H	G by POS
1948 **STL A**	10	24	2	0	1	0	0.0	2	2	1	4	0	.083	.167	5	0	OF-5
1949	7	6	0	0	0	0	0.0	0	0	1	2	0	.000	.000	3	0	OF-3
1950	128	369	83	24	0	13	3.5	42	62	38	58	0	.225	.396	32	4	OF-94
1951	109	333	79	19	0	15	4.5	40	44	27	49	1	.237	.429	10	1	OF-100
1952 2 teams			**BOS**	A	(15G –	.100)		**WAS**	A	(61G –	.238)						
" total	76	230	52	8	6	6	2.6	26	32	33	25	0	.226	.391	8	0	OF-69
1953 **WAS A**	12	33	7	1	0	0	0.0	0	3	2	3	0	.212	.242	5	1	OF-7
6 yrs.	342	995	223	52	7	34	3.4	110	143	102	141	1	.224	.393	63	6	OF-278

Roy Wood

WOOD, ROY WINTON (Woody)
B. Aug. 29, 1892, Monticello, Ark.   D. Apr. 6, 1974, Fayetteville, Ark.
BR TR 6'   175 lbs.

	G	AB	H	2B	3B	HR	HR%	R	RBI	BB	SO	SB	BA	SA	PH AB	PH H	G by POS
1913 **PIT N**	14	35	10	4	0	0	0.0	4	2	1	8	0	.286	.400	3	0	OF-8, 1B-1
1914 **CLE A**	72	220	52	6	3	1	0.5	24	15	13	26	6	.236	.305	10	2	OF-41, 1B-20
1915	33	78	15	2	1	0	0.0	5	3	2	13	1	.192	.244	8	1	1B-21, OF-2
3 yrs.	119	333	77	12	4	1	0.3	33	20	16	47	7	.231	.300	21	3	OF-51, 1B-42

Larry Woodall

WOODALL, CHARLES LAWRENCE
B. July 26, 1894, Staunton, Va.   D. May 6, 1963, Boston, Mass.
BR TR 5'9"   165 lbs.

	G	AB	H	2B	3B	HR	HR%	R	RBI	BB	SO	SB	BA	SA	PH AB	PH H	G by POS
1920 **DET A**	18	49	12	1	0	0	0.0	4	5	2	6	0	.245	.265	2	0	C-15
1921	46	80	29	4	1	0	0.0	10	14	6	7	1	.363	.438	18	5	C-24
1922	50	125	43	2	2	0	0.0	19	18	8	11	0	.344	.392	11	4	C-39
1923	71	148	41	12	2	1	0.7	20	19	22	9	2	.277	.405	9	4	C-60
1924	67	165	51	9	2	0	0.0	23	24	21	5	0	.309	.388	4	0	C-62
1925	75	171	35	4	1	0	0.0	20	13	24	8	1	.205	.240	0	0	C-75
1926	67	146	34	5	0	0	0.0	18	15	15	2	0	.233	.267	5	1	C-59
1927	88	246	69	8	6	0	0.0	28	39	37	9	9	.280	.362	2	0	C-86
1928	65	186	39	5	1	0	0.0	19	13	24	10	3	.210	.247	3	0	C-62
1929	1	1	0	0	0	0	0.0	0	0	0	0	0	.000	.000	1	0	
10 yrs.	548	1317	353	50	15	1	0.1	161	160	159	67	16	.268	.331	55	14	C-482

Darrell Woodard

WOODARD, DARRELL LEE
B. Dec. 10, 1956, Wilma, Ark.
BR TR 5'11"   160 lbs.

	G	AB	H	2B	3B	HR	HR%	R	RBI	BB	SO	SB	BA	SA	PH AB	PH H	G by POS
1978 **OAK A**	33	9	0	0	0	0	0.0	10	0	1	1	3	.000	.000	0	0	2B-14, DH-1, 3B-1

Red Woodhead

WOODHEAD, JAMES
B. July, 1851, Chelsea, Mass.   D. Sept. 7, 1881, Boston, Mass.

	G	AB	H	2B	3B	HR	HR%	R	RBI	BB	SO	SB	BA	SA	PH AB	PH H	G by POS
1879 **SYR N**	34	131	21	1	0	0	0.0	4	2	0	23		.160	.168	0	0	3B-34

	G	AB	H	2B	3B	HR	HR %	R	RBI	BB	SO	SB	BA	SA	Pinch Hit AB	Pinch Hit H	G by POS

Gene Woodling

WOODLING, EUGENE RICHARD
B. Aug. 16, 1922, Akron, Ohio
BL TR 5'9½" 195 lbs.

	G	AB	H	2B	3B	HR	HR %	R	RBI	BB	SO	SB	BA	SA	AB	H	G by POS
1943 CLE A	8	25	8	2	1	1	4.0	5	5	1	3	0	.320	.600	2	1	OF-6
1946	61	133	25	1	4	0	0.0	8	9	16	13	1	.188	.256	21	3	OF-37
1947 PIT N	22	79	21	2	2	0	0.0	7	10	7	5	0	.266	.342	1	0	OF-21
1949 NY A	112	296	80	13	7	5	1.7	60	44	52	21	2	.270	.412	13	2	OF-98
1950	122	449	127	20	10	6	1.3	81	60	69	31	5	.283	.412	4	0	OF-118
1951	120	420	118	15	8	15	3.6	65	71	62	37	0	.281	.462	5	1	OF-116
1952	122	408	126	19	6	12	2.9	58	63	59	31	1	.309	.473	5	2	OF-118
1953	125	395	121	26	4	10	2.5	64	58	82	29	2	.306	.468	11	5	OF-119
1954	97	304	76	12	5	3	1.0	33	40	53	35	3	.250	.352	10	3	OF-89
1955 2 teams	BAL A (47G – .221)							CLE A (79G – .278)									
" total	126	404	104	21	3	8	2.0	55	53	60	33	3	.257	.384	13	2	OF-117
1956 CLE A	100	317	83	17	0	8	2.5	56	38	69	29	2	.262	.391	13	3	OF-85
1957	133	430	138	25	2	19	4.4	74	78	64	35	0	.321	.521	22	5	OF-113
1958 BAL A	133	413	114	16	1	15	3.6	57	65	66	49	4	.276	.429	19	5	OF-116
1959	140	440	132	22	2	14	3.2	63	77	78	35	1	.300	.455	18	10	OF-124
1960	140	435	123	18	3	11	2.5	68	62	84	40	3	.283	.414	18	8	OF-124
1961 WAS A	110	342	107	16	4	10	2.9	39	57	50	24	1	.313	.471	20	7	OF-90
1962 2 teams	WAS A (44G – .280)							NY N (81G – .274)									
" total	125	297	82	12	1	10	3.4	37	40	48	27	1	.276	.424	39	8	OF-78
17 yrs.	1796	5587	1585	257	63	147	2.6	830	830	920	477	29	.284	.431	234	65	OF-1569

WORLD SERIES

	G	AB	H	2B	3B	HR	HR %	R	RBI	BB	SO	SB	BA	SA	AB	H	G by POS
1949 NY A	3	10	4	3	0	0	0.0	4	0	3	0	0	.400	.700	0	0	OF-3
1950	4	14	6	0	0	0	0.0	2	1	2	0	0	.429	.429	1	0	OF-4
1951	6	18	3	1	1	1	5.6	6	1	5	3	0	.167	.500	1	0	OF-5
1952	7	23	8	1	1	1	4.3	4	1	3	3	0	.348	.609	1	1	OF-6
1953	6	20	6	0	0	1	5.0	5	3	6	2	0	.300	.450	0	0	OF-6
5 yrs.	26	85	27	5	2	3	3.5	21	6	19	8	0	.318	.529	3	1	OF-24
								10th		10th							

Orville Woodruff

WOODRUFF, ORVILLE (Sam)
B. Dec. 27, 1876, Chilo, Ohio   D. July 22, 1937, Cincinnati, Ohio
BR TR 5'9" 160 lbs.

	G	AB	H	2B	3B	HR	HR %	R	RBI	BB	SO	SB	BA	SA	AB	H	G by POS
1904 CIN N	87	306	58	14	3	0	0.0	20	20	19		9	.190	.255	0	0	3B-61, 2B-17, SS-8, OF-1
1910	21	61	9	1	0	0	0.0	6	2	7	8	2	.148	.164	0	0	3B-17, 2B-4
2 yrs.	108	367	67	15	3	0	0.0	26	22	26	8	11	.183	.240	0	0	3B-78, 2B-21, SS-8, OF-1

Pete Woodruff

WOODRUFF, PETER FRANK
B. Richmond, Va.   Deceased.
BR TR

	G	AB	H	2B	3B	HR	HR %	R	RBI	BB	SO	SB	BA	SA	AB	H	G by POS
1899 NY N	20	61	15	1	1	2	3.3	11	7	9		3	.246	.393	0	0	OF-19, 1B-1

Al Woods

WOODS, ALVIS
B. Aug. 8, 1953, Oakland, Calif.
BL TL 6'3" 190 lbs.

	G	AB	H	2B	3B	HR	HR %	R	RBI	BB	SO	SB	BA	SA	AB	H	G by POS
1977 TOR A	122	440	125	17	4	6	1.4	58	35	36	38	8	.284	.382	4	2	OF-115, DH-4
1978	62	220	53	12	3	3	1.4	19	25	11	23	1	.241	.364	3	1	OF-60
1979	132	436	121	24	4	5	1.1	57	36	40	28	6	.278	.385	2	0	OF-127, DH-2
1980	100	373	112	18	2	15	4.0	54	47	37	35	4	.300	.480	10	2	OF-88, DH-13
1981	85	288	71	15	0	1	0.3	20	21	19	31	3	.247	.309	8	2	OF-77, DH-2
1982	85	201	47	11	1	3	1.5	20	24	21	20	1	.234	.343	20	3	OF-64, DH-10
6 yrs.	586	1958	529	97	14	33	1.7	228	188	164	175	23	.270	.385	47	10	OF-531, DH-31

Gary Woods

WOODS, GARY LEE
B. July 20, 1954, Santa Barbara, Calif.
BR TR 6'2" 185 lbs.

	G	AB	H	2B	3B	HR	HR %	R	RBI	BB	SO	SB	BA	SA	AB	H	G by POS
1976 OAK A	6	8	1	0	0	0	0.0	0	0	0	3	0	.125	.125	2	0	OF-4, DH-1
1977 TOR A	60	227	49	9	1	0	0.0	21	17	7	38	5	.216	.264	1	1	OF-60
1978	8	19	3	1	0	0	0.0	1	0	1	1	1	.158	.211	1	0	OF-6
1980 HOU N	19	53	20	5	0	2	3.8	8	15	2	9	1	.377	.585	5	3	OF-14
1981	54	110	23	4	1	0	0.0	10	12	11	22	2	.209	.264	15	3	OF-40
1982 CHI N	117	245	66	15	1	4	1.6	28	30	21	48	3	.269	.388	22	4	OF-103
1983	93	190	46	9	0	4	2.1	25	22	15	27	5	.242	.353	31	6	OF-73, 2B-1
1984	87	98	23	4	1	3	3.1	13	10	15	21	2	.235	.388	31	7	OF-62, 2B-3
8 yrs.	444	950	231	47	4	13	1.4	106	106	72	169	19	.243	.342	108	24	OF-362, 2B-4, DH-1

DIVISIONAL PLAYOFF SERIES

	G	AB	H	2B	3B	HR	HR %	R	RBI	BB	SO	SB	BA	SA	AB	H	G by POS
1981 HOU N	2	2	0	0	0	0	0.0	0	0	0	1	0	.000	.000	2	0	

LEAGUE CHAMPIONSHIP SERIES

	G	AB	H	2B	3B	HR	HR %	R	RBI	BB	SO	SB	BA	SA	AB	H	G by POS
1980 HOU N	4	8	2	0	0	0	0.0	0	1	1	3	1	.250	.250	2	0	OF-3
1984 CHI N	1	1	0	0	0	0	0.0	0	0	0	1	0	.000	.000	1	0	OF-1
2 yrs.	5	9	2	0	0	0	0.0	0	1	1	4	1	.222	.222	3	0	OF-4

Jim Woods

WOODS, JAMES JEROME (Woody)
B. Sept. 17, 1939, Chicago, Ill.
BR TR 6' 175 lbs.

	G	AB	H	2B	3B	HR	HR %	R	RBI	BB	SO	SB	BA	SA	AB	H	G by POS
1957 CHI N	2	0	0	0	0	0	–	1	0	0	0	0	–	–	0	0	
1960 PHI N	11	34	6	0	0	1	2.9	4	3	3	13	0	.176	.265	0	0	3B-11
1961	23	48	11	3	0	2	4.2	6	9	4	15	0	.229	.417	10	3	3B-15
3 yrs.	36	82	17	3	0	3	3.7	11	12	7	28	0	.207	.354	10	3	3B-26

Ron Woods

WOODS, RONALD LAWRENCE
B. Feb. 1, 1943, Hamilton, Ohio
BR TR 5'10" 168 lbs.

	G	AB	H	2B	3B	HR	HR %	R	RBI	BB	SO	SB	BA	SA	AB	H	G by POS
1969 2 teams	DET A (17G – .267)							NY A (72G – .175)									
" total	89	186	34	5	2	2	1.1	21	10	24	32	2	.183	.263	11	0	OF-74
1970 NY A	95	225	51	5	3	8	3.6	30	27	33	35	4	.227	.382	19	3	OF-78
1971 2 teams	NY A (25G – .250)							MON N (51G – .297)									
" total	76	170	49	8	2	3	1.2	30	19	23	20	0	.288	.406	28	5	OF-54
1972 MON N	97	221	57	5	1	10	4.5	21	31	22	33	3	.258	.425	36	7	OF-73
1973	135	318	73	11	3	3	0.9	45	31	56	34	12	.230	.311	28	6	OF-114
1974	90	127	26	0	0	1	0.8	15	12	17	17	6	.205	.228	31	4	OF-61
6 yrs.	582	1247	290	34	12	26	2.1	162	130	175	171	27	.233	.342	153	25	OF-454

	G	AB	H	2B	3B	HR	HR %	R	RBI	BB	SO	SB	BA	SA	Pinch Hit AB	Pinch Hit H	G by POS

Walt Woods

WOODS, WALTER SYDNEY 5'9½" 165 lbs.
B. Apr. 28, 1875, Rye, N. H.   D. Oct. 30, 1951, Portsmouth, N. H.

	G	AB	H	2B	3B	HR	HR %	R	RBI	BB	SO	SB	BA	SA	AB	H	G by POS
1898 CHI N	48	154	27	1	0	0	0.0	16	8	4		3	.175	.182	0	0	P-27, OF-11, 2B-6, SS-3, 3B-3
1899 LOU N	42	126	19	1	1	1	0.8	15	14	10		5	.151	.198	0	0	P-26, 2B-11, SS-3, OF-2
1900 PIT N	1	1	0	0	0	0	0.0	0	0	0		0	.000	.000	0	0	P-1
3 yrs.	91	281	46	2	1	1	0.4	31	22	14		8	.164	.189	0	0	P-54, 2B-17, OF-13, SS-6, 3B-3

Woody Woodward

WOODWARD, WILLIAM FREDERICK BR TR 6'2" 180 lbs.
B. Sept. 23, 1942, Miami, Fla.

	G	AB	H	2B	3B	HR	HR %	R	RBI	BB	SO	SB	BA	SA	AB	H	G by POS
1963 MIL N	10	2	0	0	0	0	0.0	1	0	0	0	0	.000	.000	1	0	SS-5
1964	77	115	24	2	1	0	0.0	18	11	6	28	0	.209	.243	2	0	2B-40, SS-18, 3B-7, 1B-1
1965	112	265	55	7	4	0	0.0	17	11	10	50	2	.208	.264	2	0	SS-107, 2B-8
1966 ATL N	144	455	120	23	3	0	0.0	46	43	37	54	2	.264	.327	1	0	2B-79, SS-73
1967	136	429	97	15	2	0	0.0	30	25	37	51	0	.226	.270	1	0	2B-120, SS-16
1968 2 teams		ATL	N	(12G –	.167)		CIN	N	(56G –	.244)							
" total	68	143	33	3	0	0	0.0	15	11	8	29	2	.231	.252	5	0	SS-47, 2B-10, 3B-2, 1B-1
1969 CIN N	97	241	63	12	0	0	0.0	36	15	24	40	3	.261	.311	0	0	SS-93, 2B-2
1970	100	264	59	8	3	1	0.4	23	14	20	21	1	.223	.288	2	1	SS-77, 3B-20, 2B-10, 1B-2
1971	136	273	66	9	1	0	0.0	22	18	27	28	4	.242	.282	3	1	SS-85, 3B-63, 2B-9
9 yrs.	880	2187	517	79	14	1	0.0	208	148	169	301	14	.236	.287	17	2	SS-521, 2B-278, 3B-92, 1B-4

LEAGUE CHAMPIONSHIP SERIES

	G	AB	H	2B	3B	HR	HR %	R	RBI	BB	SO	SB	BA	SA	AB	H	G by POS
1970 CIN N	3	10	1	0	0	0	0.0	0	0	1	0	0	.100	.100	0	0	SS-3

WORLD SERIES

	G	AB	H	2B	3B	HR	HR %	R	RBI	BB	SO	SB	BA	SA	AB	H	G by POS
1970 CIN N	4	5	1	0	0	0	0.0	0	0	0	0	0	.200	.200	1	1	SS-3

Earl Wooten

WOOTEN, EARL HAZWELL (Junior) BR TL 5'11" 160 lbs.
B. Jan. 16, 1924, Pelzer, S. C.

	G	AB	H	2B	3B	HR	HR %	R	RBI	BB	SO	SB	BA	SA	AB	H	G by POS
1947 WAS A	6	24	2	0	0	0	0.0	0	1	0	4	1	.083	.083	0	0	OF-6
1948	88	258	66	8	3	1	0.4	34	23	24	21	2	.256	.322	8	2	OF-73, 1B-6, P-1
2 yrs.	94	282	68	8	3	1	0.4	34	24	24	25	3	.241	.301	8	2	OF-79, 1B-6, P-1

Chuck Workman

WORKMAN, CHARLES THOMAS BL TR 6' 175 lbs.
B. Jan. 6, 1915, Leeton, Mo.   D. Jan. 3, 1953, Kansas City, Mo.

	G	AB	H	2B	3B	HR	HR %	R	RBI	BB	SO	SB	BA	SA	AB	H	G by POS
1938 CLE A	2	5	2	0	0	0	0.0	1	0	0	0	0	.400	.400	1	0	OF-1
1941	9	4	0	0	0	0	0.0	2	0	1	1	0	.000	.000	4	0	
1943 BOS N	153	615	153	17	1	10	1.6	71	67	53	72	12	.249	.328	0	0	OF-149, 1B-3, 3B-1
1944	140	418	87	18	3	11	2.6	46	53	42	41	1	.208	.344	16	4	OF-103, 3B-19
1945	139	514	141	16	2	25	4.9	77	87	51	58	9	.274	.459	6	0	3B-107, OF-24
1946 2 teams		BOS	N	(25G –	.167)		PIT	N	(58G –	.221)							
" total	83	193	40	6	1	4	2.1	16	23	14	30	2	.207	.311	24	7	OF-52, 3B-1
6 yrs.	526	1749	423	57	7	50	2.9	213	230	161	202	24	.242	.368	51	11	OF-329, 3B-128, 1B-3

Hank Workman

WORKMAN, HENRY KILGARIFF BL TR 6'1" 185 lbs.
B. Feb. 5, 1926, Los Angeles, Calif.

	G	AB	H	2B	3B	HR	HR %	R	RBI	BB	SO	SB	BA	SA	AB	H	G by POS
1950 NY A	2	5	1	0	0	0	0.0	0	0	1	1	0	.200	.200	1	0	1B-1

Red Worthington

WORTHINGTON, ROBERT LEE (Bob) BR TR 5'11" 170 lbs.
B. Apr. 24, 1906, Alhambra, Calif.   D. Dec. 8, 1963, Sepulveda, Calif.

	G	AB	H	2B	3B	HR	HR %	R	RBI	BB	SO	SB	BA	SA	AB	H	G by POS
1931 BOS N	128	491	143	25	10	4	0.8	47	44	26	38	1	.291	.407	4	0	OF-124
1932	105	435	132	35	8	8	1.8	62	61	15	24	1	.303	.476	1	0	OF-104
1933	17	45	7	4	0	0	0.0	3	0	1	3	0	.156	.244	7	0	OF-10
1934 2 teams		BOS	N	(41G –	.246)		STL	N	(1G –	.000)							
" total	42	66	16	5	0	0	0.0	6	6	6	6	0	.242	.318	27	8	OF-11
4 yrs.	292	1037	298	69	18	12	1.2	118	111	48	71	2	.287	.423	39	8	OF-249

Chuck Wortman

WORTMAN, WILLIAM LEWIS BR TR 5'7" 150 lbs.
B. Jan. 5, 1892, Baltimore, Md.   D. Aug. 19, 1977, Las Vegas, Nev.

	G	AB	H	2B	3B	HR	HR %	R	RBI	BB	SO	SB	BA	SA	AB	H	G by POS
1916 CHI N	69	234	47	4	2	2	0.9	17	16	18	22	4	.201	.261	0	0	SS-69
1917	75	190	33	4	1	0	0.0	24	9	18	23	6	.174	.205	0	0	SS-65, 3B-1, 2B-1
1918	17	17	2	0	0	1	5.9	4	3	1	2	3	.118	.294	0	0	2B-8, SS-4
3 yrs.	161	441	82	8	3	3	0.7	45	28	37	47	13	.186	.238	0	0	SS-138, 2B-9, 3B-1

WORLD SERIES

	G	AB	H	2B	3B	HR	HR %	R	RBI	BB	SO	SB	BA	SA	AB	H	G by POS
1918 CHI N	1	1	0	0	0	0	0.0	0	0	0	0	0	.000	.000	0	0	2B-1

Ron Wotus

WOTUS, RONALD ALLAN BR TR 6'1" 165 lbs.
B. Mar. 3, 1961, Colchester, Conn.

	G	AB	H	2B	3B	HR	HR %	R	RBI	BB	SO	SB	BA	SA	AB	H	G by POS
1983 PIT N	5	3	0	0	0	0	0.0	0	0	0	1	0	.000	.000	2	0	SS-2, 2B-1
1984	27	55	12	6	0	0	0.0	4	2	6	8	0	.218	.327	2	1	SS-17, 2B-7
2 yrs.	32	58	12	6	0	0	0.0	4	2	6	9	0	.207	.310	4	1	SS-19, 2B-8

Jimmy Woulfe

WOULFE, JAMES JOSEPH TR 5'11"
B. Nov. 25, 1856, New Orleans, La.   D. Dec. 19, 1924, New Orleans, La.

	G	AB	H	2B	3B	HR	HR %	R	RBI	BB	SO	SB	BA	SA	AB	H	G by POS
1884 2 teams		CIN	AA	(8G –	.147)		PIT	AA	(15G –	.113)							
" total	23	87	11	1	1	0	0.0	10		1			.126	.161	0	0	OF-22, 3B-1

Ab Wright

WRIGHT, ALBERT OWEN BR TR 6'1½" 190 lbs.
B. Nov. 16, 1905, Terlton, Okla.

	G	AB	H	2B	3B	HR	HR %	R	RBI	BB	SO	SB	BA	SA	AB	H	G by POS
1935 CLE A	67	160	38	11	1	2	1.3	17	18	10	17	2	.238	.356	20	3	OF-47
1944 BOS N	71	195	50	9	0	7	3.6	20	35	18	31	0	.256	.410	23	5	OF-47
2 yrs.	138	355	88	20	1	9	2.5	37	53	28	48	2	.248	.386	43	8	OF-94

	G	AB	H	2B	3B	HR	HR %	R	RBI	BB	SO	SB	BA	SA	Pinch Hit AB	Pinch Hit H	G by POS

Al Wright

WRIGHT, ALBERT EDGAR   BR TR 6'2"   168 lbs.
B. Nov. 11, 1912, San Francisco, Calif.

	G	AB	H	2B	3B	HR	HR%	R	RBI	BB	SO	SB	BA	SA	PH AB	PH H	G by POS
1933 BOS N	4	1	1	0	0	0	0.0	0	0	0	0	0	1.000	1.000	0	0	2B-3

Bill Wright

WRIGHT, WILLIAM H.
Deceased.

	G	AB	H	2B	3B	HR	HR%	R	RBI	BB	SO	SB	BA	SA	PH AB	PH H	G by POS
1887 WAS N	1	3	2	0	0	0	0.0	0	0	0	0	0	.667	.667	0	0	C-1

Ceylon Wright

WRIGHT, EDWARD YATMAN   BL TR 5'9"   150 lbs.
B. Aug. 16, 1893, Minneapolis, Minn.   D. Nov. 7, 1947, Hines, Ill.

	G	AB	H	2B	3B	HR	HR%	R	RBI	BB	SO	SB	BA	SA	PH AB	PH H	G by POS
1916 CHI A	8	18	0	0	0	0	0.0	0	0	1	7	0	.000	.000	0	0	SS-8

Dick Wright

WRIGHT, WILLIAM JAMES   BR TR 5'10"   170 lbs.
B. May 5, 1890, Worcester, N. Y.   D. Jan. 24, 1952, Bethlehem, Pa.

	G	AB	H	2B	3B	HR	HR%	R	RBI	BB	SO	SB	BA	SA	PH AB	PH H	G by POS
1915 BKN F	4	5	0	0	0	0	0.0	0	0	0		0	.000	.000	1	0	C-3

George Wright

WRIGHT, GEORGE   BR TR 5'9½"   150 lbs.
Brother of Harry Wright.   Brother of Sam Wright.
B. Jan. 28, 1847, Yonkers, N. Y.   D. Aug. 21, 1937, Boston, Mass.
Manager 1879.
Hall of Fame 1937.

	G	AB	H	2B	3B	HR	HR%	R	RBI	BB	SO	SB	BA	SA	PH AB	PH H	G by POS
1876 BOS N	70	**335**	100	18	6	1	0.3	72	34	8	9		.299	.397	0	0	SS-68, 2B-2, P-1
1877	61	**290**	80	15	1	0	0.0	58	35	9	15		.276	.334	0	0	2B-58, SS-3
1878	59	267	60	5	1	0	0.0	35	12	6	22		.225	.251	0	0	SS-59
1879 PRO N	85	388	107	15	10	1	0.3	79	42	13	20		.276	.374	0	0	SS-85
1880 BOS N	1	4	1	0	0	0	0.0	2	0	0	0		.250	.250	0	0	SS-1
1881	7	25	5	0	0	0	0.0	4	0	3	1		.200	.200	0	0	SS-7
1882 PRO N	46	185	30	1	2	0	0.0	14		4	36		.162	.189	0	0	SS-46
7 yrs.	329	1494	383	54	20	2	0.1	264	123	43	103		.256	.323	0	0	SS-269, 2B-60, P-1

George Wright

WRIGHT, GEORGE DEWITT   BR TR 5'11"   180 lbs.
B. Dec. 12, 1958, Oklahoma City, Okla.

	G	AB	H	2B	3B	HR	HR%	R	RBI	BB	SO	SB	BA	SA	PH AB	PH H	G by POS
1982 TEX A	150	557	147	20	5	11	2.0	69	50	30	78	3	.264	.377	0	0	OF-149
1983	162	634	175	28	6	18	2.8	79	80	41	82	8	.276	.424	2	0	OF-161
1984	101	383	93	19	4	9	2.3	40	48	15	54	0	.243	.384	2	0	OF-80, DH-18
3 yrs.	413	1574	415	67	15	38	2.4	188	178	86	214	11	.264	.398	4	0	OF-390, DH-18

Glenn Wright

WRIGHT, FORREST GLENN (Buckshot)   BR TR 5'11"   170 lbs.
B. Feb. 6, 1901, Archie, Mo.   D. Apr. 6, 1984, Olathe, Kans.

	G	AB	H	2B	3B	HR	HR%	R	RBI	BB	SO	SB	BA	SA	PH AB	PH H	G by POS
1924 PIT N	153	**616**	177	28	18	7	1.1	80	111	27	52	14	.287	.425	0	0	SS-153
1925	153	614	189	32	10	18	2.9	97	121	31	32	3	.308	.480	0	0	SS-153, 3B-1
1926	119	458	141	15	15	8	1.7	73	77	19	26	6	.308	.459	3	0	SS-116
1927	143	570	160	26	4	9	1.6	78	105	39	46	4	.281	.388	0	0	SS-143
1928	108	407	126	20	8	8	2.0	63	66	21	53	3	.310	.457	6	1	SS-101, OF-1, 1B-1
1929 BKN N	24	25	5	0	0	1	4.0	4	6	3	6	0	.200	.320	17	2	SS-3
1930	135	532	171	28	12	22	4.1	83	126	32	70	2	.321	.543	1	0	SS-134
1931	77	268	76	9	4	9	3.4	36	32	14	35	1	.284	.448	2	0	SS-75
1932	127	446	122	31	5	10	2.2	50	60	12	57	4	.274	.433	4	0	SS-122, 1B-2
1933	71	192	49	13	0	1	0.5	19	18	11	24	1	.255	.339	9	2	SS-51, 1B-9, 3B-2
1935 CHI A	9	25	3	1	0	0	0.0	1	1	0	6	0	.120	.160	2	0	2B-7
11 yrs.	1119	4153	1219	203	76	93	2.2	584	723	209	407	38	.294	.446	44	5	SS-1051, 1B-12, 2B-7, 3B-3, OF-1

WORLD SERIES

	G	AB	H	2B	3B	HR	HR%	R	RBI	BB	SO	SB	BA	SA	PH AB	PH H	G by POS
1925 PIT N	7	27	5	1	0	1	3.7	3	3	1	4	0	.185	.333	0	0	SS-7
1927	4	13	2	0	0	0	0.0	1	2	0	0	0	.154	.154	0	0	SS-4
2 yrs.	11	40	7	1	0	1	2.5	4	5	1	4	0	.175	.275	0	0	SS-11

Harry Wright

WRIGHT, WILLIAM HENRY   BR TR 5'9½"   157 lbs.
Brother of Sam Wright.   Brother of George Wright.
B. Jan. 10, 1835, Sheffield, England   D. Oct. 3, 1895, Atlantic City, N. J.
Manager 1871-93.
Hall of Fame 1953.

	G	AB	H	2B	3B	HR	HR%	R	RBI	BB	SO	SB	BA	SA	PH AB	PH H	G by POS
1876 BOS N	1	3	0	0	0	0	0.0	0	0	0	1		.000	.000	0	0	OF-1
1877	1	4	0	0	0	0	0.0	0	0	0	1		.000	.000	0	0	OF-1
2 yrs.	2	7	0	0	0	0	0.0	0	0	0	2		.000	.000	0	0	OF-2

Joe Wright

WRIGHT, JOSEPH   TL 5'8"   175 lbs.
B. 1873, Pittsburgh, Pa.   Deceased.

	G	AB	H	2B	3B	HR	HR%	R	RBI	BB	SO	SB	BA	SA	PH AB	PH H	G by POS
1895 LOU N	60	228	63	10	4	1	0.4	30	30	12	28	7	.276	.368	0	0	OF-59, C-1
1896 2 teams		LOU N (2G – .286)				PIT N (15G – .308)											
" total	17	59	18	2	1	0	0.0	5	6	1	3	1	.305	.373	2	1	OF-14, 3B-1
2 yrs.	77	287	81	12	5	1	0.3	35	36	13	31	8	.282	.369	2	1	OF-73, 3B-1, C-1

Pat Wright

WRIGHT, PATRICK FRANCIS   BB TR 6'2"   190 lbs.
B. July 5, 1865, Pottsville, Pa.   D. May 29, 1943, Springfield, Ill.

	G	AB	H	2B	3B	HR	HR%	R	RBI	BB	SO	SB	BA	SA	PH AB	PH H	G by POS
1890 CHI N	1	2	0	0	0	0	0.0	0	0	1	0	0	.000	.000	0	0	2B-1

Rasty Wright

WRIGHT, WILLIAM SMITH   6'1"
B. Jan. 31, 1863, Birmingham, Mich.   D. Oct. 14, 1922, Duluth, Minn.

	G	AB	H	2B	3B	HR	HR%	R	RBI	BB	SO	SB	BA	SA	PH AB	PH H	G by POS
1890 2 teams		SYR AA (88G – .305)				CLE N (13G – .111)											
" total	101	393	111	11	6	0	0.0	89	2	81	4	33	.282	.341	0	0	OF-101

Sam Wright

WRIGHT, SAMUEL   BR TR 5'7½"   146 lbs.
Brother of Harry Wright.   Brother of George Wright.
B. Nov. 25, 1848, New York, N. Y.   D. May 6, 1928, Boston, Mass.

	G	AB	H	2B	3B	HR	HR%	R	RBI	BB	SO	SB	BA	SA	PH AB	PH H	G by POS
1876 BOS N	2	8	1	0	0	0	0.0	0	0	0	0		.125	.125	0	0	SS-2

	G	AB	H	2B	3B	HR	HR %	R	RBI	BB	SO	SB	BA	SA	Pinch Hit AB	Pinch Hit H	G by POS

Sam Wright continued

	G	AB	H	2B	3B	HR	HR%	R	RBI	BB	SO	SB	BA	SA	AB	H	G by POS
1880 CIN N	9	34	3	0	0	0	0.0	0	0	0	5		.088	.088	0	0	SS-9
1881 BOS N	1	4	1	0	0	0	0.0	0	0	0	0		.250	.250	0	0	SS-1
3 yrs.	12	46	5	0	0	0	0.0	0	0	0	5		.109	.109	0	0	SS-12

Taffy Wright

WRIGHT, TAFT SHEDRON
B. Aug. 10, 1911, Tabor City, N. C.   D. Oct. 22, 1981, Orlando, Fla.   BL TR 5'10"   180 lbs.

	G	AB	H	2B	3B	HR	HR%	R	RBI	BB	SO	SB	BA	SA	AB	H	G by POS
1938 WAS A	100	263	92	18	10	2	0.8	37	36	13	17	1	.350	.517	39	13	OF-60
1939	129	499	154	29	11	4	0.8	77	93	38	19	1	.309	.435	6	3	OF-123
1940 CHI A	147	581	196	31	9	5	0.9	79	88	43	25	4	.337	.448	2	1	OF-144
1941	136	513	165	35	5	10	1.9	71	97	60	27	5	.322	.468	1	0	OF-134
1942	85	300	100	13	5	0	0.0	43	47	48	9	1	.333	.410	4	1	OF-81
1946	115	422	116	19	4	7	1.7	46	52	42	17	10	.275	.389	7	2	OF-107
1947	124	401	130	13	0	4	1.0	48	54	48	17	8	.324	.387	18	3	OF-100
1948	134	455	127	15	6	4	0.9	50	61	39	18	2	.279	.365	19	6	OF-114
1949 PHI A	59	149	35	2	5	2	1.3	14	25	16	6	0	.235	.356	19	3	OF-35
9 yrs.	1029	3583	1115	175	55	38	1.1	465	553	347	155	32	.311	.423	115	32	OF-898

Tom Wright

WRIGHT, THOMAS EVERETTE
B. Sept. 22, 1923, Shelby, N. C.   BL TR 5'11½" 180 lbs.

	G	AB	H	2B	3B	HR	HR%	R	RBI	BB	SO	SB	BA	SA	AB	H	G by POS
1948 BOS A	3	2	1	0	1	0	0.0	1	0	0	0	0	.500	1.500	2	1	
1949	5	4	1	1	0	0	0.0	1	1	1	1	0	.250	.500	4	1	
1950	54	107	34	7	0	0	0.0	17	20	6	18	0	.318	.383	28	7	OF-24
1951	28	63	14	1	1	1	1.6	8	9	11	8	0	.222	.317	10	1	OF-18
1952 2 teams	STL	A (29G –	.242)		CHI	A	(60G –	.258)									
" total	89	198	50	10	2	2	1.0	21	27	28	36	2	.253	.354	34	10	OF-52
1953 CHI A	77	132	33	5	3	2	1.5	14	25	12	21	0	.250	.379	42	13	OF-33
1954 WAS A	76	171	42	4	4	1	0.6	13	17	18	38	0	.246	.333	32	8	OF-43
1955	7	7	0	0	0	0	0.0	0	0	0	1	0	.000	.000	7	0	
1956	2	1	0	0	0	0	0.0	0	0	0	0	0	.000	.000	1	0	
9 yrs.	341	685	175	28	11	6	0.9	75	99	76	123	2	.255	.355	160	41	OF-170

Russ Wrightstone

WRIGHTSTONE, RUSSELL GUY
B. Mar. 18, 1893, Bowmansdale, Pa.   D. Feb. 25, 1969, Harrisburg, Pa.   BL TR 5'10½" 176 lbs.

	G	AB	H	2B	3B	HR	HR%	R	RBI	BB	SO	SB	BA	SA	AB	H	G by POS
1920 PHI N	76	206	54	6	1	3	1.5	23	17	10	25	3	.262	.345	16	4	3B-56, SS-2, 2B-1
1921	109	372	110	13	4	9	2.4	59	51	18	20	4	.296	.425	12	2	3B-54, OF-37, 2B-4
1922	99	331	101	18	6	5	1.5	56	33	28	17	4	.305	.441	20	3	3B-40, SS-35, 1B-2
1923	119	392	107	21	7	7	1.8	59	57	21	19	5	.273	.416	16	5	3B-72, SS-21, 2B-9
1924	118	388	119	24	4	7	1.8	55	58	27	15	5	.307	.443	9	2	3B-97, 2B-9, SS-5, OF-1
1925	72	286	99	18	5	14	4.9	48	61	19	18	0	.346	.591	7	6	OF-45, SS-12, 3B-11, 2B-10, 1B-6
1926	112	368	113	23	1	7	1.9	55	57	27	11	5	.307	.432	4	2	1B-53, 3B-37, 2B-13, OF-5
1927	141	533	163	24	5	6	1.1	62	75	48	20	9	.306	.403	3	1	1B-136, 3B-1, 2B-1
1928 2 teams	PHI	N (33G –	.209)		NY	N	(30G –	.160)									
" total	63	116	23	5	1	2	1.7	10	16	17	7	0	.198	.310	28	4	OF-26, 1B-6
9 yrs.	909	2992	889	152	34	60	2.0	427	425	215	152	35	.297	.431	115	28	3B-368, 1B-203, OF-114, SS-75, 2B-47

Zeke Wrigley

WRIGLEY, GEORGE WATSON
B. Jan. 18, 1874, Philadelphia, Pa.   D. Sept. 28, 1952, Philadelphia, Pa.   5'8½"   150 lbs.

	G	AB	H	2B	3B	HR	HR%	R	RBI	BB	SO	SB	BA	SA	AB	H	G by POS
1896 WAS N	5	9	1	0	0	0	0.0	1	2	1	1	0	.111	.111	1	0	2B-3, SS-1
1897	104	388	110	14	8	3	0.8	65	64	21		5	.284	.384	0	0	OF-36, SS-33, 3B-30, 2B-9
1898	111	400	98	9	10	2	0.5	50	39	20		10	.245	.333	0	0	SS-97, 2B-11, OF-3, 3B-1
1899 2 teams	NY	N (4G –	.200)		BKN	N	(15G –	.204)									
" total	19	64	13	2	2	0	0.0	5	12	4		3	.203	.297	0	0	SS-14, 3B-5
4 yrs.	239	861	222	25	20	5	0.6	121	117	46		18	.258	.351	1	0	SS-145, OF-39, 3B-36, 2B-23

Yats Wuestling

WUESTLING, GEORGE
B. Oct. 18, 1903, St. Louis, Mo.   D. Apr. 26, 1970, St. Louis, Mo.   BR TR 5'11"   167 lbs.

	G	AB	H	2B	3B	HR	HR%	R	RBI	BB	SO	SB	BA	SA	AB	H	G by POS
1929 DET A	54	150	30	4	1	0	0.0	13	16	9	24	0	.200	.240	0	0	SS-52, 3B-1, 2B-1
1930 2 teams	DET	A (4G –	.000)		NY	A	(25G –	.190)									
" total	29	67	11	0	1	0	0.0	5	3	6	17	0	.164	.194	1	0	SS-25, 3B-3
2 yrs.	83	217	41	4	2	0	0.0	18	19	15	41	0	.189	.226	1	0	SS-77, 3B-4, 2B-1

Joe Wyatt

WYATT, LORAL JOHN
B. Apr. 6, 1901, Petersburg, Ind.   D. Dec. 5, 1970, Oblong, Ill.   BR TR 6'1"   175 lbs.

	G	AB	H	2B	3B	HR	HR%	R	RBI	BB	SO	SB	BA	SA	AB	H	G by POS
1924 CLE A	4	11	2	0	0	0	0.0	1	1	2	1	0	.182	.182	0	0	OF-4

Ren Wylie

WYLIE, JAMES RENWICK
B. Dec. 14, 1861, Elizabeth, Pa.   D. Aug. 17, 1951, Wilkinsburg, Pa.   BR TR 5'11"   155 lbs.

	G	AB	H	2B	3B	HR	HR%	R	RBI	BB	SO	SB	BA	SA	AB	H	G by POS
1882 PIT AA	1	3	0	0	0	0	0.0	0		0			.000	.000	0	0	OF-1

Frank Wyman

WYMAN, FRANK C.
B. May 10, 1862, Haverhill, Mass.   D. Feb. 4, 1916, Everett, Mass.

	G	AB	H	2B	3B	HR	HR%	R	RBI	BB	SO	SB	BA	SA	AB	H	G by POS
1884 2 teams	KC	U (30G –	.218)		C-P	U	(2G –	.375)									
" total	32	132	30	4	0	0	0.0	17		3			.227	.258	0	0	OF-25, 1B-5, 3B-3, P-3

Butch Wynegar

WYNEGAR, HAROLD DELANO
B. Mar. 14, 1956, York, Pa.   BB TR 6'1"   190 lbs.

	G	AB	H	2B	3B	HR	HR%	R	RBI	BB	SO	SB	BA	SA	AB	H	G by POS
1976 MIN A	149	534	139	21	2	10	1.9	58	69	79	63	0	.260	.363	3	1	C-137, DH-15
1977	144	532	139	22	3	10	1.9	76	79	68	61	2	.261	.370	5	2	C-142, 3B-1
1978	135	454	100	22	1	4	0.9	36	45	47	42	1	.229	.308	8	1	C-131, 3B-1
1979	149	504	136	20	0	7	1.4	74	57	74	36	2	.270	.351	2	0	C-146, DH-2
1980	146	486	124	18	3	5	1.0	61	57	63	36	3	.255	.335	8	2	C-142, DH-1

	G	AB	H	2B	3B	HR	HR %	R	RBI	BB	SO	SB	BA	SA	Pinch Hit AB	H	G by POS

Butch Wynegar continued

		G	AB	H	2B	3B	HR	HR %	R	RBI	BB	SO	SB	BA	SA	Pinch Hit AB	H	G by POS
1981		47	150	37	5	0	0	0.0	11	10	17	9	0	.247	.280	2	0	C-37, DH-9
1982 2 teams		MIN A (24G – .209)					NY A (63G – .293)											
" total		87	277	74	12	1	4	1.4	36	28	50	33	0	.267	.361	2	0	C-86
1983 NY A		94	301	89	18	2	6	2.0	40	42	52	29	1	.296	.429	4	0	C-93
1984		129	442	118	13	1	6	1.4	48	45	64	36	1	.267	.342	7	1	C-126
9 yrs.		1080	3680	960	151	13	52	1.4	440	432	514	345	10	.261	.351	41	7	C-1040, DH-27, 3B-2

Early Wynn

WYNN, EARLY (Gus)
B. Jan. 6, 1920, Hartford, Ala.
Hall of Fame 1971.

BB TR 6'   190 lbs.

BR 1939-44

		G	AB	H	2B	3B	HR	HR %	R	RBI	BB	SO	SB	BA	SA	Pinch Hit AB	H	G by POS
1939 WAS A		3	6	1	0	0	0	0.0	0	1	1	1	0	.167	.167	0	0	P-3
1941		5	15	2	1	0	0	0.0	1	0	0	5	0	.133	.200	0	0	P-5
1942		30	69	15	2	0	0	0.0	4	7	3	13	0	.217	.246	0	0	P-30
1943		38	98	29	3	1	1	1.0	6	11	1	11	0	.296	.378	1	0	P-37
1944		43	92	19	2	0	1	1.1	4	6	3	21	0	.207	.261	11	1	P-33
1946		25	47	15	2	0	1	2.1	4	9	5	7	0	.319	.426	6	3	P-17
1947		54	120	33	6	0	2	1.7	6	13	1	19	0	.275	.375	20	6	P-33
1948		73	106	23	3	1	0	0.0	9	16	14	22	0	.217	.264	32	3	P-33
1949 CLE A		35	70	10	1	0	1	1.4	3	7	4	10	0	.143	.200	7	0	P-26
1950		39	77	18	5	1	2	2.6	12	10	10	12	0	.234	.403	5	1	P-32
1951		41	108	20	8	1	1	0.9	8	13	7	9	0	.185	.306	3	0	P-37
1952		44	99	22	2	0	0	0.0	5	10	9	15	0	.222	.242	2	1	P-42
1953		37	91	25	2	0	3	3.3	11	10	7	17	0	.275	.396	1	0	P-36
1954		40	93	17	3	0	0	0.0	10	4	7	13	0	.183	.215	0	0	P-40
1955		34	84	15	3	0	1	1.2	8	7	6	17	0	.179	.250	2	0	P-32
1956		38	101	23	5	0	1	1.0	5	15	7	22	1	.228	.307	0	0	P-38
1957		40	86	10	0	0	0	0.0	4	4	11	23	0	.116	.116	0	0	P-40
1958 CHI A		40	75	15	1	0	0	0.0	7	11	10	25	0	.200	.213	0	0	P-40
1959		37	90	22	7	0	2	2.2	11	8	9	18	0	.244	.389	0	0	P-37
1960		36	75	15	2	1	1	1.3	8	7	14	17	0	.200	.293	0	0	P-36
1961		17	37	6	0	0	0	0.0	4	2	3	11	0	.162	.162	0	0	P-17
1962		27	54	7	1	0	0	0.0	5	2	7	17	0	.130	.148	0	0	P-27
1963 CLE A		20	11	3	0	0	0	0.0	1	0	2	5	0	.273	.273	0	0	P-20
23 yrs.		796	1704	365	59	5	17	1.0	136	173	141	330	1	.214	.285	90	15	P-691

WORLD SERIES

		G	AB	H	2B	3B	HR	HR %	R	RBI	BB	SO	SB	BA	SA	Pinch Hit AB	H	G by POS
1954 CLE A		1	2	1	1	0	0	0.0	0	0	0	1	0	.500	1.000	0	0	P-1
1959 CHI A		3	5	1	1	0	0	0.0	0	1	0	2	0	.200	.400	0	0	P-3
2 yrs.		4	7	2	2	0	0	0.0	0	1	0	3	0	.286	.571	0	0	P-4

Jimmy Wynn

WYNN, JAMES SHERMAN (The Toy Cannon)
B. Mar. 12, 1942, Cincinnati, Ohio

BR TR 5'10"   160 lbs.

		G	AB	H	2B	3B	HR	HR %	R	RBI	BB	SO	SB	BA	SA	Pinch Hit AB	H	G by POS
1963 HOU N		70	250	61	10	5	4	1.6	31	27	30	53	4	.244	.372	1	0	OF-53, SS-21, 3B-2
1964		67	219	49	7	0	5	2.3	19	18	24	58	5	.224	.324	3	0	OF-64
1965		157	564	155	30	7	22	3.9	90	73	84	126	43	.275	.470	3	0	OF-155
1966		105	418	107	21	1	18	4.3	62	62	41	81	13	.256	.440	0	0	OF-104
1967		158	594	148	29	3	37	6.2	102	107	74	137	16	.249	.495	1	0	OF-157
1968		156	542	146	23	5	26	4.8	85	67	90	131	11	.269	.474	3	0	OF-153
1969		149	495	133	17	1	33	6.7	113	87	148	142	23	.269	.507	0	0	OF-149
1970		157	554	156	32	2	27	4.9	82	88	106	96	24	.282	.493	2	1	OF-151
1971		123	404	82	16	0	7	1.7	38	45	56	63	10	.203	.295	9	1	OF-116
1972		145	542	148	29	3	24	4.4	117	90	103	99	17	.273	.470	1	0	OF-144
1973		139	481	106	14	5	20	4.2	90	55	91	102	14	.220	.395	4	0	OF-133
1974 LA N		150	535	145	17	4	32	6.0	104	108	108	104	18	.271	.497	3	0	OF-148
1975		130	412	102	16	0	18	4.4	80	58	110	77	7	.248	.417	10	0	OF-120
1976 ATL N		148	449	93	19	1	17	3.8	75	66	127	111	16	.207	.367	8	2	OF-138
1977 2 teams		NY N (30G – .143)					MIL A (36G – .197)											
" total		66	194	34	5	2	1	0.5	17	13	32	47	4	.175	.237	13	1	OF-25, DH-18
15 yrs.		1920	6653	1665	285	39	291	4.4	1105	964	1224	1427	225	.250	.436	61	5	OF-1810, SS-21, DH-18, 3B-2

LEAGUE CHAMPIONSHIP SERIES

		G	AB	H	2B	3B	HR	HR %	R	RBI	BB	SO	SB	BA	SA	Pinch Hit AB	H	G by POS
1974 LA N		4	10	2	2	0	0	0.0	4	2	9	1	1	.200	.400	0	0	OF-4

WORLD SERIES

		G	AB	H	2B	3B	HR	HR %	R	RBI	BB	SO	SB	BA	SA	Pinch Hit AB	H	G by POS
1974 LA N		5	16	3	1	0	1	6.3	1	2	4	4	0	.188	.438	0	0	OF-5

Marvell Wynne

WYNNE, MARVELL
B. Dec. 17, 1959, Chicago, Ill.

BL TL 5'11"   176 lbs.

		G	AB	H	2B	3B	HR	HR %	R	RBI	BB	SO	SB	BA	SA	Pinch Hit AB	H	G by POS
1983 PIT N		103	366	89	16	2	7	1.9	66	26	38	52	12	.243	.355	1	0	OF-102
1984		154	653	174	24	11	0	0.0	77	39	42	81	24	.266	.337	0	0	OF-154
2 yrs.		257	1019	263	40	13	7	0.7	143	65	80	133	36	.258	.343	1	0	OF-256

Johnny Wyrostek

WYROSTEK, JOHN BARNEY
B. July 12, 1919, Fairmont City, Ill.

BL TR 6'2"   180 lbs.

		G	AB	H	2B	3B	HR	HR %	R	RBI	BB	SO	SB	BA	SA	Pinch Hit AB	H	G by POS
1942 PIT N		9	35	4	0	1	0	0.0	3	3	3	2	0	.114	.171	1	0	OF-8
1943		51	79	12	3	0	0	0.0	7	1	3	15	0	.152	.190	24	4	OF-20, 3B-2, 2B-1, 1B-1
1946 PHI N		145	545	153	30	4	6	1.1	73	45	70	42	7	.281	.383	3	0	OF-142
1947		128	454	124	24	7	5	1.1	68	51	61	45	7	.273	.390	1	0	OF-126
1948 CIN N		136	512	140	24	9	17	3.3	74	76	52	63	7	.273	.455	5	0	OF-130
1949		134	474	118	20	4	9	1.9	54	46	58	63	7	.249	.365	5	0	OF-129
1950		131	509	145	34	5	8	1.6	70	76	52	38	1	.285	.418	1	1	OF-129, 1B-4
1951		142	537	167	31	9	2	0.4	52	61	54	54	2	.311	.391	3	2	OF-139
1952 2 teams		CIN N (30G – .236)					PHI N (98G – .274)											
" total		128	427	113	17	6	2	0.5	57	47	62	33	2	.265	.347	11	2	OF-117, 1B-1
1953 PHI N		125	409	111	14	2	6	1.5	42	47	38	43	0	.271	.359	15	2	OF-110

	G	AB	H	2B	3B	HR	HR%	R	RBI	BB	SO	SB	BA	SA	Pinch Hit AB	Pinch Hit H	G by POS

Johnny Wyrostek continued

	G	AB	H	2B	3B	HR	HR%	R	RBI	BB	SO	SB	BA	SA	AB	H	G by POS
1954	92	259	62	12	4	3	1.2	28	28	29	39	0	.239	.351	17	5	OF-55, 1B-22
11 yrs.	1221	4240	1149	209	45	58	1.4	525	481	482	437	33	.271	.383	86	16	OF-1105, 1B-28, 3B-2, 2B-1

Henry Yaik

YAIK, HENRY   5'11" 185 lbs.
B. Mar. 1, 1864, Detroit, Mich.   D. Sept. 21, 1935, Detroit, Mich.

	G	AB	H	2B	3B	HR	HR%	R	RBI	BB	SO	SB	BA	SA	AB	H	G by POS
1888 PIT N	2	6	2	0	0	0	0.0	0	1	1	0	0	.333	.333	0	0	OF-1, C-1

Ad Yale

YALE, WILLIAM M.
B. Apr. 17, 1870, Bristol, Conn.   D. Apr. 27, 1948, Bridgeport, Conn.

	G	AB	H	2B	3B	HR	HR%	R	RBI	BB	SO	SB	BA	SA	AB	H	G by POS
1905 BKN N	4	13	1	0	0	0	0.0	1	1	1		0	.077	.077	0	0	1B-4

Hugh Yancy

YANCY, HUGH JR   BR TR 5'11" 170 lbs.
B. Oct. 16, 1949, Sarasota, Fla.

	G	AB	H	2B	3B	HR	HR%	R	RBI	BB	SO	SB	BA	SA	AB	H	G by POS
1972 CHI A	3	9	1	0	0	0	0.0	0	0	0	0	0	.111	.111	0	0	3B-3
1974	1	0	0	0	0	0	–	0	0	0	0	0	–	–	0	0	DH-1
1976	3	10	1	1	0	0	0.0	0	0	0	3	0	.100	.200	0	0	2B-3
3 yrs.	7	19	2	1	0	0	0.0	0	0	0	3	0	.105	.158	0	0	3B-3, 2B-3, DH-1

George Yankowski

YANKOWSKI, GEORGE EDWARD   BR TR 6' 180 lbs.
B. Nov. 19, 1922, Cambridge, Mass.

	G	AB	H	2B	3B	HR	HR%	R	RBI	BB	SO	SB	BA	SA	AB	H	G by POS
1942 PHI A	6	13	2	1	0	0	0.0	0	2	0	2	0	.154	.231	0	0	C-6
1949 CHI A	12	18	3	1	0	0	0.0	0	2	0	2	0	.167	.222	6	0	C-6
2 yrs.	18	31	5	2	0	0	0.0	0	4	0	4	0	.161	.226	6	0	C-12

George Yantz

YANTZ, GEORGE WEBB   BR TR 5'6½" 168 lbs.
B. July 27, 1886, Louisville, Ky.   D. Feb. 26, 1967, Louisville, Ky.

	G	AB	H	2B	3B	HR	HR%	R	RBI	BB	SO	SB	BA	SA	AB	H	G by POS
1912 CHI N	1	1	1	0	0	0	0.0	0	0	0	0	0	1.000	1.000	0	0	C-1

Yam Yaryan

YARYAN, CLARENCE EVERETT   BR TR 5'10½" 180 lbs.
B. Nov. 5, 1892, Knowlton, Iowa   D. Nov. 16, 1964, Birmingham, Ala.

	G	AB	H	2B	3B	HR	HR%	R	RBI	BB	SO	SB	BA	SA	AB	H	G by POS
1921 CHI A	45	102	31	8	2	0	0.0	11	15	9	16	0	.304	.422	10	1	C-34
1922	36	71	14	2	0	2	2.8	9	9	6	10	1	.197	.310	8	0	C-25
2 yrs.	81	173	45	10	2	2	1.2	20	24	15	26	1	.260	.376	18	1	C-59

Carl Yastrzemski

YASTRZEMSKI, CARL MICHAEL (Yaz)   BL TR 5'11" 175 lbs.
B. Aug. 22, 1939, Southampton, N. Y.

	G	AB	H	2B	3B	HR	HR%	R	RBI	BB	SO	SB	BA	SA	AB	H	G by POS
1961 BOS A	148	583	155	31	6	11	1.9	71	80	50	96	6	.266	.396	1	0	OF-147
1962	160	646	191	43	6	19	2.9	99	94	66	82	7	.296	.469	0	0	OF-160
1963	151	570	183	40	3	14	2.5	91	68	95	72	8	.321	.475	0	0	OF-151
1964	151	567	164	29	9	15	2.6	77	67	75	90	6	.289	.451	0	0	OF-148, 3B-2
1965	133	494	154	45	3	20	4.0	78	72	70	58	7	.312	.536	3	0	OF-130
1966	160	594	165	39	2	16	2.7	81	80	84	60	8	.278	.431	3	1	OF-158
1967	161	579	189	31	4	44	7.6	112	121	91	69	10	.326	.622	0	0	OF-161
1968	157	539	162	32	2	23	4.3	90	74	119	90	13	.301	.495	0	0	OF-155, 1B-3
1969	162	603	154	28	2	40	6.6	96	111	101	91	15	.255	.507	0	0	OF-143, 1B-22
1970	161	566	186	29	0	40	7.1	125	102	128	66	23	.329	.592	1	0	1B-94, OF-69
1971	148	508	129	21	2	15	3.0	75	70	106	60	8	.254	.392	2	2	OF-146
1972	125	455	120	18	2	12	2.6	70	68	67	44	5	.264	.391	1	0	OF-83, 1B-42
1973	152	540	160	25	4	19	3.5	82	95	105	58	9	.296	.463	1	0	1B-107, 3B-31, OF-14
1974	148	515	155	25	2	15	2.9	93	79	104	48	12	.301	.445	0	0	1B-84, OF-63, DH-4
1975	149	543	146	30	1	14	2.6	91	60	87	67	8	.269	.405	1	0	1B-140, OF-8, DH-2
1976	155	546	146	23	2	21	3.8	71	102	80	67	5	.267	.432	1	0	1B-94, OF-51, DH-10
1977	150	558	165	27	3	28	5.0	99	102	73	40	11	.296	.505	0	0	OF-140, 1B-7, DH-6
1978	144	523	145	21	2	17	3.3	70	81	76	44	4	.277	.423	1	0	OF-71, 1B-50, DH-27
1979	147	518	140	28	1	21	4.1	69	87	62	46	3	.270	.450	3	2	DH-56, 1B-51, OF-36
1980	105	364	100	21	1	15	4.1	49	50	44	38	0	.275	.462	6	0	DH-49, OF-39, 1B-16
1981	91	338	83	14	1	7	2.1	36	53	49	28	0	.246	.355	3	0	DH-48, 1B-39
1982	131	459	126	22	1	16	3.5	53	72	59	50	0	.275	.431	15	1	DH-102, 1B-14, OF-2
1983	119	380	101	24	0	10	2.6	38	56	54	29	0	.266	.408	10	2	DH-91, OF-1
23 yrs.	3308	11988	3419	646	59	452	3.8	1816	1844	1845	1393	168	.285	.462	52	8	OF-2076, 1B-765, DH-411, 3B-33
	2nd	3rd	7th	7th					9th	4th							

LEAGUE CHAMPIONSHIP SERIES

	G	AB	H	2B	3B	HR	HR%	R	RBI	BB	SO	SB	BA	SA	AB	H	G by POS
1975 BOS A	3	11	5	1	0	1	9.1	4	2	1	1	0	.455	.818	0	0	OF-3

WORLD SERIES

	G	AB	H	2B	3B	HR	HR%	R	RBI	BB	SO	SB	BA	SA	AB	H	G by POS
1967 BOS A	7	25	10	2	0	3	12.0	4	5	4	1	0	.400	.840	0	0	OF-7
1975	7	29	9	0	0	0	0.0	7	4	4	1	0	.310	.310	0	0	1B-4
2 yrs.	14	54	19	2	0	3	5.6	11	9	8	2	0	.352	.556	0	0	OF-7, 1B-4
													9th				

Al Yates

YATES, ALBERT ARTHUR (Bunny)   BR TR 6'2" 210 lbs.
B. Apr. 26, 1945, Jersey City, N. J.

	G	AB	H	2B	3B	HR	HR%	R	RBI	BB	SO	SB	BA	SA	AB	H	G by POS
1971 MIL A	24	47	13	2	0	1	2.1	5	4	3	7	1	.277	.383	11	3	OF-12

Emil Yde

YDE, EMIL OGDEN   BB TL 5'11" 165 lbs.
B. Jan. 28, 1900, Great Lakes, Ill.   BL 1925
D. Dec. 5, 1968, Leesburg, Fla.

	G	AB	H	2B	3B	HR	HR%	R	RBI	BB	SO	SB	BA	SA	AB	H	G by POS
1924 PIT N	50	88	21	1	3	1	1.1	8	9	0	13	0	.239	.352	13	3	P-33
1925	47	89	17	4	1	0	0.0	11	11	2	13	1	.191	.258	4	0	P-33
1926	43	74	17	5	2	0	0.0	11	4	5	7	0	.230	.351	0	0	P-37
1927	23	18	3	0	1	0	0.0	8	1	0	1	0	.167	.278	4	1	P-9
1929 DET A	46	48	16	1	1	0	0.0	8	3	3	6	0	.333	.396	13	5	P-29
5 yrs.	209	317	74	11	8	1	0.3	46	28	10	40	1	.233	.328	34	9	P-141

	G	AB	H	2B	3B	HR	HR%	R	RBI	BB	SO	SB	BA	SA	Pinch Hit AB	Pinch Hit H	G by POS

Emil Yde continued

WORLD SERIES

	G	AB	H	2B	3B	HR	HR%	R	RBI	BB	SO	SB	BA	SA	PH AB	PH H	G by POS
1925 PIT N	2	1	0	0	0	0	0.0	1	0	0	0	0	.000	.000	0	0	P-1
1927	1	0	0	0	0	0	–	1	0	0	0	0	–	–	1	0	
2 yrs.	3	1	0	0	0	0	0.0	2	0	0	0	0	.000	.000	1	0	P-1

Bert Yeabsley

YEABSLEY, ROBERT WATKINS BR TR 5'9½" 175 lbs.
B. Dec. 17, 1893, Philadelphia, Pa. D. Feb. 8, 1961, Philadelphia, Pa.

	G	AB	H	2B	3B	HR	HR%	R	RBI	BB	SO	SB	BA	SA	PH AB	PH H	G by POS
1919 PHI N	3	0	0	0	0	0	–	0	0	1	0	0	–	–	0	0	

George Yeager

YEAGER, GEORGE E. BR TR 5'10" 190 lbs.
B. June 5, 1874, Cincinnati, Ohio D. July 5, 1940, Cincinnati, Ohio

	G	AB	H	2B	3B	HR	HR%	R	RBI	BB	SO	SB	BA	SA	PH AB	PH H	G by POS
1896 BOS N	2	5	1	0	0	0	0.0	1	0	0	1	0	.200	.200	0	0	1B-2
1897	30	95	23	2	3	2	2.1	20	15	7		2	.242	.389	2	0	C-13, OF-10, 2B-4, 3B-1
1898	68	221	59	13	1	3	1.4	37	24	16		1	.267	.376	3	2	C-37, 1B-17, OF-9, SS-2
1899	3	8	1	0	0	0	0.0	1	0	1		0	.125	.125	0	0	OF-2, C-1
1901 2 teams	CLE	A	(39G –	.223)		PIT	N	(26G –	.264)								
" total	65	230	55	7	1	0	0.0	22	24	8		3	.239	.278	5	0	C-45, 1B-6, 3B-4, OF-3, 2B-2
1902 2 teams	NY	N	(38G –	.204)		BAL	A	(11G –	.184)								
" total	49	146	29	3	1	0	0.0	9	10	13		1	.199	.233	7	1	C-38, 1B-3, OF-1
6 yrs.	217	705	168	25	6	5	0.7	90	73	45	1	7	.238	.312	17	3	C-134, 1B-28, OF-25, 2B-6, 3B-5, SS-2

Joe Yeager

YEAGER, JOSEPH F. (Little Joe) TR
B. Aug. 28, 1875, Philadelphia, Pa. D. July 2, 1937, Detroit, Mich.

	G	AB	H	2B	3B	HR	HR%	R	RBI	BB	SO	SB	BA	SA	PH AB	PH H	G by POS
1898 BKN N	43	134	23	5	1	0	0.0	12	15	7		1	.172	.224	0	0	P-36, OF-4, SS-2, 2B-1
1899	23	47	9	0	1	0	0.0	12	4	6		0	.191	.234	0	0	SS-11, P-10, OF-1, 3B-1
1900	3	9	3	0	0	0	0.0	0	0	0		0	.333	.333	0	0	P-2, 3B-1
1901 DET A	41	125	37	7	1	2	1.6	18	17	4		3	.296	.416	2	0	P-26, SS-12, 2B-1
1902	50	161	39	6	5	1	0.6	17	23	5		1	.242	.360	1	0	P-19, OF-13, 2B-12, SS-3, 3B-1
1903	109	402	103	15	6	0	0.0	36	43	18		9	.256	.323	0	0	3B-107, SS-1, P-1
1905 NY A	115	401	107	16	7	0	0.0	53	42	25		8	.267	.342	3	2	3B-90, SS-21
1906	57	123	37	6	1	0	0.0	20	12	13		3	.301	.366	18	3	SS-22, 2B-13, 3B-3
1907 STL A	123	436	104	21	7	1	0.2	32	44	31		11	.239	.326	4	1	3B-92, 2B-17, SS-10
1908	10	15	5	1	0	0	0.0	3	1	1		2	.333	.400	5	1	2B-4, SS-1
10 yrs.	574	1853	467	77	29	4	0.2	203	201	110		37	.252	.331	33	7	3B-295, P-94, SS-83, 2B-48, OF-18

Steve Yeager

YEAGER, STEPHEN WAYNE BR TR 6' 190 lbs.
B. Nov. 24, 1948, Huntington, W. Va.

	G	AB	H	2B	3B	HR	HR%	R	RBI	BB	SO	SB	BA	SA	PH AB	PH H	G by POS
1972 LA N	35	106	29	0	1	4	3.8	18	15	16	26	0	.274	.406	0	0	C-35
1973	54	134	34	5	0	2	1.5	18	10	15	33	1	.254	.336	4	1	C-50
1974	94	316	84	16	1	12	3.8	41	41	32	77	2	.266	.437	0	0	C-93
1975	135	452	103	16	1	12	2.7	34	54	40	75	2	.228	.347	0	0	C-135
1976	117	359	77	11	3	11	3.1	42	35	30	84	3	.214	.354	1	1	C-115
1977	125	387	99	21	2	16	4.1	53	55	43	84	1	.256	.444	3	0	C-123
1978	94	228	44	7	0	4	1.8	19	23	36	41	0	.193	.276	4	1	C-91
1979	105	310	67	9	2	13	4.2	33	41	29	68	1	.216	.384	2	2	C-103
1980	96	227	48	8	0	2	0.9	20	20	20	54	2	.211	.273	4	1	C-95
1981	42	86	18	2	0	3	3.5	5	7	6	14	0	.209	.337	5	2	C-40
1982	82	196	48	5	2	2	1.0	13	18	13	28	0	.245	.321	9	2	C-76
1983	113	335	68	8	3	15	4.5	31	41	23	57	1	.203	.379	2	0	C-112
1984	74	197	45	4	0	4	2.0	16	29	20	38	1	.228	.310	17	4	C-65
13 yrs.	1166	3333	764	112	15	100	3.0	343	389	323	679	14	.229	.362	51	14	C-1133

DIVISIONAL PLAYOFF SERIES

	G	AB	H	2B	3B	HR	HR%	R	RBI	BB	SO	SB	BA	SA	PH AB	PH H	G by POS
1981 LA N	2	5	2	1	0	0	0.0	1	0	0	1	0	.400	.600	1	1	C-2

LEAGUE CHAMPIONSHIP SERIES

	G	AB	H	2B	3B	HR	HR%	R	RBI	BB	SO	SB	BA	SA	PH AB	PH H	G by POS
1974 LA N	3	9	0	0	0	0	0.0	1	0	3	3	1	.000	.000	0	0	C-3
1977	4	13	3	0	0	0	0.0	1	2	1	3	0	.231	.231	0	0	C-4
1978	4	13	3	0	0	1	7.7	2	2	2	2	1	.231	.462	0	0	C-4
1981	1	2	1	0	0	0	0.0	1	0	0	0	0	.500	.500	1	1	C-1
1983	2	6	1	1	0	0	0.0	0	0	0	0	0	.167	.333	0	0	C-2
5 yrs.	14	43	8	1	0	1	2.3	5	4	6	8	2	.186	.279	1	1	C-14

WORLD SERIES

	G	AB	H	2B	3B	HR	HR%	R	RBI	BB	SO	SB	BA	SA	PH AB	PH H	G by POS
1974 LA N	4	11	4	1	0	0	0.0	0	1	1	4	0	.364	.455	0	0	C-4
1977	6	19	6	1	0	2	10.5	2	5	1	1	0	.316	.684	0	0	C-6
1978	5	13	3	1	0	0	0.0	2	0	1	2	0	.231	.308	0	0	C-5
1981	6	14	4	1	0	2	14.3	2	4	0	2	0	.286	.786	0	0	C-6
4 yrs.	21	57	17	4	0	4	7.0 9th	6	10	3	9	0	.298	.579	0	0	C-21

Archie Yelle

YELLE, ARCHIE JOSEPH BR TR 5'10½" 170 lbs.
B. June 11, 1892, Saginaw, Mich. D. May 2, 1983, Woodland, Calif.

	G	AB	H	2B	3B	HR	HR%	R	RBI	BB	SO	SB	BA	SA	PH AB	PH H	G by POS
1917 DET A	25	51	7	1	0	0	0.0	4	0	5	4	2	.137	.157	1	0	C-24
1918	56	144	25	3	0	0	0.0	7	7	9	15	0	.174	.194	4	1	C-52
1919	5	4	0	0	0	0	0.0	1	0	1	0	0	.000	.000	0	0	C-5
3 yrs.	86	199	32	4	0	0	0.0	12	7	15	19	2	.161	.181	5	1	C-81

Steve Yerkes

YERKES, STEPHEN DOUGLAS BR TR 5'9" 165 lbs.
B. May 15, 1888, Hatboro, Pa. D. Jan. 31, 1971, Lansdale, Pa.

	G	AB	H	2B	3B	HR	HR%	R	RBI	BB	SO	SB	BA	SA	PH AB	PH H	G by POS
1909 BOS A	5	2	1	0	0	0	0.0	0	0	0		0	.500	.500	2	1	SS-3
1911	142	502	140	24	3	1	0.2	70	57	52		14	.279	.345	0	0	SS-116, 2B-14, 3B-11
1912	131	523	132	22	6	0	0.0	73	42	41		4	.252	.317	0	0	2B-131
1913	137	487	130	30	6	1	0.2	67	48	50	32	11	.267	.359	7	1	2B-129

	G	AB	H	2B	3B	HR	HR %	R	RBI	BB	SO	SB	BA	SA	Pinch Hit AB	Pinch Hit H	G by POS

Steve Yerkes continued

	G	AB	H	2B	3B	HR	HR %	R	RBI	BB	SO	SB	BA	SA	AB	H	G by POS
1914 2 teams	BOS A (92G – .218)					PIT F (39G – .338)											
" total	131	435	112	26	7	2	0.5	41	48	25	23	7	.257	.363	0	0	2B-91, SS-39
1915 PIT F	121	434	125	17	8	1	0.2	44	49	30		17	.288	.371	0	0	2B-114, SS-8
1916 CHI N	44	137	36	6	2	1	0.7	12	10	9	7	1	.263	.358	3	1	2B-41
7 yrs.	711	2520	676	125	32	6	0.2	307	254	207	62	54	.268	.350	12	3	2B-520, SS-166, 3B-11

WORLD SERIES

	G	AB	H	2B	3B	HR	HR %	R	RBI	BB	SO	SB	BA	SA	AB	H	G by POS
1912 BOS A	8	32	8	0	2	0	0.0	3	4	2	3	0	.250	.375	0	0	2B-8

Tom Yewcic

YEWCIC, THOMAS J. (Kibby)
B. May 9, 1932, Conemaugh, Pa.　　　BR　TR　5'11"　180 lbs.

	G	AB	H	2B	3B	HR	HR %	R	RBI	BB	SO	SB	BA	SA	AB	H	G by POS
1957 DET A	1	1	0	0	0	0	0.0	0	0	0	0	0	.000	.000	0	0	C-1

Ed Yewell

YEWELL, EDWIN LEONARD
B. Aug. 22, 1862, Washington, D.C.　　D. Sept. 15, 1940, Washington, D.C.

	G	AB	H	2B	3B	HR	HR %	R	RBI	BB	SO	SB	BA	SA	AB	H	G by POS
1884 2 teams	WAS AA (27G – .247)					WAS U (1G – .000)											
" total	28	97	23	3	1	0	0.0	14		1			.237	.289	0	0	2B-11, OF-8, 3B-8, SS-2

Earl Yingling

YINGLING, EARL HERSHEY (Chink)
B. Oct. 29, 1888, Chillicothe, Ohio　　D. Oct. 2, 1962, Columbus, Ohio　　BL　TL　5'11½"　180 lbs.

	G	AB	H	2B	3B	HR	HR %	R	RBI	BB	SO	SB	BA	SA	AB	H	G by POS
1911 CLE A	5	11	3	0	0	0	0.0	1	2	1		0	.273	.273	0	0	P-4
1912 BKN N	25	64	16	2	1	0	0.0	9	3	4	6	0	.250	.313	0	0	P-25
1913	40	60	23	1	0	0	0.0	11	5	9	8	0	.383	.400	11	4	P-26
1914 CIN N	61	120	23	2	0	1	0.8	9	11	9	15	3	.192	.233	13	2	P-34, OF-13
1918 WAS A	8	15	7	0	0	0	0.0	1	2	2	1	0	.467	.467	3	1	P-5
5 yrs.	139	270	72	5	1	1	0.4	31	23	25	30	3	.267	.304	27	7	P-94, OF-13

Joe Yingling

YINGLING, JOSEPH GRANVILLE
B. July 26, 1866, Westminster, Md.　　D. Oct. 24, 1946, Manchester, Md.　　BR　TL　5'7"　145 lbs.

	G	AB	H	2B	3B	HR	HR %	R	RBI	BB	SO	SB	BA	SA	AB	H	G by POS
1886 WAS N	1	2	0	0	0	0	0.0	0	0	0		1	.000	.000	0	0	P-1
1894 PHI N	1	4	1	0	0	0	0.0	0	0	0		0	.250	.250	0	0	SS-1
2 yrs.	2	6	1	0	0	0	0.0	0	0	0		2	.167	.167	0	0	SS-1, P-1

Bill Yohe

YOHE, WILLIAM CLYDE
B. Sept. 2, 1878, Mt. Elere, Ill.　　D. Dec. 24, 1938, Bremerton, Wash.　　TR

	G	AB	H	2B	3B	HR	HR %	R	RBI	BB	SO	SB	BA	SA	AB	H	G by POS
1909 WAS A	21	72	15	2	0	0	0.0	6	4	3		2	.208	.236	2	1	3B-19

Rudy York

YORK, RUDOLPH PRESTON
B. Aug. 17, 1913, Ragland, Ala.　　D. Feb. 2, 1970, Rome, Ga.　　BR　TR　6'1"　209 lbs.
Manager 1959.

	G	AB	H	2B	3B	HR	HR %	R	RBI	BB	SO	SB	BA	SA	AB	H	G by POS
1934 DET A	3	6	1	0	0	0	0.0	0	0	1	3	0	.167	.167	2	1	C-2
1937	104	375	115	18	3	35	9.3	72	103	41	52	3	.307	.651	7	1	C-54, 3B-41
1938	135	463	138	27	2	33	7.1	85	127	92	74	1	.298	.579	3	0	C-116, OF-14, 1B-1
1939	102	329	101	16	1	20	6.1	66	68	41	50	5	.307	.544	16	2	C-67, 1B-19
1940	155	588	186	46	6	33	5.6	105	134	89	88	3	.316	.583	0	0	1B-155
1941	155	590	153	29	3	27	4.6	91	111	92	88	3	.259	.456	0	0	1B-155
1942	153	577	150	26	4	21	3.6	81	90	73	71	3	.260	.428	1	1	1B-152
1943	155	571	155	22	11	34	6.0	90	118	84	88	5	.271	.527	0	0	1B-155
1944	151	583	161	27	7	18	3.1	77	98	68	73	5	.276	.439	0	0	1B-151
1945	155	595	157	25	5	18	3.0	71	87	59	85	6	.264	.413	0	0	1B-155
1946 BOS A	154	579	160	30	6	17	2.9	78	119	86	93	1	.276	.437	0	0	1B-154
1947 2 teams	BOS A (48G – .212)					CHI A (102G – .243)											
" total	150	584	136	25	4	21	3.6	56	91	58	87	1	.233	.397	0	0	1B-150
1948 PHI A	31	51	8	0	0	0	0.0	4	6	7	15	0	.157	.157	18	2	1B-14
13 yrs.	1603	5891	1621	291	52	277	4.7	876	1152	791	867	38	.275	.483	47	7	1B-1261, C-239, 3B-41, OF-14

WORLD SERIES

	G	AB	H	2B	3B	HR	HR %	R	RBI	BB	SO	SB	BA	SA	AB	H	G by POS
1940 DET A	7	26	6	0	1	1	3.8	3	2	4	7	0	.231	.423	0	0	1B-7
1945	7	28	5	1	0	0	0.0	1	3	3	4	0	.179	.214	0	0	1B-7
1946 BOS A	7	23	6	1	1	2	8.7	6	5	6	4	0	.261	.652	0	0	1B-7
3 yrs.	21	77	17	2	2	3	3.9	10	10	13	15	0	.221	.416	0	0	1B-21

Tom York

YORK, THOMAS J.
B. July 13, 1851, Brooklyn, N.Y.　　D. Feb. 17, 1936, New York, N.Y.　　BL　5'9"　165 lbs.

	G	AB	H	2B	3B	HR	HR %	R	RBI	BB	SO	SB	BA	SA	AB	H	G by POS
1876 HAR N	67	263	68	12	7	1	0.4	47	39	10	4		.259	.369	0	0	OF-67
1877	56	237	67	16	7	1	0.4	43	37	3	11		.283	.422	0	0	OF-56
1878 PRO N	62	269	83	19	10	1	0.4	56	26	8	19		.309	.465	0	0	OF-62
1879	81	342	106	25	5	1	0.3	69	50	19	28		.310	.421	0	0	OF-81
1880	53	203	43	9	2	0	0.0	21	18	8	29		.212	.276	0	0	OF-53
1881	85	316	96	23	5	2	0.6	57	47	29	26		.304	.427	0	0	OF-85
1882	81	321	86	23	7	1	0.3	48		19	14		.268	.393	0	0	OF-81
1883 CLE N	100	381	99	29	5	2	0.5	56		37	55		.260	.378	0	0	OF-100
1884 BAL AA	83	314	70	14	7	1	0.3	64		34			.223	.322	0	0	OF-83
1885	22	87	23	4	2	0	0.0	6			8		.264	.356	0	0	OF-22
10 yrs.	690	2733	741	174	57	10	0.4	467	217	175	186		.271	.387	0	0	OF-690

Tony York

YORK, ANTHONY BATTON
B. Nov. 27, 1912, Irene, Tex.　　D. Apr. 18, 1970, Hillsboro, Tex.　　BR　TR　5'10"　165 lbs.

	G	AB	H	2B	3B	HR	HR %	R	RBI	BB	SO	SB	BA	SA	AB	H	G by POS
1944 CHI N	28	85	20	1	0	0	0.0	4	7	4	11	0	.235	.247	0	0	SS-15, 3B-12

Eddie Yost

YOST, EDWARD FREDERICK (The Walking Man)
B. Oct. 13, 1926, Brooklyn, N.Y.　　BR　TR　5'10"　170 lbs.

	G	AB	H	2B	3B	HR	HR %	R	RBI	BB	SO	SB	BA	SA	AB	H	G by POS
1944 WAS A	7	14	2	0	0	0	0.0	3	0	1	2	0	.143	.143	0	0	3B-3, SS-2
1946	8	25	2	1	0	0	0.0	2	1	5	5	2	.080	.120	1	0	3B-7
1947	115	428	102	17	3	0	0.0	52	14	45	57	3	.238	.292	0	0	3B-114

	G	AB	H	2B	3B	HR	HR%	R	RBI	BB	SO	SB	BA	SA	Pinch Hit AB	Pinch Hit H	G by POS

Eddie Yost continued

	G	AB	H	2B	3B	HR	HR%	R	RBI	BB	SO	SB	BA	SA	AB	H	G by POS
1948	145	555	138	32	11	2	0.4	74	50	82	51	4	.249	.357	0	0	3B-145
1949	124	435	110	19	7	9	2.1	57	45	91	41	3	.253	.391	1	0	3B-122
1950	155	573	169	26	2	11	1.9	114	58	141	63	6	.295	.405	0	0	3B-155
1951	154	568	161	36	4	12	2.1	109	65	126	55	6	.283	.424	0	0	3B-152, OF-3
1952	157	587	137	32	3	12	2.0	92	49	129	73	4	.233	.359	0	0	3B-157
1953	152	577	157	30	7	9	1.6	107	45	123	59	7	.272	.395	0	0	3B-152
1954	155	539	138	26	4	11	2.0	101	47	131	71	7	.256	.380	0	0	3B-155
1955	122	375	91	17	5	7	1.9	64	48	95	54	4	.243	.371	14	3	3B-107
1956	152	515	119	17	2	11	2.1	94	53	151	82	8	.231	.336	9	0	3B-135, OF-8
1957	110	414	104	13	5	9	2.2	47	38	73	49	1	.251	.372	4	0	3B-107
1958	134	406	91	16	0	8	2.0	55	37	81	43	3	.224	.323	15	3	3B-114, OF-4, 1B-2
1959 DET A	148	521	145	19	0	21	4.0	115	61	135	77	9	.278	.436	3	0	3B-146, 2B-1
1960	143	497	129	23	2	14	2.8	78	47	125	69	5	.260	.398	5	1	3B-142
1961 LA A	76	213	43	4	0	3	1.4	29	15	50	48	0	.202	.263	8	1	3B-67
1962	52	104	25	9	1	0	0.0	22	10	30	21	0	.240	.346	16	1	3B-28, 1B-7
18 yrs.	2109	7346	1863	337	56	139	1.9	1215	683	1614 7th	920	72	.254	.371	76	9	3B-2008, OF-15, 1B-9, SS-2, 2B-1

Ned Yost

YOST, EDGAR FREDERICK
B. Aug. 19, 1955, Eureka, Calif.   BR TR 6'1"   190 lbs.

	G	AB	H	2B	3B	HR	HR%	R	RBI	BB	SO	SB	BA	SA	AB	H	G by POS
1980 MIL A	15	31	5	0	0	0	0.0	0	0	0	6	0	.161	.161	0	0	C-15
1981	18	27	6	0	0	3	11.1	4	3	3	6	0	.222	.556	0	0	C-16
1982	40	98	27	6	3	1	1.0	13	8	7	20	3	.276	.429	1	0	C-39, DH-1
1983	61	196	44	5	1	6	3.1	21	28	5	36	1	.224	.352	1	1	C-61
1984 TEX A	80	242	44	4	0	6	2.5	15	25	6	47	1	.182	.273	3	0	C-78
5 yrs.	214	594	126	15	4	16	2.7	53	64	21	115	5	.212	.332	5	1	C-209, DH-1

WORLD SERIES
	G	AB	H	2B	3B	HR	HR%	R	RBI	BB	SO	SB	BA	SA	AB	H	G by POS
1982 MIL A	1	0	0	0	0	0	–	0	0	1	0	0	–	–	0	0	C-1

Elmer Yoter

YOTER, ELMER ELLSWORTH
B. June 26, 1900, Carlisle, Pa.   D. July 26, 1966, Camp Hill, Pa.   BR TR 5'7"   155 lbs.

	G	AB	H	2B	3B	HR	HR%	R	RBI	BB	SO	SB	BA	SA	AB	H	G by POS
1921 PHI A	3	3	0	0	0	0	0.0	0	0	0	1	0	.000	.000	3	0	3B-19
1924 CLE A	19	66	18	1	1	0	0.0	3	7	5	8	0	.273	.318	0	0	3B-19
1927 CHI N	13	27	6	1	1	0	0.0	2	5	4	4	0	.222	.333	1	0	3B-11
1928	1	0	0	0	0	0	–	0	0	0	0	0	–	–	0	0	3B-1
4 yrs.	36	96	24	2	2	0	0.0	5	12	9	13	0	.250	.313	4	0	3B-31

Babe Young

YOUNG, NORMAN ROBERT
B. July 1, 1915, Astoria, N. Y.   D. Dec. 25, 1983, Everett, Mass.   BL TL 6'2½"   185 lbs.

	G	AB	H	2B	3B	HR	HR%	R	RBI	BB	SO	SB	BA	SA	AB	H	G by POS
1936 NY N	1	1	0	0	0	0	0.0	0	0	0	0	0	.000	.000	1	0	1B-22
1939	22	75	23	4	0	3	4.0	9	14	5	6	0	.307	.480	0	0	1B-22
1940	149	556	159	27	4	17	3.1	75	101	69	28	4	.286	.441	2	0	1B-147
1941	152	574	152	28	5	25	4.4	90	104	66	39	1	.265	.462	1	1	1B-150
1942	101	287	80	17	1	11	3.8	37	59	34	22	1	.279	.460	27	6	OF-54, 1B-18
1946	104	291	81	11	0	7	2.4	30	33	30	21	3	.278	.388	32	5	1B-49, OF-24
1947 2 teams	NY	N (14G – .071)				CIN	N (95G – .283)										
" total	109	378	104	22	3	14	3.7	55	79	35	27	0	.275	.460	16	2	1B-93
1948 2 teams	CIN	N (49G – .231)				STL	N (41G – .243)										
" total	90	241	57	12	4	2	0.8	25	25	35	18	0	.237	.344	18	3	1B-66, OF-1
8 yrs.	728	2403	656	121	17	79	3.3	320	415	274	161	9	.273	.436	97	17	1B-545, OF-79

Bobby Young

YOUNG, ROBERT GEORGE
B. Jan. 22, 1925, Granite, Md.   BL TR 6'1"   175 lbs.

	G	AB	H	2B	3B	HR	HR%	R	RBI	BB	SO	SB	BA	SA	AB	H	G by POS
1948 STL N	3	1	0	0	0	0	0.0	0	0	0	1	0	.000	.000	1	0	3B-1
1951 STL A	147	611	159	13	9	1	0.2	75	31	44	51	8	.260	.316	0	0	2B-147
1952	149	575	142	15	9	4	0.7	59	39	56	48	3	.247	.325	1	1	2B-149
1953	148	537	137	22	2	4	0.7	48	25	41	40	2	.255	.326	0	0	2B-148
1954 BAL A	130	432	106	13	6	4	0.9	43	24	54	42	4	.245	.331	8	1	2B-127
1955 2 teams	BAL	A (59G – .199)				CLE	A (18G – .311)										
" total	77	231	51	4	1	0	0.4	12	14	12	25	1	.221	.260	7	2	2B-69, 3B-1
1956 CLE A	1	0	0	0	0	0	–	0	0	0	0	0	–	–	0	0	
1958 PHI N	32	60	14	1	1	1	1.7	7	4	1	5	0	.233	.333	9	2	2B-21
8 yrs.	687	2447	609	68	28	15	0.6	244	137	208	212	18	.249	.318	26	6	2B-661, 3B-2

Del Young

YOUNG, DELMAR EDWARD
Son of Del Young.
B. May 11, 1912, Cleveland, Ohio   D. Dec. 8, 1979, San Francisco, Calif.   BB TR 6'   172 lbs.

	G	AB	H	2B	3B	HR	HR%	R	RBI	BB	SO	SB	BA	SA	AB	H	G by POS
1937 PHI N	109	360	70	9	2	0	0.0	36	24	18	55	6	.194	.231	0	0	2B-108
1938	108	340	78	13	2	0	0.0	27	31	20	35	0	.229	.279	2	0	SS-87, 2B-17
1939	77	217	57	9	2	3	1.4	22	20	8	24	1	.263	.364	7	1	SS-55, 2B-17
1940	15	33	8	0	1	0	0.0	2	1	2	1	0	.242	.303	0	0	SS-6, 2B-5
4 yrs.	309	950	213	31	7	3	0.3	87	76	48	115	7	.224	.281	9	1	SS-148, 2B-147

Del Young

YOUNG, DELMER JOHN
Father of Del Young.
B. Oct. 24, 1885, Macon, Mo.   D. Dec. 17, 1959, Cleveland, Ohio   BL TR 5'11½"   195 lbs.

	G	AB	H	2B	3B	HR	HR%	R	RBI	BB	SO	SB	BA	SA	AB	H	G by POS
1909 CIN N	2	7	2	0	0	0	0.0	0	1	1		0	.286	.286	0	0	OF-2
1914 BUF F	80	174	48	5	5	4	2.3	17	22	3		0	.276	.431	37	7	OF-41
1915	12	15	2	0	0	0	0.0	0	0	1		1	.133	.133	9	1	OF-3
3 yrs.	94	196	52	5	5	4	2.0	17	23	5		1	.265	.403	46	8	OF-46

Dick Young

YOUNG, RICHARD ENNIS
B. June 3, 1928, Seattle, Wash.   BL TR 5'11"   175 lbs.
BB 1952

	G	AB	H	2B	3B	HR	HR%	R	RBI	BB	SO	SB	BA	SA	AB	H	G by POS
1951 PHI N	15	68	16	5	0	0	0.0	7	2	3	6	0	.235	.309	0	0	2B-15

	G	AB	H	2B	3B	HR	HR %	R	RBI	BB	SO	SB	BA	SA	Pinch Hit AB	Pinch Hit H	G by POS

Dick Young continued

	G	AB	H	2B	3B	HR	HR %	R	RBI	BB	SO	SB	BA	SA	AB	H	G by POS
1952	5	9	2	1	0	0	0.0	3	0	1	3	1	.222	.333	2	0	2B-2
2 yrs.	20	77	18	6	0	0	0.0	10	2	4	9	1	.234	.312	2	0	2B-17

Don Young

YOUNG, DONALD WAYNE   BR TR 6'2"   185 lbs.
B. Oct. 18, 1945, Houston, Tex.

	G	AB	H	2B	3B	HR	HR %	R	RBI	BB	SO	SB	BA	SA	AB	H	G by POS
1965 CHI N	11	35	2	0	0	1	2.9	1	2	0	11	0	.057	.143	3	1	OF-11
1969	101	272	65	12	3	6	2.2	36	27	38	74	1	.239	.371	0	0	OF-100
2 yrs.	112	307	67	12	3	7	2.3	37	29	38	85	1	.218	.345	3	1	OF-111

George Young

YOUNG, GEORGE JOSEPH   BL TR 6'   185 lbs.
B. Apr. 1, 1890, Brooklyn, N. Y.   D. Mar. 13, 1950, New York, N. Y.

	G	AB	H	2B	3B	HR	HR %	R	RBI	BB	SO	SB	BA	SA	AB	H	G by POS
1913 CLE A	2	2	0	0	0	0	0.0	0	0	0	0	0	.000	.000	2	0	

Herman Young

YOUNG, HERMAN JOHN   BR TR 5'8"   155 lbs.
B. Apr. 14, 1886, Roxbury, Mass.   D. Dec. 13, 1966, Ipswich, Mass.

	G	AB	H	2B	3B	HR	HR %	R	RBI	BB	SO	SB	BA	SA	AB	H	G by POS
1911 BOS N	9	25	6	0	0	0	0.0	2	0	0	3	0	.240	.240	1	0	3B-5, SS-3

John Young

YOUNG, JOHN THOMAS   BL TL 6'3"   210 lbs.
B. Feb. 9, 1949, Los Angeles, Calif.

	G	AB	H	2B	3B	HR	HR %	R	RBI	BB	SO	SB	BA	SA	AB	H	G by POS
1971 DET A	2	4	2	1	0	0	0.0	1	1	0	0	0	.500	.750	1	0	1B-1

Mike Young

YOUNG, MICHAEL DARSEN   BL TL 6'3"   197 lbs.
B. Mar. 20, 1960, Oakland, Calif.

	G	AB	H	2B	3B	HR	HR %	R	RBI	BB	SO	SB	BA	SA	AB	H	G by POS
1982 BAL A	6	2	0	0	0	0	0.0	2	0	0	1	0	.000	.000	2	0	DH-2, OF-1
1983	25	36	6	2	1	0	0.0	5	2	2	8	1	.167	.278	5	0	OF-22, DH-3
1984	123	401	101	17	2	17	4.2	59	52	58	110	6	.252	.431	7	2	OF-115, DH-1
3 yrs.	154	439	107	19	3	17	3.9	66	54	60	119	7	.244	.417	14	2	OF-138, DH-6

Pep Young

YOUNG, LEMUEL FLOYD   BR TR 5'9"   162 lbs.
B. Aug. 29, 1907, Jamestown, N. C.   D. Jan. 14, 1962, Jamestown, N. C.

	G	AB	H	2B	3B	HR	HR %	R	RBI	BB	SO	SB	BA	SA	AB	H	G by POS
1933 PIT N	25	20	6	1	1	0	0.0	3	0	0	5	0	.300	.450	20	5	SS-1, 2B-1
1934	19	17	4	0	0	0	0.0	3	2	0	6	0	.235	.235	4	0	SS-2, 2B-1
1935	128	494	131	25	10	7	1.4	60	82	21	59	2	.265	.399	0	0	2B-107, OF-6, 3B-6, SS-4
1936	125	475	118	23	10	6	1.3	47	77	29	52	3	.248	.377	1	0	2B-123
1937	113	408	106	20	3	9	2.2	43	54	26	63	4	.260	.390	2	1	SS-45, 3B-39, 2B-30
1938	149	562	156	36	5	4	0.7	58	79	40	64	7	.278	.381	0	0	2B-149
1939	84	293	81	14	3	3	1.0	34	29	23	29	1	.276	.375	0	0	2B-84
1940	54	136	34	8	2	1	.7	19	20	12	23	1	.250	.382	7	1	2B-33, SS-7, 3B-5
1941 2 teams		CIN N (4G – .167)			STL N (2G – .000)												
" total	6	14	2	0	0	0	0.0	2	0	0	3	0	.143	.143	3	0	3B-3
1945 STL N	27	47	7	1	0	1	2.1	5	4	1	8	0	.149	.234	5	0	SS-11, 3B-9, 2B-3
10 yrs.	730	2466	645	128	34	32	1.3	274	347	152	312	18	.262	.380	42	7	2B-532, SS-70, 3B-62, OF-6

Ralph Young

YOUNG, RALPH STUART   BB TR 5'5"   165 lbs.
B. Sept. 19, 1890, Philadelphia, Pa.   D. Jan. 24, 1965, Philadelphia, Pa.

	G	AB	H	2B	3B	HR	HR %	R	RBI	BB	SO	SB	BA	SA	AB	H	G by POS
1913 NY A	7	15	1	0	0	0	0.0	2	0	3	3	2	.067	.067	0	0	SS-7
1915 DET A	123	378	92	6	5	0	0.0	44	31	53	31	12	.243	.286	0	0	2B-119
1916	153	528	139	16	6	1	0.2	60	45	62	43	20	.263	.322	0	0	2B-146, SS-6, 3B-1
1917	141	503	116	18	2	1	0.2	64	35	61	35	8	.231	.280	0	0	2B-141
1918	91	298	56	7	1	0	0.0	31	21	54	17	15	.188	.218	0	0	2B-91
1919	125	456	96	13	5	1	0.2	63	25	53	32	8	.211	.268	0	0	2B-121, SS-4
1920	150	594	173	21	6	0	0.0	84	33	85	30	8	.291	.347	0	0	2B-150
1921	107	401	120	8	3	0	0.0	70	29	69	23	11	.299	.334	1	0	2B-106
1922 PHI A	125	470	105	19	2	1	0.2	62	35	55	21	8	.223	.279	5	2	2B-120
9 yrs.	1022	3643	898	108	30	4	0.1	480	254	495	235	92	.247	.296	6	2	2B-994, SS-17, 3B-1

Russ Young

YOUNG, RUSSELL CHARLES   BB TR 5'11½" 190 lbs.
B. Sept. 15, 1902, Bryan, Ohio

	G	AB	H	2B	3B	HR	HR %	R	RBI	BB	SO	SB	BA	SA	AB	H	G by POS
1931 STL A	16	34	4	0	0	1	2.9	2	2	2	4	0	.118	.206	0	0	C-16

Joel Youngblood

YOUNGBLOOD, JOEL RANDOLPH   BR TR 5'11"   175 lbs.
B. Aug. 28, 1951, Houston, Tex.

	G	AB	H	2B	3B	HR	HR %	R	RBI	BB	SO	SB	BA	SA	AB	H	G by POS
1976 CIN N	55	57	11	1	1	0	0.0	8	1	2	8	1	.193	.246	33	5	OF-9, 3B-6, 2B-1, C-1
1977 2 teams		STL N (25G – .185)			NY N (70G – .253)												
" total	95	209	51	13	1	0	0.0	17	12	16	45	1	.244	.316	22	5	OF-33, 2B-33, 3B-16
1978 NY N	113	266	67	12	8	7	2.6	40	30	16	39	4	.252	.436	23	7	OF-50, 2B-39, 3B-9, SS-1
1979	158	590	162	37	5	16	2.7	90	60	60	84	18	.275	.436	4	1	OF-147, 2B-13, 3B-12
1980	146	514	142	26	2	8	1.6	58	69	52	69	14	.276	.381	13	7	OF-121, 3B-21, 2B-6
1981	43	143	50	10	2	4	2.8	16	25	12	19	2	.350	.531	3	0	OF-41
1982 2 teams		NY N (80G – .257)			MON N (40G – .200)												
" total	120	292	70	14	2	3	1.0	37	29	17	58	2	.240	.318	15	2	OF-98, 2B-8, SS-1, 3B-1
1983 SF N	124	373	109	20	3	17	4.6	59	53	33	59	7	.292	.499	20	4	2B-64, 3B-28, OF-22
1984	134	469	119	17	1	10	2.1	50	51	48	86	5	.254	.358	6	1	3B-117, OF-11, 2B-5
9 yrs.	988	2913	781	150	23	65	2.2	375	330	256	467	54	.268	.402	139	32	OF-532, 3B-210, 2B-169, SS-2, C-1

Henry Youngman

YOUNGMAN, HENRY
B. 1865, Indiana, Pa.   D. Jan. 24, 1936, Pittsburgh, Pa.

	G	AB	H	2B	3B	HR	HR %	R	RBI	BB	SO	SB	BA	SA	AB	H	G by POS
1890 PIT N	13	47	6	1	1	0	0.0	6	4	6	9	1	.128	.191	0	0	3B-7, 2B-6

	G	AB	H	2B	3B	HR	HR %	R	RBI	BB	SO	SB	BA	SA	Pinch Hit AB	Pinch Hit H	G by POS

Ross Youngs

YOUNGS, ROSS MIDDLEBROOK (Pep)
BL TR 5'8" 162 lbs.
Also known as Royce Youngs.
B. Apr. 10, 1897, Shiner, Tex.   D. Oct. 22, 1927, San Antonio, Tex.
Hall of Fame 1972.

Year	Team	Lg	G	AB	H	2B	3B	HR	HR%	R	RBI	BB	SO	SB	BA	SA	PH AB	PH H	G by POS
1917	NY	N	7	26	9	2	3	0	0.0	5	1	1	5	1	.346	.654	0	0	OF-7
1918			121	474	143	16	8	1	0.2	70	25	44	49	10	.302	.376	1	0	OF-120
1919			130	489	152	31	7	2	0.4	73	43	51	47	24	.311	.415	0	0	OF-130
1920			153	581	204	27	14	6	1.0	92	78	75	55	18	.351	.477	0	0	OF-153
1921			141	504	165	24	16	3	0.6	90	102	71	47	21	.327	.456	4	2	OF-137
1922			149	559	185	34	10	7	1.3	105	86	55	50	17	.331	.465	1	0	OF-147
1923			152	596	200	33	12	3	0.5	121	87	73	36	13	.336	.446	0	0	OF-152
1924			133	526	187	33	12	10	1.9	112	74	77	31	11	.356	.521	1	0	OF-132, 2B-2
1925			130	500	132	24	6	6	1.2	82	53	66	51	17	.264	.372	1	0	OF-127, 2B-3
1926			95	372	114	12	5	4	1.1	62	43	37	19	21	.306	.398	1	1	OF-94
10 yrs.			1211	4627	1491	236	93	42	0.9	812	592	550	390	153	.322	.441	9	3	OF-1199, 2B-5

WORLD SERIES

Year	Team	Lg	G	AB	H	2B	3B	HR	HR%	R	RBI	BB	SO	SB	BA	SA	PH AB	PH H	G by POS
1921	NY	N	8	25	7	1	1	0	0.0	3	3	7	2	2	.280	.400	0	0	OF-8
1922			5	16	6	0	0	0	0.0	2	2	3	1	0	.375	.375	0	0	OF-5
1923			6	23	8	0	0	1	4.3	2	3	2	0	0	.348	.478	0	0	OF-6
1924			7	27	5	1	0	0	0.0	3	1	5	6	1	.185	.222	0	0	OF-7
4 yrs.			26	91	26	2	1	1	1.1	10	9	17	9	3	.286	.363	0	0	OF-26

Eddie Yount

YOUNT, FLOYD EDWIN
BR TR 6'1" 185 lbs.
B. Dec. 19, 1916, Newton, N. C.   D. Oct. 26, 1973, Newton, N. C.

Year	Team	Lg	G	AB	H	2B	3B	HR	HR%	R	RBI	BB	SO	SB	BA	SA	PH AB	PH H	G by POS
1937	PHI	A	4	7	2	0	0	0	0.0	1	1	0	1	0	.286	.286	2	0	OF-2
1939	PIT	N	2	2	0	0	0	0	0.0	0	0	0	2	0	.000	.000	2	0	
2 yrs.			6	9	2	0	0	0	0.0	1	1	0	3	0	.222	.222	4	0	OF-2

Robin Yount

YOUNT, ROBIN R.
BR TR 6' 165 lbs.
Brother of Larry Yount.
B. Sept. 16, 1955, Woodland Hills, Calif.

Year	Team	Lg	G	AB	H	2B	3B	HR	HR%	R	RBI	BB	SO	SB	BA	SA	PH AB	PH H	G by POS
1974	MIL	A	107	344	86	14	5	3	0.9	48	26	12	46	7	.250	.346	0	0	SS-107
1975			147	558	149	28	2	8	1.4	67	52	33	69	12	.267	.367	2	0	SS-145
1976			161	638	161	19	3	2	0.3	59	54	38	69	16	.252	.301	0	0	SS-161, OF-1
1977			154	605	174	34	4	4	0.7	66	49	41	80	16	.288	.377	3	1	SS-153
1978			127	502	147	23	9	9	1.8	66	71	24	43	16	.293	.428	2	1	SS-125
1979			149	577	154	26	5	8	1.4	72	51	35	52	11	.267	.371	0	0	SS-149
1980			143	611	179	49	10	23	3.8	121	87	26	67	20	.293	.519	2	0	SS-133, DH-9
1981			96	377	103	15	5	10	2.7	50	49	22	37	4	.273	.419	1	1	SS-93, DH-3
1982			156	635	210	46	12	29	4.6	129	114	54	63	14	.331	.578	2	1	SS-154, DH-1
1983			149	578	178	42	10	17	2.9	102	80	72	58	12	.308	.503	2	2	SS-139, DH-8
1984			160	624	186	27	7	16	2.6	105	80	67	67	14	.298	.441	0	0	SS-120, DH-39
11 yrs.			1549	6049	1727	323	72	129	2.1	885	713	424	651	142	.286	.427	14	6	SS-1479, DH-60, OF-1

DIVISIONAL PLAYOFF SERIES

Year	Team	Lg	G	AB	H	2B	3B	HR	HR%	R	RBI	BB	SO	SB	BA	SA	PH AB	PH H	G by POS
1981	MIL	A	5	19	6	0	1	0	0.0	4	1	2	2	1	.316	.421	0	0	SS-5

LEAGUE CHAMPIONSHIP SERIES

Year	Team	Lg	G	AB	H	2B	3B	HR	HR%	R	RBI	BB	SO	SB	BA	SA	PH AB	PH H	G by POS
1982	MIL	A	5	16	4	0	0	0	0.0	1	0	5	0	0	.250	.250	0	0	SS-5

WORLD SERIES

Year	Team	Lg	G	AB	H	2B	3B	HR	HR%	R	RBI	BB	SO	SB	BA	SA	PH AB	PH H	G by POS
1982	MIL	A	7	29	12	3	0	1	3.4	6	6	2	2	0	.414	.621	0	0	SS-7

Jeff Yurak

YURAK, JEFFREY LYNN
BB TR 6'3" 195 lbs.
B. Feb. 26, 1954, Pasadena, Calif.

Year	Team	Lg	G	AB	H	2B	3B	HR	HR%	R	RBI	BB	SO	SB	BA	SA	PH AB	PH H	G by POS
1978	MIL	A	5	5	0	0	0	0	0.0	0	0	1	0	0	.000	.000	3	0	OF-1

Sal Yvars

YVARS, SALVADOR ANTHONY
BR TR 5'10" 187 lbs.
B. Feb. 20, 1924, New York, N. Y.

Year	Team	Lg	G	AB	H	2B	3B	HR	HR%	R	RBI	BB	SO	SB	BA	SA	PH AB	PH H	G by POS
1947	NY	N	1	5	1	0	0	0	0.0	0	0	0	2	0	.200	.200	0	0	C-1
1948			15	38	8	1	0	1	2.6	4	6	3	1	0	.211	.316	0	0	C-15
1949			3	8	0	0	0	0	0.0	0	0	1	1	0	.000	.000	1	0	C-2
1950			9	14	2	0	0	0	0.0	0	0	1	2	0	.143	.143	0	0	C-9
1951			25	41	13	2	0	2	4.9	9	3	5	7	0	.317	.512	2	0	C-23
1952			66	151	37	3	0	4	2.6	15	18	10	16	0	.245	.344	7	1	C-59
1953	2 teams		NY	N	(23G – .277)		STL	N	(30G – .246)										
"	total		53	104	27	2	0	1	1.0	5	7	11	7	0	.260	.308	9	1	C-46
1954	STL	N	38	57	14	4	0	2	3.5	8	8	6	5	1	.246	.421	18	4	C-21
8 yrs.			210	418	102	12	0	10	2.4	41	42	37	41	1	.244	.344	37	6	C-176

WORLD SERIES

Year	Team	Lg	G	AB	H	2B	3B	HR	HR%	R	RBI	BB	SO	SB	BA	SA	PH AB	PH H	G by POS
1951	NY	N	1	1	0	0	0	0	0.0	0	0	0	0	0	.000	.000	1	0	

Elmer Zacher

ZACHER, ELMER HENRY (Silver)
BR TR
B. Sept. 17, 1883, Buffalo, N. Y.   D. Dec. 20, 1944, Buffalo, N. Y.

Year	Team	Lg	G	AB	H	2B	3B	HR	HR%	R	RBI	BB	SO	SB	BA	SA	PH AB	PH H	G by POS
1910	2 teams		NY	N	(1G – .000)		STL	N	(47G – .212)										
"	total		48	132	28	5	1	0	0.0	7	10	10	19	3	.212	.265	9	2	OF-37, 2B-1

Fred Zahner

ZAHNER, FREDERICK JOSEPH
BR TR
B. June 5, 1870, Louisville, Ky.   D. July 24, 1900, Louisville, Ky.

Year	Team	Lg	G	AB	H	2B	3B	HR	HR%	R	RBI	BB	SO	SB	BA	SA	PH AB	PH H	G by POS
1894	LOU	N	13	45	9	0	1	0	0.0	7	3	3	5	2	.200	.244	0	0	C-10, OF-2, 1B-1
1895			21	49	11	1	1	0	0.0	7	6	6	4	0	.224	.286	0	0	C-21
2 yrs.			34	94	20	1	2	0	0.0	14	9	9	9	2	.213	.266	0	0	C-31, OF-2, 1B-1

Frankie Zak

ZAK, FRANK THOMAS
BR TR 5'10" 150 lbs.
B. Feb. 22, 1922, Passaic, N. J.   D. Feb. 6, 1972, Passaic, N. J.

Year	Team	Lg	G	AB	H	2B	3B	HR	HR%	R	RBI	BB	SO	SB	BA	SA	PH AB	PH H	G by POS
1944	PIT	N	87	160	48	3	1	0	0.0	33	11	22	18	6	.300	.331	0	0	SS-67
1945			15	28	4	2	0	0	0.0	2	3	3	5	0	.143	.214	0	0	SS-10, 2B-1
1946			21	20	4	0	0	0	0.0	8	0	1	0	0	.200	.200	0	0	SS-10
3 yrs.			123	208	56	5	1	0	0.0	43	14	26	23	6	.269	.303	0	0	SS-87, 2B-1

	G	AB	H	2B	3B	HR	HR %	R	RBI	BB	SO	SB	BA	SA	Pinch Hit AB	Pinch Hit H	G by POS

Jack Zalusky

ZALUSKY, JOHN FRANCIS
B. June 22, 1879, Minneapolis, Minn.   D. Aug. 11, 1935, Minneapolis, Minn.
BR TR 5'11½" 172 lbs.

	G	AB	H	2B	3B	HR	HR%	R	RBI	BB	SO	SB	BA	SA	PH AB	PH H	G by POS
1903 NY A	7	16	5	0	0	0	0.0	2	1	1		0	.313	.313	0	0	C-6, 1B-1

Joe Zapustas

ZAPUSTAS, JOSEPH JOHN
B. July 25, 1907, Boston, Mass.
BR TR 6'1" 185 lbs.

	G	AB	H	2B	3B	HR	HR%	R	RBI	BB	SO	SB	BA	SA	PH AB	PH H	G by POS
1933 PHI A	2	5	1	0	0	0	0.0	0	0	0	0	0	.200	.200	0	0	OF-2

Jose Zardon

ZARDON, JOSE ANTONIO SANCHEZ
B. May 20, 1923, Havana, Cuba
BR TR 6' 150 lbs.

	G	AB	H	2B	3B	HR	HR%	R	RBI	BB	SO	SB	BA	SA	PH AB	PH H	G by POS
1945 WAS A	54	131	38	5	3	0	0.0	13	13	7	11	3	.290	.374	2	0	OF-43

Al Zarilla

ZARILLA, ALLEN LEE (Zeke)
B. May 1, 1919, Los Angeles, Calif.
BL TR 5'11" 180 lbs.

	G	AB	H	2B	3B	HR	HR%	R	RBI	BB	SO	SB	BA	SA	PH AB	PH H	G by POS
1943 STL A	70	228	58	7	1	2	0.9	27	17	17	20	1	.254	.320	11	4	OF-60
1944	100	288	86	13	6	6	2.1	43	45	29	33	1	.299	.448	15	2	OF-79
1946	125	371	96	14	9	4	1.1	46	43	27	37	3	.259	.377	15	1	OF-107
1947	127	380	85	15	6	3	0.8	34	38	40	45	3	.224	.318	16	0	OF-110
1948	144	529	174	39	3	12	2.3	77	74	48	48	11	.329	.482	9	3	OF-136
1949 2 teams	STL A (15G – .250)			BOS A (124G – .281)													
" total	139	530	147	33	4	10	1.9	78	77	56	53	5	.277	.411	2	0	OF-137
1950 BOS A	130	471	153	32	10	9	1.9	92	74	76	47	2	.325	.493	1	0	OF-128
1951 CHI A	120	382	98	21	2	10	2.6	56	60	60	57	2	.257	.401	3	0	OF-117
1952 3 teams	CHI A (39G – .232)			STL A (48G – .238)				BOS A (21G – .183)									
" total	108	289	65	10	2	5	1.7	43	24	48	29	5	.225	.325	18	1	OF-86
1953 BOS A	57	67	13	2	0	0	0.0	11	4	14	13	0	.194	.224	30	4	OF-18
10 yrs.	1120	3535	975	186	43	61	1.7	507	456	415	382	33	.276	.405	120	15	OF-978

WORLD SERIES

	G	AB	H	2B	3B	HR	HR%	R	RBI	BB	SO	SB	BA	SA	PH AB	PH H	G by POS
1 yr.	4	10	1	0	0	0	0.0	1	1	0	4	0	.100	.100	2	0	OF-3

Norm Zauchin

ZAUCHIN, NORBERT HENRY
B. Nov. 17, 1929, Royal Oak, Mich.
BR TR 6'4½" 220 lbs.

	G	AB	H	2B	3B	HR	HR%	R	RBI	BB	SO	SB	BA	SA	PH AB	PH H	G by POS
1951 BOS A	5	12	2	1	0	0	0.0	0	0	0	4	0	.167	.250	1	0	1B-4
1955	130	477	114	10	0	27	5.7	65	93	69	105	3	.239	.430	4	2	1B-126
1956	44	84	18	2	0	2	2.4	12	11	14	22	0	.214	.310	12	1	1B-31
1957	52	91	24	3	0	3	3.3	11	14	9	13	0	.264	.396	21	4	1B-36
1958 WAS A	96	303	69	8	2	15	5.0	35	37	38	68	0	.228	.416	5	1	1B-91
1959	19	71	15	4	0	3	4.2	11	4	7	14	2	.211	.394	0	0	1B-19
6 yrs.	346	1038	242	28	2	50	4.8	134	159	137	226	5	.233	.408	43	8	1B-307

Joe Zdeb

ZDEB, JOSEPH EDMUND
B. June 27, 1953, Mendota, Ill.
BR TR 5'11" 185 lbs.

	G	AB	H	2B	3B	HR	HR%	R	RBI	BB	SO	SB	BA	SA	PH AB	PH H	G by POS
1977 KC A	105	195	58	5	2	2	1.0	26	23	16	23	6	.297	.374	22	7	OF-93, 3B-1, DH
1978	60	127	32	2	3	0	0.0	18	11	7	18	3	.252	.315	17	3	OF-52, 3B-1, 2B-1, DH
1979	15	23	4	1	1	0	0.0	3	0	2	4	1	.174	.304	8	1	OF-9
3 yrs.	180	345	94	8	6	2	0.6	47	34	25	45	10	.272	.348	47	11	OF-154, 3B-2, 2B-1

LEAGUE CHAMPIONSHIP SERIES

	G	AB	H	2B	3B	HR	HR%	R	RBI	BB	SO	SB	BA	SA	PH AB	PH H	G by POS
1 yr.	4	9	0	0	0	0	0.0	0	0	0	2	1	.000	.000	1	0	OF-4

Dave Zearfoss

ZEARFOSS, DAVID WILLIAM TILDEN
B. Jan. 1, 1868, Schenectady, N.Y.   D. Sept. 12, 1945, Wilmington, Del.
TR

	G	AB	H	2B	3B	HR	HR%	R	RBI	BB	SO	SB	BA	SA	PH AB	PH H	G by POS
1896 NY N	19	60	13	1	1	0	0.0	5	6	5	5	2	.217	.267	0	0	C-19
1897	5	10	3	0	1	0	0.0	1	0	1		0	.300	.500	0	0	C-5
1898	1	1	1	0	0	0	0.0	0	0	0		0	1.000	1.000	0	0	C-1
1904 STL N	27	80	17	2	0	0	0.0	7	9	10		0	.213	.238	1	0	C-25
1905	20	51	8	0	1	0	0.0	2	2	4		0	.157	.196	1	0	C-19
5 yrs.	72	202	42	3	3	0	0.0	15	17	19	5	2	.208	.252	2	0	C-69

George Zeber

ZEBER, GEORGE WILLIAM
B. Aug. 29, 1950, Ellwood City, Pa.
BB TR 5'11" 170 lbs.

	G	AB	H	2B	3B	HR	HR%	R	RBI	BB	SO	SB	BA	SA	PH AB	PH H	G by POS
1977 NY A	25	65	21	3	0	3	4.6	8	10	9	11	0	.323	.508	1	0	2B-21, SS-2, 3B-2, DH
1978	3	6	0	0	0	0	0.0	0	0	0	0	0	.000	.000	1	0	2B-1
2 yrs.	28	71	21	3	0	3	4.2	8	10	9	11	0	.296	.465	2	0	2B-22, SS-2, 3B-2

WORLD SERIES

	G	AB	H	2B	3B	HR	HR%	R	RBI	BB	SO	SB	BA	SA	PH AB	PH H	G by POS
1 yr.	2	2	0	0	0	0	0.0	0	0	0	2	0	.000	.000	2	0	

Rollie Zeider

ZEIDER, ROLLIE HUBERT (Bunions)
B. Nov. 16, 1883, Auburn, Ind.   D. Sept. 12, 1967, Garrett, Ind.
BR TR 5'10" 162 lbs.

	G	AB	H	2B	3B	HR	HR%	R	RBI	BB	SO	SB	BA	SA	PH AB	PH H	G by POS
1910 CHI A	136	498	108	9	2	0	0.0	57	31	62		49	.217	.243	0	0	2B-87, SS-45, 3B-4
1911	73	217	55	3	0	2	0.9	39	21	29		28	.253	.295	8	4	1B-29, SS-17, 3B-10, 2B-9
1912	129	420	103	12	0	2	0.5	57	42	50		47	.245	.329	3	1	1B-66, 3B-56, SS-1
1913 2 teams	CHI A (13G – .350)			NY A (49G – .233)													
" total	62	179	44	2	0	0	0.0	19	14	29	10	6	.246	.257	2	0	SS-23, 2B-20, 3B-8, 1B-7
1914 CHI F	119	452	124	13	2	1	0.2	60	36	44	35		.274	.319	1	0	3B-117, SS-1
1915	129	494	112	22	2	0	0.0	65	34	43	16		.227	.279	0	0	2B-83, 3B-30, SS-21
1916 CHI N	98	345	81	11	2	1	0.3	29	22	26	26	9	.235	.287	1	0	3B-55, 2B-33, OF-7, SS-5, 1B-2
1917	108	354	86	14	2	0	0.0	36	27	28	30	17	.243	.294	15	2	SS-48, 3B-26, 2B-24, OF-1, 1B-1
1918	82	251	56	3	2	0	0.0	31	26	23	20	16	.223	.251	7	1	2B-79, 3B-1, 1B-1
9 yrs.	936	3210	769	89	22	5	0.2	393	253	334	86	223	.240	.286	37	8	2B-335, 3B-307, SS-161, 1B-106, OF-8

	G	AB	H	2B	3B	HR	HR %	R	RBI	BB	SO	SB	BA	SA	Pinch Hit AB	H	G by POS

Rollie Zeider continued

WORLD SERIES

	G	AB	H	2B	3B	HR	HR%	R	RBI	BB	SO	SB	BA	SA	AB	H	G by POS
1918 CHI N	2	0	0	0	0	0	–	0	0	2	0	0	–	–	0	0	3B-2

Bart Zeller

ZELLER, BARTON WALLACE
B. July 22, 1941, Chicago Heights, Ill.   BR TR 6'1"   185 lbs.

	G	AB	H	2B	3B	HR	HR%	R	RBI	BB	SO	SB	BA	SA	AB	H	G by POS
1970 STL N	1	0	0	0	0	0	–	0	0	0	0	0	–	–	0	0	C-1

Gus Zernial

ZERNIAL, GUS EDWARD (Ozark Ike)
B. June 27, 1923, Beaumont, Tex.   BR TR 6'2½"   210 lbs.

	G	AB	H	2B	3B	HR	HR%	R	RBI	BB	SO	SB	BA	SA	AB	H	G by POS
1949 CHI A	73	198	63	17	2	5	2.5	29	38	15	26	0	.318	.500	25	8	OF-46
1950	143	543	152	16	4	29	5.3	75	93	38	110	0	.280	.484	5	1	OF-137
1951 2 teams	CHI	A (4G – .105)			PHI	A	(139G – .274)										
" total	143	571	153	30	5	33	5.8	92	129	63	101	2	.268	.511	1	1	OF-142
1952 PHI A	145	549	144	15	1	29	5.3	76	100	70	87	5	.262	.452	3	1	OF-141
1953	147	556	158	21	3	42	7.6	85	108	57	79	4	.284	.559	4	3	OF-141
1954	97	336	84	8	2	14	4.2	42	62	30	60	0	.250	.411	6	2	OF-90, 1B-2
1955 KC A	120	413	105	9	3	30	7.3	62	84	30	90	1	.254	.508	17	2	OF-103
1956	109	272	61	12	0	16	5.9	36	44	33	66	2	.224	.445	35	4	OF-69
1957	131	437	103	20	1	27	6.2	56	69	34	84	1	.236	.471	17	4	OF-113, 1B-1
1958 DET A	66	124	40	7	1	5	4.0	8	23	6	25	0	.323	.516	38	15	OF-24
1959	60	132	30	4	0	7	5.3	11	26	7	27	0	.227	.417	27	6	1B-32, OF-1
11 yrs.	1234	4131	1093	159	22	237	5.7	572	776	383	755	15	.265	.486	178	47	OF-1007, 1B-35

Ed Zieber

Playing record listed under Ed Whiting

Charlie Ziegler

ZIEGLER, CHARLES W.
B. Feb. 2, 1875, Canton, Ohio   D. Mar. 16, 1904, Canton, Ohio

	G	AB	H	2B	3B	HR	HR%	R	RBI	BB	SO	SB	BA	SA	AB	H	G by POS
1899 CLE N	2	8	2	0	0	0	0.0	2	0	0		0	.250	.250	0	0	SS-1, 2B-1
1900 PHI N	3	11	3	0	0	0	0.0	0	1	0		0	.273	.273	0	0	3B-3
2 yrs.	5	19	5	0	0	0	0.0	2	1	0		0	.263	.263	0	0	3B-3, SS-1, 2B-1

Benny Zientara

ZIENTARA, BENEDICT JOSEPH
B. Feb. 14, 1920, Chicago, Ill.   BR TR 5'8"   150 lbs.

	G	AB	H	2B	3B	HR	HR%	R	RBI	BB	SO	SB	BA	SA	AB	H	G by POS
1941 CIN N	9	21	6	0	0	0	0.0	3	2	1	3	0	.286	.286	0	0	2B-6
1946	78	280	81	10	2	0	0.0	26	16	14	11	3	.289	.339	0	0	2B-39, 3B-36
1947	117	418	108	18	1	2	0.5	60	24	23	23	2	.258	.321	9	5	2B-100, 3B-13
1948	74	187	35	1	2	0	0.0	17	7	12	11	0	.187	.214	7	1	2B-60, 3B-3, SS-2
4 yrs.	278	906	230	29	5	2	0.2	106	49	50	48	5	.254	.304	16	6	2B-205, 3B-52, SS-2

Bill Zies

ZIES, WILLIAM
Deceased.

	G	AB	H	2B	3B	HR	HR%	R	RBI	BB	SO	SB	BA	SA	AB	H	G by POS
1891 STL AA	2	3	1	0	0	0	0.0	0	0	0	0	0	.333	.333	0	0	C-2

Chief Zimmer

ZIMMER, CHARLES LOUIS
B. Nov. 23, 1860, Marietta, Ohio   D. Aug. 22, 1949, Cleveland, Ohio   BR TR 6'   190 lbs.
Manager 1903.

	G	AB	H	2B	3B	HR	HR%	R	RBI	BB	SO	SB	BA	SA	AB	H	G by POS
1884 DET N	8	29	2	1	0	0	0.0	0		1	14		.069	.103	0	0	C-6, OF-2
1886 NY AA	6	19	3	0	0	0	0.0	1		1			.158	.158	0	0	C-6
1887 CLE AA	14	52	12	5	0	0	0.0	9		4		1	.231	.327	0	0	C-12, 1B-2
1888	65	212	51	11	4	0	0.0	27	22	18		15	.241	.330	0	0	C-59, OF-3, 1B-3, SS-1
1889 CLE N	84	259	67	9	9	1	0.4	47	21	44	35	14	.259	.375	0	0	C-81, 1B-3
1890	125	444	95	16	6	2	0.5	54	57	46	54	15	.214	.291	0	0	C-125
1891	116	440	112	21	4	3	0.7	55	69	33	49	15	.255	.341	0	0	C-116, 3B-1
1892	111	413	108	29	13	1	0.2	63	64	32	47	18	.262	.402	0	0	C-111
1893	57	227	70	13	7	2	0.9	27	41	16	15	4	.308	.454	1	0	C-56, 3B-1
1894	90	341	97	20	5	4	1.2	55	65	17	31	14	.284	.408	1	0	C-89
1895	88	315	107	21	5	5	1.6	60	56	33	30	14	.340	.467	1	0	C-84, 1B-3
1896	91	336	93	18	3	3	0.9	46	46	31	48	4	.277	.375	0	0	C-91, 3B-1
1897	80	294	93	22	3	0	0.0	50	40	25		8	.316	.412	0	0	C-80
1898	20	63	15	2	0	0	0.0	5	4	5		2	.238	.270	1	0	C-19
1899 2 teams	CLE	N (20G – .342)			LOU	N	(75G – .298)										
" total	95	335	103	13	4	4	1.2	52	43	27		10	.307	.406	2	1	C-82, 1B-11
1900 PIT N	82	271	80	7	10	0	0.0	27	35	17		4	.295	.395	2	0	C-78, 1B-2
1901	69	236	52	7	3	0	0.0	17	21	20		6	.220	.275	1	1	C-68
1902	42	142	38	4	2	0	0.0	13	17	11		4	.268	.324	0	0	C-41, 1B-1
1903 PHI N	37	118	26	3	1	1	0.8	9	19	9		3	.220	.288	2	1	C-35
19 yrs.	1280	4546	1224	222	76	26	0.6	617	619	390	323	151	.269	.369	11	3	C-1239, 1B-25, OF-5, 3B-3, SS-1

Don Zimmer

ZIMMER, DONALD WILLIAM
B. Jan. 17, 1931, Cincinnati, Ohio   BR TR 5'9"   165 lbs.
Manager 1972-73, 1976-82.

	G	AB	H	2B	3B	HR	HR%	R	RBI	BB	SO	SB	BA	SA	AB	H	G by POS
1954 BKN N	24	33	6	0	1	0	0.0	3	0	3	8	2	.182	.242	2	0	SS-13
1955	88	280	67	10	1	15	5.4	38	50	19	66	5	.239	.443	3	0	2B-62, SS-21, 3B-8
1956	17	20	6	1	0	0	0.0	4	2	0	7	0	.300	.350	0	0	SS-8, 3B-3, 2B-1
1957	84	269	59	9	1	6	2.2	23	19	16	63	1	.219	.327	1	0	3B-39, SS-37, 2B-5
1958 LA N	127	455	119	15	2	17	3.7	52	60	28	92	14	.262	.415	1	0	SS-114, 3B-12, OF-1, 2B-1
1959	97	249	41	7	1	4	1.6	21	28	37	56	3	.165	.249	4	1	SS-88, 3B-5, 2B-1
1960 CHI N	132	368	95	16	7	6	1.6	37	35	27	56	8	.258	.389	13	3	2B-75, 3B-45, SS-5, OF-2
1961	128	477	120	25	4	13	2.7	57	40	25	70	5	.252	.403	8	1	2B-116, 3B-5, OF-1
1962 2 teams	NY	N (14G – .077)			CIN	N	(63G – .250)										
" total	77	244	52	12	2	2	0.8	19	17	17	40	1	.213	.303	9	4	3B-57, 2B-17, SS-1

	G	AB	H	2B	3B	HR	HR %	R	RBI	BB	SO	SB	BA	SA	Pinch Hit AB	Pinch Hit H	G by POS

Don Zimmer continued

		G	AB	H	2B	3B	HR	HR%	R	RBI	BB	SO	SB	BA	SA	PH AB	PH H	G by POS
1963 2 teams	LA N (22G – .217)						WAS A (83G – .248)											
" total	105	321	79	13	1	14	4.4	41	46	21	67	3	.246	.424	14	5	3B-88, 2B-3, SS-1
1964 WAS A	121	341	84	16	2	12	3.5	38	38	27	94	1	.246	.411	38	10	3B-87, OF-4, C-2, 2B-1
1965	95	226	45	6	0	2	0.9	20	17	26	59	2	.199	.252	27	5	3B-36, C-33, 2B-12
12 yrs.	1095	3283	773	130	22	91	2.8	353	352	246	678	45	.235	.372	120	29	3B-385, 2B-294, SS-288, C-35, OF-8

WORLD SERIES

	G	AB	H	2B	3B	HR	HR%	R	RBI	BB	SO	SB	BA	SA	PH AB	PH H	G by POS
1955 BKN N	4	9	2	0	0	0	0.0	0	2	2	5	0	.222	.222	1	0	2B-4
1959 LA N	1	1	0	0	0	0	0.0	0	0	0	0	0	.000	.000	0	0	SS-1
2 yrs.	5	10	2	0	0	0	0.0	0	2	2	5	0	.200	.200	1	0	2B-4, SS-1

Bill Zimmerman

ZIMMERMAN, WILLIAM H.   BR TR 5'8½" 172 lbs.
B. Jan. 20, 1889, Kengen, Germany   D. Oct. 4, 1952, Newark, N. J.

	G	AB	H	2B	3B	HR	HR%	R	RBI	BB	SO	SB	BA	SA	PH AB	PH H	G by POS
1915 BKN N	22	57	16	2	0	0	0.0	3	7	4	8	1	.281	.316	3	0	OF-18

Eddie Zimmerman

ZIMMERMAN, EDWARD DESMOND (Zimmie)   BR TR
B. Jan. 4, 1883, Oceanic, N. J.   D. May 6, 1945, Allentown, Pa.

	G	AB	H	2B	3B	HR	HR%	R	RBI	BB	SO	SB	BA	SA	PH AB	PH H	G by POS
1906 STL N	5	14	3	0	0	0	0.0	0	1	0		0	.214	.214	0	0	3B-5
1911 BKN N	122	417	77	10	7	3	0.7	31	36	34	37	9	.185	.264	0	0	3B-122
2 yrs.	127	431	80	10	7	3	0.7	31	37	34	37	9	.186	.262	0	0	3B-127

Heinie Zimmerman

ZIMMERMAN, HENRY   BR TR 5'11½" 176 lbs.
B. Feb. 9, 1887, New York, N. Y.   D. Mar. 14, 1969, New York, N. Y.

		G	AB	H	2B	3B	HR	HR%	R	RBI	BB	SO	SB	BA	SA	PH AB	PH H	G by POS
1907 CHI N		5	9	2	1	0	0	0.0	0	1	0		0	.222	.333	0	0	2B-4, OF-1, SS-1
1908		46	113	33	4	1	0	0.0	17	9	1	2	0	.292	.345	15	2	2B-20, OF-8, SS-1, 3B-1
1909		65	183	50	9	2	0	0.0	23	21	3		7	.273	.344	18	0	3B-27, 3B-16, SS-12
1910		99	335	95	16	6	3	0.9	35	38	20	36	7	.284	.394	12	3	2B-33, SS-26, 3B-22, OF-4, 1B-1
1911		143	535	164	22	17	9	1.7	80	85	25	50	23	.307	.462	4	1	2B-108, 3B-20, 1B-11
1912		145	557	207	41	14	14	2.5	95	103	38	60	23	.372	.571	2	0	3B-121, 1B-22
1913		127	447	140	28	12	9	2.0	69	95	41	40	18	.313	.490	1	0	3B-125
1914		146	564	167	36	12	4	0.7	75	87	20	46	17	.296	.424	1	1	3B-119, SS-15, 2B-12
1915		139	520	138	28	11	3	0.6	65	62	21	33	19	.265	.379	1	1	2B-100, 3B-36, SS-4
1916 2 teams	CHI N (107G – .291)	147						NY N (40G – .272)										
" total		147	549	157	29	5	6	1.1	76	83	23	43	24	.286	.390	4	1	3B-115, 2B-14, SS-4
1917 NY N		150	585	174	22	9	5	0.9	61	102	16	43	13	.297	.391	0	0	3B-149, 2B-5
1918		121	463	126	19	10	1	0.2	43	56	13	23	14	.272	.363	1	1	3B-100, 1B-19
1919		123	444	113	20	6	4	0.9	56	58	21	30	8	.255	.354	0	0	3B-123
13 yrs.		1456	5304	1566	275	105	58	1.1	695	800	242	404	175	.295	.419	59	16	3B-947, 2B-323, SS-63, 1B-53, OF-13

WORLD SERIES

	G	AB	H	2B	3B	HR	HR%	R	RBI	BB	SO	SB	BA	SA	PH AB	PH H	G by POS
1907 CHI N	1	1	0	0	0	0	0.0	0	0	0	1	0	.000	.000	0	0	2B-1
1910	5	17	4	1	0	0	0.0	0	2	1	3	1	.235	.294	0	0	2B-5
1917 NY N	6	25	3	0	1	0	0.0	1	0	0	0	0	.120	.200	0	0	3B-6
3 yrs.	12	43	7	1	1	0	0.0	1	2	1	4	1	.163	.233	0	0	3B-6, 2B-6

Jerry Zimmerman

ZIMMERMAN, GERALD ROBERT   BR TR 6'2" 185 lbs.
B. Sept. 21, 1934, Omaha, Neb.

	G	AB	H	2B	3B	HR	HR%	R	RBI	BB	SO	SB	BA	SA	PH AB	PH H	G by POS
1961 CIN N	76	204	42	5	0	0	0.0	8	10	11	21	1	.206	.230	0	0	C-76
1962 MIN A	34	62	17	4	0	0	0.0	8	7	3	5	0	.274	.339	0	0	C-34
1963	39	56	13	1	0	0	0.0	3	3	2	8	0	.232	.250	1	0	C-39
1964	63	120	24	3	0	0	0.0	6	12	10	15	0	.200	.225	3	0	C-63
1965	83	154	33	1	1	1	0.6	8	11	12	23	0	.214	.253	0	0	C-82
1966	60	119	30	4	1	1	0.8	11	15	15	23	2	.252	.328	0	0	C-59
1967	104	234	39	5	0	1	0.4	13	12	22	49	0	.167	.192	0	0	C-104
1968	24	45	5	1	0	0	0.0	3	2	3	10	0	.111	.133	0	0	C-24
8 yrs.	483	994	203	22	2	3	0.3	60	72	78	154	1	.204	.239	6	0	C-481

WORLD SERIES

	G	AB	H	2B	3B	HR	HR%	R	RBI	BB	SO	SB	BA	SA	PH AB	PH H	G by POS
1961 CIN N	2	0	0	0	0	0	–	0	0	0	0	0	–	–	0	0	C-2
1965 MIN A	2	1	0	0	0	0	0.0	0	0	0	0	0	.000	.000	0	0	C-2
2 yrs.	4	1	0	0	0	0	0.0	0	0	0	0	0	.000	.000	0	0	C-4

Roy Zimmerman

ZIMMERMAN, ROY FRANKLIN   BL TL 6'2" 187 lbs.
B. Sept. 13, 1916, Pine Grove, Pa.

	G	AB	H	2B	3B	HR	HR%	R	RBI	BB	SO	SB	BA	SA	PH AB	PH H	G by POS
1945 NY N	27	98	27	1	0	5	5.1	14	15	5	16	1	.276	.439	1	0	1B-25, OF-1

Frank Zinn

ZINN, FRANK   5'9" 160 lbs.
B. 1866, Pennsylvania   Deceased.

	G	AB	H	2B	3B	HR	HR%	R	RBI	BB	SO	SB	BA	SA	PH AB	PH H	G by POS
1888 PHI AA	2	7	0	0	0	0	0.0	0	0	1		0	.000	.000	0	0	C-2

Guy Zinn

ZINN, GUY   BL TR 5'10½" 170 lbs.
B. Feb. 13, 1887, Hallbrook, W. Va.   D. Oct. 6, 1949, Clarksburg, W. Va.

	G	AB	H	2B	3B	HR	HR%	R	RBI	BB	SO	SB	BA	SA	PH AB	PH H	G by POS
1911 NY A	9	27	4	0	2	0	0.0	5	1	4		0	.148	.296	1	0	OF-8
1912	106	401	105	15	10	6	1.5	56	55	50		17	.262	.394	0	0	OF-106
1913 BOS N	36	138	41	8	2	1	0.7	15	15	4	23	3	.297	.406	1	0	OF-35
1914 BAL F	61	225	63	10	6	3	1.3	30	25	16		6	.280	.418	3	1	OF-57
1915	102	312	84	18	3	5	1.6	30	43	35		2	.269	.394	9	1	OF-88
5 yrs.	314	1103	297	51	23	15	1.4	136	139	109	23	28	.269	.398	14	2	OF-294

Bud Zipfel

ZIPFEL, MARION SYLVESTER   BL TR 6'3" 200 lbs.
B. Nov. 18, 1938, Belleville, Ill.

	G	AB	H	2B	3B	HR	HR%	R	RBI	BB	SO	SB	BA	SA	PH AB	PH H	G by POS
1961 WAS A	50	170	34	7	5	4	2.4	17	18	15	49	1	.200	.371	5	0	1B-44
1962	68	184	44	4	1	6	3.3	21	21	17	43	1	.239	.370	18	2	1B-26, OF-23
2 yrs.	118	354	78	11	6	10	2.8	38	39	32	92	2	.220	.370	23	2	1B-70, OF-23

	G	AB	H	2B	3B	HR	HR %	R	RBI	BB	SO	SB	BA	SA	Pinch Hit AB	Pinch Hit H	G by POS

Richie Zisk

ZISK, RICHARD WALTER
B. Feb. 6, 1949, Brooklyn, N. Y. BR TR 6'1" 200 lbs.

Year/Team	G	AB	H	2B	3B	HR	HR %	R	RBI	BB	SO	SB	BA	SA	PH AB	PH H	G by POS
1971 PIT N	7	15	3	1	0	1	6.7	2	2	4	7	0	.200	.467	1	0	OF-6
1972	17	37	7	3	0	0	0.0	4	4	7	10	0	.189	.270	5	1	OF-12
1973	103	333	108	23	7	10	3.0	44	54	21	63	0	.324	.526	19	4	OF-84
1974	149	536	168	30	3	17	3.2	75	100	65	91	1	.313	.476	9	4	OF-141
1975	147	504	146	27	3	20	4.0	69	75	68	109	0	.290	.474	6	0	OF-140
1976	155	581	168	35	2	21	3.6	91	89	52	96	1	.289	.465	3	2	OF-152
1977 CHI A	141	531	154	17	6	30	5.6	78	101	55	98	0	.290	.514	3	0	OF-109, DH-28
1978 TEX A	140	511	134	19	1	22	4.3	68	85	58	76	3	.262	.432	1	0	OF-90, DH-49
1979	144	503	132	21	1	18	3.6	69	64	57	75	1	.262	.416	7	2	OF-134, DH-3
1980	135	448	130	17	1	19	4.2	48	77	39	72	0	.290	.460	19	3	DH-86, OF-37
1981 SEA A	94	357	111	12	1	16	4.5	42	43	28	63	0	.311	.485	1	0	DH-93
1982	131	503	147	28	1	21	4.2	61	62	49	89	2	.292	.477	0	0	DH-130
1983	90	285	69	12	0	12	4.2	30	36	30	61	0	.242	.411	10	2	DH-84
13 yrs.	1453	5144	1477	245	26	207	4.0	681	792	533	910	8	.287	.466	84	18	OF-905, DH-473

LEAGUE CHAMPIONSHIP SERIES

Year/Team	G	AB	H	2B	3B	HR	HR %	R	RBI	BB	SO	SB	BA	SA	PH AB	PH H	G by POS
1974 PIT N	3	10	3	0	0	0	0.0	1	0	0	3	0	.300	.300	1	1	OF-2
1975	3	10	5	1	0	0	0.0	0	0	2	2	0	.500	.600	0	0	OF-3
2 yrs.	6	20	8	1	0	0	0.0	1	0	2	5	0	.400	.450	1	1	OF-5

Billy Zitzmann

ZITZMANN, WILLIAM ARTHUR
B. Nov. 19, 1897, Long Island City, N. Y. BR TR 5'10½" 175 lbs.

Year/Team	G	AB	H	2B	3B	HR	HR %	R	RBI	BB	SO	SB	BA	SA	PH AB	PH H	G by POS
1919 2 teams	PIT N (11G – .192)				CIN N (2G – .000)												
" total	13	27	5	1	0	0	0.0	5	2	0	6	2	.185	.222	3	0	OF-9
1925 CIN N	104	301	76	13	3	0	0.0	53	21	35	22	11	.252	.316	6	1	OF-89, SS-1
1926	53	94	23	2	1	0	0.0	21	3	6	7	3	.245	.287	3	0	OF-31
1927	88	232	66	10	4	0	0.0	47	24	20	18	9	.284	.362	0	0	OF-60, SS-8, 3B-3
1928	101	266	79	9	3	3	1.1	53	33	13	22	13	.297	.387	3	0	OF-78, 3B-1
1929	47	84	19	3	0	0	0.0	18	6	9	10	4	.226	.262	1	1	OF-22, 1B-5
6 yrs.	406	1004	268	38	11	3	0.3	197	89	83	85	42	.267	.336	16	2	OF-289, SS-9, 1B-5, 3B-4

Frank Zupo

ZUPO, FRANK JOSEPH (Noodles)
B. Aug. 29, 1939, San Francisco, Calif. BL TR 5'11" 182 lbs.

Year/Team	G	AB	H	2B	3B	HR	HR %	R	RBI	BB	SO	SB	BA	SA	PH AB	PH H	G by POS
1957 BAL A	10	12	1	0	0	0	0.0	2	0	1	4	0	.083	.083	4	0	C-8
1958	1	2	0	0	0	0	0.0	0	0	0	1	0	.000	.000	0	0	C-1
1961	5	4	2	1	0	0	0.0	1	0	1	1	0	.500	.750	0	0	C-4
3 yrs.	16	18	3	1	0	0	0.0	3	0	2	6	0	.167	.222	4	0	C-13

Paul Zuvella

ZUVELLA, PAUL
B. Oct. 31, 1958, San Mateo, Calif. BR TR 6' 173 lbs.

Year/Team	G	AB	H	2B	3B	HR	HR %	R	RBI	BB	SO	SB	BA	SA	PH AB	PH H	G by POS
1982 ATL N	2	1	0	0	0	0	0.0	0	0	0	0	0	.000	.000	0	0	SS-1
1983	3	5	0	0	0	0	0.0	0	0	2	1	0	.000	.000	1	0	SS-2
1984	11	25	5	1	0	0	0.0	2	1	2	3	0	.200	.240	0	0	SS-6, 2B-6
3 yrs.	16	31	5	1	0	0	0.0	2	1	4	4	0	.161	.194	1	0	SS-9, 2B-6

Dutch Zwilling

ZWILLING, EDWARD HARRISON
B. Nov. 2, 1888, St. Louis, Mo. D. Mar. 27, 1978, La Crescenta, Calif. BL TL 5'6½" 160 lbs.

Year/Team	G	AB	H	2B	3B	HR	HR %	R	RBI	BB	SO	SB	BA	SA	PH AB	PH H	G by POS
1910 CHI A	27	87	16	5	0	0	0.0	7	5	11		1	.184	.241	0	0	OF-27
1914 CHI F	154	592	185	38	8	15	2.5	91	95	46		21	.313	.480	0	0	OF-154
1915	150	548	157	32	7	13	2.4	65	94	67		24	.286	.442	0	0	OF-148, 1B-3
1916 CHI N	35	53	6	1	0	1	1.9	4	8	4	6	0	.113	.189	23	4	OF-10
4 yrs.	366	1280	364	76	15	29	2.3	167	202	128	6	46	.284	.435	24	4	OF-339, 1B-3

PART NINE

Pitcher Register

ALPHABETICAL LIST OF EVERY MAN WHO EVER

PITCHED IN THE MAJOR LEAGUES

AND HIS PITCHING RECORD AND SIGNIFICANT

BATTING RECORD

Pitcher Register

The Pitcher Register is an alphabetical list of every man who pitched in the major leagues from 1876 through today. Included are lifetime totals of League Championship Series and World Series.

Much of this information has never been compiled, especially for the period 1876 through 1919. All information and abbreviations that may appear unfamiliar are explained in the sample format presented below. John Doe, the player used in the sample, is fictitious and serves only to illustrate the information.

	W	L	PCT	ERA	G	GS	CG	IP	H	BB	SO	ShO	Relief Pitching W	L	SV	BATTING AB	H	HR	BA

John Doe

DOE, JOHN LEE (Slim)   TR 6'2"   165 lbs.
Played as John Cherry part of 1900.
Born John Lee Doughnut.   Brother of Bill Doe.
B. Jan. 1,1850, New York, N. Y.   D. July 1, 1955, New York, N. Y.
Manager 1908-15.
Hall of Fame 1946.

Year	Team	Lg	W	L	PCT	ERA	G	GS	CG	IP	H	BB	SO	ShO	W	L	SV	AB	H	HR	BA
1884	STL	U	4	2	.667	3.40	26	0	0	54.2	41	38	40	0	1	1	0	28	12	0	.226
1885	LOU	AA	14	10	.583	4.12	40	19	10	207.2	193	76	70	0	0	1	0	43	33	0	.289
1886	CLE	N	10	5	.667	4.08	40	8	4	117	110	55	77	0	0	1	1	40	16	1	.165
1887	BOS	N	9	3	.750	3.38	27	5	2	88	90	36	34	0	2	3	2	40	12	0	.141
1888	NY	N	13	4	.765	4.17	39	4	0	110	121	50	**236**	0	0	1	0	16	6	0	.273
1889	3 teams					DET N (10G 4-2)			PIT N (2G 0-0)			PHI N (10G 4-0)									
"	total		8	2	.800	4.25	22	2	2	91.1	90	41	43	0	0	0	0	3	3	0	.333
1890	NY	P	13	6	.684	4.43	38	0	0	61.1	57	28	30	0	1	0	1	34	17	0	.185
1900	CHI	N	18	4	.818	3.71	35	1	0	63.1	58	15	23	0	0	0	2	35	13	1	.146
1901	BAL	A	18	4	.818	1.98¹	35	0	0	77.1	68	40	29	0	3	0	0	25	16	0	.254
1906	BOS	N	14	10	.583	3.41	31	0	0	58	66	23	24	0	1	3	0	37	16	1	.286
1907			13	4	.765	2.51	37	0	0	68	44	30	31	0	1	1	0	9	2	0	.182
1908			0	0	–	3.38	1	1	0	8	8	1	1	0	3	1	3	33	7	0	.226
1914	CHI	F	3	1	.750	2.78	6	0	0	54.2	41	28	9	0	2	3	3	19	2	0	.222
13 yrs.			137	55	.714	3.50	377	40	18	1059.1	987	461	647	0	21	17	15	492	216	3	.212
																	8th				

LEAGUE CHAMPIONSHIP SERIES

2 yrs.	1	1	.500	4.76	4	0	0	22.2	26	8	16	8	0	0	0	0	0	0	–

WORLD SERIES

1 yr.	2	0	1.000	1.00	2	2	2	18	7	4	13	0	0	0	0	7	0	0	.000

PLAYER INFORMATION

John Doe — This shortened version of the player's full name is the name most familiar to the fans. All players in this section are alphabetically arranged by the last name part of this name.

DOE, JOHN LEE — Player's full name. The arrangement is last name first, then first and middle name(s).

(Slim) — Player's nickname. Any name or names appearing in parentheses indicates a nickname.

The player's throwing style. Doe, for instance, threw right handed. | TR

Player's height. | 6'2"

Player's average playing weight. | 165 lbs

The player at one time in his major league career played under another name and can be found only in box scores or newspaper stories under that name. | Played as John Cherry part of 1900

The name the player was given at birth. (For the most part, the player never used this name while playing in the major leagues, but, if he did, it would be listed as "played as," which is explained above under the heading "Played as John Cherry part of 1900.") | Born John Lee Doughnut

The player's brother. (Relatives indicated here are fathers, sons, brothers, grandfathers, and grandsons who played or managed in the major leagues and the National Association.) | Brother of Bill Doe

Date and place of birth. | B. Jan. 1, 1850, New York, N.Y.

Date and place of death. (For those players who are listed simply as "deceased," it means that, although no certification of death or other information is presently available, it is reasonably certain they are dead.) | D. July 1, 1955, New York, N.Y.

Doe also served as a major league manager. All men who were managers can be found also in the Manager Register, where their complete managerial record is shown. | Manager 1908–15

Doe was elected to the Baseball Hall of Fame in 1946. | Hall of Fame 1946

COLUMN HEADINGS INFORMATION

	W	L	PCT	ERA	G	GS	CG	IP	H	BB	SO	ShO	Relief Pitching			BATTING			
													W	L	SV	AB	H	HR	BA

Total Pitching (including all starting and relief appearances)

W	Wins
L	Losses
PCT	Winning Percentage
ERA	Earned Run Average
G	Games Pitched In
GS	Games Started
CG	Complete Games
IP	Innings Pitched
H	Hits Allowed
BB	Bases on Balls Allowed
SO	Strikeouts
ShO	Shutouts

Relief Pitching

W	Wins
L	Losses
SV	Saves

Batting

AB	At Bats
H	Hits
HR	Home Runs
BA	Batting Average

TEAM AND LEAGUE INFORMATION

1884	STL	U
1885	LOU	AA
1886	CLE	N
1887	BOS	N
1888	NY	N
1889	3 teams	
"	total	
1890	NY	P
1900	CHI	N
1901	BAL	A
1906	BOS	N
1907		
1908		
1914	CHI	F
13	yrs.	

1889 3 teams DET N (10G 4–2)   PIT N (2G 0–0)   PHI N (10G 4–0)

" total 8 2 .800 | 4.25 | 22 2 2 | 91.1 90 | 41 43 | 0 | 8 | 11

Doe's record has been exaggerated so that his playing career spans all the years of the six different major leagues. Directly alongside the year and team information is the symbol for the league:

N   National League (1876 to date)
A   American League (1901 to date)
F   Federal League (1914–15)
AA   American Association (1882–91)
P   Players' League (1890)
U   Union Association (1884)

STL   The abbreviation of the city in which the team played.
Doe, for example, played for St. Louis in 1884. All teams in
this section are listed by an abbreviation of the city in which
the team played. The abbreviations follow:

ALT	Altoona	NWK	Newark
ATL	Atlanta	NY	New York
BAL	Baltimore	OAK	Oakland
BKN	Brooklyn	PHI	Philadelphia
BOS	Boston	PIT	Pittsburgh
BUF	Buffalo	PRO	Providence
CAL	California	RIC	Richmond
CHI	Chicago	ROC	Rochester
CIN	Cincinnati	SD	San Diego
CLE	Cleveland	SEA	Seattle
COL	Columbus	SF	San Francisco
DET	Detroit	STL	St. Louis
HAR	Hartford	STP	St. Paul
HOU	Houston	SYR	Syracuse
IND	Indianapolis	TEX	Texas
KC	Kansas City	TOL	Toledo
LA	Los Angeles	TOR	Toronto
LOU	Louisville	TRO	Troy
MIL	Milwaukee	WAS	Washington
MIN	Minnesota	WIL	Wilmington
MON	Montreal	WOR	Worcester

Three franchises in the history of major league baseball
changed their location during the season. These teams are designated by the first letter of the two cities they represented. They
are:

B-B   Brooklyn-Baltimore (American Association, 1890)
C-M   Cincinnati-Milwaukee (American Association, 1891)
C-P   Chicago-Pittsburgh (Union Association, 1884)

Blank space appearing beneath a team and league indicates
that the team and league are the same. Doe, for example, played
for Boston in the National League from 1906 through 1908.

3 Teams Total. Indicates a player played for more than one
team in the same year. Doe played for three teams in 1889.
The number of games he played and his wins and losses for
each team are also shown. Directly beneath this line, following
the word "total," is Doe's combined record for all three teams
for 1889.

Total Playing Years. This information, which appears as the first item on the pitcher's lifetime total line, indicates the total number of years in which he pitched at least one game. Doe, for example, pitched in at least one game for 13 years.

STATISTICAL INFORMATION

	W	L	PCT	ERA	G	GS	CG	IP	H	BB	SO	ShO	Relief Pitching W	L	SV	BATTING AB	H	HR	BA

John Doe

DOE, JOHN LEE (Slim)   TR 6'2"   165 lbs.
Played as John Cherry part of 1900.
Born John Lee Doughnut.   Brother of Bill Doe.
B. Jan. 1,1850, New York, N. Y.   D. July 1, 1955, New York, N. Y.
Hall of Fame 1946.

Year	Team	Lg	W	L	PCT	ERA	G	GS	CG	IP	H	BB	SO	ShO	RP W	RP L	SV	AB	H	HR	BA
1884	STL	U	4	2	.667	3.40	26	0	0	54.2	41	38	40	0	1	0	0	4	0	0	.000
1885	LOU	AA	14	10	.583	4.12	40	19	10	207.2	193	76	70	0	1	0	1	16	2	0	.111
1886	CLE	N	10	5	.667	4.08	40	8	4	117	110	55	77	0	0	1	0	10	0	0	.000
1887	BOS	N	9	3	.750	3.38	27	5	2	88	90	36	34	0	2	2	5	44	3	0	.214
1888	NY	N	13	4	.765	4.17	39	4	0	110	121	50	**236**	0	0	0	0	3	0	0	–
1889	3 teams		DET N (10G 4-2)				PIT N (2G 0-0)			PHI N (10G 4-0)											
"	total		8	2	.800	4.25	22	2	2	91.1	90	41	43	0	2	1	10	37	1	0	.036
1890	NY	P	13	6	.684	4.43	38	0	0	61.1	57	28	30	0	4	4	8	45	0	0	.000
1900	CHI	N	18	4	.818	3.71	35	1	0	63.1	58	15	23	0	4	2	3	42	2	0	.027
1901	BAL	A	18	4	.818	**1.98**	35	0	0	77.1	68	40	29	0	0	2	0	38	10	0	.132
1906	BOS	N	14	10	.583	3.41	31	0	0	58	66	23	24	0	0	0	1	32	3	0	.057
1907			13	4	.765	2.51	37	0	0	68	44	30	31	0	0	1	0	31	1	0	.500
1908			0	0	–	3.38	1	1	0	8	8	1	1	0	1	2	3	25	0	0	.000
1914	CHI	F	3	1	.750	2.78	6	0	0	54.2	41	28	9	0	1	0	1	41	2	0	.400
13 yrs.			137	55	.714	3.50	377	40	18	1059.1	987	461	647	0	16	18	32	*			
																	8th				

Partial Innings Pitched. These are shown in the Innings Pitched column, and are indicated by a ".1" or ".2" after the total. Doe, for example, pitched 54⅔ innings in 1884.

League Leaders. Statistics that appear in bold faced print indicate the pitcher led his league that year in a particular statistical category. Doe, for example, led the National League in earned run average in 1901. When there is a tie for league lead, the figures for all the men who tied are shown in bold face.

All-time Single Season Leaders. (Starts with 1893, the first year that the pitcher's box was moved to its present distance of 60 feet 6 inches.) Indicated by the small number that appears next to the statistic. Doe, for example, is shown by a small number "1" next to his earned run average in 1901. This means he is first on the all-time major league list for having the lowest earned run average in a single season. All pitchers who tied for first are also shown by the same number.

Lifetime Leaders. Indicated by the figure that appears beneath the line showing the pitcher's lifetime totals. Doe has an "8th" shown below his lifetime Saves total. This means that, lifetime, Doe ranks eighth among major league pitchers in Saves. Once again, only the top ten are indicated, and players who are tied receive the same number.

Meaningless Averages. Indicated by the use of a dash (—). In the case of Doe, a dash is shown for his 1908 winning percentage. This means that although he pitched in one game he never had a decision. A percentage of .000 would mean that he had at least one loss.

Estimated Earned Run Averages. Any time an earned run average appears in italics, it indicates that not all the earned runs allowed by the pitcher are known, and the information had to be estimated. Doe's 1885 earned run average, for example, appears in italics. It is known that Doe's team, Louisville, allowed 560 runs in 112 games. Of these games, it is known that in 90 of them Louisville allowed 420 runs of which 315 or 75% were earned. Doe pitched 207⅔ innings in 40 games and allowed 134 runs. In 35 of these games, it is known that he allowed 118 runs of which 83 were earned. By multiplying the team's known ratio of earned runs to total runs (75%), by Doe's 16 (134 minus 118) remaining runs allowed, a figure of 12 additional estimated earned runs is calculated. This means that Doe allowed an estimated total of 95 earned runs in 207⅔ innings, for an estimated earned run average of 4.12. In all cases at least 50% of the runs allowed by the team were "known" as a basis for estimating earned run averages. (Any time the symbol "infinity" (∞) is shown for a pitcher's earned run average, it means that the pitcher allowed one or more earned runs during a season without retiring a batter.)

League Leader Qualifications. Throughout baseball there have been different rules used to determine the minimum appearances necessary to qualify for league leader in categories concerning averages (Batting Average, Earned Run Average, etc.). For the rules and the years they were in effect, see Appendix C.

Traded League Leaders. An asterisk (*) next to a bold-faced number indicates that the player led the league in a particular category, but since he played in more than one league that year, the number does not indicate his league-leading total or average.

Batting Statistics. Because a pitcher's batting statistics are of relatively minor importance—and the Designated Hitter rule may eliminate pitchers' batting entirely—only the most significant statistics are given: number of hits, home runs, and batting average.

An asterisk (*) shown in the lifetime batting totals means that the pitcher's complete year-by-year and lifetime batting record is listed in the Player Register.

	W	L	PCT	ERA	G	GS	CG	IP	H	BB	SO	ShO	Relief Pitching			BATTING			
													W	L	SV	AB	H	HR	BA
DIVISIONAL PLAYOFF SERIES																			
1 yr.	0	0	–	0.00	1	0	0	1	0	0	0	0	0	0	0	0	0	0	–
LEAGUE CHAMPIONSHIP SERIES																			
2 yrs.	1	1	.500	4.76	4	0	0	22.2	26	8	16	8	0	0	0	0	0	0	–
WORLD SERIES																			
1 yr.	2	0	1.000	1.00	2	2	2	18	7	4	13	0	0	0	0	7	0	0	.000
											9th								

World Series Lifetime Leaders. Indicated by the figure that appears beneath the pitcher's lifetime totals. Doe has a "9th" shown below his lifetime strike out total. This means that, lifetime, Doe ranks ninth among major league pitchers for striking out the most batters in total World Series play. Pitchers who tied for a position in the top ten are shown by the same number, so that, if two men tied for fourth and fifth place, the appropriate information for both men would be followed by the small number "4," and the next man would be considered sixth in the ranking.

	W	L	PCT	ERA	G	GS	CG	IP	H	BB	SO	ShO	Relief Pitching W	L	SV	BATTING AB	H	HR	BA

Don Aase

AASE, DONALD WILLIAM B. Sept. 8, 1954, Orange, Calif. BR TR 6'3" 190 lbs.

	W	L	PCT	ERA	G	GS	CG	IP	H	BB	SO	ShO	W	L	SV	AB	H	HR	BA
1977 BOS A	6	2	.750	3.12	13	13	4	92.1	85	19	49	2	0	0	0	0	0	0	—
1978 CAL A	11	8	.579	4.03	29	29	6	178.2	185	80	93	1	0	0	0	0	0	0	—
1979	9	10	.474	4.82	37	28	7	185	200	77	96	1	1	1	2	0	0	0	—
1980	8	13	.381	4.06	40	21	5	175	193	66	74	1	3	0	2	0	0	0	—
1981	4	4	.500	2.35	39	0	0	65	56	24	38	0	4	4	11	0	0	0	—
1982	3	3	.500	3.46	24	0	0	52	45	23	40	1	3	3	4	0	0	0	—
1984	4	1	.800	1.62	23	0	0	39	30	19	28	0	4	1	8	0	0	0	—
7 yrs.	45	41	.523	3.82	205	91	22	787	794	308	418	5	15	9	27	0	0	0	—

LEAGUE CHAMPIONSHIP SERIES

	W	L	PCT	ERA	G	GS	CG	IP	H	BB	SO	ShO	W	L	SV	AB	H	HR	BA
1979 CAL A	1	0	1.000	1.80	2	0	0	5	4	2	6	0	1	0	0	0	0	0	—

Bert Abbey

ABBEY, BERT WOOD B. Nov. 29, 1869, Essex, Vt. D. June 11, 1962, Essex Junction, Vt. BR TR 5'11" 175 lbs.

	W	L	PCT	ERA	G	GS	CG	IP	H	BB	SO	ShO	W	L	SV	AB	H	HR	BA
1892 WAS N	5	18	.217	3.45	27	23	19	195.2	207	76	77	0	0	2	1	75	9	0	.120
1893 CHI N	2	4	.333	5.46	7	7	5	56	74	20	6	0	0	0	0	26	6	0	.231
1894	2	7	.222	5.18	11	11	10	92	119	37	24	0	0	0	0	39	5	0	.128
1895 2 teams	CHI N (1G 0–1)				BKN N (8G 5–2)														
" total	5	3	.625	4.35	9	7	6	60	76	11	17	0	1	0	0	22	6	0	.273
1896 BKN N	8	8	.500	5.15	25	18	12	164.1	210	48	37	0	1	1	0	63	12	0	.190
5 yrs.	22	40	.355	4.52	79	66	52	568	686	192	161	0	2	3	1	225	38	0	.169

Charlie Abbey

ABBEY, CHARLES S. B. Oct., 1868, Falls City, Neb. Deceased. BL 5'8½" 169 lbs.

	W	L	PCT	ERA	G	GS	CG	IP	H	BB	SO	ShO	W	L	SV	AB	H	HR	BA
1896 WAS N	0	0	—	4.50	1	0	0	2	6	0	0	0	0	0	0	*			

Dan Abbott

ABBOTT, LEANDER FRANKLIN (Big Dan) B. May 16, 1862, Portage, Ohio D. Feb. 13, 1930, Ottawa Lake, Mich. BR TR 5'11" 190 lbs.

	W	L	PCT	ERA	G	GS	CG	IP	H	BB	SO	ShO	W	L	SV	AB	H	HR	BA
1890 TOL AA	0	2	.000	6.23	3	1	1	19	8	1	0	0	0	1	1	7	1	0	.143

Glenn Abbott

ABBOTT, WILLIAM GLENN B. Feb. 16, 1951, Little Rock, Ark. BR TR 6'6" 200 lbs.

	W	L	PCT	ERA	G	GS	CG	IP	H	BB	SO	ShO	W	L	SV	AB	H	HR	BA
1973 OAK A	1	0	1.000	3.86	5	3	1	18.2	16	7	6	0	0	0	0	0	0	0	—
1974	5	7	.417	3.00	19	17	3	96	89	34	38	0	0	0	0	0	0	0	—
1975	5	5	.500	4.25	30	15	3	114.1	109	50	51	1	2	0	0	0	0	0	—
1976	2	4	.333	5.52	19	10	0	62	87	16	27	0	1	1	0	0	0	0	—
1977 SEA A	12	13	.480	4.46	36	34	7	204	212	56	100	0	0	0	0	0	0	0	—
1978	7	15	.318	5.27	29	28	8	155.1	191	44	67	1	0	0	0	0	0	0	—
1979	4	10	.286	5.15	23	19	3	117	138	38	25	0	0	0	0	0	0	0	—
1980	12	12	.500	4.10	31	31	7	215	228	49	78	2	0	0	0	0	0	0	—
1981	4	9	.308	3.95	22	20	1	130	127	28	35	0	0	0	0	0	0	0	—
1983 2 teams	SEA A (14G 5–3)				DET A (7G 2–1)														
" total	7	4	.636	3.63	21	21	2	129	146	22	49	1	0	0	0	0	0	0	—
1984 DET A	3	4	.429	5.93	13	8	1	44	62	8	8	0	1	1	0	0	0	0	—
11 yrs.	62	83	.428	4.39	248	206	37	1285.1	1405	352	484	5	4	2	0	0	0	0	—

LEAGUE CHAMPIONSHIP SERIES

	W	L	PCT	ERA	G	GS	CG	IP	H	BB	SO	ShO	W	L	SV	AB	H	HR	BA
1975 OAK A	0	0	—	0.00	1	0	0	1	0	0	1	0	0	0	0	0	0	0	—

Al Aber

ABER, ALBERT JULIUS (Lefty) B. July 31, 1927, Cleveland, Ohio BL TL 6'2" 195 lbs.

	W	L	PCT	ERA	G	GS	CG	IP	H	BB	SO	ShO	W	L	SV	AB	H	HR	BA
1950 CLE A	1	0	1.000	2.00	1	1	1	9	5	4	4	0	0	0	0	2	0	0	.000
1953 2 teams	CLE A (6G 1–1)				DET A (17G 4–3)														
" total	5	4	.556	4.71	23	10	2	72.2	69	50	38	0	3	1	0	23	3	0	.130
1954 DET A	5	11	.313	3.97	32	18	4	124.2	121	40	54	0	0	1	3	39	5	0	.128
1955	6	3	.667	3.38	39	1	0	80	86	28	37	0	6	3	3	17	1	0	.059
1956	4	4	.500	3.43	42	0	0	63	65	25	21	0	4	4	7	10	3	0	.300
1957 2 teams	DET A (28G 3–3)				KC A (3G 0–0)														
" total	3	3	.500	7.20	31	0	0	40	52	13	15	0	3	3	1	9	2	0	.222
6 yrs.	24	25	.490	4.18	168	30	7	389.1	398	160	169	0	16	12	14	100	14	0	.140

Bill Abernathie

ABERNATHIE, WILLIAM EDWARD B. Jan. 30, 1929, Torrance, Calif. BR TR 5'10" 190 lbs.

	W	L	PCT	ERA	G	GS	CG	IP	H	BB	SO	ShO	W	L	SV	AB	H	HR	BA
1952 CLE A	0	0	—	13.50	1	0	0	2	4	1	0	1	0	0	0	1	0	0	.000

Tal Abernathy

ABERNATHY, TALMADGE LAFAYETTE (Tal) B. Oct. 30, 1921, Bynum, N. C. BR TL 6'2" 210 lbs.

	W	L	PCT	ERA	G	GS	CG	IP	H	BB	SO	ShO	W	L	SV	AB	H	HR	BA
1942 PHI A	0	0	—	10.13	1	0	0	2.2	2	3	1	0	0	0	0	0	0	0	—
1943	0	3	.000	12.89	5	2	1	14.2	24	13	10	0	0	1	0	4	1	0	.250
1944	0	0	—	3.00	1	0	0	3	5	1	2	0	0	0	0	1	0	0	.000
3 yrs.	0	3	.000	11.07	7	2	1	20.1	31	17	13	0	0	1	0	5	1	0	.200

Ted Abernathy

ABERNATHY, THEODORE WADE B. Mar. 6, 1933, Stanley, N. C. BR TR 6'4" 215 lbs.

	W	L	PCT	ERA	G	GS	CG	IP	H	BB	SO	ShO	W	L	SV	AB	H	HR	BA
1955 WAS A	5	9	.357	5.96	40	14	3	119.1	136	67	79	2	1	1	0	26	4	0	.154
1956	1	3	.250	4.15	5	4	2	30.1	35	10	18	0	0	0	0	11	2	0	.182
1957	2	10	.167	6.78	26	16	2	85	100	65	50	0	1	0	0	24	4	0	.167
1960	0	0	—	12.00	2	0	0	3	4	4	1	0	0	0	0	1	1	0	1.000
1963 CLE A	7	2	.778	2.88	43	0	0	59.1	54	29	47	0	7	2	12	5	2	0	.400
1964	2	6	.250	4.33	53	0	0	72.2	66	46	57	0	2	6	11	6	0	0	.000
1965 CHI N	4	6	.400	2.57	84	0	0	136.1	113	56	104	0	4	6	31	18	3	0	.167
1966 2 teams	CHI N (20G 1–3)				ATL N (38G 4–4)														
" total	5	7	.417	4.55	58	0	0	93	84	53	60	0	5	7	8	12	2	0	.167
1967 CIN N	6	3	.667	1.27	70	0	0	106.1	63	41	88	0	6	3	28	17	1	0	.059
1968	10	7	.588	2.46	78	0	0	135.1	111	55	64	0	10	7	13	17	0	0	.000
1969 CHI N	4	3	.571	3.18	56	0	0	85	75	42	55	0	4	3	3	8	2	0	.250

	W	L	PCT	ERA	G	GS	CG	IP	H	BB	SO	ShO	Relief Pitching W	L	SV	BATTING AB	H	HR	BA

Ted Abernathy continued

1970 3 teams	CHI	N (11G 0–0)		STL	N (11G 1–0)		KC	A	(36G 9–3)										
" total	10	3	.769	2.59	58	0	0	83.1	65	55	59	0	10	3	14	17	3	0	.176
1971 KC A	4	6	.400	2.56	63	0	0	81	60	50	55	0	4	6	23	13	1	0	.077
1972	3	4	.429	1.71	45	0	0	58	44	19	28	0	3	4	5	6	0	0	.000
14 yrs.	63	69	.477	3.46	681	34	7	1148	1010	592	765	2	57	48	148	181	25	0	.138

Woody Abernathy

ABERNATHY, VIRGIL WOODROW
B. Feb. 1, 1915, Forest City, N. C.   BL TL 6'   170 lbs.

1946 NY N	1	1	.500	3.38	15	1	0	40	32	10	6	0	1	0	1	8	0	0	.000
1947	0	0	–	9.00	1	0	0	2	4	1	0	0	0	0	0	0	0	0	–
2 yrs.	1	1	.500	3.64	16	1	0	42	36	11	6	0	1	0	1	8	0	0	.000

Harry Ables

ABLES, HARRY TERRELL (Hal, Hans)
B. Oct. 4, 1884, Terrell, Tex.   D. Feb. 8, 1951, San Antonio, Tex.   BR TL 6'2½"   200 lbs.

1905 STL A	0	3	.000	3.82	6	3	1	30.2	37	13	11	0	0	0	0	10	0	0	.000
1909 CLE A	1	1	.500	2.12	5	3	3	29.2	26	10	24	0	0	0	0	12	0	0	.000
1911 NY A	0	1	.000	9.82	3	2	0	11	16	7	6	0	0	0	0	4	0	0	.000
3 yrs.	1	5	.167	4.04	14	8	4	71.1	79	30	41	0	0	0	0	26	0	0	.000

George Abrams

ABRAMS, GEORGE ALLEN
B. Nov. 9, 1897, Seattle, Wash.   BR TR 5'9"   170 lbs.

1923 CIN N	0	0	–	9.64	3	0	0	4.2	10	3	1	0	0	0	0	1	1	0	1.000

Jim Acker

ACKER, JAMES AUSTIN
B. Sept. 24, 1958, Freer, Tex.   BR TR 6'2"   210 lbs.

1983 TOR A	5	1	.833	4.33	38	5	0	97.2	103	38	44	0	2	1	1	0	0	0	–
1984	3	5	.375	4.38	32	3	0	72	79	25	33	0	3	4	1	0	0	0	–
2 yrs.	8	6	.571	4.35	70	8	0	169.2	182	63	77	0	5	5	2	0	0	0	–

Tom Acker

ACKER, THOMAS JAMES (Shoulders)
B. Mar. 7, 1930, Paterson, N. J.   BR TR 6'4"   215 lbs.

1956 CIN N	4	3	.571	2.37	29	7	1	83.2	60	29	54	1	1	2	1	19	1	0	.053
1957	10	5	.667	4.97	49	6	1	108.2	122	41	67	0	7	4	4	19	1	0	.053
1958	4	3	.571	4.55	38	10	3	124.2	126	43	90	0	0	1	1	30	2	0	.067
1959	1	2	.333	4.12	37	0	0	63.1	57	37	45	0	1	2	2	9	1	0	.111
4 yrs.	19	13	.594	4.12	153	23	5	380.1	365	150	256	1	9	9	8	77	5	0	.065

Fritz Ackley

ACKLEY, FLORIAN FREDERICK
B. Apr. 10, 1937, Hayward, Wis.   BL TR 6'1½"   202 lbs.

1963 CHI A	1	0	1.000	2.08	2	2	0	13	7	7	11	0	0	0	0	5	1	0	.200
1964	0	0	–	8.53	3	2	0	6.1	10	4	6	0	0	0	0	1	1	0	1.000
2 yrs.	1	0	1.000	4.19	5	4	0	19.1	17	11	17	0	0	0	0	6	2	0	.333

Cy Acosta

ACOSTA, CECILIO (Cy)
B. Nov. 22, 1946, El Sabino, Mexico   BR TR 5'10"   165 lbs.

1972 CHI A	3	0	1.000	1.56	26	0	0	34.2	25	17	28	0	3	0	5	4	0	0	.000
1973	10	6	.625	2.23	48	0	0	97	66	39	60	0	10	6	18	1	0	0	.000
1974	0	3	.000	3.72	27	0	0	46	43	18	19	0	0	3	3	2	0	0	.000
1975 PHI N	0	0	–	6.00	6	0	0	9	9	3	2	0	0	0	1	0	0	0	–
4 yrs.	13	9	.591	2.65	107	0	0	186.2	143	77	109	0	13	9	27	7	0	0	.000

Ed Acosta

ACOSTA, EDUARDO ELIXBETH LOPEZ
B. Mar. 9, 1944, Boquete, Panama   BB TR 6'5"   215 lbs.

1970 PIT N	0	0	–	12.00	3	0	0	3	5	2	1	0	0	0	1	0	0	0	–
1971 SD N	3	3	.500	2.74	8	6	3	46	43	7	16	1	0	1	0	17	0	0	.000
1972	3	6	.333	4.45	46	2	0	89	105	30	53	0	2	5	0	12	1	0	.083
3 yrs.	6	9	.400	4.04	57	8	3	138	153	39	70	1	2	6	1	29	1	0	.034

Jose Acosta

ACOSTA, JOSE
Brother of Merito Acosta.
B. Mar. 4, 1891, Havana, Cuba   BR TR 5'6"   134 lbs.

1920 WAS A	5	4	.556	4.03	17	5	4	82.2	92	26	9	1	2	2	1	25	6	0	.240
1921	5	4	.556	4.36	33	7	2	115.2	148	36	30	0	3	1	3	30	2	0	.067
1922 CHI A	0	2	.000	8.40	5	1	0	15	25	6	6	0	0	1	0	5	1	0	.200
3 yrs.	10	10	.500	4.51	55	13	6	213.1	265	68	45	1	5	4	4	60	9	0	.150

Ace Adams

ADAMS, ACE TOWNSEND
B. Mar. 2, 1912, Willows, Calif.   BR TR 5'10½"   182 lbs.

1941 NY N	4	1	.800	4.82	38	0	0	71	84	35	18	0	4	1	1	12	1	0	.083
1942	7	4	.636	1.84	61	0	0	88	69	31	33	0	7	4	11	10	1	0	.100
1943	11	7	.611	2.82	70	3	1	140.1	121	55	46	0	9	7	9	32	4	0	.125
1944	8	11	.421	4.25	65	4	1	137.2	149	58	32	0	6	9	13	29	3	0	.103
1945	11	9	.550	3.42	65	0	0	113	109	44	39	0	11	9	15	16	3	0	.188
1946	0	1	.000	16.88	3	0	0	2.2	9	1	3	0	0	1	0	0	0	0	–
6 yrs.	41	33	.554	3.47	302	7	2	552.2	541	224	171	0	37	31	49	99	12	0	.121

Babe Adams

ADAMS, CHARLES BENJAMIN
B. May 18, 1882, Tipton, Ind.   D. July 27, 1968, Silver Spring, Md.   BL TR 5'11½"   185 lbs.

1906 STL N	0	1	.000	13.50	1	1	0	4	9	2	0	0	0	0	0	1	0	0	.000
1907 PIT N	0	2	.000	6.95	4	3	1	22	40	3	11	0	0	0	0	7	2	0	.286
1909	12	3	.800	1.11	25	12	7	130	88	23	65	3	6	0	2	39	2	0	.051
1910	18	9	.667	2.24	34	30	16	245	217	60	101	3	0	1	0	83	16	0	.193
1911	22	12	.647	2.33	40	37	24	293.1	253	42	133	7	0	0	0	103	26	0	.252
1912	11	8	.579	2.91	28	21	11	170.1	169	35	63	2	1	1	0	53	12	0	.226
1913	21	10	.677	2.15	43	37	24	313.2	271	49	144	4	0	1	0	114	33	0	.289

	W	L	PCT	ERA	G	GS	CG	IP	H	BB	SO	ShO	Relief Pitching W	L	SV	BATTING AB	H	HR	BA

Babe Adams continued

	W	L	PCT	ERA	G	GS	CG	IP	H	BB	SO	ShO	W	L	SV	AB	H	HR	BA
1914	13	16	.448	2.51	40	35	19	283	253	39	91	3	0	1	1	97	16	1	.165
1915	14	14	.500	2.87	40	30	17	245	229	34	62	2	2	3	2	85	12	0	.141
1916	2	9	.182	5.72	16	10	4	72.1	91	12	22	1	0	1	0	22	6	0	.273
1918	1	1	.500	1.19	3	3	2	22.2	15	4	6	1	0	0	0	9	3	0	.333
1919	17	10	.630	1.98	34	29	23	263.1	213	23	92	7	1	0	1	92	17	0	.185
1920	17	13	.567	2.16	35	33	19	263	240	18	84	8	0	0	2	89	13	1	.146
1921	14	5	.737	2.64	25	20	11	160	155	18	55	2	3	0	0	63	16	0	.254
1922	8	11	.421	3.57	27	19	12	171.1	191	15	39	4	1	3	0	56	16	1	.286
1923	13	7	.650	4.42	26	22	11	158.2	196	25	38	0	1	1	1	55	15	0	.273
1924	3	1	.750	1.13	9	3	2	39.2	31	3	5	0	1	1	0	11	2	0	.182
1925	6	5	.545	5.42	33	10	3	101.1	129	17	18	0	3	1	3	31	7	0	.226
1926	2	3	.400	6.14	19	0	0	36.2	51	8	7	0	2	3	3	9	2	0	.222
19 yrs.	194	140	.581	2.76	482	355	206	2995.1	2841	430	1036	47	21	17	15	1019	216	3	.212

WORLD SERIES

	W	L	PCT	ERA	G	GS	CG	IP	H	BB	SO	ShO	W	L	SV	AB	H	HR	BA
1909 PIT N	3	0	1.000	1.33	3	3	3	27	18	6	11	1	0	0	0	9	0	0	.000
1925	0	0	–	0.00	1	0	0	1	2	0	0	0	0	0	0	0	0	0	–
2 yrs.	3	0	1.000	1.29	4	3	3	28	20	6	11	1	0	0	0	9	0	0	.000
			1st	9th															

Bob Adams

ADAMS, ROBERT ANDREW   BR TR 6'½" 165 lbs.
B. Jan. 20, 1907, Birmingham, Ala.   D. Mar. 6, 1970, Jacksonville, Fla.

	W	L	PCT	ERA	G	GS	CG	IP	H	BB	SO	ShO	W	L	SV	AB	H	HR	BA
1931 PHI N	0	1	.000	9.00	1	1	0	6	14	1	3	0	0	0	0	3	0	0	.000
1932	0	0	–	1.50	4	0	0	6	7	2	2	0	0	0	0	0	0	0	–
2 yrs.	0	1	.000	5.25	5	1	0	12	21	3	5	0	0	0	0	3	0	0	.000

Bob Adams

ADAMS, ROBERT BURDETTE   BR TR 5'11" 168 lbs.
B. July 24, 1901, Holyoke, Mass.

	W	L	PCT	ERA	G	GS	CG	IP	H	BB	SO	ShO	W	L	SV	AB	H	HR	BA
1925 BOS A	0	0	–	7.94	2	0	0	5.2	8	3	1	0	0	0	0	3	1	0	.333

Dan Adams

ADAMS, DANIEL LESLIE (Rube)   BR TR 5'10" 160 lbs.
B. June 19, 1887, St. Louis, Mo.   D. Oct. 6, 1964, St. Louis, Mo.

	W	L	PCT	ERA	G	GS	CG	IP	H	BB	SO	ShO	W	L	SV	AB	H	HR	BA
1914 KC F	3	9	.250	3.51	36	14	6	136	141	52	38	0	1	1	3	46	7	1	.152
1915	0	2	.000	4.63	11	2	0	35	41	13	16	0	0	0	0	9	1	0	.111
2 yrs.	3	11	.214	3.74	47	16	6	171	182	65	54	0	1	1	3	55	8	1	.145

Joe Adams

ADAMS, JOSEPH EDWARD (Wagon Tongue)   BR TL 6' 190 lbs.
B. Oct. 28, 1877, Cowden, Ill.   D. Oct. 8, 1952, Montgomery City, Mo.

	W	L	PCT	ERA	G	GS	CG	IP	H	BB	SO	ShO	W	L	SV	AB	H	HR	BA
1902 STL N	0	0	–	9.00	1	0	0	4	9	2	0	0	0	0	0	2	0	0	.000

Karl Adams

ADAMS, KARL TUTWILER (Rebel)   BR TR 6'2" 170 lbs.
B. Aug. 11, 1891, Columbus, Ga.   D. Sept. 17, 1967, Everett, Wash.

	W	L	PCT	ERA	G	GS	CG	IP	H	BB	SO	ShO	W	L	SV	AB	H	HR	BA
1914 CIN N	0	0	–	9.00	4	0	0	8	14	5	5	0	0	0	0	2	1	0	.500
1915 CHI N	1	9	.100	4.71	26	12	3	107	105	43	57	0	0	1	0	30	0	0	.000
2 yrs.	1	9	.100	5.01	30	12	3	115	119	48	62	0	0	1	0	32	1	0	.031

Red Adams

ADAMS, CHARLES DWIGHT   BR TR 6' 185 lbs.
B. Oct. 7, 1921, Parlier, Calif.

	W	L	PCT	ERA	G	GS	CG	IP	H	BB	SO	ShO	W	L	SV	AB	H	HR	BA
1946 CHI N	0	1	.000	8.25	8	0	0	12	18	7	8	0	0	1	0	1	0	0	.000

Rick Adams

ADAMS, REUBEN ALEXANDER   BL TL 6' 165 lbs.
B. Dec. 24, 1878, Paris, Tex.   D. Mar. 10, 1955, Paris, Tex.

	W	L	PCT	ERA	G	GS	CG	IP	H	BB	SO	ShO	W	L	SV	AB	H	HR	BA
1905 WAS A	2	4	.333	3.59	11	6	3	62.2	63	24	25	1	1	0	0	23	4	0	.174

Willie Adams

ADAMS, JAMES IRVIN   BR TR 6'4" 180 lbs.
B. Sept. 27, 1890, Clearfield, Pa.   D. June 18, 1937, Albany, N. Y.

	W	L	PCT	ERA	G	GS	CG	IP	H	BB	SO	ShO	W	L	SV	AB	H	HR	BA
1912 STL A	2	3	.400	3.88	13	5	0	46.1	50	19	16	0	1	0	0	13	0	0	.000
1913	0	0	–	10.00	4	0	0	9	12	4	5	0	0	0	0	1	0	0	.000
1914 PIT F	3	1	.750	3.74	15	2	1	55.1	70	22	14	0	2	0	0	15	1	0	.067
1918 PHI A	5	12	.294	4.42	32	14	7	169	164	97	39	0	3	0	0	57	8	0	.140
1919	0	0	–	3.86	1	0	0	4.2	7	2	0	0	0	0	0	2	0	0	.000
5 yrs.	10	16	.385	4.37	65	21	8	284.1	303	144	74	0	6	0	0	88	9	0	.102

Mike Adamson

ADAMSON, JOHN MICHAEL   BR TR 6'2" 185 lbs.
B. Sept. 13, 1947, San Diego, Calif.

	W	L	PCT	ERA	G	GS	CG	IP	H	BB	SO	ShO	W	L	SV	AB	H	HR	BA
1967 BAL A	0	1	.000	8.38	3	2	0	9.2	9	12	8	0	0	0	0	2	1	0	.500
1968	0	2	.000	9.39	2	2	0	7.2	9	4	4	0	0	0	0	3	1	0	.333
1969	0	1	.000	4.50	6	0	0	8	10	6	2	0	0	1	0	1	0	0	.000
3 yrs.	0	4	.000	7.46	11	4	0	25.1	28	22	14	0	0	1	0	6	2	0	.333

Dewey Adkins

ADKINS, JOHN DEWEY   BR TR 6'2" 195 lbs.
B. May 11, 1918, Norcatur, Kans.

	W	L	PCT	ERA	G	GS	CG	IP	H	BB	SO	ShO	W	L	SV	AB	H	HR	BA
1942 WAS A	0	0	–	9.95	1	1	0	6.1	7	6	3	0	0	0	0	2	1	0	.500
1943	0	0	–	2.61	7	0	0	10.1	9	5	1	0	0	0	0	0	0	0	–
1949 CHI N	2	4	.333	5.68	30	5	1	82.1	98	39	43	0	1	1	0	20	4	1	.200
3 yrs.	2	4	.333	5.64	38	6	1	99	114	50	47	0	1	1	0	22	5	1	.227

Doc Adkins

ADKINS, MERLE THERON (Babe)   BR TR 5'10½" 220 lbs.
B. Aug. 5, 1872, Troy, Wis.   D. Feb. 21, 1934, Durham, N. C.

	W	L	PCT	ERA	G	GS	CG	IP	H	BB	SO	ShO	W	L	SV	AB	H	HR	BA
1902 BOS A	1	1	.500	4.05	4	2	1	20	30	7	3	0	0	0	0	9	2	0	.222
1903 NY A	0	0	–	7.71	2	1	0	7	10	5	0	0	0	0	1	3	0	0	.000
2 yrs.	1	1	.500	5.00	6	3	1	27	40	12	3	0	0	0	1	12	2	0	.167

	W	L	PCT	ERA	G	GS	CG	IP	H	BB	SO	ShO	Relief Pitching W	L	SV	BATTING AB	H	HR	BA

Grady Adkins

ADKINS, GRADY EMMETT (Butcher Boy)   BR TR 5'11" 175 lbs.
B. June 29, 1897, Jacksonville, Ark.   D. Mar. 31, 1966, Little Rock, Ark.

Year/Team	W	L	PCT	ERA	G	GS	CG	IP	H	BB	SO	ShO	W	L	SV	AB	H	HR	BA
1928 CHI A	10	16	.385	3.73	36	27	14	224.2	233	89	54	0	3	1	1	70	10	0	.143
1929	2	11	.154	5.33	31	15	5	138.1	168	67	24	0	0	1	0	46	11	0	.239
2 yrs.	12	27	.308	4.34	67	42	19	363	401	156	78	0	3	2	1	116	21	0	.181

Juan Agosto

AGOSTO, JUAN ROBERTO   BL TL 6' 175 lbs.
B. Feb. 23, 1958, Rio Piedras, Puerto Rico

Year/Team	W	L	PCT	ERA	G	GS	CG	IP	H	BB	SO	ShO	W	L	SV	AB	H	HR	BA
1981 CHI A	0	0	—	4.50	2	0	0	6	5	0	3	0	0	0	0	0	0	0	—
1982	0	0	—	18.00	1	0	0	2	7	0	1	0	0	0	0	0	0	0	—
1983	2	2	.500	4.10	39	0	0	41.2	41	11	29	0	2	2	7	0	0	0	—
1984	2	1	.667	3.09	49	0	0	55.1	54	34	26	0	2	1	7	0	0	0	—
4 yrs.	4	3	.571	3.86	91	0	0	105	107	45	59	0	4	3	14	0	0	0	—

LEAGUE CHAMPIONSHIP SERIES

| 1983 CHI A | 0 | 0 | — | 0.00 | 1 | 0 | 0 | .1 | 0 | 0 | 0 | 0 | 0 | 0 | 0 | 0 | 0 | 0 | — |

Hank Aguirre

AGUIRRE, HENRY JOHN   BR TL 6'4" 205 lbs.
B. Jan. 31, 1932, Azusa, Calif.   BB 1965-68

Year/Team	W	L	PCT	ERA	G	GS	CG	IP	H	BB	SO	ShO	W	L	SV	AB	H	HR	BA
1955 CLE A	2	0	1.000	1.42	4	1	1	12.2	6	12	6	1	1	0	1	4	0	0	.000
1956	3	5	.375	3.72	16	9	2	65.1	63	27	31	1	1	0	1	18	2	0	.111
1957	1	1	.500	5.75	10	1	0	20.1	26	13	9	0	0	1	0	4	0	0	.000
1958 DET A	3	4	.429	3.75	44	3	0	69.2	67	27	38	0	2	2	5	14	3	0	.214
1959	0	0	—	3.38	3	0	0	2.2	4	3	3	0	0	0	0	0	0	0	—
1960	5	3	.625	2.85	37	6	1	94.2	75	30	80	0	2	1	10	28	1	0	.036
1961	4	4	.500	3.25	45	0	0	55.1	44	38	32	0	4	4	8	9	0	0	.000
1962	16	8	.667	2.21	42	22	11	216	162	65	156	2	4	2	3	75	2	0	.027
1963	14	15	.483	3.67	38	33	14	225.2	222	68	134	3	0	2	0	76	10	0	.132
1964	5	10	.333	3.79	32	27	3	161.2	134	59	88	0	0	0	1	53	3	0	.057
1965	14	10	.583	3.59	32	32	10	208.1	185	60	141	2	0	0	0	70	6	0	.086
1966	3	9	.250	3.82	30	14	2	103.2	104	26	50	0	0	3	0	25	3	0	.120
1967	0	1	.000	2.40	31	1	0	41.1	34	17	33	0	0	1	0	2	1	0	.500
1968 LA N	1	2	.333	0.69	25	0	0	39	32	13	25	0	1	2	3	3	0	0	.000
1969 CHI N	1	0	1.000	2.60	41	0	0	45	45	12	19	0	1	0	1	5	2	0	.400
1970	3	0	1.000	4.50	17	0	0	14	13	9	11	0	3	0	1	2	0	0	.000
16 yrs.	75	72	.510	3.25	447	149	44	1375.1	1216	479	856	9	19	18	33	388	33	0	.085

Eddie Ainsmith

AINSMITH, EDWARD WILBUR   BR TR 5'11" 180 lbs.
B. Feb. 4, 1890, Cambridge, Mass.   D. Sept. 6, 1981, Fort Lauderdale, Fla.

Year/Team	W	L	PCT	ERA	G	GS	CG	IP	H	BB	SO	ShO	W	L	SV	AB	H	HR	BA
1913 WAS A	0	0	—	54.00	1	0	0	.1	2	0	0	0	0	0	0	*			

Raleigh Aitchison

AITCHISON, RALEIGH LEONIDAS (Redskin)   BR TL 5'11½" 175 lbs.
B. Dec. 5, 1887, Tyndall, S. D.   D. Sept. 26, 1958, Columbus, Kans.

Year/Team	W	L	PCT	ERA	G	GS	CG	IP	H	BB	SO	ShO	W	L	SV	AB	H	HR	BA
1911 BKN N	0	1	.000	0.00	1	0	0	1.1	1	1	0	0	0	1	0	0	0	0	—
1914	12	7	.632	2.66	26	17	8	172.1	156	60	87	3	1	2	0	51	10	0	.196
1915	0	4	.000	4.96	7	5	2	32.2	36	6	14	0	0	0	0	8	0	0	.000
3 yrs.	12	12	.500	3.01	34	22	10	206.1	193	67	101	3	1	3	0	59	10	0	.169

Jack Aker

AKER, JACK DELANE (Chief)   BR TR 6'2" 190 lbs.
B. July 13, 1940, Tulare, Calif.

Year/Team	W	L	PCT	ERA	G	GS	CG	IP	H	BB	SO	ShO	W	L	SV	AB	H	HR	BA
1964 KC A	0	1	.000	8.82	9	0	0	16.1	17	10	7	0	0	1	0	3	0	0	.000
1965	4	3	.571	3.16	34	0	0	51.1	45	18	26	0	4	3	3	8	0	0	.000
1966	8	4	.667	1.99	66	0	0	113	81	28	68	0	8	4	32	21	2	0	.095
1967	3	8	.273	4.30	57	0	0	88	87	32	65	0	3	8	12	8	1	0	.125
1968 OAK A	4	4	.500	4.10	54	0	0	74.2	72	33	44	0	4	4	11	7	1	0	.143
1969 2 teams		SEA	A	(15G 0–2)		NY	A	(38G 8–4)											
" total	8	6	.571	3.17	53	0	0	82.1	76	35	47	0	8	6	14	10	1	0	.100
1970 NY A	4	2	.667	2.06	41	0	0	70	57	20	36	0	4	2	16	16	1	0	.063
1971	4	4	.500	2.57	41	0	0	56	48	26	24	0	4	4	4	3	0	0	.000
1972 2 teams		NY	A	(4G 0–0)		CHI	N	(48G 6–6)											
" total	6	6	.500	2.96	52	0	0	73	70	26	37	0	6	6	17	6	0	0	.000
1973 CHI N	4	5	.444	4.08	47	0	0	64	76	23	25	0	4	5	12	7	0	0	.000
1974 2 teams		ATL	N	(17G 0–1)		NY	N	(24G 2–1)											
" total	2	2	.500	3.57	41	0	0	58	50	23	25	0	2	2	2	3	1	0	.333
11 yrs.	47	45	.511	3.28	495	0	0	746.2	679	274	404	0	47	45	123	92	7	0	.076

Jerry Akers

AKERS, ALBERT EARL   BR TR 5'11" 175 lbs.
B. Nov. 1, 1887, Shelbyville, Ind.   D. May 15, 1979, Bay Pines, Fla.

Year/Team	W	L	PCT	ERA	G	GS	CG	IP	H	BB	SO	ShO	W	L	SV	AB	H	HR	BA
1912 WAS A	1	1	.500	4.87	5	1	0	20.1	24	15	11	0	1	0	0	6	2	0	.333

Joe Albanese

ALBANESE, JOSEPH PETER   BR TR 6'3" 215 lbs.
B. June 26, 1933, New York, N. Y.

Year/Team	W	L	PCT	ERA	G	GS	CG	IP	H	BB	SO	ShO	W	L	SV	AB	H	HR	BA
1958 WAS A	0	0	—	4.50	6	0	0	6	8	2	3	0	0	0	0	0	0	0	—

Cy Alberts

ALBERTS, FREDERICK JOSEPH   BR TR 6' 230 lbs.
B. Jan. 14, 1882, Grand Rapids, Mich.   D. Aug. 27, 1917, Fort Wayne, Ind.

Year/Team	W	L	PCT	ERA	G	GS	CG	IP	H	BB	SO	ShO	W	L	SV	AB	H	HR	BA
1910 STL N	1	2	.333	6.18	4	3	2	27.2	35	20	10	0	0	0	0	7	0	0	.000

Ed Albosta

ALBOSTA, EDWARD JOHN (Rube)   BR TR 6'1" 175 lbs.
B. Oct. 27, 1918, Saginaw, Mich.

Year/Team	W	L	PCT	ERA	G	GS	CG	IP	H	BB	SO	ShO	W	L	SV	AB	H	HR	BA
1941 BKN N	0	2	.000	6.23	2	2	0	13	11	8	5	0	0	0	0	4	0	0	.000
1946 PIT N	0	6	.000	6.09	17	6	0	39.2	41	35	19	0	0	1	0	8	1	0	.125
2 yrs.	0	8	.000	6.15	19	8	0	52.2	52	43	24	0	0	1	0	12	1	0	.083

	W	L	PCT	ERA	G	GS	CG	IP	H	BB	SO	ShO	Relief Pitching W	L	SV	BATTING AB	H	HR	BA

Ed Albrecht

ALBRECHT, EDWARD ARTHUR
B. Feb. 28, 1929, St. Louis County, Mo.   D. Dec. 29, 1979, Centerville, Iowa   BR TR 5'10½" 165 lbs.

	W	L	PCT	ERA	G	GS	CG	IP	H	BB	SO	ShO	W	L	SV	AB	H	HR	BA
1949 STL A	1	0	1.000	5.40	1	1	1	5	1	4	1	0	0	0	0	2	0	0	.000
1950	0	1	.000	5.40	2	1	0	6.2	6	7	1	0	0	1	0	1	0	0	.000
2 yrs.	1	1	.500	5.40	3	2	1	11.2	7	11	2	0	0	1	0	3	0	0	.000

Vic Albury

ALBURY, VICTOR
B. May 12, 1947, Key West, Fla.   BL TL 6'   190 lbs.

	W	L	PCT	ERA	G	GS	CG	IP	H	BB	SO	ShO	W	L	SV	AB	H	HR	BA
1973 MIN A	1	0	1.000	2.70	14	0	0	23.1	13	19	13	0	1	0	0	0	0	0	—
1974	8	9	.471	4.12	32	22	4	164	159	80	85	1	1	0	0	0	0	0	—
1975	6	7	.462	4.53	32	15	2	135	115	97	72	0	3	0	1	1	0	0	.000
1976	3	1	.750	3.58	23	0	0	50.1	51	24	23	0	3	1	0	0	0	0	—
4 yrs.	18	17	.514	4.11	101	37	6	372.2	338	220	193	1	8	1	1	1	0	0	.000

Santo Alcala

ALCALA, SANTO
B. Dec. 23, 1952, San Pedro, Dominican Republic   BR TR 6'5"   195 lbs.

	W	L	PCT	ERA	G	GS	CG	IP	H	BB	SO	ShO	W	L	SV	AB	H	HR	BA
1976 CIN N	11	4	.733	4.70	30	21	3	132	131	67	67	1	0	0	0	43	6	0	.140
1977 2 teams		CIN	N (7G 1–1)			MON	N (31G 2–6)												
" total	3	7	.300	4.83	38	12	0	117.1	126	54	73	0	1	0	2	28	2	1	.071
2 yrs.	14	11	.560	4.76	68	33	3	249.1	257	121	140	1	1	0	2	71	8	1	.113

Dale Alderson

ALDERSON, DALE LEONARD
B. Mar. 9, 1918, Belden, Neb.   D. Feb. 12, 1982, Garden Grove, Calif.   BR TR 5'10" 190 lbs.

	W	L	PCT	ERA	G	GS	CG	IP	H	BB	SO	ShO	W	L	SV	AB	H	HR	BA
1943 CHI N	0	1	.000	6.43	4	2	0	14	21	3	4	0	0	0	0	3	0	0	.000
1944	0	0	—	6.65	12	1	0	21.2	31	9	7	0	0	0	0	4	0	0	.000
2 yrs.	0	1	.000	6.56	16	3	0	35.2	52	12	11	0	0	0	0	7	0	0	.000

Vic Aldridge

ALDRIDGE, VICTOR EDDINGTON
B. Oct. 25, 1893, Indian Springs, Ind.   D. Apr. 17, 1973, Terre Haute, Ind.   BR TR 5'9½" 175 lbs.

	W	L	PCT	ERA	G	GS	CG	IP	H	BB	SO	ShO	W	L	SV	AB	H	HR	BA
1917 CHI N	6	6	.500	3.12	30	6	1	106.2	100	37	44	1	5	1	2	29	4	0	.138
1918	0	1	.000	1.46	3	0	0	12.1	11	6	10	0	0	1	0	3	1	0	.333
1922	16	15	.516	3.52	36	34	20	258.1	287	56	66	2	1	0	0	100	26	0	.260
1923	16	9	.640	3.48	30	30	15	217	209	67	64	2	0	0	0	71	19	0	.268
1924	15	12	.556	3.50	32	32	20	244.1	261	80	74	0	0	0	0	85	15	0	.176
1925 PIT N	15	7	.682	3.63	30	26	14	213.1	218	74	88	1	2	0	0	86	20	1	.233
1926	10	13	.435	4.07	30	26	12	190	204	73	61	1	0	1	1	71	16	0	.225
1927	15	10	.600	4.25	35	34	17	239.1	248	74	86	1	0	0	1	96	21	0	.219
1928 NY N	4	7	.364	4.83	22	17	3	119.1	133	45	33	0	0	0	2	40	11	1	.275
9 yrs.	97	80	.548	3.76	248	205	102	1600.2	1671	512	526	8	8	3	6	581	133	2	.229

WORLD SERIES

	W	L	PCT	ERA	G	GS	CG	IP	H	BB	SO	ShO	W	L	SV	AB	H	HR	BA
1925 PIT N	2	0	1.000	3.93	3	3	2	18.1	18	9	9	0	0	0	0	7	0	0	.000
1927	0	1	.000	7.36	1	1	0	7.1	10	4	4	0	0	0	0	2	0	0	.000
2 yrs.	2	1	.667	4.91	4	4	2	25.2	28	13	13	0	0	0	0	9	0	0	.000

Bob Alexander

ALEXANDER, ROBERT SOMERVILLE
B. Aug. 7, 1922, Vancouver, B. C., Canada   BR TR 6'2½" 205 lbs.

	W	L	PCT	ERA	G	GS	CG	IP	H	BB	SO	ShO	W	L	SV	AB	H	HR	BA
1955 BAL A	1	0	1.000	13.50	4	0	0	4	8	2	1	0	1	0	0	0	0	0	—
1957 CLE A	0	1	.000	9.00	5	0	0	7	10	5	1	0	0	1	0	1	0	0	.000
2 yrs.	1	1	.500	10.64	9	0	0	11	18	7	2	0	1	1	0	1	0	0	.000

Doyle Alexander

ALEXANDER, DOYLE LAFAYETTE
B. Sept. 4, 1950, Cordova, Ala.   BR TR 6'3"   190 lbs.

	W	L	PCT	ERA	G	GS	CG	IP	H	BB	SO	ShO	W	L	SV	AB	H	HR	BA
1971 LA N	6	6	.500	3.82	17	12	4	92	105	18	30	0	1	0	0	33	9	0	.273
1972 BAL A	6	8	.429	2.45	35	9	2	106.1	78	30	49	2	4	5	2	25	2	0	.080
1973	12	8	.600	3.86	29	26	10	175	169	52	63	0	1	0	0	0	0	0	—
1974	6	9	.400	4.03	30	12	2	114	127	43	40	0	3	2	0	0	0	0	—
1975	8	8	.500	3.04	32	11	3	133.1	127	47	46	1	3	4	1	0	0	0	—
1976 2 teams		BAL	A (11G 3–4)			NY	A (19G 10–5)												
" total	13	9	.591	3.36	30	25	7	201	172	63	58	3	2	0	0	0	0	0	—
1977 TEX A	17	11	.607	3.65	34	34	12	237	221	82	82	1	0	0	0	0	0	0	—
1978	9	10	.474	3.86	31	28	7	191	198	71	81	1	0	0	0	0	0	0	—
1979	5	7	.417	4.46	23	18	0	113	114	69	50	0	0	0	0	0	0	0	—
1980 ATL N	14	11	.560	4.19	35	35	7	232	227	74	114	1	0	0	0	83	15	0	.181
1981 SF N	11	7	.611	2.90	24	24	1	152	156	44	77	1	0	0	0	51	9	0	.176
1982 NY A	1	7	.125	6.08	16	10	0	66.2	81	14	26	0	0	0	0	0	0	0	—
1983 2 teams		NY	A (8G 0–2)			TOR	A (17G 7–6)												
" total	7	8	.467	4.41	25	20	5	145	157	33	63	0	1	0	0	0	0	0	—
1984 TOR A	17	6	.739	3.13	36	35	11	261.2	238	59	139	2	0	0	0	0	0	0	—
14 yrs.	132	115	.534	3.70	397	300	71	2220	2170	699	918	12	15	11	3	192	35	0	.182

LEAGUE CHAMPIONSHIP SERIES

	W	L	PCT	ERA	G	GS	CG	IP	H	BB	SO	ShO	W	L	SV	AB	H	HR	BA
1973 BAL A	0	1	.000	4.91	1	1	0	3.2	5	1	1	0	0	0	0	0	0	0	—

WORLD SERIES

	W	L	PCT	ERA	G	GS	CG	IP	H	BB	SO	ShO	W	L	SV	AB	H	HR	BA
1976 NY A	0	1	.000	7.50	1	1	0	6	9	2	1	0	0	0	0	0	0	0	—

Grover Alexander

ALEXANDER, GROVER CLEVELAND (Pete)
B. Feb. 26, 1887, Elba, Neb.   D. Nov. 4, 1950, St. Paul, Neb.   BR TR 6'1"   185 lbs.
Hall of Fame 1938.

	W	L	PCT	ERA	G	GS	CG	IP	H	BB	SO	ShO	W	L	SV	AB	H	HR	BA
1911 PHI N	28	13	.683	2.57	48	37	31	367	285	129	227	7	4	2	3	138	24	0	.174
1912	19	17	.528	2.81	46	34	26	310.1	289	105	195	3	3	2	2	102	19	2	.186
1913	22	8	.733	2.79	47	35	23	306.1	288	75	159	9	4	2	2	103	13	0	.126
1914	27	15	.643	2.38	46	39	32	355	327	76	214	6	4	1	1	137	32	0	.234
1915	31	10	.756	1.22	49	42	36	376.1	253	64	241	12	1	1	3	130	22	1	.169
1916	33	12	.733	1.55	48	45	38	388.2	323	50	167	16¹	0	0	3	138	33	0	.239
1917	30	13	.698	1.86	45	44	35	387.2	336	58	201	8	0	0	0	139	30	1	.216
1918 CHI N	2	1	.667	1.73	3	3	3	26	19	3	15	0	0	0	0	10	1	0	.100
1919	16	11	.593	1.72	30	27	20	235	180	38	121	9	0	1	1	70	12	0	.171

	W	L	PCT	ERA	G	GS	CG	IP	H	BB	SO	ShO	Relief Pitching W	L	SV	BATTING AB	H	HR	BA

Grover Alexander continued

	W	L	PCT	ERA	G	GS	CG	IP	H	BB	SO	ShO	W	L	SV	AB	H	HR	BA
1920	27	14	.659	1.91	46	40	33	363.1	335	69	173	7	1	0	5	118	27	1	.229
1921	15	13	.536	3.39	31	29	21	252	286	33	77	3	0	0	1	95	29	1	.305
1922	16	13	.552	3.63	33	31	20	245.2	283	34	48	1	1	0	1	85	15	0	.176
1923	22	12	.647	3.19	39	36	26	305	308	30	72	3	0	1	2	111	24	1	.216
1924	12	5	.706	3.03	21	20	12	169.1	183	25	33	0	0	1	0	65	15	1	.231
1925	15	11	.577	3.39	32	30	20	236	270	29	63	1	0	1	0	79	19	2	.241
1926 2 teams			CHI	N	(7G 3–3)		STL	N	(23G 9–7)										
" total	12	10	.545	3.05	30	23	15	200.1	191	31	47	2	2	1	2	65	13	0	.200
1927 STL N	21	10	.677	2.52	37	30	22	268	261	38	48	2	2	1	3	94	23	0	.245
1928	16	9	.640	3.36	34	31	18	243.2	262	37	59	1	0	0	2	86	25	1	.291
1929	9	8	.529	3.89	22	19	8	132	149	23	33	0	1	1	0	41	2	0	.049
1930 PHI N	0	3	.000	9.14	9	3	0	21.2	40	6	6	0	0	2	0	4	0	0	.000
20 yrs.	373	208	.642	2.56	696	598	439	5189.1	4868	953	2199	90	23	17	31	1810	378	11	.209
	3rd										6th		2nd						

WORLD SERIES																			
1915 PHI N	1	1	.500	1.53	2	2	2	17.2	14	4	10	0	0	0	0	5	1	0	.200
1926 STL N	2	0	1.000	0.89	3	2	2	20.1	12	4	17	0	0	0	1	7	0	0	.000
1928	0	1	.000	19.80	2	1	0	5	10	4	2	0	0	0	0	1	0	0	.000
3 yrs.	3	2	.600	3.35	7	5	4	43	36	12	29	0	0	0	1	13	1	0	.077

Brian Allard

ALLARD, BRIAN MARSHALL
B. Jan. 3, 1958, Spring Valley, Ill.   BR TR 6'1"   175 lbs.

	W	L	PCT	ERA	G	GS	CG	IP	H	BB	SO	ShO	W	L	SV	AB	H	HR	BA
1979 TEX A	1	3	.250	4.36	7	4	2	33	36	13	14	0	0	0	0	0	0	0	—
1980	0	1	.000	5.79	5	2	0	14	13	10	10	0	0	0	0	0	0	0	—
1981 SEA A	3	2	.600	3.75	7	7	1	48	48	8	20	0	0	0	0	0	0	0	—
3 yrs.	4	6	.400	4.26	19	13	3	95	97	31	44	0	0	0	0	0	0	0	—

Bob Allen

ALLEN, ROBERT EARL
B. July 2, 1914, Smithville, Tenn.   BR TR 6'1½"   158 lbs.

	W	L	PCT	ERA	G	GS	CG	IP	H	BB	SO	ShO	W	L	SV	AB	H	HR	BA
1937 PHI N	0	1	.000	6.75	3	1	0	12	18	8	8	0	0	0	0	3	1	0	.333

Bob Allen

ALLEN, ROBERT GRAY
B. Oct. 23, 1937, Tatum, Tex.   BL TL 6'2"   175 lbs.

	W	L	PCT	ERA	G	GS	CG	IP	H	BB	SO	ShO	W	L	SV	AB	H	HR	BA
1961 CLE A	3	2	.600	3.75	48	0	0	81.2	96	40	42	0	3	2	3	12	2	0	.167
1962	1	1	.500	5.87	30	0	0	30.2	29	25	23	0	1	1	4	5	0	0	.000
1963	1	2	.333	4.66	43	0	0	56	58	29	51	0	1	2	2	5	1	0	.200
1966	2	2	.500	4.21	36	0	0	51.1	56	13	33	0	2	2	5	9	1	0	.111
1967	0	5	.000	2.98	47	0	0	54.1	49	25	50	0	0	5	5	0	0	0	—
5 yrs.	7	12	.368	4.11	204	0	0	274	288	132	199	0	7	12	19	31	4	0	.129

Frank Allen

ALLEN, FRANK LEON
B. Aug. 26, 1888, Newbern, Ala.   D. July 30, 1933, Gainesville, Ala.   BR TL 5'9"   175 lbs.

	W	L	PCT	ERA	G	GS	CG	IP	H	BB	SO	ShO	W	L	SV	AB	H	HR	BA
1912 BKN N	3	9	.250	3.63	20	15	5	109	119	57	58	1	0	0	0	36	6	1	.167
1913	4	18	.182	2.83	34	25	11	174.2	144	81	82	0	1	3	2	51	7	1	.137
1914 2 teams			BKN	N	(36G 8–14)		PIT	F	(1G 1–0)										
" total	9	14	.391	3.18	37	22	11	178.1	174	57	71	1	1	2	0	49	7	0	.143
1915 PIT F	23	12	.657	2.51	41	37	24	283.1	230	100	127	6	1	1	0	89	7	0	.079
1916 BOS N	8	2	.800	2.07	19	14	7	113	102	31	63	2	1	0	1	34	7	0	.206
1917	3	11	.214	3.94	29	14	2	112	124	47	56	0	0	4	0	29	5	0	.172
6 yrs.	50	66	.431	2.93	180	127	60	970.1	893	373	457	10	3	10	3	288	39	2	.135

John Allen

ALLEN, JOHN MARSHALL
B. Oct. 27, 1890, Berkeley Springs, W. Va.   D. Sept. 24, 1967, Hagerstown, Md.   BR TR 6'1"   170 lbs.

	W	L	PCT	ERA	G	GS	CG	IP	H	BB	SO	ShO	W	L	SV	AB	H	HR	BA
1914 BAL F	0	0	—	18.00	1	0	0	2	2	2	2	0	0	0	0	0	0	0	—

Johnny Allen

ALLEN, JOHN THOMAS
B. Sept. 30, 1905, Lenoir, N. C.   D. Mar. 29, 1959, St. Petersburg, Fla.   BR TR 5'11½"   180 lbs.

	W	L	PCT	ERA	G	GS	CG	IP	H	BB	SO	ShO	W	L	SV	AB	H	HR	BA
1932 NY A	17	4	.810	3.70	33	21	13	192	162	76	109	3	4	0	4	73	9	1	.123
1933	15	7	.682	4.39	25	24	10	184.2	171	87	119	1	0	0	1	72	13	0	.181
1934	5	2	.714	2.89	13	10	4	71.2	62	32	54	0	0	0	0	26	5	0	.192
1935	13	6	.684	3.61	23	18	12	167	149	58	113	2	0	0	0	67	15	1	.224
1936 CLE A	20	10	.667	3.44	36	31	19	243	234	97	165	4	2	1	1	87	14	0	.161
1937	15	1	.938	2.55	24	20	14	173	157	60	87	0	0	0	0	67	6	0	.090
1938	14	8	.636	4.19	30	27	13	200	189	81	112	0	1	1	0	79	20	1	.253
1939	9	7	.563	4.58	28	26	9	175	199	56	79	2	0	0	0	71	16	0	.225
1940	9	8	.529	3.44	32	17	5	138.2	126	48	62	3	3	1	5	48	10	0	.208
1941 2 teams			STL	A	(20G 2–5)		BKN	N	(11G 3–0)										
" total	5	5	.500	4.71	31	13	3	124.1	127	41	48	0	1	3	1	42	4	1	.095
1942 BKN N	10	6	.625	3.20	27	15	5	118	106	39	50	1	1	3	3	39	7	0	.179
1943 2 teams			BKN	N	(17G 5–1)		NY	N	(15G 1–3)										
" total	6	4	.600	3.65	32	1	0	79	79	39	39	0	6	4	3	21	3	0	.143
1944 NY N	4	7	.364	4.07	18	13	2	84	88	24	33	1	0	0	0	24	2	0	.083
13 yrs.	142	75	.654	3.75	352	241	109	1950.1	1849	738	1070	17	18	13	18	716	124	4	.173

WORLD SERIES																			
1932 NY A	0	0	—	40.50	1	1	0	.2	5	0	0	0	0	0	0	0	0	0	—
1941 BKN N	0	0	—	0.00	3	0	0	3.2	1	3	6	0	0	0	0	0	0	0	—
2 yrs.	0	0	—	6.23	4	1	0	4.1	6	3	6	0	0	0	0	0	0	0	—

Lloyd Allen

ALLEN, LLOYD CECIL
B. May 8, 1950, Merced, Calif.   BR TR 6'1"   185 lbs.

	W	L	PCT	ERA	G	GS	CG	IP	H	BB	SO	ShO	W	L	SV	AB	H	HR	BA
1969 CAL A	0	1	.000	5.40	4	1	0	10	5	10	5	0	0	0	0	2	1	0	.500
1970	1	1	.500	2.63	8	2	0	24	23	11	12	0	0	0	0	4	0	0	.000
1971	4	6	.400	2.49	54	1	0	94	75	40	72	0	4	6	15	17	5	1	.294
1972	3	7	.300	3.49	42	6	0	85	76	55	53	0	3	3	5	17	2	0	.118

	W	L	PCT	ERA	G	GS	CG	IP	H	BB	SO	ShO	Relief Pitching W	L	SV	BATTING AB	H	HR	BA

Lloyd Allen continued

	W	L	PCT	ERA	G	GS	CG	IP	H	BB	SO	ShO	W	L	SV	AB	H	HR	BA
1973 2 teams			CAL	A (5G 0-0)		TEX	A (23G 0-6)												
" total	0	6	.000	9.42	28	5	0	49.2	73	44	29	0	0	2	2	0	0	0	–
1974 2 teams			TEX	A (14G 0-1)		CHI	A (6G 0-1)												
" total	0	2	.000	7.45	20	2	0	29	31	30	21	0	0	2	0	0	0	0	–
1975 CHI A	0	2	.000	11.81	3	2	0	5.1	8	6	2	0	0	0	0	0	0	0	–
7 yrs.	8	25	.242	4.70	159	19	0	297	291	196	194	0	7	13	22	40	8	1	.200

Myron Allen

ALLEN, MYRON SMITH BR TR 5'8" 150 lbs.
B. Mar. 22, 1854, Kingston, N. Y.   D. Mar. 8, 1924, Kingston, N. Y.

	W	L	PCT	ERA	G	GS	CG	IP	H	BB	SO	ShO	W	L	SV	AB	H	HR	BA
1883 NY N	0	1	.000	1.13	1	1	1	8	8	3	0	0	0	0	0	4	0	0	.000
1887 CLE AA	1	0	1.000	1.86	2	0	0	9.2	9	3	1	0	1	0	0	463	128	4	.276
1888 KC AA	0	2	.000	2.50	2	2	2	18	17	1	2	0	0	0	0	136	29	0	.213
3 yrs.	1	3	.250	2.02	5	3	3	35.2	34	7	3	0	1	0	0	*			

Neil Allen

ALLEN, NEIL PATRICK BR TR 6'3" 185 lbs.
B. Jan. 24, 1958, Kansas City, Kans.

	W	L	PCT	ERA	G	GS	CG	IP	H	BB	SO	ShO	W	L	SV	AB	H	HR	BA
1979 NY N	6	10	.375	3.55	50	5	0	99	100	47	65	0	6	6	8	14	0	0	.000
1980	7	10	.412	3.71	59	0	0	97	87	40	79	0	7	10	22	14	2	0	.143
1981	7	6	.538	2.96	43	0	0	67	64	26	50	0	7	6	18	5	1	0	.200
1982	3	7	.300	3.06	50	0	0	64.2	65	30	59	0	3	7	19	6	1	0	.167
1983 2 teams			NY	N (21G 2-7)		STL	N (25G 10-6)												
" total	12	13	.480	3.94	46	22	5	175.2	179	84	106	3	3	5	2	49	5	0	.102
1984 STL N	9	6	.600	3.55	57	1	0	119	105	49	66	0	9	5	3	25	6	0	.240
6 yrs.	44	52	.458	3.57	305	28	5	622.1	600	276	425	3	35	39	72	113	15	0	.133

Doug Allison

ALLISON, DOUGLAS L. BR TR 5'10½" 160 lbs.
Brother of Art Allison.
B. 1846, Philadelphia, Pa.   D. Dec. 19, 1916, Washington, D. C.

	W	L	PCT	ERA	G	GS	CG	IP	H	BB	SO	ShO	W	L	SV	AB	H	HR	BA
1878 PRO N	0	0	–	1.80	1	0	0	5	5	11	1	0	0	0	0	*			

Mack Allison

ALLISON, MACK PENDLETON BR TR 6'1" 185 lbs.
B. Jan. 23, 1887, Owensboro, Ky.   D. Mar. 13, 1964, St. Joseph, Mo.

	W	L	PCT	ERA	G	GS	CG	IP	H	BB	SO	ShO	W	L	SV	AB	H	HR	BA
1911 STL A	2	1	.667	2.05	3	3	3	26.1	24	5	2	0	0	0	0	10	2	0	.200
1912	6	17	.261	3.62	31	20	11	169	171	49	43	1	0	3	1	52	7	0	.135
1913	1	3	.250	2.28	11	4	3	51.1	52	13	12	0	0	0	0	14	0	0	.000
3 yrs.	9	21	.300	3.17	45	27	17	246.2	247	67	57	1	0	3	1	76	9	0	.118

Luis Aloma

ALOMA, LUIS (Witto) BR TR 6'2" 195 lbs.
B. June 19, 1923, Havana, Cuba

	W	L	PCT	ERA	G	GS	CG	IP	H	BB	SO	ShO	W	L	SV	AB	H	HR	BA
1950 CHI A	7	2	.778	3.80	42	0	0	87.2	77	53	49	0	7	2	4	15	1	0	.067
1951	6	0	1.000	1.82	25	1	1	69.1	52	24	25	1	5	0	3	20	7	0	.350
1952	3	1	.750	4.28	25	0	0	40	42	11	18	0	3	1	6	7	0	0	.000
1953	2	0	1.000	4.70	24	0	0	38.1	41	23	23	0	2	0	2	6	0	0	.000
4 yrs.	18	3	.857	3.44	116	1	1	235.1	212	111	115	1	17	3	15	48	8	0	.167

Matty Alou

ALOU, MATEO ROJAS BL TL 5'9" 160 lbs.
Brother of Jesus Alou.   Brother of Felipe Alou.
B. Dec. 22, 1938, Haina, Dominican Republic

	W	L	PCT	ERA	G	GS	CG	IP	H	BB	SO	ShO	W	L	SV	AB	H	HR	BA
1965 SF N	0	0	–	0.00	1	0	0	2	3	1	3	0	0	0	0	*			

Porfirio Altamirano

ALTAMIRANO, PORFIRIO BR TR 6' 175 lbs.
B. May 17, 1952, Esteli, Nicaragua

	W	L	PCT	ERA	G	GS	CG	IP	H	BB	SO	ShO	W	L	SV	AB	H	HR	BA
1982 PHI N	5	1	.833	4.15	29	0	0	39	41	14	26	0	5	1	2	4	1	0	.250
1983	2	3	.400	3.70	31	0	0	41.1	38	15	24	0	2	3	0	2	0	0	.000
1984 CHI N	0	0	–	4.76	5	0	0	11.1	8	1	7	0	0	0	0	2	0	0	.000
3 yrs.	7	4	.636	4.03	65	0	0	91.2	87	30	57	0	7	4	2	8	1	0	.125

Ernie Alten

ALTEN, ERNEST MATTHIAS (Lefty) BR TL 6' 175 lbs.
B. Dec. 1, 1894, Avon, Ohio   D. Sept. 9, 1981, Napa, Calif.

	W	L	PCT	ERA	G	GS	CG	IP	H	BB	SO	ShO	W	L	SV	AB	H	HR	BA
1920 DET A	0	1	.000	9.00	14	0	0	23	40	9	4	0	0	0	0	3	0	0	.000

Nick Altrock

ALTROCK, NICHOLAS BB TL 5'10" 197 lbs.
B. Sept. 15, 1876, Cincinnati, Ohio   D. Jan. 20, 1965, Washington, D. C.

	W	L	PCT	ERA	G	GS	CG	IP	H	BB	SO	ShO	W	L	SV	AB	H	HR	BA
1898 LOU N	3	3	.500	4.50	11	7	6	70	89	21	13	0	0	0	0	29	7	0	.241
1902 BOS A	0	2	.000	2.00	3	2	1	18	19	7	5	0	0	0	1	8	0	0	.000
1903 2 teams			BOS	A (1G 0-1)		CHI	A (12G 4-3)												
" total	4	4	.500	2.85	13	9	7	79	72	23	22	0	0	0	0	33	11	0	.333
1904 CHI A	19	14	.576	2.96	38	36	31	307	274	48	87	6	0	0	1	111	22	1	.198
1905	22	12	.647	1.88	38	34	31	315.2	274	63	97	3	2	1	0	114	14	0	.123
1906	20	13	.606	2.06	38	30	25	287.2	269	42	99	4	5	1	0	100	16	0	.160
1907	7	13	.350	2.57	30	21	15	213.2	210	31	61	1	2	1	2	72	13	0	.181
1908	5	7	.417	2.71	23	13	8	136	127	18	21	1	1	0	2	49	10	0	.204
1909 2 teams			CHI	A (1G 0-1)		WAS	A (9G 1-3)												
" total	1	4	.200	5.36	10	6	3	47	71	6	11	0	0	0	0	22	1	0	.045
1912 WAS A	0	1	.000	13.50	1	0	0	1.1	1	2	0	0	0	1	0	1	0	0	.000
1913	0	0	–	4.82	4	0	0	9.1	7	4	2	0	0	0	0	1	0	0	.000
1914	0	0	–	0.00	1	0	0	1	3	0	0	0	0	0	0	0	0	0	–
1915	0	0	–	9.00	1	0	0	3	7	1	2	0	0	0	1	1	0	0	.000
1918	1	2	.333	2.96	5	3	1	24.1	24	6	5	0	0	0	0	8	1	1	.125
1919	0	0	–	∞	1	0	0		4	0	0	0	0	0	0	0	0	0	–
1924	0	0	–	0.00	1	0	0	2	4	0	0	0	0	0	0	1	1	1	1.000
1929	0	0	–	0.00	1	0	0		0	0	0	0	0	0	0	1	1	0	1.000
1931	0	0	–	0.00	0	0	0		0	0	0	0	0	0	0	1	0	0	–
1933	0	0	–	0.00	0	0	0		0	0	0	0	0	0	0	1	0	0	.000
19 yrs.	82	75	.522	2.67	218	161	128	1515	1455	272	425	16	10	4	7	552	97	2	.176

	W	L	PCT	ERA	G	GS	CG	IP	H	BB	SO	ShO	Relief Pitching W	L	SV	BATTING AB	H	HR	BA

Nick Altrock continued

WORLD SERIES

	W	L	PCT	ERA	G	GS	CG	IP	H	BB	SO	ShO	W	L	SV	AB	H	HR	BA
1906 CHI A	1	1	.500	1.00	2	2	2	18	11	2	5	0	0	0	0	4	1	0	.250

Jose Alvarez

ALVAREZ, JOSE LINO   BR TR 5'11" 175 lbs.
B. Apr. 12, 1956, Tampa, Fla.

	W	L	PCT	ERA	G	GS	CG	IP	H	BB	SO	ShO	W	L	SV	AB	H	HR	BA
1981 ATL N	0	0	–	0.00	1	0	0	2	0	0	2	0	0	0	0	0	0	0	–
1982	0	0	–	4.70	7	0	0	7.2	8	2	6	0	0	0	0	0	0	0	–
2 yrs.	0	0	–	3.72	8	0	0	9.2	8	2	8	0	0	0	0	0	0	0	–

Red Ames

AMES, LEON KESSLING   BB TR 5'10½" 185 lbs.
B. Aug. 2, 1882, Warren, Ohio   D. Oct. 8, 1936, Warren, Ohio

	W	L	PCT	ERA	G	GS	CG	IP	H	BB	SO	ShO	W	L	SV	AB	H	HR	BA
1903 NY N	2	0	1.000	1.29	2	2	2	14	5	8	14	1	0	0	0	6	0	0	.000
1904	4	6	.400	2.27	16	13	11	115	94	38	93	1	0	0	3	40	5	0	.125
1905	22	8	.733	2.74	34	31	21	263	220	105	198	2	1	0	0	97	14	0	.144
1906	12	10	.545	2.66	31	25	15	203.1	166	93	156	1	1	0	1	61	4	0	.066
1907	10	12	.455	2.16	39	26	17	233.1	184	108	146	2	0	3	1	69	12	1	.174
1908	7	4	.636	1.81	18	15	5	114.1	96	27	81	0	1	0	0	36	7	0	.194
1909	15	10	.600	2.70	34	26	20	240	214	81	156	2	1	0	0	81	6	0	.074
1910	12	11	.522	2.22	33	23	13	190.1	161	63	94	3	0	3	0	62	11	1	.177
1911	11	10	.524	2.68	34	23	13	205	170	54	118	1	2	1	1	64	6	0	.094
1912	11	5	.688	2.46	33	22	9	179	194	35	83	2	1	0	2	58	13	0	.224
1913 2 teams			NY	N (8G 2–1)			CIN	N (31G 11–13)											
" total	13	14	.481	2.78	39	29	14	227	220	78	110	1	2	1	3	72	8	0	.111
1914 CIN N	15	23	.395	2.64	47	36	18	297	274	94	118	4	1	4	6	94	12	1	.128
1915 2 teams			CIN	N (17G 2–4)			STL	N (15G 9–3)											
" total	11	7	.611	3.23	32	21	12	181.1	175	56	74	3	0	0	2	55	5	0	.091
1916 STL N	11	16	.407	2.64	45	22	10	228	225	57	98	2	4	5	7	68	12	0	.176
1917	15	10	.600	2.71	43	19	10	209	189	57	62	2	8	2	3	64	12	0	.188
1918	9	14	.391	2.31	27	25	17	206.2	192	52	68	0	0	0	1	64	10	0	.156
1919 2 teams			STL	N (23G 3–5)			PHI	N (3G 0–2)											
" total	3	7	.300	5.13	26	9	2	86	114	28	23	0	2	0	2	23	6	0	.261
17 yrs.	183	167	.523	2.63	533	367	209	3192.1	2893	1034	1702	27	24	19	33	1014	143	3	.141

WORLD SERIES

	W	L	PCT	ERA	G	GS	CG	IP	H	BB	SO	ShO	W	L	SV	AB	H	HR	BA
1905 NY N	0	0	–	0.00	1	0	0	1	1	1	1	0	0	0	0	0	0	0	–
1911	0	1	.000	2.25	2	1	0	8	6	1	6	0	0	0	0	2	1	0	.500
1912	0	0	–	4.50	1	0	0	2	3	1	0	0	0	0	0	0	0	0	–
3 yrs.	0	1	.000	2.45	4	1	0	11	10	3	7	0	0	0	0	2	1	0	.500

Doc Amole

AMOLE, MORRIS GEORGE   TL 5'9" 165 lbs.
B. July 5, 1878, Coatesville, Pa.   D. Mar. 7, 1912, Wilmington, Del.

	W	L	PCT	ERA	G	GS	CG	IP	H	BB	SO	ShO	W	L	SV	AB	H	HR	BA
1897 BAL N	4	4	.500	2.57	11	7	6	70	67	17	19	0	1	0	0	28	3	0	.107
1898 WAS N	0	6	.000	7.84	7	5	4	49.1	83	22	11	0	0	1	0	20	2	0	.100
2 yrs.	4	10	.286	4.75	18	12	10	119.1	150	39	30	0	1	1	0	48	5	0	.104

Vincente Amor

AMOR, VINCENTE ALVAREZ   BR TR 6'3" 182 lbs.
B. Aug. 8, 1932, Havana, Cuba

	W	L	PCT	ERA	G	GS	CG	IP	H	BB	SO	ShO	W	L	SV	AB	H	HR	BA
1955 CHI N	0	1	.000	4.50	4	0	0	6	11	3	3	0	0	1	0	0	0	0	–
1957 CIN N	1	2	.333	5.93	9	4	1	27.1	39	10	9	0	0	1	0	6	1	0	.167
2 yrs.	1	3	.250	5.67	13	4	1	33.1	50	13	12	0	0	2	0	6	1	0	.167

Walter Ancker

ANCKER, WALTER (Gee, Liver)   BR TR 6'1" 190 lbs.
B. Apr. 10, 1894, New York, N. Y.   D. Feb. 13, 1954, Englewood, N. J.

	W	L	PCT	ERA	G	GS	CG	IP	H	BB	SO	ShO	W	L	SV	AB	H	HR	BA
1915 PHI A	0	0	–	3.57	4	1	0	17.2	19	17	4	0	0	0	0	6	0	0	.000

Larry Andersen

ANDERSEN, LARRY EUGENE   BR TR 6'3" 200 lbs.
B. May 6, 1953, Portland, Ore.

	W	L	PCT	ERA	G	GS	CG	IP	H	BB	SO	ShO	W	L	SV	AB	H	HR	BA
1975 CLE A	0	0	–	4.76	3	0	0	5.2	4	2	4	0	0	0	0	0	0	0	–
1977	0	1	.000	3.21	11	0	0	14	10	9	8	0	0	1	0	0	0	0	–
1979	0	0	–	7.41	8	0	0	17	25	4	7	0	0	0	0	0	0	0	–
1981 SEA A	3	3	.500	2.65	41	0	0	68	57	18	40	0	3	3	5	0	0	0	–
1982	0	0	–	5.99	40	1	0	79.2	100	23	32	0	0	0	1	0	0	0	–
1983 PHI N	1	0	1.000	2.39	17	0	0	26.1	19	9	14	0	1	0	0	2	0	0	.000
1984	3	7	.300	2.38	64	0	0	90.2	85	25	54	0	3	7	4	4	0	0	.000
7 yrs.	7	11	.389	3.76	184	1	0	301.1	300	90	159	0	7	10	10	6	0	0	.000

WORLD SERIES

	W	L	PCT	ERA	G	GS	CG	IP	H	BB	SO	ShO	W	L	SV	AB	H	HR	BA
1983 PHI N	0	0	–	2.25	2	0	0	4	4	0	1	0	0	0	0	0	0	0	–

Bill Anderson

ANDERSON, WILLIAM
B. Taylorsville, Ky.   Deceased.

	W	L	PCT	ERA	G	GS	CG	IP	H	BB	SO	ShO	W	L	SV	AB	H	HR	BA
1889 LOU AA	0	1	.000	10.13	1	1	1	8	10	6	2	0	0	0	0	3	1	0	.333

Bill Anderson

ANDERSON, WILLIAM EDWARD (Lefty)   BR TL 6'1" 165 lbs.
B. Dec. 3, 1895, Boston, Mass.

	W	L	PCT	ERA	G	GS	CG	IP	H	BB	SO	ShO	W	L	SV	AB	H	HR	BA
1925 BOS N	0	0	–	10.13	2	0	0	2.2	5	2	1	0	0	0	0	1	0	0	.000

Bob Anderson

ANDERSON, ROBERT CARL   BR TR 6'4½" 210 lbs.
B. Sept. 29, 1935, East Chicago, Ind.

	W	L	PCT	ERA	G	GS	CG	IP	H	BB	SO	ShO	W	L	SV	AB	H	HR	BA
1957 CHI N	0	1	.000	7.71	8	0	0	16.1	20	8	7	0	0	1	0	4	0	0	.000
1958	3	3	.500	3.97	17	8	2	65.2	61	29	51	0	0	0	0	17	2	0	.118
1959	12	13	.480	4.13	37	36	7	235.1	245	77	113	1	0	0	0	80	6	0	.075
1960	9	11	.450	4.11	38	30	5	203.2	201	68	115	0	0	1	1	71	12	0	.169
1961	7	10	.412	4.26	57	12	1	152	162	56	96	0	4	3	8	42	6	2	.143
1962	2	7	.222	5.02	57	4	0	107.2	111	60	82	0	1	6	4	23	3	0	.130

	W	L	PCT	ERA	G	GS	CG	IP	H	BB	SO	ShO	Relief Pitching W	L	SV	BATTING AB	H	HR	BA

Bob Anderson continued

	W	L	PCT	ERA	G	GS	CG	IP	H	BB	SO	ShO	W	L	SV	AB	H	HR	BA
1963 DET A	3	1	.750	3.30	32	3	0	60	58	21	38	0	2	0	0	9	4	0	.444
7 yrs.	36	46	.439	4.26	246	93	15	840.2	858	319	502	1	7	11	13	246	33	2	.134

Bud Anderson

ANDERSON, KARL ADAM
B. May 27, 1956, Westbury, N. Y.　　BR TR 6'3" 210 lbs.

	W	L	PCT	ERA	G	GS	CG	IP	H	BB	SO	ShO	W	L	SV	AB	H	HR	BA
1982 CLE A	3	4	.429	3.35	25	5	1	80.2	84	30	44	0	2	1	0	0	0	0	—
1983	1	6	.143	4.08	39	1	0	68.1	64	32	32	0	1	5	7	0	0	0	—
2 yrs.	4	10	.286	3.68	64	6	1	149	148	62	76	0	3	6	7	0	0	0	—

Craig Anderson

ANDERSON, NORMAN CRAIG
B. July 1, 1938, Washington, D. C.　　BR TR 6'2" 205 lbs.

	W	L	PCT	ERA	G	GS	CG	IP	H	BB	SO	ShO	W	L	SV	AB	H	HR	BA
1961 STL N	4	3	.571	3.26	25	0	0	38.2	38	12	21	0	4	3	1	9	3	0	.333
1962 NY N	3	17	.150	5.35	50	14	2	131.1	150	63	62	0	3	6	4	32	3	0	.094
1963	0	2	.000	8.68	3	2	0	9.1	17	3	6	0	0	0	0	3	1	0	.333
1964	0	1	.000	5.54	4	1	0	13	21	3	5	0	0	0	0	3	0	0	.000
4 yrs.	7	23	.233	5.10	82	17	2	192.1	226	81	94	0	7	9	5	47	7	0	.149

Dave Anderson

ANDERSON, DAVID S
B. Oct. 10, 1868, Chester, Pa.　D. Mar. 22, 1897, Chester, Pa.　　TL

	W	L	PCT	ERA	G	GS	CG	IP	H	BB	SO	ShO	W	L	SV	AB	H	HR	BA
1889 PHI N	0	1	.000	7.43	5	2	1	23	30	14	8	0	0	0	0	11	2	0	.182
1890 2 teams				PHI N (3G 1–1)		PIT N (13G 2–11)													
" total	3	12	.200	5.09	16	15	14	127.1	147	60	48	0	0	0	0	51	4	0	.078
2 yrs.	3	13	.188	5.45	21	17	15	150.1	177	74	56	0	0	0	0	62	6	0	.097

Fred Anderson

ANDERSON, JOHN FRED (Spitball)
B. Dec. 11, 1885, Calahan, N. C.　D. Nov. 8, 1957, Winston-Salem, N. C.　　BR TR 6'2" 180 lbs.

	W	L	PCT	ERA	G	GS	CG	IP	H	BB	SO	ShO	W	L	SV	AB	H	HR	BA
1909 BOS A	0	0	—	1.13	1	1	0	8	3	1	5	0	0	0	0	3	0	0	.000
1913	0	6	.000	5.97	10	8	4	57.1	84	21	32	0	0	0	0	20	1	0	.050
1914 BUF F	13	16	.448	3.08	37	28	21	260.1	243	64	144	2	1	2	0	90	17	0	.189
1915	19	13	.594	2.51	36	28	14	240	192	72	142	5	4	0	0	80	12	0	.150
1916 NY N	9	13	.409	3.40	38	27	13	188	206	38	98	2	0	1	2	58	8	0	.138
1917	8	8	.500	1.44	38	18	8	162	122	34	69	1	2	1	3	42	3	0	.071
1918	4	2	.667	2.67	18	4	2	70.2	62	17	24	1	2	1	3	19	0	0	.000
7 yrs.	53	58	.477	2.86	178	114	62	986.1	912	247	514	11	9	5	8	312	41	0	.131

WORLD SERIES

	W	L	PCT	ERA	G	GS	CG	IP	H	BB	SO	ShO	W	L	SV	AB	H	HR	BA
1917 NY N	0	1	.000	18.00	1	0	0	2	5	0	3	0	0	1	0	0	0	0	—

John Anderson

ANDERSON, JOHN CHARLES
B. Nov. 23, 1932, St. Paul, Minn.　　BR TR 6'1" 190 lbs.

	W	L	PCT	ERA	G	GS	CG	IP	H	BB	SO	ShO	W	L	SV	AB	H	HR	BA
1958 PHI N	0	0	—	7.88	5	1	0	16	26	4	9	0	0	0	0	3	0	0	.000
1960 BAL A	0	0	—	13.50	4	0	0	4.2	8	4	1	0	0	0	0	0	0	0	—
1962 2 teams				STL N (5G 0–0)		HOU N (10G 0–0)													
" total	0	0	—	4.13	15	0	0	24	30	6	9	0	0	0	1	2	0	0	.000
3 yrs.	0	0	—	6.45	24	1	0	44.2	64	14	19	0	0	0	1	5	0	0	.000

Larry Anderson

ANDERSON, LAWRENCE DENNIS
B. Dec. 3, 1952, Pico Rivera, Calif.　　BR TR 6'3" 190 lbs.

	W	L	PCT	ERA	G	GS	CG	IP	H	BB	SO	ShO	W	L	SV	AB	H	HR	BA
1974 MIL A	0	0	—	0.00	2	0	0	2	2	1	3	0	0	0	0	0	0	0	—
1975	1	0	1.000	5.04	8	1	1	30.1	36	6	13	1	0	0	0	0	0	0	—
1977 CHI A	1	3	.250	9.00	6	0	0	9	10	15	7	0	1	3	0	0	0	0	—
3 yrs.	2	3	.400	5.66	16	1	1	41.1	48	22	23	1	1	3	0	0	0	0	—

Mike Anderson

ANDERSON, MICHAEL ALLEN
B. June 22, 1951, Florence, S. C.　　BR TR 6'2" 200 lbs.

	W	L	PCT	ERA	G	GS	CG	IP	H	BB	SO	ShO	W	L	SV	AB	H	HR	BA
1979 PHI N	0	0	—	0.00	1	0	0	1	2	0	2	0	0	0	0	*			

Red Anderson

ANDERSON, ARNOLD REVOLA
B. June 19, 1912, Lawton, Iowa　D. Aug. 7, 1972, Sioux City, Iowa　　BR TR 6'3" 210 lbs.

	W	L	PCT	ERA	G	GS	CG	IP	H	BB	SO	ShO	W	L	SV	AB	H	HR	BA
1937 WAS A	0	1	.000	6.75	2	1	0	10.2	11	11	3	0	0	0	0	3	0	0	.000
1940	1	1	.500	3.86	2	2	2	14	12	5	3	0	0	0	0	5	3	0	.600
1941	4	6	.400	4.18	32	6	1	112	127	53	34	0	2	3	0	31	8	0	.258
3 yrs.	5	8	.385	4.35	36	9	3	136.2	150	69	40	0	2	3	0	39	11	0	.282

Rick Anderson

ANDERSON, RICHARD LEE
B. Dec. 25, 1953, Inglewood, Calif.　　BR TR 6'2" 210 lbs.

	W	L	PCT	ERA	G	GS	CG	IP	H	BB	SO	ShO	W	L	SV	AB	H	HR	BA
1979 NY A	0	0	—	4.50	1	0	0	2	1	4	0	0	0	0	0	0	0	0	—
1980 SEA A	0	0	—	3.60	5	2	0	10	8	10	7	0	0	0	0	0	0	0	—
2 yrs.	0	0	—	3.75	6	2	0	12	9	14	7	0	0	0	0	0	0	0	—

Varney Anderson

ANDERSON, VARNEY SAMUEL
B. June 18, 1866, Geneva, Ill.　D. Nov. 5, 1941, Rockford, Ill.　　5'10" 165 lbs.

	W	L	PCT	ERA	G	GS	CG	IP	H	BB	SO	ShO	W	L	SV	AB	H	HR	BA
1889 IND N	0	1	.000	4.50	2	1	1	12	13	9	3	0	0	0	0	5	0	0	.000
1894 WAS N	0	2	.000	7.07	2	2	2	14	15	6	3	0	0	0	0	7	3	0	.429
1895	9	16	.360	5.89	29	25	18	204.2	288	97	35	0	0	0	0	97	28	0	.289
1896	0	1	.000	13.00	2	2	1	9	23	3	0	0	0	0	0	5	3	0	.600
4 yrs.	9	20	.310	6.16	35	30	22	239.2	339	115	41	0	0	0	0	114	34	0	.298

Walter Anderson

ANDERSON, WALTER CARL (Lefty)
B. Sept. 25, 1897, Grand Rapids, Mich.　　BL TL 6'2" 160 lbs.

	W	L	PCT	ERA	G	GS	CG	IP	H	BB	SO	ShO	W	L	SV	AB	H	HR	BA
1917 PHI A	0	0	—	3.03	14	2	0	38.2	32	21	10	0	0	0	0	7	3	0	.429
1919	1	0	1.000	3.86	3	0	0	14	13	8	10	0	1	0	0	4	0	0	.000
2 yrs.	1	0	1.000	3.25	17	2	0	52.2	45	29	20	0	1	0	0	11	3	0	.273

	W	L	PCT	ERA	G	GS	CG	IP	H	BB	SO	ShO	Relief Pitching W	L	SV	AB	H	HR	BA

Wingo Anderson

ANDERSON, WINGO CHARLIE BR TL 5'10½" 150 lbs.
B. Aug. 13, 1886, Alvarado, Tex.   D. Dec. 19, 1950, Fort Worth, Tex.

	W	L	PCT	ERA	G	GS	CG	IP	H	BB	SO	ShO	W	L	SV	AB	H	HR	BA
1910 CIN N	0	0	–	4.67	7	2	0	17.1	16	17	11	0	0	0	0	5	1	0	.200

John Andre

ANDRE, JOHN EDWARD (Long John) BL TR 6'4" 200 lbs.
B. Jan. 3, 1923, Brockton, Mass.   D. Nov. 25, 1976, Centerville, Mass.

	W	L	PCT	ERA	G	GS	CG	IP	H	BB	SO	ShO	W	L	SV	AB	H	HR	BA
1955 CHI N	0	1	.000	5.80	22	3	0	45	45	28	19	0	0	1	1	9	1	0	.111

Elbert Andrews

ANDREWS, ELBERT DeVORE BL TR 6' 175 lbs.
B. Dec. 11, 1901, Greenwood, S. C.   D. Nov. 25, 1979, Greenwood, S. C.

	W	L	PCT	ERA	G	GS	CG	IP	H	BB	SO	ShO	W	L	SV	AB	H	HR	BA
1925 PHI A	0	0	–	10.13	6	0	0	8	12	11	0	0	0	0	0	0	0	0	–

Hub Andrews

ANDREWS, HUBERT CARL (Tuny) BR TR 6' 170 lbs.
B. Aug. 31, 1922, Burbank, Okla.

	W	L	PCT	ERA	G	GS	CG	IP	H	BB	SO	ShO	W	L	SV	AB	H	HR	BA
1947 NY N	0	0	–	6.23	7	0	0	8.2	14	4	2	0	0	0	0	0	0	0	–
1948	0	0	–	0.00	1	0	0	3	3	0	0	0	0	0	0	0	0	0	–
2 yrs.	0	0	–	4.63	8	0	0	11.2	17	4	2	0	0	0	0	0	0	0	–

Ivy Andrews

ANDREWS, IVY PAUL (Poison) BR TR 6'1" 200 lbs.
B. May 6, 1907, Dora, Ala.   D. Nov. 23, 1970, Dora, Ala.

	W	L	PCT	ERA	G	GS	CG	IP	H	BB	SO	ShO	W	L	SV	AB	H	HR	BA
1931 NY A	2	0	1.000	4.19	7	3	1	34.1	36	8	10	0	1	0	0	11	2	0	.182
1932 2 teams			NY	A	(4G 2–1)	BOS	A	(25G 8–6)											
" total	10	7	.588	3.52	29	20	9	166.1	164	62	37	0	2	1	0	60	9	0	.150
1933 BOS A	7	13	.350	4.95	34	17	5	140	157	61	37	0	3	2	1	42	9	0	.214
1934 STL A	4	11	.267	4.66	43	13	2	139	166	65	51	0	2	4	3	40	14	0	.350
1935	13	7	.650	3.54	50	20	10	213.1	231	53	43	0	3	2	1	68	9	0	.132
1936	7	12	.368	4.84	36	25	11	191.1	221	50	33	0	0	0	1	59	10	0	.169
1937 2 teams			CLE	A	(20G 3–4)	NY	A	(11G 3–2)											
" total	6	6	.500	3.81	31	9	4	108.2	125	26	33	2	3	2	1	27	4	0	.148
1938 NY A	1	3	.250	3.00	19	1	1	48	51	17	13	0	1	2	1	12	2	0	.167
8 yrs.	50	59	.459	4.14	249	108	43	1041	1151	342	257	2	15	13	8	319	59	0	.185

WORLD SERIES

	W	L	PCT	ERA	G	GS	CG	IP	H	BB	SO	ShO	W	L	SV	AB	H	HR	BA
1937 NY A	0	0	–	3.18	1	0	0	5.2	6	4	1	0	0	0	0	2	0	0	.000

John Andrews

ANDREWS, JOHN RICHARD BL TL 5'10" 175 lbs.
B. Feb. 9, 1949, Monterey Park, Calif.

	W	L	PCT	ERA	G	GS	CG	IP	H	BB	SO	ShO	W	L	SV	AB	H	HR	BA
1973 STL N	1	1	.500	4.42	16	0	0	18.1	16	11	5	0	1	1	0	2	1	0	.500

Nate Andrews

ANDREWS, NATHAN HARDY BR TR 6' 195 lbs.
B. Sept. 30, 1913, Pembroke, N. C.

	W	L	PCT	ERA	G	GS	CG	IP	H	BB	SO	ShO	W	L	SV	AB	H	HR	BA
1937 STL N	0	0	–	4.00	4	1	0	9	12	3	6	0	0	0	0	0	0	0	–
1939	1	2	.333	6.75	11	1	0	16	24	12	6	0	1	1	0	2	0	0	.000
1940 CLE A	0	1	.000	6.00	6	0	0	12	16	6	3	0	0	1	0	0	0	0	–
1941	0	0	–	11.57	2	0	0	2.1	3	2	1	0	0	0	0	1	0	0	.000
1943 BOS N	14	20	.412	2.57	36	34	23	283.2	253	75	80	3	0	2	0	90	14	0	.156
1944	16	15	.516	3.22	37	34	16	257.1	263	74	76	3	1	0	2	88	10	0	.114
1945	7	12	.368	4.58	21	19	8	137.2	160	52	26	0	0	1	0	43	9	0	.209
1946 2 teams			CIN	N	(7G 2–4)	NY	N	(3G 1–0)											
" total	3	4	.429	4.39	10	9	4	55.1	67	12	18	0	0	0	0	16	2	0	.125
8 yrs.	41	54	.432	3.46	127	98	51	773.1	798	236	216	6	2	5	2	240	35	0	.146

Fred Andrus

ANDRUS, FREDERICK HOTHAM BR TR 6'2" 185 lbs.
B. Aug. 23, 1850, Washington, Mich.   D. Nov. 10, 1937, Detroit, Mich.

	W	L	PCT	ERA	G	GS	CG	IP	H	BB	SO	ShO	W	L	SV	AB	H	HR	BA
1884 CHI N	1	0	1.000	2.00	1	1	1	9	11	2	2	0	0	0	0	*			

Joaquin Andujar

ANDUJAR, JOAQUIN BR TR 6' 170 lbs.
B. Dec. 21, 1952, San Pedro de Macoris, Dominican Republic

	W	L	PCT	ERA	G	GS	CG	IP	H	BB	SO	ShO	W	L	SV	AB	H	HR	BA
1976 HOU N	9	10	.474	3.61	28	25	9	172	163	75	59	4	0	0	0	57	8	0	.140
1977	11	8	.579	3.68	26	25	4	159	149	64	69	1	0	0	0	53	10	0	.189
1978	5	7	.417	3.41	35	13	2	111	88	58	55	0	2	3	1	23	3	0	.130
1979	12	12	.500	3.43	46	23	8	194	168	88	77	0	3	2	4	57	5	2	.088
1980	3	8	.273	3.91	35	14	0	122	132	43	75	0	0	2	2	29	5	1	.172
1981 2 teams			HOU	N	(9G 2–3)	STL	N	(11G 6–1)											
" total	8	4	.667	4.10	20	11	1	79	85	23	37	0	1	1	0	23	0	0	.000
1982 STL N	15	10	.600	2.47	38	37	9	265.2	237	50	137	5	0	0	0	95	15	0	.158
1983	6	16	.273	4.16	39	34	5	225	215	75	125	2	0	0	1	73	6	0	.082
1984	20	14	.588	3.34	36	36	12	261.1	218	70	147	4	0	0	0	84	11	2	.131
9 yrs.	89	89	.500	3.47	303	218	50	1589	1455	546	781	16	6	8	8	494	63	5	.128

LEAGUE CHAMPIONSHIP SERIES

	W	L	PCT	ERA	G	GS	CG	IP	H	BB	SO	ShO	W	L	SV	AB	H	HR	BA
1980 HOU N	0	0	–	0.00	1	0	0	1	0	1	0	0	0	0	1	0	0	0	–
1982 STL N	1	0	1.000	2.70	1	1	0	6.2	6	2	4	0	0	0	0	1	0	0	.000
2 yrs.	1	0	1.000	2.35	2	1	0	7.2	6	3	4	0	0	0	1	1	0	0	.000

WORLD SERIES

	W	L	PCT	ERA	G	GS	CG	IP	H	BB	SO	ShO	W	L	SV	AB	H	HR	BA
1982 STL N	2	0	1.000	1.35	2	2	0	13.1	10	1	4	0	0	0	0	0	0	0	–

Norm Angelini

ANGELINI, NORMAN STANLEY BL TL 5'11" 175 lbs.
B. Sept. 24, 1947, San Francisco, Calif.

	W	L	PCT	ERA	G	GS	CG	IP	H	BB	SO	ShO	W	L	SV	AB	H	HR	BA
1972 KC A	2	1	.667	2.25	21	0	0	16	13	12	16	0	2	1	2	2	0	0	.000
1973	0	0	–	4.50	7	0	0	4	2	7	3	0	0	0	1	0	0	0	–
2 yrs.	2	1	.667	2.70	28	0	0	20	15	19	19	0	2	1	3	2	0	0	.000

Cap Anson

ANSON, ADRIAN CONSTANTINE (Pop) BR TR 6' 202 lbs.
B. Apr. 17, 1852, Marshalltown, Iowa   D. Apr. 14, 1922, Chicago, Ill.
Manager 1879-98.
Hall of Fame 1939.

	W	L	PCT	ERA	G	GS	CG	IP	H	BB	SO	ShO	W	L	SV	AB	H	HR	BA
1883 CHI N	0	0	–	0.00	2	0	0	3	1	1	0	0	0	0	1	413	127	0	.308

	W	L	PCT	ERA	G	GS	CG	IP	H	BB	SO	ShO	Relief Pitching W	L	SV	BATTING AB	H	HR	BA

Cap Anson continued

	W	L	PCT	ERA	G	GS	CG	IP	H	BB	SO	ShO	W	L	SV	AB	H	HR	BA
1884	0	1	.000	18.00	1	0	0	1	3	1	1	0	0	1	0	475	159	21	.335
2 yrs.	0	1	.000	4.50	3	0	0	4	4	2	1	0	0	1	1	*			

Johnny Antonelli

ANTONELLI, JOHN AUGUST
B. Apr. 12, 1930, Rochester, N. Y.   BL TL 6'1½" 185 lbs.

	W	L	PCT	ERA	G	GS	CG	IP	H	BB	SO	ShO	W	L	SV	AB	H	HR	BA
1948 BOS N	0	0	—	2.25	4	0	0	4	3	2	0	0	0	0	1	0	0	0	—
1949	3	7	.300	3.56	22	10	3	96	99	42	48	1	0	1	0	25	3	0	.120
1950	2	3	.400	5.93	20	6	2	57.2	81	22	33	1	0	0	0	16	2	0	.125
1953 MIL N	12	12	.500	3.18	31	26	11	175.1	167	71	131	2	2	1	1	62	11	0	.177
1954 NY N	21	7	**.750**	**2.30**	39	37	18	258.2	209	94	152	6	0	0	2	98	16	2	.163
1955	14	16	.467	3.33	38	34	14	235.1	206	82	143	2	0	0	1	82	17	4	.207
1956	20	13	.606	2.86	41	36	15	258.1	225	75	145	6	3	0	1	89	14	3	.157
1957	12	18	.400	3.77	40	30	8	212.1	228	67	114	3	3	1	0	72	11	3	.153
1958 SF N	16	13	.552	3.28	41	34	13	241.2	216	87	143	0	1	1	3	84	19	1	.226
1959	19	10	.655	3.10	40	38	17	282	247	76	165	4	0	0	1	101	16	2	.158
1960	6	7	.462	3.77	41	10	1	112.1	106	47	57	1	4	2	11	34	8	0	.235
1961 2 teams			CLE A (11G 0–4)			MIL N (9G 1–0)													
" total	1	4	.200	6.75	20	7	0	58.2	84	21	31	0	1	0	0	16	4	0	.250
12 yrs.	126	110	.534	3.34	377	268	102	1992.1	1870	687	1162	26	14	6	21	679	121	15	.178
WORLD SERIES																			
1954 NY N	1	0	1.000	0.84	2	1	1	10.2	8	7	12	0	0	0	1	3	0	0	.000

Bob Apodaca

APODACA, ROBERT JOHN
B. Jan. 31, 1950, Los Angeles, Calif.   BR TR 5'10" 175 lbs.

	W	L	PCT	ERA	G	GS	CG	IP	H	BB	SO	ShO	W	L	SV	AB	H	HR	BA
1973 NY N	0	0	—	∞	1	0	0		2	0	0	0	0	0	0	0	0	0	—
1974	6	6	.500	3.50	35	8	1	103	92	42	54	0	1	5	3	25	3	0	.120
1975	3	4	.429	1.48	46	0	0	85	66	28	45	0	3	4	13	11	4	0	.364
1976	3	7	.300	2.80	43	3	0	90	71	29	45	0	3	5	5	16	2	0	.125
1977	4	8	.333	3.43	59	0	0	84	83	30	53	0	4	8	5	6	1	0	.167
5 yrs.	16	25	.390	2.86	184	11	1	362	312	131	197	0	11	22	26	58	10	0	.172

Luis Aponte

APONTE, LUIS EDUARDO
Also known as Luis Eduardo Yuripa.
B. June 14, 1954, Lel Tigre, Venezuela   BR TR 6' 180 lbs.

	W	L	PCT	ERA	G	GS	CG	IP	H	BB	SO	ShO	W	L	SV	AB	H	HR	BA
1980 BOS A	0	0	—	1.29	4	0	0	7	6	2	1	0	0	0	0	0	0	0	—
1981	1	0	1.000	0.56	7	0	0	16	11	3	11	0	1	0	1	0	0	0	—
1982	2	2	.500	3.18	40	0	0	85	78	25	44	0	2	2	3	0	0	0	—
1983	5	4	.556	3.63	34	0	0	62	74	23	32	0	5	4	3	0	0	0	—
1984 CLE A	1	0	1.000	4.11	25	0	0	50.1	53	15	25	0	1	0	0	0	0	0	—
5 yrs.	9	6	.600	3.27	110	0	0	220.1	222	68	113	0	9	6	7	0	0	0	—

Fred Applegate

APPLEGATE, FREDERICK ROMAINE (Snitz)
B. May 9, 1879, Bradford, Pa.   D. Apr. 21, 1968, Williamsport, Pa.   BR TR 6'2" 180 lbs.

	W	L	PCT	ERA	G	GS	CG	IP	H	BB	SO	ShO	W	L	SV	AB	H	HR	BA
1904 PHI A	1	2	.333	6.43	3	3	3	21	29	8	12	0	0	0	0	7	2	0	.286

Ed Appleton

APPLETON, EDWARD SAM (Whitey)
B. Feb. 29, 1892, Arlington, Tex.   D. Jan. 27, 1932, Arlington, Tex.   BR TR 6'½" 173 lbs.

	W	L	PCT	ERA	G	GS	CG	IP	H	BB	SO	ShO	W	L	SV	AB	H	HR	BA
1915 BKN N	4	10	.286	3.32	34	10	5	138.1	133	66	50	0	1	4	0	44	7	0	.159
1916	1	2	.333	3.06	14	3	1	47	49	18	14	0	1	0	1	12	2	0	.167
2 yrs.	5	12	.294	3.25	48	13	6	185.1	182	84	64	0	2	4	1	56	9	0	.161

Pete Appleton

APPLETON, PETER WILLIAM
Played as Pete Jablonowski 1927-33.   Also known as Peter William Jablonowski.
B. May 20, 1904, Terryville, Conn.   D. Jan. 18, 1974, Trenton, N. J.   BR TR 5'11" 180 lbs.

	W	L	PCT	ERA	G	GS	CG	IP	H	BB	SO	ShO	W	L	SV	AB	H	HR	BA
1927 CIN N	2	1	.667	1.82	6	2	2	29.2	29	17	3	0	0	0	0	11	6	0	.545
1928	3	4	.429	4.68	31	1	0	82.2	101	22	20	0	3	4	0	31	10	0	.323
1930 CLE A	8	7	.533	4.02	39	7	2	118.2	122	53	45	0	6	5	1	40	8	0	.200
1931	4	4	.500	4.63	29	4	3	79.2	100	29	25	0	1	3	0	24	5	0	.208
1932 2 teams			CLE A (4G 0–0)			BOS A (11G 0–3)													
" total	0	3	.000	5.29	15	3	0	51	60	29	16	0	0	0	0	17	3	0	.176
1933 NY A	0	0	—	0.00	1	0	0	2	3	1	0	0	0	0	0	0	0	0	—
1936 WAS A	14	9	.609	3.53	38	20	12	201.2	199	77	77	1	4	1	3	76	19	0	.250
1937	8	15	.348	4.39	35	18	7	168	167	72	62	4	3	4	2	59	11	0	.186
1938	7	9	.438	4.60	43	10	5	164.1	175	61	62	0	3	4	5	59	15	0	.254
1939	5	10	.333	4.56	40	4	2	102.2	104	48	50	0	4	7	6	25	4	0	.160
1940 CHI A	4	0	1.000	5.62	25	0	0	57.2	54	28	21	0	4	0	5	17	3	0	.176
1941	0	3	.000	5.27	13	0	0	27.1	27	17	12	0	0	3	1	4	1	0	.250
1942 2 teams			CHI A (4G 0–0)			STL A (14G 1–1)													
" total	1	1	.500	3.37	18	0	0	32	27	14	14	0	1	1	2	6	1	0	.167
1945 2 teams			STL A (2G 0–0)			WAS A (6G 1–0)													
" total	1	0	1.000	4.56	8	2	1	23.2	19	18	13	0	0	0	1	5	1	0	.200
14 yrs.	57	66	.463	4.30	341	71	34	1141	1187	486	420	6	29	32	26	374	87	0	.233

Fred Archer

ARCHER, FREDERICK MARVIN (Lefty)
B. Mar. 7, 1912, Johnson City, Tenn.   D. Oct. 31, 1981, Charlotte, N. C.   BL TL 6' 193 lbs.

	W	L	PCT	ERA	G	GS	CG	IP	H	BB	SO	ShO	W	L	SV	AB	H	HR	BA
1936 PHI A	2	3	.400	6.38	6	5	2	36.2	41	15	9	0	0	0	0	15	4	0	.267
1937	0	0	—	6.00	1	0	0	3	4	0	2	0	0	0	0	0	0	0	—
2 yrs.	2	3	.400	6.35	7	5	2	39.2	45	15	11	0	0	0	0	15	4	0	.267

Jim Archer

ARCHER, JAMES WILLIAM
B. May 25, 1932, Max Meadows, Va.   BR TL 6' 190 lbs.

	W	L	PCT	ERA	G	GS	CG	IP	H	BB	SO	ShO	W	L	SV	AB	H	HR	BA
1961 KC A	9	15	.375	3.20	39	27	9	205.1	204	60	110	2	1	1	5	63	4	0	.063
1962	0	1	.000	9.43	18	1	0	27.2	40	10	12	0	0	0	0	1	1	0	1.000
2 yrs.	9	16	.360	3.94	57	28	9	233	244	70	122	2	1	1	5	64	5	0	.078

	W	L	PCT	ERA	G	GS	CG	IP	H	BB	SO	ShO	Relief Pitching W	L	SV	AB	BATTING H	HR	BA

Rugger Ardizoia

ARDIZOIA, RINALDO JOSEPH
B. Nov. 20, 1919, Oleggio, Italy
BR TR 5'11" 180 lbs.

	W	L	PCT	ERA	G	GS	CG	IP	H	BB	SO	ShO	W	L	SV	AB	H	HR	BA
1947 NY A	0	0	—	9.00	1	0	0	2	4	1	0	0	0	0	0	0	0	0	—

Frank Arellanes

ARELLANES, FRANK JULIAN
B. Jan. 28, 1882, Santa Cruz, Calif.   D. Dec. 14, 1918, San Jose, Calif.
BR TR 6' 180 lbs.

	W	L	PCT	ERA	G	GS	CG	IP	H	BB	SO	ShO	W	L	SV	AB	H	HR	BA
1908 BOS A	4	3	.571	1.82	11	8	6	79.1	60	18	33	1	0	0	0	30	5	0	.167
1909	16	12	.571	2.18	45	30	17	230.2	192	43	82	1	3	2	8	78	13	0	.167
1910	4	7	.364	2.88	18	13	2	100	106	24	33	0	1	1	0	34	6	1	.176
3 yrs.	24	22	.522	2.28	74	51	25	410	358	85	148	2	4	3	8	142	24	1	.169

Rudy Arias

ARIAS, RODOLFO MARTINEZ
B. June 6, 1931, Mordoza Las Villas, Cuba
BL TL 5'10" 165 lbs.

	W	L	PCT	ERA	G	GS	CG	IP	H	BB	SO	ShO	W	L	SV	AB	H	HR	BA
1959 CHI A	2	0	1.000	4.09	34	0	0	44	49	20	28	0	2	0	2	4	0	0	.000

Don Arlich

ARLICH, DONALD LOUIS
B. Feb. 15, 1943, Wayne, Mich.
BL TL 6'2" 185 lbs.

	W	L	PCT	ERA	G	GS	CG	IP	H	BB	SO	ShO	W	L	SV	AB	H	HR	BA
1965 HOU N	0	0	—	3.00	1	1	0	6	5	1	0	0	0	0	0	2	0	0	.000
1966	0	1	.000	15.75	7	0	0	4	11	4	1	0	0	1	0	1	0	0	.000
2 yrs.	0	1	.000	8.10	8	1	0	10	16	5	1	0	0	1	0	3	0	0	.000

Steve Arlin

ARLIN, STEPHEN RALPH
B. Sept. 25, 1945, Seattle, Wash.
BR TR 6'3½" 195 lbs.

	W	L	PCT	ERA	G	GS	CG	IP	H	BB	SO	ShO	W	L	SV	AB	H	HR	BA
1969 SD N	0	1	.000	9.00	4	1	0	11	13	9	9	0	0	0	0	2	0	0	.000
1970	1	0	1.000	2.77	2	2	1	13	11	8	3	1	0	0	0	5	0	0	.000
1971	9	19	.321	3.47	36	34	10	228	211	103	156	4	0	0	0	73	9	0	.123
1972	10	21	.323	3.60	38	37	12	250	217	122	159	3	1	0	0	72	11	0	.153
1973	11	14	.440	5.10	34	27	7	180	196	72	98	3	2	1	0	60	10	0	.167
1974 2 teams			SD	N (16G 1–7)			CLE	A	(11G 2–5)											
" total	3	12	.200	6.17	27	22	2	108	144	59	38	0	0	0	0	18	2	0	.111
6 yrs.	34	67	.337	4.32	141	123	32	790	792	373	463	11	3	1	1	230	32	0	.139

Orville Armbrust

ARMBRUST, ORVILLE MARTIN
B. Mar. 2, 1910, Beirne, Ark.   D. Oct. 2, 1967, Mobile, Ala.
BR TR 5'10" 195 lbs.

	W	L	PCT	ERA	G	GS	CG	IP	H	BB	SO	ShO	W	L	SV	AB	H	HR	BA
1934 WAS A	1	0	1.000	2.13	3	2	0	12.2	10	3	3	0	0	0	0	4	0	0	.000

Howard Armstrong

ARMSTRONG, HOWARD ELMER
B. Dec. 2, 1889, East Claridon, Ohio   D. Mar. 8, 1926, Canisteo, N. Y.
BR TR 5'9" 165 lbs.

	W	L	PCT	ERA	G	GS	CG	IP	H	BB	SO	ShO	W	L	SV	AB	H	HR	BA
1911 PHI N	0	1	.000	0.00	1	0	0	3	1	1	0	0	0	1	0	1	0	0	.000

Mike Armstrong

ARMSTRONG, MICHAEL DENNIS
B. Mar. 7, 1954, Glen Cove, N. Y.
BR TR 6'3" 193 lbs.

	W	L	PCT	ERA	G	GS	CG	IP	H	BB	SO	ShO	W	L	SV	AB	H	HR	BA
1980 SD N	0	0	—	5.79	11	0	0	14	16	13	14	0	0	0	0	3	0	0	.000
1981	0	2	.000	6.00	10	0	0	12	14	11	9	0	0	2	0	0	0	0	—
1982 KC A	5	5	.500	3.20	52	0	0	112.2	88	43	75	0	5	5	6	0	0	0	—
1983	10	7	.588	3.86	58	0	0	102.2	86	45	52	0	10	7	3	0	0	0	—
1984 NY A	3	2	.600	3.48	36	0	0	54.1	47	26	43	0	3	2	1	0	0	0	—
5 yrs.	18	16	.529	3.71	167	0	0	295.2	251	138	193	0	18	16	10	3	0	0	.000

Orie Arntzen

ARNTZEN, ORIE EDGAR (Old Folks)
B. Oct. 18, 1909, Beverly, Ill.   D. Jan. 28, 1970, Cedar Rapids, Iowa
BR TR 6'1" 200 lbs.

	W	L	PCT	ERA	G	GS	CG	IP	H	BB	SO	ShO	W	L	SV	AB	H	HR	BA
1943 PHI A	4	13	.235	4.22	32	20	9	164.1	172	69	66	0	0	0	0	50	8	0	.160

Jerry Arrigo

ARRIGO, GERALD WILLIAM
B. June 12, 1941, Chicago, Ill.
BL TL 6'1" 185 lbs.

	W	L	PCT	ERA	G	GS	CG	IP	H	BB	SO	ShO	W	L	SV	AB	H	HR	BA
1961 MIN A	0	1	.000	10.24	7	2	0	9.2	9	10	6	0	0	0	0	2	1	0	.500
1962	0	0	—	18.00	1	0	0	1	3	1	1	0	0	0	0	0	0	0	—
1963	1	2	.333	2.87	5	1	0	15.2	12	4	13	0	1	1	0	4	0	0	.000
1964	7	4	.636	3.84	41	12	2	105.1	97	45	96	1	3	2	1	29	5	0	.172
1965 CIN N	2	4	.333	6.17	27	5	0	54	75	30	43	0	1	2	2	12	2	1	.167
1966 2 teams			CIN	N (3G 0–0)			NY	N	(17G 3–3)											
" total	3	3	.500	3.91	20	5	0	50.2	54	19	31	0	2	0	0	11	5	0	.455
1967 CIN N	6	6	.500	3.16	32	5	1	74	61	35	56	1	4	3	1	19	4	0	.211
1968	12	10	.545	3.33	36	31	5	205.1	181	77	140	1	1	0	0	67	5	0	.075
1969	4	7	.364	4.14	20	16	1	91.1	89	61	35	0	0	0	0	31	5	0	.161
1970 CHI A	0	3	.000	13.15	5	3	0	13	24	9	12	0	0	0	0	4	0	0	.000
10 yrs.	35	40	.467	4.14	194	80	9	620	605	291	433	3	12	8	4	179	27	1	.151

Fernando Arroyo

ARROYO, FERNANDO
B. Mar. 21, 1952, Sacramento, Calif.
BR TR 6'2" 180 lbs.

	W	L	PCT	ERA	G	GS	CG	IP	H	BB	SO	ShO	W	L	SV	AB	H	HR	BA
1975 DET A	2	1	.667	4.56	14	2	1	53.1	56	22	25	0	1	0	0	0	0	0	—
1977	8	18	.308	4.18	38	28	8	209	227	52	60	1	1	2	0	0	0	0	—
1978	0	0	—	8.31	2	0	0	4.1	8	0	1	0	0	0	0	0	0	0	—
1979	1	1	.500	8.25	6	0	0	12	17	4	7	0	1	1	0	0	0	0	—
1980 MIN A	6	6	.500	4.70	21	11	1	92	97	32	27	1	2	0	0	0	0	0	—
1981	7	10	.412	3.94	23	19	2	128	144	34	39	0	0	0	0	0	0	0	—
1982 2 teams			MIN	A (6G 0–1)			OAK	A	(10G 0–0)											
" total	0	1	.000	5.25	16	0	0	36	40	13	13	0	0	1	0	0	0	0	—
7 yrs.	24	37	.393	4.44	120	60	12	534.2	589	157	172	2	5	4	0	0	0	0	—

Luis Arroyo

ARROYO, LUIS ENRIQUE (Yo-Yo)
B. Feb. 18, 1927, Penuelas, Puerto Rico
BL TL 5'8½" 178 lbs.

	W	L	PCT	ERA	G	GS	CG	IP	H	BB	SO	ShO	W	L	SV	AB	H	HR	BA
1955 STL N	11	8	.579	4.19	35	24	9	159	162	63	68	1	1	0	0	56	13	1	.232
1956 PIT N	3	3	.500	4.71	18	2	1	28.2	36	12	17	0	2	2	0	4	2	0	.500
1957	3	11	.214	4.68	54	10	0	130.2	151	31	101	0	3	5	1	32	5	0	.156
1959 CIN N	1	0	1.000	3.95	10	0	0	13.2	17	11	8	0	1	0	0	2	0	0	.000
1960 NY A	5	1	.833	2.88	29	0	0	40.2	30	22	29	0	5	1	7	5	0	0	.000

	W	L	PCT	ERA	G	GS	CG	IP	H	BB	SO	ShO	Relief Pitching W	L	SV	Batting AB	H	HR	BA

Luis Arroyo continued

	W	L	PCT	ERA	G	GS	CG	IP	H	BB	SO	ShO	W	L	SV	AB	H	HR	BA
1961	15	5	.750	2.19	65	0	0	119	83	49	87	0	15	5	29	25	7	0	.280
1962	1	3	.250	4.81	27	0	0	33.2	33	17	21	0	1	3	7	4	2	0	.500
1963	1	1	.500	13.50	6	0	0	6	12	3	5	0	1	1	0	0	0	0	—
8 yrs.	40	32	.556	3.93	244	36	10	531.1	524	208	336	1	29	17	44	128	29	1	.227
WORLD SERIES																			
1960 NY A	0	0	—	13.50	1	0	0	.2	2	0	1	0	0	0	0	1	0	0	.000
1961	1	0	1.000	2.25	2	0	0	4	4	2	3	0	1	0	0	0	0	0	—
2 yrs.	1	0	1.000	3.86	3	0	0	4.2	6	2	4	0	1	0	0	1	0	0	.000

Rudy Arroyo

ARROYO, RUDOLPH JR
B. June 19, 1950, New York, N. Y.   BR TL 6'2"   195 lbs.

	W	L	PCT	ERA	G	GS	CG	IP	H	BB	SO	ShO	W	L	SV	AB	H	HR	BA
1971 STL N	0	1	.000	5.25	9	0	0	12	18	5	5	0	0	1	0	1	0	0	.000

Harry Arundel

ARUNDEL, HARRY
Brother of Tug Arundel.
B. 1855, Philadelphia, Pa.   D. Mar. 25, 1904, Cleveland, Ohio

	W	L	PCT	ERA	G	GS	CG	IP	H	BB	SO	ShO	W	L	SV	AB	H	HR	BA
1882 PIT AA	4	10	.286	4.65	14	14	13	120	155	23	47	0	0	0	0	53	10	0	.189
1884 PRO N	1	0	1.000	1.00	1	1	1	9	8	4	4	0	0	0	0	3	1	0	.333
2 yrs.	5	10	.333	4.40	15	15	14	129	163	27	51	0	0	0	0	56	11	0	.196

Ken Ash

ASH, KENNETH LOWTHER
B. Sept. 16, 1901, Anmoore, W. Va.   D. Nov. 15, 1979, Clarksburg, W. Va.   BR TR 5'11"   165 lbs.

	W	L	PCT	ERA	G	GS	CG	IP	H	BB	SO	ShO	W	L	SV	AB	H	HR	BA
1925 CHI A	0	0	—	9.00	2	0	0	4	7	0	0	0	0	0	0	0	0	0	—
1928 CIN N	3	3	.500	6.50	8	5	2	36	43	13	6	0	1	0	0	14	1	0	.071
1929	1	5	.167	4.83	29	7	2	82	91	30	26	0	1	1	2	21	3	0	.143
1930	2	0	1.000	3.43	16	1	1	39.1	37	16	15	0	1	0	0	11	2	0	.182
4 yrs.	6	8	.429	4.96	55	13	5	161.1	178	59	47	0	3	1	2	46	6	0	.130

Keith Atherton

ATHERTON, KEITH ROWE
B. Feb. 19, 1959, Mathews, Va.   BR TR 6'3"   190 lbs.

	W	L	PCT	ERA	G	GS	CG	IP	H	BB	SO	ShO	W	L	SV	AB	H	HR	BA
1983 OAK A	2	5	.286	2.77	29	0	0	68.1	53	23	40	0	2	5	4	1	0	0	.000
1984	7	6	.538	4.33	57	1	0	104	110	39	58	0	7	6	2	0	0	0	—
2 yrs.	9	11	.450	3.71	86	1	0	172.1	163	62	98	0	9	11	6	1	0	0	.000

Jim Atkins

ATKINS, JAMES CURTIS (Buddy)
B. Mar. 10, 1921, Birmingham, Ala.   BL TR 6'3"   205 lbs.

	W	L	PCT	ERA	G	GS	CG	IP	H	BB	SO	ShO	W	L	SV	AB	H	HR	BA
1950 BOS A	0	0	—	3.86	1	0	0	4.2	4	4	0	0	0	0	0	2	0	0	.000
1952	0	1	.000	3.48	3	1	0	10.1	11	7	2	0	0	0	0	3	2	0	.667
2 yrs.	0	1	.000	3.60	4	1	0	15	15	11	2	0	0	0	0	5	2	0	.400

Tommy Atkins

ATKINS, FRANCIS MONTGOMERY
B. Dec. 9, 1887, Ponca, Neb.   D. May 7, 1956, Cleveland, Ohio   BL TL 5'10½"   165 lbs.

	W	L	PCT	ERA	G	GS	CG	IP	H	BB	SO	ShO	W	L	SV	AB	H	HR	BA
1909 PHI A	0	0	—	4.50	1	1	0	6	6	5	4	0	0	0	0	2	0	0	.000
1910	3	2	.600	2.68	15	3	2	57	53	23	29	0	1	1	2	17	2	0	.118
2 yrs.	3	2	.600	2.86	16	4	2	63	59	28	33	0	1	1	2	19	2	0	.105

Bill Atkinson

ATKINSON, WILLIAM CECIL
Also known as Glenn Atkinson.
B. Oct. 4, 1954, Chatham, Ontario, Canada   BL TR 5'7"   165 lbs.

	W	L	PCT	ERA	G	GS	CG	IP	H	BB	SO	ShO	W	L	SV	AB	H	HR	BA
1976 MON N	0	0	—	0.00	4	0	0	5	3	1	4	0	0	0	0	0	0	0	—
1977	7	2	.778	3.36	55	0	0	83	72	29	56	0	7	2	7	5	1	0	.200
1978	2	2	.500	4.40	29	0	0	45	45	28	32	0	2	2	3	4	2	0	.500
1979	2	0	1.000	1.93	10	0	0	14	9	4	7	0	2	0	1	1	0	0	.000
4 yrs.	11	4	.733	3.43	98	0	0	147	129	62	99	0	11	4	11	10	3	0	.300

Al Atkisson

ATKISSON, ALBERT W.
B. Mar. 9, 1861, Clinton, Ill.   D. June 17, 1952, McNatt, Mo.   5'11½"   165 lbs.

	W	L	PCT	ERA	G	GS	CG	IP	H	BB	SO	ShO	W	L	SV	AB	H	HR	BA
1884 4 teams	PHI	AA (22G 11–11)		C–P	U	(16G 6–10)		BAL	U	(8G 3–5)		U	(0G 0–0)						
" total	20	26	.435	3.36	46	46	44	393.2	373	54	247	2	0	0	0	180	34	0	.189
1886 PHI AA	25	17	.595	3.95	45	45	44	396.2	414	101	154	1	0	0	0	148	18	0	.122
1887	6	8	.429	5.92	15	15	11	124.2	156	54	34	0	0	0	0	59	12	1	.203
3 yrs.	51	51	.500	3.96	106	106	99	915	943	209	435	3	0	0	0	387	64	1	.165

Jerry Augustine

AUGUSTINE, GERALD LEE
B. July 24, 1952, Green Bay, Wis.   BL TL 6'   185 lbs.

	W	L	PCT	ERA	G	GS	CG	IP	H	BB	SO	ShO	W	L	SV	AB	H	HR	BA
1975 MIL A	2	0	1.000	3.04	5	3	1	26.2	26	12	8	0	0	0	0	0	0	0	—
1976	9	12	.429	3.30	39	24	5	171.2	167	56	59	3	1	1	0	0	0	0	—
1977	12	18	.400	4.48	33	33	10	209	222	72	68	1	0	0	0	0	0	0	—
1978	13	12	.520	4.54	35	30	9	188.1	204	61	59	2	1	0	0	0	0	0	—
1979	9	6	.600	3.45	43	2	0	86	95	30	41	0	9	5	5	0	0	0	—
1980	4	3	.571	4.50	39	1	0	70	83	36	22	0	4	2	2	0	0	0	—
1981	2	2	.500	4.28	27	2	0	61	75	18	26	0	1	1	2	0	0	0	—
1982	1	3	.250	5.08	20	2	1	62	63	26	22	0	1	1	0	0	0	0	—
1983	3	3	.500	5.74	34	7	1	64.1	89	25	40	0	1	1	2	0	0	0	—
1984	0	0	—	0.00	4	0	0	5.1	4	0	3	0	0	0	0	0	0	0	—
10 yrs.	55	59	.482	4.23	279	104	27	944.1	1028	340	348	6	18	11	11	0	0	0	—

Eldon Auker

AUKER, ELDON LeROY (Big Six)
B. Sept. 21, 1910, Norcatur, Kans.   BR TR 6'2"   194 lbs.

	W	L	PCT	ERA	G	GS	CG	IP	H	BB	SO	ShO	W	L	SV	AB	H	HR	BA
1933 DET A	3	3	.500	5.24	15	6	2	55	63	25	17	1	0	1	0	17	2	0	.118
1934	15	7	.682	3.42	43	18	10	205	234	56	86	2	6	4	1	74	11	0	.149
1935	18	7	.720	3.83	36	25	13	195	213	61	63	2	3	0	0	74	16	0	.216
1936	13	16	.448	4.89	35	31	14	215.1	263	83	66	2	0	0	0	78	24	0	.308
1937	17	9	.654	3.88	39	32	19	252.2	250	97	73	1	0	1	1	91	18	3	.198
1938	11	10	.524	5.27	27	24	12	160.2	184	56	46	1	0	1	0	57	5	0	.088

	W	L	PCT	ERA	G	GS	CG	IP	H	BB	SO	ShO	Relief Pitching			BATTING			BA
													W	L	SV	AB	H	HR	

Eldon Auker continued

	W	L	PCT	ERA	G	GS	CG	IP	H	BB	SO	ShO	W	L	SV	AB	H	HR	BA
1939 BOS A	9	10	.474	5.36	31	25	6	151	183	61	43	1	1	0	0	53	12	2	.226
1940 STL A	16	11	.593	3.96	38	35	20	263.2	299	96	78	2	0	0	0	89	19	1	.213
1941	14	15	.483	5.50	34	31	13	216	268	85	60	0	1	2	0	80	10	0	.125
1942	14	13	.519	4.08	35	34	17	249	273	86	62	2	0	0	0	87	14	0	.161
10 yrs.	130	101	.563	4.42	333	261	126	1963.1	2230	706	594	14	11	9	2	700	131	6	.187
WORLD SERIES																			
1934 DET A	1	1	.500	5.56	2	2	1	11.1	16	5	2	0	0	0	0	4	0	0	.000
1935	0	0	–	3.00	1	1	0	6	6	2	1	0	0	0	0	2	0	0	.000
2 yrs.	1	1	.500	4.67	3	3	1	17.1	22	7	3	0	0	0	0	6	0	0	.000

Dennis Aust

AUST, DENNIS KAY
B. Nov. 25, 1940, Tecumseh, Neb.

BR TR 5'11" 180 lbs.

	W	L	PCT	ERA	G	GS	CG	IP	H	BB	SO	ShO	W	L	SV	AB	H	HR	BA
1965 STL N	0	0	–	4.91	6	0	0	7.1	6	2	7	0	0	0	1	1	0	0	.000
1966	0	1	.000	6.52	9	0	0	9.2	12	6	7	0	0	1	1	1	0	0	.000
2 yrs.	0	1	.000	5.82	15	0	0	17	18	8	14	0	0	1	2	2	0	0	.000

Rick Austin

AUSTIN, RICK GERALD
B. Oct. 27, 1946, Seattle, Wash.

BR TL 6'4" 190 lbs.

	W	L	PCT	ERA	G	GS	CG	IP	H	BB	SO	ShO	W	L	SV	AB	H	HR	BA
1970 CLE A	2	5	.286	4.76	31	8	1	68	74	26	53	1	1	1	3	18	2	0	.111
1971	0	0	–	5.09	23	0	0	23	25	20	20	0	0	0	1	1	0	0	.000
1975 MIL A	2	3	.400	4.05	32	0	0	40	32	32	30	0	2	3	2	0	0	0	–
1976	0	0	–	5.06	3	0	0	5.1	10	0	3	0	0	0	0	0	0	0	–
4 yrs.	4	8	.333	4.62	89	8	1	136.1	141	78	106	1	3	4	6	19	2	0	.105

Al Autry

AUTRY, ALBERT JR.
B. Feb. 29, 1952, Modesto, Calif.

BR TR 6'5" 225 lbs.

	W	L	PCT	ERA	G	GS	CG	IP	H	BB	SO	ShO	W	L	SV	AB	H	HR	BA
1976 ATL N	1	0	1.000	5.40	1	1	0	5	4	3	3	0	0	0	0	2	0	0	.000

Jim Avrea

AVREA, JAMES EPHERIUM (Jay)
B. July 6, 1920, Cleburne, Tex.

BR TR 6'1½" 175 lbs.

	W	L	PCT	ERA	G	GS	CG	IP	H	BB	SO	ShO	W	L	SV	AB	H	HR	BA
1950 CIN N	0	0	–	3.38	2	0	0	5.1	6	3	2	0	0	0	0	2	0	0	.000

Jake Aydelott

AYDELOTT, JACOB STUART
B. July 6, 1861, North Manchester, Ind.   D. Oct. 22, 1926, Detroit, Mich.

6'   180 lbs.

	W	L	PCT	ERA	G	GS	CG	IP	H	BB	SO	ShO	W	L	SV	AB	H	HR	BA
1884 IND AA	5	7	.417	4.92	12	12	11	106	129	29	30	0	0	0	0	44	5	0	.114
1886 PHI AA	0	2	.000	4.00	2	2	2	18	21	12	5	0	0	0	0	6	0	0	.000
2 yrs.	5	9	.357	4.79	14	14	13	124	150	41	35	0	0	0	0	50	5	0	.100

Doc Ayers

AYERS, YANCY WYATT
B. May 20, 1890, Fancy Gap, Va.   D. May 26, 1968, Draper, Va.

BR TR

	W	L	PCT	ERA	G	GS	CG	IP	H	BB	SO	ShO	W	L	SV	AB	H	HR	BA
1913 WAS A	1	1	.500	1.53	4	2	1	17.2	12	4	17	1	0	0	1	7	0	0	.000
1914	12	15	.444	2.54	49	31	8	265.1	221	54	148	3	3	2	3	83	14	0	.169
1915	14	9	.609	2.21	40	16	8	211.1	178	38	96	2	5	4	3	63	12	0	.190
1916	5	9	.357	3.78	43	17	7	157	173	52	69	0	0	2	2	43	6	0	.140
1917	11	10	.524	2.17	40	15	12	207.2	192	59	78	3	5	4	1	63	13	0	.206
1918	10	12	.455	2.83	39	24	11	219.2	215	63	67	4	3	2	3	66	10	0	.152
1919 2 teams					WAS	A (11G 1–6)		DET	A	(24G 5–3)									
" total	6	9	.400	2.75	35	10	3	137.1	140	45	44	1	4	3	0	36	8	0	.222
1920 DET A	7	14	.333	3.88	46	22	9	208.2	217	62	103	3	0	2	1	59	9	0	.153
1921	0	0	–	9.00	2	1	0	4	9	2	0	0	0	0	0	0	0	0	–
9 yrs.	66	79	.455	2.84	298	138	59	1428.2	1357	379	622	17	20	19	14	420	72	0	.171

Bill Ayres

AYRES, WILLIAM OSCAR
B. Sept. 27, 1919, Newnan, Ga.   D. Sept. 24, 1980, Newnan, Ga.

BR TR 6'3" 185 lbs.

	W	L	PCT	ERA	G	GS	CG	IP	H	BB	SO	ShO	W	L	SV	AB	H	HR	BA
1947 NY N	0	3	.000	8.15	13	4	0	35.1	46	14	22	0	0	0	1	8	2	0	.250

Bob Babcock

BABCOCK, ROBERT ERNEST
B. Aug. 25, 1949, New Castle, Pa.

BR TR 6'5" 210 lbs.

	W	L	PCT	ERA	G	GS	CG	IP	H	BB	SO	ShO	W	L	SV	AB	H	HR	BA
1979 TEX A	0	0	–	10.80	4	0	0	5	7	7	6	0	0	0	0	0	0	0	–
1980	1	2	.333	4.70	19	0	0	23	20	8	15	0	1	2	0	0	0	0	–
1981	1	1	.500	2.17	16	0	0	29	21	16	18	0	1	1	0	0	0	0	–
3 yrs.	2	3	.400	3.95	39	0	0	57	48	31	39	0	2	3	0	0	0	0	–

Johnny Babich

BABICH, JOHN CHARLES
B. May 14, 1913, Albion, Calif.

BR TR 6'1½" 185 lbs.

	W	L	PCT	ERA	G	GS	CG	IP	H	BB	SO	ShO	W	L	SV	AB	H	HR	BA
1934 BKN N	7	11	.389	4.20	25	19	7	135	148	51	62	0	0	2	1	50	7	0	.140
1935	7	14	.333	6.66	37	24	7	143.1	191	52	55	2	0	3	0	49	9	0	.184
1936 BOS N	0	0	–	10.50	3	0	0	6	11	6	1	0	0	0	0	1	0	0	.000
1940 PHI A	14	13	.519	3.73	31	30	16	229.1	222	80	94	1	0	0	0	86	10	0	.116
1941	2	7	.222	6.09	16	14	4	78.1	85	31	19	0	0	1	0	25	10	0	.400
5 yrs.	30	45	.400	4.93	112	87	34	592	657	220	231	3	0	6	1	211	36	0	.171

Les Backman

BACKMAN, LESTER JOHN
B. Mar. 20, 1888, Cleves, Ohio   D. Nov. 8, 1975, Cincinnati, Ohio

BR TR 6'½" 195 lbs.

	W	L	PCT	ERA	G	GS	CG	IP	H	BB	SO	ShO	W	L	SV	AB	H	HR	BA
1909 STL N	3	11	.214	4.14	21	14	8	128.1	146	39	35	0	0	0	0	39	4	0	.103
1910	6	7	.462	3.03	26	11	6	116	117	53	41	0	4	2	1	35	4	0	.114
2 yrs.	9	18	.333	3.61	47	25	14	244.1	263	92	76	0	4	2	1	74	8	0	.108

Eddie Bacon

BACON, EDGAR SUTER
B. Apr. 8, 1895, Frankfort, Ky.   D. Oct. 2, 1963, Frankfort, Ky.

	W	L	PCT	ERA	G	GS	CG	IP	H	BB	SO	ShO	W	L	SV	AB	H	HR	BA
1917 PHI A	0	0	–	6.00	1	0	0	6	5	7	0	0	0	0	0	0	0	0	*	

	W	L	PCT	ERA	G	GS	CG	IP	H	BB	SO	ShO	Relief Pitching W	L	SV	BATTING AB	H	HR	BA

Mike Bacsik

BACSIK, MICHAEL JAMES
B. Apr. 1, 1952, Dallas, Tex. BR TR 6'2" 180 lbs.

	W	L	PCT	ERA	G	GS	CG	IP	H	BB	SO	ShO	W	L	SV	AB	H	HR	BA
1975 TEX A	1	2	.333	3.71	7	3	0	26.2	28	9	13	0	0	0	0	0	0	0	–
1976	3	2	.600	4.25	23	0	0	55	66	26	21	0	3	2	0	0	0	0	–
1977	0	0	–	22.50	2	0	0	2	9	0	1	0	0	0	0	0	0	0	–
1979 MIN A	4	2	.667	4.36	31	0	0	66	61	29	33	0	4	2	0	0	0	0	–
1980	0	0	–	4.30	10	0	0	23	26	11	9	0	0	0	0	0	0	0	–
5 yrs.	8	6	.571	4.43	73	3	0	172.2	190	75	77	0	7	4	0	0	0	0	–

Fred Baczewski

BACZEWSKI, FREDERIC JOHN (Lefty) BL TL 6'2½" 185 lbs.
B. May 15, 1926, St. Paul, Minn. D. Nov. 14, 1976, Culver City, Calif.

	W	L	PCT	ERA	G	GS	CG	IP	H	BB	SO	ShO	W	L	SV	AB	H	HR	BA
1953 2 teams	CHI	N	(9G 0–0)			CIN	N	(24G 11–4)											
" total	11	4	.733	3.64	33	18	10	148.1	145	58	61	1	1	0	1	47	9	1	.191
1954 CIN N	6	6	.500	5.26	29	22	4	130	159	53	43	1	0	0	0	42	3	0	.071
1955	0	0	–	18.00	1	0	0	1	2	0	0	0	0	0	0	0	0	0	–
3 yrs.	17	10	.630	4.45	63	40	14	279.1	306	111	104	2	1	0	1	89	12	1	.135

Loren Bader

BADER, LOREN VERNE (King) BL TR 6' 175 lbs.
B. Apr. 27, 1888, Astoria, Ill. D. June 2, 1973, Leroy, Kans.

	W	L	PCT	ERA	G	GS	CG	IP	H	BB	SO	ShO	W	L	SV	AB	H	HR	BA
1912 NY N	2	0	1.000	0.90	2	1	1	10	9	6	3	0	1	0	0	3	0	0	.000
1917 BOS A	2	0	1.000	2.35	15	1	0	38.1	48	18	14	0	1	0	1	10	3	0	.300
1918	1	3	.250	3.33	5	4	2	27	26	12	10	1	0	0	0	9	1	0	.111
3 yrs.	5	3	.625	2.51	22	6	3	75.1	83	36	27	1	2	0	1	22	4	0	.182

Ed Baecht

BAECHT, EDWARD JOSEPH BR TR 6'3" 195 lbs.
B. May 15, 1907, Paden, Okla. D. Aug. 15, 1957, Grafton, Ill.

	W	L	PCT	ERA	G	GS	CG	IP	H	BB	SO	ShO	W	L	SV	AB	H	HR	BA
1926 PHI N	2	0	1.000	6.11	28	1	1	56	73	28	14	0	1	0	0	14	2	0	.143
1927	0	1	.000	12.00	1	1	0	6	12	2	0	0	0	0	0	2	0	0	.000
1928	1	1	.500	6.00	9	1	0	24	37	9	10	0	1	0	0	7	1	0	.143
1931 CHI N	2	4	.333	3.76	22	6	2	67	64	32	34	0	1	1	0	18	5	0	.278
1932	0	0	–	0.00	1	0	0	1	1	1	0	0	0	0	0	0	0	0	–
1937 STL A	0	0	–	12.79	3	0	0	6.1	13	6	3	0	0	0	0	1	0	0	.000
6 yrs.	5	6	.455	5.56	64	9	3	160.1	200	78	61	0	3	1	0	42	8	0	.190

Jim Bagby

BAGBY, JAMES CHARLES JACOB, SR. (Sarge) BB TR 6' 170 lbs.
Father of Jim Bagby.
B. Oct. 5, 1887, Barnett, Ga. D. July 28, 1954, Marietta, Ga.

	W	L	PCT	ERA	G	GS	CG	IP	H	BB	SO	ShO	W	L	SV	AB	H	HR	BA
1912 CIN N	2	0	1.000	3.12	5	1	0	17.1	17	9	10	0	2	0	0	5	0	0	.000
1916 CLE A	16	16	.500	2.55	48	27	14	278.2	253	67	88	3	5	6	5	90	15	0	.167
1917	23	13	.639	1.96	49	37	26	320.2	277	73	83	8	1	1	7	108	25	0	.231
1918	17	16	.515	2.69	45	31	23	271.1	274	78	57	2	2	2	6	99	21	0	.212
1919	17	11	.607	2.80	35	32	21	241.1	258	44	61	0	0	0	3	89	23	1	.258
1920	31	12	.721	2.89	48	39	30	339.2	338	79	73	3	6	1	0	131	33	1	.252
1921	14	12	.538	4.70	40	26	12	191.2	238	44	37	0	3	2	4	76	15	0	.197
1922	4	4	.500	6.32	25	10	4	98.1	134	39	25	0	1	0	1	42	11	0	.262
1923 PIT N	3	2	.600	5.24	21	6	2	68.2	95	25	16	0	1	1	3	20	1	0	.050
9 yrs.	127	87	.593	3.10	316	209	132	1827.2	1884	458	450	16	21	13	29	660	144	2	.218

WORLD SERIES

	W	L	PCT	ERA	G	GS	CG	IP	H	BB	SO	ShO	W	L	SV	AB	H	HR	BA
1920 CLE A	1	1	.500	1.80	2	2	1	15	20	1	3	0	0	0	0	6	2	1	.333

Jim Bagby

BAGBY, JAMES CHARLES JACOB, JR. BR TR 6'2" 170 lbs.
Son of Jim Bagby.
B. Sept. 8, 1916, Cleveland, Ohio

	W	L	PCT	ERA	G	GS	CG	IP	H	BB	SO	ShO	W	L	SV	AB	H	HR	BA
1938 BOS A	15	11	.577	4.21	43	25	10	198.2	218	90	73	1	4	1	2	67	13	0	.194
1939	5	5	.500	7.09	21	11	3	80	119	36	35	0	2	1	0	34	10	1	.294
1940	10	16	.385	4.73	36	21	6	182.2	217	83	57	1	5	5	2	74	15	0	.203
1941 CLE A	9	15	.375	4.04	33	27	12	200.2	214	76	53	0	0	0	2	74	18	0	.243
1942	17	9	.654	2.96	38	35	16	270.2	267	64	54	4	0	0	1	95	18	1	.189
1943	17	14	.548	3.10	36	33	16	273	248	80	70	3	1	0	0	112	30	0	.268
1944	4	5	.444	4.33	13	10	2	79	101	34	12	0	2	0	0	31	7	1	.226
1945	8	11	.421	3.73	25	19	11	159.1	171	59	38	3	0	1	1	58	17	0	.293
1946 BOS A	7	6	.538	3.71	21	11	6	106.2	117	49	16	1	0	1	0	42	5	0	.119
1947 PIT N	5	4	.556	4.67	37	6	2	115.2	143	37	23	0	2	2	0	32	7	0	.219
10 yrs.	97	96	.503	3.96	303	198	84	1666.1	1815	608	431	13	16	11	9	619	140	3	.226

WORLD SERIES

	W	L	PCT	ERA	G	GS	CG	IP	H	BB	SO	ShO	W	L	SV	AB	H	HR	BA
1946 BOS A	0	0	–	3.00	1	0	0	3	6	1	1	0	0	0	0	1	0	0	.000

Stan Bahnsen

BAHNSEN, STANLEY RAYMOND BR TR 6'2" 185 lbs.
B. Dec. 15, 1944, Council Bluffs, Iowa

	W	L	PCT	ERA	G	GS	CG	IP	H	BB	SO	ShO	W	L	SV	AB	H	HR	BA
1966 NY A	1	1	.500	3.52	4	3	1	23	15	7	16	0	0	0	1	7	1	0	.143
1968	17	12	.586	2.05	37	34	10	267.1	216	68	162	1	0	1	0	81	4	0	.049
1969	9	16	.360	3.83	40	33	5	220.2	222	90	130	2	1	2	1	60	5	0	.083
1970	14	11	.560	3.32	36	35	6	233	227	75	116	2	0	0	0	74	11	0	.149
1971	14	12	.538	3.35	36	34	14	242	221	72	110	3	0	0	0	79	12	0	.152
1972 CHI A	21	16	.568	3.60	43	41	5	252.1	263	73	157	1	0	0	0	92	14	0	.152
1973	18	21	.462	3.57	42	42	14	282.1	290	117	120	4	0	0	0	0	0	0	–
1974	12	15	.444	4.71	38	35	10	216	230	110	102	1	1	1	0	0	0	0	–
1975 2 teams	CHI	A	(12G 4–6)			OAK	A	(21G 6–7)											
" total	10	13	.435	4.36	33	28	4	167.1	166	77	80	0	0	0	0	1	0	0	.000
1976 OAK A	8	7	.533	3.34	35	14	1	143	124	43	82	1	3	2	0	0	0	0	–
1977 2 teams	OAK	A	(11G 1–2)			MON	N	(23G 8–9)											
" total	9	11	.450	5.01	34	24	3	149	166	51	79	1	0	1	0	42	5	0	.119
1978 MON N	1	5	.167	3.84	44	1	0	75	74	31	44	0	1	5	7	11	1	0	.091
1979	3	1	.750	3.16	55	0	0	94	80	42	71	0	3	1	5	14	1	1	.071
1980	7	6	.538	3.07	57	0	0	91	80	33	48	0	7	6	4	9	1	0	.111
1981	2	1	.667	4.96	25	3	0	49	45	24	28	0	1	1	1	9	1	0	.111

	W	L	PCT	ERA	G	GS	CG	IP	H	BB	SO	ShO	Relief Pitching W	L	SV	BATTING AB	H	HR	BA

Stan Bahnsen continued

1982 2 teams		CAL	A	(7G 0–1)		PHI	N	(8G 0–0)											
" total	0	1	.000	2.74	15	0	0	23	21	11	14	0	0	1	0	0	0	0	–
16 yrs.	146	149	.495	3.61	574	327	73	2528	2440	924	1359	16	18	20	20	479	56	1	.117

DIVISIONAL PLAYOFF SERIES

1981 MON N	0	0	–	0.00	1	0	0	1.1	1	1	1	0	0	0	0	0	0	0	–

Ed Bahr

BAHR, EDSON GARFIELD   BR TR 6'1½" 172 lbs.
B. Oct. 16, 1919, Rouleau, Sask., Canada

1946 PIT N	8	6	.571	2.63	27	14	7	136.2	128	52	44	0	0	0	0	45	8	0	.178
1947	3	5	.375	4.59	19	11	1	82.1	82	43	25	0	1	1	0	23	2	0	.087
2 yrs.	11	11	.500	3.37	46	25	8	219	210	95	69	0	1	1	0	68	10	0	.147

Grover Baichley

BAICHLEY, GROVER CLEVELAND   BR TR 5'9½" 165 lbs.
B. Jan. 7, 1890, Toledo, Ill.   D. June 30, 1956, San Jose, Calif.

1914 STL A	0	0	–	5.14	4	0	0	7	9	3	3	0	0	0	0	1	0	0	.000

Bill Bailey

BAILEY, WILLIAM F.   BL TL 5'11" 165 lbs.
B. Apr. 12, 1889, Fort Smith, Ark.   D. Nov. 2, 1926, Austin, Tex.

1907 STL A	4	1	.800	2.42	6	5	3	48.1	39	15	17	0	0	0	0	20	3	0	.150
1908	3	5	.375	3.04	22	12	7	106.2	85	50	42	0	0	0	0	34	3	0	.088
1909	9	10	.474	2.44	32	20	17	199	174	75	114	1	1	0	0	77	22	0	.286
1910	3	18	.143	3.32	34	20	13	192.1	186	97	90	0	3	1	0	63	13	0	.206
1911	0	3	.000	4.55	7	2	2	31.2	42	16	8	0	0	1	0	11	0	0	.000
1912	0	1	.000	9.28	3	2	0	10.2	15	10	2	0	0	0	0	2	1	0	.500
1914 BAL F	6	9	.400	3.08	19	18	10	128.2	106	68	131	1	1	0	0	43	7	0	.163
1915 2 teams		BAL	F	(36G 5–19)		CHI	F	(5G 3–1)											
" total	8	20	.286	4.27	41	28	14	223.2	202	125	122	5	1	4	0	74	17	0	.230
1918 DET A	1	2	.333	5.97	8	4	1	37.2	53	26	13	0	0	0	0	13	1	0	.077
1921 STL N	2	5	.286	4.26	19	6	3	74	95	22	20	1	1	2	0	22	2	0	.091
1922	0	2	.000	5.40	12	0	0	31.2	38	23	11	0	0	2	0	7	2	0	.286
11 yrs.	36	76	.321	3.57	203	117	70	1084.1	1035	527	570	8	7	10	0	366	71	0	.194

Harvey Bailey

BAILEY, HARVEY FRANCIS   TL
B. Nov. 24, 1876, Adrian, Mich.   D. July 10, 1922, Toledo, Ohio

1899 BOS N	6	4	.600	3.95	12	11	8	86.2	83	35	26	0	1	0	0	34	8	0	.235
1900	0	0	–	4.95	4	1	0	20	24	11	9	0	0	0	0	9	2	0	.222
2 yrs.	6	4	.600	4.13	16	12	8	106.2	107	46	35	0	1	0	0	43	10	0	.233

Howard Bailey

BAILEY, HOWARD LEE   BR TL 6' 195 lbs.
B. July 31, 1958, Grand Haven, Mich.

1981 DET A	1	4	.200	7.30	9	5	0	37	45	13	17	0	0	0	0	0	0	0	–
1982	0	0	–	0.00	8	0	0	10	6	2	3	0	0	0	1	0	0	0	–
1983	5	5	.500	4.88	33	3	0	72	69	25	21	0	4	3	0	0	0	0	–
3 yrs.	6	9	.400	5.22	50	8	0	119	120	40	41	0	4	3	1	0	0	0	–

Jim Bailey

BAILEY, JAMES HOPKINS   BB TL 6'2½" 210 lbs.
Brother of Ed Bailey.
B. Dec. 16, 1934, Strawberry Plains, Tenn.

1959 CIN N	0	1	.000	6.17	3	1	0	11.2	17	6	7	0	0	0	0	3	0	0	.000

King Bailey

BAILEY, LEMUEL   BL TL 6' 185 lbs.
B. Cincinnati, Ohio   D. June 2, 1952

1895 CIN N	1	0	1.000	5.63	1	1	1	8	13	0	0	0	0	0	0	4	2	0	.500

Steve Bailey

BAILEY, STEVEN JOHN   BR TR 6'1" 194 lbs.
B. Feb. 12, 1942, Bronx, N. Y.

1967 CLE A	2	5	.286	3.90	32	1	0	64.2	62	42	46	0	2	4	2	10	0	0	.000
1968	0	1	.000	3.60	2	1	0	5	4	2	1	0	0	0	0	0	0	0	–
2 yrs.	2	6	.250	3.88	34	2	0	69.2	66	44	47	0	2	4	2	10	0	0	.000

Sweetbreads Bailey

BAILEY, ABRAHAM LINCOLN   BR TR 6' 184 lbs.
B. Feb. 12, 1895, Joliet, Ill.   D. Sept. 27, 1939, Joliet, Ill.

1919 CHI N	3	5	.375	3.15	21	5	0	71.1	75	20	19	0	3	2	0	18	7	0	.389
1920	1	2	.333	7.12	21	1	0	36.2	38	11	8	0	0	1	0	7	1	0	.143
1921 2 teams		CHI	N	(3G 0–0)		BKN	N	(7G 0–0)											
" total	0	0	–	4.91	10	0	0	29.1	41	9	8	0	0	0	0	5	0	0	.000
3 yrs.	4	7	.364	4.59	52	6	0	137.1	154	40	35	0	3	3	0	30	8	0	.267

Bob Bailor

BAILOR, ROBERT MICHAEL   BR TR 5'11" 170 lbs.
B. July 10, 1951, Connellsville, Pa.

1980 TOR A	0	0	–	9.00	3	0	0	2	4	1	0	0	0	0	0	*			

Loren Bain

BAIN, HERBERT LOREN   BR TR 6' 190 lbs.
B. July 4, 1922, Staples, Minn.

1945 NY N	0	0	–	7.88	3	0	0	8	10	4	1	0	0	0	0	3	1	0	.333

Doug Bair

BAIR, CHARLES DOUGLAS   BR TR 6' 180 lbs.
B. Aug. 22, 1949, Defiance, Ohio

1976 PIT N	0	0	–	5.68	4	0	0	6.1	4	5	4	0	0	0	0	0	0	0	–
1977 OAK A	4	6	.400	3.47	45	0	0	83	78	57	68	0	4	6	8	0	0	0	–
1978 CIN N	7	6	.538	1.98	70	0	0	100	87	38	91	0	7	6	28	14	2	0	.143
1979	11	7	.611	4.31	65	0	0	94	93	51	86	0	11	7	16	8	0	0	.000
1980	3	6	.333	4.24	61	0	0	85	91	39	62	0	3	6	6	2	0	0	.000

	W	L	PCT	ERA	G	GS	CG	IP	H	BB	SO	ShO	W	L	SV	AB	H	HR	BA

Doug Bair continued

	W	L	PCT	ERA	G	GS	CG	IP	H	BB	SO	ShO	W	L	SV	AB	H	HR	BA
1981 2 teams	CIN	N	(24G 2–2)		STL	N	(11G 2–0)												
" total	4	2	.667	5.10	35	0	0	54.2	55	19	30	0	4	2	1	6	1	1	.167
1982 STL N	5	3	.625	2.55	63	0	0	91.2	69	36	68	0	5	3	8	13	1	0	.077
1983 2 teams	STL	N	(26G 1–1)		DET	A	(27G 7–3)												
" total	8	4	.667	3.59	53	1	0	85.1	75	32	60	0	7	4	5	2	0	0	.000
1984 DET A	5	3	.625	3.75	47	1	0	93.2	82	36	57	0	5	2	4	0	0	0	–
9 yrs.	47	37	.560	3.54	443	2	0	693.2	634	313	526	0	46	36	76	45	4	1	.089

LEAGUE CHAMPIONSHIP SERIES

	W	L	PCT	ERA	G	GS	CG	IP	H	BB	SO	ShO	W	L	SV	AB	H	HR	BA
1979 CIN N	0	1	.000	9.00	1	0	0	1	2	1	0	0	0	1	0	0	0	0	–
1982 STL N	0	0	–	0.00	1	0	0	1	2	3	0	0	0	0	0	0	0	0	–
2 yrs.	0	1	.000	4.50	2	0	0	2	4	4	0	0	0	1	0	0	0	0	–

WORLD SERIES

	W	L	PCT	ERA	G	GS	CG	IP	H	BB	SO	ShO	W	L	SV	AB	H	HR	BA
1982 STL N	0	1	.000	9.00	3	0	0	2	2	2	3	0	0	1	0	0	0	0	–
1984 DET A	0	0	–	0.00	1	0	0	.2	0	0	1	0	0	0	0	0	0	0	–
2 yrs.	0	1	.000	6.75	4	0	0	2.2	2	2	4	0	0	1	0	0	0	0	–

Bob Baird

BAIRD, ROBERT ALLEN   BL TL 6'4"   195 lbs.
B. Jan. 16, 1942, Knoxville, Tenn.   D. Apr. 16, 1974, Chattanooga, Tenn.

	W	L	PCT	ERA	G	GS	CG	IP	H	BB	SO	ShO	W	L	SV	AB	H	HR	BA
1962 WAS A	0	1	.000	6.75	3	3	0	10.2	13	8	3	0	0	0	0	3	0	0	.000
1963	0	3	.000	7.71	5	3	0	11.2	12	7	7	0	0	0	0	3	1	0	.333
2 yrs.	0	4	.000	7.25	8	6	0	22.1	25	15	10	0	0	0	0	6	1	0	.167

Jersey Bakely

BAKELY, EDWARD ENOCH   BR TR
B. Apr. 17, 1864, Blackwood, N. J.   D. Feb. 17, 1915, Philadelphia, Pa.

	W	L	PCT	ERA	G	GS	CG	IP	H	BB	SO	ShO	W	L	SV	AB	H	HR	BA
1883 PHI AA	5	3	.625	3.23	8	8	7	61.1	65	12	14	0	0	0	0	26	5	0	.192
1884 3 teams	PHI	U	(39G 14–25)		WIL	U	(2G 0–2)		KC	U	(5G 2–3)								
" total	16	30	.348	4.29	46	45	43	394.2	443	81	226	0	0	1	0	192	25	0	.130
1888 CLE AA	25	33	.431	2.97	61	61	60	532.2	518	128	212	4	0	0	0	194	26	1	.134
1889 CLE N	12	22	.353	2.96	36	34	33	304.1	296	106	105	2	0	1	0	111	15	1	.135
1890 CLE P	13	25	.342	4.47	43	38	32	326.1	412	147	67	0	0	0	0	138	28	0	.203
1891 2 teams	WAS	AA	(13G 2–10)		BAL	AA	(8G 4–2)												
" total	6	12	.333	4.24	21	18	16	163.1	175	90	45	0	1	0	0	66	12	0	.182
6 yrs.	77	125	.381	3.66	215	204	191	1782.2	1909	564	669	7	1	2	0	727	111	2	.153

Dave Bakenhaster

BAKENHASTER, DAVID LEE   BR TR 5'10"   168 lbs.
B. Mar. 5, 1945, Columbus, Ohio

	W	L	PCT	ERA	G	GS	CG	IP	H	BB	SO	ShO	W	L	SV	AB	H	HR	BA
1964 STL N	0	0	–	6.00	2	0	0	3	9	1	0	0	0	0	0	0	0	0	–

Al Baker

BAKER, ALBERT JONES   BR TR 5'11"   170 lbs.
B. Feb. 28, 1906, Batesville, Miss.   D. Nov. 6, 1982, Kenedy, Tex.

	W	L	PCT	ERA	G	GS	CG	IP	H	BB	SO	ShO	W	L	SV	AB	H	HR	BA
1938 BOS A	0	0	–	9.39	3	0	0	7.2	13	2	2	0	0	0	0	4	0	0	.000

Bock Baker

BAKER, CHARLES
B. July 17, 1878, Troy, N. Y.

	W	L	PCT	ERA	G	GS	CG	IP	H	BB	SO	ShO	W	L	SV	AB	H	HR	BA
1901 2 teams	CLE	A	(1G 0–1)		PHI	A	(1G 0–1)												
" total	0	2	.000	7.71	2	2	1	14	29	12	1	0	0	0	0	7	1	0	.143

Ernie Baker

BAKER, ERNEST GOULD   BR TR 5'10"   160 lbs.
B. Aug. 8, 1875, Concord, Mich.   D. Oct. 25, 1945, Homer, Mich.

	W	L	PCT	ERA	G	GS	CG	IP	H	BB	SO	ShO	W	L	SV	AB	H	HR	BA
1905 CIN N	0	0	–	4.50	1	0	0	4	7	0	1	0	0	0	0	2	0	0	.000

Jesse Baker

BAKER, JESSE ORMOND   BL TL 5'11"   188 lbs.
Also known as Jesse Ormond Silverman.
B. June 3, 1888, Steilacoom, Wash.   D. Sept. 26, 1972, Tacoma, Wash.

	W	L	PCT	ERA	G	GS	CG	IP	H	BB	SO	ShO	W	L	SV	AB	H	HR	BA
1911 CHI A	2	7	.222	3.93	22	8	3	94	101	30	51	0	1	0	1	29	3	0	.103

Kirtley Baker

BAKER, KIRTLEY (Whitey)   BR TR 5'9"   160 lbs.
B. June 24, 1869, Aurora, Ind.   D. Apr. 15, 1927, Covington, Ky.

	W	L	PCT	ERA	G	GS	CG	IP	H	BB	SO	ShO	W	L	SV	AB	H	HR	BA
1890 PIT N	3	19	.136	5.60	25	21	19	178.1	209	86	76	2	1	0	0	68	10	0	.147
1893 BAL N	3	8	.273	8.44	15	12	8	91.2	138	58	26	0	0	0	0	57	17	0	.298
1894	0	1	.000	∞	1	0	0		1	2	0	0	0	1	0	4	0	0	.000
1898 WAS N	2	3	.400	3.06	6	5	4	47	56	18	7	0	0	0	0	18	5	0	.278
1899	1	7	.125	6.83	11	6	3	54	79	22	6	0	1	1	0	19	3	0	.158
5 yrs.	9	38	.191	6.28	58	44	34	371	483	186	115	2	2	2	0	166	35	0	.211

Neal Baker

BAKER, NEAL VERNON   BR TR 6'1"   175 lbs.
B. Apr. 30, 1904, LaPorte, Tex.   D. Jan. 5, 1982, Houston, Tex.

	W	L	PCT	ERA	G	GS	CG	IP	H	BB	SO	ShO	W	L	SV	AB	H	HR	BA
1927 PHI A	0	0	–	5.71	5	2	0	17.1	27	7	3	0	0	0	0	6	1	0	.167

Norm Baker

BAKER, NORMAN LESLIE (Bones)
B. Oct. 14, 1864, Philadelphia, Pa.   D. Feb. 20, 1949, Hurffville, N. J.

	W	L	PCT	ERA	G	GS	CG	IP	H	BB	SO	ShO	W	L	SV	AB	H	HR	BA
1883 PIT AA	0	2	.000	3.32	3	3	2	19	24	11	5	0	0	0	0	12	0	0	.000
1885 LOU AA	13	12	.520	3.40	25	24	24	217	210	69	79	1	1	0	0	87	18	0	.207
1890 B-B AA	1	1	.500	3.71	2	2	2	17	16	6	10	0	0	0	0	7	0	0	.000
3 yrs.	14	15	.483	3.42	30	29	28	253	250	86	94	1	1	0	0	106	18	0	.170

Steve Baker

BAKER, STEVEN BYRNE   BR TR 6'   185 lbs.
B. Aug. 30, 1956, Eugene, Ore.

	W	L	PCT	ERA	G	GS	CG	IP	H	BB	SO	ShO	W	L	SV	AB	H	HR	BA
1978 DET A	2	4	.333	4.55	15	10	0	63.1	66	42	39	0	1	1	0	0	0	0	–
1979	1	7	.125	6.64	21	12	0	84	97	51	54	0	0	1	1	0	0	0	–
1982 OAK A	1	1	.500	4.56	5	3	0	25.2	30	4	14	0	0	0	0	0	0	0	–
1983 2 teams	OAK	A	(35G 3–3)		STL	N	(8G 0–1)												
" total	3	4	.429	3.94	43	1	0	64	69	30	24	0	3	3	5	0	0	0	–
4 yrs.	7	16	.304	5.13	84	26	0	237	262	127	131	0	4	5	6	0	0	0	–

	W	L	PCT	ERA	G	GS	CG	IP	H	BB	SO	ShO	Relief Pitching W	L	SV	BATTING AB	H	HR	BA

Tom Baker

BAKER, THOMAS CALVIN (Rattlesnake)
B. June 11, 1915, Victoria, Tex.
BR TR 6'1½" 180 lbs.

	W	L	PCT	ERA	G	GS	CG	IP	H	BB	SO	ShO	W	L	SV	AB	H	HR	BA
1935 BKN N	1	0	1.000	4.29	11	1	1	42	48	20	10	0	1	0	0	19	9	0	.474
1936	1	8	.111	4.72	35	8	2	87.2	98	48	35	0	1	2	2	30	7	0	.233
1937 2 teams			BKN	N (7G 0–1)		NY	N (13G 1–0)												
" total	1	1	.500	5.03	20	0	0	39.1	44	21	13	0	1	1	0	9	2	0	.222
1938 NY N	0	0	–	6.75	2	0	0	4	5	3	0	0	0	0	0	0	0	0	–
4 yrs.	3	9	.250	4.73	68	9	3	173	195	92	58	0	3	3	2	58	18	0	.310

Tom Baker

BAKER, THOMAS HENRY
B. May 6, 1934, Port Townsend, Wash.   D. Mar. 9, 1980, Port Townsend, Wash.
BL TL 6' 195 lbs.

	W	L	PCT	ERA	G	GS	CG	IP	H	BB	SO	ShO	W	L	SV	AB	H	HR	BA
1963 CHI N	0	1	.000	3.00	10	1	0	18	20	7	14	0	0	0	0	3	0	0	.000

Mike Balas

BALAS, MITCHELL FRANCIS
Born Mitchell Francis Balaski.
B. May 17, 1910, Lowell, Mass.
BR TR 6' 195 lbs.

	W	L	PCT	ERA	G	GS	CG	IP	H	BB	SO	ShO	W	L	SV	AB	H	HR	BA
1938 BOS N	0	0	–	6.75	1	0	0	1.1	3	0	0	0	0	0	0	0	0	0	–

Jack Baldschun

BALDSCHUN, JACK EDWARD
B. Oct. 16, 1936, Greenville, Ohio
BR TR 6'1" 175 lbs.

	W	L	PCT	ERA	G	GS	CG	IP	H	BB	SO	ShO	W	L	SV	AB	H	HR	BA
1961 PHI N	5	3	.625	3.88	65	0	0	99.2	90	49	59	0	5	3	3	11	0	0	.000
1962	12	7	.632	2.96	67	0	0	112.2	95	58	95	0	12	7	13	16	1	0	.063
1963	11	7	.611	2.30	65	0	0	113.2	99	42	89	0	11	7	16	20	0	0	.000
1964	6	9	.400	3.12	71	0	0	118.1	111	40	96	0	6	9	21	16	4	0	.250
1965	5	8	.385	3.82	65	0	0	99	102	42	81	0	5	8	6	7	0	0	.000
1966 CIN N	1	5	.167	5.49	42	0	0	57.1	71	25	44	0	1	5	0	3	1	0	.333
1967	0	0	–	4.15	9	0	0	13	15	9	12	0	0	0	0	1	0	0	.000
1969 SD N	7	2	.778	4.79	61	0	0	77	80	29	67	0	7	2	1	4	1	0	.250
1970	1	0	1.000	10.38	12	0	0	13	24	4	12	0	1	0	0	0	0	0	–
9 yrs.	48	41	.539	3.70	457	0	0	703.2	687	298	555	0	48	41	60	78	7	0	.090

Dave Baldwin

BALDWIN, DAVID GEORGE
B. Mar. 30, 1938, Tucson, Ariz.
BR TR 6'2" 200 lbs.

	W	L	PCT	ERA	G	GS	CG	IP	H	BB	SO	ShO	W	L	SV	AB	H	HR	BA
1966 WAS A	0	0	–	3.86	4	0	0	7	8	1	4	0	0	0	0	0	0	0	–
1967	2	4	.333	1.70	58	0	0	68.2	53	20	52	0	2	4	12	4	0	0	.000
1968	0	2	.000	4.07	40	0	0	42	40	12	30	0	0	2	5	2	0	0	.000
1969	2	4	.333	4.05	43	0	0	66.2	57	34	51	0	2	4	4	7	0	0	.000
1970 MIL A	2	1	.667	2.57	28	0	0	35	25	18	26	0	2	1	1	2	1	0	.500
1973 CHI A	0	0	–	3.60	3	0	0	5	7	4	1	0	0	0	0	0	0	0	–
6 yrs.	6	11	.353	3.09	176	0	0	224.1	190	89	164	0	6	11	22	15	1	0	.067

Harry Baldwin

BALDWIN, HOWARD EDWARD
B. June 30, 1900, Baltimore, Md.   D. Jan. 23, 1958, Baltimore, Md.
BR TR 5'11" 160 lbs.

	W	L	PCT	ERA	G	GS	CG	IP	H	BB	SO	ShO	W	L	SV	AB	H	HR	BA
1924 NY N	3	1	.750	4.28	10	2	1	33.2	42	11	5	0	2	0	0	11	4	0	.364
1925	0	0	–	9.00	1	0	0	1	3	1	0	0	0	0	0	0	0	0	–
2 yrs.	3	1	.750	4.41	11	2	1	34.2	45	12	5	0	2	0	0	11	4	0	.364

WORLD SERIES

	W	L	PCT	ERA	G	GS	CG	IP	H	BB	SO	ShO	W	L	SV	AB	H	HR	BA
1924 NY N	0	0	–	0.00	1	0	0	2	1	0	1	0	0	0	0	0	0	0	–

Kid Baldwin

BALDWIN, CLARENCE GEOGHAN
B. Nov. 1, 1864, Newport, Ky.   D. July 10, 1897, Cincinnati, Ohio
BR TR 5'6" 147 lbs.

	W	L	PCT	ERA	G	GS	CG	IP	H	BB	SO	ShO	W	L	SV	AB	H	HR	BA
1885 CIN AA	0	0	–	9.00	2	1	0	4	5	6	1	0	0	0	0	*			

Lady Baldwin

BALDWIN, CHARLES BUSTED
B. Apr. 10, 1859, Ormel, N.Y.   D. Mar. 7, 1937, Hastings, Mich.
BL TL 5'11" 170 lbs.

	W	L	PCT	ERA	G	GS	CG	IP	H	BB	SO	ShO	W	L	SV	AB	H	HR	BA
1884 MIL U	1	1	.500	2.65	2	2	2	17	7	1	21	0	0	0	0	27	6	0	.222
1885 DET N	11	9	.550	1.86	21	20	19	179.1	137	28	135	1	0	0	1	124	30	0	.242
1886	42	13	.764	2.24	56	56	55	487	371	100	323	7	0	0	0	204	41	0	.201
1887	13	10	.565	3.84	24	24	24	211	225	61	60	1	0	0	0	85	23	0	.271
1888	3	3	.500	5.43	6	6	5	53	76	15	26	0	0	0	0	23	6	0	.261
1890 2 teams			BKN	P (2G 1–0)		BUF	P (7G 2–5)												
" total	3	5	.375	4.78	9	8	7	69.2	105	28	17	0	0	0	0	31	8	0	.258
6 yrs.	73	41	.640	2.85	118	116	112	1017	921	233	582	9	0	0	1	494	114	0	.231

Mark Baldwin

BALDWIN, MARCUS ELMORE (Fido)
B. Oct. 29, 1865, Pittsburgh, Pa.   D. Nov. 10, 1929, Pittsburgh, Pa.
BR TR 6' 190 lbs.

	W	L	PCT	ERA	G	GS	CG	IP	H	BB	SO	ShO	W	L	SV	AB	H	HR	BA
1887 CHI N	18	17	.514	3.40	40	39	35	334	329	122	164	1	0	0	1	139	26	4	.187
1888	13	15	.464	2.76	30	30	27	251	241	99	157	2	0	0	0	106	16	1	.151
1889 COL AA	27	34	.443	3.61	63	59	54	513.2	458	274	368	6	1	2	1	208	39	2	.188
1890 CHI P	32	24	.571	3.31	59	57	54	501	498	249	211	1	2	0	0	215	45	1	.209
1891 PIT N	22	28	.440	2.76	53	50	48	437.2	385	227	197	2	1	0	0	177	27	1	.153
1892	26	27	.491	3.47	56	53	45	440.1	447	194	157	0	2	0	0	178	18	1	.101
1893 2 teams			PIT	N (1G 0–0)		NY	N (45G 16–20)												
" total	16	20	.444	4.15	46	40	33	333.2	341	142	100	2	2	1	2	135	17	0	.126
7 yrs.	154	165	.483	3.36	347	328	296	2811.1	2699	1307	1354	14	8	3	4	1158	188	10	.162

O. F. Baldwin

BALDWIN, O. F.
B. Youngstown, Ohio

	W	L	PCT	ERA	G	GS	CG	IP	H	BB	SO	ShO	W	L	SV	AB	H	HR	BA
1908 STL N	1	3	.250	6.14	4	4	0	14.2	16	11	5	0	0	0	0	6	0	0	.000

Rick Baldwin

BALDWIN, RICKEY ALAN
B. June 1, 1953, Fresno, Calif.
BR TL 6'3" 180 lbs.

	W	L	PCT	ERA	G	GS	CG	IP	H	BB	SO	ShO	W	L	SV	AB	H	HR	BA
1975 NY N	3	5	.375	3.34	54	0	0	97	97	34	54	0	3	5	6	15	3	0	.200
1976	0	0	–	2.35	11	0	0	23	14	10	9	0	0	0	0	3	1	0	.333
1977	1	2	.333	4.43	40	0	0	63	62	31	23	0	1	2	1	4	2	0	.500
3 yrs.	4	7	.364	3.59	105	0	0	183	173	75	86	0	4	7	7	22	6	0	.273

	W	L	PCT	ERA	G	GS	CG	IP	H	BB	SO	ShO	Relief Pitching W	L	SV	BATTING AB	H	HR	BA

Jay Baller

BALLER, JAY SCOTT
B. Oct. 6, 1960, Stayton, Ohio

BR TR 6'6" 215 lbs.

	W	L	PCT	ERA	G	GS	CG	IP	H	BB	SO	ShO	W	L	SV	AB	H	HR	BA
1982 PHI N	0	0	–	3.38	4	1	0	8	7	2	7	0	0	0	0	0	0	0	–

Mark Ballinger

BALLINGER, MARK ALLEN
B. Jan. 31, 1949, Glendale, Calif.

BR TR 6'6" 205 lbs.

	W	L	PCT	ERA	G	GS	CG	IP	H	BB	SO	ShO	W	L	SV	AB	H	HR	BA
1971 CLE A	1	2	.333	4.63	18	0	0	35	30	13	25	0	1	2	0	5	1	0	.200

Win Ballou

BALLOU, NOBLE WINFIELD (Old Pard)
B. Nov. 30, 1897, Mount Morgan, Ky.   D. Jan. 30, 1963, San Francisco, Calif.

BR TR 5'10½" 170 lbs.

	W	L	PCT	ERA	G	GS	CG	IP	H	BB	SO	ShO	W	L	SV	AB	H	HR	BA
1925 WAS A	1	1	.500	4.55	10	1	1	27.2	38	13	13	0	1	0	0	7	1	0	.143
1926 STL A	11	10	.524	4.79	43	13	5	154	186	71	59	0	6	3	2	42	2	1	.048
1927	5	6	.455	4.78	21	11	4	90.1	105	46	17	0	2	1	0	28	1	0	.036
1929 BKN N	2	3	.400	6.71	25	1	0	57.2	69	38	20	0	2	2	0	16	1	0	.063
4 yrs.	19	20	.487	5.11	99	26	10	329.2	398	168	109	0	11	6	2	93	5	1	.054

WORLD SERIES

	W	L	PCT	ERA	G	GS	CG	IP	H	BB	SO	ShO	W	L	SV	AB	H	HR	BA
1925 WAS A	0	0	–	0.00	2	0	0	1.2	0	1	1	0	0	0	0	0	0	0	–

Tony Balsamo

BALSAMO, ANTHONY FRED
B. Nov. 21, 1937, Brooklyn, N. Y.

BR TR 6'2" 185 lbs.

	W	L	PCT	ERA	G	GS	CG	IP	H	BB	SO	ShO	W	L	SV	AB	H	HR	BA
1962 CHI N	0	1	.000	6.44	18	0	0	29.1	34	20	27	0	0	1	0	5	1	0	.200

George Bamberger

BAMBERGER, GEORGE IRVIN
B. Aug. 1, 1925, Staten Island, N. Y.
Manager 1978-80, 1982-83.

BR TR 6' 175 lbs.

	W	L	PCT	ERA	G	GS	CG	IP	H	BB	SO	ShO	W	L	SV	AB	H	HR	BA
1951 NY N	0	0	–	18.00	2	0	0	2	4	2	1	0	0	0	0	0	0	0	–
1952	0	0	–	9.00	5	0	0	4	6	6	0	0	0	0	0	0	0	0	–
1959 BAL A	0	0	–	7.56	3	1	0	8.1	15	2	2	0	0	0	1	2	0	0	.000
3 yrs.	0	0	–	9.42	10	1	0	14.1	25	10	3	0	0	0	1	2	0	0	.000

Sal Bando

BANDO, SALVATORE LEONARD
Brother of Chris Bando.
B. Feb. 13, 1944, Cleveland, Ohio

BR TR 6' 195 lbs.

	W	L	PCT	ERA	G	GS	CG	IP	H	BB	SO	ShO	W	L	SV	AB	H	HR	BA
1979 MIL A	0	0	–	6.00	1	0	0	3	3	0	0	0	0	0	0	*			

Eddie Bane

BANE, EDWARD LEE
B. Mar. 22, 1952, Great Lakes, Ill.

BR TL 5'9" 160 lbs.

	W	L	PCT	ERA	G	GS	CG	IP	H	BB	SO	ShO	W	L	SV	AB	H	HR	BA
1973 MIN A	0	5	.000	4.92	23	6	0	60.1	62	30	42	0	0	2	2	0	0	0	–
1975	3	1	.750	2.86	4	4	0	28.1	28	15	14	0	0	0	0	0	0	0	–
1976	4	7	.364	5.11	17	15	1	79.1	92	39	24	0	0	0	0	0	0	0	–
3 yrs.	7	13	.350	4.66	44	25	1	168	182	84	80	0	0	2	2	0	0	0	–

Dick Baney

BANEY, RICHARD LEE
B. Nov. 1, 1946, Fullerton, Calif.

BR TR 6' 185 lbs.

	W	L	PCT	ERA	G	GS	CG	IP	H	BB	SO	ShO	W	L	SV	AB	H	HR	BA
1969 SEA A	1	0	1.000	3.86	9	1	0	18.2	21	7	9	0	0	0	0	2	0	0	.000
1973 CIN N	2	1	.667	2.93	11	1	0	30.2	26	6	17	0	1	1	2	9	2	0	.222
1974	1	0	1.000	5.49	22	1	0	41	51	17	12	0	1	0	1	5	0	0	.000
3 yrs.	4	1	.800	4.28	42	3	0	90.1	98	30	38	0	2	1	3	16	2	0	.125

Dan Bankhead

BANKHEAD, DANIEL ROBERT
B. May 3, 1920, Empire, Ala.   D. May 2, 1976, Houston, Tex.

BR TR 6'1" 184 lbs.

	W	L	PCT	ERA	G	GS	CG	IP	H	BB	SO	ShO	W	L	SV	AB	H	HR	BA
1947 BKN N	0	0	–	7.20	4	0	0	10	15	8	6	0	0	0	1	4	1	1	.250
1950	9	4	.692	5.50	41	12	2	129.1	119	88	96	1	5	1	3	39	9	0	.231
1951	0	1	.000	15.43	7	1	0	14	27	14	9	0	0	0	0	2	0	0	.000
3 yrs.	9	5	.643	6.52	52	13	2	153.1	161	110	111	1	5	1	4	45	10	1	.222

Bill Banks

BANKS, WILLIAM JOHN
Born William John Yerrick.
B. Feb. 26, 1873, Danville, Pa.   D. Sept. 8, 1936, Danville, Pa.

5'11" 150 lbs.

	W	L	PCT	ERA	G	GS	CG	IP	H	BB	SO	ShO	W	L	SV	AB	H	HR	BA
1895 BOS N	1	0	1.000	0.00	1	1	0	7	7	4	4	0	0	0	0	3	0	0	.000
1896	0	3	.000	10.57	4	3	2	23	42	13	6	0	0	0	0	11	3	0	.273
2 yrs.	1	3	.250	8.10	5	4	2	30	49	17	10	0	0	0	0	14	3	0	.214

Floyd Bannister

BANNISTER, FLOYD FRANKLIN
B. June 10, 1955, Pierre, S. D.

BL TL 6'1" 190 lbs.

	W	L	PCT	ERA	G	GS	CG	IP	H	BB	SO	ShO	W	L	SV	AB	H	HR	BA
1977 HOU N	8	9	.471	4.03	24	23	4	143	138	68	112	1	0	0	0	48	9	0	.188
1978	3	9	.250	4.83	28	16	2	110	120	63	94	2	0	0	0	31	5	0	.161
1979 SEA A	10	15	.400	4.05	30	30	6	182	185	68	115	2	0	0	0	0	0	0	–
1980	9	13	.409	3.47	32	32	8	218	200	66	155	0	0	0	0	0	0	0	–
1981	9	9	.500	4.46	21	20	5	121	128	39	85	2	0	0	0	0	0	0	–
1982	12	13	.480	3.43	35	35	5	247	225	77	**209**	3	0	0	0	0	0	0	–
1983 CHI A	16	10	.615	3.35	34	34	5	217.1	191	71	193	2	0	0	0	0	0	0	–
1984	14	11	.560	4.83	34	33	4	218	211	80	152	0	0	0	0	1	0	0	.000
8 yrs.	81	89	.476	3.96	238	223	39	1456.1	1398	532	1115	12	0	0	0	80	14	0	.175

LEAGUE CHAMPIONSHIP SERIES

	W	L	PCT	ERA	G	GS	CG	IP	H	BB	SO	ShO	W	L	SV	AB	H	HR	BA
1983 CHI A	0	1	.000	4.50	1	1	0	6	5	1	5	0	0	0	0	0	0	0	–

Jimmy Bannon

BANNON, JAMES HENRY (Foxy Grandpa)
Brother of Tom Bannon.
B. May 5, 1871, Amesbury, Mass.   D. Mar. 24, 1948, Glen Rock, N. J.

BR TR 5'5" 160 lbs.

	W	L	PCT	ERA	G	GS	CG	IP	H	BB	SO	ShO	W	L	SV	AB	H	HR	BA
1893 STL N	0	1	.000	22.50	1	1	0	4	10	5	1	0	0	0	0	107	36	0	.336
1894 BOS N	0	0	–	0.00	1	0	0	2	4	1	0	0	0	0	0	494	166	13	.336
1895	0	0	–	6.00	1	0	0	3	4	2	1	0	0	0	0	489	171	6	.350
3 yrs.	0	1	.000	12.00	3	1	0	9	18	8	2	0	0	0	0	*			

	W	L	PCT	ERA	G	GS	CG	IP	H	BB	SO	ShO	Relief Pitching W	L	SV	BATTING AB	H	HR	BA

Jack Banta

BANTA, JOHN KAY   BL TR 6'2½" 175 lbs.
B. June 24, 1925, Hutchinson, Kans.

	W	L	PCT	ERA	G	GS	CG	IP	H	BB	SO	ShO	W	L	SV	AB	H	HR	BA
1947 BKN N	0	1	.000	7.04	3	1	0	7.2	7	4	3	0	0	1	0	2	0	0	.000
1948	0	1	.000	8.10	2	1	0	3.1	5	5	1	0	0	0	0	1	0	0	.000
1949	10	6	.625	3.37	48	12	2	152.1	125	68	97	1	6	2	3	46	5	0	.109
1950	4	4	.500	4.35	16	5	1	41.1	39	36	15	0	2	3	2	12	2	0	.167
4 yrs.	14	12	.538	3.78	69	19	3	204.2	176	113	116	1	8	6	5	61	7	0	.115
WORLD SERIES																			
1949 BKN N	0	0	—	3.18	3	0	0	5.2	5	1	4	0	0	0	0	1	0	0	.000

Steve Barber

BARBER, STEPHEN DAVID   BL TL 6' 195 lbs.
B. Feb. 22, 1939, Takoma Park, Md.

	W	L	PCT	ERA	G	GS	CG	IP	H	BB	SO	ShO	W	L	SV	AB	H	HR	BA
1960 BAL A	10	7	.588	3.22	36	27	6	181.2	148	113	112	1	0	1	2	54	3	0	.056
1961	18	12	.600	3.33	37	34	14	248.1	194	130	150	8	0	0	1	80	13	2	.163
1962	9	6	.600	3.46	28	19	5	140.1	145	61	89	2	0	0	0	42	3	0	.071
1963	20	13	.606	2.75	39	36	11	258.2	253	92	180	2	0	1	0	87	12	1	.138
1964	9	13	.409	3.84	36	26	4	157	144	81	118	0	1	1	1	47	7	1	.149
1965	15	10	.600	2.69	37	34	7	220.2	177	81	130	2	1	1	0	65	5	1	.077
1966	10	5	.667	2.30	25	22	5	133.1	104	49	91	3	0	0	0	44	3	0	.068
1967 2 teams		BAL	A (15G 4–9)		NY	A	(17G 6–9)												
" total	10	18	.357	4.07	32	32	4	172.1	150	115	118	2	0	0	0	51	7	0	.137
1968 NY A	6	5	.545	3.23	20	19	3	128.1	127	64	87	1	0	0	0	39	2	0	.051
1969 SEA A	4	7	.364	4.80	25	16	0	86.1	99	48	69	0	0	0	0	25	5	0	.200
1970 2 teams		CHI	N (5G 0–1)		ATL	N	(5G 0–1)												
" total	2	2	.000	6.20	10	2	0	20.1	27	11	14	0	0	1	0	4	1	0	.250
1971 ATL N	3	1	.750	4.80	39	3	0	75	92	25	40	0	3	0	2	13	2	0	.154
1972 2 teams		ATL	N (5G 0–0)		CAL	A	(34G 4–4)												
" total	4	4	.500	2.80	39	3	0	74	55	36	40	0	3	4	2	12	2	0	.167
1973 CAL A	3	2	.600	3.53	50	1	0	89.1	90	32	58	0	3	2	4	0	0	0	—
1974 SF N	0	1	.000	5.14	13	0	0	14	13	12	13	0	0	1	1	0	0	0	—
15 yrs.	121	106	.533	3.36	466	272	59	1999.2	1818	950	1309	21	11	12	13	563	65	5	.115

Steve Barber

BARBER, STEVEN LEE   BR TR 6'1" 190 lbs.
B. Mar. 13, 1948, Grand Rapids, Mich.

	W	L	PCT	ERA	G	GS	CG	IP	H	BB	SO	ShO	W	L	SV	AB	H	HR	BA
1970 MIN A	0	0	—	4.67	18	0	0	27	26	18	14	0	0	0	2	2	0	0	.000
1971	1	0	1.000	6.00	4	2	0	12	8	13	4	0	1	0	0	5	0	0	.000
2 yrs.	1	0	1.000	5.08	22	2	0	39	34	31	18	0	1	0	2	7	0	0	.000

Frank Barberich

BARBERICH, FRANK FREDERICK   BB TR 5'10½" 175 lbs.
B. Feb. 3, 1882, New Town, N.Y.   D. May 1, 1965, Ocala, Fla.

	W	L	PCT	ERA	G	GS	CG	IP	H	BB	SO	ShO	W	L	SV	AB	H	HR	BA
1907 BOS N	1	1	.500	5.84	2	2	1	12.1	19	5	1	0	0	0	0	4	0	0	.000
1910 BOS A	0	0	—	7.20	2	0	0	5	7	2	0	0	0	0	0	1	0	0	.000
2 yrs.	1	1	.500	6.23	4	2	1	17.1	26	7	1	0	0	0	0	5	0	0	.000

Curt Barclay

BARCLAY, CURTIS CORDELL   BR TR 6'3" 210 lbs.
B. Aug. 22, 1931, Chicago, Ill.

	W	L	PCT	ERA	G	GS	CG	IP	H	BB	SO	ShO	W	L	SV	AB	H	HR	BA
1957 NY N	9	9	.500	3.44	37	28	5	183	196	48	67	2	2	0	0	58	11	0	.190
1958 SF N	1	0	1.000	2.81	6	1	0	16	16	5	6	0	1	0	0	6	4	0	.667
1959	0	0	—	54.00	1	0	0	.1	2	2	0	0	0	0	0	0	0	0	—
3 yrs.	10	9	.526	3.48	44	29	5	199.1	214	55	73	2	3	0	0	64	15	0	.234

Ray Bare

BARE, RAYMOND DOUGLAS   BR TR 6'2" 185 lbs.
B. Apr. 15, 1949, Miami, Fla.

	W	L	PCT	ERA	G	GS	CG	IP	H	BB	SO	ShO	W	L	SV	AB	H	HR	BA
1972 STL N	0	1	.000	0.54	14	0	0	16.2	18	6	5	0	0	1	1	0	0	0	—
1974	1	2	.333	6.00	10	3	0	24	25	9	6	0	1	0	0	5	1	0	.200
1975 DET A	8	13	.381	4.48	29	21	6	150.2	174	47	71	1	2	0	0	0	0	0	—
1976	7	8	.467	4.63	30	21	3	134	157	51	59	2	0	0	0	0	0	0	—
1977	0	2	.000	12.86	5	4	0	14	24	7	4	0	0	0	0	0	0	0	—
5 yrs.	16	26	.381	4.80	88	49	9	339.1	398	120	145	3	3	1	1	5	1	0	.200

Clyde Barfoot

BARFOOT, CLYDE RAYMOND   BR TR 6' 170 lbs.
B. July 8, 1891, Richmond, Va.   D. Mar. 11, 1971, Highland Park, Calif.

	W	L	PCT	ERA	G	GS	CG	IP	H	BB	SO	ShO	W	L	SV	AB	H	HR	BA
1922 STL N	4	5	.444	4.21	42	2	1	117.2	139	30	19	0	3	4	2	34	12	0	.353
1923	3	3	.500	3.73	33	2	1	101.1	112	27	23	1	2	3	1	37	7	0	.189
1926 DET A	1	2	.333	4.88	11	1	0	31.1	42	9	7	0	1	1	2	5	1	0	.200
3 yrs.	8	10	.444	4.10	86	5	2	250.1	293	66	49	1	6	8	5	76	20	0	.263

Cy Barger

BARGER, EROS BOLIVAR   BL TR 6' 160 lbs.
B. May 18, 1885, Jamestown, Ky.   D. Sept. 23, 1964, Columbia, Ky.

	W	L	PCT	ERA	G	GS	CG	IP	H	BB	SO	ShO	W	L	SV	AB	H	HR	BA
1906 NY A	0	0	—	10.13	2	1	0	5.1	7	3	3	0	0	0	0	3	1	0	.333
1907	0	0	—	3.00	1	0	0	6	10	1	0	0	0	0	0	2	0	0	.000
1910 BKN N	15	15	.500	2.88	35	30	25	271.2	267	107	87	2	1	0	1	104	24	0	.231
1911	11	15	.423	3.52	30	30	21	217.1	224	71	60	1	0	0	0	145	33	0	.228
1912	1	9	.100	5.46	16	11	6	94	120	42	30	0	0	0	0	37	7	0	.189
1914 PIT F	10	16	.385	4.34	33	26	18	228.1	252	63	70	1	1	1	1	83	17	0	.205
1915	10	7	.588	2.29	34	13	8	153	130	47	47	1	4	1	5	54	15	0	.278
7 yrs.	47	62	.431	3.56	151	111	78	975.2	1010	334	297	5	6	2	8	*			

Greg Barger

BARGER, GREGORY ROBERT   BR TR 6'3" 190 lbs.
B. Jan. 27, 1959, Inglewood, Calif.

	W	L	PCT	ERA	G	GS	CG	IP	H	BB	SO	ShO	W	L	SV	AB	H	HR	BA
1983 MON N	2	0	1.000	6.75	8	3	0	20	23	8	9	0	0	0	0	6	1	0	.167
1984	0	1	.000	7.88	3	1	0	8	8	7	2	0	0	0	0	1	0	0	.000
2 yrs.	2	1	.667	7.07	11	4	0	28	31	15	11	0	0	0	0	7	1	0	.143

	W	L	PCT	ERA	G	GS	CG	IP	H	BB	SO	ShO	Relief Pitching W	L	SV	BATTING AB	H	HR	BA

Len Barker

BARKER, LEONARD HAROLD
B. July 7, 1955, Ft. Knox, Ky.   BR   TR   6'5"   225 lbs.

	W	L	PCT	ERA	G	GS	CG	IP	H	BB	SO	ShO	W	L	SV	AB	H	HR	BA
1976 TEX A	1	0	1.000	2.40	2	2	1	15	7	6	7	0	0	0	0	0	0	0	—
1977	4	1	.800	2.68	15	3	0	47	36	24	51	0	3	0	1	0	0	0	—
1978	1	5	.167	4.82	29	0	0	52.1	63	29	33	0	1	5	4	0	0	0	—
1979 CLE A	6	6	.500	4.93	29	19	2	137	146	70	93	0	0	0	0	0	0	0	—
1980	19	12	.613	4.17	36	36	8	246	237	92	187	1	0	0	0	0	0	0	—
1981	8	7	.533	3.92	22	22	9	154	150	46	127	3	0	0	0	0	0	0	—
1982	15	11	.577	3.90	33	33	10	244.2	211	88	187	1	0	0	0	0	0	0	—
1983 2 teams		CLE	A (24G 8–13)		ATL	N (6G 1–3)													
" total	9	16	.360	4.88	30	30	4	182.2	181	66	126	1	0	0	0	8	1	0	.125
1984 ATL N	7	8	.467	3.85	21	20	1	126.1	120	38	95	0	0	0	0	38	2	0	.053
9 yrs.	70	66	.515	4.19	217	165	35	1205	1151	459	906	6	4	5	5	46	3	0	.065

Jeff Barkley

BARKLEY, JEFFREY CARVER
B. Nov. 21, 1959, Hickory, N. C.   BB   TR   6'3"   178 lbs.

	W	L	PCT	ERA	G	GS	CG	IP	H	BB	SO	ShO	W	L	SV	AB	H	HR	BA
1984 CLE A	0	0	—	6.75	3	0	0	4	6	1	4	0	0	0	0	0	0	0	—

Mike Barlow

BARLOW, MICHAEL ROSWELL
B. Apr. 30, 1948, Stamford, N. Y.   BL   TR   6'6"   210 lbs.

	W	L	PCT	ERA	G	GS	CG	IP	H	BB	SO	ShO	W	L	SV	AB	H	HR	BA
1975 STL N	0	0	—	4.50	9	0	0	8	11	3	2	0	0	0	0	0	0	0	—
1976 HOU N	2	2	.500	4.50	16	0	0	22	27	17	11	0	2	2	0	3	0	0	.000
1977 CAL A	4	2	.667	4.58	20	1	0	59	53	27	25	0	3	1	1	0	0	0	—
1978	0	0	—	4.50	1	0	0	2	3	0	1	0	0	0	0	0	0	0	—
1979	1	1	.500	5.13	35	0	0	86	106	30	33	0	1	1	0	0	0	0	—
1980 TOR A	3	1	.750	4.09	40	1	0	55	57	21	19	0	2	1	5	0	0	0	—
1981	0	0	—	4.20	12	0	0	15	22	6	5	0	0	0	0	0	0	0	—
7 yrs.	10	6	.625	4.63	133	2	0	247	279	104	96	0	8	5	6	3	0	0	.000

LEAGUE CHAMPIONSHIP SERIES

	W	L	PCT	ERA	G	GS	CG	IP	H	BB	SO	ShO	W	L	SV	AB	H	HR	BA
1979 CAL A	0	0	—	0.00	1	0	0	1	0	0	0	0	0	0	0	0	0	0	—

Charlie Barnabe

BARNABE, CHARLES EDWARD
B. June 12, 1900, Russell Gulch, Colo.   D. Aug. 16, 1977, Waco, Tex.   BL   TL   5'11½" 164 lbs.

	W	L	PCT	ERA	G	GS	CG	IP	H	BB	SO	ShO	W	L	SV	AB	H	HR	BA
1927 CHI A	0	5	.000	5.31	17	5	1	61	86	20	5	0	0	2	0	19	3	0	.158
1928	0	2	.000	6.52	7	2	0	9.2	17	0	3	0	0	0	0	8	4	1	.500
2 yrs.	0	7	.000	5.48	24	7	1	70.2	103	20	8	0	0	2	0	27	7	1	.259

Bob Barnes

BARNES, ROBERT AVERY (Lefty)
B. Jan. 6, 1902, Washburn, Ill.   BL   TL   5'11½" 150 lbs.

	W	L	PCT	ERA	G	GS	CG	IP	H	BB	SO	ShO	W	L	SV	AB	H	HR	BA
1924 CHI A	0	0	—	19.29	2	0	0	4.2	14	1	1	0	0	0	0	2	0	0	.000

Frank Barnes

BARNES, FRANK
B. Aug. 26, 1928, Longwood, Miss.   BR   TR   6'   170 lbs.

	W	L	PCT	ERA	G	GS	CG	IP	H	BB	SO	ShO	W	L	SV	AB	H	HR	BA
1957 STL N	0	1	.000	4.50	3	1	0	10	13	9	5	0	0	0	0	2	0	0	.000
1958	1	1	.500	7.58	8	1	0	19	19	16	17	0	1	1	0	6	1	0	.167
1960	0	1	.000	3.52	4	1	0	7.2	8	9	8	0	0	0	1	2	0	0	.000
3 yrs.	1	3	.250	5.89	15	3	0	36.2	40	34	30	0	1	1	1	10	1	0	.100

Frank Barnes

BARNES, FRANK SAMUEL (Lefty)
B. Jan. 9, 1900, Dallas, Tex.   D. Sept. 27, 1967, Houston, Tex.   BL   TL   6'2½" 195 lbs.

	W	L	PCT	ERA	G	GS	CG	IP	H	BB	SO	ShO	W	L	SV	AB	H	HR	BA
1929 DET A	0	1	.000	7.20	4	1	0	5	10	3	0	0	0	0	0	1	0	0	.000
1930 NY A	0	1	.000	8.03	2	2	0	12.1	13	13	2	0	0	0	0	6	2	0	.333
2 yrs.	0	2	.000	7.79	6	3	0	17.1	23	16	2	0	0	0	0	7	2	0	.286

Jesse Barnes

BARNES, JESSE LAWRENCE
Brother of Virgil Barnes.
B. Aug. 26, 1892, Perkins, Okla.   D. Sept. 9, 1961, Santa Rosa, N. M.   BL   TR   6'   170 lbs.

	W	L	PCT	ERA	G	GS	CG	IP	H	BB	SO	ShO	W	L	SV	AB	H	HR	BA
1915 BOS N	4	0	1.000	1.39	9	3	2	45.1	41	10	16	0	1	0	0	17	3	0	.176
1916	6	14	.300	2.37	33	18	9	163	154	37	55	3	1	4	1	48	9	0	.188
1917	13	21	.382	2.68	50	33	27	295	261	50	107	2	0	3	1	101	24	0	.238
1918 NY N	6	1	.857	1.81	9	9	4	54.2	53	13	12	2	0	0	0	18	4	0	.222
1919	25	9	.735	2.40	38	34	23	295.2	263	35	92	4	2	1	1	120	32	0	.267
1920	20	15	.571	2.64	43	35	23	292.2	271	56	63	2	3	2	0	108	22	0	.204
1921	15	9	.625	3.10	42	31	15	258.2	298	44	56	1	1	1	6	92	19	0	.207
1922	13	8	.619	3.51	37	30	14	212.2	236	38	52	2	0	1	0	77	14	0	.182
1923 2 teams		NY	N (12G 3–1)		BOS	N (31G 10–14)													
" total	13	15	.464	3.31	43	27	13	231.1	252	56	53	5	2	4	3	79	13	0	.165
1924 BOS N	15	20	.429	3.23	37	32	21	267.2	292	53	49	4	1	2	0	90	20	0	.222
1925	11	16	.407	4.53	32	28	17	216.1	255	63	55	0	0	1	0	81	16	1	.198
1926 BKN N	10	11	.476	5.24	31	24	10	158	204	35	29	1	0	0	1	59	14	0	.237
1927	2	10	.167	5.72	18	10	2	78.2	106	25	14	0	1	2	0	23	5	0	.217
13 yrs.	153	149	.507	3.22	422	314	180	2569.2	2686	515	653	26	12	21	13	913	195	1	.214

WORLD SERIES

	W	L	PCT	ERA	G	GS	CG	IP	H	BB	SO	ShO	W	L	SV	AB	H	HR	BA
1921 NY N	2	0	1.000	1.65	3	0	0	16.1	6	6	18	0	2	0	0	9	4	0	.444
1922	0	0	—	1.80	1	0	0	10	8	2	6	0	0	0	0	4	0	0	.000
2 yrs.	2	0	1.000	1.71	4	1	1	26.1	14	8	24	0	2	0	0	13	4	0	.308
				1st									2nd						

Junie Barnes

BARNES, JUNE SHOAF (Lefty)
B. June 14, 1911, Churchland, N. C.   D. Dec. 31, 1963, Jacksonville, N. C.   BL   TL   5'11½" 170 lbs.

	W	L	PCT	ERA	G	GS	CG	IP	H	BB	SO	ShO	W	L	SV	AB	H	HR	BA
1934 CIN N	0	0	—	0.00	2	0	0	.1	0	1	0	0	0	0	0	0	0	0	—

Rich Barnes

BARNES, RICHARD MONROE
B. July 21, 1959, Palm Beach, Fla.   BB   TL   6'4"   180 lbs.

	W	L	PCT	ERA	G	GS	CG	IP	H	BB	SO	ShO	W	L	SV	AB	H	HR	BA
1982 CHI A	0	2	.000	4.76	6	2	0	17	21	4	6	0	0	0	1	0	0	0	—

	W	L	PCT	ERA	G	GS	CG	IP	H	BB	SO	ShO	Relief Pitching W L SV			BATTING AB H HR			BA

Rich Barnes continued

	W	L	PCT	ERA	G	GS	CG	IP	H	BB	SO	ShO	W	L	SV	AB	H	HR	BA
1983 CLE A	1	1	.500	6.94	4	2	0	11.2	18	10	2	0	1	0	0	0	0	0	–
2 yrs.	1	3	.250	5.65	10	4	0	28.2	39	14	8	0	1	0	1	0	0	0	–

Ross Barnes

BARNES, ROSCOE CHARLES   BR TR 5'8½" 145 lbs.
B. May 8, 1850, Mt. Morris, N.Y.   D. Feb. 5, 1915, Chicago, Ill.

	W	L	PCT	ERA	G	GS	CG	IP	H	BB	SO	ShO	W	L	SV	AB	H	HR	BA
1876 CHI N	0	0	–	20.25	1	0	0	1.1	7	0	0	0	0	0	0	*			

Virgil Barnes

BARNES, VIRGIL JENNINGS (Zeke)   BR TR 6' 165 lbs.
Brother of Jesse Barnes.
B. Mar. 5, 1897, Ontario, Kans.   D. July 24, 1958, Wichita, Kans.

	W	L	PCT	ERA	G	GS	CG	IP	H	BB	SO	ShO	W	L	SV	AB	H	HR	BA
1919 NY N	0	0	–	18.00	1	0	0	2	6	1	1	0	0	0	0	0	0	0	–
1920	0	1	.000	3.86	1	1	0	7	9	1	2	0	0	0	0	1	0	0	.000
1922	1	0	1.000	3.48	22	3	1	51.2	46	11	16	0	0	0	2	12	2	0	.167
1923	2	3	.400	3.91	22	2	0	53	59	19	6	0	0	3	1	14	0	0	.000
1924	16	10	.615	3.06	35	29	15	229.1	239	57	59	1	1	2	3	77	14	0	.182
1925	15	11	.577	3.53	32	27	17	221.2	242	53	53	1	1	1	2	89	9	0	.101
1926	8	13	.381	2.87	31	25	9	185	183	56	54	2	0	0	1	56	3	0	.054
1927	14	11	.560	3.98	35	29	12	228.2	251	51	66	2	2	2	2	83	9	0	.108
1928 2 teams			NY	N (10G 3–3)		BOS	N (16G 2–7)												
" total	5	10	.333	5.45	26	19	4	115.2	157	44	18	1	0	1	0	39	3	0	.077
9 yrs.	61	59	.508	3.66	205	135	58	1094	1192	293	275	7	4	9	11	371	40	0	.108

WORLD SERIES

	W	L	PCT	ERA	G	GS	CG	IP	H	BB	SO	ShO	W	L	SV	AB	H	HR	BA
1923 NY N	0	0	–	0.00	2	0	0	4.2	4	0	4	0	0	0	0	1	0	0	.000
1924	0	1	.000	5.68	2	2	0	12.2	15	1	9	0	0	0	0	4	0	0	.000
2 yrs.	0	1	.000	4.15	4	2	0	17.1	19	1	13	0	0	0	0	5	0	0	.000

Rex Barney

BARNEY, REX EDWARD   BR TR 6'3" 185 lbs.
B. Dec. 19, 1924, Omaha, Neb.

	W	L	PCT	ERA	G	GS	CG	IP	H	BB	SO	ShO	W	L	SV	AB	H	HR	BA
1943 BKN N	2	2	.500	6.35	9	8	1	45.1	36	41	23	0	0	1	0	18	1	0	.056
1946	2	5	.286	5.87	16	9	1	53.2	46	51	36	0	0	0	0	17	4	0	.235
1947	5	2	.714	4.98	28	9	0	77.2	66	59	36	0	2	0	0	27	3	0	.111
1948	15	13	.536	3.10	44	34	12	246.2	193	122	138	4	1	3	0	84	14	0	.167
1949	9	8	.529	4.41	38	20	6	140.2	108	89	80	2	2	3	1	47	10	0	.213
1950	2	1	.667	6.42	20	1	0	33.2	25	48	23	0	2	1	0	8	1	0	.125
6 yrs.	35	31	.530	4.34	155	81	20	597.2	474	410	336	6	7	8	1	201	33	0	.164

WORLD SERIES

	W	L	PCT	ERA	G	GS	CG	IP	H	BB	SO	ShO	W	L	SV	AB	H	HR	BA
1947 BKN N	0	1	.000	2.70	3	1	0	6.2	4	10	3	0	0	0	0	1	0	0	.000
1949	0	1	.000	16.88	1	1	0	2.2	3	6	2	0	0	0	0	0	0	0	–
2 yrs.	0	2	.000	6.75	4	2	0	9.1	7	16	5	0	0	0	0	1	0	0	.000

Ed Barnhart

BARNHART, EDGAR VERNON   BL TR 5'10" 160 lbs.
B. Sept. 16, 1904, Providence, Mo.

	W	L	PCT	ERA	G	GS	CG	IP	H	BB	SO	ShO	W	L	SV	AB	H	HR	BA
1924 STL A	0	0	–	0.00	1	0	0	1	0	2	0	0	0	0	0	0	0	0	–

Les Barnhart

BARNHART, LESLIE EARL   BR TR 6' 180 lbs.
B. Feb. 23, 1905, Hoxie, Kans.   D. Oct. 7, 1971, Scottsdale, Ariz.

	W	L	PCT	ERA	G	GS	CG	IP	H	BB	SO	ShO	W	L	SV	AB	H	HR	BA
1928 CLE A	0	1	.000	7.00	2	1	0	9	13	4	1	0	0	0	0	2	1	0	.500
1930	1	0	1.000	6.48	1	1	0	8.1	12	4	1	0	0	0	0	3	0	0	.000
2 yrs.	1	1	.500	6.75	3	2	0	17.1	25	8	2	0	0	0	0	5	1	0	.200

George Barnicle

BARNICLE, GEORGE BERNARD   BR TR 6'2" 175 lbs.
B. Aug. 26, 1917, Fitchburg, Mass.

	W	L	PCT	ERA	G	GS	CG	IP	H	BB	SO	ShO	W	L	SV	AB	H	HR	BA
1939 BOS N	2	2	.500	4.91	6	1	0	18.1	16	8	15	0	2	1	0	5	0	0	.000
1940	1	0	1.000	7.44	13	2	1	32.2	28	31	11	0	0	0	0	11	0	0	.000
1941	0	1	.000	6.75	1	1	0	6.2	5	4	2	0	0	0	0	2	0	0	.000
3 yrs.	3	3	.500	6.55	20	4	1	57.2	49	43	28	0	2	1	0	18	0	0	.000

Ed Barnowski

BARNOWSKI, EDWARD ANTHONY   BR TR 6'2" 195 lbs.
B. Aug. 23, 1945, Scranton, Pa.

	W	L	PCT	ERA	G	GS	CG	IP	H	BB	SO	ShO	W	L	SV	AB	H	HR	BA
1965 BAL A	0	0	–	2.08	4	0	0	4.1	3	7	6	0	0	0	0	0	0	0	–
1966	0	0	–	3.00	2	0	0	3	4	1	2	0	0	0	0	0	0	0	–
2 yrs.	0	0	–	2.45	6	0	0	7.1	7	8	8	0	0	0	0	0	0	0	–

Salome Barojas

BAROJAS, SALOME   BR TR 5'9" 160 lbs.
B. June 16, 1957, Corova Vera Cruz, Mexico

	W	L	PCT	ERA	G	GS	CG	IP	H	BB	SO	ShO	W	L	SV	AB	H	HR	BA
1982 CHI A	6	6	.500	3.54	61	0	0	106.2	96	46	56	0	6	6	21	0	0	0	–
1983	3	3	.500	2.47	52	0	0	87.1	70	32	38	0	3	3	12	0	0	0	–
1984 2 teams			CHI	A (24G 3–2)		SEA	A (19G 6–5)												
" total	9	7	.563	4.15	43	14	0	134.1	136	60	55	0	3	3	2	0	0	0	–
3 yrs.	18	16	.529	3.51	156	14	0	328.1	302	138	149	0	12	12	35	0	0	0	–

LEAGUE CHAMPIONSHIP SERIES

	W	L	PCT	ERA	G	GS	CG	IP	H	BB	SO	ShO	W	L	SV	AB	H	HR	BA
1983 CHI A	0	0	–	18.00	2	0	0	1	4	0	0	0	0	0	0	0	0	0	–

Bob Barr

BARR, ROBERT ALEXANDER   BR TR 6' 175 lbs.
B. Mar. 12, 1908, Newton, Mass.

	W	L	PCT	ERA	G	GS	CG	IP	H	BB	SO	ShO	W	L	SV	AB	H	HR	BA
1935 BKN N	0	0	–	3.86	2	0	0	2.1	5	2	0	0	0	0	0	0	0	0	–

Bob Barr

BARR, ROBERT McCLELLAND   192 lbs.
B. 1856, Washington, D.C.   D. Mar. 11, 1930, Washington, D.C.

	W	L	PCT	ERA	G	GS	CG	IP	H	BB	SO	ShO	W	L	SV	AB	H	HR	BA
1883 PIT AA	6	18	.250	4.38	26	23	19	203.1	263	28	81	0	0	1	1	142	35	0	.246
1884 2 teams			WAS	AA (32G 9–23)		IND	AA (16G 3–11)												
" total	12	34	.261	3.94	48	48	47	413	471	50	207	2	0	0	0	200	32	2	.160
1886 WAS N	3	18	.143	4.30	22	22	21	190.2	216	54	80	1	0	0	0	79	13	0	.165
1890 ROC AA	28	24	.538	3.25	57	54	52	493.1	458	219	209	3	1	0	0	201	36	2	.179

	W	L	PCT	ERA	G	GS	CG	IP	H	BB	SO	ShO	Relief Pitching W	L	SV	BATTING AB	H	HR	BA

Bob Barr continued

	W	L	PCT	ERA	G	GS	CG	IP	H	BB	SO	ShO	W	L	SV	AB	H	HR	BA
1891 NY N	0	4	.000	5.33	5	4	2	27	47	12	11	0	0	0	0	11	1	0	.091
5 yrs.	49	98	.333	3.83	158	151	141	1327.1	1455	363	588	6	1	1	1	*			

Jim Barr

BARR, JAMES LELAND
B. Feb. 10, 1948, Lynwood, Calif.
BR TR 6'3" 205 lbs.

	W	L	PCT	ERA	G	GS	CG	IP	H	BB	SO	ShO	W	L	SV	AB	H	HR	BA
1971 SF N	1	1	.500	3.60	17	0	0	35	33	5	16	0	1	1	0	4	0	0	.000
1972	8	10	.444	2.87	44	18	8	179	166	41	86	2	0	3	2	49	9	0	.184
1973	11	17	.393	3.82	41	33	8	231	240	49	88	3	1	1	2	66	10	0	.152
1974	13	9	.591	2.74	44	27	11	240	223	47	84	5	2	0	2	71	18	1	.254
1975	13	14	.481	3.06	35	33	12	244	244	58	77	2	2	0	0	76	9	0	.118
1976	15	12	.556	2.89	37	37	8	252.1	260	60	75	3	0	0	0	74	12	0	.162
1977	12	16	.429	4.77	38	38	6	234	286	56	97	2	0	0	0	76	10	0	.132
1978	8	11	.421	3.53	32	25	5	163	180	35	44	2	0	0	0	50	5	0	.100
1979 CAL A	10	12	.455	4.20	36	25	5	197	217	55	69	0	2	1	0	0	0	0	—
1980	1	4	.200	5.56	24	7	0	68	90	23	22	0	0	0	1	0	0	0	—
1982 SF N	4	3	.571	3.29	53	9	1	128.2	125	24	36	1	1	2	2	32	8	0	.250
1983	5	3	.625	3.98	53	0	0	92.2	106	20	47	0	5	3	2	15	2	0	.133
12 yrs.	101	112	.474	3.56	454	252	64	2064.2	2170	469	741	20	14	11	12	513	83	1	.162

LEAGUE CHAMPIONSHIP SERIES

	W	L	PCT	ERA	G	GS	CG	IP	H	BB	SO	ShO	W	L	SV	AB	H	HR	BA
1971 SF N	0	0	—	9.00	1	0	0	1	3	0	2	0	0	0	0	1	0	0	.000

Steve Barr

BARR, STEVEN CHARLES
B. Sept. 8, 1951, St. Louis, Mo.
BL TL 6'4" 200 lbs.

	W	L	PCT	ERA	G	GS	CG	IP	H	BB	SO	ShO	W	L	SV	AB	H	HR	BA
1974 BOS A	1	0	1.000	4.00	1	1	1	9	7	6	3	0	0	0	0	0	0	0	—
1975	0	1	.000	2.57	3	2	0	7	11	7	2	0	0	0	0	0	0	0	—
1976 TEX A	2	6	.250	5.56	20	10	3	68	70	44	27	0	0	1	0	0	0	0	—
3 yrs.	3	7	.300	5.14	24	13	4	84	88	57	32	0	0	1	0	0	0	0	—

Bill Barrett

BARRETT, WILLIAM JOSEPH (Whispering Bill)
B. May 28, 1900, Cambridge, Mass. D. Jan. 26, 1951, Cambridge, Mass.
BR TR 6' 175 lbs.

	W	L	PCT	ERA	G	GS	CG	IP	H	BB	SO	ShO	W	L	SV	AB	H	HR	BA
1921 PHI A	1	0	1.000	7.20	4	0	0	5	2	9	2	0	1	0	0	*			

Dick Barrett

BARRETT, TRACEY SOUTER (Kewpie)
Played as Dick Oliver 1933.
B. Sept. 28, 1906, Montoursville, Pa. D. Oct. 30, 1966, Seattle, Wash.
BR TR 5'9" 175 lbs.

	W	L	PCT	ERA	G	GS	CG	IP	H	BB	SO	ShO	W	L	SV	AB	H	HR	BA
1933 PHI A	4	4	.500	5.76	15	7	3	70.1	74	49	26	0	0	0	0	21	6	0	.286
1934 BOS N	1	3	.250	6.68	15	3	0	32.1	50	12	14	0	1	1	0	7	1	0	.143
1943 2 teams			CHI	N (15G 0–4)		PHI	N (23G 10–9)												
" total	10	13	.435	2.90	38	24	10	214.1	189	79	85	2	0	0	1	58	8	0	.138
1944 PHI N	12	18	.400	3.86	37	27	11	221.1	223	88	74	1	3	2	0	74	16	0	.216
1945	7	20	.259	5.43	36	30	8	190.2	216	92	72	0	1	2	1	62	9	0	.145
5 yrs.	34	58	.370	4.30	141	91	32	729	752	320	271	3	5	5	2	222	40	0	.180

Frank Barrett

BARRETT, FRANCIS JOSEPH (Red)
B. July 1, 1913, Fort Lauderdale, Fla.
BR TR 6'2" 173 lbs.

	W	L	PCT	ERA	G	GS	CG	IP	H	BB	SO	ShO	W	L	SV	AB	H	HR	BA
1939 STL N	0	1	.000	5.40	1	0	0	1.2	1	1	3	0	0	1	0	0'	0	0	—
1944 BOS A	8	7	.533	3.69	38	2	0	90.1	93	42	40	0	7	6	8	28	4	0	.143
1945	4	3	.571	2.62	37	0	0	86	77	29	35	0	4	3	3	20	5	0	.250
1946 BOS N	2	4	.333	5.09	23	0	0	35.1	35	17	12	0	2	4	1	6	0	0	.000
1950 PIT N	1	2	.333	4.15	5	0	0	4.1	5	1	0	0	1	2	0	0	0	0	—
5 yrs.	15	17	.469	3.51	104	2	0	217.2	211	90	90	0	14	16	12	54	9	0	.167

Red Barrett

BARRETT, CHARLES HENRY
B. Feb. 14, 1915, Santa Barbara, Calif.
BR TR 5'11" 183 lbs.

	W	L	PCT	ERA	G	GS	CG	IP	H	BB	SO	ShO	W	L	SV	AB	H	HR	BA
1937 CIN N	0	0	—	1.42	1	0	0	6.1	5	2	1	0	0	0	0	3	0	0	.000
1938	2	0	1.000	3.14	6	2	2	28.2	28	15	5	0	0	0	0	7	1	0	.143
1939	0	0	—	1.69	2	0	0	5.1	5	1	1	0	0	0	0	0	0	0	.000
1940	1	0	1.000	6.75	3	0	0	2.2	5	1	0	0	1	0	0	0	0	0	—
1943 BOS N	12	18	.400	3.18	38	31	14	255	240	63	64	3	0	2	0	81	11	0	.136
1944	9	16	.360	4.06	42	30	11	230.1	257	63	54	1	1	0	3	75	13	0	.173
1945 2 teams			BOS	N (9G 2–3)		STL	N (36G 21–9)												
" total	23	12	.657	3.00	45	34	24	284.2	287	54	76	3	1	3	2	98	12	0	.122
1946 STL N	3	2	.600	4.03	23	9	1	67	75	24	22	1	1	0	2	17	1	0	.059
1947 BOS N	11	12	.478	3.55	36	30	12	210.2	200	53	53	3	0	1	1	72	8	0	.111
1948	7	8	.467	3.65	34	13	3	128.1	132	26	40	0	2	3	0	39	7	0	.179
1949	1	1	.500	5.68	23	0	0	44.1	58	10	17	0	1	1	0	5	1	0	.200
11 yrs.	69	69	.500	3.53	253	149	67	1263.1	1292	312	333	11	6	13	7	398	54	0	.136

WORLD SERIES

	W	L	PCT	ERA	G	GS	CG	IP	H	BB	SO	ShO	W	L	SV	AB	H	HR	BA
1948 BOS N	0	0	—	0.00	2	0	0	3.2	1	0	1	0	0	0	0	0	0	0	—

Francisco Barrios

BARRIOS, FRANCISCO JAVIER
Also known as Francisco Javier Jimenez.
B. June 10, 1953, Hermosillo, Mexico D. Apr. 9, 1982, Hermosillo, Mexico
BR TR 5'11" 155 lbs.

	W	L	PCT	ERA	G	GS	CG	IP	H	BB	SO	ShO	W	L	SV	AB	H	HR	BA
1974 CHI A	0	0	—	27.00	2	0	0	2	7	2	2	0	0	0	0	0	0	0	—
1976	5	9	.357	4.31	35	14	6	142	136	46	81	0	1	3	3	0	0	0	—
1977	14	7	.667	4.13	33	31	9	231	241	58	119	0	1	0	0	0	0	0	—
1978	9	15	.375	4.05	33	32	9	195.2	180	85	79	2	0	0	0	0	0	0	—
1979	8	3	.727	3.60	15	15	2	95	88	33	28	0	0	0	0	0	0	0	—
1980	1	1	.500	5.06	3	3	0	16	21	8	2	0	0	0	0	0	0	0	—
1981	1	3	.250	4.00	8	7	1	36	45	14	12	0	0	0	0	0	0	0	—
7 yrs.	38	38	.500	4.15	129	102	27	717.2	718	246	323	2	2	3	3	0	0	0	—

	W	L	PCT	ERA	G	GS	CG	IP	H	BB	SO	ShO	Relief Pitching W	L	SV	BATTING AB	H	HR	BA

Frank Barron

BARRON, FRANK JOHN
B. Aug. 6, 1890, St. Mary's, W. Va.   D. Sept. 18, 1964, St. Mary's, W. Va.   BL TL 6'1"   175 lbs.

| 1914 WAS A | 0 | 0 | – | 0.00 | 1 | 0 | 0 | 1 | 1 | 0 | 1 | 0 | 0 | 0 | 0 | 0 | 0 | 0 | – |

Ed Barry

BARRY, EDWARD (Jumbo)
B. Oct. 2, 1882, Madison, Wis.   D. June 19, 1920, Montague, Mass.   TL

1905 BOS A	1	2	.333	2.88	7	5	2	40.2	38	15	18	0	0	0	0	11	1	0	.091
1906	0	3	.000	6.00	3	3	3	21	23	5	10	0	0	0	0	9	1	0	.111
1907	0	1	.000	2.08	2	2	1	17.1	13	5	6	0	0	0	0	3	0	0	.000
3 yrs.	1	6	.143	3.53	12	10	6	79	74	25	34	0	0	0	0	23	2	0	.087

Hardin Barry

BARRY, HARDIN (Finn)
B. Mar. 26, 1891, Susanville, Calif.   D. Nov. 5, 1969, Carson City, Nev.   BR TR 6'   185 lbs.

| 1912 PHI A | 0 | 0 | – | 7.62 | 3 | 0 | 0 | 13 | 18 | 4 | 3 | 0 | 0 | 0 | 0 | 4 | 0 | 0 | .000 |

Tom Barry

BARRY, THOMAS ARTHUR
B. Apr. 10, 1879, St. Louis, Mo.   D. June 4, 1946, St. Louis, Mo.

| 1904 PHI N | 0 | 1 | .000 | 40.50 | 1 | 1 | 0 | .2 | 6 | 1 | 1 | 0 | 0 | 0 | 0 | 0 | 0 | 0 | – |

Bob Barthelson

BARTHELSON, ROBERT EDWARD
B. July 15, 1924, New Haven, Conn.   BR TR 6'   185 lbs.

| 1944 NY N | 1 | 1 | .500 | 4.66 | 7 | 1 | 0 | 9.2 | 13 | 5 | 4 | 0 | 1 | 1 | 0 | 0 | 0 | 0 | – |

John Barthold

BARTHOLD, JOHN FRANCIS (Hans)
B. Apr. 14, 1882, Philadelphia, Pa.   D. Nov. 4, 1946, Fairview Village, Pa.   BB TR 5'11"   180 lbs.

| 1904 PHI N | 0 | 0 | – | 5.06 | 4 | 0 | 0 | 10.2 | 12 | 8 | 5 | 0 | 0 | 0 | 0 | 3 | 1 | 0 | .333 |

Les Bartholomew

BARTHOLOMEW, LESTER JUSTIN
B. Apr. 4, 1903, Madison, Wis.   D. Sept. 19, 1972, Barrington, Ill.   BR TL 5'11½"   195 lbs.

1928 PIT N	0	0	–	7.15	6	0	0	22.2	31	9	6	0	0	0	0	7	1	0	.143
1932 CHI A	0	0	–	5.06	3	0	0	5.1	5	6	1	0	0	0	0	1	0	0	.000
2 yrs.	0	0	–	6.75	9	0	0	28	36	15	7	0	0	0	0	8	1	0	.125

Bill Bartley

BARTLEY, WILLIAM JACKSON
B. Jan. 8, 1885, Cincinnati, Ohio   D. May 17, 1965, Cincinnati, Ohio   BR TR 5'11½"   190 lbs.

1903 NY N	0	0	–	0.00	1	0	0	3	3	4	2	0	0	0	0	1	0	0	.000
1906 PHI A	0	0	–	9.35	3	0	0	8.2	10	6	6	0	0	0	1	3	1	0	.333
1907	0	1	.000	2.24	15	3	2	56.1	44	19	16	0	0	1	0	21	2	0	.095
3 yrs.	0	1	.000	3.04	19	3	2	68	57	29	24	0	0	1	1	25	3	0	.120

Charlie Bartson

BARTSON, CHARLES FRANKLIN
B. Mar. 13, 1865, Peoria, Ill.   D. June 9, 1936, Peoria, Ill.   6'   170 lbs.

| 1890 CHI P | 8 | 10 | .444 | 4.26 | 25 | 19 | 16 | 188 | 222 | 66 | 47 | 0 | 1 | 0 | 1 | 75 | 13 | 0 | .173 |

Jim Baskette

BASKETTE, JAMES BLAINE (Big Jim)
B. Dec. 10, 1887, Athens, Tenn.   D. July 30, 1942, Athens, Tenn.   BR TR 6'2"   185 lbs.

1911 CLE A	1	2	.333	3.38	4	2	2	21.1	21	9	8	0	0	1	0	6	2	0	.333
1912	8	4	.667	3.18	29	11	7	116	109	46	51	1	2	1	1	40	5	0	.125
1913	0	0	–	5.79	2	1	0	4.2	8	2	0	0	0	0	0	1	1	0	1.000
3 yrs.	9	6	.600	3.30	35	14	9	142	138	57	59	1	2	2	1	47	8	0	.170

Dick Bass

BASS, RICHARD WILLIAM
B. July 7, 1906, Rogersville, Tenn.   BR TR 6'2"   175 lbs.

| 1939 WAS A | 0 | 1 | .000 | 6.75 | 1 | 1 | 0 | 8 | 7 | 6 | 1 | 0 | 0 | 0 | 0 | 2 | 0 | 0 | .000 |

Norm Bass

BASS, NORMAN DELANEY
B. Jan. 21, 1939, Laurel, Miss.   BR TR 6'3"   205 lbs.

1961 KC A	11	11	.500	4.69	40	23	6	170.2	164	82	74	2	0	1	0	59	7	1	.119
1962	2	6	.250	6.09	22	10	0	75.1	96	46	33	0	1	1	0	22	1	0	.045
1963	0	0	–	11.74	3	1	0	7.2	11	9	4	0	0	0	0	1	0	0	.000
3 yrs.	13	17	.433	5.32	65	34	6	253.2	271	137	111	2	1	2	0	82	8	1	.098

Charlie Bastian

BASTIAN, CHARLES J.
B. July 4, 1860, Philadelphia, Pa.   D. Jan. 18, 1932, Pennsauken, N. J.   BR TR 5'6½"   145 lbs.

| 1884 WIL U | 0 | 0 | – | 3.00 | 1 | 0 | 0 | 6 | 6 | 0 | 2 | 0 | 0 | 0 | 0 | * | | |

Joe Batchelder

BATCHELDER, JOSEPH EDMUND (Win)
B. July 11, 1898, Wenham, Mass.   BR TL 5'7"   165 lbs.

1923 BOS N	1	0	1.000	7.00	4	1	1	9	12	1	2	0	0	0	0	1	0	0	.000
1924	0	0	–	3.86	3	0	0	4.2	4	2	2	0	0	0	0	1	0	0	.000
1925	0	0	–	5.14	4	0	0	7	10	1	2	0	0	0	0	1	0	0	.000
3 yrs.	1	0	1.000	5.66	11	1	1	20.2	26	4	6	0	0	0	0	3	0	0	.000

Bush Bates

BATES, BUSH
Deceased.

| 1889 KC AA | 0 | 1 | .000 | 13.50 | 1 | 1 | 1 | 8 | 15 | 5 | 3 | 0 | 0 | 0 | 0 | 4 | 0 | 0 | .000 |

Dick Bates

BATES, CHARLES RICHARD
B. Oct. 7, 1945, McArthur, Ohio   BL TR 6'   190 lbs.

| 1969 SEA A | 0 | 0 | – | 27.00 | 1 | 0 | 0 | 1.2 | 3 | 3 | 1 | 0 | 0 | 0 | 0 | 0 | 0 | 0 | – |

Frank Bates

BATES, FRANK CHARLES
B. Chattanooga, Tenn.   Deceased.

| 1898 CLE N | 2 | 1 | .667 | 3.10 | 4 | 4 | 4 | 29 | 30 | 11 | 5 | 0 | 0 | 0 | 0 | 9 | 1 | 0 | .111 |

	W	L	PCT	ERA	G	GS	CG	IP	H	BB	SO	ShO	Relief Pitching W	L	SV	BATTING AB	H	HR	BA

Frank Bates continued

	W	L	PCT	ERA	G	GS	CG	IP	H	BB	SO	ShO	W	L	SV	AB	H	HR	BA
1899 2 teams	STL	N	(2G 0-0)	CLE	N	(20G 1-18)													
" total	1	18	.053	6.90	22	19	17	161.2	246	110	13	0	0	0	0	68	15	0	.221
2 yrs.	3	19	.136	6.33	26	23	21	190.2	276	121	18	0	0	0	0	77	16	0	.208

Joe Battin

BATTIN, JOSEPH V.   BR TR
B. Nov. 11, 1851, Philadelphia, Pa.   D. Oct. 11, 1937, Akron, Ohio
Manager 1883-84.

	W	L	PCT	ERA	G	GS	CG	IP	H	BB	SO	ShO	W	L	SV	AB	H	HR	BA
1877 STL N	0	0	–	4.91	1	0	0	3.2	3	1	1	0	0	0	0	226	45	1	.199
1883 PIT AA	0	0	–	2.25	2	0	0	4	9	1	0	0	0	0	0	388	83	1	.214
2 yrs.	0	0	–	3.52	3	0	0	7.2	12	2	1	0	0	0	0	*			

Chris Batton

BATTON, CHRISTOPHER SEAN   BR TR 6'4"   195 lbs.
B. Aug. 24, 1954, Los Angeles, Calif.

	W	L	PCT	ERA	G	GS	CG	IP	H	BB	SO	ShO	W	L	SV	AB	H	HR	BA
1976 OAK A	0	0	–	9.00	2	1	0	4	5	3	4	0	0	0	0	0	0	0	–

Lou Bauer

BAUER, LOUIS WALTER (Kid)   BR TR 6'   175 lbs.
B. Nov. 30, 1898, Egg Harbor City, N. J.   D. Feb. 4, 1978, Pomona, N. J.

	W	L	PCT	ERA	G	GS	CG	IP	H	BB	SO	ShO	W	L	SV	AB	H	HR	BA
1918 PHI A	0	0	–	∞	1	0	0	0	0	2	0	0	0	0	0	0	0	0	–

Al Bauers

BAUERS, ALBERT J.   TL
B. 1850, Columbus, Ohio   D. Sept. 6, 1913, Wilkes-Barre, Pa.

	W	L	PCT	ERA	G	GS	CG	IP	H	BB	SO	ShO	W	L	SV	AB	H	HR	BA
1884 COL AA	1	2	.333	4.68	3	3	3	25	22	14	13	0	0	0	0	11	3	0	.273
1886 STL N	0	4	.000	5.97	4	4	3	28.2	31	27	13	0	0	0	0	12	2	0	.167
2 yrs.	1	6	.143	5.37	7	7	6	53.2	53	41	26	0	0	0	0	23	5	0	.217

Russ Bauers

BAUERS, RUSSELL LEE   BL TR 6'3"   195 lbs.
B. May 10, 1914, Townsend, Wis.

	W	L	PCT	ERA	G	GS	CG	IP	H	BB	SO	ShO	W	L	SV	AB	H	HR	BA
1936 PIT N	0	0	–	33.75	1	1	0	1.1	2	4	0	0	0	0	0	0	0	0	–
1937	13	6	.684	2.88	34	19	11	187.2	174	80	118	2	3	1	1	69	15	0	.217
1938	13	14	.481	3.07	40	34	12	243	207	99	117	3	1	2	3	88	21	0	.239
1939	2	4	.333	3.35	15	8	1	53.2	46	25	12	0	1	1	1	19	4	0	.211
1940	0	2	.000	7.63	15	2	0	30.2	42	18	11	0	0	0	0	7	2	0	.286
1941	1	3	.250	5.54	8	5	1	37.1	40	25	20	0	0	0	0	14	5	0	.357
1946 CHI N	2	1	.667	3.53	15	2	2	43.1	45	19	22	0	1	0	1	10	3	0	.300
1950 STL A	0	0	–	4.50	1	0	0	2	6	1	0	0	0	0	0	0	0	0	–
8 yrs.	31	30	.508	3.53	129	71	27	599	562	271	300	5	6	4	6	207	50	0	.242

Frank Baumann

BAUMANN, FRANK MATT (The Beau)   BL TL 6'   205 lbs.
B. July 1, 1933, St. Louis, Mo.

	W	L	PCT	ERA	G	GS	CG	IP	H	BB	SO	ShO	W	L	SV	AB	H	HR	BA
1955 BOS A	2	1	.667	5.82	7	5	0	34	38	17	27	0	1	0	0	13	3	0	.231
1956	2	1	.667	3.28	7	1	0	24.2	22	14	18	0	1	1	0	9	3	0	.333
1957	1	0	1.000	3.75	4	1	0	12	13	3	7	0	0	0	0	2	1	0	.500
1958	2	2	.500	4.47	10	7	2	52.1	56	27	31	0	0	0	0	14	3	0	.214
1959	6	4	.600	4.05	26	10	2	95.2	96	55	48	0	2	0	1	29	6	0	.207
1960 CHI A	13	6	.684	2.67	44	20	7	185.1	169	53	71	2	6	3	3	52	8	0	.154
1961	10	13	.435	5.61	53	23	5	187.2	249	59	75	1	4	4	3	61	16	2	.262
1962	7	6	.538	3.38	40	10	3	119.2	117	36	55	1	4	2	4	30	8	0	.267
1963	2	1	.667	3.04	24	1	0	50.1	52	17	31	0	2	0	1	11	1	0	.091
1964	0	3	.000	6.19	22	0	0	32	40	16	19	0	0	3	1	4	0	0	.000
1965 CHI N	0	1	.000	7.36	4	0	0	3.2	4	3	2	0	0	1	0	0	0	0	–
11 yrs.	45	38	.542	4.11	241	78	19	797.1	856	300	384	4	20	13	13	225	49	2	.218

George Baumgardner

BAUMGARDNER, GEORGE WASHINGTON   BL TR 5'11"   178 lbs.
B. July 22, 1891, Barbourville, W. Va.   D. Dec. 13, 1970, Barbourville, W. Va.

	W	L	PCT	ERA	G	GS	CG	IP	H	BB	SO	ShO	W	L	SV	AB	H	HR	BA
1912 STL A	11	14	.440	3.38	30	26	18	218.1	222	79	102	2	0	1	0	76	11	0	.145
1913	10	19	.345	3.13	38	31	23	253.1	267	84	78	2	0	0	1	78	13	0	.167
1914	14	13	.519	2.79	45	18	9	183.2	152	84	93	3	6	5	3	53	7	0	.132
1915	0	2	.000	4.43	7	1	1	22.1	29	11	6	0	0	1	0	6	0	0	.000
1916	1	0	1.000	7.88	4	2	0	8	12	5	4	0	0	0	0	2	0	0	.000
5 yrs.	36	48	.429	3.22	124	78	51	685.2	682	263	283	7	6	7	4	215	31	0	.144

Ross Baumgarten

BAUMGARTEN, ROSS   BL TL 6'1"   180 lbs.
Also known as Antonio Baumgarten.
B. May 27, 1955, Highland Park, Ill.

	W	L	PCT	ERA	G	GS	CG	IP	H	BB	SO	ShO	W	L	SV	AB	H	HR	BA
1978 CHI A	2	2	.500	5.87	7	4	1	23	29	9	15	1	0	0	0	0	0	0	–
1979	13	8	.619	3.53	28	28	4	191	175	83	72	3	0	0	0	0	0	0	–
1980	2	12	.143	3.44	24	23	3	136	127	52	66	1	0	0	0	0	0	0	–
1981	5	9	.357	4.06	19	19	2	102	101	40	52	1	0	0	0	0	0	0	–
1982 PIT N	0	5	.000	6.55	12	10	0	44	60	27	17	0	0	0	0	12	1	0	.083
5 yrs.	22	36	.379	3.99	90	84	10	496	492	211	222	6	0	0	0	12	1	0	.083

Harry Baumgartner

BAUMGARTNER, HARRY E   BR TR 5'11"   175 lbs.
B. Oct. 8, 1892, S. Pittsburg, Tenn.   D. Dec. 3, 1930, Augusta, Ga.

	W	L	PCT	ERA	G	GS	CG	IP	H	BB	SO	ShO	W	L	SV	AB	H	HR	BA
1920 DET A	0	1	.000	4.00	9	0	0	18	18	6	7	0	0	1	0	4	1	0	.250

Stan Baumgartner

BAUMGARTNER, STANWOOD FULTON   BL TL 6'   175 lbs.
B. Dec. 14, 1894, Houston, Tex.   D. Oct. 4, 1955, Philadelphia, Pa.

	W	L	PCT	ERA	G	GS	CG	IP	H	BB	SO	ShO	W	L	SV	AB	H	HR	BA
1914 PHI N	3	2	.600	3.28	15	3	2	60.1	60	16	24	1	3	0	0	19	1	0	.053
1915	0	2	.000	2.42	16	1	0	48.1	38	23	27	0	0	1	0	12	1	0	.083
1916	0	0	–	2.25	1	0	0	4	5	1	0	0	0	0	0	1	0	0	.000
1921	3	6	.333	7.02	22	7	2	66.2	103	22	13	0	2	0	0	30	6	0	.200
1922	1	1	.500	6.52	6	1	0	9.2	18	5	2	0	1	0	0	3	1	0	.333
1924 PHI A	13	6	.684	2.88	36	16	12	181	181	73	45	1	4	1	4	60	13	0	.217
1925	6	3	.667	3.57	37	11	2	113.1	120	35	18	1	2	1	3	30	7	0	.233

	W	L	PCT	ERA	G	GS	CG	IP	H	BB	SO	ShO	Relief Pitching W	L	SV	BATTING AB	H	HR	BA

Stan Baumgartner continued

	W	L	PCT	ERA	G	GS	CG	IP	H	BB	SO	ShO	W	L	SV	AB	H	HR	BA
1926	1	1	.500	4.03	10	1	0	22.1	28	10	0	0	1	1	0	3	1	0	.333
8 yrs.	27	21	.563	3.70	143	40	18	505.2	553	185	129	3	13	4	7	158	30	0	.190

George Bausewine

BAUSEWINE, GEORGE W.   6'2"
B. Mar. 22, 1869, Philadelphia, Pa.   D. July 29, 1947, Norristown, Pa.

	W	L	PCT	ERA	G	GS	CG	IP	H	BB	SO	ShO	W	L	SV	AB	H	HR	BA
1889 PHI AA	1	4	.200	3.90	7	6	6	55.1	64	33	18	0	0	0	0	21	1	0	.048

Ed Bauta

BAUTA, EDUARDO GALVEZ   BR TR 6'3"   200 lbs.
B. Jan. 6, 1935, Florida Camaguey, Cuba

	W	L	PCT	ERA	G	GS	CG	IP	H	BB	SO	ShO	W	L	SV	AB	H	HR	BA
1960 STL N	0	0	–	6.32	9	0	0	15.2	14	11	6	0	0	0	1	1	0	0	.000
1961	2	0	1.000	1.40	13	0	0	19.1	12	5	12	0	2	0	5	4	2	0	.500
1962	1	0	1.000	5.01	20	0	0	32.1	28	21	25	0	1	0	1	4	1	0	.250
1963 2 teams		STL	N (38G 3–4)		NY	N	(9G 0–0)												
" total	3	4	.429	4.27	47	0	0	71.2	77	30	43	0	3	4	3	8	0	0	.000
1964 NY N	0	2	.000	5.40	8	0	0	10	17	3	3	0	0	2	1	0	0	0	–
5 yrs.	6	6	.500	4.35	97	0	0	149	148	70	89	0	6	6	11	17	3	0	.176

Bill Bayne

BAYNE, WILLIAM LEAR (Beverly)   BL TL 5'9"   160 lbs.
B. Apr. 18, 1899, Pittsburgh, Pa.   D. May 22, 1981, St. Louis, Mo.

	W	L	PCT	ERA	G	GS	CG	IP	H	BB	SO	ShO	W	L	SV	AB	H	HR	BA
1919 STL A	1	1	.500	5.25	2	2	1	12	16	6	0	0	0	0	0	5	2	0	.400
1920	5	6	.455	3.70	18	13	6	99.2	102	41	38	1	0	0	0	35	6	0	.171
1921	11	5	.688	4.72	47	14	7	164	167	80	82	1	5	1	3	60	18	1	.300
1922	4	5	.444	4.56	26	9	3	92.2	86	37	38	0	1	2	2	30	7	0	.233
1923	2	2	.500	4.50	19	2	0	46	49	31	15	0	2	1	0	13	3	0	.231
1924	1	3	.250	4.17	21	3	0	49.2	46	28	20	0	1	2	0	14	6	0	.429
1928 CLE A	2	5	.286	5.13	37	6	3	108.2	128	43	39	0	0	3	3	30	11	0	.367
1929 BOS A	5	5	.500	6.72	27	6	2	84.1	111	29	26	0	4	0	0	25	8	0	.320
1930	0	0	–	4.50	1	0	0	4	5	1	1	0	0	0	0	2	1	0	.500
9 yrs.	31	32	.492	4.82	198	55	22	661	710	296	259	2	13	9	8	214	62	1	.290

Walter Beall

BEALL, WALTER ESAU   BR TR 5'10"   178 lbs.
B. July 29, 1899, Washington, D. C.   D. Jan. 28, 1959, Suitland, Md.

	W	L	PCT	ERA	G	GS	CG	IP	H	BB	SO	ShO	W	L	SV	AB	H	HR	BA
1924 NY A	2	0	1.000	3.52	4	2	0	23	19	17	18	0	1	0	0	7	1	0	.143
1925	0	1	.000	12.71	8	1	0	11.1	11	19	8	0	0	0	0	3	0	0	.000
1926	2	4	.333	3.53	20	9	1	81.2	71	68	56	0	0	0	1	22	3	0	.136
1927	0	0	–	9.00	1	0	0	1	1	0	0	0	0	0	0	0	0	0	–
1929 WAS A	1	0	1.000	3.86	3	0	0	7	8	7	3	0	1	0	0	3	0	0	.000
5 yrs.	5	5	.500	4.43	36	12	1	124	110	111	85	0	2	0	1	35	4	0	.114

Alex Beam

BEAM, ALEXANDER RODGER
B. Nov. 21, 1870, Johnstown, Pa.   D. Apr. 17, 1938, Nogales, Ariz.

	W	L	PCT	ERA	G	GS	CG	IP	H	BB	SO	ShO	W	L	SV	AB	H	HR	BA
1889 PIT N	1	1	.500	6.50	2	2	2	18	11	15	1	0	0	0	0	6	1	0	.167

Ernie Beam

BEAM, ERNEST JOSEPH
B. Mar. 17, 1867, Mansfield, Ohio   D. Sept. 12, 1918, Mansfield, Ohio

	W	L	PCT	ERA	G	GS	CG	IP	H	BB	SO	ShO	W	L	SV	AB	H	HR	BA
1895 PHI N	0	2	.000	11.31	9	1	1	24.2	33	25	3	0	0	1	3	11	2	0	.182

Charlie Beamon

BEAMON, CHARLES ALONZO   BR TR 5'11"   195 lbs.
Father of Charlie Beamon.
B. Dec. 25, 1934, Oakland, Calif.

	W	L	PCT	ERA	G	GS	CG	IP	H	BB	SO	ShO	W	L	SV	AB	H	HR	BA
1956 BAL A	2	0	1.000	1.38	2	1	1	13	9	8	14	1	1	0	0	5	0	0	.000
1957	0	0	–	5.19	4	1	0	8.2	8	7	5	0	0	0	0	2	0	0	.000
1958	1	3	.250	4.35	21	3	0	49.2	47	21	26	0	1	1	0	10	0	0	.000
3 yrs.	3	3	.500	3.91	27	5	1	71.1	64	36	45	1	2	1	0	17	0	0	.000

Belve Bean

BEAN, BEVERIC BENTON (Bill)   BR TR 6'1½"   197 lbs.
B. Apr. 23, 1905, Mullin, Tex.

	W	L	PCT	ERA	G	GS	CG	IP	H	BB	SO	ShO	W	L	SV	AB	H	HR	BA
1930 CLE A	3	3	.500	5.45	23	3	2	74.1	99	32	19	0	3	1	2	26	9	0	.346
1931	0	1	.000	6.43	4	0	0	7	11	4	3	0	0	1	0	1	0	0	.000
1933	1	2	.333	5.25	27	2	0	70.1	80	20	41	0	1	1	0	22	4	0	.182
1934	5	1	.833	3.86	21	1	0	51.1	53	21	20	0	5	0	0	15	3	0	.200
1935 2 teams		CLE	A (1G 0–0)		WAS	A	(10G 2–0)												
" total	2	0	1.000	7.31	11	2	0	32	45	19	6	0	2	0	0	8	3	1	.375
5 yrs.	11	7	.611	5.32	86	8	2	235	288	96	89	0	11	3	2	72	19	1	.264

Dave Beard

BEARD, CHARLES DAVID   BL TR 6'5"   190 lbs.
B. Oct. 2, 1959, Chamblee, Ga.

	W	L	PCT	ERA	G	GS	CG	IP	H	BB	SO	ShO	W	L	SV	AB	H	HR	BA
1980 OAK A	0	1	.000	3.38	13	0	0	16	12	7	12	0	0	1	1	0	0	0	–
1981	1	1	.500	2.77	8	0	0	13	9	4	15	0	1	1	3	0	0	0	–
1982	10	9	.526	3.44	54	2	0	91.2	85	35	73	0	10	7	11	0	0	0	–
1983	5	5	.500	5.61	43	0	0	61	55	36	40	0	5	5	10	0	0	0	–
1984 SEA A	3	2	.600	5.80	43	0	0	76	88	33	40	0	3	2	5	0	0	0	–
5 yrs.	19	18	.514	4.61	161	2	0	257.2	249	115	180	0	19	16	30	0	0	0	–

DIVISIONAL PLAYOFF SERIES
	W	L	PCT	ERA	G	GS	CG	IP	H	BB	SO	ShO	W	L	SV	AB	H	HR	BA
1981 OAK A	0	0	–	0.00	1	0	0	1.1	0	0	2	0	0	0	1	0	0	0	–

LEAGUE CHAMPIONSHIP SERIES
	W	L	PCT	ERA	G	GS	CG	IP	H	BB	SO	ShO	W	L	SV	AB	H	HR	BA
1981 OAK A	0	0	–	40.50	1	0	0	.2	5	0	0	0	0	0	0	0	0	0	–

Mike Beard

BEARD, MICHAEL RICHARD   BL TL 6'1"   185 lbs.
B. June 21, 1950, Little Rock, Ark.

	W	L	PCT	ERA	G	GS	CG	IP	H	BB	SO	ShO	W	L	SV	AB	H	HR	BA
1974 ATL N	0	0	–	3.00	6	0	0	9	5	1	7	0	0	0	0	0	0	0	–
1975	4	0	1.000	3.21	34	2	0	70	71	28	27	0	4	0	0	9	1	0	.111
1976	0	2	.000	4.24	30	0	0	34	38	14	8	0	0	2	1	1	0	0	.000

	W	L	PCT	ERA	G	GS	CG	IP	H	BB	SO	ShO	Relief Pitching W	L	SV	BATTING AB	H	HR	BA

Mike Beard continued

	W	L	PCT	ERA	G	GS	CG	IP	H	BB	SO	ShO	W	L	SV	AB	H	HR	BA
1977	0	0	–	9.00	4	0	0	5	14	2	1	0	0	0	0	0	0	0	–
4 yrs.	4	2	.667	3.74	74	2	0	118	128	45	43	0	4	2	1	10	1	0	.100

Ralph Beard

BEARD, RALPH WILLIAM
B. Feb. 11, 1929, Cincinnati, Ohio   BR TR 6'5"   200 lbs.

	W	L	PCT	ERA	G	GS	CG	IP	H	BB	SO	ShO	W	L	SV	AB	H	HR	BA
1954 STL N	0	4	.000	3.72	13	10	0	58	62	28	17	0	0	0	0	17	1	0	.059

Gene Bearden

BEARDEN, HENRY EUGENE
B. Sept. 5, 1920, Lexa, Ark.   BL TL 6'4"   198 lbs.

	W	L	PCT	ERA	G	GS	CG	IP	H	BB	SO	ShO	W	L	SV	AB	H	HR	BA
1947 CLE A	0	0	–	81.00	1	0	0	.1	2	1	0	0	0	0	0	0	0	0	–
1948	20	7	.741	2.43	37	29	15	229.2	187	106	80	6	0	2	1	90	23	2	.256
1949	8	8	.500	5.10	32	19	5	127	140	92	41	0	1	1	0	45	5	0	.111
1950 2 teams		CLE	A (14G 1–3)		WAS	A (12G 3–5)													
" total	4	8	.333	4.99	26	12	4	113.2	138	65	30	0	1	2	0	35	7	0	.200
1951 2 teams		WAS	A (1G 0–0)		DET	A (37G 3–4)													
" total	3	4	.429	4.64	38	5	2	108.2	118	60	39	1	1	2	0	32	6	2	.188
1952 STL A	7	8	.467	4.30	34	16	3	150.2	158	78	45	0	1	2	0	65	23	0	.354
1953 CHI A	3	3	.500	2.93	25	3	0	58.1	48	33	24	0	3	1	0	21	4	0	.190
7 yrs.	45	38	.542	3.96	193	84	29	788.1	791	435	259	7	7	10	1	288	68	4	.236

WORLD SERIES

	W	L	PCT	ERA	G	GS	CG	IP	H	BB	SO	ShO	W	L	SV	AB	H	HR	BA
1948 CLE A	1	0	1.000	0.00	2	1	1	10.2	6	1	4	1	0	0	1	4	2	0	.500

Gary Beare

BEARE, GARY RAY
B. Aug. 22, 1952, San Diego, Calif.   BR TR 6'4"   205 lbs.

	W	L	PCT	ERA	G	GS	CG	IP	H	BB	SO	ShO	W	L	SV	AB	H	HR	BA
1976 MIL A	2	3	.400	3.29	6	5	2	41	43	15	32	0	0	0	0	0	0	0	–
1977	3	3	.500	6.41	17	6	0	59	63	38	32	0	2	0	0	0	0	0	–
2 yrs.	5	6	.455	5.13	23	11	2	100	106	53	64	0	2	0	0	0	0	0	–

Larry Bearnarth

BEARNARTH, LAWRENCE DONALD
B. Sept. 11, 1941, New York, N. Y.   BR TR 6'2"   203 lbs.

	W	L	PCT	ERA	G	GS	CG	IP	H	BB	SO	ShO	W	L	SV	AB	H	HR	BA
1963 NY N	3	8	.273	3.42	58	0	0	126.1	127	47	48	0	3	7	4	30	6	0	.200
1964	5	5	.500	4.15	44	1	0	78	79	38	31	0	5	4	3	14	2	0	.143
1965	3	5	.375	4.60	40	3	0	60.2	75	28	16	0	3	3	1	9	1	0	.111
1966	2	3	.400	4.45	29	1	0	54.2	59	20	27	0	2	2	0	9	1	0	.111
1971 MIL A	0	0	–	18.00	2	0	0	3	10	2	2	0	0	0	0	0	0	0	–
5 yrs.	13	21	.382	4.13	173	7	0	322.2	350	135	124	0	13	16	8	62	10	0	.161

Ed Beatin

BEATIN, EBENEZER AMBROSE
B. Aug. 10, 1866, Baltimore, Md.   D. May 9, 1925, Baltimore, Md.   BR TR   160 lbs.

	W	L	PCT	ERA	G	GS	CG	IP	H	BB	SO	ShO	W	L	SV	AB	H	HR	BA
1887 DET N	1	1	.500	4.00	2	2	2	18	13	8	6	0	0	0	0	7	0	0	.000
1888	5	7	.417	2.86	12	12	12	107	111	16	44	0	0	0	0	56	14	2	.250
1889 CLE N	20	15	.571	3.57	36	36	35	317.2	316	141	126	3	0	0	0	121	14	1	.116
1890	22	31	.415	3.83	54	54	53	474.1	518	186	155	1	0	0	0	191	27	1	.141
1891	0	3	.000	5.28	5	4	2	29	39	21	4	0	0	0	0	13	1	0	.077
5 yrs.	48	57	.457	3.68	109	108	104	946	997	372	335	4	0	0	0	388	56	4	.144

Jim Beattie

BEATTIE, JAMES LOUIS
B. July 4, 1954, Hampton, Va.   BR TR 6'5"   210 lbs.

	W	L	PCT	ERA	G	GS	CG	IP	H	BB	SO	ShO	W	L	SV	AB	H	HR	BA
1978 NY A	6	9	.400	3.73	25	22	0	128	123	51	65	0	0	0	0	0	0	0	–
1979	3	6	.333	5.21	15	13	1	76	85	41	32	1	0	0	0	0	0	0	–
1980 SEA A	5	15	.250	4.86	33	29	3	187	205	98	67	0	0	1	0	0	0	0	–
1981	3	2	.600	2.96	13	9	0	67	59	18	36	0	0	0	1	0	0	0	–
1982	8	12	.400	3.34	28	26	6	172.1	149	65	140	1	0	0	0	0	0	0	–
1983	10	15	.400	3.84	30	29	8	196.2	197	66	132	2	0	0	0	0	0	0	–
1984	12	16	.429	3.41	32	32	12	211	206	75	119	2	0	0	0	0	0	0	–
7 yrs.	47	75	.385	3.88	176	160	30	1038	1024	414	591	6	0	1	1	0	0	0	–

LEAGUE CHAMPIONSHIP SERIES

	W	L	PCT	ERA	G	GS	CG	IP	H	BB	SO	ShO	W	L	SV	AB	H	HR	BA
1978 NY A	1	0	1.000	1.69	1	1	0	5.1	2	5	3	0	0	0	0	0	0	0	–

WORLD SERIES

	W	L	PCT	ERA	G	GS	CG	IP	H	BB	SO	ShO	W	L	SV	AB	H	HR	BA
1978 NY A	1	0	1.000	2.00	1	1	1	9	9	4	8	0	0	0	0	0	0	0	–

Johnny Beazley

BEAZLEY, JOHN ANDREW
B. May 25, 1918, Nashville, Tenn.   BR TR 6'1½"   190 lbs.

	W	L	PCT	ERA	G	GS	CG	IP	H	BB	SO	ShO	W	L	SV	AB	H	HR	BA
1941 STL N	1	0	1.000	1.00	1	1	1	9	10	3	4	0	0	0	0	3	0	0	.000
1942	21	6	.778	2.13	43	23	13	215.1	181	73	91	3	6	3	3	73	10	0	.137
1946	7	5	.583	4.46	19	18	5	103	109	55	36	0	0	0	0	33	8	0	.242
1947 BOS N	2	0	1.000	4.40	9	2	2	28.2	30	19	12	0	0	0	0	7	0	0	.000
1948	0	1	.000	4.50	3	2	0	16	19	7	4	0	0	0	0	4	0	0	.000
1949	0	0	–	0.00	1	0	0	2	0	0	0	0	0	0	0	0	0	0	–
6 yrs.	31	12	.721	3.01	76	46	21	374	349	157	147	3	6	3	3	120	18	0	.150

WORLD SERIES

	W	L	PCT	ERA	G	GS	CG	IP	H	BB	SO	ShO	W	L	SV	AB	H	HR	BA
1942 STL N	2	0	1.000	2.50	2	2	2	18	17	3	6	0	0	0	0	7	1	0	.143
1946	0	0	–	0.00	1	0	0	1	1	0	1	0	0	0	0	0	0	0	–
2 yrs.	2	0	1.000	2.37	3	2	2	19	18	3	7	0	0	0	0	7	1	0	.143

Buck Becannon

BECANNON, JAMES MELVILLE
B. Aug. 22, 1859, New York, N. Y.   D. Nov. 5, 1923, New York, N. Y.   5'10"   165 lbs.

	W	L	PCT	ERA	G	GS	CG	IP	H	BB	SO	ShO	W	L	SV	AB	H	HR	BA
1884 NY AA	1	0	1.000	1.50	1	1	1	6	2	2	2	0	0	0	0	3	0	0	.000
1885	2	8	.200	6.25	10	10	10	85	108	24	13	0	0	0	0	33	10	0	.303
1887 NY N	0	0	–	0.00	0	0	0	0	0	0	0	0	0	0	0	5	0	0	.000
3 yrs.	3	8	.273	5.93	11	11	11	91	110	26	15	0	0	0	0	41	10	0	.244

	W	L	PCT	ERA	G	GS	CG	IP	H	BB	SO	ShO	Relief Pitching W	L	SV	BATTING AB	H	HR	BA

Boom-Boom Beck

BECK, WALTER WILLIAM   BR TR 6'2"   200 lbs.
B. Oct. 16, 1904, Decatur, Ill.

	W	L	PCT	ERA	G	GS	CG	IP	H	BB	SO	ShO	W	L	SV	AB	H	HR	BA
1924 STL A	0	0	—	0.00	1	0	0	1	2	1	0	0	0	0	0	0	0	0	—
1927	1	0	1.000	5.56	3	1	1	11.1	15	5	6	0	0	0	0	4	1	0	.250
1928	2	3	.400	4.41	16	4	2	49	52	20	17	0	1	0	0	14	6	0	.429
1933 BKN N	12	20	.375	3.54	43	35	15	257	270	69	89	3	1	1	1	95	18	0	.189
1934	2	6	.250	7.42	22	9	2	57	72	32	24	0	1	1	0	17	4	0	.235
1939 PHI N	7	14	.333	4.73	34	16	12	182.2	203	64	77	0	3	4	3	68	9	0	.132
1940	4	9	.308	4.31	29	15	4	129.1	147	41	38	0	2	0	0	36	2	0	.056
1941	1	9	.100	4.63	34	7	2	95.1	104	35	34	0	0	3	0	25	3	0	.120
1942	0	1	.000	4.75	26	1	0	53	69	17	10	0	0	0	0	12	4	0	.333
1943	0	0	—	9.88	4	0	0	13.2	24	5	3	0	0	0	0	4	2	0	.500
1944 DET A	1	2	.333	3.89	28	2	0	74	67	27	25	0	1	1	1	22	7	0	.318
1945 2 teams					CIN N (11G 2–4)			PIT N (14G 6–1)											
" total	8	5	.615	2.68	25	11	6	110.2	96	26	29	0	2	1	1	30	5	0	.167
12 yrs.	38	69	.355	4.30	265	101	44	1034	1121	342	352	3	11	11	6	327	61	0	.187

Frank Beck

BECK, FRANK J.   TR
B. 1862, Poughkeepsie, N. Y.   Deceased.

	W	L	PCT	ERA	G	GS	CG	IP	H	BB	SO	ShO	W	L	SV	AB	H	HR	BA
1884 2 teams					PIT AA (3G 0–3)			BAL U (2G 0–2)											
" total	0	5	.000	6.62	5	5	4	34	50	10	18	0	0	0	0	32	6	0	.188

George Beck

BECK, GEORGE F.   BR TR 5'11"   162 lbs.
B. 1889, Moline, Ill.

	W	L	PCT	ERA	G	GS	CG	IP	H	BB	SO	ShO	W	L	SV	AB	H	HR	BA
1914 CLE A	0	0	—	0.00	1	0	0	1	1	0	0	0	0	0	0	0	0	0	—

Rich Beck

BECK, RICHARD HENRY   BB TR 6'3"   190 lbs.
B. Jan. 21, 1941, Pasco, Wash.

	W	L	PCT	ERA	G	GS	CG	IP	H	BB	SO	ShO	W	L	SV	AB	H	HR	BA
1965 NY A	2	1*	.667	2.14	3	3	1	21	22	7	10	1	0	0	0	7	0	0	.000

Bob Becker

BECKER, ROBERT CHARLES   TL
B. Aug. 15, 1875, Syracuse, N. Y.   D. Oct. 11, 1951, Syracuse, N. Y.

	W	L	PCT	ERA	G	GS	CG	IP	H	BB	SO	ShO	W	L	SV	AB	H	HR	BA
1897 PHI N	0	2	.000	5.63	5	2	2	24	32	7	10	0	0	0	0	9	1	0	.111
1898	0	0	—	10.80	1	0	0	5	6	5	0	0	0	0	0	1	0	0	.000
2 yrs.	0	2	.000	6.52	6	2	2	29	38	12	10	0	0	0	0	10	1	0	.100

Charlie Becker

BECKER, CHARLES S. (Buck)   BL TL 6'2"   180 lbs.
B. Oct. 14, 1888, Washington, D. C.   D. July 30, 1928, Washington, D. C.

	W	L	PCT	ERA	G	GS	CG	IP	H	BB	SO	ShO	W	L	SV	AB	H	HR	BA
1911 WAS A	3	5	.375	4.04	11	5	5	71.1	80	23	31	1	0	3	0	22	5	0	.227
1912	0	0	—	3.00	4	0	0	9	8	6	5	0	0	0	0	2	1	0	.500
2 yrs.	3	5	.375	3.92	15	5	5	80.1	88	29	36	1	0	3	0	24	6	0	.250

Jake Beckley

BECKLEY, JACOB PETER (Eagle Eye)   BL TL 5'10"   200 lbs.
B. Aug. 4, 1867, Hannibal, Mo.   D. June 25, 1918, Kansas City, Mo.
Hall of Fame 1971.

	W	L	PCT	ERA	G	GS	CG	IP	H	BB	SO	ShO	W	L	SV	AB	H	HR	BA
1902 CIN N	0	1	.000	6.75	1	1	0	4	9	1	2	0	0	0	0	*			

Jim Beckman

BECKMAN, JAMES JOSEPH   BR TR 5'10"   172 lbs.
B. Mar. 1, 1905, Cincinnati, Ohio

	W	L	PCT	ERA	G	GS	CG	IP	H	BB	SO	ShO	W	L	SV	AB	H	HR	BA
1927 CIN N	0	1	.000	5.84	4	1	0	12.1	18	6	0	0	0	0	0	1	0	0	.000
1928	0	1	.000	5.87	6	0	0	15.1	19	9	4	0	0	1	0	3	0	0	.000
2 yrs.	0	2	.000	5.86	10	1	0	27.2	37	15	4	0	0	1	0	4	0	0	.000

Bill Beckmann

BECKMANN, WILLIAM ALOYS   BR TR 6'   175 lbs.
B. Dec. 8, 1907, Clayton, Mo.

	W	L	PCT	ERA	G	GS	CG	IP	H	BB	SO	ShO	W	L	SV	AB	H	HR	BA
1939 PHI A	7	11	.389	5.39	27	19	7	155.1	198	41	20	2	2	0	0	52	13	0	.250
1940	8	4	.667	4.17	34	9	6	127.1	132	35	47	2	3	2	1	39	8	0	.205
1941	5	9	.357	4.75	22	15	4	130	141	33	28	0	3	0	1	47	9	0	.191
1942 2 teams					PHI A (5G 0–1)			STL N (2G 1–0)											
" total	1	1	.500	5.27	7	1	0	27.1	28	10	13	0	1	0	0	5	2	0	.400
4 yrs.	21	25	.457	4.79	90	44	17	440	499	119	108	4	9	2	2	143	32	0	.224

Joe Beckwith

BECKWITH, THOMAS JOSEPH   BL TR 6'3"   180 lbs.
B. Jan. 28, 1955, Auburn, Ala.

	W	L	PCT	ERA	G	GS	CG	IP	H	BB	SO	ShO	W	L	SV	AB	H	HR	BA
1979 LA N	1	2	.333	4.38	17	0	0	37	42	15	28	0	1	2	2	5	0	0	.000
1980	3	3	.500	1.95	38	0	0	60	60	23	40	0	3	3	0	2	0	0	.000
1982	2	1	.667	2.70	19	1	0	40	38	14	33	0	2	1	1	7	0	0	.000
1983	3	4	.429	3.55	42	3	0	71	73	35	50	0	3	2	1	5	1	0	.200
1984 KC A	8	4	.667	3.40	49	1	0	100.2	92	25	75	0	8	3	2	0	0	0	—
5 yrs.	17	14	.548	3.18	165	5	0	308.2	305	112	226	0	17	11	6	19	1	0	.053

LEAGUE CHAMPIONSHIP SERIES
	W	L	PCT	ERA	G	GS	CG	IP	H	BB	SO	ShO	W	L	SV	AB	H	HR	BA
1983 LA N	0	0	—	0.00	2	0	0	2.1	1	2	3	0	0	0	0	0	0	0	—

Julio Becquer

BECQUER, JULIO VILLEGAS   BL TL 5'11½"   178 lbs.
B. Dec. 20, 1931, Havana, Cuba

	W	L	PCT	ERA	G	GS	CG	IP	H	BB	SO	ShO	W	L	SV	AB	H	HR	BA
1960 WAS A	0	0	—	9.00	1	0	0	1	1	0	0	0	0	0	0	298	75	4	.252
1961 MIN A	0	0	—	20.25	1	0	0	1.1	4	1	0	0	0	0	0	92	20	5	.217
2 yrs.	0	0	—	15.43	2	0	0	2.1	5	1	0	0	0	0	0	*			

Phil Bedgood

BEDGOOD, PHILLIP BURLETTE   BR TR 6'3"   218 lbs.
B. Mar. 8, 1899, Harrison, Ga.   D. May 8, 1927, Fort Pierce, Fla.

	W	L	PCT	ERA	G	GS	CG	IP	H	BB	SO	ShO	W	L	SV	AB	H	HR	BA
1922 CLE A	1	0	1.000	4.00	1	1	1	9	7	4	5	0	0	0	0	2	0	0	.000
1923	0	2	.000	5.30	9	2	0	18.2	16	14	7	0	0	1	0	4	1	0	.250
2 yrs.	1	2	.333	4.88	10	3	1	27.2	23	18	12	0	0	1	0	6	1	0	.167

	W	L	PCT	ERA	G	GS	CG	IP	H	BB	SO	ShO	Relief Pitching W	L	SV	BATTING AB	H	HR	BA

Hugh Bedient

BEDIENT, HUGH CARPENTER
B. Oct. 23, 1889, Gerry, N. Y. D. July 21, 1965, Jamestown, N. Y. BR TR 6' 185 lbs.

	W	L	PCT	ERA	G	GS	CG	IP	H	BB	SO	ShO	W	L	SV	AB	H	HR	BA
1912 BOS A	20	9	.690	2.92	41	28	19	231	206	55	122	0	6	0	2	73	14	0	.192
1913	15	14	.517	2.78	43	29	19	259	255	67	122	1	3	1	5	80	10	0	.125
1914	8	12	.400	3.60	42	16	7	177.1	185	45	70	1	3	5	2	50	5	0	.100
1915 BUF F	15	18	.455	3.17	53	30	16	269.1	284	69	106	2	3	1	10	83	9	0	.108
4 yrs.	58	53	.523	3.08	179	103	61	936.2	930	236	420	4	15	7	19	286	38	0	.133
WORLD SERIES																			
1912 BOS A	1	0	1.000	0.50	4	2	1	18	10	7	7	0	0	0	0	6	0	0	.000

Andy Bednar

BEDNAR, ANDREW JACKSON
B. Aug. 16, 1908, Streator, Ill. D. Nov. 26, 1937, Graham, Tex. BR TR 5'10½" 180 lbs.

	W	L	PCT	ERA	G	GS	CG	IP	H	BB	SO	ShO	W	L	SV	AB	H	HR	BA
1930 PIT N	0	0	–	27.00	2	0	0	1.1	4	1	1	0	0	0	0	0	0	0	–
1931	0	0	–	11.25	3	0	0	4	10	0	2	0	0	0	0	0	0	0	–
2 yrs.	0	0	–	15.19	5	0	0	5.1	14	1	3	0	0	0	0	0	0	0	–

Steve Bedrosian

BEDROSIAN, STEPHEN WAYNE
B. Dec. 6, 1957, Methuen, Mass. BR TR 6'3" 200 lbs.

	W	L	PCT	ERA	G	GS	CG	IP	H	BB	SO	ShO	W	L	SV	AB	H	HR	BA
1981 ATL N	1	2	.333	4.50	15	1	0	24	15	15	9	0	1	1	0	2	0	0	.000
1982	8	6	.571	2.42	64	3	0	137.2	102	57	123	0	7	4	11	26	1	0	.038
1983	9	10	.474	3.60	70	1	0	120	100	51	114	0	9	10	19	19	2	0	.105
1984	9	6	.600	2.37	40	4	0	83.2	65	33	81	0	6	5	11	17	2	0	.118
4 yrs.	27	24	.529	2.93	189	9	0	365.1	282	156	327	0	23	20	41	64	5	0	.078
LEAGUE CHAMPIONSHIP SERIES																			
1982 ATL N	0	0	–	18.00	2	0	0	1	3	1	2	0	0	0	0	0	0	0	–

Fred Beebe

BEEBE, FREDERICK LEONARD
B. Dec. 31, 1880, Lincoln, Neb. D. Oct. 30, 1957, LaGrange, Ill. BR TR 6'1" 190 lbs.

	W	L	PCT	ERA	G	GS	CG	IP	H	BB	SO	ShO	W	L	SV	AB	H	HR	BA
1906 2 teams			CHI N (14G 7–1)				STL N (20G 9–9)												
" total	16	10	.615	2.93	34	25	20	230.2	171	100	171	1	3	0	1	87	13	0	.149
1907 STL N	7	19	.269	2.72	31	29	24	238.1	192	109	141	4	1	0	0	86	11	0	.128
1908	5	13	.278	2.63	29	19	12	174.1	134	66	72	0	0	1	0	56	7	0	.125
1909	15	21	.417	2.82	44	34	18	287.2	256	104	105	1	2	3	1	108	18	0	.167
1910 CIN N	12	15	.444	3.07	35	26	11	214.1	193	94	93	2	3	0	0	73	12	0	.164
1911 PHI N	3	3	.500	4.47	9	8	3	48.1	52	24	20	0	0	0	0	19	5	0	.263
1916 CLE A	5	3	.625	2.41	20	12	5	100.2	92	37	32	1	0	0	2	28	6	0	.214
7 yrs.	63	84	.429	2.86	202	153	93	1294.1	1090	534	634	9	9	4	4	457	72	0	.158

Ed Beecher

BEECHER, EDWARD H.
B. July 2, 1859, Guilford, Conn. D. Sept. 12, 1935, Hartford, Conn. 5'10" 185 lbs.

	W	L	PCT	ERA	G	GS	CG	IP	H	BB	SO	ShO	W	L	SV	AB	H	HR	BA
1890 BUF P	0	0	–	12.00	1	0	0	6	10	3	0	0	0	0	0	*			

Roy Beecher

BEECHER, LeROY (Colonel)
B. May 10, 1884, Swanton, Ohio D. Oct. 11, 1952, Toledo, Ohio BL TR 6'2" 180 lbs.

	W	L	PCT	ERA	G	GS	CG	IP	H	BB	SO	ShO	W	L	SV	AB	H	HR	BA
1907 NY N	0	2	.000	2.57	2	2	2	14	17	6	5	0	0	0	0	5	0	0	.000
1908	0	0	–	7.94	2	0	0	5.2	11	3	0	0	0	0	1	3	1	0	.333
2 yrs.	0	2	.000	4.12	4	2	2	19.2	28	9	5	0	0	0	1	8	1	0	.125

Andy Beene

BEENE, RAMON ANDREW
B. Oct. 13, 1956, Freeport, Tex. BR TR 6'3" 205 lbs.

	W	L	PCT	ERA	G	GS	CG	IP	H	BB	SO	ShO	W	L	SV	AB	H	HR	BA
1983 MIL A	0	0	–	4.50	1	0	0	2	3	1	0	0	0	0	0	0	0	0	–
1984	0	2	.000	11.09	5	3	0	18.2	28	9	11	0	0	0	0	0	0	0	–
2 yrs.	0	2	.000	10.45	6	3	0	20.2	31	10	11	0	0	0	0	0	0	0	–

Fred Beene

BEENE, FREDERICK RAY
B. Nov. 24, 1942, Angleton, Tex. BB TR 5'9" 155 lbs.

	W	L	PCT	ERA	G	GS	CG	IP	H	BB	SO	ShO	W	L	SV	AB	H	HR	BA
1968 BAL A	0	0	–	9.00	1	0	0	1	2	1	1	0	0	0	0	0	0	0	–
1969	0	0	–	0.00	2	0	0	2.2	2	1	0	0	0	0	0	0	0	0	–
1970	0	0	–	6.00	4	0	0	6	8	5	4	0	0	0	0	0	0	0	–
1972 NY A	1	3	.250	2.33	29	1	0	58	55	24	37	0	1	3	3	9	0	0	.000
1973	6	0	1.000	1.68	19	1	0	91	67	27	49	0	4	0	1	0	0	0	–
1974 2 teams			NY A (6G 0–0)				CLE A (32G 4–4)												
" total	4	4	.500	4.66	38	0	0	83	77	28	45	0	4	4	3	0	0	0	–
1975 CLE A	1	0	1.000	6.94	19	1	0	46.2	63	25	20	0	1	0	1	0	0	0	–
7 yrs.	12	7	.632	3.62	112	6	0	288.1	274	111	156	0	10	7	8	9	0	0	.000

Clarence Beers

BEERS, CLARENCE SCOTT
B. Dec. 9, 1918, El Dorado, Kans. BR TR 6' 175 lbs.

	W	L	PCT	ERA	G	GS	CG	IP	H	BB	SO	ShO	W	L	SV	AB	H	HR	BA
1948 STL N	0	0	–	13.50	1	0	0	.2	3	1	0	0	0	0	0	0	0	0	–

Joe Beggs

BEGGS, JOSEPH STANLEY
B. Nov. 4, 1910, Rankin, Pa. D. July 19, 1983, Indianapolis, Ind. BR TR 6'1" 182 lbs.

	W	L	PCT	ERA	G	GS	CG	IP	H	BB	SO	ShO	W	L	SV	AB	H	HR	BA
1938 NY A	3	2	.600	5.40	14	9	4	58.1	69	20	8	0	0	0	0	20	5	0	.250
1940 CIN N	12	3	.800	2.00	37	1	0	76.2	68	21	25	0	12	3	7	21	4	0	.190
1941	4	3	.571	3.79	37	0	0	57	57	27	19	0	4	3	5	10	3	0	.300
1942	6	5	.545	2.13	38	0	0	88.2	65	33	24	0	6	5	8	21	0	0	.000
1943	7	6	.538	2.34	39	4	4	115.1	120	25	28	2	4	5	6	35	5	0	.143
1944	1	0	1.000	2.00	1	1	1	9	8	0	2	0	0	0	0	4	0	0	.000
1946	12	10	.545	2.32	28	22	14	190	175	39	38	2	0	1	1	63	14	0	.222
1947 2 teams			CIN N (11G 0–3)				NY N (32G 3–3)												
" total	3	6	.333	4.58	43	4	0	98.1	123	24	34	0	3	3	2	24	2	0	.083
1948 NY N	0	0	–	0.00	1	0	0	.1	2	0	0	0	0	0	0	0	0	0	–
9 yrs.	48	35	.578	2.96	238	41	23	693.2	687	189	178	4	29	20	29	198	33	0	.167
WORLD SERIES																			
1940 CIN N	0	0	–	9.00	1	0	0	1	3	0	1	0	0	0	0	0	0	0	–

	W	L	PCT	ERA	G	GS	CG	IP	H	BB	SO	ShO	Relief Pitching W	L	SV	BATTING AB	H	HR	BA

Ed Begley

BEGLEY, EDWARD N.
B. 1863, New York, N. Y.   D. July 24, 1919, Waterbury, Conn.

	W	L	PCT	ERA	G	GS	CG	IP	H	BB	SO	ShO	W	L	SV	AB	H	HR	BA
1884 NY N	12	18	.400	4.16	31	30	30	266	296	99	104	0	0	0	0	121	22	0	.182
1885 NY AA	4	9	.308	4.93	15	14	10	115	131	48	44	0	0	0	0	52	9	1	.173
2 yrs.	16	27	.372	4.39	46	44	40	381	427	147	148	0	0	0	0	173	31	1	.179

Petie Behan

BEHAN, CHARLES FREDERICK   BR TR 5'10"   160 lbs.
B. Dec. 11, 1887, Dallas City, Pa.   D. Jan. 22, 1957, Bradford, Pa.

	W	L	PCT	ERA	G	GS	CG	IP	H	BB	SO	ShO	W	L	SV	AB	H	HR	BA
1921 PHI N	0	1	.000	5.91	2	2	1	10.2	17	1	3	0	0	0	0	4	0	0	.000
1922	4	2	.667	2.47	7	5	3	47.1	49	14	13	1	1	0	0	20	5	0	.250
1923	3	12	.200	5.50	31	17	5	131	182	57	27	0	0	1	2	43	8	0	.186
3 yrs.	7	15	.318	4.76	40	24	9	189	248	72	43	1	1	1	2	67	13	0	.194

Rick Behenna

BEHENNA, RICHARD KIPP   BR TR 6'2"   170 lbs.
B. Mar. 6, 1960, Miami, Fla.

	W	L	PCT	ERA	G	GS	CG	IP	H	BB	SO	ShO	W	L	SV	AB	H	HR	BA
1983 2 teams	ATL N (14G 3–3)					CLE	A	(5G 0–2)											
" total	3	5	.375	4.41	19	10	0	63.1	59	26	26	0	0	2	0	12	4	1	.333
1984 CLE A	0	3	.000	13.97	3	3	0	9.2	17	8	6	0	0	0	0	0	0	0	—
2 yrs.	3	8	.273	5.67	22	13	0	73	76	34	32	0	0	2	0	12	4	1	.333

Mel Behney

BEHNEY, MELVIN BRIAN   BL TL 6'2"   180 lbs.
B. Sept. 2, 1947, Newark, N. J.

	W	L	PCT	ERA	G	GS	CG	IP	H	BB	SO	ShO	W	L	SV	AB	H	HR	BA
1970 CIN N	0	2	.000	4.50	5	1	0	16	15	8	2	0	0	1	0	1	0	0	.000

Hank Behrman

BEHRMAN, HENRY BERNARD   BR TR 5'11"   174 lbs.
B. June 27, 1921, Brooklyn, N. Y.

	W	L	PCT	ERA	G	GS	CG	IP	H	BB	SO	ShO	W	L	SV	AB	H	HR	BA
1946 BKN N	11	5	.688	2.93	47	11	2	150.2	138	69	78	0	6	1	4	42	4	0	.095
1947 2 teams	PIT N (10G 0–2)					BKN	N	(40G 5–3)											
" total	5	5	.500	6.25	50	8	0	116.2	130	65	44	0	1	4	8	32	6	0	.188
1948 BKN N	5	4	.556	4.05	34	4	2	91	95	42	42	1	3	2	7	28	3	0	.107
1949 NY N	3	3	.500	4.92	43	4	1	71.1	64	52	25	1	2	2	0	13	1	0	.077
4 yrs.	24	17	.585	4.40	174	27	5	429.2	427	228	189	2	12	9	19	115	14	0	.122

WORLD SERIES
	W	L	PCT	ERA	G	GS	CG	IP	H	BB	SO	ShO	W	L	SV	AB	H	HR	BA
1947 BKN N	0	0	—	7.11	5	0	0	6.1	9	5	3	0	0	0	0	0	0	0	—

Bo Belinsky

BELINSKY, ROBERT   BL TL 6'2"   191 lbs.
B. Dec. 7, 1936, New York, N. Y.

	W	L	PCT	ERA	G	GS	CG	IP	H	BB	SO	ShO	W	L	SV	AB	H	HR	BA
1962 LA A	10	11	.476	3.56	33	31	5	187.1	149	122	145	3	0	0	1	60	10	0	.167
1963	2	9	.182	5.75	13	13	2	76.2	78	35	60	0	0	0	0	27	2	0	.074
1964	9	8	.529	2.86	23	22	4	135.1	120	49	91	1	0	0	0	42	4	0	.095
1965 PHI N	4	9	.308	4.84	30	14	3	109.2	103	48	71	0	1	1	1	32	6	0	.188
1966	0	2	.000	2.93	9	1	0	15.1	14	5	8	0	0	0	0	3	1	0	.333
1967 HOU N	3	9	.250	4.68	27	18	0	115.1	112	54	80	0	0	1	0	39	3	0	.077
1969 PIT N	0	3	.000	4.50	8	3	0	18	17	14	15	0	0	0	0	2	0	0	.000
1970 CIN N	0	0	—	4.50	3	0	0	8	10	6	6	0	0	0	0	1	1	0	1.000
8 yrs.	28	51	.354	4.10	146	102	14	665.2	603	333	476	4	1	4	2	206	27	0	.131

Bill Bell

BELL, WILLIAM SAMUEL (Ding Dong)   BR TR 6'3"   200 lbs.
B. Oct. 24, 1933, Goldsboro, N. C.   D. Oct. 11, 1962, Durham, N. C.

	W	L	PCT	ERA	G	GS	CG	IP	H	BB	SO	ShO	W	L	SV	AB	H	HR	BA
1952 PIT N	0	1	.000	4.60	4	1	0	15.2	16	13	4	0	0	0	0	4	0	0	.000
1955	0	0	—	0.00	1	0	0	1	0	1	0	0	0	0	0	0	0	0	—
2 yrs.	0	1	.000	4.32	5	1	0	16.2	16	14	4	0	0	0	0	4	0	0	.000

Charlie Bell

BELL, CHARLES C.
Brother of Frank Bell.
B. Aug. 12, 1868, Cincinnati, Ohio   D. Feb. 7, 1937, Cincinnati, Ohio

	W	L	PCT	ERA	G	GS	CG	IP	H	BB	SO	ShO	W	L	SV	AB	H	HR	BA
1889 KC AA	1	0	1.000	1.00	1	1	1	9	4	3	3	0	0	0	0	6	1	0	.167
1891 2 teams	LOU AA (10G 2–6)					C-M	AA	(1G 1–0)											
" total	3	6	.333	4.19	11	10	9	86	95	23	17	0	0	0	0	32	3	0	.094
2 yrs.	4	6	.400	3.88	12	11	10	95	99	26	20	0	0	0	0	38	4	0	.105

Gary Bell

BELL, GARY   BR TR 6'1"   196 lbs.
B. Nov. 17, 1936, San Antonio, Tex.

	W	L	PCT	ERA	G	GS	CG	IP	H	BB	SO	ShO	W	L	SV	AB	H	HR	BA
1958 CLE A	12	10	.545	3.31	33	23	10	182	141	73	110	0	1	2	1	56	11	0	.196
1959	16	11	.593	4.04	44	28	12	234	208	105	136	1	3	1	5	75	18	0	.240
1960	9	10	.474	4.13	28	23	6	154.2	139	82	109	2	0	0	1	47	7	0	.149
1961	12	16	.429	4.10	34	34	11	228.1	214	100	163	2	0	0	0	81	16	0	.198
1962	10	9	.526	4.26	57	6	1	107.2	104	52	80	0	9	6	12	24	5	0	.208
1963	8	5	.615	2.95	58	7	0	119	91	52	98	0	7	1	5	26	3	0	.115
1964	8	6	.571	4.33	56	2	0	106	106	53	89	0	7	5	4	16	6	0	.375
1965	6	5	.545	3.04	60	0	0	103.2	86	50	86	0	6	5	17	16	1	1	.063
1966	14	15	.483	3.22	40	29	12	254.1	211	79	194	1	1	0	0	76	10	0	.132
1967 2 teams	CLE A (9G 1–5)					BOS	A	(29G 12–8)											
" total	13	13	.500	3.31	38	33	9	226	193	71	154	0	0	0	3	74	12	0	.162
1968 BOS A	11	11	.500	3.12	35	27	9	199.1	177	68	103	3	1	1	1	59	13	0	.220
1969 2 teams	SEA A (13G 2–6)					CHI	A	(23G 0–0)											
" total	2	6	.250	5.31	36	13	1	100	124	57	56	1	0	0	2	19	3	0	.158
12 yrs.	121	117	.508	3.68	519	233	71	2015	1794	842	1378	9	35	21	51	569	105	1	.185

WORLD SERIES
	W	L	PCT	ERA	G	GS	CG	IP	H	BB	SO	ShO	W	L	SV	AB	H	HR	BA
1967 BOS A	0	1	.000	5.06	3	1	0	5.1	8	1	1	0	0	0	1	0	0	0	—

George Bell

BELL, GEORGE GLENN (Farmer)   BR TR 6'   195 lbs.
B. Nov. 2, 1874, Bronx, N. Y.   D. Dec. 25, 1941, New York, N. Y.

	W	L	PCT	ERA	G	GS	CG	IP	H	BB	SO	ShO	W	L	SV	AB	H	HR	BA
1907 BKN N	8	16	.333	2.25	35	27	20	263.2	222	77	88	3	1	1	1	84	8	0	.095
1908	4	15	.211	3.59	29	22	12	155.1	162	45	63	2	0	1	1	47	8	0	.170
1909	16	15	.516	2.71	33	30	29	256	236	73	95	6	1	0	1	90	15	0	.167

	W	L	PCT	ERA	G	GS	CG	IP	H	BB	SO	ShO	Relief Pitching W	L	SV	BATTING AB	H	HR	BA

George Bell continued

	W	L	PCT	ERA	G	GS	CG	IP	H	BB	SO	ShO	W	L	SV	AB	H	HR	BA
1910	10	27	.270	2.64	44	36	25	310	267	82	102	4	0	3	1	97	13	0	.134
1911	5	6	.455	4.28	19	12	6	101	123	28	28	2	1	0	0	33	4	0	.121
5 yrs.	43	79	.352	2.85	160	127	92	1086	1010	305	376	17	3	5	4	351	48	0	.137

Hi Bell

BELL, HERMAN S   BR TR 6'   185 lbs.
B. July 16, 1897, Louisville, Ky.   D. June 7, 1949, Glendale, Calif.

	W	L	PCT	ERA	G	GS	CG	IP	H	BB	SO	ShO	W	L	SV	AB	H	HR	BA
1924 STL N	3	8	.273	4.92	28	11	5	113.1	124	29	29	0	0	1	1	31	2	0	.065
1926	6	6	.500	3.18	27	8	3	85	82	17	27	0	3	2	2	25	3	0	.120
1927	1	3	.250	3.92	25	1	0	57.1	71	22	31	0	1	2	0	11	1	0	.091
1929	0	2	.000	6.92	7	0	0	13	19	4	4	0	0	2	0	3	0	0	.000
1930	4	3	.571	3.90	39	9	2	115.1	143	23	42	0	3	1	8	26	2	0	.077
1932 NY N	8	4	.667	3.68	35	10	3	120	132	16	25	0	3	1	2	34	3	0	.088
1933	6	5	.545	2.05	38	7	1	105.1	100	20	24	1	4	2	5	29	4	0	.138
1934	4	3	.571	3.67	22	2	0	54	72	12	9	0	4	2	6	19	2	0	.105
8 yrs.	32	34	.485	3.69	221	48	14	663.1	743	143	191	1	18	13	24	178	17	0	.096

WORLD SERIES

	W	L	PCT	ERA	G	GS	CG	IP	H	BB	SO	ShO	W	L	SV	AB	H	HR	BA
1926 STL N	0	0	—	9.00	1	0	0	2	4	1	1	0	0	0	0	0	0	0	—
1930	0	0	—	0.00	1	0	0	1	0	0	0	0	0	0	0	0	0	0	—
1933 NY N	0	0	—	0.00	1	0	0	1	0	0	0	0	0	0	0	0	0	0	—
3 yrs.	0	0	—	4.50	3	0	0	4	4	1	1	0	0	0	0	0	0	0	—

Jerry Bell

BELL, JERRY HOUSTON   BB TR 6'4"   190 lbs.
B. Oct. 6, 1947, Madison, Tenn.

	W	L	PCT	ERA	G	GS	CG	IP	H	BB	SO	ShO	W	L	SV	AB	H	HR	BA
1971 MIL A	2	1	.667	3.00	8	0	0	15	10	6	8	0	2	1	0	0	0	0	—
1972	5	1	.833	1.65	25	3	0	71	50	33	20	0	2	1	0	14	1	0	.071
1973	9	9	.500	3.97	31	25	8	183.2	185	70	57	0	1	2	1	0	0	0	—
1974	1	0	1.000	2.57	5	0	0	14	17	5	4	0	1	0	0	0	0	0	—
4 yrs.	17	11	.607	3.27	69	28	8	283.2	262	114	89	0	6	4	1	14	1	0	.071

Ralph Bell

BELL, RALPH ALBERT   BL TL 5'11½" 170 lbs.
B. Nov. 16, 1890, Kohoka, Mo.   D. Oct. 18, 1959, Burlington, Iowa

	W	L	PCT	ERA	G	GS	CG	IP	H	BB	SO	ShO	W	L	SV	AB	H	HR	BA
1912 CHI A	0	0	—	9.00	3	0	0	6	8	8	5	0	0	0	0	2	0	0	.000

Chief Bender

BENDER, CHARLES ALBERT   BR TR 6'2"   185 lbs.
B. May 5, 1883, Brainerd, Minn.   D. May 22, 1954, Philadelphia, Pa.
Hall of Fame 1953.

	W	L	PCT	ERA	G	GS	CG	IP	H	BB	SO	ShO	W	L	SV	AB	H	HR	BA
1903 PHI A	17	15	.531	3.07	36	33	29	270	239	65	127	2	1	1	0	120	22	0	.183
1904	10	11	.476	2.87	29	20	18	203.2	167	59	149	4	2	0	0	79	18	0	.228
1905	16	10	.615	2.83	35	23	17	229	193	90	142	4	7	1	0	92	20	0	.217
1906	15	10	.600	2.53	36	27	24	238.1	208	48	159	0	1	0	3	99	25	3	.253
1907	16	8	.667	2.05	33	24	20	219.1	185	34	112	4	0	2	3	100	23	0	.230
1908	8	9	.471	1.75	18	17	14	138.2	121	21	85	2	0	0	1	50	11	0	.220
1909	18	8	.692	1.66	34	29	24	250	196	45	161	5	0	0	1	93	20	0	.215
1910	23	5	.821	1.58	30	28	25	250	182	47	155	3	1	0	0	93	25	0	.269
1911	17	5	.773	2.16	31	24	16	216.1	198	58	114	3	2	1	3	79	13	0	.165
1912	13	8	.619	2.74	27	19	12	171	169	33	90	1	2	3	2	60	9	0	.150
1913	21	10	.677	2.21	48	22	16	236.2	208	59	135	2	6	5	3	78	12	0	.154
1914	17	3	.850	2.26	28	23	14	179	159	55	107	7	1	1	2	62	9	1	.145
1915 BAL F	4	16	.200	3.99	26	23	15	178.1	198	37	89	0	0	1	1	60	16	1	.267
1916 PHI N	7	7	.500	3.74	27	13	4	122.2	137	34	43	0	2	1	3	43	12	0	.279
1917	8	2	.800	1.67	20	10	8	113	84	26	43	4	0	0	2	39	8	1	.205
1925 CHI A	0	0	—	18.00	1	0	0	1	1	1	0	0	0	0	0	0	0	0	—
16 yrs.	210	127	.623	2.46	459	335	256	3017	2645	712	1711	41	25	16	24	*			

WORLD SERIES

	W	L	PCT	ERA	G	GS	CG	IP	H	BB	SO	ShO	W	L	SV	AB	H	HR	BA
1905 PHI A	1	1	.500	1.06	2	2	2	17	9	6	13	1	0	0	0	5	0	0	.000
1910	1	1	.500	1.93	2	2	2	18.2	12	4	14	0	0	0	0	6	2	0	.333
1911	2	1	.667	1.04	3	3	3	26	16	8	20	0	0	0	0	11	1	0	.091
1913	2	0	1.000	4.00	2	2	2	18	19	1	9	0	0	0	0	8	0	0	.000
1914	0	1	.000	10.13	1	1	0	5.1	8	2	3	0	0	0	0	2	0	0	.000
5 yrs.	6	4	.600	2.44	10	10	9	85	64	21	59	1	0	0	0	32	3	0	.094
	5th	7th				4th	2nd	4th	5th		6th								

Ray Benge

BENGE, RAYMOND ADELPHIA (Silent Cal)   BR TR 5'9½" 160 lbs.
B. Apr. 22, 1902, Jacksonville, Tex.

	W	L	PCT	ERA	G	GS	CG	IP	H	BB	SO	ShO	W	L	SV	AB	H	HR	BA
1925 CLE A	1	0	1.000	1.54	2	2	1	11.2	9	3	3	1	0	0	0	5	2	0	.400
1926	1	0	1.000	3.86	8	0	0	11.2	15	4	3	0	1	0	0	3	1	0	.333
1928 PHI N	8	18	.308	4.55	40	28	12	201.2	219	88	68	1	2	0	1	58	12	0	.207
1929	11	15	.423	6.29	38	26	9	199	255	77	78	2	0	3	4	74	15	0	.203
1930	11	15	.423	5.70	38	29	14	225.2	305	81	70	0	0	3	1	88	18	0	.205
1931	14	18	.438	3.17	38	31	16	247	251	61	117	2	1	2	2	88	18	0	.205
1932	13	12	.520	4.05	41	28	13	222.1	247	58	89	2	0	6	6	75	13	0	.173
1933 BKN N	10	17	.370	3.42	37	30	16	228.2	238	55	74	2	0	1	1	76	14	1	.184
1934	14	12	.538	4.32	36	32	14	227	252	61	64	1	1	0	0	89	15	0	.169
1935	9	9	.500	4.48	23	17	5	124.2	142	47	39	1	1	1	1	47	9	0	.191
1936 2 teams		BOS	N (21G 7–9)		PHI	N	(15G 1–4)												
" total	8	13	.381	5.49	36	25	2	160.2	231	57	45	0	1	0	1	53	6	0	.113
1938 CIN N	1	1	.500	4.11	9	0	0	15.1	13	6	5	0	1	1	2	3	1	0	.333
12 yrs.	101	130	.437	4.52	346	248	102	1875.1	2177	598	655	12	8	11	19	659	124	1	.188

Henry Benn

BENN, HENRY OMER   BR TR 6'   190 lbs.
B. Jan. 25, 1890, Viola, Wis.   D. June 4, 1967, Madison, Wis.

	W	L	PCT	ERA	G	GS	CG	IP	H	BB	SO	ShO	W	L	SV	AB	H	HR	BA
1914 CLE A	0	0	—	0.00	1	0	0	1	0	1	0	0	0	0	0	0	0	0	—

	W	L	PCT	ERA	G	GS	CG	IP	H	BB	SO	ShO	Relief Pitching W	L	SV	BATTING AB	H	HR	BA

Bugs Bennett

BENNETT, JOSEPH HARLEY BR TR 5'9½" 163 lbs.
Played as Bugs Morris 1921. Also known as Joseph Harley Morris.
B. Apr. 19, 1892, Kansas City, Mo. D. Nov. 21, 1957, Noel, Mo.

	W	L	PCT	ERA	G	GS	CG	IP	H	BB	SO	ShO	W	L	SV	AB	H	HR	BA
1918 STL A	0	2	.000	3.48	4	2	0	10.1	12	7	0	0	0	0	0	4	1	0	.250
1921 2 teams			CHI	A (3G 0–3)	STL	A	(3G 0–0)												
" total	0	3	.000	8.10	6	3	1	23.1	30	22	5	0	0	1	0	7	3	0	.429
2 yrs.	0	5	.000	6.68	10	5	1	33.2	42	29	5	0	0	1	0	11	4	0	.364

Dave Bennett

BENNETT, DAVID HANS BR TR 6'5" 195 lbs.
Brother of Dennis Bennett.
B. Nov. 7, 1945, Berkeley, Calif.

	W	L	PCT	ERA	G	GS	CG	IP	H	BB	SO	ShO	W	L	SV	AB	H	HR	BA
1964 PHI N	0	0	–	9.00	1	0	0	1	2	0	1	0	0	0	0	0	0	0	–

Dennis Bennett

BENNETT, DENNIS JOHN BL TL 6'3" 192 lbs.
Brother of Dave Bennett.
B. Oct. 5, 1939, Oakland, Calif.

	W	L	PCT	ERA	G	GS	CG	IP	H	BB	SO	ShO	W	L	SV	AB	H	HR	BA
1962 PHI N	9	9	.500	3.81	31	24	7	174.2	144	68	149	2	1	0	3	63	8	1	.127
1963	9	5	.643	2.64	23	16	6	119.1	102	33	82	1	1	0	1	40	9	1	.225
1964	12	14	.462	3.68	41	32	7	208	222	58	125	2	1	0	1	66	13	0	.197
1965 BOS A	5	7	.417	4.38	34	18	3	141.2	152	53	85	0	1	0	0	39	7	0	.179
1966	3	3	.500	3.24	16	13	0	75	75	23	47	0	0	0	0	23	3	1	.130
1967 2 teams			BOS	A (13G 4–3)	NY	N	(8G 1–1)												
" total	5	4	.556	4.22	21	17	4	96	109	29	48	1	0	0	0	33	5	1	.152
1968 CAL A	0	5	.000	3.54	16	7	1	48.1	46	17	36	0	0	1	1	13	1	0	.077
7 yrs.	43	47	.478	3.69	182	127	28	863	850	281	572	6	4	1	6	277	46	4	.166

Frank Bennett

BENNETT, FRANCIS ALLEN (Chip) BR TR 5'10½" 163 lbs.
B. Oct. 27, 1904, Mardela Springs, Md. D. Mar. 18, 1966, New Castle, Del.

	W	L	PCT	ERA	G	GS	CG	IP	H	BB	SO	ShO	W	L	SV	AB	H	HR	BA
1927 BOS A	0	1	.000	2.92	4	1	0	12.1	15	6	1	0	0	0	0	3	0	0	.000
1928	0	0	–	0.00	1	0	0	1	1	0	0	0	0	0	0	0	0	0	–
2 yrs.	0	1	.000	2.70	5	1	0	13.1	16	6	1	0	0	0	0	3	0	0	.000

Allen Benson

BENSON, ALLEN WILBERT (Bullet Ben) BR TR 6'1" 185 lbs.
B. Mar. 28, 1908, Hurley, S. D.

	W	L	PCT	ERA	G	GS	CG	IP	H	BB	SO	ShO	W	L	SV	AB	H	HR	BA
1934 WAS A	0	1	.000	12.10	2	2	0	9.2	19	5	4	0	0	0	0	3	0	0	.000

Jack Bentley

BENTLEY, JOHN NEEDLES BL TL 5'11½" 200 lbs.
B. Mar. 8, 1895, Sandy Spring, Md. D. Oct. 24, 1969, Downey, Md.

	W	L	PCT	ERA	G	GS	CG	IP	H	BB	SO	ShO	W	L	SV	AB	H	HR	BA
1913 WAS A	1	0	1.000	0.00	3	1	0	11	5	2	5	0	0	0	1	3	0	0	.000
1914	5	7	.417	2.37	30	12	3	125.1	110	53	55	2	0	1	4	40	11	0	.275
1915	0	2	.000	0.79	4	2	0	11.1	8	3	0	0	0	0	0	2	0	0	.000
1916	0	0	–	0.00	2	0	0	1.1	0	1	1	0	0	0	0	0	0	0	–
1923 NY N	13	8	.619	4.48	31	26	12	183	198	67	80	1	0	1	3	89	38	1	.427
1924	16	5	.762	3.78	28	24	13	188	196	56	60	1	1	0	1	98	26	0	.265
1925	11	9	.550	5.04	28	22	11	157	200	59	47	0	1	0	0	99	30	3	.303
1926 2 teams			PHI	N (7G 0–2)	NY	N	(1G 0–0)												
" total	0	2	.000	7.57	8	3	0	27.1	37	12	8	0	0	0	0	244	63	2	.258
1927 NY N	0	0	–	2.79	4	0	0	9.2	7	10	3	0	0	0	0	9	2	1	.222
9 yrs.	46	33	.582	4.01	138	90	39	714	761	263	259	4	2	2	9	*			

WORLD SERIES

	W	L	PCT	ERA	G	GS	CG	IP	H	BB	SO	ShO	W	L	SV	AB	H	HR	BA
1923 NY N	0	1	.000	9.45	2	1	0	6.2	10	4	1	0	0	0	0	5	3	0	.600
1924	1	2	.333	3.18	3	2	1	17	18	8	10	0	0	1	0	7	2	1	.286
2 yrs.	1	3	.250	4.94	5	3	1	23.2	28	12	11	0	0	1	0	12	5	1	.417

Al Benton

BENTON, JOHN ALTON BR TR 6'5½" 215 lbs.
B. Mar. 18, 1911, Noble, Okla. D. Apr. 14, 1968, Lynwood, Calif.

	W	L	PCT	ERA	G	GS	CG	IP	H	BB	SO	ShO	W	L	SV	AB	H	HR	BA
1934 PHI A	7	9	.438	4.88	32	21	7	155	145	88	58	0	1	1	1	55	6	0	.109
1935	3	4	.429	7.67	27	9	0	78.2	110	47	42	0	3	1	0	25	1	0	.040
1938 DET A	5	3	.625	3.30	19	10	6	95.1	93	39	33	0	0	0	0	33	4	0	.121
1939	6	8	.429	4.56	37	16	3	150	182	58	67	0	1	3	5	44	4	0	.091
1940	6	10	.375	4.42	42	0	0	79.1	93	36	50	0	6	10	17	17	0	0	.000
1941	15	6	.714	2.97	38	14	7	157.2	130	65	63	1	6	2	7	50	3	0	.060
1942	7	13	.350	2.90	35	30	9	226.2	210	84	110	1	0	1	2	67	5	0	.075
1945	13	8	.619	2.02	31	27	12	191.2	175	63	76	5	1	1	3	63	4	0	.063
1946	11	7	.611	3.65	28	15	6	140.2	132	58	60	1	1	2	1	49	9	0	.184
1947	6	7	.462	4.40	31	14	4	133	147	61	33	0	1	0	7	39	6	0	.154
1948	2	2	.500	5.68	30	0	0	44.1	45	36	18	0	2	2	3	11	2	0	.182
1949 CLE A	9	6	.600	2.12	40	11	4	135.2	116	51	41	2	4	0	10	38	5	0	.132
1950	4	2	.667	3.57	36	0	0	63	57	30	26	0	4	2	4	12	1	0	.083
1952 BOS A	4	3	.571	2.39	24	0	0	37.2	37	17	20	0	4	3	6	9	0	0	.000
14 yrs.	98	88	.527	3.66	450	167	58	1688.2	1672	733	697	10	33	28	66	512	50	0	.098

WORLD SERIES

	W	L	PCT	ERA	G	GS	CG	IP	H	BB	SO	ShO	W	L	SV	AB	H	HR	BA
1945 DET A	0	0	–	1.93	3	0	0	4.2	6	0	5	0	0	0	0	0	0	0	–

Larry Benton

BENTON, LAWRENCE JAMES BR TR 5'11" 165 lbs.
B. Nov. 20, 1897, St. Louis, Mo. D. Apr. 3, 1953, Cincinnati, Ohio

	W	L	PCT	ERA	G	GS	CG	IP	H	BB	SO	ShO	W	L	SV	AB	H	HR	BA
1923 BOS N	5	9	.357	4.99	35	9	2	128	141	57	42	0	4	4	0	31	5	0	.161
1924	5	7	.417	4.15	30	13	4	128	129	64	41	0	1	0	1	33	3	0	.091
1925	14	7	.667	3.09	31	21	16	183.1	170	70	49	2	1	1	1	58	14	0	.241
1926	14	14	.500	3.85	43	27	12	231.2	244	81	103	1	3	2	1	78	12	0	.154
1927 2 teams			BOS	N (11G 4–2)	NY	N	(29G 13–5)												
" total	17	7	.708	4.09	40	33	11	233.1	255	81	90	1	3	1	2	68	12	0	.176
1928 NY N	25	9	.735	2.73	42	35	28	310.1	299	71	90	2	0	1	4	112	16	0	.143
1929	11	17	.393	4.10	39	30	14	237	276	61	63	0	1	3	0	86	9	1	.105
1930 2 teams			NY	N (8G 1–3)	CIN	N	(35G 7–12)												
" total	8	15	.348	5.50	43	26	10	207.2	288	59	63	0	2	1	2	72	14	1	.194
1931 CIN N	10	15	.400	3.35	38	23	12	204.1	240	53	35	2	3	1	2	66	11	0	.167

	W	L	PCT	ERA	G	GS	CG	IP	H	BB	SO	ShO	Relief Pitching W	L	SV	BATTING AB	H	HR	BA

Larry Benton continued

	W	L	PCT	ERA	G	GS	CG	IP	H	BB	SO	ShO	W	L	SV	AB	H	HR	BA
1932	6	13	.316	4.31	35	21	7	179.2	201	27	35	0	1	1	2	54	11	0	.204
1933	10	11	.476	3.71	34	19	7	152.2	160	36	33	2	1	4	2	53	9	0	.170
1934	0	1	.000	6.52	16	1	0	29	53	7	5	0	0	0	2	7	2	0	.286
1935 BOS N	2	3	.400	6.88	29	0	0	72	103	24	21	0	2	3	0	20	4	0	.200
13 yrs.	127	128	.498	4.03	455	258	123	2297	2559	691	670	13	21	19	22	738	122	2	.165

Rube Benton

BENTON, JOHN CLEBON   BR TL 6'1"   190 lbs.
B. June 27, 1887, Clinton, N. C.   D. Dec. 12, 1937, Dothan, Ala.

	W	L	PCT	ERA	G	GS	CG	IP	H	BB	SO	ShO	W	L	SV	AB	H	HR	BA
1910 CIN N	1	1	.500	4.74	12	2	0	38	44	23	15	0	0	0	0	11	1	0	.091
1911	3	3	.500	2.01	6	6	5	44.2	44	23	28	0	0	0	0	14	2	0	.143
1912	18	21	.462	3.10	50	39	22	302	316	118	162	2	3	1	2	104	14	0	.135
1913	11	7	.611	3.49	23	22	9	144.1	140	60	68	1	1	0	0	48	10	0	.208
1914	17	18	.486	2.96	41	31	16	271	223	95	121	5	2	3	2	91	13	0	.143
1915 2 teams			CIN	N (35G 9–13)			NY	N (10G 4–5)											
" total	13	18	.419	3.19	45	28	9	237	222	76	109	2	4	3	5	76	16	0	.211
1916 NY N	16	8	.667	2.87	38	30	15	238.2	210	58	115	3	2	0	2	78	7	0	.090
1917	15	9	.625	2.72	35	25	14	215	190	41	70	3	0	2	3	72	12	0	.167
1918	1	2	.333	1.88	3	3	2	24	17	3	9	0	0	0	0	7	1	0	.143
1919	17	11	.607	2.63	35	28	11	209	181	52	53	1	3	0	2	67	13	1	.194
1920	9	16	.360	3.03	33	25	12	193.1	222	31	52	4	0	3	2	65	6	0	.092
1921	5	2	.714	2.88	18	9	3	72	72	17	11	1	0	1	0	21	3	0	.143
1923 CIN N	14	10	.583	3.66	33	26	15	219	243	57	59	0	0	0	1	80	23	0	.288
1924	7	9	.438	2.77	32	15	6	162.2	166	24	42	1	1	1	1	46	12	0	.261
1925	9	10	.474	4.05	33	16	6	146.2	182	34	36	1	2	2	1	45	9	0	.200
15 yrs.	156	145	.518	3.09	437	305	145	2517.1	2472	712	950	24	18	16	21	825	142	1	.172

WORLD SERIES

	W	L	PCT	ERA	G	GS	CG	IP	H	BB	SO	ShO	W	L	SV	AB	H	HR	BA
1917 NY N	1	1	.500	0.00	2	2	1	14	9	1	8	1	0	0	0	4	0	0	.000

Sid Benton

BENTON, SIDNEY WRIGHT   BR TR 6'2"   170 lbs.
B. Aug. 4, 1894, Buckner, Ark.   D. Mar. 8, 1977, Fayetteville, Ark.

	W	L	PCT	ERA	G	GS	CG	IP	H	BB	SO	ShO	W	L	SV	AB	H	HR	BA
1922 STL N	0	0	–	0.00	1	0	0	0	0	2	0	0	0	0	0	*			

Joe Benz

BENZ, JOSEPH LOUIS (Blitzen)   BR TR 6'1½"   196 lbs.
B. Jan. 21, 1886, New Alsace, Ind.   D. Apr. 23, 1957, Chicago, Ill.

	W	L	PCT	ERA	G	GS	CG	IP	H	BB	SO	ShO	W	L	SV	AB	H	HR	BA
1911 CHI A	3	2	.600	2.26	12	6	2	55.2	52	13	28	0	1	0	0	17	1	0	.059
1912	13	17	.433	2.92	41	31	12	237.2	230	70	96	3	2	2	0	76	10	0	.132
1913	7	10	.412	2.74	33	17	6	151	146	59	79	1	3	0	1	50	9	0	.180
1914	14	19	.424	2.26	48	35	16	283.1	245	66	142	4	3	0	2	92	12	0	.130
1915	15	11	.577	2.11	39	28	17	238.1	209	43	81	2	0	2	0	79	10	0	.127
1916	9	5	.643	2.03	28	16	6	142	108	32	57	4	1	1	0	46	3	0	.065
1917	7	3	.700	2.47	19	13	7	94.2	76	23	25	2	0	1	0	30	5	0	.167
1918	8	8	.500	2.51	29	17	10	154	156	28	30	1	1	1	0	51	11	0	.216
1919	0	0	–	0.00	1	0	0	2	2	0	0	0	0	0	0	0	0	0	–
9 yrs.	76	75	.503	2.42	250	163	76	1358.2	1224	334	538	17	11	7	3	441	61	0	.138

Juan Berenguer

BERENGUER, JUAN BAUTISTA   BR TR 5'11"   186 lbs.
B. Nov. 30, 1954, Aguadulce, Panama

	W	L	PCT	ERA	G	GS	CG	IP	H	BB	SO	ShO	W	L	SV	AB	H	HR	BA
1978 NY N	0	2	.000	8.31	5	3	0	13	17	11	8	0	0	0	0	3	0	0	.000
1979	1	1	.500	2.90	5	5	0	31	28	12	25	0	0	0	0	7	1	0	.143
1980	0	1	.000	6.00	4	0	0	9	9	10	7	0	0	1	0	0	0	0	–
1981 2 teams			KC	A (8G 0–4)			TOR	A (12G 2–9)											
" total	2	13	.133	5.24	20	14	1	91	84	51	49	0	0	0	0	0	0	0	–
1982 DET A	0	0	–	6.75	2	1	0	6.2	5	9	8	0	0	0	0	0	0	0	–
1983	9	5	.643	3.14	37	19	2	157.2	110	71	129	1	0	0	1	0	0	0	–
1984	11	10	.524	3.48	31	27	2	168.1	146	79	118	1	0	0	0	0	0	0	–
7 yrs.	23	32	.418	3.89	106	69	5	476.2	399	243	344	2	2	3	1	10	1	0	.100

Bruce Berenyi

BERENYI, BRUCE MICHAEL   BR TR 6'3"   205 lbs.
B. Aug. 21, 1954, Bryan, Ohio

	W	L	PCT	ERA	G	GS	CG	IP	H	BB	SO	ShO	W	L	SV	AB	H	HR	BA
1980 CIN N	2	2	.500	7.71	6	6	0	28	34	23	19	0	0	0	0	7	0	0	.000
1981	9	6	.600	3.50	21	20	5	126	97	77	106	3	0	0	0	42	8	0	.190
1982	9	18	.333	3.36	34	34	4	222.1	208	96	157	1	0	0	0	62	15	0	.242
1983	9	14	.391	3.86	32	31	4	186.1	173	102	151	1	0	0	0	55	12	0	.218
1984 2 teams			CIN	N (13G 3–7)			NY	N (19G 9–6)											
" total	12	13	.480	4.45	32	30	0	166	163	95	134	0	1	0	0	53	10	0	.189
5 yrs.	41	53	.436	3.93	125	121	13	728.2	675	393	567	5	1	0	0	219	45	0	.205

Bill Bergen

BERGEN, WILLIAM ALOYSIUS   BR TR 6'   184 lbs.
Brother of Marty Bergen.
B. June 13, 1873, N. Brookfield, Mass.   D. Dec. 19, 1943, Worcester, Mass.

	W	L	PCT	ERA	G	GS	CG	IP	H	BB	SO	ShO	W	L	SV	AB	H	HR	BA
1902 CIN N	1	1	.500	2.40	2	2	1	15	11	6	4	0	0	0	0	*			

Heinie Berger

BERGER, CHARLES   TR 5'9½"
B. Jan. 7, 1882, LaSalle, Ill.   D. Feb. 10, 1954, Lakewood, Ohio

	W	L	PCT	ERA	G	GS	CG	IP	H	BB	SO	ShO	W	L	SV	AB	H	HR	BA
1907 CLE A	3	3	.500	2.99	14	7	5	87.1	74	20	50	1	1	0	0	28	5	0	.179
1908	13	8	.619	2.12	29	24	16	199.1	152	66	101	0	0	0	0	74	8	0	.108
1909	13	14	.481	2.63	34	29	19	257	221	58	162	4	0	0	1	83	11	0	.133
1910	3	4	.429	3.03	13	8	2	65.1	57	32	24	0	1	1	0	21	3	0	.143
4 yrs.	32	29	.525	2.56	90	68	42	609	504	176	337	5	2	1	1	206	27	0	.131

Jack Berly

BERLY, JOHN CHAMBERS   BR TR 5'11½" 190 lbs.
B. May 24, 1903, Natchitoches, La.   D. June 26, 1977, Houston, Tex.

	W	L	PCT	ERA	G	GS	CG	IP	H	BB	SO	ShO	W	L	SV	AB	H	HR	BA
1924 STL N	0	0	–	5.63	4	0	0	8	8	4	2	0	0	0	0	2	0	0	.000
1931 NY N	7	8	.467	3.88	27	11	4	111.1	114	51	45	1	2	4	0	35	6	0	.171
1932 PHI N	1	2	.333	7.63	21	1	1	46	61	21	15	0	1	1	2	10	0	0	.000

	W	L	PCT	ERA	G	GS	CG	IP	H	BB	SO	ShO	Relief Pitching W	L	SV	BATTING AB	H	HR	BA

Jack Berly continued

	W	L	PCT	ERA	G	GS	CG	IP	H	BB	SO	ShO	W	L	SV	AB	H	HR	BA
1933	2	3	.400	5.04	13	6	1	50	62	22	4	1	0	0	0	13	4	0	.308
4 yrs.	10	13	.435	5.02	65	18	6	215.1	245	98	66	2	3	5	2	60	10	0	.167

Vic Bernal

BERNAL, VICTOR HUGO　　　　　　　　BR TR 6'1"　175 lbs.
B. Oct. 6, 1953, Los Angeles, Calif.

	W	L	PCT	ERA	G	GS	CG	IP	H	BB	SO	ShO	W	L	SV	AB	H	HR	BA
1977 SD N	1	1	.500	5.40	15	0	0	20	23	9	6	0	1	1	0	1	0	0	.000

Dwight Bernard

BERNARD, DWIGHT VERN　　　　　　　BR TR 6'2"　170 lbs.
B. May 31, 1952, Mt. Vernon, Ill.

	W	L	PCT	ERA	G	GS	CG	IP	H	BB	SO	ShO	W	L	SV	AB	H	HR	BA
1978 NY N	1	4	.200	4.31	30	1	0	48	54	27	26	0	1	3	0	5	1	0	.200
1979	0	3	.000	4.70	32	1	0	44	59	26	20	0	0	2	0	0	0	0	–
1981 MIL A	0	0	–	3.60	6	0	0	5	5	6	1	0	0	0	0	0	0	0	–
1982	3	1	.750	3.76	47	0	0	79	78	27	45	0	3	1	6	0	0	0	–
4 yrs.	4	8	.333	4.14	115	2	0	176	196	86	92	0	4	6	6	5	1	0	.200

DIVISIONAL PLAYOFF SERIES
	W	L	PCT	ERA	G	GS	CG	IP	H	BB	SO	ShO	W	L	SV	AB	H	HR	BA
1981 MIL A	0	0	–	0.00	2	0	0	2.1	0	0	0	0	0	0	0	0	0	0	–

LEAGUE CHAMPIONSHIP SERIES
	W	L	PCT	ERA	G	GS	CG	IP	H	BB	SO	ShO	W	L	SV	AB	H	HR	BA
1982 MIL A	0	0	–	0.00	1	0	0	1	0	0	0	0	0	0	0	0	0	0	–

WORLD SERIES
	W	L	PCT	ERA	G	GS	CG	IP	H	BB	SO	ShO	W	L	SV	AB	H	HR	BA
1982 MIL A	0	0	–	0.00	1	0	0	1	0	1	0	0	0	0	0	0	0	0	–

Joe Bernard

BERNARD, JOSEPH
B. Unknown.

	W	L	PCT	ERA	G	GS	CG	IP	H	BB	SO	ShO	W	L	SV	AB	H	HR	BA
1909 STL N	0	0	–	0.00	1	0	1	1	2	2	0	0	0	0	0	0	0	0	–

Bill Bernhard

BERNHARD, WILLIAM HENRY (Strawberry Bill)　　BB TR 6'1"　205 lbs.
B. Mar. 15, 1871, Clarence, N. Y.　D. Mar. 30, 1949, San Diego, Calif.

	W	L	PCT	ERA	G	GS	CG	IP	H	BB	SO	ShO	W	L	SV	AB	H	HR	BA
1899 PHI N	6	6	.500	2.65	21	12	10	132.1	120	36	23	1	1	1	0	54	13	0	.241
1900	15	10	.600	4.77	32	27	20	218.2	284	74	49	0	2	0	2	91	14	0	.154
1901 PHI A	17	10	.630	4.52	31	27	26	257	328	50	58	1	1	0	0	107	20	0	.187
1902 2 teams			PHI A (1G 1–0)		CLE A (27G 17–5)														
" total	18	5	.783	2.15	28	25	23	226	176	37	58	3	1	0	1	94	18	0	.191
1903 CLE A	14	6	.700	2.12	20	19	18	165.2	151	21	60	3	0	1	0	65	12	0	.185
1904	23	13	.639	2.13	38	37	35	320.2	323	55	137	4	1	0	0	124	22	0	.177
1905	7	13	.350	3.36	22	19	17	174.1	185	34	56	0	2	0	0	69	6	0	.087
1906	16	15	.516	2.54	31	30	23	255.1	235	47	85	2	1	0	0	99	21	0	.212
1907	0	4	.000	3.21	8	4	3	42	58	11	19	0	0	0	0	15	3	0	.200
9 yrs.	116	82	.586	3.04	231	200	175	1792	1860	365	545	14	9	2	3	718	129	0	.180

Walter Bernhardt

BERNHARDT, WALTER JACOB (Sarah)　　　　BR TR 6'2"　195 lbs.
B. May 20, 1893, Pleasant Valley, Pa.　D. July 26, 1958, Watertown, N. Y.

	W	L	PCT	ERA	G	GS	CG	IP	H	BB	SO	ShO	W	L	SV	AB	H	HR	BA
1918 NY A	0	0	–	0.00	1	0	0	.2	0	0	0	0	0	0	0	0	0	0	–

Joe Berry

BERRY, JONAS ARTHUR (Jittery Joe)　　　　BR TR 5'10½" 145 lbs.
B. Dec. 16, 1904, Huntsville, Ark.　D. Sept. 27, 1958, Anaheim, Calif.

	W	L	PCT	ERA	G	GS	CG	IP	H	BB	SO	ShO	W	L	SV	AB	H	HR	BA
1942 CHI N	0	0	–	18.00	2	0	0	7	7	2	1	0	0	0	0	0	0	0	–
1944 PHI A	10	8	.556	1.94	53	0	0	111.1	78	23	44	0	10	8	12	25	3	0	.120
1945	8	7	.533	2.35	52	0	0	130.1	114	38	51	0	8	7	5	35	5	0	.143
1946 2 teams			PHI A (5G 0–1)		CLE A (21G 3–6)														
" total	3	7	.300	3.22	26	0	0	50.1	47	24	21	0	3	7	1	10	3	0	.300
4 yrs.	21	22	.488	2.45	133	0	0	294	246	87	117	0	21	22	18	70	11	0	.157

Frank Bertaina

BERTAINA, FRANK LOUIS　　　　　　　BL TL 5'11"　177 lbs.
B. Apr. 14, 1944, San Francisco, Calif.

	W	L	PCT	ERA	G	GS	CG	IP	H	BB	SO	ShO	W	L	SV	AB	H	HR	BA
1964 BAL A	1	0	1.000	2.77	6	4	1	26	18	13	18	1	0	0	0	5	0	0	.000
1965	0	0	–	6.00	2	1	0	6	9	4	5	0	0	0	0	1	0	0	.000
1966	2	5	.286	3.13	16	9	0	63.1	52	36	46	0	1	0	0	19	2	0	.105
1967 2 teams			BAL A (5G 1–1)		WAS A (18G 6–5)														
" total	7	6	.538	2.99	23	19	4	117.1	107	51	86	4	0	0	0	44	3	0	.068
1968 WAS A	7	13	.350	4.66	27	23	1	127.1	133	69	81	0	0	0	0	38	5	0	.132
1969 2 teams			WAS A (14G 1–3)		BAL A (3G 0–0)														
" total	1	3	.250	5.62	17	5	0	41.2	44	26	30	0	0	3	0	12	5	1	.417
1970 STL N	1	2	.333	3.19	8	5	0	31	36	15	14	0	0	0	0	7	1	0	.143
7 yrs.	19	29	.396	3.84	99	66	6	412.2	399	214	280	5	1	3	0	126	16	1	.127

Lefty Bertrand

BERTRAND, ROMAN MATHIAS　　　　　BR TL 6'　180 lbs.
B. Feb. 28, 1909, Cobden, Minn.

	W	L	PCT	ERA	G	GS	CG	IP	H	BB	SO	ShO	W	L	SV	AB	H	HR	BA
1936 PHI N	0	0	–	9.00	1	0	0	2	3	2	1	0	0	0	0	0	0	0	–

Fred Besana

BESANA, FREDERICK CYRIL　　　　　　BR TL 6'3½"　200 lbs.
B. Apr. 5, 1931, Lincoln, Calif.

	W	L	PCT	ERA	G	GS	CG	IP	H	BB	SO	ShO	W	L	SV	AB	H	HR	BA
1956 BAL A	1	0	1.000	5.60	7	2	0	17.2	22	14	7	0	0	0	0	4	0	0	.000

Herman Besse

BESSE, HERMAN (Long Herm)　　　　　BL TL 6'2"　190 lbs.
B. Aug. 16, 1911, St. Louis, Mo.　D. Aug. 13, 1972, Los Angeles, Calif.

	W	L	PCT	ERA	G	GS	CG	IP	H	BB	SO	ShO	W	L	SV	AB	H	HR	BA
1940 PHI A	0	3	.000	8.83	17	5	0	53	70	34	19	0	0	0	0	19	5	0	.263
1941	2	0	1.000	10.07	6	2	1	19.2	28	12	8	0	1	0	0	5	1	0	.200
1942	2	9	.182	6.50	30	14	4	133	163	69	78	0	0	1	1	53	12	0	.226
1943	1	1	.500	3.31	5	1	0	16.1	18	4	3	0	0	0	0	8	0	0	.000
1946	0	2	.000	5.23	7	3	0	20.2	19	9	10	0	0	1	0	5	0	0	.000
5 yrs.	5	15	.250	6.97	65	25	5	242.2	298	128	118	0	1	2	1	90	18	0	.200

	W	L	PCT	ERA	G	GS	CG	IP	H	BB	SO	ShO	Relief Pitching W	L	SV	BATTING AB	H	HR	BA

Don Bessent

BESSENT, FRED DONALD (The Weasel)
B. Mar. 13, 1931, Jacksonville, Fla.   BR TR 6'   175 lbs.

	W	L	PCT	ERA	G	GS	CG	IP	H	BB	SO	ShO	W	L	SV	AB	H	HR	BA
1955 BKN N	8	1	.889	2.70	24	2	1	63.1	51	21	29	0	6	1	3	20	2	0	.100
1956	4	3	.571	2.50	38	0	0	79.1	63	31	52	0	4	3	9	18	2	0	.111
1957	1	3	.250	5.73	27	0	0	44	58	19	24	0	1	3	0	4	1	0	.250
1958 LA N	1	0	1.000	3.33	19	0	0	24.1	24	17	13	0	1	0	0	2	0	0	.000
4 yrs.	14	7	.667	3.33	108	2	1	211	196	88	118	0	12	7	12	44	5	0	.114
WORLD SERIES																			
1955 BKN N	0	0	–	0.00	3	0	0	3.1	3	1	1	0	0	0	0	1	0	0	.000
1956	1	0	1.000	1.80	2	0	0	10	8	3	5	0	1	0	0	2	1	0	.500
2 yrs.	1	0	1.000	1.35	5	0	0	13.1	11	4	6	0	1	0	0	3	1	0	.333

Karl Best

BEST, KARL JON
B. Mar. 6, 1959, Aberdeen, Wash.   BR TR 6'4"   200 lbs.

	W	L	PCT	ERA	G	GS	CG	IP	H	BB	SO	ShO	W	L	SV	AB	H	HR	BA
1983 SEA A	0	1	.000	13.50	4	0	0	5.1	14	5	3	0	0	1	0	0	0	0	–
1984	1	1	.500	3.00	5	0	0	6	7	0	6	0	1	1	0	0	0	0	–
2 yrs.	1	2	.333	7.94	9	0	0	11.1	21	5	9	0	1	2	0	0	0	0	–

Jim Bethke

BETHKE, JAMES CHARLES
B. Nov. 5, 1946, Falls City, Neb.   BR TR 6'3"   185 lbs.

	W	L	PCT	ERA	G	GS	CG	IP	H	BB	SO	ShO	W	L	SV	AB	H	HR	BA
1965 NY N	2	0	1.000	4.28	25	0	0	40	41	22	19	0	2	0	0	4	0	0	.000

Jeff Bettendorf

BETTENDORF, JEFFREY ALLEN
B. Dec. 10, 1961, Lompoc, Calif.   BR TR 6'3"   180 lbs.

	W	L	PCT	ERA	G	GS	CG	IP	H	BB	SO	ShO	W	L	SV	AB	H	HR	BA
1984 OAK A	0	0	–	4.66	3	0	0	9.2	9	5	5	0	0	0	1	0	0	0	–

Hal Betts

BETTS, HAROLD MATTHEW
B. June 14, 1881, Alliance, Ohio   D. May 22, 1946, San Antonio, Tex.   BR TR 5'10"   200 lbs.

	W	L	PCT	ERA	G	GS	CG	IP	H	BB	SO	ShO	W	L	SV	AB	H	HR	BA
1903 STL N	0	1	.000	10.00	1	1	1	9	11	5	2	0	0	0	0	3	0	0	.000
1913 CIN N	0	0	–	2.70	1	0	0	3.1	1	3	0	0	0	0	0	1	0	0	.000
2 yrs.	0	1	.000	8.03	2	1	1	12.1	12	8	2	0	0	0	0	4	0	0	.000

Huck Betts

BETTS, WALTER MARTIN
B. Feb. 18, 1897, Millsboro, Del.   BL TR 5'11"   170 lbs.

	W	L	PCT	ERA	G	GS	CG	IP	H	BB	SO	ShO	W	L	SV	AB	H	HR	BA
1920 PHI N	1	1	.500	3.57	27	4	1	88.1	86	33	18	0	0	1	0	25	2	0	.080
1921	3	7	.300	4.47	32	2	1	100.2	141	14	28	0	3	5	4	30	8	0	.267
1922	1	0	1.000	9.60	7	0	0	15	23	8	4	0	1	0	0	4	0	0	.000
1923	2	4	.333	3.09	19	4	3	84.1	100	14	18	0	0	1	1	31	3	0	.097
1924	7	10	.412	4.30	37	9	2	144.1	160	42	46	0	5	5	2	45	7	0	.156
1925	4	5	.444	5.55	35	7	1	97.1	146	38	28	0	3	1	1	34	10	0	.294
1932 BOS N	13	11	.542	2.80	31	27	16	221.2	229	35	32	3	2	0	1	79	19	0	.241
1933	11	11	.500	2.79	35	26	17	242	225	55	40	2	0	1	4	76	17	0	.224
1934	17	10	.630	4.06	40	27	10	213	258	42	69	2	3	1	3	69	13	0	.188
1935	2	9	.182	5.47	44	19	2	159.2	213	40	40	1	1	2	0	44	7	0	.159
10 yrs.	61	68	.473	3.93	307	125	53	1366.1	1581	321	323	8	18	17	16	437	86	0	.197

Bill Bevens

BEVENS, FLOYD CLIFFORD
B. Oct. 21, 1916, Hubbard, Ore.   BR TR 6'3½"   210 lbs.

	W	L	PCT	ERA	G	GS	CG	IP	H	BB	SO	ShO	W	L	SV	AB	H	HR	BA
1944 NY A	4	1	.800	2.68	8	5	3	43.2	44	13	16	0	0	0	0	16	1	0	.063
1945	13	9	.591	3.67	29	25	14	184	174	68	76	2	0	1	0	63	7	1	.111
1946	16	13	.552	2.23	31	31	18	249.2	213	78	120	3	0	0	0	84	7	2	.083
1947	7	13	.350	3.82	28	23	11	165	167	77	77	1	1	1	0	58	7	0	.121
4 yrs.	40	36	.526	3.08	96	84	46	642.1	598	236	289	6	1	2	0	221	22	3	.100
WORLD SERIES																			
1947 NY A	0	1	.000	2.38	2	1	1	11.1	3	11	7	0	0	0	0	4	0	0	.000

Lou Bevil

BEVIL, LOUIS EUGENE
Also known as Louis Eugene Bevilacqua.
B. Nov. 27, 1921, Nelson, Ill.   D. Feb. 1, 1973, Dixon, Ill.   BB TR 5'11½" 190 lbs.

	W	L	PCT	ERA	G	GS	CG	IP	H	BB	SO	ShO	W	L	SV	AB	H	HR	BA
1942 WAS A	0	1	.000	6.52	4	1	0	9.2	9	11	2	0	0	0	0	3	0	0	.000

Charlie Beville

BEVILLE, CLARENCE BENJAMIN (Candy)
B. Aug. 28, 1877, Colusa, Calif.   D. Jan. 5, 1937, Yountville, Calif.

	W	L	PCT	ERA	G	GS	CG	IP	H	BB	SO	ShO	W	L	SV	AB	H	HR	BA
1901 BOS A	0	2	.000	4.00	2	2	1	9	8	9	1	0	0	0	0	7	2	0	.286

Jim Bibby

BIBBY, JAMES BLAIR
B. Oct. 29, 1944, Franklinton, N. C.   BR TR 6'5"   235 lbs.

	W	L	PCT	ERA	G	GS	CG	IP	H	BB	SO	ShO	W	L	SV	AB	H	HR	BA
1972 STL N	1	3	.250	3.35	6	6	0	40.1	29	19	28	0	0	0	0	8	1	0	.125
1973 2 teams			STL	N (6G 0-2)		TEX	A	(26G 9-10)											
" total	9	12	.429	3.77	32	26	11	196	140	123	167	2	0	0	1	2	0	0	.000
1974 TEX A	19	19	.500	4.74	41	41	11	264	255	113	149	5	0	0	0	0	0	0	–
1975 2 teams			TEX	A (12G 2-6)		CLE	A	(24G 5-9)											
" total	7	15	.318	3.88	36	24	6	181	172	78	93	1	1	3	1	0	0	0	–
1976 CLE A	13	7	.650	3.20	34	21	4	163	162	56	84	3	3	1	1	0	0	0	–
1977	12	13	.480	3.57	37	30	9	207	197	73	141	2	0	1	2	0	0	0	–
1978 PIT N	8	7	.533	3.53	34	14	3	107	100	39	72	2	3	2	1	31	4	1	.129
1979	12	4	.750	2.80	34	17	4	138	110	47	103	1	2	1	0	45	8	2	.178
1980	19	6	.760	3.33	35	34	6	238	210	88	144	1	1	0	0	77	12	1	.156
1981	6	3	.667	2.49	14	14	2	94	79	26	48	2	0	0	0	28	4	1	.143
1983	5	12	.294	6.69	29	12	0	78	92	51	44	0	3	4	2	18	2	0	.111
1984 TEX A	0	0	–	4.41	8	0	0	16.1	19	10	6	0	0	0	0	0	0	0	–
12 yrs.	111	101	.524	3.76	340	239	56	1722.2	1565	723	1079	19	13	12	8	209	31	5	.148
LEAGUE CHAMPIONSHIP SERIES																			
1979 PIT N	0	0	–	1.29	1	1	0	7	4	4	5	0	0	0	0	0	0	0	–
WORLD SERIES																			
1979 PIT N	0	0	–	2.61	2	2	0	10.1	10	2	10	0	0	0	0	4	0	0	.000

	W	L	PCT	ERA	G	GS	CG	IP	H	BB	SO	ShO	Relief Pitching W	L	SV	BATTING AB	H	HR	BA

Vern Bickford

BICKFORD, VERNON EDGELL   BR TR 6'   180 lbs.
B. Aug. 17, 1920, Hellier, Ky.   D. May 6, 1960, Concord, Va.

	W	L	PCT	ERA	G	GS	CG	IP	H	BB	SO	ShO	W	L	SV	AB	H	HR	BA
1948 BOS N	11	5	.688	3.27	33	22	10	146	125	63	60	1	0	1	1	49	10	0	.204
1949	16	11	.593	4.25	37	36	15	230.2	246	106	101	2	0	1	0	81	15	0	.185
1950	19	14	.576	3.47	40	39	27	311.2	293	122	126	2	0	0	0	116	16	0	.138
1951	11	9	.550	3.12	25	20	12	164.2	146	76	76	3	0	2	0	52	6	0	.115
1952	7	12	.368	3.74	26	22	7	161.1	165	64	62	1	0	0	0	51	9	0	.176
1953 MIL N	2	5	.286	5.28	20	9	2	58	60	35	25	0	1	0	1	15	1	0	.067
1954 BAL A	0	1	.000	9.00	1	1	0	4	5	1	0	0	0	0	0	1	0	0	.000
7 yrs.	66	57	.537	3.71	182	149	73	1076.1	1040	467	450	9	1	4	2	365	57	0	.156
WORLD SERIES																			
1948 BOS N	0	1	.000	2.70	1	1	0	3.1	4	5	1	0	0	0	0	0	0	0	—

Dan Bickham

BICKHAM, DANIEL DENISON   BR TR 5'10"   160 lbs.
B. Oct. 31, 1864, Dayton, Ohio   D. Mar. 3, 1951, Dayton, Ohio

	W	L	PCT	ERA	G	GS	CG	IP	H	BB	SO	ShO	W	L	SV	AB	H	HR	BA
1886 CIN AA	1	0	1.000	3.00	1	1	1	9	13	3	6	0	0	0	0	3	1	0	.333

Charlie Bicknell

BICKNELL, CHARLES STEPHEN (Bud)   BR TR 5'11"   170 lbs.
B. July 27, 1928, Plainfield, N. J.

	W	L	PCT	ERA	G	GS	CG	IP	H	BB	SO	ShO	W	L	SV	AB	H	HR	BA
1948 PHI N	0	1	.000	5.96	17	1	0	25.2	29	17	5	0	0	0	0	5	0	0	.000
1949	0	0	—	7.62	13	0	0	28.1	32	17	4	0	0	0	0	1	0	0	.000
2 yrs.	0	1	.000	6.83	30	1	0	54	61	34	9	0	0	0	0	6	0	0	.000

Mike Bielecki

BIELECKI, MICHAEL JOSEPH   BR TR 6'3"   180 lbs.
B. July 31, 1959, Baltimore, Md.

	W	L	PCT	ERA	G	GS	CG	IP	H	BB	SO	ShO	W	L	SV	AB	H	HR	BA
1984 PIT N	0	0	—	0.00	4	0	0	4.1	4	0	1	0	0	0	0	0	0	0	—

Harry Biemiller

BIEMILLER, HARRY LEE   BR TR 6'1"   171 lbs.
B. Oct. 9, 1897, Baltimore, Md.   D. May 25, 1965, Orlando, Fla.

	W	L	PCT	ERA	G	GS	CG	IP	H	BB	SO	ShO	W	L	SV	AB	H	HR	BA
1920 WAS A	1	0	1.000	4.76	5	2	1	17	21	13	10	0	0	0	0	4	0	0	.000
1925 CIN N	0	1	.000	4.02	23	1	0	47	45	21	9	0	0	0	2	9	0	0	.000
2 yrs.	1	1	.500	4.22	28	3	1	64	66	34	19	0	0	0	2	13	0	0	.000

Lou Bierbauer

BIERBAUER, LOUIS W.   BR TR 5'8"   140 lbs.
Also appeared in box score as Bauer
B. Sept. 28, 1865, Erie, Pa.   D. Jan. 31, 1926, Erie, Pa.

	W	L	PCT	ERA	G	GS	CG	IP	H	BB	SO	ShO	W	L	SV	AB	H	HR	BA
1886 PHI AA	0	0	—	4.22	2	0	0	10.2	8	5	1	0	0	0	0	522	118	2	.226
1887	0	0	—	0.00	1	0	0	1	0	0	1	0	0	0	1	530	144	1	.272
1888	0	0	—	0.00	1	0	0	3	5	0	3	0	0	0	0	535	143	0	.267
3 yrs.	0	0	—	3.07	4	0	0	14.2	13	5	5	0	0	0	1	*			

Lyle Bigbee

BIGBEE, LYLE RANDOLPH (Al)   BL TR 6'   180 lbs.
Brother of Carson Bigbee.
B. Aug. 22, 1893, Sweet Home, Ore.   D. Aug. 5, 1942, Portland, Ore.

	W	L	PCT	ERA	G	GS	CG	IP	H	BB	SO	ShO	W	L	SV	AB	H	HR	BA
1920 PHI A	0	3	.000	8.00	12	0	0	45	66	25	12	0	0	3	0	70	13	1	.186
1921 PIT N	0	0	—	1.13	5	0	0	8	4	4	1	0	0	0	0	2	0	0	.000
2 yrs.	0	3	.000	6.96	17	0	0	53	70	29	13	0	0	3	0	*			

Charlie Biggs

BIGGS, CHARLES ORVAL   BR TR 6'1"   185 lbs.
B. Sept. 15, 1906, French Lick, Ind.   D. May 24, 1954, French Lick, Ind.

	W	L	PCT	ERA	G	GS	CG	IP	H	BB	SO	ShO	W	L	SV	AB	H	HR	BA
1932 CHI A	1	1	.500	6.93	6	4	0	24.2	32	12	1	0	0	0	0	9	1	0	.111

Larry Biittner

BIITTNER, LARRY DAVID   BL TL 6'2"   205 lbs.
B. July 27, 1946, Pocahontas, Iowa

	W	L	PCT	ERA	G	GS	CG	IP	H	BB	SO	ShO	W	L	SV	AB	H	HR	BA
1977 CHI N	0	0	—	54.00	1	0	0	1	5	1	3	0	0	0	0	*			

Jim Bilbrey

BILBREY, JAMES MELVIN   BR TR 6'2½"   205 lbs.
B. Apr. 20, 1924, Rickman, Tenn.

	W	L	PCT	ERA	G	GS	CG	IP	H	BB	SO	ShO	W	L	SV	AB	H	HR	BA
1949 STL A	0	0	—	18.00	1	0	0	1	1	3	0	0	0	0	0	0	0	0	—

Emil Bildilli

BILDILLI, EMIL (Hill Billy)   BR TL 5'10"   170 lbs.
B. Sept. 16, 1912, Diamond, Ind.   D. Sept. 16, 1946, Hartford City, Ind.

	W	L	PCT	ERA	G	GS	CG	IP	H	BB	SO	ShO	W	L	SV	AB	H	HR	BA
1937 STL A	0	1	.000	10.13	4	1	0	8	12	3	2	0	0	0	0	2	0	0	.000
1938	1	2	.333	7.06	5	3	2	21.2	33	11	11	0	0	0	0	8	2	0	.250
1939	1	1	.500	3.32	2	2	2	19	21	6	8	0	0	0	0	5	0	0	.000
1940	2	4	.333	5.57	28	11	3	97	113	52	32	0	0	0	1	30	6	0	.200
1941	0	0	—	11.57	2	0	0	2.1	5	3	2	0	0	0	0	0	0	0	—
5 yrs.	4	8	.333	5.84	41	17	7	148	184	75	55	0	0	0	1	45	8	0	.178

Harry Billiard

BILLIARD, HARRY PREE (Pre)   BR TR 6'   190 lbs.
B. Nov. 11, 1883, Monroe, Ind.   D. June 3, 1923, Wooster, Ohio

	W	L	PCT	ERA	G	GS	CG	IP	H	BB	SO	ShO	W	L	SV	AB	H	HR	BA
1908 NY A	0	0	—	2.57	5	0	0	14	13	13	9	0	0	0	0	5	1	0	.200
1914 IND F	9	8	.529	3.72	32	16	5	125.2	117	63	45	0	4	2	1	38	7	0	.184
1915 NWK F	1	0	1.000	5.72	14	2	0	28.1	32	28	7	0	1	0	0	6	2	0	.333
3 yrs.	10	8	.556	3.96	51	18	5	168	162	104	61	0	5	2	1	49	10	0	.204

Jack Billingham

BILLINGHAM, JOHN EUGENE   BR TR 6'4"   195 lbs.
B. Feb. 21, 1943, Orlando, Fla.

	W	L	PCT	ERA	G	GS	CG	IP	H	BB	SO	ShO	W	L	SV	AB	H	HR	BA
1968 LA N	3	0	1.000	2.14	50	1	0	71.1	54	30	46	0	3	0	8	3	0	0	.000
1969 HOU N	6	7	.462	4.23	52	4	1	83	92	29	71	0	0	0	2	14	1	0	.071
1970	13	9	.591	3.97	46	24	8	188	190	63	134	2	2	0	0	58	6	0	.103
1971	10	16	.385	3.39	33	33	8	228	205	68	139	3	0	0	0	73	9	0	.123
1972 CIN N	12	12	.500	3.18	36	31	8	217.2	197	64	137	4	0	0	1	71	5	0	.070
1973	19	10	.655	3.04	40	40	16	293.1	257	95	155	7	0	0	0	93	6	0	.065
1974	19	11	.633	3.95	36	35	8	212	233	64	103	3	1	0	0	67	5	0	.075

	W	L	PCT	ERA	G	GS	CG	IP	H	BB	SO	ShO	Relief Pitching W	L	SV	BATTING AB	H	HR	BA

Jack Billingham continued

	W	L	PCT	ERA	G	GS	CG	IP	H	BB	SO	ShO	W	L	SV	AB	H	HR	BA
1975	15	10	.600	4.11	33	32	5	208	222	76	79	0	0	0	0	65	7	0	.108
1976	12	10	.545	4.32	34	29	5	177	190	62	76	2	1	1	1	59	14	0	.237
1977	10	10	.500	5.22	36	23	3	162	195	56	76	2	1	2	0	56	9	0	.161
1978 DET A	15	8	.652	3.88	30	30	10	201.2	218	65	59	4	0	0	0	0	0	0	–
1979	10	7	.588	3.30	35	19	2	158	163	60	59	0	3	2	3	0	0	0	–
1980 2 teams		DET	A (8G 0-0)			BOS	A (7G 1-3)												
" total	1	3	.250	10.45	15	4	0	31	56	18	7	0	0	0	0	0	0	0	–
13 yrs.	145	113	.562	3.83	476	305	74	2231	2272	750	1141	27	11	5	15	559	62	0	.111
LEAGUE CHAMPIONSHIP SERIES																			
1972 CIN N	0	0	–	3.86	1	1	0	4.2	5	2	4	0	0	0	0	2	0	0	.000
1973	0	1	.000	4.50	2	2	0	12	9	4	9	0	0	0	0	3	0	0	.000
2 yrs.	0	1	.000	4.32	3	3	0	16.2	14	6	13	0	0	0	0	5	0	0	.000
WORLD SERIES																			
1972 CIN N	1	0	1.000	0.00	3	2	0	13.2	6	4	11	0	0	0	1	5	0	0	.000
1975	0	0	–	1.00	3	1	0	9	8	5	7	0	0	0	0	2	0	0	.000
1976	1	0	1.000	0.00	1	0	0	2.2	0	0	1	0	1	0	0	0	0	0	–
3 yrs.	2	0	1.000	0.36	7	3	0	25.1	14	9	19	0	1	0	1	7	0	0	.000
				1st		1st													

Haskell Billings

BILLINGS, HASKELL CLARK   BR TR 5'11"   180 lbs.
B. Sept. 27, 1907, New York, N. Y.   D. Dec. 26, 1983, Greenbrae, Calif.

	W	L	PCT	ERA	G	GS	CG	IP	H	BB	SO	ShO	W	L	SV	AB	H	HR	BA
1927 DET A	5	4	.556	4.84	10	9	5	67	64	39	18	0	0	1	0	27	7	0	.259
1928	5	10	.333	5.12	21	16	3	110.2	118	59	48	1	0	0	0	35	10	0	.286
1929	0	1	.000	5.12	8	0	0	19.1	27	9	1	0	0	1	0	6	0	0	.000
3 yrs.	10	15	.400	5.03	39	25	8	197	209	107	67	1	0	2	0	68	17	0	.250

Doug Bird

BIRD, JAMES DOUGLAS   BR TR 6'4"   180 lbs.
B. Mar. 5, 1950, Corona, Calif.

	W	L	PCT	ERA	G	GS	CG	IP	H	BB	SO	ShO	W	L	SV	AB	H	HR	BA
1973 KC A	4	4	.500	3.00	54	0	0	102	81	30	84	0	4	4	20	0	0	0	–
1974	7	6	.538	2.74	55	1	1	92	100	27	62	0	7	5	10	0	0	0	–
1975	9	6	.600	3.25	51	4	0	105.1	100	40	81	0	9	5	11	0	0	0	–
1976	12	10	.545	3.36	39	27	2	198	191	31	107	1	3	0	2	0	0	0	–
1977	11	4	.733	3.89	53	5	0	118	120	29	83	0	10	3	14	0	0	0	–
1978	6	6	.500	5.29	40	6	0	98.2	110	31	48	0	5	3	1	0	0	0	–
1979 PHI N	2	0	1.000	5.16	32	1	1	61	73	16	33	0	1	0	0	6	1	0	.167
1980 NY A	3	0	1.000	2.65	22	1	0	51	47	14	17	0	2	0	1	0	0	0	–
1981 2 teams		NY	A (17G 5-1)			CHI	N (12G 4-5)												
" total	9	6	.600	3.23	29	16	2	128	130	32	62	1	2	0	0	20	2	0	.100
1982 CHI N	9	14	.391	5.14	35	33	2	191	230	30	71	1	0	0	0	56	8	0	.143
1983 BOS A	1	4	.200	6.65	22	6	0	67.2	91	16	33	0	0	1	1	0	0	0	–
11 yrs.	73	60	.549	3.99	432	100	8	1212.2	1273	296	681	3	43	21	60	82	11	0	.134
LEAGUE CHAMPIONSHIP SERIES																			
1976 KC A	1	0	1.000	1.93	1	0	0	4.2	4	0	1	0	1	0	0	0	0	0	–
1977	0	0	–	0.00	3	0	0	2	4	0	1	0	0	0	0	0	0	0	–
1978	0	1	.000	9.00	2	0	0	1	2	0	1	0	0	1	0	0	0	0	–
3 yrs.	1	1	.500	2.35	6	0	0	7.2	10	0	3	0	1	1	0	0	0	0	–

Red Bird

BIRD, JAMES EDWARD   BL TL 5'11"   170 lbs.
B. Apr. 25, 1890, Stephenville, Tex.   D. Mar. 23, 1972, Murfeesboro, Ark.

	W	L	PCT	ERA	G	GS	CG	IP	H	BB	SO	ShO	W	L	SV	AB	H	HR	BA
1921 WAS A	0	0	–	5.40	1	0	0	5	5	1	2	0	0	0	0	1	0	0	.000

Ralph Birkofer

BIRKOFER, RALPH JOSEPH (Lefty)   BL TL 5'11"   213 lbs.
B. Nov. 5, 1908, Cincinnati, Ohio   D. Mar. 16, 1971, Cincinnati, Ohio

	W	L	PCT	ERA	G	GS	CG	IP	H	BB	SO	ShO	W	L	SV	AB	H	HR	BA
1933 PIT N	4	2	.667	2.31	9	8	3	50.2	43	17	20	1	0	0	0	22	7	0	.318
1934	11	12	.478	4.10	41	24	11	204	227	66	71	0	2	1	1	75	17	0	.227
1935	9	7	.563	4.07	37	18	8	150.1	173	42	80	1	2	0	1	58	14	0	.241
1936	7	5	.583	4.69	34	13	2	109.1	130	41	44	0	6	2	0	41	9	0	.220
1937 BKN N	0	2	.000	6.67	11	1	0	29.2	45	9	9	0	0	1	0	11	3	0	.273
5 yrs.	31	28	.525	4.19	132	64	24	544	618	175	224	2	10	4	2	207	50	0	.242

Babe Birrer

BIRRER, WERNER JOSEPH   BR TR 6'   195 lbs.
B. July 4, 1928, Buffalo, N. Y.

	W	L	PCT	ERA	G	GS	CG	IP	H	BB	SO	ShO	W	L	SV	AB	H	HR	BA
1955 DET A	4	3	.571	4.15	36	3	1	80.1	77	29	28	0	3	1	3	19	3	2	.158
1956 BAL A	0	0	–	6.75	4	0	0	5.1	9	1	1	0	0	0	0	1	0	0	.000
1958 LA N	0	0	–	4.50	16	0	0	34	43	7	16	0	0	0	1	7	4	0	.571
3 yrs.	4	3	.571	4.36	56	3	1	119.2	129	37	45	0	3	1	4	27	7	2	.259

Frank Biscan

BISCAN, FRANK STEPHEN (Porky)   BL TL 5'11"   190 lbs.
B. Mar. 13, 1920, Mt. Olive, Ill.   D. May 22, 1959, St. Louis, Mo.

	W	L	PCT	ERA	G	GS	CG	IP	H	BB	SO	ShO	W	L	SV	AB	H	HR	BA
1942 STL A	0	1	.000	2.33	11	0	0	27	13	11	10	0	0	1	0	6	0	0	.000
1946	1	1	.500	5.16	16	0	0	22.2	28	22	9	0	1	1	1	3	0	0	.000
1948	6	7	.462	6.11	47	4	1	98.2	129	71	45	0	6	5	2	26	5	0	.192
3 yrs.	7	9	.438	5.28	74	4	1	148.1	170	104	64	0	7	7	4	35	5	0	.143

Bill Bishop

BISHOP, WILLIAM HENRY (Lefty)   BL TL 5'8"   170 lbs.
B. Oct. 22, 1900, Clearfield, Pa.   D. Feb. 14, 1956, St. Joseph, Mo.

	W	L	PCT	ERA	G	GS	CG	IP	H	BB	SO	ShO	W	L	SV	AB	H	HR	BA
1921 PHI A	0	0	–	9.00	2	0	0	7	8	10	4	0	0	0	0	3	0	0	.000

Bill Bishop

BISHOP, WILLIAM ROBINSON
B. Dec. 27, 1869, Adamsburg, Pa.   D. Dec. 15, 1932, Pittsburgh, Pa.

	W	L	PCT	ERA	G	GS	CG	IP	H	BB	SO	ShO	W	L	SV	AB	H	HR	BA
1886 PIT AA	0	1	.000	3.18	2	2	2	17	17	11	4	0	0	0	0	7	1	0	.143
1887 PIT N	0	3	.000	13.33	3	3	3	27	45	22	4	0	0	0	0	9	0	0	.000
1889 CHI N	0	0	–	18.00	2	0	0	3	6	6	1	0	0	0	2	1	0	0	.000
3 yrs.	0	4	.000	9.96	7	5	5	47	68	39	9	0	0	0	2	17	1	0	.059

	W	L	PCT	ERA	G	GS	CG	IP	H	BB	SO	ShO	Relief Pitching W	L	SV	BATTING AB	H	HR	BA

Charlie Bishop

BISHOP, CHARLES TULLER   BR TR 6'2"   195 lbs.
B. Jan. 1, 1924, Atlanta, Ga.

	W	L	PCT	ERA	G	GS	CG	IP	H	BB	SO	ShO	W	L	SV	AB	H	HR	BA
1952 PHI A	2	2	.500	6.46	6	5	1	30.2	29	24	17	0	0	0	0	9	1	0	.111
1953	3	14	.176	5.66	39	20	1	160.2	174	86	66	1	2	1	2	56	5	0	.089
1954	4	6	.400	4.41	20	12	4	96	98	50	34	0	0	0	1	33	4	0	.121
1955 KC A	1	0	1.000	5.40	4	0	0	6.2	6	8	4	0	1	0	0	2	1	0	.500
4 yrs.	10	22	.313	5.33	69	37	6	294	307	168	121	1	3	1	3	100	11	0	.110

Jim Bishop

BISHOP, JAMES MORTON   BR TR 6'   185 lbs.
B. Jan. 28, 1898, Montgomery City, Mo.   D. Sept. 17, 1973, Montgomery City, Mo.

	W	L	PCT	ERA	G	GS	CG	IP	H	BB	SO	ShO	W	L	SV	AB	H	HR	BA
1923 PHI N	0	3	.000	6.34	15	0	0	32.2	48	11	5	0	0	3	1	10	0	0	.000
1924	0	1	.000	6.48	7	1	0	16.2	24	7	3	0	0	0	0	5	1	0	.200
2 yrs.	0	4	.000	6.39	22	1	0	49.1	72	18	8	0	0	3	1	15	1	0	.067

Lloyd Bishop

BISHOP, LLOYD CLIFTON   BR TR 6'   180 lbs.
B. Apr. 25, 1890, Wichita, Kans.   D. June 18, 1968, Wichita, Kans.

	W	L	PCT	ERA	G	GS	CG	IP	H	BB	SO	ShO	W	L	SV	AB	H	HR	BA
1914 CLE A	0	1	.000	5.63	3	1	0	8	14	3	1	0	0	0	0	2	0	0	.000

Hi Bithorn

BITHORN, HIRAM GABRIEL   BR TR 6'1"   200 lbs.
B. Mar. 18, 1916, Santurce, Puerto Rico   D. Jan. 1, 1952, El Mante, Mexico

	W	L	PCT	ERA	G	GS	CG	IP	H	BB	SO	ShO	W	L	SV	AB	H	HR	BA
1942 CHI N	9	14	.391	3.68	38	16	9	171.1	191	81	65	0	3	5	2	57	7	0	.123
1943	18	12	.600	2.60	39	30	19	249.2	226	65	86	7	1	1	2	92	16	0	.174
1946	6	5	.545	3.84	26	7	2	86.2	97	25	34	1	4	2	1	28	5	0	.179
1947 CHI A	1	0	1.000	0.00	2	0	0	2	2	0	0	0	1	0	0	0	0	0	—
4 yrs.	34	31	.523	3.16	105	53	30	509.2	516	171	185	8	9	8	5	177	28	0	.158

Jim Bivin

BIVIN, JAMES NATHANIEL   BR TR 6'   155 lbs.
B. Dec. 11, 1909, Jackson, Miss.   D. Nov. 7, 1982, Pueblo, Colo.

	W	L	PCT	ERA	G	GS	CG	IP	H	BB	SO	ShO	W	L	SV	AB	H	HR	BA
1935 PHI N	2	9	.182	5.79	47	14	0	161.2	220	65	54	0	2	1	1	48	7	0	.146

Bill Black

BLACK, WILLIAM CARROLL (Bud)   BR TR 6'3"   197 lbs.
B. July 9, 1932, St. Louis, Mo.

	W	L	PCT	ERA	G	GS	CG	IP	H	BB	SO	ShO	W	L	SV	AB	H	HR	BA
1952 DET A	0	1	.000	10.57	2	2	0	7.2	14	5	0	0	0	0	0	3	0	0	.000
1955	1	1	.500	1.26	3	2	1	14.1	12	8	7	1	0	1	0	4	1	0	.250
1956	1	1	.500	3.60	5	1	0	10	10	5	7	0	1	0	0	2	0	0	.000
3 yrs.	2	3	.400	4.22	10	5	1	32	36	18	14	1	1	1	0	9	1	0	.111

Bob Black

BLACK, ROBERT BENJAMIM
B. Dec. 10, 1864, Cincinnati, Ohio   D. Mar. 21, 1933, Sioux City, Iowa

	W	L	PCT	ERA	G	GS	CG	IP	H	BB	SO	ShO	W	L	SV	AB	H	HR	BA
1884 KC U	4	9	.308	3.22	16	15	13	123	127	17	93	0	0	0	0	*			

Bud Black

BLACK, HARRY RALSTON   BL TL 6'2"   180 lbs.
B. June 30, 1957, San Mateo, Calif.

	W	L	PCT	ERA	G	GS	CG	IP	H	BB	SO	ShO	W	L	SV	AB	H	HR	BA
1981 SEA A	0	0	—	0.00	2	0	0	1	2	3	0	0	0	0	0	0	0	0	—
1982 KC A	4	6	.400	4.58	22	14	0	88.1	92	34	40	0	0	0	0	0	0	0	—
1983	10	7	.588	3.79	24	24	3	161.1	159	43	58	0	0	0	0	0	0	0	—
1984	17	12	.586	3.12	35	35	8	257	226	64	140	1	0	0	0	0	0	0	—
4 yrs.	31	25	.554	3.58	83	73	11	507.2	479	144	238	1	0	0	0	0	0	0	—

LEAGUE CHAMPIONSHIP SERIES

	W	L	PCT	ERA	G	GS	CG	IP	H	BB	SO	ShO	W	L	SV	AB	H	HR	BA
1984 KC A	0	1	.000	7.20	1	1	0	5	7	1	3	0	0	0	0	0	0	0	—

Dave Black

BLACK, DAVID   BL TL 6'2"   175 lbs.
B. Apr. 19, 1892, Chicago, Ill.   D. Oct. 27, 1936, Pittsburgh, Pa.

	W	L	PCT	ERA	G	GS	CG	IP	H	BB	SO	ShO	W	L	SV	AB	H	HR	BA
1914 CHI F	1	0	1.000	6.12	8	1	1	25	28	4	19	0	0	0	0	12	4	0	.333
1915 2 teams					CHI F (25G 6–7)			BAL F (8G 1–3)											
" total	7	10	.412	2.72	33	14	3	155.1	136	48	53	0	1	4	0	49	7	0	.143
1923 BOS A	0	0	—	0.00	2	0	0	1	2	0	0	0	0	0	0	0	0	0	—
3 yrs.	8	10	.444	3.18	43	15	4	181.1	166	52	72	0	1	4	0	61	11	0	.180

Don Black

BLACK, DONALD PAUL   BR TR 6'   185 lbs.
B. July 20, 1916, Salix, Iowa   D. Apr. 21, 1959, Cuyahoga Falls, Ohio

	W	L	PCT	ERA	G	GS	CG	IP	H	BB	SO	ShO	W	L	SV	AB	H	HR	BA
1943 PHI A	6	16	.273	4.20	33	26	12	208	193	110	65	1	1	0	1	69	13	0	.188
1944	10	12	.455	4.06	29	27	8	177.1	177	75	78	0	0	0	0	59	11	0	.186
1945	5	11	.313	5.17	26	18	8	125.1	154	69	47	0	2	1	0	37	6	0	.162
1946 CLE A	1	2	.333	4.53	18	4	0	43.2	45	21	15	0	0	0	0	10	2	0	.200
1947	10	12	.455	3.92	30	28	8	190.2	177	85	72	3	0	0	1	66	12	0	.182
1948	2	2	.500	5.37	18	10	1	52	57	40	16	0	0	1	0	15	3	0	.200
6 yrs.	34	55	.382	4.35	154	113	37	797	803	400	293	4	3	2	1	256	47	0	.184

Joe Black

BLACK, JOSEPH   BR TR 6'2"   220 lbs.
B. Feb. 8, 1924, Plainfield, N. J.

	W	L	PCT	ERA	G	GS	CG	IP	H	BB	SO	ShO	W	L	SV	AB	H	HR	BA
1952 BKN N	15	4	.789	2.15	56	2	1	142.1	102	41	85	0	14	3	15	36	5	0	.139
1953	6	3	.667	5.33	34	3	0	72.2	74	27	42	0	6	2	5	17	4	0	.235
1954	0	0	—	11.57	5	0	0	7	11	5	3	0	0	0	0	0	0	0	—
1955 2 teams					BKN N (6G 1–0)			CIN N (32G 5–2)											
" total	6	2	.750	4.05	38	11	1	117.2	121	30	63	0	3	0	3	33	4	0	.121
1956 CIN N	3	2	.600	4.52	32	0	0	61.2	61	25	27	0	3	2	2	10	0	0	.000
1957 WAS A	0	1	.000	7.11	7	0	0	12.2	22	1	2	0	0	1	0	0	0	0	—
6 yrs.	30	12	.714	3.91	172	16	2	414	391	129	222	0	26	8	25	96	13	0	.135

WORLD SERIES

	W	L	PCT	ERA	G	GS	CG	IP	H	BB	SO	ShO	W	L	SV	AB	H	HR	BA
1952 BKN N	1	2	.333	2.53	3	3	1	21.1	15	8	9	0	0	0	0	6	0	0	.000
1953	0	0	—	9.00	1	0	0	1	1	0	2	0	0	0	0	0	0	0	—
2 yrs.	1	2	.333	2.82	4	3	1	22.1	16	8	11	0	0	0	0	6	0	0	.000

	W	L	PCT	ERA	G	GS	CG	IP	H	BB	SO	ShO	Relief Pitching W	L	SV	AB	H	HR	BA

Babe Blackburn

BLACKBURN, FOSTER EDWIN
B. Jan. 6, 1895, Chicago, Ill.   D. Mar. 9, 1984, New Port Richey, Fla.   BR TR 6'   200 lbs.

	W	L	PCT	ERA	G	GS	CG	IP	H	BB	SO	ShO	W	L	SV	AB	H	HR	BA
1915 KC F	0	1	.000	8.62	7	2	0	15.2	19	13	7	0	0	0	0	4	0	0	.000
1921 CHI A	0	0	–	0.00	1	0	0	1	0	1	0	0	0	0	0	0	0	0	–
2 yrs.	0	1	.000	8.10	8	2	0	16.2	19	14	7	0	0	0	0	4	0	0	.000

George Blackburn

BLACKBURN, GEORGE W.
B. Sept. 21, 1871, Ozark, Mo.   Deceased.   5'10"   180 lbs.

	W	L	PCT	ERA	G	GS	CG	IP	H	BB	SO	ShO	W	L	SV	AB	H	HR	BA
1897 BAL N	2	2	.500	6.82	5	4	3	33	34	12	1	0	0	0	0	13	1	0	.077

Jim Blackburn

BLACKBURN, JAMES RAY (Bones)
B. June 19, 1924, Warsaw, Ky.   D. Oct. 26, 1969, Cincinnati, Ohio   BR TR 6'4"   175 lbs.

	W	L	PCT	ERA	G	GS	CG	IP	H	BB	SO	ShO	W	L	SV	AB	H	HR	BA
1948 CIN N	0	2	.000	4.18	16	0	0	32.1	38	14	10	0	0	2	0	6	0	0	.000
1951	0	0	–	17.18	2	0	0	3.2	8	2	1	0	0	0	0	0	0	0	–
2 yrs.	0	2	.000	5.50	18	0	0	36	46	16	11	0	0	2	0	6	0	0	.000

Ron Blackburn

BLACKBURNE, RONALD HAMILTON
B. Apr. 23, 1935, Mt. Airy, N. C.   BR TR 6'½"   160 lbs.

	W	L	PCT	ERA	G	GS	CG	IP	H	BB	SO	ShO	W	L	SV	AB	H	HR	BA
1958 PIT N	2	1	.667	3.39	38	2	0	63.2	61	27	31	0	2	0	3	7	2	0	.286
1959	1	1	.500	3.65	26	0	0	44.1	50	15	19	0	1	1	1	5	1	1	.200
2 yrs.	3	2	.600	3.50	64	2	0	108	111	42	50	0	3	1	4	12	3	1	.250

Lena Blackburne

BLACKBURNE, RUSSELL AUBREY (Slats)
B. Oct. 23, 1886, Clifton Heights, Pa.   D. Feb. 29, 1968, Riverside, N. J.   BR TR 5'11"   160 lbs.
Manager 1928-29.

	W	L	PCT	ERA	G	GS	CG	IP	H	BB	SO	ShO	W	L	SV	AB	H	HR	BA
1929 CHI A	0	0	–	0.00	1	0	0	.1	1	0	0	0	0	0	0	*			

Ewell Blackwell

BLACKWELL, EWELL (The Whip)
B. Oct. 23, 1922, Fresno, Calif.   BR TR 6'6"   195 lbs.

	W	L	PCT	ERA	G	GS	CG	IP	H	BB	SO	ShO	W	L	SV	AB	H	HR	BA
1942 CIN N	0	0	–	6.00	2	0	0	3	3	3	1	0	0	0	0	1	0	0	.000
1946	9	13	.409	2.45	33	25	10	194.1	160	79	100	6	0	0	0	56	6	0	.107
1947	22	8	.733	2.47	33	33	23	273	227	95	193	6	0	0	0	106	13	0	.123
1948	7	9	.438	4.54	22	20	4	138.2	134	52	114	1	0	0	1	48	11	0	.229
1949	5	5	.500	4.23	30	4	0	76.2	80	34	55	0	4	3	1	19	4	0	.211
1950	17	15	.531	2.97	40	32	18	261	203	112	188	1	1	1	4	89	13	0	.146
1951	16	15	.516	3.45	38	32	11	232.1	204	97	120	2	2	1	2	82	24	1	.293
1952 2 teams	CIN N (23G 3–12)				NY A (5G 1–0)														
" total	4	12	.250	4.73	28	19	3	118	119	72	55	0	0	1	1	37	6	0	.162
1953 NY A	0	1	.000	3.66	8	4	0	19.2	17	13	11	0	0	1	0	5	0	0	.000
1955 KC A	0	1	.000	6.75	2	0	0	4	3	5	2	0	0	1	0	0	0	0	–
10 yrs.	82	78	.513	3.30	236	169	69	1320.2	1150	562	839	16	7	7	11	443	77	1	.174

WORLD SERIES

	W	L	PCT	ERA	G	GS	CG	IP	H	BB	SO	ShO	W	L	SV	AB	H	HR	BA
1952 NY A	0	0	–	7.20	1	1	0	5	4	3	4	0	0	0	0	1	0	0	.000

George Blaeholder

BLAEHOLDER, GEORGE FRANKLIN
B. Jan. 26, 1904, Orange, Calif.   D. Dec. 29, 1947, Garden Grove, Calif.   BR TR 5'11"   175 lbs.

	W	L	PCT	ERA	G	GS	CG	IP	H	BB	SO	ShO	W	L	SV	AB	H	HR	BA
1925 STL A	0	0	–	31.50	2	0	0	2	6	1	1	0	0	0	0	0	0	0	–
1927	0	1	.000	5.00	1	1	1	9	8	4	2	0	0	0	0	3	1	0	.333
1928	10	15	.400	4.37	38	26	9	214.1	235	52	87	1	1	0	3	71	15	2	.211
1929	14	15	.483	4.18	42	24	13	222	237	61	72	4	4	3	2	74	9	1	.122
1930	11	13	.458	4.61	37	23	10	191.1	235	46	70	1	1	2	4	65	12	0	.185
1931	11	15	.423	4.53	35	32	13	226.1	280	56	79	1	0	1	0	77	11	0	.143
1932	14	14	.500	4.70	42	36	16	258.1	304	76	80	1	0	1	0	88	12	0	.136
1933	15	19	.441	4.72	38	36	14	255.2	283	69	63	3	2	0	0	77	14	0	.182
1934	14	18	.438	4.22	39	33	14	234.1	276	68	66	1	2	1	3	75	7	0	.093
1935 2 teams	STL A (6G 1–1)				PHI A (23G 6–10)														
" total	7	11	.389	4.32	29	24	10	166.2	198	55	22	1	0	0	0	50	2	0	.040
1936 CLE A	8	4	.667	5.09	35	16	6	134.1	158	47	30	0	2	0	0	46	6	0	.130
11 yrs.	104	125	.454	4.54	338	251	106	1914.1	2220	535	572	13	12	9	12	626	89	3	.142

Bill Blair

BLAIR, WILLIAM ELLSWORTH
B. Sept. 17, 1863, Pittsburgh, Pa.   D. Feb. 22, 1890, Pittsburgh, Pa.   TL 5'8½"   172 lbs.

	W	L	PCT	ERA	G	GS	CG	IP	H	BB	SO	ShO	W	L	SV	AB	H	HR	BA
1888 PHI AA	1	3	.250	2.61	4	4	3	31	29	8	16	0	0	0	0	13	4	0	.308

Dennis Blair

BLAIR, DENNIS HERMAN
B. June 5, 1954, Middletown, Ohio   BR TR 6'5"   182 lbs.

	W	L	PCT	ERA	G	GS	CG	IP	H	BB	SO	ShO	W	L	SV	AB	H	HR	BA
1974 MON N	11	7	.611	3.27	22	22	4	146	113	72	76	1	0	0	0	51	6	0	.118
1975	8	15	.348	3.81	30	27	1	163	150	106	82	0	0	0	0	49	7	0	.143
1976	0	2	.000	4.02	5	4	1	15.2	21	11	9	0	0	0	0	4	0	0	.000
1980 SD N	0	1	.000	6.43	5	1	0	14	18	3	11	0	0	1	0	5	1	0	.200
4 yrs.	19	25	.432	3.69	62	54	6	338.2	302	192	178	1	0	1	0	109	14	0	.128

Dick Blaisdell

BLAISDELL, HOWARD CARLETON
B. June 18, 1862, Bradford, Mass.   D. Aug. 20, 1886, Malden, Mass.

	W	L	PCT	ERA	G	GS	CG	IP	H	BB	SO	ShO	W	L	SV	AB	H	HR	BA
1884 KC U	0	3	.000	8.65	3	3	3	26	49	4	8	0	0	0	0	16	5	0	.313

Ed Blake

BLAKE, EDWARD JAMES
B. Dec. 23, 1925, East St. Louis, Ill.   BR TR 5'11"   175 lbs.

	W	L	PCT	ERA	G	GS	CG	IP	H	BB	SO	ShO	W	L	SV	AB	H	HR	BA
1951 CIN N	0	0	–	11.25	3	0	0	4	10	1	1	0	0	0	0	0	0	0	–
1952	0	0	–	0.00	2	0	0	3	3	0	0	0	0	0	0	0	0	0	–
1953	0	0	–	∞	1	0	0	0	1	1	0	0	0	0	0	0	0	0	–
1957 KC A	0	0	–	5.40	2	0	0	1.2	1	2	1	0	0	0	0	0	0	0	–
4 yrs.	0	0	–	8.31	8	0	0	8.2	15	4	1	0	0	0	0	0	0	0	–

	W	L	PCT	ERA	G	GS	CG	IP	H	BB	SO	ShO	Relief Pitching W	L	SV	BATTING AB	H	HR	BA

Sheriff Blake

BLAKE, JOHN FREDERICK
B. Sept. 17, 1899, Ansted, W. Va.
D. Oct. 31, 1982, Beckley, W. Va.

BL TR 6' 180 lbs.
BR 1920,1925-27, BB 1937

	W	L	PCT	ERA	G	GS	CG	IP	H	BB	SO	ShO	W	L	SV	AB	H	HR	BA
1920 PIT N	0	0	–	8.10	6	0	0	13.1	21	6	7	0	0	0	0	4	1	0	.250
1924 CHI N	6	6	.500	4.57	29	11	4	106.1	123	44	42	0	2	2	1	31	9	0	.290
1925	10	18	.357	4.86	36	31	14	231.1	260	114	93	0	0	1	2	79	12	0	.152
1926	11	12	.478	3.60	39	27	11	197.2	204	92	95	4	1	1	1	65	14	0	.215
1927	13	14	.481	3.29	32	27	13	224.1	238	82	64	2	0	3	0	83	16	0	.193
1928	17	11	.607	2.47	34	29	16	240.2	209	101	78	4	3	0	1	88	19	0	.216
1929	14	13	.519	4.29	35	30	13	218.1	244	103	70	1	0	0	1	81	14	0	.173
1930	10	14	.417	4.82	34	24	7	186.2	213	99	80	0	2	2	0	66	15	0	.227
1931 2 teams	CHI	N	(16G 0–4)		PHI	N	(14G 4–5)												
" total	4	9	.308	5.43	30	14	1	121	154	61	60	0	0	3	1	41	14	0	.341
1937 2 teams	STL	A	(15G 2–2)		STL	N	(14G 0–3)												
" total	2	5	.286	5.49	29	3	2	80.1	100	38	32	0	2	3	1	20	4	0	.200
10 yrs.	87	102	.460	4.13	304	196	81	1620	1766	740	621	11	10	15	8	558	118	0	.211
WORLD SERIES																			
1929 CHI N	0	1	.000	13.50	2	0	0	1.1	4	0	1	0	0	1	0	1	1	0	1.000

Al Blanche

BLANCHE, PROSPER ALBERT
Born Prosper Albert Belangio.
B. Sept. 21, 1909, Somerville, Mass.

BR TR 6' 178 lbs.

	W	L	PCT	ERA	G	GS	CG	IP	H	BB	SO	ShO	W	L	SV	AB	H	HR	BA
1935 BOS N	0	0	–	1.56	6	0	0	17.1	14	5	4	0	0	0	0	6	1	0	.167
1936	0	1	.000	6.19	11	0	0	16	20	8	4	0	0	1	1	4	1	0	.250
2 yrs.	0	1	.000	3.78	17	0	0	33.1	34	13	8	0	0	1	1	10	2	0	.200

Gil Blanco

BLANCO, GILBERT HENRY
B. Dec. 15, 1945, Phoenix, Ariz.

BL TL 6'5" 205 lbs.

	W	L	PCT	ERA	G	GS	CG	IP	H	BB	SO	ShO	W	L	SV	AB	H	HR	BA
1965 NY A	1	1	.500	3.98	17	1	0	20.1	16	12	14	0	1	0	0	0	0	0	–
1966 KC A	2	4	.333	4.70	11	8	0	38.1	31	36	21	0	0	0	0	12	2	0	.167
2 yrs.	3	5	.375	4.45	28	9	0	58.2	47	48	35	0	1	0	0	12	2	0	.167

Fred Blanding

BLANDING, FRED JAMES (Fritz)
B. Feb. 8, 1888, Redlands, Calif.   D. July 16, 1950, Salem, Va.

BR TR 6' 185 lbs.

	W	L	PCT	ERA	G	GS	CG	IP	H	BB	SO	ShO	W	L	SV	AB	H	HR	BA
1910 CLE A	2	2	.500	2.78	6	5	4	45.1	43	12	25	1	0	0	0	18	2	0	.111
1911	7	11	.389	3.68	29	16	11	176	190	60	80	0	4	1	2	65	17	0	.262
1912	18	14	.563	2.92	39	31	23	262	259	79	75	1	3	0	1	93	21	1	.226
1913	15	10	.600	2.55	41	22	14	215	234	72	63	3	4	1	0	86	21	0	.244
1914	3	9	.250	3.96	29	12	5	116	133	54	35	0	0	1	1	39	4	0	.103
5 yrs.	45	46	.495	3.13	144	86	57	814.1	859	277	278	5	11	3	4	301	65	1	.216

Fred Blank

BLANK, FREDERICK AUGUST
B. June 18, 1874, DeSoto, Mo.   D. Feb. 5, 1936, St. Louis, Mo.

BL TL 6'½" 175 lbs.

	W	L	PCT	ERA	G	GS	CG	IP	H	BB	SO	ShO	W	L	SV	AB	H	HR	BA
1894 CIN N	0	1	.000	4.50	1	1	1	8	5	9	1	0	0	0	0	3	0	0	.000

Homer Blankenship

BLANKENSHIP, HOMER (Si)
Brother of Ted Blankenship.
B. Aug. 4, 1902, Bonham, Tex.   D. June 22, 1974, Longview, Tex.

BR TR 6' 185 lbs.

	W	L	PCT	ERA	G	GS	CG	IP	H	BB	SO	ShO	W	L	SV	AB	H	HR	BA
1922 CHI A	0	0	–	4.85	4	0	0	13	21	5	3	0	0	0	0	4	0	0	.000
1923	1	1	.500	3.60	4	0	0	5	9	1	1	0	1	1	1	0	0	0	–
1928 PIT N	0	2	.000	5.82	5	2	1	21.2	27	9	6	0	0	0	0	8	3	0	.375
3 yrs.	1	3	.250	5.22	13	2	1	39.2	57	15	10	0	1	1	1	12	3	0	.250

Ted Blankenship

BLANKENSHIP, THEODORE
Brother of Homer Blankenship.
B. May 10, 1901, Bonham, Tex.   D. Jan. 14, 1945, Atoko, Okla.

BR TR 6'1" 170 lbs.

	W	L	PCT	ERA	G	GS	CG	IP	H	BB	SO	ShO	W	L	SV	AB	H	HR	BA
1922 CHI A	8	10	.444	3.81	24	15	7	127.2	124	47	42	0	3	1	1	41	7	0	.171
1923	9	14	.391	4.27	44	23	9	208.2	219	100	57	1	3	3	0	76	16	3	.211
1924	7	6	.538	5.17	25	11	7	125.1	167	38	36	0	1	3	1	46	15	1	.326
1925	17	8	.680	3.16	40	23	16	222	218	69	81	3	3	3	1	88	18	2	.205
1926	13	10	.565	3.61	29	26	15	209.1	217	65	66	1	1	0	1	76	10	0	.132
1927	12	17	.414	5.06	37	34	11	236.2	280	74	51	3	0	0	0	80	15	3	.188
1928	9	11	.450	4.61	27	22	8	158	186	80	36	0	0	0	0	59	10	0	.169
1929	0	2	.000	8.84	8	1	0	18.1	28	9	7	0	0	1	0	4	1	0	.250
1930	2	1	.667	9.20	7	1	0	14.2	23	7	2	0	2	0	0	5	1	0	.200
9 yrs.	77	79	.494	4.32	241	156	73	1320.2	1462	489	378	8	13	11	4	475	93	9	.196

Cy Blanton

BLANTON, DARRELL ELIJAH
B. July 6, 1908, Waurika, Okla.   D. Sept. 13, 1945, Norman, Okla.

BL TR 5'11½" 180 lbs.

	W	L	PCT	ERA	G	GS	CG	IP	H	BB	SO	ShO	W	L	SV	AB	H	HR	BA
1934 PIT N	0	1	.000	3.38	1	1	0	8	5	4	5	0	0	0	0	1	0	0	.000
1935	18	13	.581	2.58	35	31	23	254.1	220	55	142	4	1	2	1	97	13	0	.134
1936	13	15	.464	3.51	44	32	15	235.2	235	55	127	4	0	5	3	84	13	0	.155
1937	14	12	.538	3.30	34	34	14	242.2	250	76	143	4	0	0	0	85	14	0	.165
1938	11	7	.611	3.70	29	26	10	172.2	190	46	80	1	0	0	0	64	13	0	.203
1939	2	3	.400	4.29	10	6	1	42	45	10	11	0	0	0	0	14	4	0	.286
1940 PHI N	4	3	.571	4.32	13	10	5	77	82	21	24	0	0	0	0	24	2	0	.083
1941	6	13	.316	4.51	28	25	7	163.2	186	57	64	1	0	0	0	51	6	0	.118
1942	0	4	.000	5.64	6	3	0	22.1	30	13	15	0	0	1	0	8	1	0	.125
9 yrs.	68	71	.489	3.55	202	168	75	1218.1	1243	337	611	14	1	8	4	428	66	0	.154

Wade Blasingame

BLASINGAME, WADE ALLEN
B. Nov. 22, 1943, Deming, N. M.

BL TL 6'1" 185 lbs.

	W	L	PCT	ERA	G	GS	CG	IP	H	BB	SO	ShO	W	L	SV	AB	H	HR	BA
1963 MIL N	0	0	–	12.00	2	0	0	3	7	2	6	0	0	0	0	0	0	0	–
1964	9	5	.643	4.24	28	13	3	116.2	113	51	70	1	1	1	2	40	7	1	.175
1965	16	10	.615	3.77	38	36	10	224.2	200	116	117	1	1	0	1	81	15	1	.185
1966 ATL N	3	7	.300	5.32	16	12	0	67.2	71	25	34	0	0	0	0	23	5	0	.217

	W	L	PCT	ERA	G	GS	CG	IP	H	BB	SO	ShO	Relief Pitching W	L	SV	AB	BATTING H	HR	BA

Wade Blasingame continued

	W	L	PCT	ERA	G	GS	CG	IP	H	BB	SO	ShO	W	L	SV	AB	H	HR	BA
1967 2 teams			ATL	N (10G 1–0)		HOU	N (15G 4–7)												
" total	5	7	.417	5.63	25	18	0	102.1	118	48	66	0	1	0	0	29	5	0	.172
1968 HOU N	1	2	.333	4.75	22	2	0	36	45	10	22	0	1	2	1	5	0	0	.000
1969	0	5	.000	5.37	26	5	0	52	66	33	33	0	0	0	1	12	0	0	.000
1970	3	3	.500	3.46	13	13	1	78	76	23	55	0	0	0	0	24	2	0	.083
1971	9	11	.450	4.61	30	28	2	158	177	45	93	0	0	0	0	49	10	1	.204
1972 2 teams			HOU	N (10G 0–0)		NY	A (12G 0–1)												
" total	0	1	.000	5.76	22	1	0	25	18	19	16	0	0	0	0	2	0	0	.000
10 yrs.	46	51	.474	4.52	222	128	16	863.1	891	372	512	2	4	3	5	265	44	3	.166

Steve Blass

BLASS, STEPHEN ROBERT   BR TR 6'   165 lbs.
B. Apr. 18, 1942, Cannan, Conn.

	W	L	PCT	ERA	G	GS	CG	IP	H	BB	SO	ShO	W	L	SV	AB	H	HR	BA
1964 PIT N	5	8	.385	4.04	24	13	3	104.2	107	45	67	1	1	1	0	30	2	0	.067
1966	11	7	.611	3.87	34	25	1	155.2	173	46	76	0	2	1	0	52	12	0	.231
1967	6	8	.429	3.55	32	16	2	126.2	126	47	72	0	1	1	0	39	5	0	.128
1968	18	6	.750	2.12	33	31	12	220.1	191	57	132	7	0	0	0	80	11	0	.138
1969	16	10	.615	4.46	38	32	9	210	207	86	147	0	0	0	2	84	21	1	.250
1970	10	12	.455	3.52	31	31	6	197	187	73	120	1	0	0	0	70	8	0	.114
1971	15	8	.652	2.85	33	33	12	240	226	68	136	5	0	0	0	83	10	0	.120
1972	19	8	.704	2.49	33	32	11	249.2	227	84	117	2	0	0	0	82	15	0	.183
1973	3	9	.250	9.85	23	18	1	88.2	109	84	27	0	0	0	0	24	10	0	.417
1974	0	0	–	9.00	1	0	0	5	5	7	2	0	0	0	0	2	0	0	.000
10 yrs.	103	76	.575	3.63	282	231	57	1597.2	1558	597	896	16	4	3	2	546	94	1	.172

LEAGUE CHAMPIONSHIP SERIES

	W	L	PCT	ERA	G	GS	CG	IP	H	BB	SO	ShO	W	L	SV	AB	H	HR	BA
1971 PIT N	0	1	.000	11.57	2	2	0	7	14	2	11	0	0	0	0	1	0	0	.000
1972	1	0	1.000	1.72	2	2	0	15.2	12	6	5	0	0	0	0	6	0	0	.000
2 yrs.	1	1	.500	4.76	4	4	0	22.2	26	8	16	0	0	0	0	7	0	0	.000

WORLD SERIES

	W	L	PCT	ERA	G	GS	CG	IP	H	BB	SO	ShO	W	L	SV	AB	H	HR	BA
1971 PIT N	2	0	1.000	1.00	2	2	2	18	7	4	13	0	0	0	0	7	0	0	.000

Steve Blateric

BLATERIC, STEPHEN LAWRENCE   BR TR 6'3"   200 lbs.
B. Mar. 20, 1944, Denver, Colo.

	W	L	PCT	ERA	G	GS	CG	IP	H	BB	SO	ShO	W	L	SV	AB	H	HR	BA
1971 CIN N	0	0	–	12.00	2	0	0	3	5	0	4	0	0	0	0	0	0	0	–
1972 NY A	0	0	–	0.00	1	0	0	4	2	0	4	0	0	0	0	1	0	0	.000
1975 CAL A	0	0	–	6.23	2	0	0	4.1	9	1	5	0	0	0	0	0	0	0	–
3 yrs.	0	0	–	5.56	5	0	0	11.1	16	1	13	0	0	0	0	1	0	0	.000

Henry Blauvelt

BLAUVELT, HENRY RUSSELL
B. Apr. 8, 1873, Nyack, N.Y.   D. Dec. 28, 1926, Portland, Ore.

	W	L	PCT	ERA	G	GS	CG	IP	H	BB	SO	ShO	W	L	SV	AB	H	HR	BA
1890 ROC AA	0	0	–	10.22	2	0	0	12.1	19	8	5	0	0	0	0	6	3	0	.500

Bob Blaylock

BLAYLOCK, ROBERT EDWARD   BR TR 6'1"   185 lbs.
B. June 28, 1935, Chattanooga, Okla.

	W	L	PCT	ERA	G	GS	CG	IP	H	BB	SO	ShO	W	L	SV	AB	H	HR	BA
1956 STL N	1	6	.143	6.37	14	6	0	41	45	24	39	0	1	1	0	11	1	0	.091
1959	0	1	.000	4.00	3	1	0	9	8	3	3	0	0	1	0	1	0	0	.000
2 yrs.	1	7	.125	5.94	17	7	0	50	53	27	42	0	1	2	0	12	1	0	.083

Gary Blaylock

BLAYLOCK, GARY NELSON   BR TR 6'   196 lbs.
B. Oct. 11, 1931, Clarkton, Mo.

	W	L	PCT	ERA	G	GS	CG	IP	H	BB	SO	ShO	W	L	SV	AB	H	HR	BA
1959 2 teams			STL	N (26G 4–5)		NY	A (15G 0–0)												
" total	4	6	.400	4.80	41	13	3	125.2	147	58	81	0	1	1	0	36	5	2	.139

Ray Blemker

BLEMKER, RAYMOND (Buddy)   BR TL 5'11"   190 lbs.
B. Aug. 9, 1937, Huntingburg, Ind.

	W	L	PCT	ERA	G	GS	CG	IP	H	BB	SO	ShO	W	L	SV	AB	H	HR	BA
1960 KC A	0	0	–	27.00	1	0	0	1.2	3	2	0	0	0	0	0	0	0	0	–

Clarence Blethen

BLETHEN, CLARENCE WALDO (Climax)   BL TR 5'11"   165 lbs.
B. July 11, 1893, Dover-Foxcroft, Me.   D. Apr. 11, 1973, Frederick, Md.

	W	L	PCT	ERA	G	GS	CG	IP	H	BB	SO	ShO	W	L	SV	AB	H	HR	BA
1923 BOS A	0	0	–	7.13	5	0	0	17.2	29	7	2	0	0	0	0	6	0	0	.000
1929 BKN N	0	0	–	9.00	2	0	0	2	4	3	0	0	0	0	0	0	0	0	–
2 yrs.	0	0	–	7.32	7	0	0	19.2	33	10	2	0	0	0	0	6	0	0	.000

Bob Blewett

BLEWETT, ROBERT LAWRENCE   BL TL 5'11"   170 lbs.
B. June 28, 1877, Fond du Lac, Wis.   D. Mar. 17, 1958, Sedro Wooley, Wash.

	W	L	PCT	ERA	G	GS	CG	IP	H	BB	SO	ShO	W	L	SV	AB	H	HR	BA
1902 NY N	0	2	.000	4.82	5	3	2	28	39	7	8	0	0	0	0	10	0	0	.000

Elmer Bliss

BLISS, ELMER WARD   BL TR 6'   180 lbs.
B. Mar. 9, 1875, Penfield, Pa.   D. Mar. 18, 1962, Bradford, Pa.

	W	L	PCT	ERA	G	GS	CG	IP	H	BB	SO	ShO	W	L	SV	AB	H	HR	BA
1903 NY A	1	0	1.000	0.00	1	0	0	5	4	0	2	0	1	0	0	3	0	0	.000

Joe Blong

BLONG, JOSEPH MYLES   BR TR
B. Sept. 17, 1853, St. Louis, Mo.   D. Sept. 22, 1892, St. Louis, Mo.

	W	L	PCT	ERA	G	GS	CG	IP	H	BB	SO	ShO	W	L	SV	AB	H	HR	BA
1876 STL N	0	0	–	0.00	1	0	0	4	2	1	0	0	0	0	0	264	62	0	.235
1877	10	9	.526	2.74	25	21	17	187.1	203	38	51	0	0	0	0	218	47	0	.216
2 yrs.	10	9	.526	2.68	26	21	17	191.1	205	39	51	0	0	0	0	*			

Vida Blue

BLUE, VIDA ROCHELLE   BB TL 6'   189 lbs.
B. July 28, 1949, Mansfield, La.

	W	L	PCT	ERA	G	GS	CG	IP	H	BB	SO	ShO	W	L	SV	AB	H	HR	BA
1969 OAK A	1	1	.500	6.21	12	4	0	42	49	18	24	0	0	0	0	10	0	0	.000
1970	2	0	1.000	2.09	6	6	2	39	20	12	35	2	0	0	0	15	3	1	.200
1971	24	8	.750	1.82	39	39	24	312	209	88	301	8	0	0	0	102	12	0	.118
1972	6	10	.375	2.80	25	23	5	151.1	117	48	111	4	0	1	0	45	2	0	.044
1973	20	9	.690	3.28	37	37	13	263.2	214	105	158	4	0	0	0	1	0	0	.000
1974	17	15	.531	3.26	40	40	12	282	246	98	174	1	0	0	0	0	0	0	–

	W	L	PCT	ERA	G	GS	CG	IP	H	BB	SO	ShO	Relief Pitching W	L	SV	BATTING AB	H	HR	BA

Vida Blue   continued

	W	L	PCT	ERA	G	GS	CG	IP	H	BB	SO	ShO	W	L	SV	AB	H	HR	BA
1975	22	11	.667	3.01	39	38	13	278	243	99	189	2	0	0	1	0	0	0	–
1976	18	13	.581	2.36	37	37	20	298	268	63	166	6	0	0	0	0	0	0	–
1977	14	19	.424	3.83	38	38	16	280	284	86	157	1	0	0	0	1	0	0	.000
1978 SF N	18	10	.643	2.79	35	35	9	258	233	70	171	4	0	0	0	79	6	1	.076
1979	14	14	.500	5.01	34	34	10	237	246	111	138	0	0	0	0	83	10	1	.120
1980	14	10	.583	2.97	31	31	10	224	202	61	129	3	0	0	0	68	5	0	.074
1981	8	6	.571	2.45	18	18	1	125	97	54	63	0	0	0	0	35	7	0	.200
1982 KC A	13	12	.520	3.78	31	31	6	181	163	80	103	2	0	0	0	0	0	0	–
1983	0	5	.000	6.01	19	14	1	85.1	96	35	53	0	0	0	0	0	0	0	–
15 yrs.	191	143	.572	3.21	441	425	142	3056.1	2687	1028	1972	37	0	1	2	439	45	3	.103

LEAGUE CHAMPIONSHIP SERIES

	W	L	PCT	ERA	G	GS	CG	IP	H	BB	SO	ShO	W	L	SV	AB	H	HR	BA
1971 OAK A	0	1	.000	6.43	1	1	0	7	7	2	8	0	0	0	0	3	0	0	.000
1972	0	0	–	0.00	4	0	0	5.1	4	1	5	0	0	0	1	1	0	0	.000
1973	0	1	.000	10.29	2	2	0	7	8	5	3	0	0	0	0	0	0	0	–
1974	1	0	1.000	0.00	1	1	1	9	2	0	7	1	0	0	0	0	0	0	–
1975	0	0	–	9.00	1	1	0	3	6	0	2	0	0	0	0	0	0	0	–
5 yrs.	1	2	.333	4.60	9	5	1	31.1	27	8	25	1	0	0	1	4	0	0	.000

WORLD SERIES

	W	L	PCT	ERA	G	GS	CG	IP	H	BB	SO	ShO	W	L	SV	AB	H	HR	BA
1972 OAK A	0	1	.000	4.15	4	1	0	8.2	8	5	5	0	0	0	1	1	0	0	.000
1973	0	1	.000	4.91	2	2	0	11	10	3	8	0	0	0	0	4	0	0	.000
1974	0	1	.000	3.29	2	2	0	13.2	10	7	9	0	0	0	0	4	0	0	.000
3 yrs.	0	3	.000	4.05	8	5	0	33.1	28	15	22	0	0	0	1	9	0	0	.000

Jim Bluejacket

BLUEJACKET, JAMES   BR TR 6'2½" 200 lbs.
Born James Smith.
B. July 8, 1887, Adair, Okla.   D. Mar. 26, 1947, Pekin, Ill.

	W	L	PCT	ERA	G	GS	CG	IP	H	BB	SO	ShO	W	L	SV	AB	H	HR	BA
1914 BKN F	4	5	.444	3.76	17	7	3	67	77	19	29	1	1	1	1	22	3	0	.136
1915	9	11	.450	3.15	24	21	10	162.2	155	75	48	2	1	0	0	61	8	0	.131
1916 CIN N	0	1	.000	7.71	3	2	0	7	12	3	1	0	0	0	0	2	0	0	.000
3 yrs.	13	17	.433	3.46	44	30	13	236.2	244	97	78	3	2	1	1	85	11	0	.129

Clint Blume

BLUME, CLINTON WILLIS   BR TR 5'11" 175 lbs.
B. Oct. 17, 1900, Brooklyn, N. Y.   D. June 12, 1973, Islip, N. Y.

	W	L	PCT	ERA	G	GS	CG	IP	H	BB	SO	ShO	W	L	SV	AB	H	HR	BA
1922 NY N	1	0	1.000	1.00	1	1	0	9	7	1	2	0	0	0	0	1	1	0	1.000
1923	2	0	1.000	3.75	12	1	0	24	22	20	2	0	2	0	0	5	0	0	.000
2 yrs.	3	0	1.000	3.00	13	2	1	33	29	21	4	0	2	0	0	6	1	0	.167

Bert Blyleven

BLYLEVEN, RIK AALBERT   BR TR 6'3" 200 lbs.
B. Apr. 6, 1951, Zeist, Holland

	W	L	PCT	ERA	G	GS	CG	IP	H	BB	SO	ShO	W	L	SV	AB	H	HR	BA
1970 MIN A	10	9	.526	3.18	27	25	5	164	143	47	135	1	0	0	0	50	7	0	.140
1971	16	15	.516	2.82	38	38	17	278	267	59	224	5	0	0	0	91	12	0	.132
1972	17	17	.500	2.73	39	38	11	287	247	69	228	3	0	1	0	94	15	0	.160
1973	20	17	.541	2.52	40	40	25	325	296	67	258	9	0	0	0	0	0	0	–
1974	17	17	.500	2.66	37	37	19	281	244	77	249	3	0	0	0	0	0	0	–
1975	15	10	.600	3.00	35	35	20	275.2	219	84	233	3	0	0	0	0	0	0	–
1976 2 teams		MIN	A	(12G 4–5)		TEX	A	(24G 9–11)											
" total	13	16	.448	2.87	36	36	18	297.2	283	81	219	6	0	0	0	0	0	0	–
1977 TEX A	14	12	.538	2.72	30	30	15	235	181	69	182	5	0	0	0	0	0	0	–
1978 PIT N	14	10	.583	3.02	34	34	11	244	217	66	182	4	0	0	0	85	11	0	.129
1979	12	5	.706	3.61	37	37	4	237	238	92	172	0	0	0	0	70	9	0	.129
1980	8	13	.381	3.82	34	32	5	217	219	59	168	2	0	0	0	61	5	0	.082
1981 CLE A	11	7	.611	2.89	20	20	9	159	145	40	107	1	0	0	0	0	0	0	–
1982	2	2	.500	4.87	4	4	0	20.1	16	11	19	0	0	0	0	0	0	0	–
1983	7	10	.412	3.91	24	24	5	156.1	160	44	123	0	0	0	0	0	0	0	–
1984	19	7	.731	2.87	33	32	12	245	204	74	170	4	0	0	0	0	0	0	–
15 yrs.	195	167	.539	3.00	468	462	176	3422	3079	939	2669	46	0	2	0	451	59	0	.131

LEAGUE CHAMPIONSHIP SERIES

	W	L	PCT	ERA	G	GS	CG	IP	H	BB	SO	ShO	W	L	SV	AB	H	HR	BA
1970 MIN A	0	0	–	0.00	1	0	0	2	2	0	2	0	0	0	0	0	0	0	–
1979 PIT N	1	0	1.000	1.00	1	1	1	9	8	0	9	0	0	0	0	3	1	0	.333
2 yrs.	1	0	1.000	0.82	2	1	1	11	10	0	11	0	0	0	0	3	1	0	.333

WORLD SERIES

	W	L	PCT	ERA	G	GS	CG	IP	H	BB	SO	ShO	W	L	SV	AB	H	HR	BA
1979 PIT N	1	0	1.000	1.80	2	1	0	10	8	3	4	0	0	0	0	3	0	0	.000

Mike Blyzka

BLYZKA, MICHAEL JOHN   BR TR 5'11½" 190 lbs.
B. Dec. 25, 1928, Hamtramck, Mich.

	W	L	PCT	ERA	G	GS	CG	IP	H	BB	SO	ShO	W	L	SV	AB	H	HR	BA
1953 STL A	2	6	.250	6.39	33	9	2	94.1	110	56	23	0	1	1	0	23	0	0	.000
1954 BAL A	1	5	.167	4.69	37	0	0	86.1	83	51	35	0	1	5	1	15	2	0	.133
2 yrs.	3	11	.214	5.58	70	9	2	180.2	193	107	58	0	2	6	1	38	2	0	.053

Charlie Boardman

BOARDMAN, CHARLES LOUIS   BL TL 6'2½" 194 lbs.
B. Mar. 27, 1893, Seneca Falls, N. Y.   D. Aug. 10, 1968, Sacramento, Calif.

	W	L	PCT	ERA	G	GS	CG	IP	H	BB	SO	ShO	W	L	SV	AB	H	HR	BA
1913 PHI A	0	2	.000	2.00	2	2	1	9	10	6	4	0	0	0	0	3	0	0	.000
1914	0	0	–	4.91	2	0	0	7.1	10	4	2	0	0	0	0	2	0	0	.000
1915 STL N	1	0	1.000	1.42	3	1	1	19	12	15	7	0	0	0	0	7	2	0	.286
3 yrs.	1	2	.333	2.29	7	3	2	35.1	32	25	13	0	0	0	0	12	2	0	.167

Mike Boddicker

BODDICKER, MICHAEL JAMES   BR TR 5'11" 172 lbs.
B. Aug. 23, 1957, Cedar Rapids, Iowa

	W	L	PCT	ERA	G	GS	CG	IP	H	BB	SO	ShO	W	L	SV	AB	H	HR	BA
1980 BAL A	0	1	.000	6.43	1	1	0	7	6	5	4	0	0	0	0	0	0	0	–
1981	0	0	–	4.50	2	0	0	6	6	2	2	0	0	0	0	0	0	0	–
1982	1	0	1.000	3.51	7	0	0	25.2	25	12	20	0	1	0	0	0	0	0	–
1983	16	8	.667	2.77	27	26	10	179	141	52	120	5	0	0	0	0	0	0	–
1984	20	11	.645	2.79	34	34	16	261.1	218	81	128	4	0	0	0	0	0	0	–
5 yrs.	37	20	.649	2.89	71	61	26	479	396	152	274	9	1	0	0	0	0	0	–

	W	L	PCT	ERA	G	GS	CG	IP	H	BB	SO	ShO	Relief Pitching W	L	SV	BATTING AB	H	HR	BA

Mike Boddicker continued

LEAGUE CHAMPIONSHIP SERIES

	W	L	PCT	ERA	G	GS	CG	IP	H	BB	SO	ShO	W	L	SV	AB	H	HR	BA
1983 BAL A	1	0	1.000	0.00	1	1	1	9	5	3	14	1	0	0	0	0	0	0	–

WORLD SERIES

	W	L	PCT	ERA	G	GS	CG	IP	H	BB	SO	ShO	W	L	SV	AB	H	HR	BA
1983 BAL A	1	0	1.000	0.00	1	1	1	9	3	0	6	0	0	0	0	3	0	0	.000

George Boehler

BOEHLER, GEORGE HENRY
B. Jan. 2, 1892, Lawrenceburg, Ind.   D. June 23, 1958, Lawrenceburg, Ind.
BR TR 6'2" 180 lbs.

	W	L	PCT	ERA	G	GS	CG	IP	H	BB	SO	ShO	W	L	SV	AB	H	HR	BA
1912 DET A	0	2	.000	6.68	4	4	2	31	49	14	13	0	0	0	0	10	1	0	.100
1913	0	1	.000	6.75	1	1	1	8	11	6	2	0	0	0	0	3	1	0	.333
1914	2	3	.400	3.57	18	6	2	63	54	48	37	0	0	1	0	17	3	0	.176
1915	1	1	.500	1.80	8	0	0	15	19	4	7	0	1	1	0	4	3	0	.750
1916	1	1	.500	4.73	5	2	1	13.1	12	9	8	0	0	0	0	3	0	0	.000
1920 STL N	1	0	1.000	7.71	3	1	0	7	10	4	2	0	0	0	0	1	0	0	.000
1921	0	0	–	0.00	1	0	0	1	1	0	0	0	0	0	0	0	0	0	–
1923 PIT N	1	3	.250	6.04	10	3	1	28.1	33	26	12	0	0	1	0	10	3	0	.300
1926 BKN N	1	0	1.000	4.41	10	1	0	34.2	42	23	10	0	0	0	0	12	3	0	.250
9 yrs.	6	12	.333	4.74	60	18	7	201.1	231	134	91	0	1	3	0	60	14	0	.233

Joe Boehling

BOEHLING, JOHN JOSEPH
B. Mar. 20, 1891, Richmond, Va.   D. Sept. 8, 1941, Richmond, Va.
BL TL 5'11" 168 lbs.

	W	L	PCT	ERA	G	GS	CG	IP	H	BB	SO	ShO	W	L	SV	AB	H	HR	BA
1912 WAS A	0	0	–	7.20	3	0	0	5	4	6	2	0	0	0	0	0	0	0	–
1913	17	7	.708	2.14	38	25	18	235.1	197	82	110	3	2	0	4	86	19	0	.221
1914	12	8	.600	3.03	27	24	14	196	180	76	91	2	0	1	1	71	17	0	.239
1915	14	13	.519	3.22	40	32	14	229.1	217	119	108	2	0	3	0	75	13	1	.173
1916 2 teams			WAS	A	(27G 9–11)			CLE	A	(12G 2–4)									
" total	11	15	.423	2.97	39	28	10	200.1	197	77	70	2	2	2	0	60	12	0	.200
1917 CLE A	1	6	.143	4.66	12	7	1	46.1	50	16	11	0	0	1	0	16	3	0	.188
1920	0	1	.000	4.85	3	2	0	13	16	10	4	0	0	0	0	3	2	0	.667
7 yrs.	55	50	.524	2.97	162	118	57	925.1	861	386	396	9	4	7	5	311	66	1	.212

Larry Boerner

BOERNER, LAWRENCE HYER
B. Jan. 21, 1905, Staunton, Va.   D. Oct. 16, 1969, Staunton, Va.
BR TR 6'4½" 175 lbs.

	W	L	PCT	ERA	G	GS	CG	IP	H	BB	SO	ShO	W	L	SV	AB	H	HR	BA
1932 BOS A	0	4	.000	5.02	21	5	0	61	71	37	19	0	0	0	0	17	0	0	.000

John Bogart

BOGART, JOHN RENZIE (Big John)
B. Sept. 21, 1900, Bloomsburg, Pa.
BR TR 6'2" 195 lbs.

	W	L	PCT	ERA	G	GS	CG	IP	H	BB	SO	ShO	W	L	SV	AB	H	HR	BA
1920 DET A	2	1	.667	3.04	4	3	0	23.2	16	18	5	0	1	0	0	8	2	0	.250

Ray Boggs

BOGGS, RAYMOND JOSEPH (Lefty)
B. Dec. 12, 1904, Reamsville, Kans.
BL TL 6'½" 170 lbs.

	W	L	PCT	ERA	G	GS	CG	IP	H	BB	SO	ShO	W	L	SV	AB	H	HR	BA
1928 BOS N	0	0	–	5.40	4	0	0	5	2	7	0	0	0	0	0	0	0	0	–

Tommy Boggs

BOGGS, THOMAS WINTON
B. Oct. 25, 1955, Poughkeepsie, N. Y.
BR TR 6'2" 195 lbs.

	W	L	PCT	ERA	G	GS	CG	IP	H	BB	SO	ShO	W	L	SV	AB	H	HR	BA
1976 TEX A	1	7	.125	3.50	13	13	3	90	87	34	36	0	0	0	0	0	0	0	–
1977	0	3	.000	6.00	6	6	0	27	40	12	15	0	0	0	0	0	0	0	–
1978 ATL N	2	8	.200	6.71	16	12	1	59	80	26	21	1	0	0	0	18	3	1	.167
1979	0	2	.000	6.23	3	2	0	13	21	4	1	0	0	0	0	4	1	0	.250
1980	12	9	.571	3.42	32	26	4	192	180	46	84	3	0	0	0	63	10	0	.159
1981	3	13	.188	4.09	25	24	2	143	140	54	81	0	0	1	0	46	7	0	.152
1982	2	2	.500	3.30	10	10	0	46.1	43	22	29	0	0	0	0	17	4	0	.235
1983	0	0	–	5.68	5	0	0	6.1	8	1	5	0	0	0	0	0	0	0	–
8 yrs.	20	44	.313	4.14	110	94	10	576.2	599	199	272	4	0	1	0	148	25	1	.169

Warren Bogle

BOGLE, WARREN FREDERICK
B. Oct. 19, 1946, Passaic, N. J.
BL TL 6'4" 220 lbs.

	W	L	PCT	ERA	G	GS	CG	IP	H	BB	SO	ShO	W	L	SV	AB	H	HR	BA
1968 OAK A	0	0	–	4.30	16	1	0	23	26	8	26	0	0	0	0	5	0	0	.000

Pat Bohen

BOHEN, LEO IGNATIUS
B. Oct. 20, 1891, Oakland, Iowa   D. Apr. 8, 1942, Napa, Calif.
BR TR 5'10" 160 lbs.

	W	L	PCT	ERA	G	GS	CG	IP	H	BB	SO	ShO	W	L	SV	AB	H	HR	BA
1913 PHI A	0	1	.000	1.13	1	1	1	8	3	2	5	0	0	0	0	3	0	0	.000
1914 PIT N	0	0	–	18.00	1	0	0	1	2	2	0	0	0	0	0	1	0	0	.000
2 yrs.	0	1	.000	3.00	2	1	1	9	5	4	5	0	0	0	0	4	0	0	.000

Charlie Bohn

BOHN, CHARLES
B. 1857, Cleveland, Ohio   D. Aug. 1, 1903, Cleveland, Ohio

	W	L	PCT	ERA	G	GS	CG	IP	H	BB	SO	ShO	W	L	SV	AB	H	HR	BA
1882 LOU AA	1	1	.500	3.00	2	2	1	18	21	3	1	0	0	0	0	13	2	0	.154

John Bohnet

BOHNET, JOHN KELLY
B. Jan. 18, 1961, Pasadena, Calif.
BB TL 6' 180 lbs.

	W	L	PCT	ERA	G	GS	CG	IP	H	BB	SO	ShO	W	L	SV	AB	H	HR	BA
1982 CLE A	0	0	–	6.94	3	3	0	11.2	11	7	4	0	0	0	0	0	0	0	–

Danny Boitano

BOITANO, DANNY JON
B. Mar. 22, 1953, Sacramento, Calif.
BR TR 6' 185 lbs.

	W	L	PCT	ERA	G	GS	CG	IP	H	BB	SO	ShO	W	L	SV	AB	H	HR	BA
1978 PHI N	0	0	–	0.00	1	0	0	5	0	1	0	0	0	0	0	0	0	0	–
1979 MIL A	0	0	–	1.50	5	0	0	6	6	3	5	0	0	0	0	0	0	0	–
1980	0	1	.000	8.00	11	0	0	18	26	6	11	0	0	1	0	0	0	0	–
1981 NY N	2	1	.667	5.63	15	0	0	16	21	5	8	0	2	1	0	0	0	0	–
1982 TEX A	0	0	–	5.34	19	0	0	30.1	33	13	28	0	0	0	0	0	0	0	–
5 yrs.	2	2	.500	5.68	51	0	0	71.1	86	28	52	0	2	0	0	0	0	0	–

	W	L	PCT	ERA	G	GS	CG	IP	H	BB	SO	ShO	Relief Pitching W	L	SV	BATTING AB	H	HR	BA

Dick Bokelmann

BOKELMANN, RICHARD WERNER
B. Oct. 26, 1926, Arlington Heights, Ill.   BR TR 6'½" 180 lbs.

	W	L	PCT	ERA	G	GS	CG	IP	H	BB	SO	ShO	W	L	SV	AB	H	HR	BA
1951 STL N	3	3	.500	3.78	20	1	0	52.1	49	31	22	0	3	2	3	14	0	0	.000
1952	0	1	.000	9.24	11	0	0	12.2	20	7	5	0	0	1	0	0	0	0	–
1953	0	0	–	6.00	3	0	0	3	4	0	0	0	0	0	0	0	0	0	–
3 yrs.	3	4	.429	4.90	34	1	0	68	73	38	27	0	3	3	3	14	0	0	.000

Joe Bokina

BOKINA, JOSEPH
B. Apr. 4, 1910, Northampton, Mass.   BR TR 6' 184 lbs.

	W	L	PCT	ERA	G	GS	CG	IP	H	BB	SO	ShO	W	L	SV	AB	H	HR	BA
1936 WAS A	0	2	.000	8.64	5	1	0	8.1	15	6	5	0	0	1	0	1	0	0	.000

Bernie Boland

BOLAND, BERNARD ANTHONY
B. Jan. 21, 1892, Rochester, N. Y.   D. Sept. 12, 1973, Detroit, Mich.   BR TR 5'8½" 168 lbs.

	W	L	PCT	ERA	G	GS	CG	IP	H	BB	SO	ShO	W	L	SV	AB	H	HR	BA
1915 DET A	13	7	.650	3.11	45	18	8	202.2	167	75	72	1	4	2	2	63	11	0	.175
1916	10	3	.769	3.94	46	9	5	130.1	111	73	59	1	5	0	3	32	8	0	.250
1917	16	11	.593	2.68	43	28	13	238	192	95	89	3	2	2	6	72	4	0	.056
1918	14	10	.583	2.65	29	25	14	204	176	67	63	4	1	1	0	69	12	0	.174
1919	14	16	.467	3.04	35	30	18	242.2	222	80	71	1	1	1	1	74	8	0	.108
1920	0	2	.000	7.79	4	3	1	17.1	23	14	4	0	0	0	0	7	1	0	.143
1921 STL A	1	4	.200	8.89	8	6	0	28.1	34	28	6	0	0	0	0	10	1	0	.100
7 yrs.	68	53	.562	3.24	210	119	59	1063.1	925	432	364	10	13	6	12	327	45	0	.138

Bill Bolden

BOLDEN, WILLIAM HORACE (Big Bill)
B. May 9, 1893, Dandridge, Tenn.   D. Dec. 8, 1966, Jefferson City, Tenn.   BR TR 6'4" 200 lbs.

	W	L	PCT	ERA	G	GS	CG	IP	H	BB	SO	ShO	W	L	SV	AB	H	HR	BA
1919 STL N	0	1	.000	5.25	3	1	0	12	17	4	4	0	0	0	0	3	1	0	.333

Stew Bolen

BOLEN, STEWART O'NEILL
B. Oct. 12, 1902, Jackson, Ala.   D. Aug. 30, 1969, Mobile, Ala.   BL TL 5'11" 180 lbs.

	W	L	PCT	ERA	G	GS	CG	IP	H	BB	SO	ShO	W	L	SV	AB	H	HR	BA
1926 STL A	0	0	–	6.14	5	0	0	14.2	21	6	7	0	0	0	0	4	2	0	.500
1927	0	1	.000	8.38	3	1	1	9.2	14	5	7	0	0	0	0	3	1	0	.333
1931 PHI N	3	12	.200	6.39	28	16	2	98.2	117	63	55	0	1	2	0	32	5	0	.156
1932	0	0	–	2.81	5	0	0	16	18	10	3	0	0	0	0	7	1	0	.143
4 yrs.	3	13	.188	6.09	41	17	3	139	170	84	72	0	1	2	0	46	9	0	.196

Bobby Bolin

BOLIN, BOBBY DONALD
B. Jan. 29, 1939, Smyrna, S. C.   BR TR 6'4" 185 lbs.

	W	L	PCT	ERA	G	GS	CG	IP	H	BB	SO	ShO	W	L	SV	AB	H	HR	BA
1961 SF N	2	2	.500	3.19	37	1	0	48	37	37	48	0	2	2	5	7	2	0	.286
1962	7	3	.700	3.62	41	5	2	92	84	35	74	0	3	2	5	23	6	0	.261
1963	10	6	.625	3.28	47	12	2	137.1	128	57	134	0	7	2	7	35	5	1	.143
1964	6	9	.400	3.25	38	23	5	174.2	143	77	146	3	1	0	1	50	5	0	.100
1965	14	6	.700	2.76	45	13	2	163	125	56	135	0	8	1	2	54	9	1	.167
1966	11	10	.524	2.89	36	34	10	224.1	174	70	143	4	0	0	1	76	13	2	.171
1967	6	8	.429	4.88	37	15	0	120	120	50	69	0	4	0	0	33	8	0	.242
1968	10	5	.667	1.99	34	19	6	176.2	128	46	126	3	2	0	0	55	5	0	.091
1969	7	7	.500	4.44	30	22	2	146	149	49	102	0	0	0	0	39	6	1	.154
1970 2 teams					MIL A (32G 5–11)			BOS A (6G 2–0)											
" total	7	11	.389	4.63	38	20	3	140	133	72	89	0	3	2	3	37	7	1	.189
1971 BOS A	5	3	.625	4.24	52	0	0	70	74	24	51	0	5	3	6	12	3	0	.250
1972	0	1	.000	2.90	21	0	0	31	24	11	27	0	0	1	5	2	0	0	.000
1973	3	4	.429	2.72	39	0	0	53	45	13	31	0	3	4	15	0	0	0	–
13 yrs.	88	75	.540	3.40	495	164	32	1576	1364	597	1175	10	38	17	50	423	69	6	.163
WORLD SERIES																			
1962 SF N	0	0	–	6.75	2	0	0	2.2	4	2	2	0	0	0	0	0	0	0	–

Greg Bollo

BOLLO, GREGORY GENE
B. Nov. 16, 1943, Detroit, Mich.   BR TR 6'4" 183 lbs.

	W	L	PCT	ERA	G	GS	CG	IP	H	BB	SO	ShO	W	L	SV	AB	H	HR	BA
1965 CHI A	0	0	–	3.57	15	0	0	22.2	12	9	16	0	0	0	0	0	0	0	–
1966	0	1	.000	2.57	3	1	0	7	7	3	4	0	0	0	0	1	0	0	.000
2 yrs.	0	1	.000	3.34	18	1	0	29.2	19	12	20	0	0	0	0	1	0	0	.000

Mark Bomback

BOMBACK, MARK VICTOR
B. Apr. 14, 1953, Portsmouth, Va.   BR TR 5'11" 170 lbs.

	W	L	PCT	ERA	G	GS	CG	IP	H	BB	SO	ShO	W	L	SV	AB	H	HR	BA
1978 MIL A	0	0	–	16.20	2	1	0	1.2	5	1	1	0	0	0	0	0	0	0	–
1980 NY N	10	8	.556	4.09	36	25	2	163	191	49	68	1	2	0	0	43	10	0	.233
1981 TOR A	5	5	.500	3.90	20	11	0	90	84	35	33	0	0	0	0	0	0	0	–
1982	1	5	.167	6.03	16	8	0	59.2	87	25	22	0	0	0	0	0	0	0	–
4 yrs.	16	18	.471	4.47	74	45	2	314.1	367	110	124	1	2	0	0	43	10	0	.233

Tommy Bond

BOND, THOMAS HENRY
B. Apr. 2, 1856, Granard, Ireland   D. Jan. 24, 1941, Boston, Mass.
Manager 1882.   BR TR 5'7½" 160 lbs.

	W	L	PCT	ERA	G	GS	CG	IP	H	BB	SO	ShO	W	L	SV	AB	H	HR	BA
1876 HAR N	31	13	.705	1.68	45	45	45	408	355	13	88	6	0	0	0	182	50	0	.275
1877 BOS N	40	17	.702	2.11	58	58	58	521	530	36	170	6	0	0	0	259	59	0	.228
1878	40	19	.678	2.06	59	59	57	532.2	571	33	182	9	0	0	0	236	50	0	.212
1879	43	19	.694	1.96	64	64	59	555.1	543	24	155	12	0	0	0	257	62	0	.241
1880	26	29	.473	2.67	63	57	49	493	559	45	118	3	0	2	0	282	62	0	.220
1881	0	3	.000	4.26	3	3	2	25.1	40	2	2	0	0	0	0	10	2	0	.200
1882 WOR N	0	1	.000	4.38	2	2	0	12.1	12	7	2	0	0	0	0	30	4	0	.133
1884 2 teams					BOS U (23G 13–9)			IND AA (5G 0–5)											
" total	13	14	.481	3.49	28	26	24	232	247	18	143	0	1	0	0	185	51	0	.276
8 yrs.	193	115	.627	2.25	322	314	294	2779.2	2857	178	860	36	1	2	0	*			
				9th															

	W	L	PCT	ERA	G	GS	CG	IP	H	BB	SO	ShO	Relief Pitching W	L	SV	BATTING AB	H	HR	BA

Julio Bonetti

BONETTI, JULIO G.
B. July 14, 1911, Genoa, Italy   D. June 17, 1952, Belmont, Calif.   BR TR 6'   180 lbs.

	W	L	PCT	ERA	G	GS	CG	IP	H	BB	SO	ShO	W	L	SV	AB	H	HR	BA
1937 STL A	4	11	.267	5.84	28	16	7	143.1	190	60	43	0	2	0	1	47	7	0	.149
1938	2	3	.400	6.35	17	0	0	28.1	41	13	7	0	2	3	0	8	0	0	.000
1940 CHI N	0	0	–	20.25	1	0	0	1.1	3	4	0	0	0	0	0	0	0	0	–
3 yrs.	6	14	.300	6.03	46	16	7	173	234	77	50	0	4	3	1	55	7	0	.127

Hank Boney

BONEY, HENRY TATE
B. Oct. 28, 1903, Wallace, N. C.   BL TR 5'11"   176 lbs.

	W	L	PCT	ERA	G	GS	CG	IP	H	BB	SO	ShO	W	L	SV	AB	H	HR	BA
1927 NY N	0	0	–	2.25	3	0	0	4	4	2	0	0	0	0	0	0	0	0	–

Bill Bonham

BONHAM, WILLIAM GORDON
B. Oct. 1, 1948, Glendale, Calif.   BR TR 6'3"   190 lbs.

	W	L	PCT	ERA	G	GS	CG	IP	H	BB	SO	ShO	W	L	SV	AB	H	HR	BA
1971 CHI N	2	1	.667	4.65	33	2	0	60	63	36	41	0	2	0	0	12	2	0	.167
1972	1	1	.500	3.10	19	4	0	58	56	25	49	0	0	0	4	14	4	0	.286
1973	7	5	.583	3.02	44	15	3	152	126	64	121	0	3	0	6	43	4	0	.093
1974	11	22	.333	3.85	44	36	10	243	246	109	191	2	1	2	1	84	12	0	.143
1975	13	15	.464	4.72	38	36	7	229	254	109	165	2	0	1	0	82	15	0	.183
1976	9	13	.409	4.27	32	31	3	196	215	96	110	0	0	0	0	65	13	0	.200
1977	10	13	.435	4.35	34	34	1	215	207	82	134	0	0	0	0	65	15	0	.231
1978 CIN N	11	5	.688	3.54	23	23	1	140	151	50	83	0	0	0	0	43	8	0	.186
1979	9	7	.563	3.78	29	29	2	176	173	60	78	0	0	0	0	57	8	0	.140
1980	2	1	.667	4.74	4	4	0	19	21	5	13	0	0	0	0	6	0	0	.000
10 yrs.	75	83	.475	4.00	300	214	27	1488	1512	636	985	4	6	3	11	471	81	0	.172

Ernie Bonham

BONHAM, ERNEST EDWARD (Tiny)
B. Aug. 16, 1913, Ione, Calif.   D. Sept. 15, 1949, Pittsburgh, Pa.   BR TR 6'2"   215 lbs.

	W	L	PCT	ERA	G	GS	CG	IP	H	BB	SO	ShO	W	L	SV	AB	H	HR	BA
1940 NY A	9	3	.750	1.90	12	12	10	99.1	83	13	37	3	0	0	0	37	7	0	.189
1941	9	6	.600	2.98	23	14	7	126.2	118	31	43	1	1	0	2	50	8	0	.160
1942	21	5	.808	2.27	28	27	22	226	199	24	71	6	1	0	0	74	9	0	.122
1943	15	8	.652	2.27	28	26	17	225.2	197	52	71	4	0	0	1	76	15	0	.197
1944	12	9	.571	2.99	26	25	17	213.2	228	41	54	1	0	0	0	75	10	0	.133
1945	8	11	.421	3.29	23	23	12	180.2	186	22	42	0	0	0	0	63	15	0	.238
1946	5	8	.385	3.70	18	14	6	104.2	97	23	30	2	0	0	3	31	4	0	.129
1947 PIT N	11	8	.579	3.85	33	18	7	149.2	167	35	63	3	3	1	3	45	7	0	.156
1948	6	10	.375	4.31	22	20	7	135.2	145	23	42	0	0	0	0	49	8	0	.163
1949	7	4	.636	4.25	18	14	5	89	81	23	25	1	1	0	0	22	1	0	.045
10 yrs.	103	72	.589	3.06	231	193	110	1551	1501	287	478	21	6	1	9	522	84	0	.161

WORLD SERIES

	W	L	PCT	ERA	G	GS	CG	IP	H	BB	SO	ShO	W	L	SV	AB	H	HR	BA
1941 NY A	1	0	1.000	1.00	1	1	1	9	4	2	2	0	0	0	0	4	0	0	.000
1942	0	1	.000	4.09	2	1	1	11	9	3	3	0	0	0	0	2	0	0	.000
1943	0	1	.000	4.50	1	1	0	8	6	3	9	0	0	0	0	2	0	0	.000
3 yrs.	1	2	.333	3.21	4	3	2	28	19	8	14	0	0	0	0	8	0	0	.000

Joe Bonikowski

BONIKOWSKI, JOSEPH PETER
B. Jan. 16, 1941, Philadelphia, Pa.   BR TR 6'   175 lbs.

	W	L	PCT	ERA	G	GS	CG	IP	H	BB	SO	ShO	W	L	SV	AB	H	HR	BA
1962 MIN A	5	7	.417	3.88	30	13	3	99.2	95	38	45	0	2	1	2	27	4	0	.148

Bill Bonness

BONNESS, WILLIAM JOHN (Lefty)
B. Dec. 15, 1923, Cleveland, Ohio   D. Dec. 3, 1977, Detroit, Mich.   BR TL 6'4"   200 lbs.

	W	L	PCT	ERA	G	GS	CG	IP	H	BB	SO	ShO	W	L	SV	AB	H	HR	BA
1944 CLE A	0	1	.000	7.71	2	1	0	7	11	5	1	0	0	0	0	3	0	0	.000

Gus Bono

BONO, ADLAI WENDELL
B. Aug. 29, 1894, Doe Run, Mo.   D. Dec. 3, 1948, Dearborn, Mich.   BR TR 5'11"   175 lbs.

	W	L	PCT	ERA	G	GS	CG	IP	H	BB	SO	ShO	W	L	SV	AB	H	HR	BA
1920 WAS A	0	2	.000	8.76	4	1	0	12.1	17	6	4	0	0	1	0	3	0	0	.000

Greg Booker

BOOKER, GREGORY SCOTT
B. June 22, 1960, Lynchburg, Va.   BR TR 6'6"   230 lbs.

	W	L	PCT	ERA	G	GS	CG	IP	H	BB	SO	ShO	W	L	SV	AB	H	HR	BA
1983 SD N	0	1	.000	7.71	6	1	0	11.2	18	9	5	0	0	0	0	0	0	0	.000
1984	1	1	.500	3.30	32	1	0	57.1	67	27	28	0	1	1	0	7	2	0	.286
2 yrs.	1	2	.333	4.04	38	2	0	69	85	36	33	0	1	1	0	8	2	0	.250

LEAGUE CHAMPIONSHIP SERIES

	W	L	PCT	ERA	G	GS	CG	IP	H	BB	SO	ShO	W	L	SV	AB	H	HR	BA
1984 SD N	0	0	–	0.00	1	0	0	2	2	1	2	0	0	0	0	0	0	0	–

WORLD SERIES

	W	L	PCT	ERA	G	GS	CG	IP	H	BB	SO	ShO	W	L	SV	AB	H	HR	BA
1984 SD N	0	0	–	9.00	1	0	0	1	0	4	0	0	0	0	0	0	0	0	–

Red Booles

BOOLES, SEABRON JESSE
B. July 14, 1880, Bernice, La.   D. Mar. 16, 1955, Monroe, La.   BL TL 5'10"   150 lbs.

	W	L	PCT	ERA	G	GS	CG	IP	H	BB	SO	ShO	W	L	SV	AB	H	HR	BA
1909 CLE A	0	1	.000	1.99	4	1	0	22.2	20	8	6	0	0	0	0	6	1	0	.167

Danny Boone

BOONE, DANNY HUGH
B. Jan. 14, 1954, Long Beach, Calif.   BL TL 5'8"   150 lbs.

	W	L	PCT	ERA	G	GS	CG	IP	H	BB	SO	ShO	W	L	SV	AB	H	HR	BA
1981 SD N	1	0	1.000	2.86	37	0	0	63	63	21	43	0	1	0	2	4	2	0	.500
1982 2 teams			SD N (10G 1–0)				HOU N (10G 0–1)												
" total	1	1	.500	4.71	20	0	0	28.2	28	7	12	0	1	1	2	6	1	0	.167
2 yrs.	2	1	.667	3.44	57	0	0	91.2	91	28	55	0	2	1	4	10	3	0	.300

Danny Boone

BOONE, JAMES ALBERT
Brother of Ike Boone.
B. Jan. 19, 1895, Samantha, Ala.   D. May 11, 1968, Tuscaloosa, Ala.   BR TR 6'2"   190 lbs.

	W	L	PCT	ERA	G	GS	CG	IP	H	BB	SO	ShO	W	L	SV	AB	H	HR	BA
1919 PHI A	0	1	.000	6.75	3	2	0	14.2	24	10	1	0	0	0	0	4	0	0	.000
1921 DET A	0	0	–	0.00	1	0	0	2	1	2	0	0	0	0	1	1	0	0	.000
1922 CLE A	4	6	.400	4.06	11	10	4	75.1	87	19	9	2	0	1	0	26	5	0	.192
1923	4	6	.400	6.01	27	4	2	70.1	93	31	15	0	3	3	0	19	4	0	.211
4 yrs.	8	13	.381	5.10	42	16	6	162.1	205	62	25	2	3	4	1	50	9	0	.180

	W	L	PCT	ERA	G	GS	CG	IP	H	BB	SO	ShO	Relief Pitching W	L	SV	BATTING AB	H	HR	BA

George Boone

BOONE, GEORGE MORRIS
B. Mar. 1, 1871, Louisville, Ky.   D. Sept. 24, 1910, Louisville, Ky.

	W	L	PCT	ERA	G	GS	CG	IP	H	BB	SO	ShO	W	L	SV	AB	H	HR	BA
1891 LOU AA	0	0	–	7.80	4	1	0	15	15	9	4	0	0	0	1	6	2	0	.333

Amos Booth

BOOTH, AMOS SMITH (The Darling)   BR TR
B. Sept. 14, 1853, Cincinnati, Ohio   D. July 1, 1921, Miamisburg, Ohio

	W	L	PCT	ERA	G	GS	CG	IP	H	BB	SO	ShO	W	L	SV	AB	H	HR	BA
1876 CIN N	0	1	.000	9.31	3	1	0	9.2	22	0	0	0	0	0	0	272	71	0	.261
1877	1	7	.125	3.56	12	8	6	86	114	13	18	0	0	0	0	157	27	0	.172
2 yrs.	1	8	.111	4.14	15	9	6	95.2	136	13	18	0	0	0	0	*			

Eddie Booth

BOOTH, EDWARD H.
B. Brooklyn, N. Y.   Deceased.

	W	L	PCT	ERA	G	GS	CG	IP	H	BB	SO	ShO	W	L	SV	AB	H	HR	BA
1876 NY N	0	0	–	10.80	1	0	0	5	16	0	0	0	0	0	0	*			

John Boozer

BOOZER, JOHN MORGAN   BR TR 6'3"   205 lbs.
B. July 6, 1939, Columbia, S. C.

	W	L	PCT	ERA	G	GS	CG	IP	H	BB	SO	ShO	W	L	SV	AB	H	HR	BA
1962 PHI N	0	0	–	5.75	9	0	0	20.1	22	10	13	0	0	0	0	1	0	0	.000
1963	3	4	.429	2.93	26	8	2	83	67	33	69	0	2	0	1	21	3	0	.143
1964	3	4	.429	5.07	22	3	0	60.1	64	18	51	0	2	2	2	13	1	0	.077
1966	0	0	–	6.75	2	2	0	5.1	8	3	5	0	0	0	0	2	0	0	.000
1967	5	4	.556	4.10	28	7	1	74.2	86	24	48	0	2	1	1	19	4	0	.211
1968	2	2	.500	3.67	38	0	0	68.2	76	15	49	0	2	2	5	9	1	0	.111
1969	1	2	.333	4.28	46	2	0	82	91	36	47	0	0	0	6	9	3	0	.333
7 yrs.	14	16	.467	4.09	171	22	3	394.1	414	139	282	0	8	5	15	74	12	0	.162

Pedro Borbon

BORBON, PEDRO RODRIGUEZ   BR TR 6'2"   185 lbs.
B. Dec. 2, 1946, Valverde De Mao, Dominican Republic

	W	L	PCT	ERA	G	GS	CG	IP	H	BB	SO	ShO	W	L	SV	AB	H	HR	BA
1969 CAL A	2	3	.400	6.15	22	0	0	41	55	11	20	0	2	3	0	3	0	0	.000
1970 CIN N	0	2	.000	6.88	12	1	0	17	21	6	6	0	0	1	0	3	0	0	.000
1971	0	0	–	4.50	3	0	0	4	3	1	4	0	0	0	0	0	0	0	–
1972	8	3	.727	3.17	62	2	0	122	115	32	48	0	8	3	11	21	1	0	.048
1973	11	4	.733	2.15	80	0	0	121.1	137	35	60	0	11	4	14	15	5	0	.333
1974	10	7	.588	3.24	73	0	0	139	133	32	53	0	10	7	14	26	5	0	.192
1975	9	5	.643	2.95	67	0	0	125	145	21	29	0	9	5	5	24	7	0	.292
1976	4	3	.571	3.35	69	1	0	121	135	31	53	0	4	2	8	18	4	0	.222
1977	10	5	.667	3.19	73	0	0	127	131	24	48	0	10	5	18	22	4	0	.182
1978	8	2	.800	5.00	62	0	0	99	102	27	35	0	8	2	4	11	2	0	.182
1979 2 teams			CIN	N (30G 2–2)		SF	N	(30G 4–3)											
" total	6	5	.545	4.17	60	0	0	90.2	104	21	49	0	6	5	5	9	3	0	.333
1980 STL N	1	0	1.000	3.79	10	0	0	19	17	10	4	0	1	0	1	4	1	0	.250
12 yrs.	69	39	.639	3.52	593	4	0	1026	1098	251	409	0	69	37	80	156	32	0	.205

LEAGUE CHAMPIONSHIP SERIES

	W	L	PCT	ERA	G	GS	CG	IP	H	BB	SO	ShO	W	L	SV	AB	H	HR	BA
1972 CIN N	0	0	–	2.08	3	0	0	4.1	2	0	1	0	0	0	0	0	0	0	–
1973	1	0	1.000	0.00	4	0	0	4.2	3	0	3	0	1	0	1	0	0	0	–
1975	0	0	–	0.00	1	0	0	1	0	1	0	0	0	0	1	0	0	0	–
1976	0	0	–	0.00	2	0	0	4.1	4	0	1	0	0	0	0	2	0	0	.000
4 yrs.	1	0	1.000	0.63	10	0	0	14.1	9	1	5	0	1	0	2	2	0	0	.000

WORLD SERIES

	W	L	PCT	ERA	G	GS	CG	IP	H	BB	SO	ShO	W	L	SV	AB	H	HR	BA
1972 CIN N	0	1	.000	3.86	6	0	0	7	7	2	4	0	0	1	0	0	0	0	–
1975	0	0	–	6.00	3	0	0	3	3	2	1	0	0	0	0	1	0	0	.000
1976	0	0	–	0.00	1	0	0	1.2	0	0	0	0	0	0	0	0	0	0	–
3 yrs.	0	1	.000	3.86	10	0	0	11.2	10	4	5	0	0	1	0	1	0	0	.000

George Borchers

BORCHERS, GEORGE BERNARD   5'10"   180 lbs.
B. Apr. 18, 1869, Sacramento, Calif.   D. Oct. 24, 1938, Sacramento, Calif.

	W	L	PCT	ERA	G	GS	CG	IP	H	BB	SO	ShO	W	L	SV	AB	H	HR	BA
1888 CHI N	4	4	.500	3.49	10	10	7	67	67	29	26	1	0	0	0	33	2	0	.061
1895 LOU N	0	1	.000	27.00	1	1	0	.2	1	3	0	0	0	0	0	0	0	0	–
2 yrs.	4	5	.444	3.72	11	11	7	67.2	68	32	26	1	0	0	0	33	2	0	.061

Joe Borden

BORDEN, JOSEPH EMLEY   BR TR 5'9"   140 lbs.
B. May 9, 1854, Jacobstown, N. J.   D. Oct. 14, 1929, Yeadon, Pa.

	W	L	PCT	ERA	G	GS	CG	IP	H	BB	SO	ShO	W	L	SV	AB	H	HR	BA
1876 BOS N	11	12	.478	2.89	29	24	16	218.1	257	51	34	2	0	1	1	121	25	0	.207

Rich Bordi

BORDI, RICHARD ALBERT   BR TR 6'7"   210 lbs.
B. Apr. 18, 1959, San Francisco, Calif.

	W	L	PCT	ERA	G	GS	CG	IP	H	BB	SO	ShO	W	L	SV	AB	H	HR	BA
1980 OAK A	0	0	–	4.50	1	0	0	2	4	0	0	0	0	0	0	0	0	0	–
1981	0	0	–	0.00	2	0	0	2	1	1	0	0	0	0	0	0	0	0	–
1982 SEA A	0	2	.000	8.31	7	2	0	13	18	1	10	0	0	0	0	0	0	0	–
1983 CHI N	0	2	.000	4.97	11	1	0	25.1	34	12	20	0	0	1	1	4	0	0	.000
1984	5	2	.714	3.46	31	7	0	83.1	78	20	41	0	1	1	4	19	1	0	.053
5 yrs.	5	6	.455	4.23	52	10	0	125.2	135	34	71	0	1	2	5	23	1	0	.043

Bill Bordley

BORDLEY, WILLIAM CHARLES   BL TL 6'3"   195 lbs.
B. Jan. 9, 1958, Rolling Hills Est., Calif.

	W	L	PCT	ERA	G	GS	CG	IP	H	BB	SO	ShO	W	L	SV	AB	H	HR	BA
1980 SF N	2	3	.400	4.65	8	6	0	31	34	21	11	0	0	0	0	6	1	0	.167

Paul Boris

BORIS, PAUL STANLEY   BR TR 6'2"   200 lbs.
B. Dec. 13, 1955, Irvington, N. J.

	W	L	PCT	ERA	G	GS	CG	IP	H	BB	SO	ShO	W	L	SV	AB	H	HR	BA
1982 MIN A	1	2	.333	3.99	23	0	0	49.2	46	19	30	0	1	2	0	0	0	0	–

Frank Bork

BORK, FRANK BERNARD   BR TL 6'2"   175 lbs.
B. July 13, 1940, Buffalo, N. Y.

	W	L	PCT	ERA	G	GS	CG	IP	H	BB	SO	ShO	W	L	SV	AB	H	HR	BA
1964 PIT N	2	2	.500	4.07	33	2	0	42	51	11	31	0	1	1	2	5	1	0	.200

	W	L	PCT	ERA	G	GS	CG	IP	H	BB	SO	ShO	W	L	SV	AB	H	HR	BA
													Relief Pitching			**BATTING**			

Tom Borland

BORLAND, THOMAS BRUCE (Spike)
B. Feb. 14, 1933, El Dorado, Kans.   BL TL 6'3"   172 lbs.

	W	L	PCT	ERA	G	GS	CG	IP	H	BB	SO	ShO	W	L	SV	AB	H	HR	BA
1960 **BOS A**	0	4	.000	6.53	26	4	0	51	67	23	32	0	0	1	3	13	0	0	.000
1961	0	0	–	18.00	1	0	0	1	3	0	0	0	0	0	0	0	0	0	–
2 yrs.	0	4	.000	6.75	27	4	0	52	70	23	32	0	0	1	3	13	0	0	.000

Hank Borowy

BOROWY, HENRY LUDWIG
B. May 12, 1916, Bloomfield, N. J.   BR TR 6'   175 lbs.

	W	L	PCT	ERA	G	GS	CG	IP	H	BB	SO	ShO	W	L	SV	AB	H	HR	BA
1942 **NY A**	15	4	.789	2.52	25	21	13	178.1	157	66	85	4	1	0	1	70	11	0	.157
1943	14	9	.609	2.82	29	27	14	217.1	195	72	113	3	1	0	0	74	15	0	.203
1944	17	12	.586	2.64	35	30	19	252.2	224	88	107	3	0	0	2	90	12	0	.133
1945 2 teams			**NY A** (18G 10–5)				**CHI N** (15G 11–2)												
" total	21	7	.750	2.65*	33	32	18	254.2	212	105	82	2	0	0	1	91	18	0	.198
1946 **CHI N**	12	10	.545	3.76	32	28	8	201	220	61	95	1	1	0	0	72	13	0	.181
1947	8	12	.400	4.38	40	25	7	183	190	63	75	1	1	1	2	56	7	0	.125
1948	5	10	.333	4.89	39	17	2	127	156	49	50	1	1	0	1	36	8	0	.222
1949 **PHI N**	12	12	.500	4.19	28	28	12	193.1	188	63	43	2	0	0	0	61	13	0	.213
1950 3 teams			**PHI N** (3G 0–0)				**PIT N** (11G 1–3)				**DET A** (13G 1–1)								
" total	2	4	.333	4.83	27	5	1	63.1	60	29	24	0	2	1	0	13	2	0	.154
1951 **DET A**	2	2	.500	6.95	26	1	0	45.1	58	27	16	0	2	2	0	8	0	0	.000
10 yrs.	108	82	.568	3.50	314	214	94	1716	1660	623	690	17	9	4	7	571	99	0	.173

WORLD SERIES

	W	L	PCT	ERA	G	GS	CG	IP	H	BB	SO	ShO	W	L	SV	AB	H	HR	BA
1942 **NY A**	0	0	–	18.00	1	1	0	3	6	3	1	0	0	0	0	1	0	0	.000
1943	1	0	1.000	2.25	1	1	0	8	6	3	4	0	0	0	0	2	1	0	.500
1945 **CHI N**	2	2	.500	4.00	4	3	1	18	21	6	8	1	1	0	0	5	1	0	.200
3 yrs.	3	2	.600	4.97	6	5	1	29	33	12	13	1	1	0	0	8	2	0	.250

Dick Bosman

BOSMAN, RICHARD ALLEN
B. Feb. 17, 1944, Kenosha, Wis.   BR TR 6'2"   195 lbs.

	W	L	PCT	ERA	G	GS	CG	IP	H	BB	SO	ShO	W	L	SV	AB	H	HR	BA
1966 **WAS A**	2	6	.250	7.62	13	7	0	39	60	12	20	0	0	3	0	12	3	0	.250
1967	3	1	.750	1.75	7	7	2	51.1	38	10	25	1	0	0	0	15	3	0	.200
1968	2	9	.182	3.69	46	10	0	139	139	35	63	0	1	7	1	30	6	0	.200
1969	14	5	.737	2.19	31	26	5	193	156	39	99	2	1	0	1	64	6	0	.094
1970	16	12	.571	3.00	36	34	7	231	212	71	134	3	0	0	0	80	11	0	.138
1971	12	16	.429	3.72	35	35	7	237	245	71	113	1	0	0	0	75	7	0	.093
1972 **TEX A**	8	10	.444	3.64	29	29	1	173	183	48	105	1	0	0	0	53	5	0	.094
1973 2 teams			**TEX A** (7G 2–5)				**CLE A** (22G 1–8)												
" total	3	13	.188	5.64	29	24	3	137.1	172	46	55	1	0	0	0	0	0	0	–
1974 **CLE A**	7	5	.583	4.11	25	18	2	127	126	29	56	1	0	0	0	0	0	0	–
1975 2 teams			**CLE A** (6G 0–2)				**OAK A** (22G 11–4)												
" total	11	6	.647	3.63	28	24	2	151.1	145	32	53	0	0	0	0	0	0	0	–
1976 **OAK A**	4	2	.667	4.10	27	15	0	112	118	19	34	0	1	0	0	0	0	0	–
11 yrs.	82	85	.491	3.67	306	229	29	1591	1594	412	757	10	3	10	2	329	41	0	.125

LEAGUE CHAMPIONSHIP SERIES

	W	L	PCT	ERA	G	GS	CG	IP	H	BB	SO	ShO	W	L	SV	AB	H	HR	BA
1975 **OAK A**	0	0	–	0.00	1	0	0	.1	0	0	0	0	0	0	0	0	0	0	–

Mel Bosser

BOSSER, MELVIN EDWARD
B. Feb. 8, 1920, Johnstown, Pa.   BR TR 6'   173 lbs.

	W	L	PCT	ERA	G	GS	CG	IP	H	BB	SO	ShO	W	L	SV	AB	H	HR	BA
1945 **CIN N**	2	0	1.000	3.31	7	1	0	16.1	9	17	3	0	1	0	0	4	0	0	.000

Andy Boswell

BOSWELL, ANDREW COTTRELL
B. Sept. 5, 1874, New Gretna, N. J.   D. Feb. 3, 1936, Ocean City, N. J.

	W	L	PCT	ERA	G	GS	CG	IP	H	BB	SO	ShO	W	L	SV	AB	H	HR	BA
1895 2 teams			**NY N** (5G 2–2)				**WAS N** (6G 1–2)												
" total	3	4	.429	5.91	11	7	6	64	85	41	30	0	0	0	0	30	7	0	.233

Dave Boswell

BOSWELL, DAVID WILSON
B. Jan. 20, 1945, Baltimore, Md.   BR TR 6'3"   185 lbs.

	W	L	PCT	ERA	G	GS	CG	IP	H	BB	SO	ShO	W	L	SV	AB	H	HR	BA
1964 **MIN A**	2	0	1.000	4.24	4	4	0	23.1	21	12	25	0	0	0	0	9	2	0	.222
1965	6	5	.545	3.40	27	12	1	106	77	46	85	0	1	2	0	38	12	0	.316
1966	12	5	.706	3.14	28	21	8	169.1	120	65	173	1	0	0	0	63	9	0	.143
1967	14	12	.538	3.27	37	32	11	222.2	162	107	204	3	0	0	0	73	16	1	.219
1968	10	13	.435	3.32	34	28	7	190	148	87	143	2	0	0	0	60	14	1	.233
1969	20	12	.625	3.23	39	38	10	256.1	215	99	190	0	0	0	0	94	16	2	.170
1970	3	7	.300	6.39	18	15	0	69	80	44	45	0	0	0	0	25	4	0	.160
1971 2 teams			**DET A** (3G 0–0)				**BAL A** (15G 1–2)												
" total	1	2	.333	4.66	18	2	0	29	35	21	17	0	1	1	0	5	1	0	.200
8 yrs.	68	56	.548	3.52	205	151	37	1065.2	858	481	882	6	2	3	0	367	74	4	.202

LEAGUE CHAMPIONSHIP SERIES

	W	L	PCT	ERA	G	GS	CG	IP	H	BB	SO	ShO	W	L	SV	AB	H	HR	BA
1969 **MIN A**	0	1	.000	0.84	1	1	0	10.2	7	7	4	0	0	0	0	4	0	0	.000

WORLD SERIES

	W	L	PCT	ERA	G	GS	CG	IP	H	BB	SO	ShO	W	L	SV	AB	H	HR	BA
1965 **MIN A**	0	0	–	3.38	1	0	0	2.2	3	2	3	0	0	0	0	0	0	0	–

Dick Botelho

BOTELHO, DEREK WAYNE
B. Aug. 2, 1956, Long Beach, Calif.   BR TR 6'2"   160 lbs.

	W	L	PCT	ERA	G	GS	CG	IP	H	BB	SO	ShO	W	L	SV	AB	H	HR	BA
1982 **KC A**	2	1	.667	4.13	8	4	0	24	25	8	12	0	0	0	0	0	0	0	–

Ralph Botting

BOTTING, RALPH WAYNE
B. May 12, 1955, Houlton, Me.   BL TL 6'   195 lbs.

	W	L	PCT	ERA	G	GS	CG	IP	H	BB	SO	ShO	W	L	SV	AB	H	HR	BA
1979 **CAL A**	2	0	1.000	8.70	12	1	0	30	46	15	22	0	1	0	0	0	0	0	–
1980	0	3	.000	5.88	6	6	0	26	40	13	12	0	0	0	0	0	0	0	–
2 yrs.	2	3	.400	7.39	18	7	0	56	86	28	34	0	1	0	0	0	0	0	–

Bob Botz

BOTZ, ROBERT ALLEN (Butterball)
B. Apr. 28, 1935, Milwaukee, Wis.   BR TR 5'11"   170 lbs.

	W	L	PCT	ERA	G	GS	CG	IP	H	BB	SO	ShO	W	L	SV	AB	H	HR	BA
1962 **LA A**	2	1	.667	3.43	35	0	0	63	71	11	24	0	2	1	2	9	0	0	.000

	W	L	PCT	ERA	G	GS	CG	IP	H	BB	SO	ShO	Relief Pitching W	L	SV	BATTING AB	H	HR	BA

Carl Bouldin

BOULDIN, CARL EDWARD
B. Sept. 17, 1939, Germantown, Ky.

BB TR 6'2" 180 lbs.
BL 1961

	W	L	PCT	ERA	G	GS	CG	IP	H	BB	SO	ShO	W	L	SV	AB	H	HR	BA
1961 WAS A	0	1	.000	16.20	2	1	0	3.1	9	2	2	0	0	0	0	1	0	0	.000
1962	1	2	.333	5.85	6	3	1	20	26	9	12	0	0	1	0	7	0	0	.000
1963	2	2	.500	5.79	10	3	0	23.1	31	8	10	0	2	0	0	7	0	0	.000
1964	0	3	.000	5.40	9	3	0	25	30	11	12	0	0	1	0	6	0	0	.000
4 yrs.	3	8	.273	6.15	27	10	1	71.2	96	30	36	0	2	2	0	21	0	0	.000

Jake Boultes

BOULTES, JAKE JOHN
B. Aug. 6, 1884, St. Louis, Mo.   D. Dec. 24, 1955, St. Louis, Mo.

TR

	W	L	PCT	ERA	G	GS	CG	IP	H	BB	SO	ShO	W	L	SV	AB	H	HR	BA
1907 BOS N	5	9	.357	2.71	24	12	11	139.2	140	50	49	0	2	0	0	68	9	0	.132
1908	3	5	.375	3.01	17	5	1	74.2	80	8	28	0	2	2	0	21	3	0	.143
1909	0	0	–	6.75	1	0	0	8	9	0	1	0	0	0	0	3	1	0	.333
3 yrs.	8	14	.364	2.96	42	17	12	222.1	229	58	78	0	4	2	0	92	13	0	.141

Jim Bouton

BOUTON, JAMES ALAN (Bulldog)
B. Mar. 8, 1939, Newark, N. J.

BR TR 6' 170 lbs.

	W	L	PCT	ERA	G	GS	CG	IP	H	BB	SO	ShO	W	L	SV	AB	H	HR	BA
1962 NY A	7	7	.500	3.99	36	16	3	133	124	59	71	1	3	1	2	32	2	0	.063
1963	21	7	.750	2.53	40	30	12	249.1	191	87	148	6	3	1	1	83	6	0	.072
1964	18	13	.581	3.02	38	37	11	271.1	227	60	125	4	0	0	0	100	13	0	.130
1965	4	15	.211	4.82	30	25	2	151.1	158	60	97	0	0	1	0	43	4	0	.093
1966	3	8	.273	2.69	24	19	3	120.1	117	38	65	0	0	1	1	38	4	0	.105
1967	1	0	1.000	4.67	17	1	0	44.1	47	18	31	0	1	0	0	7	0	0	.000
1968	1	1	.500	3.68	12	3	1	44	49	9	24	0	0	0	0	7	0	0	.000
1969 2 teams		SEA	A (57G 2–1)		HOU	N (16G 0–2)													
" total	2	3	.400	3.95	73	2	1	123	109	50	100	0	2	1	2	13	0	0	.000
1970 HOU N	4	6	.400	5.42	29	6	1	73	84	33	49	0	2	4	0	17	6	0	.353
1978 ATL N	1	3	.250	4.97	5	5	0	29	25	21	10	0	0	0	0	7	0	0	.000
10 yrs.	62	63	.496	3.57	304	144	34	1238.2	1131	435	720	11	11	9	6	347	35	0	.101
WORLD SERIES																			
1963 NY A	0	1	.000	1.29	1	1	0	7	4	5	4	0	0	0	0	2	0	0	.000
1964	2	0	1.000	1.56	2	2	1	17.1	15	5	7	0	0	0	0	7	1	0	.143
2 yrs.	2	1	.667	1.48	3	3	1	24.1	19	10	11	0	0	0	0	9	1	0	.111

Cy Bowen

BOWEN, SUTHERLAND McCOY
B. Feb. 17, 1871, Kingston, Ind.   D. Jan. 25, 1925, Greensburg, Ind.

BR TR 6' 175 lbs.

	W	L	PCT	ERA	G	GS	CG	IP	H	BB	SO	ShO	W	L	SV	AB	H	HR	BA
1896 NY N	0	1	.000	6.00	2	1	1	12	12	9	3	0	0	0	0	3	1	0	.333

Frank Bowerman

BOWERMAN, FRANK EUGENE (Mike)
B. Dec. 5, 1868, Romeo, Mich.   D. Nov. 30, 1948, Romeo, Mich.
Manager 1909.

BR TR 5'11" 185 lbs.

	W	L	PCT	ERA	G	GS	CG	IP	H	BB	SO	ShO	W	L	SV	AB	H	HR	BA
1904 NY N	0	0	–	9.00	1	0	0	3	3	1	0	0	0	0	0	*			

Stew Bowers

BOWERS, STEWART COLE (Doc)
B. Feb. 26, 1915, New Freedom, Pa.

BB TR 6' 170 lbs.

	W	L	PCT	ERA	G	GS	CG	IP	H	BB	SO	ShO	W	L	SV	AB	H	HR	BA
1935 BOS A	2	1	.667	3.42	10	2	1	23.2	26	17	5	0	1	0	0	5	1	0	.200
1936	0	0	–	9.53	5	0	0	5.2	10	2	0	0	0	0	0	0	0	0	–
2 yrs.	2	1	.667	4.60	15	2	1	29.1	36	19	5	0	1	0	0	5	1	0	.200

Grant Bowler

BOWLER, GRANT TIERNEY (Moose)
B. Oct. 24, 1907, Denver, Colo.   D. June 25, 1968, Denver, Colo.

BR TR 6' 190 lbs.

	W	L	PCT	ERA	G	GS	CG	IP	H	BB	SO	ShO	W	L	SV	AB	H	HR	BA
1931 CHI A	0	1	.000	5.35	13	3	1	35.1	40	24	15	0	0	0	0	10	1	0	.100
1932	0	0	–	15.63	4	0	0	6.1	15	3	2	0	0	0	0	2	0	0	.000
2 yrs.	0	1	.000	6.91	17	3	1	41.2	55	27	17	0	0	0	0	12	1	0	.083

Charlie Bowles

BOWLES, CHARLES JAMES
B. Mar. 15, 1917, Norwood, Mass.

BR TR 6'3" 180 lbs.

	W	L	PCT	ERA	G	GS	CG	IP	H	BB	SO	ShO	W	L	SV	AB	H	HR	BA
1943 PHI A	1	1	.500	3.00	2	2	2	18	17	4	6	0	0	0	0	8	1	0	.125
1945	0	3	.000	5.13	8	4	1	33.1	35	23	11	0	0	1	0	21	5	0	.238
2 yrs.	1	4	.200	4.38	10	6	3	51.1	52	27	17	0	0	1	0	29	6	0	.207

Emmett Bowles

BOWLES, EMMETT JEROME (Chief)
B. Aug. 2, 1898, Wanette, Okla.   D. Sept. 3, 1959, Flagstaff, Ariz.

BR TR 6' 180 lbs.

	W	L	PCT	ERA	G	GS	CG	IP	H	BB	SO	ShO	W	L	SV	AB	H	HR	BA
1922 CHI A	0	0	–	27.00	1	0	0	1	2	1	0	0	0	0	0	0	0	0	–

Abe Bowman

BOWMAN, ALVAH EDSON
B. Jan. 25, 1893, Greenup, Ill.   D. Oct. 11, 1979, Longview, Tex.

BR TR 6'1" 190 lbs.

	W	L	PCT	ERA	G	GS	CG	IP	H	BB	SO	ShO	W	L	SV	AB	H	HR	BA
1914 CLE A	2	7	.222	4.46	22	10	2	72.2	74	45	27	1	1	0	0	21	1	0	.048
1915	0	1	.000	20.25	2	1	0	1.1	1	3	0	0	0	0	0	0	0	0	–
2 yrs.	2	8	.200	4.74	24	11	2	74	75	48	27	1	1	0	0	21	1	0	.048

Bob Bowman

BOWMAN, ROBERT JAMES
B. Oct. 3, 1910, Keystone, W. Va.   D. Sept. 4, 1972, Bluefield, W. Va.

BR TR 5'10½" 160 lbs.

	W	L	PCT	ERA	G	GS	CG	IP	H	BB	SO	ShO	W	L	SV	AB	H	HR	BA
1939 STL N	13	5	.722	2.60	51	15	4	169.1	141	60	78	2	7	0	9	47	4	0	.085
1940	7	5	.583	4.33	28	17	7	114.1	118	43	43	0	0	2	0	33	2	0	.061
1941 NY N	6	7	.462	5.71	29	6	2	80.1	100	36	25	0	4	4	1	21	1	1	.048
1942 CHI N	0	0	–	0.00	1	0	0	1	1	0	0	0	0	0	0	0	0	0	–
4 yrs.	26	17	.605	3.82	109	38	13	365	360	139	146	2	11	6	10	101	7	1	.069

Bob Bowman

BOWMAN, ROBERT LEROY
B. May 10, 1931, Laytonville, Calif.

BR TR 6'1" 195 lbs.

	W	L	PCT	ERA	G	GS	CG	IP	H	BB	SO	ShO	W	L	SV	AB	H	HR	BA
1959 PHI N	0	1	.000	6.00	5	0	0	6	5	5	0	0	0	1	0	*			

	W	L	PCT	ERA	G	GS	CG	IP	H	BB	SO	ShO	W	L	SV	AB	H	HR	BA

Joe Bowman

BOWMAN, JOSEPH EMIL
B. June 17, 1910, Argentine, Kans.
BL TR 6'2" 190 lbs.

	W	L	PCT	ERA	G	GS	CG	IP	H	BB	SO	ShO	W	L	SV	AB	H	HR	BA
1932 PHI A	0	1	.000	8.18	7	0	0	11	14	6	4	0	0	1	0	1	1	0	1.000
1934 NY N	5	4	.556	3.61	30	10	3	107.1	119	36	36	0	1	1	3	29	5	0	.172
1935 PHI N	7	10	.412	4.25	33	17	6	148.1	157	56	58	1	2	3	1	67	13	1	.194
1936	9	20	.310	5.04	40	28	12	203.2	243	53	80	0	1	3	1	77	15	0	.195
1937 PIT N	8	8	.500	4.57	30	19	7	128	161	35	38	0	1	1	1	47	10	0	.213
1938	3	4	.429	4.65	17	1	0	60	68	20	25	0	3	3	1	21	7	0	.333
1939	10	14	.417	4.48	37	27	10	184.2	217	43	58	1	1	0	1	96	33	0	.344
1940	9	10	.474	4.46	32	24	10	187.2	209	66	57	0	2	0	2	90	22	1	.244
1941	3	2	.600	2.99	18	7	1	69.1	77	28	22	1	1	1	1	31	8	0	.258
1944 BOS A	12	8	.600	4.81	26	24	10	168.1	175	64	53	1	0	0	0	100	20	0	.200
1945 2 teams		BOS	A (3G 0–2)		CIN	N	(25G 11–13)												
" total	11	15	.423	3.92	28	27	15	197.1	216	77	71	1	0	0	0	80	7	0	.088
11 yrs.	77	96	.445	4.40	298	184	74	1465.2	1656	484	502	5	12	13	11	*			

Roger Bowman

BOWMAN, ROGER CLINTON
B. Aug. 18, 1927, Amsterdam, N. Y.
BR TL 6' 175 lbs.

	W	L	PCT	ERA	G	GS	CG	IP	H	BB	SO	ShO	W	L	SV	AB	H	HR	BA
1949 NY N	0	0	—	4.26	2	2	0	6.1	6	7	4	0	0	0	0	2	0	0	.000
1951	2	4	.333	6.15	9	5	0	26.1	35	22	24	0	1	1	0	6	0	0	.000
1952	0	0	—	12.00	2	1	0	3	6	3	3	0	0	0	0	1	0	0	.000
1953 PIT N	0	4	.000	4.82	30	2	0	65.1	65	29	36	0	0	2	0	7	2	0	.286
1955	0	3	.000	8.64	7	2	0	16.2	25	10	8	0	0	1	0	2	1	0	.500
5 yrs.	2	11	.154	5.81	50	12	0	117.2	137	71	75	0	1	4	0	18	3	0	.167

Sumner Bowman

BOWMAN, SUMNER SALLADE
B. Feb. 9, 1867, Millersburg, Pa.   D. Jan. 11, 1954, Millersburg, Pa.
BL TL 6' 160 lbs.

	W	L	PCT	ERA	G	GS	CG	IP	H	BB	SO	ShO	W	L	SV	AB	H	HR	BA
1890 2 teams		PHI	N (1G 0–0)		PIT	N	(9G 2–5)												
" total	2	5	.286	6.75	10	8	8	78.2	111	52	24	0	0	0	0	40	12	0	.300
1891 PHI AA	2	5	.286	3.44	8	8	8	68	73	37	22	0	0	0	0	54	13	0	.241
2 yrs.	4	10	.286	5.22	18	16	14	146.2	184	89	46	0	0	0	0	94	25	0	.266

Ted Bowsfield

BOWSFIELD, EDWARD OLIVER
B. Jan. 10, 1936, Vernon B. C., Canada
BR TL 6'1" 190 lbs.

	W	L	PCT	ERA	G	GS	CG	IP	H	BB	SO	ShO	W	L	SV	AB	H	HR	BA
1958 BOS A	4	2	.667	3.84	16	10	2	65.2	58	36	38	0	1	0	0	26	4	0	.154
1959	0	1	.000	15.00	5	2	0	9	16	9	4	0	0	0	0	1	0	0	.000
1960 2 teams		BOS	A (17G 1–2)		CLE	A	(11G 3–4)												
" total	4	6	.400	5.11	28	8	1	61.2	67	33	32	1	1	2	2	14	2	0	.143
1961 LA A	11	8	.579	3.73	41	21	4	157	154	63	88	1	2	1	0	51	7	0	.137
1962	9	8	.529	4.40	34	25	1	139	154	40	52	0	1	1	1	37	6	0	.162
1963 KC A	5	7	.417	4.45	41	11	2	111.1	115	47	67	1	2	2	3	23	1	0	.043
1964	4	7	.364	4.10	50	9	2	118.2	135	31	45	1	2	2	0	21	2	0	.095
7 yrs.	37	39	.487	4.35	215	86	12	662.1	699	259	326	4	9	8	6	173	22	0	.127

Gary Boyd

BOYD, GARY LEE
B. Aug. 22, 1946, Pasadena, Calif.
BR TR 6'4" 200 lbs.

	W	L	PCT	ERA	G	GS	CG	IP	H	BB	SO	ShO	W	L	SV	AB	H	HR	BA
1969 CLE A	0	2	.000	9.00	8	3	0	11	8	14	9	0	0	0	0	1	0	0	.000

Jake Boyd

BOYD, JACOB HENRY
B. Jan. 19, 1874, Martinsburgh, W. Va.   D. Aug. 12, 1932, Gettysburg, Pa.
TL

	W	L	PCT	ERA	G	GS	CG	IP	H	BB	SO	ShO	W	L	SV	AB	H	HR	BA
1894 WAS N	0	3	.000	8.53	3	3	3	19	37	14	3	0	0	0	0	21	3	0	.143
1895	2	11	.154	7.07	14	12	8	85.1	126	35	16	0	1	0	0	157	42	1	.268
1896	1	2	.333	6.75	4	2	2	32	45	15	6	0	0	1	0	13	1	0	.077
3 yrs.	3	16	.158	7.20	21	17	13	136.1	208	64	25	0	1	1	0	*			

Oil Can Boyd

BOYD, DENNIS RAY
B. Oct. 6, 1959, Meridian, Miss.
BR TR 6'2" 160 lbs.

	W	L	PCT	ERA	G	GS	CG	IP	H	BB	SO	ShO	W	L	SV	AB	H	HR	BA
1982 BOS A	0	1	.000	5.40	3	1	0	8.1	11	2	2	0	0	0	0	0	0	0	—
1983	4	8	.333	3.28	15	13	5	98.2	103	23	43	0	0	0	0	0	0	0	—
1984	12	12	.500	4.37	29	26	10	197.2	207	53	134	3	0	1	0	0	0	0	—
3 yrs.	16	21	.432	4.05	47	40	15	304.2	321	78	179	3	0	1	0	0	0	0	—

Ray Boyd

BOYD, RAYMOND C.
B. Feb. 11, 1887, Hortonville, Ind.   D. Feb. 11, 1920, Hortonville, Ind.
BR TR 5'10" 160 lbs.

	W	L	PCT	ERA	G	GS	CG	IP	H	BB	SO	ShO	W	L	SV	AB	H	HR	BA
1910 STL A	0	2	.000	4.40	3	2	1	14.1	16	5	6	0	0	0	0	5	1	0	.200
1911 CIN N	3	2	.600	2.66	7	4	3	44	34	19	20	0	1	0	1	12	1	0	.083
2 yrs.	3	4	.429	3.09	10	6	4	58.1	50	24	26	0	1	0	1	17	2	0	.118

Cloyd Boyer

BOYER, CLOYD VICTOR (Junior)
Brother of Ken Boyer.   Brother of Clete Boyer.
B. Sept. 1, 1927, Alba, Mo.
BR TR 6'1" 188 lbs.

	W	L	PCT	ERA	G	GS	CG	IP	H	BB	SO	ShO	W	L	SV	AB	H	HR	BA
1949 STL N	0	0	—	10.80	3	1	0	3.1	5	7	0	0	0	0	0	0	0	0	—
1950	7	7	.500	3.52	36	14	6	120.1	105	49	82	2	2	1	1	33	6	0	.182
1951	2	5	.286	5.26	19	8	1	63.1	68	46	40	0	1	2	1	20	4	0	.200
1952	6	6	.500	4.24	23	14	4	110.1	108	47	44	2	0	0	0	38	8	0	.211
1955 KC A	5	5	.500	6.22	30	11	2	98.1	107	69	32	0	1	1	0	29	2	0	.069
5 yrs.	20	23	.465	4.73	111	48	13	395.2	393	218	198	4	4	4	2	120	20	0	.167

Henry Boyle

BOYLE, HENRY J. (Handsome Henry)
B. Sept. 20, 1860, Philadelphia, Pa.   D. May 25, 1932, Philadelphia, Pa.
TR

	W	L	PCT	ERA	G	GS	CG	IP	H	BB	SO	ShO	W	L	SV	AB	H	HR	BA
1884 STL U	15	3	.833	1.74	19	16	16	150	118	10	88	2	1	1	1	262	68	4	.260
1885 STL N	16	24	.400	2.75	42	39	39	366.2	346	100	133	1	1	0	0	258	52	1	.202
1886	9	15	.375	2.24	25	24	23	165	183	46	101	2	1	0	0	108	27	1	.250
1887 IND N	13	24	.351	3.65	39	39	37	328	356	69	85	0	1	0	0	141	27	2	.191
1888	15	22	.405	3.26	37	37	36	323	315	58	98	3	0	0	0	125	18	1	.144
1889	21	23	.477	3.92	46	45	38	378.2	422	95	97	2	1	0	0	155	38	1	.245
6 yrs.	89	111	.445	3.14	208	200	189	1711.1	1740	378	602	10	4	1	1	*			

	W	L	PCT	ERA	G	GS	CG	IP	H	BB	SO	ShO	Relief Pitching W	L	SV	BATTING AB	H	HR	BA

Harry Boyles

BOYLES, HARRY (Stretch)
B. Nov. 29, 1911, Granite City, Ill.　　　　　　　BR TR 6'5"　185 lbs.

	W	L	PCT	ERA	G	GS	CG	IP	H	BB	SO	ShO	W	L	SV	AB	H	HR	BA
1938 CHI A	0	4	.000	5.22	9	2	1	29.1	31	25	18	0	0	2	1	8	1	0	.125
1939	0	0	–	10.80	2	0	0	3.1	4	6	1	0	0	0	0	1	0	0	.000
2 yrs.	0	4	.000	5.79	11	2	1	32.2	35	31	19	0	0	2	1	9	1	0	.111

Gene Brabender

BRABENDER, EUGENE MATHEW
B. Aug. 16, 1941, Madison, Wis.　　　　　　　BR TR 6'5½"　225 lbs.

	W	L	PCT	ERA	G	GS	CG	IP	H	BB	SO	ShO	W	L	SV	AB	H	HR	BA
1966 BAL A	4	3	.571	3.55	31	1	0	71	57	29	62	0	3	3	2	13	1	0	.077
1967	6	4	.600	3.35	14	14	3	94	77	23	71	1	0	0	0	28	2	0	.071
1968	6	7	.462	3.32	37	15	3	124.2	116	48	92	2	1	1	3	35	3	1	.086
1969 SEA A	13	14	.481	4.36	40	29	7	202.1	193	103	139	1	0	2	0	70	9	1	.129
1970 MIL A	6	15	.286	6.00	29	21	2	129	127	79	76	0	1	1	1	41	4	0	.098
5 yrs.	35	43	.449	4.25	151	80	15	621	570	282	440	4	5	7	6	187	19	2	.102

Jack Bracken

BRACKEN, JOHN JAMES
B. Apr. 14, 1881, Cleveland, Ohio　　D. July 16, 1954, Highland Park, Mich.　　　BR TR 5'11"　175 lbs.

	W	L	PCT	ERA	G	GS	CG	IP	H	BB	SO	ShO	W	L	SV	AB	H	HR	BA
1901 CLE A	4	8	.333	6.21	12	12	11	100	137	31	18	0	0	0	0	44	10	0	.227

John Brackinridge

BRACKINRIDGE, JOHN CALHOUN
B. Dec. 24, 1880, Harrisburg, Pa.　　D. Mar. 20, 1953, Harrisburg, Pa.

	W	L	PCT	ERA	G	GS	CG	IP	H	BB	SO	ShO	W	L	SV	AB	H	HR	BA
1904 PHI N	0	1	.000	5.56	7	1	0	34	37	16	11	0	0	0	0	13	2	0	.154

Don Bradey

BRADEY, DONALD EUGENE
B. Oct. 4, 1934, Charlotte, N. C.　　　　　　　BR TR 5'9"　180 lbs.

	W	L	PCT	ERA	G	GS	CG	IP	H	BB	SO	ShO	W	L	SV	AB	H	HR	BA
1964 HOU N	0	2	.000	19.29	3	1	0	2.1	6	3	2	0	0	1	0	0	0	0	–

Bill Bradford

BRADFORD, WILLIAM D
B. Aug. 28, 1921, Choctaw, Ark.　　　　　　　BR TR 6'2"　180 lbs.

	W	L	PCT	ERA	G	GS	CG	IP	H	BB	SO	ShO	W	L	SV	AB	H	HR	BA
1956 KC A	0	0	–	9.00	1	0	0	2	2	1	0	0	0	0	0	0	0	0	–

Larry Bradford

BRADFORD, LARRY
B. Dec. 21, 1951, Chicago, Ill.　　　　　　　BR TL 6'1"　200 lbs.

	W	L	PCT	ERA	G	GS	CG	IP	H	BB	SO	ShO	W	L	SV	AB	H	HR	BA
1977 ATL N	0	0	–	3.00	2	0	0	3	3	0	1	0	0	0	0	0	0	0	–
1979	1	0	1.000	0.95	21	0	0	19	11	10	11	0	1	0	2	1	0	0	.000
1980	3	4	.429	2.45	56	0	0	55	49	22	32	0	3	4	4	3	0	0	.000
1981	2	0	1.000	3.67	25	0	0	27	26	12	14	0	2	0	1	1	1	0	1.000
4 yrs.	6	4	.600	2.51	104	0	0	104	89	44	58	0	6	4	7	5	1	0	.200

Bert Bradley

BRADLEY, STEVEN BERT
B. Dec. 23, 1957, Athens, Ga.　　　　　　　BB TR 6'1"　190 lbs.

	W	L	PCT	ERA	G	GS	CG	IP	H	BB	SO	ShO	W	L	SV	AB	H	HR	BA
1983 OAK A	0	0	–	6.48	6	0	0	8.1	14	4	3	0	0	0	0	0	0	0	–

Bill Bradley

BRADLEY, WILLIAM JOSEPH
B. Feb. 13, 1878, Cleveland, Ohio　　D. Mar. 11, 1954, Cleveland, Ohio
Manager 1914.　　　　　　　BR TR 6'　185 lbs.

	W	L	PCT	ERA	G	GS	CG	IP	H	BB	SO	ShO	W	L	SV	AB	H	HR	BA
1901 CLE A	0	0	–	0.00	1	0	0	1	0	4	0	0	0	0	0	*			

Foghorn Bradley

BRADLEY, GEORGE H.
B. July 1, 1855, Milford, Mass.　　D. Apr. 3, 1900, Philadelphia, Pa.　　　BR TR

	W	L	PCT	ERA	G	GS	CG	IP	H	BB	SO	ShO	W	L	SV	AB	H	HR	BA
1876 BOS N	9	10	.474	2.49	22	21	16	173.1	201	16	16	1	0	0	1	82	19	0	.232

Fred Bradley

BRADLEY, FREDERICK LANGDON
B. July 31, 1920, Parsons, Kans.　　　　　　　BR TR 6'1"　180 lbs.

	W	L	PCT	ERA	G	GS	CG	IP	H	BB	SO	ShO	W	L	SV	AB	H	HR	BA
1948 CHI A	0	0	–	4.60	8	0	0	15.2	11	4	2	0	0	0	0	1	0	0	.000
1949	0	0	–	13.50	1	1	0	2	4	3	0	0	0	0	0	1	0	0	.000
2 yrs.	0	0	–	5.60	9	1	0	17.2	15	7	2	0	0	0	0	2	0	0	.000

George Bradley

BRADLEY, GEORGE WASHINGTON (Grin)
B. July 13, 1852, Reading, Pa.　　D. Oct. 2, 1931, Philadelphia, Pa.　　　BR TR 5'10½"　175 lbs.

	W	L	PCT	ERA	G	GS	CG	IP	H	BB	SO	ShO	W	L	SV	AB	H	HR	BA
1876 STL N	45	19	.703	1.23	64	64	63	573	470	38	103	16	0	0	0	265	66	0	.249
1877 CHI N	18	23	.439	3.31	50	44	35	394	452	39	59	2	1	0	0	214	52	0	.243
1879 TRO N	13	40	.245	2.85	54	54	53	487	590	26	133	3	0	0	0	251	62	0	.247
1880 PRO N	12	9	.571	1.38	28	20	16	196	158	6	54	4	3	1	1	309	70	0	.227
1881 CLE N	2	4	.333	3.88	6	6	5	51	70	3	6	0	0	0	0	245	60	2	.245
1882	7	10	.412	3.73	18	16	15	147	164	22	32	0	0	0	0	115	21	0	.183
1883 PHI AA	16	7	.696	3.15	26	23	22	214.1	215	22	56	0	0	0	0	328	78	1	.238
1884 CIN U	25	15	.625	2.71	41	38	36	342	350	23	168	3	1	1	0	226	43	0	.190
1886 PHI AA	0	0	–	0.00	0	0	0	0	0	0	0	0	0	0	0	48	4	0	.083
1888 BAL AA	0	0	–	0.00	0	0	0	0	0	0	0	0	0	0	0	3	0	0	.000
10 yrs.	138	127	.521	2.50	287	265	245	2404.1	2469	179	611	28	5	2	1	*			

Herb Bradley

BRADLEY, HERBERT THEODORE
B. Jan. 3, 1903, Agenda, Kans.　　D. Oct. 16, 1959, Clay City, Kans.　　　BR TR 6'　170 lbs.

	W	L	PCT	ERA	G	GS	CG	IP	H	BB	SO	ShO	W	L	SV	AB	H	HR	BA
1927 BOS A	1	1	.500	3.13	6	2	2	23	16	7	6	0	0	0	0	7	3	0	.429
1928	0	3	.000	7.23	15	5	1	47.1	64	16	14	1	0	0	0	13	2	0	.154
1929	0	0	–	6.75	3	0	0	4	7	2	0	0	0	0	0	1	0	0	.000
3 yrs.	1	4	.200	5.93	24	7	3	74.1	87	25	20	1	0	0	0	21	5	0	.238

Tom Bradley

BRADLEY, THOMAS WILLIAM
B. Mar. 16, 1947, Asheville, N. C.　　　　　　　BR TR 6'2½"　180 lbs.

	W	L	PCT	ERA	G	GS	CG	IP	H	BB	SO	ShO	W	L	SV	AB	H	HR	BA
1969 CAL A	0	1	.000	27.00	3	0	0	2	9	0	2	0	0	1	0	0	0	0	–
1970	2	5	.286	4.11	17	11	1	70	71	33	53	1	0	0	0	18	3	0	.167
1971 CHI A	15	15	.500	2.96	45	39	7	286	273	74	206	6	0	0	2	96	15	1	.156
1972	15	14	.517	2.98	40	40	11	260	225	65	209	2	0	0	0	91	12	0	.132
1973 SF N	13	12	.520	3.90	35	34	6	223.2	212	69	136	1	0	0	0	77	15	0	.195

	W	L	PCT	ERA	G	GS	CG	IP	H	BB	SO	ShO	Relief Pitching W	L	SV	BATTING AB	H	HR	BA

Tom Bradley continued

	W	L	PCT	ERA	G	GS	CG	IP	H	BB	SO	ShO	W	L	SV	AB	H	HR	BA
1974	8	11	.421	5.17	30	21	2	134	152	52	72	0	0	1	0	40	3	0	.075
1975	2	3	.400	6.21	13	6	0	42	57	18	13	0	0	0	0	10	0	0	.000
7 yrs.	55	61	.474	3.72	183	151	27	1017.2	999	311	691	10	0	3	2	332	48	1	.145

Joe Bradshaw

BRADSHAW, JOSEPH SIAH
B. Aug. 17, 1897, Dyersburg, Tenn.   BR TR 6'2½" 200 lbs.

	W	L	PCT	ERA	G	GS	CG	IP	H	BB	SO	ShO	W	L	SV	AB	H	HR	BA
1929 BKN N	0	0	—	4.50	2	0	0	4	3	4	1	0	0	0	0	0	0	0	—

Bill Brady

BRADY, WILLIAM A.
B. 1888   D. Apr. 12, 1917   TR

	W	L	PCT	ERA	G	GS	CG	IP	H	BB	SO	ShO	W	L	SV	AB	H	HR	BA
1912 BOS N	0	0	—	0.00	1	0	0	1	2	0	0	0	0	0	0	0	0	0	—

Charlie Brady

BRADY, CHARLES
B. Clayton, N. J.

	W	L	PCT	ERA	G	GS	CG	IP	H	BB	SO	ShO	W	L	SV	AB	H	HR	BA
1905 PHI N	1	1	.500	3.46	2	2	2	13	19	2	3	0	0	0	0	5	1	0	.200
1906 PIT N	1	1	.500	2.35	3	2	1	23	30	4	14	0	0	1	0	10	1	0	.100
1907	0	0	—	0.00	1	0	0	2	2	1	0	0	0	0	0	0	0	0	—
3 yrs.	2	2	.500	2.61	6	4	3	38	51	7	17	0	0	1	0	15	2	0	.133

Jim Brady

BRADY, JAMES JOSEPH (Diamond Jim)
B. Mar. 2, 1936, Jersey City, N. J.   BL TL 6'2" 185 lbs.

	W	L	PCT	ERA	G	GS	CG	IP	H	BB	SO	ShO	W	L	SV	AB	H	HR	BA
1956 DET A	0	0	—	28.42	6	0	0	6.1	15	11	3	0	0	0	0	0	0	0	—

King Brady

BRADY, JAMES WARD
B. May 28, 1881, Monroeville, N. Y.   D. Aug. 21, 1947, Albany, N. Y.   BL TR

	W	L	PCT	ERA	G	GS	CG	IP	H	BB	SO	ShO	W	L	SV	AB	H	HR	BA
1908 BOS A	1	0	1.000	0.00	1	1	1	9	8	0	3	1	0	0	0	2	0	0	.000
1912 BOS N	0	0	—	20.25	2	0	0	2.2	5	3	0	0	0	0	0	1	0	0	.000
2 yrs.	1	0	1.000	4.63	3	1	1	11.2	13	3	3	1	0	0	0	3	0	0	.000

Neal Brady

BRADY, CORNELIUS JOSEPH
B. Mar. 4, 1897, Covington, Ky.   D. June 19, 1947, Fort Mitchell, Ky.   BR TR 6'½" 197 lbs.

	W	L	PCT	ERA	G	GS	CG	IP	H	BB	SO	ShO	W	L	SV	AB	H	HR	BA
1915 NY A	0	0	—	3.12	2	1	0	8.2	9	7	6	0	0	0	0	4	0	0	.000
1917	1	0	1.000	2.00	2	1	0	9	6	5	4	0	0	0	0	2	1	0	.500
1925 CIN N	1	3	.250	4.66	20	3	2	63.2	73	20	12	0	0	1	1	25	6	0	.240
3 yrs.	2	3	.400	4.20	24	5	2	81.1	88	32	22	0	0	1	1	31	7	0	.226

Dick Braggins

BRAGGINS, RICHARD REALF
B. Dec. 25, 1879, Mercer, Pa.   D. Aug. 16, 1963, Lake Wales, Fla.   BR TR 5'11" 170 lbs.

	W	L	PCT	ERA	G	GS	CG	IP	H	BB	SO	ShO	W	L	SV	AB	H	HR	BA
1901 CLE A	1	2	.333	4.78	4	3	2	32	44	15	1	0	0	0	0	13	2	0	.154

Al Braithwood

BRAITHWOOD, ALFRED
B. Feb. 15, 1892, Braceville, Ill.   D. Nov. 24, 1960, Rowlesburg, W. Va.   BR TL 6'1½" 145 lbs.

	W	L	PCT	ERA	G	GS	CG	IP	H	BB	SO	ShO	W	L	SV	AB	H	HR	BA
1915 PIT F	0	0	—	0.00	2	0	0	3	0	2	0	0	0	0	0	0	0	0	—

Erv Brame

BRAME, ERVIN BECKHAM
B. Oct. 12, 1901, Big Rock, Tenn.   D. Nov. 22, 1949, Hopkinsville, Ky.   BL TR 6'2" 190 lbs.

	W	L	PCT	ERA	G	GS	CG	IP	H	BB	SO	ShO	W	L	SV	AB	H	HR	BA
1928 PIT N	7	4	.636	5.08	24	11	6	95.2	110	44	22	0	0	1	0	49	13	1	.265
1929	16	11	.593	4.55	38	28	19	229.2	250	71	68	1	2	0	0	116	36	4	.310
1930	17	8	.680	4.70	32	29	22	235.2	291	56	55	0	1	0	1	116	41	3	.353
1931	9	13	.409	4.21	26	21	15	179.2	211	45	33	2	2	1	0	95	26	0	.274
1932	3	1	.750	7.41	23	3	0	51	84	16	10	0	3	0	0	20	5	0	.250
5 yrs.	52	37	.584	4.76	142	92	62	791.2	946	232	188	3	8	2	1	*			

Ralph Branca

BRANCA, RALPH THEODORE JOSEPH (Hawk)
B. Jan. 6, 1926, Mt. Vernon, N. Y.   BR TR 6'3" 220 lbs.

	W	L	PCT	ERA	G	GS	CG	IP	H	BB	SO	ShO	W	L	SV	AB	H	HR	BA
1944 BKN N	0	2	.000	7.05	21	1	0	44.2	46	32	16	0	0	1	1	6	0	0	.000
1945	5	6	.455	3.04	16	15	7	109.2	73	79	69	0	0	0	1	40	4	0	.100
1946	3	1	.750	3.88	24	10	2	67.1	62	41	42	2	0	1	3	18	2	0	.111
1947	21	12	.636	2.67	43	36	15	280	251	98	148	4	3	1	1	97	12	0	.124
1948	14	9	.609	3.51	36	28	11	215.2	189	80	122	1	1	0	1	74	15	0	.203
1949	13	5	.722	4.39	34	27	9	186.2	181	91	109	2	0	1	1	62	5	0	.081
1950	7	9	.438	4.69	43	15	5	142	152	55	100	0	2	4	7	34	4	2	.118
1951	13	12	.520	3.26	42	27	13	204	180	85	118	3	1	2	3	63	11	0	.175
1952	4	2	.667	3.84	16	7	2	61	52	21	26	0	1	0	0	19	3	0	.158
1953 2 teams		BKN	N (7G 0–0)		DET	A	(17G 4–7)												
" total	4	7	.364	4.70	24	14	7	113	113	36	55	0	1	0	0	34	4	0	.118
1954 2 teams		DET	A (17G 3–3)		NY	A	(5G 1–0)												
" total	4	3	.571	5.12	22	8	0	58	72	43	22	0	2	3	0	17	6	0	.353
1956 BKN N	0	0	—	0.00	1	0	0	2	1	2	2	0	0	0	0	0	0	0	—
12 yrs.	88	68	.564	3.79	322	188	71	1484	1372	663	829	12	10	13	19	464	66	2	.142

WORLD SERIES

	W	L	PCT	ERA	G	GS	CG	IP	H	BB	SO	ShO	W	L	SV	AB	H	HR	BA
1947 BKN N	1	1	.500	8.64	3	1	0	8.1	12	5	8	0	1	0	0	4	0	0	.000
1949	0	1	.000	4.15	1	1	0	8.2	4	4	6	0	0	0	0	3	0	0	.000
2 yrs.	1	2	.333	6.35	4	2	0	17	16	9	14	0	1	0	0	7	0	0	.000

Harvey Branch

BRANCH, HARVEY ALFRED
B. Feb. 8, 1939, Memphis, Tenn.   BR TL 6' 175 lbs.

	W	L	PCT	ERA	G	GS	CG	IP	H	BB	SO	ShO	W	L	SV	AB	H	HR	BA
1962 STL N	0	1	.000	5.40	1	1	0	5	5	5	2	0	0	0	0	1	0	0	.000

Norm Branch

BRANCH, NORMAN DOWNS (Red)
B. Mar. 22, 1915, Spokane, Wash.   D. Nov. 21, 1971, Novasota, Tex.   BR TR 6'3" 200 lbs.

	W	L	PCT	ERA	G	GS	CG	IP	H	BB	SO	ShO	W	L	SV	AB	H	HR	BA
1941 NY A	5	1	.833	2.87	27	0	0	47	37	26	28	0	5	1	2	10	0	0	.000
1942	0	1	.000	6.32	10	0	0	15.2	18	16	13	0	0	1	2	3	1	0	.333
2 yrs.	5	2	.714	3.73	37	0	0	62.2	55	42	41	0	5	2	4	13	1	0	.077

	W	L	PCT	ERA	G	GS	CG	IP	H	BB	SO	ShO	Relief Pitching W	L	SV	BATTING AB	H	HR	BA

Roy Branch

BRANCH, ROY
B. July 12, 1953, St. Louis, Mo.
BR TR 6' 175 lbs.

	W	L	PCT	ERA	G	GS	CG	IP	H	BB	SO	ShO	W	L	SV	AB	H	HR	BA
1979 SEA A	0	1	.000	8.18	2	2	0	11	12	7	6	0	0	0	0	0	0	0	–

Chick Brandom

BRANDOM, CHESTER MILTON
B. Mar. 31, 1887, Oklahoma City, Okla.   D. Oct. 7, 1958, Santa Ana, Calif.
TR 5'8" 161 lbs.

	W	L	PCT	ERA	G	GS	CG	IP	H	BB	SO	ShO	W	L	SV	AB	H	HR	BA
1908 PIT N	1	0	1.000	0.53	3	1	1	17	13	4	8	0	1	0	0	7	1	0	.143
1909	1	0	1.000	1.11	13	2	0	40.2	33	10	21	0	1	0	2	10	1	0	.100
1915 NWK F	1	1	.500	3.40	16	1	1	50.1	55	15	15	0	0	1	0	10	2	0	.200
3 yrs.	3	1	.750	2.08	32	4	2	108	101	29	44	0	2	1	2	27	4	0	.148

Darrell Brandon

BRANDON, DARRELL G (Bucky)
B. July 8, 1940, Nacogdoches, Tex.
BR TR 6'2" 200 lbs.

	W	L	PCT	ERA	G	GS	CG	IP	H	BB	SO	ShO	W	L	SV	AB	H	HR	BA
1966 BOS A	8	8	.500	3.31	40	17	5	157.2	129	70	101	2	1	1	2	44	8	0	.182
1967	5	11	.313	4.17	39	19	2	157.2	147	59	96	0	2	3	3	43	8	0	.186
1968	0	0	–	6.39	8	0	0	12.2	19	9	10	0	0	0	0	1	0	0	.000
1969 2 teams			SEA	A (8G 0–1)		MIN	A	(3G 0–0)											
" total	1	0	1.000	7.36	11	1	0	18.1	20	19	11	0	0	0	0	1	0	0	.000
1971 PHI N	6	6	.500	3.90	52	0	0	83	81	47	44	0	6	6	4	13	2	0	.154
1972	7	7	.500	3.45	42	6	0	104.1	106	46	67	0	7	4	2	15	1	0	.067
1973	2	4	.333	5.43	36	0	0	56.1	54	25	25	0	2	4	2	5	1	0	.200
7 yrs.	28	37	.431	4.04	228	43	7	590	556	275	354	2	18	17	13	122	20	0	.164

Bill Brandt

BRANDT, WILLIAM GEORGE
B. Mar. 21, 1918, Aurora, Ind.   D. May 16, 1958, Fort Wayne, Ind.
BR TR 5'8½" 170 lbs.

	W	L	PCT	ERA	G	GS	CG	IP	H	BB	SO	ShO	W	L	SV	AB	H	HR	BA
1941 PIT N	0	1	.000	3.86	2	1	0	7	5	3	0	0	0	0	0	1	0	0	.000
1942	1	1	.500	4.96	3	3	1	16.1	23	5	4	0	0	0	0	7	1	0	.143
1943	4	1	.800	3.14	29	3	0	57.1	57	19	17	0	3	0	0	7	1	0	.143
3 yrs.	5	3	.625	3.57	34	7	1	80.2	85	27	21	0	3	0	0	15	2	0	.133

Ed Brandt

BRANDT, EDWARD ARTHUR
B. Feb. 17, 1905, Spokane, Wash.   D. Nov. 1, 1944, Spokane, Wash.
BL TL 6'1" 190 lbs.

	W	L	PCT	ERA	G	GS	CG	IP	H	BB	SO	ShO	W	L	SV	AB	H	HR	BA
1928 BOS N	9	21	.300	5.07	38	31	12	225.1	234	109	84	1	1	2	0	70	17	0	.243
1929	8	13	.381	5.53	26	21	13	167.2	196	83	50	0	1	1	0	64	15	0	.234
1930	4	11	.267	5.01	41	13	4	147.1	168	59	65	1	2	2	1	50	12	0	.240
1931	18	11	.621	2.92	33	29	23	250	228	77	112	3	0	1	2	82	21	0	.256
1932	16	16	.500	3.97	35	31	19	254	271	57	79	2	1	2	1	92	19	0	.207
1933	18	14	.563	2.60	41	32	23	287.2	256	77	104	3	1	1	4	97	30	0	.309
1934	16	14	.533	3.53	40	28	20	255	249	83	106	3	2	2	5	96	23	0	.240
1935	5	19	.208	5.00	29	25	12	174.2	224	66	67	0	0	2	0	62	13	0	.210
1936 BKN N	11	13	.458	3.50	38	29	12	234	246	65	104	1	1	1	2	84	16	0	.190
1937 PIT N	11	10	.524	3.11	33	25	7	176.1	177	67	74	3	0	1	2	59	10	0	.169
1938	5	4	.556	3.46	24	13	5	96.1	93	35	38	1	1	1	0	37	11	0	.297
11 yrs.	121	146	.453	3.86	378	277	150	2268.1	2342	778	877	18	10	16	17	793	187	0	.236

Roy Brashear

BRASHEAR, ROY PARKS
Brother of Kitty Brashear.
B. Jan. 3, 1874, Ashtabula, Ohio   D. Apr. 20, 1951, Los Angeles, Calif.
BR TR

	W	L	PCT	ERA	G	GS	CG	IP	H	BB	SO	ShO	W	L	SV	AB	H	HR	BA
1899 LOU N	1	0	1.000	4.50	3	0	0	8	8	2	5	0	1	0	0	*			

John Braun

BRAUN, JOHN PAUL
B. Dec. 26, 1939, Madison, Wis.
BR TR 6'5" 218 lbs.

	W	L	PCT	ERA	G	GS	CG	IP	H	BB	SO	ShO	W	L	SV	AB	H	HR	BA
1964 MIL N	0	0	–	0.00	1	0	0	2	2	1	1	0	0	0	0	0	0	0	–

Garland Braxton

BRAXTON, EDGAR GARLAND
B. June 10, 1900, Snow Camp, N. C.
D. Feb. 25, 1966, Norfolk, Va.
BL TL 5'11" 152 lbs.
BB 1925-26,1933

	W	L	PCT	ERA	G	GS	CG	IP	H	BB	SO	ShO	W	L	SV	AB	H	HR	BA
1921 BOS N	1	3	.250	4.82	17	2	0	37.1	44	17	16	0	1	1	0	7	0	0	.000
1922	1	2	.333	3.38	25	4	2	66.2	75	24	15	0	0	1	0	16	1	0	.063
1925 NY A	1	1	.500	6.52	3	2	0	19.1	26	5	11	0	0	0	0	6	2	0	.333
1926	5	1	.833	2.67	37	1	0	67.1	71	19	30	0	5	1	2	20	6	0	.300
1927 WAS A	10	9	.526	2.95	58	2	0	155.1	143	33	95	0	10	7	13	39	9	0	.231
1928	13	11	.542	2.51	38	24	15	218.1	177	44	94	2	1	3	6	72	9	0	.125
1929	12	10	.545	4.85	37	20	9	182	219	51	59	0	4	1	4	54	8	0	.148
1930 2 teams			WAS	A (15G 3–2)		CHI	A	(19G 4–10)											
" total	7	12	.368	5.72	34	10	2	118	149	42	51	0	5	4	6	28	2	0	.071
1931 2 teams			CHI	A (17G 0–3)		STL	A	(11G 0–0)											
" total	0	3	.000	7.85	28	4	0	65.1	98	33	35	0	0	1	1	14	3	0	.214
1933 STL A	0	1	.000	9.72	5	1	0	8.1	11	8	5	0	0	0	0	1	0	0	.000
10 yrs.	50	53	.485	4.13	282	70	28	938	1013	276	411	2	26	19	32	257	40	0	.156

Al Brazle

BRAZLE, ALPHA EUGENE (Cotton)
B. Oct. 13, 1913, Loyal, Okla.   D. Oct. 24, 1973, Grand Junction, Colo.
BL TL 6'2" 185 lbs.

	W	L	PCT	ERA	G	GS	CG	IP	H	BB	SO	ShO	W	L	SV	AB	H	HR	BA
1943 STL N	8	2	.800	1.53	13	9	8	88	74	29	26	1	1	0	0	32	9	0	.281
1946	11	10	.524	3.29	37	15	6	153.1	152	55	58	2	4	2	0	52	11	0	.212
1947	14	8	.636	2.84	44	19	7	168	186	48	85	0	4	1	4	64	14	0	.219
1948	10	6	.625	3.80	42	23	6	156.1	171	50	55	3	3	0	1	55	8	0	.145
1949	14	8	.636	3.18	39	25	9	206.1	208	61	75	1	3	0	0	82	11	0	.134
1950	11	9	.550	4.10	46	12	3	164.2	188	80	47	0	5	4	6	61	13	0	.213
1951	6	5	.545	3.09	56	8	5	154.1	139	61	66	0	2	2	7	46	5	0	.109
1952	12	5	.706	2.72	46	6	3	109.1	75	42	55	2	8	3	16	32	4	0	.125
1953	6	7	.462	4.21	60	0	0	92	101	43	57	0	6	7	18	15	5	0	.333
1954	5	4	.556	4.16	58	0	0	84.1	93	24	30	0	5	4	8	14	0	0	.000
10 yrs.	97	64	.602	3.31	441	117	47	1376.2	1387	493	554	9	41	23	60	453	80	0	.177

WORLD SERIES

	W	L	PCT	ERA	G	GS	CG	IP	H	BB	SO	ShO	W	L	SV	AB	H	HR	BA
1943 STL N	0	1	.000	3.68	1	1	0	7.1	5	2	4	0	0	0	0	3	0	0	.000

	W	L	PCT	ERA	G	GS	CG	IP	H	BB	SO	ShO	Relief Pitching W	L	SV	BATTING AB	H	HR	BA

Al Brazle continued

	W	L	PCT	ERA	G	GS	CG	IP	H	BB	SO	ShO	W	L	SV	AB	H	HR	BA
1946	0	1	.000	5.40	1	0	0	6.2	7	6	4	0	0	1	0	2	0	0	.000
2 yrs.	0	2	.000	4.50	2	1	0	14	12	8	8	0	0	1	0	5	0	0	.000

Harry Brecheen

BRECHEEN, HARRY DAVID (The Cat) BL TL 5'10" 160 lbs.
B. Oct. 14, 1914, Broken Bow, Okla.

	W	L	PCT	ERA	G	GS	CG	IP	H	BB	SO	ShO	W	L	SV	AB	H	HR	BA
1940 STL N	0	0	–	0.00	3	0	0	3.1	2	2	4	0	0	0	0	0	0	0	–
1943	9	6	.600	2.26	29	13	8	135.1	98	39	68	1	4	1	4	42	8	0	.190
1944	16	5	.762	2.85	30	22	13	189.1	174	46	88	3	3	0	0	68	11	0	.162
1945	14	4	.778	2.52	24	18	13	157.1	136	44	63	3	2	1	2	57	7	0	.123
1946	15	15	.500	2.49	36	30	14	231.1	212	67	117	5	0	0	3	83	11	0	.133
1947	16	11	.593	3.30	29	28	18	223.1	220	66	89	1	0	0	1	83	20	0	.241
1948	20	7	.741	2.24	33	30	21	233.1	193	49	149	7	0	0	1	82	12	0	.146
1949	14	11	.560	3.35	32	31	14	214.2	207	65	88	2	0	0	1	77	21	0	.273
1950	8	11	.421	3.80	27	23	12	163.1	151	45	80	2	0	1	0	58	14	1	.241
1951	8	4	.667	3.25	24	16	5	138.2	134	54	57	0	2	0	2	55	12	1	.218
1952	7	5	.583	3.32	25	13	4	100.1	82	28	54	1	2	1	2	29	6	0	.207
1953 STL A	5	13	.278	3.07	26	16	3	117.1	122	31	44	0	2	3	1	39	7	0	.179
12 yrs.	132	92	.589	2.92	318	240	125	1907.2	1731	536	901	25	15	8	18	673	129	2	.192

WORLD SERIES

	W	L	PCT	ERA	G	GS	CG	IP	H	BB	SO	ShO	W	L	SV	AB	H	HR	BA
1943 STL N	0	1	.000	2.45	3	0	0	3.2	5	3	3	0	0	1	0	0	0	0	–
1944	1	0	1.000	1.00	1	1	1	9	9	4	4	0	0	0	0	4	0	0	.000
1946	3	0	1.000	0.45	3	2	2	20	14	5	11	1	1	0	0	8	1	0	.125
3 yrs.	4	1	.800	0.83 **2nd**	7	3	3	32.2	28	12	18	1	1	1	0	12	1	0	.083

Bill Breckinridge

BRECKINRIDGE, WILLIAM ROBERTSON BR TR 5'11" 175 lbs.
B. Oct. 16, 1907, Tulsa, Okla. D. Aug. 23, 1958, Tulsa, Okla.

	W	L	PCT	ERA	G	GS	CG	IP	H	BB	SO	ShO	W	L	SV	AB	H	HR	BA
1929 PHI A	0	0	–	8.10	3	1	0	10	10	16	2	0	0	0	0	4	0	0	.000

Fred Breining

BREINING, FRED LAWRENCE BR TR 6'4" 185 lbs.
B. Nov. 15, 1955, San Francisco, Calif.

	W	L	PCT	ERA	G	GS	CG	IP	H	BB	SO	ShO	W	L	SV	AB	H	HR	BA
1980 SF N	0	0	–	5.14	5	0	0	7	8	4	3	0	0	0	0	0	0	0	–
1981	5	2	.714	2.54	45	1	0	78	66	38	37	0	5	2	1	11	0	0	.000
1982	11	6	.647	3.08	54	9	2	143.1	146	52	98	0	6	3	0	29	6	0	.207
1983	11	12	.478	3.82	32	32	6	202.2	202	60	117	0	0	0	0	67	10	0	.149
1984 MON N	0	0	–	1.35	4	0	0	6.2	4	5	5	0	0	0	0	1	0	0	.000
5 yrs.	27	20	.574	3.33	140	42	8	437.2	426	159	260	0	11	5	1	108	16	0	.148

Alonzo Breitenstein

BREITENSTEIN, ALONZO
B. Nov. 9, 1857, Utica, N. Y. D. June 19, 1932, Utica, N. Y.

	W	L	PCT	ERA	G	GS	CG	IP	H	BB	SO	ShO	W	L	SV	AB	H	HR	BA
1883 PHI N	0	1	.000	9.00	1	1	0	5	8	2	0	0	0	0	0	2	0	0	.000

Ted Breitenstein

BREITENSTEIN, THEODORE P. BL TL 5'9" 167 lbs.
B. June 1, 1869, St. Louis, Mo. D. May 3, 1935, St. Louis, Mo.

	W	L	PCT	ERA	G	GS	CG	IP	H	BB	SO	ShO	W	L	SV	AB	H	HR	BA
1891 STL AA	2	0	1.000	2.20	6	1	1	28.2	15	14	13	1	1	0	1	12	0	0	.000
1892 STL N	14	20	.412	4.69	39	32	28	282.1	280	148	126	1	0	0	0	131	16	0	.122
1893	19	20	.487	3.18	48	42	38	382.2	359	156	102	1	0	3	0	160	29	1	.181
1894	27	25	.519	4.79	56	50	46	447.1	497	191	140	1	2	0	0	182	40	0	.220
1895	18	30	.375	4.44	54	50	46	429.2	458	178	127	1	0	1	1	218	42	0	.193
1896	18	26	.409	4.48	44	43	37	339.2	376	138	114	1	1	0	0	162	42	0	.259
1897 CIN N	23	12	.657	3.62	40	39	32	320.1	345	91	98	2	0	0	0	124	33	0	.266
1898	21	14	.600	3.42	39	37	32	315.2	313	123	68	3	1	0	0	121	26	0	.215
1899	14	10	.583	3.59	26	24	21	210.2	219	71	59	0	1	0	0	105	37	1	.352
1900	10	10	.500	3.65	24	20	18	192.1	205	79	39	1	1	1	0	126	24	2	.190
1901 STL N	0	3	.000	6.60	3	3	1	15	24	14	3	0	0	0	0	6	2	0	.333
11 yrs.	166	170	.494	4.04	379	341	300	2964.1	3091	1203	889	12	7	5	3	*			

Ad Brennan

BRENNAN, ADDISON FOSTER BL TL 5'11" 170 lbs.
B. July 18, 1881, LaHarpe, Kans. D. Jan. 7, 1962, Kansas City, Mo.

	W	L	PCT	ERA	G	GS	CG	IP	H	BB	SO	ShO	W	L	SV	AB	H	HR	BA
1910 PHI N	3	0	1.000	2.33	19	5	2	73.1	72	28	28	0	1	0	0	25	7	0	.280
1911	2	1	.667	3.57	9	3	1	22.2	22	12	12	0	1	0	0	9	2	0	.222
1912	11	9	.550	3.57	27	19	13	174	185	49	78	1	2	1	2	59	15	1	.254
1913	14	12	.538	2.39	40	25	12	207	204	46	94	1	4	1	1	67	11	0	.164
1914 CHI F	5	4	.556	3.57	16	11	5	85.2	84	21	31	1	0	1	0	32	8	0	.250
1915	3	9	.250	3.74	19	13	7	106	117	30	40	2	0	0	0	27	5	0	.185
1918 2 teams			WAS A	(2G 0–0)		CLE A	(1G 0–0)												
" total	0	0	–	4.32	3	1	0	8.1	10	8	0	0	0	0	0	1	0	0	.000
7 yrs.	38	35	.521	3.11	129	77	40	677	694	194	283	5	8	3	3	220	48	1	.218

Don Brennan

BRENNAN, JAMES DONALD BR TR 6' 210 lbs.
B. Dec. 2, 1903, Augusta, Me. D. Apr. 26, 1953, Boston, Mass.

	W	L	PCT	ERA	G	GS	CG	IP	H	BB	SO	ShO	W	L	SV	AB	H	HR	BA
1933 NY A	5	1	.833	4.98	18	10	3	85	92	47	46	0	0	1	3	27	7	0	.259
1934 CIN N	4	3	.571	3.81	28	7	2	78	89	35	31	0	2	1	2	22	5	0	.227
1935	5	5	.500	3.15	38	5	2	114.1	101	44	48	0	3	3	5	30	3	0	.100
1936	5	2	.714	4.39	41	4	0	94.1	117	35	40	0	5	2	9	25	2	0	.080
1937 2 teams			CIN N	(10G 1–1)		NY N	(6G 1–0)												
" total	2	1	.667	6.75	16	0	0	25.1	37	19	7	0	2	1	0	6	0	0	.000
5 yrs.	21	12	.636	4.19	141	26	7	397	436	180	172	0	12	8	19	110	17	0	.155

WORLD SERIES

	W	L	PCT	ERA	G	GS	CG	IP	H	BB	SO	ShO	W	L	SV	AB	H	HR	BA
1937 NY N	0	0	–	0.00	2	0	0	3	1	1	1	0	0	0	0	0	0	0	–

	W	L	PCT	ERA	G	GS	CG	IP	H	BB	SO	ShO	Relief Pitching W	L	SV	BATTING AB	H	HR	BA

Tom Brennan

BRENNAN, THOMAS MARTIN
B. Oct. 30, 1952, Chicago, Ill.
BR TR 6'1" 180 lbs.

	W	L	PCT	ERA	G	GS	CG	IP	H	BB	SO	ShO	W	L	SV	AB	H	HR	BA
1981 CLE A	2	2	.500	3.19	7	6	1	48	49	14	15	0	0	0	0	0	0	0	—
1982	4	2	.667	4.27	30	4	0	92.2	112	10	46	0	1	2	2	0	0	0	—
1983	2	2	.500	3.86	11	5	1	39.2	45	8	21	1	0	0	0	0	0	0	—
1984 CHI A	0	1	.000	4.05	4	1	0	6.2	8	3	3	0	0	0	0	0	0	0	—
4 yrs.	8	7	.533	3.90	52	16	2	187	214	35	85	1	1	2	2	0	0	0	—

Jim Brenneman

BRENNEMAN, JAMES LeROY
B. Feb. 13, 1941, San Diego, Calif.
BR TR 6'2" 180 lbs.

	W	L	PCT	ERA	G	GS	CG	IP	H	BB	SO	ShO	W	L	SV	AB	H	HR	BA
1965 NY A	0	0	—	18.00	3	0	0	2	5	3	2	0	0	0	0	0	0	0	—

Bert Brenner

BRENNER, DELBERT HENRY (Dutch)
B. July 18, 1887, Minneapolis, Minn.   D. Apr. 11, 1971, St. Louis Park, Minn.
BR TR 6' 175 lbs.

	W	L	PCT	ERA	G	GS	CG	IP	H	BB	SO	ShO	W	L	SV	AB	H	HR	BA
1912 CLE A	1	0	1.000	2.77	2	1	1	13	14	4	3	0	0	0	0	5	0	0	.000

Lynn Brenton

BRENTON, LYNN DAVIS (Buck, Herb)
B. Oct. 7, 1889, Peoria, Ill.   D. Oct. 14, 1968, Los Angeles, Calif.
BR TR 5'10" 165 lbs.

	W	L	PCT	ERA	G	GS	CG	IP	H	BB	SO	ShO	W	L	SV	AB	H	HR	BA
1913 CLE A	0	0	—	9.00	1	0	0	2	4	0	2	0	0	0	0	0	0	0	—
1915	2	3	.400	3.35	11	5	1	51	60	20	18	1	0	0	0	17	2	0	.118
1920 CIN N	2	1	.667	4.91	5	1	1	18.1	17	4	13	0	1	1	1	8	2	0	.250
1921	1	8	.111	4.05	17	9	2	60	80	17	19	0	0	0	1	15	2	0	.133
4 yrs.	5	12	.294	3.97	34	15	4	131.1	161	41	52	1	1	1	2	40	6	0	.150

Roger Bresnahan

BRESNAHAN, ROGER PHILIP (The Duke of Tralee)
B. June 11, 1879, Toledo, Ohio   D. Dec. 4, 1944, Toledo, Ohio
Manager 1909-12, 1915.
Hall of Fame 1945.
BR TR 5'9" 200 lbs.

	W	L	PCT	ERA	G	GS	CG	IP	H	BB	SO	ShO	W	L	SV	AB	H	HR	BA
1897 WAS N	4	0	1.000	3.95	6	5	3	41	52	10	12	1	0	0	0	16	6	0	.375
1901 BAL N	0	1	.000	6.00	2	1	0	6	10	4	3	0	0	0	0	293	77	1	.263
1910 STL N	0	0	—	0.00	1	0	0	3.1	6	1	0	0	0	0	0	234	65	0	.278
3 yrs.	4	1	.800	3.93	9	6	3	50.1	68	15	15	1	0	0	0	*			

Rube Bressler

BRESSLER, RAYMOND BLOOM
B. Oct. 23, 1894, Coder, Pa.   D. Nov. 7, 1966, Cincinnati, Ohio
BR TL 6' 187 lbs.

	W	L	PCT	ERA	G	GS	CG	IP	H	BB	SO	ShO	W	L	SV	AB	H	HR	BA
1914 PHI A	10	4	.714	1.77	29	10	8	147.2	112	56	96	1	3	2	2	51	11	0	.216
1915	4	17	.190	5.20	32	20	7	178.1	183	118	69	1	0	4	0	55	8	1	.145
1916	0	2	.000	6.60	4	2	0	15	16	14	8	0	0	0	0	5	1	0	.200
1917 CIN N	0	0	—	6.00	2	1	0	9	15	5	2	0	0	0	0	5	1	0	.200
1918	8	5	.615	2.46	17	13	10	128	124	39	37	0	1	0	0	62	17	0	.274
1919	2	4	.333	3.46	13	4	1	41.2	37	8	13	0	2	1	0	165	34	2	.206
1920	2	0	1.000	1.77	10	2	1	20.1	24	2	4	1	1	0	0	30	8	0	.267
7 yrs.	26	32	.448	3.40	107	52	27	540	511	242	229	3	7	7	2	*			

Herb Brett

BRETT, HERBERT JAMES (Duke)
B. May 23, 1900, Lawrenceville, Va.   D. Nov. 25, 1974, St. Petersburg, Fla.
BR TR 6' 175 lbs.

	W	L	PCT	ERA	G	GS	CG	IP	H	BB	SO	ShO	W	L	SV	AB	H	HR	BA
1924 CHI N	0	0	—	5.06	1	1	0	5.1	6	7	1	0	0	0	0	2	0	0	.000
1925	1	1	.500	3.63	10	1	0	17.1	12	3	6	0	1	0	0	1	0	0	.000
2 yrs.	1	1	.500	3.97	11	2	0	22.2	18	10	7	0	1	0	0	3	0	0	.000

Ken Brett

BRETT, KENNETH ALVIN
Brother of George Brett.
B. Sept. 18, 1948, Brooklyn, N. Y.
BL TL 6' 190 lbs.

	W	L	PCT	ERA	G	GS	CG	IP	H	BB	SO	ShO	W	L	SV	AB	H	HR	BA
1967 BOS A	0	0	—	4.50	1	0	0	2	3	0	2	0	0	0	0	0	0	0	—
1969	2	3	.400	5.26	8	8	0	39.1	41	22	23	0	0	0	0	10	3	1	.300
1970	8	9	.471	4.08	41	14	1	139	118	79	155	1	3	5	2	41	13	2	.317
1971	0	3	.000	5.34	29	2	0	59	57	35	57	0	0	2	1	10	2	0	.200
1972 MIL A	7	12	.368	4.53	26	22	2	133	121	49	74	1	0	0	0	44	10	0	.227
1973 PHI N	13	9	.591	3.44	31	25	10	211.2	206	74	111	1	1	1	0	80	20	4	.250
1974 PIT N	13	9	.591	3.30	27	27	10	191	192	52	96	3	0	0	0	87	27	2	.310
1975	9	5	.643	3.36	23	16	4	118	110	43	47	1	1	1	0	52	12	1	.231
1976 2 teams	NY	A	(2G 0–0)		CHI	A	(27G 10–12)												
" total	10	12	.455	3.28	29	26	16	203	173	76	92	1	0	0	2	12	1	0	.083
1977 2 teams	CHI	A	(13G 6–4)		CAL	A	(21G 7–10)												
" total	13	14	.481	4.52	34	34	7	225	258	53	80	0	0	0	0	0	0	0	—
1978 CAL A	3	5	.375	4.95	31	10	1	100	100	42	43	1	1	0	0	0	0	0	—
1979 2 teams	MIN	A	(9G 0–0)		LA	N	(30G 4–3)												
" total	4	3	.571	3.75	39	0	0	60	68	18	16	0	4	3	2	11	3	0	.273
1980 KC A	0	0	—	0.00	8	0	0	13	8	5	4	0	0	0	1	0	0	0	—
1981	1	1	.500	4.22	22	0	0	32	35	14	7	0	1	1	2	0	0	0	—
14 yrs.	83	85	.494	3.93	349	184	51	1526	1490	562	807	9	11	13	11	*			

LEAGUE CHAMPIONSHIP SERIES

	W	L	PCT	ERA	G	GS	CG	IP	H	BB	SO	ShO	W	L	SV	AB	H	HR	BA
1974 PIT N	0	0	—	7.71	1	0	0	2.1	3	2	1	0	0	0	0	1	0	0	.000
1975	0	0	—	0.00	2	0	0	2.1	1	0	1	0	0	0	0	0	0	0	—
2 yrs.	0	0	—	3.86	3	0	0	4.2	4	2	2	0	0	0	0	1	0	0	.000

WORLD SERIES

	W	L	PCT	ERA	G	GS	CG	IP	H	BB	SO	ShO	W	L	SV	AB	H	HR	BA
1967 BOS A	0	0	—	0.00	2	0	0	1.1	0	1	1	0	0	0	0	0	0	0	—

Marv Breuer

BREUER, MARVIN HOWARD (Baby Face)
B. Apr. 29, 1914, Rolla, Mo.
BR TR 6'2" 185 lbs.

	W	L	PCT	ERA	G	GS	CG	IP	H	BB	SO	ShO	W	L	SV	AB	H	HR	BA
1939 NY A	0	0	—	9.00	1	0	0	1	2	1	0	0	0	0	0	0	0	0	—
1940	8	9	.471	4.55	27	22	10	164	175	61	71	0	1	0	0	54	2	0	.037
1941	9	7	.563	4.09	26	18	7	141	131	49	77	1	2	1	2	46	4	0	.087
1942	8	9	.471	3.07	27	19	6	164.1	157	37	72	0	2	2	1	54	3	0	.056
1943	0	1	.000	8.36	5	1	0	14	22	6	6	0	0	0	0	3	1	0	.333
5 yrs.	25	26	.490	4.03	86	60	23	484.1	487	154	226	1	5	3	3	157	10	0	.064

WORLD SERIES

	W	L	PCT	ERA	G	GS	CG	IP	H	BB	SO	ShO	W	L	SV	AB	H	HR	BA
1941 NY A	0	0	—	0.00	1	0	0	3	3	1	2	0	0	0	0	1	0	0	.000

	W	L	PCT	ERA	G	GS	CG	IP	H	BB	SO	ShO	Relief Pitching W	L	SV	BATTING AB	H	HR	BA

Marv Breuer continued

	W	L	PCT	ERA	G	GS	CG	IP	H	BB	SO	ShO	W	L	SV	AB	H	HR	BA
1942	0	0	—	0.00	1	0	0	2	0	0	0	0	0	0	0	0	0	0	—
2 yrs.	0	0	—	0.00	2	0	0	3	5	1	2	0	0	0	0	1	0	0	.000

Jack Brewer

BREWER, JOHN HERNDON (Buddy)
B. July 21, 1919, Los Angeles, Calif.　　　BR TR 6'2"　170 lbs.

	W	L	PCT	ERA	G	GS	CG	IP	H	BB	SO	ShO	W	L	SV	AB	H	HR	BA
1944 NY N	1	4	.200	5.56	14	7	2	55	66	16	21	0	0	0	0	19	4	0	.211
1945	8	6	.571	3.83	28	21	8	159.2	162	58	49	0	0	1	0	56	10	0	.179
1946	0	0	—	13.50	1	0	0	2	3	2	3	0	0	0	0	0	0	0	—
3 yrs.	9	10	.474	4.36	43	28	10	216.2	231	76	73	0	0	1	0	75	14	0	.187

Jim Brewer

BREWER, JAMES THOMAS
B. Nov. 14, 1937, Merced, Calif.　　　BL TL 6'1"　186 lbs.

	W	L	PCT	ERA	G	GS	CG	IP	H	BB	SO	ShO	W	L	SV	AB	H	HR	BA
1960 CHI N	0	3	.000	5.82	5	4	0	21.2	25	6	7	0	0	0	0	6	1	0	.167
1961	1	7	.125	5.82	36	11	0	86.2	116	21	57	0	0	1	0	22	4	0	.182
1962	0	1	.000	9.53	6	1	0	5.2	10	3	1	0	0	1	0	0	0	0	—
1963	3	2	.600	4.89	29	1	0	49.2	59	15	35	0	3	1	0	6	0	0	.000
1964 LA N	4	3	.571	3.00	34	5	1	93	79	25	63	1	2	2	1	22	6	0	.273
1965	3	2	.600	1.82	19	2	0	49.1	33	28	31	0	3	1	2	10	0	0	.000
1966	0	2	.000	3.68	13	0	0	22	17	11	8	0	0	2	2	0	0	0	—
1967	5	4	.556	2.68	30	11	0	100.2	78	31	74	0	1	0	1	22	1	0	.045
1968	8	3	.727	2.49	54	0	0	76	59	33	75	0	8	3	14	9	2	0	.222
1969	7	6	.538	2.56	59	0	0	88	71	41	92	0	7	6	20	11	1	0	.091
1970	7	6	.538	3.13	58	0	0	89	66	33	91	0	7	6	24	12	1	0	.083
1971	6	5	.545	1.89	55	0	0	81	55	24	66	0	6	5	22	9	3	0	.333
1972	8	7	.533	1.26	51	0	0	78.1	41	25	69	0	8	7	17	1	0	0	.000
1973	6	8	.429	3.01	56	0	0	71.2	58	25	56	0	6	8	20	5	2	0	.400
1974	4	4	.500	2.54	24	0	0	39	29	10	26	0	4	4	0	2	0	0	.000
1975 2 teams			LA	N	(21G	3–1)		CAL	A	(21G	1–0)								
" total	4	1	.800	3.46	42	0	0	67.2	82	23	43	0	4	1	7	3	0	0	.000
1976 CAL A	3	1	.750	2.70	13	0	0	20	20	6	16	0	3	1	2	0	0	0	—
17 yrs.	69	65	.515	3.07	584	35	1	1039.1	898	360	810	1	62	49	132	140	21	0	.150

WORLD SERIES

	W	L	PCT	ERA	G	GS	CG	IP	H	BB	SO	ShO	W	L	SV	AB	H	HR	BA
1965 LA N	0	0	—	4.50	1	0	0	2	3	0	1	0	0	0	0	0	0	0	—
1966	0	0	—	0.00	1	0	0	1	0	0	1	0	0	0	0	0	0	0	—
1974	0	0	—	0.00	1	0	0	.1	0	0	1	0	0	0	0	0	0	0	—
3 yrs.	0	0	—	2.70	3	0	0	3.1	3	0	3	0	0	0	0	0	0	0	—

Tom Brewer

BREWER, THOMAS AUSTIN
B. Sept. 3, 1931, Wadesboro, N. C.　　　BR TR 6'1"　175 lbs.

	W	L	PCT	ERA	G	GS	CG	IP	H	BB	SO	ShO	W	L	SV	AB	H	HR	BA
1954 BOS A	10	9	.526	4.65	33	23	7	162.2	152	95	69	0	0	0	0	60	16	0	.267
1955	11	10	.524	4.20	31	28	9	192.2	198	87	91	2	1	0	0	73	11	0	.151
1956	19	9	.679	3.50	32	32	15	244.1	200	112	127	4	0	0	0	94	28	1	.298
1957	16	13	.552	3.85	32	32	15	238.1	225	93	128	2	0	0	0	94	19	0	.202
1958	12	12	.500	3.72	33	32	10	227.1	227	93	124	1	1	0	0	82	16	0	.195
1959	10	12	.455	3.76	36	32	11	215.1	219	88	121	3	0	0	2	72	8	1	.111
1960	10	15	.400	4.82	34	29	8	186.2	220	72	60	1	0	1	1	62	12	1	.194
1961	3	2	.600	3.43	10	9	0	42	37	29	13	0	0	0	0	14	4	0	.286
8 yrs.	91	82	.526	4.00	241	217	75	1509.1	1478	669	733	13	2	1	3	551	114	3	.207

Alan Brice

BRICE, ALAN HEALEY
B. Oct. 1, 1937, New York, N. Y.　　　BR TR 6'5"　215 lbs.

	W	L	PCT	ERA	G	GS	CG	IP	H	BB	SO	ShO	W	L	SV	AB	H	HR	BA
1961 CHI A	0	1	.000	0.00	3	0	0	3.1	4	3	3	0	0	1	0	0	0	0	—

Ralph Brickner

BRICKNER, RALPH HAROLD (Brick)
B. May 2, 1925, Cincinnati, Ohio　　　BR TR 6'3½" 215 lbs.

	W	L	PCT	ERA	G	GS	CG	IP	H	BB	SO	ShO	W	L	SV	AB	H	HR	BA
1952 BOS A	3	1	.750	2.18	14	1	0	33	32	11	9	0	3	1	1	8	2	0	.250

Marshall Bridges

BRIDGES, MARSHALL (Sheriff)
B. June 2, 1931, Jackson, Miss.　　　BR TL 6'1"　165 lbs.
BB 1959-61

	W	L	PCT	ERA	G	GS	CG	IP	H	BB	SO	ShO	W	L	SV	AB	H	HR	BA
1959 STL N	6	3	.667	4.26	27	4	1	76	67	37	76	0	4	2	1	23	5	1	.217
1960 2 teams			STL	N	(20G	2–2)		CIN	N	(14G	4–0)								
" total	6	2	.750	2.38	34	0	0	56.2	47	23	53	0	6	1	3	10	1	0	.100
1961 CIN N	0	1	.000	7.84	13	0	0	20.2	26	11	17	0	0	1	0	2	0	0	.000
1962 NY A	8	4	.667	3.14	52	0	0	71.2	49	48	66	0	8	4	18	14	0	0	.000
1963	2	0	1.000	3.82	23	0	0	33	27	30	35	0	2	0	1	0	0	0	—
1964 WAS A	0	3	.000	5.70	17	0	0	30	37	17	16	0	0	3	2	3	0	0	.000
1965	1	2	.333	2.67	40	0	0	57.1	62	25	39	0	1	2	0	7	1	0	.143
7 yrs.	23	15	.605	3.75	206	5	1	345.1	315	191	302	0	21	13	25	59	7	1	.119

WORLD SERIES

	W	L	PCT	ERA	G	GS	CG	IP	H	BB	SO	ShO	W	L	SV	AB	H	HR	BA
1962 NY A	0	0	—	4.91	2	0	0	3.2	4	2	3	0	0	0	0	0	0	0	—

Tommy Bridges

BRIDGES, THOMAS JEFFERSON DAVIS
B. Dec. 28, 1906, Gordonsville, Tenn.　D. Apr. 19, 1968, Nashville, Tenn.　BR TR 5'10½" 155 lbs.

	W	L	PCT	ERA	G	GS	CG	IP	H	BB	SO	ShO	W	L	SV	AB	H	HR	BA
1930 DET A	3	2	.600	4.06	8	5	2	37.2	28	23	17	0	0	0	0	10	3	0	.300
1931	8	16	.333	4.99	35	23	15	173	182	108	105	2	1	2	0	54	8	0	.148
1932	14	12	.538	3.36	34	26	10	201	174	119	108	4	2	2	1	67	11	0	.164
1933	14	12	.538	3.09	33	28	17	233	192	110	120	2	1	0	2	78	16	0	.205
1934	22	11	.667	3.67	36	35	23	275	249	104	151	3	0	0	1	98	12	0	.122
1935	21	10	.677	3.51	36	34	23	274.1	277	113	163	4	0	1	1	109	26	0	.239
1936	23	11	.676	3.60	39	38	26	294.2	289	115	175	3	0	0	0	118	25	0	.212
1937	15	12	.556	4.07	34	31	18	245.1	267	91	138	3	1	0	0	96	23	0	.240
1938	13	9	.591	4.59	25	20	13	151	171	58	101	0	1	3	1	54	7	0	.130
1939	17	7	.708	3.50	29	26	16	198	186	61	129	2	0	0	2	71	14	0	.197
1940	12	9	.571	3.37	29	28	12	197.2	171	88	133	2	1	0	0	68	12	0	.176

	W	L	PCT	ERA	G	GS	CG	IP	H	BB	SO	ShO	Relief Pitching W	L	SV	BATTING AB	H	HR	BA

Tommy Bridges continued

	W	L	PCT	ERA	G	GS	CG	IP	H	BB	SO	ShO	W	L	SV	AB	H	HR	BA
1941	9	12	.429	3.41	25	22	10	147.2	128	70	90	1	1	0	0	47	4	0	.085
1942	9	7	.563	2.74	23	22	11	174	164	61	97	2	0	0	1	63	6	0	.095
1943	12	7	.632	2.39	25	22	11	191.2	159	61	124	3	0	1	0	64	14	0	.219
1945	1	0	1.000	3.27	4	1	0	11	14	2	6	0	0	0	0	3	0	0	.000
1946	1	1	.500	5.91	9	1	0	21.1	24	8	17	0	0	1	1	3	0	0	.000
16 yrs.	194	138	.584	3.57	424	362	207	2826.1	2675	1192	1674	33	8	10	10	1003	181	0	.180

WORLD SERIES

	W	L	PCT	ERA	G	GS	CG	IP	H	BB	SO	ShO	W	L	SV	AB	H	HR	BA
1934 DET A	1	1	.500	3.63	3	2	1	17.1	21	1	12	0	0	0	0	7	1	0	.143
1935	2	0	1.000	2.50	2	2	2	18	18	4	9	0	0	0	0	8	1	0	.125
1940	1	0	1.000	3.00	1	1	1	9	10	1	5	0	0	0	0	3	0	0	.000
1945	0	0	–	16.20	1	0	0	1.2	3	3	1	0	0	0	0	0	0	0	–
4 yrs.	4	1	.800	3.52	7	5	4	46	52	9	27	0	0	0	0	18	2	0	.111

Buttons Briggs

BRIGGS, HERBERT THEODORE   BR TR 6'1"   180 lbs.
B. July 8, 1875, Poughkeepsie, N. Y.   D. Feb. 18, 1911, Cleveland, Ohio

	W	L	PCT	ERA	G	GS	CG	IP	H	BB	SO	ShO	W	L	SV	AB	H	HR	BA
1896 CHI N	12	8	.600	4.31	26	21	19	194	202	108	84	0	0	1	1	78	10	0	.128
1897	4	17	.190	5.26	22	22	21	186.2	246	85	60	0	0	0	0	81	13	0	.160
1898	1	3	.250	5.70	4	4	3	30	38	10	14	0	0	0	0	14	6	0	.429
1904	19	11	.633	2.05	34	30	28	277	252	77	112	3	1	0	2	94	16	1	.170
1905	8	8	.500	2.14	20	20	13	168	141	52	68	5	0	0	0	57	3	0	.053
5 yrs.	44	47	.484	3.41	106	97	84	855.2	879	332	338	8	1	1	3	324	48	1	.148

Johnny Briggs

BRIGGS, JONATHAN TIFT   BR TR 5'10"   175 lbs.
B. Jan. 24, 1934, Natoma, Calif.

	W	L	PCT	ERA	G	GS	CG	IP	H	BB	SO	ShO	W	L	SV	AB	H	HR	BA
1956 CHI N	0	0	–	1.69	3	0	0	5.1	5	4	1	0	0	0	0	0	0	0	–
1957	0	1	.000	12.46	3	0	0	4.1	7	3	1	0	0	1	0	0	0	0	–
1958	5	5	.500	4.52	20	17	3	95.2	99	45	46	1	0	0	0	35	9	0	.257
1959 CLE A	0	1	.000	2.13	4	1	0	12.2	12	3	5	0	0	0	0	2	0	0	.000
1960 2 teams			CLE A (21G 4–2)		KC	A	(8G 0–2)												
" total	4	4	.500	6.42	29	3	0	47.2	51	27	27	0	1	2	1	11	1	0	.091
5 yrs.	9	11	.450	5.00	59	21	3	165.2	174	82	80	1	1	3	1	48	10	0	.208

Nellie Briles

BRILES, NELSON KELLEY   BR TR 5'11"   195 lbs.
B. Aug. 5, 1943, Dorris, Calif.

	W	L	PCT	ERA	G	GS	CG	IP	H	BB	SO	ShO	W	L	SV	AB	H	HR	BA
1965 STL N	3	3	.500	3.50	37	2	0	82.1	79	26	52	0	2	2	4	15	2	0	.133
1966	4	15	.211	3.21	49	17	0	154	162	54	100	0	1	6	6	38	3	0	.079
1967	14	5	.737	2.43	49	14	6	155.1	139	40	94	2	4	3	6	40	6	0	.150
1968	19	11	.633	2.81	33	33	13	243.2	251	55	141	4	0	0	0	80	11	0	.138
1969	15	13	.536	3.51	36	33	10	228	218	63	126	3	0	0	0	76	8	1	.105
1970	6	7	.462	6.22	30	19	1	107	129	36	59	1	1	2	0	39	7	0	.179
1971 PIT N	8	4	.667	3.04	37	14	4	136	131	35	76	2	1	2	1	39	10	1	.256
1972	14	11	.560	3.08	28	27	9	195.2	185	43	120	2	1	0	0	70	11	0	.157
1973	14	13	.519	2.84	33	33	7	218.2	201	51	94	1	0	0	0	72	14	1	.194
1974 KC A	5	7	.417	4.02	18	17	3	103	118	21	41	0	0	0	0	0	0	0	–
1975	6	6	.500	4.26	24	16	3	112	127	25	73	0	1	0	2	0	0	0	–
1976 TEX A	11	9	.550	3.26	32	31	7	210	224	47	98	1	0	0	1	0	0	0	–
1977 2 teams			TEX A (30G 6–4)		BAL	A	(2G 0–0)												
" total	6	4	.600	4.17	32	15	2	112.1	119	30	59	1	2	0	2	0	0	0	–
1978 BAL A	4	4	.500	4.64	16	8	1	54.1	58	21	30	0	3	0	0	0	0	0	–
14 yrs.	129	112	.535	3.43	454	279	64	2112.1	2141	547	1163	17	16	15	22	469	72	3	.154

LEAGUE CHAMPIONSHIP SERIES

	W	L	PCT	ERA	G	GS	CG	IP	H	BB	SO	ShO	W	L	SV	AB	H	HR	BA
1972 PIT N	0	0	–	3.00	1	1	0	6	6	1	3	0	0	0	0	0	0	0	.000

WORLD SERIES

	W	L	PCT	ERA	G	GS	CG	IP	H	BB	SO	ShO	W	L	SV	AB	H	HR	BA
1967 STL N	1	0	1.000	1.64	2	1	1	11	7	1	4	0	0	0	0	3	0	0	.000
1968	0	1	.000	5.56	2	2	0	11.1	13	4	7	0	0	0	0	4	0	0	.000
1971 PIT N	1	0	1.000	0.00	1	1	1	9	2	2	2	1	0	0	0	2	1	0	.500
3 yrs.	2	1	.667	2.59	5	4	2	31.1	22	7	13	1	0	0	0	9	1	0	.111

Frank Brill

BRILL, FRANCIS HASBROUCK   BR TR 6'1"   180 lbs.
Born Francis Hasbrouck Briell.
B. Mar. 30, 1864, Astoria, N. Y.   D. Nov. 19, 1944, Flushing, N. Y.

	W	L	PCT	ERA	G	GS	CG	IP	H	BB	SO	ShO	W	L	SV	AB	H	HR	BA
1884 DET N	2	10	.167	5.50	12	12	12	103	148	26	18	1	0	0	0	44	6	0	.136

Jim Brillheart

BRILLHEART, JAMES BENSON (Buck)   BR TL 5'11"   170 lbs.
B. Sept. 28, 1903, Dublin, Va.   D. Sept. 2, 1972, Radford, Va.

	W	L	PCT	ERA	G	GS	CG	IP	H	BB	SO	ShO	W	L	SV	AB	H	HR	BA
1922 WAS A	4	6	.400	3.61	31	10	3	119.2	120	72	47	0	0	2	1	36	3	0	.083
1923	0	1	.000	7.00	12	0	0	18	27	12	8	0	0	1	0	2	0	0	.000
1927 CHI N	4	2	.667	4.13	32	12	4	128.2	140	38	36	0	0	0	0	44	1	0	.023
1931 BOS A	0	0	–	5.49	11	1	0	19.2	27	15	7	0	0	0	0	4	2	1	.500
4 yrs.	8	9	.471	4.19	86	23	7	286	314	137	98	0	0	3	1	86	6	1	.070

Lou Brissie

BRISSIE, LELAND VICTOR   BL TL 6'4½"   210 lbs.
B. June 5, 1924, Anderson, S. C.

	W	L	PCT	ERA	G	GS	CG	IP	H	BB	SO	ShO	W	L	SV	AB	H	HR	BA
1947 PHI A	0	1	.000	6.43	1	1	0	7	9	5	4	0	0	0	0	2	0	0	.000
1948	14	10	.583	4.13	39	26	11	194	202	95	127	0	4	2	5	76	18	0	.237
1949	16	11	.593	4.28	34	29	18	229.1	220	118	118	0	1	0	3	90	24	0	.267
1950	7	19	.269	4.02	46	31	15	246	237	117	101	2	0	1	8	87	15	0	.172
1951 2 teams			PHI A (2G 0–2)		CLE	A	(54G 4–3)												
" total	4	5	.444	3.58	56	6	1	125.2	110	69	53	0	3	1	9	28	7	0	.250
1952 CLE A	3	2	.600	3.48	42	1	0	82.2	68	34	28	0	3	1	2	12	3	0	.250
1953	0	0	–	7.62	16	0	0	13	21	13	5	0	0	0	2	0	0	0	–
7 yrs.	44	48	.478	4.07	234	93	45	897.2	867	451	436	2	11	5	29	295	67	0	.227

	W	L	PCT	ERA	G	GS	CG	IP	H	BB	SO	ShO	Relief Pitching W	L	SV	BATTING AB	H	HR	BA

John Brittin

BRITTIN, JOHN ALBERT
B. Mar. 4, 1924, Athens, Ill.
BR TR 5'11" 175 lbs.

	W	L	PCT	ERA	G	GS	CG	IP	H	BB	SO	ShO	W	L	SV	AB	H	HR	BA
1950 PHI N	0	0	–	4.50	3	0	0	4	2	3	3	0	0	0	0	0	0	0	–
1951	0	0	–	9.00	3	0	0	4	5	6	3	0	0	0	0	0	0	0	–
2 yrs.	0	0	–	6.75	6	0	0	8	7	9	6	0	0	0	0	0	0	0	–

Jim Britton

BRITTON, JAMES ALAN
B. Mar. 25, 1944, North Tonawanda, N. Y.
BR TR 6'5" 225 lbs.

	W	L	PCT	ERA	G	GS	CG	IP	H	BB	SO	ShO	W	L	SV	AB	H	HR	BA
1967 ATL N	0	2	.000	6.08	2	2	0	13.1	15	2	4	0	0	0	0	4	0	0	.000
1968	4	6	.400	3.09	34	9	2	90.1	81	34	61	2	2	2	3	21	3	0	.143
1969	7	5	.583	3.78	24	13	2	88	69	49	60	1	0	0	1	21	4	0	.190
1971 MON N	2	3	.400	5.67	16	6	0	46	49	27	23	0	1	0	0	9	0	0	.000
4 yrs.	13	16	.448	4.01	76	30	4	237.2	214	112	148	3	3	2	4	55	7	0	.127
LEAGUE CHAMPIONSHIP SERIES																			
1969 ATL N	0	0	–	0.00	1	0	0	.1	0	1	0	0	0	0	0	0	0	0	–

Tony Brizzolara

BRIZZOLARA, ANTHONY JOHN
B. Jan. 14, 1957, Santa Monica, Calif.
BR TR 6'5" 215 lbs.

	W	L	PCT	ERA	G	GS	CG	IP	H	BB	SO	ShO	W	L	SV	AB	H	HR	BA
1979 ATL N	6	9	.400	5.30	20	19	2	107	133	33	64	0	0	0	0	35	1	0	.029
1983	1	0	1.000	3.54	14	0	0	20.1	22	6	17	0	1	0	1	0	0	0	–
1984	1	2	.333	5.28	10	4	0	29	33	13	17	0	0	1	0	7	0	0	.000
3 yrs.	8	11	.421	5.07	44	23	2	156.1	188	52	98	0	1	1	1	42	1	0	.024

Johnny Broaca

BROACA, JOHN JOSEPH
B. Oct. 3, 1909, Lawrence, Mass.
BR TR 5'11" 190 lbs.

	W	L	PCT	ERA	G	GS	CG	IP	H	BB	SO	ShO	W	L	SV	AB	H	HR	BA
1934 NY A	12	9	.571	4.16	26	24	13	177.1	203	65	74	1	0	0	0	66	2	0	.030
1935	15	7	.682	3.58	29	27	14	201	199	79	78	2	1	1	0	80	12	0	.150
1936	12	7	.632	4.24	37	27	12	206	235	66	84	1	0	0	3	82	9	0	.110
1937	1	4	.200	4.70	7	6	3	44	58	17	9	0	0	0	0	14	0	0	.000
1939 CLE A	4	2	.667	4.70	22	2	0	46	53	28	13	0	4	1	0	12	0	0	.000
5 yrs.	44	29	.603	4.08	121	86	42	674.1	748	255	258	4	5	2	3	254	23	0	.091

Pete Broberg

BROBERG, PETER SVEN
B. Mar. 2, 1950, West Palm Beach, Fla.
BR TR 6'3" 205 lbs.

	W	L	PCT	ERA	G	GS	CG	IP	H	BB	SO	ShO	W	L	SV	AB	H	HR	BA
1971 WAS A	5	9	.357	3.46	18	18	7	125	104	53	89	1	0	0	0	44	5	1	.114
1972 TEX A	5	12	.294	4.30	39	25	3	175.2	153	85	133	2	0	0	1	51	4	0	.078
1973	5	9	.357	5.60	22	20	6	119	130	66	57	1	0	0	0	0	0	0	–
1974	0	4	.000	8.07	12	2	0	29	29	13	15	0	0	2	0	0	0	0	–
1975 MIL A	14	16	.467	4.13	38	32	7	220.1	219	106	100	2	2	0	0	0	0	0	–
1976	1	7	.125	4.97	20	11	1	92.1	99	72	28	0	0	0	0	0	0	0	–
1977 CHI N	1	2	.333	4.75	22	0	0	36	34	18	20	0	1	2	0	6	0	0	.000
1978 OAK A	10	12	.455	4.62	35	26	2	165.2	174	65	94	0	2	1	0	0	0	0	–
8 yrs.	41	71	.366	4.56	206	134	26	963	942	478	536	6	5	5	1	101	9	1	.089

Lew Brockett

BROCKETT, LEWIS ALBERT (King)
B. July 23, 1880, Brownsville, Ill. D. Sept. 19, 1960, Norris City, Ill.
BR TR 5'10½" 168 lbs.

	W	L	PCT	ERA	G	GS	CG	IP	H	BB	SO	ShO	W	L	SV	AB	H	HR	BA
1907 NY A	1	2	.333	6.22	8	4	1	46.1	58	26	13	0	0	0	0	22	4	0	.182
1909	10	8	.556	2.37	26	18	10	152	148	59	70	3	2	0	1	60	17	0	.283
1911	2	4	.333	4.66	16	8	2	75.1	73	39	25	0	1	1	0	39	12	0	.308
3 yrs.	13	14	.481	3.65	50	30	13	273.2	279	124	108	3	3	1	1	121	33	0	.273

Dick Brodowski

BRODOWSKI, RICHARD STANLEY
B. July 26, 1932, Bayonne, N. J.
BR TR 6'1" 182 lbs.

	W	L	PCT	ERA	G	GS	CG	IP	H	BB	SO	ShO	W	L	SV	AB	H	HR	BA
1952 BOS A	5	5	.500	4.40	20	12	4	114.2	111	50	42	0	0	1	0	39	8	1	.205
1955	1	0	1.000	5.63	16	0	0	32	36	25	10	0	1	0	0	10	5	1	.500
1956 WAS A	0	3	.000	9.17	7	3	1	17.2	31	12	8	0	0	0	0	5	0	0	.000
1957	0	1	.000	11.12	6	0	0	11.1	12	10	4	0	0	1	0	1	0	0	.000
1958 CLE A	1	0	1.000	0.00	5	0	0	10	3	6	12	0	1	0	0	1	0	0	.000
1959	2	2	.500	1.80	18	0	0	30	19	21	9	0	2	2	5	6	2	0	.333
6 yrs.	9	11	.450	4.76	72	15	5	215.2	212	124	85	0	4	4	5	62	15	2	.242

Ernie Broglio

BROGLIO, ERNEST GILBERT
B. Aug. 27, 1935, Berkeley, Calif.
BR TR 6'2" 200 lbs.

	W	L	PCT	ERA	G	GS	CG	IP	H	BB	SO	ShO	W	L	SV	AB	H	HR	BA
1959 STL N	7	12	.368	4.72	35	25	6	181.1	174	89	133	3	0	3	0	61	6	0	.098
1960	21	9	.700	2.74	52	24	9	226.1	172	100	188	3	7	2	0	68	14	0	.206
1961	9	12	.429	4.12	29	26	7	174.2	166	75	113	2	0	1	0	62	9	0	.145
1962	12	9	.571	3.00	34	30	11	222.1	193	93	132	4	1	1	0	72	10	0	.139
1963	18	8	.692	2.99	39	35	11	250	202	90	145	5	2	1	0	89	10	0	.112
1964 2 teams				STL	N	(11G 3–5)		CHI	N	(18G 4–7)									
" total	7	12	.368	3.82	29	27	6	169.2	176	56	82	1	0	0	1	56	12	0	.214
1965 CHI N	1	6	.143	6.93	26	6	0	50.2	63	46	22	0	1	3	0	4	0	0	.000
1966	2	6	.250	6.35	15	11	2	62.1	70	38	34	0	0	0	1	19	7	0	.368
8 yrs.	77	74	.510	3.74	259	184	52	1337.1	1216	587	849	18	11	11	2	431	68	0	.158

Ken Brondell

BRONDELL, KENNETH LeROY
B. Oct. 17, 1921, Bradshaw, Neb.
BR TR 6'1" 195 lbs.

	W	L	PCT	ERA	G	GS	CG	IP	H	BB	SO	ShO	W	L	SV	AB	H	HR	BA
1944 NY N	0	1	.000	8.38	7	2	1	19.1	27	8	1	0	0	0	0	4	0	0	.000

Jim Bronstad

BRONSTAD, JAMES WARREN
B. June 22, 1936, Fort Worth, Tex.
BR TR 6'3" 196 lbs.

	W	L	PCT	ERA	G	GS	CG	IP	H	BB	SO	ShO	W	L	SV	AB	H	HR	BA
1959 NY A	0	3	.000	5.22	16	3	0	29.1	34	13	14	0	0	1	2	5	0	0	.000
1963 WAS A	1	3	.250	5.65	25	0	0	57.1	66	22	22	0	1	3	1	12	0	0	.000
1964	0	1	.000	5.14	4	0	0	7	10	2	9	0	0	1	0	0	0	0	–
3 yrs.	1	7	.125	5.48	45	3	0	93.2	110	37	45	0	1	5	3	17	0	0	.000

	W	L	PCT	ERA	G	GS	CG	IP	H	BB	SO	ShO	Relief Pitching W	L	SV	BATTING AB	H	HR	BA

Ed Brookens

BROOKENS, EDWARD DWAIN (Ike)
B. Nov. 3, 1949, Chambersburg, Pa.   BR TR 6'5"   170 lbs.

	W	L	PCT	ERA	G	GS	CG	IP	H	BB	SO	ShO	W	L	SV	AB	H	HR	BA
1975 DET A	0	0	–	5.40	3	0	0	10	11	5	8	0	0	0	0	0	0	0	–

Harry Brooks

BROOKS, HARRY FRANK
B. Nov. 30, 1865, Philadelphia, Pa.   D. Dec. 5, 1945, Philadelphia, Pa.

	W	L	PCT	ERA	G	GS	CG	IP	H	BB	SO	ShO	W	L	SV	AB	H	HR	BA
1886 NY AA	0	1	.000	36.00	1	1	0	2	9	2	0	0	0	0	0	1	0	0	.000

Jim Brosnan

BROSNAN, JAMES PATRICK (Professor)
B. Oct. 24, 1929, Cincinnati, Ohio   BR TR 6'4"   197 lbs.

	W	L	PCT	ERA	G	GS	CG	IP	H	BB	SO	ShO	W	L	SV	AB	H	HR	BA
1954 CHI N	1	0	1.000	9.45	18	0	0	33.1	44	18	17	0	1	0	0	8	1	0	.125
1956	5	9	.357	3.79	30	10	1	95	95	45	51	1	3	4	1	22	4	0	.182
1957	5	5	.500	3.38	41	5	1	98.2	79	46	73	0	4	4	0	20	5	0	.250
1958 2 teams			CHI N (8G 3–4)				STL N (33G 8–4)												
" total	11	8	.579	3.35	41	20	4	166.2	148	79	89	0	4	1	7	50	5	0	.100
1959 2 teams			STL N (20G 1–3)				CIN N (26G 8–3)												
" total	9	6	.600	3.79	46	10	1	116.1	113	41	74	1	5	3	4	30	3	0	.100
1960 CIN N	7	2	.778	2.36	57	2	0	99	79	22	62	0	7	2	12	15	3	1	.200
1961	10	4	.714	3.04	53	0	0	80	77	18	40	0	10	4	16	13	2	0	.154
1962	4	4	.500	3.34	48	0	0	64.2	76	18	51	0	4	4	13	6	0	0	.000
1963 2 teams			CIN N (6G 0–1)				CHI A (45G 3–8)												
" total	3	9	.250	3.13	51	0	0	77.2	79	25	50	0	3	9	14	13	4	0	.308
9 yrs.	55	47	.539	3.54	385	47	7	831.1	790	312	507	2	41	31	67	177	27	1	.153

WORLD SERIES

	W	L	PCT	ERA	G	GS	CG	IP	H	BB	SO	ShO	W	L	SV	AB	H	HR	BA
1961 CIN N	0	0	–	7.50	3	0	0	6	9	4	5	0	0	0	0	0	0	0	–

Frank Brosseau

BROSSEAU, FRANKLIN LEE
B. July 31, 1944, Drayton, N. D.   BR TR 6'1"   180 lbs.

	W	L	PCT	ERA	G	GS	CG	IP	H	BB	SO	ShO	W	L	SV	AB	H	HR	BA
1969 PIT N	0	0	–	9.00	2	0	0	2	2	2	2	0	0	0	0	0	0	0	–
1971	0	0	–	0.00	1	0	0	2	1	0	0	0	0	0	0	0	0	0	–
2 yrs.	0	0	–	4.50	3	0	0	4	3	2	2	0	0	0	0	0	0	0	–

Dan Brouthers

BROUTHERS, DENNIS JOSEPH (Big Dan)
B. May 8, 1858, Sylvan Lake, N. Y.   D. Aug. 2, 1932, East Orange, N. J.
Hall of Fame 1945.   BL TL 6'2"   207 lbs.

	W	L	PCT	ERA	G	GS	CG	IP	H	BB	SO	ShO	W	L	SV	AB	H	HR	BA
1879 TRO N	0	2	.000	5.57	3	2	2	21	35	8	6	0	0	0	0	168	46	4	.274
1883 BUF N	0	0	–	31.50	1	0	0	2	9	3	2	0	0	0	0	425	159	3	.374
2 yrs.	0	2	.000	7.83	4	2	2	23	44	11	8	0	0	0	0	*			

Frank Brower

BROWER, FRANCIS WILLARD (Turkeyfoot)
B. Mar. 26, 1893, Gainesville, Va.   D. Nov. 20, 1960, Baltimore, Md.   BL TR 6'2"   180 lbs.

	W	L	PCT	ERA	G	GS	CG	IP	H	BB	SO	ShO	W	L	SV	AB	H	HR	BA
1924 CLE A	0	0	–	0.93	4	0	0	9.2	7	4	0	0	0	0	0	*			

Alton Brown

BROWN, ALTON LEO (Deacon)
B. Apr. 16, 1925, Norfolk, Va.   BR TR 6'2"   195 lbs.

	W	L	PCT	ERA	G	GS	CG	IP	H	BB	SO	ShO	W	L	SV	AB	H	HR	BA
1951 WAS A	0	0	–	9.26	7	0	0	11.2	14	12	7	0	0	0	0	1	0	0	.000

Boardwalk Brown

BROWN, CARROLL WILLIAM
B. Feb. 20, 1889, Woodbury, N. J.   D. Feb. 8, 1977, Burlington, N. J.   BR TR 6'2"   195 lbs.

	W	L	PCT	ERA	G	GS	CG	IP	H	BB	SO	ShO	W	L	SV	AB	H	HR	BA
1911 PHI A	0	1	.000	4.50	2	1	1	12	12	2	6	0	0	0	0	4	0	0	.000
1912	13	11	.542	3.66	34	24	16	199	204	87	64	3	2	2	1	76	11	0	.145
1913	17	11	.607	2.94	43	35	11	235.1	200	87	70	3	1	3	1	82	13	1	.159
1914 2 teams			PHI A (15G 1–6)				NY A (20G 5–5)												
" total	6	11	.353	3.54	35	22	10	188.1	187	68	77	0	1	1	1	64	8	0	.125
1915 NY A	2	6	.250	4.10	19	10	5	96.2	95	47	34	0	0	0	1	32	6	0	.188
5 yrs.	38	40	.487	3.47	133	92	43	731.1	698	291	251	6	4	6	4	258	38	1	.147

Bob Brown

BROWN, ROBERT M.
B. 1891   BR TR 5'6"   165 lbs.

	W	L	PCT	ERA	G	GS	CG	IP	H	BB	SO	ShO	W	L	SV	AB	H	HR	BA
1914 BUF F	1	0	1.000	3.44	15	1	0	36.2	39	16	13	0	1	0	2	9	2	0	.222

Bob Brown

BROWN, ROBERT MURRAY
B. Apr. 1, 1911, Dorchester, Mass.   BR TR 6'1"   190 lbs.

	W	L	PCT	ERA	G	GS	CG	IP	H	BB	SO	ShO	W	L	SV	AB	H	HR	BA
1930 BOS N	0	0	–	10.50	3	0	0	6	10	8	1	0	0	0	0	2	0	0	.000
1931	0	1	.000	8.53	3	1	0	6.1	9	3	2	0	0	0	0	2	1	0	.500
1932	14	7	.667	3.30	35	28	9	213	187	104	110	0	3	0	1	67	13	0	.194
1933	0	0	–	2.70	5	0	0	6.2	6	3	3	0	0	0	0	2	0	0	.000
1934	1	3	.250	5.71	16	8	2	58.1	59	36	21	1	0	0	0	21	5	0	.238
1935	1	8	.111	6.37	15	10	2	65	79	36	17	1	0	1	0	19	2	0	.105
1936	0	2	.000	5.40	2	2	0	8.1	10	3	5	0	0	0	0	2	0	0	.000
7 yrs.	16	21	.432	4.48	79	49	13	363.2	360	193	159	2	3	1	1	115	21	0	.183

Buster Brown

BROWN, CHARLES EDWARD
B. Aug. 31, 1881, Boone, Iowa   D. Feb. 9, 1914, Sioux City, Iowa   BR TR

	W	L	PCT	ERA	G	GS	CG	IP	H	BB	SO	ShO	W	L	SV	AB	H	HR	BA
1905 STL N	8	11	.421	2.97	23	21	17	179	172	62	57	0	0	0	0	65	6	0	.092
1906	8	16	.333	2.64	32	27	21	238.1	208	112	109	0	0	1	0	85	14	1	.165
1907 2 teams			STL N (21G 9–6)				PHI N (9G 1–6)												
" total	10	12	.455	2.74	30	24	19	193.2	175	101	55	4	0	0	0	79	17	0	.215
1908 PHI N	0	0	–	2.57	3	0	0	7	9	5	3	0	0	0	0	5	1	0	.200
1909 2 teams			PHI N (7G 0–0)				BOS N (18G 4–10)												
" total	4	10	.286	3.16	25	18	8	148.1	130	72	42	2	0	0	0	57	7	0	.123
1910 BOS N	9	23	.281	2.67	46	29	16	263	251	94	88	1	3	5	2	81	16	1	.198
1911	8	18	.308	4.29	42	25	13	241	258	116	76	0	2	1	2	84	21	1	.250
1912	4	15	.211	4.01	31	21	13	168.1	146	66	68	0	0	1	0	61	13	0	.213
1913	0	0	–	4.73	2	0	0	13.1	19	3	3	0	0	0	0	5	0	0	.000
9 yrs.	51	105	.327	3.20	234	165	107	1452	1368	631	501	10	5	8	4	522	95	3	.182

	W	L	PCT	ERA	G	GS	CG	IP	H	BB	SO	ShO	Relief Pitching W	L	SV	BATTING AB	H	HR	BA

Charlie Brown

BROWN, CHARLES E.   TL
B. 1878, Baltimore, Md.   Deceased.

	W	L	PCT	ERA	G	GS	CG	IP	H	BB	SO	ShO	W	L	SV	AB	H	HR	BA
1897 CLE N	1	2	.333	7.77	4	4	2	24.1	30	17	8	0	0	0	0	11	3	0	.273

Clint Brown

BROWN, CLINTON HAROLD   BL TR 6'1"   190 lbs.
B. July 8, 1903, Blackash, Pa.   D. Dec. 31, 1955, Rocky River, Ohio

	W	L	PCT	ERA	G	GS	CG	IP	H	BB	SO	ShO	W	L	SV	AB	H	HR	BA
1928 CLE A	0	1	.000	4.91	2	1	1	11	14	2	2	0	0	0	0	5	1	0	.200
1929	0	2	.000	3.31	3	1	1	16.1	18	6	1	0	0	1	0	7	0	0	.000
1930	11	12	.478	4.97	35	31	16	213.2	271	51	54	2	0	0	1	73	18	0	.247
1931	11	15	.423	4.71	39	33	12	233.1	284	55	50	2	0	0	0	87	15	0	.172
1932	15	12	.556	4.08	37	32	21	262.2	298	50	59	1	0	0	1	100	25	2	.250
1933	11	12	.478	3.41	33	23	10	185	202	34	47	2	1	1	1	62	9	0	.145
1934	4	3	.571	5.90	17	2	0	50.1	83	14	15	0	4	2	1	17	5	0	.294
1935	4	3	.571	5.14	23	5	1	49	61	14	20	0	3	0	2	10	2	0	.200
1936 CHI A	6	2	.750	4.99	38	2	0	83	106	24	19	0	6	1	5	25	4	0	.160
1937	7	7	.500	3.42	53	0	0	100	92	36	51	0	7	7	18	18	4	0	.222
1938	1	3	.250	4.61	8	0	0	13.2	16	9	2	0	1	3	2	2	1	0	.500
1939	11	10	.524	3.88	61	0	0	118.1	127	27	41	0	11	10	18	19	4	0	.211
1940	4	6	.400	3.68	37	0	0	66	75	16	23	0	4	6	10	14	1	0	.071
1941 CLE A	3	3	.500	3.27	41	0	0	74.1	77	28	22	0	3	3	5	17	2	0	.118
1942	1	1	.500	6.00	7	0	0	9	16	2	4	0	1	1	0	1	0	0	.000
15 yrs.	89	92	.492	4.26	434	130	62	1485.2	1740	368	410	7	41	35	64	457	91	2	.199

Curly Brown

BROWN, CHARLES ROY (Lefty)   BL TL 5'10½" 165 lbs.
B. Dec. 9, 1888, Spring Hill, Kans.   D. June 10, 1968, Spring Hill, Kans.

	W	L	PCT	ERA	G	GS	CG	IP	H	BB	SO	ShO	W	L	SV	AB	H	HR	BA
1911 STL A	1	2	.333	2.74	3	2	2	23	22	5	8	0	1	0	0	9	0	0	.000
1912	1	3	.250	4.87	16	5	2	64.2	69	35	28	1	0	1	0	24	5	0	.208
1913	1	1	.500	2.57	2	2	2	14	12	4	3	0	0	0	0	5	2	0	.400
1915 CIN N	0	2	.000	4.67	7	3	0	27	26	6	13	0	0	0	0	11	4	0	.364
4 yrs.	3	8	.273	4.20	28	12	6	128.2	129	50	52	1	1	1	0	49	11	0	.224

Curt Brown

BROWN, CURTIS STEVEN   BR TR 6'3"   165 lbs.
B. Jan. 15, 1960, Ft. Lauderdale, Fla.

	W	L	PCT	ERA	G	GS	CG	IP	H	BB	SO	ShO	W	L	SV	AB	H	HR	BA
1983 CAL A	1	1	.500	7.31	10	0	0	16	25	4	7	0	1	1	0	0	0	0	–
1984 NY A	1	1	.500	2.70	13	0	0	16.2	18	4	10	0	1	1	0	0	0	0	–
2 yrs.	2	2	.500	4.96	23	0	0	32.2	43	8	17	0	2	2	0	0	0	0	–

Ed Brown

BROWN, EDWARD P.   TR
B. Chicago, Ill.   Deceased.
Manager 1882.

	W	L	PCT	ERA	G	GS	CG	IP	H	BB	SO	ShO	W	L	SV	AB	H	HR	BA
1882 STL AA	0	0	–	0.00	1	0	0	2	2	0	1	0	0	0	0	60	11	0	.183
1884 TOL AA	0	1	.000	9.00	1	1	1	9	19	4	1	0	0	0	0	153	27	0	.176
2 yrs.	0	1	.000	7.36	2	1	1	11	21	4	2	0	0	0	0	*			

Elmer Brown

BROWN, ELMER YOUNG (Shook)   BL TR 5'11½" 172 lbs.
B. Mar. 25, 1883, Southport, Ind.   D. Jan. 23, 1955, Indianapolis, Ind.

	W	L	PCT	ERA	G	GS	CG	IP	H	BB	SO	ShO	W	L	SV	AB	H	HR	BA
1911 STL A	1	1	.500	6.61	5	3	1	16.1	16	14	5	1	0	0	0	7	1	0	.143
1912	5	8	.385	2.99	23	11	2	120.1	122	42	45	1	1	2	0	36	6	0	.167
1913 BKN N	0	0	–	2.08	3	1	0	13	6	10	6	0	0	0	0	4	0	0	.000
1914	2	2	.500	3.93	11	4	1	36.2	33	23	22	0	2	2	0	12	1	0	.083
1915	0	0	–	9.00	1	0	0	2	4	3	1	0	0	0	0	0	0	0	–
5 yrs.	8	11	.421	3.49	43	19	4	188.1	181	92	79	2	3	4	0	59	8	0	.136

Hal Brown

BROWN, HECTOR HAROLD (Skinny)   BR TR 6'2"   180 lbs.
B. Dec. 11, 1924, Greensboro, N. C.

	W	L	PCT	ERA	G	GS	CG	IP	H	BB	SO	ShO	W	L	SV	AB	H	HR	BA
1951 CHI A	0	0	–	9.35	3	0	0	8.2	15	4	4	0	0	0	0	2	2	0	1.000
1952	2	3	.400	4.23	24	8	1	72.1	82	21	31	0	0	0	0	19	3	1	.158
1953 BOS A	11	6	.647	4.65	30	25	6	166.1	177	57	62	1	0	1	0	58	17	1	.293
1954	1	8	.111	4.12	40	5	1	118	126	41	66	0	1	4	0	24	3	0	.125
1955 2 teams				BOS	A	(2G 1–0)		BAL	A	(15G 0–4)									
" total	1	4	.200	3.98	17	5	1	61	53	28	28	0	1	1	0	17	1	0	.059
1956 BAL A	9	7	.563	4.04	35	14	4	151.2	142	37	57	1	3	2	2	42	8	0	.190
1957	7	8	.467	3.90	25	20	7	150	132	37	62	2	0	0	1	48	10	0	.208
1958	7	5	.583	3.07	19	17	4	96.2	96	20	44	2	0	0	1	27	4	0	.148
1959	11	9	.550	3.79	31	21	2	164	158	32	81	0	1	0	3	42	2	0	.048
1960	12	5	.706	3.06	30	20	6	159	155	22	66	1	4	1	0	44	8	0	.182
1961	10	6	.625	3.19	27	23	6	166.2	153	33	61	3	0	1	1	50	7	0	.140
1962 2 teams				BAL	A	(22G 6–4)		NY	A	(2G 0–1)									
" total	6	5	.545	4.29	24	12	0	92.1	97	23	27	0	2	2	1	29	8	0	.276
1963 HOU N	5	11	.313	3.31	26	20	6	141.1	137	8	68	3	1	0	0	43	4	0	.093
1964	3	15	.167	3.95	27	21	3	132	154	26	53	0	1	0	1	39	5	0	.128
14 yrs.	85	92	.480	3.81	358	211	47	1680	1677	389	710	13	14	12	11	484	82	2	.169

Jackie Brown

BROWN, JACKIE GENE   BR TR 6'1"   195 lbs.
Brother of Paul Brown.
B. May 31, 1943, Holdenville, Okla.

	W	L	PCT	ERA	G	GS	CG	IP	H	BB	SO	ShO	W	L	SV	AB	H	HR	BA
1970 WAS A	2	2	.500	3.95	24	5	1	57	49	37	47	0	1	0	0	13	2	0	.154
1971	3	4	.429	5.94	14	9	0	47	60	27	21	0	0	0	0	15	2	0	.133
1973 TEX A	5	5	.500	3.90	25	3	2	67	82	25	45	1	3	5	2	0	0	0	–
1974	13	12	.520	3.57	35	26	9	217	219	74	134	2	1	1	0	0	0	0	–
1975 2 teams				TEX	A	(17G 5–5)		CLE	A	(25G 1–2)									
" total	6	7	.462	4.25	42	10	3	139.2	142	64	76	1	3	4	1	0	0	0	–
1976 CLE A	9	11	.450	4.25	32	27	5	180	193	55	104	2	2	0	0	0	0	0	–
1977 MON N	9	12	.429	4.50	42	25	6	186	189	71	89	2	1	0	0	56	7	0	.125
7 yrs.	47	53	.470	4.18	214	105	26	893.2	934	353	516	8	11	10	3	84	11	0	.131

	W	L	PCT	ERA	G	GS	CG	IP	H	BB	SO	ShO	Relief Pitching W	L	SV	BATTING AB	H	HR	BA

Jim Brown

BROWN, JAMES W. H.
B. Dec. 12, 1860, Clinton County, Pa.   D. Apr. 6, 1908, Williamsport, Pa.

	W	L	PCT	ERA	G	GS	CG	IP	H	BB	SO	ShO	W	L	SV	AB	H	HR	BA
1884 3 teams	**ALT** U (11G 1–9)				**NY** N (1G 0–1)			**STP** U (6G 1–4)											
" total	2	14	.125	*4.84*	18	18	12	119	152	58	61	1	0	0	0	107	27	1	.252
1886 PHI AA	0	1	.000	3.24	1	1	1	8.1	9	3	4	0	0	0	0	3	0	0	.000
2 yrs.	2	15	.118	4.74	19	19	13	127.1	161	61	65	1	0	0	0	110	27	1	.245

Joe Brown

BROWN, JOSEPH E.
B. Apr. 4, 1859, Warren, Pa.   D. June 28, 1888, Warren, Pa.

	W	L	PCT	ERA	G	GS	CG	IP	H	BB	SO	ShO	W	L	SV	AB	H	HR	BA
1884 CHI N	4	2	.667	*4.68*	7	6	5	50	56	7	27	0	0	0	0	61	13	0	.213
1885 BAL AA	0	4	.000	*5.68*	4	4	4	38	52	4	9	0	0	0	0	19	3	0	.158
2 yrs.	4	6	.400	5.11	11	10	9	88	108	11	36	0	0	0	0	80	16	0	.200

Joe Brown

BROWN, JOSEPH HENRY   BR TR 6'   176 lbs.
B. July 3, 1900, Little Rock, Ark.   D. Mar. 7, 1950, Los Angeles, Calif.

	W	L	PCT	ERA	G	GS	CG	IP	H	BB	SO	ShO	W	L	SV	AB	H	HR	BA
1927 CHI A	0	0	–	∞	1	0	0	2	1	0	0	0	0	0	0	0	0	0	–

John Brown

BROWN, JOHN J.
B. Trenton, N. J.   Deceased.

	W	L	PCT	ERA	G	GS	CG	IP	H	BB	SO	ShO	W	L	SV	AB	H	HR	BA
1897 BKN N	0	1	.000	7.20	1	1	0	5	7	4	0	0	0	0	0	2	1	0	.500

Jophery Brown

BROWN, JOPHERY CLIFFORD   BL TR 6'2"   190 lbs.
B. Jan. 22, 1945, Grambling, La.

	W	L	PCT	ERA	G	GS	CG	IP	H	BB	SO	ShO	W	L	SV	AB	H	HR	BA
1968 CHI N	0	0	–	4.50	1	0	0	2	2	1	0	0	0	0	0	0	0	0	–

Jumbo Brown

BROWN, WALTER GEORGE   BR TR 6'4"   295 lbs.
B. Apr. 30, 1907, Greene, R. I.   D. Oct. 2, 1966, Freeport, N. Y.

	W	L	PCT	ERA	G	GS	CG	IP	H	BB	SO	ShO	W	L	SV	AB	H	HR	BA
1925 CHI N	0	0	–	3.00	2	0	0	6	5	4	0	0	0	0	0	1	0	0	.000
1927 CLE A	0	2	.000	6.27	8	0	0	18.2	19	26	8	0	0	2	0	3	2	0	.667
1928	0	1	.000	6.75	5	0	0	14.2	19	15	12	0	0	1	0	3	2	0	.667
1932 NY A	5	2	.714	4.45	19	3	3	56.2	58	30	31	1	2	1	1	23	4	0	.174
1933	7	5	.583	5.23	21	8	1	74	78	52	55	0	3	3	0	28	5	0	.179
1935	6	5	.545	3.61	20	8	3	87.1	94	37	41	0	2	1	0	32	10	0	.313
1936	1	4	.200	5.91	20	3	0	64	69	29	19	0	1	2	1	19	0	0	.000
1937 2 teams	**CIN** N (4G 1–0)				**NY** N (4G 1–0)														
" total	2	0	1.000	4.91	8	1	0	18.1	21	8	8	0	1	0	0	2	0	0	.000
1938 NY N	5	3	.625	1.80	43	0	0	90	65	28	42	0	5	3	5	16	3	0	.188
1939	4	0	1.000	4.15	31	0	0	56.1	69	25	24	0	4	0	7	11	4	0	.364
1940	2	4	.333	3.42	41	0	0	55.1	49	25	31	0	2	4	7	10	1	0	.100
1941	1	5	.167	3.32	31	0	0	57	49	21	30	0	1	5	8	9	1	0	.111
12 yrs.	33	31	.516	4.06	249	23	7	598.1	619	300	301	1	21	23	29	157	32	0	.204

Lew Brown

BROWN, LEWIS J. (Blower)   BR TR 5'10½" 185 lbs.
B. Feb. 1, 1858, Leominster, Mass.   D. Jan. 16, 1889, Boston, Mass.

	W	L	PCT	ERA	G	GS	CG	IP	H	BB	SO	ShO	W	L	SV	AB	H	HR	BA
1878 PRO N	0	0	–	18.00	1	0	0	1	0	4	0	0	0	0	0	243	74	1	.305
1884 BOS U	0	0	–	36.00	1	0	0	1	6	1	0	0	0	0	1	325	75	1	.231
2 yrs.	0	0	–	27.00	2	0	0	2	6	5	0	0	0	0	1	*			

Lloyd Brown

BROWN, LLOYD ANDREW (Gimpy)   BL TL 5'9"   170 lbs.
B. Dec. 25, 1904, Beeville, Tex.   D. Jan. 14, 1974, Opalocka, Fla.

	W	L	PCT	ERA	G	GS	CG	IP	H	BB	SO	ShO	W	L	SV	AB	H	HR	BA
1925 BKN N	0	3	.000	4.12	17	5	1	63.1	79	25	23	0	0	0	0	23	2	0	.087
1928 WAS A	4	4	.500	4.04	27	10	2	107	112	40	38	0	2	0	1	31	5	0	.161
1929	8	7	.533	4.18	40	15	7	168	186	69	48	1	4	4	0	50	11	0	.220
1930	16	12	.571	4.25	38	22	10	197	220	65	59	1	6	2	0	65	14	1	.215
1931	15	14	.517	3.20	42	32	15	258.2	256	79	79	1	1	2	0	96	22	0	.229
1932	15	12	.556	4.44	46	24	10	202.2	239	55	53	2	4	2	5	70	7	0	.100
1933 2 teams	**STL** A (8G 1–6)				**BOS** A (33G 8–11)														
" total	9	17	.346	4.63	41	27	9	202.1	237	81	44	2	0	3	1	68	19	2	.279
1934 CLE A	5	10	.333	3.85	38	15	5	117	116	51	39	0	3	1	6	30	7	0	.233
1935	8	7	.533	3.61	42	8	4	122	123	37	45	2	0	2	4	37	4	0	.108
1936	8	10	.444	4.17	24	16	12	140.1	166	45	34	1	1	1	1	45	10	1	.222
1937	2	6	.250	6.55	31	5	2	77	107	27	32	0	1	2	0	24	4	0	.167
1940 PHI N	1	3	.250	6.21	18	2	0	37.2	58	16	16	0	0	3	3	13	1	0	.077
12 yrs.	91	105	.464	4.20	404	181	77	1693	1899	590	510	10	22	22	21	552	106	4	.192

Mace Brown

BROWN, MACE STANLEY   BR TR 6'1"   190 lbs.
B. May 21, 1909, North English, Iowa

	W	L	PCT	ERA	G	GS	CG	IP	H	BB	SO	ShO	W	L	SV	AB	H	HR	BA
1935 PIT N	4	1	.800	3.59	18	5	2	72.2	84	22	28	0	1	0	0	24	4	0	.167
1936	10	11	.476	3.87	47	10	3	165	178	55	56	0	6	4	3	60	10	0	.167
1937	7	2	.778	4.18	50	2	0	107.2	109	45	60	0	6	1	7	30	9	0	.300
1938	15	9	.625	3.80	51	2	0	132.2	155	44	55	0	15	8	5	38	5	0	.132
1939	9	13	.409	3.37	47	19	8	200.1	232	52	71	1	4	7	3	64	7	0	.109
1940	10	9	.526	3.49	48	17	5	172.2	181	49	73	2	5	2	7	52	6	0	.115
1941 2 teams	**PIT** N (1G 0–0)				**BKN** N (24G 3–2)														
" total	3	2	.600	3.07	25	0	0	44	33	26	22	0	3	2	3	8	0	0	.000
1942 BOS A	9	3	.750	3.43	34	0	0	60.1	56	28	20	0	9	3	6	15	1	0	.067
1943	6	6	.500	2.12	49	0	0	93.1	71	51	40	0	6	6	9	17	1	0	.059
1946	3	1	.750	2.05	18	0	0	26.1	26	16	10	0	3	1	1	5	0	0	.000
10 yrs.	76	57	.571	3.47	387	55	18	1075	1125	388	435	3	56	30	48	313	43	0	.137

WORLD SERIES

	W	L	PCT	ERA	G	GS	CG	IP	H	BB	SO	ShO	W	L	SV	AB	H	HR	BA
1946 BOS A	0	0	–	27.00	1	0	0	1	4	1	0	0	0	0	0	0	0	0	–

Mark Brown

BROWN, MARK ANTHONY   BB TR 6'2"   190 lbs.
B. July 13, 1959, Bellows Falls, Vt.

	W	L	PCT	ERA	G	GS	CG	IP	H	BB	SO	ShO	W	L	SV	AB	H	HR	BA
1984 BAL A	1	2	.333	3.91	9	0	0	23	22	7	10	0	1	2	0	0	0	0	–

	W	L	PCT	ERA	G	GS	CG	IP	H	BB	SO	ShO	Relief Pitching W	L	SV	BATTING AB	H	HR	BA

Mike Brown
BROWN, MICHAEL GARY BR TR 6'2" 195 lbs.
B. Mar. 4, 1959, Camden, N. J.

Year	W	L	PCT	ERA	G	GS	CG	IP	H	BB	SO	ShO	W	L	SV	AB	H	HR	BA
1982 BOS A	1	0	1.000	0.00	3	0	0	6	7	1	4	0	1	0	0	0	0	0	—
1983	6	6	.500	4.67	19	18	3	104	110	43	35	1	0	0	0	0	0	0	—
1984	1	8	.111	6.85	15	11	0	67	104	19	32	0	0	0	0	0	0	0	—
3 yrs.	8	14	.364	5.34	37	29	3	177	221	63	71	1	1	0	0	0	0	0	—

Myrl Brown
BROWN, MYRL LINCOLN BR TR 5'11" 172 lbs.
B. Oct. 10, 1894, Waynesboro, Pa.   D. Feb. 23, 1981, Harrisburg, Pa.

Year	W	L	PCT	ERA	G	GS	CG	IP	H	BB	SO	ShO	W	L	SV	AB	H	HR	BA
1922 PIT N	3	1	.750	5.97	7	5	2	34.2	42	13	9	0	0	1	0	11	3	0	.273

Norm Brown
BROWN, NORMAN BB TR 6'3" 180 lbs.
B. Feb. 1, 1919, Evergreen, N. C.

Year	W	L	PCT	ERA	G	GS	CG	IP	H	BB	SO	ShO	W	L	SV	AB	H	HR	BA
1943 PHI A	0	0	—	0.00	1	1	0	7	5	0	1	0	0	0	0	3	0	0	.000
1946	0	1	.000	6.14	4	0	0	7.1	8	6	3	0	0	1	0	0	0	0	—
2 yrs.	0	1	.000	3.14	5	1	0	14.1	13	6	4	0	0	1	0	3	0	0	.000

Paul Brown
BROWN, PAUL DWAYNE BR TR 6'1" 190 lbs.
Brother of Jackie Brown.
B. June 18, 1941, Fort Smith, Ark.

Year	W	L	PCT	ERA	G	GS	CG	IP	H	BB	SO	ShO	W	L	SV	AB	H	HR	BA
1961 PHI N	0	1	.000	8.10	5	1	0	10	13	8	1	0	0	0	0	2	1	0	.500
1962	0	6	.000	5.94	23	9	0	63.2	74	33	29	0	0	0	1	13	2	0	.154
1963	0	1	.000	4.11	6	2	0	15.1	15	5	11	0	0	0	0	2	1	0	.500
1968	0	0	—	9.00	2	0	0	4	6	1	4	0	0	0	0	0	0	0	—
4 yrs.	0	8	.000	6.00	36	12	0	93	108	47	45	0	0	0	1	17	4	0	.235

Ray Brown
BROWN, PAUL PERCIVAL
B. Jan. 30, 1889, Chicago, Ill.   D. May 29, 1955, Los Angeles, Calif.

Year	W	L	PCT	ERA	G	GS	CG	IP	H	BB	SO	ShO	W	L	SV	AB	H	HR	BA
1909 CHI N	1	0	1.000	2.00	1	1	1	9	5	4	2	0	0	0	0	3	0	0	.000

Scott Brown
BROWN, SCOTT EDWARD BR TR 6'2" 220 lbs.
B. Aug. 31, 1956, DeQuincy, La.

Year	W	L	PCT	ERA	G	GS	CG	IP	H	BB	SO	ShO	W	L	SV	AB	H	HR	BA
1981 CIN N	1	0	1.000	2.77	10	0	0	13	16	1	7	0	1	0	0	1	0	0	.000

Steve Brown
BROWN, STEVEN ELBERT BR TR 6'6" 213 lbs.
B. Feb. 12, 1957, San Francisco, Calif.

Year	W	L	PCT	ERA	G	GS	CG	IP	H	BB	SO	ShO	W	L	SV	AB	H	HR	BA
1983 CAL A	2	3	.400	3.52	12	4	2	46	45	16	23	1	1	1	0	0	0	0	—
1984	0	1	.000	9.00	3	3	0	11	16	9	5	0	0	0	0	0	0	0	—
2 yrs.	2	4	.333	4.58	15	7	2	57	61	25	28	1	1	1	0	0	0	0	—

Stub Brown
BROWN, RICHARD P. TL 6'2" 220 lbs.
B. Aug. 3, 1870, Baltimore, Md.   D. Mar. 11, 1948, Baltimore, Md.

Year	W	L	PCT	ERA	G	GS	CG	IP	H	BB	SO	ShO	W	L	SV	AB	H	HR	BA
1893 BAL N	0	0	—	6.00	2	0	0	9	13	5	0	0	0	0	0	5	1	0	.200
1894	4	0	1.000	4.89	9	6	3	49.2	59	24	8	0	0	0	0	23	2	0	.087
1897 CIN N	0	1	.000	4.15	2	1	1	13	17	8	2	0	0	0	0	5	0	0	.000
3 yrs.	4	1	.800	4.90	13	7	4	71.2	89	37	10	0	0	0	0	33	3	0	.091

Three Finger Brown
BROWN, MORDECAI PETER CENTENNIAL (Miner) BB TR 5'10" 175 lbs.
B. Oct. 19, 1876, Nyesville, Ind.   D. Feb. 14, 1948, Terre Haute, Ind.
Manager 1914.
Hall of Fame 1949.

Year	W	L	PCT	ERA	G	GS	CG	IP	H	BB	SO	ShO	W	L	SV	AB	H	HR	BA
1903 STL N	9	13	.409	2.60	26	24	19	201	231	59	83	1	0	0	0	77	15	0	.195
1904 CHI N	15	10	.600	1.86	26	23	21	212.1	155	50	81	4	2	0	1	89	19	0	.213
1905	18	12	.600	2.17	30	24	24	249	219	44	89	4	2	2	0	93	13	1	.140
1906	26	6	.813	**1.04**	36	32	27	277.1	198	61	144	**10**	1	0	3	98	20	0	.204
1907	20	6	.769	1.39	34	27	20	233	180	40	107	6	1	0	3	85	13	1	.153
1908	29	9	.763	1.47	44	31	27	312.1	214	49	123	9	4	1	5	121	25	0	.207
1909	**27**	9	.750	1.31	50	34	**32**	**342.2**	246	53	172	8	1	1	7	125	22	0	.176
1910	25	13	.658	1.86	46	31	**27**	295.1	256	64	143	7	2	2	7	103	18	0	.175
1911	21	11	.656	2.80	**53**	27	21	270	267	55	129	0	5	3	**13**	91	23	0	.253
1912	5	6	.455	2.64	15	8	5	88.2	92	20	34	2	2	3	0	31	9	0	.290
1913 CIN N	11	12	.478	2.91	39	16	11	173.1	174	44	41	1	4	3	6	54	11	0	.204
1914 2 teams	STL F (26G 12–6)			BKN F (9G 2–5)															
" total	14	11	.560	3.52	35	26	18	232.2	235	61	113	2	1	2	0	78	19	0	.244
1915 CHI F	17	8	.680	2.09	35	25	18	236.1	189	64	95	3	3	2	3	82	24	0	.293
1916 CHI N	2	3	.400	3.91	12	4	2	48.1	52	9	21	0	1	0	0	16	4	0	.250
14 yrs.	239	129	.649	2.06	481	332	272	3172.1	2708	673	1375	57	29	19	48	1143	235	2	.206
				3rd								8th							

WORLD SERIES

Year	W	L	PCT	ERA	G	GS	CG	IP	H	BB	SO	ShO	W	L	SV	AB	H	HR	BA
1906 CHI N	1	2	.333	3.66	3	3	2	19.2	14	4	12	1	0	0	0	6	2	0	.333
1907	1	0	1.000	0.00	1	1	1	9	7	1	4	1	0	0	0	3	0	0	.000
1908	2	0	1.000	0.00	2	1	1	11	6	1	5	1	1	0	0	4	0	0	.000
1910	1	2	.333	5.00	3	2	1	18	23	7	14	0	1	0	0	7	0	0	.000
4 yrs.	5	4	.556	2.81	9	7	5	57.2	50	13	35	3	2	0	0	20	2	0	.100
	8th	7th					10th					2nd	2nd						

Tom Brown
BROWN, THOMAS DALE BR TR 6'1" 170 lbs.
B. Aug. 10, 1949, Lafayette, Ind.

Year	W	L	PCT	ERA	G	GS	CG	IP	H	BB	SO	ShO	W	L	SV	AB	H	HR	BA
1978 SEA A	0	0	—	4.15	6	0	0	13	14	4	8	0	0	0	0	0	0	0	—

Tom Brown
BROWN, THOMAS T. BL TR 5'10" 168 lbs.
B. Sept. 21, 1860, Liverpool, England   D. Oct. 27, 1927, Washington, D. C.
Manager 1897-98.

Year	W	L	PCT	ERA	G	GS	CG	IP	H	BB	SO	ShO	W	L	SV	AB	H	HR	BA
1882 BAL AA	0	0	—	1.08	2	0	0	8.1	13	6	2	0	0	0	0	181	55	1	.304
1883 COL AA	0	1	.000	5.79	3	1	1	14	14	10	6	0	0	0	0	420	115	5	.274
1884	2	1	.667	7.11	4	1	0	19	27	7	5	0	2	1	0	451	123	5	.273

	W	L	PCT	ERA	G	GS	CG	IP	H	BB	SO	ShO	Relief Pitching W	L	SV	BATTING AB	H	HR	BA

Tom Brown continued

	W	L	PCT	ERA	G	GS	CG	IP	H	BB	SO	ShO	W	L	SV	AB	H	HR	BA
1885 PIT AA	0	0	–	3.00	2	0	0	6	0	3	2	0	0	0	0	437	134	4	.307
1886	0	0	–	9.00	1	0	0	2	2	5	1	0	0	0	0	460	131	1	.285
5 yrs.	2	2	.500	5.29	12	1	1	49.1	56	31	16	0	2	1	0	*			

Walter Brown

BROWN, WALTER IRVING   BR TR 5'11"   175 lbs.
B. Apr. 23, 1915, Jamestown, N. Y.

	W	L	PCT	ERA	G	GS	CG	IP	H	BB	SO	ShO	W	L	SV	AB	H	HR	BA
1947 STL A	1	0	1.000	4.89	19	0	0	46	50	28	10	0	1	0	0	11	0	0	.000

Cal Browning

BROWNING, CALVIN DUANE   BL TL 5'11"   190 lbs.
B. Mar. 16, 1938, Burns Flat, Okla.

	W	L	PCT	ERA	G	GS	CG	IP	H	BB	SO	ShO	W	L	SV	AB	H	HR	BA
1960 STL N	0	0	–	40.50	1	0	0	.2	5	1	0	0	0	0	0	0	0	0	–

Frank Browning

BROWNING, FRANK   BR TR 5'5"   145 lbs.
B. Oct. 29, 1882, Falmouth, Ky.   D. May 19, 1948, San Antonio, Tex.

	W	L	PCT	ERA	G	GS	CG	IP	H	BB	SO	ShO	W	L	SV	AB	H	HR	BA
1910 DET A	2	2	.500	3.00	11	6	2	42	51	10	16	0	0	1	3	14	0	0	.000

Pete Browning

BROWNING, LOUIS ROGERS (The Gladiator)   BR TR 6'   180 lbs.
B. June 17, 1861, Louisville, Ky.   D. Sept. 10, 1905, Louisville, Ky.

	W	L	PCT	ERA	G	GS	CG	IP	H	BB	SO	ShO	W	L	SV	AB	H	HR	BA
1884 LOU AA	0	1	.000	54.00	1	1	0	.1	2	2	0	0	0	0	0	*			

Tom Browning

BROWNING, THOMAS LEO   BL TL 6'1"   180 lbs.
B. Apr. 28, 1960, Casper, Wyo.

	W	L	PCT	ERA	G	GS	CG	IP	H	BB	SO	ShO	W	L	SV	AB	H	HR	BA
1984 CIN N	1	0	1.000	1.54	3	3	0	23.1	27	5	14	0	0	0	0	7	1	0	.143

Bruce Brubaker

BRUBAKER, BRUCE ELLSWORTH   BR TR 6'1"   198 lbs.
B. Dec. 29, 1941, Harrisburg, Pa.

	W	L	PCT	ERA	G	GS	CG	IP	H	BB	SO	ShO	W	L	SV	AB	H	HR	BA
1967 LA N	0	0	–	20.25	1	0	0	1.1	3	0	2	0	0	0	0	0	0	0	–
1970 MIL A	0	0	–	9.00	1	0	0	2	2	1	0	0	0	0	0	0	0	0	–
2 yrs.	0	0	–	13.50	2	0	0	3.1	5	1	2	0	0	0	0	0	0	0	–

Bob Bruce

BRUCE, ROBERT JAMES   BR TR 6'3"   200 lbs.
B. May 16, 1933, Detroit, Mich.

	W	L	PCT	ERA	G	GS	CG	IP	H	BB	SO	ShO	W	L	SV	AB	H	HR	BA
1959 DET A	0	1	.000	9.00	2	1	0	2	2	3	1	0	0	0	0	0	0	0	–
1960	4	7	.364	3.74	34	15	1	130	127	56	76	0	0	2	0	39	7	0	.179
1961	1	2	.333	4.43	14	6	0	44.2	57	24	25	0	0	1	0	9	1	0	.111
1962 HOU N	10	9	.526	4.06	32	27	6	175	164	82	135	0	1	0	0	55	11	0	.200
1963	5	9	.357	3.59	30	25	1	170.1	162	60	123	1	0	0	0	55	7	0	.127
1964	15	9	.625	2.76	35	29	9	202.1	191	33	135	4	1	0	0	63	12	0	.190
1965	9	18	.333	3.72	35	34	7	229.2	241	38	145	1	0	0	0	74	9	0	.122
1966	3	13	.188	5.34	25	23	1	129.2	160	29	71	0	0	1	0	39	3	0	.077
1967 ATL N	2	3	.400	4.89	12	7	1	38.2	42	15	22	0	0	1	1	12	2	0	.167
9 yrs.	49	71	.408	3.85	219	167	26	1122.1	1146	340	733	6	2	5	1	346	52	0	.150

Lou Bruce

BRUCE, LOUIS   BL TR 5'5"   145 lbs.
B. Jan. 16, 1877, St. Regis, N. Y.   D. Feb. 9, 1968, Ilion, N. Y.

	W	L	PCT	ERA	G	GS	CG	IP	H	BB	SO	ShO	W	L	SV	AB	H	HR	BA
1904 PHI A	0	0	–	4.91	2	0	0	11	11	2	2	0	0	0	0	*			

Fred Bruckbauer

BRUCKBAUER, FREDERICK JOHN   BR TR 6'1"   185 lbs.
B. May 27, 1938, New Ulm, Minn.

	W	L	PCT	ERA	G	GS	CG	IP	H	BB	SO	ShO	W	L	SV	AB	H	HR	BA
1961 MIN A	0	0	–	∞	1	0	0	3	1	0	0	0	0	0	0	0	0	0	–

Andy Bruckmiller

BRUCKMILLER, ANDREW   BR TR 5'11"   175 lbs.
B. Jan. 1, 1882, Pittsburgh, Pa.   D. Jan. 12, 1970, McKeesport, Pa.

	W	L	PCT	ERA	G	GS	CG	IP	H	BB	SO	ShO	W	L	SV	AB	H	HR	BA
1905 DET A	0	0	–	27.00	1	0	0	4	1	1	1	0	0	0	0	1	0	0	.000

Mike Bruhert

BRUHERT, MICHAEL EDWIN   BR TR 6'6"   220 lbs.
B. June 24, 1951, Jamaica, N. Y.

	W	L	PCT	ERA	G	GS	CG	IP	H	BB	SO	ShO	W	L	SV	AB	H	HR	BA
1978 NY N	4	11	.267	4.77	27	22	1	134	171	34	56	1	0	0	0	40	3	0	.075

Jack Bruner

BRUNER, JACK RAYMOND (Pappy)   BL TL 6'1"   185 lbs.
B. July 1, 1924, Waterloo, Iowa

	W	L	PCT	ERA	G	GS	CG	IP	H	BB	SO	ShO	W	L	SV	AB	H	HR	BA
1949 CHI A	1	2	.333	8.22	4	2	0	7.2	10	8	4	0	1	0	0	1	0	0	.000
1950 2 teams	CHI A (9G 0–0)					STL A (13G 1–2)													
" total	1	2	.333	4.37	22	1	0	47.1	43	37	24	0	1	1	1	10	0	0	.000
2 yrs.	2	4	.333	4.91	26	3	0	55	53	45	28	0	2	1	1	11	0	0	.000

Roy Bruner

BRUNER, WALTER ROY   BR TR 6'   165 lbs.
B. Feb. 10, 1917, Cecilia, Ky.

	W	L	PCT	ERA	G	GS	CG	IP	H	BB	SO	ShO	W	L	SV	AB	H	HR	BA
1939 PHI N	0	4	.000	6.67	4	4	2	27	38	13	11	0	0	0	0	9	1	0	.111
1940	0	0	–	5.68	2	0	0	6.1	5	6	4	0	0	0	0	2	1	0	.500
1941	0	3	.000	4.91	13	1	0	29.1	37	25	13	0	0	2	0	6	0	0	.000
3 yrs.	0	7	.000	5.74	19	5	2	62.2	80	44	28	0	0	2	0	17	2	0	.118

George Brunet

BRUNET, GEORGE STUART (Lefty)   BR TL 6'1"   195 lbs.
B. June 8, 1935, Houghton, Mich.

	W	L	PCT	ERA	G	GS	CG	IP	H	BB	SO	ShO	W	L	SV	AB	H	HR	BA
1956 KC A	0	0	–	7.00	6	1	0	9	10	11	5	0.	0	0	0	2	0	0	.000
1957	0	1	.000	5.56	4	2	0	11.1	13	4	3	0	0	0	0	2	0	0	.000
1959	0	0	–	11.57	2	0	0	4.2	10	7	7	0	0	0	0	0	0	0	–
1960 2 teams	KC A (3G 0–2)					MIL N (17G 2–0)													
" total	2	2	.500	4.95	20	0	0	60	65	32	43	0	1	0	0	14	1	0	.071
1961 MIL N	0	0	–	5.40	5	0	0	5	7	2	0	0	0	0	0	0	0	0	–
1962 HOU N	2	4	.333	4.50	17	11	2	54	62	21	36	0	0	0	0	17	1	0	.059

	W	L	PCT	ERA	G	GS	CG	IP	H	BB	SO	ShO	Relief Pitching W	L	SV	BATTING AB	H	HR	BA

George Brunet continued

	W	L	PCT	ERA	G	GS	CG	IP	H	BB	SO	ShO	W	L	SV	AB	H	HR	BA
1963 2 teams	HOU	N	(5G 0–3)		BAL	A	(16G 0–1)												
" total	0	4	.000	6.06	21	2	0	32.2	49	15	24	0	0	2	1	4	0	0	.000
1964 LA A	2	2	.500	3.61	10	7	0	42.1	38	25	36	0	0	0	0	11	2	0	.182
1965 CAL A	9	11	.450	2.56	41	26	8	197	149	69	141	3	1	1	2	56	3	0	.054
1966	13	13	.500	3.31	41	32	8	212	183	106	148	2	1	2	0	68	7	1	.103
1967	11	19	.367	3.31	40	37	7	250	203	90	165	2	0	1	1	78	6	0	.077
1968	13	17	.433	2.86	39	36	8	245.1	191	68	132	5	0	1	0	74	6	0	.081
1969 2 teams	CAL	A	(23G 6–7)		SEA	A	(12G 2–5)												
" total	8	12	.400	4.44	35	30	4	164.1	168	67	93	2	0	0	0	47	4	1	.085
1970 2 teams	WAS	A	(24G 8–6)		PIT	N	(12G 1–1)												
" total	9	7	.563	4.20	36	21	2	135	143	57	84	1	2	2	0	42	6	1	.143
1971 STL N	0	1	.000	6.00	7	0	0	9	12	7	4	0	0	1	0	3	1	0	.333
15 yrs.	69	93	.426	3.62	324	213	39	1431.2	1303	581	921	15	5	10	4	418	37	3	.089

Tom Bruno

BRUNO, THOMAS MICHAEL
B. Jan. 26, 1953, Chicago, Ill. BR TR 6'5" 210 lbs.

	W	L	PCT	ERA	G	GS	CG	IP	H	BB	SO	ShO	W	L	SV	AB	H	HR	BA
1976 KC A	1	0	1.000	6.88	12	0	0	17	20	9	11	0	1	0	0	0	0	0	–
1977 TOR A	0	1	.000	8.00	12	0	0	18	30	13	9	0	0	1	0	0	0	0	–
1978 STL N	4	3	.571	1.98	18	3	0	50	38	17	33	0	3	2	1	12	1	0	.083
1979	2	3	.400	4.26	27	1	0	38	37	22	27	0	2	2	0	5	1	0	.200
4 yrs.	7	7	.500	4.24	69	4	0	123	125	61	80	0	6	5	1	17	2	0	.118

Warren Brusstar

BRUSSTAR, WARREN SCOTT
B. Feb. 2, 1952, Oakland, Calif. BR TR 6'3" 200 lbs.

	W	L	PCT	ERA	G	GS	CG	IP	H	BB	SO	ShO	W	L	SV	AB	H	HR	BA
1977 PHI N	7	2	.778	2.66	46	0	0	71	64	24	46	0	7	2	3	6	0	0	.000
1978	6	3	.667	2.33	58	0	0	89	74	30	60	0	6	3	0	7	1	0	.143
1979	1	0	1.000	7.07	13	0	0	14	23	4	3	0	1	0	1	0	0	0	–
1980	2	2	.500	3.69	26	0	0	39	42	13	21	0	2	2	0	1	0	0	.000
1981	0	1	.000	4.50	14	0	0	12	12	10	8	0	0	1	0	0	0	0	–
1982 2 teams	PHI	N	(22G 2–3)		CHI	A	(10G 2–0)												
" total	4	3	.571	4.17	32	0	0	41	50	8	19	0	4	3	2	2	0	0	.000
1983 CHI N	3	1	.750	2.35	59	0	0	80.1	67	37	46	0	3	1	1	4	0	0	.000
1984	1	1	.500	3.11	41	0	0	63.2	57	21	36	0	1	1	3	5	1	0	.200
8 yrs.	24	13	.649	3.05	289	0	0	410	389	147	239	0	24	13	10	25	2	0	.080

DIVISIONAL PLAYOFF SERIES

	W	L	PCT	ERA	G	GS	CG	IP	H	BB	SO	ShO	W	L	SV	AB	H	HR	BA
1981 PHI N	0	0	–	4.91	2	0	0	3.2	5	1	3	0	0	0	0	0	0	0	–

LEAGUE CHAMPIONSHIP SERIES

	W	L	PCT	ERA	G	GS	CG	IP	H	BB	SO	ShO	W	L	SV	AB	H	HR	BA
1977 PHI N	0	0	–	3.38	2	0	0	2.2	2	1	2	0	0	0	0	0	0	0	–
1978	0	0	–	0.00	3	0	0	2.2	2	1	0	0	0	0	0	0	0	0	–
1980	1	0	1.000	3.38	2	0	0	2.2	1	1	0	0	1	0	0	1	0	0	.000
1984 CHI N	0	0	–	0.00	3	0	0	4.2	6	0	1	0	0	0	0	1	0	0	.000
4 yrs.	1	0	1.000	1.42	10	0	0	12.2	11	3	3	0	1	0	0	2	0	0	.000

WORLD SERIES

	W	L	PCT	ERA	G	GS	CG	IP	H	BB	SO	ShO	W	L	SV	AB	H	HR	BA
1980 PHI N	0	0	–	0.00	1	0	0	2.1	0	1	0	0	0	0	0	0	0	0	–

Clay Bryant

BRYANT, CLAIBORNE HENRY
B. Nov. 16, 1911, Madison Heights, Va. BR TR 6'2½" 195 lbs.

	W	L	PCT	ERA	G	GS	CG	IP	H	BB	SO	ShO	W	L	SV	AB	H	HR	BA
1935 CHI N	1	2	.333	5.16	9	1	0	22.2	34	7	13	0	1	2	2	6	2	1	.333
1936	1	2	.333	3.30	26	0	0	57.1	57	24	35	0	1	2	0	12	5	0	.417
1937	9	3	.750	4.26	38	10	4	135.1	117	78	75	1	7	0	3	45	14	1	.311
1938	19	11	.633	3.10	44	30	17	270.1	235	125	135	3	4	1	2	106	24	3	.226
1939	2	1	.667	5.74	4	4	2	31.1	42	14	9	0	0	0	0	14	3	0	.214
1940	0	1	.000	4.78	8	0	0	26.1	26	14	5	0	0	1	0	9	3	0	.333
6 yrs.	32	20	.615	3.73	129	45	23	543.1	511	262	272	4	13	6	7	192	51	5	.266

WORLD SERIES

	W	L	PCT	ERA	G	GS	CG	IP	H	BB	SO	ShO	W	L	SV	AB	H	HR	BA
1938 CHI N	0	1	.000	6.75	1	1	0	5.1	6	5	3	0	0	0	0	2	0	0	.000

Ron Bryant

BRYANT, RONALD RAYMOND (Bear)
B. Nov. 12, 1947, Redlands, Calif. BB TL 6' 190 lbs.

	W	L	PCT	ERA	G	GS	CG	IP	H	BB	SO	ShO	W	L	SV	AB	H	HR	BA
1967 SF N	0	0	–	4.50	1	0	0	4	3	0	2	0	0	0	0	1	0	0	.000
1969	4	3	.571	4.34	16	8	0	58	60	25	30	0	0	0	1	16	3	0	.188
1970	5	8	.385	4.78	34	11	1	96	103	38	66	0	3	2	0	27	3	0	.111
1971	7	10	.412	3.79	27	22	3	140	146	49	79	2	0	1	0	50	10	0	.200
1972	14	7	.667	2.90	35	28	11	214	176	77	107	4	0	1	0	70	12	0	.171
1973	24	12	.667	3.54	41	39	8	269.2	240	115	143	0	1	0	0	95	16	0	.168
1974	3	15	.167	5.60	41	23	0	127	142	68	75	0	0	0	0	31	4	0	.129
1975 STL N	0	1	.000	16.00	10	1	0	9	20	7	7	0	0	0	0	1	0	0	.000
8 yrs.	57	56	.504	4.02	205	132	23	917.2	890	379	509	6	5	3	1	291	48	0	.165

LEAGUE CHAMPIONSHIP SERIES

	W	L	PCT	ERA	G	GS	CG	IP	H	BB	SO	ShO	W	L	SV	AB	H	HR	BA
1971 SF N	0	0	–	4.50	1	0	0	2	1	1	2	0	0	0	0	0	0	0	–

Charlie Brynan

BRYNAN, CHARLES RULEY (Tod)
B. July, 1863, Philadelphia, Pa.   D. May 10, 1925, Philadelphia, Pa. BR TR

	W	L	PCT	ERA	G	GS	CG	IP	H	BB	SO	ShO	W	L	SV	AB	H	HR	BA
1888 CHI N	2	1	.667	6.48	3	3	2	25	29	7	11	0	0	0	0	11	2	0	.182
1891 BOS N	0	1	.000	54.00	1	1	0	1	4	3	0	0	0	0	0	0	0	0	–
2 yrs.	2	2	.500	8.31	4	4	2	26	33	10	11	0	0	0	0	11	2	0	.182

Jim Buchanan

BUCHANAN, JAMES FORREST (Buck)
B. July 1, 1876, Chatham Hill, Va.   D. June 15, 1949, Randolph, Neb. BL TR 5'10½" 170 lbs.

	W	L	PCT	ERA	G	GS	CG	IP	H	BB	SO	ShO	W	L	SV	AB	H	HR	BA
1905 STL A	5	10	.333	3.50	22	15	12	141.1	149	27	54	1	0	1	2	46	7	0	.152

	W	L	PCT	ERA	G	GS	CG	IP	H	BB	SO	ShO	Relief Pitching W	L	SV	BATTING AB	H	HR	BA

Garland Buckeye

BUCKEYE, GARLAND MAIERS (Gob)
B. Oct. 16, 1897, Heron Lake, Minn.
D. Nov. 14, 1975, Stone Lake, Wis.
BL TL 6'   260 lbs.
BB 1918,1927

	W	L	PCT	ERA	G	GS	CG	IP	H	BB	SO	ShO	W	L	SV	AB	H	HR	BA
1918 WAS A	0	0	–	18.00	1	0	0	2	3	6	2	0	0	0	0	0	0	0	–
1925 CLE A	13	8	.619	3.65	30	18	11	153	161	58	49	1	3	2	0	62	14	3	.226
1926	6	9	.400	3.10	32	18	5	165.2	160	69	36	1	2	1	0	60	12	2	.200
1927	10	17	.370	3.96	35	25	13	204.2	231	74	38	2	1	3	1	71	19	0	.268
1928 2 teams	CLE	A	(9G 1–5)		NY	N	(1G 0–0)												
" total	1	5	.167	7.32	10	6	0	39.1	67	7	9	0	0	1	0	11	2	0	.182
5 yrs.	30	39	.435	3.90	108	67	29	564.2	622	214	134	4	6	7	1	204	47	5	.230

Ed Buckingham

BUCKINGHAM, EDWARD TAYLOR
B. May 12, 1874, Bridgeport, Conn.   D. July 30, 1942, Bridgeport, Conn.

	W	L	PCT	ERA	G	GS	CG	IP	H	BB	SO	ShO	W	L	SV	AB	H	HR	BA
1895 WAS N	0	0	–	6.00	1	1	0	3	6	2	1	0	0	0	0	1	0	0	.000

Jess Buckles

BUCKLES, JESS ROBERT (Jim)
B. May 20, 1890, LaVerne, Calif.   D. Aug. 2, 1975, Westminster, Calif.
BL TL 6'2½"   205 lbs.

	W	L	PCT	ERA	G	GS	CG	IP	H	BB	SO	ShO	W	L	SV	AB	H	HR	BA
1916 NY A	0	0	–	2.25	2	0	0	4	3	1	2	0	0	0	0	1	0	0	.000

John Buckley

BUCKLEY, JOHN EDWARD
B. Mar. 20, 1870, Marlboro, Mass.   D. May 3, 1942, Westborough, Mass.
BL

	W	L	PCT	ERA	G	GS	CG	IP	H	BB	SO	ShO	W	L	SV	AB	H	HR	BA
1890 BUF P	1	3	.250	7.68	4	4	4	34	49	16	4	0	0	0	0	15	0	0	.000

Mike Budnick

BUDNICK, MICHAEL JOE
B. Sept. 15, 1919, Astoria, Ore.
BR TR 6'1"   200 lbs.

	W	L	PCT	ERA	G	GS	CG	IP	H	BB	SO	ShO	W	L	SV	AB	H	HR	BA
1946 NY N	2	3	.400	3.16	35	7	1	88.1	75	48	36	1	2	3	3	20	6	1	.300
1947	0	0	–	10.50	7	1	0	12	16	10	6	0	0	0	0	4	1	0	.250
2 yrs.	2	3	.400	4.04	42	8	1	100.1	91	58	42	1	2	3	3	24	7	1	.292

Charlie Buffinton

BUFFINTON, CHARLES G.
B. June 14, 1861, Fall River, Mass.   D. Sept. 23, 1907, Fall River, Mass.
Manager 1890.
BR TR 6'1"   180 lbs.

	W	L	PCT	ERA	G	GS	CG	IP	H	BB	SO	ShO	W	L	SV	AB	H	HR	BA
1882 BOS N	2	3	.400	4.07	5	5	4	42	53	14	17	1	0	0	0	50	13	0	.260
1883	24	13	.649	3.03	43	41	34	333	346	51	188	5	1	0	1	341	81	1	.238
1884	47	16	.746	2.15	67	67	63	587	506	76	417	8	0	0	0	352	94	1	.267
1885	22	27	.449	2.88	51	50	49	434.1	425	112	242	6	0	0	0	338	81	1	.240
1886	8	10	.444	4.59	18	17	16	151	203	39	47	0	0	0	0	176	51	1	.290
1887 PHI N	21	17	.553	3.66	40	38	35	332.1	352	92	160	1	1	0	0	269	72	1	.268
1888	28	17	.622	1.91	46	46	43	400.1	324	59	199	6	0	0	0	160	29	0	.181
1889	27	17	.614	3.24	47	43	37	380	390	121	153	2	3	0	0	154	32	0	.208
1890 PHI P	19	14	.576	3.81	36	33	28	283.1	312	126	89	0	1	0	1	150	41	1	.273
1891 BOS AA	28	9	.757	2.55	48	43	33	363.2	303	120	158	4	1	0	3	181	34	1	.188
1892 BAL N	5	8	.385	4.92	13	13	9	97	130	46	30	0	0	0	0	43	15	0	.349
11 yrs.	231	151	.605	2.96	414	396	351	3404	3344	856	1700	33	7	0	5	*			

Bob Buhl

BUHL, ROBERT RAY
B. Aug. 12, 1928, Saginaw, Mich.
BR TR 6'2"   180 lbs.
BB 1958-60,1966

	W	L	PCT	ERA	G	GS	CG	IP	H	BB	SO	ShO	W	L	SV	AB	H	HR	BA
1953 MIL N	13	8	.619	2.97	30	18	8	154.1	133	73	83	3	4	2	0	53	6	0	.113
1954	2	7	.222	4.00	31	14	2	110.1	117	65	57	1	0	2	3	31	1	0	.032
1955	13	11	.542	3.21	38	27	11	201.2	168	109	117	1	1	1	1	57	6	0	.105
1956	18	8	.692	3.32	38	33	13	216.2	190	105	86	2	1	0	0	73	7	0	.096
1957	18	7	.720	2.74	34	31	14	216.2	191	121	117	2	0	0	0	73	6	0	.082
1958	5	2	.714	3.45	11	10	3	73	74	30	27	0	0	0	1	25	5	0	.200
1959	15	9	.625	2.86	31	25	12	198	181	74	105	4	0	1	0	70	4	0	.057
1960	16	9	.640	3.09	36	33	11	238.2	202	103	121	2	1	0	0	89	14	0	.157
1961	9	10	.474	4.11	32	28	9	188.1	180	98	77	1	0	0	0	60	4	0	.067
1962 2 teams	MIL	N	(1G 0–1)		CHI	N	(34G 12–13)												
" total	12	14	.462	3.87	35	31	8	214	210	98	110	1	0	0	0	70	0	0	.000
1963 CHI N	11	14	.440	3.38	37	34	6	226	229	62	108	0	0	0	0	74	8	0	.108
1964	15	14	.517	3.83	36	35	11	227.2	208	68	107	3	0	0	0	73	7	0	.096
1965	13	11	.542	4.39	32	31	2	184.1	207	57	92	0	0	0	0	67	4	0	.060
1966 2 teams	CHI	N	(1G 0–0)		PHI	N	(32G 6–8)												
" total	6	8	.429	4.96	33	19	1	134.1	160	40	60	0	2	2	1	42	4	0	.095
1967 PHI N	0	0	–	13.50	3	0	0	2.2	6	2	1	0	0	0	0	0	0	0	–
15 yrs.	166	132	.557	3.55	457	369	111	2586.2	2446	1105	1268	20	9	8	6	857	76	0	.089
WORLD SERIES																			
1957 MIL N	0	1	.000	10.80	2	2	0	3.1	6	6	4	0	0	0	0	1	0	0	.000

Cy Buker

BUKER, CYRIL OWEN
B. Feb. 5, 1919, Greenwood, Wis.
BL TR 5'11"   190 lbs.

	W	L	PCT	ERA	G	GS	CG	IP	H	BB	SO	ShO	W	L	SV	AB	H	HR	BA
1945 BKN N	7	2	.778	3.30	42	4	0	87.1	90	45	48	0	2	0	5	16	3	0	.188

Red Bullock

BULLOCK, MALTON JOSEPH
B. Oct. 12, 1912, Biloxi, Miss.
BL TL 6'1"   192 lbs.

	W	L	PCT	ERA	G	GS	CG	IP	H	BB	SO	ShO	W	L	SV	AB	H	HR	BA
1936 PHI A	0	2	.000	14.04	12	2	0	16.2	19	37	7	0	0	0	1	4	0	0	.000

Wally Bunker

BUNKER, WALLACE EDWARD
B. Jan. 25, 1945, Seattle, Wash.
BR TR 6'2"   197 lbs.

	W	L	PCT	ERA	G	GS	CG	IP	H	BB	SO	ShO	W	L	SV	AB	H	HR	BA
1963 BAL A	0	1	.000	13.50	1	1	0	4	10	3	1	0	0	0	0	2	1	0	.500
1964	19	5	.792	2.69	29	29	12	214	161	62	96	1	0	0	0	72	5	0	.069
1965	10	8	.556	3.38	34	27	4	189	170	58	84	1	0	0	2	55	4	0	.073
1966	10	6	.625	4.29	29	24	3	142.2	151	48	89	0	0	1	0	48	5	0	.104
1967	3	7	.300	4.09	29	9	1	88	83	31	51	0	1	2	1	26	2	0	.077
1968	2	0	1.000	2.41	18	10	2	71	59	14	44	1	0	0	0	18	2	0	.111
1969 KC A	12	11	.522	3.23	35	31	10	222.2	198	62	130	1	1	0	2	70	10	0	.143
1970	2	11	.154	4.20	24	15	2	122	109	50	59	1	0	1	0	31	2	0	.065

	W	L	PCT	ERA	G	GS	CG	IP	H	BB	SO	ShO	Relief Pitching W	L	SV	BATTING AB	H	HR	BA

Wally Bunker *continued*

	W	L	PCT	ERA	G	GS	CG	IP	H	BB	SO	ShO	W	L	SV	AB	H	HR	BA
1971	2	3	.400	5.06	7	6	0	32	35	6	15	0	0	0	0	9	0	0	.000
9 yrs.	60	52	.536	3.51	206	152	34	1085.1	976	334	569	5	2	4	5	331	31	0	.094
WORLD SERIES																			
1966 BAL A	1	0	1.000	0.00	1	1	1	9	6	1	6	1	0	0	0	2	0	0	.000

Jim Bunning

BUNNING, JAMES PAUL DAVID
B. Oct. 23, 1931, Southgate, Ky.   BR TR 6'3"   190 lbs.

	W	L	PCT	ERA	G	GS	CG	IP	H	BB	SO	ShO	W	L	SV	AB	H	HR	BA
1955 DET A	3	5	.375	6.35	15	8	0	51	59	32	37	0	2	0	1	15	3	0	.200
1956	5	1	.833	3.71	15	3	0	53.1	55	28	34	0	4	0	1	18	6	0	.333
1957	20	8	.714	2.69	45	30	14	267.1	214	72	182	1	2	1	1	94	20	1	.213
1958	14	12	.538	3.52	35	34	10	219.2	188	79	177	3	0	0	0	75	14	0	.187
1959	17	13	.567	3.89	40	35	14	249.2	220	75	201	1	0	1	1	89	17	1	.191
1960	11	14	.440	2.79	36	34	10	252	217	64	201	3	0	0	0	81	13	0	.160
1961	17	11	.607	3.19	38	37	12	268	232	71	194	4	0	0	1	100	13	0	.130
1962	19	10	.655	3.59	41	35	12	258	262	74	184	2	0	0	6	95	23	1	.242
1963	12	13	.480	3.88	39	35	6	248.1	245	69	196	2	0	0	1	84	13	0	.155
1964 PHI N	19	8	.704	2.63	41	39	13	284.1	248	46	219	5	0	0	2	99	12	0	.121
1965	19	9	.679	2.60	39	39	15	291	253	62	268	7	0	0	0	103	22	1	.214
1966	19	14	.576	2.41	43	41	16	314	260	55	252	5	1	0	1	106	19	0	.179
1967	17	15	.531	2.29	40	40	16	302.1	241	73	253	6	0	0	0	104	17	2	.163
1968 PIT N	4	14	.222	3.88	27	26	3	160	168	48	95	1	0	0	0	51	5	0	.098
1969 2 teams			PIT	N	(25G 10–9)		LA	N	(9G 3–1)										
" total	13	10	.565	3.69	34	34	5	212.1	212	59	157	0	0	0	0	65	4	0	.062
1970 PHI N	10	15	.400	4.11	34	33	4	219	233	56	147	0	0	0	0	71	9	0	.127
1971	5	12	.294	5.48	29	16	1	110	126	37	58	0	0	2	1	25	3	1	.120
17 yrs.	224	184	.549	3.27	591	519	151	3760.1	3433	1000	2855	40	9	4	16	1275	213	7	.167
											10th								

Bill Burbach

BURBACH, WILLIAM DAVID
B. Aug. 22, 1947, Dickeyville, Wis.   BR TR 6'4"   215 lbs.

	W	L	PCT	ERA	G	GS	CG	IP	H	BB	SO	ShO	W	L	SV	AB	H	HR	BA
1969 NY A	6	8	.429	3.65	31	24	2	140.2	112	102	82	1	1	0	0	40	4	0	.100
1970	0	2	.000	10.06	4	4	0	17	23	9	10	0	0	0	0	5	0	0	.000
1971	0	1	.000	12.00	2	0	0	3	6	5	3	0	0	1	0	2	0	0	.000
3 yrs.	6	11	.353	4.48	37	28	2	160.2	141	116	95	1	1	1	0	47	4	0	.085

Larry Burchart

BURCHART, LARRY WAYNE
B. Feb. 8, 1946, Tulsa, Okla.   BR TR 6'3"   205 lbs.

	W	L	PCT	ERA	G	GS	CG	IP	H	BB	SO	ShO	W	L	SV	AB	H	HR	BA
1969 CLE A	0	2	.000	4.25	29	0	0	42.1	42	24	26	0	0	2	0	0	0	0	—

Fred Burchell

BURCHELL, FREDERICK DUFF
B. July 14, 1879, Perth Amboy, N. J.   D. Nov. 20, 1951, Jordan, N. Y.   BL TL

	W	L	PCT	ERA	G	GS	CG	IP	H	BB	SO	ShO	W	L	SV	AB	H	HR	BA
1903 PHI N	0	3	.000	2.86	6	3	2	44	48	14	12	0	0	0	0	16	3	0	.188
1907 BOS A	0	1	.000	2.70	2	1	0	10	8	2	6	0	0	0	0	5	1	0	.200
1908	10	8	.556	2.96	31	19	9	179.2	161	65	94	0	1	1	0	69	17	0	.246
1909	3	3	.500	2.94	10	5	1	52	51	11	12	0	1	0	0	19	3	0	.158
4 yrs.	13	15	.464	2.93	49	28	12	285.2	268	92	124	0	2	1	0	109	24	0	.220

Freddie Burdette

BURDETTE, FREDDIE THOMASON
B. Sept. 15, 1936, Moultrie, Ga.   BR TR 6'1"   170 lbs.

	W	L	PCT	ERA	G	GS	CG	IP	H	BB	SO	ShO	W	L	SV	AB	H	HR	BA
1962 CHI N	0	0	—	3.72	8	0	0	9.2	5	8	5	0	0	0	1	1	0	0	.000
1963	0	0	—	3.86	4	0	0	4.2	5	2	1	0	0	0	0	0	0	0	—
1964	1	0	1.000	3.15	18	0	0	20	17	10	4	0	1	0	0	1	1	0	1.000
3 yrs.	1	0	1.000	3.41	30	0	0	34.1	27	20	10	0	1	0	1	2	1	0	.500

Lew Burdette

BURDETTE, SELVA LEWIS
B. Nov. 22, 1926, Nitro, W. Va.   BR TR 6'2"   180 lbs.

	W	L	PCT	ERA	G	GS	CG	IP	H	BB	SO	ShO	W	L	SV	AB	H	HR	BA
1950 NY A	0	0	—	6.75	2	0	0	1.1	3	0	0	0	0	0	0	0	0	0	—
1951 BOS N	0	0	—	6.23	3	0	0	4.1	6	5	1	0	0	0	0	1	0	0	.000
1952	6	11	.353	3.61	45	9	5	137	138	47	47	0	2	8	7	35	4	0	.114
1953 MIL N	15	5	.750	3.24	46	13	6	175	177	56	58	1	8	0	8	53	9	0	.170
1954	15	14	.517	2.76	38	32	13	238	224	62	79	4	1	1	0	79	7	0	.089
1955	13	8	.619	4.03	42	33	11	230	253	73	70	2	2	1	0	86	20	0	.233
1956	19	10	.655	2.70	39	35	16	256.1	234	52	110	6	0	0	1	86	16	0	.186
1957	17	9	.654	3.72	37	33	14	256.2	260	59	78	1	2	1	0	88	13	2	.148
1958	20	10	.667	2.91	40	36	19	275.1	279	50	113	3	2	0	0	99	24	3	.242
1959	21	15	.583	4.07	41	39	20	289.2	312	38	105	4	0	0	1	104	21	0	.202
1960	19	13	.594	3.36	45	32	18	275.2	277	35	83	4	3	2	4	91	16	2	.176
1961	18	11	.621	4.00	40	36	14	272.1	295	33	92	3	2	0	0	103	21	3	.204
1962	10	9	.526	4.89	37	19	6	143.2	172	23	59	1	3	1	2	51	9	0	.176
1963 2 teams			MIL	N	(15G 6–5)		STL	N	(21G 3–8)										
" total	9	13	.409	3.70	36	27	7	182.2	177	40	73	1	1	2	2	57	4	0	.070
1964 2 teams			STL	N	(8G 1–0)		CHI	N	(28G 9–9)										
" total	10	9	.526	4.66	36	17	8	141	162	22	43	2	2	1	0	44	12	2	.273
1965 2 teams			CHI	N	(7G 0–2)		PHI	N	(19G 3–3)										
" total	3	5	.375	5.44	26	12	1	91	121	21	28	1	0	0	0	26	8	0	.308
1966 CAL A	7	2	.778	3.39	54	0	0	79.2	80	12	27	0	7	2	5	8	1	0	.125
1967	1	0	1.000	4.91	19	0	0	18.1	16	0	8	0	1	0	1	0	0	0	—
18 yrs.	203	144	.585	3.66	626	373	158	3068	3186	628	1074	33	36	19	31	1011	185	12	.183
WORLD SERIES																			
1957 MIL N	3	0	1.000	0.67	3	3	3	27	21	4	13	2	0	0	0	8	0	0	.000
1958	1	2	.333	5.64	3	3	1	22.1	22	4	12	0	0	0	0	9	1	1	.111
2 yrs.	4	2	.667	2.92	6	6	4	49.1	43	8	25	2	0	0	0	17	1	1	.059
											4th								

	W	L	PCT	ERA	G	GS	CG	IP	H	BB	SO	ShO	Relief Pitching W	L	SV	BATTING AB	H	HR	BA

Bill Burdick

BURDICK, WILLIAM BYRON   BR TR
B. Oct. 11, 1859, Austin, Minn.   D. Oct. 23, 1949, Spokane, Wash.

	W	L	PCT	ERA	G	GS	CG	IP	H	BB	SO	ShO	W	L	SV	AB	H	HR	BA
1888 **IND N**	10	10	.500	2.81	20	20	20	176	168	43	55	0	0	0	0	68	10	0	.147
1889	2	4	.333	4.53	10	4	2	45.2	58	13	16	0	0	2	1	17	2	0	.118
2 yrs.	12	14	.462	3.17	30	24	22	221.2	226	56	71	0	0	2	1	85	12	0	.141

Tom Burgmeier

BURGMEIER, THOMAS HENRY (Bugs)   BL TL 5'11" 185 lbs.
B. Aug. 2, 1943, St. Paul, Minn.

	W	L	PCT	ERA	G	GS	CG	IP	H	BB	SO	ShO	W	L	SV	AB	H	HR	BA
1968 **CAL A**	1	4	.200	4.33	56	2	0	72.2	65	24	33	0	1	2	5	2	0	0	.000
1969 **KC A**	3	1	.750	4.17	31	0	0	54	67	21	23	0	3	1	0	18	3	0	.167
1970	6	6	.500	3.18	41	0	0	68	59	23	43	0	6	6	1	14	2	0	.143
1971	9	7	.563	1.74	67	0	0	88	71	30	44	0	9	7	17	20	5	0	.250
1972	6	2	.750	4.25	51	0	0	55	67	33	18	0	6	2	9	12	4	0	.333
1973	0	0	–	5.40	6	0	0	10	13	4	4	0	0	0	1	0	0	0	–
1974 **MIN A**	5	3	.625	4.52	50	0	0	91.2	92	26	34	0	5	3	4	0	0	0	–
1975	5	8	.385	3.09	46	0	0	75.2	76	23	41	0	5	8	11	0	0	0	–
1976	8	1	.889	2.50	57	0	0	115.1	95	29	45	0	8	1	1	0	0	0	–
1977	6	4	.600	5.10	61	0	0	97	113	33	35	0	6	4	7	0	0	0	–
1978 **BOS A**	2	1	.667	4.40	35	1	0	61.1	74	23	24	0	2	1	4	0	0	0	–
1979	3	2	.600	2.73	44	0	0	89	89	16	60	0	3	2	4	0	0	0	–
1980	5	4	.556	2.00	62	0	0	99	87	20	54	0	5	4	24	0	0	0	–
1981	4	5	.444	2.85	32	0	0	60	61	17	35	0	4	5	6	0	0	0	–
1982	7	0	1.000	2.29	40	0	0	102.1	98	22	44	0	7	0	2	0	0	0	–
1983 **OAK A**	6	7	.462	2.81	49	0	0	96	89	32	39	0	6	7	4	0	0	0	–
1984	3	0	1.000	2.35	17	0	0	23	15	8	8	0	3	0	2	0	0	0	–
17 yrs.	79	55	.590	3.23	745	3	0	1258	1231	384	584	0	79	53	102	66	14	0	.212

Sandy Burk

BURK, CHARLES SANFORD   BR TR
B. Apr. 22, 1887, Columbus, Ohio   D. Oct. 11, 1934, Brooklyn, N. Y.

	W	L	PCT	ERA	G	GS	CG	IP	H	BB	SO	ShO	W	L	SV	AB	H	HR	BA
1910 **BKN N**	0	3	.000	6.05	4	3	1	19.1	17	27	14	0	0	0	0	5	0	0	.000
1911	1	3	.250	5.12	13	7	1	58	54	47	15	0	0	0	0	19	2	0	.105
1912 2 teams		BKN	N (2G 0–0)		STL	N (12G 1–3)													
" total	1	3	.250	2.55	14	4	2	53	46	15	19	0	0	1	1	15	1	0	.067
1913 **STL N**	1	2	.333	5.14	19	5	0	70	81	33	29	0	0	2	1	22	2	0	.091
1915 **PIT F**	2	0	1.000	1.00	2	2	1	18	8	11	9	0	0	0	0	6	1	0	.167
5 yrs.	5	11	.313	4.25	52	21	5	218.1	206	133	86	0	0	3	2	67	6	0	.090

Elmer Burkart

BURKART, ELMER ROBERT (Swede)   BR TR 6'2" 190 lbs.
B. Feb. 1, 1917, Torresdale, Pa.

	W	L	PCT	ERA	G	GS	CG	IP	H	BB	SO	ShO	W	L	SV	AB	H	HR	BA
1936 **PHI N**	0	0	–	3.52	2	2	0	7.2	4	12	2	0	0	0	0	2	0	0	.000
1937	0	0	–	6.19	7	0	0	16	20	9	4	0	0	0	0	6	0	0	.000
1938	0	1	.000	4.50	2	1	1	10	12	3	1	0	0	0	0	3	0	0	.000
1939	1	0	1.000	4.32	5	0	0	8.1	11	2	2	0	1	0	0	1	1	0	1.000
4 yrs.	1	1	.500	4.93	16	3	1	42	47	26	9	0	1	0	0	12	1	0	.083

Billy Burke

BURKE, WILLIAM IGNATIUS   BL TL 5'10" 165 lbs.
B. July 11, 1889, Clinton, Mass.   D. Feb. 9, 1967, Worcester, Mass.

	W	L	PCT	ERA	G	GS	CG	IP	H	BB	SO	ShO	W	L	SV	AB	H	HR	BA
1910 **BOS N**	1	0	1.000	4.08	19	1	1	64	68	29	22	0	1	0	0	21	4	0	.190
1911	0	1	.000	18.90	2	1	0	3.1	6	5	1	0	0	0	0	1	1	0	1.000
2 yrs.	1	1	.500	4.81	21	2	1	67.1	74	34	23	0	0	0	0	22	5	0	.227

Bobby Burke

BURKE, ROBERT JAMES (Lefty)   BL TL 6'½" 150 lbs.
B. Jan. 23, 1907, Joliet, Ill.   D. Feb. 8, 1971, Joliet, Ill.

	W	L	PCT	ERA	G	GS	CG	IP	H	BB	SO	ShO	W	L	SV	AB	H	HR	BA
1927 **WAS A**	3	2	.600	3.96	36	6	1	100	92	32	21	0	1	0	0	24	3	0	.125
1928	2	4	.333	3.90	26	7	2	85.1	87	18	27	1	0	1	0	20	5	0	.250
1929	6	8	.429	4.79	37	17	4	141	154	55	51	0	1	1	0	43	6	0	.140
1930	3	4	.429	3.63	24	4	2	74.1	62	29	35	0	1	2	3	23	4	0	.174
1931	8	3	.727	4.27	30	13	3	128.2	124	50	38	1	3	0	2	47	10	0	.213
1932	3	6	.333	5.14	22	10	2	91	98	44	32	0	1	0	0	25	5	0	.200
1933	4	3	.571	3.23	25	6	4	64	64	31	28	1	0	1	0	17	4	0	.235
1934	8	8	.500	3.21	37	15	7	168	155	72	52	1	2	2	0	57	13	0	.228
1935	1	8	.111	7.46	15	10	2	66.1	90	27	16	0	0	0	0	22	4	0	.182
1937 **PHI N**	0	0	–	∞	2	0	0		1	2	0	0	0	0	0	0	0	0	–
10 yrs.	38	46	.452	4.29	254	88	27	918.2	927	360	300	4	9	7	5	278	54	0	.194

John Burke

BURKE, JOHN PATRICK
B. Jan. 27, 1877, Hazleton, Pa.   D. Aug. 4, 1950, Jersey City, N. J.

	W	L	PCT	ERA	G	GS	CG	IP	H	BB	SO	ShO	W	L	SV	AB	H	HR	BA
1902 **NY N**	0	1	.000	5.79	2	1	1	14	21	3	3	0	0	0	0	*			

Steve Burke

BURKE, STEVEN MICHAEL   BR TR 6'2" 200 lbs.
B. Mar. 5, 1955, Stockton, Calif.

	W	L	PCT	ERA	G	GS	CG	IP	H	BB	SO	ShO	W	L	SV	AB	H	HR	BA
1977 **SEA A**	0	1	.000	2.81	6	0	0	16	12	7	6	0	0	1	0	0	0	0	–
1978	0	1	.000	3.49	18	0	0	49	46	24	16	0	0	1	0	0	0	0	–
2 yrs.	0	2	.000	3.32	24	0	0	65	58	31	22	0	0	2	0	0	0	0	–

Walter Burke

BURKE, WALTER R.   6' 200 lbs.
B. Calif.   D. Mar. 4, 1911, Memphis, Tenn.

	W	L	PCT	ERA	G	GS	CG	IP	H	BB	SO	ShO	W	L	SV	AB	H	HR	BA
1882 **BUF N**	0	1	.000	11.25	1	1	0	4	10	0	0	0	0	0	0	4	0	0	.000
1883	0	0	–	5.63	1	1	0	8	9	3	1	0	0	0	0	5	1	0	.200
1884 **BOS U**	19	15	.559	2.85	38	36	34	322	326	31	255	0	1	0	0	184	41	0	.223
1887 **DET N**	0	1	.000	6.00	2	2	1	15	21	5	3	0	0	0	0	8	2	0	.250
4 yrs.	19	17	.528	3.15	42	40	35	349	366	39	259	0	1	0	0	201	44	0	.219

	W	L	PCT	ERA	G	GS	CG	IP	H	BB	SO	ShO	Relief Pitching W	L	SV	BATTING AB	H	HR	BA

Jesse Burkett

BURKETT, JESSE CAIL (The Crab)   BL TL 5'8"   155 lbs.
B. Dec. 4, 1868, Wheeling, W. Va.   D. May 27, 1953, Worcester, Mass.
Hall of Fame 1946.

	W	L	PCT	ERA	G	GS	CG	IP	H	BB	SO	ShO	W	L	SV	AB	H	HR	BA
1890 NY N	3	10	.231	5.57	21	12	6	118	134	92	82	0	2	0	0	401	124	4	.309
1894 CLE N	0	0	–	4.50	1	0	0	4	6	1	0	0	0	0	0	523	187	8	.358
1902 STL A	0	1	.000	9.00	1	0	0	1	4	1	2	0	0	1	0	549	168	5	.306
3 yrs.	3	11	.214	5.56	23	12	6	123	144	94	84	0	2	1	0	*			

Ken Burkhart

BURKHART, KENNETH WILLIAM   BR TR 6'1"   190 lbs.
Born Kenneth William Burkhardt.
B. Nov. 18, 1916, Knoxville, Tenn.

	W	L	PCT	ERA	G	GS	CG	IP	H	BB	SO	ShO	W	L	SV	AB	H	HR	BA
1945 STL N	19	8	**.704**	2.90	42	22	12	217.1	206	66	67	4	6	1	2	72	13	0	.181
1946	6	3	.667	2.88	25	13	5	100	111	36	32	2	1	1	2	34	5	0	.147
1947	3	6	.333	5.21	34	6	1	95	108	23	44	0	1	3	1	24	3	0	.125
1948 2 teams			STL	N (20G 0-0)		CIN	N	(16G 0-3)												
" total	0	3	.000	6.27	36	0	0	79	92	30	30	0	0	3	1	13	4	1	.308
1949 CIN N	0	0	–	3.18	11	0	0	28.1	29	10	8	0	0	0	1	7	2	0	.286
5 yrs.	28	20	.583	3.84	148	41	18	519.2	546	165	181	6	8	8	7	150	27	1	.180

Wally Burnette

BURNETTE, WALLACE HARPER   BR TR 6'½"   178 lbs.
B. June 20, 1929, Blairs, Va.

	W	L	PCT	ERA	G	GS	CG	IP	H	BB	SO	ShO	W	L	SV	AB	H	HR	BA
1956 KC A	6	8	.429	2.89	18	14	4	121.1	115	39	54	1	2	1	0	39	2	0	.051
1957	7	12	.368	4.30	38	9	1	113	115	44	57	0	5	6	1	32	8	0	.250
1958	1	1	.500	3.49	12	4	0	28.1	29	14	11	0	0	0	0	6	1	0	.167
3 yrs.	14	21	.400	3.56	68	27	5	262.2	259	97	122	1	7	7	1	77	11	0	.143

Bill Burns

BURNS, WILLIAM THOMAS (Sleepy Bill)   BB TL 6'2"   195 lbs.
B. Jan. 29, 1880, San Saba, Tex.   D. June 6, 1953, Ramona, Calif.

	W	L	PCT	ERA	G	GS	CG	IP	H	BB	SO	ShO	W	L	SV	AB	H	HR	BA
1908 WAS A	6	11	.353	1.69	23	19	11	165	135	18	55	2	0	1	0	54	8	0	.148
1909 2 teams		WAS	A (6G 1-1)		CHI	A	(22G 7-13)													
" total	8	14	.364	1.86	28	23	9	203.2	194	42	65	3	1	1	0	69	12	0	.174
1910 2 teams		CHI	A (1G 0-0)		CIN	N	(31G 8-13)													
" total	8	13	.381	3.47	32	21	13	179	183	50	57	2	0	3	0	61	16	0	.262
1911 2 teams		CIN	N (6G 1-0)		PHI	N	(21G 6-10)													
" total	7	10	.412	3.38	27	17	8	138.2	149	29	52	3	1	2	1	47	9	0	.191
1912 DET A	1	4	.200	5.35	6	5	2	38.2	52	9	6	0	0	0	0	13	3	0	.231
5 yrs.	30	52	.366	2.69	116	85	43	725	713	148	235	10	2	7	1	244	48	0	.197

Britt Burns

BURNS, ROBERT BRITT   BR TL 6'5"   215 lbs.
B. June 8, 1959, Houston, Tex.

	W	L	PCT	ERA	G	GS	CG	IP	H	BB	SO	ShO	W	L	SV	AB	H	HR	BA
1978 CHI A	0	2	.000	12.91	2	2	0	7.2	14	3	3	0	0	0	0	0	0	0	–
1979	0	0	–	5.40	6	0	0	5	10	1	2	0	0	0	0	0	0	0	–
1980	15	13	.536	2.84	34	32	11	238	213	63	133	1	1	0	0	0	0	0	–
1981	10	6	.625	2.64	24	23	5	157	139	49	108	1	0	0	0	0	0	0	–
1982	13	5	.722	4.04	28	28	5	169.1	168	67	116	1	0	0	0	0	0	0	–
1983	10	11	.476	3.58	29	26	8	173.2	165	55	115	4	1	0	0	0	0	0	–
1984	4	12	.250	5.00	34	16	2	117	130	45	85	0	1	2	3	0	0	0	–
7 yrs.	52	49	.515	3.58	157	127	31	867.2	839	283	562	7	3	2	3	0	0	0	–

LEAGUE CHAMPIONSHIP SERIES

	W	L	PCT	ERA	G	GS	CG	IP	H	BB	SO	ShO	W	L	SV	AB	H	HR	BA
1983 CHI A	0	1	.000	0.96	1	1	0	9.1	6	5	8	0	0	0	0	0	0	0	–

Denny Burns

BURNS, DENNIS   BR TR 5'10"   180 lbs.
B. May 24, 1898, Tiff City, Mo.   D. May 21, 1969, Tulsa, Okla.

	W	L	PCT	ERA	G	GS	CG	IP	H	BB	SO	ShO	W	L	SV	AB	H	HR	BA
1923 PHI A	2	1	.667	2.00	4	3	2	27	21	7	8	0	0	0	0	9	1	0	.111
1924	6	8	.429	5.08	37	17	7	154	191	68	26	0	0	1	1	42	6	0	.143
2 yrs.	8	9	.471	4.62	41	20	9	181	212	75	34	0	0	1	1	51	7	0	.137

Dick Burns

BURNS, RICHARD SIMON   TL   140 lbs.
B. Dec. 26, 1863, Holyoke, Mass.   D. Nov. 18, 1937, Holyoke, Mass.

	W	L	PCT	ERA	G	GS	CG	IP	H	BB	SO	ShO	W	L	SV	AB	H	HR	BA
1883 DET N	2	12	.143	4.51	17	13	13	127.2	172	33	30	0	0	1	0	140	26	0	.186
1884 CIN U	23	15	.605	2.46	40	40	34	329.2	298	47	167	1	0	0	0	350	107	4	.306
1885 STL N	0	0	–	9.00	1	0	0	3	3	0	2	0	0	0	0	54	12	0	.222
3 yrs.	25	27	.481	3.07	58	53	47	460.1	473	80	199	1	0	1	0	*			

Farmer Burns

BURNS, JAMES   TR
B. Ashtabula, Ohio

	W	L	PCT	ERA	G	GS	CG	IP	H	BB	SO	ShO	W	L	SV	AB	H	HR	BA
1901 STL N	0	0	–	9.00	1	0	0	1	2	1	0	0	0	0	0	0	0	0	–

Oyster Burns

BURNS, THOMAS P.   BR TR 5'8"   183 lbs.
B. Sept. 6, 1864, Philadelphia, Pa.   D. Nov. 11, 1928, Brooklyn, N. Y.

	W	L	PCT	ERA	G	GS	CG	IP	H	BB	SO	ShO	W	L	SV	AB	H	HR	BA
1884 BAL AA	0	0	–	3.00	2	0	0	9	12	2	6	0	0	0	1	138	40	6	.290
1885	7	4	.636	3.58	15	11	10	105.2	112	21	30	1	0	0	3	321	74	5	.231
1887	1	0	1.000	9.53	3	0	0	11.1	16	4	2	0	1	0	0	551	188	10	.341
1888	0	1	.000	4.26	5	0	0	12.2	12	3	2	0	0	1	0	528	158	6	.299
4 yrs.	8	5	.615	4.09	25	11	10	138.2	152	30	40	1	1	1	4	*			

Tom Burns

BURNS, THOMAS EVERETT   BL TR 5'9"   165 lbs.
B. Mar. 30, 1857, Honesdale, Pa.   D. Mar. 19, 1902, Jersey City, N. J.
Manager 1892, 1898-99.

	W	L	PCT	ERA	G	GS	CG	IP	H	BB	SO	ShO	W	L	SV	AB	H	HR	BA
1880 CHI N	0	0	–	0.00	1	0	0	1.1	2	2	1	0	0	0	0	*			

Pete Burnside

BURNSIDE, PETER WILLITS   BR TL 6'2"   180 lbs.
B. July 2, 1930, Evanston, Ill.

	W	L	PCT	ERA	G	GS	CG	IP	H	BB	SO	ShO	W	L	SV	AB	H	HR	BA
1955 NY N	1	0	1.000	2.84	2	2	1	12.2	10	9	2	0	0	0	0	5	1	0	.200
1957	1	4	.200	8.80	10	9	1	30.2	47	13	18	0	0	1	0	9	0	0	.000
1958 SF N	0	0	–	6.75	6	1	0	10.2	20	5	4	0	0	0	0	0	0	0	–
1959 DET A	1	3	.250	3.77	30	0	0	62	55	25	49	0	1	3	1	10	0	0	.000

	W	L	PCT	ERA	G	GS	CG	IP	H	BB	SO	ShO	Relief Pitching W	L	SV	BATTING AB	H	HR	BA

Pete Burnside continued

	W	L	PCT	ERA	G	GS	CG	IP	H	BB	SO	ShO	W	L	SV	AB	H	HR	BA
1960	7	7	.500	4.28	31	15	2	113.2	122	50	71	0	3	1	2	27	4	0	.148
1961 WAS A	4	9	.308	4.53	33	16	4	113.1	106	51	56	0	0	0	2	34	2	0	.059
1962	5	11	.313	4.45	40	20	6	149.2	152	51	74	0	0	1	2	35	2	0	.057
1963 2 teams			BAL	A (6G 0–1)		WAS	A	(38G 0–1)											
" total	0	2	.000	6.03	44	1	0	74.2	95	26	29	0	0	1	0	12	1	0	.083
8 yrs.	19	36	.345	4.81	196	64	14	567.1	607	230	303	3	4	7	7	132	10	0	.076

Sheldon Burnside

BURNSIDE, SHELDON JOHN
B. Dec. 22, 1954, South Bend, Ind.   BR TL 6'5"   200 lbs.

	W	L	PCT	ERA	G	GS	CG	IP	H	BB	SO	ShO	W	L	SV	AB	H	HR	BA
1978 DET A	0	0	–	9.00	2	0	0	4	4	2	3	0	0	0	0	0	0	0	–
1979	1	1	.500	6.43	10	0	0	21	28	8	13	0	1	1	0	0	0	0	–
1980 CIN N	1	0	1.000	1.80	7	0	0	5	6	1	2	0	1	0	0	1	0	0	.000
3 yrs.	2	1	.667	6.00	19	0	0	30	38	11	18	0	2	1	0	1	0	0	.000

George Burpo

BURPO, GEORGE HARVIE
B. June 19, 1922, Jenkins, Ky.   BR TL 6'   195 lbs.

	W	L	PCT	ERA	G	GS	CG	IP	H	BB	SO	ShO	W	L	SV	AB	H	HR	BA
1946 CIN N	0	0	–	15.43	2	0	0	2.1	4	5	1	0	0	0	0	0	0	0	–

Harry Burrell

BURRELL, HARRY J.
B. 1866, E. Weymouth, Mass.   D. Dec. 11, 1914, Omaha, Neb.

	W	L	PCT	ERA	G	GS	CG	IP	H	BB	SO	ShO	W	L	SV	AB	H	HR	BA
1891 STL AA	5	2	.714	4.81	7	4	3	43	51	21	19	0	3	0	0	22	5	0	.227

Al Burris

BURRIS, ALVA BURTON
B. Jan. 28, 1874, Warwick, Md.   D. Mar. 24, 1938, Salisbury, Md.

	W	L	PCT	ERA	G	GS	CG	IP	H	BB	SO	ShO	W	L	SV	AB	H	HR	BA
1894 PHI N	0	0	–	18.00	1	0	0	5	14	2	0	0	0	0	0	4	2	0	.500

Ray Burris

BURRIS, BERTRAM RAY
B. Aug. 22, 1950, Idabel, Okla.   BR TR 6'5"   200 lbs.

	W	L	PCT	ERA	G	GS	CG	IP	H	BB	SO	ShO	W	L	SV	AB	H	HR	BA
1973 CHI N	1	1	.500	2.91	31	1	0	65	65	27	57	0	0	1	0	7	1	0	.143
1974	3	5	.375	6.60	40	5	0	75	91	26	40	0	3	1	1	13	1	0	.077
1975	15	10	.600	4.12	36	35	8	238	259	73	108	2	0	0	0	82	15	0	.183
1976	15	13	.536	3.11	37	36	10	249	251	70	112	4	0	0	0	81	9	0	.111
1977	14	16	.467	4.72	39	39	5	221	270	67	105	1	0	0	0	69	12	1	.174
1978	7	13	.350	4.75	40	32	4	199	210	79	94	1	1	1	1	61	7	0	.115
1979 3 teams			CHI	N (14G 0–0)		NY	A	(15G 1–3)		NY	N	(4G 0–2)							
" total	1	5	.167	5.30	33	4	0	71.1	84	31	43	0	1	3	0	7	1	0	.143
1980 NY N	7	13	.350	4.02	29	29	1	170	181	54	83	0	0	0	0	51	5	0	.098
1981 MON N	9	7	.563	3.04	22	21	4	136	117	41	52	0	0	0	0	37	7	0	.189
1982	4	14	.222	4.73	37	15	2	123.2	143	53	55	0	4	3	2	28	5	0	.179
1983	4	7	.364	3.68	40	17	2	154	139	56	100	1	1	2	0	39	9	0	.231
1984 OAK A	13	10	.565	3.15	34	28	5	211.2	193	90	93	1	1	0	0	0	0	0	–
12 yrs.	93	114	.449	4.04	418	262	41	1913.2	2003	667	942	10	11	11	4	475	72	1	.152

DIVISIONAL PLAYOFF SERIES

	W	L	PCT	ERA	G	GS	CG	IP	H	BB	SO	ShO	W	L	SV	AB	H	HR	BA
1981 MON N	0	1	.000	5.06	1	1	0	5.1	7	4	4	0	0	0	0	2	0	0	.000

LEAGUE CHAMPIONSHIP SERIES

	W	L	PCT	ERA	G	GS	CG	IP	H	BB	SO	ShO	W	L	SV	AB	H	HR	BA
1981 MON N	1	0	1.000	0.53	2	2	1	17	10	3	4	1	0	0	0	6	0	0	.000

John Burrows

BURROWS, JOHN
B. Oct. 30, 1913, Winnfield, La.   BR TL 5'10"   200 lbs.

	W	L	PCT	ERA	G	GS	CG	IP	H	BB	SO	ShO	W	L	SV	AB	H	HR	BA
1943 2 teams			PHI	A (4G 0–1)		CHI	N	(23G 0–2)											
" total	0	3	.000	4.69	27	2	0	40.1	33	25	21	0	0	1	2	4	2	0	.500
1944 CHI N	0	0	–	18.00	3	0	0	3	7	3	1	0	0	0	0	0	0	0	–
2 yrs.	0	3	.000	5.61	30	2	0	43.1	40	28	22	0	0	1	2	4	2	0	.500

Jim Burton

BURTON, JAMES SCOTT
B. Oct. 27, 1949, Royal Oak, Mich.   BR TL 6'3"   195 lbs.

	W	L	PCT	ERA	G	GS	CG	IP	H	BB	SO	ShO	W	L	SV	AB	H	HR	BA
1975 BOS A	1	2	.333	2.89	29	4	0	53	58	19	39	0	1	0	1	0	0	0	–
1977	0	0	–	0.00	1	0	0	2.2	2	1	3	0	0	0	0	0	0	0	–
2 yrs.	1	2	.333	2.75	30	4	0	55.2	60	20	42	0	1	0	1	0	0	0	–

WORLD SERIES

	W	L	PCT	ERA	G	GS	CG	IP	H	BB	SO	ShO	W	L	SV	AB	H	HR	BA
1975 BOS A	0	1	.000	9.00	2	0	0	1	1	3	0	0	0	1	0	0	0	0	–

Moe Burtschy

BURTSCHY, EDWARD FRANK
B. Apr. 18, 1922, Cincinnati, Ohio   BR TR 6'3"   208 lbs.

	W	L	PCT	ERA	G	GS	CG	IP	H	BB	SO	ShO	W	L	SV	AB	H	HR	BA
1950 PHI A	0	1	.000	7.11	9	1	0	19	22	21	12	0	0	0	0	5	0	0	.000
1951	0	0	–	5.29	7	0	0	17	18	12	4	0	0	0	0	3	1	0	.333
1954	5	4	.556	3.80	46	0	0	94.2	80	53	54	0	5	4	4	17	2	0	.118
1955 KC A	2	0	1.000	10.32	7	0	0	11.1	17	10	9	0	2	0	0	3	1	0	.333
1956	3	1	.750	3.95	21	0	0	43.1	41	30	18	0	3	1	0	8	1	0	.125
5 yrs.	10	6	.625	4.71	90	1	0	185.1	178	126	97	0	10	5	4	36	5	0	.139

Bill Burwell

BURWELL, WILLIAM EDWIN
B. Mar. 27, 1895, Jarbalo, Kans.   D. June 11, 1973, Ormond Beach, Fla.   BL TR 5'11"   175 lbs.
Manager 1947.

	W	L	PCT	ERA	G	GS	CG	IP	H	BB	SO	ShO	W	L	SV	AB	H	HR	BA
1920 STL A	6	4	.600	3.65	33	2	0	113.1	133	42	30	0	6	3	4	42	7	0	.167
1921	2	4	.333	5.12	33	3	1	84.1	102	29	17	0	1	3	2	25	6	0	.240
1928 PIT N	1	0	1.000	5.23	4	1	0	20.2	18	8	2	0	1	0	0	9	2	0	.222
3 yrs.	9	8	.529	4.37	70	6	1	218.1	253	79	49	0	8	6	6	76	15	0	.197

Dick Burwell

BURWELL, RICHARD MATTHEW
B. Jan. 23, 1940, Alton, Ill.   BR TR 6'1"   190 lbs.

	W	L	PCT	ERA	G	GS	CG	IP	H	BB	SO	ShO	W	L	SV	AB	H	HR	BA
1960 CHI N	0	0	–	5.59	3	1	0	9.2	11	7	1	0	0	0	0	3	1	0	.333
1961	0	0	–	9.00	2	0	0	4	6	4	0	0	0	0	0	1	0	0	.000
2 yrs.	0	0	–	6.59	5	1	0	13.2	17	11	1	0	0	0	0	4	1	0	.250

	W	L	PCT	ERA	G	GS	CG	IP	H	BB	SO	ShO	Relief Pitching			BATTING			BA
													W	L	SV	AB	H	HR	

Steve Busby

BUSBY, STEVEN LEE   BR TR 6'2"   205 lbs.
B. Sept. 29, 1949, Burbank, Calif.

	W	L	PCT	ERA	G	GS	CG	IP	H	BB	SO	ShO	W	L	SV	AB	H	HR	BA
1972 KC A	3	1	.750	1.58	5	5	3	40	28	8	31	0	0	0	0	15	3	0	.200
1973	16	15	.516	4.24	37	37	7	238	246	105	174	1	0	0	0	0	0	0	—
1974	22	14	.611	3.39	38	38	20	292.1	284	92	198	3	0	0	0	0	0	0	—
1975	18	12	.600	3.08	34	34	18	260.1	233	81	160	3	0	0	0	0	0	0	—
1976	3	3	.500	4.38	13	13	1	72	58	49	29	0	0	0	0	0	0	0	—
1978	1	0	1.000	7.59	7	5	0	21.1	24	15	10	0	0	0	0	0	0	0	—
1979	6	6	.500	3.64	22	12	4	94	71	64	45	0	1	2	0	0	0	0	—
1980	1	3	.250	6.21	11	6	0	42	59	19	12	0	0	0	0	0	0	0	—
8 yrs.	70	54	.565	3.72	167	150	53	1060	1003	433	659	7	1	2	0	15	3	0	.200

Don Buschhorn

BUSCHHORN, DONALD LEE   BL TR 6'   170 lbs.
B. Apr. 29, 1946, Independence, Mo.

	W	L	PCT	ERA	G	GS	CG	IP	H	BB	SO	ShO	W	L	SV	AB	H	HR	BA
1965 KC A	0	1	.000	4.35	12	3	0	31	36	8	9	0	0	0	0	4	2	0	.500

Guy Bush

BUSH, GUY TERRELL (The Mississippi Mudcat)   BR TR 6'   175 lbs.
B. Aug. 23, 1901, Aberdeen, Miss.

	W	L	PCT	ERA	G	GS	CG	IP	H	BB	SO	ShO	W	L	SV	AB	H	HR	BA
1923 CHI N	0	0	—	0.00	1	0	0	1	1	0	2	0	0	0	0	0	0	0	—
1924	2	5	.286	4.02	16	8	4	80.2	91	24	36	0	0	1	0	26	4	0	.154
1925	6	13	.316	4.30	42	15	5	182	213	52	76	0	4	2	4	57	11	0	.193
1926	13	9	.591	2.86	35	16	7	157.1	149	42	32	2	6	2	2	48	8	0	.167
1927	10	10	.500	3.03	36	22	9	193.1	177	79	62	1	3	0	2	65	8	0	.123
1928	15	6	.714	3.83	42	24	9	204.1	229	86	61	2	4	0	2	73	6	0	.082
1929	18	7	.720	3.66	50	29	18	270.2	277	107	82	2	2	1	8	91	15	0	.165
1930	15	10	.600	6.20	46	25	11	225	291	86	75	0	3	2	3	78	22	0	.282
1931	16	8	.667	4.49	39	24	14	180.1	190	66	54	1	4	0	2	57	7	0	.123
1932	19	11	.633	3.21	40	30	15	238.2	262	70	73	1	4	2	0	84	15	0	.179
1933	20	12	.625	2.75	41	32	20	258.2	261	68	84	4	1	1	2	88	11	0	.125
1934	18	10	.643	3.83	40	27	15	209.1	213	54	75	1	3	1	2	70	16	0	.229
1935 PIT N	11	11	.500	4.32	41	25	8	204.1	237	40	42	1	5	1	2	63	8	0	.127
1936 2 teams			PIT N (16G 1–3)				BOS N (15G 4–5)												
" total	5	8	.385	4.10	31	11	5	125	147	31	38	0	2	3	1	34	6	0	.176
1937 BOS N	8	15	.348	3.54	32	20	11	180.2	201	48	56	1	2	3	1	54	6	0	.111
1938 STL N	0	1	.000	5.06	9	0	0	5.1	6	3	1	0	0	1	1	0	0	0	—
1945 CIN N	0	0	—	8.31	4	0	0	4.1	5	3	1	0	0	0	1	0	0	0	—
17 yrs.	176	136	.564	3.86	542	308	151	2721	2950	859	850	16	43	20	34	888	143	0	.161

WORLD SERIES

	W	L	PCT	ERA	G	GS	CG	IP	H	BB	SO	ShO	W	L	SV	AB	H	HR	BA
1929 CHI N	1	0	1.000	0.82	2	1	1	11	12	2	4	0	0	0	0	3	0	0	.000
1932	0	1	.000	14.29	2	2	0	5.2	5	6	2	0	0	0	0	0	0	0	.000
2 yrs.	1	1	.500	5.40	4	3	1	16.2	17	8	6	0	0	0	0	3	0	0	.000

Joe Bush

BUSH, LESLIE AMBROSE (Bullet Joe)   BR TR 5'9"   173 lbs.
B. Nov. 27, 1892, Brainerd, Minn.   D. Nov. 1, 1974, Ft. Lauderdale, Fla.

	W	L	PCT	ERA	G	GS	CG	IP	H	BB	SO	ShO	W	L	SV	AB	H	HR	BA
1912 PHI A	0	0	—	7.88	1	1	0	8	14	4	3	0	0	0	0	4	2	0	.500
1913	14	6	.700	3.82	39	15	5	200.1	199	66	81	1	7	1	3	70	11	0	.157
1914	16	12	.571	3.06	38	22	14	206	184	81	109	2	4	2	3	74	14	1	.189
1915	5	15	.250	4.14	25	18	8	145.2	137	89	89	0	1	3	0	49	7	0	.143
1916	15	24	.385	2.57	40	33	25	286.2	222	130	157	8	1	5	0	100	14	0	.140
1917	11	17	.393	2.47	37	31	17	233.1	207	111	121	4	1	0	2	80	16	0	.200
1918 BOS A	15	15	.500	2.11	36	31	26	272.2	241	91	125	7	0	0	0	98	27	0	.276
1919	0	0	—	5.00	3	2	0	9	11	4	3	0	0	0	0	5	2	0	.400
1920	15	15	.500	4.25	35	32	18	243.2	287	94	88	0	1	0	1	102	25	0	.245
1921	16	9	.640	3.50	37	31	20	254.1	244	93	96	3	0	0	1	120	39	0	.325
1922 NY A	26	7	.788	3.31	39	30	20	255.1	240	85	92	0	4	1	3	95	31	0	.326
1923	19	15	.559	3.43	37	30	23	275.2	263	117	125	3	2	2	0	113	31	2	.274
1924	17	16	.515	3.57	39	31	19	252	262	109	80	3	1	5	1	124	42	1	.339
1925 STL A	14	14	.500	4.97	33	28	15	213.2	239	91	63	2	2	1	0	102	26	2	.255
1926 2 teams			WAS A (12G 1–8)				PIT N (19G 6–6)												
" total	7	14	.333	4.45	31	22	12	182	180	70	65	2	0	1	3	79	20	1	.253
1927 2 teams			PIT N (5G 1–2)				NY N (3G 1–1)												
" total	2	3	.400	9.64	8	5	1	18.2	32	10	7	0	1	0	0	9	5	0	.556
1928 PHI A	2	1	.667	5.09	11	2	1	35.1	39	18	15	0	1	0	1	15	1	0	.067
17 yrs.	194	183	.515	3.51	489	364	224	3092.1	3001	1263	1319	35	26	21	20	*			

WORLD SERIES

	W	L	PCT	ERA	G	GS	CG	IP	H	BB	SO	ShO	W	L	SV	AB	H	HR	BA
1913 PHI A	1	0	1.000	1.00	1	1	1	9	5	4	3	0	0	0	0	4	1	0	.250
1914	0	1	.000	3.27	1	1	1	11	9	4	4	0	0	0	0	5	0	0	.000
1918 BOS A	0	1	.000	3.00	2	1	1	9	7	3	0	0	0	0	0	2	0	0	.000
1922 NY A	0	2	.000	4.80	2	2	1	15	21	5	6	0	0	0	0	6	1	0	.167
1923	1	1	.500	1.08	3	1	1	16.2	7	4	5	0	0	1	0	7	3	0	.429
5 yrs.	2	5	.286	2.67	9	6	5	60.2	49	20	18	0	0	1	1	24	5	0	.208
		2nd					10th												

Jack Bushelman

BUSHELMAN, JOHN FRANCIS   BR TR 6'2"   175 lbs.
B. Aug. 29, 1885, Cincinnati, Ohio   D. Oct. 26, 1955, Gate City, Va.

	W	L	PCT	ERA	G	GS	CG	IP	H	BB	SO	ShO	W	L	SV	AB	H	HR	BA
1909 CIN N	0	1	.000	2.57	1	1	1	7	7	4	3	0	0	0	0	1	0	0	.000
1911 BOS A	1	0	1.000	3.00	3	1	1	12	8	10	5	0	0	0	0	3	0	0	.000
1912	0	1	.000	4.70	3	0	0	7.2	9	5	5	0	0	0	0	3	0	0	.000
3 yrs.	1	2	.333	3.38	7	2	2	26.2	24	19	13	0	0	0	0	7	0	0	.000

Frank Bushey

BUSHEY, FRANCIS CLYDE   BR TR 6'   180 lbs.
B. Aug. 1, 1906, Wheaton, Kans.   D. Mar. 18, 1972, Topeka, Kans.

	W	L	PCT	ERA	G	GS	CG	IP	H	BB	SO	ShO	W	L	SV	AB	H	HR	BA
1927 BOS A	0	0	—	6.75	1	0	0	1.1	2	2	0	0	0	0	0	0	0	0	—
1930	0	1	.000	6.30	11	0	0	30	34	15	4	0	0	1	0	9	1	0	.111
2 yrs.	0	1	.000	6.32	12	0	0	31.1	36	17	4	0	0	1	0	9	1	0	.111

	W	L	PCT	ERA	G	GS	CG	IP	H	BB	SO	ShO	Relief Pitching W	L	SV	BATTING AB	H	HR	BA

Tom Buskey

BUSKEY, THOMAS WILLIAM
B. Feb. 20, 1947, Harrisburg, Pa.   BR TR 6'3"   200 lbs.

	W	L	PCT	ERA	G	GS	CG	IP	H	BB	SO	ShO	W	L	SV	AB	H	HR	BA
1973 NY A	0	1	.000	5.40	8	0	0	16.2	18	4	8	0	0	1	1	0	0	0	–
1974 2 teams			NY A	(4G 0–1)			CLE A	(51G 2–6)											
" total	2	7	.222	3.38	55	0	0	98.2	103	36	43	0	2	7	18	0	0	0	–
1975 CLE A	5	3	.625	2.57	50	0	0	77	69	29	29	0	5	3	7	0	0	0	–
1976	5	4	.556	3.64	39	0	0	94	88	34	32	0	5	4	1	0	0	0	–
1977	0	0	–	5.29	21	0	0	34	45	8	15	0	0	0	0	0	0	0	–
1978 TOR A	0	1	.000	3.38	8	0	0	13.1	14	4	7	0	0	1	0	0	0	0	–
1979	6	10	.375	3.42	44	0	0	79	74	25	44	0	6	10	7	0	0	0	–
1980	3	1	.750	4.43	33	0	0	67	68	26	34	0	3	1	0	0	0	0	–
8 yrs.	21	27	.438	3.66	258	0	0	479.2	479	166	212	0	21	27	34	0	0	0	–

John Butcher

BUTCHER, JOHN DANIEL
B. Mar. 8, 1957, Glendale, Calif.   BR TR 6'4"   185 lbs.

	W	L	PCT	ERA	G	GS	CG	IP	H	BB	SO	ShO	W	L	SV	AB	H	HR	BA
1980 TEX A	3	3	.500	4.11	6	6	1	35	34	13	27	0	0	0	0	0	0	0	–
1981	1	2	.333	1.61	5	3	1	28	18	8	19	1	0	0	0	0	0	0	–
1982	1	5	.167	4.87	18	13	2	94.1	102	34	39	0	0	0	1	0	0	0	–
1983	6	6	.500	3.51	36	6	1	123	128	41	58	1	3	4	5	0	0	0	–
1984 MIN A	13	11	.542	3.44	34	34	8	225	242	53	83	1	0	0	0	0	0	0	–
5 yrs.	24	27	.471	3.67	99	62	13	505.1	524	149	226	3	3	4	6	0	0	0	–

Max Butcher

BUTCHER, ALBERT MAXWELL
B. Sept. 21, 1910, Holden, W. Va.   D. Sept. 15, 1957, Man, W. Va.   BR TR 6'2"   220 lbs.

	W	L	PCT	ERA	G	GS	CG	IP	H	BB	SO	ShO	W	L	SV	AB	H	HR	BA
1936 BKN N	6	6	.500	3.96	38	15	5	147.2	154	59	55	0	2	0	2	48	6	0	.125
1937	11	15	.423	4.27	39	24	8	191.2	203	75	57	1	5	0	0	62	10	0	.161
1938 2 teams			BKN	N	(24G 5–4)			PHI	N	(12G 4–8)									
" total	9	12	.429	4.47	36	20	14	171	198	70	50	1	1	2	2	60	13	1	.217
1939 2 teams			PHI	N	(19G 2–13)			PIT	N	(14G 4–4)									
" total	6	17	.261	4.62	33	28	8	191	235	74	48	2	0	1	0	69	10	0	.145
1940 PIT N	8	9	.471	6.01	35	24	6	136.1	161	46	40	2	0	0	2	50	15	0	.300
1941	17	12	.586	3.05	33	32	19	236	249	66	61	0	0	1	0	82	15	0	.183
1942	5	8	.385	2.93	24	18	9	150.2	144	44	49	0	0	0	1	49	7	0	.143
1943	10	8	.556	2.60	33	21	10	193.2	191	57	45	2	1	0	1	61	10	0	.164
1944	13	11	.542	3.12	35	27	13	199	216	46	43	5	1	0	1	63	12	0	.190
1945	10	8	.556	3.03	28	20	12	169.1	184	46	37	2	2	0	0	54	12	0	.222
10 yrs.	95	106	.473	3.73	334	229	104	1786.1	1935	583	485	15	12	4	9	598	110	1	.184

Bill Butland

BUTLAND, WILBURN RUE
B. Mar. 22, 1918, Terre Haute, Ind.   BR TR 6'5"   185 lbs.

	W	L	PCT	ERA	G	GS	CG	IP	H	BB	SO	ShO	W	L	SV	AB	H	HR	BA
1940 BOS A	1	2	.333	5.57	3	3	1	21	27	10	5	0	0	0	0	7	0	0	.000
1942	7	1	.875	2.51	23	10	6	111.1	85	33	46	2	0	0	1	28	1	0	.036
1946	1	0	1.000	11.02	5	2	0	16.1	23	13	10	0	0	0	0	4	1	0	.250
1947	0	0	–	4.50	1	0	0	2	3	0	1	0	0	0	0	0	0	0	–
4 yrs.	9	3	.750	3.88	32	15	7	150.2	138	56	62	2	0	0	1	39	2	0	.051

Bill Butler

BUTLER, WILLIAM FRANKLIN
B. Mar. 12, 1947, Hyattsville, Md.   BL TL 6'2"   210 lbs.

	W	L	PCT	ERA	G	GS	CG	IP	H	BB	SO	ShO	W	L	SV	AB	H	HR	BA
1969 KC A	9	10	.474	3.90	34	29	5	193.2	174	91	156	4	0	0	0	60	3	0	.050
1970	4	12	.250	3.77	25	25	2	141	117	87	75	1	0	0	0	44	2	0	.045
1971	1	2	.333	3.48	14	6	0	44	45	18	32	0	0	0	0	12	1	0	.083
1972 CLE A	0	0	–	1.50	6	2	0	12	9	10	6	0	0	0	0	1	0	0	.000
1974 MIN A	4	6	.400	4.09	26	12	2	99	91	56	79	0	1	0	1	0	0	0	–
1975	5	4	.556	5.95	23	8	1	81.2	100	35	55	0	2	2	0	0	0	0	–
1977	0	1	.000	6.86	6	4	0	21	19	15	5	0	0	0	0	0	0	0	–
7 yrs.	23	35	.397	4.21	134	86	10	592.1	555	312	408	5	3	2	1	117	6	0	.051

Cecil Butler

BUTLER, CECIL DEAN (Slewfoot)
B. Oct. 23, 1937, Dallas, Ga.   BR TR 6'4"   195 lbs.

	W	L	PCT	ERA	G	GS	CG	IP	H	BB	SO	ShO	W	L	SV	AB	H	HR	BA
1962 MIL N	2	0	1.000	2.61	9	2	1	31	26	9	22	0	1	0	0	8	0	0	.000
1964	0	0	–	8.31	2	0	0	4.1	7	0	2	0	0	0	0	0	0	0	–
2 yrs.	2	0	1.000	3.31	11	2	1	35.1	33	9	24	0	1	0	0	8	0	0	.000

Charlie Butler

BUTLER, CHARLES THOMAS (Lefty)
B. May 12, 1905, Green Cove Springs, Fla.   D. May 10, 1964, Brunswick, Ga.   BR TL 6'1½"   210 lbs.

	W	L	PCT	ERA	G	GS	CG	IP	H	BB	SO	ShO	W	L	SV	AB	H	HR	BA
1933 PHI N	0	0	–	9.00	1	0	0	1	1	2	0	0	0	0	0	0	0	0	–

Ike Butler

BUTLER, ISAAC BURR
B. Aug. 22, 1873, Langston, Mich.   D. Mar. 17, 1948, Oakland, Calif.   TR

	W	L	PCT	ERA	G	GS	CG	IP	H	BB	SO	ShO	W	L	SV	AB	H	HR	BA
1902 BAL A	1	10	.091	5.34	16	14	12	116.1	168	45	13	0	0	0	0	53	6	0	.113

Tom Butters

BUTTERS, THOMAS ARDEN
B. Apr. 8, 1938, Delaware, Ohio   BR TR 6'2"   195 lbs.

	W	L	PCT	ERA	G	GS	CG	IP	H	BB	SO	ShO	W	L	SV	AB	H	HR	BA
1962 PIT N	0	0	–	1.50	4	0	0	6	5	6	10	0	0	0	0	0	0	0	–
1963	0	0	–	4.41	6	1	0	16.1	15	8	11	0	0	0	0	3	1	0	.333
1964	2	2	.500	2.38	28	4	0	64.1	52	37	58	0	0	0	0	11	2	0	.182
1965	0	1	.000	7.00	5	0	0	9	9	5	6	0	0	1	0	1	0	0	.000
4 yrs.	2	3	.400	3.10	43	5	0	95.2	81	56	85	0	0	1	0	15	3	0	.200

Ralph Buxton

BUXTON, RALPH STANLEY (Buck)
B. June 7, 1911, Wayburn, Sask., Canada   BR TR 5'11½"   163 lbs.

	W	L	PCT	ERA	G	GS	CG	IP	H	BB	SO	ShO	W	L	SV	AB	H	HR	BA
1938 PHI A	0	1	.000	4.82	5	0	0	9.1	12	5	9	0	0	1	0	1	0	0	.000
1949 NY A	0	1	.000	4.05	14	0	0	26.2	22	16	14	0	0	1	2	3	0	0	.000
2 yrs.	0	2	.000	4.25	19	0	0	36	34	21	23	0	0	2	2	4	0	0	.000

	W	L	PCT	ERA	G	GS	CG	IP	H	BB	SO	ShO	Relief Pitching W	L	SV	BATTING AB	H	HR	BA

John Buzhardt

BUZHARDT, JOHN WILLIAM
B. Aug. 15, 1936, Prosperity, S. C.   BR TR 6'2½" 195 lbs.

	W	L	PCT	ERA	G	GS	CG	IP	H	BB	SO	ShO	W	L	SV	AB	H	HR	BA
1958 CHI N	3	0	1.000	1.85	6	2	1	24.1	16	7	9	0	1	0	0	8	1	0	.125
1959	4	5	.444	4.97	31	10	1	101.1	107	29	33	1	1	2	0	29	2	0	.069
1960 PHI N	5	16	.238	3.86	30	29	5	200.1	198	68	73	0	0	0	0	62	10	0	.161
1961	6	18	.250	4.49	41	27	6	202.1	200	65	92	1	0	2	0	57	6	0	.105
1962 CHI A	8	12	.400	4.19	28	25	8	152.1	156	59	64	2	1	0	0	51	6	0	.118
1963	9	4	.692	2.42	19	18	6	126.1	100	31	59	3	0	0	0	48	4	0	.083
1964	10	8	.556	2.98	31	25	8	160	150	35	97	3	0	0	0	54	11	0	.204
1965	13	8	.619	3.01	32	30	4	188.2	167	56	108	1	0	1	1	56	7	0	.125
1966	6	11	.353	3.83	33	22	5	150.1	144	30	66	4	1	2	1	43	5	0	.116
1967 3 teams			CHI A	(28G 3–9)			BAL A	(7G 0–1)			HOU N	(1G 0–0)							
" total	3	10	.231	4.01	36	8	0	101	114	42	40	0	1	5	0	21	4	0	.190
1968 HOU N	4	4	.500	3.12	39	4	0	83.2	73	35	37	0	3	3	5	16	4	0	.250
11 yrs.	71	96	.425	3.66	326	200	44	1490.2	1425	457	678	15	8	15	7	445	60	0	.135

Bud Byerly

BYERLY, ELDRED WILLIAM
B. Oct. 26, 1920, Webster Groves, Mo.   BR TR 6'2½" 185 lbs.

	W	L	PCT	ERA	G	GS	CG	IP	H	BB	SO	ShO	W	L	SV	AB	H	HR	BA
1943 STL N	1	0	1.000	3.46	2	2	0	13	14	5	6	0	0	0	0	3	0	0	.000
1944	2	2	.500	3.40	9	4	2	42.1	37	20	13	0	1	0	0	12	2	0	.167
1945	4	5	.444	4.74	33	8	2	95	111	41	39	0	2	1	0	23	5	0	.217
1950 CIN N	0	1	.000	2.45	4	1	0	14.2	12	4	5	0	0	0	0	3	0	0	.000
1951	2	1	.667	3.27	40	0	0	66	69	25	28	0	2	1	0	6	0	0	.000
1952	0	1	.000	5.11	12	2	0	24.2	29	7	14	0	0	0	1	5	1	0	.200
1956 WAS A	2	4	.333	2.96	25	0	0	51.2	45	14	19	0	2	4	4	11	1	0	.091
1957	6	6	.500	3.13	47	0	0	95	94	22	39	0	6	6	6	15	1	0	.067
1958 2 teams			WAS A	(17G 2–0)			BOS A	(18G 1–2)											
" total	3	2	.600	3.98	35	0	0	54.1	65	18	29	0	3	2	1	6	0	0	.000
1959 SF N	1	0	1.000	1.38	11	0	0	13	11	5	4	0	1	0	0	0	0	0	–
1960	1	0	1.000	5.32	19	0	0	22	32	6	13	0	1	0	2	1	0	0	.000
11 yrs.	22	22	.500	3.70	237	17	4	491.2	519	167	209	0	18	14	14	85	10	0	.118

WORLD SERIES

	W	L	PCT	ERA	G	GS	CG	IP	H	BB	SO	ShO	W	L	SV	AB	H	HR	BA
1944 STL N	0	0	–	0.00	1	0	0	1.1	0	0	1	0	0	0	0	0	0	0	–

Harry Byrd

BYRD, HARRY GLADWIN
B. Feb. 3, 1925, Darlington, S. C.   BR TR 6'1" 188 lbs. BB 1955

	W	L	PCT	ERA	G	GS	CG	IP	H	BB	SO	ShO	W	L	SV	AB	H	HR	BA
1950 PHI A	0	0	–	16.88	6	0	0	10.2	25	9	2	0	0	0	0	2	0	0	.000
1952	15	15	.500	3.31	37	28	15	228.1	244	98	116	3	0	2	2	75	10	0	.133
1953	11	20	.355	5.51	40	37	11	236.2	279	115	122	2	0	1	0	81	18	0	.222
1954 NY A	9	7	.563	2.99	25	21	5	132.1	131	43	52	1	0	0	0	46	9	0	.196
1955 2 teams			BAL A	(14G 3–2)			CHI A	(25G 4–6)											
" total	7	8	.467	4.61	39	20	2	156.1	149	58	69	2	1	1	2	49	5	0	.102
1956 CHI A	0	1	.000	10.38	3	1	0	4.1	9	4	0	0	0	0	0	1	0	0	.000
1957 DET A	4	3	.571	3.36	37	1	0	59	53	28	20	0	4	3	5	8	0	0	.000
7 yrs.	46	54	.460	4.35	187	108	33	827.2	890	355	381	8	5	7	9	262	42	0	.160

Jeff Byrd

BYRD, JEFFREY ALLAN
B. Nov. 11, 1956, La Mesa, Calif.   BR TR 6'3" 195 lbs.

	W	L	PCT	ERA	G	GS	CG	IP	H	BB	SO	ShO	W	L	SV	AB	H	HR	BA
1977 TOR A	2	13	.133	6.21	17	17	1	87	98	68	40	0	0	0	0	0	0	0	–

Jerry Byrne

BYRNE, GERALD WILFORD
B. Feb. 2, 1907, Parnell, Mich.   D. Aug. 11, 1955, Lansing, Mich.   BR TR 6' 170 lbs.

	W	L	PCT	ERA	G	GS	CG	IP	H	BB	SO	ShO	W	L	SV	AB	H	HR	BA
1929 CHI A	0	1	.000	7.36	3	1	0	7.1	11	6	1	0	0	0	0	2	0	0	.000

Tommy Byrne

BYRNE, THOMAS JOSEPH
B. Dec. 31, 1919, Baltimore, Md.   BL TL 6'1" 182 lbs.

	W	L	PCT	ERA	G	GS	CG	IP	H	BB	SO	ShO	W	L	SV	AB	H	HR	BA
1943 NY A	2	1	.667	6.54	11	2	0	31.2	28	35	22	0	2	0	0	11	1	0	.091
1946	0	1	.000	5.79	4	1	0	9.1	7	8	5	0	0	0	0	9	2	0	.222
1947	0	0	–	4.15	4	1	0	4.1	5	6	2	0	0	0	0	0	0	0	–
1948	8	5	.615	3.30	31	11	5	133.2	79	101	93	1	2	1	2	46	15	1	.326
1949	15	7	.682	3.72	32	30	12	196	125	179	129	3	0	1	0	83	16	0	.193
1950	15	9	.625	4.74	31	31	10	203.1	188	160	118	2	0	0	0	81	22	2	.272
1951 2 teams			NY A	(9G 2–1)			STL A	(19G 4–10)											
" total	6	11	.353	4.26	28	20	7	143.2	120	150	71	2	2	0	0	66	18	2	.273
1952 STL A	7	14	.333	4.68	29	24	14	196	182	112	91	0	1	0	0	84	21	1	.250
1953 2 teams			CHI A	(6G 2–0)			WAS A	(6G 0–5)											
" total	2	5	.286	6.16	12	11	2	49.2	53	48	26	0	0	1	0	35	4	1	.114
1954 NY A	3	2	.600	2.70	5	5	4	40	36	19	24	1	0	0	0	19	7	0	.368
1955	16	5	.762	3.15	27	22	9	160	137	87	76	3	1	0	2	78	16	1	.205
1956	7	3	.700	3.36	37	8	1	109.2	108	72	52	0	6	2	6	52	14	3	.269
1957	4	6	.400	4.36	30	4	1	84.2	70	60	57	0	4	4	2	37	7	3	.189
13 yrs.	85	69	.552	4.11	281	170	65	1362	1138	1037	766	12	18	9	12	*			

WORLD SERIES

	W	L	PCT	ERA	G	GS	CG	IP	H	BB	SO	ShO	W	L	SV	AB	H	HR	BA
1949 NY A	0	0	–	2.70	1	0	0	3.1	2	2	1	0	0	0	0	1	1	0	1.000
1955	1	1	.500	1.88	2	2	1	14.1	8	8	8	0	0	0	0	6	1	0	.167
1956	0	0	–	0.00	1	0	0	.1	1	0	1	0	0	0	0	1	0	0	.000
1957	0	0	–	5.40	2	0	0	3.1	1	2	1	0	0	0	0	2	1	0	.500
4 yrs.	1	1	.500	2.53	6	2	1	21.1	12	12	11	0	0	0	0	10	3	0	.300

Marty Bystrom

BYSTROM, MARTIN EUGENE
B. July 26, 1958, Miami, Fla.   BR TR 6'5" 200 lbs.

	W	L	PCT	ERA	G	GS	CG	IP	H	BB	SO	ShO	W	L	SV	AB	H	HR	BA
1980 PHI N	5	0	1.000	1.50	6	5	1	36	26	9	21	1	1	0	0	14	1	0	.071
1981	4	3	.571	3.33	9	9	1	54	55	16	24	0	0	0	0	17	2	0	.118
1982	5	6	.455	4.85	19	16	1	89	93	35	50	0	0	0	0	24	3	0	.125
1983	6	9	.400	4.60	24	23	1	119.1	136	44	87	1	0	0	0	38	9	0	.237
1984 2 teams			PHI N	(11G 4–4)			NY A	(7G 2–2)											
" total	6	6	.500	4.22	18	18	0	96	100	35	60	0	0	0	0	19	3	0	.158
5 yrs.	26	24	.520	4.11	76	71	4	394.1	410	139	242	2	1	0	0	112	18	0	.161

	W	L	PCT	ERA	G	GS	CG	IP	H	BB	SO	ShO	Relief Pitching W	L	SV	BATTING AB	H	HR	BA

Marty Bystrom continued

LEAGUE CHAMPIONSHIP SERIES

	W	L	PCT	ERA	G	GS	CG	IP	H	BB	SO	ShO	W	L	SV	AB	H	HR	BA
1980 PHI N	0	0	–	1.69	1	1	0	5.1	7	2	1	0	0	0	0	2	0	0	.000

WORLD SERIES

1980 PHI N	0	0	–	5.40	1	1	0	5	10	1	4	0	0	0	0	0	0	0	–
1983	0	0	–	0.00	1	0	0	1	0	0	1	0	0	0	0	0	0	0	–
2 yrs.	0	0	–	4.50	2	1	0	6	10	1	5	0	0	0	0	0	0	0	–

Leon Cadore

CADORE, LEON JOSEPH BR TR 6'1" 190 lbs.
B. Nov. 20, 1890, Chicago, Ill. D. Mar. 16, 1958, Spokane, Wash.

	W	L	PCT	ERA	G	GS	CG	IP	H	BB	SO	ShO	W	L	SV	AB	H	HR	BA
1915 BKN N	0	2	.000	5.57	7	2	1	21	28	8	12	0	0	0	0	6	0	0	.000
1916	0	0	–	4.50	1	0	0	6	10	0	2	0	0	0	0	3	0	0	.000
1917	13	13	.500	2.45	37	30	21	264	231	63	115	1	0	0	3	92	24	0	.261
1918	1	0	1.000	0.53	2	2	1	17	6	2	5	1	0	0	0	4	0	0	.000
1919	14	12	.538	2.37	35	27	16	250.2	228	39	94	3	2	0	0	87	14	0	.161
1920	15	14	.517	2.62	35	30	16	254.1	256	56	79	4	1	1	0	91	20	2	.220
1921	13	14	.481	4.17	35	30	12	211.2	243	46	79	1	1	2	0	75	14	1	.187
1922	8	15	.348	4.35	29	21	13	190.1	224	57	49	0	4	0	0	71	19	2	.268
1923 2 teams		BKN	N	(8G 4–1)			CHI	A	(1G 0–1)										
" total	4	2	.667	4.46	9	5	3	38.1	45	15	8	0	1	0	0	13	1	0	.077
1924 NY N	0	0	–	0.00	2	0	0	4	2	3	2	0	0	0	0	0	0	0	–
10 yrs.	68	72	.486	3.14	192	147	83	1257.1	1273	289	445	10	9	3	3	442	92	5	.208

WORLD SERIES

1920 BKN N	0	1	.000	9.00	2	1	0	2	4	1	1	0	0	0	0	0	0	0	–

Charlie Cady

CADY, CHARLES B.
B. Dec., 1865, Chicago, Ill. D. June 9, 1909, Kankakee, Ill.

	W	L	PCT	ERA	G	GS	CG	IP	H	BB	SO	ShO	W	L	SV	AB	H	HR	BA
1883 CLE N	0	1	.000	7.88	1	1	1	8	13	4	5	0	0	0	0	11	0	0	.000
1884 C-P U	3	1	.750	2.83	4	4	4	35	37	13	15	0	0	0	0	23	2	0	.087
2 yrs.	3	2	.600	3.77	5	5	5	43	50	17	20	0	0	0	0	*			

John Cahill

CAHILL, JOHN FRANCIS PATRICK (Patsy) BR
B. Philadelphia, Pa. D. Nov. 1, 1901, Pleasanton, Calif.

	W	L	PCT	ERA	G	GS	CG	IP	H	BB	SO	ShO	W	L	SV	AB	H	HR	BA
1884 COL AA	1	0	1.000	5.06	2	1	1	16	15	4	1	0	0	0	0	210	46	0	.219
1886 STL N	1	0	1.000	3.00	2	0	0	12	11	3	2	0	1	0	0	463	92	1	.199
1887 IND N	0	2	.000	14.32	6	1	1	22	40	19	5	0	0	1	0	263	54	0	.205
3 yrs.	2	2	.500	8.64	10	2	2	50	66	26	8	0	1	1	0	*			

Bob Cain

CAIN, ROBERT MAX (Sugar) BL TL 6' 165 lbs.
B. Oct. 16, 1924, Longford, Kans.

	W	L	PCT	ERA	G	GS	CG	IP	H	BB	SO	ShO	W	L	SV	AB	H	HR	BA
1949 CHI A	0	0	–	2.45	6	0	0	11	7	5	5	0	0	0	1	3	0	0	.000
1950	9	12	.429	3.93	34	23	11	171.2	153	109	77	1	1	1	2	61	12	0	.197
1951 2 teams		CHI	A	(4G 1–2)			DET	A	(35G 11–10)										
" total	12	12	.500	4.56	39	26	7	175.2	160	95	61	1	2	2	2	62	16	0	.258
1952 STL A	12	10	.545	4.13	29	27	8	170	169	62	70	1	0	0	2	58	8	0	.138
1953	4	10	.286	6.23	32	13	1	99.2	129	45	36	0	0	4	1	30	6	0	.200
1954 CHI A	0	0	–	0.00	0	0	0	0	0	0	0	0	0	0	0	0	0	0	–
6 yrs.	37	44	.457	4.50	140	89	27	628	618	316	249	3	3	7	8	214	42	0	.196

Les Cain

CAIN, LESLIE BL TL 6'1" 200 lbs.
B. Jan. 13, 1948, San Luis Obispo, Calif.

	W	L	PCT	ERA	G	GS	CG	IP	H	BB	SO	ShO	W	L	SV	AB	H	HR	BA
1968 DET A	1	0	1.000	3.00	8	4	0	24	25	20	13	0	0	0	0	7	1	0	.143
1970	12	7	.632	3.83	29	29	5	181	167	98	156	0	0	0	0	68	11	1	.162
1971	10	9	.526	4.34	26	26	3	145	121	91	118	1	0	0	0	55	8	1	.145
1972	0	3	.000	3.75	5	5	0	24	18	16	16	0	0	0	0	7	1	0	.143
4 yrs.	23	19	.548	3.97	68	64	8	374	331	225	303	1	0	0	0	137	21	2	.153

Sugar Cain

CAIN, MERRITT PATRICK BL TR 5'11" 190 lbs.
B. Apr. 5, 1907, Macon, Ga. BR 1932, BB 1933
D. Apr. 3, 1975, Atlanta, Ga.

	W	L	PCT	ERA	G	GS	CG	IP	H	BB	SO	ShO	W	L	SV	AB	H	HR	BA
1932 PHI A	3	4	.429	5.00	10	6	3	45	42	28	24	0	1	0	0	12	3	0	.250
1933	13	12	.520	4.25	38	32	16	218	244	137	43	1	0	1	1	80	16	0	.200
1934	9	17	.346	4.41	36	32	15	230.2	235	128	66	0	1	1	0	82	13	0	.159
1935 2 teams		PHI	A	(6G 0–5)			STL	A	(31G 9–8)										
" total	9	13	.409	5.44	37	29	8	193.2	236	123	73	0	0	1	0	65	11	0	.169
1936 2 teams		STL	A	(4G 1–1)			CHI	A	(30G 14–10)										
" total	15	11	.577	4.89	34	29	15	211.2	248	84	50	1	1	1	0	75	9	0	.120
1937 CHI A	4	2	.667	6.16	18	6	1	68.2	88	51	17	0	3	0	0	22	4	0	.182
1938	0	1	.000	4.58	5	3	0	19.2	26	18	6	0	0	0	0	8	0	0	.000
7 yrs.	53	60	.469	4.83	178	137	58	987.1	1119	569	279	2	6	4	1	344	56	0	.163

Charlie Caldwell

CALDWELL, CHARLES WILLIAM BR TR 5'11" 190 lbs.
B. Aug. 2, 1901, Bristol, Va. D. Nov. 1, 1957, Princeton, N. J.

	W	L	PCT	ERA	G	GS	CG	IP	H	BB	SO	ShO	W	L	SV	AB	H	HR	BA
1925 NY A	0	0	–	16.88	3	0	0	2.2	7	3	1	0	0	0	0	1	0	0	.000

Earl Caldwell

CALDWELL, EARL WELTON (Teach) BR TR 6'1" 178 lbs.
B. Apr. 9, 1905, Sparks, Tex. D. Sept. 15, 1981, Mission, Tex.

	W	L	PCT	ERA	G	GS	CG	IP	H	BB	SO	ShO	W	L	SV	AB	H	HR	BA
1928 PHI N	1	4	.200	5.71	5	5	1	34.2	46	17	6	1	0	0	0	9	1	0	.111
1935 STL A	3	2	.600	3.68	6	5	3	36.2	34	17	5	1	0	0	0	11	2	0	.182
1936	7	16	.304	6.00	41	25	10	189	252	83	59	2	0	2	2	58	11	1	.190
1937	0	0	–	6.83	9	2	0	29	39	13	8	0	0	0	0	9	2	0	.222
1945 CHI A	6	7	.462	3.59	27	11	5	105.1	108	37	45	1	1	3	4	37	8	0	.216
1946	13	4	.765	2.08	39	0	0	90.2	60	29	42	0	13	4	8	18	3	0	.167
1947	1	4	.200	3.64	40	0	0	54.1	53	30	22	0	1	4	8	7	0	0	.000
1948 2 teams		CHI	A	(25G 1–5)			BOS	A	(8G 1–1)										
" total	2	6	.250	6.75	33	1	0	48	64	33	15	0	2	5	3	8	1	0	.125
8 yrs.	33	43	.434	4.69	200	49	18	587.2	656	259	202	5	17	18	25	157	28	1	.178

	W	L	PCT	ERA	G	GS	CG	IP	H	BB	SO	ShO	Relief Pitching W	L	SV	BATTING AB	H	HR	BA

Mike Caldwell

CALDWELL, RALPH MICHAEL
B. Jan. 22, 1949, Tarboro, N. C.   BR TL 6'   185 lbs.

	W	L	PCT	ERA	G	GS	CG	IP	H	BB	SO	ShO	W	L	SV	AB	H	HR	BA
1971 SD N	1	0	1.000	0.00	6	0	0	7	4	3	5	0	1	0	0	1	1	0	1.000
1972	7	11	.389	4.01	42	20	4	163.2	183	49	102	2	2	2	2	50	7	0	.140
1973	5	14	.263	3.74	55	13	3	149	146	53	86	1	2	5	10	35	5	0	.143
1974 SF N	14	5	.737	2.95	31	27	6	189	176	63	83	2	1	0	0	63	9	0	.143
1975	7	13	.350	4.80	38	21	4	163	194	48	57	0	1	2	1	44	7	0	.159
1976	1	7	.125	4.86	50	9	0	107.1	145	20	55	0	1	3	2	19	3	0	.158
1977 2 teams			CIN	N (14G 0-0)			MIL	A (21G 5-8)											
" total	5	8	.385	4.46	35	12	2	119	126	44	49	0	1	0	1	4	2	0	.500
1978 MIL A	22	9	.710	2.36	37	34	23	293.1	258	54	131	6	0	0	1	0	0	0	–
1979	16	6	.727	3.29	30	30	16	235	252	39	89	4	0	0	0	0	0	0	–
1980	13	11	.542	4.04	34	33	11	225	248	56	74	2	0	0	1	0	0	0	–
1981	11	9	.550	3.94	24	23	3	144	151	38	41	0	0	0	0	0	0	0	–
1982	17	13	.567	3.91	35	34	12	258	269	58	75	3	0	0	0	0	0	0	–
1983	12	11	.522	4.53	32	32	10	228.1	269	51	58	2	0	0	0	0	0	0	–
1984	6	13	.316	4.64	26	19	4	126	160	21	34	1	0	0	0	0	0	0	–
14 yrs.	137	130	.513	3.81	475	307	98	2407.2	2581	597	939	23	9	14	18	216	34	0	.157

DIVISIONAL PLAYOFF SERIES
| 1981 MIL A | 0 | 1 | .000 | 4.32 | 2 | 1 | 0 | 8.1 | 9 | 0 | 4 | 0 | 0 | 0 | 0 | 0 | 0 | 0 | – |

LEAGUE CHAMPIONSHIP SERIES
| 1982 MIL A | 0 | 1 | .000 | 15.00 | 1 | 1 | 0 | 3 | 7 | 1 | 2 | 0 | 0 | 0 | 0 | 0 | 0 | 0 | – |

WORLD SERIES
| 1982 MIL A | 2 | 0 | 1.000 | 2.04 | 3 | 2 | 1 | 17.2 | 19 | 3 | 6 | 1 | 0 | 0 | 0 | 0 | 0 | 0 | – |

Ralph Caldwell

CALDWELL, RALPH GRANT (Lefty)
B. Jan. 18, 1884, Philadelphia, Pa.   D. Aug. 5, 1969, Trenton, N. J.   BL TL 5'9"   155 lbs.

	W	L	PCT	ERA	G	GS	CG	IP	H	BB	SO	ShO	W	L	SV	AB	H	HR	BA
1904 PHI N	2	2	.500	4.17	6	5	5	41	40	15	30	0	0	0	0	18	8	0	.444
1905	1	2	.333	4.24	7	2	1	34	44	7	29	0	0	1	1	15	0	0	.000
2 yrs.	3	4	.429	4.20	13	7	6	75	84	22	59	0	0	1	1	33	8	0	.242

Ray Caldwell

CALDWELL, RAYMOND BENJAMIN (Slim)
B. Apr. 26, 1888, Corydon, Pa.   D. Aug. 17, 1967, Salamanca, N. Y.   BL TR 6'2"   190 lbs.

	W	L	PCT	ERA	G	GS	CG	IP	H	BB	SO	ShO	W	L	SV	AB	H	HR	BA
1910 NY A	1	0	1.000	3.72	6	2	1	19.1	19	9	17	0	0	0	1	6	0	0	.000
1911	14	14	.500	3.35	41	27	19	255	240	79	145	1	4	2	1	147	40	0	.272
1912	8	16	.333	4.47	30	26	13	183.1	196	67	95	3	0	1	0	76	18	0	.237
1913	9	8	.529	2.41	27	16	15	164.1	131	60	87	2	0	1	1	97	28	0	.289
1914	17	9	.654	1.94	31	23	22	213	153	51	92	5	2	1	1	113	22	0	.195
1915	19	16	.543	2.89	36	35	31	305	266	107	130	3	0	1	0	144	35	4	.243
1916	5	12	.294	2.99	21	18	14	165.2	142	65	76	1	0	1	0	93	19	0	.204
1917	13	16	.448	2.86	32	29	21	236	199	76	102	1	3	0	0	124	32	2	.258
1918	9	8	.529	3.06	24	21	14	176.2	173	62	59	1	0	1	1	151	44	1	.291
1919 2 teams			BOS	A (18G 7-4)			CLE	A (6G 5-1)											
" total	12	5	.706	2.98	24	18	10	139	121	49	46	2	1	1	0	71	21	0	.296
1920 CLE A	20	10	.667	3.86	34	33	20	237.2	286	63	80	0	0	0	0	89	19	0	.213
1921	6	6	.500	4.90	37	13	5	147	159	49	76	1	2	3	4	53	11	1	.208
12 yrs.	133	120	.526	3.21	343	261	185	2242	2085	737	1005	20	12	12	9	*			

WORLD SERIES
| 1920 CLE A | 0 | 1 | .000 | 27.00 | 1 | 1 | 0 | .1 | 2 | 1 | 0 | 0 | 0 | 0 | 0 | 0 | 0 | 0 | – |

Jeff Calhoun

CALHOUN, JEFFREY WILTON
B. Apr. 11, 1958, LaGrange, La.   BL TL 6'2"   190 lbs.

	W	L	PCT	ERA	G	GS	CG	IP	H	BB	SO	ShO	W	L	SV	AB	H	HR	BA
1984 HOU N	0	1	.000	1.17	9	0	0	15.1	5	2	11	0	0	1	0	0	0	0	–

Fred Caligiuri

CALIGIURI, FREDERICK JOHN
B. Oct. 22, 1918, West Hickory, Pa.   BR TR 6'   190 lbs.

	W	L	PCT	ERA	G	GS	CG	IP	H	BB	SO	ShO	W	L	SV	AB	H	HR	BA
1941 PHI A	2	2	.500	2.93	5	5	4	43	45	14	7	0	0	0	0	20	4	0	.200
1942	0	3	.000	6.38	13	2	0	36.2	45	18	20	0	0	1	1	12	1	0	.083
2 yrs.	2	5	.286	4.52	18	7	4	79.2	90	32	27	0	0	1	1	32	5	0	.156

Will Calihan

CALIHAN, WILLIAM T.
B. 1869, Rochester, N. Y.   D. Dec. 20, 1917, Rochester, N. Y.

	W	L	PCT	ERA	G	GS	CG	IP	H	BB	SO	ShO	W	L	SV	AB	H	HR	BA
1890 ROC AA	18	15	.545	3.28	37	36	31	296.1	276	125	127	0	0	0	0	159	23	1	.145
1891 PHI AA	6	6	.500	6.43	13	11	11	112	151	47	28	0	1	0	0	56	11	0	.196
2 yrs.	24	21	.533	4.14	50	47	42	408.1	427	172	155	0	1	0	0	215	34	1	.158

Ben Callahan

CALLAHAN, BENJAMIN FRANKLIN III
B. May 19, 1957, Mt. Airy, N. C.   BR TR 6'7"   230 lbs.

	W	L	PCT	ERA	G	GS	CG	IP	H	BB	SO	ShO	W	L	SV	AB	H	HR	BA
1983 OAK A	1	2	.333	12.54	4	2	0	18	5	2	0	0	1	0	0	0	0	0	–

Jim Callahan

CALLAHAN, JAMES W.
B. Moberly, Mo.   Deceased.

	W	L	PCT	ERA	G	GS	CG	IP	H	BB	SO	ShO	W	L	SV	AB	H	HR	BA
1898 STL N	0	2	.000	16.20	2	2	1	8.1	18	7	2	0	0	0	0	4	0	0	.000

Joe Callahan

CALLAHAN, JOSEPH THOMAS
B. Oct. 8, 1916, East Boston, Mass.   D. May 24, 1949, South Boston, Mass.   BR TR 6'2"   170 lbs.

	W	L	PCT	ERA	G	GS	CG	IP	H	BB	SO	ShO	W	L	SV	AB	H	HR	BA
1939 BOS N	1	0	1.000	3.12	4	1	1	17.1	17	3	8	0	0	0	0	4	0	0	.000
1940	0	2	.000	10.20	6	2	0	15	20	13	3	0	0	0	0	5	0	0	.000
2 yrs.	1	2	.333	6.40	10	3	1	32.1	37	16	11	0	0	0	0	9	-0	0	.000

Nixey Callahan

CALLAHAN, JAMES JOSEPH
B. Mar. 18, 1874, Fitchburg, Mass.   D. Oct. 4, 1934, Boston, Mass.   BR TR 5'10½" 180 lbs.
Manager 1903-04, 1912-14, 1916-17.

	W	L	PCT	ERA	G	GS	CG	IP	H	BB	SO	ShO	W	L	SV	AB	H	HR	BA
1894 PHI N	1	2	.333	9.89	9	2	1	33.2	64	17	9	0	1	0	2	21	5	0	.238
1897 CHI N	12	9	.571	4.03	23	22	21	189.2	221	55	52	1	0	1	0	360	105	3	.292

	W	L	PCT	ERA	G	GS	CG	IP	H	BB	SO	ShO	Relief Pitching W	L	SV	BATTING AB	H	HR	BA

Nixey Callahan continued

	W	L	PCT	ERA	G	GS	CG	IP	H	BB	SO	ShO	W	L	SV	AB	H	HR	BA
1898	20	10	.667	2.46	31	31	30	274.1	267	71	73	2	0	0	0	164	43	0	.262
1899	21	12	.636	3.06	35	34	33	294.1	327	76	77	3	1	0	0	150	39	0	.260
1900	13	16	.448	3.82	32	32	32	285.1	347	74	77	2	0	0	0	115	27	0	.235
1901 CHI A	15	8	.652	2.42	27	22	20	215.1	195	50	70	1	1	2	0	118	39	1	.331
1902	16	14	.533	3.60	35	31	29	282.1	287	89	75	2	1	0	0	218	51	0	.234
1903	1	2	.333	4.50	3	3	3	28	40	5	12	0	0	0	0	439	128	2	.292
8 yrs.	99	73	.576	3.39	195	177	169	1603	1748	437	445	11	4	3	2	*			

Ray Callahan

CALLAHAN, RAY JAMES (Pat)　　　　　　　BL TL 5'10½" 170 lbs.
B. Aug. 29, 1891, Ashland, Wis.　　D. Jan. 23, 1973, Olympia, Wash.

	W	L	PCT	ERA	G	GS	CG	IP	H	BB	SO	ShO	W	L	SV	AB	H	HR	BA
1915 CIN N	0	0	—	8.53	3	0	0	6.1	12	1	4	0	0	0	0	3	1	0	.333

Dick Calmus

CALMUS, RICHARD LEE　　　　　　　BR TR 6'4" 187 lbs.
B. Jan. 7, 1944, Los Angeles, Calif.

	W	L	PCT	ERA	G	GS	CG	IP	H	BB	SO	ShO	W	L	SV	AB	H	HR	BA
1963 LA N	3	1	.750	2.66	21	1	0	44	32	16	25	0	3	0	0	6	0	0	.000
1967 CHI N	0	0	—	8.31	1	1	0	4.1	5	0	1	0	0	0	0	2	1	0	.500
2 yrs.	3	1	.750	3.17	22	2	0	48.1	37	16	26	0	3	0	0	8	1	0	.125

Mark Calvert

CALVERT, MARK　　　　　　　BR TR 6'1" 195 lbs.
B. Sept. 29, 1956, Tulsa, Okla.

	W	L	PCT	ERA	G	GS	CG	IP	H	BB	SO	ShO	W	L	SV	AB	H	HR	BA
1983 SF N	1	4	.200	6.27	18	4	0	37.1	46	34	14	0	0	2	0	8	0	0	.000
1984	2	4	.333	5.06	10	5	1	32	40	9	5	0	0	1	0	8	0	0	.000
2 yrs.	3	8	.273	5.71	28	9	1	69.1	86	43	19	0	0	3	0	16	0	0	.000

Paul Calvert

CALVERT, PAUL LEO EMILE　　　　　　　BR TR 6' 175 lbs.
B. Oct. 6, 1917, Montreal, Que., Canada

	W	L	PCT	ERA	G	GS	CG	IP	H	BB	SO	ShO	W	L	SV	AB	H	HR	BA
1942 CLE A	0	0	—	0.00	1	0	0	2	0	2	2	0	0	0	0	0	0	0	—
1943	0	0	—	4.32	5	0	0	8.1	6	6	2	0	0	0	0	1	0	0	.000
1944	1	3	.250	4.56	35	4	0	77	89	38	31	0	0	2	0	15	4	0	.267
1945	0	0	—	13.50	1	0	0	1.1	3	1	1	0	0	0	0	0	0	0	—
1949 WAS A	6	17	.261	5.43	34	23	5	160.2	175	86	52	0	1	2	1	51	7	0	.137
1950 DET A	2	2	.500	6.31	32	0	0	51.1	71	25	14	0	2	2	4	7	0	0	.000
1951	0	0	—	0.00	1	0	0	1	0	0	0	0	0	0	0	0	0	0	—
7 yrs.	9	22	.290	5.31	109	27	5	301.2	345	158	102	0	3	6	5	74	11	0	.149

Ernie Camacho

CAMACHO, ERNIE CARLOS　　　　　　　BR TR 6'1" 180 lbs.
B. Feb. 1, 1956, Salinas, Calif.

	W	L	PCT	ERA	G	GS	CG	IP	H	BB	SO	ShO	W	L	SV	AB	H	HR	BA
1980 OAK A	0	0	—	6.75	5	0	0	12	20	5	9	0	0	0	0	0	0	0	—
1981 PIT N	0	1	.000	4.91	7	3	0	22	23	15	11	0	0	0	0	4	0	0	.000
1983 CLE A	0	1	.000	5.06	4	0	0	5.1	5	2	2	0	0	1	0	0	0	0	—
1984	5	9	.357	2.43	69	0	0	100	83	37	48	0	5	9	23	0	0	0	—
4 yrs.	5	11	.313	3.29	85	3	0	139.1	131	59	70	0	5	10	23	4	0	0	.000

Fred Cambria

CAMBRIA, FREDERICK DENNIS　　　　　　　BR TR 6'2" 195 lbs.
B. Jan. 22, 1948, Cambria Heights, N. Y.

	W	L	PCT	ERA	G	GS	CG	IP	H	BB	SO	ShO	W	L	SV	AB	H	HR	BA
1970 PIT N	1	2	.333	3.55	6	5	0	33	37	12	14	0	0	0	0	10	2	0	.200

John Cameron

CAMERON, JOHN S. (Happy Jack)
B. Aug. 1, 1879, Truro, Nova Scotia, Canada　　D. June 15, 1964, West Roxbury, Mass.

	W	L	PCT	ERA	G	GS	CG	IP	H	BB	SO	ShO	W	L	SV	AB	H	HR	BA
1906 BOS N	0	0	—	0.00	2	1	0	6	4	6	2	0	0	0	0	*			

Harry Camnitz

CAMNITZ, HENRY RICHARDSON　　　　　　　BR TR 6'1" 168 lbs.
Brother of Howie Camnitz.
B. Oct. 26, 1884, McKinney, Ky.　　D. Jan. 6, 1951, Louisville, Ky.

	W	L	PCT	ERA	G	GS	CG	IP	H	BB	SO	ShO	W	L	SV	AB	H	HR	BA
1909 PIT N	0	0	—	4.50	1	0	0	4	6	1	1	0	0	0	0	2	0	0	.000
1911 STL N	1	0	1.000	0.00	2	0	0	2	0	1	2	0	1	0	0	0	0	0	—
2 yrs.	1	0	1.000	3.00	3	0	0	6	6	2	3	0	1	0	0	2	0	0	.000

Howie Camnitz

CAMNITZ, SAMUEL HOWARD (Red)　　　　　　　BL TR 5'9" 169 lbs.
Brother of Harry Camnitz.
B. Aug. 22, 1881, Covington, Ky.　　D. Mar. 2, 1960, Louisville, Ky.

	W	L	PCT	ERA	G	GS	CG	IP	H	BB	SO	ShO	W	L	SV	AB	H	HR	BA
1904 PIT N	1	3	.250	4.22	10	2	2	49	48	20	21	0	1	1	0	16	1	0	.063
1906	1	0	1.000	2.00	2	1	1	9	6	5	5	1	0	0	0	3	0	0	.000
1907	13	8	.619	2.15	31	19	15	180	135	59	85	4	3	2	1	60	3	0	.050
1908	16	9	.640	1.56	38	26	17	236.2	182	69	118	3	0	0	2	72	6	0	.083
1909	25	6	.806	1.62	41	30	20	283	207	68	133	5	7	0	3	87	12	0	.138
1910	12	13	.480	3.22	38	31	16	260	246	61	120	1	2	0	2	88	11	1	.125
1911	20	15	.571	3.13	40	33	18	267.2	245	84	139	1	3	2	0	84	12	0	.143
1912	12	12	.647	2.83	41	32	22	276.2	256	82	121	2	5	0	2	98	23	0	.235
1913 2 teams		PIT N	(36G 6–17)		PHI	N	(9G 3–3)												
" total	9	20	.310	3.73	45	27	6	241.1	252	107	85	1	3	5	3	75	10	0	.133
1914 PIT F	14	18	.438	3.23	36	34	20	262	256	90	82	1	0	1	1	87	14	0	.161
1915	0	2	.000	4.50	4	2	0	20	19	11	6	0	0	1	0	7	0	0	.000
11 yrs.	133	106	.556	2.75	326	237	137	2085.1	1852	656	915	19	24	12	14	677	92	1	.136

WORLD SERIES

	W	L	PCT	ERA	G	GS	CG	IP	H	BB	SO	ShO	W	L	SV	AB	H	HR	BA
1909 PIT N	0	1	.000	12.27	2	1	0	3.2	8	2	2	0	0	0	0	1	0	0	.000

Kid Camp

CAMP, WINFIELD SCOTT　　　　　　　6' 160 lbs.
Brother of Llewellan Camp.
B. 1870, Columbus, Ohio　　D. Mar. 2, 1895, Omaha, Neb.

	W	L	PCT	ERA	G	GS	CG	IP	H	BB	SO	ShO	W	L	SV	AB	H	HR	BA
1892 PIT N	0	1	.000	6.26	4	1	1	23	31	9	6	0	0	0	0	11	1	0	.091
1894 CHI N	0	1	.000	6.55	3	2	2	22	34	12	6	0	0	0	0	11	0	0	.000
2 yrs.	0	2	.000	6.40	7	3	3	45	65	21	12	0	0	0	0	22	1	0	.045

	W	L	PCT	ERA	G	GS	CG	IP	H	BB	SO	ShO	Relief Pitching W	L	SV	BATTING AB	H	HR	BA

Rick Camp

CAMP, RICK LAMAR
B. June 10, 1953, Trion, Ga.
BR TR 6'1" 195 lbs.

	W	L	PCT	ERA	G	GS	CG	IP	H	BB	SO	ShO	W	L	SV	AB	H	HR	BA
1976 ATL N	0	1	.000	6.55	5	1	0	11	13	2	6	0	0	0	0	2	0	0	.000
1977	6	3	.667	3.99	54	0	0	79	89	47	51	0	6	3	10	6	0	0	.000
1978	2	4	.333	3.77	42	4	0	74	99	32	23	0	0	4	0	8	0	0	.000
1980	6	4	.600	1.92	77	0	0	108	92	29	33	0	6	4	22	9	1	0	.111
1981	9	3	.750	1.78	48	0	0	76	68	12	47	0	9	3	17	12	0	0	.000
1982	11	13	.458	3.65	51	21	3	177.1	199	52	68	0	4	3	5	41	1	0	.024
1983	10	9	.526	3.79	40	16	1	140	146	38	61	0	4	2	0	39	3	0	.077
1984	8	6	.571	3.27	31	21	1	148.2	134	63	69	0	1	0	0	45	5	0	.111
8 yrs.	52	43	.547	3.28	348	63	5	814	840	275	358	0	30	19	54	162	10	0	.062

LEAGUE CHAMPIONSHIP SERIES

	W	L	PCT	ERA	G	GS	CG	IP	H	BB	SO	ShO	W	L	SV	AB	H	HR	BA
1982 ATL N	0	1	.000	36.00	1	1	0	1	4	1	0	0	0	0	0	0	0	0	

Bert Campaneris

CAMPANERIS, BLANCO DAGOBERTO
Born Blanco Dagoberto Campaneria.
B. Mar. 9, 1942, Pueblo Nuevo, Cuba
BR TR 5'10" 160 lbs.

	W	L	PCT	ERA	G	GS	CG	IP	H	BB	SO	ShO	W	L	SV	AB	H	HR	BA
1965 KC A	0	0	–	9.00	1	0	0	1	2	1	2	1	0	0	0	0	*		

Archie Campbell

CAMPBELL, ARCHIBALD STEWART
B. Oct. 20, 1903, Maplewood, N. J.
BR TR 6'1" 180 lbs.

	W	L	PCT	ERA	G	GS	CG	IP	H	BB	SO	ShO	W	L	SV	AB	H	HR	BA
1928 NY A	0	1	.000	5.25	13	1	0	24	30	11	9	0	0	1	2	4	1	0	.250
1929 WAS A	0	1	.000	15.75	4	0	0	4	10	5	1	0	0	1	0	0	0	0	
1930 CIN N	2	4	.333	5.43	23	3	1	58	71	31	19	0	1	2	4	15	4	0	.267
3 yrs.	2	6	.250	5.86	40	4	1	86	111	47	29	0	1	4	6	19	5	0	.263

Bill Campbell

CAMPBELL, WILLIAM RICHARD
B. Aug. 9, 1948, Highland Park, Mich.
BR TR 6'3" 185 lbs.

	W	L	PCT	ERA	G	GS	CG	IP	H	BB	SO	ShO	W	L	SV	AB	H	HR	BA
1973 MIN A	3	3	.500	3.14	28	2	0	51.2	44	20	42	0	3	1	7	0	0	0	–
1974	8	7	.533	2.63	63	0	0	120	109	55	89	0	8	7	19	0	0	0	–
1975	4	6	.400	3.79	47	7	2	121	119	46	76	1	1	4	5	1	0	0	.000
1976	17	5	.773	3.01	78	0	0	167.2	145	62	115	0	17	5	20	0	0	0	–
1977 BOS A	13	9	.591	2.96	69	0	0	140	112	60	114	0	13	9	31	0	0	0	–
1978	7	5	.583	3.91	29	0	0	50.2	42	17	47	0	7	5	4	0	0	0	–
1979	3	4	.429	4.25	41	0	0	55	55	23	25	0	3	4	9	0	0	0	–
1980	4	0	1.000	4.83	23	0	0	41	44	22	17	0	4	0	0	0	0	0	–
1981	1	1	.500	3.19	30	0	0	48	45	20	37	0	1	1	7	0	0	0	–
1982 CHI N	3	6	.333	3.69	62	0	0	100	89	40	71	0	3	6	8	7	1	0	.143
1983	6	8	.429	4.49	82	0	0	122.1	128	49	97	0	6	8	8	10	1	0	.100
1984 PHI N	6	5	.545	3.43	57	0	0	81.1	68	35	52	0	6	5	1	1	0	0	.000
12 yrs.	75	59	.560	3.49	609	9	2	1098.2	1020	449	782	1	72	55	119	19	2	0	.105

Billy Campbell

CAMPBELL, WILLIAM JAMES
B. Nov. 4, 1873, Pittsburgh, Pa.   D. Oct. 7, 1957, Cincinnati, Ohio
BL TL 5'10" 165 lbs.

	W	L	PCT	ERA	G	GS	CG	IP	H	BB	SO	ShO	W	L	SV	AB	H	HR	BA
1905 STL N	1	1	.500	7.41	2	2	2	17	27	7	2	0	0	0	0	7	1	0	.143
1907 CIN N	3	0	1.000	2.14	3	3	3	21	19	3	4	0	0	0	0	8	2	0	.250
1908	12	13	.480	3.79	35	24	19	221.1	203	44	73	2	2	1	1	72	6	0	.083
1909	7	11	.389	2.67	30	15	7	148.1	162	39	37	0	1	4	2	43	6	0	.140
4 yrs.	23	25	.479	2.80	70	44	31	407.2	411	93	116	2	3	5	3	130	15	0	.115

Dave Campbell

CAMPBELL, DAVID ALAN
B. Sept. 3, 1951, Princeton, Ind.
BR TR 6'3" 210 lbs.

	W	L	PCT	ERA	G	GS	CG	IP	H	BB	SO	ShO	W	L	SV	AB	H	HR	BA
1977 ATL N	0	6	.000	3.03	65	0	0	89	78	33	42	0	0	6	13	12	1	0	.083
1978	4	4	.500	4.83	53	0	0	69	67	49	45	0	4	4	1	0	0	0	–
2 yrs.	4	10	.286	3.82	118	0	0	158	145	82	87	0	4	10	14	12	1	0	.083

John Campbell

CAMPBELL, JOHN MILLARD
B. Sept. 13, 1907, Washington, D. C.
BR TR 6'1½" 184 lbs.

	W	L	PCT	ERA	G	GS	CG	IP	H	BB	SO	ShO	W	L	SV	AB	H	HR	BA
1933 WAS A	0	0	–	0.00	1	0	0	1	1	1	0	0	0	0	0	0	0	0	–

Card Camper

CAMPER, CARDELL
B. July 6, 1952, Boley, Okla.
BR TR 6'3" 208 lbs.

	W	L	PCT	ERA	G	GS	CG	IP	H	BB	SO	ShO	W	L	SV	AB	H	HR	BA
1977 CLE A	1	0	1.000	4.00	3	1	0	9	7	4	9	0	0	0	0	0	0	0	–

Sal Campfield

CAMPFIELD, WILLIAM HOLTON
B. Feb. 19, 1868, Meadville, Pa.   D. May 16, 1952, Meadville, Pa.
6'3"

	W	L	PCT	ERA	G	GS	CG	IP	H	BB	SO	ShO	W	L	SV	AB	H	HR	BA
1896 NY N	1	1	.500	4.00	6	2	2	27	31	6	6	0	0	0	0	12	2	0	.167

Sal Campisi

CAMPISI, SALVATORE JOHN
B. Aug. 11, 1942, Brooklyn, N. Y.
BR TR 6'2" 210 lbs.

	W	L	PCT	ERA	G	GS	CG	IP	H	BB	SO	ShO	W	L	SV	AB	H	HR	BA
1969 STL N	1	0	1.000	0.90	7	0	0	10	4	6	7	0	1	0	0	0	0	0	–
1970	2	2	.500	2.94	37	0	0	49	53	37	26	0	2	2	4	1	0	0	.000
1971 MIN A	0	0	–	4.50	6	0	0	4	5	4	2	0	0	0	0	0	0	0	–
3 yrs.	3	2	.600	2.71	50	0	0	63	62	47	35	0	3	2	4	1	0	0	.000

Hugh Canavan

CANAVAN, HUGH EDWARD (Hugo)
B. May 13, 1897, Worcester, Mass.   D. Sept. 4, 1967, Boston, Mass.
BL TL 5'8" 160 lbs.

	W	L	PCT	ERA	G	GS	CG	IP	H	BB	SO	ShO	W	L	SV	AB	H	HR	BA
1918 BOS N	0	4	.000	6.36	11	3	3	46.2	70	15	18	0	0	1	0	21	2	0	.095

John Candelaria

CANDELARIA, JOHN ROBERT
B. Nov. 6, 1953, New York, N. Y.
BL TL 6'7" 205 lbs.

	W	L	PCT	ERA	G	GS	CG	IP	H	BB	SO	ShO	W	L	SV	AB	H	HR	BA
1975 PIT N	8	6	.571	2.75	18	18	4	121	95	36	95	1	0	0	0	43	6	0	.140
1976	16	7	.696	3.15	32	31	11	220	173	60	138	4	0	0	1	76	14	0	.184
1977	20	5	.800	2.34	33	33	6	231	197	50	133	1	0	0	0	80	18	0	.225
1978	12	11	.522	3.24	30	29	3	189	191	49	94	1	0	0	1	52	9	0	.173

	W	L	PCT	ERA	G	GS	CG	IP	H	BB	SO	ShO	Relief Pitching W	L	SV	Batting AB	H	HR	BA

John Candelaria continued

	W	L	PCT	ERA	G	GS	CG	IP	H	BB	SO	ShO	W	L	SV	AB	H	HR	BA
1979	14	9	.609	3.22	33	30	8	207	201	41	101	0	0	1	0	68	9	0	.132
1980	11	14	.440	4.02	35	34	7	233	246	50	97	0	0	0	1	77	15	0	.195
1981	2	2	.500	3.51	6	6	0	41	42	11	14	0	0	0	0	13	3	0	.231
1982	12	7	.632	2.94	31	30	1	174.2	166	37	133	1	0	0	1	54	12	0	.222
1983	15	8	.652	3.23	33	32	2	197.2	191	45	157	0	0	0	0	65	9	0	.138
1984	12	11	.522	2.72	33	28	3	185.1	179	34	133	1	0	1	2	62	8	1	.129
10 yrs.	122	80	.604	3.10	284	271	45	1799.2	1681	413	1095	9	0	2	6	590	103	1	.175
LEAGUE CHAMPIONSHIP SERIES																			
1975 PIT N	0	0	—	3.52	1	1	0	7.2	3	2	14	0	0	0	0	3	0	0	.000
1979	0	0	—	2.57	1	1	0	7	5	1	4	0	0	0	0	3	0	0	.000
2 yrs.	0	0	—	3.07	2	2	0	14.2	8	3	18	0	0	0	0	6	0	0	.000
WORLD SERIES																			
1979 PIT N	1	1	.500	5.00	2	2	0	9	14	2	4	0	0	0	0	3	1	0	.333

Milo Candini

CANDINI, MILO CAIN
B. Aug. 3, 1917, Manteca, Calif.   BR TR 6'   187 lbs.

	W	L	PCT	ERA	G	GS	CG	IP	H	BB	SO	ShO	W	L	SV	AB	H	HR	BA
1943 WAS A	11	7	.611	2.49	28	21	8	166	144	65	67	3	2	0	1	56	9	1	.161
1944	6	7	.462	4.11	28	10	4	103	110	49	31	2	1	4	1	32	10	0	.313
1946	2	0	1.000	2.08	9	0	0	21.2	15	4	6	0	2	0	1	6	2	0	.333
1947	3	4	.429	5.17	38	2	0	87	96	35	31	0	3	2	1	18	3	0	.167
1948	2	3	.400	5.15	35	4	1	94.1	96	63	23	0	2	1	3	22	8	0	.364
1949	0	0	—	4.76	3	0	0	5.2	4	1	1	0	0	0	1	1	1	0	1.000
1950 PHI N	1	0	1.000	2.70	18	0	0	30	32	15	10	0	1	0	0	6	1	0	.167
1951	1	0	1.000	6.00	15	0	0	30	33	18	14	0	1	0	0	3	1	0	.333
8 yrs.	26	21	.553	3.92	174	37	13	537.2	530	250	183	5	12	7	8	144	35	1	.243

Tom Candiotti

CANDIOTTI, THOMAS C.
B. Aug. 31, 1957, Walnut Creek, Calif.   BR TR 6'3"   205 lbs.

	W	L	PCT	ERA	G	GS	CG	IP	H	BB	SO	ShO	W	L	SV	AB	H	HR	BA
1983 MIL A	4	4	.500	3.23	10	8	2	55.2	62	16	21	1	0	0	0	0	0	0	—
1984	2	2	.500	5.29	8	6	0	32.1	38	10	23	0	0	0	0	0	0	0	—
2 yrs.	6	6	.500	3.99	18	14	2	88	100	26	44	1	0	0	0	0	0	0	—

John Caneira

CANEIRA, JOHN CASCAES
B. Oct. 7, 1952, Naugatuck, Conn.   BR TR 6'3"   180 lbs.

	W	L	PCT	ERA	G	GS	CG	IP	H	BB	SO	ShO	W	L	SV	AB	H	HR	BA
1977 CAL A	2	2	.500	4.08	6	4	0	28.2	27	16	17	0	0	0	0	0	0	0	—
1978	0	0	—	7.04	2	2	0	7.2	8	3	0	0	0	0	0	0	0	0	—
2 yrs.	2	2	.500	4.71	8	6	0	36.1	35	19	17	0	0	0	0	0	0	0	—

Guy Cantrell

CANTRELL, DEWEY GUY (Gunner)
B. Apr. 9, 1904, Clarita, Okla.   D. Jan. 31, 1961, McAlester, Okla.   BR TR 6'   190 lbs.

	W	L	PCT	ERA	G	GS	CG	IP	H	BB	SO	ShO	W	L	SV	AB	H	HR	BA
1925 BKN N	1	0	1.000	3.00	14	3	1	36	42	14	13	0	0	0	0	9	0	0	.000
1927 2 teams		BKN	N (6G 0–0)				PHI	A (2G 0–2)											
" total	0	2	.000	4.18	8	2	2	28	35	13	12	0	0	0	0	9	2	0	.222
1930 DET A	1	5	.167	5.66	16	2	0	35	38	20	20	0	1	3	0	9	0	0	.000
3 yrs.	2	7	.222	4.27	38	7	4	99	115	47	45	0	1	3	0	27	2	0	.074

Ben Cantwell

CANTWELL, BENJAMIN CALDWELL
B. Apr. 13, 1902, Milan, Tenn.   D. Dec. 4, 1962, Salem, Mo.   BR TR 6'1"   168 lbs.

	W	L	PCT	ERA	G	GS	CG	IP	H	BB	SO	ShO	W	L	SV	AB	H	HR	BA
1927 NY N	1	1	.500	4.12	5	2	1	19.2	26	2	6	0	0	0	0	8	2	0	.250
1928 2 teams		NY	N (7G 1–0)				BOS	N (22G 3–3)											
" total	4	3	.571	4.98	29	10	3	108.1	132	40	18	0	1	0	1	33	7	0	.212
1929 BOS N	4	13	.235	4.47	27	20	8	157	171	52	25	0	1	0	2	50	9	0	.180
1930	9	15	.375	4.88	31	21	10	173.1	213	45	43	0	4	1	2	63	19	0	.302
1931	7	9	.438	3.63	33	16	9	156.1	160	34	32	2	1	1	2	57	13	0	.228
1932	13	11	.542	2.96	37	9	3	146	133	33	33	1	12	8	5	50	14	0	.280
1933	20	10	.667	2.62	40	29	18	254.2	242	54	57	2	4	1	2	85	12	0	.141
1934	5	11	.313	4.33	27	19	6	143.1	163	34	45	1	1	0	5	43	12	0	.279
1935	4	25	.138	4.61	39	24	13	210.2	235	44	34	0	1	5	0	67	19	0	.284
1936	9	9	.500	3.04	34	12	4	133.1	127	35	42	0	6	3	2	41	8	0	.195
1937 2 teams		NY	N (9G 0–1)				BKN	N (13G 0–0)											
" total	0	1	.000	5.17	14	1	0	31.1	38	9	13	0	0	0	0	6	1	0	.167
11 yrs.	76	108	.413	3.91	316	163	75	1534	1640	382	348	6	31	19	21	503	116	0	.231

Mike Cantwell

CANTWELL, MICHAEL JOSEPH
Brother of Tom Cantwell.
B. Jan. 15, 1896, Washington, D. C.   D. Jan. 5, 1953, Oteen, N. C.   BL TL 5'10"   155 lbs.

	W	L	PCT	ERA	G	GS	CG	IP	H	BB	SO	ShO	W	L	SV	AB	H	HR	BA
1916 NY A	0	0	—	0.00	1	0	0	2	0	2	0	0	0	0	0	0	0	0	—
1919 PHI N	1	3	.250	5.60	5	3	2	27.1	36	9	6	0	0	1	0	9	2	0	.222
1920	0	3	.000	3.86	5	1	0	23.1	25	15	8	0	0	2	0	7	1	0	.143
3 yrs.	1	6	.143	4.61	11	4	2	52.2	61	26	14	0	0	3	0	16	3	0	.188

Tom Cantwell

CANTWELL, THOMAS ALOYSIUS
Brother of Mike Cantwell.
B. Dec. 23, 1888, Washington, D. C.   D. Apr. 1, 1968, Washington, D. C.   BR TR 6'1"   175 lbs.

	W	L	PCT	ERA	G	GS	CG	IP	H	BB	SO	ShO	W	L	SV	AB	H	HR	BA
1909 CIN N	1	0	1.000	1.66	6	1	1	21.2	16	7	7	0	1	0	0	5	3	0	.600
1910	0	0	—	13.50	2	0	0	1.1	2	3	0	0	0	0	0	0	0	0	—
2 yrs.	1	0	1.000	2.35	8	1	1	23	18	10	7	0	1	0	0	5	3	0	.600

Doug Capilla

CAPILLA, DOUGLAS EDMUND
B. Jan. 7, 1952, Honolulu, Hawaii   BL TL 5'11"   160 lbs.

	W	L	PCT	ERA	G	GS	CG	IP	H	BB	SO	ShO	W	L	SV	AB	H	HR	BA
1976 STL N	0	1	.000	5.40	7	0	0	8.1	8	4	5	0	0	0	0	0	0	0	—
1977 2 teams		STL	N (2G 0–0)				CIN	N (22G 7–8)											
" total	7	8	.467	4.47	24	16	1	108.2	96	61	75	0	0	0	0	34	2	0	.059
1978 CIN N	0	1	.000	9.82	6	3	0	11	14	11	9	0	0	0	0	2	0	0	.000

	W	L	PCT	ERA	G	GS	CG	IP	H	BB	SO	ShO	Relief Pitching W	L	SV	BATTING AB	H	HR	BA

Doug Capilla continued

	W	L	PCT	ERA	G	GS	CG	IP	H	BB	SO	ShO	W	L	SV	AB	H	HR	BA
1979 2 teams		CIN	N	(5G 1–0)	CHI	N	(13G 0–1)												
" total	1	1	.500	4.18	18	1	0	23.2	21	12	10	0	1	0	0	1	1	0	1.000
1980 CHI N	2	8	.200	4.10	39	11	0	90	82	51	51	0	1	0	0	21	4	0	.190
1981	1	0	1.000	3.18	42	0	0	51	52	34	28	0	1	0	0	3	0	0	.000
6 yrs.	12	18	.400	4.34	136	31	3	292.2	273	173	178	0	4	0	0	61	7	0	.115

George Cappuzzello

CAPPUZZELLO, GEORGE ANGELO
B. Jan. 15, 1954, Youngstown, Ohio   BR TL 6' 175 lbs.

	W	L	PCT	ERA	G	GS	CG	IP	H	BB	SO	ShO	W	L	SV	AB	H	HR	BA
1981 DET A	1	1	.500	3.44	18	3	0	34	28	18	19	0	1	0	1	0	0	0	–
1982 HOU N	0	1	.000	2.79	17	0	0	19.1	16	7	13	0	0	1	0	1	0	0	.000
2 yrs.	1	2	.333	3.21	35	3	0	53.1	44	25	32	0	1	1	1	1	0	0	.000

Buzz Capra

CAPRA, LEE WILLIAM
B. Oct. 1, 1947, Chicago, Ill.   BR TR 5'10" 168 lbs.

	W	L	PCT	ERA	G	GS	CG	IP	H	BB	SO	ShO	W	L	SV	AB	H	HR	BA
1971 NY N	0	1	.000	9.00	3	0	0	5	3	5	6	0	0	1	0	0	0	0	.000
1972	3	2	.600	4.58	14	6	0	53	50	27	45	0	0	0	0	12	3	0	.250
1973	2	7	.222	3.86	24	0	0	42	35	28	35	0	2	7	4	2	0	0	.000
1974 ATL N	16	8	.667	**2.28**	39	27	11	217	163	84	137	5	1	2	1	67	11	0	.164
1975	4	7	.364	4.27	12	12	5	78	77	28	35	0	0	0	0	23	1	0	.043
1976	0	1	.000	9.00	5	0	0	9	9	6	4	0	0	1	0	0	0	0	–
1977	6	11	.353	5.37	45	16	0	139	142	80	100	0	4	3	0	36	4	0	.111
7 yrs.	31	37	.456	3.88	142	61	16	543	479	258	362	5	7	14	5	141	19	0	.135

Pat Caraway

CARAWAY, CECIL BRADFORD
B. Sept. 26, 1906, Gordon, Tex.   D. June 9, 1974, El Paso, Tex.   BL TL 6'4" 175 lbs.

	W	L	PCT	ERA	G	GS	CG	IP	H	BB	SO	ShO	W	L	SV	AB	H	HR	BA
1930 CHI A	10	10	.500	3.86	38	21	9	193.1	194	57	83	1	2	1	1	64	11	0	.172
1931	10	**24**	.294	6.22	51	32	11	220	268	101	55	1	1	3	2	72	14	0	.194
1932	2	6	.250	6.82	19	9	1	64.2	80	37	13	0	0	1	0	21	3	0	.143
3 yrs.	22	40	.355	5.35	108	62	21	478	542	195	151	2	3	5	3	157	28	0	.178

John Carden

CARDEN, JOHN BRUTON
B. May 19, 1921, Killeen, Tex.   D. Feb. 8, 1949, Near Mexia, Tex.   BR TR 6'5" 210 lbs.

	W	L	PCT	ERA	G	GS	CG	IP	H	BB	SO	ShO	W	L	SV	AB	H	HR	BA
1946 NY N	0	0	–	22.50	1	0	0	2	4	4	1	0	0	0	0	0	0	0	–

Conrad Cardinal

CARDINAL, CONRAD SETH
B. Mar. 30, 1942, Brooklyn, N. Y.   BR TR 6'1" 190 lbs.

	W	L	PCT	ERA	G	GS	CG	IP	H	BB	SO	ShO	W	L	SV	AB	H	HR	BA
1963 HOU N	0	1	.000	6.08	6	1	0	13.1	15	7	7	0	0	0	0	2	0	0	.000

Ben Cardoni

CARDONI, ARMOND JOSEPH (Big Ben)
B. Aug. 21, 1920, Jessup, Pa.   D. Apr. 2, 1969, Jessup, Pa.   BR TR 6'3" 195 lbs.

	W	L	PCT	ERA	G	GS	CG	IP	H	BB	SO	ShO	W	L	SV	AB	H	HR	BA
1943 BOS N	0	0	–	6.43	11	0	0	28	38	14	5	0	0	0	1	7	0	0	.000
1944	0	6	.000	3.93	22	5	1	75.2	83	37	24	0	0	2	0	17	4	0	.235
1945	0	0	–	9.00	3	0	0	4	6	3	5	0	0	0	0	0	0	0	–
3 yrs.	0	6	.000	4.76	36	5	1	107.2	127	54	34	0	0	2	1	24	4	0	.167

Don Cardwell

CARDWELL, DONALD EUGENE
B. Dec. 7, 1935, Winston-Salem, N. C.   BR TR 6'4" 210 lbs.

	W	L	PCT	ERA	G	GS	CG	IP	H	BB	SO	ShO	W	L	SV	AB	H	HR	BA
1957 PHI N	4	8	.333	4.91	30	19	5	128.1	122	42	92	1	0	0	1	35	7	1	.200
1958	3	6	.333	4.51	16	14	3	107.2	99	37	77	0	0	0	0	38	8	0	.211
1959	9	10	.474	4.06	25	22	5	153	135	65	106	1	0	1	0	55	3	1	.055
1960 2 teams		PHI	N	(5G 1–2)	CHI	N	(31G 8–14)												
" total	9	16	.360	4.38	36	30	6	205.1	194	79	150	1	1	2	0	77	16	5	.208
1961 CHI N	15	14	.517	3.82	39	**38**	13	259.1	243	88	156	3	0	1	0	95	10	3	.105
1962	7	16	.304	4.92	41	29	6	195.2	205	60	104	1	1	0	4	61	9	0	.148
1963 PIT N	13	15	.464	3.07	33	32	7	213.2	195	52	112	2	1	0	0	71	6	0	.085
1964	1	2	.333	2.79	4	4	1	19.1	15	7	10	1	0	0	0	7	1	0	.143
1965	13	10	.565	3.18	37	34	12	240.1	214	59	107	2	0	0	0	74	12	2	.162
1966	6	6	.500	4.60	32	14	1	101.2	112	27	60	0	3	0	1	29	3	0	.103
1967 NY N	5	9	.357	3.57	26	16	3	118.1	112	39	71	3	1	0	0	38	6	1	.158
1968	7	13	.350	2.95	29	25	5	180	156	50	82	1	0	0	1	61	3	1	.049
1969	8	10	.444	3.01	30	21	4	152.1	145	47	60	0	1	1	0	47	8	1	.170
1970 2 teams		NY	N	(16G 0–2)	ATL	N	(16G 2–1)												
" total	2	3	.400	7.69	32	8	0	48	62	19	24	1	0	0	0	10	2	0	.200
14 yrs.	102	138	.425	3.92	410	301	72	2123	2009	671	1211	17	9	7	7	698	94	15	.135

WORLD SERIES

	W	L	PCT	ERA	G	GS	CG	IP	H	BB	SO	ShO	W	L	SV	AB	H	HR	BA
1969 NY N	0	0	–	0.00	1	0	0	1	0	0	0	0	0	0	0	0	0	0	–

Tex Carleton

CARLETON, JAMES OTTO
B. Aug. 19, 1906, Comanche, Tex.
D. Jan. 11, 1977, Fort Worth, Tex.   BB TR 6'1½" 180 lbs. BR 1933–34

	W	L	PCT	ERA	G	GS	CG	IP	H	BB	SO	ShO	W	L	SV	AB	H	HR	BA
1932 STL N	10	13	.435	4.08	44	22	9	196.1	198	70	113	3	3	2	0	60	9	1	.150
1933	17	11	.607	3.38	44	33	15	277	263	97	147	4	1	1	3	91	17	1	.187
1934	16	11	.593	4.26	40	31	16	240.2	260	52	103	0	1	2	2	88	17	1	.193
1935 CHI N	11	8	.579	3.89	31	22	8	171	169	60	84	0	2	2	1	62	8	0	.129
1936	14	10	.583	3.65	35	26	12	197.1	204	67	88	4	2	1	1	60	14	3	.233
1937	16	8	.667	3.15	32	27	18	208.1	183	94	105	4	0	0	0	71	12	0	.169
1938	10	9	.526	5.42	33	24	9	167.2	213	74	80	0	2	1	0	65	15	0	.231
1940 BKN N	6	6	.500	3.81	34	17	4	149	140	47	88	1	2	1	2	43	8	0	.186
8 yrs.	100	76	.568	3.91	293	202	91	1607.1	1630	561	808	16	12	10	9	540	100	6	.185

WORLD SERIES

	W	L	PCT	ERA	G	GS	CG	IP	H	BB	SO	ShO	W	L	SV	AB	H	HR	BA
1934 STL N	0	0	–	7.36	2	1	0	3.2	5	2	2	0	0	0	0	1	0	0	.000
1935 CHI N	0	1	.000	1.29	1	1	0	7	6	7	4	0	0	0	0	1	0	0	.000
1938	0	0	–	∞	1	0	0	1	2	0	0	0	0	0	0	0	0	0	–
3 yrs.	0	1	.000	5.06	4	2	0	10.2	12	11	6	0	0	0	0	2	0	0	.000

	W	L	PCT	ERA	G	GS	CG	IP	H	BB	SO	ShO	Relief Pitching W	L	SV	BATTING AB	H	HR	BA

Cisco Carlos

CARLOS, FRANCISCO MANUEL
B. Sept. 17, 1940, Monrovia, Calif.
BR TR 6'3" 205 lbs.

	W	L	PCT	ERA	G	GS	CG	IP	H	BB	SO	ShO	W	L	SV	AB	H	HR	BA
1967 CHI A	2	0	1.000	0.86	8	7	1	41.2	23	9	27	1	0	0	0	16	1	0	.063
1968	4	14	.222	3.90	29	21	0	122.1	121	37	57	0	0	0	0	31	2	0	.065
1969 2 teams			CHI A (25G 4-3)				WAS A (6G 1-1)												
" total	5	4	.556	5.37	31	8	0	67	75	29	33	0	3	2	0	15	1	0	.067
1970 WAS A	0	0	–	1.50	5	0	0	6	3	4	2	0	0	0	0	0	0	0	–
4 yrs.	11	18	.379	3.72	73	36	1	237	222	79	119	1	3	2	0	62	4	0	.065

Don Carlsen

CARLSEN, DONALD HERBERT
B. Oct. 15, 1926, Chicago, Ill.
BR TR 6'1" 175 lbs.

	W	L	PCT	ERA	G	GS	CG	IP	H	BB	SO	ShO	W	L	SV	AB	H	HR	BA
1948 CHI N	0	0	–	36.00	1	0	0	1	5	2	1	0	0	0	0	0	0	0	–
1951 PIT N	2	3	.400	4.19	7	6	2	43	50	14	20	0	0	0	0	16	4	0	.250
1952	0	1	.000	10.80	5	1	0	10	20	5	2	0	0	0	0	3	1	0	.333
3 yrs.	2	4	.333	6.00	13	7	2	54	75	21	23	0	0	0	0	19	5	0	.263

Hal Carlson

CARLSON, HAROLD GUST
B. May 17, 1892, Rockford, Ill.   D. May 28, 1930, Chicago, Ill.
BR TR 6' 180 lbs.

	W	L	PCT	ERA	G	GS	CG	IP	H	BB	SO	ShO	W	L	SV	AB	H	HR	BA
1917 PIT N	7	11	.389	2.90	34	17	9	161.1	140	49	68	1	3	2	1	49	6	0	.122
1918	0	1	.000	3.75	3	2	0	12	12	5	5	0	0	0	0	5	1	0	.200
1919	8	10	.444	2.23	22	14	7	141	114	39	49	1	3	1	0	43	7	0	.163
1920	14	13	.519	3.36	39	31	16	246.2	262	63	62	3	1	0	3	85	23	0	.271
1921	4	8	.333	4.27	31	10	3	109.2	121	23	37	0	1	3	4	34	10	0	.294
1922	9	12	.429	5.70	39	18	6	145.1	193	58	64	0	2	4	2	56	15	1	.268
1923	0	0	–	4.73	4	0	0	13.1	19	2	4	0	0	0	0	5	0	0	.000
1924 PHI N	8	17	.320	4.86	38	24	12	203.2	267	55	66	1	1	3	2	76	21	0	.276
1925	13	14	.481	4.23	35	32	18	234	281	52	80	4	0	1	0	93	17	2	.183
1926	17	12	.586	3.23	35	34	20	267.1	293	47	55	3	0	0	0	96	23	0	.240
1927 2 teams			PHI N (11G 4-5)				CHI N (27G 12-8)												
" total	16	13	.552	3.70	38	31	19	248	281	45	40	2	1	0	1	92	17	0	.185
1928 CHI N	3	2	.600	5.91	20	5	2	56.1	74	15	11	0	1	0	4	19	5	0	.263
1929	11	5	.688	5.16	31	14	6	111.2	131	31	35	2	2	2	2	39	9	0	.231
1930	4	2	.667	5.05	8	6	3	51.2	68	14	14	0	1	0	0	20	5	0	.250
14 yrs.	114	120	.487	3.97	377	238	121	2002	2256	498	590	17	16	16	19	712	159	5	.223

WORLD SERIES																			
1929 CHI N	0	0	–	6.75	2	0	0	4	7	1	3	0	0	0	0	0	0	0	–

Leon Carlson

CARLSON, LEON ALTON (Swede)
B. Feb. 17, 1895, Jamestown, N. Y.   D. Sept. 15, 1961, Jamestown, N. Y.
BR TR 6'3" 195 lbs.

	W	L	PCT	ERA	G	GS	CG	IP	H	BB	SO	ShO	W	L	SV	AB	H	HR	BA
1920 WAS A	0	0	–	3.65	3	0	0	12.1	14	2	3	0	0	0	0	6	1	0	.167

Steve Carlton

CARLTON, STEPHEN NORMAN (Lefty)
B. Dec. 22, 1944, Miami, Fla.
BL TL 6'4" 210 lbs.

	W	L	PCT	ERA	G	GS	CG	IP	H	BB	SO	ShO	W	L	SV	AB	H	HR	BA
1965 STL N	0	0	–	2.52	15	2	0	25	27	8	21	0	0	0	0	0	0	0	.000
1966	3	3	.500	3.12	9	9	2	52	56	18	25	1	0	0	0	15	4	0	.267
1967	14	9	.609	2.98	30	28	11	193	173	62	168	2	0	1	1	72	11	0	.153
1968	13	11	.542	2.99	34	33	10	232	214	61	162	5	0	1	0	73	12	2	.164
1969	17	11	.607	2.17	31	31	12	236	185	93	210	2	0	0	0	80	17	1	.213
1970	10	19	.345	3.72	34	33	13	254	239	109	193	2	0	0	0	80	16	0	.200
1971	20	9	.690	3.56	37	36	18	273	275	98	172	4	0	0	0	96	17	0	.177
1972 PHI N	27	10	.730	1.97	41	41	30	346.1	257	87	310	8	0	0	0	117	23	1	.197
1973	13	20	.394	3.90	40	40	18	293.1	293	113	223	3	0	0	0	100	16	2	.160
1974	16	13	.552	3.22	39	39	17	291	249	136	240	1	0	0	0	102	25	0	.245
1975	15	14	.517	3.56	37	37	14	255	217	104	192	3	0	0	0	90	14	0	.156
1976	20	7	.741	3.13	35	35	13	252.2	224	72	195	2	0	0	0	92	20	0	.217
1977	23	10	.697	2.64	36	36	17	283	229	89	198	2	0	0	0	97	26	3	.268
1978	16	13	.552	2.84	34	34	12	247	228	63	161	3	0	0	0	86	25	0	.291
1979	18	11	.621	3.62	35	35	13	251	202	89	213	4	0	0	0	94	21	0	.223
1980	24	9	.727	2.34	38	38	13	304	243	90	286	3	0	0	0	101	19	0	.188
1981	13	4	.765	2.42	24	24	10	190	152	62	179	1	0	0	0	67	9	0	.134
1982	23	11	.676	3.10	38	38	19	295.2	253	86	286	6	0	0	0	101	22	2	.218
1983	15	16	.484	3.11	37	37	8	283.2	277	84	275	3	0	0	0	97	19	0	.196
1984	13	7	.650	3.58	33	33	1	229	214	79	163	0	0	0	0	84	16	1	.190
20 yrs.	313	207	.602	3.04	657	639	251	4786.2	4207	1603	3872	55	0	2	1	1646	332	12	.202
										6th	2nd								

DIVISIONAL PLAYOFF SERIES																			
1981 PHI N	0	2	.000	3.86	2	2	0	14	14	8	13	0	0	0	0	4	1	0	.250

LEAGUE CHAMPIONSHIP SERIES																			
1976 PHI N	0	1	.000	5.14	1	1	0	7	8	5	6	0	0	0	0	2	0	0	.000
1977	0	1	.000	6.94	2	2	0	11.2	13	8	6	0	0	0	0	4	2	0	.500
1978	1	0	1.000	4.00	1	1	1	9	8	2	8	0	0	0	0	4	2	1	.500
1980	1	0	1.000	2.19	2	2	0	12.1	11	8	6	0	0	0	0	4	0	0	.000
1983	2	0	1.000	0.66	2	2	0	13.2	13	5	13	0	0	0	0	5	1	0	.200
5 yrs.	4	2	.667	3.52	8	8	1	53.2	53	28	39	0	0	0	0	19	5	1	.263

WORLD SERIES																			
1967 STL N	0	1	.000	0.00	1	1	0	6	3	2	5	0	0	0	0	1	0	0	.000
1968	0	0	–	6.75	2	0	0	4	7	1	3	0	0	0	0	0	0	0	–
1980 PHI N	2	0	1.000	2.40	2	2	0	15	14	9	17	0	0	0	0	0	0	0	–
1983	0	1	.000	2.70	1	1	0	6.2	5	3	7	0	0	0	0	3	0	0	.000
4 yrs.	2	2	.500	2.56	6	4	0	31.2	29	15	32	0	0	0	0	4	0	0	.000

Don Carman

CARMAN, DONALD WAYNE
B. Aug. 14, 1959, Oklahoma City, Okla.
BL TL 6'3" 190 lbs.

	W	L	PCT	ERA	G	GS	CG	IP	H	BB	SO	ShO	W	L	SV	AB	H	HR	BA
1983 PHI N	0	0	–	0.00	1	0	0	1	0	0	0	0	0	0	1	0	0	0	–
1984	0	1	.000	5.40	11	0	0	13.1	14	6	16	0	0	1	0	1	0	0	.000
2 yrs.	0	1	.000	5.02	12	0	0	14.1	14	6	16	0	0	1	1	1	0	0	.000

	W	L	PCT	ERA	G	GS	CG	IP	H	BB	SO	ShO	Relief Pitching W	L	SV	BATTING AB	H	HR	BA

Chet Carmichael

CARMICHAEL, CHESTER KELLER
B. Jan. 9, 1888, Muncie, Ind.   D. Aug. 23, 1960, Rochester, N. Y.   BR TR 5'11½" 200 lbs.

	W	L	PCT	ERA	G	GS	CG	IP	H	BB	SO	ShO	W	L	SV	AB	H	HR	BA
1909 **CIN N**	0	0	–	0.00	2	0	0	7	9	3	2	0	0	0	0	2	0	0	.000

Eddie Carnett

CARNETT, EDWIN ELLIOTT (Lefty)
B. Oct. 21, 1916, Springfield, Mo.   BL TL 6' 185 lbs.

	W	L	PCT	ERA	G	GS	CG	IP	H	BB	SO	ShO	W	L	SV	AB	H	HR	BA
1941 **BOS N**	0	0	–	20.25	2	0	0	1.1	4	3	2	0	0	0	0	0	0	0	–
1944 **CHI A**	0	0	–	9.00	2	0	0	2	3	0	1	0	0	0	0	457	126	1	.276
1945 **CLE A**	0	0	–	0.00	2	0	0	2	0	0	1	0	0	0	0	73	16	0	.219
3 yrs.	0	0	–	8.44	6	0	0	5.1	7	3	4	0	0	0	0	*			

Pat Carney

CARNEY, PATRICK JOSEPH (Doc)
B. Aug. 7, 1876, Holyoke, Mass.   D. Jan. 9, 1953, Worcester, Mass.   BL TL 6' 200 lbs.

	W	L	PCT	ERA	G	GS	CG	IP	H	BB	SO	ShO	W	L	SV	AB	H	HR	BA
1902 **BOS N**	0	1	.000	9.00	2	1	0	5	6	3	3	0	0	0	0	522	141	2	.270
1903	4	5	.444	4.04	10	9	9	78	93	31	29	0	1	0	0	392	94	1	.240
1904	0	3	.000	5.81	4	2	1	26.1	40	12	5	0	0	2	0	279	57	0	.204
3 yrs.	4	9	.308	4.69	16	12	10	109.1	139	46	37	0	1	2	0	*			

Bob Carpenter

CARPENTER, ROBERT LOUIS
B. Dec. 12, 1917, Chicago, Ill.   BR TR 6'3" 195 lbs.

	W	L	PCT	ERA	G	GS	CG	IP	H	BB	SO	ShO	W	L	SV	AB	H	HR	BA
1940 **NY N**	2	0	1.000	2.73	5	3	2	33	29	14	25	0	0	0	0	10	1	0	.100
1941	11	6	.647	3.83	29	19	8	131.2	138	42	42	1	1	0	2	45	7	0	.156
1942	11	10	.524	3.15	28	25	12	185.2	192	51	53	2	1	1	0	65	12	0	.185
1946	1	3	.250	4.85	12	6	1	39	37	18	13	1	0	0	0	10	1	0	.100
1947 **2 teams**		**NY**	**N**	(2G 0–0)		**CHI**	**N**	(4G 0–1)											
" total	0	1	.000	6.97	6	1	0	10.1	15	7	1	0	0	0	0	1	1	0	1.000
5 yrs.	25	20	.556	3.60	80	54	23	399.2	411	132	134	4	2	1	2	131	22	0	.168

Lew Carpenter

CARPENTER, LEWIS EMMETT
B. Aug. 16, 1913, Woodstock, Ga.   D. Apr. 25, 1979, Marietta, Ga.   BR TR 6'2" 195 lbs.

	W	L	PCT	ERA	G	GS	CG	IP	H	BB	SO	ShO	W	L	SV	AB	H	HR	BA
1943 **WAS A**	0	0	–	0.00	4	0	0	3.1	1	4	1	0	0	0	0	0	0	0	–

Paul Carpenter

CARPENTER, PAUL CALVIN
B. Aug. 12, 1894, Granville, Ohio   D. Mar. 14, 1968, Newark, Ohio   BR TR 5'11" 165 lbs.

	W	L	PCT	ERA	G	GS	CG	IP	H	BB	SO	ShO	W	L	SV	AB	H	HR	BA
1916 **PIT N**	0	0	–	1.17	5	0	0	7.2	8	4	5	0	0	0	0	2	0	0	.000

Frank Carpin

CARPIN, FRANK DOMINIC
B. Sept. 14, 1938, Brooklyn, N. Y.   BL TL 5'10" 172 lbs.

	W	L	PCT	ERA	G	GS	CG	IP	H	BB	SO	ShO	W	L	SV	AB	H	HR	BA
1965 **PIT N**	3	1	.750	3.18	39	0	0	39.2	35	24	27	0	3	1	4	1	0	0	.000
1966 **HOU N**	1	0	1.000	7.50	10	0	0	6	9	6	2	0	1	0	0	0	0	0	–
2 yrs.	4	1	.800	3.74	49	0	0	45.2	44	30	29	0	4	1	4	1	0	0	.000

Alex Carrasquel

CARRASQUEL, ALEJANDRO ALEXANDER APARICIO ELROY
B. July 24, 1912, Caracas, Venezuela   D. Aug. 19, 1969, Caracas, Venezuela   BR TR 6'1" 182 lbs.

	W	L	PCT	ERA	G	GS	CG	IP	H	BB	SO	ShO	W	L	SV	AB	H	HR	BA
1939 **WAS A**	5	9	.357	4.69	40	17	7	159.1	165	68	41	0	1	1	3	42	7	1	.167
1940	6	2	.750	4.88	28	0	0	48	42	29	19	0	6	2	0	7	0	0	.000
1941	6	2	.750	3.44	35	5	4	96.2	103	49	30	0	4	1	2	21	2	0	.095
1942	7	7	.500	3.43	35	15	7	152.1	161	53	40	1	1	4	4	44	6	0	.136
1943	11	7	.611	3.68	39	13	4	144.1	160	54	48	1	5	3	5	43	8	0	.186
1944	8	7	.533	3.43	43	7	3	134	143	50	35	0	5	3	2	36	7	0	.194
1945	7	5	.583	2.71	35	7	5	122.2	105	40	38	2	4	3	1	36	3	0	.083
1949 **CHI A**	0	0	–	14.73	3	0	0	3.2	8	4	1	0	0	0	0	0	0	0	–
8 yrs.	50	39	.562	3.73	258	64	30	861	887	347	252	4	26	15	16	229	33	1	.144

Bill Carrick

CARRICK, WILLIAM MARTIN (Doughnut Bill)
B. Sept. 5, 1873, Erie, Pa.   D. Mar. 7, 1932, Philadelphia, Pa.   TR

	W	L	PCT	ERA	G	GS	CG	IP	H	BB	SO	ShO	W	L	SV	AB	H	HR	BA
1898 **NY N**	3	1	.750	3.40	5	4	4	39.2	39	21	10	0	0	0	0	18	3	0	.167
1899	16	26	.381	4.65	44	43	40	361.2	485	122	60	3	0	0	0	130	18	0	.138
1900	19	22	.463	3.53	45	41	32	341.2	415	92	63	1	2	1	0	115	20	0	.174
1901 **WAS A**	14	23	.378	3.75	42	37	34	324	367	93	70	0	1	0	0	126	20	0	.159
1902	11	17	.393	4.86	31	30	28	257.2	344	72	36	0	0	0	0	108	20	0	.185
5 yrs.	63	89	.414	4.14	167	155	138	1324.2	1650	400	239	4	3	2	0	497	81	0	.163

Don Carrithers

CARRITHERS, DONALD GEORGE
B. Sept. 15, 1949, Lynwood, Calif.   BR TR 6'2" 180 lbs.

	W	L	PCT	ERA	G	GS	CG	IP	H	BB	SO	ShO	W	L	SV	AB	H	HR	BA
1970 **SF N**	2	1	.667	7.36	11	2	0	22	31	14	14	0	2	0	0	6	0	0	.000
1971	5	3	.625	4.05	22	12	2	80	77	37	41	1	1	0	1	17	3	0	.176
1972	4	8	.333	5.80	25	14	2	90	108	42	42	1	0	1	1	29	6	0	.207
1973	1	2	.333	4.81	25	3	0	58	64	35	36	0	1	0	0	16	4	0	.250
1974 **MON N**	5	2	.714	3.00	22	3	0	60	56	17	31	0	4	0	1	14	4	0	.286
1975	5	3	.625	3.30	19	14	5	101	90	38	37	2	0	0	0	34	6	0	.176
1976	6	12	.333	4.43	34	19	2	140.1	153	78	71	0	1	1	0	37	4	0	.108
1977 **MIN A**	0	1	.000	7.07	7	0	0	14	16	6	3	0	0	1	0	0	0	0	–
8 yrs.	28	32	.467	4.46	165	67	11	565.1	595	267	275	4	9	3	3	153	27	0	.176

LEAGUE CHAMPIONSHIP SERIES

	W	L	PCT	ERA	G	GS	CG	IP	H	BB	SO	ShO	W	L	SV	AB	H	HR	BA
1971 **SF N**	0	0	–	∞	1	0	0	0	3	0	0	0	0	0	0	0	0	0	–

Clay Carroll

CARROLL, CLAY PALMER (Hawk)
B. May 2, 1941, Clanton, Ala.   BR TR 6'1" 178 lbs.

	W	L	PCT	ERA	G	GS	CG	IP	H	BB	SO	ShO	W	L	SV	AB	H	HR	BA
1964 **MIL N**	2	0	1.000	1.77	11	1	0	20.1	15	3	17	0	2	0	1	2	0	0	.000
1965	0	1	.000	4.41	19	1	0	34.2	35	13	16	0	0	1	1	5	0	0	.000
1966 **ATL N**	8	7	.533	2.37	73	3	0	144.1	127	29	67	0	8	7	11	30	3	0	.100
1967	6	12	.333	3.47	51	1	0	93	111	29	35	0	3	8	0	16	1	0	.063
1968 **2 teams**		**ATL**	**N**	(10G 0–1)		**CIN**	**N**	(58G 7–7)											
" total	7	8	.467	2.69	68	1	0	144	128	38	71	0	7	8	17	29	6	0	.207

	W	L	PCT	ERA	G	GS	CG	IP	H	BB	SO	ShO	Relief Pitching W	L	SV	BATTING AB	H	HR	BA

Clay Carroll continued

	W	L	PCT	ERA	G	GS	CG	IP	H	BB	SO	ShO	W	L	SV	AB	H	HR	BA
1969 CIN N	12	6	.667	3.52	71	4	0	151	149	78	90	0	11	6	7	29	6	1	.207
1970	9	4	.692	2.60	65	0	0	104	104	27	63	0	9	4	16	14	1	0	.071
1971	10	4	.714	2.49	61	0	0	94	78	42	64	0	10	4	15	10	1	0	.100
1972	6	4	.600	2.25	65	0	0	96	89	32	51	0	6	4	37	11	2	0	.182
1973	8	8	.500	3.69	53	5	0	92.2	111	34	41	0	6	8	14	14	3	0	.214
1974	12	5	.706	2.14	57	3	0	101	96	30	46	0	10	4	6	18	3	0	.167
1975	7	5	.583	2.63	56	2	0	96	93	32	44	0	7	5	7	19	0	0	.000
1976 CHI A	4	4	.500	2.57	29	0	0	77	67	24	38	0	4	4	6	0	0	0	–
1977 2 teams			CHI	A (8G 1–3)				STL	N	(51G 4–2)									
" total	5	5	.500	2.76	59	1	0	101	91	28	38	0	5	5	5	11	1	0	.091
1978 PIT N	0	0	–	2.25	2	0	0	4	2	3	0	0	0	0	0	0	0	0	–
15 yrs.	96	73	.568	2.94	731	28	1	1353	1296	442	681	0	88	68	143	208	27	1	.130
														9th					

LEAGUE CHAMPIONSHIP SERIES																			
1970 CIN N	0	0	–	0.00	2	0	0	1.1	2	0	2	0	0	0	1	0	0	0	–
1972	1	1	.500	3.38	2	0	0	2.2	2	3	0	0	1	1	0	0	0	0	–
1973	1	0	1.000	1.29	3	0	0	7	5	1	2	0	1	0	0	0	0	0	–
1975	0	0	–	0.00	1	0	0	1	0	1	1	0	0	0	0	0	0	0	–
4 yrs.	2	1	.667	1.50	8	0	0	12	9	5	5	0	2	1	1	0	0	0	–

WORLD SERIES																			
1970 CIN N	1	0	1.000	0.00	4	0	0	9	5	2	11	0	1	0	0	1	0	0	.000
1972	0	1	.000	1.59	5	0	0	5.2	6	4	3	0	0	1	1	0	0	0	–
1975	1	0	1.000	3.18	5	0	0	5.2	4	2	3	0	1	0	0	0	0	0	–
3 yrs.	2	1	.667	1.33	14	0	0	20.1	15	8	17	0	2	1	1	1	0	0	.000
				5th										2nd					

Dick Carroll

CARROLL, RICHARD THOMAS   6'2"
B. July 21, 1884, Cleveland, Ohio   D. Nov. 22, 1945, Cleveland, Ohio

	W	L	PCT	ERA	G	GS	CG	IP	H	BB	SO	ShO	W	L	SV	AB	H	HR	BA
1909 NY A	0	0	–	3.60	2	1	0	5	7	1	1	0	0	0	0	2	1	0	.500

Ed Carroll

CARROLL, EDGAR FLEISCHER   BR TR 6'3"   185 lbs.
B. July 27, 1907, Baltimore, Md.

	W	L	PCT	ERA	G	GS	CG	IP	H	BB	SO	ShO	W	L	SV	AB	H	HR	BA
1929 BOS A	1	0	1.000	5.61	24	3	0	67.1	77	20	13	0	0	0	0	16	1	0	.063

Ownie Carroll

CARROLL, OWEN THOMAS   BR TR 5'10½" 165 lbs.
B. Nov. 11, 1902, Kearny, N. J.   D. June 18, 1975, Orange, N. J.

	W	L	PCT	ERA	G	GS	CG	IP	H	BB	SO	ShO	W	L	SV	AB	H	HR	BA
1925 DET A	3	1	.750	3.76	10	4	1	40.2	46	28	12	0	1	0	0	16	6	0	.375
1927	10	6	.625	3.98	31	15	8	172	186	73	41	0	3	0	0	69	12	0	.174
1928	16	12	.571	3.27	34	28	19	231	219	87	51	2	2	2	2	98	19	0	.194
1929	9	17	.346	4.63	34	26	12	202	249	86	54	0	2	3	1	74	17	0	.230
1930 3 teams			DET	A (6G 0–5)				NY	A	(10G 0–1)			CIN	N	(3G 0–1)				
" total	0	7	.000	7.39	19	6	1	67	96	30	12	0	0	3	0	22	4	0	.182
1931 CIN N	3	9	.250	5.53	29	12	4	107.1	135	51	24	0	1	2	0	34	7	0	.206
1932	10	19	.345	4.50	32	26	15	210	245	44	55	0	1	0	1	77	16	0	.208
1933 BKN N	13	15	.464	3.78	33	31	11	226.1	248	54	45	0	0	0	0	74	11	0	.149
1934	1	3	.250	6.42	26	5	0	74.1	108	33	17	0	1	0	1	25	6	0	.240
9 yrs.	65	89	.422	4.43	248	153	71	1330.2	1532	486	311	2	11	10	5	489	98	0	.200

Tom Carroll

CARROLL, THOMAS MICHAEL   BL TR 6'3"   190 lbs.
B. Nov. 5, 1952, Utica, N. Y.

	W	L	PCT	ERA	G	GS	CG	IP	H	BB	SO	ShO	W	L	SV	AB	H	HR	BA
1974 CIN N	4	3	.571	3.69	16	13	0	78	68	44	37	0	0	0	0	26	4	0	.154
1975	4	1	.800	4.98	12	7	0	47	52	26	14	0	1	1	0	14	0	0	.000
2 yrs.	8	4	.667	4.18	28	20	0	125	120	70	51	0	1	1	0	40	4	0	.100

Kid Carsey

CARSEY, WILFRED   BR TR 5'7"   168 lbs.
B. Oct. 22, 1870, New York, N. Y.   D. Mar. 29, 1960, Miami, Fla.

	W	L	PCT	ERA	G	GS	CG	IP	H	BB	SO	ShO	W	L	SV	AB	H	HR	BA
1891 WAS AA	14	37	.275	4.99	54	53	46	415	513	161	174	1	1	0	0	187	28	0	.150
1892 PHI N	19	16	.543	3.12	43	34	30	317.2	320	104	76	1	2	0	1	131	20	1	.153
1893	20	15	.571	4.81	39	35	30	318.1	375	124	50	1	1	2	0	145	27	0	.186
1894	18	12	.600	5.56	35	31	26	277	349	102	41	0	0	1	1	125	34	0	.272
1895	24	16	.600	4.92	44	40	35	342.1	460	118	64	0	1	1	1	141	41	0	.291
1896	11	11	.500	5.62	27	21	18	187.1	273	72	36	1	2	0	1	81	18	0	.222
1897 2 teams			PHI	N (4G 2–1)				STL	N	(12G 3–8)									
" total	5	9	.357	5.81	16	15	13	127	168	47	15	0	0	0	0	56	16	0	.286
1898 STL N	2	12	.143	6.33	20	13	10	123.2	177	37	10	0	0	1	0	105	21	1	.200
1899 2 teams			CLE	N (10G 1–8)				WAS	N	(4G 1–2)									
" total	2	10	.167	5.15	14	12	10	106.2	136	28	14	0	1	0	0	65	16	0	.246
1901 BKN N	1	0	1.000	10.29	2	0	0	7	9	3	4	0	1	0	0	2	0	0	.000
10 yrs.	116	138	.457	4.95	294	256	218	2222	2780	796	484	4	9	5	3	*			

Alex Carson

CARSON, ALBERT JAMES (Soldier)   TR
B. Aug. 22, 1882, Chicago, Ill.   D. Nov. 26, 1962, San Diego, Calif.

	W	L	PCT	ERA	G	GS	CG	IP	H	BB	SO	ShO	W	L	SV	AB	H	HR	BA
1910 CHI N	0	0	–	4.05	2	0	0	6.2	6	1	2	0	0	0	0	1	0	0	.000

Arnold Carter

CARTER, ARNOLD LEE (Lefty)   BL TL 5'10"   170 lbs.
B. Mar. 14, 1920, Rainelle, W. Va.

	W	L	PCT	ERA	G	GS	CG	IP	H	BB	SO	ShO	W	L	SV	AB	H	HR	BA
1944 CIN N	11	7	.611	2.61	33	18	9	148.1	143	40	33	3	1	1	3	48	12	2	.250
1945	2	4	.333	3.09	13	6	2	46.2	54	13	4	1	1	0	0	17	3	0	.176
2 yrs.	13	11	.542	2.72	46	24	11	195	197	53	37	4	2	1	3	65	15	2	.231

Nick Carter

CARTER, CONRAD POWELL   BL TR 5'8"   126 lbs.
B. May 19, 1879, Oatlands, Va.   D. Nov. 23, 1961, Grasonville, Md.

	W	L	PCT	ERA	G	GS	CG	IP	H	BB	SO	ShO	W	L	SV	AB	H	HR	BA
1908 PHI A	2	5	.286	2.97	14	6	2	60.2	58	17	17	0	2	1	0	20	2	0	.100

	W	L	PCT	ERA	G	GS	CG	IP	H	BB	SO	ShO	Relief Pitching W	L	SV	BATTING AB	H	HR	BA

Paul Carter

CARTER, PAUL WARREN (Nick)
B. May 1, 1894, Lake Park, Ga.   BL TR 6'3"   175 lbs.

	W	L	PCT	ERA	G	GS	CG	IP	H	BB	SO	ShO	RP W	L	SV	AB	H	HR	BA
1914 CLE A	1	3	.250	2.92	5	4	1	24.2	35	5	9	0	0	0	0	7	0	0	.000
1915	1	1	.500	3.21	11	2	2	42	44	18	14	0	0	0	0	14	3	0	.214
1916 CHI N	2	2	.500	2.75	8	5	2	36	26	17	14	0	0	0	0	12	2	0	.167
1917	5	8	.385	3.26	23	13	6	113.1	115	19	34	0	1	2	2	33	6	0	.182
1918	4	1	.800	2.71	21	4	1	73	78	19	13	0	3	0	1	25	6	0	.240
1919	5	4	.556	2.65	28	7	2	85	81	28	17	0	3	0	1	26	7	0	.269
1920	3	6	.333	4.67	31	8	2	106	131	36	14	0	1	2	2	35	6	0	.171
7 yrs.	21	25	.457	3.32	127	43	16	480	510	142	115	0	8	4	6	152	30	0	.197

Sol Carter

CARTER, SOLOMON MOBLEY (Buck)
B. Dec. 23, 1908, Picayune, Miss.   BR TR 6'   178 lbs.

	W	L	PCT	ERA	G	GS	CG	IP	H	BB	SO	ShO	RP W	L	SV	AB	H	HR	BA
1931 PHI A	0	0	-	19.29	2	0	0	2.1	4	4	1	0	0	0	0	0	0	0	-

Bob Caruthers

CARUTHERS, ROBERT LEE (Parisian Bob)
B. Jan. 5, 1864, Memphis, Tenn.   D. Aug. 5, 1911, Peoria, Ill.   BL TR 5'7"   138 lbs.

	W	L	PCT	ERA	G	GS	CG	IP	H	BB	SO	ShO	RP W	L	SV	AB	H	HR	BA
1884 STL AA	7	2	.778	2.61	13	7	7	82.2	61	15	58	0	3	0	0	82	21	2	.256
1885	40	13	.755	2.07	53	53	53	482.1	430	57	190	6	0	0	0	222	50	1	.225
1886	30	14	.682	2.32	44	43	42	387.1	323	86	166	2	1	0	0	317	106	4	.334
1887	29	9	.763	3.30	39	39	39	341	337	61	74	2	0	0	0	364	130	8	.357
1888 BKN AA	29	15	.659	2.39	44	43	42	391.2	337	53	140	4	1	0	0	335	77	5	.230
1889	40	11	.784	3.13	56	50	46	445	444	104	118	7	4	0	1	172	43	0	.250
1890 BKN N	23	11	.676	3.09	37	33	30	300	292	87	64	2	1	0	0	238	63	1	.265
1891	18	14	.563	3.12	38	32	29	297	323	107	69	2	1	0	1	171	48	2	.281
1892 STL N	2	8	.200	5.84	16	10	10	101.2	131	27	21	0	0	2	1	513	142	3	.277
9 yrs.	218	97	.692	2.83	340	310	298	2828.2	2678	597	900	25	11	2	3	*			
			1st																

Scott Cary

CARY, SCOTT RUSSELL (Red)
B. Apr. 11, 1923, Kendallville, Ind.   BL TL 5'11½"   168 lbs.

	W	L	PCT	ERA	G	GS	CG	IP	H	BB	SO	ShO	RP W	L	SV	AB	H	HR	BA
1947 WAS A	3	1	.750	5.93	23	3	1	54.2	73	20	25	0	1	0	0	13	1	0	.077

Jerry Casale

CASALE, JERRY JOSEPH
B. Sept. 27, 1933, Brooklyn, N.Y.   BR TR 6'2"   200 lbs.

	W	L	PCT	ERA	G	GS	CG	IP	H	BB	SO	ShO	RP W	L	SV	AB	H	HR	BA
1958 BOS A	0	0	-	0.00	2	0	0	3	1	2	3	0	0	0	0	0	0	0	-
1959	13	8	.619	4.31	31	26	9	179.2	162	89	93	3	1	0	0	59	10	3	.169
1960	2	9	.182	6.17	29	14	1	96.1	113	67	54	0	0	0	0	33	9	0	.273
1961 2 teams			LA	A (13G 1–5)		DET	A (3G 0–0)												
" total	1	5	.167	6.26	16	1	0	54.2	67	28	41	0	0	0	1	16	6	1	.375
1962 DET A	1	2	.333	4.66	18	1	0	36.2	33	18	16	0	1	2	0	8	0	0	.000
5 yrs.	17	24	.415	5.08	96	49	10	370.1	376	204	207	3	2	2	1	116	25	4	.216

Joe Cascarella

CASCARELLA, JOSEPH THOMAS (Crooning Joe)
B. June 28, 1907, Philadelphia, Pa.   BR TR 5'10½"   175 lbs.

	W	L	PCT	ERA	G	GS	CG	IP	H	BB	SO	ShO	RP W	L	SV	AB	H	HR	BA
1934 PHI A	12	15	.444	4.68	42	22	9	194.1	214	104	71	2	7	3	1	64	6	0	.094
1935 2 teams			PHI	A (9G 1–6)		BOS	A (6G 0–3)												
" total	1	9	.100	5.84	15	7	0	49.1	54	33	24	0	1	3	0	10	1	0	.100
1936 2 teams			BOS	A (10G 0–2)		WAS	A (22G 9–8)												
" total	9	10	.474	4.44	32	17	7	160	174	63	41	1	2	3	1	53	7	0	.132
1937 2 teams			WAS	A (10G 0–5)		CIN	N (11G 1–2)												
" total	1	7	.125	5.68	21	7	3	76	94	45	26	0	0	1	2	20	3	0	.150
1938 CIN N	4	7	.364	4.57	33	1	0	61	66	22	30	0	4	6	4	18	3	0	.167
5 yrs.	27	48	.360	4.84	143	54	20	540.2	602	267	192	3	14	16	8	165	20	0	.121

Charlie Case

CASE, CHARLES EMMETT
B. Sept. 7, 1879, Rural, Ohio   D. Apr. 16, 1964, Clermont, Ohio   BR TR 6'   170 lbs.

	W	L	PCT	ERA	G	GS	CG	IP	H	BB	SO	ShO	RP W	L	SV	AB	H	HR	BA
1901 CIN N	1	2	.333	4.67	3	3	3	27	34	6	5	0	0	0	0	10	1	0	.100
1904 PIT N	10	5	.667	2.94	18	17	14	141	129	31	49	3	0	0	0	53	9	0	.170
1905	12	10	.545	2.57	31	24	18	217	202	66	57	3	1	0	1	68	7	0	.103
1906	1	1	.500	5.73	2	2	1	11	8	5	3	0	0	0	0	2	1	0	.500
4 yrs.	24	18	.571	2.93	54	46	36	396	373	108	114	6	1	0	1	133	18	0	.135

Bill Casey

CASEY, WILLIAM B.
B. St. Louis, Mo.   Deceased.

	W	L	PCT	ERA	G	GS	CG	IP	H	BB	SO	ShO	RP W	L	SV	AB	H	HR	BA
1887 PHI AA	0	0	-	18.00	1	0	0	1	4	1	0	0	0	0	0	0	0	0	-

Dan Casey

CASEY, DANIEL MAURICE
Brother of Dennis Casey.
B. Oct. 2, 1865, Binghamton, N.Y.   D. Feb. 8, 1943, Washington, D.C.   BR TL

	W	L	PCT	ERA	G	GS	CG	IP	H	BB	SO	ShO	RP W	L	SV	AB	H	HR	BA
1884 WIL U	1	1	.500	1.00	2	2	2	18	23	4	10	0	0	0	0	6	1	0	.167
1885 DET N	4	8	.333	3.29	12	12	12	104	105	35	79	1	0	0	0	43	5	0	.116
1886 PHI N	24	18	.571	2.41	44	44	39	369	326	104	193	4	0	0	0	151	23	0	.152
1887	28	13	.683	2.86	45	45	43	390.1	377	115	119	4	0	0	0	164	27	1	.165
1888	14	18	.438	3.15	33	33	31	285.2	298	48	108	1	0	0	0	118	18	0	.153
1889	6	10	.375	3.77	20	20	15	152.2	170	72	65	1	0	0	0	68	15	0	.221
1890 SYR AA	19	22	.463	4.14	45	42	40	360.2	365	165	169	2	0	0	0	160	26	0	.163
7 yrs.	96	90	.516	3.18	201	198	182	1680.1	1664	543	743	13	0	0	0	710	115	1	.162

Hugh Casey

CASEY, HUGH THOMAS
B. Oct. 14, 1913, Atlanta, Ga.   D. July 3, 1951, Atlanta, Ga.   BR TR 6'1"   207 lbs.

	W	L	PCT	ERA	G	GS	CG	IP	H	BB	SO	ShO	RP W	L	SV	AB	H	HR	BA
1935 CHI N	0	0	-	3.86	13	0	0	25.2	29	14	10	0	0	0	0	6	1	0	.167
1939 BKN N	15	10	.600	2.93	40	25	15	227.1	228	54	79	0	2	1	1	74	15	0	.203
1940	11	8	.579	3.62	44	10	5	154	136	51	53	2	6	5	2	36	9	0	.250
1941	14	11	.560	3.89	45	18	4	162	155	57	61	1	8	4	7	50	6	0	.120
1942	6	3	.667	2.25	50	2	0	112	91	44	54	0	6	1	13	27	4	0	.148
1946	11	5	.688	1.99	46	1	0	99.2	101	33	31	0	11	4	5	22	3	0	.136

	W	L	PCT	ERA	G	GS	CG	IP	H	BB	SO	ShO	Relief Pitching W	L	SV	BATTING AB	H	HR	BA

Hugh Casey *continued*

	W	L	PCT	ERA	G	GS	CG	IP	H	BB	SO	ShO	W	L	SV	AB	H	HR	BA
1947	10	4	.714	3.99	46	0	0	76.2	75	29	40	0	10	4	18	18	1	0	.056
1948	3	0	1.000	8.00	22	0	0	36	59	17	7	0	3	0	4	7	0	0	.000
1949 2 teams			PIT N (33G 4–1)			NY	A	(4G 1–0)											
" total	5	1	.833	5.24	37	0	0	46.1	61	22	14	0	5	1	5	4	1	0	.250
9 yrs.	75	42	.641	3.45	343	56	24	939.2	935	321	349	3	51	20	55	244	40	0	.164

WORLD SERIES
	W	L	PCT	ERA	G	GS	CG	IP	H	BB	SO	ShO	W	L	SV	AB	H	HR	BA
1941 BKN N	0	2	.000	3.38	3	0	0	5.1	9	2	1	0	0	2	0	2	1	0	.500
1947	2	0	1.000	0.87	6	0	0	10.1	5	1	3	0	2	0	1	1	0	0	.000
2 yrs.	2	2	.500	1.72	9	0	0	15.2	14	3	4	0	2	2	1	3	1	0	.333
													2nd	2nd					

Jay Cashion

CASHION, JAY CARL   BL TR 6'2"   200 lbs.
B. June 6, 1891, Mecklenburg, N. C.   D. Nov. 17, 1935, Lake Millicent, Wis.

	W	L	PCT	ERA	G	GS	CG	IP	H	BB	SO	ShO	W	L	SV	AB	H	HR	BA
1911 WAS A	1	5	.167	4.16	11	9	5	71.1	67	47	26	0	0	0	0	37	12	0	.324
1912	10	6	.625	3.17	26	17	13	170.1	150	103	84	1	1	0	1	103	22	2	.214
1913	1	1	.500	6.23	4	3	0	8.2	7	14	3	0	0	0	0	12	3	0	.250
1914	0	1	.000	10.80	2	1	0	5	4	6	1	0	0	0	0	1	0	0	.000
4 yrs.	12	13	.480	3.70	43	30	18	255.1	228	170	114	1	1	0	1	*			

Craig Caskey

CASKEY, CRAIG DOUGLAS   BR TL 5'11"   185 lbs.
B. Dec. 11, 1949, Visalia, Calif.

	W	L	PCT	ERA	G	GS	CG	IP	H	BB	SO	ShO	W	L	SV	AB	H	HR	BA
1973 MON N	0	0	—	5.65	9	1	0	14.1	15	4	6	0	0	0	0	1	0	0	.000

Ed Cassian

CASSIAN, EDWIN   5'8"   160 lbs.
B. Conn.   Deceased.

	W	L	PCT	ERA	G	GS	CG	IP	H	BB	SO	ShO	W	L	SV	AB	H	HR	BA
1891 2 teams			PHI N (6G 1–3)			WAS	AA	(7G 2–4)											
" total	3	7	.300	4.45	13	9	8	91	113	51	24	0	1	0	0	43	11	0	.256

John Cassidy

CASSIDY, JOHN P.   BR TL 5'8"   168 lbs.
B. 1857, Brooklyn, N. Y.   D. July 2, 1891, Brooklyn, N. Y.

	W	L	PCT	ERA	G	GS	CG	IP	H	BB	SO	ShO	W	L	SV	AB	H	HR	BA
1877 HAR N	1	1	.500	5.00	2	2	2	18	24	1	2	0	0	0	0	*			

George Caster

CASTER, GEORGE JASPER   BR TR 6'1½"   180 lbs.
B. Aug. 4, 1907, Colton, Calif.   D. Dec. 18, 1955, Lakewood, Calif.

	W	L	PCT	ERA	G	GS	CG	IP	H	BB	SO	ShO	W	L	SV	AB	H	HR	BA
1934 PHI A	3	2	.600	3.41	5	3	2	37	32	14	15	0	1	1	0	15	4	0	.267
1935	1	4	.200	6.25	25	1	0	63.1	86	37	24	0	1	3	1	22	5	0	.227
1937	12	19	.387	4.43	34	33	19	231.2	227	107	100	3	0	0	0	90	19	0	.211
1938	16	20	.444	4.37	42	40	20	280.1	310	117	112	2	0	0	1	101	20	0	.198
1939	9	9	.500	4.90	28	17	7	136	144	45	59	1	2	0	0	43	9	0	.209
1940	4	19	.174	6.56	36	24	11	178.1	234	69	75	0	1	1	2	62	8	0	.129
1941 STL A	3	7	.300	5.00	32	9	3	104.1	105	37	36	0	0	1	3	29	3	0	.103
1942	8	2	.800	2.81	39	0	0	80	62	39	34	0	8	2	5	15	1	0	.067
1943	6	8	.429	2.12	35	0	0	76.1	69	41	43	0	6	8	8	22	3	0	.136
1944	6	6	.500	2.44	42	0	0	81	91	33	46	0	6	6	12	20	5	0	.250
1945 2 teams			STL A (10G 1–2)			DET	A	(22G 5–1)											
" total	6	3	.667	4.57	32	0	0	67	67	34	32	0	6	3	3	14	3	0	.214
1946 DET A	2	1	.667	5.66	26	0	0	41.1	42	24	19	0	2	1	4	7	1	0	.143
12 yrs.	76	100	.432	4.54	376	127	62	1376.2	1469	597	595	6	33	26	39	440	81	0	.184

WORLD SERIES
	W	L	PCT	ERA	G	GS	CG	IP	H	BB	SO	ShO	W	L	SV	AB	H	HR	BA
1945 DET A	0	0	—	0.00	1	0	0	.2	0	0	1	0	0	0	0	0	0	0	—

Bobby Castillo

CASTILLO, ROBERT ERNIE   BR TR 5'10"   170 lbs.
B. Apr. 18, 1955, Los Angeles, Calif.

	W	L	PCT	ERA	G	GS	CG	IP	H	BB	SO	ShO	W	L	SV	AB	H	HR	BA
1977 LA N	1	0	1.000	4.09	6	1	0	11	12	2	7	0	1	0	0	1	0	0	.000
1978	0	4	.000	3.97	18	0	0	34	28	33	30	0	0	3	1	7	0	0	.000
1979	2	0	1.000	1.13	19	0	0	24	26	13	25	0	2	0	7	3	0	0	.000
1980	8	6	.571	2.76	61	0	0	98	70	45	60	0	8	6	5	9	1	0	.111
1981	2	4	.333	5.29	34	1	0	51	50	24	35	0	2	4	5	9	4	0	.444
1982 MIN A	13	11	.542	3.66	40	25	6	218.2	194	85	123	1	2	1	0	0	0	0	—
1983	8	12	.400	4.77	27	25	3	158.1	170	65	90	0	1	0	0	0	0	0	—
1984	2	1	.667	1.78	10	2	0	25.1	14	19	7	0	1	0	0	0	0	0	—
8 yrs.	36	38	.486	3.79	215	54	9	620.1	564	286	377	1	16	14	18	29	5	0	.172

LEAGUE CHAMPIONSHIP SERIES
	W	L	PCT	ERA	G	GS	CG	IP	H	BB	SO	ShO	W	L	SV	AB	H	HR	BA
1981 LA N	0	0	—	0.00	1	0	0	1	0	0	1	0	0	0	0	0	0	0	—

WORLD SERIES
	W	L	PCT	ERA	G	GS	CG	IP	H	BB	SO	ShO	W	L	SV	AB	H	HR	BA
1981 LA N	0	0	—	9.00	1	0	0	1	0	5	0	0	0	0	0	0	0	0	—

Manny Castillo

CASTILLO, ESTEBAN MANUEL   BB TR 5'9"   160 lbs.
Also known as Antonio Castillo.
B. Apr. 1, 1957, Santo Domingo, Dominican Republic

	W	L	PCT	ERA	G	GS	CG	IP	H	BB	SO	ShO	W	L	SV	AB	H	HR	BA
1983 SEA A	0	0	—	23.63	1	0	0	2.2	8	3	2	0	0	0	0	*			

Slick Castleman

CASTLEMAN, CLYDELL   BR TR 6'   185 lbs.
B. Sept. 8, 1913, Donelson, Tenn.

	W	L	PCT	ERA	G	GS	CG	IP	H	BB	SO	ShO	W	L	SV	AB	H	HR	BA
1934 NY N	1	0	1.000	5.40	7	1	0	16.2	18	10	5	0	1	0	0	4	1	0	.250
1935	15	6	.714	4.09	29	25	9	173.2	186	64	64	1	2	0	0	67	12	1	.179
1936	4	7	.364	5.64	29	12	2	111.2	148	56	54	1	3	0	1	39	5	1	.128
1937	11	6	.647	3.31	23	23	10	160.1	148	33	78	2	0	0	0	57	4	0	.070
1938	4	5	.444	4.17	21	14	0	90.2	108	37	18	0	1	0	0	31	3	0	.097
1939	1	2	.333	4.54	12	4	0	33.2	36	23	6	0	1	0	0	9	3	0	.333
6 yrs.	36	26	.581	4.25	121	79	25	586.2	644	223	225	4	7	0	1	207	28	2	.135

WORLD SERIES
	W	L	PCT	ERA	G	GS	CG	IP	H	BB	SO	ShO	W	L	SV	AB	H	HR	BA
1936 NY N	0	0	—	2.08	1	0	0	4.1	3	2	5	0	0	0	0	2	1	0	.500

	W	L	PCT	ERA	G	GS	CG	IP	H	BB	SO	ShO	Relief Pitching W	L	SV	BATTING AB	H	HR	BA

Roy Castleton

CASTLETON, ROYAL EUGENE
B. July 26, 1885, Salt Lake City, Utah   D. June 24, 1967, Los Angeles, Calif.
BL TL 5'11"   167 lbs.

	W	L	PCT	ERA	G	GS	CG	IP	H	BB	SO	ShO	W	L	SV	AB	H	HR	BA
1907 NY A	1	1	.500	2.81	3	2	1	16	11	3	3	0	0	0	0	5	0	0	.000
1909 CIN N	1	1	.500	1.93	4	1	1	14	14	6	5	0	0	1	0	3	2	0	.667
1910	1	2	.333	3.29	4	2	1	13.2	15	6	5	0	0	2	0	5	0	0	.000
3 yrs.	3	4	.429	2.68	11	5	3	43.2	40	15	13	0	0	3	0	13	2	0	.154

Paul Castner

CASTNER, PAUL HENRY (Lefty)
B. Feb. 16, 1897, St. Paul, Minn.
BL TL 5'11"   187 lbs.

	W	L	PCT	ERA	G	GS	CG	IP	H	BB	SO	ShO	W	L	SV	AB	H	HR	BA
1923 CHI A	0	0	—	6.30	6	0	0	10	14	5	0	0	0	0	0	3	0	0	.000

Bill Castro

CASTRO, WILLIAMS RADHAMES (Checo)
B. Dec. 13, 1953, Santiago, Dominican Republic
BR TR 5'11"   170 lbs.

	W	L	PCT	ERA	G	GS	CG	IP	H	BB	SO	ShO	W	L	SV	AB	H	HR	BA
1974 MIL A	0	0	—	4.50	8	0	0	18	19	5	10	0	0	0	0	0	0	0	—
1975	3	2	.600	2.52	18	5	0	75	78	17	25	0	1	0	1	0	0	0	—
1976	4	6	.400	3.45	39	0	0	70.1	70	19	23	0	4	6	8	0	0	0	—
1977	8	6	.571	4.17	51	0	0	69	76	23	28	0	8	6	13	0	0	0	—
1978	5	4	.556	1.81	42	0	0	49.2	43	14	17	0	5	4	8	0	0	0	—
1979	3	1	.750	2.05	39	0	0	44	40	13	10	0	3	1	6	0	0	0	—
1980	2	4	.333	2.79	56	0	0	84	89	17	32	0	2	4	8	0	0	0	—
1981 NY A	1	1	.500	3.79	11	0	0	19	26	5	4	0	1	1	0	0	0	0	—
1982 KC A	3	2	.600	3.45	21	4	0	75.2	72	20	37	0	1	1	1	0	0	0	—
1983	2	0	1.000	6.64	18	0	0	40.2	51	12	17	0	2	0	0	0	0	0	—
10 yrs.	31	26	.544	3.33	303	9	0	545.1	564	145	203	0	27	23	45	0	0	0	—

Eli Cates

CATES, ELI ELDO
B. Jan. 26, 1877, Greensfork, Ind.   D. May 29, 1964, Richmond, Ind.
BR TR 5'9½"   175 lbs.

	W	L	PCT	ERA	G	GS	CG	IP	H	BB	SO	ShO	W	L	SV	AB	H	HR	BA
1908 WAS A	4	8	.333	2.51	19	10	7	114.2	112	32	33	0	1	2	0	*			

Ted Cather

CATHER, THEODORE P
B. May 20, 1889, Chester, Pa.   D. Apr. 9, 1945, Charlestown, Md.
BR TR 5'10½"   178 lbs.

	W	L	PCT	ERA	G	GS	CG	IP	H	BB	SO	ShO	W	L	SV	AB	H	HR	BA
1913 STL N	0	0	—	54.00	1	0	0	.1	1	2	0	0	0	0	0	*			

Hardin Cathey

CATHEY, HARDIN (Abner)
B. July 6, 1919, Burns, Tenn.
BR TR 6'   190 lbs.

	W	L	PCT	ERA	G	GS	CG	IP	H	BB	SO	ShO	W	L	SV	AB	H	HR	BA
1942 WAS A	1	1	.500	7.42	12	2	0	30.1	44	16	8	0	0	1	0	8	3	0	.375

Keefe Cato

CATO, JOHN KEEFE
B. May 6, 1958, Yonkers, N. Y.
BR TR 6'1"   180 lbs.

	W	L	PCT	ERA	G	GS	CG	IP	H	BB	SO	ShO	W	L	SV	AB	H	HR	BA
1983 CIN N	1	0	1.000	2.45	4	0	0	3.2	2	1	3	0	1	0	0	0	0	0	—
1984	0	1	.000	8.04	8	0	0	15.2	22	4	12	0	0	1	1	4	2	0	.500
2 yrs.	1	1	.500	6.98	12	0	0	19.1	24	5	15	0	1	1	1	4	2	0	.500

John Cattanach

CATTANACH, JOHN L.
B. May 10, 1863, Providence, R. I.   D. Nov. 10, 1926, Providence, R. I.
190 lbs.

	W	L	PCT	ERA	G	GS	CG	IP	H	BB	SO	ShO	W	L	SV	AB	H	HR	BA
1884 2 teams		PRO	N (1G 0–0)		STL	U	(2G 1–1)												
" total	1	1	.500	3.68	3	3	2	22	14	8	15	0	0	0	0	11	0	0	.000

Bill Caudill

CAUDILL, WILLIAM HOLLAND
B. July 13, 1956, Santa Monica, Calif.
BR TR 6'1"   190 lbs.

	W	L	PCT	ERA	G	GS	CG	IP	H	BB	SO	ShO	W	L	SV	AB	H	HR	BA
1979 CHI N	1	7	.125	4.80	29	12	0	90	89	41	104	0	1	0	0	17	1	0	.059
1980	4	6	.400	2.18	72	2	0	128	100	59	112	0	4	6	1	9	2	0	.222
1981	1	5	.167	5.83	30	10	0	71	87	31	45	0	0	0	0	14	2	0	.143
1982 SEA A	12	9	.571	2.35	70	0	0	95.2	65	35	111	0	12	9	26	0	0	0	—
1983	2	8	.200	4.71	63	0	0	72.2	70	38	73	0	2	8	26	0	0	0	—
1984 OAK A	9	7	.563	2.71	68	0	0	96.1	77	31	89	0	9	7	36	1	0	0	.000
6 yrs.	29	42	.408	3.53	332	24	0	553.2	488	235	534	0	28	30	89	41	5	0	.122

Red Causey

CAUSEY, CECIL ALGERNON
B. Aug. 11, 1893, Seville, Fla.   D. Nov. 11, 1960, Tampa, Fla.
BL TR 6'1"   160 lbs.

	W	L	PCT	ERA	G	GS	CG	IP	H	BB	SO	ShO	W	L	SV	AB	H	HR	BA
1918 NY N	11	6	.647	2.79	29	18	10	158.1	143	42	48	2	2	2	2	48	6	0	.125
1919 2 teams		NY	N (19G 9–3)		BOS	N	(10G 4–5)												
" total	13	8	.619	4.03	29	26	9	174	180	58	39	0	1	0	0	59	7	0	.119
1920 PHI N	7	14	.333	4.32	35	26	11	181.1	203	79	30	1	0	2	3	59	11	0	.186
1921 2 teams		PHI	N (7G 3–3)		NY	N	(7G 1–1)												
" total	4	4	.500	2.76	14	8	4	65.1	71	17	9	0	1	0	0	23	4	0	.174
1922 NY N	4	3	.571	3.18	24	2	1	70.2	69	34	13	0	3	2	1	21	5	0	.238
5 yrs.	39	35	.527	3.59	131	80	35	649.2	666	230	139	3	6	7	6	210	33	0	.157

Pug Cavet

CAVET, TILLER H.
B. Dec. 26, 1889, McGregor, Tex.   D. Aug. 4, 1966, San Luis Obispo, Calif.
BL TL 6'3"   176 lbs.

	W	L	PCT	ERA	G	GS	CG	IP	H	BB	SO	ShO	W	L	SV	AB	H	HR	BA
1911 DET A	0	0	—	4.50	1	0	0	4	6	1	1	0	0	0	0	1	0	0	.000
1914	7	7	.500	2.44	31	14	6	151.1	129	44	51	1	2	0	2	47	5	0	.106
1915	4	2	.667	4.06	17	7	2	71	83	22	26	0	1	1	1	24	6	0	.250
3 yrs.	11	9	.550	2.98	49	22	8	226.1	218	67	78	1	3	1	3	72	11	0	.153

Art Ceccarelli

CECCARELLI, ARTHUR EDWARD (Chic)
B. Apr. 2, 1930, New Haven, Conn.
BR TL 6'   190 lbs.
BB 1957

	W	L	PCT	ERA	G	GS	CG	IP	H	BB	SO	ShO	W	L	SV	AB	H	HR	BA
1955 KC A	4	7	.364	5.31	31	16	3	123.2	123	71	68	1	1	0	0	38	3	0	.079
1956	0	1	.000	7.20	3	2	0	10	13	4	2	0	0	0	0	3	0	0	.000
1957 BAL A	0	5	.000	4.50	20	8	1	58	62	31	30	0	0	0	0	14	0	0	.000
1959 CHI N	5	5	.500	4.76	18	15	4	102	95	37	56	2	0	0	0	33	3	0	.091
1960	0	0	—	5.54	7	1	0	13	16	4	10	0	0	0	0	0	0	0	—
5 yrs.	9	18	.333	5.05	79	42	8	306.2	309	147	166	3	1	0	0	88	6	0	.068

	W	L	PCT	ERA	G	GS	CG	IP	H	BB	SO	ShO	Relief Pitching W	L	SV	Batting AB	H	HR	BA

Rex Cecil

CECIL, REX HOLSTON   BL TR 6'3"   195 lbs.
B. Oct. 8, 1916, Lindsay, Okla.   D. Oct. 30, 1966, Long Beach, Calif.

	W	L	PCT	ERA	G	GS	CG	IP	H	BB	SO	ShO	W	L	SV	AB	H	HR	BA
1944 BOS A	4	5	.444	5.16	11	9	4	61	72	33	33	0	1	0	0	18	5	0	.278
1945	2	5	.286	5.20	7	7	1	45	46	27	30	0	0	0	0	20	6	0	.300
2 yrs.	6	10	.375	5.18	18	16	5	106	118	60	63	0	1	0	0	38	11	0	.289

Pete Center

CENTER, MARVIN EARL   BR TR 6'4"   190 lbs.
B. Apr. 22, 1912, Hazel Green, Ky.

	W	L	PCT	ERA	G	GS	CG	IP	H	BB	SO	ShO	W	L	SV	AB	H	HR	BA
1942 CLE A	0	0	–	16.20	1	0	0	3.1	7	4	0	0	0	0	0	1	0	0	.000
1943	1	2	.333	2.76	24	1	0	42.1	29	18	10	0	1	2	1	5	0	0	.000
1945	6	3	.667	3.99	31	8	2	85.2	89	28	34	0	3	2	1	22	2	0	.091
1946	0	2	.000	4.97	21	0	0	29	29	20	6	0	0	2	1	3	0	0	.000
4 yrs.	7	7	.500	4.10	77	9	2	160.1	154	70	50	0	4	6	3	31	2	0	.065

Leon Chagnon

CHAGNON, LEON WILBUR (Shag)   BR TR 6'   182 lbs.
B. Sept. 28, 1902, Pittsfield, N. H.   D. July 30, 1953, Amesbury, Mass.

	W	L	PCT	ERA	G	GS	CG	IP	H	BB	SO	ShO	W	L	SV	AB	H	HR	BA
1929 PIT N	0	0	–	9.00	1	1	0	7	11	1	4	0	0	0	0	2	0	0	.000
1930	0	3	.000	6.82	18	4	3	62	92	23	27	0	0	0	0	20	4	0	.200
1932	9	6	.600	3.94	30	10	4	128	140	34	52	1	5	1	0	40	9	0	.225
1933	6	4	.600	3.69	39	5	1	100	100	17	35	0	5	2	1	21	1	0	.048
1934	4	1	.800	4.81	33	1	0	58	68	24	19	0	4	1	1	13	3	0	.231
1935 NY N	0	2	.000	3.52	14	1	0	38.1	32	5	16	0	0	1	1	9	0	0	.000
6 yrs.	19	16	.543	4.51	135	22	8	393.1	443	104	153	1	14	5	3	105	17	0	.162

Bob Chakales

CHAKALES, ROBERT EDWARD (Chick)   BR TR 6'1"   185 lbs.
B. Aug. 10, 1927, Asheville, N. C.

	W	L	PCT	ERA	G	GS	CG	IP	H	BB	SO	ShO	W	L	SV	AB	H	HR	BA
1951 CLE A	3	4	.429	4.74	17	10	2	68.1	80	43	32	1	0	0	0	20	7	1	.350
1952	1	2	.333	9.75	5	1	0	12	19	8	7	0	0	2	0	4	2	0	.500
1953	0	2	.000	2.67	7	3	1	27	28	10	6	0	0	0	0	7	2	0	.286
1954 2 teams					CLE A (3G 2-0)			BAL A (38G 3-7)											
" total	5	7	.417	3.43	41	6	0	99.2	85	55	47	0	5	4	3	25	9	0	.360
1955 2 teams					CHI A (7G 0-0)			WAS A (29G 2-3)											
" total	2	3	.400	4.57	36	0	0	67	66	31	34	0	2	3	0	10	0	0	.000
1956 WAS A	4	4	.500	4.03	43	1	0	96	94	57	33	0	4	4	4	20	3	0	.150
1957 2 teams					WAS A (4G 0-1)			BOS A (18G 0-2)											
" total	0	3	.000	7.15	22	2	0	50.1	73	21	28	0	0	3	3	10	3	0	.300
7 yrs.	15	25	.375	4.54	171	23	3	420.1	445	225	187	1	11	16	10	96	26	1	.271

George Chalmers

CHALMERS, GEORGE W. (Dut)   BR TR 6'1"   189 lbs.
B. June 7, 1888, Edinburgh, Scotland   D. Aug. 5, 1960, Bronx, N. Y.

	W	L	PCT	ERA	G	GS	CG	IP	H	BB	SO	ShO	W	L	SV	AB	H	HR	BA
1910 PHI N	1	1	.500	5.32	4	3	2	22	11	11	12	0	0	0	0	7	1	0	.143
1911	13	10	.565	3.11	38	22	11	208.2	196	101	101	3	4	1	4	73	13	0	.178
1912	3	4	.429	3.28	12	8	3	57.2	64	37	22	0	0	1	0	16	3	0	.188
1913	3	10	.231	4.81	26	13	4	116	133	51	46	0	1	2	1	33	7	0	.212
1914	0	3	.000	5.50	3	2	1	18	23	15	6	0	0	1	0	6	0	0	.000
1915	8	9	.471	2.48	26	20	13	170.1	159	45	82	1	0	1	1	59	10	0	.169
1916	1	4	.200	3.19	12	8	2	53.2	49	19	21	0	0	0	0	15	0	0	.000
7 yrs.	29	41	.414	3.41	121	76	36	646.1	645	279	290	4	5	6	6	209	34	0	.163
WORLD SERIES																			
1915 PHI N	0	1	.000	2.25	1	1	1	8	8	3	6	0	0	0	0	3	1	0	.333

Bill Chamberlain

CHAMBERLAIN, WILLIAM VINCENT   BR TL 5'10½" 173 lbs.
B. Apr. 21, 1909, Stoughton, Mass.

	W	L	PCT	ERA	G	GS	CG	IP	H	BB	SO	ShO	W	L	SV	AB	H	HR	BA
1932 CHI A	0	5	.000	4.57	12	5	0	41.1	39	25	11	0	0	0	0	10	1	0	.100

Craig Chamberlain

CHAMBERLAIN, CRAIG PHILLIP   BR TR 6'1"   190 lbs.
B. Feb. 2, 1957, Hollywood, Calif.

	W	L	PCT	ERA	G	GS	CG	IP	H	BB	SO	ShO	W	L	SV	AB	H	HR	BA
1979 KC A	4	4	.500	3.73	10	10	4	70	68	18	30	0	0	0	0	0	0	0	–
1980	0	1	.000	7.00	5	0	0	9	10	5	3	0	0	1	0	0	0	0	–
2 yrs.	4	5	.444	4.10	15	10	4	79	78	23	33	0	0	1	0	0	0	0	–

Icebox Chamberlain

CHAMBERLAIN, ELTON P.   BR TR 5'9"   168 lbs.
B. Nov. 5, 1867, Warsaw, N. Y.   D. Sept. 24, 1929, Baltimore, Md.

	W	L	PCT	ERA	G	GS	CG	IP	H	BB	SO	ShO	W	L	SV	AB	H	HR	BA
1886 LOU AA	0	3	.000	6.61	4	4	4	31.1	39	17	18	0	0	0	0	19	3	0	.158
1887	18	16	.529	3.79	36	36	35	309	340	117	118	1	0	0	0	131	26	1	.198
1888 2 teams					LOU AA (24G 11-9)			STL AA (14G 11-2)											
" total	25	11	.694	2.19	38	38	34	308	238	86	176	2	0	0	0	144	23	1	.160
1889 STL AA	32	15	.681	2.97	53	51	44	421.2	376	165	202	2	0	0	1	171	34	2	.199
1890 2 teams					STL AA (5G 3-1)			COL AA (25G 12-6)											
" total	25	7	.682	2.83	30	26	22	210	175	96	128	0	0	0	0	80	17	0	.213
1891 PHI AA	22	23	.489	4.22	49	46	44	405.2	397	206	204	0	0	1	0	176	33	2	.188
1892 CIN N	19	23	.452	3.39	52	49	43	406.1	391	170	169	2	0	1	0	160	36	2	.225
1893	16	12	.571	3.73	34	27	19	241	248	112	59	1	3	1	0	97	19	0	.196
1894	10	9	.526	5.77	23	22	18	177.2	220	91	57	1	0	0	0	70	22	1	.314
1896 CLE N	0	1	.000	7.36	2	1	0	11	21	5	2	0	0	0	0	3	0	0	.000
10 yrs.	157	120	.567	3.57	321	301	264	2521.2	2445	1065	1133	15	4	2	1	1051	213	9	.203

Bill Chambers

CHAMBERS, WILLIAM CHRISTOPHER   BR TR 5'9"   185 lbs.
B. Sept. 13, 1889, Cameron, W. Va.   D. Mar. 27, 1962, Fort Wayne, Ind.

	W	L	PCT	ERA	G	GS	CG	IP	H	BB	SO	ShO	W	L	SV	AB	H	HR	BA
1910 STL N	0	0	–	0.00	1	0	0	1	1	0	0	0	0	0	0	0	0	0	–

Cliff Chambers

CHAMBERS, CLIFFORD DAY (Lefty)   BL TL 6'3"   208 lbs.
B. Jan. 10, 1922, Portland, Ore.

	W	L	PCT	ERA	G	GS	CG	IP	H	BB	SO	ShO	W	L	SV	AB	H	HR	BA
1948 CHI N	2	9	.182	4.43	29	12	3	103.2	100	48	51	1	0	2	0	30	4	0	.133
1949 PIT N	13	7	.650	3.96	34	21	10	177.1	186	58	93	1	1	0	0	55	13	0	.236
1950	12	15	.444	4.30	37	33	11	249.1	262	92	93	2	1	2	0	90	26	2	.289

	W	L	PCT	ERA	G	GS	CG	IP	H	BB	SO	ShO	Relief Pitching W	L	SV	BATTING AB	H	HR	BA

Cliff Chambers continued

	W	L	PCT	ERA	G	GS	CG	IP	H	BB	SO	ShO	W	L	SV	AB	H	HR	BA
1951 **2 teams**	PIT **N** (10G 3–6)			STL **N** (21G 11–6)															
" total	14	12	.538	4.38	31	26	11	189	184	87	64	2	1	2	0	70	15	1	.214
1952 **STL N**	4	4	.500	4.12	26	13	2	98.1	110	33	47	1	0	0	1	32	9	0	.281
1953	3	6	.333	4.86	32	8	0	79.2	82	43	26	0	2	2	0	17	2	0	.118
6 yrs.	48	53	.475	4.29	189	113	37	897.1	924	361	374	7	5	8	1	294	69	3	.235

John Chambers

CHAMBERS, JOHN MONROE
B. Sept. 9, 1910, Copperhill, Tenn.   D. May 11, 1977, Palatka, Fla.   BL TR 6'2" 190 lbs.

	W	L	PCT	ERA	G	GS	CG	IP	H	BB	SO	ShO	W	L	SV	AB	H	HR	BA
1937 **STL N**	0	0	–	18.00	2	0	0	2	5	2	1	0	0	0	0	0	0	0	–

Rome Chambers

CHAMBERS, ROME J.
B. Kernersville, N. C.   BL TL 6'2"

	W	L	PCT	ERA	G	GS	CG	IP	H	BB	SO	ShO	W	L	SV	AB	H	HR	BA
1900 **BOS N**	0	0	–	11.25	1	0	0	4	5	5	2	0	0	0	1	1	0	0	.000

Billy Champion

CHAMPION, BUFORD BILLY
B. Sept. 18, 1947, Shelby, N. C.   BR TR 6'4" 188 lbs.

	W	L	PCT	ERA	G	GS	CG	IP	H	BB	SO	ShO	W	L	SV	AB	H	HR	BA
1969 **PHI N**	5	10	.333	5.00	23	20	4	117	130	63	70	2	0	0	1	35	6	0	.171
1970	0	2	.000	9.00	7	1	0	14	21	10	12	0	0	1	0	3	0	0	.000
1971	3	5	.375	4.38	37	9	0	109	100	48	49	0	0	0	0	27	3	0	.111
1972	4	14	.222	5.09	30	22	2	132.2	155	54	54	0	0	1	0	34	5	1	.147
1973 **MIL A**	5	8	.385	3.70	37	11	2	136.1	139	62	67	0	4	3	1	0	0	0	–
1974	11	4	.733	3.61	31	23	2	162	168	49	60	0	0	0	0	0	0	0	–
1975	6	6	.500	5.89	27	13	3	110	125	55	40	1	1	1	0	0	0	0	–
1976	0	1	.000	7.13	10	3	0	24	35	13	8	0	0	0	0	0	0	0	–
8 yrs.	34	50	.405	4.68	202	102	13	805	873	354	360	3	5	6	2	99	14	1	.141

Dean Chance

CHANCE, WILMER DEAN
B. June 1, 1941, Wayne, Ohio   BR TR 6'3" 200 lbs.

	W	L	PCT	ERA	G	GS	CG	IP	H	BB	SO	ShO	W	L	SV	AB	H	HR	BA
1961 **LA A**	0	2	.000	6.87	5	4	0	18.1	33	5	11	0	0	0	0	5	0	0	.000
1962	14	10	.583	2.96	50	24	6	206.2	195	66	127	2	5	2	8	65	4	0	.062
1963	13	18	.419	3.19	45	35	6	248	229	90	168	2	2	1	3	80	12	0	.150
1964	20	9	.690	1.65	46	35	15	278.1	194	86	207	11	2	1	4	89	7	0	.079
1965 **CAL A**	15	10	.600	3.15	36	33	10	225.2	197	101	164	4	0	2	0	75	7	0	.093
1966	12	17	.414	3.08	41	37	11	259.2	206	114	180	2	0	2	1	76	2	0	.026
1967 **MIN A**	20	14	.588	2.73	41	39	18	283.2	244	68	220	5	0	0	1	92	3	0	.033
1968	16	16	.500	2.53	43	39	15	292	224	63	234	6	0	0	1	93	5	0	.054
1969	5	4	.556	2.95	20	15	1	88.1	76	35	50	0	1	0	0	24	1	0	.042
1970 **2 teams**	CLE **A** (45G 9–8)			NY **N** (3G 0–1)															
" total	9	9	.500	4.36	48	19	1	157	175	61	109	1	4	2	5	42	3	0	.071
1971 **DET A**	4	6	.400	3.50	31	14	0	90	91	50	64	0	3	0	0	21	0	0	.000
11 yrs.	128	115	.527	2.92	406	294	83	2147.2	1864	739	1534	33	17	10	23	662	44	0	.066

LEAGUE CHAMPIONSHIP SERIES

	W	L	PCT	ERA	G	GS	CG	IP	H	BB	SO	ShO	W	L	SV	AB	H	HR	BA
1969 **MIN A**	0	0	–	13.50	1	0	0	2	4	0	2	0	0	0	0	0	0	0	–

Ed Chandler

CHANDLER, EDWARD OLIVER
B. Feb. 17, 1922, Pinson, Ala.   BR TR 6'2" 190 lbs.

	W	L	PCT	ERA	G	GS	CG	IP	H	BB	SO	ShO	W	L	SV	AB	H	HR	BA
1947 **BKN N**	0	1	.000	6.37	15	1	0	29.2	31	12	8	0	0	0	1	2	0	0	.000

Spud Chandler

CHANDLER, SPURGEON FERDINAND
B. Sept. 12, 1907, Commerce, Ga.   BR TR 6' 181 lbs.

	W	L	PCT	ERA	G	GS	CG	IP	H	BB	SO	ShO	W	L	SV	AB	H	HR	BA
1937 **NY A**	7	4	.636	2.84	12	10	6	82.1	79	20	31	2	0	1	0	30	4	0	.133
1938	14	5	.737	4.03	23	23	14	172	183	47	36	2	0	0	0	69	14	3	.203
1939	3	0	1.000	2.84	11	0	0	19	26	9	4	0	3	0	0	5	2	0	.400
1940	8	7	.533	4.60	27	24	8	172	184	60	56	1	0	0	0	60	9	2	.150
1941	10	4	.714	3.19	28	20	11	163.2	146	60	60	4	0	0	4	60	11	0	.183
1942	16	5	.762	2.38	24	24	17	200.2	176	74	74	3	0	0	0	71	15	0	.211
1943	20	4	.833	1.64	30	30	20	253	197	54	134	5	0	0	0	97	25	2	.258
1944	0	0	–	4.50	1	1	0	6	6	1	1	0	0	0	0	1	0	0	.000
1945	2	1	.667	4.65	4	4	3	31	30	7	12	1	0	0	0	12	4	0	.333
1946	20	8	.714	2.10	34	32	20	257.1	200	90	138	6	0	0	2	94	14	0	.149
1947	9	5	.643	2.46	17	16	13	128	100	41	68	2	0	0	0	49	12	2	.245
11 yrs.	109	43	.717	2.84	211	184	109	1485	1327	463	614	26	3	1	6	548	110	9	.201

WORLD SERIES

	W	L	PCT	ERA	G	GS	CG	IP	H	BB	SO	ShO	W	L	SV	AB	H	HR	BA
1941 **NY A**	0	1	.000	3.60	1	1	0	5	4	2	2	0	0	0	0	2	1	0	.500
1942	0	1	.000	1.08	2	1	0	8.1	5	1	3	0	0	0	1	2	0	0	.000
1943	2	0	1.000	0.50	2	2	2	18	17	3	10	1	0	0	0	6	1	0	.167
1947	0	0	–	9.00	1	0	0	2	2	3	1	0	0	0	0	0	0	0	–
4 yrs.	2	2	.500	1.62	6	4	2	33.1	28	9	16	1	0	0	1	10	2	0	.200

Estey Chaney

CHANEY, ESTEY CLYON
B. Jan. 29, 1891, Hadley, Pa.   D. Feb. 5, 1952, Cleveland, Ohio   BR TR 5'11" 170 lbs.

	W	L	PCT	ERA	G	GS	CG	IP	H	BB	SO	ShO	W	L	SV	AB	H	HR	BA
1913 **BOS A**	0	0	–	9.00	1	0	0	1	1	2	0	0	0	0	0	0	0	0	–
1914 **BKN F**	0	0	–	6.75	1	0	0	4	7	2	1	0	0	0	0	1	0	0	.000
2 yrs.	0	0	–	7.20	2	0	0	5	8	4	1	0	0	0	0	1	0	0	.000

Tiny Chaplin

CHAPLIN, JAMES BAILEY
B. July 13, 1905, Los Angeles, Calif.   D. Mar. 25, 1939, National City, Calif.   BR TR 6'1" 195 lbs.

	W	L	PCT	ERA	G	GS	CG	IP	H	BB	SO	ShO	W	L	SV	AB	H	HR	BA
1928 **NY N**	0	2	.000	4.50	12	1	0	24	27	8	5	0	0	2	0	5	0	0	.000
1930	2	6	.250	5.18	19	8	3	73	89	16	20	0	0	2	1	19	2	1	.105
1931	2	1	.667	3.19	16	3	1	42.1	39	16	7	0	0	0	0	11	2	0	.182
1936 **BOS N**	10	15	.400	4.12	40	31	14	231.1	273	62	86	0	1	0	2	84	17	0	.202
4 yrs.	14	24	.368	4.25	87	43	18	370.2	428	102	118	0	1	4	4	119	21	1	.176

	W	L	PCT	ERA	G	GS	CG	IP	H	BB	SO	ShO	W	L	SV	AB	H	HR	BA
													Relief Pitching			BATTING			

Ben Chapman

CHAPMAN, WILLIAM BENJAMIN   BR TR 6'   190 lbs.
B. Dec. 25, 1908, Nashville, Tenn.
Manager 1945-48.

	W	L	PCT	ERA	G	GS	CG	IP	H	BB	SO	ShO	W	L	SV	AB	H	HR	BA
1944 BKN N	5	3	.625	3.40	11	9	6	79.1	75	33	37	0	0	1	0	38	14	0	.368
1945 2 teams		BKN	N (10G 3–3)		PHI	N (3G 0–0)													
" total	3	3	.500	5.79	13	7	2	60.2	71	38	27	0	1	0	0	73	19	0	.260
1946 PHI N	0	0	–	0.00	1	0	0	1.1	1	0	1	0	0	0	0	1	0	0	.000
3 yrs.	8	6	.571	4.39	25	16	8	141.1	147	71	65	0	1	1	0	*			

Ed Chapman

CHAPMAN, EDWIN VOLNEY   BB TR 6'1"   185 lbs.
Brother of Calvin Chapman.
B. Nov. 28, 1905, Courtland, Miss.

	W	L	PCT	ERA	G	GS	CG	IP	H	BB	SO	ShO	W	L	SV	AB	H	HR	BA
1933 WAS A	0	0	–	8.00	6	1	0	9	10	2	4	0	0	0	0	3	0	0	.000

Fred Chapman

CHAPMAN, FREDERICK JOSEPH   BR TR 5'8"   165 lbs.
B. Nov. 25, 1872, Little Cooley, Pa.   D. Dec. 14, 1957, Union City, Pa.

	W	L	PCT	ERA	G	GS	CG	IP	H	BB	SO	ShO	W	L	SV	AB	H	HR	BA
1887 PHI AA	0	0	–	7.20	1	1	1	5	8	2	4	0	0	0	0	2	0	0	.000

Bill Chappelle

CHAPPELLE, WILLIAM HOGAN (Big Bill)   BR TR 6'2"   206 lbs.
B. Mar. 22, 1884, Waterloo, N. Y.   D. Dec. 31, 1944, Mineola, N. Y.

	W	L	PCT	ERA	G	GS	CG	IP	H	BB	SO	ShO	W	L	SV	AB	H	HR	BA
1908 BOS N	2	4	.333	1.79	13	7	3	70.1	60	17	23	1	0	0	0	21	1	0	.048
1909 2 teams		BOS	N (5G 1–1)		CIN	N (1G 0–0)													
" total	1	1	.500	1.91	6	3	2	33	36	13	8	0	0	0	1	12	4	1	.333
1914 BKN F	4	2	.667	3.15	16	6	4	74.1	71	29	31	0	0	1	0	23	0	0	.000
3 yrs.	7	7	.500	2.38	35	16	9	177.2	167	59	62	1	0	1	1	56	5	1	.089

Pete Charton

CHARTON, FRANK LANE   BL TR 6'2"   190 lbs.
B. Dec. 21, 1942, Jackson, Tenn.

	W	L	PCT	ERA	G	GS	CG	IP	H	BB	SO	ShO	W	L	SV	AB	H	HR	BA
1964 BOS A	0	2	.000	5.26	25	5	0	65	67	24	37	0	0	0	0	10	1	0	.100

Ken Chase

CHASE, KENDALL FAY (Lefty)   BR TL 6'2"   210 lbs.
B. Oct. 6, 1913, Oneonta, N. Y.

	W	L	PCT	ERA	G	GS	CG	IP	H	BB	SO	ShO	W	L	SV	AB	H	HR	BA
1936 WAS A	0	0	–	11.57	1	0	0	2.1	2	4	1	0	0	0	0	1	1	0	1.000
1937	4	3	.571	4.13	14	9	4	76.1	74	60	43	0	0	0	0	29	1	0	.034
1938	9	10	.474	5.58	32	21	7	150	151	113	64	0	2	1	1	48	10	0	.208
1939	10	19	.345	3.80	32	31	15	232	215	114	118	1	1	0	0	89	15	0	.169
1940	15	17	.469	3.23	35	34	20	261.2	260	143	129	1	0	0	0	92	15	1	.163
1941	6	18	.250	5.08	33	30	8	205.2	228	115	98	1	1	0	0	74	11	0	.149
1942 BOS A	5	1	.833	3.81	13	10	4	80.1	82	41	34	0	0	0	0	33	6	0	.182
1943 2 teams		BOS	A (7G 0–4)		NY	N (21G 4–12)													
" total	4	16	.200	4.60	28	25	4	156.2	176	104	95	1	0	0	0	53	10	0	.189
8 yrs.	53	84	.387	4.27	188	160	62	1165	1188	694	582	4	4	2	1	419	69	1	.165

Jim Chatterton

CHATTERTON, JAMES M.
B. Oct. 14, 1864, Brooklyn, N. Y.   D. Dec. 18, 1944, Malden, Mass.

	W	L	PCT	ERA	G	GS	CG	IP	H	BB	SO	ShO	W	L	SV	AB	H	HR	BA
1884 KC U	0	1	.000	3.60	1	1	0	5	11	2	2	0	0	0	0	*			

Nestor Chavez

CHAVEZ, NESTOR ISAIAS SILVA   BR TR 6'   170 lbs.
B. July 6, 1947, Chacao Miranda, Venezuela   D. Mar. 16, 1969, Maracaibo, Venezuela

	W	L	PCT	ERA	G	GS	CG	IP	H	BB	SO	ShO	W	L	SV	AB	H	HR	BA
1967 SF N	1	0	1.000	0.00	2	0	0	5	4	3	3	0	1	0	0	1	0	0	.000

Dave Cheadle

CHEADLE, DAVID BAIRD   BL TL 6'2"   203 lbs.
B. Feb. 19, 1952, Greensboro, N. C.

	W	L	PCT	ERA	G	GS	CG	IP	H	BB	SO	ShO	W	L	SV	AB	H	HR	BA
1973 ATL N	0	1	.000	18.00	2	0	0	2	2	3	2	0	0	1	0	0	0	0	–

Charlie Chech

CHECH, CHARLES WILLIAM   BR TR 5'11½" 190 lbs.
B. Apr. 27, 1879, Madison, Wis.   D. Jan. 31, 1938, Los Angeles, Calif.

	W	L	PCT	ERA	G	GS	CG	IP	H	BB	SO	ShO	W	L	SV	AB	H	HR	BA
1905 CIN N	14	15	.483	2.89	39	25	20	268	300	77	79	1	2	3	0	89	17	0	.191
1906	1	4	.200	2.32	11	5	5	66	59	24	17	0	0	0	3	25	5	0	.200
1908 CLE A	11	7	.611	1.74	27	20	14	165.2	136	34	51	4	0	0	0	48	5	0	.104
1909 BOS A	7	5	.583	2.95	17	13	6	106.2	107	27	40	1	2	1	0	36	3	0	.083
4 yrs.	33	31	.516	2.52	94	63	45	606.1	602	162	187	6	4	4	3	198	30	0	.152

Virgil Cheeves

CHEEVES, VIRGIL EARL (Chief)   BR TR 6'   195 lbs.
B. Feb. 12, 1901, Oklahoma City, Okla.

	W	L	PCT	ERA	G	GS	CG	IP	H	BB	SO	ShO	W	L	SV	AB	H	HR	BA
1920 CHI N	0	0	–	3.50	5	2	0	18	16	7	9	0	0	0	0	4	0	0	.000
1921	11	12	.478	4.64	37	22	9	163	192	47	39	1	3	1	0	48	8	0	.167
1922	12	11	.522	4.09	39	23	9	182.2	195	76	40	1	3	3	2	62	13	1	.210
1923	3	4	.429	6.18	19	8	0	71.1	89	37	13	0	3	1	0	23	4	0	.174
1924 CLE A	0	0	–	7.79	8	1	0	17.1	26	17	2	0	0	0	0	4	1	0	.250
1927 NY N	0	0	–	4.26	3	0	0	6.1	8	4	1	0	0	0	0	0	0	0	–
6 yrs.	26	27	.491	4.73	111	56	18	458.2	526	188	98	2	9	5	2	141	26	1	.184

Italo Chelini

CHELINI, ITALO VINCENT (Lefty)   BL TL 5'10½" 175 lbs.
B. Oct. 10, 1914, San Francisco, Calif.   D. Aug. 25, 1972, San Francisco, Calif.

	W	L	PCT	ERA	G	GS	CG	IP	H	BB	SO	ShO	W	L	SV	AB	H	HR	BA
1935 CHI A	0	0	–	12.60	2	0	0	5	7	4	1	0	0	0	0	2	1	0	.500
1936	4	3	.571	4.95	18	6	5	83.2	100	30	16	0	1	0	0	32	5	0	.156
1937	0	1	.000	10.38	4	0	0	8.2	15	0	3	0	0	0	0	1	0	0	.000
3 yrs.	4	4	.500	5.83	24	6	5	97.1	122	34	20	0	1	0	0	35	6	0	.171

Larry Cheney

CHENEY, LAURANCE RUSSELL   BR TR 6'1½" 185 lbs.
B. May 2, 1886, Belleville, Kans.   D. Jan. 6, 1969, Daytona Beach, Fla.

	W	L	PCT	ERA	G	GS	CG	IP	H	BB	SO	ShO	W	L	SV	AB	H	HR	BA
1911 CHI N	1	0	1.000	0.00	3	1	0	10	8	3	11	0	0	0	0	4	1	0	.250
1912	26	10	.722	2.85	42	37	28	303.1	262	111	140	4	2	0	0	106	24	1	.226
1913	21	14	.600	2.57	54	36	25	305	271	98	136	2	4	0	11	104	20	0	.192
1914	20	18	.526	2.54	50	40	21	311.1	239	140	157	6	3	0	5	100	18	0	.180

	W	L	PCT	ERA	G	GS	CG	IP	H	BB	SO	ShO	W	L	SV	AB	H	HR	BA
													Relief Pitching			BATTING			

Larry Cheney continued

		W	L	PCT	ERA	G	GS	CG	IP	H	BB	SO	ShO	W	L	SV	AB	H	HR	BA
1915 2 teams	CHI N (25G 8–9)	BKN	N	(5G 0–2)																
" total	8 11	.421	3.24	30	22	7	158.1	136	72	79	2	2	2	0	47	7	0	.149		
1916 BKN N	18 12	.600	1.92	41	32	15	253	178	105	166	5	2	3	0	79	9	0	.114		
1917	8 12	.400	2.35	35	24	14	210.1	185	73	102	1	1	0	2	68	14	0	.206		
1918	11 13	.458	3.00	32	21	15	200.2	177	74	83	0	3	2	1	66	16	0	.242		
1919 3 teams	BKN N (9G 1–3)	BOS	N	(8G 0–2)	PHI	N	(9G 2–5)													
" total	3 10	.231	4.18	26	12	7	129.1	149	57	52	0	1	1	0	43	6	0	.140		
9 yrs.	116 100	.537	2.70	313	225	132	1881.1	1605	733	926	20	18	8	19	617	115	1	.186		

WORLD SERIES

| 1916 BKN N | 0 | 0 | – | 3.00 | 1 | 0 | 0 | 3 | 4 | 1 | 5 | 0 | 0 | 0 | 0 | 0 | 0 | 0 | – |

Tom Cheney

CHENEY, THOMAS EDGAR
B. Oct. 14, 1934, Morgan, Ga.
BR TR 5'11" 170 lbs.

	W	L	PCT	ERA	G	GS	CG	IP	H	BB	SO	ShO	W	L	SV	AB	H	HR	BA
1957 STL N	0	1	.000	5.00	4	3	0	9	6	15	10	0	0	0	0	2	0	0	.000
1959	0	1	.000	6.94	11	2	0	11.2	17	11	8	0	0	1	0	0	0	0	–
1960 PIT N	2	2	.500	3.98	11	8	1	52	44	33	35	1	0	0	0	17	3	0	.176
1961 2 teams	PIT	N	(1G 0–0)	WAS	A	(10G 1–3)													
" total	1	3	.250	10.01	11	7	0	29.2	33	30	20	0	0	0	0	8	4	0	.500
1962 WAS A	7	9	.438	3.17	37	23	4	173.1	134	97	147	3	0	1	1	48	3	0	.063
1963	8	9	.471	2.71	23	21	7	136.1	99	40	97	4	0	0	0	46	5	0	.109
1964	1	3	.250	3.70	15	6	1	48.2	45	13	25	0	0	0	1	12	3	0	.250
1966	0	1	.000	5.06	3	1	0	5.1	4	6	3	0	0	0	0	0	0	0	–
8 yrs.	19	29	.396	3.77	115	71	13	466	382	245	345	8	0	2	2	133	18	0	.135

WORLD SERIES

| 1960 PIT N | 0 | 0 | – | 4.50 | 3 | 0 | 0 | 4 | 4 | 1 | 6 | 0 | 0 | 0 | 0 | 0 | 0 | 0 | – |

Jack Chesbro

CHESBRO, JOHN DWIGHT (Happy Jack)
B. June 5, 1874, North Adams, Mass. D. Nov. 6, 1931, Conway, Mass.
Hall of Fame 1946.
BR TR 5'9" 180 lbs.

	W	L	PCT	ERA	G	GS	CG	IP	H	BB	SO	ShO	W	L	SV	AB	H	HR	BA
1899 PIT N	6	10	.375	4.11	19	17	15	149	165	59	28	0	0	0	0	58	9	0	.155
1900	14	13	.519	3.67	32	26	20	215.2	220	79	56	3	1	1	3	85	15	0	.176
1901	21	10	.677	2.38	36	28	26	287.2	261	52	129	6	2	1	1	116	25	1	.216
1902	28	6	.824	2.17	35	33	31	286.1	242	62	136	8	1	0	1	112	20	0	.179
1903 NY A	21	15	.583	2.77	40	36	33	324.2	300	74	147	1	0	1	0	124	23	2	.185
1904	41[1]	12	.774	1.82	55	51	48	454.2	338	88	239	6	3	0	0	174	41	1	.236
1905	19	15	.559	2.20	41	38	24	303.1	262	71	156	3	1	1	0	112	21	0	.188
1906	24	16	.600	2.96	49	42	24	325	314	75	152	4	3	0	0	125	26	1	.208
1907	10	10	.500	2.53	30	25	17	206	192	46	78	1	0	0	0	72	15	0	.208
1908	14	20	.412	2.93	45	31	21	289	271	67	124	3	3	0	0	102	18	0	.176
1909 2 teams	NY	A	(9G 0–4)	BOS	A	(1G 0–1)													
" total	0	5	.000	6.14	10	5	2	55.2	77	17	20	0	0	0	0	19	4	0	.211
11 yrs.	198	132	.600	2.68	392	332	261	2897	2642	690	1265	35	14	4	4	1099	217	5	.197

Bob Chesnes

CHESNES, ROBERT VINCENT
B. May 6, 1921, Oakland, Calif. D. May 23, 1979, Everett, Wash.
BB TR 6' 180 lbs.

	W	L	PCT	ERA	G	GS	CG	IP	H	BB	SO	ShO	W	L	SV	AB	H	HR	BA
1948 PIT N	14	6	.700	3.57	25	23	15	194.1	180	90	69	0	0	0	0	91	25	1	.275
1949	7	13	.350	5.88	27	25	8	145.1	153	82	49	1	0	0	1	68	17	1	.250
1950	3	3	.500	5.54	9	7	2	39	44	17	12	0	1	0	0	13	2	0	.154
3 yrs.	24	22	.522	4.66	61	55	25	378.2	377	189	130	1	1	0	1	172	44	2	.256

Mitch Chetkovich

CHETKOVICH, MITCHELL
B. July 21, 1918, Fairpoint, Ohio D. Aug. 24, 1971, Grass Valley, Calif.
BR TR 6'3½" 208 lbs.

	W	L	PCT	ERA	G	GS	CG	IP	H	BB	SO	ShO	W	L	SV	AB	H	HR	BA
1945 PHI N	0	0	–	0.00	4	0	0	3	2	3	0	0	0	0	0	0	0	0	–

Tony Chevez

CHEVEZ, ANTONIO SILVIO
B. June 20, 1954, Telica, Nicaragua
BR TR 5'11" 177 lbs.

	W	L	PCT	ERA	G	GS	CG	IP	H	BB	SO	ShO	W	L	SV	AB	H	HR	BA
1977 BAL A	0	0	–	12.38	4	0	0	8	10	8	7	0	0	0	0	0	0	0	–

Floyd Chiffer

CHIFFER, FLOYD JOHN
B. Apr. 20, 1956, Glen Cove, N. Y.
BR TR 6'2" 180 lbs.

	W	L	PCT	ERA	G	GS	CG	IP	H	BB	SO	ShO	W	L	SV	AB	H	HR	BA
1982 SD N	4	3	.571	2.95	51	0	0	79.1	73	34	48	0	4	3	4	8	0	0	.000
1983	0	2	.000	3.18	15	0	0	22.2	17	10	15	0	0	2	1	1	0	0	.000
1984	1	0	1.000	7.71	15	1	0	28	42	16	20	0	1	0	0	3	0	0	.000
3 yrs.	5	5	.500	4.02	81	1	0	130	132	60	83	0	5	5	5	12	0	0	.000

Harry Child

CHILD, HARRY PATRICK
Born Harry Patrick Chesley.
B. May 23, 1905, Baltimore, Md. D. Nov. 9, 1972, Alexandria, Va.
BB TR 5'11" 175 lbs.

	W	L	PCT	ERA	G	GS	CG	IP	H	BB	SO	ShO	W	L	SV	AB	H	HR	BA
1930 WAS A	0	0	–	6.30	5	0	0	10	10	5	5	0	0	0	0	4	1	0	.250

Childers

CHILDERS,
B. St. Louis, Mo. Deceased.

	W	L	PCT	ERA	G	GS	CG	IP	H	BB	SO	ShO	W	L	SV	AB	H	HR	BA
1895 LOU N	0	0	–	∞	1	0	0	2	5	0	0	0	0	0	0	0	0	–	

Bob Chipman

CHIPMAN, ROBERT HOWARD (Mr. Chips)
B. Oct. 11, 1918, Brooklyn, N. Y. D. Nov. 8, 1973, Huntington, N. Y.
BL TL 6'2" 190 lbs.

	W	L	PCT	ERA	G	GS	CG	IP	H	BB	SO	ShO	W	L	SV	AB	H	HR	BA
1941 BKN N	1	0	1.000	0.00	1	0	0	5	3	1	3	0	1	0	0	3	0	0	.000
1942	0	0	–	0.00	2	0	0	1.1	1	2	1	0	0	0	0	0	0	0	–
1943	0	0	–	0.00	1	0	0	1.2	2	2	0	0	0	0	0	0	0	0	–
1944 2 teams	BKN	N	(11G 3–1)	CHI	N	(26G 9–9)													
" total	12	10	.545	3.65	37	24	9	165.1	185	64	61	1	2	3	2	59	7	0	.119
1945 CHI N	4	5	.444	3.50	25	10	3	72	63	34	29	1	0	1	0	17	3	0	.176
1946	6	5	.545	3.13	34	10	5	109.1	103	54	42	3	1	0	2	33	2	0	.061
1947	7	6	.538	3.68	32	17	5	134.2	135	66	51	1	1	0	0	44	4	0	.091
1948	2	1	.667	3.58	34	3	0	60.1	73	24	16	0	2	0	4	16	4	0	.250

	W	L	PCT	ERA	G	GS	CG	IP	H	BB	SO	ShO	Relief Pitching W	L	SV	BATTING AB	H	HR	BA

Bob Chipman continued

	W	L	PCT	ERA	G	GS	CG	IP	H	BB	SO	ShO	W	L	SV	AB	H	HR	BA
1949	7	8	.467	3.97	38	11	3	113.1	110	63	46	1	3	2	1	24	3	0	.125
1950 **BOS N**	7	7	.500	4.43	27	12	4	124	127	37	40	0	2	1	1	39	6	0	.154
1951	4	3	.571	4.85	33	0	0	52	59	19	17	0	4	3	4	10	1	0	.100
1952	1	1	.500	2.81	29	0	0	41.2	28	20	16	0	1	1	0	5	2	0	.400
12 yrs.	51	46	.526	3.72	293	87	29	880.2	889	386	322	7	17	11	14	250	32	0	.128

WORLD SERIES
| 1945 **CHI N** | 0 | 0 | — | 0.00 | 1 | 0 | 0 | .1 | 0 | 1 | 0 | 0 | 0 | 0 | 0 | 0 | 0 | 0 | — |

Nels Chittum

CHITTUM, NELSON BOYD
B. Mar. 25, 1933, Harrisonburg, Va.   BR TR 6'1"   180 lbs.

	W	L	PCT	ERA	G	GS	CG	IP	H	BB	SO	ShO	W	L	SV	AB	H	HR	BA
1958 **STL N**	0	1	.000	6.44	13	2	0	29.1	31	7	13	0	0	0	0	4	1	0	.250
1959 **BOS A**	3	0	1.000	1.19	21	0	0	30.1	29	11	12	0	3	0	0	5	1	0	.200
1960	0	0	—	4.32	6	0	0	8.1	8	6	5	0	0	0	0	1	0	0	.000
3 yrs.	3	1	.750	3.84	40	2	0	68	68	24	30	0	3	0	0	10	2	0	.200

Bob Chlupsa

CHLUPSA, ROBERT JOSEPH
B. Sept. 16, 1945, New York, N.Y.   BR TR 6'7"   215 lbs.

	W	L	PCT	ERA	G	GS	CG	IP	H	BB	SO	ShO	W	L	SV	AB	H	HR	BA
1970 **STL N**	0	2	.000	9.00	14	0	0	16	26	9	10	0	0	2	0	0	0	0	—
1971	0	0	—	9.00	1	0	0	2	3	0	1	0	0	0	0	0	0	0	—
2 yrs.	0	2	.000	9.00	15	0	0	18	29	9	11	0	0	2	0	0	0	0	—

Don Choate

CHOATE, DONALD LEON
B. July 2, 1938, Potosi, Mo.   BR TR 6'   185 lbs.

	W	L	PCT	ERA	G	GS	CG	IP	H	BB	SO	ShO	W	L	SV	AB	H	HR	BA
1960 **SF N**	0	0	—	2.25	4	0	0	8	7	4	7	0	0	0	0	0	0	0	—

Chief Chouneau

CHOUNEAU, WILLIAM
Born William Cadreau.
B. Sept. 2, 1889, Cloquet, Minn.   D. Sept. 17, 1948, Cloquet, Minn.   BR TR 5'9"   150 lbs.

	W	L	PCT	ERA	G	GS	CG	IP	H	BB	SO	ShO	W	L	SV	AB	H	HR	BA
1910 **CHI A**	0	1	.000	3.38	1	1	0	5.1	7	0	1	0	0	0	0	1	0	0	.000

Mike Chris

CHRIS, MICHAEL
B. Oct. 8, 1957, Santa Monica, Calif.   BL TL 6'3"   180 lbs.

	W	L	PCT	ERA	G	GS	CG	IP	H	BB	SO	ShO	W	L	SV	AB	H	HR	BA
1979 **DET A**	3	3	.500	6.92	13	8	0	39	46	21	31	0	0	0	0	0	0	0	—
1982 **SF N**	0	2	.000	4.85	9	6	0	26	23	26	10	0	0	0	0	7	1	0	.143
1983	0	0	—	8.10	7	0	0	13.1	16	16	5	0	0	0	0	2	0	0	.000
3 yrs.	3	5	.375	6.43	29	14	0	78.1	85	63	46	0	0	0	0	9	1	0	.111

Gary Christenson

CHRISTENSON, GARY RICHARD
B. May 5, 1953, New Hyde Park, N.Y.   BL TL 6'5"   200 lbs.

	W	L	PCT	ERA	G	GS	CG	IP	H	BB	SO	ShO	W	L	SV	AB	H	HR	BA
1979 **KC A**	0	0	—	3.27	6	0	0	11	10	2	4	0	0	0	0	0	0	0	—
1980	3	0	1.000	5.23	24	0	0	31	35	18	16	0	3	0	1	0	0	0	—
2 yrs.	3	0	1.000	4.71	30	0	0	42	45	20	20	0	3	0	1	0	0	0	—

Larry Christenson

CHRISTENSON, LARRY RICHARD
B. Nov. 10, 1953, Everett, Wash.   BR TR 6'4"   215 lbs.

	W	L	PCT	ERA	G	GS	CG	IP	H	BB	SO	ShO	W	L	SV	AB	H	HR	BA
1973 **PHI N**	1	4	.200	6.55	10	9	1	34.1	53	20	11	0	0	0	0	10	0	0	.000
1974	1	1	.500	4.30	10	1	0	23	20	15	18	0	1	0	2	4	0	0	.000
1975	11	6	.647	3.66	29	26	5	172	149	45	88	2	0	0	1	57	14	2	.246
1976	13	8	.619	3.68	32	29	2	168.2	199	42	54	0	0	0	0	51	10	2	.196
1977	19	6	.760	4.07	34	34	5	219	229	69	118	1	0	0	0	74	10	3	.135
1978	13	14	.481	3.24	33	33	9	228	209	47	131	3	0	0	0	67	5	1	.075
1979	5	10	.333	4.50	19	17	2	106	118	30	53	0	0	0	0	31	9	1	.290
1980	5	1	.833	4.01	14	14	0	74	62	27	49	0	0	0	0	19	7	1	.368
1981	4	7	.364	3.53	20	15	0	107	108	30	70	0	1	1	1	30	3	0	.100
1982	9	10	.474	3.47	33	33	3	223	212	53	145	0	0	0	0	67	5	1	.075
1983	2	4	.333	3.91	9	9	0	48.1	42	17	44	0	0	0	0	17	1	0	.059
11 yrs.	83	71	.539	3.79	243	220	27	1403.1	1401	395	781	6	2	1	4	427	64	11	.150

DIVISIONAL PLAYOFF SERIES
| 1981 **PHI N** | 1 | 0 | 1.000 | 1.50 | 1 | 1 | 0 | 6 | 4 | 1 | 8 | 0 | 0 | 0 | 0 | 2 | 0 | 0 | .000 |

LEAGUE CHAMPIONSHIP SERIES
1977 **PHI N**	0	0	—	8.10	1	1	0	3.1	7	0	2	0	0	0	0	0	0	0	—
1978	0	1	.000	12.46	1	1	0	4.1	7	1	3	0	0	0	0	1	0	0	.000
1980	0	0	—	4.05	2	1	0	6.2	5	5	2	0	0	0	0	2	0	0	.000
3 yrs.	0	1	.000	7.53	4	3	0	14.1	19	6	7	0	0	0	0	3	0	0	.000

WORLD SERIES
| 1980 **PHI N** | 0 | 1 | .000 | 108.00 | 1 | 1 | 0 | .1 | 5 | 0 | 0 | 0 | 0 | 0 | 0 | 0 | 0 | 0 | — |

Clay Christiansen

CHRISTIANSEN, CLAY
B. June 28, 1958, Wichita, Kans.   BR TR 6'4"   215 lbs.

	W	L	PCT	ERA	G	GS	CG	IP	H	BB	SO	ShO	W	L	SV	AB	H	HR	BA
1984 **NY A**	2	4	.333	6.05	24	1	0	38.2	50	12	27	0	2	3	2	0	0	0	—

Russ Christopher

CHRISTOPHER, RUSSELL ORMAND
Brother of Lloyd Christopher.
B. Sept. 12, 1917, Richmond, Calif.   D. Dec. 5, 1954, Richmond, Calif.   BR TR 6'3½"   170 lbs.

	W	L	PCT	ERA	G	GS	CG	IP	H	BB	SO	ShO	W	L	SV	AB	H	HR	BA
1942 **PHI A**	4	13	.235	3.82	30	18	10	165	154	99	58	0	0	1	1	56	5	0	.089
1943	5	8	.385	3.45	24	15	5	133	120	58	56	0	1	3	2	45	7	0	.156
1944	14	14	.500	2.97	35	24	13	215.1	200	63	84	1	2	1	1	81	18	1	.222
1945	13	13	.500	3.17	33	27	17	227.1	213	75	100	2	1	0	2	76	13	1	.171
1946	5	7	.417	4.30	30	13	1	119.1	119	44	79	0	1	0	0	36	5	0	.139
1947	10	7	.588	2.90	44	0	0	80.2	70	33	33	0	10	7	12	16	2	0	.125
1948 **CLE A**	3	2	.600	2.90	45	0	0	59	55	27	14	0	3	2	17	6	0	0	.000
7 yrs.	54	64	.458	3.37	241	97	46	999.2	931	399	424	3	17	16	35	316	50	2	.158

WORLD SERIES
| 1948 **CLE A** | 0 | 0 | — | ∞ | 1 | 0 | 0 | 2 | 0 | 0 | 0 | 0 | 0 | 0 | 0 | 0 | 0 | 0 | — |

	W	L	PCT	ERA	G	GS	CG	IP	H	BB	SO	ShO	Relief Pitching W	L	SV	BATTING AB	H	HR	BA

Bubba Church

CHURCH, EMORY NICHOLAS
B. Sept. 12, 1924, Birmingham, Ala.
BR TR 6' 180 lbs.

	W	L	PCT	ERA	G	GS	CG	IP	H	BB	SO	ShO	W	L	SV	AB	H	HR	BA
1950 PHI N	8	6	.571	2.73	31	18	8	142	113	56	50	2	0	0	1	44	8	0	.182
1951	15	11	.577	3.53	38	33	15	247	246	90	104	4	1	1	1	86	22	1	.256
1952 2 teams			.357	PHI N (2G 0-0)		CIN N (29G 5-9)													
" total	5	9	.357	4.55	31	23	5	158.1	184	49	50	1	0	0	0	51	12	1	.235
1953 2 teams			.467	CIN N (11G 3-3)		CHI N (27G 4-5)													
" total	7	8	.467	5.29	38	18	3	148	170	68	59	0	2	2	1	48	11	1	.229
1954 CHI N	1	3	.250	9.82	7	3	1	14.2	21	13	8	0	0	1	0	5	0	0	.000
1955	0	0	—	5.40	2	0	0	3.1	4	1	3	0	0	0	1	1	0	0	.000
6 yrs.	36	37	.493	4.10	147	95	32	713.1	738	277	274	7	3	4	4	235	53	3	.226

Len Church

CHURCH, LEONARD
B. Mar. 21, 1942, Chicago, Ill.
BB TR 6' 190 lbs.

	W	L	PCT	ERA	G	GS	CG	IP	H	BB	SO	ShO	W	L	SV	AB	H	HR	BA
1966 CHI N	0	1	.000	7.50	4	0	0	6	10	7	3	0	0	1	0	1	0	0	.000

Chuck Churn

CHURN, CLARENCE NOTTINGHAM
B. Feb. 1, 1930, Bridgetown, Va.
BR TR 6'3" 205 lbs.

	W	L	PCT	ERA	G	GS	CG	IP	H	BB	SO	ShO	W	L	SV	AB	H	HR	BA
1957 PIT N	0	0	—	4.32	5	0	0	8.1	9	4	4	0	0	0	0	1	0	0	.000
1958 CLE A	0	0	—	6.23	6	0	0	8.2	12	5	4	0	0	0	0	0	0	0	
1959 LA N	3	2	.600	4.99	14	0	0	30.2	28	10	24	0	3	2	1	6	1	0	.167
3 yrs.	3	2	.600	5.10	25	0	0	47.2	49	19	32	0	3	2	1	7	1	0	.143

WORLD SERIES

	W	L	PCT	ERA	G	GS	CG	IP	H	BB	SO	ShO	W	L	SV	AB	H	HR	BA
1959 LA N	0	0	—	27.00	1	0	0	.2	5	0	0	0	0	0	0	0	0	0	

Al Cicotte

CICOTTE, ALVA WARREN (Bozo)
B. Dec. 23, 1929, Melvindale, Mich. D. Nov. 29, 1982, Westland, Mich.
BR TR 6'3" 185 lbs.

	W	L	PCT	ERA	G	GS	CG	IP	H	BB	SO	ShO	W	L	SV	AB	H	HR	BA
1957 NY A	2	2	.500	3.03	20	2	0	65.1	57	30	36	0	2	0	2	20	3	0	.150
1958 2 teams			.429	WAS A (8G 0-3)		DET A (14G 3-1)													
" total	3	4	.429	4.06	22	6	0	71	86	29	35	0	2	1	0	27	5	0	.185
1959 CLE A	3	1	.750	5.32	26	1	0	44	46	25	23	0	3	1	1	3	1	0	.333
1961 STL N	2	6	.250	5.28	29	7	0	75	83	34	51	0	2	3	1	21	6	0	.286
1962 HOU N	0	0	—	3.86	5	0	0	4.2	8	1	4	0	0	0	0	0	0	0	
5 yrs.	10	13	.435	4.36	102	16	0	260	280	119	149	0	9	5	4	71	15	0	.211

Eddie Cicotte

CICOTTE, EDWARD VICTOR
B. June 19, 1884, Detroit, Mich. D. May 5, 1969, Detroit, Mich.
BB TR 5'9" 175 lbs.

	W	L	PCT	ERA	G	GS	CG	IP	H	BB	SO	ShO	W	L	SV	AB	H	HR	BA
1905 DET A	1	1	.500	3.50	3	1	1	18	25	5	6	0	0	1	0	7	3	0	.429
1908 BOS A	11	12	.478	2.43	39	24	17	207.1	198	59	95	2	1	2	2	72	17	0	.236
1909	13	5	.722	1.97	27	15	10	159.2	117	56	82	1	4	0	2	49	11	0	.224
1910	15	11	.577	2.74	36	30	20	250	213	86	104	4	1	0	0	85	12	0	.141
1911	11	15	.423	2.81	35	25	16	221	236	73	106	1	2	2	0	71	10	0	.141
1912 2 teams			.500	BOS A (9G 1-3)		CHI A (20G 9-7)													
" total	10	10	.500	3.50	29	24	15	198	217	52	90	1	0	1	0	69	15	0	.217
1913 CHI A	18	12	.600	1.58	41	30	18	268	224	73	121	3	2	0	1	91	13	0	.143
1914	11	16	.407	2.04	45	29	15	269.1	220	72	122	4	1	0	3	86	14	0	.163
1915	13	12	.520	3.02	39	26	15	223.1	216	48	106	1	0	2	3	67	14	0	.209
1916	15	7	.682	1.78	44	19	11	187	138	70	91	2	3	2	5	57	12	0	.211
1917	28	12	.700	1.53	49	35	29	346.2	246	70	150	7	5	1	4	112	20	0	.179
1918	12	19	.387	2.64	38	30	24	266	275	40	104	1	3	1	2	86	14	0	.163
1919	29	7	.806	1.82	40	35	30	306.2	256	49	110	5	2	1	1	99	20	0	.202
1920	21	10	.677	3.26	37	35	28	303.1	316	74	87	4	0	0	2	112	22	0	.196
14 yrs.	208	149	.583	2.37	502	358	249	3224.1	2897	827	1374	36	24	13	25	1063	197	0	.185

WORLD SERIES

	W	L	PCT	ERA	G	GS	CG	IP	H	BB	SO	ShO	W	L	SV	AB	H	HR	BA
1917 CHI A	1	1	.500	1.96	3	2	2	23	23	2	13	0	0	0	0	7	1	0	.143
1919	1	2	.333	2.91	3	3	2	21.2	19	5	7	0	0	0	0	8	0	0	.000
2 yrs.	2	3	.400	2.42	6	5	4	44.2	42	7	20	0	0	0	0	15	1	0	.067

Pete Cimino

CIMINO, PETER WILLIAM
B. Oct. 17, 1942, Philadelphia, Pa.
BR TR 6'2" 195 lbs.

	W	L	PCT	ERA	G	GS	CG	IP	H	BB	SO	ShO	W	L	SV	AB	H	HR	BA
1965 MIN A	0	0	—	0.00	1	0	0	1	0	0	0	0	0	0	0	0	0	0	
1966	2	5	.286	2.92	35	0	0	64.2	53	30	57	0	2	5	4	6	0	0	.000
1967 CAL A	3	3	.500	3.26	46	1	0	88.1	73	31	80	0	3	3	1	12	5	0	.417
1968	0	0	—	2.57	4	0	0	7	7	4	2	0	0	0	0	0	0	0	
4 yrs.	5	8	.385	3.07	86	1	0	161	133	65	139	0	5	8	5	18	5	0	.278

Lou Ciola

CIOLA, LOUIS ALEXANDER
B. Sept. 6, 1922, Norfolk, Va.
BR TR 5'9" 165 lbs.

	W	L	PCT	ERA	G	GS	CG	IP	H	BB	SO	ShO	W	L	SV	AB	H	HR	BA
1943 PHI A	1	3	.250	5.56	12	3	2	43.2	48	22	7	0	0	1	0	18	3	0	.167

Galen Cisco

CISCO, GALEN BERNARD
B. Mar. 7, 1937, St. Mary's, Ohio
BR TR 6' 200 lbs.

	W	L	PCT	ERA	G	GS	CG	IP	H	BB	SO	ShO	W	L	SV	AB	H	HR	BA
1961 BOS A	2	4	.333	6.71	17	8	0	52.1	67	28	26	0	1	0	0	10	1	0	.100
1962 2 teams			.385	BOS A (23G 4-7)		NY N (4G 1-1)													
" total	5	8	.385	6.07	27	11	2	102.1	110	61	56	0	1	1	0	32	2	0	.063
1963 NY N	7	15	.318	4.34	51	17	1	155.2	165	64	81	0	5	3	0	38	5	0	.132
1964	6	19	.240	3.62	36	25	5	191.2	182	54	78	2	0	3	0	54	6	0	.111
1965	4	8	.333	4.49	35	17	1	112.1	119	51	58	1	0	0	0	27	7	0	.259
1967 BOS A	0	1	.000	3.63	11	0	0	22.1	21	8	8	0	0	1	1	3	0	0	.000
1969 KC A	1	1	.500	3.63	15	0	0	22.1	17	15	18	0	1	1	1	0	0	0	
7 yrs.	25	56	.309	4.56	192	78	9	659	681	281	325	3	8	9	2	164	21	0	.128

Ralph Citarella

CITARELLA, RALPH ALEXANDER
B. Feb. 7, 1958, East Orange, N. J.
BR TR 6' 175 lbs.

	W	L	PCT	ERA	G	GS	CG	IP	H	BB	SO	ShO	W	L	SV	AB	H	HR	BA
1983 STL N	0	0	—	1.64	6	0	0	11	8	3	4	0	0	0	0	1	0	0	.000
1984	0	1	.000	3.63	10	2	0	22.1	20	7	15	0	0	0	0	4	1	0	.250
2 yrs.	0	1	.000	2.97	16	2	0	33.1	28	10	19	0	0	0	0	5	1	0	.200

	W	L	PCT	ERA	G	GS	CG	IP	H	BB	SO	ShO	Relief Pitching W	L	SV	BATTING AB	H	HR	BA

Bobby Clack

CLACK, ROBERT S. (Gentlemanly Bobby)   BR TR 5'9"   153 lbs.
Born Robert S. Clark.
B. 1851, Brooklyn, N. Y.   D. Oct. 22, 1933, Danvers, Mass.

	W	L	PCT	ERA	G	GS	CG	IP	H	BB	SO	ShO	W	L	SV	AB	H	HR	BA
1876 CIN N	0	0	—	4.50	1	0	0	2	2	0	0	0	0	0	0	*			

Jim Clancy

CLANCY, JAMES   BR TR 6'2"   185 lbs.
B. Dec. 18, 1955, Chicago, Ill.

	W	L	PCT	ERA	G	GS	CG	IP	H	BB	SO	ShO	W	L	SV	AB	H	HR	BA
1977 TOR A	4	9	.308	5.03	13	13	4	77	80	47	44	1	0	0	0	0	0	0	—
1978	10	12	.455	4.09	31	30	7	193.2	199	91	106	0	0	0	0	0	0	0	—
1979	2	7	.222	5.48	12	11	2	64	65	31	33	0	0	0	0	0	0	0	—
1980	13	16	.448	3.30	34	34	15	251	217	128	152	2	0	0	0	0	0	0	—
1981	6	12	.333	4.90	22	22	2	125	126	64	56	0	0	0	0	0	0	0	—
1982	16	14	.533	3.71	40	40	11	266.2	251	77	139	3	0	0	0	0	0	0	—
1983	15	11	.577	3.91	34	34	11	223	238	61	99	1	0	0	0	0	0	0	—
1984	13	15	.464	5.12	36	36	5	219.2	249	88	118	0	0	0	0	0	0	0	—
8 yrs.	79	96	.451	4.20	222	220	57	1420	1425	587	747	7	0	0	0	0	0	0	—

Bill Clark

CLARK, WILLIAM WINFIELD (Win)   BR TR 5'10"   175 lbs.
B. Apr. 11, 1875, Circleville, Ohio   D. Apr. 15, 1959, Los Angeles, Calif.

	W	L	PCT	ERA	G	GS	CG	IP	H	BB	SO	ShO	W	L	SV	AB	H	HR	BA
1897 LOU N	1	1	.500	4.15	3	2	2	21.2	30	1	1	0	0	0	0	*			

Bob Clark

CLARK, ROBERT WILLIAM   BR TR 6'3"   188 lbs.
B. Aug. 22, 1897, Newport, Pa.   D. May 18, 1944, Carlsbad, N. M.

	W	L	PCT	ERA	G	GS	CG	IP	H	BB	SO	ShO	W	L	SV	AB	H	HR	BA
1920 CLE A	1	2	.333	3.43	11	2	2	42	59	13	8	1	0	1	0	10	2	0	.200
1921	0	0	—	14.46	5	0	0	9.1	23	6	2	0	0	0	0	3	0	0	.000
2 yrs.	1	2	.333	5.44	16	2	2	51.1	82	19	10	1	0	1	0	13	2	0	.154

Bryan Clark

CLARK, BRYAN DONALD   BL TL 6'2"   185 lbs.
B. July 12, 1956, Madera, Calif.

	W	L	PCT	ERA	G	GS	CG	IP	H	BB	SO	ShO	W	L	SV	AB	H	HR	BA
1981 SEA A	2	5	.286	4.35	29	9	1	93	92	55	52	0	2	1	2	0	0	0	—
1982	5	2	.714	2.75	37	5	1	114.2	104	58	70	1	2	1	0	0	0	0	—
1983	7	10	.412	3.94	41	17	2	162.1	160	72	76	0	4	2	0	0	0	0	—
1984 TOR A	1	2	.333	5.91	20	3	0	45.2	66	22	21	0	1	1	0	0	0	0	—
4 yrs.	15	19	.441	3.92	127	34	4	415.2	422	207	219	1	9	5	2	0	0	0	—

Ed Clark

CLARK, EDWARD C.
B. Cincinnati, Ohio   Deceased.

	W	L	PCT	ERA	G	GS	CG	IP	H	BB	SO	ShO	W	L	SV	AB	H	HR	BA
1886 PHI AA	0	1	.000	6.75	1	1	1	8	10	2	2	0	0	0	0	2	0	0	.000
1891 COL AA	0	0	—	0.00	1	0	0	2	2	0	1	0	0	0	0	1	0	0	.000
2 yrs.	0	1	.000	5.40	2	1	1	10	12	2	3	0	0	0	0	3	0	0	.000

George Clark

CLARK, GEORGE MYRON   BR TL 6'   190 lbs.
B. May 19, 1891, Smithland, Iowa   D. Nov. 14, 1940, Sioux City, Iowa

	W	L	PCT	ERA	G	GS	CG	IP	H	BB	SO	ShO	W	L	SV	AB	H	HR	BA
1913 NY A	0	1	.000	9.00	11	1	0	19	22	19	5	0	0	0	0	4	2	0	.500

Ginger Clark

CLARK, HARVEY DANIEL   BR TR 5'11"   165 lbs.
B. Mar. 7, 1879, Wooster, Ohio   D. May 10, 1943, Lake Charles, La.

	W	L	PCT	ERA	G	GS	CG	IP	H	BB	SO	ShO	W	L	SV	AB	H	HR	BA
1902 CLE A	1	0	1.000	6.00	1	0	0	6	10	3	1	0	1	0	0	4	2	0	.500

Mike Clark

CLARK, MICHAEL JOHN   BR TR 6'4"   190 lbs.
B. Feb. 12, 1922, Camden, N. J.

	W	L	PCT	ERA	G	GS	CG	IP	H	BB	SO	ShO	W	L	SV	AB	H	HR	BA
1952 STL N	2	0	1.000	6.04	12	4	0	25.1	32	14	10	0	2	0	0	5	0	0	.000
1953	1	0	1.000	4.79	23	2	0	35.2	46	21	17	0	0	0	1	6	0	0	.000
2 yrs.	3	0	1.000	5.31	35	6	0	61	78	35	27	0	2	0	1	11	0	0	.000

Otie Clark

CLARK, WIL⁻IAM OTIS   BR TR 6'1½"   190 lbs.
B. May 22, 1918, Boscobel, Wis.

	W	L	PCT	ERA	G	GS	CG	IP	H	BB	SO	ShO	W	L	SV	AB	H	HR	BA
1945 BOS A	4	4	.500	3.06	12	9	4	82.1	86	19	20	1	0	0	0	24	5	0	.208

Phil Clark

CLARK, PHILIP JAMES   BR TR 6'3"   210 lbs.
B. Oct. 3, 1932, Albany, Ga.

	W	L	PCT	ERA	G	GS	CG	IP	H	BB	SO	ShO	W	L	SV	AB	H	HR	BA
1958 STL N	0	1	.000	3.52	7	0	0	7.2	11	3	1	0	0	1	1	1	0	0	.000
1959	0	1	.000	12.86	7	0	0	7	8	8	5	0	0	1	0	0	0	0	—
2 yrs.	0	2	.000	7.98	14	0	0	14.2	19	11	6	0	0	2	1	1	0	0	.000

Rickey Clark

CLARK, RICKEY CHARLES   BR TR 6'2"   170 lbs.
B. Mar. 21, 1946, Mt. Clemens, Mich.

	W	L	PCT	ERA	G	GS	CG	IP	H	BB	SO	ShO	W	L	SV	AB	H	HR	BA
1967 CAL A	12	11	.522	2.59	32	30	1	174	144	69	81	1	1	0	0	50	2	0	.040
1968	1	11	.083	3.53	21	17	0	94.1	74	54	60	0	0	0	0	28	3	0	.107
1969	0	0	—	5.59	6	1	0	9.2	12	7	6	0	0	0	0	2	1	0	.500
1971	2	1	.667	2.86	11	7	1	44	36	28	28	1	0	0	1	15	4	0	.267
1972	4	9	.308	4.50	26	15	2	110	105	55	61	0	0	1	1	31	3	0	.097
5 yrs.	19	32	.373	3.38	96	70	4	432	371	213	236	2	1	1	2	126	13	0	.103

Spider Clark

CLARK, OWEN F.   TR 5'10"   150 lbs.
B. Sept. 16, 1867, Brooklyn, N. Y.   D. Feb. 8, 1892, Brooklyn, N. Y.

	W	L	PCT	ERA	G	GS	CG	IP	H	BB	SO	ShO	W	L	SV	AB	H	HR	BA
1890 BUF P	0	0	—	6.75	1	0	0	4	8	2	2	0	0	0	0	*			

Watty Clark

CLARK, WILLIAM WATSON   BL TL 6'½"   175 lbs.
B. May 16, 1902, St. Joseph, La.   D. Mar. 4, 1972, Clearwater, Fla.

	W	L	PCT	ERA	G	GS	CG	IP	H	BB	SO	ShO	W	L	SV	AB	H	HR	BA
1924 CLE A	1	3	.250	7.01	12	1	0	25.2	38	14	6	0	1	2	0	9	2	0	.222
1927 BKN N	7	2	.778	2.32	27	3	1	73.2	74	19	32	0	5	2	2	21	3	0	.143
1928	12	9	.571	2.68	40	19	10	194.2	193	50	85	2	2	4	3	66	10	0	.152
1929	16	19	.457	3.74	41	36	19	279	295	71	140	3	0	3	1	97	16	0	.165
1930	13	13	.500	4.19	44	24	9	200	209	38	81	1	4	1	6	68	14	1	.206
1931	14	10	.583	3.20	34	28	16	233.1	243	52	96	3	1	0	1	84	21	0	.250

	W	L	PCT	ERA	G	GS	CG	IP	H	BB	SO	ShO	Relief Pitching W	L	SV	BATTING AB	H	HR	BA

Watty Clark continued

	W	L	PCT	ERA	G	GS	CG	IP	H	BB	SO	ShO	W	L	SV	AB	H	HR	BA
1932	20	12	.625	3.49	40	36	19	273	282	49	99	2	1	0	0	97	21	0	.216
1933 2 teams					BKN N (11G 2–4)			NY N (16G 3–4)											
" total	5	8	.385	4.75	27	13	4	94.2	119	17	25	1	2	1	1	24	5	0	.208
1934 2 teams					NY N (5G 1–2)			BKN N (17G 2–0)											
" total	3	2	.600	5.93	22	5	1	44	63	14	16	0	1	0	0	14	2	0	.143
1935 BKN N	13	8	.619	3.30	33	25	11	207	215	28	35	1	4	0	0	79	14	0	.177
1936	7	11	.389	4.43	33	16	1	120	162	28	28	1	3	2	2	39	9	0	.231
1937	0	0	–	7.71	2	0	0	2.1	4	3	0	0	0	0	0	0	0	0	–
12 yrs.	111	97	.534	3.66	355	206	91	1747.1	1897	383	643	14	24	15	16	598	117	1	.196

Alan Clarke

CLARKE, ALAN THOMAS (Lefty) BL TL 5'11" 180 lbs.
B. Mar. 8, 1896, Clarksville, Md. D. Mar. 11, 1975, Cheverly, Mass.

	W	L	PCT	ERA	G	GS	CG	IP	H	BB	SO	ShO	W	L	SV	AB	H	HR	BA
1921 CIN N	0	1	.000	5.40	1	1	1	5	7	2	1	0	0	0	0	1	0	0	.000

Dad Clarke

CLARKE, WILLIAM H. BB TR
B. Jan. 7, 1865, Oswego, N. Y. D. June 3, 1911, Lorain, Ohio

	W	L	PCT	ERA	G	GS	CG	IP	H	BB	SO	ShO	W	L	SV	AB	H	HR	BA
1888 CHI N	1	0	1.000	5.06	2	2	1	16	23	6	6	0	0	0	0	7	2	1	.286
1891 COL AA	1	2	.333	6.86	4	3	2	21	30	16	2	0	0	0	0	9	1	0	.111
1894 NY N	3	4	.429	4.93	15	6	5	84	114	26	15	0	0	1	1	37	8	0	.216
1895	18	15	.545	3.39	37	30	27	281.2	336	60	67	1	1	4	1	121	29	0	.240
1896	17	24	.415	4.26	48	40	33	351	431	60	66	1	2	0	1	147	30	0	.204
1897 2 teams					NY N (6G 2–1)			LOU N (4G 1–3)											
" total	3	4	.429	4.92	10	8	6	64	87	20	16	0	1	0	0	30	5	0	.167
1898 LOU N	0	1	.000	5.00	1	1	1	10	10	2	1	0	0	0	0	3	0	0	.000
7 yrs.	43	50	.462	4.17	117	90	75	826.2	1031	190	173	2	3	5	3	354	75	1	.212

Henry Clarke

CLARKE, HENRY TEFFT BR TR
B. Aug. 4, 1875, Bellevue, Neb. D. Mar. 28, 1950, Colorado Springs, Colo.

	W	L	PCT	ERA	G	GS	CG	IP	H	BB	SO	ShO	W	L	SV	AB	H	HR	BA
1897 CLE N	0	4	.000	5.87	5	4	3	30.2	32	12	3	0	0	0	0	25	7	0	.280
1898 CHI N	1	0	1.000	2.00	1	1	1	9	8	5	1	0	0	0	0	4	1	0	.250
2 yrs.	1	4	.200	4.99	6	5	4	39.2	40	17	4	0	0	0	0	29	8	0	.276

Rufe Clarke

CLARKE, RUFUS RIVERS BR TR 6'1" 203 lbs.
Brother of Sumpter Clarke.
B. Apr. 13, 1900, Estill, S. C. D. Feb. 8, 1983, Columbia, S. C.

	W	L	PCT	ERA	G	GS	CG	IP	H	BB	SO	ShO	W	L	SV	AB	H	HR	BA
1923 DET A	1	1	.500	4.50	5	0	0	6	6	6	2	0	1	1	0	0	0	0	–
1924	0	0	–	3.38	2	0	0	5.1	3	5	1	0	0	0	0	1	0	0	.000
2 yrs.	1	1	.500	3.97	7	0	0	11.1	9	11	3	0	1	1	0	1	0	0	.000

Stan Clarke

CLARKE, STANLEY MARTIN BR TL 6'1" 180 lbs.
B. Aug. 9, 1960, Toledo, Ohio

	W	L	PCT	ERA	G	GS	CG	IP	H	BB	SO	ShO	W	L	SV	AB	H	HR	BA
1983 TOR A	1	1	.500	3.27	10	0	0	11	10	5	7	0	1	1	0	0	0	0	–

Webbo Clarke

CLARKE, VIBERT ERNESTO BL TL 6' 165 lbs.
B. June 8, 1928, Cristobal, Canal Zone D. June 14, 1970, Cristobal, Canal Zone

	W	L	PCT	ERA	G	GS	CG	IP	H	BB	SO	ShO	W	L	SV	AB	H	HR	BA
1955 WAS A	0	0	–	4.64	7	2	0	21.1	17	14	9	0	0	0	0	6	1	0	.167

Bill Clarkson

CLARKSON, WILLIAM HENRY (Blackie) BR TR 5'11" 160 lbs.
B. Sept. 27, 1898, Portsmouth, Va. D. Aug. 27, 1971, Raleigh, N. C.

	W	L	PCT	ERA	G	GS	CG	IP	H	BB	SO	ShO	W	L	SV	AB	H	HR	BA
1927 NY N	3	9	.250	4.36	26	7	2	86.2	92	52	28	0	3	2	2	20	1	0	.050
1928 2 teams					NY N (4G 0–0)			BOS N (19G 0–2)											
" total	0	2	.000	6.92	23	2	1	40.1	63	23	11	0	0	0	0	3	0	0	.000
1929 BOS N	0	1	.000	10.29	2	0	0	7	16	4	0	0	0	0	0	2	1	0	.500
3 yrs.	3	12	.200	5.44	51	9	3	134	171	79	39	0	3	2	2	25	2	0	.080

Dad Clarkson

CLARKSON, ARTHUR HAMILTON BR TR 5'10" 165 lbs.
Brother of Walter Clarkson. Brother of John Clarkson.
B. Aug. 31, 1866, Cambridge, Mass. D. Feb. 6, 1911, Cambridge, Mass.

	W	L	PCT	ERA	G	GS	CG	IP	H	BB	SO	ShO	W	L	SV	AB	H	HR	BA
1891 NY N	1	2	.333	2.89	5	2	1	28	24	18	11	0	1	0	0	9	4	0	.444
1892 BOS N	1	0	1.000	1.29	1	1	1	7	5	3	0	0	0	0	0	3	0	0	.000
1893 STL N	12	9	.571	3.48	24	21	17	186.1	194	79	37	1	1	0	0	75	10	0	.133
1894	8	17	.320	6.36	32	32	24	233.1	318	117	46	1	0	0	0	88	16	0	.182
1895 2 teams					STL N (7G 1–6)			BAL N (20G 12–3)											
" total	13	9	.591	4.92	27	21	17	203	260	90	32	0	2	1	0	80	9	1	.113
1896 BAL N	4	2	.667	4.98	7	4	3	47	72	18	7	0	2	0	0	18	5	0	.278
6 yrs.	39	39	.500	4.90	96	81	63	704.2	873	325	133	2	6	1	0	273	44	1	.161

John Clarkson

CLARKSON, JOHN GIBSON BR TR 5'10" 150 lbs.
Brother of Dad Clarkson. Brother of Walter Clarkson.
B. July 1, 1861, Cambridge, Mass. D. Feb. 4, 1909, Cambridge, Mass.
Hall of Fame 1963.

	W	L	PCT	ERA	G	GS	CG	IP	H	BB	SO	ShO	W	L	SV	AB	H	HR	BA
1882 WOR N	1	2	.333	4.50	3	3	2	24	49	2	3	0	0	0	0	11	4	0	.364
1884 CHI N	10	3	.769	2.14	14	13	12	118	94	25	102	0	0	0	0	84	22	3	.262
1885	53	16	.768	1.85	70	70	68	623	497	97	318	10	0	0	0	283	61	4	.216
1886	35	17	.673	2.41	55	55	50	466.2	419	86	340	3	0	0	0	210	49	3	.233
1887	38	21	.644	3.08	60	59	56	523	513	92	237	2	1	0	0	215	52	6	.242
1888 BOS N	33	20	.623	2.76	54	54	53	483.1	448	119	223	3	0	0	0	205	40	1	.195
1889	49	19	.721	2.73	73	72	68	620	589	203	284	8	0	0	1	262	54	2	.206
1890	25	18	.581	3.27	44	44	43	383	370	140	138	2	0	0	0	173	43	2	.249
1891	33	19	.635	2.79	55	51	47	460.2	435	154	141	3	0	1	3	187	42	0	.225
1892 2 teams					BOS N (16G 8–6)			CLE N (29G 17–10)											
" total	25	16	.610	2.48	45	44	42	389	350	132	139	5	0	0	1	158	27	1	.171
1893 CLE N	16	17	.485	4.45	36	35	31	295	358	95	62	0	0	1	0	131	27	1	.206
1894	8	9	.471	4.42	22	18	13	150.2	173	46	28	1	0	2	0	55	11	1	.200
12 yrs.	326	177	.648	2.81	531	518	485	4536.1	4295	1191	2015	37	1	4	5	*			
	10th						8th												

	W	L	PCT	ERA	G	GS	CG	IP	H	BB	SO	ShO	Relief Pitching W	L	SV	BATTING AB	H	HR	BA

Walter Clarkson

CLARKSON, WALTER HAMILTON BR TR 5'10" 150 lbs.
Brother of John Clarkson.   Brother of Dad Clarkson.
B. Nov. 3, 1878, Cambridge, Mass.   D. Oct. 10, 1946, Cambridge, Mass.

	W	L	PCT	ERA	G	GS	CG	IP	H	BB	SO	ShO	W	L	SV	AB	H	HR	BA
1904 NY A	1	2	.333	5.02	13	4	2	66.1	63	25	43	0	1	0	1	26	7	0	.269
1905	3	3	.500	3.91	9	4	3	46	40	13	35	0	2	1	0	19	1	0	.053
1906	9	4	.692	2.32	32	16	9	151	135	55	64	3	1	0	0	51	8	0	.157
1907 2 teams		NY	A (5G 1–1)		CLE	A (17G 4–6)													
" total	5	7	.417	2.67	22	12	9	108	96	37	35	1	1	0	0	35	3	0	.086
1908 CLE A	0	0	—	10.80	2	1	0	3.1	6	2	1	0	0	0	0	1	1	0	1.000
5 yrs.	18	16	.529	3.17	78	37	23	374.2	340	132	178	4	5	1	1	132	20	0	.152

Gowell Claset

CLASET, GOWELL SYLVESTER (Lefty) BB TL 6'3½" 210 lbs.
B. Nov. 16, 1907, Battle Creek, Mich.   D. Mar. 8, 1981, St. Petersburg, Fla.

	W	L	PCT	ERA	G	GS	CG	IP	H	BB	SO	ShO	W	L	SV	AB	H	HR	BA
1933 PHI A	2	0	1.000	9.53	8	1	0	11.1	23	11	1	0	2	0	0	2	1	0	.500

Fritz Clausen

CLAUSEN, FREDERICK WILLIAM BR TL 5'11" 190 lbs.
B. Apr. 26, 1869, New York, N. Y.   D. Feb. 11, 1960, Memphis, Tenn.

	W	L	PCT	ERA	G	GS	CG	IP	H	BB	SO	ShO	W	L	SV	AB	H	HR	BA
1892 LOU N	9	13	.409	3.06	24	24	24	200	181	87	94	2	0	0	0	84	13	0	.155
1893 2 teams		LOU	N (5G 1–4)		CHI	N (10G 6–2)													
" total	7	6	.538	3.96	15	14	11	109	112	61	35	0	0	0	0	47	7	0	.149
1894 CHI N	0	1	.000	10.38	1	1	0	4.1	5	3	1	0	0	0	0	1	0	0	.000
1896 LOU N	0	2	.000	6.55	2	2	1	11	17	6	4	0	0	0	0	4	0	0	.000
4 yrs.	16	22	.421	3.58	42	41	36	324.1	315	157	134	2	0	0	1	136	20	0	.147

Al Clauss

CLAUSS, ALBERT STANLEY (Lefty) BL TL 5'10½" 178 lbs.
B. June 24, 1891, New Haven, Conn.   D. Sept. 13, 1952, New Haven, Conn.

	W	L	PCT	ERA	G	GS	CG	IP	H	BB	SO	ShO	W	L	SV	AB	H	HR	BA
1913 DET A	0	1	.000	4.73	5	1	0	13.1	11	12	1	0	0	0	0	4	0	0	.000

Ken Clay

CLAY, KENNETH EARL BR TR 6'3" 185 lbs.
B. Apr. 6, 1954, Lynchburg, Va.

	W	L	PCT	ERA	G	GS	CG	IP	H	BB	SO	ShO	W	L	SV	AB	H	HR	BA
1977 NY A	2	3	.400	4.34	21	3	0	56	53	24	20	0	2	1	1	0	0	0	—
1978	3	4	.429	4.28	28	6	0	75.2	89	21	32	0	3	4	0	0	0	0	—
1979	1	7	.125	5.42	32	5	0	78	88	25	28	0	1	3	2	0	0	0	—
1980 TEX A	2	3	.400	4.60	8	8	0	43	43	29	17	0	0	0	0	0	0	0	—
1981 SEA A	2	7	.222	4.63	22	14	0	101	116	42	32	0	0	1	0	0	0	0	—
5 yrs.	10	24	.294	4.68	111	36	0	353.2	389	141	129	0	6	9	3	0	0	0	—

LEAGUE CHAMPIONSHIP SERIES
	W	L	PCT	ERA	G	GS	CG	IP	H	BB	SO	ShO	W	L	SV	AB	H	HR	BA
1978 NY A	0	0	—	0.00	1	0	0	3.2	0	3	2	0	0	0	1	0	0	0	—

WORLD SERIES
	W	L	PCT	ERA	G	GS	CG	IP	H	BB	SO	ShO	W	L	SV	AB	H	HR	BA
1977 NY A	0	0	—	2.45	2	0	0	3.2	2	1	0	0	0	0	0	0	0	0	—
1978	0	0	—	11.57	1	0	0	2.1	4	2	2	0	0	0	0	0	0	0	—
2 yrs.	0	0	—	6.00	3	0	0	6	6	3	2	0	0	0	0	0	0	0	—

Mark Clear

CLEAR, MARK ALAN BR TR 6'4" 200 lbs.
B. May 27, 1956, Los Angeles, Calif.

	W	L	PCT	ERA	G	GS	CG	IP	H	BB	SO	ShO	W	L	SV	AB	H	HR	BA
1979 CAL A	11	5	.688	3.63	52	0	0	109	87	68	98	0	11	5	14	0	0	0	—
1980	11	11	.500	3.31	58	0	0	106	82	65	105	0	11	11	9	0	0	0	—
1981 BOS A	8	3	.727	4.09	34	0	0	77	69	51	82	0	8	3	9	0	0	0	—
1982	14	9	.609	3.00	55	0	0	105	92	61	109	0	14	9	14	0	0	0	—
1983	4	5	.444	6.28	48	0	0	96	101	68	81	0	4	5	4	0	0	0	—
1984	8	3	.727	4.03	47	0	0	67	47	70	76	0	8	3	8	0	0	0	—
6 yrs.	56	36	.609	4.02	294	0	0	560	478	383	551	0	56	36	58	0	0	0	—

LEAGUE CHAMPIONSHIP SERIES
	W	L	PCT	ERA	G	GS	CG	IP	H	BB	SO	ShO	W	L	SV	AB	H	HR	BA
1979 CAL A	0	0	—	4.76	1	0	0	5.2	4	2	3	0	0	0	0	0	0	0	—

Joe Cleary

CLEARY, JOSEPH CHRISTOPHER (Fire) BR TR 5'9" 145 lbs.
B. Dec. 3, 1919, Cork City, Eire, Ireland

	W	L	PCT	ERA	G	GS	CG	IP	H	BB	SO	ShO	W	L	SV	AB	H	HR	BA
1945 WAS A	0	0	—	189.00	1	0	0	.1	5	3	1	0	0	0	0	0	0	0	—

Roger Clemens

CLEMENS, WILLIAM ROGER BR TR 6'4" 205 lbs.
B. Aug. 4, 1962, Dayton, Ohio

	W	L	PCT	ERA	G	GS	CG	IP	H	BB	SO	ShO	W	L	SV	AB	H	HR	BA
1984 BOS A	9	4	.692	4.32	21	20	5	133.1	146	29	126	1	0	0	0	0	0	0	—

Bill Clemensen

CLEMENSEN, WILLIAM MELVILLE BR TR 6'1" 193 lbs.
B. June 20, 1919, New Brunswick, N. J.

	W	L	PCT	ERA	G	GS	CG	IP	H	BB	SO	ShO	W	L	SV	AB	H	HR	BA
1939 PIT N	0	1	.000	7.33	12	1	0	27	32	20	73	0	0	0	0	6	2	0	.333
1941	1	0	1.000	2.77	2	1	1	13	7	7	4	0	0	0	0	4	0	0	.000
1946	0	0	—	0.00	1	0	0	2	0	0	2	0	0	0	0	0	0	0	—
3 yrs.	1	1	.500	5.57	15	2	1	42	39	27	79	0	0	0	0	10	2	0	.200

Lance Clemons

CLEMONS, LANCE LEVIS BL TL 6'2" 205 lbs.
B. July 6, 1947, Philadelphia, Pa.

	W	L	PCT	ERA	G	GS	CG	IP	H	BB	SO	ShO	W	L	SV	AB	H	HR	BA
1971 KC A	1	0	1.000	4.13	10	3	0	24	26	12	20	0	1	0	0	7	2	1	.286
1972 STL N	0	1	.000	10.13	3	1	0	5.1	8	5	2	0	0	0	0	1	0	0	.000
1974 BOS A	1	0	1.000	10.50	6	0	0	6	8	4	1	0	1	0	0	0	0	0	—
3 yrs.	2	1	.667	6.11	19	4	0	35.1	42	21	23	0	2	0	0	8	2	1	.250

Reggie Cleveland

CLEVELAND, REGINALD LESLIE BR TR 6'1" 195 lbs.
B. May 23, 1948, Swift Current, Sask., Canada

	W	L	PCT	ERA	G	GS	CG	IP	H	BB	SO	ShO	W	L	SV	AB	H	HR	BA
1969 STL N	0	0	—	9.00	1	1	0	4	7	1	3	0	0	0	0	1	0	0	.000
1970	0	4	.000	7.62	16	1	0	26	31	18	22	0	0	3	0	4	1	0	.250
1971	12	12	.500	4.01	34	34	10	222	238	53	148	2	0	0	0	82	14	0	.171
1972	14	15	.483	3.94	33	33	11	230.2	229	60	153	3	0	0	0	71	17	0	.239
1973	14	10	.583	3.01	32	32	6	224	211	61	122	3	0	0	0	74	17	0	.230
1974 BOS A	12	14	.462	4.32	41	27	10	221	234	69	103	0	2	1	0	0	0	0	—
1975	13	9	.591	4.43	31	20	3	170.2	173	52	78	1	3	1	0	0	0	0	—

	W	L	PCT	ERA	G	GS	CG	IP	H	BB	SO	ShO	Relief Pitching W	L	SV	BATTING AB	H	HR	BA

Reggie Cleveland continued

	W	L	PCT	ERA	G	GS	CG	IP	H	BB	SO	ShO	W	L	SV	AB	H	HR	BA
1976	10	9	.526	3.07	41	14	3	170	159	61	76	0	4	4	2	0	0	0	–
1977	11	8	.579	4.26	36	27	9	190.1	211	43	85	1	0	0	2	0	0	0	–
1978 2 teams		BOS	A (1G 0–1)			TEX	A (53G 5–7)												
" total	5	8	.385	3.08	54	0	0	76	66	23	46	0	5	8	12	0	0	0	–
1979 MIL A	1	5	.167	6.71	29	1	0	55	77	23	22	0	1	4	4	0	0	0	–
1980	11	9	.550	3.74	45	13	5	154	150	49	54	0	7	4	4	0	0	0	–
1981	2	3	.400	5.12	35	0	0	65	57	30	18	0	2	3	1	0	0	0	–
13 yrs.	105	106	.498	4.02	428	203	57	1808.2	1843	543	930	12	24	28	25	232	49	0	.211

LEAGUE CHAMPIONSHIP SERIES

1975 BOS A	0	0	–	5.40	1	1	0	5	7	1	2	0	0	0	0	0	0	0	–

WORLD SERIES

1975 BOS A	0	1	.000	6.75	3	1	0	6.2	7	3	5	0	0	0	0	2	0	0	.000

Tex Clevenger

CLEVENGER, TRUMAN EUGENE
B. July 9, 1932, Visalia, Calif.
BR TR 6'1" 180 lbs.

	W	L	PCT	ERA	G	GS	CG	IP	H	BB	SO	ShO	W	L	SV	AB	H	HR	BA
1954 BOS A	2	4	.333	4.79	23	8	1	67.2	67	29	43	0	1	0	0	14	3	0	.214
1956 WAS A	0	0	–	5.40	20	1	0	31.2	33	21	17	0	0	0	0	2	0	0	.000
1957	7	6	.538	4.19	52	9	2	139.2	139	47	75	0	5	4	8	33	7	0	.212
1958	9	9	.500	4.35	55	4	0	124	119	50	70	0	0	3	6	22	3	0	.136
1959	8	5	.615	3.91	50	7	2	117.1	114	51	71	2	5	2	8	23	4	0	.174
1960	5	11	.313	4.20	53	11	1	128.2	150	49	49	0	3	4	7	22	2	0	.091
1961 2 teams		LA	A (12G 2–1)			NY	A (21G 1–1)												
" total	3	2	.600	3.78	33	0	0	47.2	48	34	25	0	3	2	1	7	1	0	.143
1962 NY A	2	0	1.000	2.84	21	0	0	38	36	17	11	0	2	0	0	4	0	0	.000
8 yrs.	36	37	.493	4.18	307	40	6	694.2	706	298	361	2	19	15	30	127	20	0	.157

Stew Cliburn

CLIBURN, STEWART WALKER
Brother of Stan Cliburn.
B. Dec. 19, 1956, Jackson, Miss.
BR TR 6' 195 lbs.

	W	L	PCT	ERA	G	GS	CG	IP	H	BB	SO	ShO	W	L	SV	AB	H	HR	BA
1984 CAL A	0	0	–	13.50	1	0	0	2	3	1	1	0	0	0	0	0	0	0	–

Jim Clinton

CLINTON, JAMES LAWRENCE (Big Jim)
B. Aug. 10, 1850, New York, N. Y. D. Sept. 3, 1921, Brooklyn, N. Y.
Manager 1872.
BR TR 5'8½" 174 lbs.

	W	L	PCT	ERA	G	GS	CG	IP	H	BB	SO	ShO	W	L	SV	AB	H	HR	BA
1876 LOU N	0	1	.000	6.00	1	1	1	9	12	0	1	0	0	0	0	*			

Tony Cloninger

CLONINGER, TONY LEE
B. Aug. 13, 1940, Lincoln, N. C.
BR TR 6' 210 lbs.

	W	L	PCT	ERA	G	GS	CG	IP	H	BB	SO	ShO	W	L	SV	AB	H	HR	BA
1961 MIL N	7	2	.778	5.25	19	10	3	84	84	33	51	0	2	0	0	30	5	0	.167
1962	8	3	.727	4.30	24	15	4	111	113	46	69	1	0	0	0	39	4	0	.103
1963	9	11	.450	3.78	41	18	4	145.1	131	63	100	2	2	4	1	37	5	0	.135
1964	19	14	.576	3.56	38	34	15	242.2	206	82	163	3	1	0	2	87	21	0	.241
1965	24	11	.686	3.29	40	38	16	279	247	119	211	1	0	0	1	105	17	1	.162
1966 ATL N	14	11	.560	4.12	39	38	11	257.2	253	116	178	1	0	0	1	111	26	5	.234
1967	4	7	.364	5.17	16	16	1	76.2	85	31	55	0	0	0	0	25	5	0	.200
1968 2 teams		ATL	N (8G 1–3)			CIN	N (17G 4–3)												
" total	5	6	.455	4.08	25	18	2	110.1	96	59	72	2	1	2	0	38	7	2	.184
1969 CIN N	11	17	.393	5.02	35	34	6	190	184	103	103	2	0	0	0	72	12	1	.167
1970	9	7	.563	3.83	30	18	0	148	136	78	56	0	1	1	1	47	10	2	.213
1971	3	6	.333	3.90	28	8	1	97	79	49	51	1	0	2	0	27	7	0	.259
1972 STL N	0	2	.000	5.19	17	0	0	26	29	19	11	0	0	2	0	3	0	0	.000
12 yrs.	113	97	.538	4.07	352	247	63	1767.2	1643	798	1120	13	7	11	6	621	119	11	.192

LEAGUE CHAMPIONSHIP SERIES

1970 CIN N	0	0	–	3.60	1	1	0	5	7	4	1	0	0	0	0	1	0	0	.000

WORLD SERIES

1970 CIN N	0	1	.000	7.36	2	1	0	7.1	10	5	4	0	0	0	0	2	0	0	.000

Al Closter

CLOSTER, ALAN EDWARD
B. June 15, 1943, Creighton, Neb.
BL TL 6'2" 190 lbs.

	W	L	PCT	ERA	G	GS	CG	IP	H	BB	SO	ShO	W	L	SV	AB	H	HR	BA
1966 WAS A	0	0	–	0.00	1	0	0	.1	1	2	0	0	0	0	0	0	0	0	–
1971 NY A	2	2	.500	5.14	14	1	0	28	33	13	22	0	2	1	0	6	0	0	.000
1972	0	0	–	13.50	2	0	0	2	2	4	2	0	0	0	0	1	0	0	.000
1973 ATL N	0	0	–	15.75	4	0	0	4	7	4	2	0	0	0	0	0	0	0	–
4 yrs.	2	2	.500	6.82	21	1	0	34.1	43	23	26	0	2	1	0	7	0	0	.000

Ed Clough

CLOUGH, EDGAR GEORGE (Spec)
B. Oct. 11, 1905, Wiconisco, Pa. D. Jan. 30, 1944, Harrisburg, Pa.
BL TL 6' 188 lbs.

	W	L	PCT	ERA	G	GS	CG	IP	H	BB	SO	ShO	W	L	SV	AB	H	HR	BA
1925 STL N	0	1	.000	8.10	3	1	0	10	11	5	3	0	0	0	0	4	1	0	.250
1926	0	0	–	22.50	1	0	0	2	5	3	0	0	0	0	0	1	0	0	.000
2 yrs.	0	1	.000	10.50	4	1	0	12	16	8	3	0	0	0	0	*			

Bill Clowers

CLOWERS, WILLIAM PERRY
B. 1898, San Marcos, Tex. D. Jan. 13, 1978, Sweeney, Tex.
BL TL 5'11" 175 lbs.

	W	L	PCT	ERA	G	GS	CG	IP	H	BB	SO	ShO	W	L	SV	AB	H	HR	BA
1926 BOS A	0	0	–	0.00	2	0	0	1.2	2	0	0	0	0	0	0	0	0	0	–

David Clyde

CLYDE, DAVID EUGENE
B. Apr. 22, 1955, Houston, Tex.
BL TL 6'1½" 180 lbs.

	W	L	PCT	ERA	G	GS	CG	IP	H	BB	SO	ShO	W	L	SV	AB	H	HR	BA
1973 TEX A	4	8	.333	5.03	18	18	0	93	106	54	74	0	0	0	0	0	0	0	–
1974	3	9	.250	4.38	28	21	4	117	129	47	52	0	0	0	0	0	0	0	–
1975	0	1	.000	5.72	1	1	0	7	6	6	2	0	0	0	0	0	0	0	–
1978 CLE A	8	11	.421	4.28	28	25	5	153.1	166	60	83	0	0	0	0	0	0	0	–
1979	3	4	.429	5.87	9	8	1	46	50	13	17	0	0	0	0	0	0	0	–
5 yrs.	18	33	.353	4.63	84	73	10	416.1	457	180	228	0	0	0	0	0	0	0	–

	W	L	PCT	ERA	G	GS	CG	IP	H	BB	SO	ShO	Relief Pitching W	L	SV	BATTING AB	H	HR	BA

Tom Clyde

CLYDE, THOMAS KNOX
B. Aug. 17, 1923, Wachapreague, Va.   BR TR 6'3"   195 lbs.

	W	L	PCT	ERA	G	GS	CG	IP	H	BB	SO	ShO	W	L	SV	AB	H	HR	BA
1943 PHI A	0	0	–	9.00	4	0	0	6	7	4	0	0	0	0	0	2	0	0	.000

Andy Coakley

COAKLEY, ANDREW JAMES
Played as Jack McAllister 1902.
B. Nov. 20, 1882, Providence, R. I.   D. Sept. 27, 1963, New York, N. Y.   BL TR 6'   165 lbs.

	W	L	PCT	ERA	G	GS	CG	IP	H	BB	SO	ShO	W	L	SV	AB	H	HR	BA
1902 PHI A	2	1	.667	2.67	3	3	3	27	25	9	9	0	0	0	0	8	3	0	.375
1903	0	3	.000	5.50	6	3	2	37.2	48	11	20	0	0	0	0	15	3	0	.200
1904	4	4	.500	2.03	8	8	8	62	50	23	33	2	0	0	0	23	2	0	.087
1905	20	7	.741	1.84	35	31	22	255	227	73	145	3	1	0	0	90	13	0	.144
1906	7	8	.467	3.14	22	16	10	149	144	44	59	0	1	0	0	49	7	0	.143
1907 CIN N	17	16	.515	2.34	37	30	21	265.1	269	79	89	1	4	1	1	84	6	0	.071
1908 2 teams			CIN	N (32G 8–18)		CHI	N (4G 2–0)												
" total	10	18	.357	1.78	36	31	22	262.2	233	70	68	5	0	1	2	82	7	0	.085
1909 CHI N	0	1	.000	18.00	1	1	0	2	7	3	1	0	0	0	0	0	0	0	–
1911 NY A	0	1	.000	5.40	2	1	1	11.2	20	2	4	0	0	0	0	4	1	0	.250
9 yrs.	60	59	.504	2.36	150	124	89	1072.1	1023	314	428	11	6	2	3	355	42	0	.118

WORLD SERIES
| 1905 PHI A | 0 | 1 | .000 | 2.00 | 1 | 1 | 1 | 9 | 9 | 5 | 2 | 0 | 0 | 0 | 0 | 2 | 0 | 0 | .000 |

Jim Coates

COATES, JAMES ALTON
B. Aug. 4, 1932, Farnham, Va.   BR TR 6'4"   192 lbs.

	W	L	PCT	ERA	G	GS	CG	IP	H	BB	SO	ShO	W	L	SV	AB	H	HR	BA
1956 NY A	0	0	–	13.50	2	0	0	1	4	0	0	0	0	0	0	0	0	0	–
1959	6	1	.857	2.87	37	4	2	100.1	89	36	64	0	4	1	3	21	2	0	.095
1960	13	3	.813	4.28	35	18	6	149.1	139	66	73	2	4	0	1	48	12	0	.250
1961	11	5	.688	3.44	43	11	4	141.1	128	53	80	1	6	2	5	35	1	0	.029
1962	7	6	.538	4.44	50	6	0	117.2	119	50	67	0	7	5	6	32	4	0	.125
1963 2 teams			WAS	A (20G 2–4)		CIN	N (9G 0–0)												
" total	2	4	.333	5.34	29	2	0	60.2	72	28	42	0	2	4	0	9	0	0	.000
1965 CAL A	2	0	1.000	3.54	17	0	0	28	23	16	15	0	2	0	3	1	0	0	.000
1966	1	1	.500	3.98	9	4	1	31.2	32	10	16	1	0	0	0	11	1	0	.091
1967	1	2	.333	4.30	25	1	0	52.1	47	23	39	0	1	1	0	3	1	0	.333
9 yrs.	43	22	.662	4.00	247	46	13	683.1	650	286	396	4	26	13	18	160	21	0	.131

WORLD SERIES
1960 NY A	0	0	–	5.68	3	0	0	6.1	6	1	3	0	0	0	0	1	0	0	.000
1961	0	0	–	0.00	1	0	0	4	1	1	2	0	0	0	1	1	0	0	.000
1962	0	1	.000	6.75	2	0	0	2.2	1	1	3	0	0	0	0	0	0	0	–
3 yrs.	0	1	.000	4.15	6	0	0	13	8	3	8	0	0	0	1	2	0	0	.000

George Cobb

COBB, GEORGE WASHINGTON
B. San Francisco, Calif.   Deceased.

	W	L	PCT	ERA	G	GS	CG	IP	H	BB	SO	ShO	W	L	SV	AB	H	HR	BA
1892 BAL N	10	37	.213	4.86	53	47	42	394.1	495	140	159	0	1	1	0	172	36	1	.209

Herb Cobb

COBB, HERBERT EDWARD
B. Aug. 6, 1904, Pinetops, N. C.   D. Jan. 8, 1980, Tarboro, N. C.   BR TR 5'11"   150 lbs.

	W	L	PCT	ERA	G	GS	CG	IP	H	BB	SO	ShO	W	L	SV	AB	H	HR	BA
1929 STL A	0	0	–	36.00	1	0	0	1	3	1	0	0	0	0	0	0	0	0	–

Ty Cobb

COBB, TYRUS RAYMOND (The Georgia Peach)
B. Dec. 18, 1886, Narrows, Ga.   D. July 17, 1961, Atlanta, Ga.   BL TR 6'1"   175 lbs.
Manager 1921-26.
Hall of Fame 1936.

	W	L	PCT	ERA	G	GS	CG	IP	H	BB	SO	ShO	W	L	SV	AB	H	HR	BA
1918 DET A	0	0	–	4.50	2	0	0	4	6	2	0	0	0	0	0	421	161	3	.382
1925	0	0	–	0.00	1	0	0	1	0	0	0	0	0	0	1	415	157	12	.378
2 yrs.	0	0	–	3.60	3	0	0	5	6	2	0	0	0	0	1	*			

Jaime Cocanower

COCANOWER, JAMES STANLEY
B. Feb. 14, 1957, Balboa Hgts., Canal Zone   BR TR 6'4"   200 lbs.

	W	L	PCT	ERA	G	GS	CG	IP	H	BB	SO	ShO	W	L	SV	AB	H	HR	BA
1983 MIL A	2	0	1.000	1.80	5	3	1	30	21	12	8	0	0	0	0	0	0	0	–
1984	8	16	.333	4.02	33	27	1	174.2	188	78	65	0	0	2	0	0	0	0	–
2 yrs.	10	16	.385	3.69	38	30	2	204.2	209	90	73	0	0	2	0	0	0	0	–

Al Cochran

COCHRAN, ALVIN JACKSON (Goat)
B. Jan. 31, 1891, Concord, Ga.   D. May 23, 1947, Atlanta, Ga.   BR TR 5'10"   175 lbs.

	W	L	PCT	ERA	G	GS	CG	IP	H	BB	SO	ShO	W	L	SV	AB	H	HR	BA
1915 CIN N	0	0	–	9.00	1	0	0	2	5	0	1	0	0	0	0	0	0	0	–

Gene Cocreham

COCREHAM, EUGENE
B. Nov. 14, 1884, Luling, Tex.   D. Dec. 27, 1945, Luling, Tex.   BR TR 6'3½"   192 lbs.

	W	L	PCT	ERA	G	GS	CG	IP	H	BB	SO	ShO	W	L	SV	AB	H	HR	BA
1913 BOS N	0	1	.000	7.56	7	1	0	8.1	13	4	3	0	0	0	0	4	0	0	.000
1914	3	4	.429	4.84	15	3	1	44.2	48	27	15	0	2	2	0	10	1	0	.100
1915	0	0	–	5.40	1	0	0	1.2	3	0	0	0	0	0	0	0	0	0	–
3 yrs.	3	5	.375	5.27	17	4	1	54.2	64	31	18	0	2	2	0	14	1	0	.071

Chris Codiroli

CODIROLI, CHRISTOPHER ALLEN
B. Mar. 26, 1958, Oxnard, Calif.   BR TR 6'   165 lbs.

	W	L	PCT	ERA	G	GS	CG	IP	H	BB	SO	ShO	W	L	SV	AB	H	HR	BA
1982 OAK A	1	2	.333	4.32	3	3	0	16.2	16	4	5	0	0	0	0	0	0	0	–
1983	12	12	.500	4.46	37	31	7	205.2	208	72	85	2	1	1	1	0	0	0	–
1984	6	4	.600	5.84	28	14	1	89.1	111	34	44	0	0	0	1	0	0	0	–
3 yrs.	19	18	.514	4.85	68	48	8	311.2	335	110	134	2	1	1	2	0	0	0	–

Dick Coffman

COFFMAN, SAMUEL RICHARD
Brother of Slick Coffman.
B. Dec. 18, 1906, Veto, Ala.   D. Mar. 24, 1972, Athens, Ala.   BR TR 6'2"   195 lbs.

	W	L	PCT	ERA	G	GS	CG	IP	H	BB	SO	ShO	W	L	SV	AB	H	HR	BA
1927 WAS A	0	1	.000	3.38	5	2	0	16	20	2	5	0	0	0	0	3	1	0	.333
1928 STL A	4	5	.444	6.09	29	7	3	85.2	122	37	25	0	0	1	1	23	1	0	.043
1929	1	1	.500	5.98	27	3	1	52.2	61	14	11	1	0	1	1	7	0	0	.000

	W	L	PCT	ERA	G	GS	CG	IP	H	BB	SO	ShO	Relief Pitching W	L	SV	BATTING AB	H	HR	BA

Dick Coffman continued

	W	L	PCT	ERA	G	GS	CG	IP	H	BB	SO	ShO	W	L	SV	AB	H	HR	BA
1930	8	18	.308	5.14	38	30	12	196	250	69	54	1	1	1	1	66	9	0	.136
1931	9	13	.409	3.88	32	17	11	169.1	159	51	39	2	2	4	1	51	4	0	.078
1932 2 teams			STL	A	(9G 5–3)		WAS	A	(22G 1–6)										
" total	6	9	.400	4.06	31	15	5	137.1	158	52	31	2	1	1	0	44	3	0	.068
1933 STL A	3	7	.300	5.89	21	13	3	81	114	39	19	1	0	1	1	27	1	0	.037
1934	9	10	.474	4.53	40	21	6	173	212	59	55	1	2	0	3	51	11	0	.216
1935	5	11	.313	6.14	41	18	5	143.2	206	46	34	0	1	3	3	41	6	0	.146
1936 NY N	7	5	.583	3.90	42	2	0	101.2	119	23	26	0	7	3	7	20	4	0	.200
1937	8	3	.727	3.04	42	1	0	80	93	31	30	0	8	3	3	19	7	0	.368
1938	8	4	.667	3.48	51	3	1	111.1	116	21	21	1	7	2	12	28	2	0	.071
1939	1	2	.333	3.08	28	0	0	38	50	6	9	0	1	2	3	4	0	0	.000
1940 BOS N	1	5	.167	5.40	31	0	0	48.1	63	11	11	0	1	5	3	12	1	0	.083
1945 PHI N	2	1	.667	5.13	14	0	0	26.1	39	2	2	0	2	1	0	4	1	0	.250
15 yrs.	72	95	.431	4.65	472	132	47	1460.1	1782	463	372	9	33	28	38	400	51	0	.128

WORLD SERIES

	W	L	PCT	ERA	G	GS	CG	IP	H	BB	SO	ShO	W	L	SV	AB	H	HR	BA
1936 NY N	0	0	–	32.40	2	0	0	1.2	5	1	1	0	0	0	0	0	0	0	–
1937	0	0	–	4.15	2	0	0	4.1	2	5	1	0	0	0	0	1	0	0	.000
2 yrs.	0	0	–	12.00	4	0	0	6	7	6	2	0	0	0	0	1	0	0	.000

Slick Coffman

COFFMAN, GEORGE DAVID
Brother of Dick Coffman.
B. Dec. 11, 1910, Veto, Ala.
BR TR 6' 155 lbs.

	W	L	PCT	ERA	G	GS	CG	IP	H	BB	SO	ShO	W	L	SV	AB	H	HR	BA
1937 DET A	7	5	.583	4.37	28	5	1	101	121	39	22	0	5	3	0	29	5	0	.172
1938	4	4	.500	6.02	39	6	1	95.2	120	48	31	0	3	1	2	24	4	0	.167
1939	2	1	.667	6.38	23	1	0	42.1	51	22	10	0	2	1	0	5	0	0	.000
1940 STL A	2	2	.500	6.27	31	4	1	74.2	108	23	26	0	1	0	1	15	3	0	.200
4 yrs.	15	12	.556	5.60	121	16	3	313.2	400	132	89	0	11	5	3	73	12	0	.164

Dick Cogan

COGAN, RICHARD HENRY
B. Dec. 5, 1871, Paterson, N. J.   D. May 2, 1948, Paterson, N. J.
BR TR 5'7" 150 lbs.

	W	L	PCT	ERA	G	GS	CG	IP	H	BB	SO	ShO	W	L	SV	AB	H	HR	BA
1897 BAL N	0	0	–	13.50	1	0	0	2	4	2	0	0	0	0	0	1	0	0	.000
1899 CHI N	2	3	.400	4.30	5	5	5	44	54	24	9	0	0	0	0	25	5	0	.200
1900 NY N	0	0	–	6.75	2	0	0	8	10	6	1	0	0	0	0	8	1	0	.125
3 yrs.	2	3	.400	5.00	8	5	5	54	68	32	10	0	0	0	0	34	6	0	.176

Hy Cohen

COHEN, HYMAN
B. Jan. 29, 1931, Brooklyn, N. Y.
BR TR 6'5" 215 lbs.

	W	L	PCT	ERA	G	GS	CG	IP	H	BB	SO	ShO	W	L	SV	AB	H	HR	BA
1955 CHI N	0	0	–	7.94	7	1	0	17	28	10	4	0	0	0	0	3	0	0	.000

Sid Cohen

COHEN, SYDNEY HARRY
Brother of Andy Cohen.
B. May 7, 1908, Baltimore, Md.
BB TL 5'11" 180 lbs.

	W	L	PCT	ERA	G	GS	CG	IP	H	BB	SO	ShO	W	L	SV	AB	H	HR	BA
1934 WAS A	1	1	.500	7.50	3	2	2	18	25	6	6	0	0	0	0	11	3	0	.273
1936	0	2	.000	5.25	19	1	0	36	44	14	21	0	0	1	1	8	0	0	.000
1937	2	4	.333	3.11	33	0	0	55	64	17	22	0	2	4	4	14	2	0	.143
3 yrs.	3	7	.300	4.54	55	3	2	109	133	37	49	0	2	5	5	33	5	0	.152

Rocky Colavito

COLAVITO, ROCCO DOMENICO
B. Aug. 10, 1933, New York, N. Y.
BR TR 6'3" 190 lbs.

	W	L	PCT	ERA	G	GS	CG	IP	H	BB	SO	ShO	W	L	SV	AB	H	HR	BA
1958 CLE A	0	0	–	0.00	1	0	0	3	0	3	1	0	0	0	0	489	148	41	.303
1968 NY A	1	0	1.000	0.00	1	0	0	2.2	1	2	1	0	1	0	0	204	43	8	.211
2 yrs.	1	0	1.000	0.00	2	0	0	5.2	1	5	2	0	1	0	0	*			

Vince Colbert

COLBERT, VINCENT NORMAN
B. Dec. 20, 1945, Washington, D. C.
BR TR 6'4" 200 lbs.

	W	L	PCT	ERA	G	GS	CG	IP	H	BB	SO	ShO	W	L	SV	AB	H	HR	BA
1970 CLE A	1	1	.500	7.26	23	0	0	31	37	16	17	0	1	1	2	2	0	0	.000
1971	7	6	.538	3.97	50	10	2	143	140	71	74	0	2	1	2	29	4	0	.138
1972	1	7	.125	4.56	22	11	1	75	74	38	36	1	0	0	0	20	4	0	.200
3 yrs.	9	14	.391	4.55	95	21	3	249	251	125	127	1	3	2	4	51	8	0	.157

Jim Colborn

COLBORN, JAMES WILLIAM
B. May 22, 1946, Santa Paula, Calif.
BR TR 6' 185 lbs.

	W	L	PCT	ERA	G	GS	CG	IP	H	BB	SO	ShO	W	L	SV	AB	H	HR	BA
1969 CHI N	1	0	1.000	3.00	6	2	0	15	15	9	4	0	0	0	0	3	0	0	.000
1970	3	1	.750	3.58	34	5	0	73	88	23	50	0	2	0	4	15	1	0	.067
1971	0	1	.000	7.20	14	0	0	10	18	3	2	0	0	1	0	0	0	0	–
1972 MIL A	7	7	.500	3.10	39	12	4	148	135	43	97	1	2	0	0	37	3	0	.081
1973	20	12	.625	3.18	43	36	22	314.1	297	87	135	4	2	0	1	0	0		–
1974	10	13	.435	4.06	33	31	10	224	230	60	83	1	1	0	0	0	0		–
1975	11	13	.458	4.27	36	29	8	206.1	215	65	79	1	0	1	2	0	0		–
1976	9	15	.375	3.71	32	32	7	225.2	232	54	101	0	0	0	0	0	0		–
1977 KC A	18	14	.563	3.62	36	35	6	239	233	81	103	1	0	0	0	0	0		–
1978 2 teams			KC	A	(8G 1–2)		SEA	A	(20G 3–10)										
" total	4	12	.250	5.26	28	22	3	142	156	50	34	0	0	0	0	0	0		–
10 yrs.	83	88	.485	3.80	301	204	60	1597.1	1619	475	688	8	7	2	7	55	4	0	.073

Tom Colcolough

COLCOLOUGH, THOMAS BERNARD
B. Oct. 8, 1870, Charleston, S. C.   D. Dec. 10, 1919, Charleston, S. C.
BR TR 5'10" 189 lbs.

	W	L	PCT	ERA	G	GS	CG	IP	H	BB	SO	ShO	W	L	SV	AB	H	HR	BA
1893 PIT N	2	0	1.000	4.12	8	3	1	43.2	45	32	7	0	1	0	1	14	2	0	.143
1894	8	5	.615	7.08	22	14	11	148.2	207	70	29	0	1	0	0	70	14	0	.200
1895	1	1	.500	5.60	6	5	2	35.1	38	21	15	0	0	0	0	15	5	0	.333
1899 NY N	4	5	.444	3.97	11	8	7	81.2	85	41	14	0	1	0	0	37	10	0	.270
4 yrs.	15	11	.577	5.67	47	30	21	309.1	375	164	65	0	3	0	1	136	31	0	.228

	W	L	PCT	ERA	G	GS	CG	IP	H	BB	SO	ShO	Relief Pitching W	L	SV	Batting AB	H	HR	BA

Bert Cole

COLE, ALBERT GEORGE
B. July 1, 1896, San Francisco, Calif.   D. May 30, 1975, San Mateo, Calif.
BL TL 6'1"   180 lbs.

	W	L	PCT	ERA	G	GS	CG	IP	H	BB	SO	ShO	W	L	SV	AB	H	HR	BA
1921 DET A	7	4	.636	4.27	20	11	7	109.2	134	36	22	1	1	0	1	46	13	0	.283
1922	1	6	.143	4.88	23	5	2	79.1	105	39	21	1	0	3	0	25	4	0	.160
1923	13	5	.722	4.14	52	13	5	163	183	61	32	1	5	2	5	55	14	1	.255
1924	3	9	.250	4.69	28	11	2	109.1	135	35	16	1	1	2	2	37	10	0	.270
1925 2 teams			DET	A	(14G 2–3)		CLE	A	(13G 1–1)										
" total	3	4	.429	6.03	27	4	1	77.2	99	40	16	0	2	2	2	24	5	0	.208
1927 CHI A	1	4	.200	4.73	27	2	0	66.2	79	19	12	0	1	3	0	18	3	0	.167
6 yrs.	28	32	.467	4.67	177	46	17	605.2	735	230	119	4	10	12	10	205	49	1	.239

Dave Cole

COLE, DAVID BRUCE
B. Aug. 29, 1930, Williamsport, Md.
BR TR 6'2"   175 lbs.

	W	L	PCT	ERA	G	GS	CG	IP	H	BB	SO	ShO	W	L	SV	AB	H	HR	BA
1950 BOS N	0	1	.000	1.13	4	0	0	8	7	3	8	0	0	1	0	1	0	0	.000
1951	2	4	.333	4.26	23	7	1	67.2	64	64	33	0	0	2	0	17	6	1	.353
1952	1	1	.500	4.03	22	3	0	44.2	38	42	22	0	0	0	0	8	0	0	.000
1953 MIL N	0	1	.000	8.59	10	0	0	14.2	17	14	13	0	0	1	0	2	1	1	.500
1954 CHI N	3	8	.273	5.36	18	14	2	84	74	62	37	1	0	0	0	28	6	1	.214
1955 PHI N	0	3	.000	6.38	7	3	0	18.1	21	14	6	0	0	0	0	5	1	0	.200
6 yrs.	6	18	.250	4.93	84	27	3	237.1	221	199	119	1	0	4	0	61	14	3	.230

Ed Cole

COLE, EDWARD WILLIAM
Born Edward William Kisleauskas.
B. Mar. 22, 1909, Wilkes-Barre, Pa.
BR TR 5'11"   170 lbs.

	W	L	PCT	ERA	G	GS	CG	IP	H	BB	SO	ShO	W	L	SV	AB	H	HR	BA
1938 STL A	1	5	.167	5.18	36	6	1	88.2	116	48	26	0	0	2	3	21	3	0	.143
1939	0	2	.000	7.11	6	0	0	6.1	8	6	5	0	0	2	0	1	0	0	.000
2 yrs.	1	7	.125	5.31	42	6	1	95	124	54	31	0	0	4	3	22	3	0	.136

King Cole

COLE, LEONARD LESLIE
B. Apr. 15, 1886, Toledo, Iowa   D. Jan. 6, 1916, Bay City, Mich.
BR TR

	W	L	PCT	ERA	G	GS	CG	IP	H	BB	SO	ShO	W	L	SV	AB	H	HR	BA
1909 CHI N	1	0	1.000	0.00	1	1	1	9	6	3	1	1	0	0	0	4	3	0	.750
1910	20	4	.833	1.80	33	29	21	239.2	174	130	114	4	2	0	0	91	21	0	.231
1911	18	7	.720	3.13	32	27	13	221.1	188	99	101	2	1	1	0	79	12	0	.152
1912 2 teams			CHI	N	(8G 1–2)		PIT	N	(12G 2–2)										
" total	3	4	.429	7.68	20	7	2	68	97	26	20	0	1	1	0	20	4	0	.200
1914 NY A	11	9	.550	3.30	33	15	8	141.2	151	51	43	2	5	2	0	42	2	0	.048
1915	3	3	.500	3.18	10	6	2	51	41	22	19	0	1	0	1	13	1	0	.077
6 yrs.	56	27	.675	3.12	129	85	47	730.2	657	331	298	9	10	4	1	249	43	0	.173

WORLD SERIES
| 1910 CHI N | 0 | 0 | – | 3.38 | 1 | 1 | 0 | 8 | 10 | 3 | 5 | 0 | 0 | 0 | 0 | 2 | 0 | 0 | .000 |

Joe Coleman

COLEMAN, JOSEPH HOWARD
Son of Joe Coleman.
B. Feb. 3, 1947, Boston, Mass.
BR TR 6'3"   175 lbs.

	W	L	PCT	ERA	G	GS	CG	IP	H	BB	SO	ShO	W	L	SV	AB	H	HR	BA
1965 WAS A	2	0	1.000	1.50	2	2	2	18	9	8	7	0	0	0	0	6	0	0	.000
1966	1	0	1.000	2.00	1	1	1	9	6	2	4	0	0	0	0	3	0	0	.000
1967	8	9	.471	4.63	28	22	3	134	154	47	77	0	0	1	0	36	2	0	.056
1968	12	16	.429	3.27	33	33	12	223	212	51	139	2	0	0	0	70	9	0	.129
1969	12	13	.480	3.27	40	36	12	247.2	222	100	182	4	0	0	1	84	9	0	.107
1970	8	12	.400	3.58	39	29	6	219	190	89	152	1	0	0	0	67	8	0	.119
1971 DET A	20	9	.690	3.15	39	38	16	286	241	96	236	3	0	0	0	96	9	0	.094
1972	19	14	.576	2.80	40	39	9	279.2	216	110	222	3	0	0	0	82	9	0	.110
1973	23	15	.605	3.53	40	40	13	288	283	93	202	2	0	0	0	0	0	0	–
1974	14	12	.538	4.31	41	41	11	286	272	158	177	2	0	0	0	0	0	0	–
1975	10	18	.357	5.55	31	31	6	201	234	85	125	1	0	0	0	0	0	0	–
1976 2 teams			DET	A	(12G 2–5)		CHI	N	(39G 2–8)										
" total	4	13	.235	4.44	51	16	1	146	152	69	104	0	2	5	4	13	2	0	.154
1977 OAK A	4	4	.500	2.95	43	12	2	128	114	49	55	0	0	2	2	0	0	0	–
1978 2 teams			OAK	A	(10G 3–0)		TOR	A	(31G 2–0)										
" total	5	0	1.000	3.78	41	0	0	81	79	35	32	0	5	0	0	0	0	0	–
1979 2 teams			SF	N	(5G 0–0)		PIT	N	(10G 0–0)										
" total	0	0	–	5.18	15	0	0	24.1	32	11	14	0	0	0	0	5	1	0	.200
15 yrs.	142	135	.513	3.69	484	340	94	2570.2	2416	1003	1728	18	7	6	7	462	49	0	.106

LEAGUE CHAMPIONSHIP SERIES
| 1972 DET A | 1 | 0 | 1.000 | 0.00 | 1 | 1 | 1 | 9 | 7 | 3 | 14 | 1 | 0 | 0 | 0 | 2 | 1 | 0 | .500 |

Joe Coleman

COLEMAN, JOSEPH PATRICK
Father of Joe Coleman.
B. July 30, 1922, Medford, Mass.
BR TR 6'2½"   200 lbs.

	W	L	PCT	ERA	G	GS	CG	IP	H	BB	SO	ShO	W	L	SV	AB	H	HR	BA
1942 PHI A	0	1	.000	3.00	1	0	0	6	8	1	0	0	0	1	0	4	0	0	.000
1946	0	2	.000	5.54	4	2	0	13	19	8	8	0	0	0	0	5	2	0	.400
1947	6	12	.333	4.32	32	21	9	160.1	171	62	65	2	1	1	1	48	7	0	.146
1948	14	13	.519	4.09	33	29	13	215.2	224	90	86	3	0	1	0	74	9	0	.122
1949	13	14	.481	3.86	33	30	18	240.1	249	127	109	1	1	0	1	79	14	1	.177
1950	0	5	.000	8.50	15	6	2	54	74	50	12	0	0	1	0	17	1	1	.059
1951	1	6	.143	5.98	28	9	1	96.1	117	59	34	0	0	2	1	27	7	0	.259
1953	3	4	.429	4.00	21	9	2	90	85	49	18	1	0	0	0	28	8	0	.286
1954 BAL A	13	17	.433	3.50	33	32	15	221.1	184	96	103	4	0	1	0	74	13	2	.176
1955 2 teams			BAL	A	(6G 0–1)		DET	A	(17G 2–1)										
" total	2	2	.500	5.59	23	2	0	37	41	24	9	0	2	1	3	7	5	0	.714
10 yrs.	52	76	.406	4.38	223	140	60	1134	1172	566	444	11	4	6	6	363	66	4	.182

John Coleman

COLEMAN, JOHN
B. Bristol, Pa.   Deceased.

	W	L	PCT	ERA	G	GS	CG	IP	H	BB	SO	ShO	W	L	SV	AB	H	HR	BA
1890 PHI N	0	1	.000	21.60	1	1	0	1.2	4	3	2	0	0	0	0	0	0	0	–

	W	L	PCT	ERA	G	GS	CG	IP	H	BB	SO	ShO	Relief Pitching W	L	SV	BATTING AB	H	HR	BA

John Coleman

COLEMAN, JOHN
B. 1870, Jefferson City, Mo.   Deceased.

TL

	W	L	PCT	ERA	G	GS	CG	IP	H	BB	SO	ShO	W	L	SV	AB	H	HR	BA
1895 STL N	0	1	.000	13.50	1	1	1	8	12	8	5	0	0	0	0	5	1	0	.200

John Coleman

COLEMAN, JOHN FRANCIS
B. Mar. 6, 1863, Saratoga Springs, N. Y.
D. May 31, 1922, Detroit, Mich.

BL TR 5'9½" 165 lbs.
BB 1887

	W	L	PCT	ERA	G	GS	CG	IP	H	BB	SO	ShO	W	L	SV	AB	H	HR	BA
1883 PHI N	12	48	.200	4.87	65	61	59	538.1	772	48	159	3	0	1	0	354	83	0	.234
1884 2 teams		PHI	N (21G 5–15)		PHI	AA (3G 0–2)													
" total	5	17	.227	4.72	24	21	16	175.1	244	24	42	1	1	0	0	278	64	2	.230
1885 PHI AA	2	2	.500	3.43	8	3	3	60.1	82	5	12	0	1	0	0	398	119	2	.299
1886	1	1	.500	2.61	3	1	1	20.2	18	5	2	0	0	1	0	535	136	0	.254
1889	3	2	.600	2.91	5	5	4	34	38	14	6	0	0	0	0	19	1	0	.053
1890 PIT N	0	2	.000	9.64	2	2	1	14	28	6	3	0	0	0	0	11	2	0	.182
6 yrs.	23	72	.242	4.68	107	93	84	842.2	1182	102	224	4	2	2	0	*			

Percy Coleman

COLEMAN, PIERCE D.
B. Oct. 15, 1876, Mason, Ohio   D. Feb. 16, 1948, Van Nuys, Calif.

	W	L	PCT	ERA	G	GS	CG	IP	H	BB	SO	ShO	W	L	SV	AB	H	HR	BA
1897 STL N	1	3	.250	8.16	12	4	2	57.1	99	32	10	0	0	0	0	28	6	0	.214
1898 CIN N	0	1	.000	3.00	1	1	1	9	13	3	2	0	0	0	0	3	0	0	.000
2 yrs.	1	4	.200	7.46	13	5	3	66.1	112	35	12	0	0	0	0	31	6	0	.194

Rip Coleman

COLEMAN, WALTER GARY
B. July 31, 1931, Troy, N. Y.

BL TL 6'2" 185 lbs.

	W	L	PCT	ERA	G	GS	CG	IP	H	BB	SO	ShO	W	L	SV	AB	H	HR	BA
1955 NY A	2	1	.667	5.28	10	6	0	29	40	16	15	0	0	0	1	10	2	0	.200
1956	3	5	.375	3.67	29	9	0	88.1	97	42	42	0	1	3	2	24	1	0	.042
1957 KC A	0	7	.000	5.93	19	6	1	41	53	25	15	1	0	4	0	9	0	0	.000
1959 2 teams		KC	A (29G 2–10)		BAL	A (3G 0–0)													
" total	2	10	.167	4.34	32	11	2	85	89	36	58	0	0	4	2	25	2	0	.080
1960 BAL A	0	2	.000	11.25	5	1	0	4	8	5	0	0	0	1	0	1	0	0	.000
5 yrs.	7	25	.219	4.58	95	33	3	247.1	287	124	130	1	1	12	5	69	5	0	.072
WORLD SERIES																			
1955 NY A	0	0	–	9.00	1	0	0	1	5	0	1	0	0	0	0	0	0	0	–

Allan Collamore

COLLAMORE, ALLAN EDWARD
B. June 5, 1887, Worcester, Mass.   D. Aug. 8, 1980, Battle Creek, Mich.

BR TR 6' 170 lbs.

	W	L	PCT	ERA	G	GS	CG	IP	H	BB	SO	ShO	W	L	SV	AB	H	HR	BA
1911 PHI A	0	1	.000	36.00	2	0	0	2	6	3	1	0	0	0	0				–
1914 CLE A	3	7	.300	3.25	27	8	3	105.1	100	49	32	0	1	1	0	32	3	0	.094
1915	2	5	.286	2.38	11	6	5	64.1	52	22	15	2	0	1	0	23	4	0	.174
3 yrs.	5	13	.278	3.30	40	14	8	171.2	158	74	48	2	1	3	0	55	7	0	.127

Hap Collard

COLLARD, EARL CLINTON
B. Aug. 29, 1898, Williams, Ariz.   D. July 7, 1968, Jamestown, Calif.

BR TR 6' 170 lbs.

	W	L	PCT	ERA	G	GS	CG	IP	H	BB	SO	ShO	W	L	SV	AB	H	HR	BA
1927 CLE A	0	0	–	5.06	4	0	0	5.1	8	3	2	0	0	0	0	0	0	0	–
1928	0	0	–	2.25	1	0	0	4	4	4	1	0	0	0	0	1	1	0	1.000
1930 PHI N	6	12	.333	6.80	30	15	4	127	188	39	25	0	2	2	0	44	9	0	.205
3 yrs.	6	12	.333	6.60	35	15	4	136.1	200	46	28	0	2	2	0	45	10	0	.222

Orlin Collier

COLLIER, ORLIN EDWARD
B. Feb. 17, 1907, East Prairie, Mo.   D. Sept. 9, 1944, Memphis, Tenn.

BR TR 5'11½" 180 lbs.

	W	L	PCT	ERA	G	GS	CG	IP	H	BB	SO	ShO	W	L	SV	AB	H	HR	BA
1931 DET A	0	1	.000	7.84	2	2	0	10.1	17	7	3	0	0	0	0	3	0	0	.000

Harry Colliflower

COLLIFLOWER, JAMES HARRY
B. Mar. 11, 1869, Petersville, Md.   D. Aug. 14, 1961, Washington, D. C.

5'11½" 175 lbs.

	W	L	PCT	ERA	G	GS	CG	IP	H	BB	SO	ShO	W	L	SV	AB	H	HR	BA
1899 CLE N	1	11	.083	8.17	14	12	11	98	152	41	8	0	0	0	0	76	23	0	.303

Don Collins

COLLINS, DONALD EDWARD
B. Sept. 15, 1952, Lyons, Ga.

BR TL 6'2" 195 lbs.

	W	L	PCT	ERA	G	GS	CG	IP	H	BB	SO	ShO	W	L	SV	AB	H	HR	BA
1977 ATL N	3	9	.250	5.07	40	6	0	71	82	41	27	0	3	3	2	11	0	0	.000
1980 CLE A	0	0	–	7.50	4	0	0	6	9	7	0	0	0	0	0	0	0	0	–
2 yrs.	3	9	.250	5.26	44	6	0	77	91	48	27	0	3	3	2	11	0	0	.000

Orth Collins

COLLINS, ORTH STEIN (Buck)
B. Apr. 27, 1880, Lafayette, Ind.   D. Dec. 13, 1949, Fort Lauderdale, Fla.

BL TR 6' 150 lbs.

	W	L	PCT	ERA	G	GS	CG	IP	H	BB	SO	ShO	W	L	SV	AB	H	HR	BA
1909 WAS A	0	0	–	0.00	1	0	0	1	0	0	1	0	0	0	0	*			

Phil Collins

COLLINS, PHILIP EUGENE (Fidgety Phil)
B. Aug. 27, 1901, Chicago, Ill.   D. Aug. 14, 1948, Chicago, Ill.

BR TR 6' 170 lbs.

	W	L	PCT	ERA	G	GS	CG	IP	H	BB	SO	ShO	W	L	SV	AB	H	HR	BA
1923 CHI N	1	0	1.000	3.60	1	1	0	5	8	1	2	0	0	0	0	2	0	0	.000
1929 PHI N	9	7	.563	5.75	43	11	3	153.1	172	83	61	0	7	2	5	58	11	1	.190
1930	16	11	.593	4.78	47	25	17	239	287	86	87	1	3	1	3	87	22	3	.253
1931	12	16	.429	3.86	42	27	16	240.1	268	83	73	2	0	2	4	95	16	0	.168
1932	14	12	.538	5.27	43	21	6	184.1	231	65	66	0	5	3	3	68	18	0	.265
1933	8	13	.381	4.11	42	13	5	151	178	57	40	1	3	6	6	53	7	0	.132
1934	13	18	.419	4.18	45	32	15	254	277	87	72	0	4	1	1	88	15	0	.170
1935 2 teams		PHI	N (3G 0–2)		STL	N (26G 7–6)													
" total	7	8	.467	5.64	29	7	1	97.1	120	35	22	0	3	2	2	31	4	0	.129
8 yrs.	80	85	.485	4.66	292	141	64	1324.1	1541	497	423	4	25	17	24	482	93	4	.193

Ray Collins

COLLINS, RAYMOND WILLISTON
B. Feb. 11, 1887, Colchester, Vt.   D. Jan. 9, 1970, Burlington, Vt.

BL TL 6'1" 185 lbs.

	W	L	PCT	ERA	G	GS	CG	IP	H	BB	SO	ShO	W	L	SV	AB	H	HR	BA
1909 BOS A	4	3	.571	2.81	12	8	4	73.2	70	18	31	2	0	0	0	23	3	0	.130
1910	13	11	.542	1.62	35	26	18	244.2	205	41	109	4	1	0	1	84	15	0	.179
1911	11	12	.478	2.39	31	24	14	203.2	189	46	88	0	2	1	1	60	9	0	.150
1912	13	8	.619	2.53	27	23	17	199.1	192	42	82	4	0	0	0	65	11	0	.169
1913	19	8	.704	2.63	30	30	19	246.2	242	37	88	3	0	0	0	80	12	1	.150

	W	L	PCT	ERA	G	GS	CG	IP	H	BB	SO	ShO	Relief Pitching W	L	SV	BATTING AB	H	HR	BA

Ray Collins continued

	W	L	PCT	ERA	G	GS	CG	IP	H	BB	SO	ShO	W	L	SV	AB	H	HR	BA
1914	20	13	.606	2.51	39	30	16	272.1	252	56	72	6	5	1	0	79	11	0	.139
1915	4	7	.364	4.30	25	9	2	104.2	101	31	43	0	2	2	2	28	8	0	.286
7 yrs.	84	62	.575	2.51	199	150	90	1345	1251	271	513	19	10	4	4	419	69	1	.165

WORLD SERIES
1912 BOS A	0	0	—	1.88	2	1	0	14.1	14	0	6	0	0	0	0	5	0	0	.000

Rip Collins

COLLINS, HARRY WARREN
B. Feb. 26, 1896, Weatherford, Tex.
D. May 27, 1968, Bryan, Tex.

BR TR 6'1" 205 lbs.
BL 1920, BB 1921-23

	W	L	PCT	ERA	G	GS	CG	IP	H	BB	SO	ShO	W	L	SV	AB	H	HR	BA
1920 NY A	14	8	.636	3.17	36	20	12	187.1	171	79	66	3	4	0	1	62	8	0	.129
1921	11	5	.688	5.44	28	16	7	137.1	158	78	64	2	1	2	0	56	11	0	.196
1922 BOS A	14	11	.560	3.76	32	29	15	210.2	219	103	69	3	0	0	0	76	12	0	.158
1923 DET A	3	7	.300	4.87	17	13	3	92.1	104	32	25	1	0	0	0	27	3	0	.111
1924	14	7	.667	3.21	34	30	11	216	199	63	75	1	0	0	0	76	11	0	.145
1925	6	11	.353	4.56	26	20	5	140	149	52	33	0	0	0	0	42	5	0	.119
1926	8	8	.500	2.73	30	13	5	122	128	44	44	3	2	3	1	39	6	0	.154
1927	13	7	.650	4.69	30	25	10	172.2	207	59	37	1	1	0	0	54	11	0	.204
1929 STL A	11	6	.647	4.00	26	20	10	155.1	162	73	47	1	1	1	1	62	17	1	.274
1930	9	7	.563	4.35	35	20	6	171.2	168	63	75	1	0	0	2	54	7	0	.130
1931	5	5	.500	3.79	17	14	2	107	130	38	34	0	0	1	0	34	5	0	.147
11 yrs.	108	82	.568	3.99	311	220	86	1712.1	1795	684	569	16	9	7	5	582	96	1	.165

WORLD SERIES
1921 NY A	0	0	—	54.00	1	0	0	.2	4	1	0	0	0	0	0	0	0	0	—

Jackie Collum

COLLUM, JACK DEAN
B. June 21, 1927, Victor, Iowa

BL TL 5'7½" 160 lbs.

	W	L	PCT	ERA	G	GS	CG	IP	H	BB	SO	ShO	W	L	SV	AB	H	HR	BA
1951 STL N	2	1	.667	1.59	3	2	1	17	11	10	5	1	0	1	0	7	3	0	.429
1952	0	0	—	0.00	2	0	0	3	2	1	0	0	0	0	0	0	0	0	—
1953 2 teams		STL N (7G 0-0)			CIN N (30G 7-11)														
" total	7	11	.389	3.97	37	12	4	136	138	43	56	1	3	3	3	39	10	0	.256
1954 CIN N	7	3	.700	3.74	36	2	1	79.1	86	32	28	0	7	2	0	13	3	1	.231
1955	9	8	.529	3.63	32	17	5	134	128	37	49	0	2	1	1	40	10	0	.250
1956 STL N	6	2	.750	4.20	38	1	0	60	63	27	17	0	6	2	7	14	3	0	.214
1957 2 teams		CHI N (9G 1-1)			BKN N (3G 0-0)														
" total	1	1	.500	7.20	12	0	0	15	15	10	10	0	1	1	0	0	0	0	.000
1958 LA N	0	0	—	8.10	2	0	0	3.1	4	2	0	0	0	0	0	1	0	0	.000
1962 2 teams		MIN A (8G 0-2)			CLE A (1G 0-0)														
" total	0	2	.000	11.34	9	3	0	16.2	33	11	6	0	0	0	0	4	0	0	.000
9 yrs.	32	28	.533	4.15	171	37	11	464.1	480	173	171	2	19	10	12	118	29	1	.246

Dick Colpaert

COLPAERT, RICHARD CHARLES
B. Jan. 3, 1944, Freaser, Mich.

BR TR 5'10" 182 lbs.

	W	L	PCT	ERA	G	GS	CG	IP	H	BB	SO	ShO	W	L	SV	AB	H	HR	BA
1970 PIT N	1	0	1.000	5.73	8	0	0	11	9	8	6	0	1	0	0	0	0	0	—

Loyd Colson

COLSON, LOYD ALBERT
B. Nov. 4, 1947, Wellington, Tex.

BR TR 6'1" 190 lbs.

	W	L	PCT	ERA	G	GS	CG	IP	H	BB	SO	ShO	W	L	SV	AB	H	HR	BA
1970 NY A	0	0	—	4.50	1	0	0	2	3	0	3	0	0	0	0	0	0	0	—

Larry Colton

COLTON, LAWRENCE ROBERT
B. June 8, 1942, Los Angeles, Calif.

BL TR 6'3" 200 lbs.

	W	L	PCT	ERA	G	GS	CG	IP	H	BB	SO	ShO	W	L	SV	AB	H	HR	BA
1968 PHI N	0	0	—	4.50	1	0	0	2	3	0	2	0	0	0	0	0	0	0	—

Jeff Combe

COMBE, GEOFFREY WADE
B. Feb. 1, 1956, Melrose, Mass.

BR TR 6'2" 185 lbs.

	W	L	PCT	ERA	G	GS	CG	IP	H	BB	SO	ShO	W	L	SV	AB	H	HR	BA
1980 CIN N	0	0	—	10.29	4	0	0	7	9	4	10	0	0	0	0	0	0	0	—
1981	1	0	1.000	7.50	14	0	0	18	27	10	9	0	1	0	0	0	0	0	—
2 yrs.	1	0	1.000	8.28	18	0	0	25	36	14	19	0	1	0	0	0	0	0	—

Jorge Comellas

COMELLAS, JORGE (Pancho)
B. Dec. 7, 1916, Havana, Cuba

BR TR 6' 185 lbs.

	W	L	PCT	ERA	G	GS	CG	IP	H	BB	SO	ShO	W	L	SV	AB	H	HR	BA
1945 CHI N	0	2	.000	4.50	7	1	0	12	11	6	6	0	0	1	0	3	0	0	.000

Steve Comer

COMER, STEPHEN MICHAEL
B. Jan. 13, 1954, Minneapolis, Minn.

BB TR 6'3" 195 lbs.

	W	L	PCT	ERA	G	GS	CG	IP	H	BB	SO	ShO	W	L	SV	AB	H	HR	BA
1978 TEX A	11	5	.688	2.30	30	11	3	117.1	107	37	65	2	5	2	1	0	0	0	—
1979	17	12	.586	3.68	36	36	6	242	230	84	86	1	0	0	0	0	0	0	—
1980	2	4	.333	7.93	12	11	0	42	65	22	9	0	0	0	0	0	0	0	—
1981	8	2	.800	2.57	36	1	0	77	70	31	22	0	8	1	6	0	0	0	—
1982	1	6	.143	5.10	37	3	1	97	133	36	23	0	0	4	6	0	0	0	—
1983 PHI N	1	0	1.000	5.19	3	1	0	8.2	11	3	1	0	0	0	0	1	0	0	.000
1984 CLE A	4	8	.333	5.68	22	20	1	117.1	146	39	39	0	0	0	0	0	0	0	—
7 yrs.	44	37	.543	4.13	176	83	11	701.1	762	252	245	3	13	7	13	1	0	0	.000

Charlie Comiskey

COMISKEY, CHARLES ALBERT (Commy, The Old Roman)
B. Aug. 15, 1859, Chicago, Ill. D. Oct. 26, 1931, Eagle River, Wis.
Manager 1883, 1885-94.
Hall of Fame 1939.

BR TR 6' 180 lbs.

	W	L	PCT	ERA	G	GS	CG	IP	H	BB	SO	ShO	W	L	SV	AB	H	HR	BA
1882 STL AA	0	1	.000	0.00	2	1	1	8	12	3	2	0	0	0	0	329	80	1	.243
1884	0	0	—	2.25	1	0	0	4	1	0	4	0	0	0	0	460	110	2	.239
1889	0	0	—	0.00	1	0	0	.1	0	0	0	0	0	0	0	587	168	3	.286
3 yrs.	0	1	.000	0.73	4	1	1	12.1	13	3	6	0	0	0	0	*			

	W	L	PCT	ERA	G	GS	CG	IP	H	BB	SO	ShO	W	L	SV	AB	H	HR	BA

Clint Compton

COMPTON, ROBERT CLINTON
B. Nov. 1, 1950, Montgomery, Ala.
BL TL 5'11" 185 lbs.

Year/Team	W	L	PCT	ERA	G	GS	CG	IP	H	BB	SO	ShO	W	L	SV	AB	H	HR	BA
1972 CHI N	0	0	–	9.00	1	0	0	2	2	2	2	0	0	0	0	0	0	0	–

Jack Compton

COMPTON, HARRY LEROY
B. Mar. 9, 1882, Lancaster, Ohio   D. July 4, 1974, Lancaster, Ohio
BR TR 5'9" 157 lbs.

Year/Team	W	L	PCT	ERA	G	GS	CG	IP	H	BB	SO	ShO	W	L	SV	AB	H	HR	BA
1911 CIN N	0	1	.000	3.91	8	3	0	25.1	19	15	6	0	0	1	1	6	2	0	.333

Keith Comstock

COMSTOCK, KEITH MARTIN
B. Dec. 23, 1955, San Francisco, Calif.
BL TL 6' 160 lbs.

Year/Team	W	L	PCT	ERA	G	GS	CG	IP	H	BB	SO	ShO	W	L	SV	AB	H	HR	BA
1984 MIN A	0	0	–	8.53	4	0	0	6.1	6	4	2	0	0	0	0	0	0	0	–

Ralph Comstock

COMSTOCK, RALPH REMICK (Commy)
B. Nov. 24, 1890, Sylvania, Ohio   D. Sept. 13, 1966, Toledo, Ohio
BR TR 5'10" 168 lbs.

Year/Team	W	L	PCT	ERA	G	GS	CG	IP	H	BB	SO	ShO	W	L	SV	AB	H	HR	BA
1913 DET A	2	5	.286	5.37	10	7	1	60.1	90	16	37	0	0	0	1	22	5	0	.227
1915 2 teams	BOS A (3G 1–0)				PIT F (12G 3–3)														
" total	4	3	.571	3.06	15	7	3	61.2	54	9	19	0	1	0	2	18	0	0	.000
1918 PIT N	5	6	.455	3.00	15	8	6	81	78	14	44	0	2	1	1	26	5	0	.192
3 yrs.	11	14	.440	3.72	40	22	10	203	222	39	100	0	3	1	4	66	10	0	.152

Bob Cone

CONE, ROBERT EARL (Ike)
B. Feb. 27, 1894, Galveston, Tex.   D. May 24, 1955, Galveston, Tex.

Year/Team	W	L	PCT	ERA	G	GS	CG	IP	H	BB	SO	ShO	W	L	SV	AB	H	HR	BA
1915 PHI A	0	0	–	40.50	1	1	0	.2	5	0	0	0	0	0	0	0	0	0	–

Dick Conger

CONGER, RICHARD
B. Apr. 3, 1921, Los Angeles, Calif.   D. Feb. 16, 1970, Arcadia, Calif.
BR TR 6' 185 lbs.

Year/Team	W	L	PCT	ERA	G	GS	CG	IP	H	BB	SO	ShO	W	L	SV	AB	H	HR	BA
1940 DET A	1	0	1.000	3.00	2	0	0	3	2	3	1	0	1	0	0	0	0	0	–
1941 PIT N	0	0	–	0.00	2	1	0	4	3	3	2	0	0	0	0	0	0	0	–
1942	0	0	–	2.16	2	1	0	8.1	9	5	3	0	0	0	0	3	0	0	.000
1943 PHI N	2	7	.222	6.09	13	10	2	54.2	72	24	18	0	0	0	0	16	1	0	.063
4 yrs.	3	7	.300	5.14	19	12	2	70	86	35	24	0	1	0	0	19	1	0	.053

Red Conkwright

CONKWRIGHT, ALLEN HOWARD (Red)
B. Dec. 4, 1896, Sedalia, Mo.
BR TR 5'10" 170 lbs.

Year/Team	W	L	PCT	ERA	G	GS	CG	IP	H	BB	SO	ShO	W	L	SV	AB	H	HR	BA
1920 DET A	2	1	.667	6.98	5	2	0	19.1	29	16	4	0	2	0	1	4	1	0	.250

Bob Conley

CONLEY, ROBERT BURNS
B. Feb. 1, 1934, Knott County, Ky.
BR TR 6'1" 188 lbs.

Year/Team	W	L	PCT	ERA	G	GS	CG	IP	H	BB	SO	ShO	W	L	SV	AB	H	HR	BA
1958 PHI N	0	0	–	7.56	2	2	0	8.1	9	1	0	0	0	0	0	1	0	0	.000

Ed Conley

CONLEY, EDWARD J.
B. July 10, 1864, Sandwich, Mass.   D. Oct. 16, 1894, Cumberland, R. I.
5'11½"

Year/Team	W	L	PCT	ERA	G	GS	CG	IP	H	BB	SO	ShO	W	L	SV	AB	H	HR	BA
1884 PRO N	4	4	.500	2.15	8	8	8	71	63	22	33	1	0	0	0	28	4	0	.143

Gene Conley

CONLEY, DONALD EUGENE
B. Nov. 10, 1930, Muskogee, Okla.
BR TR 6'8" 225 lbs.

Year/Team	W	L	PCT	ERA	G	GS	CG	IP	H	BB	SO	ShO	W	L	SV	AB	H	HR	BA
1952 BOS N	0	3	.000	7.82	4	3	0	12.2	23	9	6	0	0	0	0	5	2	0	.400
1954 MIL N	14	9	.609	2.96	28	27	12	194.1	171	79	113	2	1	0	0	77	12	0	.156
1955	11	7	.611	4.16	22	21	10	158	152	52	107	0	0	1	0	54	11	0	.204
1956	8	9	.471	3.13	31	19	5	158.1	169	52	68	1	1	2	3	45	7	0	.156
1957	9	9	.500	3.16	35	18	6	148	133	64	61	1	4	1	1	46	9	0	.196
1958	0	6	.000	4.88	26	7	0	72	89	17	53	0	0	3	2	16	3	1	.188
1959 PHI N	12	7	.632	3.00	25	22	12	180	159	42	102	3	0	0	1	67	16	0	.239
1960	8	14	.364	3.68	29	25	9	183.1	192	42	117	2	1	0	0	63	8	1	.127
1961 BOS A	11	14	.440	4.91	33	30	6	199.2	229	65	113	2	0	1	1	73	16	2	.219
1962	15	14	.517	3.95	34	33	9	241.2	238	68	134	2	0	0	1	87	18	1	.207
1963	3	4	.429	6.64	9	9	0	40.2	51	21	14	0	0	0	0	15	3	0	.200
11 yrs.	91	96	.487	3.82	276	214	69	1588.2	1606	511	888	13	7	8	9	548	105	5	.192

WORLD SERIES

Year/Team	W	L	PCT	ERA	G	GS	CG	IP	H	BB	SO	ShO	W	L	SV	AB	H	HR	BA
1957 MIL N	0	0	–	10.80	1	0	0	1.2	2	1	0	0	0	0	0	0	0	0	–

Snipe Conley

CONLEY, JAMES PATRICK
B. Apr. 25, 1894, Cressona, Pa.   D. Jan. 7, 1978, DeSoto, Tex.
BR TR 5'11½" 179 lbs.

Year/Team	W	L	PCT	ERA	G	GS	CG	IP	H	BB	SO	ShO	W	L	SV	AB	H	HR	BA
1914 BAL F	5	8	.385	2.52	35	11	4	125	112	47	86	2	1	3	0	35	4	0	.114
1915	1	4	.200	4.29	25	6	4	86	97	32	40	0	0	1	0	24	6	0	.250
1918 CIN N	2	0	1.000	5.27	5	0	0	13.2	17	5	2	0	2	0	1	4	1	0	.250
3 yrs.	8	12	.400	3.36	65	17	8	224.2	226	84	128	2	3	4	1	63	11	0	.175

Bert Conn

CONN, ALBERT THOMAS
B. Sept. 22, 1879, Philadelphia, Pa.   D. Nov. 2, 1944, Philadelphia, Pa.
TR

Year/Team	W	L	PCT	ERA	G	GS	CG	IP	H	BB	SO	ShO	W	L	SV	AB	H	HR	BA
1898 PHI N	0	1	.000	6.43	1	1	0	7	13	2	3	0	0	0	0	3	1	0	.333
1900	0	2	.000	8.31	4	1	1	17.1	29	16	2	0	0	1	0	9	3	0	.333
2 yrs.	0	3	.000	7.77	5	2	1	24.1	42	18	5	0	0	1	0	*			

Sarge Connally

CONNALLY, GEORGE WALTER
B. Aug. 31, 1898, McGregor, Tex.   D. Jan. 27, 1978, Temple, Tex.
BR TR 5'11" 170 lbs.

Year/Team	W	L	PCT	ERA	G	GS	CG	IP	H	BB	SO	ShO	W	L	SV	AB	H	HR	BA
1921 CHI A	0	1	.000	6.45	5	2	0	22.1	29	10	6	0	0	0	0	8	4	0	.500
1923	0	0	–	6.23	3	0	0	8.2	7	12	3	0	0	0	0	3	1	0	.333
1924	7	13	.350	4.05	44	13	6	160	177	68	55	0	5	5	6	50	11	0	.220
1925	6	7	.462	4.64	40	2	0	104.2	122	58	45	0	5	6	8	28	7	0	.250
1926	6	5	.545	3.16	31	8	5	108.1	128	35	47	0	2	4	3	32	5	0	.156
1927	10	15	.400	4.08	43	18	11	198.1	217	83	58	1	5	3	5	67	22	0	.328
1928	2	5	.286	4.84	28	5	1	74.1	89	29	28	0	1	4	2	19	2	0	.105
1929	0	0	–	4.76	11	0	0	11.1	13	8	1	0	0	0	0	0	0	0	–
1931 CLE A	5	5	.500	4.20	17	9	5	85.2	87	50	37	0	2	0	1	27	5	0	.185

	W	L	PCT	ERA	G	GS	CG	IP	H	BB	SO	ShO	Relief Pitching W	L	SV	BATTING AB	H	HR	BA

Sarge Connally continued

	W	L	PCT	ERA	G	GS	CG	IP	H	BB	SO	ShO	W	L	SV	AB	H	HR	BA
1932	8	6	.571	4.33	35	7	4	112.1	119	42	32	1	4	4	3	40	7	1	.175
1933	5	3	.625	4.89	41	3	1	103	112	49	30	0	4	2	1	26	6	0	.231
1934	0	0	–	5.06	5	0	0	5.1	4	5	1	0	0	0	1	1	0	0	.000
12 yrs.	49	60	.450	4.30	303	67	33	994.1	1104	449	345	2	28	28	31	301	70	1	.233

Bill Connelly

CONNELLY, WILLIAM WIRT (Wild Bill)
B. June 29, 1925, Alberta, Va. D. Nov. 27, 1980, Richmond, Va.
BL TR 6' 175 lbs.

	W	L	PCT	ERA	G	GS	CG	IP	H	BB	SO	ShO	W	L	SV	AB	H	HR	BA
1945 PHI A	1	1	.500	4.50	2	1	0	8	7	8	0	0	1	0	0	1	0	0	.000
1950 2 teams			CHI A	(2G 0–0)		DET A	(2G 0–0)												
" total	0	0	–	8.53	4	0	0	6.1	9	3	1	0	0	0	0	1	0	0	.000
1952 NY N	5	0	1.000	4.55	11	4	0	31.2	22	25	22	0	2	0	0	11	4	0	.364
1953	0	1	.000	11.07	8	2	0	20.1	33	17	11	0	0	0	0	6	0	0	.000
4 yrs.	6	2	.750	6.92	25	7	0	66.1	71	53	34	0	3	0	0	19	4	0	.211

Ed Connolly

CONNOLLY, EDWARD JOSEPH
Son of Ed Connolly.
B. Dec. 3, 1939, Brooklyn, N. Y.
BL TL 6'1" 190 lbs.

	W	L	PCT	ERA	G	GS	CG	IP	H	BB	SO	ShO	W	L	SV	AB	H	HR	BA
1964 BOS A	4	11	.267	4.91	27	15	1	80.2	80	64	73	1	0	1	0	18	3	0	.167
1967 CLE A	2	1	.667	7.48	15	4	0	49.1	63	34	45	0	1	0	0	11	2	0	.182
2 yrs.	6	12	.333	5.88	42	19	1	130	143	98	118	1	1	1	0	29	5	0	.172

John Connor

CONNOR, JOHN
B. 1853, Scotland D. Oct. 13, 1932, Boston, Mass.

	W	L	PCT	ERA	G	GS	CG	IP	H	BB	SO	ShO	W	L	SV	AB	H	HR	BA
1884 BOS N	1	4	.200	3.15	7	7	7	60	70	18	29	0	0	0	0	25	2	0	.080
1885 2 teams			BUF N	(1G 0–1)		LOU AA	(4G 1–3)												
" total	1	4	.200	4.70	5	5	5	44	57	14	19	0	0	0	0	17	2	0	.118
2 yrs.	2	8	.200	3.81	12	12	12	104	127	32	48	0	0	0	0	42	4	0	.095

Bill Connors

CONNORS, WILLIAM JOSEPH
B. Nov. 2, 1941, Schenectady, N. Y.
BR TR 6'1" 180 lbs.

	W	L	PCT	ERA	G	GS	CG	IP	H	BB	SO	ShO	W	L	SV	AB	H	HR	BA
1966 CHI N	0	0	.000	7.31	11	0	0	16	20	7	3	0	0	0	0	0	0	0	–
1967 NY N	0	0	–	6.23	6	1	0	13	8	5	13	0	0	0	0	1	0	0	.000
1968	0	1	.000	9.00	9	0	0	14	21	7	8	0	0	1	0	1	1	0	1.000
3 yrs.	0	2	.000	7.53	26	1	0	43	49	19	24	0	0	2	0	2	1	0	.500

Joe Connors

CONNORS, JOSEPH P.
B. Philadelphia, Pa. Deceased.

	W	L	PCT	ERA	G	GS	CG	IP	H	BB	SO	ShO	W	L	SV	AB	H	HR	BA
1884 2 teams			ALT U	(1G 0–1)		KC U	(2G 0–1)												
" total	0	2	.000	5.57	3	2	2	21	42	5	1	0	0	0	0	22	2	0	.091

Ted Conovar

CONOVAR, THEODORE
B. Mar. 10, 1868, Lexington, Ky. D. July 27, 1910, Paris, Ky.
BR TR 5'10½" 165 lbs.

	W	L	PCT	ERA	G	GS	CG	IP	H	BB	SO	ShO	W	L	SV	AB	H	HR	BA
1889 CIN AA	0	0	–	13.50	1	0	0	2	4	2	1	0	0	0	1	0	0	0	–

Tim Conroy

CONROY, TIMOTHY JAMES
B. Apr. 3, 1960, Monroeville, Pa.
BL TL 6' 178 lbs.

	W	L	PCT	ERA	G	GS	CG	IP	H	BB	SO	ShO	W	L	SV	AB	H	HR	BA
1978 OAK A	0	0	–	7.71	2	2	0	4.2	3	9	0	0	0	0	0	0	0	0	–
1982	2	2	.500	3.55	5	5	1	25.1	20	18	17	0	0	0	0	0	0	0	–
1983	7	10	.412	3.94	39	18	3	162.1	141	98	112	1	2	0	0	0	0	0	–
1984	1	6	.143	5.23	38	14	0	93	82	63	69	0	0	0	0	0	0	0	–
4 yrs.	10	18	.357	4.38	84	39	4	285.1	246	188	198	1	2	0	0	0	0	0	–

Jim Constable

CONSTABLE, JIMMY LEE (Sheriff)
B. June 14, 1933, Jonesboro, Tenn.
BB TL 6'1" 185 lbs.

	W	L	PCT	ERA	G	GS	CG	IP	H	BB	SO	ShO	W	L	SV	AB	H	HR	BA
1956 NY N	0	0	–	14.54	3	0	0	4.1	9	7	1	0	0	0	0	0	0	0	–
1957	1	1	.500	2.86	16	0	0	28.1	27	7	13	0	1	1	0	5	0	0	.000
1958 3 teams			SF N	(9G 1–0)		CLE A	(6G 0–1)		WAS A	(15G 0–1)									
" total	1	2	.333	6.40	30	4	0	45	56	22	32	0	1	1	1	7	4	0	.571
1962 MIL N	1	1	.500	2.00	3	2	1	18	14	4	12	1	0	0	1	5	0	0	.000
1963 SF N	0	0	–	3.86	4	0	0	2.1	3	1	1	0	0	0	0	0	0	0	–
5 yrs.	3	4	.429	4.87	56	6	1	98	109	41	59	1	2	2	2	17	4	0	.235

Sandy Consuegra

CONSUEGRA, SANDALIO SIMEON CASTELLON
B. Sept. 3, 1920, Potrerillo, Cuba
BR TR 5'11" 165 lbs.

	W	L	PCT	ERA	G	GS	CG	IP	H	BB	SO	ShO	W	L	SV	AB	H	HR	BA
1950 WAS A	7	8	.467	4.40	21	18	8	124.2	132	57	38	2	0	0	2	40	7	0	.175
1951	7	8	.467	4.01	40	12	5	146	140	63	31	0	2	5	3	43	10	0	.233
1952	6	0	1.000	3.05	30	2	0	73.2	80	27	19	0	5	0	5	17	3	0	.176
1953 2 teams			WAS A	(4G 0–0)		CHI A	(29G 7–5)												
" total	7	5	.583	2.86	33	13	5	129	131	32	30	1	3	0	3	35	2	0	.057
1954 CHI A	16	3	.842	2.69	39	17	3	154	142	35	31	2	8	0	3	48	11	0	.229
1955	6	5	.545	2.64	44	7	3	126.1	120	18	35	0	3	3	7	29	3	0	.103
1956 2 teams			CHI A	(28G 1–2)		BAL A	(4G 1–1)												
" total	2	3	.400	4.98	32	2	0	47	55	13	8	0	1	1	3	6	1	0	.167
1957 2 teams			BAL A	(5G 0–0)		NY N	(4G 0–0)												
" total	0	0	–	2.08	9	0	0	8.2	11	1	1	0	0	0	0	0	0	0	–
8 yrs.	51	32	.614	3.37	248	71	24	809.1	811	246	193	5	22	9	26	218	37	0	.170

Nardi Contreras

CONTRERAS, ARNALDO JUAN
B. Sept. 19, 1951, Tampa, Fla.
BB TR 6'2" 193 lbs.

	W	L	PCT	ERA	G	GS	CG	IP	H	BB	SO	ShO	W	L	SV	AB	H	HR	BA
1980 CHI A	0	0	–	5.79	8	0	0	14	18	7	8	0	0	0	0	0	0	0	–

Dick Conway

CONWAY, RICHARD BUTLER
Brother of Bill Conway.
B. 1865, Lowell, Mass. D. Sept. 9, 1926, Lowell, Mass.
TR 5'7½" 140 lbs.

	W	L	PCT	ERA	G	GS	CG	IP	H	BB	SO	ShO	W	L	SV	AB	H	HR	BA
1886 BAL AA	2	7	.222	6.81	9	9	8	76.2	106	43	64	0	0	0	0	34	7	0	.206

	W	L	PCT	ERA	G	GS	CG	IP	H	BB	SO	ShO	Relief Pitching W	L	SV	Batting AB	H	HR	BA

Dick Conway continued

	W	L	PCT	ERA	G	GS	CG	IP	H	BB	SO	ShO	W	L	SV	AB	H	HR	BA
1887 BOS N	9	15	.375	4.66	26	26	25	222.1	249	86	45	0	0	0	0	145	36	0	.248
1888	4	2	.667	2.38	6	6	6	53	49	8	12	0	0	0	0	25	4	0	.160
3 yrs.	15	24	.385	4.78	41	41	39	352	404	137	121	0	0	0	0	204	47	0	.230

Jim Conway

CONWAY, JAMES P.
Brother of Pete Conway.
B. Clifton, Pa.   Deceased.   TR

	W	L	PCT	ERA	G	GS	CG	IP	H	BB	SO	ShO	W	L	SV	AB	H	HR	BA
1884 BKN AA	3	9	.250	4.44	13	13	10	105.1	132	15	25	0	0	0	0	47	6	0	.128
1885 PHI AA	0	1	.000	7.30	2	2	1	12.1	19	2	0	0	0	0	0	6	0	0	.000
1889 KC AA	19	19	.500	3.25	41	37	33	335	334	90	115	0	1	0	0	149	31	0	.208
3 yrs.	22	29	.431	3.64	56	52	44	452.2	485	107	140	0	1	0	0	202	37	0	.183

Pat Conway

CONWAY, JEROME PATRICK
B. June 7, 1901, Holyoke, Mass.   D. Apr. 16, 1980, Holyoke, Mass.   BL TL 6'2"   190 lbs.

	W	L	PCT	ERA	G	GS	CG	IP	H	BB	SO	ShO	W	L	SV	AB	H	HR	BA
1920 WAS A	0	0	—	0.00	1	0	0	2	1	1	0	0	0	0	0	0	0	0	—

Pete Conway

CONWAY, PETER J.
Brother of Jim Conway.
B. Oct. 30, 1866, Burmont, Pa.   D. Jan. 13, 1903, Clifton Heights, Pa.   BR TR 5'10½"

	W	L	PCT	ERA	G	GS	CG	IP	H	BB	SO	ShO	W	L	SV	AB	H	HR	BA
1885 BUF N	10	17	.370	4.67	27	27	26	210	256	44	94	0	0	0	0	90	10	1	.111
1886 2 teams			KC	N (23G 5–15)			DET	N (11G 6–5)											
" total	11	20	.355	4.95	34	31	30	271	329	86	116	0	0	0	0	237	55	3	.232
1887 DET N	8	9	.471	2.90	17	17	16	146	132	47	40	0	0	0	0	95	22	1	.232
1888	30	14	.682	2.26	45	45	43	391	315	90	176	4	0	0	0	167	46	3	.275
1889 PIT N	2	1	.667	4.91	3	3	2	22	26	16	2	0	0	0	0	10	1	1	.100
5 yrs.	61	61	.500	3.59	126	123	117	1040	1058	250	428	4	0	0	0	*			

Joe Conzelman

CONZELMAN, JOSEPH HARRISON
B. July 14, 1885, Bristol, Conn.   D. Apr. 17, 1979, Mountain Brook, Ala.   BR TR 6'   170 lbs.

	W	L	PCT	ERA	G	GS	CG	IP	H	BB	SO	ShO	W	L	SV	AB	H	HR	BA
1913 PIT N	0	1	.000	1.20	3	2	1	15	13	5	9	0	0	0	0	4	0	0	.000
1914	5	6	.455	2.94	33	9	4	101	88	40	39	1	2	2	1	27	3	0	.111
1915	1	1	.500	3.42	18	1	0	47.1	41	20	22	0	1	0	0	11	1	0	.091
3 yrs.	6	8	.429	2.92	54	12	5	163.1	142	65	70	1	3	2	1	42	4	0	.095

Earl Cook

COOK, EARL DAVIS
B. Dec. 10, 1908, Stouffville, Ont., Canada   BR TR 6'   195 lbs.

	W	L	PCT	ERA	G	GS	CG	IP	H	BB	SO	ShO	W	L	SV	AB	H	HR	BA
1941 DET A	0	0	—	4.50	1	0	0	2	4	0	1	0	0	0	0	0	0	0	—

Rollin Cook

COOK, ROLLIN EDWARD
B. Oct. 5, 1890, Toledo, Ohio   D. Aug. 11, 1975, Toledo, Ohio   BR TR 5'9"   152 lbs.

	W	L	PCT	ERA	G	GS	CG	IP	H	BB	SO	ShO	W	L	SV	AB	H	HR	BA
1915 STL A	0	0	—	7.24	5	0	0	13.2	16	9	7	0	0	0	0	4	1	0	.250

Ron Cook

COOK, RONALD WAYNE
B. July 11, 1947, Jefferson, Tex.   BL TL 6'1"   175 lbs.

	W	L	PCT	ERA	G	GS	CG	IP	H	BB	SO	ShO	W	L	SV	AB	H	HR	BA
1970 HOU N	4	4	.500	3.73	41	7	0	82	80	42	50	0	3	1	2	17	4	0	.235
1971	0	4	.000	4.85	5	4	0	26	23	8	10	0	0	0	0	8	2	0	.250
2 yrs.	4	8	.333	4.00	46	11	0	108	103	50	60	0	3	1	2	25	6	0	.240

Bobby Coombs

COOMBS, RAYMOND FRANKLIN
B. Feb. 2, 1908, Goodwins Mills, Me.   BR TR 5'9½"   160 lbs.

	W	L	PCT	ERA	G	GS	CG	IP	H	BB	SO	ShO	W	L	SV	AB	H	HR	BA
1933 PHI A	0	1	.000	7.47	21	0	0	31.1	47	20	8	0	0	1	2	5	2	0	.400
1943 NY N	0	1	.000	12.94	9	0	0	16	33	8	5	0	0	1	0	2	0	0	.000
2 yrs.	0	2	.000	9.32	30	0	0	47.1	80	28	13	0	0	2	2	7	2	0	.286

Danny Coombs

COOMBS, DANIEL BERNARD
B. Mar. 23, 1942, Lincoln, Me.   BR TL 6'4"   200 lbs.
BL 1967

	W	L	PCT	ERA	G	GS	CG	IP	H	BB	SO	ShO	W	L	SV	AB	H	HR	BA
1963 HOU N	0	0	—	27.00	1	0	0	.1	3	0	0	0	0	0	0	0	0	0	—
1964	1	1	.500	5.00	7	1	0	18	21	10	14	0	0	1	0	4	0	0	.000
1965	0	2	.000	4.79	26	3	0	47	54	23	35	0	0	0	0	9	1	0	.111
1966	0	0	—	3.38	2	0	0	2.2	4	0	3	0	0	0	0	1	0	0	.000
1967	3	0	1.000	3.33	6	2	0	24.1	21	9	23	0	3	0	0	8	1	0	.125
1968	4	3	.571	3.28	40	2	0	46.2	52	17	29	0	3	2	2	10	4	0	.400
1969	0	1	.000	6.75	8	0	0	8	12	2	3	0	0	1	0	2	0	0	.000
1970 SD N	10	14	.417	3.30	35	27	5	188	185	76	105	1	2	1	0	52	5	0	.096
1971	1	6	.143	6.21	19	7	0	58	81	25	37	0	0	1	0	14	3	0	.214
9 yrs.	19	27	.413	4.08	144	42	5	393	433	162	249	1	8	7	2	100	14	0	.140

Jack Coombs

COOMBS, JOHN WESLEY (Colby Jack)
B. Nov. 18, 1882, LeGrand, Iowa   D. Apr. 15, 1957, LeGrand, Iowa   BB TR 6'   185 lbs.
Manager 1919.

	W	L	PCT	ERA	G	GS	CG	IP	H	BB	SO	ShO	W	L	SV	AB	H	HR	BA
1906 PHI A	10	10	.500	2.50	23	18	13	173	144	68	90	1	2	2	0	67	16	0	.239
1907	6	9	.400	3.12	23	17	10	132.2	109	64	73	2	0	0	2	48	8	1	.167
1908	7	5	.583	2.00	26	18	10	153	130	64	80	4	1	0	0	220	56	1	.255
1909	12	11	.522	2.32	31	25	19	205.2	156	73	97	6	0	3	1	83	14	0	.169
1910	31	9	.775	1.30	45	38	35	353	248	115	224	13	4	1	1	132	29	0	.220
1911	28	12	.700	3.53	47	40	26	336.2	360	119	185	1	3	1	2	141	45	2	.319
1912	21	10	.677	3.29	40	32	23	262.1	227	94	120	1	3	0	2	110	28	0	.255
1913	1	0	1.000	10.13	2	2	0	5.1	5	6	0	0	0	0	0	3	1	0	.333
1914	0	1	.000	4.50	2	2	0	8	8	3	1	0	0	0	0	11	3	0	.273
1915 BKN N	15	10	.600	2.58	29	24	17	195.2	166	91	56	2	2	1	0	75	21	0	.280
1916	13	8	.619	2.66	27	21	10	159	136	44	47	3	2	0	0	61	11	0	.180
1917	7	11	.389	3.96	31	14	9	141	147	49	34	0	3	2	0	44	10	0	.227
1918	8	14	.364	3.81	27	22	16	189	191	49	44	2	1	0	0	113	19	0	.168

	W	L	PCT	ERA	G	GS	CG	IP	H	BB	SO	ShO	Relief Pitching			BATTING			
													W	L	SV	AB	H	HR	BA

Jack Coombs continued

	W	L	PCT	ERA	G	GS	CG	IP	H	BB	SO	ShO	W	L	SV	AB	H	HR	BA
1920 DET A	0	0	–	3.18	2	0	0	5.2	7	2	1	0	0	0	0	2	0	0	.000
14 yrs.	159	110	.591	2.78	355	273	188	2320	2034	841	1052	35	21	10	8	*			
WORLD SERIES																			
1910 PHI A	3	0	1.000	3.33	3	3	3	27	23	14	17	0	0	0	0	13	5	0	.385
1911	1	0	1.000	1.35	2	2	1	20	11	6	16	0	0	0	0	8	2	0	.250
1916 BKN N	1	0	1.000	4.26	1	1	0	6.1	7	1	1	0	0	0	0	3	1	0	.333
3 yrs.	5	0	1.000	2.70	6	6	4	53.1	41	21	34	0	0	0	0	24	8	0	.333
		8th		1st															

Bill Cooney

COONEY, WILLIAM A.   TR
B. Apr. 4, 1887, Boston, Mass.   D. Nov. 6, 1928, Roxbury, Mass.

	W	L	PCT	ERA	G	GS	CG	IP	H	BB	SO	ShO	W	L	SV	AB	H	HR	BA
1909 BOS N	0	0	–	1.42	3	0	0	6.1	4	2	3	0	0	0	0	*			

Bob Cooney

COONEY, ROBERT DANIEL   BR TR 5'11"   160 lbs.
B. July 12, 1907, Glens Falls, N. Y.   D. May 4, 1976, Glens Falls, N. Y.

	W	L	PCT	ERA	G	GS	CG	IP	H	BB	SO	ShO	W	L	SV	AB	H	HR	BA
1931 STL A	0	3	.000	4.12	5	4	1	39.1	46	20	13	0	0	0	0	13	5	0	.385
1932	1	2	.333	6.97	23	3	1	71	94	36	23	0	0	0	1	22	0	0	.000
2 yrs.	1	5	.167	5.95	28	7	2	110.1	140	56	36	0	0	0	1	35	5	0	.143

Johnny Cooney

COONEY, JOHN WALTER   BR TL 5'10"   165 lbs.
Son of Jimmy Cooney.   Brother of Jimmy Cooney.
B. Mar. 18, 1901, Cranston, R. I.

	W	L	PCT	ERA	G	GS	CG	IP	H	BB	SO	ShO	W	L	SV	AB	H	HR	BA
1921 BOS N	0	1	.000	3.92	8	1	0	20.2	19	10	9	0	0	0	0	5	1	0	.200
1922	1	2	.333	2.16	4	3	1	25	19	6	7	0	0	0	0	8	0	0	.000
1923	3	5	.375	3.31	23	8	5	98	92	22	23	2	0	0	0	66	25	0	.379
1924	8	9	.471	3.18	34	19	12	181	176	50	67	2	0	0	2	130	33	0	.254
1925	14	14	.500	3.48	31	29	20	245.2	267	50	65	2	2	0	0	103	33	0	.320
1926	3	3	.500	4.00	19	8	3	83.1	106	29	23	1	1	1	0	126	38	0	.302
1928	3	7	.300	4.32	24	6	2	89.2	106	31	18	0	2	2	1	41	7	0	.171
1929	2	3	.400	5.00	14	2	1	45	57	22	11	0	1	3	3	72	23	0	.319
1930	0	0	–	18.00	2	0	0	7	16	3	1	0	0	0	0	3	0	0	.000
9 yrs.	34	44	.436	3.72	159	76	44	795.1	858	223	224	7	6	6	6	*			

William Coons

COONS, WILBUR K.
B. Mar. 21, 1855, Philadelphia, Pa.   D. Aug. 30, 1915, Burlington, N. J.

	W	L	PCT	ERA	G	GS	CG	IP	H	BB	SO	ShO	W	L	SV	AB	H	HR	BA
1876 PHI N	0	0	–	5.14	2	0	0	7	9	0	0	0	0	0	0	*			

Cal Cooper

COOPER, CALVIN ASA   BR TR 6'2½"   180 lbs.
B. Aug. 11, 1922, Great Falls, S. C.

	W	L	PCT	ERA	G	GS	CG	IP	H	BB	SO	ShO	W	L	SV	AB	H	HR	BA
1948 WAS A	0	0	–	45.00	1	0	0	1	5	1	0	0	0	0	0	0	0	0	–

Don Cooper

COOPER, DONALD JAMES   BR TR 6'1"   185 lbs.
B. Feb. 15, 1957, New York, N. Y.

	W	L	PCT	ERA	G	GS	CG	IP	H	BB	SO	ShO	W	L	SV	AB	H	HR	BA
1981 MIN A	1	5	.167	4.27	27	2	0	59	61	32	33	0	1	3	0	0	0	0	–
1982	0	1	.000	9.53	6	1	0	11.1	14	11	5	0	0	0	0	0	0	0	–
1983 TOR A	0	0	–	6.75	4	0	0	5.1	8	0	5	0	0	0	0	0	0	0	–
3 yrs.	1	6	.143	5.23	37	3	0	75.2	83	43	43	0	1	3	0	0	0	0	–

Guy Cooper

COOPER, GUY EVANS (Rebel)   BL TR 6'1"   185 lbs.
B. Jan. 28, 1893, Rome, Ga.   D. Aug. 2, 1951, Santa Monica, Calif.

	W	L	PCT	ERA	G	GS	CG	IP	H	BB	SO	ShO	W	L	SV	AB	H	HR	BA
1914 2 teams			NY	A (1G 0–0)		BOS	A (9G 1–1)												
" total	1	1	.500	5.76	10	1	0	25	26	11	8	0	0	1	0	8	0	0	.000
1915 BOS A	0	0	–	0.00	1	0	0	2	0	2	0	0	0	0	0	0	0	0	–
2 yrs.	1	1	.500	5.33	11	1	0	27	26	13	8	0	0	1	0	8	0	0	.000

Mort Cooper

COOPER, MORTON CECIL   BR TR 6'2"   210 lbs.
Brother of Walker Cooper.
B. Mar. 2, 1913, Atherton, Mo.   D. Nov. 17, 1958, Little Rock, Ark.

	W	L	PCT	ERA	G	GS	CG	IP	H	BB	SO	ShO	W	L	SV	AB	H	HR	BA
1938 STL N	2	1	.667	3.04	4	3	1	23.2	17	12	11	0	0	0	1	9	2	0	.222
1939	12	6	.667	3.25	45	26	7	210.2	208	97	130	2	2	0	4	69	16	2	.232
1940	11	12	.478	3.63	38	29	16	230.2	225	86	95	3	1	0	3	83	13	0	.157
1941	13	9	.591	3.91	29	25	12	186.2	175	69	118	0	1	0	0	70	13	0	.186
1942	22	7	.759	1.78	37	35	22	278.2	207	68	152	10	0	1	0	103	19	0	.184
1943	21	8	.724	2.30	37	32	24	274	228	79	141	6	1	1	3	100	17	1	.170
1944	22	7	.759	2.46	34	33	22	252.1	227	60	97	7	0	0	1	94	19	0	.202
1945 2 teams			STL	N (4G 2–0)		BOS	N (20G 7–4)												
" total	9	4	.692	2.92	24	14	5	101.2	97	34	59	1	3	2	1	32	8	1	.250
1946 BOS N	13	11	.542	3.12	28	27	15	199	181	39	83	4	0	0	1	67	14	1	.209
1947 2 teams			BOS	N (10G 2–5)		NY	N (8G 1–5)												
" total	3	10	.231	5.40	18	15	4	83.1	99	26	27	0	1	0	0	27	6	1	.222
1949 CHI N	0	0	–	∞	1	0	0	0	2	1	0	0	0	0	0	0	0	0	–
11 yrs.	128	75	.631	2.97	295	239	128	1840.2	1666	571	913	33	9	4	14	654	127	6	.194
WORLD SERIES																			
1942 STL N	0	1	.000	5.54	2	2	0	13	17	4	9	0	0	0	0	5	1	0	.200
1943	1	1	.500	2.81	2	2	1	16	11	3	10	0	0	0	0	5	0	0	.000
1944	1	1	.500	1.13	2	2	1	16	9	5	16	1	0	0	0	4	0	0	.000
3 yrs.	2	3	.400	3.00	6	6	2	45	37	12	35	1	0	0	0	14	1	0	.071

Pat Cooper

COOPER, ORGE PATTERSON   BR TR 6'3"   180 lbs.
B. Nov. 26, 1917, Albermarle, N. C.

	W	L	PCT	ERA	G	GS	CG	IP	H	BB	SO	ShO	W	L	SV	AB	H	HR	BA
1946 PHI A	0	0	–	0.00	1	0	0	1	1	1	0	0	0	0	0	*			

	W	L	PCT	ERA	G	GS	CG	IP	H	BB	SO	ShO	Relief Pitching W	L	SV	BATTING AB	H	HR	BA

Wilbur Cooper

COOPER, ARLEY WILBUR
B. Feb. 24, 1892, Bearsville, W. Va.   D. Aug. 7, 1973, Encino, Calif.   BR TL 5'11½" 165 lbs.

	W	L	PCT	ERA	G	GS	CG	IP	H	BB	SO	ShO	W	L	SV	AB	H	HR	BA
1912 PIT N	3	0	1.000	1.66	6	4	3	38	32	15	30	2	0	0	0	13	2	0	.154
1913	5	3	.625	3.29	30	9	3	93	98	45	39	1	3	1	0	26	2	0	.077
1914	16	15	.516	2.13	40	34	19	266.2	246	79	102	0	0	1	0	92	19	0	.207
1915	5	16	.238	3.30	38	21	11	185.2	180	52	71	1	1	0	4	60	7	0	.117
1916	12	11	.522	1.87	42	23	16	246	189	74	111	2	4	0	2	79	17	0	.215
1917	17	11	.607	2.36	40	34	23	297.2	276	54	99	7	1	0	1	103	21	0	.204
1918	19	14	.576	2.11	38	29	26	273.1	219	65	117	3	4	1	3	95	23	0	.242
1919	19	13	.594	2.67	35	32	27	286.2	229	74	106	4	1	0	1	101	29	0	.287
1920	24	15	.615	2.39	44	37	28	327	307	52	114	3	2	1	2	113	25	0	.221
1921	22	14	.611	3.25	38	38	29	327	341	80	134	2	0	0	0	122	31	0	.254
1922	23	14	.622	3.18	41	37	27	294.2	330	61	129	4	0	1	0	108	29	4	.269
1923	17	19	.472	3.57	39	38	26	294.2	331	71	77	1	1	0	0	107	28	0	.262
1924	20	14	.588	3.28	38	35	25	268.2	296	40	62	4	1	0	1	104	36	0	.346
1925 CHI N	12	14	.462	4.28	32	26	13	212.1	249	61	41	0	3	1	0	82	17	2	.207
1926 2 teams		CHI	N	(8G 2–1)		DET	A	(8G 0–4)											
" total	2	5	.286	5.77	16	3	1	68.2	92	30	20	2	0	1	0	22	7	0	.318
15 yrs.	216	178	.548	2.89	517	408	279	3480	3415	853	1252	36	21	7	14	1227	293	6	.239

Mays Copeland

COPELAND, MAYS
B. Aug. 31, 1913, Mt. View, Ark.   BR TR 6' 180 lbs.

	W	L	PCT	ERA	G	GS	CG	IP	H	BB	SO	ShO	W	L	SV	AB	H	HR	BA
1935 STL N	0	0	—	13.50	1	0	0	.2	2	0	0	0	0	0	0	0	0	0	—

Henry Coppola

COPPOLA, HENRY PETER
B. Aug. 6, 1912, East Douglas, Mass.   BR TR 5'11" 175 lbs.

	W	L	PCT	ERA	G	GS	CG	IP	H	BB	SO	ShO	W	L	SV	AB	H	HR	BA
1935 WAS A	3	4	.429	5.92	19	5	2	59.1	72	29	19	1	1	2	0	14	1	0	.071
1936	0	0	—	4.50	6	0	0	14	17	12	2	0	0	0	1	3	1	0	.333
2 yrs.	3	4	.429	5.65	25	5	2	73.1	89	41	21	1	1	2	1	17	2	0	.118

Doug Corbett

CORBETT, DOUGLAS MITCHELL
B. Nov. 4, 1952, Sarasota, Fla.   BR TR 6'1" 185 lbs.

	W	L	PCT	ERA	G	GS	CG	IP	H	BB	SO	ShO	W	L	SV	AB	H	HR	BA
1980 MIN A	8	6	.571	1.99	73	0	0	136	102	42	89	0	8	6	23	0	0	0	—
1981	2	6	.250	2.56	54	0	0	88	80	34	60	0	2	6	17	0	0	0	—
1982 2 teams		MIN	A	(10G 0–2)		CAL	A	(33G 1–7)											
" total	1	9	.100	5.13	43	0	0	79	73	35	52	0	1	9	11	0	0	0	—
1983 CAL A	1	1	.500	3.63	11	0	0	17.1	26	4	18	0	1	1	0	0	0	0	—
1984	5	1	.833	2.12	45	0	0	85	76	30	48	0	4	1	4	0	0	0	—
5 yrs.	17	23	.425	2.82	226	1	0	405.1	357	145	267	0	16	23	55	0	0	0	—

Joe Corbett

CORBETT, JOSEPH A.
B. Dec. 4, 1875, San Francisco, Calif.   D. May 2, 1945, San Francisco, Calif.   BR TR 5'10"

	W	L	PCT	ERA	G	GS	CG	IP	H	BB	SO	ShO	W	L	SV	AB	H	HR	BA
1895 WAS N	0	2	.000	5.68	3	3	3	19	26	9	3	0	0	0	0	15	2	0	.133
1896 BAL N	3	0	1.000	2.20	8	3	3	41	31	17	28	0	0	0	1	22	6	0	.273
1897	24	8	.750	3.11	37	37	34	313	330	115	149	1	0	0	0	150	37	0	.247
1904 STL N	5	9	.357	4.39	14	14	12	108.2	110	51	68	0	0	0	0	43	9	0	.209
4 yrs.	32	19	.627	3.42	62	57	52	481.2	497	192	248	1	0	0	1	230	54	0	.235

Ray Corbin

CORBIN, ALTON RAY
B. Feb. 12, 1949, Live Oak, Fla.   BR TR 6'2" 200 lbs.

	W	L	PCT	ERA	G	GS	CG	IP	H	BB	SO	ShO	W	L	SV	AB	H	HR	BA
1971 MIN A	8	11	.421	4.11	52	11	2	140	141	70	83	0	6	4	3	34	7	0	.206
1972	8	9	.471	2.61	31	19	5	162	135	53	83	3	2	0	0	49	4	0	.082
1973	8	5	.615	3.03	51	7	1	148.1	124	60	83	0	4	5	14	0	0	0	—
1974	7	6	.538	5.30	29	15	1	112	133	40	50	0	3	1	0	0	0	0	—
1975	5	7	.417	5.12	18	11	3	89.2	105	38	49	0	2	0	0	0	0	0	—
5 yrs.	36	38	.486	3.84	181	63	12	652	638	261	348	3	17	10	17	83	11	0	.133

John Corcoran

CORCORAN, JOHN H.
B. Lowell, Mass.   Deceased.

	W	L	PCT	ERA	G	GS	CG	IP	H	BB	SO	ShO	W	L	SV	AB	H	HR	BA
1884 BKN AA	0	0	—	0.00	1	0	0	1	0	1	0	0	0	0	0	*			

Larry Corcoran

CORCORAN, LAWRENCE J.
Brother of Mike Corcoran.
B. Aug. 10, 1859, Brooklyn, N. Y.   D. Oct. 14, 1891, Newark, N. J.   TR

	W	L	PCT	ERA	G	GS	CG	IP	H	BB	SO	ShO	W	L	SV	AB	H	HR	BA
1880 CHI N	43	14	.754	1.95	63	60	57	536.1	404	99	268	5	0	0	2	286	66	0	.231
1881	31	14	.689	2.31	45	44	39	396.2	380	78	150	4	1	0	0	189	42	0	.222
1882	27	13	.675	1.95	40	40	39	355.2	281	63	170	3	0	0	0	169	35	1	.207
1883	34	20	.630	2.49	56	53	51	473.2	483	82	216	3	1	0	0	263	55	0	.209
1884	35	23	.603	2.40	60	59	57	516.2	473	116	272	7	0	1	0	251	61	0	.243
1885 2 teams		CHI	N	(7G 5–2)		NY	N	(3G 2–1)											
" total	7	3	.700	3.42	10	10	8	84.1	87	35	20	1	0	0	0	36	11	0	.306
1886 WAS N	0	1	.000	5.79	2	1	1	14	16	4	3	0	0	0	0	85	15	0	.176
1887 IND N	0	2	.000	12.60	2	2	1	15	23	19	4	0	0	0	0	10	2	0	.200
8 yrs.	177	90	.663	2.36	278	269	257	2392.1	2147	496	1103	23	2	1	2	*			
			8th																

Mike Corcoran

CORCORAN, MICHAEL
Brother of Larry Corcoran.
Deceased.

	W	L	PCT	ERA	G	GS	CG	IP	H	BB	SO	ShO	W	L	SV	AB	H	HR	BA
1884 CHI N	0	1	.000	4.00	1	1	1	9	16	7	2	0	0	0	0	3	0	0	.000

Ed Corey

COREY, EDWARD NORMAN
Born Edward Norman Cohen.
B. July 13, 1899, Chicago, Ill.   D. Sept. 17, 1970, Kenosha, Wis.   BR TR 6' 170 lbs.

	W	L	PCT	ERA	G	GS	CG	IP	H	BB	SO	ShO	W	L	SV	AB	H	HR	BA
1918 CHI A	0	0	—	4.50	1	0	0	2	2	1	0	0	0	0	0	1	0	0	.000

	W	L	PCT	ERA	G	GS	CG	IP	H	BB	SO	ShO	Relief Pitching W	L	SV	BATTING AB	H	HR	BA

Fred Corey

COREY, FREDERICK HARRISON   BR TR
B. 1857, S. Kingston, R. I.   D. Nov. 27, 1912, Providence, R. I.

	W	L	PCT	ERA	G	GS	CG	IP	H	BB	SO	ShO	W	L	SV	AB	H	HR	BA
1878 PRO N	1	2	.333	2.35	5	5	2	23	22	7	7	0	0	0	0	21	3	0	.143
1880 WOR N	8	9	.471	2.43	25	17	9	148.1	131	16	47	2	0	1	2	138	24	0	.174
1881	6	15	.286	3.72	23	21	20	188.2	231	31	33	1	0	0	0	203	45	0	.222
1882	1	13	.071	3.56	21	14	12	139	180	19	36	0	0	1	0	255	63	0	.247
1883 PHI AA	10	7	.588	3.40	18	16	15	148.1	182	24	42	0	0	1	0	298	77	1	.258
1885	1	0	1.000	7.00	1	1	1	9	18	1	3	0	0	0	0	384	94	1	.245
6 yrs.	27	46	.370	3.32	93	74	59	656.1	764	98	168	3	0	3	2	*			

Pop Corkhill

CORKHILL, JOHN STEWART   BL TR   5'10"   180 lbs.
B. Apr. 11, 1858, Parkesburg, Pa.   D. Apr. 4, 1921, Pennsauken, N. J.

	W	L	PCT	ERA	G	GS	CG	IP	H	BB	SO	ShO	W	L	SV	AB	H	HR	BA
1884 CIN AA	1	0	1.000	1.80	1	0	0	5	1	2	4	0	1	0	0	452	124	4	.274
1885	1	4	.200	3.65	8	1	0	37	36	10	12	0	1	3	1	440	111	1	.252
1886	0	0	—	13.50	1	0	0	.2	1	0	1	0	0	0	0	540	143	4	.265
1887	1	0	1.000	5.52	5	0	0	14.2	22	5	3	0	1	0	0	541	168	5	.311
1888	0	0	—	10.80	2	0	0	5	8	0	1	0	0	0	1	561	160	2	.285
5 yrs.	3	4	.429	4.62	17	1	0	62.1	68	17	21	0	3	3	2	*			

Mike Corkins

CORKINS, MICHAEL PATRICK   BR TR   6'1"   190 lbs.
B. May 25, 1946, Riverside, Calif.

	W	L	PCT	ERA	G	GS	CG	IP	H	BB	SO	ShO	W	L	SV	AB	H	HR	BA
1969 SD N	1	3	.250	8.47	6	4	0	17	27	8	13	0	0	0	0	3	0	0	.000
1970	5	6	.455	4.62	24	18	1	111	109	79	75	0	0	0	0	37	8	1	.216
1971	0	0	—	3.46	8	0	0	13	14	6	16	0	0	0	0	0	0	0	—
1972	6	9	.400	3.54	47	9	2	140	125	62	108	1	4	3	6	38	9	1	.237
1973	5	8	.385	4.50	47	11	2	122	130	61	82	0	2	3	3	33	7	3	.212
1974	2	2	.500	4.82	25	2	0	56	53	32	41	0	2	1	0	8	0	0	.000
6 yrs.	19	28	.404	4.39	157	44	5	459	458	248	335	1	8	7	9	119	24	5	.202

Mardie Cornejo

CORNEJO, NEIVES MARDIE   BR TR   6'3"   200 lbs.
B. Aug. 5, 1951, Wellington, Kans.

	W	L	PCT	ERA	G	GS	CG	IP	H	BB	SO	ShO	W	L	SV	AB	H	HR	BA
1978 NY N	4	2	.667	2.43	25	0	0	37	37	14	17	0	4	2	3	0	0	0	—

Jeff Cornell

CORNELL, JEFFREY RAY   BL TR   6'   170 lbs.
B. Feb. 10, 1957, Kansas City, Mo.

	W	L	PCT	ERA	G	GS	CG	IP	H	BB	SO	ShO	W	L	SV	AB	H	HR	BA
1984 SF N	1	3	.250	6.10	23	0	0	38.1	51	22	19	0	1	3	0	4	0	0	.000

Terry Cornutt

CORNUTT, TERRY STANTON   BR TR   6'2"   195 lbs.
B. Oct. 2, 1952, Roseburg, Ore.

	W	L	PCT	ERA	G	GS	CG	IP	H	BB	SO	ShO	W	L	SV	AB	H	HR	BA
1977 SF N	1	2	.333	3.89	28	1	0	44	38	22	23	0	1	1	0	1	0	0	.000
1978	0	0	—	0.00	1	0	0	3	1	0	0	0	0	0	0	0	0	0	—
2 yrs.	1	2	.333	3.64	29	1	0	47	39	22	23	0	1	1	0	1	0	0	.000

Frank Corridon

CORRIDON, FRANK J. (Fiddler)   BR TR
B. Nov. 25, 1880, Newport, R. I.   D. Feb. 21, 1941, Syracuse, N. Y.

	W	L	PCT	ERA	G	GS	CG	IP	H	BB	SO	ShO	W	L	SV	AB	H	HR	BA
1904 2 teams		CHI	N (12G 5–5)		PHI	N (12G 6–5)													
" total	11	10	.524	2.64	24	21	20	194.2	176	65	78	1	1	1	0	93	19	0	.204
1905 PHI N	10	13	.435	3.48	35	26	18	212	203	57	79	1	1	1	1	72	15	1	.208
1907	18	14	.563	2.46	37	32	23	274	228	89	131	3	0	1	1	97	16	0	.165
1908	14	10	.583	2.51	27	24	18	208.1	178	48	50	2	0	0	1	73	9	0	.123
1909	11	7	.611	2.11	27	19	11	171	147	61	69	3	1	1	0	59	11	0	.186
1910 STL N	6	14	.300	3.81	30	18	9	156	168	55	51	0	1	2	2	51	10	0	.196
6 yrs.	70	68	.507	2.80	180	140	99	1216	1100	375	458	10	4	6	5	445	80	1	.180

Barry Cort

CORT, BARRY LEE   BR TR   6'5"   210 lbs.
B. Apr. 15, 1956, Toronto, Ontario, Canada

	W	L	PCT	ERA	G	GS	CG	IP	H	BB	SO	ShO	W	L	SV	AB	H	HR	BA
1977 MIL A	1	1	.500	3.38	7	3	1	24	25	9	17	0	0	0	0	0	0	0	—

Al Corwin

CORWIN, ELMER NATHAN   BR TR   6'1"   170 lbs.
B. Dec. 3, 1926, Newburgh, N. Y.

	W	L	PCT	ERA	G	GS	CG	IP	H	BB	SO	ShO	W	L	SV	AB	H	HR	BA
1951 NY N	5	1	.833	3.66	15	8	3	59	49	21	30	1	1	0	0	20	1	0	.050
1952	6	1	.857	2.66	21	7	1	67.2	58	36	36	0	3	0	2	21	2	0	.095
1953	6	4	.600	4.98	48	7	2	106.2	122	68	49	1	4	2	2	32	9	2	.281
1954	1	3	.250	4.02	20	0	0	31.1	35	14	14	0	1	3	0	3	0	0	.000
1955	0	0	—	4.01	13	0	0	24.2	25	17	13	0	0	1	1	3	0	0	.000
5 yrs.	18	10	.643	3.98	117	22	6	289.1	289	156	142	2	9	6	5	79	12	2	.152
WORLD SERIES																			
1951 NY N	0	0	—	0.00	1	0	0	1.2	1	1	1	0	0	0	0	0	0	0	—

Mike Cosgrove

COSGROVE, MICHAEL JOHN   BL TL   6'1"   170 lbs.
B. Feb. 17, 1951, Phoenix, Ariz.

	W	L	PCT	ERA	G	GS	CG	IP	H	BB	SO	ShO	W	L	SV	AB	H	HR	BA
1972 HOU N	0	1	.000	4.61	7	1	0	13.2	16	3	7	0	0	0	1	2	0	0	.000
1973	1	1	.500	1.80	13	0	0	10	11	8	2	0	1	1	0	0	0	0	—
1974	7	3	.700	3.49	45	0	0	90.1	76	39	47	0	7	3	2	18	1	0	.056
1975	1	2	.333	3.04	32	3	1	71	62	37	32	0	0	1	5	13	2	0	.154
1976	3	4	.429	5.50	22	16	1	90	106	58	34	1	0	0	0	23	2	0	.087
5 yrs.	12	11	.522	4.03	119	20	2	275	271	145	122	1	8	5	8	56	5	0	.089

Jim Cosman

COSMAN, JAMES HENRY   BR TR   6'4½"   211 lbs.
B. Feb. 19, 1943, Brockport, N. Y.

	W	L	PCT	ERA	G	GS	CG	IP	H	BB	SO	ShO	W	L	SV	AB	H	HR	BA
1966 STL N	1	0	1.000	0.00	1	1	1	9	2	2	5	1	0	0	0	3	0	0	.000
1967	1	0	1.000	3.16	10	5	0	31.1	21	24	11	0	0	0	0	8	1	0	.125
1970 CHI N	0	0	—	27.00	1	0	0	1	3	1	0	0	0	0	0	0	0	0	—
3 yrs.	2	0	1.000	3.05	12	6	1	41.1	26	27	16	1	0	0	0	11	1	0	.091

	W	L	PCT	ERA	G	GS	CG	IP	H	BB	SO	ShO	Relief Pitching W	L	SV	BATTING AB	H	HR	BA

Dan Cotter

COTTER, DANIEL JOSEPH   BR TR
B. Apr. 14, 1867, Boston, Mass.   D. Sept. 4, 1935, Boston, Mass.

	W	L	PCT	ERA	G	GS	CG	IP	H	BB	SO	ShO	W	L	SV	AB	H	HR	BA
1890 BUF P	0	1	.000	14.00	1	1	1	9	18	7	0	0	0	0	0	4	0	0	.000

Ensign Cottrell

COTTRELL, ENSIGN STOVER   BL TL 5'9½"   173 lbs.
B. Aug. 29, 1888, Hoosick Falls, N. Y.   D. Feb. 27, 1947, Syracuse, N. Y.

	W	L	PCT	ERA	G	GS	CG	IP	H	BB	SO	ShO	W	L	SV	AB	H	HR	BA
1911 PIT N	0	0	—	9.00	1	0	0	1	4	1	0	0	0	0	0	0	0	0	—
1912 CHI N	0	0	—	9.00	1	0	0	4	8	1	1	0	0	0	0	1	0	0	.000
1913 PHI A	1	0	1.000	5.40	2	1	1	10	15	2	3	0	0	0	0	4	1	0	.250
1914 BOS N	0	1	.000	9.00	1	0	1	1	2	3	1	0	0	0	0	0	0	0	—
1915 NY A	0	1	.000	3.38	7	0	0	21.1	29	7	7	0	0	1	0	7	0	0	.000
5 yrs.	1	2	.333	4.82	12	2	1	37.1	58	14	12	0	0	1	0	12	1	0	.083

Johnny Couch

COUCH, JOHN DANIEL   BL TR 6'   180 lbs.
B. Mar. 31, 1891, Vaughn, Mont.   D. Dec. 8, 1975, Palo Alto, Calif.

	W	L	PCT	ERA	G	GS	CG	IP	H	BB	SO	ShO	W	L	SV	AB	H	HR	BA
1917 DET A	0	0	—	2.70	3	0	0	13.1	13	1	1	0	0	0	0	4	0	0	.000
1922 CIN N	16	9	.640	3.89	43	34	18	264	301	56	45	2	1	0	1	91	12	0	.132
1923 2 teams		CIN	N (19G 2–7)		PHI	N (11G 2–4)													
" total	4	11	.267	5.63	30	15	3	134.1	189	36	32	0	0	1	0	47	10	0	.213
1924 PHI N	4	8	.333	4.73	37	6	3	137	170	39	23	0	4	3	3	49	10	2	.204
1925	5	6	.455	5.44	34	7	2	94.1	112	39	11	1	4	0	2	31	5	1	.161
5 yrs.	29	34	.460	4.63	147	62	26	643	785	171	112	3	9	4	6	222	37	3	.167

Mike Couchee

COUCHEE, MICHAEL EUGENE   BR TR 5'11"   185 lbs.
B. Dec. 4, 1957, San Jose, Calif.

	W	L	PCT	ERA	G	GS	CG	IP	H	BB	SO	ShO	W	L	SV	AB	H	HR	BA
1983 SD N	0	1	.000	5.14	8	0	0	14	12	6	5	0	0	1	0	2	1	0	.500

Ed Coughlin

COUGHLIN, EDWARD E.
B. Aug. 5, 1861, Hartford, Conn.   D. Dec. 25, 1952, Hartford, Conn.

	W	L	PCT	ERA	G	GS	CG	IP	H	BB	SO	ShO	W	L	SV	AB	H	HR	BA
1884 BUF N	0	0	—	∞	1	0	0		3	0	0	0	0	0	0	4	1	0	.250

Roscoe Coughlin

COUGHLIN, WILLIAM E.   TR
B. Mar. 15, 1868, Walpole, Mass.   D. Mar. 20, 1951, Chelsea, Mass.

	W	L	PCT	ERA	G	GS	CG	IP	H	BB	SO	ShO	W	L	SV	AB	H	HR	BA
1890 CHI N	4	4	.500	4.26	11	10	10	95	102	40	29	0	0	0	0	39	10	0	.256
1891 NY N	3	3	.500	3.84	8	7	6	61	74	23	22	0	0	0	0	23	3	0	.130
2 yrs.	7	7	.500	4.10	19	17	16	156	176	63	51	0	0	0	0	62	13	0	.210

Fritz Coumbe

COUMBE, FREDERICK NICHOLAS   BL TL 6'   152 lbs.
B. Dec. 13, 1889, Antrim, Pa.   D. Mar. 21, 1978, Paradise, Calif.

	W	L	PCT	ERA	G	GS	CG	IP	H	BB	SO	ShO	W	L	SV	AB	H	HR	BA
1914 2 teams		BOS	A (17G 1–2)		CLE	A (14G 1–5)													
" total	2	7	.222	2.29	31	10	3	117.2	108	32	39	0	1	1	1	41	8	0	.195
1915 CLE A	4	7	.364	3.47	30	12	4	114	123	37	37	1	1	0	2	37	10	0	.270
1916	7	5	.583	2.02	29	13	7	120.1	121	27	39	2	2	0	0	35	2	0	.057
1917	8	6	.571	2.14	34	10	4	134.1	119	35	30	1	3	1	5	39	6	0	.154
1918	13	7	.650	3.00	30	17	9	150	164	52	41	0	3	2	3	56	12	0	.214
1919	1	1	.500	5.32	8	2	0	23.2	32	9	7	0	0	1	1	6	3	0	.500
1920 CIN N	0	1	.000	4.91	3	0	0	14.2	17	4	7	0	0	1	0	13	3	1	.231
1921	3	4	.429	3.22	28	6	3	86.2	89	21	12	0	1	1	1	25	8	0	.320
8 yrs.	38	38	.500	2.79	193	70	30	761.1	773	217	212	4	11	7	13	252	52	1	.206

Henry Courtney

COURTNEY, HARRY SEYMOUR   BB TL 6'4"   185 lbs.
B. Nov. 19, 1898, Asheville, N. C.   D. Dec. 11, 1954, Lyme, Conn.

	W	L	PCT	ERA	G	GS	CG	IP	H	BB	SO	ShO	W	L	SV	AB	H	HR	BA
1919 WAS A	3	0	1.000	2.73	4	3	3	26.1	25	19	6	1	0	0	0	10	2	0	.200
1920	8	11	.421	4.74	37	24	10	188	223	77	48	1	0	2	0	69	16	1	.232
1921	6	9	.400	5.63	30	15	3	132.2	159	71	26	0	1	1	1	47	14	0	.298
1922 2 teams		WAS	A (5G 0–0)		CHI	A (18G 5–6)													
" total	5	6	.455	4.81	23	11	5	97.1	111	46	32	0	1	0	0	37	9	0	.243
4 yrs.	22	26	.458	4.90	94	53	21	444.1	518	213	112	2	2	3	1	163	41	1	.252

Harry Coveleski

COVELESKI, HARRY FRANK (The Giant Killer)   BB TL 6'   180 lbs.
Born Harry Frank Kowalewski.   Brother of Stan Coveleski.
B. Apr. 23, 1886, Shamokin, Pa.   D. Aug. 4, 1950, Shamokin, Pa.

	W	L	PCT	ERA	G	GS	CG	IP	H	BB	SO	ShO	W	L	SV	AB	H	HR	BA
1907 PHI N	1	0	1.000	0.00	4	0	0	20	10	3	6	0	1	0	0	8	0	0	.000
1908	4	1	.800	1.24	6	5	5	43.2	29	12	22	2	0	0	0	15	2	0	.133
1909	6	10	.375	2.74	24	17	8	121.2	109	49	56	2	1	0	1	37	4	0	.108
1910 CIN N	1	1	.500	5.26	7	4	2	39.1	35	42	27	0	0	0	0	16	1	0	.063
1914 DET A	22	12	.647	2.49	44	36	23	303.1	251	100	124	5	2	1	2	95	23	0	.242
1915	22	13	.629	2.45	50	38	20	312.2	271	87	150	1	4	2	4	103	18	0	.175
1916	21	11	.656	1.97	44	39	22	324.1	278	63	108	3	1	1	2	118	25	0	.212
1917	4	6	.400	2.61	16	11	2	69	70	14	15	0	1	0	0	22	5	0	.227
1918	0	1	.000	3.86	3	1	1	14	17	6	3	0	0	0	0	4	1	0	.250
9 yrs.	81	55	.596	2.39	198	151	83	1248	1070	376	511	13	10	4	9	418	79	0	.189

Stan Coveleski

COVELESKI, STANLEY ANTHONY   BR TR 5'11"   166 lbs.
Born Stanislaus Kowalewski.   Brother of Harry Coveleski.
B. July 13, 1889, Shamokin, Pa.   D. Mar. 20, 1984, South Bend, Ind.
Hall of Fame 1969.

	W	L	PCT	ERA	G	GS	CG	IP	H	BB	SO	ShO	W	L	SV	AB	H	HR	BA
1912 PHI A	2	1	.667	3.43	5	2	2	21	18	4	9	1	1	0	0	7	1	0	.143
1916 CLE A	15	13	.536	3.41	45	27	11	232	247	58	76	1	2	4	3	75	13	1	.173
1917	19	14	.576	1.81	45	36	24	298.1	202	94	133	9	1	2	4	97	13	0	.134
1918	22	13	.629	1.82	38	33	25	311	261	76	87	2	1	1	1	110	21	0	.191
1919	24	12	.667	2.52	43	34	24	296	286	60	118	4	1	4	4	94	20	0	.213
1920	24	14	.632	2.49	41	37	26	315	284	65	133	3	1	0	2	111	25	0	.225
1921	23	13	.639	3.36	43	40	29	315.2	341	84	99	2	0	0	2	116	18	0	.155
1922	17	14	.548	3.32	35	33	21	276.2	292	64	98	3	0	0	2	99	10	0	.101
1923	13	14	.481	2.76	33	31	17	228	251	42	54	5	0	0	2	79	7	0	.089
1924	15	16	.484	4.04	37	33	18	240.1	286	73	58	2	2	1	0	82	11	0	.134

	W	L	PCT	ERA	G	GS	CG	IP	H	BB	SO	ShO	Relief Pitching W	L	SV	BATTING AB	H	HR	BA

Stan Coveleski continued

	W	L	PCT	ERA	G	GS	CG	IP	H	BB	SO	ShO	W	L	SV	AB	H	HR	BA
1925 WAS A	20	5	.800	2.84	32	32	15	241	230	73	58	3	0	0	0	81	9	0	.111
1926	14	11	.560	3.12	36	34	11	245.1	272	81	50	3	0	0	1	82	17	0	.207
1927	2	1	.667	3.14	5	4	0	14.1	13	8	3	0	0	0	0	6	2	0	.333
1928 NY A	5	1	.833	5.74	12	8	2	58	72	20	5	0	0	0	0	19	1	0	.053
14 yrs.	215	142	.602	2.88	450	384	225	3092.2	3055	802	981	38	9	12	21	1058	168	1	.159
WORLD SERIES																			
1920 CLE A	3	0	1.000	0.67	3	3	3	27	15	2	8	1	0	0	0	10	1	0	.100
1925 WAS A	0	2	.000	3.77	2	2	1	14.1	16	5	3	0	0	0	0	3	0	0	.000
2 yrs.	3	2	.600	1.74	5	5	4	41.1	31	7	11	1	0	0	0	13	1	0	.077

Chet Covington

COVINGTON, CHESTER ROGERS (Chesty)   BB TL 6'2"   225 lbs.
B. Nov. 6, 1910, Cairo, Ill.   D. June 11, 1976, Pembroke Park, Fla.

	W	L	PCT	ERA	G	GS	CG	IP	H	BB	SO	ShO	W	L	SV	AB	H	HR	BA
1944 PHI N	1	1	.500	4.66	19	0	0	38.2	46	8	13	0	1	1	0	6	0	0	.000

Tex Covington

COVINGTON, WILLIAM WILKES   BL TR 6'1"   175 lbs.
Brother of Sam Covington.
B. Mar. 19, 1887, Henryville, Tenn.   D. Dec. 10, 1931, Denison, Tex.

	W	L	PCT	ERA	G	GS	CG	IP	H	BB	SO	ShO	W	L	SV	AB	H	HR	BA
1911 DET A	7	1	.875	4.09	17	6	5	83.2	94	33	29	0	2	0	0	32	6	0	.188
1912	3	4	.429	4.12	14	9	2	63.1	58	30	19	1	0	0	0	15	2	0	.133
2 yrs.	10	5	.667	4.10	31	15	7	147	152	63	48	1	2	0	0	47	8	0	.170

Joe Cowley

COWLEY, JOE ALAN   BR TR 6'5"   205 lbs.
B. Aug. 15, 1958, Lexington, Ky.

	W	L	PCT	ERA	G	GS	CG	IP	H	BB	SO	ShO	W	L	SV	AB	H	HR	BA
1982 ATL N	1	2	.333	4.47	17	8	0	52.1	53	16	27	0	1	0	1	15	3	0	.200
1984 NY A	9	2	.818	3.56	16	11	3	83.1	75	31	71	1	1	2	0	0	0	0	–
2 yrs.	10	4	.714	3.91	33	19	3	135.2	128	47	98	1	2	2	0	15	3	0	.200

Bill Cox

COX, WILLIAM DONALD   BR TR 6'1"   185 lbs.
B. June 23, 1913, Ashmore, Ill.

	W	L	PCT	ERA	G	GS	CG	IP	H	BB	SO	ShO	W	L	SV	AB	H	HR	BA
1936 STL N	0	0	–	6.75	2	0	0	2.2	4	1	1	0	0	0	0	0	0	0	–
1937 CHI A	1	0	1.000	0.71	3	2	1	12.2	9	5	8	0	0	0	0	4	1	0	.250
1938 2 teams		CHI	A (7G 0–2)		STL	A (22G 1–4)													
" total	1	6	.143	6.99	29	8	1	74.2	92	48	21	0	0	1	0	19	1	0	.053
1939 STL A	0	2	.000	9.64	4	2	1	9.1	10	8	8	0	0	0	0	1	0	0	.000
1940	0	1	.000	7.27	12	0	0	17.1	23	12	7	0	0	1	0	1	0	0	.000
5 yrs.	2	9	.182	6.56	50	12	3	116.2	138	74	45	0	0	2	0	25	2	0	.080

Casey Cox

COX, JOSEPH CASEY   BR TR 6'5"   200 lbs.
B. July 3, 1941, Long Beach, Calif.

	W	L	PCT	ERA	G	GS	CG	IP	H	BB	SO	ShO	W	L	SV	AB	H	HR	BA
1966 WAS A	4	5	.444	3.50	66	0	0	113	104	35	46	0	4	5	7	8	0	0	.000
1967	7	4	.636	2.96	54	0	0	73	67	21	32	0	7	4	1	3	0	0	.000
1968	0	1	.000	2.35	4	0	0	7.2	7	0	4	0	0	1	0	0	0	0	–
1969	12	7	.632	2.78	52	13	4	171.2	161	64	73	0	7	3	0	47	5	0	.106
1970	8	12	.400	4.45	37	30	1	192	211	44	68	0	0	0	1	58	7	0	.121
1971	5	7	.417	3.99	54	11	0	124	131	40	43	0	5	4	7	26	2	0	.077
1972 2 teams		TEX	A (35G 3–5)		NY	A (5G 0–1)													
" total	3	6	.333	4.44	40	5	0	77	86	29	31	0	2	2	4	9	1	0	.111
1973 NY A	0	0	–	6.00	1	0	0	3	5	1	0	0	0	0	0	0	0	0	–
8 yrs.	39	42	.481	3.70	308	59	5	761.1	772	234	297	0	25	19	20	151	15	0	.099

Danny Cox

COX, DANNY BRADFORD   BR TR 6'4"   220 lbs.
B. Sept. 21, 1959, North Hampton, England

	W	L	PCT	ERA	G	GS	CG	IP	H	BB	SO	ShO	W	L	SV	AB	H	HR	BA
1983 STL N	3	6	.333	3.25	12	12	0	83	92	23	36	0	0	0	0	27	2	0	.074
1984	9	11	.450	4.03	29	27	1	156.1	171	54	70	1	1	0	0	53	7	0	.132
2 yrs.	12	17	.414	3.76	41	39	1	239.1	263	77	106	1	1	0	0	80	9	0	.113

Ernie Cox

COX, ERNEST THOMPSON (Elmer)   BL TR 6'1"   180 lbs.
B. Feb. 19, 1894, Birmingham, Ala.   D. Apr. 29, 1974, Birmingham, Ala.

	W	L	PCT	ERA	G	GS	CG	IP	H	BB	SO	ShO	W	L	SV	AB	H	HR	BA
1922 CHI A	0	0	–	18.00	1	0	0	1	1	2	0	0	0	0	0	0	0	0	–

George Cox

COX, GEORGE MELVIN   BR TR 6'1"   170 lbs.
B. Nov. 15, 1904, Sherman, Tex.

	W	L	PCT	ERA	G	GS	CG	IP	H	BB	SO	ShO	W	L	SV	AB	H	HR	BA
1928 CHI A	1	2	.333	5.26	26	2	0	89	110	39	22	0	1	1	0	26	2	0	.077

Glenn Cox

COX, GLENN MELVIN (Jingles)   BR TR 6'2"   210 lbs.
B. Feb. 3, 1931, Montebello, Calif.

	W	L	PCT	ERA	G	GS	CG	IP	H	BB	SO	ShO	W	L	SV	AB	H	HR	BA
1955 KC A	0	2	.000	30.86	2	2	0	2.1	11	1	2	0	0	0	0	1	0	0	.000
1956	0	2	.000	4.24	3	3	1	23.1	15	22	6	0	0	0	0	7	0	0	.000
1957	1	0	1.000	5.02	10	0	0	14.1	18	9	8	0	1	0	0	2	0	0	.000
1958	0	0	–	9.82	2	0	0	3.2	6	3	1	0	0	0	0	0	0	0	–
4 yrs.	1	4	.200	6.39	17	5	1	43.2	50	35	17	0	1	0	0	10	0	0	.000

Les Cox

COX, LESLIE WARREN   BR TR 6'   164 lbs.
B. Aug. 14, 1905, Junction, Tex.   D. Nov. 14, 1934, San Angelo, Tex.

	W	L	PCT	ERA	G	GS	CG	IP	H	BB	SO	ShO	W	L	SV	AB	H	HR	BA
1926 CHI A	0	1	.000	5.40	2	0	0	5	6	5	3	0	0	1	0	2	1	0	.500

Red Cox

COX, PLATEAU REX   BL TR 6'2"   190 lbs.
B. Feb. 16, 1895, Laurel Springs, N. C.   D. Oct. 15, 1984, Roanoke, Va.

	W	L	PCT	ERA	G	GS	CG	IP	H	BB	SO	ShO	W	L	SV	AB	H	HR	BA
1920 DET A	0	0	–	5.40	3	0	0	5	9	3	1	0	0	0	0	1	0	0	.000

Terry Cox

COX, TERRY LEE   BR TR 6'5"   215 lbs.
B. Mar. 30, 1949, Odessa, Tex.

	W	L	PCT	ERA	G	GS	CG	IP	H	BB	SO	ShO	W	L	SV	AB	H	HR	BA
1970 CAL A	0	0	–	4.50	3	0	0	2	4	0	3	0	0	0	0	0	0	0	–

	W	L	PCT	ERA	G	GS	CG	IP	H	BB	SO	ShO	Relief Pitching W	L	SV	BATTING AB	H	HR	BA

Bill Coyle

COYLE, WILLIAM CLAUDE   TR
B. Pittsburgh, Pa.   Deceased.

	W	L	PCT	ERA	G	GS	CG	IP	H	BB	SO	ShO	W	L	SV	AB	H	HR	BA
1893 BOS N	0	1	.000	9.00	2	1	0	8	14	3	2	0	0	0	0	4	0	0	.000

Charlie Cozart

COZART, CHARLES RHUBIN   BR TL 6'   190 lbs.
B. Oct. 17, 1919, Lenoir, N. C.

	W	L	PCT	ERA	G	GS	CG	IP	H	BB	SO	ShO	W	L	SV	AB	H	HR	BA
1945 BOS N	1	0	1.000	10.13	5	0	0	8	10	15	4	0	1	0	0	2	0	0	.000

Jim Crabb

CRABB, JAMES ROY   BR TR 5'11"   160 lbs.
B. Aug. 23, 1890, Monticello, Iowa   D. Mar. 30, 1940, Lewistown, Mont.

	W	L	PCT	ERA	G	GS	CG	IP	H	BB	SO	ShO	W	L	SV	AB	H	HR	BA
1912 2 teams			CHI A (2G 0–1)			PHI A (7G 2–4)													
" total	2	5	.286	3.29	9	8	3	52	54	21	15	0	0	0	0	19	0	0	.000

George Crable

CRABLE, GEORGE E.   BL TL 6'1"   190 lbs.
B. 1886, Brooklyn, N. Y.

	W	L	PCT	ERA	G	GS	CG	IP	H	BB	SO	ShO	W	L	SV	AB	H	HR	BA
1910 BKN N	0	0	–	4.91	2	1	1	7.1	5	5	3	0	0	0	0	2	0	0	.000

Walter Craddock

CRADDOCK, WALTER ANDERSON   BR TL 5'11½"   176 lbs.
B. Mar. 25, 1932, Pax, W. Va.   D. July 6, 1980, Parma Heights, Ohio

	W	L	PCT	ERA	G	GS	CG	IP	H	BB	SO	ShO	W	L	SV	AB	H	HR	BA
1955 KC A	0	2	.000	7.80	4	2	0	15	18	10	9	0	0	1	0	5	0	0	.000
1956	0	2	.000	6.75	2	2	0	9.1	9	10	8	0	0	0	0	2	0	0	.000
1958	0	3	.000	5.89	23	1	0	36.2	41	20	22	0	0	2	0	2	0	0	.000
3 yrs.	0	7	.000	6.49	29	5	0	61	68	40	39	0	0	3	0	9	0	0	.000

Molly Craft

CRAFT, MAURICE MONTAGUE   BR TR 6'2"   165 lbs.
B. Nov. 28, 1895, Portsmouth, Va.   D. Oct. 25, 1978, Los Angeles, Calif.

	W	L	PCT	ERA	G	GS	CG	IP	H	BB	SO	ShO	W	L	SV	AB	H	HR	BA
1916 WAS A	0	1	.000	3.27	2	1	1	11	12	6	9	0	0	0	0	4	0	0	.000
1917	0	0	–	3.86	8	0	0	14	17	8	2	0	0	0	1	2	1	0	.500
1918	0	0	–	1.29	3	0	0	7	5	1	5	0	0	0	0	2	0	0	.000
1919	0	3	.000	3.88	16	2	0	48.2	59	18	17	0	0	2	0	18	2	0	.111
4 yrs.	0	4	.000	3.57	29	3	1	80.2	93	33	33	0	0	2	1	26	3	0	.115

Howard Craghead

CRAGHEAD, HOWARD OLIVER (Judge)   BR TR 6'2"   200 lbs.
B. May 25, 1908, Selma, Calif.   D. July 15, 1962, San Zieloe, Calif.

	W	L	PCT	ERA	G	GS	CG	IP	H	BB	SO	ShO	W	L	SV	AB	H	HR	BA
1931 CLE A	0	0	–	6.35	4	0	0	5.2	8	2	2	0	0	0	0	0	0	0	–
1933	0	0	–	6.23	11	0	0	17.1	19	10	2	0	0	0	0	3	0	0	.000
2 yrs.	0	0	–	6.26	15	0	0	23	27	12	4	0	0	0	0	3	0	0	.000

George Craig

CRAIG, GEORGE McCARTHY (Lefty)   TL
B. Nov. 15, 1887, Philadelphia, Pa.   D. Apr. 23, 1911, Indianapolis, Ind.

	W	L	PCT	ERA	G	GS	CG	IP	H	BB	SO	ShO	W	L	SV	AB	H	HR	BA
1907 PHI A	0	0	–	10.80	2	0	0	1.2	2	3	0	0	0	0	0	1	0	0	.000

Pete Craig

CRAIG, PETER JOEL   BL TR 6'5"   220 lbs.
B. July 10, 1940, La Salle, Ont., Canada

	W	L	PCT	ERA	G	GS	CG	IP	H	BB	SO	ShO	W	L	SV	AB	H	HR	BA
1964 WAS A	0	0	–	48.60	2	1	0	1.2	8	4	0	0	0	0	0	0	0	0	–
1965	0	3	.000	8.16	3	3	0	14.1	18	8	2	0	0	0	0	3	2	0	.667
1966	0	0	–	4.50	1	0	0	2	2	1	1	0	0	0	0	0	0	0	–
3 yrs.	0	3	.000	11.50	6	4	0	18	28	13	3	0	0	0	0	3	2	0	.667

Roger Craig

CRAIG, ROGER LEE   BR TR 6'4"   185 lbs.
B. Feb. 17, 1931, Durham, N. C.
Manager 1978-79.

	W	L	PCT	ERA	G	GS	CG	IP	H	BB	SO	ShO	W	L	SV	AB	H	HR	BA
1955 BKN N	5	3	.625	2.78	21	10	3	90.2	81	43	48	0	0	1	2	26	2	0	.077
1956	12	11	.522	3.71	35	32	8	199	169	87	109	2	0	2	1	61	1	0	.016
1957	6	9	.400	4.61	32	13	1	111.1	102	47	69	0	4	2	0	29	4	0	.138
1958 LA N	2	1	.667	4.50	9	2	1	32	30	12	16	0	0	1	0	9	0	0	.000
1959	11	5	.688	2.06	29	17	7	152.2	122	45	76	4	2	0	0	52	3	0	.058
1960	8	3	.727	3.27	21	15	6	115.2	99	43	69	1	1	0	0	36	2	0	.056
1961	5	6	.455	6.15	40	14	2	112.2	130	52	63	0	2	1	2	27	4	0	.148
1962 NY N	10	24	.294	4.51	42	33	13	233.1	261	70	118	0	4	2	3	76	4	0	.053
1963	5	22	.185	3.78	46	31	14	236	249	58	108	0	0	1	2	69	6	0	.087
1964 STL N	7	9	.438	3.25	39	19	3	166	180	35	84	0	2	1	5	48	10	0	.208
1965 CIN N	1	4	.200	3.64	40	0	0	64.1	74	25	30	0	1	4	3	11	2	0	.182
1966 PHI N	2	1	.667	5.56	14	0	0	22.2	31	5	13	0	2	1	1	4	0	0	.000
12 yrs.	74	98	.430	3.83	368	186	58	1536.1	1528	522	803	7	18	16	19	448	38	0	.085
WORLD SERIES																			
1955 BKN N	1	0	1.000	3.00	1	1	0	6	4	5	4	0	0	0	0	0	0	0	–
1956	0	1	.000	12.00	2	1	0	6	10	3	4	0	0	0	0	2	1	0	.500
1959 LA N	0	1	.000	8.68	2	2	0	9.1	15	5	8	0	0	0	0	3	0	0	.000
1964 STL N	1	0	1.000	0.00	2	0	0	5	2	3	9	0	1	0	0	1	0	0	.000
4 yrs.	2	2	.500	6.49	7	4	0	26.1	31	16	25	0	1	0	0	6	1	0	.167

Jerry Cram

CRAM, GERALD ALLEN   BR TR 6'   180 lbs.
B. Dec. 9, 1947, Los Angeles, Calif.

	W	L	PCT	ERA	G	GS	CG	IP	H	BB	SO	ShO	W	L	SV	AB	H	HR	BA
1969 KC A	0	1	.000	3.24	5	2	0	16.2	15	6	10	0	0	0	0	3	0	0	.000
1974 NY N	0	1	.000	1.64	10	0	0	22	22	4	8	0	0	1	0	3	1	0	.333
1975	0	1	.000	5.40	4	0	0	5	7	2	2	0	0	1	0	0	0	0	–
1976 KC A	0	0	–	6.75	4	0	0	4	8	1	2	0	0	0	0	0	0	0	–
4 yrs.	0	3	.000	3.02	23	2	0	47.2	52	13	22	0	0	2	0	6	1	0	.167

Bill Cramer

CRAMER, WILLIAM WENDELL   BR TR
B. May 21, 1891, Bedford, Ind.   D. Sept. 11, 1966, Fort Wayne, Ind.

	W	L	PCT	ERA	G	GS	CG	IP	H	BB	SO	ShO	W	L	SV	AB	H	HR	BA
1912 CIN N	0	0	–	0.00	1	0	0	2.1	6	0	2	0	0	0	0	1	0	0	.000

	W	L	PCT	ERA	G	GS	CG	IP	H	BB	SO	ShO	Relief Pitching W	L	SV	BATTING AB	H	HR	BA

Doc Cramer

CRAMER, ROGER MAXWELL (Flit)
B. July 22, 1905, Beach Haven, N. J.
BL TR 6'2" 185 lbs.

	W	L	PCT	ERA	G	GS	CG	IP	H	BB	SO	ShO	W	L	SV	AB	H	HR	BA
1938 BOS A	0	0	–	4.50	1	0	0	4	3	3	1	0	0	0	0	*			

Doc Crandall

CRANDALL, JAMES OTIS
B. Oct. 8, 1887, Wadena, Ind.   D. Aug. 17, 1951, Bell, Calif.
BR TR 5'10½" 180 lbs.

	W	L	PCT	ERA	G	GS	CG	IP	H	BB	SO	ShO	W	L	SV	AB	H	HR	BA
1908 NY N	12	12	.500	2.93	32	24	13	214.2	198	59	77	0	2	1	0	72	16	2	.222
1909	6	4	.600	2.88	30	7	4	122	117	33	55	0	5	1	4	41	10	1	.244
1910	17	4	.810	2.56	42	18	13	207.2	194	43	73	2	7	1	4	73	25	1	.342
1911	15	5	.750	2.63	41	15	9	198.2	199	51	94	2	7	0	5	113	27	2	.239
1912	13	7	.650	3.61	37	10	7	162	181	35	60	0	6	5	2	80	25	0	.313
1913	4	4	.500	2.86	35	3	2	97.2	102	24	42	0	3	3	6	49	15	0	.306
1914 STL F	12	9	.571	3.54	27	21	18	196	194	52	84	1	1	0	0	278	86	2	.309
1915	21	15	.583	2.59	51	33	22	312.2	307	77	117	4	6	3	0	141	40	1	.284
1916 STL A	0	0	–	27.00	2	0	0	1.1	7	1	0	0	0	0	0	12	1	0	.083
1918 BOS N	1	2	.333	2.38	5	3	3	34	39	4	4	0	0	0	0	28	8	0	.286
10 yrs.	101	62	.620	2.92	302	134	91	1546.2	1538	379	606	9	37	14	21	*			

WORLD SERIES	W	L	PCT	ERA	G	GS	CG	IP	H	BB	SO	ShO	W	L	SV	AB	H	HR	BA
1911 NY N	1	0	1.000	0.00	2	0	0	4	2	0	2	0	1	0	0	2	1	0	.500
1912	0	0	–	0.00	1	0	0	2	1	0	2	0	0	0	0	1	0	0	.000
1913	0	0	–	3.86	2	0	0	4.2	4	0	2	0	0	0	0	4	0	0	.000
3 yrs.	1	0	1.000	1.69	5	0	0	10.2	7	0	6	0	1	0	0	7	1	0	.143

Cannonball Crane

CRANE, EDWARD NICHOLAS
B. May, 1862, Boston, Mass.   D. Sept. 19, 1896, Rochester, N. Y.
BR TR 5'10½" 204 lbs.

	W	L	PCT	ERA	G	GS	CG	IP	H	BB	SO	ShO	W	L	SV	AB	H	HR	BA
1884 BOS U	0	2	.000	4.00	4	2	1	18	17	6	13	0	0	0	0	428	122	12	.285
1885 BUF N	0	0	–	0.00	0	0	0	0	0	0	0	0	0	0	0	53	14	2	.264
1886 WAS N	1	7	.125	7.20	10	8	7	70	91	53	39	1	0	0	0	292	50	0	.171
1888 NY N	5	6	.455	2.43	12	11	11	92.2	70	40	58	1	0	0	1	37	6	1	.162
1889	14	10	.583	3.68	29	25	23	230	221	136	130	0	1	1	0	103	21	2	.204
1890 NY P	16	18	.471	4.63	43	35	28	330.1	323	210	117	0	1	1	0	146	46	0	.315
1891 2 teams			C-M	AA (32G 14–14)				CIN N (15G 4–8)											
" total	18	22	.450	2.97	47	44	36	366.2	350	203	173	2	0	0	0	156	22	1	.141
1892 NY N	16	24	.400	3.80	47	43	35	364.1	350	189	174	2	0	1	1	163	40	0	.245
1893 2 teams			NY	N (10G 2–4)				BKN N (2G 0–2)											
" total	2	6	.250	6.89	12	9	5	78.1	103	50	16	0	0	0	0	31	14	0	.452
9 yrs.	72	95	.431	3.99	204	177	146	1550.1	1525	887	720	6	2	3	2	*			

Jim Crawford

CRAWFORD, JAMES FREDERICK
B. Sept. 29, 1950, Chicago, Ill.
BL TL 6'3" 200 lbs.

	W	L	PCT	ERA	G	GS	CG	IP	H	BB	SO	ShO	W	L	SV	AB	H	HR	BA
1973 HOU N	2	4	.333	4.50	48	0	0	70	69	33	56	0	2	4	6	13	3	0	.231
1975	3	5	.375	3.62	44	2	0	87	92	37	37	0	3	4	4	17	5	0	.294
1976 DET A	1	8	.111	4.53	32	5	1	109.1	115	43	68	0	0	6	2	0	0	0	–
1977	7	8	.467	4.79	37	7	0	126	156	50	91	0	5	4	1	0	0	0	–
1978	2	3	.400	4.35	20	0	0	39.1	45	19	24	0	2	3	0	0	0	0	–
5 yrs.	15	28	.349	4.40	181	14	1	431.2	477	182	276	0	12	21	13	30	8	0	.267

Larry Crawford

CRAWFORD, CHARLES LOWRIE
B. Apr. 27, 1914, Swissvale, Pa.
BL TL 6'1" 165 lbs.

	W	L	PCT	ERA	G	GS	CG	IP	H	BB	SO	ShO	W	L	SV	AB	H	HR	BA
1937 PHI N	0	0	–	15.00	6	0	0	6	12	1	2	0	0	0	0	0	0	0	–

Steve Crawford

CRAWFORD, STEPHEN RAY
B. Apr. 29, 1958, Pryor, Okla.
BR TR 6'5" 225 lbs.

	W	L	PCT	ERA	G	GS	CG	IP	H	BB	SO	ShO	W	L	SV	AB	H	HR	BA
1980 BOS A	2	0	1.000	3.66	6	4	2	32	41	8	10	0	0	0	0	0	0	0	–
1981	0	5	.000	4.97	14	11	0	58	69	18	29	0	0	0	0	0	0	0	–
1982	1	0	1.000	2.00	5	0	0	9	14	0	2	0	1	0	0	0	0	0	–
1984	5	0	1.000	3.34	35	0	0	62	69	21	21	0	5	0	1	0	0	0	–
4 yrs.	8	5	.615	3.91	60	15	2	161	193	47	62	0	6	0	1	0	0	0	–

Jack Creel

CREEL, JACK DALTON (Tex)
B. Apr. 23, 1916, Kyle, Tex.
BR TR 6' 165 lbs.

	W	L	PCT	ERA	G	GS	CG	IP	H	BB	SO	ShO	W	L	SV	AB	H	HR	BA
1945 STL N	5	4	.556	4.14	26	8	2	87	78	45	34	0	2	0	2	26	2	0	.077

Keith Creel

CREEL, STEVEN KEITH
B. Feb. 4, 1959, Dallas, Tex.
BR TR 6'2" 180 lbs.

	W	L	PCT	ERA	G	GS	CG	IP	H	BB	SO	ShO	W	L	SV	AB	H	HR	BA
1982 KC A	1	4	.200	5.40	9	6	0	41.2	43	25	13	0	0	0	0	0	0	0	–
1983	2	5	.286	6.35	25	10	1	89.1	116	35	31	0	0	1	0	0	0	0	–
2 yrs.	3	9	.250	6.05	34	16	1	131	159	60	44	0	0	1	0	0	0	0	–

Bob Cremins

CREMINS, ROBERT ANTHONY (Lefty)
B. Feb. 15, 1906, Pelham Manor, N. Y.
BL TL 5'11" 160 lbs.

	W	L	PCT	ERA	G	GS	CG	IP	H	BB	SO	ShO	W	L	SV	AB	H	HR	BA
1927 BOS A	0	0	–	5.06	4	0	0	5.1	5	3	0	0	0	0	0	0	0	0	–

Walker Cress

CRESS, WALKER JAMES (Foots)
B. Mar. 6, 1917, Ben Hur, Va.
BR TR 6'5" 205 lbs.

	W	L	PCT	ERA	G	GS	CG	IP	H	BB	SO	ShO	W	L	SV	AB	H	HR	BA
1948 CIN N	0	1	.000	4.50	30	2	1	60	60	42	33	0	0	0	0	8	4	0	.500
1949	0	0	–	0.00	3	0	0	2	2	3	0	0	0	0	0	0	0	0	–
2 yrs.	0	1	.000	4.35	33	2	1	62	62	45	33	0	0	0	0	8	4	0	.500

Jerry Crider

CRIDER, JERRY STEPHEN
B. Sept. 2, 1941, Sioux Falls, S. D.
BR TR 6'2" 200 lbs.

	W	L	PCT	ERA	G	GS	CG	IP	H	BB	SO	ShO	W	L	SV	AB	H	HR	BA
1969 MIN A	1	0	1.000	4.71	21	1	0	28.2	31	15	16	0	1	0	1	9	4	0	.444
1970 CHI A	4	7	.364	4.45	32	8	0	91	101	34	40	0	2	2	4	24	2	0	.083
2 yrs.	5	7	.417	4.51	53	9	0	119.2	132	49	56	0	3	2	5	33	6	0	.182

	W	L	PCT	ERA	G	GS	CG	IP	H	BB	SO	ShO	Relief Pitching W	L	SV	BATTING AB	H	HR	BA

Jack Crimian

CRIMIAN, JOHN MELVIN
B. Feb. 17, 1926, Philadelphia, Pa. — BR TR 5'10" 180 lbs.

	W	L	PCT	ERA	G	GS	CG	IP	H	BB	SO	ShO	W	L	SV	AB	H	HR	BA
1951 STL N	1	0	1.000	9.00	11	0	0	17	24	8	5	0	1	0	1	3	1	0	.333
1952	0	0	–	9.72	5	0	0	8.1	15	4	4	0	0	0	0	1	0	0	.000
1956 KC A	4	8	.333	5.51	54	7	0	129	129	49	59	0	3	3	3	22	5	0	.227
1957 DET A	0	1	.000	12.71	4	0	0	5.2	9	4	1	0	0	1	0	0	0	0	–
4 yrs.	5	9	.357	6.36	74	7	0	160	177	65	69	0	4	4	4	26	6	0	.231

Dode Criss

CRISS, DODE
B. Mar. 12, 1885, Sherman, Miss. D. Sept. 8, 1955, Sherman, Miss. — BL TR 6'2" 200 lbs.

	W	L	PCT	ERA	G	GS	CG	IP	H	BB	SO	ShO	W	L	SV	AB	H	HR	BA
1908 STL A	0	1	.000	6.50	9	1	0	18	15	13	9	0	0	1	0	82	28	0	.341
1909	1	5	.167	3.42	11	6	3	55.1	53	32	43	0	0	1	0	48	14	0	.292
1910	2	1	.667	1.40	6	0	0	19.1	12	9	9	0	2	1	0	91	21	1	.231
1911	0	2	.000	8.35	4	2	0	18.1	24	10	9	0	0	0	0	83	21	2	.253
4 yrs.	3	9	.250	4.38	30	9	3	111	104	64	70	0	2	3	0	*			

Bill Cristall

CRISTALL, WILLIAM ARTHUR (Lefty)
B. Sept. 12, 1878, Odessa, Russia D. Jan. 28, 1939, Buffalo, N. Y. — BL TL 5'7" 147 lbs.

	W	L	PCT	ERA	G	GS	CG	IP	H	BB	SO	ShO	W	L	SV	AB	H	HR	BA
1901 CLE A	1	5	.167	4.84	6	6	5	48.1	54	30	12	1	0	0	0	20	7	0	.350

Leo Cristante

CRISTANTE, LEO DANTE
B. Dec. 10, 1926, Detroit, Mich. D. Aug. 24, 1977, Dearborn, Mich. — BR TR 6'1" 205 lbs.

	W	L	PCT	ERA	G	GS	CG	IP	H	BB	SO	ShO	W	L	SV	AB	H	HR	BA
1951 PHI N	1	1	.500	4.91	10	1	0	22	28	9	6	0	1	0	0	6	1	0	.167
1955 DET A	0	1	.000	3.19	20	1	0	36.2	37	14	9	0	0	1	0	7	0	0	.000
2 yrs.	1	2	.333	3.84	30	2	0	58.2	65	23	15	0	1	1	0	13	1	0	.077

Morrie Critchley

CRITCHLEY, MORRIS ARTHUR
B. Mar. 26, 1850, New London, Conn. D. Mar. 6, 1910, Pittsburgh, Pa. — 6'1" 190 lbs.

	W	L	PCT	ERA	G	GS	CG	IP	H	BB	SO	ShO	W	L	SV	AB	H	HR	BA
1882 2 teams								PIT AA (1G 1–0)		STL AA (4G 0–4)									
" total	1	4	.200	3.35	5	5	5	43	50	8	5	1	0	0	0	19	3	0	.158

Claude Crocker

CROCKER, CLAUDE ARTHUR
B. July 20, 1924, Caroleen, N. Y. — BR TR 6'2" 185 lbs.

	W	L	PCT	ERA	G	GS	CG	IP	H	BB	SO	ShO	W	L	SV	AB	H	HR	BA
1944 BKN N	0	0	–	10.80	2	0	0	3.1	6	5	1	0	0	0	0	1	1	0	1.000
1945	0	0	–	0.00	1	0	0	2	2	1	1	0	0	0	1	0	0	0	–
2 yrs.	0	0	–	6.75	3	0	0	5.1	8	6	2	0	0	0	1	1	1	0	1.000

Ray Crone

CRONE, RAYMOND HAYES
B. Aug. 7, 1931, Memphis, Tenn. — BR TR 6'2" 165 lbs.

	W	L	PCT	ERA	G	GS	CG	IP	H	BB	SO	ShO	W	L	SV	AB	H	HR	BA
1954 MIL N	1	0	1.000	2.02	19	2	1	49	44	19	33	0	0	0	1	10	2	0	.200
1955	10	9	.526	3.46	33	15	6	140.1	117	42	76	1	5	2	0	44	7	0	.159
1956	11	10	.524	3.87	35	21	6	169.2	173	44	73	0	1	2	2	49	6	0	.122
1957 2 teams								MIL N (11G 3–1)		NY N (25G 4–8)									
" total	7	9	.438	4.36	36	22	4	163	185	55	71	0	0	1	1	51	3	0	.059
1958 SF N	1	2	.333	6.75	14	1	0	24	35	13	7	0	1	2	0	2	0	0	.000
5 yrs.	30	30	.500	3.87	137	61	17	546	554	173	260	1	7	7	4	156	18	0	.115

John Cronin

CRONIN, JOHN J.
B. May 26, 1874, Staten Island, N. Y. D. July 13, 1929, Middletown, N. Y. — BR TR 6' 200 lbs.

	W	L	PCT	ERA	G	GS	CG	IP	H	BB	SO	ShO	W	L	SV	AB	H	HR	BA
1895 BKN N	0	0	–	10.80	2	0	0	5	10	3	1	0	0	0	2	2	1	0	.500
1898 PIT N	2	2	.500	3.54	4	4	2	28	35	8	9	1	0	0	0	10	1	0	.100
1899 CIN N	2	2	.500	5.49	5	5	4	41	56	16	9	0	0	0	0	17	2	0	.118
1901 DET A	13	15	.464	3.89	30	28	21	219.2	261	42	62	1	1	0	0	85	21	0	.247
1902 3 teams								DET A (4G 0–0)		BAL A (10G 3–5)		NY N (13G 5–6)						
" total	8	11	.421	3.09	27	20	19	207	197	50	77	0	0	0	0	99	15	0	.152
1903 NY N	6	4	.600	3.81	20	11	8	115.2	130	37	50	0	1	0	1	46	9	0	.196
1904 BKN N	12	23	.343	2.70	40	34	33	307	284	79	110	4	1	1	0	108	17	0	.157
7 yrs.	43	57	.430	3.40	128	102	88	923.1	973	235	318	6	3	1	3	367	66	0	.180

George Crosby

CROSBY, GEORGE WASHINGTON
B. Chicago, Ill. D. Jan. 9, 1913, San Francisco, Calif.

	W	L	PCT	ERA	G	GS	CG	IP	H	BB	SO	ShO	W	L	SV	AB	H	HR	BA
1884 CHI N	1	2	.333	3.54	3	3	3	28	27	12	11	0	0	0	0	13	4	1	.308

Ken Crosby

CROSBY, KENNETH STEWART
B. Dec. 16, 1947, New Denver, B. C., Canada — BR TR 6'2" 179 lbs.

	W	L	PCT	ERA	G	GS	CG	IP	H	BB	SO	ShO	W	L	SV	AB	H	HR	BA
1975 CHI N	1	0	1.000	3.38	9	0	0	8	10	7	6	0	1	0	0	0	0	0	–
1976	0	0	–	12.00	7	1	0	12	20	8	5	0	0	0	0	2	1	0	.500
2 yrs.	1	0	1.000	8.55	16	1	0	20	30	15	11	0	1	0	0	2	1	0	.500

Lem Cross

CROSS, GEORGE LEWIS
B. Jan. 9, 1872, Manchester, N. H. D. Oct. 9, 1930, Manchester, N. H. — 5'9" 155 lbs.

	W	L	PCT	ERA	G	GS	CG	IP	H	BB	SO	ShO	W	L	SV	AB	H	HR	BA
1893 CIN N	0	2	.000	5.57	3	3	2	21	24	9	7	0	0	0	0	6	2	0	.333
1894	3	4	.429	8.49	8	7	3	53	94	21	11	0	0	1	0	26	6	0	.231
2 yrs.	3	6	.333	7.66	11	10	5	74	118	30	18	0	0	1	0	32	8	0	.250

Dug Crothers

CROTHERS, DOUGLAS
B. Nov. 16, 1859, Natchez, Miss. D. Mar. 29, 1907, St. Louis, Mo. — BR TR

	W	L	PCT	ERA	G	GS	CG	IP	H	BB	SO	ShO	W	L	SV	AB	H	HR	BA
1884 KC U	1	2	.333	1.80	3	3	3	25	26	6	11	0	0	0	0	15	2	0	.133
1885 NY AA	7	11	.389	5.08	18	18	18	154	192	49	40	1	0	0	0	51	8	0	.157
2 yrs.	8	13	.381	4.63	21	21	21	179	218	55	51	1	0	0	0	66	10	0	.152

Bill Crouch

CROUCH, WILLIAM ELMER (Skip)
Father of Bill Crouch.
B. Dec. 3, 1886, Marshallton, Del. — BL TL 6'1" 210 lbs.

	W	L	PCT	ERA	G	GS	CG	IP	H	BB	SO	ShO	W	L	SV	AB	H	HR	BA
1910 STL A	0	0	–	3.38	1	1	1	8	6	7	2	0	0	0	0	3	0	0	.000

	W	L	PCT	ERA	G	GS	CG	IP	H	BB	SO	ShO	Relief Pitching W	L	SV	BATTING AB	H	HR	BA

Bill Crouch

CROUCH, WILLIAM ELMER
Son of Bill Crouch.
B. Aug. 20, 1910, Wilmington, Del.   D. Dec. 26, 1980, Howell, Mich.
BB TR 6'1"   180 lbs.

	W	L	PCT	ERA	G	GS	CG	IP	H	BB	SO	ShO	W	L	SV	AB	H	HR	BA
1939 BKN N	4	0	1.000	2.58	6	3	3	38.1	37	14	10	0	1	0	0	15	2	0	.133
1941 2 teams			PHI N (20G 2–3)			STL N (18G 1–2)														
" total	3	5	.375	3.81	38	9	1	104	110	31	41	0	0	2	7	24	1	0	.042
1945 STL N	1	0	1.000	3.38	6	0	0	13.1	12	7	4	0	1	0	0	2	0	0	.000
3 yrs.	8	5	.615	3.47	50	12	4	155.2	159	52	55	0	2	2	7	41	3	0	.073

General Crowder

CROWDER, ALVIN FLOYD
B. Jan. 11, 1899, Winston-Salem, N. C.   D. Apr. 3, 1972, Winston Salem, N. C.
BL TR 5'10"   170 lbs.

	W	L	PCT	ERA	G	GS	CG	IP	H	BB	SO	ShO	W	L	SV	AB	H	HR	BA
1926 WAS A	7	4	.636	3.96	19	12	6	100	97	60	26	0	1	0	1	38	9	0	.237
1927 2 teams			WAS A (15G 4–7)			STL A (21G 3–5)														
" total	7	12	.368	4.79	36	19	6	141	129	84	52	3	2	1	3	45	9	0	.200
1928 STL A	21	5	.808	3.69	41	31	19	244	238	91	99	1	0	0	2	80	15	0	.188
1929	17	15	.531	3.92	40	34	19	266.2	272	93	79	4	1	0	4	96	18	0	.188
1930 2 teams			STL A (13G 3–7)			WAS A (27G 15–9)														
" total	18	16	.529	3.89	40	35	25	279.2	276	96	107	1	0	0	2	101	17	0	.168
1931 WAS A	18	11	.621	3.88	44	26	13	234.1	255	72	85	1	4	2	2	88	19	0	.216
1932	26	13	.667	3.33	50	39	21	327	319	77	103	3	5	0	1	122	27	0	.221
1933	24	15	.615	3.97	52	35	17	299.1	311	81	110	0	4	4	4	102	19	0	.186
1934 2 teams			WAS A (29G 4–10)			DET A (9G 5–1)														
" total	9	11	.450	5.75	38	22	7	167.1	223	58	69	1	1	4	3	62	11	0	.177
1935 DET A	16	10	.615	4.26	33	32	16	241	269	67	59	2	0	0	0	93	17	0	.183
1936	4	3	.571	8.39	9	7	1	44	64	21	10	0	1	0	0	20	3	0	.150
11 yrs.	167	115	.592	4.12	402	292	150	2344.1	2453	800	799	16	19	11	22	847	164	0	.194
WORLD SERIES																			
1933 WAS A	0	1	.000	7.36	2	2	0	11	16	5	7	0	0	0	0	4	1	0	.250
1934 DET A	0	1	.000	1.50	2	1	0	6	6	1	2	0	0	0	0	1	0	0	.000
1935	1	0	1.000	1.00	1	1	1	9	5	3	5	0	0	0	0	3	1	0	.333
3 yrs.	1	2	.333	3.81	5	4	1	26	27	9	14	0	0	0	0	8	2	0	.250

Billy Crowell

CROWELL, WILLIAM THEODORE
B. Nov. 6, 1865, Cincinnati, Ohio   D. July 23, 1935, Fort Worth, Tex.
BR TR 5'8½"   160 lbs.

	W	L	PCT	ERA	G	GS	CG	IP	H	BB	SO	ShO	W	L	SV	AB	H	HR	BA
1887 CLE AA	14	31	.311	4.88	45	45	45	389.1	541	138	72	1	0	0	0	156	22	0	.141
1888 2 teams			CLE AA (18G 5–13)			LOU AA (1G 0–1)														
" total	5	14	.263	5.81	19	19	17	159.2	224	67	66	0	0	0	0	61	5	0	.082
2 yrs.	19	45	.297	5.15	64	64	62	549	765	205	138	1	0	0	0	217	27	0	.124

Cap Crowell

CROWELL, MINOT JOY
B. Sept. 5, 1892, Roxbury, Mass.   D. Sept. 30, 1962, Central Falls, R. I.
BR TR 6'1"   178 lbs.

	W	L	PCT	ERA	G	GS	CG	IP	H	BB	SO	ShO	W	L	SV	AB	H	HR	BA
1915 PHI A	2	6	.250	5.47	10	8	4	54.1	56	47	15	0	0	0	0	22	5	0	.227
1916	0	5	.000	4.76	9	6	1	39.2	43	34	15	0	0	0	0	12	0	0	.000
2 yrs.	2	11	.154	5.17	19	14	5	94	99	81	30	0	0	0	0	34	5	0	.147

Woody Crowson

CROWSON, THOMAS WOODROW
B. Sept. 9, 1918, Fuquay Springs, N. C.   D. Aug. 14, 1947, Mayodan, N. C.
BR TR 6'2"   185 lbs.

	W	L	PCT	ERA	G	GS	CG	IP	H	BB	SO	ShO	W	L	SV	AB	H	HR	BA
1945 PHI A	0	0	—	6.00	1	0	0	3	2	3	2	0	0	0	0	1	0	0	.000

Cal Crum

CRUM, CALVIN CARL
B. July 27, 1890, Mattoon, Ill.   D. Dec. 7, 1945, Tulsa, Okla.
BR TR 6'1"   175 lbs.

	W	L	PCT	ERA	G	GS	CG	IP	H	BB	SO	ShO	W	L	SV	AB	H	HR	BA
1917 BOS N	0	0	—	0.00	1	0	0	1	1	1	0	0	0	0	0	0	0	0	—
1918	0	1	.000	15.43	1	1	0	2.1	6	3	0	0	0	0	0	1	0	0	.000
2 yrs.	0	1	.000	10.80	2	1	0	3.1	7	4	0	0	0	0	0	1	0	0	.000

Roy Crumpler

CRUMPLER, ROY MAXTON
B. July 8, 1896, Clinton, N. C.   D. Oct. 6, 1969, Fayetteville, N. C.
BL TL 6'1"   195 lbs.

	W	L	PCT	ERA	G	GS	CG	IP	H	BB	SO	ShO	W	L	SV	AB	H	HR	BA
1920 DET A	1	0	1.000	5.54	3	2	1	13	17	11	2	0	0	0	0	9	3	0	.333
1925 PHI N	0	0	—	7.71	3	1	0	4.2	8	2	1	0	0	0	0	2	0	0	.000
2 yrs.	1	0	1.000	6.11	6	3	1	17.2	25	13	3	0	0	0	0	11	3	0	.273

Dick Crutcher

CRUTCHER, RICHARD LOUIS
B. Nov. 25, 1889, Frankfort, Ky.   D. June 19, 1952, Frankfort, Ky.
BR TR 5'9"   148 lbs.

	W	L	PCT	ERA	G	GS	CG	IP	H	BB	SO	ShO	W	L	SV	AB	H	HR	BA
1914 BOS N	5	6	.455	3.46	33	15	5	158.2	169	66	48	1	2	2	0	54	8	0	.148
1915	2	2	.500	4.33	14	4	1	43.2	50	16	17	0	1	0	2	13	3	0	.231
2 yrs.	7	8	.467	3.65	47	19	6	202.1	219	82	65	1	3	2	2	67	11	0	.164

Todd Cruz

CRUZ, TODD RUBEN
B. Nov. 23, 1955, Highland Park, Mich.
BR TR 6'   175 lbs.

	W	L	PCT	ERA	G	GS	CG	IP	H	BB	SO	ShO	W	L	SV	AB	H	HR	BA
1984 BAL A	0	0	—	0.00	1	0	0	1	0	1	0	0	0	0	0	*			

Victor Cruz

CRUZ, VICTOR MANUEL
B. Dec. 24, 1957, Rancho Viejo, Dominican Republic
BR TR 5'9"   174 lbs.

	W	L	PCT	ERA	G	GS	CG	IP	H	BB	SO	ShO	W	L	SV	AB	H	HR	BA
1978 TOR A	7	3	.700	1.71	32	0	0	47.1	28	36	51	0	7	3	9	0	0	0	—
1979 CLE A	3	9	.250	4.22	6t	0	0	79	70	44	63	0	3	9	10	0	0	0	—
1980	6	7	.462	3.45	55	0	0	86	71	27	88	0	6	7	12	0	0	0	—
1981 PIT N	1	1	.500	2.65	22	0	0	34	33	15	28	0	1	1	1	4	0	0	.000
1983 TEX A	1	3	.250	1.44	17	0	0	25	16	10	18	0	1	3	5	0	0	0	—
5 yrs.	18	23	.439	3.08	187	0	0	271.1	218	132	248	0	18	23	37	4	0	0	.000

Cookie Cuccurullo

CUCCURULLO, ARTHUR JOSEPH
B. Feb. 8, 1918, Asbury Park, N. J.   D. Jan. 23, 1983, West Orange, N. J.
BL TL 5'10"   168 lbs.

	W	L	PCT	ERA	G	GS	CG	IP	H	BB	SO	ShO	W	L	SV	AB	H	HR	BA
1943 PIT N	0	1	.000	6.43	1	0	0	7	10	3	3	0	0	0	0	0	0	0	—
1944	2	1	.667	4.06	32	4	0	106.1	110	44	31	0	2	1	4	38	14	0	.368
1945	1	3	.250	5.24	29	4	0	56.2	68	34	17	0	1	1	1	14	3	0	.214
3 yrs.	3	5	.375	4.55	62	9	0	170	188	81	51	0	3	2	5	52	17	0	.327

	W	L	PCT	ERA	G	GS	CG	IP	H	BB	SO	ShO	Relief Pitching W	L	SV	BATTING AB	H	HR	BA

Jim Cudworth

CUDWORTH, JAMES ALARIC   BR TR 6'   165 lbs.
B. Aug. 22, 1858, Fairhaven, Mass.   D. Dec. 21, 1943, Middleboro, Mass.

	W	L	PCT	ERA	G	GS	CG	IP	H	BB	SO	ShO	W	L	SV	AB	H	HR	BA
1884 KC U	0	0	–	4.24	2	1	1	17	19	3	6	0	0	0	0	*			

Bobby Cuellar

CUELLAR, ROBERT   BR TR 5'11"   188 lbs.
B. Aug. 20, 1952, Alice, Tex.

1977 TEX A	0	0	–	1.29	4	0	0	7	4	2	3	0	0	0	0	0	0	0	–

Charlie Cuellar

CUELLAR, JESUS PATRACIS   BR TR 5'11"   183 lbs.
B. Sept. 24, 1917, Ybor City, Fla.

1950 CHI A	0	0	–	33.75	2	0	0	1.1	6	3	1	0	0	0	0	0	0	0	–

Mike Cuellar

CUELLAR, MIGUEL SANTANA   BL TL 6'   165 lbs.
B. May 8, 1937, Las Villas, Cuba

	W	L	PCT	ERA	G	GS	CG	IP	H	BB	SO	ShO	W	L	SV	AB	H	HR	BA
1959 CIN N	0	0	–	15.75	2	0	0	4	7	4	5	0	0	0	0	1	0	0	.000
1964 STL N	5	5	.500	4.50	32	7	1	72	80	33	56	0	3	0	4	18	0	0	.000
1965 HOU N	1	4	.200	3.54	25	4	0	56	55	21	46	0	1	1	2	12	0	0	.000
1966	12	10	.545	2.22	38	28	11	227.1	193	52	175	1	3	1	2	71	8	1	.113
1967	16	11	.593	3.03	36	32	16	246.1	233	63	203	3	1	0	1	93	13	0	.140
1968	8	11	.421	2.74	28	24	11	170.2	152	45	133	2	0	1	1	57	11	1	.193
1969 BAL A	23	11	.676	2.38	39	39	18	290.2	213	79	182	5	0	0	0	103	12	0	.117
1970	**24**	8	**.750**	3.47	40	**40**	**21**	298	273	69	190	4	0	0	0	112	10	2	.089
1971	20	9	.690	3.08	38	38	21	292	250	78	124	4	0	0	0	107	11	1	.103
1972	18	12	.600	2.57	35	35	17	248.1	197	71	132	4	0	0	0	87	11	2	.126
1973	18	13	.581	3.27	38	38	17	267	265	84	140	2	0	0	0	0	0	0	–
1974	22	10	**.688**	3.11	38	38	20	269	253	86	106	5	0	0	0	0	0	0	–
1975	14	12	.538	3.66	36	36	17	256	229	84	105	5	0	0	0	0	0	0	–
1976	4	13	.235	4.96	26	19	2	107	129	50	32	1	0	2	1	0	0	0	–
1977 CAL A	0	1	.000	18.90	2	1	0	3.1	9	3	3	0	0	0	0	0	0	0	–
15 yrs.	185	130	.587	3.14	453	379	172	2807.2	2538	822	1632	36	8	5	11	661	76	7	.115

LEAGUE CHAMPIONSHIP SERIES

1969 BAL A	0	0	–	2.25	1	1	0	8	3	1	7	0	0	0	0	2	0	0	.000
1970	0	0	–	12.46	1	1	0	4.1	10	1	2	0	0	0	0	2	1	1	.500
1971	1	0	1.000	1.00	1	1	1	9	6	1	2	0	0	0	0	3	1	0	.333
1973	0	1	.000	1.80	1	1	1	10	4	3	11	0	0	0	0	0	0	0	–
1974	1	1	.500	2.84	2	2	0	12.2	9	13	6	0	0	0	0	0	0	0	–
5 yrs.	2	2	.500	3.07	6	6	2	44	32	19	28	0	0	0	0	7	2	1	.286

WORLD SERIES

1969 BAL A	1	0	1.000	1.13	2	2	1	16	13	4	13	0	0	0	0	5	2	0	.400
1970	1	0	1.000	3.18	2	2	1	11.1	10	2	5	0	0	0	0	4	0	0	.000
1971	0	2	.000	3.86	2	2	0	14	11	6	10	0	0	0	0	3	0	0	.000
3 yrs.	2	2	.500	2.61	6	6	2	41.1	34	12	28	0	0	0	0	12	2	0	.167

Berto Cueto

CUETO, DAGOBERTO CONCEPCION   BR TR 6'4"   170 lbs.
B. Aug. 14, 1937, San Luis Pinar, Cuba

1961 MIN A	1	3	.250	7.17	7	5	0	21.1	27	10	5	0	1	1	0	5	0	0	.000

Jack Cullen

CULLEN, JOHN PATRICK   BR TR 5'11"   170 lbs.
B. Oct. 6, 1939, Newark, N. J.

1962 NY A	0	0	–	0.00	2	0	0	3	2	2	2	0	0	0	1	0	0	0	–
1965	3	4	.429	3.05	12	9	2	59	59	21	25	1	0	0	0	20	3	0	.150
1966	1	0	1.000	3.97	5	0	0	11.1	11	5	7	0	1	0	0	3	0	0	.000
3 yrs.	4	4	.500	3.07	19	9	2	73.1	72	28	34	1	1	0	1	23	3	0	.130

Nick Cullop

CULLOP, HENRY NICHOLAS (Tomato Face)   BR TR 6'   200 lbs.
B. Oct. 16, 1900, St. Louis, Mo.   D. Dec. 8, 1978, Westerville, Ohio

1927 CLE A	0	0	–	9.00	1	0	0	3	3	0	0	0	0	0	0	*			

Nick Cullop

CULLOP, NORMAN ANDREW   BR TL 5'11½"   172 lbs.
B. Sept. 17, 1887, Chilhowie, Va.   D. Apr. 15, 1961, Tazewell, Va.

1913 CLE A	3	7	.300	4.42	23	8	4	97.2	105	35	30	0	1	3	0	31	4	0	.129
1914 2 teams			CLE	A (1G 0–1)			KC	F (44G 14–17)											
" total	14	18	.438	2.35	45	36	22	299	260	88	152	4	1	2	1	100	14	0	.140
1915 KC F	22	11	.667	2.44	44	36	22	302.1	278	67	111	3	2	0	2	96	18	0	.188
1916 NY A	13	6	.684	2.05	28	22	9	167	151	32	77	0	2	0	1	55	6	0	.109
1917	5	9	.357	3.32	30	18	5	146.1	161	31	27	2	1	1	1	44	7	0	.159
1921 STL A	0	2	.000	8.49	4	1	0	11.2	18	6	3	0	0	1	0	3	0	0	.000
6 yrs.	57	53	.518	2.73	174	121	62	1024	973	259	400	9	7	7	5	329	49	0	.149

Bud Culloton

CULLOTON, BERNARD ALOYSIUS   BR TR 5'8½"   148 lbs.
B. May 19, 1896, Kingston, N. Y.   D. Nov. 9, 1976, Kingston, N. Y.

1925 PIT N	0	1	.000	2.57	9	1	0	21	19	1	3	0	0	0	0	3	0	0	.000
1926	0	0	–	7.36	4	0	0	3.2	3	6	1	0	0	0	0	0	0	0	–
2 yrs.	0	1	.000	3.28	13	1	0	24.2	22	7	4	0	0	0	0	3	0	0	.000

Bill Culp

CULP, WILLIAM EDWARD   BB TR 6'1½"   165 lbs.
B. June 11, 1887, Bellaire, Ohio   D. Sept. 3, 1969, Arnold, Pa.

1910 PHI N	0	0	–	8.10	4	0	0	6.2	8	4	4	0	0	0	1	2	0	0	.000

Ray Culp

CULP, RAY LEONARD   BR TR 6'   200 lbs.
B. Aug. 6, 1941, Elgin, Tex.

1963 PHI N	14	11	.560	2.97	34	30	10	203.1	148	**102**	176	5	2	1	0	66	9	0	.136
1964	8	7	.533	4.13	30	19	3	135	139	56	96	1	1	0	0	44	5	0	.114
1965	14	10	.583	3.22	33	30	11	204.1	188	78	134	2	1	1	0	68	6	0	.088
1966	7	4	.636	5.04	34	12	1	110.2	106	53	100	0	4	0	1	26	2	0	.077
1967 CHI N	8	11	.421	3.89	30	22	4	152.2	138	59	111	1	1	1	0	51	5	0	.098

	W	L	PCT	ERA	G	GS	CG	IP	H	BB	SO	ShO	Relief Pitching W	L	SV	BATTING AB	H	HR	BA

Ray Culp continued

	W	L	PCT	ERA	G	GS	CG	IP	H	BB	SO	ShO	W	L	SV	AB	H	HR	BA
1968 BOS A	16	6	.727	2.91	35	30	11	216.1	166	82	190	6	0	0	0	70	8	0	.114
1969	17	8	.680	3.81	32	32	9	227	195	79	172	2	0	0	0	79	12	1	.152
1970	17	14	.548	3.05	33	33	15	251	211	91	197	1	0	0	0	97	12	0	.124
1971	14	16	.467	3.61	35	35	12	242	236	67	151	3	0	0	0	68	8	0	.118
1972	5	8	.385	4.46	16	16	4	105	104	53	52	1	0	0	0	33	7	0	.212
1973	2	6	.250	4.50	10	9	0	50	46	32	32	0	0	0	0	0	0	0	–
11 yrs.	122	101	.547	3.58	322	268	80	1897.1	1677	752	1411	22	9	3	1	602	74	1	.123

George Culver

CULVER, GEORGE RAYMOND　　　BR TR 6'2" 185 lbs.
B. July 8, 1943, Salinas, Calif.

	W	L	PCT	ERA	G	GS	CG	IP	H	BB	SO	ShO	W	L	SV	AB	H	HR	BA
1966 CLE A	0	2	.000	8.38	5	1	0	9.2	15	7	6	0	0	1	0	2	0	0	.000
1967	7	3	.700	3.96	53	1	0	75	71	31	41	0	7	2	3	4	1	0	.250
1968 CIN N	11	16	.407	3.23	42	35	5	226	229	84	114	2	2	0	2	66	8	0	.121
1969	5	7	.417	4.28	32	13	0	101	117	52	58	0	0	0	4	31	3	0	.097
1970 2 teams			STL	N	(11G 3–3)			HOU	N	(32G 3–3)									
" total	6	6	.500	3.98	43	7	2	101.2	108	45	54	0	3	6	3	21	4	0	.190
1971 HOU N	5	8	.385	2.65	59	0	0	95	89	38	57	0	5	8	7	11	1	0	.091
1972	6	2	.750	3.05	45	0	0	97.1	73	43	82	0	6	2	2	19	3	0	.158
1973 2 teams			LA	N	(28G 4–4)			PHI	N	(14G 3–1)									
" total	7	5	.583	3.56	42	0	0	60.2	71	36	30	0	7	5	2	4	0	0	.000
1974 PHI N	1	0	1.000	6.55	14	0	0	22	20	16	9	0	1	0	0	3	0	0	.000
9 yrs.	48	49	.495	3.62	335	57	7	788.1	793	352	451	2	31	24	23	161	20	0	.124

John Cumberland

CUMBERLAND, JOHN SHELDON　　　BR TL 6' 185 lbs.
B. May 10, 1947, Westbrook, Me.

	W	L	PCT	ERA	G	GS	CG	IP	H	BB	SO	ShO	W	L	SV	AB	H	HR	BA
1968 NY A	0	0	–	9.00	1	0	0	2	3	1	1	0	0	0	0	0	0	0	–
1969	0	0	–	4.50	2	0	0	4	3	4	0	0	0	0	0	0	0	0	–
1970 2 teams			NY	A	(15G 3–4)			SF	N	(7G 2–0)									
" total	5	4	.556	3.48	22	8	1	75	68	19	44	0	3	0	0	18	1	0	.056
1971 SF N	9	6	.600	2.92	45	21	5	185	153	55	65	2	2	0	2	59	7	0	.119
1972 2 teams			SF	N	(9G 0–4)			STL	N	(14G 1–1)									
" total	1	5	.167	7.71	23	7	0	46.2	61	14	15	0	1	0	0	14	1	0	.071
1974 CAL A	0	1	.000	3.68	17	0	0	22	24	10	12	0	0	1	0	0	0	0	–
6 yrs.	15	16	.484	3.82	110	36	6	334.2	312	103	137	2	6	1	2	91	9	0	.099

LEAGUE CHAMPIONSHIP SERIES
| 1971 SF N | 0 | 1 | .000 | 9.00 | 1 | 1 | 0 | 3 | 7 | 1 | 4 | 0 | 0 | 0 | 0 | 0 | 0 | 0 | – |

Candy Cummings

CUMMINGS, WILLIAM ARTHUR　　　BR TR 5'9" 120 lbs.
B. Oct. 18, 1848, Ware, Mass.　　D. May 16, 1924, Toledo, Ohio
Hall of Fame 1939.

	W	L	PCT	ERA	G	GS	CG	IP	H	BB	SO	ShO	W	L	SV	AB	H	HR	BA
1876 HAR N	16	8	.667	1.67	24	24	24	216	215	14	26	5	0	0	0	105	17	0	.162
1877 CIN N	5	14	.263	4.34	19	19	16	155.2	219	13	11	0	0	0	0	70	14	0	.200
2 yrs.	21	22	.488	2.78	43	43	40	371.2	434	27	37	5	0	0	0	175	31	0	.177

Bert Cunningham

CUNNINGHAM, ELLSWORTH ELMER　　　BR TR
B. Nov. 25, 1866, Wilmington, Del.　　D. May 14, 1952, Cragmere, Del.

	W	L	PCT	ERA	G	GS	CG	IP	H	BB	SO	ShO	W	L	SV	AB	H	HR	BA
1887 BKN AA	0	2	.000	5.09	3	3	3	23	26	13	8	0	0	0	0	8	0	0	.000
1888 BAL AA	22	29	.431	3.39	51	51	50	453.1	412	157	186	0	0	0	0	177	33	1	.186
1889	16	19	.457	4.87	39	33	29	279.1	306	141	140	0	2	0	1	131	27	0	.206
1890 2 teams			PHI	P	(14G 3–9)			BUF	P	(25G 9–15)									
" total	12	24	.333	5.63	39	36	35	319.2	384	201	111	2	0	1	0	153	29	0	.190
1891 BAL AA	11	14	.440	4.01	30	25	21	237.2	241	138	59	0	1	0	0	100	15	1	.150
1895 LOU N	11	16	.407	4.75	31	28	24	231	299	104	49	1	0	0	0	100	30	0	.300
1896	7	14	.333	5.09	27	20	17	189.1	242	74	37	0	0	1	1	88	22	0	.250
1897	14	13	.519	4.14	29	27	25	234.2	286	72	49	0	2	0	0	93	22	2	.237
1898	28	15	.651	3.16	44	42	41	362	387	65	34	0	0	1	0	140	32	1	.229
1899	17	17	.500	3.84	39	37	33	323.2	385	75	36	1	0	0	0	154	40	2	.260
1900 CHI N	4	3	.571	4.36	8	7	7	64	84	21	7	0	0	0	0	27	4	0	.148
1901	0	1	.000	5.00	1	1	1	9	11	3	2	0	0	0	0	1	0	0	.000
12 yrs.	142	167	.460	4.22	341	310	286	2726.2	3063	1064	718	4	5	4	2	1172	254	9	.217

Bruce Cunningham

CUNNINGHAM, BRUCE LEE　　　BR TR 5'10½" 165 lbs.
B. Sept. 29, 1905, San Francisco, Calif.　　D. Mar. 8, 1984, Hayward, Calif.

	W	L	PCT	ERA	G	GS	CG	IP	H	BB	SO	ShO	W	L	SV	AB	H	HR	BA
1929 BOS N	4	6	.400	4.52	17	8	4	91.2	100	32	22	0	1	1	1	27	4	0	.148
1930	5	6	.455	5.48	36	6	2	106.2	121	41	28	0	3	2	0	31	6	0	.194
1931	3	12	.200	4.48	33	16	6	136.2	157	54	32	1	0	3	1	42	3	0	.071
1932	1	0	1.000	3.45	18	3	0	47	50	19	21	0	1	0	0	9	2	0	.222
4 yrs.	13	24	.351	4.64	104	33	12	382	428	146	103	1	5	6	2	109	15	0	.138

George Cunningham

CUNNINGHAM, GEORGE HAROLD　　　BR TR 5'11" 185 lbs.
B. July 13, 1894, Sturgeon Lake, Minn.　　D. Mar. 10, 1972, Chattanooga, Tenn.

	W	L	PCT	ERA	G	GS	CG	IP	H	BB	SO	ShO	W	L	SV	AB	H	HR	BA
1916 DET A	7	10	.412	2.75	35	14	5	150.1	146	74	68	0	2	1	2	41	11	0	.268
1917	2	7	.222	2.91	44	8	4	139	113	51	49	0	2	5	4	34	6	1	.176
1918	6	7	.462	3.15	27	14	10	140	131	38	39	0	2	0	1	112	25	0	.223
1919	1	1	.500	4.91	17	0	0	47.2	54	15	11	0	1	1	1	23	5	0	.217
1921	0	0	–	0.00	0	0	0	0	0	0	0	0	0	0	0	*			–
5 yrs.	16	25	.390	3.13	123	36	19	477	444	178	167	0	7	3	8				

Mike Cunningham

CUNNINGHAM, MODY　　　BR TR 5'10½" 175 lbs.
B. June 14, 1882, Lancaster, S. C.　　D. Dec. 10, 1969, Lancaster, S. C.

	W	L	PCT	ERA	G	GS	CG	IP	H	BB	SO	ShO	W	L	SV	AB	H	HR	BA
1906 PHI A	1	0	1.000	3.21	5	1	1	28	29	9	15	0	0	0	0	12	4	0	.333

Nig Cuppy

CUPPY, GEORGE JOSEPH　　　BR TR 5'7" 160 lbs.
Born George Maceo Koppe.
B. July 3, 1869, Logansport, Ind.　　D. July 27, 1922, Elkhart, Ind.

	W	L	PCT	ERA	G	GS	CG	IP	H	BB	SO	ShO	W	L	SV	AB	H	HR	BA
1892 CLE N	28	13	.683	2.51	47	42	38	376	333	121	103	1	0	0	1	168	36	0	.214

	W	L	PCT	ERA	G	GS	CG	IP	H	BB	SO	ShO	Relief Pitching W	L	SV	BATTING AB	H	HR	BA

Nig Cuppy continued

	W	L	PCT	ERA	G	GS	CG	IP	H	BB	SO	ShO	W	L	SV	AB	H	HR	BA
1893	17	10	.630	4.47	31	30	24	243.2	316	75	39	0	0	0	0	109	27	0	.248
1894	24	15	.615	4.56	43	33	29	316	381	128	65	3	8	0	0	135	35	0	.259
1895	26	14	.650	3.54	47	40	36	353	384	95	91	1	3	0	2	140	40	0	.286
1896	25	14	.641	3.12	46	40	35	358	388	75	86	1	2	0	1	141	38	1	.270
1897	10	6	.625	3.18	19	17	13	138.2	150	26	23	1	0	0	0	55	8	0	.145
1898	9	8	.529	3.30	18	15	13	128	147	25	27	1	1	2	0	48	5	0	.104
1899 STL N	11	8	.579	3.15	21	21	18	171.2	203	26	25	1	0	0	0	70	13	0	.186
1900 BOS N	8	4	.667	3.08	17	13	9	105.1	107	24	23	0	1	0	1	42	11	0	.262
1901 BOS A	4	6	.400	4.15	13	11	9	93.1	111	14	22	0	0	0	0	49	10	0	.204
10 yrs.	162	98	.623	3.48	302	262	224	2283.2	2520	609	504	9	15	2	5	957	223	1	.233

Sam Curran

CURRAN, SIMON FRANCIS
B. Oct. 30, 1874, Dorchester, Mass.   D. May 19, 1936, Dorchester, Mass.

	W	L	PCT	ERA	G	GS	CG	IP	H	BB	SO	ShO	W	L	SV	AB	H	HR	BA
1902 BOS N	0	0	—	1.35	1	0	0	6.2	6	0	3	0	0	0	0	2	0	0	.000

Lafayette Currence

CURRENCE, DELANCY LAFAYETTE   BB   TL   5'11"   175 lbs.
B. Dec. 3, 1951, Rock Hill, S. C.

	W	L	PCT	ERA	G	GS	CG	IP	H	BB	SO	ShO	W	L	SV	AB	H	HR	BA
1975 MIL A	0	2	.000	7.71	8	1	0	18.2	25	14	7	0	0	1	0	0	0	0	—

Bill Currie

CURRIE, WILLIAM CLEVELAND   BR   TR   6'   175 lbs.
B. Nov. 29, 1928, Leary, Ga.

	W	L	PCT	ERA	G	GS	CG	IP	H	BB	SO	ShO	W	L	SV	AB	H	HR	BA
1955 WAS A	0	0	—	12.46	3	0	0	4.1	7	2	2	0	0	0	0	0	0	0	—

Clarence Currie

CURRIE, CLARENCE F.   BR   TR
B. Dec. 30, 1878, Glencoe, Ont., Canada   D. July 15, 1941, Little Chute, Wis.

	W	L	PCT	ERA	G	GS	CG	IP	H	BB	SO	ShO	W	L	SV	AB	H	HR	BA
1902 2 teams		CIN	N (10G 3–4)		STL	N (15G 6–5)													
" total	9	9	.500	3.10	25	18	15	183	192	48	49	2	0	0	0	70	11	0	.157
1903 2 teams		STL	N (22G 4–12)		CHI	N (6G 1–2)													
" total	5	14	.263	3.82	28	19	15	181.1	190	69	61	1	2	1	2	59	9	0	.153
2 yrs.	14	23	.378	3.46	53	37	30	364.1	382	117	110	3	2	1	2	129	20	0	.155

Murphy Currie

CURRIE, MURPHY ARCHIBALD   BR   TR   5'11½"   185 lbs.
B. Aug. 31, 1893, Fayetteville, N. C.   D. June 22, 1939, Asheboro, N. C.

	W	L	PCT	ERA	G	GS	CG	IP	H	BB	SO	ShO	W	L	SV	AB	H	HR	BA
1916 STL N	0	0	—	1.88	6	0	0	14.1	7	9	8	0	0	0	0	3	0	0	.000

George Curry

CURRY, GEORGE JAMES (Soldier Boy)   BR   TR   6'   185 lbs.
B. Dec. 21, 1888, Bridgeport, Conn.   D. Oct. 5, 1963, Stratford, Conn.

	W	L	PCT	ERA	G	GS	CG	IP	H	BB	SO	ShO	W	L	SV	AB	H	HR	BA
1911 STL A	0	3	.000	7.47	3	3	0	15.2	19	24	2	0	0	0	0	5	0	0	.000

Wes Curry

CURRY, WESLEY
B. Apr. 1, 1860, Wilmington, Del.   D. May 20, 1933, Philadelphia, Pa.

	W	L	PCT	ERA	G	GS	CG	IP	H	BB	SO	ShO	W	L	SV	AB	H	HR	BA
1884 RIC AA	0	2	.000	5.06	2	2	2	16	15	3	1	0	0	0	0	8	2	0	.250

Cliff Curtis

CURTIS, CLIFTON GARFIELD   BR   TR
B. July 3, 1883, Delaware, Ohio   D. Apr. 23, 1943, Newark, Ohio

	W	L	PCT	ERA	G	GS	CG	IP	H	BB	SO	ShO	W	L	SV	AB	H	HR	BA
1909 BOS N	4	5	.444	1.41	10	9	8	83	53	30	22	2	0	1	0	29	1	0	.034
1910	6	24	.200	3.55	43	37	12	251	251	124	75	2	0	1	2	82	12	0	.146
1911 3 teams		BOS	N (12G 1–8)		CHI	N (4G 1–2)		PHI	N (8G 2–1)										
" total	4	11	.267	3.77	24	15	8	129	131	54	40	1	1	2	1	45	12	0	.267
1912 2 teams		PHI	N (10G 2–5)		BKN	N (19G 4–7)													
" total	6	12	.333	3.67	29	17	5	130	127	54	42	0	1	2	0	41	8	0	.195
1913 BKN N	8	9	.471	3.26	30	16	5	151.2	145	55	57	0	3	1	1	49	6	0	.122
5 yrs.	28	61	.315	3.31	136	94	38	744.2	707	317	236	5	5	7	4	246	39	0	.159

Jack Curtis

CURTIS, JACK PATRICK   BL   TL   5'10"   175 lbs.
B. Jan. 11, 1937, Rhodhiss, N. C.

	W	L	PCT	ERA	G	GS	CG	IP	H	BB	SO	ShO	W	L	SV	AB	H	HR	BA
1961 CHI N	10	13	.435	4.89	31	27	6	180.1	220	51	57	0	0	0	0	60	10	2	.167
1962 2 teams		CHI	N (4G 0–2)		MIL	N (30G 4–4)													
" total	4	6	.400	4.04	34	8	0	93.2	100	33	48	0	4	3	1	22	5	0	.227
1963 CLE A	0	0	—	18.00	4	0	0	5	8	5	3	0	0	0	0	0	0	0	—
3 yrs.	14	19	.424	4.84	69	35	6	279	328	89	108	0	4	3	1	82	15	2	.183

John Curtis

CURTIS, JOHN DUFFIELD II   BL   TL   6'1"   175 lbs.
B. Mar. 9, 1948, Newton, Mass.

	W	L	PCT	ERA	G	GS	CG	IP	H	BB	SO	ShO	W	L	SV	AB	H	HR	BA
1970 BOS A	0	0	—	13.50	1	0	0	2	4	1	1	0	0	0	0	0	0	0	—
1971	2	2	.500	3.12	5	3	1	26	30	6	19	0	1	0	0	9	1	0	.111
1972	11	8	.579	3.73	26	21	8	154.1	161	50	106	3	1	0	0	53	5	0	.094
1973	13	13	.500	3.58	35	30	10	221	225	83	101	4	0	0	0	0	0	0	—
1974 STL N	10	14	.417	3.78	33	29	5	195	199	83	89	2	0	1	1	63	10	0	.159
1975	8	9	.471	3.43	39	14	4	147	151	65	67	0	0	1	1	38	8	0	.211
1976	6	11	.353	4.50	37	15	3	134	139	65	52	1	0	3	1	35	7	0	.200
1977 SF N	3	3	.500	5.49	43	9	1	77	95	48	47	1	1	1	1	13	3	0	.231
1978	4	3	.571	3.71	46	0	0	63	60	29	38	0	4	3	1	2	0	0	.000
1979	10	9	.526	4.17	27	18	3	121	121	42	85	2	1	2	0	34	5	0	.147
1980 SD N	10	8	.556	3.51	30	27	6	187	184	67	71	0	0	0	0	62	12	0	.194
1981	2	6	.250	5.10	28	8	0	67	70	30	31	0	2	4	0	13	1	0	.077
1982 2 teams		SD	N (26G 8–6)		CAL	A (8G 0–1)													
" total	8	7	.533	4.24	34	18	1	128.1	137	49	64	1	1	2	1	37	11	0	.297
1983 CAL A	1	2	.333	3.80	37	3	0	90	89	40	36	0	1	1	5	0	0	0	—
1984	1	2	.333	4.40	17	0	0	28.2	30	11	18	0	1	2	0	0	0	0	—
15 yrs.	89	97	.478	3.96	438	199	42	1641.1	1695	669	825	14	13	20	11	359	63	0	.175

	W	L	PCT	ERA	G	GS	CG	IP	H	BB	SO	ShO	Relief Pitching W	L	SV	BATTING AB	H	HR	BA

Vern Curtis — CURTIS, VERNON EUGENE (Turk) B. May 24, 1920, Cairo, Ill. — BR TR 6' 170 lbs.

	W	L	PCT	ERA	G	GS	CG	IP	H	BB	SO	ShO	W	L	SV	AB	H	HR	BA
1943 WAS A	0	0	–	6.75	2	0	0	4	3	6	1	0	0	0	0	0	0	0	–
1944	0	1	.000	2.79	3	1	0	9.2	8	3	2	0	0	0	0	2	0	0	.000
1946	0	0	–	7.16	11	0	0	16.1	19	10	7	0	0	0	0	2	0	0	.000
3 yrs.	0	1	.000	5.70	16	1	0	30	30	19	10	0	0	0	0	4	0	0	.000

Ed Cushman — CUSHMAN, EDGAR LEANDER B. Mar. 27, 1852, Eaglesville, Ohio D. Sept. 26, 1915, Erie, Pa. — BR TL

	W	L	PCT	ERA	G	GS	CG	IP	H	BB	SO	ShO	W	L	SV	AB	H	HR	BA
1883 BUF N	3	3	.500	3.93	7	7	5	50.1	61	17	34	0	0	0	0	23	5	0	.217
1884 MIL U	4	0	1.000	1.00	4	4	4	36	10	3	47	2	0	0	0	11	1	0	.091
1885 2 teams			PHI	AA (10G 3–7)	NY	AA (22G 8–14)													
" total	11	21	.344	3.01	32	32	32	278	259	50	170	0	0	0	0	106	17	0	.160
1886 NY AA	17	20	.459	3.12	38	37	37	325.2	278	99	167	2	0	0	0	126	19	0	.151
1887	10	14	.417	5.97	26	26	25	220	310	83	64	0	0	0	0	93	23	0	.247
1890 TOL AA	17	21	.447	4.19	40	38	34	315.2	346	107	125	0	0	1	1	130	13	0	.100
6 yrs.	62	79	.440	3.86	147	144	137	1225.2	1264	359	607	4	0	1	1	489	78	0	.160

Harv Cushman — CUSHMAN, HARVEY BARNES B. July 10, 1877, Rockland, Me. D. Dec. 27, 1920, Ensworth, Pa.

	W	L	PCT	ERA	G	GS	CG	IP	H	BB	SO	ShO	W	L	SV	AB	H	HR	BA
1902 PIT N	0	4	.000	7.36	4	3	1	25.2	30	31	12	0	0	0	0	10	2	0	.200

Mike Cvengros — CVENGROS, MICHAEL JOHN B. Dec. 1, 1901, Hot Springs, Ark. D. Aug. 2, 1970, Hotsprings, Ark. — BL TL 5'8" 159 lbs.

	W	L	PCT	ERA	G	GS	CG	IP	H	BB	SO	ShO	W	L	SV	AB	H	HR	BA
1922 NY N	0	1	.000	4.00	1	1	1	9	6	3	3	0	0	0	0	3	0	0	.000
1923 CHI A	12	13	.480	4.39	41	26	14	215.1	216	107	86	0	2	1	3	74	15	0	.203
1924	3	12	.200	5.88	26	15	2	105.2	119	67	36	0	1	3	0	30	6	0	.200
1925	3	9	.250	4.30	22	11	4	104.2	109	55	32	0	1	2	0	33	5	0	.152
1927 PIT N	2	1	.667	3.35	23	4	0	53.2	55	24	21	0	2	0	1	19	3	0	.158
1929 CHI N	5	4	.556	4.64	32	2	0	64	82	29	23	0	5	4	2	15	6	0	.400
6 yrs.	25	40	.385	4.58	145	59	21	552.1	587	285	201	0	11	10	6	174	35	0	.201

WORLD SERIES

	W	L	PCT	ERA	G	GS	CG	IP	H	BB	SO	ShO	W	L	SV	AB	H	HR	BA
1927 PIT N	0	0	–	3.86	2	0	0	2.1	3	0	2	0	0	0	0	0	0	0	–

John D'Acquisto — D'ACQUISTO, JOHN FRANCIS B. Dec. 24, 1951, San Diego, Calif. — BR TR 6'2" 205 lbs.

	W	L	PCT	ERA	G	GS	CG	IP	H	BB	SO	ShO	W	L	SV	AB	H	HR	BA
1973 SF N	1	1	.500	3.54	7	3	1	28	23	19	29	0	0	0	0	9	0	0	.000
1974	12	14	.462	3.77	38	36	5	215	182	124	167	1	0	0	0	71	8	1	.113
1975	2	4	.333	10.29	10	6	0	28	29	34	22	0	1	0	0	7	0	0	.000
1976	3	8	.273	5.35	28	19	0	106	93	102	53	0	0	0	0	26	7	0	.269
1977 2 teams			STL	N (3G 0–0)	SD	N (17G 1–2)													
" total	1	2	.333	6.54	20	14	0	52.1	54	57	54	0	1	0	0	8	0	0	.000
1978 SD N	4	3	.571	2.13	45	3	0	93	60	56	104	0	3	2	10	21	4	0	.190
1979	9	13	.409	4.90	51	11	1	134	140	86	97	1	5	7	2	31	4	0	.129
1980 2 teams			SD	N (39G 2–3)	MON	N (11G 0–2)													
" total	2	5	.286	3.38	50	0	0	88	81	45	59	0	2	5	3	0	0	0	.000
1981 CAL A	0	0	–	10.89	6	0	0	19	26	12	8	0	0	0	0	0	0	0	–
1982 OAK A	0	1	.000	5.29	11	0	0	17	20	9	7	0	0	1	0	0	0	0	–
10 yrs.	34	51	.400	4.56	266	92	7	780.1	708	544	600	2	12	15	15	181	23	1	.127

John Dagenhard — DAGENHARD, JOHN DOUGLAS B. Apr. 25, 1917, Magnolia, Ohio — BR TR 6'2" 195 lbs.

	W	L	PCT	ERA	G	GS	CG	IP	H	BB	SO	ShO	W	L	SV	AB	H	HR	BA
1943 BOS N	1	0	1.000	0.00	2	1	1	11	9	4	2	0	0	0	0	3	0	0	.000

Pete Daglia — DAGLIA, PETER GEORGE (Rig Pete) B. Feb. 28, 1906, Napa, Calif. D. Mar. 11, 1952, Willits, Calif. — BR TR 6'1" 200 lbs.

	W	L	PCT	ERA	G	GS	CG	IP	H	BB	SO	ShO	W	L	SV	AB	H	HR	BA
1932 CHI A	2	4	.333	5.76	12	5	2	50	67	20	16	0	1	0	0	13	1	0	.077

Jay Dahl — DAHL, JAY STEVEN B. Dec. 6, 1945, San Bernardino, Calif. D. June 20, 1965, Salisbury, N. C. — BB TL 5'10" 183 lbs.

	W	L	PCT	ERA	G	GS	CG	IP	H	BB	SO	ShO	W	L	SV	AB	H	HR	BA
1963 HOU N	0	1	.000	16.88	1	1	0	2.2	7	0	0	0	0	0	0	0	0	0	–

Jerry Dahlke — DAHLKE, JEROME ALEX (Joe) B. June 8, 1930, Marathon, Wis. — BR TR 6' 180 lbs.

	W	L	PCT	ERA	G	GS	CG	IP	H	BB	SO	ShO	W	L	SV	AB	H	HR	BA
1956 CHI A	0	0	–	19.29	5	0	0	2.1	5	6	1	0	0	0	0	0	0	0	–

Bill Dailey — DAILEY, WILLIAM GARLAND B. May 13, 1935, Arlington, Va. — BR TR 6'3" 185 lbs.

	W	L	PCT	ERA	G	GS	CG	IP	H	BB	SO	ShO	W	L	SV	AB	H	HR	BA
1961 CLE A	1	0	1.000	0.95	12	0	0	19	16	6	7	0	1	0	0	2	0	0	.000
1962	2	2	.500	3.59	27	0	0	42.2	43	17	24	0	2	2	1	3	0	0	.000
1963 MIN A	6	3	.667	1.99	66	0	0	108.2	80	19	72	0	6	3	21	21	5	1	.238
1964	1	2	.333	8.22	14	0	0	15.1	23	17	6	0	1	2	0	0	0	0	–
4 yrs.	10	7	.588	2.76	119	0	0	185.2	162	59	109	0	10	7	22	26	5	1	.192

Sam Dailey — DAILEY, SAMUEL LAURENCE B. Mar. 31, 1904, Oakford, Ill. D. Dec. 2, 1979, Columbia, S. C. — BR TR 5'11" 168 lbs.

	W	L	PCT	ERA	G	GS	CG	IP	H	BB	SO	ShO	W	L	SV	AB	H	HR	BA
1929 PHI N	2	2	.500	7.54	20	5	0	51.1	74	23	18	0	2	0	0	17	1	0	.059

Ed Daily — DAILY, EDWARD M. Brother of Con Daily. B. Sept. 7, 1862, Providence, R. I. D. Oct. 21, 1891, Washington, D. C. — BR TR

	W	L	PCT	ERA	G	GS	CG	IP	H	BB	SO	ShO	W	L	SV	AB	H	HR	BA
1885 PHI N	26	23	.531	2.21	50	50	49	440	370	90	140	4	0	0	0	184	38	1	.207
1886	16	9	.640	3.06	27	23	22	218	211	59	95	1	3	0	0	309	70	4	.227
1887 2 teams			PHI	N (6G 0–4)	WAS	N (1G 0–1)													
" total	0	5	.000	7.26	7	6	5	48.1	57	31	10	0	0	0	0	417	108	3	.259
1888 WAS N	2	7	.222	4.89	9	8	8	73.2	88	19	20	0	0	1	0	453	102	2	.225
1889 COL AA	0	0	–	21.60	2	0	0	1.2	1	4	2	0	0	0	1	578	148	3	.256

	W	L	PCT	ERA	G	GS	CG	IP	H	BB	SO	ShO	Relief Pitching W	L	SV	BATTING AB	H	HR	BA

Ed Daily continued

	W	L	PCT	ERA	G	GS	CG	IP	H	BB	SO	ShO	W	L	SV	AB	H	HR	BA
1890 3 teams	B-B	AA	(27G 10–15)		NY	N	(2G 2–0)	LOU	AA	(12G 6–3)									
" total	18	18	.500	3.39	41	38	37	344.2	341	129	113	1	2	0	0	489	116	1	.237
1891 LOU AA	4	8	.333	5.74	15	14	11	111.1	149	48	27	0	0	0	0	143	34	0	.238
7 yrs.	66	70	.485	3.39	151	139	132	1237.2	1217	380	407	6	5	1	1	*			

One Arm Daily

DAILY, HUGH IGNATIUS
B. 1857, Baltimore, Md.   Deceased.
BR TR 6'2" 180 lbs.

	W	L	PCT	ERA	G	GS	CG	IP	H	BB	SO	ShO	W	L	SV	AB	H	HR	BA
1882 BUF N	15	14	.517	2.99	29	29	29	255.2	246	70	116	0	0	0	0	110	18	0	.164
1883 CLE N	23	19	.548	2.42	45	43	40	378.2	360	99	171	4	0	1	1	142	18	0	.127
1884 3 teams	C–P	U	(56G 27–29)		WAS	U	(2G 1–1)		U	(0G 0–0)									
" total	28	30	.483	2.80	58	58	56	500.2	446	72	483	4	0	0	0	201	43	0	.214
1885 STL N	3	8	.273	3.94	11	11	10	91.1	92	44	31	1	0	0	0	35	3	0	.086
1886 WAS N	0	6	.000	7.35	6	6	6	49	69	40	15	0	0	0	0	16	2	0	.125
1887 CLE AA	4	12	.250	3.67	16	16	16	139.2	181	44	30	0	0	0	0	58	4	0	.069
6 yrs.	73	89	.451	3.05	165	163	157	1415	1394	369	846	9	0	1	1	562	88	0	.157

Vince Daily

DAILY, VINCENT PERRY
B. Dec. 25, 1864, Osceola, Pa.   D. Nov. 14, 1919, Hornell, N. Y.

	W	L	PCT	ERA	G	GS	CG	IP	H	BB	SO	ShO	W	L	SV	AB	H	HR	BA
1890 CLE N	0	1	.000	7.71	2	1	0	7	12	7	0	0	0	0	0	*			

Bruce Dal Canton

Dal CANTON, JOHN BRUCE
B. June 15, 1942, California, Pa.
BR TR 6'2" 205 lbs.

	W	L	PCT	ERA	G	GS	CG	IP	H	BB	SO	ShO	W	L	SV	AB	H	HR	BA
1967 PIT N	2	1	.667	1.88	8	2	1	24	19	10	13	0	2	0	0	6	2	0	.333
1968	1	1	.500	2.12	7	0	0	17	7	6	8	0	1	1	2	3	0	0	.000
1969	8	2	.800	3.35	57	0	0	86	79	49	56	0	8	2	5	10	3	0	.300
1970	9	4	.692	4.55	41	6	1	85	94	39	53	0	6	3	1	16	0	0	.000
1971 KC A	8	6	.571	3.45	25	22	2	141	144	44	58	0	0	0	0	46	4	0	.087
1972	6	6	.500	3.40	35	16	1	132.1	135	29	75	0	2	2	2	41	4	0	.098
1973	8	3	.571	4.82	32	3	1	97	108	46	38	0	3	1	3	0	0	0	–
1974	8	10	.444	3.14	31	22	9	175	135	82	96	2	2	2	0	0	0	0	–
1975 2 teams		KC	A	(4G 0–2)		ATL	N	(26G 2–7)											
" total	2	9	.182	4.76	30	11	0	75.2	86	31	43	0	2	2	3	19	2	0	.105
1976 ATL N	3	5	.375	3.58	42	1	0	73	67	42	36	0	3	4	1	9	2	0	.222
1977 CHI A	0	2	.000	3.75	8	0	0	24	20	13	9	0	0	2	2	0	0	0	–
11 yrs.	51	49	.510	3.68	316	83	15	930	894	391	485	2	29	19	19	150	17	0	.113

Gene Dale

DALE, EMMETT EUGENE
B. June 16, 1889, St. Louis, Mo.   D. Mar. 20, 1958, St. Louis, Mo.
BR TR 6'3" 179 lbs.

	W	L	PCT	ERA	G	GS	CG	IP	H	BB	SO	ShO	W	L	SV	AB	H	HR	BA
1911 STL N	0	2	.000	6.75	5	2	0	14.2	13	16	13	0	0	0	0	5	2	0	.400
1912	0	5	.000	6.57	19	3	1	61.2	76	51	37	0	0	2	0	22	6	0	.273
1915 CIN N	18	17	.514	2.46	49	35	20	296.2	256	107	104	4	3	2	3	91	20	0	.220
1916	3	4	.429	5.17	17	5	2	69.2	80	33	23	0	2	1	0	21	3	0	.143
4 yrs.	21	28	.429	3.60	90	45	23	442.2	425	207	177	4	5	5	3	139	31	0	.223

Bill Daley

DALEY, WILLIAM
B. June 27, 1868, Poughkeepsie, N. Y.   D. May 4, 1922, Poughkeepsie, N. Y.
TL

	W	L	PCT	ERA	G	GS	CG	IP	H	BB	SO	ShO	W	L	SV	AB	H	HR	BA
1889 BOS N	3	3	.500	4.31	9	7	4	48	34	43	40	0	0	0	0	20	3	0	.150
1890 BOS P	18	8	.692	3.60	34	25	19	235	246	167	110	2	4	0	2	110	17	2	.155
1891 BOS AA	8	6	.571	2.98	19	11	10	126.2	119	81	68	0	1	2	2	59	10	0	.169
3 yrs.	29	17	.630	3.49	62	43	33	409.2	399	291	218	2	5	2	4	189	30	2	.159

Buddy Daley

DALEY, LEAVITT LEO
B. Oct. 7, 1932, Orange, Calif.
BL TL 6'1" 185 lbs.

	W	L	PCT	ERA	G	GS	CG	IP	H	BB	SO	ShO	W	L	SV	AB	H	HR	BA
1955 CLE A	0	1	.000	6.43	2	1	0	7	10	1	2	0	0	0	0	2	0	0	.000
1956	1	0	1.000	6.20	14	0	0	20.1	21	14	13	0	1	0	0	2	0	0	.000
1957	2	8	.200	4.43	34	10	1	87.1	99	40	54	0	0	2	2	20	4	0	.200
1958 KC A	3	2	.600	3.31	26	5	1	70.2	67	19	39	0	2	0	0	16	2	0	.125
1959	16	13	.552	3.16	39	29	12	216.1	212	62	125	2	1	2	1	78	23	0	.295
1960	16	16	.500	4.56	37	35	13	231	234	96	126	1	1	1	0	75	12	0	.160
1961 2 teams		KC	A	(16G 4–8)		NY	A	(23G 8–9)											
" total	12	17	.414	4.28	39	27	9	193.1	211	73	119	0	1	3	1	63	8	0	.127
1962 NY A	7	5	.583	3.59	43	6	0	105.1	105	21	55	0	5	3	4	27	5	0	.185
1963	0	0	–	0.00	1	0	0	1	2	0	0	0	0	0	0	0	0	0	–
1964	3	2	.600	4.63	13	3	0	35	37	25	16	0	0	2	1	8	2	0	.250
10 yrs.	60	64	.484	4.03	248	116	36	967.1	998	351	549	3	11	13	10	291	56	0	.192
WORLD SERIES																			
1961 NY A	1	0	1.000	0.00	2	0	0	7	5	0	3	0	1	0	0	1	0	0	.000
1962	0	0	–	0.00	1	0	0	1	1	1	0	0	0	0	0	0	0	0	–
2 yrs.	1	0	1.000	0.00	3	0	0	8	6	1	3	0	1	0	0	1	0	0	.000

George Daly

DALY, GEORGE JOSEPH (Pecks)
B. July 28, 1887, Buffalo, N. Y.   D. Dec. 12, 1957, Buffalo, N. Y.
BR TR 5'10½" 175 lbs.

	W	L	PCT	ERA	G	GS	CG	IP	H	BB	SO	ShO	W	L	SV	AB	H	HR	BA
1909 NY N	0	3	.000	6.00	3	3	3	21	31	8	8	0	0	0	0	9	1	0	.111

Bill Damman

DAMMAN, WILLIAM HENRY (Wee Willie)
B. Aug. 9, 1872, Chicago, Ill.   D. Dec. 6, 1948, Lynnhaven, Va.
BL TL 5'7" 155 lbs.

	W	L	PCT	ERA	G	GS	CG	IP	H	BB	SO	ShO	W	L	SV	AB	H	HR	BA
1897 CIN N	6	4	.600	4.74	16	11	7	95	122	37	21	1	1	0	0	31	5	0	.161
1898	16	10	.615	3.61	35	22	16	224.2	277	67	51	2	4	2	2	82	16	0	.195
1899	2	1	.667	4.88	9	5	3	48	74	11	2	1	0	0	1	18	1	0	.056
3 yrs.	24	15	.615	4.06	60	38	26	367.2	473	115	74	4	5	3	3	131	22	0	.168

Lee Daney

DANEY, ARTHUR LEE
Also known as Arthur Lee Whitehorn.
B. July 9, 1905, Talihina, Okla.
BR TR 5'11" 165 lbs.

	W	L	PCT	ERA	G	GS	CG	IP	H	BB	SO	ShO	W	L	SV	AB	H	HR	BA
1928 PHI A	0	0	–	0.00	1	0	0	1	1	1	0	0	0	0	0	0	0	0	–

	W	L	PCT	ERA	G	GS	CG	IP	H	BB	SO	ShO	Relief Pitching W	L	SV	BATTING AB	H	HR	BA

Dave Danforth

DANFORTH, DAVID CHARLES (Dauntless Dave)   BL TL 6'   167 lbs.
B. Mar. 7, 1890, Granger, Tex.   D. Sept. 19, 1970, Baltimore, Md.

	W	L	PCT	ERA	G	GS	CG	IP	H	BB	SO	ShO	W	L	SV	AB	H	HR	BA
1911 PHI A	4	1	.800	3.74	14	2	1	33.2	29	17	21	0	3	0	1	6	1	0	.167
1912	0	0	–	3.98	3	0	0	20.1	26	12	8	0	0	0	0	8	2	0	.250
1916 CHI A	6	5	.545	3.27	28	8	1	93.2	87	37	49	0	5	0	2	23	2	0	.087
1917	11	6	.647	2.65	50	9	1	173	155	74	79	1	6	3	9	46	6	0	.130
1918	6	15	.286	3.43	39	13	5	139	148	40	48	0	6	6	2	42	6	0	.143
1919	1	2	.333	7.78	15	1	0	41.2	58	20	17	0	1	1	1	9	1	0	.111
1922 STL A	5	2	.714	3.28	20	10	3	79.2	93	38	48	0	0	1	0	23	2	0	.087
1923	16	14	.533	3.94	38	29	16	226.1	221	87	96	1	1	2	1	71	15	0	.211
1924	15	12	.556	4.51	41	27	12	219.2	246	69	65	1	3	2	4	76	13	0	.171
1925	7	9	.438	4.36	38	15	5	159	172	61	53	0	3	2	2	46	8	0	.174
10 yrs.	71	66	.518	3.89	286	114	44	1186	1235	455	484	3	28	16	23	350	56	0	.160

WORLD SERIES

	W	L	PCT	ERA	G	GS	CG	IP	H	BB	SO	ShO	W	L	SV	AB	H	HR	BA
1917 CHI A	0	0	–	18.00	1	0	0	1	3	0	2	0	0	0	0	0	0	0	–

Chuck Daniel

DANIEL, CHARLES EDWARD   BR TR 6'2"   195 lbs.
B. Sept. 17, 1933, Bluffton, Ark.

	W	L	PCT	ERA	G	GS	CG	IP	H	BB	SO	ShO	W	L	SV	AB	H	HR	BA
1957 DET A	0	0	–	7.71	1	0	0	2.1	3	0	2	0	0	0	0	0	0	0	–

Bennie Daniels

DANIELS, BENNIE   BL TR 6'1½"   193 lbs.
B. June 17, 1932, Tuscaloosa, Ala.

	W	L	PCT	ERA	G	GS	CG	IP	H	BB	SO	ShO	W	L	SV	AB	H	HR	BA
1957 PIT N	0	1	.000	1.29	1	1	0	7	5	3	2	0	0	0	0	2	0	0	.000
1958	0	3	.000	5.53	8	5	1	27.2	31	15	7	0	0	0	0	8	1	0	.125
1959	7	9	.438	5.45	34	12	0	100.2	115	39	67	0	4	3	1	29	9	1	.310
1960	1	3	.250	7.81	10	6	0	40.1	52	17	16	0	0	0	0	16	3	0	.188
1961 WAS A	12	11	.522	3.44	32	28	12	212	184	80	110	1	0	1	0	76	15	2	.197
1962	7	16	.304	4.85	44	21	3	161.1	172	68	66	1	3	3	2	46	6	0	.130
1963	5	10	.333	4.38	35	24	6	168.2	163	58	88	1	0	0	1	46	7	0	.152
1964	8	10	.444	3.70	33	24	3	163	147	64	73	2	1	0	0	47	6	1	.128
1965	5	13	.278	4.72	33	18	1	116.1	135	39	42	0	2	1	1	30	4	0	.133
9 yrs.	45	76	.372	4.44	230	139	26	997	1004	383	471	5	10	8	5	300	51	5	.170

Charlie Daniels

DANIELS, CHARLES L.   B. July 1, 1861, Roxbury, Mass.   D. Feb. 9, 1938, Boston, Mass.

	W	L	PCT	ERA	G	GS	CG	IP	H	BB	SO	ShO	W	L	SV	AB	H	HR	BA
1884 BOS U	0	2	.000	4.32	2	2	2	16.2	20	2	12	0	0	0	0	11	3	0	.273

Pete Daniels

DANIELS, PETER J.   BL
B. Apr. 8, 1864, County Cavan, Ireland   D. Feb. 13, 1928, Indianapolis, Ind.

	W	L	PCT	ERA	G	GS	CG	IP	H	BB	SO	ShO	W	L	SV	AB	H	HR	BA
1890 PIT N	1	2	.333	7.07	4	4	3	28	40	12	8	0	0	0	0	12	4	0	.333
1898 STL N	1	6	.143	3.62	10	6	3	54.2	62	14	13	0	1	0	0	17	3	0	.176
2 yrs.	2	8	.200	4.79	14	10	6	82.2	102	26	21	0	1	0	0	29	7	0	.241

George Darby

DARBY, GEORGE WILLIAM (Deek)   BR TR 5'10½" 160 lbs.
B. Feb. 6, 1869, Kansas City, Mo.   D. Feb. 25, 1937, Sacramento, Calif.

	W	L	PCT	ERA	G	GS	CG	IP	H	BB	SO	ShO	W	L	SV	AB	H	HR	BA
1893 CIN N	1	1	.500	7.76	4	3	2	29	41	18	6	0	0	0	0	10	3	0	.300

Pat Darcy

DARCY, PATRICK LEONARD   BR TR 6'3"   175 lbs.
B. May 12, 1950, Troy, Ohio

	W	L	PCT	ERA	G	GS	CG	IP	H	BB	SO	ShO	W	L	SV	AB	H	HR	BA
1974 CIN N	1	0	1.000	3.71	6	2	0	17	17	8	14	0	0	0	0	3	1	0	.333
1975	11	5	.688	3.57	27	22	1	131	134	59	46	0	2	0	1	47	4	0	.085
1976	2	3	.400	6.23	11	4	0	39	41	22	15	0	0	1	2	11	2	0	.182
3 yrs.	14	8	.636	4.14	44	28	1	187	192	89	75	0	2	1	3	61	7	0	.115

WORLD SERIES

	W	L	PCT	ERA	G	GS	CG	IP	H	BB	SO	ShO	W	L	SV	AB	H	HR	BA
1975 CIN N	0	1	.000	4.50	2	0	0	4	3	2	1	0	0	0	0	1	0	0	.000

Alvin Dark

DARK, ALVIN RALPH (Blackie)   BR TR 5'11"   185 lbs.
B. Jan. 7, 1922, Comanche, Okla.
Manager 1961-64, 1966-71, 1974-75, 1977.

	W	L	PCT	ERA	G	GS	CG	IP	H	BB	SO	ShO	W	L	SV	AB	H	HR	BA
1953 NY N	0	0	–	18.00	1	1	0	1	1	1	0	0	0	0	0	*			

Ron Darling

DARLING, RONALD MAURICE JR.   BR TR 6'3"   205 lbs.
B. Aug. 19, 1960, Honolulu, Hawaii

	W	L	PCT	ERA	G	GS	CG	IP	H	BB	SO	ShO	W	L	SV	AB	H	HR	BA
1983 NY N	1	3	.250	2.80	5	5	1	35.1	31	17	23	0	0	0	0	10	1	0	.100
1984	12	9	.571	3.81	33	33	2	205.2	179	104	136	2	0	0	0	67	10	0	.149
2 yrs.	13	12	.520	3.66	38	38	3	241	210	121	159	2	0	0	0	77	11	0	.143

Bob Darnell

DARNELL, ROBERT JACK   BR TR 5'10"   175 lbs.
B. Nov. 6, 1930, Wewoka, Okla.

	W	L	PCT	ERA	G	GS	CG	IP	H	BB	SO	ShO	W	L	SV	AB	H	HR	BA
1954 BKN N	0	0	–	3.14	6	1	0	14.1	15	7	5	0	0	0	0	2	0	0	.000
1956	0	0	–	0.00	1	0	0	1.1	1	0	0	0	0	0	0	0	0	0	–
2 yrs.	0	0	–	2.87	7	1	0	15.2	16	7	5	0	0	0	0	2	0	0	.000

Mike Darr

DARR, MICHAEL EDWARD   BR TR 6'4"   190 lbs.
B. Mar. 23, 1956, Pomona, Calif.

	W	L	PCT	ERA	G	GS	CG	IP	H	BB	SO	ShO	W	L	SV	AB	H	HR	BA
1977 TOR A	0	1	.000	45.00	1	1	0	1	3	4	1	0	0	0	0	0	0	0	–

George Darrow

DARROW, GEORGE OLIVER   BL TL 6'   180 lbs.
B. July 12, 1903, Beloit, Kans.   D. Mar. 24, 1983, Sun City, Ariz.

	W	L	PCT	ERA	G	GS	CG	IP	H	BB	SO	ShO	W	L	SV	AB	H	HR	BA
1934 PHI N	2	6	.250	5.51	17	8	2	49	57	28	14	0	1	1	1	15	2	0	.133

Bobby Darwin

DARWIN, ARTHUR BOBBY LEE   BR TR 6'2"   190 lbs.
B. Feb. 16, 1943, Los Angeles, Calif.

	W	L	PCT	ERA	G	GS	CG	IP	H	BB	SO	ShO	W	L	SV	AB	H	HR	BA
1962 LA A	0	1	.000	10.80	1	1	0	3.1	8	4	6	0	0	0	0	1	0	0	.000

	W	L	PCT	ERA	G	GS	CG	IP	H	BB	SO	ShO	Relief Pitching W	L	SV	BATTING AB	H	HR	BA

Bobby Darwin continued

	W	L	PCT	ERA	G	GS	CG	IP	H	BB	SO	ShO	W	L	SV	AB	H	HR	BA
1969 LA N	0	0	–	9.00	3	0	0	4	4	5	0	0	0	0	0	0	0	0	–
2 yrs.	0	1	.000	9.82	4	1	0	7.1	9	6	0		0	0	0	*			–

Danny Darwin

DARWIN, DANNY WAYNE
B. Oct. 25, 1955, Bonham, Tex.   BR TR 6'3" 185 lbs.

	W	L	PCT	ERA	G	GS	CG	IP	H	BB	SO	ShO	W	L	SV	AB	H	HR	BA
1978 TEX A	1	0	1.000	4.15	3	1	0	8.2	11	1	8	0	1	0	0	0	0	0	–
1979	4	4	.500	4.04	20	6	1	78	50	30	58	0	1	3	0	0	0	0	–
1980	13	4	.765	2.62	53	2	0	110	98	50	104	0	12	3	8	0	0	0	–
1981	9	9	.500	3.64	22	22	6	146	115	57	98	2	0	0	0	0	0	0	–
1982	10	8	.556	3.44	56	1	0	89	95	37	61	0	10	7	7	0	0	0	–
1983	8	13	.381	3.49	28	26	9	183	175	62	92	2	0	0	0	0	0	0	–
1984	8	12	.400	3.94	35	32	5	223.2	249	54	123	1	0	0	0	0	0	0	–
7 yrs.	53	50	.515	3.57	217	90	21	838.1	793	291	544	5	24	13	15	0	0	0	–

Lee Dashner

DASHNER, LEE CLAIRE (Lefty)
B. Apr. 25, 1887, Renault, Ill.   D. Dec. 16, 1959, El Dorado, Kans.   BB TL 5'11½" 192 lbs.

	W	L	PCT	ERA	G	GS	CG	IP	H	BB	SO	ShO	W	L	SV	AB	H	HR	BA
1913 CLE A	0	0	–	5.40	1	0	0	1.2	0	0	2	0	0	0	0	0	0	0	–

Frank Dasso

DASSO, FRANCIS JOSEPH NICHOLAS
B. Aug. 31, 1917, Chicago, Ill.   BR TR 5'11½" 185 lbs.

	W	L	PCT	ERA	G	GS	CG	IP	H	BB	SO	ShO	W	L	SV	AB	H	HR	BA
1945 CIN N	4	5	.444	3.67	16	12	6	95.2	89	53	39	0	1	1	0	31	5	0	.161
1946	0	0	–	27.00	2	0	0	1	2	2	1	0	0	0	0	0	0	0	–
2 yrs.	4	5	.444	3.91	18	12	6	96.2	91	55	40	0	1	1	0	31	5	0	.161

Dan Daub

DAUB, DANIEL WILLIAM (Mickey)
B. Jan. 12, 1868, Middletown, Ohio   D. Mar. 25, 1951, Bradenton, Fla.   BR TR 5'10" 160 lbs.

	W	L	PCT	ERA	G	GS	CG	IP	H	BB	SO	ShO	W	L	SV	AB	H	HR	BA
1892 CIN N	1	2	.333	2.88	4	3	2	25	23	13	7	0	0	0	0	7	0	0	.000
1893 BKN N	6	6	.500	3.84	12	12	12	103	104	61	25	0	0	0	0	42	8	0	.190
1894	9	12	.429	6.32	33	26	14	215	283	90	45	0	0	0	0	92	16	0	.174
1895	10	10	.500	4.29	25	21	16	184.2	212	51	36	0	1	0	0	71	14	0	.197
1896	12	11	.522	3.60	32	24	18	225	255	63	53	0	2	0	0	84	19	0	.226
1897	6	11	.353	6.08	19	16	11	137.2	180	48	19	0	2	1	0	49	11	0	.224
6 yrs.	44	52	.458	4.79	125	102	73	890.1	1057	326	185	0	5	1	0	345	68	0	.197

Hooks Dauss

DAUSS, GEORGE AUGUST
B. Sept. 22, 1889, Indianapolis, Ind.   D. July 27, 1963, St. Louis, Mo.   BR TR 5'10½" 168 lbs.

	W	L	PCT	ERA	G	GS	CG	IP	H	BB	SO	ShO	W	L	SV	AB	H	HR	BA
1912 DET A	1	1	.500	3.18	2	2	2	17	11	9	7	0	0	0	0	4	1	0	.250
1913	13	12	.520	2.68	33	29	22	225	188	82	107	2	0	1	1	79	14	0	.177
1914	18	15	.545	2.86	45	35	22	302	286	87	150	3	1	2	4	97	21	1	.216
1915	24	13	.649	2.50	46	35	27	309.2	261	112	132	1	3	2	2	103	15	0	.146
1916	19	12	.613	3.21	39	29	18	238.2	220	90	95	1	4	0	4	72	16	1	.222
1917	17	14	.548	2.43	37	31	22	270.2	243	87	102	6	1	0	1	87	11	0	.126
1918	12	16	.429	2.99	33	26	21	249.2	243	58	73	1	1	3	3	77	14	0	.182
1919	21	9	.700	3.55	34	32	22	256.1	262	63	73	2	1	0	0	97	14	0	.144
1920	13	21	.382	3.56	38	32	18	270.1	308	84	82	0	1	3	0	83	14	0	.169
1921	10	15	.400	4.33	32	28	16	233	275	81	68	0	1	1	1	88	23	1	.261
1922	13	13	.500	4.20	39	25	12	218.2	251	59	78	1	5	1	4	72	15	1	.208
1923	21	13	.618	3.62	50	39	22	316	331	78	105	4	1	1	3	104	24	0	.231
1924	12	11	.522	4.59	40	10	5	131.1	155	40	44	0	8	5	6	38	5	0	.132
1925	16	11	.593	3.16	35	30	16	228	238	85	58	1	2	1	1	81	15	1	.185
1926	11	7	.611	4.20	35	5	0	124.1	135	49	27	0	11	4	9	42	10	1	.238
15 yrs.	221	183	.547	3.32	538	388	245	3390.2	3407	1064	1201	22	40	23	40	1124	212	6	.189

Vic Davalillo

DAVALILLO, VICTOR JOSE
Brother of Yo-Yo Davalillo.
B. July 31, 1939, Cabimas, Venezuela   BL TL 5'7" 150 lbs.

	W	L	PCT	ERA	G	GS	CG	IP	H	BB	SO	ShO	W	L	SV	AB	H	HR	BA
1969 STL N	0	0	–	∞	2	0	0	2	2	0	0	0	0	0	0	*			

Claude Davenport

DAVENPORT, CLAUDE EDWIN
Brother of Dave Davenport.
B. May 28, 1898, Runge, Tex.   D. June 13, 1976, Corpus Christi, Tex.   BR TR 6'6" 193 lbs.

	W	L	PCT	ERA	G	GS	CG	IP	H	BB	SO	ShO	W	L	SV	AB	H	HR	BA
1920 NY N	0	0	–	4.50	1	0	0	2	2	1	0	0	0	0	0	1	0	0	.000

Dave Davenport

DAVENPORT, ARTHUR DAVID W. (Big Dave)
Brother of Claude Davenport.
B. Feb. 20, 1890, DeRidder, La.   D. Oct. 16, 1954, El Dorado, Ark.   BR TR 6'6" 220 lbs.

	W	L	PCT	ERA	G	GS	CG	IP	H	BB	SO	ShO	W	L	SV	AB	H	HR	BA
1914 2 teams	CIN N (10G 2–2)				STL F (33G 8–13)														
" total	10	15	.400	3.27	43	32	16	269.2	242	110	164	3	0	4	6	86	8	0	.093
1915 STL F	22	18	.550	2.20	55	46	30	392.2	300	96	229	10	0	2	1	130	12	0	.092
1916 STL A	12	11	.522	2.85	59	31	13	290.2	267	100	129	1	2	3	2	73	10	0	.137
1917	17	17	.500	3.08	47	39	19	280.2	273	105	100	2	0	0	2	92	9	0	.098
1918	10	11	.476	3.25	31	22	12	180	182	69	60	2	0	0	1	52	7	1	.135
1919	3	11	.214	3.94	24	16	5	123.1	135	41	37	0	1	1	0	39	3	0	.077
6 yrs.	74	83	.471	2.93	259	186	95	1537	1399	521	719	18	3	10	12	472	49	1	.104

Lum Davenport

DAVENPORT, JOUBERT LUM
B. June 27, 1900, Tucson, Ariz.   D. Apr. 21, 1961, Dallas, Tex.   BL TL 6'1" 165 lbs.

	W	L	PCT	ERA	G	GS	CG	IP	H	BB	SO	ShO	W	L	SV	AB	H	HR	BA
1921 CHI A	0	3	.000	6.88	13	2	0	35.1	41	32	9	0	0	2	0	17	7	0	.412
1922	1	1	.500	10.80	9	1	0	16.2	14	13	9	0	0	1	0	3	0	0	.000
1923	0	0	–	6.23	2	0	0	4.1	7	4	1	0	0	0	0	1	1	0	1.000
1924	0	0	–	0.00	1	0	0	2	1	2	1	0	0	0	0	0	0	0	–
4 yrs.	1	4	.200	7.71	25	3	0	58.1	63	51	20	0	0	3	0	21	8	0	.381

	W	L	PCT	ERA	G	GS	CG	IP	H	BB	SO	ShO	Relief Pitching W	L	SV	BATTING AB	H	HR	BA

Mike Davey

DAVEY, MICHAEL GERARD BL TR 6'2" 190 lbs.
B. June 2, 1952, Spokane, Wash.

	W	L	PCT	ERA	G	GS	CG	IP	H	BB	SO	ShO	W	L	SV	AB	H	HR	BA
1977 ATL N	0	0	–	5.06	16	0	0	16	19	9	7	0	0	0	2	1	0	0	.000
1978	0	0	–	0.00	3	0	0	3	1	1	0	0	0	0	0	0	0	0	–
2 yrs.	0	0	–	4.26	19	0	0	19	20	10	7	0	0	0	2	1	0	0	.000

Ray Daviault

DAVIAULT, RAYMOND JOSEPH ROBERT BR TR 6'1" 170 lbs.
B. May 27, 1934, Montreal, Que., Canada

	W	L	PCT	ERA	G	GS	CG	IP	H	BB	SO	ShO	W	L	SV	AB	H	HR	BA
1962 NY N	1	5	.167	6.22	36	3	0	81	92	48	51	0	1	3	0	15	1	0	.067

Ted Davidson

DAVIDSON, THOMAS EUGENE BR TL 6' 192 lbs.
B. Oct. 4, 1939, Las Vegas, Nev.

	W	L	PCT	ERA	G	GS	CG	IP	H	BB	SO	ShO	W	L	SV	AB	H	HR	BA
1965 CIN N	4	3	.571	2.23	24	1	0	68.2	57	17	54	0	3	3	1	17	0	0	.000
1966	5	4	.556	3.90	54	0	0	85.1	82	23	54	0	5	4	4	12	0	0	.000
1967	1	0	1.000	4.15	9	0	0	13	13	3	6	0	1	0	0	0	0	0	–
1968 2 teams				CIN N (23G 1–0)			ATL N (4G 0–0)												
" total	1	0	1.000	6.35	27	0	0	28.1	37	11	10	0	1	0	0	2	0	0	.000
4 yrs.	11	7	.611	3.69	114	1	0	195.1	189	54	124	0	10	7	5	31	0	0	.000

Jerry Davie

DAVIE, GERALD LEE BR TR 6' 180 lbs.
B. Feb. 10, 1933, Detroit, Mich.

	W	L	PCT	ERA	G	GS	CG	IP	H	BB	SO	ShO	W	L	SV	AB	H	HR	BA
1959 DET A	2	2	.500	4.17	11	5	1	36.2	40	17	20	0	0	0	0	10	4	0	.400

Chick Davies

DAVIES, LLOYD GARRISON BL TL 5'8" 145 lbs.
B. Mar. 6, 1892, Peabody, Mass. D. Sept. 5, 1973, Middletown, Conn.

	W	L	PCT	ERA	G	GS	CG	IP	H	BB	SO	ShO	W	L	SV	AB	H	HR	BA
1914 PHI A	1	0	1.000	1.00	1	1	1	9	8	3	4	0	0	0	0	46	11	0	.239
1915	1	2	.333	8.80	4	2	0	15.1	20	12	2	0	1	0	0	132	24	0	.182
1925 NY N	0	0	–	6.14	2	1	0	7.1	13	4	5	0	0	0	0	6	0	0	.000
1926	2	4	.333	3.94	38	1	0	89	96	35	27	0	2	3	6	18	4	0	.222
4 yrs.	4	6	.400	4.48	45	5	1	120.2	137	54	38	0	3	3	6	*			

George Davies

DAVIES, GEORGE WASHINGTON 180 lbs.
B. Feb. 22, 1868, Columbus, Wis. D. Sept. 22, 1906, Waterloo, Wis.

	W	L	PCT	ERA	G	GS	CG	IP	H	BB	SO	ShO	W	L	SV	AB	H	HR	BA
1891 C-M AA	7	5	.583	2.65	12	12	12	102	94	35	61	1	0	0	0	37	9	0	.243
1892 CLE N	10	16	.385	2.59	26	26	23	215.2	201	69	95	0	0	0	0	87	12	0	.138
1893 2 teams				CLE N (3G 0–2)			NY N (5G 1–1)												
" total	1	3	.250	7.71	8	4	2	51.1	69	23	10	0	0	1	0	18	6	0	.333
3 yrs.	18	24	.429	3.32	46	42	37	369	364	127	166	1	0	1	0	142	27	0	.190

Bob Davis

DAVIS, ROBERT EDWARD BR TR 6' 170 lbs.
B. Sept. 11, 1933, New York, N. Y.

	W	L	PCT	ERA	G	GS	CG	IP	H	BB	SO	ShO	W	L	SV	AB	H	HR	BA
1958 KC A	0	4	.000	7.84	8	4	0	31	45	12	22	0	0	0	0	6	1	0	.167
1960	0	0	–	3.66	21	0	0	32	31	22	28	0	0	0	1	4	1	0	.250
2 yrs.	0	4	.000	5.71	29	4	0	63	76	34	50	0	0	0	1	10	2	0	.200

Bud Davis

DAVIS, JOHN WILBUR (Country) BL TR 6' 207 lbs.
B. Dec. 7, 1889, Merry Point, Va. D. May 26, 1967, Williamsburg, Va.

	W	L	PCT	ERA	G	GS	CG	IP	H	BB	SO	ShO	W	L	SV	AB	H	HR	BA
1915 PHI A	0	2	.000	4.05	18	2	2	66.2	65	59	18	0	0	0	0	26	8	0	.308

Curt Davis

DAVIS, CURTIS BENTON (Coonskin) BR TR 6'2" 185 lbs.
B. Sept. 7, 1903, Greenfield, Mo. D. Oct. 13, 1965, Covina, Calif.

	W	L	PCT	ERA	G	GS	CG	IP	H	BB	SO	ShO	W	L	SV	AB	H	HR	BA
1934 PHI N	19	17	.528	2.95	51	31	18	274.1	283	60	99	3	6	2	5	95	20	1	.211
1935	16	14	.533	3.66	44	27	19	231	264	47	74	3	2	2	2	75	13	1	.173
1936 2 teams				PHI N (10G 2–4)			CHI N (24G 11–9)												
" total	13	13	.500	3.46	34	28	13	213.1	217	50	70	0	1	2	1	79	12	0	.152
1937 CHI N	10	5	.667	4.08	28	14	8	123.2	138	30	32	0	1	1	1	40	12	1	.300
1938 STL N	12	8	.600	3.63	40	21	8	173.1	187	27	36	2	4	0	3	57	13	3	.228
1939	22	16	.579	3.63	49	31	13	248	279	48	70	3	3	5	7	105	40	1	.381
1940 2 teams				STL N (14G 0–4)			BKN N (22G 8–7)												
" total	8	11	.421	4.19	36	22	9	191	208	38	58	0	1	1	3	66	6	0	.091
1941 BKN N	13	7	.650	2.97	28	16	10	154.1	141	27	50	5	2	3	2	59	11	2	.186
1942	15	6	.714	2.36	32	26	13	206	179	51	60	5	1	0	2	68	12	0	.176
1943	10	13	.435	3.78	31	21	8	164.1	182	39	47	2	3	1	3	55	9	0	.164
1944	10	11	.476	3.34	31	23	12	194	207	39	49	1	1	0	4	63	10	0	.159
1945	10	10	.500	3.25	24	18	10	149.2	171	21	39	0	0	2	0	51	7	1	.137
1946	0	0	–	13.50	1	0	0	2	3	2	0	0	0	0	0	0	0	0	–
13 yrs.	158	131	.547	3.42	429	281	141	2325	2459	479	684	24	25	19	33	813	165	11	.203

WORLD SERIES

	W	L	PCT	ERA	G	GS	CG	IP	H	BB	SO	ShO	W	L	SV	AB	H	HR	BA
1941 BKN N	0	1	.000	5.06	1	1	0	5.1	6	3	1	0	0	0	0	2	0	0	.000

Daisy Davis

DAVIS, JOHN A.
B. 1858, Boston, Mass. Deceased.

	W	L	PCT	ERA	G	GS	CG	IP	H	BB	SO	ShO	W	L	SV	AB	H	HR	BA
1884 2 teams				STL AA (25G 10–12)			BOS N (4G 1–3)												
" total	11	15	.423	3.57	29	28	23	229.1	246	43	156	1	0	0	0	103	15	0	.146
1885 BOS N	5	6	.455	4.29	11	11	10	94.1	110	28	30	1	0	0	0	37	7	0	.189
2 yrs.	16	21	.432	3.78	40	39	33	323.2	356	71	186	2	0	0	0	140	22	0	.157

Dixie Davis

DAVIS, FRANK TALMADGE BR TR 5'11" 155 lbs.
B. Oct. 12, 1890, Wilson Mills, N. C. D. Feb. 4, 1944, Raleigh, N. C.

	W	L	PCT	ERA	G	GS	CG	IP	H	BB	SO	ShO	W	L	SV	AB	H	HR	BA
1912 CIN N	0	1	.000	2.70	7	0	0	26.2	25	16	12	0	0	1	0	10	2	0	.200
1915 CHI A	0	0	–	0.00	2	0	0	3	2	2	2	0	0	0	0	0	0	0	–
1918 PHI N	0	2	.000	3.06	17	2	1	47	43	30	18	0	0	0	0	9	0	0	.000
1920 STL A	18	12	.600	3.17	38	31	22	269.1	250	149	85	0	1	0	0	94	25	0	.266
1921	16	16	.500	4.44	40	36	20	265.1	279	123	100	2	0	0	0	95	20	0	.211
1922	11	6	.647	4.08	25	25	7	174.1	162	87	65	0	0	0	0	59	8	0	.136
1923	4	6	.400	3.62	19	17	5	109.1	106	63	36	1	0	0	0	40	10	0	.250

	W	L	PCT	ERA	G	GS	CG	IP	H	BB	SO	ShO	Relief Pitching W	L	SV	BATTING AB	H	HR	BA

Dixie Davis continued

	W	L	PCT	ERA	G	GS	CG	IP	H	BB	SO	ShO	W	L	SV	AB	H	HR	BA
1924	11	13	.458	4.10	29	24	11	160.1	159	72	45	5	1	0	0	46	7	0	.152
1925	12	7	.632	4.59	35	23	9	180.1	192	106	58	0	2	1	1	64	11	0	.172
1926	3	8	.273	4.66	27	7	2	83	93	40	39	0	3	3	1	24	4	0	.167
10 yrs.	75	71	.514	3.97	239	165	77	1318.2	1311	688	460	10	7	5	2	441	87	0	.197

George Davis

DAVIS, GEORGE ALLEN (Iron) BB TR 5'10½" 175 lbs.
B. Mar. 9, 1890, Lancaster, N. Y. D. June 4, 1961, Buffalo, N. Y.

	W	L	PCT	ERA	G	GS	CG	IP	H	BB	SO	ShO	W	L	SV	AB	H	HR	BA
1912 NY A	1	4	.200	6.50	10	7	5	54	61	28	22	0	0	0	0	18	2	0	.111
1913 BOS N	0	0	–	4.50	2	0	0	8	7	5	3	0	0	0	0	2	0	0	.000
1914	3	3	.500	3.40	9	6	4	55.2	42	26	26	1	0	0	0	18	3	0	.167
1915	3	3	.500	3.80	15	9	4	73.1	85	19	26	0	0	0	0	23	6	0	.261
4 yrs.	7	10	.412	4.48	36	22	13	191	195	78	77	1	0	0	0	61	11	0	.180

George Davis

DAVIS, GEORGE STACEY BB TR 5'9" 180 lbs.
B. Aug. 23, 1870, Cohoes, N. Y. D. Oct. 17, 1940, Philadelphia, Pa.
Manager 1895, 1900-01.

	W	L	PCT	ERA	G	GS	CG	IP	H	BB	SO	ShO	W	L	SV	AB	H	HR	BA
1891 CLE N	0	1	.000	15.75	3	0	0	4	8	3	4	0	0	1	1	*			

Jim Davis

DAVIS, JAMES BENNETT BB TL 6' 180 lbs.
B. Sept. 15, 1924, Red Bluff, Calif.

	W	L	PCT	ERA	G	GS	CG	IP	H	BB	SO	ShO	W	L	SV	AB	H	HR	BA
1954 CHI N	11	7	.611	3.52	46	12	2	127.2	114	51	58	0	6	2	4	32	2	0	.063
1955	7	11	.389	4.44	42	16	0	133.2	122	58	62	0	5	3	3	37	1	0	.027
1956	5	7	.417	3.66	46	11	2	120.1	116	59	66	1	3	2	2	28	5	0	.179
1957 2 teams	STL N (10G 0–1)				NY	N (10G 1–0)													
" total	1	1	.500	5.84	20	0	0	24.2	31	11	11	0	1	1	1	2	1	0	.500
4 yrs.	24	26	.480	4.01	154	39	4	406.1	383	179	197	1	15	8	10	99	9	0	.091

Mark Davis

DAVIS, MARK WILLIAM BL TL 6'3" 180 lbs.
B. Oct. 19, 1960, Livermore, Calif.

	W	L	PCT	ERA	G	GS	CG	IP	H	BB	SO	ShO	W	L	SV	AB	H	HR	BA
1980 PHI N	0	0	–	2.57	2	1	0	7	4	5	5	0	0	0	0	2	1	0	.500
1981	1	4	.200	7.74	9	9	0	43	49	24	29	0	0	0	0	11	1	0	.091
1983 SF N	6	4	.600	3.49	20	20	2	111	93	50	83	2	0	0	0	30	4	0	.133
1984	5	17	.227	5.36	46	27	1	174.2	201	54	124	0	3	4	0	46	6	0	.130
4 yrs.	12	25	.324	4.99	77	57	3	335.2	347	133	241	2	3	4	0	89	12	0	.135

Peaches Davis

DAVIS, RAY THOMAS BL TR 6'3½" 190 lbs.
B. May 31, 1905, Glen Rose, Tex.

	W	L	PCT	ERA	G	GS	CG	IP	H	BB	SO	ShO	W	L	SV	AB	H	HR	BA
1936 CIN N	8	8	.500	3.58	26	15	5	125.2	139	36	32	0	2	1	5	43	7	0	.163
1937	11	13	.458	3.59	42	24	11	218	252	51	59	1	1	3	3	78	10	0	.128
1938	7	12	.368	3.97	29	19	11	167.2	193	40	28	1	1	2	1	61	15	0	.246
1939	1	0	1.000	6.46	20	0	0	30.2	43	11	4	0	1	0	2	3	1	0	.333
4 yrs.	27	33	.450	3.87	117	58	27	542	627	138	123	2	5	6	11	185	33	0	.178

Ron Davis

DAVIS, RONALD GENE BR TR 6'4" 205 lbs.
B. Aug. 6, 1955, Houston, Tex.

	W	L	PCT	ERA	G	GS	CG	IP	H	BB	SO	ShO	W	L	SV	AB	H	HR	BA
1978 NY A	0	0	–	11.57	4	0	0	2.1	3	3	0	0	0	0	0	0	0	0	–
1979	14	2	.875	2.86	44	0	0	85	84	28	43	0	14	2	9	1	0	0	.000
1980	9	3	.750	2.95	53	0	0	131	121	32	65	0	9	3	7	1	0	0	.000
1981	4	5	.444	2.71	43	0	0	73	47	25	83	0	4	5	6	0	0	0	–
1982 MIN A	3	9	.250	4.42	63	0	0	106	106	47	89	0	3	9	22	0	0	0	–
1983	5	8	.385	3.34	66	0	0	89	89	33	84	0	5	8	30	0	0	0	–
1984	7	11	.389	4.55	64	0	0	83	79	41	74	0	7	11	29	0	0	0	–
7 yrs.	42	38	.525	3.51	337	0	0	569.1	529	209	438	0	42	38	103	2	0	0	.000

DIVISIONAL PLAYOFF SERIES

	W	L	PCT	ERA	G	GS	CG	IP	H	BB	SO	ShO	W	L	SV	AB	H	HR	BA
1981 NY A	1	0	1.000	0.00	3	0	0	6	1	2	6	0	1	0	0	0	0	0	–

LEAGUE CHAMPIONSHIP SERIES

	W	L	PCT	ERA	G	GS	CG	IP	H	BB	SO	ShO	W	L	SV	AB	H	HR	BA
1980 NY A	0	0	–	2.25	1	0	0	4	3	1	3	0	0	0	0	0	0	0	–
1981	0	0	–	0.00	2	0	0	3.1	0	2	4	0	0	0	0	0	0	0	–
2 yrs.	0	0	–	1.23	3	0	0	7.1	3	3	7	0	0	0	0	0	0	0	–

WORLD SERIES

	W	L	PCT	ERA	G	GS	CG	IP	H	BB	SO	ShO	W	L	SV	AB	H	HR	BA
1981 NY A	0	0	–	23.14	4	0	0	2.1	4	5	4	0	0	0	0	0	0	0	–

Storm Davis

DAVIS, GEORGE EARL BR TR 6'4" 210 lbs.
B. Dec. 26, 1961, Dallas, Tex.

	W	L	PCT	ERA	G	GS	CG	IP	H	BB	SO	ShO	W	L	SV	AB	H	HR	BA
1982 BAL A	8	4	.667	3.49	29	8	1	100.2	96	28	67	0	3	2	0	0	0	0	–
1983	13	7	.650	3.59	34	29	6	200.1	180	64	125	0	0	0	0	0	0	0	–
1984	14	9	.609	3.12	35	31	10	225	205	71	105	2	0	1	1	0	0	0	–
3 yrs.	35	20	.636	3.37	98	68	17	526	481	163	297	3	3	3	1	0	0	0	–

LEAGUE CHAMPIONSHIP SERIES

	W	L	PCT	ERA	G	GS	CG	IP	H	BB	SO	ShO	W	L	SV	AB	H	HR	BA
1983 BAL A	0	0	–	0.00	1	1	0	6	5	2	2	0	0	0	0	0	0	0	–

WORLD SERIES

	W	L	PCT	ERA	G	GS	CG	IP	H	BB	SO	ShO	W	L	SV	AB	H	HR	BA
1983 BAL A	1	0	1.000	5.40	1	1	0	5	6	1	3	0	0	0	0	2	0	0	.000

Wiley Davis

DAVIS, WILEY ANDERSON BR TR 5'10" 165 lbs.
B. Aug. 1, 1875, Seymour, Tenn. D. Sept. 22, 1942, Detroit, Mich.

	W	L	PCT	ERA	G	GS	CG	IP	H	BB	SO	ShO	W	L	SV	AB	H	HR	BA
1896 CIN N	1	1	.500	8.31	2	0	0	4.1	8	2	1	0	1	1	0	1	0	0	.000

Woody Davis

DAVIS, WOODROW WILSON (Babe) BL TR 6'1" 200 lbs.
B. Apr. 25, 1913, Nicholas, Ga.

	W	L	PCT	ERA	G	GS	CG	IP	H	BB	SO	ShO	W	L	SV	AB	H	HR	BA
1938 DET A	0	0	–	1.50	2	0	0	6	3	4	1	0	0	0	0	1	0	0	.000

	W	L	PCT	ERA	G	GS	CG	IP	H	BB	SO	ShO	Relief Pitching W	L	SV	BATTING AB	H	HR	BA

Mike Davison

DAVISON, MICHAEL LYNN
B. Aug. 4, 1945, Galesburg, Ill.
BL TL 6'1"   170 lbs.

	W	L	PCT	ERA	G	GS	CG	IP	H	BB	SO	ShO	W	L	SV	AB	H	HR	BA
1969 SF N	0	0	–	4.50	1	0	0	2	2	0	2	0	0	0	0	0	0	0	–
1970	3	5	.375	6.50	31	0	0	36	46	22	21	0	3	5	1	1	0	0	.000
2 yrs.	3	5	.375	6.39	32	0	0	38	48	22	23	0	3	5	1	1	0	0	.000

Bill Dawley

DAWLEY, WILLIAM CHESTER
B. Feb. 6, 1958, Norwich, Conn.
BR TR 6'4"   205 lbs.

	W	L	PCT	ERA	G	GS	CG	IP	H	BB	SO	ShO	W	L	SV	AB	H	HR	BA
1983 HOU N	6	6	.500	2.82	48	0	0	79.2	51	22	60	0	6	6	14	9	2	0	.222
1984	11	4	.733	1.93	60	0	0	98	82	35	47	0	11	4	5	9	3	0	.333
2 yrs.	17	10	.630	2.33	108	0	0	177.2	133	57	107	0	17	10	19	18	5	0	.278

Joe Dawson

DAWSON, RALPH FENTON
B. 1897, Bow, Wash.   D. Jan. 4, 1978, Longview, Tex.
BR TR 5'11"   182 lbs.

	W	L	PCT	ERA	G	GS	CG	IP	H	BB	SO	ShO	W	L	SV	AB	H	HR	BA
1924 CLE A	1	2	.333	6.64	4	4	0	20.1	24	21	7	0	0	0	0	7	2	0	.286
1927 PIT N	3	7	.300	4.46	20	7	4	80.2	80	32	17	0	2	2	0	25	5	0	.200
1928	7	7	.500	3.29	31	7	1	128.2	116	56	36	0	5	2	3	43	12	0	.279
1929	0	1	.000	8.31	4	0	0	8.2	13	3	2	0	0	1	0	2	1	0	.500
4 yrs.	11	17	.393	4.15	59	18	5	238.1	233	112	62	0	7	5	3	77	20	0	.260
WORLD SERIES																			
1927 PIT N	0	0	–	0.00	1	0	0	1	0	1	0	0	0	0	0	0	0	0	–

Rex Dawson

DAWSON, REXFORD PAUL
B. Feb. 10, 1889, Skagit County, Wash.   D. Oct. 20, 1958, Indianapolis, Ind.
BL TR 6'   185 lbs.

	W	L	PCT	ERA	G	GS	CG	IP	H	BB	SO	ShO	W	L	SV	AB	H	HR	BA
1913 WAS A	0	0	–	0.00	1	0	0	1	1	0	0	0	0	0	0	0	0	0	–

Bill Day

DAY, WILLIAM
B. July 28, 1867, Wilmington, Del.   D. Aug. 16, 1923, Wilmington, Del.
TR

	W	L	PCT	ERA	G	GS	CG	IP	H	BB	SO	ShO	W	L	SV	AB	H	HR	BA
1889 PHI N	0	3	.000	5.21	4	3	2	19	16	23	20	0	0	0	0	10	0	0	.000
1890 2 teams					PHI N	(4G 1–1)			PIT N	(6G 0–6)									
" total	1	7	.125	4.52	10	8	8	73.2	92	36	19	0	0	0	0	33	2	0	.061
2 yrs.	1	10	.091	4.66	14	11	10	92.2	108	59	39	0	0	0	0	43	2	0	.047

Pea Ridge Day

DAY, CLYDE HENRY
B. Aug. 27, 1899, Pea Ridge, Ark.   D. Mar. 21, 1934, Kansas City, Mo.
BR TR 6'   190 lbs.

	W	L	PCT	ERA	G	GS	CG	IP	H	BB	SO	ShO	W	L	SV	AB	H	HR	BA
1924 STL N	1	1	.500	4.58	3	3	1	17.2	22	6	3	0	0	0	0	8	1	0	.125
1925	2	4	.333	6.30	17	4	2	40	53	7	13	0	1	1	1	13	2	0	.154
1926 CIN N	0	0	–	7.36	4	0	0	7.1	13	2	2	0	0	0	0	2	0	0	.000
1931 BKN N	2	2	.500	4.55	22	2	1	57.1	75	13	30	0	2	0	1	18	4	0	.222
4 yrs.	5	7	.417	5.30	46	9	3	122.1	163	28	48	0	3	1	2	41	7	0	.171

Ken Dayley

DAYLEY, KENNETH GRANT
B. Feb. 25, 1959, Jerome, Ida.
BL TL 6'   178 lbs.

	W	L	PCT	ERA	G	GS	CG	IP	H	BB	SO	ShO	W	L	SV	AB	H	HR	BA
1982 ATL N	5	6	.455	4.54	20	11	0	71.1	79	25	34	0	2	0	0	20	5	0	.250
1983	5	8	.385	4.30	24	16	0	104.2	100	39	70	0	1	2	0	32	7	0	.219
1984 2 teams					ATL N	(4G 0–3)			STL N	(3G 0–2)									
" total	0	5	.000	7.99	7	6	0	23.2	44	11	10	0	0	0	0	4	2	0	.500
3 yrs.	10	19	.345	4.82	51	33	0	199.2	223	75	114	0	3	2	0	56	14	0	.250

Ren Deagle

DEAGLE, LORENZO BURROUGHS
B. June 26, 1858, New York, N.Y.   D. Dec. 24, 1937, Kansas City, Mo.
BR TR 5'9"   190 lbs.

	W	L	PCT	ERA	G	GS	CG	IP	H	BB	SO	ShO	W	L	SV	AB	H	HR	BA
1883 CIN AA	10	8	.556	2.31	18	18	17	148	136	34	46	1	0	0	0	70	9	0	.129
1884 2 teams					CIN AA	(3G 3–1)			LOU AA	(12G 4–6)									
" total	7	7	.500	3.26	16	16	12	121.1	119	22	35	1	0	0	0	58	6	0	.103
2 yrs.	17	15	.531	2.74	34	34	29	269.1	255	56	81	2	0	0	0	128	15	0	.117

Cot Deal

DEAL, ELLIS FERGASON
B. Jan. 23, 1923, Arapaho, Okla.
BB TR 5'10½" 185 lbs.
BL 1947-48

	W	L	PCT	ERA	G	GS	CG	IP	H	BB	SO	ShO	W	L	SV	AB	H	HR	BA
1947 BOS A	0	1	.000	9.24	5	2	0	12.2	20	7	6	0	0	0	0	4	2	0	.500
1948	1	0	1.000	0.00	4	0	0	4	3	3	2	0	1	0	0	0	0	0	–
1950 STL N	0	0	–	18.00	3	0	0	1	3	2	1	0	0	0	0	0	0	0	–
1954	2	3	.400	6.28	33	0	0	71.2	85	36	25	0	2	3	1	20	2	1	.100
4 yrs.	3	4	.429	6.55	45	2	0	89.1	111	48	34	0	3	3	1	24	4	1	.167

Chubby Dean

DEAN, ALFRED LOVILL
B. Aug. 24, 1916, Mt. Airy, N.C.   D. Dec. 21, 1970, Riverside, N.J.
BL TL 5'11"   181 lbs.

	W	L	PCT	ERA	G	GS	CG	IP	H	BB	SO	ShO	W	L	SV	AB	H	HR	BA
1937 PHI A	1	0	1.000	4.00	2	1	0	9	7	6	4	0	0	0	0	309	81	2	.262
1938	2	1	.667	3.52	6	1	0	23	22	15	3	0	2	0	0	20	6	0	.300
1939	5	8	.385	5.25	54	1	0	116.2	132	80	39	0	5	7	7	77	27	0	.351
1940	6	13	.316	6.61	30	19	8	159.1	220	63	38	1	1	3	1	90	26	0	.289
1941 2 teams					PHI A	(18G 2–4)			CLE A	(8G 1–4)									
" total	3	8	.273	5.44	26	15	4	129	147	59	36	0	1	0	0	62	13	0	.210
1942 CLE A	8	11	.421	3.81	27	22	8	172.2	170	66	46	0	2	0	1	101	27	0	.267
1943	5	5	.500	4.50	17	9	3	76	83	34	29	0	1	2	0	46	9	0	.196
7 yrs.	30	46	.395	5.08	162	68	23	685.2	781	323	195	1	12	12	9	*			

Dizzy Dean

DEAN, JAY HANNA
Brother of Paul Dean.
B. Jan. 16, 1911, Lucas, Ark.   D. July 17, 1974, Reno, Nev.
Hall of Fame 1953.
BR TR 6'2"   182 lbs.

	W	L	PCT	ERA	G	GS	CG	IP	H	BB	SO	ShO	W	L	SV	AB	H	HR	BA
1930 STL N	1	0	1.000	1.00	1	1	1	9	3	3	5	0	0	0	0	3	1	0	.333
1932	18	15	.545	3.30	46	33	16	286	280	102	191	4	0	3	2	97	25	2	.258
1933	20	18	.526	3.04	48	34	26	293	279	64	199	3	1	3	4	105	19	1	.181
1934	30	7	.811	2.66	50	33	24	311.2	288	75	195	7	4	2	7	118	29	2	.246
1935	28	12	.700	3.11	50	36	29	324.1	326	82	182	3	4	3	5	128	30	2	.234
1936	24	13	.649	3.17	51	34	28	315	310	53	195	2	2	3	11	121	27	0	.223
1937	13	10	.565	2.69	27	25	17	197.1	206	33	120	4	0	1	1	66	15	1	.227

	W	L	PCT	ERA	G	GS	CG	IP	H	BB	SO	ShO	Relief Pitching W	L	SV	BATTING AB	H	HR	BA

Dizzy Dean continued

	W	L	PCT	ERA	G	GS	CG	IP	H	BB	SO	ShO	W	L	SV	AB	H	HR	BA
1938 CHI N	7	1	.875	1.81	13	10	3	74.2	63	8	22	1	0	0	0	26	5	0	.192
1939	6	4	.600	3.36	19	13	7	96.1	98	17	27	2	0	1	0	34	5	0	.147
1940	3	3	.500	5.17	10	9	3	54	68	20	18	0	0	0	0	18	4	0	.222
1941	0	0	—	18.00	1	1	0	1	3	0	1	0	0	0	0	0	0	0	—
1947 STL A	0	0	—	0.00	1	1	0	4	3	1	0	0	0	0	0	1	1	0	1.000
12 yrs.	150	83	.644	3.03	317	230	154	1966.1	1927	458	1155	26	11	16	30	717	161	8	.225

WORLD SERIES

	W	L	PCT	ERA	G	GS	CG	IP	H	BB	SO	ShO	W	L	SV	AB	H	HR	BA
1934 STL N	2	1	.667	1.73	3	3	2	26	20	5	17	1	0	0	0	12	3	0	.250
1938 CHI N	0	1	.000	6.48	2	1	0	8.1	8	1	2	0	0	0	0	3	2	0	.667
2 yrs.	2	2	.500	2.88	5	4	2	34.1	28	6	19	1	0	0	0	15	5	0	.333

Dory Dean

DEAN, CHARLES WILSON
B. Nov. 6, 1852, Cincinnati, Ohio   D. May 4, 1935, Nashville, Tenn.   BR TR 5'10"   160 lbs.

	W	L	PCT	ERA	G	GS	CG	IP	H	BB	SO	ShO	W	L	SV	AB	H	HR	BA
1876 CIN N	4	26	.133	3.73	30	30	26	262.2	397	24	22	0	0	0	0	138	36	0	.261

Harry Dean

DEAN, JAMES HARRY
B. May 12, 1915, Rockmart, Ga.   D. June 1, 1960, Rockmart, Ga.   BR TR 6'4"   185 lbs.

	W	L	PCT	ERA	G	GS	CG	IP	H	BB	SO	ShO	W	L	SV	AB	H	HR	BA
1941 WAS A	0	0	—	4.50	2	0	0	2	2	3	0	0	0	0	0	0	0	0	—

Paul Dean

DEAN, PAUL DEE (Daffy)
Brother of Dizzy Dean.
B. Aug. 14, 1913, Lucas, Ark.   D. Mar. 17, 1981, Springdale, Ark.   BR TR 6'   175 lbs.

	W	L	PCT	ERA	G	GS	CG	IP	H	BB	SO	ShO	W	L	SV	AB	H	HR	BA
1934 STL N	19	11	.633	3.43	39	26	16	233.1	225	52	150	5	2	4	2	83	20	0	.241
1935	19	12	.613	3.37	46	33	19	269.2	261	55	143	2	3	1	5	90	12	0	.133
1936	5	5	.500	4.60	17	14	5	92	113	20	28	0	0	1	1	34	2	0	.059
1937	0	0	—	∞	1	0	0	1	1	2	0	0	0	0	0	0	0	0	—
1938	3	1	.750	2.61	5	4	2	31	37	5	14	1	0	0	0	11	2	0	.182
1939	0	1	.000	6.07	16	2	0	43	54	10	16	0	0	0	0	9	1	0	.111
1940 NY N	4	4	.500	3.90	27	7	2	99.1	110	29	32	0	2	3	0	26	3	0	.115
1941	0	0	—	3.18	5	0	0	5.2	8	3	3	0	0	0	0	0	0	0	—
1943 STL A	0	0	—	3.38	3	1	0	13.1	16	3	1	0	0	0	0	3	0	0	.000
9 yrs.	50	34	.595	3.75	159	87	44	787.1	825	179	387	8	7	9	8	256	40	0	.156

WORLD SERIES

	W	L	PCT	ERA	G	GS	CG	IP	H	BB	SO	ShO	W	L	SV	AB	H	HR	BA
1934 STL N	2	0	1.000	1.00	2	2	2	18	15	7	11	0	0	0	0	6	1	0	.167

Wayland Dean

DEAN, WAYLAND OGDEN
B. June 20, 1903, Richwood, W. Va.
D. Apr. 10, 1930, Huntington, W. Va.   BB TR 6'2"   178 lbs.
BL 1926-27

	W	L	PCT	ERA	G	GS	CG	IP	H	BB	SO	ShO	W	L	SV	AB	H	HR	BA
1924 NY N	6	12	.333	5.01	26	20	6	125.2	139	45	39	0	1	2	0	40	8	2	.200
1925	10	7	.588	4.64	33	14	6	151.1	169	50	53	1	5	1	1	51	12	1	.235
1926 PHI N	8	16	.333	6.10	33	26	15	163.2	245	89	52	1	0	2	0	102	27	3	.265
1927 2 teams						PHI N (2G 0-1)			CHI N (2G 0-0)											
" total	0	1	.000	7.20	4	0	0	5	6	4	3	0	0	1	0	3	2	0	.667
4 yrs.	24	36	.400	5.31	96	60	27	445.2	559	188	147	2	6	6	1	*			

WORLD SERIES

	W	L	PCT	ERA	G	GS	CG	IP	H	BB	SO	ShO	W	L	SV	AB	H	HR	BA
1924 NY N	0	0	—	4.50	1	0	0	2	3	0	2	0	0	0	0	0	0	0	—

Denny DeBarr

DeBARR, DENNIS LEE
B. Jan. 16, 1953, Cheyenne, Wyo.   BL TL 6'2"   190 lbs.

	W	L	PCT	ERA	G	GS	CG	IP	H	BB	SO	ShO	W	L	SV	AB	H	HR	BA
1977 TOR A	0	1	.000	6.00	14	0	0	21	29	8	10	0	0	1	0	0	0	0	—

Joe DeBerry

DeBERRY, JOSEPH GADDY
B. Nov. 29, 1896, Mt. Gilead, N. C.   D. Oct. 9, 1944, Southern Pines, N. C.   BL TR 6'1"   175 lbs.

	W	L	PCT	ERA	G	GS	CG	IP	H	BB	SO	ShO	W	L	SV	AB	H	HR	BA
1920 STL A	2	4	.333	4.94	10	7	3	54.2	65	20	12	1	0	1	0	18	3	0	.167
1921	0	1	.000	6.57	10	1	0	12.1	15	10	1	0	0	0	0	2	0	0	.000
2 yrs.	2	5	.286	5.24	20	8	3	67	80	30	13	1	0	1	0	20	3	0	.150

Dave DeBusschere

DeBUSSCHERE, DAVID ALBERT
B. Oct. 16, 1940, Detroit, Mich.   BR TR 6'6"   225 lbs.

	W	L	PCT	ERA	G	GS	CG	IP	H	BB	SO	ShO	W	L	SV	AB	H	HR	BA
1962 CHI A	0	0	—	2.00	12	0	0	18	5	23	8	0	0	0	0	0	0	0	—
1963	3	4	.429	3.09	24	10	1	84.1	80	34	53	1	0	0	0	22	1	0	.045
2 yrs.	3	4	.429	2.90	36	10	1	102.1	85	57	61	1	0	0	0	22	1	0	.045

Art Decatur

DECATUR, ARTHUR RUE
B. Jan. 14, 1894, Cleveland, Ohio   D. Apr. 25, 1966, Talladega, Ala.   BR TR 6'1"   190 lbs.

	W	L	PCT	ERA	G	GS	CG	IP	H	BB	SO	ShO	W	L	SV	AB	H	HR	BA
1922 BKN N	3	4	.429	2.77	29	2	1	87.2	87	29	31	0	3	3	1	25	2	0	.080
1923	3	3	.500	2.67	36	5	2	104.2	115	34	27	0	2	0	3	21	0	0	.000
1924	10	9	.526	4.07	31	10	4	128.1	158	28	39	0	7	2	1	44	5	0	.114
1925 2 teams						BKN N (1G 0-0)			PHI N (25G 4-13)											
" total	4	13	.235	5.37	26	15	4	129	173	35	31	0	0	4	2	41	2	0	.049
1926 PHI N	0	0	—	6.00	2	1	0	3	6	2	0	0	0	0	0	1	0	0	.000
1927	3	5	.375	7.26	29	3	0	96.2	130	20	27	0	3	3	0	27	6	0	.222
6 yrs.	23	34	.404	4.47	153	36	11	549.1	669	148	155	0	15	12	7	159	15	0	.094

Joe Decker

DECKER, GEORGE HENRY
B. June 16, 1947, Storm Lake, Iowa   BR TR 5'11"   183 lbs.

	W	L	PCT	ERA	G	GS	CG	IP	H	BB	SO	ShO	W	L	SV	AB	H	HR	BA
1969 CHI N	1	0	1.000	3.00	4	1	0	12	10	6	13	0	0	0	0	2	0	0	.000
1970	2	7	.222	4.62	24	17	1	109	108	56	79	0	0	0	0	34	6	1	.176
1971	3	2	.600	4.70	21	4	0	46	62	25	37	0	0	0	0	8	2	0	.250
1972	1	0	1.000	2.08	5	1	0	13	9	4	7	0	0	0	0	2	0	0	.000
1973 MIN A	10	10	.500	4.17	29	24	6	170.1	167	88	109	3	0	0	0	0	0	0	—
1974	16	14	.533	3.29	37	37	11	249	234	97	158	1	0	0	0	0	0	0	—
1975	1	3	.250	8.54	10	7	1	26.1	25	36	8	0	0	0	0	0	0	0	—
1976	2	7	.222	5.28	13	12	0	58	60	51	35	0	0	0	0	0	0	0	—

	W	L	PCT	ERA	G	GS	CG	IP	H	BB	SO	ShO	Relief Pitching W	L	SV	BATTING AB	H	HR	BA

Joe Decker continued

	W	L	PCT	ERA	G	GS	CG	IP	H	BB	SO	ShO	W	L	SV	AB	H	HR	BA
1979 SEA A	0	1	.000	4.33	9	2	0	27	27	14	12	0	0	0	0	0	0	0	–
9 yrs.	36	44	.450	4.17	152	105	19	710.2	702	377	458	4	2	0	0	46	8	1	.174

Marty Decker

DECKER, DEE MARTIN
B. June 7, 1957, Upland, Calif.
BR TR 5'11" 170 lbs.

	W	L	PCT	ERA	G	GS	CG	IP	H	BB	SO	ShO	W	L	SV	AB	H	HR	BA
1983 SD N	0	0	–	2.08	4	0	0	8.2	5	3	9	0	0	0	0	0	0	0	–

Jeff Dedmon

DEDMON, JEFFREY LINDEN
B. Mar. 4, 1960, Torrance, Calif.
BR TR 6'3" 185 lbs.

	W	L	PCT	ERA	G	GS	CG	IP	H	BB	SO	ShO	W	L	SV	AB	H	HR	BA
1983 ATL N	0	0	–	13.50	5	0	0	4	10	0	3	0	0	0	0	0	0	0	–
1984	4	3	.571	3.78	54	0	0	81	86	35	51	0	4	3	4	6	0	0	.000
2 yrs.	4	3	.571	4.24	59	0	0	85	96	35	54	0	4	3	4	6	0	0	.000

Dummy Deegan

DEEGAN, W. JOHN
B. New York, N. Y.

	W	L	PCT	ERA	G	GS	CG	IP	H	BB	SO	ShO	W	L	SV	AB	H	HR	BA
1901 NY N	0	2	.000	6.35	2	1	1	17	27	6	8	0	0	1	0	5	0	0	.000

John Deering

DEERING, JOHN THOMAS
B. June 25, 1878, Lynn, Mass.   D. Feb. 15, 1943, Beverly, Mass.
TR

	W	L	PCT	ERA	G	GS	CG	IP	H	BB	SO	ShO	W	L	SV	AB	H	HR	BA
1903 2 teams		DET A	(10G 3–4)		NY	A	(9G 3–3)												
" total	6	7	.462	3.80	19	15	11	120.2	136	42	28	1	0	0	0	47	9	0	.191

Mike DeGerick

DeGERICK, MICHAEL ARTHUR
B. Apr. 1, 1943, New York, N. Y.
BR TR 6'2" 178 lbs.

	W	L	PCT	ERA	G	GS	CG	IP	H	BB	SO	ShO	W	L	SV	AB	H	HR	BA
1961 CHI A	0	0	–	5.40	1	0	0	1.2	2	1	0	0	0	0	0	0	0	0	–
1962	0	0	–	0.00	1	0	0	1	1	1	0	0	0	0	0	0	0	0	–
2 yrs.	0	0	–	3.38	2	0	0	2.2	3	2	0	0	0	0	0	0	0	0	–

Pep Deininger

DEININGER, OTTO CHARLES
B. Oct. 10, 1877, Wasseralfingen, Germany   D. Sept. 25, 1950, Boston, Mass.
BL TL 5'8½" 180 lbs.

	W	L	PCT	ERA	G	GS	CG	IP	H	BB	SO	ShO	W	L	SV	AB	H	HR	BA
1902 BOS A	0	0	–	9.75	2	1	0	12	19	9	2	0	0	0	0	*		

Tommy de la Cruz

de la CRUZ, TOMAS
B. Sept. 18, 1914, Marianao, Cuba   D. Sept. 6, 1958, Havana, Cuba
BR TR 6'1" 168 lbs.

	W	L	PCT	ERA	G	GS	CG	IP	H	BB	SO	ShO	W	L	SV	AB	H	HR	BA
1944 CIN N	9	9	.500	3.25	34	20	9	191.1	170	45	65	0	2	1	1	58	9	0	.155

Jim Delahanty

DELAHANTY, JAMES CHRISTOPHER
Brother of Ed Delahanty.   Brother of Frank Delahanty.
Brother of Tom Delahanty.   Brother of Joe Delahanty.
B. June 20, 1879, Cleveland, Ohio   D. Oct. 17, 1953, Cleveland, Ohio
BR TR 5'10½" 170 lbs.

	W	L	PCT	ERA	G	GS	CG	IP	H	BB	SO	ShO	W	L	SV	AB	H	HR	BA
1904 BOS N	0	0	–	0.00	1	0	0	3.1	5	1	0	0	0	0	0	499	142	3	.285
1905	0	0	–	4.50	1	1	0	2	5	0	1	0	0	0	0	461	119	5	.258
2 yrs.	0	0	–	1.69	2	1	0	5.1	10	1	1	0	0	0	0	*		

Art Delaney

DELANEY, ARTHUR DEWEY (Swede)
Also known as Arthur Dewey Helenius.
B. Jan. 5, 1895, Greensboro, N. C.   D. May 2, 1970, Hayward, Calif.
BR TR 5'10½" 178 lbs.

	W	L	PCT	ERA	G	GS	CG	IP	H	BB	SO	ShO	W	L	SV	AB	H	HR	BA
1924 STL N	1	0	1.000	1.80	8	1	1	20	19	6	2	0	0	0	0	7	2	0	.286
1928 BOS N	9	17	.346	3.79	39	22	8	192.1	197	56	45	0	4	3	2	63	9	0	.143
1929	3	5	.375	6.12	20	8	3	75	103	35	17	1	1	1	0	21	3	1	.143
3 yrs.	13	22	.371	4.26	67	31	12	287.1	319	97	64	1	5	4	2	91	14	1	.154

Jose DeLeon

DeLEON, JOSE
Also known as Jose Chestaro.
B. Dec. 20, 1960, La Vega, Dominican Republic
BR TR 6'3" 195 lbs.

	W	L	PCT	ERA	G	GS	CG	IP	H	BB	SO	ShO	W	L	SV	AB	H	HR	BA
1983 PIT N	7	3	.700	2.83	15	15	3	108	75	47	118	2	0	0	0	34	2	0	.059
1984	7	13	.350	3.74	30	28	5	192.1	147	92	153	1	1	0	0	59	5	0	.085
2 yrs.	14	16	.467	3.42	45	43	8	300.1	222	139	271	3	1	0	0	93	7	0	.075

Luis DeLeon

DeLEON, LUIS ANTONIO
B. Aug. 19, 1958, Ponce, Puerto Rico
BR TR 6'1" 153 lbs.

	W	L	PCT	ERA	G	GS	CG	IP	H	BB	SO	ShO	W	L	SV	AB	H	HR	BA
1981 STL N	0	1	.000	2.40	10	0	0	15	11	3	8	0	0	1	0	1	0	0	.000
1982 SD N	9	5	.643	2.03	61	0	0	102	77	16	60	0	9	5	15	11	1	0	.091
1983	6	6	.500	2.68	63	0	0	111	89	27	90	0	6	6	13	14	2	0	.143
1984	2	2	.500	5.48	32	0	0	42.2	44	12	44	0	2	2	0	4	0	0	.000
4 yrs.	17	14	.548	2.86	166	0	0	270.2	221	58	202	0	17	14	28	30	3	0	.100

Flame Delhi

DELHI, LEE WILLIAM
B. Nov. 2, 1890, Harqua Hala, Ariz.   D. May 9, 1966, San Rafael, Calif.
BR TR 6'2½" 198 lbs.

	W	L	PCT	ERA	G	GS	CG	IP	H	BB	SO	ShO	W	L	SV	AB	H	HR	BA
1912 CHI A	0	0	–	9.00	1	0	0	3	7	3	2	0	0	0	0	0	0	0	–

Wheezer Dell

DELL, WILLIAM GEORGE
B. June 11, 1887, Tuscarora, Nev.   D. Aug. 24, 1966, Independence, Calif.
BR TR 6'4" 210 lbs.

	W	L	PCT	ERA	G	GS	CG	IP	H	BB	SO	ShO	W	L	SV	AB	H	HR	BA
1912 STL N	0	0	–	11.57	3	0	0	2.1	3	3	0	0	0	0	0	66	10	0	.152
1915 BKN N	11	10	.524	2.34	40	24	12	215	166	100	94	4	2	0	1	44	4	0	.091
1916	8	9	.471	2.26	32	16	9	155	143	43	76	2	2	1	1	16	1	0	.063
1917	0	4	.000	3.72	17	4	0	58	55	25	28	0	0	1	1	0	0	0	.119
4 yrs.	19	23	.452	2.55	92	44	21	430.1	367	171	198	6	4	2	3	126	15	0	.119

WORLD SERIES																			
1916 BKN N	0	0	–	0.00	1	0	0	1	1	0	0	0	0	0	0	0	0	0	–

	W	L	PCT	ERA	G	GS	CG	IP	H	BB	SO	ShO	Relief Pitching W	L	SV	Batting AB	H	HR	BA

Ike Delock

DELOCK, IVAN MARTIN
B. Nov. 11, 1929, Highland Park, Mich. BR TR 5'11" 175 lbs.

	W	L	PCT	ERA	G	GS	CG	IP	H	BB	SO	ShO	W	L	SV	AB	H	HR	BA
1952 BOS A	4	9	.308	4.26	39	7	1	95	88	50	46	1	2	5	5	22	1	0	.045
1953	3	1	.750	4.44	23	1	0	48.2	60	20	22	0	2	1	1	10	1	0	.100
1955	9	7	.563	3.76	29	18	6	143.2	136	61	88	0	1	1	3	49	7	0	.143
1956	13	7	.650	4.21	48	8	1	128.1	122	80	105	0	11	2	9	29	3	0	.103
1957	9	8	.529	3.83	49	2	0	94	80	45	62	0	9	6	11	21	1	0	.048
1958	14	8	.636	3.38	31	19	9	160	155	56	82	1	4	0	2	48	3	0	.063
1959	11	6	.647	2.95	28	17	4	134.1	120	62	55	0	5	0	0	47	3	0	.064
1960	9	10	.474	4.73	24	23	3	129.1	145	52	49	1	0	0	0	43	5	1	.116
1961	6	9	.400	4.90	28	28	3	156	185	52	80	1	0	0	0	48	5	0	.104
1962	4	5	.444	3.75	17	13	4	86.1	89	24	49	2	0	0	0	23	2	0	.087
1963 2 teams			BOS	A (6G 1–2)			BAL	A (7G 1–3)											
" total	2	5	.286	4.76	13	11	1	62.1	56	28	34	0	0	0	0	21	0	0	.000
11 yrs.	84	75	.528	4.03	329	147	32	1238	1236	530	672	6	34	15	31	361	31	1	.086

Ramon de los Santos

de los SANTOS, RAMON GENERO
B. Jan. 19, 1949, Santo Domingo, Dominican Republic BL TL 6' 175 lbs.

	W	L	PCT	ERA	G	GS	CG	IP	H	BB	SO	ShO	W	L	SV	AB	H	HR	BA
1974 HOU N	1	1	.500	2.25	12	0	0	12	11	9	7	0	1	1	0	0	0	0	—

Al Demaree

DEMAREE, ALBERT WENTWORTH
B. Sept. 8, 1886, Quincy, Ill. D. Apr. 30, 1962, Long Beach, Calif. BL TR 6' 170 lbs.

	W	L	PCT	ERA	G	GS	CG	IP	H	BB	SO	ShO	W	L	SV	AB	H	HR	BA
1912 NY N	1	0	1.000	1.69	2	2	1	16	17	2	11	1	0	0	0	5	0	0	.000
1913	13	4	.765	2.21	31	24	11	199.2	176	38	76	3	0	1	2	66	7	0	.106
1914	10	17	.370	3.09	38	30	13	224	219	77	89	2	0	2	0	68	9	0	.132
1915 PHI N	14	11	.560	3.05	32	26	13	209.2	201	58	69	3	0	1	1	68	12	0	.176
1916	19	14	.576	2.62	39	35	25	285	252	48	130	4	2	0	1	101	11	0	.109
1917 2 teams			CHI	N (24G 5–9)			NY	N (15G 4–5)											
" total	9	14	.391	2.58	39	29	7	219.2	195	54	66	1	2	0	1	59	7	0	.119
1918 NY N	8	6	.571	2.47	26	14	8	142	143	25	39	2	0	1	1	47	6	0	.128
1919 BOS N	6	6	.500	3.80	25	13	6	128	147	35	34	0	2	1	3	42	2	0	.048
8 yrs.	80	72	.526	2.77	232	173	84	1424	1350	337	514	16	6	6	9	456	54	0	.118

WORLD SERIES

	W	L	PCT	ERA	G	GS	CG	IP	H	BB	SO	ShO	W	L	SV	AB	H	HR	BA
1913 NY N	0	1	.000	4.50	1	1	0	4	7	1	0	0	0	0	0	1	0	0	.000

Fred Demarris

DEMARRIS, FRED
B. 1865, Nashua, N. H. Deceased. TR

	W	L	PCT	ERA	G	GS	CG	IP	H	BB	SO	ShO	W	L	SV	AB	H	HR	BA
1890 CHI N	0	0	—	0.00	1	0	0	2	1	1	1	0	0	0	0	2	0	0	.000

Larry Demery

DEMERY, LAWRENCE CALVIN
B. June 4, 1953, Bakersfield, Calif. BR TR 6' 170 lbs.

	W	L	PCT	ERA	G	GS	CG	IP	H	BB	SO	ShO	W	L	SV	AB	H	HR	BA
1974 PIT N	6	6	.500	4.26	19	15	2	95	95	51	51	0	0	0	0	33	5	0	.152
1975	7	5	.583	2.90	45	8	1	115	95	43	59	0	4	3	4	24	3	0	.125
1976	10	7	.588	3.17	36	15	4	145	123	58	72	1	4	1	2	40	5	0	.125
1977	6	5	.545	5.10	39	8	0	90	100	47	35	0	3	2	1	20	3	0	.150
4 yrs.	29	23	.558	3.72	139	46	7	445	413	199	217	1	11	6	7	117	16	0	.137

LEAGUE CHAMPIONSHIP SERIES

	W	L	PCT	ERA	G	GS	CG	IP	H	BB	SO	ShO	W	L	SV	AB	H	HR	BA
1974 PIT N	0	0	—	27.00	2	0	0	1	3	2	0	0	0	0	0	0	0	0	—
1975	0	0	—	18.00	1	0	0	2	4	1	1	0	0	0	0	0	0	0	—
2 yrs.	0	0	—	21.00	3	0	0	3	7	3	1	0	0	0	0	0	0	0	—

Don De Mola

De MOLA, DONALD JOHN
B. July 5, 1952, Glen Cove, N. Y. BR TR 6'2" 185 lbs.

	W	L	PCT	ERA	G	GS	CG	IP	H	BB	SO	ShO	W	L	SV	AB	H	HR	BA
1974 MON N	1	0	1.000	3.10	25	1	0	58	46	21	47	0	1	0	0	4	0	0	.000
1975	4	7	.364	4.13	60	0	0	98	92	42	63	0	4	7	1	8	0	0	.000
2 yrs.	5	7	.417	3.75	85	1	0	156	138	63	110	0	5	7	1	12	0	0	.000

Ben DeMott

DeMOTT, BENYEW HARRISON
B. Apr. 2, 1889, Green Village, N. J. D. July 5, 1963, Somerville, N. J. BR TR 6' 192 lbs.

	W	L	PCT	ERA	G	GS	CG	IP	H	BB	SO	ShO	W	L	SV	AB	H	HR	BA
1910 CLE A	0	3	.000	5.40	6	4	1	28.1	90	8	13	0	0	0	0	14	3	0	.214
1911	0	1	.000	12.27	1	1	0	3.2	10	2	2	0	0	0	0	4	0	0	.000
2 yrs.	0	4	.000	6.19	7	5	1	32	100	10	15	0	0	0	0	18	3	0	.167

Con Dempsey

DEMPSEY, CORNELIUS FRANCIS
B. Sept. 16, 1923, San Francisco, Calif. BR TR 6'4" 190 lbs.

	W	L	PCT	ERA	G	GS	CG	IP	H	BB	SO	ShO	W	L	SV	AB	H	HR	BA
1951 PIT N	0	2	.000	9.00	3	2	0	7	11	4	3	0	0	0	0	1	0	0	.000

Mark Dempsey

DEMPSEY, MARK S
B. Dec. 17, 1957, Dayton, Ohio BR TR 6'6" 215 lbs.

	W	L	PCT	ERA	G	GS	CG	IP	H	BB	SO	ShO	W	L	SV	AB	H	HR	BA
1982 SF N	0	0	—	7.94	3	1	0	5.2	11	2	4	0	0	0	0	1	0	0	.000

Bill Denehy

DENEHY, WILLIAM FRANCIS
B. Mar. 31, 1946, Middletown, Conn. BR TR 6'3" 200 lbs.

	W	L	PCT	ERA	G	GS	CG	IP	H	BB	SO	ShO	W	L	SV	AB	H	HR	BA
1967 NY N	1	7	.125	4.70	15	8	0	53.2	51	29	35	0	0	0	0	9	0	0	.000
1968 WAS A	0	0	—	9.00	3	0	0	2	4	4	1	0	0	0	0	0	0	0	—
1971 DET A	0	3	.000	4.22	31	1	0	49	47	28	27	0	0	2	1	2	0	0	.000
3 yrs.	1	10	.091	4.56	49	9	0	104.2	102	61	63	0	0	2	1	11	0	0	.000

Brian Denman

DENMAN, BRIAN JOHN
B. Feb. 12, 1956, Minneapolis, Minn. BR TR 6'4" 215 lbs.

	W	L	PCT	ERA	G	GS	CG	IP	H	BB	SO	ShO	W	L	SV	AB	H	HR	BA
1982 BOS A	3	4	.429	4.78	9	9	2	49	55	9	9	1	0	0	0	0	0	0	—

Don Dennis

DENNIS, DONALD RAY
B. Mar. 3, 1942, Uniontown, Kans. BR TR 6'2" 190 lbs.

	W	L	PCT	ERA	G	GS	CG	IP	H	BB	SO	ShO	W	L	SV	AB	H	HR	BA
1965 STL N	2	3	.400	2.29	41	0	0	55	47	16	29	0	2	3	6	5	2	0	.400

	W	L	PCT	ERA	G	GS	CG	IP	H	BB	SO	ShO	Relief Pitching W	L	SV	BATTING AB	H	HR	BA

Don Dennis continued

	W	L	PCT	ERA	G	GS	CG	IP	H	BB	SO	ShO	W	L	SV	AB	H	HR	BA
1966	4	2	.667	4.98	38	1	0	59.2	73	17	25	0	4	2	2	12	1	0	.083
2 yrs.	6	5	.545	3.69	79	1	0	114.2	120	33	54	0	6	5	8	17	3	0	.176

Jerry Denny

DENNY, JEREMIAH DENNIS   BR TR 5'11½" 180 lbs.
Born Jeremiah Dennis Eldridge.
B. Mar. 16, 1859, New York, N.Y.   D. Aug. 16, 1927, Houston, Tex.

	W	L	PCT	ERA	G	GS	CG	IP	H	BB	SO	ShO	W	L	SV	AB	H	HR	BA
1888 IND N	0	0	—	9.00	1	0	0	4	5	4	1	0	0	0	0	*			

John Denny

DENNY, JOHN ALLEN   BR TR 6'3" 185 lbs.
B. Nov. 8, 1952, Prescott, Ariz.

	W	L	PCT	ERA	G	GS	CG	IP	H	BB	SO	ShO	W	L	SV	AB	H	HR	BA
1974 STL N	0	0	—	0.00	2	0	0	2	3	0	1	0	0	0	0	0	0	0	—
1975	10	7	.588	3.97	25	24	3	136	149	51	72	2	0	0	0	44	10	0	.227
1976	11	9	.550	2.52	30	30	8	207	189	74	74	3	0	0	0	67	15	0	.224
1977	8	8	.500	4.50	26	26	3	150	165	62	60	1	0	0	0	51	5	0	.098
1978	14	11	.560	2.96	33	33	11	234	200	74	103	2	0	0	0	73	13	0	.178
1979	8	11	.421	4.85	31	31	5	206	206	100	99	2	0	0	0	70	9	0	.129
1980 CLE A	8	6	.571	4.38	16	16	4	109	116	47	59	1	0	0	0	0	0	0	—
1981	10	6	.625	3.14	19	19	6	146	139	66	94	3	0	0	0	0	0	0	—
1982 2 teams			CLE A (21G 6–11)		PHI N (4G 0–2)														
" total	6	13	.316	4.87	25	25	5	160.2	144	83	113	0	0	0	0	6	1	0	.167
1983 PHI N	19	6	.760	2.37	36	36	7	242.2	229	53	139	1	0	0	0	77	13	0	.169
1984	7	7	.500	2.45	22	22	2	154.1	122	29	94	0	0	0	0	47	9	0	.191
11 yrs.	101	84	.546	3.49	265	262	54	1747.2	1662	639	908	15	0	0	0	435	75	0	.172

LEAGUE CHAMPIONSHIP SERIES

	W	L	PCT	ERA	G	GS	CG	IP	H	BB	SO	ShO	W	L	SV	AB	H	HR	BA
1983 PHI N	0	1	.000	0.00	1	1	0	6	5	3	3	0	0	0	0	1	0	0	.000

WORLD SERIES

	W	L	PCT	ERA	G	GS	CG	IP	H	BB	SO	ShO	W	L	SV	AB	H	HR	BA
1983 PHI N	1	1	.500	3.46	2	2	0	13	12	3	9	0	0	0	0	5	1	0	.200

Eddie Dent

DENT, ELLIOTT ESTILL   BR TR 6'1" 190 lbs.
B. Dec. 8, 1887, Baltimore, Md.   D. Nov. 25, 1974, Birmingham, Ala.

	W	L	PCT	ERA	G	GS	CG	IP	H	BB	SO	ShO	W	L	SV	AB	H	HR	BA
1909 BKN N	2	4	.333	4.29	6	5	4	42	47	15	17	0	0	1	0	15	1	0	.067
1911	2	1	.667	3.69	5	3	1	31.2	30	10	3	0	0	0	0	10	1	0	.100
1912	0	0	—	36.00	1	0	0	1	4	1	1	0	0	0	0	1	0	0	.000
3 yrs.	4	5	.444	4.46	12	8	5	74.2	81	26	21	0	0	1	0	26	2	0	.077

Roger Denzer

DENZER, ROGER (Peaceful Valley)   BL TR 6' 180 lbs.
B. Oct. 5, 1871, LeSeuer, Minn.   D. Sept. 18, 1949, LeSeuer, Minn.

	W	L	PCT	ERA	G	GS	CG	IP	H	BB	SO	ShO	W	L	SV	AB	H	HR	BA
1897 CHI N	2	8	.200	5.13	12	10	8	94.2	125	34	17	0	1	1	0	39	6	0	.154
1901 NY N	2	5	.286	3.36	11	9	3	61.2	69	5	22	1	0	0	0	22	2	0	.091
2 yrs.	4	13	.235	4.43	23	19	11	156.1	194	39	39	1	1	1	0	61	8	0	.131

George Derby

DERBY, GEORGE H.   BL TR 6' 175 lbs.
B. July 6, 1857, Webster, Mass.   D. July 4, 1925, Philadelphia, Pa.

	W	L	PCT	ERA	G	GS	CG	IP	H	BB	SO	ShO	W	L	SV	AB	H	HR	BA
1881 DET N	29	26	.527	2.20	56	55	55	494.2	505	86	212	9	0	0	0	236	44	0	.186
1882	17	20	.459	3.26	40	39	38	362	386	81	182	3	0	0	0	149	29	0	.195
1883 BUF N	2	10	.167	5.85	14	13	12	107.2	173	15	34	0	0	0	1	59	14	0	.237
3 yrs.	48	56	.462	3.01	110	107	105	964.1	1064	182	428	12	0	0	1	444	87	0	.196

Paul Derringer

DERRINGER, PAUL (Duke, 'Oom Paul)   BR TR 6'3½" 205 lbs.
B. Oct. 17, 1906, Springfield, Ky.

	W	L	PCT	ERA	G	GS	CG	IP	H	BB	SO	ShO	W	L	SV	AB	H	HR	BA
1931 STL N	18	8	.692	3.36	35	23	15	211.2	225	65	134	4	4	0	2	72	7	0	.097
1932	11	14	.440	4.05	39	30	14	233.1	296	67	78	1	1	1	0	73	13	0	.178
1933 2 teams			STL N (3G 0–2)		CIN N (33G 7–25)														
" total	7	27	.206	3.30	36	33	17	248	264	60	89	2	0	1	1	81	14	0	.173
1934 CIN N	15	21	.417	3.59	47	31	18	261	297	59	122	1	2	4	4	92	18	0	.196
1935	22	13	.629	3.51	45	33	20	276.2	295	49	120	3	3	2	2	93	13	0	.140
1936	19	19	.500	4.02	51	37	13	282.1	331	42	121	2	1	3	5	90	18	0	.200
1937	10	14	.417	4.04	43	26	12	222.2	240	55	94	1	1	4	1	80	16	0	.200
1938	21	14	.600	2.93	41	37	26	307	315	49	132	4	0	0	3	119	21	2	.176
1939	25	7	.781	2.93	38	35	28	301	321	35	128	5	1	0	0	110	23	0	.209
1940	20	12	.625	3.06	37	37	26	296.2	280	48	115	3	0	0	0	108	18	0	.167
1941	12	14	.462	3.31	29	28	17	228.1	233	54	76	2	0	0	1	84	13	0	.155
1942	10	11	.476	3.06	29	27	13	208.2	203	49	68	1	0	0	0	68	9	0	.132
1943 CHI N	10	14	.417	3.57	32	22	10	174	184	39	75	2	1	2	3	58	13	0	.224
1944	7	13	.350	4.15	42	16	7	180	205	39	69	0	2	5	3	57	9	0	.158
1945 CHI N	16	11	.593	3.45	35	30	15	213.2	223	51	86	1	1	0	4	75	15	0	.200
15 yrs.	223	212	.513	3.46	579	445	251	3645	3912	761	1507	32	17	22	29	1260	220	2	.175

WORLD SERIES

	W	L	PCT	ERA	G	GS	CG	IP	H	BB	SO	ShO	W	L	SV	AB	H	HR	BA
1931 STL N	0	2	.000	4.26	3	2	0	12.2	14	7	14	0	0	0	0	2	0	0	.000
1939 CIN N	0	1	.000	2.35	2	1	1	15.1	9	3	9	0	0	0	0	5	1	0	.200
1940	2	1	.667	2.79	3	3	2	19.1	17	10	6	0	0	0	0	7	0	0	.000
1945 CHI N	0	0	—	6.75	3	0	0	5.1	5	7	1	0	0	0	0	14	1	0	—
4 yrs.	2	4	.333	3.42	11	7	3	52.2	45	27	30	0	0	0	0	14	1	0	.071
			7th								10th							6th	

Jim Derrington

DERRINGTON, CHARLES JAMES (Blackie)   BL TL 6'3" 190 lbs.
B. Nov. 29, 1939, Compton, Calif.

	W	L	PCT	ERA	G	GS	CG	IP	H	BB	SO	ShO	W	L	SV	AB	H	HR	BA
1956 CHI A	0	1	.000	7.50	1	1	0	6	9	6	3	0	0	0	0	2	1	0	.500
1957	0	1	.000	4.86	20	5	0	37	29	29	14	0	0	0	0	4	0	0	.000
2 yrs.	0	2	.000	5.23	21	6	0	43	38	35	17	0	0	0	0	6	1	0	.167

	W	L	PCT	ERA	G	GS	CG	IP	H	BB	SO	ShO	W	L	SV	AB	H	HR	BA
													Relief Pitching			Batting			

Jim Deshaies

DESHAIES, JAMES J.
B. June 23, 1960, Massena, N. Y. BL TL 6'4" 222 lbs.

	W	L	PCT	ERA	G	GS	CG	IP	H	BB	SO	ShO	W	L	SV	AB	H	HR	BA
1984 NY A	0	1	.000	11.57	2	2	0	7	14	7	5	0	0	0	0	0	0	0	–

Jimmie DeShong

DeSHONG, JAMES BROOKLYN
B. Nov. 30, 1909, Harrisburg, Pa. BR TR 5'11" 165 lbs.

	W	L	PCT	ERA	G	GS	CG	IP	H	BB	SO	ShO	W	L	SV	AB	H	HR	BA
1932 PHI A	0	0	–	11.70	6	0	0	10	17	9	5	0	0	0	0	3	0	0	.000
1934 NY A	6	7	.462	4.11	31	12	6	133.2	126	56	40	0	0	2	3	42	8	0	.190
1935	4	1	.800	3.26	29	3	0	69	64	33	30	0	3	1	3	14	1	0	.071
1936 WAS A	18	10	.643	4.63	34	31	16	223.2	255	96	59	2	0	1	2	79	15	0	.190
1937	14	15	.483	4.90	37	34	20	264.1	290	124	86	0	1	0	1	94	19	0	.202
1938	5	8	.385	6.58	31	14	1	131.1	160	83	41	0	1	2	0	46	12	0	.261
1939	0	3	.000	8.63	7	6	1	40.2	56	31	12	0	0	0	0	15	3	0	.200
7 yrs.	47	44	.516	5.08	175	100	44	872.2	968	432	273	2	5	6	9	293	58	0	.198

Shorty DesJardien

DesJARDIEN, PAUL RAYMOND
B. Aug. 24, 1893, Coffeyville, Kans. D. Mar. 7, 1956, Monrovia, Calif. BR TR 6'4½" 205 lbs.

	W	L	PCT	ERA	G	GS	CG	IP	H	BB	SO	ShO	W	L	SV	AB	H	HR	BA
1916 CLE A	0	0	–	18.00	1	0	0	1	1	1	1	0	0	0	0	0	0	0	–

Rube Dessau

DESSAU, FRANK ROLLAND
B. Mar. 29, 1883, New Galilee, Pa. D. May 6, 1952, York, Pa. BB TR 5'11" 175 lbs.

	W	L	PCT	ERA	G	GS	CG	IP	H	BB	SO	ShO	W	L	SV	AB	H	HR	BA
1907 BOS N	0	1	.000	10.61	2	2	1	9.1	13	10	1	0	0	0	0	4	0	0	.000
1910 BKN N	2	3	.400	5.79	19	0	0	51.1	67	29	24	0	2	3	0	15	1	0	.067
2 yrs.	2	4	.333	6.53	21	2	1	60.2	80	39	25	0	2	3	0	19	1	0	.053

Tom Dettore

DETTORE, THOMAS ANTHONY
B. Nov. 17, 1947, Canonsburg, Pa. BL TR 6'4". 200 lbs.

	W	L	PCT	ERA	G	GS	CG	IP	H	BB	SO	ShO	W	L	SV	AB	H	HR	BA
1973 PIT N	0	1	.000	5.96	12	1	0	22.2	33	14	13	0	0	0	0	4	0	0	.000
1974 CHI N	3	5	.375	4.15	16	9	0	65	64	31	43	0	1	0	0	20	5	0	.250
1975	5	4	.556	5.40	36	5	0	85	88	31	46	0	4	3	0	24	6	0	.250
1976	0	1	.000	10.29	4	0	0	7	11	2	4	0	0	1	0	0	0	0	–
4 yrs.	8	11	.421	5.21	68	15	0	179.2	196	78	106	0	5	4	0	48	11	0	.229

Mel Deutsch

DEUTSCH, MELVIN ELLIOTT
B. July 26, 1915, Caldwell, Tex. BR TR 6'4" 215 lbs.

	W	L	PCT	ERA	G	GS	CG	IP	H	BB	SO	ShO	W	L	SV	AB	H	HR	BA
1946 BOS A	0	0	–	5.68	3	0	0	6.1	7	3	2	0	0	0	0	2	0	0	.000

Charlie Devens

DEVENS, CHARLES
B. Jan. 1, 1910, Milton, Mass. BR TR 6'1" 180 lbs.

	W	L	PCT	ERA	G	GS	CG	IP	H	BB	SO	ShO	W	L	SV	AB	H	HR	BA
1932 NY A	1	0	1.000	2.00	1	1	1	9	6	7	4	0	0	0	0	2	0	0	.000
1933	3	3	.500	4.35	14	8	2	62	59	50	23	0	1	1	0	21	2	0	.095
1934	1	0	1.000	1.64	1	1	1	11	9	5	4	0	0	0	0	2	1	0	.500
3 yrs.	5	3	.625	3.73	16	10	4	82	74	62	31	0	1	1	0	25	3	0	.120

Adrian Devine

DEVINE, PAUL ADRIAN
B. Dec. 2, 1951, Galveston, Tex. BR TR 6'4" 185 lbs.

	W	L	PCT	ERA	G	GS	CG	IP	H	BB	SO	ShO	W	L	SV	AB	H	HR	BA
1973 ATL N	2	3	.400	6.47	24	1	0	32	45	12	15	0	2	2	4	4	1	0	.250
1975	1	0	1.000	4.50	5	2	0	16	19	7	8	0	0	0	0	5	0	0	.000
1976	5	6	.455	3.21	48	1	0	73	72	26	48	0	5	6	9	14	0	0	.000
1977 TEX A	11	6	.647	3.57	56	2	0	106	102	31	67	0	9	6	15	0	0	0	–
1978 ATL N	5	4	.556	5.95	31	6	0	65	84	25	26	0	2	2	3	11	1	0	.091
1979	1	2	.333	3.22	40	0	0	67	84	25	22	0	1	2	0	7	0	0	.000
1980 TEX A	1	1	.500	4.82	13	0	0	28	49	9	8	0	1	1	0	0	0	0	–
7 yrs.	26	22	.542	4.21	217	12	0	387	455	135	194	0	20	19	31	41	2	0	.049

Jim Devine

DEVINE, WALTER JAMES
B. Oct. 5, 1858, Brooklyn, N. Y. D. Jan. 11, 1905, Syracuse, N. Y.

	W	L	PCT	ERA	G	GS	CG	IP	H	BB	SO	ShO	W	L	SV	AB	H	HR	BA
1883 BAL AA	1	1	.500	7.36	2	2	1	11	15	1	3	0	0	0	0	9	2	0	.222
1886 NY N	0	0	–	0.00	0	0	0	0	0	0	0	0	0	0	0	3	0	0	.000
2 yrs.	1	1	.500	7.36	2	2	1	11	15	1	3	0	0	0	0	12	2	0	.167

Hal Deviney

DEVINEY, HAROLD JOHN
B. 1891, Newton, Mass. D. Jan. 4, 1933, Westwood, Mass. BR TR

	W	L	PCT	ERA	G	GS	CG	IP	H	BB	SO	ShO	W	L	SV	AB	H	HR	BA
1920 BOS A	0	0	–	15.00	1	0	0	3	7	2	0	0	0	0	0	2	2	0	1.000

Jim Devlin

DEVLIN, JAMES ALEXANDER
B. 1849, Philadelphia, Pa. D. Oct. 10, 1883, Philadelphia, Pa. BR TR 5'11" 175 lbs.

	W	L	PCT	ERA	G	GS	CG	IP	H	BB	SO	ShO	W	L	SV	AB	H	HR	BA
1876 LOU N	30	35	.462	1.56	68	68	66	622	566	37	122	5	0	0	0	298	94	0	.315
1877	35	25	.583	2.25	61	61	61	559	617	41	141	4	0	0	0	268	72	1	.269
2 yrs.	65	60	.520	1.89	129	129	127	1181	1183	78	263	9	0	0	0	566	166	1	.293

Jim Devlin

DEVLIN, JAMES H.
B. Apr. 16, 1866, Troy, N. Y. D. Dec. 14, 1900, Troy, N. Y. TL

	W	L	PCT	ERA	G	GS	CG	IP	H	BB	SO	ShO	W	L	SV	AB	H	HR	BA
1886 NY N	0	0	–	18.00	1	0	0	2	3	4	2	0	0	0	1	1	0	0	.000
1887 PHI N	0	2	.000	6.00	2	2	2	18	20	10	6	0	0	0	0	6	2	0	.333
1888 STL AA	6	5	.545	3.19	11	11	10	90.1	82	20	45	0	0	0	0	37	11	0	.297
1889	5	3	.625	2.40	9	8	5	60	56	24	37	0	1	0	0	26	5	0	.192
4 yrs.	11	10	.524	3.38	23	21	17	170.1	161	58	90	0	1	0	1	70	18	0	.257

Charlie Dewald

DEWALD, CHARLES H.
B. 1867, Newark, N. J. D. Aug. 22, 1904, Cleveland, Ohio TL

	W	L	PCT	ERA	G	GS	CG	IP	H	BB	SO	ShO	W	L	SV	AB	H	HR	BA
1890 CLE P	2	0	1.000	0.64	2	2	2	14	13	5	6	0	0	0	0	8	3	0	.375

	W	L	PCT	ERA	G	GS	CG	IP	H	BB	SO	ShO	Relief W	Relief L	SV	AB	H	HR	BA

Carlos Diaz

DIAZ, CARLOS ANTONIO
B. Jan. 7, 1958, Kapeotte, Hawaii
BR TL 6' 170 lbs.

	W	L	PCT	ERA	G	GS	CG	IP	H	BB	SO	ShO	W	L	SV	AB	H	HR	BA
1982 2 teams	ATL	N	(19G 3-2)		NY	N	(4G 0-0)												
" total	3	2	.600	4.03	23	0	0	29	37	13	16	0	3	2	1	3	0	0	.000
1983 NY N	3	1	.750	2.05	54	0	0	83.1	62	35	64	0	3	1	2	5	0	0	.000
1984 LA N	1	0	1.000	5.49	37	0	0	41	47	24	36	0	1	0	1	1	0	0	.000
3 yrs.	7	3	.700	3.35	114	0	0	153.1	146	72	116	0	7	3	4	9	0	0	.000

Pedro Dibut

DIBUT, PEDRO
Also known as Pedro Villafana.
B. Nov. 18, 1892, Cienfuegos, Cuba   D. Dec. 4, 1979, Hialeah, Fla.
BR TR 5'8" 190 lbs.

	W	L	PCT	ERA	G	GS	CG	IP	H	BB	SO	ShO	W	L	SV	AB	H	HR	BA
1924 CIN N	3	0	1.000	2.21	7	2	2	36.2	24	12	15	0	1	0	0	11	3	0	.273
1925	0	0		∞	1	0	0	0	3	0	0	0	0	0	0	0	0	0	
2 yrs.	3	0	1.000	2.70	8	2	2	36.2	27	12	15	0	1	0	0	11	3	0	.273

Leo Dickerman

DICKERMAN, LEO LOUIS
B. Oct. 31, 1896, DeSoto, Mo.   D. Apr. 30, 1982, Atkins, Ark.
BR TR 6'4" 192 lbs.

	W	L	PCT	ERA	G	GS	CG	IP	H	BB	SO	ShO	W	L	SV	AB	H	HR	BA
1923 BKN N	8	12	.400	3.59	35	20	7	165.2	185	71	57	1	2	1	0	52	13	2	.250
1924 2 teams	BKN	N	(7G 0-0)		STL	N	(18G 7-4)												
" total	7	4	.636	2.84	25	15	8	139.1	128	67	37	1	0	0	0	45	10	0	.222
1925 STL N	4	11	.267	5.58	29	20	7	130.2	135	79	40	2	0	0	1	44	5	0	.114
3 yrs.	19	27	.413	3.95	89	55	22	435.2	448	217	134	4	2	1	1	141	28	2	.199

George Dickerson

DICKERSON, GEORGE CLARK
B. Dec. 1, 1892, Renner, Tex.   D. July 9, 1938, Los Angeles, Calif.
BR TR 6'1" 170 lbs.

	W	L	PCT	ERA	G	GS	CG	IP	H	BB	SO	ShO	W	L	SV	AB	H	HR	BA
1917 CLE A	0	0	-	0.00	1	0	0	1	0	1	0	0	0	0	0	0	0	0	-

Emerson Dickman

DICKMAN, GEORGE EMERSON
B. Nov. 12, 1914, Buffalo, N. Y.   D. Apr. 27, 1981, New York, N. Y.
BR TR 6'2" 175 lbs.

	W	L	PCT	ERA	G	GS	CG	IP	H	BB	SO	ShO	W	L	SV	AB	H	HR	BA
1936 BOS A	0	0	-	9.00	1	0	0	1	2	1	2	0	0	0	0	-	-	-	-
1938	5	5	.500	5.28	32	11	3	104	117	54	22	1	2	0	0	35	10	1	.286
1939	8	3	.727	4.43	48	1	0	113.2	126	43	46	0	8	3	5	36	2	0	.056
1940	8	6	.571	6.03	35	9	2	100	121	38	40	0	5	1	3	28	3	0	.107
1941	1	1	.500	6.39	9	3	1	31	37	17	16	0	0	0	0	11	1	0	.091
5 yrs.	22	15	.595	5.33	125	24	6	349.2	403	153	126	1	15	4	8	110	16	1	.145

Jim Dickson

DICKSON, JAMES EDWARD
B. Apr. 20, 1938, Portland, Ore.
BL TR 6'1" 185 lbs.

	W	L	PCT	ERA	G	GS	CG	IP	H	BB	SO	ShO	W	L	SV	AB	H	HR	BA
1963 HOU N	0	1	.000	6.14	13	0	0	14.2	22	2	6	0	0	1	2	1	0	0	.000
1964 CIN N	1	0	1.000	7.20	4	0	0	5	8	5	4	0	1	0	0	0	0	0	-
1965 KC A	3	2	.600	3.47	68	0	0	85.2	68	47	54	0	3	2	0	2	0	0	.000
1966	1	0	1.000	5.35	24	1	0	37	37	23	20	0	1	0	1	4	1	0	.250
4 yrs.	5	3	.625	4.36	109	1	0	142.1	135	77	86	0	5	3	3	7	1	0	.143

Murry Dickson

DICKSON, MURRY MONROE
B. Aug. 21, 1916, Tracy, Mo.
BR TR 5'10½" 157 lbs.

	W	L	PCT	ERA	G	GS	CG	IP	H	BB	SO	ShO	W	L	SV	AB	H	HR	BA
1939 STL N	0	0	-	0.00	1	0	0	3.2	1	1	2	0	0	0	0	1	0	0	.000
1940	0	0	-	16.20	1	1	0	1.2	5	1	0	0	0	0	0	0	0	0	-
1942	6	3	.667	2.91	36	7	2	120.2	91	61	66	0	4	1	2	42	8	0	.190
1943	8	2	.800	3.58	31	7	2	115.2	114	49	44	0	2	2	0	34	9	0	.265
1946	15	6	.714	2.88	47	19	12	184.1	160	56	82	2	4	2	1	65	18	0	.277
1947	13	16	.448	3.07	47	25	11	231.2	211	88	111	4	3	2	3	80	17	0	.213
1948	12	16	.429	4.14	42	29	11	252.1	257	85	113	1	2	4	1	96	27	0	.281
1949 PIT N	12	14	.462	3.29	44	20	11	224.1	216	80	89	2	3	5	0	84	17	0	.202
1950	10	15	.400	3.80	51	22	8	225	227	83	76	0	5	3	3	82	21	0	.256
1951	20	16	.556	4.02	45	35	19	288.2	294	101	112	3	4	2	2	110	30	1	.273
1952	14	21	.400	3.57	43	34	21	277.2	278	76	112	2	2	0	2	107	24	0	.224
1953	10	19	.345	4.53	45	26	10	200.2	240	58	88	1	2	4	4	61	7	0	.115
1954 PHI N	10	20	.333	3.78	40	31	12	226.1	256	73	64	4	1	1	3	79	15	0	.190
1955	12	11	.522	3.50	36	28	12	216	190	82	92	4	1	0	0	82	18	1	.220
1956 2 teams	PHI	N	(3G 0-3)		STL	N	(28G 13-8)												
" total	13	11	.542	3.28	31	30	12	219.1	195	69	110	3	0	1	0	86	22	0	.256
1957 STL N	5	3	.625	4.14	14	13	3	74	87	25	29	1	0	0	0	27	6	0	.222
1958 2 teams	KC	A	(27G 9-5)		NY	N	(6G 1-2)												
" total	10	7	.588	3.70	33	11	3	119.1	117	43	55	0	7	3	2	42	11	1	.262
1959 KC A	2	1	.667	4.94	38	0	0	71	85	27	36	0	2	1	0	17	3	0	.176
18 yrs.	172	181	.487	3.66	625	338	149	3052.1	3024	1058	1281	27	42	32	23	1095	253	3	.231

WORLD SERIES																			
1943 STL N	0	0	-	0.00	1	0	0	.2	1	0	1	0	0	0	0	5	2	0	.400
1946	0	1	.000	3.86	2	2	0	14	11	4	7	0	0	0	0	0	0	0	-
1958 NY A	0	0	-	4.50	2	0	0	4	4	1	0	0	0	0	0	0	0	0	-
3 yrs.	0	1	.000	3.86	5	2	0	18.2	15	5	8	0	0	0	0	5	2	0	.400

Walt Dickson

DICKSON, WALTER R. (Hickory)
B. Dec. 3, 1878, New Summerfield, Tex.   D. Feb. 9, 1918, Ardmore, Okla.
BR TR 6'1" 185 lbs.

	W	L	PCT	ERA	G	GS	CG	IP	H	BB	SO	ShO	W	L	SV	AB	H	HR	BA
1910 NY N	1	0	1.000	5.46	12	1	0	29.2	31	9	9	0	1	0	0	4	1	0	.250
1912 BOS N	3	19	.136	3.86	36	20	9	189	233	61	47	1	2	4	0	60	10	0	.167
1913	6	7	.462	3.23	19	15	8	128	118	45	47	0	0	1	0	45	8	0	.178
1914 PIT F	9	21	.300	3.16	40	32	19	256.2	262	74	63	3	0	2	1	83	7	0	.084
1915	6	5	.545	4.19	27	11	4	96.2	115	33	36	0	2	2	0	31	4	0	.129
5 yrs.	25	52	.325	3.60	134	79	40	700	759	222	202	4	5	9	1	223	30	0	.135

George Diehl

DIEHL, GEORGE KRAUSE
B. Feb. 25, 1918, Allentown, Pa.
BR TR 6'2" 196 lbs.

	W	L	PCT	ERA	G	GS	CG	IP	H	BB	SO	ShO	W	L	SV	AB	H	HR	BA
1942 BOS N	0	0	-	2.45	1	0	0	3.2	2	2	0	0	0	0	0	1	0	0	.000
1943	0	0	-	4.50	1	0	0	4	4	3	1	0	0	0	0	1	0	0	.000
2 yrs.	0	0	-	3.52	2	0	0	7.2	6	5	1	0	0	0	0	2	0	0	.000

Larry Dierker

DIERKER, LAWRENCE EDWARD
B. Sept. 22, 1946, Hollywood, Calif. BR TR 6'4" 190 lbs.

	W	L	PCT	ERA	G	GS	CG	IP	H	BB	SO	ShO	Relief Pitching W	L	SV	BATTING AB	H	HR	BA
1964 HOU N	0	1	.000	2.00	3	1	0	9	7	3	5	0	0	0	0	3	0	0	.000
1965	7	8	.467	3.50	26	19	1	146.2	135	37	109	0	1	0	0	50	5	1	.100
1966	10	8	.556	3.18	29	28	8	187	173	45	108	2	0	0	0	67	10	1	.149
1967	6	5	.545	3.36	15	15	4	99	95	25	68	0	0	0	0	31	7	0	.226
1968	12	15	.444	3.31	32	32	10	233.2	206	89	161	1	0	0	0	73	5	0	.068
1969	20	13	.606	2.33	39	37	20	305	240	72	232	4	0	0	0	118	17	1	.144
1970	16	12	.571	3.87	37	36	17	270	263	82	191	2	0	0	0	92	16	0	.174
1971	12	6	.667	2.72	24	23	6	159	150	33	91	2	0	0	1	54	4	0	.074
1972	15	8	.652	3.40	31	31	12	214.2	209	51	115	5	0	0	0	78	13	0	.167
1973	1	1	.500	4.33	14	3	0	27	27	13	18	0	1	0	0	4	0	0	.000
1974	11	10	.524	2.89	33	33	7	224	189	82	150	3	0	0	0	71	14	0	.197
1975	14	16	.467	4.00	34	34	14	232	225	91	127	2	0	0	0	76	7	0	.092
1976	13	14	.481	3.69	28	28	7	188	171	72	112	4	0	0	0	64	9	1	.141
1977 STL N	2	6	.250	4.62	11	9	0	39	40	16	6	0	0	0	0	8	0	0	.000
14 yrs.	139	123	.531	3.30	356	329	106	2334	2130	711	1493	25	2	0	1	789	107	4	.136

Bill Dietrich

DIETRICH, WILLIAM JOHN (Bullfrog)
B. Mar. 29, 1910, Philadelphia, Pa. D. June 20, 1978, Philadelphia, Pa. BR TR 6' 185 lbs.

	W	L	PCT	ERA	G	GS	CG	IP	H	BB	SO	ShO	Relief Pitching W	L	SV	BATTING AB	H	HR	BA
1933 PHI A	0	1	.000	5.82	8	1	0	17	13	19	4	0	0	0	0	3	1	0	.333
1934	11	12	.478	4.68	39	23	14	207.2	201	114	88	4	0	2	3	72	15	1	.208
1935	7	13	.350	5.39	43	15	8	185.1	203	101	59	1	4	3	3	60	5	0	.083
1936 3 teams			PHI A (21G 4–6)				WAS A (5G 0–1)				CHI A (14G 4–4)								
" total	8	11	.421	5.75	40	15	6	162.2	197	82	77	1	4	3	3	57	11	0	.193
1937 CHI A	8	10	.444	4.90	29	20	7	143.1	162	72	62	1	1	0	1	44	8	0	.182
1938	2	4	.333	5.44	8	7	1	48	49	31	11	0	0	0	0	16	1	0	.063
1939	7	8	.467	5.22	25	19	2	127.2	134	56	43	0	1	0	0	37	8	1	.216
1940	10	6	.625	4.03	23	17	6	149.2	154	65	43	1	1	0	0	50	12	1	.240
1941	5	8	.385	5.35	19	15	4	109.1	114	50	26	1	0	1	0	34	3	0	.088
1942	6	11	.353	4.89	26	23	6	160	173	70	39	0	0	0	0	48	5	0	.104
1943	12	10	.545	2.80	26	26	12	186.2	180	53	52	2	0	0	0	56	8	1	.143
1944	16	17	.485	3.62	36	36	15	246	269	68	70	2	0	0	0	77	9	1	.117
1945	7	10	.412	4.19	18	16	6	122.1	136	36	43	4	0	2	0	36	6	0	.167
1946	3	3	.500	2.61	11	9	3	62	63	24	20	0	0	0	1	19	1	0	.053
1947 PHI A	5	2	.714	3.12	11	9	2	60.2	48	40	18	1	1	0	0	16	1	0	.063
1948	1	2	.333	5.87	4	2	0	15.1	21	9	5	0	1	0	0	2	0	0	.000
16 yrs.	108	128	.458	4.48	366	253	92	2003.2	2117	890	660	18	13	11	11	627	94	5	.150

Dutch Dietz

DIETZ, LLOYD ARTHUR
B. Feb. 12, 1912, Cincinnati, Ohio. D. Oct. 29, 1972, Beaumont, Tex. BR TR 5'11½" 180 lbs.

	W	L	PCT	ERA	G	GS	CG	IP	H	BB	SO	ShO	Relief Pitching W	L	SV	BATTING AB	H	HR	BA
1940 PIT N	0	1	.000	5.87	4	2	0	15.1	12	4	8	0	0	0	0	7	1	0	.143
1941	7	2	.778	2.33	33	6	4	100.1	88	33	22	1	4	0	1	25	4	0	.160
1942	6	9	.400	3.95	40	13	3	134.1	139	57	35	0	2	2	3	35	7	0	.200
1943 2 teams			PIT N (8G 0–3)				PHI N (21G 1–1)												
" total	1	4	.200	6.40	29	0	0	45	54	19	14	0	1	4	2	6	1	0	.167
4 yrs.	14	16	.467	3.87	106	21	7	295	303	113	79	1	7	6	6	73	13	0	.178

Reese Diggs

DIGGS, REESE WILSON (Diggsy)
B. Sept. 22, 1915, Mathews, Va. D. Oct. 30, 1978, Baltimore, Md. BB TR 6'2" 180 lbs.

	W	L	PCT	ERA	G	GS	CG	IP	H	BB	SO	ShO	Relief Pitching W	L	SV	BATTING AB	H	HR	BA
1934 WAS A	1	2	.333	6.75	4	3	2	21.1	26	15	2	0	0	0	0	8	2	0	.250

Jack DiLauro

DiLAURO, JACK EDWARD
B. May 3, 1943, Akron, Ohio. BB TL 6'2" 185 lbs.

	W	L	PCT	ERA	G	GS	CG	IP	H	BB	SO	ShO	Relief Pitching W	L	SV	BATTING AB	H	HR	BA
1969 NY N	1	4	.200	2.40	23	4	0	63.2	50	18	27	0	1	1	1	12	0	0	.000
1970 HOU N	1	3	.250	4.24	42	0	0	34	34	17	23	0	1	3	3	2	0	0	.000
2 yrs.	2	7	.222	3.04	65	4	0	97.2	84	35	50	0	2	4	4	14	0	0	.000

Harley Dillinger

DILLINGER, HARLEY HUGH (Hoke, Lefty)
B. Oct. 30, 1894, Pomeroy, Ohio. D. Jan. 8, 1959, Cleveland, Ohio. BR TL 5'11" 175 lbs.

	W	L	PCT	ERA	G	GS	CG	IP	H	BB	SO	ShO	Relief Pitching W	L	SV	BATTING AB	H	HR	BA
1914 CLE A	0	1	.000	4.54	11	1	0	33.2	41	25	11	0	0	0	0	10	0	0	.000

Bill Dillman

DILLMAN, WILLIAM HOWARD
B. May 25, 1945, Trenton, N. J. BR TR 6'2" 180 lbs.

	W	L	PCT	ERA	G	GS	CG	IP	H	BB	SO	ShO	Relief Pitching W	L	SV	BATTING AB	H	HR	BA
1967 BAL A	5	9	.357	4.35	32	15	2	124	115	33	69	1	2	0	3	31	5	0	.161
1970 MON N	2	3	.400	5.23	18	0	0	31	28	18	17	0	2	3	0	2	0	0	.000
2 yrs.	7	12	.368	4.53	50	15	2	155	143	51	86	1	4	3	3	33	5	0	.152

Steve Dillon

DILLON, STEPHEN EDWARD
B. Mar. 20, 1943, Bronx, N. Y. BL TL 5'10" 160 lbs.

	W	L	PCT	ERA	G	GS	CG	IP	H	BB	SO	ShO	Relief Pitching W	L	SV	BATTING AB	H	HR	BA
1963 NY N	0	0	—	10.80	1	0	0	1.2	3	0	1	0	0	0	0	0	0	0	—
1964	0	0	—	9.00	2	0	0	3	4	2	2	0	0	0	0	0	0	0	—
2 yrs.	0	0	—	9.64	3	0	0	4.2	7	2	3	0	0	0	0	0	0	0	—

Bill Dinneen

DINNEEN, WILLIAM HENRY (Big Bill)
B. Apr. 5, 1876, Syracuse, N. Y. D. Jan. 13, 1955, Syracuse, N. Y. BR TR 6'1" 190 lbs.

	W	L	PCT	ERA	G	GS	CG	IP	H	BB	SO	ShO	Relief Pitching W	L	SV	BATTING AB	H	HR	BA
1898 WAS N	9	16	.360	4.00	29	27	22	218.1	238	88	83	0	1	0	0	80	8	0	.100
1899	14	18	.438	3.93	37	35	30	291	350	106	91	0	0	2	0	119	36	0	.303
1900 BOS N	20	14	.588	3.12	40	37	33	320.2	304	105	107	1	0	0	0	125	35	0	.280
1901	16	19	.457	2.94	37	34	31	309.1	295	77	141	0	1	0	0	147	31	1	.211
1902 BOS A	21	21	.500	2.93	42	42	39	371.1	348	99	136	2	0	0	0	141	18	0	.128
1903	21	13	.618	2.26	37	33	32	299	255	66	148	6	0	1	2	106	17	0	.160
1904	23	14	.622	2.20	37	37	37	335.2	283	63	153	5	0	0	0	120	25	0	.208
1905	12	15	.444	3.73	31	29	23	243.2	235	50	97	2	1	0	1	88	13	0	.148
1906	8	19	.296	2.92	28	27	22	218.2	209	52	60	1	0	0	0	63	7	0	.111

	W	L	PCT	ERA	G	GS	CG	IP	H	BB	SO	ShO	Relief Pitching W	L	SV	BATTING AB	H	HR	BA

Bill Dinneen continued

	W	L	PCT	ERA	G	GS	CG	IP	H	BB	SO	ShO	W	L	SV	AB	H	HR	BA
1907 2 teams			BOS	A (5G 0–4)			STL	A (24G 7–10)											
" total	7	14	.333	2.92	29	21	18	188	195	41	46	2	0	1	4	59	10	0	.169
1908 STL A	14	7	.667	2.10	27	16	11	167	133	53	39	2	4	1	0	59	12	0	.203
1909	6	7	.462	3.46	17	13	8	112	112	29	26	3	1	0	0	36	7	0	.194
12 yrs.	171	177	.491	3.01	391	351	306	3074.2	2957	829	1127	24	8	5	7	1143	219	1	.192
WORLD SERIES																			
1903 BOS A	3	1	.750	2.06	4	4	4	35	29	8	28	2 4th	0	0	0	12	3	0	.250

Ron Diorio

DIORIO, RONALD MICHAEL BR TR 6'6" 212 lbs.
B. July 15, 1946, Waterbury, Conn.

	W	L	PCT	ERA	G	GS	CG	IP	H	BB	SO	ShO	W	L	SV	AB	H	HR	BA
1973 PHI N	0	0	–	2.33	23	0	0	19.1	18	6	11	0	0	0	1	0	0	0	–
1974	0	0	–	18.00	2	0	0	1	2	1	0	0	0	0	0	0	0	0	–
2 yrs.	0	0	–	3.10	25	0	0	20.1	20	7	11	0	0	0	1	0	0	0	–

Frank DiPino

DiPINO, FRANK MICHAEL BL TL 5'10" 175 lbs.
B. Oct. 22, 1956, Syracuse, N. Y.

	W	L	PCT	ERA	G	GS	CG	IP	H	BB	SO	ShO	W	L	SV	AB	H	HR	BA
1981 MIL A	0	0	–	0.00	2	0	0	2	0	3	3	0	0	0	0	0	0	0	–
1982 HOU N	2	2	.500	6.04	6	6	0	28.1	32	11	25	0	0	0	0	8	0	0	.000
1983	3	4	.429	2.65	53	0	0	71.1	52	20	67	0	3	4	20	6	1	0	.167
1984	4	9	.308	3.35	57	0	0	75.1	74	36	65	0	4	9	14	10	0	0	.000
4 yrs.	9	15	.375	3.46	118	6	0	177	158	70	160	0	7	13	34	24	1	0	.042

George Disch

DISCH, GEORGE CHARLES
B. Mar. 15, 1879, Lincoln, Mo. D. Aug. 25, 1950, Rapid City, S. D.

	W	L	PCT	ERA	G	GS	CG	IP	H	BB	SO	ShO	W	L	SV	AB	H	HR	BA
1905 DET A	0	2	.000	2.64	8	3	1	47.2	43	8	14	0	0	1	0	19	2	0	.105

Alec Distaso

DISTASO, ALEC JOHN BR TR 6'2" 200 lbs.
B. Dec. 23, 1948, Los Angeles, Calif.

	W	L	PCT	ERA	G	GS	CG	IP	H	BB	SO	ShO	W	L	SV	AB	H	HR	BA
1969 CHI N	0	0	–	3.60	2	0	0	5	6	1	1	0	0	0	0	0	0	0	–

Art Ditmar

DITMAR, ARTHUR JOHN BR TR 6'2" 185 lbs.
B. Apr. 3, 1929, Winthrop, Mass.

	W	L	PCT	ERA	G	GS	CG	IP	H	BB	SO	ShO	W	L	SV	AB	H	HR	BA
1954 PHI A	1	4	.200	6.41	14	5	0	39.1	50	36	14	0	0	2	0	8	1	0	.125
1955 KC A	12	12	.500	5.03	35	22	7	175.1	180	86	79	1	3	2	1	62	13	1	.210
1956	12	22	.353	4.42	44	34	14	254.1	254	108	126	2	3	1	1	91	13	1	.143
1957 NY A	8	3	.727	3.25	46	11	0	127.1	128	35	64	0	6	1	6	35	7	0	.200
1958	9	8	.529	3.42	38	13	4	139.2	124	38	52	0	4	4	4	44	11	0	.250
1959	13	9	.591	2.90	38	25	7	202	156	52	96	1	1	1	1	76	15	1	.197
1960	15	9	.625	3.06	34	28	8	200	195	56	65	1	1	2	0	69	11	0	.159
1961 2 teams			NY	A (12G 2–3)			KC	A (20G 0–5)											
" total	2	8	.200	5.15	32	13	1	108.1	119	37	43	0	2	2	1	31	3	0	.097
1962 KC A	0	2	.000	6.65	6	5	0	21.2	31	13	13	0	0	0	0	6	1	0	.167
9 yrs.	72	77	.483	3.98	287	156	41	1268	1237	461	552	5	18	15	14	422	75	2	.178
WORLD SERIES																			
1957 NY A	0	0	–	0.00	2	0	0	6	2	0	2	0	0	0	0	1	0	0	.000
1958	0	0	–	0.00	1	0	0	3.2	2	0	2	0	0	0	0	1	0	0	.000
1960	0	2	.000	21.60	2	2	0	1.2	6	1	0	0	0	0	0	0	0	0	–
3 yrs.	0	2	.000	3.18	5	2	0	11.1	10	1	4	0	0	0	0	2	0	0	.000

Ken Dixon

DIXON, KENNETH JOHN BB TR 5'10" 175 lbs.
B. Oct. 17, 1960, Monroe, Va.

	W	L	PCT	ERA	G	GS	CG	IP	H	BB	SO	ShO	W	L	SV	AB	H	HR	BA
1984 BAL A	0	1	.000	4.15	2	2	0	13	14	4	8	0	0	0	0	0	0	0	–

Sonny Dixon

DIXON, JOHN CRAIG BB TR 6'2½" 205 lbs.
B. Nov. 5, 1924, Charlotte, N. C.

	W	L	PCT	ERA	G	GS	CG	IP	H	BB	SO	ShO	W	L	SV	AB	H	HR	BA
1953 WAS A	5	8	.385	3.75	43	6	3	120	123	31	40	0	0	2	3	26	4	0	.154
1954 2 teams			WAS	A (16G 1–2)			PHI	A (38G 5–7)											
" total	6	9	.400	4.47	54	6	1	137	162	39	49	0	4	6	5	34	7	0	.206
1955 KC A	0	0	–	16.20	2	0	0	1.2	6	0	0	0	0	0	0	0	0	0	–
1956 NY A	0	1	.000	2.08	3	0	0	4.1	5	5	1	0	0	1	1	1	0	0	.000
4 yrs.	11	18	.379	4.17	102	12	4	263	296	75	90	0	4	9	9	61	11	0	.180

Tom Dixon

DIXON, THOMAS EARL BR TR 6' 180 lbs.
B. Apr. 23, 1955, Orlando, Fla.

	W	L	PCT	ERA	G	GS	CG	IP	H	BB	SO	ShO	W	L	SV	AB	H	HR	BA
1977 HOU N	1	0	1.000	3.30	9	4	1	30	40	7	15	0	0	0	0	7	0	0	.000
1978	7	11	.389	3.99	30	19	3	140	140	40	66	2	2	0	1	40	4	0	.100
1979	1	2	.333	6.58	19	1	0	26	39	15	9	0	1	2	0	1	1	0	1.000
1983 MON N	0	1	.000	9.82	4	0	0	3.2	6	1	4	0	0	1	0	0	0	0	–
4 yrs.	9	14	.391	4.33	62	24	4	199.2	225	63	94	2	3	3	1	48	5	0	.104

Bill Doak

DOAK, WILLIAM LEOPOLD (Spittin' Bill) BR TR 6'½" 165 lbs.
B. Jan. 28, 1891, Pittsburgh, Pa. D. Nov. 26, 1954, Bradenton, Fla.

	W	L	PCT	ERA	G	GS	CG	IP	H	BB	SO	ShO	W	L	SV	AB	H	HR	BA
1912 CIN N	0	0	–	4.50	1	1	0	2	4	1	0	0	0	0	0	0	0	0	–
1913 STL N	2	8	.200	3.10	15	12	5	93	79	39	51	1	0	0	0	31	1	0	.032
1914	20	6	.769	1.72	36	33	16	256	193	87	118	7	1	0	0	85	10	0	.118
1915	16	18	.471	2.64	38	36	19	276	263	85	124	3	0	0	1	86	15	0	.174
1916	12	8	.600	2.63	29	26	11	192	177	55	82	3	0	0	0	62	8	0	.129
1917	16	20	.444	3.10	44	37	16	281.1	257	85	111	3	2	1	2	95	12	0	.126
1918	9	15	.375	2.43	31	23	16	211	191	60	74	1	0	2	1	66	12	0	.182
1919	13	14	.481	3.11	31	29	13	202.2	182	55	69	3	1	0	0	64	7	0	.109
1920	20	12	.625	2.53	39	37	20	270	256	80	90	5	0	0	1	88	10	0	.114
1921	15	6	.714	2.59	32	28	13	208.2	224	37	83	1	1	0	1	70	10	0	.143
1922	11	13	.458	5.54	37	29	8	180.1	222	69	73	2	1	1	2	54	7	0	.130

	W	L	PCT	ERA	G	GS	CG	IP	H	BB	SO	ShO	Relief Pitching W	L	SV	BATTING AB	H	HR	BA

Bill Doak continued

	W	L	PCT	ERA	G	GS	CG	IP	H	BB	SO	ShO	W	L	SV	AB	H	HR	BA
1923	8	13	.381	3.26	30	26	7	185	199	69	53	3	0	3	0	67	3	0	.045
1924 2 teams			STL	N	(11G 2–1)		BKN	N	(21G 11–5)										
" total	13	6	.684	3.10	32	17	8	171.1	155	49	39	2	4	2	3	61	11	1	.180
1927 BKN N	11	8	.579	3.48	27	20	6	145	153	40	32	1	3	0	0	47	6	0	.128
1928	3	8	.273	3.26	28	12	4	99.1	104	35	12	1	1	2	3	27	3	0	.111
1929 STL N	1	2	.333	12.00	3	2	0	9	17	5	3	0	0	1	0	2	0	0	.000
16 yrs.	170	157	.520	2.98	453	368	162	2782.2	2676	851	1014	36	14	12	15	905	115	1	.127

Walt Doane

DOANE, WALTER RUDOLPH
B. Mar. 12, 1887, Bellevue, Ida. D. Oct. 20, 1935, Coatesville, Pa. BL TR 6' 165 lbs.

	W	L	PCT	ERA	G	GS	CG	IP	H	BB	SO	ShO	W	L	SV	AB	H	HR	BA
1909 CLE A	0	1	.000	5.40	1	1	0	5	10	1	2	0	0	0	0	9	1	0	.111
1910	0	0	–	5.60	6	0	0	17.2	31	8	7	0	0	0	0	7	2	0	.286
2 yrs.	0	1	.000	5.56	7	1	0	22.2	41	9	9	0	0	0	0	16	3	0	.188

John Dobb

DOBB, JOHN KENNETH (Lefty)
B. Nov. 15, 1901, Muskegon, Mich. BR TL 6'2" 180 lbs.

	W	L	PCT	ERA	G	GS	CG	IP	H	BB	SO	ShO	W	L	SV	AB	H	HR	BA
1924 CHI A	0	0	–	9.00	2	0	0	2	4	1	2	0	0	0	0	0	0	0	–

Ray Dobens

DOBENS, RAYMOND JOSEPH (Lefty)
B. July 28, 1906, Nashua, N. H. D. Apr. 21, 1980, Stuart, Fla. BL TL 5'8" 165 lbs.

	W	L	PCT	ERA	G	GS	CG	IP	H	BB	SO	ShO	W	L	SV	AB	H	HR	BA
1929 BOS A	0	0	–	3.81	11	2	0	28.1	32	9	4	0	0	0	0	8	3	0	.375

Jess Dobernic

DOBERNIC, ANDREW JOSEPH
B. Nov. 20, 1917, Mt. Olive, Ill. BR TR 5'10" 170 lbs.

	W	L	PCT	ERA	G	GS	CG	IP	H	BB	SO	ShO	W	L	SV	AB	H	HR	BA
1939 CHI A	0	1	.000	13.50	4	0	0	3.1	3	6	1	0	0	1	0	1	0	0	.000
1948 CHI N	7	2	.778	3.15	54	0	0	85.2	67	40	48	0	7	2	1	10	2	0	.200
1949 2 teams			CHI	N	(4G 0–0)		CIN	N	(14G 0–0)										
" total	0	0	–	11.57	18	0	0	23.1	37	20	6	0	0	0	0	2	0	0	.000
3 yrs.	7	3	.700	5.21	76	0	0	112.1	107	66	55	0	7	3	1	13	2	0	.154

Chuck Dobson

DOBSON, CHARLES THOMAS
B. Jan. 10, 1944, Kansas City, Mo. BR TR 6'4" 200 lbs.

	W	L	PCT	ERA	G	GS	CG	IP	H	BB	SO	ShO	W	L	SV	AB	H	HR	BA
1966 KC A	4	6	.400	4.09	14	14	1	83.2	71	50	61	0	0	0	0	26	3	0	.115
1967	10	10	.500	3.69	32	29	4	197.2	172	75	110	1	0	0	0	72	13	0	.181
1968 OAK A	12	14	.462	3.00	35	34	11	225.1	197	80	168	3	0	0	0	75	15	0	.200
1969	15	13	.536	3.86	35	35	11	235.1	244	80	137	1	0	0	0	79	8	0	.101
1970	16	15	.516	3.74	41	40	13	267	230	92	149	5	0	1	0	93	11	0	.118
1971	15	5	.750	3.81	30	30	7	189	185	71	100	1	0	0	0	66	13	0	.197
1973	0	1	.000	7.71	1	1	0	2.1	6	2	3	0	0	0	0	0	0	0	–
1974 CAL A	2	3	.400	5.70	5	5	2	30	39	13	16	0	0	0	0	0	0	0	–
1975	0	2	.000	6.75	9	2	0	28	30	13	14	0	0	1	0	0	0	0	–
9 yrs.	74	69	.517	3.78	202	190	49	1258.1	1174	476	758	11	0	2	0	411	63	0	.153

Joe Dobson

DOBSON, JOSEPH GORDON (Burrhead)
B. Jan. 20, 1917, Durant, Okla. BR TR 6'2" 197 lbs.

	W	L	PCT	ERA	G	GS	CG	IP	H	BB	SO	ShO	W	L	SV	AB	H	HR	BA
1939 CLE A	2	3	.400	5.88	35	3	0	78	87	51	27	0	2	1	1	18	1	0	.056
1940	3	7	.300	4.95	40	7	2	100	101	48	57	1	2	3	3	24	3	0	.125
1941 BOS A	12	5	.706	4.49	27	18	7	134.1	136	67	69	1	2	1	0	47	7	1	.149
1942	11	9	.550	3.30	30	23	10	182.2	155	68	72	3	1	1	0	69	10	0	.145
1943	7	11	.389	3.12	25	20	9	164.1	144	57	63	3	0	1	0	52	5	0	.096
1946	13	7	.650	3.24	32	24	9	166.2	148	68	91	1	2	0	0	50	5	0	.100
1947	18	8	.692	2.95	33	31	15	228.2	203	73	110	1	0	0	0	77	16	0	.208
1948	16	10	.615	3.56	38	32	16	245.1	237	92	116	5	0	2	2	84	17	1	.202
1949	14	12	.538	3.85	33	27	12	212.2	219	97	87	2	2	1	2	68	10	0	.147
1950	15	10	.600	4.18	39	27	12	206.2	217	81	81	1	2	0	0	70	15	0	.214
1951 CHI A	7	6	.538	3.62	28	21	6	146.2	136	51	67	0	0	0	3	46	3	0	.065
1952	14	10	.583	2.51	29	25	11	200.2	164	60	101	3	1	1	1	63	12	0	.190
1953	5	5	.500	3.67	23	15	3	100.2	96	37	50	1	0	0	1	29	2	0	.069
1954 BOS A	0	0	–	6.75	2	0	0	2.2	5	1	1	0	0	0	0	0	0	0	–
14 yrs.	137	103	.571	3.62	414	273	112	2170	2048	851	992	22	14	10	18	697	106	2	.152
WORLD SERIES																			
1946 BOS A	1	0	1.000	0.00	3	1	1	12.2	4	3	10	0	0	0	0	3	0	0	.000

Pat Dobson

DOBSON, PATRICK EDWARD
B. Feb. 12, 1942, Depew, N. Y. BR TR 6'3" 190 lbs.

	W	L	PCT	ERA	G	GS	CG	IP	H	BB	SO	ShO	W	L	SV	AB	H	HR	BA
1967 DET A	1	2	.333	2.92	28	1	0	49.1	38	27	34	0	1	1	0	5	0	0	.000
1968	5	8	.385	2.66	47	10	2	125	89	48	93	1	3	3	7	28	4	0	.143
1969	5	10	.333	3.60	49	9	1	105	100	39	64	0	3	6	9	22	2	0	.091
1970 SD N	14	15	.483	3.76	40	34	8	251	257	78	185	1	0	0	0	71	10	0	.141
1971 BAL A	20	8	.714	2.90	38	37	18	282	248	63	187	4	0	0	1	91	10	0	.110
1972	16	18	.471	2.65	38	36	13	268.1	220	69	161	3	0	0	0	85	12	0	.141
1973 2 teams			ATL	N	(12G 3–7)		NY	A	(22G 9–8)										
" total	12	15	.444	4.40	34	31	7	200.1	223	53	93	2	2	0	0	15	1	0	.067
1974 NY A	19	15	.559	3.07	39	39	12	281	282	75	157	2	0	0	0	0	0	0	–
1975	11	14	.440	4.07	33	30	7	207.2	205	83	129	1	0	0	0	0	0	0	–
1976 CLE A	16	12	.571	3.48	35	35	6	217	226	65	117	0	0	0	0	0	0	0	–
1977	3	12	.200	6.16	33	17	0	133	155	65	81	0	0	0	0	0	0	0	–
11 yrs.	122	129	.486	3.54	414	279	74	2119.2	2043	665	1301	14	10	12	19	317	39	0	.123
WORLD SERIES																			
1968 DET A	0	0	–	3.86	3	0	0	4.2	5	1	0	0	0	0	0	0	0	0	–
1971 BAL A	0	0	–	4.05	3	0	0	6.2	13	4	6	0	0	0	0	2	0	0	.000
2 yrs.	0	0	–	3.97	6	1	0	11.1	18	5	6	0	0	0	0	2	0	0	.000

	W	L	PCT	ERA	G	GS	CG	IP	H	BB	SO	ShO	Relief Pitching W	L	SV	BATTING AB	H	HR	BA

George Dockins

DOCKINS, GEORGE WOODROW (Lefty)
B. May 5, 1917, Clyde, Kans.   BL TL 6'   175 lbs.

	W	L	PCT	ERA	G	GS	CG	IP	H	BB	SO	ShO	W	L	SV	AB	H	HR	BA
1945 STL N	8	6	.571	3.21	31	12	5	126.1	132	38	33	2	3	4	0	34	6	0	.176
1947 BKN N	0	0	–	11.81	4	0	0	5.1	10	2	1	0	0	0	0	1	0	0	.000
2 yrs.	8	6	.571	3.55	35	12	5	131.2	142	40	34	2	3	4	0	35	6	0	.171

Sam Dodge

DODGE, SAMUEL EDWARD
B. Dec. 19, 1889, Philadelphia, Pa.   BR TR 6'1"   170 lbs.

	W	L	PCT	ERA	G	GS	CG	IP	H	BB	SO	ShO	W	L	SV	AB	H	HR	BA
1921 BOS A	0	0	–	9.00	1	0	0	1	1	1	0	0	0	0	0	0	0	0	–
1922	0	0	–	4.50	3	0	0	6	11	3	3	0	0	0	0	2	0	0	.000
2 yrs.	0	0	–	5.14	4	0	0	7	12	4	3	0	0	0	0	2	0	0	.000

Al Doe

DOE, ALFRED GEORGE (Count)
B. Apr. 18, 1864, Rockport, Mass.   D. Oct. 4, 1938, Quincy, Mass.

1890 2 teams	BUF	P	(1G 0–1)		PIT	P	(1G 0–0)												
" total	0	1	.000	9.00	2	1	1	10	14	9	4	0	0	0	0	4	1	0	.250

Ed Doheny

DOHENY, EDWARD R.
B. Nov. 24, 1874, Northfield, Vt.   D. Dec. 29, 1916, Medfield, Mass.   BL TL 5'10½" 165 lbs.

	W	L	PCT	ERA	G	GS	CG	IP	H	BB	SO	ShO	W	L	SV	AB	H	HR	BA
1895 NY N	0	3	.000	6.66	3	3	3	25.2	37	19	9	0	0	0	0	10	1	0	.100
1896	6	7	.462	4.49	17	15	9	108.1	112	59	39	0	0	0	0	40	6	0	.150
1897	4	4	.500	2.12	10	10	10	85	69	45	37	0	0	0	0	35	7	0	.200
1898	7	19	.269	3.68	28	27	23	213	238	101	96	0	0	1	0	86	14	2	.163
1899	14	17	.452	4.51	35	33	30	265.1	282	156	115	1	0	0	0	112	27	0	.241
1900	4	14	.222	5.45	20	18	12	133.2	148	96	44	0	1	0	0	54	12	0	.222
1901 2 teams	NY	N	(10G 2–5)		PIT	N	(11G 6–2)												
" total	8	7	.533	3.23	21	16	12	150.2	156	39	64	1	0	1	0	55	13	0	.236
1902 PIT N	16	4	.800	2.53	22	21	19	188.1	161	61	88	2	0	0	2	77	12	1	.156
1903	16	8	.667	3.19	27	25	22	222.2	209	89	75	2	0	0	2	91	19	0	.209
9 yrs.	75	83	.475	3.75	183	168	140	1392.2	1412	665	567	6	1	2	2	560	111	3	.198

Cozy Dolan

DOLAN, PATRICK HENRY
B. Dec. 3, 1872, Cambridge, Mass.   D. Mar. 29, 1907, Louisville, Ky.   BL TL 5'10"   160 lbs.

	W	L	PCT	ERA	G	GS	CG	IP	H	BB	SO	ShO	W	L	SV	AB	H	HR	BA
1895 BOS N	11	7	.611	4.27	25	21	18	198.1	215	67	47	3	0	0	1	83	20	0	.241
1896	1	4	.200	4.83	6	5	3	41	55	27	14	0	0	0	0	14	2	0	.143
1905	0	1	.000	9.00	2	0	0	4	7	1	1	0	0	1	0	510	137	3	.269
1906	0	1	.000	4.50	2	0	0	12	12	6	7	0	0	1	0	549	136	0	.248
4 yrs.	12	13	.480	4.44	35	26	21	255.1	289	101	69	3	0	2	1	*			

John Dolan

DOLAN, JOHN
B. Sept. 12, 1867, Newport, Ky.   D. May 8, 1948, Springfield, Ohio   TR 5'10"   170 lbs.

	W	L	PCT	ERA	G	GS	CG	IP	H	BB	SO	ShO	W	L	SV	AB	H	HR	BA
1890 CIN N	1	1	.500	4.50	2	2	2	18	17	10	9	0	0	0	0	8	1	0	.125
1891 COL AA	12	11	.522	4.16	27	24	19	203.1	216	84	68	0	0	0	0	78	7	1	.090
1892 WAS N	2	2	.500	4.38	5	4	3	37	39	15	8	0	0	0	1	13	3	0	.231
1893 STL N	0	2	.000	4.15	3	1	1	17.1	26	7	1	0	0	0	0	7	1	1	.143
1895 CHI N	0	1	.000	6.55	2	2	1	11	16	6	1	0	0	0	0	3	0	0	.000
5 yrs.	15	17	.469	4.30	39	33	26	286.2	314	122	87	0	0	0	1	109	12	2	.110

Tom Dolan

DOLAN, THOMAS J.
B. Jan. 10, 1859, New York, N. Y.   D. Jan. 16, 1913, St. Louis, Mo.   BR TR

	W	L	PCT	ERA	G	GS	CG	IP	H	BB	SO	ShO	W	L	SV	AB	H	HR	BA
1883 STL AA	0	0	–	4.50	1	0	0	4	4	0	0	0	0	0	0	*			

Art Doll

DOLL, ARTHUR JAMES (Moose)
B. May 7, 1913, Chicago, Ill.   D. Apr. 28, 1978, Calumet City, Ill.   BR TR 6'1"   190 lbs.

	W	L	PCT	ERA	G	GS	CG	IP	H	BB	SO	ShO	W	L	SV	AB	H	HR	BA
1935 BOS N	0	0	–	0.00	0	0	0	0	0	0	0	0	0	0	0	10	1	0	.100
1936	0	1	.000	3.38	1	1	0	8	11	2	0	0	0	0	0	2	0	0	.000
1938	0	0	–	2.25	3	0	0	4	4	3	1	0	0	0	0	1	1	0	1.000
3 yrs.	0	1	.000	3.00	4	1	0	12	15	5	3	0	0	0	0	13	2	0	.154

Deacon Donahue

DONAHUE, JOHN STEPHEN MICHAEL
B. June 23, 1920, Chicago, Ill.   BR TR 6'   175 lbs.

	W	L	PCT	ERA	G	GS	CG	IP	H	BB	SO	ShO	W	L	SV	AB	H	HR	BA
1943 PHI N	0	0	–	4.50	2	0	0	4	4	1	1	0	0	0	0	0	0	0	–
1944	0	2	.000	7.71	6	0	0	9.1	18	2	2	0	0	2	0	1	0	0	.000
2 yrs.	0	2	.000	6.75	8	0	0	13.1	22	3	3	0	0	2	0	1	0	0	.000

Red Donahue

DONAHUE, FRANCIS ROSTELL
B. Jan. 23, 1873, Waterbury, Conn.   D. Aug. 25, 1913, Philadelphia, Pa.   BR TR

	W	L	PCT	ERA	G	GS	CG	IP	H	BB	SO	ShO	W	L	SV	AB	H	HR	BA
1893 NY N	0	0	–	9.00	2	0	0	5	8	3	1	0	0	0	1	2	0	0	.000
1895 STL N	0	1	.000	6.75	1	1	1	8	9	3	2	0	0	0	0	3	0	0	.000
1896	7	24	.226	5.80	32	32	28	267	376	98	70	0	0	0	0	107	17	0	.159
1897	11	33[1]	.250	6.13	46	42	38	348	484	106	62	1	1	2	1	155	33	1	.213
1898 PHI N	17	17	.500	3.55	35	35	33	284.1	327	80	57	1	0	0	0	112	16	0	.143
1899	21	8	.724	3.39	35	31	27	279	292	63	51	4	1	1	0	111	20	0	.180
1900	15	10	.600	3.60	32	24	21	240	299	50	41	2	3	1	0	90	20	0	.222
1901	21	13	.618	2.60	35	34	34	304.1	307	60	89	1	1	0	0	117	11	0	.094
1902 STL A	22	11	.667	2.76	35	34	33	316.1	322	65	63	2	1	0	0	118	11	0	.093
1903 2 teams	STL	A	(16G 8–7)		CLE	A	(16G 7–9)												
" total	15	16	.484	2.59	32	30	28	267.2	287	34	96	4	1	1	0	104	16	0	.154
1904 CLE A	19	14	.576	2.40	35	32	30	277	281	49	127	6	1	1	0	101	17	0	.168
1905	6	12	.333	3.40	20	18	13	137.2	132	25	45	1	0	0	0	53	4	0	.075
1906 DET A	13	14	.481	2.73	28	28	26	241	260	54	82	3	0	0	0	81	10	0	.123
13 yrs.	167	173	.491	3.61	368	341	312	2975.1	3384	690	788	25	9	6	2	1154	175	1	.152

Atley Donald

DONALD, RICHARD ATLEY (Swampy)
B. Aug. 19, 1910, Morton, Miss.   BL TR 6'1"   186 lbs.

	W	L	PCT	ERA	G	GS	CG	IP	H	BB	SO	ShO	W	L	SV	AB	H	HR	BA
1938 NY A	0	1	.000	5.25	2	2	0	12	7	14	6	0	0	0	0	6	1	0	.167
1939	13	3	.813	3.71	24	20	11	153	144	60	55	1	1	0	1	60	15	0	.250

	W	L	PCT	ERA	G	GS	CG	IP	H	BB	SO	ShO	Relief Pitching W	L	SV	BATTING AB	H	HR	BA

Atley Donald continued

	W	L	PCT	ERA	G	GS	CG	IP	H	BB	SO	ShO	W	L	SV	AB	H	HR	BA
1940	8	3	.727	3.03	24	11	6	118.2	113	59	60	1	2	0	0	41	6	0	.146
1941	9	5	.643	3.57	22	20	10	159	141	69	71	0	0	0	0	62	5	0	.081
1942	11	3	.786	3.11	20	19	10	147.2	133	45	53	1	0	0	0	61	9	0	.148
1943	6	4	.600	4.60	22	15	2	119.1	134	38	57	0	0	0	0	47	6	0	.128
1944	13	10	.565	3.34	30	19	9	159	173	59	48	0	2	0	0	55	10	0	.182
1945	5	4	.556	2.97	9	9	6	63.2	62	25	19	2	3	4	0	24	5	1	.208
8 yrs.	65	33	.663	3.52	153	115	54	932.1	907	369	369	5	8	4	1	356	57	1	.160
WORLD SERIES																			
1941 NY A	0	0	—	9.00	1	1	0	4	6	3	2	0	0	0	0	2	0	0	.000
1942	0	1	.000	6.00	1	0	0	3	3	2	1	0	0	1	0	2	0	0	.000
2 yrs.	0	1	.000	7.71	2	1	0	7	9	5	3	0	0	1	0	4	0	0	.000

Ed Donalds

DONALDS, EDWARD ALEXANDER (Skipper)   BR TR 5'11"   180 lbs.
B. June 22, 1885, Bidwell, Ohio   D. July 3, 1950, Columbus, Ohio

	W	L	PCT	ERA	G	GS	CG	IP	H	BB	SO	ShO	W	L	SV	AB	H	HR	BA
1912 CIN N	1	0	1.000	4.50	1	0	0	4	7	0	1	0	1	0	0	1	0	0	.000

Mike Donlin

DONLIN, MICHAEL JOSEPH (Turkey Mike)   BL TL 5'9"   170 lbs.
B. May 30, 1878, Erie, Pa.   D. Sept. 24, 1933, Hollywood, Calif.

	W	L	PCT	ERA	G	GS	CG	IP	H	BB	SO	ShO	W	L	SV	AB	H	HR	BA
1899 STL N	0	1	.000	7.63	3	1	0	15.1	15	14	6	0	0	0	0	267	88	6	.330
1902 CIN N	0	0	—	0.00	1	0	0	1	1	0	0	0	0	0	0	143	42	0	.294
2 yrs.	0	1	.000	7.16	4	1	0	16.1	16	14	6	0	0	0	0	*			

Blix Donnelly

DONNELLY, SYLVESTER URBAN   BR TR 5'10"   166 lbs.
B. Jan. 21, 1914, Olivia, Minn.   D. June 20, 1976, Olivia, Minn.

	W	L	PCT	ERA	G	GS	CG	IP	H	BB	SO	ShO	W	L	SV	AB	H	HR	BA
1944 STL N	2	1	.667	2.12	27	4	2	76.1	61	34	45	1	0	1	2	16	1	0	.063
1945	8	10	.444	3.52	31	23	9	166.1	157	87	76	4	0	1	2	54	7	0	.130
1946 2 teams			STL N (13G 1-2)		PHI	N (12G 3-4)													
" total	4	6	.400	3.10	25	8	2	90	81	34	49	0	1	2	1	25	7	0	.280
1947 PHI N	4	6	.400	2.98	38	10	5	120.2	113	46	31	1	0	3	5	32	2	0	.063
1948	5	7	.417	3.69	26	19	8	131.2	125	49	46	1	0	0	2	45	10	0	.222
1949	2	1	.667	5.06	23	10	1	78.1	84	40	36	0	1	0	0	23	4	0	.174
1950	2	4	.333	4.29	14	1	0	21	30	10	10	0	2	3	0	5	1	0	.200
1951 BOS N	0	1	.000	7.36	6	0	0	7.1	8	6	3	0	0	1	0	1	0	0	.000
8 yrs.	27	36	.429	3.49	190	75	27	691.2	659	306	296	7	4	11	12	201	32	0	.159
WORLD SERIES																			
1944 STL N	1	0	1.000	0.00	2	0	0	6	2	1	9	0	1	0	0	1	0	0	.000

Ed Donnelly

DONNELLY, EDWARD   BR TR 6'1"   205 lbs.
B. July 29, 1880, Hampton, N. Y.   D. Nov. 28, 1957, Rutland, Vt.

	W	L	PCT	ERA	G	GS	CG	IP	H	BB	SO	ShO	W	L	SV	AB	H	HR	BA
1911 BOS N	3	2	.600	2.45	5	4	4	36.2	33	9	16	1	0	1	0	14	1	0	.071
1912	5	10	.333	4.35	37	18	10	184.1	225	72	67	0	0	1	0	69	19	0	.275
2 yrs.	8	12	.400	4.03	42	22	14	221	258	81	83	1	0	2	0	83	20	0	.241

Ed Donnelly

DONNELLY, EDWARD VINCENT   BR TR 6'   175 lbs.
B. Dec. 10, 1934, Allen, Mich.

	W	L	PCT	ERA	G	GS	CG	IP	H	BB	SO	ShO	W	L	SV	AB	H	HR	BA
1959 CHI N	1	1	.500	3.14	9	0	0	14.1	18	9	6	0	1	1	0	0	0	0	—

Frank Donnelly

DONNELLY, FRANKLIN MARION   BR TR
B. Oct. 7, 1869, Tamaroa, Ill.   D. Feb. 3, 1953, Canton, Ill.

	W	L	PCT	ERA	G	GS	CG	IP	H	BB	SO	ShO	W	L	SV	AB	H	HR	BA
1893 CHI N	3	1	.750	5.36	7	5	3	42	51	17	6	0	0	0	2	18	8	0	.444

Jim Donohue

DONOHUE, JAMES THOMAS   BR TR 6'4"   190 lbs.
B. Oct. 31, 1938, St. Louis, Mo.

	W	L	PCT	ERA	G	GS	CG	IP	H	BB	SO	ShO	W	L	SV	AB	H	HR	BA
1961 2 teams			DET A (14G 1-1)		LA	A (38G 4-6)													
" total	5	7	.417	4.18	52	7	0	120.2	116	65	99	0	5	5	6	28	4	0	.143
1962 2 teams			LA A (12G 1-0)		MIN	A (6G 0-1)													
" total	1	1	.500	4.67	18	2	0	34.2	36	17	17	0	1	1	1	6	1	0	.167
2 yrs.	6	8	.429	4.29	70	9	0	155.1	152	82	116	0	6	6	7	34	5	0	.147

Pete Donohue

DONOHUE, PETER JOSEPH   BR TR 6'2"   185 lbs.
B. Nov. 5, 1900, Athens, Tex.

	W	L	PCT	ERA	G	GS	CG	IP	H	BB	SO	ShO	W	L	SV	AB	H	HR	BA
1921 CIN N	7	6	.538	3.35	21	11	7	118.1	117	26	44	0	1	2	1	38	8	1	.211
1922	18	9	.667	3.12	33	30	18	242	257	43	66	2	0	1	1	88	16	0	.182
1923	21	15	.583	3.38	42	36	19	274.1	304	68	84	2	2	0	3	96	24	1	.250
1924	16	9	.640	3.60	35	32	16	222.1	248	36	72	3	0	1	0	73	14	1	.192
1925	21	14	.600	3.08	42	38	27	301	310	49	78	3	1	0	2	109	32	1	.294
1926	20	14	.588	3.37	47	38	17	285.2	298	39	73	5	4	0	2	106	33	0	.311
1927	6	16	.273	4.11	33	24	12	190.2	253	32	48	1	0	1	1	64	16	0	.250
1928	7	11	.389	4.74	23	18	8	150	180	32	37	0	1	0	0	48	7	1	.146
1929	10	13	.435	5.42	32	24	7	177.2	243	51	30	0	2	0	0	60	20	0	.333
1930 2 teams			CIN N (8G 1-3)		NY	N (18G 7-6)													
" total	8	9	.471	6.17	26	16	6	121	188	31	30	0	1	2	2	43	10	1	.233
1931 2 teams			NY N (4G 0-1)		CLE	A (2G 0-0)													
" total	0	1	.000	6.48	6	1	0	16.2	23	9	8	0	0	0	0	4	0	0	.000
1932 BOS A	0	1	.000	7.82	4	2	0	12.2	18	6	1	0	0	0	0	3	0	0	.000
12 yrs.	134	118	.532	3.87	344	270	137	2112.1	2439	422	571	16	12	7	12	732	180	6	.246

Lino Donoso

DONOSO, LINO GALATA   BL TL 5'11"   160 lbs.
B. Sept. 23, 1922, Havana, Cuba

	W	L	PCT	ERA	G	GS	CG	IP	H	BB	SO	ShO	W	L	SV	AB	H	HR	BA
1955 PIT N	4	6	.400	5.31	25	9	3	95	106	35	38	0	1	2	1	27	5	0	.185
1956	0	0	—	0.00	3	0	0	1.2	2	1	1	0	0	0	0	0	0	0	—
2 yrs.	4	6	.400	5.21	28	9	3	96.2	108	36	39	0	1	2	1	27	5	0	.185

	W	L	PCT	ERA	G	GS	CG	IP	H	BB	SO	ShO	Relief Pitching W	L	SV	AB	H	HR	BA

Bill Donovan

DONOVAN, WILLARD EARL
B. July 6, 1916, Maywood, Ill.　　　　　　　　　　BR TL 6'2"　　198 lbs.

	W	L	PCT	ERA	G	GS	CG	IP	H	BB	SO	ShO	W	L	SV	AB	H	HR	BA
1942 BOS N	3	6	.333	3.43	31	10	2	89.1	97	32	23	1	1	0	0	25	6	0	.240
1943	1	0	1.000	1.84	7	0	0	14.2	17	9	1	0	1	0	0	3	1	0	.333
2 yrs.	4	6	.400	3.20	38	10	2	104	114	41	24	1	2	0	0	28	7	0	.250

Dick Donovan

DONOVAN, RICHARD EDWARD
B. Dec. 7, 1927, Boston, Mass.　　　　　　　　　　BL TR 6'3"　　190 lbs.

	W	L	PCT	ERA	G	GS	CG	IP	H	BB	SO	ShO	W	L	SV	AB	H	HR	BA
1950 BOS N	0	2	.000	8.19	10	3	0	29.2	28	34	9	0	0	0	0	6	1	0	.167
1951	0	0	–	5.27	8	2	0	13.2	17	11	4	0	0	0	0	3	1	0	.333
1952	0	2	.000	5.54	7	2	0	13	18	12	6	0	0	0	1	3	0	0	.000
1954 DET A	0	0	–	10.50	2	0	0	6	9	5	2	0	0	0	0	1	0	0	.000
1955 CHI A	15	9	.625	3.32	29	24	11	187	186	48	88	5	2	1	0	76	17	1	.224
1956	12	10	.545	3.64	34	31	14	234.2	212	59	120	3	0	0	0	90	20	3	.222
1957	16	6	.727	2.77	28	28	16	220.2	203	45	88	2	0	0	0	83	12	3	.145
1958	15	14	.517	3.01	34	34	16	248	240	53	127	4	0	0	0	61	8	1	.131
1959	9	10	.474	3.66	31	29	5	179.2	171	58	71	1	0	0	0	23	3	0	.130
1960	6	1	.857	5.38	33	8	0	78.2	87	25	30	0	5	0	3	56	10	1	.179
1961 WAS A	10	10	.500	2.40	23	22	11	168.2	138	35	62	2	0	0	0	89	16	4	.180
1962 CLE A	20	10	.667	3.59	34	34	16	250.2	255	47	94	5	0	0	0	69	9	1	.130
1963	11	13	.458	4.24	30	30	7	206	211	28	84	3	0	0	1	48	7	1	.146
1964	7	9	.438	4.55	30	23	5	158.1	181	29	83	0	0	0	0	6	0	0	.000
1965	1	3	.250	5.96	12	3	0	22.2	32	6	12	0	0	1	0				
15 yrs.	122	99	.552	3.67	345	273	101	2017.1	1988	495	880	25	7	2	5	694	113	15	.163

WORLD SERIES
| 1959 CHI A | 0 | 1 | .000 | 5.40 | 3 | 1 | 0 | 8.1 | 4 | 3 | 5 | 0 | 0 | 0 | 1 | 3 | 1 | 0 | .333 |

Tom Donovan

DONOVAN, THOMAS JOSEPH
Brother of Jerry Donovan.　　　　　　　　　　　　BR TR
B. July 7, 1879, Lock Haven, Pa.　　D. Feb. 20, 1955, Williamsport, Pa.

	W	L	PCT	ERA	G	GS	CG	IP	H	BB	SO	ShO	W	L	SV	AB	H	HR	BA
1901 CLE A	0	0	–	5.14	1	0	0	7	16	3	0	0	0	0	0	*			

Wild Bill Donovan

DONOVAN, WILLIAM EDWARD
B. Oct. 13, 1876, Lawrence, Mass.　　D. Dec. 9, 1923, Forsyth, N. Y.　　BR TR 5'11"　　190 lbs.
Manager 1915-17, 1921.

	W	L	PCT	ERA	G	GS	CG	IP	H	BB	SO	ShO	W	L	SV	AB	H	HR	BA
1898 WAS N	1	6	.143	4.30	17	7	6	88	88	69	36	0	0	0	0	103	17	1	.165
1899 BKN N	1	2	.333	4.32	5	2	2	25	35	13	11	0	0	1	1	13	3	0	.231
1900	1	2	.333	6.68	5	4	2	31	36	18	13	0	0	0	0	13	0	0	.000
1901	25	15	.625	2.77	45	38	36	351	324	152	226	2	4	0	1	135	23	2	.170
1902	17	15	.531	2.78	35	33	30	297.2	250	111	170	4	0	0	1	161	27	1	.168
1903 DET A	17	16	.515	2.29	35	34	34	307	247	95	187	4	0	0	0	124	30	0	.242
1904	17	16	.515	2.46	34	34	30	293	251	94	137	3	0	0	0	140	38	1	.271
1905	18	15	.545	2.60	34	32	27	280.2	236	101	135	5	1	1	0	130	25	0	.192
1906	9	15	.375	3.15	25	25	22	211.2	221	72	85	0	0	0	0	91	11	0	.121
1907	25	4	.862	2.19	32	28	27	271	222	82	123	3	2	0	1	109	29	0	.266
1908	18	7	.720	2.08	29	28	25	242.2	210	53	141	6	0	0	0	82	13	0	.159
1909	8	7	.533	2.31	21	17	13	140.1	121	60	76	4	0	0	2	45	9	0	.200
1910	17	7	.708	2.42	26	23	20	208.2	184	61	107	3	1	0	0	69	10	0	.145
1911	10	9	.526	3.31	20	19	15	168.1	160	64	81	1	1	0	0	60	12	1	.200
1912	1	0	1.000	0.90	3	1	0	10	5	2	6	0	0	0	0	13	1	0	.077
1915 NY A	0	3	.000	4.81	9	1	0	33.2	35	10	17	0	0	2	0	12	1	0	.083
1916	0	0	–	0.00	1	0	0	1	1	1	1	0	0	0	0	0	0	0	–
1918 DET A	0	1	1.000	1.50	2	1	0	6	5	1	1	0	0	0	0	2	1	0	.500
18 yrs.	186	139	.572	2.69	378	327	289	2966.2	2631	1059	1552	35	9	4	6	*			

WORLD SERIES
1907 DET A	0	1	.000	1.29	2	2	2	21	17	5	16	0	0	0	0	8	0	0	.000
1908	0	2	.000	4.24	2	2	2	17	17	4	10	0	0	0	0	4	0	0	.000
1909	1	1	.500	3.00	2	2	1	12	7	8	7	0	0	0	0	4	0	0	.000
3 yrs.	1	4	.200	2.70	6	6	5	50	41	17	33	0	0	0	0	16	0	0	.000
			7th									10th							

John Doran

DORAN, JOHN F.
B. 1870, N. J.　Deceased.　　　　　　　　　　　　TL 5'11"　　175 lbs.

	W	L	PCT	ERA	G	GS	CG	IP	H	BB	SO	ShO	W	L	SV	AB	H	HR	BA
1891 LOU AA	5	10	.333	5.43	15	14	12	126	160	75	55	1	0	1	0	53	10	0	.189

Mike Dorgan

DORGAN, MICHAEL CORNELIUS
Brother of Jerry Dorgan.　　　　　　　　　　　　TR 5'9"　　180 lbs.
B. Oct. 2, 1853, Middletown, Conn.　　D. Apr. 26, 1909, Hartford, Conn.
Manager 1879.

	W	L	PCT	ERA	G	GS	CG	IP	H	BB	SO	ShO	W	L	SV	AB	H	HR	BA
1879 SYR N	0	0	–	2.25	2	0	0	12	13	2	8	0	0	0	0	270	72	1	.267
1880 PRO N	0	0	–	1.13	1	0	0	8	4	0	2	0	0	0	0	321	79	0	.246
1883 NY N	0	1	.000	3.86	1	1	1	7	8	6	3	0	0	0	0	261	61	0	.234
1884	8	6	.571	3.50	14	14	12	113	98	51	90	0	0	0	0	341	94	1	.276
4 yrs.	8	7	.533	3.28	18	15	13	140	123	59	103	0	0	0	0	*			

Harry Dorish

DORISH, HARRY (Fritz)
B. July 13, 1921, Swoyersville, Pa.　　　　　　　BR TR 5'11"　　204 lbs.

	W	L	PCT	ERA	G	GS	CG	IP	H	BB	SO	ShO	W	L	SV	AB	H	HR	BA
1947 BOS A	7	8	.467	4.70	41	9	2	136	149	54	50	0	4	3	2	35	5	0	.143
1948	0	1	.000	5.65	9	0	0	14.1	18	6	5	0	0	1	0	4	1	0	.250
1949	0	0	–	2.35	5	0	0	7.2	7	1	5	0	0	0	0	0	0	0	–
1950 STL A	4	9	.308	6.44	29	13	4	109	162	36	36	0	1	2	0	31	5	0	.161
1951 CHI A	5	6	.455	3.54	32	4	2	96.2	101	31	29	1	3	5	0	31	8	0	.258
1952	8	4	.667	2.47	39	1	1	91	66	42	47	0	7	4	11	22	2	0	.091
1953	10	6	.625	3.40	55	6	2	145.2	140	52	69	0	7	4	18	41	7	0	.171
1954	6	4	.600	2.72	37	6	2	109	88	29	48	1	2	2	6	27	3	0	.111

	W	L	PCT	ERA	G	GS	CG	IP	H	BB	SO	ShO	Relief Pitching W	L	SV	BATTING AB	H	HR	BA

Harry Dorish continued

1955 2 teams			CHI	A (13G 2–0)	BAL	A	(35G 3–3)												
" total	5	3	.625	2.83	48	1	0	82.2	74	37	28	0	5	2	7	13	1	0	.077
1956 2 teams			BAL	A (13G 0–0)	BOS	A	(15G 0–2)												
" total	0	2	.000	3.83	28	0	0	42.1	45	13	15	0	0	2	0	0	0	0	–
10 yrs.	45	43	.511	3.83	323	40	13	834.1	850	301	332	2	29	25	44	204	32	0	.157

Gus Dorner

DORNER, AUGUSTUS
B. Aug. 18, 1876, Chambersburg, Pa.   D. May 4, 1956, Chambersburg, Pa.   BR TR 5'10"   176 lbs.

1902 CLE A	3	1	.750	1.25	4	4	4	36	33	13	5	1	0	0	0	13	5	0	.385
1903	4	5	.444	3.30	12	8	4	73.2	83	24	28	2	1	1	0	25	2	0	.080
1906 2 teams			CIN	N (2G 1–1)	BOS	N	(34G 8–25)												
" total	9	26	.257	3.73	36	33	30	272.1	280	107	109	0	1	1	0	105	14	0	.133
1907 BOS N	12	16	.429	3.12	36	31	24	271.1	253	92	85	2	1	0	0	92	12	0	.130
1908	8	19	.296	3.54	38	28	14	216.1	176	77	41	3	2	0	0	67	12	0	.179
1909	1	2	.333	2.55	5	2	0	24.2	17	17	7	0	0	1	0	6	1	0	.167
6 yrs.	37	69	.349	3.33	131	106	76	894.1	842	330	275	8	5	3	1	308	46	0	.149

Bert Dorr

DORR, CHARLES ALBERT
B. Feb. 22, 1862, New York, N. Y.   D. June 16, 1914, Dickinson Township, N. Y.

1882 STL AA	2	6	.250	2.59	8	8	8	66	53	1	34	0	0	0	0	26	4	0	.154

Cal Dorsett

DORSETT, CALVIN LEAVELL (Preacher)
B. June 10, 1916, Greenville, Tex.   D. Oct. 22, 1970, Elk City, Okla.   BR TR 6'   180 lbs.

1940 CLE A	0	0	–	9.00	1	0	0	1	1	0	0	0	0	0	0	0	0	0	–
1941	0	1	.000	10.32	5	2	0	11.1	21	10	5	0	0	0	0	2	0	0	.000
1947	0	0	–	27.00	2	0	0	1.1	3	3	1	0	0	0	0	0	0	0	–
3 yrs.	0	1	.000	11.85	8	2	0	13.2	25	13	6	0	0	0	0	2	0	0	.000

Jerry Dorsey

DORSEY, MICHAEL JEREMIAH
B. 1854, Auburn, N. Y.   D. Nov. 3, 1938, Auburn, N. Y.

1884 BAL U	0	1	.000	9.00	1	1	0	4	7	0	3	0	0	0	0	3	0	0	.000

Jim Dorsey

DORSEY, JAMES EDWARD
B. Aug. 2, 1955, Oak Park, Ill.   BR TR 6'3"   200 lbs.

1980 CAL A	1	2	.333	9.00	4	4	0	16	25	8	8	0	0	0	0	0	0	0	–
1984 BOS A	0	0	–	10.13	2	0	0	2.2	6	2	4	0	0	0	0	0	0	0	–
2 yrs.	1	2	.333	9.16	6	4	0	18.2	31	10	12	0	0	0	0	0	0	0	–

Jack Doscher

DOSCHER, JOHN HENRY
Son of Herm Doscher.
B. July 27, 1880, Troy, N. Y.   D. May 27, 1971, Ridgefield Park, N. J.   BR TR 6'1"

1903 2 teams			CHI	N (1G 0–1)	BKN	N	(3G 0–0)												
" total	0	1	.000	9.00	4	1	0	10	14	11	9	0	0	0	0	4	0	0	.000
1904 BKN N	0	1	.000	0.00	2	0	0	6.1	1	1	2	0	0	0	0	2	1	0	.500
1905	1	5	.167	3.17	12	7	6	71	60	30	33	0	0	0	0	24	2	0	.083
1906	0	1	.000	1.29	2	1	1	14	12	4	10	0	0	0	0	5	0	0	.000
1908 CIN N	1	3	.250	1.83	7	4	3	44.1	31	22	7	0	0	0	0	15	2	0	.133
5 yrs.	2	11	.154	2.84	27	13	10	145.2	118	68	61	0	0	0	0	50	5	0	.100

Rich Dotson

DOTSON, RICHARD ELLIOTT
B. Jan. 10, 1959, Cincinnati, Ohio   BR TR 6'1"   190 lbs.

1979 CHI A	2	0	1.000	3.75	5	5	1	24	28	6	13	1	0	0	0	0	0	0	–
1980	12	10	.545	4.27	33	32	8	198	185	87	109	0	0	0	0	0	0	0	–
1981	9	8	.529	3.77	24	24	5	141	145	49	73	4	0	0	0	0	0	0	–
1982	11	15	.423	3.84	34	31	3	196.2	219	73	109	1	0	0	0	0	0	0	–
1983	22	7	.759	3.23	35	35	8	240	209	106	137	1	0	0	0	0	0	0	–
1984	14	15	.483	3.59	32	32	14	245.2	216	103	120	1	0	0	0	0	0	0	–
6 yrs.	70	55	.560	3.71	163	159	39	1045.1	1002	424	561	8	0	0	0	0	0	0	–

LEAGUE CHAMPIONSHIP SERIES

1983 CHI A	0	1	.000	10.80	1	1	0	5	6	3	3	0	0	0	0	0	0	0	–

Gary Dotter

DOTTER, GARY RICHARD
B. Aug. 7, 1942, St. Louis, Mo.   BL TL 6'1"   180 lbs.

1961 MIN A	0	0	–	9.00	2	0	0	6	6	4	2	0	0	0	0	1	0	0	.000
1963	0	0	–	0.00	2	0	0	2	0	0	2	0	0	0	0	0	0	0	–
1964	0	0	–	2.08	3	0	0	4.1	3	3	6	0	0	0	0	0	0	0	–
3 yrs.	0	0	–	5.11	7	0	0	12.1	9	7	10	0	0	0	0	1	0	0	.000

Babe Doty

DOTY, ELMER L.
B. Dec. 17, 1867, Genoa, Ohio   D. Nov. 20, 1929, Toledo, Ohio   BL TR 6'   160 lbs.

1890 TOL AA	1	0	1.000	1.00	1	1	1	9	9	1	4	0	0	0	0	3	0	0	.000

Tom Dougherty

DOUGHERTY, THOMAS JAMES (Sugar Boy)
B. May 30, 1881, Chicago, Ill.   D. Nov. 6, 1953, Milwaukee, Wis.   BL TR

1904 CHI A	1	0	1.000	0.00	1	0	0	2	0	0	0	0	1	0	0	1	0	0	.000

Larry Douglas

DOUGLAS, HOWARD LAWRENCE (Doug)
B. June 5, 1890, Jellico, Tenn.   D. Nov. 4, 1949, Jellico, Tenn.   BR TR 6'3"   175 lbs.

1915 BAL F	0	0	–	3.00	2	0	0	3	3	2	1	0	0	0	0	0	0	0	–

Phil Douglas

DOUGLAS, PHILLIP BROOKS (Shufflin' Phil)
B. June 17, 1890, Cedartown, Ga.   D. Aug. 1, 1952, Sequatchie Valley, Tenn.   BR TR 6'5"   210 lbs.

1912 CHI A	0	1	.000	7.30	3	1	0	12.1	21	6	7	0	0	0	0	2	0	0	.000
1914 CIN N	11	18	.379	2.56	45	25	13	239.1	186	92	121	0	4	4	1	73	10	0	.137

	W	L	PCT	ERA	G	GS	CG	IP	H	BB	SO	ShO	Relief Pitching W	L	SV	BATTING AB	H	HR	BA

Phil Douglas continued

1915 3 teams	CIN	N	(8G 1–5)		BKN	N	(20G 5–5)	CHI	N	(4G 1–1)									
" total	7	11	.389	3.25	32	24	7	188.1	174	47	110	2	0	0	0	64	8	0	.125
1917 CHI N	14	20	.412	2.55	51	37	20	293.1	269	50	151	5	3	0	1	89	11	0	.124
1918	9	9	.500	2.13	25	19	11	156.2	145	31	51	2	1	1	2	55	14	0	.255
1919 2 teams	CHI	N	(25G 10–6)		NY	N	(8G 2–4)									66	8	0	.121
" total	12	10	.545	2.03	33	25	12	213	186	40	84	4	2	0	0	73	11	0	.151
1920 NY N	14	10	.583	2.71	46	21	10	226	225	55	71	3	4	5	2	81	16	1	.198
1921	15	10	.600	4.22	40	27	13	221.2	266	55	55	3	2	1	2	58	12	1	.207
1922	11	4	.733	2.63	24	21	9	157.2	154	35	33	1	1	0	0	58	12	1	.207
9 yrs.	93	93	.500	2.80	299	200	95	1708.1	1626	411	683	20	17	11	8	561	90	2	.160

WORLD SERIES

1918 CHI N	0	1	.000	0.00	1	0	0	1	1	0	0	0	0	1	0	0	0	0	–
1921 NY N	2	1	.667	2.08	3	3	2	26	24	5	17	0	0	0	0	7	0	0	.000
2 yrs.	2	2	.500	2.00	4	3	2	27	25	5	17	0	0	1	0	7	0	0	.000

Whammy Douglas

DOUGLAS, CHARLES WILLIAM   BR TR 6'2" 185 lbs.
B. Feb. 17, 1935, Carrboro, N. C.

1957 PIT N	3	3	.500	3.26	11	8	0	47	48	30	28	0	0	0	0	16	1	0	.063

Skip Dowd

DOWD, JAMES JOSEPH   BR TR 5'10½" 160 lbs.
B. Feb. 16, 1889, Holyoke, Mass.   D. Dec. 20, 1960, Holyoke, Mass.

1910 PIT N	0	0	–	0.00	1	0	0	2	4	2	1	0	0	0	0	0	0	0	–

Dave Dowling

DOWLING, DAVID BARCLAY   BR TL 6'2" 181 lbs.
B. Aug. 23, 1942, St. Louis, Mo.

1964 STL N	0	0	–	0.00	1	0	0	1	2	0	0	0	0	0	0	0	0	0	–
1966 CHI N	1	0	1.000	2.00	1	1	1	9	10	0	3	0	0	0	0	2	0	0	.000
2 yrs.	1	0	1.000	1.80	2	1	1	10	12	0	3	0	0	0	0	2	0	0	.000

Pete Dowling

DOWLING, HENRY PETER   TL
B. Ky.   D. June 30, 1905, Hot Lake, Ore.

1897 LOU N	1	2	.333	5.88	4	4	2	26	39	8	3	0	0	0	0	10	2	0	.200
1898	13	20	.394	4.16	36	32	30	285.2	284	120	84	0	1	1	0	107	21	0	.196
1899	13	17	.433	3.11	34	32	29	289.2	321	93	88	0	1	0	0	116	27	0	.233
1901 2 teams	MIL	A	(10G 1–4)		CLE	A	(33G 11–22)									118	20	1	.169
" total	12	26	.316	4.15	43	34	31	306	340	118	124	2	0	4	1	351	70	1	.199
4 yrs.	39	65	.375	3.87	117	102	92	907.1	984	339	299	2	2	5	1	351	70	1	.199

Al Downing

DOWNING, ALPHONSO ERWIN   BR TL 5'11" 175 lbs.
B. June 28, 1941, Trenton, N. J.

1961 NY A	0	1	.000	8.00	5	1	0	9	7	12	12	0	0	0	0	1	0	0	.000
1962	0	0	–	0.00	1	0	0	1	0	1	0	0	0	0	0	0	0	0	–
1963	13	5	.722	2.56	24	22	10	175.2	114	80	171	4	0	1	0	58	6	0	.103
1964	13	8	.619	3.47	37	35	11	244	201	120	217	1	0	0	2	85	15	0	.176
1965	12	14	.462	3.40	35	32	8	212	185	105	179	2	0	0	0	74	8	1	.108
1966	10	11	.476	3.56	30	30	1	200	178	79	152	0	0	0	0	70	7	0	.100
1967	14	10	.583	2.63	31	28	10	201.2	158	61	171	4	2	0	0	66	8	1	.121
1968	3	3	.500	3.52	15	12	1	61.1	54	20	40	0	0	0	0	17	3	0	.176
1969	7	5	.583	3.38	30	15	5	130.2	117	49	85	1	1	1	0	44	6	0	.136
1970 2 teams	OAK	A	(10G 3–3)		MIL	A	(17G 2–10)									35	4	0	.114
" total	5	13	.278	3.52	27	22	2	135.1	118	81	79	0	0	0	0	92	16	0	.174
1971 LA N	20	9	.690	2.68	37	36	12	262	245	84	136	5	0	0	0	66	8	0	.121
1972	9	9	.500	2.98	31	30	7	202.2	196	67	117	4	0	0	0	57	5	0	.088
1973	9	9	.500	3.31	30	28	5	193	155	68	124	2	1	0	0	29	5	0	.172
1974	5	6	.455	3.67	21	16	1	98	94	45	63	1	0	0	0	29	5	0	.172
1975	2	1	.667	2.88	22	6	0	75	59	28	39	0	2	1	1	16	0	0	.000
1976	1	2	.333	3.86	17	3	0	46.2	43	18	30	0	1	1	0	6	0	0	.000
1977	0	1	.000	6.75	12	1	0	20	22	16	23	0	0	1	0	1	0	0	.000
17 yrs.	123	107	.535	3.22	405	317	73	2268	1946	933	1639	24	7	5	3	717	91	2	.127

LEAGUE CHAMPIONSHIP SERIES

1974 LA N	0	0	–	0.00	1	0	0	4	1	1	0	0	0	0	0	1	0	0	.000

WORLD SERIES

1963 NY A	0	1	.000	5.40	1	1	0	5	7	1	6	0	0	0	0	1	0	0	.000
1964	0	1	.000	8.22	3	1	0	7.2	9	2	5	0	0	0	0	2	0	0	.000
1974 LA N	0	1	.000	2.45	1	1	0	3.2	4	4	3	0	0	0	0	1	0	0	.000
3 yrs.	0	3	.000	6.06	5	3	0	16.1	20	7	14	0	0	0	0	4	0	0	.000

Dave Downs

DOWNS, DAVID RALPH   BR TR 6'5" 220 lbs.
B. June 21, 1952, Logan, Utah

1972 PHI N	1	1	.500	2.74	4	4	1	23	25	3	5	1	0	0	0	8	2	0	.250

Tom Dowse

DOWSE, THOMAS JOSEPH   BR TR 5'11" 175 lbs.
B. Aug. 12, 1867, Ireland   D. Dec. 14, 1946, Riverside, Calif.

1890 CLE N	0	0	–	5.40	1	0	0	5	6	1	0	0	0	0	0	*			

Carl Doyle

DOYLE, WILLIAM CARL   BR TR 6'1" 185 lbs.
B. July 30, 1912, Knoxville, Tenn.   D. Sept. 4, 1951, Knoxville, Tenn.

1935 PHI A	2	7	.222	5.99	14	9	3	79.2	86	72	34	0	0	1	0	30	4	0	.133
1936	0	3	.000	10.94	8	6	1	38.2	66	29	12	0	0	0	0	15	4	0	.267
1939 BKN N	1	2	.333	1.02	5	1	1	17.2	8	7	7	1	0	2	1	6	1	0	.167
1940 2 teams	BKN	N	(3G 0–0)		STL	N	(21G 3–3)									31	7	1	.226
" total	3	3	.500	7.27	24	5	1	86.2	117	47	48	0	2	2	1	82	16	1	.195
4 yrs.	6	15	.286	6.95	51	21	6	222.2	277	155	101	1	2	5	2	82	16	1	.195

	W	L	PCT	ERA	G	GS	CG	IP	H	BB	SO	ShO	Relief Pitching W	L	SV	BATTING AB	H	HR	BA

Ed Doyle

DOYLE, EDWARD H.
B. 1853, Ill. D. Feb. 6, 1929, Havre, Mont.

	W	L	PCT	ERA	G	GS	CG	IP	H	BB	SO	ShO	W	L	SV	AB	H	HR	BA
1882 STL AA	0	3	.000	2.63	3	3	3	24	41	3	5	0	0	0	0	11	2	0	.182

Jess Doyle

DOYLE, JESSE HERBERT BR TR 5'11" 175 lbs.
B. Apr. 14, 1898, Knoxville, Tenn. D. Apr. 15, 1961, Belleville, Ill.

	W	L	PCT	ERA	G	GS	CG	IP	H	BB	SO	ShO	W	L	SV	AB	H	HR	BA
1925 DET A	4	7	.364	5.93	45	3	0	118.1	158	50	31	0	4	5	8	33	8	2	.242
1926	0	0	–	4.15	2	0	0	4.1	6	1	2	0	0	0	1	1	1	0	1.000
1927	0	0	–	8.03	7	0	0	12.1	16	5	5	0	0	0	0	3	1	0	.333
1931 STL A	0	0	–	27.00	1	0	0	1	3	1	0	0	0	0	0	0	0	0	–
4 yrs.	4	7	.364	6.22	55	3	0	136	183	57	38	0	4	5	9	37	10	2	.270

Paul Doyle

DOYLE, PAUL SINNOTT BL TL 5'11" 172 lbs.
B. Oct. 2, 1939, Philadelphia, Pa.

	W	L	PCT	ERA	G	GS	CG	IP	H	BB	SO	ShO	W	L	SV	AB	H	HR	BA
1969 ATL N	2	0	1.000	2.08	36	0	0	39	31	16	25	0	2	0	4	3	0	0	.000
1970 2 teams						CAL A (40G 3–1)			SD N (9G 0–2)											
" total	3	3	.500	5.33	49	0	0	49	52	27	36	0	3	3	7	4	0	0	.000
1972 CAL A	0	0	–	0.00	2	0	0	2	2	3	4	0	0	0	0	0	0	0	–
3 yrs.	5	3	.625	3.80	87	0	0	90	85	46	65	0	5	3	11	7	0	0	.000

LEAGUE CHAMPIONSHIP SERIES

	W	L	PCT	ERA	G	GS	CG	IP	H	BB	SO	ShO	W	L	SV	AB	H	HR	BA
1969 ATL N	0	0	–	0.00	1	0	0	1	2	1	3	0	0	0	0	0	0	0	–

Slow Joe Doyle

DOYLE, JUDD BRUCE BL TR 5'8" 150 lbs.
B. Sept. 15, 1881, Clay Center, Kans. D. Nov. 21, 1947, Tannersville, N. H.

	W	L	PCT	ERA	G	GS	CG	IP	H	BB	SO	ShO	W	L	SV	AB	H	HR	BA
1906 NY A	2	2	.500	2.38	9	6	3	45.1	34	13	28	2	0	0	0	14	3	0	.214
1907	11	11	.500	2.65	29	23	15	193.2	169	67	94	1	1	0	1	58	8	0	.138
1908	1	1	.500	2.63	12	4	2	48	42	14	20	1	0	0	0	14	3	0	.214
1909	8	6	.571	2.58	17	15	8	125.2	103	37	57	3	0	0	0	42	7	0	.167
1910 2 teams						NY A (3G 0–2)			CIN N (5G 0–0)											
" total	0	2	–	7.23	8	2	1	23.2	35	16	10	0	0	0	0	7	1	0	.143
5 yrs.	22	22	.500	2.85	75	50	29	436.1	383	147	209	7	1	0	1	135	22	0	.163

Buzz Dozier

DOZIER, WILLIAM JOSEPH BR TR 6'3" 185 lbs.
B. Aug. 31, 1927, Waco, Tex.

	W	L	PCT	ERA	G	GS	CG	IP	H	BB	SO	ShO	W	L	SV	AB	H	HR	BA
1947 WAS A	0	0	–	0.00	2	0	0	4.2	2	1	2	0	0	0	0	1	0	0	.000
1949	0	0	–	11.37	2	0	0	6.1	12	6	1	0	0	0	0	2	0	0	.000
2 yrs.	0	0	–	6.55	4	0	0	11	14	7	3	0	0	0	0	3	0	0	.000

Moe Drabowsky

DRABOWSKY, MYRON WALTER BR TR 6'3" 190 lbs.
B. July 21, 1935, Ozanna, Poland

	W	L	PCT	ERA	G	GS	CG	IP	H	BB	SO	ShO	W	L	SV	AB	H	HR	BA
1956 CHI N	2	4	.333	2.47	9	7	3	51	37	39	36	0	0	0	0	16	4	0	.250
1957	13	15	.464	3.53	36	33	12	239.2	214	94	170	2	0	0	0	82	15	1	.183
1958	9	11	.450	4.51	22	20	4	125.2	118	73	77	1	0	0	0	45	7	0	.156
1959	5	10	.333	4.13	31	23	3	141.2	138	75	70	1	1	1	0	45	5	0	.111
1960	3	1	.750	6.44	32	7	0	50.1	71	23	26	0	2	0	1	6	0	0	.000
1961 MIL N	0	2	.000	4.62	16	0	0	25.1	26	18	5	0	0	2	2	4	1	0	.250
1962 2 teams						CIN N (23G 2–6)			KC A (10G 1–1)											
" total	3	7	.300	5.03	33	13	1	111	113	41	75	0	1	1	1	23	1	0	.043
1963 KC A	7	13	.350	3.05	26	22	9	174.1	135	64	109	2	0	0	0	62	10	2	.161
1964	5	13	.278	5.29	53	21	1	168.1	176	72	119	0	1	2	1	43	1	0	.023
1965	1	5	.167	4.42	14	5	0	38.2	44	18	25	0	1	2	0	11	1	0	.091
1966 BAL A	6	0	1.000	2.81	44	3	0	96	62	29	98	0	5	0	7	22	8	0	.364
1967	7	5	.583	1.60	43	0	0	95.1	66	25	96	0	7	5	12	20	7	0	.350
1968	4	4	.500	1.91	45	0	0	61.1	35	25	46	0	4	4	7	7	2	0	.286
1969 KC A	11	9	.550	2.94	52	0	0	98	68	30	76	0	11	9	11	17	4	0	.235
1970 2 teams						KC A (24G 1–2)			BAL A (21G 4–2)											
" total	5	4	.556	3.52	45	0	0	69	58	27	59	0	5	4	3	9	1	0	.111
1971 STL N	6	1	.857	3.45	51	0	0	60	45	33	49	0	6	1	8	6	1	0	.167
1972 2 teams						STL N (30G 1–1)			CHI A (7G 0–0)											
" total	1	1	.500	2.57	37	0	0	35	35	16	26	0	1	1	2	2	0	0	.000
17 yrs.	88	105	.456	3.71	589	154	33	1640.2	1441	702	1162	6	45	32	55	420	68	3	.162

WORLD SERIES

	W	L	PCT	ERA	G	GS	CG	IP	H	BB	SO	ShO	W	L	SV	AB	H	HR	BA
1966 BAL A	1	0	1.000	0.00	1	0	0	6.2	1	2	11	0	1	0	0	2	0	0	.000
1970	0	0	–	2.70	2	0	0	3.1	2	1	1	0	0	0	0	1	0	0	.000
2 yrs.	1	0	1.000	0.90	3	0	0	10	3	3	12	0	1	0	0	3	0	0	.000

Dick Drago

DRAGO, RICHARD ANTHONY BR TR 6'1" 190 lbs.
B. June 25, 1945, Toledo, Ohio

	W	L	PCT	ERA	G	GS	CG	IP	H	BB	SO	ShO	W	L	SV	AB	H	HR	BA
1969 KC A	11	13	.458	3.77	41	26	10	200.2	190	65	108	2	0	1	1	52	3	0	.058
1970	9	15	.375	3.75	35	34	7	240	239	72	127	1	0	0	0	76	4	0	.053
1971	17	11	.607	2.99	35	34	15	241	251	46	127	4	0	0	0	77	10	0	.130
1972	12	17	.414	3.01	34	33	11	239.1	230	51	135	2	0	0	0	68	4	0	.059
1973	12	14	.462	4.23	37	33	10	212.2	252	76	98	1	0	0	0	0	0	0	–
1974 BOS A	7	10	.412	3.48	33	18	8	176	165	56	90	0	1	3	3	0	0	0	–
1975	2	2	.500	3.84	40	2	0	72.2	69	31	43	0	2	2	15	0	0	0	–
1976 CAL A	7	8	.467	4.42	44	0	0	79.1	80	31	43	0	7	8	6	0	0	0	–
1977 2 teams						CAL A (13G 0–1)			BAL A (36G 6–3)											
" total	6	4	.600	3.41	49	0	0	60.2	71	18	35	0	6	4	5	0	0	0	–
1978 BOS A	4	4	.500	3.03	37	1	0	77.1	71	32	42	0	4	4	7	0	0	0	–
1979	10	6	.625	3.03	53	1	0	89	85	21	67	0	10	6	13	0	0	0	–
1980	7	7	.500	4.13	43	7	1	133	127	44	63	0	4	4	3	0	0	0	.000
1981 SEA A	4	6	.400	5.50	39	0	0	54	71	15	27	0	4	6	5	0	0	0	–
13 yrs.	108	117	.480	3.62	519	189	62	1875.2	1901	558	987	10	38	38	58	274	21	0	.077

LEAGUE CHAMPIONSHIP SERIES

	W	L	PCT	ERA	G	GS	CG	IP	H	BB	SO	ShO	W	L	SV	AB	H	HR	BA
1975 BOS A	0	0	–	0.00	2	0	0	4.2	2	1	2	0	0	0	2	0	0	0	–

WORLD SERIES

	W	L	PCT	ERA	G	GS	CG	IP	H	BB	SO	ShO	W	L	SV	AB	H	HR	BA
1975 BOS A	0	1	.000	2.25	2	0	0	4	3	1	1	0	0	1	0	0	0	0	–

	W	L	PCT	ERA	G	GS	CG	IP	H	BB	SO	ShO	Relief Pitching W	L	SV	BATTING AB	H	HR	BA

Logan Drake

DRAKE, LOGAN GAFFNEY
B. Dec. 26, 1900, Spartanburg, S. C.   D. June 1, 1940, Columbia, S. C.   BR TR 5'10½" 165 lbs.

	W	L	PCT	ERA	G	GS	CG	IP	H	BB	SO	ShO	W	L	SV	AB	H	HR	BA
1922 CLE A	0	0	–	3.00	1	0	0	3	4	2	1	0	0	0	0	1	0	0	.000
1923	0	0	–	4.15	4	0	0	4.1	2	5	2	0	0	0	0	0	0	0	–
1924	0	1	.000	10.32	5	1	0	11.1	18	10	8	0	0	0	0	1	0	0	.000
3 yrs.	0	1	.000	7.71	10	1	0	18.2	24	17	11	0	0	0	0	2	0	0	.000

Tom Drake

DRAKE, THOMAS KENDALL
B. Aug. 7, 1914, Birmingham, Ala.   BR TR 6'1"   185 lbs.

	W	L	PCT	ERA	G	GS	CG	IP	H	BB	SO	ShO	W	L	SV	AB	H	HR	BA
1939 CLE A	0	1	.000	9.00	8	1	0	15	23	19	1	0	0	1	0	2	0	0	.000
1941 BKN N	1	1	.500	4.38	10	2	0	24.2	26	9	12	0	0	0	0	5	2	0	.400
2 yrs.	1	2	.333	6.13	18	3	0	39.2	49	28	13	0	0	1	0	7	2	0	.286

Dave Dravecky

DRAVECKY, DAVID FRANCIS
B. Feb. 14, 1956, Youngstown, Ohio   BR TL 6'1"   195 lbs.

	W	L	PCT	ERA	G	GS	CG	IP	H	BB	SO	ShO	W	L	SV	AB	H	HR	BA
1982 SD N	5	3	.625	2.57	31	10	0	105	86	33	59	0	1	1	2	23	3	0	.130
1983	14	10	.583	3.58	28	28	9	183.2	181	44	74	1	0	0	0	61	6	0	.098
1984	9	8	.529	2.93	50	14	3	156.2	125	51	71	2	4	4	8	41	4	0	.098
3 yrs.	28	21	.571	3.11	109	52	12	445.1	392	128	204	3	5	5	10	125	13	0	.104
LEAGUE CHAMPIONSHIP SERIES																			
1984 SD N	0	0	–	0.00	3	0	0	6	2	0	5	0	0	0	0	0	0	0	–
WORLD SERIES																			
1984 SD N	0	0	–	0.00	2	0	0	4.2	3	1	5	0	0	0	0	0	0	0	–

Clem Dreisewerd

DREISEWERD, CLEMENT JOHN (Steamboat)
B. Jan. 24, 1916, Old Monroe, Mo.   BL TL 6'1½"   195 lbs.

	W	L	PCT	ERA	G	GS	CG	IP	H	BB	SO	ShO	W	L	SV	AB	H	HR	BA
1944 BOS A	2	4	.333	4.07	7	7	3	48.2	52	9	9	0	0	0	0	16	3	0	.188
1945	0	1	.000	4.66	2	2	0	9.2	13	2	3	0	0	0	0	3	0	0	.000
1946	4	1	.800	4.18	20	1	0	47.1	50	15	19	0	3	1	0	10	0	0	.000
1948 2 teams			STL	A (13G 0–2)			NY	N (4G 0–0)											
" total	0	2	.000	5.66	17	0	0	35	45	13	8	0	0	2	2	9	1	0	.111
4 yrs.	6	8	.429	4.54	46	10	3	140.2	160	39	39	0	3	3	2	38	4	0	.105
WORLD SERIES																			
1946 BOS A	0	0	–	0.00	1	0	0	.1	0	0	0	0	0	0	0	0	0	0	–

Bob Dresser

DRESSER, ROBERT NICHOLSON
B. Oct. 4, 1878, Newton, Mass.   D. July 27, 1924, Duxbury, Mass.   BL TL

	W	L	PCT	ERA	G	GS	CG	IP	H	BB	SO	ShO	W	L	SV	AB	H	HR	BA
1902 BOS N	0	1	.000	3.00	1	1	1	9	12	1	0	8	0	0	0	4	1	0	.250

Rob Dressler

DRESSLER, ROBERT ALAN
B. Feb. 2, 1954, Portland, Ore.   BR TR 6'3"   180 lbs.

	W	L	PCT	ERA	G	GS	CG	IP	H	BB	SO	ShO	W	L	SV	AB	H	HR	BA
1975 SF N	1	0	1.000	1.13	3	2	1	16	17	4	6	0	0	0	0	4	0	0	.000
1976	3	10	.231	4.43	25	19	0	107.2	125	35	33	0	1	0	0	31	4	0	.129
1978 STL N	1	0	1.000	2.08	3	2	0	13	12	4	4	0	0	0	0	3	0	0	.000
1979 SEA A	3	2	.600	4.93	21	11	2	104	134	22	36	0	0	0	0	0	0	0	–
1980	4	10	.286	3.99	30	14	3	149	161	33	50	0	0	3	0	0	0	0	–
5 yrs.	11	23	.324	4.18	82	48	6	389.2	449	98	129	0	1	3	0	38	4	0	.105

Dave Drew

DREW, DAVID
Deceased.

	W	L	PCT	ERA	G	GS	CG	IP	H	BB	SO	ShO	W	L	SV	AB	H	HR	BA
1884 PHI U	0	1	.000	3.86	1	0	0	7	7	0	2	0	0	1	0	*			

Karl Drews

DREWS, KARL AUGUST
B. Feb. 22, 1920, Staten Island, N. Y.   D. Aug. 13, 1963, Dania, Fla.   BR TR 6'4½"   192 lbs.

	W	L	PCT	ERA	G	GS	CG	IP	H	BB	SO	ShO	W	L	SV	AB	H	HR	BA
1946 NY A	1	1	.000	8.53	3	1	0	6.1	6	6	4	0	0	0	0	1	0	0	.000
1947	6	6	.500	4.91	30	10	0	91.2	92	55	45	0	4	0	1	27	1	0	.037
1948 2 teams			NY	A (19G 2–3)			STL	A (20G 3–2)											
" total	5	5	.500	5.92	39	4	0	76	78	69	22	0	4	4	3	15	0	0	.000
1949 STL A	4	12	.250	6.64	31	23	3	139.2	180	66	35	1	0	1	0	46	0	0	.000
1951 PHI N	1	0	1.000	6.26	5	3	1	23	29	7	13	0	0	0	0	8	2	0	.250
1952	14	15	.483	2.72	33	30	15	228.2	213	52	96	5	1	0	0	82	9	0	.110
1953	9	10	.474	4.52	47	27	6	185.1	218	50	72	0	0	1	3	59	7	0	.119
1954 2 teams			PHI	N (8G 1–0)			CIN	N (22G 4–4)											
" total	5	4	.556	5.92	30	9	1	76	97	27	35	1	2	1	0	16	2	0	.125
8 yrs.	44	53	.454	4.76	218	107	26	826.2	913	332	322	7	11	7	7	254	21	0	.083
WORLD SERIES																			
1947 NY A	0	0	–	3.00	2	0	0	3	2	1	0	0	0	0	0	2	0	0	–

Denny Driscoll

DRISCOLL, JOHN F.
B. Nov. 19, 1855, Lowell, Mass.   D. July 11, 1886, Lowell, Mass.   5'10½" 160 lbs.

	W	L	PCT	ERA	G	GS	CG	IP	H	BB	SO	ShO	W	L	SV	AB	H	HR	BA
1880 BUF N	1	3	.250	3.89	6	4	4	41.2	48	9	17	0	0	0	0	65	10	0	.154
1882 PIT AA	13	9	.591	1.21	23	23	23	201	162	12	59	0	0	0	0	80	11	0	.138
1883	18	21	.462	3.99	41	40	35	336.1	427	39	79	1	0	0	0	148	27	0	.182
1884 LOU AA	6	6	.500	3.44	13	13	10	102	110	7	16	0	0	0	0	48	9	0	.188
1885 BUF N	0	0	–	0.00	0	0	0	0	0	0	0	0	0	0	0	19	3	0	.158
5 yrs.	38	39	.494	3.08	83	80	72	681	747	67	171	1	0	0	0	*			

Mike Driscoll

DRISCOLL, MICHAEL COLUMBUS
B. Oct. 19, 1892, Rockland, Mass.   D. Mar. 21, 1953, Foxboro, Mass.   BR TR 6'1"   160 lbs.

	W	L	PCT	ERA	G	GS	CG	IP	H	BB	SO	ShO	W	L	SV	AB	H	HR	BA
1916 PHI A	0	1	.000	5.40	1	0	0	5	6	2	0	0	0	1	0	2	0	0	.000

Tom Drohan

DROHAN, THOMAS F
B. Aug. 26, 1887, Fall River, Mass.   D. Sept. 17, 1926, Kewanee, Ill.   BR TR 5'10"   175 lbs.

	W	L	PCT	ERA	G	GS	CG	IP	H	BB	SO	ShO	W	L	SV	AB	H	HR	BA
1913 WAS A	0	0	–	9.00	2	0	0	2	5	0	2	0	0	0	0	0	0	0	–

	W	L	PCT	ERA	G	GS	CG	IP	H	BB	SO	ShO	Relief Pitching W	L	SV	BATTING AB	H	HR	BA

Dick Drott

DROTT, RICHARD FRED (Hummer)
B. July 1, 1936, Cincinnati, Ohio — BR TR 6' 185 lbs.

	W	L	PCT	ERA	G	GS	CG	IP	H	BB	SO	ShO	W	L	SV	AB	H	HR	BA
1957 CHI N	15	11	.577	3.58	38	32	7	229	200	129	170	3	2	0	0	80	8	0	.100
1958	7	11	.389	5.43	39	31	4	167.1	156	99	127	0	0	0	0	55	15	0	.273
1959	1	2	.333	5.93	8	6	1	27.1	25	26	15	1	0	0	0	8	1	0	.125
1960	0	6	.000	7.16	23	9	0	55.1	63	42	32	0	0	0	0	10	1	0	.100
1961	1	4	.200	4.22	35	8	0	98	75	51	48	0	1	1	0	22	6	0	.273
1962 HOU N	1	0	1.000	7.62	6	1	0	13	12	9	10	0	0	0	0	4	0	0	.000
1963	2	12	.143	4.98	27	14	2	97.2	95	49	58	1	0	2	0	23	3	0	.130
7 yrs.	27	46	.370	4.78	176	101	14	687.2	626	405	460	5	3	3	0	202	34	0	.168

Louis Drucke

DRUCKE, LOUIS FRANK
B. Dec. 3, 1888, Waco, Tex. D. Sept. 22, 1955, Waco, Tex. — BR TR 6'1" 188 lbs.

	W	L	PCT	ERA	G	GS	CG	IP	H	BB	SO	ShO	W	L	SV	AB	H	HR	BA
1909 NY N	2	1	.667	2.25	3	3	2	24	20	13	8	0	0	0	0	8	1	0	.125
1910	12	10	.545	2.47	34	27	15	215.1	174	82	151	0	1	0	0	70	15	1	.214
1911	4	4	.500	4.04	15	10	4	75.2	83	41	42	0	0	0	0	23	2	0	.087
1912	0	0	—	13.50	1	0	0	2	5	1	0	0	0	0	1	0	0	0	—
4 yrs.	18	15	.545	2.90	53	40	21	317	282	137	201	0	1	0	1	101	18	1	.178

Carl Druhot

DRUHOT, CARL A.
B. Sept. 1, 1882, Ohio D. Feb. 11, 1918, Portland, Ore. — BL TL 5'7" 150 lbs.

	W	L	PCT	ERA	G	GS	CG	IP	H	BB	SO	ShO	W	L	SV	AB	H	HR	BA
1906 2 teams			CIN N	(4G 2-2)		STL N	(15G 6-7)												
" total	8	9	.471	2.90	19	16	13	155.1	144	53	59	1	2	0	0	65	15	0	.231
1907 STL N	0	1	.000	15.43	1	1	0	2.1	3	4	1	0	0	0	0	0	0	0	—
2 yrs.	8	10	.444	3.08	20	17	13	157.2	147	57	60	1	2	0	0	65	15	0	.231

Don Drysdale

DRYSDALE, DONALD SCOTT (Big D)
B. July 23, 1936, Van Nuys, Calif. — BR TR 6'5" 190 lbs.
Hall of Fame 1984.

	W	L	PCT	ERA	G	GS	CG	IP	H	BB	SO	ShO	W	L	SV	AB	H	HR	BA
1956 BKN N	5	5	.500	2.64	25	12	2	99	95	31	55	0	1	0	0	26	5	1	.192
1957	17	9	.654	2.69	34	29	9	221	197	61	148	4	2	1	0	73	9	2	.123
1958 LA N	12	13	.480	4.17	44	29	6	211.2	214	72	131	1	1	1	0	66	15	7	.227
1959	17	13	.567	3.46	44	36	15	270.2	237	93	242	4	1	2	2	91	15	4	.165
1960	15	14	.517	2.84	41	36	15	269	214	72	246	5	1	1	2	83	13	0	.157
1961	13	10	.565	3.69	40	37	10	244	236	83	182	3	0	0	0	83	16	5	.193
1962	25	9	.735	2.83	43	41	19	314.1	272	78	232	2	0	1	1	111	22	0	.198
1963	19	17	.528	2.63	42	42	17	315.1	287	57	251	3	0	0	0	96	16	0	.167
1964	18	16	.529	2.18	40	40	21	321.1	242	68	237	5	0	0	0	110	19	1	.173
1965	23	12	.657	2.77	44	42	20	308.1	270	66	210	7	0	0	1	130	39	7	.300
1966	13	16	.448	3.42	40	40	11	273.2	279	45	177	3	0	0	0	106	20	2	.189
1967	13	16	.448	2.74	38	38	9	282	269	60	196	3	0	0	0	93	12	0	.129
1968	14	12	.538	2.15	31	31	12	239	201	56	155	8	0	0	0	79	14	0	.177
1969	5	4	.556	4.43	12	12	1	63	71	13	24	1	0	0	0	22	3	0	.136
14 yrs.	209	166	.557	2.95	518	465	167	3432.1	3084	855	2486	49	6	6	6	1169	218	29	.186

WORLD SERIES

	W	L	PCT	ERA	G	GS	CG	IP	H	BB	SO	ShO	W	L	SV	AB	H	HR	BA
1956 BKN N	0	0	—	9.00	1	0	0	2	2	1	1	0	0	0	0	0	0	0	
1959 LA N	1	0	1.000	1.29	1	1	0	7	11	4	5	0	0	0	0	2	0	0	.000
1963	1	0	1.000	0.00	1	1	1	9	3	1	9	1	0	0	0	1	0	0	.000
1965	1	1	.500	3.86	2	2	1	11.2	12	3	15	0	0	0	0	5	0	0	.000
1966	0	2	.000	4.50	2	2	1	10	8	3	6	0	0	0	0	2	0	0	.000
5 yrs.	3	3	.500	2.95	7	6	3	39.2	36	12	36	1	0	0	0	10	0	0	.000

Monk Dubiel

DUBIEL, WALTER JOHN
B. Feb. 12, 1919, Hartford, Conn. D. Oct. 25, 1969, Hartford, Conn. — BR TR 6' 190 lbs.

	W	L	PCT	ERA	G	GS	CG	IP	H	BB	SO	ShO	W	L	SV	AB	H	HR	BA
1944 NY A	13	13	.500	3.38	30	28	19	232	217	86	79	3	1	0	0	83	15	0	.181
1945	10	9	.526	4.64	26	20	9	151.1	157	62	45	1	1	1	0	58	16	1	.276
1948 PHI N	8	10	.444	3.89	37	17	6	150.1	139	58	42	2	1	3	4	42	7	0	.167
1949 CHI N	6	9	.400	4.14	32	20	3	147.2	142	54	52	1	1	1	4	35	10	0	.286
1950	6	10	.375	4.16	39	12	4	142.2	152	67	51	2	3	3	2	45	9	0	.200
1951	2	2	.500	2.30	22	0	0	54.2	46	22	19	0	2	1	1	12	0	0	.000
1952	0	0	—	0.00	1	0	0	.2	1	0	1	0	0	0	0	0	0	0	—
7 yrs.	45	53	.459	3.87	187	97	41	879.1	854	349	289	9	9	10	11	275	57	1	.207

Jean Dubuc

DUBUC, JEAN JOSEPH OCTAVE (Chauncey)
Born Jean Baptiste Arthur Dubuc.
B. Sept. 15, 1888, St. Johnsbury, Vt. D. Aug. 29, 1958, Ft. Myers, Fla. — BR TR 5'10½" 185 lbs.

	W	L	PCT	ERA	G	GS	CG	IP	H	BB	SO	ShO	W	L	SV	AB	H	HR	BA
1908 CIN N	5	6	.455	2.74	15	9	7	85.1	62	41	32	1	2	0	0	29	4	0	.138
1909	3	5	.375	3.66	19	5	2	71.1	72	46	19	0	2	2	2	18	3	0	.167
1912 DET A	17	10	.630	2.77	37	26	23	250	217	109	97	2	1	1	3	108	29	1	.269
1913	15	14	.517	2.89	36	28	22	242.2	228	91	73	1	0	2	2	135	36	2	.267
1914	13	14	.481	3.46	36	27	15	224	216	76	70	2	2	0	1	124	28	1	.226
1915	17	12	.586	3.21	39	33	22	258	231	88	74	5	0	2	2	112	23	0	.205
1916	10	10	.500	2.96	36	16	8	170.1	134	84	40	1	5	2	1	78	20	0	.256
1918 BOS A	0	1	.000	4.22	2	1	1	10.2	11	5	1	0	0	0	0	6	1	0	.167
1919 NY N	6	4	.600	2.66	36	5	1	132	119	37	32	0	6	4	3	42	6	0	.143
9 yrs.	86	76	.531	3.04	256	150	101	1444.1	1290	577	438	12	18	13	14	*			

Jim Duckworth

DUCKWORTH, JAMES RAYMOND
B. May 24, 1939, National City, Calif. — BR TR 6'4" 194 lbs.

	W	L	PCT	ERA	G	GS	CG	IP	H	BB	SO	ShO	W	L	SV	AB	H	HR	BA
1963 WAS A	4	12	.250	6.04	37	15	2	120.2	131	67	66	0	2	3	0	27	0	0	.000
1964	1	6	.143	4.34	30	2	0	56	52	25	56	0	1	4	3	9	2	0	.222
1965	2	2	.500	3.94	17	8	0	64	45	36	74	0	0	0	0	18	0	0	.000
1966 2 teams			WAS	A (5G 0-3)		KC	A (8G 0-2)												
" total	0	5	.000	6.84	13	4	0	26.1	28	20	24	0	0	2	1	5	0	0	.000
4 yrs.	7	25	.219	5.26	97	29	2	267	256	148	220	0	3	9	4	59	2	0	.034

	W	L	PCT	ERA	G	GS	CG	IP	H	BB	SO	ShO	Relief Pitching W	L	SV	BATTING AB	H	HR	BA

Clise Dudley

DUDLEY, ELZIE CLISE   BL TR 6'1"   195 lbs.
B. Aug. 8, 1903, Graham, N. C.

	W	L	PCT	ERA	G	GS	CG	IP	H	BB	SO	ShO	W	L	SV	AB	H	HR	BA
1929 BKN N	6	14	.300	5.69	35	21	8	156.2	202	64	33	1	1	2	0	51	5	2	.098
1930	2	4	.333	6.35	21	7	2	66.2	103	27	18	0	0	0	1	24	5	0	.208
1931 PHI N	8	14	.364	3.52	30	24	8	179	206	56	50	0	0	0	0	84	18	0	.214
1932	1	1	.500	7.13	13	0	0	17.2	23	8	5	0	1	1	1	14	4	1	.286
1933 PIT N	0	0	—	135.00	1	0	0	.1	6	1	0	0	0	0	0	0	0	0	—
5 yrs.	17	33	.340	5.03	100	52	18	420.1	540	156	106	1	2	3	2	173	32	3	.185

Hal Dues

DUES, HAL JOSEPH   BR TR 6'3"   180 lbs.
B. Sept. 22, 1954, LaMarque, Tex.

	W	L	PCT	ERA	G	GS	CG	IP	H	BB	SO	ShO	W	L	SV	AB	H	HR	BA
1977 MON N	1	1	.500	4.30	6	4	0	23	26	9	9	0	0	0	0	5	0	0	.000
1978	5	6	.455	2.36	25	12	1	99	85	42	36	0	1	1	1	31	6	0	.194
1980	0	1	.000	6.75	6	1	0	12	17	4	2	0	0	1	0	3	0	0	.000
3 yrs.	6	8	.429	3.09	37	17	1	134	128	55	47	0	1	2	1	39	6	0	.154

Larry Duff

DUFF, CECIL ELBA   BL TR 6'1"   175 lbs.
B. Nov. 30, 1896, Radersburg, Mont.   D. Nov. 10, 1969, Bend, Ore.

	W	L	PCT	ERA	G	GS	CG	IP	H	BB	SO	ShO	W	L	SV	AB	H	HR	BA
1922 CHI A	1	1	.500	4.97	3	1	2	12.2	16	3	7	0	1	0	0	5	2	0	.400

Jim Duffalo

DUFFALO, JAMES FRANCIS   BR TR 6'1"   175 lbs.
B. Nov. 25, 1935, Helvetia, Pa.

	W	L	PCT	ERA	G	GS	CG	IP	H	BB	SO	ShO	W	L	SV	AB	H	HR	BA
1961 SF N	5	1	.833	4.23	24	4	1	61.2	59	32	37	0	3	0	1	17	5	1	.294
1962	1	2	.333	3.64	24	2	0	42	42	23	29	0	1	1	0	6	0	0	.000
1963	4	2	.667	2.87	34	5	0	75.1	56	37	55	0	3	0	2	18	2	0	.111
1964	5	1	.833	2.92	35	3	1	74	57	31	55	0	4	1	3	14	1	0	.071
1965 2 teams			SF	N	(2G 0–1)		CIN	N	(22G 0–1)										
" total	0	2	.000	3.63	24	0	0	44.2	34	32	34	0	0	2	0	8	0	0	.000
5 yrs.	15	8	.652	3.39	141	14	2	297.2	248	155	210	0	11	4	6	63	8	1	.127

John Duffie

DUFFIE, JOHN BROWN   BR TR 6'7"   210 lbs.
B. Oct. 4, 1945, Greenwood, S. C.

	W	L	PCT	ERA	G	GS	CG	IP	H	BB	SO	ShO	W	L	SV	AB	H	HR	BA
1967 LA N	0	2	.000	2.79	2	2	0	9.2	11	4	6	0	0	0	0	2	0	0	.000

Bernie Duffy

DUFFY, BERNARD ALLEN   BR TR 5'11"   180 lbs.
B. Aug. 18, 1893, Vinson, Okla.   D. Feb. 9, 1962, Abilene, Tex.

	W	L	PCT	ERA	G	GS	CG	IP	H	BB	SO	ShO	W	L	SV	AB	H	HR	BA
1913 PIT N	0	0	—	5.56	3	2	0	11.1	18	3	8	0	0	0	0	4	1	0	.250

Dan Dugan

DUGAN, DANIEL PHILLIP   BL TL 6'1½"   187 lbs.
B. Feb. 22, 1907, Plainfield, N. J.   D. June 25, 1968, Greenbrook, N. J.

	W	L	PCT	ERA	G	GS	CG	IP	H	BB	SO	ShO	W	L	SV	AB	H	HR	BA
1928 CHI A	0	0	—	0.00	1	0	0	.1	0	0	0	0	0	0	0	0	0	0	—
1929	1	4	.200	6.65	19	2	0	65	77	19	15	0	1	2	1	20	3	0	.150
2 yrs.	1	4	.200	6.61	20	2	0	65.1	77	19	15	0	1	2	1	20	3	0	.150

Ed Dugan

DUGAN, EDWARD JOHN   TR
Brother of Bill Dugan.
B. 1864, Brooklyn, N. Y.   D. July 19, 1943, Sea Cliff, N. J.

	W	L	PCT	ERA	G	GS	CG	IP	H	BB	SO	ShO	W	L	SV	AB	H	HR	BA
1884 RIC AA	5	14	.263	4.49	20	20	20	166.1	196	15	60	0	0	0	0	76	8	0	.105

Bill Duggleby

DUGGLEBY, WILLIAM JAMES (Frosty Bill)   TR
B. Mar. 16, 1874, Utica, N. Y.   D. Aug. 30, 1944, Redfield, N. Y.

	W	L	PCT	ERA	G	GS	CG	IP	H	BB	SO	ShO	W	L	SV	AB	H	HR	BA
1898 PHI N	3	3	.500	5.50	9	5	4	54	70	18	12	0	1	0	0	21	5	1	.238
1901	19	12	.613	2.87	34	28	25	275.2	294	40	94	5	1	1	0	111	19	0	.171
1902 2 teams			PHI	A	(2G 1–1)		PHI	N	(33G 11–17)										
" total	12	18	.400	3.36	35	30	27	275.2	301	61	64	0	1	0	0	105	17	0	.162
1903 PHI N	13	18	.419	3.75	36	30	28	264.1	318	79	57	3	1	0	1	104	24	0	.231
1904	12	13	.480	3.78	32	27	22	223.2	265	53	55	2	1	1	1	82	14	2	.171
1905	18	17	.514	2.46	38	36	27	289	270	83	75	1	1	1	0	101	11	1	.109
1906	13	19	.406	2.25	42	30	22	280.1	241	66	83	5	1	2	2	99	14	2	.141
1907 2 teams			PHI	N	(5G 0–2)		PIT	N	(9G 2–2)										
" total	2	4	.333	4.67	14	5	3	69.1	77	23	12	1	1	0	0	22	3	0	.136
8 yrs.	92	104	.469	3.19	240	191	158	1732	1836	423	452	17	8	5	4	645	107	6	.166

Martin Duke

DUKE, MARTIN F.   TL
B. Columbus, Ohio   D. Dec. 31, 1898, Minneapolis, Minn.

	W	L	PCT	ERA	G	GS	CG	IP	H	BB	SO	ShO	W	L	SV	AB	H	HR	BA
1891 WAS AA	0	3	.000	7.43	4	3	2	23	36	19	5	0	0	0	0	9	1	0	.111

Jan Dukes

DUKES, JAN NOBLE   BL TL 5'11"   175 lbs.
B. Aug. 16, 1945, Cheyenne, Wyo.

	W	L	PCT	ERA	G	GS	CG	IP	H	BB	SO	ShO	W	L	SV	AB	H	HR	BA
1969 WAS A	0	2	.000	2.45	8	0	0	11	8	4	3	0	0	2	0	1	0	0	.000
1970	0	0	—	2.57	5	0	0	7	6	1	4	0	0	0	0	1	0	0	.000
1972 TEX A	0	0	—	4.50	3	0	0	2	1	5	0	0	0	0	0	0	0	0	—
3 yrs.	0	2	.000	2.70	16	0	0	20	15	10	7	0	0	2	0	2	0	0	.000

Tom Dukes

DUKES, THOMAS EARL   BR TR 6'2"   185 lbs.
B. Aug. 31, 1942, Knoxville, Tenn.

	W	L	PCT	ERA	G	GS	CG	IP	H	BB	SO	ShO	W	L	SV	AB	H	HR	BA
1967 HOU N	0	2	.000	5.32	17	0	0	23.2	25	11	23	0	0	2	1	2	1	0	.500
1968	2	2	.500	4.27	43	0	0	52.2	62	28	37	0	2	2	4	4	0	0	.000
1969 SD N	1	0	1.000	7.36	13	0	0	22	26	10	15	0	1	0	1	1	0	0	.000
1970	1	6	.143	4.04	53	0	0	69	62	25	56	0	1	6	10	7	0	0	.000
1971 BAL A	1	5	.167	3.55	28	0	0	38	40	8	30	0	1	5	4	7	1	0	.143
1972 CAL A	0	1	.000	1.64	7	0	0	11	11	0	8	0	0	1	1	0	0	0	—
6 yrs.	5	16	.238	4.37	161	0	0	216.1	226	82	169	0	5	16	21	21	2	0	.095

WORLD SERIES

	W	L	PCT	ERA	G	GS	CG	IP	H	BB	SO	ShO	W	L	SV	AB	H	HR	BA
1971 BAL A	0	0	—	0.00	2	0	0	4	2	0	1	0	0	0	0	0	0	0	—

	W	L	PCT	ERA	G	GS	CG	IP	H	BB	SO	ShO	Relief Pitching W	L	SV	BATTING AB	H	HR	BA

Bob Duliba

DULIBA, ROBERT JOHN
B. Jan. 9, 1935, Glen Lyon, Pa. BR TR 5'10" 180 lbs.

	W	L	PCT	ERA	G	GS	CG	IP	H	BB	SO	ShO	W	L	SV	AB	H	HR	BA
1959 STL N	0	1	.000	2.78	11	0	0	22.2	19	12	14	0	0	1	1	4	0	0	.000
1960	4	4	.500	4.20	27	0	0	40.2	49	16	23	0	4	4	0	5	1	0	.200
1962	2	0	1.000	2.06	28	0	0	39.1	33	17	22	0	2	0	2	4	0	0	.000
1963 LA A	1	1	.500	1.17	6	0	0	7.2	3	6	4	0	1	1	1	1	0	0	.000
1964	6	4	.600	3.59	58	0	0	72.2	80	22	33	0	6	4	9	5	0	0	.000
1965 BOS A	4	2	.667	3.78	39	0	0	64.1	60	22	27	0	4	2	1	7	0	0	.000
1967 KC A	0	0	—	6.52	7	0	0	9.2	13	1	6	0	0	0	0	0	0	0	—
7 yrs.	17	12	.586	3.47	176	0	0	257	257	96	129	0	17	12	14	26	1	0	.038

George Dumont

DUMONT, GEORGE HENRY (Pea Soup)
B. Nov. 13, 1895, Minneapolis, Minn. D. Oct. 13, 1956, Minneapolis, Minn. BR TR 5'11" 163 lbs.

	W	L	PCT	ERA	G	GS	CG	IP	H	BB	SO	ShO	W	L	SV	AB	H	HR	BA
1915 WAS A	2	1	.667	2.03	6	4	3	40	23	12	18	2	0	0	0	12	2	0	.167
1916	2	3	.400	3.06	17	5	2	53	37	17	21	0	0	1	1	14	1	0	.071
1917	5	14	.263	2.55	37	23	8	204.2	171	76	65	2	2	1	2	58	2	0	.034
1918	1	1	.500	5.14	4	1	1	14	18	6	12	0	1	0	0	3	1	0	.333
1919 BOS A	0	4	.000	4.33	13	2	0	35.1	45	19	12	0	0	3	0	7	0	0	.000
5 yrs.	10	23	.303	2.85	77	35	14	347	294	130	128	4	3	5	3	94	6	0	.064

Dan Dumoulin

DUMOULIN, DANIEL LYNN
B. Aug. 20, 1953, Kokomo, Ind. BR TR 6' 175 lbs.

	W	L	PCT	ERA	G	GS	CG	IP	H	BB	SO	ShO	W	L	SV	AB	H	HR	BA
1977 CIN N	0	0	—	14.40	5	0	0	5	12	3	5	0	0	0	0	0	0	0	—
1978	1	0	1.000	1.80	3	0	0	5	7	3	2	0	1	0	0	0	0	0	—
2 yrs.	1	0	1.000	8.10	8	0	0	10	19	6	7	0	1	0	0	0	0	0	—

Nick Dumovich

DUMOVICH, NICHOLAS
B. Jan. 2, 1902, Sacramento, Calif. D. Dec., 1979, Laguna Hills, Calif. BL TL 6' 170 lbs.

	W	L	PCT	ERA	G	GS	CG	IP	H	BB	SO	ShO	W	L	SV	AB	H	HR	BA
1923 CHI N	3	5	.375	4.60	28	8	1	94	118	45	23	0	2	1	1	29	7	0	.241

Ed Dundon

DUNDON, EDWARD JOSEPH (Dummy)
B. July 10, 1859, Columbus, Ohio D. Aug. 18, 1893, Columbus, Ohio

	W	L	PCT	ERA	G	GS	CG	IP	H	BB	SO	ShO	W	L	SV	AB	H	HR	BA
1883 COL AA	3	16	.158	4.48	20	19	16	166.2	213	38	31	0	0	0	0	93	15	0	.161
1884	6	4	.600	3.78	11	9	7	81	85	15	37	0	1	0	0	86	12	0	.140
2 yrs.	9	20	.310	4.25	31	28	23	247.2	298	53	68	0	1	0	0	*			

Jim Dunegan

DUNEGAN, JAMES WILLIAM JR
B. Aug. 6, 1947, Burlington, Iowa BR TR 6'1" 205 lbs.

	W	L	PCT	ERA	G	GS	CG	IP	H	BB	SO	ShO	W	L	SV	AB	H	HR	BA
1970 CHI N	0	2	.000	4.85	7	0	0	13	13	12	3	0	0	2	0	4	1	0	.250

Wiley Dunham

DUNHAM, HENRY HUSTON
B. Jan. 30, 1877, Piketon, Ohio D. Jan. 16, 1934, Cleveland, Ohio 6'1" 180 lbs.

	W	L	PCT	ERA	G	GS	CG	IP	H	BB	SO	ShO	W	L	SV	AB	H	HR	BA
1902 STL N	2	3	.400	5.68	7	5	3	38	47	13	15	0	0	0	1	12	1	0	.083

Davey Dunkle

DUNKLE, EDWARD PERKS
B. Aug. 19, 1872, Philipsburg, Pa. D. Nov. 19, 1941, Lock Haven, Pa. BB TR 6'2" 220 lbs.

	W	L	PCT	ERA	G	GS	CG	IP	H	BB	SO	ShO	W	L	SV	AB	H	HR	BA
1897 PHI N	5	2	.714	3.48	7	7	7	62	72	23	9	0	0	0	0	23	4	0	.174
1898	1	4	.200	6.98	12	7	4	68.1	83	38	21	0	0	0	0	28	6	0	.214
1899 WAS N	0	2	.000	10.04	4	2	2	26	46	14	9	0	0	0	0	11	3	0	.273
1903 2 teams					CHI	(12G 4–4)		WAS	A	(14G 5–9)									
" total	9	13	.409	4.16	26	20	16	190.1	207	64	77	0	2	0	1	74	14	0	.189
1904 WAS A	2	9	.182	4.96	12	11	7	74.1	95	23	23	0	0	0	0	28	4	0	.143
5 yrs.	17	30	.362	5.02	61	47	36	421	503	162	139	0	2	0	1	164	31	0	.189

Fred Dunlap

DUNLAP, FREDERICK C. (Sure Shot)
B. May 21, 1859, Philadelphia, Pa. D. Dec. 1, 1902, Philadelphia, Pa. BR TR 5'8" 165 lbs.
Manager 1889.

	W	L	PCT	ERA	G	GS	CG	IP	H	BB	SO	ShO	W	L	SV	AB	H	HR	BA
1884 STL U	0	0	—	13.50	1	0	0	.2	2	0	1	0	0	0	1	449	185	13	.412
1887 DET N	0	0	—	4.50	1	0	0	2	4	0	1	0	0	0	0	272	72	5	.265
2 yrs.	0	0	—	6.75	2	0	0	2.2	6	0	2	0	0	0	1	*			

Jack Dunleavy

DUNLEAVY, JOHN FRANCIS
B. Sept. 14, 1879, Harrison, N. J. D. Apr. 12, 1944, South Norwalk, Conn. 5'6½" 145 lbs.

	W	L	PCT	ERA	G	GS	CG	IP	H	BB	SO	ShO	W	L	SV	AB	H	HR	BA
1903 STL N	6	8	.429	4.06	14	13	9	102	101	57	51	0	1	0	0	193	48	0	.249
1904	1	4	.200	4.42	7	5	5	55	63	23	28	0	0	0	0	172	40	1	.233
2 yrs.	7	12	.368	4.18	21	18	14	157	164	80	79	0	1	0	0	*			

Jack Dunn

DUNN, JOHN JOSEPH
B. Oct. 6, 1872, Meadville, Pa. D. Oct. 22, 1928, Towson, Md. BR TR 5'9"

	W	L	PCT	ERA	G	GS	CG	IP	H	BB	SO	ShO	W	L	SV	AB	H	HR	BA
1897 BKN N	14	9	.609	4.57	25	21	21	216.2	251	66	26	0	1	1	0	131	29	0	.221
1898	16	21	.432	3.60	41	37	31	322.2	352	82	66	0	2	0	0	167	41	0	.246
1899	23	13	.639	3.70	41	34	29	299.1	323	86	48	2	2	1	2	122	30	0	.246
1900 2 teams					BKN	N	(10G 3–4)	PHI	N	(10G 5–5)									
" total	8	9	.471	5.16	20	16	14	143	175	57	18	1	1	1	0	59	16	0	.271
1901 2 teams					PHI	N	(2G 0–1)	BAL	A	(9G 3–3)									
" total	3	4	.429	4.90	11	8	6	64.1	85	28	6	0	0	0	0	363	91	0	.251
1902 NY N	0	3	.000	3.71	3	2	2	26.2	28	12	6	0	0	1	0	342	72	0	.211
1904	0	0	—	4.50	1	0	0	4	3	3	3	0	0	0	1	181	56	1	.309
7 yrs.	64	59	.520	4.11	142	118	103	1076.2	1217	334	171	3	6	4	3	*			

Jim Dunn

DUNN, JAMES WILLIAM (Bill)
B. Feb. 25, 1931, Valdosta, Ga. BR TR 6'½" 185 lbs.

	W	L	PCT	ERA	G	GS	CG	IP	H	BB	SO	ShO	W	L	SV	AB	H	HR	BA
1952 PIT N	0	0	—	3.38	3	0	0	5.1	4	3	2	0	0	0	0	1	0	0	.000

	W	L	PCT	ERA	G	GS	CG	IP	H	BB	SO	ShO	Relief Pitching W	L	SV	AB	H	HR	BA

Andy Dunning

DUNNING, ANDREW JACKSON BR TR 6' 175 lbs.
B. Aug. 12, 1871, New York, N. Y. D. June 21, 1952, New York, N. Y.

	W	L	PCT	ERA	G	GS	CG	IP	H	BB	SO	ShO	W	L	SV	AB	H	HR	BA
1889 PIT N	0	2	.000	7.00	2	2	1	18	20	16	4	0	0	0	0	7	0	0	.000
1891 NY N	0	1	.000	4.50	1	1	0	2	3	3	2	0	0	0	0	0	0	0	—
2 yrs.	0	3	.000	6.75	3	3	2	20	23	19	6	0	0	0	0	7	0	0	.000

Steve Dunning

DUNNING, STEVEN JOHN BR TR 6'2" 205 lbs.
B. May 15, 1949, Denver, Colo.

	W	L	PCT	ERA	G	GS	CG	IP	H	BB	SO	ShO	W	L	SV	AB	H	HR	BA
1970 CLE A	4	9	.308	4.98	19	17	0	94	93	54	77	0	0	0	0	31	5	0	.161
1971	8	14	.364	4.50	31	29	3	184	173	109	132	1	0	0	1	55	10	1	.182
1972	6	4	.600	3.26	16	16	1	105	98	43	52	0	0	0	0	33	9	3	.273
1973 2 teams				CLE A (4G 0–2)				TEX A (23G 2–6)											
" total	2	8	.200	5.53	27	15	2	112.1	118	65	48	0	0	0	0	0	0	0	—
1974 TEX A	0	0	—	22.50	1	0	0	2	3	3	1	0	0	0	0	0	0	0	—
1976 2 teams				CAL A (4G 0–0)				MON N (32G 2–6)											
" total	2	6	.250	4.35	36	7	1	97.1	102	39	76	0	0	2	0	15	2	0	.133
1977 OAK A	1	0	1.000	4.00	6	0	0	18	17	10	4	0	1	0	0	0	0	0	—
7 yrs.	23	41	.359	4.57	136	84	7	612.2	604	323	390	1	1	2	1	134	26	4	.194

Frank Dupee

DUPEE, FRANK OLIVER 6'1" 200 lbs.
B. Apr. 29, 1877, Monkton, Vt. D. Aug. 14, 1956, Portland, Me.

	W	L	PCT	ERA	G	GS	CG	IP	H	BB	SO	ShO	W	L	SV	AB	H	HR	BA
1901 CHI A	0	1	.000	∞	1	1	0	0	0	3	0	0	0	0	0	0	0	0	—

Mike Dupree

DUPREE, MICHAEL DENNIS BR TR 6'1" 185 lbs.
B. May 29, 1953, Kansas City, Kans.

	W	L	PCT	ERA	G	GS	CG	IP	H	BB	SO	ShO	W	L	SV	AB	H	HR	BA
1976 SD N	0	0	—	9.19	12	0	0	15.2	18	7	5	0	0	0	0	1	1	0	1.000

Kid Durbin

DURBIN, BLAINE ALPHONSUS BL TL 5'8" 155 lbs.
B. Sept. 10, 1886, Lamar, Kans. D. Sept. 11, 1943, Kirkwood, Mo.

	W	L	PCT	ERA	G	GS	CG	IP	H	BB	SO	ShO	W	L	SV	AB	H	HR	BA
1907 CHI N	0	1	.000	5.40	5	1	1	16.2	14	10	5	0	0	0	1	*			

Ryne Duren

DUREN, RINOLD GEORGE BR TR 6'2" 190 lbs.
B. Feb. 22, 1929, Cazenovia, Wis.

	W	L	PCT	ERA	G	GS	CG	IP	H	BB	SO	ShO	W	L	SV	AB	H	HR	BA
1954 BAL A	0	0	—	9.00	1	0	0	2	3	1	2	0	0	0	0	0	0	0	—
1957 KC A	0	3	.000	5.27	14	6	0	42.2	37	30	37	0	0	0	1	14	1	0	.071
1958 NY A	6	4	.600	2.02	44	1	0	75.2	40	43	87	0	6	4	20	13	1	0	.077
1959	3	6	.333	1.88	41	0	0	76.2	49	43	96	0	3	6	14	14	0	0	.000
1960	3	4	.429	4.96	42	1	0	49	27	49	67	0	3	4	9	6	0	0	.000
1961 2 teams				NY A (4G 0–1)				LA A (40G 6–12)											
" total	6	13	.316	5.19	44	14	1	104	89	79	115	1	4	9	2	25	1	0	.040
1962 LA A	2	9	.182	4.42	42	3	0	71.1	53	57	74	0	2	8	8	15	1	0	.067
1963 PHI N	6	2	.750	3.30	33	7	1	87.1	65	52	84	0	3	1	2	21	3	0	.143
1964 2 teams				PHI N (2G 0–0)				CIN N (26G 0–2)											
" total	0	2	.000	3.09	28	0	0	46.2	46	16	44	0	0	2	1	0	0	0	.000
1965 2 teams				PHI N (6G 0–0)				WAS N (16G 1–1)											
" total	1	1	.500	5.56	22	0	0	34	34	22	24	0	1	1	0	1	0	0	.000
10 yrs.	27	44	.380	3.83	311	32	2	589.1	443	392	630	1	22	35	57	114	7	0	.061
WORLD SERIES																			
1958 NY A	1	1	.500	1.93	3	0	0	9.1	7	6	14	0	1	1	1	3	0	0	.000
1960	0	0	—	2.25	2	0	0	4	2	1	5	0	0	0	0	0	0	0	—
2 yrs.	1	1	.500	2.03	5	0	0	13.1	9	7	19	0	1	1	1	3	0	0	.000

Bull Durham

DURHAM, LOUIS STAUB (Judge, Whitey) TR 5'10"
Born Louis Raphael Staub.
B. June 27, 1877, New Oxford, Pa. D. June 28, 1960, Bentley, Kans.

	W	L	PCT	ERA	G	GS	CG	IP	H	BB	SO	ShO	W	L	SV	AB	H	HR	BA
1904 BKN N	1	0	1.000	3.27	2	2	1	11	10	5	1	0	0	0	0	4	1	0	.250
1907 WAS A	0	0	—	12.60	2	0	0	5	10	4	1	0	0	0	0	1	0	0	.000
1908 NY N	0	0	—	9.00	1	0	0	2	2	1	2	0	0	0	0	0	0	0	—
1909	0	0	—	3.27	4	0	0	11	15	2	2	0	0	0	1	2	0	0	.000
4 yrs.	1	0	1.000	5.28	9	2	1	29	37	12	6	0	0	0	1	7	1	0	.143

Don Durham

DURHAM, DONALD GARY (Bull) BR TR 6' 170 lbs.
B. Mar. 21, 1949, Yosemite, Ky.

	W	L	PCT	ERA	G	GS	CG	IP	H	BB	SO	ShO	W	L	SV	AB	H	HR	BA
1972 STL N	2	7	.222	4.34	10	8	1	47.2	42	22	35	0	0	1	0	14	7	2	.500
1973 TEX A	0	4	.000	7.65	15	4	0	40	49	23	23	0	0	0	1	0	0	0	—
2 yrs.	2	11	.154	5.85	25	12	1	87.2	91	45	58	0	0	1	1	14	7	2	.500

Ed Durham

DURHAM, EDWARD FANT (Bull) BL TR 5'11" 170 lbs.
B. Aug. 17, 1907, Chester, S. C. D. Apr. 27, 1976, Chester, S. C.

	W	L	PCT	ERA	G	GS	CG	IP	H	BB	SO	ShO	W	L	SV	AB	H	HR	BA
1929 BOS A	1	0	1.000	9.27	14	1	0	22.1	34	14	6	0	0	0	0	4	0	0	.000
1930	4	15	.211	4.69	33	12	6	140	144	43	28	1	2	5	1	41	4	0	.098
1931	8	10	.444	4.25	38	15	7	165.1	175	50	53	2	2	3	0	54	3	0	.056
1932	6	13	.316	3.80	34	22	4	175.1	187	49	52	0	2	1	0	57	7	0	.123
1933 CHI A	10	6	.625	4.48	24	21	6	138.2	137	46	65	0	1	0	0	46	10	0	.217
5 yrs.	29	44	.397	4.45	143	71	23	641.2	677	202	204	3	7	9	1	202	24	0	.119

Jimmy Durham

DURHAM, JAMES GARFIELD BR TR 6' 175 lbs.
B. Oct. 7, 1881, Douglass, Kans. D. May 7, 1949, Coffeyville, Kans.

	W	L	PCT	ERA	G	GS	CG	IP	H	BB	SO	ShO	W	L	SV	AB	H	HR	BA
1902 CHI A	1	1	.500	5.85	3	3	3	20	21	16	3	0	0	0	0	15	1	0	.067

Dick Durning

DURNING, RICHARD KNOTT BL TL 6'2" 178 lbs.
B. Oct. 10, 1892, Louisville, Ky. D. Sept. 23, 1948, Castle Point, N. Y.

	W	L	PCT	ERA	G	GS	CG	IP	H	BB	SO	ShO	W	L	SV	AB	H	HR	BA
1917 BKN N	0	0	—	0.00	1	0	0	1	0	0	0	0	0	0	0	0	0	0	—
1918	0	0	—	13.50	1	0	0	2	3	4	0	0	0	0	0	0	0	0	—
2 yrs.	0	0	—	9.00	2	0	0	3	3	4	0	0	0	0	0	0	0	0	—

	W	L	PCT	ERA	G	GS	CG	IP	H	BB	SO	ShO	Relief Pitching W	L	SV	BATTING AB	H	HR	BA

Jesse Duryea

DURYEA, JAMES WHITNEY (Cyclone Jim)
B. Sept. 7, 1862, Osage, Iowa   D. Aug. 7, 1942, Algona, Iowa   BR TR 5'10"   175 lbs.

	W	L	PCT	ERA	G	GS	CG	IP	H	BB	SO	ShO	W	L	SV	AB	H	HR	BA
1889 CIN AA	32	19	.627	2.56	53	48	38	401	372	127	183	2	2	2	1	162	44	0	.272
1890 CIN N	16	12	.571	2.92	33	32	29	274	270	60	108	2	0	0	0	99	15	1	.152
1891 2 teams	CIN	N	(10G 1–9)		STL	AA	(3G 1–1)												
" total	0	10	.167	4.90	13	13	10	101	120	35	36	0	0	0	0	43	5	0	.116
1892 2 teams	CIN	N	(9G 2–5)		WAS	N	(18G 3–10)												
" total	5	15	.250	2.82	27	22	18	195	157	71	69	1	1	1	2	77	9	0	.117
1893 WAS N	4	10	.286	7.54	17	15	9	117	182	56	20	0	0	1	0	47	13	0	.277
5 yrs.	59	66	.472	3.45	143	130	104	1088	1101	349	416	5	3	4	3	428	86	1	.201

Erv Dusak

DUSAK, ERVIN FRANK (Four Sack)
B. July 29, 1920, Chicago, Ill.   BR TR 6'2"   185 lbs.

	W	L	PCT	ERA	G	GS	CG	IP	H	BB	SO	ShO	W	L	SV	AB	H	HR	BA
1948 STL N	0	0	—	0.00	1	0	0	1	0	1	0	0	0	0	0	311	65	6	.209
1950	0	2	.000	3.72	14	2	0	36.1	27	27	16	0	0	0	0	12	1	0	.083
1951 2 teams	STL	N	(5G 0–0)		PIT	N	(3G 0–1)												
" total	0	1	.000	9.18	8	1	0	16.2	24	16	10	0	0	0	1	41	13	2	.317
3 yrs.	0	3	.000	5.33	23	3	0	54	51	44	26	0	0	0	1	*			

Carl Duser

DUSER, CARL ROBERT
B. July 22, 1932, Hazleton, Pa.   BL TL 6'1"   175 lbs.

	W	L	PCT	ERA	G	GS	CG	IP	H	BB	SO	ShO	W	L	SV	AB	H	HR	BA
1956 KC A	1	1	.500	9.00	2	2	0	6	14	2	5	0	0	0	0	3	0	0	.000
1958	0	0		4.50	1	0	0	2	5	1	0	0	0	0	0	0	0	0	
2 yrs.	1	1	.500	7.88	3	2	0	8	19	3	5	0	0	0	0	3	0	0	.000

Bob Dustal

DUSTAL, ROBERT ANDREW
B. Sept. 28, 1935, Sayreville, N. J.   BR TR 6'   172 lbs.

	W	L	PCT	ERA	G	GS	CG	IP	H	BB	SO	ShO	W	L	SV	AB	H	HR	BA
1963 DET A	0	1	.000	9.00	7	0	0	10	5	4	0	0	0	1	0	0	0	0	—

Bill Duzen

DUZEN, WILLIAM GEORGE
B. Feb. 21, 1870, Buffalo, N. Y.   D. Mar. 11, 1944, Buffalo, N. Y.   BR TR 5'11"   165 lbs.

	W	L	PCT	ERA	G	GS	CG	IP	H	BB	SO	ShO	W	L	SV	AB	H	HR	BA
1890 BUF P	0	2	.000	13.85	2	2	2	13	20	14	5	0	0	0	0	4	1	0	.250

Frank Dwyer

DWYER, JOHN FRANCIS
B. Mar. 25, 1868, Lee, Mass.   D. Feb. 4, 1943, Pittsfield, Mass.   BR TR 5'8"   145 lbs.
Manager 1902.

	W	L	PCT	ERA	G	GS	CG	IP	H	BB	SO	ShO	W	L	SV	AB	H	HR	BA
1888 CHI N	4	1	.800	1.07	5	5	5	42	32	9	17	1	0	0	0	21	4	0	.190
1889	16	13	.552	3.59	32	30	27	276	307	72	63	0	1	0	0	135	27	1	.200
1890 CHI P	3	6	.333	6.23	12	6	6	69.1	98	25	17	0	2	1	1	53	14	0	.264
1891 C-M AA	19	23	.452	3.98	45	41	39	375	424	145	128	1	0	1	0	181	49	0	.271
1892 2 teams	STL	N	(10G 2–8)		CIN	N	(33G 19–10)												
" total	21	18	.538	2.98	43	37	30	323.1	341	73	61	3	2	1	1	154	23	0	.149
1893 CIN N	18	15	.545	4.13	37	30	28	287.1	332	93	53	1	2	2	2	120	24	1	.200
1894	19	22	.463	5.07	45	40	34	348	471	106	49	1	1	1	1	172	46	2	.267
1895	18	15	.545	4.24	37	31	23	280.1	355	74	46	2	2	3	0	113	30	1	.265
1896	24	11	.686	3.15	36	34	30	288.2	321	60	57	3	1	0	1	110	29	0	.264
1897	18	13	.581	3.78	37	31	22	247.1	315	56	41	0	3	1	0	94	25	0	.266
1898	16	10	.615	3.04	31	28	24	240	257	42	29	0	1	0	0	85	12	0	.141
1899	0	5	.000	5.51	5	5	2	32.2	48	9	2	0	0	0	0	11	4	0	.364
12 yrs.	176	152	.537	3.85	365	318	270	2810	3301	764	563	12	15	10	6	*			

Ben Dyer

DYER, BENJAMIN FRANKLIN
B. Feb. 13, 1893, Chicago, Ill.   D. Aug. 7, 1959, Kenosha, Wis.   BR TR 5'10"   170 lbs.

	W	L	PCT	ERA	G	GS	CG	IP	H	BB	SO	ShO	W	L	SV	AB	H	HR	BA
1918 DET A	0	0	—	0.00	2	0	0	1.2	0	1	0	0	0	0	0	*			

Eddie Dyer

DYER, EDWIN HAWLEY
B. Oct. 11, 1900, Morgan City, La.   D. Apr. 20, 1964, Houston, Tex.   BL TL 5'11½" 168 lbs.
Manager 1946-50.

	W	L	PCT	ERA	G	GS	CG	IP	H	BB	SO	ShO	W	L	SV	AB	H	HR	BA
1922 STL N	0	0	—	2.45	2	0	0	3.2	7	0	3	0	0	0	0	3	1	0	.333
1923	2	1	.667	4.09	4	3	2	22	30	5	7	1	0	0	0	45	12	2	.267
1924	8	11	.421	4.61	29	15	7	136.2	174	51	23	1	3	2	0	76	18	0	.237
1925	4	3	.571	4.15	27	5	1	82.1	93	24	25	0	3	2	3	31	3	0	.097
1926	1	0	1.000	11.57	6	0	0	9.1	7	14	4	0	1	0	0	2	1	0	.500
1927	0	0		18.00	1	0	0	2	5	2	1	0	0	0	0	0	0	0	—
6 yrs.	15	15	.500	4.75	69	23	10	256	316	96	63	2	7	4	3	*			

Jimmy Dygert

DYGERT, JAMES HENRY (Sunny Jim)
B. July 5, 1884, Utica, N. Y.   D. Feb. 8, 1936, New Orleans, La.   BR TR 5'10"   185 lbs.

	W	L	PCT	ERA	G	GS	CG	IP	H	BB	SO	ShO	W	L	SV	AB	H	HR	BA
1905 PHI A	1	4	.200	4.33	6	3	2	35.1	41	11	24	0	1	1	0	15	4	0	.267
1906	11	13	.458	2.70	35	25	15	213.2	175	91	106	4	2	2	0	74	13	1	.176
1907	21	8	.724	2.34	42	28	18	261.2	200	85	151	5	3	2	1	94	12	0	.128
1908	11	15	.423	2.87	41	27	15	238.2	184	97	164	5	2	1	1	75	6	0	.080
1909	9	5	.643	2.42	32	12	6	137.1	117	50	79	1	3	1	0	42	9	0	.214
1910	4	4	.500	2.54	19	8	6	99.1	81	49	59	1	0	0	0	36	3	0	.083
6 yrs.	57	49	.538	2.65	175	103	62	986	798	383	583	16	11	7	2	336	47	1	.140

Jimmy Dykes

DYKES, JAMES JOSEPH
B. Nov. 10, 1896, Philadelphia, Pa.   D. June 15, 1976, Philadelphia, Pa.   BR TR 5'9"   185 lbs.
Manager 1934-46, 1951-54, 1958-61.

	W	L	PCT	ERA	G	GS	CG	IP	H	BB	SO	ShO	W	L	SV	AB	H	HR	BA
1927 PHI A	0	0	—	4.50	2	0	0	2	2	1	0	0	0	0	0	*			

Arnie Earley

EARLEY, ARNOLD CARL
B. June 4, 1933, Lincoln Park, Mich.   BL TL 6'1"   195 lbs.

	W	L	PCT	ERA	G	GS	CG	IP	H	BB	SO	ShO	W	L	SV	AB	H	HR	BA
1960 BOS A	1	1	.000	15.75	2	0	0	4	9	4	5	0	0	1	0	1	0	0	.000
1961	2	4	.333	3.99	33	0	0	49.2	42	34	44	0	2	4	7	6	0	0	.000
1962	4	5	.444	5.80	38	3	0	68.1	76	46	59	0	3	3	5	10	2	0	.200
1963	3	7	.300	4.75	53	4	0	115.2	124	43	97	0	1	5	1	18	5	0	.278

	W	L	PCT	ERA	G	GS	CG	IP	H	BB	SO	ShO	Relief Pitching W	L	SV	BATTING AB	H	HR	BA

Arnie Earley continued

	W	L	PCT	ERA	G	GS	CG	IP	H	BB	SO	ShO	W	L	SV	AB	H	HR	BA
1964	1	1	.500	2.68	25	3	1	50.1	51	18	45	0	0	0	1	9	1	0	.111
1965	0	1	.000	3.63	57	0	0	74.1	79	29	47	0	0	1	0	6	0	0	.000
1966 CHI N	2	1	.667	3.57	13	0	0	17.2	14	9	12	0	2	1	0	1	0	0	.000
1967 HOU N	0	0	—	27.00	2	0	0	1.1	5	1	1	0	0	0	0	0	0	0	—
8 yrs.	12	20	.375	4.48	223	10	1	381.1	400	184	310	0	8	15	14	51	8	0	.157

Tom Earley

EARLEY, THOMAS FRANCIS ALOYSIUS (Chick)   BR TR 6'   180 lbs.
B. Feb. 19, 1917, Roxbury, Mass.

	W	L	PCT	ERA	G	GS	CG	IP	H	BB	SO	ShO	W	L	SV	AB	H	HR	BA
1938 BOS N	1	0	1.000	3.27	2	1	1	11	8	1	4	0	0	0	0	4	0	0	.000
1939	1	4	.200	4.73	14	2	0	40	49	19	9	0	0	3	1	10	3	0	.300
1940	2	0	1.000	3.86	4	1	1	16.1	16	3	5	1	1	0	0	5	2	0	.400
1941	6	8	.429	2.53	33	13	6	138.2	120	46	54	1	1	1	3	47	11	0	.234
1942	6	11	.353	4.71	27	18	6	112.2	120	55	28	0	1	1	1	34	4	0	.118
1945	2	1	.667	4.61	11	2	1	41	36	19	4	0	1	0	0	14	3	0	.214
6 yrs.	18	24	.429	3.78	91	37	15	359.2	349	143	104	2	4	6	5	114	23	0	.202

George Earnshaw

EARNSHAW, GEORGE LIVINGSTON (Moose)   BR TR 6'4"   210 lbs.
B. Feb. 15, 1900, New York, N. Y.   D. Dec. 1, 1976, Little Rock, Ark.

	W	L	PCT	ERA	G	GS	CG	IP	H	BB	SO	ShO	W	L	SV	AB	H	HR	BA
1928 PHI A	7	7	.500	3.81	26	22	7	158.1	143	100	117	3	0	1	0	57	14	0	.246
1929	24	8	.750	3.29	44	33	13	254.2	233	125	149	3	3	0	1	87	15	1	.172
1930	22	13	.629	4.44	49	39	20	296	299	139	193	3	2	2	2	114	26	0	.228
1931	21	7	.750	3.67	43	33	23	281.2	255	75	152	3	1	0	6	114	30	2	.263
1932	19	13	.594	4.77	36	33	21	245.1	262	94	109	1	1	1	0	91	26	0	.286
1933	5	10	.333	5.97	21	18	4	117.2	153	58	37	0	1	0	0	44	8	0	.182
1934 CHI A	14	11	.560	4.52	33	30	14	227	242	104	97	2	0	1	0	79	16	0	.203
1935 2 teams		CHI	A (3G 1–2)		BKN	N (25G 8–12)													
" total	9	14	.391	4.60	28	25	6	184	201	64	80	2	1	1	0	67	15	0	.224
1936 2 teams		BKN	N (19G 4–9)		STL	N (20G 2–1)													
" total	6	10	.375	5.73	39	19	5	150.2	193	50	71	1	3	0	2	51	12	0	.235
9 yrs.	127	93	.577	4.38	319	249	115	1915.1	1981	809	1005	18	12	5	12	704	162	3	.230

WORLD SERIES	W	L	PCT	ERA	G	GS	CG	IP	H	BB	SO	ShO	W	L	SV	AB	H	HR	BA
1929 PHI A	1	1	.500	2.63	2	2	1	13.2	14	6	17	0	0	0	0	5	0	0	.000
1930	2	0	1.000	0.72	3	3	2	25	13	7	19	0	0	0	0	9	0	0	.000
1931	1	2	.333	1.88	3	3	2	24	12	4	20	1	0	0	0	8	0	0	.000
3 yrs.	4	3	.571	1.58	8	8	5	62.2	39	17	56	1	0	0	0	22	0	0	.000
					10th	10th					7th								

Mal Eason

EASON, MALCOLM WAYNE (Kid)   TR
B. Mar. 13, 1879, Brookville, Pa.   D. Apr. 16, 1970, Douglas, Ariz.

	W	L	PCT	ERA	G	GS	CG	IP	H	BB	SO	ShO	W	L	SV	AB	H	HR	BA
1900 CHI N	1	0	1.000	1.00	1	1	1	9	9	3	2	0	0	0	0	3	0	0	.000
1901	8	17	.320	3.59	27	25	23	220.2	246	60	68	1	0	0	0	87	12	0	.138
1902 2 teams		CHI	N (2G 1–1)		BOS	N (27G 9–14)													
" total	10	15	.400	2.61	29	28	22	224.1	258	61	54	2	0	0	0	77	7	0	.091
1903 DET A	2	5	.286	3.36	7	6	6	56.1	60	19	21	1	0	1	0	20	2	0	.100
1905 BKN N	5	21	.192	4.30	27	27	20	207	230	72	64	3	0	0	0	81	14	0	.173
1906	10	17	.370	3.25	34	26	18	227	212	74	64	3	1	0	0	88	8	0	.091
6 yrs.	36	75	.324	3.39	125	113	90	944.1	1015	289	273	10	1	1	0	356	43	0	.121

Carl East

EAST, CARLTON WILLIAM   BL TR 6'2"   178 lbs.
B. Aug. 27, 1894, Marietta, Ga.   D. Jan. 15, 1953, Whitesburg, Ga.

	W	L	PCT	ERA	G	GS	CG	IP	H	BB	SO	ShO	W	L	SV	AB	H	HR	BA
1915 STL A	0	0	—	16.20	1	1	0	3.1	6	2	1	0	0	0	0	*			

Hugh East

EAST, GORDON HUGH   BR TR 6'2"   185 lbs.
B. July 7, 1919, Birmingham, Ala.   D. Nov. 2, 1981, Charleston, S. C.

	W	L	PCT	ERA	G	GS	CG	IP	H	BB	SO	ShO	W	L	SV	AB	H	HR	BA
1941 NY N	1	1	.500	3.45	2	2	0	15.2	19	9	4	0	0	0	0	9	2	0	.222
1942	0	2	.000	9.82	4	1	0	7.1	15	7	2	0	0	1	0	2	1	1	.500
1943	1	3	.250	5.36	13	5	1	40.1	51	25	21	0	0	0	0	13	1	0	.077
3 yrs.	2	6	.250	5.40	19	8	1	63.1	85	41	27	0	0	1	0	24	4	1	.167

Jamie Easterly

EASTERLY, JAMES MORRIS   BB TL 5'9"   180 lbs.
B. Feb. 17, 1953, Houston, Tex.

	W	L	PCT	ERA	G	GS	CG	IP	H	BB	SO	ShO	W	L	SV	AB	H	HR	BA
1974 ATL N	0	0	—	15.00	3	0	0	3	6	4	0	0	0	0	0	0	0	0	—
1975	2	9	.182	4.96	21	13	0	69	73	42	34	0	0	0	0	18	1	0	.056
1976	1	1	.500	4.91	4	4	0	22	23	13	11	0	0	0	0	9	1	0	.111
1977	2	4	.333	6.10	22	5	0	59	72	30	37	0	0	2	1	15	4	0	.267
1978	3	6	.333	5.65	37	6	0	78	91	45	42	0	2	3	1	19	4	0	.211
1979	0	0	—	12.00	4	0	0	3	7	3	3	0	0	0	0	0	0	0	—
1981 MIL A	3	3	.500	3.19	44	0	0	62	46	34	31	0	3	3	4	0	0	0	—
1982	0	2	.000	4.70	28	0	0	30.2	39	15	16	0	0	2	2	0	0	0	—
1983 2 teams		MIL	A (12G 0–1)		CLE	A (41G 4–2)													
" total	4	3	.571	3.67	53	0	0	68.2	83	32	45	0	4	3	4	1	0	0	.000
1984 CLE A	3	1	.750	3.38	26	1	0	69.1	74	23	42	0	3	1	2	0	0	0	—
10 yrs.	18	29	.383	4.65	242	29	0	464.2	514	241	261	0	12	14	14	62	10	0	.161

DIVISIONAL PLAYOFF SERIES	W	L	PCT	ERA	G	GS	CG	IP	H	BB	SO	ShO	W	L	SV	AB	H	HR	BA
1981 MIL A	0	0	—	6.75	2	0	0	1.1	2	1	0	0	0	0	0	0	0	0	—

Jack Easton

EASTON, JOHN E.
B. Feb. 28, 1867, Bridgeport, Ohio   D. Nov. 28, 1903, Steubenville, Ohio

	W	L	PCT	ERA	G	GS	CG	IP	H	BB	SO	ShO	W	L	SV	AB	H	HR	BA
1889 COL AA	1	0	1.000	3.50	4	1	1	18	13	21	7	0	0	0	1	7	0	0	.000
1890	15	14	.517	3.52	37	29	23	255.2	213	125	147	0	2	1	1	107	19	0	.178
1891 2 teams		COL	AA (20G 5–12)		STL	AA (7G 3–2)													
" total	8	14	.364	4.59	27	24	19	198	208	86	87	0	0	0	0	102	20	0	.196
1892 STL N	2	0	1.000	6.39	5	2	2	31	38	26	4	0	0	0	0	17	3	0	.176
1894 PIT N	0	1	.000	4.12	3	1	1	19.2	26	4	1	0	0	0	0	5	0	0	.000
5 yrs.	26	29	.473	4.12	76	57	46	522.1	498	262	246	0	2	1	2	238	42	0	.176

	W	L	PCT	ERA	G	GS	CG	IP	H	BB	SO	ShO	Relief Pitching W	L	SV	BATTING AB	H	HR	BA

Rawley Eastwick

EASTWICK, RAWLINS JACKSON
B. Oct. 24, 1950, Camden, N. J.   BR TR 6'3"   180 lbs.

	W	L	PCT	ERA	G	GS	CG	IP	H	BB	SO	ShO	RP W	L	SV	AB	H	HR	BA
1974 CIN N	0	0	–	2.00	8	0	0	18	12	5	14	0	0	0	2	1	0	0	.000
1975	5	3	.625	2.60	58	0	0	90	77	25	61	0	5	3	22	15	1	0	.067
1976	11	5	.688	2.08	71	0	0	108	93	27	70	0	11	5	26	17	0	0	.000
1977 2 teams		CIN N (23G 2–2)			STL N (41G 3–7)														
" total	5	9	.357	3.90	64	1	0	97	114	29	47	0	11	5	11	11	3	0	.273
1978 2 teams		NY A (8G 2–1)			PHI N (22G 2–1)														
" total	4	2	.667	3.76	30	0	0	64.2	53	22	27	0	4	2	0	3	0	0	.000
1979 PHI N	3	6	.333	4.88	51	0	0	83	90	25	47	0	3	6	6	7	0	0	.000
1980 KC A	0	1	.000	5.32	14	0	0	22	37	8	5	0	0	1	0	0	0	0	–
1981 CHI N	0	1	.000	2.30	30	0	0	43	43	15	24	0	0	1	1	2	0	0	.000
8 yrs.	28	27	.509	3.30	326	1	0	525.2	519	156	295	0	27	25	68	56	4	0	.071
LEAGUE CHAMPIONSHIP SERIES																			
1975 CIN N	1	0	1.000	0.00	2	0	0	3.2	2	2	1	0	1	0	1	0	0	0	–
1976	1	0	1.000	12.00	2	0	0	3	7	2	1	0	1	0	0	0	0	0	–
1978 PHI N	0	0	–	9.00	1	0	0	1	3	0	1	0	0	0	0	0	0	0	–
3 yrs.	2	0	1.000	5.87	5	0	0	7.2	12	4	3	0	2	0	1	0	0	0	–
WORLD SERIES																			
1975 CIN N	2	0	1.000	2.25	5	0	0	8	6	3	4	0	2	0	1	1	0	0	.000

2nd

Craig Eaton

EATON, CRAIG
B. Sept. 7, 1954, Cincinnati, Ohio   BR TR 5'11"   175 lbs.

	W	L	PCT	ERA	G	GS	CG	IP	H	BB	SO	ShO	RP W	L	SV	AB	H	HR	BA
1979 KC A	0	0	–	2.70	5	0	0	10	8	3	4	0	0	0	0	0	0	0	–

Zeb Eaton

EATON, ZEBULON VANCE (Red)
B. Feb. 2, 1920, Cooleemee, N. C.   BR TR 5'10"   185 lbs.

	W	L	PCT	ERA	G	GS	CG	IP	H	BB	SO	ShO	RP W	L	SV	AB	H	HR	BA
1944 DET A	0	0	–	5.74	6	0	0	15.2	19	8	4	0	0	0	0	10	1	0	.100
1945	4	2	.667	4.05	17	3	0	53.1	48	40	15	0	3	0	0	32	8	2	.250
2 yrs.	4	2	.667	4.43	23	3	0	69	67	48	19	0	3	0	0	42	9	2	.214

Vallie Eaves

EAVES, VALLIE ENNIS (Chief)
B. Sept. 6, 1911, Allen, Okla.   D. Apr. 19, 1960, Norman, Okla.   BR TR 6'2½"   180 lbs.

	W	L	PCT	ERA	G	GS	CG	IP	H	BB	SO	ShO	RP W	L	SV	AB	H	HR	BA
1935 PHI A	1	2	.333	5.14	3	3	1	14	12	15	6	0	0	0	0	4	0	0	.000
1939 CHI A	0	1	.000	4.63	2	1	1	11.2	11	8	5	0	0	0	0	6	2	0	.333
1940	0	2	.000	6.75	5	3	0	18.2	22	24	11	0	0	0	0	5	0	0	.000
1941 CHI N	3	3	.500	3.53	12	7	4	58.2	56	21	24	0	1	0	0	20	2	0	.100
1942	0	0	–	9.00	2	0	0	3	4	2	0	0	0	0	0	0	0	0	–
5 yrs.	4	8	.333	4.58	24	14	6	106	105	70	46	0	1	0	0	35	4	0	.114

Eddie Eayrs

EAYRS, EDWIN
B. Nov. 10, 1890, Blackstone, Mass.   D. Nov. 30, 1969, Warwick, R. I.   BL TL 5'7"   160 lbs.

	W	L	PCT	ERA	G	GS	CG	IP	H	BB	SO	ShO	RP W	L	SV	AB	H	HR	BA
1913 PIT N	0	0	–	2.25	2	0	0	8	8	6	5	0	0	0	0	6	1	0	.167
1920 BOS N	1	2	.333	5.47	7	3	0	26.1	36	12	7	0	0	0	0	244	80	1	.328
1921	0	0	–	17.36	2	0	0	4.2	9	9	1	0	0	0	0	21	2	0	.095
3 yrs.	1	2	.333	6.23	11	3	0	39	53	27	13	0	0	0	0	*			

Harry Eccles

ECCLES, HARRY JOSIAH (Buggs)
B. July 9, 1893, Kennedy, N. Y.   D. June 2, 1955, Jamestown, N. Y.   BL TL 6'2"   170 lbs.

	W	L	PCT	ERA	G	GS	CG	IP	H	BB	SO	ShO	RP W	L	SV	AB	H	HR	BA
1915 PHI A	0	1	.000	6.86	5	1	0	21	18	6	13	0	0	0	1	6	1	0	.167

Dennis Eckersley

ECKERSLEY, DENNIS LEE
B. Oct. 3, 1954, Oakland, Calif.   BR TR 6'2"   190 lbs.

	W	L	PCT	ERA	G	GS	CG	IP	H	BB	SO	ShO	RP W	L	SV	AB	H	HR	BA
1975 CLE A	13	7	.650	2.60	34	24	6	186.2	147	90	152	2	1	0	2	0	0	0	–
1976	13	12	.520	3.44	36	30	9	199	155	78	200	3	0	1	1	0	0	0	–
1977	14	13	.519	3.53	33	33	12	247	214	54	191	3	0	0	0	0	0	0	–
1978 BOS A	20	8	.714	2.99	35	35	16	268.1	258	71	162	3	0	0	0	0	0	0	–
1979	17	10	.630	2.99	33	33	17	247	234	59	150	2	0	0	0	0	0	0	–
1980	12	14	.462	4.27	30	30	8	198	188	44	121	0	0	0	0	0	0	0	–
1981	9	8	.529	4.27	23	23	8	154	160	35	79	2	0	0	0	0	0	0	–
1982	13	13	.500	3.73	33	33	11	224.1	228	43	127	3	0	0	0	0	0	0	–
1983	9	13	.409	5.61	28	28	2	176.1	223	39	77	0	0	0	0	0	0	0	–
1984 2 teams		BOS A (9G 4–4)			CHI N (24G 10–8)														
" total	14	12	.538	3.60	33	33	4	225	223	49	114	0	0	0	0	55	6	0	.109
10 yrs.	134	110	.549	3.63	318	302	93	2125.2	2030	562	1373	18	1	1	3	55	6	0	.109
LEAGUE CHAMPIONSHIP SERIES																			
1984 CHI N	0	1	.000	8.44	1	1	0	5.1	9	0	0	0	0	0	0	2	0	0	.000

Al Eckert

ECKERT, ALBERT GEORGE (Obbie)
B. May 17, 1906, Milwaukee, Wis.   D. Apr. 20, 1974, Milwaukee, Wis.   BL TL 5'10"   174 lbs.

	W	L	PCT	ERA	G	GS	CG	IP	H	BB	SO	ShO	RP W	L	SV	AB	H	HR	BA
1930 CIN N	0	1	.000	7.20	2	1	0	5	7	4	1	0	0	0	0	1	0	0	.000
1931	0	1	.000	9.16	14	1	0	18.2	26	9	5	0	0	0	0	3	1	0	.333
1935 STL N	0	0	–	12.00	2	0	0	3	7	1	1	0	0	0	0	0	0	0	–
3 yrs.	0	2	.000	9.11	18	2	0	26.2	40	14	7	0	0	0	0	4	1	0	.250

Charlie Eckert

ECKERT, CHARLES WILLIAM (Buzz)
B. Aug. 8, 1897, Philadelphia, Pa.   BR TR 5'11½"   180 lbs.

	W	L	PCT	ERA	G	GS	CG	IP	H	BB	SO	ShO	RP W	L	SV	AB	H	HR	BA
1919 PHI A	0	1	.000	3.94	2	1	1	16	17	3	6	0	0	0	0	6	1	0	.167
1920	0	0	–	4.76	2	1	0	5.2	8	1	1	0	0	0	0	1	0	0	.000
1922	0	2	.000	4.68	21	0	0	50	61	23	15	0	0	2	0	11	1	0	.091
3 yrs.	0	3	.000	4.52	25	1	1	71.2	86	27	22	0	0	2	0	18	2	0	.111

	W	L	PCT	ERA	G	GS	CG	IP	H	BB	SO	ShO	Relief Pitching W	L	SV	BATTING AB	H	HR	BA

Don Eddy

EDDY, DONALD EUGENE
B. Oct. 25, 1946, Mason City, Iowa
BR TL 5'11" 170 lbs.

	W	L	PCT	ERA	G	GS	CG	IP	H	BB	SO	ShO	W	L	SV	AB	H	HR	BA
1970 CHI A	0	0	–	2.25	7	0	0	12	10	6	9	0	0	0	0	0	0	0	–
1971	0	2	.000	2.35	22	0	0	23	19	19	14	0	0	2	0	1	1	0	1.000
2 yrs.	0	2	.000	2.31	29	0	0	35	29	25	23	0	0	2	0	1	1	0	1.000

Steve Eddy

EDDY, STEVEN ALLEN
B. Aug. 21, 1957, Sterling, Ill.
BR TR 6'2" 185 lbs.

	W	L	PCT	ERA	G	GS	CG	IP	H	BB	SO	ShO	W	L	SV	AB	H	HR	BA
1979 CAL A	1	1	.500	4.78	7	4	0	32	36	20	7	0	0	0	0	0	0	0	–

Ed Edelen

EDELEN, EDWARD JOSEPH (Doc)
B. Mar. 16, 1912, Bryantown, Md. D. Feb. 1, 1982, LaPlata, Md.
BR TR 6' 191 lbs.

	W	L	PCT	ERA	G	GS	CG	IP	H	BB	SO	ShO	W	L	SV	AB	H	HR	BA
1932 WAS A	0	0	–	20.25	2	0	0	1.1	0	6	0	0	0	0	0	0	0	0	–

Joe Edelen

EDELEN, BENNY JOE
B. Sept. 16, 1955, Durant, Okla.
BR TR 6' 165 lbs.

	W	L	PCT	ERA	G	GS	CG	IP	H	BB	SO	ShO	W	L	SV	AB	H	HR	BA
1981 2 teams		STL	N (13G 1–0)			CIN	N	(5G 1–0)											
" total	2	0	1.000	5.70	18	0	0	30	34	3	15	0	2	0	0	5	1	0	.200
1982 CIN N	0	0	–	8.80	9	0	0	15.1	22	8	11	0	0	0	0	2	1	0	.500
2 yrs.	2	0	1.000	6.75	27	0	0	45.1	56	11	26	0	2	0	0	7	2	0	.286

John Edelman

EDELMAN, JOHN ROGERS
B. July 27, 1935, Philadelphia, Pa.
BR TR 6'3" 185 lbs.

	W	L	PCT	ERA	G	GS	CG	IP	H	BB	SO	ShO	W	L	SV	AB	H	HR	BA
1955 MIL N	0	0	–	11.12	5	0	0	5.2	7	8	3	0	0	0	0	0	0	0	–

Charlie Eden

EDEN, CHARLES M.
B. Jan. 18, 1855, Lexington, Ky. D. Sept. 17, 1920, Cincinnati, Ohio
BR TR

	W	L	PCT	ERA	G	GS	CG	IP	H	BB	SO	ShO	W	L	SV	AB	H	HR	BA
1884 PIT AA	0	1	.000	6.00	2	1	1	12	12	3	3	0	0	0	0	122	33	1	.270
1885	1	2	.333	5.17	4	1	0	15.2	22	3	5	0	1	1	0	405	103	0	.254
2 yrs.	1	3	.250	5.53	6	2	1	27.2	34	6	8	0	1	1	0	*			

Butch Edge

EDGE, CLAUDE LEE JR.
B. July 18, 1956, Houston, Tex.
BR TR 6'3" 203 lbs.

	W	L	PCT	ERA	G	GS	CG	IP	H	BB	SO	ShO	W	L	SV	AB	H	HR	BA
1979 TOR A	3	4	.429	5.19	9	9	1	52	60	24	19	0	0	0	0	0	0	0	–

Bill Edgerton

EDGERTON, WILLIAM ALBERT
B. Aug. 16, 1941, South Bend, Ind.
BL TL 6'2" 185 lbs.

	W	L	PCT	ERA	G	GS	CG	IP	H	BB	SO	ShO	W	L	SV	AB	H	HR	BA
1966 KC A	0	1	.000	3.24	6	1	0	8.1	10	7	3	0	0	1	0	0	0	0	–
1967	1	0	1.000	2.16	7	0	0	8.1	11	3	6	0	1	0	0	0	0	0	–
1969 SEA A	0	1	.000	13.50	4	0	0	4	10	0	2	0	0	1	0	0	0	0	–
3 yrs.	1	2	.333	4.79	17	1	0	20.2	31	10	11	0	1	2	0	0	0	0	–

George Edmondson

EDMONDSON, GEORGE HENDERSON
B. May 18, 1896, Waxahachie, Tex. D. July 11, 1973, Waco, Tex.
BR TR 6'1" 179 lbs.

	W	L	PCT	ERA	G	GS	CG	IP	H	BB	SO	ShO	W	L	SV	AB	H	HR	BA
1922 CLE A	0	0	–	9.00	2	0	0	2	4	0	0	0	0	0	0	0	0	0	.000
1923	0	0	–	11.25	1	0	0	4	8	3	0	0	0	0	0	0	0	0	.333
1924	0	0	–	9.00	5	1	0	8	10	5	3	0	0	0	0	3	1	0	.250
3 yrs.	0	0	–	9.64	8	1	0	14	22	8	3	0	0	0	0	4	1	0	.250

Paul Edmondson

EDMONDSON, PAUL MICHAEL
B. Feb. 12, 1943, Kansas City, Kans. D. Feb. 13, 1970, Santa Barbara, Calif.
BR TR 6'5" 195 lbs.

	W	L	PCT	ERA	G	GS	CG	IP	H	BB	SO	ShO	W	L	SV	AB	H	HR	BA
1969 CHI A	1	6	.143	3.70	14	13	1	87.2	72	39	46	0	0	1	0	29	5	0	.172

Sam Edmondston

EDMONDSTON, SAMUEL SHERWOOD
B. Aug. 30, 1883, Washington, D. C. D. Apr. 12, 1979, Corpus Christi, Tex.
BL TL 5'11½" 185 lbs.

	W	L	PCT	ERA	G	GS	CG	IP	H	BB	SO	ShO	W	L	SV	AB	H	HR	BA
1906 WAS A	0	1	.000	4.50	2	1	1	10	10	2	0	0	0	0	0	3	1	0	.333
1907	0	0	–	9.00	1	0	0	3	8	1	0	0	0	0	0	2	0	0	.000
2 yrs.	0	1	.000	5.54	3	1	1	13	18	3	0	0	0	0	0	5	1	0	.200

Foster Edwards

EDWARDS, FOSTER HAMILTON (Eddie)
B. Sept. 1, 1903, Holstein, Iowa D. Jan. 4, 1980, Orleans, Mass.
BR TR 6'4" 178 lbs.

	W	L	PCT	ERA	G	GS	CG	IP	H	BB	SO	ShO	W	L	SV	AB	H	HR	BA
1925 BOS N	0	0	–	9.00	1	0	0	2	6	1	1	0	0	0	0	0	0	0	–
1926	2	0	1.000	0.72	3	3	1	25	20	13	4	0	0	0	0	9	0	0	.000
1927	2	8	.200	4.99	29	11	1	92	95	45	37	0	1	0	0	22	1	0	.045
1928	2	1	.667	5.66	21	3	2	49.1	67	23	17	0	0	0	0	11	1	0	.091
1930 NY A	0	0	–	21.60	2	0	0	1.2	5	2	1	0	0	0	0	0	0	0	–
5 yrs.	6	9	.400	4.76	56	17	4	170	193	84	60	0	1	0	0	42	2	0	.048

Jim Joe Edwards

EDWARDS, JAMES CORBETTE
B. Dec. 14, 1894, Banner, Miss. D. Jan. 19, 1965, Calhoun County, Miss.
BR TL 6'2" 185 lbs.

	W	L	PCT	ERA	G	GS	CG	IP	H	BB	SO	ShO	W	L	SV	AB	H	HR	BA
1922 CLE A	3	8	.273	4.70	25	7	0	88	113	40	44	0	2	3	0	23	2	0	.087
1923	10	10	.500	3.71	38	21	7	179.1	200	75	68	1	0	3	1	59	7	0	.119
1924	4	3	.571	2.84	10	7	5	57	64	34	15	1	0	0	0	20	3	0	.150
1925 2 teams		CLE	A (13G 0–3)			CHI	A	(9G 1–2)											
" total	1	5	.167	5.86	22	7	2	81.1	106	46	32	1	0	2	0	26	4	0	.154
1926 CHI A	6	9	.400	4.18	32	16	8	142	140	63	41	3	2	3	1	46	5	0	.109
1928 CIN N	2	2	.500	7.59	18	1	0	32	43	20	11	0	1	2	2	10	3	0	.300
6 yrs.	26	37	.413	4.41	145	59	22	579.2	666	278	211	6	5	13	4	184	24	0	.130

Sherman Edwards

EDWARDS, SHERMAN STANLEY
B. July 25, 1909, Mt. Ida, Ark.
BR TR 6'1" 170 lbs.

	W	L	PCT	ERA	G	GS	CG	IP	H	BB	SO	ShO	W	L	SV	AB	H	HR	BA
1934 CIN N	0	0	–	3.00	1	0	0	3	4	1	1	0	0	0	0	0	0	0	.000

	W	L	PCT	ERA	G	GS	CG	IP	H	BB	SO	ShO	Relief Pitching W	L	SV	BATTING AB	H	HR	BA

Harry Eells

EELLS, HARRY ARCHIBALD
B. Feb. 14, 1882, Ida Grove, Iowa   D. Oct. 15, 1940, San Francisco, Calif.
TR 5'10" 170 lbs.

	W	L	PCT	ERA	G	GS	CG	IP	H	BB	SO	ShO	RW	RL	SV	AB	H	HR	BA
1906 CLE A	4	5	.444	2.61	14	8	6	86.1	77	48	35	1	0	1	0	32	6	0	.188

Dick Egan

EGAN, RICHARD WALLIS
B. Mar. 24, 1937, Berkeley, Calif.
BL TL 6'4" 193 lbs.

	W	L	PCT	ERA	G	GS	CG	IP	H	BB	SO	ShO	RW	RL	SV	AB	H	HR	BA
1963 DET A	0	1	.000	5.14	20	0	0	21	25	3	16	0	0	1	0	0	0	0	—
1964	0	0	—	4.46	23	0	0	34.1	33	17	21	0	0	0	2	3	0	0	.000
1966 CAL A	0	0	—	4.40	11	0	0	14.1	17	6	11	0	0	0	0	1	0	0	.000
1967 LA N	1	1	.500	6.25	20	0	0	31.2	34	15	20	0	1	1	0	1	0	0	.000
4 yrs.	1	2	.333	5.15	74	0	0	101.1	109	41	68	0	1	2	2	5	0	0	.000

Jim Egan

EGAN, JAMES (Troy Terrier)
B. 1838, Ansonia, Conn.   D. Sept. 26, 1884, New Haven, Conn.
TB

	W	L	PCT	ERA	G	GS	CG	IP	H	BB	SO	ShO	RW	RL	SV	AB	H	HR	BA
1882 TRO N	4	6	.400	4.14	12	10	10	100	133	24	20	0	0	0	0	*			

Rip Egan

EGAN, JOHN JOSEPH
B. July 9, 1871, Philadelphia, Pa.   D. Dec. 22, 1950, Cranston, R. I.
5'11" 168 lbs.

	W	L	PCT	ERA	G	GS	CG	IP	H	BB	SO	ShO	RW	RL	SV	AB	H	HR	BA
1894 WAS N	0	0	—	10.80	1	0	0	5	8	2	2	0	0	0	0	3	0	0	.000

Wish Egan

EGAN, ALOYSIUS JEROME
B. June 16, 1881, Evart, Mich.   D. Apr. 13, 1951, Detroit, Mich.
BR TR 6'3" 185 lbs.

	W	L	PCT	ERA	G	GS	CG	IP	H	BB	SO	ShO	RW	RL	SV	AB	H	HR	BA
1902 DET A	0	2	.000	2.86	3	3	2	22	23	6	0	0	0	0	0	8	2	0	.250
1905 STL N	6	15	.286	3.58	23	19	18	171	189	39	29	0	0	2	0	59	6	0	.102
1906	2	9	.182	4.59	16	12	7	86.1	97	27	23	0	0	1	0	29	2	0	.069
3 yrs.	8	26	.235	3.83	42	34	27	279.1	309	72	52	0	0	3	0	96	10	0	.104

Howard Ehmke

EHMKE, HOWARD JONATHAN (Bob)
B. Apr. 24, 1894, Silver Creek, N. Y.
D. Mar. 17, 1959, Philadelphia, Pa.
BR TR 6'3" 190 lbs.
BB 1923

	W	L	PCT	ERA	G	GS	CG	IP	H	BB	SO	ShO	RW	RL	SV	AB	H	HR	BA
1915 BUF F	0	2	.000	5.53	18	2	0	53.2	69	25	18	0	0	0	0	12	0	0	.000
1916 DET A	3	1	.750	3.13	5	4	4	37.1	34	15	15	0	0	0	0	14	2	0	.143
1917	10	15	.400	2.97	35	25	13	206	174	88	90	4	0	1	2	69	17	0	.246
1919	17	10	.630	3.18	33	31	20	248.2	255	107	79	2	1	0	0	91	23	0	.253
1920	15	18	.455	3.29	38	33	23	268.1	250	124	98	2	0	1	3	105	25	0	.238
1921	13	14	.481	4.54	30	22	13	196.1	220	81	68	1	3	2	0	74	21	0	.284
1922	17	17	.500	4.22	45	30	16	279.2	299	101	108	1	7	1	1	102	16	0	.157
1923 BOS A	20	17	.541	3.78	43	39	28	316.2	318	119	121	2	0	0	3	112	25	0	.223
1924	19	17	.528	3.46	45	36	26	315	324	81	119	4	2	1	4	126	28	0	.222
1925	9	20	.310	3.73	34	31	22	260.2	285	85	95	0	0	1	1	88	13	0	.148
1926 2 teams					BOS	A	(14G 3–10)		PHI	A	(20G 12–4)								
" total	15	14	.517	3.86	34	32	17	244.2	240	95	93	2	1	0	0	80	12	0	.150
1927 PHI A	12	10	.545	4.22	30	27	10	189.2	200	60	68	1	1	0	0	68	14	0	.206
1928	9	8	.529	3.62	23	18	5	139.1	135	44	34	1	0	2	0	46	11	0	.239
1929	7	2	.778	3.29	11	8	2	54.2	48	15	20	0	2	0	0	19	2	0	.105
1930	0	1	.000	11.70	3	1	0	10	22	2	4	0	0	0	0	3	1	0	.333
15 yrs.	166	166	.500	3.75	427	339	199	2820.2	2873	1042	1030	20	17	9	14	1009	210	0	.208

WORLD SERIES

	W	L	PCT	ERA	G	GS	CG	IP	H	BB	SO	ShO	RW	RL	SV	AB	H	HR	BA
1929 PHI A	1	0	1.000	1.42	2	2	1	12.2	14	3	13	0	0	0	0	5	1	0	.200

Red Ehret

EHRET, PHILIP SYDNEY
B. Aug. 31, 1868, Louisville, Ky.   D. July 28, 1940, Cincinnati, Ohio
BR TR 6' 175 lbs.

	W	L	PCT	ERA	G	GS	CG	IP	H	BB	SO	ShO	RW	RL	SV	AB	H	HR	BA
1888 KC AA	3	2	.600	3.98	7	6	5	52	58	22	12	0	0	0	0	63	12	0	.190
1889 LOU AA	10	29	.256	4.80	45	38	35	364	441	115	135	1	0	2	0	258	65	1	.252
1890	25	14	.641	2.53	43	38	35	359	351	79	174	4	1	1	2	146	31	0	.212
1891	13	13	.500	3.47	26	24	23	220.2	225	70	76	2	0	2	0	91	22	0	.242
1892 PIT N	16	20	.444	2.65	39	36	32	316	290	83	101	0	0	1	0	132	34	0	.258
1893	18	18	.500	3.44	39	35	32	314.1	322	115	70	4	1	2	0	136	24	1	.176
1894	19	21	.475	5.14	46	38	31	346.2	441	128	102	1	5	0	0	135	23	0	.170
1895 STL N	6	19	.240	6.02	37	32	18	231.2	360	88	55	0	1	0	0	96	21	1	.219
1896 CIN N	18	14	.563	3.42	34	33	29	276.2	298	74	60	2	1	0	0	102	20	1	.196
1897	8	10	.444	4.78	34	19	11	184.1	256	47	43	0	2	1	2	66	13	0	.197
1898 LOU N	3	7	.300	5.76	12	10	9	89	130	20	20	0	0	0	0	40	9	0	.225
11 yrs.	139	167	.454	4.02	362	309	260	2754.1	3172	841	848	14	11	9	4	*			

Rube Ehrhardt

EHRHARDT, WELTON CLAUDE
B. Nov. 20, 1894, Beecher, Ill.   D. Apr. 27, 1980, Chicago Heights, Ill.
BR TR 6'2" 190 lbs.

	W	L	PCT	ERA	G	GS	CG	IP	H	BB	SO	ShO	RW	RL	SV	AB	H	HR	BA
1924 BKN N	5	3	.625	2.26	15	9	6	83.2	71	17	13	2	0	0	0	29	4	0	.138
1925	10	14	.417	5.03	36	24	12	207.2	239	62	47	0	1	3	1	71	15	1	.211
1926	2	5	.286	3.90	44	1	0	97	101	35	25	0	2	4	4	24	6	0	.250
1927	3	7	.300	3.57	46	3	2	95.2	90	37	22	0	2	6	2	24	6	0	.250
1928	1	3	.250	4.67	28	2	1	54	74	27	12	0	1	2	0	14	4	0	.286
1929 CIN N	1	2	.333	4.74	24	1	1	49.1	58	22	9	1	0	2	1	11	2	0	.182
6 yrs.	22	34	.393	4.15	193	40	22	587.1	633	200	128	3	5	17	10	173	37	1	.214

Hack Eibel

EIBEL, HENRY H.
B. Dec. 6, 1893, Brooklyn, N. Y.   D. Oct. 16, 1945, Macon, Ga.
BL

	W	L	PCT	ERA	G	GS	CG	IP	H	BB	SO	ShO	RW	RL	SV	AB	H	HR	BA
1920 BOS A	0	0	—	3.48	3	0	0	10.1	10	3	5	0	0	0	0	*			

Juan Eichelberger

EICHELBERGER, JUAN TYRONE
B. Oct. 21, 1953, St. Louis, Mo.
BR TR 6'2" 195 lbs.

	W	L	PCT	ERA	G	GS	CG	IP	H	BB	SO	ShO	RW	RL	SV	AB	H	HR	BA
1978 SD N	0	0	—	12.00	3	0	0	3	4	2	2	0	0	0	0	0	0	0	—
1979	1	1	.500	3.43	3	3	1	21	15	11	12	0	0	0	0	5	2	0	.400
1980	4	2	.667	3.64	15	13	0	89	73	55	43	0	1	0	0	27	3	0	.111
1981	8	8	.500	3.51	25	24	3	141	136	74	81	1	0	0	0	46	4	0	.087
1982	7	14	.333	4.20	31	24	8	177.2	171	72	74	0	0	2	0	55	5	0	.091

	W	L	PCT	ERA	G	GS	CG	IP	H	BB	SO	ShO	W	L	SV	AB	H	HR	BA

Juan Eichelberger continued

	W	L	PCT	ERA	G	GS	CG	IP	H	BB	SO	ShO	W	L	SV	AB	H	HR	BA
1983 CLE A	4	11	.267	4.90	28	15	2	134	132	59	56	0	1	0	0	0	0	0	—
6 yrs.	24	36	.400	4.12	105	79	14	565.2	531	273	268	1	2	2	0	133	14	0	.105

Mark Eichhorn

EICHHORN, MARK ANTHONY
B. Nov. 21, 1960, San Jose, Calif.
BR TR 6'3" 180 lbs.

	W	L	PCT	ERA	G	GS	CG	IP	H	BB	SO	ShO	W	L	SV	AB	H	HR	BA
1982 TOR A	0	3	.000	5.45	7	7	0	38	40	14	16	0	0	0	0	0	0	0	—

Dave Eilers

EILERS, DAVID LOUIS
B. Dec. 3, 1936, Oldenberg, Tex.
BR TR 5'11" 188 lbs.

	W	L	PCT	ERA	G	GS	CG	IP	H	BB	SO	ShO	W	L	SV	AB	H	HR	BA
1964 MIL N	0	0	—	4.70	6	0	0	7.2	11	1	1	0	0	0	0	0	0	0	—
1965 2 teams			MIL	N (6G 0–0)			NY	N (11G 1–1)											
" total	1	1	.500	5.40	17	0	0	21.2	28	4	10	0	1	1	2	1	1	0	1.000
1966 NY N	1	1	.500	4.67	23	0	0	34.2	39	7	14	0	1	1	0	1	0	0	.000
1967 HOU N	6	4	.600	3.94	35	0	0	59.1	68	17	27	0	6	4	1	7	0	0	.000
4 yrs.	8	6	.571	4.45	81	0	0	123.1	146	29	52	0	8	6	3	9	1	0	.111

Jake Eisenhardt

EISENHARDT, JACOB HENRY (Hank)
B. Oct. 3, 1922, Perkasie, Pa.
BL TL 6'3½" 195 lbs.

	W	L	PCT	ERA	G	GS	CG	IP	H	BB	SO	ShO	W	L	SV	AB	H	HR	BA
1944 CIN N	0	0	—	0.00	1	0	0	.1	0	1	0	0	0	0	0	0	0	0	—

Harry Eisenstat

EISENSTAT, HARRY
B. Oct. 10, 1915, Brooklyn, N. Y.
BL TL 5'11" 180 lbs.

	W	L	PCT	ERA	G	GS	CG	IP	H	BB	SO	ShO	W	L	SV	AB	H	HR	BA
1935 BKN N	0	1	.000	13.50	2	0	0	4.2	9	2	2	0	0	1	0	1	0	0	.000
1936	1	2	.333	5.65	5	2	1	14.1	22	6	5	0	0	1	0	3	1	0	.333
1937	3	3	.500	3.97	13	4	0	47.2	61	11	12	0	2	1	0	11	0	0	.000
1938 DET A	9	6	.600	3.73	32	9	5	125.1	131	29	37	0	6	5	4	36	5	0	.139
1939 2 teams			DET	A (10G 2–2)			CLE	A (26G 6–7)											
" total	8	9	.471	4.12	36	13	5	133.1	148	32	44	1	4	2	2	40	11	0	.275
1940 CLE A	1	4	.200	3.14	27	3	0	71.2	78	12	27	0	1	2	4	22	6	0	.273
1941	1	1	.500	4.24	21	0	0	34	43	16	11	0	1	1	2	6	2	0	.333
1942	2	1	.667	2.45	29	1	0	47.2	58	6	19	0	2	0	2	4	1	0	.250
8 yrs.	25	27	.481	3.84	165	32	11	478.2	550	114	157	1	16	13	14	123	26	0	.211

Ed Eiteljorg

EITELJORG, EDWARD HENRY
B. Oct. 14, 1871, Berlin, Germany   D. Dec. 7, 1942, Greencastle, Ind.
BR TR 6'2" 190 lbs.

	W	L	PCT	ERA	G	GS	CG	IP	H	BB	SO	ShO	W	L	SV	AB	H	HR	BA
1890 CHI N	0	1	.000	22.50	1	1	0	2	5	1	1	0	0	0	0	1	0	0	.000
1891 WAS AA	1	5	.167	6.16	8	7	6	61.1	79	41	23	0	0	0	0	26	5	0	.192
2 yrs.	1	6	.143	6.68	9	8	6	63.1	84	42	24	0	0	0	0	27	5	0	.185

Heinie Elder

ELDER, HENRY KNOX
B. Aug. 23, 1890, Seattle, Wash.   D. Nov. 13, 1958, Long Beach, Calif.
BL TL

	W	L	PCT	ERA	G	GS	CG	IP	H	BB	SO	ShO	W	L	SV	AB	H	HR	BA
1913 DET A	0	0	—	8.10	1	0	0	3.1	4	5	0	0	0	0	0	1	0	0	.000

Hod Eller

ELLER, HORACE OWEN
B. July 5, 1894, Muncie, Ind.   D. July 18, 1961, Indianapolis, Ind.
BR TR 5'11½" 185 lbs.

	W	L	PCT	ERA	G	GS	CG	IP	H	BB	SO	ShO	W	L	SV	AB	H	HR	BA
1917 CIN N	10	5	.667	2.36	37	11	7	152.1	131	37	77	1	4	1	1	45	6	0	.133
1918	16	12	.571	2.36	37	22	14	217.2	205	59	84	0	7	1	1	70	11	0	.157
1919	20	9	.690	2.39	38	30	16	248.1	216	50	137	7	3	0	2	93	26	1	.280
1920	13	12	.520	2.95	35	22	15	210.1	208	52	76	2	2	1	0	87	22	0	.253
1921	2	2	.500	4.98	13	3	0	34.1	46	15	7	0	0	2	1	13	3	0	.231
5 yrs.	61	40	.604	2.62	160	88	52	863	806	213	381	10	16	5	5	308	68	1	.221

WORLD SERIES

	W	L	PCT	ERA	G	GS	CG	IP	H	BB	SO	ShO	W	L	SV	AB	H	HR	BA
1919 CIN N	2	0	1.000	2.00	2	2	2	18	13	2	15	1	0	0	0	7	2	0	.286

Joe Ellick

ELLICK, JOSEPH J.
B. Apr. 3, 1854, Cincinnati, Ohio   D. Apr. 21, 1923, Kansas City, Mo.
Manager 1884.

	W	L	PCT	ERA	G	GS	CG	IP	H	BB	SO	ShO	W	L	SV	AB	H	HR	BA
1878 MIL N	0	1	.000	3.00	1	0	0	3	1	1	0	0	0	1	0	*			

Bruce Ellingsen

ELLINGSEN, H. BRUCE (Little Pod)
B. Apr. 26, 1949, Pocatello, Ida.
BL TL 6' 180 lbs.

	W	L	PCT	ERA	G	GS	CG	IP	H	BB	SO	ShO	W	L	SV	AB	H	HR	BA
1974 CLE A	1	1	.500	3.21	16	2	0	42	45	17	16	0	1	0	0	0	0	0	—

Claude Elliott

ELLIOTT, CLAUDE JUDSON
B. Nov. 17, 1879, Pardeeville, Wis.   D. June 21, 1923, Pardeeville, Wis.
BR TR 6' 190 lbs.

	W	L	PCT	ERA	G	GS	CG	IP	H	BB	SO	ShO	W	L	SV	AB	H	HR	BA
1904 2 teams			CIN	N (9G 3–1)			NY	N (3G 0–2)											
" total	3	3	.500	2.97	12	7	5	72.2	74	26	27	1	0	0	0	29	6	1	.207
1905 NY N	1	1	.500	4.03	10	2	2	38	41	12	20	0	0	0	6	16	3	0	.188
2 yrs.	4	4	.500	3.33	22	9	7	110.2	115	38	47	1	0	0	6	45	9	1	.200

Glenn Elliott

ELLIOTT, HERBERT GLENN (Lefty)
B. Nov. 11, 1919, Sapulpa, Okla.   D. July 27, 1969, Portland, Ore.
BL TL 5'11" 175 lbs.

	W	L	PCT	ERA	G	GS	CG	IP	H	BB	SO	ShO	W	L	SV	AB	H	HR	BA
1947 BOS N	0	1	.000	4.74	11	0	0	19	18	11	8	0	0	1	1	2	1	0	.500
1948	1	0	1.000	3.00	1	1	0	3	5	1	2	0	0	0	0	2	0	0	.000
1949	3	4	.429	3.95	22	6	1	68.1	70	27	15	0	2	0	0	17	1	0	.059
3 yrs.	4	5	.444	4.08	34	7	1	90.1	93	39	25	0	2	1	1	21	2	0	.095

Hal Elliott

ELLIOTT, HAROLD WILLIAM (Ace)
B. May 29, 1899, Mt. Clemens, Mich.   D. Apr. 25, 1963, Honolulu, Hawaii
BR TR 6'1½" 170 lbs.

	W	L	PCT	ERA	G	GS	CG	IP	H	BB	SO	ShO	W	L	SV	AB	H	HR	BA
1929 PHI N	3	7	.300	6.06	40	8	2	114.1	146	59	32	0	2	2	2	30	5	0	.167
1930	6	11	.353	7.67	48	11	2	117.1	191	58	37	0	5	2	0	32	3	0	.094
1931	0	2	.000	9.55	16	4	0	33	46	19	8	0	0	1	2	9	1	0	.111
1932	2	4	.333	5.77	16	7	0	57.2	70	38	13	0	1	1	0	18	3	0	.167
4 yrs.	11	24	.314	6.95	120	30	4	322.1	453	174	90	0	8	6	4	89	12	0	.135

	W	L	PCT	ERA	G	GS	CG	IP	H	BB	SO	ShO	Relief Pitching W	L	SV	BATTING AB	H	HR	BA

Jumbo Elliott

ELLIOTT, JAMES THOMAS
B. Oct. 22, 1900, St. Louis, Mo.   D. Jan. 7, 1970, Terre Haute, Ind.   BR TL 6'3"   235 lbs.

	W	L	PCT	ERA	G	GS	CG	IP	H	BB	SO	ShO	W	L	SV	AB	H	HR	BA
1923 **STL A**	0	0	—	27.00	1	0	0	1	1	3	0	0	0	0	0	0	0	0	
1925 **BKN N**	0	2	.000	8.44	3	1	0	10.2	17	9	3	0	0	1	0	4	0	0	.000
1927	6	13	.316	3.30	30	21	12	188.1	188	60	99	2	0	2	3	64	9	0	.141
1928	9	14	.391	3.89	41	21	7	192	194	64	74	2	2	4	1	68	12	3	.176
1929	1	2	.333	6.63	6	3	0	19	21	16	7	0	0	0	0	4	1	0	.250
1930	10	7	.588	3.95	35	21	6	198.1	204	70	59	2	3	0	1	68	10	1	.147
1931 **PHI N**	19	14	.576	4.27	52	30	12	249	288	83	99	2	3	0	5	90	11	0	.122
1932	11	10	.524	5.42	39	22	8	166	210	47	62	0	2	3	0	61	12	0	.197
1933	6	10	.375	3.84	35	21	6	161.2	188	49	43	0	1	0	2	52	12	0	.231
1934 **2 teams**			PHI	N (3G 0–1)			BOS	N (7G 1–1)											
" total	1	2	.333	6.97	10	4	0	20.2	27	13	7	0	0	1	0	5	1	0	.200
10 yrs.	63	74	.460	4.24	252	144	51	1206.2	1338	414	453	8	11	11	12	416	68	4	.163

Dock Ellis

ELLIS, DOCK PHILLIP
B. Mar. 11, 1945, Los Angeles, Calif.   BB TR 6'3"   205 lbs.

	W	L	PCT	ERA	G	GS	CG	IP	H	BB	SO	ShO	W	L	SV	AB	H	HR	BA
1968 **PIT N**	6	5	.545	2.50	26	10	2	104.1	82	38	52	0	1	2	0	29	2	0	.069
1969	11	17	.393	3.58	35	33	8	219	206	76	173	2	0	0	0	68	6	0	.088
1970	13	10	.565	3.21	30	30	9	202	194	87	128	4	0	0	0	70	7	0	.100
1971	19	9	.679	3.05	31	31	11	227	207	63	137	2	0	0	0	79	16	0	.203
1972	15	7	.682	2.70	25	25	4	163.1	156	33	96	1	0	0	0	59	9	0	.153
1973	12	14	.462	3.05	28	28	3	192	176	55	122	1	0	0	0	65	7	0	.108
1974	12	9	.571	3.15	26	26	9	177	163	41	91	0	0	0	0	56	12	0	.214
1975	8	9	.471	3.79	27	24	5	140	163	43	69	2	0	0	0	36	4	0	.111
1976 **NY A**	17	8	.680	3.19	32	32	8	211.2	195	76	65	1	0	0	0	0	0	0	—
1977 **3 teams**			NY	A (3G 1–1)			OAK	A (7G 1–5)			TEX	A (23G 10–6)							
" total	12	12	.500	3.64	33	32	8	212.2	211	64	106	1	0	0	1	0	0	0	—
1978 **TEX A**	9	7	.563	4.20	22	22	3	141.1	131	46	45	0	1	0	0	0	0	0	—
1979 **3 teams**			TEX	A (10G 1–5)			NY	N (17G 3–7)			PIT	N (3G 0–0)							
" total	4	12	.250	5.83	30	24	1	139	183	52	52	0	1	0	0	27	2	0	.074
12 yrs.	138	119	.537	3.45	345	317	71	2129.1	2067	674	1136	14	2	2	1	489	65	0	.133

LEAGUE CHAMPIONSHIP SERIES

	W	L	PCT	ERA	G	GS	CG	IP	H	BB	SO	ShO	W	L	SV	AB	H	HR	BA
1970 **PIT N**	0	1	.000	2.79	1	1	0	9.2	9	4	1	0	0	0	0	2	0	0	.000
1971	1	0	1.000	3.60	1	1	0	5	6	4	1	0	0	0	0	3	0	0	.000
1972	0	1	.000	0.00	1	1	0	5	5	1	3	0	0	0	0	1	0	0	.000
1975	0	0	—	0.00	1	0	0	2	2	0	2	0	0	0	0	0	0	0	—
1976 **NY A**	1	0	1.000	3.38	1	1	0	8	6	2	5	0	0	0	0	0	0	0	—
5 yrs.	2	2	.500	2.43	5	4	0	29.2	28	11	12	0	0	0	0	6	0	0	.000

WORLD SERIES

	W	L	PCT	ERA	G	GS	CG	IP	H	BB	SO	ShO	W	L	SV	AB	H	HR	BA
1971 **PIT N**	0	1	.000	15.43	1	1	0	2.1	4	1	1	0	0	0	0	1	0	0	.000
1976 **NY A**	0	1	.000	10.80	1	1	0	3.1	7	0	1	0	0	0	0	0	0	0	—
2 yrs.	0	2	.000	12.71	2	2	0	5.2	11	1	2	0	0	0	0	1	0	0	.000

Jim Ellis

ELLIS, JAMES RUSSELL
B. Mar. 25, 1945, Tulare, Calif.   BR TL 6'2"   185 lbs.

	W	L	PCT	ERA	G	GS	CG	IP	H	BB	SO	ShO	W	L	SV	AB	H	HR	BA
1967 **CHI N**	1	1	.500	3.24	8	5	0	16.2	20	9	8	0	0	1	0	5	1	0	.200
1969 **STL N**	0	0	—	1.80	2	1	0	5	7	3	0	0	0	0	0	0	0	0	—
2 yrs.	1	1	.500	2.91	10	2	0	21.2	27	12	8	0	0	1	0	5	1	0	.200

Sammy Ellis

ELLIS, SAMUEL JOSEPH
B. Feb. 11, 1941, Youngstown, Ohio   BL TR 6'1"   175 lbs.

	W	L	PCT	ERA	G	GS	CG	IP	H	BB	SO	ShO	W	L	SV	AB	H	HR	BA
1962 **CIN N**	2	2	.500	6.75	8	4	0	28	29	29	27	0	0	0	0	10	2	0	.200
1964	10	3	.769	2.57	52	5	2	122.1	101	28	125	0	7	2	14	24	2	0	.083
1965	22	10	.688	3.79	44	39	15	263.2	222	104	183	2	2	0	2	96	12	0	.125
1966	12	19	.387	5.29	41	36	7	221	226	78	154	0	1	0	0	70	8	0	.114
1967	8	11	.421	3.84	32	27	8	175.2	197	67	80	1	0	0	0	49	4	0	.082
1968 **CAL A**	9	10	.474	3.95	42	24	3	164	150	56	93	0	1	1	2	44	2	0	.045
1969 **CHI A**	0	3	.000	5.83	10	5	0	29.1	42	16	15	0	0	1	0	6	1	0	.167
7 yrs.	63	58	.521	4.15	229	140	35	1004	967	378	677	3	11	4	18	299	31	0	.104

George Ellison

ELLISON, GEORGE RUSSELL
B. Jan. 24, 1895, California   D. Jan. 20, 1978, San Francisco, Calif.   BR TR 6'3"   185 lbs.

	W	L	PCT	ERA	G	GS	CG	IP	H	BB	SO	ShO	W	L	SV	AB	H	HR	BA
1920 **CLE A**	0	0	—	0.00	1	0	0	1	0	2	1	0	0	0	0	0	0	0	—

Dick Ellsworth

ELLSWORTH, RICHARD CLARK
B. Mar. 22, 1940, Lusk, Wyo.   BL TL 6'3½"   180 lbs.

	W	L	PCT	ERA	G	GS	CG	IP	H	BB	SO	ShO	W	L	SV	AB	H	HR	BA
1958 **CHI N**	0	1	.000	15.43	1	1	0	2.1	4	3	0	0	0	0	0	1	0	0	.000
1960	7	13	.350	3.72	31	27	6	176.2	170	72	94	0	0	0	0	48	2	0	.042
1961	10	11	.476	3.86	37	31	7	186.2	213	48	91	1	1	0	0	56	2	0	.036
1962	9	20	.310	5.09	37	33	6	208.2	241	77	113	0	1	1	0	62	7	0	.113
1963	22	10	.688	2.11	37	37	19	290.2	223	75	185	4	0	0	0	94	9	0	.096
1964	14	18	.438	3.75	37	36	16	256.2	267	71	148	1	0	1	0	87	4	0	.046
1965	14	15	.483	3.81	36	34	8	222.1	227	57	130	4	0	1	0	73	7	0	.096
1966	8	22	.267	3.98	38	37	9	269.1	321	51	144	0	0	0	1	90	14	0	.156
1967 **PHI N**	6	7	.462	4.38	32	21	3	125.1	152	36	45	1	0	0	0	37	4	0	.108
1968 **BOS A**	16	7	.696	3.03	31	28	10	196	196	37	106	1	1	0	0	72	4	0	.056
1969 **2 teams**			BOS	A (2G 0–0)			CLE	A (34G 6–9)											
" total	6	9	.400	4.10	36	24	3	147	178	44	52	1	0	0	0	48	6	0	.125
1970 **2 teams**			CLE	A (29G 3–3)			MIL	A (14G 0–0)											
" total	3	3	.500	3.79	43	16	0	59.1	60	17	22	0	3	2	3	4	0	0	.000
1971 **MIL A**	0	1	.000	4.80	11	0	0	15	22	7	10	0	0	1	0	1	0	0	.000
13 yrs.	115	137	.456	3.72	407	310	87	2156	2274	595	1140	9	7	5	5	673	59	0	.088

	W	L	PCT	ERA	G	GS	CG	IP	H	BB	SO	ShO	Relief Pitching W	L	SV	BATTING AB	H	HR	BA

Don Elston

ELSTON, DONALD RAY
B. Apr. 26, 1929, Campbellstown, Ohio   BR TR 6' 165 lbs.

Year/Team	W	L	PCT	ERA	G	GS	CG	IP	H	BB	SO	ShO	RP W	L	SV	AB	H	HR	BA
1953 CHI N	0	1	.000	14.40	2	1	0	5	11	0	2	0	0	0	0	1	0	0	.000
1957 2 teams					BKN N (1G 0–0)			CHI N (39G 6–7)											
" total	6	7	.462	3.54	40	14	2	145	140	55	103	0	3	1	8	37	4	0	.108
1958 CHI N	9	8	.529	2.88	69	0	0	97	75	39	84	0	9	8	10	14	5	0	.357
1959	10	8	.556	3.32	65	0	0	97.2	77	46	82	0	10	8	13	19	4	0	.211
1960	8	9	.471	3.40	60	0	0	127	109	55	85	0	8	9	11	24	3	0	.125
1961	6	7	.462	5.59	58	0	0	93.1	108	45	59	0	6	7	8	11	2	0	.182
1962	4	8	.333	2.44	57	0	0	66.1	57	32	37	0	4	8	8	8	0	0	.000
1963	4	1	.800	2.83	51	0	0	70	57	21	41	0	4	1	4	4	0	0	.000
1964	2	5	.286	5.30	48	0	0	54.1	68	34	26	0	2	5	1	6	1	0	.167
9 yrs.	49	54	.476	3.69	450	15	2	755.2	702	327	519	0	46	47	63	124	19	0	.153

Bones Ely

ELY, FREDERICK WILLIAM
B. June 7, 1863, Girard, Pa.   D. Jan. 10, 1952, Berkeley, Calif.   BR TR 6'1" 155 lbs.

Year/Team	W	L	PCT	ERA	G	GS	CG	IP	H	BB	SO	ShO	RP W	L	SV	AB	H	HR	BA
1884 BUF N	0	1	.000	14.40	1	1	0	5	17	5	4	0	0	0	0	4	0	0	.000
1886 LOU AA	0	4	.000	5.32	6	4	4	44	53	26	28	0	0	0	1	32	5	0	.156
1890 SYR AA	0	0	–	22.50	1	0	0	2	7	0	0	0	0	0	0	496	130	0	.262
1894 STL N	0	0	–	0.00	1	0	0	1	0	3	0	0	0	0	0	510	156	12	.306
4 yrs.	0	5	.000	6.75	9	5	4	52	77	34	32	0	0	0	1	*			

Harry Ely

ELY, HARRY
B. Unknown.

Year/Team	W	L	PCT	ERA	G	GS	CG	IP	H	BB	SO	ShO	RP W	L	SV	AB	H	HR	BA
1892 BAL N	0	1	.000	7.71	1	1	1	7	14	7	0	0	0	0	0	3	0	0	.000

Red Embree

EMBREE, CHARLES WILLARD
B. Aug. 30, 1917, El Monte, Calif.   BR TR 6' 165 lbs.

Year/Team	W	L	PCT	ERA	G	GS	CG	IP	H	BB	SO	ShO	RP W	L	SV	AB	H	HR	BA
1941 CLE A	0	1	.000	6.75	1	1	0	4	7	3	4	0	0	0	0	1	0	0	.000
1942	3	4	.429	3.86	19	6	2	63	58	31	44	0	2	1	0	15	2	0	.133
1944	0	1	.000	13.50	3	1	0	3.1	2	5	4	0	0	0	0	0	0	0	–
1945	4	4	.500	1.93	8	8	5	70	56	26	42	1	0	0	0	21	3	0	.143
1946	8	12	.400	3.47	28	26	8	200	170	79	87	0	1	0	0	70	13	0	.186
1947	8	10	.444	3.15	27	21	6	162.2	137	67	56	0	2	0	0	52	9	0	.173
1948 NY A	5	3	.625	3.76	20	8	4	76.2	77	30	25	0	0	1	0	27	4	0	.148
1949 STL A	3	13	.188	5.37	35	19	4	127.1	146	89	24	0	0	1	1	37	6	0	.162
8 yrs.	31	48	.392	3.72	141	90	29	707	653	330	286	1	5	3	1	223	37	0	.166

Slim Embry

EMBRY, CHARLES AKIN
B. Aug. 17, 1901, Columbia, Tenn.   D. Oct. 10, 1947, Nashville, Tenn.   BR TR 6'4½" 195 lbs.

Year/Team	W	L	PCT	ERA	G	GS	CG	IP	H	BB	SO	ShO	RP W	L	SV	AB	H	HR	BA
1923 CHI A	0	0	–	10.13	1	0	0	2.2	7	2	1	0	0	0	0	0	0	0	–

Charlie Emig

EMIG, CHARLES H.
B. Bellevue, Ky.   Deceased.

Year/Team	W	L	PCT	ERA	G	GS	CG	IP	H	BB	SO	ShO	RP W	L	SV	AB	H	HR	BA
1896 LOU N	0	1	.000	7.88	1	1	1	8	12	7	1	0	0	0	0	3	0	0	.000

Slim Emmerich

EMMERICH, WILLIAM PETER
B. Sept. 29, 1919, Allentown, Pa.   BR TR 6'1" 170 lbs.

Year/Team	W	L	PCT	ERA	G	GS	CG	IP	H	BB	SO	ShO	RP W	L	SV	AB	H	HR	BA
1945 NY N	4	4	.500	4.86	31	7	1	100	111	33	27	0	3	0	0	25	3	0	.120
1946	0	0	–	4.50	2	0	0	4	6	0	1	0	0	0	0	0	0	0	–
2 yrs.	4	4	.500	4.85	33	7	1	104	117	33	28	0	3	0	0	25	3	0	.120

Bob Emslie

EMSLIE, ROBERT DANIEL
B. Jan. 27, 1859, Guelph, Ont., Canada   D. Apr. 26, 1943, St. Thomas, Ont., Canada   TR

Year/Team	W	L	PCT	ERA	G	GS	CG	IP	H	BB	SO	ShO	RP W	L	SV	AB	H	HR	BA
1883 BAL AA	9	13	.409	3.17	24	23	21	201.1	188	41	62	1	0	0	0	97	16	0	.165
1884	32	17	.653	2.75	50	50	50	455.1	419	88	264	4	0	0	0	195	37	0	.190
1885 2 teams					BAL AA (13G 3–10)			PHI A (4G 0–4)											
" total	3	14	.176	4.71	17	17	14	135.2	168	36	36	0	0	0	0	63	13	0	.206
3 yrs.	44	44	.500	3.19	91	90	85	792.1	775	165	362	5	0	0	0	355	66	0	.186

Joe Engel

ENGEL, JOSEPH WILLIAM
B. Mar. 12, 1893, Washington, D.C.   D. June 12, 1969, Chattanooga, Tenn.   BR TR 6'2" 193 lbs.

Year/Team	W	L	PCT	ERA	G	GS	CG	IP	H	BB	SO	ShO	RP W	L	SV	AB	H	HR	BA
1912 WAS A	2	5	.286	3.96	17	10	2	75	70	50	29	0	1	0	1	17	1	0	.059
1913	8	9	.471	3.06	36	23	6	164.2	124	85	70	2	1	0	0	49	3	0	.061
1914	7	5	.583	2.97	35	15	1	124.1	108	75	41	0	2	1	3	28	3	0	.107
1915	0	3	.000	3.21	11	3	0	33.2	30	19	9	0	0	0	0	6	0	0	.000
1917 CIN N	0	1	.000	5.63	1	1	1	8	12	6	2	0	0	0	0	3	0	0	.000
1919 CLE A	0	0	–	∞	1	0	0	0	3	3	0	0	0	0	0	0	0	0	–
1920 WAS A	0	0	–	21.60	1	0	0	1.2	4	4	0	0	0	0	0	1	0	0	.000
7 yrs.	17	23	.425	3.38	102	52	10	407.1	344	242	151	2	4	1	4	104	7	0	.067

Rick Engle

ENGLE, RICHARD DOUGLAS
B. Apr. 7, 1957, Corbin, Ky.   BL TL 5'11½" 181 lbs.

Year/Team	W	L	PCT	ERA	G	GS	CG	IP	H	BB	SO	ShO	RP W	L	SV	AB	H	HR	BA
1981 MON N	0	0	–	18.00	1	0	0	1	2	1	2	0	0	0	0	0	0	0	–

Jack Enright

ENRIGHT, JACKSON PERCY
B. Nov. 25, 1895, Fort Worth, Tex.   D. Aug. 18, 1975, Pompano Beach, Fla.   BR TR 5'11" 177 lbs.

Year/Team	W	L	PCT	ERA	G	GS	CG	IP	H	BB	SO	ShO	RP W	L	SV	AB	H	HR	BA
1917 NY A	0	1	.000	5.40	1	1	0	5	5	3	1	0	0	0	0	1	0	0	.000

Terry Enyart

ENYART, TERRY GENE
B. Oct. 10, 1950, Ironton, Ohio   BR TL 6'2" 190 lbs.

Year/Team	W	L	PCT	ERA	G	GS	CG	IP	H	BB	SO	ShO	RP W	L	SV	AB	H	HR	BA
1974 MON N	0	0	–	13.50	2	0	0	2	4	4	2	0	0	0	0	0	0	0	–

	W	L	PCT	ERA	G	GS	CG	IP	H	BB	SO	ShO	Relief Pitching W	L	SV	BATTING AB	H	HR	BA

Johnny Enzmann

ENZMANN, JOHN
B. Mar. 4, 1890, Brooklyn, N. Y.   D. Mar. 14, 1984, Riverhead, N. Y.
BR TR 5'10"   165 lbs.

	W	L	PCT	ERA	G	GS	CG	IP	H	BB	SO	ShO	W	L	SV	AB	H	HR	BA
1914 BKN N	1	0	1.000	4.74	7	1	0	19	21	8	5	0	0	0	0	6	0	0	.000
1918 CLE A	5	7	.417	2.37	30	14	8	136.2	130	29	38	0	1	1	2	47	7	0	.149
1919	3	2	.600	2.28	14	4	2	55.1	67	8	13	0	1	1	0	15	2	0	.133
1920 PHI N	2	3	.400	3.84	16	1	1	58.2	79	16	35	0	1	2	0	24	4	0	.167
4 yrs.	11	12	.478	2.84	67	20	11	269.2	297	61	91	0	3	4	2	92	13	0	.141

Al Epperly

EPPERLY, ALBERT PAUL (Pard)
B. May 7, 1918, Glidden, Iowa
BL TR 6'2"   194 lbs.

	W	L	PCT	ERA	G	GS	CG	IP	H	BB	SO	ShO	W	L	SV	AB	H	HR	BA
1938 CHI N	2	0	1.000	3.67	9	4	1	27	28	15	10	0	0	0	0	8	2	0	.250
1950 BKN N	0	0	—	5.00	5	0	0	9	14	5	3	0	0	0	0	0	0	0	—
2 yrs.	2	0	1.000	4.00	14	4	1	36	42	20	13	0	0	0	0	8	2	0	.250

Joe Erardi

ERARDI, JOSEPH GREGORY
B. May 31, 1954, Liverpool, N. Y.
BR TR 6'1"   190 lbs.

	W	L	PCT	ERA	G	GS	CG	IP	H	BB	SO	ShO	W	L	SV	AB	H	HR	BA
1977 SEA A	0	1	.000	6.00	5	0	0	9	12	6	5	0	0	1	0	0	0	0	—

Eddie Erautt

ERAUTT, JOSEPH MICHAEL
Brother of Joe Erautt.
B. Sept. 26, 1924, Portland, Ore.   D. Oct. 6, 1976, Portland, Ore.
BR TR 5'11½" 185 lbs.

	W	L	PCT	ERA	G	GS	CG	IP	H	BB	SO	ShO	W	L	SV	AB	H	HR	BA
1947 CIN N	4	9	.308	5.07	36	10	2	119	146	53	43	0	3	2	0	29	2	0	.069
1948	0	0	—	6.00	2	0	0	3	3	1	0	0	0	0	0	0	0	0	—
1949	4	11	.267	3.36	39	9	1	112.2	99	61	43	0	3	5	1	23	4	0	.174
1950	4	2	.667	5.65	33	2	1	65.1	82	22	35	0	3	1	1	13	2	0	.154
1951	0	0	—	5.72	30	0	0	39.1	50	23	20	0	0	0	0	3	0	0	.000
1953 2 teams			CIN	N	(4G	0–0)		STL	N	(20G	3–1)									
" total	3	1	.750	6.25	24	1	0	40.1	54	19	16	0	3	0	0	7	1	0	.143
6 yrs.	15	23	.395	4.86	164	22	4	379.2	434	179	157	0	12	8	2	75	9	0	.120

Don Erickson

ERICKSON, DON LEE
B. Dec. 13, 1931, Springfield, Ill.
BR TR 6'   175 lbs.

	W	L	PCT	ERA	G	GS	CG	IP	H	BB	SO	ShO	W	L	SV	AB	H	HR	BA
1958 PHI N	0	1	.000	4.63	9	0	0	11.2	11	9	9	0	0	1	1	1	0	0	.000

Eric Erickson

ERICKSON, ERIC GEORGE ADOLPH
B. Mar. 13, 1892, Gothenburg, Sweden   D. May 19, 1965, Jamestown, N. Y.
BR TR 6'2"   190 lbs.

	W	L	PCT	ERA	G	GS	CG	IP	H	BB	SO	ShO	W	L	SV	AB	H	HR	BA
1914 NY N	0	1	.000	0.00	1	1	0	5	8	3	3	0	0	0	0	1	0	0	.000
1916 DET A	0	0	—	2.81	8	0	0	16	13	8	7	0	0	0	0	4	0	0	.000
1918	4	5	.444	2.48	12	9	8	94.1	81	29	48	0	0	1	1	33	4	0	.121
1919 2 teams			DET	A	(3G	0–2)		WAS	A	(20G	6–11)									
" total	6	13	.316	4.23	23	17	7	146.2	147	73	90	1	1	1	0	53	8	0	.151
1920 WAS A	12	16	.429	3.84	39	28	12	239.1	231	128	87	0	2	3	1	83	23	1	.277
1921	8	10	.444	3.62	32	22	9	179	181	65	71	3	0	1	0	60	9	0	.150
1922	4	12	.250	4.96	30	17	6	141.2	144	73	61	2	0	1	2	45	6	0	.133
7 yrs.	34	57	.374	3.85	145	94	42	822	805	379	367	6	3	7	4	279	50	1	.179

Hal Erickson

ERICKSON, HAROLD JAMES
B. July 17, 1919, Portland, Ore.
BR TR 6'5"   230 lbs.

	W	L	PCT	ERA	G	GS	CG	IP	H	BB	SO	ShO	W	L	SV	AB	H	HR	BA
1953 DET A	0	1	.000	4.73	18	0	0	32.1	43	10	19	0	0	1	1	4	0	0	.000

Paul Erickson

ERICKSON, PAUL WALFORD (Li'l Abner)
B. Dec. 14, 1915, Zion, Ill.
BR TR 6'2½" 200 lbs.

	W	L	PCT	ERA	G	GS	CG	IP	H	BB	SO	ShO	W	L	SV	AB	H	HR	BA
1941 CHI N	5	7	.417	3.70	32	15	7	141	126	64	85	1	0	0	1	46	7	1	.152
1942	1	6	.143	5.43	18	7	1	63	70	41	26	0	1	0	0	21	3	0	.143
1943	1	3	.250	6.12	15	4	0	42.2	47	22	24	0	0	1	0	15	3	0	.200
1944	5	9	.357	3.55	33	15	5	124.1	113	67	82	3	5	8	1	36	2	1	.056
1945	7	4	.636	3.32	28	9	3	108.1	94	48	53	0	2	2	3	32	5	0	.156
1946	9	7	.563	2.43	32	14	5	137	119	65	70	1	2	0	0	40	2	0	.050
1947	7	12	.368	4.34	40	20	6	174	179	93	82	0	3	1	1	60	15	1	.250
1948 3 teams			CHI	N	(3G	0–0)	PHI	N	(4G	2–0)		NY	N	(2G	0–0)					
" total	2	0	1.000	5.25	9	2	0	24	26	25	10	0	0	0	0	8	1	0	.125
8 yrs.	37	48	.435	3.86	207	86	27	814.1	774	425	432	5	13	12	6	258	38	3	.147
WORLD SERIES																			
1945 CHI N	0	0	—	3.86	4	0	0	7	8	3	5	0	0	0	0	0	0	0	—

Ralph Erickson

ERICKSON, RALPH LEIF
B. June 25, 1904, Dubois, Ida.
BL TL 6'1"   175 lbs.

	W	L	PCT	ERA	G	GS	CG	IP	H	BB	SO	ShO	W	L	SV	AB	H	HR	BA
1929 PIT N	0	0	—	27.00	1	0	0	1	2	2	0	0	0	0	0	0	0	0	—
1930	1	0	1.000	7.07	7	0	0	14	21	10	2	0	1	0	0	4	1	0	.250
2 yrs.	1	0	1.000	8.40	8	0	0	15	23	12	2	0	1	0	0	4	1	0	.250

Roger Erickson

ERICKSON, ROGER FARRELL
B. Aug. 30, 1956, Springfield, Ill.
BR TR 6'3"   180 lbs.

	W	L	PCT	ERA	G	GS	CG	IP	H	BB	SO	ShO	W	L	SV	AB	H	HR	BA
1978 MIN A	14	13	.519	3.96	37	37	14	265.2	268	79	121	0	0	0	0	0	0	0	—
1979	3	10	.231	5.63	24	21	0	123	154	48	47	0	0	1	0	0	0	0	—
1980	3	13	.350	3.25	32	27	7	191	198	56	97	0	0	0	0	0	0	0	—
1981	3	8	.273	3.86	14	14	1	91	93	31	44	0	0	0	0	0	0	0	—
1982 2 teams			MIN	A	(7G	4–3)		NY	A	(16G	4–5)									
" total	8	8	.500	4.61	23	18	2	111.1	142	29	49	0	0	0	1	0	0	0	—
1983 NY A	1	1	.500	4.32	5	0	0	16.2	13	8	7	0	0	0	0	0	0	0	—
6 yrs.	35	53	.398	4.14	135	117	24	798.2	868	251	365	0	0	2	1	0	0	0	—

Dick Errickson

ERRICKSON, RICHARD MERRIWELL (Lief)
B. Mar. 4, 1914, Vineland, N. J.
BL TR 6'1"   175 lbs.

	W	L	PCT	ERA	G	GS	CG	IP	H	BB	SO	ShO	W	L	SV	AB	H	HR	BA
1938 BOS N	9	7	.563	3.15	34	10	6	122.2	113	56	40	1	3	3	1	35	4	0	.114
1939	6	9	.400	4.00	28	11	3	128.1	143	54	33	0	1	3	1	44	10	0	.227
1940	12	13	.480	3.16	34	29	17	236.1	241	90	34	3	0	0	4	83	13	0	.157

	W	L	PCT	ERA	G	GS	CG	IP	H	BB	SO	ShO	Relief Pitching W	L	SV	BATTING AB	H	HR	BA

Dick Errickson continued

	W	L	PCT	ERA	G	GS	CG	IP	H	BB	SO	ShO	W	L	SV	AB	H	HR	BA
1941	6	12	.333	4.78	38	23	5	165.2	192	62	45	2	1	1	1	45	8	0	.178
1942 2 teams			**BOS**	**N** (21G 2–5)				**CHI**	**N** (13G 1–1)										
" total	3	6	.333	4.75	34	4	0	83.1	115	28	24	0	1	4	1	21	2	0	.095
5 yrs.	36	47	.434	3.85	168	77	31	736.1	804	290	176	6	6	11	13	228	37	0	.162

Carl Erskine

ERSKINE, CARL DANIEL (Oisk)
B. Dec. 13, 1926, Anderson, Ind.

BR TR 5'10" 165 lbs.

	W	L	PCT	ERA	G	GS	CG	IP	H	BB	SO	ShO	W	L	SV	AB	H	HR	BA
1948 BKN N	6	3	.667	3.23	17	9	3	64	51	35	29	0	3	1	0	21	2	0	.095
1949	8	1	.889	4.63	22	3	2	79.2	68	51	49	0	6	1	0	26	3	0	.115
1950	7	6	.538	4.72	22	13	3	103	109	35	50	0	1	0	1	37	9	0	.243
1951	16	12	.571	4.46	46	19	7	189.2	206	78	95	0	9	7	4	61	8	0	.131
1952	14	6	.700	2.70	33	26	10	206.2	167	71	131	4	1	1	2	66	10	0	.152
1953	20	6	**.769**	3.54	39	33	16	246.2	213	95	187	4	1	0	3	93	20	0	.215
1954	18	15	.545	4.15	38	37	12	260.1	239	92	166	2	0	0	1	88	14	0	.159
1955	11	8	.579	3.79	31	29	7	194.2	185	64	84	2	1	0	1	74	15	1	.203
1956	13	11	.542	4.25	31	28	8	186.1	189	57	95	1	2	1	0	66	8	0	.121
1957	5	3	.625	3.55	15	7	1	66	62	20	26	0	1	0	0	22	2	0	.091
1958 LA N	4	4	.500	5.13	31	9	2	98.1	115	35	54	1	1	1	0	27	1	0	.037
1959	0	3	.000	7.71	10	3	0	23.1	33	13	15	0	0	1	0	7	0	0	.000
12 yrs.	122	78	.610	4.00	335	216	71	1718.2	1637	646	981	14	26	12	13	588	92	1	.156

WORLD SERIES																			
1949 BKN N	0	0	—	16.20	2	0	0	1.2	3	1	0	0	0	0	0	0	0	0	—
1952	1	1	.500	4.50	3	2	1	18	12	10	10	0	0	0	0	6	0	0	.000
1953	1	0	1.000	5.79	3	3	1	14	14	9	16	0	0	0	0	4	1	0	.250
1955	0	0	—	9.00	1	1	0	3	3	2	3	0	0	0	0	1	0	0	.000
1956	0	1	.000	5.40	2	1	0	5	4	2	2	0	0	0	0	1	0	0	.000
5 yrs.	2	2	.500	5.83	11	7	2	41.2	36	24	31	0	0	0	0	12	1	0	.083
					10th														

Ernesto Escarrega

ESCARREGA, CHICO ERNESTO
B. Dec. 27, 1949, Los Mochis, Mexico

BR TR 5'10" 196 lbs.

	W	L	PCT	ERA	G	GS	CG	IP	H	BB	SO	ShO	W	L	SV	AB	H	HR	BA
1982 CHI A	1	3	.250	3.67	38	2	0	73.2	73	16	33	0	1	1	1	0	0	0	—

Duke Esper

ESPER, CHARLES H.
B. July 28, 1868, Salem, N. J.   D. Aug. 31, 1910, Philadelphia, Pa.

TL 5'11½" 185 lbs.

	W	L	PCT	ERA	G	GS	CG	IP	H	BB	SO	ShO	W	L	SV	AB	H	HR	BA
1890 3 teams			**PHI**	**AA** (18G 8–9)				**PIT**	**N** (2G 0–2)				**PHI**	**N** (5G 5–0)					
" total	13	11	.542	*4.55*	25	23	20	201.2	234	93	88	1	1	0	0	87	22	0	.253
1891 PHI N	20	15	.571	3.56	39	36	25	296	302	121	108	1	1	0	1	123	27	0	.220
1892 2 teams			**PHI**	**N** (21G 12–6)				**PIT**	**N** (3G 2–0)										
" total	14	6	.700	3.63	24	21	15	178.2	189	70	50	0	1	0	1	79	17	1	.215
1893 WAS N	12	28	.300	4.71	42	36	34	334.1	442	156	78	0	2	2	0	143	41	0	.287
1894 2 teams			**WAS**	**N** (19G 5–10)				**BAL**	**N** (16G 10–2)										
" total	15	12	.556	5.86	35	24	15	224.1	298	76	52	0	3	2	2	102	26	1	.255
1895 BAL N	10	12	.455	3.92	34	25	16	218.1	248	79	39	1	1	4	1	90	16	0	.178
1896	14	5	.737	3.58	20	18	14	155.2	168	39	19	1	2	0	0	66	13	0	.197
1897 STL N	1	6	.143	5.28	8	8	7	61.1	95	12	8	0	0	0	0	25	8	0	.320
1898	3	5	.375	5.98	10	8	6	64.2	86	22	14	0	0	0	0	27	10	0	.370
9 yrs.	102	100	.505	4.40	237	199	152	1735	2062	668	456	4	11	8	5	742	180	2	.243

Nino Espinosa

ESPINOSA, ANULFO ACEVEDO
B. Aug. 15, 1953, Villa Altagracia, Dominican Republic

BR TR 6' 165 lbs.

	W	L	PCT	ERA	G	GS	CG	IP	H	BB	SO	ShO	W	L	SV	AB	H	HR	BA
1974 NY N	0	0	—	5.00	2	1	0	9	12	0	2	0	0	0	0	2	1	0	.500
1975	0	1	.000	18.00	2	0	0	3	8	1	2	0	0	1	0	0	0	0	—
1976	4	4	.500	3.64	12	5	0	42	41	13	30	0	2	2	0	9	0	0	.000
1977	10	13	.435	3.42	32	29	7	200	188	55	105	1	1	0	0	62	8	0	.129
1978	11	15	.423	4.72	32	32	6	204	230	75	76	1	0	0	0	67	14	0	.209
1979 PHI N	14	12	.538	3.65	33	33	8	212	211	65	88	3	0	0	0	72	14	0	.194
1980	3	5	.375	3.79	12	12	1	76	73	19	13	0	0	0	0	26	3	0	.115
1981 2 teams			**PHI**	**N** (14G 2–5)				**TOR**	**A** (1G 0–0)										
" total	2	5	.286	6.12	15	14	2	75	102	24	22	0	0	0	0	20	4	0	.200
8 yrs.	44	55	.444	4.17	140	126	24	821	865	252	338	5	3	3	0	258	44	0	.171

Mark Esser

ESSER, MARK GERALD
B. Apr. 1, 1956, Erie, Pa.

BR TL 6'1" 190 lbs.

	W	L	PCT	ERA	G	GS	CG	IP	H	BB	SO	ShO	W	L	SV	AB	H	HR	BA
1979 CHI A	0	0	—	13.50	2	0	0	2	2	4	1	0	0	0	0	0	0	0	—

Bill Essick

ESSICK, WILLIAM EARL (Vinegar Bill)
B. Dec. 18, 1881, Grand Ridge, Ill.   D. Oct. 11, 1951, Los Angeles, Calif.

TR

	W	L	PCT	ERA	G	GS	CG	IP	H	BB	SO	ShO	W	L	SV	AB	H	HR	BA
1906 CIN N	2	1	.667	2.97	6	4	3	39.1	39	16	16	0	0	0	0	13	1	0	.077
1907	0	2	.000	2.91	3	2	2	21.2	23	8	7	0	0	0	0	8	0	0	.000
2 yrs.	2	3	.400	2.95	9	6	5	61	62	24	23	0	0	0	0	21	1	0	.048

Dick Estelle

ESTELLE, RICHARD HENRY
B. Jan. 18, 1942, Lakewood, N. J.

BB TL 6'2" 170 lbs.

	W	L	PCT	ERA	G	GS	CG	IP	H	BB	SO	ShO	W	L	SV	AB	H	HR	BA
1964 SF N	1	2	.333	3.02	6	6	0	41.2	39	23	23	0	0	0	0	15	1	0	.067
1965	0	0	—	3.97	6	1	0	11.1	12	8	6	0	0	0	0	1	0	0	.000
2 yrs.	1	2	.333	3.23	12	7	0	53	51	31	29	0	0	0	0	16	1	0	.063

George Estock

ESTOCK, GEORGE JOHN
B. Nov. 2, 1924, Stirling, N. J.

BR TR 6' 185 lbs.

	W	L	PCT	ERA	G	GS	CG	IP	H	BB	SO	ShO	W	L	SV	AB	H	HR	BA
1951 BOS N	0	1	.000	4.33	37	1	0	60.1	56	37	11	0	0	0	3	7	2	0	.286

	W	L	PCT	ERA	G	GS	CG	IP	H	BB	SO	ShO	Relief Pitching W	L	SV	BATTING AB	H	HR	BA

Chuck Estrada

ESTRADA, CHARLES LEONARD
B. Feb. 15, 1938, San Luis Obispo, Calif.　　BR TR 6'1"　185 lbs.

	W	L	PCT	ERA	G	GS	CG	IP	H	BB	SO	ShO	W	L	SV	AB	H	HR	BA
1960 BAL A	18	11	.621	3.58	36	25	12	208.2	162	101	144	1	5	2	2	64	9	0	.141
1961	15	9	.625	3.69	33	31	6	212	159	132	160	1	0	0	0	70	8	0	.114
1962	9	17	.346	3.83	34	33	6	223.1	199	121	165	0	0	0	0	66	10	1	.152
1963	3	2	.600	4.60	8	7	0	31.1	26	19	16	0	0	0	0	10	1	0	.100
1964	3	2	.600	5.27	17	6	0	54.2	62	21	32	0	1	2	0	14	2	0	.143
1966 CHI N	1	1	.500	7.30	9	1	0	12.1	16	5	3	0	0	0	0	3	0	0	.000
1967 NY N	1	2	.333	9.41	9	2	0	22	28	17	15	0	1	0	0	5	0	0	.000
7 yrs.	50	44	.532	4.07	146	105	24	764.1	652	416	535	2	7	4	2	232	30	1	.129

Oscar Estrada

ESTRADA, OSCAR
B. Feb. 15, 1904, Havana, Cuba　　D. Jan. 2, 1978, Havana, Cuba　　BL TL 5'8"　160 lbs.

	W	L	PCT	ERA	G	GS	CG	IP	H	BB	SO	ShO	W	L	SV	AB	H	HR	BA
1929 STL A	0	0	—	0.00	1	0	0	1	1	1	0	0	0	0	0	0	0	0	—

John Eubank

EUBANK, JOHN FRANKLIN (Honest John)
B. Sept. 9, 1872, Servia, Ind.　　D. Nov. 3, 1958, Bellevue, Mich.　　BL TR 6'2"　215 lbs.

	W	L	PCT	ERA	G	GS	CG	IP	H	BB	SO	ShO	W	L	SV	AB	H	HR	BA
1905 DET A	1	0	1.000	2.08	3	2	0	17.1	13	3	1	0	1	0	0	11	4	0	.364
1906	4	10	.286	3.53	24	12	7	135	147	35	38	1	1	1	2	60	12	0	.200
1907	3	3	.500	2.67	15	8	4	81	88	20	17	1	0	0	0	31	4	0	.129
3 yrs.	8	13	.381	3.12	42	22	11	233.1	248	58	56	2	2	1	2	102	20	0	.196

Uel Eubanks

EUBANKS, UEL MELVIN (Poss)
B. Feb. 14, 1903, Quinlan, Tex.　　D. Nov. 21, 1954, Dallas, Tex.　　BR TR 6'3"　175 lbs.

	W	L	PCT	ERA	G	GS	CG	IP	H	BB	SO	ShO	W	L	SV	AB	H	HR	BA
1922 CHI N	0	0	—	27.00	2	0	0	1.2	5	4	1	0	0	0	0	1	1	0	1.000

Art Evans

EVANS, WILLIAM ARTHUR
B. Aug. 3, 1911, Elvins, Mo.　　D. Jan. 8, 1952, Wichita, Kans.　　BB TL 6'1½"　181 lbs.

	W	L	PCT	ERA	G	GS	CG	IP	H	BB	SO	ShO	W	L	SV	AB	H	HR	BA
1932 CHI A	0	0	—	3.00	7	0	0	18	19	10	6	0	0	0	0	5	0	0	.000

Bill Evans

EVANS, WILLIAM JAMES
B. Feb. 10, 1893, Reidsville, N. C.　　D. Dec. 21, 1946, Burlington, N. C.　　BR TR 6'　175 lbs.

	W	L	PCT	ERA	G	GS	CG	IP	H	BB	SO	ShO	W	L	SV	AB	H	HR	BA
1916 PIT N	2	5	.286	3.00	13	6	3	63	57	16	21	0	1	0	0	20	3	0	.150
1917	0	4	.000	3.38	8	2	1	26.2	24	14	5	0	0	2	0	9	1	0	.111
1919	0	4	.000	5.65	7	3	2	36.2	41	18	15	0	0	1	0	11	0	0	.000
3 yrs.	2	13	.133	3.85	28	11	6	126.1	122	48	41	0	1	3	0	40	4	0	.100

Bill Evans

EVANS, WILLIAM LAWRENCE
B. Mar. 25, 1919, Childress, Tex.　　BR TR 6'2"　180 lbs.

	W	L	PCT	ERA	G	GS	CG	IP	H	BB	SO	ShO	W	L	SV	AB	H	HR	BA
1949 CHI A	0	1	.000	7.11	4	0	0	6.1	6	8	1	0	0	1	0	1	0	0	.000
1951 BOS A	0	0	—	4.11	9	0	0	15.1	15	8	3	0	0	0	0	4	0	0	.000
2 yrs.	0	1	.000	4.98	13	0	0	21.2	21	16	4	0	0	1	0	5	0	0	.000

Chick Evans

EVANS, CHARLES FRANKLIN
B. Oct. 15, 1889, Arlington, Vt.　　D. Sept. 2, 1916, Schenectady, N. Y.　　BR TR

	W	L	PCT	ERA	G	GS	CG	IP	H	BB	SO	ShO	W	L	SV	AB	H	HR	BA
1909 BOS N	0	3	.000	4.57	4	3	1	21.2	25	14	11	0	0	0	0	9	0	0	.000
1910	1	1	.500	5.23	13	1	0	31	28	27	12	0	1	0	0	10	1	0	.100
2 yrs.	1	4	.200	4.96	17	4	1	52.2	53	41	23	0	1	0	0	19	1	0	.053

Jake Evans

EVANS, JACOB (Bloody Jake)
B. Baltimore, Md.　　D. Feb. 3, 1907, Baltimore, Md.　　5'8"　154 lbs.

	W	L	PCT	ERA	G	GS	CG	IP	H	BB	SO	ShO	W	L	SV	AB	H	HR	BA
1880 TRO N	0	0	—	13.50	1	0	0	4	11	0	0	0	0	0	0	180	46	0	.256
1882 WOR N	0	1	.000	5.63	1	1	1	8	13	0	2	0	0	0	0	334	71	0	.213
1883 CLE N	0	0	—	0.00	1	0	0	3	0	0	1	0	0	0	0	332	79	0	.238
3 yrs.	0	1	.000	6.60	3	1	1	15	24	0	3	0	0	0	0	*			

Red Evans

EVANS, RUSSELL EDISON
B. Nov. 12, 1906, Chicago, Ill.　　D. June 18, 1982, Lakeview, Ark.　　BR TR 5'11"　168 lbs.

	W	L	PCT	ERA	G	GS	CG	IP	H	BB	SO	ShO	W	L	SV	AB	H	HR	BA
1936 CHI A	0	3	.000	7.61	17	0	0	47.1	70	22	19	0	0	3	1	15	2	0	.133
1939 BKN N	1	8	.111	5.18	24	6	0	64.1	74	26	28	0	1	2	1	13	4	0	.308
2 yrs.	1	11	.083	6.21	41	6	0	111.2	144	48	47	0	1	5	2	28	6	0	.214

Roy Evans

EVANS, ROY
B. Mar. 19, 1874, Knoxville, Tenn.　　D. Aug. 15, 1915, Galveston, Tex.　　BR TR 6'　180 lbs.

	W	L	PCT	ERA	G	GS	CG	IP	H	BB	SO	ShO	W	L	SV	AB	H	HR	BA
1897 2 teams			STL	N	(3G 0–0)			LOU	N	(9G 5–4)									
" total	5	4	.556	5.10	12	8	6	72.1	99	37	24	0	0	1	0	26	3	0	.115
1898 WAS N	3	3	.500	3.38	7	4	4	50.2	50	25	11	0	0	0	0	19	1	0	.053
1899	3	4	.429	5.67	7	7	6	54	60	25	27	0	0	0	0	20	4	0	.200
1902 2 teams			NY	N	(13G 8–13)			BKN	N	(5G 5–6)									
" total	13	19	.406	3.00	36	28	28	273.1	277	91	83	2	2	3	0	88	17	0	.193
1903 2 teams			BKN	N	(15G 4–8)			STL	A	(7G 0–4)									
" total	4	12	.250	3.57	22	19	13	164	187	55	66	0	1	1	0	48	7	0	.146
5 yrs.	28	42	.400	3.66	84	68	57	614.1	673	233	211	2	3	5	0	201	32	0	.159

Leon Everitt

EVERITT, EDWARD LEON
B. Jan. 12, 1947, Marshall, Tex.　　BL TR 6'1½"　195 lbs.

	W	L	PCT	ERA	G	GS	CG	IP	H	BB	SO	ShO	W	L	SV	AB	H	HR	BA
1969 SD N	0	1	.000	7.88	5	0	0	16	18	12	11	0	0	0	0	3	0	0	.000

Bob Ewing

EWING, GEORGE LEMUEL (Long Bob)
B. Apr. 24, 1873, New Hampshire, Ohio　　D. June 20, 1947, Wapakoneta, Ohio　　BR TR 6'1½"　170 lbs.

	W	L	PCT	ERA	G	GS	CG	IP	H	BB	SO	ShO	W	L	SV	AB	H	HR	BA
1902 CIN N	6	6	.500	2.98	15	12	10	117.2	126	47	44	0	0	0	0	71	12	0	.169
1903	14	13	.519	2.77	29	28	27	246.2	254	64	104	1	0	0	1	95	24	0	.253
1904	11	13	.458	2.46	26	24	22	212	198	58	99	0	1	0	0	97	25	1	.258
1905	20	11	.645	2.51	40	34	30	312	284	79	164	4	3	0	0	122	32	0	.262
1906	13	14	.481	2.38	33	32	26	287.2	248	60	145	2	0	1	0	101	14	1	.139
1907	17	19	.472	1.73	41	37	32	332.2	279	85	147	2	1	1	0	123	19	1	.154

	W	L	PCT	ERA	G	GS	CG	IP	H	BB	SO	ShO	Relief Pitching W	L	SV	BATTING AB	H	HR	BA

Bob Ewing continued

	W	L	PCT	ERA	G	GS	CG	IP	H	BB	SO	ShO	W	L	SV	AB	H	HR	BA
1908	17	15	.531	2.21	37	32	23	293.2	247	57	95	4	1	1	3	94	14	0	.149
1909	11	12	.478	2.43	31	29	14	218.1	195	63	86	2	0	1	0	73	8	0	.110
1910 PHI N	16	14	.533	3.00	34	32	20	255.1	235	86	102	4	0	1	0	90	20	0	.222
1911	0	1	.000	7.88	4	3	1	24	29	14	12	0	0	0	0	6	2	0	.333
1912 STL N	0	0	–	0.00	1	1	0	1.1	2	1	0	0	0	0	0	0	0	0	–
11 yrs.	125	118	.514	2.49	291	264	205	2301.1	2097	614	998	19	6	5	4	872	170	3	.195

Buck Ewing

EWING, WILLIAM
Brother of John Ewing.
B. Oct. 17, 1859, Hoaglands, Ohio   D. Oct. 20, 1906, Cincinnati, Ohio
Manager 1890, 1895-1900.
Hall of Fame 1939.

BR TR 5'10"   188 lbs.

	W	L	PCT	ERA	G	GS	CG	IP	H	BB	SO	ShO	W	L	SV	AB	H	HR	BA
1882 TRO N	0	0	–	9.00	1	0	0	1	2	1	0	0	0	0	0	328	89	2	.271
1884 NY N	0	1	.000	1.13	1	1	1	8	7	4	3	0	0	0	0	382	106	3	.277
1885	0	1	.000	4.50	1	0	0	2	4	3	0	0	0	1	0	342	104	6	.304
1888	1	0	1.000	2.57	2	0	0	7	8	4	6	0	1	0	0	415	127	6	.306
1889	2	0	1.000	4.05	3	2	2	20	23	8	12	0	0	0	0	407	133	4	.327
1890 NY P	0	1	.000	4.00	1	1	1	9	11	3	2	0	0	0	0	352	119	8	.338
6 yrs.	3	3	.500	3.45	9	4	4	47	55	23	23	0	1	1	0	*			

John Ewing

EWING, JOHN
Brother of Buck Ewing.
B. June 1, 1863, Cincinnati, Ohio   D. Apr. 23, 1895, Denver, Colo.

TR

	W	L	PCT	ERA	G	GS	CG	IP	H	BB	SO	ShO	W	L	SV	AB	H	HR	BA
1883 STL AA	0	0	–	0.00	0	0	0	0	0	0	0	0	0	0	0	5	0	0	.000
1884 CIN U	0	0	–	0.00	0	0	0	0	0	0	0	0	0	0	0	9	1	0	.111
1888 LOU AA	8	13	.381	2.83	21	21	21	191	175	34	87	2	0	0	0	79	16	0	.203
1889	6	30	.167	4.87	40	39	37	331	407	147	155	1	0	0	0	134	23	0	.172
1890 NY P	18	12	.600	4.24	35	31	27	267.1	293	104	145	1	1	0	2	114	24	2	.211
1891 NY N	21	8	.724	2.27	33	30	28	269.1	237	105	138	5	1	0	0	113	23	0	.204
6 yrs.	53	63	.457	3.68	129	121	113	1058.2	1112	390	525	9	2	0	2	454	87	2	.192

George Eyrich

EYRICH, GEORGE LINCOLN
B. Mar. 3, 1925, Reading, Pa.

BR TR 5'11"   175 lbs.

	W	L	PCT	ERA	G	GS	CG	IP	H	BB	SO	ShO	W	L	SV	AB	H	HR	BA
1943 PHI N	0	0	–	3.38	9	0	0	18.2	23	9	5	0	0	0	0	2	0	0	.000

Red Faber

FABER, URBAN CLARENCE
B. Sept. 6, 1888, Cascade, Iowa
D. Sept. 25, 1976, Chicago, Ill.
Hall of Fame 1964.

BB TR 6'2"   180 lbs.
BR 1925

	W	L	PCT	ERA	G	GS	CG	IP	H	BB	SO	ShO	W	L	SV	AB	H	HR	BA
1914 CHI A	10	9	.526	2.68	40	20	11	181.1	154	64	88	2	2	2	4	55	8	0	.145
1915	24	14	.632	2.55	50	32	22	299.2	264	99	182	3	5	4	2	84	11	0	.131
1916	17	9	.654	2.02	35	25	15	205.1	167	61	87	3	2	1	1	63	6	0	.095
1917	16	13	.552	1.92	41	29	16	248	224	85	84	3	2	3	3	69	4	0	.058
1918	4	1	.800	1.23	11	9	5	80.2	70	23	26	1	0	0	1	24	1	0	.042
1919	11	9	.550	3.83	25	20	9	162.1	185	45	45	0	3	0	0	54	10	0	.185
1920	23	13	.639	2.99	40	39	28	319	332	88	108	2	0	0	1	104	11	0	.106
1921	25	15	.625	2.48	43	39	32	330.2	293	87	124	4	1	1	1	108	16	0	.148
1922	21	17	.553	2.80	43	38	31	353	334	83	148	4	1	1	2	125	25	0	.200
1923	14	11	.560	3.41	32	31	15	232.1	233	62	91	2	0	1	0	69	15	1	.217
1924	9	11	.450	3.85	21	20	9	161.1	173	58	47	0	0	1	0	54	8	0	.148
1925	12	11	.522	3.78	34	32	16	238	266	59	71	1	1	1	0	77	8	0	.104
1926	15	9	.652	3.56	27	25	13	184.2	203	57	65	1	0	2	0	60	9	0	.150
1927	4	7	.364	4.55	18	15	6	110.2	131	41	39	0	0	0	0	37	10	0	.270
1928	13	9	.591	3.75	27	27	16	201.1	223	68	43	2	0	0	0	70	8	1	.114
1929	13	13	.500	3.88	31	31	15	234	241	61	68	1	0	0	0	78	10	1	.128
1930	8	13	.381	4.21	29	26	10	169	188	49	62	0	0	0	1	49	2	0	.041
1931	10	14	.417	3.82	44	19	5	184	210	57	49	1	5	2	1	53	4	0	.075
1932	2	11	.154	3.74	42	5	0	106	123	38	26	0	2	6	6	18	4	0	.222
1933	3	4	.429	3.44	36	2	0	86.1	92	28	18	0	3	2	5	18	0	0	.000
20 yrs.	254	212	.545	3.15	669	484	274	4087.2	4106	1213	1471	30	27	27	28	1269	170	3	.134

WORLD SERIES

	W	L	PCT	ERA	G	GS	CG	IP	H	BB	SO	ShO	W	L	SV	AB	H	HR	BA
1917 CHI A	3	1	.750	2.33	4	3	2	27	21	3	9	0	1	0	0	7	1	0	.143

Roy Face

FACE, ELROY LEON
B. Feb. 20, 1928, Stephentown, N.Y.

BB TR 5'8"   155 lbs.
BR 1953-59

	W	L	PCT	ERA	G	GS	CG	IP	H	BB	SO	ShO	W	L	SV	AB	H	HR	BA
1953 PIT N	6	8	.429	6.58	41	13	2	119	145	30	56	0	3	2	0	30	4	0	.133
1955	5	7	.417	3.58	42	10	4	125.2	128	40	84	0	1	1	5	26	3	0	.115
1956	12	13	.480	3.52	68	3	0	135.1	131	42	96	0	11	12	6	26	5	0	.192
1957	4	6	.400	3.07	59	1	0	93.2	97	24	53	0	4	6	10	16	2	0	.125
1958	5	2	.714	2.89	57	0	0	84	77	22	47	0	5	2	20	7	0	0	.000
1959	18	1	.947 [1]	2.70	57	0	0	93.1	91	25	69	0	18 [1]	1	10	13	3	0	.231
1960	10	8	.556	2.90	68	0	0	114.2	93	29	72	0	10	8	24	17	7	0	.412
1961	6	12	.333	3.82	62	0	0	92	94	10	55	0	6	12	17	11	3	0	.273
1962	8	7	.533	1.88	63	0	0	91	74	18	45	0	8	7	28	12	1	0	.083
1963	3	9	.250	3.23	56	0	0	69.2	75	19	41	0	3	9	16	8	2	0	.250
1964	3	3	.500	5.20	55	0	0	79.2	82	27	63	0	3	3	4	4	0	0	.000
1965	5	2	.714	2.66	16	0	0	20.1	20	7	19	0	5	2	0	1	0	0	.000
1966	6	6	.500	2.70	54	0	0	70	68	24	67	0	6	6	18	11	0	0	.000
1967	7	5	.583	2.42	61	0	0	74.1	62	22	41	0	7	5	17	6	0	0	.000
1968 2 teams			PIT	N	(43G 2-4)		DET	A	(2G 0-0)										
" total	2	4	.333	2.55	45	0	0	53	48	8	35	0	2	4	13	4	0	0	.000
1969 MON N	4	2	.667	3.94	44	0	0	59.1	62	15	34	0	4	2	5	2	1	0	.500
16 yrs.	104	95	.523	3.48	848 8th	27	6	1375	1347	362	877	0	96 5th	82	193 6th	194	31	0	.160

WORLD SERIES

	W	L	PCT	ERA	G	GS	CG	IP	H	BB	SO	ShO	W	L	SV	AB	H	HR	BA
1960 PIT N	0	0	–	5.23	4	0	0	10.1	9	2	4	0	0	0	3 4th	3	0	0	.000

	W	L	PCT	ERA	G	GS	CG	IP	H	BB	SO	ShO	Relief Pitching W	L	SV	BATTING AB	H	HR	BA

Tony Faeth

FAETH, ANTHONY JOSEPH   BR TR 6'   180 lbs.
B. July 9, 1893, Aberdeen, S. D.   D. Dec. 22, 1982, St Paul, Minn.

	W	L	PCT	ERA	G	GS	CG	IP	H	BB	SO	ShO	W	L	SV	AB	H	HR	BA
1919 CLE A	0	0	–	0.49	6	0	0	18.1	13	10	7	0	0	0	0	4	0	0	.000
1920	0	0	–	4.32	13	0	0	25	31	20	14	0	0	0	0	5	0	0	.000
2 yrs.	0	0	–	2.70	19	0	0	43.1	44	30	21	0	0	0	0	9	0	0	.000

Bill Fagan

FAGAN, WILLIAM A. (Clinkers)   TL
B. Feb. 15, 1869, Troy, N. Y.   D. Mar. 21, 1930, Troy, N. Y.

	W	L	PCT	ERA	G	GS	CG	IP	H	BB	SO	ShO	W	L	SV	AB	H	HR	BA
1887 NY AA	1	4	.200	4.00	6	6	6	45	55	24	12	0	0	0	0	21	3	0	.143
1888 KC AA	5	11	.313	5.69	17	17	15	142.1	179	75	49	0	0	0	0	65	14	0	.215
2 yrs.	6	15	.286	5.28	23	23	21	187.1	234	99	61	0	0	0	0	86	17	0	.198

Everett Fagan

FAGAN, EVERETT JOSEPH   BR TR 6'   195 lbs.
B. Jan. 13, 1918, Pottersville, N. J.   D. Feb. 16, 1983, Morristown, N. J.

	W	L	PCT	ERA	G	GS	CG	IP	H	BB	SO	ShO	W	L	SV	AB	H	HR	BA
1943 PHI A	2	6	.250	6.27	18	2	0	37.1	41	14	9	0	2	4	3	7	0	0	.000
1946	0	1	.000	4.80	20	0	0	45	47	24	12	0	0	1	0	14	4	0	.286
2 yrs.	2	7	.222	5.47	38	2	0	82.1	88	38	21	0	2	5	3	21	4	0	.190

Frank Fahey

FAHEY, FRANCIS RAYMOND   BB TR 6'1"   190 lbs.
B. Jan. 22, 1896, Milford, Mass.   D. Mar. 19, 1954, Uxbridge, Mass.

	W	L	PCT	ERA	G	GS	CG	IP	H	BB	SO	ShO	W	L	SV	AB	H	HR	BA
1918 PHI A	0	0	–	6.00	3	0	0	9	5	14	1	0	0	0	0	*			

Red Fahr

FAHR, GERALD WARREN   BR TR 6'5"   185 lbs.
B. Dec. 9, 1924, Marmaduke, Ark.

	W	L	PCT	ERA	G	GS	CG	IP	H	BB	SO	ShO	W	L	SV	AB	H	HR	BA
1951 CLE A	0	0	–	4.76	5	0	0	5.2	11	2	0	0	0	0	0	0	0	0	–

Pete Fahrer

FAHRER, CLARENCE WILLIE   BL TR 6'   190 lbs.
B. Mar. 10, 1890, Holgate, Ohio   D. June 10, 1967, Fremont, Mich.

	W	L	PCT	ERA	G	GS	CG	IP	H	BB	SO	ShO	W	L	SV	AB	H	HR	BA
1914 CIN N	0	0	–	1.13	5	0	0	8	8	4	2	0	0	0	0	1	0	0	.000

Jim Fairbank

FAIRBANK, JAMES LEE (Smoky, Lee)   BR TR 5'10"   185 lbs.
B. Mar. 17, 1881, Deansboro, N. Y.   D. Dec. 27, 1955, Utica, N. Y.

	W	L	PCT	ERA	G	GS	CG	IP	H	BB	SO	ShO	W	L	SV	AB	H	HR	BA
1903 PHI A	1	1	.500	4.88	4	1	1	24	33	12	10	0	0	1	0	10	1	0	.100
1904	0	1	.000	6.35	3	1	1	17	19	13	6	0	0	0	0	6	0	0	.000
2 yrs.	1	2	.333	5.49	7	2	2	41	52	25	16	0	0	1	0	16	1	0	.063

Rags Faircloth

FAIRCLOTH, JAMES LAMAR   BR TR 5'11"   160 lbs.
B. Aug. 19, 1892, Kenton, Tenn.   D. Oct. 5, 1953, Tucson, Ariz.

	W	L	PCT	ERA	G	GS	CG	IP	H	BB	SO	ShO	W	L	SV	AB	H	HR	BA
1919 PHI N	0	0	–	9.00	2	0	0	5	2	5	0	0	0	0	0	0	0	0	–

Pete Falcone

FALCONE, PETER   BL TL 6'2"   185 lbs.
B. Oct. 1, 1953, Brooklyn, N. Y.

	W	L	PCT	ERA	G	GS	CG	IP	H	BB	SO	ShO	W	L	SV	AB	H	HR	BA
1975 SF N	12	11	.522	4.17	34	32	3	190	171	111	131	1	0	0	0	65	4	0	.062
1976 STL N	12	16	.429	3.23	32	32	9	212	173	93	138	2	0	0	0	62	8	0	.129
1977	4	8	.333	5.44	27	22	1	124	130	61	75	1	0	1	1	41	10	0	.244
1978	2	7	.222	5.76	19	14	0	75	94	48	28	0	0	0	0	21	5	0	.238
1979 NY N	6	14	.300	4.16	33	31	1	184	194	76	113	1	0	0	0	52	9	0	.173
1980	7	10	.412	4.53	37	23	1	157	163	58	109	0	1	1	1	41	6	0	.146
1981	5	3	.625	2.56	35	9	3	95	84	36	56	1	2	1	1	22	4	1	.182
1982	8	10	.444	3.84	40	23	3	171	159	71	101	0	1	1	2	53	6	0	.113
1983 ATL N	9	4	.692	3.63	33	15	2	106.2	102	60	59	0	3	1	0	26	3	0	.115
1984	5	7	.417	4.13	35	16	2	120	115	57	55	1	1	0	2	33	7	0	.212
10 yrs.	70	90	.438	4.07	325	217	25	1434.2	1385	671	865	7	8	5	7	416	62	1	.149

Chet Falk

FALK, CHESTER EMANUEL (Spot)   BL TL 6'2"   170 lbs.
Brother of Bibb Falk.
B. May 15, 1905, Austin, Tex.

	W	L	PCT	ERA	G	GS	CG	IP	H	BB	SO	ShO	W	L	SV	AB	H	HR	BA
1925 STL A	0	0	–	8.28	13	0	0	25	38	17	7	0	0	0	0	8	5	0	.625
1926	4	4	.500	5.35	18	8	3	74	95	27	7	0	1	0	0	31	6	0	.194
1927	1	0	1.000	5.74	9	0	0	15.2	25	10	2	0	1	0	0	5	1	0	.200
3 yrs.	5	4	.556	6.04	40	8	3	114.2	158	54	16	0	2	0	0	44	12	0	.273

Cy Falkenberg

FALKENBERG, FREDERICK PETER   BR TR 6'5"   180 lbs.
B. Dec. 17, 1880, Chicago, Ill.   D. Apr. 14, 1961, San Francisco, Calif.

	W	L	PCT	ERA	G	GS	CG	IP	H	BB	SO	ShO	W	L	SV	AB	H	HR	BA
1903 PIT N	2	4	.333	3.86	10	6	3	56	65	32	24	0	0	0	0	21	4	0	.190
1905 WAS A	7	1	.875	3.82	12	10	6	75.1	71	31	35	2	1	0	0	32	4	0	.125
1906	14	20	.412	2.86	40	36	30	298.2	277	108	178	2	0	0	1	106	18	1	.170
1907	6	17	.261	2.35	32	24	17	233.2	195	77	108	1	0	2	0	86	12	0	.140
1908 2 teams								WAS A (17G 6–2)				CLE A (8G 2–4)							
" total	8	6	.571	2.65	25	15	7	129	122	31	51	1	1	0	0	44	8	0	.182
1909 CLE A	10	9	.526	2.40	24	18	13	165	135	50	82	2	0	1	0	52	9	0	.173
1910	14	13	.519	2.95	37	29	18	256.2	246	75	107	3	3	0	1	82	15	0	.183
1911	8	5	.615	3.29	15	13	7	106.2	117	24	46	0	0	1	1	40	7	0	.175
1913	23	10	.697	2.22	39	36	23	276	238	88	166	6	0	0	0	84	10	0	.119
1914 IND F	25	18	.581	2.22	49	43	33	377.1	332	89	236	9	0	2	3	125	21	0	.168
1915 2 teams								NWK F (25G 9–11)				BKN F (7G 3–3)							
" total	12	14	.462	2.86	32	28	19	220	206	59	96	1	4	0	0	72	4	0	.056
1917 PHI A	2	6	.250	3.35	15	8	4	80.2	86	26	35	0	0	1	0	27	5	0	.185
12 yrs.	131	123	.516	2.68	330	266	180	2275	2090	690	1164	27	6	7	7	771	117	1	.152

Ed Fallenstin

FALLENSTIN, EDWARD JOSEPH (Jack)   BR TR 6'3"   180 lbs.
Also known as Edward Joseph Valestin.
B. Dec. 22, 1908, Newark, N. J.   D. Nov. 24, 1971, Orange, N. J.

	W	L	PCT	ERA	G	GS	CG	IP	H	BB	SO	ShO	W	L	SV	AB	H	HR	BA
1931 PHI N	0	0	–	7.13	24	0	0	41.2	56	26	15	0	0	0	0	5	1	0	.200
1933 BOS N	2	1	.667	3.60	9	4	1	35	43	13	5	1	0	0	0	8	3	0	.375
2 yrs.	2	1	.667	5.52	33	4	1	76.2	99	39	20	1	0	0	0	13	4	0	.308

	W	L	PCT	ERA	G	GS	CG	IP	H	BB	SO	ShO	Relief Pitching W	L	SV	AB	H	HR	BA

Bob Fallon

FALLON, ROBERT JOSEPH   BL TL 6'3"   200 lbs.
B. Feb. 18, 1960, New York, N. Y.

	W	L	PCT	ERA	G	GS	CG	IP	H	BB	SO	ShO	W	L	SV	AB	H	HR	BA
1984 CHI A	0	0	—	3.68	3	3	0	14.2	12	11	10	0	0	0	0	0	0	0	—

Cliff Fannin

FANNIN, CLIFFORD BRYSON (Mule)   BL TR 6'   170 lbs.
B. May 13, 1924, Louisa, Ky.   D. Dec. 11, 1966, Sandusky, Ohio

	W	L	PCT	ERA	G	GS	CG	IP	H	BB	SO	ShO	W	L	SV	AB	H	HR	BA
1945 STL A	0	0	—	2.61	5	0	0	10.1	8	5	5	0	0	0	0	1	0	0	.000
1946	5	2	.714	3.01	27	7	4	86.2	76	42	52	1	0	0	2	31	5	0	.161
1947	6	8	.429	3.58	26	18	6	145.2	134	77	77	2	0	0	1	46	9	0	.196
1948	10	14	.417	4.17	34	29	10	213.2	198	104	102	3	0	0	1	65	11	0	.169
1949	8	14	.364	6.17	30	25	5	143	177	93	57	0	0	2	1	55	9	0	.164
1950	5	9	.357	6.53	25	16	3	102	116	58	42	0	2	1	1	34	6	0	.176
1951	0	2	.000	6.46	7	1	0	15.1	20	5	11	0	0	2	0	4	1	0	.250
1952	0	2	.000	12.67	10	2	0	16.1	34	9	6	0	0	0	0	1	0	0	.000
8 yrs.	34	51	.400	4.85	164	98	28	733	763	393	352	6	2	5	6	237	41	0	.173

Jack Fanning

FANNING, JOHN JACOB
B. 1863, South Orange, N. J.   D. June 10, 1917, Aberdeen, Wash.

	W	L	PCT	ERA	G	GS	CG	IP	H	BB	SO	ShO	W	L	SV	AB	H	HR	BA
1889 IND N	0	1	.000	18.00	1	1	0	3	3	2	0	0	0	0	0	1	0	0	.000
1894 PHI N	1	3	.250	8.07	5	4	2	32.1	45	20	7	0	0	0	0	13	2	0	.154
2 yrs.	1	4	.200	8.37	6	5	2	33.1	48	22	7	0	0	0	0	14	2	0	.143

Harry Fanok

FANOK, HARRY MICHAEL (The Flame Thrower)   BB TR 6'   180 lbs.
B. May 11, 1940, Whippany, N. J.

	W	L	PCT	ERA	G	GS	CG	IP	H	BB	SO	ShO	W	L	SV	AB	H	HR	BA
1963 STL N	2	1	.667	5.26	12	0	0	25.2	24	21	25	0	2	1	1	5	2	0	.400
1964	0	0	—	5.87	4	0	0	7.2	5	3	10	0	0	0	0	1	0	0	.000
2 yrs.	2	1	.667	5.40	16	0	0	33.1	29	24	35	0	2	1	1	6	2	0	.333

Frank Fanovich

FANOVICH, FRANK JOSEPH (Lefty)   BL TL 5'11"   180 lbs.
B. Jan. 11, 1922, New York, N. Y.

	W	L	PCT	ERA	G	GS	CG	IP	H	BB	SO	ShO	W	L	SV	AB	H	HR	BA
1949 CIN N	0	2	.000	5.40	29	1	0	43.1	44	28	27	0	0	1	0	4	0	0	.000
1953 PHI A	0	3	.000	5.55	26	3	0	61.2	62	37	37	0	0	1	0	11	2	0	.182
2 yrs.	0	5	.000	5.49	55	4	0	105	106	65	64	0	0	2	0	15	2	0	.133

Harry Fanwell

FANWELL, HARRY CLAYTON   BB TR 6'   175 lbs.
B. Oct. 16, 1886, Patapsco, Md.   D. July 16, 1965, Baltimore, Md.

	W	L	PCT	ERA	G	GS	CG	IP	H	BB	SO	ShO	W	L	SV	AB	H	HR	BA
1910 CLE A	2	9	.182	3.62	17	11	5	92	87	38	30	1	1	0	0	30	1	0	.033

Ed Farmer

FARMER, EDWARD JOSEPH   BR TR 6'5"   200 lbs.
B. Oct. 18, 1949, Evergreen Park, Ill.

	W	L	PCT	ERA	G	GS	CG	IP	H	BB	SO	ShO	W	L	SV	AB	H	HR	BA
1971 CLE A	5	4	.556	4.33	43	4	0	79	77	41	48	0	5	2	4	14	1	0	.071
1972	2	5	.286	4.43	46	1	0	61	51	27	33	0	2	4	7	7	1	0	.143
1973 2 teams			CLE A (16G 0-2)				DET A (24G 3-0)												
" total	3	2	.600	4.91	40	0	0	62.1	77	32	38	0	3	2	3	0	0	0	—
1974 PHI N	2	1	.667	8.42	14	3	0	31	41	27	20	0	1	0	0	9	1	0	.111
1977 BAL A	0	0	—	∞	1	0	0	0	1	1	0	0	0	0	0	0	0	0	—
1978 MIL A	1	0	1.000	0.82	3	0	0	11	7	4	6	0	1	0	1	0	0	0	—
1979 2 teams			TEX A (11G 2-0)				CHI A (42G 3-7)												
" total	5	7	.417	3.00	53	5	0	114	96	53	73	0	5	7	14	0	0	0	—
1980 CHI A	7	9	.438	3.33	64	0	0	100	92	56	54	0	7	9	30	0	0	0	—
1981	3	3	.500	4.58	42	0	0	53	53	34	42	0	3	3	10	0	0	0	—
1982 PHI N	2	6	.250	4.86	47	4	0	76	66	50	58	0	1	4	6	11	0	0	.000
1983 2 teams			PHI N (12G 0-6)				OAK A (5G 0-0)												
" total	0	6	.000	5.35	17	4	0	37	50	20	23	0	0	3	0	6	1	0	.167
11 yrs.	30	43	.411	4.30	370	21	0	624.1	611	345	395	0	28	34	75	47	4	0	.085

Jimmy Farr

FARR, JAMES ALFRED   BR TR 6'1"   195 lbs.
B. May 18, 1956, Waverly, N. Y.

	W	L	PCT	ERA	G	GS	CG	IP	H	BB	SO	ShO	W	L	SV	AB	H	HR	BA
1982 TEX A	0	0	—	2.50	5	0	0	18	20	7	6	0	0	0	0	0	0	0	—

Steve Farr

FARR, STEVEN MICHAEL   BR TR 5'10"   190 lbs.
B. Dec. 12, 1956, Portland, Ore.

	W	L	PCT	ERA	G	GS	CG	IP	H	BB	SO	ShO	W	L	SV	AB	H	HR	BA
1984 CLE A	3	11	.214	4.58	31	16	0	116	106	46	83	0	1	2	1	0	0	0	—

Dick Farrell

FARRELL, RICHARD JOSEPH (Turk)   BR TR 6'4"   215 lbs.
B. Apr. 8, 1934, Boston, Mass.   D. June 11, 1977, Great Yarmouth, England

	W	L	PCT	ERA	G	GS	CG	IP	H	BB	SO	ShO	W	L	SV	AB	H	HR	BA
1956 PHI N	0	1	.000	12.46	7	1	0	4.1	6	3	0	0	0	0	0	1	0	0	.000
1957	10	2	.833	2.38	52	0	0	83.1	74	36	54	0	10	2	10	9	1	1	.111
1958	8	9	.471	3.35	54	0	0	94	84	40	73	0	8	9	11	24	5	0	.208
1959	1	6	.143	4.74	38	0	0	57	61	25	31	0	1	6	6	6	1	0	.167
1960	10	6	.625	2.70	59	0	0	103.1	88	29	70	0	10	6	11	15	3	0	.200
1961 2 teams			PHI N (5G 2-1)				LA N (50G 6-6)												
" total	8	7	.533	5.20	55	0	0	98.2	117	49	90	0	8	7	10	20	1	0	.050
1962 HOU N	10	20	.333	3.02	43	29	11	241.2	210	55	203	2	2	4	4	78	14	2	.179
1963	14	13	.519	3.02	34	26	12	202.1	161	35	141	0	3	1	1	63	9	0	.143
1964	11	10	.524	3.27	32	27	7	198.1	196	52	117	0	1	0	0	69	5	0	.072
1965	11	11	.500	3.50	33	29	8	208.1	202	35	122	3	1	0	1	74	10	0	.135
1966	6	10	.375	4.60	32	21	3	152.2	167	28	101	0	2	0	2	48	7	1	.146
1967 2 teams			HOU N (7G 1-0)				PHI N (50G 9-6)												
" total	10	6	.625	2.34	57	1	0	103.2	87	22	78	0	10	5	12	20	2	0	.100
1968 PHI N	4	6	.400	3.48	54	0	0	82.2	83	32	57	0	4	6	12	6	1	0	.167
1969	3	4	.429	4.01	46	0	0	74	92	27	40	0	3	4	3	3	0	0	.000
14 yrs.	106	111	.488	3.45	590	134	41	1704.1	1628	468	1177	5	62	51	83	436	59	4	.135

	W	L	PCT	ERA	G	GS	CG	IP	H	BB	SO	ShO	Relief Pitching			BATTING			BA
													W	L	SV	AB	H	HR	

Kerby Farrell

FARRELL, MAJOR KERBY
B. Sept. 3, 1913, Leapwood, Tenn. D. Dec. 17, 1975, Nashville, Tenn.
Manager 1957. BL TL 5'11" 172 lbs.

	W	L	PCT	ERA	G	GS	CG	IP	H	BB	SO	ShO	W	L	SV	AB	H	HR	BA
1943 BOS N	0	1	.000	4.30	5	0	0	23	24	9	4	0	0	1	0	*			

Fast

FAST,
B. Milwaukee, Wis. Deceased.

	W	L	PCT	ERA	G	GS	CG	IP	H	BB	SO	ShO	W	L	SV	AB	H	HR	BA
1887 IND N	0	1	.000	10.34	4	2	1	15.2	25	8	0	0	0	0	1	11	2	0	.182

Darcy Fast

FAST, DARCY RAE
B. Mar. 10, 1947, Dallas, Ore. BL TL 6'3" 195 lbs.

	W	L	PCT	ERA	G	GS	CG	IP	H	BB	SO	ShO	W	L	SV	AB	H	HR	BA
1968 CHI N	0	1	.000	5.40	8	1	0	10	8	8	10	0	0	1	0	3	0	0	.000

Jack Faszholz

FASZHOLZ, JOHN EDWARD (Preacher)
B. Apr. 11, 1927, St. Louis, Mo. BR TR 6'3" 205 lbs.

	W	L	PCT	ERA	G	GS	CG	IP	H	BB	SO	ShO	W	L	SV	AB	H	HR	BA
1953 STL N	0	0	—	6.94	4	1	0	11.2	16	1	7	0	0	0	0	3	0	0	.000

Bill Faul

FAUL, WILLIAM ALVAN
B. Apr. 21, 1940, Cincinnati, Ohio BR TR 5'10" 184 lbs.

	W	L	PCT	ERA	G	GS	CG	IP	H	BB	SO	ShO	W	L	SV	AB	H	HR	BA
1962 DET A	0	0	—	32.40	1	0	0	1.2	4	3	2	0	0	0	0	0	0	0	—
1963	5	6	.455	4.64	28	10	2	97	93	48	64	0	0	0	0	27	4	0	.148
1964	0	0	—	10.80	1	1	0	5	5	2	1	0	1	1	1	2	0	0	.000
1965 CHI N	6	6	.500	3.54	17	16	5	96.2	83	18	59	3	0	0	0	30	3	0	.100
1966	1	4	.200	5.08	17	6	1	51.1	47	18	32	0	0	0	0	13	0	0	.000
1970 SF N	0	0	—	7.20	7	0	0	10	15	6	6	0	0	0	1	0	0	0	—
6 yrs.	12	16	.429	4.71	71	33	8	261.2	247	95	164	3	1	1	2	72	7	0	.097

Jim Faulkner

FAULKNER, JAMES LeROY (Lefty)
B. July 27, 1899, Beatrice, Neb.
D. June 1, 1962, West Palm Beach, Fla. BB TL 6'3" 190 lbs. BL 1927

	W	L	PCT	ERA	G	GS	CG	IP	H	BB	SO	ShO	W	L	SV	AB	H	HR	BA
1927 NY N	1	0	1.000	3.72	3	1	0	9.2	13	5	2	0	0	0	0	2	1	0	.500
1928	9	8	.529	3.53	38	8	3	117.1	131	41	32	0	7	6	2	39	9	0	.231
1930 BKN N	0	0	—	81.00	2	1	0	.1	2	1	0	0	0	0	1	0	0	0	—
3 yrs.	10	8	.556	3.75	43	10	3	127.1	146	47	34	0	7	6	3	41	10	0	.244

Buck Fausett

FAUSETT, ROBERT SHAW (Leaky)
B. Apr. 8, 1908, Sheridan, Ark. BL TR 5'10" 170 lbs.

	W	L	PCT	ERA	G	GS	CG	IP	H	BB	SO	ShO	W	L	SV	AB	H	HR	BA
1944 CIN N	0	0	—	5.91	2	0	0	10.2	13	7	3	0	0	0	0	*			

Charlie Faust

FAUST, CHARLES VICTOR (Victory)
B. Oct. 9, 1880, Marion, Kans. D. June 18, 1915, Fort Steilacoom, Wash.

	W	L	PCT	ERA	G	GS	CG	IP	H	BB	SO	ShO	W	L	SV	AB	H	HR	BA
1911 NY N	0	0	—	4.50	2	0	0	2	2	1	0	0	0	0	0	0	0	0	—

Cayt Fauver

FAUVER, CLAYTON KING (Pop)
B. Aug. 1, 1872, North Eaton, Ohio D. Mar. 3, 1942, Chatsworth, Ga. BB TR 5'10"

	W	L	PCT	ERA	G	GS	CG	IP	H	BB	SO	ShO	W	L	SV	AB	H	HR	BA
1899 LOU N	1	0	1.000	0.00	1	1	1	9	11	2	1	0	0	0	0	4	0	0	.000

Vern Fear

FEAR, LUVERN CARL
B. Aug. 21, 1924, Everly, Iowa D. Sept. 6, 1976, Spencer, Iowa BB TR 6' 170 lbs.

	W	L	PCT	ERA	G	GS	CG	IP	H	BB	SO	ShO	W	L	SV	AB	H	HR	BA
1952 CHI N	0	0	—	7.88	4	0	0	8	9	3	4	0	0	0	0	1	0	0	.000

Jack Fee

FEE, JOHN
B. 1870, Carbondale, Pa. D. Mar. 3, 1913, Carbondale, Pa.

	W	L	PCT	ERA	G	GS	CG	IP	H	BB	SO	ShO	W	L	SV	AB	H	HR	BA
1889 IND N	2	2	.500	4.28	7	3	2	40	39	31	10	0	1	0	0	21	3	0	.143

Harry Feldman

FELDMAN, HARRY
B. Nov. 10, 1919, New York, N.Y. D. Mar. 16, 1962, Ft. Smith, Ark. BR TR 6' 175 lbs.

	W	L	PCT	ERA	G	GS	CG	IP	H	BB	SO	ShO	W	L	SV	AB	H	HR	BA
1941 NY N	1	1	.500	3.98	3	3	1	20.1	21	6	9	1	0	0	0	6	1	0	.167
1942	7	1	.875	3.16	31	6	2	114	100	73	49	1	6	0	0	39	11	1	.282
1943	4	5	.444	4.30	31	10	1	104.2	114	58	49	0	2	0	0	30	4	0	.133
1944	11	13	.458	4.16	40	27	8	205.1	214	91	70	1	2	2	2	73	15	0	.205
1945	12	13	.480	3.27	35	30	10	217.2	213	69	74	3	0	2	1	72	7	1	.097
1946	0	2	.000	18.00	3	2	0	4	9	3	3	0	0	0	0	1	0	0	.000
6 yrs.	35	35	.500	3.80	143	78	22	666	671	300	254	6	10	4	3	221	38	2	.172

Harry Felix

FELIX, HARRY
B. 1870, Brooklyn, N.Y. D. Oct. 17, 1961, Miami, Fla. TR 5'7½" 160 lbs.

	W	L	PCT	ERA	G	GS	CG	IP	H	BB	SO	ShO	W	L	SV	AB	H	HR	BA
1901 NY N	0	0	—	0.00	1	0	0	2	3	0	0	0	0	0	0	1	0	0	.000
1902 PHI N	1	3	.250	5.60	9	5	3	45	61	11	10	0	0	0	0	37	5	0	.135
2 yrs.	1	3	.250	5.36	10	5	3	47	64	11	10	0	0	0	0	38	5	0	.132

Bob Feller

FELLER, ROBERT WILLIAM ANDREW (Rapid Robert)
B. Nov. 3, 1918, Van Meter, Iowa BR TR 6' 185 lbs.
Hall of Fame 1962.

	W	L	PCT	ERA	G	GS	CG	IP	H	BB	SO	ShO	W	L	SV	AB	H	HR	BA
1936 CLE A	5	3	.625	3.34	14	8	5	62	52	47	76	0	0	0	1	22	3	0	.136
1937	9	7	.563	3.39	26	19	9	148.2	116	106	150	0	2	0	1	53	9	0	.170
1938	17	11	.607	4.08	39	36	20	277.2	225	208	240	2	0	1	1	94	17	0	.181
1939	24	9	.727	2.85	39	35	24	296.2	227	142	246	4	1	0	1	99	21	0	.212
1940	27	11	.711	2.61	43	37	31	320.1	245	118	261	4	1	1	4	115	18	2	.157
1941	25	13	.658	3.15	44	40	28	343	284	194	260	6	0	1	2	120	18	1	.150
1945	5	3	.625	2.50	9	9	7	72	50	35	59	1	0	0	0	25	4	0	.160
1946	26	15	.634	2.18	48	42	36	371.1	277	153	348	10	0	0	4	124	16	0	.129
1947	20	11	.645	2.68	42	37	20	299	230	127	196	5	0	1	3	98	18	0	.184
1948	19	15	.559	3.56	44	38	18	280.1	255	116	164	3	0	1	3	95	9	0	.095
1949	15	14	.517	3.75	36	28	15	211	198	84	108	0	1	0	0	72	17	2	.236

	W	L	PCT	ERA	G	GS	CG	IP	H	BB	SO	ShO	Relief Pitching W	L	SV	BATTING AB	H	HR	BA

Bob Feller continued

	W	L	PCT	ERA	G	GS	CG	IP	H	BB	SO	ShO	W	L	SV	AB	H	HR	BA
1950	16	11	.593	3.43	35	34	16	247	230	103	119	3	0	1	0	83	10	2	.120
1951	22	8	.733	3.50	33	32	16	249.2	239	95	111	4	0	1	0	81	10	0	.123
1952	9	13	.409	4.74	30	30	11	191.2	219	83	81	1	0	0	0	60	7	1	.117
1953	10	7	.588	3.59	25	25	10	175.2	163	60	60	1	0	0	0	56	6	0	.107
1954	13	3	.813	3.09	19	19	9	140	127	39	59	1	0	0	0	48	9	0	.188
1955	4	4	.500	3.47	25	11	2	83	71	31	25	1	1	0	0	21	1	0	.048
1956	0	4	.000	4.97	19	4	2	58	63	23	18	0	0	1	1	16	0	0	.000
18 yrs.	266	162	.621	3.25	570	484	279	3827	3271	1764 3rd	2581	46	6	8	21	1282	193	8	.151

WORLD SERIES
	W	L	PCT	ERA	G	GS	CG	IP	H	BB	SO	ShO	W	L	SV	AB	H	HR	BA
1948 CLE A	0	2	.000	5.02	2	2	1	14.1	10	5	7	0	0	0	0	4	0	0	.000

Terry Felton

FELTON, TERRY LANE
B. Oct. 29, 1957, Texarkana, Tex.   BR TR 6'1"   180 lbs.

	W	L	PCT	ERA	G	GS	CG	IP	H	BB	SO	ShO	W	L	SV	AB	H	HR	BA
1979 MIN A	0	0	–	0.00	1	0	0	2	0	0	1	0	0	0	0	0	0	0	–
1980	0	3	.000	7.00	5	4	0	18	20	9	14	0	0	0	0	0	0	0	–
1981	0	0	–	54.00	1	0	0	1	4	2	1	0	0	0	0	0	0	0	–
1982	0	13	.000	4.99	48	6	0	117.1	99	76	92	0	0	9	3	0	0	0	–
4 yrs.	0	16	.000	5.53	55	10	0	138.1	123	87	108	0	0	9	3	0	0	0	–

Hod Fenner

FENNER, HORACE ALFRED
B. July 12, 1897, Martin, Mich.   D. Nov. 20, 1954, Detroit, Mich.   BR TR 5'10½" 165 lbs.

	W	L	PCT	ERA	G	GS	CG	IP	H	BB	SO	ShO	W	L	SV	AB	H	HR	BA
1921 CHI A	0	0	–	7.71	2	1	0	7	14	3	1	0	0	0	0	2	0	0	.000

Stan Ferens

FERENS, STANLEY (Lefty)
B. Mar. 5, 1915, Wendell, Pa.   BB TL 5'11"   170 lbs.

	W	L	PCT	ERA	G	GS	CG	IP	H	BB	SO	ShO	W	L	SV	AB	H	HR	BA
1942 STL A	3	4	.429	3.78	19	3	1	69	76	21	23	0	2	3	0	21	3	0	.143
1946	2	9	.182	4.50	34	6	1	88	100	38	28	0	1	5	0	24	4	0	.167
2 yrs.	5	13	.278	4.18	53	9	2	157	176	59	51	0	3	8	0	45	7	0	.156

Alex Ferguson

FERGUSON, JAMES ALEXANDER
B. Feb. 16, 1897, Montclair, N. J.   D. Apr. 26, 1976, Sepulveda, Calif.   BR TR 6'   180 lbs.

	W	L	PCT	ERA	G	GS	CG	IP	H	BB	SO	ShO	W	L	SV	AB	H	HR	BA
1918 NY A	0	0	–	0.00	1	0	0	1.2	2	2	1	0	0	0	0	1	0	0	.000
1921	3	1	.750	5.91	17	4	1	56.1	64	27	9	0	1	0	1	19	4	0	.211
1922 BOS A	9	16	.360	4.31	39	27	10	198.1	201	62	44	1	3	0	2	65	6	0	.092
1923	9	13	.409	4.04	34	27	11	198.1	229	67	72	0	1	0	0	62	6	0	.097
1924	14	17	.452	3.79	40	32	15	235	257	107	78	0	3	1	2	85	11	0	.129
1925 3 teams																			
" total	9	5	.643	6.18	33	15	3	125.1	157	70	49	0	3	2	2	39	3	0	.077
1926 WAS A	3	4	.429	7.74	19	4	0	47.2	69	18	16	0	2	1	1	11	2	0	.182
1927 PHI N	8	16	.333	4.84	31	31	16	227	280	65	73	0	0	0	0	70	7	0	.100
1928	5	10	.333	5.67	34	19	5	131.2	162	48	50	1	1	0	2	39	1	0	.026
1929 2 teams																			
" total	1	3	.250	13.50	8	1	1	14.2	26	11	4	0	0	0	0	5	1	0	.200
10 yrs.	61	85	.418	4.91	256	166	62	1236	1447	477	396	2	14	5	10	396	41	0	.104

1925 3 teams BOS A (5G 0–2) NY A (21G 4–2) WAS A (7G 5–1)
1929 2 teams PHI N (5G 1–2) BKN N (3G 0–1)

WORLD SERIES
	W	L	PCT	ERA	G	GS	CG	IP	H	BB	SO	ShO	W	L	SV	AB	H	HR	BA
1925 WAS A	1	1	.500	3.21	2	2	2	14	13	6	11	0	0	0	0	4	0	0	.000

Bob Ferguson

FERGUSON, ROBERT LESTER
B. Apr. 18, 1919, Birmingham, Ala.   BR TR 6'1½" 180 lbs.

	W	L	PCT	ERA	G	GS	CG	IP	H	BB	SO	ShO	W	L	SV	AB	H	HR	BA
1944 CIN N	0	3	.000	9.00	9	2	0	16	24	10	9	0	0	3	1	3	1	0	.333

Bob Ferguson

FERGUSON, ROBERT V. (Death to Flying Things)
B. Jan. 31, 1845, Brooklyn, N. Y.   D. May 3, 1894, Brooklyn, N. Y.   BB TR 5'9½" 149 lbs.
Manager 1871-84, 1886-87.

	W	L	PCT	ERA	G	GS	CG	IP	H	BB	SO	ShO	W	L	SV	AB	H	HR	BA
1877 HAR N	1	1	.500	3.96	3	2	2	25	38	2	1	0	0	0	0	254	65	0	.256
1883 PHI N	0	0	–	9.00	1	0	0	1	2	0	0	0	0	0	0	329	85	0	.258
2 yrs.	1	1	.500	4.15	4	2	2	26	40	2	1	0	0	0	0	*			

Charlie Ferguson

FERGUSON, CHARLES AUGUSTUS
B. May 10, 1875, Okemos, Mich.   D. May 17, 1931, Sault Ste. Marie, Mich.   TR 5'11"

	W	L	PCT	ERA	G	GS	CG	IP	H	BB	SO	ShO	W	L	SV	AB	H	HR	BA
1901 CHI N	0	0	–	0.00	1	0	0	2	1	2	0	0	0	0	0	1	0	0	.000

Charlie Ferguson

FERGUSON, CHARLES J.
B. Apr. 17, 1863, Charlottesville, Va.   D. Apr. 29, 1888, Philadelphia, Pa.   BB TR 6'   165 lbs.

	W	L	PCT	ERA	G	GS	CG	IP	H	BB	SO	ShO	W	L	SV	AB	H	HR	BA
1884 PHI N	21	25	.457	3.54	50	47	46	416.2	443	93	194	2	0	0	1	203	50	0	.246
1885	26	20	.565	2.22	48	45	45	405	345	81	197	5	1	1	0	235	72	1	.306
1886	30	9	.769	1.98	48	45	43	395.2	317	69	212	4	0	0	2	261	66	2	.253
1887	22	10	.688	3.00	37	33	31	297.1	297	47	125	2	1	0	1	264	89	3	.337
4 yrs.	99	64	.607	2.67	183	170	165	1514.2	1402	290	728	13	2	1	4	*			

George Ferguson

FERGUSON, GEORGE CECIL
B. Aug. 19, 1886, Ellsworth, Ind.   D. Sept. 5, 1943, Orlando, Fla.

	W	L	PCT	ERA	G	GS	CG	IP	H	BB	SO	ShO	W	L	SV	AB	H	HR	BA
1906 NY N	2	1	.667	2.58	22	1	1	52.1	43	24	32	1	2	1	6	15	5	0	.333
1907	3	1	.750	2.11	15	5	4	64	63	20	37	0	0	1	1	18	1	0	.056
1908 BOS N	12	11	.522	2.47	37	20	13	208	168	84	98	3	3	3	2	65	11	0	.169
1909	5	23	.179	3.73	36	30	19	226.2	235	83	87	3	0	0	0	73	15	0	.205
1910	8	7	.533	3.80	26	14	10	123	110	58	40	1	2	2	0	40	7	1	.175
1911	1	3	.250	9.75	6	3	0	24	40	12	4	0	1	0	0	7	2	0	.286
6 yrs.	31	46	.403	3.34	142	73	47	698	659	281	298	8	8	6	7	218	41	1	.188

	W	L	PCT	ERA	G	GS	CG	IP	H	BB	SO	ShO	Relief Pitching W	L	SV	BATTING AB	H	HR	BA

Sid Fernandez

FERNANDEZ, CHARLES SID
B. Oct. 12, 1962, Honolulu, Hawaii
BL TL 6'1" 220 lbs.

	W	L	PCT	ERA	G	GS	CG	IP	H	BB	SO	ShO	W	L	SV	AB	H	HR	BA
1983 LA N	0	1	.000	6.00	2	1	0	6	7	7	9	0	0	0	0	1	1	0	1.000
1984 NY N	6	6	.500	3.50	15	15	0	90	74	34	62	0	0	0	0	28	5	0	.179
2 yrs.	6	7	.462	3.66	17	16	0	96	81	41	71	0	0	0	0	29	6	0	.207

Don Ferrarese

FERRARESE, DONALD HUGH (Midget)
B. June 19, 1929, Oakland, Calif.
BR TL 5'9" 170 lbs.

	W	L	PCT	ERA	G	GS	CG	IP	H	BB	SO	ShO	W	L	SV	AB	H	HR	BA
1955 BAL A	0	0	–	3.00	6	0	0	9	8	11	5	0	0	0	0	1	0	0	.000
1956	4	10	.286	5.03	36	14	3	102	86	64	81	1	2	2	2	28	1	0	.036
1957	1	1	.500	4.74	8	2	0	19	14	12	13	0	1	0	0	3	0	0	.000
1958 CLE A	3	4	.429	3.71	28	10	2	94.2	91	46	62	0	2	1	1	26	3	0	.115
1959	5	3	.625	3.20	15	10	4	76	58	51	45	0	0	0	0	27	7	0	.259
1960 CHI A	0	1	.000	18.00	5	0	0	4	8	9	4	0	0	1	0	2	1	0	.500
1961 PHI N	5	12	.294	3.76	42	14	3	138.2	120	68	89	1	2	3	1	35	6	0	.171
1962 2 teams			PHI	N (5G 0–1)		STL	N	(38G 1–4)											
" total	1	5	.167	3.27	43	0	0	63.1	64	34	51	0	1	5	1	6	2	1	.333
8 yrs.	19	36	.345	4.00	183	50	12	506.2	449	295	350	2	8	12	5	128	20	1	.156

Bill Ferrazzi

FERRAZZI, WILLIAM JOSEPH
B. Apr. 19, 1907, West Quincy, Mass.
BR TR 6'2½" 200 lbs.

	W	L	PCT	ERA	G	GS	CG	IP	H	BB	SO	ShO	W	L	SV	AB	H	HR	BA
1935 PHI A	1	2	.333	5.14	3	2	0	7	7	5	0	0	1	0	0	1	0	0	.000

Wes Ferrell

FERRELL, WESLEY CHEEK
Brother of Rick Ferrell.
B. Feb. 2, 1908, Greensboro, N. C.   D. Dec. 9, 1976, Sarasota, Fla.
BR TR 6'2" 195 lbs.

	W	L	PCT	ERA	G	GS	CG	IP	H	BB	SO	ShO	W	L	SV	AB	H	HR	BA
1927 CLE A	0	0	–	27.00	1	0	0	1	3	2	0	0	0	0	0	0	0	0	–
1928	0	2	.000	2.25	2	2	1	16	15	5	4	0	0	0	0	4	1	0	.250
1929	21	10	.677	3.60	43	25	18	242.2	256	109	100	1	4	2	5	93	22	1	.237
1930	25	13	.658	3.31	43	35	25	296.2	299	106	143	1	2	1	3	118	35	0	.297
1931	22	12	.647	3.75	40	35	27	276.1	276	130	123	2	1	1	3	116	37	9	.319
1932	23	13	.639	3.66	38	34	26	287.2	299	104	105	3	1	2	1	128	31	2	.242
1933	11	12	.478	4.21	28	26	16	201	225	70	41	1	0	0	0	140	38	7	.271
1934 BOS A	14	5	.737	3.63	26	23	17	181	205	49	67	1	1	0	1	78	22	4	.282
1935	25	14	.641	3.52	41	38	31	322.1	336	108	110	3	0	3	0	150	52	7	.347
1936	20	15	.571	4.19	39	38	28	301	330	119	106	3	0	0	0	135	36	5	.267
1937 2 teams			BOS	A (12G 3–6)		WAS	A	(25G 11–13)											
" total	14	19	.424	4.90	37	35	26	281	325	122	123	0	0	0	0	139	39	1	.281
1938 2 teams			WAS	A (23G 13–8)		NY	A	(5G 2–2)											
" total	15	10	.600	6.28	28	26	10	179	245	86	43	0	1	0	0	61	13	1	.213
1939 NY A	1	2	.333	4.66	3	3	1	19.1	14	17	6	0	0	0	0	8	1	0	.125
1940 BKN N	0	0	–	6.75	1	0	0	4	4	4	4	0	0	0	0	2	0	0	.000
1941 BOS N	2	1	.667	5.14	4	3	1	14	13	9	10	0	1	0	0	4	2	1	.500
15 yrs.	193	128	.601	4.04	374	323	227	2623	2845	1040	985	17	11	9	13	*			

Tom Ferrick

FERRICK, THOMAS JEROME
B. Jan. 6, 1915, New York, N. Y.
BR TR 6'2½" 220 lbs.

	W	L	PCT	ERA	G	GS	CG	IP	H	BB	SO	ShO	W	L	SV	AB	H	HR	BA
1941 PHI A	8	10	.444	3.77	36	4	2	119.1	130	33	30	1	1	2	7	44	9	0	.205
1942 CLE A	3	2	.600	1.99	31	2	2	81.1	56	32	28	0	2	1	3	19	4	0	.211
1946 2 teams			CLE	A (9G 0–0)		STL	A	(25G 4–1)											
" total	4	1	.800	3.58	34	0	0	50.1	51	9	22	0	4	1	6	7	2	0	.286
1947 WAS A	1	7	.125	3.15	31	0	0	60	57	20	23	0	1	7	9	10	1	0	.100
1948	2	5	.286	4.15	37	0	0	73.2	75	38	34	0	2	5	10	15	1	0	.067
1949 STL A	6	4	.600	3.88	50	0	0	104.1	102	41	34	0	6	4	6	21	3	0	.143
1950 2 teams			STL	A (16G 1–3)		NY	A	(30G 8–4)											
" total	9	7	.563	3.79	46	0	0	80.2	73	29	26	0	9	7	11	18	3	0	.167
1951 2 teams			NY	A (9G 1–1)		WAS	A	(22G 2–0)											
" total	3	1	.750	3.52	31	0	0	53.2	57	14	20	0	3	1	3	8	3	0	.375
1952 WAS A	4	3	.571	3.02	27	0	0	50.2	53	11	28	0	4	3	1	5	1	0	.200
9 yrs.	40	40	.500	3.47	323	7	4	674	654	227	245	1	32	31	56	147	27	0	.184

WORLD SERIES

	W	L	PCT	ERA	G	GS	CG	IP	H	BB	SO	ShO	W	L	SV	AB	H	HR	BA
1950 NY A	1	0	1.000	0.00	1	0	0	1	1	1	0	0	1	0	0	0	0	0	–

Bob Ferris

FERRIS, ROBERT EUGENE
B. May 7, 1955, Arlington, Va.
BR TR 6'6" 225 lbs.

	W	L	PCT	ERA	G	GS	CG	IP	H	BB	SO	ShO	W	L	SV	AB	H	HR	BA
1979 CAL A	0	0	–	1.50	2	0	0	6	5	3	2	0	0	0	0	0	0	0	–
1980	0	2	.000	6.00	5	3	0	15	23	9	4	0	0	0	0	0	0	0	–
2 yrs.	0	2	.000	4.71	7	3	0	21	28	12	6	0	0	0	0	0	0	0	–

Boo Ferriss

FERRISS, DAVID MEADOW
B. Dec. 5, 1921, Shaw, Miss.
BL TR 6'2" 208 lbs.

	W	L	PCT	ERA	G	GS	CG	IP	H	BB	SO	ShO	W	L	SV	AB	H	HR	BA
1945 BOS A	21	10	.677	2.96	35	31	26	264.2	263	85	94	5	1	0	2	120	32	1	.267
1946	25	6	.806	3.25	40	35	26	274	274	71	106	6	1	0	3	115	24	0	.209
1947	12	11	.522	4.04	33	28	14	218.1	241	92	64	1	0	1	0	99	27	0	.273
1948	7	3	.700	5.23	31	9	1	115.1	127	61	30	0	1	1	3	37	9	0	.243
1949	0	0	–	4.05	4	0	0	6.2	7	4	1	0	0	0	0	1	1	0	1.000
1950	0	0	–	18.00	1	0	0	1	2	1	1	0	0	0	0	0	0	0	–
6 yrs.	65	30	.684	3.64	144	103	67	880	914	314	296	12	7	2	8	*			

WORLD SERIES

	W	L	PCT	ERA	G	GS	CG	IP	H	BB	SO	ShO	W	L	SV	AB	H	HR	BA
1946 BOS A	1	0	1.000	2.03	2	2	1	13.1	13	2	4	1	0	0	0	6	0	0	.000

Cy Ferry

FERRY, ALFRED JOSEPH
Brother of Jack Ferry.
B. Sept. 27, 1878, Hudson, N. Y.   D. Sept. 27, 1938, Pittsfield, Mass.
BR TR 6'1" 170 lbs.

	W	L	PCT	ERA	G	GS	CG	IP	H	BB	SO	ShO	W	L	SV	AB	H	HR	BA
1904 DET A	0	1	.000	6.23	3	1	1	13	12	11	4	0	0	0	0	6	2	0	.333
1905 CLE A	0	0	–	13.50	1	1	0	2	3	0	2	0	0	0	0	1	0	0	.000
2 yrs.	0	1	.000	7.20	4	2	1	15	15	11	6	0	0	0	0	7	2	0	.286

	W	L	PCT	ERA	G	GS	CG	IP	H	BB	SO	ShO	Relief Pitching W	L	SV	BATTING AB	H	HR	BA

Jack Ferry

FERRY, JOHN FRANCIS
Brother of Cy Ferry.
B. Apr. 7, 1887, Pittsfield, Mass. D. Aug. 29, 1954, Pittsfield, Mass.
BR TR 5'11" 175 lbs.

	W	L	PCT	ERA	G	GS	CG	IP	H	BB	SO	ShO	W	L	SV	AB	H	HR	BA
1910 PIT N	1	2	.333	2.32	6	3	2	31	26	8	12	0	0	0	0	9	3	0	.333
1911	6	4	.600	3.15	26	8	4	85.2	83	27	32	1	2	4	3	29	9	0	.310
1912	2	0	1.000	3.00	11	3	1	39	33	23	10	1	0	0	1	13	1	0	.077
1913	1	0	1.000	5.40	4	0	0	5	4	2	2	0	1	0	0	0	0	0	-
4 yrs.	10	6	.625	3.02	47	14	7	160.2	146	60	56	2	3	4	4	51	13	0	.255

Alex Ferson

FERSON, ALEXANDER (Colonel)
B. July 14, 1866, Philadelphia, Pa. D. Dec. 5, 1957, Boston, Mass.
TR 5'9" 165 lbs.

	W	L	PCT	ERA	G	GS	CG	IP	H	BB	SO	ShO	W	L	SV	AB	H	HR	BA
1889 WAS N	17	17	.500	3.90	36	34	28	288.1	319	105	85	1	1	0	0	114	13	0	.114
1890 BUF P	1	7	.125	5.45	10	10	7	71	88	40	13	0	0	0	0	32	7	0	.219
1892 BAL N	0	1	.000	11.00	2	1	1	9	17	6	8	0	0	0	0	4	0	0	.000
3 yrs.	18	25	.419	4.37	48	45	36	368.1	424	151	106	1	1	0	0	150	20	0	.133

Lou Fette

FETTE, LOUIS HENRY
B. Mar. 15, 1907, Alma, Mo. D. Jan. 3, 1981, Warrensburg, Mo.
BR TR 6'1½" 200 lbs.

	W	L	PCT	ERA	G	GS	CG	IP	H	BB	SO	ShO	W	L	SV	AB	H	HR	BA
1937 BOS N	20	10	.667	2.88	35	33	23	259	243	81	70	5	0	1	0	92	22	0	.239
1938	11	13	.458	3.15	33	32	17	239.2	235	79	83	3	0	0	1	85	16	0	.188
1939	10	10	.500	2.96	27	26	11	146	123	61	35	6	0	0	0	49	3	0	.061
1940 2 teams				BOS	N (7G 0–5)			BKN	N (2G 0–0)										
" total	0	5	.000	5.09	9	5	0	35.1	41	20	2	0	0	0	0	8	3	0	.375
1945 BOS N	0	2	.000	5.73	5	1	0	11	16	7	4	0	0	1	0	2	0	0	.000
5 yrs.	41	40	.506	3.15	109	97	51	691	658	248	194	14	0	2	1	236	44	0	.186

John Fick

FICK, JOHN RALPH
B. May 18, 1921, Baltimore, Md. D. June 9, 1958, Somers Point, N. J.
BL TL 5'10" 150 lbs.

	W	L	PCT	ERA	G	GS	CG	IP	H	BB	SO	ShO	W	L	SV	AB	H	HR	BA
1944 PHI N	0	0	-	3.38	4	0	0	5.1	3	3	2	0	0	0	0	0	0	0	-

Mark Fidrych

FIDRYCH, MARK STEVEN (The Bird)
B. Aug. 14, 1954, Worcester, Mass.
BR TR 6'3" 175 lbs.

	W	L	PCT	ERA	G	GS	CG	IP	H	BB	SO	ShO	W	L	SV	AB	H	HR	BA
1976 DET A	19	9	.679	2.34	31	29	24	250	217	53	97	4	0	0	0	0	0	0	-
1977	6	4	.600	2.89	11	11	7	81	82	12	42	1	0	0	0	0	0	0	-
1978	2	0	1.000	2.45	3	3	2	22	17	5	10	0	0	0	0	0	0	0	-
1979	0	3	.000	10.20	4	4	0	15	23	9	5	0	0	0	0	0	0	0	-
1980	2	3	.400	5.73	9	9	1	44	58	20	16	0	0	0	0	0	0	0	-
5 yrs.	29	19	.604	3.10	58	56	34	412	397	99	170	5	0	0	0	0	0	0	-

Clarence Fieber

FIEBER, CLARENCE THOMAS (Lefty)
B. Sept. 4, 1913, San Francisco, Calif.
BL TL 6'4" 187 lbs.

	W	L	PCT	ERA	G	GS	CG	IP	H	BB	SO	ShO	W	L	SV	AB	H	HR	BA
1932 CHI A	1	0	1.000	1.69	3	0	0	5.1	6	3	1	0	1	0	0	0	0	0	-

Jim Field

FIELD, JAMES C.
B. Apr. 24, 1863, Philadelphia, Pa. D. May 13, 1953, Atlantic City, N. J.

	W	L	PCT	ERA	G	GS	CG	IP	H	BB	SO	ShO	W	L	SV	AB	H	HR	BA
1890 ROC AA	1	0	1.000	2.79	2	1	1	9.2	7	4	2	0	0	0	1	*			

Jocko Fields

FIELDS, JOHN JOSEPH
B. Oct. 20, 1864, Cork, Ireland D. Oct. 14, 1950, Jersey City, N. J.
BR TR 5'10" 160 lbs.

	W	L	PCT	ERA	G	GS	CG	IP	H	BB	SO	ShO	W	L	SV	AB	H	HR	BA
1887 PIT N	0	0	-	0.00	1	0	0	1	0	2	0	0	0	0	0	*			

Lou Fiene

FIENE, LOUIS HENRY (Big Finn)
B. Dec. 29, 1884, Fort Dodge, Iowa D. Dec. 22, 1964, Chicago, Ill.
BR TR 6' 175 lbs.

	W	L	PCT	ERA	G	GS	CG	IP	H	BB	SO	ShO	W	L	SV	AB	H	HR	BA
1906 CHI A	1	1	.500	2.90	6	2	1	31	35	9	12	0	0	0	0	10	2	0	.200
1907	0	1	.000	4.15	6	1	1	26	30	7	15	0	0	0	1	11	2	0	.182
1908	0	1	.000	4.00	1	1	1	9	9	1	3	0	0	0	0	3	0	0	.000
1909	2	5	.286	4.13	13	6	4	72	75	18	24	0	1	0	1	29	2	0	.069
4 yrs.	3	8	.273	3.85	26	10	7	138	149	35	54	0	1	0	1	53	6	0	.113

Dan Fife

FIFE, DANIEL WAYNE
B. Oct. 5, 1949, Harrisburg, Ill.
BR TR 6'3" 175 lbs.

	W	L	PCT	ERA	G	GS	CG	IP	H	BB	SO	ShO	W	L	SV	AB	H	HR	BA
1973 MIN A	3	2	.600	4.35	10	7	1	51.2	54	29	18	0	0	0	0	0	0	0	-
1974	0	0	-	17.36	4	0	0	4.2	10	4	3	0	0	0	0	0	0	0	-
2 yrs.	3	2	.600	5.43	14	7	1	56.1	64	33	21	0	0	0	0	0	0	0	-

Jack Fifield

FIFIELD, JOHN PROCTOR
B. Oct. 5, 1871, Enfield, N. H. D. Nov. 27, 1939, Syracuse, N. Y.
BR TR 5'11" 160 lbs.

	W	L	PCT	ERA	G	GS	CG	IP	H	BB	SO	ShO	W	L	SV	AB	H	HR	BA
1897 PHI N	5	18	.217	5.51	27	26	21	210.2	263	80	38	0	0	0	0	77	18	2	.234
1898	11	9	.550	3.31	21	21	18	171.1	170	60	31	2	0	0	0	64	7	0	.109
1899 2 teams				PHI	N (14G 3–8)			WAS	N (6G 2–4)										
" total	5	12	.294	4.77	20	17	15	139.2	183	53	20	1	0	0	1	55	13	0	.236
3 yrs.	21	39	.350	4.59	68	64	54	521.2	616	193	89	3	0	0	1	196	38	2	.194

Frank Figgemeier

FIGGEMEIER, FRANK Y.
B. Apr. 22, 1874, St. Louis, Mo. D. Apr. 15, 1915, St. Louis, Mo.

	W	L	PCT	ERA	G	GS	CG	IP	H	BB	SO	ShO	W	L	SV	AB	H	HR	BA
1894 PHI N	0	1	.000	11.25	1	1	1	8	12	4	2	0	0	0	0	3	1	0	.333

Ed Figueroa

FIGUEROA, EDUARDO
Also known as Eduardo Padilla.
B. Oct. 14, 1948, Ciales, Puerto Rico
BR TR 6'1" 190 lbs.

	W	L	PCT	ERA	G	GS	CG	IP	H	BB	SO	ShO	W	L	SV	AB	H	HR	BA
1974 CAL A	2	8	.200	3.69	25	12	5	105	119	36	49	1	0	0	0	0	0	0	-
1975	16	13	.552	2.91	33	32	16	244.2	213	84	139	2	0	0	0	0	0	0	-
1976 NY A	19	10	.655	3.02	34	34	14	256.2	237	94	119	4	0	0	0	0	0	0	-
1977	16	11	.593	3.58	32	32	12	239	228	75	104	2	0	0	0	0	0	0	-
1978	20	9	.690	2.99	35	35	12	253	233	77	92	2	0	0	0	0	0	0	-
1979	4	6	.400	4.11	16	16	4	105	109	35	42	1	0	0	0	0	0	0	-

	W	L	PCT	ERA	G	GS	CG	IP	H	BB	SO	ShO	Relief Pitching W	L	SV	BATTING AB	H	HR	BA

Ed Figueroa continued

	W	L	PCT	ERA	G	GS	CG	IP	H	BB	SO	ShO	W	L	SV	AB	H	HR	BA
1980 2 teams	NY A (15G 3–3)				TEX	A	(8G 0–7)												
" total	3	10	.231	6.52	23	17	0	98	152	36	25	0	0	0	1	0	0	0	–
1981 OAK A	0	0	–	5.63	2	1	0	8	8	6	1	0	0	0	0	0	0	0	–
8 yrs.	80	67	.544	3.51	200	179	63	1309.1	1299	443	571	12	0	0	1	0	0	0	–
LEAGUE CHAMPIONSHIP SERIES																			
1976 NY A	0	1	.000	5.84	2	2	0	12.1	14	2	5	0	0	0	0	0	0	0	–
1977	0	0	–	10.80	1	1	0	3.1	5	2	3	0	0	0	0	0	0	0	–
1978	0	1	.000	27.00	1	1	0	1	5	0	0	0	0	0	0	0	0	0	–
3 yrs.	0	2	.000	8.10	4	4	0	16.2	24	4	8	0	0	0	0	0	0	0	–
WORLD SERIES																			
1976 NY A	0	1	.000	5.63	1	1	0	8	6	5	2	0	0	0	0	0	0	0	–
1978	0	1	.000	8.10	2	2	0	6.2	9	5	2	0	0	0	0	0	0	0	–
2 yrs.	0	2	.000	6.75	3	3	0	14.2	15	10	4	0	0	0	0	0	0	0	–

Tom Filer

FILER, THOMAS CARSON
B. Dec. 1, 1956, Philadelphia, Pa.   BR TR 6'1" 195 lbs.

	W	L	PCT	ERA	G	GS	CG	IP	H	BB	SO	ShO	W	L	SV	AB	H	HR	BA
1982 CHI N	1	2	.333	5.53	8	8	0	40.2	50	18	15	0	0	0	0	12	1	0	.083

Eddie Files

FILES, CHARLES EDWARD
B. May 19, 1883, Portland, Me.   D. May 10, 1954, Cornish, Me.   BR TR

	W	L	PCT	ERA	G	GS	CG	IP	H	BB	SO	ShO	W	L	SV	AB	H	HR	BA
1908 PHI A	0	0	–	6.00	2	0	0	9	8	3	6	0	0	0	0	3	0	0	.000

Marc Filley

FILLEY, MARCUS LUCIUS
B. Feb. 28, 1912, Troy, N. Y.   BR TR 5'11" 172 lbs.

	W	L	PCT	ERA	G	GS	CG	IP	H	BB	SO	ShO	W	L	SV	AB	H	HR	BA
1934 WAS A	0	0	–	27.00	1	0	0	.1	2	0	0	0	0	0	0	0	0	0	–

Dana Fillingim

FILLINGIM, DANA
B. Nov. 6, 1893, Columbus, Ga.   D. Feb. 3, 1961, Tuskegee, Ala.   BL TR 5'10" 175 lbs.

	W	L	PCT	ERA	G	GS	CG	IP	H	BB	SO	ShO	W	L	SV	AB	H	HR	BA
1915 PHI A	0	5	.000	3.43	8	4	1	39.1	42	32	17	0	0	1	0	12	2	0	.167
1918 BOS N	7	6	.538	2.23	14	13	10	113	99	28	29	4	0	0	0	42	9	0	.214
1919	6	13	.316	3.38	32	19	9	186.1	185	39	50	0	2	0	2	65	16	0	.246
1920	12	21	.364	3.11	37	30	22	272	292	79	66	2	1	2	0	92	16	0	.174
1921	15	10	.600	3.45	44	22	11	239.2	249	56	54	3	4	1	1	85	21	2	.247
1922	5	9	.357	4.54	25	12	5	117	143	37	25	1	1	3	2	38	6	0	.158
1923	1	9	.100	5.20	35	12	1	100.1	141	36	27	0	1	1	0	31	7	0	.226
1925 PHI N	1	0	1.000	10.38	5	1	0	8.2	19	6	2	0	1	0	0	3	0	0	.000
8 yrs.	47	73	.392	3.56	200	113	59	1076.1	1170	313	270	10	10	8	5	368	77	2	.209

Pete Filson

FILSON, WILLIAM PETER
B. Sept. 28, 1958, Darby, Pa.   BB TL 6'1" 185 lbs.

	W	L	PCT	ERA	G	GS	CG	IP	H	BB	SO	ShO	W	L	SV	AB	H	HR	BA
1982 MIN A	0	2	.000	8.76	5	3	0	12.1	17	8	10	0	0	0	0	0	0	0	–
1983	4	1	.800	3.40	26	8	0	90	87	29	49	0	1	0	1	0	0	0	–
1984	6	5	.545	4.10	55	7	0	118.2	106	54	59	0	4	3	1	0	0	0	–
3 yrs.	10	8	.556	4.07	86	18	0	221	210	91	118	0	5	3	2	0	0	0	–

Joel Finch

FINCH, JOEL D.
B. Aug. 20, 1956, South Bend, Ind.   BR TR 6'2" 175 lbs.

	W	L	PCT	ERA	G	GS	CG	IP	H	BB	SO	ShO	W	L	SV	AB	H	HR	BA
1979 BOS A	0	3	.000	4.89	15	7	0	57	65	25	25	0	0	0	0	1	0	0	.000

Bill Fincher

FINCHER, WILLIAM ALLEN
B. May 26, 1894, Atlanta, Ga.   D. May 8, 1946, Shreveport, La.   BR TR 6'1" 180 lbs.

	W	L	PCT	ERA	G	GS	CG	IP	H	BB	SO	ShO	W	L	SV	AB	H	HR	BA
1916 STL A	0	1	.000	2.14	12	1	0	21	22	7	5	0	0	0	0	4	1	0	.250

Tom Fine

FINE, THOMAS MORGAN
B. Oct. 10, 1914, Cleburne, Tex.   BB TR 6' 180 lbs.

	W	L	PCT	ERA	G	GS	CG	IP	H	BB	SO	ShO	W	L	SV	AB	H	HR	BA
1947 BOS A	1	2	.333	5.50	9	7	1	36	41	19	10	0	0	0	0	9	3	0	.333
1950 STL A	0	1	.000	8.10	14	0	0	36.2	53	25	6	0	0	1	0	12	4	0	.333
2 yrs.	1	3	.250	6.81	23	7	1	72.2	94	44	16	0	0	1	0	21	7	0	.333

Rollie Fingers

FINGERS, ROLAND GLEN
B. Aug. 25, 1946, Steubenville, Ohio   BR TR 6'4" 190 lbs.

	W	L	PCT	ERA	G	GS	CG	IP	H	BB	SO	ShO	W	L	SV	AB	H	HR	BA
1968 OAK A	0	0	–	27.00	1	0	0	1.1	4	1	0	0	0	0	0	0	0	0	–
1969	6	7	.462	3.71	60	8	1	119	116	41	61	1	4	3	12	25	5	0	.200
1970	7	9	.438	3.65	45	19	1	148	137	48	79	0	3	2	2	39	4	1	.103
1971	4	6	.400	3.00	48	8	2	129	94	30	98	1	3	3	17	33	7	0	.212
1972	11	9	.550	2.51	65	0	0	111.1	85	32	113	0	11	9	21	19	6	1	.316
1973	7	8	.467	1.92	62	2	0	126.2	107	39	110	0	7	6	22	1	0	0	.000
1974	9	5	.643	2.65	76	0	0	119	104	29	95	0	9	5	18	0	0	0	–
1975	10	6	.625	2.98	75	0	0	126.2	95	33	115	0	10	6	24	1	0	0	.000
1976	13	11	.542	2.47	70	0	0	135	118	40	113	0	13	11	20	0	0	0	–
1977 SD N	8	9	.471	3.00	78	0	0	132	123	36	113	0	8	9	35	20	1	0	.050
1978	6	13	.316	2.52	67	0	0	107	84	29	72	0	6	13	37	12	2	0	.167
1979	9	9	.500	4.50	54	0	0	84	91	37	65	0	9	9	13	12	1	0	.083
1980	11	9	.550	2.80	66	0	0	103	101	32	69	0	11	9	23	18	5	0	.278
1981 MIL A	6	3	.667	1.04	47	0	0	78	55	13	61	0	6	3	28	0	0	0	–
1982	5	6	.455	2.60	50	0	0	79.2	63	20	71	0	5	6	29	0	0	0	–
1984	1	2	.333	1.96	33	0	0	46	38	13	40	0	1	2	23	0	0	0	–
16 yrs.	113	112	.502	2.83	897 6th	37	4	1645.2	1415	473	1275	2	106 3rd	96	324 1st	180	31	2	.172

DIVISIONAL PLAYOFF SERIES																			
1981 MIL A	1	0	1.000	3.86	3	0	0	4.2	7	1	5	0	1	0	1	0	0	0	–

LEAGUE CHAMPIONSHIP SERIES																			
1971 OAK A	0	0	–	7.71	2	0	0	2.1	2	1	2	0	0	0	0	0	0	0	–

	W	L	PCT	ERA	G	GS	CG	IP	H	BB	SO	ShO	Relief Pitching W	L	SV	BATTING AB	H	HR	BA

Rollie Fingers continued

	W	L	PCT	ERA	G	GS	CG	IP	H	BB	SO	ShO	W	L	SV	AB	H	HR	BA
1972	1	0	1.000	1.69	3	0	0	5.1	4	1	3	0	1	0	0	1	0	0	.000
1973	0	1	.000	1.93	3	0	0	4.2	4	2	4	0	0	1	1	0	0	0	–
1974	0	0	–	3.00	2	0	0	3	3	1	3	0	0	0	1	0	0	0	–
1975	0	1	.000	6.75	1	0	0	4	5	1	3	0	0	1	0	0	0	0	–
5 yrs.	1	2	.333	3.72	11	0	0	19.1	18	6	15	0	1	2	2	1	0	0	.000
WORLD SERIES																			
1972 **OAK A**	1	1	.500	1.74	6	0	0	10.1	4	4	11	0	1	1	2	1	0	0	.000
1973	0	1	.000	0.66	6	0	0	13.2	13	4	8	0	0	1	2	3	1	0	.333
1974	1	0	1.000	1.93	4	0	0	9.1	8	2	6	0	1	0	2	2	0	0	.000
3 yrs.	2	2	.500	1.35	16	0	0	33.1	25	10	25	0	2	2	6	6	1	0	.167
					2nd								2nd	2nd	1st				

Herman Fink

FINK, HERMAN ADAM   BR TR 6'2"   198 lbs.
B. Aug. 22, 1911, Concord, N. C.   D. Aug. 24, 1980, Salisbury, N. C.

	W	L	PCT	ERA	G	GS	CG	IP	H	BB	SO	ShO	W	L	SV	AB	H	HR	BA
1935 **PHI A**	0	3	.000	9.19	5	3	0	15.2	18	10	2	0	0	0	0	5	1	0	.200
1936	8	16	.333	5.39	34	24	9	188.2	222	78	53	0	0	2	3	64	8	0	.125
1937	2	1	.667	4.05	28	3	1	80	82	35	18	0	2	0	1	24	5	0	.208
3 yrs.	10	20	.333	5.22	67	30	10	284.1	322	123	73	0	2	2	4	93	14	0	.151

Pembroke Finlayson

FINLAYSON, PEMBROKE   BR TR
B. July 31, 1888, Cheraw, S. C.   D. Mar. 6, 1912, Brooklyn, N. Y.

	W	L	PCT	ERA	G	GS	CG	IP	H	BB	SO	ShO	W	L	SV	AB	H	HR	BA
1908 **BKN N**	0	0	–	135.00	1	0	0	.1	0	4	0	0	0	0	0	0	0	0	–
1909	0	0	–	5.14	1	0	0	7	7	4	2	0	0	0	0	3	0	0	.000
2 yrs.	0	0	–	11.05	2	0	0	7.1	7	8	2	0	0	0	0	3	0	0	.000

Happy Finneran

FINNERAN, JOSEPH IGNATIUS (Smokey Joe)   BB TR 5'10½"   169 lbs.
B. Oct. 29, 1891, East Orange, N. J.   D. Feb. 3, 1942, Orange, N. J.

	W	L	PCT	ERA	G	GS	CG	IP	H	BB	SO	ShO	W	L	SV	AB	H	HR	BA
1912 **PHI N**	0	2	.000	2.53	14	4	0	46.1	50	10	10	0	0	1	1	10	2	0	.200
1913	0	0	–	7.20	3	0	0	5	12	2	0	0	0	0	0	3	2	0	.667
1914 **BKN F**	12	11	.522	3.18	27	23	13	175.1	153	60	54	2	1	0	1	55	7	0	.127
1915	12	13	.480	2.80	37	24	12	215.1	197	87	68	1	3	2	0	74	11	0	.149
1918 2 teams			DET	A (5G 0–2)	NY	A	(23G 3–6)												
" total	3	8	.273	4.43	28	15	4	128	156	43	36	0	1	0	1	42	9	0	.214
5 yrs.	27	34	.443	3.30	109	66	29	570	568	202	168	3	5	3	3	184	31	0	.168

Steve Fireovid

FIREOVID, STEPHEN JOHN   BB TR 6'2"   195 lbs.
B. June 6, 1957, Bryan, Ohio

	W	L	PCT	ERA	G	GS	CG	IP	H	BB	SO	ShO	W	L	SV	AB	H	HR	BA
1981 **SD N**	0	1	.000	2.77	5	4	0	26	30	7	11	0	0	0	0	7	1	0	.143
1983	0	0	–	1.80	3	0	0	5	4	2	1	0	0	0	0	0	0	0	–
1984 **PHI N**	0	0	–	1.59	6	0	0	5.2	4	0	3	0	0	0	0	0	0	0	–
3 yrs.	0	1	.000	2.45	14	4	0	36.2	38	9	15	0	0	0	0	7	1	0	.143

Ted Firth

FIRTH, JOHN EDWARD
B. Philadelphia, Pa.   D. June 23, 1902, Tewksberry, Mass.

	W	L	PCT	ERA	G	GS	CG	IP	H	BB	SO	ShO	W	L	SV	AB	H	HR	BA
1884 **RIC AA**	0	1	.000	8.00	1	1	1	9	14	5	0	0	0	0	0	3	1	0	.333

Bill Fischer

FISCHER, WILLIAM CHARLES   BR TR 6'   190 lbs.
B. Oct. 11, 1930, Wausau, Wis.

	W	L	PCT	ERA	G	GS	CG	IP	H	BB	SO	ShO	W	L	SV	AB	H	HR	BA
1956 **CHI A**	0	0	–	21.60	3	0	0	1.2	6	1	2	0	0	0	0	0	0	0	–
1957	7	8	.467	3.48	33	11	3	124	139	35	48	1	3	4	1	40	6	0	.150
1958 3 teams			CHI	A (17G 2–3)	DET	A	(22G 2–4)	WAS	A	(3G 0–3)									
" total	4	10	.286	6.34	42	6	0	88	113	31	42	0	2	6	2	13	2	0	.154
1959 **WAS A**	9	11	.450	4.28	34	29	6	187.1	211	43	62	1	0	0	0	54	7	0	.130
1960 2 teams			WAS	A (20G 3–5)	DET	A	(20G 5–3)												
" total	8	8	.500	4.30	40	13	2	132	135	35	55	0	2	1	0	30	7	1	.233
1961 2 teams			DET	A (26G 3–2)	KC	A	(15G 1–0)												
" total	4	2	.667	4.66	41	1	0	67.2	80	23	30	0	4	1	5	9	0	0	.000
1962 **KC A**	4	12	.250	3.95	34	16	5	127.2	150	38	50	0	1	0	2	38	4	0	.105
1963	4	6	.400	3.57	45	2	0	95.2	86	29	34	0	9	6	3	15	1	0	.067
1964 **MIN A**	0	1	.000	7.36	9	0	0	7.1	16	5	2	0	0	1	0	0	0	0	–
9 yrs.	45	58	.437	4.34	281	78	16	831.1	936	240	313	2	21	19	13	199	27	1	.136

Carl Fischer

FISCHER, CHARLES WILLIAM   BR TL 6'   180 lbs.
B. Nov. 5, 1905, Medina, N. Y.   D. Dec. 10, 1963, Medina, N. Y.

	W	L	PCT	ERA	G	GS	CG	IP	H	BB	SO	ShO	W	L	SV	AB	H	HR	BA
1930 **WAS A**	1	1	.500	4.86	8	4	1	33.1	37	18	21	0	0	0	1	9	0	0	.000
1931	13	9	.591	4.38	46	23	7	191	207	80	96	0	2	0	3	66	8	0	.121
1932 2 teams			WAS	A (12G 3–2)	STL	A	(24G 3–7)												
" total	6	9	.400	5.36	36	18	5	147.2	179	76	58	1	1	0	1	49	12	0	.245
1933 **DET A**	11	15	.423	3.55	35	22	9	182.2	176	84	93	0	5	1	3	62	9	0	.145
1934	6	4	.600	4.37	20	15	4	94.2	107	38	39	1	1	1	1	31	2	0	.065
1935 2 teams			DET	A (3G 0–1)	CHI	A	(24G 5–5)												
" total	5	6	.455	6.17	27	12	3	100.2	118	44	38	1	2	1	0	23	4	0	.174
1937 2 teams			CLE	A (2G 0–1)	WAS	A	(17G 4–5)												
" total	4	6	.400	4.58	19	11	2	72.2	76	32	31	0	0	2	2	22	3	0	.136
7 yrs.	46	50	.479	4.63	191	105	31	822.2	900	372	376	3	11	5	11	262	38	0	.145

Hank Fischer

FISCHER, HENRY WILLIAM (Bulldog)   BR TR 6'   190 lbs.
B. Jan. 11, 1940, Yonkers, N. Y.

	W	L	PCT	ERA	G	GS	CG	IP	H	BB	SO	ShO	W	L	SV	AB	H	HR	BA
1962 **MIL N**	2	3	.400	5.30	29	0	0	37.1	43	20	29	0	2	3	4	4	0	0	.000
1963	4	3	.571	4.96	31	6	1	74.1	74	28	72	0	1	3	0	19	2	0	.105
1964	11	10	.524	4.01	37	28	9	168.1	177	39	99	5	0	0	2	52	8	0	.154
1965	8	9	.471	3.89	31	19	2	122.2	126	39	79	0	1	0	0	37	4	0	.108
1966 3 teams			ATL	N (14G 2–3)	CIN	N	(11G 0–6)	BOS	A	(6G 2–3)									
" total	4	12	.250	4.53	31	22	1	117.1	143	40	72	0	0	0	0	33	3	0	.091
1967 **BOS A**	1	2	.333	2.36	9	2	1	26.2	24	8	18	0	0	1	1	7	1	0	.143
6 yrs.	30	39	.435	4.23	168	77	14	546.2	587	174	369	5	4	7	7	152	18	0	.118

	W	L	PCT	ERA	G	GS	CG	IP	H	BB	SO	ShO	W	L	SV	AB	H	HR	BA
													Relief Pitching			**BATTING**			

Rube Fischer

FISCHER, REUBEN WALTER   BR TR 6'4"   190 lbs.
B. Sept. 19, 1916, Carlock, S. D.

	W	L	PCT	ERA	G	GS	CG	IP	H	BB	SO	ShO	W	L	SV	AB	H	HR	BA
1941 NY N	1	0	1.000	2.45	2	1	1	11	10	6	9	0	0	0	0	3	1	0	.333
1943	5	10	.333	4.61	22	17	4	130.2	140	59	47	0	1	0	1	43	11	1	.256
1944	6	14	.300	5.18	38	18	2	128.2	128	87	39	1	3	4	2	40	5	0	.125
1945	3	8	.273	5.63	31	4	0	76.2	90	49	27	0	2	5	1	19	4	1	.211
1946	1	2	.333	6.31	15	1	0	35.2	48	21	14	0	1	2	0	9	1	0	.111
5 yrs.	16	34	.320	5.10	108	41	7	382.2	416	222	136	1	7	11	4	114	22	2	.193

Leo Fishel

FISHEL, LEO   BR TR 6'   175 lbs.
B. Dec. 13, 1877, Babylon, N. Y.   D. May 19, 1960, Hempstead, N. Y.

	W	L	PCT	ERA	G	GS	CG	IP	H	BB	SO	ShO	W	L	SV	AB	H	HR	BA
1899 NY N	0	1	.000	6.00	1	1	1	9	9	6	6	0	0	0	0	4	1	0	.250

Fisher

FISHER,
B. Johnstown, Pa.   Deceased.

	W	L	PCT	ERA	G	GS	CG	IP	H	BB	SO	ShO	W	L	SV	AB	H	HR	BA
1884 PHI U	1	7	.125	3.57	8	8	8	70.2	76	13	42	0	0	0	0	65	10	0	.154
1885 BUF N	0	1	.000	5.00	1	1	1	9	10	2	4	0	0	0	0	4	0	0	.000
2 yrs.	1	8	.111	3.73	9	9	9	79.2	86	15	46	0	0	0	0	*			

Chauncey Fisher

FISHER, CHAUNCEY BURR (Peach)   BR TR 5'11"   175 lbs.
Brother of Tom Fisher.
B. Jan. 8, 1872, Anderson, Ind.   D. Apr. 27, 1939, Los Angeles, Calif.

	W	L	PCT	ERA	G	GS	CG	IP	H	BB	SO	ShO	W	L	SV	AB	H	HR	BA
1893 CLE N	0	2	.000	5.50	2	2	1	18	26	9	9	0	0	0	0	8	2	0	.250
1894 2 teams				CLE N (3G 0–2)				CIN N (11G 2–8)											
" total	2	10	.167	7.76	14	13	10	102	156	49	14	0	0	0	0	47	10	1	.213
1896 CIN N	10	7	.588	4.45	27	15	13	159.2	199	36	25	2	2	2	2	57	14	0	.246
1897 BKN N	9	7	.563	4.23	20	13	11	149	184	43	31	1	2	1	1	59	12	0	.203
1901 2 teams				NY N (1G 0–1)				STL N (1G 0–0)											
" total	0	1	.000	15.43	2	1	0	7	18	3	1	0	0	0	0	3	0	0	.000
5 yrs.	21	27	.438	5.37	65	44	36	435.2	583	140	80	3	4	3	3	174	38	1	.218

Cherokee Fisher

FISHER, WILLIAM CHARLES   BR TR 5'9"   164 lbs.
B. Dec., 1845, Philadelphia, Pa.   D. Sept. 26, 1912, New York, N. Y.

	W	L	PCT	ERA	G	GS	CG	IP	H	BB	SO	ShO	W	L	SV	AB	H	HR	BA
1876 CIN N	4	20	.167	3.02	28	24	22	229.1	294	6	29	0	0	0	0	129	32	0	.248
1877 CHI N	0	0	–	0.00	0	0	0	0	0	0	0	0	0	0	0	4	0	0	.000
1878 PRO N	0	1	.000	4.00	1	1	1	9	14	0	2	0	0	0	0	3	0	0	.000
3 yrs.	4	21	.160	3.06	29	25	23	238.1	308	6	31	0	0	0	0	136	32	0	.235

Clarence Fisher

FISHER, CLARENCE HENRY   BR TR 6'   174 lbs.
B. Aug. 27, 1898, Letart, W. Va.   D. Nov. 2, 1965, Point Pleasant, W. Va.

	W	L	PCT	ERA	G	GS	CG	IP	H	BB	SO	ShO	W	L	SV	AB	H	HR	BA
1919 WAS A	0	0	–	13.50	2	0	0	4	8	3	1	0	0	0	0	1	0	0	–
1920	0	1	.000	9.82	2	0	0	3.2	5	5	0	0	0	1	0	1	0	0	.000
2 yrs.	0	1	.000	11.74	4	0	0	7.2	13	8	1	0	0	1	0	1	0	0	.000

Don Fisher

FISHER, DONALD RAYMOND   BR TR 6'   210 lbs.
B. Feb. 6, 1916, Cleveland, Ohio   D. July 29, 1973, Mayfield Heights, Ohio

	W	L	PCT	ERA	G	GS	CG	IP	H	BB	SO	ShO	W	L	SV	AB	H	HR	BA
1945 NY N	1	0	1.000	2.00	2	1	1	18	12	7	4	1	0	0	0	7	1	0	.143

Ed Fisher

FISHER, EDWARD FREDERICK   BR TR 6'2"   200 lbs.
B. Oct. 31, 1876, Wayne, Mich.   D. July 24, 1951, Spokane, Wash.

	W	L	PCT	ERA	G	GS	CG	IP	H	BB	SO	ShO	W	L	SV	AB	H	HR	BA
1902 DET A	0	0	–	0.00	1	0	0	4	4	1	0	0	0	0	0	2	0	0	.000

Eddie Fisher

FISHER, EDDIE GENE   BR TR 6'2½"   200 lbs.
B. July 16, 1936, Shreveport, La.

	W	L	PCT	ERA	G	GS	CG	IP	H	BB	SO	ShO	W	L	SV	AB	H	HR	BA
1959 SF N	2	6	.250	7.88	17	5	0	40	57	8	15	0	0	4	1	8	0	0	.000
1960	1	0	1.000	3.55	9	1	1	12.2	11	2	7	0	0	0	0	5	3	0	.600
1961	0	2	.000	5.35	15	1	0	33.2	36	9	16	0	0	2	1	7	1	0	.143
1962 CHI A	9	5	.643	3.10	57	12	2	182.2	169	45	88	1	4	3	5	46	6	0	.130
1963	9	8	.529	3.95	33	15	2	120.2	114	28	67	1	2	3	0	36	5	0	.139
1964	6	3	.667	3.02	59	2	0	125	86	32	74	0	6	3	9	18	3	0	.167
1965	15	7	.682	2.40	82	0	0	165.1	118	43	90	0	15	7	24	29	4	0	.138
1966 2 teams				CHI A (23G 1–3)				BAL A (44G 5–3)											
" total	6	6	.500	2.52	67	0	0	107	87	36	57	0	6	6	19	15	2	0	.133
1967 BAL A	4	3	.571	3.61	46	0	0	89.2	82	26	53	0	4	3	1	5	1	0	.200
1968 CLE A	4	2	.667	2.85	54	0	0	94.2	87	17	42	0	4	2	4	12	0	0	.000
1969 CAL A	3	2	.600	3.63	52	1	0	96.2	100	28	47	0	2	2	2	13	0	0	.000
1970	4	4	.500	3.05	67	2	0	130	117	35	74	0	4	4	8	11	1	0	.091
1971	10	8	.556	2.72	57	3	0	119	92	50	82	0	9	6	3	16	1	0	.063
1972 2 teams				CAL A (43G 4–5)				CHI A (6G 0–1)											
" total	4	6	.400	3.91	49	5	0	103.2	104	40	42	0	4	3	4	24	4	0	.083
1973 2 teams				CHI A (26G 6–7)				STL N (6G 2–1)											
" total	8	8	.500	4.67	32	16	2	117.2	138	39	58	0	2	1	0	1	1	0	1.000
15 yrs.	85	70	.548	3.41	690	63	7	1538.1	1398	438	812	2	56	46	81	246	30	0	.122

Fritz Fisher

FISHER, FREDERICK BROWN   BL TL 6'1"   180 lbs.
B. Nov. 28, 1941, Adrian, Mich.

	W	L	PCT	ERA	G	GS	CG	IP	H	BB	SO	ShO	W	L	SV	AB	H	HR	BA
1964 DET A	0	0	–	108.00	1	0	0	.1	2	2	1	0	0	0	0	0	0	0	–

Harry Fisher

FISHER, HARRY DEVEREUX   BL TR 6'   180 lbs.
B. Jan. 3, 1926, Newbury, Ont., Canada   D. Sept. 20, 1981, Waterloo, Ont., Canada

	W	L	PCT	ERA	G	GS	CG	IP	H	BB	SO	ShO	W	L	SV	AB	H	HR	BA
1952 PIT N	1	2	.333	6.87	8	3	0	18.1	17	13	5	0	0	0	0	*			

Jack Fisher

FISHER, JOHN HOWARD (Fat Jack)   BR TR 6'2"   215 lbs.
B. Mar. 4, 1939, Frostburg, Md.

	W	L	PCT	ERA	G	GS	CG	IP	H	BB	SO	ShO	W	L	SV	AB	H	HR	BA
1959 BAL A	1	6	.143	3.05	27	7	1	88.2	76	38	52	1	0	2	2	23	3	0	.130
1960	12	11	.522	3.41	40	20	8	197.2	174	78	99	3	6	3	2	60	11	1	.183

	W	L	PCT	ERA	G	GS	CG	IP	H	BB	SO	ShO	Relief Pitching W	L	SV	BATTING AB	H	HR	BA

Jack Fisher continued

	W	L	PCT	ERA	G	GS	CG	IP	H	BB	SO	ShO	W	L	SV	AB	H	HR	BA
1961	10	13	.435	3.90	36	25	10	196	205	75	118	1	0	4	1	56	5	0	.089
1962	7	9	.438	5.09	32	25	4	152	173	56	81	0	0	1	1	49	5	0	.102
1963 SF N	6	10	.375	4.58	36	12	2	116	132	38	57	0	3	2	1	29	3	0	.103
1964 NY N	10	17	.370	4.23	40	34	8	227.2	256	56	115	1	0	2	0	76	12	0	.158
1965	8	24	.250	3.94	43	36	10	253.2	252	68	116	0	0	2	1	78	12	0	.154
1966	11	14	.440	3.68	38	33	10	230	229	54	127	2	1	0	0	67	6	0	.090
1967	9	18	.333	4.70	39	30	7	220.1	251	64	117	1	1	1	0	70	7	0	.100
1968 CHI A	8	13	.381	2.99	35	28	2	180.2	176	48	80	0	0	1	0	53	6	0	.113
1969 CIN N	4	4	.500	5.50	34	15	0	113	137	30	55	0	1	0	1	33	4	0	.121
11 yrs.	86	139	.382	4.06	400	265	62	1975.2	2061	605	1017	9	12	18	9	594	74	1	.125

Maury Fisher

FISHER, MAURICE WAYNE   BR TR 6'5" 210 lbs.
B. Feb. 16, 1931, Uniondale, Ind.

	W	L	PCT	ERA	G	GS	CG	IP	H	BB	SO	ShO	W	L	SV	AB	H	HR	BA
1955 CIN N	0	0	–	6.75	1	0	0	2.2	5	2	1	0	0	0	0	1	0	0	.000

Ray Fisher

FISHER, RAYMOND LYLE   BR TR 5'11½" 180 lbs.
B. Oct. 4, 1887, Middlebury, Vt.   D. Nov. 3, 1982, Ann Arbor, Mich.

	W	L	PCT	ERA	G	GS	CG	IP	H	BB	SO	ShO	W	L	SV	AB	H	HR	BA
1910 NY A	5	3	.625	2.92	17	7	3	92.1	95	18	42	0	1	0	1	29	3	0	.103
1911	10	11	.476	3.25	29	22	8	171.2	178	55	99	2	2	1	0	59	7	1	.119
1912	2	8	.200	5.88	17	13	5	90.1	107	32	47	0	1	0	0	31	2	0	.065
1913	12	16	.429	3.18	43	31	14	246.1	244	71	92	1	0	1	1	79	22	0	.278
1914	10	12	.455	2.28	29	26	17	209	177	61	86	2	0	0	1	65	9	0	.138
1915	18	11	.621	2.11	30	28	20	247.2	219	62	97	4	2	0	0	83	9	0	.108
1916	11	8	.579	3.17	31	21	9	179	191	51	56	1	2	1	2	62	11	0	.177
1917	8	9	.471	2.19	23	18	12	144	126	43	64	3	0	0	0	50	9	1	.180
1919 CIN N	14	5	.737	2.17	26	20	12	174.1	141	38	41	5	1	0	1	59	16	0	.271
1920	10	11	.476	2.73	33	22	10	201	189	50	56	1	1	0	1	70	17	0	.243
10 yrs.	100	94	.515	2.82	278	208	110	1755.2	1667	481	680	19	10	3	7	587	105	2	.179

WORLD SERIES

	W	L	PCT	ERA	G	GS	CG	IP	H	BB	SO	ShO	W	L	SV	AB	H	HR	BA
1919 CIN N	0	1	.000	2.35	2	1	0	7.2	7	2	2	0	0	0	0	2	1	0	.500

Tom Fisher

FISHER, THOMAS CHALMERS (Red)   BR TR 5'10½" 185 lbs.
Brother of Chauncey Fisher.
B. Nov. 1, 1880, Anderson, Ind.   D. Sept. 3, 1972, Anderson, Ind.

	W	L	PCT	ERA	G	GS	CG	IP	H	BB	SO	ShO	W	L	SV	AB	H	HR	BA
1904 BOS N	6	15	.286	4.25	31	21	19	214	257	82	84	3	0	1	0	99	21	2	.212

Tom Fisher

FISHER, THOMAS GENE   BR TR 6' 180 lbs.
B. Apr. 4, 1943, Cleveland, Ohio

	W	L	PCT	ERA	G	GS	CG	IP	H	BB	SO	ShO	W	L	SV	AB	H	HR	BA
1967 BAL A	0	0	–	0.00	2	0	0	3.1	2	2	1	0	0	0	0	0	0	0	–

Max Fiske

FISKE, MAXIMILIAN PATRICK (Mox Ski)   BR TR 5'11" 185 lbs.
B. Oct. 10, 1889, Chicago, Ill.   D. May 28, 1928, Chicago, Ill.

	W	L	PCT	ERA	G	GS	CG	IP	H	BB	SO	ShO	W	L	SV	AB	H	HR	BA
1914 CHI F	12	9	.571	3.14	38	22	7	198	161	59	87	0	4	1	0	68	16	0	.235

Paul Fittery

FITTERY, PAUL CLARENCE   BB TL 5'8" 168 lbs.
B. Oct. 10, 1887, Lebanon, Pa.   D. Jan. 28, 1974, Cartersville, Ga.

	W	L	PCT	ERA	G	GS	CG	IP	H	BB	SO	ShO	W	L	SV	AB	H	HR	BA
1914 CIN N	0	2	.000	3.09	8	4	2	43.2	41	12	21	0	0	0	0	17	1	0	.059
1917 PHI N	1	1	.500	4.53	17	2	1	55.2	69	27	13	0	0	0	0	22	2	0	.091
2 yrs.	1	3	.250	3.90	25	6	3	99.1	110	39	34	0	0	0	0	39	3	0	.077

John Fitzgerald

FITZGERALD, JOHN FRANCIS   BL TL 6'3" 190 lbs.
B. Sept. 15, 1933, Brooklyn, N.Y.

	W	L	PCT	ERA	G	GS	CG	IP	H	BB	SO	ShO	W	L	SV	AB	H	HR	BA
1958 SF N	0	0	–	3.00	1	1	0	3	1	1	3	0	0	0	0	1	0	0	.000

John Fitzgerald

FITZGERALD, JOHN H.
B. May 30, 1870, Natick, Mass.   D. Mar. 21, 1921, Boston, Mass.

	W	L	PCT	ERA	G	GS	CG	IP	H	BB	SO	ShO	W	L	SV	AB	H	HR	BA
1890 ROC AA	3	8	.273	4.04	11	11	8	78	77	45	35	1	0	0	0	31	6	0	.194
1891 BOS AA	1	1	.500	5.63	6	3	2	32	49	11	16	0	0	0	1	14	1	0	.071
2 yrs.	4	9	.308	4.50	17	14	10	110	126	56	51	1	0	0	1	45	7	0	.156

John Fitzgerald

FITZGERALD, JOHN T.
B. Leadville, Colo.   Deceased.

	W	L	PCT	ERA	G	GS	CG	IP	H	BB	SO	ShO	W	L	SV	AB	H	HR	BA
1891 LOU AA	14	18	.438	3.59	33	32	29	276	280	95	111	3	0	1	0	112	19	1	.170
1892 LOU N	1	3	.250	4.24	4	4	4	34	45	11	3	0	0	0	0	15	2	0	.133
2 yrs.	15	21	.417	3.66	37	36	33	310	325	106	114	3	0	1	0	127	21	1	.165

Paul Fitzke

FITZKE, PAUL FREDERICK HERMAN (Bob)   BR TR 5'11½" 185 lbs.
B. July 30, 1900, LaCrosse, Wis.   D. June 30, 1950, Sacramento, Calif.

	W	L	PCT	ERA	G	GS	CG	IP	H	BB	SO	ShO	W	L	SV	AB	H	HR	BA
1924 CLE A	0	0	–	4.50	1	0	0	4	5	3	1	0	0	0	0	1	0	0	.000

Al Fitzmorris

FITZMORRIS, ALAN JAMES   BB TR 6'2" 190 lbs.
B. Mar. 21, 1946, Buffalo, N.Y.

	W	L	PCT	ERA	G	GS	CG	IP	H	BB	SO	ShO	W	L	SV	AB	H	HR	BA
1969 KC A	1	1	.500	4.22	7	0	0	10.2	9	4	3	0	1	1	2	1	0	0	.000
1970	8	5	.615	4.42	43	11	2	118	112	52	47	0	4	1	1	31	9	0	.290
1971	7	5	.583	4.18	36	15	2	127	112	55	53	1	0	0	0	44	11	0	.250
1972	2	5	.286	3.74	38	2	0	101	99	28	51	0	2	3	3	23	4	0	.174
1973	8	3	.727	2.83	15	13	3	89	88	25	26	1	1	0	0	0	0	0	–
1974	13	6	.684	2.79	34	27	9	190	189	63	53	4	0	0	1	0	0	0	–
1975	16	12	.571	3.57	35	35	11	242	239	76	78	3	0	0	0	0	0	0	–
1976	15	11	.577	3.07	35	33	8	220	227	56	80	2	0	0	0	0	0	0	–
1977 CLE A	6	10	.375	5.41	29	21	1	133	164	53	54	0	1	0	0	0	0	0	–
1978 2 teams			CLE A (7G 0–1)			CAL A (9G 1–0)													
" total	1	1	.500	3.13	16	0	0	46	45	21	13	0	0	1	0	0	0	0	–
10 yrs.	77	59	.566	3.65	288	159	36	1276.2	1284	433	458	11	9	6	7	99	24	0	.242

	W	L	PCT	ERA	G	GS	CG	IP	H	BB	SO	ShO	Relief Pitching W	L	SV	BATTING AB	H	HR	BA

Freddie Fitzsimmons

FITZSIMMONS, FREDERICK LANDIS (Fat Freddie) BR TR 5'11" 185 lbs.
B. July 28, 1901, Mishawaka, Ind. D. Nov. 18, 1979, Yucca Valley, Calif.
Manager 1943-45.

	W	L	PCT	ERA	G	GS	CG	IP	H	BB	SO	ShO	W	L	SV	AB	H	HR	BA
1925 NY N	6	3	.667	2.65	10	8	6	74.2	70	18	17	1	1	0	0	29	9	0	.310
1926	14	10	.583	2.88	37	26	12	219	224	58	48	0	1	2	0	86	11	0	.128
1927	17	10	.630	3.72	42	31	14	244.2	260	67	78	1	2	1	3	87	18	0	.207
1928	20	9	.690	3.68	40	32	16	261.1	264	65	67	1	4	0	1	94	18	0	.191
1929	15	11	.577	4.10	37	31	14	221.2	242	66	55	4	1	0	1	82	15	0	.183
1930	19	7	**.731**	4.25	41	29	17	224.1	230	59	76	1	3	0	1	83	22	2	.265
1931	18	11	.621	3.05	35	33	19	253.2	242	62	78	4	0	1	0	92	21	4	.228
1932	11	11	.500	4.43	35	31	11	237.2	287	83	65	0	0	0	0	86	19	2	.221
1933	16	11	.593	2.90	36	35	13	251.2	243	72	65	1	0	0	0	95	19	2	.200
1934	18	14	.563	3.04	38	37	14	263.1	266	51	73	3	0	0	1	95	22	2	.232
1935	4	8	.333	4.02	18	15	6	94	104	22	23	**4**	0	0	0	31	8	0	.258
1936	10	7	.588	3.32	28	17	7	141	147	39	35	0	1	2	2	47	7	0	.149
1937 2 teams		NY	N (6G 2-2)		BKN	N (13G 4-8)													
" total	6	10	.375	4.35	19	17	5	118	119	40	42	1	1	0	0	40	8	1	.200
1938 BKN N	11	8	.579	3.02	27	26	12	202.2	205	43	78	3	0	0	0	70	12	0	.171
1939	7	9	.438	3.87	27	20	5	151.1	178	28	44	0	1	1	3	47	11	1	.234
1940	16	2	**.889**	2.81	20	18	11	134.1	120	25	35	4	1	0	1	47	5	0	.106
1941	6	1	.857	2.07	13	12	3	82.2	78	26	19	1	1	0	0	28	4	0	.143
1942	0	0	—	15.00	1	1	0	3	6	1	0	0	0	0	0	2	1	0	.500
1943	3	4	.429	5.44	9	7	1	44.2	50	21	12	0	0	1	0	14	1	0	.071
19 yrs.	217	146	.598	3.51	513	426	186	3223.2	3335	846	870	29	17	8	13	1155	231	14	.200

WORLD SERIES

	W	L	PCT	ERA	G	GS	CG	IP	H	BB	SO	ShO	W	L	SV	AB	H	HR	BA
1933 NY N	0	1	.000	5.14	1	1	0	7	9	0	2	0	0	0	0	2	1	0	.500
1936	0	2	.000	5.40	2	2	1	11.2	13	2	6	0	0	0	0	4	2	0	.500
1941 BKN N	0	0	—	0.00	1	1	0	7	4	3	1	0	0	0	0	2	0	0	.000
3 yrs.	0	3	.000	3.86	4	4	1	25.2	26	5	9	0	0	0	0	8	3	0	.375

Patsy Flaherty

FLAHERTY, PATRICK JOSEPH BL TL
B. June 29, 1876, Carnegie, Pa. D. Jan. 23, 1968, Alexandria, La.

	W	L	PCT	ERA	G	GS	CG	IP	H	BB	SO	ShO	W	L	SV	AB	H	HR	BA
1899 LOU N	2	3	.400	2.31	5	4	4	39	41	5	5	0				24	5	0	.208
1900 PIT N	0	0	—	6.14	4	1	0	22	30	9	5	0	0	0	0	9	1	0	.111
1903 CHI A	11	25	.306	3.74	40	34	29	293.2	338	50	65	2	2	1	1	102	14	0	.137
1904 2 teams		CHI	A (5G 1-2)		PIT	N (29G 19-9)													
" total	20	11	.645	2.05	34	33	32	285	246	69	68	5	0	0	0	116	26	2	.224
1905 PIT N	9	10	.474	3.49	27	20	15	188	197	49	44	0	0	1	1	76	15	0	.197
1907 BOS N	12	15	.444	2.70	27	25	23	217	197	59	34	0	1	1	0	115	22	2	.191
1908	12	18	.400	3.25	31	31	21	244	221	81	50	0	0	0	0	86	12	0	.140
1910 PHI N	0	0	—	0.00	1	0	0	.1	1	1	0	0	0	0	0	2	1	0	.500
1911 BOS N	0	2	.000	7.07	4	2	1	14	21	8	0	0	0	0	0	94	27	2	.287
9 yrs.	66	84	.440	3.10	173	150	125	1303	1292	331	271	7	4	3	2	*			

Mike Flanagan

FLANAGAN, MICHAEL KENDALL BL TL 6' 180 lbs.
B. Dec. 16, 1951, Manchester, N. H.

	W	L	PCT	ERA	G	GS	CG	IP	H	BB	SO	ShO	W	L	SV	AB	H	HR	BA
1975 BAL A	0	1	.000	2.79	2	1	0	9.2	9	6	7	0	0	0	0	0	0	0	—
1976	3	5	.375	4.13	20	10	4	85	83	33	56	0	0	3	0	0	0	0	—
1977	15	10	.600	3.64	36	33	15	235	235	70	149	2	0	1	1	0	0	0	—
1978	19	15	.559	4.03	40	**40**	17	281.1	271	87	167	2	0	0	0	0	0	0	—
1979	**23**	9	.719	3.08	39	38	16	266	245	70	190	**5**	0	0	0	0	0	0	—
1980	16	13	.552	4.12	37	37	12	251	**278**	71	128	2	0	0	0	0	0	0	—
1981	9	6	.600	4.19	20	20	3	116	108	37	72	2	0	0	0	0	0	0	—
1982	15	11	.577	3.97	36	35	11	236	233	76	103	1	0	0	0	0	0	0	—
1983	12	4	.750	3.30	20	20	3	125.1	135	31	50	1	0	0	0	0	0	0	—
1984	13	13	.500	3.53	34	34	10	226.2	213	81	115	2	0	0	0	0	0	0	—
10 yrs.	125	87	.590	3.74	284	268	91	1832	1810	562	1037	17	0	4	1	0	0	0	—

LEAGUE CHAMPIONSHIP SERIES

	W	L	PCT	ERA	G	GS	CG	IP	H	BB	SO	ShO	W	L	SV	AB	H	HR	BA
1979 BAL A	1	0	1.000	5.14	1	1	0	7	6	1	2	0	0	0	0	0	0	0	—
1983	1	0	1.000	1.80	1	1	0	5	5	0	1	0	0	0	0	0	0	0	—
2 yrs.	2	0	1.000	3.75	2	2	0	12	11	1	3	0	0	0	0	0	0	0	—

WORLD SERIES

	W	L	PCT	ERA	G	GS	CG	IP	H	BB	SO	ShO	W	L	SV	AB	H	HR	BA
1979 BAL A	1	1	.500	3.00	3	2	1	15	18	2	13	0	0	0	0	5	0	0	.000
1983	0	0	—	4.50	1	1	0	4	6	1	1	0	0	0	0	1	0	0	.000
2 yrs.	1	1	.500	3.32	4	3	1	19	24	3	14	0	0	0	0	6	0	0	.000

Ray Flanigan

FLANIGAN, RAYMOND ARTHUR BR TR 6' 190 lbs.
B. Jan. 8, 1923, Morgantown, W. Va.

	W	L	PCT	ERA	G	GS	CG	IP	H	BB	SO	ShO	W	L	SV	AB	H	HR	BA
1946 CLE A	0	1	.000	11.00	3	1	0	9	11	8	2	0	0	0	0	2	1	0	.500

Tom Flanigan

FLANIGAN, THOMAS ANTHONY BR TL 6'3" 175 lbs.
B. Sept. 6, 1934, Cincinnati, Ohio

	W	L	PCT	ERA	G	GS	CG	IP	H	BB	SO	ShO	W	L	SV	AB	H	HR	BA
1954 CHI A	0	0	—	0.00	2	0	0	1.2	1	1	0	0	0	0	0	0	0	0	—
1958 STL N	0	0	—	9.00	1	0	0	1	2	1	0	0	0	0	0	0	0	0	—
2 yrs.	0	0	—	3.38	3	0	0	2.2	3	2	0	0	0	0	0	0	0	0	—

Jack Flater

FLATER, JOHN WILLIAM BR TR 5'10" 175 lbs.
B. Sept. 22, 1883, Sandymount, Md. D. Mar. 20, 1970, Westminster, Md.

	W	L	PCT	ERA	G	GS	CG	IP	H	BB	SO	ShO	W	L	SV	AB	H	HR	BA
1908 PHI A	1	3	.250	2.06	5	3	3	39.1	35	12	8	0	1	0	0	15	2	0	.133

John Flavin

FLAVIN, JOHN THOMAS BL TL 6'2" 208 lbs.
B. May 7, 1942, Albany, Calif.

	W	L	PCT	ERA	G	GS	CG	IP	H	BB	SO	ShO	W	L	SV	AB	H	HR	BA
1964 CHI N	0	1	.000	13.50	5	1	0	4.2	11	3	5	0	0	0	0	1	0	0	.000

	W	L	PCT	ERA	G	GS	CG	IP	H	BB	SO	ShO	Relief Pitching W	L	SV	Batting AB	H	HR	BA

Bill Fleming

FLEMING, LESLIE FLETCHARD
B. July 31, 1913, Rowland, Calif.   BR TR 6'   190 lbs.

	W	L	PCT	ERA	G	GS	CG	IP	H	BB	SO	ShO	W	L	SV	AB	H	HR	BA
1940 BOS A	1	2	.333	4.86	10	6	1	46.1	53	20	24	0	0	1	0	13	0	0	.000
1941	1	1	.500	3.92	16	1	0	41.1	32	24	20	0	1	1	1	9	2	0	.222
1942 CHI N	5	6	.455	3.01	33	14	4	134.1	117	63	59	2	0	1	2	39	2	0	.051
1943	0	1	.000	6.40	11	0	0	32.1	40	12	12	0	0	1	0	8	0	0	.000
1944	9	10	.474	3.13	39	18	9	158.1	163	62	42	1	6	10	0	53	9	0	.170
1946	0	1	.000	6.14	14	1	0	29.1	37	12	10	0	0	0	0	3	0	0	.000
6 yrs.	16	21	.432	3.79	123	40	14	442	442	193	167	3	7	14	3	125	13	0	.104

Sam Fletcher

FLETCHER, SAMUEL S.
B. Altoona, Pa.   TR 6'2"   210 lbs.

	W	L	PCT	ERA	G	GS	CG	IP	H	BB	SO	ShO	W	L	SV	AB	H	HR	BA
1909 BKN N	0	1	.000	8.00	1	1	1	9	13	2	5	0	0	0	0	3	0	0	.000
1912 CIN N	0	0	–	12.10	2	0	0	9.2	15	11	3	0	0	0	0	4	2	0	.500
2 yrs.	0	1	.000	10.13	3	1	1	18.2	28	13	8	0	0	0	0	7	2	0	.286

Tom Fletcher

FLETCHER, THOMAS WAYNE
B. June 28, 1942, Elmira, N. Y.   BB TL 6'   170 lbs.

	W	L	PCT	ERA	G	GS	CG	IP	H	BB	SO	ShO	W	L	SV	AB	H	HR	BA
1962 DET A	0	0	–	0.00	1	0	0	2	2	2	1	0	0	0	0	0	0	0	–

Van Fletcher

FLETCHER, ALFRED VANOIDE
B. Aug. 6, 1924, East Bend, N. C.   BR TR 6'2"   185 lbs.

	W	L	PCT	ERA	G	GS	CG	IP	H	BB	SO	ShO	W	L	SV	AB	H	HR	BA
1955 DET A	0	0	–	3.00	9	0	0	12	13	2	4	0	0	0	0	0	0	0	–

John Flinn

FLINN, JOHN RICHARD
B. Sept. 2, 1954, Merced, Calif.   BR TR 6'   175 lbs.

	W	L	PCT	ERA	G	GS	CG	IP	H	BB	SO	ShO	W	L	SV	AB	H	HR	BA
1978 BAL A	1	1	.500	8.04	13	0	0	15.2	24	13	8	0	1	1	0	0	0	0	–
1979	0	0	–	0.00	4	0	0	3	2	1	0	0	0	0	0	0	0	0	–
1980 MIL A	2	1	.667	3.89	20	1	0	37	31	20	15	0	2	1	2	0	0	0	–
1982 BAL A	2	0	1.000	1.32	5	0	0	13.2	13	3	13	0	2	0	0	0	0	0	–
4 yrs.	5	2	.714	4.15	42	1	0	69.1	70	37	36	0	5	2	2	0	0	0	–

Hilly Flitcraft

FLITCRAFT, HILDRETH MILTON
B. Aug. 21, 1923, Woodstown, N. J.   BL TL 6'2"   180 lbs.

	W	L	PCT	ERA	G	GS	CG	IP	H	BB	SO	ShO	W	L	SV	AB	H	HR	BA
1942 PHI N	0	0	–	8.10	3	0	0	3.1	6	2	1	0	0	0	0	0	0	0	–

Mort Flohr

FLOHR, MORITZ HERMAN (Dutch)
B. Aug. 15, 1911, Canisteo, N. Y.   BL TL 6'   173 lbs.

	W	L	PCT	ERA	G	GS	CG	IP	H	BB	SO	ShO	W	L	SV	AB	H	HR	BA
1934 PHI A	0	2	.000	5.87	14	3	0	30.2	34	33	6	0	0	0	0	12	4	0	.333

Jesse Flores

FLORES, JESSE SANDOVAL
B. Nov. 2, 1914, Guadalajara, Mexico   BR TR 5'10"   175 lbs.

	W	L	PCT	ERA	G	GS	CG	IP	H	BB	SO	ShO	W	L	SV	AB	H	HR	BA
1942 CHI N	0	1	.000	3.38	4	0	0	5.1	5	2	6	0	0	1	0	0	0	0	–
1943 PHI A	12	14	.462	3.11	31	27	13	231.1	208	70	113	0	1	2	0	80	14	0	.175
1944	9	11	.450	3.39	27	25	11	185.2	172	49	65	2	0	0	0	64	11	0	.172
1945	7	10	.412	3.43	29	24	9	191.1	180	63	52	4	0	2	1	61	9	0	.148
1946	9	7	.563	2.32	29	15	8	155	147	38	48	4	0	0	1	44	11	0	.250
1947	4	13	.235	3.39	28	20	4	151.1	139	59	41	0	1	0	0	44	10	0	.227
1950 CLE A	3	3	.500	3.74	28	2	1	53	53	25	27	1	0	0	4	11	0	0	.000
7 yrs.	44	59	.427	3.18	176	113	46	973	904	306	352	11	2	5	6	304	55	0	.181

Ben Flowers

FLOWERS, BENNETT
B. June 15, 1927, Wilson, N. C.   BR TR 6'4"   195 lbs.

	W	L	PCT	ERA	G	GS	CG	IP	H	BB	SO	ShO	W	L	SV	AB	H	HR	BA
1951 BOS A	0	0	–	0.00	1	0	0	3	2	1	2	0	0	0	0	1	0	0	.000
1953	1	4	.200	3.86	32	6	1	79.1	87	24	36	1	0	0	3	19	3	0	.158
1955 2 teams			DET A	(4G 0–0)			STL N	(4G 1–0)											
" total	1	0	1.000	4.05	8	4	0	33.1	32	14	21	0	0	0	0	11	1	0	.091
1956 2 teams			STL N	(3G 1–1)			PHI N	(32G 0–2)											
" total	1	3	.250	5.98	35	3	0	52.2	69	15	27	0	0	2	0	5	0	0	.000
4 yrs.	3	7	.300	4.49	76	13	1	168.1	190	54	86	1	0	2	3	36	4	0	.111

Wes Flowers

FLOWERS, CHARLES WESLEY
B. Aug. 13, 1913, Vanndale, Ark.   BL TL 6'1½"   190 lbs.

	W	L	PCT	ERA	G	GS	CG	IP	H	BB	SO	ShO	W	L	SV	AB	H	HR	BA
1940 BKN N	1	1	.500	3.43	5	2	0	21	23	10	8	0	1	0	0	5	1	0	.200
1944	1	1	.500	7.79	9	1	0	17.1	26	13	3	0	0	1	0	5	3	0	.600
2 yrs.	2	2	.500	5.40	14	3	0	38.1	49	23	11	0	1	1	0	10	4	0	.400

Carney Flynn

FLYNN, CORNELIUS FRANCIS XAVIER
B. Jan. 23, 1875, Cincinnati, Ohio   D. Feb. 10, 1947, Cincinnati, Ohio   BL TL 5'11"   165 lbs.

	W	L	PCT	ERA	G	GS	CG	IP	H	BB	SO	ShO	W	L	SV	AB	H	HR	BA
1894 CIN N	0	2	.000	17.61	2	1	0	7.2	16	10	4	0	0	1	0	3	0	0	.000
1896 2 teams			NY N	(3G 0–2)			WAS N	(4G 0–1)											
" total	0	3	.000	9.68	7	3	2	30.2	61	18	7	0	0	0	0	12	4	1	.333
2 yrs.	0	5	.000	11.27	9	4	2	38.1	77	28	11	0	0	1	0	15	4	1	.267

Jocko Flynn

FLYNN, JOHN A.
B. June 30, 1864, Lawrence, Mass.   D. Dec. 30, 1907, Lawrence, Mass.   5'6½"   143 lbs.

	W	L	PCT	ERA	G	GS	CG	IP	H	BB	SO	ShO	W	L	SV	AB	H	HR	BA
1886 CHI N	24	6	.800	2.24	32	29	28	257	207	63	146	2	1	0	1	205	41	4	.200
1887	0	0	–	0.00	0	0	0	0	0	0	0	0	0	0	0	0	0	0	–
2 yrs.	24	6	.800	2.24	32	29	28	257	207	63	146	2	1	0	1	*			

Stu Flythe

FLYTHE, STUART McGUIRE
B. Dec. 5, 1911, Conway, N. C.   D. Oct. 18, 1963, Durham, N. C.   BR TR 6'2"   175 lbs.

	W	L	PCT	ERA	G	GS	CG	IP	H	BB	SO	ShO	W	L	SV	AB	H	HR	BA
1936 PHI A	0	0	–	13.04	17	3	0	39.1	49	61	14	0	0	0	0	15	4	0	.267

	W	L	PCT	ERA	G	GS	CG	IP	H	BB	SO	ShO	Relief Pitching W	L	SV	BATTING AB	H	HR	BA

Gene Fodge

FODGE, EUGENE ARLAN (Suds)
B. July 9, 1931, South Bend, Ind.
BR TR 6' 175 lbs.

	W	L	PCT	ERA	G	GS	CG	IP	H	BB	SO	ShO	RW	RL	SV	AB	H	HR	BA
1958 CHI N	1	1	.500	4.76	16	4	1	39.2	47	11	15	0	0	0	0	7	0	0	.000

Jim Fogarty

FOGARTY, JAMES G.
Brother of Joe Fogarty.
B. Feb. 12, 1864, San Francisco, Calif. D. May 20, 1891, Philadelphia, Pa.
Manager 1890.
BR TR 5'6½" 180 lbs.

	W	L	PCT	ERA	G	GS	CG	IP	H	BB	SO	ShO	RW	RL	SV	AB	H	HR	BA
1884 PHI N	0	0	–	0.00	1	0	0	1	2	0	1	0	0	0	0	378	80	1	.212
1886	0	1	.000	0.00	1	0	0	6	7	0	4	0	0	1	0	280	82	3	.293
1887	0	0	–	9.00	1	0	0	3	3	1	0	0	0	0	0	495	129	8	.261
1889	0	0	–	9.00	4	0	0	4	4	2	0	0	0	0	0	499	129	3	.259
4 yrs.	0	1	.000	4.50	7	0	0	14	16	3	5	0	0	1	0	*			

Curry Foley

FOLEY, CHARLES JOSEPH
B. Jan. 14, 1856, Milltown, Ireland D. Oct. 20, 1898, Boston, Mass.
TL 180 lbs.

	W	L	PCT	ERA	G	GS	CG	IP	H	BB	SO	ShO	RW	RL	SV	AB	H	HR	BA
1879 BOS N	9	9	.500	2.51	21	16	16	161.2	175	15	57	0	2	0	1	146	46	0	.315
1880	14	14	.500	3.89	36	28	21	238	264	40	68	0	1	1	0	332	97	2	.292
1881 BUF N	3	4	.429	5.27	10	6	2	41	70	5	2	0	1	0	0	375	96	1	.256
1882	0	0	–	18.00	1	0	0	1	2	0	0	0	0	0	0	341	104	3	.305
1883	1	0	1.000	0.00	1	0	0	1	0	4	0	0	1	0	0	111	30	0	.270
5 yrs.	27	27	.500	3.54	69	50	39	442.2	511	64	127	0	5	1	1	*			

John Foley

FOLEY, JOHN J.
B. Hannibal, Mo. Deceased.
TL

	W	L	PCT	ERA	G	GS	CG	IP	H	BB	SO	ShO	RW	RL	SV	AB	H	HR	BA
1885 PRO N	0	1	.000	4.50	1	1	1	8	6	5	2	0	0	0	0	2	0	0	.000

Rich Folkers

FOLKERS, RICHARD NEVIN
B. Oct. 17, 1946, Waterloo, Iowa
BL TL 6'2" 180 lbs.

	W	L	PCT	ERA	G	GS	CG	IP	H	BB	SO	ShO	RW	RL	SV	AB	H	HR	BA
1970 NY N	0	2	.000	6.52	16	1	0	29	36	25	15	0	0	1	2	6	2	0	.333
1972 STL N	1	0	1.000	3.38	9	0	0	13.1	12	5	7	0	1	0	0	1	0	0	.000
1973	4	4	.500	3.61	34	9	1	82.1	74	34	44	0	1	0	3	20	2	0	.100
1974	6	2	.750	3.00	55	0	0	90	65	38	57	0	6	2	2	10	1	0	.100
1975 SD N	6	11	.353	4.18	45	15	4	142	155	39	87	0	1	3	0	36	6	0	.167
1976	2	3	.400	5.28	33	3	0	59.2	67	25	26	0	2	0	0	4	0	0	.000
1977 MIL N	0	1	.000	4.50	3	0	0	6	7	4	6	0	0	1	0	0	0	0	–
7 yrs.	19	23	.452	4.11	195	28	5	422.1	416	170	242	0	11	7	7	77	11	0	.143

Lew Fonseca

FONSECA, LEWIS ALBERT
B. Jan. 21, 1899, Oakland, Calif.
Manager 1932-34.
BR TR 5'10½" 180 lbs.

	W	L	PCT	ERA	G	GS	CG	IP	H	BB	SO	ShO	RW	RL	SV	AB	H	HR	BA
1932 CHI A	0	0	–	0.00	1	0	0	1	0	0	0	0	0	0	0	*			

Ray Fontenot

FONTENOT, SILTON RAY
B. Aug. 8, 1957, Lake Charles, La.
BL TL 6' 175 lbs.

	W	L	PCT	ERA	G	GS	CG	IP	H	BB	SO	ShO	RW	RL	SV	AB	H	HR	BA
1983 NY N	8	2	.800	3.33	15	15	3	97.1	101	25	27	1	0	0	0	0	0	0	–
1984	8	9	.471	3.61	33	24	0	169.1	189	58	85	0	1	0	0	0	0	0	–
2 yrs.	16	11	.593	3.51	48	39	3	266.2	290	83	112	1	1	0	0	0	0	0	–

Jim Foor

FOOR, JAMES EMERSON
B. Jan. 13, 1949, St Louis, Mo.
BL TL 6'2" 170 lbs.

	W	L	PCT	ERA	G	GS	CG	IP	H	BB	SO	ShO	RW	RL	SV	AB	H	HR	BA
1971 DET A	0	0	–	18.00	3	0	0	1	2	4	2	0	0	0	0	0	0	0	–
1972	1	0	1.000	13.50	7	0	0	4	6	6	2	0	1	0	0	0	0	0	–
1973 PIT N	0	0	–	0.00	3	0	0	1.1	2	1	1	0	0	0	0	0	0	0	–
3 yrs.	1	0	1.000	11.37	13	0	0	6.1	10	11	5	0	1	0	0	0	0	0	–

Dave Ford

FORD, DAVID ALAN
B. Dec. 29, 1956, Cleveland, Ohio
BR TR 6'4" 190 lbs.

	W	L	PCT	ERA	G	GS	CG	IP	H	BB	SO	ShO	RW	RL	SV	AB	H	HR	BA
1978 BAL A	1	0	1.000	0.00	2	1	0	15	10	2	5	0	0	0	0	0	0	0	–
1979	2	1	.667	2.10	9	2	0	30	23	7	7	0	1	1	2	0	0	0	–
1980	1	3	.250	4.24	25	3	1	70	66	13	22	0	0	1	1	0	0	0	–
1981	1	2	.333	6.53	15	2	0	40	61	10	12	0	1	1	0	0	0	0	–
4 yrs.	5	6	.455	4.01	51	8	1	155	160	32	46	0	2	3	3	0	0	0	–

Gene Ford

FORD, EUGENE MATTHEW
B. June 23, 1912, Fort Dodge, Iowa D. Sept. 7, 1970, Emmetsburg, Iowa
BR TR 6'2" 195 lbs.

	W	L	PCT	ERA	G	GS	CG	IP	H	BB	SO	ShO	RW	RL	SV	AB	H	HR	BA
1936 BOS N	0	0	–	13.50	2	1	0	2	2	3	0	0	0	0	0	0	0	0	–
1938 CHI A	0	0	–	10.29	4	0	0	14	21	12	2	0	0	0	0	6	1	0	.167
2 yrs.	0	0	–	10.69	6	1	0	16	23	15	2	0	0	0	0	6	1	0	.167

Gene Ford

FORD, EUGENE WYMAN
Brother of Russ Ford.
B. Apr. 16, 1881, Milton, N. S., Canada D. Aug. 23, 1973, Dunedin, Fla.
BR TR 6' 170 lbs.

	W	L	PCT	ERA	G	GS	CG	IP	H	BB	SO	ShO	RW	RL	SV	AB	H	HR	BA
1905 DET A	0	1	.000	5.66	7	1	1	35	51	14	20	0	0	0	0	10	0	0	.000

Russ Ford

FORD, RUSSELL WILLIAM
Brother of Gene Ford.
B. Apr. 25, 1883, Brandon, Man., Canada D. Jan. 24, 1960, Rockingham, N. C.
BR TR 5'11" 175 lbs.

	W	L	PCT	ERA	G	GS	CG	IP	H	BB	SO	ShO	RW	RL	SV	AB	H	HR	BA
1909 NY A	0	0	–	9.00	1	0	0	3	4	4	2	0	0	0	0	1	0	0	.000
1910	26	6	.813	1.65	36	33	29	299.2	194	70	209	8	0	0	1	96	20	0	.208
1911	22	11	.667	2.27	37	33	26	281.1	251	76	158	1	2	1	0	102	20	0	.196
1912	13	21	.382	3.55	36	35	30	291.2	317	79	112	0	0	0	0	112	32	1	.286
1913	12	18	.400	2.66	33	28	15	237	244	58	72	1	3	0	2	74	12	0	.162
1914 BUF F	20	6	.769	1.82	35	26	19	247.1	190	41	123	5	0	2	6	78	10	0	.128
1915	5	9	.357	4.52	21	15	7	127.1	140	48	34	0	0	1	0	43	12	0	.279
7 yrs.	98	71	.580	2.59	199	170	126	1487.1	1340	376	710	15	5	4	9	506	106	1	.209

	W	L	PCT	ERA	G	GS	CG	IP	H	BB	SO	ShO	Relief Pitching			BATTING			
													W	L	SV	AB	H	HR	BA

Tom Ford

FORD, THOMAS WALTER
B. 1866, Chattanooga, Tenn.   Deceased.

5'10½" 155 lbs.

	W	L	PCT	ERA	G	GS	CG	IP	H	BB	SO	ShO	W	L	SV	AB	H	HR	BA
1890 2 teams			COL	AA (1G 0–0)	B-B	AA	(7G 0–6)												
" total	0	6	.000	4.94	8	6	6	51	70	35	12	0	0	0	0	31	1	0	.032

Wenty Ford

FORD, PERCIVAL EDMUND
Also known as Wentworth Ford.
B. Nov. 25, 1946, Nassau, Bahamas   D. July 8, 1980, Nassau, Bahamas

BR TR 5'11" 165 lbs.

	W	L	PCT	ERA	G	GS	CG	IP	H	BB	SO	ShO	W	L	SV	AB	H	HR	BA
1973 ATL N	1	2	.333	5.63	4	2	1	16	17	8	4	0	0	1	0	5	2	0	.400

Whitey Ford

FORD, EDWARD CHARLES (The Chairman of the Board)
B. Oct. 21, 1928, New York, N. Y.
Hall of Fame 1974.

BL TL 5'10" 178 lbs.

	W	L	PCT	ERA	G	GS	CG	IP	H	BB	SO	ShO	W	L	SV	AB	H	HR	BA
1950 NY A	9	1	.900	2.81	20	12	7	112	87	52	59	2	0	1	1	36	7	0	.194
1953	18	6	.750	3.00	32	30	11	207	187	110	110	3	0	0	0	75	20	0	.267
1954	16	8	.667	2.82	34	28	11	210.2	170	101	125	3	2	2	1	62	10	0	.161
1955	18	7	.720	2.63	39	33	18	253.2	188	113	137	5	0	1	2	86	14	1	.163
1956	19	6	.760	2.47	31	30	18	225.2	187	84	141	2	0	0	1	78	17	0	.218
1957	11	5	.688	2.57	24	17	5	129.1	114	53	84	0	3	0	0	42	6	0	.143
1958	14	7	.667	2.01	30	29	15	219.1	174	62	145	7	0	0	1	73	15	0	.205
1959	16	10	.615	3.04	35	29	9	204	194	89	114	2	2	2	1	65	15	1	.231
1960	12	9	.571	3.08	33	29	8	192.2	168	65	85	4	0	0	0	53	8	0	.151
1961	25	4	.862	3.21	39	39	11	283	242	92	209	3	0	0	0	96	17	0	.177
1962	17	8	.680	2.90	38	37	7	257.2	243	69	160	0	0	0	1	85	10	0	.118
1963	24	7	.774	2.74	38	37	13	269.1	240	56	189	3	0	0	1	92	13	1	.141
1964	17	6	.739	2.13	39	36	12	244.2	212	57	172	8	0	0	1	67	8	0	.119
1965	16	13	.552	3.24	37	36	9	244.1	241	50	162	2	0	0	1	82	15	0	.183
1966	2	5	.286	2.47	22	9	0	73	79	24	43	0	2	1	0	18	0	0	.000
1967	2	4	.333	1.64	7	7	2	44	40	9	21	1	0	0	0	13	2	0	.154
16 yrs.	236	106	.690	2.75	498	438	156	3170.1	2766	1086	1956	45	9	7	10	1023	177	3	.173
				3rd															

WORLD SERIES

	W	L	PCT	ERA	G	GS	CG	IP	H	BB	SO	ShO	W	L	SV	AB	H	HR	BA
1950 NY A	1	0	1.000	0.00	1	1	0	8.2	7	1	7	0	0	0	0	3	0	0	.000
1953	0	1	.000	4.50	2	2	0	8	9	2	7	0	0	0	0	3	1	0	.333
1955	2	0	1.000	2.12	2	2	1	17	13	8	10	0	0	0	0	6	0	0	.000
1956	1	1	.500	5.25	2	2	1	12	14	2	8	0	0	0	0	4	1	0	.250
1957	1	1	.500	1.13	2	2	1	16	11	5	7	0	0	0	0	5	0	0	.000
1958	0	1	.000	4.11	3	3	0	15.1	19	5	16	0	0	0	0	4	0	0	.000
1960	2	0	1.000	0.00	2	2	2	18	11	2	8	2	0	0	0	8	2	0	.250
1961	2	0	1.000	0.00	2	2	1	14	6	1	7	1	0	0	0	5	0	0	.000
1962	1	1	.500	4.12	3	3	1	19.2	24	4	12	0	0	0	0	7	0	0	.000
1963	0	2	.000	4.50	2	2	0	12	10	3	8	0	0	0	0	3	0	0	.000
1964	0	1	.000	8.44	1	1	0	5.1	8	1	4	0	0	0	0	1	1	0	1.000
11 yrs.	10	8	.556	2.71	22	22	7	146	132	34	94	3	0	0	0	49	4	0	.082
	1st	1st					1st	1st	4th	1st	1st	1st	1st 2nd						

Bill Foreman

FOREMAN, WILLIAM ORANGE
B. Oct. 10, 1886, Venango, Pa.   D. Oct. 3, 1958, Uniontown, Pa.

5'11" 180 lbs.

	W	L	PCT	ERA	G	GS	CG	IP	H	BB	SO	ShO	W	L	SV	AB	H	HR	BA
1909 WAS A	0	2	.000	4.91	2	2	1	11	8	7	2	0	0	0	0	3	1	0	.333
1910	0	0		13.50	1	0	0	.2	1	0	0	0	0	0	0	0	0	0	—
2 yrs.	0	2	.000	5.40	3	2	1	11.2	9	7	2	0	0	0	0	3	1	0	.333

Brownie Foreman

FOREMAN, JOHN DAVIS
Brother of Frank Foreman.
B. Aug. 6, 1875, Baltimore, Md.   D. Dec. 10, 1926, Baltimore, Md.

BL TL 5'8" 150 lbs.

	W	L	PCT	ERA	G	GS	CG	IP	H	BB	SO	ShO	W	L	SV	AB	H	HR	BA
1895 PIT N	8	6	.571	3.22	19	16	12	139.2	131	64	54	0	0	0	2	46	3	0	.065
1896 2 teams	3	7	.300	8.81	PIT	N	(9G 3–3)	CIN	N	(4G 0–4)									
" total	3	7	.300	8.81	13	12	7	79.2	112	51	22	0	0	1	0	28	4	0	.143
2 yrs.	11	13	.458	5.25	32	28	19	219.1	243	115	76	0	0	1	2	74	7	0	.095

Frank Foreman

FOREMAN, FRANCIS ISAIAH
Brother of Brownie Foreman.
B. May 1, 1863, Baltimore, Md.   D. Nov. 19, 1957, Baltimore, Md.

BR TR 6' 160 lbs.

	W	L	PCT	ERA	G	GS	CG	IP	H	BB	SO	ShO	W	L	SV	AB	H	HR	BA
1884 2 teams			C-P	U (3G 1–2)	KC	U	(1G 0–1)												
" total	1	3	.250	4.50	4	4	2	26	40	4	15	0	0	0	0	14	1	0	.071
1885 BAL AA	1	2	.667	3.00	3	3	2	27	33	9	11	0	0	0	0	14	4	0	.286
1889	23	21	.523	3.52	51	48	43	414	364	137	180	5	0	0	0	181	26	1	.144
1890 CIN N	13	10	.565	3.95	25	24	20	198.1	201	89	57	0	0	0	0	75	10	1	.133
1891	18	21	.462	3.73	43	41	39	345.1	381	142	170	1	0	0	1	157	35	4	.223
1892 2 teams			WAS	N (11G 2–4)	BAL	N	(4G 0–3)												
" total	2	7	.222	4.34	15	10	6	85	93	48	21	0	0	0	0	51	17	1	.333
1893 NY N	0	1	.000	27.00	2	1	0	5.2	19	10	0	0	0	0	0	3	0	0	.000
1895 CIN N	11	14	.440	4.11	32	27	19	219	253	92	55	0	0	1	1	94	29	2	.309
1896	15	6	.714	3.68	27	23	18	190.2	214	62	38	1	1	1	1	76	19	0	.250
1901 2 teams			BOS	A (1G 0–1)	BAL	A	(24G 12–6)												
" total	12	7	.632	3.88	25	23	19	199.1	233	60	42	1	0	0	1	84	26	0	.310
1902 BAL A	0	2	.000	6.06	2	2	2	16.1	28	6	2	0	0	0	0	7	3	0	.429
11 yrs.	97	93	.511	3.94	229	206	170	1726.2	1859	659	591	8	1	2	4	756	170	9	.225

Happy Foreman

FOREMAN, AUGUST
B. July 20, 1897, Memphis, Tenn.   D. Feb. 13, 1953, New York, N. Y.

BL TL 5'7" 160 lbs.

	W	L	PCT	ERA	G	GS	CG	IP	H	BB	SO	ShO	W	L	SV	AB	H	HR	BA
1924 CHI A	0	0	—	2.25	3	0	0	4	7	4	1	0	0	0	0	2	0	0	.000
1926 BOS A	0	0	—	3.68	3	0	0	7.1	3	5	3	0	0	0	0	2	0	0	.000
2 yrs.	0	0	—	3.18	6	0	0	11.1	10	9	4	0	0	0	0	2	0	0	.000

	W	L	PCT	ERA	G	GS	CG	IP	H	BB	SO	ShO	Relief Pitching W	L	SV	BATTING AB	H	HR	BA

Mike Fornieles

FORNIELES, JOSE MIGUEL TORRES   BR TR 5'11"   155 lbs.
B. Jan. 18, 1932, Havana, Cuba

	W	L	PCT	ERA	G	GS	CG	IP	H	BB	SO	ShO	W	L	SV	AB	H	HR	BA
1952 **WAS A**	2	2	.500	1.37	4	2	2	26.1	13	11	12	1	1	1	0	10	0	0	.000
1953 **CHI A**	8	7	.533	3.59	39	16	5	153	160	61	72	0	4	1	3	41	4	0	.098
1954	1	2	.333	4.29	15	6	0	42	41	14	18	0	1	1	1	11	3	0	.273
1955	6	3	.667	3.86	26	9	2	86.1	84	29	23	0	3	1	2	29	3	0	.103
1956 **2 teams**							**CHI A** (6G 0–1)			**BAL A** (30G 4–7)									
" total	4	8	.333	4.05	36	11	1	126.2	131	31	59	1	3	2	1	35	6	0	.171
1957 **2 teams**							**BAL A** (15G 2–6)			**BOS A** (25G 8–7)									
" total	10	13	.435	3.75	40	22	8	182.1	193	55	107	2	3	3	2	62	11	0	.177
1958 **BOS A**	4	6	.400	4.96	37	7	1	110.2	123	33	49	0	3	3	1	29	6	0	.207
1959	5	3	.625	3.07	46	0	0	82	77	29	54	0	5	3	11	19	3	0	.158
1960	10	5	.667	2.64	**70**	0	0	109	86	49	64	0	10	5	**14**	15	6	0	.400
1961	9	8	.529	4.68	57	2	1	119.1	121	54	70	0	8	7	15	32	5	1	.156
1962	3	6	.333	5.36	42	1	0	82.1	96	37	36	0	3	5	5	16	3	0	.188
1963 **2 teams**							**BOS A** (9G 0–0)			**MIN A** (11G 1–1)									
" total	1	1	.500	5.40	20	0	0	36.2	40	18	12	0	1	1	0	9	2	0	.222
12 yrs.	63	64	.496	3.96	432	76	20	1156.2	1165	421	576	4	45	33	55	308	52	1	.169

Bob Forsch

FORSCH, ROBERT HERBERT   BR TR 6'4"   200 lbs.
Brother of Ken Forsch.
B. Jan. 13, 1950, Sacramento, Calif.

	W	L	PCT	ERA	G	GS	CG	IP	H	BB	SO	ShO	W	L	SV	AB	H	HR	BA
1974 **STL N**	7	4	.636	2.97	19	14	5	100	84	34	39	2	0	0	0	29	7	0	.241
1975	15	10	.600	2.86	34	34	7	230	213	70	108	4	0	0	0	78	24	1	.308
1976	8	10	.444	3.94	33	32	2	194	209	71	76	0	0	1	0	62	11	1	.177
1977	20	7	.741	3.48	35	35	8	217	210	69	95	2	0	0	0	72	12	0	.167
1978	11	17	.393	3.69	34	34	7	234	205	97	114	3	0	0	0	83	15	1	.181
1979	11	11	.500	3.82	33	32	7	219	215	52	92	1	0	0	0	73	8	0	.110
1980	11	10	.524	3.77	31	31	8	215	225	33	87	0	0	0	0	78	23	3	.295
1981	10	5	.667	3.19	20	20	1	124	106	29	41	0	0	0	0	41	5	0	.122
1982	15	9	.625	3.48	36	34	6	233	238	54	69	2	0	0	1	73	15	0	.205
1983	10	12	.455	4.28	34	30	6	187	190	54	56	2	1	0	0	54	13	1	.241
1984	2	5	.286	6.02	16	11	1	52.1	64	19	21	0	1	0	0	16	4	0	.250
11 yrs.	120	100	.545	3.64	325	307	58	2005.1	1959	582	798	16	2	1	1	659	137	7	.208

LEAGUE CHAMPIONSHIP SERIES
	W	L	PCT	ERA	G	GS	CG	IP	H	BB	SO	ShO	W	L	SV	AB	H	HR	BA
1982 **STL N**	1	0	1.000	0.00	1	1	1	9	3	0	6	1	0	0	0	3	2	0	.667

WORLD SERIES
	W	L	PCT	ERA	G	GS	CG	IP	H	BB	SO	ShO	W	L	SV	AB	H	HR	BA
1982 **STL N**	0	2	.000	4.97	2	2	0	12.2	18	3	4	0	0	0	0	0	0	0	–

Ken Forsch

FORSCH, KENNETH ROTH   BR TR 6'4"   195 lbs.
Brother of Bob Forsch.
B. Sept. 8, 1946, Sacramento, Calif.

	W	L	PCT	ERA	G	GS	CG	IP	H	BB	SO	ShO	W	L	SV	AB	H	HR	BA
1970 **HOU N**	1	2	.333	5.63	4	4	1	24	28	5	13	0	0	0	0	6	0	0	.000
1971	8	8	.500	2.54	33	23	7	188	162	53	131	2	0	0	0	59	8	0	.136
1972	6	8	.429	3.91	30	24	1	156.1	163	62	113	0	0	0	0	41	6	0	.146
1973	9	12	.429	4.20	46	26	5	201.1	197	74	149	0	1	3	4	62	4	0	.065
1974	8	7	.533	2.80	70	0	0	103	98	37	48	0	8	7	10	7	0	0	.000
1975	4	8	.333	3.22	34	9	2	109	114	30	54	0	2	3	2	22	1	0	.045
1976	4	3	.571	2.15	52	0	0	92	76	26	49	0	4	3	19	11	1	0	.091
1977	5	8	.385	2.72	42	5	0	86	80	28	45	0	5	5	8	13	1	0	.077
1978	10	6	.625	2.71	52	6	4	133	136	37	71	2	6	4	7	27	5	0	.185
1979	11	6	.647	3.03	26	24	10	178	155	35	58	2	1	0	0	58	8	0	.138
1980	12	13	.480	3.20	32	32	6	222	230	41	84	3	0	0	0	77	18	0	.234
1981 **CAL A**	11	7	.611	2.88	20	20	10	153	143	27	55	4	0	0	0	0	0	0	–
1982	13	11	.542	3.87	37	35	12	228	225	57	73	4	2	0	0	0	0	0	–
1983	11	12	.478	4.06	31	31	11	219.1	226	61	81	1	0	0	0	0	0	0	–
1984	1	1	.500	2.20	2	2	1	16.1	14	3	10	0	0	0	0	0	0	0	–
15 yrs.	114	112	.504	3.32	511	241	70	2109.1	2047	576	1034	18	29	25	50	383	52	0	.136

LEAGUE CHAMPIONSHIP SERIES
	W	L	PCT	ERA	G	GS	CG	IP	H	BB	SO	ShO	W	L	SV	AB	H	HR	BA
1980 **HOU N**	0	1	.000	4.15	2	1	1	8.2	10	1	6	0	0	0	0	2	2	0	1.000

Terry Forster

FORSTER, TERRY JAY   BL TL 6'3"   200 lbs.
B. Jan. 14, 1952, Sioux Falls, S. D.

	W	L	PCT	ERA	G	GS	CG	IP	H	BB	SO	ShO	W	L	SV	AB	H	HR	BA
1971 **CHI A**	2	3	.400	3.96	45	3	0	50	46	23	48	0	2	2	1	5	2	0	.400
1972	6	5	.545	2.25	62	0	0	100	75	44	104	0	6	5	29	19	10	0	.526
1973	6	11	.353	3.23	51	12	4	172.2	174	78	120	0	3	4	16	1	0	0	.000
1974	7	8	.467	3.63	59	1	0	134	120	48	105	0	7	7	24	0	0	0	–
1975	3	3	.500	2.19	17	1	0	37	30	24	32	0	3	3	4	0	0	0	–
1976	2	12	.143	4.38	29	16	1	111	126	41	70	0	0	5	1	0	0	0	–
1977 **PIT N**	6	4	.600	4.45	33	6	0	87	90	32	58	0	4	1	1	26	9	0	.346
1978 **LA N**	5	4	.556	1.94	47	0	0	65	56	23	46	0	5	4	22	8	4	0	.500
1979	1	2	.333	5.63	17	0	0	16	18	11	8	0	1	2	2	0	0	0	–
1980	0	0	–	3.00	9	0	0	12	10	4	2	0	0	0	0	0	0	0	–
1981	0	1	.000	4.06	21	0	0	31	37	15	17	0	0	1	0	2	0	0	.000
1982	6	5	.455	3.04	56	0	0	83	66	31	52	0	5	6	3	2	0	0	.000
1983 **ATL N**	3	2	.600	2.16	56	0	0	79.1	60	31	54	0	3	2	13	8	4	0	.500
1984	2	0	1.000	2.70	25	0	0	26.2	30	7	10	0	2	0	5	3	2	0	.667
14 yrs.	48	61	.440	3.28	527	39	5	1004.2	938	412	726	0	41	42	121	74	31	0	.419

DIVISIONAL PLAYOFF SERIES
	W	L	PCT	ERA	G	GS	CG	IP	H	BB	SO	ShO	W	L	SV	AB	H	HR	BA
1981 **LA N**	0	0	–	0.00	1	0	0	.1	0	0	0	0	0	0	0	0	0	0	–

LEAGUE CHAMPIONSHIP SERIES
	W	L	PCT	ERA	G	GS	CG	IP	H	BB	SO	ShO	W	L	SV	AB	H	HR	BA
1978 **LA N**	1	0	1.000	0.00	1	0	0	1	1	0	2	0	1	0	0	0	0	0	–
1981	0	0	–	0.00	1	0	0	.1	0	0	1	0	0	0	0	0	0	0	–
2 yrs.	1	0	1.000	0.00	2	0	0	1.1	1	0	3	0	1	0	0	0	0	0	–

WORLD SERIES
	W	L	PCT	ERA	G	GS	CG	IP	H	BB	SO	ShO	W	L	SV	AB	H	HR	BA
1978 **LA N**	0	0	–	0.00	3	0	0	4	5	1	6	0	0	0	0	0	0	0	–

	W	L	PCT	ERA	G	GS	CG	IP	H	BB	SO	ShO	Relief Pitching W	L	SV	BATTING AB	H	HR	BA

Terry Forster continued

1981	0	0	—	0.00	2	0	0	2	1	3	0	0	0	0	0	0	0	0	—
2 yrs.	0	0	—	0.00	5	0	0	6	6	4	6	0	0	0	0	0	0	0	—

Gary Fortune

FORTUNE, GARRETT REESE
B. Oct. 11, 1894, High Point, N. C.   D. Sept. 23, 1955, Washington, D. C.   BB TR 5'11½'' 176 lbs.

1916 PHI N	0	1	.000	3.60	1	1	0	5	2	4	3	0	0	0	0	2	0	0	.000
1918	0	2	.000	8.13	5	2	1	31	41	19	10	0	0	0	0	10	2	0	.200
1920 BOS A	0	2	.000	5.83	14	3	1	41.2	46	23	10	0	0	1	0	12	2	0	.167
3 yrs.	0	5	.000	6.61	20	6	2	77.2	89	46	23	0	0	1	0	24	4	0	.167

Jerry Fosnow

FOSNOW, GERALD EUGENE
B. Sept. 21, 1940, Deshler, Ohio   BR TL 6'4'' 195 lbs.

1964 MIN A	0	1	.000	10.97	7	0	0	10.2	13	8	9	0	0	1	0	0	0	0	—
1965	3	3	.500	4.44	29	0	0	46.2	33	25	35	0	3	3	2	5	0	0	.000
2 yrs.	3	4	.429	5.65	36	0	0	57.1	46	33	44	0	3	4	2	5	0	0	.000

Larry Foss

FOSS, LARRY CURTIS
B. Apr. 18, 1936, Castleton, Kans.   BR TR 6'2'' 187 lbs.

1961 PIT N	1	1	.500	5.87	3	3	0	15.1	15	11	9	0	0	0	0	6	1	0	.167
1962 NY N	0	1	.000	4.63	5	1	0	11.2	17	7	3	0	0	0	0	1	0	0	.000
2 yrs.	1	2	.333	5.33	8	4	0	27	32	18	12	0	0	0	0	7	1	0	.143

Alan Foster

FOSTER, ALAN BENTON
B. Dec. 8, 1946, Pasadena, Calif.   BR TR 6' 180 lbs.

1967 LA N	0	1	.000	2.16	4	2	0	16.2	10	3	15	0	0	0	0	4	0	0	.000
1968	1	1	.500	1.72	3	3	0	15.2	11	2	10	0	0	0	0	4	1	0	.250
1969	3	9	.250	4.37	24	15	2	103	119	29	59	2	0	0	0	27	2	0	.074
1970	10	13	.435	4.25	33	33	7	199	200	81	83	1	0	0	0	64	7	0	.109
1971 CLE A	8	12	.400	4.15	36	26	3	182	158	82	97	0	1	0	0	51	2	0	.039
1972 CAL A	0	1	.000	4.85	8	0	0	13	12	6	11	0	0	1	0	0	0	0	—
1973 STL N	13	9	.591	3.14	35	29	6	203.2	195	63	106	2	0	2	0	68	13	0	.191
1974	7	10	.412	3.89	31	25	5	162	167	61	78	1	0	0	0	48	8	0	.167
1975 SD N	3	1	.750	2.40	17	4	1	45	41	21	20	0	0	1	0	11	1	0	.091
1976	3	6	.333	3.22	26	11	2	86.2	75	35	22	0	0	0	0	18	1	0	.056
10 yrs.	48	63	.432	3.73	217	148	26	1026.2	988	383	501	6	2	3	0	295	35	0	.119

Larry Foster

FOSTER, LARRY LYNN
B. Dec. 24, 1937, Lansing, Mich.   BL TR 6' 185 lbs.

1963 DET A	0	0	—	13.50	1	0	0	2	4	1	1	0	0	0	0	0	0	0	—

Rube Foster

FOSTER, GEORGE
B. Jan. 5, 1889, Lehigh, Okla.   D. Mar. 1, 1976, Bukoshe, Okla.   BR TR 5'7½'' 170 lbs.

1913 BOS A	3	4	.429	3.16	19	8	4	68.1	64	28	36	1	0	0	0	21	2	0	.095
1914	14	8	.636	1.65	32	27	17	212.2	162	52	92	5	0	0	0	63	11	0	.175
1915	19	8	.704	2.11	37	33	22	255.1	217	86	82	5	0	0	1	83	23	1	.277
1916	14	7	.667	3.06	33	19	9	182.1	173	86	53	3	4	0	2	62	11	0	.177
1917	8	7	.533	2.53	17	16	9	124.2	108	53	34	1	0	1	0	41	11	0	.268
5 yrs.	58	34	.630	2.35	138	103	61	843.1	724	305	297	15	4	1	3	270	58	1	.215

WORLD SERIES																			
1915 BOS A	2	0	1.000	2.00	2	2	2	18	12	2	13	0	0	0	0	8	4	0	.500
1916	0	0	—	0.00	1	0	0	3	3	0	1	0	0	0	0	1	0	0	.000
2 yrs.	2	0	1.000	1.71	3	2	2	21	15	2	14	0	0	0	0	9	4	0	.444

Slim Foster

FOSTER, EDDY LEE
B. 1885, Birmingham, Ala.   D. Mar. 1, 1929, Montgomery, Ala.   BR TR 6'1''

1908 CLE A	1	0	1.000	2.14	6	1	1	21	16	12	11	0	0	0	2	6	0	0	.000

Steve Foucault

FOUCAULT, STEVEN RAYMOND
B. Oct. 3, 1949, Duluth, Minn.   BL TR 6' 205 lbs.

1973 TEX A	2	4	.333	3.86	32	0	0	56	54	31	28	0	2	4	8	0	0	0	—
1974	8	9	.471	2.25	69	0	0	144	123	40	106	0	8	9	12	0	0	0	—
1975	8	4	.667	4.12	59	0	0	107	96	55	56	0	8	4	10	0	0	0	—
1976	8	8	.500	3.32	46	0	0	76	68	25	41	0	8	8	5	0	0	0	—
1977 DET A	7	7	.500	3.16	44	0	0	74	64	17	58	0	7	7	13	0	0	0	—
1978 2 teams			DET	A	(24G 2–4)				KC	A	(3G 0–0)								
" total	2	4	.333	3.23	27	0	0	39	53	22	18	0	2	4	4	0	0	0	—
6 yrs.	35	36	.493	3.21	277	0	0	496	458	190	307	0	35	36	52	0	0	0	—

Henry Fournier

FOURNIER, JULIUS HENRY (Frenchy)
B. Aug. 8, 1865, Syracuse, N. Y.   D. Dec. 8, 1945, Detroit, Mich.   TL

1894 CIN N	1	3	.250	5.40	6	4	4	45	71	20	5	0	0	0	0	19	2	0	.105

Jack Fournier

FOURNIER, JOHN FRANK (Jacques)
B. Sept. 28, 1892, Au Sable, Mich.   D. Sept. 5, 1973, Tacoma, Wash.   BL TR 6' 195 lbs.

1922 STL N	0	0	—	0.00	1	0	0	1	0	0	0	0	0	0	0	*		

Dave Foutz

FOUTZ, DAVID LUTHER (Scissors)
B. Sept. 7, 1856, Carroll County, Md.   D. Mar. 5, 1897, Waverly, Md.   BR TR 6'2'' 161 lbs.
Manager 1893-96.

1884 STL AA	15	6	.714	2.18	25	25	19	206.2	167	36	95	2	0	0	0	119	27	0	.227
1885	33	14	.702	2.63	47	46	46	407.2	351	92	147	2	1	0	0	238	59	0	.248
1886	41	16	.719	2.11	59	57	55	504	418	144	283	11	1	0	1	414	116	3	.280
1887	25	12	.676	3.87	40	38	36	339.1	369	90	94	1	0	0	0	423	151	4	.357
1888 BKN AA	12	7	.632	2.51	23	19	19	176	146	35	73	0	0	0	0	563	156	3	.277

	W	L	PCT	ERA	G	GS	CG	IP	H	BB	SO	ShO	Relief Pitching W	L	SV	BATTING AB	H	HR	BA

Dave Foutz continued

	W	L	PCT	ERA	G	GS	CG	IP	H	BB	SO	ShO	W	L	SV	AB	H	HR	BA
1889	3	0	1.000	4.37	12	4	3	59.2	70	19	21	0	0	0	0	553	153	7	.277
1890 BKN N	2	1	.667	1.86	5	2	2	29	29	6	4	0	1	0	2	509	154	5	.303
1891	3	2	.600	3.29	6	5	5	52	51	16	14	0	0	0	0	521	134	2	.257
1892	13	8	.619	3.41	27	20	17	203	210	63	56	0	0	2	1	220	41	1	.186
1893	0	0	–	7.50	6	0	0	18	28	8	3	0	0	0	0	557	137	7	.246
1894	0	0	–	13.50	1	0	0	2	4	1	0	0	0	0	0	293	90	0	.307
11 yrs.	147	66	.690 2nd	2.84	251	216	202	1997.1	1843	510	790	16	3	2	4	*			

Art Fowler

FOWLER, JOHN ARTHUR
Brother of Jesse Fowler.
B. July 3, 1922, Converse, S. C.   BR TR 5'11" 180 lbs.

	W	L	PCT	ERA	G	GS	CG	IP	H	BB	SO	ShO	W	L	SV	AB	H	HR	BA
1954 CIN N	12	10	.545	3.83	40	29	8	227.2	256	85	93	1	1	2	0	60	6	0	.100
1955	11	10	.524	3.90	46	28	8	207.2	198	63	94	3	1	0	2	60	12	0	.200
1956	11	11	.500	4.05	45	23	8	177.2	191	35	86	0	3	1	1	48	7	0	.146
1957	3	0	1.000	6.47	33	7	1	87.2	111	24	45	0	1	0	0	17	3	0	.176
1959 LA N	3	4	.429	5.31	36	0	0	61	70	23	47	0	3	4	2	12	1	0	.083
1961 LA A	5	8	.385	3.64	53	3	0	89	68	29	78	0	5	6	11	13	1	0	.077
1962	4	3	.571	2.81	48	0	0	77	67	25	38	0	4	3	5	11	3	0	.273
1963	5	3	.625	2.42	57	0	0	89.1	70	19	53	0	5	3	10	9	2	0	.222
1964	0	2	.000	10.29	4	0	0	7	8	5	5	0	0	2	1	1	0	0	.000
9 yrs.	54	51	.514	4.03	362	90	25	1024	1039	308	539	4	23	21	32	231	35	0	.152

Dick Fowler

FOWLER, RICHARD JOHN
B. Mar. 30, 1921, Toronto, Ont., Canada   D. May 22, 1972, Oneonta, N. Y.   BR TR 6'4½" 215 lbs.

	W	L	PCT	ERA	G	GS	CG	IP	H	BB	SO	ShO	W	L	SV	AB	H	HR	BA
1941 PHI A	1	2	.333	3.38	4	3	1	24	26	8	8	0	0	1	0	9	0	0	.000
1942	6	11	.353	4.95	31	17	4	140	159	45	38	0	2	2	1	50	8	0	.160
1945	1	2	.333	4.82	7	3	2	37.1	41	18	21	1	0	1	0	18	8	0	.444
1946	9	16	.360	3.28	32	28	14	205.2	213	75	89	1	0	0	0	71	13	0	.183
1947	12	11	.522	2.81	36	31	16	227.1	210	85	75	3	1	1	0	82	14	0	.171
1948	15	8	.652	3.78	29	26	16	204.2	221	76	50	2	0	0	2	82	14	1	.171
1949	15	11	.577	3.75	31	28	15	213.2	210	115	43	4	1	0	1	77	18	0	.234
1950	1	5	.167	6.48	11	9	2	66.2	75	56	15	0	0	0	0	26	5	0	.192
1951	5	11	.313	5.62	22	22	4	125	141	72	29	0	0	0	0	42	8	0	.190
1952	1	2	.333	6.44	18	3	1	58.2	71	28	14	0	0	0	0	15	0	0	.000
10 yrs.	66	79	.455	4.11	221	170	75	1303	1367	578	382	11	4	5	4	472	88	1	.186

Jesse Fowler

FOWLER, JESSE (Pete)
Brother of Art Fowler.
B. Oct. 30, 1898, Spartanburg, S. C.   D. Sept. 23, 1973, Columbia, S. C.   BR TL 5'10½" 158 lbs.

	W	L	PCT	ERA	G	GS	CG	IP	H	BB	SO	ShO	W	L	SV	AB	H	HR	BA
1924 STL N	1	1	.500	4.41	13	3	0	32.2	28	18	5	0	1	0	0	9	2	0	.222

Alan Fowlkes

FOWLKES, ALAN KIM
B. Aug. 8, 1958, Brawley, Calif.   BR TR 6'2" 190 lbs.

	W	L	PCT	ERA	G	GS	CG	IP	H	BB	SO	ShO	W	L	SV	AB	H	HR	BA
1982 SF N	4	2	.667	5.19	21	15	1	85	111	24	50	0	0	0	0	26	3	0	.115

Henry Fox

FOX, HENRY
Born Henry Fuchs.
B. Nov., 1874, Pennsylvania   D. June 6, 1927, Scranton, Pa.

	W	L	PCT	ERA	G	GS	CG	IP	H	BB	SO	ShO	W	L	SV	AB	H	HR	BA
1902 PHI N	0	0	–	18.00	1	0	0	1	2	1	1	0	0	0	1	0	0	0	–

Howie Fox

FOX, HOWARD FRANCIS
B. Mar. 1, 1921, Coburg, Ore.   D. Oct. 9, 1955, San Antonio, Tex.   BR TR 6'3" 210 lbs.

	W	L	PCT	ERA	G	GS	CG	IP	H	BB	SO	ShO	W	L	SV	AB	H	HR	BA
1944 CIN N	0	0	–	0.00	2	0	0	2.1	2	0	0	0	0	0	0	1	0	0	.000
1945	8	13	.381	4.93	45	15	7	164.1	169	77	54	0	4	2	0	46	13	0	.283
1946	0	0	–	18.00	4	0	0	5	12	5	1	0	0	0	0	0	0	0	–
1948	6	9	.400	4.53	34	24	5	171	185	62	63	0	0	0	1	60	12	0	.200
1949	6	19	.240	3.98	38	30	9	215	221	77	60	0	1	0	0	72	17	0	.236
1950	11	8	.579	4.33	34	22	10	187	196	85	64	1	0	0	0	63	11	1	.175
1951	9	14	.391	3.83	40	30	9	228	239	69	57	0	1	1	2	70	8	1	.114
1952 PHI N	2	7	.222	5.08	13	11	2	62	70	26	16	0	0	0	2	21	1	0	.048
1954 BAL A	1	2	.333	3.67	38	0	0	73.2	80	34	27	0	1	2	2	16	4	0	.250
9 yrs.	43	72	.374	4.33	248	132	42	1108.1	1174	435	342	5	7	7	6	349	66	2	.189

John Fox

FOX, JOHN JOSEPH
B. Feb. 7, 1859, Roxbury, Mass.   D. Apr. 18, 1893, Boston, Mass.

	W	L	PCT	ERA	G	GS	CG	IP	H	BB	SO	ShO	W	L	SV	AB	H	HR	BA
1881 BOS N	6	8	.429	3.33	17	16	12	124.1	144	39	30	0	0	0	0	118	21	0	.178
1883 BAL AA	6	13	.316	4.03	20	19	18	165.1	209	32	49	0	0	0	0	92	14	0	.152
1884 PIT AA	1	6	.143	5.64	7	7	7	59	76	16	22	0	0	0	0	25	6	0	.240
1886 WAS N	0	1	.000	9.00	1	1	1	8	11	11	3	0	0	0	0	3	1	0	.333
4 yrs.	13	28	.317	4.16	45	43	38	356.2	440	98	104	0	0	0	0	238	42	0	.176

Terry Fox

FOX, TERRENCE EDWARD
B. July 31, 1935, Chicago, Ill.   BR TR 6' 175 lbs.

	W	L	PCT	ERA	G	GS	CG	IP	H	BB	SO	ShO	W	L	SV	AB	H	HR	BA
1960 MIL N	0	0	–	4.32	5	0	0	8.1	6	6	5	0	0	0	0	1	0	0	.000
1961 DET A	5	2	.714	1.41	39	0	0	57.1	42	16	32	0	5	2	12	12	2	0	.167
1962	3	1	.750	1.71	44	0	0	58	48	16	23	0	3	1	16	8	2	0	.250
1963	8	6	.571	3.59	46	0	0	80.1	81	20	35	0	8	6	11	11	1	0	.091
1964	4	3	.571	3.39	32	0	0	61	77	16	28	0	4	3	5	12	3	0	.250
1965	6	4	.600	2.78	42	0	0	77.2	59	31	34	0	6	4	10	15	0	0	.000
1966 2 teams			DET A	(4G 0–1)			PHI N	(36G 3–2)											
" total	3	3	.500	4.80	40	0	0	54.1	66	19	28	0	3	3	5	6	0	0	.000
7 yrs.	29	19	.604	2.99	248	0	0	397	379	124	185	0	29	19	59	65	8	0	.123

Bill Foxen

FOXEN, WILLIAM ALOYSIUS   BL TL 5'11½" 165 lbs.
B. May 31, 1884, Tenafly, N. J.   D. Apr. 17, 1937, Brooklyn, N. Y.

		W	L	PCT	ERA	G	GS	CG	IP	H	BB	SO	ShO	W	L	SV	AB	H	HR	BA
1908	PHI N	7	7	.500	1.95	22	16	10	147.1	126	53	52	2	0	0	0	53	5	0	.094
1909		3	7	.300	3.35	18	7	5	83.1	65	32	37	1	0	3	0	24	5	1	.208
1910	2 teams			PHI	N (16G 5–5)			CHI	N (2G 0–0)											
"	total	5	5	.500	2.94	18	9	5	82.2	80	43	35	0	2	0	0	25	4	0	.160
1911	CHI N	1	1	.500	2.08	3	1	0	13	12	12	6	0	0	0	0	4	1	0	.250
4 yrs.		16	20	.444	2.56	61	33	20	326.1	283	140	130	3	2	3	0	106	15	1	.142

Jimmie Foxx

FOXX, JAMES EMORY (Double X, The Beast)   BR TR 6' 195 lbs.
B. Oct. 22, 1907, Sudlersville, Md.   D. July 21, 1967, Miami, Fla.
Hall of Fame 1951.

		W	L	PCT	ERA	G	GS	CG	IP	H	BB	SO	ShO	W	L	SV	AB	H	HR	BA
1939	BOS A	0	0	–	0.00	1	0	0	1	0	0	1	0	0	0	0	467	168	35	.360
1945	PHI N	1	0	1.000	1.59	9	2	0	22.2	13	14	10	0	0	0	0	224	60	7	.268
2 yrs.		1	0	1.000	1.52	10	2	0	23.2	13	14	11	0	0	0	0	*			

Paul Foytack

FOYTACK, PAUL EUGENE   BR TR 5'11" 175 lbs.
B. Nov. 16, 1930, Scranton, Pa.

		W	L	PCT	ERA	G	GS	CG	IP	H	BB	SO	ShO	W	L	SV	AB	H	HR	BA
1953	DET A	0	0	–	11.17	6	0	0	9.2	15	9	7	0	0	0	0	1	0	0	.000
1955		0	1	.000	5.26	22	1	0	49.2	48	36	38	0	0	0	0	11	1	0	.091
1956		15	13	.536	3.59	43	33	16	256	211	142	184	1	1	0	1	90	11	0	.122
1957		14	11	.560	3.14	38	27	8	212	175	104	118	1	3	2	1	63	14	0	.222
1958		15	13	.536	3.44	39	33	16	230	198	77	135	2	0	0	1	75	18	0	.240
1959		14	14	.500	4.64	39	37	11	240.1	239	64	110	2	0	0	1	81	9	0	.111
1960		2	11	.154	6.14	28	13	1	96.2	108	49	38	0	0	4	2	25	7	0	.280
1961		11	10	.524	3.93	32	20	6	169.2	152	56	89	0	3	2	0	54	12	1	.222
1962		10	7	.588	4.39	29	21	5	143.2	145	86	63	1	2	0	0	42	6	0	.143
1963	2 teams			DET	A (9G 0–1)			LA	A (25G 5–5)											
"	total	5	6	.455	4.70	34	8	0	88	86	37	44	0	2	2	1	19	4	0	.211
1964	LA A	0	1	.000	15.43	2	0	0	2.1	4	2	1	0	0	1	0	0	0	0	–
11 yrs.		86	87	.497	4.14	312	193	63	1498	1381	662	827	7	11	11	7	461	82	1	.178

Ken Frailing

FRAILING, KENNETH DOUGLAS   BL TL 6' 190 lbs.
B. Jan. 19, 1948, Marion, Wis.

		W	L	PCT	ERA	G	GS	CG	IP	H	BB	SO	ShO	W	L	SV	AB	H	HR	BA
1972	CHI A	1	0	1.000	3.00	4	0	0	3	3	1	1	0	1	0	0	0	0	0	–
1973		0	0	–	1.96	10	0	0	18.1	18	7	15	0	0	0	0	0	0	0	–
1974	CHI N	6	9	.400	3.89	55	16	1	125	150	43	71	0	1	2	1	31	8	0	.258
1975		2	5	.286	5.43	41	0	0	53	61	26	39	0	2	5	1	7	1	0	.143
1976		1	2	.333	2.37	6	3	0	19	20	5	10	0	1	0	0	3	0	0	.000
5 yrs.		10	16	.385	3.96	116	19	1	218.1	252	82	136	0	5	7	2	41	9	0	.220

Ossie France

FRANCE, OSMAN B.
B. Oct. 4, 1859, Greentown, Ohio   D. May 2, 1947, Akron, Ohio

		W	L	PCT	ERA	G	GS	CG	IP	H	BB	SO	ShO	W	L	SV	AB	H	HR	BA
1890	CHI N	0	0	–	13.50	1	1	0	2	3	2	0	0	0	0	0	1	0	0	.000

Earl Francis

FRANCIS, EARL COLEMAN   BR TR 6'2" 210 lbs.
B. July 14, 1936, Slab Fork, W. Va.

		W	L	PCT	ERA	G	GS	CG	IP	H	BB	SO	ShO	W	L	SV	AB	H	HR	BA
1960	PIT N	1	0	1.000	2.00	7	0	0	18	14	4	8	0	1	0	0	5	0	0	.000
1961		2	8	.200	4.21	23	15	0	102.2	110	47	53	0	0	1	0	28	3	0	.107
1962		9	8	.529	3.07	36	23	5	176	153	83	121	1	2	0	0	61	10	1	.164
1963		4	6	.400	4.53	33	13	0	97.1	107	43	72	0	2	0	0	26	8	0	.308
1964		0	1	.000	8.53	2	1	0	6.1	7	1	6	0	0	0	0	1	0	0	.000
1965	STL N	0	0	–	5.06	2	0	0	5.1	7	3	3	0	0	0	0	1	0	0	.000
6 yrs.		16	23	.410	3.77	103	52	5	405.2	398	181	263	1	5	1	0	122	21	1	.172

Ray Francis

FRANCIS, RAY JAMES   BL TL 6'1½" 182 lbs.
B. Mar. 8, 1893, Sherman, Tex.   D. July 6, 1934, Atlanta, Ga.

		W	L	PCT	ERA	G	GS	CG	IP	H	BB	SO	ShO	W	L	SV	AB	H	HR	BA
1922	WAS A	7	18	.280	4.28	39	26	15	225	265	66	64	2	0	3	2	78	13	0	.167
1923	DET A	5	8	.385	4.42	33	6	0	79.1	95	28	27	0	1	3	1	21	3	0	.143
1925	2 teams			NY	A (4G 0–0)			BOS	A (6G 0–2)											
"	total	0	2	.000	7.71	10	4	0	32.2	49	16	5	0	0	0	0	8	1	0	.125
3 yrs.		12	28	.300	4.65	82	36	15	337	409	110	96	2	1	6	3	107	17	0	.159

John Franco

FRANCO, JOHN ANTHONY   BL TL 5'10" 175 lbs.
B. Sept. 17, 1960, Brooklyn, N. Y.

		W	L	PCT	ERA	G	GS	CG	IP	H	BB	SO	ShO	W	L	SV	AB	H	HR	BA
1984	CIN N	6	2	.750	2.61	54	0	0	79.1	74	36	55	0	6	2	4	3	0	0	.000

Charlie Frank

FRANK, CHARLES
B. May 30, 1870, Mobile, Ala.   D. May 24, 1922, Memphis, Tenn.

		W	L	PCT	ERA	G	GS	CG	IP	H	BB	SO	ShO	W	L	SV	AB	H	HR	BA
1894	STL N	0	0	–	15.00	2	0	0	3	6	7	1	0	0	0	0	*			

Fred Frankhouse

FRANKHOUSE, FREDRICK MELOY   BR TR 5'11" 175 lbs.
B. Apr. 9, 1904, Port Royal, Pa.

		W	L	PCT	ERA	G	GS	CG	IP	H	BB	SO	ShO	W	L	SV	AB	H	HR	BA
1927	STL N	5	1	.833	2.70	6	6	5	50	41	16	20	1	0	0	0	20	5	0	.250
1928		3	2	.600	3.96	21	10	1	84	91	36	29	0	0	0	1	27	5	0	.185
1929		7	2	.778	4.12	30	12	6	133.1	149	43	37	0	1	0	1	52	15	1	.288
1930	2 teams			STL	N (8G 2–3)			BOS	N (27G 7–6)											
"	total	9	9	.500	5.87	35	12	3	130.1	169	54	34	1	5	3	0	44	14	0	.318
1931	BOS N	8	8	.500	4.03	26	15	6	127.1	125	43	50	0	0	1	1	40	6	0	.150
1932		4	6	.400	3.56	37	6	3	108.2	113	45	35	0	2	3	0	30	3	0	.100
1933		16	15	.516	3.16	43	30	14	244.2	249	77	83	2	2	2	2	80	19	0	.238
1934		17	9	.654	3.20	37	31	13	233.2	239	77	78	2	0	0	1	85	17	0	.200
1935		11	15	.423	4.76	40	29	10	230.2	278	81	64	1	0	0	0	76	20	0	.263
1936	BKN N	13	10	.565	3.65	41	31	9	234.1	236	89	84	1	1	1	2	91	13	0	.143
1937		10	13	.435	4.27	33	26	9	179.1	214	78	64	1	2	1	0	58	11	0	.190
1938		3	5	.375	4.04	30	8	2	93.2	92	44	32	1	2	1	0	26	4	0	.154

	W	L	PCT	ERA	G	GS	CG	IP	H	BB	SO	ShO	Relief Pitching W	L	SV	BATTING AB	H	HR	BA

Fred Frankhouse continued

	W	L	PCT	ERA	G	GS	CG	IP	H	BB	SO	ShO	W	L	SV	AB	H	HR	BA
1939 BOS N	0	2	.000	2.61	23	0	0	38	37	18	12	0	0	2	4	7	0	0	.000
13 yrs.	106	97	.522	3.92	402	216	81	1888	2033	701	622	10	15	14	12	636	132	1	.208

Jack Franklin

FRANKLIN, JAMES WILFORD
B. Oct. 20, 1919, Paris, Ill.   BR TR 5'11½" 170 lbs.

	W	L	PCT	ERA	G	GS	CG	IP	H	BB	SO	ShO	W	L	SV	AB	H	HR	BA
1944 BKN N	0	0	—	13.50	1	0	0	2	2	4	0	0	0	0	0	0	0	0	—

Jay Franklin

FRANKLIN, JOHN WILLIAM
B. Mar. 16, 1953, Arlington, Va.   BR TR 6'2" 180 lbs.

	W	L	PCT	ERA	G	GS	CG	IP	H	BB	SO	ShO	W	L	SV	AB	H	HR	BA
1971 SD N	0	1	.000	6.00	3	1	0	6	5	4	4	0	0	0	0	1	0	0	.000

Chick Fraser

FRASER, CHARLES CARROLTON
B. Mar. 17, 1871, Chicago, Ill.   D. May 8, 1940, Wendell, Ida.   BR TR 5'10½" 188 lbs.

	W	L	PCT	ERA	G	GS	CG	IP	H	BB	SO	ShO	W	L	SV	AB	H	HR	BA
1896 LOU N	13	25	.342	4.87	43	38	36	349.1	396	166	91	0	0	2	1	146	22	0	.151
1897	15	17	.469	4.09	35	34	32	286.1	332	133	70	0	1	0	0	112	18	2	.161
1898 2 teams			LOU	N (26G 7–19)			CLE	N (6G 2–3)											
" total	9	22	.290	5.36	32	32	26	245	279	112	77	1	0	0	0	94	17	0	.181
1899 PHI N	21	13	.618	3.36	35	33	29	270.2	278	85	68	4	0	1	0	117	21	0	.179
1900	16	10	.615	3.14	29	26	22	223.1	250	93	58	1	0	0	0	85	22	0	.259
1901 PHI A	22	16	.579	3.81	40	37	35	331	344	132	110	2	1	0	0	139	26	0	.187
1902 PHI N	12	13	.480	3.42	27	26	24	224	238	74	97	3	0	1	0	86	15	0	.174
1903	12	17	.414	4.50	31	29	26	250	260	97	104	1	0	1	0	93	19	1	.204
1904	14	24	.368	3.25	42	36	32	302	287	100	127	1	2	1	1	110	17	0	.155
1905 BOS N	14	21	.400	3.29	39	38	35	334	320	149	130	2	0	0	0	156	35	0	.224
1906 CIN N	10	20	.333	2.67	31	28	25	236	221	80	58	2	1	2	0	82	14	0	.171
1907 CHI N	8	5	.615	2.28	22	15	9	138.1	112	46	41	2	4	0	0	45	3	0	.067
1908	11	9	.550	2.27	26	17	11	162.2	141	61	66	2	3	0	2	50	6	0	.120
1909	0	0	—	0.00	1	0	0	3	2	4	1	0	0	0	0	3	0	0	.000
14 yrs.	177	212	.455	3.68	433	389	342	3355.2	3460	1332	1098	22	12	8	5	1316	235	3	.179

George Frazier

FRAZIER, GEORGE ALLEN
B. Oct. 13, 1954, Oklahoma City, Okla.   BR TR 6'5" 205 lbs.

	W	L	PCT	ERA	G	GS	CG	IP	H	BB	SO	ShO	W	L	SV	AB	H	HR	BA
1978 STL N	0	3	.000	4.09	14	0	0	22	22	6	8	0	0	3	0	3	1	0	.333
1979	2	4	.333	4.50	25	0	0	32	35	12	14	0	2	4	0	1	0	0	.000
1980	1	4	.200	2.74	22	0	0	23	24	7	11	0	1	4	3	0	0	0	—
1981 NY A	0	1	.000	1.61	16	0	0	28	26	11	17	0	0	1	3	0	0	0	—
1982	4	4	.500	3.47	63	0	0	111.2	103	39	69	0	4	4	1	0	0	0	—
1983	4	4	.500	3.43	61	0	0	115.1	94	45	78	0	4	4	8	0	0	0	—
1984 2 teams			CLE	A (22G 3–2)			CHI	N (37G 6–3)											
" total	9	5	.643	3.92	59	0	0	108	98	40	82	0	9	5	4	7	2	0	.286
7 yrs.	20	25	.444	3.52	260	0	0	440	402	160	279	0	20	25	19	11	3	0	.273
LEAGUE CHAMPIONSHIP SERIES																			
1981 NY A	1	0	1.000	0.00	1	0	0	5.2	5	1	5	0	1	0	0	0	0	0	—
1984 CHI N	0	0	—	10.80	1	0	0	1.2	2	0	1	0	0	0	0	0	0	0	—
2 yrs.	1	0	1.000	2.45	2	0	0	7.1	7	1	6	0	1	0	0	0	0	0	—
WORLD SERIES																			
1981 NY A	0	3	.000	17.18	3	0	0	3.2	9	3	2	0	0	3	0	2	0	0	.000
															1st				

Vic Frazier

FRAZIER, VICTOR PATRICK
B. Aug. 5, 1904, Ruston, La.   D. Jan. 10, 1977, Jacksonville, Tex.   BR TR 6' 182 lbs.

	W	L	PCT	ERA	G	GS	CG	IP	H	BB	SO	ShO	W	L	SV	AB	H	HR	BA
1931 CHI A	13	15	.464	4.46	46	29	13	254	258	127	87	2	1	1	4	86	18	0	.209
1932	3	13	.188	6.23	29	21	4	146	180	70	33	0	1	0	1	44	4	0	.091
1933 2 teams			CHI	A (10G 1–1)			DET	A (20G 5–5)											
" total	6	6	.500	7.00	30	15	4	124.2	161	70	30	0	0	2	0	41	7	0	.171
1934 DET A	3	3	.250	5.96	8	2	0	22.2	30	12	11	0	1	2	0	7	2	0	.286
1937 BOS N	0	0	—	5.63	3	0	0	8	12	1	2	0	0	0	0	1	0	0	.000
1939 CHI A	0	1	.000	10.27	10	1	0	23.2	45	11	7	0	0	0	0	7	2	0	.286
6 yrs.	23	38	.377	5.77	126	68	21	579	686	291	170	2	2	6	4	186	33	0	.177

Buck Freeman

FREEMAN, ALEXANDER VERNON
B. July 5, 1893, Mart, Tex.   BB TR 5'10" 167 lbs.   BR 1922
D. Feb. 21, 1953, Fort Sam Houston, Tex.

	W	L	PCT	ERA	G	GS	CG	IP	H	BB	SO	ShO	W	L	SV	AB	H	HR	BA
1921 CHI N	9	10	.474	4.11	38	20	6	177.1	189	70	42	0	4	2	3	53	11	0	.208
1922	0	1	.000	8.77	11	1	0	25.2	47	10	10	0	0	2	1	8	1	0	.125
2 yrs.	9	11	.450	4.70	49	21	6	203	236	80	52	0	4	4	4	61	12	0	.197

Buck Freeman

FREEMAN, JOHN FRANK
B. Oct. 30, 1871, Catasauqua, Pa.   D. June 25, 1949, Wilkes-Barre, Pa.   BL TL 5'11" 160 lbs.

	W	L	PCT	ERA	G	GS	CG	IP	H	BB	SO	ShO	W	L	SV	AB	H	HR	BA
1891 WAS AA	3	2	.600	3.89	5	4	4	44	35	33	28	0	1	0	0	18	4	0	.222
1899 WAS N	0	0	—	7.71	2	0	0	7	15	3	0	0	0	0	0	588	187	25	.318
2 yrs.	3	2	.600	4.41	7	4	4	51	50	36	28	0	1	0	0	*			

Harvey Freeman

FREEMAN, HARVEY BAYARD
B. Dec. 22, 1897, Mottville, Mich.   D. Jan. 10, 1970, Kalamazoo, Mich.   BR TR 5'10" 145 lbs.

	W	L	PCT	ERA	G	GS	CG	IP	H	BB	SO	ShO	W	L	SV	AB	H	HR	BA
1921 PHI A	1	4	.200	7.24	18	4	2	51	65	35	5	0	0	1	0	12	1	0	.083

Hersh Freeman

FREEMAN, HERSHELL BASKIN (Buster)
B. July 1, 1928, Gadsden, Ala.   BR TR 6'3" 220 lbs.

	W	L	PCT	ERA	G	GS	CG	IP	H	BB	SO	ShO	W	L	SV	AB	H	HR	BA
1952 BOS A	1	0	1.000	3.29	4	1	1	13.2	13	5	5	0	0	0	0	4	2	0	.500
1953	1	4	.200	5.54	18	2	0	39	50	17	15	0	1	2	0	11	1	0	.091
1955 2 teams			BOS	A (2G 0–0)			CIN	N (52G 7–4)											
" total	7	4	.636	2.12	54	0	0	93.1	95	31	38	0	7	4	11	18	3	1	.167
1956 CIN N	14	5	.737	3.40	64	0	0	108.2	112	34	50	0	14	5	18	18	1	0	.056

	W	L	PCT	ERA	G	GS	CG	IP	H	BB	SO	ShO	Relief Pitching W	L	SV	BATTING AB	H	HR	BA

Hersh Freeman continued

1957	7	2	.778	4.52	52	0	0	83.2	90	14	36	0	7	2	8	10	2	0	.200
1958 2 teams		CIN	N (3G 0–0)		CHI	N	(9G 0–1)												
" total	0	1	.000	6.53	12	0	0	20.2	27	8	14	0	0	1	0	2	0	0	.000
6 yrs.	30	16	.652	3.74	204	3	1	359	387	109	158	0	29	14	37	63	9	1	.143

Jimmy Freeman

FREEMAN, JIMMY LEE
B. June 29, 1951, Carlsbad, N. M.

BL TL 6'4"   180 lbs.

1972 ATL N	2	2	.500	6.00	6	6	1	36	40	22	18	0	0	0	0	13	1	0	.077
1973	0	2	.000	7.78	13	5	0	37	50	25	20	0	0	0	1	13	2	0	.154
2 yrs.	2	4	.333	6.90	19	11	1	73	90	47	38	0	0	0	1	26	3	0	.115

Julie Freeman

FREEMAN, JULIUS BENJAMIN
B. Nov. 7, 1868, Missouri   D. June 10, 1921, St. Louis, Mo.

| 1888 STL AA | 0 | 1 | .000 | 4.26 | 1 | 1 | 0 | 6.1 | 7 | 4 | 1 | 0 | 0 | 0 | 0 | 3 | 1 | 0 | .333 |

Mark Freeman

FREEMAN, MARK PRICE
B. Dec. 7, 1930, Memphis, Tenn.

BR TR 6'4"   220 lbs.

1959 2 teams		NY	A (1G 0–0)		KC	A	(3G 0–0)												
" total	0	0	–	5.06	4	1	0	10.2	12	5	5	0	0	0	0	2	0	0	.000
1960 CHI N	3	3	.500	5.63	30	8	1	76.2	70	33	50	0	1	2	1	20	3	0	.150
2 yrs.	3	3	.500	5.56	34	9	1	87.1	82	38	55	0	1	2	1	22	3	0	.136

Jake Freeze

FREEZE, CARL ALEXANDER
B. Apr. 25, 1900, Huntington, Ark.   D. Apr. 9, 1983, San Angelo, Tex.

BR TR 5'8"   105 lbs.

| 1925 CHI A | 0 | 0 | – | 2.45 | 2 | 0 | 0 | 3.2 | 5 | 3 | 1 | 0 | 0 | 0 | 0 | 1 | 0 | 0 | .000 |

Dave Freisleben

FREISLEBEN, DAVID JAMES
B. Oct. 31, 1951, Coraopolis, Pa.

BR TR 5'11"   195 lbs.

1974 SD N	9	14	.391	3.65	33	31	6	212	194	112	130	2	0	0	0	64	11	0	.172
1975	5	14	.263	4.28	36	27	4	181	206	82	77	1	0	0	0	48	4	0	.083
1976	10	13	.435	3.51	34	24	6	172	163	66	81	3	2	1	1	37	7	0	.189
1977	7	9	.438	4.60	33	23	1	139	140	71	72	0	1	1	0	37	5	0	.135
1978 2 teams		SD	N (12G 0–3)		CLE	A	(12G 1–4)												
" total	1	7	.125	6.69	24	14	0	71.1	93	46	35	0	0	1	0	6	0	0	.000
1979 TOR A	2	3	.400	4.95	42	2	0	91	101	53	35	0	2	3	3	0	0	0	–
6 yrs.	34	60	.362	4.29	202	121	17	866.1	897	430	430	6	5	5	4	192	27	0	.141

Tony Freitas

FREITAS, ANTONIO
B. May 5, 1908, Mill Valley, Calif.

BR TL 5'8"   161 lbs.

1932 PHI A	12	5	.706	3.83	23	18	10	150.1	150	48	31	1	1	2	0	54	8	0	.148
1933	2	4	.333	7.27	19	9	2	64.1	90	24	15	0	0	1	1	16	1	0	.063
1934 CIN N	6	12	.333	4.01	30	18	5	152.2	194	25	37	0	1	2	1	47	9	0	.191
1935	5	10	.333	4.57	31	18	5	143.2	174	38	51	0	0	1	2	46	6	0	.130
1936	0	2	.000	1.29	4	0	0	7	6	2	1	0	0	2	0	2	0	0	.000
5 yrs.	25	33	.431	4.48	107	63	22	518	614	137	135	1	2	8	4	165	24	0	.145

Larry French

FRENCH, LAWRENCE ROBERT
B. Nov. 1, 1907, Visalia, Calif.

BR TL 6'1"   195 lbs.
BB 1934,1940–42

1929 PIT N	7	5	.583	4.90	30	13	6	123	130	62	49	0	2	1	1	42	8	0	.190
1930	17	18	.486	4.36	42	35	21	274.2	325	89	90	3	1	1	1	91	22	0	.242
1931	15	13	.536	3.26	39	33	20	275.2	301	70	73	1	1	0	1	95	17	0	.179
1932	18	16	.529	3.02	47	33	20	274.1	301	62	72	3	2	2	4	92	19	0	.207
1933	18	13	.581	2.72	47	35	21	291.1	290	55	88	5	1	2	1	101	15	0	.149
1934	12	18	.400	3.58	49	35	16	263.2	299	59	103	3	1	4	1	84	16	0	.190
1935 CHI N	17	10	.630	2.96	42	30	16	246.1	279	44	90	4	1	3	2	85	12	0	.141
1936	18	9	.667	3.39	43	28	16	252.1	262	54	104	4	3	2	3	85	18	0	.212
1937	16	10	.615	3.98	42	28	11	208	229	65	100	4	3	1	0	71	9	0	.127
1938	10	19	.345	3.80	43	27	10	201.1	210	62	83	3	2	4	0	62	13	0	.210
1939	15	8	.652	3.29	36	21	10	194	205	50	98	2	4	0	1	73	14	1	.192
1940	14	14	.500	3.29	40	33	18	246	240	64	107	3	1	1	2	85	14	0	.165
1941 2 teams		CHI	N (26G 5–14)		BKN	N	(6G 0–0)												
" total	5	14	.263	4.51	32	19	6	153.2	177	47	68	1	1	0	0	51	10	0	.196
1942 BKN N	15	4	.789	1.83	38	14	8	147.2	127	36	62	4	7	1	0	40	12	0	.300
14 yrs.	197	171	.535	3.44	570	384	199	3152	3375	819	1187	40	30	22	17	1057	199	1	.188

WORLD SERIES

1935 CHI N	0	2	.000	3.38	2	1	1	10.2	15	2	8	0	0	1	0	4	1	0	.250
1938	0	0	–	2.70	3	0	0	3.1	1	1	2	0	0	0	0	0	0	0	–
1941 BKN N	0	0	–	0.00	2	0	0	1	0	0	0	0	0	0	0	0	0	0	–
3 yrs.	0	2	.000	3.00	7	1	1	15	16	3	10	0	0	1	0	4	1	0	.250

Benny Frey

FREY, BENJAMIN RUDOLPH
B. Apr. 6, 1906, Dexter, Mich.   D. Nov. 1, 1937, Jackson, Mich.

BR TR 5'10"   165 lbs.

1929 CIN N	1	2	.333	4.13	3	3	2	24	29	8	1	0	0	0	0	8	3	0	.375
1930	11	18	.379	4.70	44	28	14	245	295	62	43	2	2	2	1	88	25	0	.284
1931	8	12	.400	4.92	34	17	7	133.2	166	36	19	1	3	0	2	44	14	0	.318
1932 2 teams		STL	N (2G 0–2)		CIN	N	(28G 4–10)												
" total	4	12	.250	4.49	30	15	5	134.1	165	32	27	0	1	2	0	45	9	0	.200
1933 CIN N	6	4	.600	3.82	37	9	1	132	144	21	12	1	4	0	0	42	11	0	.262
1934	11	16	.407	3.52	39	30	12	245.1	288	42	33	2	1	1	2	82	14	0	.171
1935	6	10	.375	6.85	38	13	3	114.1	164	32	24	1	3	2	2	32	11	0	.344
1936	10	8	.556	4.25	31	12	5	131.1	164	30	20	0	4	2	0	44	11	0	.250
8 yrs.	57	82	.410	4.50	256	127	49	1160	1415	263	179	7	18	9	7	385	98	0	.255

	W	L	PCT	ERA	G	GS	CG	IP	H	BB	SO	ShO	Relief Pitching W	L	SV	BATTING AB	H	HR	BA

Barney Friberg

FRIBERG, AUGUSTAF BERNHARDT
Also known as Bernard Albert Friberg.
B. Aug. 18, 1899, Manchester, N. H.   D. Dec. 8, 1958, Swampscott, Mass.
BR TR 5'11" 178 lbs.

Year	W	L	PCT	ERA	G	GS	CG	IP	H	BB	SO	ShO	RW	RL	SV	AB	H	HR	BA
1925 PHI N	0	0	–	4.50	1	0	0	4	4	3	1	0	0	0	0	*			

Marion Fricano

FRICANO, MARION JOHN
B. July 15, 1923, Brant, N. Y.   D. May 18, 1976, Tijuana, Mexico
BR TR 6' 170 lbs.

Year	W	L	PCT	ERA	G	GS	CG	IP	H	BB	SO	ShO	RW	RL	SV	AB	H	HR	BA
1952 PHI A	1	0	1.000	1.80	2	0	0	5	5	1	0	0	1	0	0	0	0	0	
1953	9	12	.429	3.88	39	23	10	211	206	90	67	0	1	0	0	69	10	0	.145
1954	5	11	.313	5.16	37	20	4	151.2	163	64	43	0	1	0	1	41	4	0	.098
1955 KC A	0	0	–	3.15	10	0	0	20	19	9	5	0	0	0	0	3	2	0	.667
4 yrs.	15	23	.395	4.32	88	43	14	387.2	393	164	115	0	3	0	1	113	16	0	.142

Skipper Friday

FRIDAY, GRIER WILLIAM
B. Oct. 24, 1896, Lincolnton, N. C.   D. Aug. 25, 1962, Gastonia, N. C.
BR TR 5'11" 170 lbs.

Year	W	L	PCT	ERA	G	GS	CG	IP	H	BB	SO	ShO	RW	RL	SV	AB	H	HR	BA
1923 WAS A	0	1	.000	6.90	7	2	1	30	35	22	9	0	0	0	0	9	2	0	.222

Cy Fried

FRIED, ARTHUR EDWIN
B. July 23, 1897, San Antonio, Tex.   D. Oct. 10, 1970, San Antonio, Tex.
BL TL 5'11½" 150 lbs.

Year	W	L	PCT	ERA	G	GS	CG	IP	H	BB	SO	ShO	RW	RL	SV	AB	H	HR	BA
1920 DET A	0	0	–	16.20	2	0	0	1.2	3	4	0	0	0	0	0	0	0	0	

Bob Friedrichs

FRIEDRICHS, ROBERT GEORGE
B. Aug. 30, 1906, Cincinnati, Ohio
BR TR 5'11½" 165 lbs.

Year	W	L	PCT	ERA	G	GS	CG	IP	H	BB	SO	ShO	RW	RL	SV	AB	H	HR	BA
1932 WAS A	0	0	–	11.25	2	0	0	4	4	7	2	0	0	0	0	1	0	0	.000

Bill Friel

FRIEL, WILLIAM EDWARD
Brother of Pat Friel.
B. Apr. 1, 1876, Renovo, Pa.   D. Dec. 24, 1959, St. Louis, Mo.
BL TR

Year	W	L	PCT	ERA	G	GS	CG	IP	H	BB	SO	ShO	RW	RL	SV	AB	H	HR	BA
1902 STL A	0	0	–	4.50	1	0	0	4	4	0	0	0	0	0	0	*			

Bob Friend

FRIEND, ROBERT BARTMESS (Warrior)
B. Nov. 24, 1930, Lafayette, Ind.
BR TR 6' 190 lbs.

Year	W	L	PCT	ERA	G	GS	CG	IP	H	BB	SO	ShO	RW	RL	SV	AB	H	HR	BA
1951 PIT N	6	10	.375	4.27	34	22	3	149.2	173	68	41	1	0	1	0	44	4	0	.091
1952	7	17	.292	4.18	35	23	6	185	186	84	75	1	2	2	0	52	3	0	.058
1953	8	11	.421	4.90	32	24	8	170.2	193	57	66	0	0	1	0	52	7	0	.135
1954	7	12	.368	5.07	35	20	4	170.1	204	58	73	2	1	1	2	51	14	1	.275
1955	14	9	.609	2.83	44	20	9	200.1	178	52	98	2	5	1	2	61	10	0	.164
1956	17	17	.500	3.46	49	42	19	314.1	310	85	166	4	0	0	3	97	16	1	.165
1957	14	18	.438	3.38	40	38	17	277	273	68	143	3	0	1	0	87	16	0	.184
1958	22	14	.611	3.68	38	38	16	274	299	61	135	1	0	0	0	94	10	0	.106
1959	8	19	.296	4.03	35	35	7	234.2	267	52	104	2	0	0	0	73	12	0	.164
1960	18	12	.600	3.00	38	37	16	275.2	266	45	183	4	0	0	1	88	6	0	.068
1961	14	19	.424	3.85	41	35	10	236	271	45	108	1	1	1	1	79	11	0	.139
1962	18	14	.563	3.06	39	36	13	261.2	280	53	144	5	0	0	1	91	11	0	.121
1963	17	16	.515	2.34	39	38	12	268.2	236	44	144	4	1	0	0	86	9	0	.105
1964	13	18	.419	3.33	35	35	13	240.1	253	50	128	3	0	0	0	71	5	0	.070
1965	8	12	.400	3.24	34	34	8	222	221	47	74	2	0	0	0	71	3	0	.042
1966 2 teams				NY	A	(12G 1–4)		NY	N	(22G 5–8)									
" total	6	12	.333	4.55	34	20	2	130.2	162	25	52	1		4	1	40	1	0	.025
16 yrs.	197	230	.461	3.58	602	497	163	3611	3772	894	1734	36	11	12	11	1137	138	2	.121

WORLD SERIES

Year	W	L	PCT	ERA	G	GS	CG	IP	H	BB	SO	ShO	RW	RL	SV	AB	H	HR	BA
1960 PIT N	0	2	.000	13.50	3	2	0	6	13	3	7	0	0	0	0	1	0	0	.000

Danny Friend

FRIEND, DANIEL SEBASTIAN
B. Apr. 18, 1873, Cincinnati, Ohio   D. June 1, 1942, Chillicothe, Ohio
TL 5'9" 175 lbs.

Year	W	L	PCT	ERA	G	GS	CG	IP	H	BB	SO	ShO	RW	RL	SV	AB	H	HR	BA
1895 CHI N	2	2	.500	5.27	5	5	5	41	50	14	10	0	0	0	0	17	4	0	.235
1896	18	14	.563	4.74	36	33	28	290.2	298	139	86	1	1	1	0	126	30	1	.238
1897	12	11	.522	4.52	24	24	23	203	244	86	58	0	0	0	0	88	25	0	.284
1898	0	2	.000	5.29	2	2	2	17	20	10	4	0	0	0	0	7	2	0	.286
4 yrs.	32	29	.525	4.71	67	64	58	551.2	612	249	158	1	1	1	0	238	61	1	.256

Pete Fries

FRIES, PETER MARTIN
B. Oct. 30, 1857, Scranton, Pa.   D. July 30, 1937, Chicago, Ill.
BL TL 5'8" 160 lbs.

Year	W	L	PCT	ERA	G	GS	CG	IP	H	BB	SO	ShO	RW	RL	SV	AB	H	HR	BA
1883 COL AA	0	3	.000	6.48	3	3	3	25	34	14	7	0	0	0	0	10	3	0	.300
1884 IND AA	0	0	–	0.00	0	0	0	0	0	0	0	0	0	0	0	3	1	0	.333
2 yrs.	0	3	.000	6.48	3	3	3	25	34	14	7	0	0	0	0	13	4	0	.308

John Frill

FRILL, JOHN EDMOND
B. Apr. 3, 1879, Reading, Pa.   D. Sept. 29, 1918, Westerly, R. I.
BR TL 5'10½" 170 lbs.

Year	W	L	PCT	ERA	G	GS	CG	IP	H	BB	SO	ShO	RW	RL	SV	AB	H	HR	BA
1910 NY A	2	2	.500	4.47	10	5	3	48.1	55	5	27	1	0	0	1	18	2	0	.111
1912 2 teams				STL	A	(3G 0–1)		CIN	N	(3G 1–0)									
" total	1	1	.500	9.31	6	5	0	19.1	35	2	6	0	0	0	0	6	2	0	.333
2 yrs.	3	3	.500	5.85	16	10	3	67.2	90	7	33	1	0	0	1	24	4	0	.167

Danny Frisella

FRISELLA, DANIEL VINCENT (Bear)
B. Mar. 4, 1946, San Francisco, Calif.   D. Jan. 1, 1977, Phoenix, Ariz.
BL TR 6' 185 lbs.

Year	W	L	PCT	ERA	G	GS	CG	IP	H	BB	SO	ShO	RW	RL	SV	AB	H	HR	BA
1967 NY N	1	6	.143	3.41	14	11	0	74	68	33	51	0	0	0	0	23	2	0	.087
1968	2	4	.333	3.91	19	4	0	50.2	53	19	47	0	0	2	2	12	1	0	.083
1969	0	0	–	7.71	3	0	0	4.2	8	3	5	0	0	0	0	1	0	0	.000
1970	8	3	.727	3.00	30	1	0	66	49	34	54	0	7	3	1	13	4	0	.308
1971	8	5	.615	1.98	53	0	0	91	76	30	93	0	8	5	12	13	3	0	.231
1972	5	8	.385	3.34	39	0	0	67.1	63	20	46	0	5	8	9	7	2	0	.286
1973 ATL N	1	2	.333	4.20	42	0	0	45	40	23	27	0	1	2	8	2	1	0	.500
1974	3	4	.429	5.14	36	1	0	42	37	28	27	0	3	4	6	1	0	0	.000
1975 SD N	1	6	.143	3.12	65	0	0	98	86	51	67	0	1	6	9	5	1	0	.200

	W	L	PCT	ERA	G	GS	CG	IP	H	BB	SO	ShO	Relief Pitching W	L	SV	BATTING AB	H	HR	BA

John Gabler

GABLER, JOHN RICHARD (Gabe)
B. Oct. 2, 1930, Kansas City, Mo.
BL TR 6'2"   165 lbs.
BB 1960

	W	L	PCT	ERA	G	GS	CG	IP	H	BB	SO	ShO	W	L	SV	AB	H	HR	BA
1959 NY A	1	1	.500	2.79	3	1	0	19.1	21	10	11	0	1	0	0	6	0	0	.000
1960	3	3	.500	4.15	21	4	0	52	46	32	19	0	2	1	1	11	1	0	.091
1961 WAS A	3	8	.273	4.86	29	9	0	92.2	104	37	33	0	2	2	4	25	5	0	.200
3 yrs.	7	12	.368	4.39	53	14	0	164	171	79	63	0	5	3	5	42	6	0	.143

Ken Gables

GABLES, KENNETH HARLIN
B. Jan. 21, 1919, Walnut Grove, Mo.   D. Jan. 2, 1960, Walnut Grove, Mo.
BR TR 5'11"   210 lbs.

	W	L	PCT	ERA	G	GS	CG	IP	H	BB	SO	ShO	W	L	SV	AB	H	HR	BA
1945 PIT N	11	7	.611	4.15	29	16	6	138.2	139	46	49	0	5	1	1	39	4	0	.103
1946	2	4	.333	5.27	32	7	0	100.2	113	52	39	0	1	0	1	24	6	0	.250
1947	0	0	–	54.00	1	0	0	.1	3	0	0	0	0	0	0	0	0	0	–
3 yrs.	13	11	.542	4.69	62	23	6	239.2	255	98	88	0	6	1	2	63	10	0	.159

John Gaddy

GADDY, JOHN WILSON (Sheriff)
B. Feb. 5, 1914, Wadesboro, N. C.   D. May 3, 1966, Albermarle, N. C.
BR TR 6'½"   182 lbs.

	W	L	PCT	ERA	G	GS	CG	IP	H	BB	SO	ShO	W	L	SV	AB	H	HR	BA
1938 BKN N	2	0	1.000	0.69	2	2	1	13	13	4	3	0	0	0	0	6	0	0	.000

Brent Gaff

GAFF, BRENT ALLEN (Willy)
B. Oct. 5, 1958, Fort Wayne, Ind.
BR TR 6'1"   185 lbs.

	W	L	PCT	ERA	G	GS	CG	IP	H	BB	SO	ShO	W	L	SV	AB	H	HR	BA
1982 NY N	0	3	.000	4.55	7	5	0	31.2	41	10	14	0	0	0	0	8	0	0	.000
1983	1	0	1.000	6.10	4	0	0	10.1	18	1	4	0	1	0	0	3	0	0	.000
1984	3	2	.600	3.63	47	0	0	84.1	77	36	42	0	3	2	1	6	0	0	.000
3 yrs.	4	5	.444	4.06	58	5	0	126.1	136	47	60	0	4	2	1	17	0	0	.000

Charlie Gagus

GAGUS, CHARLES FREDERICK
Also known as Charles Frederick Geggus.
B. Mar. 25, 1862, San Francisco, Calif.   D. Jan. 16, 1917, San Francisco, Calif.

	W	L	PCT	ERA	G	GS	CG	IP	H	BB	SO	ShO	W	L	SV	AB	H	HR	BA
1884 WAS U	10	9	.526	2.54	23	21	19	177.1	143	38	156	0	0	0	0	154	38	0	.247

Nemo Gaines

GAINES, WILLARD ROLAND
B. Dec. 23, 1897, Alexandria, Va.   D. Jan. 26, 1979, Warrentown, Va.
BL TL 6'   180 lbs.

	W	L	PCT	ERA	G	GS	CG	IP	H	BB	SO	ShO	W	L	SV	AB	H	HR	BA
1921 WAS A	0	0	–	0.00	4	0	0	4.2	5	1	1	0	0	0	0	1	0	0	.000

Fred Gaiser

GAISER, FREDERICK JACOB
B. Aug. 31, 1885, Stuttgart, Germany   D. Oct. 9, 1918, Trenton, N. J.

	W	L	PCT	ERA	G	GS	CG	IP	H	BB	SO	ShO	W	L	SV	AB	H	HR	BA
1908 STL N	0	0	–	7.71	1	0	0	2.1	4	3	2	0	0	0	0	1	0	0	.000

Bob Galasso

GALASSO, ROBERT JOSEPH
B. Jan. 13, 1952, Connellsville, Pa.
BL TR 6'1"   205 lbs.

	W	L	PCT	ERA	G	GS	CG	IP	H	BB	SO	ShO	W	L	SV	AB	H	HR	BA
1977 SEA A	0	6	.000	9.00	11	7	0	35	57	8	21	0	0	1	0	0	0	0	–
1979 MIL A	3	1	.750	4.41	31	0	0	51	64	26	28	0	3	1	3	0	0	0	–
1981 SEA A	1	1	.500	4.78	13	1	0	32	32	13	14	0	0	0	1	0	0	0	–
3 yrs.	4	8	.333	5.87	55	8	0	118	153	47	63	0	3	2	4	0	0	0	–

Milt Galatzer

GALATZER, MILTON
B. May 4, 1907, Chicago, Ill.   D. Jan. 29, 1976, San Francisco, Calif.
BL TL 5'10"   168 lbs.

	W	L	PCT	ERA	G	GS	CG	IP	H	BB	SO	ShO	W	L	SV	AB	H	HR	BA
1936 CLE A	0	0	–	4.50	1	0	0	6	7	5	3	0	0	0	0	*			

Rich Gale

GALE, RICHARD BLACKWELL
B. Jan. 19, 1954, Littleton, N. H.
BR TR 6'7"   225 lbs.

	W	L	PCT	ERA	G	GS	CG	IP	H	BB	SO	ShO	W	L	SV	AB	H	HR	BA
1978 KC A	14	8	.636	3.09	31	30	9	192.1	171	100	88	3	0	0	0	0	0	0	–
1979	9	10	.474	5.64	34	31	2	182	197	99	103	1	0	0	0	0	0	0	–
1980	13	9	.591	3.91	32	28	6	191	169	78	97	1	0	2	1	0	0	0	–
1981	6	6	.500	5.38	19	15	2	102	107	38	47	0	1	0	0	0	0	0	–
1982 SF N	7	14	.333	4.23	33	29	2	170.1	193	81	102	0	1	2	0	48	6	1	.125
1983 CIN N	4	6	.400	5.82	33	7	0	89.2	103	43	53	0	2	1	1	20	3	1	.150
1984 BOS A	2	3	.400	5.56	13	4	0	43.2	57	18	28	0	1	2	0	0	0	0	–
7 yrs.	55	56	.495	4.53	195	144	21	971	997	457	518	5	5	7	2	68	9	2	.132

WORLD SERIES

	W	L	PCT	ERA	G	GS	CG	IP	H	BB	SO	ShO	W	L	SV	AB	H	HR	BA
1980 KC A	0	1	.000	4.26	2	2	0	6.1	11	4	4	0	0	0	0	0	0	0	–

Denny Galehouse

GALEHOUSE, DENNIS WARD
B. Dec. 7, 1911, Marshallville, Ohio
BR TR 6'1"   195 lbs.

	W	L	PCT	ERA	G	GS	CG	IP	H	BB	SO	ShO	W	L	SV	AB	H	HR	BA
1934 CLE A	0	0	–	18.00	1	0	0	1	2	1	0	0	0	0	0	0	0	0	–
1935	1	0	1.000	9.00	5	1	1	13	16	9	8	0	0	0	0	4	1	0	.250
1936	8	7	.533	4.85	36	15	11	148.1	161	68	71	0	2	1	1	47	8	0	.170
1937	9	14	.391	4.57	36	29	7	200.2	238	83	78	0	2	0	3	72	15	0	.208
1938	7	8	.467	4.34	36	12	5	114	119	65	66	0	4	5	3	39	6	0	.154
1939 BOS A	9	10	.474	4.54	30	18	6	146.2	160	52	68	1	3	1	0	47	3	0	.064
1940	6	6	.500	5.18	25	20	5	120	155	41	53	0	0	0	0	39	3	0	.077
1941 STL A	9	10	.474	3.64	30	24	11	190.1	183	68	61	2	1	0	0	68	13	0	.191
1942	12	12	.500	3.62	32	28	12	191.1	193	79	75	3	0	0	1	72	14	0	.194
1943	11	11	.500	2.77	31	28	14	224	217	74	114	2	0	1	1	72	9	0	.125
1944	9	10	.474	3.12	24	19	6	153	162	44	80	2	1	1	0	48	3	0	.063
1946	8	12	.400	3.65	30	24	11	180	194	52	90	2	0	0	0	55	5	0	.091
1947 2 teams			STL	A (9G 1–3)		BOS	A	(21G 11–7)											
" total	12	10	.545	3.82	30	25	11	181.1	192	50	49	3	0	0	1	60	5	0	.083
1948 BOS A	8	8	.500	4.00	27	15	6	137.1	152	46	38	1	4	1	3	42	7	0	.167
1949	0	0	–	13.50	2	0	0	2	4	3	0	0	0	0	0	0	0	0	–
15 yrs.	109	118	.480	3.98	375	258	106	2003	2148	735	851	17	17	10	13	665	92	0	.138

WORLD SERIES

	W	L	PCT	ERA	G	GS	CG	IP	H	BB	SO	ShO	W	L	SV	AB	H	HR	BA
1944 STL A	1	1	.500	1.50	2	2	2	18	13	5	15	0	0	0	0	5	1	0	.200

	W	L	PCT	ERA	G	GS	CG	IP	H	BB	SO	ShO	Relief Pitching W	L	SV	BATTING AB	H	HR	BA

Bill Gallagher

GALLAGHER, WILLIAM JOHN
B. Philadelphia, Pa.   Deceased.

	W	L	PCT	ERA	G	GS	CG	IP	H	BB	SO	ShO	W	L	SV	AB	H	HR	BA
1883 BAL AA	0	5	.000	5.40	7	5	4	51.2	79	6	19	0	0	0	0	69	10	0	.145
1884 PHI U	1	2	.333	3.24	3	3	3	25	32	4	12	0	0	0	0	11	1	0	.091
2 yrs.	1	7	.125	4.70	10	8	7	76.2	111	10	31	0	0	0	0	*			

Doug Gallagher

GALLAGHER, DOUGLAS EUGENE   BR TL 6'3½" 195 lbs.
B. Feb. 21, 1940, Fremont, Ohio

	W	L	PCT	ERA	G	GS	CG	IP	H	BB	SO	ShO	W	L	SV	AB	H	HR	BA
1962 DET A	0	4	.000	4.68	9	2	0	25	31	15	14	0	0	2	1	6	2	0	.333

Ed Gallagher

GALLAGHER, EDWARD MICHAEL (Lefty)   BB TL 6'2" 197 lbs.
B. Nov. 28, 1910, Dorchester, Mass.   D. Dec. 22, 1981, Hyannis, Mass.

	W	L	PCT	ERA	G	GS	CG	IP	H	BB	SO	ShO	W	L	SV	AB	H	HR	BA
1932 BOS A	0	3	.000	12.55	9	3	0	23.2	30	28	6	0	0	0	0	5	0	0	.000

Bert Gallia

GALLIA, MELVIN ALLYS   BR TR 6' 165 lbs.
B. Oct. 14, 1891, Beeville, Tex.   D. Mar. 19, 1976, Devine, Tex.

	W	L	PCT	ERA	G	GS	CG	IP	H	BB	SO	ShO	W	L	SV	AB	H	HR	BA
1912 WAS A	0	0	–	0.00	2	0	0	2	0	3	0	0	0	0	0	0	0	0	–
1913	1	5	.167	4.13	31	4	0	96	85	46	46	0	1	2	3	23	2	0	.087
1914	0	0	–	4.50	2	0	0	6	3	4	4	0	0	0	0	2	0	0	.000
1915	17	11	.607	2.29	43	29	14	259.2	220	64	130	3	4	1	1	85	14	0	.165
1916	17	12	.586	2.76	49	31	13	283.2	278	99	120	1	4	3	2	93	18	0	.194
1917	9	13	.409	2.99	42	23	9	207.2	191	93	84	1	3	4	1	67	14	0	.209
1918 STL A	8	6	.571	3.48	19	17	10	124	126	61	48	1	0	0	0	46	6	0	.130
1919	11	14	.440	3.60	34	25	14	222.1	220	92	83	1	1	2	2	72	11	1	.153
1920 2 teams			STL	A	(2G 0–1)		PHI	N	(18G 2–6)										
" total	2	7	.222	4.64	20	6	1	75.2	87	32	35	0	2	1	2	24	4	0	.167
9 yrs.	65	68	.489	3.14	242	135	61	1277	1210	494	550	7	15	13	11	412	69	1	.167

Phil Gallivan

GALLIVAN, PHILIP JOSEPH   BR TR 6' 180 lbs.
B. May 29, 1907, Seattle, Wash.   D. Nov. 24, 1969, St. Paul, Minn.

	W	L	PCT	ERA	G	GS	CG	IP	H	BB	SO	ShO	W	L	SV	AB	H	HR	BA
1931 BKN N	0	1	.000	5.28	6	1	0	15.1	23	7	1	0	0	0	0	3	0	0	.000
1932 CHI A	1	3	.250	7.56	13	3	1	33.1	49	24	12	0	1	0	0	8	3	0	.375
1934	4	7	.364	5.61	35	7	3	126.2	155	64	55	0	4	4	1	40	9	0	.225
3 yrs.	5	11	.313	5.95	54	11	4	175.1	227	95	68	0	5	4	1	51	12	0	.235

Lou Galvin

GALVIN, LOUIS
Brother of Pud Galvin.
B. Haverhill, Mass.   D. June 17, 1895, Mass.

	W	L	PCT	ERA	G	GS	CG	IP	H	BB	SO	ShO	W	L	SV	AB	H	HR	BA
1884 STP U	0	2	.000	2.88	3	3	3	25	21	10	17	0	0	0	0	9	2	0	.222

Pud Galvin

GALVIN, JAMES FRANCIS (Gentle Jeems, The Little Steam Engine)
BR TR 5'8" 190 lbs.
Brother of Lou Galvin.
B. Dec. 25, 1855, St. Louis, Mo.   D. Mar. 7, 1902, Pittsburgh, Pa.
Manager 1885.
Hall of Fame 1965.

	W	L	PCT	ERA	G	GS	CG	IP	H	BB	SO	ShO	W	L	SV	AB	H	HR	BA
1879 BUF N	37	27	.578	2.28	66	66	65	593	585	31	136	6	0	0	0	265	66	0	.249
1880	20	37	.351	2.71	58	54	46	458.2	528	32	128	5	0	2	0	241	51	0	.212
1881	29	24	.547	2.37	56	53	48	474	546	46	136	5	0	0	0	236	50	0	.212
1882	28	23	.549	3.17	52	51	48	445.1	476	40	162	3	0	0	0	206	44	0	.214
1883	46	29	.613	2.72	76	75	72	656.1	676	50	279	5	1	0	0	322	71	1	.220
1884	46	22	.676	1.99	72	72	71	636.1	566	63	369	12	0	0	0	274	49	0	.179
1885 2 teams			BUF	N	(33G 13–19)		PIT	AA	(11G 3–7)										
" total	16	26	.381	3.99	44	43	40	372.1	453	44	120	3	0	0	1	160	27	1	.169
1886 PIT AA	29	21	.580	2.67	50	50	49	434.2	457	75	72	2	0	0	0	194	49	0	.253
1887 PIT N	28	21	.571	3.29	49	48	47	440.2	490	67	76	3	1	0	0	193	41	2	.212
1888	23	25	.479	2.63	50	50	49	437.1	446	53	107	6	0	0	0	175	25	1	.143
1889	23	16	.590	4.17	41	40	38	341	392	78	77	4	0	0	0	150	28	0	.187
1890 PIT P	12	13	.480	4.35	26	25	23	217	275	49	35	1	1	0	0	97	20	0	.206
1891 PIT N	14	13	.519	2.88	33	31	23	246.2	256	62	46	2	0	0	0	109	18	0	.165
1892 2 teams			PIT	N	(12G 5–7)		STL	N	(12G 5–7)										
" total	10	13	.435	2.92	24	24	20	188	206	54	56	0	0	0	0	80	7	0	.088
14 yrs.	361	310	.538	2.87	697	682	639	5941.1	6352	744	1799	57	3	2	1	*			
	6th	2nd				2nd		2nd				8th							

Bob Gamble

GAMBLE, ROBERT J.   5'10" 155 lbs.
B. Feb., 1867, Hazleton, Pa.   Deceased.

	W	L	PCT	ERA	G	GS	CG	IP	H	BB	SO	ShO	W	L	SV	AB	H	HR	BA
1888 PHI AA	0	1	.000	8.00	1	1	1	9	10	3	2	0	0	0	0	3	1	0	.333

Bill Gannon

GANNON, WILLIAM G.
B. New Haven, Conn.   D. Apr. 26, 1927, Ft. Worth, Tex.

	W	L	PCT	ERA	G	GS	CG	IP	H	BB	SO	ShO	W	L	SV	AB	H	HR	BA
1898 STL N	0	1	.000	11.00	1	1	1	9	13	5	2	0	0	0	0	*			

Gussie Gannon

GANNON, JAMES EDWARD   BL TL 5'11" 154 lbs.
B. Nov. 26, 1873, Erie, Pa.   D. Apr. 12, 1966, Erie, Pa.

	W	L	PCT	ERA	G	GS	CG	IP	H	BB	SO	ShO	W	L	SV	AB	H	HR	BA
1895 PIT N	0	0	–	1.80	1	0	0	5	7	2	0	0	0	0	0	2	0	0	.000

Jim Gantner

GANTNER, JAMES ELMER   BL TR 6' 180 lbs.
B. Jan. 5, 1953, Fond du Lac, Wis.

	W	L	PCT	ERA	G	GS	CG	IP	H	BB	SO	ShO	W	L	SV	AB	H	HR	BA
1979 MIL A	0	0	–	0.00	1	0	0	1	2	0	0	0	0	0	0	*			

John Ganzel

GANZEL, JOHN HENRY   BR TR 6'½" 195 lbs.
Brother of Charlie Ganzel.
B. Apr. 7, 1874, Kalamazoo, Mich.   D. Jan. 14, 1959, Orlando, Fla.
Manager 1908, 1915.

	W	L	PCT	ERA	G	GS	CG	IP	H	BB	SO	ShO	W	L	SV	AB	H	HR	BA
1898 PIT N	0	0	–	0.00	1	0	0	0	0	0	0	0	0	0	0	*			

	W	L	PCT	ERA	G	GS	CG	IP	H	BB	SO	ShO	Relief Pitching W	L	SV	Batting AB	H	HR	BA

Bob Garber

GARBER, ROBERT MITCHELL
B. Sept. 10, 1928, Hunker, Pa.
BR TR 6'1" 190 lbs.

	W	L	PCT	ERA	G	GS	CG	IP	H	BB	SO	ShO	W	L	SV	AB	H	HR	BA
1956 PIT N	0	0	—	2.25	2	0	0	4	3	3	3	0	0	0	0	0	0	0	—

Gene Garber

GARBER, HENRY EUGENE
B. Nov. 13, 1947, Elizabethtown, Pa.
BR TR 5'10" 175 lbs.

	W	L	PCT	ERA	G	GS	CG	IP	H	BB	SO	ShO	W	L	SV	AB	H	HR	BA
1969 PIT N	0	0	—	5.40	2	1	0	5	6	1	3	0	0	0	0	1	0	0	.000
1970	0	3	.000	5.32	14	0	0	22	22	10	7	0	0	3	0	3	2	0	.667
1971	0	0	—	7.50	4	0	0	6	7	3	3	0	0	0	0	1	0	0	.000
1973 KC A	9	9	.500	4.24	48	8	4	153	164	49	60	0	7	4	11	0	0	0	—
1974 2 teams			KC	A (17G 1–2)			PHI	N	(34G 4–0)											
" total	5	2	.714	3.08	51	0	0	76	74	44	41	0	5	2	5	3	0	0	.000
1975 PHI N	10	12	.455	3.60	71	0	0	110	103	27	69	0	10	12	14	12	2	0	.167
1976	9	3	.750	2.82	59	0	0	92.2	78	30	92	0	9	3	11	7	2	0	.286
1977	8	6	.571	2.36	64	0	0	103	82	23	78	0	8	6	19	10	0	0	.000
1978 2 teams			PHI	N (22G 2–1)			ATL	N	(43G 4–4)											
" total	6	5	.545	2.15	65	0	0	117	84	24	85	0	6	5	25	14	1	0	.071
1979 ATL N	6	16	.273	4.33	68	0	0	106	121	24	56	0	6	16¹	25	10	3	0	.300
1980	5	5	.500	3.84	68	0	0	82	95	24	51	0	5	5	7	2	1	0	.500
1981	4	6	.400	2.59	35	0	0	59	49	20	34	0	4	6	2	5	0	0	.000
1982	8	10	.444	2.34	69	0	0	119.1	100	32	68	0	8	10	30	15	2	0	.133
1983	4	5	.444	4.60	43	0	0	60.2	72	23	45	0	4	5	9	3	0	0	.000
1984	3	6	.333	3.06	62	0	0	106	103	24	55	0	3	6	11	14	2	0	.143
15 yrs.	77	88	.467	3.31	723	9	4	1217.2	1160	358	747	0	75	83	169	100	15	0	.150
LEAGUE CHAMPIONSHIP SERIES																			
1976 PHI N	0	1	.000	13.50	2	0	0	.2	2	1	0	0	0	1	0	0	0	0	—
1977	1	1	.500	3.38	3	0	0	5.1	4	0	3	0	1	1	0	0	0	0	—
1982 ATL N	0	1	.000	8.10	2	0	0	3.1	4	1	3	0	0	1	0	1	0	0	.000
3 yrs.	1	3	.250	5.79	7	0	0	9.1	10	2	6	0	1	3	0	1	0	0	.000

Mike Garcia

GARCIA, EDWARD MIGUEL (The Big Bear)
B. Nov. 17, 1923, San Gabriel, Calif.
BR TR 6'1" 195 lbs.

	W	L	PCT	ERA	G	GS	CG	IP	H	BB	SO	ShO	W	L	SV	AB	H	HR	BA
1948 CLE A	0	0	—	0.00	1	0	0	2	3	0	1	0	0	0	0	0	0	0	.235
1949	14	5	.737	2.36	41	20	8	175.2	154	60	94	5	3	1	2	51	12	1	.235
1950	11	11	.500	3.86	33	29	11	184	191	74	76	0	0	0	0	65	13	0	.200
1951	20	13	.606	3.15	47	30	15	254	239	82	118	1	3	2	6	85	18	1	.212
1952	22	11	.667	2.37	46	36	19	292.1	284	87	143	6	1	2	4	95	13	0	.137
1953	18	9	.667	3.25	38	35	21	271.2	260	81	134	3	0	0	0	96	24	0	.250
1954	19	8	.704	2.64	45	34	13	258.2	220	71	129	5	0	0	5	81	11	0	.136
1955	11	13	.458	4.02	38	31	6	210.2	230	56	120	2	0	2	3	69	15	0	.217
1956	11	12	.478	3.78	35	30	8	197.2	213	74	119	4	0	1	0	61	7	0	.115
1957	12	8	.600	3.75	38	27	9	211.1	221	73	110	1	1	0	0	75	12	0	.160
1958	1	0	1.000	9.00	6	1	0	8	15	7	2	0	1	0	0	1	0	0	.000
1959	3	6	.333	4.00	29	8	1	72	72	31	49	0	3	3	1	14	1	0	.071
1960 CHI A	0	0	—	4.58	15	0	0	17.2	23	10	8	0	0	0	2	3	1	0	.333
1961 WAS A	0	1	.000	4.74	16	0	0	19	23	13	14	0	0	1	0	0	0	0	—
14 yrs.	142	97	.594	3.27	428	281	111	2174.2	2148	719	1117	27	12	13	23	696	127	2	.182
WORLD SERIES																			
1954 CLE A	0	1	.000	5.40	2	1	0	5	6	4	4	0	0	0	0	0	0	0	—

Ralph Garcia

GARCIA, RALPH
B. Dec. 14, 1948, Los Angeles, Calif.
BR TR 6' 195 lbs.

	W	L	PCT	ERA	G	GS	CG	IP	H	BB	SO	ShO	W	L	SV	AB	H	HR	BA
1972 SD N	0	0	—	1.80	3	0	0	5	4	3	3	0	0	0	0	0	0	0	—
1974	0	0	—	6.30	8	0	0	10	15	7	9	0	0	0	0	0	0	0	—
2 yrs.	0	0	—	4.80	11	0	0	15	19	10	12	0	0	0	0	0	0	0	—

Ramon Garcia

GARCIA, RAMON GARCIA
B. Mar. 5, 1924, La Esperanza, Cuba
BR TR 5'10" 170 lbs.

	W	L	PCT	ERA	G	GS	CG	IP	H	BB	SO	ShO	W	L	SV	AB	H	HR	BA
1948 WAS A	0	0	—	17.18	4	0	0	3.2	11	4	2	0	0	0	0	1	1	0	1.000

Art Gardiner

GARDINER, ARTHUR CECIL
B. Dec. 26, 1899, Brooklyn, N. Y.   D. Oct. 21, 1954, Copiage, N. Y.
BR TR

	W	L	PCT	ERA	G	GS	CG	IP	H	BB	SO	ShO	W	L	SV	AB	H	HR	BA
1923 PHI N	0	0	—	0.00	1	0	0	1	1	1	0	0	0	0	0	0	0	0	—

Fred Gardner

GARDNER, FREDERICK
B. Palmer, Mass.   Deceased.

	W	L	PCT	ERA	G	GS	CG	IP	H	BB	SO	ShO	W	L	SV	AB	H	HR	BA
1887 BAL AA	0	1	.000	11.08	3	2	1	13	23	10	3	0	0	0	0	11	3	0	.273

Gid Gardner

GARDNER, FRANKLIN W.
B. Aug. 1, 1859, Cambridge, Mass.   D. Aug. 1, 1914, Cambridge, Mass.

	W	L	PCT	ERA	G	GS	CG	IP	H	BB	SO	ShO	W	L	SV	AB	H	HR	BA
1879 TRO N	0	2	.000	5.79	2	2	2	14	27	0	3	0	0	0	0	6	1	0	.167
1880 CLE N	1	8	.111	2.57	9	9	9	77	80	20	21	0	0	0	0	32	6	0	.188
1883 BAL AA	1	0	1.000	5.14	2	0	0	7	9	1	2	0	1	0	0	161	44	1	.273
1884 C-P U	0	1	.000	6.00	1	1	0	6	10	1	4	0	0	0	0	326	76	2	.233
1885 BAL AA	0	1	.000	10.00	1	1	1	9	16	6	3	0	0	0	0	170	37	0	.218
5 yrs.	2	12	.143	3.90	15	13	12	113	142	28	33	0	1	0	0	*			

Glenn Gardner

GARDNER, MILES GLENN
B. Jan. 25, 1916, Burnsville, N. C.   D. July 7, 1964, Rochester, N. Y.
BR TR 5'11" 180 lbs.

	W	L	PCT	ERA	G	GS	CG	IP	H	BB	SO	ShO	W	L	SV	AB	H	HR	BA
1945 STL N	3	1	.750	3.29	17	4	2	54.2	50	27	20	1	1	1	1	21	7	0	.333

Harry Gardner

GARDNER, HARRY RAY
B. July 1, 1887, Quincy, Mich.   D. Aug. 2, 1961, Canby, Ore.
TR

	W	L	PCT	ERA	G	GS	CG	IP	H	BB	SO	ShO	W	L	SV	AB	H	HR	BA
1911 PIT N	1	1	.500	4.50	13	3	2	42	39	20	24	0	0	0	2	14	3	0	.214
1912	0	0	—	0.00	1	0	0	.1	3	1	0	0	0	0	0	0	0	0	—
2 yrs.	1	1	.500	4.46	14	3	2	42.1	42	21	24	0	0	0	2	14	3	0	.214

	W	L	PCT	ERA	G	GS	CG	IP	H	BB	SO	ShO	Relief Pitching W	L	SV	BATTING AB	H	HR	BA

Jim Gardner

GARDNER, JAMES ANDERSON
B. Oct. 4, 1874, Pittsburgh, Pa.   D. Apr. 24, 1905, Pittsburgh, Pa.   TR

	W	L	PCT	ERA	G	GS	CG	IP	H	BB	SO	ShO	W	L	SV	AB	H	HR	BA
1895 PIT N	8	2	.800	2.64	11	10	8	85.1	99	27	31	0	0	0	0	34	9	0	.265
1897	5	5	.500	5.19	14	11	8	95.1	115	32	35	0	1	0	0	76	12	1	.158
1898	10	13	.435	3.21	25	22	19	185.1	179	48	41	1	0	1	0	91	14	0	.154
1899	1	0	1.000	7.52	6	3	0	32.1	52	13	2	0	0	0	0	13	3	0	.231
1902 CHI N	1	2	.333	2.88	3	3	2	25	23	10	6	0	0	0	0	10	2	0	.200
5 yrs.	25	22	.532	3.85	59	49	37	423.1	468	130	115	1	1	1	0	224	40	1	.179

Rob Gardner

GARDNER, RICHARD FRANK
B. Dec. 19, 1944, Binghamton, N. Y.   BR TL 6'1"   176 lbs.

	W	L	PCT	ERA	G	GS	CG	IP	H	BB	SO	ShO	W	L	SV	AB	H	HR	BA
1965 NY N	0	2	.000	3.21	5	4	0	28	23	7	19	0	0	0	0	7	0	0	.000
1966	4	8	.333	5.12	41	17	3	133.2	147	64	74	0	1	1	1	41	7	0	.171
1967 CHI N	0	2	.000	3.98	18	5	0	31.2	33	6	16	0	0	0	0	6	0	0	.000
1968 CLE A	0	0	—	6.75	5	0	0	2.2	5	2	6	0	0	0	0	0	0	0	—
1970 NY A	1	0	1.000	5.14	1	1	0	7	8	4	6	0	0	0	0	3	1	0	.333
1971 2 teams	OAK	A	(4G 0–0)		NY	A	(2G 0–0)												
" total	0	0	—	2.53	6	1	0	10.2	11	5	7	0	0	0	0	2	1	0	.500
1972 NY A	8	5	.615	3.06	20	14	1	97	91	28	58	0	0	1	0	28	3	0	.107
1973 2 teams	MIL	A	(10G 1–1)		OAK	A	(3G 0–0)												
" total	1	1	.500	8.10	13	0	0	20	27	17	7	0	1	1	1	0	0	0	—
8 yrs.	14	18	.438	4.35	109	42	4	330.2	345	133	193	0	2	3	2	87	12	0	.138

Wes Gardner

GARDNER, WESLEY
B. Apr. 29, 1961, Benton, Ark.   BR TR 6'4"   195 lbs.

	W	L	PCT	ERA	G	GS	CG	IP	H	BB	SO	ShO	W	L	SV	AB	H	HR	BA
1984 NY N	1	1	.500	6.39	21	0	0	25.1	34	8	19	0	1	1	1	1	0	0	.000

Bill Garfield

GARFIELD, WILLIAM MILTON
B. Oct. 26, 1867, Sheffield, Ohio   D. Dec. 16, 1941, Danville, Ill.   BR TR 5'11½"   160 lbs.

	W	L	PCT	ERA	G	GS	CG	IP	H	BB	SO	ShO	W	L	SV	AB	H	HR	BA
1889 PIT N	0	2	.000	7.76	4	2	2	29	45	17	4	0	0	0	0	13	0	0	.000
1890 CLE N	1	7	.125	4.89	9	8	7	70	91	35	16	0	0	0	0	26	4	0	.154
2 yrs.	1	9	.100	5.73	13	10	9	99	136	52	20	0	0	0	0	39	4	0	.103

Bob Garibaldi

GARIBALDI, ROBERT ROY
B. Mar. 3, 1942, Stockton, Calif.   BL TR 6'4"   210 lbs.

	W	L	PCT	ERA	G	GS	CG	IP	H	BB	SO	ShO	W	L	SV	AB	H	HR	BA
1962 SF N	0	0	—	5.11	9	0	0	12.1	13	5	9	0	0	0	1	1	0	0	.000
1963	0	1	.000	1.13	4	0	0	8	8	4	4	0	0	1	1	1	0	0	.000
1966	0	0	—	0.00	1	0	0	1	1	0	0	0	0	0	0	0	0	0	—
1969	0	1	.000	1.80	1	1	0	5	6	2	1	0	0	0	0	2	0	0	.000
4 yrs.	0	2	.000	3.08	15	1	0	26.1	28	11	14	0	0	1	2	4	0	0	.000

Lou Garland

GARLAND, LOUIS LYMAN
B. July 16, 1905, Archie, Mo.   BR TR 6'2½"   200 lbs.

	W	L	PCT	ERA	G	GS	CG	IP	H	BB	SO	ShO	W	L	SV	AB	H	HR	BA
1931 CHI A	0	2	.000	10.26	7	2	0	16.2	30	14	4	0	0	2	0	3	0	0	.000

Wayne Garland

GARLAND, MARCUS WAYNE
B. Oct. 26, 1950, Nashville, Tenn.   BR TR 6'   195 lbs.

	W	L	PCT	ERA	G	GS	CG	IP	H	BB	SO	ShO	W	L	SV	AB	H	HR	BA
1973 BAL A	0	1	.000	3.94	4	1	0	16	14	7	10	0	0	0	0	0	0	0	—
1974	5	5	.500	2.97	20	6	0	91	68	26	40	0	3	1	1	0	0	0	—
1975	2	5	.286	3.71	29	1	0	87.1	80	31	46	0	2	5	4	0	0	0	—
1976	20	7	.741	2.68	38	25	14	232	224	64	113	4	4	0	1	0	0	0	—
1977 CLE A	13	19	.406	3.59	38	38	21	283	281	88	118	1	0	0	0	0	0	0	—
1978	2	3	.400	7.89	6	6	0	29.2	43	16	13	0	0	0	0	0	0	0	—
1979	4	10	.286	5.21	18	14	2	95	120	34	40	0	1	1	0	0	0	0	—
1980	6	9	.400	4.62	25	20	4	150	163	48	55	1	0	0	0	0	0	0	—
1981	3	7	.300	5.79	12	10	2	56	89	14	15	1	0	0	0	0	0	0	—
9 yrs.	55	66	.455	3.89	190	121	43	1040	1082	328	450	7	10	7	6	0	0	0	—

LEAGUE CHAMPIONSHIP SERIES

	W	L	PCT	ERA	G	GS	CG	IP	H	BB	SO	ShO	W	L	SV	AB	H	HR	BA
1974 BAL A	0	0	—	0.00	1	0	0	.2	1	1	1	0	0	0	0	0	0	0	—

Mike Garman

GARMAN, MICHAEL DOUGLAS
B. Sept. 16, 1949, Caldwell, Ida.   BR TR 6'3"   195 lbs.

	W	L	PCT	ERA	G	GS	CG	IP	H	BB	SO	ShO	W	L	SV	AB	H	HR	BA
1969 BOS A	1	0	1.000	4.38	2	2	0	12.1	13	10	10	0	0	0	0	5	2	0	.400
1971	1	1	.500	3.79	3	3	0	19	15	9	6	0	0	0	0	6	2	0	.333
1972	0	1	.000	12.00	3	1	0	3	4	2	1	0	0	0	0	0	0	0	—
1973	0	0	—	5.32	12	0	0	22	32	15	9	0	0	0	0	0	0	0	—
1974 STL N	7	2	.778	2.63	64	0	0	82	66	27	45	0	7	2	6	10	1	0	.100
1975	3	8	.273	2.39	66	0	0	79	73	48	48	0	3	8	10	0	0	0	.000
1976 CHI N	2	4	.333	4.97	47	2	0	76	79	35	37	0	2	2	1	7	0	0	.000
1977 LA N	4	4	.500	2.71	49	0	0	63	60	22	29	0	4	4	12	7	0	0	.000
1978 2 teams	LA	N	(10G 0–1)		MON	N	(47G 4–6)												
" total	4	7	.364	4.40	57	0	0	77.2	69	34	28	0	4	7	13	5	0	0	.000
9 yrs.	22	27	.449	3.63	303	8	0	434	411	202	213	0	20	23	42	42	5	0	.119

LEAGUE CHAMPIONSHIP SERIES

	W	L	PCT	ERA	G	GS	CG	IP	H	BB	SO	ShO	W	L	SV	AB	H	HR	BA
1977 LA N	0	0	—	0.00	2	0	0	1.1	0	1	1	0	0	0	1	0	0	0	—

WORLD SERIES

	W	L	PCT	ERA	G	GS	CG	IP	H	BB	SO	ShO	W	L	SV	AB	H	HR	BA
1977 LA N	0	0	—	0.00	2	0	0	4	2	1	3	0	0	0	0	0	0	0	—

Willie Garoni

GARONI, WILLIAM
B. July 28, 1877, Fort Lee, N. J.   D. Sept. 9, 1914, Fort Lee, N. J.   BR TR 6'1"   165 lbs.

	W	L	PCT	ERA	G	GS	CG	IP	H	BB	SO	ShO	W	L	SV	AB	H	HR	BA
1899 NY N	0	1	.000	4.50	3	1	1	10	12	2	2	0	0	0	0	4	0	0	.000

Scott Garrelts

GARRELTS, SCOTT WILLIAM
B. Oct. 30, 1961, Urbana, Ill.   BR TR 6'4"   200 lbs.

	W	L	PCT	ERA	G	GS	CG	IP	H	BB	SO	ShO	W	L	SV	AB	H	HR	BA
1982 SF N	0	0	—	13.50	1	0	0	2	3	2	4	0	0	0	0	0	0	0	—
1983	2	2	.500	2.52	5	5	1	35.2	33	19	16	1	0	0	0	9	2	0	.222

	W	L	PCT	ERA	G	GS	CG	IP	H	BB	SO	ShO	Relief Pitching W	L	SV	Batting AB	H	HR	BA

Scott Garrelts continued

	W	L	PCT	ERA	G	GS	CG	IP	H	BB	SO	ShO	W	L	SV	AB	H	HR	BA
1984	2	3	.400	5.65	21	3	0	43	45	34	32	0	2	3	0	10	1	0	.100
3 yrs.	4	5	.444	4.46	27	8	1	80.2	81	55	52	1	2	3	0	19	3	0	.158

Clarence Garrett

GARRETT, CLARENCE RAYMOND (Laz)
B. Mar. 6, 1891, Reader, W. Va.   D. Feb. 11, 1977, Moundsville, W. Va.
BR TR 6'5½" 185 lbs.

	W	L	PCT	ERA	G	GS	CG	IP	H	BB	SO	ShO	W	L	SV	AB	H	HR	BA
1915 CLE A	2	2	.500	2.31	4	4	2	23.1	19	6	5	0	0	0	0	8	0	0	.000

Greg Garrett

GARRETT, GREGORY
B. Mar. 12, 1948, Newhall, Calif.
BB TL 6' 200 lbs.

	W	L	PCT	ERA	G	GS	CG	IP	H	BB	SO	ShO	W	L	SV	AB	H	HR	BA
1970 CAL A	5	6	.455	2.64	32	7	0	75	48	44	53	0	4	0	0	15	1	0	.067
1971 CIN N	0	1	.000	1.00	2	1	0	9	7	10	2	0	0	1	0	3	1	0	.333
2 yrs.	5	7	.417	2.46	34	8	0	84	55	54	55	0	4	3	0	18	2	0	.111

Cliff Garrison

GARRISON, CLIFFORD WILLIAM
B. Aug. 13, 1905, Belmont, Okla.
BR TR 6' 195 lbs.

	W	L	PCT	ERA	G	GS	CG	IP	H	BB	SO	ShO	W	L	SV	AB	H	HR	BA
1928 BOS A	0	0	-	7.88	6	0	0	16	22	6	0	0	0	0	0	3	0	0	.000

Jim Garry

GARRY, JAMES THOMAS
B. Sept. 21, 1869, Great Barrington, Mass.   D. Jan. 15, 1917, Pittsfield, Mass.

	W	L	PCT	ERA	G	GS	CG	IP	H	BB	SO	ShO	W	L	SV	AB	H	HR	BA
1893 BOS N	0	1	.000	63.00	1	0	0	1	5	4	2	0	0	1	0	1	0	0	.000

Ned Garver

GARVER, NED FRANKLIN
B. Dec. 25, 1925, Ney, Ohio
BR TR 5'10½" 180 lbs.

	W	L	PCT	ERA	G	GS	CG	IP	H	BB	SO	ShO	W	L	SV	AB	H	HR	BA
1948 STL A	7	11	.389	3.41	38	24	7	198	200	95	75	0	1	0	5	66	19	1	.288
1949	12	17	.414	3.98	41	32	16	223.2	245	102	70	1	3	0	3	75	14	0	.187
1950	13	18	.419	3.39	37	31	22	260	264	108	85	2	1	2	0	91	26	1	.286
1951	20	12	.625	3.73	33	30	24	246	237	96	84	1	2	1	0	95	29	1	.305
1952 2 teams			.444		STL	A	(21G 7-10)	DET	A	(1G 1-0)									
" total	8	10	.444	3.60	22	22	8	157.2	139	58	63	2	0	0	0	51	9	0	.176
1953 DET A	11	11	.500	4.45	30	26	13	198.1	228	66	69	0	1	0	1	72	11	1	.153
1954	14	11	.560	2.81	35	32	16	246.1	216	62	93	3	0	0	1	79	13	0	.165
1955	12	16	.429	3.98	33	32	16	230.2	251	67	83	1	0	0	0	76	17	1	.224
1956	0	2	.000	4.08	6	3	1	17.2	15	13	6	0	0	0	0	5	0	0	.000
1957 KC A	6	13	.316	3.84	24	23	6	145.1	120	55	61	1	0	0	0	44	8	0	.182
1958	12	11	.522	4.03	31	28	10	201	192	66	72	3	0	0	1	69	12	0	.174
1959	10	13	.435	3.71	32	30	9	201.1	214	42	61	2	0	0	1	71	20	2	.282
1960	4	9	.308	3.83	28	15	5	122.1	110	35	50	2	0	0	0	27	2	0	.074
1961 LA A	0	3	.000	5.59	12	2	0	29	40	16	9	0	0	1	0	6	0	0	.000
14 yrs.	129	157	.451	3.73	402	330	153	2477.1	2471	881	881	18	8	4	12	827	180	7	.218

Jerry Garvin

GARVIN, THEODORE JARED
B. Oct. 21, 1955, Oakland, Calif.
BL TL 6'3" 195 lbs.

	W	L	PCT	ERA	G	GS	CG	IP	H	BB	SO	ShO	W	L	SV	AB	H	HR	BA
1977 TOR A	10	18	.357	4.19	34	34	12	245	247	85	127	1	0	0	0	0	0	0	-
1978	4	12	.250	5.54	26	22	3	144.2	189	48	67	0	0	0	0	0	0	0	-
1979	0	1	.000	2.74	8	1	0	23	15	10	14	0	0	1	0	0	0	0	-
1980	4	7	.364	2.28	61	0	0	83	70	27	52	0	4	7	8	0	0	0	-
1981	1	2	.333	3.40	35	4	0	53	46	23	25	0	1	1	0	0	0	0	-
1982	1	1	.500	7.25	32	4	0	58.1	81	26	35	0	1	1	0	0	0	0	-
6 yrs.	20	41	.328	4.42	196	65	15	607	648	219	320	1	6	10	8	0	0	0	-

Ned Garvin

GARVIN, VIRGIL LEE
B. Jan. 1, 1874, Navasota, Tex.   D. June 16, 1908, Fresno, Calif.
TR 6'3½" 160 lbs.

	W	L	PCT	ERA	G	GS	CG	IP	H	BB	SO	ShO	W	L	SV	AB	H	HR	BA
1896 PHI N	0	1	.000	7.62	2	1	1	13	19	7	4	0	0	0	0	6	0	0	.000
1899 CHI N	9	13	.409	2.85	24	23	22	199	202	42	69	4	0	0	0	71	11	0	.155
1900	10	18	.357	2.41	30	28	25	246.1	225	63	107	1	0	1	0	91	14	0	.154
1901 MIL A	7	20	.259	3.46	37	27	22	257.1	258	90	122	1	0	0	2	93	10	0	.108
1902 2 teams					CHI	A	(23G 10-10)	BKN	N	(2G 1-1)									
" total	11	11	.500	2.09	25	21	18	193.1	184	47	62	3	1	0	0	66	10	0	.152
1903 BKN N	15	18	.455	3.08	38	34	30	298	277	84	154	2	0	1	2	106	8	0	.075
1904 2 teams					BKN	N	(23G 5-15)	NY	A	(2G 0-1)									
" total	5	16	.238	1.72	25	24	16	193.2	155	80	94	2	0	0	0	67	8	0	.119
7 yrs.	57	97	.370	2.72	181	158	134	1400.2	1320	413	612	13	1	2	4	500	61	0	.122

Harry Gaspar

GASPAR, HARRY LAMBERT
B. Apr. 28, 1883, Kingsley, Iowa   D. May 14, 1940, Orange, Calif.
BR TR 6' 180 lbs.

	W	L	PCT	ERA	G	GS	CG	IP	H	BB	SO	ShO	W	L	SV	AB	H	HR	BA
1909 CIN N	18	11	.621	2.01	44	29	19	260	228	57	65	4	2	2	2	82	10	0	.122
1910	15	17	.469	2.59	48	31	16	275	257	75	74	4	1	1	5	87	10	0	.115
1911	10	17	.370	3.30	44	32	11	253.2	272	69	76	2	2	2	3	85	13	0	.153
1912	1	3	.250	4.17	7	6	2	38.2	38	16	13	1	0	1	0	12	3	0	.250
4 yrs.	44	48	.478	2.69	143	98	48	825.1	795	217	228	11	5	6	10	266	36	0	.135

Charlie Gassaway

GASSAWAY, CHARLES CASON (Sheriff)
B. Aug. 12, 1918, Gassaway, Tenn.
BL TL 6'2½" 210 lbs.

	W	L	PCT	ERA	G	GS	CG	IP	H	BB	SO	ShO	W	L	SV	AB	H	HR	BA
1944 CHI N	0	1	.000	7.71	2	2	0	11.2	20	10	7	0	0	0	0	4	1	0	.250
1945 PHI A	4	7	.364	3.74	24	11	4	118	114	55	50	0	0	0	0	39	6	0	.154
1946 CLE A	1	1	.500	3.91	13	6	0	50.2	54	26	23	0	0	0	0	15	1	0	.067
3 yrs.	5	9	.357	4.04	39	19	4	180.1	188	91	80	0	0	0	0	58	8	0	.138

Milt Gaston

GASTON, NATHANIEL MILTON
Brother of Alex Gaston.
B. Jan. 27, 1896, Ridgefield Park, N. J.
BR TR 6'1" 185 lbs.
BB 1933

	W	L	PCT	ERA	G	GS	CG	IP	H	BB	SO	ShO	W	L	SV	AB	H	HR	BA
1924 NY A	5	3	.625	4.50	29	2	0	86	92	44	24	0	5	1	1	27	6	0	.222
1925 STL A	15	14	.517	4.41	42	30	16	238.2	284	101	84	0	3	3	1	80	21	1	.263
1926	10	18	.357	4.33	32	28	14	214.1	227	101	39	1	0	2	0	78	13	1	.167
1927	13	17	.433	5.00	37	30	21	254	275	100	77	0	0	2	1	96	25	3	.260

	W	L	PCT	ERA	G	GS	CG	IP	H	BB	SO	ShO	Relief Pitching W	L	SV	BATTING AB	H	HR	BA

Milt Gaston continued

	W	L	PCT	ERA	G	GS	CG	IP	H	BB	SO	ShO	W	L	SV	AB	H	HR	BA
1928 WAS A	6	12	.333	5.51	28	22	8	148.2	179	53	45	3	0	1	0	49	7	0	.143
1929 BOS A	12	19	.387	3.73	39	29	20	243.2	265	81	83	1	2	3	2	78	15	1	.192
1930	13	20	.394	3.92	38	34	20	273	272	98	99	2	0	1	2	98	20	0	.204
1931	2	13	.133	4.46	23	18	4	119	137	41	33	0	0	0	0	38	6	0	.158
1932 CHI A	7	17	.292	4.00	28	25	7	166.2	183	73	44	1	0	1	1	60	14	0	.233
1933	8	12	.400	4.85	30	25	7	167	177	60	39	1	0	0	0	52	8	0	.154
1934	6	19	.240	5.85	29	28	10	194	247	84	48	1	0	0	0	68	10	0	.147
11 yrs.	97	164	.372	4.55	355	271	127	2105	2338	836	615	10	10	14	8	724	145	6	.200

Welcome Gaston

GASTON, WELCOME THORNBURG   TL
B. Dec. 19, 1872, Guernsey County, Ohio   D. Dec. 13, 1944, Columbus, Ohio

	W	L	PCT	ERA	G	GS	CG	IP	H	BB	SO	ShO	W	L	SV	AB	H	HR	BA
1898 BKN N	1	1	.500	2.81	2	2	2	16	17	9	0	0	0	0	0	8	1	0	.125
1899	0	0	—	3.00	1	0	0	3	3	4	0	0	0	0	0	1	1	0	1.000
2 yrs.	1	1	.500	2.84	3	2	2	19	20	13	0	0	0	0	0	9	2	0	.222

Hank Gastright

GASTRIGHT, HENRY CARL   BR TR 6'2"   190 lbs.
Born Henry Carl Gastreich.
B. Mar. 29, 1865, Covington, Ky.   D. Oct. 9, 1937, Cold Springs, Ky.

	W	L	PCT	ERA	G	GS	CG	IP	H	BB	SO	ShO	W	L	SV	AB	H	HR	BA
1889 COL AA	10	16	.385	4.57	32	26	21	222.2	255	104	115	0	0	0	0	94	17	0	.181
1890	30	14	.682	2.94	48	45	41	401.1	312	135	199	4	3	0	0	169	36	0	.213
1891	12	19	.387	3.78	35	33	28	283.2	280	136	109	1	0	1	0	117	23	0	.197
1892 WAS N	3	3	.500	5.08	11	7	6	79.2	94	38	32	0	0	0	0	29	4	0	.138
1893 2 teams		PIT	N	(9G 3–1)		BOS	N	(19G 12–4)											
" total	15	5	.750	5.44	28	23	19	215	253	115	39	0	2	0	0	92	14	0	.152
1894 BKN N	2	6	.250	6.39	16	8	6	93	135	55	20	1	0	2	2	41	7	0	.171
1896 CIN N	0	0	—	4.50	1	0	0	6	8	1	0	0	0	0	0	2	0	0	.000
7 yrs.	72	63	.533	4.20	171	142	121	1301.1	1337	584	514	6	5	4	2	544	101	0	.186

Aubrey Gatewood

GATEWOOD, AUBREY LEE   BR TR 6'1"   170 lbs.
B. Nov. 17, 1938, Little Rock, Ark.

	W	L	PCT	ERA	G	GS	CG	IP	H	BB	SO	ShO	W	L	SV	AB	H	HR	BA
1963 LA A	1	1	.500	1.50	4	3	1	24	12	16	13	0	0	0	0	8	0	0	.000
1964	3	3	.500	2.24	15	7	0	60.1	59	12	25	0	1	1	0	20	2	0	.100
1965 CAL A	4	5	.444	3.42	46	3	0	92	91	37	37	0	4	3	0	14	3	0	.214
1970 ATL N	0	0	—	4.50	3	0	0	2	4	2	0	0	0	0	0	0	0	0	—
4 yrs.	8	9	.471	2.78	68	13	1	178.1	166	67	75	0	5	4	0	42	5	0	.119

Chippy Gaw

GAW, GEORGE JOSEPH   BR TR 5'11"   180 lbs.
B. Mar. 13, 1892, Auburndale, Mass.   D. May 26, 1968, Boston, Mass.

	W	L	PCT	ERA	G	GS	CG	IP	H	BB	SO	ShO	W	L	SV	AB	H	HR	BA
1920 CHI N	1	1	.500	4.85	6	1	0	13	16	3	4	0	1	0	0	4	1	0	.250

Dale Gear

GEAR, DALE DUDLEY   BR TR 5'11"   165 lbs.
B. Feb. 2, 1872, Lone Elm, Kans.   D. Sept. 23, 1951, Topeka, Kans.

	W	L	PCT	ERA	G	GS	CG	IP	H	BB	SO	ShO	W	L	SV	AB	H	HR	BA
1896 CLE N	0	2	.000	5.48	3	2	2	23	35	6	6	0	0	0	0	15	6	0	.400
1901 WAS A	4	11	.267	4.03	24	16	14	163	199	22	35	1	1	1	0	199	47	0	.236
2 yrs.	4	13	.235	4.21	27	18	16	186	234	28	41	1	1	1	0	*			

Dinty Gearin

GEARIN, DENNIS JOHN   BL TL 5'4"   148 lbs.
B. Oct. 15, 1897, Providence, R. I.   D. Mar. 11, 1959, Providence, R. I.

	W	L	PCT	ERA	G	GS	CG	IP	H	BB	SO	ShO	W	L	SV	AB	H	HR	BA
1923 NY N	1	1	.500	3.38	6	2	1	24	23	10	9	0	1	0	0	7	2	0	.286
1924 2 teams		NY	N	(6G 1–2)		BOS	N	(1G 0–1)											
" total	1	3	.250	4.03	7	4	2	29	33	18	4	0	1	0	0	9	3	0	.333
2 yrs.	2	4	.333	3.74	13	6	3	53	56	28	13	0	1	1	0	16	5	0	.313

Bob Geary

GEARY, ROBERT NORTON (Speed)   BR TR 5'11"   168 lbs.
B. May 10, 1891, Cincinnati, Ohio   D. Jan. 3, 1980, Cincinnati, Ohio

	W	L	PCT	ERA	G	GS	CG	IP	H	BB	SO	ShO	W	L	SV	AB	H	HR	BA
1918 PHI A	2	5	.286	2.69	16	7	6	87	94	31	22	2	0	0	4	27	4	0	.148
1919	0	3	.000	4.73	9	2	1	32.1	32	18	9	0	0	1	0	10	5	0	.500
1921 CIN N	1	1	.500	4.34	10	1	0	29	38	2	10	0	0	1	0	8	2	0	.250
3 yrs.	3	9	.250	3.46	35	10	7	148.1	164	51	41	2	0	2	4	45	11	0	.244

Bob Gebhard

GEBHARD, ROBERT HENRY   BR TR 6'2"   210 lbs.
B. Jan. 3, 1943, Lamberton, Minn.

	W	L	PCT	ERA	G	GS	CG	IP	H	BB	SO	ShO	W	L	SV	AB	H	HR	BA
1971 MIN A	1	2	.333	3.00	17	0	0	18	17	11	13	0	1	2	0	0	0	0	—
1972	0	1	.000	8.57	13	0	0	21	36	13	13	0	0	1	1	0	0	0	—
1974 MON N	0	0	—	4.50	1	0	0	2	5	0	0	0	0	0	0	0	0	0	—
3 yrs.	1	3	.250	5.93	31	0	0	41	58	24	26	0	1	3	1	0	0	0	—

Pete Gebrian

GEBRIAN, PETER (Gabe)   BR TR 6'   170 lbs.
B. Aug. 10, 1923, Bayonne, N. J.

	W	L	PCT	ERA	G	GS	CG	IP	H	BB	SO	ShO	W	L	SV	AB	H	HR	BA
1947 CHI A	2	3	.400	4.48	27	4	0	66.1	61	33	17	0	2	0	5	13	0	0	.000

Jim Geddes

GEDDES, JAMES LEE   BR TR 6'2"   200 lbs.
B. Mar. 23, 1949, Columbus, Ohio

	W	L	PCT	ERA	G	GS	CG	IP	H	BB	SO	ShO	W	L	SV	AB	H	HR	BA
1972 CHI A	0	0	—	6.97	5	1	0	10.1	12	10	3	0	0	0	0	1	0	0	.000
1973	0	0	—	2.87	6	1	0	15.2	14	14	7	0	0	0	0	0	0	0	—
2 yrs.	0	0	—	4.50	11	2	0	26	26	24	10	0	0	0	0	1	0	0	.000

Joe Gedeon

GEDEON, ELMER JOSEPH   BR TR 6'   167 lbs.
B. Dec. 5, 1893, Sacramento, Calif.   D. May 19, 1941, San Francisco, Calif.

	W	L	PCT	ERA	G	GS	CG	IP	H	BB	SO	ShO	W	L	SV	AB	H	HR	BA
1913 WAS A	0	0	—	0.00	1	0	0	0	0	0	0	0	0	0	1	*			

	W	L	PCT	ERA	G	GS	CG	IP	H	BB	SO	ShO	Relief Pitching W	L	SV	BATTING AB	H	HR	BA

Johnny Gee

GEE, JOHN ALEXANDER (Whiz)
B. Dec. 7, 1915, Syracuse, N. Y.   BL TL 6'9"   225 lbs.

	W	L	PCT	ERA	G	GS	CG	IP	H	BB	SO	ShO	W	L	SV	AB	H	HR	BA
1939 PIT N	1	2	.333	4.12	3	3	1	19.2	20	10	16	0	0	0	0	6	0	0	.000
1941	0	2	.000	6.14	3	2	0	7.1	10	5	2	0	0	0	0	3	1	0	.333
1943	4	4	.500	4.28	15	10	2	82	89	27	18	0	2	0	0	26	3	0	.115
1944 2 teams			PIT N (4G 0–0)		NY		N	(4G 0–0)											
" total	0	0	–	4.96	8	0	0	16.1	25	5	6	0	0	0	0	2	1	0	.500
1945 NY N	0	0	–	9.00	2	0	0	3	5	2	1	0	0	0	1	1	0	0	.000
1946	2	4	.333	3.99	13	6	1	47.1	60	15	22	0	0	0	1	13	3	0	.231
6 yrs.	7	12	.368	4.41	44	21	4	175.2	209	64	65	0	2	0	1	51	8	0	.157

Billy Geer

GEER, WILLIAM HENRY
Also known as Harrison Harrelson.
B. Aug. 13, 1849, Syracuse, N. Y.   D. Jan. 5, 1922, Syracuse, N. Y.   TR 5'8"   160 lbs.

	W	L	PCT	ERA	G	GS	CG	IP	H	BB	SO	ShO	W	L	SV	AB	H	HR	BA
1884 BKN AA	0	0	–	12.60	2	0	0	5	14	3	1	0	0	0	0	*			

Henry Gehring

GEHRING, HENRY
B. Jan. 24, 1881, St. Paul, Minn.   D. Apr. 18, 1912, Kansas City, Mo.   BR TR

	W	L	PCT	ERA	G	GS	CG	IP	H	BB	SO	ShO	W	L	SV	AB	H	HR	BA
1907 WAS A	3	7	.300	3.31	15	9	8	87	92	14	31	2	0	1	0	44	9	1	.205
1908	0	1	.000	14.40	3	1	0	5	9	2	0	0	0	0	0	4	2	0	.500
2 yrs.	3	8	.273	3.91	18	10	8	92	101	16	31	2	0	1	0	48	11	1	.229

Paul Gehrman

GEHRMAN, PAUL ARTHUR (Dutch)
B. May 3, 1912, Mt. Angel, Ore.   BR TR 6'   195 lbs.

	W	L	PCT	ERA	G	GS	CG	IP	H	BB	SO	ShO	W	L	SV	AB	H	HR	BA
1937 CIN N	0	1	.000	2.89	2	1	0	9.1	11	5	1	0	0	0	0	3	0	0	.000

Gary Geiger

GEIGER, GARY MERLE
B. Apr. 4, 1937, Sand Ridge, Ill.   BL TR 6'   168 lbs.

	W	L	PCT	ERA	G	GS	CG	IP	H	BB	SO	ShO	W	L	SV	AB	H	HR	BA
1958 CLE A	0	0	–	9.00	1	0	0	2	2	1	2	0	0	0	0	*			

Bill Geis

GEIS, WILLIAM J
Brother of Emil Geis.
B. Mar. 20, 1867, Chicago, Ill.   D. Oct. 4, 1911, Chicago, Ill.   5'10"   164 lbs.

	W	L	PCT	ERA	G	GS	CG	IP	H	BB	SO	ShO	W	L	SV	AB	H	HR	BA
1884 DET N	0	0	–	14.40	1	0	0	5	14	2	1	0	0	0	0	*			

Emil Geis

GEIS, EMIL AUGUST
Brother of Bill Geis.
B. Chicago, Ill.   Deceased.   BR

	W	L	PCT	ERA	G	GS	CG	IP	H	BB	SO	ShO	W	L	SV	AB	H	HR	BA
1887 CHI N	0	1	.000	8.00	1	1	1	9	17	3	4	0	0	0	0	*			

Dave Geisel

GEISEL, JOHN DAVID
B. Jan. 18, 1955, Windber, Pa.   BL TL 6'3"   210 lbs.

	W	L	PCT	ERA	G	GS	CG	IP	H	BB	SO	ShO	W	L	SV	AB	H	HR	BA
1978 CHI N	1	0	1.000	4.30	18	1	0	23	27	11	15	0	0	0	0	3	0	0	.000
1979	0	0	–	0.60	7	0	0	15	10	4	5	0	0	0	0	1	0	0	.000
1981	2	0	1.000	0.56	11	2	0	16	11	10	7	0	2	0	0	3	0	0	.000
1982 TOR A	1	1	.500	3.98	16	2	0	31.2	32	17	22	0	1	0	0	0	0	0	–
1983	0	3	.000	4.64	47	0	0	52.1	47	31	50	0	0	3	5	0	0	0	–
1984 SEA A	1	1	.500	4.15	20	3	0	43.1	47	9	28	0	1	0	3	0	0	0	–
6 yrs.	5	5	.500	3.67	119	8	0	181.1	174	82	127	0	4	3	8	7	0	0	.000

Vern Geishert

GEISHERT, VERNON WILLIAM
B. Jan. 10, 1946, Madison, Wis.   BR TR 6'1"   215 lbs.

	W	L	PCT	ERA	G	GS	CG	IP	H	BB	SO	ShO	W	L	SV	AB	H	HR	BA
1969 CAL A	1	1	.500	4.65	11	3	0	31	32	7	18	0	1	0	1	9	0	0	.000

Emil Geiss

GEISS, EMIL MICHAEL
B. Mar., 1861, Villmer, Germany   Deceased.

	W	L	PCT	ERA	G	GS	CG	IP	H	BB	SO	ShO	W	L	SV	AB	H	HR	BA
1882 BAL AA	4	9	.308	4.80	13	13	10	95.2	84	22	10	1	0	0	0	41	6	0	.146

Charley Gelbert

GELBERT, CHARLES MAGNUS
B. Jan. 26, 1906, Scranton, Pa.   D. Jan. 13, 1967, Easton, Pa.   BR TR 5'11"   170 lbs.

	W	L	PCT	ERA	G	GS	CG	IP	H	BB	SO	ShO	W	L	SV	AB	H	HR	BA
1940 WAS A	0	0	–	9.00	2	0	0	4	5	3	1	0	0	0	0	*			

John Gelnar

GELNAR, JOHN RICHARD
B. June 25, 1943, Granite, Okla.   BR TR 6'2"   185 lbs.

	W	L	PCT	ERA	G	GS	CG	IP	H	BB	SO	ShO	W	L	SV	AB	H	HR	BA
1964 PIT N	0	0	–	5.00	7	0	0	9	11	1	4	0	0	0	0	0	0	0	–
1967	0	1	.000	8.05	10	1	0	19	30	11	5	0	0	0	0	6	1	0	.167
1969 SEA A	3	10	.231	3.31	39	10	0	108.2	103	26	69	0	2	3	3	19	1	0	.053
1970 MIL A	4	3	.571	4.21	53	0	0	92	98	23	48	0	4	3	4	12	1	0	.083
1971	0	0	–	18.00	2	0	0	1	3	1	0	0	0	0	0	0	0	0	–
5 yrs.	7	14	.333	4.19	111	11	0	229.2	245	62	126	0	6	6	7	37	3	0	.081

Joe Genewich

GENEWICH, JOSEPH EDWARD
B. Jan. 15, 1897, Elmira, N. Y.   BR TR 6'   174 lbs.

	W	L	PCT	ERA	G	GS	CG	IP	H	BB	SO	ShO	W	L	SV	AB	H	HR	BA
1922 BOS N	0	2	.000	7.04	6	2	1	23	29	11	4	0	0	0	0	6	1	0	.167
1923	13	14	.481	3.72	43	24	12	227.1	272	46	54	1	1	4	1	77	19	0	.247
1924	10	19	.345	5.21	34	27	11	200.1	258	65	43	2	2	1	1	60	10	0	.167
1925	12	10	.545	3.99	34	21	10	169	185	41	34	0	3	2	0	55	15	0	.273
1926	8	16	.333	3.88	37	26	12	216	239	63	59	2	1	1	2	67	11	0	.164
1927	11	8	.579	3.83	40	19	7	181	199	54	38	0	5	0	1	57	11	0	.193
1928 2 teams			BOS N (13G 3–7)		NY		N	(26G 11–4)											
" total	14	11	.560	3.50	39	29	14	239	224	72	52	2	1	1	3	90	14	0	.156
1929 NY N	5	7	.300	6.78	21	9	1	85	133	30	19	0	2	3	1	32	12	0	.375
1930	2	5	.286	5.61	18	9	3	61	71	20	13	0	0	0	3	20	3	0	.150
9 yrs.	73	92	.442	4.29	272	166	71	1401.2	1610	402	316	7	15	12	12	464	96	0	.207

	W	L	PCT	ERA	G	GS	CG	IP	H	BB	SO	ShO	Relief Pitching W	L	SV	BATTING AB	H	HR	BA

Gary Gentry

GENTRY, GARY EDWARD
B. Oct. 6, 1946, Phoenix, Ariz.　　　　　BR TR 6'　170 lbs.

	W	L	PCT	ERA	G	GS	CG	IP	H	BB	SO	ShO	W	L	SV	AB	H	HR	BA
1969 NY N	13	12	.520	3.43	35	35	6	233.2	192	81	154	3	0	0	0	74	6	0	.081
1970	9	9	.500	3.69	32	29	5	188	155	86	134	2	0	1	1	59	4	0	.068
1971	12	11	.522	3.24	32	31	8	203	167	82	155	3	0	0	0	68	5	0	.074
1972	7	10	.412	4.01	32	26	3	164	153	75	120	0	0	0	0	48	5	0	.104
1973 ATL N	4	6	.400	3.41	16	14	3	87	74	35	42	0	0	0	1	30	7	0	.233
1974	0	0	–	1.29	3	1	0	7	4	2	0	0	0	0	0	1	0	0	.000
1975	1	1	.500	4.95	7	2	0	20	25	8	10	0	1	0	0	5	0	0	.000
7 yrs.	46	49	.484	3.56	157	138	25	902.2	770	369	615	8	1	1	2	285	27	0	.095

LEAGUE CHAMPIONSHIP SERIES

	W	L	PCT	ERA	G	GS	CG	IP	H	BB	SO	ShO	W	L	SV	AB	H	HR	BA
1969 NY N	0	0	–	9.00	1	1	0	2	5	1	1	0	0	0	0	0	0	0	–

WORLD SERIES

	W	L	PCT	ERA	G	GS	CG	IP	H	BB	SO	ShO	W	L	SV	AB	H	HR	BA
1969 NY N	1	0	1.000	0.00	1	1	0	6.2	3	5	4	0	0	0	0	3	1	0	.333

Rufe Gentry

GENTRY, JAMES RUFFUS
B. May 18, 1918, Winston-Salem, N. C.　　　　BR TR 6'1"　180 lbs.

	W	L	PCT	ERA	G	GS	CG	IP	H	BB	SO	ShO	W	L	SV	AB	H	HR	BA
1943 DET A	1	3	.250	3.68	4	4	2	29.1	30	12	8	1	0	0	0	10	0	0	.000
1944	12	14	.462	4.24	37	30	10	203.2	211	108	68	4	2	0	0	76	15	0	.197
1946	0	0	–	15.00	2	0	0	3	4	7	1	0	0	0	0	0	0	0	–
1947	0	0	–	81.00	1	0	0	.1	1	2	0	0	0	0	0	0	0	0	–
1948	0	0	–	2.70	4	0	0	6.2	5	5	1	0	0	0	0	1	1	0	1.000
5 yrs.	13	17	.433	4.37	48	34	12	243	251	134	78	4	2	0	0	87	16	0	.184

Bill George

GEORGE, WILLIAM M.
B. Jan. 27, 1865, Bellaire, Ohio　　D. Aug. 23, 1916, Wheeling, W. Va.　BR TL 5'8"　165 lbs.

	W	L	PCT	ERA	G	GS	CG	IP	H	BB	SO	ShO	W	L	SV	AB	H	HR	BA
1887 NY N	3	9	.250	5.25	13	13	11	108	126	89	49	0	0	0	0	53	9	0	.170
1888	3	1	.750	1.34	4	3	3	33.2	18	11	26	1	1	0	0	39	9	1	.231
1889	0	0	–	7.88	2	0	0	8	11	3	3	0	0	0	0	32	8	0	.250
3 yrs.	6	10	.375	4.51	19	16	14	149.2	155	103	78	1	1	0	0	124	26	1	.210

Lefty George

GEORGE, THOMAS EDWARD
B. Aug. 13, 1886, Pittsburgh, Pa.　　D. May 13, 1955, York, Pa.　BL TL 6'　155 lbs.

	W	L	PCT	ERA	G	GS	CG	IP	H	BB	SO	ShO	W	L	SV	AB	H	HR	BA
1911 STL A	4	9	.308	4.18	27	13	6	116.1	136	51	23	1	2	1	0	44	5	0	.114
1912 CLE A	0	5	.000	4.87	11	5	2	44.1	69	18	18	0	0	0	0	14	3	0	.214
1915 CIN N	2	2	.500	3.86	5	3	2	28	24	8	11	1	1	0	0	12	4	0	.333
1918 BOS N	1	5	.167	2.32	9	5	4	54.1	56	21	22	0	0	1	0	22	2	0	.091
4 yrs.	7	21	.250	3.85	52	26	14	243	285	98	74	2	3	2	0	92	14	0	.152

Oscar Georgy

GEORGY, OSCAR JOHN
B. Nov. 25, 1916, New Orleans, La.　　　　BR TR 6'3½"　180 lbs.

	W	L	PCT	ERA	G	GS	CG	IP	H	BB	SO	ShO	W	L	SV	AB	H	HR	BA
1938 NY N	0	0	–	18.00	1	0	0	2	1	0	0	0	0	0	0	0	0	0	–

Jug Gerard

GERARD, DAVID FREDERICK
B. Aug. 6, 1936, New York, N. Y.　　　　BR TR 6'2"　205 lbs.

	W	L	PCT	ERA	G	GS	CG	IP	H	BB	SO	ShO	W	L	SV	AB	H	HR	BA
1962 CHI N	2	3	.400	4.91	39	0	0	58.2	67	28	30	0	2	3	3	8	3	0	.375

George Gerberman

GERBERMAN, GEORGE ALOIS
B. Mar. 8, 1942, El Campo, Tex.　　　　BR TR 6'　180 lbs.

	W	L	PCT	ERA	G	GS	CG	IP	H	BB	SO	ShO	W	L	SV	AB	H	HR	BA
1962 CHI N	0	0	–	1.69	1	1	0	5.1	3	5	1	0	0	0	0	1	0	0	.000

Allen Gerhardt

GERHARDT, ALLEN RUSSELL (Rusty)
B. Aug. 13, 1950, Baltimore, Md.　　　　BB TL 5'9"　175 lbs.

	W	L	PCT	ERA	G	GS	CG	IP	H	BB	SO	ShO	W	L	SV	AB	H	HR	BA
1974 SD N	2	1	.667	7.00	23	1	0	36	44	17	22	0	1	1	1	6	1	0	.167

Al Gerheauser

GERHEAUSER, ALBERT (Lefty)
B. June 24, 1917, St. Louis, Mo.　　D. May 28, 1972, Springfield, Mo.　BL TL 6'3"　190 lbs.

	W	L	PCT	ERA	G	GS	CG	IP	H	BB	SO	ShO	W	L	SV	AB	H	HR	BA
1943 PHI N	10	19	.345	3.60	38	31	11	215	222	70	92	2	1	1	0	71	8	0	.113
1944	8	16	.333	4.58	30	29	10	182.2	210	65	66	2	0	0	0	65	15	1	.231
1945 PIT N	5	10	.333	3.91	22	14	5	140.1	170	54	55	0	2	3	1	48	12	0	.250
1946	2	2	.500	3.97	35	3	1	81.2	92	25	32	0	2	1	0	21	7	0	.333
1948 STL A	0	3	.000	7.33	14	2	0	23.1	32	10	10	0	0	1	0	6	2	0	.333
5 yrs.	25	50	.333	4.13	149	79	27	643	726	224	255	4	5	6	1	211	44	1	.209

Steve Gerkin

GERKIN, STEPHEN PAUL (Splinter)
B. Nov. 19, 1915, Grafton, W. Va.　　D. Nov. 8, 1978, Bay Pines, Fla.　BR TR 6'1"　162 lbs.

	W	L	PCT	ERA	G	GS	CG	IP	H	BB	SO	ShO	W	L	SV	AB	H	HR	BA
1945 PHI A	0	12	.000	3.62	21	12	3	102	112	27	25	0	0	3	0	34	2	0	.059

Les German

GERMAN, LESTER STANLEY
B. Aug. 17, 1870, Mechanicsville, Md.　　D. June 10, 1934, Lanham, Md.　5'10"　143 lbs.

	W	L	PCT	ERA	G	GS	CG	IP	H	BB	SO	ShO	W	L	SV	AB	H	HR	BA
1890 B-B AA	5	11	.313	4.83	17	16	15	132.1	147	54	37	0	1	0	0	51	6	0	.118
1893 NY N	8	8	.500	4.14	20	18	14	152	162	70	35	0	1	1	0	74	23	0	.311
1894	9	8	.529	5.78	23	15	10	134	178	66	17	0	2	1	1	57	17	0	.298
1895	7	11	.389	5.96	23	18	16	178.1	243	78	36	0	0	2	0	111	29	2	.261
1896 2 teams							NY N (1G 0–0)		WAS N (28G 2–20)										
" total	2	20	.091	6.43	29	20	14	169.1	249	75	20	0	1	3	1	71	16	1	.225
1897 WAS N	3	5	.375	5.59	15	5	4	83.2	117	33	2	0	2	1	0	44	15	0	.341
6 yrs.	34	63	.351	5.49	129	92	73	849.2	1096	376	147	0	7	9	2	408	106	3	.260

Ed Gerner

GERNER, EDWIN FREDERICK (Lefty)
B. July 22, 1897, Philadelphia, Pa.　　D. May 15, 1970, Philadelphia, Pa.　BL TL 5'8½"　175 lbs.

	W	L	PCT	ERA	G	GS	CG	IP	H	BB	SO	ShO	W	L	SV	AB	H	HR	BA
1919 CIN N	1	0	1.000	3.18	5	1	0	17	22	3	2	0	0	0	0	6	1	0	.167

	W	L	PCT	ERA	G	GS	CG	IP	H	BB	SO	ShO	Relief Pitching W	L	SV	BATTING AB	H	HR	BA

Lefty Gervais

GERVAIS, LUCIEN EDWARD   BL TL 5'10"   165 lbs.
B. July 6, 1890, Grover, Wis.   D. Oct. 19, 1950, Olive View, Calif.

| 1913 BOS N | 0 | 1 | .000 | 5.74 | 5 | 2 | 1 | 15.2 | 18 | 4 | 1 | 0 | 0 | 0 | 0 | 5 | 0 | 0 | .000 |

Charlie Gessner

GESSNER, CHARLES J.
B. Philadelphia, Pa.   Deceased.

| 1886 PHI AA | 0 | 1 | .000 | 9.00 | 1 | 1 | 1 | 8 | 13 | 5 | 0 | 0 | 0 | 0 | 0 | 4 | 1 | 0 | .250 |

Al Gettel

GETTEL, ALLEN JONES   BR TR 6'3½"   200 lbs.
B. Sept. 17, 1917, Norfolk, Va.

1945 NY A	9	8	.529	3.90	27	17	9	154.2	141	53	67	0	0	0	3	57	16	0	.281
1946	6	7	.462	2.97	26	11	5	103	89	40	54	2	3	0	0	32	4	0	.125
1947 CLE A	11	10	.524	3.20	31	21	9	149	122	62	64	2	1	2	0	51	15	0	.294
1948 2 teams		CLE	A	(5G 0–1)	CHI	A	(22G 8–10)												
" total	8	11	.421	4.68	27	21	7	155.2	169	70	53	0	0	2	1	57	13	0	.228
1949 2 teams		CHI	A	(19G 2–5)	WAS	A	(16G 0–2)												
" total	2	7	.222	6.08	35	8	1	97.2	112	50	29	1	1	4	2	26	3	0	.115
1951 NY N	1	2	.333	4.87	30	1	0	57.1	52	25	36	0	1	2	0	12	1	0	.083
1955 STL N	1	0	1.000	9.00	8	0	0	17	26	10	7	0	1	0	0	6	3	0	.500
7 yrs.	38	45	.458	4.28	184	79	31	734.1	711	310	310	5	7	10	6	241	55	0	.228

Charlie Gettig

GETTIG, CHARLES HENRY
Also known as Charles Henry Gettinger.   Brother of Tom Gettinger.
B. Dec., 1870, Cumberland, Md.   Deceased.

1896 NY N	1	0	1.000	9.64	4	1	1	14	20	8	5	0	0	0	1	9	3	0	.333
1897	1	1	.500	5.21	3	2	2	19	23	9	7	0	0	0	0	75	15	0	.200
1898	6	3	.667	3.83	17	8	7	115	141	39	14	0	1	1	0	196	49	0	.250
1899	7	8	.467	4.43	18	15	12	128	161	54	25	0	0	0	0	97	24	0	.247
4 yrs.	15	12	.556	4.50	42	26	22	276	345	110	51	0	1	1	1	*			

Tom Gettinger

GETTINGER, THOMAS L   BL TL 5'10"   180 lbs.
Brother of Charlie Gettig.
B. 1870, Mobile, Ala.   Deceased.

| 1895 LOU N | 0 | 0 | – | 7.11 | 2 | 0 | 0 | 6.1 | 13 | 1 | 0 | 0 | 0 | 0 | 0 | * | | | |

Charlie Getzien

GETZIEN, CHARLES H. (Pretzels)   BR TR 6'   172 lbs.
B. Feb. 14, 1868, Chicago, Ill.   D. June 19, 1932, Chicago, Ill.

1884 DET N	5	12	.294	1.95	17	17	17	147.1	118	25	107	1	0	0	0	55	6	0	.109
1885	12	25	.324	3.03	37	37	37	330	360	92	110	1	0	0	0	137	29	0	.212
1886	30	11	.732	3.03	43	43	42	386.2	388	85	172	1	0	0	0	165	29	0	.176
1887	29	13	.690	3.73	43	42	41	366.2	373	106	135	2	1	0	0	156	29	1	.186
1888	19	25	.432	3.05	46	46	45	404	411	54	202	2	0	0	0	167	41	1	.246
1889 IND N	18	22	.450	4.54	45	44	36	349	395	100	139	0	0	0	1	139	25	2	.180
1890 BOS N	23	17	.575	3.19	40	40	39	350	342	82	140	4	0	0	0	147	34	2	.231
1891 2 teams		BOS	N	(11G 4–5)	CLE	N	(1G 0–1)												
" total	4	6	.400	4.22	12	10	8	98	124	27	33	0	0	0	0	45	7	1	.156
1892 STL N	1	8	.385	5.67	13	13	12	108	159	31	32	0	0	0	0	45	9	1	.200
9 yrs.	145	139	.511	3.46	296	292	277	2539.2	2670	602	1070	11	1	0	1	1056	209	8	.198

Rube Geyer

GEYER, JACOB BOWMAN   TR
B. Mar. 22, 1885, Allegheny, Pa. D. Oct. 12, 1962, Wahkon, Minn.

1910 STL N	0	1	.000	4.50	4	0	0	4	5	3	5	0	0	1	0	1	0	0	.000
1911	9	6	.600	3.27	29	11	7	148.2	141	56	46	1	3	2	0	57	13	0	.228
1912	7	14	.333	3.28	41	18	6	181	191	84	61	0	4	3	0	53	11	0	.208
1913	1	5	.167	5.26	30	4	2	78.2	83	38	21	0	0	2	1	22	2	0	.091
4 yrs.	17	26	.395	3.67	104	33	15	412.1	420	181	133	1	7	8	1	133	26	0	.195

Tony Ghelfi

GHELFI, ANTHONY PAUL   BR TR 6'1"   175 lbs.
B. Aug. 23, 1961, La Crosse, Wis.

| 1983 PHI N | 1 | 1 | .500 | 3.14 | 3 | 3 | 0 | 14.1 | 15 | 6 | 14 | 0 | 0 | 0 | 0 | 4 | 1 | 0 | .250 |

Bob Giallombardo

GIALLOMBARDO, ROBERT PAUL   BL TL 6'   175 lbs.
B. May 20, 1937, Brooklyn, N. Y.

| 1958 LA N | 1 | 1 | .500 | 3.76 | 6 | 5 | 0 | 26.1 | 29 | 15 | 14 | 0 | 0 | 0 | 0 | 6 | 1 | 0 | .167 |

Joe Giard

GIARD, JOSEPH OSCAR (Peco)   BL TL 5'10½" 170 lbs.
B. Oct. 7, 1898, Ware, Mass.   D. July 10, 1956, Worcester, Mass.

1925 STL A	10	5	.667	5.04	30	21	9	160.2	179	87	43	4	0	0	0	53	3	0	.057
1926	3	10	.231	7.00	22	16	2	90	113	67	18	0	0	1	0	29	8	0	.276
1927 NY A	0	0	–	8.00	16	0	0	27	38	19	10	0	0	0	0	7	2	0	.286
3 yrs.	13	15	.464	5.96	68	37	11	277.2	330	173	71	4	0	1	0	89	13	0	.146

Joe Gibbon

GIBBON, JOSEPH CHARLES   BR TL 6'4"   210 lbs.
B. Apr. 10, 1936, Hickory, Miss.   BB 1967-68

1960 PIT N	4	2	.667	4.03	27	9	0	80.1	87	31	60	0	3	0	0	19	4	0	.211
1961	13	10	.565	3.32	30	29	7	195.1	185	57	145	3	0	0	0	59	8	0	.136
1962	3	4	.429	3.63	19	8	0	57	53	24	26	0	1	1	0	17	3	0	.176
1963	5	12	.294	3.30	37	22	5	147.1	147	54	110	0	1	1	0	43	4	0	.093
1964	10	7	.588	3.68	28	24	3	146.2	145	54	97	0	1	0	0	47	12	0	.255
1965	4	9	.308	4.51	31	15	1	105.2	85	34	63	0	3	1	1	26	3	0	.115
1966 SF N	4	6	.400	3.67	37	10	1	81	86	16	48	0	1	3	1	15	3	0	.200
1967	6	2	.750	3.07	28	10	3	82	65	33	63	1	1	0	1	24	1	0	.042
1968	2	3	.333	1.58	29	0	0	40	33	19	22	0	1	2	1	1	0	0	.000
1969 2 teams		SF	N	(16G 1–3)	PIT	N	(35G 5–1)												
" total	6	4	.600	2.40	51	0	0	71.1	53	30	44	0	6	4	11	8	0	0	.000
1970 PIT N	0	1	.000	4.83	41	0	0	41	44	24	26	0	0	1	5	3	0	0	.000
1971 CIN N	5	6	.455	2.95	50	0	0	64	54	32	34	0	5	6	11	1	0	0	.000

	W	L	PCT	ERA	G	GS	CG	IP	H	BB	SO	ShO	Relief Pitching W	L	SV	BATTING AB	H	HR	BA

Joe Gibbon continued

1972 2 teams	CIN	N	(2G 0–0)		HOU	N	(9G 0–0)												
" total	0	0	–	11.74	11	0	0	7.2	16	6	5	0	0	0	0	0	0	0	–
13 yrs.	61	65	.484	3.52	419	127	20	1119.1	1053	414	743	4	23	19	32	263	38	0	.144

LEAGUE CHAMPIONSHIP SERIES

1970 PIT N	0	0	–	0.00	2	0	0	.1	1	0	1	0	0	0	0	0	0	0	–

WORLD SERIES

1960 PIT N	0	0	–	9.00	2	0	0	3	4	1	2	0	0	0	0	0	0	0	–

Bob Gibson

GIBSON, ROBERT (Hoot)
B. Nov. 9, 1935, Omaha, Neb.
Hall of Fame 1981.

BR TR 6'1" 189 lbs.

	W	L	PCT	ERA	G	GS	CG	IP	H	BB	SO	ShO	W	L	SV	AB	H	HR	BA
1959 STL N	3	5	.375	3.33	13	9	2	75.2	77	39	48	1	1	0	0	26	3	0	.115
1960	3	6	.333	5.61	27	12	2	86.2	97	48	69	0	1	0	0	28	5	0	.179
1961	13	12	.520	3.24	35	27	10	211.1	186	119	166	2	0	1	1	66	13	1	.197
1962	15	13	.536	2.85	32	30	15	233.2	174	95	208	5	1	0	1	76	20	2	.263
1963	18	9	.667	3.39	36	33	14	254.2	224	96	204	2	1	0	0	87	18	3	.207
1964	19	12	.613	3.01	40	36	17	287.1	250	86	245	2	1	1	1	96	15	0	.156
1965	20	12	.625	3.07	38	36	20	299	243	103	270	6	0	0	1	104	25	5	.240
1966	21	12	.636	2.44	35	35	20	280.1	210	78	225	5	0	0	0	100	20	1	.200
1967	13	7	.650	2.98	24	24	10	175.1	151	40	147	2	0	0	0	60	8	0	.133
1968	22	9	.710	1.12	34	34	28	304.2	198	62	268	13	0	0	0	94	16	0	.170
1969	20	13	.606	2.18	35	35	28	314	251	95	269	4	0	0	0	118	29	1	.246
1970	23	7	.767	3.12	34	34	23	294	262	88	274	3	0	0	0	109	33	2	.303
1971	16	13	.552	3.04	31	31	20	246	215	76	185	5	0	0	0	87	15	2	.172
1972	19	11	.633	2.46	34	34	23	278	226	88	208	4	0	0	0	103	20	5	.194
1973	12	10	.545	2.77	25	25	13	195	159	57	142	1	0	0	0	65	12	2	.185
1974	11	13	.458	3.83	33	33	9	240	236	104	129	1	0	0	0	81	17	0	.210
1975	3	10	.231	5.04	22	14	1	109	120	62	60	0	1	2	2	28	5	0	.179
17 yrs.	251	174	.591	2.91	528	482	255	3884.2	3279	1336	3117 8th	56	6	4	6	1328	274	24	.206

WORLD SERIES

	W	L	PCT	ERA	G	GS	CG	IP	H	BB	SO	ShO	W	L	SV	AB	H	HR	BA
1964 STL N	2	1	.667	3.00	3	3	2	27	23	8	31	0	0	0	0	9	2	0	.222
1967	3	0	1.000	1.00	3	3	3	27	14	5	26	1	0	0	0	11	1	1	.091
1968	2	1	.667	1.67	3	3	3	27	18	4	35	1	0	0	0	8	1	1	.125
3 yrs. 2nd	7	2	.778	1.89 6th	9 3rd	9 6th	8 9th	81	55	17	92 2nd	2 4th	0	0	0	28	4	2	.143

Bob Gibson

GIBSON, ROBERT LOUIS
B. June 19, 1957, Philadelphia, Pa.

BR TR 6' 195 lbs.

	W	L	PCT	ERA	G	GS	CG	IP	H	BB	SO	ShO	W	L	SV	AB	H	HR	BA
1983 MIL A	3	4	.429	3.90	27	7	0	80.2	71	46	46	0	1	2	2	0	0	0	–
1984	2	5	.286	4.96	18	9	1	69	61	47	54	1	0	0	0	0	0	0	–
2 yrs.	5	9	.357	4.39	45	16	1	149.2	132	93	100	1	1	2	2	0	0	0	–

Bob Gibson

GIBSON, ROBERT MURRAY
B. Aug. 20, 1869, Duncansville, Pa.   D. Dec. 19, 1949, Pittsburgh, Pa.

BR TR 6'3" 185 lbs.

1890 2 teams	CHI	N	(1G 1–0)		PIT	N	(3G 0–3)												
" total	1	3	.250	9.86	4	4	3	21	30	25	4	0	0	0	0	17	3	0	.176

Norwood Gibson

GIBSON, NORWOOD R.
B. Mar. 11, 1877, Peoria, Ill.   D. July 7, 1959, Peoria, Ill.

TR 5'10" 165 lbs.

	W	L	PCT	ERA	G	GS	CG	IP	H	BB	SO	ShO	W	L	SV	AB	H	HR	BA
1903 BOS A	13	9	.591	3.19	24	21	17	183.1	166	65	76	2	1	0	0	64	17	0	.266
1904	17	14	.548	2.21	33	32	29	273	216	81	112	1	0	0	0	92	6	0	.065
1905	4	7	.364	3.69	23	17	9	134	118	55	67	0	0	1	0	45	4	0	.089
1906	0	2	.000	5.30	5	2	1	18.2	25	7	3	0	0	0	0	5	1	0	.200
4 yrs.	34	32	.515	2.93	85	72	56	609	525	208	258	3	1	1	0	206	28	0	.136

Sam Gibson

GIBSON, SAMUEL BRAXTON
B. Aug. 5, 1899, King, N. C.   D. Jan. 31, 1983, High Point, N. C.

BL TR 6'2" 198 lbs.

	W	L	PCT	ERA	G	GS	CG	IP	H	BB	SO	ShO	W	L	SV	AB	H	HR	BA
1926 DET A	12	9	.571	3.48	35	24	16	196.1	199	75	61	2	1	0	2	72	18	0	.250
1927	11	12	.478	3.69	33	26	11	190.1	201	86	76	0	0	2	0	66	14	0	.212
1928	5	8	.385	5.42	20	18	5	119.2	155	52	29	1	0	0	0	42	12	0	.286
1930 NY A	0	1	.000	15.00	2	2	0	6	14	6	3	0	0	0	0	3	1	0	.333
1932 NY N	4	8	.333	4.85	41	5	1	81.2	107	30	39	1	2	5	3	19	5	0	.263
5 yrs.	32	38	.457	4.24	131	75	33	594	676	249	208	4	3	7	5	202	50	0	.248

George Gick

GICK, GEORGE EDWARD
B. Oct. 18, 1915, Dunnington, Ind.

BB TR 6' 190 lbs.

	W	L	PCT	ERA	G	GS	CG	IP	H	BB	SO	ShO	W	L	SV	AB	H	HR	BA
1937 CHI A	0	0	–	0.00	1	0	0	2	0	1	0	0	0	0	1	0	0	0	–
1938	0	0	–	0.00	1	0	0	1	0	0	1	0	0	0	0	0	0	0	–
2 yrs.	0	0	–	0.00	2	0	0	3	0	1	1	0	0	0	1	0	0	0	–

Jim Gideon

GIDEON, JAMES LESLIE
B. Sept. 26, 1953, Taylor, Tex.

BR TR 6'3" 190 lbs.

	W	L	PCT	ERA	G	GS	CG	IP	H	BB	SO	ShO	W	L	SV	AB	H	HR	BA
1975 TEX A	0	0	–	7.94	1	1	0	5.2	7	5	2	0	0	0	0	0	0	0	–

Floyd Giebell

GIEBELL, FLOYD GEORGE
B. Dec. 10, 1909, Pennsboro, W. Va.

BL TR 6'2½" 172 lbs.

	W	L	PCT	ERA	G	GS	CG	IP	H	BB	SO	ShO	W	L	SV	AB	H	HR	BA
1939 DET A	1	1	.500	2.93	9	0	0	15.1	19	12	9	0	1	1	0	2	0	0	.000
1940	2	0	1.000	1.00	2	2	2	18	14	4	11	1	0	0	0	6	0	0	.000
1941	0	0	–	6.03	17	2	0	34.1	45	26	10	0	0	0	0	6	2	0	.333
3 yrs.	3	1	.750	3.99	28	4	2	67.2	78	42	30	1	1	1	0	14	2	0	.143

	W	L	PCT	ERA	G	GS	CG	IP	H	BB	SO	ShO	Relief Pitching W	L	SV	BATTING AB	H	HR	BA

Paul Giel

GIEL, PAUL ROBERT
B. Sept. 29, 1932, Winona, Minn. — BR TR 5'11" 185 lbs.

	W	L	PCT	ERA	G	GS	CG	IP	H	BB	SO	ShO	W	L	SV	AB	H	HR	BA
1954 NY N	0	0	—	8.31	6	0	0	4.1	8	2	4	0	0	0	0	0	0	0	—
1955	4	4	.500	3.39	34	2	0	82.1	70	50	47	0	4	3	0	19	1	0	.053
1958 SF N	4	5	.444	4.70	29	9	0	92	89	55	55	0	2	0	0	27	2	0	.074
1959 PIT N	0	0	—	14.09	4	0	0	7.2	17	6	3	0	0	0	0	0	0	0	—
1960	2	0	1.000	5.73	16	0	0	33	35	15	21	0	2	0	0	7	0	0	.000
1961 2 teams		MIN	A	(12G 1–0)		KC	A	(1G 0–0)											
" total	1	0	1.000	12.00	13	0	0	21	30	20	15	0	1	0	0	2	1	0	.500
6 yrs.	11	9	.550	5.39	102	11	0	240.1	249	148	145	0	9	3	0	55	4	0	.073

Bob Giggie

GIGGIE, ROBERT THOMAS
B. Aug. 13, 1933, Dorchester, Mass. — BR TR 6'1" 200 lbs.

	W	L	PCT	ERA	G	GS	CG	IP	H	BB	SO	ShO	W	L	SV	AB	H	HR	BA
1959 MIL N	1	0	1.000	4.05	13	0	0	20	24	10	15	0	1	0	1	1	0	0	.000
1960 2 teams		MIL	N	(3G 0–0)		KC	A	(10G 1–0)											
" total	1	0	1.000	5.48	13	0	0	23	29	19	13	0	1	0	0	2	0	0	.000
1962 KC A	1	1	.500	6.28	4	2	0	14.1	17	3	4	0	0	0	0	4	0	0	.000
3 yrs.	3	1	.750	5.18	30	2	0	57.1	70	32	32	0	2	0	1	7	0	0	.000

Bill Gilbert

GILBERT, WILLIAM
B. Havre de Grace, Md. Deceased. — 6' 180 lbs.

	W	L	PCT	ERA	G	GS	CG	IP	H	BB	SO	ShO	W	L	SV	AB	H	HR	BA
1892 BAL N	0	1	.000	5.79	2	1	1	14	14	17	5	0	0	0	0	6	2	0	.333

Joe Gilbert

GILBERT, JOE DENNIS
B. Apr. 20, 1952, Jasper, Tex. — BR TL 6'1" 167 lbs.

	W	L	PCT	ERA	G	GS	CG	IP	H	BB	SO	ShO	W	L	SV	AB	H	HR	BA
1972 MON N	0	1	.000	8.45	22	0	0	33	41	18	25	0	0	1	0	3	0	0	.000
1973	1	2	.333	4.97	21	0	0	29	30	19	17	0	1	2	1	2	0	0	.000
2 yrs.	1	3	.250	6.82	43	0	0	62	71	37	42	0	1	3	1	5	0	0	.000

Bill Gilbreth

GILBRETH, WILLIAM FREEMAN
B. Sept. 3, 1947, Abilene, Tex. — BL TL 6' 180 lbs.

	W	L	PCT	ERA	G	GS	CG	IP	H	BB	SO	ShO	W	L	SV	AB	H	HR	BA
1971 DET A	2	1	.667	4.80	9	5	2	30	28	21	14	0	0	0	0	11	2	0	.182
1972	0	0	—	16.20	2	0	0	5	10	4	2	0	0	0	0	1	0	0	.000
1974 CAL A	0	0	—	13.50	3	0	0	1.1	2	1	0	0	0	0	0	0	0	0	—
3 yrs.	2	1	.667	6.69	14	5	2	36.1	40	26	16	0	0	0	0	12	2	0	.167

Bob Gilks

GILKS, ROBERT JAMES
B. July 2, 1867, Cincinnati, Ohio D. Aug. 20, 1944, Brunswick, Ga. — BR TR 5'8" 178 lbs.

	W	L	PCT	ERA	G	GS	CG	IP	H	BB	SO	ShO	W	L	SV	AB	H	HR	BA
1887 CLE AA	7	5	.583	3.08	13	13	12	108	104	42	28	1	0	0	0	83	26	0	.313
1888	0	2	.000	8.14	4	2	2	21	26	8	3	0	0	0	1	484	111	1	.229
1890 CLE N	2	2	.500	4.26	4	3	3	31.2	34	9	5	0	1	0	0	544	116	0	.213
3 yrs.	9	9	.500	3.98	21	18	17	160.2	164	59	36	1	1	0	1	*			

Ed Gill

GILL, EDWARD JAMES
B. Aug. 7, 1895, Somerville, Mass. — BR TR 5'10" 165 lbs.

	W	L	PCT	ERA	G	GS	CG	IP	H	BB	SO	ShO	W	L	SV	AB	H	HR	BA
1919 WAS A	1	1	.500	4.82	16	2	0	37.1	38	21	7	0	0	1	0	7	0	0	.000

George Gill

GILL, GEORGE LLOYD
B. Feb. 13, 1909, Catchings, Miss. — BR TR 6'1" 185 lbs.

	W	L	PCT	ERA	G	GS	CG	IP	H	BB	SO	ShO	W	L	SV	AB	H	HR	BA
1937 DET A	11	4	.733	4.51	31	10	4	127.2	146	42	40	1	7	1	1	50	7	0	.140
1938	12	9	.571	4.12	24	23	13	164	195	50	30	1	0	0	0	57	6	0	.105
1939 2 teams		DET	A	(3G 0–1)		STL	A	(27G 1–12)											
" total	1	13	.071	7.21	30	12	5	103.2	153	37	25	0	0	4	0	28	4	0	.143
3 yrs.	24	26	.480	5.05	85	45	22	395.1	494	129	95	2	7	5	1	135	17	0	.126

Haddie Gill

GILL, HAROLD EDMUND
B. Jan. 23, 1899, Brockton, Mass. D. Aug. 1, 1932, Brockton, Mass. — BL TL 5'10½" 145 lbs.

	W	L	PCT	ERA	G	GS	CG	IP	H	BB	SO	ShO	W	L	SV	AB	H	HR	BA
1923 CIN N	0	0	—	0.00	1	0	0	1	1	1	1	0	0	0	0	0	0	0	—

Claral Gillenwater

GILLENWATER, CLARAL LEWIS
B. May 20, 1900, Simes, Ind. D. Feb. 26, 1978, Pensacola, Fla. — BR TR 6' 187 lbs.

	W	L	PCT	ERA	G	GS	CG	IP	H	BB	SO	ShO	W	L	SV	AB	H	HR	BA
1923 CHI A	1	3	.250	5.48	5	3	1	21.1	28	6	2	1	1	1	0	6	0	0	.000

Bob Gillespie

GILLESPIE, ROBERT WILLIAM (Bunch)
B. Oct. 8, 1918, Columbus, Ohio — BR TR 6'4" 187 lbs.

	W	L	PCT	ERA	G	GS	CG	IP	H	BB	SO	ShO	W	L	SV	AB	H	HR	BA
1944 DET A	0	1	.000	6.55	7	0	0	11	7	12	4	0	0	1	0	2	0	0	.000
1947 CHI A	5	8	.385	4.73	25	17	1	118	133	53	36	0	0	0	0	33	2	0	.061
1948	0	4	.000	5.13	25	6	1	72	81	33	19	0	0	0	0	16	0	0	.000
1950 BOS A	0	0	—	20.25	1	0	0	1.1	2	4	0	0	0	0	0	0	0	0	—
4 yrs.	5	13	.278	5.07	58	23	2	202.1	223	102	59	0	0	1	0	51	2	0	.039

John Gillespie

GILLESPIE, JOHN PATRICK (Silent John)
B. Feb. 25, 1900, Oakland, Calif. D. Feb. 15, 1954, Vallejo, Calif. — BR TR 5'11½" 172 lbs.

	W	L	PCT	ERA	G	GS	CG	IP	H	BB	SO	ShO	W	L	SV	AB	H	HR	BA
1922 CIN N	3	3	.500	4.52	31	4	1	77.2	84	29	21	0	2	2	0	15	2	0	.133

Paul Gilliford

GILLIFORD, PAUL GANT (Gorilla)
B. Jan. 12, 1945, Bryn Mawr, Pa. — BR TL 5'11" 210 lbs.

	W	L	PCT	ERA	G	GS	CG	IP	H	BB	SO	ShO	W	L	SV	AB	H	HR	BA
1967 BAL A	0	0	—	12.00	2	0	0	3	6	1	2	0	0	0	0	0	0	0	—

Jack Gilligan

GILLIGAN, JOHN PATRICK
B. Oct. 18, 1884, Chicago, Ill. D. Nov. 19, 1980, Modesto, Calif. — BB TR 6' 190 lbs.

	W	L	PCT	ERA	G	GS	CG	IP	H	BB	SO	ShO	W	L	SV	AB	H	HR	BA
1909 STL A	1	2	.333	5.48	3	3	3	23	28	9	4	0	0	0	0	9	1	0	.111
1910	0	3	.000	3.66	9	5	2	39.1	37	28	10	0	0	1	0	15	3	0	.200
2 yrs.	1	5	.167	4.33	12	8	5	62.1	65	37	14	0	0	1	0	24	4	0	.167

	W	L	PCT	ERA	G	GS	CG	IP	H	BB	SO	ShO	Relief Pitching W	L	SV	BATTING AB	H	HR	BA

Frank Gilmore

GILMORE, FRANK T.
B. Apr. 27, 1864, Webster, Mass.   D. July 22, 1929, Hartford, Conn.   BR

	W	L	PCT	ERA	G	GS	CG	IP	H	BB	SO	ShO	W	L	SV	AB	H	HR	BA
1886 WAS N	4	4	.500	2.52	9	9	9	75	57	22	75	1	0	0	0	29	0	0	.000
1887	7	20	.259	3.87	28	27	27	234.2	247	92	114	1	0	0	0	93	6	0	.065
1888	1	9	.100	6.59	12	11	10	95.2	131	29	23	0	0	0	0	41	1	0	.024
3 yrs.	12	33	.267	4.26	49	47	46	405.1	435	143	212	2	0	0	0	163	7	0	.043

Len Gilmore

GILMORE, LEONARD PRESTON (Meow)
B. Nov. 3, 1917, Clinton, Ind.   BR TR 6'3"   175 lbs.

	W	L	PCT	ERA	G	GS	CG	IP	H	BB	SO	ShO	W	L	SV	AB	H	HR	BA
1944 PIT N	0	1	.000	7.88	1	1	1	8	13	0	0	0	0	0	0	2	0	0	.000

George Gilpatrick

GILPATRICK, GEORGE F.
B. Feb. 28, 1875, Holden, Mo.   D. Dec. 15, 1941, Kansas City, Mo.

	W	L	PCT	ERA	G	GS	CG	IP	H	BB	SO	ShO	W	L	SV	AB	H	HR	BA
1898 STL N	0	2	.000	6.94	7	3	1	35	42	19	12	0	0	0	0	16	2	0	.125

John Gilroy

GILROY, JOHN M.
B. Oct. 26, 1869, Washington, D. C.   D. Aug. 4, 1897, Norfolk, Va.

	W	L	PCT	ERA	G	GS	CG	IP	H	BB	SO	ShO	W	L	SV	AB	H	HR	BA
1895 WAS N	1	4	.200	6.53	8	4	2	41.1	63	24	2	0	0	1	0	29	7	0	.241
1896	0	0	–	0.00	1	0	0	2	0	1	0	0	0	0	0	1	0	0	.000
2 yrs.	1	4	.200	6.23	9	4	2	43.1	63	25	2	0	0	1	0	30	7	0	.233

Hal Gilson

GILSON, HAROLD (Lefty)
B. Feb. 9, 1942, Los Angeles, Calif.   BR TL 6'5"   195 lbs.

	W	L	PCT	ERA	G	GS	CG	IP	H	BB	SO	ShO	W	L	SV	AB	H	HR	BA
1968 2 teams	STL N (13G 0–2)				HOU N (2G 0–0)														
" total	0	2	.000	4.97	15	0	0	25.1	34	12	20	0	0	2	2	4	0	0	.000

Billy Ging

GING, WILLIAM JOSEPH
B. Nov. 7, 1872, Elmira, N. Y.   D. Sept. 14, 1950, Elmira, N. Y.   BR TR 5'10"   170 lbs.

	W	L	PCT	ERA	G	GS	CG	IP	H	BB	SO	ShO	W	L	SV	AB	H	HR	BA
1899 BOS N	1	0	1.000	1.13	1	1	1	8	5	1	2	0	0	0	0	2	0	0	.000

Joe Gingras

GINGRAS, JOSEPH JOHN ELZEAD
B. Jan. 10, 1894, New York, N. Y.   D. Sept. 6, 1947, Jersey City, N. J.   BR TR 6'2"   188 lbs.

	W	L	PCT	ERA	G	GS	CG	IP	H	BB	SO	ShO	W	L	SV	AB	H	HR	BA
1915 KC F	0	0	–	6.75	2	0	0	4	6	1	2	0	0	0	1	1	0	0	.000

Charlie Girard

GIRARD, CHARLES AUGUST
B. Dec. 16, 1884, Brooklyn, N. Y.   D. Aug. 6, 1936, Brooklyn, N. Y.   BR TR 5'10"   175 lbs.

	W	L	PCT	ERA	G	GS	CG	IP	H	BB	SO	ShO	W	L	SV	AB	H	HR	BA
1910 PHI N	0	2	.000	6.41	7	1	0	26.2	33	12	11	0	0	1	0	8	1	0	.125

Dave Giusti

GIUSTI, DAVID JOHN
B. Nov. 27, 1939, Seneca Falls, N. Y.   BR TR 5'11"   190 lbs.

	W	L	PCT	ERA	G	GS	CG	IP	H	BB	SO	ShO	W	L	SV	AB	H	HR	BA
1962 HOU N	2	3	.400	5.62	22	5	0	73.2	82	30	43	0	2	0	0	24	7	0	.292
1964	0	0	–	3.16	8	0	0	25.2	24	8	16	0	0	0	0	7	2	0	.286
1965	8	7	.533	4.32	38	13	4	131.1	132	46	92	1	4	3	3	35	6	1	.171
1966	15	14	.517	4.20	34	33	9	210	215	54	131	4	0	0	0	74	17	0	.230
1967	11	15	.423	4.18	37	33	8	221.2	231	58	157	1	0	1	1	84	13	3	.155
1968	11	14	.440	3.19	37	34	12	251	226	67	186	2	0	0	1	82	15	0	.183
1969 STL N	3	7	.300	3.60	22	12	2	100	96	37	62	1	0	0	0	25	5	0	.200
1970 PIT N	9	3	.750	3.06	66	1	0	103	98	39	85	0	9	3	26	16	3	0	.188
1971	5	6	.455	2.93	58	0	0	86	79	31	55	0	5	6	30	17	1	0	.059
1972	7	4	.636	1.93	54	0	0	74.2	59	20	54	0	7	4	22	10	0	0	.000
1973	9	2	.818	2.37	67	0	0	98.2	89	37	64	0	9	2	20	13	4	0	.308
1974	7	5	.583	3.31	64	2	0	106	101	40	53	0	6	5	12	9	1	0	.111
1975	5	4	.556	2.93	61	0	0	92	79	42	38	0	5	4	17	10	3	0	.300
1976	5	4	.556	4.32	40	0	0	58.1	59	27	24	0	5	4	6	4	0	0	.000
1977 2 teams	CHI N (20G 0–2)				OAK A (40G 3–3)														
" total	3	5	.375	3.92	60	0	0	85	84	34	43	0	3	5	7	2	0	0	.000
15 yrs.	100	93	.518	3.60	668	133	35	1717	1654	570	1103	9	55	37	145	412	77	4	.187

LEAGUE CHAMPIONSHIP SERIES

	W	L	PCT	ERA	G	GS	CG	IP	H	BB	SO	ShO	W	L	SV	AB	H	HR	BA
1970 PIT N	0	0	–	3.86	2	0	0	2.1	3	1	1	0	0	0	0	0	0	0	–
1971	0	0	–	0.00	4	0	0	5.1	1	2	3	0	0	0	3	1	0	0	.000
1972	0	1	.000	6.75	3	0	0	2.2	5	0	3	0	0	1	1	1	0	0	.000
1974	0	1	.000	21.60	3	0	0	3.1	13	5	1	0	0	1	0	0	0	0	–
1975	0	0	–	0.00	1	1	0	1.1	0	0	1	0	0	0	0	0	0	0	–
5 yrs.	0	2	.000	6.60	13	1	0	15	22	8	9	0	0	2	4	2	0	0	.000

WORLD SERIES

	W	L	PCT	ERA	G	GS	CG	IP	H	BB	SO	ShO	W	L	SV	AB	H	HR	BA
1971 PIT N	0	0	–	0.00	3	0	0	5.1	3	2	4	0	0	0	1	0	0	0	–

Fred Gladding

GLADDING, FRED EARL
B. June 28, 1936, Flat Rock, Mich.   BL TR 6'1"   220 lbs.

	W	L	PCT	ERA	G	GS	CG	IP	H	BB	SO	ShO	W	L	SV	AB	H	HR	BA
1961 DET A	1	0	1.000	3.31	8	0	0	16.1	18	11	11	0	1	0	0	3	0	0	.000
1962	0	0	–	0.00	6	0	0	5	3	2	4	0	0	0	0	0	0	0	–
1963	1	1	.500	1.98	22	0	0	27.1	19	14	24	0	1	1	7	1	0	0	.000
1964	7	4	.636	3.07	42	0	0	67.1	57	27	59	0	7	4	7	9	0	0	.000
1965	6	2	.750	2.83	46	0	0	70	63	29	43	0	6	2	5	7	0	0	.000
1966	5	0	1.000	3.28	51	0	0	74	62	29	57	0	5	0	2	2	0	0	.000
1967	6	4	.600	1.99	42	1	0	77	62	19	64	0	6	4	12	18	0	0	.000
1968 HOU N	0	0	–	14.54	7	0	0	4.1	8	3	2	0	0	0	2	0	0	0	–
1969	4	8	.333	4.19	57	0	0	73	83	27	40	0	4	8	29	10	1	0	.100
1970	7	4	.636	4.06	63	0	0	71	84	24	46	0	7	4	18	6	0	0	.000
1971	4	5	.444	2.12	48	0	0	51	51	22	17	0	4	5	12	2	0	0	.000
1972	5	6	.455	2.77	42	0	0	48.2	38	12	18	0	5	6	14	5	0	0	.000
1973	2	0	1.000	4.50	16	0	0	16	18	4	9	0	2	0	1	0	0	0	–
13 yrs.	48	34	.585	3.13	450	1	0	601	566	223	394	0	48	34	109	63	1	0	.016

	W	L	PCT	ERA	G	GS	CG	IP	H	BB	SO	ShO	Relief Pitching W	L	SV	BATTING AB	H	HR	BA

Fred Glade

GLADE, FREDERICK MONROE
B. Jan. 25, 1876, Dubuque, Iowa   D. Nov. 21, 1934, Grand Island, Neb.
BR TR 6'1"   200 lbs.

	W	L	PCT	ERA	G	GS	CG	IP	H	BB	SO	ShO	W	L	SV	AB	H	HR	BA
1902 CHI N	0	1	.000	9.00	1	1	1	8	13	3	3	0	0	0	0	3	1	0	.333
1904 STL A	18	15	.545	2.27	35	34	30	289	248	58	156	6	0	0	1	102	19	0	.186
1905	6	25	.194	2.81	32	32	28	275	257	58	127	2	0	0	0	98	9	0	.092
1906	15	14	.517	2.36	35	32	28	266.2	215	59	96	4	0	0	1	95	13	0	.137
1907	13	9	.591	2.67	24	22	18	202	187	45	71	2	0	1	0	73	15	0	.205
1908 NY A	0	4	.000	4.22	5	5	2	32	30	14	11	0	0	0	0	10	0	0	.000
6 yrs.	52	68	.433	2.62	132	126	107	1072.2	950	237	464	14	0	1	2	381	57	0	.150

John Glaiser

GLAISER, JOHN BURKE (Bert)
B. July 28, 1894, Yoakum, Tex.   D. Mar. 7, 1959, Houston, Tex.
BR TR 5'8"   165 lbs.

	W	L	PCT	ERA	G	GS	CG	IP	H	BB	SO	ShO	W	L	SV	AB	H	HR	BA
1920 DET A	0	0	–	6.35	9	1	0	17	23	8	3	0	0	0	1	3	0	0	.000

Tom Glass

GLASS, THOMAS JOSEPH
B. Apr. 29, 1898, Greensboro, N. C.
BR TR 6'3"   170 lbs.

	W	L	PCT	ERA	G	GS	CG	IP	H	BB	SO	ShO	W	L	SV	AB	H	HR	BA
1925 PHI A	1	0	1.000	5.40	2	0	0	5	9	0	2	0	1	0	0	2	0	0	.000

Jack Glasscock

GLASSCOCK, JOHN WESLEY (Pebbly Jack)
B. July 22, 1859, Wheeling, W. Va.   D. Feb. 24, 1947, Wheeling, W. Va.
Manager 1889.
BR TR 5'8"   160 lbs.

	W	L	PCT	ERA	G	GS	CG	IP	H	BB	SO	ShO	W	L	SV	AB	H	HR	BA
1884 CLE N	0	0	–	5.40	2	0	0	5	8	2	1	0	0	0	0	453	142	3	.313
1887 IND N	0	0	–	0.00	1	0	0	1	0	0	1	0	0	0	0	483	142	0	.294
1888	0	0	–	54.00	1	0	0	.1	1	2	1	0	0	0	0	442	119	1	.269
1889	0	0	–	0.00	1	0	0	.2	3	3	0	0	0	0	0	582	205	7	.352
4 yrs.	0	0	–	6.43	5	0	0	7	12	7	3	0	0	0	0				

Luke Glavenich

GLAVENICH, LUKE FRANK
B. Jan. 17, 1893, Jackson, Calif.   D. May 22, 1935, Stockton, Calif.
BR TR 5'9½"   189 lbs.

	W	L	PCT	ERA	G	GS	CG	IP	H	BB	SO	ShO	W	L	SV	AB	H	HR	BA
1913 CLE A	0	0	–	9.00	1	0	0	1	3	3	1	0	0	0	0	0	0	0	–

Ralph Glaze

GLAZE, DANIEL RALPH
B. Mar. 13, 1881, Denver, Colo.   D. Oct. 31, 1968, Atascadero, Calif.
BR TR 5'9"   165 lbs.

	W	L	PCT	ERA	G	GS	CG	IP	H	BB	SO	ShO	W	L	SV	AB	H	HR	BA
1906 BOS A	4	6	.400	3.59	19	10	7	123	110	32	56	0	0	0	0	55	10	0	.182
1907	8	13	.381	2.32	32	21	11	182.1	150	48	68	1	0	2	0	61	11	1	.180
1908	2	2	.500	3.38	10	3	2	34.2	43	5	13	0	0	1	0	13	1	0	.077
3 yrs.	14	21	.400	2.89	61	34	20	340	303	85	137	1	0	3	0	129	22	1	.171

Whitey Glazner

GLAZNER, CHARLES FRANKLIN
B. Sept. 17, 1893, Sycamore, Ala.
BR TR 5'9"   165 lbs.

	W	L	PCT	ERA	G	GS	CG	IP	H	BB	SO	ShO	W	L	SV	AB	H	HR	BA
1920 PIT N	0	0	–	3.12	2	0	0	8.2	9	2	1	0	0	0	0	3	0	0	.000
1921	14	5	.737	2.77	36	25	15	234	214	58	88	0	0	1	1	76	10	0	.132
1922	11	12	.478	4.38	34	26	10	193	238	52	77	1	1	0	1	65	16	1	.246
1923 2 teams			PIT	N	(7G 2–1)		PHI	N	(28G 7–14)										
" total	9	15	.375	4.47	35	27	13	191.1	224	74	59	3	0	1	2	65	13	1	.200
1924 PHI N	7	16	.304	5.92	35	24	8	156.2	210	63	41	2	2	2	0	51	8	0	.157
5 yrs.	41	48	.461	4.21	142	102	46	783.2	895	249	266	6	3	4	4	260	47	2	.181

Bill Gleason

GLEASON, WILLIAM
B. 1868, Cleveland, Ohio   D. Dec. 2, 1893, Cleveland, Ohio

	W	L	PCT	ERA	G	GS	CG	IP	H	BB	SO	ShO	W	L	SV	AB	H	HR	BA
1890 CLE P	0	1	.000	27.00	1	1	0	4	14	6	0	0	0	0	0	2	0	0	.000

Joe Gleason

GLEASON, JOSEPH PAUL
B. July 9, 1895, Phelps, N. Y.
BR TR 5'10½" 175 lbs.

	W	L	PCT	ERA	G	GS	CG	IP	H	BB	SO	ShO	W	L	SV	AB	H	HR	BA
1920 WAS A	0	0	–	13.50	3	0	0	8	14	6	2	0	0	0	0	2	0	0	.000
1922	2	3	.400	4.65	8	5	3	40.2	53	18	12	0	0	1	0	14	2	0	.143
2 yrs.	2	3	.400	6.10	11	5	3	48.2	67	24	14	0	0	1	0	16	2	0	.125

Kid Gleason

GLEASON, WILLIAM J.
Brother of Harry Gleason.
B. Oct. 26, 1866, Camden, N. J.   D. Jan. 2, 1933, Philadelphia, Pa.
Manager 1919-23.
BL TR 5'7"   158 lbs.

	W	L	PCT	ERA	G	GS	CG	IP	H	BB	SO	ShO	W	L	SV	AB	H	HR	BA
1888 PHI N	7	16	.304	2.84	24	23	23	199.2	199	53	89	1	0	0	0	83	17	0	.205
1889	9	15	.375	5.58	29	21	15	205	242	97	64	0	2	2	1	99	25	0	.253
1890	38	17	.691	2.63	60	55	54	506	479	167	222	6	1	0	2	224	47	0	.210
1891	24	22	.522	3.51	53	44	40	418	431	165	100	1	1	2	1	214	53	0	.248
1892 STL N	16	24	.400	3.33	47	45	43	400	389	151	133	2	1	0	0	233	50	3	.215
1893	21	25	.457	4.61	48	45	37	380.1	436	187	86	1	1	1	1	199	51	0	.256
1894 2 teams			STL	N	(8G 2–6)		BAL	N	(21G 15–5)										
" total	17	11	.607	4.85	29	28	25	230	299	65	44	0	0	0	0	114	37	0	.325
1895 BAL N	2	4	.333	6.97	9	5	3	50.1	77	21	6	0	1	2	1	421	130	0	.309
8 yrs.	134	134	.500	3.79	299	266	240	2389.1	2552	906	744	11	6	7	6				

Jerry Gleaton

GLEATON, JERRY DON
B. Sept. 14, 1957, Brownwood, Tex.
BL TL 6'3"   205 lbs.

	W	L	PCT	ERA	G	GS	CG	IP	H	BB	SO	ShO	W	L	SV	AB	H	HR	BA
1979 TEX A	0	1	.000	6.30	5	2	0	10	15	2	2	0	0	0	0	0	0	0	–
1980	0	0	–	2.57	5	0	0	7	5	4	2	0	0	0	0	0	0	0	–
1981 SEA A	4	7	.364	4.76	20	13	1	85	88	38	31	0	0	0	0	0	0	0	–
1982	0	0	–	13.50	3	0	0	4.2	7	2	1	0	0	0	0	0	0	0	–
1984 CHI A	1	2	.333	3.44	11	1	0	18.1	20	6	4	0	1	1	2	0	0	0	–
5 yrs.	5	10	.333	4.90	44	16	1	125	135	52	40	0	1	1	2	0	0	0	–

Martin Glendon

GLENDON, MARTIN J.
B. Feb. 8, 1877, Milwaukee, Wis.   D. Nov. 6, 1950, Chicago, Ill.
5'11"   180 lbs.

	W	L	PCT	ERA	G	GS	CG	IP	H	BB	SO	ShO	W	L	SV	AB	H	HR	BA
1902 CIN N	0	1	.000	12.00	1	1	0	3	5	4	0	0	0	0	0	0	0	0	.000
1903 CLE A	1	2	.333	0.98	3	3	3	27.2	20	7	9	0	0	0	0	8	0	0	.000
2 yrs.	1	3	.250	2.05	4	4	3	30.2	25	11	9	0	0	0	0	9	0	0	.000

	W	L	PCT	ERA	G	GS	CG	IP	H	BB	SO	ShO	Relief Pitching W	L	SV	BATTING AB	H	HR	BA

Bob Glenn

GLENN, BURDETTE
B. June 16, 1894, West Sunbury, Pa.   D. June 3, 1977, Richmond, Calif.

	W	L	PCT	ERA	G	GS	CG	IP	H	BB	SO	ShO	W	L	SV	AB	H	HR	BA
1920 STL N	0	0	–	0.00	2	0	0	2	2	2	0	0	0	0	0	0	0	0	–

Sal Gliatto

GLIATTO, SALVADOR MICHAEL
B. May 7, 1902, Chicago, Ill.   BB TR 5'8½"   150 lbs.

	W	L	PCT	ERA	G	GS	CG	IP	H	BB	SO	ShO	W	L	SV	AB	H	HR	BA
1930 CLE A	0	0	–	6.60	8	0	0	15	21	9	7	0	0	0	2	2	0	0	.000

Ed Glynn

GLYNN, EDWARD PAUL
B. June 3, 1953, New York, N. Y.   BR TL 6'2"   180 lbs.

	W	L	PCT	ERA	G	GS	CG	IP	H	BB	SO	ShO	W	L	SV	AB	H	HR	BA
1975 DET A	0	2	.000	4.30	3	1	0	14.2	11	8	8	0	0	1	0	0	0	0	–
1976	1	3	.250	6.00	5	4	1	24	22	20	17	0	0	0	0	0	0	0	–
1977	2	1	.667	5.33	8	3	0	27	36	12	13	0	0	0	0	0	0	0	–
1978	0	0	–	3.07	10	0	0	14.2	11	4	9	0	0	0	0	0	0	0	–
1979 NY N	1	4	.200	3.00	46	0	0	60	57	40	32	0	1	4	7	4	0	0	.000
1980	3	3	.500	4.15	38	0	0	52	49	23	32	0	3	3	1	6	0	0	.000
1981 CLE A	0	0	–	1.13	4	0	0	8	5	4	4	0	0	0	0	0	0	0	–
1982	5	2	.714	4.17	47	0	0	49.2	43	30	54	0	5	2	4	0	0	0	–
1983	0	2	.000	5.84	11	0	0	12.1	22	6	13	0	2	0	0	0	0	0	–
9 yrs.	12	17	.414	4.12	172	8	1	262.1	256	147	182	0	10	12	12	10	0	0	.000

Jot Goar

GOAR, JOSHUA MERCER
B. Jan. 31, 1870, New Lisbon, Ind.   D. Apr. 4, 1947, New Castle, Ind.   BR TR 5'9"   160 lbs.

	W	L	PCT	ERA	G	GS	CG	IP	H	BB	SO	ShO	W	L	SV	AB	H	HR	BA
1896 PIT N	0	1	.000	16.88	3	0	0	13.1	36	8	3	0	0	1	0	6	1	0	.167
1898 CIN N	0	0	–	9.00	1	0	0	2	4	1	0	0	0	0	0	0	0	0	–
2 yrs.	0	1	.000	15.85	4	0	0	15.1	40	9	3	0	0	1	0	6	1	0	.167

George Goetz

GOETZ, GEORGE BURT
B. Greencastle, Ind.   Deceased.

	W	L	PCT	ERA	G	GS	CG	IP	H	BB	SO	ShO	W	L	SV	AB	H	HR	BA
1889 BAL AA	1	0	1.000	4.00	1	1	0	9	12	0	2	0	0	0	0	4	0	0	.000

John Goetz

GOETZ, JOHN HARDY
B. Oct. 24, 1937, Goetzville, Mich.   BR TR 6'   185 lbs.

	W	L	PCT	ERA	G	GS	CG	IP	H	BB	SO	ShO	W	L	SV	AB	H	HR	BA
1960 CHI N	0	0	–	12.79	4	0	0	6.1	10	4	6	0	0	0	0	1	0	0	.000

Bill Gogolewski

GOGOLEWSKI, WILLIAM JOSEPH
B. Oct. 26, 1947, Oshkosh, Wis.   BL TR 6'4"   190 lbs.

	W	L	PCT	ERA	G	GS	CG	IP	H	BB	SO	ShO	W	L	SV	AB	H	HR	BA
1970 WAS A	2	2	.500	4.76	8	5	0	34	33	25	19	0	0	0	0	7	0	0	.000
1971	6	5	.545	2.76	27	17	4	124	112	39	70	1	0	0	0	32	5	0	.156
1972 TEX A	4	11	.267	4.23	36	21	2	151	136	58	95	1	0	1	2	40	5	0	.125
1973	3	6	.333	4.21	49	1	0	124	139	48	77	0	3	6	6	0	0	0	–
1974 CLE A	0	0	–	4.50	5	0	0	14	15	2	3	0	0	0	0	0	0	0	–
1975 CHI A	0	0	–	5.24	19	0	0	55	61	28	37	0	0	0	2	0	0	0	–
6 yrs.	15	24	.385	4.02	144	44	6	502	496	200	301	2	3	7	10	79	10	0	.127

Jim Golden

GOLDEN, JAMES EDWARD
B. Mar. 20, 1936, Eldon, Mo.   BL TR 6'   175 lbs.

	W	L	PCT	ERA	G	GS	CG	IP	H	BB	SO	ShO	W	L	SV	AB	H	HR	BA
1960 LA N	1	0	1.000	6.43	1	1	0	7	6	4	4	0	0	0	0	3	1	0	.333
1961	1	1	.500	5.79	28	0	0	42	52	20	18	0	1	1	0	3	0	0	.000
1962 HOU N	7	11	.389	4.07	37	18	5	152.2	163	50	88	2	2	1	1	54	12	0	.222
1963	0	1	.000	5.68	3	1	0	6.1	12	2	5	0	0	0	0	0	0	0	–
4 yrs.	9	13	.409	4.54	69	20	5	208	233	76	115	2	3	2	1	60	13	0	.217

Mike Golden

GOLDEN, MICHAEL HENRY
B. Sept. 11, 1851, Shirley, Mass.   D. Jan. 11, 1929, Rockford, Ill.   BR TR 5'7"   166 lbs.

	W	L	PCT	ERA	G	GS	CG	IP	H	BB	SO	ShO	W	L	SV	AB	H	HR	BA
1878 MIL N	3	13	188	4.14	22	18	15	161	217	33	52	0	0	0	0	*			

Roy Golden

GOLDEN, ROY KRAMER
B. July 12, 1888, Madisonville, Ohio   D. Oct. 4, 1961, Norwood, Ohio   TR

	W	L	PCT	ERA	G	GS	CG	IP	H	BB	SO	ShO	W	L	SV	AB	H	HR	BA
1910 STL N	2	3	.400	4.43	7	6	3	42.2	44	33	31	0	0	0	0	15	4	0	.267
1911	4	9	.308	5.02	30	25	6	148.2	127	129	81	0	0	0	0	44	5	0	.114
2 yrs.	6	12	.333	4.89	37	31	9	191.1	171	162	112	0	0	0	0	59	9	0	.153

Fred Goldsmith

GOLDSMITH, FRED ERNEST
B. May 15, 1852, New Haven, Conn.   D. Mar. 28, 1939, Berkley, Mich.   BR TR 6'1"   195 lbs.

	W	L	PCT	ERA	G	GS	CG	IP	H	BB	SO	ShO	W	L	SV	AB	H	HR	BA
1879 TRO N	2	4	.333	1.57	8	7	7	63	61	1	31	0	0	0	0	38	9	0	.237
1880 CHI N	21	3	.875	1.75	26	24	22	210.1	189	18	90	4	0	0	0	142	37	0	.261
1881	24	13	.649	2.59	39	39	37	330	328	44	76	5	0	0	1	158	38	0	.241
1882	28	16	.636	2.42	44	44	44	405	377	38	109	4	0	0	0	183	42	0	.230
1883	25	19	.568	3.15	46	45	40	383.1	456	39	82	2	0	0	0	235	52	1	.221
1884 2 teams				CHI N (21G 9–11)				BAL AA (4G 3–1)											
" total	12	12	.500	4.05	25	25	23	218	274	31	45	1	0	0	0	95	13	2	.137
6 yrs.	112	67	.626	2.73	188	184	173	1609.2	1685	171	433	16	0	0	1	*			

Hal Goldsmith

GOLDSMITH, HAROLD EUGENE
B. Aug. 18, 1898, Peconic, N. Y.   BR TR 6'   174 lbs.

	W	L	PCT	ERA	G	GS	CG	IP	H	BB	SO	ShO	W	L	SV	AB	H	HR	BA
1926 BOS N	5	7	.417	4.37	19	15	5	101	135	28	16	0	1	1	0	38	8	0	.211
1927	1	3	.250	3.52	22	5	1	71.2	83	26	13	0	0	1	1	21	5	0	.238
1928	0	0	–	3.24	4	0	0	8.1	14	1	1	0	0	0	0	2	0	0	.000
1929 STL N	0	0	–	6.75	2	0	0	4	3	1	0	0	0	0	0	1	0	0	.000
4 yrs.	6	10	.375	4.04	47	20	6	185	235	56	30	0	1	2	1	62	13	0	.210

Izzy Goldstein

GOLDSTEIN, ISADORE
B. June 6, 1908, New York, N. Y.   BB TR 6'   160 lbs.

	W	L	PCT	ERA	G	GS	CG	IP	H	BB	SO	ShO	W	L	SV	AB	H	HR	BA
1932 DET A	3	2	.600	4.47	16	6	2	56.1	63	41	14	0	0	0	0	17	5	0	.294

	W	L	PCT	ERA	G	GS	CG	IP	H	BB	SO	ShO	Relief Pitching W	L	SV	BATTING AB	H	HR	BA

Dave Goltz

GOLTZ, DAVID ALLAN
B. June 23, 1949, Pelican Rapids, Minn.　　　　　　　BR TR 6'4"　　200 lbs.

	W	L	PCT	ERA	G	GS	CG	IP	H	BB	SO	ShO	W	L	SV	AB	H	HR	BA
1972 MIN A	3	3	.500	2.67	15	11	2	91	75	26	38	0	0	0	1	29	3	0	.103
1973	6	4	.600	5.25	32	10	1	106.1	138	32	66	0	3	0	1	0	0	0	–
1974	10	10	.500	3.26	28	24	5	174	192	45	89	1	1	0	1	0	0	0	–
1975	14	14	.500	3.67	32	32	15	243	235	72	128	1	0	0	0	0	0	0	–
1976	14	14	.500	3.36	36	35	13	249.1	239	91	133	4	0	0	0	0	0	0	–
1977	**20**	11	.645	3.36	39	**39**	19	303	**284**	91	186	2	0	0	0	0	0	0	–
1978	15	10	.600	2.49	29	29	13	220.1	209	67	116	2	0	0	0	0	0	0	–
1979	14	13	.519	4.16	36	35	12	251	**282**	69	132	1	0	0	0	0	0	0	–
1980 LA N	7	11	.389	4.32	35	27	2	171	198	59	91	2	0	0	1	47	6	0	.128
1981	2	7	.222	4.09	26	8	0	77	83	25	48	0	1	3	1	17	1	0	.059
1982 2 teams		LA	N (2G 0–1)				CAL	A (28G 8–5)											
" total	8	6	.571	4.12	30	8	1	89.2	88	32	52	0	4	4	3	1	0	0	.000
1983 CAL A	0	6	.000	6.22	15	6	0	63.2	81	37	27	0	0	2	0	0	0	0	–
12 yrs.	113	109	.509	3.69	353	264	83	2039.1	2104	646	1106	13	9	9	8	94	10	0	.106

LEAGUE CHAMPIONSHIP SERIES
| 1982 CAL A | 0 | 0 | – | 7.36 | 1 | 0 | 0 | 3.2 | 4 | 2 | 2 | 0 | 0 | 0 | 0 | 0 | 0 | 0 | – |

WORLD SERIES
| 1981 LA N | 0 | 0 | – | 5.40 | 2 | 0 | 0 | 3.1 | 4 | 1 | 2 | 0 | 0 | 0 | 0 | 0 | 0 | 0 | – |

Lefty Gomez

GOMEZ, VERNON LOUIS (Goofy, The Gay Castillion)　　　BL TL 6'2"　　173 lbs.
B. Nov. 26, 1909, Rodeo, Calif.
Hall of Fame 1972.

	W	L	PCT	ERA	G	GS	CG	IP	H	BB	SO	ShO	W	L	SV	AB	H	HR	BA
1930 NY A	2	5	.286	5.55	15	6	2	60	66	28	22	0	0	2	1	20	3	0	.150
1931	21	9	.700	2.63	40	26	17	243	206	85	150	1	3	2	3	83	11	0	.133
1932	24	7	.774	4.21	37	31	21	265.1	266	105	176	1	1	2	1	104	18	0	.173
1933	16	10	.615	3.18	35	30	14	234.2	218	106	**163**	4	0	2	2	80	9	0	.113
1934	**26**	5	**.839**	**2.33**	38	33	**25**	281.2	223	96	**158**	6	1	2	1	99	13	0	.131
1935	12	15	.444	3.18	34	30	15	246	223	86	138	2	0	1	1	83	10	0	.120
1936	13	7	.650	4.39	31	30	10	188.2	184	122	105	0	0	0	0	69	10	0	.145
1937	**21**	11	.656	**2.33**	34	34	25	278.1	233	93	**194**	6	0	0	0	105	21	0	.200
1938	18	12	.600	3.35	32	32	20	239	239	99	129	4	0	0	0	86	13	0	.151
1939	12	8	.600	3.41	26	26	14	198	173	84	102	2	0	0	0	73	11	0	.151
1940	3	3	.500	6.59	9	5	0	27.1	37	18	14	0	0	1	0	9	0	0	.000
1941	15	5	**.750**	3.74	23	23	8	156.1	151	103	76	2	0	0	0	59	9	0	.153
1942	6	4	.600	4.28	13	13	2	80	67	65	41	0	0	0	0	33	5	0	.152
1943 WAS A	0	1	.000	5.79	1	1	0	4.2	4	5	0	0	0	0	0	1	0	0	.000
14 yrs.	189	102	.649	3.34	368	320	173	2503	2290	1095	1468	28	5	12	9	904	133	0	.147

WORLD SERIES
1932 NY A	1	0	1.000	1.00	1	1	1	9	9	1	8	0	0	0	0	3	0	0	.000
1936	2	0	1.000	4.70	2	2	1	15.1	14	11	9	0	0	0	0	8	2	0	.250
1937	2	0	1.000	1.50	2	2	2	18	16	2	8	0	0	0	0	6	1	0	.167
1938	1	0	1.000	3.86	1	1	0	7	9	1	5	0	0	0	0	2	0	0	.000
1939	0	0	–	9.00	1	1	0	1	3	0	1	0	0	0	0	1	0	0	.000
5 yrs.	6	0	1.000	2.86	7	7	4	50.1	51	15	31	0	0	0	0	20	3	0	.150
	5th		**1st**																

Luis Gomez

GOMEZ, JOSE LUIS
Born Jose Luis Gomez Sanchez.　　　　　　　　　　BR TR 5'9"　　150 lbs.
B. Aug. 19, 1951, Los Angeles, Calif.

	W	L	PCT	ERA	G	GS	CG	IP	H	BB	SO	ShO	W	L	SV	AB	H	HR	BA
1981 ATL N	0	0	–	27.00	1	0	0	1	3	2	0	0	0	0	0	*			

Ruben Gomez

GOMEZ, RUBEN COLON　　　　　　　　　　　　　BR TR 6'　　170 lbs.
B. July 13, 1927, Arroyo, Puerto Rico

	W	L	PCT	ERA	G	GS	CG	IP	H	BB	SO	ShO	W	L	SV	AB	H	HR	BA
1953 NY N	13	11	.542	3.40	29	26	13	204	166	101	113	3	0	0	0	72	15	0	.208
1954	17	9	.654	2.88	37	32	10	221.2	202	109	106	4	0	2	0	81	14	2	.173
1955	9	10	.474	4.56	33	31	9	185.1	207	63	79	3	0	1	1	60	18	0	.300
1956	7	17	.292	4.58	40	31	4	196.1	191	77	76	2	1	0	0	60	11	0	.183
1957	15	13	.536	3.78	38	36	16	238.1	233	71	92	1	0	0	0	87	16	1	.184
1958 SF N	10	12	.455	4.38	42	30	8	207.2	204	77	112	1	0	2	1	70	14	0	.200
1959 PHI N	3	8	.273	6.10	20	12	2	72.1	90	24	37	1	1	1	1	17	3	0	.176
1960	0	3	.000	5.33	22			52.1	68	9	24	0	0	3	1	12	1	0	.083
1962 2 teams		CLE	A (15G 1–2)				MIN	A (6G 1–1)											
" total	2	3	.400	4.45	21	6	1	64.2	67	36	29	0	0	1	1	18	3	0	.167
1967 PHI N	0	0	–	3.97	7	0	0	11.1	8	7	9	0	0	0	0	0	0	0	–
10 yrs.	76	86	.469	4.09	289	205	63	1454	1436	574	677	15	2	10	5	477	95	3	.199

WORLD SERIES
| 1954 NY N | 1 | 0 | 1.000 | 2.45 | 1 | 1 | 0 | 7.1 | 4 | 3 | 2 | 0 | 0 | 0 | 0 | 4 | 0 | 0 | .000 |

Joe Gonzales

GONZALES, JOSE MADRID　　　　　　　　　　　BR TR 5'9"　　175 lbs.
B. Mar. 19, 1915, San Francisco, Calif.

	W	L	PCT	ERA	G	GS	CG	IP	H	BB	SO	ShO	W	L	SV	AB	H	HR	BA
1937 BOS A	1	2	.333	4.35	8	2	2	31	37	11	11	0	1	0	0	10	0	0	.000

Julio Gonzales

GONZALES, JULIO ENRIQUE　　　　　　　　　　BR TR 5'11"　　150 lbs.
B. Dec. 20, 1920, Havana, Cuba

	W	L	PCT	ERA	G	GS	CG	IP	H	BB	SO	ShO	W	L	SV	AB	H	HR	BA
1949 WAS A	0	0	–	4.72	13	0	0	34.1	33	27	5	0	0	0	0	5	1	0	.200

Vince Gonzales

GONZALES, WENCESLAO O'REILLY　　　　　　　BL TL 6'1"　　165 lbs.
B. Sept. 28, 1925, Quivican, Cuba　　D. Mar. 11, 1981, Ciudad Del Carmen, Mexico

	W	L	PCT	ERA	G	GS	CG	IP	H	BB	SO	ShO	W	L	SV	AB	H	HR	BA
1955 WAS A	0	0	–	27.00	1	0	0	2	6	3	1	0	0	0	0	0	0	0	

	W	L	PCT	ERA	G	GS	CG	IP	H	BB	SO	ShO	Relief Pitching W	L	SV	BATTING AB	H	HR	BA

Ralph Good

GOOD, RALPH NELSON
B. Apr. 25, 1886, Monticello, Me.   D. Nov. 24, 1965, Waterville, Me.
BR TR 6'   165 lbs.

	W	L	PCT	ERA	G	GS	CG	IP	H	BB	SO	ShO	W	L	SV	AB	H	HR	BA
1910 BOS N	0	0	—	2.00	2	0	0	9	6	2	4	0	0	0	0	3	0	0	.000

Wilbur Good

GOOD, WILBUR DAVID (Lefty)
B. Sept. 28, 1885, Punxsutawney, Pa.   D. Dec. 30, 1963, Brooksville, Fla.
BL TL 5'6"   165 lbs.

	W	L	PCT	ERA	G	GS	CG	IP	H	BB	SO	ShO	W	L	SV	AB	H	HR	BA
1905 NY A	0	2	.000	4.74	5	2	0	19	18	14	13	0	0	0	0	*			

Herb Goodall

GOODALL, HERBERT FRANK
B. Aug. 10, 1866, Mansfield, Pa.   D. Jan. 20, 1938, Mansfield, Pa.
BR TR 5'9"   180 lbs.

	W	L	PCT	ERA	G	GS	CG	IP	H	BB	SO	ShO	W	L	SV	AB	H	HR	BA
1890 LOU AA	8	5	.615	3.39	18	13	8	109	94	51	46	1	0	0	4	45	19	0	.422

John Goodell

GOODELL, JOHN HENRY WILLIAM (Lefty)
B. Apr. 5, 1907, Muskogee, Okla.
BR TL 5'10"   165 lbs.

	W	L	PCT	ERA	G	GS	CG	IP	H	BB	SO	ShO	W	L	SV	AB	H	HR	BA
1928 CHI A	0	0	—	18.00	2	0	0	3	6	2	0	0	0	0	0	0	0	0	

Dwight Gooden

GOODEN, DWIGHT EUGENE
B. Nov. 16, 1964, Tampa, Fla.
BR TR 6'2"   190 lbs.

	W	L	PCT	ERA	G	GS	CG	IP	H	BB	SO	ShO	W	L	SV	AB	H	HR	BA
1984 NY N	17	9	.654	2.60	31	31	7	218	161	73	**276**	3	0	0	0	70	14	0	.200

Art Goodwin

GOODWIN, ARTHUR INGRAM
B. Feb. 27, 1877, Greene County, Pa.   D. June 19, 1943, Franklin Township, Pa.

	W	L	PCT	ERA	G	GS	CG	IP	H	BB	SO	ShO	W	L	SV	AB	H	HR	BA
1905 NY A	0	0	—	81.00	1	0	0	.1	2	2	0	0	0	0	0	0	0	0	—

Clyde Goodwin

GOODWIN, CLYDE SAMUEL
B. Nov. 12, 1886, Shade, Ohio   D. Oct. 12, 1963, Dayton, Ohio
BR TR 5'11"   145 lbs.

	W	L	PCT	ERA	G	GS	CG	IP	H	BB	SO	ShO	W	L	SV	AB	H	HR	BA
1906 WAS A	0	2	.000	4.43	4	3	1	22.1	20	13	9	0	0	0	0	5	1	0	.200

Jim Goodwin

GOODWIN, JAMES PATRICK
B. Aug. 15, 1926, St. Louis, Mo.
BL TL 6'1"   170 lbs.

	W	L	PCT	ERA	G	GS	CG	IP	H	BB	SO	ShO	W	L	SV	AB	H	HR	BA
1948 CHI A	0	0	—	8.71	8	1	0	10.1	9	12	3	0	0	0	1	2	1	0	.500

Marv Goodwin

GOODWIN, MARVIN MARDO
B. Jan. 16, 1893, Richmond, Vt.   D. Oct. 22, 1925, Houston, Tex.
BR TR 5'11"   168 lbs.

	W	L	PCT	ERA	G	GS	CG	IP	H	BB	SO	ShO	W	L	SV	AB	H	HR	BA
1916 WAS A	0	0	—	3.18	3	0	0	5.2	5	3	1	0	0	0	0	1	0	0	.000
1917 STL N	6	4	.600	2.21	14	12	6	85.1	70	19	38	3	0	1	0	23	4	0	.174
1919	11	9	.550	2.51	33	17	7	179	163	33	48	0	3	3	0	60	12	0	.200
1920	3	8	.273	4.95	32	12	3	116.1	153	28	23	0	1	1	1	35	7	0	.200
1921	1	2	.333	3.72	14	4	1	36.1	47	9	7	0	0	0	1	6	0	0	.000
1922	0	0	—	2.25	2	0	0	4	3	3	0	0	0	0	0	0	0	0	—
1925 CIN N	0	2	.000	4.79	4	3	2	20.2	26	5	4	0	0	0	0	4	1	0	.250
7 yrs.	21	25	.457	3.30	102	48	19	447.1	467	100	121	3	4	5	2	129	24	0	.186

Ray Gordonier

GORDONIER, RAYMOND CHARLES
B. Apr. 11, 1892, Rochester, N. Y.
D. Nov. 15, 1960, Rochester, N. Y.
BR TR 5'8½"   170 lbs.
BB 1922

	W	L	PCT	ERA	G	GS	CG	IP	H	BB	SO	ShO	W	L	SV	AB	H	HR	BA
1921 BKN N	1	0	1.000	5.25	3	3	0	12	10	8	4	0	0	0	0	4	1	0	.250
1922	0	0	—	8.74	5	0	0	11.1	13	8	5	0	0	0	0	2	0	0	.000
2 yrs.	1	0	1.000	6.94	8	3	0	23.1	23	16	9	0	0	0	0	6	1	0	.167

Charlie Gorin

GORIN, CHARLES PERRY
B. Feb. 6, 1928, Waco, Tex.
BL TL 5'10"   165 lbs.

	W	L	PCT	ERA	G	GS	CG	IP	H	BB	SO	ShO	W	L	SV	AB	H	HR	BA
1954 MIL N	0	1	.000	1.86	5	0	0	9.2	5	6	12	0	0	1	0	3	0	0	.000
1955	0	0	—	54.00	2	0	0	.1	1	3	0	0	0	0	0	0	0	0	—
2 yrs.	0	1	.000	3.60	7	0	0	10	6	9	12	0	0	1	0	3	0	0	.000

Jack Gorman

GORMAN, JOHN F. (Stooping Jack)
B. 1859, St. Louis, Mo.   D. Sept. 9, 1889, St. Louis, Mo.

	W	L	PCT	ERA	G	GS	CG	IP	H	BB	SO	ShO	W	L	SV	AB	H	HR	BA
1884 PIT AA	1	2	.333	4.68	3	3	3	25	22	5	10	0	0	0	0	*			

Tom Gorman

GORMAN, THOMAS ALOYSIUS
B. Jan. 4, 1925, New York, N. Y.
BR TR 6'1"   190 lbs.

	W	L	PCT	ERA	G	GS	CG	IP	H	BB	SO	ShO	W	L	SV	AB	H	HR	BA
1952 NY A	6	2	.750	4.60	12	6	1	60.2	63	22	31	1	3	0	1	23	2	0	.087
1953	4	5	.444	3.39	40	1	0	77	65	32	38	0	4	4	6	15	2	0	.133
1954	0	0	—	2.21	23	0	0	36.2	30	14	31	0	0	0	2	4	0	0	.000
1955 KC A	7	6	.538	3.55	57	0	0	109	98	36	46	0	7	6	18	24	2	0	.083
1956	9	10	.474	3.83	52	13	1	171.1	168	68	56	0	6	3	3	39	2	0	.051
1957	5	9	.357	3.83	38	12	3	124.2	125	33	66	1	1	5	3	33	4	0	.121
1958	4	4	.500	3.51	50	1	0	89.2	86	20	44	0	4	3	8	17	2	0	.118
1959	1	0	1.000	7.08	17	0	0	20.1	24	14	9	0	1	0	1	0	0	0	—
8 yrs.	36	36	.500	3.77	289	33	5	689.1	659	239	321	2	26	21	42	155	14	0	.090
WORLD SERIES																			
1952 NY A	0	0	—	0.00	1	0	0	.2	1	0	0	0	0	0	0	0	0	0	—
1953	0	0	—	3.00	1	0	0	3	4	0	1	0	0	0	0	1	0	0	.000
2 yrs.	0	0	—	2.45	2	0	0	3.2	5	0	1	0	0	0	0	1	0	0	.000

Tom Gorman

GORMAN, THOMAS DAVID (Big Tom)
B. Mar. 16, 1916, New York, N. Y.
BR TL 6'2"   200 lbs.

	W	L	PCT	ERA	G	GS	CG	IP	H	BB	SO	ShO	W	L	SV	AB	H	HR	BA
1939 NY N	0	0	—	7.20	4	0	0	5	7	1	2	0	0	0	0	1	0	0	.000

Tom Gorman

GORMAN, THOMAS PATRICK
B. Dec. 12, 1957, Woodburn, Ore.
BL TL 6'4"   194 lbs.

	W	L	PCT	ERA	G	GS	CG	IP	H	BB	SO	ShO	W	L	SV	AB	H	HR	BA
1981 MON N	0	0	—	4.20	9	0	0	15	12	6	13	0	0	0	0	0	0	0	—

	W	L	PCT	ERA	G	GS	CG	IP	H	BB	SO	ShO	Relief Pitching W	L	SV	BATTING AB	H	HR	BA

Tom Gorman continued

	W	L	PCT	ERA	G	GS	CG	IP	H	BB	SO	ShO	W	L	SV	AB	H	HR	BA
1982 **2 teams**			**MON** N (5G 1–0)			**NY**	N (3G 0–1)												
" total	1	1	.500	2.76	8	1	0	16.1	16	4	13	0	1	0	0	1	0	0	.000
1983 NY N	1	4	.200	4.93	25	4	0	49.1	45	15	30	0	1	0	0	4	1	0	.250
1984	6	0	1.000	2.97	36	0	0	57.2	51	13	40	0	6	0	0	3	0	0	.000
4 yrs.	8	5	.615	3.77	78	5	0	138.1	124	38	96	0	8	0	0	8	1	0	.125

Ed Gormley

GORMLEY, EDWARD JOSEPH   TL
B. Lansford, Pa.   D. July 2, 1950, Summit Hill, Pa.

	W	L	PCT	ERA	G	GS	CG	IP	H	BB	SO	ShO	W	L	SV	AB	H	HR	BA
1891 PHI N	0	1	.000	5.63	1	1	1	8	10	5	2	0	0	0	0	4	0	0	.000

Hank Gornicki

GORNICKI, FRANK TED   BR TR 6'   145 lbs.
B. Jan. 14, 1911, Niagara Falls, N. Y.

	W	L	PCT	ERA	G	GS	CG	IP	H	BB	SO	ShO	W	L	SV	AB	H	HR	BA
1941 **2 teams**			**STL** N (4G 1–0)			**CHI**	N (1G 0–0)												
" total	1	0	1.000	3.38	5	1	1	13.1	9	9	8	1	0	0	0	4	1	0	.250
1942 PIT N	5	6	.455	2.57	25	14	7	112	89	40	48	2	0	0	2	35	4	1	.114
1943	9	13	.409	3.98	42	18	4	147	165	47	63	1	3	3	4	40	7	0	.175
1946	0	0	–	3.55	7	0	0	12.2	12	11	4	0	0	0	0	3	0	0	.000
4 yrs.	15	19	.441	3.38	79	33	12	285	275	107	123	4	3	3	6	82	12	1	.146

Johnny Gorsica

GORSICA, JOHN JOSEPH PERRY   BR TR 6'2"   180 lbs.
Born John Joseph Perry Gorczyca.
B. Mar. 29, 1915, Bayonne, N. J.

	W	L	PCT	ERA	G	GS	CG	IP	H	BB	SO	ShO	W	L	SV	AB	H	HR	BA
1940 DET A	7	7	.500	4.33	29	20	5	160	170	57	68	2	0	0	0	62	12	1	.194
1941	9	11	.450	4.47	33	21	8	171	193	55	59	1	4	1	2	57	17	0	.298
1942	3	2	.600	4.75	28	0	0	53	63	26	19	0	3	2	4	10	1	0	.100
1943	4	5	.444	3.36	35	4	1	96.1	88	40	45	0	4	3	5	23	4	0	.174
1944	6	14	.300	4.11	34	19	8	162	192	32	47	1	1	2	4	52	7	0	.135
1946	0	0	–	4.56	14	0	0	23.2	28	11	14	0	0	0	1	3	2	0	.667
1947	2	0	1.000	3.75	31	0	0	57.2	44	26	20	0	2	0	1	10	2	0	.200
7 yrs.	31	39	.443	4.18	204	64	22	723.2	778	247	272	4	14	8	17	217	45	1	.207

WORLD SERIES

	W	L	PCT	ERA	G	GS	CG	IP	H	BB	SO	ShO	W	L	SV	AB	H	HR	BA
1940 DET A	0	0	–	0.79	2	0	0	11.1	6	4	4	0	0	0	0	4	0	0	.000

Goose Gossage

GOSSAGE, RICHARD MICHAEL   BR TR 6'3"   180 lbs.
B. July 5, 1951, Colorado Springs, Colo.

	W	L	PCT	ERA	G	GS	CG	IP	H	BB	SO	ShO	W	L	SV	AB	H	HR	BA
1972 CHI A	7	1	.875	4.28	36	1	0	80	72	44	57	0	7	0	2	16	0	0	.000
1973	0	4	.000	7.43	20	4	1	49.2	57	37	33	0	0	0	0	0	0	0	–
1974	4	6	.400	4.15	39	3	0	89	92	47	64	0	4	5	1	0	0	0	–
1975	9	8	.529	1.84	62	0	0	141.2	99	70	130	0	9	8	26	0	0	0	–
1976	9	17	.346	3.94	31	29	15	224	214	90	135	0	0	1	1	0	0	0	–
1977 PIT N	11	9	.550	1.62	72	0	0	133	78	49	151	0	11	9	26	23	5	0	.217
1978 NY A	10	11	.476	2.01	63	0	0	134.1	87	59	122	0	10	11	27	0	0	0	–
1979	5	3	.625	2.64	36	0	0	58	48	19	41	0	5	3	18	0	0	0	–
1980	6	2	.750	2.27	64	0	0	99	74	37	103	0	6	2	33	0	0	0	–
1981	3	2	.600	0.77	32	0	0	47	22	14	48	0	3	2	20	0	0	0	–
1982	4	5	.444	2.23	56	0	0	93	63	28	102	0	4	5	30	0	0	0	–
1983	13	5	.722	2.27	57	0	0	87.1	82	25	90	0	13	5	22	0	0	0	–
1984 SD N	10	6	.625	2.90	62	0	0	102.1	75	36	84	0	10	6	25	22	4	0	.182
13 yrs.	91	79	.535	2.86	630	37	16	1338.1	1063	555	1160	0	82 10th	57	231 4th	61	9	0	.148

DIVISIONAL PLAYOFF SERIES

	W	L	PCT	ERA	G	GS	CG	IP	H	BB	SO	ShO	W	L	SV	AB	H	HR	BA
1981 NY A	0	0	–	0.00	3	0	0	6.2	3	2	8	0	0	0	3	0	0	0	–

LEAGUE CHAMPIONSHIP SERIES

	W	L	PCT	ERA	G	GS	CG	IP	H	BB	SO	ShO	W	L	SV	AB	H	HR	BA
1978 NY A	1	0	1.000	4.50	2	0	0	4	3	0	3	0	1	0	1	0	0	0	–
1980	0	1	.000	54.00	1	0	0	.1	3	0	0	0	0	1	0	0	0	0	–
1981	0	0	–	0.00	2	0	0	2.2	1	0	2	0	0	0	1	0	0	0	–
1984 SD N	0	0	–	4.50	3	0	0	4	5	1	5	0	0	0	1	0	0	0	–
4 yrs.	1	1	.500	4.91	8	0	0	11	12	1	10	0	1	1	3	0	0	0	–

WORLD SERIES

	W	L	PCT	ERA	G	GS	CG	IP	H	BB	SO	ShO	W	L	SV	AB	H	HR	BA
1978 NY A	1	0	1.000	0.00	3	0	0	6	1	1	4	0	1	0	0	0	0	0	–
1981	0	0	–	0.00	3	0	0	5	2	2	5	0	0	0	2	1	0	0	.000
1984 SD N	0	0	–	13.50	2	0	0	2.2	3	1	2	0	0	0	0	0	0	0	–
3 yrs.	1	0	1.000	2.63	8	0	0	13.2	6	4	11	0	1	0	2	1	0	0	.000

Jim Gott

GOTT, JAMES WILLIAM   BR TR 6'4"   200 lbs.
B. Aug. 3, 1959, Hollywood, Calif.

	W	L	PCT	ERA	G	GS	CG	IP	H	BB	SO	ShO	W	L	SV	AB	H	HR	BA
1982 TOR A	5	10	.333	4.43	30	23	1	136	134	66	82	1	0	0	0	0	0	0	–
1983	9	14	.391	4.74	34	30	6	176.2	195	68	121	1	0	1	0	0	0	0	–
1984	7	6	.538	4.02	35	12	1	109.2	93	49	73	1	2	1	2	0	0	0	–
3 yrs.	21	30	.412	4.45	99	65	8	422.1	422	183	276	3	2	2	2	0	0	0	–

Ted Goulait

GOULAIT, THEODORE LEE (Snooze)   BR TR 5'9½"   172 lbs.
B. Aug. 11, 1889, St. Clair, Mich.   D. July 15, 1936, St. Clair, Mich.

	W	L	PCT	ERA	G	GS	CG	IP	H	BB	SO	ShO	W	L	SV	AB	H	HR	BA
1912 NY N	0	0	–	6.43	1	1	1	7	11	4	6	0	0	0	0	2	1	0	.500

Al Gould

GOULD, ALBERT FRANK (Pudgy)   BR TR 5'6½"   160 lbs.
B. Jan. 20, 1893, Muscatine, Iowa   D. Aug. 8, 1982, San Jose, Calif.

	W	L	PCT	ERA	G	GS	CG	IP	H	BB	SO	ShO	W	L	SV	AB	H	HR	BA
1916 CLE A	5	7	.417	2.53	30	9	6	106.2	101	40	41	1	0	3	1	29	3	0	.103
1917	4	4	.500	3.64	27	7	1	94	95	52	24	0	2	1	0	24	5	0	.208
2 yrs.	9	11	.450	3.05	57	16	7	200.2	196	92	65	1	2	4	1	53	8	0	.151

	W	L	PCT	ERA	G	GS	CG	IP	H	BB	SO	ShO	Relief Pitching W	L	SV	BATTING AB	H	HR	BA

Charlie Gould

GOULD, CHARLES HARVEY   BR TR 6'   172 lbs.
B. Aug. 21, 1847, Cincinnati, Ohio   D. Apr. 10, 1917, Flushing, N. Y.
Manager 1875-76.

	W	L	PCT	ERA	G	GS	CG	IP	H	BB	SO	ShO	W	L	SV	AB	H	HR	BA
1876 CIN N	0	0	–	0.00	2	0	0	4.1	10	0	0	0	0	0	0	*			

Larry Gowell

GOWELL, LAWRENCE CLYDE   BR TR 6'2"   182 lbs.
B. May 2, 1948, Lewiston, Me.

	W	L	PCT	ERA	G	GS	CG	IP	H	BB	SO	ShO	W	L	SV	AB	H	HR	BA
1972 NY A	0	1	.000	1.29	2	1	0	7	3	2	7	0	0	0	0	1	1	0	1.000

Al Grabowski

GRABOWSKI, ALFONS FRANCIS (Hook)   BL TL 5'11½" 175 lbs.
Brother of Reggie Grabowski.
B. Sept. 4, 1901, Syracuse, N. Y.   D. Oct. 29, 1966, Memphis, N. Y.

	W	L	PCT	ERA	G	GS	CG	IP	H	BB	SO	ShO	W	L	SV	AB	H	HR	BA
1929 STL N	3	2	.600	2.52	6	6	4	50	44	8	22	2	0	0	0	16	4	0	.250
1930	6	4	.600	4.84	33	8	1	106	121	50	45	0	2	3	1	33	12	0	.364
2 yrs.	9	6	.600	4.10	39	14	5	156	165	58	67	2	2	3	1	49	16	0	.327

Reggie Grabowski

GRABOWSKI, REGINALD JOHN   BR TR 6'½"   185 lbs.
Brother of Al Grabowski.
B. July 16, 1907, Syracuse, N. Y.   D. Apr. 2, 1955, Syracuse, N. Y.

	W	L	PCT	ERA	G	GS	CG	IP	H	BB	SO	ShO	W	L	SV	AB	H	HR	BA
1932 PHI N	2	2	.500	3.67	14	2	0	34.1	38	22	15	0	2	1	0	6	0	0	.000
1933	1	3	.250	2.44	10	5	4	48	38	10	9	1	0	0	0	16	2	0	.125
1934	1	3	.250	9.23	27	5	0	65.1	114	23	13	0	1	0	0	18	1	0	.056
3 yrs.	4	8	.333	5.73	51	12	4	147.2	190	55	37	1	3	1	0	40	3	0	.075

John Graff

GRAFF, JOHN F.
B. Philadelphia, Pa.   Deceased.

	W	L	PCT	ERA	G	GS	CG	IP	H	BB	SO	ShO	W	L	SV	AB	H	HR	BA
1893 WAS N	0	1	.000	11.25	2	1	1	12	21	13	4	0	0	0	0	5	1	0	.200

Bill Graham

GRAHAM, WILLIAM ALBERT   BR TR 6'3"   217 lbs.
B. Jan. 21, 1937, Flemingsburg, Ky.

	W	L	PCT	ERA	G	GS	CG	IP	H	BB	SO	ShO	W	L	SV	AB	H	HR	BA
1966 DET A	0	0	–	0.00	1	0	0	2	2	0	2	0	0	0	0	0	0	0	–
1967 NY N	1	2	.333	2.63	5	3	1	27.1	20	11	14	0	0	0	0	8	1	0	.125
2 yrs.	1	2	.333	2.45	6	3	1	29.1	22	11	16	0	0	0	0	8	1	0	.125

Bill Graham

GRAHAM, WILLIAM JAMES   TL 6'
B. July 22, 1884, Owosso, Mich.   D. Feb. 15, 1936, Holt, Mich.

	W	L	PCT	ERA	G	GS	CG	IP	H	BB	SO	ShO	W	L	SV	AB	H	HR	BA
1908 STL A	6	7	.462	2.30	21	13	7	117.1	104	32	47	0	3	1	0	42	5	0	.119
1909	8	14	.364	3.12	34	21	13	187.1	171	60	82	3	2	2	1	63	10	0	.159
1910	0	8	.000	3.56	9	6	1	43	46	13	12	0	0	0	0	13	2	0	.154
3 yrs.	14	29	.326	2.90	64	40	21	347.2	321	105	141	3	5	5	1	118	17	0	.144

Kyle Graham

GRAHAM, KYLE (Skinny)   BR TR 6'2"   172 lbs.
B. Aug. 14, 1899, Oak Grove, Ala.   D. Dec. 1, 1973, Oak Grove, Ala.

	W	L	PCT	ERA	G	GS	CG	IP	H	BB	SO	ShO	W	L	SV	AB	H	HR	BA
1924 BOS N	0	4	.000	3.82	5	4	1	33	33	11	15	0	0	0	0	7	0	0	.000
1925	7	12	.368	4.41	34	23	5	157	177	62	32	0	1	1	1	44	6	0	.136
1926	3	3	.500	7.93	15	4	1	36.1	54	19	7	0	2	2	0	12	2	0	.167
1929 DET A	1	3	.250	5.57	13	6	2	51.2	70	33	7	0	0	1	1	19	2	1	.105
4 yrs.	11	22	.333	5.02	67	37	9	278	334	125	61	0	3	4	2	82	10	1	.122

Oscar Graham

GRAHAM, OSCAR M.   TL
B. July 20, 1878, Plattsmouth, Neb.   D. Oct. 15, 1931, Moline, Ill.

	W	L	PCT	ERA	G	GS	CG	IP	H	BB	SO	ShO	W	L	SV	AB	H	HR	BA
1907 WAS A	4	9	.308	3.98	20	14	6	104	116	29	44	0	0	1	0	48	11	1	.229

Peaches Graham

GRAHAM, GEORGE FREDERICK   BR TR 5'9"   180 lbs.
Father of Jack Graham.
B. Mar. 23, 1880, Aledo, Ill.   D. July 25, 1939, Long Beach, Calif.

	W	L	PCT	ERA	G	GS	CG	IP	H	BB	SO	ShO	W	L	SV	AB	H	HR	BA
1903 CHI N	0	1	.000	5.40	1	0	1	5	9	3	4	0	0	0	0	*			

Tommy Gramly

GRAMLY, BERT THOMAS   BR TR 6'3"   175 lbs.
B. Apr. 19, 1945, Dallas, Tex.

	W	L	PCT	ERA	G	GS	CG	IP	H	BB	SO	ShO	W	L	SV	AB	H	HR	BA
1968 CLE A	0	1	.000	2.70	3	0	0	3.1	3	2	1	0	0	1	0	0	0	0	–

Henry Grampp

GRAMPP, HENRY EKHARDT   BR TR 6'1"   185 lbs.
B. Sept. 28, 1903, New York, N. Y.

	W	L	PCT	ERA	G	GS	CG	IP	H	BB	SO	ShO	W	L	SV	AB	H	HR	BA
1927 CHI N	0	0	–	9.00	2	0	0	3	4	1	3	0	0	0	0	0	0	0	–
1929	0	1	.000	27.00	1	1	0	2	4	3	0	0	0	0	0	0	0	0	–
2 yrs.	0	1	.000	16.20	3	1	0	5	8	4	3	0	0	0	0	0	0	0	–

Jack Graney

GRANEY, JOHN GLADSTONE   BL TL 5'9"   180 lbs.
B. June 10, 1886, St. Thomas, Ont., Canada   D. Apr. 20, 1978, Louisiana, Mo.

	W	L	PCT	ERA	G	GS	CG	IP	H	BB	SO	ShO	W	L	SV	AB	H	HR	BA
1908 CLE A	0	0	–	5.40	2	0	0	3.1	1	1	0	0	0	0	0	*			

Wayne Granger

GRANGER, WAYNE ALLAN   BR TR 6'2"   165 lbs.
B. Mar. 15, 1944, Springfield, Mass.

	W	L	PCT	ERA	G	GS	CG	IP	H	BB	SO	ShO	W	L	SV	AB	H	HR	BA
1968 STL N	4	2	.667	2.25	34	0	0	44	40	12	27	0	4	2	4	5	1	0	.200
1969 CIN N	9	6	.600	2.79	90	0	0	145	143	40	68	0	9	6	27	21	2	0	.095
1970	6	5	.545	2.65	67	0	0	85	79	27	38	0	6	5	35	10	1	0	.100
1971	7	6	.538	3.33	70	0	0	100	94	28	51	0	7	6	11	7	1	1	.143
1972 MIN A	4	6	.400	3.00	63	0	0	90	83	28	45	0	4	6	19	10	2	0	.200
1973 2 teams				STL	N (33G 2-4)			NY	A (7G 0-1)										
" total	2	5	.286	3.63	40	0	0	62	69	24	24	0	2	5	5	3	0	0	.000
1974 CHI A	0	0	–	7.88	9	0	0	8	16	3	4	0	0	0	0	0	0	0	–
1975 HOU N	2	5	.286	3.65	55	0	0	74	76	23	30	0	2	5	5	9	0	0	.000
1976 MON N	1	0	1.000	3.66	27	0	0	32	32	16	16	0	1	0	2	3	0	0	.000
9 yrs.	35	35	.500	3.14	451	0	0	640	632	201	303	0	35	35	108	68	7	1	.103

LEAGUE CHAMPIONSHIP SERIES

	W	L	PCT	ERA	G	GS	CG	IP	H	BB	SO	ShO	W	L	SV	AB	H	HR	BA
1970 CIN N	0	0	–	0.00	1	0	0	.2	1	0	0	0	0	0	0	0	0	0	–

	W	L	PCT	ERA	G	GS	CG	IP	H	BB	SO	ShO	Relief Pitching W	L	SV	BATTING AB	H	HR	BA

Wayne Granger continued

WORLD SERIES

	W	L	PCT	ERA	G	GS	CG	IP	H	BB	SO	ShO	W	L	SV	AB	H	HR	BA
1968 STL N	0	0	–	0.00	1	0	0	2	0	1	1	0	0	0	0	0	0	0	–
1970 CIN N	0	0	–	33.75	2	0	0	1.1	7	1	1	0	0	0	0	0	0	0	–
2 yrs.	0	0	–	13.50	3	0	0	3.1	7	2	2	0	0	0	0	0	0	0	–

George Grant

GRANT, GEORGE ADDISON
B. Jan. 6, 1903, East Tallassee, Ala.
BR TR 5'11½" 175 lbs.

	W	L	PCT	ERA	G	GS	CG	IP	H	BB	SO	ShO	W	L	SV	AB	H	HR	BA
1923 STL A	0	0	–	5.19	4	0	0	8.2	15	3	2	0	0	0	0	2	0	0	.000
1924	1	2	.333	6.26	21	2	0	50.1	67	25	11	0	1	0	0	13	0	0	.000
1925	0	2	.000	6.06	12	0	0	16.1	26	8	7	0	0	2	0	4	1	0	.250
1927 CLE A	4	6	.400	4.46	25	3	2	74.2	85	40	19	0	3	4	1	21	2	0	.095
1928	10	8	.556	5.04	28	18	6	155.1	196	76	39	1	2	1	0	60	11	0	.183
1929	0	2	.000	10.50	12	0	0	24	41	23	5	0	0	2	0	2	0	0	.000
1931 PIT N	0	0	–	7.41	11	0	0	17	28	7	6	0	0	0	0	2	0	0	.000
7 yrs.	15	20	.429	5.64	113	23	8	346.1	458	182	89	1	6	9	1	104	14	0	.135

Jim Grant

GRANT, JAMES RONALD
B. Aug. 4, 1894, Coalville, Iowa
BR TL 5'11" 180 lbs.

	W	L	PCT	ERA	G	GS	CG	IP	H	BB	SO	ShO	W	L	SV	AB	H	HR	BA
1923 PHI N	0	0	–	13.50	2	0	0	4	10	4	0	0	0	0	0	1	0	0	.000

Mark Grant

GRANT, MARK ANDREW
B. Oct. 24, 1963, Aurora, Ill.
BR TR 6'2" 205 lbs.

	W	L	PCT	ERA	G	GS	CG	IP	H	BB	SO	ShO	W	L	SV	AB	H	HR	BA
1984 SF N	1	4	.200	6.37	11	10	0	53.2	56	19	32	0	0	0	1	17	0	0	.000

Mudcat Grant

GRANT, JAMES TIMOTHY
B. Aug. 13, 1935, Lacoochee, Fla.
BR TR 6'1" 186 lbs.

	W	L	PCT	ERA	G	GS	CG	IP	H	BB	SO	ShO	W	L	SV	AB	H	HR	BA
1958 CLE A	10	11	.476	3.84	44	28	11	204	173	104	111	1	2	2	4	66	5	0	.076
1959	10	7	.588	4.14	38	19	6	165.1	140	81	85	1	1	1	3	55	11	1	.200
1960	9	8	.529	4.40	33	19	5	159.2	147	78	75	0	1	3	0	57	16	0	.281
1961	15	9	.625	3.86	35	35	11	244.2	207	109	146	3	0	0	0	88	15	1	.170
1962	7	10	.412	4.27	26	23	6	149.2	128	81	90	1	0	0	0	53	8	0	.151
1963	13	14	.481	3.69	38	32	10	229.1	213	87	157	2	1	0	1	69	13	1	.188
1964 2 teams								CLE A (13G 3–4)					MIN A (26G 11–9)						
" total	14	13	.519	3.67	39	32	11	228	244	61	118	1	1	0	1	82	16	2	.195
1965 MIN A	21	7	.750	3.30	41	39	14	270.1	252	61	142	6	1	0	0	97	15	0	.155
1966	13	13	.500	3.25	35	35	10	249	248	49	110	3	0	0	0	78	15	0	.192
1967	5	6	.455	4.72	27	14	2	95.1	121	17	50	0	0	0	0	28	5	0	.179
1968 LA N	6	4	.600	2.08	37	4	1	95	77	19	35	0	5	2	3	31	4	1	.129
1969 2 teams								MON N (11G 1–6)					STL N (30G 7–5)						
" total	8	11	.421	4.42	41	13	2	114	126	36	55	0	0	0	7	33	7	0	.212
1970 2 teams								OAK A (72G 6–2)					PIT N (8G 2–1)						
" total	8	3	.727	1.87	80	0	0	135	112	32	58	0	8	3	24	11	2	0	.182
1971 2 teams								PIT N (42G 5–3)					OAK A (15G 1–0)						
" total	6	3	.667	3.18	57	0	0	102	104	34	35	0	6	3	10	11	3	0	.273
14 yrs.	145	119	.549	3.63	571	293	89	2441.1	2292	849	1267	18	25	15	53	759	135	6	.178

LEAGUE CHAMPIONSHIP SERIES

	W	L	PCT	ERA	G	GS	CG	IP	H	BB	SO	ShO	W	L	SV	AB	H	HR	BA
1971 OAK A	0	0	–	0.00	1	0	0	2	3	0	2	0	0	0	0	0	0	0	–

WORLD SERIES

	W	L	PCT	ERA	G	GS	CG	IP	H	BB	SO	ShO	W	L	SV	AB	H	HR	BA
1965 MIN A	2	1	.667	2.74	3	3	2	23	22	2	12	0	0	0	0	8	2	1	.250

Dick Grapenthin

GRAPENTHIN, RICHARD RAY
B. Apr. 16, 1958, Linn Grove, Iowa
BR TR 6'2" 190 lbs.

	W	L	PCT	ERA	G	GS	CG	IP	H	BB	SO	ShO	W	L	SV	AB	H	HR	BA
1983 MON N	0	1	.000	9.00	1	0	0	4	4	1	3	0	0	1	0	1	0	0	.000
1984	1	2	.333	3.52	13	1	0	23	19	7	9	0	1	1	2	5	1	0	.200
2 yrs.	1	3	.250	4.33	14	1	0	27	23	8	12	0	1	2	2	6	1	0	.167

Lou Grasmick

GRASMICK, LOUIS JUNIOR
B. Sept. 11, 1924, Baltimore, Md.
BR TR 6' 195 lbs.

	W	L	PCT	ERA	G	GS	CG	IP	H	BB	SO	ShO	W	L	SV	AB	H	HR	BA
1948 PHI N	0	0	–	7.20	2	0	0	5	3	8	2	0	0	0	0	1	1	0	1.000

Don Grate

GRATE, DONALD (Buckeye)
B. Aug. 27, 1923, Greenfield, Ohio
BR TR 6'2½" 180 lbs.

	W	L	PCT	ERA	G	GS	CG	IP	H	BB	SO	ShO	W	L	SV	AB	H	HR	BA
1945 PHI N	0	1	.000	17.28	4	2	0	8.1	18	12	6	0	0	0	0	3	0	0	.000
1946	1	0	1.000	1.13	3	0	0	8	4	2	2	0	1	0	0	1	0	0	.000
2 yrs.	1	1	.500	9.37	7	2	0	16.1	22	14	8	0	1	0	0	4	0	0	.000

Frank Graves

GRAVES, FRANK M.
B. Nov. 2, 1860, Cincinnati, Ohio   Deceased.
6' 163 lbs.

	W	L	PCT	ERA	G	GS	CG	IP	H	BB	SO	ShO	W	L	SV	AB	H	HR	BA
1886 STL N	0	0	–	9.00	1	0	0	7	10	1	2	0	0	0	0	*		

Charlie Gray

GRAY, CHARLES
B. 1867, Indianapolis, Ind.   Deceased.

	W	L	PCT	ERA	G	GS	CG	IP	H	BB	SO	ShO	W	L	SV	AB	H	HR	BA
1890 PIT N	1	4	.200	7.55	5	4	3	31	48	24	10	0	1	0	0	15	3	0	.200

Chummy Gray

GRAY, GEORGE EDWARD
B. July 17, 1873, Rockland, Me.   D. Aug. 14, 1913, Rockland, Me.
TR 5'11½" 163 lbs.

	W	L	PCT	ERA	G	GS	CG	IP	H	BB	SO	ShO	W	L	SV	AB	H	HR	BA
1899 PIT N	3	3	.500	3.44	9	7	6	70.2	85	24	9	0	0	0	0	26	1	0	.038

Dave Gray

GRAY, DAVID ALEXANDER
B. Jan. 7, 1943, Ogden, Utah
BR TR 6'1" 190 lbs.

	W	L	PCT	ERA	G	GS	CG	IP	H	BB	SO	ShO	W	L	SV	AB	H	HR	BA
1964 BOS A	0	0	–	9.00	9	1	0	13	18	20	17	0	0	0	0	1	1	0	1.000

	W	L	PCT	ERA	G	GS	CG	IP	H	BB	SO	ShO	Relief Pitching W	L	SV	BATTING AB	H	HR	BA

Dolly Gray

GRAY, WILLIAM DENTON BL TL 6'2" 160 lbs.
B. Dec. 4, 1878, Ishpeming, Mich.   D. Apr. 4, 1956, Yuba City, Calif.

	W	L	PCT	ERA	G	GS	CG	IP	H	BB	SO	ShO	W	L	SV	AB	H	HR	BA
1909 WAS A	5	19	.208	3.59	36	26	19	218	210	77	87	0	0	0	0	89	13	0	.146
1910	8	19	.296	2.63	34	29	21	229	216	64	84	3	0	2	0	85	21	0	.247
1911	2	13	.133	5.06	28	15	6	121	160	40	42	0	0	3	0	44	10	0	.227
3 yrs.	15	51	.227	3.52	98	70	46	568	586	181	213	3	0	5	0	218	44	0	.202

John Gray

GRAY, JOHN LEONARD BR TR 6'4" 226 lbs.
B. Dec. 11, 1927, West Palm Beach, Fla.

	W	L	PCT	ERA	G	GS	CG	IP	H	BB	SO	ShO	W	L	SV	AB	H	HR	BA
1954 PHI A	3	12	.200	6.51	18	16	5	105	111	91	51	0	0	0	0	34	1	0	.029
1955 KC A	0	3	.000	6.41	8	5	0	26.2	28	24	11	0	0	0	0	8	1	0	.125
1957 CLE A	1	3	.250	5.85	7	3	1	20	21	13	3	1	0	1	0	4	0	0	.000
1958 PHI N	0	0	—	4.15	15	0	0	17.1	12	14	10	0	0	0	0	1	0	0	.000
4 yrs.	4	18	.182	6.18	48	24	6	169	172	142	75	1	0	1	0	47	2	0	.043

Sam Gray

GRAY, SAMUEL DAVID (Sad Sam) BR TR 5'10" 175 lbs.
B. Oct. 15, 1897, Van Alstyne, Tex.   D. Apr. 16, 1953, McKinney, Tex.

	W	L	PCT	ERA	G	GS	CG	IP	H	BB	SO	ShO	W	L	SV	AB	H	HR	BA
1924 PHI A	8	7	.533	3.98	34	19	8	151.2	169	89	54	2	1	0	2	57	10	0	.175
1925	16	8	.667	3.40	32	28	14	195.2	199	63	80	4	0	0	3	67	12	0	.179
1926	11	12	.478	3.64	38	18	5	150.2	164	50	82	0	4	3	0	51	11	0	.216
1927	9	6	.600	4.60	38	14	3	141	162	53	54	1	2	2	3	42	8	0	.190
1928 STL A	20	12	.625	3.19	35	31	21	262.2	256	86	102	2	1	0	3	101	19	1	.188
1929	18	15	.545	3.72	43	37	23	305	336	96	109	4	1	0	1	103	19	0	.184
1930	4	15	.211	6.28	27	24	7	167.2	215	52	51	0	0	1	0	54	11	0	.204
1931	11	24	.314	5.09	43	37	13	258	323	54	88	0	1	1	2	79	14	1	.177
1932	8	12	.400	4.53	52	18	7	206.2	250	53	79	3	2	1	4	62	13	0	.210
1933	7	4	.636	4.10	38	6	0	112	131	45	36	0	4	4	4	32	7	0	.219
10 yrs.	112	115	.493	4.20	380	232	101	1951	2205	641	735	16	16	12	22	648	124	2	.191

Ted Gray

GRAY, TED GLENN BB TL 5'11" 175 lbs.
B. Dec. 31, 1924, Detroit, Mich.

	W	L	PCT	ERA	G	GS	CG	IP	H	BB	SO	ShO	W	L	SV	AB	H	HR	BA
1946 DET A	0	2	.000	8.49	3	2	0	11.2	17	5	5	0	0	0	1	3	0	0	.000
1948	6	2	.750	4.22	26	11	3	85.1	73	72	60	1	0	0	0	29	7	0	.241
1949	10	10	.500	3.51	34	27	8	195	163	103	96	3	0	0	1	63	8	0	.127
1950	10	7	.588	4.40	27	21	7	149.1	139	72	102	0	1	0	1	50	7	0	.140
1951	7	14	.333	4.06	34	28	9	197.1	194	95	131	1	0	1	1	63	9	0	.143
1952	12	17	.414	4.14	35	32	13	224	212	101	138	2	0	0	0	76	13	0	.171
1953	10	15	.400	4.60	30	28	8	176	166	76	115	0	0	0	0	61	14	0	.230
1954	3	5	.375	5.38	19	10	2	72	70	56	29	0	0	0	0	22	1	0	.045
1955 4 teams				CHI A (2G 0-0)				CLE A (2G 0-0)			NY A (1G 0-0)				BAL A (9G 1-2)				
" total	1	2	.333	9.64	14	3	0	23.1	38	15	11	0	1	1	0	3	0	0	.000
9 yrs.	59	74	.444	4.37	222	162	50	1134	1072	595	687	7	2	2	4	370	59	0	.159

Eli Grba

GRBA, ELI BR TR 6'2" 205 lbs.
B. Aug. 9, 1934, Chicago, Ill.

	W	L	PCT	ERA	G	GS	CG	IP	H	BB	SO	ShO	W	L	SV	AB	H	HR	BA
1959 NY A	2	5	.286	6.44	19	6	0	50.1	52	39	23	0	1	1	0	14	3	0	.214
1960	6	4	.600	3.68	24	9	1	80.2	65	46	32	0	5	0	1	21	5	1	.238
1961 LA A	11	13	.458	4.25	40	30	8	211.2	197	114	105	0	2	1	2	64	15	2	.234
1962	8	9	.471	4.54	40	29	1	176.1	185	75	90	0	0	0	1	58	12	1	.207
1963	1	2	.333	4.67	12	1	0	17.1	14	10	5	0	1	1	0	3	0	0	.000
5 yrs.	28	33	.459	4.48	135	75	10	536.1	513	284	255	0	9	3	4	160	35	4	.219

Bill Greason

GREASON, WILLIAM HENRY (Booster) BR TR 5'10" 170 lbs.
B. Sept. 3, 1924, Atlanta, Ga.

	W	L	PCT	ERA	G	GS	CG	IP	H	BB	SO	ShO	W	L	SV	AB	H	HR	BA
1954 STL N	0	1	.000	13.50	3	2	0	4	8	4	2	0	0	0	0	1	0	0	.000

Chris Green

GREEN, CHRISTOPHER DeWAYNE BL TL 6'2" 180 lbs.
B. Sept. 5, 1961, Los Angeles, Calif.

	W	L	PCT	ERA	G	GS	CG	IP	H	BB	SO	ShO	W	L	SV	AB	H	HR	BA
1984 PIT N	0	0	—	6.00	4	0	0	3	5	1	3	0	0	0	0	0	0	0	—

Dallas Green

GREEN, GEORGE DALLAS BL TR 6'5" 210 lbs.
B. Aug. 4, 1934, Newport, Del.
Manager 1979-81.

	W	L	PCT	ERA	G	GS	CG	IP	H	BB	SO	ShO	W	L	SV	AB	H	HR	BA
1960 PHI N	3	6	.333	4.06	23	10	5	108.2	100	44	51	1	0	1	0	34	7	0	.206
1961	2	4	.333	4.85	42	10	1	128	160	47	51	0	1	1	1	33	5	0	.152
1962	6	6	.500	3.83	37	10	2	129.1	145	43	58	0	3	1	1	32	2	0	.063
1963	7	5	.583	3.23	40	14	4	120	134	38	68	0	3	0	2	35	3	0	.086
1964	2	1	.667	5.79	25	0	0	42	63	14	21	0	2	1	0	3	0	0	.000
1965 WAS A	0	0	—	3.14	6	2	0	14.1	14	3	6	0	0	0	0	4	0	0	.000
1966 NY N	0	0	—	5.40	4	0	0	5	6	2	1	0	0	0	0	0	0	0	—
1967 PHI N	0	0	—	9.00	8	0	0	15	25	6	12	0	0	0	0	1	0	0	.000
8 yrs.	20	22	.476	4.26	185	46	12	562.1	647	197	268	2	9	4	4	142	17	0	.120

Ed Green

GREEN, EDWARD M.
B. 1850, Toronto, Canada   D. Mar. 22, 1917, Ogden, Utah

	W	L	PCT	ERA	G	GS	CG	IP	H	BB	SO	ShO	W	L	SV	AB	H	HR	BA
1890 PHI AA	7	15	.318	5.80	25	22	20	191	267	94	56	1	0	0	1	126	15	0	.119

Freddie Green

GREEN, FRED ALLEN BR TL 6'4" 190 lbs.
B. Sept. 14, 1933, Titusville, N. J.

	W	L	PCT	ERA	G	GS	CG	IP	H	BB	SO	ShO	W	L	SV	AB	H	HR	BA
1959 PIT N	1	2	.333	3.13	17	0	0	37.1	37	15	20	0	1	1	1	6	0	0	.000
1960	8	4	.667	3.21	45	0	0	70	61	33	49	0	8	4	3	8	3	2	.375
1961	0	0	—	4.79	13	0	0	20.2	27	9	4	0	0	0	0	3	0	0	.000
1962 WAS A	0	1	.000	6.43	5	0	0	7	7	6	2	0	0	1	0	0	0	0	—
1964 PIT N	0	0	—	1.23	8	0	0	7.1	10	0	2	0	0	0	0	0	0	0	—
5 yrs.	9	7	.563	3.48	88	0	0	142.1	142	63	77	0	9	6	4	17	3	2	.176
WORLD SERIES																			
1960 PIT N	0	0	—	22.50	3	0	0	4	11	1	3	0	0	0	0	1	0	0	.000

	W	L	PCT	ERA	G	GS	CG	IP	H	BB	SO	ShO	Relief Pitching W	L	SV	BATTING AB	H	HR	BA

Harvey Green

GREEN, HARVEY GEORGE (Buck)
B. Feb. 9, 1915, Kenosha, Wis. D. July 24, 1970, Franklin, La. BB TR 6'4" 187 lbs.

	W	L	PCT	ERA	G	GS	CG	IP	H	BB	SO	ShO	W	L	SV	AB	H	HR	BA
1935 BKN N	0	0	–	9.00	2	0	0	1	2	3	0	0	0	0	0	0	0	0	–

Julius Green

GREEN, JULIUS FOUST
Also known as Henry Green.
B. June 25, 1902, Greensboro, N. C. D. Mar. 19, 1974, San Clemente, Calif. BL TR 6'2½" 185 lbs.

	W	L	PCT	ERA	G	GS	CG	IP	H	BB	SO	ShO	W	L	SV	AB	H	HR	BA
1928 PHI N	0	0	–	9.00	1	0	0	2	5	0	0	0	0	0	0	6	3	0	.500
1929	0	0	–	19.76	5	0	0	13.2	33	9	4	0	0	0	0	19	4	0	.211
2 yrs.	0	0	–	18.38	6	0	0	15.2	38	9	4	0	0	0	0	*			

Nelson Greene

GREENE, NELSON GEORGE (Lefty)
B. Sept. 20, 1900, Philadelphia, Pa. D. Apr. 6, 1983, Lebanon, Pa. BL TL 6' 185 lbs.

	W	L	PCT	ERA	G	GS	CG	IP	H	BB	SO	ShO	W	L	SV	AB	H	HR	BA
1924 BKN N	0	1	.000	4.00	4	1	0	9	14	2	3	0	0	0	0	1	0	0	.000
1925	2	0	1.000	10.64	11	0	0	22	45	7	4	0	2	0	1	7	2	0	.286
2 yrs.	2	1	.667	8.71	15	1	0	31	59	9	7	0	2	0	1	8	2	0	.250

Kent Greenfield

GREENFIELD, KENT
B. July 1, 1902, Guthrie, Ky. D. Mar. 14, 1978, Guthrie, Ky. BR TR 6'1" 180 lbs.

	W	L	PCT	ERA	G	GS	CG	IP	H	BB	SO	ShO	W	L	SV	AB	H	HR	BA
1924 NY N	0	1	.000	15.00	1	1	0	3	9	1	1	0	0	0	0	0	0	0	–
1925	12	8	.600	3.88	29	21	12	171.2	195	64	66	0	1	0	0	62	5	0	.081
1926	13	12	.520	3.96	39	28	8	222.2	206	82	74	1	2	3	1	65	6	0	.092
1927 2 teams		NY	N (12G 2–2)		BOS	N (27G 11–14)													
" total	13	16	.448	4.37	39	27	11	210	242	72	63	1	2	2	0	66	11	0	.167
1928 BOS N	3	11	.214	5.32	32	23	5	143.2	173	60	30	0	0	0	0	38	2	0	.053
1929 2 teams		BOS	N (6G 0–0)		BKN	N (6G 0–0)													
" total	0	0	–	9.99	12	2	0	24.1	46	18	8	0	0	0	0	6	0	0	.000
6 yrs.	41	48	.461	4.54	152	102	36	775.1	871	297	242	2	5	5	1	237	24	0	.101

John Greening

GREENING, JOHN A.
Born John A. Greenig.
B. Philadelphia, Pa. Deceased.

	W	L	PCT	ERA	G	GS	CG	IP	H	BB	SO	ShO	W	L	SV	AB	H	HR	BA
1888 WAS N	0	1	.000	11.00	1	1	1	9	17	4	2	0	0	0	0	3	0	0	.000

Bob Greenwood

GREENWOOD, ROBERT CHANDLER (Greenie)
B. Mar. 13, 1928, Cananea Sonora, Mexico. BR TR 6'4" 205 lbs.

	W	L	PCT	ERA	G	GS	CG	IP	H	BB	SO	ShO	W	L	SV	AB	H	HR	BA
1954 PHI N	1	2	.333	3.19	11	4	0	36.2	28	18	9	0	0	0	0	9	0	0	.000
1955	0	0	–	15.43	1	0	0	2.1	7	0	0	0	0	0	0	1	0	0	.000
2 yrs.	1	2	.333	3.92	12	4	0	39	35	18	9	0	0	0	0	10	0	0	.000

Dave Gregg

GREGG, DAVID CHARLES (Highpockets)
Brother of Vean Gregg.
B. Mar. 14, 1891, Chehalis, Wash. D. Nov. 12, 1965, Clarkston, Wash. BR TR 6'1" 185 lbs.

	W	L	PCT	ERA	G	GS	CG	IP	H	BB	SO	ShO	W	L	SV	AB	H	HR	BA
1913 CLE A	0	0	–	18.00	1	0	0	1	2	0	0	0	0	0	0	0	0	0	–

Hal Gregg

GREGG, HAROLD DANA
B. July 11, 1921, Anaheim, Calif. BR TR 6'3½" 195 lbs.

	W	L	PCT	ERA	G	GS	CG	IP	H	BB	SO	ShO	W	L	SV	AB	H	HR	BA
1943 BKN N	0	3	.000	9.64	5	4	0	18.2	21	21	7	0	0	0	0	2	0	0	.000
1944	9	16	.360	5.46	39	31	6	197.2	201	137	92	0	1	0	2	68	14	0	.206
1945	18	13	.581	3.47	42	34	13	254.1	221	120	139	2	1	2	2	91	20	1	.220
1946	6	4	.600	2.99	26	16	4	117.1	103	44	54	2	1	1	2	32	4	0	.125
1947	4	5	.444	5.87	37	16	2	104.1	115	55	59	1	1	0	1	34	9	0	.265
1948 PIT N	2	4	.333	4.60	22	8	1	74.1	72	34	25	0	0	2	1	22	6	1	.273
1949	1	1	.500	3.38	8	1	0	18.2	20	8	9	0	1	0	0	5	0	0	.000
1950	0	1	.000	13.50	5	1	0	5.1	10	7	3	0	0	0	0	1	0	0	.000
1952 NY N	0	1	.000	4.71	16	4	1	36.1	42	17	13	0	0	0	1	8	1	0	.125
9 yrs.	40	48	.455	4.54	200	115	27	827	805	443	401	5	5	5	9	263	54	2	.205

WORLD SERIES

	W	L	PCT	ERA	G	GS	CG	IP	H	BB	SO	ShO	W	L	SV	AB	H	HR	BA
1947 BKN N	0	1	.000	3.55	3	1	0	12.2	9	8	10	0	0	0	0	3	0	0	.000

Vean Gregg

GREGG, SYLVEANUS AUGUSTUS
Brother of Dave Gregg.
B. Apr. 13, 1885, Chehalis, Wash. D. July 29, 1964, Aberdeen, Wash. BR TL 6'1" 185 lbs.

	W	L	PCT	ERA	G	GS	CG	IP	H	BB	SO	ShO	W	L	SV	AB	H	HR	BA
1911 CLE A	23	7	.767	1.81	34	26	22	244	172	86	125	5	5	0	0	85	14	0	.165
1912	20	13	.606	2.59	37	34	26	271.1	242	90	184	1	0	1	2	97	17	0	.175
1913	20	13	.606	2.24	44	34	23	285.2	258	124	166	3	2	0	3	99	13	0	.131
1914 2 teams		CLE	A (17G 9–3)		BOS	A (12G 3–4)													
" total	12	7	.632	3.44	29	21	10	165	159	85	80	1	2	0	0	52	10	0	.192
1915 BOS A	4	2	.667	3.36	18	9	3	75	71	32	43	1	0	0	3	20	7	0	.350
1916	2	5	.286	3.01	21	7	3	77.2	71	30	41	0	1	1	0	18	2	0	.111
1918 PHI A	8	14	.364	3.12	30	25	17	199.1	180	67	63	3	0	0	2	71	12	0	.169
1925 WAS A	2	2	.500	4.12	26	5	1	74.1	87	38	18	0	1	1	2	14	3	0	.214
8 yrs.	91	63	.591	2.70	239	161	105	1392.1	1240	552	720	14	11	3	12	456	78	0	.171

Frank Gregory

GREGORY, FRANK ERNST
B. July 25, 1890, Beloit, Wis. D. Nov. 5, 1955, Beloit, Wis. BR TR 5'11" 185 lbs.

	W	L	PCT	ERA	G	GS	CG	IP	H	BB	SO	ShO	W	L	SV	AB	H	HR	BA
1912 CIN N	2	0	1.000	4.60	4	2	1	15.2	19	7	4	0	1	0	0	5	1	0	.200

Howie Gregory

GREGORY, HOWARD WATTERSON
B. Nov. 18, 1886, Hannibal, Mo. D. May 30, 1970, Tulsa, Okla. BL TR 6' 175 lbs.

	W	L	PCT	ERA	G	GS	CG	IP	H	BB	SO	ShO	W	L	SV	AB	H	HR	BA
1911 STL A	0	1	.000	5.14	3	1	0	7	11	4	1	0	0	0	0	2	0	0	.000

Lee Gregory

GREGORY, GROVER LeROY
B. June 2, 1938, Bakersfield, Calif. BL TL 6'1" 180 lbs.

	W	L	PCT	ERA	G	GS	CG	IP	H	BB	SO	ShO	W	L	SV	AB	H	HR	BA
1964 CHI N	0	0	–	3.50	11	0	0	18	23	5	8	0	0	0	0	13	1	0	.077

	W	L	PCT	ERA	G	GS	CG	IP	H	BB	SO	ShO	Relief Pitching W	L	SV	BATTING AB	H	HR	BA

Paul Gregory

GREGORY, PAUL EDWIN (Pop)
B. July 9, 1908, Tomnolen, Miss. — BR TR 6'2" 180 lbs.

	W	L	PCT	ERA	G	GS	CG	IP	H	BB	SO	ShO	W	L	SV	AB	H	HR	BA
1932 CHI A	5	3	.625	4.51	33	9	3	117.2	125	51	39	0	2	0	0	38	3	0	.079
1933	4	11	.267	4.95	23	17	5	103.2	124	47	18	0	0	0	0	35	5	0	.143
2 yrs.	9	14	.391	4.72	56	26	8	221.1	249	98	57	0	2	0	0	73	8	0	.110

Bill Greif

GREIF, WILLIAM BRILEY
B. Apr. 25, 1950, Ft Stockton, Tex. — BB TR 6'4" 196 lbs.

	W	L	PCT	ERA	G	GS	CG	IP	H	BB	SO	ShO	W	L	SV	AB	H	HR	BA
1971 HOU N	1	1	.500	5.06	7	3	0	16	18	8	14	0	1	0	0	3	1	0	.333
1972 SD N	5	16	.238	5.60	34	22	2	125.1	143	47	91	1	1	0	2	33	1	0	.030
1973	10	17	.370	3.21	36	31	9	199.1	181	62	120	3	0	0	1	61	6	0	.098
1974	9	19	.321	4.66	43	35	7	226	244	95	137	1	0	0	1	56	4	0	.071
1975	4	6	.400	3.88	59	1	0	72	74	38	43	0	4	6	9	1	0	0	.000
1976 2 teams	SD N (5G 1–3)				STL N (47G 1–5)														
" total	2	8	.200	5.26	52	5	0	77	87	37	37	0	1	5	6	12	0	0	.000
6 yrs.	31	67	.316	4.41	231	97	18	715.2	747	287	442	5	7	11	19	166	12	0	.072

Bill Grevell

GREVELL, WILLIAM
B. Mar. 5, 1898, Williamstown, N. J. D. June 21, 1923, Springfield Twp., Pa. — BR TR 5'11" 170 lbs.

	W	L	PCT	ERA	G	GS	CG	IP	H	BB	SO	ShO	W	L	SV	AB	H	HR	BA
1919 PHI A	0	0	–	14.25	5	2	0	12	15	18	3	0	0	0	0	5	0	0	.000

Lee Griffeth

GRIFFETH, LEON CLIFFORD
B. May 20, 1925, Carmel, N. Y. — BB TL 5'11½" 180 lbs.

	W	L	PCT	ERA	G	GS	CG	IP	H	BB	SO	ShO	W	L	SV	AB	H	HR	BA
1946 PHI A	0	0	–	2.93	10	0	0	15.1	13	6	4	0	0	0	0	1	0	0	.000

Hank Griffin

GRIFFIN, JAMES LINTON
B. July 11, 1886, Whitehouse, Tex. D. Feb. 11, 1950, Terrell, Tex. — BR TR 6' 170 lbs.

	W	L	PCT	ERA	G	GS	CG	IP	H	BB	SO	ShO	W	L	SV	AB	H	HR	BA
1911 2 teams	CHI N (1G 0–0)				BOS N (15G 0–6)														
" total	0	6	.000	5.38	16	7	1	83.2	97	37	31	0	0	1	0	30	7	0	.233
1912 BOS N	0	0	–	27.00	3	0	0	1.2	3	3	0	0	0	0	0	0	0	0	–
2 yrs.	0	6	.000	5.80	19	7	1	85.1	100	40	31	0	0	1	0	30	7	0	.233

Marty Griffin

GRIFFIN, MARTIN JOHN
B. Sept. 2, 1901, San Francisco, Calif. D. Nov. 19, 1951, Los Angeles, Calif. — BR TR 6'2" 200 lbs.

	W	L	PCT	ERA	G	GS	CG	IP	H	BB	SO	ShO	W	L	SV	AB	H	HR	BA
1928 BOS A	0	3	.000	5.02	11	3	0	37.2	42	17	9	0	0	0	0	13	4	0	.308

Mike Griffin

GRIFFIN, MICHAEL LEROY
B. June 26, 1957, Colusa, Calif. — BR TR 6'4" 195 lbs.

	W	L	PCT	ERA	G	GS	CG	IP	H	BB	SO	ShO	W	L	SV	AB	H	HR	BA
1979 NY A	0	0	–	4.50	3	0	0	4	5	2	5	0	0	0	1	0	0	0	–
1980	2	4	.333	4.83	13	9	0	54	64	23	25	0	0	1	0	0	0	0	–
1981 2 teams	NY A (2G 0–0)				CHI N (16G 2–5)														
" total	2	5	.286	4.34	18	9	0	56	69	9	24	0	0	0	1	13	2	0	.154
1982 SD N	0	1	.000	3.48	7	0	0	10.1	9	3	4	0	0	1	0	1	0	0	.000
4 yrs.	4	10	.286	4.49	41	18	0	124.1	147	37	58	0	0	2	2	14	2	0	.143

Pat Griffin

GRIFFIN, PATRICK RICHARD
B. May 6, 1893, Niles, Ohio D. June 7, 1927, Youngstown, Ohio — BR TR 6'2" 180 lbs.

	W	L	PCT	ERA	G	GS	CG	IP	H	BB	SO	ShO	W	L	SV	AB	H	HR	BA
1914 CIN N	0	0	–	9.00	1	0	0	1	3	2	0	0	0	0	0	0	0	0	–

Tom Griffin

GRIFFIN, THOMAS JAMES
B. Feb. 22, 1948, Los Angeles, Calif. — BR TR 6'3" 210 lbs.

	W	L	PCT	ERA	G	GS	CG	IP	H	BB	SO	ShO	W	L	SV	AB	H	HR	BA
1969 HOU N	11	10	.524	3.54	31	31	6	188	156	93	200	3	0	0	0	62	9	2	.145
1970	3	13	.188	5.76	23	20	2	111	118	72	72	1	0	0	0	33	2	0	.061
1971	0	6	.000	4.74	10	6	0	38	44	20	29	0	0	2	0	9	1	0	.111
1972	5	4	.556	3.24	39	5	1	94.1	92	38	83	1	4	1	3	25	7	1	.280
1973	4	6	.400	4.15	25	12	4	99.2	83	46	69	0	0	1	0	28	3	1	.107
1974	14	10	.583	3.54	34	34	8	211	202	89	110	3	0	0	0	68	20	2	.294
1975	3	8	.273	5.35	17	13	3	79	89	46	56	1	0	0	0	22	3	0	.136
1976 2 teams	HOU N (20G 5–3)				SD N (11G 4–3)														
" total	9	6	.600	4.10	31	13	2	112	100	79	69	0	5	1	0	31	2	0	.065
1977 SD N	6	9	.400	4.47	38	20	0	151	144	88	79	0	2	1	0	45	6	2	.133
1978 CAL A	3	4	.429	4.02	24	4	0	56	63	31	35	0	3	1	0	0	0	0	–
1979 SF N	5	6	.455	3.93	59	3	0	94	83	46	82	0	5	3	2	14	1	0	.071
1980	5	1	.833	2.75	42	4	0	108	80	49	79	0	3	1	0	18	2	1	.111
1981	8	8	.500	3.77	22	22	3	129	121	57	83	1	0	0	0	41	8	1	.195
1982 PIT N	1	3	.250	8.87	6	2	0	22.1	32	15	8	0	0	0	0	9	2	0	.222
14 yrs.	77	94	.450	4.07	401	191	29	1493.1	1407	769	1054	10	22	11	5	405	66	10	.163

Clark Griffith

GRIFFITH, CLARK CALVIN (The Old Fox)
B. Nov. 20, 1869, Stringtown, Mo. D. Oct. 27, 1955, Washington, D. C. — BR TR 5'6½" 156 lbs.
Manager 1901-20.
Hall of Fame 1946.

	W	L	PCT	ERA	G	GS	CG	IP	H	BB	SO	ShO	W	L	SV	AB	H	HR	BA
1891 2 teams	STL AA (27G 14–6)				BOS AA (7G 3–1)														
" total	17	7	.708	3.74	34	21	15	226.1	242	73	88	0	7	0	0	100	16	2	.160
1893 CHI N	1	1	.500	5.03	4	2	2	19.2	24	5	9	0	0	1	0	11	2	0	.182
1894	21	11	.656	4.92	36	30	28	261.1	328	85	71	0	3	3	0	142	33	0	.232
1895	25	13	.658	3.93	42	41	39	353	434	91	79	0	1	0	0	144	46	1	.319
1896	22	13	.629	3.54	36	35	35	317.2	370	70	81	0	0	0	0	135	36	1	.267
1897	21	19	.525	3.72	41	38	38	343.2	410	86	102	1	1	0	1	162	38	0	.235
1898	26	10	.722	1.88	38	38	36	325.2	305	64	97	4	0	0	0	122	20	0	.164
1899	22	13	.629	2.79	38	38	35	319.2	329	65	73	0	0	0	0	120	31	0	.258
1900	14	13	.519	3.05	30	30	27	248	245	51	61	0	4	0	0	95	24	1	.253
1901 CHI A	24	7	.774	2.67	35	30	26	266.2	275	50	67	5	3	0	1	89	27	2	.303
1902	15	9	.625	4.19	28	24	20	212.2	247	47	51	3	2	0	0	92	20	0	.217
1903 NY A	14	11	.560	2.70	25	24	22	213	201	33	69	3	1	0	0	69	11	1	.159
1904	7	5	.583	2.87	16	11	8	100.1	91	16	36	1	1	0	0	42	6	0	.143

	W	L	PCT	ERA	G	GS	CG	IP	H	BB	SO	ShO	Relief Pitching W	L	SV	BATTING AB	H	HR	BA

Connie Grob

GROB, CONRAD GEORGE
B. Nov. 9, 1932, Cross Plains, Wis.   BL TR 6'½" 180 lbs.

	W	L	PCT	ERA	G	GS	CG	IP	H	BB	SO	ShO	W	L	SV	AB	H	HR	BA
1956 WAS A	4	5	.444	7.83	37	1	0	79.1	121	26	27	0	4	5	1	18	6	0	.333

Johnny Grodzicki

GRODZICKI, JOHN
B. Feb. 26, 1917, Nanticoke, Pa.   BR TR 6'2" 200 lbs.

	W	L	PCT	ERA	G	GS	CG	IP	H	BB	SO	ShO	W	L	SV	AB	H	HR	BA
1941 STL N	2	1	.667	1.35	5	1	0	13.1	6	11	10	0	2	0	0	2	0	0	.000
1946	0	0	–	9.00	3	0	0	4	4	4	2	0	0	0	0	0	0	0	–
1947	0	1	.000	5.40	16	0	0	23.1	21	19	8	0	0	1	0	1	0	0	.000
3 yrs.	2	2	.500	4.43	24	1	0	40.2	31	34	20	0	2	1	0	3	0	0	.000

Steve Gromek

GROMEK, STEPHEN JOSEPH
B. Jan. 15, 1920, Hamtramck, Mich.   BB TR 6'2" 180 lbs.
BR 1941-49

	W	L	PCT	ERA	G	GS	CG	IP	H	BB	SO	ShO	W	L	SV	AB	H	HR	BA
1941 CLE A	1	1	.500	4.24	9	2	1	23.1	25	11	19	0	0	0	2	6	1	0	.167
1942	2	0	1.000	3.65	14	0	0	44.1	46	23	14	0	2	0	0	15	5	0	.333
1943	0	0	–	9.00	3	0	0	4	6	0	4	0	0	0	0	2	2	0	1.000
1944	10	9	.526	2.56	35	21	12	203.2	160	70	115	2	0	1	1	73	19	0	.260
1945	19	9	.679	2.55	33	30	21	251	229	66	101	3	0	1	1	91	21	0	.231
1946	5	15	.250	4.33	29	21	5	153.2	159	47	75	2	0	2	4	56	11	0	.196
1947	3	5	.375	3.74	29	7	0	84.1	77	36	39	0	1	3	4	22	7	0	.318
1948	9	3	.750	2.84	38	9	4	130	109	51	50	1	3	1	2	41	6	0	.146
1949	4	6	.400	3.33	27	12	3	92	86	40	22	0	1	2	0	24	4	0	.167
1950	10	7	.588	3.65	31	13	4	113.1	94	36	43	1	4	0	0	38	6	0	.158
1951	7	4	.636	2.77	27	8	4	107.1	98	29	40	0	3	2	1	27	8	0	.296
1952	7	7	.500	3.67	29	13	3	122.2	109	28	65	1	1	1	1	30	3	0	.100
1953 2 teams		CLE	A (5G 1–1)			DET	A	(19G 6–8)											
" total	7	9	.438	4.41	24	18	6	136.2	149	39	67	1	1	0	1	43	3	0	.070
1954 DET A	18	16	.529	2.74	36	32	17	252.2	236	57	102	4	2	0	1	79	15	0	.190
1955	13	10	.565	3.98	28	25	8	181	183	37	73	2	2	0	0	54	9	0	.167
1956	8	6	.571	4.28	40	13	4	141	142	47	64	0	3	0	4	27	4	0	.148
1957	0	1	.000	6.08	15	1	0	23.2	32	13	11	0	0	1	0	2	0	0	.000
17 yrs.	123	108	.532	3.41	447	225	92	2064.2	1940	630	904	17	23	14	23	630	124	0	.197

WORLD SERIES

	W	L	PCT	ERA	G	GS	CG	IP	H	BB	SO	ShO	W	L	SV	AB	H	HR	BA
1948 CLE A	1	0	1.000	1.00	1	1	1	9	7	1	2	0	0	0	0	3	0	0	.000

Bob Groom

GROOM, ROBERT
B. Sept. 12, 1884, Belleville, Ill.   D. Feb. 19, 1948, Belleville, Ill.   BR TR 6'2" 175 lbs.

	W	L	PCT	ERA	G	GS	CG	IP	H	BB	SO	ShO	W	L	SV	AB	H	HR	BA
1909 WAS A	7	26	.212	2.87	44	31	17	260.2	218	105	131	1	2	1	0	88	8	0	.091
1910	12	17	.414	2.76	34	30	22	257.2	255	77	98	3	0	2	0	92	11	0	.120
1911	13	17	.433	3.82	37	32	20	254.2	280	67	135	2	1	0	2	82	11	0	.134
1912	24	13	.649	2.62	43	40	28	316	287	94	179	2	0	2	1	103	12	0	.117
1913	16	16	.500	3.23	37	36	17	264.1	258	81	156	4	0	1	0	92	15	0	.163
1914 STL F	13	20	.394	3.24	42	34	23	280.2	281	75	167	1	0	3	1	94	15	0	.160
1915	12	11	.522	3.27	37	26	11	209	200	73	111	4	2	0	1	66	10	0	.152
1916 STL A	13	9	.591	2.57	41	26	6	217.1	174	98	92	1	2	1	4	63	7	0	.111
1917	8	19	.296	2.94	38	28	11	232.2	193	95	82	4	1	1	3	72	8	0	.111
1918 CLE A	2	2	.500	7.06	14	5	0	43.1	70	18	8	0	1	0	0	12	1	0	.083
10 yrs.	120	150	.444	3.10	367	288	155	2336.1	2216	783	1159	22	9	11	12	764	98	0	.128

Don Gross

GROSS, DONALD JOHN
B. June 30, 1931, Weidman, Mich.   BL TL 5'11" 186 lbs.

	W	L	PCT	ERA	G	GS	CG	IP	H	BB	SO	ShO	W	L	SV	AB	H	HR	BA
1955 CIN N	4	5	.444	4.14	17	11	2	67.1	79	16	33	1	0	2	0	19	3	0	.158
1956	3	0	1.000	1.95	19	7	2	69.1	69	20	47	0	0	0	0	19	2	0	.105
1957	7	9	.438	4.31	43	16	5	148.1	152	33	73	0	1	4	1	46	5	0	.109
1958 PIT N	5	7	.417	3.98	40	3	0	74.2	67	38	59	0	5	5	7	18	1	0	.056
1959	1	1	.500	3.55	21	0	0	33	28	10	15	0	1	1	2	2	0	0	.000
1960	0	0	–	3.38	5	0	0	5.1	5	0	3	0	0	0	0	0	0	0	–
6 yrs.	20	22	.476	3.73	145	37	9	398	400	117	230	1	7	12	10	104	11	0	.106

Kevin Gross

GROSS, KEVIN FRANK
B. June 8, 1961, Downey, Calif.   BR TR 6'5" 200 lbs.

	W	L	PCT	ERA	G	GS	CG	IP	H	BB	SO	ShO	W	L	SV	AB	H	HR	BA
1983 PHI N	4	6	.400	3.56	17	17	1	96	100	35	66	1	0	0	0	33	3	0	.091
1984	8	5	.615	4.12	44	14	1	129	140	44	84	0	4	0	1	30	2	0	.067
2 yrs.	12	11	.522	3.88	61	31	2	225	240	79	150	1	4	0	1	63	5	0	.079

Wayne Gross

GROSS, WAYNE DALE
B. Jan. 14, 1952, Riverside, Calif.   BL TR 6'2" 210 lbs.

	W	L	PCT	ERA	G	GS	CG	IP	H	BB	SO	ShO	W	L	SV	AB	H	HR	BA
1983 OAK A	0	0	–	0.00	1	0	0	2.1	2	1	0	0	0	0	0	*			

Harley Grossman

GROSSMAN, HARLEY JOSEPH
B. May 5, 1930, Evansville, Ind.   BR TR 6' 170 lbs.

	W	L	PCT	ERA	G	GS	CG	IP	H	BB	SO	ShO	W	L	SV	AB	H	HR	BA
1952 WAS A	0	0	–	54.00	1	0	0	.1	2	0	0	0	0	0	0	0	0	0	–

Ed Groth

GROTH, EDWARD JOHN
B. Dec. 24, 1885, Cedarburg, Wis.   D. May 23, 1950, Milwaukee, Wis.   BR TR 6'2" 175 lbs.

	W	L	PCT	ERA	G	GS	CG	IP	H	BB	SO	ShO	W	L	SV	AB	H	HR	BA
1904 CHI N	0	2	.000	5.63	3	2	2	16	22	6	9	0	0	0	1	6	0	0	.000

Ernie Groth

GROTH, ERNEST WILLIAM
B. May 3, 1922, Beaver Falls, Pa.   BR TR 5'9" 185 lbs.

	W	L	PCT	ERA	G	GS	CG	IP	H	BB	SO	ShO	W	L	SV	AB	H	HR	BA
1947 CLE A	0	0	–	0.00	2	0	0	1.1	0	1	0	0	0	0	0	0	0	0	–
1948	0	0	–	9.00	1	0	0	1	1	2	0	0	0	0	0	0	0	0	–
1949 CHI A	0	1	.000	5.40	3	0	0	5	2	3	1	0	0	1	0	0	0	0	–
3 yrs.	0	1	.000	4.91	6	0	0	7.1	3	6	2	0	0	1	0	0	0	0	–

	W	L	PCT	ERA	G	GS	CG	IP	H	BB	SO	ShO	Relief Pitching W	L	SV	Batting AB	H	HR	BA

Lefty Grove

GROVE, ROBERT MOSES (Mose)
B. Mar. 6, 1900, Lonaconing, Md.   D. May 23, 1975, Norwalk, Ohio
Hall of Fame 1947.
BL TL 6'3" 190 lbs.

	W	L	PCT	ERA	G	GS	CG	IP	H	BB	SO	ShO	W	L	SV	AB	H	HR	BA
1925 PHI A	10	13	.435	4.75	45	18	5	197	207	131	116	0	5	3	1	65	8	0	.123
1926	13	13	.500	2.51	45	33	20	258	227	101	194	1	1	1	6	81	8	0	.099
1927	20	12	.625	3.19	51	28	14	262.1	251	79	174	1	3	5	9	80	10	2	.125
1928	24	8	.750	2.58	39	31	24	261.2	228	64	183	4	1	0	4	88	15	1	.170
1929	20	6	.769	2.81	42	37	21	275.1	278	81	170	2	0	0	4	102	22	1	.216
1930	28	5	.848	2.54	50	32	22	291	273	60	209	2	5	2	9	110	22	2	.200
1931	31	4	.886	2.06	41	30	27	288.2	249	62	175	4	4	1	5	115	23	0	.200
1932	25	10	.714	2.84	44	30	27	291.2	269	79	188	4	3	2	7	107	18	4	.168
1933	24	8	.750	3.20	45	28	21	275.1	280	83	114	2	6	2	6	105	9	1	.086
1934 BOS A	8	8	.500	6.50	22	11	5	109.1	149	32	43	0	3	3	0	37	6	1	.162
1935	20	12	.625	2.70	35	30	23	273	269	65	121	2	2	1	1	89	7	1	.079
1936	17	12	.586	2.81	35	30	22	253.1	237	65	130	6	0	2	2	80	11	0	.138
1937	17	9	.654	3.02	32	32	21	262	269	83	153	3	0	0	0	91	13	0	.143
1938	14	4	.778	3.08	24	21	12	163.2	169	52	99	1	0	0	1	54	8	0	.148
1939	15	4	.789	2.54	23	23	17	191	180	58	81	2	0	0	0	67	9	1	.134
1940	7	6	.538	3.99	22	21	9	153.1	159	50	62	1	0	0	0	53	8	1	.151
1941	7	7	.500	4.37	21	21	10	134	155	42	54	0	0	0	0	45	5	0	.111
17 yrs.	300	141	.680	3.06	616	456	300	3940.2	3849	1187	2266	35	33	22	55	1369	202	15	.148
				5th															

WORLD SERIES

	W	L	PCT	ERA	G	GS	CG	IP	H	BB	SO	ShO	W	L	SV	AB	H	HR	BA
1929 PHI A	0	0	—	0.00	2	0	0	6.1	3	1	10	0	0	0	2	2	0	0	.000
1930	2	1	.667	1.42	3	2	2	19	15	3	10	0	1	0	0	6	0	0	.000
1931	2	1	.667	2.42	3	3	2	26	28	2	16	0	0	0	0	10	0	0	.000
3 yrs.	4	2	.667	1.75	8	5	4	51.1	46	6	36	0	1	0	2	18	0	0	.000

Orval Grove

GROVE, LeROY ORVAL
B. Aug. 29, 1919, Mineral, Kans.
BR TR 6'3" 196 lbs.

	W	L	PCT	ERA	G	GS	CG	IP	H	BB	SO	ShO	W	L	SV	AB	H	HR	BA
1940 CHI A	0	0	—	3.00	3	0	0	6	4	4	1	0	0	0	0	0	0	0	.000
1941	0	0	—	10.29	2	0	0	7	9	5	5	0	0	0	0	2	0	0	.000
1942	4	6	.400	5.16	12	8	4	66.1	77	33	21	0	1	1	0	22	5	1	.227
1943	15	9	.625	2.75	32	25	18	216.1	192	72	76	3	1	0	2	66	12	0	.182
1944	14	15	.483	3.72	34	33	11	234.2	237	71	105	2	1	0	0	77	8	0	.104
1945	14	12	.538	3.44	33	30	16	217	217	68	54	4	0	0	1	71	7	0	.099
1946	8	13	.381	3.02	33	26	10	205.1	213	78	60	1	0	0	0	65	7	0	.108
1947	6	8	.429	4.44	25	19	6	135.2	158	70	33	1	0	0	0	48	7	0	.146
1948	2	10	.167	6.16	32	11	1	87.2	110	42	18	0	1	2	1	21	2	0	.095
1949	0	0	—	54.00	1	0	0	.2	4	1	1	0	0	0	0	0	0	0	—
10 yrs.	63	73	.463	3.78	207	152	66	1176.2	1237	444	374	11	4	3	4	373	48	1	.129

Charlie Grover

GROVER, CHARLES BERT (Bugs)
B. June 20, 1891, Vanceton, Ohio   D. May 24, 1971, Emmett Township, Mich.
BL TR 6'1½" 185 lbs.

	W	L	PCT	ERA	G	GS	CG	IP	H	BB	SO	ShO	W	L	SV	AB	H	HR	BA
1913 DET A	0	0	—	3.38	2	1	0	10.2	9	7	2	0	0	0	0	3	0	0	.000

Tom Grubbs

GRUBBS, THOMAS DILLARD (Judge)
B. Feb. 22, 1894, Mt. Sterling, Ky.
BR TR 6'2" 165 lbs.

	W	L	PCT	ERA	G	GS	CG	IP	H	BB	SO	ShO	W	L	SV	AB	H	HR	BA
1920 NY N	0	1	.000	7.20	1	0	5	9	0	0	0	0	0	0	0	1	0	0	.000

Henry Gruber

GRUBER, HENRY JOHN
B. Dec. 14, 1864, New Haven, Conn.   D. Sept. 26, 1932, New Haven, Conn.
BR TL

	W	L	PCT	ERA	G	GS	CG	IP	H	BB	SO	ShO	W	L	SV	AB	H	HR	BA
1887 DET N	4	3	.571	2.74	7	7	7	62.1	63	21	12	0	0	0	0	24	4	0	.167
1888	11	14	.440	2.29	27	25	25	240	196	41	71	3	1	1	0	92	13	0	.141
1889 CLE N	7	16	.304	3.64	25	23	23	205	198	94	74	0	1	0	1	69	7	0	.101
1890 CLE P	21	23	.477	4.27	48	44	39	383.1	464	204	110	1	0	0	1	163	36	0	.221
1891 CLE N	17	22	.436	4.13	44	40	35	348.2	407	119	79	1	2	1	0	141	23	1	.163
5 yrs.	60	78	.435	3.67	151	139	129	1239.1	1328	479	346	5	4	2	2	489	83	1	.170

Al Grunwald

GRUNWALD, ALFRED HENRY (Stretch)
B. Feb. 13, 1930, Los Angeles, Calif.
BL TL 6'4" 210 lbs.

	W	L	PCT	ERA	G	GS	CG	IP	H	BB	SO	ShO	W	L	SV	AB	H	HR	BA
1955 PIT N	0	0	—	4.70	3	0	0	7.2	7	7	2	0	0	0	0	4	2	0	.500
1959 KC A	0	1	.000	7.94	6	1	0	11.1	18	11	9	0	0	0	1	4	0	0	.000
2 yrs.	0	1	.000	6.63	9	1	0	19	25	18	11	0	0	0	1	8	2	0	.250

Joe Grzenda

GRZENDA, JOSEPH CHARLES
B. June 8, 1937, Scranton, Pa.
BR TL 6'2" 180 lbs.

	W	L	PCT	ERA	G	GS	CG	IP	H	BB	SO	ShO	W	L	SV	AB	H	HR	BA
1961 DET A	1	0	1.000	7.94	4	0	0	5.2	9	2	0	0	1	0	0	1	1	0	1.000
1964 KC A	0	2	.000	5.40	20	0	0	25	34	13	17	0	0	2	0	2	0	0	.000
1966	0	2	.000	3.27	21	0	0	22	28	12	14	0	0	2	0	1	0	0	.000
1967 NY N	0	0	—	2.16	11	0	0	16.2	14	8	9	0	0	0	1	1	0	0	.000
1969 MIN A	4	1	.800	3.88	38	0	0	48.2	52	17	24	0	4	1	3	5	0	0	.000
1970 WAS A	3	6	.333	4.98	49	3	0	85	86	34	38	0	2	5	6	12	0	0	.000
1971	5	2	.714	1.93	46	0	0	70	54	17	56	0	5	2	5	7	1	0	.143
1972 STL N	1	0	1.000	5.71	30	0	0	34.2	46	17	15	0	1	0	0	1	0	0	.000
8 yrs.	14	13	.519	4.01	219	3	0	307.2	323	120	173	0	13	12	14	30	2	0	.067

LEAGUE CHAMPIONSHIP SERIES

	W	L	PCT	ERA	G	GS	CG	IP	H	BB	SO	ShO	W	L	SV	AB	H	HR	BA
1969 MIN A	0	0	—	0.00	1	0	0	.2	0	0	1	0	0	0	0	0	0	0	—

Cecilio Guante

GUANTE, CECILIO
Also known as Cecilio Magallanes.
B. Feb. 1, 1961, Villa Hella, Dominican Republic
BR TR 6'3" 185 lbs.

	W	L	PCT	ERA	G	GS	CG	IP	H	BB	SO	ShO	W	L	SV	AB	H	HR	BA
1982 PIT N	0	0	—	3.33	10	0	0	27	28	5	26	0	0	0	0	5	0	0	.000
1983	2	6	.250	3.32	49	0	0	100.1	90	46	82	0	2	6	9	22	2	0	.091
1984	2	3	.400	2.61	27	0	0	41.1	32	16	30	0	2	3	2	4	0	0	.000
3 yrs.	4	9	.308	3.15	86	0	0	168.2	150	67	138	0	4	9	11	31	2	0	.065

	W	L	PCT	ERA	G	GS	CG	IP	H	BB	SO	ShO	Relief Pitching W	L	SV	BATTING AB	H	HR	BA

Mark Gubicza

GUBICZA, MARK STEVEN
B. Aug. 14, 1962, Philadelphia, Pa.
BR TR 6'5" 215 lbs.

	W	L	PCT	ERA	G	GS	CG	IP	H	BB	SO	ShO	W	L	SV	AB	H	HR	BA
1984 KC A	10	14	.417	4.05	29	29	4	189	172	75	111	2	0	0	0	0	0	0	–

Marv Gudat

GUDAT, MARVIN JOHN
B. Aug. 27, 1905, Coliad, Tex.   D. Mar. 1, 1954, Los Angeles, Calif.
BL TL 5'11" 176 lbs.

	W	L	PCT	ERA	G	GS	CG	IP	H	BB	SO	ShO	W	L	SV	AB	H	HR	BA
1929 CIN N	1	1	.500	3.38	7	2	2	26.2	29	4	0	0	0	0	0	10	2	0	.200
1932 CHI N	0	0	–	0.00	1	0	0	1	1	0	2	0	0	0	0	94	24	1	.255
2 yrs.	1	1	.500	3.25	8	2	2	27.2	30	4	2	0	0	0	0	*			

Whitey Guese

GUESE, THEODORE
B. Jan. 24, 1872, New Bremen, Ohio   D. Apr. 8, 1951, Wapakoneta, Ohio
BR TR 6'½" 200 lbs.

	W	L	PCT	ERA	G	GS	CG	IP	H	BB	SO	ShO	W	L	SV	AB	H	HR	BA
1901 CIN N	1	4	.200	6.09	6	5	4	44.1	62	14	11	0	0	0	0	15	3	0	.200

Lee Guetterman

GUETTERMAN, ARTHUR LEE
B. Nov. 22, 1956, Chattanooga, Tenn.
BL TL 6'8" 225 lbs.

	W	L	PCT	ERA	G	GS	CG	IP	H	BB	SO	ShO	W	L	SV	AB	H	HR	BA
1984 SEA A	0	0	–	4.15	3	1	0	4.1	9	2	2	0	0	0	0	0	0	0	–

Ron Guidry

GUIDRY, RONALD AMES (Louisiana Lightning, Gator)
B. Aug. 28, 1950, Carencero, La.
BL TL 5'11" 161 lbs.

	W	L	PCT	ERA	G	GS	CG	IP	H	BB	SO	ShO	W	L	SV	AB	H	HR	BA
1975 NY A	0	1	.000	3.45	10	1	0	15.2	15	9	15	0	0	0	0	0	0	0	–
1976	0	0	–	5.63	7	0	0	16	20	4	12	0	0	0	0	0	0	0	–
1977	16	7	.696	2.82	31	25	9	211	174	65	176	5	1	0	1	0	0	0	–
1978	25	3	.893	1.74	35	35	16	273.2	187	72	248	9	0	0	0	0	0	0	–
1979	18	8	.692	2.78	33	30	15	236	203	71	201	2	1	0	2	0	0	0	–
1980	17	10	.630	3.56	37	29	5	220	215	80	166	3	1	1	1	0	0	0	–
1981	11	5	.688	2.76	23	21	0	127	100	26	104	0	0	0	0	0	0	0	–
1982	14	8	.636	3.81	34	33	6	222	216	69	162	1	0	0	0	0	0	0	–
1983	21	9	.700	3.42	31	31	21	250.1	232	60	156	3	0	0	0	0	0	0	–
1984	10	11	.476	4.51	29	28	5	195.2	223	44	127	1	0	0	0	0	0	0	–
10 yrs.	132	62	.680 4th	3.16	270	233	77	1767.1	1585	500	1367	24	3	1	4	0	0	0	–

DIVISIONAL PLAYOFF SERIES

	W	L	PCT	ERA	G	GS	CG	IP	H	BB	SO	ShO	W	L	SV	AB	H	HR	BA
1981 NY A	0	0	–	5.40	2	2	0	8.1	11	3	8	0	0	0	0	0	0	0	–

LEAGUE CHAMPIONSHIP SERIES

	W	L	PCT	ERA	G	GS	CG	IP	H	BB	SO	ShO	W	L	SV	AB	H	HR	BA
1977 NY A	1	0	1.000	3.97	2	2	1	11.1	9	3	8	0	0	0	0	0	0	0	–
1978	1	0	1.000	1.13	1	1	0	8	7	1	7	0	0	0	0	0	0	0	–
1980	0	1	.000	12.00	1	1	0	3	5	4	2	0	0	0	0	0	0	0	–
3 yrs.	2	1	.667	4.03	4	4	1	22.1	21	8	17	0	0	0	0	0	0	0	–

WORLD SERIES

	W	L	PCT	ERA	G	GS	CG	IP	H	BB	SO	ShO	W	L	SV	AB	H	HR	BA
1977 NY A	1	0	1.000	2.00	1	1	1	9	4	3	7	0	0	0	0	2	0	0	.000
1978	1	0	1.000	1.00	1	1	1	9	8	7	4	0	0	0	0	0	0	0	–
1981	1	1	.500	1.93	2	2	0	14	8	4	15	0	0	0	0	5	0	0	.000
3 yrs.	3	1	.750	1.69	4	4	2	32	20	14	26	0	0	0	0	7	0	0	.000

Skip Guinn

GUINN, DRANNON EUGENE
B. Oct. 25, 1944, St. Charles, Mo.
BR TL 5'10" 180 lbs.

	W	L	PCT	ERA	G	GS	CG	IP	H	BB	SO	ShO	W	L	SV	AB	H	HR	BA
1968 ATL N	0	0	–	3.60	3	0	0	5	3	3	4	0	0	0	0	0	0	0	–
1969 HOU N	1	2	.333	6.67	28	0	0	27	34	21	33	0	1	2	0	3	0	0	.000
1971	0	0	–	0.00	4	0	0	5	1	3	3	0	0	0	1	0	0	0	–
3 yrs.	1	2	.333	5.35	35	0	0	37	38	27	40	0	1	2	1	3	0	0	.000

Witt Guise

GUISE, WITT ORISON (Lefty)
B. Sept. 18, 1908, Driggs, Ark.   D. Aug. 13, 1968, Little Rock, Ark.
BL TL 6'2" 172 lbs.

	W	L	PCT	ERA	G	GS	CG	IP	H	BB	SO	ShO	W	L	SV	AB	H	HR	BA
1940 CIN N	0	0	–	1.17	2	0	0	7.2	8	5	1	0	0	0	0	3	1	0	.333

Don Gullett

GULLETT, DONALD EDWARD
B. Jan. 5, 1951, Lynn, Ky.
BR TL 6' 190 lbs.

	W	L	PCT	ERA	G	GS	CG	IP	H	BB	SO	ShO	W	L	SV	AB	H	HR	BA
1970 CIN N	5	2	.714	2.42	44	2	0	78	54	44	76	0	4	1	6	19	4	0	.211
1971	16	6	.727	2.64	35	31	4	218	196	64	107	3	0	0	0	75	9	0	.120
1972	9	10	.474	3.94	31	16	2	134.2	127	43	96	0	3	2	2	38	8	0	.211
1973	18	8	.692	3.51	45	30	7	228.1	198	69	153	4	4	4	2	64	12	0	.188
1974	17	11	.607	3.04	36	35	10	243	201	88	183	3	0	1	0	80	19	0	.238
1975	15	4	.789	2.42	22	22	8	160	127	56	98	3	0	0	0	62	14	0	.226
1976	11	3	.786	3.00	23	20	4	126	119	48	64	0	1	0	1	44	8	0	.182
1977 NY A	14	4	.778	3.59	22	22	7	158	137	69	116	1	0	0	0	0	0	0	–
1978	4	2	.667	3.63	8	8	2	44.2	46	20	28	0	0	0	0	0	0	0	–
9 yrs.	109	50	.686	3.11	266	186	44	1390.2	1205	501	921	14	12	8	11	382	74	0	.194

LEAGUE CHAMPIONSHIP SERIES

	W	L	PCT	ERA	G	GS	CG	IP	H	BB	SO	ShO	W	L	SV	AB	H	HR	BA
1970 CIN N	0	0	–	0.00	2	0	0	3.2	1	2	3	0	0	0	2	1	0	0	.000
1972	0	1	.000	8.00	2	2	0	9	12	0	5	0	0	0	0	2	1	0	.500
1973	0	1	.000	2.00	3	1	0	9	4	3	6	0	0	0	0	1	0	0	.000
1975	1	0	1.000	3.00	1	1	1	9	8	2	5	0	0	0	0	4	2	1	.500
1976	1	0	1.000	1.13	1	1	0	8	2	3	4	0	0	0	0	4	2	0	.500
1977 NY A	0	1	.000	18.00	1	1	0	2	4	2	0	0	0	0	0	0	0	0	–
6 yrs.	2	3	.400	3.98	10	6	1	40.2	31	12	23	0	0	0	2	12	5	1	.417

WORLD SERIES

	W	L	PCT	ERA	G	GS	CG	IP	H	BB	SO	ShO	W	L	SV	AB	H	HR	BA
1970 CIN N	0	0	–	1.35	3	0	0	6.2	5	4	4	0	0	0	0	1	0	0	.000
1972	0	0	–	1.29	1	0	0	7	5	2	4	0	0	0	0	2	0	0	.000
1975	1	1	.500	4.34	3	3	0	18.2	19	10	15	0	0	0	0	7	2	0	.286
1976	1	0	1.000	1.23	1	1	0	7.1	5	3	4	0	0	0	0	2	0	0	.000
1977 NY A	0	1	.000	6.39	2	2	0	12.2	13	7	10	0	0	0	0	0	0	0	–
5 yrs.	2	2	.500	3.61	10	7	0	52.1	47	26	37	0	0	0	0	12	2	0	.167
											8th								

	W	L	PCT	ERA	G	GS	CG	IP	H	BB	SO	ShO	Relief Pitching W	L	SV	BATTING AB	H	HR	BA

Bill Gullickson

GULLICKSON, WILLIAM LEE
B. Feb. 20, 1959, Marshall, Minn.
BR TR 6'3" 200 lbs.

	W	L	PCT	ERA	G	GS	CG	IP	H	BB	SO	ShO	W	L	SV	AB	H	HR	BA
1979 MON N	0	0	–	0.00	1	0	0	1	2	0	0	0	0	0	0	0	0	0	–
1980	10	5	.667	3.00	24	19	5	141	127	50	120	2	0	1	0	40	7	0	.175
1981	7	9	.438	2.81	22	22	3	157	142	34	115	2	0	0	0	46	7	0	.152
1982	12	14	.462	3.57	34	34	6	236.2	231	61	155	0	0	0	0	82	10	0	.122
1983	17	12	.586	3.75	34	34	10	242.1	230	59	120	1	0	0	0	82	11	1	.134
1984	12	9	.571	3.61	32	32	3	226.2	230	37	100	0	0	0	0	73	8	0	.110
6 yrs.	58	49	.542	3.42	147	141	27	1004.2	962	241	610	5	0	1	0	323	43	1	.133
DIVISIONAL PLAYOFF SERIES																			
1981 MON N	1	0	1.000	1.17	1	1	0	7.2	6	1	3	0	0	0	0	3	0	0	.000
LEAGUE CHAMPIONSHIP SERIES																			
1981 MON N	0	2	.000	2.51	2	2	0	14.1	12	6	12	0	0	0	0	3	0	0	.000

Ad Gumbert

GUMBERT, ADDISON COURTNEY
Brother of Billy Gumbert.
B. Oct. 10, 1868, Pittsburgh, Pa.   D. Apr. 23, 1925, Pittsburgh, Pa.
BR TR 5'10" 200 lbs.

	W	L	PCT	ERA	G	GS	CG	IP	H	BB	SO	ShO	W	L	SV	AB	H	HR	BA
1888 CHI N	3	3	.500	3.14	6	6	5	48.2	44	10	16	0	0	0	0	24	8	0	.333
1889	16	13	.552	3.62	31	28	25	246.1	258	76	91	2	2	0	0	153	44	7	.288
1890 BOS P	22	11	.667	3.96	39	33	27	277.1	338	86	81	1	3	1	0	145	35	3	.241
1891 CHI N	17	11	.607	3.58	32	31	24	256.1	282	90	73	1	0	0	0	105	32	0	.305
1892	22	19	.537	3.41	46	45	39	382.2	399	107	118	0	0	0	0	178	42	1	.236
1893 PIT N	11	7	.611	5.15	22	20	16	162.2	207	78	40	2	1	0	0	95	21	0	.221
1894	15	14	.517	6.02	37	31	26	269	372	84	65	0	1	0	0	113	33	1	.292
1895 BKN N	11	16	.407	5.08	33	26	19	234	288	69	45	0	1	1	1	97	35	2	.361
1896 2 teams					BKN	N	(5G 0–4)		PHI	N	(11G 5–3)								
" total	5	7	.417	4.32	16	14	9	108.1	133	34	17	1	0	0	0	45	11	1	.244
9 yrs.	122	101	.547	4.27	262	234	191	1985.1	2321	634	546	7	8	2	1	*			

Billy Gumbert

GUMBERT, WILLIAM SKEEN
Brother of Ad Gumbert.
B. Aug. 8, 1865, Pittsburgh, Pa.   D. Apr. 13, 1946, Pittsburgh, Pa.
BR TR 6'1½" 200 lbs.

	W	L	PCT	ERA	G	GS	CG	IP	H	BB	SO	ShO	W	L	SV	AB	H	HR	BA
1890 PIT N	4	6	.400	5.22	10	10	8	79.1	96	31	18	0	0	0	0	37	9	1	.243
1892	3	2	.600	1.36	6	3	2	39.2	30	23	3	0	1	1	0	18	2	0	.111
1893 LOU N	0	0	–	27.00	1	1	0	.2	2	5	0	0	0	0	0	1	1	0	1.000
3 yrs.	7	8	.467	4.06	17	14	10	119.2	128	59	21	0	1	1	0	56	12	1	.214

Harry Gumbert

GUMBERT, HARRY EDWARD (Gunboat)
B. Nov. 5, 1909, Elizabeth, Pa.
BR TR 6'2" 185 lbs.

	W	L	PCT	ERA	G	GS	CG	IP	H	BB	SO	ShO	W	L	SV	AB	H	HR	BA
1935 NY N	1	2	.333	6.08	6	3	1	23.2	35	10	11	0	0	0	0	8	0	0	.000
1936	11	3	.786	3.90	39	15	1	140.2	157	54	52	0	4	0	0	44	11	0	.250
1937	10	11	.476	3.68	34	24	10	200.1	194	62	65	1	0	0	1	72	13	1	.181
1938	15	13	.536	4.01	38	33	14	235.2	238	84	84	1	0	0	0	84	13	0	.155
1939	18	11	.621	4.32	36	34	14	243.2	257	81	81	2	0	1	0	90	18	0	.200
1940	12	14	.462	3.76	35	30	14	237	230	81	77	2	2	0	2	87	17	1	.195
1941 2 teams					NY	N	(5G 1–1)		STL	N	(33G 11–5)								
" total	12	6	.667	3.06	38	22	9	176.2	173	48	62	3	4	0	1	65	19	2	.292
1942 STL N	9	5	.643	3.26	38	19	5	163	156	59	52	0	4	0	5	54	6	0	.111
1943	10	5	.667	2.84	21	19	7	133	115	32	40	2	0	0	0	45	7	0	.156
1944 2 teams					STL	N	(10G 4–2)		CIN	N	(24G 10–8)								
" total	14	10	.583	3.07	34	26	14	216.2	217	59	56	2	1	2	3	73	9	0	.123
1946 CIN N	6	8	.429	3.24	36	10	5	119.1	112	42	44	0	4	0	4	32	8	0	.250
1947	10	10	.500	3.89	46	0	0	90.1	88	47	43	0	10	10	10	22	6	0	.273
1948	10	8	.556	3.47	61	0	0	106.1	123	34	25	0	10	8	17	25	1	1	.040
1949 2 teams					CIN	N	(29G 4–3)		PIT	N	(16G 1–4)								
" total	5	7	.417	5.64	45	0	0	68.2	88	26	17	0	5	7	5	6	1	0	.167
1950 PIT N	0	0	–	5.40	5	0	0	1.2	3	2	0	0	0	0	0	1	1	0	1.000
15 yrs.	143	113	.559	3.68	508	235	94	2156.2	2186	721	709	13	44	28	48	708	130	5	.184
WORLD SERIES																			
1936 NY N	0	0	–	36.00	2	0	0	2	7	4	2	0	0	0	0	0	0	0	–
1937	0	0	–	27.00	2	0	0	1.1	4	1	1	0	0	0	0	0	0	0	–
1942 STL N	0	0	–	0.00	2	0	0	.2	1	0	0	0	0	0	0	0	0	0	–
3 yrs.	0	0	–	27.00	6	0	0	4	12	5	3	0	0	0	0	0	0	0	–

Dave Gumpert

GUMPERT, DAVID LAWRENCE
B. May 5, 1958, South Haven, Mich.
BR TR 6'3" 190 lbs.

	W	L	PCT	ERA	G	GS	CG	IP	H	BB	SO	ShO	W	L	SV	AB	H	HR	BA
1982 DET A	0	0	–	27.00	5	1	0	2	7	2	0	0	0	0	1	0	0	0	–
1983	0	2	.000	2.64	26	0	0	44.1	43	7	14	0	0	2	2	0	0	0	–
2 yrs.	0	2	.000	3.69	31	1	0	46.1	50	9	14	0	0	2	3	0	0	0	–

Randy Gumpert

GUMPERT, RANDALL PENNINGTON
B. Jan. 23, 1918, Monocacy, Pa.
BR TR 6'3" 185 lbs.

	W	L	PCT	ERA	G	GS	CG	IP	H	BB	SO	ShO	W	L	SV	AB	H	HR	BA
1936 PHI A	1	2	.333	4.76	22	3	2	62.1	74	32	9	0	0	0	2	22	6	0	.273
1937	0	0	–	12.00	10	1	0	12	16	15	5	0	0	0	0	3	1	0	.333
1938	0	2	.000	10.95	4	2	0	12.1	24	10	1	0	0	0	0	4	1	0	.250
1946 NY A	11	3	.786	2.31	33	12	4	132.2	113	32	63	0	3	0	1	47	6	0	.128
1947	4	1	.800	5.43	24	6	2	56.1	71	28	25	0	1	0	0	14	1	0	.071
1948 2 teams					NY	A	(15G 1–0)		CHI	A	(16G 2–6)								
" total	3	6	.333	3.60	31	11	6	122.1	130	19	43	1	1	3	0	29	4	0	.138
1949 CHI A	13	16	.448	3.81	34	32	18	234	223	83	78	3	0	0	1	84	16	0	.190
1950	5	12	.294	4.75	40	17	6	155.1	165	58	48	1	2	2	0	42	3	0	.071
1951	9	8	.529	4.32	33	16	7	141.2	156	34	45	1	2	3	2	45	15	0	.333
1952 2 teams					BOS	A	(10G 1–0)		WAS	A	(20G 4–9)								
" total	5	9	.357	4.22	30	13	2	123.2	127	35	35	0	2	1	1	39	7	0	.179
10 yrs.	51	59	.464	4.17	261	113	47	1052.2	1099	346	352	6	11	10	7	329	60	0	.182

	W	L	PCT	ERA	G	GS	CG	IP	H	BB	SO	ShO	Relief Pitching W	L	SV	BATTING AB	H	HR	BA

Red Gunkel

GUNKEL, WOODWARD WILLIAM   BB TR 5'8"   158 lbs.
B. Apr. 15, 1894, Sheffield, Ill.   D. Apr. 19, 1954, Chicago, Ill.

	W	L	PCT	ERA	G	GS	CG	IP	H	BB	SO	ShO	W	L	SV	AB	H	HR	BA
1916 CLE A	0	0	–	0.00	1	0	0	1	0	1	1	0	0	0	0	0	0	0	–

Larry Gura

GURA, LAWRENCE CYRIL   BL TL 6'   170 lbs.
B. Nov. 26, 1947, Joliet, Ill.

	W	L	PCT	ERA	G	GS	CG	IP	H	BB	SO	ShO	W	L	SV	AB	H	HR	BA
1970 CHI N	1	3	.250	3.79	20	3	1	38	35	23	21	0	0	1	1	10	0	0	.000
1971	0	0	–	6.00	6	0	0	3	6	1	2	0	0	0	1	1	0	0	.000
1972	0	0	–	3.75	7	0	0	12	11	3	13	0	0	0	0	1	0	0	.000
1973	2	4	.333	4.85	21	7	0	65	79	11	43	0	0	0	0	15	3	0	.200
1974 NY A	5	1	.833	2.41	8	8	4	56	54	12	17	0	0	0	0	0	0	0	–
1975	7	8	.467	3.51	26	20	5	151.1	173	41	65	0	0	0	0	0	0	0	–
1976 KC A	4	0	1.000	2.29	20	2	1	63	47	20	22	1	3	0	1	0	0	0	–
1977	8	5	.615	3.14	52	6	1	106	108	28	46	1	5	3	10	0	0	0	–
1978	16	4	.800	2.72	35	26	8	221.2	183	60	81	2	2	0	0	0	0	0	–
1979	13	12	.520	4.46	39	33	7	234	226	73	85	1	1	0	0	0	0	0	–
1980	18	10	.643	2.96	36	36	16	283	272	76	113	4	0	0	0	0	0	0	–
1981	11	8	.579	2.72	23	23	12	172	139	35	61	2	0	0	0	0	0	0	–
1982	18	12	.600	4.03	37	37	8	248	251	64	98	3	0	0	0	0	0	0	–
1983	11	18	.379	4.90	34	31	5	200.1	220	76	57	0	0	0	0	0	0	0	–
1984	12	9	.571	5.18	31	25	3	168.2	175	67	68	0	1	0	0	0	0	0	–
15 yrs.	126	94	.573	3.69	395	257	71	2022	1979	590	792	14	13	4	13	27	3	0	.111

DIVISIONAL PLAYOFF SERIES

	W	L	PCT	ERA	G	GS	CG	IP	H	BB	SO	ShO	W	L	SV	AB	H	HR	BA
1981 KC A	0	1	.000	7.36	1	1	0	3.2	7	3	3	0	0	0	0	0	0	0	–

LEAGUE CHAMPIONSHIP SERIES

	W	L	PCT	ERA	G	GS	CG	IP	H	BB	SO	ShO	W	L	SV	AB	H	HR	BA
1976 KC A	0	1	.000	4.22	2	2	0	10.2	18	1	4	0	0	0	0	0	0	0	–
1977	0	1	.000	18.00	2	1	0	2	7	1	2	0	0	0	0	0	0	0	–
1978	1	0	1.000	2.84	1	1	0	6.1	8	2	2	0	0	0	0	0	0	0	–
1980	1	0	1.000	2.00	1	1	1	9	10	1	4	0	0	0	0	0	0	0	–
4 yrs.	2	2	.500	4.18	6	5	1	28	43	5	12	0	0	0	0	0	0	0	–

WORLD SERIES

	W	L	PCT	ERA	G	GS	CG	IP	H	BB	SO	ShO	W	L	SV	AB	H	HR	BA
1980 KC A	0	0	–	2.19	2	2	0	12.1	8	3	4	0	0	0	0	0	0	0	–

Charlie Guth

GUTH, CHARLES J.
B. 1856, Chicago, Ill.   D. July, 1883, Chicago, Ill.

	W	L	PCT	ERA	G	GS	CG	IP	H	BB	SO	ShO	W	L	SV	AB	H	HR	BA
1880 CHI N	1	0	1.000	5.00	1	1	1	9	12	1	7	0	0	0	0	4	1	0	.250

Santiago Guzman

GUZMAN, SANTIAGO DONOVAN   BR TR 6'2"   180 lbs.
B. July 25, 1949, San Pedro De Macoris, Dominican Republic

	W	L	PCT	ERA	G	GS	CG	IP	H	BB	SO	ShO	W	L	SV	AB	H	HR	BA
1969 STL N	0	1	.000	5.14	1	1	0	7	9	3	7	0	0	0	0	3	1	0	.333
1970	1	1	.500	7.07	8	3	1	14	14	13	9	0	0	1	0	5	1	0	.200
1971	0	0	–	0.00	2	1	0	10	6	2	13	0	0	0	0	1	0	0	.000
1972	0	0	–	9.00	1	0	0	1	1	0	0	0	0	0	0	0	0	0	–
4 yrs.	1	2	.333	4.50	12	5	1	32	30	18	29	0	0	1	0	9	2	0	.222

Bruno Haas

HAAS, BRUNO PHILIP (Boon)   BB TL 5'10"   180 lbs.
B. May 5, 1891, Worcester, Mass.   D. June 5, 1952, Sarasota, Fla.

	W	L	PCT	ERA	G	GS	CG	IP	H	BB	SO	ShO	W	L	SV	AB	H	HR	BA
1915 PHI A	0	1	.000	11.93	6	2	1	14.1	23	28	7	0	0	0	0	18	1	0	.056

Moose Haas

HAAS, BRYAN EDMUND   BR TR 6'   180 lbs.
B. Apr. 22, 1956, Baltimore, Md.

	W	L	PCT	ERA	G	GS	CG	IP	H	BB	SO	ShO	W	L	SV	AB	H	HR	BA
1976 MIL A	0	1	.000	3.94	5	2	0	16	12	12	9	0	0	0	0	0	0	0	–
1977	10	12	.455	4.32	32	32	6	198	195	84	113	0	0	0	0	0	0	0	–
1978	2	3	.400	6.16	7	6	2	30.2	33	8	32	0	0	0	1	0	0	0	–
1979	11	11	.500	4.77	29	28	8	185	198	59	95	1	0	0	0	0	0	0	–
1980	16	15	.516	3.11	33	33	14	252	246	56	146	3	0	0	0	0	0	0	–
1981	11	7	.611	4.47	24	22	5	137	146	40	64	0	1	0	0	0	0	0	–
1982	11	8	.579	4.47	32	27	3	193.1	232	39	104	0	1	0	1	0	0	0	–
1983	13	3	.813	3.27	25	25	7	179	170	42	75	3	0	0	0	0	0	0	–
1984	9	11	.450	3.99	31	30	4	189.1	205	43	84	0	0	0	0	0	0	0	–
9 yrs.	83	71	.539	4.05	218	205	49	1380.1	1437	383	722	7	2	0	2	0	0	0	–

DIVISIONAL PLAYOFF SERIES

	W	L	PCT	ERA	G	GS	CG	IP	H	BB	SO	ShO	W	L	SV	AB	H	HR	BA
1981 MIL A	0	2	.000	9.45	2	2	0	6.2	13	1	1	0	0	0	0	0	0	0	–

LEAGUE CHAMPIONSHIP SERIES

	W	L	PCT	ERA	G	GS	CG	IP	H	BB	SO	ShO	W	L	SV	AB	H	HR	BA
1982 MIL A	1	0	1.000	4.91	1	1	0	7.1	5	5	7	0	0	0	0	0	0	0	–

WORLD SERIES

	W	L	PCT	ERA	G	GS	CG	IP	H	BB	SO	ShO	W	L	SV	AB	H	HR	BA
1982 MIL A	0	0	–	7.36	2	1	0	7.1	8	3	4	0	0	0	0	0	0	0	–

Bob Habenicht

HABENICHT, ROBERT JULIUS (Hobby)   BR TR 6'2"   185 lbs.
B. Feb. 13, 1926, St. Louis, Mo.   D. Dec. 24, 1980, Richmond, Va.

	W	L	PCT	ERA	G	GS	CG	IP	H	BB	SO	ShO	W	L	SV	AB	H	HR	BA
1951 STL N	0	0	–	7.20	3	0	0	5	5	9	1	0	0	0	0	1	0	0	.000
1953 STL N	0	0	–	5.40	1	0	0	1.2	1	1	1	0	0	0	0	0	0	0	–
2 yrs.	0	0	–	6.75	4	0	0	6.2	6	10	2	0	0	0	0	1	0	0	.000

Warren Hacker

HACKER, WARREN LOUIS   BR TR 6'1"   185 lbs.
B. Nov. 21, 1924, Marissa, Ill.

	W	L	PCT	ERA	G	GS	CG	IP	H	BB	SO	ShO	W	L	SV	AB	H	HR	BA
1948 CHI N	0	1	.000	21.00	3	1	0	3	7	3	0	0	0	0	0	0	0	0	–
1949	5	8	.385	4.23	30	12	3	125.2	141	53	40	0	3	1	0	38	7	0	.184
1950	0	1	.000	5.28	5	3	1	15.1	20	8	5	0	0	0	1	5	0	0	.000
1951	0	0	–	13.50	2	0	0	1.1	3	0	2	0	0	0	0	0	0	0	–
1952	15	9	.625	2.58	33	20	12	185	144	31	84	5	2	2	1	58	7	0	.121
1953	12	19	.387	4.38	39	32	9	221.2	225	54	106	0	1	2	2	78	17	0	.218
1954	6	13	.316	4.25	39	18	4	158.2	157	37	80	1	1	6	2	55	13	0	.236
1955	11	15	.423	4.27	35	30	13	213	202	43	80	0	1	0	3	72	18	0	.250

	W	L	PCT	ERA	G	GS	CG	IP	H	BB	SO	ShO	Relief Pitching W	L	SV	BATTING AB	H	HR	BA

Warren Hacker continued

	W	L	PCT	ERA	G	GS	CG	IP	H	BB	SO	ShO	W	L	SV	AB	H	HR	BA
1956	3	13	.188	4.66	34	24	4	168	190	44	65	0	0	0	0	54	8	0	.148
1957 2 teams			CIN	N	(15G 3–2)		PHI	N	(20G 4–4)										
" total	7	6	.538	4.76	35	9	1	117.1	122	31	51	0	1	0	0	31	7	0	.226
1958 PHI N	0	1	.000	7.41	9	1	0	17	24	8	4	0	0	0	0	1	0	0	.000
1961 CHI A	3	3	.500	3.77	42	0	0	57.1	62	8	40	0	3	3	8	9	1	0	.111
12 yrs.	62	89	.411	4.21	306	157	47	1283.1	1297	320	557	6	12	14	17	401	78	0	.195

Jim Hackett

HACKETT, JAMES JOSEPH (Sunny Jim)   BR TR 6'2"   185 lbs.
B. Oct. 1, 1877, Jacksonville, Ill.   D. Mar. 28, 1961, Douglas, Mich.

	W	L	PCT	ERA	G	GS	CG	IP	H	BB	SO	ShO	W	L	SV	AB	H	HR	BA
1902 STL N	0	3	.000	6.23	4	3	3	30.1	46	16	7	0	0	0	0	21	6	0	.286
1903	1	4	.200	3.72	7	6	5	48.1	47	18	21	0	0	0	1	351	80	0	.228
2 yrs.	1	7	.125	4.69	11	9	8	78.2	93	34	28	0	0	0	1	*			

Harvey Haddix

HADDIX, HARVEY (The Kitten)   BL TL 5'9½"   170 lbs.
B. Sept. 18, 1925, Medway, Ohio

	W	L	PCT	ERA	G	GS	CG	IP	H	BB	SO	ShO	W	L	SV	AB	H	HR	BA
1952 STL N	2	2	.500	2.79	7	6	3	42	31	10	31	0	0	0	0	14	3	0	.214
1953	20	9	.690	3.06	36	33	19	253	220	69	163	6	0	0	1	97	28	1	.289
1954	18	13	.581	3.57	43	35	13	259.2	247	77	184	3	1	1	4	93	18	0	.194
1955	12	16	.429	4.46	37	30	9	208	216	62	150	2	1	1	1	73	12	1	.164
1956 2 teams			STL	N	(4G 1–0)		PHI	N	(31G 12–8)										
" total	13	8	.619	3.67	35	30	12	230.1	224	65	170	3	0	0	2	102	24	0	.235
1957 PHI N	10	13	.435	4.06	27	25	8	170.2	176	39	136	1	1	0	0	68	21	0	.309
1958 CIN N	8	7	.533	3.52	29	26	8	184	191	43	110	1	0	0	0	61	11	1	.180
1959 PIT N	12	12	.500	3.13	31	29	14	224.1	189	49	149	2	0	0	1	83	12	0	.145
1960	11	10	.524	3.97	29	28	4	172.1	189	38	101	0	0	0	0	67	17	0	.254
1961	10	6	.625	4.10	29	22	5	156	159	41	99	2	3	0	0	56	8	0	.143
1962	9	6	.600	4.20	28	20	4	141.1	146	42	101	0	2	1	0	52	13	1	.250
1963	3	4	.429	3.34	49	1	0	70	67	20	70	0	3	4	1	11	2	0	.182
1964 BAL A	5	5	.500	2.31	49	0	0	89.2	68	23	90	0	5	5	10	19	0	0	.000
1965	3	2	.600	3.48	24	0	0	33.2	31	23	21	0	3	1	2	2	0	0	.000
14 yrs.	136	113	.546	3.63	453	285	99	2235	2154	601	1575	20	19	14	21	*			

WORLD SERIES
	W	L	PCT	ERA	G	GS	CG	IP	H	BB	SO	ShO	W	L	SV	AB	H	HR	BA
1960 PIT N	2	0	1.000	2.45	2	1	0	7.1	6	2	6	0	1	0	0	3	1	0	.333

George Haddock

HADDOCK, GEORGE SILAS (Gentleman George)   TR 5'11"   155 lbs.
B. Dec. 25, 1866, Portsmouth, N. H.   D. Apr. 18, 1926, Boston, Mass.

	W	L	PCT	ERA	G	GS	CG	IP	H	BB	SO	ShO	W	L	SV	AB	H	HR	BA
1888 WAS N	0	2	.000	2.25	2	2	2	16	9	2	3	0	0	0	0	5	1	0	.200
1889	11	19	.367	4.20	33	31	30	276.1	299	123	106	0	0	0	0	112	25	2	.223
1890 BUF P	9	26	.257	5.76	35	34	31	290.2	366	149	123	0	1	0	0	146	36	0	.247
1891 BOS AA	34	11	.756	2.49	51	47	37	379.2	330	137	169	5	2	0	1	185	45	3	.243
1892 BKN N	29	13	.690	3.14	46	44	39	381.1	340	163	153	3	0	0	1	158	28	0	.177
1893	8	9	.471	5.60	23	20	12	151	193	89	37	0	1	0	0	85	24	1	.282
1894 2 teams			PHI	N	(10G 4–3)		WAS	N	(4G 0–4)										
" total	4	7	.364	6.78	14	11	9	85	113	51	8	0	0	0	0	45	8	0	.178
7 yrs.	95	87	.522	4.07	204	189	160	1580	1650	714	599	8	4	0	2	*			

Bump Hadley

HADLEY, IRVING DARIUS   BR TR 5'11"   190 lbs.
B. July 5, 1904, Lynn, Mass.   D. Feb. 15, 1963, Lynn, Mass.

	W	L	PCT	ERA	G	GS	CG	IP	H	BB	SO	ShO	W	L	SV	AB	H	HR	BA
1926 WAS A	0	0	–	12.00	1	0	0	3	6	2	0	0	0	0	0	0	0	0	–
1927	14	6	.700	2.85	30	27	13	198.2	177	86	60	0	0	0	0	70	19	0	.271
1928	12	13	.480	3.54	33	31	16	231.2	236	100	80	3	0	0	0	81	17	0	.210
1929	6	16	.273	5.65	37	27	6	194.1	196	85	98	1	0	4	0	62	6	0	.097
1930	15	11	.577	3.73	42	34	15	260.1	242	105	162	1	1	1	2	93	21	0	.226
1931	11	10	.524	3.06	55	11	2	179.2	145	92	124	1	8	5	8	54	9	0	.167
1932 2 teams			CHI	A	(3G 1–1)		STL	A	(40G 13–20)										
" total	14	21	.400	5.40	43	35	13	248.1	261	171	145	1	0	3	2	84	23	0	.274
1933 STL A	15	20	.429	3.92	45	36	19	316.2	309	141	149	2	2	1	3	109	17	0	.156
1934	10	16	.385	4.35	39	32	7	213	212	127	79	2	0	2	1	64	13	0	.203
1935 WAS A	10	15	.400	4.92	35	32	13	230.1	268	102	77	0	0	0	0	77	15	0	.195
1936 NY A	14	4	.778	4.35	31	17	8	173.2	194	89	74	1	3	1	1	68	16	0	.235
1937	11	8	.579	5.30	29	25	6	178.1	199	83	70	0	0	1	0	65	11	0	.169
1938	9	8	.529	3.60	29	17	8	167.1	165	66	61	1	1	1	1	54	5	0	.093
1939	12	6	.667	2.98	26	18	7	154	132	85	65	1	2	0	2	62	11	0	.177
1940	3	5	.375	5.74	25	2	0	80	88	52	39	0	3	3	2	27	3	0	.111
1941 2 teams			NY	N	(3G 1–0)		PHI	A	(25G 4–6)										
" total	5	6	.455	5.15	28	11	1	115.1	150	56	35	0	1	3	0	34	4	0	.118
16 yrs.	161	165	.494	4.25	528	355	134	2944.2	2980	1442	1318	14	21	23	25	1004	190	0	.189
											10th								

WORLD SERIES
	W	L	PCT	ERA	G	GS	CG	IP	H	BB	SO	ShO	W	L	SV	AB	H	HR	BA
1936 NY A	1	0	1.000	1.13	1	1	0	8	10	1	2	0	0	0	0	2	0	0	.000
1937	0	1	.000	33.75	1	1	0	1.1	6	0	0	0	0	0	0	0	0	0	–
1939	1	0	1.000	2.25	1	0	0	8	7	3	2	0	1	0	0	3	0	0	.000
3 yrs.	2	1	.667	4.15	3	2	0	17.1	23	4	4	0	1	0	0	5	0	0	.000

Mickey Haefner

HAEFNER, MILTON ARNOLD   BL TL 5'8"   160 lbs.
B. Oct. 9, 1912, Lenzburg, Ill.

	W	L	PCT	ERA	G	GS	CG	IP	H	BB	SO	ShO	W	L	SV	AB	H	HR	BA
1943 WAS A	11	5	.688	2.29	36	13	8	165.1	126	60	65	1	3	1	6	45	6	0	.133
1944	12	15	.444	3.04	31	28	18	228	221	71	86	3	0	1	1	70	11	0	.157
1945	16	14	.533	3.47	37	28	19	238.1	226	69	83	1	2	0	3	82	20	0	.244
1946	14	11	.560	2.85	33	29	17	227.2	220	80	85	2	0	1	1	74	15	0	.203
1947	10	14	.417	3.64	31	28	14	193	195	85	77	4	0	0	1	59	8	0	.136
1948	5	13	.278	4.02	28	20	4	147.2	151	61	45	0	1	1	0	43	7	0	.163
1949 2 teams			WAS	A	(19G 5–5)		CHI	A	(14G 4–6)										
" total	9	11	.450	4.40	33	24	8	172	169	94	40	2	0	1	1	48	11	0	.229

	W	L	PCT	ERA	G	GS	CG	IP	H	BB	SO	ShO	Relief Pitching W	L	SV	BATTING AB	H	HR	BA

Mickey Haefner continued

1950 2 teams	CHI	A	(24G 1-6)		BOS	N	(8G 0-2)												
" total	1	8	.111	5.70	32	11	3	94.2	106	57	27	0	0	0	0	27	6	0	.222
8 yrs.	78	91	.462	3.50	261	179	91	1466.2	1414	577	508	13	6	5	13	448	84	0	.188

Bud Hafey

HAFEY, DANIEL ALBERT   BR TR 6'   185 lbs.
Brother of Tom Hafey.
B. Aug. 6, 1912, Berkeley, Calif.

	W	L	PCT	ERA	G	GS	CG	IP	H	BB	SO	ShO	W	L	SV	AB	H	HR	BA
1939 PHI N	0	0	–	33.75	2	0	0	1.1	7	1	1	0	0	0	0	*			

Leo Hafford

HAFFORD, LEO EDGAR   6'   170 lbs.
B. Sept. 17, 1883, Somerville, Mass.   D. Oct. 2, 1911, Willimantic, Conn.

	W	L	PCT	ERA	G	GS	CG	IP	H	BB	SO	ShO	W	L	SV	AB	H	HR	BA
1906 CIN N	1	1	.500	0.95	3	1	1	19	13	11	5	0	0	1	0	9	2	0	.222

Art Hagan

HAGAN, ARTHUR CHARLES
B. Mar. 17, 1863, Providence, R. I.   D. Mar. 25, 1936, Providence, R. I.

	W	L	PCT	ERA	G	GS	CG	IP	H	BB	SO	ShO	W	L	SV	AB	H	HR	BA
1883 2 teams	PHI	N	(17G 1-14)		BUF	N	(2G 0-2)												
" total	1	16	.059	5.27	19	18	16	152	224	39	46	0	0	0	0	66	6	0	.091
1884 BUF N	1	2	.333	5.88	3	3	3	26	53	4	4	0	0	0	0	13	4	0	.308
2 yrs.	2	18	.100	5.36	22	21	19	178	277	43	50	0	0	0	0	79	10	0	.127

Casey Hageman

HAGEMAN, KURT MORITZ   BR TR 5'10½" 186 lbs.
B. May 12, 1887, Mt. Oliver, Pa.   D. Apr. 1, 1964, New Bedford, Pa.

	W	L	PCT	ERA	G	GS	CG	IP	H	BB	SO	ShO	W	L	SV	AB	H	HR	BA
1911 BOS A	0	2	.000	2.12	2	2	2	17	16	5	8	0	0	0	0	4	0	0	.000
1912	0	0	–	27.00	2	1	0	1.1	5	3	1	0	0	0	0	0	0	0	–
1914 2 teams	STL	N	(12G 1-4)		CHI	N	(16G 2-1)												
" total	3	5	.375	2.91	28	8	1	102	87	32	38	0	2	1	1	31	9	0	.290
3 yrs.	3	7	.300	3.07	32	11	3	120.1	108	40	47	0	2	1	1	35	9	0	.257

Kevin Hagen

HAGEN, KEVIN EUGENE   BR TR 6'2"   180 lbs.
B. Mar. 8, 1960, Renton, Wash.

	W	L	PCT	ERA	G	GS	CG	IP	H	BB	SO	ShO	W	L	SV	AB	H	HR	BA
1983 STL N	2	2	.500	4.84	9	4	0	22.1	34	7	7	0	0	1	0	5	0	0	.000
1984	1	0	1.000	2.45	4	0	0	7.1	9	1	2	0	1	0	0	0	0	0	–
2 yrs.	3	2	.600	4.25	13	4	0	29.2	43	8	9	0	1	1	0	5	0	0	.000

Rip Hagerman

HAGERMAN, ZERIAH ZEQUIEL   BR TR
B. June 20, 1888, Linden, Kans.   D. Jan. 30, 1930, Albuquerque, N. M.

	W	L	PCT	ERA	G	GS	CG	IP	H	BB	SO	ShO	W	L	SV	AB	H	HR	BA
1909 CHI N	4	4	.500	1.82	13	7	4	79	64	28	32	1	1	0	0	23	3	0	.130
1914 CLE A	9	15	.375	3.09	37	26	12	198	189	118	112	3	1	2	0	61	1	0	.016
1915	6	14	.300	3.52	29	22	7	151	156	77	69	0	1	1	0	38	4	0	.105
1916	0	0	–	12.27	2	0	0	3.2	5	2	1	0	0	0	0	1	0	0	.000
4 yrs.	19	33	.365	3.09	81	55	23	431.2	414	225	214	4	3	3	0	123	8	0	.065

Fred Hahn

HAHN, FREDERICK ALOYS   BR TL 6'3"   174 lbs.
B. Feb. 16, 1929, Nyack, N. Y.

	W	L	PCT	ERA	G	GS	CG	IP	H	BB	SO	ShO	W	L	SV	AB	H	HR	BA
1952 STL N	0	0	–	0.00	1	0	0	2	2	1	0	0	0	0	0	0	0	0	–

Noodles Hahn

HAHN, FRANK GEORGE   BL TL 5'9"   160 lbs.
B. Apr. 29, 1879, Nashville, Tenn.   D. Feb. 6, 1960, Asheville, N. C.

	W	L	PCT	ERA	G	GS	CG	IP	H	BB	SO	ShO	W	L	SV	AB	H	HR	BA
1899 CIN N	23	7	.767	2.68	38	34	32	309	280	68	145	4	1	0	0	109	16	0	.147
1900	16	19	.457	3.29	38	36	28	303.1	296	88	127	4	0	1	0	111	23	2	.207
1901	22	19	.537	2.71	42	42	41	375.1	370	69	239	2	0	0	0	141	24	0	.170
1902	22	12	.647	1.76	36	35	34	312	274	57	138	6	0	0	0	119	22	0	.185
1903	22	12	.647	2.52	34	34	34	296	297	47	127	5	0	0	0	112	18	0	.161
1904	16	18	.471	2.06	35	34	33	297.2	258	35	98	2	1	0	0	99	17	0	.172
1905	5	3	.625	2.81	13	8	5	77	85	9	17	1	1	0	0	24	4	0	.167
1906 NY A	3	2	.600	3.86	6	6	3	42	38	6	17	1	0	0	0	12	4	0	.333
8 yrs.	129	92	.584	2.55	242	229	210	2012.1	1898	379	908	25	3	1	0	727	128	2	.176

Hal Haid

HAID, HAROLD AUGUSTINE   BR TR 5'10½" 150 lbs.
B. Dec. 21, 1897, Barberton, Ohio   D. Aug. 13, 1952, Los Angeles, Calif.

	W	L	PCT	ERA	G	GS	CG	IP	H	BB	SO	ShO	W	L	SV	AB	H	HR	BA
1919 STL A	0	0	–	18.00	1	0	0	2	5	3	1	0	0	0	0	0	0	0	–
1928 STL N	2	2	.500	2.30	27	0	0	47	39	11	21	0	2	2	5	8	3	0	.375
1929	9	9	.500	4.07	38	12	8	154.2	171	66	41	0	4	3	4	49	4	0	.082
1930	2	0	.600	4.09	20	0	0	33	38	14	13	0	3	0	2	3	0	0	.000
1931 BOS N	0	2	.000	4.50	27	0	0	56	59	16	20	0	0	2	1	8	1	0	.125
1933 CHI A	0	0	–	7.98	6	0	0	14.2	18	13	7	0	0	0	0	4	1	0	.250
6 yrs.	14	15	.483	4.16	119	12	8	307.1	330	123	103	0	9	9	12	72	9	0	.125

Jesse Haines

HAINES, JESSE JOSEPH (Pop)   BR TR 6'   190 lbs.
B. July 22, 1893, Clayton, Ohio   D. Aug. 5, 1978, Dayton, Ohio
Hall of Fame 1970.

	W	L	PCT	ERA	G	GS	CG	IP	H	BB	SO	ShO	W	L	SV	AB	H	HR	BA
1918 CIN N	0	0	–	1.80	1	0	0	5	5	1	2	0	0	0	0	1	1	0	1.000
1920 STL N	13	20	.394	2.98	47	37	19	301.2	303	80	120	4	2	2	2	108	19	1	.176
1921	18	12	.600	3.50	37	29	14	244.1	261	56	84	3	3	0	0	94	17	0	.181
1922	11	9	.550	3.84	29	26	11	183	207	45	62	2	0	1	0	72	12	0	.167
1923	20	13	.606	3.11	37	36	23	266	283	75	73	1	1	0	0	99	20	0	.202
1924	8	19	.296	4.41	35	31	16	222.2	275	66	69	1	0	1	0	74	14	0	.189
1925	13	14	.481	4.57	29	25	15	207	234	52	63	0	1	1	0	74	13	0	.176
1926	13	4	.765	3.25	33	21	14	183	186	48	46	3	0	0	0	61	13	0	.213
1927	24	10	.706	2.72	38	36	25	300.2	273	77	89	6	1	0	1	114	23	0	.202
1928	20	8	.714	3.18	33	28	20	240.1	238	72	77	1	1	1	0	87	16	0	.184
1929	13	10	.565	5.71	28	25	12	179.2	230	73	59	0	0	0	0	69	11	1	.159
1930	13	8	.619	4.30	29	24	14	182	215	54	68	0	0	0	1	65	16	0	.246
1931	12	3	.800	3.02	19	17	8	122.1	134	28	27	2	1	0	0	45	6	0	.133

	W	L	PCT	ERA	G	GS	CG	IP	H	BB	SO	ShO	Relief Pitching W	L	SV	BATTING AB	H	HR	BA

Jesse Haines continued

	W	L	PCT	ERA	G	GS	CG	IP	H	BB	SO	ShO	W	L	SV	AB	H	HR	BA
1932	3	5	.375	4.75	20	10	4	85.1	116	16	27	1	0	1	0	27	5	1	.185
1933	9	6	.600	2.50	32	10	5	115.1	113	37	37	0	5	2	1	30	2	0	.067
1934	4	4	.500	3.50	37	6	0	90	86	19	17	0	4	2	1	19	3	0	.158
1935	6	5	.545	3.59	30	12	3	115.1	110	28	24	0	1	2	2	33	9	0	.273
1936	7	5	.583	3.90	25	9	4	99.1	110	21	19	0	4	1	1	30	5	0	.167
1937	3	3	.500	4.52	16	6	2	65.2	81	23	18	0	1	0	0	22	4	0	.182
19 yrs.	210	158	.571	3.64	555	388	209	3208.2	3460	871	981	24	25	14	10	1124	209	3	.186

WORLD SERIES

	W	L	PCT	ERA	G	GS	CG	IP	H	BB	SO	ShO	W	L	SV	AB	H	HR	BA
1926 STL N	2	0	1.000	1.08	3	2	1	16.2	13	9	5	1	0	0	0	5	3	1	.600
1928	0	1	.000	4.50	1	1	0	6	6	3	3	0	0	0	0	2	0	0	.000
1930	1	0	1.000	1.00	1	1	1	9	4	4	2	0	0	0	0	2	1	0	.500
1934	0	0	–	0.00	1	0	0	.2	1	0	2	0	0	0	0	0	0	0	–
4 yrs.	3	1	.750	1.67	6	4	2	32.1	24	16	12	1	0	0	0	9	4	1	.444

Jim Haislip

HAISLIP, JAMES CLIFTON　　　　　　　　　　　BR TR 6'1"　186 lbs.
B. Aug. 4, 1891, Farmersville, Tex.　D. Jan. 22, 1970, Dallas, Tex.

	W	L	PCT	ERA	G	GS	CG	IP	H	BB	SO	ShO	W	L	SV	AB	H	HR	BA
1913 PHI N	0	0	–	6.00	1	0	0	3	4	3	0	0	0	0	0	1	0	0	.000

Ed Halbriter

HALBRITER, EDWARD L.
B. Feb. 2, 1860, Auburn, N.Y.　D. Aug. 9, 1936, Los Angeles, Calif.

	W	L	PCT	ERA	G	GS	CG	IP	H	BB	SO	ShO	W	L	SV	AB	H	HR	BA
1882 PHI AA	0	1	.000	7.88	1	1	1	8	17	4	4	0	0	0	0	4	0	0	.000

Dad Hale

HALE, RAY LUTHER　　　　　　　　　　　　　　BR TR 5'10"　180 lbs.
B. Feb. 18, 1879, Allegan, Mich.　D. Feb. 1, 1946, Allegan, Mich.

	W	L	PCT	ERA	G	GS	CG	IP	H	BB	SO	ShO	W	L	SV	AB	H	HR	BA
1902 2 teams	BOS	N (8G 1–3)		BAL	A	(3G 0–1)													
" total	1	4	.200	5.90	11	8	4	61	90	24	18	0	0	0	0	20	0	0	.000

Ed Halicki

HALICKI, EDWARD LOUIS　　　　　　　　　　　BR TR 6'7"　220 lbs.
B. Oct. 4, 1950, Newark, N.J.

	W	L	PCT	ERA	G	GS	CG	IP	H	BB	SO	ShO	W	L	SV	AB	H	HR	BA
1974 SF N	1	8	.111	4.26	16	11	2	74	84	31	40	0	0	0	0	25	6	1	.240
1975	9	13	.409	3.49	24	23	7	160	143	59	153	2	0	0	0	53	6	0	.113
1976	12	14	.462	3.62	32	31	8	186.1	171	61	130	4	1	0	0	53	9	0	.170
1977	16	12	.571	3.31	37	37	7	258	241	70	168	2	0	0	0	85	15	2	.176
1978	9	10	.474	2.85	29	28	9	199	166	45	105	4	0	0	1	66	9	0	.136
1979	5	8	.385	4.57	33	19	3	126	134	47	81	1	0	0	0	34	7	0	.206
1980 2 teams	SF	N (11G 0–0)		CAL	A	(10G 3–1)													
" total	3	1	.750	5.10	21	8	0	60	68	21	30	0	0	0	0	6	1	0	.167
7 yrs.	55	66	.455	3.62	192	157	36	1063.1	1007	334	707	13	1	0	1	322	53	3	.165

Bert Hall

HALL, HERBERT ERNEST　　　　　　　　　　　BR TR 5'10"　178 lbs.
B. Oct. 15, 1888, Portland, Ore.　D. July 18, 1948, Seattle, Wash.

	W	L	PCT	ERA	G	GS	CG	IP	H	BB	SO	ShO	W	L	SV	AB	H	HR	BA
1911 PHI N	0	1	.000	4.00	7	1	0	18	19	13	8	0	0	1	0	3	1	0	.333

Bill Hall

HALL, WILLIAM BERNARD　　　　　　　　　　　BR TR 6'2"　250 lbs.
B. Feb. 22, 1894, Charleston, W. Va.　D. Aug. 15, 1947, Newport, Ky.

	W	L	PCT	ERA	G	GS	CG	IP	H	BB	SO	ShO	W	L	SV	AB	H	HR	BA
1913 BKN N	0	0	–	5.79	3	0	0	4.2	5	4	5	3	0	0	0	1	0	0	.000

Bob Hall

HALL, ROBERT LEWIS　　　　　　　　　　　　BR TR 6'2"　195 lbs.
B. Dec. 22, 1923, Swissvale, Pa.　D. Apr. 12, 1983, St Petersburg, Fla.

	W	L	PCT	ERA	G	GS	CG	IP	H	BB	SO	ShO	W	L	SV	AB	H	HR	BA
1949 BOS N	6	4	.600	4.36	31	6	2	74.1	77	41	43	0	5	0	0	22	8	0	.364
1950	0	2	.000	6.97	21	4	0	50.1	58	33	22	0	0	1	0	12	1	0	.083
1953 PIT N	3	12	.200	5.39	37	17	6	152	172	72	68	1	0	1	1	38	6	1	.158
3 yrs.	9	18	.333	5.40	89	27	8	276.2	307	146	133	1	5	2	1	72	15	1	.208

Charley Hall

HALL, CHARLES LOUIS (Sea Lion)　　　　　　BL TR 6'2"　185 lbs.
Born Carlos Clolo.
B. July 27, 1885, Ventura, Calif.　D. Dec. 6, 1943, Ventura, Calif.

	W	L	PCT	ERA	G	GS	CG	IP	H	BB	SO	ShO	W	L	SV	AB	H	HR	BA
1906 CIN N	4	6	.400	3.32	14	9	9	95	86	50	49	1	0	1	1	47	6	0	.128
1907	4	2	.667	2.51	11	8	5	68	51	43	25	0	1	0	0	26	7	0	.269
1909 BOS A	6	4	.600	2.56	11	7	3	59.2	59	17	27	0	3	0	0	19	3	0	.158
1910	12	9	.571	1.91	35	16	13	188.2	142	73	95	0	6	1	2	82	17	0	.207
1911	8	7	.533	3.73	32	10	6	147.1	149	72	83	0	4	3	4	64	9	1	.141
1912	15	8	.652	3.02	34	21	9	191	178	70	83	2	6	0	2	75	20	1	.267
1913	4	4	.500	3.43	35	4	2	105	97	46	48	0	4	0	3	42	9	0	.214
1916 STL N	0	4	.000	5.48	10	5	2	42.2	45	14	15	0	0	0	1	14	2	0	.143
1918 DET A	0	1	.000	6.75	6	1	0	13.1	14	6	2	0	0	0	0	2	0	0	.000
9 yrs.	53	45	.541	3.08	188	81	49	910.2	821	391	427	3	24	5	13	*			

WORLD SERIES

	W	L	PCT	ERA	G	GS	CG	IP	H	BB	SO	ShO	W	L	SV	AB	H	HR	BA
1912 BOS A	0	0	–	3.38	2	0	0	10.2	11	9	1	0	0	0	0	4	3	0	.750

Dick Hall

HALL, RICHARD WALLACE　　　　　　　　　　BR TR 6'6"　200 lbs.
B. Sept. 27, 1930, St. Louis, Mo.

	W	L	PCT	ERA	G	GS	CG	IP	H	BB	SO	ShO	W	L	SV	AB	H	HR	BA
1952 PIT N	0	0	–	0.00	0	0	0	0	0	0	0	0	0	0	0	80	11	0	.138
1953	0	0	–	0.00	0	0	0	0	0	0	0	0	0	0	0	24	4	0	.167
1954	0	0	–	0.00	0	0	0	0	0	0	0	0	0	0	0	310	74	2	.239
1955	6	6	.500	3.91	15	13	4	94.1	92	28	46	0	0	0	1	40	7	1	.175
1956	0	7	.000	4.76	19	9	1	62.1	64	21	27	0	0	1	1	29	10	0	.345
1957	0	0	–	10.80	8	0	0	10	17	5	7	0	0	0	0	1	0	0	.000
1959	0	0	–	3.12	2	0	0	8.2	12	1	3	0	0	0	0	2	0	0	.000
1960 KC A	8	13	.381	4.05	29	28	9	182.1	183	38	79	1	0	1	0	56	6	0	.107
1961 BAL A	7	5	.583	3.09	29	13	4	122.1	102	30	92	2	2	1	4	36	5	0	.139
1962	6	6	.500	2.28	43	6	1	118.1	102	19	71	0	4	3	6	24	4	0	.167
1963	5	5	.500	2.98	47	3	0	111.2	91	16	74	0	5	2	12	28	13	1	.464

	W	L	PCT	ERA	G	GS	CG	IP	H	BB	SO	ShO	Relief Pitching W	L	SV	BATTING AB	H	HR	BA

Dick Hall continued

	W	L	PCT	ERA	G	GS	CG	IP	H	BB	SO	ShO	W	L	SV	AB	H	HR	BA
1964	9	1	.900	1.85	45	0	0	87.2	58	16	52	0	9	1	7	16	2	0	.125
1965	11	8	.579	3.07	48	0	0	93.2	84	11	79	0	11	8	12	15	5	0	.333
1966	6	2	.750	3.95	32	0	0	66	59	8	44	0	6	2	7	12	2	0	.167
1967 PHI N	10	8	.556	2.20	48	1	1	86	83	12	49	0	9	8	8	14	1	0	.071
1968	4	1	.800	4.89	32	0	0	46	53	5	31	0	4	1	0	3	1	0	.333
1969 BAL A	5	2	.714	1.92	39	0	0	65.2	49	9	31	0	5	2	6	7	2	0	.286
1970	10	5	.667	3.10	32	0	0	61	51	6	30	0	10	5	3	12	1	0	.083
1971	6	6	.500	5.02	27	0	0	43	52	11	26	0	6	6	1	5	2	0	.400
19 yrs.	93	75	.554	3.32	495	74	20	1259	1152	236	741	3	71	41	68	*			

LEAGUE CHAMPIONSHIP SERIES

	W	L	PCT	ERA	G	GS	CG	IP	H	BB	SO	ShO	W	L	SV	AB	H	HR	BA
1969 BAL A	1	0	1.000	0.00	1	0	0	.2	0	0	1	0	1	0	0	0	0	0	–
1970	1	0	1.000	0.00	1	0	0	4.2	1	0	3	0	1	0	0	2	1	0	.500
2 yrs.	2	0	1.000	0.00	2	0	0	5.1	1	0	4	0	2	0	0	2	1	0	.500

WORLD SERIES

	W	L	PCT	ERA	G	GS	CG	IP	H	BB	SO	ShO	W	L	SV	AB	H	HR	BA
1969 BAL A	0	1	.000	0.00	1	0	0	1	1	0	0	0	0	1	0	0	0	0	–
1970	0	0	–	0.00	1	0	0	2.1	0	0	0	0	0	0	1	1	0	0	.000
1971	0	0	–	0.00	1	0	0		1	1	0	0	0	0	1	0	0	0	–
3 yrs.	0	1	.000	0.00	3	0	0	3.1	2	1	0	0	0	1	2	1	0	0	.000

Herb Hall

HALL, HERBERT SILAS (Iron Duke)
B. June 5, 1894, Steelville, Ill.   D. July 3, 1970, Fresno, Calif.   BB TR 6'4"   220 lbs.

	W	L	PCT	ERA	G	GS	CG	IP	H	BB	SO	ShO	W	L	SV	AB	H	HR	BA
1918 DET A	0	0	–	15.00	3	0	0	6	12	7	1	0	0	0	0	1	0	0	.000

Johnny Hall

HALL, JOHN SYLVESTER
B. Jan. 9, 1924, Muskogee, Okla.   BR TR 6'2½"   170 lbs.

	W	L	PCT	ERA	G	GS	CG	IP	H	BB	SO	ShO	W	L	SV	AB	H	HR	BA
1948 BKN N	0	0	–	6.23	3	0	0	4.1	4	2	2	0	0	0	0	0	0	0	–

Marc Hall

HALL, MARCUS
B. Aug. 12, 1887, Joplin, Mo.   D. Feb. 24, 1915, Joplin, Mo.   BR TR

	W	L	PCT	ERA	G	GS	CG	IP	H	BB	SO	ShO	W	L	SV	AB	H	HR	BA
1910 STL A	1	7	.125	4.27	8	7	5	46.1	50	31	25	0	1	0	0	15	1	0	.067
1913 DET A	10	12	.455	3.27	30	21	8	165	154	79	69	1	2	3	0	45	4	0	.089
1914	4	6	.400	2.69	25	8	1	90.1	88	27	18	0	0	3	0	23	1	0	.043
3 yrs.	15	25	.375	3.25	63	36	14	301.2	292	137	112	1	3	6	0	83	6	0	.072

Tom Hall

HALL, THOMAS EDWARD (The Blade)
B. Nov. 23, 1947, Thomasville, N. C.   BL TL 6'   150 lbs.

	W	L	PCT	ERA	G	GS	CG	IP	H	BB	SO	ShO	W	L	SV	AB	H	HR	BA
1968 MIN A	2	1	.667	2.43	8	4	0	29.2	27	12	18	0	1	0	0	9	0	0	.000
1969	8	7	.533	3.33	31	18	5	140.2	129	50	92	2	0	2	0	43	8	0	.186
1970	11	6	.647	2.55	52	11	1	155	94	66	184	0	4	2	4	34	9	0	.265
1971	4	7	.364	3.32	48	11	0	130	104	58	137	0	3	3	9	30	3	0	.100
1972 CIN N	10	1	.909	2.61	47	7	1	124.1	77	56	134	1	7	1	8	20	1	0	.045
1973	8	5	.615	3.47	54	1	0	103.2	74	48	96	0	7	3	8	22	1	0	.045
1974	3	1	.750	4.08	40	1	0	64	54	30	48	0	2	1	1	5	0	0	.000
1975 2 teams								CIN N (2G 0–0)			NY N (34G 4–3)								
" total	4	3	.571	4.57	36	4	0	63	60	33	51	0	2	2	1	5	2	0	.400
1976 2 teams								NY N (5G 1–1)			KC A (31G 1–1)								
" total	2	2	.500	4.63	36	0	0	35	33	23	27	0	2	2	1	0	0	0	–
1977 KC A	0	0	–	3.38	6	0	0	8	4	6	10	0	0	0	0	0	0	0	–
10 yrs.	52	33	.612	3.27	358	63	7	853.1	656	382	797	3	28	16	32	192	31	0	.161

LEAGUE CHAMPIONSHIP SERIES

	W	L	PCT	ERA	G	GS	CG	IP	H	BB	SO	ShO	W	L	SV	AB	H	HR	BA
1969 MIN A	0	0	–	0.00	1	0	0	.2	0	0	0	0	0	0	0	0	0	0	–
1970	0	1	.000	6.75	2	1	0	5.1	6	4	6	0	0	0	0	1	0	0	.000
1972 CIN N	1	0	1.000	1.23	2	0	0	7.1	3	3	8	0	1	0	0	1	0	0	.000
1973	0	0	–	67.50	3	0	0	.2	3	4	1	0	0	0	0	0	0	0	–
1976 KC A	0	0	–	0.00	1	0	0	.1	1	0	0	0	0	0	0	0	0	0	–
5 yrs.	1	1	.500	6.28	9	1	0	14.1	13	11	15	0	1	0	0	2	0	0	.000

WORLD SERIES

	W	L	PCT	ERA	G	GS	CG	IP	H	BB	SO	ShO	W	L	SV	AB	H	HR	BA
1972 CIN N	0	0	–	0.00	4	0	0	8.1	6	2	7	0	0	0	1	2	0	0	.000

John Halla

HALLA, JOHN ARTHUR
B. May 13, 1884, St. Louis, Mo.   D. Sept. 30, 1947, Redondo Beach, Calif.   BL TL

	W	L	PCT	ERA	G	GS	CG	IP	H	BB	SO	ShO	W	L	SV	AB	H	HR	BA
1905 CLE A	0	0	–	2.84	3	0	0	12.2	12	0	4	0	0	0	0	4	1	0	.250

Bill Hallahan

HALLAHAN, WILLIAM ANTHONY (Wild Bill)
B. Aug. 4, 1902, Binghamton, N. Y.   D. July 8, 1981, Binghamton, N. Y.   BR TL 5'10½" 170 lbs.

	W	L	PCT	ERA	G	GS	CG	IP	H	BB	SO	ShO	W	L	SV	AB	H	HR	BA
1925 STL N	1	0	1.000	3.52	6	0	0	15.1	14	11	8	0	1	0	0	3	1	0	.333
1926	1	4	.200	3.65	19	3	0	56.2	45	32	28	0	1	2	0	16	4	0	.250
1929	4	4	.500	4.42	20	12	5	93.2	94	60	52	0	0	0	0	26	4	0	.154
1930	15	9	.625	4.66	35	32	13	237.1	233	126	177	2	0	0	2	81	10	0	.123
1931	19	9	.679	3.29	37	30	16	248.2	242	112	159	3	1	1	4	81	8	0	.099
1932	12	7	.632	3.11	25	22	13	176.1	169	69	108	1	1	0	0	56	12	0	.214
1933	16	13	.552	3.50	36	32	16	244.1	245	98	93	2	1	1	0	80	12	0	.150
1934	8	12	.400	4.26	32	26	10	162.2	195	66	70	2	0	2	0	55	10	0	.182
1935	15	8	.652	3.42	40	23	8	181.1	196	57	73	2	3	2	1	56	8	1	.143
1936 2 teams								STL N (9G 2–2)			CIN N (23G 5–9)								
" total	7	11	.389	4.76	32	25	6	172	178	77	48	2	0	2	0	56	14	1	.250
1937 CIN N	3	9	.250	6.14	21	9	2	63	90	29	18	0	1	3	0	21	2	0	.095
1938 PHI N	1	8	.111	5.46	21	10	1	89	107	45	22	0	0	0	0	26	5	0	.192
12 yrs.	102	94	.520	4.03	324	224	90	1740.1	1808	782	856	14	9	14	8	557	90	2	.162

WORLD SERIES

	W	L	PCT	ERA	G	GS	CG	IP	H	BB	SO	ShO	W	L	SV	AB	H	HR	BA
1926 STL N	0	0	–	4.50	1	0	0	2	2	3	1	0	0	0	0	0	0	0	–
1930	1	1	.500	1.64	2	2	1	11	9	8	8	1	0	0	0	2	0	0	.000
1931	2	0	1.000	0.49	3	2	2	18.1	12	8	11	1	0	0	0	6	0	0	.000

	W	L	PCT	ERA	G	GS	CG	IP	H	BB	SO	ShO	Relief Pitching W	L	SV	BATTING AB	H	HR	BA

Bill Hallahan continued

	W	L	PCT	ERA	G	GS	CG	IP	H	BB	SO	ShO	W	L	SV	AB	H	HR	BA
1934	0	0	–	2.16	1	1	0	8.1	6	4	6	0	0	0	0	3	0	0	.000
4 yrs.	3	1	.750	1.36	7	5	3	39.2	29	23	27	2	0	0	1	11	0	0	.000
												4th							

Jack Hallett

HALLETT, JACK PRICE   BR TR 6'4"   215 lbs.
B. Nov. 13, 1913, Toledo, Ohio   D. June 11, 1982, Toledo, Ohio

	W	L	PCT	ERA	G	GS	CG	IP	H	BB	SO	ShO	W	L	SV	AB	H	HR	BA
1940 CHI A	1	1	.500	6.43	2	2	1	14	15	6	9	0	0	0	0	5	2	0	.400
1941	5	5	.500	6.03	22	6	3	74.2	96	38	25	0	3	1	0	26	4	0	.154
1942 PIT N	0	1	.000	4.84	3	3	2	22.1	23	8	16	0	0	0	0	8	3	1	.375
1943	1	2	.333	1.70	9	4	2	47.2	36	11	11	1	0	1	0	14	4	0	.286
1946	5	7	.417	3.29	35	9	3	115	107	39	64	1	3	2	0	26	6	0	.231
1948 NY N	0	0	–	4.50	2	0	0	4	3	4	3	0	0	0	0	1	0	0	.000
6 yrs.	12	16	.429	4.05	73	24	11	277.2	280	106	128	2	6	4	0	80	19	1	.238

Bill Hallman

HALLMAN, WILLIAM WILSON   BR TR 5'8"
B. Mar. 30, 1867, Pittsburgh, Pa.   D. Sept. 11, 1920, Philadelphia, Pa.
Manager 1897.

	W	L	PCT	ERA	G	GS	CG	IP	H	BB	SO	ShO	W	L	SV	AB	H	HR	BA
1896 PHI N	0	0	–	18.00	1	0	0	2	4	2	0	0	0	0	0	*			

Charlie Hallstrom

HALLSTROM, CHARLES E. (Swedish Wonder)
B. Jan. 22, 1864, Jonkaping, Sweden   D. May 6, 1949, Chicago, Ill.

	W	L	PCT	ERA	G	GS	CG	IP	H	BB	SO	ShO	W	L	SV	AB	H	HR	BA
1885 PRO N	0	1	.000	11.00	1	1	1	9	18	6	0	0	0	0	0	4	0	0	.000

Doc Hamann

HAMANN, ELMER JOSEPH   BR TR 6'1"   180 lbs.
B. Dec. 21, 1900, New Ulm, Minn.   D. Jan. 11, 1973, Milwaukee, Wis.

	W	L	PCT	ERA	G	GS	CG	IP	H	BB	SO	ShO	W	L	SV	AB	H	HR	BA
1922 CLE A	0	0	–	∞	1	0	0		3	3	0	0	0	0	0	0	0	0	–

Roger Hambright

HAMBRIGHT, ROGER DEE   BR TR 5'10"   180 lbs.
B. Mar. 26, 1949, Sunnywise, Wash.

	W	L	PCT	ERA	G	GS	CG	IP	H	BB	SO	ShO	W	L	SV	AB	H	HR	BA
1971 NY A	3	1	.750	4.33	18	0	0	27	22	10	14	0	3	1	2	2	1	0	.500

John Hamill

HAMILL, JOHN ALEXANDER CHARLES   BR TR 5'8"   158 lbs.
B. Dec. 18, 1860, New York, N. Y.   D. Dec. 6, 1911, Bristol, R. I.

	W	L	PCT	ERA	G	GS	CG	IP	H	BB	SO	ShO	W	L	SV	AB	H	HR	BA
1884 WAS AA	2	17	.105	4.48	19	19	18	156.2	197	43	50	1	0	0	0	71	7	0	.099

Dave Hamilton

HAMILTON, DAVID EDWARD   BL TL 6'   180 lbs.
B. Dec. 14, 1947, Seattle, Wash.

	W	L	PCT	ERA	G	GS	CG	IP	H	BB	SO	ShO	W	L	SV	AB	H	HR	BA
1972 OAK A	6	6	.500	2.93	25	14	1	101.1	94	31	55	0	0	1	0	26	4	0	.154
1973	6	4	.600	4.39	16	11	1	69.2	74	24	34	0	1	0	0	0	0	0	–
1974	7	4	.636	3.15	29	18	1	117	104	48	69	1	1	0	0	0	0	0	–
1975 2 teams					OAK	A (11G 1–2)		CHI	A (30G 6–5)										
" total	7	7	.500	3.25	41	5	0	105.1	105	47	71	0	7	4	6	0	0	0	–
1976 CHI A	6	6	.500	3.60	45	1	0	90	81	45	62	0	5	6	10	0	0	0	–
1977	4	5	.444	3.63	55	0	0	67	71	33	45	0	4	5	9	0	0	0	–
1978 2 teams					STL	N (13G 0–0)		PIT	N (16G 0–2)										
" total	0	2	.000	4.46	29	0	0	40.1	39	18	23	0	0	2	1	7	0	0	.000
1979	3	4	.429	3.69	40	7	1	83	80	43	52	0	2	0	5	0	0	0	–
1980	0	3	.000	11.40	21	1	0	30	44	28	23	0	0	3	0	0	0	0	–
9 yrs.	39	41	.488	3.85	301	57	4	703.2	692	317	434	1	20	21	31	33	4	0	.121
LEAGUE CHAMPIONSHIP SERIES																			
1972 OAK A	0	0	–	0.00	1	0	0		1	1	0	0	0	0	0	0	0	0	–
WORLD SERIES																			
1972 OAK A	0	0	–	27.00	2	0	0	1.1	3	1	1	0	0	0	0	0	0	0	–

Earl Hamilton

HAMILTON, EARL ANDREW   BL TL 5'8"   160 lbs.
B. July 19, 1891, Gibson City, Ill.   D. Nov. 17, 1968, Anaheim, Calif.

	W	L	PCT	ERA	G	GS	CG	IP	H	BB	SO	ShO	W	L	SV	AB	H	HR	BA
1911 STL A	5	12	.294	3.97	32	17	10	177	191	69	55	1	1	1	0	56	6	0	.107
1912	11	14	.440	3.24	41	26	17	249.2	228	86	139	1	1	1	2	73	13	0	.178
1913	13	12	.520	2.57	31	24	19	217.1	197	83	101	3	0	2	1	74	10	0	.135
1914	17	18	.486	2.50	44	35	20	302.1	265	100	111	5	1	2	2	85	15	0	.176
1915	9	17	.346	2.87	35	27	13	204	203	69	63	1	0	1	0	62	7	0	.113
1916 3 teams					STL	A (1G 0–0)		DET	A (5G 1–2)			STL	A (22G 5–7)						
" total	6	9	.400	3.12	28	17	5	132.2	135	52	32	0	2	2	0	37	1	0	.027
1917 STL A	0	9	.000	3.14	27	8	2	83	86	41	19	0	0	3	1	19	7	0	.368
1918 PIT N	6	0	1.000	0.83	14	6	6	54	47	13	20	1	0	0	0	21	6	0	.286
1919	8	11	.421	3.31	28	19	10	160.1	167	49	39	1	1	0	1	52	7	0	.135
1920	10	13	.435	3.24	39	23	12	230.2	223	69	74	0	3	2	3	67	10	0	.149
1921	13	15	.464	3.36	35	30	12	225	237	58	59	2	0	3	0	75	12	0	.160
1922	11	7	.611	3.99	33	14	9	160	183	40	34	1	3	3	2	58	9	0	.155
1923	7	9	.438	3.77	28	15	5	141	148	42	42	0	2	3	1	52	9	0	.173
1924 PHI N	0	1	.000	10.50	3	0	0	6	9	2	2	0	0	1	0	2	0	0	.000
14 yrs.	116	147	.441	3.16	410	261	140	2343	2319	773	790	16	14	24	13	733	112	0	.153

Jack Hamilton

HAMILTON, JACK EDWIN (Hairbreadth Harry)   BR TR 6'   200 lbs.
B. Dec. 25, 1938, Burlington, Iowa

	W	L	PCT	ERA	G	GS	CG	IP	H	BB	SO	ShO	W	L	SV	AB	H	HR	BA
1962 PHI N	9	12	.429	5.09	41	26	4	182	185	107	101	1	2	0	2	54	3	0	.056
1963	2	1	.667	5.40	19	1	0	30	22	17	23	0	2	0	1	3	0	0	.000
1964 DET A	1	1	.000	8.40	5	0	0	15	24	8	5	0	0	0	0	3	0	0	.000
1965	1	1	.500	14.54	4	1	0	4.1	6	4	3	0	1	0	0	0	0	0	–
1966 NY N	6	13	.316	3.93	57	13	3	148.2	138	88	93	1	2	6	13	38	5	0	.132
1967 2 teams					NY	N (17G 2–0)		CAL	A (26G 9–6)										
" total	11	6	.647	3.35	43	21	0	150.2	128	79	96	0	3	0	1	43	7	0	.163
1968 CAL A	3	1	.750	3.32	21	2	1	38	34	15	18	0	2	0	2	7	1	0	.143
1969 2 teams					CLE	A (20G 0–2)		CHI	A (8G 0–3)										
" total	0	5	.000	6.49	28	0	0	43	60	30	18	0	0	5	1	2	0	0	.000
8 yrs.	32	40	.444	4.53	218	65	8	611.2	597	348	357	2	12	11	20	150	16	1	.107

		W	L	PCT	ERA	G	GS	CG	IP	H	BB	SO	ShO	Relief Pitching W	L	SV	BATTING AB	H	HR	BA

Steve Hamilton

HAMILTON, STEVE ABSHER
B. Nov. 30, 1935, Columbia, Ky.
BL TL 6'6" 190 lbs.

		W	L	PCT	ERA	G	GS	CG	IP	H	BB	SO	ShO	W	L	SV	AB	H	HR	BA
1961	CLE A	0	0	–	2.70	2	0	0	3.1	2	3	4	0	0	0	0	1	1	0	1.000
1962	WAS A	3	8	.273	3.77	41	10	1	107.1	103	39	83	0	2	4	2	26	2	0	.077
1963	2 teams			WAS	A (3G 0–1)				NY	A (34G 5–1)											
"	total	5	2	.714	2.94	37	0	0	64.1	54	26	64	0	5	2	5	14	4	0	.286
1964	NY A	7	2	.778	3.28	30	3	1	60.1	55	15	49	0	5	2	3	20	4	0	.200
1965		3	1	.750	1.39	46	1	0	58.1	47	16	51	0	3	1	5	6	1	0	.167
1966		8	3	.727	3.00	44	3	1	90	69	22	57	1	7	2	3	19	1	0	.053
1967		2	4	.333	3.48	44	0	0	62	57	23	55	0	2	4	4	9	1	0	.111
1968		2	2	.500	2.13	40	0	0	50.2	37	13	42	0	2	2	11	3	0	0	.000
1969		3	4	.429	3.32	38	0	0	57	39	21	39	0	3	4	2	5	0	0	.000
1970	2 teams			NY	A (35G 4–3)				CHI	A (3G 0–0)											
"	total	4	3	.571	2.98	38	0	0	48.1	40	17	36	0	4	3	3	6	0	0	.000
1971	SF N	2	2	.500	3.00	39	0	0	45	29	11	38	0	2	2	4	2	0	0	.000
1972	CHI N	1	0	1.000	4.76	22	0	0	17	24	8	13	0	1	0	0	1	0	0	.000
12 yrs.		40	31	.563	3.05	421	17	3	663.2	556	214	531	1	36	26	42	112	14	0	.125

LEAGUE CHAMPIONSHIP SERIES

1971	SF	N	0	0	–	9.00	1	0	0	1	1	0	3	0	0	0	0	0	0	0	–

WORLD SERIES

1963	NY A	0	0	–	0.00	1	0	0	1	0	0	1	0	0	0	0	0	0	0	–
1964		0	0		4.50	2	0	0	2	3	0	2	0	0	0	1	0	0	0	–
2 yrs.		0	0	–	3.00	3	0	0	3	3	0	3	0	0	0	1	0	0	0	–

Luke Hamlin

HAMLIN, LUKE DANIEL (Hot Potato)
B. July 3, 1906, Terris Center, Mich.   D. Feb. 18, 1978, Clare, Mich.
BL TR 6'2" 168 lbs.

		W	L	PCT	ERA	G	GS	CG	IP	H	BB	SO	ShO	W	L	SV	AB	H	HR	BA
1933	DET A	1	0	1.000	4.86	3	3	0	16.2	20	10	10	0	0	0	0	5	2	0	.400
1934		2	3	.400	5.38	20	5	1	75.1	87	44	30	0	0	3	1	26	6	0	.231
1937	BKN N	11	13	.458	3.59	39	25	11	185.2	183	48	93	1	2	2	1	59	11	0	.186
1938		12	15	.444	3.68	44	30	10	237.1	243	65	97	3	1	1	6	78	11	0	.141
1939		20	13	.606	3.64	40	36	19	269.2	255	54	88	2	2	0	0	103	13	1	.126
1940		9	8	.529	3.06	33	25	9	182.1	183	34	91	2	0	0	0	58	5	0	.086
1941		8	8	.500	4.24	30	20	5	136	139	41	58	1	1	0	1	41	6	0	.146
1942	PIT N	4	4	.500	3.94	23	14	6	112	128	19	38	1	0	0	0	37	9	0	.243
1944	PHI N	6	12	.333	3.74	29	23	9	190	204	38	58	2	0	1	0	56	13	0	.232
9 yrs.		73	76	.490	3.77	261	181	70	1405	1442	353	563	12	6	7	9	463	76	1	.164

Pete Hamm

HAMM, PETER WHITFIELD
B. Sept. 20, 1947, Buffalo, N. Y.
BR TR 6'5" 210 lbs.

		W	L	PCT	ERA	G	GS	CG	IP	H	BB	SO	ShO	W	L	SV	AB	H	HR	BA
1970	MIN A	0	2	.000	5.63	10	0	0	16	17	7	3	0	0	2	0	1	0	0	.000
1971		2	4	.333	6.75	13	8	1	44	55	18	16	0	0	1	0	11	3	0	.273
2 yrs.		2	6	.250	6.45	23	8	1	60	72	25	19	0	0	3	0	12	3	0	.250

Atlee Hammaker

HAMMAKER, ATLEE CHARLTON
B. Jan. 24, 1958, Carmel, Calif.
BB TL 6'3" 200 lbs.

		W	L	PCT	ERA	G	GS	CG	IP	H	BB	SO	ShO	W	L	SV	AB	H	HR	BA
1981	KC A	1	3	.250	5.54	10	6	0	39	44	12	11	0	0	0	0	0	0	0	–
1982	SF N	12	8	.600	4.11	29	27	4	175	189	28	102	1	0	0	0	59	4	0	.068
1983		10	9	.526	2.25	23	23	8	172.1	147	32	127	3	0	0	0	59	6	0	.102
1984		2	0	1.000	2.18	6	6	0	33	32	9	24	0	0	0	0	11	2	0	.182
4 yrs.		25	20	.556	3.33	68	62	12	419.1	412	81	264	4	0	0	0	129	12	0	.093

Granny Hamner

HAMNER, GRANVILLE WILBUR
Brother of Garvin Hamner.
B. Apr. 26, 1927, Richmond, Va.
BR TR 5'10" 163 lbs.

		W	L	PCT	ERA	G	GS	CG	IP	H	BB	SO	ShO	W	L	SV	AB	H	HR	BA
1956	PHI N	0	1	.000	4.32	3	1	0	8.1	10	2	4	0	0	0	0	401	90	4	.224
1957		0	0	–	0.00	1	0	0	1	1	0	1	0	0	0	0	502	114	10	.227
1962	KC A	0	1	.000	9.00	3	0	0	4	10	6	0	0	0	1	0	0	0	0	–
3 yrs.		0	2	.000	5.40	7	1	0	13.1	21	8	5	0	0	1	0	*			

Ralph Hamner

HAMNER, RALPH CONANT (Bruz)
B. Sept. 12, 1916, Gibsland, La.
BR TR 6'3" 165 lbs.

		W	L	PCT	ERA	G	GS	CG	IP	H	BB	SO	ShO	W	L	SV	AB	H	HR	BA
1946	CHI A	2	7	.222	4.42	25	7	1	71.1	80	39	29	0	0	0	1	18	3	0	.167
1947	CHI N	2	4	.333	2.52	3	3	2	25	24	16	14	0	0	0	0	8	1	0	.125
1948		5	9	.357	4.69	27	17	5	111.1	110	69	53	0	0	1	0	33	6	1	.182
1949		0	2	.000	8.76	6	1	0	12.1	22	8	3	0	0	1	0	2	0	0	.000
4 yrs.		8	20	.286	4.58	61	28	8	220	236	132	99	0	0	2	1	61	10	1	.164

Garry Hancock

HANCOCK, RONALD GARRY
B. Jan. 23, 1954, Tampa, Fla.
BL TL 6' 175 lbs.

		W	L	PCT	ERA	G	GS	CG	IP	H	BB	SO	ShO	W	L	SV	AB	H	HR	BA
1984	OAK A	0	0	–	0.00	1	0	0	1.1	0	0	0	0	0	0	0	*			

Rich Hand

HAND, RICHARD ALLEN
B. July 10, 1948, Bellevue, Wash.
BR TR 6'1" 185 lbs.

		W	L	PCT	ERA	G	GS	CG	IP	H	BB	SO	ShO	W	L	SV	AB	H	HR	BA
1970	CLE A	6	13	.316	3.83	35	25	3	160	132	69	110	1	0	1	3	41	6	0	.146
1971		6	12	.000	5.75	15	12	0	61	74	38	26	0	0	1	0	16	2	0	.125
1972	TEX A	10	14	.417	3.32	30	28	2	170.2	139	103	109	1	0	0	0	52	8	0	.154
1973	2 teams			TEX	A (8G 2–3)				CAL	N (16G 4–3)											
"	total	6	6	.500	4.39	24	13	1	96.1	107	40	33	0	2	0	0	0	0	0	–
4 yrs.		24	39	.381	4.00	104	78	6	488	452	250	278	2	2	2	3	109	16	0	.147

Jim Handiboe

HANDIBOE, JAMES EDWARD (Nick)
B. July 17, 1866, Columbus, Ohio   D. Nov. 8, 1942, Columbus, Ohio
BR TR 5'11" 160 lbs.

		W	L	PCT	ERA	G	GS	CG	IP	H	BB	SO	ShO	W	L	SV	AB	H	HR	BA
1886	PIT AA	7	7	.500	3.32	14	14	12	114	82	33	83	1	0	0	0	44	5	0	.114

	W	L	PCT	ERA	G	GS	CG	IP	H	BB	SO	ShO	Relief Pitching W	L	SV	BATTING AB	H	HR	BA

Vern Handrahan

HANDRAHAN, JAMES VERNON
B. Nov. 27, 1938, Charlottetown, P. E. I., Canada — BL TR 6'2" 185 lbs.

	W	L	PCT	ERA	G	GS	CG	IP	H	BB	SO	ShO	W	L	SV	AB	H	HR	BA
1964 KC A	0	1	.000	6.06	18	1	0	35.2	33	25	18	0	0	0	0	9	2	0	.222
1966	0	1	.000	4.26	16	1	0	25.1	20	15	18	0	0	0	1	3	0	0	.000
2 yrs.	0	2	.000	5.31	34	2	0	61	53	40	36	0	0	0	1	12	2	0	.167

Bill Hands

HANDS, WILLIAM ALFRED
B. May 6, 1940, Rutherford, N. J. — BR TR 6'2" 185 lbs.

	W	L	PCT	ERA	G	GS	CG	IP	H	BB	SO	ShO	W	L	SV	AB	H	HR	BA
1965 SF N	0	2	.000	16.50	4	2	0	6	13	6	5	0	0	0	0	1	0	0	.000
1966 CHI N	8	13	.381	4.58	41	26	0	159	168	59	93	0	4	0	2	49	2	0	.041
1967	7	8	.467	2.46	49	11	3	150	134	48	84	1	3	6	6	38	4	0	.105
1968	16	10	.615	2.89	38	34	11	258.2	221	36	148	4	0	1	0	82	5	0	.061
1969	20	14	.588	2.49	41	41	18	300	268	73	181	3	0	0	0	98	9	0	.092
1970	18	15	.545	3.70	39	38	12	265	278	76	170	2	0	0	1	75	10	0	.133
1971	12	18	.400	3.42	36	35	14	242	248	50	128	1	0	0	0	72	6	0	.083
1972	11	8	.579	2.99	32	28	6	189.1	168	47	96	3	0	1	0	57	1	0	.018
1973 MIN A	7	10	.412	3.49	39	15	3	142	138	41	78	1	2	3	2	0	0		–
1974 2 teams	MIN A (35G 4–5)				TEX A (2G 2–0)														
" total	6	5	.545	4.19	37	12	1	129	141	28	78	1	2	0	3	0	0		–
1975 TEX A	6	7	.462	4.02	18	18	4	109.2	118	28	67	1	0	0	0	0	0		–
11 yrs.	111	110	.502	3.35	374	260	72	1950.2	1895	492	1128	17	11	11	14	472	37	0	.078

Don Hankins

HANKINS, DONALD WAYNE
B. Feb. 9, 1902, Pendleton, Ind. D. May 16, 1963, Winston-Salem, N. C. — BR TR 6'3" 183 lbs.

	W	L	PCT	ERA	G	GS	CG	IP	H	BB	SO	ShO	W	L	SV	AB	H	HR	BA
1927 DET A	2	1	.667	6.48	20	1	0	41.2	67	13	10	0	2	0	2	7	1	0	.143

Frank Hankinson

HANKINSON, FRANK EDWARD
B. Apr. 29, 1856, New York, N. Y. D. Apr. 5, 1911, Palisades Park, N. J. — BR TR 5'11" 168 lbs.

	W	L	PCT	ERA	G	GS	CG	IP	H	BB	SO	ShO	W	L	SV	AB	H	HR	BA
1878 CHI N	0	1	.000	6.00	1	1	1	9	11	0	4	0	0	0	0	240	64	1	.267
1879	15	10	.600	2.50	26	25	25	230.2	248	27	69	2	1	0	0	171	31	0	.181
1880 CLE N	1	1	.500	1.08	4	2	2	25	20	3	8	0	0	0	1	263	55	1	.209
1885 NY AA	0	0	–	4.50	1	0	0	2	2	1	0	0	0	0	0	362	81	2	.224
4 yrs.	16	12	.571	2.50	32	28	28	266.2	281	31	81	2	1	0	1	*			

Jim Hanley

HANLEY, JAMES PATRICK
B. Oct. 13, 1885, Providence, R. I. D. May 1, 1961, Elmhurst, N. Y. —

	W	L	PCT	ERA	G	GS	CG	IP	H	BB	SO	ShO	W	L	SV	AB	H	HR	BA
1913 NY A	0	0	–	6.75	1	0	0	4	5	4	2	0	0	0	0	1	0	0	.000

Preston Hanna

HANNA, PRESTON LEE
B. Sept. 10, 1954, Pensacola, Fla. — BR TR 6'1" 195 lbs.

	W	L	PCT	ERA	G	GS	CG	IP	H	BB	SO	ShO	W	L	SV	AB	H	HR	BA
1975 ATL N	0	0	–	1.50	4	0	0	6	7	5	2	0	0	0	0	0	0	0	–
1976	0	0	–	4.50	5	0	0	8	11	4	3	0	0	0	0	1	0	0	.000
1977	2	6	.250	4.95	17	9	1	60	69	34	37	0	0	0	0	14	1	0	.071
1978	7	13	.350	5.14	29	28	0	140	132	93	90	0	0	0	1	49	9	1	.184
1979	1	1	.500	3.00	6	4	0	24	27	15	15	0	0	0	0	6	0	0	.000
1980	2	0	1.000	3.19	32	2	0	79	63	44	35	0	1	0	0	14	2	0	.143
1981	2	1	.667	6.43	20	1	0	35	45	23	22	0	2	0	0	4	1	0	.250
1982 2 teams	ATL N (20G 3–0)				OAK A (23G 0–4)														
" total	3	4	.429	4.80	43	3	1	84.1	90	61	49	0	3	2	0	5	2	0	.400
8 yrs.	17	25	.405	4.62	156	47	2	436.1	444	279	253	0	6	2	1	93	15	1	.161

Gerry Hannahs

HANNAHS, GERALD ELLIS
B. Mar. 6, 1953, Binghamton, N. Y. — BL TL 6'3" 210 lbs.

	W	L	PCT	ERA	G	GS	CG	IP	H	BB	SO	ShO	W	L	SV	AB	H	HR	BA
1976 MON N	2	0	1.000	6.75	3	3	0	16	20	12	10	0	0	0	0	8	3	0	.375
1977	1	5	.167	4.86	8	7	0	37	43	17	21	0	0	0	0	7	0	0	.000
1978 LA N	0	0	–	9.00	1	0	0	2	3	0	5	0	0	0	0	0	0	0	–
1979	0	2	.000	3.38	4	2	0	16	10	13	6	0	0	0	1	4	1	0	.250
4 yrs.	3	7	.300	5.07	16	12	0	71	76	42	42	0	0	0	1	19	4	0	.211

Jim Hannan

HANNAN, JAMES JOHN
B. Jan. 7, 1940, Jersey City, N. J. — BR TR 6'3" 205 lbs.

	W	L	PCT	ERA	G	GS	CG	IP	H	BB	SO	ShO	W	L	SV	AB	H	HR	BA
1962 WAS A	2	4	.333	3.31	42	3	0	68	56	49	39	0	1	2	4	11	1	0	.091
1963	2	2	.500	4.88	13	2	0	27.2	23	17	14	0	1	1	0	6	0	0	.000
1964	4	7	.364	4.16	49	7	0	106	108	45	67	0	4	2	3	20	3	0	.150
1965	1	1	.500	4.91	4	1	1	14.2	18	6	5	1	0	1	0	3	0	0	.000
1966	3	9	.250	4.26	30	18	2	114	125	59	68	0	0	1	0	30	2	0	.067
1967	1	1	.500	5.40	8	2	0	21.2	28	7	14	0	0	0	0	4	0	0	.000
1968	10	6	.625	3.01	25	22	4	140.1	147	50	75	1	0	0	0	47	3	0	.064
1969	7	6	.538	3.64	35	28	1	158.1	138	91	72	1	0	0	0	52	6	0	.115
1970	9	11	.450	4.01	42	17	1	128	119	54	61	1	4	3	0	31	4	0	.129
1971 2 teams	DET A (7G 1–0)				MIL A (21G 1–1)														
" total	2	1	.667	4.57	28	1	0	43.1	45	28	23	0	2	0	0	5	0	0	.000
10 yrs.	41	48	.461	3.88	276	101	9	822	807	406	438	4	13	10	7	209	19	0	.091

Loy Hanning

HANNING, LOY VERNON
B. Oct. 18, 1917, Bunker, Mo. — BR TR 6'2" 175 lbs.

	W	L	PCT	ERA	G	GS	CG	IP	H	BB	SO	ShO	W	L	SV	AB	H	HR	BA
1939 STL A	0	1	.000	3.60	4	1	0	10	6	4	8	0	0	0	0	1	0	0	.000
1942	1	1	.500	7.79	11	0	0	17.1	26	12	9	0	1	1	0	4	1	0	.250
2 yrs.	1	2	.333	6.26	15	1	0	27.1	32	16	17	0	1	1	0	5	1	0	.200

Andy Hansen

HANSEN, ANDREW VIGGO (Swede)
B. Nov. 12, 1924, Lake Worth, Fla. — BR TR 6'3" 185 lbs.

	W	L	PCT	ERA	G	GS	CG	IP	H	BB	SO	ShO	W	L	SV	AB	H	HR	BA
1944 NY N	3	3	.500	6.49	23	4	0	52.2	63	32	15	0	3	0	1	12	2	0	.167
1945	4	3	.571	4.66	23	13	4	92.2	98	28	37	0	0	0	3	25	0	0	.000
1947	1	5	.167	4.37	27	9	1	82.1	78	38	18	0	0	1	0	21	4	0	.190
1948	5	3	.625	2.97	36	9	3	100	96	36	27	0	2	0	4	20	1	0	.050
1949	2	6	.250	4.61	33	2	0	66.1	58	28	26	0	2	5	4	12	0	0	.000

	W	L	PCT	ERA	G	GS	CG	IP	H	BB	SO	ShO	Relief Pitching W	L	SV	BATTING AB	H	HR	BA

Mickey Hughes
HUGHES, MICHAEL J.
Brother of Jim Hughes.
B. Oct. 25, 1866, New York, N. Y.   D. Apr. 10, 1931, Jersey City, N. J.
TR

Year	W	L	PCT	ERA	G	GS	CG	IP	H	BB	SO	ShO	W	L	SV	AB	H	HR	BA
1888 BKN AA	25	13	.658	2.13	40	40	40	363	281	98	159	2	0	0	0	139	19	0	.137
1889	9	8	.529	4.35	20	17	13	153	172	86	54	0	0	1	0	68	12	0	.176
1890 2 teams			BKN	N (9G 4–4)	PHI	AA (6G 1–3)													
" total	5	7	.417	5.27	15	13	10	107.2	141	51	37	0	0	1	0	42	3	0	.071
3 yrs.	39	28	.582	3.22	75	70	63	623.2	594	235	250	2	0	2	0	249	34	0	.137

Tom Hughes
HUGHES, THOMAS EDWARD   BL TR 6'2" 180 lbs.
B. Sept. 13, 1934, Ancon, Canal Zone

Year	W	L	PCT	ERA	G	GS	CG	IP	H	BB	SO	ShO	W	L	SV	AB	H	HR	BA
1959 STL N	0	2	.000	15.75	2	2	0	4	9	2	2	0	0	0	0	1	0	0	.000

Tom Hughes
HUGHES, THOMAS L.   BR TR 6'2" 175 lbs.
B. Jan. 28, 1884, Coal Creek, Colo.   D. Nov. 1, 1961, Los Angeles, Calif.

Year	W	L	PCT	ERA	G	GS	CG	IP	H	BB	SO	ShO	W	L	SV	AB	H	HR	BA
1906 NY A	1	0	1.000	4.20	3	1	1	15	11	1	5	0	0	0	0	5	1	0	.200
1907	2	0	1.000	2.67	4	3	2	27	16	11	10	0	0	0	0	7	1	0	.143
1909	7	8	.467	2.65	24	16	9	118.2	109	37	69	2	1	0	1	39	5	1	.128
1910	7	9	.438	3.50	23	15	11	151.2	153	37	64	0	1	1	1	55	9	0	.164
1914 BOS N	1	0	1.000	2.65	2	2	1	17	14	4	11	0	0	0	0	7	0	0	.000
1915	16	14	.533	2.12	50	25	17	280.1	208	58	171	4	6	0	5	90	9	1	.100
1916	16	3	.842	2.35	40	14	7	161	121	51	97	1	9	2	5	52	10	0	.192
1917	5	3	.625	1.95	11	8	6	74	54	30	40	2	0	0	0	24	0	0	.000
1918	0	2	.000	3.44	3	3	1	18.1	17	6	9	0	0	0	0	6	2	1	.333
9 yrs.	55	39	.585	2.56	160	87	55	863	703	235	476	9	17	3	12	285	37	3	.130

Tommy Hughes
HUGHES, THOMAS OWEN   BR TR 6'1" 190 lbs.
B. Oct. 7, 1919, Wilkes-Barre, Pa.

Year	W	L	PCT	ERA	G	GS	CG	IP	H	BB	SO	ShO	W	L	SV	AB	H	HR	BA
1941 PHI N	9	14	.391	4.45	34	24	5	170	187	82	59	2	3	2	0	55	11	0	.200
1942	12	18	.400	3.06	40	31	19	253	224	99	77	0	1	0	1	80	8	0	.100
1946	6	9	.400	4.38	29	13	3	111	123	44	34	2	2	0	1	31	3	0	.097
1947	4	11	.267	3.47	29	15	4	127	121	59	44	1	1	1	1	40	2	0	.050
1948 CIN N	0	4	.000	9.00	12	4	0	27	43	24	7	0	0	0	0	7	1	0	.143
5 yrs.	31	56	.356	3.92	144	87	31	688	698	308	221	5	7	3	3	213	25	0	.117

Vern Hughes
HUGHES, VERNON ALEXANDER (Lefty)   BL TL 5'10" 155 lbs.
B. Apr. 15, 1893, Etna, Pa.   D. Sept. 26, 1961, Sewickley, Pa.

Year	W	L	PCT	ERA	G	GS	CG	IP	H	BB	SO	ShO	W	L	SV	AB	H	HR	BA
1914 BAL F	0	0	–	3.18	3	0	0	5.2	5	3	0	0	0	0	0	1	0	0	.000

Jim Hughey
HUGHEY, JAMES ULYSSES (Cold Water Jim)   TR
B. Mar. 8, 1869, Coldwater, Mich.   D. Mar. 29, 1945, Coldwater, Mich.

Year	W	L	PCT	ERA	G	GS	CG	IP	H	BB	SO	ShO	W	L	SV	AB	H	HR	BA
1891 C-M AA	1	0	1.000	3.00	2	1	1	15	18	3	9	0	0	0	0	7	1	0	.143
1893 CHI N	0	1	.000	11.00	2	2	1	9	14	3	4	0	0	0	0	2	0	0	.000
1896 PIT N	6	8	.429	4.99	25	14	11	155	171	67	48	0	2	0	0	65	14	0	.215
1897	6	10	.375	5.06	25	17	13	149.1	193	45	38	0	1	1	1	63	8	0	.127
1898 STL N	7	24	.226	3.93	35	33	31	283.2	325	71	74	0	0	0	0	97	11	1	.113
1899 CLE N	4	30	.118	5.41	36	34	32	283	403	88	54	0	0	2	0	111	18	0	.162
1900 STL N	5	7	.417	5.19	20	12	11	112.2	147	40	23	0	0	0	0	41	7	0	.171
7 yrs.	29	80	.266	4.87	145	113	100	1007.2	1271	317	250	0	3	3	1	386	59	1	.153

Tex Hughson
HUGHSON, CECIL CARLTON   BR TR 6'3" 198 lbs.
B. Feb. 9, 1916, Kyle, Tex.

Year	W	L	PCT	ERA	G	GS	CG	IP	H	BB	SO	ShO	W	L	SV	AB	H	HR	BA
1941 BOS A	5	3	.625	4.13	12	8	4	61	70	13	22	0	1	0	0	17	1	0	.059
1942	22	6	.786	2.59	38	30	22	281	258	75	113	4	0	0	4	102	18	0	.176
1943	12	15	.444	2.64	35	32	20	266	242	73	114	4	0	1	2	86	9	0	.105
1944	18	5	.783	2.26	28	23	19	203.1	172	41	112	2	0	0	5	66	10	0	.152
1946	20	11	.645	2.75	39	35	21	278	252	51	172	6	0	0	3	91	12	0	.132
1947	12	11	.522	3.33	29	26	13	189.1	173	71	119	3	1	0	0	61	2	0	.033
1948	3	1	.750	5.12	15	0	0	19.1	21	7	6	0	3	1	0	2	0	0	.000
1949	4	2	.667	5.33	29	2	0	77.2	82	41	35	0	4	1	3	21	1	0	.045
8 yrs.	96	54	.640	2.94	225	156	99	1375.2	1270	372	693	19	9	3	17	447	53	0	.119

WORLD SERIES

Year	W	L	PCT	ERA	G	GS	CG	IP	H	BB	SO	ShO	W	L	SV	AB	H	HR	BA
1946 BOS A	0	1	.000	3.14	3	2	0	14.1	14	3	8	0	0	0	0	3	1	0	.333

Mark Huismann
HUISMANN, MARK LAWRENCE   BR TR 6'3" 195 lbs.
B. May 11, 1958, Littleton, Colo.

Year	W	L	PCT	ERA	G	GS	CG	IP	H	BB	SO	ShO	W	L	SV	AB	H	HR	BA
1983 KC A	2	1	.667	5.58	13	0	0	30.2	29	17	20	0	2	1	0	0	0	0	–
1984	3	3	.500	4.08	38	0	0	75	83	21	54	0	3	3	3	0	0	0	–
2 yrs.	5	4	.556	4.51	51	0	0	105.2	112	38	74	0	5	4	3	0	0	0	–

LEAGUE CHAMPIONSHIP SERIES

Year	W	L	PCT	ERA	G	GS	CG	IP	H	BB	SO	ShO	W	L	SV	AB	H	HR	BA
1984 KC A	0	0	–	10.13	1	0	0	2.2	6	1	2	0	2	0	0	0	0	0	–

Harry Hulihan
HULIHAN, HARRY JOSEPH   BR TL 5'11" 170 lbs.
B. Apr. 18, 1899, Rutland, Vt.   D. Sept. 11, 1980, Rutland, Vt.

Year	W	L	PCT	ERA	G	GS	CG	IP	H	BB	SO	ShO	W	L	SV	AB	H	HR	BA
1922 BOS N	2	3	.400	3.15	7	6	2	40	40	26	16	0	0	0	0	13	2	0	.154

Jim Hulvey
HULVEY, JAMES HENSEL   BB TR 6' 180 lbs.
B. July 18, 1897, Mt. Sidney, Va.   D. Apr. 9, 1982, Mount Sidney, Va.

Year	W	L	PCT	ERA	G	GS	CG	IP	H	BB	SO	ShO	W	L	SV	AB	H	HR	BA
1923 PHI A	0	1	.000	7.71	1	1	0	7	10	2	2	0	0	0	0	2	1	0	.500

Tom Hume
HUME, THOMAS HUBERT   BR TR 6'1" 185 lbs.
B. Mar. 29, 1953, Cincinnati, Ohio

Year	W	L	PCT	ERA	G	GS	CG	IP	H	BB	SO	ShO	W	L	SV	AB	H	HR	BA
1977 CIN N	3	3	.500	7.12	14	5	0	43	54	17	22	0	1	0	0	10	2	1	.200
1978	8	11	.421	4.14	42	23	3	174	198	50	90	0	2	0	1	45	3	0	.067
1979	10	9	.526	2.76	57	12	2	163	162	33	80	0	5	5	17	23	4	0	.174

	W	L	PCT	ERA	G	GS	CG	IP	H	BB	SO	ShO	Relief Pitching W	L	SV	BATTING AB	H	HR	BA

Tom Hume continued

	W	L	PCT	ERA	G	GS	CG	IP	H	BB	SO	ShO	W	L	SV	AB	H	HR	BA
1980	9	10	.474	2.56	78	0	0	137	121	38	68	0	9	10	25	16	3	0	.188
1981	9	4	.692	3.44	51	0	0	68	63	31	27	0	9	4	13	4	0	0	.000
1982	2	6	.250	3.11	46	0	0	63.2	57	21	22	0	2	6	17	5	0	0	.000
1983	3	5	.375	4.77	48	0	0	66	66	41	34	0	3	5	9	5	0	0	.000
1984	4	13	.235	5.64	54	8	0	113.1	142	41	59	0	3	8	3	22	3	0	.136
8 yrs.	48	61	.440	3.88	390	48	5	828	863	272	402	0	33	39	85	153	19	1	.124

LEAGUE CHAMPIONSHIP SERIES

	W	L	PCT	ERA	G	GS	CG	IP	H	BB	SO	ShO	W	L	SV	AB	H	HR	BA
1979 CIN N	0	1	.000	6.75	3	0	0	4	6	0	2	0	0	1	0	1	0	0	.000

Bill Humphrey

HUMPHREY, BYRON WILLIAM
B. June 17, 1911, Vienna, Mo. BR TR 6' 180 lbs.

	W	L	PCT	ERA	G	GS	CG	IP	H	BB	SO	ShO	W	L	SV	AB	H	HR	BA
1938 BOS A	0	0	—	9.00	2	0	0	2	5	1	0	0	0	0	0	0	0	0	—

Bob Humphreys

HUMPHREYS, ROBERT WILLIAM
B. Aug. 18, 1935, Covington, Va. BR TR 5'11" 165 lbs.

	W	L	PCT	ERA	G	GS	CG	IP	H	BB	SO	ShO	W	L	SV	AB	H	HR	BA
1962 DET A	0	1	.000	7.20	4	0	0	5	8	2	3	0	0	1	1	0	0	0	—
1963 STL N	0	1	.000	5.06	9	0	0	10.2	11	7	8	0	0	1	0	0	0	0	—
1964	2	0	1.000	2.53	28	0	0	42.2	32	15	36	0	2	0	2	4	1	0	.250
1965 CHI N	2	0	1.000	3.15	41	0	0	65.2	59	27	38	0	2	0	0	3	0	0	.000
1966 WAS A	7	3	.700	2.82	58	1	0	111.2	91	28	88	0	6	3	3	12	2	0	.167
1967	6	2	.750	4.17	48	2	0	105.2	93	41	54	0	5	1	4	15	2	0	.133
1968	5	7	.417	3.69	56	0	0	92.2	78	30	56	0	5	7	2	5	2	0	.400
1969	3	3	.500	3.05	47	0	0	79.2	69	38	43	0	3	3	5	13	1	0	.077
1970 2 teams																			
WAS A (5G 0-0) MIL A (23G 2-4)																			
" total	2	4	.333	2.92	28	0	0	52.1	41	31	38	0	2	4	3	9	0	0	.000
9 yrs.	27	21	.563	3.36	319	4	0	566	482	219	364	0	25	20	20	61	8	0	.131

WORLD SERIES

	W	L	PCT	ERA	G	GS	CG	IP	H	BB	SO	ShO	W	L	SV	AB	H	HR	BA
1964 STL N	0	0	—	0.00	1	0	0	1	0	0	1	0	0	0	0	0	0	0	—

Bert Humphries

HUMPHRIES, ALBERT
B. Sept. 26, 1880, California, Pa. D. Sept. 21, 1945, Orlando, Fla. BR TR 5'11½" 182 lbs.

	W	L	PCT	ERA	G	GS	CG	IP	H	BB	SO	ShO	W	L	SV	AB	H	HR	BA
1910 PHI N	0	0	—	4.66	5	0	0	9.2	13	3	3	0	0	0	1	2	0	0	.000
1911 2 teams																			
PHI N (11G 3-1) CIN N (14G 4-3)																			
" total	7	4	.636	3.06	25	12	5	106	118	28	29	0	0	1	1	31	6	0	.194
1912 CIN N	9	11	.450	3.23	30	15	9	158.2	162	36	58	0	4	3	2	51	7	0	.137
1913 CHI N	16	4	.800	2.69	28	20	13	181	169	24	61	2	2	1	0	62	12	0	.194
1914	10	11	.476	2.68	34	22	8	171	162	37	62	2	2	0	0	55	13	0	.236
1915	8	13	.381	2.31	31	22	10	171.2	183	23	45	4	1	1	2	46	8	0	.174
6 yrs.	50	43	.538	2.79	153	91	45	798	807	151	258	9	9	6	6	247	46	0	.186

John Humphries

HUMPHRIES, JOHN WILLIAM
B. June 23, 1915, Clifton Forge, Va. D. June 24, 1965, New Orleans, La. BR TR 6'1" 185 lbs.

	W	L	PCT	ERA	G	GS	CG	IP	H	BB	SO	ShO	W	L	SV	AB	H	HR	BA
1938 CLE A	9	8	.529	5.23	45	6	1	103.1	105	63	56	0	8	3	6	29	3	0	.103
1939	2	4	.333	8.26	15	1	0	28.1	30	32	12	0	2	3	2	7	0	0	.000
1940	0	2	.000	8.29	19	1	1	33.2	35	29	17	0	0	1	1	6	0	0	.000
1941 CHI A	4	2	.667	1.84	14	6	4	73.1	63	22	25	4	0	0	1	23	2	0	.087
1942	12	12	.500	2.68	28	28	17	228.1	227	59	71	2	0	0	0	80	18	0	.225
1943	11	11	.500	3.30	28	27	8	188.1	198	54	51	2	0	0	0	69	20	0	.290
1944	8	10	.444	3.67	30	20	8	169	170	57	42	0	2	1	1	53	10	0	.189
1945	6	14	.300	4.24	22	21	10	153	172	48	33	1	0	0	1	54	8	0	.148
1946 PHI N	0	0	—	4.01	10	1	0	24.2	24	9	10	0	0	0	0	8	2	0	.250
9 yrs.	52	63	.452	3.78	211	111	49	1002	1024	373	317	9	12	8	12	329	63	0	.191

Ben Hunt

HUNT, BENJAMIN FRANKLIN (Highpockets)
B. 1888, Eufaula, Okla. BL TL

	W	L	PCT	ERA	G	GS	CG	IP	H	BB	SO	ShO	W	L	SV	AB	H	HR	BA
1910 BOS A	2	3	.400	4.05	7	7	3	46.2	45	20	19	0	0	0	0	18	1	0	.056
1913 STL N	0	1	.000	3.38	2	1	0	8	6	9	6	0	0	0	0	2	0	0	.000
2 yrs.	2	4	.333	3.95	9	8	3	54.2	51	29	25	0	0	0	0	20	1	0	.050

Ken Hunt

HUNT, KENNETH RAYMOND
B. Dec. 14, 1938, Ogden, Utah BR TR 6'4" 200 lbs.

	W	L	PCT	ERA	G	GS	CG	IP	H	BB	SO	ShO	W	L	SV	AB	H	HR	BA
1961 CIN N	9	10	.474	3.96	29	22	4	136.1	130	66	75	0	0	0	0	39	7	0	.179

WORLD SERIES

	W	L	PCT	ERA	G	GS	CG	IP	H	BB	SO	ShO	W	L	SV	AB	H	HR	BA
1961 CIN N	0	0	—	0.00	1	0	0	1	0	1	1	0	0	0	0	0	0	0	—

Catfish Hunter

HUNTER, JAMES AUGUSTUS
B. Apr. 18, 1946, Hertford, N. C. BR TR 6' 190 lbs.

	W	L	PCT	ERA	G	GS	CG	IP	H	BB	SO	ShO	W	L	SV	AB	H	HR	BA
1965 KC A	8	8	.500	4.26	32	20	3	133	124	46	82	2	1	0	0	40	6	0	.150
1966	9	11	.450	4.02	30	25	4	176.2	158	64	103	0	0	0	0	59	9	0	.153
1967	13	17	.433	2.81	35	35	13	259.2	209	84	196	5	0	0	0	92	18	2	.196
1968 OAK A	13	13	.500	3.35	36	34	11	234	210	69	172	2	0	0	0	82	19	1	.232
1969	12	15	.444	3.35	38	35	10	247	210	85	150	3	0	0	0	85	19	1	.224
1970	18	14	.563	3.81	40	40	9	262	253	74	178	1	0	0	0	90	18	0	.200
1971	21	11	.656	2.96	37	37	16	274	225	80	181	4	0	0	0	103	36	1	.350
1972	21	7	.750	2.04	38	37	16	295	200	70	191	5	1	0	0	105	23	0	.219
1973	21	5	.808	3.34	36	36	11	256.1	222	69	124	3	0	0	0	1	1	0	1.000
1974	25	12	.676	2.49	41	41	23	318	268	46	143	6	0	0	0	0	0	0	—
1975 NY A	23	14	.622	2.58	39	39	30	328	248	83	177	7	0	0	0	0	0	0	—
1976	17	15	.531	3.53	36	36	21	298.2	268	68	173	2	0	0	0	0	0	0	—
1977	9	9	.500	4.72	22	22	8	143	137	47	52	1	0	0	0	1	0	0	.000
1978	12	6	.667	3.58	21	20	5	118	98	35	56	1	0	0	0	0	0	0	—
1979	2	9	.182	5.31	19	19	1	105	128	34	34	0	0	0	0	0	0	0	—
15 yrs.	224	166	.574	3.26	500	476	181	3448.1	2958	954	2012	42	2	0	0	658	149	6	.226

LEAGUE CHAMPIONSHIP SERIES

	W	L	PCT	ERA	G	GS	CG	IP	H	BB	SO	ShO	W	L	SV	AB	H	HR	BA
1971 OAK A	0	1	.000	5.63	1	1	0	8	7	2	6	0	0	0	0	3	0	0	.000

	W	L	PCT	ERA	G	GS	CG	IP	H	BB	SO	ShO	Relief Pitching W	L	SV	BATTING AB	H	HR	BA

Catfish Hunter continued

	W	L	PCT	ERA	G	GS	CG	IP	H	BB	SO	ShO	W	L	SV	AB	H	HR	BA
1972	0	0	–	1.17	2	2	0	15.1	10	5	9	0	0	0	0	6	1	0	.167
1973	2	0	1.000	1.65	2	2	1	16.1	12	5	6	0	0	0	0	0	0	0	–
1974	1	1	.500	4.63	2	2	1	11.2	11	2	6	0	0	0	0	0	0	0	–
1976 NY A	1	1	.500	4.50	2	2	1	12	10	1	5	0	0	0	0	0	0	0	–
1978	0	0	–	4.50	1	1	0	6	7	3	5	0	0	0	0	0	0	0	–
6 yrs.	4	3	.571	3.25	10	10	3	69.1	57	18	37	0	0	0	0	9	1	0	.111

WORLD SERIES

	W	L	PCT	ERA	G	GS	CG	IP	H	BB	SO	ShO	W	L	SV	AB	H	HR	BA
1972 OAK A	2	0	1.000	2.81	3	2	0	16	12	6	11	0	0	0	0	5	1	0	.200
1973	1	0	1.000	2.03	2	2	0	13.1	11	4	6	0	0	0	0	5	0	0	.000
1974	1	0	1.000	1.17	2	1	0	7.2	5	2	5	0	0	0	1	2	0	0	.000
1976 NY A	0	1	.000	3.12	1	1	1	8.2	10	4	5	0	0	0	0	0	0	0	–
1977	0	1	.000	10.38	2	1	0	4.1	6	0	1	0	0	0	0	0	0	0	–
1978	1	1	.500	4.15	2	2	0	13	13	1	5	0	0	0	0	12	1	0	.083
6 yrs.	5	3	.625	3.29	12	9	1	63	57	17	33	0	0	0	1	12	1	0	.083
	8th				7th	6th		10th			7th								

George Hunter

HUNTER, GEORGE HENRY
Brother of Bill Hunter.
B. July 8, 1886, Buffalo, N. Y. D. Jan. 11, 1968, Harrisburg, Pa.
    BB TL 5'8½" 165 lbs.

	W	L	PCT	ERA	G	GS	CG	IP	H	BB	SO	ShO	W	L	SV	AB	H	HR	BA
1909 BKN N	4	10	.286	2.46	16	13	10	113.1	104	38	43	0	1	2	0	*			

Lem Hunter

HUNTER, ROBERT LEMUEL
B. Jan. 14, 1863, Warren, Ohio D. Nov. 9, 1956, West Lafayette, Ohio

	W	L	PCT	ERA	G	GS	CG	IP	H	BB	SO	ShO	W	L	SV	AB	H	HR	BA
1883 CLE N	0	0	–	1.42	1	0	0	6.1	10	2	4	0	0	0	0	4	1	0	.250

Willard Hunter

HUNTER, WILLARD MITCHELL
B. Mar. 18, 1934, Newark, N. J.
    BR TL 6'2" 180 lbs.

	W	L	PCT	ERA	G	GS	CG	IP	H	BB	SO	ShO	W	L	SV	AB	H	HR	BA
1962 2 teams					LA N (1G 0–0)			NY N (27G 1–6)											
" total	1	6	.143	6.65	28	6	1	65	73	38	41	0	1	0	1	13	3	0	.231
1963				4.41	41	0	0	49	54	9	22	0	3	3	5	1	1	0	1.000
1964 NY N	3	3	.500													14	4	0	.286
2 yrs.	4	9	.308	5.68	69	6	1	114	127	47	63	0	4	3	5	14	4	0	.286

Walter Huntzinger

HUNTZINGER, WALTER HENRY (Shakes)
B. Feb. 6, 1899, Pottsville, Pa. D. Aug. 11, 1981, Upper Darby, Pa.
    BR TR 6' 150 lbs.

	W	L	PCT	ERA	G	GS	CG	IP	H	BB	SO	ShO	W	L	SV	AB	H	HR	BA
1923 NY N	0	1	.000	7.88	2	1	0	8	9	1	2	0	0	1	0	2	0	0	.000
1924	1	1	.500	4.45	12	2	0	32.1	41	9	6	0	0	0	1	8	4	0	.500
1925	5	1	.833	3.50	26	1	0	64.1	68	17	19	0	5	1	0	11	1	0	.091
1926 2 teams					STL N (9G 0–4)			CHI N (11G 1–1)											
" total	1	5	.167	2.73	20	4	2	62.2	61	22	13	0	1	2	2	15	1	0	.067
4 yrs.	7	8	.467	3.60	60	8	2	167.1	179	49	40	0	6	4	3	36	6	0	.167

Tom Hurd

HURD, THOMAS CARR (Whitey)
B. May 27, 1924, Danville, Va. D. Sept. 5, 1982, Waterloo, Iowa
    BR TR 5'9" 155 lbs.

	W	L	PCT	ERA	G	GS	CG	IP	H	BB	SO	ShO	W	L	SV	AB	H	HR	BA
1954 BOS A	2	0	1.000	3.03	16	0	0	29.2	21	14	14	0	2	0	1	3	1	0	.333
1955	8	6	.571	3.01	43	0	0	80.2	72	38	48	0	8	6	5	14	1	0	.071
1956	3	4	.429	5.33	40	0	0	76	84	47	34	0	3	4	5	12	6	0	.500
3 yrs.	13	10	.565	3.96	99	0	0	186.1	177	97	96	0	13	10	11	29	8	0	.276

Bruce Hurst

HURST, BRUCE VEE
B. Mar. 24, 1958, St. George, Utah
    BL TL 6'4" 200 lbs.

	W	L	PCT	ERA	G	GS	CG	IP	H	BB	SO	ShO	W	L	SV	AB	H	HR	BA
1980 BOS A	2	2	.500	9.00	12	7	0	31	39	16	16	0	0	0	0	0	0	0	–
1981	2	0	1.000	4.30	5	5	0	23	23	12	11	0	0	0	0	0	0	0	–
1982	3	7	.300	5.77	28	19	0	117	161	40	53	0	0	1	0	0	0	0	–
1983	12	12	.500	4.09	33	32	6	211.1	241	62	115	2	0	0	0	0	0	0	–
1984	12	12	.500	3.92	33	33	9	218	232	88	136	2	0	0	0	0	0	0	–
5 yrs.	31	33	.484	4.62	111	96	15	600.1	696	218	331	4	0	1	0	0	0	0	–

Bill Husted

HUSTED, WILLIAM J.
B. Oct. 9, 1867, Gloucester, N. J. Deceased.

	W	L	PCT	ERA	G	GS	CG	IP	H	BB	SO	ShO	W	L	SV	AB	H	HR	BA
1890 PHI P	5	12	.294	4.88	18	17	12	129	148	67	33	0	0	0	0	56	6	0	.107

Bert Husting

HUSTING, BERTHOLD JUNEAU (Pete)
B. Mar. 6, 1878, Fond du Lac, Wis. D. Sept. 3, 1948, Milwaukee, Wis.
    BR TR

	W	L	PCT	ERA	G	GS	CG	IP	H	BB	SO	ShO	W	L	SV	AB	H	HR	BA
1900 PIT N	0	0	–	5.63	2	0	0	8	10	5	7	0	0	0	0	3	0	0	.000
1901 MIL A	10	15	.400	4.27	34	26	19	217.1	234	95	67	0	1	1	1	94	19	1	.202
1902 2 teams					BOS A (1G 0–1)			PHI A (32G 14–5)											
" total	14	6	.700	3.99	33	28	18	212	255	99	48	1	1	0	0	86	14	0	.163
3 yrs.	24	21	.533	4.16	69	54	37	437.1	499	199	122	1	2	1	1	183	33	1	.180

Johnny Hutchings

HUTCHINGS, JOHN RICHARD JOSEPH
B. Apr. 14, 1916, Chicago, Ill.
D. Apr. 27, 1963, Indianapolis, Ind.
    BB TR 6'2" 250 lbs.
    BR 1944,1946

	W	L	PCT	ERA	G	GS	CG	IP	H	BB	SO	ShO	W	L	SV	AB	H	HR	BA
1940 CIN N	2	1	.667	3.50	19	4	0	54	53	18	18	0	2	0	0	13	2	0	.154
1941 2 teams					CIN N (8G 0–0)			BOS N (36G 1–6)											
" total	1	6	.143	4.13	44	7	1	106.2	122	26	41	1	0	2	0	27	4	0	.148
1942 BOS N	1	0	1.000	4.39	20	3	0	65.2	66	34	27	0	0	0	1	20	1	0	.050
1944	1	4	.200	3.97	14	7	1	56.2	66	26	26	0	0	0	0	15	1	0	.067
1945	7	6	.538	3.75	57	12	3	185	173	75	99	2	3	3	3	54	13	0	.241
1946	0	1	.000	9.00	1	1	0	3	5	1	1	0	0	1	0	1	0	0	.000
6 yrs.	12	18	.400	3.96	155	34	5	471	474	180	212	3	5	6	6	130	21	0	.162

WORLD SERIES

	W	L	PCT	ERA	G	GS	CG	IP	H	BB	SO	ShO	W	L	SV	AB	H	HR	BA
1940 CIN N	0	0	–	9.00	1	0	0	1	2	1	0	0	0	0	0	0	0	0	–

	W	L	PCT	ERA	G	GS	CG	IP	H	BB	SO	ShO	W	L	SV	AB	H	HR	BA
													Relief Pitching			BATTING			

Fred Hutchinson

HUTCHINSON, FREDERICK CHARLES
B. Aug. 12, 1919, Seattle, Wash. D. Nov. 12, 1964, Bradenton, Fla.
Manager 1952-54, 1956-64.   BL TR 6'2" 190 lbs.

Year	Team	W	L	PCT	ERA	G	GS	CG	IP	H	BB	SO	ShO	W	L	SV	AB	H	HR	BA
1939	DET A	3	6	.333	5.21	13	12	3	84.2	95	51	22	0	0	0	0	34	13	0	.382
1940		3	7	.300	5.68	17	10	1	76	85	26	32	0	1	2	0	30	8	0	.267
1941		0	0	–	0.00	0	0	0	0	0	0	0	0	0	0	0	2	0	0	.000
1946		14	11	.560	3.09	28	26	16	207	184	66	138	3	0	0	0	89	28	0	.315
1947		18	10	.643	3.03	33	25	18	219.2	211	61	113	3	2	1	2	106	32	2	.302
1948		13	11	.542	4.32	33	28	15	221	223	48	92	0	0	0	0	112	23	1	.205
1949		15	7	.682	2.96	33	21	9	188.2	167	52	54	4	3	2	1	73	18	0	.247
1950		17	8	.680	3.96	39	26	10	231.2	269	48	71	1	4	1	0	95	31	0	.326
1951		10	10	.500	3.68	31	20	9	188.1	204	27	53	2	4	1	2	85	16	0	.188
1952		2	1	.667	3.38	12	1	0	37.1	40	9	12	0	2	0	0	18	1	0	.056
1953		0	0	–	2.79	3	0	0	9.2	9	0	4	0	0	0	0	6	1	1	.167
11 yrs.		95	71	.572	3.73	242	169	81	1464	1487	388	591	13	16	7	7	*			

WORLD SERIES

| 1940 | DET A | 0 | 0 | – | 9.00 | 1 | 0 | 0 | 1 | 1 | 1 | 1 | 0 | 0 | 0 | 0 | 0 | 0 | 0 | – |

Ira Hutchinson

HUTCHINSON, IRA KENDALL
B. Aug. 31, 1910, Chicago, Ill. D. Aug. 21, 1973, Chicago, Ill.   BR TR 5'10½" 180 lbs.

Year	Team	W	L	PCT	ERA	G	GS	CG	IP	H	BB	SO	ShO	W	L	SV	AB	H	HR	BA
1933	CHI A	0	0	–	13.50	1	1	0	4	7	3	2	0	0	0	0	2	1	0	.500
1937	BOS N	4	6	.400	3.73	31	8	1	91.2	99	35	29	0	4	0	0	26	3	0	.115
1938		9	8	.529	2.74	36	12	4	151	150	61	38	1	5	3	4	52	9	0	.173
1939	BKN N	5	2	.714	4.34	41	1	0	105.2	103	51	46	0	5	2	1	27	1	0	.037
1940	STL N	4	2	.667	3.13	20	2	1	63.1	68	19	19	0	2	2	1	18	4	0	.222
1941		1	5	.167	3.86	29	0	0	46.2	32	19	19	0	1	5	5	8	2	0	.250
1944	BOS N	9	7	.563	4.21	40	8	1	119.2	136	53	22	1	6	4	1	29	4	0	.138
1945		2	3	.400	5.02	11	0	0	28.2	33	8	4	0	2	3	1	9	0	0	.000
8 yrs.		34	33	.507	3.76	209	32	7	610.2	628	249	179	2	25	19	13	171	24	0	.140

Jim Hutchinson

HUTCHINSON, JAMES F.
B. 1863 D. Dec. 24, 1941, New York, N. Y.

Year	Team	W	L	PCT	ERA	G	GS	CG	IP	H	BB	SO	ShO	W	L	SV	AB	H	HR	BA
1884	KC U	1	1	.500	2.65	2	2	2	17	14	1	5	0	0	0	0	8	2	0	.250

Bill Hutchison

HUTCHISON, WILLIAM FORREST (Wild Bill)
B. Dec. 17, 1859, New Haven, Conn. D. Mar. 19, 1926, Kansas City, Mo.   BR TR 5'9" 175 lbs.

Year	Team	W	L	PCT	ERA	G	GS	CG	IP	H	BB	SO	ShO	W	L	SV	AB	H	HR	BA
1889	CHI N	16	17	.485	3.54	37	36	33	318	306	117	136	3	0	0	0	133	21	1	.158
1890		42	25	.627	2.70	71	66	65	603	505	199	289	5	1	1	2	261	53	2	.203
1891		43	19	.694	2.81	66	58	56	561	508	178	261	4	7	0	1	243	45	2	.185
1892		37	34	.521	2.74	75	71	67	627	572	187	316	5	1	2	0	263	57	1	.217
1893		16	23	.410	4.75	44	40	38	348.1	420	156	80	2	0	1	0	162	41	0	.253
1894		14	15	.483	6.06	36	34	28	277.2	373	140	59	0	1	0	0	136	42	6	.309
1895		13	21	.382	4.73	38	35	30	291	371	129	85	2	0	0	0	126	25	0	.198
1897	STL N	1	4	.200	6.08	6	5	2	40	55	22	5	0	0	0	0	18	5	0	.278
8 yrs.		182	158	.535	3.59	373	345	319	3066	3110	1128	1231	21	10	4	3	1342	289	12	.215

Herb Hutson

HUTSON, GEORGE HERBERT
B. July 17, 1949, Savannah, Ga.   BR TR 6'2" 205 lbs.

Year	Team	W	L	PCT	ERA	G	GS	CG	IP	H	BB	SO	ShO	W	L	SV	AB	H	HR	BA
1974	CHI N	0	2	.000	3.41	20	2	0	29	24	15	22	0	0	0	0	2	0	0	.000

Tom Hutton

HUTTON, THOMAS GEORGE
B. Apr. 20, 1946, Los Angeles, Calif.   BL TL 5'11" 180 lbs.

Year	Team	W	L	PCT	ERA	G	GS	CG	IP	H	BB	SO	ShO	W	L	SV	AB	H	HR	BA
1980	MON N	0	0	–	27.00	1	0	0	1	3	1	1	0	0	0	0	*			

Dick Hyde

HYDE, RICHARD ELDE
B. Aug. 3, 1928, Hindsboro, Ill.   BR TR 5'11" 170 lbs.

Year	Team	W	L	PCT	ERA	G	GS	CG	IP	H	BB	SO	ShO	W	L	SV	AB	H	HR	BA
1955	WAS A	0	0	–	4.50	3	0	0	2	2	1	1	0	0	0	0	0	0	0	–
1957		4	3	.571	4.12	52	2	0	109.1	104	56	46	0	4	3	1	18	3	0	.167
1958		10	3	.769	1.75	53	0	0	103	82	35	49	0	10	3	18	18	0	0	.000
1959		2	5	.286	4.97	32	0	0	54.1	56	27	29	0	2	5	4	6	0	0	.000
1960		0	1	.000	4.15	9	0	0	8.2	11	5	4	0	0	1	0	0	0	0	–
1961	BAL A	1	2	.333	5.57	15	0	0	21	18	13	15	0	1	2	0	1	1	0	1.000
6 yrs.		17	14	.548	3.56	169	2	0	298.1	273	137	144	0	17	14	23	43	4	0	.093

Jim Hyndman

HYNDMAN, JAMES WILLIAM
B. 1864, Kingston, Pa. Deceased.

Year	Team	W	L	PCT	ERA	G	GS	CG	IP	H	BB	SO	ShO	W	L	SV	AB	H	HR	BA
1886	PHI AA	0	1	.000	27.00	1	1	0	2	5	5	1	0	0	0	0	4	0	0	.000

Pat Hynes

HYNES, PATRICK J.
B. Mar. 12, 1884, St. Louis, Mo. D. Mar. 12, 1907, St. Louis, Mo.   TL

Year	Team	W	L	PCT	ERA	G	GS	CG	IP	H	BB	SO	ShO	W	L	SV	AB	H	HR	BA
1903	STL N	0	1	.000	4.00	1	1	1	9	10	6	1	0	0	0	0	3	0	0	.000
1904	STL A	1	0	1.000	6.23	5	2	1	26	35	7	6	0	0	0	0	254	60	0	.236
2 yrs.		1	1	.500	5.66	6	3	2	35	45	13	7	0	0	0	0	*			

Ham Iburg

IBURG, HERMAN EDWARD
B. Oct. 29, 1877, San Francisco, Calif. D. Feb. 11, 1945, San Francisco, Calif.   TR 5'11½" 165 lbs.

Year	Team	W	L	PCT	ERA	G	GS	CG	IP	H	BB	SO	ShO	W	L	SV	AB	H	HR	BA
1902	PHI N	11	18	.379	3.89	30	30	20	236	286	62	106	1	0	0	0	87	12	0	.138

Gary Ignasiak

IGNASIAK, GARY RAYMOND
B. Sept. 1, 1949, Mt. Clemens, Mich.   BR TL 5'11" 185 lbs.

Year	Team	W	L	PCT	ERA	G	GS	CG	IP	H	BB	SO	ShO	W	L	SV	AB	H	HR	BA
1973	DET A	0	0	–	3.60	3	0	0	5	5	3	4	0	0	0	0	0	0	0	–

	W	L	PCT	ERA	G	GS	CG	IP	H	BB	SO	ShO	Relief Pitching W	L	SV	BATTING AB	H	HR	BA

Doc Imlay

IMLAY, HARRY MILLER
B. Jan. 12, 1889, Allentown, N. J.   D. Oct. 7, 1948, Bordentown, N. J.
BR TR 5'11"   168 lbs.

	W	L	PCT	ERA	G	GS	CG	IP	H	BB	SO	ShO	W	L	SV	AB	H	HR	BA
1913 PHI N	0	0	—	7.24	9	0	0	13.2	19	7	7	0	0	0	0	3	0	0	.000

Bob Ingersoll

INGERSOLL, ROBERT RANDOLPH
B. Jan. 8, 1883, Rapid City, S. D.   D. Jan. 13, 1927, Minneapolis, Minn.
BR TR 5'11½" 175 lbs.

	W	L	PCT	ERA	G	GS	CG	IP	H	BB	SO	ShO	W	L	SV	AB	H	HR	BA
1914 CIN N	0	0	—	3.00	4	0	0	6	5	5	2	0	0	0	0	1	1	0	1.000

Bert Inks

INKS, ALBERT JOHN
B. Jan. 27, 1871, Ligonier, Ind.   D. Oct. 3, 1941, Ligonier, Ind.
BL TL 6'3"   175 lbs.

	W	L	PCT	ERA	G	GS	CG	IP	H	BB	SO	ShO	W	L	SV	AB	H	HR	BA
1891 BKN N	3	10	.231	4.02	13	13	11	96.1	99	43	47	1	0	0	0	35	10	0	.286
1892 2 teams					BKN	N (9G 4-2)		WAS	N	(3G 1-2)									
" total	5	4	.556	4.22	12	11	7	79	77	43	36	1	0	0	0	35	13	0	.371
1894 2 teams					BAL	N (22G 9-4)		LOU	N	(8G 2-6)									
" total	11	10	.524	5.84	30	23	18	192.2	268	88	38	0	1	0	1	84	30	0	.357
1895 LOU N	7	20	.259	6.40	28	27	21	205.1	294	78	42	0	0	0	0	84	21	0	.250
1896 2 teams					PHI	N (3G 0-1)		CIN	N	(3G 1-1)									
" total	1	2	.333	5.64	6	4	2	30.1	42	14	4	0	0	0	0	12	1	0	.083
5 yrs.	27	46	.370	5.52	89	77	59	603.2	780	266	167	2	1	0	1	250	75	0	.300

Hooks Iott

IOTT, CLARENCE EUGENE
B. Dec. 3, 1919, Mountain Grove, Mo.   D. Aug. 17, 1980, St. Petersburg, Fla.
BB TL 6'2"   200 lbs.

	W	L	PCT	ERA	G	GS	CG	IP	H	BB	SO	ShO	W	L	SV	AB	H	HR	BA
1941 STL A	0	0	—	9.00	2	0	0	2	2	1	1	0	0	0	0	0	0	0	—
1947 2 teams					STL	A (4G 0-1)		NY	N	(20G 3-8)									
" total	3	9	.250	7.00	24	9	2	79.2	82	66	52	1	1	5	0	23	3	0	.130
2 yrs.	3	9	.250	7.05	26	9	2	81.2	84	67	53	1	1	5	0	23	3	0	.130

Arthur Irwin

IRWIN, ARTHUR ALBERT
Brother of John Irwin.
B. Feb. 14, 1858, Toronto, Ont., Canada   D. July 16, 1921, Atlantic Ocean
Manager 1889, 1891-92, 1894-96, 1898-99.
BL TR 5'8½"   158 lbs.

	W	L	PCT	ERA	G	GS	CG	IP	H	BB	SO	ShO	W	L	SV	AB	H	HR	BA
1884 PRO N	0	0	—	3.00	1	0	0	3	5	1	0	0	0	0	0	404	97	2	.240
1889 PHI N	0	0	—	0.00	1	0	0	1	1	0	0	0	0	0	0	386	89	0	.231
2 yrs.	0	0	—	2.25	2	0	0	4	6	1	0	0	0	0	0	*			

Bill Irwin

IRWIN, WILLIAM FRANKLIN (Phil)
B. Sept. 16, 1859, Neville, Ohio   D. Aug. 7, 1933, Ft. Thomas, Ky.
BR TR 6'   195 lbs.

	W	L	PCT	ERA	G	GS	CG	IP	H	BB	SO	ShO	W	L	SV	AB	H	HR	BA
1886 CIN AA	0	2	.000	5.82	2	2	2	17	18	8	6	0	0	0	0	6	0	0	.000

Frank Isbell

ISBELL, WILLIAM FRANK (Bald Eagle)
B. Aug. 21, 1875, Delavan, N. Y.   D. July 15, 1941, Wichita, Kans.
BL TR 5'11"   190 lbs.

	W	L	PCT	ERA	G	GS	CG	IP	H	BB	SO	ShO	W	L	SV	AB	H	HR	BA
1898 CHI N	4	7	.364	3.56	13	9	7	81	86	42	16	0	1	1	0	159	37	0	.233
1901 CHI A	0	0	—	9.00	1	0	0	1	2	0	0	0	0	0	0	556	143	3	.257
1902	0	0	—	9.00	1	1	0	1	3	1	1	0	0	0	0	515	130	4	.252
1906	0	0	—	0.00	1	0	0	2	1	0	2	0	0	0	0	549	153	0	.279
1907	0	0	—	0.00	1	0	0	.1	0	0	0	0	0	0	0	486	118	0	.243
5 yrs.	4	7	.364	3.59	17	10	7	85.1	92	43	19	0	1	1	0	*			

Al Jackson

JACKSON, ALVIN NEAL
B. Dec. 25, 1935, Waco, Tex.
BL TL 5'10"   169 lbs.

	W	L	PCT	ERA	G	GS	CG	IP	H	BB	SO	ShO	W	L	SV	AB	H	HR	BA
1959 PIT N	0	0	—	6.50	8	3	0	18	30	8	13	0	0	0	0	5	1	0	.200
1961	1	0	1.000	3.42	3	2	1	23.2	20	4	15	0	0	0	0	8	0	0	.000
1962 NY N	8	20	.286	4.40	36	33	12	231.1	244	78	118	4	0	0	0	73	5	0	.068
1963	13	17	.433	3.96	37	34	11	227	237	84	142	0	1	0	1	79	16	0	.203
1964	11	16	.407	4.26	40	31	11	213.1	229	60	112	3	2	0	1	72	11	1	.153
1965	8	20	.286	4.34	37	31	7	205.1	217	61	120	3	0	0	1	60	7	0	.117
1966 STL N	13	15	.464	2.51	36	30	11	232.2	222	45	90	3	1	1	0	74	13	0	.176
1967	9	4	.692	3.95	38	11	1	107	117	29	43	1	4	1	1	31	8	0	.258
1968 NY N	3	7	.300	3.69	25	9	0	92.2	88	17	59	0	1	1	3	28	7	0	.250
1969 2 teams					NY	N (9G 0-0)		CIN	N	(33G 1-0)									
" total	1	0	1.000	6.81	42	0	0	38.1	45	21	26	0	1	0	3	5	1	0	.200
10 yrs.	67	99	.404	3.98	302	184	54	1389.1	1449	407	738	14	9	3	10	435	69	1	.159

Charlie Jackson

JACKSON, CHARLES BERNARD
B. Aug. 4, 1876, Versailles, Ohio   D. Nov. 23, 1957, Scottsbluff, Neb.

	W	L	PCT	ERA	G	GS	CG	IP	H	BB	SO	ShO	W	L	SV	AB	H	HR	BA
1905 DET A	0	2	.000	5.73	2	2	1	11	14	7	3	0	0	0	0	4	1	0	.250

Danny Jackson

JACKSON, DANNY LYNN
B. Jan. 5, 1962, San Antonio, Tex.
BR TL 6'   190 lbs.

	W	L	PCT	ERA	G	GS	CG	IP	H	BB	SO	ShO	W	L	SV	AB	H	HR	BA
1983 KC A	1	1	.500	5.21	4	3	0	19	26	6	9	0	1	0	0	0	0	0	
1984	2	6	.250	4.26	15	11	1	76	84	35	40	0	1	0	0	0	0	0	
2 yrs.	3	7	.300	4.45	19	14	1	95	110	41	49	0	2	0	0	0	0	0	

Darrell Jackson

JACKSON, DARRELL PRESTON
B. Apr. 3, 1956, Los Angeles, Calif.
BL TL 5'10"   150 lbs.

	W	L	PCT	ERA	G	GS	CG	IP	H	BB	SO	ShO	W	L	SV	AB	H	HR	BA
1978 MIN A	4	6	.400	4.48	19	15	1	92.1	89	48	54	1	0	0	0	0	0	0	
1979	4	4	.500	4.30	24	8	1	69	89	26	43	0	1	0	0	0	0	0	
1980	9	9	.500	3.87	32	25	1	172	161	69	90	0	0	0	1	0	0	0	
1981	3	3	.500	4.36	14	5	0	33	35	19	26	0	1	1	0	0	0	0	
1982	0	5	.000	6.25	13	7	0	44.2	51	24	16	0	0	1	0	0	0	0	
5 yrs.	20	27	.426	4.38	102	60	3	411	425	186	229	1	2	2	1	0	0	0	

Grant Jackson

JACKSON, GRANT DWIGHT (Buck)
B. Sept. 28, 1942, Fostoria, Ohio
BR TL 6'   180 lbs.
BB 1967, BL 1968

	W	L	PCT	ERA	G	GS	CG	IP	H	BB	SO	ShO	W	L	SV	AB	H	HR	BA
1965 PHI N	1	1	.500	7.24	6	2	0	13.2	17	5	15	0	1	1	0	0	0	0	.000
1966	0	0	—	5.40	2	0	0	1.2	2	3	0	0	0	0	0	0	0	0	—
1967	2	3	.400	3.84	43	4	0	84.1	86	43	83	0	2	1	0	15	2	0	.133

	W	L	PCT	ERA	G	GS	CG	IP	H	BB	SO	ShO	Relief Pitching W	L	SV	BATTING AB	H	HR	BA

Grant Jackson continued

	W	L	PCT	ERA	G	GS	CG	IP	H	BB	SO	ShO	W	L	SV	AB	H	HR	BA
1968	1	6	.143	2.95	33	6	1	61	59	20	49	0	0	3	1	10	3	0	.300
1969	14	18	.438	3.34	38	35	13	253	237	92	180	4	0	0	1	86	12	1	.140
1970	5	15	.250	5.28	32	23	1	150	170	61	104	0	2	0	0	44	4	0	.091
1971 BAL A	4	3	.571	3.12	29	9	0	78	72	20	51	0	0	0	0	22	2	1	.091
1972	1	1	.500	2.63	32	0	0	41	33	9	34	0	1	1	8	4	0	0	.000
1973	8	0	1.000	1.91	45	0	0	80	54	24	47	0	8	0	9	0	0	0	—
1974	6	4	.600	2.55	49	0	0	67	48	22	56	0	6	4	12	0	0	0	—
1975	4	3	.571	3.35	41	0	0	48.1	42	21	39	0	4	3	7	0	0	0	—
1976 2 teams					BAL A (13G 1–1)		NY A (21G 6–0)												
" total	7	1	.875	2.54	34	2	1	78	57	25	39	1	5	1	4	0	0	0	—
1977 PIT N	5	3	.625	3.86	49	2	0	91	81	39	41	0	5	2	4	18	6	0	.333
1978	7	5	.583	3.27	60	0	0	77	89	32	45	0	7	5	5	12	3	0	.250
1979	8	5	.615	2.96	72	0	0	82	67	35	39	0	8	5	14	9	0	0	.000
1980	8	4	.667	2.92	61	0	0	71	71	20	31	0	8	4	9	10	0	0	.000
1981 2 teams					PIT N (35G 1–2)		MON N (10G 1–0)												
" total	2	2	.500	3.77	45	0	0	43	44	19	21	0	2	2	4	2	0	0	.000
1982 2 teams					KC A (20G 3–1)		PIT N (1G 0–0)												
" total	3	1	.750	5.31	21	0	0	39	43	21	15	0	3	1	0	0	0	0	—
18 yrs.	86	75	.534	3.46	692	83	16	1359	1272	511	889	5	62	33	79	236	32	2	.136

LEAGUE CHAMPIONSHIP SERIES

	W	L	PCT	ERA	G	GS	CG	IP	H	BB	SO	ShO	W	L	SV	AB	H	HR	BA
1973 BAL A	1	0	1.000	0.00	2	0	0	3	0	1	0	0	1	0	0	0	0	0	—
1974	0	0	—	0.00	1	0	0	.1	1	0	1	0	0	0	0	0	0	0	—
1976 NY A	0	0	—	8.10	2	0	0	3.1	4	1	3	0	0	0	0	0	0	0	—
1979 PIT N	1	0	1.000	0.00	2	0	0	2	1	1	2	0	1	0	0	1	0	0	.000
4 yrs.	2	0	1.000	3.12	7	0	0	8.2	6	3	6	0	2	0	0	1	0	0	.000

WORLD SERIES

	W	L	PCT	ERA	G	GS	CG	IP	H	BB	SO	ShO	W	L	SV	AB	H	HR	BA
1971 BAL A	0	0	—	0.00	1	0	0	.2	0	1	0	0	0	0	0	0	0	0	—
1976 NY A	0	0	—	4.91	1	0	0	3.2	4	0	3	0	0	0	0	0	0	0	—
1979 PIT N	1	0	1.000	0.00	4	0	0	4.2	1	2	2	0	1	0	0	0	0	0	.000
3 yrs.	1	0	1.000	2.00	6	0	0	9	5	3	5	0	1	0	0	0	0	0	.000

John Jackson

JACKSON, JOHN LEWIS
B. July 15, 1909, Wynnefield, Pa.   D. Oct. 24, 1956, Somers Point, N. J.
BR TR 6'2" 180 lbs.

	W	L	PCT	ERA	G	GS	CG	IP	H	BB	SO	ShO	W	L	SV	AB	H	HR	BA
1933 PHI N	2	2	.500	6.00	10	7	1	54	74	35	11	0	0	0	0	21	3	0	.143

Larry Jackson

JACKSON, LAWRENCE CURTIS
B. June 2, 1931, Nampa, Ida.
BR TR 6'1½" 175 lbs.

	W	L	PCT	ERA	G	GS	CG	IP	H	BB	SO	ShO	W	L	SV	AB	H	HR	BA
1955 STL N	9	14	.391	4.31	37	25	4	177.1	189	72	88	1	4	2	2	57	3	0	.053
1956	2	2	.500	4.11	51	1	0	85.1	75	45	50	0	2	1	9	11	1	0	.091
1957	15	9	.625	3.47	41	22	6	210.1	196	57	96	2	7	2	1	72	13	0	.181
1958	13	13	.500	3.68	49	23	11	198	211	51	124	1	2	5	8	60	9	0	.150
1959	14	13	.519	3.30	40	37	12	256	271	64	145	3	0	1	0	80	9	0	.113
1960	18	13	.581	3.48	43	38	14	282	277	70	171	3	0	2	0	95	20	0	.211
1961	14	11	.560	3.75	33	28	9	211	203	56	113	3	0	1	0	74	13	0	.176
1962	16	11	.593	3.75	36	35	11	252.1	267	64	112	2	0	0	0	89	15	0	.169
1963 CHI N	14	18	.438	2.55	37	37	13	275	256	54	153	4	0	0	0	87	17	0	.195
1964	24	11	.686	3.14	40	38	19	297.2	265	58	148	3	0	1	0	114	20	0	.175
1965	14	21	.400	3.85	39	39	12	257.1	268	57	131	4	0	0	0	86	11	1	.128
1966 2 teams					CHI N (3G 0–2)		PHI N (35G 15–13)												
" total	15	15	.500	3.32	38	35	12	255	257	62	112	5	1	0	0	92	13	1	.141
1967 PHI N	13	15	.464	3.10	40	37	11	261.2	242	54	139	4	1	0	0	87	14	0	.161
1968	13	17	.433	2.77	34	34	12	243.2	229	60	127	2	0	0	0	85	12	0	.141
14 yrs.	194	183	.515	3.40	558	429	149	3262.2	3206	824	1709	37	17	15	20	1089	170	2	.156

Mike Jackson

JACKSON, MICHAEL WARREN
B. Mar. 27, 1946, Paterson, N. J.
BL TL 6'3" 190 lbs.

	W	L	PCT	ERA	G	GS	CG	IP	H	BB	SO	ShO	W	L	SV	AB	H	HR	BA
1970 PHI N	1	1	.500	1.50	5	0	0	6	4	4	4	0	1	1	0	1	1	0	1.000
1971 STL N	0	0	—	0.00	1	0	0	1	6	1	0	0	0	0	0	1	0	0	.000
1972 KC A	1	2	.333	6.30	7	3	0	20	24	14	15	0	0	1	0	5	0	0	.000
1973 2 teams					KC A (9G 0–0)		CLE A (1G 0–0)												
" total	0	0	—	6.65	10	0	0	23	26	20	14	0	0	0	0	0	0	0	—
4 yrs.	2	3	.400	5.76	23	3	0	50	57	39	33	0	1	2	0	7	1	0	.143

Roy Lee Jackson

JACKSON, ROY LEE
B. May 1, 1954, Opelika, Ala.
BR TR 6'2" 190 lbs.

	W	L	PCT	ERA	G	GS	CG	IP	H	BB	SO	ShO	W	L	SV	AB	H	HR	BA
1977 NY N	0	2	.000	6.00	4	4	0	24	25	15	13	0	0	0	0	6	0	0	.000
1978	0	0	—	9.00	4	2	0	13	21	6	6	0	0	0	0	3	2	0	.667
1979	1	0	1.000	2.25	8	0	0	16	11	5	10	0	1	0	0	1	1	0	1.000
1980	1	7	.125	4.18	24	8	1	71	78	20	58	0	0	1	1	16	3	0	.188
1981 TOR A	1	2	.333	2.61	39	0	0	62	65	25	27	0	1	2	7	0	0	0	—
1982	8	8	.500	3.06	48	2	0	97	77	31	71	0	8	7	6	0	0	0	—
1983	8	3	.727	4.50	49	0	0	92	92	41	48	0	8	3	7	0	0	0	—
1984	7	8	.467	3.56	54	0	0	86	73	31	58	0	7	8	10	0	0	0	—
8 yrs.	26	30	.464	3.85	230	16	2	461	442	174	291	0	25	21	31	26	6	0	.231

Art Jacobs

JACOBS, ARTHUR EDWARD
B. Aug. 28, 1902, Luckey, Ohio   D. June 8, 1967, Inglewood, Calif.
BL TL 5'10" 170 lbs.

	W	L	PCT	ERA	G	GS	CG	IP	H	BB	SO	ShO	W	L	SV	AB	H	HR	BA
1939 CIN N	0	0	—	9.00	1	0	0	1	2	1	0	0	0	0	1	0	0	0	—

Bucky Jacobs

JACOBS, NEWTON SMITH
B. Mar. 21, 1913, Altavista, Va.
BR TR 5'11" 155 lbs.

	W	L	PCT	ERA	G	GS	CG	IP	H	BB	SO	ShO	W	L	SV	AB	H	HR	BA
1937 WAS A	1	1	.500	4.84	11	1	0	22.1	26	11	8	0	1	0	0	5	0	0	.000
1939	0	0	—	0.00	2	0	0	3	1	0	1	0	0	0	0	1	0	0	.000
1940	0	1	.000	6.00	9	0	0	15	16	9	6	0	0	1	0	0	0	0	—
3 yrs.	1	2	.333	4.91	22	1	0	40.1	43	20	15	0	1	1	0	6	0	0	.000

	W	L	PCT	ERA	G	GS	CG	IP	H	BB	SO	ShO	Relief Pitching W	L	SV	BATTING AB	H	HR	BA

Elmer Jacobs

JACOBS, WILLIAM ELMER
B. Aug. 10, 1892, Salem, Mo.   D. Feb. 10, 1958, Salem, Mo.
BR TR 6'   165 lbs.

	W	L	PCT	ERA	G	GS	CG	IP	H	BB	SO	ShO	W	L	SV	AB	H	HR	BA
1914 PHI N	1	3	.250	4.80	14	7	1	50.2	65	20	17	0	0	0	0	14	0	0	.000
1916 PIT N	6	10	.375	2.94	34	17	8	153	151	38	46	0	2	1	0	40	3	0	.075
1917	6	19	.240	2.81	38	25	10	227.1	214	76	58	1	1	3	2	67	12	0	.179
1918 2 teams	PIT N	(8G 0–1)		PHI	N	(18G 9–5)													
" total	9	6	.600	2.95	26	18	12	146.1	122	56	35	4	0	1	1	45	8	0	.178
1919 2 teams	PHI N	(17G 6–10)		STL	N	(17G 3–6)													
" total	9	16	.360	3.32	34	23	7	214	231	69	68	1	2	1	1	68	16	0	.235
1920 STL N	4	8	.333	5.21	23	9	1	77.2	91	33	21	0	2	2	1	26	5	0	.192
1924 CHI N	11	12	.478	3.74	38	22	13	190.1	181	72	50	1	2	2	1	54	6	0	.111
1925	2	3	.400	5.17	18	4	1	55.2	63	22	19	1	1	2	1	13	3	0	.231
1927 CHI A	2	4	.333	4.60	25	8	2	74.1	105	37	22	1	0	0	0	20	3	0	.150
9 yrs.	50	81	.382	3.55	250	133	65	1189.1	1223	423	336	9	10	12	7	347	56	0	.161

Tony Jacobs

JACOBS, ANTHONY ROBERT
B. Aug. 5, 1925, Dixmoor, Ill.   D. Dec. 21, 1980, Nashville, Tenn.
BB TR 5'9"   150 lbs.

	W	L	PCT	ERA	G	GS	CG	IP	H	BB	SO	ShO	W	L	SV	AB	H	HR	BA
1948 CHI N	0	0	–	4.50	1	0	0	2	3	0	2	0	0	0	0	0	0	0	–
1955 STL N	0	0	–	18.00	1	0	0	2	6	1	1	0	0	0	0	1	0	0	.000
2 yrs.	0	0	–	11.25	2	0	0	4	9	1	3	0	0	0	0	1	0	0	.000

Beany Jacobson

JACOBSON, ALBERT L.
Born Albin L. Jacobson.
B. June 5, 1881, Port Washington, Wis.   D. Jan. 31, 1933, Decatur, Ill.
BL TL 6'   170 lbs.

	W	L	PCT	ERA	G	GS	CG	IP	H	BB	SO	ShO	W	L	SV	AB	H	HR	BA
1904 WAS A	6	23	.207	3.55	33	30	23	253.2	276	57	75	1	0	1	0	88	8	0	.091
1905	9	9	.500	3.30	22	17	12	144.1	139	35	50	0	1	1	0	44	7	0	.159
1906 STL A	9	9	.500	2.50	24	15	12	155	146	27	53	0	2	1	0	58	5	0	.086
1907 2 teams	STL A	(7G 1–6)		BOS	A	(2G 0–0)													
" total	1	6	.143	3.19	9	8	6	59.1	57	29	17	0	0	0	0	18	4	0	.222
4 yrs.	25	47	.347	3.19	88	70	53	612.1	618	148	195	1	3	3	0	208	24	0	.115

Larry Jacobus

JACOBUS, STUART LOUIS
B. Dec. 13, 1893, Cincinnati, Ohio   D. Aug. 19, 1965, North College Hill, Ohio
BB TR 6'2"   186 lbs.

	W	L	PCT	ERA	G	GS	CG	IP	H	BB	SO	ShO	W	L	SV	AB	H	HR	BA
1918 CIN N	0	1	.000	5.71	5	0	0	17.1	25	1	8	0	0	1	0	5	0	0	.000

Pat Jacquez

JACQUEZ, PAT THOMAS
B. Apr. 23, 1947, Stockton, Calif.
BR TR 6'   200 lbs.

	W	L	PCT	ERA	G	GS	CG	IP	H	BB	SO	ShO	W	L	SV	AB	H	HR	BA
1971 CHI A	0	0	–	4.50	2	0	0	2	4	2	1	0	0	0	0	0	0	0	.000

Paul Jaeckel

JAECKEL, PAUL HENRY (Jake)
B. Apr. 1, 1942, East Los Angeles, Calif.
BR TR 5'10"   170 lbs.

	W	L	PCT	ERA	G	GS	CG	IP	H	BB	SO	ShO	W	L	SV	AB	H	HR	BA
1964 CHI N	1	0	1.000	0.00	4	0	0	8	3	2	1	0	1	0	1	1	0	0	.000

Charlie Jaeger

JAEGER, CHARLES THOMAS
B. Apr. 17, 1875, Ottawa, Ill.   D. Sept. 27, 1942, Ottawa, Ill.
BR TR 6'

	W	L	PCT	ERA	G	GS	CG	IP	H	BB	SO	ShO	W	L	SV	AB	H	HR	BA
1904 DET A	3	3	.500	2.57	8	6	5	49	49	15	13	0	0	0	0	17	1	0	.059

Joe Jaeger

JAEGER, JOSEPH PETER
B. Mar. 3, 1895, St. Cloud, Minn.   D. Dec. 13, 1963, Hampton, Iowa
BR TR 6'3"   180 lbs.

	W	L	PCT	ERA	G	GS	CG	IP	H	BB	SO	ShO	W	L	SV	AB	H	HR	BA
1920 CHI N	0	0	–	12.00	2	0	0	3	6	4	0	0	0	0	0	1	0	0	.000

Sig Jakucki

JAKUCKI, SIGMUND (Jack)
B. Aug. 20, 1909, Camden, N. J.   D. May 28, 1979, Galveston, Tex.
BR TR 6'2½"   198 lbs.

	W	L	PCT	ERA	G	GS	CG	IP	H	BB	SO	ShO	W	L	SV	AB	H	HR	BA
1936 STL A	0	3	.000	8.71	7	2	0	20.2	32	12	9	0	0	1	0	6	0	0	.000
1944	13	9	.591	3.55	35	24	12	198	211	54	67	4	1	2	3	73	11	1	.151
1945	12	10	.545	3.51	30	24	15	192.1	188	65	55	1	2	0	2	70	13	2	.186
3 yrs.	25	22	.532	3.79	72	50	27	411	431	131	131	5	3	3	5	149	24	3	.161

WORLD SERIES
| 1944 STL A | 0 | 1 | .000 | 9.00 | 1 | 1 | 0 | 3 | 5 | 0 | 4 | 0 | 0 | 0 | 0 | 0 | 0 | 0 | – |

Charlie Jamerson

JAMERSON, CHARLES DEWEY (Lefty)
B. Jan. 26, 1900, Enfield, Ill.   D. Aug. 4, 1980, Mockville, N. C.
BL TL 6'1"   195 lbs.

	W	L	PCT	ERA	G	GS	CG	IP	H	BB	SO	ShO	W	L	SV	AB	H	HR	BA
1924 BOS A	0	0	–	18.00	1	0	0	1	1	3	0	0	0	0	0	0	0	0	–

Bill James

JAMES, WILLIAM HENRY (Big Bill)
B. Jan. 20, 1888, Ann Arbor, Mich.   D. May 24, 1942, Venice, Calif.
BB TR 6'4"   195 lbs.

	W	L	PCT	ERA	G	GS	CG	IP	H	BB	SO	ShO	W	L	SV	AB	H	HR	BA
1911 CLE A	2	4	.333	4.88	8	6	4	51.2	58	32	21	0	0	0	0	17	1	0	.059
1912	2	0	–	4.61	3	0	0	13.2	15	9	5	0	0	0	0	3	0	0	.000
1914 STL A	15	14	.517	2.85	44	35	20	284	269	109	109	3	0	0	1	89	10	0	.112
1915 2 teams	STL A	(34G 7–10)		DET	A	(11G 7–3)													
" total	14	13	.519	3.26	45	32	11	237.1	212	125	82	1	2	0	1	63	14	0	.222
1916 DET A	8	12	.400	3.68	30	8	8	151.2	141	79	61	0	2	1	1	44	3	0	.068
1917	13	10	.565	2.09	34	23	10	198	163	96	62	2	2	1	1	57	12	0	.211
1918	6	11	.353	3.76	19	18	8	122	127	68	42	1	1	0	0	39	6	0	.109
1919 3 teams	DET A	(2G 1–0)		BOS	A	(13G 3–5)		CHI	A	(5G 3–2)									
" total	7	7	.500	3.71	20	13	7	121.1	129	58	26	2	2	0	0	39	6	0	.154
8 yrs.	65	71	.478	3.20	203	147	68	1179.2	1114	576	408	9	7	3	4	358	51	0	.142

WORLD SERIES
| 1919 CHI A | 0 | 0 | – | 5.79 | 1 | 0 | 0 | 4.2 | 8 | 3 | 2 | 0 | 0 | 0 | 0 | 0 | 0 | 0 | .000 |

Bill James

JAMES, WILLIAM LAWRENCE (Seattle Bill)
B. Mar. 12, 1892, Iowa Hill, Calif.   D. Mar. 10, 1971, Oroville, Calif.
BL TR 6'3"   196 lbs.

	W	L	PCT	ERA	G	GS	CG	IP	H	BB	SO	ShO	W	L	SV	AB	H	HR	BA
1913 BOS N	6	10	.375	2.79	24	14	10	135.2	134	57	73	1	1	0	1	47	12	0	.255
1914	26	7	.788	1.90	46	37	30	332.1	261	118	156	4	1	1	2	129	33	0	.256
1915	5	4	.556	3.03	13	10	4	68.1	68	22	23	0	0	1	0	21	1	0	.048

	W	L	PCT	ERA	G	GS	CG	IP	H	BB	SO	ShO	Relief Pitching			BATTING			
													W	L	SV	AB	H	HR	BA

Bill James continued

	W	L	PCT	ERA	G	GS	CG	IP	H	BB	SO	ShO	W	L	SV	AB	H	HR	BA
1919	0	0	–	3.38	1	0	0	5.1	6	2	1	0	0	0	0	2	0	0	.000
4 yrs.	37	21	.638	2.28	84	61	44	541.2	469	199	253	5	2	3	2	199	46	0	.231

WORLD SERIES

	W	L	PCT	ERA	G	GS	CG	IP	H	BB	SO	ShO	W	L	SV	AB	H	HR	BA
1914 BOS N	2	0	1.000	0.00	2	1	1	11	2	6	9	1	1	0	0	4	0	0	.000

Bob James   JAMES, ROBERT HARVEY
B. Aug. 15, 1958, Glendale, Calif.   BR TR 6'4"   215 lbs.

	W	L	PCT	ERA	G	GS	CG	IP	H	BB	SO	ShO	W	L	SV	AB	H	HR	BA
1978 MON N	0	1	.000	9.00	4	1	0	4	4	4	3	0	0	0	0	0	0	0	–
1979	0	0	–	13.50	2	0	0	2	2	3	1	0	0	0	0	0	0	0	–
1982 2 teams	MON	N	(7G 0–0)		DET	A	(12G 0–2)												
" total	0	2	.000	5.34	19	1	0	28.2	32	16	31	0	0	2	0	0	0	0	–
1983 2 teams	DET	A	(4G 0–0)		MON	N	(27G 1–0)												
" total	1	0	1.000	3.50	31	0	0	54	42	26	60	0	1	0	7	7	2	0	.286
1984 MON N	6	6	.500	3.66	62	0	0	96	92	45	91	0	6	6	10	14	2	0	.143
5 yrs.	7	9	.438	4.09	118	2	0	184.2	172	94	186	0	7	8	17	21	4	0	.190

Jeff James   JAMES, JEFFREY LYNN (Jesse)
B. Sept. 29, 1941, Indianapolis, Ind.   BR TR 6'3"   195 lbs.

	W	L	PCT	ERA	G	GS	CG	IP	H	BB	SO	ShO	W	L	SV	AB	H	HR	BA
1968 PHI N	4	4	.500	4.28	29	13	1	115.2	112	46	83	1	0	0	0	33	4	0	.121
1969	2	2	.500	5.34	6	5	1	32	36	14	21	0	0	0	0	11	2	0	.182
2 yrs.	6	6	.500	4.51	35	18	2	147.2	148	60	104	1	0	0	0	44	6	0	.136

Johnny James   JAMES, JOHN PHILLIP
B. July 23, 1933, Bonner's Ferry, Ida.   BL TR 5'10"   160 lbs.

	W	L	PCT	ERA	G	GS	CG	IP	H	BB	SO	ShO	W	L	SV	AB	H	HR	BA
1958 NY A	0	0	–	0.00	1	0	0	3	2	4	1	0	0	0	0	1	0	0	.000
1960	5	1	.833	4.36	28	0	0	43.1	38	26	29	0	5	1	2	3	0	0	.000
1961 2 teams	NY	A	(1G 0–0)		LA	A	(36G 0–2)												
" total	0	2	.000	5.20	37	3	0	72.2	67	54	43	0	0	1	0	13	0	0	.000
3 yrs.	5	3	.625	4.76	66	3	0	119	107	84	73	0	5	2	2	17	0	0	.000

Lefty James   JAMES, WILLIAM A.
B. July 1, 1889, Glenroy, Ohio   D. May 3, 1933, Portsmouth, Ohio   BR TL 5'11½" 175 lbs.

	W	L	PCT	ERA	G	GS	CG	IP	H	BB	SO	ShO	W	L	SV	AB	H	HR	BA
1912 CLE A	0	1	.000	7.50	3	1	0	6	8	4	2	0	0	0	1	3	0	0	.000
1913	2	2	.500	3.00	11	4	4	39	42	9	18	0	0	1	0	13	3	0	.231
1914	0	3	.000	3.20	17	6	1	50.2	44	32	16	0	0	1	0	12	0	0	.000
3 yrs.	2	6	.250	3.39	31	11	5	95.2	94	45	36	0	0	2	1	28	3	0	.107

Rick James   JAMES, RICHARD LEE
B. Oct. 11, 1947, Sheffield, Ala.   BR TR 6'2½"   205 lbs.

	W	L	PCT	ERA	G	GS	CG	IP	H	BB	SO	ShO	W	L	SV	AB	H	HR	BA
1967 CHI N	0	1	.000	13.50	3	1	0	4.2	9	2	2	0	0	0	0	1	0	0	.000

Charlie Jamieson   JAMIESON, CHARLES DEVINE
B. Feb. 7, 1893, Paterson, N. J.   D. Oct. 27, 1969, Paterson, N. J.   BL TL 5'8½"   165 lbs.

	W	L	PCT	ERA	G	GS	CG	IP	H	BB	SO	ShO	W	L	SV	AB	H	HR	BA
1916 WAS A	0	0	–	4.50	1	0	0	4	2	3	2	0	0	0	0	145	36	0	.248
1917	0	0	–	38.57	1	0	0	2.1	10	2	1	0	0	0	0	382	98	0	.257
1918 PHI A	2	1	.667	4.30	5	2	1	23	24	13	2	0	1	0	0	416	84	0	.202
1919 CLE A	0	0	–	5.54	4	1	0	13	12	8	0	0	0	0	0	17	6	0	.353
1922	0	0	–	3.18	2	0	0	5.2	7	4	2	0	0	0	0	567	183	3	.323
5 yrs.	2	1	.667	6.19	13	3	1	48	55	30	7	0	1	0	0	*			

Gerry Janeski   JANESKI, GERALD JOSEPH
B. Apr. 18, 1946, Pasadena, Calif.   BR TR 6'4"   205 lbs.

	W	L	PCT	ERA	G	GS	CG	IP	H	BB	SO	ShO	W	L	SV	AB	H	HR	BA
1970 CHI A	10	17	.370	4.76	35	35	4	206	247	63	79	1	0	0	0	66	5	0	.076
1971 WAS A	1	5	.167	4.94	23	10	0	62	72	34	19	0	1	0	1	14	3	0	.214
1972 TEX A	0	1	.000	2.77	4	1	0	13	11	7	7	0	0	0	0	2	0	0	.000
3 yrs.	11	23	.324	4.71	62	46	4	281	330	104	105	1	1	0	1	82	8	0	.098

Larry Jansen   JANSEN, LAWRENCE JOSEPH
B. July 16, 1920, Verboort, Ore.   BR TR 6'2"   190 lbs.

	W	L	PCT	ERA	G	GS	CG	IP	H	BB	SO	ShO	W	L	SV	AB	H	HR	BA
1947 NY N	21	5	.808	3.16	42	30	20	248	241	57	104	1	1	1	1	86	16	0	.186
1948	18	12	.600	3.61	42	36	15	277	283	54	126	4	1	0	1	95	13	0	.137
1949	15	16	.484	3.85	37	35	17	259.2	271	62	113	3	0	1	0	97	16	0	.165
1950	19	13	.594	3.01	40	35	21	275	238	55	161	5	0	0	0	96	16	1	.167
1951	23	11	.676	3.04	39	34	18	278.1	254	56	145	3	4	1	0	96	9	0	.094
1952	11	11	.500	4.09	34	27	8	167.1	183	47	74	1	1	0	2	45	8	0	.178
1953	11	16	.407	4.14	36	26	6	184.2	185	55	88	0	2	1	1	60	8	0	.133
1954	2	2	.500	5.98	13	7	0	40.2	57	15	15	0	1	1	0	14	4	0	.286
1956 CIN N	2	3	.400	5.19	8	7	2	34.2	39	9	16	0	0	1	1	11	0	0	.000
9 yrs.	122	89	.578	3.58	291	237	107	1765.1	1751	410	842	17	10	5	10	600	90	1	.150

WORLD SERIES

	W	L	PCT	ERA	G	GS	CG	IP	H	BB	SO	ShO	W	L	SV	AB	H	HR	BA
1951 NY N	0	2	.000	6.30	3	2	0	10	8	4	6	0	0	0	0	2	0	0	.000

Pat Jarvis   JARVIS, ROBERT PATRICK
B. Mar. 18, 1941, Carlyle, Ill.   BR TR 5'10½" 180 lbs.

	W	L	PCT	ERA	G	GS	CG	IP	H	BB	SO	ShO	W	L	SV	AB	H	HR	BA
1966 ATL N	6	2	.750	2.31	10	9	3	62.1	46	12	41	1	0	0	0	22	0	0	.000
1967	15	10	.600	3.66	32	30	7	194	195	62	118	1	0	0	0	71	6	0	.085
1968	16	12	.571	2.60	34	34	14	256	202	50	157	1	2	0	0	71	10	0	.141
1969	13	11	.542	4.44	37	33	4	217	204	73	123	1	0	0	0	85	12	0	.113
1970	16	16	.500	3.61	36	34	11	254	240	72	173	1	0	1	0	82	15	0	.183
1971	6	14	.300	4.11	35	23	3	162	162	51	68	3	2	1	1	47	5	0	.106
1972	11	7	.611	4.09	37	6	0	99	94	44	56	0	8	5	2	24	3	0	.125
1973 MON N	2	1	.667	3.20	28	0	0	39.1	37	16	19	0	2	1	0	3	0	0	.000
8 yrs.	85	73	.538	3.58	249	169	42	1283.2	1180	380	755	8	14	8	3	405	49	0	.121

LEAGUE CHAMPIONSHIP SERIES

	W	L	PCT	ERA	G	GS	CG	IP	H	BB	SO	ShO	W	L	SV	AB	H	HR	BA
1969 ATL N	0	1	.000	12.46	1	1	0	4.1	10	0	6	0	0	0	0	2	0	0	.000

	W	L	PCT	ERA	G	GS	CG	IP	H	BB	SO	ShO	RP W	RP L	SV	AB	H	HR	BA

Ray Jarvis

JARVIS, RAYMOND ARNOLD
B. May 10, 1946, Providence, R. I. — BR TR 6'2" 198 lbs.

	W	L	PCT	ERA	G	GS	CG	IP	H	BB	SO	ShO	RP W	RP L	SV	AB	H	HR	BA
1969 BOS A	5	6	.455	4.75	29	12	2	100.1	105	43	36	0	2	0	1	29	2	0	.069
1970	0	1	.000	3.94	15	0	0	16	17	14	8	0	0	1	0	0	0	0	—
2 yrs.	5	7	.417	4.64	44	12	2	116.1	122	57	44	0	2	1	1	29	2	0	.069

Hi Jasper

JASPER, HARRY W.
B. May 24, 1887, St. Louis, Mo.   D. May 22, 1937, St. Louis, Mo. — BR TR 5'11" 180 lbs.

	W	L	PCT	ERA	G	GS	CG	IP	H	BB	SO	ShO	RP W	RP L	SV	AB	H	HR	BA
1914 CHI A	1	0	1.000	3.34	16	0	0	32.1	22	20	19	0	1	0	0	5	0	0	.000
1915	0	1	.000	4.60	3	2	1	15.2	8	9	15	0	0	0	0	7	2	0	.286
1916 STL N	5	6	.455	3.28	21	11	2	107	97	42	37	0	3	1	1	33	7	1	.212
1919 CLE A	4	5	.444	3.59	12	10	5	82.2	83	28	25	0	1	0	0	29	3	0	.103
4 yrs.	10	12	.455	3.48	52	23	8	237.2	210	99	96	0	5	1	1	74	12	1	.162

Larry Jaster

JASTER, LARRY EDWARD
B. Jan. 13, 1944, Midland, Mich. — BL TL 6'3" 190 lbs.

	W	L	PCT	ERA	G	GS	CG	IP	H	BB	SO	ShO	RP W	RP L	SV	AB	H	HR	BA
1965 STL N	3	0	1.000	1.61	4	3	3	28	21	7	10	0	0	0	0	10	2	0	.200
1966	11	5	.688	3.26	26	21	6	151.2	124	45	92	5	1	0	0	45	8	1	.178
1967	9	7	.563	3.01	34	23	2	152.1	141	44	87	1	1	0	3	50	5	0	.100
1968	9	13	.409	3.51	31	21	3	153.2	153	38	70	1	2	1	0	43	6	1	.140
1969 MON N	1	6	.143	5.49	24	11	1	77	95	28	39	0	0	0	0	19	8	0	.421
1970 ATL N	1	1	.500	6.95	14	0	0	22	33	8	9	0	1	0	0	3	0	0	.000
1972	1	1	.500	5.25	5	1	0	12	12	8	6	0	1	0	0	1	0	0	.000
7 yrs.	35	33	.515	3.65	138	80	15	596.2	579	178	313	7	6	2	3	171	29	2	.170

WORLD SERIES

	W	L	PCT	ERA	G	GS	CG	IP	H	BB	SO	ShO	RP W	RP L	SV	AB	H	HR	BA
1967 STL N	0	0	—	0.00	1	0	0	.1	2	0	0	0	0	0	0	0	0	0	—
1968	0	0	—	∞	1	0	0		2	1	0	0	0	0	0	0	0	0	—
2 yrs.	0	0	—	81.00	2	0	0	.1	4	1	0	0	0	0	0	0	0	0	—

Al Javery

JAVERY, ALVA WILLIAM (Bear Tracks)
B. June 5, 1918, Worcester, Mass.   D. Sept. 13, 1977, Woodstock, Conn. — BR TR 6'3" 183 lbs.

	W	L	PCT	ERA	G	GS	CG	IP	H	BB	SO	ShO	RP W	RP L	SV	AB	H	HR	BA
1940 BOS N	2	4	.333	5.51	29	4	1	83.1	99	36	42	0	2	3	1	23	2	0	.087
1941	10	11	.476	4.31	34	23	9	160.2	181	65	54	1	2	4	1	58	6	0	.103
1942	12	16	.429	3.03	42	37	19	261	251	78	85	5	0	0	0	86	9	0	.105
1943	17	16	.515	3.21	41	35	19	303	288	99	134	5	2	3	0	104	17	0	.163
1944	10	19	.345	3.54	40	33	11	254	248	118	137	3	2	0	3	79	12	0	.152
1945	2	7	.222	6.28	17	14	2	77.1	92	51	18	1	0	1	0	29	6	0	.207
1946	0	1	.000	13.50	2	1	0	3.1	5	5	0	0	0	0	0	1	0	0	.000
7 yrs.	53	74	.417	3.80	205	147	61	1142.2	1164	452	470	15	8	7	5	380	52	0	.137

Joey Jay

JAY, JOSEPH RICHARD
B. Aug. 15, 1935, Middletown, Conn. — BB TR 6'4" 228 lbs.   BR 1953

	W	L	PCT	ERA	G	GS	CG	IP	H	BB	SO	ShO	RP W	RP L	SV	AB	H	HR	BA
1953 MIL N	1	0	1.000	0.00	3	1	1	10	6	5	4	1	0	0	0	3	0	0	.000
1954	1	0	1.000	6.50	15	1	0	18	21	16	13	0	1	0	0	0	0	0	—
1955	0	0	—	4.74	12	1	0	19	23	13	3	0	0	0	0	3	2	0	.667
1957	0	0	—	0.00	1	0	0	.2	0	0	0	0	0	0	1	0	0	0	—
1958	7	5	.583	2.14	18	12	6	96.2	60	45	74	3	0	0	0	32	3	0	.094
1959	6	11	.353	4.09	34	19	4	136.1	130	64	88	1	1	2	0	35	3	0	.086
1960	9	8	.529	3.24	32	11	3	133.1	128	59	90	0	3	5	1	45	7	0	.156
1961 CIN N	21	10	.677	3.53	34	34	14	247.1	217	92	157	4	1	0	0	89	8	0	.090
1962	21	14	.600	3.76	39	37	16	273	269	100	155	1	1	0	0	90	15	2	.167
1963	7	18	.280	4.29	30	22	4	170	172	73	116	1	2	3	1	50	8	0	.160
1964	11	11	.500	3.39	34	23	10	183	167	36	134	0	2	0	2	53	3	0	.057
1965	9	8	.529	4.22	37	24	4	155.2	150	63	102	1	2	1	1	49	2	0	.041
1966 2 teams		CIN N (12G 6-2)				ATL N (9G 0-4)													
" total	6	6	.500	5.05	21	18	1	103.1	117	43	63	1	0	0	0	34	4	0	.118
13 yrs.	99	91	.521	3.77	310	203	63	1546.1	1460	607	999	16	12	11	7	483	55	2	.114

WORLD SERIES

	W	L	PCT	ERA	G	GS	CG	IP	H	BB	SO	ShO	RP W	RP L	SV	AB	H	HR	BA
1961 CIN N	1	1	.500	5.59	2	2	1	9.2	8	6	6	0	0	0	0	4	0	0	.000

Tex Jeanes

JEANES, ERNEST LEE
B. Dec. 19, 1900, Maypearl, Tex.   D. Apr. 5, 1973, Longview, Tex. — BR TR 6' 176 lbs.

	W	L	PCT	ERA	G	GS	CG	IP	H	BB	SO	ShO	RP W	RP L	SV	AB	H	HR	BA
1922 CLE A	0	0	—	0.00	1	0	0	0	1	0	0	0	0	0	0	1	0	0	.000
1927 NY N	0	0	—	9.00	1	0	0	2	2	0	0	0	0	0	0	20	6	0	.300
2 yrs.	0	0	—	9.00	2	0	0	2	3	0	0	0	0	0	0	*			

George Jeffcoat

JEFFCOAT, GEORGE EDWARD
Brother of Hal Jeffcoat.
B. Dec. 24, 1913, New Brookland, S. C.   D. Oct. 13, 1978, Leesville, S. C. — BR TR 5'11½" 175 lbs.

	W	L	PCT	ERA	G	GS	CG	IP	H	BB	SO	ShO	RP W	RP L	SV	AB	H	HR	BA
1936 BKN N	5	6	.455	4.52	40	5	3	95.2	84	63	46	0	4	3	3	23	3	0	.130
1937	1	3	.250	5.13	21	3	1	54.1	58	27	29	1	1	2	0	12	0	0	.000
1939	0	0	—	0.00	1	0	0	2	2	0	1	0	0	0	0	0	0	0	—
1943 BOS N	1	2	.333	3.06	8	1	0	17.2	15	10	10	0	0	2	0	4	2	0	.500
4 yrs.	7	11	.389	4.51	70	9	4	169.2	159	100	86	1	5	7	3	39	5	0	.128

Hal Jeffcoat

JEFFCOAT, HAROLD BENTLEY
Brother of George Jeffcoat.
B. Sept. 6, 1924, West Columbia, S. C. — BR TR 5'10½" 185 lbs.

	W	L	PCT	ERA	G	GS	CG	IP	H	BB	SO	ShO	RP W	RP L	SV	AB	H	HR	BA
1954 CHI N	5	6	.455	5.19	43	3	1	104	110	58	35	0	4	4	7	31	8	1	.258
1955	8	6	.571	2.95	50	1	0	100.2	107	53	32	0	8	6	6	23	4	1	.174
1956 CIN N	8	2	.800	3.84	38	16	2	171	189	55	55	0	2	0	2	54	8	0	.148
1957	12	13	.480	4.52	37	31	10	207	236	46	63	1	0	1	0	69	14	4	.203
1958	6	8	.429	3.72	49	0	0	75	76	26	35	0	6	8	9	9	5	0	.556
1959 2 teams		CIN N (17G 0-1)				STL N (11G 0-1)													
" total	0	2	.000	5.95	28	0	0	39.1	54	19	19	0	0	2	1	4	1	0	.250
6 yrs.	39	37	.513	4.22	245	51	13	697	772	257	239	1	20	21	25	*			

	W	L	PCT	ERA	G	GS	CG	IP	H	BB	SO	ShO	Relief Pitching W	L	SV	BATTING AB	H	HR	BA

Mike Jeffcoat

JEFFCOAT, JAMES MICHAEL
B. Aug. 3, 1959, Pine Bluff, Ark.   BL TL 6'2"   185 lbs.

Year	W	L	PCT	ERA	G	GS	CG	IP	H	BB	SO	ShO	W	L	SV	AB	H	HR	BA
1983 CLE A	1	3	.250	3.31	11	2	0	32.2	32	13	9	0	1	1	0	0	0	0	—
1984	5	2	.714	2.99	63	1	0	75.1	82	24	41	0	4	2	1	0	0	0	—
2 yrs.	6	5	.545	3.08	74	3	0	108	114	37	50	0	5	3	1	0	0	0	—

Jesse Jefferson

JEFFERSON, JESSE HARRISON
B. Mar. 3, 1950, Midlothian, Va.   BR TR 6'3"   188 lbs.

Year	W	L	PCT	ERA	G	GS	CG	IP	H	BB	SO	ShO	W	L	SV	AB	H	HR	BA
1973 BAL A	6	5	.545	4.10	18	15	3	101	104	46	52	0	1	0	0	0	0	0	—
1974	1	0	1.000	4.42	20	2	0	57	55	38	31	0	0	0	0	0	0	0	—
1975 2 teams						BAL A (4G 0–2)			CHI A (22G 5–9)										
" total	5	11	.313	4.92	26	21	1	115.1	105	102	71	0	0	2	0	0	0	0	—
1976 CHI A	2	5	.286	8.56	19	9	0	62	86	42	30	0	0	1	0	0	0	0	—
1977 TOR A	9	17	.346	4.31	33	33	8	217	224	83	114	0	0	0	0	0	0	0	—
1978	7	16	.304	4.38	31	30	9	211.2	214	86	97	2	0	0	0	0	0	0	—
1979	2	10	.167	5.51	34	10	2	116	150	45	43	0	0	3	1	0	0	0	—
1980 2 teams						TOR A (29G 4–13)			PIT N (1G 1–0)										
" total	5	13	.278	5.23	30	19	2	129	133	54	57	2	1	1	0	1	0	0	.000
1981 CAL A	2	4	.333	3.62	26	5	0	77	80	24	27	0	1	0	0	0	0	0	—
9 yrs.	39	81	.325	4.81	237	144	25	1086	1151	520	522	4	3	7	1	1	0	0	.000

Ferguson Jenkins

JENKINS, FERGUSON ARTHUR
B. Dec. 13, 1943, Chatham, Ont., Canada   BR TR 6'5"   205 lbs.

Year	W	L	PCT	ERA	G	GS	CG	IP	H	BB	SO	ShO	W	L	SV	AB	H	HR	BA
1965 PHI N	2	1	.667	2.19	7	0	0	12.1	7	2	10	0	2	1	1	1	0	0	.000
1966 2 teams						PHI N (1G 0–0)			CHI N (60G 6–8)										
" total	6	8	.429	3.32	61	12	2	184.1	150	52	150	1	2	5	5	51	7	1	.137
1967 CHI N	20	13	.606	2.80	38	38	20	289.1	230	83	236	3	0	0	0	93	14	0	.151
1968	20	15	.571	2.63	40	40	20	308	255	65	260	3	0	0	0	100	16	1	.160
1969	21	15	.583	3.21	43	42	23	311	284	71	273	7	0	0	0	108	15	1	.139
1970	22	16	.579	3.39	40	39	24	313	265	60	274	3	0	0	1	113	14	3	.124
1971	24	13	.649	2.77	39	39	30	325	304	37	263	3	0	0	0	115	28	6	.243
1972	20	12	.625	3.21	36	36	23	289	253	62	184	5	0	0	0	109	20	1	.183
1973	14	16	.467	3.89	38	38	7	271	267	57	170	2	0	0	0	84	10	0	.119
1974 TEX A	25	12	.676	2.83	41	41	29	328	286	45	225	6	0	0	0	2	1	0	.500
1975	17	18	.486	3.93	37	37	22	270	261	56	157	4	0	0	0	0	0	0	—
1976 BOS A	12	11	.522	3.27	30	29	12	209	201	43	142	2	1	0	0	0	0	0	—
1977	10	10	.500	3.68	28	28	11	193	190	36	105	1	0	0	0	0	0	0	—
1978 TEX A	18	8	.692	3.04	34	30	16	249	228	41	157	4	0	1	0	0	0	0	—
1979	16	14	.533	4.07	37	37	10	259	252	81	164	3	0	0	0	0	0	0	—
1980	12	12	.500	3.77	29	29	12	198	190	52	129	1	0	0	0	0	0	0	—
1981	5	8	.385	4.50	19	16	1	106	122	40	63	0	0	1	0	0	0	0	—
1982 CHI N	14	15	.483	3.15	34	34	4	217.1	221	68	134	1	0	0	0	67	10	0	.149
1983	6	9	.400	4.30	33	29	1	167.1	176	46	96	1	0	0	0	53	13	0	.245
19 yrs.	284	226	.557	3.34	664	594	267	4499.2	4142	997	3192	49	5	8	7	896	148	13	.165
												7th							

Jack Jenkins

JENKINS, WARREN WASHINGTON
B. Dec. 22, 1942, Covington, Va.   BR TR 6'2"   195 lbs.

Year	W	L	PCT	ERA	G	GS	CG	IP	H	BB	SO	ShO	W	L	SV	AB	H	HR	BA
1962 WAS A	0	1	.000	4.05	3	1	1	13.1	12	7	10	0	0	0	0	4	0	0	.000
1963	0	2	.000	5.84	4	2	0	12.1	16	12	5	0	0	0	0	3	1	0	.333
1969 LA N	0	0	—	0.00	1	0	0	1	0	0	1	0	0	0	0	0	0	0	—
3 yrs.	0	3	.000	4.73	8	3	1	26.2	28	19	16	0	0	0	0	7	1	0	.143

Bill Jensen

JENSEN, WILLIAM CHRISTIAN
B. Nov. 17, 1889, Philadelphia, Pa.   D. Mar. 27, 1917, Philadelphia, Pa.   BL TR 5'11½"   170 lbs.

Year	W	L	PCT	ERA	G	GS	CG	IP	H	BB	SO	ShO	W	L	SV	AB	H	HR	BA
1912 DET A	1	2	.333	5.40	4	3	1	25	30	14	4	0	0	0	0	11	0	0	.000
1914 PHI A	0	1	.000	2.00	1	1	1	9	7	2	1	0	0	0	0	2	0	0	.000
2 yrs.	1	3	.250	4.50	5	4	2	34	37	16	5	0	0	0	0	13	0	0	.000

Virgil Jester

JESTER, VIRGIL MILTON
B. July 23, 1927, Denver, Colo.   BR TR 5'11"   188 lbs.

Year	W	L	PCT	ERA	G	GS	CG	IP	H	BB	SO	ShO	W	L	SV	AB	H	HR	BA
1952 BOS N	3	5	.375	3.33	19	8	4	73	80	23	25	1	0	0	0	19	4	0	.211
1953 MIL N	0	0	—	22.50	2	0	0	2	4	4	0	0	0	0	0	0	0	0	—
2 yrs.	3	5	.375	3.84	21	8	4	75	84	27	25	1	0	0	0	19	4	0	.211

Juan Jimenez

JIMENEZ, JUAN ANTONIO
B. Mar. 8, 1949, La Vega, Dominican Republic   BR TR 6'1"   165 lbs.

Year	W	L	PCT	ERA	G	GS	CG	IP	H	BB	SO	ShO	W	L	SV	AB	H	HR	BA
1974 PIT N	0	0	—	6.75	4	0	0	4	6	2	2	0	0	0	0	0	0	0	—

Tommy John

JOHN, THOMAS EDWARD
B. May 22, 1943, Terre Haute, Ind.   BR TL 6'3"   180 lbs.

Year	W	L	PCT	ERA	G	GS	CG	IP	H	BB	SO	ShO	W	L	SV	AB	H	HR	BA
1963 CLE A	0	2	.000	2.21	6	3	0	20.1	23	6	9	0	0	0	0	6	0	0	.000
1964	2	9	.182	3.91	25	14	2	94.1	97	35	65	1	0	0	0	24	5	0	.208
1965 CHI A	14	7	.667	3.09	39	27	6	183.2	162	58	126	1	1	1	3	59	10	1	.169
1966	14	11	.560	2.62	34	33	10	223	195	57	138	5	0	0	0	69	10	2	.145
1967	10	13	.435	2.47	31	29	9	178.1	143	47	110	6	0	1	0	51	8	0	.157
1968	10	5	.667	1.98	25	25	5	177.1	135	49	117	1	0	0	0	62	12	1	.194
1969	9	11	.450	3.25	33	33	6	232.1	230	90	128	2	0	0	0	79	9	0	.114
1970	12	17	.414	3.28	37	37	10	269	253	101	138	3	0	0	0	84	17	0	.202
1971	13	16	.448	3.62	38	35	10	229	244	58	131	3	0	0	0	69	10	0	.145
1972 LA N	11	5	.688	2.89	29	29	4	186.2	172	40	117	1	0	0	0	63	10	0	.159
1973	16	7	.696	3.10	36	31	4	218	202	50	116	2	0	0	0	74	15	0	.203
1974	13	3	.813	2.59	22	22	5	153	133	42	78	3	0	0	0	51	6	0	.118
1976	10	10	.500	3.09	31	31	6	207	207	61	91	2	0	0	0	64	7	0	.109
1977	20	7	.741	2.78	31	31	11	220	225	50	123	3	0	0	0	79	14	1	.177
1978	17	10	.630	3.30	33	30	7	213	230	53	124	0	1	0	0	66	8	0	.121
1979 NY A	21	9	.700	2.97	37	36	17	276	268	65	111	3	1	0	0	0	0	0	—

	W	L	PCT	ERA	G	GS	CG	IP	H	BB	SO	ShO	Relief Pitching W	L	SV	BATTING AB	H	HR	BA

Tommy John continued

	W	L	PCT	ERA	G	GS	CG	IP	H	BB	SO	ShO	W	L	SV	AB	H	HR	BA
1980	22	9	.710	3.43	36	36	16	265	270	56	78	6	0	0	0	0	0	0	–
1981	9	8	.529	2.64	20	20	7	140	135	39	50	0	0	0	0	0	0	0	–
1982 2 teams								NY	A	(30G	10–10)		CAL	A	(7G 4–2)				
" total	14	12	.538	3.69	37	33	10	221.2	239	39	68	2	0	0	0	0	0	0	–
1983 CAL A	11	13	.458	4.33	34	34	9	234.2	287	49	65	0	0	0	0	0	0	0	–
1984	7	13	.350	4.52	32	29	4	181.1	223	56	47	1	0	0	0	0	0	0	–
21 yrs.	255	197	.564	3.19	646	598	158	4123.2	4073	1101	2030	45	3	2	4	900	141	5	.157

DIVISIONAL PLAYOFF SERIES
	W	L	PCT	ERA	G	GS	CG	IP	H	BB	SO	ShO	W	L	SV	AB	H	HR	BA
1981 NY A	0	1	.000	6.43	1	1	0	7	8	2	0	0	0	0	0	0	0	0	–

LEAGUE CHAMPIONSHIP SERIES
	W	L	PCT	ERA	G	GS	CG	IP	H	BB	SO	ShO	W	L	SV	AB	H	HR	BA
1977 LA N	1	0	1.000	0.66	2	2	1	13.2	11	5	11	0	0	0	0	5	1	0	.200
1978	1	0	1.000	0.00	1	1	1	9	4	2	4	1	0	0	0	3	0	0	.000
1980 NY A	0	0	–	2.70	1	1	0	6.2	8	1	3	0	0	0	0	0	0	0	–
1981	1	0	1.000	1.50	1	1	0	6	6	1	3	0	0	0	0	0	0	0	–
1982 CAL A	1	1	.500	5.11	2	2	1	12.1	11	6	6	0	0	0	0	8	1	0	.125
5 yrs.	4	1	.800	2.08	7	7	3	47.2	40	15	27	1	0	0	0	16	2	0	.125

WORLD SERIES
	W	L	PCT	ERA	G	GS	CG	IP	H	BB	SO	ShO	W	L	SV	AB	H	HR	BA
1977 LA N	0	1	.000	6.00	1	1	0	6	9	3	7	0	0	0	0	2	0	0	.000
1978	1	0	1.000	3.07	2	2	0	14.2	14	4	6	0	0	0	0	2	0	0	.000
1981 NY A	1	0	1.000	0.69	3	2	0	13	11	0	8	0	0	0	0	4	0	0	.000
3 yrs.	2	1	.667	2.67	6	5	0	33.2	34	7	21	0	0	0	0	8	0	0	.000

Augie Johns

JOHNS, AUGUSTUS FRANCIS (Lefty)
B. Sept. 10, 1899, St. Louis, Mo.   D. Sept. 12, 1975, San Antonio, Tex.
    BL   TL   5'8½"   170 lbs.

	W	L	PCT	ERA	G	GS	CG	IP	H	BB	SO	ShO	W	L	SV	AB	H	HR	BA
1926 DET A	6	4	.600	5.35	35	14	3	112.2	117	69	40	1	2	0	1	28	4	0	.143
1927	0	0	–	9.00	1	0	0	1	1	1	1	0	0	0	0	0	0	0	–
2 yrs.	6	4	.600	5.38	36	14	3	113.2	118	70	41	1	2	0	1	28	4	0	.143

Ollie Johns

JOHNS, OLIVER TRACY
B. Aug. 21, 1879, Trenton, Ohio   D. June 17, 1961, Hamilton, Ohio
    BL   TL

	W	L	PCT	ERA	G	GS	CG	IP	H	BB	SO	ShO	W	L	SV	AB	H	HR	BA
1905 CIN N	1	0	1.000	3.50	4	1	1	18	31	4	8	0	0	0	1	5	1	0	.200

Abe Johnson

JOHNSON, ABRAHAM
B. London, Ont., Canada   Deceased.

	W	L	PCT	ERA	G	GS	CG	IP	H	BB	SO	ShO	W	L	SV	AB	H	HR	BA
1893 CHI N	0	0	–	36.00	1	0	0	1	2	2	0	0	0	0	1	0	0	0	–

Adam Johnson

JOHNSON, ADAM RANKIN, SR. (Tex)
Father of Adam Johnson.
B. Feb. 4, 1888, Burnet, Tex.   D. July 2, 1972, Williamsport, Pa.
    BR   TR   6'1½"   185 lbs.

	W	L	PCT	ERA	G	GS	CG	IP	H	BB	SO	ShO	W	L	SV	AB	H	HR	BA
1914 2 teams			BOS	A	(16G	4–9)		CHI	F	(16G	9–5)								
" total	13	14	.481	2.26	32	27	16	219.1	180	63	84	4	1	1	0	67	8	0	.119
1915 2 teams			CHI	F	(11G	2–4)		BAL	F	(23G	7–11)								
" total	9	15	.375	3.64	34	25	15	207.2	201	81	81	2	1	2	2	73	9	0	.123
1918 STL N	1	1	.500	2.74	6	1	0	23	20	7	4	0	1	0	0	4	1	0	.250
3 yrs.	23	30	.434	2.92	72	53	31	450	401	151	169	6	3	3	2	144	18	0	.125

Adam Johnson

JOHNSON, ADAM RANKIN, JR.
Son of Adam Johnson.
B. Mar. 1, 1917, Hayden, Ariz.
    BR   TR   6'3"   177 lbs.

	W	L	PCT	ERA	G	GS	CG	IP	H	BB	SO	ShO	W	L	SV	AB	H	HR	BA
1941 PHI A	1	0	1.000	3.60	7	0	0	10	14	3	0	0	1	0	0	1	0	0	.000

Art Johnson

JOHNSON, ARTHUR GILBERT
B. Feb. 15, 1897, Warren, Pa.   D. June 7, 1982, Sarasota, Fla.
    BR   TL   6'1"   167 lbs.

	W	L	PCT	ERA	G	GS	CG	IP	H	BB	SO	ShO	W	L	SV	AB	H	HR	BA
1927 NY N	0	0	–	0.00	1	0	0	3	1	0	0	0	0	0	0	0	0	0	–

Art Johnson

JOHNSON, ARTHUR HENRY (Lefty)
B. July 16, 1916, Winchester, Mass.
    BL   TL   6'2"   185 lbs.

	W	L	PCT	ERA	G	GS	CG	IP	H	BB	SO	ShO	W	L	SV	AB	H	HR	BA
1940 BOS N	0	1	.000	10.50	2	1	0	6	10	3	1	0	0	0	0	1	0	0	.000
1941	7	15	.318	3.53	43	18	6	183.1	189	71	70	0	1	4	1	55	8	0	.145
1942	0	0	–	1.42	4	0	0	6.1	4	5	0	0	0	0	0	1	0	0	.000
3 yrs.	7	16	.304	3.68	49	19	6	195.2	203	79	71	0	1	4	1	57	8	0	.140

Bart Johnson

JOHNSON, CLAIR BARTH
B. Jan. 3, 1950, Torrance, Calif.
    BR   TR   6'5"   190 lbs.

	W	L	PCT	ERA	G	GS	CG	IP	H	BB	SO	ShO	W	L	SV	AB	H	HR	BA
1969 CHI A	1	3	.250	3.22	4	3	0	22.1	22	6	18	0	0	1	0	6	1	0	.167
1970	4	7	.364	4.80	18	15	2	90	92	46	71	1	0	0	0	29	8	0	.276
1971	12	10	.545	2.93	53	16	4	178	148	111	153	0	4	4	14	57	11	0	.193
1972	0	3	.000	9.22	9	0	0	13.2	18	13	9	0	0	3	1	1	0	0	.000
1973	3	3	.500	4.13	22	9	0	80.2	76	40	56	0	1	0	0	0	0	0	–
1974	10	4	.714	2.73	18	18	8	122	105	32	76	2	0	0	0	0	0	0	–
1976	9	16	.360	4.73	32	32	8	211	231	62	91	3	0	0	0	0	0	0	–
1977	4	5	.444	4.01	29	4	0	92	114	38	46	0	3	3	2	0	0	0	–
8 yrs.	43	51	.457	3.93	185	97	22	809.2	806	348	520	6	8	10	17	93	20	0	.215

Ben Johnson

JOHNSON, BENJAMIN FRANKLIN
B. May 16, 1931, Greenwood, S. C.
    BR   TR   6'2"   190 lbs.

	W	L	PCT	ERA	G	GS	CG	IP	H	BB	SO	ShO	W	L	SV	AB	H	HR	BA
1959 CHI N	0	0	–	2.16	4	2	0	16.2	17	4	6	0	0	0	0	4	0	0	.000
1960	2	1	.667	4.91	17	0	0	29.1	39	11	9	0	2	1	1	2	0	0	.000
2 yrs.	2	1	.667	3.91	21	2	0	46	56	15	15	0	2	1	1	6	0	0	.000

Bill Johnson

JOHNSON, WILLIAM C.
B. Oct. 6, 1956, Wilmington, Del.
    BR   TR   6'5"   205 lbs.

	W	L	PCT	ERA	G	GS	CG	IP	H	BB	SO	ShO	W	L	SV	AB	H	HR	BA
1983 CHI N	1	0	1.000	4.38	10	0	0	12.1	17	3	4	0	1	0	0	0	0	0	–

	W	L	PCT	ERA	G	GS	CG	IP	H	BB	SO	ShO	Relief Pitching W	L	SV	BATTING AB	H	HR	BA

Bill Johnson continued

	W	L	PCT	ERA	G	GS	CG	IP	H	BB	SO	ShO	W	L	SV	AB	H	HR	BA
1984	0	0	—	1.69	4	0	0	5.1	4	1	3	0	0	0	0	0	0	0	—
2 yrs.	1	0	1.000	3.57	14	0	0	17.2	21	4	7	0	1	0	0	0	0	0	—

Bob Johnson

JOHNSON, ROBERT DALE
B. Apr. 25, 1943, Aurora, Ill. BL TR 6'4" 220 lbs.

	W	L	PCT	ERA	G	GS	CG	IP	H	BB	SO	ShO	W	L	SV	AB	H	HR	BA
1969 NY N	0	0	—	0.00	2	0	0	1.2	1	1	1	0	0	0	0	0	0	0	—
1970 KC A	8	13	.381	3.07	40	26	10	214	178	82	206	1	0	1	4	57	6	0	.105
1971 PIT N	9	10	.474	3.45	31	27	7	175	170	55	101	1	0	0	0	48	3	0	.063
1972	4	4	.500	2.96	31	11	1	115.2	98	46	79	0	2	2	3	35	5	0	.143
1973	4	2	.667	3.62	50	2	0	92	98	34	68	0	4	1	4	14	0	0	.000
1974 CLE A	3	4	.429	4.38	14	10	0	72	75	37	36	0	0	0	0	0	0	0	—
1977 ATL N	0	1	.000	7.36	15	0	0	22	24	14	16	0	0	1	0	3	1	0	.333
7 yrs.	28	34	.452	3.48	183	76	18	692.1	644	269	507	2	6	5	12	157	15	0	.096
LEAGUE CHAMPIONSHIP SERIES																			
1971 PIT N	1	0	1.000	0.00	1	1	0	8	5	3	7	0	0	0	0	2	0	0	.000
1972	0	0	—	3.00	2	0	0	6	4	2	7	0	0	0	0	1	0	0	.000
2 yrs.	1	0	1.000	1.29	3	1	0	14	9	5	14	0	0	0	0	3	0	0	.000
WORLD SERIES																			
1971 PIT N	0	1	.000	9.00	2	1	0	5	5	3	3	0	0	0	0	3	0	0	.000

Chet Johnson

JOHNSON, CHESTER LILLIS
Brother of Earl Johnson.
B. Aug. 1, 1917, Redmond, Wash. D. Apr. 10, 1983, Seattle, Wash. BL TL 6' 175 lbs.

	W	L	PCT	ERA	G	GS	CG	IP	H	BB	SO	ShO	W	L	SV	AB	H	HR	BA
1946 STL A	0	0	—	5.00	5	3	0	18	20	13	8	0	0	0	0	6	0	0	.000

Chief Johnson

JOHNSON, GEORGE MURPHY
B. Mar. 25, 1887, Winnebago, Neb. D. June 12, 1922, Des Moines, Iowa BR TR 5'11½" 190 lbs.

	W	L	PCT	ERA	G	GS	CG	IP	H	BB	SO	ShO	W	L	SV	AB	H	HR	BA
1913 CIN N	14	16	.467	3.01	44	31	13	269	251	86	107	3	2	2	0	88	10	1	.114
1914 2 teams	CIN N (1G 0–0)				KC F (20G 9–10)														
" total	9	10	.474	3.26	21	20	12	138	163	35	79	2	0	0	0	49	6	1	.122
1915 KC F	18	17	.514	2.75	46	34	19	281.1	253	71	118	4	4	0	1	87	11	1	.126
3 yrs.	41	43	.488	2.95	111	85	44	688.1	667	192	304	9	6	2	1	224	27	3	.121

Connie Johnson

JOHNSON, CLIFFORD
B. Dec. 27, 1922, Stone Mountain, Ga. BR TR 6'4" 200 lbs.

	W	L	PCT	ERA	G	GS	CG	IP	H	BB	SO	ShO	W	L	SV	AB	H	HR	BA
1953 CHI A	4	4	.500	3.56	14	10	2	60.2	55	38	44	1	0	0	0	20	1	0	.050
1955	7	4	.636	3.45	17	16	5	99	95	52	72	2	0	0	0	33	5	0	.152
1956 2 teams	CHI A (5G 0–1)				BAL A (26G 9–10)														
" total	9	11	.450	3.44	31	27	9	196	176	69	136	2	0	0	0	61	15	0	.246
1957 BAL A	14	11	.560	3.20	35	30	14	242	212	66	177	3	0	1	0	89	12	0	.135
1958	6	9	.400	3.88	26	17	4	118.1	116	32	68	0	1	1	1	34	7	0	.206
5 yrs.	40	39	.506	3.44	123	100	34	716	654	257	497	8	1	2	1	237	40	0	.169

Dave Johnson

JOHNSON, DAVID CHARLES
B. Oct. 4, 1948, Abilene, Tex. BR TR 6'1" 183 lbs.

	W	L	PCT	ERA	G	GS	CG	IP	H	BB	SO	ShO	W	L	SV	AB	H	HR	BA
1974 BAL A	2	2	.500	3.00	11	0	0	15	17	5	6	0	2	2	2	0	0	0	—
1975	0	1	.000	4.15	6	0	0	8.2	8	7	4	0	0	1	0	0	0	0	—
1977 MIN A	2	5	.286	4.56	30	6	0	73	86	23	33	0	1	3	0	0	0	0	—
1978	0	2	.000	7.50	6	1	0	12	15	9	7	0	0	1	0	0	0	0	—
4 yrs.	4	10	.286	4.64	53	7	0	108.2	126	44	50	0	3	7	2	0	0	0	—

Don Johnson

JOHNSON, DONALD ROY
B. Nov. 12, 1926, Portland, Ore. BR TR 6'3" 200 lbs.

	W	L	PCT	ERA	G	GS	CG	IP	H	BB	SO	ShO	W	L	SV	AB	H	HR	BA
1947 NY A	4	3	.571	3.64	15	8	2	54.1	57	23	16	0	1	1	0	13	0	0	.000
1950 2 teams	NY A (8G 1–0)				STL A (25G 5–6)														
" total	6	6	.500	6.71	33	12	4	114	161	67	40	0	2	0	1	32	2	0	.063
1951 2 teams	STL A (6G 0–1)				WAS A (21G 7–11)														
" total	7	12	.368	4.76	27	23	8	158.2	165	76	60	1	0	0	0	50	5	0	.100
1952 WAS A	0	5	.000	4.43	29	6	0	69	80	33	37	0	0	2	2	13	1	0	.077
1954 CHI A	8	7	.533	3.13	46	16	3	144	129	43	68	3	2	3	7	35	1	0	.029
1955 BAL A	2	4	.333	5.82	31	5	0	68	89	35	27	0	2	1	1	10	0	0	.000
1958 SF N	0	1	.000	6.26	17	0	0	23	31	8	14	0	0	1	0	2	0	0	.000
7 yrs.	27	38	.415	4.78	198	70	17	631	712	285	262	4	7	8	12	155	9	0	.058

Earl Johnson

JOHNSON, EARL DOUGLAS (Lefty)
Brother of Chet Johnson.
B. Apr. 2, 1919, Redmond, Wash. BL TL 6'3" 190 lbs.

	W	L	PCT	ERA	G	GS	CG	IP	H	BB	SO	ShO	W	L	SV	AB	H	HR	BA
1940 BOS A	6	2	.750	4.09	17	10	2	70.1	69	39	26	0	2	1	0	27	2	0	.074
1941	4	5	.444	4.52	17	12	4	93.2	90	51	46	0	1	0	0	34	10	0	.294
1946	5	4	.556	3.71	29	5	1	80	78	39	40	1	5	3	3	22	5	0	.227
1947	12	11	.522	2.97	45	17	6	142.1	129	62	65	1	4	3	8	44	12	0	.273
1948	10	4	.714	4.53	35	3	1	91.1	98	42	45	0	9	2	5	31	3	0	.097
1949	3	6	.333	7.48	19	3	0	49.1	65	29	20	0	3	4	0	11	0	0	.000
1950	0	0	—	7.24	11	0	0	13.2	18	8	6	0	0	0	0	2	0	0	.000
1951 DET A	0	0	—	6.35	6	0	0	5.2	9	2	2	0	0	0	0	0	0	0	—
8 yrs.	40	32	.556	4.30	179	50	14	546.1	556	272	250	4	24	13	17	171	32	0	.187
WORLD SERIES																			
1946 BOS A	1	0	1.000	2.70	3	0	0	3.1	1	2	1	0	1	0	0	0	0	0	.000

Ellis Johnson

JOHNSON, ELLIS WATT
B. Dec. 8, 1892, Minneapolis, Minn. D. Jan. 14, 1965, Minneapolis, Minn. BR TR 6'½" 180 lbs.

	W	L	PCT	ERA	G	GS	CG	IP	H	BB	SO	ShO	W	L	SV	AB	H	HR	BA
1912 CHI A	0	0	—	3.29	4	0	0	13.2	11	10	8	0	0	0	0	3	0	0	.000
1915	0	0	—	9.00	1	0	0	2	3	0	3	0	0	0	0	0	0	0	—

	W	L	PCT	ERA	G	GS	CG	IP	H	BB	SO	ShO	Relief Pitching			BATTING			
													W	L	SV	AB	H	HR	BA

Ellis Johnson *continued*

	W	L	PCT	ERA	G	GS	CG	IP	H	BB	SO	ShO	W	L	SV	AB	H	HR	BA
1917 PHI A	0	2	.000	7.24	4	2	0	13.2	15	5	8	0	0	0	0	1	0	0	.000
3 yrs.	0	2	.000	5.52	9	2	0	29.1	29	15	19	0	0	0	0	4	0	0	.000

Ernie Johnson

JOHNSON, ERNEST THORWALD BR TR 6'3½" 190 lbs.
B. June 16, 1924, Brattleboro, Vt.

	W	L	PCT	ERA	G	GS	CG	IP	H	BB	SO	ShO	W	L	SV	AB	H	HR	BA
1950 BOS N	2	0	1.000	6.97	16	1	0	20.2	37	13	15	0	2	0	0	2	1	0	.500
1952	6	3	.667	4.11	29	10	2	92	100	31	45	1	2	0	1	22	2	0	.091
1953 MIL N	4	3	.571	2.67	36	1	0	81	79	22	36	0	4	2	0	14	1	0	.071
1954	5	2	.714	2.81	40	4	1	99.1	77	34	68	0	4	1	2	13	3	0	.231
1955	5	7	.417	3.42	40	2	0	92	81	55	43	0	5	5	4	20	2	0	.100
1956	4	3	.571	3.71	36	0	0	51	54	21	26	0	4	3	6	4	1	0	.250
1957	7	3	.700	3.88	30	0	0	65	67	26	44	0	7	3	4	17	6	1	.353
1958	3	1	.750	8.10	15	0	0	23.1	35	10	13	0	3	1	1	2	0	0	.000
1959 BAL A	4	1	.800	4.11	31	1	0	50.1	57	19	29	0	4	1	1	6	2	0	.333
9 yrs.	40	23	.635	3.77	273	19	3	574.2	587	231	319	1	35	16	19	100	18	1	.180

WORLD SERIES
| 1957 MIL N | 0 | 1 | .000 | 1.29 | 3 | 0 | 0 | 7 | 2 | 1 | 8 | 0 | 0 | 1 | 0 | 1 | 0 | 0 | .000 |

Fred Johnson

JOHNSON, FREDERICK EDWARD (Cactus) BR TR 6' 185 lbs.
B. Mar. 5, 1897, Hanley, Tex. D. June 14, 1973, Kerrville, Tex.

	W	L	PCT	ERA	G	GS	CG	IP	H	BB	SO	ShO	W	L	SV	AB	H	HR	BA
1922 NY N	0	2	.000	4.00	2	2	1	18	20	1	8	0	0	0	0	4	0	0	.000
1923	2	0	1.000	4.24	3	2	1	17	11	7	5	0	1	0	0	6	0	0	.000
1938 STL A	3	7	.300	5.61	17	6	3	69	91	27	24	0	0	5	3	25	6	0	.240
1939	0	1	.000	6.43	5	2	1	14	23	9	2	0	0	0	0	4	0	0	.000
4 yrs.	5	10	.333	5.26	27	12	6	118	145	44	39	0	1	5	3	39	6	0	.154

Hank Johnson

JOHNSON, HENRY WARD BR TR 5'11½" 175 lbs.
B. May 21, 1906, Bradenton, Fla. BB 1933
D. Aug. 20, 1982, Bradenton, Fla.

	W	L	PCT	ERA	G	GS	CG	IP	H	BB	SO	ShO	W	L	SV	AB	H	HR	BA
1925 NY A	1	3	.250	6.85	24	4	2	67	88	37	25	1	0	1	0	17	1	0	.059
1926	0	0	–	18.00	1	0	0	1	2	2	0	0	0	0	1	0	0	0	.000
1928	14	9	.609	4.30	31	22	10	199	188	104	110	1	2	0	0	79	19	1	.241
1929	3	3	.500	5.06	12	8	2	42.2	37	39	24	0	0	0	0	14	1	0	.071
1930	14	11	.560	4.67	44	15	7	175.1	177	104	115	1	9	5	2	64	17	1	.266
1931	13	8	.619	4.72	40	23	8	196.1	176	102	106	0	3	1	4	77	15	0	.195
1932	2	2	.500	4.88	5	4	2	31.1	34	15	27	0	0	0	0	13	3	0	.231
1933 BOS A	6	8	.571	4.06	25	21	7	155.1	156	74	65	0	0	2	1	52	12	0	.231
1934	6	8	.429	5.36	31	14	7	124.1	162	53	66	1	0	0	0	43	10	0	.233
1935	2	1	.667	5.52	13	2	0	31	41	14	14	0	2	0	1	8	0	0	.000
1936 PHI A	2	0	1.000	7.71	3	3	0	11.2	16	10	6	0	0	0	0	4	1	0	.250
1939 CIN N	0	3	.000	2.01	20	0	0	31.1	30	13	10	0	0	3	1	5	2	0	.400
12 yrs.	63	56	.529	4.75	249	116	45	1066.1	1107	567	568	4	16	12	11	376	81	2	.215

Jerry Johnson

JOHNSON, JERRY MICHAEL BR TR 6'3" 200 lbs.
B. Dec. 3, 1943, Miami, Fla.

	W	L	PCT	ERA	G	GS	CG	IP	H	BB	SO	ShO	W	L	SV	AB	H	HR	BA
1968 PHI N	4	4	.500	3.24	16	11	2	80.2	82	29	40	0	0	0	0	25	2	0	.080
1969	6	13	.316	4.29	33	21	4	147	151	57	82	2	0	0	1	43	9	0	.209
1970 2 teams			STL N	(7G 2–0)		SF N	(33G 3–4)												
" total	5	4	.556	4.11	40	4	2	76.2	73	41	49	0	5	3	4	16	1	0	.063
1971 SF N	12	9	.571	2.97	67	0	0	109	93	48	85	0	12	9	18	13	2	0	.154
1972	8	6	.571	4.44	48	0	0	73	73	40	57	0	8	6	8	9	0	0	.000
1973 CLE A	6	5	.455	6.18	39	1	0	59.2	70	39	46	0	5	6	5	0	0	0	–
1974 HOU N	2	1	.667	4.80	34	0	0	45	47	24	32	0	2	1	0	1	0	0	.000
1975 SD N	3	1	.750	5.17	21	4	0	54	60	31	18	0	2	0	0	12	1	0	.083
1976	1	3	.250	5.31	24	1	0	39	39	26	27	0	0	2	0	3	0	0	.000
1977 TOR A	2	4	.333	4.60	43	0	0	86	91	54	54	0	2	4	5	0	0	0	–
10 yrs.	48	51	.485	4.31	365	39	6	770	779	389	489	2	36	31	41	122	15	0	.123

LEAGUE CHAMPIONSHIP SERIES
| 1971 SF N | 0 | 0 | – | 13.50 | 1 | 0 | 0 | 1.1 | 1 | 1 | 2 | 0 | 0 | 0 | 0 | 0 | 0 | 0 | – |

Jim Johnson

JOHNSON, JAMES BRIAN BL TL 5'11" 175 lbs.
B. Nov. 3, 1945, Muskegon, Mich.

	W	L	PCT	ERA	G	GS	CG	IP	H	BB	SO	ShO	W	L	SV	AB	H	HR	BA
1970 SF N	1	0	1.000	7.71	3	0	0	7	8	5	2	0	1	0	0	2	0	0	.000

Jing Johnson

JOHNSON, RUSSELL CONWELL BR TR 5'9" 172 lbs.
B. Oct. 9, 1894, Parker Ford, Pa. D. Dec. 6, 1950, Pottstown, Pa.

	W	L	PCT	ERA	G	GS	CG	IP	H	BB	SO	ShO	W	L	SV	AB	H	HR	BA
1916 PHI A	2	8	.200	3.74	12	12	8	84.1	90	39	25	0	0	0	0	27	2	1	.074
1917	9	12	.429	2.78	34	23	13	191	184	56	55	0	0	0	0	59	12	0	.203
1919	9	15	.375	3.61	34	25	12	202	222	62	67	0	2	1	0	72	14	1	.194
1927	4	2	.667	3.48	17	3	2	51.2	42	16	16	0	2	1	2	12	2	0	.167
1928	0	0	–	5.06	3	0	0	10.2	13	5	3	0	0	0	0	4	2	0	.500
5 yrs.	24	37	.393	3.35	100	63	35	539.2	551	178	166	0	4	2	0	174	32	2	.184

John Johnson

JOHNSON, JOHN LOUIS (Youngy) TL
Born John Louis Mercer.
B. Nov. 18, 1869, N. Cohocton, N.Y. D. Jan. 28, 1941, Kansas City, Mo.

	W	L	PCT	ERA	G	GS	CG	IP	H	BB	SO	ShO	W	L	SV	AB	H	HR	BA
1894 PHI N	1	1	.500	6.06	4	3	2	32.2	44	15	10	0	0	0	0	16	3	0	.188

John Henry Johnson

JOHNSON, JOHN HENRY BL TL 6'2" 190 lbs.
B. Aug. 21, 1956, Houston, Tex.

	W	L	PCT	ERA	G	GS	CG	IP	H	BB	SO	ShO	W	L	SV	AB	H	HR	BA
1978 OAK A	11	10	.524	3.39	33	30	7	186	164	82	91	2	0	0	0	0	0	0	–
1979 2 teams			OAK A	(14G 2–8)		TEX A	(17G 2–6)												
" total	4	14	.222	4.63	31	25	2	167	168	72	96	1	0	0	0	0	0	0	–
1980 TEX A	2	2	.500	2.31	33	0	0	39	27	15	44	0	2	2	4	0	0	0	–

	W	L	PCT	ERA	G	GS	CG	IP	H	BB	SO	ShO	Relief Pitching W	L	SV	BATTING AB	H	HR	BA

John Henry Johnson continued

	W	L	PCT	ERA	G	GS	CG	IP	H	BB	SO	ShO	W	L	SV	AB	H	HR	BA
1981	3	1	.750	2.63	24	0	0	24	19	6	8	0	3	1	2	0	0	0	–
1983 BOS A	3	2	.600	3.71	34	1	0	53.1	58	20	51	0	3	1	1	0	0	0	–
1984	1	2	.333	3.53	30	3	0	63.2	64	27	57	0	1	1	1	0	0	0	–
6 yrs.	24	31	.436	3.71	185	59	9	533	500	222	347	2	10	5	8	0	0	0	–

Johnny Johnson

JOHNSON, JOHN CLIFFORD (Swede)
B. Sept. 29, 1914, Belmore, Ohio — BL TL 6' 182 lbs.

	W	L	PCT	ERA	G	GS	CG	IP	H	BB	SO	ShO	W	L	SV	AB	H	HR	BA
1944 NY A	0	2	.000	4.05	22	1	0	26.2	25	24	11	0	0	1	3	6	3	0	.500
1945 CHI A	3	0	1.000	4.26	29	0	0	69.2	85	35	38	0	3	0	4	14	4	0	.286
2 yrs.	3	2	.600	4.20	51	1	0	96.1	110	59	49	0	3	1	7	20	7	0	.350

Ken Johnson

JOHNSON, KENNETH TRAVIS
B. June 16, 1933, West Palm Beach, Fla. — BR TR 6'4" 210 lbs.

	W	L	PCT	ERA	G	GS	CG	IP	H	BB	SO	ShO	W	L	SV	AB	H	HR	BA
1958 KC A	0	0	–	27.00	2	0	0	2.1	6	3	1	0	0	0	0	0	0	0	–
1959	1	1	.500	4.09	2	2	0	11	11	5	8	0	0	0	0	3	0	0	.000
1960	5	10	.333	4.26	42	6	2	120.1	120	45	83	0	3	6	3	30	5	0	.167
1961 2 teams	KC A (6G 0–4)				CIN N (15G 6–2)														
" total	6	6	.500	4.00	21	12	3	92.1	82	29	46	1	0	3	1	26	6	0	.231
1962 HOU N	7	16	.304	3.84	33	31	9	197	195	46	178	1	0	0	0	52	4	0	.077
1963	11	17	.393	2.65	37	32	6	224	204	50	148	1	1	1	1	74	5	0	.068
1964	11	16	.407	3.63	35	35	7	218	209	44	117	1	0	0	0	76	6	1	.079
1965 2 teams	HOU N (8G 3–2)				MIL N (29G 13–8)														
" total	16	10	.615	3.42	37	34	9	231.1	217	48	151	1	0	0	2	79	9	0	.114
1966 ATL N	14	8	.636	3.30	32	31	11	215.2	213	46	105	2	0	0	0	70	10	1	.143
1967	13	9	.591	2.74	29	29	6	210.1	191	38	85	0	0	0	0	71	9	0	.127
1968	5	8	.385	3.47	31	16	1	135	145	25	57	0	1	2	0	40	7	0	.175
1969 3 teams	ATL N (9G 0–1)				NY A (12G 1–2)			CHI N (9G 1–2)											
" total	2	5	.286	3.89	30	3	0	74	68	33	59	0	1	2	2	13	0	0	.000
1970 MON N	0	0	–	7.50	3	0	0	6	9	1	4	0	0	0	0	0	0	0	–
13 yrs.	91	106	.462	3.46	334	231	50	1737.1	1670	413	1042	7	6	14	9	534	61	2	.114

WORLD SERIES

	W	L	PCT	ERA	G	GS	CG	IP	H	BB	SO	ShO	W	L	SV	AB	H	HR	BA
1961 CIN N	0	0	–	0.00	1	0	0	.2	0	0	0	0	0	0	0	0	0	0	–

Ken Johnson

JOHNSON, KENNETH WANDERSEE (Hooks)
B. Jan. 14, 1923, Topeka, Kans. — BL TL 6'1" 185 lbs.

	W	L	PCT	ERA	G	GS	CG	IP	H	BB	SO	ShO	W	L	SV	AB	H	HR	BA
1947 STL N	1	0	1.000	0.00	2	1	1	10	2	5	8	0	0	0	0	4	2	0	.500
1948	2	4	.333	4.76	13	4	1	45.1	43	30	20	0	2	1	0	20	6	0	.300
1949	0	1	.000	6.42	14	2	0	33.2	29	35	18	0	0	0	0	8	2	0	.250
1950 2 teams	STL N (2G 0–0)				PHI N (14G 4–1)														
" total	4	1	.800	3.88	16	8	3	62.2	62	46	33	1	1	0	0	19	3	0	.158
1951 PHI N	5	8	.385	4.57	20	18	4	106.1	103	68	58	3	1	0	0	35	5	0	.143
1952 DET A	0	0	–	6.35	9	1	0	11.1	12	11	10	0	0	0	0	3	1	0	.333
6 yrs.	12	14	.462	4.58	74	34	8	269.1	251	195	147	4	3	1	0	89	19	0	.213

Lloyd Johnson

JOHNSON, LLOYD WILLIAM (Eppa)
B. Dec. 24, 1910, Santa Rosa, Calif. D. Oct. 8, 1980, Stockton, Calif. — BL TL 6'4" 204 lbs.

	W	L	PCT	ERA	G	GS	CG	IP	H	BB	SO	ShO	W	L	SV	AB	H	HR	BA
1934 PIT N	0	0	–	0.00	1	0	0	1	1	0	0	0	0	0	0	0	0	0	–

Mike Johnson

JOHNSON, MICHAEL NORTON
B. Mar. 2, 1951, Slayton, Minn. — BR TR 6'1" 185 lbs.

	W	L	PCT	ERA	G	GS	CG	IP	H	BB	SO	ShO	W	L	SV	AB	H	HR	BA
1974 SD N	0	2	.000	4.71	18	0	0	21	29	15	15	0	0	2	0	0	0	0	–

Roy Johnson

JOHNSON, ROY (Hardrock)
B. Oct. 1, 1895, Madill, Okla. — BR TR 6' 185 lbs.

	W	L	PCT	ERA	G	GS	CG	IP	H	BB	SO	ShO	W	L	SV	AB	H	HR	BA
1918 PHI A	1	5	.167	3.42	10	8	3	50	47	27	14	0	0	1	0	15	1	0	.067

Si Johnson

JOHNSON, SILAS KENNETH
B. Oct. 5, 1906, Marseilles, Ill. — BR TR 5'11½" 185 lbs.

	W	L	PCT	ERA	G	GS	CG	IP	H	BB	SO	ShO	W	L	SV	AB	H	HR	BA
1928 CIN N	0	0	–	4.35	3	0	0	10.1	9	5	1	0	0	0	0	4	1	0	.250
1929	0	0	–	4.50	1	0	0	2	2	1	0	0	0	0	0	0	0	0	–
1930	3	1	.750	4.94	35	3	0	78.1	86	31	47	0	2	1	0	17	4	0	.235
1931	11	19	.367	3.77	42	33	14	262.1	273	74	95	0	2	0	2	87	13	0	.149
1932	13	15	.464	3.27	42	27	14	245	246	57	94	2	1	0	2	80	10	0	.125
1933	7	18	.280	3.49	34	28	14	211.1	212	54	51	4	0	0	1	72	3	0	.042
1934	7	22	.241	5.22	46	31	9	215.2	264	84	89	0	0	2	3	72	10	0	.139
1935	5	11	.313	6.23	30	20	4	130	155	59	40	1	0	0	0	41	1	0	.024
1936 2 teams	CIN N (2G 0–0)				STL N (12G 5–3)														
" total	5	3	.625	4.93	14	9	3	65.2	89	11	23	1	1	1	0	21	4	0	.190
1937 STL N	12	12	.500	3.32	38	21	12	192.1	222	43	64	1	3	3	1	65	9	0	.138
1938	0	3	.000	7.47	6	3	0	15.2	27	6	4	0	0	0	0	1	0	0	.000
1940 PHI N	5	14	.263	4.88	37	14	5	138.1	145	42	58	0	1	6	1	43	6	0	.140
1941	5	12	.294	4.52	39	21	6	163.1	207	54	80	1	0	3	2	47	7	0	.149
1942	8	19	.296	3.69	39	26	10	195.1	198	72	78	1	1	1	0	58	6	0	.103
1943	8	3	.727	3.27	21	9	3	113	110	25	46	1	0	2	3	33	6	0	.182
1946 2 teams	PHI N (1G 0–0)				BOS N (28G 6–5)														
" total	6	5	.545	2.77	29	12	5	130	141	35	43	1	0	0	1	38	6	0	.158
1947 BOS N	6	8	.429	4.23	36	10	3	112.2	124	34	27	0	2	2	3	30	1	0	.033
17 yrs.	101	165	.380	4.09	492	272	108	2281.1	2510	687	840	13	11	15	15	709	87	0	.123

Syl Johnson

JOHNSON, SYLVESTER W.
B. Dec. 31, 1900, Portland, Ore. — BR TR 5'11½" 180 lbs.

	W	L	PCT	ERA	G	GS	CG	IP	H	BB	SO	ShO	W	L	SV	AB	H	HR	BA
1922 DET A	7	3	.700	3.71	29	8	3	97	99	30	29	0	3	1	1	36	8	0	.222
1923	12	7	.632	3.98	37	18	7	176.1	181	47	93	1	5	2	0	62	10	1	.161
1924	5	4	.556	4.93	29	9	2	104	117	42	55	0	2	2	3	34	7	0	.206
1925	0	2	.000	3.46	6	0	0	13	11	10	5	0	0	2	0	3	0	0	.000

		W	L	PCT	ERA	G	GS	CG	IP	H	BB	SO	ShO	Relief Pitching W	L	SV	BATTING AB	H	HR	BA

Syl Johnson continued

		W	L	PCT	ERA	G	GS	CG	IP	H	BB	SO	ShO	W	L	SV	AB	H	HR	BA
1926	STL N	0	3	.000	4.22	19	6	1	49	54	15	10	0	0	0	1	12	0	0	.000
1927		0	0	–	6.00	2	0	0	3	3	0	2	0	0	0	0	0	0	0	–
1928		8	4	.667	3.90	34	6	2	120	117	33	66	0	4	2	3	38	6	0	.158
1929		13	7	.650	3.60	42	19	12	182.1	186	56	80	3	3	2	3	60	7	1	.117
1930		12	10	.545	4.65	32	24	12	187.2	215	38	92	2	1	2	1	70	15	0	.214
1931		11	9	.550	3.00	32	24	12	186	186	29	82	2	1	0	2	60	14	0	.233
1932		5	14	.263	4.92	32	22	7	164.2	199	35	70	1	1	1	2	51	10	0	.196
1933		3	3	.500	4.29	35	1	0	84	89	16	28	0	2	3	3	21	5	0	.238
1934	2 teams			CIN N	(2G 0–0)				PHI N	(42G 5–9)										
"	total	5	9	.357	3.46	44	10	4	140.1	131	24	54	3	2	5	3	43	9	1	.209
1935	PHI N	10	8	.556	3.56	37	18	8	174.2	182	31	89	1	3	1	6	58	14	1	.241
1936		5	7	.417	4.30	39	8	1	111	129	29	48	0	1	4	7	36	9	0	.250
1937		4	10	.286	5.02	32	15	4	138	155	22	46	0	1	2	3	48	7	0	.146
1938		2	7	.222	4.23	22	6	2	83	87	11	21	0	1	3	0	29	1	0	.034
1939		8	8	.500	3.81	22	14	6	111	112	15	37	0	2	0	2	33	5	0	.152
1940		2	2	.500	4.20	17	2	2	40.2	37	5	13	0	0	2	2	8	0	0	.000
19 yrs.		112	117	.489	4.06	542	210	82	2165.2	2290	488	920	13	33	33	43	702	127	4	.181
WORLD SERIES																				
1928	STL N	0	0	–	4.50	2	0	0	2	4	1	1	0	0	0	0	0	0	0	–
1930		0	0	–	7.20	2	0	0	5	4	3	4	0	0	0	0	0	0	0	–
1931		0	1	.000	3.00	3	1	0	9	10	1	6	0	0	0	0	2	0	0	.000
3 yrs.		0	1	.000	4.50	7	1	0	16	18	5	11	0	0	0	0	2	0	0	.000

Tom Johnson

JOHNSON, THOMAS G.
B. Scranton, Pa.   Deceased.

		W	L	PCT	ERA	G	GS	CG	IP	H	BB	SO	ShO	W	L	SV	AB	H	HR	BA
1897	PHI N	1	2	.333	4.66	5	2	1	29	39	12	7	0	0	0	0	13	1	0	.077
1899	NY N	0	0	–	0.00	1	0	0	2	0	2	1	0	0	0	0	1	0	0	.000
2 yrs.		1	2	.333	4.35	6	2	1	31	39	14	8	0	1	0	0	14	1	0	.071

Tom Johnson

JOHNSON, THOMAS RAYMOND   BR TR 6'1"   185 lbs.
B. Apr. 2, 1951, St. Paul, Minn.

		W	L	PCT	ERA	G	GS	CG	IP	H	BB	SO	ShO	W	L	SV	AB	H	HR	BA
1974	MIN A	2	0	1.000	0.00	7	0	0	7	4	0	4	0	2	0	1	0	0	0	–
1975		1	2	.333	4.19	18	0	0	38.2	40	21	17	0	1	2	3	0	0	0	–
1976		3	1	.750	2.61	18	1	0	48.1	44	8	37	0	3	0	0	0	0	0	–
1977		16	7	.696	3.12	71	0	0	147	152	47	87	0	16	7	15	0	0	0	–
1978		1	4	.200	5.51	18	0	0	32.2	42	17	21	0	1	4	3	0	0	0	–
5 yrs.		23	14	.622	3.39	129	1	0	273.2	282	93	166	0	23	13	22	0	0	0	–

Vic Johnson

JOHNSON, VICTOR OSCAR   BR TL 6'   160 lbs.
B. Aug. 3, 1920, Eau Claire, Wis.

		W	L	PCT	ERA	G	GS	CG	IP	H	BB	SO	ShO	W	L	SV	AB	H	HR	BA
1944	BOS A	0	3	.000	6.26	7	5	0	27.1	42	15	7	0	0	0	0	10	0	0	.000
1945		6	4	.600	4.01	26	9	4	85.1	90	46	21	1	3	0	2	30	5	0	.167
1946	CLE A	0	1	.000	9.22	9	1	0	13.2	20	8	3	0	0	0	0	2	0	0	.000
3 yrs.		6	8	.429	5.06	42	15	4	126.1	152	69	31	1	3	0	2	42	5	0	.119

Walter Johnson

JOHNSON, WALTER PERRY (The Big Train, Barney)   BR TR 6'1"   200 lbs.
B. Nov. 6, 1887, Humboldt, Kans.   D. Dec. 10, 1946, Washington, D. C.
Manager 1929-35.
Hall of Fame 1936.

		W	L	PCT	ERA	G	GS	CG	IP	H	BB	SO	ShO	W	L	SV	AB	H	HR	BA
1907	WAS A	5	9	.357	1.87	14	12	11	110.2	98	17	70	2	0	2	0	36	4	0	.111
1908		14	14	.500	1.64	36	29	23	257.1	194	53	160	6	0	1	1	79	13	0	.165
1909		13	25	.342	2.21	40	36	27	297	247	84	164	4	1	2	1	101	13	1	.129
1910		25	17	.595	1.35	45	42	38	373	269	76	313	8	1	1	1	137	24	2	.175
1911		25	13	.658	1.89	40	37	36	323.1	292	70	207	6	1	1	1	128	30	1	.234
1912		32	12	.727	1.39	50	37	34	368	259	76	303	7	5	2	2	144	38	2	.264
1913		36	7	.837	1.09	47	36	29	346	230	38	243	11	7	0	2	134	35	2	.261
1914		28	18	.609	1.72	51	40	33	371.2	287	74	225	9	4	3	1	136	30	3	.221
1915		27	13	.675	1.55	47	39	35	336.2	258	56	203	7	2	0	4	147	34	2	.231
1916		25	20	.556	1.89	48	38	36	371	290	132	228	3	4	3	1	142	33	1	.232
1917		23	16	.590	2.30	47	34	30	328	259	67	188	8	5	1	3	130	33	0	.254
1918		23	13	.639	1.27	39	29	29	325	241	70	162	8	3	4	3	150	40	1	.267
1919		20	14	.588	1.49	39	29	27	290.1	235	51	147	7	2	4	2	125	24	1	.192
1920		8	10	.444	3.13	21	15	12	143.2	135	27	78	4	1	2	3	69	18	1	.261
1921		17	14	.548	3.51	35	32	25	264	265	92	143	1	1	1	1	111	30	0	.270
1922		15	16	.484	2.99	41	31	23	280	283	99	105	4	1	1	4	108	22	1	.204
1923		17	12	.586	3.54	43	35	18	262	267	69	130	3	1	0	4	93	18	0	.194
1924		23	7	.767	2.72	38	38	20	277.2	233	77	158	6	0	0	0	113	32	1	.283
1925		20	7	.741	3.07	30	29	16	229	211	78	108	3	1	0	0	97	42	2	.433
1926		15	16	.484	3.61	33	33	22	261.2	259	73	125	2	0	0	0	103	20	1	.194
1927		5	6	.455	5.10	18	15	7	107.2	113	26	48	1	0	0	0	46	16	2	.348
21 yrs.		416	279	.599	2.17	802	666	531	5923.2	4925	1405	3508	110	40	30	34	*			
		2nd	3rd		7th	10th		5th			3rd		4th	1st							
WORLD SERIES																				
1924	WAS A	1	2	.333	2.63	3	2	2	24	30	11	20	0	1	0	0	9	1	0	.111
1925		2	1	.667	2.08	3	3	3	26	26	4	15	1	0	0	0	11	1	0	.091
2 yrs.		3	3	.500	2.34	6	5	5	50	56	15	35	1	1	0	0	20	2	0	.100
							10th			8th										

Roy Joiner

JOINER, ROY MERRILL (Pop)   BL TL 6'   170 lbs.
B. Oct. 30, 1906, Red Bluff, Calif.

		W	L	PCT	ERA	G	GS	CG	IP	H	BB	SO	ShO	W	L	SV	AB	H	HR	BA
1934	CHI N	0	1	.000	8.21	20	2	0	34	61	8	9	0	0	0	0	10	2	0	.200
1935		0	0	–	5.40	2	0	0	3.1	6	2	0	0	0	0	0	1	0	0	.000
1940	NY N	3	2	.600	3.40	30	2	0	53	66	17	25	0	2	1	1	11	3	0	.273
3 yrs.		3	3	.500	5.28	52	4	0	90.1	133	27	34	0	2	1	1	22	5	0	.227

	W	L	PCT	ERA	G	GS	CG	IP	H	BB	SO	ShO	Relief Pitching W	L	SV	BATTING AB	H	HR	BA

Dave Jolly

JOLLY, DAVID (Gabby)
B. Oct. 14, 1924, Stony Point, N. C. D. May 27, 1963, Statesville, N. C. BR TR 6' 170 lbs.

	W	L	PCT	ERA	G	GS	CG	IP	H	BB	SO	ShO	W	L	SV	AB	H	HR	BA
1953 MIL N	0	1	.000	3.52	24	0	0	38.1	34	27	23	0	0	1	0	2	1	0	.500
1954	11	6	.647	2.43	47	1	0	111.1	87	64	62	0	11	6	10	31	9	1	.290
1955	2	3	.400	5.71	36	0	0	58.1	58	51	23	0	2	3	1	6	1	0	.167
1956	2	3	.400	3.74	29	0	0	45.2	39	35	20	0	2	3	7	4	0	0	.000
1957	1	1	.500	5.02	23	0	0	37.2	37	21	27	0	1	1	1	5	3	0	.600
5 yrs.	16	14	.533	3.77	159	1	0	291.1	255	198	155	0	16	14	19	48	14	1	.292

Al Jones

JONES, ALFORNIA
B. Feb. 10, 1959, Charleston, Miss. BR TR 6'4" 210 lbs.

1983 CHI A	0	0	–	3.86	2	0	0	2.1	3	2	2	0	0	0	0	0	0	0	–
1984	1	1	.500	4.43	20	0	0	20.1	23	11	15	0	1	1	5	0	0	0	–
2 yrs.	1	1	.500	4.37	22	0	0	22.2	26	13	17	0	1	1	5	0	0	0	–

Alex Jones

JONES, ALEXANDER H.
B. Dec. 25, 1867, Pittsburgh, Pa. D. Apr. 4, 1941, Woodville, Pa. TL

1889 PIT N	1	0	1.000	3.00	1	1	1	9	7	1	10	0	0	0	0	5	1	0	.200
1892 2 teams			LOU	N (18G 5–11)			WAS	N	(4G 0–3)										
" total	5	14	.263	3.42	22	20	16	173.2	163	70	51	1	0	1	0	66	11	0	.167
1894 PHI N	1	0	1.000	2.00	1	1	1	9	10	0	2	0	0	0	0	4	1	0	.250
1903 DET A	0	1	.000	12.46	2	2	0	8.2	19	6	2	0	0	0	0	4	0	0	.000
4 yrs.	7	15	.318	3.73	26	24	18	200.1	199	77	65	1	0	1	0	79	13	0	.165

Art Jones

JONES, ARTHUR LENOX
B. Feb. 7, 1906, Kershaw, S. C. D. Nov. 25, 1980, Columbia, S. C. BR TR 6' 165 lbs.

1932 BKN N	0	0	–	18.00	1	0	0	2	1	2	1	0	0	0	0	0	0	0	–

Broadway Jones

JONES, JESSE FRANK
B. Nov. 15, 1898, Millsboro, Del. D. Sept. 7, 1977, Lewes, Del. BR TR 5'9" 154 lbs.

1923 PHI N	0	0	–	9.00	3	0	0	8	5	7	1	0	0	0	0	2	1	0	.500

Bumpus Jones

JONES, CHARLES LEANDER
B. Jan. 1, 1870, Cedarville, Ohio D. June 25, 1938, Xenia, Ohio BR TR

1892 CIN N	1	0	1.000	0.00	1	1	1	9	0	4	3	0	0	0	0	2	0	0	.000
1893 2 teams			CIN	N (6G 1–3)			NY	N	(1G 0–1)										
" total	1	4	.200	10.19	7	6	2	32.2	42	33	7	0	1	0	0	16	4	0	.250
2 yrs.	2	4	.333	7.99	8	7	3	41.2	42	37	10	0	1	0	0	18	4	0	.222

Charley Jones

JONES, CHARLES WESLEY
Also known as Benjamin Wesley Rippay.
B. Apr. 3, 1850, Alamance County, N. C. Deceased. BR TR 5'11½" 202 lbs.

1887 CIN AA	0	0	–	3.00	2	0	0	3	2	4	0	0	0	0	0	*			

Cowboy Jones

JONES, ALBERT EDWARD (Bronco)
B. Aug. 23, 1874, Golden, Colo. D. Feb. 8, 1958, Inglewood, Calif. BL TL 5'11" 160 lbs.

1898 CLE N	4	4	.500	3.00	9	9	7	72	76	29	26	0	0	0	0	28	2	0	.071
1899 STL N	6	5	.545	3.59	12	12	9	85.1	111	22	28	0	0	0	0	29	5	0	.172
1900	13	19	.406	3.54	39	36	29	292.2	334	82	68	3	0	0	0	117	21	0	.179
1901	2	6	.250	4.48	10	9	7	76.1	97	22	25	0	0	0	0	27	4	0	.148
4 yrs.	25	34	.424	3.61	70	66	52	526.1	618	155	147	3	0	2	0	201	32	0	.159

Dale Jones

JONES, DALE ELDON (Nubs)
B. Dec. 17, 1918, Marquette, Neb. D. Nov. 8, 1980, Orlando, Fla. BR TR 6'1" 172 lbs.

1941 PHI N	0	1	.000	7.56	2	1	0	8.1	13	6	2	0	0	0	0	3	1	0	.333

Deacon Jones

JONES, CARROLL ELMER
B. Dec. 20, 1893, Arcadia, Kans. D. Dec. 28, 1952, Pittsburg, Kans. BR TR 6'1" 174 lbs.

1916 DET A	0	0	–	2.57	1	0	0	7	7	5	2	0	0	0	0	2	0	0	.000
1917	4	4	.500	2.92	24	6	2	77	69	26	28	0	2	2	0	15	0	0	.000
1918	3	1	.750	3.09	21	4	1	67	60	38	15	0	2	0	0	27	5	0	.185
3 yrs.	7	5	.583	2.98	46	10	3	151	136	69	45	0	4	2	0	44	5	0	.114

Dick Jones

JONES, DECATUR POINDEXTER
B. May 22, 1902, Meadville, Miss. BL TR 6' 184 lbs.

1926 WAS A	2	1	.667	4.29	4	3	1	21	20	11	3	0	0	0	0	10	2	0	.200
1927	0	0	–	21.60	2	0	0	3.1	8	5	1	0	0	0	0	0	0	0	–
2 yrs.	2	1	.667	6.66	6	3	1	24.1	28	16	4	0	0	0	0	10	2	0	.200

Doug Jones

JONES, DOUGLAS REID
B. June 24, 1957, Lebanon, Ind. BR TR 6'2" 170 lbs.

1982 MIL A	0	0	–	10.13	4	0	0	2.2	5	1	1	0	0	0	0	0	0	0	–

Earl Jones

JONES, EARL LESLIE (Lefty)
B. June 11, 1919, Fresno, Calif. BL TL 5'10½" 190 lbs.

1945 STL A	0	0	–	2.54	10	0	0	28.1	18	18	13	0	0	0	0	10	2	0	.200

Elijah Jones

JONES, ELIJAH ALBERT
B. Jan. 27, 1882, Oxford, Mich. D. Apr. 28, 1943, Pontiac, Mich. BR TR

1907 DET A	0	1	.000	5.06	4	1	1	16	23	4	9	0	0	0	0	4	0	0	.000
1909	1	1	.500	2.70	2	2	0	10	10	0	2	0	0	0	1	4	1	0	.250
2 yrs.	1	2	.333	4.15	6	3	1	26	33	4	11	0	0	0	1	8	1	0	.125

	W	L	PCT	ERA	G	GS	CG	IP	H	BB	SO	ShO	Relief Pitching W	L	SV	BATTING AB	H	HR	BA

Gary Jones

JONES, GARY HOWELL
Brother of Steve Jones.
B. June 12, 1945, Huntington Park, Calif.
BL TL 6' 191 lbs.

	W	L	PCT	ERA	G	GS	CG	IP	H	BB	SO	ShO	W	L	SV	AB	H	HR	BA
1970 NY A	0	0	—	0.00	2	0	0	2	3	1	2	0	0	0	0	0	0	0	—
1971	0	0	—	9.00	12	0	0	14	19	7	10	0	0	0	0	1	0	0	.000
2 yrs.	0	0	—	7.88	14	0	0	16	22	8	12	0	0	0	0	1	0	0	.000

Gordon Jones

JONES, GORDON BASSETT
B. Apr. 2, 1930, Portland, Ore.
BR TR 6' 185 lbs.

	W	L	PCT	ERA	G	GS	CG	IP	H	BB	SO	ShO	W	L	SV	AB	H	HR	BA
1954 STL N	4	4	.500	2.00	11	10	4	81	78	19	48	2	0	0	0	24	3	0	.125
1955	1	4	.200	5.84	15	9	0	57	66	28	46	0	0	1	0	14	1	0	.071
1956	0	2	.000	5.56	5	1	0	11.1	14	5	6	0	0	1	0	2	0	0	.000
1957 NY N	0	1	.000	6.17	10	0	0	11.2	16	3	5	0	0	1	0	2	1	0	.500
1958 SF N	3	1	.750	2.37	11	1	0	30.1	33	5	8	0	2	1	1	7	0	0	.000
1959	3	2	.600	4.33	31	0	0	43.2	45	19	29	0	3	2	2	4	0	0	.000
1960 BAL A	1	1	.500	4.42	29	0	0	55	59	13	30	0	1	1	2	5	2	0	.400
1961	0	0	—	5.40	3	0	0	5	5	0	4	0	0	0	1	0	0	0	—
1962 KC A	3	2	.600	6.34	21	0	0	32.2	31	14	28	0	3	2	6	5	0	0	.000
1964 HOU N	0	1	.000	4.14	34	0	0	50	58	14	28	0	0	1	0	4	1	0	.250
1965	0	0	—	0.00	1	0	0	1	0	0	0	0	0	0	0	0	0	0	—
11 yrs.	15	18	.455	4.16	171	21	4	378.2	405	120	232	2	9	10	12	67	8	0	.119

Henry Jones

JONES, HENRY M. (Baldy)
B. Cadillac, Mich. Deceased.

	W	L	PCT	ERA	G	GS	CG	IP	H	BB	SO	ShO	W	L	SV	AB	H	HR	BA
1890 PIT N	2	1	.667	3.48	5	4	2	31	35	14	13	0	0	0	0	*			

Jeff Jones

JONES, JEFFREY ALLEN
B. July 29, 1956, Detroit, Mich.
BR TR 6'3" 210 lbs.

	W	L	PCT	ERA	G	GS	CG	IP	H	BB	SO	ShO	W	L	SV	AB	H	HR	BA
1980 OAK A	1	3	.250	2.86	35	0	0	44	32	26	34	0	1	3	5	0	0	0	—
1981	4	1	.800	3.39	33	0	0	61	51	40	43	0	4	1	3	0	0	0	—
1982	3	1	.750	5.11	18	2	0	37	44	26	18	0	1	1	0	0	0	0	—
1983	1	1	.500	5.76	13	1	0	29.2	43	8	14	0	1	1	0	0	0	0	—
1984	0	3	.000	3.55	13	0	0	33	31	12	19	0	0	3	0	0	0	0	—
5 yrs.	9	9	.500	3.96	112	3	0	204.2	201	112	128	0	8	9	8	0	0	0	—

LEAGUE CHAMPIONSHIP SERIES

	W	L	PCT	ERA	G	GS	CG	IP	H	BB	SO	ShO	W	L	SV	AB	H	HR	BA
1981 OAK A	0	0	—	4.50	1	0	0	2	2	1	0	0	0	0	0	0	0	0	—

Jim Jones

JONES, JAMES TILFORD (Sheriff)
B. Dec. 25, 1876, London, Ky. D. May 6, 1953, London, Ky.
5'10" 150 lbs.

	W	L	PCT	ERA	G	GS	CG	IP	H	BB	SO	ShO	W	L	SV	AB	H	HR	BA
1897 LOU N	0	0	—	18.90	1	0	0	6.2	19	5	0	0	0	0	0	4	1	0	.250
1901 NY N	0	1	.000	10.80	1	1	1	5	6	2	3	0	0	0	0	91	19	0	.209
2 yrs.	0	1	.000	15.43	2	1	1	11.2	25	7	3	0	0	0	0	*			

Johnny Jones

JONES, JOHN PAUL
B. Aug. 25, 1894, Arcadia, La. D. June 5, 1980, Ruston, La.
BR TR 6'1" 151 lbs.

	W	L	PCT	ERA	G	GS	CG	IP	H	BB	SO	ShO	W	L	SV	AB	H	HR	BA
1919 NY N	0	0	—	5.40	2	0	0	6.2	9	3	3	0	0	0	1	3	0	0	.000
1920 BOS N	1	0	1.000	6.52	3	1	0	9.2	16	5	6	0	0	0	0	4	1	0	.250
2 yrs.	1	0	1.000	6.06	5	1	0	16.1	25	8	9	0	0	0	1	7	1	0	.143

Jumping Jack Jones

JONES, DANIEL ALBION
B. Oct. 23, 1860, Litchfield, Conn. D. Oct. 19, 1936, Wallingford, Conn.
TR

	W	L	PCT	ERA	G	GS	CG	IP	H	BB	SO	ShO	W	L	SV	AB	H	HR	BA
1883 2 teams					DET N (12G 6–5)				PHI AA (7G 5–2)										
" total	11	7	.611	3.14	19	19	16	157.2	161	25	61	0	0	0	0	67	14	0	.209

Ken Jones

JONES, KENNETH FREDERICK (Broadway)
B. Apr. 13, 1904, Dover, N. J.
BR TR 6'3" 193 lbs.

	W	L	PCT	ERA	G	GS	CG	IP	H	BB	SO	ShO	W	L	SV	AB	H	HR	BA
1924 DET A	0	0	—	0.00	1	0	0	2	1	1	0	0	0	0	0	0	0	0	—
1930 BOS N	0	1	.000	5.95	8	1	0	19.2	28	4	4	0	0	0	0	5	1	0	.200
2 yrs.	0	1	.000	5.40	9	1	0	21.2	29	5	4	0	0	0	0	5	1	0	.200

Mike Jones

JONES, MICHAEL
B. Hamilton, Ont., Canada D. Mar. 24, 1894, Hamilton, Ont., Canada
TL

	W	L	PCT	ERA	G	GS	CG	IP	H	BB	SO	ShO	W	L	SV	AB	H	HR	BA
1890 LOU AA	2	0	1.000	3.27	3	3	2	22	21	9	6	0	0	0	0	9	4	0	.444

Mike Jones

JONES, MICHAEL CARL
B. July 30, 1959, Rochester, N. Y.
BL TL 6'6" 215 lbs.

	W	L	PCT	ERA	G	GS	CG	IP	H	BB	SO	ShO	W	L	SV	AB	H	HR	BA
1980 KC A	0	1	.000	10.80	3	1	0	5	6	5	2	0	0	0	0	0	0	0	—
1981	6	3	.667	3.20	12	11	0	76	74	28	29	0	0	0	0	0	0	0	—
1984	2	3	.400	4.89	23	12	0	81	86	36	43	0	0	0	0	0	0	0	—
3 yrs.	8	7	.533	4.28	38	24	0	162	166	69	74	0	0	0	0	0	0	0	—

DIVISIONAL PLAYOFF SERIES

	W	L	PCT	ERA	G	GS	CG	IP	H	BB	SO	ShO	W	L	SV	AB	H	HR	BA
1981 KC A	0	1	.000	2.25	1	1	0	8	9	1	2	0	0	0	0	0	0	0	—

LEAGUE CHAMPIONSHIP SERIES

	W	L	PCT	ERA	G	GS	CG	IP	H	BB	SO	ShO	W	L	SV	AB	H	HR	BA
1984 KC A	0	0	—	6.75	1	0	0	1.1	1	1	0	0	0	0	0	0	0	0	—

Odell Jones

JONES, ODELL
B. Jan. 13, 1953, Tulare, Calif.
BR TR 6'3" 175 lbs.

	W	L	PCT	ERA	G	GS	CG	IP	H	BB	SO	ShO	W	L	SV	AB	H	HR	BA
1975 PIT N	0	0	—	0.00	2	0	0	3	1	0	2	0	0	0	0	0	0	0	—
1977	3	7	.300	5.08	34	15	1	108	118	31	66	0	1	1	0	28	4	0	.143
1978	2	0	1.000	2.00	3	1	0	9	7	4	10	0	1	0	0	1	0	0	.000
1979 SEA A	3	11	.214	6.05	25	19	3	119	151	58	72	0	0	2	0	0	0	0	—
1981 PIT N	4	5	.444	3.33	13	8	0	54	51	23	30	0	1	1	0	10	2	0	.200
1983 TEX A	3	6	.333	3.09	42	0	0	67	56	22	50	0	3	6	10	0	0	0	—
1984	2	4	.333	3.64	33	0	0	59.1	62	23	28	0	2	4	2	0	0	0	—
7 yrs.	17	33	.340	4.51	152	43	4	419.1	446	161	258	0	8	14	12	39	6	0	.154

	W	L	PCT	ERA	G	GS	CG	IP	H	BB	SO	ShO	Relief Pitching W	L	SV	BATTING AB	H	HR	BA

Oscar Jones

JONES, OSCAR WINFIELD (Flip Flap)
B. Jan. 21, 1879, London Grove, Pa.   D. Oct. 8, 1946, Perkasie, Pa.
BR TR 5'7"   163 lbs.

	W	L	PCT	ERA	G	GS	CG	IP	H	BB	SO	ShO	W	L	SV	AB	H	HR	BA
1903 BKN N	20	16	.556	2.94	38	36	31	324.1	320	77	95	4	0	1	0	125	32	0	.256
1904	17	25	.405	2.75	46	41	38	377	387	92	96	0	1	0	0	137	24	0	.175
1905	8	15	.348	4.66	29	20	14	174	197	56	66	0	2	1	1	65	13	0	.200
3 yrs.	45	56	.446	3.20	113	97	83	875.1	904	225	257	4	3	2	1	327	69	0	.211

Percy Jones

JONES, PERCY LEE
B. Oct. 28, 1899, Harwood, Tex.
BR TL 5'11½"   175 lbs.

	W	L	PCT	ERA	G	GS	CG	IP	H	BB	SO	ShO	W	L	SV	AB	H	HR	BA
1920 CHI N	0	0	—	11.57	4	0	0	7	15	3	0	0	0	0	0	2	0	0	.000
1921	3	5	.375	4.56	32	5	1	98.2	116	39	46	0	2	3	0	27	6	0	.222
1922	8	9	.471	4.72	44	26	7	164	197	69	46	2	2	0	1	47	4	0	.085
1925	6	6	.500	4.65	28	13	6	124	123	71	60	1	2	1	0	39	6	0	.154
1926	12	7	.632	3.09	30	20	10	160.1	151	90	80	2	4	0	2	50	13	0	.260
1927	7	8	.467	4.07	30	11	5	112.2	123	72	37	1	3	1	0	40	14	0	.350
1928	10	6	.625	4.03	39	18	9	154	164	56	41	1	3	0	3	56	11	0	.196
1929 BOS N	7	15	.318	4.64	35	22	11	188.1	219	84	69	1	2	1	0	61	9	0	.148
1930 PIT N	0	1	.000	6.63	9	2	0	19	26	11	3	0	0	0	0	2	0	0	.000
9 yrs.	53	57	.482	4.33	251	117	49	1028	1134	495	382	8	18	6	6	324	63	0	.194

Randy Jones

JONES, RANDALL LEO
B. Jan. 12, 1950, Fullerton, Calif.
BR TL 6'   178 lbs.

	W	L	PCT	ERA	G	GS	CG	IP	H	BB	SO	ShO	W	L	SV	AB	H	HR	BA
1973 SD N	7	6	.538	3.16	20	19	6	139.2	129	37	77	1	0	0	0	48	8	0	.167
1974	8	22	.267	4.46	40	34	4	208	217	78	124	1	0	1	2	65	10	0	.154
1975	20	12	.625	2.24	37	36	18	285	242	56	103	6	1	0	0	83	11	0	.133
1976	22	14	.611	2.74	40	40	25	315.1	274	50	93	5	0	0	0	103	6	0	.058
1977	6	12	.333	4.59	27	25	1	147	173	36	44	0	0	0	0	43	5	0	.116
1978	13	14	.481	2.88	37	36	7	253	263	64	71	2	1	1	0	82	15	0	.183
1979	11	12	.478	3.63	39	39	6	263	257	64	112	0	0	0	0	86	15	0	.174
1980	5	13	.278	3.92	24	24	4	154	165	29	53	3	0	0	0	45	3	0	.067
1981 NY N	1	8	.111	4.88	13	12	0	59	65	38	14	0	0	0	0	17	2	0	.118
1982	7	10	.412	4.60	28	20	2	107.2	130	51	44	1	0	0	0	27	4	0	.148
10 yrs.	100	123	.448	3.42	305	285	73	1931.2	1915	503	735	19	2	2	2	599	79	0	.132

Rick Jones

JONES, THOMAS FREDERICK
B. Apr. 16, 1955, Jacksonville, Fla.
BL TL 6'5"   190 lbs.

	W	L	PCT	ERA	G	GS	CG	IP	H	BB	SO	ShO	W	L	SV	AB	H	HR	BA
1976 BOS A	5	3	.625	3.38	24	14	1	104	133	26	45	0	1	0	0	0	0	0	—
1977 SEA A	1	4	.200	5.14	10	10	0	42	47	37	16	0	0	0	0	0	0	0	—
1978	0	2	.000	5.84	3	2	0	12.1	17	7	11	0	0	0	0	0	0	0	—
3 yrs.	6	9	.400	4.04	37	26	1	158.1	197	70	72	0	1	0	0	0	0	0	—

Sad Sam Jones

JONES, SAMUEL POND
B. July 26, 1892, Woodsfield, Ohio   D. July 6, 1966, Barnesville, Ohio
BR TR 6'   170 lbs.

	W	L	PCT	ERA	G	GS	CG	IP	H	BB	SO	ShO	W	L	SV	AB	H	HR	BA
1914 CLE A	0	0	—	2.70	1	0	0	3.1	2	2	0	0	0	0	0	2	1	0	.500
1915	4	9	.308	3.65	48	9	2	145.2	131	63	42	0	2	3	4	32	5	0	.156
1916 BOS A	0	1	.000	3.67	12	0	0	27	25	10	7	0	0	1	1	6	2	0	.333
1917	0	1	.000	4.41	9	1	0	16.1	15	6	5	0	0	0	1	4	0	0	.000
1918	16	5	.762	2.25	24	21	16	184	151	70	44	5	0	0	0	57	10	0	.175
1919	12	20	.375	3.75	35	31	21	245	258	95	67	5	0	3	1	81	11	0	.136
1920	13	16	.448	3.94	37	33	20	274	302	79	86	3	0	2	0	92	20	0	.217
1921	23	16	.590	3.22	40	38	25	298.2	318	78	98	5	1	0	1	100	24	2	.240
1922 NY A	13	13	.500	3.67	45	28	21	260	270	76	81	0	1	0	8	87	23	1	.264
1923	21	8	.724	3.63	39	27	18	243	239	69	68	3	2	2	4	85	19	0	.224
1924	9	6	.600	3.63	36	21	8	178.2	187	76	53	3	2	1	3	51	9	1	.176
1925	15	21	.417	4.63	43	31	14	246.2	267	104	92	1	4	3	2	80	13	0	.163
1926	9	8	.529	4.98	39	23	6	161	186	80	69	1	2	1	5	49	10	0	.204
1927 STL A	8	14	.364	4.32	30	26	11	189.2	211	102	72	0	0	0	0	55	6	0	.109
1928 WAS A	17	7	.708	2.84	30	27	19	224.2	209	78	63	4	0	0	0	79	20	2	.253
1929	9	9	.500	3.92	24	24	8	153.2	156	49	36	1	0	0	0	51	8	0	.157
1930	15	7	.682	4.07	25	25	14	183.1	195	61	60	1	0	0	0	61	9	0	.148
1931	9	10	.474	4.32	25	24	8	148	185	47	58	1	0	0	0	48	15	0	.313
1932 CHI A	10	15	.400	4.22	30	28	10	200.1	217	75	64	0	2	0	0	57	11	0	.193
1933	10	12	.455	3.36	27	25	11	176.2	181	65	60	2	0	1	0	58	9	0	.155
1934	8	12	.400	5.11	27	26	11	183.1	217	60	60	1	0	0	0	60	12	0	.200
1935	8	7	.533	4.05	21	19	7	140	162	51	38	0	0	0	0	48	8	0	.167
22 yrs.	229	217	.513	3.84	647	487	250	3883	4084	1396	1223	36	16	17	31	1243	245	6	.197

WORLD SERIES

	W	L	PCT	ERA	G	GS	CG	IP	H	BB	SO	ShO	W	L	SV	AB	H	HR	BA
1918 BOS A	0	1	.000	3.00	1	1	1	9	7	5	5	1	0	0	0	1	0	0	.000
1922 NY A	0	0	—	0.00	2	0	0	2	1	1	0	0	0	0	0	0	0	0	—
1923	0	1	.000	0.90	2	1	0	10	5	2	3	0	0	0	0	2	0	0	.000
1926	0	0	—	9.00	1	0	0	1	2	1	1	0	0	0	1	0	0	0	—
4 yrs.	0	2	.000	2.05	6	2	1	22	15	9	9	1	0	0	1	3	0	0	.000

Sam Jones

JONES, SAMUEL (Toothpick Sam, Sad Sam)
B. Dec. 14, 1925, Stewartsville, Ohio   D. Nov. 5, 1971, Morgantown, W. Va.
BR TR 6'4"   192 lbs.

	W	L	PCT	ERA	G	GS	CG	IP	H	BB	SO	ShO	W	L	SV	AB	H	HR	BA
1951 CLE A	0	1	.000	2.08	2	1	0	8.2	5	4	4	0	0	0	0	0	0	0	—
1952	2	3	.400	7.25	14	4	0	36	38	37	28	0	1	0	1	10	1	0	.100
1955 CHI N	14	20	.412	4.10	36	34	12	241.2	175	185	198	4	1	1	0	77	14	0	.182
1956	9	14	.391	3.91	33	28	8	188.2	155	115	176	2	1	0	0	57	10	0	.175
1957 STL N	12	9	.571	3.60	28	27	10	182.2	164	71	154	2	1	0	0	63	10	0	.159
1958	14	13	.519	2.88	35	35	14	250	204	107	225	2	0	0	0	90	9	0	.100
1959 SF N	21	15	.583	2.83	50	35	16	270.2	232	109	209	4	4	1	4	85	11	0	.129
1960	18	14	.563	3.19	39	35	13	234	200	91	190	3	2	1	0	80	16	0	.200
1961	8	8	.500	4.49	37	17	2	128.1	134	57	105	0	1	1	1	36	5	0	.139
1962 DET A	2	4	.333	3.65	30	6	1	81.1	77	35	73	0	1	1	1	21	2	0	.095
1963 STL N	2	0	1.000	9.00	11	0	0	11	15	5	8	0	2	0	0	1	0	0	.000

	W	L	PCT	ERA	G	GS	CG	IP	H	BB	SO	ShO	Relief Pitching W	L	SV	BATTING AB	H	HR	BA

Sam Jones continued

	W	L	PCT	ERA	G	GS	CG	IP	H	BB	SO	ShO	W	L	SV	AB	H	HR	BA
1964 BAL A	0	0	—	2.61	7	0	0	10.1	5	5	6	0	0	0	0	0	0	0	—
12 yrs.	102	101	.502	3.59	322	222	76	1643.1	1403	822	1376	17	15	5	9	522	78	1	.149

Sheldon Jones

JONES, SHELDON LESLIE (Available)　　　　　　BR TR 6'　　180 lbs.
B. Feb. 2, 1922, Tecumseh, Neb.

	W	L	PCT	ERA	G	GS	CG	IP	H	BB	SO	ShO	W	L	SV	AB	H	HR	BA
1946 NY N	1	2	.333	3.21	6	4	1	28	21	17	24	0	0	0	0	8	2	0	.250
1947	2	2	.500	3.88	15	6	0	55.2	51	29	24	0	2	0	0	16	2	0	.125
1948	16	8	.667	3.35	55	21	8	201.1	204	90	82	2	5	4	5	64	13	0	.203
1949	15	12	.556	3.34	42	27	11	207.1	198	88	79	1	5	0	0	66	8	0	.121
1950	13	16	.448	4.61	40	28	11	199	188	90	97	2	2	3	2	57	6	0	.105
1951	6	11	.353	4.26	41	12	2	120.1	119	52	58	0	4	4	4	31	3	0	.097
1952 BOS N	1	4	.200	4.76	39	1	0	70	81	31	40	0	1	3	1	8	1	0	.125
1953 CHI N	0	2	.000	5.40	22	2	0	38.1	47	16	9	0	0	1	0	7	0	0	.000
8 yrs.	54	57	.486	3.96	260	101	33	920	909	413	413	5	19	15	12	257	35	0	.136

WORLD SERIES
| 1951 NY N | 0 | 0 | — | 2.08 | 2 | 0 | 0 | 4.1 | 5 | 1 | 2 | 0 | 0 | 0 | 1 | 0 | 0 | 0 | — |

Sherman Jones

JONES, SHERMAN JARVIS (Roadblock)　　　　　　BL TR 6'4"　　205 lbs.
B. Feb. 10, 1935, Winton, N. C.

	W	L	PCT	ERA	G	GS	CG	IP	H	BB	SO	ShO	W	L	SV	AB	H	HR	BA
1960 SF N	1	1	.500	3.09	16	0	0	32	37	11	10	0	1	1	1	7	2	0	.286
1961 CIN N	1	1	.500	4.42	24	2	0	55	51	27	32	0	1	2	2	11	2	0	.182
1962 NY N	0	4	.000	7.71	8	3	0	23.1	31	8	11	0	0	0	0	7	3	0	.429
3 yrs.	2	6	.250	4.73	48	5	0	110.1	119	46	53	0	1	3	3	25	7	0	.280

WORLD SERIES
| 1961 CIN N | 0 | 0 | — | 0.00 | 1 | 0 | 0 | .2 | 0 | 0 | 0 | 0 | 0 | 0 | 0 | 0 | 0 | 0 | — |

Steve Jones

JONES, STEVEN HOWELL　　　　　　BL TL 5'10"　　175 lbs.
Brother of Gary Jones.
B. Apr. 22, 1941, Huntington Park, Calif.

	W	L	PCT	ERA	G	GS	CG	IP	H	BB	SO	ShO	W	L	SV	AB	H	HR	BA
1967 CHI A	2	2	.500	4.21	11	3	0	25.2	21	12	17	0	1	0	0	4	1	0	.250
1968 WAS A	1	2	.333	5.91	7	0	0	10.2	8	7	11	0	1	2	0	1	0	0	.000
1969 KC A	2	3	.400	4.23	20	4	0	44.2	45	24	31	0	0	1	0	8	1	0	.125
3 yrs.	5	7	.417	4.44	38	7	0	81	74	43	59	0	2	3	0	13	2	0	.154

Tim Jones

JONES, TIMOTHY BRYON　　　　　　BR TR 6'5"　　220 lbs.
B. Jan. 24, 1954, Sacramento, Calif.

	W	L	PCT	ERA	G	GS	CG	IP	H	BB	SO	ShO	W	L	SV	AB	H	HR	BA
1977 PIT N	1	0	1.000	0.00	3	1	0	10	4	3	5	0	0	0	0	2	0	0	.000

Claude Jonnard

JONNARD, CLAUDE ALFRED　　　　　　BR TR 6'1"　　165 lbs.
Brother of Bubber Jonnard.
B. Nov. 23, 1897, Nashville, Tenn.　　　D. Aug. 27, 1959, Nashville, Tenn.

	W	L	PCT	ERA	G	GS	CG	IP	H	BB	SO	ShO	W	L	SV	AB	H	HR	BA
1921 NY N	0	0	—	0.00	1	0	0	4	4	0	7	0	0	0	1	1	0	0	.000
1922	6	1	.857	3.84	33	0	0	96	96	28	44	0	6	1	5	24	1	0	.042
1923	4	3	.571	3.28	45	1	1	96	105	35	45	0	3	3	5	26	1	0	.038
1924	4	5	.444	2.41	34	3	1	89.2	80	24	40	0	4	3	5	22	1	0	.045
1926 STL A	2	0	2.000	6.00	12	3	0	36	46	24	13	0	0	0	1	7	0	0	.000
1929 CHI N	0	1	.000	7.48	12	2	0	27.2	41	11	11	0	0	0	0	10	2	0	.200
6 yrs.	14	12	.538	3.79	137	9	2	349.1	372	122	160	0	13	7	17	90	5	0	.056

WORLD SERIES
1923 NY N	0	0	—	0.00	2	0	0	2	1	1	1	0	0	0	0	0	0	0	—
1924	0	0	—	0.00	1	0	0	0	0	1	0	0	0	0	0	0	0	0	—
2 yrs.	0	0	—	0.00	3	0	0	2	1	2	1	0	0	0	0	0	0	0	—

Charlie Jordan

JORDAN, CHARLES T.
B. Oct. 4, 1871, Baltimore, Md.　　　D. June 1, 1928, Hazleton, Pa.

	W	L	PCT	ERA	G	GS	CG	IP	H	BB	SO	ShO	W	L	SV	AB	H	HR	BA
1896 PHI N	0	0	—	7.71	2	0	0	4.2	9	2	3	0	0	0	0	2	1	0	.500

Harry Jordan

JORDAN, HARRY J.
B. Feb. 14, 1873, Pittsburgh, Pa.　　　D. Mar. 1, 1920, Pittsburgh, Pa.

	W	L	PCT	ERA	G	GS	CG	IP	H	BB	SO	ShO	W	L	SV	AB	H	HR	BA
1894 PIT N	1	0	1.000	4.00	1	1	1	9	10	2	1	0	0	0	0	3	0	0	.000
1895	0	2	.000	4.24	2	2	2	17	24	6	4	0	0	0	0	7	2	0	.286
2 yrs.	1	2	.333	4.15	3	3	3	26	34	8	5	0	0	0	0	10	2	0	.200

Milt Jordan

JORDAN, MILTON MIGNOT　　　　　　BR TR 6'2½"　　207 lbs.
B. May 24, 1927, Mineral Springs, Pa.

	W	L	PCT	ERA	G	GS	CG	IP	H	BB	SO	ShO	W	L	SV	AB	H	HR	BA
1953 DET A	0	1	.000	5.82	8	1	0	17	26	5	4	0	0	0	0	2	1	0	.500

Niles Jordan

JORDAN, NILES CHAPMAN　　　　　　BL TL 5'11"　　180 lbs.
B. Dec. 1, 1925, Lyman, Wash.

	W	L	PCT	ERA	G	GS	CG	IP	H	BB	SO	ShO	W	L	SV	AB	H	HR	BA
1951 PHI N	2	3	.400	3.19	5	5	2	36.2	35	8	11	1	0	0	0	13	1	0	.077
1952 CIN N	0	1	.000	9.95	3	1	0	6.1	14	3	2	0	0	0	0	1	0	0	.000
2 yrs.	2	4	.333	4.19	8	6	2	43	49	11	13	1	0	0	0	14	1	0	.071

Rip Jordan

JORDAN, RAYMOND WILLIS (Lanky)　　　　　　BL TR 6'　　172 lbs.
B. Sept. 28, 1889, Portland, Me.　　　D. June 5, 1960, Meriden, Conn.

	W	L	PCT	ERA	G	GS	CG	IP	H	BB	SO	ShO	W	L	SV	AB	H	HR	BA
1912 CHI A	0	0	—	6.10	3	0	0	10.1	13	0	0	0	0	0	0	4	0	0	.000
1919 WAS A	0	0	—	11.25	1	1	0	4	6	2	2	0	0	0	0	1	0	0	.000
2 yrs.	0	0	—	7.53	4	1	0	14.1	19	2	2	0	0	0	0	5	0	0	.000

Orville Jorgens

JORGENS, ORVILLE EDWARD　　　　　　BR TR 6'1"　　180 lbs.
Brother of Arndt Jorgens.
B. June 4, 1908, Rockford, Ill.

	W	L	PCT	ERA	G	GS	CG	IP	H	BB	SO	ShO	W	L	SV	AB	H	HR	BA
1935 PHI N	10	15	.400	4.83	53	24	6	188.1	216	96	57	0	4	3	2	62	6	0	.097

	W	L	PCT	ERA	G	GS	CG	IP	H	BB	SO	ShO	Relief Pitching W	L	SV	BATTING AB	H	HR	BA

Orville Jorgens continued

	W	L	PCT	ERA	G	GS	CG	IP	H	BB	SO	ShO	W	L	SV	AB	H	HR	BA
1936	8	8	.500	4.79	39	21	4	167.1	196	69	58	0	0	1	0	60	12	0	.200
1937	3	4	.429	4.41	52	11	1	140.2	159	68	34	0	2	0	3	35	5	0	.143
3 yrs.	21	27	.438	4.70	144	56	11	496.1	571	233	149	0	6	4	5	157	23	0	.146

Addie Joss

JOSS, ADRIAN   BR TR 6'3"   185 lbs.
B. Apr. 12, 1880, Juneau, Wis.   D. Apr. 14, 1911, Toledo, Ohio
Hall of Fame 1978.

	W	L	PCT	ERA	G	GS	CG	IP	H	BB	SO	ShO	W	L	SV	AB	H	HR	BA
1902 CLE A	17	13	.567	2.77	32	29	28	269.1	225	75	106	5	1	0	0	103	12	0	.117
1903	18	13	.581	2.15	32	31	31	292.2	239	43	126	3	0	0	0	117	22	0	.188
1904	14	10	.583	1.59	25	24	20	192.1	160	30	83	6	0	1	0	76	10	0	.132
1905	20	12	.625	2.01	33	32	31	286	246	46	132	3	0	1	0	94	13	0	.138
1906	21	9	.700	1.72	34	31	28	282	220	43	106	9	0	1	1	100	21	0	.210
1907	27	11	.711	1.83	42	38	34	338.2	279	54	127	6	2	0	2	114	13	0	.114
1908	24	11	.686	1.16	42	35	29	325	232	30	130	9	2	0	0	97	15	0	.155
1909	14	13	.519	1.71	33	28	24	242.2	198	31	67	4	0	1	0	80	8	1	.100
1910	5	5	.500	2.26	13	12	9	107.1	96	18	49	1	0	0	0	36	4	0	.111
9 yrs.	160	97	.623	1.88 2nd	286	260	234	2336	1895	370	926	46	5	4	5	817	118	1	.144

Bob Joyce

JOYCE, ROBERT EMMETT   BR TR 6'1"   180 lbs.
B. Jan. 14, 1915, Stockton, Calif.   D. Dec. 10, 1981, San Francisco, Calif.

	W	L	PCT	ERA	G	GS	CG	IP	H	BB	SO	ShO	W	L	SV	AB	H	HR	BA
1939 PHI A	3	5	.375	6.69	30	6	1	107.2	156	37	25	0	3	1	0	35	3	0	.086
1946 NY N	3	4	.429	5.34	14	7	2	60.2	79	20	24	0	0	0	0	19	3	1	.158
2 yrs.	6	9	.400	6.20	44	13	3	168.1	235	57	49	0	3	1	0	54	6	1	.111

Dick Joyce

JOYCE, RICHARD EDWARD   BL TL 6'5"   225 lbs.
B. Nov. 18, 1943, Portland, Me.

	W	L	PCT	ERA	G	GS	CG	IP	H	BB	SO	ShO	W	L	SV	AB	H	HR	BA
1965 KC A	0	1	.000	2.77	5	3	0	13	12	4	7	0	0	0	0	4	0	0	.000

Mike Joyce

JOYCE, MICHAEL LEWIS   BR TR 6'2"   193 lbs.
B. Feb. 12, 1941, Detroit, Mich.

	W	L	PCT	ERA	G	GS	CG	IP	H	BB	SO	ShO	W	L	SV	AB	H	HR	BA
1962 CHI A	2	1	.667	3.32	25	1	0	43.1	40	14	9	0	2	1	2	7	3	0	.429
1963	0	0		8.44	6	0	0	10.2	13	8	7	0	0	0	0	0	0	0	
2 yrs.	2	1	.667	4.33	31	1	0	54	53	22	16	0	2	1	2	7	3	0	.429

Oscar Judd

JUDD, THOMAS WILLIAM OSCAR (Ossie)   BL TL 6'½"   180 lbs.
B. Feb. 14, 1908, Rebecca, Ont., Canada

	W	L	PCT	ERA	G	GS	CG	IP	H	BB	SO	ShO	W	L	SV	AB	H	HR	BA
1941 BOS A	0	0		8.76	7	0	0	12.1	15	10	5	0	0	0	0	4	2	0	.500
1942	8	10	.444	3.89	31	19	11	150.1	135	90	70	0	0	2	2	67	18	2	.269
1943	11	6	.647	2.90	23	20	8	155.1	131	69	53	1	0	1	0	54	14	0	.259
1944	1	1	.500	3.60	9	6	1	30	30	15	9	0	0	0	0	11	2	0	.182
1945 2 teams		BOS A (2G 0–1)			PHI N (23G 5–4)														
" total	5	5	.500	4.13	25	10	3	89.1	90	43	41	1	0	0	2	32	9	0	.281
1946 PHI N	11	12	.478	3.53	30	24	12	173.1	169	90	65	1	0	1	2	79	25	1	.316
1947	4	15	.211	4.60	32	19	8	146.2	155	69	54	1	0	2	0	64	12	0	.188
1948	0	2	.000	6.91	4	1	0	14.1	19	11	7	0	0	2	0	6	1	0	.167
8 yrs.	40	51	.440	3.90	161	99	43	771.2	744	397	304	4	0	8	7	*			

Ralph Judd

JUDD, RALPH WESLEY   BL TR 5'10"   170 lbs.
B. Dec. 7, 1901, Perrysburg, Ohio   D. May 6, 1957, Lapeer, Mich.

	W	L	PCT	ERA	G	GS	CG	IP	H	BB	SO	ShO	W	L	SV	AB	H	HR	BA
1927 WAS A	0	0	—	6.75	1	0	0	4	8	2	2	0	0	0	0	1	0	0	.000
1929 NY N	3	0	1.000	2.66	18	0	0	50.2	49	11	21	0	3	0	0	14	0	0	.000
1930	0	0	—	5.87	2	0	0	7.2	13	3	0	0	0	0	0	3	0	0	.000
3 yrs.	3	0	1.000	3.32	21	0	0	62.1	70	16	23	0	3	0	0	18	0	0	.000

Howie Judson

JUDSON, HOWARD KOLLS   BR TR 6'1"   195 lbs.
B. Feb. 16, 1926, Hebron, Ill.

	W	L	PCT	ERA	G	GS	CG	IP	H	BB	SO	ShO	W	L	SV	AB	H	HR	BA
1948 CHI A	4	5	.444	4.78	40	5	1	107.1	102	56	38	0	4	2	8	29	3	0	.103
1949	1	14	.067	4.58	26	12	3	108	114	70	36	0	0	4	1	31	2	0	.065
1950	2	3	.400	3.94	46	3	1	112	105	63	34	0	2	2	0	20	2	0	.100
1951	5	6	.455	3.77	27	14	3	121.2	124	55	43	0	0	1	1	33	4	0	.121
1952	0	1	.000	4.24	21	0	0	34	30	22	15	0	0	1	1	4	0	0	.000
1953 CIN N	0	1	.000	5.59	10	0	0	38.2	58	11	11	0	0	0	0	9	1	0	.111
1954	5	7	.417	3.95	37	0	0	93.1	86	42	27	0	1	3	3	24	2	0	.083
7 yrs.	17	37	.315	4.29	207	48	8	615	619	319	204	0	7	13	14	150	14	0	.093

Ken Jungels

JUNGELS, KENNETH PETER (Curly)   BR TR 6'1"   180 lbs.
B. June 23, 1916, Aurora, Ill.   D. Sept. 9, 1975, West Bend, Wis.

	W	L	PCT	ERA	G	GS	CG	IP	H	BB	SO	ShO	W	L	SV	AB	H	HR	BA
1937 CLE A	0	0	—	0.00	2	0	0	9	5	2	0	0	0	0	0	0	0	0	—
1938	1	0	1.000	8.80	9	0	0	15.1	21	18	7	0	1	0	0	5	0	0	.000
1940	0	0	—	2.70	2	0	0	3.1	3	1	1	0	0	0	0	0	0	0	.000
1941	0	0	—	7.24	6	0	0	13.2	17	8	6	0	0	0	0	2	0	0	.000
1942 PIT N	0	0	—	6.59	6	0	0	13.2	12	4	7	0	0	0	0	2	1	0	.500
5 yrs.	1	0	1.000	6.80	25	0	0	49	56	32	21	0	1	0	0	10	1	0	.100

Mike Jurewicz

JUREWICZ, MICHAEL ALLEN   BB TL 6'3"   205 lbs.
B. Sept. 20, 1945, Buffalo, N. Y.

	W	L	PCT	ERA	G	GS	CG	IP	H	BB	SO	ShO	W	L	SV	AB	H	HR	BA
1965 NY A	0	0	—	7.71	2	0	0	2.1	5	1	2	0	0	0	0	0	0	0	—

Al Jurisich

JURISICH, ALVIN JOSEPH   BR TR 6'2"   193 lbs.
B. Aug. 25, 1921, New Orleans, La.   D. Nov. 3, 1981, New Orleans, La.

	W	L	PCT	ERA	G	GS	CG	IP	H	BB	SO	ShO	W	L	SV	AB	H	HR	BA
1944 STL N	7	9	.438	3.39	30	14	5	130	102	65	53	2	2	0	1	45	8	0	.178
1945	3	3	.500	5.15	27	6	1	71.2	61	41	42	0	1	1	0	23	2	0	.087
1946 PHI N	4	3	.571	3.69	13	10	2	68.1	71	31	34	1	0	0	1	23	3	0	.130

	W	L	PCT	ERA	G	GS	CG	IP	H	BB	SO	ShO	Relief Pitching W	L	SV	BATTING AB	H	HR	BA

Al Jurisich continued

	W	L	PCT	ERA	G	GS	CG	IP	H	BB	SO	ShO	W	L	SV	AB	H	HR	BA
1947	1	7	.125	4.94	34	12	5	118.1	110	52	48	0	1	2	3	31	1	0	.032
4 yrs.	15	22	.405	4.24	104	42	13	388.1	344	189	177	3	4	3	5	122	14	0	.115

WORLD SERIES

	W	L	PCT	ERA	G	GS	CG	IP	H	BB	SO	ShO	W	L	SV	AB	H	HR	BA
1944 STL N	0	0	–	27.00	1	0	0	.2	2	1	0	0	0	0	0	0	0	0	–

Walt Justis

JUSTIS, WALTER NEWTON (Smoke)
B. Aug. 17, 1883, Moores Hill, Ind.   D. Oct. 4, 1941, Lawrenceburg, Ind.   BR TR 5'11½" 195 lbs.

	W	L	PCT	ERA	G	GS	CG	IP	H	BB	SO	ShO	W	L	SV	AB	H	HR	BA
1905 DET A	0	0	–	8.10	2	0	0	3.1	4	6	0	0	0	0	0	0	0	0	–

Earl Juul

JUUL, EARL HERBERT
B. May 21, 1893, Chicago, Ill.   D. Jan. 4, 1942, Chicago, Ill.   BR TR 5'9½" 150 lbs.

	W	L	PCT	ERA	G	GS	CG	IP	H	BB	SO	ShO	W	L	SV	AB	H	HR	BA
1914 BKN F	0	3	.000	6.21	9	3	0	29	26	31	16	0	0	0	0	9	2	0	.222

Herb Juul

JUUL, HERBERT VICTOR
B. Feb. 2, 1886, Chicago, Ill.   D. Nov. 14, 1928, Chicago, Ill.   TL 5'11" 150 lbs.

	W	L	PCT	ERA	G	GS	CG	IP	H	BB	SO	ShO	W	L	SV	AB	H	HR	BA
1911 CIN N	0	0	–	4.50	1	0	0	4	3	4	2	0	0	0	0	2	0	0	.000

Jim Kaat

KAAT, JAMES LEE
B. Nov. 7, 1938, Zeeland, Mich.   BL TL 6'4½" 205 lbs.

	W	L	PCT	ERA	G	GS	CG	IP	H	BB	SO	ShO	W	L	SV	AB	H	HR	BA
1959 WAS A	0	2	.000	12.60	3	2	0	5	7	4	2	0	0	0	0	1	0	0	.000
1960	1	5	.167	5.58	13	9	0	50	48	31	25	0	0	0	0	14	2	0	.143
1961 MIN A	9	17	.346	3.90	36	29	8	200.2	188	82	122	1	0	1	0	63	15	0	.238
1962	18	14	.563	3.14	39	35	16	269	243	75	173	5	1	0	1	100	18	1	.180
1963	10	10	.500	4.19	31	27	7	178.1	195	38	105	1	0	1	1	61	8	1	.131
1964	17	11	.607	3.22	36	34	13	243	231	60	171	0	0	1	1	83	14	3	.169
1965	18	11	.621	2.83	42	42	7	264.1	267	63	154	2	0	0	2	93	23	1	.247
1966	25	13	.658	2.75	41	41	19	304.2	271	55	205	3	0	0	0	118	23	2	.195
1967	16	13	.552	3.04	42	38	13	263.1	269	42	211	2	0	0	0	99	17	1	.172
1968	14	12	.538	2.94	30	29	9	208	192	40	130	2	0	0	0	77	12	0	.156
1969	14	13	.519	3.49	40	32	10	242.1	252	75	139	0	3	1	1	87	18	2	.207
1970	14	10	.583	3.56	45	34	4	230	244	58	120	1	1	0	0	76	15	1	.197
1971	13	14	.481	3.32	39	38	15	260	275	47	137	4	0	0	0	93	15	0	.161
1972	10	2	.833	2.07	15	15	5	113	94	20	64	0	0	0	0	45	13	2	.289
1973 2 teams			MIN A (29G 11–12)				CHI A (7G 4–1)												
" total	15	13	.536	4.37	36	35	10	224.1	250	43	109	3	1	0	0	0	0	0	–
1974 CHI A	21	13	.618	2.92	42	39	15	277	263	63	142	3	1	0	0	1	0	0	.000
1975	20	14	.588	3.11	43	41	12	303.2	321	77	142	1	0	0	0	0	0	0	–
1976 PHI N	12	14	.462	3.48	35	35	7	227.2	241	32	83	1	0	1	0	79	14	1	.177
1977	6	11	.353	5.40	35	27	2	160	211	40	55	0	0	0	0	53	10	0	.189
1978	8	5	.615	4.11	26	24	2	140	150	32	48	1	0	0	0	48	7	0	.146
1979 2 teams			PHI N (3G 1–0)				NY A (40G 2–3)												
" total	3	3	.500	3.95	43	2	0	66	73	19	25	0	3	3	2	1	0	0	.000
1980 2 teams			NY A (4G 0–1)				STL N (49G 8–7)												
" total	8	8	.500	3.93	53	14	6	135	148	37	37	0	3	3	4	35	5	1	.143
1981 STL N	6	6	.500	3.40	41	1	0	53	60	17	8	0	6	5	4	8	3	0	.375
1982	5	3	.625	4.08	62	2	0	75	79	23	35	0	5	3	2	12	0	0	.000
1983	0	0	–	3.89	24	0	0	34.2	48	10	19	0	0	0	0	4	0	0	.000
25 yrs.	283	237	.544	3.45	898	625	180	4528	4620	1083	2461	31	24	19	18	1251	232	16	.185
					5th														

LEAGUE CHAMPIONSHIP SERIES

	W	L	PCT	ERA	G	GS	CG	IP	H	BB	SO	ShO	W	L	SV	AB	H	HR	BA
1970 MIN A	0	1	.000	9.00	1	1	0	2	6	2	1	0	0	0	0	1	0	0	.000
1976 PHI N	0	0	–	3.00	1	1	0	6	2	2	1	0	0	0	0	2	1	0	.500
2 yrs.	0	1	.000	4.50	2	2	0	8	8	4	2	0	0	0	0	3	1	0	.333

WORLD SERIES

	W	L	PCT	ERA	G	GS	CG	IP	H	BB	SO	ShO	W	L	SV	AB	H	HR	BA
1965 MIN A	1	2	.333	3.77	3	3	1	14.1	18	2	6	0	0	0	0	6	1	0	.167
1982 STL N	0	0	–	3.86	4	0	0	2.1	4	2	2	0	0	0	0	0	0	0	–
2 yrs.	1	2	.333	3.78	7	3	1	16.2	22	4	8	0	0	0	0	6	1	0	.167

George Kahler

KAHLER, GEORGE RANNELS (Krum)
B. Sept. 6, 1889, Athens, Ohio   D. Feb. 14, 1924, Battle Creek, Mich.   BR TR

	W	L	PCT	ERA	G	GS	CG	IP	H	BB	SO	ShO	W	L	SV	AB	H	HR	BA
1910 CLE A	6	4	.600	1.60	12	12	8	95.1	80	46	38	2	0	0	0	35	5	0	.143
1911	9	8	.529	3.27	30	17	10	154.1	153	66	97	0	1	0	1	54	9	0	.167
1912	12	19	.387	3.69	41	32	17	246.1	263	121	104	3	0	0	1	80	9	0	.113
1913	5	9	.357	3.14	24	15	5	117.2	118	32	43	0	0	2	0	33	2	0	.061
1914	0	1	.000	3.86	2	1	1	14	17	7	3	0	0	0	0	5	0	0	.000
5 yrs.	32	41	.438	3.17	109	77	41	627.2	631	272	285	5	1	2	2	207	25	0	.121

Don Kainer

KAINER, DONALD WAYNE
B. Sept. 3, 1955, Houston, Tex.   BR TR 6'3" 205 lbs.

	W	L	PCT	ERA	G	GS	CG	IP	H	BB	SO	ShO	W	L	SV	AB	H	HR	BA
1980 TEX A	0	0	–	1.80	4	3	0	20	22	9	10	0	0	0	0	0	0	0	–

Bob Kaiser

KAISER, ROBERT THOMAS
B. Apr. 29, 1950, Cincinnati, Ohio   BR TL 5'10" 175 lbs.

	W	L	PCT	ERA	G	GS	CG	IP	H	BB	SO	ShO	W	L	SV	AB	H	HR	BA
1971 CLE A	0	0	–	4.50	5	0	0	6	8	3	4	0	0	0	0	0	0	0	–

Don Kaiser

KAISER, CLYDE DONALD (Tiger)
B. Feb. 3, 1935, Byng, Okla.   BR TR 6'5" 195 lbs.

	W	L	PCT	ERA	G	GS	CG	IP	H	BB	SO	ShO	W	L	SV	AB	H	HR	BA
1955 CHI N	0	0	–	5.40	11	0	0	18.1	20	5	11	0	0	0	0	2	0	0	.000
1956	4	9	.308	3.59	27	22	5	150.1	144	52	74	1	0	0	0	47	2	0	.043
1957	2	6	.250	5.00	20	13	1	72	91	28	23	0	0	0	0	19	2	0	.105
3 yrs.	6	15	.286	4.15	58	35	6	240.2	255	85	108	1	0	0	0	68	4	0	.059

	W	L	PCT	ERA	G	GS	CG	IP	H	BB	SO	ShO	Relief Pitching W	L	SV	BATTING AB	H	HR	BA

George Kaiserling

KAISERLING, GEORGE
B. Aug. 15, 1890, Steubenville, Ohio   D. Mar. 2, 1918, Steubenville, Ohio   BR TR 6'   175 lbs.

	W	L	PCT	ERA	G	GS	CG	IP	H	BB	SO	ShO	W	L	SV	AB	H	HR	BA
1914 IND F	17	9	.654	3.11	37	33	20	275.1	288	72	75	1	1	1	0	98	11	0	.112
1915 NWK F	13	14	.481	2.24	41	29	16	261.1	246	73	75	5	1	0	2	79	12	0	.152
2 yrs.	30	23	.566	2.68	78	62	36	536.2	534	145	150	6	2	1	2	177	23	0	.130

Bill Kalfass

KALFASS, WILLIAM PHILIP (Lefty)
B. Mar. 3, 1916, New York, N.Y.   D. Sept. 8, 1968, Brooklyn, N.Y.   BR TL 6'3½"   190 lbs.

	W	L	PCT	ERA	G	GS	CG	IP	H	BB	SO	ShO	W	L	SV	AB	H	HR	BA
1937 PHI A	1	0	1.000	3.00	3	1	1	12	10	10	9	0	0	0	0	4	0	0	.000

Rudy Kallio

KALLIO, RUDOLPH
B. Dec. 14, 1892, Portland, Ore.   D. Apr. 6, 1979, Newport, Ore.   BR TR 5'10"   160 lbs.

	W	L	PCT	ERA	G	GS	CG	IP	H	BB	SO	ShO	W	L	SV	AB	H	HR	BA
1918 DET A	8	14	.364	3.62	30	22	10	181.1	178	76	70	2	1	2	0	56	9	0	.161
1919	0	0	—	5.64	12	1	0	22.1	28	8	3	0	0	0	1	4	0	0	.000
1925 BOS A	1	4	.200	7.71	7	4	0	18.2	28	9	2	0	0	1	0	6	2	0	.333
3 yrs.	9	18	.333	4.17	49	27	10	222.1	234	93	75	2	1	3	1	66	11	0	.167

Bob Kammeyer

KAMMEYER, ROBERT LYNN
B. Dec. 2, 1950, Kansas City, Mo.   BR TR 6'4"   210 lbs.

	W	L	PCT	ERA	G	GS	CG	IP	H	BB	SO	ShO	W	L	SV	AB	H	HR	BA
1978 NY A	0	0	—	5.82	7	0	0	21.2	24	6	11	0	0	0	0	0	0	0	—
1979	0	0	—	∞	1	0	0	0	7	0	0	0	0	0	0	0	0	0	—
2 yrs.	0	0	—	9.14	8	0	0	21.2	31	6	11	0	0	0	0	0	0	0	—

Ike Kamp

KAMP, ALPHONSE FRANCIS
B. Sept. 5, 1900, Roxbury, Mass.   D. Feb. 26, 1955, Boston, Mass.   BB TL 6'   170 lbs.

	W	L	PCT	ERA	G	GS	CG	IP	H	BB	SO	ShO	W	L	SV	AB	H	HR	BA
1924 BOS N	0	1	.000	5.14	1	1	0	7	9	5	4	0	0	0	0	1	0	0	.000
1925	2	4	.333	5.09	24	4	1	58.1	68	35	20	0	1	2	0	12	2	0	.167
2 yrs.	2	5	.286	5.10	25	5	1	65.1	77	40	24	0	1	2	0	13	2	0	.154

Harry Kane

KANE, HARRY (Klondike)
Born Harry Cohen.
B. July 27, 1883, Hamburg, Ark.   D. Sept. 15, 1932, Portland, Ore.   BL TL

	W	L	PCT	ERA	G	GS	CG	IP	H	BB	SO	ShO	W	L	SV	AB	H	HR	BA
1902 STL A	0	1	.000	5.48	4	1	1	23	34	16	7	0	0	0	0	9	1	0	.111
1903 DET A	0	2	.000	8.50	3	3	1	18	26	8	10	0	0	0	0	7	1	0	.143
1905 PHI N	1	1	.500	1.59	2	2	2	17	12	8	12	1	0	0	0	6	1	0	.167
1906	1	3	.250	3.86	6	3	2	28	28	18	14	0	1	1	0	8	0	0	.000
4 yrs.	2	7	.222	4.81	15	9	7	86	100	50	43	1	1	1	0	30	3	0	.100

Erv Kantlehner

KANTLEHNER, ERVINE LESLIE
B. July 31, 1892, San Jose, Calif.   BL TL 6'   190 lbs.

	W	L	PCT	ERA	G	GS	CG	IP	H	BB	SO	ShO	W	L	SV	AB	H	HR	BA
1914 PIT N	3	2	.600	3.09	21	5	3	67	51	39	26	2	0	0	0	15	1	0	.067
1915	5	12	.294	2.26	29	18	10	163	135	58	64	1	1	2	2	52	15	0	.288
1916 2 teams			PIT N (34G 5–15)					PHI N (3G 0–0)											
" total	5	15	.250	3.30	37	21	7	169	158	60	51	2	2	3	2	46	8	0	.174
3 yrs.	13	29	.310	2.84	87	44	20	399	344	157	141	5	3	6	4	113	24	0	.212

Paul Kardow

KARDOW, PAUL OTTO (Tex)
B. Sept. 19, 1915, Humble, Tex.   D. Apr. 27, 1968, San Antonio, Tex.   BR TR 6'6"   210 lbs.

	W	L	PCT	ERA	G	GS	CG	IP	H	BB	SO	ShO	W	L	SV	AB	H	HR	BA
1936 CLE A	0	0	—	4.50	2	0	0	2	1	2	0	0	0	0	0	0	0	0	—

Ed Karger

KARGER, EDWIN (Loose)
B. May 6, 1883, San Angelo, Tex.   D. Sept. 9, 1957, Delta, Colo.   BL TL 5'11"   185 lbs.

	W	L	PCT	ERA	G	GS	CG	IP	H	BB	SO	ShO	W	L	SV	AB	H	HR	BA
1906 2 teams			PIT N (6G 2–3)					STL N (25G 5–16)											
" total	7	19	.269	2.62	31	22	17	219.2	214	52	81	0	1	4	1	84	18	1	.214
1907 STL N	15	19	.441	2.03	38	31	28	310	251	64	132	6	1	2	1	111	19	2	.171
1908	4	9	.308	3.06	22	15	9	141.1	148	50	34	1	0	0	0	54	13	0	.241
1909 2 teams			CIN N (9G 1–3)					BOS A (12G 5–2)											
" total	6	5	.545	3.61	21	11	4	102.1	97	52	25	0	2	2	0	35	6	0	.171
1910 BOS A	11	7	.611	3.19	27	25	16	183.1	162	53	81	1	0	0	1	68	20	2	.294
1911	5	8	.385	3.37	25	18	6	131	134	42	57	1	0	0	0	47	11	1	.234
6 yrs.	48	67	.417	2.79	164	122	80	1087.2	1006	313	410	9	4	8	3	399	87	6	.218

Andy Karl

KARL, ANTON ANDREW
B. Apr. 8, 1914, Mount Vernon, N.Y.   BR TR 6'1½"   175 lbs.

	W	L	PCT	ERA	G	GS	CG	IP	H	BB	SO	ShO	W	L	SV	AB	H	HR	BA
1943 2 teams			BOS A (11G 1–1)					PHI N (9G 1–2)											
" total	2	3	.400	5.30	20	2	0	52.2	75	24	10	0	1	1	1	15	4	0	.267
1944 PHI N	3	2	.600	2.33	38	0	0	89	76	21	26	0	3	2	2	15	3	0	.200
1945	9	8	.529	2.99	67	2	1	180.2	175	50	51	0	9	6	15	49	7	0	.143
1946	3	7	.300	4.96	39	0	0	65.1	84	22	15	0	3	7	5	10	1	0	.100
1947 BOS N	2	3	.400	3.86	27	0	0	35	41	13	5	0	2	3	3	6	1	0	.167
5 yrs.	19	23	.452	3.51	191	4	1	422.2	451	130	107	0	18	19	26	95	16	0	.168

Herb Karpel

KARPEL, HERBERT (Lefty)
B. Dec. 27, 1917, Brooklyn, N.Y.   BL TL 5'9½"   180 lbs.

	W	L	PCT	ERA	G	GS	CG	IP	H	BB	SO	ShO	W	L	SV	AB	H	HR	BA
1946 NY A	0	0	—	10.80	2	0	0	3.1	4	0	0	0	0	0	0	0	0	0	—

Benn Karr

KARR, BENJAMIN JOYCE (Baldy)
B. Nov. 28, 1893, Mt. Pleasant, Miss.   D. Dec. 8, 1968, Memphis, Tenn.   BL TR 6'   175 lbs.

	W	L	PCT	ERA	G	GS	CG	IP	H	BB	SO	ShO	W	L	SV	AB	H	HR	BA
1920 BOS A	3	8	.273	4.81	26	2	0	91.2	109	24	21	0	3	6	1	75	21	1	.280
1921	8	7	.533	3.67	26	7	5	117.2	123	38	37	0	5	3	0	62	16	0	.258
1922	5	12	.294	4.47	41	13	7	183.1	212	45	41	0	0	5	1	98	21	0	.214
1925 CLE A	11	12	.478	4.78	32	24	12	197.2	248	80	41	1	0	0	0	92	24	1	.261
1926	5	6	.455	5.00	30	7	4	113.1	137	41	23	0	2	4	1	45	10	0	.222
1927	3	3	.500	5.05	22	5	1	76.2	92	32	17	0	1	0	2	20	4	0	.200
6 yrs.	35	48	.422	4.60	177	58	29	780.1	921	260	180	1	16	19	5	*			

	W	L	PCT	ERA	G	GS	CG	IP	H	BB	SO	ShO	Relief Pitching W	L	SV	BATTING AB	H	HR	BA

Jim Keenan

KEENAN, JAMES WILLIAM (Sparkplug)   BL TL 5'6"   155 lbs.
B. May 25, 1899, Avon, N. Y.   D. June 5, 1980, Seminole, Fla.

	W	L	PCT	ERA	G	GS	CG	IP	H	BB	SO	ShO	W	L	SV	AB	H	HR	BA
1920 PHI N	0	0	—	3.00	1	0	0	3	3	1	2	0	0	0	0	1	0	0	.000
1921	1	2	.333	6.68	15	2	0	32.1	48	15	7	0	1	0	0	9	0	0	.000
2 yrs.	1	2	.333	6.37	16	2	0	35.1	51	16	9	0	1	0	0	10	0	0	.000

Kid Keenan

KEENAN, HARRY LEON   TR
B. 1875, Louisville, Ky.   D. June 11, 1903, Covington, Ky.

	W	L	PCT	ERA	G	GS	CG	IP	H	BB	SO	ShO	W	L	SV	AB	H	HR	BA
1891 C-M AA	0	1	.000	0.00	1	1	1	8	6	4	5	0	0	0	0	4	2	0	.500

Harry Keener

KEENER, JOSHUA HARRY (Beans)
B. 1869, Easton, Pa.   D. Mar. 5, 1912, Easton, Pa.

	W	L	PCT	ERA	G	GS	CG	IP	H	BB	SO	ShO	W	L	SV	AB	H	HR	BA
1896 PHI N	3	11	.214	5.88	16	13	11	113.1	144	39	28	0	0	1	0	51	16	0	.314

Jeff Keener

KEENER, JEFFREY BRUCE   BL TR 6'   180 lbs.
B. Jan. 14, 1959, Pana, Ill.

	W	L	PCT	ERA	G	GS	CG	IP	H	BB	SO	ShO	W	L	SV	AB	H	HR	BA
1982 STL N	1	1	.500	1.61	19	0	0	22.1	19	19	25	0	1	1	0	0	0	0	—
1983	0	0	—	8.31	4	0	0	4.1	6	1	4	0	0	0	0	0	0	0	—
2 yrs.	1	1	.500	2.70	23	0	0	26.2	25	20	29	0	1	1	0	0	0	0	—

Joe Keener

KEENER, JOSEPH DONALD   BR TR 6'4"   200 lbs.
B. Apr. 21, 1953, San Pedro, Calif.

	W	L	PCT	ERA	G	GS	CG	IP	H	BB	SO	ShO	W	L	SV	AB	H	HR	BA
1976 MON N	0	1	.000	10.38	2	2	0	4.1	7	8	1	0	0	0	0	1	0	0	.000

Rickey Keeton

KEETON, RICKEY (Buster)   BR TR 6'2"   190 lbs.
B. Mar. 18, 1958, Cincinnati, Ohio

	W	L	PCT	ERA	G	GS	CG	IP	H	BB	SO	ShO	W	L	SV	AB	H	HR	BA
1980 MIL A	2	2	.500	4.82	5	5	0	28	35	9	8	0	0	0	0	0	0	0	—
1981	1	0	1.000	5.14	17	0	0	35	47	11	9	0	1	0	0	0	0	0	—
2 yrs.	3	2	.600	5.00	22	5	0	63	82	20	17	0	1	0	0	0	0	0	—

Frank Keffer

KEFFER, C. FRANK
B. Philadelphia, Pa.   D. Oct. 1, 1932, Chicago, Ill.

	W	L	PCT	ERA	G	GS	CG	IP	H	BB	SO	ShO	W	L	SV	AB	H	HR	BA
1890 SYR AA	1	1	.500	5.63	2	1	1	16	15	9	4	0	1	0	0	7	1	0	.143

Chet Kehn

KEHN, CHESTER LAWRENCE   BR TR 5'11"   168 lbs.
B. Oct. 30, 1921, San Diego, Calif.   D. Apr. 5, 1984, San Diego, Calif.

	W	L	PCT	ERA	G	GS	CG	IP	H	BB	SO	ShO	W	L	SV	AB	H	HR	BA
1942 BKN N	0	0	—	7.04	3	1	0	7.2	8	4	3	0	0	0	0	2	2	0	1.000

Katie Keifer

KEIFER, SHERMAN C.   BB TR
B. 1892

	W	L	PCT	ERA	G	GS	CG	IP	H	BB	SO	ShO	W	L	SV	AB	H	HR	BA
1914 IND F	1	0	1.000	2.00	1	1	1	9	6	2	2	0	0	0	0	3	1	0	.333

Mike Kekich

KEKICH, MICHAEL DENNIS   BR TL 6'1"   196 lbs.
B. Apr. 2, 1945, San Diego, Calif.

	W	L	PCT	ERA	G	GS	CG	IP	H	BB	SO	ShO	W	L	SV	AB	H	HR	BA
1965 LA N	0	1	.000	9.58	5	1	0	10.1	10	13	9	0	0	0	0	2	0	0	.000
1968	2	10	.167	3.91	25	20	1	115	116	46	84	1	0	0	0	37	3	0	.081
1969 NY A	4	6	.400	4.54	28	13	1	105	91	49	66	0	1	0	1	27	3	0	.111
1970	6	3	.667	4.82	26	14	1	99	103	55	63	0	0	0	0	32	3	0	.094
1971	10	9	.526	4.08	37	24	3	170	167	82	93	0	2	0	0	52	8	0	.154
1972	10	13	.435	3.70	29	28	2	175.1	172	76	78	0	0	0	0	59	8	0	.136
1973 2 teams		NY	A (5G 1-1)			CLE	A (16G 1-4)												
" total	2	5	.286	7.52	21	10	0	64.2	93	49	30	0	0	0	0	0	0	0	—
1975 TEX A	0	0	—	3.73	23	0	0	31.1	33	21	19	0	0	0	2	0	0	0	—
1977 SEA A	5	4	.556	5.60	41	2	0	90	90	51	55	0	5	2	3	0	0	0	—
9 yrs.	39	51	.433	4.59	235	112	8	860.2	875	442	497	1	8	2	6	209	25	0	.120

George Kelb

KELB, GEORGE FRANCIS (Pugger, Lefty)   BL TL
B. July 17, 1870, Toledo, Ohio   D. Oct. 20, 1936, Toledo, Ohio

	W	L	PCT	ERA	G	GS	CG	IP	H	BB	SO	ShO	W	L	SV	AB	H	HR	BA
1898 CLE N	0	1	.000	4.41	3	1	1	16.1	23	1	8	0	0	0	0	5	1	0	.200

Hal Kelleher

KELLEHER, HAROLD JOSEPH   BR TR 6'   165 lbs.
B. June 24, 1914, Philadelphia, Pa.

	W	L	PCT	ERA	G	GS	CG	IP	H	BB	SO	ShO	W	L	SV	AB	H	HR	BA
1935 PHI N	2	0	1.000	1.80	3	3	2	25	26	12	12	1	0	0	0	8	3	0	.375
1936	0	5	.000	5.32	14	4	1	44	60	29	13	0	0	2	0	12	2	0	.167
1937	2	4	.333	6.63	27	2	1	58.1	72	31	20	0	2	2	0	17	3	0	.176
1938	0	0	—	18.41	6	0	0	7.1	16	9	4	0	0	0	0	2	1	0	.500
4 yrs.	4	9	.308	5.95	50	9	4	134.2	174	81	49	1	2	4	0	39	9	0	.231

Ron Keller

KELLER, RONALD LEE   BR TR 6'2"   200 lbs.
B. June 3, 1943, Indianapolis, Ind.

	W	L	PCT	ERA	G	GS	CG	IP	H	BB	SO	ShO	W	L	SV	AB	H	HR	BA
1966 MIN A	0	0	—	5.06	2	0	0	5.1	7	1	1	0	0	0	0	1	0	0	.000
1968	0	1	.000	2.81	7	1	0	16	18	4	11	0	0	0	0	1	0	0	.000
2 yrs.	0	1	.000	3.38	9	1	0	21.1	25	5	12	0	0	0	0	2	0	0	.000

Al Kellett

KELLETT, ALFRED HENRY   BR TR 6'3"   200 lbs.
B. Oct. 30, 1901, Red Bank, N. J.   D. July 14, 1960, New York, N. Y.

	W	L	PCT	ERA	G	GS	CG	IP	H	BB	SO	ShO	W	L	SV	AB	H	HR	BA
1923 PHI A	0	1	.000	6.30	5	0	0	10	11	8	1	0	0	0	0	3	1	0	.333
1924 BOS A	0	0	—	∞	1	0	0	0	0	2	0	0	0	0	0	0	0	0	—
2 yrs.	0	1	.000	8.10	6	0	0	10	11	10	1	0	0	0	1	3	1	0	.333

Dick Kelley

KELLEY, RICHARD ANTHONY   BR TL 5'11½" 174 lbs.
B. Jan. 8, 1940, Brighton, Mass.

	W	L	PCT	ERA	G	GS	CG	IP	H	BB	SO	ShO	W	L	SV	AB	H	HR	BA
1964 MIL N	0	0	—	18.00	2	0	0	2	2	3	2	0	0	0	0	0	0	0	—
1965	1	1	.500	3.00	21	4	0	45	37	20	31	0	1	0	0	8	0	0	.000
1966 ATL N	7	5	.583	3.22	20	13	2	81	75	21	50	2	1	0	0	28	1	0	.036

	W	L	PCT	ERA	G	GS	CG	IP	H	BB	SO	ShO	Relief Pitching W	L	SV	Batting AB	H	HR	BA

Dick Kelley continued

	W	L	PCT	ERA	G	GS	CG	IP	H	BB	SO	ShO	W	L	SV	AB	H	HR	BA
1967	2	9	.182	3.77	39	9	1	98	88	42	75	1	1	4	2	16	4	0	.250
1968	2	4	.333	2.75	31	11	1	98.1	86	45	73	1	0	0	1	23	1	0	.043
1969 SD N	4	8	.333	3.57	27	23	1	136	113	61	96	1	0	0	0	47	5	0	.106
1971	2	3	.400	3.45	48	1	0	60	52	23	42	0	1	3	2	3	1	0	.333
7 yrs.	18	30	.375	3.39	188	61	5	520.1	453	215	369	5	3	8	5	125	12	0	.096

Harry Kelley

KELLEY, HARRY LEROY
B. Feb. 13, 1906, Parkin, Ark.   D. Mar. 23, 1958, Parkin, Ark.   BR TR 5'9½" 170 lbs.

	W	L	PCT	ERA	G	GS	CG	IP	H	BB	SO	ShO	W	L	SV	AB	H	HR	BA
1925 WAS A	1	1	.500	9.00	6	1	0	16	30	12	7	0	1	0	0	4	0	0	.000
1926	0	0	–	8.10	7	1	0	10	17	8	6	0	0	0	0	1	0	0	.000
1936 PHI A	15	12	.556	3.86	35	27	20	235.1	250	75	82	1	0	0	0	91	18	0	.198
1937	13	21	.382	5.36	41	29	14	205	267	79	68	0	2	2	3	71	16	0	.225
1938 2 teams			PHI A (4G 0–2)					WAS A (38G 9–8)											
" total	9	10	.474	5.12	42	17	7	156.1	179	56	47	2	2	1	1	50	12	0	.240
1939 WAS A	4	3	.571	4.70	15	3	2	53.2	69	14	20	0	2	2	1	15	4	0	.267
6 yrs.	42	47	.472	4.86	146	78	43	676.1	812	244	230	3	11	8	5	232	50	0	.216

Tom Kelley

KELLEY, THOMAS HENRY
B. Jan. 5, 1944, Manchester, Conn.   BR TR 6' 185 lbs.

	W	L	PCT	ERA	G	GS	CG	IP	H	BB	SO	ShO	W	L	SV	AB	H	HR	BA
1964 CLE A	0	0	–	5.59	6	0	0	9.2	9	9	7	0	0	0	0	0	0	0	–
1965	2	1	.667	2.40	4	4	1	30	19	13	31	0	0	0	0	9	2	0	.222
1966	4	8	.333	4.34	31	7	1	95.1	97	42	64	0	3	4	0	28	4	0	.143
1967	0	0	–	0.00	1	0	0	1	0	2	0	0	0	0	0	0	0	0	–
1971 ATL N	9	5	.643	2.96	28	20	5	143	140	69	68	0	0	0	0	43	2	0	.047
1972	5	7	.417	4.58	27	14	2	116	122	65	59	1	0	0	0	34	3	0	.088
1973	0	1	.000	2.77	7	0	0	13	13	7	5	0	0	1	0	2	0	0	.000
7 yrs.	20	22	.476	3.75	104	45	9	408	400	207	234	1	3	5	0	116	11	0	.095

Alex Kellner

KELLNER, ALEXANDER RAYMOND
Brother of Walt Kellner.
B. Aug. 26, 1924, Tucson, Ariz.   BR TL 6' 200 lbs.

	W	L	PCT	ERA	G	GS	CG	IP	H	BB	SO	ShO	W	L	SV	AB	H	HR	BA
1948 PHI A	0	0	–	7.83	13	1	0	23	21	16	14	0	0	0	0	5	0	0	.000
1949	20	12	.625	3.75	38	27	19	245	243	129	94	0	4	2	1	92	20	0	.217
1950	8	20	.286	5.47	36	29	15	225.1	253	112	85	0	0	1	2	80	16	0	.200
1951	11	14	.440	4.46	33	29	11	209.2	218	93	94	1	0	1	2	79	18	0	.228
1952	12	14	.462	4.36	34	33	14	231.1	223	86	105	2	0	0	0	82	17	1	.207
1953	11	12	.478	3.93	25	25	14	201.2	210	51	81	2	0	0	0	69	15	0	.217
1954	6	17	.261	5.39	27	27	8	173.2	204	88	69	1	0	0	0	55	10	0	.182
1955 KC A	11	8	.579	4.20	30	24	6	162.2	164	60	75	3	0	1	0	56	12	0	.214
1956	7	4	.636	4.32	20	17	5	91.2	103	33	44	0	1	0	0	30	6	0	.200
1957	6	5	.545	4.27	28	21	3	132.2	141	41	72	0	0	0	0	47	11	3	.234
1958 2 teams			KC A (7G 0–2)					CIN N (18G 7–3)											
" total	7	5	.583	3.35	25	13	4	115.2	114	28	64	0	3	0	0	39	11	0	.282
1959 STL N	1	1	.667	3.16	12	4	0	37	31	10	19	0	1	0	0	9	2	0	.222
12 yrs.	101	112	.474	4.41	321	250	99	1849.1	1925	747	816	9	9	5	5	643	138	4	.215

Walt Kellner

KELLNER, WALTER JOSEPH
Brother of Alex Kellner.
B. Apr. 26, 1929, Tucson, Ariz.   BR TR 6' 200 lbs.

	W	L	PCT	ERA	G	GS	CG	IP	H	BB	SO	ShO	W	L	SV	AB	H	HR	BA
1952 PHI A	0	0	–	6.75	1	0	0	4	4	3	2	0	0	0	1	1	0	0	.000
1953	0	0	–	6.00	2	0	0	3	1	4	4	0	0	0	0	0	0	0	–
2 yrs.	0	0	–	6.43	3	0	0	7	5	7	6	0	0	0	1	1	0	0	.000

Al Kellogg

KELLOGG, ALBERT CLEMENT
B. Sept. 9, 1886, Providence, R.I.   D. July 21, 1953, Portland, Ore.

	W	L	PCT	ERA	G	GS	CG	IP	H	BB	SO	ShO	W	L	SV	AB	H	HR	BA
1908 PHI A	0	2	.000	5.82	3	3	2	17	20	9	8	0	0	0	0	8	1	0	.125

Win Kellum

KELLUM, WINFORD ANSLEY
B. Apr. 11, 1876, Waterford, Ont., Canada   D. Aug. 10, 1951, Big Rapids, Mich.   BL TL 5'10" 190 lbs.

	W	L	PCT	ERA	G	GS	CG	IP	H	BB	SO	ShO	W	L	SV	AB	H	HR	BA
1901 BOS A	2	3	.400	6.38	6	6	5	48	61	7	8	0	0	0	0	18	3	0	.167
1904 CIN N	15	10	.600	2.60	31	24	22	224.2	206	46	70	1	2	1	2	82	13	0	.159
1905 STL N	3	3	.500	2.92	11	7	5	74	70	10	19	1	0	1	0	25	5	0	.200
3 yrs.	20	16	.556	3.19	48	37	32	346.2	337	63	97	2	2	2	2	125	21	0	.168

Bob Kelly

KELLY, ROBERT EDWARD
B. Oct. 4, 1927, Cleveland, Ohio   BR TR 6' 180 lbs.

	W	L	PCT	ERA	G	GS	CG	IP	H	BB	SO	ShO	W	L	SV	AB	H	HR	BA
1951 CHI N	7	4	.636	4.66	35	11	4	123.2	130	55	48	0	1	5	0	31	5	0	.161
1952	4	9	.308	3.59	31	15	3	125.1	114	46	50	2	0	3	0	37	8	0	.216
1953 2 teams			CHI N (14G 0–1)					CIN N (28G 1–2)											
" total	1	3	.250	5.40	42	5	0	83.1	98	35	35	0	0	2	2	18	2	0	.111
1958 2 teams			CIN N (2G 0–0)					CLE A (13G 0–2)											
" total	0	2	.000	5.16	15	4	0	29.2	32	16	13	0	1	0	0	4	1	0	.250
4 yrs.	12	18	.400	4.50	123	35	7	362	374	152	146	2	2	6	2	90	16	0	.178

Ed Kelly

KELLY, EDWARD LEO
B. Dec. 10, 1889, Providence, R.I.   D. Nov. 4, 1928, Red Lodge, Mont.   BR TR 5'11½" 173 lbs.

	W	L	PCT	ERA	G	GS	CG	IP	H	BB	SO	ShO	W	L	SV	AB	H	HR	BA
1914 BOS A	0	0	–	0.00	3	0	0	2.1	1	1	4	0	0	0	0	1	0	0	.000

George Kelly

KELLY, GEORGE LANGE (Highpockets)
Brother of Ren Kelly.
B. Sept. 10, 1895, San Francisco, Calif.   D. Oct. 13, 1984, San Francisco, Calif.
Hall of Fame 1973.   BR TR 6'4" 190 lbs.

	W	L	PCT	ERA	G	GS	CG	IP	H	BB	SO	ShO	W	L	SV	AB	H	HR	BA
1917 NY N	1	0	1.000	0.00	1	0	0	5	4	1	2	0	1	0	0				*

	W	L	PCT	ERA	G	GS	CG	IP	H	BB	SO	ShO	Relief Pitching W	L	SV	BATTING AB	H	HR	BA

Herb Kelly

KELLY, HERBERT BARRETT   BL TL 5'9"   160 lbs.
B. June 4, 1892, Mobile, Ala.   D. May 18, 1973, Torrance, Calif.

	W	L	PCT	ERA	G	GS	CG	IP	H	BB	SO	ShO	W	L	SV	AB	H	HR	BA
1914 PIT N	0	2	.000	2.45	5	2	2	25.2	24	7	6	0	0	0	0	9	2	0	.222
1915	1	1	.500	4.09	5	1	0	11	10	4	6	0	1	0	0	2	1	0	.500
2 yrs.	1	3	.250	2.95	10	3	2	36.2	34	11	12	0	1	0	0	11	3	0	.273

King Kelly

KELLY, MICHAEL JOSEPH   BR TR 5'10"   180 lbs.
B. Dec. 31, 1857, Troy, N. Y.   D. Nov. 8, 1894, Boston, Mass.
Manager 1890-91.
Hall of Fame 1945.

	W	L	PCT	ERA	G	GS	CG	IP	H	BB	SO	ShO	W	L	SV	AB	H	HR	BA
1880 CHI N	0	0	–	0.00	1	0	0	3	3	1	1	0	0	0	0	344	100	1	.291
1883	0	0	–	0.00	1	0	0	1	1	0	0	0	0	0	0	428	109	3	.255
1884	0	1	.000	8.44	2	0	0	5.1	12	2	1	0	0	1	0	452	160	13	.354
1887 BOS N	1	0	1.000	3.46	3	0	0	13	17	14	0	0	1	0	0	484	156	8	.322
1890 BOS P	1	0	1.000	4.50	1	0	0	2	1	2	2	0	1	0	0	340	111	4	.326
1891 C-M AA	0	1	.000	5.28	3	0	0	15.1	21	7	0	0	0	1	0	379	107	2	.282
1892 BOS N	0	0	–	1.50	1	0	0	6	8	4	0	0	0	0	0	281	53	2	.189
7 yrs.	2	2	.500	4.14	12	0	0	45.2	63	30	4	0	2	2	0	*			

Mike Kelly

KELLY, MICHAEL J.   BR TR 6'1"   178 lbs.
B. Nov. 9, 1902, St. Louis, Mo.

	W	L	PCT	ERA	G	GS	CG	IP	H	BB	SO	ShO	W	L	SV	AB	H	HR	BA
1926 PHI N	0	0	–	9.45	4	0	0	6.2	9	4	2	0	0	0	0	3	0	0	.000

Ren Kelly

KELLY, REYNOLDS JOSEPH   BR TR 6'   183 lbs.
Brother of George Kelly.
B. Nov. 18, 1899, San Francisco, Calif.   D. Aug. 24, 1963, Millbrae, Calif.

	W	L	PCT	ERA	G	GS	CG	IP	H	BB	SO	ShO	W	L	SV	AB	H	HR	BA
1923 PHI A	0	0	–	2.57	1	0	0	7	7	4	1	0	0	0	0	3	0	0	.000

Bill Kelso

KELSO, WILLIAM EUGENE   BR TR 6'4"   215 lbs.
B. Feb. 19, 1940, Kansas City, Mo.

	W	L	PCT	ERA	G	GS	CG	IP	H	BB	SO	ShO	W	L	SV	AB	H	HR	BA
1964 LA A	2	0	1.000	2.28	10	1	1	23.2	19	9	21	0	1	0	0	6	0	0	.000
1966 CAL A	1	1	.500	2.38	5	0	0	11.1	11	6	11	0	1	1	0	1	0	0	.000
1967	5	3	.625	2.97	69	0	0	112	85	63	91	0	5	2	11	19	2	0	.105
1968 CIN N	4	1	.800	3.98	35	0	0	54.1	56	15	39	0	4	1	1	8	0	0	.000
4 yrs.	12	5	.706	3.13	119	2	1	201.1	171	93	162	1	11	4	12	34	2	0	.059

Russ Kemmerer

KEMMERER, RUSSELL PAUL (Rusty, Dutch)   BR TR 6'2"   198 lbs.
B. Nov. 1, 1931, Pittsburgh, Pa.

	W	L	PCT	ERA	G	GS	CG	IP	H	BB	SO	ShO	W	L	SV	AB	H	HR	BA
1954 BOS A	5	3	.625	3.82	19	9	2	75.1	71	41	37	1	2	0	0	21	3	0	.143
1955	1	1	.500	7.27	7	2	0	17.1	18	15	13	0	1	0	0	3	0	0	.000
1957 2 teams					BOS	A (1G 0–0)		WAS	A (39G 7–11)										
" total	7	11	.389	4.95	40	26	6	176.1	219	73	82	0	1	0	0	46	3	2	.065
1958 WAS A	6	15	.286	4.61	40	30	6	224.1	234	74	111	0	0	0	0	69	11	0	.159
1959	8	17	.320	4.50	37	28	8	206	221	71	89	0	0	0	0	60	8	0	.133
1960 2 teams					WAS	A (3G 0–2)		CHI	A (36G 6–3)										
" total	6	5	.545	3.59	39	10	2	138	129	55	86	1	4	2	2	33	0	0	.000
1961 CHI A	3	3	.500	4.38	47	2	0	96.2	102	26	35	0	3	3	2	15	3	0	.200
1962 2 teams					CHI	A (20G 2–1)		HOU	N (36G 5–3)										
" total	7	4	.636	4.03	56	2	0	96	102	26	40	0	7	2	3	11	4	0	.364
1963 HOU N	0	0	–	5.65	17	0	0	36.2	48	8	12	0	0	0	1	7	2	0	.286
9 yrs.	43	59	.422	4.46	302	109	24	1066.2	1144	389	505	2	18	7	8	265	34	2	.128

Dutch Kemner

KEMNER, HERMAN JOHN   BR TR 5'10½" 175 lbs.
B. Mar. 4, 1899, Quincy, Ill.

	W	L	PCT	ERA	G	GS	CG	IP	H	BB	SO	ShO	W	L	SV	AB	H	HR	BA
1929 CIN N	0	0	–	7.63	9	0	0	15.1	19	8	10	0	0	0	1	4	1	0	.250

Ed Kenna

KENNA, EDWARD BENNINGHAUS (The Pitching Poet)   TR 6'   180 lbs.
B. Oct. 17, 1877, Charleston, W. Va.   D. Aug. 23, 1972, San Francisco, Calif.

	W	L	PCT	ERA	G	GS	CG	IP	H	BB	SO	ShO	W	L	SV	AB	H	HR	BA
1902 PHI A	1	1	.500	5.29	2	1	1	17	19	11	5	0	1	0	0	8	1	0	.125

Bill Kennedy

KENNEDY, WILLIAM AULTON (Lefty)   BL TL 6'2½"   200 lbs.
B. Mar. 14, 1921, Carnesville, Ga.   D. Apr. 9, 1983, Seattle, Wash.

	W	L	PCT	ERA	G	GS	CG	IP	H	BB	SO	ShO	W	L	SV	AB	H	HR	BA
1948 2 teams					CLE	A (6G 1–0)		STL	A (26G 7–8)										
" total	8	8	.500	5.21	32	23	3	143.1	148	117	89	0	0	0	0	47	13	0	.277
1949 STL A	4	11	.267	4.69	48	16	2	153.2	172	73	69	0	2	1	1	40	6	0	.150
1950	0	0	–	0.00	1	0	0	2	1	2	1	0	0	0	0	0	0	0	–
1951	1	5	.167	5.63	19	5	1	56	76	37	29	0	1	0	0	16	2	0	.125
1952 CHI A	2	2	.500	2.80	47	1	0	70.2	54	38	46	0	2	1	5	13	3	0	.231
1953 BOS A	0	0	–	3.70	16	0	0	24.1	24	17	14	0	0	0	2	2	1	0	.500
1956 CIN N	0	0	–	18.00	1	0	0	2	6	0	0	0	0	0	0	0	0	0	–
1957	0	2	.000	6.39	8	0	0	12.2	16	5	8	0	0	2	3	2	0	0	.000
8 yrs.	15	28	.349	4.71	172	45	6	464.2	497	289	256	0	4	6	11	120	25	0	.208

Bill Kennedy

KENNEDY, WILLIAM GORMAN   BL TL 6'1"   175 lbs.
B. Dec. 22, 1918, Alexandria, Va.

	W	L	PCT	ERA	G	GS	CG	IP	H	BB	SO	ShO	W	L	SV	AB	H	HR	BA
1942 WAS A	0	1	.000	8.00	8	2	1	18	21	10	4	0	0	0	2	4	0	0	.000
1946	1	2	.333	6.00	21	2	0	39	40	29	18	0	1	1	3	8	1	0	.125
1947	0	0	–	8.10	2	0	0	6.2	10	5	1	0	0	0	0	2	0	0	.000
3 yrs.	1	3	.250	6.79	31	4	1	63.2	71	44	23	0	1	1	5	14	1	0	.071

Brickyard Kennedy

KENNEDY, WILLIAM V.   TR
B. Oct. 7, 1868, Bellaire, Ohio   D. Sept. 23, 1915, Bellaire, Ohio

	W	L	PCT	ERA	G	GS	CG	IP	H	BB	SO	ShO	W	L	SV	AB	H	HR	BA
1892 BKN N	13	9	.591	3.86	26	21	18	191	189	95	108	1	1	0	1	85	14	0	.165
1893	26	20	.565	3.72	46	44	40	382.2	376	168	107	2	0	1	1	157	39	0	.248
1894	22	19	.537	4.92	48	41	34	360.2	445	149	107	0	4	0	2	161	49	0	.304
1895	18	13	.581	5.12	39	33	26	279.2	335	93	39	1	3	0	1	127	39	0	.307
1896	15	20	.429	4.42	42	38	28	305.2	334	130	76	1	1	0	1	122	23	0	.189

	W	L	PCT	ERA	G	GS	CG	IP	H	BB	SO	ShO	Relief Pitching W	L	SV	BATTING AB	H	HR	BA

Brickyard Kennedy continued

1897		19	22	.463	3.91	44	40	36	343.1	370	149	81	2	1	1	1	147	40	1	.272
1898		16	21	.432	3.37	40	39	38	339.1	360	123	73	0	0	0	0	135	34	0	.252
1899		22	8	.733	2.79	40	33	27	277.1	297	86	55	2	1	0	2	109	27	0	.248
1900		20	13	.606	3.91	42	35	26	292	316	111	75	2	2	0	0	123	37	0	.301
1901		3	5	.375	3.06	14	8	6	85.1	80	24	28	0	0	0	0	36	6	0	.167
1902 NY N		1	4	.200	3.96	6	6	4	38.2	44	16	9	1	0	0	0	15	4	0	.267
1903 PIT N		9	6	.600	3.45	18	15	10	125.1	130	57	39	1	0	1	0	58	21	0	.362
12 yrs.		184	160	.535	3.96	405	353	293	3021	3276	1201	797	13	12	3	9	1275	333	1	.261

WORLD SERIES

| 1903 PIT N | | 0 | 1 | .000 | 5.14 | 1 | 1 | 0 | 7 | 11 | 3 | 3 | 0 | 0 | 0 | 0 | 2 | 1 | 0 | .500 |

Monte Kennedy

KENNEDY, MONTIA CALVIN (Lefty)
B. May 11, 1922, Amelia, Va.　　　　　　　　BR TL 6'2"　　185 lbs.

1946 NY N		9	10	.474	3.42	38	27	10	186.2	153	116	71	1	0	0	1	64	15	0	.234
1947		9	12	.429	4.85	34	24	9	148.1	158	88	60	0	1	1	0	48	8	0	.167
1948		3	9	.250	4.01	25	16	7	114.1	118	57	63	1	0	0	0	31	4	0	.129
1949		12	14	.462	3.43	38	32	14	223.1	208	100	95	4	0	0	1	83	12	1	.145
1950		5	4	.556	4.72	36	17	5	114.1	120	53	41	0	2	0	2	36	2	0	.056
1951		1	2	.333	2.25	29	5	1	68	68	31	22	0	0	1	0	15	3	0	.200
1952		3	4	.429	3.32	31	6	2	83.1	73	31	48	1	2	1	0	22	2	0	.091
1953		0	0	—	7.15	18	0	0	22.2	30	19	11	0	0	0	0	2	0	0	.000
8 yrs.		42	55	.433	3.84	249	127	48	961	928	495	411	7	5	3	4	301	46	1	.153

WORLD SERIES

| 1951 NY N | | 0 | 0 | — | 6.00 | 2 | 0 | 0 | 3 | 3 | 1 | 4 | 0 | 0 | 0 | 0 | 0 | 0 | 0 | — |

Ted Kennedy

KENNEDY, THEODORE A.
B. Feb., 1865, Henry, Ill.　　D. Oct. 31, 1907, St. Louis, Mo.　　BL

1885 CHI N		7	2	.778	3.43	9	9	8	78.2	91	28	36	0	0	0	0	36	3	0	.083
1886 2 teams	PHI AA (20G 5–15)					LOU AA (4G 0–4)														
" total		5	19	.208	4.66	24	23	23	204.2	249	81	82	0	0	1	0	81	4	0	.049
2 yrs.		12	21	.364	4.32	33	32	31	283.1	340	109	118	0	0	1	0	117	7	0	.060

Vern Kennedy

KENNEDY, LLOYD VERNON
B. Mar. 20, 1907, Kansas City, Mo.　　BL TR 6'　　175 lbs.

1934 CHI A		0	2	.000	3.72	3	3	1	19.1	21	9	7	0	0	0	0	7	2	0	.286
1935		11	11	.500	3.91	31	25	16	211.2	211	95	65	2	0	1	1	73	18	0	.247
1936		21	9	.700	4.63	35	34	20	274.1	282	147	99	1	1	0	0	113	32	0	.283
1937		14	13	.519	5.09	32	30	15	221	238	124	114	1	0	1	0	87	20	2	.230
1938 DET A		12	9	.571	5.06	33	26	11	190.1	215	113	53	0	1	0	2	79	23	0	.291
1939 2 teams	DET A (4G 0–3)					STL A (33G 9–17)														
" total		9	20	.310	5.80	37	31	13	212.2	254	124	64	0	0	1	0	74	12	0	.162
1940 STL A		12	17	.414	5.59	34	32	13	222.1	263	122	70	0	1	0	0	84	25	2	.298
1941 2 teams	STL A (6G 2–4)					WAS A (17G 1–7)														
" total		3	11	.214	5.17	23	13	4	111.1	121	66	28	0	1	1	0	36	9	0	.250
1942 CLE A		4	8	.333	4.08	28	12	4	108	108	50	37	0	0	2	1	30	6	0	.200
1943		10	7	.588	2.45	28	17	8	146.2	130	59	63	1	3	1	0	52	12	0	.231
1944 2 teams	CLE A (12G 2–5)					PHI N (12G 1–5)														
" total		3	10	.231	4.64	24	17	5	114.1	126	57	40	0	1	0	0	44	8	0	.182
1945 2 teams	PHI N (12G 0–3)					CIN N (24G 5–12)														
" total		5	15	.250	4.28	36	23	11	193.2	213	83	51	1	0	2	0	64	14	0	.219
12 yrs.		104	132	.441	4.67	344	263	126	2025.2	2173	1049	691	7	8	9	5	743	181	4	.244

Art Kenney

KENNEY, ARTHUR JOSEPH
B. Apr. 29, 1916, Milford, Mass.　　BL TL 6'　　175 lbs.

| 1938 BOS N | | 0 | 0 | — | 15.43 | 2 | 0 | 0 | 2.1 | 3 | 8 | 2 | 0 | 0 | 0 | 0 | 0 | 0 | 0 | — |

Ed Kent

KENT, EDWARD C.
B. 1859, New York, N. Y.　　Deceased.　　TL 5'6½"　　152 lbs.

| 1884 TOL AA | | 0 | 1 | .000 | 6.00 | 1 | 1 | 1 | 9 | 14 | 3 | 4 | 0 | 0 | 0 | 0 | 4 | 0 | 0 | .000 |

Maury Kent

KENT, MAURICE ALLEN
B. Sept. 17, 1885, Marshalltown, Iowa　　D. Apr. 19, 1966, Iowa City, Iowa　　BB TR 6'　　168 lbs.

1912 BKN N		5	5	.500	4.84	20	9	2	93	107	46	24	1	1	1	0	35	8	0	.229
1913		0	0	—	2.45	3	0	0	7.1	5	3	1	0	0	0	0	3	0	0	.000
2 yrs.		5	5	.500	4.66	23	9	2	100.1	112	49	25	1	1	1	0	38	8	0	.211

Matt Keough

KEOUGH, MATTHEW LON
Son of Marty Keough.
B. July 3, 1955, Pomona, Calif.　　BR TR 6'3"　　190 lbs.

1977 OAK A		1	3	.250	4.81	7	6	0	43	39	22	23	0	0	0	0	0	0	0	—
1978		8	15	.348	3.24	32	32	6	197.1	178	85	108	0	0	0	0	0	0	0	—
1979		2	17	.105	5.03	30	28	7	177	220	78	95	1	0	0	0	0	0	0	—
1980		16	13	.552	2.92	34	32	20	250	218	94	121	2	0	0	0	0	0	0	—
1981		10	6	.625	3.41	19	19	10	140	125	45	60	2	0	0	0	0	0	0	—
1982		11	18	.379	5.72	34	34	10	209.1	233	101	75	2	0	0	0	0	0	0	—
1983 2 teams	OAK A (14G 2–3)					NY A (12G 3–4)														
" total		5	7	.417	5.33	26	16	0	99.2	109	51	54	0	2	0	0	0	0	0	—
7 yrs.		53	79	.402	4.18	182	167	53	1116.1	1122	476	536	7	2	0	0	0	0	0	—

LEAGUE CHAMPIONSHIP SERIES

| 1981 OAK A | | 0 | 1 | .000 | 1.08 | 1 | 1 | 0 | 8.1 | 7 | 6 | 2 | 0 | 0 | 0 | 0 | 0 | 0 | 0 | — |

	W	L	PCT	ERA	G	GS	CG	IP	H	BB	SO	ShO	Relief Pitching W	L	SV	BATTING AB	H	HR	BA

Kurt Kepshire

KEPSHIRE, KURT DAVID
B. July 3, 1959, Bridgeport, Conn.   BL TR 6'2"   195 lbs.

	W	L	PCT	ERA	G	GS	CG	IP	H	BB	SO	ShO	W	L	SV	AB	H	HR	BA
1984 STL N	6	5	.545	3.30	17	16	2	109	100	44	71	2	0	0	0	36	2	0	.056

Gus Keriazakos

KERIAZAKOS, CONSTANTINE NICHOLAS
B. July 28, 1931, West Orange, N. J.   BR TR 6'3"   187 lbs.

	W	L	PCT	ERA	G	GS	CG	IP	H	BB	SO	ShO	W	L	SV	AB	H	HR	BA
1950 CHI A	0	1	.000	19.29	1	1	0	2.1	7	5	1	0	0	0	0	1	1	0	1.000
1954 WAS A	2	3	.400	3.77	22	3	2	59.2	59	30	33	0	1	1	0	15	1	0	.067
1955 KC A	0	1	.000	12.34	5	1	0	11.2	15	7	8	0	0	1	0	3	0	0	.000
3 yrs.	2	5	.286	5.62	28	5	2	73.2	81	42	42	0	1	2	0	19	2	0	.105

Bill Kerksieck

KERKSIECK, WAYMAN WILLIAM
B. Dec. 6, 1913, Ulm, Ark.   D. Mar. 11, 1970, Little Rock, Ark.   BR TR 6'1"   183 lbs.

	W	L	PCT	ERA	G	GS	CG	IP	H	BB	SO	ShO	W	L	SV	AB	H	HR	BA
1939 PHI N	0	2	.000	7.18	23	2	1	62.2	81	32	13	0	0	0	0	12	1	0	.083

Jim Kern

KERN, JAMES LESTER
B. Mar. 15, 1949, Gladwin County, Mich.   BR TR 6'5"   185 lbs.

	W	L	PCT	ERA	G	GS	CG	IP	H	BB	SO	ShO	W	L	SV	AB	H	HR	BA
1974 CLE A	0	1	.000	4.70	4	3	1	15.1	16	14	11	0	0	0	0	0	0	0	—
1975	1	2	.333	3.77	13	7	0	71.2	60	45	55	0	0	0	0	0	0	0	—
1976	10	7	.588	2.36	50	2	0	118	91	50	111	0	9	6	15	0	0	0	—
1977	8	10	.444	3.42	60	0	0	92	85	47	91	0	8	10	18	0	0	0	—
1978	10	10	.500	3.08	58	0	0	99.1	77	58	95	0	10	10	13	1	0	0	.000
1979 TEX A	13	5	.722	1.57	71	0	0	143	99	62	136	0	13	5	29	0	0	0	—
1980	3	11	.214	4.86	38	1	0	63	65	45	40	0	3	11	2	0	0	0	—
1981	1	2	.333	2.70	23	0	0	30	21	22	20	0	1	2	6	0	0	0	—
1982 2 teams			CIN N (50G 3–5)					CHI A (13G 2–1)											
" total	5	6	.455	3.46	63	1	0	104	81	60	66	0	4	6	5	7	0	0	.000
1983 CHI A	0	0	—	0.00	1	0	0	.2	1	0	0	0	0	0	0	0	0	0	—
1984 2 teams			PHI N (8G 0–1)					MIL A (6G 1–0)											
" total	1	1	.500	7.50	14	0	0	18	26	13	12	0	1	1	0	1	0	0	.000
11 yrs.	52	55	.486	3.11	395	14	1	755	622	416	637	0	49	51	88	9	0	0	.000

Dickie Kerr

KERR, RICHARD HENRY
B. July 3, 1893, St. Louis, Mo.   D. May 4, 1963, Houston, Tex.   BL TL 5'7"   155 lbs.

	W	L	PCT	ERA	G	GS	CG	IP	H	BB	SO	ShO	W	L	SV	AB	H	HR	BA
1919 CHI A	13	7	.650	2.88	39	17	10	212.1	208	64	79	1	7	1	0	68	17	0	.250
1920	21	9	.700	3.37	45	28	20	253.2	266	72	72	3	3	1	5	90	14	0	.156
1921	19	17	.528	4.72	44	37	25	308.2	357	96	80	3	3	0	1	105	25	0	.238
1925	0	1	.000	5.15	12	2	0	36.2	45	18	4	0	0	0	0	12	4	0	.333
4 yrs.	53	34	.609	3.84	140	84	55	811.1	876	250	235	7	13	2	6	275	60	0	.218
WORLD SERIES																			
1919 CHI A	2	0	1.000	1.42	2	2	2	19	14	3	6	1	0	0	0	6	1	0	.167

Joe Kerrigan

KERRIGAN, JOSEPH THOMAS
B. Nov. 30, 1954, Philadelphia, Pa.   BR TR 6'5"   205 lbs.

	W	L	PCT	ERA	G	GS	CG	IP	H	BB	SO	ShO	W	L	SV	AB	H	HR	BA
1976 MON N	2	6	.250	3.81	38	0	0	56.2	63	23	22	0	2	6	1	2	0	0	.000
1977	3	5	.375	3.24	66	0	0	89	80	33	43	0	3	5	11	8	0	0	.000
1978 BAL A	3	1	.750	4.77	26	2	0	71.2	75	36	41	0	2	1	3	0	0	0	—
1980	0	0	—	4.50	1	0	0	2	3	0	1	0	0	0	0	0	0	0	—
4 yrs.	8	12	.400	3.90	131	2	0	219.1	221	92	107	0	7	12	15	10	0	0	.000

Rick Kester

KESTER, RICHARD LEE
B. July 7, 1946, Iola, Kans.   BR TR 6'   190 lbs.

	W	L	PCT	ERA	G	GS	CG	IP	H	BB	SO	ShO	W	L	SV	AB	H	HR	BA
1968 ATL N	0	0	—	5.68	5	0	0	6.1	8	3	9	0	0	0	0	0	0	0	—
1969	0	0	—	13.50	1	0	0	2	5	0	2	0	0	0	0	0	0	0	—
1970	0	0	—	5.63	15	0	0	32	36	19	20	0	0	0	0	9	0	0	.000
3 yrs.	0	0	—	6.02	21	0	0	40.1	49	22	31	0	0	0	0	9	0	0	.000

Gus Ketchum

KETCHUM, AUGUST FRANKLIN
B. Mar. 21, 1898, Rockwall, Tex.   BR TR 5'9½"   170 lbs.

	W	L	PCT	ERA	G	GS	CG	IP	H	BB	SO	ShO	W	L	SV	AB	H	HR	BA
1922 PHI A	0	1	.000	5.63	6	0	0	16	19	8	4	0	0	1	0	4	0	0	.000

Hank Keupper

KEUPPER, HENRY J.
B. June 24, 1887, Staunton, Ill.   D. Aug. 14, 1960, Pittsburg, Ill.   BL TL 6'1"   185 lbs.

	W	L	PCT	ERA	G	GS	CG	IP	H	BB	SO	ShO	W	L	SV	AB	H	HR	BA
1914 STL F	8	20	.286	4.27	42	25	12	213	256	49	70	1	3	1	0	68	17	0	.250

Jimmy Key

KEY, JAMES EDWARD
B. Apr. 22, 1961, Huntsville, Ala.   BR TL 6'1"   180 lbs.

	W	L	PCT	ERA	G	GS	CG	IP	H	BB	SO	ShO	W	L	SV	AB	H	HR	BA
1984 TOR A	4	5	.444	4.65	63	0	0	62	70	32	44	0	4	5	10	0	0	0	—

Joe Kiefer

KIEFER, JOSEPH WILLIAM (Smoke, Harlem Joe)
B. July 19, 1899, West Leyden, N. Y.   D. July 5, 1975, Utica, N. Y.   BR TR 5'11"   190 lbs.

	W	L	PCT	ERA	G	GS	CG	IP	H	BB	SO	ShO	W	L	SV	AB	H	HR	BA
1920 CHI A	0	1	.000	15.43	2	1	0	4.2	7	5	1	0	0	0	0	2	0	0	.000
1925 BOS A	0	2	.000	6.00	2	2	0	15	20	9	4	0	0	0	0	4	0	0	.000
1926	0	2	.000	4.80	11	1	0	30	29	16	4	0	0	1	0	7	1	0	.143
3 yrs.	0	5	.000	6.16	15	4	0	49.2	56	30	9	0	0	1	0	13	1	0	.077

Leo Kiely

KIELY, LEO PATRICK
B. Nov. 30, 1929, Hoboken, N. J.   D. Jan. 18, 1984, Montclair, N. J. BL TL 6'2"   180 lbs.

	W	L	PCT	ERA	G	GS	CG	IP	H	BB	SO	ShO	W	L	SV	AB	H	HR	BA
1951 BOS A	7	7	.500	3.34	17	16	4	113.1	106	39	46	0	0	0	0	35	5	0	.143
1954	5	8	.385	3.50	28	19	4	131	153	58	59	1	0	0	0	50	9	1	.180
1955	3	3	.500	2.80	33	4	0	90	91	37	36	0	3	2	6	26	5	0	.192
1956	2	2	.500	5.17	23	0	0	31.1	47	14	9	0	2	2	3	6	1	0	.167
1958	5	2	.714	3.00	47	0	0	81	77	18	26	0	5	2	12	13	0	0	.000
1959	3	3	.500	4.20	41	0	0	55.2	67	18	30	0	3	3	7	8	0	0	.000
1960 KC A	1	2	.333	1.74	20	0	0	20.2	21	5	6	0	1	2	1	1	0	0	.000
7 yrs.	26	27	.491	3.37	209	39	8	523	562	189	212	1	14	12	29	139	20	1	.144

	W	L	PCT	ERA	G	GS	CG	IP	H	BB	SO	ShO	Relief Pitching W	L	SV	BATTING AB	H	HR	BA

John Kiley

KILEY, JOHN FREDERICK   BL TL
B. July, 1859, South Dedham, Mass.   D. Dec. 18, 1940, Norwood, Mass.

	W	L	PCT	ERA	G	GS	CG	IP	H	BB	SO	ShO	W	L	SV	AB	H	HR	BA
1891 BOS N	0	1	.000	6.75	1	1	1	8	13	5	1	0	0	0	0	*			

Mike Kilkenny

KILKENNY, MICHAEL DAVID   BR TL 6'3½" 175 lbs.
B. Apr. 11, 1945, Toronto, Ont., Canada

	W	L	PCT	ERA	G	GS	CG	IP	H	BB	SO	ShO	W	L	SV	AB	H	HR	BA
1969 DET A	8	6	.571	3.37	39	15	6	128.1	99	63	97	4	1	1	2	37	2	0	.054
1970	7	6	.538	5.16	36	21	3	129	141	70	105	0	1	0	0	39	3	0	.077
1971	4	5	.444	5.02	30	11	2	86	83	44	47	0	0	0	1	24	2	0	.083
1972 4 teams	DET	A (1G 0-0)		OAK	A (1G 0-0)		CLE	A (22G 4-1)		SD	N (5G 0-0)								
" total	4	1	.800	3.78	29	7	1	64.1	59	42	49	0	2	0	1	14	1	0	.071
1973 CLE A	0	0	—	22.50	5	0	0	2	5	5	3	0	0	0	0	0	0	0	—
5 yrs.	23	18	.561	4.44	139	54	12	409.2	387	224	301	4	4	1	4	114	8	0	.070

Evans Killeen

KILLEEN, EVANS HENRY   BR TR 6' 190 lbs.
B. Feb. 27, 1936, Brooklyn, N. Y.

	W	L	PCT	ERA	G	GS	CG	IP	H	BB	SO	ShO	W	L	SV	AB	H	HR	BA
1959 KC A	0	0	—	4.76	4	0	0	5.2	4	4	1	0	0	0	0	0	0	0	—

Henry Killeen

KILLEEN, HENRY
B. 1871, Troy, N. Y.   Deceased.

	W	L	PCT	ERA	G	GS	CG	IP	H	BB	SO	ShO	W	L	SV	AB	H	HR	BA
1891 CLE N	0	1	.000	6.23	1	1	1	8.2	11	8	3	0	0	0	0	3	0	0	.000

Frank Killen

KILLEN, FRANK BISSELL (Lefty)   BL TL 6'1" 200 lbs.
B. Nov. 30, 1870, Pittsburgh, Pa.   D. Dec. 4, 1939, Pittsburgh, Pa.

	W	L	PCT	ERA	G	GS	CG	IP	H	BB	SO	ShO	W	L	SV	AB	H	HR	BA
1891 C-M AA	7	4	.636	1.68	11	11	11	96.2	73	51	38	2	0	0	0	35	8	0	.229
1892 WAS N	29	26	.527	3.31	60	52	46	459.2	448	182	147	2	1	3	0	186	37	4	.199
1893 PIT N	34	10	.773	3.64	55	48	38	415	401	140	99	2	5	1	0	171	47	4	.275
1894	14	11	.560	4.50	28	28	20	204	261	86	62	1	0	0	0	80	21	0	.263
1895	5	5	.500	5.49	13	11	6	95	113	57	25	0	1	1	0	38	13	0	.342
1896	29	15	.659	3.41	52	50	44	432.1	427	119	134	5	1	0	0	173	40	2	.231
1897	17	23	.425	4.46	42	41	38	337.1	417	76	99	1	0	1	0	129	32	1	.248
1898 2 teams	PIT	N (23G 10-11)		WAS	N (17G 6-9)														
" total	16	20	.444	3.68	40	39	32	306	350	70	91	0	0	0	0	120	32	0	.267
1899 2 teams	WAS	N (2G 0-2)		BOS	N (12G 7-5)														
" total	7	7	.500	4.45	14	14	12	111.1	126	30	26	0	0	0	0	46	8	0	.174
1900 CHI N	3	3	.500	4.67	6	6	6	54	65	11	4	0	0	0	0	20	3	0	.150
10 yrs.	161	124	.565	3.78	321	300	253	2511.1	2730	823	725	13	8	6	0	998	241	11	.241

Ed Killian

KILLIAN, EDWIN HENRY (Twilight Ed)   BL TL 5'11" 170 lbs.
B. Nov. 12, 1876, Racine, Wis.   D. July 18, 1928, Detroit, Mich.

	W	L	PCT	ERA	G	GS	CG	IP	H	BB	SO	ShO	W	L	SV	AB	H	HR	BA
1903 CLE A	3	4	.429	2.48	9	8	7	61.2	61	13	18	3	0	0	0	28	5	0	.179
1904 DET A	14	20	.412	2.44	40	34	32	331.2	293	93	124	4	0	2	1	126	18	0	.143
1905	23	14	.622	2.27	39	37	33	313.1	263	102	110	8	2	0	0	118	32	0	.271
1906	10	6	.625	3.43	21	16	14	149.2	165	54	47	0	1	0	0	53	9	0	.170
1907	25	13	.658	1.78	41	34	29	314	286	91	96	3	1	0	1	122	39	0	.320
1908	12	9	.571	2.99	27	23	15	180.2	170	53	47	0	0	0	1	73	10	0	.137
1909	11	9	.550	1.71	25	19	14	173.1	150	49	54	3	1	0	1	62	10	0	.161
1910	4	3	.571	3.04	11	9	5	74	75	27	20	1	0	1	0	27	4	0	.148
8 yrs.	102	78	.567	2.38	213	180	149	1598.1	1463	482	516	22	5	3	6	609	127	0	.209

WORLD SERIES

	W	L	PCT	ERA	G	GS	CG	IP	H	BB	SO	ShO	W	L	SV	AB	H	HR	BA
1907 DET A	0	0	—	2.25	1	0	0	4	3	1	1	0	0	0	0	2	1	0	.500
1908	0	0	—	7.71	1	1	0	2.1	5	3	1	0	0	0	0	0	0	0	—
2 yrs.	0	0	—	4.26	2	1	0	6.1	8	4	2	0	0	0	0	2	1	0	.500

Jack Killilay

KILLILAY, JOHN WILLIAM   BR TR 5'11" 165 lbs.
B. May 24, 1887, Leavenworth, Kans.   D. Oct. 21, 1968, Tulsa, Okla.

	W	L	PCT	ERA	G	GS	CG	IP	H	BB	SO	ShO	W	L	SV	AB	H	HR	BA
1911 BOS A	4	2	.667	3.54	14	7	1	61	65	36	28	0	2	0	0	24	1	0	.042

Matt Kilroy

KILROY, MATTHEW ALOYSIUS (Matches)   BL TL 5'9" 175 lbs.
Brother of Mike Kilroy.
B. June 21, 1866, Philadelphia, Pa.   D. Mar. 2, 1940, Philadelphia, Pa.

	W	L	PCT	ERA	G	GS	CG	IP	H	BB	SO	ShO	W	L	SV	AB	H	HR	BA
1886 BAL AA	29	34	.460	3.37	68	68	66	583	476	182	513	5	0	0	0	218	38	0	.174
1887	46	20	.697	3.07	69	69	66	589.1	585	157	217	6	0	0	0	239	59	0	.247
1888	17	21	.447	4.04	40	40	35	321	347	79	135	2	0	0	0	145	26	0	.179
1889	29	25	.537	2.85	59	56	55	480.2	476	142	217	0	0	0	0	208	57	1	.274
1890 BOS P	10	15	.400	4.26	30	27	18	217.2	268	87	48	0	2	1	0	93	20	0	.215
1891 C-M AA	1	4	.200	2.98	7	6	4	45.1	51	19	6	0	0	0	0	20	3	0	.150
1892 WAS N	1	1	.500	2.39	4	3	2	26.1	20	15	1	0	0	0	0	10	2	0	.200
1893 LOU N	3	2	.600	9.00	5	5	5	35	52	23	4	1	0	0	0	16	7	0	.438
1894	0	5	.000	3.89	8	7	3	37	46	20	11	0	0	0	0	17	2	0	.118
1898 CHI N	6	7	.462	4.31	13	11	10	100.1	119	30	18	0	1	1	0	96	22	0	.229
10 yrs.	142	134	.514	3.47	303	292	264	2435.2	2445	754	1170	19	3	2	0	*			

Mike Kilroy

KILROY, MICHAEL JOSEPH   BR TR
Brother of Matt Kilroy.
B. Nov. 4, 1872, Philadelphia, Pa.   D. Oct. 2, 1960, Philadelphia, Pa.

	W	L	PCT	ERA	G	GS	CG	IP	H	BB	SO	ShO	W	L	SV	AB	H	HR	BA
1888 BAL AA	0	1	.000	8.00	1	1	1	9	12	5	1	0	0	0	0	4	0	0	.000
1891 PHI N	0	2	.000	9.90	3	1	0	10	15	4	3	0	0	0	0	5	2	0	.400
2 yrs.	0	3	.000	9.00	4	2	1	19	27	9	4	0	0	0	0	9	2	0	.222

Newt Kimball

KIMBALL, NEWELL W.   BR TR 6'2½" 190 lbs.
B. Mar. 27, 1915, Logan, Utah

	W	L	PCT	ERA	G	GS	CG	IP	H	BB	SO	ShO	W	L	SV	AB	H	HR	BA
1937 CHI N	0	0	—	10.80	2	0	0	5	12	1	0	0	0	0	0	1	0	0	.000
1938	0	0	—	9.00	1	0	0	1	3	1	0	0	0	0	0	0	0	0	—
1940 2 teams	BKN	N (21G 3-1)		STL	N (2G 1-0)														
" total	4	1	.800	3.02	23	1	1	47.2	40	21	27	0	3	1	1	11	2	0	.182

	W	L	PCT	ERA	G	GS	CG	IP	H	BB	SO	ShO	Relief Pitching			BATTING			
													W	L	SV	AB	H	HR	BA

Newt Kimball continued

	W	L	PCT	ERA	G	GS	CG	IP	H	BB	SO	ShO	W	L	SV	AB	H	HR	BA
1941 BKN N	3	1	.750	3.63	15	5	1	52	43	29	17	0	1	0	1	14	3	0	.214
1942	2	0	1.000	3.68	14	1	0	29.1	27	19	8	0	1	0	0	5	1	0	.200
1943 2 teams			BKN	N (5G 1–1)			PHI	N (34G 1–6)											
" total	2	7	.222	3.84	39	6	2	100.2	94	47	35	0	1	4	3	19	3	0	.158
6 yrs.	11	9	.550	3.78	94	13	4	235.2	219	117	88	0	6	5	5	50	9	0	.180

Sam Kimber

KIMBER, SAMUEL JACKSON
B. Oct. 29, 1852, Philadelphia, Pa.   D. Nov. 7, 1925, Philadelphia, Pa.

BR TR 5'10½" 168 lbs.

	W	L	PCT	ERA	G	GS	CG	IP	H	BB	SO	ShO	W	L	SV	AB	H	HR	BA
1884 BKN AA	17	20	.459	3.91	40	40	40	352.1	363	69	119	3	0	0	0	138	20	0	.145
1885 PRO N	0	1	.000	11.25	1	1	1	8	15	5	4	0	0	0	0	3	0	0	.000
2 yrs.	17	21	.447	4.07	41	41	41	360.1	378	74	123	3	0	0	0	141	20	0	.142

Harry Kimberlin

KIMBERLIN, HARRY LYDLE (Murphy)
B. Mar. 13, 1909, Sullivan, Mo.

BR TR 6'3" 175 lbs.
BB 1938

	W	L	PCT	ERA	G	GS	CG	IP	H	BB	SO	ShO	W	L	SV	AB	H	HR	BA
1936 STL A	0	0	–	5.40	13	0	0	20	24	16	4	0	0	0	0	1	0	0	.000
1937	0	2	.000	2.35	3	2	1	15.1	16	9	5	0	0	0	0	5	1	0	.200
1938	0	0	–	3.38	1	1	1	8	8	3	1	0	0	0	0	1	0	0	.000
1939	1	2	.333	5.49	17	3	0	41	59	19	11	0	1	0	0	9	3	0	.333
4 yrs.	1	4	.200	4.70	34	6	2	84.1	107	47	21	0	1	0	0	16	4	0	.250

Hal Kime

KIME, HAROLD LEE (Lefty)
B. Mar. 15, 1899, West Salem, Ohio   D. May 16, 1939, Columbus, Ohio

BL TL 5'9" 160 lbs.

	W	L	PCT	ERA	G	GS	CG	IP	H	BB	SO	ShO	W	L	SV	AB	H	HR	BA
1920 STL N	0	0	–	2.57	4	0	0	7	9	2	1	0	0	0	0	1	0	0	.000

Chad Kimsey

KIMSEY, CLYDE ELIAS
B. Aug. 6, 1905, Copperhill, Tenn.   D. Dec. 3, 1942, Pryor, Okla.

BL TR 6'3½" 200 lbs.

	W	L	PCT	ERA	G	GS	CG	IP	H	BB	SO	ShO	W	L	SV	AB	H	HR	BA
1929 STL A	3	6	.333	5.04	24	3	1	64.1	88	19	13	0	1	5	1	30	8	2	.267
1930	6	10	.375	6.35	42	4	1	113.1	139	45	32	0	6	7	1	70	24	3	.343
1931	4	6	.400	4.39	42	4	0	94.1	121	27	27	0	4	5	7	37	10	2	.270
1932 2 teams			STL	A (33G 4–2)			CHI	A (7G 1–1)											
" total	5	3	.625	3.83	40	0	0	89.1	93	38	19	0	5	3	5	20	6	0	.300
1933 CHI A	4	1	.800	5.53	28	0	0	96	124	36	19	0	4	0	0	33	5	0	.152
1936 DET A	2	3	.400	4.85	22	0	0	52	58	29	11	0	2	3	3	16	5	0	.313
6 yrs.	24	29	.453	5.07	198	10	2	509.1	623	194	121	0	22	23	17	*			

Ellis Kinder

KINDER, ELLIS RAYMOND (Old Folks)
B. July 26, 1914, Atkins, Ark.   D. Oct. 16, 1968, Memphis, Tenn.

BR TR 6'3" 215 lbs.

	W	L	PCT	ERA	G	GS	CG	IP	H	BB	SO	ShO	W	L	SV	AB	H	HR	BA
1946 STL A	3	3	.500	3.32	33	7	1	86.2	78	36	59	0	0	0	1	19	1	0	.053
1947	8	15	.348	4.49	34	26	10	194.1	201	82	110	2	0	0	1	62	8	0	.129
1948 BOS A	10	7	.588	3.74	28	22	10	178	183	63	53	1	1	2	0	62	6	0	.097
1949	23	6	.793	3.36	43	30	19	252	251	99	138	6	2	1	4	92	12	0	.130
1950	14	12	.538	4.26	48	23	11	207	212	78	95	1	3	4	9	71	13	1	.183
1951	11	2	.846	2.55	63	2	1	127	108	46	84	0	10	1	14	34	4	0	.118
1952	5	6	.455	2.58	23	10	4	97.2	85	28	50	0	1	2	4	32	0	0	.000
1953	10	6	.625	1.85	69	0	0	107	84	38	39	0	10	6	27	29	11	0	.379
1954	8	8	.500	3.62	48	2	0	107	106	36	67	0	7	8	15	27	5	0	.185
1955	5	5	.500	2.84	43	0	0	66.2	57	15	31	0	5	5	18	12	3	0	.250
1956 2 teams			STL	N (22G 2–0)			CHI	A (29G 3–1)											
" total	5	1	.833	3.09	51	0	0	55.1	56	17	23	0	5	1	9	4	0	0	–
1957 CHI A	0	0	–	0.00	1	0	0	1	0	1	0	0	0	0	0	0	0	0	–
12 yrs.	102	71	.590	3.43	484	122	56	1479.2	1421	539	749	10	44	30	102	444	63	1	.142

Clyde King

KING, CLYDE EDWARD
B. May 23, 1925, Goldsboro, N. C.
Manager 1969–70, 1974–75, 1982.

BB TR 6'1" 175 lbs.

	W	L	PCT	ERA	G	GS	CG	IP	H	BB	SO	ShO	W	L	SV	AB	H	HR	BA
1944 BKN N	2	1	.667	3.09	14	3	1	43.2	42	12	14	0	0	0	0	10	2	0	.200
1945	5	5	.500	4.09	42	2	0	112.1	131	48	29	0	0	1	3	32	4	0	.125
1947	6	5	.545	2.77	29	9	2	87.2	85	29	31	0	2	2	0	26	3	0	.115
1948	0	1	.000	8.03	9	0	0	12.1	14	6	5	0	0	1	0	2	0	0	.000
1951	14	7	.667	4.15	48	3	1	121.1	118	50	33	0	13	6	6	29	4	0	.138
1952	2	0	1.000	5.06	23	0	0	42.2	56	12	17	0	2	0	0	5	0	0	.000
1953 CIN N	3	6	.333	5.21	35	4	0	76	78	32	21	0	2	4	2	10	0	0	.000
7 yrs.	32	25	.561	4.14	200	21	4	496	524	189	150	0	19	14	11	114	13	0	.114

Nellie King

KING, NELSON JOSEPH
B. Mar. 15, 1928, Shenandoah, Pa.

BR TR 6'6" 185 lbs.

	W	L	PCT	ERA	G	GS	CG	IP	H	BB	SO	ShO	W	L	SV	AB	H	HR	BA
1954 PIT N	0	0	–	5.14	4	0	0	7	10	1	3	0	0	0	0	12	0	0	–
1955	1	3	.250	2.98	17	4	0	54.1	60	14	21	0	0	1	0	6	0	0	.000
1956	4	1	.800	3.15	38	0	0	60	54	19	25	0	4	1	5	6	0	0	.000
1957	2	1	.667	4.50	36	0	0	52	69	16	23	0	2	1	1	5	0	0	.000
4 yrs.	7	5	.583	3.58	95	4	0	173.1	193	50	72	0	6	3	6	23	0	0	.000

Silver King

KING, CHARLES FREDERICK
Born Charles Frederick Koenig.
B. Jan. 11, 1868, St. Louis, Mo.   D. May 19, 1938, St. Louis, Mo.

BR TR 6' 170 lbs.

	W	L	PCT	ERA	G	GS	CG	IP	H	BB	SO	ShO	W	L	SV	AB	H	HR	BA
1886 KC N	1	3	.250	4.85	5	5	5	39	43	9	23	0	0	0	0	22	1	0	.045
1887 STL AA	34	11	.756	3.78	46	44	43	390	401	109	128	2	1	0	1	222	46	0	.207
1888	45	21	.682	1.64	66	65	64	585.2	437	76	258	6	1	0	0	207	43	0	.208
1889	33	17	.660	3.14	56	53	47	458	462	125	188	3	0	1	1	189	43	0	.228
1890 CHI P	32	22	.593	2.69	56	56	48	461	420	163	185	4	0	0	0	185	31	1	.168
1891 PIT N	14	29	.326	3.11	48	44	40	384.1	382	144	160	3	0	0	1	148	25	0	.169
1892 NY N	22	24	.478	3.24	52	47	46	419.1	397	174	177	1	1	0	0	167	35	2	.210
1893 2 teams			NY	N (7G 3–4)			CIN	N (17G 5–6)											
" total	8	10	.444	6.08	24	22	12	154	188	82	43	1	0	0	1	54	9	0	.167
1896 WAS N	10	7	.588	4.09	22	16	12	145.1	179	43	35	0	3	1	1	58	16	0	.276

	W	L	PCT	ERA	G	GS	CG	IP	H	BB	SO	ShO	Relief Pitching W	L	SV	BATTING AB	H	HR	BA

Silver King continued

	W	L	PCT	ERA	G	GS	CG	IP	H	BB	SO	ShO	W	L	SV	AB	H	HR	BA
1897	7	8	.467	4.79	23	19	12	154	196	45	32	0	0	1	1	57	11	0	.193
10 yrs.	206	152	.575	3.18	398	371	329	3190.2	3105	970	1229	20	6	3	6	*			

Brian Kingman

KINGMAN, BRIAN PAUL
B. July 27, 1954, Los Angeles, Calif.   BR TR 6'2" 200 lbs.

	W	L	PCT	ERA	G	GS	CG	IP	H	BB	SO	ShO	W	L	SV	AB	H	HR	BA
1979 OAK A	8	7	.533	4.30	18	17	5	113	113	33	58	1	1	0	0	0	0	0	—
1980	8	20	.286	3.84	32	30	10	211.	209	82	116	1	0	1	0	0	0	0	—
1981	3	6	.333	3.96	18	15	3	100	112	32	52	1	0	0	0	0	0	0	—
1982	4	12	.250	4.48	23	20	3	122.2	131	57	46	0	1	0	1	0	0	0	—
1983 SF N	0	0	—	7.71	3	0	0	4.2	10	1	1	0	0	0	0	0	0	0	—
5 yrs.	23	45	.338	4.13	94	82	21	551.1	575	205	273	3	2	1	1	0	0	0	—

LEAGUE CHAMPIONSHIP SERIES

	W	L	PCT	ERA	G	GS	CG	IP	H	BB	SO	ShO	W	L	SV	AB	H	HR	BA
1981 OAK A	0	0	—	81.00	1	0	0	.1	3	0	0	0	0	0	0	0	0	0	—

Dave Kingman

KINGMAN, DAVID ARTHUR
B. Dec. 21, 1948, Pendleton, Ore.   BR TR 6'6" 210 lbs.

	W	L	PCT	ERA	G	GS	CG	IP	H	BB	SO	ShO	W	L	SV	AB	H	HR	BA
1973 SF N	0	0	—	9.00	2	0	0	4	3	6	4	0	0	0	0	*			

Dennis Kinney

KINNEY, DENNIS PAUL
B. Feb. 26, 1952, Toledo, Ohio   BL TL 6'1" 175 lbs.

	W	L	PCT	ERA	G	GS	CG	IP	H	BB	SO	ShO	W	L	SV	AB	H	HR	BA
1978 2 teams			CLE A (18G 0–2)				SD N (7G 0–1)												
" total	0	3	.000	4.73	25	0	0	45.2	43	18	21	0	0	3	5	1	0	0	.000
1979 SD N	0	0	—	3.50	13	0	0	18	17	8	11	0	0	0	0	1	0	0	.000
1980	4	6	.400	4.23	50	0	0	83	79	37	40	0	4	6	1	12	1	0	.083
1981 DET A	0	0	—	9.00	6	0	0	4	5	4	3	0	0	0	0	0	0	0	—
1982 OAK A	0	0	—	8.31	3	0	0	4.1	9	4	0	0	0	0	0	0	0	0	—
5 yrs.	4	9	.308	4.53	97	0	0	155	153	71	75	0	4	9	6	14	1	0	.071

Walt Kinney

KINNEY, WALTER WILLIAM
B. Sept. 9, 1894, Denison, Tex.   D. July 1, 1971, Escondido, Calif.   BL TL 6'2" 186 lbs.

	W	L	PCT	ERA	G	GS	CG	IP	H	BB	SO	ShO	W	L	SV	AB	H	HR	BA
1918 BOS A	0	0	—	1.80	5	0	0	15	5	8	4	0	0	0	0	5	0	0	.000
1919 PHI A	9	15	.375	3.64	43	21	13	202.2	199	91	97	0	3	2	2	88	25	1	.284
1920	2	4	.333	3.10	10	8	5	61	59	28	19	1	0	0	0	26	9	0	.346
1923	0	1	.000	7.50	5	1	0	12	11	9	9	0	0	1	0	6	1	1	.167
4 yrs.	11	20	.355	3.59	63	30	18	290.2	274	136	129	1	3	3	2	125	35	2	.280

Mike Kinnunen

KINNUNEN, MICHAEL JOHN
B. Apr. 1, 1958, Seattle, Wash.   BL TL 6'1" 185 lbs.

	W	L	PCT	ERA	G	GS	CG	IP	H	BB	SO	ShO	W	L	SV	AB	H	HR	BA
1980 MIN A	0	0	—	5.04	21	0	0	25	29	9	8	0	0	0	0	0	0	0	—

Ed Kinsella

KINSELLA, EDWARD WILLIAM (Rube)
B. Jan. 15, 1882, Lexington, Ill.   D. Jan. 17, 1976, Bloomington, Ill.   BR TR 6'1½" 175 lbs.

	W	L	PCT	ERA	G	GS	CG	IP	H	BB	SO	ShO	W	L	SV	AB	H	HR	BA
1905 PIT N	0	1	.000	2.65	3	2	1	17	19	3	11	0	0	0	0	3	0	0	.000
1910 STL A	1	3	.250	3.78	10	5	2	50	62	16	10	0	0	0	0	12	3	0	.250
2 yrs.	1	4	.200	3.49	13	7	4	67	81	19	21	0	0	0	0	15	3	0	.200

Harry Kinzy

KINZY, HENRY HERSEL (Slim)
B. July 19, 1910, Hallsville, Tex.   BR TR 6'4" 185 lbs.

	W	L	PCT	ERA	G	GS	CG	IP	H	BB	SO	ShO	W	L	SV	AB	H	HR	BA
1934 CHI A	0	1	.000	4.98	13	2	1	34.1	38	31	12	0	0	0	0	10	3	0	.300

Fred Kipp

KIPP, FRED LEO
B. Oct. 1, 1931, Piqua, Kans.   BL TL 6'4" 200 lbs.

	W	L	PCT	ERA	G	GS	CG	IP	H	BB	SO	ShO	W	L	SV	AB	H	HR	BA
1957 BKN N	0	0	—	9.00	1	0	0	4	6	0	3	0	0	0	0	1	0	0	.000
1958 LA N	6	6	.500	5.01	40	9	0	102.1	107	45	58	0	2	3	0	36	9	0	.250
1959	0	0	—	0.00	2	0	0	2.2	2	0	1	0	0	0	0	0	0	0	—
1960 NY A	0	1	.000	6.23	4	0	0	4.1	4	0	2	0	0	1	0	0	0	0	—
4 yrs.	6	7	.462	5.08	47	9	0	113.1	119	48	64	0	2	4	0	37	9	0	.243

Thornton Kipper

KIPPER, THORNTON JOHN
B. Sept. 27, 1928, Bagley, Wis.   BR TR 6'3" 190 lbs.

	W	L	PCT	ERA	G	GS	CG	IP	H	BB	SO	ShO	W	L	SV	AB	H	HR	BA
1953 PHI N	3	3	.500	4.73	20	3	0	45.2	59	12	15	0	3	0	0	11	1	0	.091
1954	0	0	—	7.90	11	0	0	13.2	22	12	5	0	0	0	1	2	0	0	.000
1955	0	1	.000	4.99	24	0	0	39.2	47	22	15	0	0	1	0	3	1	0	.333
3 yrs.	3	4	.429	5.27	55	3	0	99	128	46	35	0	3	1	1	16	2	0	.125

Clay Kirby

KIRBY, CLAYTON LAWS
B. June 25, 1948, Washington, D. C.   BR TR 6'3" 175 lbs.

	W	L	PCT	ERA	G	GS	CG	IP	H	BB	SO	ShO	W	L	SV	AB	H	HR	BA
1969 SD N	7	20	.259	3.79	35	35	2	216	204	100	113	0	0	0	0	66	4	0	.061
1970	10	16	.385	4.52	36	34	6	215	198	120	154	1	0	0	0	74	11	0	.149
1971	15	13	.536	2.83	38	36	13	267	213	103	231	2	0	0	0	86	8	0	.093
1972	12	14	.462	3.13	34	34	9	238.2	197	116	175	2	0	0	0	74	5	0	.068
1973	8	18	.308	4.79	34	31	4	191.2	214	66	129	2	0	0	0	54	5	0	.093
1974 CIN N	12	9	.571	3.27	36	35	7	231	210	91	160	1	0	0	0	74	7	0	.095
1975	10	6	.625	4.70	26	19	1	111	113	54	48	0	2	2	0	32	6	0	.188
1976 MON N	1	8	.111	5.72	22	15	0	78.2	81	63	51	0	0	0	0	18	1	0	.056
8 yrs.	75	104	.419	3.83	261	239	42	1549	1430	713	1061	8	2	2	0	478	47	0	.098

John Kirby

KIRBY, JOHN F. (Chickenhearted)
B. Jan. 13, 1865, St. Louis, Mo.   D. Oct. 6, 1931, St. Louis, Mo.   TR 5'8" 172 lbs.

	W	L	PCT	ERA	G	GS	CG	IP	H	BB	SO	ShO	W	L	SV	AB	H	HR	BA
1884 KC U	0	1	.000	4.09	2	2	1	11	13	2	1	0	0	0	0	7	1	0	.143
1885 STL N	5	8	.385	3.55	14	14	14	129.1	118	44	46	0	0	0	0	50	3	0	.060
1886	11	25	.306	3.30	41	41	38	325	329	134	129	1	0	0	0	136	15	0	.110
1887 2 teams			IND N (8G 1–6)				CLE AA (5G 0–5)												
" total	1	11	.083	7.25	13	13	10	103	132	71	13	0	0	0	0	47	7	0	.149

	W	L	PCT	ERA	G	GS	CG	IP	H	BB	SO	ShO	Relief Pitching W	L	SV	BATTING AB	H	HR	BA

John Kirby *continued*

	W	L	PCT	ERA	G	GS	CG	IP	H	BB	SO	ShO	W	L	SV	AB	H	HR	BA
1888 KC AA	1	4	.200	4.19	5	5	5	43	48	7	11	0	0	0	0	16	1	0	.063
5 yrs.	18	49	.269	4.09	75	75	68	611.1	640	258	200	1	0	0	0	256	27	0	.105

LaRue Kirby

KIRBY, LaRUE
B. Dec. 30, 1889, Eureka, Mich. D. June 10, 1961, Lansing, Mich. BB TR 6' 185 lbs.

	W	L	PCT	ERA	G	GS	CG	IP	H	BB	SO	ShO	W	L	SV	AB	H	HR	BA
1912 NY N	1	0	1.000	5.73	3	1	1	11	13	6	2	0	0	0	0	5	1	0	.200
1915 STL F	0	0	—	5.14	1	0	0	7	7	2	7	0	0	0	0	178	38	0	.213
2 yrs.	1	0	1.000	5.50	4	1	1	18	20	8	9	0	0	0	0	*			

Mike Kircher

KIRCHER, MICHAEL ANDREW
B. Sept. 30, 1897, Rochester, N. Y. D. June 26, 1972, Rochester, N. Y. BR TL 6'1½" 185 lbs.

	W	L	PCT	ERA	G	GS	CG	IP	H	BB	SO	ShO	W	L	SV	AB	H	HR	BA
1919 PHI A	0	0	—	7.88	2	0	0	8	15	3	2	0	0	0	0	3	0	0	.000
1920 STL N	2	1	.667	5.40	9	3	1	36.2	50	5	5	0	1	0	0	11	3	0	.273
1921	0	1	.000	8.10	3	0	0	3.1	4	1	2	0	0	1	0	0	0	0	—
3 yrs.	2	2	.500	6.00	14	3	1	48	69	9	9	0	1	1	0	14	3	0	.214

Bill Kirk

KIRK, WILLIAM PARTLEMORE
B. July 19, 1935, Coatesville, Pa. BL TL 6' 165 lbs.

	W	L	PCT	ERA	G	GS	CG	IP	H	BB	SO	ShO	W	L	SV	AB	H	HR	BA
1961 KC A	0	0	—	12.00	1	0	0	3	6	1	3	0	0	0	0	0	0	0	—

Don Kirkwood

KIRKWOOD, DONALD PAUL
B. Sept. 24, 1950, Pontiac, Mich. BR TR 6'3" 175 lbs.

	W	L	PCT	ERA	G	GS	CG	IP	H	BB	SO	ShO	W	L	SV	AB	H	HR	BA
1974 CAL A	0	0	—	9.00	3	0	0	7	12	6	4	0	0	0	0	0	0	0	—
1975	6	5	.545	3.11	44	2	0	84	85	28	49	0	6	4	7	0	0	0	—
1976	6	12	.333	4.61	28	26	4	158	167	57	78	0	0	1	0	0	0	0	—
1977 2 teams			CAL A (13G 1–0)			CHI A (16G 1–1)														
" total	2	1	.667	5.15	29	0	0	57.2	69	19	34	0	2	1	1	0	0	0	—
1978 TOR A	4	5	.444	4.24	16	9	3	68	76	25	29	0	1	1	0	0	0	0	—
5 yrs.	18	23	.439	4.37	120	37	7	374.2	409	135	194	0	9	7	8	0	0	0	—

Harry Kirsch

KIRSCH, HARRY LOUIS (Casey)
B. Oct. 17, 1889, Fair Haven, Pa. D. Dec. 25, 1925, Pittsburgh, Pa. BR TR 5'11" 170 lbs.

	W	L	PCT	ERA	G	GS	CG	IP	H	BB	SO	ShO	W	L	SV	AB	H	HR	BA
1910 CLE A	0	0	—	6.00	2	0	0	3	5	1	5	0	0	0	0	0	0	0	—

Rube Kisinger

KISINGER, CHARLES SAMUEL
B. Dec. 13, 1876, Adrian, Mich. D. July 14, 1941, Huron, Ohio BR TR 6' 190 lbs.

	W	L	PCT	ERA	G	GS	CG	IP	H	BB	SO	ShO	W	L	SV	AB	H	HR	BA
1902 DET A	2	3	.400	3.12	5	5	5	43.1	48	14	7	0	0	0	0	19	3	0	.158
1903	7	9	.438	2.96	16	14	13	118.2	118	27	33	2	2	0	0	47	6	0	.128
2 yrs.	9	12	.429	3.00	21	19	18	162	166	41	40	2	2	0	0	66	9	0	.136

Bruce Kison

KISON, BRUCE EUGENE
B. Feb. 18, 1950, Pasco, Wash. BR TR 6'4" 178 lbs.

	W	L	PCT	ERA	G	GS	CG	IP	H	BB	SO	ShO	W	L	SV	AB	H	HR	BA
1971 PIT N	6	5	.545	3.41	18	13	2	95	93	36	60	0	1	1	0	31	2	0	.065
1972	9	7	.563	3.26	32	18	6	152	123	69	102	1	0	0	3	53	10	0	.189
1973	3	0	1.000	3.09	7	7	0	43.2	36	24	26	0	0	0	0	12	1	0	.083
1974	9	8	.529	3.49	40	16	1	129	123	57	71	0	4	4	2	37	4	0	.108
1975	12	11	.522	3.23	33	29	6	192	160	92	89	0	1	0	0	59	7	0	.119
1976	14	9	.609	3.08	31	29	6	193	180	52	98	1	0	0	0	59	12	0	.203
1977	9	10	.474	4.90	33	32	3	193	209	55	122	1	0	0	0	69	18	1	.261
1978	6	6	.500	3.19	28	11	0	96	81	39	62	0	2	2	0	29	4	1	.138
1979	13	7	.650	3.19	33	25	3	172	157	45	105	1	2	1	0	55	8	1	.145
1980 CAL A	3	6	.333	4.93	13	13	2	73	73	32	28	1	0	0	0	0	0	0	—
1981	1	1	.500	3.48	11	4	0	44	40	14	19	0	0	0	0	0	0	0	—
1982	10	5	.667	3.17	33	16	3	142	120	44	86	1	1	2	1	0	0	0	—
1983	11	5	.688	4.05	26	17	4	126.2	128	43	83	1	3	0	2	0	0	0	—
1984	4	5	.444	5.37	20	7	0	65.1	72	28	66	0	2	1	2	0	0	0	—
14 yrs.	110	85	.564	3.64	358	237	36	1716.2	1595	630	1017	7	16	11	11	404	66	3	.163

LEAGUE CHAMPIONSHIP SERIES

	W	L	PCT	ERA	G	GS	CG	IP	H	BB	SO	ShO	W	L	SV	AB	H	HR	BA
1971 PIT N	1	0	1.000	0.00	1	0	0	4.2	2	2	3	0	0	0	0	2	0	0	.000
1972	1	0	1.000	0.00	2	0	0	2.1	1	0	3	0	0	0	0	0	0	0	—
1974	1	0	1.000	0.00	1	1	0	6.2	2	6	5	0	0	0	0	2	0	0	.000
1975	0	0	—	4.50	1	0	0	2	2	1	1	0	0	0	0	0	0	0	—
1982 CAL A	1	0	1.000	1.93	2	2	1	14	8	3	12	0	0	0	0	5	0	0	.000
5 yrs.	4	0	1.000	1.21	7	3	1	29.2	15	12	24	0	2	0	0				

WORLD SERIES

	W	L	PCT	ERA	G	GS	CG	IP	H	BB	SO	ShO	W	L	SV	AB	H	HR	BA
1971 PIT N	1	0	1.000	0.00	2	0	0	6.1	1	2	3	0	1	0	0	2	0	0	.000
1979	0	1	.000	108.00	1	1	0	.1	3	2	0	0	0	0	0	0	0	0	—
2 yrs.	1	1	.500	5.40	3	1	0	6.2	4	4	3	0	1	0	0	2	0	0	.000

Bill Kissinger

KISSINGER, WILLIAM FRANCIS (Shang)
B. Aug. 15, 1871, Dayton, Ky. D. Apr. 20, 1929, Cincinnati, Ohio BR TR

	W	L	PCT	ERA	G	GS	CG	IP	H	BB	SO	ShO	W	L	SV	AB	H	HR	BA
1895 2 teams			BAL N (2G 1–0)			STL N (24G 4–12)														
" total	5	12	.294	6.51	26	16	10	152	240	53	34	0	2	2	0	102	25	0	.245
1896 STL N	2	9	.182	6.49	20	12	11	136	209	55	22	0	0	0	1	73	22	0	.301
1897	0	4	.000	11.49	7	4	2	31.1	51	15	5	0	0	0	0	39	13	0	.333
3 yrs.	7	25	.219	6.99	53	32	23	319.1	500	123	61	0	2	2	1	214	60	0	.280

Frank Kitson

KITSON, FRANK L
B. Apr. 11, 1872, Hopkins, Mich. D. Apr. 14, 1930, Allegan, Mich. BL TR 5'11" 165 lbs.

	W	L	PCT	ERA	G	GS	CG	IP	H	BB	SO	ShO	W	L	SV	AB	H	HR	BA
1898 BAL N	8	6	.571	3.24	17	13	13	119.1	123	35	32	1	0	1	0	86	27	0	.314
1899	22	16	.579	2.76	40	37	35	329.2	329	66	75	3	0	1	0	134	27	0	.201
1900 BKN N	15	13	.536	4.19	40	30	21	253.1	283	56	55	2	2	0	4	109	32	0	.294
1901	19	11	.633	2.98	38	32	26	280.2	312	67	127	5	1	2	2	133	35	1	.263
1902	19	12	.613	2.84	31	30	28	259.2	251	48	107	3	0	1	0	113	30	1	.265

	W	L	PCT	ERA	G	GS	CG	IP	H	BB	SO	ShO	Relief Pitching W	L	SV	BATTING AB	H	HR	BA

Frank Kitson continued

	W	L	PCT	ERA	G	GS	CG	IP	H	BB	SO	ShO	W	L	SV	AB	H	HR	BA
1903 DET A	15	16	.484	2.58	31	28	28	257.2	277	38	102	2	2	1	0	116	21	0	.181
1904	8	13	.381	3.07	26	24	19	199.2	211	38	69	0	0	0	1	72	15	1	.208
1905	12	14	.462	3.47	33	27	21	225.2	230	57	78	3	2	0	1	87	16	0	.184
1906 WAS A	6	14	.300	3.65	30	21	15	197	196	57	59	1	1	2	0	90	22	1	.244
1907 2 teams		WAS	A	(5G 0-3)		NY	A	(12G 4-0)											
" total	4	3	.571	3.39	17	7	5	93	116	26	25	0	1	0	0	31	7	0	.226
10 yrs.	128	118	.520	3.17	303	249	211	2215.2	2328	488	729	20	9	8	8	*			

Malachi Kittredge

KITTREDGE, MALACHI J.
B. Oct. 12, 1869, Clinton, Mass.   D. June 23, 1928, Gary, Ind.
Manager 1904.   BR TR 5'10"

	W	L	PCT	ERA	G	GS	CG	IP	H	BB	SO	ShO	W	L	SV	AB	H	HR	BA
1896 CHI N	0	0	—	5.40	1	0	0	1.2	2	1	0	0	0	0	0	*			

Hugo Klaerner

KLAERNER, HUGO EMIL (Dutch)
B. Oct. 15, 1908, Fredericksburg, Tex.   D. Feb. 3, 1982, Fredericksburg, Tex.   BR TR 5'11" 190 lbs.

	W	L	PCT	ERA	G	GS	CG	IP	H	BB	SO	ShO	W	L	SV	AB	H	HR	BA
1934 CHI A	0	2	.000	10.90	3	3	1	17.1	24	16	9	0	0	0	0	6	2	0	.333

Fred Klages

KLAGES, FREDERICK ANTHONY
B. Oct. 31, 1943, Ambridge, Pa.   BR TR 6'2" 185 lbs.

	W	L	PCT	ERA	G	GS	CG	IP	H	BB	SO	ShO	W	L	SV	AB	H	HR	BA
1966 CHI A	1	0	1.000	1.72	3	3	0	15.2	9	7	6	0	0	0	0	6	3	0	.500
1967	4	4	.500	3.83	11	9	0	44.2	43	16	17	0	1	0	0	12	0	0	.000
2 yrs.	5	4	.556	3.28	14	12	0	60.1	52	23	23	0	1	0	0	18	3	0	.167

Al Klawitter

KLAWITTER, ALBERT C.
B. Apr. 12, 1888, Wilkes-Barre, Pa.   D. May 2, 1950, Milwaukee, Wis.   BR TR 6' 180 lbs.

	W	L	PCT	ERA	G	GS	CG	IP	H	BB	SO	ShO	W	L	SV	AB	H	HR	BA
1909 NY N	1	1	.500	2.00	6	3	2	27	24	13	6	0	0	0	1	9	3	0	.333
1910	0	0	—	9.00	1	0	0	1	2	2	0	0	0	0	0	0	0	0	—
1913 DET A	1	2	.333	5.91	8	3	1	32	39	15	10	0	0	1	0	11	0	0	.000
3 yrs.	2	3	.400	4.20	15	6	3	60	65	30	16	0	0	1	1	20	3	0	.150

Hal Klein

KLEIN, HAROLD JOHN
B. June 8, 1923, St. Louis, Mo.   D. Dec. 10, 1957, St. Louis, Mo.   BL TL 6'2" 193 lbs.

	W	L	PCT	ERA	G	GS	CG	IP	H	BB	SO	ShO	W	L	SV	AB	H	HR	BA
1944 CLE A	1	2	.333	5.75	11	6	1	40.2	38	36	13	0	0	0	0	14	2	0	.143
1945	0	0	—	3.86	3	0	0	7	8	7	5	0	0	0	0	3	1	0	.333
2 yrs.	1	2	.333	5.48	14	6	1	47.2	46	43	18	0	0	0	0	17	3	0	.176

Ted Kleinhans

KLEINHANS, THEODORE OTTO
B. Apr. 8, 1899, Deer Park, Wis.   BR TL 6' 170 lbs.

	W	L	PCT	ERA	G	GS	CG	IP	H	BB	SO	ShO	W	L	SV	AB	H	HR	BA
1934 2 teams		PHI	N	(5G 0-0)		CIN	N	(24G 2-6)											
" total	2	6	.250	5.99	29	9	0	85.2	118	41	25	0	1	1	0	24	3	0	.125
1936 NY A	1	1	.500	5.83	19	0	0	29.1	36	23	10	0	1	1	1	6	1	0	.167
1937 CIN N	1	2	.333	2.30	7	3	1	27.1	29	12	13	0	0	0	0	8	2	0	.250
1938	0	0	—	9.00	1	0	0	1	2	0	0	0	0	0	0	0	0	0	—
4 yrs.	4	9	.308	5.27	56	12	1	143.1	185	76	48	0	2	2	1	38	6	0	.158

Nub Kleinke

KLEINKE, NORBERT GEORGE
B. May 19, 1911, Fond du Lac, Wis.   D. Mar. 16, 1950, Off Marin Coast, Calif.   BR TR 6'1" 170 lbs.

	W	L	PCT	ERA	G	GS	CG	IP	H	BB	SO	ShO	W	L	SV	AB	H	HR	BA
1935 STL N	0	0	—	4.97	4	2	0	12.2	19	3	5	0	0	0	0	2	0	0	.000
1937	1	1	.500	4.79	5	2	1	20.2	25	7	9	0	0	1	0	8	0	0	.000
2 yrs.	1	1	.500	4.86	9	4	1	33.1	44	10	14	0	0	1	0	10	0	0	.000

Ed Klepfer

KLEPFER, EDWARD LLOYD (Big Ed)
B. Mar. 17, 1888, Summerville, Pa.   D. Aug. 9, 1950, Tulsa, Okla.   BR TR 6' 185 lbs.

	W	L	PCT	ERA	G	GS	CG	IP	H	BB	SO	ShO	W	L	SV	AB	H	HR	BA
1911 NY A	0	0	—	6.75	2	0	0	4	5	2	4	0	0	0	0	1	0	0	.000
1913	0	1	.000	7.66	8	1	0	24.2	38	12	10	0	0	0	0	6	1	0	.167
1915 2 teams		CHI	A	(3G 1-0)		CLE	A	(8G 1-6)											
" total	2	6	.250	2.26	11	9	3	55.2	58	16	16	0	0	0	0	15	2	0	.133
1916 CLE A	6	6	.500	2.52	31	13	4	143	136	46	62	1	0	2	2	40	1	0	.025
1917	14	4	.778	2.37	41	27	9	213	208	55	66	0	2	1	1	62	2	0	.032
1919	0	0	—	7.36	5	0	0	7.1	12	6	7	0	0	0	0	1	0	0	.000
6 yrs.	22	17	.564	2.81	98	50	16	447.2	457	137	165	1	2	3	3	125	6	0	.048

Eddie Klieman

KLIEMAN, EDWARD FREDERICK (Babe)
B. Mar. 21, 1918, Norwood, Ohio   D. Nov. 15, 1979, Homosassa, Fla.   BR TR 6'1" 190 lbs.

	W	L	PCT	ERA	G	GS	CG	IP	H	BB	SO	ShO	W	L	SV	AB	H	HR	BA
1943 CLE A	0	1	.000	1.00	1	1	1	9	8	5	2	0	0	0	0	3	0	0	.000
1944	11	13	.458	3.38	47	19	5	178.1	185	70	44	1	5	3	5	57	6	0	.105
1945	5	8	.385	3.85	38	12	4	126.1	123	49	33	1	1	2	4	40	8	1	.200
1946	0	0	—	6.60	9	0	0	15	18	10	2	0	0	0	0	1	0	0	.000
1947	5	4	.556	3.03	58	0	0	92	78	39	21	0	5	4	17	19	2	0	.105
1948	3	2	.600	2.60	44	0	0	79.2	62	46	18	0	3	2	4	14	2	0	.143
1949 2 teams		WAS	A	(2G 0-0)		CHI	A	(18G 2-0)											
" total	2	0	1.000	4.25	20	0	0	36	41	18	10	0	2	0	3	9	3	0	.333
1950 PHI A	0	0	—	9.53	5	0	0	5.2	10	2	0	0	0	0	0	1	0	0	.000
8 yrs.	26	28	.481	3.49	222	32	10	542	525	239	130	2	16	11	33	144	21	1	.146
WORLD SERIES																			
1948 CLE A	0	0	—	∞	1	0	0		1	2	0	0	0	0	0	0	0	0	—

Ron Klimkowski

KLIMKOWSKI, RONALD BERNARDO
B. Mar. 1, 1945, Jersey City, N. J.   BR TR 6'2" 190 lbs.

	W	L	PCT	ERA	G	GS	CG	IP	H	BB	SO	ShO	W	L	SV	AB	H	HR	BA
1969 NY A	0	0	—	0.64	3	1	0	14	6	5	3	0	0	0	0	3	0	0	.000
1970	6	7	.462	2.66	45	3	1	98	80	33	40	1	5	5	1	19	1	0	.053
1971 OAK A	2	2	.500	3.40	26	0	0	45	37	23	25	0	2	2	2	5	2	0	.400
1972 NY A	0	3	.000	4.06	16	2	0	31	32	15	11	0	0	1	1	6	0	0	.000
4 yrs.	8	12	.400	2.92	90	6	1	188	155	76	79	1	7	8	4	33	3	0	.091

	W	L	PCT	ERA	G	GS	CG	IP	H	BB	SO	ShO	Relief Pitching W	L	SV	BATTING AB	H	HR	BA

Bob Kline

KLINE, ROBERT GEORGE (Junior)
B. Dec. 9, 1909, Enterprise, Ohio
BR TR 6'3" 200 lbs.

	W	L	PCT	ERA	G	GS	CG	IP	H	BB	SO	ShO	W	L	SV	AB	H	HR	BA
1930 BOS A	0	0	–	0.00	1	0	0	1	1	0	0	0	0	0	0	0	0	0	–
1931	5	5	.500	4.41	28	10	3	98	110	35	25	0	2	0	0	27	9	0	.333
1932	11	13	.458	5.28	47	19	4	172	203	76	31	1	5	2	2	54	7	0	.130
1933	7	8	.467	4.54	46	8	1	127	127	67	16	0	4	4	4	34	6	0	.176
1934 2 teams			PHI	A (20G 6–2)		WAS	A	(6G 1–0)											
" total	7	2	.778	7.21	26	0	0	43.2	60	17	15	0	7	2	1	9	3	0	.333
5 yrs.	30	28	.517	5.05	148	37	8	441.2	501	195	87	1	18	8	7	124	25	0	.202

Bobby Kline

KLINE, JOHN ROBERT
B. Jan. 27, 1929, St. Petersburg, Fla.
BR TR 6' 179 lbs.

	W	L	PCT	ERA	G	GS	CG	IP	H	BB	SO	ShO	W	L	SV	AB	H	HR	BA
1955 WAS A	0	0	–	27.00	1	0	0	4	1	0	0	0	0	0	0	*		

Ron Kline

KLINE, RONALD LEE
B. Mar. 9, 1932, Callery, Pa.
BR TR 6'3" 205 lbs.

	W	L	PCT	ERA	G	GS	CG	IP	H	BB	SO	ShO	W	L	SV	AB	H	HR	BA
1952 PIT N	0	7	.000	5.49	27	11	0	78.2	74	66	27	0	0	1	0	19	0	0	.000
1955	6	13	.316	4.15	36	19	2	136.2	161	53	48	1	2	0	2	38	5	0	.132
1956	14	18	.438	3.38	44	39	9	264	263	81	125	2	0	0	2	79	10	0	.127
1957	9	16	.360	4.04	40	31	11	205	214	61	88	2	0	1	0	66	4	0	.061
1958	13	16	.448	3.53	32	32	11	237.1	220	92	109	2	0	0	0	74	2	0	.027
1959	11	13	.458	4.26	33	29	7	186	186	70	91	0	1	0	0	59	8	0	.136
1960 STL N	4	9	.308	6.04	34	17	1	117.2	133	43	54	0	1	2	1	35	5	0	.143
1961 2 teams			LA	A (26G 3–6)		DET	A	(10G 5–3)											
" total	8	9	.471	4.14	36	20	3	161	172	61	97	1	1	3	1	49	6	0	.122
1962 DET A	3	6	.333	4.31	36	4	0	77.1	88	28	47	0	3	3	2	16	2	0	.125
1963 WAS A	3	8	.273	2.79	62	1	0	93.2	85	30	49	0	3	8	17	11	1	0	.091
1964	10	7	.588	2.32	61	0	0	81.1	81	21	40	0	10	7	14	6	1	0	.167
1965	7	6	.538	2.63	74	0	0	99.1	106	32	52	0	7	6	29	7	0	0	.000
1966	6	4	.600	2.39	63	0	0	90.1	79	17	46	0	6	4	23	6	1	0	.167
1967 MIN A	7	1	.875	3.77	54	0	0	71.2	71	15	36	0	7	1	5	5	0	0	.000
1968 PIT N	12	5	.706	1.68	56	0	0	112.2	94	31	48	0	12	5	7	16	0	0	.000
1969 3 teams			PIT	N (20G 1–3)		SF	N (7G 0–2)		BOS	A	(16G 0–1)								
" total	1	6	.143	5.19	43	0	0	59	77	28	29	0	1	6	4	5	0	0	.000
1970 ATL N	0	0	–	7.50	5	0	0	6	9	2	3	0	0	0	0	0	0	0	–
17 yrs.	114	144	.442	3.75	736	203	44	2077.2	2113	731	989	8	54	47	108	491	45	0	.092

Steve Kline

KLINE, STEVEN JACK
B. Oct. 6, 1947, Wenatchee, Wash.
BR TR 6'3" 205 lbs.

	W	L	PCT	ERA	G	GS	CG	IP	H	BB	SO	ShO	W	L	SV	AB	H	HR	BA
1970 NY A	6	6	.500	3.42	16	15	5	100	99	24	49	0	0	0	0	28	5	0	.179
1971	12	13	.480	2.96	31	30	15	222	206	37	81	1	0	0	0	66	9	0	.136
1972	16	9	.640	2.40	32	32	11	236	210	44	58	4	0	0	0	76	7	0	.092
1973	4	7	.364	4.01	14	13	2	74	76	31	19	1	0	0	0	0	0	0	–
1974 2 teams			NY	A (4G 2–2)		CLE	A	(16G 3–8)											
" total	5	10	.333	4.64	20	13	1	97	96	36	23	0	0	0	0	0	0	0	–
1977 ATL N	0	0	–	6.75	16	0	0	20	21	12	10	0	0	0	1	0	0	0	–
6 yrs.	43	45	.489	3.27	129	105	34	749	708	184	240	6	0	0	1	170	21	0	.124

Bill Kling

KLING, WILLIAM
Brother of Johnny Kling.
B. Jan. 14, 1867, Kansas City, Mo.　　D. Aug. 26, 1934, Kansas City, Mo.
BL TR 6' 190 lbs.

	W	L	PCT	ERA	G	GS	CG	IP	H	BB	SO	ShO	W	L	SV	AB	H	HR	BA
1891 PHI N	4	2	.667	4.32	12	7	4	75	90	32	26	0	0	0	0	31	6	0	.194
1892 BAL N	0	2	.000	11.45	2	2	0	11	17	7	7	0	0	0	0	4	1	0	.250
1895 LOU N	0	0	–	0.00	1	0	0	1	0	1	0	0	0	0	0	1	0	0	.000
3 yrs.	4	4	.500	5.17	15	9	4	87	107	40	33	0	0	0	0	36	7	0	.194

Bob Klinger

KLINGER, ROBERT HAROLD
B. June 4, 1908, Allenton, Mo.　　D. Aug. 19, 1977, Villa Ridge, Mo.
BR TR 6' 180 lbs.

	W	L	PCT	ERA	G	GS	CG	IP	H	BB	SO	ShO	W	L	SV	AB	H	HR	BA
1938 PIT N	12	5	.706	2.99	28	21	10	159.1	152	42	58	1	2	0	1	60	10	0	.167
1939	14	17	.452	4.36	37	33	10	225	251	81	64	2	1	1	0	84	17	0	.202
1940	8	13	.381	5.39	39	22	3	142	196	53	48	0	2	0	3	42	6	0	.143
1941	9	4	.692	3.93	35	9	3	116.2	127	30	36	0	7	0	4	32	8	0	.250
1942	8	11	.421	3.24	37	19	8	152.2	151	45	58	1	1	3	1	40	8	0	.200
1943	11	8	.579	2.72	33	25	14	195	185	58	65	3	0	0	0	65	16	0	.246
1946 BOS A	3	2	.600	2.37	28	1	0	57	49	25	16	0	3	2	9	16	5	0	.313
1947	1	1	.500	3.86	28	0	0	42	42	24	12	0	1	1	5	9	1	0	.111
8 yrs.	66	61	.520	3.68	265	130	48	1089.2	1153	358	357	7	17	9	23	348	71	0	.204

WORLD SERIES

	W	L	PCT	ERA	G	GS	CG	IP	H	BB	SO	ShO	W	L	SV	AB	H	HR	BA
1946 BOS A	0	1	.000	13.50	1	0	0	.2	2	1	0	0	0	1	0	0	0	0	–

Johnny Klippstein

KLIPPSTEIN, JOHN CALVIN
B. Oct. 17, 1927, Washington, D. C.
BR TR 6'1" 173 lbs.

	W	L	PCT	ERA	G	GS	CG	IP	H	BB	SO	ShO	W	L	SV	AB	H	HR	BA
1950 CHI N	2	9	.182	5.25	33	11	3	104.2	112	64	51	0	1	1	1	33	11	1	.333
1951	6	6	.500	4.29	35	11	1	123.2	121	53	56	1	4	0	2	37	4	1	.108
1952	9	14	.391	4.44	41	25	7	202.2	208	89	110	2	4	0	3	63	11	1	.175
1953	10	11	.476	4.83	48	20	5	167.2	169	107	113	0	2	4	6	58	9	1	.155
1954	4	11	.267	5.29	36	21	4	148	155	96	69	0	0	2	1	45	6	0	.133
1955 CIN N	9	10	.474	3.39	39	14	3	138	120	60	68	2	4	0	1	31	2	0	.065
1956	12	11	.522	4.09	37	29	11	211	219	82	86	0	3	0	0	71	7	0	.099
1957	8	11	.421	5.05	46	18	3	146	146	68	99	1	3	2	3	41	3	0	.073
1958 2 teams			CIN	N (12G 3–2)		LA	N (45G 3–5)												
" total	6	7	.462	4.10	57	4	0	123	118	58	95	0	5	6	10	28	2	0	.071
1959 LA N	4	0	1.000	5.91	28	0	0	45.2	48	33	30	0	4	0	2	7	1	0	.143
1960 CLE A	5	5	.500	2.91	49	0	0	74.1	53	35	46	0	5	5	14	14	2	0	.143
1961 WAS A	2	2	.500	6.78	42	1	0	71.2	83	43	41	0	2	1	0	7	1	0	.143
1962 CIN N	7	6	.538	4.47	40	7	0	108.2	113	64	67	0	6	3	4	24	3	0	.125
1963 PHI N	5	6	.455	1.93	49	1	0	112	80	46	86	0	5	5	8	26	1	0	.038

	W	L	PCT	ERA	G	GS	CG	IP	H	BB	SO	ShO	Relief Pitching W	L	SV	BATTING AB	H	HR	BA

Johnny Klippstein continued

	W	L	PCT	ERA	G	GS	CG	IP	H	BB	SO	ShO	W	L	SV	AB	H	HR	BA
1964 2 teams			PHI N (11G 2–1)			MIN A (33G 0–4)													
" total	2	5	.286	2.65	44	0	0	68	66	28	52	0	2	5	3	6	0	0	.000
1965 MIN A	9	3	.750	2.24	56	0	0	76.1	59	31	59	0	9	3	5	8	0	0	.000
1966	1	1	.500	3.40	26	0	0	39.2	35	20	26	0	1	1	3	3	0	0	.000
1967 DET A	0	0	–	5.40	5	0	0	6.2	6	9	1	0	0	0	0	0	0	0	–
18 yrs.	101	118	.461	4.24	711	162	37	1967.2	1911	978	1158	6	59	40	66	502	63	5	.125
WORLD SERIES																			
1959 LA N	0	0	–	0.00	1	0	0	2	1	0	2	0	0	0	0	0	0	0	–
1965 MIN A	0	0	–	0.00	2	0	0	2.2	2	2	3	0	0	0	0	0	0	0	–
2 yrs.	0	0	–	0.00	3	0	0	4.2	3	2	5	0	0	0	0	0	0	0	–

Fred Klobedanz

KLOBEDANZ, FREDERICK AUGUSTUS
B. June 13, 1871, Waterbury, Conn.   D. Apr. 12, 1940, Waterbury, Conn.   BL TL 5'11"   190 lbs.

	W	L	PCT	ERA	G	GS	CG	IP	H	BB	SO	ShO	W	L	SV	AB	H	HR	BA
1896 BOS N	6	4	.600	3.01	10	9	9	80.2	69	31	26	0	1	0	0	41	13	2	.317
1897	26	7	.788	4.60	38	37	30	309.1	344	125	92	2	0	0	0	148	48	1	.324
1898	19	10	.655	3.89	35	33	25	270.2	281	99	51	0	0	0	0	127	27	3	.213
1899	1	4	.200	4.86	5	5	4	33.1	39	9	8	0	0	0	0	11	2	1	.182
1902	1	0	1.000	1.13	1	1	1	8	9	2	4	0	0	0	0	2	1	0	.500
5 yrs.	53	25	.679	4.12	89	85	69	702	742	266	181	2	1	0	0	329	91	7	.277

Stan Klopp

KLOPP, STANLEY HAROLD (Betz)
B. Dec. 22, 1910, Womelsdorf, Pa.   D. Mar. 11, 1980, Robesonia, Pa.   BR TR 6'1½"   180 lbs.

	W	L	PCT	ERA	G	GS	CG	IP	H	BB	SO	ShO	W	L	SV	AB	H	HR	BA
1944 BOS N	1	2	.333	4.27	24	0	0	46.1	47	33	17	0	1	2	0	7	2	0	.286

Chris Knapp

KNAPP, ROBERT CHRISTIAN
B. Sept. 16, 1953, Cherry Point, N. C.   BR TR 6'5"   195 lbs.

	W	L	PCT	ERA	G	GS	CG	IP	H	BB	SO	ShO	W	L	SV	AB	H	HR	BA
1975 CHI A	0	0	–	4.50	2	0	0	4	2	4	3	0	0	0	0	0	0	0	–
1976	3	1	.750	4.85	11	6	1	52	54	32	41	0	0	1	0	0	0	0	–
1977	12	7	.632	4.81	27	26	4	146	166	61	103	0	0	0	0	0	0	0	–
1978 CAL AA	14	8	.636	4.21	30	29	6	188.1	178	67	126	0	0	0	0	0	0	0	–
1979	5	5	.500	5.51	20	18	3	98	109	35	36	0	0	0	0	0	0	0	–
1980	2	11	.154	6.15	32	20	1	117	133	51	46	0	1	1	1	0	0	0	–
6 yrs.	36	32	.529	5.00	122	99	15	603.1	642	250	355	0	1	2	1	0	0	0	–
LEAGUE CHAMPIONSHIP SERIES																			
1979 CAL A	0	1	.000	7.71	1	1	0	2.1	5	1	0	0	0	0	0	0	0	0	–

Frank Knauss

KNAUSS, FRANK H.
B. 1868, Cleveland, Ohio   Deceased.   BL TL

	W	L	PCT	ERA	G	GS	CG	IP	H	BB	SO	ShO	W	L	SV	AB	H	HR	BA
1890 COL AA	17	12	.586	2.81	37	34	28	275.2	206	106	148	3	0	0	2	106	24	1	.226
1891 CLE N	0	3	.000	7.20	3	3	1	15	23	8	6	0	0	0	0	6	1	0	.167
1892 CIN N	0	0	–	3.38	1	0	0	8	13	5	2	0	0	0	0	3	1	0	.333
1894 CLE N	0	1	.000	5.73	2	2	1	11	7	14	2	0	0	0	0	4	0	0	.000
1895 NY N	0	0	–	17.18	1	1	0	3.2	9	2	1	0	0	0	0	1	0	0	.000
5 yrs.	17	16	.515	3.30	44	40	30	313.1	258	135	159	3	0	0	2	120	26	1	.217

Rudy Kneisch

KNEISCH, RUDOLPH FRANK
B. Apr. 10, 1899, Baltimore, Md.   D. Apr. 6, 1965, Baltimore, Md.   BR TL 5'10½"   175 lbs.

	W	L	PCT	ERA	G	GS	CG	IP	H	BB	SO	ShO	W	L	SV	AB	H	HR	BA
1926 DET A	0	1	.000	2.65	2	2	1	17	18	6	4	0	0	0	0	5	0	0	.000

Phil Knell

KNELL, PHILIP LOUIS
B. Mar. 12, 1865, San Francisco, Calif.   D. June 5, 1944, Santa Monica, Calif.   BR TL

	W	L	PCT	ERA	G	GS	CG	IP	H	BB	SO	ShO	W	L	SV	AB	H	HR	BA
1888 PIT N	1	2	.333	3.76	3	3	3	26.1	20	18	15	0	0	0	0	11	1	0	.091
1890 PHI P	22	11	.667	3.83	35	31	30	286.2	287	166	99	2	2	1	0	132	29	0	.220
1891 COL AA	28	27	.509	2.92	58	52	47	462	363	226	228	5	1	2	0	215	34	0	.158
1892 2 teams			WAS N (22G 9–13)			PHI N (11G 5–5)													
" total	14	18	.438	3.78	33	30	24	250	243	111	117	1	2	0	0	102	11	0	.108
1894 2 teams			PIT N (1G 0–0)			LOU N (32G 7–21)													
" total	7	21	.250	5.49	33	28	25	254	341	110	67	0	0	0	0	116	31	1	.267
1895 2 teams			LOU N (10G 0–6)			CLE N (20G 7–5)													
" total	7	11	.389	5.76	30	19	12	173.1	224	74	49	0	2	1	0	81	17	0	.210
6 yrs.	79	90	.467	4.05	192	163	141	1452.1	1478	705	575	8	7	4	0	657	123	1	.187

Bob Knepper

KNEPPER, ROBERT WESLEY
B. May 25, 1954, Akron, Ohio   BL TL 6'3"   195 lbs.

	W	L	PCT	ERA	G	GS	CG	IP	H	BB	SO	ShO	W	L	SV	AB	H	HR	BA
1976 SF N	1	2	.333	3.24	4	4	0	25	26	7	11	0	0	0	0	9	1	0	.111
1977	11	9	.550	3.36	27	27	6	166	151	72	100	2	0	0	0	55	10	0	.182
1978	17	11	.607	2.63	36	35	16	260	218	85	147	6	0	0	0	79	5	0	.063
1979	9	12	.429	4.65	34	34	6	207	241	77	123	2	0	0	0	66	12	1	.182
1980	9	16	.360	4.10	35	33	8	215	242	61	103	1	0	0	0	66	10	0	.152
1981 HOU N	9	5	.643	2.18	22	22	6	157	128	38	75	5	0	0	0	47	7	1	.149
1982	5	15	.250	4.45	33	29	4	180	193	60	108	0	0	1	0	52	3	0	.058
1983	6	13	.316	3.19	35	29	4	203	202	71	125	3	1	1	0	66	12	1	.182
1984	15	10	.600	3.20	35	34	11	233.2	223	55	140	3	0	0	0	76	13	1	.171
9 yrs.	82	93	.469	3.47	261	247	61	1646.2	1624	526	932	22	1	2	0	516	73	4	.141
DIVISIONAL PLAYOFF SERIES																			
1981 HOU N	0	1	.000	5.40	1	1	0	5	6	2	4	0	0	0	0	0	0	0	.000

Charlie Knepper

KNEPPER, CHARLES
B. Feb. 18, 1871, Anderson, Ind.   D. Feb. 6, 1946, Muncie, Ind.   BR TR 6'4"   190 lbs.

	W	L	PCT	ERA	G	GS	CG	IP	H	BB	SO	ShO	W	L	SV	AB	H	HR	BA
1899 CLE N	4	22	.154	5.78	27	26	26	219.2	307	77	43	0	0	0	0	89	12	0	.135

	W	L	PCT	ERA	G	GS	CG	IP	H	BB	SO	ShO	Relief Pitching W	L	SV	BATTING AB	H	HR	BA

Lou Knerr

KNERR, WALLACE LUTHER
B. Aug. 21, 1921, Strasburg, Pa.   D. Mar. 23, 1980, Lancaster, Pa.   BR TR 6'1"   210 lbs.

	W	L	PCT	ERA	G	GS	CG	IP	H	BB	SO	ShO	W	L	SV	AB	H	HR	BA
1945 PHI A	5	11	.313	4.22	27	17	5	130	142	74	41	0	1	0	0	47	9	0	.191
1946	3	16	.158	5.40	30	22	6	148.1	171	67	58	0	0	1	0	50	9	0	.180
1947 WAS A	0	0	—	11.00	6	0	0	9	17	8	5	0	0	0	0	1	1	0	1.000
3 yrs.	8	27	.229	5.04	63	39	11	287.1	330	149	104	0	1	1	0	98	19	0	.194

Elmer Knetzer

KNETZER, ELMER ELLSWORTH (Baron)
B. July 22, 1885, Carrick, Pa.   D. Oct. 3, 1975, Pittsburgh, Pa.   BR TR 5'10"   180 lbs.

	W	L	PCT	ERA	G	GS	CG	IP	H	BB	SO	ShO	W	L	SV	AB	H	HR	BA
1909 BKN N	1	3	.250	3.03	5	4	3	35.2	33	22	7	0	0	0	0	12	0	0	.000
1910	7	5	.583	3.19	20	15	10	132.2	122	60	56	3	0	0	0	38	2	0	.053
1911	11	12	.478	3.49	35	20	11	204	202	93	66	3	2	3	0	62	6	0	.097
1912	7	9	.438	4.55	33	16	4	140.1	135	70	61	1	2	1	0	37	5	0	.135
1914 PIT F	19	11	.633	2.88	37	30	20	272	257	88	146	3	4	0	1	91	9	0	.099
1915	18	15	.545	2.58	41	33	22	279	256	89	120	3	1	1	3	91	12	0	.132
1916 2 teams	BOS	N	(2G 0–2)		CIN	N	(36G 5–12)												
" total	5	14	.263	3.01	38	16	12	176.1	172	47	72	0	0	5	1	52	8	0	.154
1917 CIN N	0	0	—	2.96	11	0	0	27.1	29	12	7	0	0	0	0	3	0	0	.000
8 yrs.	68	69	.496	3.15	220	134	82	1267.1	1206	481	535	13	9	10	6	386	42	0	.109

Jack Knight

KNIGHT, ELMER RUSSELL
B. Jan. 12, 1895, Pittsboro, Miss.   D. July 30, 1976, San Antonio, Tex.   BL TR 6'   175 lbs.

	W	L	PCT	ERA	G	GS	CG	IP	H	BB	SO	ShO	W	L	SV	AB	H	HR	BA
1922 STL N	0	0	—	9.00	1	1	0	4	9	3	1	0	0	0	0	2	1	0	.500
1925 PHI N	7	6	.538	6.84	33	11	4	105.1	161	36	19	0	3	2	3	44	9	0	.205
1926	3	12	.200	6.62	35	15	5	142.2	206	48	29	0	1	1	2	56	12	2	.214
1927 BOS N	0	0	—	15.00	3	0	0	3	6	2	0	0	0	0	0	0	0	0	—
4 yrs.	10	18	.357	6.85	72	27	9	255	382	89	49	0	4	3	5	102	22	2	.216

Joe Knight

KNIGHT, JONAS WILLIAM (Quiet Joe)
B. Sept. 26, 1859, Point Stanley, Ont., Canada   D. Oct. 18, 1938, St. Thomas, Ont., Canada   BL TL 5'11"   185 lbs.

	W	L	PCT	ERA	G	GS	CG	IP	H	BB	SO	ShO	W	L	SV	AB	H	HR	BA
1884 PHI N	2	4	.333	5.47	6	6	6	51	66	21	8	0	0	0	0	*			

Lon Knight

KNIGHT, ALONZO P.
B. June 16, 1853, Philadelphia, Pa.   D. Apr. 23, 1932, Philadelphia, Pa.   BR TR 5'11½" 165 lbs.
Manager 1885.

	W	L	PCT	ERA	G	GS	CG	IP	H	BB	SO	ShO	W	L	SV	AB	H	HR	BA
1876 PHI N	10	22	.313	2.62	34	32	27	282	383	34	12	0	0	0	0	240	60	0	.250
1884 PHI AA	0	1	.000	9.00	2	1	1	14	24	4	2	0	0	0	0	484	131	1	.271
1885 2 teams	PHI	AA	(1G 0–0)		PRO	N	(1G 0–0)												
" total	0	0	—	4.00	2	0	0	9	8	6	2	0	0	0	0	200	38	0	.190
3 yrs.	10	23	.303	2.95	38	33	28	305	415	44	16	0	0	0	0	*			

Hub Knolls

KNOLLS, OSCAR EDWARD
B. Dec. 18, 1883, Valparaiso, Ind.   D. July 1, 1946, Chicago, Ill.   TR

	W	L	PCT	ERA	G	GS	CG	IP	H	BB	SO	ShO	W	L	SV	AB	H	HR	BA
1906 BKN N	0	0	—	4.05	2	0	0	6.2	13	2	3	0	0	0	0	1	1	0	1.000

Jack Knott

KNOTT, JOHN HENRY
B. Mar. 2, 1907, Dallas, Tex.   D. Oct. 13, 1981, Brownwood, Tex.   BR TR 6'2½" 200 lbs.

	W	L	PCT	ERA	G	GS	CG	IP	H	BB	SO	ShO	W	L	SV	AB	H	HR	BA
1933 STL A	1	8	.111	5.01	20	9	0	82.2	88	33	19	0	0	2	0	23	7	0	.304
1934	10	3	.769	4.96	45	10	2	138	149	67	56	0	7	0	4	30	4	0	.133
1935	11	8	.579	4.60	48	19	7	187.2	219	78	45	2	5	4	7	61	7	0	.115
1936	9	17	.346	7.29	47	23	9	192.2	272	93	60	0	3	3	6	57	4	0	.070
1937	8	18	.308	4.89	38	22	8	191.1	220	91	74	0	2	5	2	57	8	0	.140
1938 2 teams	STL	A	(7G 1–2)		CHI	A	(20G 5–10)												
" total	6	12	.333	4.19	27	22	9	161	170	69	43	0	0	1	0	50	6	0	.120
1939 CHI A	11	6	.647	4.15	25	23	8	149.2	157	41	56	0	0	0	0	53	8	0	.151
1940	11	9	.550	4.56	25	23	4	158	166	52	44	2	0	0	0	57	5	0	.088
1941 PHI A	13	11	.542	4.40	27	26	11	194.1	212	81	54	0	0	0	0	65	5	0	.077
1942	2	10	.167	5.57	20	14	4	95.1	127	36	31	0	1	0	0	29	4	0	.138
1946	0	1	.000	5.68	3	0	0	6.1	7	1	2	0	0	1	0	0	0	0	—
11 yrs.	82	103	.443	4.97	325	192	62	1557	1787	642	484	4	18	16	19	482	58	0	.120

Ed Knouff

KNOUFF, EDWARD (Fred)
B. 1867, Philadelphia, Pa.   D. Sept. 14, 1900, Philadelphia, Pa.   BR TR   210 lbs.

	W	L	PCT	ERA	G	GS	CG	IP	H	BB	SO	ShO	W	L	SV	AB	H	HR	BA
1885 PHI AA	7	6	.538	3.65	14	13	12	106	103	44	43	0	0	0	0	48	9	0	.188
1886 BAL AA	0	1	.000	2.00	1	1	1	9	2	5	8	0	0	0	0	3	0	0	.000
1887 2 teams	BAL	AA	(9G 2–6)		STL	AA	(6G 4–2)												
" total	6	8	.429	6.21	15	12	12	113	119	77	45	1	0	0	0	87	19	0	.218
1888 2 teams	STL	AA	(9G 5–4)		CLE	AA	(2G 0–1)												
" total	5	5	.500	2.50	11	11	10	90	74	40	27	0	0	0	0	37	4	0	.108
1889 PHI AA	2	0	1.000	3.96	3	3	2	25	37	9	5	0	0	0	0	12	3	0	.250
5 yrs.	20	20	.500	4.17	44	43	37	343	335	175	128	1	0	0	0	187	35	0	.187

Darold Knowles

KNOWLES, DAROLD DUANE
B. Dec. 9, 1941, Brunswick, Mo.   BL TL 6'   180 lbs.

	W	L	PCT	ERA	G	GS	CG	IP	H	BB	SO	ShO	W	L	SV	AB	H	HR	BA
1965 BAL A	0	1	.000	9.20	5	1	0	14.2	14	10	12	0	0	0	0	4	0	0	.000
1966 PHI N	6	5	.545	3.05	69	0	0	100.1	98	46	88	0	6	5	13	16	4	0	.250
1967 WAS A	6	8	.429	2.70	61	1	0	113.1	91	52	85	0	6	7	14	16	1	0	.063
1968	1	1	.500	2.18	32	0	0	41.1	38	12	37	0	1	1	4	13	1	0	.250
1969	9	2	.818	2.24	53	0	0	84.1	73	31	59	0	9	2	13	13	1	0	.077
1970	2	14	.125	2.04	71	0	0	119	100	58	71	0	2	14	27	20	1	0	.050
1971 2 teams	WAS	A	(12G 2–2)		OAK	A	(43G 5–2)												
" total	7	4	.636	3.57	55	0	0	68	57	22	56	0	7	4	9	10	1	0	.100
1972 OAK A	5	1	.833	1.36	54	0	0	66	49	37	36	0	5	1	11	12	3	0	.250
1973	6	8	.429	3.09	52	5	1	99	87	49	46	1	4	5	9	0	0	0	—
1974	3	3	.500	4.25	45	1	0	53	61	35	18	0	2	3	3	0	0	0	—
1975 CHI N	6	9	.400	5.83	58	0	0	88	107	36	63	0	6	9	15	15	1	0	.067
1976	5	7	.417	2.88	58	0	0	72	61	22	39	0	5	7	9	7	1	0	.143

	W	L	PCT	ERA	G	GS	CG	IP	H	BB	SO	ShO	Relief Pitching W	L	SV	BATTING AB	H	HR	BA

Darold Knowles continued

		W	L	PCT	ERA	G	GS	CG	IP	H	BB	SO	ShO	W	L	SV	AB	H	HR	BA
1977	TEX A	5	2	.714	3.24	42	0	0	50	50	23	14	0	5	2	4	0	0	0	—
1978	MON N	3	3	.500	2.38	60	0	0	72	63	30	34	0	3	3	6	6	1	0	.167
1979	STL N	2	5	.286	4.04	48	0	0	49	54	17	22	0	2	5	6	2	0	0	.000
1980		0	1	.000	9.00	2	0	0	2	3	0	1	0	0	0	0	0	0	0	—
16 yrs.		66	74	.471	3.12	765	8	1	1092	1006	480	681	1	63	69	143	125	15	0	.120

LEAGUE CHAMPIONSHIP SERIES

| 1971 | OAK A | 0 | 0 | — | 0.00 | 1 | 0 | 0 | .1 | 1 | 0 | 0 | 0 | 0 | 0 | 0 | 0 | 0 | 0 | — |

WORLD SERIES

| 1973 | OAK A | 0 | 0 | — | 0.00 | 7 | 0 | 0 | 6.1 | 4 | 5 | 5 | 0 | 0 | 0 | 2 | 0 | 0 | 0 | — |

Tom Knowlson

KNOWLSON, THOMAS HERBERT   BR TR 5'10" 165 lbs.
B. Apr. 23, 1895, Pittsburgh, Pa.   D. Apr. 11, 1943, Miami Shores, Fla.

| 1915 | PHI A | 4 | 6 | .400 | 3.49 | 18 | 9 | 8 | 100.2 | 99 | 60 | 24 | 0 | 1 | 0 | 0 | 36 | 3 | 0 | .083 |

Bill Knowlton

KNOWLTON, WILLIAM YOUNG   BR TR
B. Aug. 18, 1892, Philadelphia, Pa.   D. Feb. 25, 1944, Philadelphia, Pa.

| 1920 | PHI A | 0 | 1 | .000 | 4.76 | 1 | 1 | 0 | 5.2 | 9 | 3 | 5 | 0 | 0 | 0 | 0 | 2 | 0 | 0 | .000 |

Kevin Kobel

KOBEL, KEVIN RICHARD   BR TL 6' 180 lbs.
B. Oct. 2, 1953, Colden, N. Y.

1973	MIL A	0	1	.000	8.64	2	1	0	8.1	9	8	4	0	0	0	0	0	0	0	—
1974		6	14	.300	3.99	34	24	3	169	166	54	74	2	0	1	0	0	0	0	—
1976		0	1	.000	11.25	3	0	0	4	6	3	1	0	0	1	0	0	0	0	—
1978	NY N	5	6	.455	2.92	32	11	1	108	95	30	51	0	0	2	0	25	4	0	.160
1979		6	8	.429	3.50	30	27	1	162	169	46	67	1	0	0	0	46	9	0	.196
1980		1	4	.200	7.13	14	1	0	24	36	11	8	0	1	4	0	2	0	0	.000
6 yrs.		18	34	.346	3.88	115	64	5	475.1	481	152	205	3	1	8	0	73	13	0	.178

Alan Koch

KOCH, ALAN GOODMAN   BR TR 6'4" 195 lbs.
B. Mar. 25, 1938, Decatur, Ala.

1963	DET A	1	1	.500	10.80	7	1	0	10	21	9	5	0	1	1	0	3	2	0	.667
1964	2 teams			.231		DET	A	(3G 0–0)					WAS	A	(32G 3–10)					
"	total	3	10		4.96	35	14	1	118	116	46	68	0	0	3	0	32	8	0	.250
2 yrs.		4	11	.267	5.41	42	15	1	128	137	55	73	0	1	4	0	35	10	0	.286

Dick Koecher

KOECHER, RICHARD FINLAY (Highpockets)   BL TL 6'5" 196 lbs.
B. Mar. 30, 1926, Philadelphia, Pa.

1946	PHI N	0	1	.000	10.13	1	1	0	2.2	7	1	2	0	0	0	0	1	0	0	.000
1947		0	2	.000	4.76	3	2	1	17	20	10	4	0	0	0	0	4	0	0	.000
1948		0	1	.000	3.00	3	0	0	6	4	3	2	0	0	1	0	0	0	0	—
3 yrs.		0	4	.000	4.91	7	3	1	25.2	31	14	8	0	0	1	0	5	0	0	.000

Mark Koenig

KOENIG, MARK ANTHONY   BB TR 6' 180 lbs.
B. July 19, 1902, San Francisco, Calif.   BL 1928

1930	DET A	0	1	.000	10.00	2	1	0	9	11	8	6	0	0	0	0	341	81	1	.238
1931		0	0	—	6.43	3	0	0	7	7	11	3	0	0	0	0	364	92	1	.253
2 yrs.		0	1	—	8.44	5	1	0	16	18	19	9	0	0	0	0	*			

Willis Koenigsmark

KOENIGSMARK, WILLIS THOMAS   BR TR 6'4" 180 lbs.
B. Feb. 27, 1896, Waterloo, Ill.   D. July 1, 1972, Waterloo, Ill.

| 1919 | STL N | 0 | 0 | — | ∞ | 1 | 0 | 0 | | 2 | 1 | 0 | 0 | 0 | 0 | 0 | 0 | 0 | 0 | — |

Elmer Koestner

KOESTNER, ELMER JOSEPH (Bob)   BR TR 6'1½" 175 lbs.
B. Nov. 30, 1885, Piper City, Ill.   D. Oct. 27, 1959, Fairbury, Ill.

1910	CLE A	5	10	.333	3.04	27	13	8	145	145	63	44	1	2	4	2	48	15	0	.313
1914	2 teams					CHI	N	(4G 0–0)					CIN	N	(5G 0–0)					
"	total	0	0	—	4.01	9	1	0	24.2	24	13	12	0	0	0	0	6	2	0	.333
2 yrs.		5	10	.333	3.18	36	14	8	169.2	169	76	56	1	2	4	2	54	17	0	.315

Joe Kohlman

KOHLMAN, JOSEPH JAMES (Blackie)   BR TR 6' 160 lbs.
B. Jan. 28, 1913, Philadelphia, Pa.   D. Mar. 16, 1974, Philadelphia, Pa.

1937	WAS A	1	0	1.000	4.15	2	2	1	13	15	3	3	0	0	0	0	5	1	0	.200
1938		0	0	—	6.28	7	0	0	14.1	12	11	5	0	0	0	0	3	0	0	.000
2 yrs.		1	0	1.000	5.27	9	2	1	27.1	27	14	8	0	0	0	0	8	1	0	.125

Eddie Kolb

KOLB, EDWARD WILLIAM   BR TR
B. July 20, 1880, Cincinnati, Ohio   Deceased.

| 1899 | CLE N | 0 | 1 | .000 | 10.13 | 1 | 1 | 1 | 8 | 18 | 5 | 1 | 0 | 0 | 0 | 0 | 4 | 1 | 0 | .250 |

Ray Kolp

KOLP, RAYMOND CARL (Jockey)   BR TR 5'10½" 187 lbs.
B. Oct. 1, 1894, New Berlin, Ohio   D. July 29, 1967, New Orleans, La.

1921	STL A	8	7	.533	4.97	37	18	5	166.2	208	51	43	1	1	2	0	55	7	0	.127
1922		14	4	.778	3.93	32	18	9	169.2	199	36	54	1	2	1	0	57	17	0	.298
1923		5	12	.294	3.89	34	17	11	171.1	178	54	44	1	0	2	1	54	6	0	.111
1924		5	7	.417	5.68	25	12	5	96.2	131	25	29	1	2	0	0	30	6	0	.200
1927	CIN N	3	3	.500	3.06	24	5	2	82.1	86	29	28	1	1	2	3	30	6	0	.200
1928		13	10	.565	3.19	44	24	12	209	219	55	61	1	3	5	1	70	15	1	.214
1929		8	10	.444	4.03	30	16	4	145.1	151	39	27	1	2	1	0	49	8	0	.163
1930		7	12	.368	4.22	37	19	5	168.1	180	34	40	2	1	2	1	49	12	1	.245
1931		4	9	.308	4.96	30	10	2	107	144	39	24	0	2	1	1	32	4	0	.125
1932		6	10	.375	3.89	32	19	7	159.2	176	27	42	2	0	1	3	49	9	0	.184
1933		6	9	.400	3.53	30	14	4	150.1	168	23	28	1	3	2	3	45	7	0	.156

	W	L	PCT	ERA	G	GS	CG	IP	H	BB	SO	ShO	Relief Pitching W	L	SV	BATTING AB	H	HR	BA

Ray Kolp continued

	W	L	PCT	ERA	G	GS	CG	IP	H	BB	SO	ShO	W	L	SV	AB	H	HR	BA
1934	0	2	.000	4.52	28	2	0	61.2	78	12	19	0	0	0	3	12	1	0	.083
12 yrs.	79	95	.454	4.08	383	174	66	1688	1918	424	439	11	17	14	18	532	98	2	.184

Hal Kolstad

KOLSTAD, HAROLD EVERETTE   BR TR 5'9"   190 lbs.
B. June 1, 1935, Rice Lake, Wis.

	W	L	PCT	ERA	G	GS	CG	IP	H	BB	SO	ShO	W	L	SV	AB	H	HR	BA
1962 BOS A	0	2	.000	5.43	27	2	0	61.1	65	35	36	0	0	2	2	18	1	0	.056
1963	0	2	.000	13.09	7	0	0	11	16	6	6	0	0	2	0	1	0	0	.000
2 yrs.	0	4	.000	6.59	34	2	0	72.1	81	41	42	0	0	4	2	19	1	0	.053

Ed Konetchy

KONETCHY, EDWARD JOSEPH (Big Ed)   BR TR 6'2½"   195 lbs.
Also appeared in box score as Koney
B. Sept. 3, 1885, LaCrosse, Wis.   D. May 27, 1947, Fort Worth, Tex.

	W	L	PCT	ERA	G	GS	CG	IP	H	BB	SO	ShO	W	L	SV	AB	H	HR	BA
1910 STL N	0	0	–	4.50	1	0	0	4	4	1	0	0	0	0	0	520	157	3	.302
1913	1	0	1.000	0.00	1	0	0	4.2	1	4	3	0	1	0	0	502	137	7	.273
1918 BOS N	0	1	.000	6.75	1	1	1	8	14	2	3	0	0	1	0	437	103	2	.236
3 yrs.	1	1	.500	4.32	3	1	1	16.2	19	7	6	0	1	1	0	*			

Doug Konieczny

KONIECZNY, DOUGLAS JAMES   BR TR 6'4"   220 lbs.
B. Sept. 27, 1951, Detroit, Mich.

	W	L	PCT	ERA	G	GS	CG	IP	H	BB	SO	ShO	W	L	SV	AB	H	HR	BA
1973 HOU N	0	1	.000	5.54	2	2	0	13	12	4	6	0	0	0	0	4	0	0	.000
1974	0	3	.000	7.88	6	3	0	16	18	12	8	0	0	0	0	4	0	0	.000
1975	6	13	.316	4.47	32	29	4	171	184	87	89	1	0	0	0	50	8	0	.160
1977	1	1	.500	6.00	4	4	0	21	26	8	7	0	0	0	0	7	1	0	.143
4 yrs.	7	18	.280	4.93	44	38	4	221	240	111	110	1	0	0	0	65	9	0	.138

Alex Konikowski

KONIKOWSKI, ALEXANDER JAMES (Whitey)   BR TR 6'1"   187 lbs.
B. June 8, 1928, Throop, Pa.

	W	L	PCT	ERA	G	GS	CG	IP	H	BB	SO	ShO	W	L	SV	AB	H	HR	BA
1948 NY N	2	3	.400	7.56	22	1	0	33.1	46	17	9	0	2	2	1	2	0	0	.000
1951	0	0	–	0.00	3	0	0	4	2	0	5	0	0	0	0	0	0	0	–
1954	0	0	–	7.50	10	0	0	12	10	12	6	0	0	0	0	1	0	0	.000
3 yrs.	2	3	.400	6.93	35	1	0	49.1	58	29	20	0	2	2	1	3	0	0	.000

WORLD SERIES

	W	L	PCT	ERA	G	GS	CG	IP	H	BB	SO	ShO	W	L	SV	AB	H	HR	BA
1951 NY N	0	0	–	0.00	1	0	0	1	1	0	0	0	0	0	0	0	0	0	–

Jim Konstanty

KONSTANTY, CASIMIR JAMES   BR TR 6'1½"   202 lbs.
B. Mar. 2, 1917, Strykersville, N. Y.   D. June 11, 1976, Oneonta, N. Y.

	W	L	PCT	ERA	G	GS	CG	IP	H	BB	SO	ShO	W	L	SV	AB	H	HR	BA
1944 CIN N	6	4	.600	2.80	20	12	5	112.2	113	33	19	1	2	1	0	34	10	0	.294
1946 BOS N	0	1	.000	5.28	10	1	0	15.1	17	7	9	0	0	0	0	2	0	0	.000
1948 PHI N	1	0	1.000	0.93	6	0	0	9.2	7	2	7	0	1	0	2	3	0	0	.000
1949	9	5	.643	3.25	53	0	0	97	98	29	43	0	9	5	7	17	3	0	.176
1950	16	7	.696	2.66	74	0	0	152	108	50	56	0	16	7	22	37	4	0	.108
1951	4	11	.267	4.05	58	0	0	115.2	127	31	27	0	4	10	9	19	3	0	.158
1952	5	3	.625	3.94	42	2	2	80	87	21	16	1	4	2	6	14	1	0	.071
1953	14	10	.583	4.43	48	19	7	170.2	198	42	45	0	4	3	5	50	11	0	.220
1954 2 teams		PHI	N (33G 2–3)			NY	A (9G 1–1)												
" total	4	4	.429	3.01	42	1	0	68.2	73	18	14	0	3	4	5	16	0	0	.000
1955 NY A	7	2	.778	2.32	45	0	0	73.2	68	24	19	0	7	2	11	8	1	0	.125
1956 2 teams		NY	A (8G 0–0)			STL	N (27G 1–1)												
" total	1	1	.500	4.65	35	0	0	50.1	61	12	13	0	1	1	7	2	0	0	.000
11 yrs.	66	48	.579	3.46	433	36	14	945.2	957	269	268	2	51	35	74	202	33	0	.163

WORLD SERIES

	W	L	PCT	ERA	G	GS	CG	IP	H	BB	SO	ShO	W	L	SV	AB	H	HR	BA
1950 PHI N	0	1	.000	2.40	3	1	0	15	9	4	3	0	0	0	0	4	1	0	.250

Ernie Koob

KOOB, ERNEST GERALD   BL TL 5'10"   160 lbs.
B. Sept. 11, 1893, Keeler, Mich.   D. Nov. 12, 1941, Lemay, Mo.

	W	L	PCT	ERA	G	GS	CG	IP	H	BB	SO	ShO	W	L	SV	AB	H	HR	BA
1915 STL A	4	5	.444	2.36	28	13	6	133.2	119	50	37	0	0	0	0	37	5	0	.135
1916	11	8	.579	2.54	33	20	10	166.2	153	56	26	2	2	1	2	41	0	0	.000
1917	6	14	.300	3.91	39	18	3	133.2	139	57	47	1	1	2	1	35	4	0	.114
1919	2	3	.400	4.64	25	4	0	66	77	23	11	0	2	1	0	15	0	0	.000
4 yrs.	23	30	.434	3.13	125	55	19	500	488	186	121	3	5	4	3	128	9	0	.070

Cal Koonce

KOONCE, CALVIN LEE   BR TR 6'1"   185 lbs.
B. Nov. 18, 1940, Fayetteville, N. C.

	W	L	PCT	ERA	G	GS	CG	IP	H	BB	SO	ShO	W	L	SV	AB	H	HR	BA
1962 CHI N	10	10	.500	3.97	35	30	3	190.2	200	86	84	1	0	0	0	64	6	0	.094
1963	2	6	.250	4.58	21	13	0	72.2	75	32	44	0	0	0	0	19	2	0	.105
1964	3	0	1.000	2.03	6	2	0	31	30	7	17	0	1	0	0	10	0	0	.000
1965	7	9	.438	3.69	38	23	3	173	181	52	88	1	0	0	0	49	5	0	.102
1966	5	5	.500	3.81	45	5	0	108.2	113	35	65	0	4	4	2	23	3	0	.130
1967 2 teams		CHI	N (34G 2–2)			NY	N (11G 3–3)												
" total	5	5	.500	3.75	45	2	0	96	97	28	52	1	2	2	2	20	2	0	.100
1968 NY N	6	4	.600	2.42	55	2	0	96.2	80	32	50	0	5	4	11	14	0	0	.000
1969	6	3	.667	4.99	40	0	0	83	85	42	48	0	6	3	7	17	4	0	.235
1970 2 teams		NY	N (13G 0–2)			BOS	A (23G 3–4)												
" total	3	6	.333	3.49	36	8	1	98	89	43	47	0	0	2	2	22	2	0	.091
1971 BOS A	0	1	.000	5.57	13	1	0	21	22	11	9	0	0	0	0	1	0	0	.000
10 yrs.	47	49	.490	3.78	334	90	9	970.2	972	368	504	3	18	15	24	239	24	0	.100

Jerry Koosman

KOOSMAN, JEROME MARTIN   BR TL 6'2"   205 lbs.
B. Dec. 23, 1943, Appleton, Minn.

	W	L	PCT	ERA	G	GS	CG	IP	H	BB	SO	ShO	W	L	SV	AB	H	HR	BA
1967 NY N	0	2	.000	6.04	9	3	0	22.1	22	19	11	0	0	0	0	2	0	0	.000
1968	19	12	.613	2.08	35	34	17	263.2	221	69	178	7	0	0	0	91	7	1	.077
1969	17	9	.654	2.28	32	32	16	241	187	68	180	6	0	0	0	84	4	0	.048
1970	12	7	.632	3.14	30	29	5	212	189	71	118	1	0	0	0	50	8	0	.160
1971	6	11	.353	3.04	26	24	4	166	160	51	96	0	0	0	0	47	4	0	.085
1972	11	12	.478	4.14	34	24	4	163	155	52	147	1	0	0	0	47	4	0	.085

	W	L	PCT	ERA	G	GS	CG	IP	H	BB	SO	ShO	Relief Pitching W	L	SV	BATTING AB	H	HR	BA

Jerry Koosman continued

	W	L	PCT	ERA	G	GS	CG	IP	H	BB	SO	ShO	W	L	SV	AB	H	HR	BA
1973	14	15	.483	2.84	35	35	12	263	234	76	156	3	0	0	0	78	8	0	.103
1974	15	11	.577	3.36	35	35	13	265	258	85	188	0	0	0	0	86	16	0	.186
1975	14	13	.519	3.41	36	34	11	240	234	98	173	4	0	0	0	78	14	0	.179
1976	21	10	.677	2.70	34	32	17	247	205	66	200	3	0	0	2	79	17	0	.215
1977	8	20	.286	3.49	32	32	6	227	195	81	192	1	0	0	0	72	8	1	.111
1978	3	15	.167	3.75	38	32	3	235	221	84	160	0	0	0	2	70	6	0	.086
1979 MIN A	20	13	.606	3.38	37	36	10	264	268	83	157	2	0	0	0	0	0	0	
1980	16	13	.552	4.04	38	34	8	243	252	69	149	0.	1	1	2	0	0	0	
1981 2 teams		MIN	A	(19G	3–9)		CHI	A	(8G	1–4)									
" total	4	13	.235	4.02	27	16	3	121	125	41	76	1	0	2	5	0	0	0	
1982 CHI A	11	7	.611	3.84	42	19	3	173.1	194	38	88	1	2	3	3	0	0	0	
1983	11	7	.611	4.77	37	24	2	169.2	176	53	90	1	1	0	2	0	0	0	
1984 PHI N	14	15	.483	3.25	36	34	3	224	232	60	137	1	0	0	0	74	8	0	.108
18 yrs.	216	205	.513	3.33	593	509	137	3740	3528	1164	2496	32	7	6	17	881	106	2	.120

LEAGUE CHAMPIONSHIP SERIES

	W	L	PCT	ERA	G	GS	CG	IP	H	BB	SO	ShO	W	L	SV	AB	H	HR	BA
1969 NY N	0	0	–	11.57	1	1	0	4.2	7	4	5	0	0	0	0	2	0	0	.000
1973	1	0	1.000	2.00	1	1	1	9	8	0	9	0	0	0	0	4	2	0	.500
1983 CHI A	0	0	–	54.00	1	0	0	.1	1	2	0	0	0	0	0	0	0	0	
3 yrs.	1	0	1.000	6.43	3	2	1	14	16	6	14	0	0	0	0	6	2	0	.333

WORLD SERIES

	W	L	PCT	ERA	G	GS	CG	IP	H	BB	SO	ShO	W	L	SV	AB	H	HR	BA
1969 NY N	2	0	1.000	2.04	2	2	1	17.2	7	4	9	0	0	0	0	7	1	0	.143
1973	1	0	1.000	3.12	2	2	0	8.2	9	7	8	0	0	0	0	4	0	0	.000
2 yrs.	3	0	1.000	2.39	4	4	1	26.1	16	11	17	0	0	0	0	11	1	0	.091
		1st																	

Howie Koplitz

KOPLITZ, HOWARD DEAN
B. May 4, 1938, Oshkosh, Wis.   BR TR 5'10½" 190 lbs.

	W	L	PCT	ERA	G	GS	CG	IP	H	BB	SO	ShO	W	L	SV	AB	H	HR	BA
1961 DET A	2	0	1.000	2.25	4	1	1	12	16	8	9	0	1	0	0	4	0	0	.000
1962	3	0	1.000	5.26	10	6	1	37.2	54	10	10	0	0	0	0	13	3	0	.231
1964 WAS A	0	0	–	4.76	6	1	0	17	20	13	9	0	0	0	0	4	0	0	.000
1965	4	7	.364	4.05	33	11	0	106.2	97	48	59	0	2	2	1	30	3	0	.100
1966	0	0	–	0.00	1	0	0	2	0	1	0	0	0	0	0	0	0	0	
5 yrs.	9	7	.563	4.21	54	19	2	175.1	187	80	87	0	3	2	1	51	6	0	.118

George Korince

KORINCE, GEORGE EUGENE (Moose)
B. Jan. 10, 1946, Ottawa, Ont., Canada   BR TR 6'3" 210 lbs.

	W	L	PCT	ERA	G	GS	CG	IP	H	BB	SO	ShO	W	L	SV	AB	H	HR	BA
1966 DET A	0	0	–	0.00	2	0	0	3	1	3	2	0	0	0	0	0	0	0	
1967	1	0	1.000	5.14	9	0	0	14	10	11	11	0	1	0	0	1	0	0	.000
2 yrs.	1	0	1.000	4.24	11	0	0	17	11	14	13	0	1	0	0	1	0	0	.000

Jim Korwan

KORWAN, JAMES
B. Mar. 4, 1874, Brooklyn, N. Y.   D. Aug., 1899, Brooklyn, N. Y.

	W	L	PCT	ERA	G	GS	CG	IP	H	BB	SO	ShO	W	L	SV	AB	H	HR	BA
1894 BKN N	0	0	–	14.40	1	0	0	5	9	5	2	0	0	0	0	2	0	0	.000
1897 CHI N	1	2	.333	5.82	5	4	3	34	47	28	12	0	0	0	0	12	0	0	.000
2 yrs.	1	2	.333	6.92	6	4	3	39	56	33	14	0	0	0	0	14	0	0	.000

Bill Koski

KOSKI, WILLIAM JOHN (T-Bone)
B. Feb. 6, 1932, Madera, Calif.   BR TR 6'4" 185 lbs.

	W	L	PCT	ERA	G	GS	CG	IP	H	BB	SO	ShO	W	L	SV	AB	H	HR	BA
1951 PIT N	0	1	.000	6.67	13	1	0	27	26	28	6	0	0	0	0	4	0	0	.000

Dave Koslo

KOSLO, GEORGE BERNARD
Born George Bernard Koslowski.
B. Mar. 31, 1920, Menasha, Wis.   D. Dec. 1, 1975, Menasha, Wis.   BL TL 5'11" 180 lbs.

	W	L	PCT	ERA	G	GS	CG	IP	H	BB	SO	ShO	W	L	SV	AB	H	HR	BA
1941 NY N	1	2	.333	1.90	4	3	2	23.2	17	10	12	0	0	0	0	9	1	0	.111
1942	3	6	.333	5.08	19	11	3	78	79	32	42	1	0	0	0	25	3	0	.120
1946	14	19	.424	3.63	40	35	17	265.1	251	101	121	3	0	1	1	88	11	0	.125
1947	15	10	.600	4.39	39	31	10	217.1	223	82	86	3	2	1	0	78	10	0	.128
1948	8	10	.444	3.87	35	18	5	149	168	62	58	3	2	2	3	44	5	0	.114
1949	11	14	.440	2.50	38	23	15	212	193	43	64	1	1	1	4	69	10	2	.145
1950	13	15	.464	3.91	40	22	7	186.2	190	68	56	2	5	3	3	65	8	1	.123
1951	10	9	.526	3.31	39	16	5	149.2	153	45	54	2	5	0	3	50	5	0	.100
1952	10	7	.588	3.19	41	17	8	166.1	154	47	67	2	2	1	5	54	2	0	.037
1953	6	12	.333	4.76	37	12	2	111.2	135	36	36	0	3	4	2	30	1	0	.033
1954 2 teams		BAL	A	(3G	0–1)		MIL	N	(12G	1–1)									
" total	1	2	.333	3.13	15	1	0	31.2	33	12	10	0	1	1	1	4	0	0	.000
1955 MIL N	0	1	.000	∞	1	0	0		1	0	0	0	0	1	0	0	0	0	–
12 yrs.	92	107	.462	3.68	348	189	74	1591.1	1597	538	606	16	21	15	22	516	56	3	.109

WORLD SERIES

	W	L	PCT	ERA	G	GS	CG	IP	H	BB	SO	ShO	W	L	SV	AB	H	HR	BA
1951 NY N	1	1	.500	3.00	2	2	1	15	12	7	6	0	0	0	0	5	0	0	.000

Joe Kostal

KOSTAL, JOSEPH
B. Mar. 17, 1876, Guelph, Ont., Canada   D. Oct. 10, 1933, Guelph, Ont., Canada   BR TR 5'6" 130 lbs.

	W	L	PCT	ERA	G	GS	CG	IP	H	BB	SO	ShO	W	L	SV	AB	H	HR	BA
1896 LOU N	0	0	–	0.00	2	0	0	4	0	0	0	0	0	0	0	0	0	0	–

Sandy Koufax

KOUFAX, SANFORD
B. Dec. 30, 1935, Brooklyn, N. Y.   BR TL 6'2" 210 lbs.
Hall of Fame 1971.

	W	L	PCT	ERA	G	GS	CG	IP	H	BB	SO	ShO	W	L	SV	AB	H	HR	BA
1955 BKN N	2	2	.500	3.02	12	5	2	41.2	33	28	30	2	0	1	0	12	0	0	.000
1956	2	4	.333	4.91	16	10	0	58.2	66	29	30	0	0	0	0	17	2	0	.118
1957	5	4	.556	3.88	34	13	2	104.1	83	51	122	0	1	0	0	26	0	0	.000
1958 LA N	11	11	.500	4.48	40	26	5	158.2	132	105	131	0	3	1	1	49	6	0	.122
1959	8	6	.571	4.05	35	23	6	153.1	136	92	173	1	0	0	2	54	6	0	.111
1960	8	13	.381	3.91	37	26	7	175	133	100	197	2	1	0	1	57	7	0	.123
1961	18	13	.581	3.52	42	35	15	255.2	212	96	269	2	1	0	1	77	5	0	.065

	W	L	PCT	ERA	G	GS	CG	IP	H	BB	SO	ShO	Relief Pitching W	L	SV	BATTING AB	H	HR	BA

Sandy Koufax continued

	W	L	PCT	ERA	G	GS	CG	IP	H	BB	SO	ShO	W	L	SV	AB	H	HR	BA
1962	14	7	.667	2.54	28	26	11	184.1	134	57	216	2	0	0	1	69	6	1	.087
1963	25	5	.833	1.88	40	40	20	311	214	58	306	11	0	0	0	110	7	1	.064
1964	19	5	.792	1.74	29	28	15	223	154	53	223	7	0	0	1	74	7	0	.095
1965	26	8	.765	2.04	43	41	27	335.2	216	71	382	8	0	0	2	113	20	0	.177
1966	27	9	.750	1.73	41	41	27	323	241	77	317	5	0	0	0	118	9	0	.076
12 yrs.	165	87	.655	2.76	397	314	137	2324.1	1754	817	2396	40	6	2	9	776	75	2	.097

WORLD SERIES																			
1959 LA N	0	1	.000	1.00	2	1	0	9	5	1	7	0	0	0	0	2	0	0	.000
1963	2	0	1.000	1.50	2	2	2	18	12	3	23	0	0	0	0	6	0	0	.000
1965	2	1	.667	0.38	3	3	2	24	13	5	29	2	0	0	0	9	1	0	.111
1966	0	1	.000	1.50	1	1	0	6	6	2	2	0	0	0	0	2	0	0	.000
4 yrs.	4	3	.571	0.95 5th	8	7	4	57	36	11	61 4th	2 4th	0	0	0	19	1	0	.053

Joe Koukalik

KOUKALIK, JOSEPH   BR TR 5'8" 160 lbs.
B. Mar. 3, 1880, Chicago, Ill.   D. Dec. 27, 1945, Chicago, Ill.

	W	L	PCT	ERA	G	GS	CG	IP	H	BB	SO	ShO	W	L	SV	AB	H	HR	BA
1904 BKN N	0	1	.000	1.13	1	1	1	8	10	4	1	0	0	0	0	3	0	0	.000

Lou Koupal

KOUPAL, LOUIS LADDIE   BR TR 5'11" 175 lbs.
B. Dec. 19, 1898, Tabor, S. D.   D. Dec. 8, 1961, San Gabriel, Calif.

	W	L	PCT	ERA	G	GS	CG	IP	H	BB	SO	ShO	W	L	SV	AB	H	HR	BA
1925 PIT N	0	0	–	9.00	6	0	0	9	14	7	0	0	0	0	0	3	0	0	.000
1926	0	2	.000	3.20	6	2	1	19.2	22	8	7	0	0	0	0	4	1	0	.250
1928 BKN N	1	0	1.000	2.41	17	1	1	37.1	43	15	10	0	0	0	1	9	1	0	.111
1929 2 teams			BKN	N (18G 0–1)			PHI	N (15G 5–5)											
" total	5	6	.455	4.96	33	14	3	127	155	54	35	0	0	6	6	46	5	0	.109
1930 PHI N	0	4	.000	8.59	13	4	1	36.2	52	17	11	0	0	1	0	12	1	0	.083
1937 STL A	4	9	.308	6.56	26	13	6	105.2	150	55	24	0	0	0	0	32	3	0	.094
6 yrs.	10	21	.323	5.58	101	34	12	335.1	436	156	87	0	0	1	7	104	11	0	.106

Fabian Kowalik

KOWALIK, FABIAN LORENZ   BR TR 5'11" 185 lbs.
B. Apr. 22, 1908, Falls City, Tex.   BL 1932, BB 1935
D. Aug. 14, 1954, Karnes City, Tex.

	W	L	PCT	ERA	G	GS	CG	IP	H	BB	SO	ShO	W	L	SV	AB	H	HR	BA
1932 CHI A	0	1	.000	6.97	2	1	0	10.1	16	4	2	0	0	0	0	13	5	0	.385
1935 CHI N	2	2	.500	4.42	20	2	1	55	60	19	20	0	2	0	1	15	3	0	.200
1936 3 teams			CHI	N (6G 0–2)			PHI	N (22G 1–5)				BOS	N (1G 0–1)						
" total	1	8	.111	5.82	29	9	3	102	142	40	20	0	0	2	1	67	15	0	.224
3 yrs.	3	11	.214	5.43	51	12	4	167.1	218	63	42	0	2	2	2	95	23	0	.242

WORLD SERIES																			
1935 CHI N	0	0	–	2.08	1	0	0	4.1	3	1	1	0	0	0	0	2	1	0	.500

Joe Krakauskas

KRAKAUSKAS, JOSEPH VICTOR LAWRENCE   BL TL 6'1" 203 lbs.
B. Mar. 28, 1915, Montreal, Que., Canada   D. July 8, 1960, Hamilton, Ont., Canada

	W	L	PCT	ERA	G	GS	CG	IP	H	BB	SO	ShO	W	L	SV	AB	H	HR	BA
1937 WAS A	4	1	.800	2.70	5	4	3	40	33	22	18	0	1	0	0	16	2	0	.125
1938	7	5	.583	3.12	29	10	5	121.1	99	88	104	1	2	1	0	33	6	0	.182
1939	11	17	.393	4.60	39	29	12	217.1	230	114	110	0	0	3	1	77	16	0	.208
1940	1	6	.143	6.44	32	10	2	109	137	73	68	0	0	2	2	32	8	0	.250
1941 CLE A	1	2	.333	4.10	12	5	0	41.2	39	29	25	0	0	1	0	13	1	0	.077
1942	0	0	–	3.86	3	0	0	7	7	4	2	0	0	0	0	2	0	0	.000
1946	2	5	.286	5.51	29	5	0	47.1	60	25	20	0	2	2	1	10	0	0	.000
7 yrs.	26	36	.419	4.53	149	63	22	583.2	605	355	347	1	5	9	4	183	33	0	.180

Jack Kralick

KRALICK, JOHN FRANCIS   BL TL 6'2" 180 lbs.
B. June 1, 1935, Youngstown, Ohio

	W	L	PCT	ERA	G	GS	CG	IP	H	BB	SO	ShO	W	L	SV	AB	H	HR	BA
1959 WAS A	0	0	–	6.57	6	0	0	12.1	13	6	7	0	0	0	0	2	0	0	.000
1960	8	6	.571	3.04	35	18	7	151	139	45	71	0	2	0	1	41	5	0	.122
1961 MIN A	13	11	.542	3.61	33	33	11	242	257	64	137	2	0	0	0	86	13	1	.151
1962	12	11	.522	3.86	39	37	7	242.2	239	61	139	1	0	0	0	89	18	2	.202
1963 2 teams			MIN	A (5G 1–4)			CLE	A (28G 13–9)											
" total	14	13	.519	3.03	33	32	11	223	215	49	129	4	0	0	0	66	12	1	.182
1964 CLE A	12	7	.632	3.21	30	29	8	190.2	196	51	119	3	0	0	0	64	10	0	.156
1965	5	11	.313	4.92	30	16	1	86	106	21	34	0	2	0	0	21	3	0	.143
1966	3	4	.429	3.82	27	4	0	68.1	69	20	31	0	3	1	0	13	1	0	.077
1967	0	2	.000	9.00	2	0	0	2	4	1	1	0	0	2	0				
9 yrs.	67	65	.508	3.56	235	169	45	1218	1238	318	668	12	7	5	1	382	62	4	.162

Steve Kraly

KRALY, STEVE CHARLES (Lefty)   BL TL 5'10" 152 lbs.
B. Apr. 18, 1929, Whiting, Ind.

	W	L	PCT	ERA	G	GS	CG	IP	H	BB	SO	ShO	W	L	SV	AB	H	HR	BA
1953 NY A	0	2	.000	3.24	5	3	0	25	19	16	8	0	0	0	1	7	0	0	.000

Jack Kramer

KRAMER, JOHN HENRY   BR TR 6'2" 190 lbs.
B. Jan. 5, 1918, New Orleans, La.

	W	L	PCT	ERA	G	GS	CG	IP	H	BB	SO	ShO	W	L	SV	AB	H	HR	BA
1939 STL A	9	16	.360	5.83	40	31	10	211.2	269	127	68	2	0	2	0	66	9	1	.136
1940	3	7	.300	6.26	16	9	1	64.2	86	26	12	0	1	2	0	20	1	0	.050
1941	4	3	.571	5.16	29	3	0	59.1	69	40	20	0	4	1	2	8	0	0	.000
1943	0	0	–	8.00	3	0	0	9	11	8	4	0	0	0	0	2	1	0	.500
1944	17	13	.567	2.49	33	31	18	257	233	75	124	1	1	0	0	85	14	2	.165
1945	10	15	.400	3.36	29	25	15	193	190	73	99	3	1	0	2	61	9	0	.148
1946	13	11	.542	3.19	31	28	13	194.2	190	68	69	3	0	0	0	59	8	0	.136
1947	11	16	.407	4.97	33	28	9	199.1	206	89	77	1	1	1	1	62	7	0	.113
1948 BOS A	18	5	.783	4.35	29	29	14	205	233	64	72	2	0	0	0	73	11	1	.151
1949	6	8	.429	5.16	21	18	7	111.2	126	49	24	2	1	1	1	35	9	0	.257
1950 NY N	3	6	.333	3.53	35	9	1	86.2	91	39	27	0	2	1	1	20	2	1	.100
1951 2 teams			NY	N (4G 0–0)			NY	A (19G 1–3)											
" total	1	3	.250	5.76	23	3	0	45.1	57	24	17	0	1	3	0	10	1	0	.100
12 yrs.	95	103	.480	4.24	322	215	88	1637.1	1761	682	613	14	12	11	7	501	72	5	.144

	W	L	PCT	ERA	G	GS	CG	IP	H	BB	SO	ShO	Relief Pitching W	L	SV	AB	H	HR	BA

Jack Kramer continued

WORLD SERIES

	W	L	PCT	ERA	G	GS	CG	IP	H	BB	SO	ShO	W	L	SV	AB	H	HR	BA
1944 STL A	1	0	1.000	0.00	2	1	1	11	9	4	12	0	0	0	0	4	0	0	.000

Gene Krapp

KRAPP, EUGENE HAMLET (Rubber) BR TR 5'7"
B. May 12, 1888, Rochester, N. Y.   D. Apr. 13, 1923, Detroit, Mich.

	W	L	PCT	ERA	G	GS	CG	IP	H	BB	SO	ShO	W	L	SV	AB	H	HR	BA
1911 CLE A	13	9	.591	3.44	34	26	14	214.2	182	136	130	1	2	0	1	74	17	0	.230
1912	2	5	.286	4.60	9	7	4	58.2	57	42	22	0	0	0	0	22	7	0	.318
1914 BUF F	14	14	.500	2.49	36	29	18	252.2	198	115	106	1	1	1	0	77	11	0	.143
1915	9	19	.321	3.51	38	30	14	231	188	123	93	1	1	0	0	70	9	0	.129
4 yrs.	38	47	.447	3.23	117	92	50	757	625	416	351	3	4	1	1	243	44	0	.181

Tex Kraus

KRAUS, JOHN WILLIAM (Texas Jack) BR TL 6'4"   190 lbs.
B. Apr. 26, 1918, San Antonio, Tex.   D. Jan. 2, 1976, San Antonio, Tex.

	W	L	PCT	ERA	G	GS	CG	IP	H	BB	SO	ShO	W	L	SV	AB	H	HR	BA
1943 PHI N	9	15	.375	3.16	34	25	10	199.2	197	78	48	1	0	0	2	60	4	0	.067
1945	4	9	.308	5.40	19	13	0	81.2	96	40	28	0	1	0	0	25	3	0	.120
1946 NY N	2	1	.667	6.12	17	1	0	25	25	15	7	0	2	1	0	3	0	0	.000
3 yrs.	15	25	.375	4.00	70	39	10	306.1	318	133	83	1	3	2	2	88	7	0	.080

Harry Krause

KRAUSE, HARRY WILLIAM (Hal) BR TL
B. July 12, 1887, San Francisco, Calif.   D. Oct. 23, 1940, San Francisco, Calif.

	W	L	PCT	ERA	G	GS	CG	IP	H	BB	SO	ShO	W	L	SV	AB	H	HR	BA
1908 PHI A	1	1	.500	2.57	4	2	2	21	20	4	10	0	0	0	0	7	0	0	.000
1909	18	8	.692	1.39	32	21	16	213	151	49	139	7	4	2	0	77	12	0	.156
1910	6	6	.500	2.88	16	11	9	112.1	99	42	60	2	0	1	0	38	8	0	.211
1911	12	8	.600	3.04	27	19	12	169	155	47	85	1	2	1	2	59	15	0	.254
1912 2 teams			PHI A	(4G 0-2)				CLE A	(2G 0-1)										
" total	0	3	.000	12.60	6	4	0	10	21	4	4	0	0	0	0	4	1	0	.250
5 yrs.	37	26	.587	2.50	85	57	39	525.1	446	146	298	10	6	4	2	185	36	0	.195

Lew Krausse

KRAUSSE, LEWIS BERNARD, SR. BR TR 6'½"   167 lbs.
Father of Lew Krausse.
B. June 8, 1912, Media, Pa.

	W	L	PCT	ERA	G	GS	CG	IP	H	BB	SO	ShO	W	L	SV	AB	H	HR	BA
1931 PHI A	1	0	1.000	3.97	3	1	1	11.1	6	6	1	0	0	0	0	2	0	0	.000
1932	4	1	.800	4.58	20	3	2	57	64	24	16	1	2	1	0	15	2	0	.133
2 yrs.	5	1	.833	4.48	23	4	3	68.1	70	30	17	1	2	1	0	17	2	0	.118

Lew Krausse

KRAUSSE, LEWIS BERNARD, JR. BR TR 6'   175 lbs.
Son of Lew Krausse.
B. Apr. 25, 1943, Media, Pa.

	W	L	PCT	ERA	G	GS	CG	IP	H	BB	SO	ShO	W	L	SV	AB	H	HR	BA
1961 KC A	2	5	.286	4.85	12	8	2	55.2	49	46	32	1	0	0	0	17	2	0	.118
1964	0	2	.000	7.36	5	4	0	14.2	22	9	9	0	0	0	0	2	0	0	.000
1965	2	4	.333	5.04	7	5	0	25	29	8	22	0	0	1	0	7	0	0	.000
1966	14	9	.609	2.99	36	22	4	177.2	144	63	87	1	1	3	3	52	8	0	.154
1967	7	17	.292	4.28	48	19	0	160	140	67	96	0	3	3	6	41	6	1	.146
1968 OAK A	10	11	.476	3.11	36	25	8	185	147	62	105	0	2	1	4	56	9	0	.161
1969	7	7	.500	4.44	43	16	4	140	134	48	85	2	1	3	7	48	8	4	.167
1970 MIL A	13	18	.419	4.75	37	35	8	216	235	67	130	1	0	0	0	65	9	0	.138
1971	8	12	.400	2.95	43	22	1	180	164	62	92	0	1	2	0	44	1	0	.023
1972 BOS A	1	3	.250	6.34	24	7	0	61	74	28	35	0	0	1	1	16	2	0	.125
1973 STL N	0	0	–	0.00	1	0	0	2	2	1	1	0	0	0	0	0	0	0	–
1974 ATL N	4	3	.571	4.16	29	4	0	67	65	32	27	0	3	1	0	6	2	1	.333
12 yrs.	68	91	.428	4.00	321	167	21	1284	1205	493	721	5	11	14	21	354	47	6	.133

Ken Kravec

KRAVEC, KENNETH PETER BL TL 6'2"   185 lbs.
B. July 29, 1951, Cleveland, Ohio

	W	L	PCT	ERA	G	GS	CG	IP	H	BB	SO	ShO	W	L	SV	AB	H	HR	BA
1975 CHI A	0	1	.000	6.23	2	1	0	4.1	1	8	1	0	0	0	0	0	0	0	–
1976	1	5	.167	4.86	9	8	1	50	49	32	38	0	0	0	0	0	0	0	–
1977	11	8	.579	4.10	26	25	6	167	161	57	125	1	0	0	0	0	0	0	–
1978	11	16	.407	4.08	30	30	7	203	188	95	154	2	0	0	0	0	0	0	–
1979	15	13	.536	3.74	36	35	10	250	208	111	132	3	0	0	1	0	0	0	–
1980	3	6	.333	6.91	20	15	0	82	100	44	37	0	0	0	0	0	0	0	–
1981 CHI N	1	6	.143	5.08	24	12	0	78	80	39	50	0	0	1	0	15	0	0	.000
1982	1	1	.500	6.12	13	2	0	25	27	18	20	0	1	1	2	3	0	0	.000
8 yrs.	43	56	.434	4.46	160	128	24	859.1	814	404	557	6	1	2	1	18	0	0	.000

Ray Krawczyk

KRAWCZYK, RAYMOND ALLEN BR TR 6'2"   190 lbs.
B. Oct. 9, 1959, Pittsburgh, Pa.

	W	L	PCT	ERA	G	GS	CG	IP	H	BB	SO	ShO	W	L	SV	AB	H	HR	BA
1984 PIT N	0	0	–	3.38	4	0	0	5.1	7	4	3	0	0	0	0	0	0	0	–

Ray Kremer

KREMER, REMY PETER (Wiz) BR TR 6'1"   190 lbs.
B. Mar. 23, 1893, Oakland, Calif.   D. Feb. 8, 1965, Pinole, Calif.

	W	L	PCT	ERA	G	GS	CG	IP	H	BB	SO	ShO	W	L	SV	AB	H	HR	BA
1924 PIT N	18	10	.643	3.19	41	30	17	259.1	262	51	64	4	3	1	3	86	13	0	.151
1925	17	8	.680	3.69	40	27	14	214.2	232	47	62	0	3	2	2	71	14	0	.197
1926	20	6	.769	2.61	37	26	18	231.1	221	51	74	3	2	0	5	83	21	1	.253
1927	19	8	.704	2.47	35	28	18	226	205	53	63	3	2	2	2	83	14	2	.169
1928	15	13	.536	4.64	34	31	17	219	253	68	61	1	0	0	0	78	14	0	.179
1929	18	10	.643	4.26	34	27	14	221.2	226	60	66	0	3	0	0	86	11	1	.128
1930	20	12	.625	5.02	39	38	18	276	366	63	58	1	0	0	0	102	16	1	.157
1931	11	15	.423	3.33	30	30	15	230	246	65	58	1	0	0	0	75	17	0	.227
1932	4	3	.571	4.29	11	10	3	56.2	61	16	6	1	0	0	0	19	2	0	.105
1933	1	0	1.000	10.35	7	0	0	20	36	9	4	0	1	0	0	4	0	0	.000
10 yrs.	143	85	.627	3.76	308	247	134	1954.2	2108	483	516	14	14	6	10	687	122	5	.178

WORLD SERIES

	W	L	PCT	ERA	G	GS	CG	IP	H	BB	SO	ShO	W	L	SV	AB	H	HR	BA
1925 PIT N	2	1	.667	3.00	3	2	2	21	17	4	9	0	1	0	0	7	1	0	.143

	W	L	PCT	ERA	G	GS	CG	IP	H	BB	SO	ShO	Relief Pitching W	L	SV	BATTING AB	H	HR	BA

Ray Kremer continued

	W	L	PCT	ERA	G	GS	CG	IP	H	BB	SO	ShO	W	L	SV	AB	H	HR	BA
1927	0	1	.000	3.60	1	1	0	5	5	3	1	0	0	0	0	2	1	0	.500
2 yrs.	2	2	.500	3.12	4	3	2	26	22	7	10	0	1	0	0	9	2	0	.222

Jim Kremmel

KREMMEL, DOUGLAS JAMES
B. Feb. 28, 1949, Columbia, Ill.   BL TL 6'   175 lbs.

	W	L	PCT	ERA	G	GS	CG	IP	H	BB	SO	ShO	W	L	SV	AB	H	HR	BA
1973 TEX A	0	2	.000	9.00	4	2	0	9	15	6	6	0	0	0	0	0	0	0	–
1974 CHI N	0	2	.000	5.23	23	2	0	31	37	18	22	0	0	1	0	3	0	0	.000
2 yrs.	0	4	.000	6.08	27	4	0	40	52	24	28	0	0	1	0	3	0	0	.000

Red Kress

KRESS, RALPH
B. Jan. 2, 1907, Columbia, Calif.   D. Nov. 29, 1962, Los Angeles, Calif.   BR TR 5'11½" 165 lbs.

	W	L	PCT	ERA	G	GS	CG	IP	H	BB	SO	ShO	W	L	SV	AB	H	HR	BA
1935 WAS A	0	0	–	12.71	3	0	0	5.2	8	5	5	0	0	0	0	252	75	2	.298
1946 NY N	0	0	–	12.27	1	0	0	3.2	5	1	1	0	0	0	0	1	0	0	.000
2 yrs.	0	0	–	12.54	4	0	0	9.1	13	6	6	0	0	0	0	*			

Lou Kretlow

KRETLOW, LOUIS HENRY
B. June 27, 1923, Apache, Okla.   BR TR 6'2"   185 lbs.

	W	L	PCT	ERA	G	GS	CG	IP	H	BB	SO	ShO	W	L	SV	AB	H	HR	BA
1946 DET A	1	0	1.000	3.00	1	1	1	9	7	2	4	0	0	0	0	4	2	0	.500
1948	2	1	.667	4.63	5	2	1	23.1	21	11	9	0	1	0	0	8	4	0	.500
1949	3	2	.600	6.16	25	10	1	76	85	69	40	0	2	1	0	26	4	0	.000
1950 2 teams			STL A	(9G 0–2)		CHI A	(11G 0–0)												
" total	0	2	.000	7.07	20	3	0	35.2	42	45	24	0	0	1	0	7	0	0	.000
1951 CHI A	6	9	.400	4.20	26	18	7	137	129	74	89	1	0	1	0	48	4	0	.083
1952	4	4	.500	2.96	19	11	4	79	52	56	63	2	0	0	1	20	1	0	.050
1953 2 teams			CHI A	(9G 0–0)		STL A	(22G 1–5)												
" total	1	5	.167	4.78	31	14	0	101.2	105	82	52	0	0	0	0	29	5	0	.172
1954 BAL A	6	11	.353	4.37	32	20	5	166.2	169	82	82	0	0	1	0	51	8	0	.157
1955	0	4	.000	8.22	15	5	0	38.1	50	27	26	0	0	0	0	11	1	0	.091
1956 KC A	4	9	.308	5.31	25	20	3	118.2	121	74	61	0	0	0	0	33	2	0	.061
10 yrs.	27	47	.365	4.87	199	104	22	785.1	781	522	450	3	3	4	1	237	27	0	.114

Rick Kreuger

KREUGER, RICHARD ALLEN
B. Nov. 3, 1948, Wyoming, Mich.   BR TL 6'2"   185 lbs.

	W	L	PCT	ERA	G	GS	CG	IP	H	BB	SO	ShO	W	L	SV	AB	H	HR	BA
1975 BOS A	0	0	–	4.50	2	0	0	4	3	1	1	0	0	0	0	0	0	0	–
1976	2	1	.667	4.06	8	4	1	31	31	16	12	0	0	0	0	0	0	0	–
1977	0	1	.000	∞	1	0	0	0	2	0	0	0	0	1	0	0	0	0	–
1978 CLE A	0	0	–	3.86	6	0	0	9.1	6	3	7	0	0	0	0	0	0	0	–
4 yrs.	2	2	.500	4.47	17	4	1	44.1	42	20	20	0	0	1	0	0	0	0	–

Frank Kreutzer

KREUTZER, FRANK JAMES
B. Feb. 7, 1939, Buffalo, N. Y.   BR TL 6'1"   175 lbs.

	W	L	PCT	ERA	G	GS	CG	IP	H	BB	SO	ShO	W	L	SV	AB	H	HR	BA
1962 CHI A	0	0	–	0.00	1	0	0	1.1	0	1	1	0	0	0	0	0	0	0	–
1963	1	1	1.000	1.80	1	1	0	5	3	1	0	0	0	0	0	2	0	0	.000
1964 2 teams			CHI A	(17G 3–1)		WAS A	(13G 2–6)												
" total	5	7	.417	4.10	30	11	0	85.2	85	41	59	0	2	2	1	19	1	0	.053
1965 WAS A	2	6	.250	4.32	33	14	2	85.1	73	54	65	1	0	1	0	22	1	1	.045
1966	0	5	.000	6.03	9	6	0	31.1	30	10	24	0	0	0	0	8	2	0	.250
1969	0	0	–	4.50	4	0	0	2	3	2	2	0	0	0	0	0	0	0	–
6 yrs.	8	18	.308	4.40	78	32	2	210.2	194	109	151	1	2	3	1	51	4	1	.078

Krieger

KRIEGER,
Deceased.

	W	L	PCT	ERA	G	GS	CG	IP	H	BB	SO	ShO	W	L	SV	AB	H	HR	BA
1884 KC U	0	1	.000	0.00	1	1	0	7	9	5	3	0	0	0	0	3	0	0	.000

Kurt Krieger

KRIEGER, KURT FERDINAND (Dutch)
B. Sept. 16, 1926, Traisen, Austria   D. Aug. 16, 1970, St. Louis, Mo.   BR TR 6'3"   212 lbs.

	W	L	PCT	ERA	G	GS	CG	IP	H	BB	SO	ShO	W	L	SV	AB	H	HR	BA
1949 STL N	0	0	–	0.00	1	0	0	1	0	0	0	0	0	0	0	0	0	0	–
1951	0	0	–	15.75	2	0	0	4	6	5	3	0	0	0	0	0	0	0	–
2 yrs.	0	0	–	12.60	3	0	0	4	6	5	3	0	0	0	0	0	0	0	–

Howie Krist

KRIST, HOWARD WILBUR (Spud)
B. Feb. 28, 1916, West Henrietta, N. Y.   BL TR 6'1"   175 lbs.

	W	L	PCT	ERA	G	GS	CG	IP	H	BB	SO	ShO	W	L	SV	AB	H	HR	BA
1937 STL N	3	1	.750	4.23	6	4	1	27.2	34	10	6	0	1	0	0	9	0	0	.000
1938	0	0	–	0.00	2	0	0	1.1	1	0	1	0	0	0	0	0	0	0	–
1941	10	0	1.000	4.03	37	8	2	114	107	35	36	0	6	0	2	38	9	0	.237
1942	13	3	.813	2.51	34	8	3	118.1	103	43	47	0	8	2	1	42	6	0	.143
1943	11	5	.688	2.90	34	17	9	164.1	141	62	57	3	2	1	3	60	10	0	.167
1946	0	2	.000	6.75	15	0	0	18.2	22	8	3	0	0	2	0	0	0	0	–
6 yrs.	37	11	.771	3.32	128	37	15	444.1	408	158	150	3	17	5	6	149	25	0	.168

WORLD SERIES

	W	L	PCT	ERA	G	GS	CG	IP	H	BB	SO	ShO	W	L	SV	AB	H	HR	BA
1943 STL N	0	0	–	0.00	1	0	0	1	1	0	0	0	0	0	0	0	0	0	–

Gus Krock

KROCK, AUGUST H.
B. May 9, 1866, Milwaukee, Wis.   D. Mar. 22, 1905, Pasadena, Calif.   TL 6'   196 lbs.

	W	L	PCT	ERA	G	GS	CG	IP	H	BB	SO	ShO	W	L	SV	AB	H	HR	BA
1888 CHI N	24	14	.632	2.44	39	39	39	339.2	295	45	161	4	0	0	0	134	22	1	.164
1889 3 teams			CHI N	(7G 3–3)		IND N	(4G 2–2)		WAS N	(6G 2–4)									
" total	7	9	.438	5.57	17	17	14	140.2	199	50	43	0	0	0	0	61	11	0	.180
1890 BUF P	0	3	.000	6.12	4	3	3	25	43	15	5	0	0	0	0	12	1	0	.083
3 yrs.	31	26	.544	3.49	60	59	56	505.1	537	110	209	4	0	0	0	207	34	1	.164

Rube Kroh

KROH, FLOYD MYRON
B. Aug. 25, 1886, Friendship, N. Y.   D. Mar. 17, 1944, New Orleans, La.   BL TL 6'2"   186 lbs.

	W	L	PCT	ERA	G	GS	CG	IP	H	BB	SO	ShO	W	L	SV	AB	H	HR	BA
1906 BOS A	1	0	1.000	0.00	1	1	1	9	2	4	5	1	0	0	0	3	0	0	.000
1907	1	4	.200	2.62	7	5	5	34.1	33	8	8	0	0	0	0	11	3	0	.273
1908 CHI N	0	0	–	1.50	2	1	0	12	9	4	11	0	0	0	0	4	0	0	.000

	W	L	PCT	ERA	G	GS	CG	IP	H	BB	SO	ShO	Relief Pitching W	L	SV	BATTING AB	H	HR	BA

Rube Kroh continued

	W	L	PCT	ERA	G	GS	CG	IP	H	BB	SO	ShO	W	L	SV	AB	H	HR	BA
1909	9	4	.692	1.65	17	13	10	120.1	97	30	51	2	0	0	0	40	6	0	.150
1910	3	1	.750	4.46	6	4	1	34.1	33	15	16	0	2	0	0	12	3	0	.250
1912 BOS N	0	0	–	5.68	3	1	0	6.1	8	6	1	0	0	0	0	2	1	0	.500
6 yrs.	14	9	.609	2.29	36	25	13	216.1	182	67	92	3	2	0	0	72	13	0	.181

Gary Kroll

KROLL, GARY MELVIN
B. July 8, 1941, Culver City, Calif. BR TR 6'6" 220 lbs.

	W	L	PCT	ERA	G	GS	CG	IP	H	BB	SO	ShO	W	L	SV	AB	H	HR	BA
1964 2 teams			PHI N (2G 0–0)					NY N (8G 0–1)											
" total	0	1	.000	4.01	10	2	0	24.2	22	17	26	0	0	0	0	3	1	0	.333
1965 NY N	6	6	.500	4.45	32	11	1	87	83	41	62	0	4	1	1	26	3	0	.115
1966 HOU N	0	0	–	3.80	10	0	0	23.2	26	11	22	0	0	0	0	3	0	0	.000
1969 CLE A	0	0	–	4.13	19	0	0	24	16	22	28	0	0	0	0	0	0	0	–
4 yrs.	6	7	.462	4.24	71	13	1	159.1	147	91	138	0	4	1	1	32	4	0	.125

Bill Krueger

KRUEGER, WILLIAM C.
B. Apr. 24, 1958, Waukegan, Ill. BL TL 6'5" 205 lbs.

	W	L	PCT	ERA	G	GS	CG	IP	H	BB	SO	ShO	W	L	SV	AB	H	HR	BA
1983 OAK A	7	6	.538	3.61	17	16	2	109.2	104	53	58	0	1	0	0	0	0	0	–
1984	10	10	.500	4.75	26	24	1	142	156	85	61	0	0	0	0	0	0	0	–
2 yrs.	17	16	.515	4.26	43	40	3	251.2	260	138	119	0	1	0	0	0	0	0	–

Abe Kruger

KRUGER, ABRAHAM
B. Feb. 14, 1885, Morris Run, Pa. D. July 4, 1962, Elmira, N. Y. BR TR 6'2" 190 lbs.

	W	L	PCT	ERA	G	GS	CG	IP	H	BB	SO	ShO	W	L	SV	AB	H	HR	BA
1908 BKN N	0	1	.000	4.26	2	1	0	6.1	5	3	2	0	0	0	0	2	0	0	.000

Mike Krukow

KRUKOW, MICHAEL EDWARD
B. Jan. 21, 1952, Long Beach, Calif. BR TR 6'5" 205 lbs.

	W	L	PCT	ERA	G	GS	CG	IP	H	BB	SO	ShO	W	L	SV	AB	H	HR	BA
1976 CHI N	0	0	–	9.00	2	0	0	4	6	2	1	0	0	0	0	1	0	0	.000
1977	8	14	.364	4.40	34	33	1	172	195	61	106	1	0	0	0	55	11	0	.200
1978	9	3	.750	3.91	27	20	3	138	125	53	81	1	0	0	0	45	11	0	.244
1979	9	9	.500	4.20	28	28	0	165	172	81	119	0	0	0	0	51	16	1	.314
1980	10	15	.400	4.39	34	34	3	205	200	80	130	0	0	0	0	65	16	1	.246
1981	9	9	.500	3.69	25	25	2	144	146	55	101	1	0	0	0	50	9	0	.180
1982 PHI N	13	11	.542	3.12	33	33	7	208	211	82	138	2	0	0	0	72	13	0	.181
1983 SF N	11	11	.500	3.95	31	31	2	184.1	189	76	136	1	0	0	0	63	16	1	.254
1984	11	12	.478	4.56	35	33	3	199.1	234	78	141	1	0	0	1	72	10	0	.139
9 yrs.	80	84	.488	4.04	249	237	21	1419.2	1478	568	953	7	0	0	1	474	102	3	.215

Al Krumm

KRUMM, ALBERT
B. Columbus, Ohio   Deceased.

	W	L	PCT	ERA	G	GS	CG	IP	H	BB	SO	ShO	W	L	SV	AB	H	HR	BA
1889 PIT N	0	1	.000	10.00	1	1	1	9	8	10	4	0	0	0	0	4	0	0	.000

Johnny Kucab

KUCAB, JOHN ALBERT
B. Dec. 17, 1919, Olyphant, Pa.   D. May 26, 1977, Youngstown, Ohio BR TR 6'2" 185 lbs.

	W	L	PCT	ERA	G	GS	CG	IP	H	BB	SO	ShO	W	L	SV	AB	H	HR	BA
1950 PHI A	1	1	.500	3.46	4	2	2	26	29	8	8	0	0	0	0	9	1	0	.111
1951	4	3	.571	4.22	30	1	0	74.2	76	23	23	0	4	2	4	16	0	0	.000
1952	0	1	.000	5.26	25	0	0	51.1	64	20	17	0	0	1	2	10	2	0	.200
3 yrs.	5	5	.500	4.44	59	3	2	152	169	51	48	0	4	3	6	35	3	0	.086

Jack Kucek

KUCEK, JOHN ANDREW
B. June 8, 1953, Newton Falls, Ohio BR TR 6'2" 200 lbs.

	W	L	PCT	ERA	G	GS	CG	IP	H	BB	SO	ShO	W	L	SV	AB	H	HR	BA
1974 CHI A	1	4	.200	5.21	9	7	0	38	48	21	25	0	0	0	0	0	0	0	–
1975	0	0	–	4.91	2	0	0	3.2	9	4	2	0	0	0	0	0	0	0	–
1976	0	0	–	9.00	2	0	0	5	9	4	2	0	0	0	0	0	0	0	–
1977	0	1	.000	3.60	8	3	0	35	35	10	25	0	0	0	0	0	0	0	–
1978	2	3	.400	3.29	10	5	3	52	42	27	30	0	0	1	0	0	0	0	–
1979 2 teams			CHI A (1G 0–0)					PHI N (4G 1–0)											
" total	1	0	1.000	7.20	5	0	0	5	6	4	2	0	1	0	0	0	0	0	–
1980 TOR A	3	8	.273	6.75	23	12	0	68	83	41	35	0	1	2	1	0	0	0	–
7 yrs.	7	16	.304	5.10	59	27	3	206.2	232	111	121	0	2	2	2	0	0	0	–

Johnny Kucks

KUCKS, JOHN CHARLES
B. July 27, 1933, Hoboken, N. J. BR TR 6'3" 170 lbs.

	W	L	PCT	ERA	G	GS	CG	IP	H	BB	SO	ShO	W	L	SV	AB	H	HR	BA
1955 NY A	8	7	.533	3.41	29	13	3	126.2	122	44	49	1	2	3	0	40	2	0	.050
1956	18	9	.667	3.85	34	31	12	224.1	223	72	67	3	2	0	0	77	11	0	.143
1957	8	10	.444	3.56	37	23	4	179.1	169	59	78	1	1	1	3	55	6	0	.109
1958	8	8	.500	3.93	34	15	4	126	132	39	46	1	2	5	4	40	5	0	.125
1959 2 teams			NY A (9G 0–1)					KC A (33G 8–11)											
" total	8	12	.400	4.34	42	24	6	168	184	51	60	1	0	1	1	49	4	0	.082
1960 KC A	4	10	.286	6.00	31	17	1	114	140	43	38	0	2	0	0	30	4	0	.133
6 yrs.	54	56	.491	4.10	207	123	30	938.1	970	308	338	7	9	10	7	291	32	0	.110
WORLD SERIES																			
1955 NY A	0	0	–	6.00	2	0	0	3	4	1	1	0	0	0	0	0	0	0	–
1956	1	0	1.000	0.82	3	1	1	11	6	3	2	1	0	0	0	3	0	0	.000
1957	0	0	–	0.00	1	0	0	.2	1	1	1	0	0	0	0	0	0	0	–
1958	0	0	–	2.08	2	0	0	4.1	4	1	0	0	0	0	0	1	1	0	1.000
4 yrs.	1	0	1.000	1.89	8	1	1	19	15	6	4	1	0	0	0	4	1	0	.250

Bert Kuczynski

KUCZYNSKI, BERNARD CARL
B. Jan. 8, 1920, Philadelphia, Pa. BR TR 6' 195 lbs.

	W	L	PCT	ERA	G	GS	CG	IP	H	BB	SO	ShO	W	L	SV	AB	H	HR	BA
1943 PHI A	0	1	.000	4.01	6	1	0	24.2	36	9	8	0	0	0	0	6	0	0	.000

Bub Kuhn

KUHN, BERNARD DANIEL
B. Oct. 12, 1899, Vicksburg, Mich. D. Nov. 20, 1956, Detroit, Mich. BL TR 6'4" 182 lbs.

	W	L	PCT	ERA	G	GS	CG	IP	H	BB	SO	ShO	W	L	SV	AB	H	HR	BA
1924 CLE A	0	1	.000	27.00	1	0	0	1	4	0	0	0	0	1	0	0	0	0	–

	W	L	PCT	ERA	G	GS	CG	IP	H	BB	SO	ShO	Relief Pitching W	L	SV	BATTING AB	H	HR	BA

Fred Kuhualua

KUHUALUA, FRED MAHELE   BL TL 5'11"   175 lbs.
B. Feb. 23, 1953, Honolulu, Hawaii

	W	L	PCT	ERA	G	GS	CG	IP	H	BB	SO	ShO	W	L	SV	AB	H	HR	BA
1977 CAL A	0	0	—	15.63	3	1	0	6.1	15	7	3	0	0	0	0	0	0	0	—
1981 SD N	1	0	1.000	2.48	5	4	0	29	28	9	16	0	0	0	0	9	1	0	.111
2 yrs.	1	0	1.000	4.84	8	5	0	35.1	43	16	19	0	0	0	0	9	1	0	.111

John Kull

KULL, JOHN A.   BR TR 6'2"   190 lbs.
B. June 24, 1882, Shenandoah, Pa.   D. Mar. 30, 1936, Schuylkill, Pa.

	W	L	PCT	ERA	G	GS	CG	IP	H	BB	SO	ShO	W	L	SV	AB	H	HR	BA
1909 PHI A	1	0	1.000	3.00	1	0	0	3	3	5	4	0	1	0	0	1	1	0	1.000

John Kume

KUME, JOHN MICHAEL   BR TR 6'1"   200 lbs.
B. May 19, 1926, Premier, W. Va.

	W	L	PCT	ERA	G	GS	CG	IP	H	BB	SO	ShO	W	L	SV	AB	H	HR	BA
1955 KC A	0	2	.000	7.99	6	4	0	23.2	35	15	7	0	0	0	0	8	1	0	.125

Bill Kunkel

KUNKEL, WILLIAM GUSTAVE JAMES   BR TR 6'1"   187 lbs.
Father of Jeff Kunkel.
B. July 7, 1936, Hoboken, N. J.

	W	L	PCT	ERA	G	GS	CG	IP	H	BB	SO	ShO	W	L	SV	AB	H	HR	BA
1961 KC A	3	4	.429	5.18	58	2	0	88.2	103	32	46	0	3	2	4	8	1	0	.125
1962	0	0	—	3.52	9	0	0	7.2	8	4	6	0	0	0	0	0	0	0	—
1963 NY A	3	2	.600	2.72	22	0	0	46.1	42	13	31	0	3	2	0	6	2	0	.333
3 yrs.	6	6	.500	4.29	89	2	0	142.2	153	49	83	0	6	4	4	14	3	0	.214

Earl Kunz

KUNZ, EARL DEWEY (Pinch)   BR TR 5'10"   170 lbs.
B. Dec. 25, 1899, Sacramento, Calif.   D. Apr. 14, 1963, Sacramento, Calif.

	W	L	PCT	ERA	G	GS	CG	IP	H	BB	SO	ShO	W	L	SV	AB	H	HR	BA
1923 PIT N	1	2	.333	5.52	21	2	1	45.2	48	24	12	0	1	1	1	12	1	0	.083

Ryan Kurosaki

KUROSAKI, RYAN YOSHITOMO   BR TR 5'10"   160 lbs.
B. July 3, 1952, Honolulu, Hawaii

	W	L	PCT	ERA	G	GS	CG	IP	H	BB	SO	ShO	W	L	SV	AB	H	HR	BA
1975 STL N	0	0	—	7.62	7	0	0	13	15	7	6	0	0	0	0	1	0	0	.000

Hal Kurtz

KURTZ, HAROLD JAMES (Bud)   BR TR 6'3"   205 lbs.
B. Aug. 20, 1943, Washington, D. C.

	W	L	PCT	ERA	G	GS	CG	IP	H	BB	SO	ShO	W	L	SV	AB	H	HR	BA
1968 CLE A	1	0	1.000	5.21	28	0	0	38	37	15	16	0	1	0	1	4	0	0	.000

Ed Kusel

KUSEL, EDWARD D.   BR TR 5'11"   185 lbs.
B. Feb. 15, 1886, Cleveland, Ohio   D. Oct. 20, 1948, Cleveland, Ohio

	W	L	PCT	ERA	G	GS	CG	IP	H	BB	SO	ShO	W	L	SV	AB	H	HR	BA
1909 STL A	0	3	.000	7.13	3	3	3	24	43	1	2	0	0	0	0	10	3	0	.300

Emil Kush

KUSH, EMIL BENEDICT   BR TR 5'11"   185 lbs.
B. Nov. 4, 1916, Chicago, Ill.   D. Nov. 25, 1969, River Grove, Ill.

	W	L	PCT	ERA	G	GS	CG	IP	H	BB	SO	ShO	W	L	SV	AB	H	HR	BA
1941 CHI N	0	0	—	2.25	2	0	0	4	2	0	2	0	0	0	0	1	0	0	.000
1942	0	0	—	0.00	1	0	0	2	1	1	1	0	0	0	0	1	0	0	.000
1946	9	2	.818	3.05	40	6	1	129.2	120	43	50	1	8	0	2	38	8	0	.211
1947	8	3	.727	3.36	47	1	1	91	80	53	44	0	7	2	5	20	5	0	.250
1948	1	4	.200	4.38	34	1	0	72	70	37	31	0	1	3	3	13	2	0	.154
1949	3	3	.500	3.78	26	0	0	47.2	51	24	22	0	3	3	2	9	3	0	.333
6 yrs.	21	12	.636	3.48	150	8	2	346.1	324	158	150	1	19	8	12	82	18	0	.220

Craig Kusick

KUSICK, CRAIG ROBERT   BR TR 6'3"   210 lbs.
B. Sept. 30, 1948, Milwaukee, Wis.

	W	L	PCT	ERA	G	GS	CG	IP	H	BB	SO	ShO	W	L	SV	AB	H	HR	BA
1979 TOR A	0	0	—	4.50	1	0	0	4	3	0	0	0	0	0	0	*			

Marty Kutyna

KUTYNA, MARION JOHN   BR TR 6'   190 lbs.
B. Nov. 14, 1932, Philadelphia, Pa.

	W	L	PCT	ERA	G	GS	CG	IP	H	BB	SO	ShO	W	L	SV	AB	H	HR	BA
1959 KC A	0	0	—	0.00	4	0	0	7.1	7	1	1	0	0	0	1	0	0	0	—
1960	3	2	.600	3.94	51	0	0	61.2	64	32	20	0	3	2	4	5	1	0	.200
1961 WAS A	6	8	.429	3.97	50	6	0	143	147	48	64	0	5	4	3	34	7	0	.206
1962	5	6	.455	4.04	54	0	0	78	83	27	25	0	5	6	0	8	1	0	.125
4 yrs.	14	16	.467	3.88	159	6	0	290	301	108	110	0	13	12	8	47	9	0	.191

Bob Kuzava

KUZAVA, ROBERT LeROY (Sarge)   BB TL 6'2"   202 lbs.
B. May 28, 1923, Wyandotte, Mich.   BR 1946

	W	L	PCT	ERA	G	GS	CG	IP	H	BB	SO	ShO	W	L	SV	AB	H	HR	BA
1946 CLE A	1	0	1.000	3.00	2	2	0	12	9	11	4	0	0	0	0	5	1	0	.200
1947	1	1	.500	4.15	4	4	1	21.2	22	9	9	1	0	0	0	9	1	0	.111
1949 CHI A	10	6	.625	4.02	29	18	9	156.2	139	91	83	1	2	0	0	56	2	0	.036
1950 2 teams					CHI A (10G 1–3)			WAS A (22G 8–7)											
" total	9	10	.474	4.33	32	29	9	199.1	199	102	105	1	0	0	0	62	6	1	.097
1951 2 teams					WAS A (8G 3–3)			NY A (23G 8–4)											
" total	11	7	.611	3.61	31	16	7	134.2	133	55	72	1	5	1	5	39	6	0	.154
1952 NY A	8	8	.500	3.45	28	12	6	133	115	63	67	1	3	2	3	43	4	0	.093
1953	6	5	.545	3.23	33	6	2	92.1	92	34	48	2	4	1	4	21	1	0	.048
1954 2 teams					NY A (20G 1–3)			BAL A (4G 1–3)											
" total	6	6	.250	4.97	24	7	0	63.1	76	29	37	0	1	1	1	13	0	0	.000
1955 2 teams					BAL A (6G 0–1)			PHI N (17G 1–0)											
" total	1	1	.500	6.25	23	5	0	44.2	57	16	18	0	1	0	0	8	1	0	.125
1957 2 teams					PIT N (4G 0–0)			STL N (3G 0–0)											
" total	0	0	—	6.23	7	0	0	4.1	7	5	3	0	0	0	0	0	0	0	—
10 yrs.	49	44	.527	4.05	213	99	34	862	849	415	446	7	15	5	13	256	22	1	.086

WORLD SERIES																			
1951 NY A	0	0	—	0.00	1	0	0	1	0	0	0	0	0	0	1	0	0	0	—
1952	0	0	—	0.00	1	0	0	2.2	0	2	2	0	0	0	1	0	0	0	.000
1953	0	0	—	13.50	1	0	0	.2	2	0	1	0	0	0	0	1	0	0	.000
3 yrs.	0	0	—	2.08	3	0	0	4.1	2	0	3	0	0	0	2	2	0	0	.000

	W	L	PCT	ERA	G	GS	CG	IP	H	BB	SO	ShO	W	L	SV	AB	H	HR	BA
													Relief Pitching			BATTING			

Clem Labine

LABINE, CLEMENT WALTER
B. Aug. 6, 1926, Lincoln, R. I.
BR TR 6' 180 lbs.

	W	L	PCT	ERA	G	GS	CG	IP	H	BB	SO	ShO	W	L	SV	AB	H	HR	BA
1950 BKN N	0	0	–	4.50	1			2	2	1	0		0	0	0	0	0	0	–
1951	5	1	.833	2.20	14	6	5	65.1	52	20	39	2	0	0	0	21	3	0	.143
1952	8	4	.667	5.14	25	9	0	77	76	47	43	0	6	1	0	22	1	0	.045
1953	11	6	.647	2.77	37	7	0	110.1	92	30	44	0	10	4	7	28	2	0	.071
1954	7	6	.538	4.15	47	2	0	108.1	101	56	43	0	6	5	5	30	1	0	.033
1955	13	5	.722	3.24	**60**	8	1	144.1	121	55	67	0	10	2	11	31	3	3	.097
1956	10	6	.625	3.35	62	3	1	115.2	111	39	75	0	9	6	19	23	2	0	.087
1957	5	7	.417	3.44	58	0	0	104.2	104	27	67	0	5	7	17	20	2	0	.100
1958 LA N	6	6	.500	4.15	52	2	0	104	112	33	43	0	5	5	14	18	1	0	.056
1959	5	10	.333	3.93	58	0	0	84.2	91	25	37	0	5	10	9	16	0	0	.000
1960 3 teams			LA N (13G 0-1)		DET A (14G 0-3)			PIT N (15G 3-0)											
" total	3	4	.429	3.65	42	0	0	66.2	74	31	42	0	3	4	6	8	1	0	.125
1961 PIT N	4	1	.800	3.69	56	1	0	92.2	102	31	49	0	4	1	8	10	1	0	.100
1962 NY N	0	0	–	11.25	3	0	0	4	5	1	2	0	0	0	0	0	0	0	–
13 yrs.	77	56	.579	3.63	513	38	7	1079.2	1043	396	551	2	63	45	96	227	17	3	.075

WORLD SERIES

	W	L	PCT	ERA	G	GS	CG	IP	H	BB	SO	ShO	W	L	SV	AB	H	HR	BA
1953 BKN N	0	2	.000	3.60	3	0	0	5	10	1	3	0	0	2	1	2	0	0	.000
1955	1	0	1.000	2.89	4	0	0	9.1	6	2	2	0	1	0	1	4	0	0	.000
1956	1	0	1.000	0.00	2	1	1	12	8	3	7	1	0	0	0	4	1	0	.250
1959 LA N	0	0	–	0.00	1	0	0	1	0	1	0	0	0	0	0	0	0	0	–
1960 PIT N	0	0	–	13.50	3	0	0	4	13	1	2	0	0	0	0	0	0	0	–
5 yrs.	2	2	.500	3.16	13	1	1	31.1	37	7	15	1	1	2	2	10	1	0	.100
				6th										2nd					

Bob Lacey

LACEY, ROBERT JOSEPH
B. Aug. 25, 1953, Fredericksburg, Va.
BR TL 6'5" 210 lbs.

	W	L	PCT	ERA	G	GS	CG	IP	H	BB	SO	ShO	W	L	SV	AB	H	HR	BA
1977 OAK A	6	8	.429	3.02	64	0	0	122	100	43	69	0	6	8	7	0	0	0	–
1978	8	9	.471	3.01	**74**	0	0	119.2	126	35	60	0	8	9	5	0	0	0	–
1979	1	5	.167	5.81	42	0	0	48	66	24	33	0	1	5	4	0	0	0	–
1980	3	2	.600	2.93	47	1	1	80	68	21	45	1	2	2	6	0	0	0	–
1981 2 teams			CLE A (14G 0-0)		TEX A (1G 0-0)														
" total	0	0	–	7.77	15	0	0	22	37	3	11	0	0	0	0	0	0	0	–
1983 CAL A	1	2	.333	5.19	8	0	0	8.2	12	0	7	0	1	2	0	0	0	0	–
1984 SF N	1	3	.250	3.88	34	1	0	51	55	13	26	0	1	2	0	6	2	0	.333
7 yrs.	20	29	.408	3.67	284	2	1	451.1	464	139	251	1	19	28	22	6	2	0	.333

Marcel Lachemann

LACHEMANN, MARCEL ERNEST
Brother of Rene Lachemann.
B. June 13, 1941, Los Angeles, Calif.
BR TR 6'1" 185 lbs.

	W	L	PCT	ERA	G	GS	CG	IP	H	BB	SO	ShO	W	L	SV	AB	H	HR	BA
1969 OAK A	4	1	.800	3.95	28	0	0	43.1	43	19	16	0	4	1	2	2	0	0	.000
1970	3	3	.500	2.79	41	0	0	58	58	18	39	0	3	3	3	8	0	0	.000
1971	0	0	–	54.00	1	0	0	1	2	1	0	0	0	0	0	0	0	0	–
3 yrs.	7	4	.636	3.45	70	0	0	101.2	103	38	55	0	7	4	5	10	0	0	.000

Al Lachowicz

LACHOWICZ, ALLEN RICHARD
B. Sept. 6, 1960, Pittsburgh, Pa.
BR TR 6'3" 185 lbs.

	W	L	PCT	ERA	G	GS	CG	IP	H	BB	SO	ShO	W	L	SV	AB	H	HR	BA
1983 TEX A	0	1	.000	2.25	2	1	0	8	9	2	8	0	0	0	0	0	0	0	–

George LaClaire

LaCLAIRE, GEORGE LEWIS
B. Oct. 18, 1886, Milton, Vt. D. Oct. 10, 1918, Farnham, Que., Canada
BR TR 5'9" 170 lbs.

	W	L	PCT	ERA	G	GS	CG	IP	H	BB	SO	ShO	W	L	SV	AB	H	HR	BA
1914 PIT F	5	2	.714	4.01	22	7	5	103.1	99	25	49	1	2	0	0	34	5	0	.147
1915 3 teams			PIT F (14G 1-0)		BUF F (1G 0-0)			BAL F (18G 2-8)											
" total	3	8	.273	2.85	33	12	7	132.2	123	36	42	1	1	2	1	37	4	0	.108
2 yrs.	8	10	.444	3.36	55	19	12	236	222	61	91	2	3	2	1	71	9	0	.127

Frank LaCorte

LaCORTE, FRANK JOSEPH
B. Oct. 13, 1951, San Jose, Calif.
BR TR 6'1" 180 lbs.

	W	L	PCT	ERA	G	GS	CG	IP	H	BB	SO	ShO	W	L	SV	AB	H	HR	BA
1975 ATL N	0	3	.000	5.14	3	2	0	14	13	6	10	0	0	1	0	5	0	0	.000
1976	3	12	.200	4.71	19	17	1	105	97	53	79	0	0	1	0	33	3	0	.091
1977	1	8	.111	11.68	14	7	0	37	67	29	28	0	0	2	0	10	2	0	.200
1978	0	1	.000	3.60	2	2	0	15	9	4	7	0	0	0	0	4	0	0	.000
1979 2 teams			ATL N (6G 0-0)		HOU N (12G 1-2)														
" total	1	2	.333	5.60	18	3	0	35.1	30	15	30	0	0	0	0	4	0	0	.000
1980 HOU N	8	5	.615	2.82	55	0	0	83	61	43	66	0	8	5	11	6	1	0	.167
1981	4	2	.667	3.64	37	0	0	42	41	21	40	0	4	2	5	3	1	0	.333
1982	1	5	.167	4.48	55	0	0	76.1	71	46	51	0	1	5	7	7	0	0	.000
1983	4	4	.500	5.06	37	0	0	53.1	35	28	48	0	4	4	3	5	1	0	.200
1984 CAL A	1	2	.333	7.06	13	1	0	29.1	33	13	13	0	0	2	0	0	0	0	–
10 yrs.	23	44	.343	5.01	253	32	1	490.1	457	258	372	0	17	22	26	77	8	0	.104

DIVISIONAL PLAYOFF SERIES

	W	L	PCT	ERA	G	GS	CG	IP	H	BB	SO	ShO	W	L	SV	AB	H	HR	BA
1981 HOU N	0	0	–	0.00	2	0	0	3.2	2	1	5	0	0	0	0	0	0	0	–

LEAGUE CHAMPIONSHIP SERIES

	W	L	PCT	ERA	G	GS	CG	IP	H	BB	SO	ShO	W	L	SV	AB	H	HR	BA
1980 HOU N	1	1	.500	3.00	2	0	0	3	7	2	2	0	1	1	0	1	0	0	.000

Mike LaCoss

LaCOSS, MICHAEL JAMES
B. May 30, 1956, Glendale, Calif.
BR TR 6'5" 185 lbs.

	W	L	PCT	ERA	G	GS	CG	IP	H	BB	SO	ShO	W	L	SV	AB	H	HR	BA
1978 CIN N	4	8	.333	4.50	16	15	2	96	104	46	31	1	0	0	0	30	2	0	.067
1979	14	8	.636	3.50	35	32	6	206	202	79	73	1	0	0	0	70	9	0	.129
1980	10	12	.455	4.63	34	29	4	169	207	68	59	2	2	0	0	55	5	0	.091
1981	4	7	.364	6.12	20	13	1	78	102	30	22	0	1	2	0	19	0	0	.000
1982 HOU N	6	6	.500	2.90	41	8	0	115	107	54	51	0	3	3	0	24	6	0	.250
1983	5	7	.417	4.43	38	17	2	138	142	56	53	0	1	1	1	35	3	0	.086
1984	7	5	.583	4.02	39	18	2	132	132	55	86	1	1	0	3	31	4	0	.129
7 yrs.	50	53	.485	4.16	223	132	17	934	996	388	375	6	8	4	5	264	29	0	.110

LEAGUE CHAMPIONSHIP SERIES

	W	L	PCT	ERA	G	GS	CG	IP	H	BB	SO	ShO	W	L	SV	AB	H	HR	BA
1979 CIN N	0	1	.000	10.80	1	1	0	1.2	1	4	0	0	0	0	0	0	0	0	–

	W	L	PCT	ERA	G	GS	CG	IP	H	BB	SO	ShO	Relief Pitching W	L	SV	BATTING AB	H	HR	BA

Pete Ladd

LADD, PETER LINWOOD (Bigfoot)
B. July 17, 1956, Portland, Me.   BR TR 6'3"   228 lbs.

	W	L	PCT	ERA	G	GS	CG	IP	H	BB	SO	ShO	W	L	SV	AB	H	HR	BA
1979 HOU N	1	1	.500	3.00	10	0	0	12	8	8	6	0	1	1	0	1	0	0	.000
1982 MIL A	1	3	.250	4.00	16	0	0	18	16	6	12	0	1	3	3	0	0	0	–
1983	3	4	.429	2.55	44	0	0	49.1	30	16	41	0	3	4	25	0	0	0	–
1984	4	9	.308	5.24	54	1	0	91	94	38	75	0	4	8	3	0	0	0	–
4 yrs.	9	17	.346	4.17	124	1	0	170.1	148	68	134	0	9	16	31	1	0	0	.000
LEAGUE CHAMPIONSHIP SERIES
1982 MIL A	0	0	–	0.00	3	0	0	3.1	0	0	5	0	0	0	2	0	0	0	–
WORLD SERIES
1982 MIL A	0	0	–	0.00	1	0	0	.2	1	2	0	0	0	0	0	0	0	0	–

Doyle Lade

LADE, DOYLE MARION (Porky)
B. Feb. 17, 1921, Fairbury, Neb.   BR TR 5'10"   183 lbs.
BB 1946-47

	W	L	PCT	ERA	G	GS	CG	IP	H	BB	SO	ShO	W	L	SV	AB	H	HR	BA
1946 CHI N	0	2	.000	4.11	3	2	0	15.1	15	3	8	0	0	1	0	5	1	0	.200
1947	11	10	.524	3.94	34	25	7	187.1	202	79	62	1	0	0	0	60	13	0	.217
1948	5	6	.455	4.02	19	12	6	87.1	99	31	29	0	0	0	0	32	5	0	.156
1949	4	5	.444	5.00	36	13	5	129.2	141	58	43	1	0	0	1	32	7	0	.219
1950	5	6	.455	4.74	34	12	2	117.2	126	50	36	0	2	1	2	35	10	0	.286
5 yrs.	25	29	.463	4.39	126	64	20	537.1	583	221	178	2	2	2	3	164	36	0	.220

Steve Ladew

LADEW, STEPHEN
B. St. Louis, Mo.   Deceased.

	W	L	PCT	ERA	G	GS	CG	IP	H	BB	SO	ShO	W	L	SV	AB	H	HR	BA
1889 KC AA	0	0	–	4.50	1	0	0	2	1	3	0	0	0	0	0	4	0	0	.000

Flip Lafferty

LAFFERTY, FRANK BERNARD
B. May 4, 1854, Scranton, Pa.   D. Feb. 8, 1910, Wilmington, Del.   TR

	W	L	PCT	ERA	G	GS	CG	IP	H	BB	SO	ShO	W	L	SV	AB	H	HR	BA
1876 PHI N	0	1	.000	0.00	1	1	1	9	5	0	0	0	0	0	0	*			

Ed Lafitte

LAFITTE, EDWARD FRANCIS (Doc)
B. Apr. 7, 1886, New Orleans, La.   D. Apr. 12, 1971, Jenkintown, Pa.   BR TR 6'2"   188 lbs.

	W	L	PCT	ERA	G	GS	CG	IP	H	BB	SO	ShO	W	L	SV	AB	H	HR	BA
1909 DET A	0	1	.000	3.86	3	1	1	14	22	2	11	0	0	0	0	4	1	0	.250
1911	11	8	.579	3.92	29	20	15	172.1	205	52	63	0	0	1	1	70	11	1	.157
1912	0	0	–	16.20	1	0	0	1.2	2	2	2	0	0	0	0	0	0	0	–
1914 BKN F	16	16	.500	2.63	42	33	23	290.2	260	127	137	0	1	2	2	101	26	1	.257
1915 2 teams				BKN F (17G 6–9)			BUF F (14G 2–2)												
" total	8	11	.421	3.80	31	21	8	168	179	79	51	0	0	1	1	70	16	0	.229
5 yrs.	35	36	.493	3.34	106	75	47	646.2	668	262	262	0	1	4	5	245	54	2	.220

Ed Lagger

LAGGER, EDWIN JOSEPH
B. July 14, 1912, Joliet, Ill.   D. Nov. 10, 1981, Joliet, Ill.   BR TR 6'3"   200 lbs.

	W	L	PCT	ERA	G	GS	CG	IP	H	BB	SO	ShO	W	L	SV	AB	H	HR	BA
1934 PHI A	0	0	–	11.00	8	0	0	18	27	14	2	0	0	0	0	6	0	0	.000

Lerrin LaGrow

LaGROW, LERRIN HARRIS
B. July 8, 1948, Phoenix, Ariz.   BR TR 6'5"   220 lbs.

	W	L	PCT	ERA	G	GS	CG	IP	H	BB	SO	ShO	W	L	SV	AB	H	HR	BA
1970 DET A	0	1	.000	7.50	10	0	0	12	16	6	7	0	0	1	0	1	0	0	.000
1972	0	1	.000	1.33	16	0	0	27	22	6	9	0	0	1	2	0	0	0	–
1973	1	5	.167	4.33	21	3	0	54	54	23	33	0	0	3	3	0	0	0	–
1974	8	19	.296	4.67	37	34	11	216	245	80	85	0	0	0	0	0	0	0	–
1975	7	14	.333	4.38	32	26	7	164.1	183	66	75	2	0	0	0	0	0	0	–
1976 STL N	0	1	.000	1.48	8	2	1	24.1	21	7	10	0	0	0	0	5	0	0	.000
1977 CHI A	7	3	.700	2.45	66	0	0	99	81	35	63	0	7	3	25	0	0	0	–
1978	6	5	.545	4.40	52	0	0	88	85	38	41	0	6	5	16	0	0	0	–
1979 2 teams			CHI A (11G 0–3)			LA N (31G 5–1)													
" total	5	4	.556	5.24	42	2	0	55	65	34	31	0	5	2	5	3	1	0	.333
1980 PHI N	0	2	.000	4.15	25	0	0	39	42	17	21	0	0	2	3	4	1	0	.250
10 yrs.	34	55	.382	4.11	309	67	19	778.2	814	312	375	2	18	17	54	13	2	0	.154
LEAGUE CHAMPIONSHIP SERIES
1972 DET A	0	0	–	0.00	1	0	0	1	0	0	1	0	0	0	0	0	0	0	–

Jeff Lahti

LAHTI, JEFFREY ALLEN
B. Oct. 8, 1956, Oregon City, Ore.   BR TR 6'   180 lbs.

	W	L	PCT	ERA	G	GS	CG	IP	H	BB	SO	ShO	W	L	SV	AB	H	HR	BA
1982 STL N	5	4	.556	3.81	33	1	0	56.2	53	21	22	0	5	3	0	13	1	0	.077
1983	3	3	.500	3.16	53	0	0	74	64	29	26	0	3	3	0	10	0	0	.000
1984	4	2	.667	3.72	63	0	0	84.2	69	34	45	0	4	2	1	6	1	0	.167
3 yrs.	12	9	.571	3.55	149	1	0	215.1	186	84	93	0	12	8	1	29	2	0	.069
WORLD SERIES
1982 STL N	0	0	–	10.80	2	0	0	1.2	4	1	1	0	0	0	0	0	0	0	–

Eddie Lake

LAKE, EDWARD ERVING
B. Mar. 18, 1916, Antioch, Calif.   BR TR 5'7"   159 lbs.

	W	L	PCT	ERA	G	GS	CG	IP	H	BB	SO	ShO	W	L	SV	AB	H	HR	BA
1944 BOS A	0	0	–	4.19	6	0	0	19.1	20	11	7	0	0	0	0	*			

Joe Lake

LAKE, JOSEPH HENRY
B. Dec. 6, 1881, Brooklyn, N. Y.   D. June 30, 1950, Brooklyn, N. Y.   BR TR 6'   185 lbs.

	W	L	PCT	ERA	G	GS	CG	IP	H	BB	SO	ShO	W	L	SV	AB	H	HR	BA
1908 NY A	9	22	.290	3.17	38	27	19	269.1	252	77	118	2	2	2	0	112	21	1	.188
1909	14	11	.560	1.88	31	26	17	215.1	180	59	117	3	2	0	1	81	14	0	.173
1910 STL A	11	17	.393	2.20	35	29	24	261.1	243	77	141	1	1	1	2	81	21	0	.259
1911	10	15	.400	3.30	30	25	14	215.1	245	40	69	2	1	1	0	80	21	0	.263
1912 2 teams			STL A (11G 1–7)			DET A (26G 9–11)													
" total	10	18	.357	3.44	37	20	16	219.2	260	55	114	0	5	4	1	81	12	1	.148
1913 DET A	8	7	.533	3.28	28	12	6	137	149	24	35	0	4	1	1	45	12	1	.267
6 yrs.	62	90	.408	2.85	199	139	96	1318	1329	332	594	8	15	9	5	480	101	3	.210

		W	L	PCT	ERA	G	GS	CG	IP	H	BB	SO	ShO	Relief W	Relief L	SV	AB	H	HR	BA

Al Lakeman

LAKEMAN, ALBERT WESLEY (Moose)   BR TR 6'2" 195 lbs.
B. Dec. 31, 1918, Cincinnati, Ohio   D. May 25, 1976, Spartanburg, S. C.

Year	Team	W	L	PCT	ERA	G	GS	CG	IP	H	BB	SO	ShO	RW	RL	SV	AB	H	HR	BA
1948	PHI N	0	0	-	13.50	1	0	0	.2	1	0	0	0	0	0	0	*			

Jack Lamabe

LAMABE, JOHN ALEXANDER   BR TR 6'1" 198 lbs.
B. Oct. 3, 1936, Farmingdale, N. Y.

Year	Team	W	L	PCT	ERA	G	GS	CG	IP	H	BB	SO	ShO	RW	RL	SV	AB	H	HR	BA
1962	PIT N	3	1	.750	2.88	46	0	0	78	70	40	56	0	3	1	2	9	0	0	.000
1963	BOS A	7	4	.636	3.15	65	2	0	151.1	139	46	93	0	7	3	6	32	3	1	.094
1964	BOS A	9	13	.409	5.89	39	25	3	177.1	235	57	109	0	1	2	1	52	6	0	.115
1965	2 teams			BOS	A (14G 0-3)		HOU	N	(3G 0-2)											
"	total	0	5	.000	6.87	17	2	0	38	51	17	23	0	0	3	0	8	1	0	.125
1966	CHI A	7	9	.438	3.93	34	17	3	121.1	116	35	67	2	2	0	0	35	2	0	.057
1967	3 teams			CHI	A (3G 1-0)		NY	N	(16G 0-3)		STL	N	(23G 3-4)							
"	total	4	7	.364	3.20	42	3	1	84.1	74	19	56	1	3	5	5	15	2	0	.133
1968	CHI N	3	2	.600	4.30	42	0	0	60.2	68	24	30	0	3	2	1	5	1	0	.200
7 yrs.		33	41	.446	4.24	285	49	7	711	753	238	434	3	19	16	15	156	15	1	.096

WORLD SERIES

Year	Team	W	L	PCT	ERA	G	GS	CG	IP	H	BB	SO	ShO	RW	RL	SV	AB	H	HR	BA
1967	STL N	0	1	.000	6.75	3	0	0	2.2	5	0	4	0	0	1	0	0	0	0	-

Al LaMacchia

LaMACCHIA, ALFRED ANTHONY   BR TR 5'10½" 190 lbs.
B. July 22, 1921, St. Louis, Mo.

Year	Team	W	L	PCT	ERA	G	GS	CG	IP	H	BB	SO	ShO	RW	RL	SV	AB	H	HR	BA
1943	STL A	0	1	.000	11.25	1	1	0	4	9	2	2	0	0	0	0	2	0	0	.000
1945		2	0	1.000		2	1	0	9	6	3	2	0	2	0	0	1	0	0	.000
1946	2 teams			STL	A (8G 0-0)		WAS	A	(2G 0-1)											
"	total	0	1	.000	7.64	10	0	0	17.2	23	9	3	0	0	1	0	3	0	0	.000
3 yrs.		2	2	.500	6.46	16	1	0	30.2	38	14	7	0	2	1	0	6	0	0	.000

Frank Lamanna

LAMANNA, FRANK (Hank)   BR TR 6'2½" 195 lbs.
B. Aug. 22, 1919, Watertown, Pa.   D. Sept. 1, 1980, Syracuse, N. Y.

Year	Team	W	L	PCT	ERA	G	GS	CG	IP	H	BB	SO	ShO	RW	RL	SV	AB	H	HR	BA
1940	BOS N	1	0	1.000	4.73	5	1	1	13.1	13	8	3	0	0	0	0	5	1	0	.200
1941		5	4	.556	5.33	35	4	0	72.2	77	56	23	0	4	2	1	32	9	0	.281
1942		0	1	.000	5.40	5	0	0	6.2	5	3	2	0	0	0	0	2	0	0	-
3 yrs.		6	5	.545	5.24	45	5	1	92.2	95	67	28	0	4	3	1	39	10	0	.256

Frank Lamanske

LAMANSKE, FRANK JAMES (Lefty)   BL TL 5'11" 170 lbs.
B. Sept. 30, 1906, Oglesby, Ill.   D. Aug. 4, 1971, Olney, Ill.

Year	Team	W	L	PCT	ERA	G	GS	CG	IP	H	BB	SO	ShO	RW	RL	SV	AB	H	HR	BA
1935	BKN N	0	0	-	7.36	2	0	0	3.2	5	1	1	0	0	0	0	1	0	0	.000

Wayne LaMaster

LaMASTER, WAYNE LEE   BL TL 5'8" 170 lbs.
B. Feb. 13, 1907, Speed, Ind.

Year	Team	W	L	PCT	ERA	G	GS	CG	IP	H	BB	SO	ShO	RW	RL	SV	AB	H	HR	BA
1937	PHI N	15	19	.441	5.31	50	30	10	220.1	255	82	135	1	3	4	4	79	15	0	.190
1938	2 teams			PHI	N (18G 4-7)		BKN	N	(3G 0-1)											
"	total	4	8	.333	7.32	21	12	1	75	97	34	38	1	0	2	0	28	10	0	.357
2 yrs.		19	27	.413	5.82	71	42	11	295.1	352	116	173	2	3	6	4	107	25	0	.234

John Lamb

LAMB, JOHN ANDREW   BR TR 6'3" 180 lbs.
B. July 20, 1946, Sharon, Conn.

Year	Team	W	L	PCT	ERA	G	GS	CG	IP	H	BB	SO	ShO	RW	RL	SV	AB	H	HR	BA
1970	PIT N	0	1	.000	2.81	23	0	0	32	23	13	24	0	0	1	3	3	0	0	.000
1971		0	0	-	0.00	2	0	0	4	3	1	1	0	0	0	0	1	0	0	.000
1973		0	1	.000	6.07	22	0	0	29.2	37	10	11	0	0	1	2	3	0	0	.000
3 yrs.		0	2	.000	4.11	47	0	0	65.2	63	24	36	0	0	2	5	7	0	0	.000

Ray Lamb

LAMB, RAYMOND RICHARD   BR TR 6'1" 170 lbs.
B. Dec. 28, 1944, Glendale, Calif.

Year	Team	W	L	PCT	ERA	G	GS	CG	IP	H	BB	SO	ShO	RW	RL	SV	AB	H	HR	BA
1969	LA N	0	1	.000	1.80	10	0	0	15	12	7	11	0	0	1	1	1	0	0	.000
1970		6	1	.857	3.79	35	0	0	57	59	27	32	0	6	1	0	4	0	0	.000
1971	CLE A	6	12	.333	3.36	43	21	3	158	147	69	91	1	0	2	1	43	4	0	.093
1972		5	6	.455	3.08	34	9	0	108	101	29	64	0	4	1	0	21	0	0	.000
1973		3	3	.500	4.60	32	1	0	86	98	42	60	0	3	2	2	0	0	0	-
5 yrs.		20	23	.465	3.54	154	31	3	424	417	174	258	1	13	7	4	69	4	0	.058

Clay Lambert

LAMBERT, CLAYTON PATRICK   BR TR 6'2" 185 lbs.
B. Mar. 26, 1917, Summit, Ill.   D. Apr. 3, 1981, Ogden, Utah

Year	Team	W	L	PCT	ERA	G	GS	CG	IP	H	BB	SO	ShO	RW	RL	SV	AB	H	HR	BA
1946	CIN N	2	2	.500	4.27	23	4	2	52.2	48	20	20	0	1	1	1	13	2	0	.154
1947		0	0	-	15.88	3	0	0	5.2	12	6	1	0	0	0	0	1	0	0	.000
2 yrs.		2	2	.500	5.40	26	4	2	58.1	60	26	21	0	1	1	1	14	2	0	.143

Gene Lambert

LAMBERT, EUGENE MARION   BR TR 5'11" 175 lbs.
B. Apr. 26, 1921, Crenshaw, Miss.

Year	Team	W	L	PCT	ERA	G	GS	CG	IP	H	BB	SO	ShO	RW	RL	SV	AB	H	HR	BA
1941	PHI N	0	1	.000	2.00	2	1	0	9	11	2	3	0	0	0	0	2	0	0	.000
1942		0	0	-	9.00	1	0	0	1	3	0	1	0	0	0	0	0	0	0	-
2 yrs.		0	1	.000	2.70	3	1	0	10	14	2	4	0	0	0	0	2	0	0	.000

Otis Lambeth

LAMBETH, OTIS LAMBETH   BR TR 6' 175 lbs.
B. May 13, 1890, Berlin, Kans.   D. June 5, 1976, Moran, Kans.

Year	Team	W	L	PCT	ERA	G	GS	CG	IP	H	BB	SO	ShO	RW	RL	SV	AB	H	HR	BA
1916	CLE A	4	3	.571	2.92	15	9	3	74	69	38	28	0	1	0	1	27	3	0	.111
1917		7	6	.538	3.14	26	10	2	97.1	97	30	27	0	3	3	2	32	6	0	.188
1918		0	0	-	6.43	2	0	0	7	10	6	3	0	0	0	0	1	1	0	1.000
3 yrs.		11	9	.550	3.18	43	19	5	178.1	176	74	58	0	4	3	3	60	10	0	.167

Fred Lamline

LAMLINE, FREDERICK ARTHUR (Dutch)   BR TR 5'11" 171 lbs.
B. Aug. 14, 1891, Port Huron, Mich.   D. Sept. 20, 1970, Port Huron, Mich.

Year	Team	W	L	PCT	ERA	G	GS	CG	IP	H	BB	SO	ShO	RW	RL	SV	AB	H	HR	BA
1912	CHI A	0	0	-	31.50	1	0	0	2	7	2	1	0	0	0	0	0	0	0	-
1915	STL N	0	0	-	2.84	4	0	0	19	21	3	11	0	0	0	0	8	1	0	.125
2 yrs.		0	0	-	5.57	5	0	0	21	28	5	12	0	0	0	0	8	1	0	.125

	W	L	PCT	ERA	G	GS	CG	IP	H	BB	SO	ShO	Relief Pitching W	L	SV	BATTING AB	H	HR	BA

Dennis Lamp

LAMP, DENNIS PATRICK   BR TR 6'4"   200 lbs.
B. Sept. 23, 1952, Los Angeles, Calif.

	W	L	PCT	ERA	G	GS	CG	IP	H	BB	SO	ShO	W	L	SV	AB	H	HR	BA
1977 CHI N	0	2	.000	6.30	11	3	0	30	43	8	12	0	0	0	0	8	3	0	.375
1978	7	15	.318	3.29	37	36	6	224	221	56	73	3	0	0	0	73	15	0	.205
1979	11	10	.524	3.51	38	32	6	200	223	46	86	1	0	0	0	58	9	0	.155
1980	10	14	.417	5.19	41	37	2	203	259	82	83	1	1	2	0	61	6	0	.098
1981 CHI A	7	6	.538	2.41	27	10	3	127	103	43	71	0	3	1	0	0	0	0	–
1982	11	8	.579	3.99	44	27	3	189.2	206	59	78	2	1	1	5	0	0	0	–
1983	7	7	.500	3.71	49	5	1	116.1	123	29	44	0	4	5	15	0	0	0	–
1984 TOR A	8	8	.500	4.55	56	4	0	85	97	38	45	0	5	7	9	0	0	0	–
8 yrs.	61	70	.466	3.88	303	154	21	1175	1275	361	492	7	14	16	29	200	33	0	.165

LEAGUE CHAMPIONSHIP SERIES
| 1983 CHI A | 0 | 0 | – | 0.00 | 3 | 0 | 0 | 2 | 0 | 2 | 1 | 0 | 0 | 0 | 0 | 0 | 0 | 0 | – |

Henry Lampe

LAMPE, HENRY JOSEPH   BR TL 5'11½" 175 lbs.
B. Sept. 19, 1872, Boston, Mass.   D. Sept. 16, 1936, Dorchester, Mass.

	W	L	PCT	ERA	G	GS	CG	IP	H	BB	SO	ShO	W	L	SV	AB	H	HR	BA
1894 BOS N	0	1	.000	11.81	2	1	0	5.1	17	7	1	0	0	0	0	2	0	0	.000
1895 PHI N	0	2	.000	7.57	7	3	2	44	68	33	18	0	0	0	0	16	2	0	.125
2 yrs.	0	3	.000	8.03	9	4	2	49.1	85	40	19	0	0	0	0	18	2	0	.111

Dick Lanahan

LANAHAN, RICHARD ANTHONY   BL TL 6'   186 lbs.
B. Sept. 27, 1913, Washington, D. C.   D. Mar. 12, 1975, Rochester, Minn.

	W	L	PCT	ERA	G	GS	CG	IP	H	BB	SO	ShO	W	L	SV	AB	H	HR	BA
1935 WAS A	0	3	.000	5.66	3	3	0	20.2	27	17	10	0	0	0	0	6	1	0	.167
1937	0	1	.000	12.71	6	2	0	11.1	16	13	2	0	0	0	0	1	0	0	.000
1940 PIT N	6	8	.429	4.25	40	8	4	108	121	42	45	0	2	6	2	34	4	0	.118
1941	0	1	.000	5.25	7	0	0	12	13	3	5	0	0	1	0	1	0	0	.000
4 yrs.	6	13	.316	5.15	56	13	4	152	177	75	62	0	2	7	2	42	5	0	.119

Gary Lance

LANCE, GARY DEAN   BB TL 6'3" 195 lbs.
B. Sept. 21, 1948, Greenville, S. C.

	W	L	PCT	ERA	G	GS	CG	IP	H	BB	SO	ShO	W	L	SV	AB	H	HR	BA
1977 KC A	0	1	.000	4.50	1	0	0	2	2	2	0	0	0	1	0	0	0	0	–

Bill Landis

LANDIS, WILLIAM HENRY   BL TL 6'2" 178 lbs.
B. Oct. 8, 1942, Hanford, Calif.

	W	L	PCT	ERA	G	GS	CG	IP	H	BB	SO	ShO	W	L	SV	AB	H	HR	BA
1963 KC A	0	0	–	0.00	1	0	0	1.2	0	1	3	0	0	0	0	0	0	0	–
1967 BOS A	1	0	1.000	5.26	18	1	0	25.2	11	11	23	0	1	0	0	2	0	0	.000
1968	3	3	.500	3.15	38	1	0	60	48	30	59	0	3	2	3	6	0	0	.000
1969	5	5	.500	5.25	45	5	0	82.1	82	49	50	0	4	3	1	11	0	0	.000
4 yrs.	9	8	.529	4.46	102	7	0	169.2	154	91	135	0	8	5	4	19	0	0	.000

Doc Landis

LANDIS, SAMUEL H.   5'11" 172 lbs.
B. Aug. 16, 1854, Philadelphia, Pa.   Deceased.

	W	L	PCT	ERA	G	GS	CG	IP	H	BB	SO	ShO	W	L	SV	AB	H	HR	BA
1882 2 teams			PHI AA (2G 1–1)			BAL AA (42G 11–27)													
" total	12	28	.300	3.32	44	41	37	358	425	47	75	0	0	0	0	187	31	0	.166

Larry Landreth

LANDRETH, LARRY ROBERT   BR TR 6'1" 175 lbs.
B. Mar. 11, 1955, Stratford, Ontario, Canada

	W	L	PCT	ERA	G	GS	CG	IP	H	BB	SO	ShO	W	L	SV	AB	H	HR	BA
1976 MON N	1	2	.333	4.09	3	3	0	11	13	10	7	0	0	0	0	3	0	0	.000
1977	0	2	.000	10.00	4	1	0	9	16	8	5	0	0	0	0	2	0	0	.000
2 yrs.	1	4	.200	6.75	7	4	0	20	29	18	12	0	0	0	0	5	0	0	.000

Joe Landrum

LANDRUM, JOSEPH BUTLER   BR TR 5'11" 180 lbs.
B. Dec. 13, 1928, Columbia, S. C.

	W	L	PCT	ERA	G	GS	CG	IP	H	BB	SO	ShO	W	L	SV	AB	H	HR	BA
1950 BKN N	0	0	–	8.10	7	0	0	6.2	12	1	5	0	0	0	1	0	0	0	–
1952	1	3	.250	5.21	9	5	2	38	46	10	17	0	0	0	0	8	1	0	.125
2 yrs.	1	3	.250	5.64	16	5	2	44.2	58	11	22	0	0	0	1	8	1	0	.125

Jerry Lane

LANE, JERALD HAL   BR TR 6'½" 205 lbs.
B. Feb. 7, 1926, Ashland, N. Y.

	W	L	PCT	ERA	G	GS	CG	IP	H	BB	SO	ShO	W	L	SV	AB	H	HR	BA
1953 WAS A	1	4	.200	4.92	20	2	0	56.2	64	16	26	0	1	2	0	9	1	0	.111
1954 CIN N	1	0	1.000	1.69	3	0	0	10.2	9	3	2	0	1	0	0	4	0	0	.000
1955	0	2	.000	4.91	8	0	0	11	11	6	5	0	0	2	1	0	0	0	–
3 yrs.	2	6	.250	4.48	31	2	0	78.1	84	25	33	0	2	4	1	13	1	0	.077

Sam Lanford

LANFORD, LEWIS GROVER   BL TR 5'9" 155 lbs.
B. Jan. 8, 1886, Woodruff, S. C.   D. Sept. 14, 1970, Woodruff, S. C.

	W	L	PCT	ERA	G	GS	CG	IP	H	BB	SO	ShO	W	L	SV	AB	H	HR	BA
1907 WAS A	0	1	.000	5.14	2	1	0	7	10	5	2	0	0	0	0	3	1	0	.333

Walt Lanfranconi

LANFRANCONI, WALTER OSWALD   BR TR 5'7½" 155 lbs.
B. Nov. 9, 1916, Barre, Vt.

	W	L	PCT	ERA	G	GS	CG	IP	H	BB	SO	ShO	W	L	SV	AB	H	HR	BA
1941 CHI N	0	1	.000	3.00	2	1	0	6	7	2	1	0	0	0	0	1	0	0	.000
1947 BOS N	4	4	.500	2.95	36	4	1	64	65	27	18	0	3	0	1	10	0	0	.000
2 yrs.	4	5	.444	2.96	38	5	1	70	72	29	19	0	3	0	1	11	0	0	.000

Chip Lang

LANG, ROBERT DAVID   BR TR 6'4" 210 lbs.
B. Aug. 21, 1952, Pittsburgh, Pa.

	W	L	PCT	ERA	G	GS	CG	IP	H	BB	SO	ShO	W	L	SV	AB	H	HR	BA
1975 MON N	0	0	–	9.00	1	1	0	2	2	3	2	0	0	0	0	0	0	0	–
1976	1	3	.250	4.19	29	2	0	62.1	56	34	30	0	0	2	0	6	1	0	.167
2 yrs.	1	3	.250	4.34	30	3	0	64.1	58	37	32	0	0	2	0	6	1	0	.167

Marty Lang

LANG, MARTIN JOHN (Lefty)   BR TL 5'11" 160 lbs.
B. Sept. 27, 1906, Hooper, Neb.   D. Jan. 13, 1968, Lakewood, Colo.

	W	L	PCT	ERA	G	GS	CG	IP	H	BB	SO	ShO	W	L	SV	AB	H	HR	BA
1930 PIT N	0	0	–	54.00	2	0	0	1.2	9	3	2	0	0	0	0	0	0	0	–

	W	L	PCT	ERA	G	GS	CG	IP	H	BB	SO	ShO	Relief Pitching W	L	SV	BATTING AB	H	HR	BA

Dick Lange

LANGE, RICHARD OTTO
B. Sept. 1, 1948, Harbor Beach, Mich. BR TR 5'10" 185 lbs.

	W	L	PCT	ERA	G	GS	CG	IP	H	BB	SO	ShO	W	L	SV	AB	H	HR	BA
1972 CAL A	0	0	–	4.50	2	1	0	8	7	2	8	0	0	0	0	3	0	0	.000
1973	2	1	.667	4.44	17	4	1	52.2	61	21	27	0	1	0	0	0	0	0	–
1974	3	8	.273	3.79	21	18	1	114	111	47	57	0	0	0	0	0	0	0	–
1975	4	6	.400	5.21	30	8	1	102	119	53	45	0	2	2	1	0	0	0	–
4 yrs.	9	15	.375	4.46	70	31	3	276.2	298	123	137	0	3	2	1	3	0	0	.000

Erv Lange

LANGE, ERWIN HENRY
B. Aug. 12, 1887, Forest Park Ill. D. Apr. 24, 1971, Maywood, Ill. BR TR 5'10" 170 lbs.

	W	L	PCT	ERA	G	GS	CG	IP	H	BB	SO	ShO	W	L	SV	AB	H	HR	BA
1914 CHI F	12	10	.545	2.23	36	22	10	190	162	55	87	2	3	1	2	51	9	0	.176

Frank Lange

LANGE, FRANK HERMAN (Seagan)
B. Oct. 28, 1883, Columbus, Wis. D. Dec. 26, 1945, Madison, Wis. BR TR 5'11" 180 lbs.

	W	L	PCT	ERA	G	GS	CG	IP	H	BB	SO	ShO	W	L	SV	AB	H	HR	BA
1910 CHI A	9	4	.692	1.65	23	15	6	130.2	93	54	98	1	1	0	0	51	13	0	.255
1911	8	8	.500	3.23	29	22	8	161.2	151	77	104	1	0	1	0	76	22	0	.289
1912	10	10	.500	3.27	31	21	11	165.1	165	68	96	2	3	1	3	65	14	0	.215
1913	1	3	.250	4.87	12	3	0	40.2	46	20	20	0	0	1	0	18	3	0	.167
4 yrs.	28	25	.528	2.96	95	61	25	498.1	455	219	318	4	4	3	3	*			

Rick Langford

LANGFORD, JAMES RICK
B. Mar. 20, 1952, Farmville, Va. BR TR 6' 180 lbs.

	W	L	PCT	ERA	G	GS	CG	IP	H	BB	SO	ShO	W	L	SV	AB	H	HR	BA
1976 PIT N	0	1	.000	6.26	12	1	0	23	27	14	17	0	0	1	0	5	1	0	.200
1977 OAK A	8	19	.296	4.02	37	31	6	208	223	73	141	1	1	0	0	0	0	0	–
1978	7	13	.350	3.43	37	24	4	175.2	169	56	92	2	1	1	0	0	0	0	–
1979	12	16	.429	4.27	34	29	14	219	233	57	101	1	1	0	0	0	0	0	–
1980	19	12	.613	3.26	35	33	**28**	**290**	276	64	102	2	1	0	0	0	0	0	–
1981	12	10	.545	3.00	24	24	**18**	195	190	58	84	2	0	0	0	0	0	0	–
1982	11	16	.407	4.21	32	31	15	237.1	265	49	79	2	0	0	0	1	0	0	.000
1983	0	4	.000	12.15	7	7	0	20	43	10	2	0	0	0	0	0	0	0	–
1984	0	0	–	8.31	3	1	0	8.2	15	2	2	0	0	0	0	0	0	0	–
9 yrs.	69	91	.431	3.90	221	181	85	1376.2	1441	383	620	10	4	2	0	6	1	0	.167

DIVISIONAL PLAYOFF SERIES

	W	L	PCT	ERA	G	GS	CG	IP	H	BB	SO	ShO	W	L	SV	AB	H	HR	BA
1981 OAK A	1	0	1.000	1.23	1	1	0	7.1	10	1	3	0	0	0	0	0	0	0	–

Mark Langston

LANGSTON, MARK EDWARD
B. Aug. 20, 1960, San Diego, Calif. BR TL 6'1" 175 lbs.

	W	L	PCT	ERA	G	GS	CG	IP	H	BB	SO	ShO	W	L	SV	AB	H	HR	BA
1984 SEA A	17	10	.630	3.40	35	33	5	225	188	**118**	**204**	2	1	0	0	0	0	0	–

Max Lanier

LANIER, HUBERT MAX
Father of Hal Lanier.
B. Aug. 18, 1915, Denton, N. C. BR TL 5'11" 180 lbs.

	W	L	PCT	ERA	G	GS	CG	IP	H	BB	SO	ShO	W	L	SV	AB	H	HR	BA
1938 STL N	0	3	.000	4.20	18	3	1	45	57	28	14	0	0	2	0	10	1	0	.100
1939	2	1	.667	2.39	7	6	2	37.2	29	13	14	0	0	0	0	14	4	0	.286
1940	9	6	.600	3.34	35	11	4	105	113	38	49	2	5	3	3	30	6	0	.200
1941	10	8	.556	2.82	35	18	8	153	126	59	93	2	2	3	3	52	10	0	.192
1942	13	8	.619	2.98	34	20	8	160	137	60	93	2	5	4	0	47	12	0	.255
1943	15	7	.682	1.90	32	25	14	213.1	195	75	123	2	2	0	3	73	12	0	.164
1944	17	12	.586	2.65	33	30	16	224.1	192	71	141	5	3	0	0	77	14	0	.182
1945	2	2	.500	1.73	4	3	3	26	22	8	16	0	0	1	0	11	2	0	.182
1946	6	0	1.000	1.93	6	6	6	56	45	19	36	2	0	0	0	25	5	0	.200
1949	5	4	.556	3.82	15	15	4	92	92	35	37	1	0	0	0	27	2	0	.074
1950	11	9	.550	3.13	27	27	10	181.1	173	68	89	2	0	0	0	68	11	0	.162
1951	11	9	.550	3.26	31	23	9	160	149	59	59	2	1	0	1	53	8	0	.151
1952 NY N	7	12	.368	3.94	37	16	6	137	124	65	47	1	2	3	5	41	11	0	.268
1953 2 teams			NY	N (3G 0–0)			STL	A (10G 0–1)											
" total	0	1	.000	7.16	13	1	0	27.2	36	22	10	0	0	0	0	7	1	0	.143
14 yrs.	108	82	.568	3.01	327	204	91	1618.1	1490	611	821	21	20	12	17	535	99	0	.185

WORLD SERIES

	W	L	PCT	ERA	G	GS	CG	IP	H	BB	SO	ShO	W	L	SV	AB	H	HR	BA
1942 STL N	1	0	1.000	0.00	2	0	0	4	3	1	1	0	1	0	0	1	1	0	1.000
1943	0	1	.000	1.76	3	2	0	15.1	13	3	13	0	0	0	0	4	1	0	.250
1944	1	0	1.000	2.19	2	2	0	12.1	8	8	11	0	0	0	0	4	2	0	.500
3 yrs.	2	1	.667	1.71	7	4	0	31.2	24	12	25	0	1	0	0	9	4	0	.444

Johnny Lanning

LANNING, JOHN YOUNG (Tobacco Chewin' Johnny)
Brother of Tom Lanning.
B. Sept. 6, 1910, Asheville, N. C. BR TR 6'1" 185 lbs.

	W	L	PCT	ERA	G	GS	CG	IP	H	BB	SO	ShO	W	L	SV	AB	H	HR	BA
1936 BOS N	7	11	.389	3.65	28	20	3	153	154	55	33	1	1	0	0	52	7	1	.135
1937	5	7	.417	3.93	32	11	4	116.2	107	40	37	1	2	0	2	33	4	0	.121
1938	8	7	.533	3.72	32	18	4	138	146	52	39	1	3	1	0	48	9	0	.188
1939	5	6	.455	3.42	37	6	3	129	120	53	45	0	3	2	4	42	6	0	.143
1940 PIT N	8	4	.667	4.05	38	7	2	115.2	119	39	42	0	5	2	2	35	7	0	.200
1941	11	11	.500	3.13	34	23	9	175.2	175	47	41	0	2	1	1	56	6	0	.107
1942	6	8	.429	3.32	34	8	2	119.1	125	26	31	1	4	2	1	29	4	0	.138
1943	4	1	.800	2.33	12	2	0	27	23	9	11	0	4	0	2	6	1	0	.167
1945	0	0	–	36.00	1	0	0	2	8	0	0	0	0	0	0	0	0	0	–
1946	4	5	.444	3.07	27	9	3	91	97	31	16	0	2	5	1	21	3	0	.143
1947 BOS N	0	0	–	9.82	3	0	0	3.2	4	6	0	0	0	0	0	0	0	0	–
11 yrs.	58	60	.492	3.58	278	104	30	1071	1078	358	295	4	26	10	13	322	47	1	.146

Les Lanning

LANNING, LESTER ALFRED (Red)
B. May 13, 1895, Harvard, Ill. D. June 13, 1962, Bristol, Conn. BL TL 5'9" 165 lbs.

	W	L	PCT	ERA	G	GS	CG	IP	H	BB	SO	ShO	W	L	SV	AB	H	HR	BA
1916 PHI A	0	3	.000	8.14	6	3	1	24.1	38	17	9	0	0	0	0	*			

	W	L	PCT	ERA	G	GS	CG	IP	H	BB	SO	ShO	Relief Pitching W	L	SV	BATTING AB	H	HR	BA

Tom Lanning

LANNING, THOMAS NEWTON   BL TL 6'1"   165 lbs.
Brother of Johnny Lanning.
B. Apr. 22, 1907, Asheville, N. C.   D. Nov. 4, 1967, Marietta, Ga.

	W	L	PCT	ERA	G	GS	CG	IP	H	BB	SO	ShO	W	L	SV	AB	H	HR	BA
1938 PHI N	0	1	.000	6.43	3	1	0	7	9	2	2	0	0	0	0	1	1	0	1.000

Gene Lansing

LANSING, EUGENE HEWITT (Jigger)   BR TR 6'1"   185 lbs.
B. Jan. 11, 1898, Albany, N. Y.   D. Jan. 18, 1945, Rensselaer, N. Y.

	W	L	PCT	ERA	G	GS	CG	IP	H	BB	SO	ShO	W	L	SV	AB	H	HR	BA
1922 BOS N	0	1	.000	5.98	15	1	0	40.2	46	22	14	0	0	1	0	11	0	0	.000

Paul LaPalme

LaPALME, PAUL EDMORE (Lefty)   BL TL 5'10"   175 lbs.
B. Dec. 14, 1923, Springfield, Mass.

	W	L	PCT	ERA	G	GS	CG	IP	H	BB	SO	ShO	W	L	SV	AB	H	HR	BA
1951 PIT N	1	5	.167	6.29	22	8	1	54.1	79	31	24	1	0	2	0	10	1	0	.100
1952	1	2	.333	3.92	31	2	0	59.2	56	37	25	0	1	2	0	10	1	0	.100
1953	8	16	.333	4.59	35	24	7	176.1	191	64	86	1	1	1	2	59	5	0	.085
1954	4	10	.286	5.52	33	15	2	120.2	147	54	57	0	1	1	0	35	5	0	.143
1955 STL N	4	3	.571	2.75	56	0	0	91.2	76	34	39	0	4	3	3	19	4	0	.211
1956 3 teams			STL N (1G 0–0)			CIN N (11G 2–4)			CHI A (29G 3–1)											
" total	5	5	.500	3.93	41	2	0	73.1	61	33	27	0	4	4	2	10	2	0	.200
1957 CHI A	1	4	.200	3.35	35	0	0	40.1	35	19	19	0	1	4	7	4	2	0	.500
7 yrs.	24	45	.348	4.42	253	51	10	616.1	645	272	277	2	12	17	14	147	20	0	.136

Andy Lapihuska

LAPIHUSKA, ANDREW (Apples)   BL TR 5'10½" 175 lbs.
B. Nov. 1, 1922, Delmont, N. J.

	W	L	PCT	ERA	G	GS	CG	IP	H	BB	SO	ShO	W	L	SV	AB	H	HR	BA
1942 PHI N	0	2	.000	5.23	3	2	0	20.2	17	13	8	0	0	0	0	7	2	0	.286
1943	0	0	–	23.14	1	0	0	2.1	5	3	0	0	0	0	0	2	0	0	.000
2 yrs.	0	2	.000	7.04	4	2	0	23	22	16	8	0	0	0	0	9	2	0	.222

Dave LaPoint

LaPOINT, DAVID JEFFREY   BL TL 6'3"   205 lbs.
B. July 29, 1959, Glens Falls, N. Y.

	W	L	PCT	ERA	G	GS	CG	IP	H	BB	SO	ShO	W	L	SV	AB	H	HR	BA
1980 MIL A	1	0	1.000	6.00	5	3	0	15	17	13	5	0	1	0	1	0	0	0	–
1981 STL N	1	0	1.000	4.09	3	2	0	11	12	2	4	0	0	0	0	5	0	0	.000
1982	9	3	.750	3.42	42	21	0	152.2	170	52	81	0	1	0	0	38	2	0	.053
1983	12	9	.571	3.95	37	29	1	191.1	191	84	113	0	2	1	0	59	9	0	.153
1984	12	10	.545	3.96	33	33	2	193	205	77	130	1	0	0	0	59	4	0	.068
5 yrs.	35	22	.614	3.87	120	88	3	563	595	228	333	1	4	1	1	161	15	0	.093

WORLD SERIES
	W	L	PCT	ERA	G	GS	CG	IP	H	BB	SO	ShO	W	L	SV	AB	H	HR	BA
1982 STL N	0	0	–	3.24	2	1	0	8.1	10	2	3	0	0	0	0	0	0	0	–

Pat Larkin

LARKIN, PATRICK C.   BL TL 6'   180 lbs.
B. June 14, 1960, Arcadia, Calif.

	W	L	PCT	ERA	G	GS	CG	IP	H	BB	SO	ShO	W	L	SV	AB	H	HR	BA
1983 SF N	0	0	–	4.35	5	0	0	10.1	13	3	6	0	0	0	0	1	0	0	.000

Steve Larkin

LARKIN, STEPHEN PATRICK   BR TR 6'1"   195 lbs.
B. Dec. 9, 1910, Cincinnati, Ohio   D. May 2, 1969, Norristown, Pa.

	W	L	PCT	ERA	G	GS	CG	IP	H	BB	SO	ShO	W	L	SV	AB	H	HR	BA
1934 DET A	0	0	–	1.50	2	1	0	6	8	5	8	0	0	0	0	3	1	0	.333

Terry Larkin

LARKIN, FRANK   BR TR
B. New York, N. Y.   Deceased.

	W	L	PCT	ERA	G	GS	CG	IP	H	BB	SO	ShO	W	L	SV	AB	H	HR	BA
1876 NY N	0	1	.000	3.00	1	1	1	9	9	0	0	0	0	0	0	4	0	0	.000
1877 HAR N	29	25	.537	2.14	56	56	55	501	510	53	96	4	0	0	0	228	52	1	.228
1878 CHI N	29	26	.527	2.24	56	56	56	506	511	31	163	1	0	0	0	226	65	0	.288
1879	31	23	.574	2.44	58	58	57	513.1	514	30	142	3	0	0	0	228	50	0	.219
1880 TRO N	0	5	.000	8.76	5	5	3	38	83	10	5	0	0	0	0	20	3	0	.150
1884 RIC AA	0	0	–	0.00	0	0	0	0	0	0	0	0	0	0	0	209	45	0	.215
6 yrs.	89	80	.527	2.43	176	176	172	1567.1	1627	124	406	8	0	0	0	*			

Dave LaRoche

LaROCHE, DAVID EUGENE   BL TL 6'2"   200 lbs.
B. May 14, 1948, Colorado Springs, Colo.

	W	L	PCT	ERA	G	GS	CG	IP	H	BB	SO	ShO	W	L	SV	AB	H	HR	BA
1970 CAL A	4	1	.800	3.42	38	0	0	50	41	21	44	0	4	1	4	8	2	0	.250
1971	5	1	.833	2.50	56	0	0	72	55	27	63	0	5	1	9	11	1	0	.091
1972 MIN A	5	7	.417	2.84	62	0	0	95	72	39	79	0	5	7	10	11	1	0	.091
1973 CHI N	4	1	.800	5.83	45	0	0	54	55	29	34	0	4	1	4	4	2	0	.500
1974	5	6	.455	4.79	49	4	0	92	103	47	49	0	4	5	5	27	9	0	.333
1975 CLE A	5	3	.625	2.19	61	0	0	82.1	61	57	94	0	5	3	17	0	0	0	–
1976	1	4	.200	2.25	61	0	0	96	57	49	104	0	1	4	21	0	0	0	–
1977 2 teams			CLE A (13G 2–2)			CAL A (46G 6–5)														
" total	8	7	.533	3.51	59	0	0	100	79	44	79	0	8	7	17	0	0	0	–
1978 CAL A	10	9	.526	2.81	59	0	0	96	73	48	70	0	10	9	25	0	0	0	–
1979	7	11	.389	5.55	53	1	0	86	107	32	59	0	6	11	10	0	0	0	–
1980	3	5	.375	4.08	52	9	1	128	122	39	89	0	2	0	4	0	0	0	–
1981 NY A	4	1	.800	2.49	26	1	0	47	38	16	24	0	4	1	0	0	0	0	–
1982	4	2	.667	3.42	25	0	0	50	54	11	31	0	4	2	0	0	0	0	–
1983	0	0	–	18.00	1	0	0	1	2	0	0	0	0	0	0	0	0	0	–
14 yrs.	65	58	.528	3.53	647	15	1	1049.1	919	459	819	0	62	52	126	61	15	0	.246

LEAGUE CHAMPIONSHIP SERIES
	W	L	PCT	ERA	G	GS	CG	IP	H	BB	SO	ShO	W	L	SV	AB	H	HR	BA
1979 CAL A	0	0	–	6.75	1	0	0	1.1	2	1	1	0	0	0	0	0	0	0	–

WORLD SERIES
	W	L	PCT	ERA	G	GS	CG	IP	H	BB	SO	ShO	W	L	SV	AB	H	HR	BA
1981 NY A	0	0	–	0.00	1	0	0	1	0	0	2	0	0	0	0	0	0	0	–

John LaRose

LaROSE, JOHN HENRY   BL TL 6'1"   185 lbs.
B. Oct. 25, 1951, Pawtucket, R. I.

	W	L	PCT	ERA	G	GS	CG	IP	H	BB	SO	ShO	W	L	SV	AB	H	HR	BA
1978 BOS A	0	0	–	22.50	1	0	0	2	3	3	0	0	0	0	0	0	0	0	–

	W	L	PCT	ERA	G	GS	CG	IP	H	BB	SO	ShO	Relief Pitching W	L	SV	BATTING AB	H	HR	BA

Don Larsen

LARSEN, DONALD JAMES
B. Aug. 7, 1929, Michigan City, Ind.
BR TR 6'4" 215 lbs.

	W	L	PCT	ERA	G	GS	CG	IP	H	BB	SO	ShO	W	L	SV	AB	H	HR	BA
1953 STL A	7	12	.368	4.16	38	22	7	192.2	201	64	96	2	1	2	2	81	23	3	.284
1954 BAL A	3	21	.125	4.37	29	28	12	201.2	213	89	80	1	0	1	0	88	22	1	.250
1955 NY A	9	2	.818	3.06	19	13	5	97	81	51	44	1	1	1	2	41	6	2	.146
1956	11	5	.688	3.26	38	20	6	179.2	133	96	107	1	2	1	1	79	19	2	.241
1957	10	4	.714	3.74	27	20	4	139.2	113	87	81	1	2	0	0	56	14	0	.250
1958	9	6	.600	3.07	19	19	5	114.1	100	52	55	3	0	0	0	49	15	4	.306
1959	6	7	.462	4.33	25	18	3	124.2	122	76	69	1	0	0	0	47	12	0	.255
1960 KC A	1	10	.091	5.38	22	15	0	83.2	97	42	43	0	0	1	0	29	6	0	.207
1961 2 teams			KC	A	(8G 1–0)		CHI	A	(25G 7–2)										
" total	8	2	.800	4.13	33	4	0	89.1	85	40	66	0	6	1	2	45	14	2	.311
1962 SF N	5	4	.556	4.38	49	0	0	86.1	83	47	58	0	5	4	11	25	5	0	.200
1963	7	7	.500	3.05	46	0	0	62	46	30	44	0	7	7	3	11	2	0	.182
1964 2 teams			SF	N	(6G 0–1)		HOU	N	(30G 4–8)										
" total	4	9	.308	2.45	36	10	2	113.2	102	26	64	1	1	4	1	32	3	0	.094
1965 2 teams			HOU	N	(1G 0–0)		BAL	A	(27G 1–2)										
" total	1	2	.333	2.88	28	2	0	59.1	61	23	41	0	1	1	1	13	3	0	.231
1967 CHI N	0	0	–	9.00	3	0	0	4	5	2	1	0	0	0	0	0	0	0	–
14 yrs.	81	91	.471	3.78	412	171	44	1548	1442	725	849	11	26	23	23	*			

WORLD SERIES

	W	L	PCT	ERA	G	GS	CG	IP	H	BB	SO	ShO	W	L	SV	AB	H	HR	BA
1955 NY A	0	1	.000	11.25	1	1	0	4	5	2	2	0	0	0	0	2	0	0	.000
1956	1	0	1.000	0.00	2	2	1	10.2	1	4	7	1	0	0	0	3	1	0	.333
1957	1	1	.500	3.72	2	1	0	9.2	8	5	6	0	1	0	0	2	0	0	.000
1958	1	0	1.000	0.96	2	2	0	9.1	9	6	9	0	0	0	0	2	0	0	.000
1962 SF N	1	0	1.000	3.86	3	0	0	2.1	1	2	0	0	1	0	0	0	0	0	–
5 yrs.	4	2	.667	2.75	10	6	1	36	24	19	24	1	2	0	0	9	1	0	.111
													2nd						

Dan Larson

LARSON, DANIEL JAMES
B. July 4, 1954, Los Angeles, Calif.
BR TR 6' 175 lbs.

	W	L	PCT	ERA	G	GS	CG	IP	H	BB	SO	ShO	W	L	SV	AB	H	HR	BA
1976 HOU N	5	8	.385	3.03	13	13	5	92	81	28	42	0	0	0	0	31	9	0	.290
1977	1	7	.125	5.79	32	10	1	98	108	45	44	0	1	2	1	28	6	0	.214
1978 PHI N	0	0	–	9.00	1	0	0	1	1	1	2	0	0	0	0	0	0	0	–
1979	1	1	.500	4.26	3	3	0	19	17	9	9	0	0	0	0	5	0	0	.000
1980	0	5	.000	3.13	12	7	0	46	46	24	17	0	0	0	0	13	2	0	.154
1981	3	0	1.000	4.18	5	4	1	28	27	15	15	0	0	0	0	9	1	0	.111
1982 CHI N	0	4	.000	5.67	12	6	0	39.2	51	18	22	0	0	0	0	11	3	0	.273
7 yrs.	10	25	.286	4.39	78	43	7	323.2	331	140	151	0	1	2	1	97	21	0	.216

Al Lary

LARY, ALFRED ALLEN
Brother of Frank Lary.
B. Sept. 26, 1929, Northport, Ala.
BR TR 6'3" 185 lbs.

	W	L	PCT	ERA	G	GS	CG	IP	H	BB	SO	ShO	W	L	SV	AB	H	HR	BA
1954 CHI N	0	0	–	3.00	1	1	0	6	3	7	4	0	0	0	0	2	1	0	.500
1955	0	0	–	0.00	0	0	0	0	0	0	0	0	0	0	0	0	0	0	–
1962	0	1	.000	7.15	15	3	0	34	42	15	18	0	0	0	0	6	1	0	.167
3 yrs.	0	1	.000	6.53	16	4	0	40	45	22	22	0	0	0	0	8	2	0	.250

Frank Lary

LARY, FRANK STRONG (Mule, The Yankee Killer)
Brother of Al Lary.
B. Apr. 10, 1930, Northport, Ala.
BR TR 5'11" 175 lbs.

	W	L	PCT	ERA	G	GS	CG	IP	H	BB	SO	ShO	W	L	SV	AB	H	HR	BA
1954 DET A	0	0	–	2.45	3	0	0	3.2	4	3	5	0	0	0	0	0	0	0	–
1955	14	15	.483	3.10	36	31	16	235	232	89	98	2	1	1	1	82	16	0	.195
1956	21	13	.618	3.15	41	38	20	294	289	116	165	3	0	0	1	103	19	1	.184
1957	11	16	.407	3.98	40	35	12	237.2	250	72	107	2	0	1	3	73	9	0	.123
1958	16	15	.516	2.90	39	34	19	260.1	249	68	131	3	0	2	1	88	15	1	.170
1959	17	10	.630	3.55	32	32	11	223	225	46	137	3	0	0	0	80	10	1	.125
1960	15	15	.500	3.51	38	36	15	274.1	262	62	149	2	0	0	1	93	17	2	.183
1961	23	9	.719	3.24	36	36	22	275.1	252	66	146	4	0	0	0	108	25	1	.231
1962	2	6	.250	5.74	17	14	2	80	98	21	41	1	0	0	0	24	4	0	.167
1963	4	9	.308	3.27	16	14	6	107.1	90	26	46	0	0	0	0	35	8	0	.229
1964 3 teams			DET	A	(6G 0–2)		NY	N	(13G 2–3)		MIL	N	(5G 1–0)						
" total	3	5	.375	5.03	24	14	3	87.2	101	24	37	1	0	0	1	27	2	0	.074
1965 2 teams			NY	N	(14G 1–3)		CHI	A	(14G 1–0)										
" total	2	3	.400	3.32	28	8	0	84	71	23	37	0	0	0	3	21	5	0	.238
12 yrs.	128	116	.525	3.49	350	292	126	2162.1	2123	616	1099	21	1	5	11	734	130	6	.177

Fred Lasher

LASHER, FREDERICK WALTER
B. Aug. 19, 1941, Poughkeepsie, N. Y.
BR TR 6'3" 190 lbs.

	W	L	PCT	ERA	G	GS	CG	IP	H	BB	SO	ShO	W	L	SV	AB	H	HR	BA
1963 MIN A	0	0	–	4.76	11	0	0	11.1	12	11	10	0	0	0	0	1	0	0	.000
1967 DET A	2	1	.667	3.90	17	0	0	30	25	11	28	0	2	1	9	9	1	0	.111
1968	5	1	.833	3.33	34	0	0	48.2	37	22	32	0	5	1	5	9	1	0	.111
1969	2	1	.667	3.07	32	0	0	44	34	22	26	0	2	1	0	4	0	0	.000
1970 2 teams			DET	A	(12G 1–3)		CLE	A	(43G 1–7)										
" total	2	10	.167	4.19	55	1	0	66.2	67	42	52	0	2	9	8	9	0	0	.000
1971 CAL A	0	0	–	36.00	2	0	0	1	4	2	0	0	0	0	0	0	0	0	–
6 yrs.	11	13	.458	3.88	151	1	0	201.2	179	110	148	0	11	12	22	32	2	0	.063

WORLD SERIES

	W	L	PCT	ERA	G	GS	CG	IP	H	BB	SO	ShO	W	L	SV	AB	H	HR	BA
1968 DET A	0	0	–	0.00	1	0	0	2	1	0	1	0	0	0	0	0	0	0	–

Bill Laskey

LASKEY, WILLIAM ALAN
B. Dec. 20, 1957, Toledo, Ohio
BR TR 6'5" 190 lbs.

	W	L	PCT	ERA	G	GS	CG	IP	H	BB	SO	ShO	W	L	SV	AB	H	HR	BA
1982 SF N	13	12	.520	3.14	32	31	7	189.1	186	43	88	1	0	0	0	62	8	0	.129
1983	13	10	.565	4.19	25	25	2	148.1	151	45	81	0	0	0	0	47	5	0	.106
1984	9	14	.391	4.33	35	34	2	207.2	222	50	71	0	0	0	0	63	4	0	.063
3 yrs.	35	36	.493	3.88	92	90	10	545.1	559	138	240	1	0	0	0	172	17	0	.099

	W	L	PCT	ERA	G	GS	CG	IP	H	BB	SO	ShO	Relief Pitching W	L	SV	BATTING AB	H	HR	BA

Bill Lasley

LASLEY, WILLARD ALMOND
B. July 13, 1902, Marietta, Ohio   BR TR 6'   175 lbs.

	W	L	PCT	ERA	G	GS	CG	IP	H	BB	SO	ShO	W	L	SV	AB	H	HR	BA
1924 STL A	0	0	–	6.75	2	0	0	4	7	2	0	0	0	0	0	1	0	0	.000

Tom Lasorda

LASORDA, THOMAS CHARLES
B. Sept. 22, 1927, Norristown, Pa.   BL TL 5'10"   175 lbs.
Manager 1976-84.

	W	L	PCT	ERA	G	GS	CG	IP	H	BB	SO	ShO	W	L	SV	AB	H	HR	BA
1954 BKN N	0	0	–	5.00	4	0	0	9	8	5	5	0	0	0	0	1	0	0	.000
1955	0	0	–	13.50	4	1	0	4	5	6	4	0	0	0	0	0	0	0	–
1956 KC A	0	4	.000	6.15	18	5	0	45.1	40	45	28	0	0	0	1	13	1	0	.077
3 yrs.	0	4	.000	6.48	26	6	0	58.1	53	56	37	0	0	0	1	14	1	0	.071

Bill Lathrop

LATHROP, WILLIAM GEORGE
B. Aug. 12, 1891, Hanover, Wis.   D. Nov. 20, 1958, Janesville, Wis.   BR TR 6'2½"   184 lbs.

	W	L	PCT	ERA	G	GS	CG	IP	H	BB	SO	ShO	W	L	SV	AB	H	HR	BA
1913 CHI A	0	1	.000	4.24	6	0	0	17	16	12	9	0	0	1	0	4	0	0	.000
1914	1	2	.333	2.64	19	1	0	47.2	41	19	7	0	1	1	0	12	0	0	.000
2 yrs.	1	3	.250	3.06	25	1	0	64.2	57	31	16	0	1	2	0	16	0	0	.000

Bill Latimore

LATIMORE, WILLIAM HERSHEL (Sloathful Bill)
B. May 5, 1884, Roxton, Tex.   D. Oct. 30, 1919, Colorado Springs, Colo.   BL TL 5'9"   165 lbs.

	W	L	PCT	ERA	G	GS	CG	IP	H	BB	SO	ShO	W	L	SV	AB	H	HR	BA
1908 CLE A	1	2	.333	4.50	4	4	1	24	24	7	5	1	0	0	0	9	4	0	.444

Barry Latman

LATMAN, ARNOLD BARRY
B. May 21, 1936, Los Angeles, Calif.   BR TR 6'3"   210 lbs.

	W	L	PCT	ERA	G	GS	CG	IP	H	BB	SO	ShO	W	L	SV	AB	H	HR	BA
1957 CHI A	1	2	.333	8.03	7	2	0	12.1	12	13	9	0	1	1	1	1	0	0	.000
1958	3	0	1.000	0.76	13	3	1	47.2	27	17	28	1	1	0	0	12	1	0	.083
1959	8	5	.615	3.75	37	21	5	156	138	72	97	2	0	0	0	47	6	0	.128
1960 CLE A	7	7	.500	4.03	31	20	4	147.1	146	72	94	0	1	1	0	41	9	0	.220
1961	13	5	.722	4.02	45	18	4	176.2	163	54	108	2	6	0	5	55	4	0	.073
1962	8	13	.381	4.17	45	21	7	179.1	179	72	117	1	2	2	5	53	10	1	.189
1963	7	12	.368	4.94	38	21	4	149.1	146	52	133	2	1	1	2	44	8	1	.182
1964 LA N	6	10	.375	3.85	40	18	2	138	128	52	81	1	3	2	2	40	5	0	.125
1965 CAL A	1	1	.500	2.84	18	0	0	31.2	30	16	18	0	1	1	0	2	0	0	.000
1966 HOU N	2	7	.222	2.71	31	9	1	103	88	35	74	1	1	2	1	26	4	0	.154
1967	3	6	.333	4.52	39	1	0	77.2	73	34	70	0	3	6	0	11	1	0	.091
11 yrs.	59	68	.465	3.91	344	134	28	1219	1130	489	829	10	20	16	16	332	48	2	.145

George Lauzerique

LAUZERIQUE, GEORGE ALBERT
B. July 22, 1947, Havana, Cuba   BR TR 6'1"   180 lbs.

	W	L	PCT	ERA	G	GS	CG	IP	H	BB	SO	ShO	W	L	SV	AB	H	HR	BA
1967 KC A	0	2	.000	2.25	3	2	0	16	11	6	10	0	0	0	0	3	0	0	.000
1968 OAK A	0	0	–	0.00	1	0	0	1	0	1	0	0	0	0	0	0	0	0	–
1969	3	4	.429	4.70	19	8	1	61.1	58	27	39	0	0	2	0	20	2	0	.100
1970 MIL A	1	2	.333	6.94	11	4	1	35	41	14	24	0	0	0	0	10	2	1	.200
4 yrs.	4	8	.333	5.00	34	14	2	113.1	110	48	73	0	0	2	0	33	4	1	.121

Gary Lavelle

LAVELLE, GARY ROBERT
B. Jan. 3, 1949, Scranton, Pa.   BB TL 6'2"   190 lbs.

	W	L	PCT	ERA	G	GS	CG	IP	H	BB	SO	ShO	W	L	SV	AB	H	HR	BA
1974 SF N	0	3	.000	2.12	10	0	0	17	14	10	12	0	0	3	0	2	0	0	.000
1975	6	3	.667	2.96	65	0	0	82	80	48	51	0	6	3	8	9	1	0	.111
1976	10	6	.625	2.69	65	0	0	110.1	102	52	71	0	10	6	12	13	1	0	.077
1977	7	7	.500	2.06	73	0	0	118	106	37	93	0	7	7	20	14	0	0	.000
1978	13	10	.565	3.31	67	0	0	98	96	44	63	0	13	10	14	15	1	0	.067
1979	7	9	.438	2.51	70	0	0	97	86	42	80	0	7	9	20	4	1	0	.250
1980	6	4	.429	3.42	62	0	0	100	106	36	66	0	6	8	9	11	0	0	.000
1981	2	6	.250	3.82	34	3	0	66	58	23	45	0	2	3	4	11	3	0	.273
1982	10	7	.588	2.67	68	0	0	104.2	97	29	76	0	10	7	8	13	2	0	.154
1983	7	4	.636	2.59	56	0	0	87	73	19	68	0	7	4	20	14	0	0	.000
1984	5	4	.556	2.76	77	0	0	101	92	42	71	0	5	4	12	5	0	0	.000
11 yrs.	73	67	.521	2.82	647	0	0	981	910	382	696	0	73	64	127	111	9	0	.081

Jimmy Lavender

LAVENDER, JAMES SANFORD
B. Mar. 25, 1884, Barnesville, Ga.   D. Jan. 12, 1960, Cartersville, Ga.   BR TR 5'11"   165 lbs.

	W	L	PCT	ERA	G	GS	CG	IP	H	BB	SO	ShO	W	L	SV	AB	H	HR	BA
1912 CHI N	16	13	.552	3.04	42	31	15	251.2	240	89	109	3	1	1	3	87	13	0	.149
1913	10	14	.417	3.66	40	20	10	204	206	98	91	0	3	2	2	68	8	0	.118
1914	11	11	.500	3.07	37	28	11	214.1	191	87	87	2	1	2	0	63	11	0	.175
1915	10	16	.385	2.58	41	24	13	220	178	67	117	1	2	4	3	67	9	0	.134
1916	10	14	.417	2.82	36	25	9	188	163	62	91	4	1	1	2	53	8	0	.151
1917 PHI N	5	8	.385	3.55	28	14	7	129.1	119	44	52	0	1	0	1	36	5	0	.139
6 yrs.	62	76	.449	3.09	224	142	65	1207.1	1097	447	547	10	9	10	11	374	54	0	.144

Chuck Laver

LAVER, JOHN CHARLES
B. 1865, Pittsburgh, Pa.   Deceased.   TR

	W	L	PCT	ERA	G	GS	CG	IP	H	BB	SO	ShO	W	L	SV	AB	H	HR	BA
1884 PIT AA	0	2	.000	7.58	3	3	2	19	23	9	8	0	0	0	0	*		

Ron Law

LAW, RONALD DAVID
B. Mar. 14, 1946, Hamilton, Ont., Canada   BR TR 6'2"   165 lbs.

	W	L	PCT	ERA	G	GS	CG	IP	H	BB	SO	ShO	W	L	SV	AB	H	HR	BA
1969 CLE A	3	4	.429	4.99	35	1	0	52.1	68	34	29	0	3	4	1	7	1	0	.143

Vern Law

LAW, VERNON SANDERS (Deacon)
Father of Vance Law.
B. Mar. 12, 1930, Meridian, Ida.   BR TR 6'2"   195 lbs.

	W	L	PCT	ERA	G	GS	CG	IP	H	BB	SO	ShO	W	L	SV	AB	H	HR	BA
1950 PIT N	7	9	.438	4.92	27	17	5	128	137	49	57	1	1	0	0	41	3	0	.073
1951	6	9	.400	4.50	28	14	2	114	109	51	41	1	3	3	2	32	11	1	.344
1954	9	13	.409	5.51	39	18	7	161.2	201	56	57	1	4	0	3	52	12	1	.231
1955	10	10	.500	3.81	43	24	8	200.2	221	61	82	1	1	1	1	63	16	1	.254
1956	8	16	.333	4.32	39	32	6	195.2	218	49	60	0	1	3	2	57	10	1	.175
1957	10	8	.556	2.87	31	25	9	172.2	172	32	55	3	2	0	1	63	12	0	.190

	W	L	PCT	ERA	G	GS	CG	IP	H	BB	SO	ShO	Relief Pitching W	L	SV	BATTING AB	H	HR	BA

Vern Law continued

	W	L	PCT	ERA	G	GS	CG	IP	H	BB	SO	ShO	W	L	SV	AB	H	HR	BA
1958	14	12	.538	3.96	35	29	6	202.1	235	39	56	1	2	0	3	62	12	2	.194
1959	18	9	.667	2.98	34	33	20	266	245	53	110	2	0	0	1	96	16	1	.167
1960	20	9	.690	3.08	35	35	18	271.2	266	40	120	3	0	0	0	94	17	1	.181
1961	3	4	.429	4.70	11	10	1	59.1	72	18	20	0	0	0	0	19	5	0	.263
1962	10	7	.588	3.94	23	20	7	139.1	156	27	78	2	0	0	0	45	14	0	.311
1963	4	5	.444	4.93	18	12	1	76.2	91	13	31	1	0	1	0	23	5	0	.217
1964	12	13	.480	3.61	35	29	7	192	203	32	93	5	0	1	0	61	19	1	.311
1965	17	9	.654	2.15	39	28	13	217.1	182	35	101	4	1	0	0	82	20	1	.244
1966	12	8	.600	4.05	31	28	8	177.2	203	24	88	4	2	0	0	66	16	1	.242
1967	2	6	.250	4.18	25	10	1	97	122	18	43	0	0	2	0	27	3	0	.111
16 yrs.	162	147	.524	3.77	483	364	119	2672	2833	597	1092	28	17	13	13	883	191	11	.216

WORLD SERIES

	W	L	PCT	ERA	G	GS	CG	IP	H	BB	SO	ShO	W	L	SV	AB	H	HR	BA
1960 PIT N	2	0	1.000	3.44	3	3	0	18.1	22	3	8	0	0	0	0	6	2	0	.333

Bob Lawrence

LAWRENCE, ROBERT ANDREW (Larry)
B. Dec. 14, 1899, Brooklyn, N. Y.   BR TR 5'11" 180 lbs.

	W	L	PCT	ERA	G	GS	CG	IP	H	BB	SO	ShO	W	L	SV	AB	H	HR	BA
1924 CHI A	0	0	—	9.00	1	0	0	1	1	1	1	0	0	0	0	0	0	0	—

Brooks Lawrence

LAWRENCE, ULYSSES BROOKS (Bull)
B. Jan. 30, 1925, Springfield, Ohio   BR TR 6' 205 lbs.

	W	L	PCT	ERA	G	GS	CG	IP	H	BB	SO	ShO	W	L	SV	AB	H	HR	BA
1954 STL N	15	6	.714	3.74	35	18	8	158.2	141	72	72	0	6	4	1	53	10	0	.189
1955	3	8	.273	6.56	46	10	2	96	102	58	52	1	1	3	1	21	2	0	.095
1956 CIN N	19	10	.655	3.99	49	30	11	218.2	210	71	96	1	6	1	0	70	11	0	.157
1957	16	13	.552	3.52	49	32	12	250.1	234	76	121	1	1	2	4	82	14	0	.171
1958	8	13	.381	4.13	46	23	6	181	194	55	74	2	5	5	5	53	6	0	.113
1959	7	12	.368	4.77	43	14	3	128.1	144	45	64	0	4	5	10	40	6	0	.150
1960	1	0	1.000	10.57	7	0	0	7.2	9	8	2	0	1	0	1	0	0	0	—
7 yrs.	69	62	.527	4.25	275	127	42	1040.2	1034	385	481	5	21	20	22	319	49	0	.154

Al Lawson

LAWSON, ALFRED WILLIAM   BR TR
B. Mar. 24, 1869, London, England   D. Nov. 29, 1954, San Antonio, Tex.

	W	L	PCT	ERA	G	GS	CG	IP	H	BB	SO	ShO	W	L	SV	AB	H	HR	BA
1890 2 teams					BOS N (1G 0–1)			PIT N	(2G 0–2)										
" total	0	3	.000	6.63	3	3	2	19	27	14	3	0	0	0	0	6	0	0	.000

Bob Lawson

LAWSON, ROBERT BAKER
B. Aug. 23, 1876, Brookneal, Va.   D. Oct. 28, 1952, Chapel Hill, N. C.

	W	L	PCT	ERA	G	GS	CG	IP	H	BB	SO	ShO	W	L	SV	AB	H	HR	BA
1901 BOS N	2	2	.500	3.33	6	4	4	46	45	28	12	0	0	0	0	27	4	1	.148
1902 BAL A	0	2	.000	4.85	3	2	1	13	21	3	5	0	0	0	0	6	1	0	.167
2 yrs.	2	4	.333	3.66	9	6	5	59	66	31	17	0	0	0	0	33	5	1	.152

Roxie Lawson

LAWSON, ALFRED VOYLE   BR TR 6' 170 lbs.
B. Apr. 13, 1906, Donnellson, Iowa   D. Apr. 9, 1977, Stockport, Iowa

	W	L	PCT	ERA	G	GS	CG	IP	H	BB	SO	ShO	W	L	SV	AB	H	HR	BA
1930 CLE A	1	2	.333	6.15	7	4	2	33.2	46	23	10	0	0	0	0	11	1	0	.091
1931	0	2	.000	7.60	17	3	0	55.2	72	36	20	0	0	0	0	14	2	0	.143
1933 DET A	0	1	.000	7.31	4	2	0	16	17	17	6	0	0	0	0	5	0	0	.000
1935	3	1	.750	1.58	7	4	4	40	34	24	16	2	0	0	0	13	4	0	.308
1936	8	6	.571	5.48	41	8	3	128	139	71	34	0	5	5	3	45	10	0	.222
1937	18	7	.720	5.26	37	29	15	217.1	236	115	68	0	3	1	1	81	21	0	.259
1938	8	9	.471	5.46	27	16	5	127	154	82	39	0	3	0	1	45	2	0	.044
1939 2 teams					DET A (2G 1–1)			STL	A (36G 3–7)										
" total	4	8	.333	5.28	38	15	5	162	188	90	47	0	2	0	0	47	8	0	.170
1940 STL A	5	3	.625	5.13	30	2	0	72	77	54	18	0	5	1	4	22	1	0	.045
9 yrs.	47	39	.547	5.37	208	83	34	851.2	963	512	258	2	18	7	11	283	49	0	.173

Steve Lawson

LAWSON, STEVEN GEORGE   BR TL 6'1" 175 lbs.
B. Dec. 28, 1950, Oakland, Calif.

	W	L	PCT	ERA	G	GS	CG	IP	H	BB	SO	ShO	W	L	SV	AB	H	HR	BA
1972 TEX A	0	0	—	2.81	13	0	0	16	13	10	13	0	0	0	1	1	1	0	1.000

Bill Laxton

LAXTON, WILLIAM HARRY   BL TL 6'1" 190 lbs.
B. Jan. 5, 1948, Camden, N. J.

	W	L	PCT	ERA	G	GS	CG	IP	H	BB	SO	ShO	W	L	SV	AB	H	HR	BA
1970 PHI N	0	0	—	13.50	2	0	0	2	2	2	2	0	0	0	0	0	0	0	—
1971 SD N	0	2	.000	6.75	18	0	0	28	32	26	23	0	0	2	0	0	0	0	—
1974	0	1	.000	4.00	30	1	0	45	37	38	40	0	0	1	0	5	1	0	.200
1976 DET A	0	5	.000	4.09	26	3	0	94.2	77	51	74	0	0	2	2	0	0	0	—
1977 2 teams					SEA A (43G 3–2)			CLE	A (2G 0–0)										
" total	3	2	.600	4.96	45	0	0	74.1	64	41	50	0	3	2	3	0	0	0	—
5 yrs.	3	10	.231	4.72	121	4	0	244	212	158	189	0	3	7	5	5	1	0	.200

Danny Lazar

LAZAR, JOHN DAN   BL TL 6'1" 190 lbs.
B. Nov. 14, 1943, East Chicago, Ind.

	W	L	PCT	ERA	G	GS	CG	IP	H	BB	SO	ShO	W	L	SV	AB	H	HR	BA
1968 CHI A	0	1	.000	4.05	8	1	0	13.1	14	4	11	0	0	0	0	2	0	0	.000
1969	0	0	—	6.53	9	3	0	20.2	21	11	9	0	0	0	0	4	0	0	.000
2 yrs.	0	1	.000	5.56	17	4	0	34	35	15	20	0	0	0	0	6	0	0	.000

Jack Lazorko

LAZORKO, JACK THOMAS   BR TR 5'11" 198 lbs.
B. Mar. 30, 1957, Hoboken, N. J.

	W	L	PCT	ERA	G	GS	CG	IP	H	BB	SO	ShO	W	L	SV	AB	H	HR	BA
1984 MIL A	0	1	.000	4.31	15	1	0	39.2	37	22	24	0	0	1	1	0	0	0	—

Charlie Lea

LEA, CHARLES WILLIAM   BR TR 6'4" 194 lbs.
B. Dec. 25, 1956, Orleans, France

	W	L	PCT	ERA	G	GS	CG	IP	H	BB	SO	ShO	W	L	SV	AB	H	HR	BA
1980 MON N	7	5	.583	3.72	21	19	0	104	103	55	56	0	0	0	0	37	3	0	.081
1981	5	4	.556	4.64	16	11	2	64	63	26	31	2	0	0	0	15	2	0	.133
1982	12	10	.545	3.24	27	27	4	177.2	145	56	115	2	0	0	0	65	8	0	.123
1983	16	11	.593	3.12	33	33	8	222	195	84	137	4	0	0	0	70	8	0	.114

	W	L	PCT	ERA	G	GS	CG	IP	H	BB	SO	ShO	Relief Pitching W	L	SV	BATTING AB	H	HR	BA

Charlie Lea continued

1984	15	10	.600	2.89	30	30	8	224.1	198	68	123	0	0	0	0	72	8	0	.111
5 yrs.	55	40	.579	3.28	127	120	22	792	704	289	462	8	0	0	0	259	29	0	.112

Rick Leach

LEACH, RICHARD MAX   BL TL 6'1"   180 lbs.
B. May 4, 1957, Ann Arbor, Mich.

1984 TOR A	0	0	—	27.00	1	0	0	1	2	2	0	0	0	0	0	*			

Terry Leach

LEACH, TERRY HESTER   BR TR 6'   215 lbs.
B. Mar. 13, 1954, Selma, Ala.

1981 NY N	1	1	.500	2.57	21	1	0	35	26	12	16	0	1	0	0	1	0	0	.000
1982	2	1	.667	4.17	21	1	1	45.1	46	18	30	1	1	1	3	8	1	0	.125
2 yrs.	3	2	.600	3.47	42	2	1	80.1	72	30	46	1	2	1	3	9	1	0	.111

Luis Leal

LEAL, LUIS ENRIQUE   BR TR 6'3"   205 lbs.
B. Mar. 21, 1957, Barquisimento, Venezuela

1980 TOR A	3	4	.429	4.50	13	10	1	60	72	31	26	0	0	0	0	0	0	0	—
1981	7	13	.350	3.67	29	19	3	130	127	44	71	0	1	3	1	0	0	0	—
1982	12	15	.444	3.93	38	38	10	249.2	250	79	111	0	0	0	0	0	0	0	—
1983	13	12	.520	4.31	35	35	7	217.1	216	65	116	1	0	0	0	0	0	0	—
1984	13	8	.619	3.89	35	35	6	222.1	221	77	134	2	0	0	0	0	0	0	—
5 yrs.	48	52	.480	4.01	150	137	27	879.1	886	296	458	3	1	3	1	0	0	0	—

King Lear

LEAR, CHARLES BERNARD   BR TR 6'   175 lbs.
B. Jan. 23, 1891, Greencastle, Pa.   D. Oct. 31, 1976, Greencastle, Pa.

1914 CIN N	1	2	.333	3.07	17	4	3	55.2	55	19	20	1	0	0	1	16	3	0	.188
1915	6	10	.375	3.01	40	15	9	167.2	169	45	46	0	1	3	0	47	8	0	.170
2 yrs.	7	12	.368	3.02	57	19	12	223.1	224	64	66	1	1	3	1	63	11	0	.175

Frank Leary

LEARY, FRANCIS PATRICK
B. Feb. 26, 1881, Wayland, Mass.   D. Oct. 4, 1907, Natick, Mass.

1907 CIN N	0	1	.000	1.13	2	1	1	8	7	6	4	0	0	1	0	2	0	0	.000

Jack Leary

LEARY, JOHN J.   TL
B. 1858, New Haven, Conn.   Deceased.

1880 BOS N	0	1	.000	15.00	1	1	0	3	8	0	1	0	0	0	0	3	0	0	.000
1881 DET N	0	2	.000	4.15	2	1	1	13	13	2	2	0	0	0	0	11	3	0	.273
1882 2 teams			PIT	AA (3G 1–0)		BAL	AA (3G 2–1)													
" total	3	1	.750	3.43	6	5	4	44.2	57	11	7	0	0	0	0	275	79	2	.287
1884 2 teams			ALT	U (3G 0–3)		C-P	U (2G 0–2)													
" total	0	5	.000	5.29	5	4	3	34	45	7	13	0	0	1	0	73	10	0	.137
4 yrs.	3	9	.250	4.56	14	12	8	94.2	123	20	23	0	0	1	0	*			

Tim Leary

LEARY, TIMOTHY JAMES   BR TR 6'3"   205 lbs.
B. Mar. 21, 1957, Santa Monica, Calif.

1981 NY N	0	0	—	0.00	1	1	0	2	0	1	3	0	0	0	0	1	0	0	.000
1983	1	1	.500	3.38	2	2	1	10.2	15	4	9	0	0	0	0	3	1	0	.333
1984	3	3	.500	4.02	20	7	0	53.2	61	18	29	0	3	0	0	10	3	1	.300
3 yrs.	4	4	.500	3.80	23	10	1	66.1	76	23	41	0	3	0	0	14	4	1	.286

Razor Ledbetter

LEDBETTER, RALPH OVERTON   BR TR 6'3"   190 lbs.
B. Dec. 8, 1894, Rutherford College, N. C.   D. Feb. 1, 1969, West Palm Beach, Fla.

1915 DET A	0	0	—	0.00	1	0	0	1	1	0	0	0	0	0	0	0	0	0	—

Bill Lee

LEE, WILLIAM CRUTCHER (Big Bill)   BR TR 6'3"   195 lbs.
B. Oct. 21, 1909, Plaquemine, La.   D. June 15, 1977, Plaquemine, La.

1934 CHI N	13	14	.481	3.40	35	29	16	214.1	218	74	104	4	0	0	1	76	10	0	.132
1935	20	6	.769	2.96	39	32	18	252	241	84	100	3	2	0	1	102	24	0	.235
1936	18	11	.621	3.31	43	33	20	258.2	238	93	102	4	1	2	1	87	12	1	.138
1937	14	15	.483	3.54	42	33	17	272.1	289	73	108	2	0	1	3	87	15	1	.172
1938	22	9	.710	2.66	44	37	19	291	281	74	121	9	1	1	2	101	20	0	.198
1939	19	15	.559	3.44	37	36	20	282.1	295	85	105	1	0	1	0	103	13	1	.126
1940	9	17	.346	5.03	37	30	9	211.1	246	70	70	1	1	1	0	76	10	0	.132
1941	8	14	.364	3.76	28	22	12	167.1	179	43	62	0	0	1	1	59	11	2	.186
1942	13	13	.500	3.85	32	30	18	219.2	221	67	75	1	0	0	0	69	11	0	.159
1943 2 teams			CHI	N (13G 3–7)		PHI	N (13G 1–5)													
" total	4	12	.250	4.01	26	19	6	139	153	48	35	0	0	0	3	43	8	0	.186
1944 PHI N	10	11	.476	3.15	31	28	11	208.1	199	57	50	3	0	0	1	72	14	0	.194
1945 2 teams			PHI	N (13G 3–6)		BOS	N (16G 6–3)													
" total	9	9	.500	3.58	29	26	8	183.2	219	66	25	1	0	0	0	55	8	0	.145
1946 BOS N	10	9	.526	4.18	25	21	8	140	148	45	32	0	1	0	0	47	8	0	.170
1947 CHI N	0	2	.000	4.50	14	2	0	24	26	14	9	0	0	0	0	3	1	0	.333
14 yrs.	169	157	.518	3.54	462	378	182	2864	2953	893	998	29	6	7	13	980	165	5	.168

WORLD SERIES																			
1935 CHI N	0	0	—	3.48	2	1	0	10.1	11	5	5	0	0	0	0	1	0	0	.000
1938	0	2	.000	2.45	2	2	0	11	15	1	8	0	0	0	0	3	0	0	.000
2 yrs.	0	2	.000	2.95	4	3	0	21.1	26	6	13	0	0	0	0	4	0	0	.000

Bill Lee

LEE, WILLIAM FRANCIS (Spaceman)   BL TL 6'3"   205 lbs.
B. Dec. 28, 1946, Burbank, Calif.

1969 BOS A	1	3	.250	4.50	20	1	0	52	56	28	45	0	1	2	0	10	0	0	.000
1970	2	2	.500	4.62	11	5	0	37	48	14	19	0	0	1	0	11	0	0	.000
1971	9	2	.818	2.74	47	3	0	102	102	46	74	0	8	2	2	23	5	0	.217
1972	7	4	.636	3.20	47	0	0	84.1	75	32	43	0	7	4	5	16	3	1	.188
1973	17	11	.607	2.74	38	33	18	285.1	275	76	120	1	1	0	0	0	0	0	—
1974	17	15	.531	3.51	38	37	16	282	320	67	95	0	0	0	0	0	0	0	—

	W	L	PCT	ERA	G	GS	CG	IP	H	BB	SO	ShO	Relief Pitching W	L	SV	BATTING AB	H	HR	BA

Bill Lee continued

	W	L	PCT	ERA	G	GS	CG	IP	H	BB	SO	ShO	W	L	SV	AB	H	HR	BA
1975	17	9	.654	3.95	41	34	17	260	274	69	78	4	0	0	0	0	0	0	–
1976	5	7	.417	5.63	24	14	1	96	124	28	29	0	1	0	3	0	0	0	–
1977	9	5	.643	4.42	27	16	4	128.1	155	29	31	0	0	1	1	0	0	0	–
1978	10	10	.500	3.46	28	24	8	177	198	59	44	1	0	0	0	0	0	0	–
1979 **MON N**	16	10	.615	3.04	33	33	6	222	230	46	59	3	0	0	0	74	16	0	.216
1980	4	6	.400	4.96	24	18	2	118	156	22	34	0	1	1	0	41	9	0	.220
1981	5	6	.455	2.93	31	7	0	89	90	14	34	0	3	3	6	22	8	1	.364
1982	0	0	–	4.38	7	0	0	12.1	19	1	8	0	0	0	0	0	0	0	–
14 yrs.	119	90	.569	3.62	416	225	72	1945.1	2122	531	713	10	22	13	19	197	41	2	.208
DIVISIONAL PLAYOFF SERIES																			
1981 **MON N**	0	0	–	0.00	1	0	0	.2	2	1	1	0	0	0	0	0	0	0	–
LEAGUE CHAMPIONSHIP SERIES																			
1981 **MON N**	0	0	–	0.00	1	0	0	.1	1	0	0	0	0	0	0	0	0	0	–
WORLD SERIES																			
1975 **BOS A**	0	0	–	3.14	2	2	0	14.1	12	3	7	0	0	0	0	6	1	0	.167

Bob Lee

LEE, ROBERT DEAN (Moose, Horse)
B. Nov. 26, 1937, Ottumwa, Iowa   BR TR 6'3"   225 lbs.

	W	L	PCT	ERA	G	GS	CG	IP	H	BB	SO	ShO	W	L	SV	AB	H	HR	BA
1964 **LA A**	6	5	.545	1.51	64	5	0	137	87	58	111	0	5	4	19	22	0	0	.000
1965 **CAL A**	9	7	.563	1.92	69	0	0	131.1	95	42	89	0	9	7	23	21	3	1	.143
1966	5	4	.556	2.74	61	0	0	101.2	90	31	46	0	5	4	16	11	0	0	.000
1967 2 teams			LA	N	(4G 0–0)		CIN	N	(27G 3–3)										
" total	3	3	.500	4.55	31	1	0	57.1	57	28	35	0	2	3	2	8	3	0	.375
1968 **CIN N**	2	4	.333	5.15	44	1	0	64.2	73	37	34	0	2	4	3	5	1	0	.200
5 yrs.	25	23	.521	2.71	269	7	0	492	402	196	315	0	23	22	63	67	7	1	.104

Don Lee

LEE, DONALD EDWARD
Son of Thornton Lee.
B. Feb. 26, 1934, Globe, Ariz.   BR TR 6'4"   205 lbs.

	W	L	PCT	ERA	G	GS	CG	IP	H	BB	SO	ShO	W	L	SV	AB	H	HR	BA
1957 **DET A**	1	3	.250	4.66	11	6	0	38.2	48	18	19	0	0	1	0	12	2	0	.167
1958	0	0	–	9.00	1	0	0	2	1	1	0	0	0	0	0	0	0	0	–
1960 **WAS A**	8	7	.533	3.44	44	20	1	165	160	64	88	0	3	2	3	43	5	1	.116
1961 **MIN A**	3	6	.333	3.52	37	10	4	115	93	35	65	0	1	0	3	30	2	0	.067
1962 2 teams			MIN	A	(9G 3–3)		LA	A	(27G 8–8)										
" total	11	11	.500	3.46	36	31	5	205.1	204	63	102	2	0	1	2	68	13	0	.191
1963 **LA A**	8	11	.421	3.68	40	22	3	154	148	51	89	2	2	0	1	45	7	0	.156
1964	5	4	.556	2.72	33	8	0	89.1	99	25	73	0	3	1	2	23	6	0	.261
1965 2 teams			CAL	A	(10G 0–1)		HOU	N	(7G 0–0)										
" total	0	1	.000	5.32	17	0	0	22	29	8	15	0	0	1	0	4	1	0	.250
1966 2 teams			HOU	N	(9G 2–0)		CHI	N	(16G 2–1)										
" total	4	1	.800	4.86	25	0	0	37	45	16	16	0	4	1	0	1	1	0	1.000
9 yrs.	40	44	.476	3.61	244	97	13	828.1	827	281	467	4	13	7	11	226	37	1	.164

Mark Lee

LEE, MARK LINDEN
B. June 14, 1953, Inglewood, Calif.   BR TR 6'4"   225 lbs.

	W	L	PCT	ERA	G	GS	CG	IP	H	BB	SO	ShO	W	L	SV	AB	H	HR	BA
1978 **SD N**	5	1	.833	3.28	56	0	0	85	74	36	31	0	5	1	2	5	0	0	.000
1979	2	4	.333	4.29	46	1	0	65	88	25	25	0	2	3	5	6	2	0	.333
1980 **PIT N**	0	1	.000	4.50	4	0	0	6	5	3	2	0	0	1	0	0	0	0	–
1981	0	2	.000	2.70	12	0	0	20	17	5	5	0	0	2	2	2	1	0	.500
4 yrs.	7	8	.467	3.63	118	1	0	176	184	69	63	0	7	7	9	13	3	0	.231

Mike Lee

LEE, MICHAEL RANDALL
B. May 19, 1941, Bell, Calif.   BL TL 6'5"   220 lbs.

	W	L	PCT	ERA	G	GS	CG	IP	H	BB	SO	ShO	W	L	SV	AB	H	HR	BA
1960 **CLE A**	0	0	–	2.00	7	0	0	9	6	11	6	0	0	0	0	0	0	0	–
1963 **LA A**	1	1	.500	3.81	6	4	0	26	30	14	11	0	0	0	0	7	0	0	.000
2 yrs.	1	1	.500	3.34	13	4	0	35	36	25	17	0	0	0	0	7	0	0	.000

Roy Lee

LEE, ROY EDWIN
B. Sept. 28, 1917, Elmira, N. Y.   BL TL 5'11½"   175 lbs.

	W	L	PCT	ERA	G	GS	CG	IP	H	BB	SO	ShO	W	L	SV	AB	H	HR	BA
1945 **NY N**	0	2	.000	11.57	3	1	0	7	8	3	0	0	0	1	0	1	0	0	.000

Thornton Lee

LEE, THORNTON STARR (Lefty)
Father of Don Lee.
B. Sept. 13, 1906, Sonoma, Calif.   BL TL 6'3"   205 lbs.

	W	L	PCT	ERA	G	GS	CG	IP	H	BB	SO	ShO	W	L	SV	AB	H	HR	BA
1933 **CLE A**	1	1	.500	4.15	3	2	2	17.1	13	11	7	0	0	0	0	8	3	0	.375
1934	1	1	.500	5.04	24	6	0	85.2	105	44	41	0	0	0	0	21	2	0	.095
1935	7	10	.412	4.04	32	20	8	180.2	179	71	81	1	2	1	1	61	12	0	.197
1936	3	5	.375	4.89	43	8	2	127	138	67	49	0	1	2	3	41	5	0	.122
1937 **CHI A**	12	10	.545	3.52	30	25	13	204.2	209	60	80	2	0	0	0	71	15	0	.211
1938	13	12	.520	3.49	33	30	18	245.1	252	94	77	1	0	1	1	97	25	4	.258
1939	15	11	.577	4.21	33	29	15	235	260	70	81	2	0	1	3	91	15	0	.165
1940	12	13	.480	3.47	28	27	24	228	223	56	87	1	0	0	0	84	23	0	.274
1941	22	11	.667	2.37	35	34	30	300.1	258	92	130	3	0	0	1	114	29	0	.254
1942	2	6	.250	3.32	11	8	6	76	82	31	25	0	0	0	0	30	6	0	.200
1943	5	9	.357	4.18	19	19	7	127	129	50	35	1	0	0	0	42	3	0	.071
1944	3	9	.250	3.02	15	14	6	113.1	105	25	39	0	0	0	0	42	4	0	.095
1945	15	12	.556	2.44	29	28	19	228.1	208	76	108	1	1	0	0	78	14	0	.179
1946	2	4	.333	3.53	7	7	2	43.1	39	23	23	0	0	0	0	15	4	0	.267
1947	3	7	.300	4.47	21	11	2	86.2	86	56	57	0	0	3	1	29	6	0	.207
1948 **NY N**	1	3	.250	4.41	11	4	1	32.2	41	12	17	0	0	1	0	11	1	0	.091
16 yrs.	117	124	.485	3.56	374	272	155	2331.1	2327	838	937	14	4	9	10	835	167	4	.200

	W	L	PCT	ERA	G	GS	CG	IP	H	BB	SO	ShO	Relief Pitching W	L	SV	BATTING AB	H	HR	BA

Tom Lee
LEE, THOMAS F.
B. June 9, 1864, Milwaukee, Wis.   D. Mar. 4, 1886, Milwaukee, Wis.

	W	L	PCT	ERA	G	GS	CG	IP	H	BB	SO	ShO	W	L	SV	AB	H	HR	BA
1884 2 teams	CHI	N (5G 1–4)		BAL	U (15G 5–8)														
" total	6	12	.333	3.50	20	19	17	167.1	176	44	95	0	0	0	0	106	26	0	.245

Watty Lee
LEE, WYATT ARNOLD   BL TL 5'10½" 171 lbs.
B. Aug. 12, 1879, Lynch's Station, Va.   D. Mar. 6, 1936, Washington, D. C.

	W	L	PCT	ERA	G	GS	CG	IP	H	BB	SO	ShO	W	L	SV	AB	H	HR	BA
1901 WAS A	16	16	.500	4.40	36	33	25	262	328	45	63	2	1	1	0	129	33	0	.256
1902	5	7	.417	5.05	13	10	10	98	118	20	24	0	1	1	0	391	100	4	.256
1903	8	12	.400	3.08	22	20	15	166.2	169	40	70	2	1	0	0	231	48	0	.208
1904 PIT N	1	2	.333	8.74	5	3	1	22.2	34	9	5	0	0	1	0	12	4	0	.333
4 yrs.	30	37	.448	4.29	76	66	51	549.1	649	114	162	4	3	3	0	*			

Sam Leever
LEEVER, SAMUEL (The Goshen Schoolmaster)   BR TR 5'10½" 175 lbs.
B. Dec. 23, 1871, Goshen, Ohio   D. May 19, 1953, Goshen, Ohio

	W	L	PCT	ERA	G	GS	CG	IP	H	BB	SO	ShO	W	L	SV	AB	H	HR	BA
1898 PIT N	1	0	1.000	2.45	5	3	2	33	26	5	15	0	0	0	0	12	3	0	.250
1899	20	23	.465	3.18	51	39	35	379	353	122	121	4	2	5	3	146	33	0	.226
1900	15	13	.536	2.71	30	29	25	232.2	236	48	84	3	0	0	0	88	18	1	.205
1901	14	5	.737	2.86	21	20	18	176	182	39	82	2	1	0	0	71	13	0	.183
1902	16	7	.696	2.39	28	26	23	222	203	31	86	4	0	0	2	90	16	0	.178
1903	25	7	.781	2.06	36	34	30	284.1	255	60	90	7	0	0	1	115	19	0	.165
1904	18	11	.621	2.17	34	32	26	253.1	224	54	63	1	1	0	0	99	26	1	.263
1905	19	6	.760	2.70	33	29	20	230	199	54	81	3	1	0	0	88	9	0	.102
1906	22	7	.759	2.32	36	31	25	260.1	232	48	76	6	1	1	0	95	20	0	.211
1907	14	9	.609	1.66	31	24	17	216.2	182	46	65	5	2	1	0	73	11	0	.151
1908	15	7	.682	2.10	38	20	14	192.2	179	41	28	4	2	2	2	61	9	0	.148
1909	8	1	.889	2.83	19	4	2	70	74	14	23	0	6	1	2	24	4	0	.167
1910	6	5	.545	2.76	26	8	4	111	104	25	33	0	3	2	2	31	2	0	.065
13 yrs.	193	101	.656 10th	2.47	388	299	241	2661	2449	587	847	39	19	12	12	993	183	2	.184

WORLD SERIES

	W	L	PCT	ERA	G	GS	CG	IP	H	BB	SO	ShO	W	L	SV	AB	H	HR	BA
1903 PIT N	0	2	.000	6.30	2	2	1	10	13	3	2	0	0	0	0	4	0	0	.000

Bill LeFebvre
LeFEBVRE, WILFRID HENRY (Lefty)   BL TL 5'11½" 180 lbs.
B. Nov. 11, 1915, Natick, R. I.

	W	L	PCT	ERA	G	GS	CG	IP	H	BB	SO	ShO	W	L	SV	AB	H	HR	BA
1938 BOS A	0	0	—	13.50	1	0	0	4	8	0	0	0	0	0	0	1	1	1	1.000
1939	1	1	.500	5.81	5	3	0	26.1	35	14	8	0	0	0	0	10	3	0	.300
1943 WAS A	2	0	1.000	4.45	6	3	1	32.1	33	16	10	0	1	0	0	14	4	0	.286
1944	2	4	.333	4.52	24	4	2	69.2	86	21	18	0	1	1	3	62	16	0	.258
4 yrs.	5	5	.500	5.03	36	10	3	132.1	162	51	36	0	2	1	3	*			

Craig Lefferts
LEFFERTS, CRAIG LINDSAY   BL TL 6'1"   180 lbs.
B. Sept. 29, 1957, Munich, West Germany

	W	L	PCT	ERA	G	GS	CG	IP	H	BB	SO	ShO	W	L	SV	AB	H	HR	BA
1983 CHI N	3	4	.429	3.13	56	5	0	89	80	29	60	0	2	3	1	18	2	0	.111
1984 SD N	3	4	.429	2.13	62	0	0	105.2	88	24	56	0	3	4	10	17	5	0	.294
2 yrs.	6	8	.429	2.59	118	5	0	194.2	168	53	116	0	5	7	11	35	7	0	.200

LEAGUE CHAMPIONSHIP SERIES

	W	L	PCT	ERA	G	GS	CG	IP	H	BB	SO	ShO	W	L	SV	AB	H	HR	BA
1984 SD N	2	0	1.000	0.00	3	0	0	4	1	1	1	0	2	0	0	0	0	0	—

WORLD SERIES

	W	L	PCT	ERA	G	GS	CG	IP	H	BB	SO	ShO	W	L	SV	AB	H	HR	BA
1984 SD N	0	0	—	0.00	3	0	0	6	2	1	7	0	0	0	1	0	0	0	—

Regis Leheny
LEHENY, REGIS FRANCIS   BL TL 6'½"   180 lbs.
B. Jan. 5, 1908, Pittsburgh, Pa.   D. Nov. 2, 1976, Pittsburgh, Pa.

	W	L	PCT	ERA	G	GS	CG	IP	H	BB	SO	ShO	W	L	SV	AB	H	HR	BA
1932 BOS A	0	0	—	16.88	2	0	0	2.2	5	3	1	0	0	0	0	1	0	0	.000

Jim Lehew
LEHEW, JAMES ANTHONY   BR TR 6'   185 lbs.
B. Aug. 19, 1937, Baltimore, Md.

	W	L	PCT	ERA	G	GS	CG	IP	H	BB	SO	ShO	W	L	SV	AB	H	HR	BA
1961 BAL A	0	0	—	0.00	2	0	0	2	1	0	0	0	0	0	0	0	0	0	—
1962	0	0	—	1.86	6	0	0	9.2	10	3	2	0	0	0	0	1	0	0	.000
2 yrs.	0	0	—	1.54	8	0	0	11.2	11	3	2	0	0	0	0	1	0	0	.000

Ken Lehman
LEHMAN, KENNETH KARL   BL TL 6'   170 lbs.
B. June 10, 1928, Seattle, Wash.

	W	L	PCT	ERA	G	GS	CG	IP	H	BB	SO	ShO	W	L	SV	AB	H	HR	BA
1952 BKN N	1	2	.333	5.28	4	3	0	15.1	19	6	7	0	1	0	0	4	0	0	.000
1956	2	3	.400	5.66	25	4	0	49.1	65	23	29	0	2	1	0	10	3	0	.300
1957 2 teams	BKN	N (3G 0–0)		BAL	A (30G 8–3)														
" total	8	3	.727	2.52	33	3	1	75	64	23	35	0	7	1	6	22	5	0	.227
1958 BAL A	2	1	.667	3.48	31	1	1	62	64	18	36	0	2	1	0	14	1	0	.071
1961 PHI N	1	1	.500	4.26	41	2	0	63.1	61	25	27	0	1	0	1	6	0	0	.000
5 yrs.	14	10	.583	3.91	134	13	2	265	273	95	134	0	13	3	7	56	9	0	.161

WORLD SERIES

	W	L	PCT	ERA	G	GS	CG	IP	H	BB	SO	ShO	W	L	SV	AB	H	HR	BA
1952 BKN N	0	0	—	0.00	1	0	0	2	2	1	0	0	0	0	0	0	0	0	—

Norm Lehr
LEHR, NORMAN CARL MICHAEL (King)   BR TR 6'   168 lbs.
B. May 28, 1901, Rochester, N. Y.   D. July 17, 1968, Livonia, N. Y.

	W	L	PCT	ERA	G	GS	CG	IP	H	BB	SO	ShO	W	L	SV	AB	H	HR	BA
1926 CLE A	0	0	—	3.07	4	0	0	14.2	11	4	4	0	0	0	0	4	0	0	.000

Hank Leiber
LEIBER, HENRY EDWARD   BR TR 6'1½" 205 lbs.
B. Jan. 17, 1911, Phoenix, Ariz.

	W	L	PCT	ERA	G	GS	CG	IP	H	BB	SO	ShO	W	L	SV	AB	H	HR	BA
1942 NY N	0	1	.000	6.00	1	1	1	9	9	5	5	0	0	0	0	*			

Charlie Leibrandt
LEIBRANDT, CHARLES LOUIS, JR.   BR TL 6'3"   195 lbs.
B. Oct. 4, 1956, Chicago, Ill.

	W	L	PCT	ERA	G	GS	CG	IP	H	BB	SO	ShO	W	L	SV	AB	H	HR	BA
1979 CIN N	0	0	—	0.00	3	0	0	4	2	2	1	0	0	0	0	0	0	0	—
1980	10	9	.526	4.24	36	27	5	174	200	54	62	2	0	0	0	56	11	0	.196

	W	L	PCT	ERA	G	GS	CG	IP	H	BB	SO	ShO	Relief Pitching W	L	SV	BATTING AB	H	HR	BA

Charlie Leibrandt continued

	W	L	PCT	ERA	G	GS	CG	IP	H	BB	SO	ShO	W	L	SV	AB	H	HR	BA
1981	1	1	.500	3.60	7	4	1	30	28	15	9	1	0	0	0	8	0	0	.000
1982	5	7	.417	5.10	36	11	0	107.2	130	48	34	0	2	1	2	25	2	0	.080
1984 KC A	11	7	.611	3.63	23	23	0	143.2	158	38	53	0	0	0	0	0	0		–
5 yrs.	27	24	.529	4.17	105	65	6	459.1	518	157	159	3	2	1	2	89	13	0	.146

LEAGUE CHAMPIONSHIP SERIES

	W	L	PCT	ERA	G	GS	CG	IP	H	BB	SO	ShO	W	L	SV	AB	H	HR	BA
1979 CIN N	0	0	–	0.00	1	0	0	.1	0	0	0	0	0	0	0	0	0	0	–
1984 KC A	0	1	.000	1.13	1	1	1	8	3	4	6	0	0	0	0	0	0	0	–
2 yrs.	0	1	.000	1.08	2	1	1	8.1	3	4	6	0	0	0	0	0	0	0	–

Lefty Leifield

LEIFIELD, ALBERT PETER   BL TL 6'1"   165 lbs.
B. Sept. 5, 1883, Trenton, Ill.   D. Oct. 10, 1970, Alexandria, Va.

	W	L	PCT	ERA	G	GS	CG	IP	H	BB	SO	ShO	W	L	SV	AB	H	HR	BA
1905 PIT N	5	2	.714	2.89	8	7	6	56	52	14	10	1	0	0	0	20	7	0	.350
1906	18	13	.581	1.87	37	31	24	255.2	214	68	111	8	3	0	1	88	11	0	.125
1907	20	16	.556	2.33	40	33	24	286	270	100	112	6	3	2	0	102	15	0	.147
1908	15	14	.517	2.10	34	26	18	218.2	168	86	87	5	2	1	2	75	17	0	.227
1909	19	8	.704	2.37	32	27	13	201.2	172	54	43	3	3	1	0	73	14	0	.192
1910	15	12	.556	2.64	40	30	13	218.1	197	67	64	3	5	0	1	60	11	0	.183
1911	16	16	.500	2.63	42	37	26	318	301	82	111	2	0	0	1	102	24	0	.235
1912 2 teams		PIT N	(6G 1–2)		CHI N	(13G 7–2)													
" total	8	4	.667	2.86	19	10	5	94.1	97	31	31	1	3	1	0	33	4	0	.121
1913 CHI N	1	1	.000	5.48	6	1	0	21.1	28	5	4	0	0	0	0	7	0	0	.000
1918 STL A	2	6	.250	2.55	15	6	3	67	61	19	22	1	1	1	0	19	1	0	.053
1919	6	4	.600	2.93	19	9	6	92	96	25	18	2	1	1	0	30	3	0	.100
1920	0	0	–	7.00	4	0	0	9	17	3	3	0	0	0	0	2	0	0	.000
12 yrs.	124	96	.564	2.47	296	217	138	1838	1673	554	616	32	21	8	5	611	107	0	.175

WORLD SERIES

	W	L	PCT	ERA	G	GS	CG	IP	H	BB	SO	ShO	W	L	SV	AB	H	HR	BA
1909 PIT N	0	1	.000	11.25	1	1	0	4	7	1	0	0	0	0	0	1	0	0	.000

Dave Leiper

LEIPER, DAVID PAUL   BL TL 6'1"   160 lbs.
B. June 1, 1960, Whittier, Calif.

	W	L	PCT	ERA	G	GS	CG	IP	H	BB	SO	ShO	W	L	SV	AB	H	HR	BA
1984 OAK A	1	0	1.000	9.00	8	0	0	7	12	5	3	0	1	0	0	0	0	0	–

Jack Leiper

LEIPER, JOHN HENRY THOMAS   TL
B. Dec. 23, 1867, Chester, Pa.   D. Aug. 23, 1960, West Goshen, Pa.

	W	L	PCT	ERA	G	GS	CG	IP	H	BB	SO	ShO	W	L	SV	AB	H	HR	BA
1891 COL AA	2	2	.500	5.40	6	5	4	45	41	39	19	0	0	0	0	21	3	0	.143

Bill Leith

LEITH, WILLIAM (Shady Bill)   TL
B. May 31, 1873, Matteawan, N. Y.   D. July 16, 1940, Beacon, N. Y.

	W	L	PCT	ERA	G	GS	CG	IP	H	BB	SO	ShO	W	L	SV	AB	H	HR	BA
1899 WAS N	0	0	–	18.00	1	0	0	2	4	2	1	0	0	0	0	1	0	0	.000

Doc Leitner

LEITNER, GEORGE ALOYSIUS   BR TR 5'11½" 185 lbs.
B. Sept. 14, 1865, Piermont, N. Y.   D. May 18, 1937, New York, N. Y.

	W	L	PCT	ERA	G	GS	CG	IP	H	BB	SO	ShO	W	L	SV	AB	H	HR	BA
1887 IND N	2	6	.250	5.68	8	8	6	65	69	41	27	0	0	0	0	27	4	0	.148

Dummy Leitner

LEITNER, GEORGE MICHAEL   BL TR 5'7"   120 lbs.
B. June 19, 1871, Parkton, Md.   D. Feb. 20, 1960, Baltimore, Md.

	W	L	PCT	ERA	G	GS	CG	IP	H	BB	SO	ShO	W	L	SV	AB	H	HR	BA
1901 2 teams		PHI A	(1G 0–0)		NY N	(2G 0–2)													
" total	0	2	.000	4.05	3	2	2	20	28	5	4	0	0	0	0	8	1	0	.125
1902 2 teams		CLE A	(1G 0–0)		CHI A	(1G 0–0)													
" total	0	0	–	7.50	2	1	0	12	20	3	0	0	0	0	0	7	1	0	.143
2 yrs.	0	2	.000	5.34	5	3	2	32	48	8	4	0	0	0	0	15	2	0	.133

Bill Lelivelt

LELIVELT, WILLIAM JOHN   BR TR 6'   195 lbs.
Brother of Jack Lelivelt.
B. Oct. 21, 1884, Chicago, Ill.   D. Feb. 14, 1968, Chicago, Ill.

	W	L	PCT	ERA	G	GS	CG	IP	H	BB	SO	ShO	W	L	SV	AB	H	HR	BA
1909 DET A	0	1	.000	4.50	4	2	1	20	27	2	4	0	0	0	1	6	2	0	.333
1910	0	1	.000	1.00	1	1	1	9	6	3	2	0	0	0	0	2	1	0	.500
2 yrs.	0	2	.000	3.41	5	3	2	29	33	5	6	0	0	0	1	8	3	0	.375

Dave Lemanczyk

LEMANCZYK, DAVID LAWRENCE   BR TR 6'4"   235 lbs.
B. Aug. 17, 1950, Syracuse, N. Y.

	W	L	PCT	ERA	G	GS	CG	IP	H	BB	SO	ShO	W	L	SV	AB	H	HR	BA
1973 DET A	0	0	–	13.50	1	0	0	2	4	0	0	0	0	0	0	0	0	0	–
1974	2	1	.667	3.99	22	3	0	79	79	44	52	0	1	0	0	0	0	0	–
1975	2	7	.222	4.46	26	6	4	109	120	46	67	0	2	1	0	0	0	0	–
1976	4	6	.400	5.11	20	10	1	81	86	34	51	0	2	0	0	0	0	0	–
1977 TOR A	13	16	.448	4.25	34	34	11	252	278	87	105	0	0	0	0	0	0	0	–
1978	4	14	.222	6.26	29	20	3	136.2	170	65	62	0	0	0	0	0	0	0	–
1979	8	10	.444	3.71	22	20	11	143	137	45	63	3	0	0	0	0	0	0	–
1980 2 teams		TOR A	(10G 2–5)		CAL A	(21G 2–4)													
" total	4	9	.308	4.75	31	10	0	110	138	42	29	0	1	3	0	0	0	0	–
8 yrs.	37	63	.370	4.62	185	103	30	912.2	1012	363	429	3	6	4	0	0	0	0	–

Denny Lemaster

LEMASTER, DENVER CLAYTON   BR TL 6'1"   182 lbs.
B. Feb. 25, 1939, Corona, Calif.

	W	L	PCT	ERA	G	GS	CG	IP	H	BB	SO	ShO	W	L	SV	AB	H	HR	BA
1962 MIL N	3	4	.429	3.01	17	12	4	86.2	75	32	69	1	0	0	0	33	4	0	.121
1963	11	14	.440	3.04	46	31	10	237	199	85	190	1	1	1	1	74	14	2	.189
1964	17	11	.607	4.15	39	35	9	221	216	75	185	3	1	0	1	67	9	0	.134
1965	7	13	.350	4.43	32	23	4	146.1	140	58	111	1	0	1	0	45	4	0	.089
1966 ATL N	11	8	.579	3.74	27	27	10	171	170	41	139	3	0	0	0	59	7	0	.119
1967	9	9	.500	3.34	31	31	8	215.1	184	72	148	2	0	0	0	67	7	0	.104
1968 HOU N	10	15	.400	2.81	33	32	7	224	231	72	146	2	0	0	0	65	2	0	.031
1969	13	17	.433	3.16	38	37	11	245	232	72	173	1	0	0	1	88	15	1	.170
1970	7	12	.368	4.56	39	21	3	162	169	65	103	0	1	1	3	45	8	1	.178
1971	0	2	.000	3.45	42	1	0	60	59	22	28	0	0	2	2	6	1	0	.167

	W	L	PCT	ERA	G	GS	CG	IP	H	BB	SO	ShO	Relief Pitching W	L	SV	BATTING AB	H	HR	BA

Denny Lemaster continued

	W	L	PCT	ERA	G	GS	CG	IP	H	BB	SO	ShO	W	L	SV	AB	H	HR	BA
1972 MON N	2	0	1.000	7.78	13	0	0	19.2	28	6	13	0	2	0	0	3	1	0	.333
11 yrs.	90	105	.462	3.58	357	249	66	1788	1703	600	1305	14	5	4	8	552	72	4	.130

Dick LeMay

LeMAY, RICHARD PAUL
B. Aug. 28, 1938, Cincinnati, Ohio
BL TL 6'3" 190 lbs.

	W	L	PCT	ERA	G	GS	CG	IP	H	BB	SO	ShO	W	L	SV	AB	H	HR	BA
1961 SF N	3	6	.333	3.56	27	5	1	83.1	65	36	54	0	2	6	3	26	2	0	.077
1962	0	1	.000	7.71	9	0	0	9.1	9	9	5	0	0	1	1	0	0	0	—
1963 CHI N	0	1	.000	5.28	9	1	0	15.1	26	4	10	0	0	1	0	2	0	0	.000
3 yrs.	3	8	.273	4.17	45	6	1	108	100	49	69	0	2	8	4	28	2	0	.071

Bob Lemon

LEMON, ROBERT GRANVILLE
B. Sept. 22, 1920, San Bernardino, Calif.
Manager 1970-72, 1977-79, 1981-82.
Hall of Fame 1976.
BL TR 6' 180 lbs.

	W	L	PCT	ERA	G	GS	CG	IP	H	BB	SO	ShO	W	L	SV	AB	H	HR	BA
1941 CLE A	0	0	—	0.00	0	0	0		0	0	0	0	0	0	0	4	1	0	.250
1942	0	0	—	0.00	0	0	0		0	0	0	0	0	0	0	5	0	0	.000
1946	4	5	.444	2.49	32	5	1	94	77	68	39	0	3	2	1	89	16	1	.180
1947	11	5	.688	3.44	37	15	6	167.1	150	97	65	1	1	2	3	56	18	2	.321
1948	20	14	.588	2.82	43	37	20	293.2	231	129	147	10	1	1	2	119	34	5	.286
1949	22	10	.688	2.99	37	33	22	279.2	211	137	138	2	1	0	1	108	29	7	.269
1950	23	11	.676	3.84	44	37	22	288	281	146	170	3	1	0	3	136	37	6	.272
1951	17	14	.548	3.52	42	34	17	263.1	244	124	132	1	0	0	2	102	21	3	.206
1952	22	11	.667	2.50	42	36	28	309.2	236	105	131	5	0	1	4	124	28	2	.226
1953	21	15	.583	3.36	41	36	23	286.2	283	110	98	5	1	1	1	112	26	2	.232
1954	23	7	.767	2.72	36	33	21	258.1	228	92	110	2	1	0	0	98	21	2	.214
1955	18	10	.643	3.88	35	31	5	211.1	218	74	100	0	1	0	2	78	19	1	.244
1956	20	14	.588	3.03	39	35	21	255.1	230	89	94	2	0	0	3	93	18	5	.194
1957	6	11	.353	4.60	21	17	2	117.1	129	64	45	0	1	2	0	46	3	1	.065
1958	0	1	.000	5.33	11	1	0	25.1	41	16	8	0	0	0	0	13	3	0	.231
15 yrs.	207	128	.618	3.23	460	350	188	2850	2559	1251	1277	31	12	10	22	*			

WORLD SERIES

	W	L	PCT	ERA	G	GS	CG	IP	H	BB	SO	ShO	W	L	SV	AB	H	HR	BA
1948 CLE A	2	0	1.000	1.65	2	2	1	16.1	16	7	6	0	0	0	0	7	0	0	.000
1954	0	2	.000	6.75	2	2	1	13.1	16	8	11	0	0	0	0	6	0	0	.000
2 yrs.	2	2	.500	3.94	4	4	2	29.2	32	15	17	0	0	0	0	13	0	0	.000

Dave Lemonds

LEMONDS, DAVID LEE
B. July 5, 1948, Charlotte, N. C.
BL TL 6'1½" 180 lbs.

	W	L	PCT	ERA	G	GS	CG	IP	H	BB	SO	ShO	W	L	SV	AB	H	HR	BA
1969 CHI N	0	1	.000	3.60	2	1	0	5	5	5	0	0	0	0	0	1	0	0	.000
1972 CHI A	4	7	.364	2.95	31	18	0	94.2	87	38	69	0	1	1	0	25	3	0	.120
2 yrs.	4	8	.333	2.98	33	19	0	99.2	92	43	69	0	1	1	0	26	3	0	.115

Mark Lemongello

LEMONGELLO, MARK
B. July 21, 1955, Jersey City, N. J.
BR TR 6'1" 180 lbs.

	W	L	PCT	ERA	G	GS	CG	IP	H	BB	SO	ShO	W	L	SV	AB	H	HR	BA
1976 HOU N	3	1	.750	2.79	4	4	1	29	26	7	9	0	0	0	0	8	0	0	.000
1977	9	14	.391	3.47	34	30	5	215	237	52	83	0	0	1	0	69	6	0	.087
1978	9	14	.391	3.94	33	30	9	210	204	66	77	1	0	0	1	64	11	0	.172
1979 TOR A	1	9	.100	6.29	18	10	2	83	97	34	40	0	1	2	0	0	0	0	—
4 yrs.	22	38	.367	4.06	89	74	17	537	564	159	209	1	1	3	1	141	17	0	.121

Ed Lennon

LENNON, EDWARD FRANCIS
B. Aug. 17, 1897, Philadelphia, Pa.   D. Sept. 13, 1947, Philadelphia, Pa.
BR TR 5'11" 170 lbs.

	W	L	PCT	ERA	G	GS	CG	IP	H	BB	SO	ShO	W	L	SV	AB	H	HR	BA
1928 PHI N	0	0	—	8.76	5	0	0	12.1	19	10	6	0	0	0	0	4	0	0	.000

Isidore Leon

LEON, ISIDORE JUAN
B. Jan. 4, 1911, Cruces Las Villas, Cuba
BR TR 5'10" 160 lbs.

	W	L	PCT	ERA	G	GS	CG	IP	H	BB	SO	ShO	W	L	SV	AB	H	HR	BA
1945 PHI N	0	4	.000	5.35	14	4	0	38.2	49	19	11	0	0	0	0	9	1	0	.111

Max Leon

LEON, MAXIMO
B. Feb. 4, 1950, Veracruz, Mexico
BR TR 5'10" 145 lbs.

	W	L	PCT	ERA	G	GS	CG	IP	H	BB	SO	ShO	W	L	SV	AB	H	HR	BA
1973 ATL N	2	2	.500	5.33	12	2	1	27	30	9	18	0	1	2	0	7	2	0	.286
1974	4	7	.364	2.64	34	2	1	75	68	14	38	1	3	6	3	15	2	0	.133
1975	2	1	.667	4.13	50	1	0	85	90	33	53	0	1	1	6	9	3	0	.333
1976	2	4	.333	2.75	30	0	0	36	32	15	16	0	2	4	3	2	0	0	.000
1977	4	4	.500	3.95	31	9	0	82	89	25	44	0	2	2	1	19	6	0	.316
1978	0	0	—	6.00	5	0	0	6	6	4	1	0	0	0	0	0	0	0	—
6 yrs.	14	18	.438	3.70	162	13	2	311	315	100	170	1	9	15	13	52	13	0	.250

Dennis Leonard

LEONARD, DENNIS PATRICK
B. May 8, 1951, Brooklyn, N. Y.
BR TR 6'1" 190 lbs.

	W	L	PCT	ERA	G	GS	CG	IP	H	BB	SO	ShO	W	L	SV	AB	H	HR	BA
1974 KC A	0	4	.000	5.32	5	4	0	22	28	12	8	0	0	0	0	0	0	0	—
1975	15	7	.682	3.77	32	30	8	212.1	212	90	146	0	1	0	0	0	0	0	—
1976	17	10	.630	3.51	35	34	16	259	247	70	150	2	0	0	0	0	0	0	—
1977	20	12	.625	3.04	38	37	21	293	246	79	244	5	0	0	1	0	0	0	—
1978	21	17	.553	3.33	40	40	20	294.2	283	78	183	4	0	0	0	0	0	0	—
1979	14	12	.538	4.08	32	32	12	226	226	56	126	5	0	0	0	0	0	0	—
1980	20	11	.645	3.79	38	38	9	280	271	80	155	3	0	0	0	0	0	0	—
1981	13	11	.542	2.99	26	26	9	202	202	41	107	2	0	0	0	0	0	0	—
1982	10	6	.625	5.10	21	21	2	130.2	145	46	58	0	0	0	0	0	0	0	—
1983	6	3	.667	3.71	10	10	1	63	69	19	31	0	0	0	0	0	0	0	—
10 yrs.	136	93	.594	3.63	277	272	98	1992.2	1929	571	1208	21	1	0	1	0	0	0	—

DIVISIONAL PLAYOFF SERIES

	W	L	PCT	ERA	G	GS	CG	IP	H	BB	SO	ShO	W	L	SV	AB	H	HR	BA
1981 KC A	0	1	.000	1.13	1	1	0	8	7	1	3	0	0	0	0	0	0	0	—

LEAGUE CHAMPIONSHIP SERIES

	W	L	PCT	ERA	G	GS	CG	IP	H	BB	SO	ShO	W	L	SV	AB	H	HR	BA
1976 KC A	0	0	—	19.29	2	2	0	2.1	9	2	0	0	0	0	0	0	0	0	—

	W	L	PCT	ERA	G	GS	CG	IP	H	BB	SO	ShO	Relief Pitching W	L	SV	AB	H	HR	BA

Dennis Leonard continued

	W	L	PCT	ERA	G	GS	CG	IP	H	BB	SO	ShO	W	L	SV	AB	H	HR	BA
1977	1	1	.500	3.00	2	1	1	9	5	2	4	0	0	1	0	0	0	0	–
1978	0	2	.000	3.75	2	2	1	12	13	2	11	0	0	0	0	0	0	0	–
1980	1	0	1.000	2.25	1	1	0	8	7	1	8	0	0	0	0	0	0	0	–
4 yrs.	2	3	.400	4.31	7	6	2	31.1	34	7	23	0	0	1	0	0	0	0	–
WORLD SERIES																			
1980 KC A	1	1	.500	6.75	2	2	0	10.2	15	2	5	0	0	0	0	0	0	0	–

Dutch Leonard

LEONARD, EMIL JOHN
B. Mar. 25, 1909, Auburn, Ill.   D. Apr. 17, 1983, Springfield, Ill.   BR TR 6'   175 lbs.

	W	L	PCT	ERA	G	GS	CG	IP	H	BB	SO	ShO	W	L	SV	AB	H	HR	BA
1933 BKN N	2	3	.400	2.93	10	3	2	40	42	10	6	0	1	1	0	11	0	0	.000
1934	14	11	.560	3.28	44	20	11	183.2	210	34	58	2	5	3	5	67	12	0	.179
1935	2	9	.182	3.92	43	11	4	137.2	152	29	41	0	0	4	8	39	1	0	.026
1936	0	0	–	3.66	16	0	0	32	34	5	8	0	0	0	1	5	2	0	.400
1938 WAS A	12	15	.444	3.43	33	31	15	223.1	221	53	68	3	1	0	0	82	19	0	.232
1939	20	8	.714	3.54	34	34	21	269.1	273	59	88	2	0	0	0	95	21	0	.221
1940	14	19	.424	3.49	35	35	23	289	328	78	124	2	0	0	0	101	16	0	.158
1941	18	13	.581	3.45	34	33	19	256	271	54	91	4	0	0	0	88	9	0	.102
1942	2	2	.500	4.11	6	5	1	35	28	5	15	1	0	0	0	10	1	0	.100
1943	11	13	.458	3.28	31	30	15	219.2	218	46	51	2	0	0	1	67	7	0	.104
1944	14	14	.500	3.06	32	31	17	229.1	222	37	62	1	0	1	0	79	18	0	.228
1945	17	7	.708	2.13	31	29	12	216	208	35	96	4	1	0	1	78	18	0	.231
1946	10	10	.500	3.56	26	23	7	161.2	182	36	62	2	0	0	0	53	9	0	.170
1947 PHI N	17	12	.586	2.68	32	29	19	235	224	57	103	3	1	1	0	80	14	0	.175
1948	12	17	.414	2.51	34	31	16	225.2	226	54	92	1	1	1	0	83	12	0	.145
1949 CHI N	7	16	.304	4.15	33	28	10	180	198	43	83	1	0	0	0	59	12	0	.203
1950	5	1	.833	3.77	35	1	0	74	70	27	28	0	4	1	6	16	1	0	.063
1951	10	6	.625	2.64	41	1	0	81.2	69	28	30	0	10	5	3	21	0	0	.000
1952	2	2	.500	2.16	45	0	0	66.2	56	24	37	0	2	2	11	10	2	0	.200
1953	2	3	.400	4.60	45	0	0	62.2	72	24	27	0	2	3	8	10	3	0	.300
20 yrs.	191	181	.513	3.25	640	375	192	3218.1	3304	738	1170	30	28	22	44	1054	177	0	.168

Dutch Leonard

LEONARD, HUBERT BENJAMIN
B. Apr. 16, 1892, Birmingham, Ohio   D. July 11, 1952, Fresno, Calif.   BL TL 5'10½" 185 lbs.

	W	L	PCT	ERA	G	GS	CG	IP	H	BB	SO	ShO	W	L	SV	AB	H	HR	BA
1913 BOS A	14	16	.467	2.39	42	27	14	259.1	245	94	144	2	3	3	1	83	15	0	.181
1914	19	5	.792	1.01¹	36	25	17	222.2	141	60	174	7	4	0	3	69	10	0	.145
1915	15	7	.682	2.36	32	21	10	183.1	130	67	116	2	4	2	0	53	14	0	.264
1916	18	12	.600	2.36	48	34	17	274	244	66	144	6	2	0	6	85	17	0	.200
1917	16	17	.485	2.17	37	36	26	294.1	257	72	144	4	0	0	1	104	9	0	.087
1918	8	6	.571	2.72	16	16	12	125.2	119	53	47	3	0	0	0	43	8	0	.186
1919 DET A	14	13	.519	2.77	29	28	18	217.1	212	65	102	4	0	1	0	71	11	0	.155
1920	10	17	.370	4.33	28	27	10	191.1	192	63	76	3	0	1	0	57	12	0	.211
1921	11	13	.458	3.75	36	32	16	245	273	63	120	1	0	2	1	82	14	0	.171
1924	3	2	.600	4.56	9	7	3	51.1	69	17	26	0	0	0	1	19	4	0	.211
1925	11	4	.733	4.51	18	18	9	125.2	143	43	65	0	0	0	0	50	10	0	.200
11 yrs.	139	112	.554	2.77	331	271	152	2190	2025	663	1158	32	13	9	13	716	124	0	.173
WORLD SERIES																			
1915 BOS A	1	0	1.000	1.00	1	1	1	9	3	0	6	0	0	0	0	3	0	0	.000
1916	1	0	1.000	1.00	1	1	1	9	5	4	3	0	0	0	0	3	0	0	.000
2 yrs.	2	0	1.000	1.00	2	2	2	18	8	4	9	0	0	0	0	6	0	0	.000

Elmer Leonard

LEONARD, ELMER ELLSWORTH (Tiny)
B. Nov. 12, 1888, Napa, Calif.   D. May 27, 1981, Napa, Calif.   BR TR 6'3½"   210 lbs.

	W	L	PCT	ERA	G	GS	CG	IP	H	BB	SO	ShO	W	L	SV	AB	H	HR	BA
1911 PHI A	2	2	.500	2.84	5	1	1	19	26	10	10	0	1	2	0	7	2	0	.286

Dave Leonhard

LEONHARD, DAVID PAUL
B. Jan. 22, 1942, Arlington, Va.   BR TR 5'11"   165 lbs.

	W	L	PCT	ERA	G	GS	CG	IP	H	BB	SO	ShO	W	L	SV	AB	H	HR	BA
1967 BAL A	0	0	–	3.14	3	2	0	14.1	11	6	9	0	0	0	0	5	0	0	.000
1968	7	7	.500	3.13	28	18	5	126.1	95	57	61	2	1	0	1	31	4	0	.129
1969	7	4	.636	2.49	37	3	1	94	78	38	37	1	6	2	1	21	2	0	.095
1970	0	0	–	5.14	23	0	0	28	32	18	14	0	0	0	1	1	0	0	.000
1971	2	3	.400	2.83	12	6	1	54	51	19	18	1	1	0	1	18	5	0	.278
1972	0	0	–	4.50	14	0	0	20	20	12	7	0	0	0	0	1	1	0	1.000
6 yrs.	16	14	.533	3.15	117	29	7	336.2	287	150	146	4	8	2	5	77	12	0	.156
WORLD SERIES																			
1969 BAL A	0	0	–	4.50	1	0	0	2	1	1	1	0	0	0	0	0	0	0	–
1971	0	0	–	0.00	1	0	0	1	0	1	0	0	0	0	0	0	0	0	–
2 yrs.	0	0	–	3.00	2	0	0	3	1	2	1	0	0	0	0	0	0	0	–

Rudy Leopold

LEOPOLD, RUDOLPH MATAS
B. July 27, 1905, Grand Cane, La.   D. Sept. 3, 1965, Baton Rouge, La.   BL TL 6'   160 lbs.

	W	L	PCT	ERA	G	GS	CG	IP	H	BB	SO	ShO	W	L	SV	AB	H	HR	BA
1928 CHI A	0	0	–	3.86	2	0	0	2.1	3	0	0	0	0	0	0	1	0	0	.000

Randy Lerch

LERCH, RANDY LOUIS
B. Oct. 9, 1954, Sacramento, Calif.   BL TL 6'5"   195 lbs.

	W	L	PCT	ERA	G	GS	CG	IP	H	BB	SO	ShO	W	L	SV	AB	H	HR	BA
1975 PHI N	0	0	–	6.43	3	0	0	7	6	1	8	0	0	0	0	0	0	0	–
1976	0	0	–	3.00	1	0	0	3	3	0	2	0	0	0	0	1	1	0	1.000
1977	10	6	.625	5.06	32	28	3	169	207	75	81	0	0	0	0	54	9	0	.167
1978	11	8	.579	3.96	33	28	6	184	183	70	96	0	0	0	0	60	15	3	.250
1979	10	13	.435	3.74	37	35	6	214	228	60	92	1	0	0	0	72	11	1	.153
1980	4	14	.222	5.16	30	22	2	150	178	55	57	0	1	0	0	45	12	0	.267
1981 MIL A	7	9	.438	4.30	23	18	1	111	134	43	53	0	2	1	0	0	0	0	–
1982 2 teams		MIL A (21G 8–7)				MON	N (6G 2–0)												
" total	10	7	.588	4.69	27	24	1	132.1	149	59	37	1	0	0	0	8	2	0	.250

	W	L	PCT	ERA	G	GS	CG	IP	H	BB	SO	ShO	Relief Pitching W	L	SV	BATTING AB	H	HR	BA

Randy Lerch continued

	W	L	PCT	ERA	G	GS	CG	IP	H	BB	SO	ShO	W	L	SV	AB	H	HR	BA
1983 2 teams	MON N (19G 1–3)				SF	N	(7G 1–0)												
" total	2	3	.400	6.02	26	5	0	49.1	54	26	30	0	1	1	0	9	2	0	.222
1984 SF N	5	3	.625	4.23	37	4	0	72.1	80	36	48	0	5	2	2	15	2	0	.133
10 yrs.	59	63	.484	4.50	249	164	18	1092	1222	425	502	2	9	4	3	264	54	4	.205
DIVISIONAL PLAYOFF SERIES																			
1981 MIL A	0	0	–	1.50	1	1	0	6	3	4	3	0	0	0	0	0	0	0	–
LEAGUE CHAMPIONSHIP SERIES																			
1978 PHI N	0	0	–	5.06	1	1	0	5.1	7	0	0	0	0	0	0	2	0	0	.000

Louis LeRoy

LeROY, LOUIS PAUL   TR
B. Feb. 18, 1879, Red Springs, Wis.   D. Oct. 10, 1944, Shawano, Wis.

	W	L	PCT	ERA	G	GS	CG	IP	H	BB	SO	ShO	W	L	SV	AB	H	HR	BA
1905 NY A	1	1	.500	3.75	3	3	2	24	26	1	8	0	0	0	0	8	1	0	.125
1906	2	0	1.000	2.22	11	2	1	44.2	33	12	28	0	1	0	1	14	2	0	.143
1910 BOS A	0	0	–	11.25	1	0	0	4	7	2	3	0	0	0	0	1	0	0	.000
3 yrs.	3	1	.750	3.22	15	5	3	72.2	66	15	39	0	1	0	1	23	3	0	.130

Barry Lersch

LERSCH, BARRY LEE   BR TR 6' 175 lbs.
B. Sept. 7, 1944, Denver, Colo.

	W	L	PCT	ERA	G	GS	CG	IP	H	BB	SO	ShO	W	L	SV	AB	H	HR	BA
1969 PHI N	0	3	.000	7.00	10	0	0	18	20	10	13	0	0	3	2	3	0	0	.000
1970	6	3	.667	3.26	42	11	3	138	119	47	92	0	2	0	3	31	2	0	.065
1971	5	14	.263	3.79	38	30	3	214	203	50	113	0	0	0	0	59	10	0	.169
1972	4	6	.400	3.04	36	8	3	100.2	86	33	48	1	0	2	0	23	0	0	.000
1973	3	6	.333	4.39	42	4	0	98.1	105	27	51	0	3	4	1	17	3	0	.176
1974 STL N	0	0	–	54.00	1	0	0	1	3	5	0	0	0	0	0	0	0	0	–
6 yrs.	18	32	.360	3.82	169	53	9	570	536	172	317	1	5	9	6	133	15	0	.113

Don Leshnock

LESHNOCK, DONALD LEE   BR TL 6'3" 195 lbs.
B. Nov. 25, 1946, Youngstown, Ohio

	W	L	PCT	ERA	G	GS	CG	IP	H	BB	SO	ShO	W	L	SV	AB	H	HR	BA
1972 DET A	0	0	–	0.00	1	0	0	1	2	0	2	0	0	0	0	0	0	0	–

Brad Lesley

LESLEY, BRADLEY JAY (The Animal)   BR TR 6'6" 220 lbs.
B. Sept. 11, 1958, Turlock, Calif.

	W	L	PCT	ERA	G	GS	CG	IP	H	BB	SO	ShO	W	L	SV	AB	H	HR	BA
1982 CIN N	0	2	.000	2.58	28	0	0	38.1	27	13	29	0	0	2	4	1	0	0	.000
1983	0	0	–	2.16	5	0	0	8.1	9	0	5	0	0	0	0	0	0	0	–
1984	0	1	.000	5.12	16	0	0	19.1	17	14	7	0	0	1	2	2	1	0	.500
3 yrs.	0	3	.000	3.27	49	0	0	66	53	27	41	0	0	3	6	3	1	0	.333

Walt Leverenz

LEVERENZ, WALTER FRED (Tiny)   BL TL 5'10" 175 lbs.
B. July 21, 1888, Chicago, Ill.   D. Mar. 19, 1973, Atascader, Calif.

	W	L	PCT	ERA	G	GS	CG	IP	H	BB	SO	ShO	W	L	SV	AB	H	HR	BA
1913 STL A	6	17	.261	2.58	30	27	13	202.2	159	89	87	2	0	0	1	68	12	0	.176
1914	1	12	.077	3.80	27	16	5	111.1	107	63	41	0	0	2	0	33	6	0	.182
1915	0	2	.000	8.00	5	1	0	9	11	8	3	0	0	1	1	1	0	0	.000
3 yrs.	7	31	.184	3.15	62	44	18	323	277	160	131	2	0	3	2	102	18	0	.176

Dixie Leverett

LEVERETT, GORHAM VANCE   BR TR 5'11" 190 lbs.
B. Mar. 29, 1894, Georgetown, Tex.   D. Feb. 20, 1957, Beaverton, Ore.

	W	L	PCT	ERA	G	GS	CG	IP	H	BB	SO	ShO	W	L	SV	AB	H	HR	BA
1922 CHI A	13	10	.565	3.32	33	27	16	224.2	224	79	60	4	0	0	1	83	21	0	.253
1923	10	13	.435	4.06	38	24	9	192.2	212	64	64	0	1	3	3	60	16	0	.267
1924	2	3	.400	5.82	21	11	4	99	123	41	29	0	0	0	0	32	6	0	.188
1926	1	1	.500	6.00	6	3	1	24	31	7	12	0	0	1	1	7	1	0	.143
1929 BOS N	3	7	.300	6.36	24	12	3	97.2	135	30	28	0	0	0	1	32	6	0	.188
5 yrs.	29	34	.460	4.50	122	77	33	638	725	221	193	4	1	4	6	214	50	0	.234

Hod Leverette

LEVERETTE, HORACE WILBUR   BR TR 6' 180 lbs.
B. Feb. 4, 1889, Shreveport, La.   D. Apr. 10, 1958, St. Petersburg, Fla.

	W	L	PCT	ERA	G	GS	CG	IP	H	BB	SO	ShO	W	L	SV	AB	H	HR	BA
1920 STL A	0	2	.000	5.23	3	2	0	10.1	9	12	0	0	0	0	0	3	0	0	.000

Dutch Levsen

LEVSEN, EMIL HENRY   BR TR 6' 180 lbs.
B. Apr. 29, 1898, Wyoming, Iowa   D. Mar. 12, 1972, Minneapolis, Minn.

	W	L	PCT	ERA	G	GS	CG	IP	H	BB	SO	ShO	W	L	SV	AB	H	HR	BA
1923 CLE A	0	0	–	0.00	3	0	0	4.1	4	0	1	0	0	0	0	1	0	0	.000
1924	1	1	.500	4.41	4	1	1	16.1	22	4	3	0	0	1	0	5	0	0	.000
1925	1	2	.333	5.55	4	3	2	24.1	30	16	9	0	0	0	0	8	2	0	.250
1926	16	13	.552	3.41	33	31	18	237.1	235	85	53	2	0	0	0	83	17	0	.205
1927	3	7	.300	5.49	25	13	2	80.1	96	37	15	1	0	1	0	25	5	0	.200
1928	0	3	.000	5.44	11	3	0	41.1	39	31	7	0	0	1	0	13	0	0	.000
6 yrs.	21	26	.447	4.17	80	51	23	404	426	173	88	3	0	5	0	135	24	0	.178

Dennis Lewallyn

LEWALLYN, DENNIS DALE   BR TR 6'4" 195 lbs.
B. Aug. 11, 1953, Pensacola, Fla.

	W	L	PCT	ERA	G	GS	CG	IP	H	BB	SO	ShO	W	L	SV	AB	H	HR	BA
1975 LA N	0	0	–	0.00	2	0	0	3	1	0	0	0	0	0	0	0	0	0	–
1976	1	1	.500	2.16	4	2	0	16.2	12	6	4	0	0	0	0	5	0	0	.000
1977	3	1	.750	4.24	5	1	0	17	22	4	8	0	2	1	1	6	0	0	.000
1978	0	0	–	0.00	2	0	0	2	2	0	0	0	0	0	0	0	0	0	–
1979	0	1	.000	5.25	7	0	0	12	19	5	1	0	0	1	0	2	1	0	.500
1980 TEX A	0	0	–	7.50	4	0	0	6	7	4	1	0	0	0	0	0	0	0	–
1981 CLE A	0	0	–	5.54	7	0	0	13	16	2	11	0	0	0	0	0	0	0	–
1982	0	1	.000	6.97	4	0	0	10.1	13	1	3	0	0	1	0	0	0	0	–
8 yrs.	4	4	.500	4.50	34	3	0	80	92	22	28	0	2	3	1	13	1	0	.077

Dan Lewandowski

LEWANDOWSKI, DANIEL WILLIAM   BR TR 6' 180 lbs.
B. Jan. 6, 1928, Buffalo, N. Y.

	W	L	PCT	ERA	G	GS	CG	IP	H	BB	SO	ShO	W	L	SV	AB	H	HR	BA
1951 STL N	0	1	.000	9.00	2	0	0	1	1	1	0	0	0	1	0	0	0	0	–

	W	L	PCT	ERA	G	GS	CG	IP	H	BB	SO	ShO	Relief Pitching W	L	SV	BATTING AB	H	HR	BA

Lewis

LEWIS,
B. Brooklyn, N. Y.   Deceased.

	W	L	PCT	ERA	G	GS	CG	IP	H	BB	SO	ShO	W	L	SV	AB	H	HR	BA
1890 BUF P	0	1	.000	60.00	1	1	0	3	13	7	1	0	0	0	0	5	1	0	.200

Bert Lewis

LEWIS, WILLIAM BURTON   BR TR 6'2"   176 lbs.
B. Oct. 3, 1895, Tonawanda, N. Y.   D. Mar. 24, 1950, Tonawanda, N. Y.

	W	L	PCT	ERA	G	GS	CG	IP	H	BB	SO	ShO	W	L	SV	AB	H	HR	BA
1924 PHI N	0	0	—	6.00	12	0	0	18	23	7	3	0	0	0	0	5	0	0	.000

Duffy Lewis

LEWIS, GEORGE EDWARD   BR TR 5'10½" 165 lbs.
B. Apr. 18, 1888, San Francisco, Calif.   D. June 17, 1979, Salem, N. H.

	W	L	PCT	ERA	G	GS	CG	IP	H	BB	SO	ShO	W	L	SV	AB	H	HR	BA
1913 BOS A	0	0	—	0.00	1	0	0	1	0	0	1	0	0	0	0	*			

Jim Lewis

LEWIS, JAMES MARTIN   BR TR 6'3"   190 lbs.
B. Oct. 12, 1955, Miami, Fla.

	W	L	PCT	ERA	G	GS	CG	IP	H	BB	SO	ShO	W	L	SV	AB	H	HR	BA
1979 SEA A	0	0	—	18.00	2	0	0	2	10	1	0	0	0	0	0	0	0	0	—
1982 NY A	0	0	—	54.00	1	0	0	.2	3	3	0	0	0	0	0	0	0	0	—
1983 MIN A	0	0	—	6.50	6	0	0	18	24	7	8	0	0	0	0	0	0	0	—
3 yrs.	0	0	—	9.15	9	0	0	20.2	37	11	8	0	0	0	0	0	0	0	—

Ted Lewis

LEWIS, EDWARD MORGAN (Parson)   BR TR 5'10½" 158 lbs.
B. Dec. 25, 1872, Machynlleth, Wales   D. May 24, 1936, Durham, N. H.

	W	L	PCT	ERA	G	GS	CG	IP	H	BB	SO	ShO	W	L	SV	AB	H	HR	BA
1896 BOS N	1	4	.200	3.24	6	5	4	41.2	37	27	12	0	0	0	0	18	2	0	.111
1897	21	12	.636	3.85	38	34	30	290	316	125	65	2	1	1	1	113	28	0	.248
1898	26	8	.765	2.90	41	33	29	313.1	267	109	72	1	3	0	2	131	37	0	.282
1899	17	11	.607	3.49	29	25	23	234.2	245	73	60	2	3	1	0	96	25	0	.260
1900	13	12	.520	4.13	30	22	19	209	215	86	66	1	4	0	0	73	10	0	.137
1901 BOS A	16	17	.485	3.53	39	34	31	316.1	299	91	103	1	0	2	1	121	21	0	.174
6 yrs.	94	64	.595	3.53	183	153	136	1405	1379	511	378	7	11	4	4	552	123	0	.223

Terry Ley

LEY, TERRENCE RICHARD   BL TL 6'   190 lbs.
B. Feb. 21, 1947, Portland, Ore.

	W	L	PCT	ERA	G	GS	CG	IP	H	BB	SO	ShO	W	L	SV	AB	H	HR	BA
1971 NY A	0	0	—	5.00	6	0	0	9	9	9	7	0	0	0	0	0	0	0	—

Al Libke

LIBKE, ALBERT WALTER (Big Al)   BL TR 6'4"   215 lbs.
B. Sept. 12, 1918, Tacoma, Wash.

	W	L	PCT	ERA	G	GS	CG	IP	H	BB	SO	ShO	W	L	SV	AB	H	HR	BA
1945 CIN N	0	0	—	0.00	4	0	0	4.1	3	3	2	0	0	0	0	449	127	4	.283
1946	0	0	—	3.60	1	1	0	5	4	3	2	0	0	0	0	431	109	5	.253
2 yrs.	0	0	—	1.93	5	1	0	9.1	7	6	4	0	0	0	0	*			

Don Liddle

LIDDLE, DONALD EUGENE   BL TL 5'10"   165 lbs.
B. May 25, 1925, Mt. Carmel, Ill.

	W	L	PCT	ERA	G	GS	CG	IP	H	BB	SO	ShO	W	L	SV	AB	H	HR	BA
1953 MIL N	7	6	.538	3.08	31	15	4	128.2	119	55	63	0	3	1	2	34	3	0	.088
1954 NY N	9	4	.692	3.06	28	19	4	126.2	100	55	44	3	1	1	0	37	7	0	.189
1955	10	4	.714	4.23	33	13	4	106.1	97	61	56	0	4	1	1	27	5	0	.185
1956 2 teams			NY	N (11G 1–2)		STL	N (14G 1–2)												
" total	2	4	.333	5.59	25	7	1	66	81	32	35	0	1	0	1	14	2	0	.143
4 yrs.	28	18	.609	3.75	117	54	13	427.2	397	203	198	3	9	3	4	112	17	0	.152
WORLD SERIES																			
1954 NY N	1	0	1.000	1.29	2	1	0	7	5	1	2	0	0	0	0	3	0	0	.000

Dutch Lieber

LIEBER, CHARLES EDWIN   BR TR 6'½"   180 lbs.
B. Feb. 1, 1909, Alameda, Calif.   D. Dec. 31, 1961, Sawtelle, Calif.

	W	L	PCT	ERA	G	GS	CG	IP	H	BB	SO	ShO	W	L	SV	AB	H	HR	BA
1935 PHI A	1	1	.500	3.09	18	1	0	46.2	45	19	14	0	1	1	2	14	2	0	.143
1936	0	1	.000	7.71	3	0	0	11.2	17	6	1	0	0	1	0	3	0	0	.000
2 yrs.	1	2	.333	4.01	21	1	0	58.1	62	25	15	0	1	2	2	17	2	0	.118

Glenn Liebhardt

LIEBHARDT, GLENN IGNATIUS (Sandy)   BR TR 5'10½" 170 lbs.
Son of Glenn Liebhardt.
B. July 31, 1910, Cleveland, Ohio

	W	L	PCT	ERA	G	GS	CG	IP	H	BB	SO	ShO	W	L	SV	AB	H	HR	BA
1930 PHI A	0	1	.000	11.00	5	0	0	9	14	8	2	0	0	0	0	2	0	0	.000
1936 STL A	0	0	—	8.78	24	0	0	55.1	98	27	20	0	0	0	0	11	0	0	.000
1938	0	0	—	6.00	2	0	0	3	4	0	1	0	0	0	0	0	0	0	—
3 yrs.	0	1	.000	8.96	31	0	0	67.1	116	35	23	0	0	1	0	13	0	0	.000

Glenn Liebhardt

LIEBHARDT, GLENN JOHN   BR TR 5'10"   175 lbs.
Father of Glenn Liebhardt.
B. Mar. 10, 1883, Milton, Ind.   D. July 13, 1956, Cleveland, Ohio

	W	L	PCT	ERA	G	GS	CG	IP	H	BB	SO	ShO	W	L	SV	AB	H	HR	BA
1906 CLE A	2	0	1.000	1.50	2	2	2	18	11	3	9	0	0	0	0	8	0	0	.000
1907	18	14	.563	2.05	38	34	27	280.1	254	85	110	4	0	0	1	87	14	0	.161
1908	15	16	.484	2.20	39	26	19	262	222	81	146	3	3	2	0	80	14	0	.175
1909	1	5	.167	2.92	12	4	1	52.1	54	16	15	0	1	1	1	15	0	0	.000
4 yrs.	36	35	.507	2.17	91	66	49	612.2	543	183	280	7	4	3	2	190	28	0	.147

Gene Lillard

LILLARD, ROBERT EUGENE   BR TR 5'10½" 178 lbs.
Brother of Bill Lillard.
B. Nov. 12, 1913, Santa Barbara, Calif.

	W	L	PCT	ERA	G	GS	CG	IP	H	BB	SO	ShO	W	L	SV	AB	H	HR	BA
1939 CHI N	3	5	.375	6.55	20	7	2	55	68	36	31	0	1	1	0	10	1	0	.100
1940 STL N	0	1	.000	13.50	2	1	0	4.2	8	4	2	0	0	1	0	0	0	0	—
2 yrs.	3	6	.333	7.09	22	8	2	59.2	76	40	33	0	1	2	0	44	8	0	.182

Jim Lillie

LILLIE, JAMES J. (Grasshopper)
B. 1862, New Haven, Conn.   D. Nov. 9, 1890, Kansas City, Mo.

	W	L	PCT	ERA	G	GS	CG	IP	H	BB	SO	ShO	W	L	SV	AB	H	HR	BA
1883 BUF N	0	1	.000	3.00	3	0	0	12	16	2	4	0	0	0	0	201	47	1	.234
1884	0	1	.000	6.23	2	1	0	13	22	5	4	0	0	0	0	471	105	3	.223
1886 KC N	0	0	—	4.50	1	0	0	6	8	1	0	0	0	0	0	416	73	0	.175
3 yrs.	0	2	.000	4.65	6	1	0	31	46	8	8	0	0	1	0	*			

	W	L	PCT	ERA	G	GS	CG	IP	H	BB	SO	ShO	Relief Pitching W	L	SV	BATTING AB	H	HR	BA

Ezra Lincoln

LINCOLN, EZRA PERRY
B. Nov. 17, 1868, Raynham, Mass.   D. May 7, 1951, Taunton, Mass.
BL TL 5'11"   160 lbs.

	W	L	PCT	ERA	G	GS	CG	IP	H	BB	SO	ShO	W	L	SV	AB	H	HR	BA
1890 2 teams					CLE N (15G 3–11)			SYR AA (3G 0–3)											
" total	3	14	.176	5.28	18	18	15	138	190	57	28	0	0	0	0	59	8	0	.136

Vive Lindaman

LINDAMAN, VIVIAN ALEXANDER
B. Oct. 28, 1877, Charles City, Iowa   D. Feb. 13, 1927, Charles City, Iowa
BL TL

	W	L	PCT	ERA	G	GS	CG	IP	H	BB	SO	ShO	W	L	SV	AB	H	HR	BA
1906 BOS N	12	23	.343	2.43	39	36	32	307.1	303	90	115	2	0	0	0	106	14	0	.132
1907	11	15	.423	3.63	34	28	24	260	252	108	90	2	0	1	1	90	11	0	.122
1908	12	16	.429	2.36	43	30	21	270.2	246	70	68	2	0	1	1	85	15	0	.176
1909	1	6	.143	4.64	15	6	6	66	75	28	13	1	0	1	0	22	6	0	.273
4 yrs.	36	60	.375	2.92	131	100	83	904	876	296	286	7	0	3	2	303	46	0	.152

Paul Lindblad

LINDBLAD, PAUL AARON
B. Aug. 9, 1941, Chanute, Kans.
BL TL 6'1"   185 lbs.

	W	L	PCT	ERA	G	GS	CG	IP	H	BB	SO	ShO	W	L	SV	AB	H	HR	BA
1965 KC A	0	1	.000	11.05	4	0	0	7.1	12	0	12	0	0	1	0	1	0	0	.000
1966	5	10	.333	4.17	38	14	0	121	138	37	69	0	2	3	1	34	5	0	.147
1967	5	8	.385	3.58	46	10	1	115.2	106	35	83	1	3	3	6	34	7	1	.206
1968 OAK A	4	3	.571	2.40	47	1	0	56.1	51	14	42	0	4	2	2	8	3	0	.375
1969	9	6	.600	4.14	60	0	0	78.1	72	33	64	0	9	6	9	12	4	0	.333
1970	8	2	.800	2.71	62	0	0	63	52	28	42	0	8	2	3	6	0	0	.000
1971 2 teams					OAK A (8G 1–0)			WAS A (43G 6–4)											
" total	7	4	.636	2.80	51	0	0	99.2	76	31	54	0	7	4	8	22	4	0	.182
1972 TEX A	5	8	.385	2.61	66	0	0	100	95	29	51	0	5	8	9	15	3	0	.200
1973 OAK A	1	5	.167	3.69	36	3	0	78	89	28	33	0	1	2	2	0	0	0	–
1974	4	4	.500	2.05	45	2	0	101	85	30	46	0	3	4	6	0	0	0	–
1975	9	1	.900	2.72	48	0	0	122.1	105	43	58	0	9	1	7	1	0	0	.000
1976	6	5	.545	3.05	65	0	0	115	111	24	37	0	6	5	5	0	0	0	–
1977 TEX A	4	5	.444	4.18	42	1	0	99	103	29	46	0	3	4	4	0	0	0	–
1978 2 teams					TEX A (18G 1–1)			NY A (7G 0–0)											
" total	1	1	.500	3.88	25	1	0	58	62	23	34	0	1	1	2	0	0	0	–
14 yrs.	68	63	.519	3.28	655	32	1	1214.2	1157	384	671	1	61	46	64	133	26	1	.195

LEAGUE CHAMPIONSHIP SERIES

	W	L	PCT	ERA	G	GS	CG	IP	H	BB	SO	ShO	W	L	SV	AB	H	HR	BA
1975 OAK A	0	0	–	0.00	2	0	0	4.2	5	1	0	0	0	0	0	0	0	0	–

WORLD SERIES

	W	L	PCT	ERA	G	GS	CG	IP	H	BB	SO	ShO	W	L	SV	AB	H	HR	BA
1973 OAK A	1	0	1.000	0.00	3	0	0	3.1	4	1	1	0	1	0	0	0	0	0	.000
1978 NY A	0	0	–	11.57	1	0	0	2.1	4	0	1	0	0	0	0	0	0	0	–
2 yrs.	1	0	1.000	4.76	4	0	0	5.2	8	1	2	0	1	0	0	0	0	0	.000

Lymie Linde

LINDE, LYMAN GILBERT
B. Sept. 20, 1920, Beaver Dam, Wis.
BR TR 5'11"   185 lbs.

	W	L	PCT	ERA	G	GS	CG	IP	H	BB	SO	ShO	W	L	SV	AB	H	HR	BA
1947 CLE A	0	0	–	27.00	1	0	0	.2	3	1	0	0	0	0	0	0	0	0	–
1948	0	0	–	5.40	3	0	0	10	9	4	0	0	0	0	0	2	0	0	.000
2 yrs.	0	0	–	6.75	4	0	0	10.2	12	5	0	0	0	0	0	2	0	0	.000

Johnny Lindell

LINDELL, JOHN HARLAN
B. Aug. 30, 1916, Greeley, Colo.
BR TR 6'4½"   217 lbs.

	W	L	PCT	ERA	G	GS	CG	IP	H	BB	SO	ShO	W	L	SV	AB	H	HR	BA
1942 NY A	2	1	.667	3.76	23	2	0	52.2	52	22	28	0	2	0	1	24	6	0	.250
1953 2 teams					PIT N (27G 5–16)			PHI N (5G 1–1)											
" total	6	17	.261	4.66	32	26	15	199	195	139	118	1	1	0	0	109	33	4	.303
2 yrs.	8	18	.308	4.47	55	28	15	251.2	247	161	146	1	3	0	1	*			

Ernie Lindeman

LINDEMAN, JOHN FREDERICK MANN
B. June 5, 1881, Philadelphia, Pa.   D. Dec. 27, 1951, Brooklyn, N. Y.
BR TR

	W	L	PCT	ERA	G	GS	CG	IP	H	BB	SO	ShO	W	L	SV	AB	H	HR	BA
1907 BOS N	0	0	–	5.68	1	1	0	6.1	6	4	3	0	0	0	0	2	1	0	.500

Carl Lindquist

LINDQUIST, CARL EMIL (Lindy)
B. May 9, 1919, Morris Run, Pa.
BR TR 6'2"   185 lbs.

	W	L	PCT	ERA	G	GS	CG	IP	H	BB	SO	ShO	W	L	SV	AB	H	HR	BA
1943 BOS N	0	2	.000	6.23	2	2	0	13	17	4	1	0	0	0	0	4	0	0	.000
1944	0	0	–	3.12	5	0	0	8.2	8	2	4	0	0	0	0	1	0	0	.000
2 yrs.	0	2	.000	4.98	7	2	0	21.2	25	6	5	0	0	0	0	5	0	0	.000

Jim Lindsey

LINDSEY, JAMES KENDRICK
B. Jan. 24, 1898, Greensburg, La.   D. Oct. 25, 1963, Jackson, La.
BR TR 6'1"   175 lbs.

	W	L	PCT	ERA	G	GS	CG	IP	H	BB	SO	ShO	W	L	SV	AB	H	HR	BA
1922 CLE A	4	5	.444	6.02	29	5	0	83.2	105	24	29	0	4	2	1	24	4	0	.167
1924	0	0	–	21.00	3	0	0	3	8	3	0	0	0	0	0	0	0	0	–
1929 STL N	1	1	.500	5.51	2	2	1	16.1	20	2	8	0	0	0	0	5	1	0	.200
1930	7	5	.583	4.43	39	6	3	105.2	131	46	50	0	4	2	5	28	8	0	.286
1931	6	4	.600	2.77	35	2	1	74.2	77	45	32	1	5	4	7	9	1	0	.111
1932	3	3	.500	4.94	38	5	0	89.1	96	38	31	0	3	2	3	21	3	0	.143
1933	0	0	–	4.50	1	0	0	2	2	1	1	0	0	0	0	0	0	0	–
1934 2 teams					CIN N (4G 0–0)			STL N (11G 0–1)											
" total	0	1	.000	6.00	15	0	0	18	25	5	9	0	0	1	1	1	0	0	.000
1937 BKN N	0	1	.000	3.52	20	0	0	38.1	43	12	15	0	0	1	2	6	1	0	.167
9 yrs.	21	20	.512	4.70	177	20	5	431	507	176	175	1	16	12	19	94	18	0	.191

WORLD SERIES

	W	L	PCT	ERA	G	GS	CG	IP	H	BB	SO	ShO	W	L	SV	AB	H	HR	BA
1930 STL N	0	0	–	1.93	2	0	0	4.2	1	1	2	0	0	0	0	1	1	0	1.000
1931	0	0	–	5.40	2	0	0	3.1	4	3	2	0	0	0	0	0	0	0	–
2 yrs.	0	0	–	3.38	4	0	0	8	5	4	4	0	0	0	0	1	1	0	1.000

Axel Lindstrom

LINDSTROM, AXEL OLAF
B. Aug. 26, 1895, Gustafsburg, Sweden   D. June 24, 1940, Asheville, N. C.
BR TR 5'10"   180 lbs.

	W	L	PCT	ERA	G	GS	CG	IP	H	BB	SO	ShO	W	L	SV	AB	H	HR	BA
1916 PHI A	0	0	–	4.50	1	0	0	4	2	0	1	0	0	0	0	2	1	0	.500

	W	L	PCT	ERA	G	GS	CG	IP	H	BB	SO	ShO	Relief Pitching W	L	SV	BATTING AB	H	HR	BA

Dick Lines

LINES, RICHARD GEORGE
B. Aug. 17, 1938, Montreal, Que., Canada
BR TL 6'1" 175 lbs.

	W	L	PCT	ERA	G	GS	CG	IP	H	BB	SO	ShO	W	L	SV	AB	H	HR	BA
1966 WAS A	5	2	.714	2.28	53	0	0	83	63	24	49	0	5	2	2	10	0	0	.000
1967	2	5	.286	3.36	54	0	0	85.2	83	24	54	0	2	5	4	9	1	0	.111
2 yrs.	7	7	.500	2.83	107	0	0	168.2	146	48	103	0	7	7	6	19	1	0	.053

Fred Link

LINK, FREDERICK THEODORE (Laddie)
B. Mar. 11, 1887, Columbus, Ohio   D. May 22, 1939, Houston, Tex.
BR TL 6' 175 lbs.

	W	L	PCT	ERA	G	GS	CG	IP	H	BB	SO	ShO	W	L	SV	AB	H	HR	BA
1910 2 teams		CLE	A (22G 5–6)		STL	A	(3G 0–1)												
" total	5	7	.417	3.42	25	16	6	139.2	139	62	57	1	1	0	1	49	8	0	.163

Ed Linke

LINKE, EDWARD KARL
B. Nov. 9, 1911, Chicago, Ill.
BR TR 5'11" 180 lbs.

	W	L	PCT	ERA	G	GS	CG	IP	H	BB	SO	ShO	W	L	SV	AB	H	HR	BA
1933 WAS A	1	0	1.000	5.06	3	2	0	16	15	11	6	0	0	0	0	6	1	0	.167
1934	2	2	.500	4.15	7	4	2	34.2	38	9	9	0	0	0	0	11	2	0	.182
1935	11	7	.611	5.01	40	22	10	178	211	80	51	1	2	1	3	68	20	1	.294
1936	1	5	.167	7.10	13	6	1	52	73	14	11	0	1	1	0	15	6	1	.400
1937	6	1	.857	5.60	36	7	0	128.2	158	59	61	0	3	1	3	46	10	0	.217
1938 STL A	1	7	.125	7.94	21	2	0	39.2	60	33	18	0	1	5	0	10	2	0	.200
6 yrs.	22	22	.500	5.61	120	43	13	449	555	206	156	1	7	8	6	156	41	2	.263

Royce Lint

LINT, ROYCE JAMES
B. Jan. 1, 1921, Birmingham, Ala.
BL TL 6'1" 165 lbs.

	W	L	PCT	ERA	G	GS	CG	IP	H	BB	SO	ShO	W	L	SV	AB	H	HR	BA
1954 STL N	2	3	.400	4.86	30	4	1	70.1	75	30	36	1	1	3	0	10	1	0	.100

Frank Linzy

LINZY, FRANK ALFRED
B. Sept. 15, 1940, Fort Gibson, Okla.
BR TR 6'1" 190 lbs.

	W	L	PCT	ERA	G	GS	CG	IP	H	BB	SO	ShO	W	L	SV	AB	H	HR	BA
1963 SF N	0	0	–	4.86	8	1	0	16.2	22	10	14	0	0	0	0	3	0	0	.000
1965	9	3	.750	1.43	57	0	0	81.2	76	23	35	0	9	3	21	18	4	1	.222
1966	7	11	.389	2.96	51	0	0	100.1	107	34	57	0	7	11	16	20	3	0	.150
1967	7	7	.500	1.51	57	0	0	95.2	67	34	38	0	7	7	17	15	0	0	.000
1968	9	8	.529	2.08	57	0	0	95.1	76	27	36	0	9	8	12	11	0	0	.000
1969	14	9	.609	3.65	58	0	0	116	129	38	62	0	14	9	11	30	8	0	.267
1970 2 teams	5	6	SF	N (20G 2–1)			STL	N	(47G 3–5)										
" total	5	6	.455	4.66	67	0	0	87	99	34	35	0	5	6	3	11	0	0	.000
1971 STL N	4	3	.571	2.14	50	0	0	59	49	27	24	0	4	3	6	4	2	0	.500
1972 MIL A	2	2	.500	3.04	47	0	0	77	70	27	24	0	2	2	12	9	1	0	.111
1973	2	6	.250	3.57	42	1	0	63	68	21	21	0	2	6	13	0	0	0	–
1974 PHI N	3	2	.600	3.24	22	0	0	25	27	7	12	0	3	2	0	0	0	0	–
11 yrs.	62	57	.521	2.85	516	2	0	816.2	790	282	358	0	62	57	111	121	18	1	.149

Angelo LiPetri

LiPETRI, MICHAEL ANGELO
B. July 6, 1930, Brooklyn, N. Y.
BR TR 6'1½" 180 lbs.

	W	L	PCT	ERA	G	GS	CG	IP	H	BB	SO	ShO	W	L	SV	AB	H	HR	BA
1956 PHI N	0	0	–	3.27	6	0	0	11	7	3	8	0	0	0	0	1	0	0	.000
1958	0	0	–	11.25	4	0	0	4	6	0	1	0	0	0	0	0	0	0	–
2 yrs.	0	0	–	5.40	10	0	0	15	13	3	9	0	0	0	0	1	0	0	.000

Tom Lipp

LIPP, THOMAS C.
B. June 4, 1870, Baltimore, Md.   D. May 30, 1932, Pittsburgh, Pa.

	W	L	PCT	ERA	G	GS	CG	IP	H	BB	SO	ShO	W	L	SV	AB	H	HR	BA
1897 PHI N	0	1	.000	15.00	1	1	0	3	8	2	1	0	0	0	0	1	1	0	1.000

Nig Lipscomb

LIPSCOMB, GERARD
B. Feb. 24, 1911, Rutherfordton, N. C.   D. Feb. 27, 1978, Huntersville, N. C.
BR TR 6' 175 lbs.

	W	L	PCT	ERA	G	GS	CG	IP	H	BB	SO	ShO	W	L	SV	AB	H	HR	BA
1937 STL A	0	0	–	6.52	3	0	0	9.2	13	5	1	0	0	0	0	*		

Hod Lisenbee

LISENBEE, HORACE MILTON
B. Sept. 23, 1898, Clarksville, Tenn.
BR TR 5'11" 170 lbs.

	W	L	PCT	ERA	G	GS	CG	IP	H	BB	SO	ShO	W	L	SV	AB	H	HR	BA
1927 WAS A	18	9	.667	3.57	39	34	17	242	221	78	105	4	2	1	0	83	11	0	.133
1928	2	6	.250	6.08	16	9	3	77	102	32	13	0	1	0	0	23	4	0	.174
1929 BOS A	0	0	–	5.19	5	0	0	8.2	10	4	2	0	0	0	0	2	0	0	.000
1930	10	17	.370	4.40	37	31	15	237.1	254	86	47	0	1	0	0	75	20	0	.267
1931	5	12	.294	5.19	41	17	6	164.2	190	49	42	0	2	1	0	53	12	0	.226
1932	4	0	.000	5.65	19	6	3	73.1	87	25	13	0	0	0	0	21	1	0	.048
1936 PHI A	1	7	.125	6.20	19	7	4	85.2	115	24	17	0	0	1	0	25	3	0	.120
1945 CIN N	1	3	.250	5.49	31	3	0	80.1	97	16	14	0	1	2	1	19	0	0	.000
8 yrs.	37	58	.389	4.81	207	107	48	969	1076	314	253	4	7	5	1	301	51	0	.169

Ad Liska

LISKA, ADOLPH JAMES
B. July 10, 1906, Dwight, Neb.
BR TR 5'11½" 160 lbs.

	W	L	PCT	ERA	G	GS	CG	IP	H	BB	SO	ShO	W	L	SV	AB	H	HR	BA
1929 WAS A	3	9	.250	4.77	24	10	4	94.1	87	42	33	0	0	3	0	29	5	0	.172
1930	9	7	.563	3.29	32	16	7	150.2	140	71	40	1	0	1	1	52	5	0	.096
1931	0	1	.000	6.75	2	0	0	4	9	1	2	0	0	0	0	1	0	0	.000
1932 PHI N	2	0	1.000	1.69	8	0	0	26.2	22	10	6	0	2	0	1	7	0	0	.000
1933	3	1	.750	4.52	45	1	0	75.2	96	26	23	0	3	1	1	14	1	0	.071
5 yrs.	17	18	.486	3.87	111	28	11	351.1	354	150	104	1	5	5	3	103	11	0	.107

Mark Littell

LITTELL, MARK ALAN
B. Jan. 17, 1953, Gideon, Mo.
BL TR 6'3" 210 lbs.

	W	L	PCT	ERA	G	GS	CG	IP	H	BB	SO	ShO	W	L	SV	AB	H	HR	BA
1973 KC A	1	3	.250	5.68	8	7	1	38	44	23	16	0	0	0	0	0	0	0	–
1975	1	2	.333	3.70	7	3	1	24.1	19	15	19	0	1	0	0	0	0	0	–
1976	8	4	.667	2.08	60	0	0	104	68	60	92	0	8	3	16	1	0	0	.000
1977	8	4	.667	3.60	48	5	0	105	73	55	106	0	6	4	12	0	0	0	.000
1978 STL N	4	8	.333	2.80	72	2	0	106	80	59	130	0	4	8	11	7	0	0	.000
1979	9	4	.692	2.20	63	0	0	82	60	39	67	0	9	4	13	14	0	0	.000
1980	0	2	.000	9.00	14	0	0	11	14	7	7	0	0	2	1	0	0	0	–
1981	1	3	.250	4.39	28	1	0	41	36	31	22	0	1	2	2	8	2	0	.250

	W	L	PCT	ERA	G	GS	CG	IP	H	BB	SO	ShO	Relief Pitching W	L	SV	BATTING AB	H	HR	BA

Marcelino Lopez

LOPEZ, MARCELINO PONS   BR TL 6'3"   195 lbs.
B. Sept. 23, 1943, Havana, Cuba

	W	L	PCT	ERA	G	GS	CG	IP	H	BB	SO	ShO	W	L	SV	AB	H	HR	BA
1963 PHI N	1	0	1.000	6.00	4	2	0	6	8	7	2	0	0	0	0	2	0	0	.000
1965 CAL A	14	13	.519	2.93	35	32	8	215.1	185	82	122	1	0	0	1	69	14	1	.203
1966	7	14	.333	3.93	37	32	6	199	188	68	132	2	0	0	1	58	11	0	.190
1967 2 teams			CAL	A (4G 0-2)			BAL	A (4G 1-0)											
" total	1	2	.333	4.73	8	7	0	26.2	26	19	21	0	0	0	0	7	1	0	.143
1969 BAL A	5	3	.625	4.41	27	4	0	69.1	65	34	57	0	4	2	0	14	3	0	.214
1970	1	1	.500	2.07	25	3	0	61	47	37	49	0	0	1	0	13	1	0	.077
1971 MIL A	2	7	.222	4.63	31	11	0	68	64	60	42	0	1	3	0	17	1	0	.059
1972 CLE A	0	0	–	5.63	4	2	0	8	8	10	1	0	0	0	0	1	0	0	.000
8 yrs.	31	40	.437	3.62	171	93	14	653.1	591	317	426	3	5	6	2	181	31	1	.171

LEAGUE CHAMPIONSHIP SERIES

	W	L	PCT	ERA	G	GS	CG	IP	H	BB	SO	ShO	W	L	SV	AB	H	HR	BA
1969 BAL A	0	0	–	0.00	1	0	0	.1	1	2	0	0	0	0	0	0	0	0	–

WORLD SERIES

	W	L	PCT	ERA	G	GS	CG	IP	H	BB	SO	ShO	W	L	SV	AB	H	HR	BA
1970 BAL A	0	0	–	0.00	1	0	0	.1	0	0	0	0	0	0	0	0	0	0	–

Ramon Lopez

LOPEZ, JOSE RAMON   BR TR 6'   175 lbs.
B. May 26, 1933, Las Villas, Cuba   D. Sept. 4, 1982, Miami, Fla.

	W	L	PCT	ERA	G	GS	CG	IP	H	BB	SO	ShO	W	L	SV	AB	H	HR	BA
1966 CAL A	0	1	.000	5.14	4	1	0	7	4	4	2	0	0	0	0	0	0	0	–

Bris Lord

LORD, BRISTOL ROBOTHAM (The Human Eyeball)   BR TR 5'9"   185 lbs.
B. Sept. 21, 1883, Upland, Pa.   D. Nov. 13, 1964, Annapolis, Md.

	W	L	PCT	ERA	G	GS	CG	IP	H	BB	SO	ShO	W	L	SV	AB	H	HR	BA
1907 PHI A	0	0	–	9.00	1	0	0	3	1	0	0	0	0	0	0	*			

Lefty Lorenzen

LORENZEN, ADOLPH ANDREAS   BL TL 5'10"   164 lbs.
B. Jan. 12, 1893, Davenport, Iowa   D. Mar. 5, 1963, Davenport, Iowa

	W	L	PCT	ERA	G	GS	CG	IP	H	BB	SO	ShO	W	L	SV	AB	H	HR	BA
1913 DET A	0	0	–	18.00	1	0	0	2	4	3	0	0	0	0	0	2	1	0	.500

Joe Lotz

LOTZ, JOSEPH PETER (Smokey)   BR TR 5'8½"   175 lbs.
B. Jan. 2, 1891, Remsen, Iowa   D. Jan. 1, 1971, Castro Valley, Calif.

	W	L	PCT	ERA	G	GS	CG	IP	H	BB	SO	ShO	W	L	SV	AB	H	HR	BA
1916 STL N	0	3	.000	4.28	12	3	1	40	31	17	18	0	0	0	0	12	4	0	.333

Art Loudell

LOUDELL, ARTHUR   BR TR 5'11"   173 lbs.
Born Arthur Laudel.
B. May 10, 1882, Latham, Mo.   D. Feb. 19, 1961, Kansas City, Mo.

	W	L	PCT	ERA	G	GS	CG	IP	H	BB	SO	ShO	W	L	SV	AB	H	HR	BA
1910 DET A	1	1	.500	3.38	5	2	1	21.1	23	14	12	0	0	0	0	7	1	0	.143

Larry Loughlin

LOUGHLIN, LARRY JOHN   BL TL 6'1"   190 lbs.
B. Aug. 16, 1941, Tacoma, Wash.

	W	L	PCT	ERA	G	GS	CG	IP	H	BB	SO	ShO	W	L	SV	AB	H	HR	BA
1967 PHI N	0	0	–	15.19	3	0	0	5.1	9	4	5	0	0	0	0	1	1	0	1.000

Don Loun

LOUN, DONALD NELSON   BR TL 6'2"   185 lbs.
B. Nov. 9, 1940, Frederick, Md.

	W	L	PCT	ERA	G	GS	CG	IP	H	BB	SO	ShO	W	L	SV	AB	H	HR	BA
1964 WAS A	1	1	.500	2.08	2	2	1	13	13	3	3	1	0	0	0	4	0	0	.000

Slim Love

LOVE, EDWARD HAUGHTON   BL TL 6'7"   195 lbs.
B. Aug. 1, 1890, Love, Mo.   D. Nov. 30, 1942, Memphis, Tenn.

	W	L	PCT	ERA	G	GS	CG	IP	H	BB	SO	ShO	W	L	SV	AB	H	HR	BA
1913 WAS A	1	0	1.000	1.62	5	1	0	16.2	14	6	5	0	0	0	1	5	1	0	.200
1916 NY A	2	0	1.000	4.91	20	1	0	47.2	46	23	21	0	1	0	0	14	0	0	.000
1917	6	5	.545	2.35	33	9	2	130.1	115	57	82	0	4	0	1	36	6	0	.167
1918	13	12	.520	3.07	38	29	13	228.2	207	116	95	1	1	1	1	74	17	0	.230
1919 DET A	6	4	.600	3.01	22	8	4	89.2	92	40	46	0	3	1	1	27	6	0	.222
1920	0	0	–	8.31	1	0	0	4.1	6	4	2	0	0	0	0	0	0	0	–
6 yrs.	28	21	.571	3.04	119	48	19	517.1	480	246	251	1	9	2	4	156	30	0	.192

Lynn Lovenguth

LOVENGUTH, LYNN RICHARD   BL TR 5'10½" 170 lbs.
B. Nov. 29, 1922, Camden, N. Y.

	W	L	PCT	ERA	G	GS	CG	IP	H	BB	SO	ShO	W	L	SV	AB	H	HR	BA
1955 PHI N	0	1	.000	4.50	14	0	0	18	17	10	14	0	0	0	0	2	0	0	.000
1957 STL N	0	1	.000	2.00	2	1	0	9	6	6	6	0	0	0	0	2	0	0	.000
2 yrs.	0	2	.000	3.67	16	1	0	27	23	16	20	0	0	1	0	4	0	0	.000

John Lovett

LOVETT, JOHN
B. May 6, 1878, Monday, Ohio   D. Dec. 5, 1937, Murray City, Iowa

	W	L	PCT	ERA	G	GS	CG	IP	H	BB	SO	ShO	W	L	SV	AB	H	HR	BA
1903 STL N	0	1	.000	5.40	3	1	0	5	6	5	3	0	0	0	0	3	1	0	.333

Tom Lovett

LOVETT, THOMAS JOSEPH   BR   158 lbs.
B. Dec. 7, 1863, Providence, R. I.   D. Mar. 20, 1928, Providence, R. I.

	W	L	PCT	ERA	G	GS	CG	IP	H	BB	SO	ShO	W	L	SV	AB	H	HR	BA
1885 PHI AA	7	8	.467	3.70	16	16	15	138.2	130	38	56	1	0	0	0	58	13	0	.224
1889 BKN AA	17	10	.630	4.32	29	28	23	229	234	65	92	1	0	0	0	100	19	2	.190
1890 BKN N	30	11	.732	2.78	44	41	39	372	327	141	124	4	1	0	0	164	33	1	.201
1891	23	19	.548	3.69	44	43	39	365.2	361	129	129	3	0	0	0	153	25	0	.163
1893	3	5	.375	6.56	14	8	6	96	134	35	15	0	1	0	1	50	9	0	.180
1894 BOS N	8	6	.571	5.97	15	13	10	104	155	36	23	0	1	1	0	49	7	1	.143
6 yrs.	88	59	.599	3.94	162	149	132	1305.1	1341	444	439	9	3	1	1	574	106	4	.185

Pete Lovrich

LOVRICH, PETER   BR TR 6'4"   200 lbs.
B. Oct. 16, 1942, Blue Island, Ill.

	W	L	PCT	ERA	G	GS	CG	IP	H	BB	SO	ShO	W	L	SV	AB	H	HR	BA
1963 KC A	1	1	.500	7.84	20	1	0	20.2	25	10	16	0	1	0	0	0	0	0	–

Grover Lowdermilk

LOWDERMILK, GROVER CLEVELAND (Slim)   BR TR 6'4"   190 lbs.
Brother of Lou Lowdermilk.
B. Jan. 15, 1885, Sandborn, Ind.   D. Mar. 31, 1968, Odin, Ill.

	W	L	PCT	ERA	G	GS	CG	IP	H	BB	SO	ShO	W	L	SV	AB	H	HR	BA
1909 STL N	0	2	.000	6.21	7	3	1	29	28	30	14	0	0	0	0	10	1	0	.100
1911	0	1	.000	7.29	11	2	1	33.1	37	33	15	0	0	0	0	9	1	0	.111

	W	L	PCT	ERA	G	GS	CG	IP	H	BB	SO	ShO	Relief Pitching W	L	SV	Batting AB	H	HR	BA

Grover Lowdermilk continued

	W	L	PCT	ERA	G	GS	CG	IP	H	BB	SO	ShO	W	L	SV	AB	H	HR	BA
1912 CHI N	0	1	.000	9.69	2	1	1	13	17	14	8	0	0	0	0	4	0	0	.000
1915 2 teams			STL	A (38G 9–17)		DET	A (7G 4–1)												
" total	13	18	.419	3.24	45	34	14	250.1	200	157	148	1	3	2	0	80	10	0	.125
1916 2 teams			DET	A (1G 0–0)		CLE	A (10G 1–5)												
" total	1	5	.167	3.14	11	9	2	51.2	52	48	28	0	0	0	0	18	3	0	.167
1917 STL A	2	1	.667	1.42	3	2	2	19	16	4	9	1	0	1	0	7	0	0	.000
1918	2	6	.250	3.15	13	11	4	80	74	38	25	0	0	0	0	28	7	0	.250
1919 2 teams			STL	A (7G 0–0)		CHI	A (20G 5–5)												
" total	5	5	.500	2.57	27	11	5	108.2	101	47	49	0	0	2	0	35	3	0	.086
1920 CHI A	0	0	—	6.75	3	0	0	5.1	9	5	0	0	0	0	0	0	0	0	—
9 yrs.	23	39	.371	3.58	122	73	30	590.1	534	376	296	2	3	5	0	191	25	0	.131

WORLD SERIES

	W	L	PCT	ERA	G	GS	CG	IP	H	BB	SO	ShO	W	L	SV	AB	H	HR	BA
1919 CHI A	0	0	—	9.00	1	0	0	1	2	1	0	0	0	0	0	0	0	0	—

Lou Lowdermilk

LOWDERMILK, LOUIS BAILEY   BR TL 6'1"   180 lbs.
Brother of Grover Lowdermilk.
B. Feb. 23, 1887, Sandborn, Ind.   D. Dec. 27, 1975, Centralia, Ill.

	W	L	PCT	ERA	G	GS	CG	IP	H	BB	SO	ShO	W	L	SV	AB	H	HR	BA
1911 STL N	3	4	.429	3.46	16	3	3	65	72	29	20	1	2	2	0	18	2	0	.111
1912	1	1	.500	3.00	4	1	1	15	14	9	2	0	0	1	1	4	1	0	.250
2 yrs.	4	5	.444	3.38	20	4	4	80	86	38	22	1	2	3	1	22	3	0	.136

Bobby Lowe

LOWE, ROBERT LINCOLN (Link)   BR TR 5'10"   150 lbs.
B. July 10, 1868, Pittsburgh, Pa.   D. Dec. 8, 1951, Detroit, Mich.
Manager 1904.

	W	L	PCT	ERA	G	GS	CG	IP	H	BB	SO	ShO	W	L	SV	AB	H	HR	BA
1891 BOS N	0	0	—	9.00	1	0	0	1	3	1	0	0	0	0	0	*			

George Lowe

LOWE, GEORGE WESLEY   BR TR 6'2"   180 lbs.
B. Apr. 25, 1895, Ridgefield Park, N. J.   D. Sept. 2, 1982, Somers Point, N. J.

	W	L	PCT	ERA	G	GS	CG	IP	H	BB	SO	ShO	W	L	SV	AB	H	HR	BA
1920 CIN N	0	0	—	0.00	1	0	0	2	1	1	0	0	0	0	0	0	0	0	—

Turk Lown

LOWN, OMAR JOSEPH   BR TR 6'   180 lbs.
B. May 30, 1924, Brooklyn, N. Y.

	W	L	PCT	ERA	G	GS	CG	IP	H	BB	SO	ShO	W	L	SV	AB	H	HR	BA
1951 CHI N	4	9	.308	5.46	31	18	3	127	80	90	39	1	1	2	0	39	8	0	.205
1952	4	11	.267	4.37	30	19	5	156.2	154	93	73	0	1	2	0	50	7	0	.140
1953	8	7	.533	5.16	49	12	2	148.1	166	84	76	0	7	3	3	48	6	0	.125
1954	0	2	.000	6.14	15	0	0	22	23	15	16	0	0	2	0	0	0	0	—
1956	9	8	.529	3.58	61	0	0	110.2	95	78	74	0	9	8	13	23	5	1	.217
1957	5	7	.417	3.77	67	0	0	93	74	51	51	0	5	7	12	10	2	0	.200
1958 3 teams			CHI	N (4G 0–0)		CIN	N (11G 0–2)		CHI	A (27G 3–3)									
" total	3	5	.375	4.31	42	0	0	56.1	63	43	53	0	3	5	8	10	3	0	.300
1959 CHI A	9	2	.818	2.89	60	0	0	93.1	73	42	63	0	9	2	15	12	3	0	.250
1960	2	3	.400	3.88	45	0	0	67.1	60	34	39	0	2	3	5	5	1	0	.200
1961	7	5	.583	2.76	59	0	0	101	87	35	50	0	7	5	11	14	0	0	.000
1962	4	2	.667	3.04	42	0	0	56.1	58	25	40	0	4	2	6	3	0	0	.000
11 yrs.	55	61	.474	4.12	504	49	10	1032	933	590	574	1	48	41	73	214	35	1	.164

WORLD SERIES

	W	L	PCT	ERA	G	GS	CG	IP	H	BB	SO	ShO	W	L	SV	AB	H	HR	BA
1959 CHI A	0	0	—	0.00	3	0	0	3.1	2	1	3	0	0	0	0	0	0	0	—

Sam Lowry

LOWRY, SAMUEL JOSEPH (Mose)   BR TR 5'11"   160 lbs.
B. Mar. 25, 1920, Philadelphia, Pa.

	W	L	PCT	ERA	G	GS	CG	IP	H	BB	SO	ShO	W	L	SV	AB	H	HR	BA
1942 PHI A	0	0	—	6.00	1	0	0	3	3	1	0	0	0	0	0	1	0	0	.000
1943	0	0	—	5.00	5	0	0	18	18	9	3	0	0	0	0	6	1	0	.167
2 yrs.	0	0	—	5.14	6	0	0	21	21	10	3	0	0	0	0	7	1	0	.143

Pat Luby

LUBY, JOHN PERKINS   TR 6'   185 lbs.
B. 1868, Charleston, S. C.   D. Apr. 24, 1899, Charleston, S. C.

	W	L	PCT	ERA	G	GS	CG	IP	H	BB	SO	ShO	W	L	SV	AB	H	HR	BA
1890 CHI N	20	9	.690	3.19	34	31	26	267.2	226	95	85	0	0	0	1	116	31	3	.267
1891	8	11	.421	4.76	30	24	18	206	221	94	52	0	1	0	1	98	24	2	.245
1892	10	17	.370	3.13	31	26	24	247.1	247	106	64	1	2	0	1	163	31	0	.190
1895 LOU N	1	5	.167	6.81	11	6	5	71.1	115	19	12	0	0	0	0	53	15	0	.283
4 yrs.	39	42	.481	3.91	106	87	73	792.1	809	314	213	1	3	0	3	*			

Gary Lucas

LUCAS, GARY PAUL   BL TL 6'5"   200 lbs.
B. Nov. 8, 1954, Riverside, Calif.

	W	L	PCT	ERA	G	GS	CG	IP	H	BB	SO	ShO	W	L	SV	AB	H	HR	BA
1980 SD N	5	8	.385	3.24	46	18	0	150	138	43	85	0	1	1	3	35	6	0	.171
1981	7	7	.500	2.00	57	0	0	90	78	36	53	0	7	7	13	10	1	0	.100
1982	1	10	.091	3.24	65	0	0	97.1	89	29	64	0	1	10	16	14	0	0	.000
1983	5	8	.385	2.87	62	0	0	91	85	34	60	0	5	8	17	12	0	0	.000
1984 MON N	0	3	.000	2.72	55	0	0	53	54	20	42	0	0	3	8	4	0	0	.000
5 yrs.	18	36	.333	2.88	285	18	0	481.1	444	162	304	0	14	29	57	75	7	0	.093

Ray Lucas

LUCAS, RAY WESLEY (Luke)   BR TR 6'2"   175 lbs.
B. Oct. 2, 1908, Springfield, Ohio   D. Oct. 9, 1969, Harrison, Mich.

	W	L	PCT	ERA	G	GS	CG	IP	H	BB	SO	ShO	W	L	SV	AB	H	HR	BA
1929 NY N	0	0	—	0.00	3	0	0	8	3	3	1	0	0	0	0	2	1	0	.500
1930	0	0	—	6.97	6	0	0	10.1	9	10	1	0	0	0	0	1	0	0	.000
1931	0	0	—	4.50	1	0	0	2	1	1	0	0	0	0	0	0	0	0	—
1933 BKN N	0	0	—	7.20	2	0	0	5	6	4	0	0	0	0	0	0	0	0	—
1934	1	1	.500	6.75	10	2	0	30.2	39	14	3	0	1	0	0	6	2	0	.333
5 yrs.	1	1	.500	5.79	22	2	0	56	58	32	5	0	1	0	1	9	3	0	.333

Red Lucas

LUCAS, CHARLES FRED (The Nashville Narcissus)   BL TR 5'9½"   170 lbs.
B. Apr. 28, 1902, Columbia, Tenn.

	W	L	PCT	ERA	G	GS	CG	IP	H	BB	SO	ShO	W	L	SV	AB	H	HR	BA
1923 NY N	0	0	—	0.00	3	0	0	5.1	9	4	3	0	0	0	0	2	0	0	.000
1924 BOS N	1	4	.200	5.16	27	4	1	83.2	112	18	30	0	1	1	0	33	11	0	.333
1926 CIN N	8	5	.615	3.68	39	11	7	154	161	30	34	0	3	1	2	76	23	0	.303

	W	L	PCT	ERA	G	GS	CG	IP	H	BB	SO	ShO	Relief Pitching W	L	SV	BATTING AB	H	HR	BA

Red Lucas continued

	W	L	PCT	ERA	G	GS	CG	IP	H	BB	SO	ShO	W	L	SV	AB	H	HR	BA
1927	18	11	.621	3.38	37	23	19	239.2	231	39	51	4	4	3	2	150	47	0	.313
1928	13	9	.591	3.39	27	19	13	167.1	164	42	35	4	3	2	1	73	23	0	.315
1929	19	12	.613	3.60	32	32	28	270	267	58	72	2	0	0	0	140	41	0	.293
1930	14	16	.467	5.38	33	28	18	210.2	270	44	53	1	0	2	1	113	38	2	.336
1931	14	13	.519	3.59	29	29	24	238	261	39	56	0	0	0	0	153	43	0	.281
1932	13	17	.433	2.94	31	31	28	269.1	261	35	63	0	0	0	0	150	43	0	.287
1933	10	16	.385	3.40	29	29	21	219.2	248	18	40	3	0	0	0	122	35	1	.287
1934 PIT N	10	9	.526	4.38	29	21	12	172.2	198	40	44	1	0	1	0	105	23	0	.219
1935	8	6	.571	3.44	20	19	8	125.2	136	23	29	2	0	0	0	66	21	0	.318
1936	15	4	.789	3.18	27	22	12	175.2	178	26	53	0	3	0	0	108	26	0	.241
1937	8	10	.444	4.27	20	20	9	126.1	150	23	20	1	0	0	0	82	22	0	.268
1938	6	3	.667	3.54	13	13	4	84	90	16	19	0	0	0	0	46	5	0	.109
15 yrs.	157	135	.538	3.72	396	301	204	2542	2736	455	602	19	14	10	7	*			

Joe Lucey

LUCEY, JOSEPH EARL (Scootch)   BR TR 6'   168 lbs.
B. Mar. 27, 1897, Holyoke, Mass.   D. July 30, 1980, Holyoke, Mass.

	W	L	PCT	ERA	G	GS	CG	IP	H	BB	SO	ShO	W	L	SV	AB	H	HR	BA
1920 NY A	0	0	–	0.00	0	0	0	0	0	0	0	0	0	0	0	3	0	0	.000
1925 BOS A	0	1	.000	9.00	7	2	0	11	18	14	2	0	0	0	0	15	2	0	.133
2 yrs.	0	1	.000	9.00	7	2	0	11	18	14	2	0	0	0	0	18	2	0	.111

Con Lucid

LUCID, CORNELIUS CECIL
B. Feb. 24, 1874, Dublin, Ireland   D. June 25, 1931, Houston, Tex.

	W	L	PCT	ERA	G	GS	CG	IP	H	BB	SO	ShO	W	L	SV	AB	H	HR	BA
1893 LOU N	0	1	.000	15.00	2	1	0	6	10	10	0	0	0	0	0	3	1	0	.333
1894 BKN N	5	3	.625	6.56	10	9	7	71.1	87	44	15	0	0	0	0	33	7	0	.212
1895 2 teams				BKN	N (21G 10–7)		PHI	N (10G 6–3)											
" total	16	10	.615	5.66	31	29	19	206.2	244	107	43	3	1	0	0	82	23	0	.280
1896 PHI N	4	4	.200	8.36	5	5	5	42	75	17	3	0	0	0	0	16	2	0	.125
1897 STL N	1	5	.167	3.67	6	6	5	49	66	26	4	0	0	0	0	17	3	0	.176
5 yrs.	23	23	.500	6.02	54	50	36	375	482	204	65	3	1	0	0	151	36	0	.238

Lou Lucier

LUCIER, LOUIS JOSEPH   BR TR 5'8"   160 lbs.
B. Mar. 23, 1918, Northbridge, Mass.

	W	L	PCT	ERA	G	GS	CG	IP	H	BB	SO	ShO	W	L	SV	AB	H	HR	BA
1943 BOS A	3	4	.429	3.89	16	9	3	74	94	33	23	0	0	0	0	20	4	0	.200
1944 2 teams				BOS	A (3G 0–0)		PHI	N (1G 0–0)											
" total	0	0	–	7.36	4	0	0	7.1	10	9	3	0	0	0	0	1	0	0	.000
1945 PHI N	0	1	.000	2.21	13	0	0	20.1	14	5	5	0	0	1	1	4	1	0	.250
3 yrs.	3	5	.375	3.81	33	9	3	101.2	118	47	31	0	0	1	1	25	5	0	.200

Howard Luckey

LUCKEY, HOWARD J.
B. Philadelphia, Pa.   Deceased.

	W	L	PCT	ERA	G	GS	CG	IP	H	BB	SO	ShO	W	L	SV	AB	H	HR	BA
1890 PHI AA	0	0	–	9.00	1	0	0	2	1	3	1	0	0	0	0	1	0	0	.000

Willie Ludolph

LUDOLPH, WILLIAM FRANCIS (Wee Willie)   BR TR 6'1½"   170 lbs.
B. Jan. 21, 1900, San Francisco, Calif.   D. Apr. 8, 1952, Oakland, Calif.

	W	L	PCT	ERA	G	GS	CG	IP	H	BB	SO	ShO	W	L	SV	AB	H	HR	BA
1924 DET A	0	0	–	4.76	3	0	0	5.2	5	2	1	0	0	0	0	1	0	0	.000

Steve Luebber

LUEBBER, STEPHEN LEE   BR TR 6'3"   185 lbs.
B. July 9, 1949, Clinton, Mo.

	W	L	PCT	ERA	G	GS	CG	IP	H	BB	SO	ShO	W	L	SV	AB	H	HR	BA
1971 MIN A	2	5	.286	5.03	18	12	0	68	73	37	35	0	1	0	1	19	1	0	.053
1972	0	0	–	0.00	2	0	0	2	3	2	1	0	0	0	0	0	0	0	–
1976	4	5	.444	4.00	38	12	2	119.1	109	62	45	1	0	1	2	0	0	0	–
1979 TOR A	0	0	–	∞	1	0	0	0	2	1	0	0	0	0	0	0	0	0	–
1981 BAL A	0	0	–	7.41	7	0	0	17	26	4	12	0	0	0	0	0	0	0	–
5 yrs.	6	10	.375	4.62	66	24	2	206.1	213	106	93	1	1	1	3	19	1	0	.053

Dick Luebke

LUEBKE, RICHARD RAYMOND   BR TL 6'4"   200 lbs.
B. Apr. 8, 1935, Chicago, Ill.   D. Dec. 4, 1974, San Diego, Calif.

	W	L	PCT	ERA	G	GS	CG	IP	H	BB	SO	ShO	W	L	SV	AB	H	HR	BA
1962 BAL A	0	1	.000	2.70	10	0	0	13.1	12	6	7	0	0	1	0	0	0	0	–

Bill Luhrsen

LUHRSEN, WILLIAM FERDINAND (Wild Bill)   BR TR 5'9"   165 lbs.
B. Apr. 14, 1884, Buckley, Ill.   D. Sept. 15, 1973, Little Rock, Ark.

	W	L	PCT	ERA	G	GS	CG	IP	H	BB	SO	ShO	W	L	SV	AB	H	HR	BA
1913 PIT N	3	1	.750	2.48	5	3	2	29	25	16	11	0	1	0	0	10	0	0	.000

Al Lukens

LUKENS, ALBERT P.
B. Nov., 1868, Pa.   Deceased.

	W	L	PCT	ERA	G	GS	CG	IP	H	BB	SO	ShO	W	L	SV	AB	H	HR	BA
1894 PHI N	0	1	.000	10.20	3	2	1	15	26	10	0	0	0	0	0	8	0	0	.000

Ralph Lumenti

LUMENTI, RALPH ANTHONY (Commuter)   BL TL 6'3"   185 lbs.
B. Dec. 21, 1936, Milford, Mass.

	W	L	PCT	ERA	G	GS	CG	IP	H	BB	SO	ShO	W	L	SV	AB	H	HR	BA
1957 WAS A	0	1	.000	6.75	3	2	0	9.1	9	5	8	0	0	0	0	2	0	0	.000
1958	1	2	.333	8.57	8	4	0	21	21	36	20	0	0	0	0	8	2	0	.250
1959	0	0	–	0.00	2	0	0	3	2	1	2	0	0	0	0	0	0	0	–
3 yrs.	1	3	.250	7.29	13	6	0	33.1	32	42	30	0	0	0	0	10	2	0	.200

Memo Luna

LUNA, GUILLERMO ROMERO   BL TL 6'   168 lbs.
B. June 25, 1930, Tacubaya, Mexico

	W	L	PCT	ERA	G	GS	CG	IP	H	BB	SO	ShO	W	L	SV	AB	H	HR	BA
1954 STL N	0	1	.000	27.00	1	1	0	.2	2	2	0	0	0	0	0	0	0	0	–

Jack Lundbom

LUNDBOM, JOHN FREDERICK   BR TR 6'2"   187 lbs.
B. Mar. 10, 1877, Manistee, Mich.   D. Oct. 31, 1949, Manistee, Mich.

	W	L	PCT	ERA	G	GS	CG	IP	H	BB	SO	ShO	W	L	SV	AB	H	HR	BA
1902 CLE A	1	1	.500	6.62	8	3	1	34	48	16	7	0	1	0	0	15	4	0	.267

	W	L	PCT	ERA	G	GS	CG	IP	H	BB	SO	ShO	Relief Pitching W	L	SV	BATTING AB	H	HR	BA

Carl Lundgren

LUNDGREN, CARL LEONARD
B. Feb. 16, 1880, Marengo, Ill.   D. Aug. 21, 1934, Marengo, Ill.   BR TR 5'11½" 175 lbs.

	W	L	PCT	ERA	G	GS	CG	IP	H	BB	SO	ShO	W	L	SV	AB	H	HR	BA
1902 CHI N	9	9	.500	1.97	18	18	17	160	158	45	68	1	0	0	0	66	7	0	.106
1903	10	9	.526	2.94	27	20	16	193	191	60	67	0	1	0	3	61	7	0	.115
1904	17	10	.630	2.60	31	27	25	242	203	77	106	2	1	0	1	90	20	0	.222
1905	13	4	.765	2.24	23	19	16	169	132	53	69	3	0	0	0	61	11	0	.180
1906	17	6	.739	2.21	27	24	21	207.2	160	89	103	5	0	0	2	67	12	0	.179
1907	18	7	.720	1.17	28	25	21	207	130	92	84	7	3	0	0	66	7	0	.106
1908	6	9	.400	4.22	23	15	9	138.2	149	56	38	1	1	0	0	47	7	0	.149
1909	0	1	.000	4.15	2	1	0	4.1	6	4	0	0	0	0	0	2	1	0	.500
8 yrs.	90	55	.621	2.42	179	149	125	1321.2	1129	476	535	19	6	0	6	460	72	0	.157

Del Lundgren

LUNDGREN, EBIN DELMAR
B. Sept. 21, 1900, Lindsborg, Kans.   BR TR 5'8" 160 lbs.

	W	L	PCT	ERA	G	GS	CG	IP	H	BB	SO	ShO	W	L	SV	AB	H	HR	BA
1924 PIT N	0	1	.000	6.48	8	1	0	16.2	25	3	4	0	0	0	0	3	0	0	.000
1926 BOS A	0	2	.000	8.07	17	1	0	29	35	24	10	0	0	1	0	4	0	0	.000
1927	5	12	.294	6.27	30	17	5	136.1	160	87	39	2	0	2	0	44	7	0	.159
3 yrs.	5	15	.250	6.58	55	19	5	182	220	114	53	2	0	3	0	51	7	0	.137

Dolf Luque

LUQUE, ADOLFO (The Pride Of Havana)
B. Aug. 4, 1890, Havana, Cuba   D. July 3, 1957, Havana, Cuba   BR TR 5'7" 160 lbs.

	W	L	PCT	ERA	G	GS	CG	IP	H	BB	SO	ShO	W	L	SV	AB	H	HR	BA
1914 BOS N	0	1	.000	4.15	2	1	1	8.2	5	4	1	0	0	0	0	2	0	0	.000
1915	0	0	–	3.60	2	1	0	5	6	4	3	0	0	0	0	2	0	0	.000
1918 CIN N	6	3	.667	3.80	12	10	9	83	84	32	26	1	0	0	0	28	9	0	.321
1919	9	3	.750	2.63	30	9	6	106	89	36	40	2	3	0	3	32	4	0	.125
1920	13	9	.591	2.51	37	23	10	207.2	168	60	72	1	1	1	1	64	17	0	.266
1921	17	19	.472	3.38	41	36	25	304	318	64	102	3	0	1	3	111	30	0	.270
1922	13	23	.361	3.31	39	32	18	261	266	72	79	0	3	2	0	86	18	0	.209
1923	27	8	.771	1.93	41	37	28	322	279	88	151	6	1	0	2	104	21	1	.202
1924	10	15	.400	3.16	31	28	13	219.1	229	53	86	2	0	1	0	73	13	1	.178
1925	16	18	.471	2.63	36	36	22	291	263	78	140	4	0	0	0	102	26	2	.255
1926	13	16	.448	3.43	34	30	16	233.2	231	77	83	1	1	1	0	78	27	0	.346
1927	13	12	.520	3.20	29	27	17	230.2	225	56	76	2	1	0	0	83	18	0	.217
1928	11	10	.524	3.57	33	29	11	234.1	254	84	72	1	0	1	1	67	8	0	.119
1929	5	16	.238	4.50	32	22	8	176	213	56	43	1	0	1	0	54	15	1	.278
1930 BKN N	14	8	.636	4.30	31	24	16	199	221	58	62	2	1	0	2	75	18	0	.240
1931	7	6	.538	4.56	19	15	5	102.2	122	27	25	0	2	0	0	30	4	0	.133
1932 NY N	6	7	.462	4.01	38	5	1	110	128	32	32	0	6	3	5	25	1	0	.040
1933	8	2	.800	2.69	35	0	0	80.1	75	19	23	0	8	2	4	19	5	0	.263
1934	4	3	.571	3.83	26	0	0	42.1	54	17	12	0	4	3	7	7	2	0	.286
1935	0	0	1.000	0.00	2	0	0	3.2	1	1	2	0	1	0	0	1	1	0	1.000
20 yrs.	193	179	.519	3.24	550	365	206	3220.1	3231	918	1130	26	32	16	28	1043	237	5	.227

WORLD SERIES

	W	L	PCT	ERA	G	GS	CG	IP	H	BB	SO	ShO	W	L	SV	AB	H	HR	BA
1919 CIN N	0	0	–	0.00	2	0	0	5	1	0	6	0	0	0	0	1	0	0	.000
1933 NY N	1	0	1.000	0.00	1	0	0	4.1	2	2	5	0	1	0	0	1	1	0	1.000
2 yrs.	1	0	1.000	0.00	3	0	0	9.1	3	2	11	0	1	0	0	2	1	0	.500

Johnny Lush

LUSH, JOHN CHARLES
B. Oct. 8, 1885, Williamsport, Pa.   D. Nov. 18, 1946, Beverly Hills, Calif.   BL TL 5'9½" 165 lbs.

	W	L	PCT	ERA	G	GS	CG	IP	H	BB	SO	ShO	W	L	SV	AB	H	HR	BA
1904 PHI N	0	6	.000	3.59	7	6	3	42.2	52	27	27	0	0	0	0	369	102	2	.276
1905	2	0	1.000	1.59	2	2	1	17	12	8	8	0	0	0	0	16	5	0	.313
1906	18	15	.545	2.37	37	35	24	281	254	119	151	5	0	0	0	212	56	0	.264
1907 2 teams					PHI	N (8G 3-5)		STL	N (20G 7-10)										
" total	10	15	.400	2.64	28	27	20	201.1	180	63	91	6	0	0	0	122	31	0	.254
1908 STL N	11	18	.379	2.12	38	32	23	250.2	221	57	93	3	1	0	1	89	15	0	.169
1909	11	18	.379	3.13	34	28	21	221.1	215	69	66	2	0	1	0	92	22	0	.239
1910	14	13	.519	3.20	36	24	13	225.1	235	70	54	1	4	3	1	93	21	0	.226
7 yrs.	66	85	.437	2.68	182	154	105	1239.1	1169	413	490	17	5	4	2	*			

Jim Lyle

LYLE, JAMES CHARLES
B. July 24, 1900, Lake, Miss.   D. Oct. 10, 1977, Williamsport, Pa.   BR TR 6'1" 180 lbs.

	W	L	PCT	ERA	G	GS	CG	IP	H	BB	SO	ShO	W	L	SV	AB	H	HR	BA
1925 WAS A	0	0	–	6.00	1	0	0	3	5	1	3	0	0	0	0	1	0	0	.000

Sparky Lyle

LYLE, ALBERT WALTER
B. July 22, 1944, DuBois, Pa.   BL TL 6'1" 182 lbs.

	W	L	PCT	ERA	G	GS	CG	IP	H	BB	SO	ShO	W	L	SV	AB	H	HR	BA
1967 BOS A	1	2	.333	2.28	27	0	0	43.1	33	14	42	0	1	2	5	8	2	0	.250
1968	6	1	.857	2.74	49	0	0	65.2	67	14	52	0	6	1	11	8	1	0	.125
1969	8	3	.727	2.54	71	0	0	102.2	91	48	93	0	8	3	17	17	2	0	.118
1970	1	7	.125	3.90	63	0	0	67	62	34	51	0	1	7	20	13	0	0	.000
1971	6	4	.600	2.77	50	0	0	52	41	23	37	0	6	4	16	3	3	0	1.000
1972 NY A	9	5	.643	1.91	59	0	0	108.1	84	29	75	0	9	5	35	21	4	0	.190
1973	5	9	.357	2.51	51	0	0	82.1	66	18	63	0	5	9	27	0	0	0	–
1974	9	3	.750	1.66	66	0	0	114	93	43	89	0	9	3	15	1	0	0	.000
1975	5	7	.417	3.12	49	0	0	89.1	94	36	65	0	5	7	6	0	0	0	–
1976	7	8	.467	2.26	64	0	0	103.2	82	42	61	0	7	8	23	0	0	0	–
1977	13	5	.722	2.17	72	0	0	137	131	33	68	0	13	5	26	0	0	0	–
1978	9	3	.750	3.47	59	0	0	111.2	116	33	33	0	9	3	9	0	0	0	–
1979 TEX A	5	8	.385	3.13	67	0	0	95	78	28	48	0	5	8	13	0	0	0	–
1980 2 teams					TEX	A (49G 3-2)		PHI	N (10G 0-0)										
" total	3	2	.600	4.26	59	0	0	95	108	34	49	0	3	2	10	0	0	0	–
1981 PHI N	9	6	.600	4.44	48	0	0	75	85	33	29	0	9	6	2	5	2	0	.400
1982 2 teams					PHI	N (34G 3-3)		CHI	A (11G 0-0)										
" total	3	3	.500	4.62	45	0	0	48.2	61	19	18	0	3	3	1	2	1	0	.500
16 yrs.	99	76	.566	2.88 4th	899	0	0	1390.2	1292	481	873	0	99 4th	76	238 3rd	78	15	0	.192

DIVISIONAL PLAYOFF SERIES

	W	L	PCT	ERA	G	GS	CG	IP	H	BB	SO	ShO	W	L	SV	AB	H	HR	BA
1981 PHI N	0	0	–	0.00	3	0	0	2.1	4	2	1	0	0	0	0	0	0	0	–

	W	L	PCT	ERA	G	GS	CG	IP	H	BB	SO	ShO	Relief Pitching W	L	SV	BATTING AB	H	HR	BA

Sparky Lyle continued

LEAGUE CHAMPIONSHIP SERIES

	W	L	PCT	ERA	G	GS	CG	IP	H	BB	SO	ShO	W	L	SV	AB	H	HR	BA
1976 NY A	0	0	–	0.00	1	0	0	1	0	1	0	0	0	0	1	0	0	0	–
1977	2	0	1.000	0.96	4	0	0	9.1	7	0	3	0	2	0	0	0	0	0	–
1978	0	0	–	13.50	1	0	0	1.1	3	0	0	0	0	0	0	0	0	0	–
3 yrs.	2	0	1.000	2.31	6	0	0	11.2	10	1	3	0	2	0	1	0	0	0	–

WORLD SERIES

	W	L	PCT	ERA	G	GS	CG	IP	H	BB	SO	ShO	W	L	SV	AB	H	HR	BA
1976 NY A	0	0	–	0.00	2	0	0	2.2	1	0	3	0	0	0	0	0	0	0	–
1977	1	0	1.000	1.93	2	0	0	4.2	2	0	2	0	1	0	0	2	0	0	.000
2 yrs.	1	0	1.000	1.23	4	0	0	7.1	3	0	5	0	1	0	0	2	0	0	.000

Adrian Lynch

LYNCH, ADRIAN RYAN   BR TR
B. Feb. 9, 1897, Laurens, Iowa   D. Mar. 16, 1934, Davenport, Iowa

	W	L	PCT	ERA	G	GS	CG	IP	H	BB	SO	ShO	W	L	SV	AB	H	HR	BA
1920 STL A	2	0	1.000	5.24	5	3	1	22.1	23	17	8	0	0	0	0	9	2	0	.222

Ed Lynch

LYNCH, EDWARD FRANCIS   BR TR 6'5"   210 lbs.
B. Feb. 25, 1956, Brooklyn, N. Y.

	W	L	PCT	ERA	G	GS	CG	IP	H	BB	SO	ShO	W	L	SV	AB	H	HR	BA
1980 NY N	1	1	.500	5.21	5	4	0	19	24	5	9	0	0	0	0	6	2	0	.333
1981	4	5	.444	2.93	17	13	0	80	79	21	27	0	0	1	0	21	3	0	.143
1982	4	8	.333	3.55	43	12	0	139.1	145	40	51	0	1	3	2	33	0	0	.000
1983	10	10	.500	4.28	30	27	1	174.2	208	41	44	0	1	0	0	52	8	0	.154
1984	9	8	.529	4.50	40	13	0	124	169	24	62	0	5	0	2	27	6	0	.222
5 yrs.	28	32	.467	3.97	135	69	1	537	625	131	193	0	7	4	4	139	19	0	.137

Jack Lynch

LYNCH, JOHN H.   BR TR
B. Feb. 5, 1855, New York, N. Y.   D. Apr. 19, 1923, Bronx, N. Y.

	W	L	PCT	ERA	G	GS	CG	IP	H	BB	SO	ShO	W	L	SV	AB	H	HR	BA
1881 BUF N	10	9	.526	3.59	20	19	17	165.2	203	29	32	0	0	0	0	78	13	0	.167
1883 NY AA	13	15	.464	4.09	29	29	29	255	263	25	119	0	0	0	0	107	20	0	.187
1884	37	14	.725	2.64	54	53	53	487	410	42	286	5	0	1	0	195	30	0	.154
1885	23	21	.523	3.61	44	43	43	379	410	42	177	1	1	0	0	153	30	0	.196
1886	20	30	.400	3.95	51	50	50	432.2	485	116	193	1	0	0	0	169	27	0	.160
1887	7	14	.333	5.10	21	21	21	187	245	36	45	0	0	0	0	83	14	0	.169
1890 B-B AA	0	1	.000	12.00	1	1	1	9	22	5	1	0	0	0	0	4	3	0	.750
7 yrs.	110	104	.514	3.69	220	216	214	1915.1	2038	295	853	8	1	1	0	789	137	0	.174

Mike Lynch

LYNCH, MICHAEL JOSEPH   BR TR
B. June 28, 1880, Holyoke, Mass.   D. Apr. 2, 1927, Garrison, N. Y.

	W	L	PCT	ERA	G	GS	CG	IP	H	BB	SO	ShO	W	L	SV	AB	H	HR	BA
1904 PIT N	15	11	.577	2.71	27	24	24	222.2	200	91	95	1	1	0	0	87	20	0	.230
1905	17	8	.680	3.80	33	22	13	206	191	107	106	0	5	1	2	81	11	0	.136
1906	6	5	.545	2.42	18	12	7	119	101	31	48	0	2	0	0	39	8	0	.205
1907 2 teams							PIT N (7G 2-2)		NY N (12G 3-6)										
" total	5	8	.385	3.00	19	14	9	108	105	52	43	0	0	0	0	39	11	0	.282
4 yrs.	43	32	.573	3.05	97	72	53	655.2	597	281	292	1	8	2	2	246	50	0	.203

Thomas Lynch

LYNCH, THOMAS S.   BL 5'11"   175 lbs.
B. 1862, Peru, Ill.   D. May 13, 1923, Peru, Ill.

	W	L	PCT	ERA	G	GS	CG	IP	H	BB	SO	ShO	W	L	SV	AB	H	HR	BA
1884 CHI N	0	0	–	2.57	1	1	0	7	7	3	2	0	0	0	0	4	0	0	.000

Red Lynn

LYNN, JAPHET MONROE   BR TR 6'   162 lbs.
B. Dec. 27, 1913, Kenney, Tex.   D. Oct. 27, 1977, Bellville, Tex.

	W	L	PCT	ERA	G	GS	CG	IP	H	BB	SO	ShO	W	L	SV	AB	H	HR	BA
1939 2 teams							DET A (4G 0-1)		NY N (26G 1-0)										
" total	1	1	.500	3.88	30	0	0	58	55	24	25	0	1	1	1	8	0	0	.000
1940 NY N	4	3	.571	3.83	33	0	0	42.1	40	24	25	0	4	3	3	4	0	0	.000
1944 CHI N	5	4	.556	4.06	22	7	4	84.1	80	37	35	1	0	2	1	29	6	0	.207
3 yrs.	10	8	.556	3.95	85	7	4	184.2	175	85	85	1	5	6	5	41	6	0	.146

Al Lyons

LYONS, ALBERT HAROLD   BR TR 6'2"   195 lbs.
B. July 18, 1918, St. Joseph, Mo.   D. Dec. 20, 1965, Inglewood, Calif.

	W	L	PCT	ERA	G	GS	CG	IP	H	BB	SO	ShO	W	L	SV	AB	H	HR	BA
1944 NY A	0	0	–	4.54	11	0	0	39.2	43	24	14	0	0	0	0	26	9	0	.346
1946	0	1	.000	5.40	2	1	0	8.1	11	6	4	0	0	1	0	4	0	0	.000
1947 2 teams							NY A (6G 1-0)		PIT N (13G 1-2)										
" total	2	2	.500	7.78	19	0	0	39.1	54	21	23	0	2	0	0	16	6	1	.375
1948 BOS N	1	0	1.000	7.82	7	0	0	12.2	17	8	5	0	1	0	0	12	2	0	.167
4 yrs.	3	3	.500	6.30	39	1	0	100	125	59	46	0	3	2	0	58	17	1	.293

George Lyons

LYONS, GEORGE TONY (Smooth)   BR TR 5'11"   180 lbs.
B. Jan. 25, 1891, Bible Grove, Ill.   D. Aug. 12, 1981, Nevada, Mo.

	W	L	PCT	ERA	G	GS	CG	IP	H	BB	SO	ShO	W	L	SV	AB	H	HR	BA
1920 STL N	2	1	.667	3.09	7	2	1	23.1	21	9	5	0	1	0	0	7	1	0	.143
1924 STL A	3	2	.600	4.93	25	6	2	76.2	95	44	25	0	1	0	0	20	5	0	.250
2 yrs.	5	3	.625	4.50	32	8	3	100	116	53	30	0	2	0	0	27	6	0	.222

Harry Lyons

LYONS, HARRY P.   BR TR 5'8½"   195 lbs.
B. Mar. 25, 1866, Chester, Pa.   D. June 30, 1912, Mauricetown, N. J.

	W	L	PCT	ERA	G	GS	CG	IP	H	BB	SO	ShO	W	L	SV	AB	H	HR	BA
1890 ROC AA	0	0	–	12.27	1	0	0	3.2	8	1	2	0	0	0	0	*			

Hersh Lyons

LYONS, HERSHEL ENGLEBERT   BR TR 5'11"   195 lbs.
B. July 23, 1915, Fresno, Calif.

	W	L	PCT	ERA	G	GS	CG	IP	H	BB	SO	ShO	W	L	SV	AB	H	HR	BA
1941 STL N	0	0	–	0.00	1	0	0	1.1	1	3	1	0	0	0	0	0	0	0	–

Ted Lyons

LYONS, THEODORE AMAR   BB TR 5'11"   200 lbs.
B. Dec. 28, 1900, Lake Charles, La.
Manager 1946-48.
Hall of Fame 1955.
BR 1925-27

	W	L	PCT	ERA	G	GS	CG	IP	H	BB	SO	ShO	W	L	SV	AB	H	HR	BA
1923 CHI A	2	1	.667	6.35	9	1	0	22.2	30	15	6	0	2	0	0	5	1	0	.200
1924	12	11	.522	4.87	41	22	12	216.1	279	72	52	0	1	1	3	77	17	0	.221

	W	L	PCT	ERA	G	GS	CG	IP	H	BB	SO	ShO	Relief Pitching W	L	SV	BATTING AB	H	HR	BA

Ted Lyons continued

	W	L	PCT	ERA	G	GS	CG	IP	H	BB	SO	ShO	W	L	SV	AB	H	HR	BA
1925	21	11	.656	3.26	43	32	19	262.2	274	83	45	5	2	2	3	97	18	0	.186
1926	18	16	.529	3.01	39	31	24	283.2	268	106	51	3	1	3	2	104	22	0	.212
1927	22	14	.611	2.84	39	34	30	307.2	291	67	71	2	0	2	2	110	28	1	.255
1928	15	14	.517	3.98	39	27	21	240	276	68	60	0	3	1	6	91	23	0	.253
1929	14	20	.412	4.10	37	31	21	259.1	276	76	57	1	1	3	2	91	20	0	.220
1930	22	15	.595	3.78	42	36	29	297.2	331	57	69	1	2	1	1	122	38	1	.311
1931	4	6	.400	4.01	22	12	7	101	117	33	16	0	1	1	0	33	5	0	.152
1932	10	15	.400	3.28	33	26	19	230.2	243	71	58	1	0	1	2	73	19	1	.260
1933	10	21	.323	4.38	36	27	14	228	260	74	74	2	4	3	1	91	26	1	.286
1934	11	13	.458	4.87	30	24	21	205.1	249	66	53	0	0	1	1	97	20	1	.206
1935	15	8	.652	3.02	23	22	19	190.2	194	56	54	1	0	1	0	82	18	0	.220
1936	10	13	.435	5.14	26	24	15	182	227	45	48	1	0	1	0	70	11	0	.157
1937	12	7	.632	4.15	22	22	11	169.1	182	45	45	0	0	0	0	57	12	0	.211
1938	9	11	.450	3.70	23	23	17	194.2	238	52	54	1	0	0	0	72	14	0	.194
1939	14	6	.700	2.76	21	21	16	172.2	162	26	65	0	0	0	0	61	18	0	.295
1940	12	8	.600	3.24	22	22	17	186.1	188	37	72	4	0	0	0	75	18	0	.240
1941	12	10	.545	3.70	22	22	19	187.1	199	37	63	2	0	0	0	74	20	0	.270
1942	14	6	.700	2.10	20	20	20	180.1	167	26	50	1	0	0	0	67	16	0	.239
1946	1	4	.200	2.32	5	5	5	42.2	38	9	10	0	0	0	0	14	0	0	.000
21 yrs.	260	230	.531	3.67	594	484	356	4161	4489	1121	1073	27	17	21	23	*			

Toby Lyons

LYONS, THOMAS A.
B. Mar. 27, 1869, Cambridge, Mass. D. Aug. 27, 1920, Boston, Mass.

	W	L	PCT	ERA	G	GS	CG	IP	H	BB	SO	ShO	W	L	SV	AB	H	HR	BA
1890 SYR AA	0	2	.000	10.48	3	3	2	22.1	40	21	6	0	0	0	0	12	4	0	.333

Rick Lysander

LYSANDER, RICHARD EUGENE
B. Feb. 21, 1953, Hunting Park, Calif. BR TR 6'2" 195 lbs.

	W	L	PCT	ERA	G	GS	CG	IP	H	BB	SO	ShO	W	L	SV	AB	H	HR	BA
1980 OAK A	0	0	–	7.71	5	0	0	14	14	4	5	0	0	0	0	0	0	0	–
1983 MIN A	5	12	.294	3.38	61	4	1	125	132	43	58	1	4	9	3	0	0	0	–
1984	4	3	.571	3.65	36	0	0	56.2	62	27	22	0	4	3	5	0	0	0	–
3 yrs.	9	15	.375	3.77	102	4	1	195.2	218	74	85	1	8	12	8	0	0	0	–

Bill Lyston

LYSTON, WILLIAM EDWARD
B. 1863, Baltimore, Md. D. Aug. 4, 1944, Baltimore, Md.

	W	L	PCT	ERA	G	GS	CG	IP	H	BB	SO	ShO	W	L	SV	AB	H	HR	BA
1891 COL AA	0	1	.000	10.50	1	1	1	6	10	6	1	0	0	0	0	2	0	0	.000
1894 CLE N	0	1	.000	9.82	1	1	0	3.2	5	4	0	0	0	0	0	2	0	0	.000
2 yrs.	0	2	.000	10.24	2	2	1	9.2	15	10	1	0	0	0	0	4	0	0	.000

Duke Maas

MAAS, DUANE FREDERICK
B. Jan. 31, 1929, Utica, Mich. D. Dec. 7, 1976, Mt. Clemens, Mich. BR TR 5'10" 170 lbs.

	W	L	PCT	ERA	G	GS	CG	IP	H	BB	SO	ShO	W	L	SV	AB	H	HR	BA
1955 DET A	5	6	.455	4.88	18	16	5	86.2	91	50	42	2	0	0	0	30	5	0	.167
1956	0	7	.000	6.54	26	7	0	63.1	81	32	34	0	0	1	0	16	3	0	.188
1957	10	14	.417	3.28	45	26	8	219.1	210	65	116	2	1	2	6	71	6	1	.085
1958 2 teams								KC A (10G 4–5)					NY A (22G 7–3)						
" total	11	8	.579	3.85	32	20	5	156.2	142	49	69	2	2	1	1	51	6	0	.118
1959 NY A	14	8	.636	4.43	38	21	3	138	149	53	67	1	5	0	4	40	5	0	.125
1960	5	1	.833	4.09	35	1	0	70.1	70	35	28	0	5	0	4	6	0	0	.000
1961	0	0	–	54.00	1	0	0	.1	2	0	0	0	0	0	0	0	0	0	–
7 yrs.	45	44	.506	4.19	195	91	21	734.2	745	284	356	7	13	5	15	214	25	1	.117

WORLD SERIES

	W	L	PCT	ERA	G	GS	CG	IP	H	BB	SO	ShO	W	L	SV	AB	H	HR	BA
1958 NY A	0	0	–	81.00	1	0	0	.1	2	1	0	0	0	0	0	0	0	0	–
1960	0	0	–	4.50	1	0	0	2	2	0	1	0	0	0	0	0	0	0	–
2 yrs.	0	0	–	15.43	2	0	0	2.1	4	1	1	0	0	0	0	0	0	0	–

Bob Mabe

MABE, ROBERT LEE
B. Oct. 8, 1929, Danville, Va. BR TR 5'11" 165 lbs.

	W	L	PCT	ERA	G	GS	CG	IP	H	BB	SO	ShO	W	L	SV	AB	H	HR	BA
1958 STL N	3	9	.250	4.51	31	13	4	111.2	113	41	74	0	1	1	0	24	1	0	.042
1959 CIN N	4	2	.667	5.46	18	1	0	29.2	29	19	8	0	4	2	3	7	0	0	.000
1960 BAL A	0	0	–	27.00	2	0	0	.2	4	1	0	0	0	0	0	0	0	0	–
3 yrs.	7	11	.389	4.82	51	14	4	142	146	61	82	0	5	3	3	31	1	0	.032

Mac MacArthur

MacARTHUR, MALCOLM
B. Jan. 19, 1862, Glasgow, S. C. D. Oct. 18, 1932, Detroit, Mich.

	W	L	PCT	ERA	G	GS	CG	IP	H	BB	SO	ShO	W	L	SV	AB	H	HR	BA
1884 IND AA	1	5	.167	5.02	6	6	6	52	57	21	19	0	0	0	0	21	2	0	.095

Frank MacCormick

MacCORMICK, FRANK LOUIS
B. Sept. 21, 1954, Jersey City, N. J. BR TR 6'4" 210 lbs.

	W	L	PCT	ERA	G	GS	CG	IP	H	BB	SO	ShO	W	L	SV	AB	H	HR	BA
1976 DET A	0	5	.000	5.73	9	8	0	33	35	34	14	0	0	0	0	3	0	0	.000
1977 SEA A	0	0	–	3.86	3	3	0	7	4	12	4	0	0	0	0	0	0	0	–
2 yrs.	0	5	.000	5.40	12	11	0	40	39	46	18	0	0	0	0	3	0	0	.000

Bill Macdonald

MACDONALD, WILLIAM PAUL
B. Mar. 28, 1929, Alameda, Calif. BR TR 5'10" 170 lbs.

	W	L	PCT	ERA	G	GS	CG	IP	H	BB	SO	ShO	W	L	SV	AB	H	HR	BA
1950 PIT N	8	10	.444	4.29	32	20	6	153	138	88	60	2	1	1	1	49	6	0	.122
1953	0	1	.000	12.27	4	1	0	7.1	12	8	4	0	0	0	0	0	0	0	–
2 yrs.	8	11	.421	4.66	36	21	6	160.1	150	96	64	2	1	1	1	49	6	0	.122

Jimmy Mace

MACE, HARRY L.
B. Washington, D. C. Deceased.

	W	L	PCT	ERA	G	GS	CG	IP	H	BB	SO	ShO	W	L	SV	AB	H	HR	BA
1891 WAS AA	0	1	.000	7.31	3	1	1	16	18	8	3	0	0	0	0	6	0	0	.000

	W	L	PCT	ERA	G	GS	CG	IP	H	BB	SO	ShO	Relief Pitching W	L	SV	BATTING AB	H	HR	BA

Danny MacFayden

MacFAYDEN, DANIEL KNOWLES (Deacon Danny) BR TR 5'11" 170 lbs.
B. June 10, 1905, North Truro, Mass. D. Aug. 26, 1972, Brunswick, Me.

	W	L	PCT	ERA	G	GS	CG	IP	H	BB	SO	ShO	W	L	SV	AB	H	HR	BA
1926 BOS A	0	1	.000	4.85	3	1	1	13	10	7	1	0	0	0	0	3	1	0	.333
1927	5	8	.385	4.27	34	16	6	160.1	176	59	42	1	2	1	2	46	13	1	.283
1928	9	15	.375	4.75	33	28	9	195	215	78	61	0	0	0	0	63	9	0	.143
1929	10	18	.357	3.62	32	26	14	221	225	81	61	4	0	2	0	74	13	0	.176
1930	11	14	.440	4.21	36	33	18	269.1	293	93	76	1	1	0	2	92	13	0	.141
1931	16	12	.571	4.02	35	32	17	230.2	263	79	74	2	1	0	0	81	10	0	.123
1932 2 teams			BOS	A (12G 1–10)			NY	A (17G 7–5)											
" total	8	15	.348	4.39	29	26	14	199	228	70	62	0	0	0	1	74	8	0	.108
1933 NY A	3	2	.600	5.88	25	6	2	90.1	120	37	28	0	0	1	0	34	1	0	.029
1934	4	3	.571	4.50	22	11	4	96	110	31	41	0	0	0	0	39	4	0	.103
1935 2 teams			CIN	N (7G 1–2)			BOS	N (28G 5–13)											
" total	6	15	.286	5.04	35	24	8	187.2	239	47	59	1	0	2	0	62	9	0	.145
1936 BOS N	17	13	.567	2.87	37	31	21	266.2	268	66	86	2	2	1	0	83	8	0	.096
1937	14	14	.500	2.93	32	32	16	246	250	60	70	2	0	0	0	83	13	0	.157
1938	14	9	.609	2.95	29	29	19	219.2	211	64	58	5	0	0	0	77	9	0	.117
1939	8	14	.364	3.90	33	28	8	191.2	221	59	46	0	0	0	0	67	12	0	.179
1940 PIT N	5	4	.556	3.55	35	8	0	91.1	112	27	24	0	4	2	2	28	5	0	.179
1941 WAS A	0	1	.000	10.29	5	0	0	7	12	5	3	0	0	1	0	0	0	0	–
1943 BOS N	2	1	.667	5.91	10	1	0	21.1	31	9	5	0	2	1	0	4	1	0	.250
17 yrs.	132	159	.454	3.96	465	332	157	2706	2984	872	797	18	12	11	9	910	129	1	.142

Chuck Machemehl

MACHEMEHL, CHARLES WALTER BR TR 6'4" 200 lbs.
B. Apr. 20, 1947, Brenham, Tex.

	W	L	PCT	ERA	G	GS	CG	IP	H	BB	SO	ShO	W	L	SV	AB	H	HR	BA
1971 CLE A	0	2	.000	6.50	14	0	0	18	16	15	9	0	0	2	3	2	1	0	.500

Bill Mack

MACK, WILLIAM FRANCIS BL TL 6'1" 155 lbs.
B. Feb. 12, 1885, Elmira, N. Y. D. Sept. 30, 1971, Elmira, N. Y.

	W	L	PCT	ERA	G	GS	CG	IP	H	BB	SO	ShO	W	L	SV	AB	H	HR	BA
1908 CHI N	0	0	–	2.84	2	0	0	6.1	5	1	2	0	0	0	0	3	2	0	.667

Frank Mack

MACK, FRANK GEORGE (Stubby) BR TR 6'1½" 180 lbs.
B. Feb. 2, 1900, Oklahoma City, Okla. D. July 2, 1971, Sacramento, Calif.

	W	L	PCT	ERA	G	GS	CG	IP	H	BB	SO	ShO	W	L	SV	AB	H	HR	BA
1922 CHI A	2	2	.500	3.67	8	4	1	34.1	36	16	11	1	0	0	0	12	3	0	.250
1923	0	1	.000	4.24	11	0	0	23.1	23	11	6	0	0	1	0	6	0	0	.000
1925	0	0	–	9.45	8	0	0	13.1	24	13	6	0	0	0	0	3	1	0	.333
3 yrs.	2	3	.400	4.94	27	4	1	71	83	40	23	1	0	1	0	21	4	0	.190

Ken MacKenzie

MacKENZIE, KENNETH PURVIS BR TL 6' 185 lbs.
B. Mar. 10, 1934, Gore Bay, Ont., Canada

	W	L	PCT	ERA	G	GS	CG	IP	H	BB	SO	ShO	W	L	SV	AB	H	HR	BA
1960 MIL N	0	1	.000	6.48	9	0	0	8.1	9	3	9	0	0	1	0	1	0	0	.000
1961	0	1	.000	5.14	5	0	0	7	8	2	5	0	0	1	0	2	0	0	.000
1962 NY N	5	4	.556	4.95	42	1	0	80	87	34	51	0	5	3	1	12	1	0	.083
1963 2 teams			NY	N (34G 3–1)			STL	N (8G 0–0)											
" total	3	1	.750	4.88	42	0	0	66.1	72	15	48	0	3	1	3	10	0	0	.000
1964 SF N	0	0	–	5.00	10	0	0	9	9	3	3	0	0	0	1	0	0	0	–
1965 HOU N	0	3	.000	3.86	21	0	0	37.1	46	6	26	0	0	3	0	11	3	0	.273
6 yrs.	8	10	.444	4.80	129	1	0	208	231	63	142	0	8	9	5	36	4	0	.111

Johnny Mackinson

MACKINSON, JOHN JOSEPH BR TR 5'10½" 160 lbs.
B. Oct. 29, 1923, Orange, N. J.

	W	L	PCT	ERA	G	GS	CG	IP	H	BB	SO	ShO	W	L	SV	AB	H	HR	BA
1953 PHI A	0	0	–	0.00	1	0	0	1.1	1	2	0	0	0	0	0	0	0	0	–
1955 STL N	0	1	.000	7.84	8	1	0	20.2	24	10	8	0	0	1	0	4	0	0	.000
2 yrs.	0	1	.000	7.36	9	1	0	22	25	12	8	0	0	1	0	4	0	0	.000

Bill MacLeod

MacLEOD, WILLIAM DANIEL BL TL 6'2" 190 lbs.
B. May 13, 1942, Gloucester, Mass.

	W	L	PCT	ERA	G	GS	CG	IP	H	BB	SO	ShO	W	L	SV	AB	H	HR	BA
1962 BOS A	0	1	.000	5.40	2	0	0	1.2	4	1	2	0	0	1	0	0	0	0	–

Max Macon

MACON, MAX CULLEN BL TL 6'3" 175 lbs.
B. Oct. 14, 1915, Pensacola, Fla.

	W	L	PCT	ERA	G	GS	CG	IP	H	BB	SO	ShO	W	L	SV	AB	H	HR	BA
1938 STL N	4	11	.267	4.11	38	12	5	129.1	133	61	39	1	2	2	2	36	11	0	.306
1940 BKN N	1	0	1.000	22.50	2	0	0	2	5	0	1	0	1	0	0	1	1	0	1.000
1942	5	3	.625	1.93	14	8	4	84	67	33	27	1	2	0	1	43	12	0	.279
1943	7	5	.583	5.96	25	9	0	77	89	32	21	0	3	2	0	55	9	0	.164
1944 BOS N	0	0	–	21.00	1	0	0	3	10	1	1	0	0	0	0	366	100	3	.273
1947	0	0	–	0.00	1	0	0	2	1	1	1	0	0	0	0	0	0	0	.000
6 yrs.	17	19	.472	4.24	81	29	9	297.1	305	128	90	2	8	4	3	*			

Harry MacPherson

MacPHERSON, HARRY WILLIAM BR TR 5'10" 150 lbs.
B. July 10, 1926, North Andover, Mass.

	W	L	PCT	ERA	G	GS	CG	IP	H	BB	SO	ShO	W	L	SV	AB	H	HR	BA
1944 BOS N	0	0	–	0.00	1	0	0	1	1	1	0	0	0	0	0	0	0	0	–

Jimmy Macullar

MACULLAR, JAMES F. (Little Mac) BR TL
B. Jan. 16, 1855, Boston, Mass. D. Apr. 8, 1924, Baltimore, Md.

	W	L	PCT	ERA	G	GS	CG	IP	H	BB	SO	ShO	W	L	SV	AB	H	HR	BA
1886 BAL AA	0	0	–	9.00	1	0	0	2	4	0	1	0	0	0	0	*			

Keith MacWhorter

MacWHORTER, KEITH BR TR 6'4" 190 lbs.
B. Dec. 30, 1955, Worcester, Mass.

	W	L	PCT	ERA	G	GS	CG	IP	H	BB	SO	ShO	W	L	SV	AB	H	HR	BA
1980 BOS A	0	3	.000	5.57	14	2	0	42	46	18	21	0	0	1	0	0	0	0	–

Kid Madden

MADDEN, MICHAEL JOSEPH TL 5'7½" 130 lbs.
B. Oct. 22, 1866, Portland, Me. D. Mar. 16, 1896, Portland, Me.

	W	L	PCT	ERA	G	GS	CG	IP	H	BB	SO	ShO	W	L	SV	AB	H	HR	BA
1887 BOS N	22	14	.611	3.79	37	37	36	321	317	122	81	3	0	0	0	132	32	1	.242
1888	7	11	.389	2.95	20	18	17	165	142	24	53	1	0	0	0	67	11	0	.164
1889	10	10	.500	4.40	22	19	18	178	194	71	64	1	1	0	1	86	25	0	.291

	W	L	PCT	ERA	G	GS	CG	IP	H	BB	SO	ShO	Relief W	Pitching L	SV	BATTING AB	H	HR	BA

Kid Madden continued

	W	L	PCT	ERA	G	GS	CG	IP	H	BB	SO	ShO	W	L	SV	AB	H	HR	BA
1890 BOS P	4	2	.667	4.79	10	7	5	62	85	25	24	1	1	0	0	38	7	0	.184
1891 2 teams	BOS	AA (1G 0–1)		BAL	AA (32G 13–12)														
" total	13	13	.500	4.19	33	28	21	232	249	94	62	1	1	0	1	110	31	1	.282
5 yrs.	56	50	.528	3.92	122	109	97	958	987	336	284	7	3	0	2	433	106	2	.245

Len Madden

MADDEN, LEONARD JOSEPH (Lefty)   BL TL 6'2"   165 lbs.
B. July 2, 1890, Toledo, Ohio   D. Sept. 9, 1949, Toledo, Ohio

	W	L	PCT	ERA	G	GS	CG	IP	H	BB	SO	ShO	W	L	SV	AB	H	HR	BA
1912 CHI N	0	1	.000	2.92	6	2	0	12.1	16	9	5	0	0	0	0	4	1	0	.250

Mike Madden

MADDEN, MICHAEL ANTHONY   BL TL 6'1"   185 lbs.
B. Jan. 13, 1958, Denver, Colo.

	W	L	PCT	ERA	G	GS	CG	IP	H	BB	SO	ShO	W	L	SV	AB	H	HR	BA
1983 HOU N	9	5	.643	3.14	28	13	0	94.2	76	45	44	0	3	0	0	22	1	0	.045
1984	2	3	.400	5.53	17	7	0	40.2	46	35	29	0	1	0	0	6	2	0	.333
2 yrs.	11	8	.579	3.86	45	20	0	135.1	122	80	73	0	4	0	0	28	3	0	.107

Nick Maddox

MADDOX, NICHOLAS   TR
B. Nov. 9, 1886, Gavanstown, Md.   D. Nov. 27, 1954, Pittsburgh, Pa.

	W	L	PCT	ERA	G	GS	CG	IP	H	BB	SO	ShO	W	L	SV	AB	H	HR	BA
1907 PIT N	5	1	.833	0.83	6	6	6	54	32	13	38	1	0	0	0	20	5	0	.250
1908	23	8	.742	2.28	36	32	22	260.2	209	90	70	4	2	0	1	94	25	0	.266
1909	13	8	.619	2.21	31	27	17	203.1	173	39	56	4	0	0	0	67	15	0	.224
1910	2	3	.400	3.40	20	7	2	87.1	73	28	29	0	1	0	0	28	6	0	.214
4 yrs.	43	20	.683	2.29	93	72	47	605.1	487	170	193	9	4	1	1	209	51	0	.244
WORLD SERIES																			
1909 PIT N	1	0	1.000	1.00	1	1	1	9	10	2	4	0	0	0	0	4	0	0	.000

Tony Madigan

MADIGAN, ANTHONY WILLIAM   TR   118 lbs.
B. 1868, Washington, D. C.   D. Dec. 4, 1954, Washington, D. C.

	W	L	PCT	ERA	G	GS	CG	IP	H	BB	SO	ShO	W	L	SV	AB	H	HR	BA
1886 WAS N	1	13	.071	5.06	14	14	13	115.2	159	44	29	0	0	0	0	48	4	0	.083

Dave Madison

MADISON, DAVID PLEDGER   BR TR 6'3"   190 lbs.
B. Feb. 1, 1921, Brooksville, Miss.

	W	L	PCT	ERA	G	GS	CG	IP	H	BB	SO	ShO	W	L	SV	AB	H	HR	BA
1950 NY A	0	0	–	6.00	2	0	0	3	3	1	1	0	0	0	0	0	0	0	–
1952 2 teams	STL	A (31G 4–2)		DET	A (10G 1–1)														
" total	5	3	.625	4.94	41	5	0	93	94	58	42	0	3	2	0	19	2	0	.105
1953 DET A	3	4	.429	6.82	32	1	0	62	76	44	27	0	3	3	0	11	1	0	.091
3 yrs.	8	7	.533	5.70	74	6	0	158	173	103	70	0	6	5	0	30	3	0	.100

Hector Maestri

MAESTRI, HECTOR ANIBAL   BR TR 5'10"   158 lbs.
B. Apr. 19, 1935, Havana, Cuba

	W	L	PCT	ERA	G	GS	CG	IP	H	BB	SO	ShO	W	L	SV	AB	H	HR	BA
1960 WAS A	0	0	–	0.00	1	0	0	2	1	1	1	0	0	0	0	0	0	0	–
1961	0	1	.000	1.50	1	1	0	6	6	2	2	0	0	0	0	1	0	0	.000
2 yrs.	0	1	.000	1.13	2	1	0	8	7	3	3	0	0	0	0	1	0	0	.000

Bill Magee

MAGEE, WILLIAM J.   TR 5'10"   154 lbs.
Born William Fitzgerald.
B. Jan. 11, 1868, Cambridge, Mass.   D. Aug. 15, 1922, Tuftonboro, N. H.

	W	L	PCT	ERA	G	GS	CG	IP	H	BB	SO	ShO	W	L	SV	AB	H	HR	BA
1897 LOU N	4	12	.250	5.39	22	16	13	155.1	186	99	44	1	0	1	0	62	13	0	.210
1898	16	15	.516	4.05	38	33	29	295.1	294	129	55	3	0	1	0	111	14	0	.126
1899 3 teams	LOU	N (12G 3–7)		PHI	N (9G 3–5)		WAS	N (8G 1–4)											
" total	7	16	.304	6.15	29	26	17	183	227	88	28	1	0	1	0	73	13	0	.178
1901 2 teams	STL	N (1G 0–0)		NY	N (6G 0–4)														
" total	0	4	.000	5.72	7	6	4	50.1	64	15	17	0	0	0	0	18	4	0	.222
1902 2 teams	NY	N (2G 0–0)		PHI	N (8G 2–4)														
" total	2	4	.333	3.68	10	7	6	58.2	66	19	17	0	0	0	0	20	4	0	.200
5 yrs.	29	51	.363	4.93	106	88	69	742.2	837	350	161	5	0	3	0	284	48	0	.169

Sal Maglie

MAGLIE, SALVATORE ANTHONY (The Barber)   BR TR 6'2"   180 lbs.
B. Apr. 26, 1917, Niagara Falls, N. Y.

	W	L	PCT	ERA	G	GS	CG	IP	H	BB	SO	ShO	W	L	SV	AB	H	HR	BA
1945 NY N	5	4	.556	2.35	13	10	7	84.1	72	22	32	3	0	1	0	30	5	0	.167
1950	18	4	.818	2.71	47	16	12	206	169	86	96	5	5	2	1	66	8	0	.121
1951	23	6	.793	2.93	42	37	22	298	254	86	146	3	1	0	4	112	17	1	.152
1952	18	8	.692	2.92	35	31	12	216	199	75	112	5	1	1	1	69	5	0	.072
1953	8	9	.471	4.15	27	24	9	145.1	158	47	80	3	0	0	0	48	13	0	.271
1954	14	6	.700	3.26	34	32	9	218.1	222	70	117	1	0	0	0	63	8	0	.127
1955 2 teams	NY	N (23G 9–5)		CLE	A (10G 0–2)														
" total	9	7	.563	3.77	33	23	6	155.1	168	55	82	0	1	0	2	45	5	0	.111
1956 2 teams	CLE	A (2G 0–0)		BKN	N (28G 13–5)														
" total	13	5	.722	2.89	30	26	9	196	160	54	110	3	0	0	0	70	9	0	.129
1957 2 teams	BKN	N (19G 6–6)		NY	A (6G 2–0)														
" total	8	6	.571	2.69	25	20	5	127.1	116	33	59	2	0	0	4	37	3	0	.081
1958 2 teams	NY	A (7G 1–1)		STL	N (10G 2–6)														
" total	3	7	.300	4.72	17	13	2	76.1	73	34	28	0	0	0	0	23	3	1	.130
10 yrs.	119	62	.657	3.15	303	232	93	1723	1591	562	862	25	8	4	14	563	76	2	.135
			9th																
WORLD SERIES																			
1951 NY N	0	1	.000	7.20	1	1	0	5	8	2	3	0	0	0	0	1	0	0	.000
1954	0	0	–	2.57	1	1	0	7	7	2	2	0	0	0	0	3	0	0	.000
1956 BKN N	1	1	.500	2.65	2	2	2	17	14	6	15	0	0	0	0	5	0	0	.000
3 yrs.	1	2	.333	3.41	4	4	2	29	29	10	20	0	0	0	0	9	0	0	.000

Jim Magnuson

MAGNUSON, JAMES ROBERT   BR TL 6'2"   190 lbs.
B. Aug. 18, 1946, Marinette, Wis.

	W	L	PCT	ERA	G	GS	CG	IP	H	BB	SO	ShO	W	L	SV	AB	H	HR	BA
1970 CHI A	1	5	.167	4.80	13	6	0	45	45	16	20	0	0	0	0	11	0	0	.000
1971	2	1	.667	4.50	15	4	0	30	30	16	11	0	0	0	0	4	0	0	.000

	W	L	PCT	ERA	G	GS	CG	IP	H	BB	SO	ShO	Relief Pitching W	L	SV	BATTING AB	H	HR	BA

Jim Magnuson continued

	W	L	PCT	ERA	G	GS	CG	IP	H	BB	SO	ShO	W	L	SV	AB	H	HR	BA
1973 NY A	0	1	.000	4.28	8	0	0	27.1	38	9	9	0	0	1	0	0	0	0	–
3 yrs.	3	7	.300	4.57	36	10	0	102.1	113	41	40	0	0	1	0	15	0	0	.000

Pete Magrini

MAGRINI, PETER ALEXANDER
B. June 8, 1942, San Francisco, Calif.   BR TR 6'   195 lbs.

	W	L	PCT	ERA	G	GS	CG	IP	H	BB	SO	ShO	W	L	SV	AB	H	HR	BA
1966 BOS A	0	1	.000	9.82	3	1	0	7.1	8	8	3	0	0	0	0	3	0	0	.000

Art Mahaffey

MAHAFFEY, ARTHUR
B. June 4, 1938, Cincinnati, Ohio   BR TR 6'1"   185 lbs.

	W	L	PCT	ERA	G	GS	CG	IP	H	BB	SO	ShO	W	L	SV	AB	H	HR	BA
1960 PHI N	7	3	.700	2.31	14	12	5	93.1	78	34	56	1	0	0	0	30	3	0	.100
1961	11	19	.367	4.10	36	32	12	219.1	205	70	158	3	0	1	0	63	8	0	.127
1962	19	14	.576	3.94	41	39	20	274	253	81	177	2	0	1	0	92	13	2	.141
1963	7	10	.412	3.99	26	22	6	149	143	48	97	1	1	0	0	50	10	0	.200
1964	12	9	.571	4.52	34	29	2	157.1	161	82	80	2	1	0	0	50	6	1	.120
1965	2	5	.286	6.21	22	9	1	71	82	32	52	0	0	0	0	21	2	0	.095
1966 STL N	1	4	.200	6.43	12	5	0	35	37	21	19	0	0	0	1	7	0	0	.000
7 yrs.	59	64	.480	4.17	185	148	46	999	959	368	639	9	2	2	1	313	42	3	.134

Roy Mahaffey

MAHAFFEY, LEE ROY (Popeye)
B. Feb. 9, 1903, Belton, S. C.   D. July 23, 1969, Anderson, S. C.   BR TR 6'   180 lbs.

	W	L	PCT	ERA	G	GS	CG	IP	H	BB	SO	ShO	W	L	SV	AB	H	HR	BA
1926 PIT N	0	0	–	0.00	4	0	0	4.2	5	1	3	0	0	0	0	2	0	0	.000
1927	1	0	1.000	7.71	2	1	0	9.1	9	9	4	0	0	0	0	5	2	0	.400
1930 PHI A	9	5	.643	5.01	33	16	6	152.2	186	53	38	0	0	0	0	59	7	1	.119
1931	15	4	.789	4.21	30	20	8	162.1	161	82	59	0	3	0	2	63	12	2	.190
1932	13	13	.500	5.09	37	28	13	222.2	245	96	106	0	2	3	0	87	15	1	.172
1933	13	10	.565	5.17	33	23	9	179.1	198	74	66	0	2	2	0	65	14	0	.215
1934	6	7	.462	5.37	34	13	4	129	142	55	37	0	2	0	2	48	13	0	.271
1935	8	4	.667	3.90	27	17	5	136	153	42	39	0	2	0	0	51	9	0	.176
1936 STL A	2	6	.250	8.10	21	9	1	60	82	40	13	0	1	0	1	16	1	0	.063
9 yrs.	67	49	.578	5.01	224	128	45	1056	1181	452	365	0	12	5	5	396	73	4	.184

WORLD SERIES

	W	L	PCT	ERA	G	GS	CG	IP	H	BB	SO	ShO	W	L	SV	AB	H	HR	BA
1931 PHI A	0	0	–	9.00	1	0	0	1	1	1	0	0	0	0	0	0	0	0	–

Lou Mahaffy

MAHAFFY, LOUIS WOOD
B. Jan. 3, 1874, Kentucky   D. Oct. 26, 1949, Torrance, Calif.   5'9"   170 lbs.

	W	L	PCT	ERA	G	GS	CG	IP	H	BB	SO	ShO	W	L	SV	AB	H	HR	BA
1898 LOU N	0	1	.000	3.00	1	1	1	9	10	5	1	0	0	0	0	4	0	0	.000

Art Mahan

MAHAN, ARTHUR LEO
B. June 8, 1913, Somerville, Mass.   BL TL 5'11"   178 lbs.

	W	L	PCT	ERA	G	GS	CG	IP	H	BB	SO	ShO	W	L	SV	AB	H	HR	BA
1940 PHI N	0	0	–	0.00	1	0	0	1	1	0	0	0	0	0	0	*			–

Mickey Mahler

MAHLER, MICHAEL JAMES
Brother of Rick Mahler.
B. July 30, 1952, Montgomery, Ala.   BB TL 6'3"   189 lbs.

	W	L	PCT	ERA	G	GS	CG	IP	H	BB	SO	ShO	W	L	SV	AB	H	HR	BA
1977 ATL N	1	2	.333	6.26	5	5	0	23	31	9	14	0	0	0	0	6	3	0	.500
1978	4	11	.267	4.67	34	21	1	135	130	66	92	0	0	0	0	41	4	0	.098
1979	5	11	.313	5.85	26	18	1	100	123	47	71	0	2	0	0	27	3	0	.111
1980 PIT N	0	0	–	63.00	2	0	0	1	4	3	1	0	0	0	0	0	0	0	–
1981 CAL A	0	0	–	0.00	6	0	0	6	1	2	5	0	0	0	0	0	0	0	–
1982	2	0	1.000	1.13	6	0	0	8	9	6	5	0	2	0	0	0	0	0	–
6 yrs.	12	24	.333	5.24	79	44	2	273	298	133	188	0	4	0	0	74	10	0	.135

Rick Mahler

MAHLER, RICHARD KEITH
Brother of Mickey Mahler.
B. Aug. 5, 1953, Austin, Tex.   BR TR 6'1"   195 lbs.

	W	L	PCT	ERA	G	GS	CG	IP	H	BB	SO	ShO	W	L	SV	AB	H	HR	BA
1979 ATL N	0	0	–	6.14	15	0	0	22	28	11	12	0	0	0	0	2	1	0	.500
1980	0	0	–	2.25	2	0	0	4	2	0	1	0	0	0	0	0	0	0	–
1981	8	6	.571	2.81	34	14	1	112	109	43	54	0	2	0	2	27	4	0	.148
1982	9	10	.474	4.21	39	33	5	205.1	213	62	105	2	0	0	0	58	11	1	.190
1983	0	0	–	5.02	10	0	0	14.1	16	9	7	0	0	0	0	2	0	0	.000
1984	13	10	.565	3.12	38	29	9	222	209	62	106	1	0	0	0	71	21	0	.296
6 yrs.	30	26	.536	3.60	138	76	15	579.2	577	187	285	3	2	0	2	160	37	1	.231

LEAGUE CHAMPIONSHIP SERIES

	W	L	PCT	ERA	G	GS	CG	IP	H	BB	SO	ShO	W	L	SV	AB	H	HR	BA
1982 ATL N	0	0	–	0.00	1	0	0	1.2	3	2	0	0	0	0	0	0	0	0	–

Al Mahon

MAHON, ALFRED GWINN (Lefty)
B. Sept. 23, 1909, Albion, Neb.   D. Dec. 26, 1977, New Haven, Conn.   BL TL 5'11"   160 lbs.

	W	L	PCT	ERA	G	GS	CG	IP	H	BB	SO	ShO	W	L	SV	AB	H	HR	BA
1930 PHI A	0	0	–	22.85	3	0	0	4.1	11	7	0	0	0	0	0	1	0	0	.000

Bob Mahoney

MAHONEY, ROBERT PAUL
B. June 20, 1928, LeRoy, Minn.   BR TR 6'1"   185 lbs.

	W	L	PCT	ERA	G	GS	CG	IP	H	BB	SO	ShO	W	L	SV	AB	H	HR	BA
1951 2 teams			CHI A (3G 0–0)			STL	A	(30G 2–5)											
" total	2	5	.286	4.52	33	4	0	87.2	91	46	33	0	2	5	0	18	4	0	.222
1952 STL A	0	0	–	18.00	3	0	0	3	8	4	1	0	0	0	0	0	0	0	–
2 yrs.	2	5	.286	4.96	36	4	0	90.2	99	50	34	0	2	5	0	18	4	0	.222

Chris Mahoney

MAHONEY, CHRISTOPHER JOHN
B. June 11, 1885, Milton, Mass.   D. July 15, 1954, Visalia, Calif.   BR TR 5'9"   160 lbs.

	W	L	PCT	ERA	G	GS	CG	IP	H	BB	SO	ShO	W	L	SV	AB	H	HR	BA
1910 BOS A	0	1	.000	3.27	2	1	0	11	16	5	6	0	0	0	1	7	1	0	.143

	W	L	PCT	ERA	G	GS	CG	IP	H	BB	SO	ShO	Relief Pitching W	L	SV	BATTING AB	H	HR	BA

Mike Mahoney

MAHONEY, GEORGE W.
B. Dec. 5, 1873, Boston, Mass.   D. Jan. 3, 1940, Boston, Mass.

	W	L	PCT	ERA	G	GS	CG	IP	H	BB	SO	ShO	W	L	SV	AB	H	HR	BA
1897 BOS N	0	0	–	18.00	1	0	0	1	3	1	1	0	0	0	0	*			

Duster Mails

MAILS, JOHN WALTER (The Great)   BL TL 6'   195 lbs.
B. Oct. 1, 1895, San Quentin, Calif.   D. July 5, 1974, San Francisco, Calif.

	W	L	PCT	ERA	G	GS	CG	IP	H	BB	SO	ShO	W	L	SV	AB	H	HR	BA
1915 BKN N	0	1	.000	3.60	2	0	0	5	6	5	3	0	0	1	0	1	0	0	.000
1916	0	1	.000	3.63	11	0	0	17.1	15	9	13	0	0	1	0	4	1	0	.250
1920 CLE A	7	0	1.000	1.85	9	8	6	63.1	54	18	25	2	0	0	0	20	4	0	.200
1921	14	8	.636	3.94	34	24	10	194.1	210	89	87	2	2	1	2	64	6	0	.094
1922	4	7	.364	5.28	26	13	4	104	122	40	54	1	1	1	0	31	5	0	.161
1925 STL N	7	7	.500	4.60	21	14	9	131	145	58	49	0	0	1	0	45	6	0	.133
1926	0	1	.000	0.00	1	0	0	1	2	1	1	0	0	1	0	0	0	0	–
7 yrs.	32	25	.561	4.10	104	59	29	516	554	220	232	5	3	6	2	165	22	0	.133
WORLD SERIES																			
1920 CLE A	1	0	1.000	0.00	2	1	1	15.2	6	6	6	1	0	0	0	5	0	0	.000

Alex Main

MAIN, MILES GRANT   BL TR 6'5"   195 lbs.
B. May 13, 1884, Montrose, Mich.   D. Dec. 29, 1965, Royal Oak, Mich.

	W	L	PCT	ERA	G	GS	CG	IP	H	BB	SO	ShO	W	L	SV	AB	H	HR	BA
1914 DET A	6	6	.500	2.67	32	12	5	138.1	131	59	55	1	1	1	3	40	4	0	.100
1915 KC F	13	14	.481	2.54	35	28	18	230	181	75	91	2	1	0	3	76	15	0	.197
1918 PHI N	2	2	.500	4.63	8	4	1	35	30	16	14	1	0	0	0	11	1	0	.091
3 yrs.	21	22	.488	2.77	75	44	24	403.1	342	150	160	4	2	1	6	127	20	0	.157

Woody Main

MAIN, FORREST HARRY   BR TR 6'3½"   195 lbs.
B. Feb. 12, 1922, Delano, Calif.

	W	L	PCT	ERA	G	GS	CG	IP	H	BB	SO	ShO	W	L	SV	AB	H	HR	BA
1948 PIT N	1	1	.500	8.33	17	0	0	27	35	19	12	0	1	1	0	2	0	0	.000
1950	1	0	1.000	4.87	12	0	0	20.1	21	11	12	0	1	0	1	5	2	0	.400
1952	2	12	.143	4.46	48	11	2	153.1	149	52	79	0	0	7	2	37	2	0	.054
1953	0	0	–	11.25	2	0	0	4	5	2	4	0	0	0	0	0	0	0	–
4 yrs.	4	13	.235	5.14	79	11	2	204.2	210	84	107	0	2	8	3	44	4	0	.091

Jim Mains

MAINS, JAMES ROYAL   BR TR 6'2"   190 lbs.
B. June 12, 1922, Bridgton, Me.   D. Mar. 17, 1969, Bridgton, Me.

	W	L	PCT	ERA	G	GS	CG	IP	H	BB	SO	ShO	W	L	SV	AB	H	HR	BA
1943 PHI A	0	1	.000	5.63	1	1	1	8	9	3	4	0	0	0	0	2	0	0	.000

Willard Mains

MAINS, WILLARD EBEN (Grasshopper)   TR 6'2"   190 lbs.
B. July 7, 1868, North Windham, Me.   D. May 23, 1923, Bridgton, Me.

	W	L	PCT	ERA	G	GS	CG	IP	H	BB	SO	ShO	W	L	SV	AB	H	HR	BA
1888 CHI N	1	1	.500	4.91	2	2	1	11	8	6	5	0	0	0	0	7	1	0	.143
1891 C-M AA	12	14	.462	3.07	32	25	20	214	210	117	78	0	1	2	0	95	25	1	.263
1896 BOS N	3	2	.600	5.48	8	5	3	42.2	43	31	13	0	0	0	1	22	6	0	.273
3 yrs.	16	17	.485	3.53	42	32	24	267.2	261	154	96	0	1	2	1	124	32	1	.258

Frank Makosky

MAKOSKY, FRANK   BR TR 6'1"   185 lbs.
B. Jan. 20, 1912, Boonton, N. J.

	W	L	PCT	ERA	G	GS	CG	IP	H	BB	SO	ShO	W	L	SV	AB	H	HR	BA
1937 NY A	5	2	.714	4.97	26	1	1	58	64	24	27	0	5	1	3	16	5	0	.313

Tom Makowski

MAKOWSKI, THOMAS ANTHONY   BR TL 5'11"   185 lbs.
B. Dec. 22, 1950, Buffalo, N. Y.

	W	L	PCT	ERA	G	GS	CG	IP	H	BB	SO	ShO	W	L	SV	AB	H	HR	BA
1975 DET A	0	0	–	4.82	3	0	0	9.1	10	9	3	0	0	0	0	0	0	0	–

Bill Malarkey

MALARKEY, WILLIAM JOHN   BR TR
B. May 4, 1872, Port Byron, Ill.   D. Dec. 12, 1956, Phoenix, Ariz.

	W	L	PCT	ERA	G	GS	CG	IP	H	BB	SO	ShO	W	L	SV	AB	H	HR	BA
1908 NY N	0	2	.000	2.57	15	0	0	35	31	10	12	0	0	2	1	4	0	0	.000

John Malarkey

MALARKEY, JOHN S.   5'11"   155 lbs.
B. May 10, 1872, Springfield, Ohio   D. Oct. 29, 1949, Cincinnati, Ohio

	W	L	PCT	ERA	G	GS	CG	IP	H	BB	SO	ShO	W	L	SV	AB	H	HR	BA
1894 WAS N	2	1	.667	4.15	3	3	3	26	42	5	3	0	0	0	0	14	1	0	.071
1895	0	8	.000	5.99	22	8	5	100.2	135	60	32	0	0	0	1	37	5	0	.135
1896	0	1	.000	1.29	1	1	0	7	9	3	0	0	0	0	0	2	1	0	.500
1899 CHI N	0	1	.000	13.00	1	1	0	9	19	5	7	0	0	0	0	5	1	0	.200
1902 BOS N	8	11	.421	2.59	21	19	18	170.1	158	58	39	1	1	0	1	62	13	1	.210
1903	11	16	.407	3.09	32	27	25	253	266	96	98	2	1	2	0	87	14	0	.161
6 yrs.	21	38	.356	3.64	80	59	52	566	629	227	179	3	1	3	3	207	35	1	.169

Cy Malis

MALIS, CYRUS SOL   BR TR 5'10"   175 lbs.
B. Feb. 26, 1907, Philadelphia, Pa.   D. Jan. 12, 1971, North Hollywood, Calif.

	W	L	PCT	ERA	G	GS	CG	IP	H	BB	SO	ShO	W	L	SV	AB	H	HR	BA
1934 PHI N	0	0	–	4.91	1	0	0	3.2	4	2	1	0	0	0	0	0	0	0	–

Mal Mallette

MALLETTE, MALCOLM FRANCIS   BL TL 6'2"   200 lbs.
B. Jan. 30, 1922, Syracuse, N. Y.

	W	L	PCT	ERA	G	GS	CG	IP	H	BB	SO	ShO	W	L	SV	AB	H	HR	BA
1950 BKN N	0	0	–	0.00	2	0	0	1.1	2	1	2	0	0	0	0	0	0	0	–

Alex Malloy

MALLOY, ARCHIBALD ALEXANDER (Lick)   BR TR 6'2"   180 lbs.
B. Oct. 31, 1886, Laurinburg, N. C.   D. Mar. 1, 1961, Ferris, Tex.

	W	L	PCT	ERA	G	GS	CG	IP	H	BB	SO	ShO	W	L	SV	AB	H	HR	BA
1910 STL A	0	6	.000	2.56	7	6	4	52.2	47	17	27	0	0	0	0	16	1	0	.063

Bob Malloy

MALLOY, PAUL AUGUSTUS   BR TR 5'11"   185 lbs.
B. May 28, 1918, Canonsburg, Pa.   D. Mar. 18, 1976, Sandusky, Ohio

	W	L	PCT	ERA	G	GS	CG	IP	H	BB	SO	ShO	W	L	SV	AB	H	HR	BA
1943 CIN N	0	0	–	6.30	6	0	0	10	14	8	4	0	0	0	0	3	2	0	.667
1944	1	1	.500	3.09	9	0	0	23.1	22	11	4	0	1	1	0	7	0	0	.000
1946	2	5	.286	2.75	27	3	1	72	71	26	24	0	1	4	2	18	5	0	.278
1947	0	0	–	18.00	1	0	0	1	3	0	1	0	0	0	0	0	0	0	–
1949 STL A	1	1	.500	2.79	5	0	0	9.2	6	7	2	0	1	1	0	3	0	0	.000
5 yrs.	4	7	.364	3.26	48	3	1	116	116	52	35	0	3	6	2	31	7	0	.226

	W	L	PCT	ERA	G	GS	CG	IP	H	BB	SO	ShO	Relief Pitching W	L	SV	BATTING AB	H	HR	BA

Herm Malloy

MALLOY, HERMAN
B. June 1, 1885, Massillon, Ohio   D. May 9, 1942, Massillon, Ohio

	W	L	PCT	ERA	G	GS	CG	IP	H	BB	SO	ShO	W	L	SV	AB	H	HR	BA
1907 DET A	0	1	.000	5.63	1	1	1	8	13	5	6	0	0	0	0	4	0	0	.000
1908	0	2	.000	3.71	3	2	2	17	20	4	8	0	0	0	0	9	3	0	.333
2 yrs.	0	3	.000	4.32	4	3	3	25	33	9	14	0	0	0	0	13	3	0	.231

Pat Malone

MALONE, PERCE LEIGH
B. Sept. 25, 1902, Altoona, Pa.
D. May 13, 1943, Altoona, Pa.
BL TR 6'   200 lbs.
BB 1935-37

	W	L	PCT	ERA	G	GS	CG	IP	H	BB	SO	ShO	W	L	SV	AB	H	HR	BA
1928 CHI N	18	13	.581	2.84	42	25	16	250.2	218	99	155	2	2	4	2	95	18	1	.189
1929	22	10	.688	3.57	40	30	19	267	283	102	166	5	4	1	2	105	22	2	.210
1930	20	9	.690	3.94	45	35	22	271.2	290	96	142	2	1	1	4	105	26	4	.248
1931	16	9	.640	3.90	36	30	12	228.1	229	88	112	2	3	0	0	79	17	1	.215
1932	15	17	.469	3.38	37	33	17	237	222	78	120	2	1	1	0	78	14	1	.179
1933	10	14	.417	3.91	31	26	13	186.1	186	59	72	2	2	0	0	63	10	0	.159
1934	14	7	.667	3.53	34	21	8	191	200	55	111	1	2	0	0	64	11	0	.172
1935 NY A	3	5	.375	5.43	29	2	0	56.1	53	33	25	0	3	4	3	15	0	0	.000
1936	12	4	.750	3.81	35	9	5	134.2	144	60	72	0	8	2	9	51	10	0	.196
1937	4	4	.500	5.48	28	9	3	92	109	35	49	0	1	3	6	33	1	0	.030
10 yrs.	134	92	.593	3.74	357	220	115	1915	1934	705	1024	16	27	16	26	688	129	9	.188

WORLD SERIES
	W	L	PCT	ERA	G	GS	CG	IP	H	BB	SO	ShO	W	L	SV	AB	H	HR	BA
1929 CHI N	0	2	.000	4.15	3	2	1	13	12	7	11	0	0	0	0	4	1	0	.250
1932	0	0		0.00	1	0	0	2.2	1	4	4	0	0	0	0	0	0	0	—
1936 NY A	0	1	.000	1.80	2	0	0	5	2	1	2	0	0	1	1	1	1	0	1.000
3 yrs.	0	3	.000	3.05	6	2	1	20.2	15	12	17	0	0	1	1	5	2	0	.400

Charlie Maloney

MALONEY, CHARLES MICHAEL
B. May 22, 1886, Cambridge, Mass.   D. Jan. 17, 1967, Somerville, Mass.

	W	L	PCT	ERA	G	GS	CG	IP	H	BB	SO	ShO	W	L	SV	AB	H	HR	BA
1908 BOS N	0	0	—	4.50	1	0	0	2	3	1	0	0	0	0	0	0	0	0	—

Jim Maloney

MALONEY, JAMES WILLIAM
B. June 2, 1940, Fresno, Calif.
BL TR 6'2"   190 lbs.

	W	L	PCT	ERA	G	GS	CG	IP	H	BB	SO	ShO	W	L	SV	AB	H	HR	BA
1960 CIN N	2	6	.250	4.66	11	10	2	63.2	61	37	48	1	0	0	0	18	2	0	.111
1961	6	7	.462	4.37	27	11	1	94.2	86	59	57	0	1	3	2	29	11	1	.379
1962	9	7	.563	3.51	22	17	3	115.1	90	66	105	0	2	0	1	43	8	0	.186
1963	23	7	.767	2.77	33	33	13	250.1	183	88	265	6	0	0	0	89	15	0	.169
1964	15	10	.600	2.71	31	31	11	216	175	83	214	2	0	0	0	73	11	1	.151
1965	20	9	.690	2.54	33	33	14	255.1	189	110	244	5	0	0	0	89	20	0	.225
1966	16	8	.667	2.80	32	32	10	224.2	174	90	216	5	0	0	0	81	18	0	.222
1967	15	11	.577	3.25	30	29	6	196.1	181	72	153	3	0	1	0	74	18	2	.243
1968	16	10	.615	3.61	33	32	8	207	183	80	181	5	1	0	0	55	11	3	.200
1969	12	5	.706	2.77	30	27	6	179	135	86	102	3	0	0	0	55	11	3	.200
1970	0	1	.000	11.12	7	3	0	17	26	15	7	0	0	0	0	3	0	0	.000
1971 CAL A	0	1	.000	5.10	13	4	0	30	35	24	13	0	0	0	0	5	1	0	.200
12 yrs.	134	84	.615	3.19	302	262	74	1849.1	1518	810	1605	30	4	4	4	628	126	7	.201

WORLD SERIES
	W	L	PCT	ERA	G	GS	CG	IP	H	BB	SO	ShO	W	L	SV	AB	H	HR	BA
1961 CIN N	0	0	—	27.00	1	0	0	.2	4	1	1	0	0	0	0	0	0	0	—

Paul Maloy

MALOY, PAUL AUGUSTUS (Biff)
B. June 4, 1892, Bascom, Ohio   D. Mar. 18, 1976, Sandusky, Ohio
BR TR 5'11"   185 lbs.

	W	L	PCT	ERA	G	GS	CG	IP	H	BB	SO	ShO	W	L	SV	AB	H	HR	BA
1913 BOS A	0	0	—	9.00	2	0	0	2	2	1	0	0	0	0	0	0	0	0	—

Gordon Maltzberger

MALTZBERGER, GORDON RALPH (Maltzy)
B. Sept. 4, 1912, Utopia, Tex.   D. Dec. 11, 1974, Rialto, Calif.
BR TR 6'   170 lbs.

	W	L	PCT	ERA	G	GS	CG	IP	H	BB	SO	ShO	W	L	SV	AB	H	HR	BA
1943 CHI A	7	4	.636	2.46	37	0	0	98.2	86	24	48	0	7	4	14	25	3	0	.120
1944	10	5	.667	2.96	46	0	0	91.1	81	19	49	0	10	5	12	22	3	0	.136
1946	2	0	1.000	1.59	19	0	0	39.2	30	6	17	0	2	0	2	6	0	0	.000
1947	1	4	.200	3.39	33	0	0	63.2	61	25	22	0	1	4	5	7	1	0	.143
4 yrs.	20	13	.606	2.70	135	0	0	293.1	258	74	136	0	20	13	33	60	7	0	.117

Al Mamaux

MAMAUX, ALBERT LEON
B. May 30, 1894, Pittsburgh, Pa.   D. Jan. 2, 1963, Santa Monica, Calif.
BR TR 6'½"   168 lbs.

	W	L	PCT	ERA	G	GS	CG	IP	H	BB	SO	ShO	W	L	SV	AB	H	HR	BA
1913 PIT N	0	0	—	3.00	1	0	0	3	2	2	2	0	0	0	0	1	0	0	.000
1914	5	2	.714	1.71	13	6	4	63	41	24	30	2	1	1	0	20	5	0	.250
1915	21	8	.724	2.04	38	31	17	251.2	182	96	152	8	3	0	0	92	15	0	.163
1916	21	15	.583	2.53	45	38	26	310	264	136	163	1	1	0	2	110	21	0	.191
1917	2	11	.154	5.25	16	13	5	85.2	92	50	22	0	0	1	0	31	7	0	.226
1918 BKN N	0	1	.000	6.75	2	1	0	8	14	2	2	0	0	0	0	2	0	0	.000
1919	10	12	.455	2.66	30	22	16	199.1	174	66	80	2	1	0	0	63	11	0	.175
1920	12	8	.600	2.69	41	18	9	190.2	172	63	101	2	5	1	4	60	10	0	.167
1921	3	3	.500	3.14	12	1	0	43	36	13	21	0	3	2	1	11	2	0	.182
1922	1	4	.200	3.70	37	7	1	87.2	97	33	35	0	1	2	3	17	4	1	.235
1923	0	2	.000	8.31	5	1	0	13	20	6	5	0	0	1	0	2	1	0	.500
1924 NY A	1	1	.500	5.68	14	2	0	38	44	20	12	0	0	1	0	13	1	0	.077
12 yrs.	76	67	.531	2.90	254	140	78	1293	1138	511	625	15	14	9	10	422	77	1	.182

WORLD SERIES
	W	L	PCT	ERA	G	GS	CG	IP	H	BB	SO	ShO	W	L	SV	AB	H	HR	BA
1920 BKN N	0	0	—	4.50	3	0	0	4	2	1	5	0	0	0	0	1	0	0	.000

Hal Manders

MANDERS, HAROLD CARL
B. June 14, 1917, Waukee, Iowa
BR TR 6'   187 lbs.

	W	L	PCT	ERA	G	GS	CG	IP	H	BB	SO	ShO	W	L	SV	AB	H	HR	BA
1941 DET A	1	0	1.000	2.35	8	0	0	15.1	13	8	7	0	1	0	0	4	0	0	.000
1942	1	0	1.000	4.09	18	0	0	33	39	15	14	0	1	0	0	4	1	0	.250
1946 2 teams			DET A (2G 0-0)			CHI N (2G 0-1)														
" total	0	1	.000	9.75	4	1	0	12	19	5	7	0	0	0	0	4	1	0	.250
3 yrs.	3	1	.750	4.77	30	1	0	60.1	71	28	28	0	3	0	0	12	2	0	.167

		W	L	PCT	ERA	G	GS	CG	IP	H	BB	SO	ShO	Relief Pitching W	L	SV	BATTING AB	H	HR	BA

Leo Mangum

MANGUM, LEO ALLAN (Blackie)
B. May 24, 1896, Durham, N. C.   D. July 9, 1974, Lima, Ohio   BR TR 6'1"   187 lbs.

		W	L	PCT	ERA	G	GS	CG	IP	H	BB	SO	ShO	W	L	SV	AB	H	HR	BA
1924	CHI A	1	4	.200	7.09	13	7	1	47	69	25	12	0	1	0	0	14	1	0	.071
1925		1	0	1.000	7.80	7	0	0	15	25	6	6	0	1	0	0	4	2	0	.500
1928	NY N	0	0	—	15.00	1	1	0	3	6	5	1	0	0	0	0	1	1	0	1.000
1932	BOS N	0	0	—	5.23	7	0	0	10.1	17	0	3	0	0	0	0	2	0	0	.000
1933		4	3	.571	3.32	25	5	2	84	93	11	28	1	2	1	0	22	2	0	.091
1934		5	3	.625	5.72	29	3	1	94.1	127	23	28	0	4	2	1	32	9	0	.281
1935		0	0	—	3.86	3	0	0	4.2	6	2	0	0	0	0	0	0	0	0	—
7 yrs.		11	10	.524	5.37	85	16	4	258.1	343	72	78	1	8	3	1	75	15	0	.200

Ernie Manning

MANNING, ERNEST DEVON (Ed)
B. Oct. 9, 1890, Florala, Ala.   D. Apr. 28, 1973, Pensacola, Fla.   BL TR 6'   175 lbs.

		W	L	PCT	ERA	G	GS	CG	IP	H	BB	SO	ShO	W	L	SV	AB	H	HR	BA
1914	STL A	0	0	—	3.60	4	0	0	10	11	3	3	0	0	0	0	4	0	0	.000

Jack Manning

MANNING, JOHN E.
B. Dec. 20, 1853, Braintree, Mass.   D. Aug. 15, 1929, Boston, Mass.   BR TR 5'8½"   158 lbs.

		W	L	PCT	ERA	G	GS	CG	IP	H	BB	SO	ShO	W	L	SV	AB	H	HR	BA
1876	BOS N	18	5	.783	2.14	34	20	13	197.1	213	32	24	0	4	0	5	288	76	2	.264
1877	CIN N	0	4	.000	6.95	10	4	2	44	83	7	6	0	0	0	1	252	80	0	.317
1878	BOS N	1	0	1.000	14.29	3	1	1	11.1	24	5	2	0	0	0	0	248	63	0	.254
3 yrs.		19	9	.679	3.53	47	25	16	252.2	320	44	32	0	4	0	6	*			

Jim Manning

MANNING, JAMES BENJAMIN
B. July 21, 1943, L'Anse, Mich.   BR TR 6'1"   185 lbs.

		W	L	PCT	ERA	G	GS	CG	IP	H	BB	SO	ShO	W	L	SV	AB	H	HR	BA
1962	MIN A	0	0	—	5.14	5	1	0	7	14	1	2	0	0	0	0	1	0	0	.000

Rube Manning

MANNING, WALTER S.
B. Apr. 29, 1883, Chambersburg, Pa.   D. Apr. 23, 1930, Williamsport, Pa.   TR

		W	L	PCT	ERA	G	GS	CG	IP	H	BB	SO	ShO	W	L	SV	AB	H	HR	BA
1907	NY A	0	1	.000	3.00	1	1	1	9	8	3	3	0	0	0	0	3	0	0	.000
1908		13	16	.448	2.94	41	26	19	245	228	86	113	2	4	1	1	91	17	0	.187
1909		7	11	.389	3.17	26	21	11	173	167	48	71	2	1	1	1	60	11	0	.183
1910		2	4	.333	3.70	16	9	4	75.1	80	25	25	0	0	0	0	26	5	0	.192
4 yrs.		22	32	.407	3.14	84	57	35	502.1	483	162	212	4	5	2	2	180	33	0	.183

Tom Mansell

MANSELL, THOMAS E.
Brother of Mike Mansell.   Brother of John Mansell.
B. Jan. 1, 1855, Auburn, N. Y.   D. Oct. 6, 1934, Auburn, N. Y.   BL   5'8"   160 lbs.

		W	L	PCT	ERA	G	GS	CG	IP	H	BB	SO	ShO	W	L	SV	AB	H	HR	BA
1883	DET N	0	0	—	16.20	1	0	0	6.2	21	5	3	0	0	0	0	*			

Lou Manske

MANSKE, LOUIS H.
B. July 4, 1884, Milwaukee, Wis.   D. Apr. 27, 1963, Milwaukee, Wis.

		W	L	PCT	ERA	G	GS	CG	IP	H	BB	SO	ShO	W	L	SV	AB	H	HR	BA
1906	PIT N	1	0	1.000	5.63	2	1	0	8	12	5	6	0	0	0	0	4	0	0	.000

Moxie Manuel

MANUEL, MARK GARFIELD
B. Oct. 16, 1881, Metropolis, Ill.   D. Apr. 26, 1924, Memphis, Tenn.

		W	L	PCT	ERA	G	GS	CG	IP	H	BB	SO	ShO	W	L	SV	AB	H	HR	BA
1905	WAS A	0	1	.000	5.40	3	1	1	10	9	3	3	0	0	1	0	4	1	0	.250
1908	CHI A	3	4	.429	3.28	18	6	3	60.1	52	25	25	0	2	1	1	16	1	0	.063
2 yrs.		3	5	.375	3.58	21	7	4	70.1	61	28	28	0	2	2	1	20	2	0	.100

Dick Manville

MANVILLE, RICHARD WESLEY
B. Dec. 25, 1926, Des Moines, Iowa   BR TR 6'5"   200 lbs.

		W	L	PCT	ERA	G	GS	CG	IP	H	BB	SO	ShO	W	L	SV	AB	H	HR	BA
1950	BOS N	0	0	—	0.00	1	0	0	2	0	3	2	0	0	0	0	0	0	0	—
1952	CHI N	0	0	—	7.94	11	0	0	17	25	12	6	0	0	0	0	2	1	0	.500
2 yrs.		0	0	—	7.11	12	0	0	19	25	15	8	0	0	0	0	2	1	0	.500

Rolla Mapel

MAPEL, ROLLA HAMILTON (Lefty)
B. Mar. 9, 1890, Lee's Summit, Mo.   D. Apr. 6, 1966, San Diego, Calif.   BL TL 5'11½" 165 lbs.

		W	L	PCT	ERA	G	GS	CG	IP	H	BB	SO	ShO	W	L	SV	AB	H	HR	BA
1919	STL A	0	3	.000	4.50	4	3	2	20	17	17	2	0	0	0	0	6	1	0	.167

Georges Maranda

MARANDA, GEORGES HENRI
B. Jan. 15, 1932, Levis, Que., Canada   BR TR 6'2"   195 lbs.

		W	L	PCT	ERA	G	GS	CG	IP	H	BB	SO	ShO	W	L	SV	AB	H	HR	BA
1960	SF N	1	4	.200	4.62	17	4	0	50.2	50	30	28	0	0	1	0	12	2	0	.167
1962	MIN A	1	3	.250	4.46	32	4	0	72.2	69	35	36	0	2	2	0	16	4	0	.250
2 yrs.		2	7	.222	4.52	49	8	0	123.1	119	65	64	0	2	3	0	28	6	0	.214

Firpo Marberry

MARBERRY, FREDRICK
B. Nov. 30, 1898, Streetman, Tex.   D. June 30, 1976, Mexia, Tex.   BR TR 6'1"   190 lbs.

		W	L	PCT	ERA	G	GS	CG	IP	H	BB	SO	ShO	W	L	SV	AB	H	HR	BA
1923	WAS A	4	0	1.000	2.82	11	4	2	44.2	42	17	18	0	0	0	0	14	2	0	.143
1924		11	12	.478	3.09	50	15	6	195.1	190	70	68	0	6	5	15	59	8	0	.136
1925		8	6	.571	3.47	55	0	0	93.1	84	45	53	0	8	6	15	19	5	0	.263
1926		12	7	.632	3.00	64	5	3	138	120	66	43	0	9	5	22	34	6	0	.176
1927		10	7	.588	4.64	56	10	2	155.1	177	68	74	0	8	2	9	41	5	0	.122
1928		13	13	.500	3.85	48	11	7	161.1	160	42	76	1	7	9	3	46	5	0	.109
1929		19	12	.613	3.06	49	26	16	250.1	233	69	121	0	3	4	11	82	19	0	.232
1930		15	5	.750	4.09	33	22	9	185	190	53	56	2	3	1	7	73	24	0	.329
1931		16	4	.800	3.45	45	25	11	219	211	63	88	2	3	1	7	82	19	1	.232
1932		8	4	.667	4.01	54	15	8	197.2	202	72	66	1	1	1	13	66	11	0	.167
1933	DET A	16	11	.593	3.29	37	32	15	238.1	232	61	84	1	2	0	2	90	11	0	.122
1934		15	5	.750	4.57	38	19	6	155.2	174	48	64	1	6	0	3	55	12	0	.218
1935		0	2	.000	4.26	5	2	1	19	22	9	7	0	0	2	0	5	1	0	.200
1936 2 teams				NY N (1G 0-0)				WAS A (5G 0-2)												
"	total	0	2	.000	3.77	6	1	0	14.1	12	3	4	0	0	1	0	3	0	0	.000
14 yrs.		147	89	.623	3.63	551	187	86	2067.1	2049	686	822	8	53	37	101	669	128	1	.191

WORLD SERIES

		W	L	PCT	ERA	G	GS	CG	IP	H	BB	SO	ShO	W	L	SV	AB	H	HR	BA
1924	WAS A	0	1	.000	1.13	4	1	0	8	9	4	10	0	0	2	1	2	0	0	.000

	W	L	PCT	ERA	G	GS	CG	IP	H	BB	SO	ShO	Relief Pitching W	L	SV	BATTING AB	H	HR	BA

Firpo Marberry continued

	W	L	PCT	ERA	G	GS	CG	IP	H	BB	SO	ShO	W	L	SV	AB	H	HR	BA
1925	0	0	–	0.00	2	0	0	2.1	3	0	2	0	0	0	1	0	0	0	–
1934 DET A	0	0	–	21.60	2	0	0	1.2	5	1	0	0	0	0	0	0	0	0	–
3 yrs.	0	1	.000	3.75	8	1	0	12	17	5	12	0	0	0	3	2	0	0	.000

4th

Walt Marbet

MARBET, WALTER WILLIAM   BR TR 6'1"   175 lbs.
B. Sept. 13, 1890, Plymouth County, Iowa   D. Sept. 24, 1956, Hohenwald, Tenn.

	W	L	PCT	ERA	G	GS	CG	IP	H	BB	SO	ShO	W	L	SV	AB	H	HR	BA
1913 STL N	0	1	.000	16.20	3	1	0	3.1	9	4	1	0	0	0	0	0	0	0	–

Phil Marchildon

MARCHILDON, PHILIP EDWARD   BR TR 5'10½" 170 lbs.
B. Oct. 25, 1913, Penetanguishene, Ont., Canada

	W	L	PCT	ERA	G	GS	CG	IP	H	BB	SO	ShO	W	L	SV	AB	H	HR	BA
1940 PHI A	0	2	.000	7.20	2	2	1	10	12	8	4	0	0	0	0	2	0	0	.000
1941	10	15	.400	3.57	30	27	14	204.1	188	118	74	1	1	1	0	66	11	0	.167
1942	17	14	.548	4.20	38	31	18	244	215	140	110	1	2	0	1	84	20	0	.238
1945	0	1	.000	4.00	3	2	0	9	5	11	2	0	0	1	0	2	1	0	.500
1946	13	16	.448	3.49	36	29	16	226.2	197	114	95	1	2	0	1	75	5	0	.067
1947	19	9	.679	3.22	35	35	21	276.2	228	141	128	2	0	0	0	98	15	1	.153
1948	9	15	.375	4.53	33	30	12	226.1	214	131	66	1	0	1	0	72	5	0	.069
1949	0	3	.000	11.81	7	6	0	16	24	19	2	0	0	0	0	6	1	0	.167
1950 BOS A	0	0	–	6.75	1	0	0	1.1	1	2	0	0	0	0	0	0	0	0	–
9 yrs.	68	75	.476	3.93	185	162	82	1214.1	1084	684	481	6	5	3	2	405	58	1	.143

Johnny Marcum

MARCUM, JOHN ALFRED (Footsie)   BL TR 5'11"   197 lbs.
B. Sept. 9, 1908, Campbellsburg, Ky.   D. Sept. 10, 1984, Louisville, Ky.

	W	L	PCT	ERA	G	GS	CG	IP	H	BB	SO	ShO	W	L	SV	AB	H	HR	BA
1933 PHI A	3	2	.600	1.95	5	5	4	37	28	20	14	2	0	0	0	12	2	0	.167
1934	14	11	.560	4.50	37	31	17	232	257	88	92	2	1	2	0	112	30	1	.268
1935	17	12	.586	4.08	39	27	19	242.2	256	83	99	2	2	0	3	119	37	2	.311
1936 BOS A	8	13	.381	4.81	31	23	9	174	194	52	57	1	1	2	1	88	18	2	.205
1937	13	11	.542	4.85	37	23	9	183.2	230	47	59	1	5	1	3	86	23	0	.267
1938	5	6	.455	4.09	15	11	7	92.1	113	25	25	0	1	0	0	37	5	0	.135
1939 2 teams		STL	A (12G 2–5)			CHI	A (19G 3–3)												
" total	5	8	.385	6.60	31	12	4	137.2	191	29	46	0	0	3	0	79	26	0	.329
7 yrs.	65	63	.508	4.66	195	132	69	1099.1	1269	344	392	8	10	8	7	*			

Leo Marentette

MARENTETTE, LEO JOHN   BR TR 6'2"   200 lbs.
B. Feb. 18, 1941, Detroit, Mich.

	W	L	PCT	ERA	G	GS	CG	IP	H	BB	SO	ShO	W	L	SV	AB	H	HR	BA
1965 DET A	0	0	–	0.00	2	0	0	3	1	1	3	0	0	0	0	0	0	0	–
1969 MON N	0	0	–	6.75	3	0	0	5.1	9	1	4	0	0	0	0	1	0	0	.000
2 yrs.	0	0	–	4.32	5	0	0	8.1	10	2	7	0	0	0	0	1	0	0	.000

Joe Margoneri

MARGONERI, JOSEPH EMANUEL   BL TL 6'   185 lbs.
B. Jan. 13, 1930, Somerset, Pa.

	W	L	PCT	ERA	G	GS	CG	IP	H	BB	SO	ShO	W	L	SV	AB	H	HR	BA
1956 NY N	6	6	.500	3.93	23	13	2	91.2	88	49	49	0	1	1	0	29	3	1	.103
1957	1	1	.500	5.24	13	2	1	34.1	44	21	18	0	0	1	0	8	0	0	.000
2 yrs.	7	7	.500	4.29	36	15	3	126	132	70	67	0	1	2	0	37	3	1	.081

Juan Marichal

MARICHAL, JUAN ANTONIO SANCHEZ (Manito, The Dominican Dandy)   BR TR 6'   185 lbs.
B. Oct. 20, 1938, Laguna Verde, Dominican Republic
Hall of Fame 1983.

	W	L	PCT	ERA	G	GS	CG	IP	H	BB	SO	ShO	W	L	SV	AB	H	HR	BA
1960 SF N	6	2	.750	2.66	11	11	6	81.1	59	28	58	1	0	0	0	31	4	0	.129
1961	13	10	.565	3.89	29	27	9	185	183	48	124	3	1	1	0	59	7	0	.119
1962	18	11	.621	3.36	37	36	18	262.2	233	90	153	3	0	0	1	89	21	0	.236
1963	25	8	.758	2.41	41	40	18	321.1	259	61	248	5	1	0	0	112	20	1	.179
1964	21	8	.724	2.48	33	33	22	269	241	52	206	4	0	0	0	97	14	0	.144
1965	22	13	.629	2.13	39	37	24	295.1	224	46	240	10	1	0	1	98	17	0	.173
1966	25	6	.806	2.23	37	36	25	307.1	228	36	222	4	1	0	0	112	28	0	.250
1967	14	10	.583	2.76	26	26	18	202.1	195	42	166	2	0	0	0	79	14	0	.177
1968	26	9	.743	2.43	38	38	30	325.2	295	46	218	5	0	0	0	123	20	0	.163
1969	21	11	.656	2.10	37	36	27	300	244	54	205	8	0	0	0	109	15	0	.138
1970	12	10	.545	4.11	34	33	14	243	269	48	123	1	0	0	0	85	5	0	.059
1971	18	11	.621	2.94	37	37	18	279	244	56	159	4	0	0	0	105	14	2	.133
1972	6	16	.273	3.71	25	24	6	165	176	46	72	0	0	1	0	51	10	0	.196
1973	11	15	.423	3.79	34	32	9	209	231	37	87	2	0	0	0	69	13	0	.188
1974 BOS A	5	1	.833	4.87	11	9	0	57.1	61	14	21	0	0	0	0	2	0	0	–
1975 LA N	0	1	.000	13.50	2	2	0	6	11	5	1	0	0	0	0	0	0	0	.000
16 yrs.	243	142	.631	2.89	471	457	244	3509.1	3153	709	2303	52	5	2	2	1221	202	4	.165
LEAGUE CHAMPIONSHIP SERIES																			
1971 SF N	0	1	.000	2.25	1	1	1	8	4	1	6	0	0	0	0	3	0	0	.000
WORLD SERIES																			
1962 SF N	0	0	–	0.00	1	1	0	4	2	1	4	0	0	0	0	2	0	0	.000

Dan Marion

MARION, DONALD G.   BR TR 6'1"   187 lbs.
B. July 31, 1890, Cleveland, Ohio   D. Jan. 19, 1933, Milwaukee, Wis.

	W	L	PCT	ERA	G	GS	CG	IP	H	BB	SO	ShO	W	L	SV	AB	H	HR	BA
1914 BKN F	3	2	.600	3.93	17	9	4	89.1	97	38	41	0	0	0	0	36	7	0	.194
1915	10	9	.526	3.20	35	25	15	208.1	193	64	46	2	0	1	0	74	13	0	.176
2 yrs.	13	11	.542	3.42	52	34	19	297.2	290	102	87	2	0	1	0	110	20	0	.182

Duke Markell

MARKELL, HARRY DUQUESNE   BR TR 6'1½" 209 lbs.
Also known as Harry Duquesne Makowsky.
B. Aug. 17, 1923, Paris, France   D. June 14, 1984, Fort Lauderdale, Fla.

	W	L	PCT	ERA	G	GS	CG	IP	H	BB	SO	ShO	W	L	SV	AB	H	HR	BA
1951 STL A	1	1	.500	6.33	5	2	1	21.1	25	20	10	0	0	0	0	6	1	0	.167

	W	L	PCT	ERA	G	GS	CG	IP	H	BB	SO	ShO	Relief Pitching W	L	SV	BATTING AB	H	HR	BA

Cliff Markle

MARKLE, CLIFFORD MONROE
B. May 3, 1894, Dravosburg, Pa.   D. May 24, 1974, Temple City, Calif.   BR TR 5'8½" 160 lbs.

	W	L	PCT	ERA	G	GS	CG	IP	H	BB	SO	ShO	W	L	SV	AB	H	HR	BA
1915 NY A	2	0	1.000	0.39	3	2	2	23	15	6	12	0	0	0	0	4	0	0	.000
1916	4	3	.571	4.53	11	7	3	45.2	41	31	14	1	0	1	0	13	0	0	.000
1921 CIN N	2	6	.250	3.76	10	6	5	67	75	20	23	0	1	1	0	24	3	0	.125
1922	4	5	.444	3.81	25	3	2	75.2	75	33	34	1	3	3	0	20	3	0	.150
1924 NY A	0	3	.000	8.87	7	3	0	23.1	29	20	7	0	0	0	0	8	0	0	.000
5 yrs.	12	17	.414	4.10	56	21	12	234.2	235	110	90	2	4	5	0	69	6	0	.087

Dick Marlowe

MARLOWE, RICHARD BURTON
B. June 27, 1929, Hickory, N. C.   D. Dec. 30, 1968, Toledo, Ohio   BR TR 6'2" 165 lbs.

	W	L	PCT	ERA	G	GS	CG	IP	H	BB	SO	ShO	W	L	SV	AB	H	HR	BA
1951 DET A	0	1	.000	32.40	2	1	0	1.2	5	2	1	0	0	0	0	0	0	0	–
1952	0	2	.000	7.36	4	1	0	11	21	3	3	0	0	1	0	2	0	0	.000
1953	6	7	.462	5.26	42	11	2	119.2	152	42	52	0	3	1	0	32	7	0	.219
1954	5	4	.556	4.18	38	2	0	84	76	40	39	0	5	2	2	18	3	0	.167
1955	1	0	1.000	1.80	4	1	1	15	12	4	9	0	0	0	1	4	0	0	.000
1956 2 teams			DET	A	(7G	1–1)		CHI	A	(1G	0–0)								
" total	1	1	.500	6.00	8	1	0	12	14	10	4	0	1	0	1	1	0	0	.000
6 yrs.	13	15	.464	4.99	98	17	3	243.1	280	101	108	0	9	4	3	57	10	0	.175

Lou Marone

MARONE, LOUIS STEPHEN
B. Dec. 3, 1945, San Diego, Calif.   BB TL 5'11" 185 lbs.

	W	L	PCT	ERA	G	GS	CG	IP	H	BB	SO	ShO	W	L	SV	AB	H	HR	BA
1969 PIT N	1	1	.500	2.57	29	0	0	35	24	13	25	0	1	1	0	0	0	0	–
1970	0	0	–	4.50	1	0	0	2	2	0	0	0	0	0	0	0	0	0	–
2 yrs.	1	1	.500	2.68	30	0	0	37	26	13	25	0	1	1	0	0	0	0	–

Jim Maroney

MARONEY, JAMES FRANCIS
B. Dec. 4, 1885, Boston, Mass.   D. Feb. 26, 1929, Philadelphia, Pa.   BL TL 6'1" 175 lbs.

	W	L	PCT	ERA	G	GS	CG	IP	H	BB	SO	ShO	W	L	SV	AB	H	HR	BA
1906 BOS N	0	3	.000	5.33	3	3	3	27	28	12	11	0	0	0	0	10	1	0	.100
1910 PHI N	1	2	.333	2.14	12	2	1	42	43	11	13	0	1	0	1	10	0	0	.000
1912 CHI N	1	1	.500	4.56	10	3	1	23.2	25	17	5	0	0	0	1	6	3	0	.500
3 yrs.	2	6	.250	3.69	25	8	5	92.2	96	40	29	0	1	0	2	26	4	0	.154

Rube Marquard

MARQUARD, RICHARD WILLIAM
B. Oct. 9, 1889, Cleveland, Ohio
D. June 1, 1980, Pikesville, Md.
Hall of Fame 1971.   BB TL 6'3" 180 lbs.   BL 1925

	W	L	PCT	ERA	G	GS	CG	IP	H	BB	SO	ShO	W	L	SV	AB	H	HR	BA
1908 NY N	0	1	.000	3.60	1	1	0	5	6	2	2	0	0	0	0	1	0	0	.000
1909	5	13	.278	2.60	29	21	8	173	155	73	109	0	2	0	0	54	8	0	.148
1910	4	4	.500	4.46	13	8	2	70.2	65	40	52	0	0	1	0	27	3	0	.111
1911	24	7	.774	2.50	45	33	22	277.2	221	106	237	5	2	1	2	104	17	1	.163
1912	26	11	.703	2.57	43	38	22	294.2	286	80	175	1	2	0	0	96	21	0	.219
1913	23	10	.697	2.50	42	33	20	288	248	49	151	4	5	0	2	105	23	0	.219
1914	12	22	.353	3.06	39	33	15	268	261	47	92	4	1	0	2	84	15	0	.179
1915 2 teams			NY	N	(27G	9–8)		BKN	N	(6G	2–2)								
" total	11	10	.524	4.04	33	23	10	193.2	207	38	92	2	4	1	2	63	7	0	.111
1916 BKN N	13	6	.684	1.58	36	20	15	205	169	38	107	2	3	0	5	63	9	0	.143
1917	19	12	.613	2.55	37	29	14	232.2	200	60	117	2	5	1	0	75	15	0	.200
1918	9	18	.333	2.64	34	29	19	239	231	59	89	4	0	0	0	76	13	0	.171
1919	3	3	.500	2.29	8	7	3	59	54	10	29	0	0	0	0	23	6	0	.261
1920	10	7	.588	3.23	28	26	10	189.2	181	35	89	1	0	0	0	59	10	0	.169
1921 CIN N	17	14	.548	3.39	39	35	18	265.2	291	50	88	2	0	1	0	95	19	0	.200
1922 BOS N	11	15	.423	5.09	39	24	7	198	255	66	57	0	3	1	1	63	14	0	.222
1923	11	14	.440	3.73	38	29	11	239	265	65	78	3	0	2	0	86	12	0	.140
1924	1	2	.333	3.00	6	6	1	36	33	13	10	0	0	0	0	11	3	0	.273
1925	2	8	.200	5.75	26	8	0	72	105	27	19	0	0	4	0	22	3	0	.136
18 yrs.	201	177	.532	3.08	536	403	197	3306.2	3233	858	1593	30	27	12	14	1107	198	1	.179
WORLD SERIES																			
1911 NY N	0	1	.000	1.54	3	2	2	11.2	9	1	8	0	0	0	0	2	0	0	.000
1912	2	0	1.000	0.50	2	2	2	18	14	2	9	0	0	0	0	4	0	0	.000
1913	0	1	.000	7.00	2	1	1	9	10	3	3	0	0	0	0	1	0	0	.000
1916 BKN N	0	2	.000	4.91	2	2	0	11	12	6	9	0	0	0	0	3	0	0	.000
1920	0	1	.000	2.00	2	1	0	9	7	3	6	0	0	0	0	1	0	0	.000
5 yrs.	2	5	.286	2.76	11	8	4	58.2	52	15	35	0	0	0	0	11	0	0	.000
		2nd			10th	10th													

Jim Marquis

MARQUIS, JAMES MILBURN
B. Nov. 18, 1900, Yoakum, Tex.   BR TR 5'11" 174 lbs.

	W	L	PCT	ERA	G	GS	CG	IP	H	BB	SO	ShO	W	L	SV	AB	H	HR	BA
1925 NY A	0	0	–	9.82	2	0	0	7.1	12	6	0	0	0	0	0	2	0	0	.000

Connie Marrero

MARRERO, CONRADO EUGENIO RAMOS
B. May 1, 1917, Sagua La Grande, Cuba   BR TR 5'7" 158 lbs.

	W	L	PCT	ERA	G	GS	CG	IP	H	BB	SO	ShO	W	L	SV	AB	H	HR	BA
1950 WAS A	6	10	.375	4.50	27	19	8	152	159	55	63	1	1	0	1	49	6	0	.122
1951	11	9	.550	3.90	25	25	16	187	198	71	66	2	0	0	0	61	10	0	.164
1952	11	8	.579	2.88	22	22	16	184.1	175	53	77	2	0	0	0	63	5	0	.079
1953	8	7	.533	3.03	22	20	10	145.2	130	48	65	2	0	0	2	48	6	0	.125
1954	3	6	.333	4.75	22	8	1	66.1	74	22	26	0	2	2	0	15	0	0	.000
5 yrs.	39	40	.494	3.67	118	94	51	735.1	736	249	297	7	3	2	3	236	27	0	.114

Buck Marrow

MARROW, CHARLES KENNON
B. Aug. 29, 1909, Tarboro, N. C.   D. Nov. 21, 1982, Newport News, Va.   BR TR 6'4" 200 lbs.

	W	L	PCT	ERA	G	GS	CG	IP	H	BB	SO	ShO	W	L	SV	AB	H	HR	BA
1932 DET A	2	5	.286	4.81	18	7	2	63.2	70	29	31	0	1	0	1	19	3	0	.158
1937 BKN N	1	2	.333	6.61	6	3	1	16.1	19	9	2	0	0	0	0	5	0	0	.000
1938	0	1	.000	4.58	15	0	0	19.2	23	11	6	0	0	1	0	1	0	0	.000
3 yrs.	3	8	.273	5.06	39	10	3	99.2	112	49	39	0	1	1	1	25	3	0	.120

	W	L	PCT	ERA	G	GS	CG	IP	H	BB	SO	ShO	W	L	SV	AB	H	HR	BA
													Relief Pitching			BATTING			

Christy Mathewson continued

	W	L	PCT	ERA	G	GS	CG	IP	H	BB	SO	ShO	W	L	SV	AB	H	HR	BA
1911	1	2	.333	2.00	3	3	2	27	25	2	13	0	0	0	0	7	2	0	.286
1912	0	2	.000	1.57	3	3	3	28.2	23	5	10	0	0	0	0	12	2	0	.167
1913	1	1	.500	0.95	2	2	2	19	14	2	7	1	0	0	0	5	3	0	.600
4 yrs.	5	5	.500	1.15	11	11	10	101.2	76	10	48	4	0	0	0	32	9	0	.281
	8th	2nd		8th	10th	2nd	1st	2nd	3rd		9th	1st							

Henry Mathewson

MATHEWSON, HENRY　　　　　　　　　　　BR TR 6'3" 175 lbs.
Brother of Christy Mathewson.
B. Dec. 24, 1886, Factoryville, Pa.　　D. July 1, 1917, Factoryville, Pa.

	W	L	PCT	ERA	G	GS	CG	IP	H	BB	SO	ShO	W	L	SV	AB	H	HR	BA
1906 NY N	0	1	.000	5.40	2	1	1	10	7	14	2	0	0	0	1	2	0	0	.000
1907	0	0	—	0.00	1	0	0	1	1	0	0	0	0	0	1	0	0	0	—
2 yrs.	0	1	.000	4.91	3	1	1	11	8	14	2	0	0	0	2	2	0	0	.000

Carl Mathias

MATHIAS, CARL LYNWOOD (Stubby)　　　BR TL 5'11" 195 lbs.
B. June 13, 1936, Bechtelsville, Pa.　　BB 1960

	W	L	PCT	ERA	G	GS	CG	IP	H	BB	SO	ShO	W	L	SV	AB	H	HR	BA
1960 CLE A	0	1	.000	3.52	7	0	0	15.1	14	8	13	0	0	1	0	1	0	0	.000
1961 WAS A	0	1	.000	11.20	4	3	0	13.2	22	4	7	0	0	0	0	5	1	0	.200
2 yrs.	0	2	.000	7.14	11	3	0	29	36	12	20	0	0	1	0	6	1	0	.167

Jon Matlack

MATLACK, JONATHAN TRUMPBOUR　　　BL TL 6'3" 205 lbs.
B. Jan. 19, 1950, West Chester, Pa.

	W	L	PCT	ERA	G	GS	CG	IP	H	BB	SO	ShO	W	L	SV	AB	H	HR	BA
1971 NY N	0	3	.000	4.14	7	6	0	37	31	15	24	0	0	0	0	11	3	0	.273
1972	15	10	.600	2.32	34	32	8	244	215	71	169	4	1	0	0	78	10	0	.128
1973	14	16	.467	3.20	34	34	14	242	210	99	205	3	0	0	0	65	9	0	.138
1974	13	15	.464	2.41	34	34	14	265	221	76	195	7	0	0	0	79	8	0	.101
1975	16	12	.571	3.38	33	32	8	229	224	58	154	3	0	0	0	70	7	0	.100
1976	17	10	.630	2.95	35	35	16	262	236	57	153	6	0	0	0	88	17	0	.193
1977	7	15	.318	4.21	26	26	5	169	175	43	123	3	0	0	0	50	3	0	.060
1978 TEX A	15	13	.536	2.27	35	33	18	270	252	51	157	2	0	0	0	0	0	0	—
1979	5	4	.556	4.13	13	13	2	85	98	15	35	0	0	0	0	0	0	0	—
1980	10	10	.500	3.68	35	34	8	235	265	48	142	1	0	0	1	0	0	0	—
1981	4	7	.364	4.15	17	16	1	104	101	41	43	1	0	0	0	0	0	0	—
1982	7	7	.500	3.53	33	14	1	147.2	158	37	78	0	2	2	1	0	0	0	—
1983	2	4	.333	4.66	25	9	2	73.1	90	27	38	0	0	1	0	0	0	0	—
13 yrs.	125	126	.498	3.18	361	318	97	2363	2276	638	1516	30	3	3	3	441	57	0	.129

LEAGUE CHAMPIONSHIP SERIES

	W	L	PCT	ERA	G	GS	CG	IP	H	BB	SO	ShO	W	L	SV	AB	H	HR	BA
1973 NY N	1	0	1.000	0.00	1	1	1	9	2	3	9	1	0	0	0	2	0	0	.000

WORLD SERIES

	W	L	PCT	ERA	G	GS	CG	IP	H	BB	SO	ShO	W	L	SV	AB	H	HR	BA
1973 NY N	1	2	.333	2.16	3	3	0	16.2	10	5	11	0	0	0	0	4	1	0	.250

Al Mattern

MATTERN, ALONZO ALBERT　　　　　　BL TR 5'10" 165 lbs.
B. June 16, 1883, West Rush, N. Y.　　D. Nov. 6, 1958, West Rush, N. Y.

	W	L	PCT	ERA	G	GS	CG	IP	H	BB	SO	ShO	W	L	SV	AB	H	HR	BA
1908 BOS N	1	3	.250	2.08	5	3	1	30.1	30	6	8	1	0	1	0	8	1	0	.125
1909	16	20	.444	2.85	47	32	24	316.1	322	108	98	2	3	4	3	101	17	0	.168
1910	16	19	.457	2.98	51	37	17	305	288	121	94	6	4	2	1	98	16	0	.163
1911	4	15	.211	4.97	33	21	11	186.1	228	63	51	0	0	2	0	63	11	0	.175
1912	0	1	.000	7.11	2	1	0	6.1	10	1	3	0	0	0	0	2	0	0	.000
5 yrs.	37	58	.389	3.37	138	94	53	844.1	878	299	254	9	7	9	4	272	45	0	.165

C. V. Matterson

MATTERSON, C. V.
B. Ohio　　Deceased.

	W	L	PCT	ERA	G	GS	CG	IP	H	BB	SO	ShO	W	L	SV	AB	H	HR	BA
1884 STL U	1	0	1.000	9.00	1	1	1	6	9	3	3	0	0	0	0	4	0	0	.000

Henry Matteson

MATTESON, HENRY EDSON　　　　　　BR TR 5'9½" 160 lbs.
B. Sept. 7, 1884, Guy's Mills, Pa.　　D. Sept. 1, 1943, Westfield, N. Y.

	W	L	PCT	ERA	G	GS	CG	IP	H	BB	SO	ShO	W	L	SV	AB	H	HR	BA
1914 PHI N	3	2	.600	3.10	15	3	2	58	58	23	28	0	2	1	0	22	4	0	.182
1918 WAS A	5	3	.625	1.73	14	6	2	67.2	57	15	17	0	3	1	0	19	2	0	.105
2 yrs.	8	5	.615	2.36	29	9	4	125.2	115	38	45	0	5	2	0	41	6	0	.146

Jim Matthews

MATTHEWS, JAMES VINCENT　　　　　BR TL 6' 170 lbs.
B. Sept. 29, 1899, Baltimore, Md.

	W	L	PCT	ERA	G	GS	CG	IP	H	BB	SO	ShO	W	L	SV	AB	H	HR	BA
1922 BOS N	0	1	.000	3.60	3	1	0	10	5	6	1	0	0	0	0	2	0	0	.000

Dale Matthewson

MATTHEWSON, DALE WESLEY　　　　　BR TR 5'11½" 145 lbs.
B. May 15, 1923, Catasauqua, Pa.

	W	L	PCT	ERA	G	GS	CG	IP	H	BB	SO	ShO	W	L	SV	AB	H	HR	BA
1943 PHI N	0	3	.000	4.85	11	1	0	26	26	8	8	0	0	2	0	2	0	0	.000
1944	0	0	—	3.94	17	1	0	32	27	16	8	0	0	0	0	3	1	0	.333
2 yrs.	0	3	.000	4.34	28	2	0	58	53	24	16	0	0	2	0	5	1	0	.200

Mike Mattimore

MATTIMORE, MICHAEL JOSEPH　　　　BL TR 5'8½" 160 lbs.
B. 1859, Renovo, Pa.　　D. Apr. 29, 1931, Butte, Mont.

	W	L	PCT	ERA	G	GS	CG	IP	H	BB	SO	ShO	W	L	SV	AB	H	HR	BA
1887 NY N	3	3	.500	2.35	7	7	6	57.1	47	28	12	1	0	0	0	32	8	0	.250
1888 PHI AA	15	10	.600	3.38	26	24	24	221	221	65	80	4	0	1	0	142	38	0	.268
1889 2 teams					PHI	AA (5G 2–1)	KC	AA (1G 0–0)											
" total	2	1	.667	5.56	6	1	1	34	46	15	7	0	2	0	1	148	29	1	.196
1890 B-B AA	6	14	.300	4.54	19	19	19	178.1	201	76	33	0	0	0	0	129	17	0	.132
4 yrs.	26	28	.481	3.83	58	51	50	490.2	515	184	132	5	2	1	1	*			

Earl Mattingly

MATTINGLY, LAURENCE EARL　　　　　BR TR 5'10½" 164 lbs.
B. Nov. 4, 1904, Newport, Md.

	W	L	PCT	ERA	G	GS	CG	IP	H	BB	SO	ShO	W	L	SV	AB	H	HR	BA
1931 BKN N	0	1	.000	2.51	8	0	0	14.1	15	10	6	0	0	1	0	3	0	0	.000

	W	L	PCT	ERA	G	GS	CG	IP	H	BB	SO	ShO	Relief Pitching			BATTING			
													W	L	SV	AB	H	HR	BA

Rick Matula
MATULA, RICHARD CARLTON
B. Nov. 22, 1953, Wharton, Tex.   BR TR 6'   190 lbs.

	W	L	PCT	ERA	G	GS	CG	IP	H	BB	SO	ShO	W	L	SV	AB	H	HR	BA
1979 ATL N	8	10	.444	4.16	28	28	1	171	193	64	67	0	0	0	0	53	5	0	.094
1980	11	13	.458	4.58	33	30	3	177	195	60	62	1	0	0	0	57	6	0	.105
1981	0	0	—	6.43	5	0	0	7	8	2	0	0	0	0	0	1	0	0	.000
3 yrs.	19	23	.452	4.41	66	58	4	355	396	126	129	1	0	0	0	111	11	0	.099

Harry Matuzak
MATUZAK, HENRY GEORGE (Matty)
B. Jan. 27, 1910, Omer, Mich.   D. Nov. 26, 1978, Fairhope, Ala.   TR 5'11½" 185 lbs.

	W	L	PCT	ERA	G	GS	CG	IP	H	BB	SO	ShO	W	L	SV	AB	H	HR	BA
1934 PHI A	0	3	.000	4.88	11	0	0	24	28	10	9	0	0	3	0	6	1	0	.167
1936	0	1	.000	7.20	6	1	0	15	21	4	8	0	0	1	0	3	0	0	.000
2 yrs.	0	4	.000	5.77	17	1	0	39	49	14	17	0	0	4	0	9	1	0	.111

Hal Mauck
MAUCK, ALFRED MARIS
B. Mar. 6, 1869, Princeton, Ind.   D. Apr. 27, 1921, Gibson County, Ind.

	W	L	PCT	ERA	G	GS	CG	IP	H	BB	SO	ShO	W	L	SV	AB	H	HR	BA
1893 CHI N	8	10	.444	4.41	23	18	12	143	168	60	23	1	2	1	0	61	9	0	.148

Al Maul
MAUL, ALBERT JOSEPH (Smiling Al)
B. Oct. 9, 1865, Philadelphia, Pa.   D. May 3, 1958, Philadelphia, Pa.   BR TR 6'   175 lbs.

	W	L	PCT	ERA	G	GS	CG	IP	H	BB	SO	ShO	W	L	SV	AB	H	HR	BA
1884 PHI U	0	1	.000	4.50	1	1	1	8	10	1	7	0	0	0	0	4	0	0	.000
1887 PHI N	4	2	.667	5.54	7	5	4	50.1	72	15	18	0	2	0	0	56	17	1	.304
1888 PIT N	0	2	.000	6.35	3	1	1	17	26	5	12	0	0	1	0	259	54	0	.208
1889	1	4	.200	9.86	6	4	4	42	64	28	11	0	0	1	0	257	71	4	.276
1890 PIT P	16	12	.571	3.79	30	28	26	246.2	258	104	81	2	0	1	0	162	42	0	.259
1891 PIT N	1	2	.333	2.31	8	3	3	39	44	16	13	0	0	0	0	149	28	0	.188
1893 WAS N	12	21	.364	5.30	37	33	29	297	355	144	72	1	1	0	0	134	34	0	.254
1894	11	15	.423	5.98	28	26	21	201.2	272	73	34	0	0	0	0	124	30	2	.242
1895	10	5	.667	2.45	16	16	14	135.2	136	37	34	0	0	0	0	72	18	0	.250
1896	5	2	.714	3.63	8	8	7	62	75	20	18	0	0	0	0	28	8	0	.286
1897 2 teams		WAS	N (1G 0–1)			BAL	N (2G 0–0)												
" total	0	1	.000	7.45	3	3	0	9.2	13	9	2	0	0	0	0	4	1	0	.250
1898 BAL N	20	6	.769	2.10	28	28	26	239.2	207	49	31	0	0	0	0	93	19	0	.204
1899 BKN N	2	0	1.000	4.50	4	4	2	26	35	6	2	0	0	0	0	11	3	0	.273
1900 PHI N	2	3	.400	6.16	5	4	3	38	53	3	6	0	1	0	0	15	3	0	.200
1901 NY N	0	2	.000	11.37	3	3	2	19	39	8	5	0	0	0	0	8	3	0	.375
15 yrs.	84	78	.519	4.43	187	167	143	1431.2	1659	518	346	4	4	3	0	*			

Ernie Maun
MAUN, ERNEST GERALD
B. Feb. 3, 1901, Clearwater, Kans.   BL TR 6'   165 lbs.

	W	L	PCT	ERA	G	GS	CG	IP	H	BB	SO	ShO	W	L	SV	AB	H	HR	BA
1924 NY N	1	1	.500	5.91	22	5	0	35	46	10	5	0	1	1	1	3	2	0	.667
1926 PHI N	1	4	.200	6.45	14	5	0	37.2	57	18	9	0	1	1	0	12	3	0	.250
2 yrs.	2	5	.286	6.19	36	5	0	72.2	103	28	14	0	2	2	1	15	5	0	.333

Dick Mauney
MAUNEY, RICHARD
B. Jan. 26, 1920, Concord, N. C.   D. Feb. 6, 1970, Albemarle, N. C.   BR TR 5'11½" 164 lbs.

	W	L	PCT	ERA	G	GS	CG	IP	H	BB	SO	ShO	W	L	SV	AB	H	HR	BA
1945 PHI N	6	10	.375	3.08	20	16	6	122.2	127	27	35	2	0	2	1	41	6	0	.146
1946	6	4	.600	2.70	24	7	3	90	98	18	31	1	3	2	2	24	4	0	.167
1947	0	0	—	3.86	9	1	0	16.1	15	7	6	0	0	1	1	2	0	0	.000
3 yrs.	12	14	.462	2.99	53	24	9	229	240	52	72	3	3	4	4	67	10	0	.149

Harry Maupin
MAUPIN, HENRY CARR
B. July 11, 1874, Wellesville, Mo.   D. Aug. 23, 1952

	W	L	PCT	ERA	G	GS	CG	IP	H	BB	SO	ShO	W	L	SV	AB	H	HR	BA
1898 STL N	0	2	.000	5.50	2	2	2	18	22	3	3	0	0	0	0	7	3	0	.429
1899 CLE N	0	3	.000	12.60	5	3	2	25	55	7	3	0	0	0	0	10	0	0	.000
2 yrs.	0	5	.000	9.63	7	5	4	43	77	10	6	0	0	0	0	17	3	0	.176

Ralph Mauriello
MAURIELLO, RALPH (Tami)
B. Aug. 25, 1934, Brooklyn, N. Y.   BR TR 6'3"   195 lbs.

	W	L	PCT	ERA	G	GS	CG	IP	H	BB	SO	ShO	W	L	SV	AB	H	HR	BA
1958 LA N	1	1	.500	4.63	3	2	0	11.2	10	8	11	0	0	0	0	4	0	0	.000

Larry Maxie
MAXIE, LARRY HANS
B. Oct. 10, 1940, Upland, Calif.   BR TR 6'4"   220 lbs.

	W	L	PCT	ERA	G	GS	CG	IP	H	BB	SO	ShO	W	L	SV	AB	H	HR	BA
1969 ATL N	0	0	—	3.00	2	0	0	3	1	1	1	0	0	0	0	0	0	0	—

Bert Maxwell
MAXWELL, JAMES ALBERT
B. Oct. 17, 1886, Texarkana, Ark.   D. Dec. 10, 1961, Brady, Tex.   BB TR

	W	L	PCT	ERA	G	GS	CG	IP	H	BB	SO	ShO	W	L	SV	AB	H	HR	BA
1906 PIT N	0	1	.000	5.63	1	1	0	8	8	2	1	0	0	0	0	3	0	0	.000
1908 PHI N	0	0	—	11.08	4	0	0	13	23	9	7	0	0	0	0	5	0	0	.000
1911 NY N	1	2	.333	2.90	4	3	3	31	37	7	8	0	0	0	0	9	1	0	.111
1914 BKN F	3	4	.429	3.28	12	8	6	71.1	76	24	19	1	0	0	1	23	2	0	.087
4 yrs.	4	7	.364	4.16	21	12	9	123.1	144	42	35	1	0	0	1	40	3	0	.075

Buckshot May
MAY, WILLIAM HERBERT
B. Dec. 13, 1899, Bakersfield, Calif.   D. Mar. 15, 1984, Bakersfield, Calif.   BL TR 6'2"   169 lbs.

	W	L	PCT	ERA	G	GS	CG	IP	H	BB	SO	ShO	W	L	SV	AB	H	HR	BA
1924 PIT N	0	0	—	0.00	1	0	0	1	2	0	1	0	0	0	0	0	0	0	—

Jakie May
MAY, FRANK SPRUIELL
B. Nov. 25, 1895, Youngville, N. C.   D. June 3, 1970, Wendell, N. C.   BR TL 5'8"   178 lbs.

	W	L	PCT	ERA	G	GS	CG	IP	H	BB	SO	ShO	W	L	SV	AB	H	HR	BA
1917 STL N	0	0	—	3.38	15	1	0	29.1	29	11	18	0	0	0	0	4	0	0	.000
1918	5	6	.455	3.83	29	16	6	152.2	149	69	61	0	2	0	0	45	3	1	.067
1919	3	12	.200	3.22	28	19	8	125.2	99	87	58	1	0	1	0	37	6	0	.162
1920	1	4	.200	3.06	16	5	3	70.2	65	37	33	0	0	1	0	22	5	0	.227
1921	1	3	.250	4.71	5	5	1	21	29	12	5	0	0	0	0	6	2	0	.333
1924 CIN N	3	3	.500	3.00	38	4	2	99	104	29	59	0	2	2	6	27	3	1	.111
1925	8	9	.471	3.87	36	12	7	137.1	146	45	74	1	2	4	2	43	8	0	.186
1926	13	9	.591	3.22	45	15	9	167.2	175	44	103	1	5	4	3	48	7	0	.146

	W	L	PCT	ERA	G	GS	CG	IP	H	BB	SO	ShO	Relief Pitching W	L	SV	BATTING AB	H	HR	BA

Jakie May continued

	W	L	PCT	ERA	G	GS	CG	IP	H	BB	SO	ShO	W	L	SV	AB	H	HR	BA
1927	15	12	.556	3.51	44	28	17	235.2	242	70	121	2	2	0	1	76	14	0	.184
1928	3	5	.375	4.42	21	11	1	79.1	99	35	39	1	2	2	1	27	8	0	.296
1929	10	14	.417	4.61	41	24	10	199	219	75	92	0	4	1	3	64	13	0	.203
1930	3	11	.214	5.77	26	18	5	112.1	147	41	44	1	0	1	0	39	5	0	.128
1931 CHI N	5	5	.500	3.87	31	4	1	79	81	43	38	0	3	4	2	22	5	0	.227
1932	2	2	.500	4.36	35	0	0	53.2	61	19	20	0	2	2	1	8	1	0	.125
14 yrs.	72	95	.431	3.88	410	162	70	1562.1	1645	617	765	7	24	22	19	468	80	2	.171

WORLD SERIES

	W	L	PCT	ERA	G	GS	CG	IP	H	BB	SO	ShO	W	L	SV	AB	H	HR	BA
1932 CHI N	0	1	.000	11.57	2	0	0	4.2	9	3	4	0	0	1	0	2	0	0	.000

Rudy May

MAY, RUDOLPH   BL TL 6'2"   205 lbs.
B. July 18, 1944, Coffeyville, Kans.

	W	L	PCT	ERA	G	GS	CG	IP	H	BB	SO	ShO	W	L	SV	AB	H	HR	BA
1965 CAL A	4	9	.308	3.92	30	19	2	124	111	78	76	1	0	0	0	30	6	0	.200
1969	10	13	.435	3.44	43	25	4	180.1	142	66	133	0	3	2	2	49	4	0	.082
1970	7	13	.350	4.00	38	34	2	209	190	81	164	2	1	1	0	69	6	0	.087
1971	11	12	.478	3.03	32	31	7	208	160	87	156	2	0	1	0	68	10	0	.147
1972	12	11	.522	2.94	35	30	10	205	162	82	169	3	1	0	1	62	7	0	.113
1973	7	17	.292	4.38	34	28	10	185	177	80	134	4	0	2	0				—
1974 2 teams		CAL	A (18G 0–1)		NY	A (17G 8–4)													
" total	8	5	.615	3.19	35	18	8	141	104	58	102	2	1	0	2	0	0	0	—
1975 NY A	14	12	.538	3.06	32	31	13	212	179	99	145	1	0	0	0	0	0	0	—
1976 2 teams		NY	A (11G 4–3)		BAL	A (24G 11–7)													
" total	15	10	.600	3.72	35	32	7	220.1	205	70	109	2	0	0	0	0	0	0	—
1977 BAL A	18	14	.563	3.61	37	37	11	252	243	78	105	4	0	0	0	0	0	0	—
1978 MON N	8	10	.444	3.88	27	23	4	144	141	42	87	1	0	1	0	42	6	0	.143
1979	10	3	.769	2.30	33	7	2	94	88	31	67	1	6	1	0	21	3	0	.143
1980 NY A	15	5	.750	**2.47**	41	17	3	175	144	39	133	1	4	2	3	0	0	0	—
1981	6	11	.353	4.14	27	22	4	148	137	41	79	0	0	1	1	0	0	0	—
1982	6	6	.500	2.89	41	6	0	106	109	14	85	0	4	3	3	0	0	0	—
1983	1	5	.167	6.87	15	0	0	18.1	22	12	16	0	1	5	0	0	0	0	—
16 yrs.	152	156	.494	3.46	535	360	87	2622	2314	958	1760	24	21	19	12	341	42	0	.123

DIVISIONAL PLAYOFF SERIES

	W	L	PCT	ERA	G	GS	CG	IP	H	BB	SO	ShO	W	L	SV	AB	H	HR	BA
1981 NY A	0	0	—	0.00	1	0	0	2	1	0	1	0	0	0	0	0	0	0	—

LEAGUE CHAMPIONSHIP SERIES

	W	L	PCT	ERA	G	GS	CG	IP	H	BB	SO	ShO	W	L	SV	AB	H	HR	BA
1980 NY A	0	1	.000	3.38	1	1	1	8	6	3	4	0	0	0	0	0	0	0	—
1981	0	0	—	8.10	1	1	0	3.1	6	0	5	0	0	0	0	0	0	0	—
2 yrs.	0	1	.000	4.76	2	2	1	11.1	12	3	9	0	0	0	0	0	0	0	—

WORLD SERIES

	W	L	PCT	ERA	G	GS	CG	IP	H	BB	SO	ShO	W	L	SV	AB	H	HR	BA
1981 NY A	0	0	—	2.84	3	0	0	6.1	5	1	5	0	0	0	0	1	0	0	.000

Ed Mayer

MAYER, EDWIN DAVID   BL TL 6'2"   185 lbs.
B. Nov. 30, 1931, San Francisco, Calif.

	W	L	PCT	ERA	G	GS	CG	IP	H	BB	SO	ShO	W	L	SV	AB	H	HR	BA
1957 CHI N	0	0	—	5.87	3	1	0	7.2	8	2	3	0	0	0	0	2	1	0	.500
1958	2	2	.500	3.80	19	0	0	23.2	15	16	14	0	2	2	1	5	1	0	.200
2 yrs.	2	2	.500	4.31	22	1	0	31.1	23	18	17	0	2	2	1	7	2	0	.286

Erskine Mayer

MAYER, JAMES ERSKINE   BR TR 6'   168 lbs.
Born James Erskine. Brother of Sam Mayer.
B. Jan. 16, 1891, Atlanta, Ga.   D. Mar. 10, 1957, Los Angeles, Calif.

	W	L	PCT	ERA	G	GS	CG	IP	H	BB	SO	ShO	W	L	SV	AB	H	HR	BA
1912 PHI N	1	1	.000	6.33	7	1	0	21.1	27	7	5	0	0	0	0	3	0	0	.000
1913	9	9	.500	3.11	39	20	7	170.2	172	46	51	2	3	1	1	50	6	0	.120
1914	21	19	.525	2.58	48	39	24	321	308	91	116	4	3	1	2	108	21	1	.194
1915	21	15	.583	2.36	43	33	20	274.2	240	59	114	2	4	1	2	88	21	1	.239
1916	7	7	.500	3.15	28	16	7	140	148	33	62	2	1	0	0	38	5	0	.132
1917	11	6	.647	2.76	28	18	11	160	160	33	64	1	1	1	0	51	10	0	.196
1918 2 teams		PHI	N (13G 7–4)		PIT	N (15G 9–3)													
" total	16	7	.696	2.65	28	27	18	227.1	230	53	41	1	0	0	0	79	15	0	.190
1919 2 teams		PIT	N (18G 5–3)		CHI	A (6G 1–3)													
" total	6	6	.500	5.30	24	12	6	112	130	23	29	0	2	1	1	36	6	0	.167
8 yrs.	91	70	.565	2.96	245	166	93	1427	1415	345	482	12	14	5	6	453	84	2	.185

WORLD SERIES

	W	L	PCT	ERA	G	GS	CG	IP	H	BB	SO	ShO	W	L	SV	AB	H	HR	BA
1915 PHI N	0	1	.000	2.38	2	2	1	11.1	16	2	7	0	0	0	0	4	0	0	.000
1919 CHI A	0	0	—	0.00	1	0	0	1	0	1	0	0	0	0	0	0	0	0	—
2 yrs.	0	1	.000	2.19	3	2	1	12.1	16	3	7	0	0	0	0	4	0	0	.000

Sam Mayer

MAYER, SAMUEL FRANKEL   BR TL 5'10"   164 lbs.
Born Samuel Frankel Erskine. Brother of Erskine Mayer.
B. Feb. 28, 1893, Atlanta, Ga.   D. July 1, 1962, Atlanta, Ga.

	W	L	PCT	ERA	G	GS	CG	IP	H	BB	SO	ShO	W	L	SV	AB	H	HR	BA
1915 WAS A	0	0	—	0.00	1	0	0	0	0	2	0	0	0	0	0	*			

Al Mays

MAYS, ALBERT C.   BR
B. May 17, 1865, Canal Dover, Ohio   D. May 7, 1905, Parkersburg, W. Va.

	W	L	PCT	ERA	G	GS	CG	IP	H	BB	SO	ShO	W	L	SV	AB	H	HR	BA
1885 LOU AA	6	11	.353	2.76	17	17	17	150	129	43	61	0	0	0	0	61	13	0	.213
1886 NY AA	11	28	.282	3.39	41	41	39	350	330	140	163	1	0	0	0	135	16	1	.119
1887	17	34	.333	4.73	52	52	50	441.1	551	136	124	0	0	0	0	221	45	2	.204
1888 BKN AA	9	9	.500	2.80	18	18	17	160.2	150	32	67	1	0	0	0	63	5	0	.079
1889 COL AA	10	7	.588	4.82	21	19	13	140	167	56	52	1	0	0	0	54	7	0	.130
1890	0	1	.000	8.00	1	1	1	9	14	8	2	0	0	0	0	3	0	0	.000
6 yrs.	53	90	.371	3.91	150	148	137	1251	1341	415	469	3	0	0	0	537	86	0	.160

Carl Mays

MAYS, CARL WILLIAM (Sub)   BL TR 5'11½" 195 lbs.
B. Nov. 12, 1891, Liberty, Ky.   D. Apr. 4, 1971, El Cajon, Calif.

	W	L	PCT	ERA	G	GS	CG	IP	H	BB	SO	ShO	W	L	SV	AB	H	HR	BA
1915 BOS A	6	5	.545	2.60	38	6	2	131.2	119	21	65	0	5	3	7	38	9	0	.237
1916	18	13	.581	2.39	44	24	14	245	208	74	76	2	6	3	3	77	18	0	.234

	W	L	PCT	ERA	G	GS	CG	IP	H	BB	SO	ShO	Relief Pitching W	L	SV	BATTING AB	H	HR	BA

Carl Mays continued

	W	L	PCT	ERA	G	GS	CG	IP	H	BB	SO	ShO	W	L	SV	AB	H	HR	BA
1917	22	9	.710	1.74	35	33	27	289	230	74	91	2	1	0	0	107	27	0	.252
1918	21	13	.618	2.21	35	33	30	293.1	230	81	114	8	0	1	0	104	30	0	.288
1919 2 teams		BOS	A (21G 5–11)			NY	A (13G 9–3)												
" total	14	14	.500	2.11	34	29	26	265	227	77	107	3	0	0	2	98	22	0	.224
1920 NY A	26	11	.703	3.06	45	37	26	312	310	84	92	6	4	0	2	109	26	0	.239
1921	27	9	.750	3.05	49	38	30	336.2	332	76	70	1	1	0	7	143	49	2	.343
1922	13	14	.481	3.60	34	29	21	240	257	50	41	1	0	1	2	92	23	0	.250
1923	5	2	.714	6.20	23	7	2	81.1	119	32	16	0	2	0	0	27	4	1	.148
1924 CIN N	20	9	.690	3.15	37	27	15	226	238	36	63	2	4	1	0	83	24	0	.289
1925	3	5	.375	3.31	12	5	3	51.2	60	13	10	0	1	2	2	16	4	0	.250
1926	19	12	.613	3.14	39	33	24	281	286	53	58	3	0	1	1	98	22	0	.224
1927	3	7	.300	3.51	14	9	6	82	89	10	17	0	1	0	0	32	13	1	.406
1928	4	1	.800	3.88	14	7	4	62.2	67	22	10	1	0	0	1	27	8	0	.296
1929 NY N	7	2	.778	4.32	37	8	1	123	140	31	32	0	6	1	4	34	12	0	.353
15 yrs.	208	126	.623	2.92	490	325	231	3020.1	2912	734	862	29	31	13	31	1085	291	5	.268
WORLD SERIES																			
1916 BOS A	0	1	.000	5.06	2	1	0	5.1	8	3	2	0	0	0	1	1	0	0	.000
1918	2	0	1.000	1.00	2	2	2	18	10	3	5	0	0	0	0	5	1	0	.200
1921 NY A	1	2	.333	1.73	3	3	3	26	20	0	9	1	0	0	0	9	1	0	.111
1922	0	1	.000	4.50	1	1	0	8	9	2	1	0	0	0	0	2	0	0	.000
4 yrs.	3	4	.429	2.20	8	7	5	57.1	47	8	17	1	0	0	1	17	2	0	.118
			7th				10th												

Jack McAdams

McADAMS, GEORGE D.
B. Dec. 17, 1886, Benton, Ark.   D. May 21, 1937, San Francisco, Calif.   BR TR 6'1½" 170 lbs.

	W	L	PCT	ERA	G	GS	CG	IP	H	BB	SO	ShO	W	L	SV	AB	H	HR	BA
1911 STL N	0	0	–	3.72	6	0	0	9.2	7	5	4	0	0	0	0	1	0	0	.000

Bill McAfee

McAFEE, WILLIAM FORT
B. Sept. 7, 1907, Smithville, Ga.   D. July 8, 1958, Culpeper, Va.   BR TR 6'2" 186 lbs.

	W	L	PCT	ERA	G	GS	CG	IP	H	BB	SO	ShO	W	L	SV	AB	H	HR	BA
1930 CHI N	0	0	–	0.00	2	0	0	1	3	2	0	0	0	0	0	0	0	0	–
1931 BOS N	0	1	.000	6.37	18	1	0	29.2	39	10	9	0	0	0	0	3	0	0	.000
1932 WAS A	6	1	.857	3.92	8	5	2	41.1	47	22	10	0	3	0	0	18	2	0	.111
1933	3	2	.600	6.62	27	1	0	53	64	21	14	0	3	0	0	15	4	1	.267
1934 STL A	1	0	1.000	5.84	28	0	0	61.2	84	26	11	0	1	0	0	16	3	0	.188
5 yrs.	10	4	.714	5.69	83	7	2	186.2	237	81	44	0	7	2	5	52	9	1	.173

Jimmy McAleer

McALEER, JAMES ROBERT
B. July 10, 1864, Youngstown, Ohio   D. Apr. 29, 1931, Youngstown, Ohio   BR TR 6' 175 lbs.
Manager 1901-11.

	W	L	PCT	ERA	G	GS	CG	IP	H	BB	SO	ShO	W	L	SV	AB	H	HR	BA
1901 CLE A	0	0	–	0.00	1	0	0	.1	2	3	0	0	0	0	0	*			

John McAleese

McALEESE, JOHN JAMES
B. Aug. 22, 1877, Sharon, Pa.   D. Nov. 15, 1950, New York, N. Y.   BR TR 5'8"

	W	L	PCT	ERA	G	GS	CG	IP	H	BB	SO	ShO	W	L	SV	AB	H	HR	BA
1901 CHI A	0	0	–	9.00	1	0	0	3	7	1	1	0	0	0	0	*			

Sport McAllister

McALLISTER, LEWIS WILLIAM
B. July 23, 1874, Austin, Miss.   D. July 18, 1962, Detroit, Mich.   BB TR 5'11" 180 lbs.

	W	L	PCT	ERA	G	GS	CG	IP	H	BB	SO	ShO	W	L	SV	AB	H	HR	BA
1896 CLE N	0	0	–	6.75	1	0	0	4	9	2	0	0	0	0	0	27	6	0	.222
1897	1	2	.333	4.50	4	3	3	28	29	9	10	0	0	0	0	137	30	0	.219
1898	3	4	.429	4.55	9	7	6	65.1	73	23	9	0	0	0	0	57	13	0	.228
1899	0	1	.000	9.56	3	1	1	16	29	10	2	0	0	0	0	418	99	1	.237
4 yrs.	4	7	.364	5.32	17	11	10	113.1	140	44	21	0	0	0	0	*			

Ernie McAnally

McANALLY, ERNEST LEE
B. Aug. 15, 1946, Pittsburg, Tex.   BR TR 6'1" 190 lbs.

	W	L	PCT	ERA	G	GS	CG	IP	H	BB	SO	ShO	W	L	SV	AB	H	HR	BA
1971 MON N	11	12	.478	3.89	31	25	8	178	150	87	98	2	0	0	0	60	7	1	.117
1972	6	15	.286	3.81	29	27	4	170	165	71	102	2	0	0	0	53	6	0	.113
1973	7	9	.438	4.04	27	24	4	147	158	54	72	0	0	0	0	49	9	0	.184
1974	6	13	.316	4.47	25	21	5	129	126	56	79	2	0	1	0	42	5	0	.119
4 yrs.	30	49	.380	4.02	112	97	21	624	599	268	351	6	0	1	0	204	27	1	.132

Jim McAndrew

McANDREW, JAMES CLEMENT
B. Jan. 11, 1945, Lost Nation, Iowa   BR TR 6'2" 185 lbs.

	W	L	PCT	ERA	G	GS	CG	IP	H	BB	SO	ShO	W	L	SV	AB	H	HR	BA
1968 NY N	4	7	.364	2.28	12	12	2	79	66	17	46	1	0	0	0	22	1	0	.045
1969	6	7	.462	3.47	27	21	4	135	112	44	90	2	0	0	0	37	5	0	.135
1970	10	14	.417	3.57	32	27	9	184	166	38	111	3	0	1	2	54	8	0	.148
1971	2	5	.286	4.40	24	10	0	90	78	32	42	0	0	1	0	23	1	0	.043
1972	11	8	.579	2.80	28	23	4	160.2	133	38	81	0	1	0	0	43	2	0	.047
1973	3	8	.273	5.38	23	12	0	80.1	109	31	38	0	0	1	1	15	2	0	.133
1974 SD N	1	4	.200	5.57	15	5	1	42	48	13	16	0	0	1	0	7	1	0	.143
7 yrs.	37	53	.411	3.65	161	110	20	771	712	213	424	6	1	4	4	201	20	0	.100

Dixie McArthur

McARTHUR, OLAND ALEXANDER
B. Feb. 1, 1892, Vernon, Ala.   BR TR 6'1" 185 lbs.

	W	L	PCT	ERA	G	GS	CG	IP	H	BB	SO	ShO	W	L	SV	AB	H	HR	BA
1914 PIT N	0	0	–	0.00	1	0	0	1	0	1	0	0	0	0	0	0	0	0	–

Tom McAvoy

McAVOY, THOMAS JOHN
B. Aug. 12, 1936, Brooklyn, N. Y.   BL TL 6'3" 200 lbs.

	W	L	PCT	ERA	G	GS	CG	IP	H	BB	SO	ShO	W	L	SV	AB	H	HR	BA
1959 WAS A	0	0	–	0.00	1	0	0	2.2	1	2	0	0	0	0	0	1	0	0	.000

Wickey McAvoy

McAVOY, JAMES EUGENE
B. Oct. 20, 1894, Rochester, N. Y.   D. July 1, 1973, Rochester, N. Y.   BR TR 5'11" 172 lbs.

	W	L	PCT	ERA	G	GS	CG	IP	H	BB	SO	ShO	W	L	SV	AB	H	HR	BA
1918 PHI A	0	0	–	0.00	1	0	0	.2	0	0	0	0	0	0	0	*			

	W	L	PCT	ERA	G	GS	CG	IP	H	BB	SO	ShO	Relief Pitching W	L	SV	BATTING AB	H	HR	BA

Lindy McDaniel continued

	W	L	PCT	ERA	G	GS	CG	IP	H	BB	SO	ShO	W	L	SV	AB	H	HR	BA
1973	12	6	.667	2.86	47	3	1	160.1	148	49	93	0	12	3	10	0	0	0	–
1974 KC A	1	4	.200	3.45	38	5	2	107	109	24	47	0	0	2	1	0	0	0	–
1975	5	1	.833	4.15	40	0	0	78	81	24	40	0	5	1	1	0	0	0	–
21 yrs.	141	119	.542	3.45	987	74	18	2140.1	2099	623	1361	2	119	87	172	376	56	3	.149
					2nd								**2nd**						

Von McDaniel

McDANIEL, MAX VON
Brother of Lindy McDaniel.
B. Apr. 18, 1939, Hollis, Okla.

BR TR 6'2½" 180 lbs.

	W	L	PCT	ERA	G	GS	CG	IP	H	BB	SO	ShO	W	L	SV	AB	H	HR	BA
1957 STL N	7	5	.583	3.22	17	13	4	86.2	71	31	45	2	1	0	0	26	0	0	.000
1958	0	0	–	13.50	2	1	0	2	5	5	0	0	0	0	0	0	0	0	–
2 yrs.	7	5	.583	3.45	19	14	4	88.2	76	36	45	2	1	0	0	26	0	0	.000

Mickey McDermott

McDERMOTT, MAURICE JOSEPH
B. Aug. 29, 1928, Poughkeepsie, N. Y.

BL TL 6'2" 170 lbs.

	W	L	PCT	ERA	G	GS	CG	IP	H	BB	SO	ShO	W	L	SV	AB	H	HR	BA
1948 BOS A	0	0	–	6.17	7	0	0	23.1	16	35	17	0	0	0	0	8	3	0	.375
1949	5	4	.556	4.05	12	12	6	80	63	52	50	2	0	0	0	33	7	0	.212
1950	7	3	.700	5.19	38	15	4	130	119	124	96	0	3	0	5	44	16	0	.364
1951	8	8	.500	3.35	34	19	9	172	141	92	127	1	0	1	3	66	18	1	.273
1952	10	9	.526	3.72	30	21	7	162	139	92	117	2	2	3	0	62	14	1	.226
1953	18	10	.643	3.01	32	30	8	206.1	169	109	92	4	0	0	0	93	28	1	.301
1954 WAS A	7	15	.318	3.44	30	26	11	196.1	172	110	95	1	0	0	1	95	19	0	.200
1955	10	10	.500	3.75	31	20	8	156	140	102	78	1	2	1	1	95	25	1	.263
1956 NY A	2	6	.250	4.24	23	9	1	87	85	47	38	0	0	0	0	52	11	1	.212
1957 KC A	1	4	.200	5.48	29	4	0	69	68	50	29	0	1	2	0	49	12	4	.245
1958 DET A	0	0	–	9.00	2	0	0	2	6	2	0	0	0	0	0	3	1	0	.333
1961 2 teams			STL N	(19G 1–0)		KC A	(4G 0–0)												
" total	1	0	1.000	5.51	23	0	0	32.2	43	25	18	0	1	0	4	19	2	0	.105
12 yrs.	69	69	.500	3.91	291	156	54	1316.2	1161	840	757	11	9	7	14	*			

WORLD SERIES

	W	L	PCT	ERA	G	GS	CG	IP	H	BB	SO	ShO	W	L	SV	AB	H	HR	BA
1956 NY A	0	0	–	3.00	1	0	0	3	2	3	3	0	0	0	0	1	1	0	1.000

Mike McDermott

McDERMOTT, MICHAEL JOSEPH
B. Sept. 7, 1862, St. Louis, Mo.   D. June 30, 1943, St. Louis, Mo.

TR 5'8" 145 lbs.

	W	L	PCT	ERA	G	GS	CG	IP	H	BB	SO	ShO	W	L	SV	AB	H	HR	BA
1889 LOU AA	1	8	.111	4.16	9	9	9	84.1	108	34	22	0	0	0	0	33	6	0	.182
1895 LOU N	4	19	.174	5.99	33	26	18	207.1	258	103	42	0	0	0	0	82	13	0	.159
1896	2	7	.222	7.34	12	10	4	65	87	44	12	1	0	0	0	27	8	0	.296
1897 2 teams			CLE N	(9G 4–5)		STL N	(4G 1–2)												
" total	5	7	.417	5.72	13	11	5	83.1	98	44	15	0	2	0	0	34	10	0	.294
4 yrs.	12	41	.226	5.79	67	56	36	440	551	225	91	1	2	0	0	176	37	0	.210

Danny McDevitt

McDEVITT, DANIEL EUGENE
B. Nov. 18, 1932, New York, N. Y.

BL TL 5'10" 175 lbs.

	W	L	PCT	ERA	G	GS	CG	IP	H	BB	SO	ShO	W	L	SV	AB	H	HR	BA
1957 BKN N	7	4	.636	3.25	22	17	5	119	105	72	90	2	0	0	0	39	6	0	.154
1958 LA N	2	6	.250	7.45	13	10	2	48.1	71	31	26	0	0	0	0	15	2	0	.133
1959	10	8	.556	3.97	39	22	6	145	149	51	106	2	1	0	4	46	5	0	.109
1960	0	4	.000	4.25	24	7	0	53	51	42	30	0	0	2	0	10	2	0	.200
1961 2 teams			NY A	(8G 1–2)		MIN A	(16G 1–0)												
" total	2	2	.500	4.08	24	3	0	39.2	38	27	23	0	2	0	1	4	0	0	.000
1962 KC A	0	3	.000	5.82	33	1	0	51	47	41	28	0	0	2	2	9	2	0	.222
6 yrs.	21	27	.438	4.40	155	60	13	456	461	264	303	4	3	4	7	123	17	0	.138

Hank McDonald

McDONALD, HENRY MONROE
B. Jan. 16, 1911, Santa Monica, Calif.   D. Oct. 17, 1982, Hemet, Calif.

BR TR 6'3½" 200 lbs.

	W	L	PCT	ERA	G	GS	CG	IP	H	BB	SO	ShO	W	L	SV	AB	H	HR	BA
1931 PHI A	2	4	.333	3.71	19	10	1	70.1	62	41	23	1	1	1	0	21	2	0	.095
1933 2 teams			PHI A	(4G 1–1)		STL A	(25G 0–4)												
" total	1	5	.167	8.02	29	6	0	70.2	97	38	23	0	1	1	0	18	2	0	.111
2 yrs.	3	9	.250	5.87	48	16	1	141	159	79	46	1	2	2	0	39	4	0	.103

Jim McDonald

McDONALD, JAMES LeROY (Hot Rod)
B. May 17, 1927, Grants Pass, Ore.

BR TR 5'10½" 185 lbs.
BB 1950-51

	W	L	PCT	ERA	G	GS	CG	IP	H	BB	SO	ShO	W	L	SV	AB	H	HR	BA
1950 BOS A	1	0	1.000	3.79	9	0	0	19	23	10	5	0	1	0	0	3	1	0	.333
1951 STL A	4	7	.364	4.07	16	11	5	84	84	46	28	0	0	0	1	29	6	0	.207
1952 NY A	3	4	.429	3.50	26	5	1	69.1	71	40	20	0	2	3	0	19	6	0	.316
1953	9	7	.563	3.82	27	18	6	129.2	128	39	43	2	1	1	0	41	4	0	.098
1954	4	1	.800	3.17	16	10	3	71	54	45	20	1	0	0	0	19	4	0	.211
1955 BAL A	3	5	.375	7.14	21	8	0	51.2	76	30	20	0	1	0	0	11	2	0	.182
1956 CHI A	0	2	.000	8.68	8	3	0	18.2	29	7	10	0	0	0	0	5	0	0	.000
1957	0	1	.000	2.01	10	0	0	22.1	18	10	12	0	0	1	0	1	0	0	.000
1958	0	0	–	19.29	3	0	0	2.1	6	4	0	0	0	0	0	0	0	0	–
9 yrs.	24	27	.471	4.27	136	55	15	468	489	231	158	3	5	5	1	128	23	0	.180

WORLD SERIES

	W	L	PCT	ERA	G	GS	CG	IP	H	BB	SO	ShO	W	L	SV	AB	H	HR	BA
1953 NY A	1	0	1.000	5.87	1	1	0	7.2	12	1	0	3	0	0	0	2	1	0	.500

John McDonald

McDONALD, JOHN JOSEPH
Born John Joseph McDonnell.
B. Jan. 27, 1883, Throop, Pa.   D. Apr. 9, 1950, Roselle, N. J.

TR 6'1" 170 lbs.

	W	L	PCT	ERA	G	GS	CG	IP	H	BB	SO	ShO	W	L	SV	AB	H	HR	BA
1907 WAS A	0	0	–	9.00	1	0	0	6	12	2	3	0	0	0	0	3	1	0	.333

John McDougal

McDOUGAL, JOHN ARCHANBOLT (Sandy)
B. Feb. 18, 1878, Buffalo, N. Y.   D. Dec. 2, 1910, Buffalo, N. Y.

	W	L	PCT	ERA	G	GS	CG	IP	H	BB	SO	ShO	W	L	SV	AB	H	HR	BA
1895 BKN N	0	0	–	12.00	1	0	0	3	3	5	2	0	0	0	1	1	0	0	.000
1905 STL N	1	4	.200	3.43	5	5	5	44.2	50	12	10	0	0	0	0	15	2	0	.133
2 yrs.	1	4	.200	3.97	6	5	5	47.2	53	17	12	0	0	0	1	16	2	0	.125

	W	L	PCT	ERA	G	GS	CG	IP	H	BB	SO	ShO	Relief Pitching W	L	SV	BATTING AB	H	HR	BA

John McDougal

McDOUGAL, JOHN H.
B. Sept. 19, 1871, Aledo, Ill.   D. Apr. 28, 1936, Galesburg, Ill.

	W	L	PCT	ERA	G	GS	CG	IP	H	BB	SO	ShO	W	L	SV	AB	H	HR	BA
1895 STL N	4	10	.286	8.32	18	14	10	114.2	187	46	23	0	0	1	0	41	6	0	.146
1896	0	1	.000	8.10	3	1	0	10	13	4	0	0	0	0	0	3	0	0	.000
2 yrs.	4	11	.267	8.30	21	15	10	124.2	200	50	23	0	0	1	0	44	6	0	.136

Sam McDowell

McDOWELL, SAMUEL EDWARD (Sudden Sam)   BL TL 6'5"   190 lbs.
B. Sept. 21, 1942, Pittsburgh, Pa.

	W	L	PCT	ERA	G	GS	CG	IP	H	BB	SO	ShO	W	L	SV	AB	H	HR	BA
1961 CLE A	0	0	–	0.00	1	1	0	6.1	3	5	5	0	0	0	0	2	0	0	.000
1962	3	7	.300	6.06	25	13	0	87.2	81	70	70	0	2	0	1	26	4	0	.154
1963	3	5	.375	4.85	14	12	3	65	63	44	63	1	0	0	0	19	4	0	.211
1964	11	6	.647	2.70	31	24	6	173.1	148	100	177	2	2	0	1	56	8	0	.143
1965	17	11	.607	2.18	42	35	14	273	178	132	325	3	1	0	4	95	12	0	.126
1966	9	8	.529	2.87	35	28	8	194.1	130	102	225	5	0	0	3	60	12	0	.200
1967	13	15	.464	3.85	37	37	10	236.1	201	123	236	1	0	0	0	82	15	1	.183
1968	15	14	.517	1.81	38	37	11	269	181	110	283	3	0	0	0	85	13	0	.153
1969	18	14	.563	2.94	39	38	18	285	222	102	279	4	0	0	1	92	16	0	.174
1970	20	12	.625	2.92	39	39	19	305	236	131	304	1	0	0	0	105	13	1	.124
1971	13	17	.433	3.39	35	31	8	215	160	153	192	2	2	0	1	73	13	0	.178
1972 SF N	10	8	.556	4.34	28	25	4	164	155	86	122	0	0	0	0	59	7	0	.119
1973 2 teams			SF	N (18G 1–2)				NY	A (16G 5–8)										
" total	6	10	.375	4.11	34	18	2	135.2	118	93	110	1	0	1	3	12	2	0	.167
1974 NY A	1	6	.143	4.69	13	7	0	48	42	41	33	0	1	1	0	4	0	0	
1975 PIT N	2	1	.667	2.83	14	1	0	35	30	20	29	0	1	0	0	8	0	0	.000
15 yrs.	141	134	.513	3.17	425	346	103	2492.2	1948	1312	2453	23	8	3	14	774	119	2	.154

Jim McElroy

McELROY, JAMES D.
B. 1863, San Francisco, Calif.   D. July 24, 1889, Needles, Calif.

	W	L	PCT	ERA	G	GS	CG	IP	H	BB	SO	ShO	W	L	SV	AB	H	HR	BA
1884 2 teams			PHI	N (13G 1–12)				WIL	U (1G 0–1)										
" total	1	13	.071	5.12	14	14	13	116	125	54	48	0	0	0	0	50	7	0	.140

Will McEnaney

McENANEY, WILLIAM HENRY   BL TL 6'   180 lbs.
B. Feb. 14, 1952, Springfield, Ohio

	W	L	PCT	ERA	G	GS	CG	IP	H	BB	SO	ShO	W	L	SV	AB	H	HR	BA
1974 CIN N	2	1	.667	4.33	24	0	0	27	24	9	13	0	2	1	2	0	0	0	–
1975	5	2	.714	2.47	70	0	0	91	92	23	48	0	5	2	15	14	0	0	.000
1976	2	6	.250	4.88	55	0	0	72	97	23	28	0	2	6	7	6	1	0	.167
1977 MON N	3	5	.375	3.93	69	0	0	87	92	22	38	0	3	5	3	8	0	0	.000
1978 PIT N	0	0	–	10.00	6	0	0	9	15	2	6	0	0	0	0	0	0	0	–
1979 STL N	0	3	.000	2.95	45	0	0	64	60	16	15	0	0	3	2	3	0	0	.000
6 yrs.	12	17	.414	3.75	269	0	0	350	380	95	148	0	12	17	29	31	1	0	.032
LEAGUE CHAMPIONSHIP SERIES																			
1975 CIN N	0	0	–	6.75	1	0	0	1.1	1	0	1	0	0	0	0	0	0	0	–
WORLD SERIES																			
1975 CIN N	0	0	–	2.70	5	0	0	6.2	3	2	5	0	0	0	1	1	1	0	1.000
1976	0	0	–	0.00	2	0	0	4.2	2	1	2	0	0	0	2	0	0	0	–
2 yrs.	0	0	–	1.59	7	0	0	11.1	5	3	7	0	0	0	3	1	1	0	1.000
												4th							

Lou McEvoy

McEVOY, LOUIS ANTHONY   BR TR 6'2½" 203 lbs.
B. May 30, 1902, Williamsburg, Kans.   D. Dec. 17, 1953, Webster Groves, Mo.

	W	L	PCT	ERA	G	GS	CG	IP	H	BB	SO	ShO	W	L	SV	AB	H	HR	BA
1930 NY A	1	3	.250	6.71	28	1	0	52.1	64	29	14	0	1	2	3	16	2	0	.125
1931	0	0	–	12.41	6	0	0	12.1	19	12	3	0	0	0	1	4	0	0	.000
2 yrs.	1	3	.250	7.79	34	1	0	64.2	83	41	17	0	1	2	4	20	2	0	.100

Barney McFadden

McFADDEN, BERNARD JOSEPH   BR TR 6'1"   195 lbs.
B. Feb. 22, 1874, Eckley, Pa.   D. Apr. 28, 1924, Mauch Chunk, Pa.

	W	L	PCT	ERA	G	GS	CG	IP	H	BB	SO	ShO	W	L	SV	AB	H	HR	BA
1901 CIN N	3	3	.500	6.07	8	5	4	46	54	40	11	0	1	1	0	20	3	0	.150
1902 PHI N	0	1	.000	8.00	1	1	1	9	14	7	3	0	0	0	0	3	0	0	.000
2 yrs.	3	4	.429	6.38	9	6	5	55	68	47	14	0	1	1	0	23	3	0	.130

Dan McFarlan

McFARLAN, ANDERSON DANIEL
Brother of Alex McFarlan.
B. Nov. 5, 1873, Gainesville, Tex.   D. Sept. 23, 1924, Louisville, Ky.

	W	L	PCT	ERA	G	GS	CG	IP	H	BB	SO	ShO	W	L	SV	AB	H	HR	BA
1895 LOU N	0	7	.000	6.65	7	7	6	46	80	15	10	0	0	0	0	21	5	0	.238
1899 2 teams			BKN	N (1G 0–0)				WAS	N (32G 8–18)										
" total	8	18	.308	4.67	33	28	22	217.2	274	67	41	1	0	0	0	88	16	0	.182
2 yrs.	8	25	.242	5.02	40	35	28	263.2	354	82	51	1	0	0	0	109	21	0	.193

Chappie McFarland

McFARLAND, CHARLES A.   TR 6'1"
Brother of Monte McFarland.
B. Mar. 13, 1875, White Hill, Ill.   D. Dec. 14, 1924, Houston, Tex.

	W	L	PCT	ERA	G	GS	CG	IP	H	BB	SO	ShO	W	L	SV	AB	H	HR	BA
1902 STL N	0	1	.000	5.73	2	1	1	11	11	3	3	0	0	0	0	4	0	0	.000
1903	9	18	.333	3.07	28	26	25	229	253	48	76	1	0	2	0	74	8	0	.108
1904	14	17	.452	3.21	32	31	28	269.1	266	56	111	1	0	0	0	99	13	0	.131
1905	8	18	.308	3.82	31	28	22	250	281	65	85	3	0	0	1	85	14	0	.165
1906 3 teams			STL	N (6G 2–1)				PIT	N (6G 1–3)					BKN	N (1G 0–1)				
" total	3	5	.375	2.87	13	10	5	81.2	82	20	32	1	0	0	0	31	7	0	.226
5 yrs.	34	59	.366	3.35	106	96	81	841	893	192	307	6	0	2	2	293	42	0	.143

Claude McFarland

McFARLAND, CLAUDE   5'9"   170 lbs.
B. Aug. 17, 1861, Fall River, Mass.   D. May 24, 1918, New Bedford, Mass.

	W	L	PCT	ERA	G	GS	CG	IP	H	BB	SO	ShO	W	L	SV	AB	H	HR	BA
1884 BAL U	0	1	.000	15.00	1	1	1	3	9	1	3	0	0	0	0	*			

Monte McFarland

McFARLAND, LAMONT A.
Brother of Chappie McFarland.
B. 1871   D. Nov. 15, 1913, Peoria, Ill.

	W	L	PCT	ERA	G	GS	CG	IP	H	BB	SO	ShO	W	L	SV	AB	H	HR	BA
1895 CHI N	2	0	1.000	5.14	2	2	2	14	21	5	5	0	0	0	0	7	1	0	.143

	W	L	PCT	ERA	G	GS	CG	IP	H	BB	SO	ShO	Relief Pitching W	L	SV	BATTING AB	H	HR	BA

Doc Medich continued

WORLD SERIES

	W	L	PCT	ERA	G	GS	CG	IP	H	BB	SO	ShO	W	L	SV	AB	H	HR	BA
1982 MIL A	0	0	–	18.00	1	0	0	2	5	1	0	0	0	0	0	0	0	0	–

Irv Medlinger

MEDLINGER, IRVING JOHN   BL TL 5'11"   185 lbs.
B. June 18, 1927, Chicago, Ill.   D. Sept. 3, 1975

	W	L	PCT	ERA	G	GS	CG	IP	H	BB	SO	ShO	W	L	SV	AB	H	HR	BA
1949 STL A	0	0	–	27.00	3	0	0	4	11	3	4	0	0	0	0	0	0	0	–
1951	0	0	–	8.38	6	0	0	9.2	10	12	5	0	0	0	0	0	0	0	–
2 yrs.	0	0	–	13.83	9	0	0	13.2	21	15	9	0	0	0	0	0	0	0	–

Pete Meegan

MEEGAN, PETER J. (Steady Pete)
B. Nov. 13, 1863, San Francisco, Calif.   D. Mar. 15, 1905, San Francisco, Calif.

	W	L	PCT	ERA	G	GS	CG	IP	H	BB	SO	ShO	W	L	SV	AB	H	HR	BA
1884 RIC AA	5	9	.357	4.37	17	17	17	140	140	27	71	1	0	0	0	59	8	0	.136
1885 PIT AA	7	8	.467	3.39	18	16	14	146	146	38	58	1	1	0	0	67	13	0	.194
2 yrs.	12	17	.414	3.87	35	33	31	286	286	65	129	2	1	0	0	126	21	0	.167

Bill Meehan

MEEHAN, WILLIAM THOMAS   BR TR 5'9"   155 lbs.
B. Sept. 3, 1889, Osceola, Pa.   D. Oct. 8, 1982, Douglas, Wyo.

	W	L	PCT	ERA	G	GS	CG	IP	H	BB	SO	ShO	W	L	SV	AB	H	HR	BA
1915 PHI A	0	1	.000	11.25	1	1	0	4	7	3	4	0	0	0	0	1	1	0	1.000

Roy Meeker

MEEKER, CHARLES ROY (Lefty)   BL TL 5'9"   175 lbs.
B. Sept. 15, 1900, Lead Mines, Mo.   D. Mar. 25, 1929, Orlando, Fla.

	W	L	PCT	ERA	G	GS	CG	IP	H	BB	SO	ShO	W	L	SV	AB	H	HR	BA
1923 PHI A	3	0	1.000	3.60	5	2	2	25	24	13	12	0	1	0	0	9	1	0	.111
1924	5	12	.294	4.68	30	14	5	146	166	81	37	1	1	2	0	48	11	0	.229
1926 CIN N	0	2	.000	6.43	7	1	1	21	24	9	5	0	0	1	0	6	0	0	.000
3 yrs.	8	14	.364	4.73	42	17	8	192	214	103	54	1	2	3	0	63	12	0	.190

Jouett Meekin

MEEKIN, JOUETT   BR TR 6'1"   180 lbs.
B. Feb. 21, 1867, New Albany, Ind.   D. Dec. 14, 1944, New Albany, Ind.

	W	L	PCT	ERA	G	GS	CG	IP	H	BB	SO	ShO	W	L	SV	AB	H	HR	BA
1891 LOU AA	10	16	.385	4.30	29	26	25	228	227	113	144	2	0	0	0	97	21	1	.216
1892 2 teams			LOU	N	(19G 7–10)			WAS	N	(14G 3–10)									
" total	10	20	.333	3.79	33	32	30	268.1	280	126	125	1	0	0	0	109	11	2	.101
1893 WAS N	10	15	.400	4.96	31	28	24	245	289	140	91	1	0	0	0	113	29	3	.257
1894 NY N	36	10	.783	3.70	52	48	40	409	404	171	133	1	1	1	2	170	48	5	.282
1895	16	11	.593	5.30	29	29	24	225.2	296	73	76	1	0	0	0	96	28	1	.292
1896	26	14	.650	3.82	42	41	34	334.1	378	127	110	0	0	1	0	144	43	2	.299
1897	20	11	.645	3.76	37	34	30	303.2	328	99	83	2	0	1	0	137	41	0	.299
1898	16	18	.471	3.77	38	37	34	320	329	108	82	1	0	0	0	129	27	0	.209
1899 2 teams			NY	N	(18G 5–11)			BOS	N	(13G 7–6)									
" total	12	17	.414	3.72	31	31	28	256.1	280	93	53	0	0	0	0	99	19	1	.192
1900 PIT N	0	2	.000	6.92	2	2	1	13	20	8	3	0	0	0	0	4	0	0	.000
10 yrs.	156	134	.538	4.07	324	308	270	2603.1	2831	1058	900	9	1	3	2	1098	267	15	.243

Phil Meeler

MEELER, CHARLES PHILIP JR.   BR TR 6'5"   215 lbs.
B. July 23, 1948, South Boston, Va.

	W	L	PCT	ERA	G	GS	CG	IP	H	BB	SO	ShO	W	L	SV	AB	H	HR	BA
1972 DET A	0	1	.000	4.50	7	0	0	8	10	7	5	0	0	1	0	2	0	0	.000

Russ Meers

MEERS, RUSSELL HARLAN (Babe)   BL TL 5'10"   170 lbs.
B. Nov. 28, 1918, Tilton, Ill.

	W	L	PCT	ERA	G	GS	CG	IP	H	BB	SO	ShO	W	L	SV	AB	H	HR	BA
1941 CHI N	0	1	.000	1.13	1	1	0	8	5	0	5	0	0	0	0	2	0	0	.000
1946	1	2	.333	3.18	7	2	0	11.1	10	10	2	0	1	0	0	1	1	0	1.000
1947	2	0	1.000	4.48	35	1	0	64.1	61	38	28	0	2	0	0	14	2	0	.143
3 yrs.	3	3	.500	3.98	43	4	0	83.2	76	48	35	0	3	0	0	17	3	0	.176

Heinie Meine

MEINE, HENRY WILLIAM (The Count of Luxemburg)   BR TR 5'11"   180 lbs.
B. May 1, 1896, St. Louis, Mo.   D. Mar. 18, 1968, St. Louis, Mo.

	W	L	PCT	ERA	G	GS	CG	IP	H	BB	SO	ShO	W	L	SV	AB	H	HR	BA
1922 STL A	0	0	–	4.50	1	0	0	4	5	2	0	0	0	0	0	1	0	0	.000
1929 PIT N	7	6	.538	4.50	22	13	7	108	120	34	19	1	1	1	1	39	4	0	.103
1930	6	8	.429	6.14	20	16	4	117.1	168	44	18	0	0	0	1	41	5	0	.122
1931	19	13	.594	2.98	36	35	22	284	278	87	58	3	0	1	0	96	14	0	.146
1932	12	9	.571	3.86	28	25	13	172.1	193	45	32	1	0	0	1	61	10	0	.164
1933	15	8	.652	3.65	32	29	12	207.1	227	50	50	2	2	0	0	75	13	0	.173
1934	7	6	.538	4.32	26	14	2	106.1	134	25	22	0	3	0	0	28	3	0	.107
7 yrs.	66	50	.569	3.95	165	132	60	999.1	1125	287	199	7	6	2	3	341	49	0	.144

Frank Meinke

MEINKE, FRANK LOUIS   170 lbs.
Father of Bob Meinke.
B. Oct. 18, 1862, Chicago, Ill.   D. Nov. 8, 1931, Chicago, Ill.

	W	L	PCT	ERA	G	GS	CG	IP	H	BB	SO	ShO	W	L	SV	AB	H	HR	BA
1884 DET N	8	22	.267	3.18	35	31	31	289	341	63	124	1	0	1	0	341	56	6	.164
1885	0	1	.000	3.60	1	1	0	5	13	4	0	0	0	0	0	3	0	0	.000
2 yrs.	8	23	.258	3.18	36	32	31	294	354	67	124	1	0	1	0	*			

Sam Mejias

MEJIAS, SAMUEL ELIAS   BR TR 6'   170 lbs.
B. May 9, 1953, Santiago, Dominican Republic

	W	L	PCT	ERA	G	GS	CG	IP	H	BB	SO	ShO	W	L	SV	AB	H	HR	BA
1978 MON N	0	0	–	0.00	1	0	0	2	0	0	0	0	0	0	0	*			

Steve Melter

MELTER, STEPHEN BLASIUS   TR 6'2"   180 lbs.
B. Jan. 2, 1886, Cherokee, Iowa   D. Jan. 28, 1962, Mishawaka, Ind.

	W	L	PCT	ERA	G	GS	CG	IP	H	BB	SO	ShO	W	L	SV	AB	H	HR	BA
1909 STL N	0	1	.000	3.50	23	1	0	64.1	79	20	24	0	0	1	1	15	2	0	.133

Cliff Melton

MELTON, CLIFFORD GEORGE (Mountain Music)   BL TL 6'5½"   203 lbs.
B. Jan. 3, 1912, Brevard, N. C.

	W	L	PCT	ERA	G	GS	CG	IP	H	BB	SO	ShO	W	L	SV	AB	H	HR	BA
1937 NY N	20	9	.690	2.61	46	27	14	248	216	55	142	2	4	1	7	82	10	0	.122
1938	14	14	.500	3.89	36	31	10	243	266	61	101	1	1	0	0	80	14	0	.175
1939	12	15	.444	3.56	41	23	9	207.1	214	65	95	2	3	2	5	66	12	0	.182

	W	L	PCT	ERA	G	GS	CG	IP	H	BB	SO	ShO	Relief Pitching W	L	SV	BATTING AB	H	HR	BA

Cliff Melton continued

1940	10	11	.476	4.91	37	21	4	166.2	185	68	91	1	3	2	2	54	12	0	.222
1941	8	11	.421	3.01	42	22	9	194.1	181	61	100	3	1	1	1	61	7	0	.115
1942	11	5	.688	2.63	23	17	12	143.2	122	33	61	2	0	0	1	47	11	0	.234
1943	9	13	.409	3.19	34	28	6	186.1	184	69	55	2	0	1	0	54	8	0	.148
1944	2	2	.500	4.06	13	10	1	64.1	78	19	15	0	0	0	0	25	3	0	.120
8 yrs.	86	80	.518	3.42	272	179	65	1453.2	1446	431	660	13	12	7	16	469	77	0	.164

WORLD SERIES
1937 NY N	0	2	.000	4.91	3	2	0	11	12	6	7	0	0	0	0	2	0	0	.000

Rube Melton

MELTON, REUBEN FRANKLIN   BR TR 6'5"   205 lbs.
B. Feb. 27, 1917, Cramerton, N. C.   D. Sept. 11, 1971, Greer, S. C.

1941 PHI N	1	5	.167	4.73	25	5	2	83.2	81	47	57	0	1	2	0	19	2	0	.105
1942	9	20	.310	3.70	42	29	10	209.1	180	114	107	1	1	1	4	65	8	1	.123
1943 BKN N	5	8	.385	3.92	30	17	4	119.1	102	79	63	2	1	1	0	38	4	0	.105
1944	9	13	.409	3.46	37	23	6	187.1	178	96	91	1	2	0	0	57	7	0	.123
1946	6	3	.667	1.99	24	12	3	99.2	72	52	44	2	1	1	1	28	3	0	.107
1947	0	1	.000	13.50	4	1	0	4.2	7	7	1	0	0	0	0	1	1	0	1.000
6 yrs.	30	50	.375	3.62	162	87	25	704	620	395	363	6	6	5	5	208	25	1	.120

Mario Mendoza

MENDOZA, MARIO   BR TR 5'11"   170 lbs.
Also known as Mario Alzpuru.
B. Dec. 26, 1950, Chihuahua, Mexico

1977 PIT N	0	0	–	13.50	1	0	0	2	3	2	0	0	0	0	0	*			

Mike Mendoza

MENDOZA, MICHAEL JOSEPH   BR TR 6'5"   215 lbs.
B. Nov. 26, 1955, Inglewood, Calif.

1979 HOU N	0	0	–	0.00	1	0	0	1	0	0	0	0	0	0	0	0	0	0	–

Jock Menefee

MENEFEE, JOHN   BR TR 6'
B. Jan. 16, 1868, West Virginia   D. Mar. 11, 1953, Belle Vernon, Pa.

1892 PIT N	0	0	–	11.25	1	0	0	4	10	2	0	0	0	0	0	3	0	0	.000
1893 LOU N	8	7	.533	4.24	15	15	14	129.1	150	40	30	1	0	0	0	73	20	0	.274
1894 2 teams			LOU	N (28G 8–17)		PIT	N	(13G 5–8)											
" total	13	25	.342	4.68	41	37	33	323.1	417	89	76	1	0	1	0	126	25	0	.198
1895 PIT N	0	1	.000	16.20	2	1	0	1.2	7	2	0	0	0	0	0	0	0	0	–
1898 NY N	0	1	.000	4.82	1	1	1	9.1	11	2	3	0	0	0	0	5	0	0	.000
1900 CHI N	9	4	.692	3.85	16	13	11	117	140	35	30	0	1	0	0	46	5	0	.109
1901	8	13	.381	3.80	21	20	19	182.1	201	34	55	0	0	1	0	152	39	0	.257
1902	12	10	.545	2.42	22	21	20	197.1	202	26	60	5	1	0	0	216	50	0	.231
1903	8	8	.500	3.00	20	17	13	147	157	38	39	1	1	1	0	64	13	0	.203
9 yrs.	58	69	.457	3.81	139	125	111	1111.1	1290	273	293	8	3	3	0	*			

Mike Meola

MEOLA, EMILE MICHAEL   BR TR 5'11"   175 lbs.
B. Oct. 19, 1905, New York, N. Y.   D. Sept. 1, 1976, Fair Lawn, N. J.

1933 BOS A	0	0	–	23.14	3	0	0	2.1	5	2	1	0	0	0	0	0	0	0	–
1936 2 teams			STL	A (9G 0–1)		BOS	A	(6G 0–2)											
" total	0	3	.000	7.30	15	3	1	40.2	58	23	14	0	0	1	1	9	2	0	.222
2 yrs.	0	3	.000	8.16	18	3	1	43	63	25	15	0	0	1	1	9	2	0	.222

John Mercer

MERCER, JOHN LOCKE   BL TL 5'10½"   155 lbs.
B. June 22, 1892, Taylortown, La.   D. Dec. 22, 1982, Shreveport, La.

1912 STL N	0	0	–	0.00	0	0	0	0	0	0	0	0	0	0	0	1	0	0	.000
1 yr.	0	0	–	0.00	1	0	0	2	1	0	0	0	0	0	0	1	0	0	.000

Mark Mercer

MERCER, MARK KENNETH   BL TL 6'5"   220 lbs.
B. May 22, 1951, Fort Bragg, N. C.

1981 TEX A	0	1	.000	4.50	7	0	0	8	7	7	8	0	0	1	2	0	0	0	–

Win Mercer

MERCER, GEORGE BARCLAY   TR 5'7"   140 lbs.
B. June 20, 1874, Chester, W. Va.   D. Jan. 12, 1903, San Francisco, Calif.

1894 WAS N	17	23	.425	3.76	49	38	30	333	431	125	69	0	2	1	3	162	46	2	.284
1895	13	23	.361	4.46	43	38	32	311	430	96	84	0	0	1	2	196	50	1	.255
1896	25	18	.581	4.13	46	45	38	366.1	456	117	94	2	1	0	0	156	38	1	.244
1897	20	20	.500	3.25	45	42	34	332	395	102	88	3	0	1	2	135	43	0	.319
1898	12	18	.400	4.81	33	30	24	233.2	309	71	52	0	0	1	0	249	80	2	.321
1899	7	14	.333	4.60	23	21	21	186	234	53	28	0	0	0	0	375	112	1	.299
1900 NY N	13	17	.433	3.86	32	29	26	242.1	303	58	39	1	0	1	0	248	73	0	.294
1901 WAS A	9	13	.409	4.56	24	22	19	179.2	217	50	31	1	0	0	1	140	42	0	.300
1902 DET A	15	18	.455	3.04	35	33	28	281.2	282	80	40	4	0	0	1	100	18	0	.180
9 yrs.	131	164	.444	3.98	330	298	252	2465.2	3057	752	525	11	3	5	9	*			

Spike Merena

MERENA, JOHN JOSEPH   BL TR 6'   185 lbs.
B. Nov. 18, 1909, Paterson, N. J.   D. Mar. 8, 1977, Bridgeport, Conn.

1934 BOS A	1	2	.333	2.92	4	3	2	24.2	20	16	7	1	0	0	0	7	1	0	.143

Ron Meridith

MERIDITH, RONALD KNOX   BL TL 6'   175 lbs.
B. Nov. 26, 1956, San Pedro, Calif.

1984 CHI N	0	0	–	3.38	3	0	0	5.1	6	2	4	0	0	0	0	0	0	0	–

	W	L	PCT	ERA	G	GS	CG	IP	H	BB	SO	ShO	Relief Pitching W	L	SV	BATTING AB	H	HR	BA

George Merritt

MERRITT, GEORGE WASHINGTON   TR 6'   160 lbs.
B. Apr. 14, 1880, Paterson, N. J.   D. Feb. 21, 1938, Memphis, Tenn.

	W	L	PCT	ERA	G	GS	CG	IP	H	BB	SO	ShO	W	L	SV	AB	H	HR	BA
1901 PIT N	3	0	1.000	4.88	3	3	3	24	28	5	5	0	0	0	0	11	3	0	.273
1903	0	0	–	2.25	1	0	0	4	4	1	2	0	0	0	0	27	4	0	.148
2 yrs.	3	0	1.000	4.50	4	3	3	28	32	6	7	0	0	0	0	*			

Jim Merritt

MERRITT, JAMES JOSEPH   BL TL 6'3"   175 lbs.
B. Dec. 9, 1943, Altadena, Calif.

	W	L	PCT	ERA	G	GS	CG	IP	H	BB	SO	ShO	W	L	SV	AB	H	HR	BA
1965 MIN A	5	4	.556	3.17	16	9	1	76.2	68	20	61	0	1	1	2	22	3	0	.136
1966	7	14	.333	3.38	31	18	5	144	112	33	124	1	0	3	3	39	4	0	.103
1967	13	7	.650	2.53	37	28	11	227.2	196	30	161	4	1	0	0	74	10	0	.135
1968	12	16	.429	3.25	38	34	11	238.1	207	52	181	1	1	0	1	71	10	0	.141
1969 CIN N	17	9	.654	4.37	42	36	8	251	269	61	144	1	0	0	0	77	11	1	.143
1970	20	12	.625	4.08	35	35	12	234	248	53	136	1	0	0	0	83	14	3	.169
1971	1	11	.083	4.37	28	11	0	107	115	31	38	0	1	2	0	29	4	0	.138
1972	1	0	1.000	4.50	4	1	0	8	13	2	4	0	1	0	0	2	0	0	.000
1973 TEX A	5	13	.278	4.05	35	19	8	160	191	34	65	1	0	2	1	0	0	0	–
1974	0	0	–	4.09	26	1	0	33	46	6	18	0	0	1	0	0	0	0	–
1975	0	0	–	0.00	5	0	0	3.2	3	0	0	0	0	0	0	0	0	0	–
11 yrs.	81	86	.485	3.65	297	192	56	1483.1	1468	322	932	9	5	8	7	397	56	4	.141

LEAGUE CHAMPIONSHIP SERIES
	W	L	PCT	ERA	G	GS	CG	IP	H	BB	SO	ShO	W	L	SV	AB	H	HR	BA
1970 CIN N	1	0	1.000	1.69	1	1	0	5.1	3	0	2	0	0	0	0	2	0	0	.000

WORLD SERIES
	W	L	PCT	ERA	G	GS	CG	IP	H	BB	SO	ShO	W	L	SV	AB	H	HR	BA
1965 MIN A	0	0	–	2.70	2	0	0	3.1	2	1	1	0	0	0	0	0	0	0	
1970 CIN N	0	1	.000	21.60	1	1	0	1.2	3	1	0	0	0	0	0	1	0	0	.000
2 yrs.	0	1	.000	9.00	3	1	0	5	5	1	1	0	0	0	0	1	0	0	.000

Lloyd Merritt

MERRITT, LLOYD WESLEY   BR TR 6'   189 lbs.
B. Apr. 8, 1933, St. Louis, Mo.

	W	L	PCT	ERA	G	GS	CG	IP	H	BB	SO	ShO	W	L	SV	AB	H	HR	BA
1957 STL N	1	2	.333	3.31	44	0	0	65.1	60	28	35	0	1	2	7	7	0	0	.000

Sam Mertes

MERTES, SAMUEL BLAIR (Sandow)   BR TR 5'10"   185 lbs.
B. Aug. 6, 1872, San Francisco, Calif.   D. Mar. 11, 1945, San Francisco, Calif.

	W	L	PCT	ERA	G	GS	CG	IP	H	BB	SO	ShO	W	L	SV	AB	H	HR	BA
1902 CHI A	1	0	1.000	1.17	1	0	0	7.2	6	0	0	0	1	0	0	*			

Jim Mertz

MERTZ, JAMES VERLIN   BR TR 5'10½" 170 lbs.
B. Aug. 10, 1916, Lima, Ohio

	W	L	PCT	ERA	G	GS	CG	IP	H	BB	SO	ShO	W	L	SV	AB	H	HR	BA
1943 WAS A	5	7	.417	4.63	33	10	2	116.2	109	58	53	0	2	1	3	38	7	0	.184

Bud Messenger

MESSENGER, ANDREW WARREN   BR TR 6'   175 lbs.
B. Feb. 1, 1898, Grand Blanc, Mich.   D. Nov. 4, 1971, Lansing, Mich.

	W	L	PCT	ERA	G	GS	CG	IP	H	BB	SO	ShO	W	L	SV	AB	H	HR	BA
1924 CLE A	2	0	1.000	4.32	5	2	1	25	28	14	4	0	1	0	0	8	1	0	.125

Andy Messersmith

MESSERSMITH, JOHN ALEXANDER   BR TR 6'1"   200 lbs.
B. Aug. 6, 1945, Toms River, N. J.

	W	L	PCT	ERA	G	GS	CG	IP	H	BB	SO	ShO	W	L	SV	AB	H	HR	BA
1968 CAL A	4	2	.667	2.21	28	5	2	81.1	44	35	74	1	2	0	4	20	2	0	.100
1969	16	11	.593	2.52	40	33	10	250	169	100	211	2	0	0	2	77	12	0	.156
1970	11	10	.524	3.00	37	26	6	195	144	78	162	1	3	0	5	70	11	1	.157
1971	20	13	.606	2.99	38	38	14	277	224	121	179	4	0	0	0	93	16	2	.172
1972	8	11	.421	2.81	25	21	10	170	125	68	142	3	0	0	2	53	10	0	.189
1973 LA N	14	10	.583	2.70	33	33	10	249.2	196	77	177	3	0	0	0	89	15	0	.169
1974	20	6	.769	2.59	39	39	13	292	227	94	221	3	0	0	0	96	23	1	.240
1975	19	14	.576	2.29	42	40	19	322	244	96	213	7	0	0	1	108	17	0	.157
1976 ATL N	11	11	.500	3.04	29	28	12	207	166	74	135	3	0	0	1	67	12	0	.179
1977	5	4	.556	4.41	16	16	1	102	101	39	69	0	0	0	0	34	4	1	.118
1978 NY A	0	3	.000	5.64	6	5	0	22.1	24	15	16	0	0	0	0	0	0	0	–
1979 LA N	2	4	.333	4.94	11	11	1	62	55	34	26	0	0	0	0	22	2	0	.091
12 yrs.	130	99	.568	2.86	344	295	98	2230.1	1719	831	1625	27	5	0	15	729	124	5	.170

LEAGUE CHAMPIONSHIP SERIES
	W	L	PCT	ERA	G	GS	CG	IP	H	BB	SO	ShO	W	L	SV	AB	H	HR	BA
1974 LA N	1	0	1.000	2.57	1	1	1	7	8	3	0	0	0	0	0	3	0	0	.000

WORLD SERIES
	W	L	PCT	ERA	G	GS	CG	IP	H	BB	SO	ShO	W	L	SV	AB	H	HR	BA
1974 LA N	0	2	.000	4.50	2	2	0	14	11	7	12	0	0	0	0	4	2	0	.500

Tom Metcalf

METCALF, THOMAS JOHN   BR TR 6'2½" 174 lbs.
B. July 16, 1940, Amherst, Wis.

	W	L	PCT	ERA	G	GS	CG	IP	H	BB	SO	ShO	W	L	SV	AB	H	HR	BA
1963 NY A	1	0	1.000	2.77	8	0	0	13	12	3	3	0	1	0	0	0	0	0	–

Dewey Metivier

METIVIER, GEORGE DEWEY   BB TR 5'11"   175 lbs.
B. May 6, 1898, Cambridge, Mass.   BL 1922
D. Mar. 2, 1947, Cambridge, Mass.

	W	L	PCT	ERA	G	GS	CG	IP	H	BB	SO	ShO	W	L	SV	AB	H	HR	BA
1922 CLE A	2	0	1.000	4.50	2	2	2	18	18	3	1	0	0	0	0	6	1	0	.167
1923	4	2	.667	6.50	26	5	1	73.1	111	38	9	0	3	1	1	20	3	0	.150
1924	1	5	.167	5.31	26	6	1	76.1	110	34	14	0	1	1	3	24	3	0	.125
3 yrs.	7	7	.500	5.74	54	13	4	167.2	239	75	24	0	4	2	4	50	7	0	.140

Butch Metzger

METZGER, CLARENCE EDWARD   BR TR 6'1"   185 lbs.
B. May 23, 1952, Lafayette, Ind.

	W	L	PCT	ERA	G	GS	CG	IP	H	BB	SO	ShO	W	L	SV	AB	H	HR	BA
1974 SF N	1	0	1.000	3.46	10	0	0	13	11	12	5	0	1	0	0	0	0	0	–
1975 SD N	1	0	1.000	7.20	4	0	0	5	6	4	6	0	1	0	0	0	0	0	–
1976	11	4	.733	2.92	77	0	0	123.1	119	52	89	0	11	4	16	8	0	0	.000
1977 2 teams		SD	N (17G 0-0)			STL	N	(58G 4-2)											
" total	4	2	.667	3.59	75	1	0	115.1	105	50	54	0	4	2	7	7	0	0	.000
1978 NY N	1	3	.250	6.57	25	0	0	37	48	22	21	0	1	3	0	0	0	0	–
5 yrs.	18	9	.667	3.74	191	1	0	293.2	289	140	175	0	18	9	23	15	0	0	.000

	W	L	PCT	ERA	G	GS	CG	IP	H	BB	SO	ShO	Relief Pitching W	L	SV	BATTING AB	H	HR	BA

Bob Meyer

MEYER, ROBERT BERNARD
B. Aug. 4, 1939, Toledo, Ohio
BR TL 6'2" 185 lbs.

	W	L	PCT	ERA	G	GS	CG	IP	H	BB	SO	ShO	W	L	SV	AB	H	HR	BA
1964 **3 teams**			**NY**	**A** (7G 0-3)		**LA**	**A** (6G 1-1)		**KC**	**A**	(9G 1-4)								
" total	2	8	.200	4.37	22	13	2	78.1	78	58	55	0	0	2	0	21	0	0	.000
1969 SEA A	0	3	.000	3.31	6	5	1	32.2	30	10	17	0	0	0	0	11	1	0	.091
1970 MIL A	0	1	.000	6.50	10	0	0	18	24	12	20	0	0	0	0	3	1	0	.333
3 yrs.	2	12	.143	4.40	38	18	3	129	132	80	92	0	0	2	0	35	2	0	.057

Jack Meyer

MEYER, JOHN ROBERT
B. Mar. 23, 1932, Philadelphia, Pa.   D. Mar. 9, 1967, Philadelphia, Pa.
BR TR 6'1" 175 lbs.

	W	L	PCT	ERA	G	GS	CG	IP	H	BB	SO	ShO	W	L	SV	AB	H	HR	BA
1955 PHI N	6	11	.353	3.43	50	5	0	110.1	75	66	97	0	5	7	16	20	2	0	.100
1956	7	11	.389	4.41	41	7	2	96	86	51	66	0	6	6	2	20	4	1	.200
1957	0	2	.000	5.73	19	2	0	37.2	44	28	34	0	0	2	0	6	1	0	.167
1958	3	6	.333	3.59	37	5	1	90.1	77	33	87	0	3	2	2	18	5	0	.278
1959	5	3	.625	3.36	47	1	1	93.2	76	53	71	0	5	2	1	14	1	0	.071
1960	3	1	.750	4.32	7	4	0	25	25	11	18	0	1	0	0	8	1	0	.125
1961	0	0	–	9.00	1	0	0	2	2	2	2	0	0	0	0	0	0	0	–
7 yrs.	24	34	.414	3.92	202	24	4	455	385	244	375	0	20	19	21	86	14	1	.163

Russ Meyer

MEYER, RUSSELL CHARLES (The Mad Monk)
B. Oct. 25, 1923, Peru, Ill.
BB TR 6'1" 175 lbs.

	W	L	PCT	ERA	G	GS	CG	IP	H	BB	SO	ShO	W	L	SV	AB	H	HR	BA
1946 CHI N	0	0	–	3.18	4	1	0	17	21	10	10	0	0	0	1	5	1	0	.200
1947	3	2	.600	3.40	23	2	1	45	43	14	22	0	3	1	0	12	3	0	.250
1948	10	10	.500	3.66	29	26	8	164.2	157	77	89	3	0	2	0	56	6	0	.107
1949 PHI N	17	8	.680	3.08	37	28	14	213	199	70	78	2	2	1	1	70	10	0	.143
1950	9	11	.450	5.30	32	25	3	159.2	193	67	74	0	1	1	1	50	7	0	.140
1951	8	9	.471	3.48	28	24	7	168	172	55	65	2	0	1	0	48	5	0	.104
1952	13	14	.481	3.14	37	32	14	232.1	235	65	92	1	0	1	0	79	7	1	.089
1953 BKN N	15	5	.750	4.56	34	32	10	191.1	201	63	106	2	0	1	0	75	11	0	.147
1954	11	6	.647	3.99	36	28	6	180.1	193	49	70	2	0	0	0	47	2	0	.043
1955	6	2	.750	5.42	18	11	2	73	86	31	26	1	1	1	0	27	1	0	.037
1956 **2 teams**			**CHI**	**N** (20G 1-6)				**CIN**	**N**	(1G 0-0)									
" total	1	6	.143	6.21	21	9	0	58	72	26	29	0	0	0	0	12	1	0	.083
1957 BOS A	0	0	–	5.40	2	1	0	5	10	3	1	0	0	0	0	1	1	0	1.000
1959 KC A	1	0	1.000	4.50	18	0	0	24	24	11	10	0	1	0	1	2	0	0	.000
13 yrs.	94	73	.563	3.99	319	219	65	1531.1	1606	541	672	13	7	10	5	484	55	1	.114

WORLD SERIES																			
1950 PHI N	0	1	.000	5.40	2	0	0	1.2	4	0	1	0	0	1	0	0	0	0	–
1953 BKN N	0	0	–	6.23	1	0	0	4.1	8	4	5	0	0	0	0	1	0	0	.000
1955	0	0	–	0.00	1	0	0	5.2	4	2	4	0	0	0	0	2	0	0	.000
3 yrs.	0	1	.000	3.09	4	0	0	11.2	16	6	10	0	0	1	0	3	0	0	.000

Levi Meyerle

MEYERLE, LEVI SAMUEL (Long Levi)
B. 1849, Philadelphia, Pa.   D. Nov. 4, 1921, Philadelphia, Pa.
BR TR 6'1" 177 lbs.

	W	L	PCT	ERA	G	GS	CG	IP	H	BB	SO	ShO	W	L	SV	AB	H	HR	BA
1876 PHI N	0	2	.000	5.00	2	2	2	18	28	1	0	0	0	0	0	*			

Gene Michael

MICHAEL, GENE RICHARD (Stick)
B. June 2, 1938, Kent, Ohio
Manager 1981-82.
BB TR 6'2" 183 lbs.

	W	L	PCT	ERA	G	GS	CG	IP	H	BB	SO	ShO	W	L	SV	AB	H	HR	BA
1968 NY A	0	0	–	0.00	1	0	0	3	5	0	3	0	0	0	0	*			

John Michaels

MICHAELS, JOHN JOSEPH
B. July 10, 1907, Bridgeport, Conn.
BL TL 5'10½" 154 lbs.

	W	L	PCT	ERA	G	GS	CG	IP	H	BB	SO	ShO	W	L	SV	AB	H	HR	BA
1932 BOS A	1	6	.143	5.13	28	8	2	80.2	101	27	16	0	0	0	0	21	3	0	.143

John Michaelson

MICHAELSON, JOHN AUGUST (Mike)
B. Aug. 12, 1893, Tivalkoski, Finland   D. Apr. 16, 1968, Woodruff, Wis.
BR TR 5'9" 165 lbs.

	W	L	PCT	ERA	G	GS	CG	IP	H	BB	SO	ShO	W	L	SV	AB	H	HR	BA
1921 CHI A	0	0	–	10.13	2	0	0	2.2	4	1	1	0	0	0	0	0	0	0	–

Glenn Mickens

MICKENS, GLENN ROGER
B. July 26, 1930, Wilmar, Calif.
BR TR 6' 175 lbs.

	W	L	PCT	ERA	G	GS	CG	IP	H	BB	SO	ShO	W	L	SV	AB	H	HR	BA
1953 BKN N	0	1	.000	11.37	4	2	0	6.1	11	4	5	0	0	0	0	2	0	0	.000

Jim Middleton

MIDDLETON, JAMES BLAINE (Rifle Jim)
B. May 28, 1899, Argos, Ind.   D. Jan. 12, 1974, Argos, Ind.
BR TR 5'11½" 165 lbs.

	W	L	PCT	ERA	G	GS	CG	IP	H	BB	SO	ShO	W	L	SV	AB	H	HR	BA
1917 NY N	1	1	.500	2.75	13	0	0	36	35	8	9	0	1	1	1	8	0	0	.000
1921 DET A	6	11	.353	5.03	38	10	2	121.2	149	44	31	0	4	8	7	34	5	0	.147
2 yrs.	7	12	.368	4.51	51	10	2	157.2	184	52	40	0	5	9	8	42	5	0	.119

John Middleton

MIDDLETON, JOHN WAYNE (Lefty)
B. Apr. 11, 1900, Mt. Calm, Tex.
BL TL 6'1" 185 lbs.

	W	L	PCT	ERA	G	GS	CG	IP	H	BB	SO	ShO	W	L	SV	AB	H	HR	BA
1922 CLE A	0	1	.000	7.36	2	1	0	7.1	8	6	2	0	0	0	0	3	1	0	.333

Dick Midkiff

MIDKIFF, RICHARD JAMES
B. Sept. 28, 1914, Gonzales, Tex.   D. Oct. 30, 1956, Temple, Tex.
BR TR 6'2" 195 lbs.

	W	L	PCT	ERA	G	GS	CG	IP	H	BB	SO	ShO	W	L	SV	AB	H	HR	BA
1938 BOS A	1	1	.500	5.09	13	2	0	35.1	43	21	10	0	1	0	0	10	2	0	.200

Pete Mikkelsen

MIKKELSEN, PETER JAMES
B. Oct. 25, 1939, Staten Island, N. Y.
BR TR 6'2" 210 lbs.

	W	L	PCT	ERA	G	GS	CG	IP	H	BB	SO	ShO	W	L	SV	AB	H	HR	BA
1964 NY A	7	4	.636	3.56	50	0	0	86	79	41	63	0	7	4	12	16	1	0	.063
1965	4	9	.308	3.28	41	3	0	82.1	78	36	69	0	4	6	1	10	1	0	.100
1966 PIT N	9	8	.529	3.07	71	0	0	126	106	51	76	0	9	8	14	20	3	0	.150
1967 **2 teams**			**PIT**	**N** (32G 1-2)		**CHI**	**N**	(7G 0-0)											
" total	1	2	.333	4.55	39	0	0	63.1	59	24	30	0	1	2	2	4	0	0	.000

	W	L	PCT	ERA	G	GS	CG	IP	H	BB	SO	ShO	Relief Pitching W	L	SV	BATTING AB	H	HR	BA

Pete Mikkelsen continued

	W	L	PCT	ERA	G	GS	CG	IP	H	BB	SO	ShO	W	L	SV	AB	H	HR	BA
1968 2 teams	CHI	N	(3G 0–0)			STL	N	(5G 0–0)											
" total	0	0	–	2.61	8	0	0	20.2	17	8	13	0	0	0	0	4	1	0	.250
1969 LA N	7	5	.583	2.78	48	0	0	81	57	30	51	0	7	5	4	6	1	0	.167
1970	4	2	.667	2.76	33	0	0	62	48	20	47	0	4	2	6	6	2	0	.333
1971	8	5	.615	3.65	41	0	0	74	67	17	46	0	8	5	5	10	2	0	.200
1972	5	5	.500	4.06	33	0	0	57.2	65	23	41	0	5	5	5	7	0	0	.000
9 yrs.	45	40	.529	3.38	364	3	0	653	576	250	436	0	45	37	49	83	11	0	.133
WORLD SERIES																			
1964 NY A	0	1	.000	5.79	4	0	0	4.2	4	2	4	0	0	1	0	0	0	0	–

John Miklos

MIKLOS, JOHN JOSEPH (Hank)
B. Nov. 27, 1910, Chicago, Ill.   BL TL 5'11" 185 lbs.

	W	L	PCT	ERA	G	GS	CG	IP	H	BB	SO	ShO	W	L	SV	AB	H	HR	BA
1944 CHI N	0	0	–	7.71	2	0	0	7	9	3	0	0	0	0	0	2	0	0	.000

Carl Miles

MILES, CARL THOMAS
B. Mar. 22, 1918, Trenton, Mo.   BB TL 5'11" 178 lbs.

	W	L	PCT	ERA	G	GS	CG	IP	H	BB	SO	ShO	W	L	SV	AB	H	HR	BA
1940 PHI A	0	0	–	13.50	2	0	0	8	9	8	6	0	0	0	0	4	3	0	.750

Jim Miles

MILES, JAMES CHARLIE
B. Aug. 8, 1943, Grenada, Miss.   BR TR 6'2" 210 lbs.

	W	L	PCT	ERA	G	GS	CG	IP	H	BB	SO	ShO	W	L	SV	AB	H	HR	BA
1968 WAS A	0	0	–	12.46	3	0	0	4.1	8	2	5	0	0	0	0	0	0	0	–
1969	0	1	.000	6.20	10	1	0	20.1	19	15	15	0	0	0	0	3	1	0	.333
2 yrs.	0	1	.000	7.30	13	1	0	24.2	27	17	20	0	0	0	0	3	1	0	.333

Johnny Miljus

MILJUS, JOHN KENNETH (Big Serb)
B. June 30, 1895, Pittsburgh, Pa.   D. Feb. 11, 1976, Polson, Mont.   BR TR 6'1" 178 lbs.

	W	L	PCT	ERA	G	GS	CG	IP	H	BB	SO	ShO	W	L	SV	AB	H	HR	BA
1915 PIT F	0	0	–	0.00	1	0	0	1	1	0	0	0	0	0	0	0	0	0	–
1917 BKN N	0	1	.000	0.60	4	1	1	15	14	8	9	0	0	0	0	5	0	0	.000
1920	1	0	1.000	3.09	9	0	0	23.1	24	4	9	0	1	0	0	6	2	0	.333
1921	6	3	.667	4.23	28	9	3	93.2	115	27	37	0	2	0	1	30	5	0	.167
1927 PIT N	8	3	.727	1.90	19	6	3	75.2	62	17	24	2	4	1	0	28	5	0	.179
1928 2 teams	PIT	N	(21G 5–7)			CLE	A	(11G 1–4)											
" total	6	11	.353	4.19	32	14	4	120.1	136	53	45	0	3	2	2	41	11	0	.268
1929 CLE A	8	8	.500	5.19	34	15	4	128.1	174	64	42	0	4	1	2	43	11	0	.256
7 yrs.	29	26	.527	3.92	127	45	15	457.1	526	173	166	2	14	4	5	153	34	0	.222
WORLD SERIES																			
1927 PIT N	0	1	.000	1.35	2	0	0	6.2	4	4	6	0	0	1	0	2	0	0	.000

Bill Miller

MILLER, WILLIAM FRANCIS (Wild Bill)
B. Apr. 12, 1910, Hannibal, Mo.   D. Feb. 26, 1982, Hannibal, Mo.   BR TR 6' 180 lbs.

	W	L	PCT	ERA	G	GS	CG	IP	H	BB	SO	ShO	W	L	SV	AB	H	HR	BA
1937 STL A	0	1	.000	13.50	1	1	0	4	7	4	1	0	0	0	0	1	0	0	.000

Bill Miller

MILLER, WILLIAM PAUL (Hooks)
B. July 26, 1926, Minersville, Pa.   BL TL 6' 175 lbs.

	W	L	PCT	ERA	G	GS	CG	IP	H	BB	SO	ShO	W	L	SV	AB	H	HR	BA
1952 NY A	4	6	.400	3.48	21	13	5	88	78	49	45	2	0	1	0	28	6	0	.214
1953	2	1	.667	4.76	13	3	0	34	46	19	17	0	1	0	1	10	2	0	.200
1954	0	1	.000	6.35	2	1	0	5.2	9	1	6	0	0	0	0	1	0	0	.000
1955 BAL A	0	1	.000	13.50	5	1	0	4	3	10	4	0	0	0	0	1	1	0	1.000
4 yrs.	6	9	.400	4.24	41	18	5	131.2	136	79	72	2	1	1	1	40	9	0	.225

Bob Miller

MILLER, ROBERT GERALD
B. July 15, 1935, Berwyn, Ill.   BR TL 6'1" 185 lbs.

	W	L	PCT	ERA	G	GS	CG	IP	H	BB	SO	ShO	W	L	SV	AB	H	HR	BA
1953 DET A	1	2	.333	5.94	13	1	0	36.1	43	21	9	0	1	1	0	8	1	0	.125
1954	1	1	.500	2.45	32	1	0	69.2	62	26	27	0	1	1	1	15	2	0	.133
1955	2	1	.667	2.49	7	3	1	25.1	26	12	11	0	0	0	0	9	2	0	.222
1956	0	2	.000	5.68	11	3	0	31.2	37	22	16	0	0	0	0	7	1	0	.143
1962 2 teams	CIN	N	(6G 0–0)			NY	N	(17G 2–2)											
" total	2	2	.500	10.17	23	0	0	25.2	38	11	12	0	2	2	0	2	0	0	.000
5 yrs.	6	8	.429	4.72	86	8	1	188.2	206	92	75	0	4	4	1	41	6	0	.146

Bob Miller

MILLER, ROBERT JOHN
B. June 16, 1926, Detroit, Mich.   BR TR 6'3" 190 lbs.

	W	L	PCT	ERA	G	GS	CG	IP	H	BB	SO	ShO	W	L	SV	AB	H	HR	BA
1949 PHI N	0	0	–	0.00	3	0	0	2.2	2	2	0	0	0	0	0	0	0	0	–
1950	11	6	.647	3.57	35	22	7	174	190	57	44	2	0	0	1	61	11	0	.180
1951	2	1	.667	6.82	17	3	0	34.1	47	18	10	0	1	1	0	7	3	0	.429
1952	0	1	.000	6.00	3	1	0	9	13	1	2	0	0	0	0	1	0	0	.000
1953	8	9	.471	4.00	35	20	8	157.1	169	42	63	3	2	1	2	55	10	0	.182
1954	7	9	.438	4.56	30	16	5	150	176	39	42	0	4	1	0	50	8	1	.160
1955	8	4	.667	2.41	40	6	0	89.2	80	28	28	0	8	4	1	18	5	0	.278
1956	3	6	.333	3.24	49	6	3	122.1	115	34	53	1	1	4	5	22	2	0	.091
1957	2	5	.286	2.69	32	1	0	60.1	61	17	12	0	2	5	6	8	2	1	.250
1958	1	1	.500	11.69	17	0	0	22.1	36	9	9	0	1	1	0	1	0	0	.000
10 yrs.	42	42	.500	3.96	261	69	23	822	889	247	263	6	19	17	15	223	41	2	.184
WORLD SERIES																			
1950 PHI N	0	1	.000	27.00	1	1	0	.1	2	0	0	0	0	0	0	0	0	0	–

Bob Miller

MILLER, ROBERT LANE
B. Feb. 18, 1939, St. Louis, Mo.   BR TR 6'1" 180 lbs.

	W	L	PCT	ERA	G	GS	CG	IP	H	BB	SO	ShO	W	L	SV	AB	H	HR	BA
1957 STL N	0	0	–	7.00	5	0	0	9	13	5	7	0	0	0	0	0	0	0	–
1959	4	3	.571	3.31	11	10	3	70.2	66	21	43	0	0	0	0	24	5	0	.208
1960	4	3	.571	3.42	15	7	0	52.2	53	17	33	0	1	0	0	14	2	0	.143
1961	1	3	.250	4.24	34	5	0	74.1	82	46	39	0	1	1	3	14	5	0	.357
1962 NY N	1	12	.077	4.89	33	21	0	143.2	146	62	91	0	0	1	1	41	5	0	.122
1963 LA N	10	8	.556	2.89	42	23	2	187	171	65	125	0	4	2	1	57	4	0	.070

	W	L	PCT	ERA	G	GS	CG	IP	H	BB	SO	ShO	Relief Pitching W	L	SV	AB	BATTING H	HR	BA

Bob Miller continued

	W	L	PCT	ERA	G	GS	CG	IP	H	BB	SO	ShO	W	L	SV	AB	H	HR	BA
1964	7	7	.500	2.62	74	2	0	137.2	115	63	94	0	6	7	9	19	3	0	.158
1965	6	7	.462	2.97	61	1	0	103	82	26	77	0	6	6	9	16	0	0	.000
1966	4	2	.667	2.77	46	0	0	84.1	70	29	58	0	4	2	5	13	1	0	.077
1967	2	9	.182	4.31	52	4	0	85.2	88	27	32	0	2	6	0	8	1	0	.125
1968 MIN A	0	3	.000	2.74	45	0	0	72.1	65	24	41	0	0	3	2	7	1	0	.143
1969	5	5	.500	3.02	48	11	1	119.1	118	32	57	0	0	4	3	31	0	0	.000
1970 3 teams			CLE A (15G 2-2)		CHI N (7G 0-0)			CHI A (15G 4-6)											
" total	6	8	.429	4.79	37	15	0	107	129	54	55	0	2	0	3	28	5	0	.179
1971 3 teams			CHI N (2G 0-0)		SD N (38G 7-3)			PIT N (16G 1-2)											
" total	8	5	.615	1.64	56	0	0	98.2	83	40	51	0	8	5	10	12	0	0	.000
1972 PIT N	5	2	.714	2.65	36	0	0	54.1	54	24	18	0	5	2	3	4	0	0	.000
1973 3 teams			DET A (22G 4-2)		SD N (18G 0-0)			NY N (1G 0-0)											
" total	4	2	.667	3.67	41	0	0	73.2	63	34	39	0	4	2	1	2	0	0	.000
1974 NY N	2	2	.500	3.58	58	0	0	78	89	39	35	0	2	2	2	9	1	0	.111
17 yrs.	69	81	.460	3.37	694	99	7	1551.1	1487	608	895	0	45	43	52	299	33	0	.110

LEAGUE CHAMPIONSHIP SERIES

	W	L	PCT	ERA	G	GS	CG	IP	H	BB	SO	ShO	W	L	SV	AB	H	HR	BA
1969 MIN A	0	1	.000	5.40	1	1	0	1.2	5	0	0	0	0	0	0	0	0	0	–
1971 PIT N	0	0	–	6.00	1	0	0	3	3	3	3	0	0	0	0	1	0	0	.000
1972	0	0	–	0.00	1	0	0	1	0	0	1	0	0	0	0	0	0	0	–
3 yrs.	0	1	.000	4.76	3	1	0	5.2	8	3	4	0	0	0	0	1	0	0	.000

WORLD SERIES

	W	L	PCT	ERA	G	GS	CG	IP	H	BB	SO	ShO	W	L	SV	AB	H	HR	BA
1965 LA N	0	0	–	0.00	2	0	0	1.1	0	0	0	0	0	0	0	0	0	0	–
1966	0	0	–	0.00	1	0	0	3	2	1	0	0	0	0	0	0	0	0	–
1971 PIT N	0	1	.000	3.86	3	0	0	4.2	7	1	2	0	0	0	0	0	0	0	–
3 yrs.	0	1	.000	2.00	6	0	0	9	9	3	3	0	0	0	0	0	0	0	–

Bob Miller

MILLER, ROBERT W.
B. 1862. Deceased.

	W	L	PCT	ERA	G	GS	CG	IP	H	BB	SO	ShO	W	L	SV	AB	H	HR	BA
1890 ROC AA	3	7	.300	4.29	13	12	11	92.1	89	26	20	0	0	0	1	40	6	0	.150
1891 WAS AA	2	5	.286	4.29	7	7	3	42	53	24	13	0	0	0	0	18	2	0	.111
2 yrs.	5	12	.294	4.29	20	19	14	134.1	142	50	33	0	0	0	1	58	8	0	.138

Burt Miller

MILLER, BURT
B. Kalamazoo, Mich. Deceased.

	W	L	PCT	ERA	G	GS	CG	IP	H	BB	SO	ShO	W	L	SV	AB	H	HR	BA
1897 LOU N	0	1	.000	7.94	4	1	1	17	32	3	3	0	0	0	0	6	1	0	.167

Cyclone Miller

MILLER, JOSEPH H.
B. Sept. 24, 1859, Springfield, Mass. D. Oct. 13, 1916, New London, Conn.   TL 5'9½" 165 lbs.

	W	L	PCT	ERA	G	GS	CG	IP	H	BB	SO	ShO	W	L	SV	AB	H	HR	BA
1884 3 teams			C-P U (1G 1-0)		PRO N (6G 2-2)			PHI N (1G 0-1)											
" total	3	3	.500	3.25	8	7	4	52.2	57	17	26	0	0	1	0	31	2	0	.065
1886 PHI AA	10	8	.556	2.97	19	19	19	169.2	158	59	99	1	0	0	0	66	9	0	.136
2 yrs.	13	11	.542	3.04	27	26	23	222.1	215	76	125	1	0	1	0	97	11	0	.113

Dyar Miller

MILLER, DYAR K
B. May 29, 1946, Batesville, Ind.   BR TR 6'1" 195 lbs.

	W	L	PCT	ERA	G	GS	CG	IP	H	BB	SO	ShO	W	L	SV	AB	H	HR	BA
1975 BAL A	6	3	.667	2.72	30	0	0	46.1	32	16	33	0	6	3	8	0	0	0	–
1976	2	4	.333	2.93	49	0	0	89	79	36	37	0	2	4	7	0	0	0	–
1977 2 teams			BAL A (12G 2-2)		CAL A (41G 4-4)														
" total	6	6	.500	3.53	53	0	0	114.2	106	40	58	0	6	6	5	0	0	0	–
1978 CAL A	6	2	.750	2.66	41	0	0	84.2	85	41	34	0	6	2	1	0	0	0	–
1979 2 teams			CAL A (14G 1-0)		TOR A (10G 0-0)														
" total	1	0	1.000	5.58	24	1	0	50	71	18	23	0	1	0	0	1	0	0	.000
1980 NY N	1	2	.333	1.93	31	0	0	42	37	11	28	0	1	2	1	1	0	0	.000
1981	1	0	1.000	3.32	23	0	0	38	49	15	22	0	1	0	0	3	1	0	.333
7 yrs.	23	17	.575	3.23	251	1	0	464.2	459	177	235	0	23	17	22	4	1	0	.250

Elmer Miller

MILLER, ELMER LeROY
B. Apr. 17, 1904, Detroit, Mich.   BL TL 5'11" 185 lbs.

	W	L	PCT	ERA	G	GS	CG	IP	H	BB	SO	ShO	W	L	SV	AB	H	HR	BA
1929 PHI N	0	1	.000	11.12	8	2	0	11.1	12	21	5	0	0	0	0	*			

Frank Miller

MILLER, FRANK LEE (Bullet)
B. Mar. 13, 1886, Salem, Mich. D. Feb. 19, 1974, Allegan, Mich.   BR TR 6' 188 lbs.

	W	L	PCT	ERA	G	GS	CG	IP	H	BB	SO	ShO	W	L	SV	AB	H	HR	BA
1913 CHI A	0	1	.000	27.00	1	1	0	1.2	4	3	2	0	0	0	0	0	0	0	–
1916 PIT N	7	10	.412	2.29	30	20	10	173	135	49	88	2	0	2	1	51	7	0	.137
1917	10	19	.345	3.13	38	28	14	224	216	60	92	5	1	2	1	76	9	0	.118
1918	11	8	.579	2.38	23	23	14	170.1	152	37	47	2	0	0	0	57	6	0	.105
1919	13	12	.520	3.03	32	26	16	201.2	170	34	59	3	0	0	0	66	7	0	.106
1922 BOS N	11	13	.458	3.51	31	23	14	200	213	60	65	2	2	1	1	68	8	0	.118
1923	0	3	.000	4.58	8	6	0	39.1	54	11	6	0	0	0	1	7	1	0	.143
7 yrs.	52	66	.441	3.01	163	127	68	1010	944	254	359	14	3	5	4	325	38	0	.117

Fred Miller

MILLER, FREDERICK HOLMAN (Speedy)
B. June 28, 1886, Fairfield, Ind. D. May 2, 1953, Brookville, Ind.   BL TL 6'2" 190 lbs.

	W	L	PCT	ERA	G	GS	CG	IP	H	BB	SO	ShO	W	L	SV	AB	H	HR	BA
1910 BKN N	1	1	.500	4.71	6	2	0	21	25	13	2	0	0	0	0	8	2	0	.250

Henry Miller

MILLER, HENRY D.
Deceased.

	W	L	PCT	ERA	G	GS	CG	IP	H	BB	SO	ShO	W	L	SV	AB	H	HR	BA
1892 CHI N	1	1	.500	6.38	4	2	2	24	29	16	15	0	0	0	0	10	3	0	.300

Jake Miller

MILLER, WALTER JACOB
Brother of Russ Miller.
B. Feb. 28, 1898, Wagram, Ohio D. Aug. 20, 1975, Venice, Fla.   BL TL 6'1" 185 lbs.

	W	L	PCT	ERA	G	GS	CG	IP	H	BB	SO	ShO	W	L	SV	AB	H	HR	BA
1924 CLE A	0	1	.000	3.00	2	2	1	12	13	5	4	0	0	0	0	5	0	0	.000
1925	10	13	.435	3.31	32	22	13	190.1	207	62	51	0	2	2	2	71	13	0	.183

	W	L	PCT	ERA	G	GS	CG	IP	H	BB	SO	ShO	Relief Pitching W	L	SV	BATTING AB	H	HR	BA

Jake Miller continued

	W	L	PCT	ERA	G	GS	CG	IP	H	BB	SO	ShO	W	L	SV	AB	H	HR	BA
1926	7	4	.636	3.27	18	11	5	82.2	99	18	24	3	2	0	1	24	2	0	.083
1927	10	8	.556	3.21	34	23	11	185.1	189	48	53	0	0	1	0	58	8	0	.138
1928	8	9	.471	4.44	25	23	8	158	203	43	37	0	0	0	0	52	7	0	.135
1929	14	12	.538	3.58	29	29	14	206	227	60	58	2	0	0	0	75	15	0	.200
1930	4	5	.444	7.13	24	9	1	88.1	147	38	31	0	2	0	0	33	10	0	.303
1931	2	1	.667	4.35	10	5	1	41.1	45	19	17	1	1	0	0	13	1	0	.077
1933 CHI A	5	6	.455	5.62	26	14	4	105.2	130	47	30	2	0	1	0	37	7	0	.189
9 yrs.	60	59	.504	4.09	200	138	58	1069.2	1260	340	305	8	7	4	3	368	63	0	.171

John Miller

MILLER, JOHN ERNEST
B. May 30, 1941, Baltimore, Md.   BR TR 6'2"   210 lbs.

	W	L	PCT	ERA	G	GS	CG	IP	H	BB	SO	ShO	W	L	SV	AB	H	HR	BA
1962 BAL A	1	1	.500	0.90	2	1	0	10	2	5	4	0	1	0	0	3	0	0	.000
1963	1	1	.500	3.18	3	2	0	17	12	14	16	0	0	0	0	6	0	0	.000
1965	6	4	.600	3.18	16	16	1	93.1	75	58	71	0	0	0	0	30	3	0	.100
1966	4	8	.333	4.74	23	16	0	100.2	92	58	81	0	2	1	0	34	4	0	.118
1967	0	0	–	7.50	2	0	0	6	7	3	6	0	0	0	0	0	0	0	–
5 yrs.	12	14	.462	3.89	46	35	1	227	188	138	178	0	3	1	0	73	7	0	.096

Ken Miller

MILLER, KENNETH ALBERT (Whitey)
B. May 2, 1915, St. Louis, Mo.   BR TR 6'1"   195 lbs.

	W	L	PCT	ERA	G	GS	CG	IP	H	BB	SO	ShO	W	L	SV	AB	H	HR	BA
1944 NY N	0	1	.000	0.00	4	0	0	5	1	4	2	0	0	1	0	1	0	0	.000

Larry Miller

MILLER, LARRY DON
B. June 19, 1937, Topeka, Kans.   BL TL 6'   195 lbs.

	W	L	PCT	ERA	G	GS	CG	IP	H	BB	SO	ShO	W	L	SV	AB	H	HR	BA
1964 LA N	4	8	.333	4.18	16	14	1	79.2	87	28	50	0	1	0	0	26	7	0	.269
1965 NY N	1	4	.200	5.02	28	5	0	57.1	66	25	36	0	1	0	0	11	2	0	.182
1966	0	2	.000	7.56	4	1	0	8.1	9	4	7	0	0	1	0	2	1	0	.500
3 yrs.	5	14	.263	4.71	48	20	1	145.1	162	57	93	0	2	1	0	39	10	0	.256

Ox Miller

MILLER, JOHN ANTHONY
B. May 4, 1915, Gause, Tex.   BR TR 6'1"   190 lbs.

	W	L	PCT	ERA	G	GS	CG	IP	H	BB	SO	ShO	W	L	SV	AB	H	HR	BA
1943 2 teams	WAS A	(3G 0–0)			STL A	(2G 0–0)													
" total	0	0	–	11.25	5	0	0	12	17	8	4	0	0	0	0	2	0	0	.000
1945 STL A	2	1	.667	1.59	4	3	3	28.1	23	5	4	0	0	0	0	11	2	0	.182
1946	1	3	.250	6.88	11	3	0	35.1	52	15	12	0	0	0	1	7	2	0	.286
1947 CHI N	1	2	.333	10.13	4	4	1	16	31	5	7	0	0	0	0	7	3	1	.429
4 yrs.	4	6	.400	6.38	24	10	4	91.2	123	33	27	0	0	0	1	27	7	1	.259

Ralph Miller

MILLER, RALPH DARWIN
B. Mar. 15, 1873, Cincinnati, Ohio   D. Cincinnati, Ohio   BR TR 5'11"   170 lbs.

	W	L	PCT	ERA	G	GS	CG	IP	H	BB	SO	ShO	W	L	SV	AB	H	HR	BA
1898 BKN N	4	14	.222	5.34	23	21	16	151.2	161	86	43	0	1	0	0	62	12	0	.194
1899 BAL N	1	3	.250	4.76	5	4	3	34	42	13	3	0	1	0	0	11	2	0	.182
2 yrs.	5	17	.227	5.24	28	25	19	185.2	203	99	46	0	2	0	0	73	14	0	.192

Ralph Miller

MILLER, RALPH HENRY (Lefty)
Brother of Bing Miller.
B. Jan. 14, 1899, Vinton, Iowa   D. Feb. 18, 1967, White Bear Lake, Minn.   BR TL 6'1½"   190 lbs.

	W	L	PCT	ERA	G	GS	CG	IP	H	BB	SO	ShO	W	L	SV	AB	H	HR	BA
1921 WAS A	0	0	–	0.00	1	0	0	1	0	0	0	0	0	0	0	0	0	0	–

Randy Miller

MILLER, RANDALL SCOTT
B. Mar. 18, 1953, Oxnard, Calif.   BR TR 6'1"   180 lbs.

	W	L	PCT	ERA	G	GS	CG	IP	H	BB	SO	ShO	W	L	SV	AB	H	HR	BA
1977 BAL A	0	0	–	27.00	1	0	0	1	4	0	0	0	0	0	0	0	0	0	–
1978 MON N	0	1	.000	10.29	5	0	0	7	11	3	6	0	0	1	0	1	0	0	.000
2 yrs.	0	1	.000	12.38	6	0	0	8	15	3	6	0	0	1	0	1	0	0	.000

Red Miller

MILLER, LEO ALPHONSO
B. Feb. 11, 1897, Philadelphia, Pa.   D. Oct. 20, 1973, Orlando, Fla.   BR TR 5'11"   195 lbs.

	W	L	PCT	ERA	G	GS	CG	IP	H	BB	SO	ShO	W	L	SV	AB	H	HR	BA
1923 PHI N	0	0	–	32.40	1	0	0	1.2	6	1	0	0	0	0	0	1	0	0	.000

Roger Miller

MILLER, ROGER WESLEY
B. Aug. 1, 1954, Connellsville, Pa.   BR TR 6'3"   200 lbs.

	W	L	PCT	ERA	G	GS	CG	IP	H	BB	SO	ShO	W	L	SV	AB	H	HR	BA
1974 MIL A	0	0	–	13.50	2	0	0	2	3	0	2	0	0	0	0	0	0	0	–

Ronnie Miller

MILLER, ROLAND ARTHUR
B. Aug. 28, 1918, Mason City, Iowa   BB TR 5'11"   167 lbs.

	W	L	PCT	ERA	G	GS	CG	IP	H	BB	SO	ShO	W	L	SV	AB	H	HR	BA
1941 WAS A	0	0	–	4.50	1	0	0	2	2	1	0	0	0	0	0	0	0	0	–

Roscoe Miller

MILLER, ROSCOE CLYDE (Roxy, Rubberlegs)
B. Dec. 2, 1876, Greenville, Ind.   D. Apr. 18, 1913, Corydon, Ind.

	W	L	PCT	ERA	G	GS	CG	IP	H	BB	SO	ShO	W	L	SV	AB	H	HR	BA
1901 DET A	23	13	.639	2.95	38	36	35	332	339	98	79	3	1	0	1	130	27	0	.208
1902 2 teams	DET A	(20G 6–12)			NY N	(10G 1–8)													
" total	7	20	.259	3.98	30	27	22	221.1	235	68	54	1	0	0	1	81	12	0	.148
1903 NY N	2	5	.286	4.13	15	8	6	85	101	24	30	0	0	0	3	31	5	0	.161
1904 PIT N	7	8	.467	3.35	19	17	11	134.1	133	39	35	2	0	0	0	46	2	0	.043
4 yrs.	39	46	.459	3.45	102	88	74	772.2	808	229	198	6	1	0	5	288	46	0	.160

Russ Miller

MILLER, RUSSELL LEWIS
Brother of Jake Miller.
B. Mar. 25, 1900, Etna, Ohio   D. Apr. 30, 1962, Bucyrus, Ohio   BR TR 5'11"   165 lbs.

	W	L	PCT	ERA	G	GS	CG	IP	H	BB	SO	ShO	W	L	SV	AB	H	HR	BA
1927 PHI N	1	1	.500	5.28	2	2	1	15.1	21	3	4	0	0	0	0	3	1	0	.333
1928	0	12	.000	5.42	33	12	1	108	137	34	19	0	0	3	1	27	4	0	.148
2 yrs.	1	13	.071	5.40	35	14	2	123.1	158	37	23	0	0	3	1	30	5	0	.167

	W	L	PCT	ERA	G	GS	CG	IP	H	BB	SO	ShO	Relief Pitching W	L	SV	Batting AB	H	HR	BA

Stu Miller

MILLER, STUART LEONARD
B. Dec. 26, 1927, Northampton, Mass.   BR TR 5'11½" 165 lbs.

	W	L	PCT	ERA	G	GS	CG	IP	H	BB	SO	ShO	W	L	SV	AB	H	HR	BA
1952 STL N	6	3	.667	2.05	12	11	6	88	63	26	64	2	1	0	0	25	3	0	.120
1953	7	8	.467	5.56	40	18	8	137.2	161	47	79	2	0	1	4	43	8	0	.186
1954	2	3	.400	5.79	19	4	0	46.2	55	29	22	0	1	2	2	13	4	0	.308
1956 2 teams			STL N	(3G 0–1)				PHI N	(24G 5–8)										
" total	5	9	.357	4.50	27	15	2	114	121	56	60	0	2	1	1	26	4	0	.154
1957 NY N	7	9	.438	3.63	38	13	0	124	110	45	60	0	6	3	1	35	2	0	.057
1958 SF N	6	9	.400	2.47	41	20	4	182	160	49	119	1	0	2	0	50	6	0	.120
1959	8	7	.533	2.84	59	9	2	167.2	164	57	95	0	7	4	8	45	2	0	.044
1960	7	6	.538	3.90	47	3	2	101.2	100	31	65	0	5	5	2	25	5	0	.200
1961	14	5	.737	2.66	63	0	0	122	95	37	89	0	14	5	17	20	4	0	.200
1962	5	8	.385	4.12	59	0	0	107	107	42	78	0	5	8	19	16	2	0	.125
1963 BAL A	5	8	.385	2.24	71	0	0	112.1	93	53	114	0	5	8	27	16	5	0	.313
1964	7	7	.500	3.06	66	0	0	97	77	34	87	0	7	7	23	9	1	0	.111
1965	14	7	.667	1.89	67	0	0	119.1	87	32	104	0	14	7	24	16	1	0	.063
1966	9	4	.692	2.25	51	0	0	92	65	22	67	0	9	4	18	19	2	0	.105
1967	3	10	.231	2.55	42	0	0	81.1	63	36	60	0	3	10	8	11	0	0	.000
1968 ATL N	0	0	–	54.00	2	0	0	.2	1	4	1	0	0	0	0	0	0	0	–
16 yrs.	105	103	.505	3.24	704	93	24	1693.1	1522	600	1164	5	79	67	154	369	49	0	.133

WORLD SERIES

	W	L	PCT	ERA	G	GS	CG	IP	H	BB	SO	ShO	W	L	SV	AB	H	HR	BA
1962 SF N	0	0	–	0.00	2	0	0	1.1	1	2	0	0	0	0	0	0	0	0	–

Walt Miller

MILLER, WALTER W.
B. Oct. 19, 1884, Gas City, Ind.   D. Mar. 1, 1956, Marion, Ind.   BR TR 5'11½" 180 lbs.

	W	L	PCT	ERA	G	GS	CG	IP	H	BB	SO	ShO	W	L	SV	AB	H	HR	BA
1911 BKN N	0	1	.000	6.55	3	2	0	11	16	6	0	0	0	0	0	4	0	0	.000

Bill Milligan

MILLIGAN, WILLIAM J.
B. Aug. 19, 1878, Buffalo, N. Y.   D. Oct. 14, 1928, Buffalo, N. Y.   BR TL 5'7"

	W	L	PCT	ERA	G	GS	CG	IP	H	BB	SO	ShO	W	L	SV	AB	H	HR	BA
1901 PHI A	0	3	.000	4.36	6	3	2	33	43	14	5	0	0	1	0	15	5	1	.333
1904 NY N	0	1	.000	5.40	5	1	1	25	36	4	6	0	0	0	2	9	1	0	.111
2 yrs.	0	4	.000	4.81	11	4	3	58	79	18	11	0	0	1	2	24	6	1	.250

Jocko Milligan

MILLIGAN, JOHN
B. Aug. 8, 1861, Philadelphia, Pa.   D. Aug. 30, 1923, Philadelphia, Pa.   BR TR 6'   195 lbs.

	W	L	PCT	ERA	G	GS	CG	IP	H	BB	SO	ShO	W	L	SV	AB	H	HR	BA
1890 PHI P	0	0	–	0.00	1	0	0		0	0	0	0	0	0	0		*		

John Milligan

MILLIGAN, JOHN ALEXANDER
B. Jan. 22, 1904, Schuylerville, N. Y.   D. May 15, 1972, Fort Pierce, Fla.   BR TL 5'10" 172 lbs.

	W	L	PCT	ERA	G	GS	CG	IP	H	BB	SO	ShO	W	L	SV	AB	H	HR	BA
1928 PHI N	2	5	.286	4.37	13	7	3	68	69	32	22	0	0	1	0	20	1	0	.050
1929	0	1	.000	16.76	8	3	0	9.2	29	10	2	0	0	1	0	3	1	0	.333
1930	1	2	.333	3.18	9	2	1	28.1	26	21	7	0	0	1	0	9	1	0	.111
1931	0	0	–	3.38	3	0	0	8	11	4	6	0	0	0	0	2	0	0	.000
1934 WAS A	0	0	–	10.13	2	0	0	2.2	6	0	1	0	0	0	0	0	0	0	–
5 yrs.	3	8	.273	5.17	35	12	4	116.2	141	67	38	0	0	3	0	34	3	0	.088

Bob Milliken

MILLIKEN, ROBERT FOGLE (Bobo)
B. Aug. 25, 1926, Majorsville, W. Va.   BR TR 6'   195 lbs.

	W	L	PCT	ERA	G	GS	CG	IP	H	BB	SO	ShO	W	L	SV	AB	H	HR	BA
1953 BKN N	8	4	.667	3.37	37	10	3	117.2	94	42	65	0	5	2	2	34	4	0	.118
1954	5	2	.714	4.02	24	3	0	62.2	58	18	25	0	5	0	2	17	3	0	.176
2 yrs.	13	6	.684	3.59	61	13	3	180.1	152	60	90	0	10	2	4	51	7	0	.137

WORLD SERIES

	W	L	PCT	ERA	G	GS	CG	IP	H	BB	SO	ShO	W	L	SV	AB	H	HR	BA
1953 BKN N	0	0	–	0.00	1	0	0	2	2	1	0	0	0	0	0	0	0	0	–

Art Mills

MILLS, ARTHUR GRANT
Son of Willie Mills.
B. Mar. 2, 1903, Utica, N. Y.   D. July 23, 1975, Utica, N. Y.   BR TR 5'10" 155 lbs.

	W	L	PCT	ERA	G	GS	CG	IP	H	BB	SO	ShO	W	L	SV	AB	H	HR	BA
1927 BOS N	0	1	.000	3.82	15	1	0	37.2	41	18	7	0	0	1	0	7	0	0	.000
1928	0	0	–	12.91	4	0	0	7.2	17	8	0	0	0	0	0	1	0	0	.000
2 yrs.	0	1	.000	5.36	19	1	0	45.1	58	26	7	0	0	1	0	8	0	0	.000

Dick Mills

MILLS, RICHARD ALLEN
B. Jan. 29, 1945, Boston, Mass.   BR TR 6'3" 195 lbs.

	W	L	PCT	ERA	G	GS	CG	IP	H	BB	SO	ShO	W	L	SV	AB	H	HR	BA
1970 BOS A	0	0	–	2.25	2	0	0	4	6	3	3	0	0	0	0	0	0	0	–

Lefty Mills

MILLS, HOWARD ROBINSON
B. May 12, 1910, Dedham, Mass.   D. Sept. 23, 1982, Riverside, Calif.   BL TL 6'1" 187 lbs.

	W	L	PCT	ERA	G	GS	CG	IP	H	BB	SO	ShO	W	L	SV	AB	H	HR	BA
1934 STL A	0	0	–	4.15	4	0	0	8.2	10	11	2	0	0	0	0	3	1	0	.333
1937	1	1	.500	6.39	2	2	1	12.2	16	10	10	0	0	0	0	5	0	0	.000
1938	10	12	.455	5.31	30	27	15	210.1	216	116	134	1	0	0	0	66	6	0	.091
1939	4	11	.267	6.55	34	14	4	144.1	147	113	103	0	2	2	2	47	11	1	.234
1940	0	6	.000	7.78	26	5	1	59	64	52	18	0	0	1	0	13	2	0	.154
5 yrs.	15	30	.333	6.06	96	48	21	435	453	302	267	1	2	3	2	134	20	1	.149

Willie Mills

MILLS, WILLIAM GRANT (Wee Willie)
Father of Art Mills.
B. Aug. 15, 1877, Schenevus, N. Y.   D. July 5, 1914, Norwood, N. Y.   BR TR 5'7" 150 lbs.

	W	L	PCT	ERA	G	GS	CG	IP	H	BB	SO	ShO	W	L	SV	AB	H	HR	BA
1901 NY N	0	2	.000	8.44	2	2	2	16	21	4	3	0	0	0	0	6	1	0	.167

Al Milnar

MILNAR, ALBERT JOSEPH (Happy)
B. Dec. 26, 1913, Cleveland, Ohio   BL TL 6'2" 195 lbs.

	W	L	PCT	ERA	G	GS	CG	IP	H	BB	SO	ShO	W	L	SV	AB	H	HR	BA
1936 CLE A	1	2	.333	7.36	4	3	1	22	26	18	9	0	0	0	0	10	3	0	.300
1938	3	1	.750	5.00	23	5	2	68.1	90	26	29	0	2	0	1	26	4	1	.154
1939	14	12	.538	3.79	37	26	12	209	212	99	76	2	2	1	3	79	20	0	.253
1940	18	10	.643	3.27	37	33	15	242.1	242	99	99	4	0	0	3	94	17	0	.181
1941	12	19	.387	4.36	35	30	9	229.1	236	116	82	1	0	3	0	82	14	2	.171

	W	L	PCT	ERA	G	GS	CG	IP	H	BB	SO	ShO	Relief Pitching W	L	SV	BATTING AB	H	HR	BA

Al Milnar continued

	W	L	PCT	ERA	G	GS	CG	IP	H	BB	SO	ShO	W	L	SV	AB	H	HR	BA
1942	6	8	.429	4.13	28	19	8	157	146	85	35	2	0	0	0	70	12	1	.171
1943 2 teams		CLE	A (16G 1–3)		STL	A	(3G 1–2)												
" total	2	5	.286	7.38	19	8	1	53.2	74	44	19	0	1	1	0	25	6	0	.240
1946 2 teams		STL	A (4G 1–1)		PHI	N	(1G 0–0)												
" total	1	1	.500	4.91	5	3	1	14.2	17	8	1	1	0	0	0	4	3	0	.750
8 yrs.	57	58	.496	4.22	188	127	49	996.1	1043	495	350	10	5	5	7	390	79	4	.203

George Milstead

MILSTEAD, GEORGE EARL (Cowboy)
B. Sept. 26, 1903, Cleburne, Tex.   D. Aug. 9, 1977, Cleburne, Tex.   BL TL 5'10"   144 lbs.

	W	L	PCT	ERA	G	GS	CG	IP	H	BB	SO	ShO	W	L	SV	AB	H	HR	BA
1924 CHI N	1	1	.500	6.07	13	2	1	29.2	41	13	6	0	0	0	0	6	1	0	.167
1925	1	1	.500	3.00	5	3	1	21	26	8	7	0	0	0	0	7	0	0	.000
1926	1	5	.167	3.58	18	4	0	55.1	63	24	14	0	1	2	2	19	1	0	.053
3 yrs.	3	7	.300	4.16	36	9	2	106	130	45	27	0	1	2	2	32	2	0	.063

Larry Milton

MILTON, SAMUEL LAWRENCE
B. May 4, 1879, Owensboro, Ky.   D. May 16, 1942, Hannibal, Mo.

	W	L	PCT	ERA	G	GS	CG	IP	H	BB	SO	ShO	W	L	SV	AB	H	HR	BA
1903 STL N	0	0	–	2.25	1	0	0	4	3	1	0	0	0	0	0	2	1	0	.500

Cotton Minahan

MINAHAN, EDMUND JOSEPH
B. Dec. 10, 1882, Springfield, Ohio   D. May 20, 1958, East Orange, N. J.   BR TR 6'   190 lbs.

	W	L	PCT	ERA	G	GS	CG	IP	H	BB	SO	ShO	W	L	SV	AB	H	HR	BA
1907 CIN N	0	2	.000	1.29	2	2	1	14	12	13	4	0	0	0	0	5	0	0	.000

Rudy Minarcin

MINARCIN, RUDY ANTHONY (Buster)
B. Mar. 25, 1930, North Vandergrift, Pa.   BR TR 6'   195 lbs.

	W	L	PCT	ERA	G	GS	CG	IP	H	BB	SO	ShO	W	L	SV	AB	H	HR	BA
1955 CIN N	5	9	.357	4.90	41	12	3	115.2	116	51	45	1	2	1	1	28	5	0	.179
1956 BOS A	1	0	1.000	2.79	3	1	0	9.2	9	8	5	0	1	0	0	2	1	0	.500
1957	0	0	–	4.43	26	0	0	44.2	44	30	20	0	0	0	2	2	0	0	.000
3 yrs.	6	9	.400	4.66	70	13	3	170	169	89	70	1	3	1	3	32	6	0	.188

Ray Miner

MINER, RAMON THEODORE (Lefty)
B. Apr. 4, 1897, Glen Falls, N. Y.   D. Sept. 15, 1963, New York, N. Y.   BR TL 5'11"   160 lbs.

	W	L	PCT	ERA	G	GS	CG	IP	H	BB	SO	ShO	W	L	SV	AB	H	HR	BA
1921 PHI A	0	0	–	36.00	1	0	0	2	3	0	0	0	0	0	0	0	0	0	–

Craig Minetto

MINETTO, CRAIG STEPHEN
Also known as Craig Stephen Briceno.
B. Apr. 25, 1954, Stockton, Calif.   BL TL 6'   185 lbs.

	W	L	PCT	ERA	G	GS	CG	IP	H	BB	SO	ShO	W	L	SV	AB	H	HR	BA
1978 OAK A	0	0	–	3.75	4	1	0	12	13	7	3	0	0	0	0	0	0	0	–
1979	1	5	.167	5.57	36	13	0	118	131	58	64	0	0	0	0	0	0	0	–
1980	0	2	.000	7.88	7	1	0	8	11	3	5	0	0	1	1	0	0	0	–
1981	0	0	–	2.57	8	0	0	7	7	4	4	0	0	0	0	0	0	0	–
4 yrs.	1	7	.125	5.40	55	15	0	145	162	72	76	0	0	1	1	0	0	0	–

Steve Mingori

MINGORI, STEVEN BERNARD
B. Feb. 29, 1944, Kansas City, Mo.   BL TL 5'10"   165 lbs.

	W	L	PCT	ERA	G	GS	CG	IP	H	BB	SO	ShO	W	L	SV	AB	H	HR	BA
1970 CLE A	1	0	1.000	2.70	21	0	0	20	17	12	16	0	1	0	1	1	0	0	.000
1971	1	2	.333	1.42	54	0	0	57	31	24	45	0	1	2	4	2	1	0	.500
1972	0	6	.000	3.95	41	0	0	57	67	36	47	0	0	6	10	8	1	0	.125
1973 2 teams		CLE	A (5G 0–0)		KC	A	(19G 3–3)												
" total	3	3	.500	3.57	24	0	0	68	69	33	50	0	3	2	1	0	0	0	–
1974 KC A	2	3	.400	2.82	36	0	0	67	53	23	43	0	2	3	2	0	0	0	–
1975	0	3	.000	2.52	36	0	0	50	42	20	25	0	0	3	2	1	0	0	.000
1976	5	5	.500	2.33	55	0	0	85	73	25	38	0	5	5	10	0	0	0	–
1977	2	4	.333	3.09	43	0	0	64	59	19	19	0	2	4	4	0	0	0	–
1978	1	4	.200	2.74	45	0	0	69	64	16	28	0	1	4	7	0	0	0	–
1979	3	3	.500	5.74	30	1	0	47	69	17	18	0	3	2	1	0	0	0	–
10 yrs.	18	33	.353	3.04	385	2	0	584	544	225	329	0	18	31	42	12	2	0	.167
LEAGUE CHAMPIONSHIP SERIES																			
1976 KC A	0	0	–	2.70	3	0	0	3.1	4	0	1	0	0	0	1	0	0	0	–
1977	0	0	–	0.00	3	0	0	1.1	0	0	1	0	0	0	0	0	0	0	–
1978	0	0	–	7.36	1	0	0	3.2	5	3	0	0	0	0	0	0	0	0	–
3 yrs.	0	0	–	4.32	7	0	0	8.1	9	3	2	0	0	0	1	0	0	0	–

Paul Minner

MINNER, PAUL EDISON (Lefty)
B. July 30, 1923, New Wilmington, Pa.   BL TL 6'5"   200 lbs.

	W	L	PCT	ERA	G	GS	CG	IP	H	BB	SO	ShO	W	L	SV	AB	H	HR	BA
1946 BKN N	0	1	.000	6.75	3	0	0	4	6	3	3	0	0	1	0	0	0	0	–
1948	4	3	.571	2.44	28	2	0	62.2	61	26	23	0	3	3	1	21	4	0	.190
1949	3	1	.750	3.80	27	1	0	47.1	49	18	17	0	3	1	2	14	3	0	.214
1950 CHI N	8	13	.381	4.11	39	24	9	190.1	217	72	99	1	0	0	4	65	14	1	.215
1951	6	17	.261	3.79	33	28	14	201.2	219	64	68	3	0	0	1	71	18	1	.254
1952	14	9	.609	3.74	28	27	12	180.2	180	54	61	2	0	0	0	64	15	1	.234
1953	12	15	.444	4.21	31	27	9	201	227	40	64	2	2	0	1	68	15	1	.221
1954	11	11	.500	3.96	32	29	12	218	236	50	79	0	0	1	1	76	13	2	.171
1955	9	9	.500	3.48	22	22	7	157.2	173	47	53	1	0	0	0	56	13	0	.232
1956	2	5	.286	6.89	10	9	1	47	60	19	14	0	0	0	0	12	3	0	.250
10 yrs.	69	84	.451	3.94	253	169	64	1310.1	1428	393	481	9	8	6	10	447	98	6	.219
WORLD SERIES																			
1949 BKN N	0	0	–	0.00	1	0	0	1	1	0	0	0	0	0	0	0	0	0	–

Don Minnick

MINNICK, DONALD ATHEY
B. Apr. 14, 1931, Lynchburg, Va.   BR TR 6'3"   195 lbs.

	W	L	PCT	ERA	G	GS	CG	IP	H	BB	SO	ShO	W	L	SV	AB	H	HR	BA
1957 WAS A	0	1	.000	4.82	2	1	0	9.1	14	2	7	0	0	0	0	2	0	0	.000

	W	L	PCT	ERA	G	GS	CG	IP	H	BB	SO	ShO	Relief Pitching W	L	SV	BATTING AB	H	HR	BA

Jim Minshall

MINSHALL, JAMES EDWARD
B. July 4, 1947, Campbell County, Ky.   BB TR 6'6"   215 lbs.

	W	L	PCT	ERA	G	GS	CG	IP	H	BB	SO	ShO	W	L	SV	AB	H	HR	BA
1974 PIT N	0	1	.000	0.00	5	0	0	4	1	2	3	0	0	1	0	0	0	0	–
1975	0	0	–	0.00	1	0	0	1	0	2	2	0	0	0	0	0	0	0	–
2 yrs.	0	1	.000	0.00	6	0	0	5	1	4	5	0	0	1	0	0	0	0	–

Greg Minton

MINTON, GREGORY BRIAN
B. July 29, 1951, Lubbock, Tex.   BB TR 6'2"   180 lbs.

	W	L	PCT	ERA	G	GS	CG	IP	H	BB	SO	ShO	W	L	SV	AB	H	HR	BA
1975 SF N	1	1	.500	6.88	4	2	0	17	19	11	6	0	0	0	0	6	0	0	.000
1976	0	3	.000	4.91	10	2	0	25.2	32	12	7	0	0	2	0	5	1	0	.200
1977	1	1	.500	4.50	2	2	0	14	14	4	5	0	0	0	0	3	1	0	.333
1978	0	1	.000	7.88	11	0	0	16	22	8	6	0	0	1	0	1	0	0	.000
1979	4	3	.571	1.80	46	0	0	80	59	27	33	0	4	3	4	4	0	0	.000
1980	4	6	.400	2.47	68	0	0	91	81	34	42	0	4	6	19	8	1	0	.125
1981	4	5	.444	2.89	55	0	0	84	84	36	29	0	4	5	21	12	0	0	.000
1982	10	4	.714	1.83	78	0	0	123	108	42	58	0	10	4	30	17	3	0	.176
1983	7	11	.389	3.54	73	0	0	106.2	117	47	38	0	7	11	22	11	6	1	.545
1984	4	9	.308	3.76	74	1	0	124.1	130	57	48	0	3	9	19	21	1	0	.048
10 yrs.	35	44	.443	3.10	421	7	0	681.2	666	278	272	0	32	41	115	88	13	1	.148

Paul Mirabella

MIRABELLA, PAUL THOMAS
B. Mar. 20, 1954, Belleville, N. J.   BL TL 6'1"   190 lbs.

	W	L	PCT	ERA	G	GS	CG	IP	H	BB	SO	ShO	W	L	SV	AB	H	HR	BA
1978 TEX A	3	2	.600	5.79	10	4	0	28	30	17	23	0	1	1	1	0	0	0	–
1979 NY A	0	4	.000	9.00	10	1	0	14	16	10	4	0	0	3	0	0	0	0	–
1980 TOR A	5	12	.294	4.33	33	22	3	131	151	66	53	1	0	0	0	0	0	0	–
1981	0	0	–	7.20	8	1	0	15	20	7	9	0	0	0	0	0	0	0	–
1982 TEX A	1	1	.500	4.80	40	0	0	50.2	46	22	29	0	1	1	3	0	0	0	–
1983 BAL A	0	0	–	5.59	3	2	0	9.2	9	7	4	0	0	0	0	0	0	0	–
1984 SEA A	2	5	.286	4.37	52	1	0	68	74	32	41	0	2	4	3	0	0	0	–
7 yrs.	11	24	.314	4.92	156	31	3	316.1	346	161	163	1	4	9	7	0	0	0	–

Bobby Mitchell

MITCHELL, ROBERT McKASHA
B. Feb. 6, 1856, Cincinnati, Ohio   D. May 1, 1933, Cincinnati, Ohio   BL TL 5'5"   135 lbs.

	W	L	PCT	ERA	G	GS	CG	IP	H	BB	SO	ShO	W	L	SV	AB	H	HR	BA
1877 CIN N	6	5	.545	3.51	12	12	11	100	123	11	41	1	0	0	0	49	10	0	.204
1878	7	2	.778	2.14	9	9	9	80	69	18	51	1	0	0	0	49	12	0	.245
1879 CLE N	7	15	.318	3.28	23	22	20	194.2	236	42	90	0	0	1	0	109	16	0	.147
1882 STL AA	0	1	.000	7.71	1	1	0	7	12	2	2	0	0	0	0	4	0	0	.000
4 yrs.	20	23	.465	3.18	45	44	40	381.2	440	73	184	2	0	1	0	211	38	0	.180

Charlie Mitchell

MITCHELL, CHARLES ROSS
B. June 24, 1962, Dickson, Tenn.   BR TR 6'3"   170 lbs.

	W	L	PCT	ERA	G	GS	CG	IP	H	BB	SO	ShO	W	L	SV	AB	H	HR	BA
1984 BOS A	0	0	–	2.76	10	0	0	16.1	14	6	7	0	0	0	0	0	0	0	–

Clarence Mitchell

MITCHELL, CLARENCE ELMER
B. Feb. 22, 1891, Franklin, Neb.   D. Nov. 6, 1963, Grand Island, Neb.   BL TL 5'11½" 190 lbs.

	W	L	PCT	ERA	G	GS	CG	IP	H	BB	SO	ShO	W	L	SV	AB	H	HR	BA
1911 DET A	1	0	1.000	8.16	5	1	0	14.1	20	7	4	0	1	0	0	4	2	0	.500
1916 CIN N	11	10	.524	3.14	29	24	17	194.2	211	45	52	1	0	1	0	117	28	0	.239
1917	9	15	.375	3.22	32	20	10	159.1	166	34	37	2	2	3	1	90	25	0	.278
1918 BKN N	0	1	.000	108.00	1	1	0	.1	4	0	0	0	0	0	0	24	6	0	.250
1919	7	5	.583	3.06	23	11	9	108.2	123	23	43	0	1	0	0	49	18	1	.367
1920	5	2	.714	3.09	19	7	3	78.2	85	23	18	1	0	1	1	107	25	0	.234
1921	11	9	.550	2.89	37	18	13	190	206	46	39	3	2	2	2	91	24	0	.264
1922	0	3	.000	14.21	5	3	0	12.2	28	7	1	0	0	0	0	155	45	3	.290
1923 PHI N	9	10	.474	4.72	29	19	8	139.1	170	46	42	1	1	1	0	78	21	1	.269
1924	6	13	.316	5.62	30	26	9	165	223	58	36	1	0	1	1	102	26	0	.255
1925	10	17	.370	5.28	32	26	12	199.1	245	51	46	1	0	1	1	92	18	0	.196
1926	9	14	.391	4.58	28	25	12	178.2	232	55	52	0	1	0	1	78	19	0	.244
1927	6	3	.667	4.79	13	12	8	94.2	99	28	17	1	0	0	0	42	10	1	.238
1928 2 teams			PHI N	(3G 0–0)			STL N	(19G 8–9)											
" total	8	9	.471	3.53	22	18	9	155.2	162	40	31	1	1	0	0	60	8	0	.133
1929 STL N	8	11	.421	4.27	25	22	16	173	221	60	39	0	0	0	0	66	18	0	.273
1930 2 teams			STL N	(1G 1–0)			NY N	(24G 10–3)											
" total	11	3	.786	4.02	25	17	5	132	156	38	41	0	1	0	0	49	13	0	.265
1931 NY N	13	11	.542	4.07	27	25	13	190.1	221	52	39	0	0	0	0	73	16	1	.219
1932	1	3	.250	4.15	8	3	1	30.1	41	11	7	0	0	1	2	10	2	0	.200
18 yrs.	125	139	.473	4.12	390	278	145	2217	2613	624	544	12	10	13	9	*			

WORLD SERIES

	W	L	PCT	ERA	G	GS	CG	IP	H	BB	SO	ShO	W	L	SV	AB	H	HR	BA
1920 BKN N	0	0	–	0.00	1	0	0	4.2	3	3	1	0	0	0	0	3	1	0	.333
1928 STL N	0	0	–	1.59	1	0	0	5.2	2	2	2	0	0	0	0	2	0	0	.000
2 yrs.	0	0	–	0.87	2	0	0	10.1	5	5	3	0	0	0	0	5	1	0	.200

Craig Mitchell

MITCHELL, CRAIG SETON
B. Apr. 14, 1954, Spokane, Wash.   BR TR 6'3"   180 lbs.

	W	L	PCT	ERA	G	GS	CG	IP	H	BB	SO	ShO	W	L	SV	AB	H	HR	BA
1975 OAK A	0	1	.000	12.27	1	1	0	3.2	6	2	2	0	0	0	0	0	0	0	–
1976	0	0	–	3.00	1	0	0	3	3	0	0	0	0	0	0	0	0	0	–
1977	0	1	.000	7.50	3	1	0	6	9	2	1	0	0	0	0	0	0	0	–
3 yrs.	0	2	.000	7.82	5	2	0	12.2	18	4	3	0	0	0	0	0	0	0	–

Fred Mitchell

MITCHELL, FREDERICK FRANCIS
Born Frederick Francis Yapp.
B. June 5, 1878, Cambridge, Mass.   D. Oct. 13, 1970, Newton, Mass.   BR TR 5'9½" 185 lbs.
Manager 1917-23.

	W	L	PCT	ERA	G	GS	CG	IP	H	BB	SO	ShO	W	L	SV	AB	H	HR	BA
1901 BOS A	6	6	.500	3.81	17	13	10	108.2	115	51	34	0	1	0	0	44	7	0	.159
1902 2 teams			BOS A	(1G 0–1)			PHI A	(18G 5–7)											
" total	5	8	.385	3.87	19	14	9	111.2	128	64	24	0	1	1	1	49	9	0	.184
1903 PHI N	11	15	.423	4.48	28	28	24	227	250	102	69	1	0	0	0	95	19	0	.200

	W	L	PCT	ERA	G	GS	CG	IP	H	BB	SO	ShO	Relief Pitching W	L	SV	BATTING AB	H	HR	BA

Fred Mitchell continued

		W	L	PCT	ERA	G	GS	CG	IP	H	BB	SO	ShO	W	L	SV	AB	H	HR	BA
1904	2 teams				PHI	N	(13G 4–7)		BKN	N	(8G 2–5)										
"	total	6	12	.333	3.56	21	21	19	174.2	206	48	45	1	0	0	0	106	24	0	.226
1905	BKN N	3	7	.300	4.78	12	10	9	96	107	38	44	0	0	0	0	79	15	0	.190
5 yrs.		31	48	.392	4.10	97	86	71	718	806	303	216	2	2	1	1	*			

Monroe Mitchell

MITCHELL, MONROE BARR
B. Sept. 11, 1901, Starkville, Miss.   D. Sept. 4, 1976, Valdosta, Ga.
BR TR 6'1½" 170 lbs.

		W	L	PCT	ERA	G	GS	CG	IP	H	BB	SO	ShO	W	L	SV	AB	H	HR	BA
1923	WAS A	2	4	.333	6.48	10	6	3	41.2	57	22	8	1	0	0	2	12	3	0	.250

Paul Mitchell

MITCHELL, PAUL MICHAEL
B. Aug. 19, 1950, Worcester, Mass.
BR TR 6'1" 195 lbs.

		W	L	PCT	ERA	G	GS	CG	IP	H	BB	SO	ShO	W	L	SV	AB	H	HR	BA
1975	BAL A	3	0	1.000	3.63	11	4	1	57	41	19	31	0	2	0	0	0	0	0	—
1976	OAK A	9	7	.563	4.25	26	26	4	142	169	30	67	1	0	0	0	0	0	0	—
1977	2 teams				OAK	A	(5G 0–3)		SEA	A	(9G 3–3)										
"	total	3	6	.333	6.41	14	12	0	53.1	71	23	25	0	0	0	0	0	0	0	—
1978	SEA A	8	14	.364	4.18	29	29	4	168	173	79	75	2	0	0	0	0	0	0	—
1979	2 teams				SEA	A	(10G 1–4)		MIL	A	(18G 3–3)										
"	total	4	7	.364	5.30	28	14	1	112	127	25	50	0	0	0	0	0	0	0	—
1980	MIL A	5	5	.500	3.54	17	11	1	89	92	15	29	1	0	0	1	0	0	0	—
6 yrs.		32	39	.451	4.45	125	96	11	621.1	673	191	277	4	2	0	1	0	0	0	—

Roy Mitchell

MITCHELL, ALBERT ROY
B. Apr. 19, 1885, Belton, Tex.   D. Sept. 8, 1959, Temple, Tex.
BR TR 5'9½" 170 lbs.

		W	L	PCT	ERA	G	GS	CG	IP	H	BB	SO	ShO	W	L	SV	AB	H	HR	BA
1910	STL A	4	2	.667	2.60	6	6	6	52	43	12	23	0	0	0	0	19	4	0	.211
1911		4	8	.333	3.84	28	12	8	133.2	134	45	40	1	1	1	0	49	11	0	.224
1912		3	4	.429	4.65	13	8	5	62	81	17	22	0	1	0	0	19	6	0	.316
1913		13	16	.448	3.01	33	27	21	245.1	265	47	59	4	2	1	1	88	13	0	.148
1914		4	5	.444	4.35	28	9	4	103.1	134	38	38	0	2	0	4	34	7	0	.206
1918	2 teams				CHI	N	(2G 0–1)		CIN	N	(5G 4–0)										
"	total	4	1	.800	2.42	7	5	3	48.1	45	9	12	2	1	0	0	16	3	0	.188
1919	CIN N	0	1	.000	2.32	7	1	0	31	32	9	10	0	0	0	0	10	0	0	.000
7 yrs.		32	37	.464	3.42	122	68	47	675.2	734	177	204	7	7	2	5	235	44	0	.187

Willie Mitchell

MITCHELL, WILLIAM
B. Dec. 1, 1889, Sardis, Miss.   D. Nov. 23, 1973, Sardis, Miss.
BR TL 6' 176 lbs.

		W	L	PCT	ERA	G	GS	CG	IP	H	BB	SO	ShO	W	L	SV	AB	H	HR	BA
1909	CLE A	1	2	.333	1.57	3	3	3	23	18	10	8	0	0	0	0	7	2	0	.286
1910		12	8	.600	2.60	35	18	11	183.2	155	55	102	1	2	2	0	63	10	0	.159
1911		7	14	.333	3.76	30	22	9	177.1	190	60	78	0	1	2	0	64	7	0	.109
1912		5	8	.385	2.80	29	15	8	163.2	149	56	94	0	1	0	1	53	6	0	.113
1913		14	8	.636	1.74	34	22	14	217	153	88	141	4	4	1	0	70	10	0	.143
1914		12	17	.414	3.19	39	32	16	257	228	124	179	3	0	1	1	81	7	0	.086
1915		11	14	.440	2.82	36	30	12	236	210	84	149	1	1	1	1	79	10	0	.127
1916	2 teams				CLE	A	(12G 2–5)		DET	A	(23G 7–5)										
"	total	9	10	.474	3.78	35	23	8	171.1	174	67	84	2	1	1	1	47	9	0	.191
1917	DET A	12	8	.600	2.19	30	22	12	185.1	172	46	80	5	0	0	0	59	7	0	.119
1918		0	1	.000	9.00	1	1	0	4	3	5	2	0	0	0	0	2	0	0	.000
1919		1	2	.333	2.86	3	1	0	13.2	12	10	4	0	0	1	0	5	1	0	.200
11 yrs.		84	92	.477	2.86	275	190	93	1632	1464	605	921	16	10	9	4	530	69	0	.130

Vinegar Bend Mizell

MIZELL, WILMER DAVID
B. Aug. 13, 1930, Leakesville, Miss.
BR TL 6'3½" 205 lbs.

		W	L	PCT	ERA	G	GS	CG	IP	H	BB	SO	ShO	W	L	SV	AB	H	HR	BA
1952	STL N	10	8	.556	3.65	30	30	7	190	171	103	146	2	0	0	0	68	3	0	.044
1953		13	11	.542	3.49	33	33	10	224.1	193	114	173	1	0	0	0	83	7	1	.084
1956		14	14	.500	3.62	33	33	11	208.2	172	92	153	3	0	0	0	75	8	0	.107
1957		8	10	.444	3.74	33	21	7	149.1	136	51	87	2	1	1	0	45	4	0	.089
1958		10	14	.417	3.42	30	29	8	189.2	178	91	80	2	0	0	0	61	7	0	.115
1959		13	10	.565	4.20	31	30	8	201.1	196	89	108	1	1	0	0	75	14	0	.187
1960	2 teams				STL	N	(9G 1–3)		PIT	N	(23G 13–5)										
"	total	14	8	.636	3.50	32	32	8	211	205	74	113	3	0	0	0	69	9	0	.130
1961	PIT N	7	10	.412	5.04	25	17	2	100	120	31	37	1	1	0	0	23	3	0	.130
1962	2 teams				PIT	N	(4G 1–1)		NY	N	(17G 0–2)										
"	total	1	3	.250	6.63	21	5	0	54.1	63	35	21	0	0	2	0	14	2	0	.143
9 yrs.		90	88	.506	3.85	268	230	61	1528.2	1434	680	918	15	3	3	0	513	57	1	.111

WORLD SERIES

		W	L	PCT	ERA	G	GS	CG	IP	H	BB	SO	ShO	W	L	SV	AB	H	HR	BA
1960	PIT N	0	1	.000	15.43	2	1	0	2.1	4	2	1	0	0	0	0	0	0	0	—

Mike Modak

MODAK, MICHAEL JOSEPH ALOYSIUS
B. May 18, 1922, Campbell, Ohio
BR TR 5'10½" 195 lbs.

		W	L	PCT	ERA	G	GS	CG	IP	H	BB	SO	ShO	W	L	SV	AB	H	HR	BA
1945	CIN N	1	2	.333	5.74	20	3	1	42.1	52	23	7	1	0	1	1	10	1	0	.100

Joe Moeller

MOELLER, JOSEPH DOUGLAS
B. Feb. 15, 1943, Blue Island, Ill.
BR TR 6'5" 192 lbs.

		W	L	PCT	ERA	G	GS	CG	IP	H	BB	SO	ShO	W	L	SV	AB	H	HR	BA
1962	LA N	6	5	.545	5.25	19	15	1	85.2	87	58	46	0	0	1	1	33	7	0	.212
1964		7	13	.350	4.21	27	24	1	145.1	153	31	97	0	0	0	0	45	3	0	.067
1966		2	4	.333	2.52	29	8	0	78.2	73	14	31	0	1	1	0	12	2	0	.167
1967		0	0	—	9.00	6	0	0	5	9	3	2	0	0	0	0	0	0	0	—
1968		1	1	.500	5.06	3	3	0	16	17	2	11	0	0	0	0	7	0	0	.000
1969		1	0	1.000	3.35	23	4	0	51	54	13	25	0	1	0	1	10	2	0	.200
1970		7	9	.438	3.93	31	19	2	135	131	43	63	1	1	0	4	39	6	0	.154
1971		2	4	.333	3.82	28	1	0	66	72	12	32	0	2	3	1	9	0	0	.000
8 yrs.		26	36	.419	4.02	166	74	4	582.2	596	176	307	1	4	5	7	155	20	0	.129

WORLD SERIES

		W	L	PCT	ERA	G	GS	CG	IP	H	BB	SO	ShO	W	L	SV	AB	H	HR	BA
1966	LA N	0	0	—	4.50	1	0	0	2	1	1	0	0	0	0	0	0	0	0	—

	W	L	PCT	ERA	G	GS	CG	IP	H	BB	SO	ShO	Relief Pitching W	L	SV	BATTING AB	H	HR	BA

Ron Moeller

MOELLER, RONALD RALPH (The Kid)
B. Oct. 13, 1938, Cincinnati, Ohio   BL TL 6'   180 lbs.

	W	L	PCT	ERA	G	GS	CG	IP	H	BB	SO	ShO	W	L	SV	AB	H	HR	BA
1956 **BAL A**	0	1	.000	4.15	4	1	0	8.2	10	3	2	0	0	0	0	1	0	0	.000
1958	0	0	–	4.15	4	0	0	4.1	6	3	3	0	0	0	0	0	0	0	–
1961 **LA A**	4	8	.333	5.83	33	18	1	112.2	122	83	87	1	0	1	0	29	6	0	.207
1963 **2 teams**			1.000	**LA A** (3G 0–0)				**WAS A** (8G 2–0)											
" total	2	0	1.000	6.33	11	3	0	27	36	11	12	0	0	0	0	9	2	0	.222
4 yrs.	6	9	.400	5.78	52	22	1	152.2	174	100	104	1	0	1	0	39	8	0	.205

Sam Moffett

MOFFETT, SAMUEL R.
Brother of Joe Moffett.
B. 1857, Wheeling, W. Va.   D. May 5, 1907, Butte, Mont.   TR

	W	L	PCT	ERA	G	GS	CG	IP	H	BB	SO	ShO	W	L	SV	AB	H	HR	BA
1884 **CLE N**	3	19	.136	*3.87*	24	22	21	197.2	236	58	84	0	0	0	0	256	47	0	.184
1887 **IND N**	1	5	.167	3.78	6	6	6	50	47	23	3	0	0	0	0	41	5	0	.122
1888	2	5	.286	4.66	7	7	6	56	62	17	7	1	0	0	0	35	4	0	.114
3 yrs.	6	29	.171	4.00	37	35	33	303.2	345	98	94	1	0	0	0	*			

Randy Moffitt

MOFFITT, RANDALL JAMES
B. Oct. 13, 1948, Long Beach, Calif.   BR TR 6'3"   190 lbs.

	W	L	PCT	ERA	G	GS	CG	IP	H	BB	SO	ShO	W	L	SV	AB	H	HR	BA
1972 **SF N**	1	5	.167	3.68	40	0	0	71	72	30	37	0	1	5	4	8	0	0	.000
1973	4	4	.500	2.43	60	0	0	100	86	31	65	0	4	4	14	17	1	0	.059
1974	5	7	.417	4.50	61	1	0	102	99	29	49	0	5	7	15	16	5	0	.313
1975	4	5	.444	3.89	55	0	0	74	73	32	39	0	4	5	11	14	3	0	.214
1976	6	6	.500	2.27	58	0	0	103	92	35	50	0	6	6	14	14	2	0	.143
1977	4	9	.308	3.58	64	0	0	88	91	39	68	0	4	9	11	3	0	0	.000
1978	8	4	.667	3.29	70	0	0	82	79	33	52	0	8	4	12	7	1	0	.143
1979	2	5	.286	7.71	28	0	0	35	53	14	16	0	2	5	2	4	0	0	.000
1980	1	1	.500	4.76	13	0	0	17	18	4	10	0	1	1	0	1	0	0	.000
1981	0	0	–	8.18	10	0	0	11	15	2	11	0	0	0	0	0	0	0	–
1982 **HOU N**	2	4	.333	3.02	30	0	0	41.2	36	13	20	0	2	4	3	2	0	0	.000
1983 **TOR A**	6	2	.750	3.77	45	0	0	57.1	52	24	38	0	6	2	10	0	0	0	–
12 yrs.	43	52	.453	3.65	534	1	0	782	766	286	455	0	43	52	96	86	12	0	.140

Herb Moford

MOFORD, HERBERT
B. Aug. 6, 1928, Brooksville, Ky.   BR TR 6'1"   175 lbs.

	W	L	PCT	ERA	G	GS	CG	IP	H	BB	SO	ShO	W	L	SV	AB	H	HR	BA
1955 **STL N**	1	1	.500	7.88	14	1	0	24	29	15	8	0	1	0	2	2	0	0	.000
1958 **DET A**	4	9	.308	3.61	25	11	6	109.2	83	42	58	0	0	2	1	37	1	0	.027
1959 **BOS A**	0	2	.000	11.42	4	2	0	8.2	10	6	7	0	0	0	0	1	0	0	.000
1962 **NY N**	0	1	.000	7.20	7	0	0	15	21	1	5	0	0	1	0	4	1	0	.250
4 yrs.	5	13	.278	5.03	50	14	6	157.1	143	64	78	0	1	3	3	44	2	0	.045

George Mogridge

MOGRIDGE, GEORGE ANTHONY
B. Feb. 18, 1889, Rochester, N. Y.   D. Mar. 4, 1962, Rochester, N. Y.   BL TL 6'2"   165 lbs.

	W	L	PCT	ERA	G	GS	CG	IP	H	BB	SO	ShO	W	L	SV	AB	H	HR	BA
1911 **CHI A**	0	2	.000	4.97	4	1	0	12.2	12	1	5	0	0	0	0	5	2	0	.400
1912	3	4	.429	4.04	17	7	2	64.2	69	35	31	0	1	1	3	16	2	0	.125
1915 **NY A**	2	3	.400	1.76	6	6	3	41	33	11	11	1	0	0	0	12	1	0	.083
1916	6	12	.333	2.31	30	21	10	194.2	174	45	66	2	1	0	0	66	14	0	.212
1917	9	11	.450	2.98	29	25	15	196.1	185	39	46	1	1	0	0	69	11	0	.159
1918	16	13	.552	2.27	45	19	13	230.1	232	43	62	1	4	7	7	79	15	0	.190
1919	10	7	.588	2.50	35	18	13	187	159	46	58	3	1	1	0	48	6	0	.125
1920	5	9	.357	4.31	26	15	7	125.1	146	36	35	0	0	1	1	42	7	0	.167
1921 **WAS A**	18	14	.563	3.00	38	36	21	288	301	66	101	4	1	0	0	98	15	0	.153
1922	18	13	.581	3.58	34	32	18	251.2	300	72	61	3	0	2	0	86	21	1	.244
1923	13	13	.500	3.11	33	28	17	211	228	56	62	3	0	1	1	75	17	0	.227
1924	16	11	.593	3.76	30	30	13	213	217	61	48	2	0	0	0	74	13	0	.176
1925 **2 teams**							**WAS A** (10G 4–3)					**STL A** (2G 1–1)							
" total	5	4	.556	3.95	12	10	4	68.1	73	23	21	0	0	1	0	23	2	0	.087
1926 **BOS N**	6	10	.375	4.50	39	10	2	142	173	36	46	0	5	3	3	46	8	0	.174
1927	6	4	.600	3.70	20	1	0	48.2	48	15	26	0	6	3	5	15	3	0	.200
15 yrs.	133	130	.506	3.20	398	259	138	2274.2	2350	565	679	20	20	21	20	754	137	1	.182

WORLD SERIES

	W	L	PCT	ERA	G	GS	CG	IP	H	BB	SO	ShO	W	L	SV	AB	H	HR	BA
1924 **WAS A**	1	0	1.000	2.25	2	1	0	12	7	6	5	0	0	0	0	5	0	0	.000

George Mohart

MOHART, BENJAMIN GEORGE
B. Mar. 6, 1892, Buffalo, N. Y.   D. Oct. 2, 1970, Silver Creek, N. Y.   BR TR 5'9"   165 lbs.

	W	L	PCT	ERA	G	GS	CG	IP	H	BB	SO	ShO	W	L	SV	AB	H	HR	BA
1920 **BKN N**	0	1	.000	1.77	13	1	0	35.2	33	7	13	0	0	0	0	8	1	0	.125
1921	0	0	–	3.86	2	0	0	7	8	1	1	0	0	0	0	2	1	0	.500
2 yrs.	0	1	.000	2.11	15	1	0	42.2	41	8	14	0	0	0	0	10	2	0	.200

Bill Moisan

MOISAN, WILLIAM JOSEPH
B. July 30, 1925, Bradford, Mass.   BL TR 6'1"   170 lbs.

	W	L	PCT	ERA	G	GS	CG	IP	H	BB	SO	ShO	W	L	SV	AB	H	HR	BA
1953 **CHI N**	0	0	–	5.40	3	0	0	5	5	2	1	0	0	0	0	0	0	0	–

Carlton Molesworth

MOLESWORTH, CARLTON
B. Feb. 15, 1876, Frederick, Md.   D. July 25, 1961, Frederick, Md.   BL TL 5'6"   200 lbs.

	W	L	PCT	ERA	G	GS	CG	IP	H	BB	SO	ShO	W	L	SV	AB	H	HR	BA
1895 **WAS N**	0	2	.000	14.63	4	3	1	16	33	15	7	0	0	0	0	7	1	0	.143

Rich Moloney

MOLONEY, RICHARD HENRY
B. June 7, 1950, Brookline, Mass.   BR TR 6'3"   185 lbs.

	W	L	PCT	ERA	G	GS	CG	IP	H	BB	SO	ShO	W	L	SV	AB	H	HR	BA
1970 **CHI A**	0	0	–	0.00	1	0	0	1	2	0	1	0	0	0	0	0	0	0	–

Vince Molyneaux

MOLYNEAUX, VINCENT LEO
B. Aug. 17, 1888, Lewiston, N. Y.   D. May 4, 1950, Stamford, Conn.   BR TR 6'   180 lbs.

	W	L	PCT	ERA	G	GS	CG	IP	H	BB	SO	ShO	W	L	SV	AB	H	HR	BA
1917 **STL A**	0	0	–	4.91	7	0	0	22	18	20	4	0	0	0	0	4	0	0	.000
1918 **BOS A**	1	0	1.000	3.38	6	0	0	10.2	3	8	1	0	1	0	0	2	0	0	.000
2 yrs.	1	0	1.000	4.41	13	0	0	32.2	21	28	5	0	1	0	0	6	0	0	.000

	W	L	PCT	ERA	G	GS	CG	IP	H	BB	SO	ShO	Relief Pitching W	L	SV	BATTING AB	H	HR	BA

Rinty Monahan

MONAHAN, EDWARD FRANCIS
B. Apr. 28, 1928, Brooklyn, N. Y.   BR TR 6'1"   195 lbs.

	W	L	PCT	ERA	G	GS	CG	IP	H	BB	SO	ShO	W	L	SV	AB	H	HR	BA
1953 PHI A	0	0	–	4.22	4	0	0	10.2	11	7	2	0	0	0	0	2	0	0	.000

Bill Monbouquette

MONBOUQUETTE, WILLIAM CHARLES
B. Aug. 11, 1936, Medford, Mass.   BR TR 5'11"   190 lbs.

	W	L	PCT	ERA	G	GS	CG	IP	H	BB	SO	ShO	W	L	SV	AB	H	HR	BA
1958 BOS A	3	4	.429	3.31	10	8	3	54.1	52	20	30	0	0	0	0	17	3	0	.176
1959	7	7	.500	4.15	34	17	4	151.2	165	33	87	0	2	1	0	46	3	0	.065
1960	14	11	.560	3.64	35	30	12	215	217	68	134	3	2	0	0	65	6	0	.092
1961	14	14	.500	3.39	32	32	12	236.1	233	100	161	1	0	0	0	69	9	0	.130
1962	15	13	.536	3.33	35	35	11	235.1	227	65	153	4	0	0	0	73	7	0	.096
1963	20	10	.667	3.81	37	36	13	266.2	258	42	174	1	0	1	0	88	10	0	.114
1964	13	14	.481	4.04	36	35	7	234	258	40	120	5	0	0	1	72	6	0	.083
1965	10	18	.357	3.70	35	35	10	228.2	239	40	110	2	0	0	0	68	4	0	.059
1966 DET A	7	8	.467	4.73	30	14	2	102.2	120	22	61	1	3	0	0	26	4	0	.154
1967 2 teams			DET	A (2G 0–0)		NY	A	(33G 6–5)											
" total	6	5	.545	2.33	35	10	2	135.1	123	17	55	1	2	1	1	32	5	0	.156
1968 2 teams			NY	A (17G 5–7)		SF	N	(7G 0–1)											
" total	5	8	.385	4.35	24	11	2	101.1	103	15	37	0	1	4	1	26	3	0	.115
11 yrs.	114	112	.504	3.68	343	263	78	1961.1	1995	462	1122	18	10	7	3	582	60	0	.103

Sid Monge

MONGE, ISIDRO PEDROZA
B. Apr. 11, 1951, Agun Prieta, Mexico   BB TL 6'2"   185 lbs.

	W	L	PCT	ERA	G	GS	CG	IP	H	BB	SO	ShO	W	L	SV	AB	H	HR	BA
1975 CAL A	0	2	.000	4.18	4	2	2	23.2	22	10	17	0	0	0	0	0	0	0	–
1976	6	7	.462	3.36	32	13	2	118	108	49	53	0	2	2	0	0	0	0	–
1977 2 teams			CAL	A (4G 0–1)		CLE	A	(33G 1–2)											
" total	1	3	.250	5.44	37	0	0	51.1	61	33	29	0	1	3	4	0	0	0	–
1978 CLE A	4	3	.571	2.76	48	2	0	84.2	71	51	54	0	4	2	6	0	0	0	–
1979	12	10	.545	2.40	76	0	0	131	96	64	108	0	12	10	19	0	0	0	–
1980	3	5	.375	3.54	67	0	0	94	80	40	60	0	3	5	14	0	0	0	–
1981	3	5	.375	4.34	31	0	0	58	58	21	41	0	3	5	4	0	0	0	–
1982 PHI N	7	1	.875	3.75	47	0	0	72	70	22	43	0	7	1	2	9	1	0	.111
1983 2 teams			PHI	N (14G 3–0)		SD	N	(47G 7–3)											
" total	10	3	.769	3.70	61	0	0	80.1	85	37	39	0	10	3	7	11	1	0	.091
1984 2 teams			SD	N (13G 2–1)		DET	A	(19G 1–0)											
" total	3	1	.750	4.41	32	0	0	51	57	29	26	0	3	1	0	1	0	0	.000
10 yrs.	49	40	.551	3.53	435	17	4	764	708	356	470	0	45	32	56	21	2	0	.095

Ed Monroe

MONROE, EDWARD OLIVER (Peck)
B. Feb. 22, 1895, Louisville, Ky.   D. Apr. 29, 1969, Louisville, Ky.   BR TR 6'5"   187 lbs.

	W	L	PCT	ERA	G	GS	CG	IP	H	BB	SO	ShO	W	L	SV	AB	H	HR	BA
1917 NY A	1	0	1.000	3.45	9	1	1	28.2	35	6	12	0	0	0	1	12	2	0	.167
1918	0	0	–	4.50	1	0	0	2	1	2	1	0	0	0	0	0	0	0	–
2 yrs.	1	0	1.000	3.52	10	1	1	30.2	36	8	13	0	0	0	1	12	2	0	.167

Larry Monroe

MONROE, LAWRENCE JAMES
B. June 20, 1956, Detroit, Mich.   BR TR 6'4"   200 lbs.

	W	L	PCT	ERA	G	GS	CG	IP	H	BB	SO	ShO	W	L	SV	AB	H	HR	BA
1976 CHI A	0	1	.000	4.09	8	2	0	22	23	13	9	0	0	0	0	0	0	0	–

Zack Monroe

MONROE, ZACHARY CHARLES
B. July 8, 1931, Peoria, Ill.   BR TR 6'   198 lbs.

	W	L	PCT	ERA	G	GS	CG	IP	H	BB	SO	ShO	W	L	SV	AB	H	HR	BA
1958 NY A	4	2	.667	3.26	21	6	1	58	57	27	18	0	1	1	1	17	2	0	.118
1959	0	0	–	5.40	3	0	0	3.1	3	2	1	0	0	0	0	0	0	0	–
2 yrs.	4	2	.667	3.38	24	6	1	61.1	60	29	19	0	1	1	1	17	2	0	.118

WORLD SERIES

	W	L	PCT	ERA	G	GS	CG	IP	H	BB	SO	ShO	W	L	SV	AB	H	HR	BA
1958 NY A	0	0	–	27.00	1	0	0	1	3	1	1	0	0	0	0	0	0	0	–

John Montague

MONTAGUE, JOHN EVANS
B. Sept. 12, 1947, Newport News, Va.   BR TR 6'2"   213 lbs.

	W	L	PCT	ERA	G	GS	CG	IP	H	BB	SO	ShO	W	L	SV	AB	H	HR	BA
1973 MON N	0	0	–	3.52	4	0	0	7.2	8	2	7	0	0	0	0	1	0	0	.000
1974	3	4	.429	3.14	46	1	0	83	73	38	43	0	3	3	3	10	1	0	.100
1975 2 teams			MON	N (12G 0–1)		PHI	N	(3G 0–0)											
" total	0	1	.000	6.35	15	0	0	22.2	31	10	10	0	0	1	2	1	0	0	.000
1977 SEA A	8	12	.400	3.44	47	15	2	182	193	75	98	0	4	2	4	0	0	0	–
1978	1	3	.250	6.18	19	0	0	43.2	52	24	14	0	1	3	2	0	0	0	–
1979 2 teams			SEA	A (41G 6–4)		CAL	N	(14G 2–0)											
" total	8	4	.667	5.51	55	1	0	134	141	56	66	0	8	3	7	0	0	0	–
1980 CAL A	4	2	.667	5.11	37	0	0	74	97	21	22	0	4	2	3	0	0	0	–
7 yrs.	24	26	.480	4.76	223	17	2	547	595	226	260	0	20	14	21	12	1	0	.083

LEAGUE CHAMPIONSHIP SERIES

	W	L	PCT	ERA	G	GS	CG	IP	H	BB	SO	ShO	W	L	SV	AB	H	HR	BA
1979 CAL A	0	1	.000	9.00	2	0	0	4	4	2	2	0	0	1	0	0	0	0	–

Aurelio Monteagudo

MONTEAGUDO, AURELIO FAUTINO CINTRA
Son of Rene Monteagudo.
B. Nov. 28, 1943, Caibarien, Cuba   BR TR 5'11"   180 lbs.

	W	L	PCT	ERA	G	GS	CG	IP	H	BB	SO	ShO	W	L	SV	AB	H	HR	BA
1963 KC A	0	0	–	2.57	4	0	0	7	4	3	3	0	0	0	0	0	0	0	.286
1964	0	4	.000	8.90	11	6	0	31.1	40	10	14	0	0	0	0	7	2	0	–
1965	0	0	–	3.86	4	0	0	7	5	4	5	0	0	0	0	0	0	0	–
1966 2 teams			KC	A (6G 0–0)		HOU	N	(10G 0–0)											
" total	0	0	–	3.86	16	0	0	28	26	18	10	0	0	0	1	1	0	0	.000
1967 CHI A	0	1	.000	20.25	1	1	0	1.1	4	2	0	0	0	0	0	0	0	0	–
1970 KC A	1	1	.500	3.00	21	0	0	27	20	9	18	0	1	1	0	2	0	0	.000
1973 CAL A	2	1	.667	4.20	15	0	0	30	23	16	8	0	2	1	3	0	0	0	–
7 yrs.	3	7	.300	5.06	72	7	0	131.2	122	62	58	0	3	2	4	10	2	0	.200

	W	L	PCT	ERA	G	GS	CG	IP	H	BB	SO	ShO	Relief Pitching W	L	SV	AB	H	HR	BA

Rene Monteagudo

MONTEAGUDO, RENE MIRANDA
Father of Aurelio Monteagudo.
B. Mar. 12, 1916, Santa Clara, Cuba   D. Sept. 14, 1973, Hialeah, Fla.
BL TL 5'7"   165 lbs.

Year	W	L	PCT	ERA	G	GS	CG	IP	H	BB	SO	ShO	RP W	L	SV	AB	H	HR	BA
1938 WAS A	1	1	.500	5.73	5	3	2	22	26	15	13	0	0	0	0	6	3	0	.500
1940	2	6	.250	6.08	27	8	3	100.2	128	52	64	0	0	1	2	33	6	0	.182
1945 PHI N	0	0	—	7.49	14	0	0	45.2	67	28	16	0	0	0	0	193	58	0	.301
3 yrs.	3	7	.300	6.42	46	11	5	168.1	221	95	93	0	0	1	2	*			

John Montefusco

MONTEFUSCO, JOHN JOSEPH (The Count)
B. May 25, 1950, Long Branch, N. J.
BR TR 6'1"   180 lbs.

Year	W	L	PCT	ERA	G	GS	CG	IP	H	BB	SO	ShO	RP W	L	SV	AB	H	HR	BA
1974 SF N	3	2	.600	4.85	7	5	1	39	41	19	34	1	1	0	0	14	4	2	.286
1975	15	9	.625	2.88	35	34	10	244	210	86	215	4	0	0	0	80	7	1	.088
1976	16	14	.533	2.84	37	36	11	253.1	224	74	172	6	0	0	0	78	8	0	.103
1977	7	12	.368	3.50	26	25	4	157	170	46	110	0	0	0	0	49	6	1	.122
1978	11	9	.550	3.80	36	36	3	239	233	68	177	0	0	0	0	70	4	0	.057
1979	3	8	.273	3.94	22	22	0	137	145	51	76	0	0	0	0	42	7	0	.167
1980	4	8	.333	4.38	22	17	1	113	120	39	85	0	1	0	0	30	1	0	.033
1981 ATL N	2	3	.400	3.51	26	9	0	77	75	27	34	0	0	0	1	15	1	0	.067
1982 SD N	10	11	.476	4.00	32	32	1	184.1	177	41	83	0	0	0	0	58	5	0	.086
1983 2 teams			SD N (31G 9–4)					NY A (6G 5–0)											
" total	14	4	.778	3.31	37	16	1	133.1	133	42	67	0	6	1	4	19	1	0	.053
1984 NY A	5	3	.625	3.58	11	11	0	55.1	55	13	23	0	0	0	0	0	0	0	—
11 yrs.	90	83	.520	3.52	291	243	32	1632.1	1583	506	1076	11	8	1	5	455	44	4	.097

Manny Montejo

MONTEJO, MANUEL (Pete)
B. Oct. 16, 1936, Havana, Cuba
BR TR 5'11"   166 lbs.

Year	W	L	PCT	ERA	G	GS	CG	IP	H	BB	SO	ShO	RP W	L	SV	AB	H	HR	BA
1961 DET A	0	0	—	3.86	12	0	0	16.1	13	6	15	0	0	0	0	0	0	0	—

Monty Montgomery

MONTGOMERY, MONTY BRYSON
B. Sept. 1, 1946, Albermarle, N. C.
BR TR 6'3"   200 lbs.

Year	W	L	PCT	ERA	G	GS	CG	IP	H	BB	SO	ShO	RP W	L	SV	AB	H	HR	BA
1971 KC A	3	0	1.000	2.14	3	2	0	21	16	3	12	0	1	0	0	7	0	0	.000
1972	3	3	.500	3.05	9	8	1	56	55	17	24	1	0	0	0	17	3	0	.176
2 yrs.	6	3	.667	2.81	12	10	1	77	71	20	36	1	1	0	0	24	3	0	.125

Ray Monzant

MONZANT, RAMON SEGUNDO
B. Jan. 4, 1933, Maracaibo, Venezuela
BR TR 6'   160 lbs.

Year	W	L	PCT	ERA	G	GS	CG	IP	H	BB	SO	ShO	RP W	L	SV	AB	H	HR	BA
1954 NY N	0	0	—	4.70	6	1	0	7.2	8	11	5	0	0	0	0	2	0	0	.000
1955	4	8	.333	3.99	28	12	3	94.2	98	43	54	0	2	1	0	24	3	0	.125
1956	1	0	1.000	4.15	4	1	1	13	8	7	11	0	0	0	0	4	0	0	.000
1957	3	2	.600	3.99	24	2	0	49.2	55	16	37	0	3	0	0	10	3	0	.300
1958 SF N	8	11	.421	4.72	43	16	4	150.2	160	57	93	1	3	5	1	49	8	0	.163
1960	0	0	—	9.00	1	0	0	1	1	0	1	0	0	0	0	0	0	0	—
6 yrs.	16	21	.432	4.38	106	32	8	316.2	330	134	201	1	8	6	1	89	14	0	.157

Leo Moon

MOON, LEO (Lefty)
B. June 22, 1899, Belmont, N. C.   D. Aug. 25, 1970, New Orleans, La.
BR TL 5'11"   165 lbs.

Year	W	L	PCT	ERA	G	GS	CG	IP	H	BB	SO	ShO	RP W	L	SV	AB	H	HR	BA
1932 CLE A	0	0	—	11.12	1	0	0	5.2	11	7	1	0	0	0	0	2	1	0	.500

Jim Mooney

MOONEY, JAMES IRVING
B. Sept. 4, 1906, Mooresburg, Tenn.   D. Apr. 27, 1979, Johnson City, Tenn.
BR TL 5'11"   168 lbs.

Year	W	L	PCT	ERA	G	GS	CG	IP	H	BB	SO	ShO	RP W	L	SV	AB	H	HR	BA
1931 NY N	7	1	.875	2.01	10	8	6	71.2	71	16	38	2	1	0	0	25	4	0	.160
1932	6	10	.375	5.05	29	18	4	124.2	154	42	37	1	0	1	0	41	5	0	.122
1933 STL N	2	5	.286	3.72	21	8	2	77.1	87	26	14	0	0	1	1	20	1	0	.050
1934	2	4	.333	5.47	32	7	1	82.1	114	49	27	0	2	0	1	19	1	0	.053
4 yrs.	17	20	.459	4.25	92	41	13	356	426	133	116	3	3	2	2	105	11	0	.105

WORLD SERIES

Year	W	L	PCT	ERA	G	GS	CG	IP	H	BB	SO	ShO	RP W	L	SV	AB	H	HR	BA
1934 STL N	0	0	—	0.00	1	0	0	1	0	0	0	0	0	0	0	0	0	0	—

Balor Moore

MOORE, BALOR LILBON
B. Jan. 25, 1951, Smithville, Tex.
BL TL 6'2"   178 lbs.

Year	W	L	PCT	ERA	G	GS	CG	IP	H	BB	SO	ShO	RP W	L	SV	AB	H	HR	BA
1970 MON N	0	2	.000	7.20	6	2	0	10	14	8	6	0	0	0	0	3	1	0	.333
1972	9	9	.500	3.47	22	22	6	147.2	122	59	161	3	0	0	0	55	8	0	.145
1973	7	16	.304	4.49	35	32	3	176.1	151	109	151	1	0	1	0	53	3	0	.057
1974	0	2	.000	3.86	8	2	0	14	13	15	16	0	0	0	0	2	0	0	.000
1977 CAL A	0	2	.000	3.97	7	3	0	22.2	28	10	14	0	0	0	0	0	0	0	—
1978 TOR A	6	9	.400	4.86	37	18	2	144.1	165	54	75	0	2	0	0	0	0	0	—
1979	5	7	.417	4.86	34	16	5	139	135	79	51	0	0	0	0	0	0	0	—
1980	1	1	.500	5.26	31	3	0	65	76	31	22	0	1	0	1	0	0	0	—
8 yrs.	28	48	.368	4.51	180	98	16	719	704	365	496	4	3	1	1	113	12	0	.106

Barry Moore

MOORE, ROBERT BARRY
B. Apr. 3, 1943, Statesville, N. C.
BL TL 6'1"   190 lbs.

Year	W	L	PCT	ERA	G	GS	CG	IP	H	BB	SO	ShO	RP W	L	SV	AB	H	HR	BA
1965 WAS A	0	0	—	0.00	1	0	0	1	1	1	0	0	0	0	0	0	0	0	—
1966	3	3	.500	3.75	12	11	1	62.1	55	39	28	0	0	0	0	19	2	0	.105
1967	7	11	.389	3.76	27	26	3	143.2	127	71	74	1	0	0	0	46	6	0	.130
1968	4	6	.400	3.37	32	18	0	117.2	116	42	56	0	0	0	3	31	3	0	.097
1969	9	8	.529	4.30	31	25	4	134	123	67	51	0	0	2	0	43	9	0	.209
1970 2 teams			CLE A (13G 3–5)					CHI A (24G 0–4)											
" total	3	9	.250	5.30	37	19	0	141	155	80	69	0	0	0	0	40	7	0	.175
6 yrs.	26	37	.413	4.16	140	99	8	599.2	577	300	278	1	0	2	3	179	27	0	.151

Bill Moore

MOORE, WILLIAM CHRISTOPHER
B. Sept. 3, 1902, Corning, N. Y.
BR TR 6'3"   195 lbs.

Year	W	L	PCT	ERA	G	GS	CG	IP	H	BB	SO	ShO	RP W	L	SV	AB	H	HR	BA
1925 DET A	0	0	—	∞	1	0	0	0	3	0	0	0	0	0	0	0	0	0	—

	W	L	PCT	ERA	G	GS	CG	IP	H	BB	SO	ShO	Relief Pitching W	L	SV	BATTING AB	H	HR	BA

Carlos Moore

MOORE, CARLOS WHITMAN   BR TR 6'1½" 180 lbs.
B. Aug. 13, 1906, Clinton, Tenn.   D. July 2, 1958, New Orleans, La.

	W	L	PCT	ERA	G	GS	CG	IP	H	BB	SO	ShO	W	L	SV	AB	H	HR	BA
1930 WAS A	0	0	–	2.31	4	0	0	11.2	9	4	2	0	0	0	0	4	0	0	.000

Cy Moore

MOORE, WILLIAM AUSTIN   BR TR 6'1" 190 lbs.
B. Feb. 7, 1905, Elberton, Ga.   D. Mar. 28, 1972, Augusta, Ga.

	W	L	PCT	ERA	G	GS	CG	IP	H	BB	SO	ShO	W	L	SV	AB	H	HR	BA
1929 BKN N	3	3	.500	5.56	32	4	0	68	87	31	17	0	2	1	2	16	3	0	.188
1930	0	0	–	0.00	1	0	0	2	2	0	0	0	0	0	0	0	0	0	–
1931	1	2	.333	3.79	23	1	1	61.2	62	13	35	0	1	1	0	13	2	0	.154
1932	0	3	.000	4.81	20	2	0	48.2	56	17	23	0	0	2	0	14	3	0	.214
1933 PHI N	8	9	.471	3.74	36	18	9	161.1	177	42	53	3	2	0	1	48	3	0	.063
1934	4	9	.308	6.47	35	15	3	126.2	163	65	55	0	2	0	0	42	6	0	.143
6 yrs.	16	26	.381	4.86	147	40	13	466.1	547	168	183	3	7	4	3	133	17	0	.128

Dee Moore

MOORE, D C   BR TR 6' 200 lbs.
B. Apr. 6, 1914, Hedley, Tex.

	W	L	PCT	ERA	G	GS	CG	IP	H	BB	SO	ShO	W	L	SV	AB	H	HR	BA
1936 CIN N	0	0	–	0.00	2	1	0	7	3	2	3	0	0	0	0	*			

Donnie Moore

MOORE, DONNIE RAY   BL TR 6' 175 lbs.
B. Feb. 13, 1954, Lubbock, Tex.

	W	L	PCT	ERA	G	GS	CG	IP	H	BB	SO	ShO	W	L	SV	AB	H	HR	BA
1975 CHI N	0	0	–	4.00	4	1	0	9	12	4	8	0	0	0	0	3	0	0	.000
1977	4	2	.667	4.04	27	1	0	49	51	18	34	0	3	2	0	10	3	0	.300
1978	9	7	.563	4.11	71	1	0	103	117	31	50	0	9	7	4	15	4	0	.267
1979	1	4	.200	5.18	39	1	0	73	95	25	43	0	1	3	1	13	2	0	.154
1980 STL N	1	1	.500	6.14	11	0	0	22	25	5	10	0	1	1	0	4	3	0	.750
1981 MIL A	0	0	–	6.75	3	0	0	4	4	4	2	0	0	0	0	0	0	0	–
1982 ATL N	3	1	.750	4.23	16	0	0	27.2	32	7	17	0	3	1	1	1	0	0	.000
1983	2	3	.400	3.67	43	0	0	68.2	72	10	41	0	2	3	6	8	4	0	.500
1984	4	5	.444	2.94	47	0	0	64.1	63	18	47	0	4	5	16	3	0	0	.000
9 yrs.	24	23	.511	4.17	261	4	0	420.2	471	122	252	0	23	22	28	57	16	0	.281

LEAGUE CHAMPIONSHIP SERIES

	W	L	PCT	ERA	G	GS	CG	IP	H	BB	SO	ShO	W	L	SV	AB	H	HR	BA
1982 ATL N	0	0	–	0.00	2	0	0	2.2	2	0	1	0	0	0	0	0	0	0	–

Earl Moore

MOORE, EARL ALONZO (Crossfire)   BR TR 6' 195 lbs.
B. July 29, 1878, Pickerington, Ohio   D. Nov. 28, 1961, Columbus, Ohio

	W	L	PCT	ERA	G	GS	CG	IP	H	BB	SO	ShO	W	L	SV	AB	H	HR	BA
1901 CLE A	16	14	.533	2.90	31	30	28	251.1	234	107	99	4	0	0	0	99	16	0	.162
1902	17	17	.500	2.95	36	34	29	293	304	101	84	4	1	0	1	113	24	0	.212
1903	19	9	.679	1.77	29	27	27	238.2	189	56	142	3	0	1	1	84	8	0	.095
1904	12	11	.522	2.25	26	24	22	227.2	186	61	139	1	0	1	0	86	12	0	.140
1905	15	15	.500	2.64	31	30	28	269	232	92	131	3	0	0	0	94	10	0	.106
1906	1	1	.500	3.94	5	4	2	29.2	27	18	8	0	0	0	0	10	0	0	.000
1907 2 teams			CLE	A (3G 1–1)			NY	A (12G 2–6)											
" total	3	7	.300	4.10	15	11	4	83.1	90	38	35	0	0	0	1	29	6	0	.207
1908 PHI N	2	1	.667	0.00	3	3	3	26	20	8	16	1	0	0	0	9	2	0	.222
1909	18	12	.600	2.10	38	34	24	299.2	238	108	173	4	2	1	0	96	9	0	.094
1910	22	15	.595	2.58	46	35	19	283	228	121	185	6	3	3	0	87	20	0	.230
1911	15	19	.441	2.63	42	36	21	308.1	265	164	174	5	0	2	1	101	11	0	.109
1912	9	14	.391	3.31	31	24	10	182.1	186	77	79	1	2	0	0	56	6	0	.107
1913 2 teams			PHI	N (12G 1–3)			CHI	N (7G 1–1)											
" total	2	4	.333	4.82	19	6	0	80.1	84	52	36	0	0	0	1	24	1	0	.042
1914 BUF F	10	14	.417	4.30	36	27	14	194.2	184	99	96	2	0	1	2	56	9	0	.161
14 yrs.	161	153	.513	2.78	388	325	231	2767	2467	1102	1397	34	8	9	7	944	134	0	.142

Euel Moore

MOORE, EUEL WALTON (Chief)   BR TR 6'2" 185 lbs.
B. May 27, 1908, Reagan, Okla.

	W	L	PCT	ERA	G	GS	CG	IP	H	BB	SO	ShO	W	L	SV	AB	H	HR	BA
1934 PHI N	5	7	.417	4.05	20	16	3	122.1	145	41	38	0	0	1	1	46	5	0	.109
1935 2 teams			PHI	N (15G 1–6)			NY	N (6G 1–0)											
" total	2	6	.250	7.45	21	8	1	48.1	72	24	18	0	1	0	1	17	6	0	.353
1936 PHI N	2	3	.400	6.96	20	5	1	54.1	76	12	19	0	0	2	1	18	4	0	.222
3 yrs.	9	16	.360	5.48	61	29	5	225	293	77	75	0	1	3	3	81	15	0	.185

Gene Moore

MOORE, EUGENE, JR. (Blue Goose)   BL TL 6'2" 185 lbs.
Father of Gene Moore.
B. Nov. 9, 1885, Lancaster, Tex.   D. Mar. 12, 1978, Jackson, Miss.

	W	L	PCT	ERA	G	GS	CG	IP	H	BB	SO	ShO	W	L	SV	AB	H	HR	BA
1909 PIT N	0	0	–	18.00	1	0	0	2	4	3	2	0	0	0	0	1	0	0	.000
1910	2	1	.667	3.12	4	1	0	17.1	19	7	9	0	2	1	0	6	0	0	.000
1912 CIN N	0	1	.000	4.91	5	2	0	14.2	17	11	6	0	0	0	1	4	0	0	.000
3 yrs.	2	2	.500	4.76	10	3	0	34	40	21	17	0	2	1	1	11	0	0	.000

George Moore

MOORE, GEORGE RAYMOND
B. Nov. 25, 1872, Cambridge, Mass.   D. Nov. 4, 1948, Hyannis, Mass.

	W	L	PCT	ERA	G	GS	CG	IP	H	BB	SO	ShO	W	L	SV	AB	H	HR	BA
1905 PIT N	0	0	–	0.00	1	0	0	3	2	0	1	0	0	0	0	1	0	0	.000

Jim Moore

MOORE, JAMES STANFORD   BR TR 6' 165 lbs.
B. Dec. 14, 1904, Prescott, Ark.   D. May 19, 1973, Seattle, Wash.

	W	L	PCT	ERA	G	GS	CG	IP	H	BB	SO	ShO	W	L	SV	AB	H	HR	BA
1928 CLE A	0	1	.000	2.00	1	1	1	9	5	5	1	0	0	0	0	3	0	0	.000
1929	0	0	–	9.53	2	0	0	5.2	6	4	0	0	0	0	0	2	0	0	.000
1930 CHI A	2	1	.667	3.60	9	5	2	40	42	12	11	0	0	0	1	13	3	0	.231
1931	0	2	.000	4.95	33	4	0	83.2	93	27	15	0	0	0	0	16	1	0	.063
1932	0	0	–	0.00	1	0	0	1	1	1	2	0	0	0	0	1	0	0	.000
5 yrs.	2	4	.333	4.52	46	10	3	139.1	147	49	29	0	0	0	1	35	4	0	.114

Mike Moore

MOORE, MICHAEL WAYNE   BR TR 6'4" 205 lbs.
B. Nov. 26, 1959, Eakly, Okla.

	W	L	PCT	ERA	G	GS	CG	IP	H	BB	SO	ShO	W	L	SV	AB	H	HR	BA
1982 SEA A	7	14	.333	5.36	28	27	1	144.1	159	79	73	1	0	0	0	0	0	0	–
1983	6	8	.429	4.71	22	21	3	128	130	60	108	2	0	0	0	0	0	0	–

	W	L	PCT	ERA	G	GS	CG	IP	H	BB	SO	ShO	Relief Pitching W	L	SV	BATTING AB	H	HR	BA

Mike Moore continued

	W	L	PCT	ERA	G	GS	CG	IP	H	BB	SO	ShO	W	L	SV	AB	H	HR	BA
1984	7	17	.292	4.97	34	33	6	212	236	85	158	0	0	0	0	0	0	0	–
3 yrs.	20	39	.339	5.02	84	81	10	484.1	525	224	339	3	0	0	0	0	0	0	–

Ray Moore

MOORE, RAYMOND LEROY (Farmer)
B. June 1, 1926, Meadows, Md.   BR TR 6'   195 lbs.

	W	L	PCT	ERA	G	GS	CG	IP	H	BB	SO	ShO	W	L	SV	AB	H	HR	BA
1952 BKN N	1	2	.333	4.76	14	2	0	28.1	29	26	11	0	1	0	0	3	0	0	.000
1953	0	1	.000	3.38	1	1	1	8	6	4	4	0	0	0	0	3	0	0	.000
1955 BAL A	10	10	.500	3.92	46	14	3	151.2	128	80	80	1	3	7	6	44	6	0	.136
1956	12	7	.632	4.18	32	27	9	185	161	99	105	1	1	1	0	70	19	2	.271
1957	11	13	.458	3.72	34	32	7	227.1	196	112	117	1	0	1	0	84	18	3	.214
1958 CHI A	9	7	.563	3.82	32	20	4	136.2	107	70	73	2	2	3	2	44	9	1	.205
1959	3	6	.333	4.12	29	8	0	89.2	86	46	49	0	2	1	0	23	2	0	.087
1960 2 teams			CHI	A	(14G 1–1)		WAS	A	(37G 3–2)										
" total	4	3	.571	3.54	51	0	0	86.1	68	38	32	0	4	3	13	16	1	0	.063
1961 MIN A	4	4	.500	3.67	46	0	0	56.1	49	38	45	0	4	4	14	4	0	0	.000
1962	8	3	.727	4.73	49	0	0	64.2	55	30	58	0	8	3	9	5	0	0	.000
1963	1	3	.250	6.98	31	1	0	38.2	50	17	38	0	1	2	2	3	1	0	.333
11 yrs.	63	59	.516	4.06	365	105	24	1072.2	935	560	612	5	26	25	46	299	56	6	.187
WORLD SERIES																			
1959 CHI A	0	0	–	9.00	1	0	0	1	1	0	1	0	0	0	0	0	0	0	–

Roy Moore

MOORE, ROY DANIEL
B. Dec. 26, 1898, Austin, Tex.
D. Apr. 5, 1951, Seattle, Wash.   BB TL 6'   185 lbs.   BL 1921,1923

	W	L	PCT	ERA	G	GS	CG	IP	H	BB	SO	ShO	W	L	SV	AB	H	HR	BA
1920 PHI A	1	13	.071	4.68	24	16	7	132.2	161	64	45	0	0	0	0	50	10	1	.200
1921	10	10	.500	4.51	29	26	12	191.2	206	122	64	0	0	0	0	74	19	3	.257
1922 2 teams			PHI	A	(15G 0–3)		DET	A	(9G 0–0)										
" total	0	3	.000	7.17	24	6	0	70.1	94	42	38	0	0	1	2	26	8	0	.308
1923 DET A	0	0	–	3.00	3	0	0	12	15	11	7	0	0	0	1	5	0	0	.000
4 yrs.	11	26	.297	4.98	80	48	19	406.2	476	239	154	0	0	1	3	155	37	4	.239

Terry Moore

MOORE, TERRY BLUFORD
B. May 27, 1912, Vernon, Ala.
Manager 1954.   BR TR 5'11"   195 lbs.

	W	L	PCT	ERA	G	GS	CG	IP	H	BB	SO	ShO	W	L	SV	AB	H	HR	BA
1939 STL N	0	0	–	0.00	1	0	0	1	0	0	1	0	0	0	0	*			

Tommy Moore

MOORE, TOMMY JOE
B. July 7, 1948, Lynwood, Calif.   BR TR 5'11"   175 lbs.

	W	L	PCT	ERA	G	GS	CG	IP	H	BB	SO	ShO	W	L	SV	AB	H	HR	BA
1972 NY N	0	0	–	2.92	3	1	0	12.1	12	1	5	0	0	0	0	3	1	0	.333
1973	0	1	.000	10.80	3	1	0	3.1	6	3	1	0	0	0	0	0	0	0	–
1975 2 teams			STL	N	(10G 0–0)		TEX	A	(12G 0–2)										
" total	0	2	.000	6.08	22	0	0	40	46	24	21	0	0	2	0	2	1	0	.500
1977 SEA A	2	1	.667	4.91	14	1	0	33	36	21	13	0	2	0	0	0	0	0	–
4 yrs.	2	4	.333	5.38	42	3	0	88.2	100	49	40	0	2	2	0	5	2	0	.400

Whitey Moore

MOORE, LLOYD ALBERT
B. June 10, 1912, Tuscarawas, Ohio   BR TR 6'1"   195 lbs.

	W	L	PCT	ERA	G	GS	CG	IP	H	BB	SO	ShO	W	L	SV	AB	H	HR	BA
1936 CIN N	1	0	1.000	5.40	1	0	0	5	3	3	4	0	1	0	0	2	0	0	.000
1937	0	3	.000	4.89	13	6	0	38.2	32	39	27	0	0	0	0	8	0	0	.000
1938	6	4	.600	3.49	19	11	3	90.1	66	42	38	1	2	0	0	26	2	0	.077
1939	13	12	.520	3.45	42	24	9	187.2	177	95	81	2	4	0	3	61	6	0	.098
1940	8	8	.500	3.63	25	15	5	116.2	100	56	60	1	2	2	1	39	5	0	.128
1941	2	1	.667	4.38	23	4	1	61.2	62	45	17	0	1	0	0	18	3	0	.167
1942 2 teams			CIN	N	(1G 0–0)		STL	N	(9G 0–1)										
" total	0	1	.000	4.05	10	0	0	13.1	10	12	1	0	0	1	0	2	0	0	.000
7 yrs.	30	29	.508	3.75	133	60	18	513.1	450	292	228	4	10	3	4	156	16	0	.103
WORLD SERIES																			
1939 CIN N	0	0	–	0.00	1	0	0	3	0	0	2	0	0	0	0	1	0	0	.000
1940	0	0	–	3.24	1	0	0	8.1	8	6	7	0	0	0	0	2	0	0	.000
2 yrs.	0	0	–	2.38	2	0	0	11.1	8	6	9	0	0	0	0	3	0	0	.000

Wilcy Moore

MOORE, WILLIAM WILCY (Cy)
B. May 20, 1897, Bonita, Tex.   D. Mar. 29, 1963, Hollis, Okla.   BR TR 6'   195 lbs.

	W	L	PCT	ERA	G	GS	CG	IP	H	BB	SO	ShO	W	L	SV	AB	H	HR	BA
1927 NY A	19	7	.731	2.28	50	12	6	213	185	59	75	1	13	3	13	75	6	1	.080
1928	4	4	.500	4.18	35	2	0	60.1	71	31	18	0	3	3	2	14	2	0	.143
1929	6	4	.600	4.06	41	0	0	62	64	19	21	0	6	4	8	15	1	0	.067
1931 BOS A	11	13	.458	3.88	53	15	8	185.1	195	55	37	1	7	2	10	56	9	0	.161
1932 2 teams			BOS	A	(37G 4–10)		NY	A	(10G 2–0)										
" total	6	10	.375	4.61	47	3	0	109.1	125	48	36	0	5	8	8	30	1	0	.033
1933 NY A	5	6	.455	5.52	35	0	0	62	92	20	17	0	5	6	8	15	2	0	.133
6 yrs.	51	44	.537	3.69	261	32	14	692	732	232	204	2	39	26	49	205	21	1	.102
WORLD SERIES																			
1927 NY A	1	0	1.000	0.84	2	1	1	10.2	11	2	2	0	0	0	1	5	1	0	.200
1932	1	0	1.000	0.00	1	0	0	5.1	2	0	1	0	1	0	0	3	1	0	.333
2 yrs.	2	0	1.000	0.56	3	1	1	16	13	2	3	0	1	0	1	8	2	0	.250

Bob Moorhead

MOORHEAD, CHARLES ROBERT
B. Jan. 23, 1938, Chambersburg, Pa.   BR TR 6'1"   208 lbs.

	W	L	PCT	ERA	G	GS	CG	IP	H	BB	SO	ShO	W	L	SV	AB	H	HR	BA
1962 NY N	0	2	.000	4.53	38	7	0	105.1	118	42	63	0	0	1	0	22	1	0	.045
1965	0	1	.000	4.40	9	0	0	14.1	16	5	5	0	0	1	0	0	0	0	–
2 yrs.	0	3	.000	4.51	47	7	0	119.2	134	47	68	0	0	2	0	22	1	0	.045

	W	L	PCT	ERA	G	GS	CG	IP	H	BB	SO	ShO	Relief W	Relief L	Relief SV	AB	H	HR	BA

Bob Moose

MOOSE, ROBERT RALPH   BR TR 6'   200 lbs.
B. Oct. 9, 1947, Export, Pa.   D. Oct. 9, 1976, Martin's Ferry, Ohio

	W	L	PCT	ERA	G	GS	CG	IP	H	BB	SO	ShO	Relief W	Relief L	Relief SV	AB	H	HR	BA
1967 PIT N	1	0	1.000	3.68	2	2	1	14.2	14	4	7	0	0	0	0	6	2	0	.333
1968	8	12	.400	2.74	38	22	3	170.2	136	41	126	3	0	4	3	54	5	0	.093
1969	14	3	.824	2.91	44	19	6	170	149	62	165	1	0	0	4	53	4	0	.075
1970	11	10	.524	3.98	28	27	9	190	186	64	119	2	0	0	0	66	12	0	.182
1971	11	7	.611	4.11	30	18	3	140	169	35	68	1	4	1	1	39	4	0	.103
1972	13	10	.565	2.91	31	30	6	226	213	47	144	3	0	0	1	71	12	0	.169
1973	12	13	.480	3.53	33	29	6	201.1	219	70	111	3	1	0	0	67	9	0	.134
1974	1	5	.167	7.50	7	6	0	36	59	7	15	0	0	0	0	11	2	0	.182
1975	2	2	.500	3.71	23	5	1	68	63	25	34	0	1	0	0	18	3	0	.167
1976	3	9	.250	3.70	53	2	0	87.2	100	32	38	0	3	7	10	12	3	1	.250
10 yrs.	76	71	.517	3.50	289	160	35	1304.1	1308	387	827	13	9	12	19	397	56	1	.141

LEAGUE CHAMPIONSHIP SERIES

	W	L	PCT	ERA	G	GS	CG	IP	H	BB	SO	ShO	Relief W	Relief L	Relief SV	AB	H	HR	BA
1970 PIT N	0	1	.000	3.52	1	1	0	7.2	4	2	4	0	0	0	0	4	0	0	.000
1971	0	0	—	0.00	1	0	0	2	0	0	0	0	0	0	0	0	0	0	—
1972	0	1	.000	54.00	2	1	0	.2	5	0	0	0	0	0	0	0	0	0	—
3 yrs.	0	2	.000	6.10	4	2	0	10.1	9	2	4	0	0	0	0	4	0	0	.000

WORLD SERIES

	W	L	PCT	ERA	G	GS	CG	IP	H	BB	SO	ShO	Relief W	Relief L	Relief SV	AB	H	HR	BA
1971 PIT N	0	0	—	6.52	3	1	0	9.2	12	2	7	0	0	0	0	2	0	0	.000

Jake Mooty

MOOTY, J T   BR TR 5'10½" 170 lbs.
B. Apr. 13, 1913, Bennett, Tex.   D. Apr. 20, 1970, Fort Worth, Tex.

	W	L	PCT	ERA	G	GS	CG	IP	H	BB	SO	ShO	Relief W	Relief L	Relief SV	AB	H	HR	BA
1936 CIN N	0	0	—	3.95	8	0	0	13.2	10	4	11	0	0	0	1	1	0	0	.000
1937	0	3	.000	8.31	14	2	0	39	54	22	11	0	0	1	1	8	0	0	.000
1940 CHI N	6	6	.500	2.92	20	12	6	114	101	49	42	0	2	0	1	38	10	0	.263
1941	8	9	.471	3.35	33	14	7	153.1	143	56	45	1	3	0	4	50	10	0	.200
1942	2	5	.286	4.70	19	10	1	84.1	89	44	28	0	0	1	1	28	6	0	.214
1943	0	0	—	0.00	2	0	0	1	2	1	1	0	0	0	0	1	0	0	—
1944 DET A	0	0	—	4.45	15	0	0	28.1	35	18	7	0	0	0	0	7	1	0	.143
7 yrs.	16	23	.410	4.03	111	38	14	433.2	434	194	145	1	5	2	8	132	27	0	.205

Carl Moran

MORAN, CARL WILLIAM (Bugs)   BR TR 6'4" 210 lbs.
B. Sept. 26, 1950, Portsmouth, Va.

	W	L	PCT	ERA	G	GS	CG	IP	H	BB	SO	ShO	Relief W	Relief L	Relief SV	AB	H	HR	BA
1974 CHI A	1	3	.250	4.70	15	5	0	46	57	23	17	0	0	1	0	0	0	0	—

Charley Moran

MORAN, CHARLES BARTHELL (Uncle Charlie)   BR TR 5'8" 180 lbs.
B. Feb. 22, 1878, Nashville, Tenn.   D. June 13, 1949, Horse Cave, Ky.

	W	L	PCT	ERA	G	GS	CG	IP	H	BB	SO	ShO	Relief W	Relief L	Relief SV	AB	H	HR	BA
1903 STL N	0	1	.000	5.25	3	2	2	24	30	19	7	0	0	0	0	*			

Harry Moran

MORAN, HARRY EDWIN   BL TL 6'1" 165 lbs.
B. Apr. 2, 1889, Slater, W. Va.   D. Nov. 28, 1962, Beckley, W. Va.

	W	L	PCT	ERA	G	GS	CG	IP	H	BB	SO	ShO	Relief W	Relief L	Relief SV	AB	H	HR	BA
1912 DET A	0	1	.000	4.91	5	2	1	14.2	19	12	3	0	0	0	0	5	1	0	.200
1914 BUF F	11	8	.579	4.27	34	16	7	154	159	53	73	2	3	1	1	51	10	0	.196
1915 NWK F	13	10	.565	2.54	34	23	13	205.2	193	66	87	2	2	0	0	61	11	0	.180
3 yrs.	24	19	.558	3.34	73	41	21	374.1	371	131	163	4	5	1	1	117	22	0	.188

Hiker Moran

MORAN, ALBERT THOMAS   BR TR 6'4½" 185 lbs.
B. Jan. 1, 1912, Rochester, N. Y.

	W	L	PCT	ERA	G	GS	CG	IP	H	BB	SO	ShO	Relief W	Relief L	Relief SV	AB	H	HR	BA
1938 BOS N	0	0	—	0.00	1	0	0	3	1	1	0	0	0	0	0	0	0	0	—
1939	1	1	.500	4.50	6	2	1	20	21	11	4	0	0	0	0	5	1	0	.200
2 yrs.	1	1	.500	3.91	7	2	1	23	22	12	4	0	0	0	0	5	1	0	.200

Sam Moran

MORAN, SAMUEL   TL
B. Sept. 16, 1870, Rochester, N. Y.   D. Aug. 29, 1897, Rochester, N. Y.

	W	L	PCT	ERA	G	GS	CG	IP	H	BB	SO	ShO	Relief W	Relief L	Relief SV	AB	H	HR	BA
1895 PIT N	2	4	.333	7.47	10	6	6	62.2	78	51	19	0	0	0	0	26	4	1	.154

Forrest More

MORE, FORREST   BR TR 6' 180 lbs.
B. Sept. 30, 1883, Hayden, Ind.   D. Aug. 17, 1968, Columbus, Ind.

	W	L	PCT	ERA	G	GS	CG	IP	H	BB	SO	ShO	Relief W	Relief L	Relief SV	AB	H	HR	BA
1909 2 teams	STL	N (15G 1-5)		BOS	N (10G 0-4)														
" total	1	9	.100	4.74	25	7	4	98.2	95	40	27	0	0	5	0	28	3	0	.107

Dave Morehead

MOREHEAD, DAVID MICHAEL (Moe)   BR TR 6'1" 185 lbs.
B. Sept. 5, 1943, San Diego, Calif.

	W	L	PCT	ERA	G	GS	CG	IP	H	BB	SO	ShO	Relief W	Relief L	Relief SV	AB	H	HR	BA
1963 BOS A	10	13	.435	3.81	29	29	6	174.2	137	99	136	1	0	0	0	57	6	0	.105
1964	8	15	.348	4.97	32	30	3	166.2	156	112	139	1	0	0	0	54	5	0	.093
1965	10	18	.357	4.06	34	33	5	192.2	157	113	163	2	0	0	0	61	8	0	.131
1966	1	2	.333	5.46	12	5	0	28	31	7	20	0	0	0	0	6	3	0	.500
1967	5	4	.556	4.34	10	9	1	47.2	48	22	40	1	1	0	0	12	1	0	.083
1968	1	4	.200	2.45	11	9	3	55	52	20	28	1	0	0	0	16	2	0	.125
1969 KC A	2	3	.400	5.73	21	2	0	33	28	28	32	0	2	1	0	2	0	0	.000
1970	3	5	.375	3.61	28	17	1	122	121	62	69	0	0	1	1	36	6	0	.167
8 yrs.	40	64	.385	4.15	177	134	19	819.2	730	463	627	6	3	2	1	244	31	0	.127

WORLD SERIES

	W	L	PCT	ERA	G	GS	CG	IP	H	BB	SO	ShO	Relief W	Relief L	Relief SV	AB	H	HR	BA
1967 BOS A	0	0	—	0.00	2	0	0	3.1	0	4	3	0	0	0	0	0	0	0	—

Seth Morehead

MOREHEAD, SETH MARVIN (Moe)   BL TL 6'½" 195 lbs.
B. Aug. 15, 1934, Houston, Tex.

	W	L	PCT	ERA	G	GS	CG	IP	H	BB	SO	ShO	Relief W	Relief L	Relief SV	AB	H	HR	BA
1957 PHI N	1	1	.500	3.68	34	1	1	58.2	57	20	36	0	0	1	1	6	0	0	.000
1958	1	6	.143	5.85	27	11	0	92.1	121	26	54	0	0	0	0	22	4	0	.182
1959 2 teams	PHI	N (3G 0-2)		CHI	N (11G 0-1)														
" total	0	3	.000	6.59	14	5	0	28.2	40	11	17	0	0	0	0	5	1	0	.200
1960 CHI N	2	9	.182	3.94	45	7	2	123.1	123	46	64	0	2	4	4	29	4	0	.138
1961 MIL N	1	0	1.000	6.46	12	0	0	15.1	16	7	13	0	1	0	0	0	0	0	—
5 yrs.	5	19	.208	4.81	132	24	3	318.1	357	110	184	0	3	5	5	62	9	0	.145

	W	L	PCT	ERA	G	GS	CG	IP	H	BB	SO	ShO	Relief Pitching W	Relief Pitching L	Relief Pitching SV	BATTING AB	BATTING H	BATTING HR	BA

Lew Moren

MOREN, LEWIS HOWARD (Hicks) BR TR 5'11" 150 lbs.
B. Aug. 4, 1883, Pittsburgh, Pa.   D. Nov. 2, 1966, Pittsburgh, Pa.

	W	L	PCT	ERA	G	GS	CG	IP	H	BB	SO	ShO	RP W	RP L	RP SV	AB	H	HR	BA
1903 PIT N	0	1	.000	9.00	1	1	1	6	9	2	2	0	0	0	0	2	0	0	.000
1904	0	0	–	9.00	1	0	0	4	7	4	0	0	0	0	0	2	0	0	.000
1907 PHI N	11	18	.379	2.54	37	31	21	255	202	101	98	3	0	1	1	74	6	0	.081
1908	8	9	.471	2.92	28	16	9	154	146	49	72	4	1	1	0	49	12	0	.245
1909	16	15	.516	2.66	39	31	19	253.2	223	91	108	2	3	3	1	90	10	0	.111
1910	13	14	.481	3.55	34	26	12	205.1	207	82	74	1	3	2	1	74	11	0	.149
6 yrs.	48	57	.457	2.95	140	105	62	878	794	329	354	10	7	7	3	291	39	0	.134

Angel Moreno

MORENO, ANGEL BL TL 5'9" 165 lbs.
B. June 6, 1956, Vera Cruz, Mexico

	W	L	PCT	ERA	G	GS	CG	IP	H	BB	SO	ShO	RP W	RP L	RP SV	AB	H	HR	BA
1981 CAL A	1	3	.250	2.90	8	4	1	31	27	14	12	0	0	0	0	0	0	0	–
1982	3	7	.300	4.74	13	8	2	49.1	55	23	22	0	0	1	1	0	0	0	–
2 yrs.	4	10	.286	4.03	21	12	3	80.1	82	37	34	0	0	1	1	0	0	0	–

Julio Moreno

MORENO, JULIO GONZALEZ BR TR 5'8" 165 lbs.
B. Jan. 28, 1921, Guines, Cuba

	W	L	PCT	ERA	G	GS	CG	IP	H	BB	SO	ShO	RP W	RP L	RP SV	AB	H	HR	BA
1950 WAS A	1	1	.500	4.64	4	3	1	21.1	22	12	7	0	0	0	0	8	1	0	.125
1951	5	11	.313	4.88	31	18	5	132.2	132	80	37	0	1	2	2	40	7	0	.175
1952	9	9	.500	3.97	26	22	7	147.1	154	52	62	0	0	1	0	49	6	0	.122
1953	3	1	.750	2.80	12	2	1	35.1	41	13	13	0	2	1	0	9	0	0	.000
4 yrs.	18	22	.450	4.25	73	45	14	336.2	349	157	119	0	3	4	2	106	14	0	.132

Roger Moret

MORET, ROGELIO BB TL 6'4" 170 lbs.
B. Sept. 16, 1949, Guayama, Puerto Rico

	W	L	PCT	ERA	G	GS	CG	IP	H	BB	SO	ShO	RP W	RP L	RP SV	AB	H	HR	BA
1970 BOS A	1	0	1.000	3.38	3	1	0	8	7	4	2	0	1	0	0	3	0	0	.000
1971	4	3	.571	2.92	13	7	4	71	50	40	47	1	0	1	0	23	2	0	.087
1972	0	0	–	3.60	3	0	0	5	5	6	4	0	0	0	0	1	0	0	.000
1973	13	2	.867	3.17	30	15	5	156	138	67	90	2	1	0	3	0	0	0	–
1974	9	10	.474	3.75	31	21	10	173	158	79	111	1	1	1	2	0	0	0	–
1975	14	3	.824	3.60	36	16	4	145	132	76	80	1	4	0	1	0	0	0	–
1976 ATL N	3	5	.375	5.03	27	12	1	77	84	27	30	0	1	0	1	23	3	0	.130
1977 TEX A	3	3	.500	3.75	18	8	0	72	59	38	39	0	1	0	4	0	0	0	–
1978	0	1	.000	4.91	7	2	0	14.2	23	2	5	0	0	0	1	0	0	0	–
9 yrs.	47	27	.635	3.67	168	82	24	721.2	656	339	408	5	8	2	12	50	5	0	.100

LEAGUE CHAMPIONSHIP SERIES

	W	L	PCT	ERA	G	GS	CG	IP	H	BB	SO	ShO	RP W	RP L	RP SV	AB	H	HR	BA
1975 BOS A	1	0	1.000	0.00	1	0	0	1	1	1	0	0	1	0	0	0	0	0	–

WORLD SERIES

	W	L	PCT	ERA	G	GS	CG	IP	H	BB	SO	ShO	RP W	RP L	RP SV	AB	H	HR	BA
1975 BOS A	0	0	–	0.00	3	0	0	1.2	2	3	1	0	0	0	0	0	0	0	–

Dave Morey

MOREY, DAVID BEALE BL TR 6' 185 lbs.
B. Feb. 25, 1889, Malden, Mass.

	W	L	PCT	ERA	G	GS	CG	IP	H	BB	SO	ShO	RP W	RP L	RP SV	AB	H	HR	BA
1913 PHI A	0	0	–	4.50	2	0	0	4	2	2	1	0	0	0	0	1	0	0	.000

Bill Morgan

MORGAN, HENRY WILLIAM
B. Oct., 1857, Washington, D. C.   Deceased.

	W	L	PCT	ERA	G	GS	CG	IP	H	BB	SO	ShO	RP W	RP L	RP SV	AB	H	HR	BA
1884 RIC AA	2	3	.400	4.15	5	5	5	39	37	2	35	0	0	0	0	*			

Cy Morgan

MORGAN, CYRIL ARLON BR TR 6' 170 lbs.
B. Dec. 11, 1896, Lakeville, Mass.   D. Sept. 11, 1946, Lakeville, Mass.

	W	L	PCT	ERA	G	GS	CG	IP	H	BB	SO	ShO	RP W	RP L	RP SV	AB	H	HR	BA
1921 BOS N	1	1	.500	6.53	17	0	0	30.1	37	17	8	0	1	1	1	5	0	0	.000
1922	0	0	–	27.00	2	0	0	1.1	8	2	0	0	0	0	0	0	0	0	–
2 yrs.	1	1	.500	7.39	19	0	0	31.2	45	19	8	0	1	1	1	5	0	0	.000

Cy Morgan

MORGAN, HARRY RICHARD BR TR 6' 175 lbs.
B. Nov. 10, 1878, Pomeroy, Ohio   D. June 28, 1962, Wheeling, W. Va.

	W	L	PCT	ERA	G	GS	CG	IP	H	BB	SO	ShO	RP W	RP L	RP SV	AB	H	HR	BA
1903 STL A	0	2	.000	4.15	2	1	1	13	12	6	6	0	0	1	0	4	1	0	.250
1904	0	2	.000	3.71	8	3	2	51	51	10	24	0	0	0	0	18	1	0	.056
1905	2	5	.286	3.61	13	8	5	77.1	82	37	44	1	0	0	0	31	8	0	.258
1907 2 teams					STL	A	(10G 2–5)	BOS	A	(16G 6–6)									
" total	8	11	.421	3.30	26	19	13	169.1	154	51	64	2	1	0	0	55	4	0	.073
1908 BOS A	14	13	.519	2.46	30	26	17	205	166	90	99	2	1	1	1	63	8	0	.127
1909 2 teams					BOS	A	(12G 6–1)	PHI	A	(28G 16–11)									
" total	18	17	.514	1.81	40	36	26	293.1	204	102	111	5	1	1	1	94	9	0	.096
1910 PHI A	18	12	.600	1.55	36	34	23	290.2	214	117	134	3	0	1	0	99	14	0	.141
1911	15	7	.682	2.70	38	30	15	249.2	217	113	136	2	1	1	1	94	15	0	.160
1912	3	8	.273	3.75	16	14	5	93.2	75	51	47	0	1	0	0	30	1	0	.033
1913 CIN N	0	1	.000	15.43	1	0	0	2.1	5	1	2	0	0	0	0	0	0	0	.000
10 yrs.	78	78	.500	2.51	210	172	107	1445.1	1180	578	667	15	5	5	3	489	61	0	.125

Mike Morgan

MORGAN, MICHAEL THOMAS BR TR 6'3" 195 lbs.
B. Oct. 8, 1959, Tulare, Calif.

	W	L	PCT	ERA	G	GS	CG	IP	H	BB	SO	ShO	RP W	RP L	RP SV	AB	H	HR	BA
1978 OAK A	0	3	.000	7.30	3	3	1	12.1	19	8	0	0	0	0	0	0	0	0	–
1979	2	10	.167	5.96	13	13	2	77	102	50	17	0	0	0	0	0	0	0	–
1982 NY A	7	11	.389	4.37	30	23	2	150.1	167	67	71	0	2	1	0	0	0	0	–
1983 TOR A	0	3	.000	5.16	16	4	0	45.1	48	21	22	0	0	1	0	0	0	0	–
4 yrs.	9	27	.250	5.05	62	43	5	285	336	146	110	0	2	2	0	0	0	0	–

Tom Morgan

MORGAN, TOM STEPHEN (Plowboy) BR TR 6'1" 180 lbs.
B. May 20, 1930, El Monte, Calif.

	W	L	PCT	ERA	G	GS	CG	IP	H	BB	SO	ShO	RP W	RP L	RP SV	AB	H	HR	BA
1951 NY A	9	3	.750	3.68	27	16	4	124.2	119	36	57	2	1	0	2	44	12	1	.273
1952	5	4	.556	3.07	16	12	4	93.2	86	33	35	1	0	0	2	33	6	1	.182
1954	11	5	.688	3.34	32	17	7	143	149	40	34	4	3	1	1	49	7	1	.143
1955	7	3	.700	3.25	40	1	0	72	72	24	17	0	7	3	10	18	4	0	.222
1956	6	7	.462	4.16	41	0	0	71.1	74	27	20	0	6	7	11	13	2	0	.154
1957 KC A	9	7	.563	4.64	46	13	5	143.2	160	61	32	0	6	2	7	33	3	0	.091

	W	L	PCT	ERA	G	GS	CG	IP	H	BB	SO	ShO	Relief Pitching W	L	SV	BATTING AB	H	HR	BA

Carl Morton continued

	W	L	PCT	ERA	G	GS	CG	IP	H	BB	SO	ShO	W	L	SV	AB	H	HR	BA
1974	16	12	.571	3.14	38	38	7	275	**293**	89	113	1	0	0	0	89	10	0	.112
1975	17	16	.515	3.50	39	39	11	278	**302**	82	78	2	0	0	0	94	15	0	.160
1976	4	9	.308	4.18	26	24	1	140	172	45	42	1	0	0	0	45	8	0	.178
8 yrs.	87	92	.486	3.73	255	242	51	1649.1	1753	565	650	13	0	0	2	551	86	7	.156

Charlie Morton

MORTON, CHARLES HAZEN
B. Oct. 12, 1854, Kingsville, Ohio   D. Dec. 13, 1921, Akron, Ohio
Manager 1884-85, 1890.

	W	L	PCT	ERA	G	GS	CG	IP	H	BB	SO	ShO	W	L	SV	AB	H	HR	BA
1884 TOL AA	0	1	.000	3.09	3	1	1	23.1	18	5	7	0	0	0	0	*			

Guy Morton

MORTON, GUY, SR. (Alabama Blossom)   BR TR 6'2"   165 lbs.
Father of Guy Morton.
B. June 1, 1893, Vernon, Ala.   D. Oct. 18, 1934, Sheffield, Ala.

	W	L	PCT	ERA	G	GS	CG	IP	H	BB	SO	ShO	W	L	SV	AB	H	HR	BA
1914 CLE A	1	13	.071	3.02	25	13	5	128	116	55	80	0	0	2	1	35	1	0	.029
1915	16	15	.516	2.14	34	27	15	240	189	60	134	6	2	2	1	82	12	0	.146
1916	12	8	.600	2.89	27	18	9	149.2	139	42	88	0	1	3	0	57	12	0	.211
1917	10	10	.500	2.74	35	18	6	161	158	59	62	1	3	3	2	47	4	0	.085
1918	14	8	.636	2.64	30	28	13	214.2	189	77	123	1	1	0	0	77	12	0	.156
1919	9	9	.500	2.81	26	20	9	147.1	128	47	64	3	1	1	0	56	9	0	.161
1920	8	6	.571	4.47	29	17	5	137	140	57	72	1	2	0	1	46	10	0	.217
1921	8	3	.727	2.76	30	6	2	107.2	98	32	45	2	5	1	0	35	6	0	.171
1922	14	9	.609	4.00	38	23	13	202.2	218	85	102	3	2	2	0	68	13	0	.191
1923	6	6	.500	4.24	33	14	3	129.1	133	56	54	2	1	1	1	44	7	0	.159
1924	0	1	.000	6.57	10	0	0	12.1	12	13	6	0	0	1	0	1	0	0	.000
11 yrs.	98	88	.527	3.13	317	184	80	1629.2	1520	583	830	19	18	16	6	548	86	0	.157

Sparrow Morton

MORTON, WILLIAM P   TL
Deceased.

	W	L	PCT	ERA	G	GS	CG	IP	H	BB	SO	ShO	W	L	SV	AB	H	HR	BA
1884 PHI N	0	2	.000	5.29	2	2	2	17	16	11	5	0	0	0	0	8	3	0	.375

Earl Moseley

MOSELEY, EARL VICTOR   BR TR 5'9½"   168 lbs.
B. Sept. 7, 1884, Middleburg, Ohio   D. July 1, 1963, Alliance, Ohio

	W	L	PCT	ERA	G	GS	CG	IP	H	BB	SO	ShO	W	L	SV	AB	H	HR	BA
1913 BOS A	9	5	.643	3.13	24	15	7	120.2	105	49	62	3	1	1	0	37	3	0	.081
1914 IND F	18	18	.500	3.47	43	38	29	316.2	303	123	205	4	1	2	1	109	12	0	.110
1915 NWK F	16	16	.500	1.91	38	32	22	268	222	99	142	5	1	2	0	88	13	0	.148
1916 CIN N	7	10	.412	3.89	31	15	7	150.1	145	69	60	0	2	2	1	46	4	0	.087
4 yrs.	50	49	.505	3.01	136	100	65	855.2	775	340	469	12	5	7	2	280	32	0	.114

Walter Moser

MOSER, WALTER FREDERICK   BR TR
B. Feb. 27, 1886, Concord, N. C.   D. Dec. 10, 1946, Philadelphia, Pa.

	W	L	PCT	ERA	G	GS	CG	IP	H	BB	SO	ShO	W	L	SV	AB	H	HR	BA
1906 PHI N	0	4	.000	3.59	6	4	4	42.2	49	15	17	0	0	0	0	14	0	0	.000
1911 2 teams			BOS A (6G 0-1)			STL A (2G 0-2)														
" total	0	3	.000	6.11	8	5	1	28	48	15	13	0	0	0	0	8	1	0	.125
2 yrs.	0	7	.000	4.58	14	9	5	70.2	97	30	30	0	0	0	0	22	1	0	.045

Paul Moskau

MOSKAU, PAUL RICHARD   BR TR 6'2"   200 lbs.
B. Dec. 20, 1953, St. Joseph, Mo.

	W	L	PCT	ERA	G	GS	CG	IP	H	BB	SO	ShO	W	L	SV	AB	H	HR	BA
1977 CIN N	6	6	.500	4.00	20	19	2	108	116	40	71	2	0	0	0	38	7	1	.184
1978	6	4	.600	3.97	26	25	2	145	139	57	88	1	0	0	1	49	10	1	.204
1979	5	4	.556	3.91	21	15	1	106	107	51	58	0	1	0	0	37	3	0	.081
1980	9	7	.563	4.00	33	19	2	153	147	41	94	1	5	0	2	44	7	0	.159
1981	2	1	.667	4.91	27	1	0	55	54	32	32	0	2	1	2	6	0	0	.000
1982 PIT N	1	3	.250	4.37	13	5	0	35	43	8	15	0	0	1	0	11	1	0	.091
1983 CHI N	3	2	.600	6.75	8	8	0	32	44	14	16	0	0	0	0	11	2	0	.182
7 yrs.	32	27	.542	4.22	148	92	7	634	650	243	374	4	8	2	5	196	30	2	.153

Jim Mosolf

MOSOLF, JAMES FREDERICK   BL TR 5'10"   186 lbs.
B. Aug. 21, 1905, Puyallup, Wash.   D. Dec. 28, 1979, Dallas, Ore.

	W	L	PCT	ERA	G	GS	CG	IP	H	BB	SO	ShO	W	L	SV	AB	H	HR	BA
1930 PIT N	0	0	-	27.00	1	0	0	.1	1	1	0	1	0	0	0	0	*		

Mal Moss

MOSS, CHARLES MALCOLM   BR TL 6'   175 lbs.
B. Apr. 18, 1905, Sullivan, Ind.   D. Feb. 5, 1983, Savannah, Ga.

	W	L	PCT	ERA	G	GS	CG	IP	H	BB	SO	ShO	W	L	SV	AB	H	HR	BA
1930 CHI N	0	0	-	6.27	12	1	0	18.2	18	14	4	0	0	0	1	11	3	0	.273

Ray Moss

MOSS, RAYMOND EARL   BR TR 6'1"   185 lbs.
B. Dec. 5, 1901, Chattanooga, Tenn.

	W	L	PCT	ERA	G	GS	CG	IP	H	BB	SO	ShO	W	L	SV	AB	H	HR	BA
1926 BKN N	0	0	-	9.00	1	0	0	1	3	0	0	0	0	0	0	1	0	0	.000
1927	1	0	1.000	3.24	1	1	0	8.1	11	1	1	0	0	0	0	3	1	0	.333
1928	0	3	.000	4.92	22	5	1	60.1	62	35	5	1	0	1	1	25	8	0	.320
1929	11	6	.647	5.04	39	20	7	182	214	81	59	2	2	1	0	66	5	0	.076
1930	9	6	.600	5.10	36	11	5	118.1	127	55	30	0	3	3	1	39	6	0	.154
1931 2 teams			BKN N (1G 0-0)			BOS N (12G 1-3)														
" total	1	3	.250	4.50	13	5	0	46	57	17	14	0	1	0	0	15	2	0	.133
6 yrs.	22	18	.550	4.95	112	42	13	416	474	189	109	3	6	5	2	149	22	0	.148

Don Mossi

MOSSI, DONALD LOUIS (The Sphinx)   BL TL 6'1"   195 lbs.
B. Jan. 11, 1929, St. Helena, Calif.

	W	L	PCT	ERA	G	GS	CG	IP	H	BB	SO	ShO	W	L	SV	AB	H	HR	BA
1954 CLE A	6	1	.857	1.94	40	5	2	93	56	39	55	0	4	0	7	19	3	0	.158
1955	4	3	.571	2.42	57	1	0	81.2	81	18	69	0	4	3	9	9	1	0	.111
1956	6	5	.545	3.59	48	3	0	87.2	79	33	59	0	0	4	11	20	3	0	.150
1957	11	10	.524	4.13	36	22	6	159	166	57	97	1	1	1	2	55	12	0	.218
1958	7	8	.467	3.90	43	5	0	101.2	106	30	55	0	7	4	3	26	3	0	.115
1959 DET A	17	9	.654	3.36	34	30	15	228	210	49	125	3	0	1	0	77	13	1	.169
1960	9	8	.529	3.47	23	22	9	158.1	158	32	69	2	1	0	0	43	5	0	.116

	W	L	PCT	ERA	G	GS	CG	IP	H	BB	SO	ShO	W	L	SV	AB	H	HR	BA
													Relief Pitching			BATTING			

Don Mossi *continued*

	W	L	PCT	ERA	G	GS	CG	IP	H	BB	SO	ShO	W	L	SV	AB	H	HR	BA
1961	15	7	.682	2.96	35	34	12	240.1	237	47	137	1	0	0	1	79	13	1	.165
1962	11	13	.458	4.19	35	27	8	180.1	195	36	121	1	0	2	1	55	9	0	.164
1963	7	7	.500	3.74	24	16	3	122.2	110	17	68	0	2	0	2	39	8	0	.205
1964 CHI A	3	1	.750	2.93	34	0	0	40	37	7	36	0	3	1	7	6	1	0	.167
1965 KC A	5	8	.385	3.74	51	0	0	55.1	59	20	41	0	5	8	7	8	0	0	.000
12 yrs.	101	80	.558	3.43	460	165	55	1548	1494	385	932	8	27	24	50	436	71	2	.163
WORLD SERIES																			
1954 CLE A	0	0	—	0.00	3	0	0	4	3	0	1	0	0	0	0	0	0	0	

Earl Mossor

MOSSOR, EARL DALTON
B. July 21, 1925, Forbes, Tenn. — BL TR 6'1" 175 lbs.

	W	L	PCT	ERA	G	GS	CG	IP	H	BB	SO	ShO	W	L	SV	AB	H	HR	BA
1951 BKN N	0	0	—	32.40	3	0	0	1.2	2	7	1	0	0	0	0	1	1	0	1.000

Glen Moulder

MOULDER, GLEN HUBERT
B. Sept. 28, 1917, Cleveland, Okla. — BR TR 6' 180 lbs.

	W	L	PCT	ERA	G	GS	CG	IP	H	BB	SO	ShO	W	L	SV	AB	H	HR	BA
1946 BKN N	0	0	—	4.50	1	0	0	2	2	1	1	0	0	0	0	0	0	0	—
1947 STL A	4	2	.667	3.82	32	2	0	73	78	43	23	0	3	1	2	17	4	0	.235
1948 CHI A	3	6	.333	6.41	33	9	0	85.2	108	54	26	0	1	2	2	20	6	0	.300
3 yrs.	7	8	.467	5.21	66	11	0	160.2	188	98	50	0	4	3	4	37	10	0	.270

Frank Mountain

MOUNTAIN, FRANK HENRY
B. May 17, 1860, Ft. Edward, N. Y.   D. Nov. 19, 1939, Schenectady, N. Y. — BR TR 5'11" 185 lbs.

	W	L	PCT	ERA	G	GS	CG	IP	H	BB	SO	ShO	W	L	SV	AB	H	HR	BA
1880 TRO N	1	1	.500	5.29	2	2	2	17	23	6	2	0	0	0	0	9	2	0	.222
1881 DET N	3	4	.429	5.25	7	7	7	60	80	18	13	0	0	0	0	25	4	0	.160
1882 3 teams		WOR	N	(5G 0–5)	PHI	AA	(8G 2–5)	WOR	N	(13G 2–11)									
" total	4	21	.160	3.76	26	26	24	213	257	46	44	0	0	0	0	122	32	2	.262
1883 COL AA	26	33	.441	3.60	59	59	57	503	546	123	159	4	0	0	0	276	60	3	.217
1884	23	17	.575	2.45	42	41	40	360.2	289	78	156	5	0	0	1	210	50	4	.238
1885 PIT AA	1	4	.200	4.30	5	5	5	46	56	24	7	0	0	0	0	20	2	0	.100
1886	0	2	.000	7.88	2	2	2	16	22	14	2	0	0	0	0	55	8	0	.145
7 yrs.	58	82	.414	3.47	143	142	137	1215.2	1273	309	383	9	0	0	1	*			

Billy Mountjoy

MOUNTJOY, WILLIAM R. (Medicine Bill)
B. 1857, Port Huron, Mich.   D. May 19, 1894, London, Ont., Canada — TR

	W	L	PCT	ERA	G	GS	CG	IP	H	BB	SO	ShO	W	L	SV	AB	H	HR	BA
1883 CIN AA	0	1	.000	2.25	1	1	1	8	9	2	3	0	0	0	0	3	0	0	.000
1884	19	12	.613	2.93	33	33	32	289	274	43	96	3	0	0	0	119	18	0	.151
1885 2 teams		CIN	AA	(17G 10–7)	BAL	AA	(6G 2–4)												
" total	12	11	.522	3.75	23	23	23	206.2	221	65	65	2	0	0	0	78	11	0	.141
3 yrs.	31	24	.564	3.25	57	57	56	503.2	504	110	164	5	0	0	0	200	29	0	.145

Charlie Moyer

MOYER, CHARLES EDWARD
B. Aug. 15, 1885, Andover, Ohio   D. Nov. 18, 1962, Jacksonville, Fla.

	W	L	PCT	ERA	G	GS	CG	IP	H	BB	SO	ShO	W	L	SV	AB	H	HR	BA
1910 WAS A	0	3	.000	3.24	6	3	2	25	13	13	4	0	0	0	0	8	1	0	.125

Ron Mrozinski

MROZINSKI, RONALD FRANK
B. Sept. 16, 1930, White Haven, Pa. — BR TL 5'11" 160 lbs.

	W	L	PCT	ERA	G	GS	CG	IP	H	BB	SO	ShO	W	L	SV	AB	H	HR	BA
1954 PHI N	1	1	.500	4.50	15	4	1	48	49	25	26	0	0	0	0	12	1	0	.083
1955	0	2	.000	6.55	22	1	0	34.1	38	19	18	0	0	1	1	4	0	0	.000
2 yrs.	1	3	.250	5.36	37	5	1	82.1	87	44	44	0	0	1	1	16	1	0	.063

Phil Mudrock

MUDROCK, PHILIP RAY
B. June 12, 1937, Louisville, Colo. — BR TR 6'1" 190 lbs.

	W	L	PCT	ERA	G	GS	CG	IP	H	BB	SO	ShO	W	L	SV	AB	H	HR	BA
1963 CHI N	0	0	—	9.00	1	0	0	1	2	0	0	0	0	0	0	0	0	0	—

Gordy Mueller

MUELLER, JOSEPH GORDON
B. Dec. 10, 1922, Baltimore, Md. — BR TR 6'4" 200 lbs.

	W	L	PCT	ERA	G	GS	CG	IP	H	BB	SO	ShO	W	L	SV	AB	H	HR	BA
1950 BOS A	0	0	—	10.29	8	0	0	7	11	13	1	0	0	0	0	1	0	0	.000

Les Mueller

MUELLER, LESLIE CLYDE
B. Mar. 4, 1919, Belleville, Ill. — BR TR 6'3" 190 lbs.

	W	L	PCT	ERA	G	GS	CG	IP	H	BB	SO	ShO	W	L	SV	AB	H	HR	BA
1941 DET A	0	0	—	4.85	4	0	0	13	9	10	8	0	0	0	0	3	0	0	.000
1945	6	8	.429	3.68	26	18	6	134.2	117	58	42	2	0	0	1	44	8	1	.182
2 yrs.	6	8	.429	3.78	30	18	6	147.2	126	68	50	2	0	0	1	47	8	1	.170
WORLD SERIES																			
1945 DET A	0	0	—	0.00	1	0	0	2	0	1	1	0	0	0	0	0	0	0	—

Willie Mueller

MUELLER, WILLARD LAWRENCE
Also known as Willard Lawrence Caceres.
B. Aug. 30, 1956, West Bend, Wis. — BR TR 6'4" 220 lbs.

	W	L	PCT	ERA	G	GS	CG	IP	H	BB	SO	ShO	W	L	SV	AB	H	HR	BA
1978 MIL A	1	0	1.000	6.39	5	0	0	12.2	16	6	6	0	1	0	0	0	0	0	—
1981	0	0	—	4.50	1	0	0	2	4	0	1	0	0	0	0	0	0	0	—
2 yrs.	1	0	1.000	6.14	6	0	0	14.2	20	6	7	0	1	0	0	0	0	0	—

Billy Muffett

MUFFETT, BILLY ARNOLD (Muff)
B. Sept. 21, 1930, Hammond, Ind. — BR TR 6'1" 198 lbs.

	W	L	PCT	ERA	G	GS	CG	IP	H	BB	SO	ShO	W	L	SV	AB	H	HR	BA
1957 STL N	3	2	.600	2.25	23	0	0	44	35	13	21	0	3	2	8	7	0	0	.000
1958	4	6	.400	4.93	35	6	1	84	107	42	41	0	3	3	5	20	4	0	.200
1959 SF N	0	0	—	5.40	5	0	0	6.2	11	3	3	0	0	0	0	0	0	0	—
1960 BOS A	6	4	.600	3.24	23	14	4	125	116	36	75	1	1	1	0	41	11	0	.268
1961	3	11	.214	5.67	38	11	2	112.2	130	36	47	0	2	3	2	23	5	1	.217
1962	0	0	—	9.00	1	1	0	4	8	2	1	0	0	0	0	1	0	0	.000
6 yrs.	16	23	.410	4.33	125	32	7	376.1	407	132	188	1	9	9	15	92	20	1	.217

	W	L	PCT	ERA	G	GS	CG	IP	H	BB	SO	ShO	Relief Pitching W	L	SV	BATTING AB	H	HR	BA

Joe Muich

MUICH, IGNATIUS ANDREW
B. Nov. 23, 1903, St. Louis, Mo.
BR TR 6'2"   175 lbs.

	W	L	PCT	ERA	G	GS	CG	IP	H	BB	SO	ShO	W	L	SV	AB	H	HR	BA
1924 BOS N	0	0	–	11.00	3	0	0	9	19	5	1	0	0	0	0	3	0	0	.000

Joe Muir

MUIR, JOSEPH ALLEN
B. Nov. 26, 1922, Oriole, Md.   D. June 25, 1980, Baltimore, Md.
BL TL 6'1"   172 lbs.

	W	L	PCT	ERA	G	GS	CG	IP	H	BB	SO	ShO	W	L	SV	AB	H	HR	BA
1951 PIT N	0	2	.000	2.76	9	1	0	16.1	11	7	5	0	0	2	0	1	0	0	.000
1952	2	3	.400	6.31	12	5	1	35.2	42	18	17	0	0	1	0	9	1	0	.111
2 yrs.	2	5	.286	5.19	21	6	1	52	53	25	22	0	0	3	0	10	1	0	.100

Hugh Mulcahy

MULCAHY, HUGH NOYES (Losing Pitcher)
B. Sept. 9, 1913, Brighton, Mass.
BR TR 6'2"   190 lbs.

	W	L	PCT	ERA	G	GS	CG	IP	H	BB	SO	ShO	W	L	SV	AB	H	HR	BA
1935 PHI N	1	5	.167	4.78	18	5	0	52.2	62	25	11	0	1	1	1	17	0	0	.000
1936	1	1	.500	3.22	3	2	2	22.1	20	12	2	0	0	0	0	8	2	0	.250
1937	8	18	.308	5.13	56	25	9	215.2	256	97	54	1	1	5	3	73	11	0	.151
1938	10	20	.333	4.61	46	34	15	267.1	294	120	90	0	1	1	1	94	16	0	.170
1939	9	16	.360	4.99	38	31	14	225.2	246	93	59	1	0	2	4	76	12	0	.158
1940	13	22	.371	3.60	36	36	21	280	283	91	82	3	0	0	0	94	19	0	.202
1945	1	3	.250	3.81	5	4	1	28.1	33	9	2	0	0	0	0	7	0	0	.000
1946	2	4	.333	4.45	16	5	1	62.2	69	33	12	0	0	2	0	16	3	0	.188
1947 PIT N	0	0	–	4.05	2	1	0	6.2	8	7	2	0	0	0	0	3	1	0	.333
9 yrs.	45	89	.336	4.49	220	143	63	1161.1	1271	487	314	5	3	11	9	388	64	0	.165

Tony Mullane

MULLANE, ANTHONY JOHN (Count, The Apollo of the Box)
B. Feb. 20, 1859, Cork, Ireland
D. Apr. 25, 1944, Chicago, Ill.
BB TB 5'10½" 165 lbs.
BL 1882

	W	L	PCT	ERA	G	GS	CG	IP	H	BB	SO	ShO	W	L	SV	AB	H	HR	BA
1881 DET N	1	4	.200	4.91	5	5	5	44	55	17	7	0	0	0	0	19	5	0	.263
1882 LOU AA	30	24	.556	1.88	55	55	51	460.1	418	78	170	5	0	0	0	303	78	0	.257
1883 STL AA	35	15	.700	2.19	53	49	49	460.2	372	74	191	3	1	0	1	307	69	0	.225
1884 TOL AA	35	25	.583	2.48	68	66	65	576	485	90	334	8	0	1	0	352	97	3	.276
1886 CIN AA	31	27	.534	3.70	63	56	55	529.2	501	166	250	1	4	0	0	324	73	0	.225
1887	31	17	.646	3.24	48	48	47	416.1	414	121	97	6	0	0	0	199	44	3	.221
1888	26	16	.619	2.84	44	42	41	380.1	341	75	186	4	1	0	1	175	44	1	.251
1889	11	9	.550	2.99	33	24	17	220	218	89	112	0	1	0	5	196	58	0	.296
1890 CIN N	12	10	.545	2.24	25	21	21	209	175	96	91	0	1	0	1	286	79	0	.276
1891	24	25	.490	3.23	51	47	42	426.1	390	187	124	1	2	2	0	209	31	0	.148
1892	21	10	.677	2.59	37	34	30	295	222	127	109	3	2	0	1	118	20	0	.169
1893 2 teams	CIN	N	(15G 6–6)	BAL	N	(34G 13–16)													
" total	19	22	.463	4.44	49	39	34	367	407	189	95	0	3	1	2	166	41	1	.247
1894 2 teams	BAL	N	(21G 8–9)	CLE	N	(4G 1–2)													
" total	9	11	.450	6.59	25	19	12	155.2	201	100	46	0	0	1	4	66	22	0	.333
13 yrs.	285	215	.570	3.05	556	505	469	4540.1	4199	1409	1812	31	15	5	15	*			
							9th												

Dick Mulligan

MULLIGAN, RICHARD CHARLES
B. Mar. 18, 1918, Wilkes-Barre, Pa.
BL TL 6'   167 lbs.

	W	L	PCT	ERA	G	GS	CG	IP	H	BB	SO	ShO	W	L	SV	AB	H	HR	BA
1941 WAS A	0	1	.000	5.00	1	1	0	9	11	2	2	0	0	0	0	3	0	0	.000
1946 2 teams	PHI	N	(19G 2–2)	BOS	N	(4G 1–0)													
" total	3	2	.600	4.24	23	5	1	70	67	36	20	0	1	0	1	15	0	0	.000
1947 BOS N	0	0	–	9.00	1	0	0	2	4	1	1	0	0	0	0	0	0	0	–
3 yrs.	3	3	.500	4.44	25	6	2	81	82	39	23	0	1	0	1	18	0	0	.000

Joe Mulligan

MULLIGAN, JOSEPH IGNATIUS (Big Joe)
B. July 31, 1913, East Weymouth, Mass.
BR TR 6'4"   210 lbs.

	W	L	PCT	ERA	G	GS	CG	IP	H	BB	SO	ShO	W	L	SV	AB	H	HR	BA
1934 BOS A	1	0	1.000	3.63	14	2	1	44.2	46	27	13	0	0	0	0	12	0	0	.000

George Mullin

MULLIN, GEORGE JOSEPH (Wabash George)
B. July 4, 1880, Toledo, Ohio   D. Jan. 7, 1944, Wabash, Ind.
BR TR 5'11"   188 lbs.

	W	L	PCT	ERA	G	GS	CG	IP	H	BB	SO	ShO	W	L	SV	AB	H	HR	BA
1902 DET A	13	16	.448	3.67	35	30	25	260	282	95	78	0	1	1	0	120	39	0	.325
1903	19	15	.559	2.25	41	36	31	320.2	284	106	170	6	1	1	2	126	35	1	.278
1904	17	23	.425	2.40	45	44	42	382.1	345	131	161	7	1	0	0	151	45	0	.298
1905	21	21	.500	2.51	44	41	35	347.2	303	138	168	1	1	1	0	135	35	0	.259
1906	21	18	.538	2.78	40	40	35	330	315	108	123	2	0	0	0	142	32	0	.225
1907	20	20	.500	2.59	46	46	35	357.1	346	106	146	5	1	0	3	157	34	0	.217
1908	17	13	.567	3.10	39	30	26	290.2	301	71	121	1	3	0	0	125	32	1	.256
1909	29	8	.784	2.22	40	35	29	303.2	258	78	124	3	4	0	1	126	27	0	.214
1910	21	12	.636	2.87	38	32	27	289	260	102	98	5	2	0	0	129	33	1	.256
1911	18	10	.643	3.07	30	29	25	234.1	245	61	87	2	0	1	0	98	28	0	.286
1912	12	17	.414	3.54	30	29	22	226	214	92	88	2	1	0	0	90	25	0	.278
1913 2 teams	DET	A	(7G 1–6)	WAS	A	(12G 3–5)													
" total	4	11	.267	3.94	19	16	7	109.2	122	43	30	0	1	0	0	41	11	0	.268
1914 IND F	14	10	.583	2.70	36	20	11	203	202	91	74	1	8	0	2	77	24	0	.312
1915 NWK F	2	2	.500	5.85	5	4	3	32.1	41	16	14	0	0	0	0	10	1	0	.100
14 yrs.	228	196	.538	2.82	488	428	353	3686.2	3518	1238	1482	35	23	5	8	*			

WORLD SERIES																			
1907 DET A	0	2	.000	2.12	2	2	1	17	16	6	7	0	0	0	0	6	0	0	.000
1908	1	0	1.000	1.00	1	1	1	9	7	1	8	0	0	0	0	3	1	0	.333
1909	2	1	.667	2.25	4	3	3	32	22	8	20	1	0	0	0	16	3	0	.188
3 yrs.	3	3	.500	2.02	7	6	6	58	45	15	35	1	0	0	0	25	4	0	.160
							6th												

Dominic Mulrenan

MULRENAN, DOMINIC JOSEPH
B. Dec. 18, 1893, Woburn, Mass.   D. July 27, 1964, Melrose, Mass.
BR TR 5'11"   170 lbs.

	W	L	PCT	ERA	G	GS	CG	IP	H	BB	SO	ShO	W	L	SV	AB	H	HR	BA
1921 CHI A	2	8	.200	7.23	12	10	3	56	84	36	10	0	0	1	0	20	3	0	.150

	W	L	PCT	ERA	G	GS	CG	IP	H	BB	SO	ShO	Relief Pitching W	L	SV	BATTING AB	H	HR	BA

Frank Mulroney

MULRONEY, FRANCIS JOSEPH
B. Apr. 8, 1903, Mallard, Iowa. BR TR 6' 170 lbs.

	W	L	PCT	ERA	G	GS	CG	IP	H	BB	SO	ShO	W	L	SV	AB	H	HR	BA
1930 BOS A	0	1	.000	3.00	2	0	0	3	3	3	0	2	0	1	0	0	0	0	

Bob Muncrief

MUNCRIEF, ROBERT CLEVELAND
B. Jan. 28, 1916, Madill, Okla. BR TR 6'2" 190 lbs.

	W	L	PCT	ERA	G	GS	CG	IP	H	BB	SO	ShO	W	L	SV	AB	H	HR	BA
1937 STL A	0	0	—	4.50	1	1	0	2	3	2	0	0	0	0	0	0	0	0	—
1939	0	0	—	15.00	2	0	0	3	7	3	1	0	0	0	0	0	0	0	—
1941	13	9	.591	3.65	36	24	12	214.1	221	53	67	2	1	0	1	76	18	0	.237
1942	6	8	.429	3.89	24	18	7	134.1	149	31	39	1	0	0	0	45	5	0	.111
1943	13	12	.520	2.81	35	27	12	205	211	48	80	3	1	1	1	66	10	0	.152
1944	13	8	.619	3.08	33	27	12	219.1	216	50	88	3	0	1	1	78	18	0	.231
1945	13	4	.765	2.72	27	15	10	145.2	132	44	54	0	3	2	1	45	3	0	.067
1946	3	12	.200	4.99	29	14	4	115.1	149	31	49	1	0	1	0	32	1	0	.031
1947	8	14	.364	4.90	31	23	7	176.1	210	51	74	0	2	1	0	57	6	0	.105
1948 CLE A	5	4	.556	3.98	21	9	1	72.1	76	31	24	1	2	0	0	18	2	0	.111
1949 2 teams			PIT N (13G 1–5)		CHI	N (34G 5–6)														
" total	6	11	.353	5.12	47	7	2	110.2	124	44	47	0	4	7	5	21	5	0	.238
1951 NY A	0	0	—	9.00	2	0	0	3	5	4	2	0	0	0	0	0	0	0	—
12 yrs.	80	82	.494	3.80	288	165	67	1401.1	1503	392	525	11	13	13	9	438	68	0	.155

WORLD SERIES

	W	L	PCT	ERA	G	GS	CG	IP	H	BB	SO	ShO	W	L	SV	AB	H	HR	BA
1944 STL A	0	1	.000	1.35	2	0	0	6.2	5	4	4	0	0	1	0	1	0	0	.000
1948 CLE A	0	0	—	0.00	1	0	0	2	1	0	0	0	0	0	0	0	0	0	—
2 yrs.	0	1	.000	1.04	3	0	0	8.2	6	4	4	0	0	1	0	1	0	0	.000

George Munger

MUNGER, GEORGE DAVID (Red)
B. Oct. 4, 1918, Houston, Tex. BR TR 6'2" 200 lbs.

	W	L	PCT	ERA	G	GS	CG	IP	H	BB	SO	ShO	W	L	SV	AB	H	HR	BA
1943 STL N	9	5	.643	3.95	32	9	5	93.1	101	42	45	0	4	2	2	28	6	0	.214
1944	11	3	.786	1.34	21	12	7	121	92	41	55	2	2	1	2	44	5	0	.114
1946	2	2	.500	3.33	10	7	2	48.2	47	12	28	0	0	0	1	16	4	0	.250
1947	16	5	.762	3.37	40	31	13	224.1	218	76	123	6	0	0	3	81	15	0	.185
1948	10	11	.476	4.50	39	25	7	166	179	74	72	2	0	2	0	50	8	0	.160
1949	15	8	.652	3.87	35	28	12	188.1	179	87	82	2	0	2	2	66	17	1	.258
1950	7	8	.467	3.90	32	20	5	154.2	158	70	61	1	1	1	0	51	7	0	.137
1951	6	4	.400	5.32	23	11	3	94.2	106	46	44	0	2	2	0	29	5	0	.172
1952 2 teams			STL N (1G 0–1)		PIT	N (5G 0–3)														
" total	0	4	.000	7.92	6	5	0	30.2	37	11	9	0	0	0	0	9	0	0	.000
1956 PIT N	3	4	.429	4.04	35	13	0	107	126	41	45	0	1	1	2	28	3	0	.107
10 yrs.	77	56	.579	3.83	273	161	54	1228.2	1243	500	564	13	10	11	12	402	70	1	.174

WORLD SERIES

	W	L	PCT	ERA	G	GS	CG	IP	H	BB	SO	ShO	W	L	SV	AB	H	HR	BA
1946 STL N	1	0	1.000	1.00	1	1	1	9	9	3	2	0	0	0	0	4	1	0	.250

Van Mungo

MUNGO, VAN LINGLE
B. June 8, 1911, Pageland, S. C. BR TR 6'2" 185 lbs.

	W	L	PCT	ERA	G	GS	CG	IP	H	BB	SO	ShO	W	L	SV	AB	H	HR	BA
1931 BKN N	3	1	.750	2.32	5	4	2	31	27	13	12	1	0	0	0	12	3	0	.250
1932	13	11	.542	4.43	39	33	11	223.1	224	115	107	1	0	1	2	79	16	0	.203
1933	16	15	.516	2.72	41	28	18	248	223	84	110	3	2	2	0	84	15	0	.179
1934	18	16	.529	3.37	45	38	22	315.1	300	104	184	3	1	1	3	121	30	0	.248
1935	16	10	.615	3.65	37	26	18	214.1	205	90	143	4	1	2	2	90	26	0	.289
1936	18	19	.486	3.35	45	37	22	311.2	275	118	238	2	1	3	3	123	22	0	.179
1937	9	11	.450	2.91	25	21	14	161	136	56	122	0	0	0	3	64	16	0	.250
1938	4	11	.267	3.92	24	18	6	133.1	133	72	72	2	1	1	0	47	9	0	.191
1939	4	5	.444	3.26	14	10	1	77.1	70	33	34	0	1	0	0	29	10	0	.345
1940	1	0	1.000	2.45	7	0	0	22	24	10	9	0	1	0	1	7	0	0	.000
1941	0	0	—	4.50	2	0	0	2	1	2	0	0	0	0	0	0	0	0	—
1942 NY N	1	2	.333	5.94	9	5	0	36.1	38	21	27	0	0	0	0	14	3	0	.214
1943	3	7	.300	3.91	45	13	2	154.1	140	79	83	2	3	7	2	44	7	0	.159
1945	14	7	.667	3.20	26	26	7	183	161	71	101	2	0	0	0	73	17	0	.233
14 yrs.	120	115	.511	3.47	364	259	123	2113	1957	868	1242	20	11	16	16	787	174	0	.221

Manny Muniz

MUNIZ, MANUEL RODRIGUEZ
B. Dec. 31, 1947, Caguas, Puerto Rico. BR TR 5'11" 190 lbs.

	W	L	PCT	ERA	G	GS	CG	IP	H	BB	SO	ShO	W	L	SV	AB	H	HR	BA
1971 PHI N	0	1	.000	7.20	5	0	0	10	9	8	6	0	0	1	0	1	0	0	.000

Scott Munninghoff

MUNNINGHOFF, SCOTT ANDREW
B. Dec. 5, 1958, Cincinnati, Ohio. BR TR 6' 175 lbs.

	W	L	PCT	ERA	G	GS	CG	IP	H	BB	SO	ShO	W	L	SV	AB	H	HR	BA
1980 PHI N	0	0	—	4.50	4	0	0	6	8	5	2	0	0	0	0	1	1	0	1.000

Les Munns

MUNNS, LESLIE ERNEST (Nemo, Big Ed)
B. Dec. 1, 1908, Fort Bragg, Calif. BR TR 6'5" 212 lbs.

	W	L	PCT	ERA	G	GS	CG	IP	H	BB	SO	ShO	W	L	SV	AB	H	HR	BA
1934 BKN N	3	7	.300	4.71	33	9	4	99.1	106	60	41	0	1	1	0	29	7	0	.241
1935	1	3	.250	5.55	21	5	0	58.1	74	33	13	0	1	0	1	16	3	0	.188
1936 STL N	0	3	.000	3.00	7	1	0	24	23	12	4	0	0	3	1	9	1	0	.111
3 yrs.	4	13	.235	4.76	61	15	4	181.2	203	105	58	0	2	4	2	54	11	0	.204

Steve Mura

MURA, STEPHEN ANDREW
B. Feb. 12, 1955, New Orleans, La. BR TR 6'2" 188 lbs.

	W	L	PCT	ERA	G	GS	CG	IP	H	BB	SO	ShO	W	L	SV	AB	H	HR	BA
1978 SD N	0	2	.000	11.25	5	2	0	8	15	5	5	0	0	0	0	1	0	0	.000
1979	4	4	.500	3.08	38	5	0	73	57	37	59	0	3	2	0	10	0	0	.000
1980	8	7	.533	3.67	37	23	3	169	149	86	109	1	0	0	2	51	7	0	.137
1981	5	14	.263	4.27	23	22	2	139	156	50	70	0	0	1	0	44	6	0	.136
1982 STL N	12	11	.522	4.05	35	30	7	184.1	196	80	84	1	0	0	0	53	3	0	.057
1983 CHI A	0	0	—	4.38	6	0	0	12.1	13	6	4	0	0	0	0	0	0	0	—
6 yrs.	29	38	.433	3.98	144	82	12	585.2	586	264	331	2	3	3	4	159	16	0	.101

	W	L	PCT	ERA	G	GS	CG	IP	H	BB	SO	ShO	Relief Pitching W	L	SV	BATTING AB	H	HR	BA

Masanori Murakami

MURAKAMI, MASANORI
B. May 6, 1944, Otsuki, Japan
BL TL 6' 180 lbs.

	W	L	PCT	ERA	G	GS	CG	IP	H	BB	SO	ShO	W	L	SV	AB	H	HR	BA
1964 SF N	1	0	1.000	1.80	9	0	0	15	8	1	15	0	1	0	1	3	0	0	.000
1965	4	1	.800	3.75	45	1	0	74.1	57	22	85	0	4	1	8	13	2	0	.154
2 yrs.	5	1	.833	3.43	54	1	0	89.1	65	23	100	0	5	1	9	16	2	0	.125

Tim Murchison

MURCHISON, THOMAS MALCOLM
B. Oct. 8, 1896, Liberty, N. C.   D. Oct. 20, 1962, Liberty, N. C.
BR TL 6' 185 lbs.

	W	L	PCT	ERA	G	GS	CG	IP	H	BB	SO	ShO	W	L	SV	AB	H	HR	BA
1917 STL N	0	0	—	0.00	1	0	0	1	0	2	2	0	0	0	0	0	0	0	—
1920 CLE A	0	0	—	0.00	2	0	0	5	3	4	0	0	0	0	0	1	0	0	.000
2 yrs.	0	0	—	0.00	3	0	0	6	3	6	2	0	0	0	0	1	0	0	.000

Red Murff

MURFF, JOHN ROBERT
B. Apr. 1, 1921, Burlington, Tex.
BR TR 6'3" 195 lbs.

	W	L	PCT	ERA	G	GS	CG	IP	H	BB	SO	ShO	W	L	SV	AB	H	HR	BA
1956 MIL N	0	0	—	4.44	14	1	0	24.1	25	7	18	0	0	0	1	5	1	0	.200
1957	2	2	.500	4.85	12	1	0	26	31	11	13	0	2	2	2	6	0	0	.000
2 yrs.	2	2	.500	4.65	26	2	0	50.1	56	18	31	0	2	2	3	11	1	0	.091

Bob Murphy

MURPHY, ROBERT J.
B. Dec. 26, 1866, Dutchess County, N. Y.   Deceased.

	W	L	PCT	ERA	G	GS	CG	IP	H	BB	SO	ShO	W	L	SV	AB	H	HR	BA
1890 NY N	1	0	1.000	5.50	3	2	1	18	23	10	8	0	0	0	0	9	1	0	.111

Con Murphy

MURPHY, CORNELIUS B. (Razzle Dazzle)
B. Oct. 15, 1863, Worcester, Mass.   D. Aug. 1, 1914, Worcester, Mass.
5'9" 130 lbs.

	W	L	PCT	ERA	G	GS	CG	IP	H	BB	SO	ShO	W	L	SV	AB	H	HR	BA
1884 2 teams	ALT	U	(14G 5–6)		PHI	N	(3G 0–3)												
" total	5	9	.357	4.38	17	13	13	137.2	178	15	56	0	1	0	0	104	14	0	.135
1890 2 teams	BKN	P	(20G 4–10)		B-B	AA	(12G 3–9)												
" total	7	19	.269	5.17	32	26	21	235	289	128	55	0	0	2	2	119	24	1	.202
2 yrs.	12	28	.300	4.88	49	39	34	372.2	467	143	111	0	1	2	2	223	38	1	.170

Danny Murphy

MURPHY, DANIEL FRANCIS
B. Aug. 23, 1942, Beverly, Mass.
BL TR 5'11" 185 lbs.

	W	L	PCT	ERA	G	GS	CG	IP	H	BB	SO	ShO	W	L	SV	AB	H	HR	BA
1960 CHI N	0	0	—	0.00	0	0	0	0	0	0	0	0	0	0	0	75	9	1	.120
1961	0	0	—	0.00	0	0	0	0	0	0	0	0	0	0	0	13	5	2	.385
1962	0	0	—	0.00	0	0	0	0	0	0	0	0	0	0	0	35	7	0	.200
1969 CHI A	2	1	.667	2.01	17	0	0	31.1	28	10	16	0	2	1	4	1	0	0	.000
1970	2	3	.400	5.67	51	0	0	81	82	49	42	0	2	3	5	6	2	0	.333
5 yrs.	4	4	.500	4.65	68	0	0	112.1	110	59	58	0	4	4	9	*			

Ed Murphy

MURPHY, EDWARD J.
B. Jan. 22, 1877, Auburn, N. Y.   D. Jan. 29, 1935, Weedsport, N. Y.
TR 6'1" 186 lbs.

	W	L	PCT	ERA	G	GS	CG	IP	H	BB	SO	ShO	W	L	SV	AB	H	HR	BA
1898 PHI N	1	2	.333	5.10	7	3	2	30	41	10	8	0	0	0	0	14	5	0	.357
1901 STL N	10	9	.526	4.20	23	21	16	165	201	32	42	0	1	0	0	64	16	1	.250
1902	9	7	.563	3.02	23	17	12	164	187	31	37	1	1	0	1	61	16	0	.262
1903	4	8	.333	3.31	15	12	9	106	108	38	16	0	1	1	0	64	13	0	.203
4 yrs.	24	26	.480	3.64	68	53	39	465	537	111	103	1	2	1	1	203	50	1	.246

Joe Murphy

MURPHY, JOSEPH AKIN
B. Sept. 7, 1866, St. Louis, Mo.   D. Mar. 28, 1951, Coral Gables, Fla.
5'11" 160 lbs.

	W	L	PCT	ERA	G	GS	CG	IP	H	BB	SO	ShO	W	L	SV	AB	H	HR	BA
1886 3 teams	CIN	AA	(5G 2–3)		STL	N	(4G 0–4)		STL	AA	(1G 1–0)								
" total	3	7	.300	6.07	10	10	9	86	100	40	25	0	0	0	0	35	3	0	.086
1887 STL AA	1	0	1.000	5.00	1	1	1	9	13	4	5	0	0	0	0	6	1	0	.167
2 yrs.	4	7	.364	5.97	11	11	10	95	113	44	30	0	0	0	0	41	4	0	.098

John Murphy

MURPHY, JOHN H.
B. Mar. 8, 1867, Philadelphia, Pa.   Deceased.

	W	L	PCT	ERA	G	GS	CG	IP	H	BB	SO	ShO	W	L	SV	AB	H	HR	BA
1884 WIL U	0	6	.000	3.00	7	6	5	48	52	2	27	0	0	0	0	31	2	0	.065

Johnny Murphy

MURPHY, JOHN JOSEPH (Fireman, Grandma, Fordham Johnny)
BR TR 6'2" 190 lbs.
B. July 14, 1908, New York, N. Y.   D. Jan. 14, 1970, New York, N. Y.

	W	L	PCT	ERA	G	GS	CG	IP	H	BB	SO	ShO	W	L	SV	AB	H	HR	BA
1932 NY A	0	0	—	16.20	2	0	0	3.1	7	3	2	0	0	0	0	1	1	0	1.000
1934	14	10	.583	3.12	40	20	10	207.2	193	76	70	0	3	2	4	71	7	0	.099
1935	10	5	.667	4.08	40	8	4	117	110	55	28	0	6	4	5	32	5	0	.156
1936	9	3	.750	3.38	27	5	2	88	90	36	34	0	5	2	5	36	13	0	.361
1937	13	4	.765	4.17	39	4	0	110	121	50	36	0	12	4	10	35	8	0	.229
1938	8	2	.800	4.24	32	2	1	91.1	90	41	43	0	8	1	11	32	2	0	.063
1939	3	6	.333	4.40	38	0	0	61.1	57	28	30	0	3	6	19	11	2	0	.182
1940	8	4	.667	3.69	35	1	0	63.1	58	15	23	0	8	4	9	13	1	0	.077
1941	8	3	.727	1.98	35	0	0	77.1	68	40	29	0	8	3	15	18	1	0	.056
1942	4	10	.286	3.41	31	0	0	58	66	23	24	0	4	10	11	13	2	0	.154
1943	12	4	.750	2.51	37	0	0	68	44	30	31	0	12	4	8	19	1	0	.053
1946	4	2	.667	3.40	27	0	0	45	40	19	19	0	4	2	7	6	0	0	.000
1947 BOS A	0	0	—	2.80	32	0	0	54.2	41	28	9	0	0	0	3	11	3	0	.273
13 yrs.	93	53	.637	3.50	415	40	17	1045	985	444	378	0	73	42	107	298	46	0	.154

WORLD SERIES

	W	L	PCT	ERA	G	GS	CG	IP	H	BB	SO	ShO	W	L	SV	AB	H	HR	BA
1936 NY A	0	0	—	3.38	1	0	0	2.2	1	1	1	0	0	0	1	2	1	0	.500
1937	0	0	—	0.00	1	0	0	.1	0	0	0	0	0	0	1	0	0	0	—
1938	0	0	—	0.00	1	0	0	2	2	1	1	0	0	0	1	0	0	0	—
1939	1	0	1.000	2.70	1	0	0	3.1	5	2	3	0	1	0	0	2	0	0	.000
1941	1	0	1.000	0.00	2	0	0	6	2	1	3	0	1	0	1	2	0	0	.000
1943	0	0	—	0.00	2	0	0	2	1	1	1	0	0	0	0				
6 yrs.	2	0	1.000	1.10	8	0	0	16.1	11	4	8	0	2	0	4	6	1	0	.167
													2nd		2nd				

	W	L	PCT	ERA	G	GS	CG	IP	H	BB	SO	ShO	W	L	SV	AB	H	HR	BA
													Relief Pitching			BATTING			

Tom Murphy

MURPHY, THOMAS ANDREW
B. Dec. 30, 1945, Cleveland, Ohio
BR TR 6'3" 185 lbs.

	W	L	PCT	ERA	G	GS	CG	IP	H	BB	SO	ShO	W	L	SV	AB	H	HR	BA
1968 CAL A	5	6	.455	2.17	15	15	3	99.1	67	28	56	0	0	0	0	28	0	0	.000
1969	10	16	.385	4.21	36	35	4	215.2	213	69	100	0	0	0	0	71	10	0	.141
1970	16	13	.552	4.24	39	38	5	227	223	81	99	2	0	0	0	76	14	1	.184
1971	6	17	.261	3.78	37	36	7	243	228	82	89	0	0	0	0	75	13	0	.173
1972 2 teams			CAL	A	(6G 0–0)			KC	A	(18G 4–4)									
" total	4	4	.500	3.36	24	9	1	80.1	90	24	36	1	1	0	1	14	0	0	.000
1973 STL N	3	7	.300	3.76	19	13	2	88.2	89	22	42	0	0	0	0	23	4	0	.174
1974 MIL A	10	10	.500	1.90	70	0	0	123	97	51	47	0	10	10	20	2	1	0	.500
1975	1	9	.100	4.60	52	0	0	72.1	85	27	32	0	1	9	20	0	0	0	—
1976 2 teams			MIL	A	(15G 0–1)			BOS	A	(37G 4–5)									
" total	4	6	.400	4.17	52	0	0	99.1	116	34	39	0	4	6	9	0	0	0	—
1977 2 teams			BOS	A	(16G 0–1)			TOR	A	(19G 2–1)									
" total	2	2	.500	4.79	35	1	0	82.2	107	30	39	0	1	2	2	0	0	0	—
1978 TOR A	6	9	.400	3.93	50	0	0	94	87	37	36	0	6	9	7	0	0	0	—
1979	1	2	.333	5.50	10	0	0	18	23	8	6	0	1	2	0	0	0	0	—
12 yrs.	68	101	.402	3.78	439	147	22	1443.1	1425	493	621	3	24	38	59	289	42	1	.145

Walter Murphy

MURPHY, WALTER JOSEPH
B. Sept. 27, 1907, New York, N.Y.
BR TR 6'1½" 180 lbs.

	W	L	PCT	ERA	G	GS	CG	IP	H	BB	SO	ShO	W	L	SV	AB	H	HR	BA
1931 BOS A	0	0	—	9.00	2	0	0	2	4	1	0	0	0	0	0	0	0	0	—

Amby Murray

MURRAY, AMBROSE JOSEPH
B. June 4, 1913, Fall River, Mass.
BL TL 5'7" 150 lbs.

	W	L	PCT	ERA	G	GS	CG	IP	H	BB	SO	ShO	W	L	SV	AB	H	HR	BA
1936 BOS N	0	0	—	4.09	4	1	0	11	15	3	2	0	0	0	0	4	1	0	.250

Dale Murray

MURRAY, DALE ALBERT
B. Feb. 2, 1950, Cuero, Tex.
BR TR 6'4" 205 lbs.

	W	L	PCT	ERA	G	GS	CG	IP	H	BB	SO	ShO	W	L	SV	AB	H	HR	BA
1974 MON N	1	1	.500	1.03	32	0	0	70	46	23	31	0	1	1	10	10	0	0	.000
1975	15	8	.652	3.97	63	0	0	111	134	39	43	0	15	8	9	14	3	0	.214
1976	4	9	.308	3.26	81	0	0	113.1	117	37	35	0	4	9	13	8	0	0	.000
1977 CIN N	7	2	.778	4.94	61	1	0	102	125	46	42	0	7	2	4	12	2	0	.167
1978 2 teams			CIN	N	(15G 1–1)			NY	N	(53G 8–5)									
" total	9	6	.600	3.78	68	0	0	119	119	53	62	0	9	6	7	10	0	0	.000
1979 2 teams			NY	N	(58G 4–8)			MON	N	(9G 1–2)									
" total	5	10	.333	4.57	67	0	0	110.1	119	55	41	0	5	10	5	8	0	0	.000
1980 MON N	0	1	.000	6.21	16	0	0	29	39	12	16	0	0	1	0	3	0	0	.000
1981 TOR A	1	0	1.000	1.20	11	0	0	15	12	5	12	0	1	0	0	0	0	0	—
1982	8	7	.533	3.16	56	0	0	111	115	32	60	0	8	7	11	0	0	0	—
1983 NY A	2	4	.333	4.48	40	0	0	94.1	113	22	45	0	2	4	1	0	0	0	—
1984	1	2	.333	4.94	19	0	0	23.2	30	5	13	0	1	2	0	0	0	0	—
11 yrs.	53	50	.515	3.82	514	1	0	898.2	969	329	400	0	53	50	60	65	5	0	.077

George Murray

MURRAY, GEORGE KING (Smiler)
B. Sept. 23, 1898, Charlotte, N.C. D. Oct. 18, 1955, Memphis, Tenn.
BR TR 6'2" 200 lbs.

	W	L	PCT	ERA	G	GS	CG	IP	H	BB	SO	ShO	W	L	SV	AB	H	HR	BA
1922 NY A	4	2	.667	3.97	22	3	0	56.2	53	26	14	0	4	1	0	18	5	1	.278
1923 BOS A	7	11	.389	4.91	39	18	5	177.2	190	87	40	0	3	1	0	55	9	0	.164
1924	2	9	.182	6.72	28	7	0	80.1	97	32	27	0	1	3	0	22	4	0	.182
1926 WAS A	6	3	.667	5.64	12	12	5	81.1	89	37	28	0	0	0	0	36	5	0	.139
1927	1	1	.500	7.00	7	3	0	18	18	15	5	0	0	1	0	6	1	0	.167
1933 CHI A	0	0	—	7.71	2	0	0	2.1	3	2	0	0	0	0	0	0	0	0	—
6 yrs.	20	26	.435	5.38	110	43	10	416.1	450	199	114	0	8	6	0	137	24	1	.175

Jim Murray

MURRAY, JAMES FRANCIS (Big Jim)
B. Dec. 31, 1900, Scranton, Pa. D. July 15, 1973, New York, N.Y.
BL TL 6'2" 200 lbs.

	W	L	PCT	ERA	G	GS	CG	IP	H	BB	SO	ShO	W	L	SV	AB	H	HR	BA
1922 BKN N	0	0	—	4.50	4	0	0	6	8	3	3	0	0	0	1	2	1	0	.500

Joe Murray

MURRAY, JOSEPH AMBROSE
B. Nov. 11, 1920, Wilkes-Barre, Pa.
BL TL 6' 165 lbs.

	W	L	PCT	ERA	G	GS	CG	IP	H	BB	SO	ShO	W	L	SV	AB	H	HR	BA
1950 PHI A	0	3	.000	5.70	8	2	0	30	34	21	8	0	0	1	0	11	0	0	.000

Pat Murray

MURRAY, PATRICK JOSEPH
B. July 18, 1897, Scottsville, N.Y.
BR TL 6' 175 lbs.

	W	L	PCT	ERA	G	GS	CG	IP	H	BB	SO	ShO	W	L	SV	AB	H	HR	BA
1919 PHI N	0	2	.000	6.29	8	1	0	34.1	50	12	11	0	0	0	0	12	0	0	.000

Dennis Musgraves

MUSGRAVES, DENNIS EUGENE
B. Dec. 25, 1943, Indianapolis, Ind.
BR TR 6'4" 188 lbs.

	W	L	PCT	ERA	G	GS	CG	IP	H	BB	SO	ShO	W	L	SV	AB	H	HR	BA
1965 NY N	0	0	—	0.56	5	1	0	16	11	7	11	0	0	0	0	2	0	0	.000

Stan Musial

MUSIAL, STANLEY FRANK (Stan the Man)
B. Nov. 21, 1920, Donora, Pa.
Hall of Fame 1969.
BL TL 6' 175 lbs.

	W	L	PCT	ERA	G	GS	CG	IP	H	BB	SO	ShO	W	L	SV	AB	H	HR	BA
1952 STL N	0	0	—	0.00	1	0	0	0	0	0	0	0	0	0	0	*			

Ron Musselman

MUSSELMAN, RALPH RONALD
B. Nov. 11, 1954, Wilmington, N.C.
BR TR 6'1" 185 lbs.

	W	L	PCT	ERA	G	GS	CG	IP	H	BB	SO	ShO	W	L	SV	AB	H	HR	BA
1982 SEA A	1	0	1.000	3.45	12	0	0	15.2	18	6	9	0	1	0	0	0	0	0	—
1984 TOR A	0	2	.000	2.11	11	0	0	21.1	18	10	9	0	0	2	1	0	0	0	—
2 yrs.	1	2	.333	2.68	23	0	0	37	36	16	18	0	1	2	1	0	0	0	—

Paul Musser

MUSSER, PAUL
B. June 24, 1889, Millheim, Pa. D. July 7, 1973, State College, Pa.
BR TR 6' 175 lbs.

	W	L	PCT	ERA	G	GS	CG	IP	H	BB	SO	ShO	W	L	SV	AB	H	HR	BA
1912 WAS A	1	0	1.000	2.61	7	2	0	20.2	16	16	10	0	0	0	1	7	0	0	.000
1919 BOS A	0	2	.000	4.12	5	4	1	19.2	26	8	14	0	0	0	0	8	0	0	.000
2 yrs.	1	2	.333	3.35	12	6	1	40.1	42	24	24	0	0	0	1	15	0	0	.000

	W	L	PCT	ERA	G	GS	CG	IP	H	BB	SO	ShO	W	L	SV	AB	H	HR	BA

Roger Nelson continued

	W	L	PCT	ERA	G	GS	CG	IP	H	BB	SO	ShO	RW	RL	SV	AB	H	HR	BA
1976 KC A	0	0	–	2.00	3	0	0	9	4	4	4	0	0	0	0	0	0	0	–
9 yrs.	29	32	.475	3.06	135	77	20	636.1	516	190	371	7	3	4	4	180	23	0	.128

LEAGUE CHAMPIONSHIP SERIES

	W	L	PCT	ERA	G	GS	CG	IP	H	BB	SO	ShO	RW	RL	SV	AB	H	HR	BA
1973 CIN N	0	0	–	0.00	1	0	0	2.1	0	1	0	0	0	0	0	1	0	0	.000

Hal Neubauer

NEUBAUER, HAROLD CHARLES   BR TR 6'3" 190 lbs.
B. May 13, 1902, Hoboken, N. J.   D. Sept. 9, 1949, Barrington, R. I.

	W	L	PCT	ERA	G	GS	CG	IP	H	BB	SO	ShO	RW	RL	SV	AB	H	HR	BA
1925 BOS A	1	0	1.000	12.19	7	0	0	10.1	17	11	4	0	1	0	0	0	0	0	–

Tex Neuer

NEUER, JOHN S.
B. June 8, 1877, Freemont, Ohio   D. Jan. 14, 1966, Northumberland, Pa.

	W	L	PCT	ERA	G	GS	CG	IP	H	BB	SO	ShO	RW	RL	SV	AB	H	HR	BA
1907 NY A	4	2	.667	2.17	7	6	6	54	40	19	22	3	0	0	0	21	2	0	.095

Dan Neumeier

NEUMEIER, DANIEL GEORGE   BR TR 6'5" 205 lbs.
B. Mar. 9, 1948, Shawano, Wis.

	W	L	PCT	ERA	G	GS	CG	IP	H	BB	SO	ShO	RW	RL	SV	AB	H	HR	BA
1972 CHI A	0	0	–	7.36	3	0	0	3.2	3	3	2	0	0	0	0	1	0	0	.000

Ernie Nevel

NEVEL, ERNIE WYRE   BR TR 5'11" 190 lbs.
B. Aug. 17, 1919, Charleston, Mo.

	W	L	PCT	ERA	G	GS	CG	IP	H	BB	SO	ShO	RW	RL	SV	AB	H	HR	BA
1950 NY A	0	1	.000	9.95	3	1	0	6.1	10	6	3	0	0	0	0	1	0	0	.000
1951	0	0	–	0.00	1	0	0	4	1	1	1	0	0	0	1	1	0	0	.000
1953 CIN N	0	0	–	6.10	10	0	0	10.1	16	1	5	0	0	0	0	0	0	0	–
3 yrs.	0	1	.000	6.10	14	1	0	20.2	27	8	9	0	0	0	1	2	0	0	.000

Ernie Nevers

NEVERS, ERNEST ALONZO   BR TR 6' 205 lbs.
B. June 11, 1903, Willow River, Minn.   D. May 3, 1976, San Rafael, Calif.

	W	L	PCT	ERA	G	GS	CG	IP	H	BB	SO	ShO	RW	RL	SV	AB	H	HR	BA
1926 STL A	2	4	.333	4.46	11	7	4	74.2	82	24	16	0	0	0	0	27	5	0	.185
1927	3	8	.273	4.94	27	5	2	94.2	105	35	22	0	3	4	2	32	7	0	.219
1928	1	0	1.000	3.00	6	0	0	9	9	2	1	0	1	0	0	1	0	0	.000
3 yrs.	6	12	.333	4.64	44	12	6	178.1	196	61	39	0	4	4	2	60	12	0	.200

Don Newcombe

NEWCOMBE, DONALD (Newk)   BR TR 6'4" 220 lbs.
B. June 14, 1926, Madison, N. J.

	W	L	PCT	ERA	G	GS	CG	IP	H	BB	SO	ShO	RW	RL	SV	AB	H	HR	BA
1949 BKN N	17	8	.680	3.17	38	31	19	244.1	223	73	149	5	0	0	1	96	22	0	.229
1950	19	11	.633	3.70	40	35	20	267.1	258	75	130	4	0	0	3	97	24	1	.247
1951	20	9	.690	3.28	40	36	18	272	235	91	164	3	1	1	0	103	23	0	.223
1954	9	8	.529	4.55	29	25	6	144.1	158	49	82	0	0	0	0	47	15	0	.319
1955	20	5	.800	3.20	34	31	17	233.2	222	38	143	1	1	0	0	117	42	7	.359
1956	27	7	.794	3.06	38	36	18	268	219	46	139	5	2	0	0	111	26	2	.234
1957	11	12	.478	3.49	28	28	12	198.2	199	33	90	4	0	0	0	74	17	1	.230
1958 2 teams						LA N (11G 0–6)					CIN N (20G 7–7)								
" total	7	13	.350	4.67	31	26	8	167.2	212	36	69	0	0	1	1	72	26	1	.361
1959 CIN N	13	8	.619	3.16	30	29	17	222	216	27	100	2	0	0	1	105	32	3	.305
1960 2 teams						CIN N (16G 4–6)					CLE A (20G 2–3)								
" total	6	9	.400	4.48	36	17	1	136.2	160	22	63	0	2	1	1	56	11	0	.196
10 yrs.	149	90	.623	3.56	344	294	136	2154.2	2102	490	1129	24	6	3	7	*			

WORLD SERIES

	W	L	PCT	ERA	G	GS	CG	IP	H	BB	SO	ShO	RW	RL	SV	AB	H	HR	BA
1949 BKN N	0	2	.000	3.09	2	2	1	11.2	10	3	11	0	0	0	0	4	0	0	.000
1955	0	1	.000	9.53	1	1	0	5.2	8	2	4	0	0	0	0	3	0	0	.000
1956	0	1	.000	21.21	2	2	0	4.2	11	3	4	0	0	0	0	1	0	0	.000
3 yrs.	0	4	.000	8.59	5	5	1	22	29	8	19	0	0	0	0	8	0	0	.000
		7th																	

Don Newhauser

NEWHAUSER, DONALD LOUIS   BR TR 6'4" 200 lbs.
B. Nov. 7, 1947, Miami, Fla.

	W	L	PCT	ERA	G	GS	CG	IP	H	BB	SO	ShO	RW	RL	SV	AB	H	HR	BA
1972 BOS A	4	2	.667	2.43	31	0	0	37	30	25	27	0	4	2	4	2	0	0	.000
1973	0	0	–	0.00	9	0	0	12	9	13	8	0	0	0	1	0	0	0	–
1974	0	1	.000	9.00	2	0	0	4	5	4	2	0	0	1	0	0	0	0	–
3 yrs.	4	3	.571	2.38	42	0	0	53	44	42	37	0	4	3	5	2	0	0	.000

Hal Newhouser

NEWHOUSER, HAROLD (Prince Hal)   BL TL 6'2" 180 lbs.
B. May 20, 1921, Detroit, Mich.

	W	L	PCT	ERA	G	GS	CG	IP	H	BB	SO	ShO	RW	RL	SV	AB	H	HR	BA
1939 DET A	0	1	.000	5.40	1	1	1	5	3	4	4	0	0	0	0	1	0	0	.000
1940	9	9	.500	4.86	28	20	7	133.1	149	76	89	0	1	0	0	40	8	0	.200
1941	9	11	.450	4.79	33	27	5	173	166	137	106	1	0	1	0	60	9	0	.150
1942	8	14	.364	2.45	38	23	11	183.2	137	114	103	1	0	2	5	52	8	0	.154
1943	8	17	.320	3.04	37	25	10	195.2	163	111	144	1	1	1	1	65	12	0	.185
1944	29	9	.763	2.22	47	34	25	312.1	264	102	187	6	4	2	2	120	29	0	.242
1945	25	9	.735	1.81	40	36	29	313.1	239	110	212	8	1	0	2	109	28	0	.257
1946	26	9	.743	1.94	37	34	29	292.1	215	98	275	6	0	1	1	103	13	2	.126
1947	17	17	.500	2.87	40	36	24	285	268	110	176	3	0	1	2	96	19	0	.198
1948	21	12	.636	3.01	39	35	19	272.1	249	99	143	2	1	1	1	92	19	0	.207
1949	18	11	.621	3.36	38	35	22	292	277	111	144	3	1	0	1	91	18	0	.198
1950	15	13	.536	4.34	35	30	15	213.2	232	81	87	1	1	0	3	74	13	0	.176
1951	6	6	.500	3.92	15	14	7	96.1	98	19	37	1	0	0	0	29	9	0	.310
1952	9	9	.500	3.74	25	19	8	154	148	47	57	0	3	0	0	46	10	0	.217
1953	0	1	.000	7.06	7	4	0	21.2	31	8	6	0	0	0	1	8	4	0	.500
1954 CLE A	7	2	.778	2.51	26	1	0	46.2	34	18	25	0	7	1	7	13	2	0	.154
1955	0	0	–	0.00	2	0	0	2.1	1	4	1	0	0	0	0				
17 yrs.	207	150	.580	3.06	488	374	212	2992.2	2674	1249	1796	33	20	10	26	999	201	2	.201

WORLD SERIES

	W	L	PCT	ERA	G	GS	CG	IP	H	BB	SO	ShO	RW	RL	SV	AB	H	HR	BA
1945 DET A	2	1	.667	6.10	3	3	2	20.2	25	4	22	0	0	0	0	8	0	0	.000

	W	L	PCT	ERA	G	GS	CG	IP	H	BB	SO	ShO	Relief Pitching W	L	SV	BATTING AB	H	HR	BA

Hal Newhouser continued

	W	L	PCT	ERA	G	GS	CG	IP	H	BB	SO	ShO	W	L	SV	AB	H	HR	BA
1954 CLE A	0	0	–	∞	1	0	0	1	1	0	0	0	0	0	0	0	0	0	
2 yrs.	2	1	.667	6.53	4	3	2	20.2	26	5	22	0	0	0	0	8	0	0	.000

Floyd Newkirk

NEWKIRK, FLOYD ELMO (Three-Finger)
Brother of Joel Newkirk.
B. July 16, 1908, Norris City, Ill.   D. Apr. 15, 1976, Clayton, Mo.
BR TR 5'11"   178 lbs.

	W	L	PCT	ERA	G	GS	CG	IP	H	BB	SO	ShO	W	L	SV	AB	H	HR	BA
1934 NY A	0	0	–	0.00	1	0	0	1	1	1	0	0	0	0	0	0	0	0	

Joel Newkirk

NEWKIRK, JOEL INEZ (Sailor)
Brother of Floyd Newkirk.
B. May 1, 1896, Kyana, Ind.   D. Jan. 22, 1966, Eldorado, Ill.
BR TR 6'   180 lbs.

	W	L	PCT	ERA	G	GS	CG	IP	H	BB	SO	ShO	W	L	SV	AB	H	HR	BA
1919 CHI N	0	0	–	13.50	1	0	0	2	2	3	1	0	0	0	0	1	0	0	.000
1920	0	1	.000	5.40	2	1	0	6.2	8	6	2	0	0	0	0	3	0	0	.000
2 yrs.	0	1	.000	7.27	3	1	0	8.2	10	9	3	0	0	0	0	4	0	0	.000

Maury Newlin

NEWLIN, MAURICE MILTON (Mickey)
B. June 22, 1914, Bloomingdale, Ind.   D. Aug. 14, 1978, Houston, Tex.
BR TR 6'   176 lbs.

	W	L	PCT	ERA	G	GS	CG	IP	H	BB	SO	ShO	W	L	SV	AB	H	HR	BA
1940 STL A	1	0	1.000	6.00	1	1	0	6	4	2	3	0	0	0	0	2	1	0	.500
1941	0	2	.000	6.51	14	0	0	27.2	43	12	10	0	0	2	1	6	0	0	.000
2 yrs.	1	2	.333	6.42	15	1	0	33.2	47	14	13	0	0	2	1	8	1	0	.125

Fred Newman

NEWMAN, FREDERICK WILLIAM
B. Feb. 21, 1942, Boston, Mass.
BR TR 6'3"   180 lbs.

	W	L	PCT	ERA	G	GS	CG	IP	H	BB	SO	ShO	W	L	SV	AB	H	HR	BA
1962 LA A	0	1	.000	9.95	4	1	0	6.1	11	3	4	0	0	0	0	1	0	0	.000
1963	1	5	.167	5.32	12	8	0	44	56	15	16	0	0	0	0	16	4	0	.250
1964	13	10	.565	2.75	32	28	7	190	177	39	83	2	0	0	0	61	11	1	.180
1965 CAL A	14	16	.467	2.93	36	36	10	260.2	225	64	109	2	0	0	0	74	7	1	.095
1966	4	7	.364	4.73	21	19	1	102.2	112	31	42	0	0	0	0	30	6	0	.200
1967	1	0	1.000	1.42	3	1	0	6.1	8	2	0	0	1	0	0	1	0	0	.000
6 yrs.	33	39	.458	3.41	108	93	18	610	589	154	254	4	1	0	0	183	28	2	.153

Jeff Newman

NEWMAN, JEFFREY LYNN
B. Sept. 11, 1948, Ft. Worth, Tex.
BR TR 6'2"   215 lbs.

	W	L	PCT	ERA	G	GS	CG	IP	H	BB	SO	ShO	W	L	SV	AB	H	HR	BA
1977 OAK A	0	0	–	0.00	1	0	0	1	1	0	0	0	0	0	0	*			

Ray Newman

NEWMAN, RAYMOND FRANCIS
B. June 20, 1945, Evansville, Ind.
BL TL 6'5"   205 lbs.

	W	L	PCT	ERA	G	GS	CG	IP	H	BB	SO	ShO	W	L	SV	AB	H	HR	BA
1971 CHI N	1	2	.333	3.55	30	0	0	38	30	17	35	0	1	2	2	6	0	0	.000
1972 MIL A	0	0	–	0.00	4	0	0	7	4	2	1	0	0	0	1	1	1	0	1.000
1973	2	1	.667	2.95	11	0	0	18.1	19	5	10	0	2	1	1	0	0	0	
3 yrs.	3	3	.500	2.98	45	0	0	63.1	53	24	46	0	3	3	4	7	1	0	.143

Bobo Newsom

NEWSOM, NORMAN LOUIS (Buck)
B. Aug. 11, 1907, Hartsville, S. C.   D. Dec. 7, 1962, Orlando, Fla.
BR TR 6'3"   200 lbs.

	W	L	PCT	ERA	G	GS	CG	IP	H	BB	SO	ShO	W	L	SV	AB	H	HR	BA
1929 BKN N	0	3	.000	10.61	3	2	0	9.1	15	5	6	0	0	1	0	2	0	0	.000
1930	0	0	–	0.00	2	0	0	3	2	2	1	0	0	0	0	0	0	0	–
1932 CHI N	0	0	–	0.00	1	0	0	1	1	0	0	0	0	0	0	0	0	0	–
1934 STL A	16	20	.444	4.01	47	32	15	262.1	259	149	135	2	3	4	5	93	17	0	.183
1935 2 teams				STL A (7G 0-6)				WAS A (28G 11-12)											
" total	11	18	.379	4.52	35	29	18	241	276	97	87	2	0	2	3	84	23	0	.274
1936 WAS A	17	15	.531	4.32	43	38	24	285.2	294	146	156	4	0	2	0	108	23	0	.213
1937 2 teams				WAS A (11G 3-4)				BOS A (30G 13-10)											
" total	16	14	.533	4.74	41	37	17	275.1	297	167	166	1	1	1	0	100	22	1	.220
1938 STL A	20	16	.556	5.08	44	40	31	329.2	334	192	226	0	0	0	1	124	31	0	.250
1939 2 teams				STL A (6G 3-1)				DET A (35G 17-10)											
" total	20	11	.645	3.58	41	37	24	291.2	272	126	192	3	0	0	2	115	22	0	.191
1940 DET A	21	5	.808	2.83	36	34	20	264	235	100	164	3	1	1	0	107	23	0	.215
1941	12	20	.375	4.60	43	36	12	250.1	265	118	175	2	1	1	2	88	9	0	.102
1942 2 teams				WAS A (30G 11-17)				BKN N (6G 2-2)											
" total	13	19	.406	4.73	36	34	17	245.2	264	106	134	3	1	0	0	86	12	0	.140
1943 3 teams				BKN N (22G 9-4)		STL A (10G 1-6)			WAS A (6G 3-3)										
" total	13	13	.500	4.22	38	27	8	217.1	220	113	123	1	4	1	0	74	18	0	.243
1944 PHI A	13	15	.464	2.82	37	33	18	265	243	82	142	2	0	0	1	88	10	0	.114
1945	8	20	.286	3.29	36	34	16	257.1	255	103	127	3	0	1	0	86	14	0	.163
1946 2 teams				PHI A (10G 3-5)				WAS A (24G 11-8)											
" total	14	13	.519	2.93	34	31	17	236.2	224	90	114	3	0	0	1	81	12	0	.148
1947 2 teams				WAS A (14G 4-6)				NY A (17G 7-5)											
" total	11	11	.500	3.34	31	28	7	199.1	208	67	82	2	0	0	0	71	11	0	.155
1948 NY N	0	4	.000	4.21	11	4	0	25.2	35	13	9	0	0	1	0	7	3	0	.429
1952 2 teams				WAS A (10G 1-1)				PHI A (14G 3-3)											
" total	4	4	.500	3.88	24	5	1	60.1	54	32	27	0	3	2	3	17	2	0	.118
1953 PHI A	2	1	.667	4.89	17	1	0	38.2	44	24	16	0	1	0	0	6	1	0	.167
20 yrs.	211	222	.487	3.98	600	483	246	3759.1	3771	1732	2082	31	15	15	21	1337	253	1	.189
										4th									

WORLD SERIES

	W	L	PCT	ERA	G	GS	CG	IP	H	BB	SO	ShO	W	L	SV	AB	H	HR	BA
1940 DET A	2	1	.667	1.38	3	3	3	26	18	4	17	1	0	0	0	10	1	0	.100
1947 NY A	0	1	.000	19.29	2	1	0	2.1	6	2	0	0	0	0	0	0	0	0	–
2 yrs.	2	2	.500	2.86	5	4	3	28.1	24	6	17	1	0	0	0	10	1	0	.100

Dick Newsome

NEWSOME, HEBER HAMPTON
B. Dec. 13, 1909, Ahoskie, N. C.   D. Dec. 15, 1965, Ahoskie, N. C.
BR TR 6'   185 lbs.

	W	L	PCT	ERA	G	GS	CG	IP	H	BB	SO	ShO	W	L	SV	AB	H	HR	BA
1941 BOS A	19	10	.655	4.13	36	29	17	213.2	235	79	58	2	2	1	0	78	19	0	.244
1942	8	10	.444	5.01	24	23	11	158	174	67	40	0	0	0	0	55	13	0	.236
1943	8	13	.381	4.49	25	22	8	154.1	166	68	40	2	0	0	0	48	7	0	.146
3 yrs.	35	33	.515	4.50	85	74	36	526	575	214	138	4	2	1	0	181	39	0	.215

	W	L	PCT	ERA	G	GS	CG	IP	H	BB	SO	ShO	Relief Pitching W	L	SV	BATTING AB	H	HR	BA

Dan O'Brien

O'BRIEN, DANIEL JOSEPH   BR TR 6'4" 215 lbs.
B. Apr. 22, 1954, St. Petersburg, Fla.

	W	L	PCT	ERA	G	GS	CG	IP	H	BB	SO	ShO	W	L	SV	AB	H	HR	BA
1978 STL N	0	2	.000	4.50	7	2	0	18	22	8	12	0	0	1	0	3	0	0	.000
1979	1	1	.500	8.18	6	0	0	11	21	3	5	0	1	1	0	2	0	0	.000
2 yrs.	1	3	.250	5.90	13	2	0	29	43	11	17	0	1	2	0	5	0	0	.000

Darby O'Brien

O'BRIEN, JOHN F.   BR TR 5'10" 165 lbs.
B. Apr. 15, 1867, Troy, N. Y.   D. Mar. 11, 1892, Troy, N. Y.

	W	L	PCT	ERA	G	GS	CG	IP	H	BB	SO	ShO	W	L	SV	AB	H	HR	BA
1888 CLE AA	11	19	.367	3.30	30	30	30	259	245	99	135	1	0	0	0	109	20	0	.183
1889 CLE N	22	17	.564	4.15	41	41	39	346.2	345	167	122	1	0	0	0	140	35	0	.250
1890 CLE P	8	16	.333	3.40	25	25	22	206.1	229	93	54	0	0	0	0	96	15	0	.156
1891 BOS AA	19	13	.594	3.65	40	30	22	268.2	300	127	87	0	3	1	1	128	30	0	.234
4 yrs.	60	65	.480	3.68	136	126	113	1080.2	1119	486	398	2	3	1	1	473	100	0	.211

Darby O'Brien

O'BRIEN, WILLIAM D.   BR TR 5'11½" 185 lbs.
B. Sept. 1, 1863, Peoria, Ill.   D. June 15, 1893, Peoria, Ill.

	W	L	PCT	ERA	G	GS	CG	IP	H	BB	SO	ShO	W	L	SV	AB	H	HR	BA
1887 NY AA	0	0	—	7.36	1	0	0	3.2	4	5	0	0	0	0	0	*			

Eddie O'Brien

O'BRIEN, EDWARD JOSEPH   BR TR 5'9" 165 lbs.
Brother of Johnny O'Brien.
B. Dec. 11, 1930, South Amboy, N. J.

	W	L	PCT	ERA	G	GS	CG	IP	H	BB	SO	ShO	W	L	SV	AB	H	HR	BA
1956 PIT N	0	0	—	0.00	1	0	0	2	1	0	0	0	0	0	0	53	14	0	.264
1957	1	0	1.000	2.19	3	1	1	12.1	11	3	10	0	0	0	0	4	0	0	.000
1958	0	0	—	13.50	1	0	0	2	4	1	1	0	0	0	0	0	0	0	—
3 yrs.	1	0	1.000	3.31	5	1	1	16.1	16	4	11	0	0	0	0	*			

Johnny O'Brien

O'BRIEN, JOHN THOMAS   BR TR 5'9" 170 lbs.
Brother of Eddie O'Brien.
B. Dec. 11, 1930, South Amboy, N. J.

	W	L	PCT	ERA	G	GS	CG	IP	H	BB	SO	ShO	W	L	SV	AB	H	HR	BA
1956 PIT N	1	0	1.000	2.84	8	0	0	19	8	9	9	0	1	0	0	104	18	0	.173
1957	0	3	.000	6.08	16	1	0	40	46	24	19	0	0	2	0	35	11	0	.314
1958 STL N	0	0	—	22.50	1	0	0	2	7	2	2	0	0	0	0	3	0	0	.000
3 yrs.	1	3	.250	5.61	25	1	0	61	61	35	30	0	1	2	0	*			

Tom O'Brien

O'BRIEN, THOMAS H.   BR TR
B. Salem, Mass.   D. Apr. 21, 1921, Worcester, Mass.

	W	L	PCT	ERA	G	GS	CG	IP	H	BB	SO	ShO	W	L	SV	AB	H	HR	BA
1887 NY AA	0	0	—	0.00	1	0	0	1	1	1	0	0	0	0	0	*			

Walter Ockey

OCKEY, WALTER ANDREW (Footie)   BR TR 6' 175 lbs.
Born Walter Andrew Okypch.
B. July 4, 1920, New York, N. Y.   D. Dec. 4, 1971, Staten Island, N. Y.

	W	L	PCT	ERA	G	GS	CG	IP	H	BB	SO	ShO	W	L	SV	AB	H	HR	BA
1944 NY N	0	0	—	3.38	2	0	0	2.2	2	2	1	0	0	0	0	0	0	0	—

Pat O'Connell

O'CONNELL, PATRICK H.   BL TR 5'11"
B. June 10, 1861, Bangor, Me.   D. Jan. 24, 1943, Lewiston, Me.

	W	L	PCT	ERA	G	GS	CG	IP	H	BB	SO	ShO	W	L	SV	AB	H	HR	BA
1886 BAL AA	0	0	—	6.00	1	0	0	3	4	2	1	0	0	0	0	*			

Andy O'Connor

O'CONNOR, ANDREW JAMES   BR TR 6' 160 lbs.
B. Sept. 14, 1884, Roxbury, Mass.   D. Sept. 26, 1980, Norwood, Mass.

	W	L	PCT	ERA	G	GS	CG	IP	H	BB	SO	ShO	W	L	SV	AB	H	HR	BA
1908 NY A	0	1	.000	10.13	1	1	1	8	15	7	5	0	0	0	0	3	0	0	.000

Frank O'Connor

O'CONNOR, FRANK HENRY   TL
B. Sept. 15, 1870, Keeseville, N. Y.   D. Dec. 26, 1913, Brattleboro, Vt.

	W	L	PCT	ERA	G	GS	CG	IP	H	BB	SO	ShO	W	L	SV	AB	H	HR	BA
1893 PHI N	0	0	—	11.25	3	1	0	4	2	9	0	0	0	0	1	2	2	1	1.000

Jack O'Connor

O'CONNOR, JACK WILLIAM   BL TL 6'3" 215 lbs.
B. June 2, 1958, Yucca Valley, Calif.

	W	L	PCT	ERA	G	GS	CG	IP	H	BB	SO	ShO	W	L	SV	AB	H	HR	BA
1981 MIN A	3	2	.600	5.91	28	0	0	35	46	30	16	0	3	2	0	0	0	0	—
1982	8	9	.471	4.29	23	19	6	126	122	57	56	1	0	0	0	0	0	0	—
1983	2	3	.400	5.86	27	8	0	83	107	36	56	0	1	0	0	0	0	0	—
1984	0	0	—	1.93	2	0	0	4.2	1	4	0	0	0	0	0	0	0	0	—
4 yrs.	13	14	.481	4.99	80	27	6	248.2	276	127	128	1	4	2	0	0	0	0	—

Hank O'Day

O'DAY, HENRY FRANCIS   TR
B. July 8, 1863, Chicago, Ill.   D. July 2, 1935, Chicago, Ill.
Manager 1912, 1914.

	W	L	PCT	ERA	G	GS	CG	IP	H	BB	SO	ShO	W	L	SV	AB	H	HR	BA
1884 TOL AA	7	28	.200	3.97	39	38	33	308.2	326	65	154	0	0	0	1	242	51	0	.211
1885 PIT AA	5	7	.417	3.67	12	12	10	103	110	16	36	0	0	0	0	49	12	0	.245
1886 WAS N	1	2	.333	1.65	6	6	6	49	41	17	47	0	0	0	0	19	1	0	.053
1887	8	20	.286	4.17	30	30	29	254.2	255	109	86	0	0	0	0	116	23	0	.198
1888	16	29	.356	3.10	46	46	46	403	359	117	186	3	0	0	0	166	23	0	.139
1889 2 teams			WAS	N (13G 2-10)		NY	N (10G 9-1)												
" total	11	11	.500	4.31	23	23	19	186	200	92	51	0	0	0	0	75	11	0	.147
1890 NY P	23	15	.605	4.21	43	35	32	329	356	163	94	1	1	0	3	150	34	1	.227
7 yrs.	71	112	.388	3.79	199	190	175	1633.1	1647	579	654	4	1	0	4	*			

Paul O'Dea

O'DEA, PAUL (Lefty)   BL TL 6' 200 lbs.
B. July 3, 1920, Cleveland, Ohio   D. Dec. 11, 1978, Cleveland, Ohio

	W	L	PCT	ERA	G	GS	CG	IP	H	BB	SO	ShO	W	L	SV	AB	H	HR	BA
1944 CLE A	0	0	—	2.08	3	0	0	4.1	5	6	0	0	0	0	0	173	55	0	.318
1945	0	0	—	13.50	1	0	0	2	4	2	0	0	0	0	0	221	52	1	.235
2 yrs.	0	0	—	5.68	4	0	0	6.1	9	8	0	0	0	0	0	*			

Billy O'Dell

O'DELL, WILLIAM OLIVER (Digger)   BB TL 5'11" 170 lbs.
B. Feb. 10, 1933, Whitmere, S. C.

	W	L	PCT	ERA	G	GS	CG	IP	H	BB	SO	ShO	W	L	SV	AB	H	HR	BA
1954 BAL A	1	1	.500	2.76	7	2	1	16.1	15	5	6	0	0	0	0	3	0	0	.000
1956	0	0	—	1.13	4	1	0	8	6	6	6	0	0	0	0	1	0	0	.000

	W	L	PCT	ERA	G	GS	CG	IP	H	BB	SO	ShO	Relief Pitching W	L	SV	BATTING AB	H	HR	BA

Billy O'Dell continued

	W	L	PCT	ERA	G	GS	CG	IP	H	BB	SO	ShO	W	L	SV	AB	H	HR	BA
1957	4	10	.286	2.69	35	15	2	140.1	107	39	97	1	0	1	4	34	5	0	.147
1958	14	11	.560	2.97	41	25	12	221.1	201	51	137	3	2	1	8	72	8	1	.111
1959	10	12	.455	2.93	38	24	6	199.1	163	67	88	2	2	4	1	60	5	1	.083
1960 SF N	8	13	.381	3.20	43	24	6	202.2	198	72	145	1	1	3	2	56	6	0	.107
1961	7	5	.583	3.59	46	14	4	130.1	132	33	110	1	3	2	2	39	4	0	.103
1962	19	14	.576	3.53	43	39	20	280.2	282	66	195	2	1	0	0	90	12	0	.133
1963	14	10	.583	3.16	36	33	10	222.1	218	70	116	3	0	1	1	78	16	0	.205
1964	8	7	.533	5.40	36	8	1	85	82	35	54	0	8	3	2	22	0	0	.000
1965 MIL N	10	6	.625	2.18	62	1	0	111.1	87	30	78	0	10	5	18	23	4	0	.174
1966 2 teams	ATL	N	(24G 2–3)		PIT	N	(37G 3–2)												
" total	5	5	.500	2.64	61	2	0	112.2	118	41	67	0	4	5	10	24	3	0	.125
1967 PIT N	5	6	.455	5.82	27	11	1	86.2	88	41	34	0	1	1	0	26	3	0	.115
13 yrs.	105	100	.512	3.29	479	199	63	1817	1697	556	1133	13	32	26	48	528	66	2	.125

WORLD SERIES

	W	L	PCT	ERA	G	GS	CG	IP	H	BB	SO	ShO	W	L	SV	AB	H	HR	BA
1962 SF N	0	1	.000	4.38	3	1	0	12.1	12	3	9	0	0	0	1	3	1	0	.333

Ted Odenwald

ODENWALD, THEODORE JOSEPH (Lefty)   BR TL 5'10" 147 lbs.
B. Jan. 4, 1902, Hudson, Wis.   D. Oct. 23, 1965, Shakopee, Minn.

	W	L	PCT	ERA	G	GS	CG	IP	H	BB	SO	ShO	W	L	SV	AB	H	HR	BA
1921 CLE A	1	0	1.000	1.56	10	0	0	17.1	16	6	4	0	1	0	0	3	0	0	.000
1922	0	0	–	40.50	1	0	0	1.1	6	2	2	0	0	0	0	0	0	0	–
2 yrs.	1	0	1.000	4.34	11	0	0	18.2	22	8	6	0	1	0	0	3	0	0	.000

Blue Moon Odom

ODOM, JOHNNY LEE   BR TR 6' 178 lbs.
B. May 29, 1945, Macon, Ga.

	W	L	PCT	ERA	G	GS	CG	IP	H	BB	SO	ShO	W	L	SV	AB	H	HR	BA
1964 KC A	1	2	.333	10.06	5	5	1	17	29	11	10	1	0	0	0	5	0	0	.000
1965	0	0	–	9.00	1	0	0	1	2	2	0	0	0	0	0	0	0	0	–
1966	5	5	.500	2.49	14	14	4	90.1	70	53	47	2	0	0	0	31	3	0	.097
1967	3	8	.273	5.04	29	17	0	103.2	94	68	67	0	0	0	0	28	8	0	.286
1968 OAK A	16	10	.615	2.45	32	31	9	231.1	179	98	143	4	0	0	0	78	17	1	.218
1969	15	6	.714	2.92	32	32	10	231.1	179	112	150	3	0	0	0	79	21	5	.266
1970	9	8	.529	3.81	29	29	4	156	128	100	88	1	0	0	0	54	13	3	.241
1971	10	12	.455	4.28	25	25	3	141	147	71	69	1	0	0	0	50	8	1	.160
1972	15	6	.714	2.50	31	30	4	194.1	164	87	86	2	0	0	0	66	8	2	.121
1973	5	12	.294	4.49	30	24	3	150.1	153	67	83	0	1	0	0	1	0	0	.000
1974	1	5	.167	3.83	34	5	1	87	85	52	52	0	1	0	1	0	0	0	–
1975 3 teams	OAK	A	(7G 0–2)		CLE	A	(3G 1–0)		ATL	N	(15G 1–7)								
" total	2	9	.182	7.22	25	13	1	77.1	101	47	44	1	0	1	0	13	1	0	.077
1976 CHI A	2	2	.500	5.79	8	4	0	28	31	20	18	0	0	0	0	0	0	0	–
13 yrs.	84	85	.497	3.70	295	229	40	1508.2	1362	788	857	15	2	1	1	405	79	12	.195

LEAGUE CHAMPIONSHIP SERIES

	W	L	PCT	ERA	G	GS	CG	IP	H	BB	SO	ShO	W	L	SV	AB	H	HR	BA
1972 OAK A	2	0	1.000	0.00	2	2	1	14	5	2	5	1	0	0	0	4	1	0	.250
1973	0	0	–	1.80	1	0	0	5	6	2	4	0	0	0	0	0	0	0	–
1974	0	0	–	0.00	1	0	0	3.1	1	0	1	0	0	0	0	0	0	0	–
3 yrs.	2	0	1.000	0.40	4	2	1	22.1	12	4	10	1	0	0	0	4	1	0	.250

WORLD SERIES

	W	L	PCT	ERA	G	GS	CG	IP	H	BB	SO	ShO	W	L	SV	AB	H	HR	BA
1972 OAK A	0	1	.000	1.59	2	2	0	11.1	5	6	13	0	0	0	0	4	0	0	.000
1973	0	0	–	3.86	2	0	0	4.2	5	2	2	0	0	0	0	1	0	0	.000
1974	1	0	1.000	0.00	2	0	0	1.1	0	1	2	0	1	0	0	0	0	0	–
3 yrs.	1	1	.500	2.08	6	2	0	17.1	10	9	17	0	1	0	0	5	0	0	.000

Dave Odom

ODOM, DAVID EVERETT (Porky)   BR TR 5'10" 185 lbs.
B. June 5, 1918, Dinuba, Calif.

	W	L	PCT	ERA	G	GS	CG	IP	H	BB	SO	ShO	W	L	SV	AB	H	HR	BA
1943 BOS N	0	3	.000	5.27	22	3	1	54.2	54	30	17	0	0	0	2	12	0	0	.000

George O'Donnell

O'DONNELL, GEORGE DANA   BR TR 6'3" 175 lbs.
B. May 27, 1929, Winchester, Ill.

	W	L	PCT	ERA	G	GS	CG	IP	H	BB	SO	ShO	W	L	SV	AB	H	HR	BA
1954 PIT N	3	9	.250	4.53	21	10	3	87.1	105	21	8	0	1	1	1	23	2	1	.087

John O'Donoghue

O'DONOGHUE, JOHN EUGENE   BR TL 6'4" 203 lbs.
B. Oct. 7, 1939, Kansas City, Mo.

	W	L	PCT	ERA	G	GS	CG	IP	H	BB	SO	ShO	W	L	SV	AB	H	HR	BA
1963 KC A	0	1	.000	1.50	1	1	0	6	6	2	1	0	0	0	0	2	0	0	.000
1964	10	14	.417	4.92	39	32	2	173.2	202	65	79	1	1	0	0	55	13	1	.236
1965	9	18	.333	3.95	34	30	4	177.2	183	66	82	1	0	2	0	55	12	1	.218
1966 CLE A	6	8	.429	3.83	32	13	2	108	109	23	49	0	2	2	0	33	5	0	.152
1967	8	9	.471	3.24	33	17	5	130.2	120	33	81	2	1	0	2	40	4	1	.100
1968 BAL A	0	0	–	6.14	16	0	0	22	34	7	11	0	0	0	2	2	0	0	.000
1969 SEA A	2	2	.500	2.96	55	0	0	70	58	37	48	0	2	2	6	13	1	0	.077
1970 2 teams	MIL	A	(25G 2–0)		MON	N	(9G 2–3)												
" total	4	3	.571	5.20	34	3	0	45	49	20	19	0	4	1	0	6	0	0	.000
1971 MON N	0	0	–	4.76	13	0	0	17	19	7	7	0	0	0	0	0	0	0	–
9 yrs.	39	55	.415	4.08	257	96	13	750	780	260	377	4	10	7	10	206	35	3	.170

Lefty O'Doul

O'DOUL, FRANCIS JOSEPH   BL TL 6' 180 lbs.
B. Mar. 4, 1897, San Francisco, Calif.   D. Dec. 7, 1969, San Francisco, Calif.

	W	L	PCT	ERA	G	GS	CG	IP	H	BB	SO	ShO	W	L	SV	AB	H	HR	BA
1919 NY A	0	0	–	3.60	3	0	0	5	7	4	2	0	0	0	0	16	4	0	.250
1920	0	0	–	4.91	2	0	0	3.2	4	2	2	0	0	0	0	12	2	0	.167
1922	0	0	–	3.38	6	0	0	16	24	12	5	0	0	0	0	9	3	0	.333
1923 BOS A	1	1	.500	5.43	23	0	0	53	69	31	10	0	1	1	0	35	5	0	.143
4 yrs.	1	1	.500	4.87	34	0	0	77.2	104	49	19	0	1	1	0	*			

Bryan Oelkers

OELKERS, BRYAN ALOIS   BL TL 6'2" 190 lbs.
B. Mar. 1, 1961, Zaragoza, Spain

	W	L	PCT	ERA	G	GS	CG	IP	H	BB	SO	ShO	W	L	SV	AB	H	HR	BA
1983 MIN A	0	5	.000	8.65	10	8	0	34.1	56	17	13	0	0	0	0	0	0	0	–

	W	L	PCT	ERA	G	GS	CG	IP	H	BB	SO	ShO	Relief Pitching W	L	SV	BATTING AB	H	HR	BA

Joe Oeschger

OESCHGER, JOSEPH CARL   BR TR 6'   190 lbs.
B. 1892, Chicago, Ill.

	W	L	PCT	ERA	G	GS	CG	IP	H	BB	SO	ShO	W	L	SV	AB	H	HR	BA
1914 PHI N	4	8	.333	3.77	32	10	5	124	129	54	47	0	3	0	1	40	3	0	.075
1915	1	0	1.000	3.42	6	1	1	23.2	21	9	8	0	0	0	0	7	0	0	.000
1916	1	0	1.000	2.37	14	0	0	30.1	18	14	17	0	1	0	0	5	0	0	.000
1917	16	14	.533	2.75	42	30	18	262	241	72	123	5	3	0	0	88	10	0	.114
1918	6	18	.250	3.03	30	23	13	184	159	83	60	2	0	3	3	60	5	0	.083
1919 3 teams			PHI	N	(5G 0–1)		NY	N	(5G 0–1)		BOS	N	(7G 4–2)						
" total	4	4	.500	3.94	17	12	6	102.2	127	39	24	1	0	1	0	38	2	0	.053
1920 BOS N	15	13	.536	3.46	38	30	20	299	294	99	80	5	0	1	0	101	18	0	.178
1921	20	14	.588	3.52	46	36	19	299	303	97	68	3	2	1	0	110	28	0	.255
1922	6	21	.222	5.06	46	23	10	195.2	234	81	51	1	2	3	1	63	12	0	.190
1923	5	15	.250	5.68	44	19	6	166.1	227	54	33	1	2	2	2	52	12	0	.231
1924 2 teams			NY	N	(10G 2–0)		PHI	N	(19G 2–7)										
" total	4	7	.364	4.01	29	10	0	94.1	123	30	18	0	2	2	0	27	8	0	.296
1925 BKN N	1	2	.333	6.08	21	3	1	37	60	19	6	0	0	1	0	8	1	0	.125
12 yrs.	83	116	.417	3.81	365	197	99	1818	1936	651	535	18	15	14	7	599	99	0	.165

Curly Ogden

OGDEN, WARREN HARVEY   BR TR 6'1½" 180 lbs.
Brother of Jack Ogden.
B. Jan. 24, 1901, Ogden, Pa.   D. Aug. 6, 1964, Chester, Pa.

	W	L	PCT	ERA	G	GS	CG	IP	H	BB	SO	ShO	W	L	SV	AB	H	HR	BA
1922 PHI A	1	4	.200	3.11	15	6	4	72.1	59	33	20	0	0	0	0	29	7	0	.241
1923	1	2	.333	5.63	18	2	0	46.1	63	32	14	0	1	0	0	17	5	0	.294
1924 2 teams			PHI	A	(5G 0–3)		WAS	A	(16G 9–5)										
" total	9	8	.529	2.83	21	17	9	120.2	97	58	27	3	0	2	0	50	13	0	.260
1925 WAS A	3	1	.750	4.50	17	4	2	42	45	18	6	1	1	0	0	12	3	0	.250
1926	4	4	.500	4.30	22	9	4	96.1	114	45	21	0	1	1	0	27	5	0	.185
5 yrs.	18	19	.486	3.79	93	38	19	377.2	378	186	88	4	3	3	0	135	33	0	.244

WORLD SERIES

	W	L	PCT	ERA	G	GS	CG	IP	H	BB	SO	ShO	W	L	SV	AB	H	HR	BA
1924 WAS A	0	0	–	0.00	1	1	0	.1	0	1	1	0	0	0	0	0	0	0	–

Jack Ogden

OGDEN, JOHN MAHLON   BR TR 6'   190 lbs.
Brother of Curly Ogden.
B. Nov. 5, 1897, Ogden, Pa.   D. Nov. 9, 1977, Philadelphia, Pa.

	W	L	PCT	ERA	G	GS	CG	IP	H	BB	SO	ShO	W	L	SV	AB	H	HR	BA
1918 NY N	0	0	–	3.12	5	0	0	8.2	8	3	1	0	0	0	0	1	0	0	.000
1928 STL N	15	16	.484	4.15	38	31	18	242.2	257	80	67	1	2	1	2	85	17	0	.200
1929	4	8	.333	4.93	34	14	7	131.1	154	44	32	0	0	2	0	45	11	0	.244
1931 CIN N	4	8	.333	2.93	22	9	3	89	79	32	24	1	1	3	1	27	4	0	.148
1932	2	2	.500	5.21	24	3	1	57	72	22	20	0	1	1	0	12	2	0	.167
5 yrs.	25	34	.424	4.24	123	57	29	528.2	570	181	144	2	4	7	3	170	34	0	.200

Joe Ogrodowski

OGRODOWSKI, JOSEPH ANTHONY   BR TR 5'11" 165 lbs.
B. Nov. 20, 1906, Hoytville, Pa.   D. June 24, 1959, Elmira, N. Y.

	W	L	PCT	ERA	G	GS	CG	IP	H	BB	SO	ShO	W	L	SV	AB	H	HR	BA
1925 BOS N	0	0	–	54.00	1	0	0	1	6	3	0	0	0	0	0	0	0	0	–

Bill O'Hara

O'HARA, WILLIAM ALEXANDER   BL TR
B. Aug. 14, 1883, Toronto, Ont., Canada   D. June 15, 1931, Jersey City, N. J.

	W	L	PCT	ERA	G	GS	CG	IP	H	BB	SO	ShO	W	L	SV	AB	H	HR	BA
1910 STL N	0	0	–	0.00	1	0	0	1	0	0	0	0	0	0	0	*			

Joe Ohl

OHL, JOSEPH EARL   BL TL
B. Jan. 10, 1888, Jobstown N. J.   D. Dec. 18, 1951, Camden, N. J.

	W	L	PCT	ERA	G	GS	CG	IP	H	BB	SO	ShO	W	L	SV	AB	H	HR	BA
1909 WAS A	0	0	–	2.08	4	0	0	8.2	7	1	2	0	0	0	0	2	0	0	.000

Bob Ojeda

OJEDA, ROBERT MICHAEL   BL TL 6'1" 185 lbs.
B. Dec. 17, 1957, Los Angeles, Calif.

	W	L	PCT	ERA	G	GS	CG	IP	H	BB	SO	ShO	W	L	SV	AB	H	HR	BA
1980 BOS A	1	1	.500	6.92	7	7	0	26	39	14	12	0	0	0	0	0	0	0	–
1981	6	2	.750	3.14	10	10	2	66	50	25	28	0	0	0	0	0	0	0	–
1982	4	6	.400	5.63	22	14	0	78.1	95	29	52	0	1	0	0	0	0	0	–
1983	12	7	.632	4.04	29	28	5	173.2	173	73	94	0	0	0	0	0	0	0	–
1984	12	12	.500	3.99	33	32	8	216.2	211	96	137	5	0	0	0	0	0	0	–
5 yrs.	35	28	.556	4.27	101	91	15	560.2	568	237	323	5	1	0	0	0	0	0	–

Frank Okrie

OKRIE, FRANK ANTHONY (Lefty)   BL TL 5'11½" 175 lbs.
Father of Len Okrie.
B. Oct. 28, 1896, Detroit, Mich.   D. Oct. 16, 1959, Detroit, Mich.

	W	L	PCT	ERA	G	GS	CG	IP	H	BB	SO	ShO	W	L	SV	AB	H	HR	BA
1920 DET A	1	2	.333	5.27	21	1	1	41	44	18	9	0	1	1	0	5	1	0	.200

Red Oldham

OLDHAM, JOHN CYRUS   BL TL 6'   176 lbs.
B. July 15, 1893, Zion, Md.   D. Jan. 28, 1961, Costa Mesa, Calif.

	W	L	PCT	ERA	G	GS	CG	IP	H	BB	SO	ShO	W	L	SV	AB	H	HR	BA
1914 DET A	2	4	.333	3.38	9	7	3	45.1	42	8	23	0	0	0	0	15	4	0	.267
1915	3	0	1.000	2.81	17	1	1	57.2	52	17	17	0	2	0	4	14	2	0	.143
1920	8	13	.381	3.85	39	23	11	215.1	248	91	62	1	1	2	1	69	12	0	.174
1921	11	14	.440	4.24	40	28	12	229.1	258	81	67	1	0	5	1	85	19	2	.224
1922	10	13	.435	4.67	43	27	9	212	256	59	72	0	1	2	3	73	19	0	.260
1925 PIT N	3	2	.600	3.91	11	4	3	53	66	18	10	0	1	0	1	18	6	0	.333
1926	2	2	.500	5.62	17	2	0	41.2	56	18	16	0	2	1	2	9	2	0	.222
7 yrs.	39	48	.448	4.15	176	93	39	854.1	978	292	267	2	7	10	12	283	64	2	.226

WORLD SERIES

	W	L	PCT	ERA	G	GS	CG	IP	H	BB	SO	ShO	W	L	SV	AB	H	HR	BA
1925 PIT N	0	0	–	0.00	1	0	0	1	0	0	2	0	0	0	1	0	0	0	–

Chi Chi Olivo

OLIVO, FREDERICO EMILIO   BR TR 6'2" 215 lbs.
Brother of Diomedes Olivo.
B. May 18, 1926, Guayubin, Dominican Republic   D. Feb. 3, 1977, Guayubin, Dominican Republic

	W	L	PCT	ERA	G	GS	CG	IP	H	BB	SO	ShO	W	L	SV	AB	H	HR	BA
1961 MIL N	0	0	–	18.00	3	0	0	2	3	5	1	0	0	0	0	0	0	0	–
1964	2	1	.667	3.75	38	0	0	60	55	21	45	0	2	1	5	4	1	0	.250
1965	0	1	.000	1.38	8	0	0	13	12	5	11	0	0	1	0	0	0	0	–

	W	L	PCT	ERA	G	GS	CG	IP	H	BB	SO	ShO	Relief Pitching W	L	SV	BATTING AB	H	HR	BA

Chi Chi Olivo continued

	W	L	PCT	ERA	G	GS	CG	IP	H	BB	SO	ShO	W	L	SV	AB	H	HR	BA
1966 ATL N	5	4	.556	4.23	47	0	0	66	59	19	41	0	5	4	7	9	1	0	.111
4 yrs.	7	6	.538	3.96	96	0	0	141	129	50	98	0	7	6	12	13	2	0	.154

Diomedes Olivo

OLIVO, DIOMEDES ANTONIO   BL TL 6'1"   195 lbs.
Brother of Chi Chi Olivo.
B. Jan. 22, 1919, Guayubin, Dominican Republic   D. Feb. 15, 1977, Santo Domingo, Dominican Republic

	W	L	PCT	ERA	G	GS	CG	IP	H	BB	SO	ShO	W	L	SV	AB	H	HR	BA
1960 PIT N	0	0	—	2.79	4	0	0	9.2	8	5	10	0	0	0	0	1	0	0	.000
1962	5	1	.833	2.77	62	1	0	84.1	88	25	66	0	5	1	7	16	3	0	.188
1963 STL N	0	5	.000	5.40	19	0	0	13.1	16	9	9	0	0	5	0	0	0	0	—
3 yrs.	5	6	.455	3.10	85	1	0	107.1	112	39	85	0	5	6	7	17	3	0	.176

Jim Ollom

OLLOM, JAMES DONALD   BL TR 6'4"   210 lbs.
B. July 8, 1945, Snohomish, Wash.   BR 1967

	W	L	PCT	ERA	G	GS	CG	IP	H	BB	SO	ShO	W	L	SV	AB	H	HR	BA
1966 MIN A	0	0	—	3.60	3	1	0	10	6	1	11	0	0	0	0	2	0	0	.000
1967	0	1	.000	5.40	21	2	0	35	33	11	17	0	0	0	0	5	1	0	.200
2 yrs.	0	1	.000	5.00	24	3	0	45	39	12	28	0	0	0	0	7	1	0	.143

Fred Olmstead

OLMSTEAD, FREDERICK WILLIAM   BR TR 5'11"   170 lbs.
B. July 3, 1883, Grand Rapids, Mich.   D. Oct. 22, 1936, Muskogee, Okla.

	W	L	PCT	ERA	G	GS	CG	IP	H	BB	SO	ShO	W	L	SV	AB	H	HR	BA
1908 CHI A	0	0	—	13.50	1	0	0	2	6	1	1	0	0	0	0	1	0	0	.000
1909	3	2	.600	1.81	8	6	5	54.2	52	12	21	0	0	0	0	21	2	0	.095
1910	10	12	.455	1.95	32	20	14	184.1	174	50	68	4	2	1	0	65	10	0	.154
1911	6	6	.500	4.21	25	11	7	117.2	146	30	45	1	3	0	2	37	7	0	.189
4 yrs.	19	20	.487	2.74	66	37	26	358.2	378	93	135	5	5	1	2	124	19	0	.153

Alan Olmsted

OLMSTED, ALAN RAY   BR TL 6'2"   195 lbs.
B. Mar. 18, 1957, St. Louis, Mo.

	W	L	PCT	ERA	G	GS	CG	IP	H	BB	SO	ShO	W	L	SV	AB	H	HR	BA
1980 STL N	1	1	.500	2.83	5	5	0	35	32	14	14	0	0	0	0	11	2	0	.182

Hank Olmsted

OLMSTED, HENRY THEODORE   BR TR 5'8½"   147 lbs.
B. Jan. 12, 1879, Bradenton, Fla.   D. Jan. 6, 1969, Brandenton, Fla.

	W	L	PCT	ERA	G	GS	CG	IP	H	BB	SO	ShO	W	L	SV	AB	H	HR	BA
1905 BOS A	1	2	.333	3.24	3	3	3	25	18	12	6	0	0	0	0	8	1	0	.125

Ole Olsen

OLSEN, ARTHUR   BR TR 5'10"   163 lbs.
B. Sept. 12, 1894, South Norwalk, Conn.   D. Sept. 12, 1980, Norwalk, Conn.

	W	L	PCT	ERA	G	GS	CG	IP	H	BB	SO	ShO	W	L	SV	AB	H	HR	BA
1922 DET A	7	6	.538	4.53	37	15	5	137	147	40	52	0	1	3	3	39	7	0	.179
1923	1	1	.500	6.31	17	2	1	41.1	42	17	12	0	0	0	0	8	1	0	.125
2 yrs.	8	7	.533	4.95	54	17	6	178.1	189	57	64	0	1	3	3	47	8	0	.170

Vern Olsen

OLSEN, VERN JARL   BR TL 6'½"   175 lbs.
B. Mar. 16, 1918, Hillsboro, Ore.

	W	L	PCT	ERA	G	GS	CG	IP	H	BB	SO	ShO	W	L	SV	AB	H	HR	BA
1939 CHI N	1	0	1.000	0.00	4	0	0	7.2	2	7	3	0	1	0	0	1	0	0	.000
1940	13	9	.591	2.97	34	20	9	172.2	172	62	71	4	2	1	0	57	15	0	.263
1941	10	8	.556	3.15	37	23	10	185.2	202	59	73	2	0	0	1	63	15	1	.238
1942	6	9	.400	4.49	32	17	4	140.1	161	55	46	1	0	1	1	48	9	0	.188
1946	0	0	—	2.79	5	0	0	9.2	10	9	8	0	0	0	0	0	0	0	—
5 yrs.	30	26	.536	3.40	112	60	23	516	547	192	201	7	3	2	2	169	39	1	.231

Ted Olson

OLSON, THEODORE OTTO   BR TR 6'½"   185 lbs.
B. Aug. 27, 1912, Quincy, Mass.   D. Dec. 9, 1980, Weymouth, Mass.

	W	L	PCT	ERA	G	GS	CG	IP	H	BB	SO	ShO	W	L	SV	AB	H	HR	BA
1936 BOS A	1	1	.500	7.36	5	3	1	18.1	24	8	5	0	0	0	0	7	1	0	.143
1937	0	0	—	7.24	11	0	0	32.1	42	15	11	0	0	0	0	10	3	0	.300
1938	0	0	—	6.43	2	0	0	7	9	2	2	0	0	0	0	1	0	0	.000
3 yrs.	1	1	.500	7.18	18	3	1	57.2	75	25	18	0	0	0	0	18	4	0	.222

Randy O'Neal

O'NEAL, RANDALL JEFFREY   BR TR 6'2"   195 lbs.
B. Aug. 30, 1960, West Palm Beach, Fla.

	W	L	PCT	ERA	G	GS	CG	IP	H	BB	SO	ShO	W	L	SV	AB	H	HR	BA
1984 DET A	2	1	.667	3.38	4	3	0	18.2	16	6	12	0	0	0	0	0	0	0	—

Skinny O'Neal

O'NEAL, ORAN HERBERT   BR TR 5'11"   160 lbs.
B. May 2, 1899, Gatewood, Mo.   D. June 2, 1981, Springfield, Mo.

	W	L	PCT	ERA	G	GS	CG	IP	H	BB	SO	ShO	W	L	SV	AB	H	HR	BA
1925 PHI N	0	0	—	9.30	11	1	0	20.1	35	12	6	0	0	0	0	6	1	0	.167
1927	0	0	—	9.00	2	0	0	5	9	2	2	0	0	0	0	1	0	0	.000
2 yrs.	0	0	—	9.24	13	1	0	25.1	44	14	8	0	0	0	0	7	1	0	.143

Ed O'Neil

O'NEIL, EDWARD J.   TR 5'11"   180 lbs.
B. Mar. 11, 1859, Fall River, Mass.   D. Sept. 30, 1892, Fall River, Mass.

	W	L	PCT	ERA	G	GS	CG	IP	H	BB	SO	ShO	W	L	SV	AB	H	HR	BA
1890 2 teams			TOL	AA (2G 0–1)			PHI	AA (6G 0–6)											
" total	0	7	.000	9.26	8	8	8	68	111	45	19	0	0	0	0	40	5	0	.125

Emmett O'Neill

O'NEILL, ROBERT EMMETT (Pinky)   BR TR 6'3"   185 lbs.
B. Jan. 13, 1918, San Mateo, Calif.

	W	L	PCT	ERA	G	GS	CG	IP	H	BB	SO	ShO	W	L	SV	AB	H	HR	BA
1943 BOS A	1	4	.200	4.53	11	5	1	57.2	56	46	20	0	1	0	0	16	3	0	.188
1944	6	11	.353	4.63	28	22	8	151.2	154	89	68	1	0	0	0	55	10	0	.182
1945	8	11	.421	5.15	24	22	10	141.2	134	117	55	1	0	0	0	50	9	1	.180
1946 2 teams			CHI	N (1G 0–0)			CHI	A (2G 0–0)											
" total	0	0	—	0.00	3	0	0	4.2	4	8	1	0	0	0	0	1	0	0	.000
4 yrs.	15	26	.366	4.76	66	49	19	355.2	348	260	144	2	1	0	0	122	22	1	.180

Harry O'Neill

O'NEILL, JOSEPH HENRY   BR TR 6'   180 lbs.
B. Feb. 19, 1897, Ridgetown, Ont., Canada   D. Sept. 5, 1969, Ridgetown, Ont., Canada

	W	L	PCT	ERA	G	GS	CG	IP	H	BB	SO	ShO	W	L	SV	AB	H	HR	BA
1922 PHI A	0	0	—	3.00	1	0	0	3	2	1	0	0	0	0	0	1	0	0	.000

	W	L	PCT	ERA	G	GS	CG	IP	H	BB	SO	ShO	Relief Pitching W	L	SV	BATTING AB	H	HR	BA

Harry O'Neill continued

	W	L	PCT	ERA	G	GS	CG	IP	H	BB	SO	ShO	W	L	SV	AB	H	HR	BA
1923	0	0	–	0.00	3	0	0	2	1	3	2	0	0	0	0	0	0	0	–
2 yrs.	0	0	–	1.80	4	0	0	5	3	4	2	0	0	0	0	1	0	0	.000

Mike O'Neill

O'NEILL, MICHAEL JOYCE   BL TL 5'11"   185 lbs.
Played as Mike Joyce 1901.   Brother of Jim O'Neill.
Brother of Jack O'Neill.   Brother of Steve O'Neill.
B. Sept. 7, 1877, Galway, Ireland   D. Aug. 12, 1959, Scranton, Pa.

	W	L	PCT	ERA	G	GS	CG	IP	H	BB	SO	ShO	W	L	SV	AB	H	HR	BA
1901 STL N	2	2	.500	1.32	5	4	4	41	29	10	16	1	0	0	0	15	6	0	.400
1902	18	14	.563	2.93	36	32	29	288.1	297	66	105	2	2	0	0	135	43	2	.319
1903	4	13	.235	4.77	19	17	12	115	184	43	39	0	0	0	0	110	25	0	.227
1904	10	14	.417	2.09	25	24	23	220	229	50	68	1	0	0	0	91	21	0	.231
1907 CIN N	0	0	–	0.00	0	0	0	0	0	0	0	0	0	0	0	29	2	0	.069
5 yrs.	34	43	.442	2.87	85	77	68	664.1	739	169	228	4	2	0	0	*			

Tip O'Neill

O'NEILL, JAMES EDWARD   BR TR 6'½"   167 lbs.
B. May 25, 1858, Woodstock, Ont., Canada   D. Dec. 31, 1915, Woodstock, Ont., Canada

	W	L	PCT	ERA	G	GS	CG	IP	H	BB	SO	ShO	W	L	SV	AB	H	HR	BA
1883 NY N	5	12	.294	4.07	19	19	15	148	182	64	55	0	0	0	0	76	15	0	.197
1884 STL AA	11	4	.733	2.68	17	14	14	141	125	51	36	0	1	0	0	297	82	3	.276
2 yrs.	16	16	.500	3.39	36	33	29	289	307	115	91	0	1	0	0	*			

Don O'Riley

O'RILEY, DONALD LEE   BR TR 6'3"   205 lbs.
B. Mar. 12, 1945, Topeka, Kans.

	W	L	PCT	ERA	G	GS	CG	IP	H	BB	SO	ShO	W	L	SV	AB	H	HR	BA
1969 KC A	1	1	.500	6.94	18	0	0	23.1	32	15	10	0	1	1	1	3	0	0	.000
1970	0	0	–	5.48	9	2	0	23	26	9	13	0	0	0	0	3	0	0	.000
2 yrs.	1	1	.500	6.22	27	2	0	46.1	58	24	23	0	1	1	1	6	0	0	.000

Jesse Orosco

OROSCO, JESSE   BR TL 6'2"   174 lbs.
B. Apr. 21, 1957, Santa Barbara, Calif.

	W	L	PCT	ERA	G	GS	CG	IP	H	BB	SO	ShO	W	L	SV	AB	H	HR	BA
1979 NY N	1	2	.333	4.89	18	2	0	35	33	22	22	0	1	2	0	6	0	0	.000
1981	0	1	.000	1.59	8	0	0	17	13	6	18	0	0	1	1	2	0	0	.000
1982	4	10	.286	2.72	54	2	0	109.1	92	40	89	0	4	8	4	14	2	0	.143
1983	13	7	.650	1.47	62	0	0	110	76	38	84	0	13	7	17	12	4	0	.333
1984	10	6	.625	2.59	60	0	0	87	58	34	85	0	10	6	31	4	1	0	.250
5 yrs.	28	26	.519	2.46	202	4	0	358.1	272	140	298	0	28	24	53	38	7	0	.184

Jim O'Rourke

O'ROURKE, JAMES HENRY (Orator Jim)   BR TR 5'8"   185 lbs.
Father of Queenie O'Rourke.
B. Aug. 24, 1852, Bridgeport, Conn.   D. Jan. 8, 1919, Bridgeport, Conn.
Manager 1881-84, 1893.
Hall of Fame 1945.

	W	L	PCT	ERA	G	GS	CG	IP	H	BB	SO	ShO	W	L	SV	AB	H	HR	BA
1883 BUF N	0	0	–	6.43	2	0	0	7	10	1	1	0	0	0	1	436	143	1	.328
1884	0	1	.000	2.84	4	0	0	12.2	7	1	3	0	0	1	1	467	162	5	.347
2 yrs.	0	1	.000	4.12	6	0	0	19.2	17	2	4	0	0	1	2	*			

Mike O'Rourke

O'ROURKE, MICHAEL J.
Deceased.

	W	L	PCT	ERA	G	GS	CG	IP	H	BB	SO	ShO	W	L	SV	AB	H	HR	BA
1890 B-B AA	1	2	.333	3.95	5	5	5	41	45	10	8	0	0	0	0	26	3	0	.115

Dave Orr

ORR, DAVID L.   BR TR
B. Sept. 29, 1859, New York, N.Y.   D. June 3, 1915, Brooklyn, N.Y.
Manager 1887.

	W	L	PCT	ERA	G	GS	CG	IP	H	BB	SO	ShO	W	L	SV	AB	H	HR	BA
1885 NY AA	0	0	–	7.20	3	0	0	10	11	5	1	0	0	0	0	*			

Joe Orrell

ORRELL, FORREST GORDON   BR TR 6'4"   210 lbs.
B. Mar. 6, 1917, National City, Calif.

	W	L	PCT	ERA	G	GS	CG	IP	H	BB	SO	ShO	W	L	SV	AB	H	HR	BA
1943 DET A	0	0	–	3.72	10	0	0	19.1	18	11	2	0	0	0	1	4	1	0	.250
1944	2	1	.667	2.42	10	2	0	22.1	26	11	10	0	1	0	0	4	1	0	.250
1945	2	3	.400	3.00	12	5	1	48	46	24	14	0	0	1	0	15	2	0	.133
3 yrs.	4	4	.500	3.01	32	7	1	89.2	90	46	26	0	1	1	1	23	4	0	.174

Phil Ortega

ORTEGA, FILOMENO CORONADO (Kemo)   BR TR 6'2"   170 lbs.
B. Oct. 7, 1939, Gilbert, Ariz.

	W	L	PCT	ERA	G	GS	CG	IP	H	BB	SO	ShO	W	L	SV	AB	H	HR	BA
1960 LA N	0	0	–	17.05	3	1	0	6.1	12	5	4	0	0	0	0	1	0	0	.000
1961	0	2	.000	5.54	4	2	1	13	10	2	15	0	0	0	0	4	1	0	.250
1962	0	2	.000	6.88	24	3	0	53.2	60	39	30	0	0	0	1	7	0	0	.000
1963	0	0	–	18.00	1	0	0	1	2	0	1	0	0	0	0	0	0	0	–
1964	7	9	.438	4.00	34	25	4	157.1	149	56	107	3	1	0	1	44	6	0	.136
1965 WAS A	12	15	.444	5.11	35	29	4	179.2	176	97	88	2	2	0	0	53	11	0	.208
1966	12	12	.500	3.92	33	31	5	197.1	158	53	121	1	1	0	0	54	3	0	.056
1967	10	10	.500	3.03	34	34	5	219.2	189	57	122	2	0	0	0	66	4	0	.061
1968	5	12	.294	4.98	31	16	1	115.2	115	62	57	1	1	3	0	24	4	0	.167
1969 CAL A	0	0	–	10.13	5	0	0	8	13	7	4	0	0	0	0	0	0	0	–
10 yrs.	46	62	.426	4.43	204	141	20	951.2	884	378	549	9	5	3	2	253	29	0	.115

Al Orth

ORTH, ALBERT LEWIS (The Curveless Wonder)   BL TR 6'   200 lbs.
B. Sept. 5, 1872, Danville, Ind.   D. Oct. 8, 1948, Lynchburg, Va.

	W	L	PCT	ERA	G	GS	CG	IP	H	BB	SO	ShO	W	L	SV	AB	H	HR	BA
1895 PHI N	9	1	.900	3.89	11	10	9	88	103	22	25	0	0	0	1	45	16	1	.356
1896	15	7	.682	4.41	25	23	19	196	244	46	23	0	2	0	0	82	21	1	.256
1897	14	19	.424	4.62	36	34	29	282.1	349	82	64	2	0	1	0	152	50	1	.329
1898	15	12	.556	3.02	32	28	25	250	290	53	52	1	0	1	0	123	36	1	.293
1899	13	3	.813	2.49	21	15	13	144.2	149	19	35	3	3	0	1	62	13	1	.210
1900	12	13	.480	3.78	33	30	24	262	302	60	68	2	1	1	1	129	40	1	.310
1901	20	12	.625	2.27	35	33	30	281.2	250	32	92	6	1	1	0	128	36	1	.281
1902 WAS A	19	18	.514	3.97	38	37	36	324	367	40	76	1	0	1	0	175	38	2	.217
1903	10	22	.313	4.34	36	32	30	279.2	326	62	88	2	0	0	2	162	49	0	.302

	W	L	PCT	ERA	G	GS	CG	IP	H	BB	SO	ShO	Relief Pitching W	L	SV	BATTING AB	H	HR	BA

Al Orth continued

		W	L	PCT	ERA	G	GS	CG	IP	H	BB	SO	ShO	W	L	SV	AB	H	HR	BA
1904	2 teams	WAS	A	(10G 3–4)		NY	A	(20G 11–6)												
"	total	14	10	.583	3.41	30	25	18	211.1	210	34	70	2	0	1	0	166	41	0	.247
1905	NY A	18	16	.529	2.86	40	37	26	305.1	273	61	121	6	1	1	0	131	24	1	.183
1906		27	17	.614	2.34	45	39	36	338.2	317	66	133	3	5	0	0	135	37	1	.274
1907		14	21	.400	2.61	36	33	21	248.2	244	53	78	2	1	2	0	105	34	1	.324
1908		2	13	.133	3.42	21	17	8	139.1	134	30	22	1	0	1	0	69	20	0	.290
1909		0	0	–	12.00	1	1	0	3	6	1	1	0	0	0	0	34	9	0	.265
	15 yrs.	202	184	.523	3.37	440	394	324	3354.2	3564	661	948	31	14	9	5	*			

Baby Ortiz

ORTIZ, OLIVIERO NUNEZ   BR TR 6'   190 lbs.
Brother of Roberto Ortiz.
B. Dec. 5, 1919, Camaguey, Cuba   D. Mar. 27, 1984, Central Senado, Camaguey, Cuba

		W	L	PCT	ERA	G	GS	CG	IP	H	BB	SO	ShO	W	L	SV	AB	H	HR	BA
1944	WAS A	0	2	.000	6.23	2	2	1	13	13	6	4	0	0	0	0	6	1	0	.167

Ossie Orwoll

ORWOLL, OSWALD CHRISTIAN   BL TL 6'   174 lbs.
B. Nov. 17, 1900, Portland, Ore.   D. May 8, 1967, Decorah, Iowa

		W	L	PCT	ERA	G	GS	CG	IP	H	BB	SO	ShO	W	L	SV	AB	H	HR	BA
1928	PHI A	6	5	.545	4.58	27	8	3	106	110	50	53	0	3	0	2	170	52	0	.306
1929		0	2	.000	4.80	12	0	0	30	32	6	12	0	0	2	1	51	13	0	.255
	2 yrs.	6	7	.462	4.63	39	8	3	136	142	56	65	0	3	2	3	*			

Bob Osborn

OSBORN, JOHN BODE   BR TR 6'1"   175 lbs.
B. Apr. 17, 1903, San Diego, Tex.   D. Apr. 19, 1960, Paris, Ark.

		W	L	PCT	ERA	G	GS	CG	IP	H	BB	SO	ShO	W	L	SV	AB	H	HR	BA
1925	CHI N	0	0	–	0.00	1	0	0	2	6	0	0	0	0	0	0	0	0	0	–
1926		6	5	.545	3.63	31	15	6	136.1	157	58	43	0	2	0	1	41	6	0	.146
1927		5	5	.500	4.18	24	12	2	107.2	125	48	45	0	1	1	0	39	8	0	.205
1929		0	0	–	3.00	3	1	0	9	8	2	1	0	0	0	0	4	1	0	.250
1930		10	6	.625	4.97	35	13	3	126.2	147	53	42	0	5	3	1	42	4	0	.095
1931	PIT N	6	1	.857	5.01	27	2	0	64.2	85	20	9	0	6	1	0	18	3	0	.167
	6 yrs.	27	17	.614	4.32	121	43	11	446.1	528	181	140	0	14	5	2	144	22	0	.153

Danny Osborn

OSBORN, DANIEL LEON   BR TR 6'2"   195 lbs.
B. June 19, 1946, Springfield, Ohio

		W	L	PCT	ERA	G	GS	CG	IP	H	BB	SO	ShO	W	L	SV	AB	H	HR	BA
1975	CHI A	3	0	1.000	4.50	24	0	0	58	57	37	38	0	3	0	0	0	0	0	–

Pat Osborn

OSBORN, LARRY PATRICK   BL TL 6'4"   195 lbs.
B. May 4, 1949, Murray, Ky.

		W	L	PCT	ERA	G	GS	CG	IP	H	BB	SO	ShO	W	L	SV	AB	H	HR	BA
1974	CIN N	0	0	–	8.00	6	0	0	9	11	4	4	0	0	0	0	2	0	0	.000
1975	MIL A	0	1	.000	6.17	6	1	0	11.2	19	9	1	0	0	0	0	0	0	0	–
	2 yrs.	0	1	.000	6.97	12	1	0	20.2	30	13	5	0	0	0	0	2	0	0	.000

Fred Osborne

OSBORNE, FREDERICK W.
B. Nevada, Ohio   Deceased.

		W	L	PCT	ERA	G	GS	CG	IP	H	BB	SO	ShO	W	L	SV	AB	H	HR	BA
1890	PIT N	0	5	.000	8.38	8	5	5	58	82	45	14	0	0	0	0	*			

Tiny Osborne

OSBORNE, EARNEST PRESTON   BL TR 6'4½"   215 lbs.
Father of Bobo Osborne.
B. Apr. 9, 1893, Porterdale, Ga.   D. Jan. 5, 1969, Atlanta, Ga.

		W	L	PCT	ERA	G	GS	CG	IP	H	BB	SO	ShO	W	L	SV	AB	H	HR	BA
1922	CHI N	9	5	.643	4.50	41	14	7	184	183	95	81	1	2	1	3	67	9	0	.134
1923		8	15	.348	4.56	37	25	8	179.2	174	89	69	1	1	3	1	60	12	0	.200
1924	2 teams	CHI	N	(2G 0–0)		BKN	N	(21G 6–5)												
"	total	6	5	.545	5.03	23	13	6	107.1	126	56	54	0	1	0	1	36	9	0	.250
1925	BKN N	8	15	.348	4.94	41	22	10	175	210	75	59	0	2	4	1	57	14	0	.246
	4 yrs.	31	40	.437	4.72	142	74	31	646	693	315	263	2	6	8	6	220	44	0	.200

Wayne Osborne

OSBORNE, WAYNE HAROLD (Ossie)   BL TR 6'2½"   172 lbs.
B. Oct. 11, 1912, Watsonville, Calif.

		W	L	PCT	ERA	G	GS	CG	IP	H	BB	SO	ShO	W	L	SV	AB	H	HR	BA
1935	PIT N	0	0	–	6.75	2	0	0	1.1	1	0	1	0	0	0	0	0	0	0	–
1936	BOS N	1	1	.500	5.85	5	3	0	20	31	9	8	0	0	0	0	8	2	0	.250
	2 yrs.	1	1	.500	5.91	7	3	0	21.1	32	9	9	0	0	0	0	8	2	0	.250

Charlie Osgood

OSGOOD, CHARLES BENJAMIN   BR TR 5'10"   180 lbs.
B. Nov. 23, 1926, Somerville, Mass.

		W	L	PCT	ERA	G	GS	CG	IP	H	BB	SO	ShO	W	L	SV	AB	H	HR	BA
1944	BKN N	0	0	–	3.00	1	0	0	3	2	3	0	0	0	0	0	0	0	0	–

Dan Osinski

OSINSKI, DANIEL   BR TR 6'1½"   190 lbs.
B. Nov. 17, 1933, Chicago, Ill.

		W	L	PCT	ERA	G	GS	CG	IP	H	BB	SO	ShO	W	L	SV	AB	H	HR	BA
1962	2 teams	KC	A	(4G 0–0)		LA	A	(33G 6–4)												
"	total	6	4	.600	3.97	37	0	0	59	53	38	48	0	6	4	4	11	0	0	.000
1963	LA A	8	8	.500	3.28	47	16	4	159.1	145	80	100	1	4	2	0	45	5	0	.111
1964		3	3	.500	3.48	47	4	1	93	87	39	88	1	2	2	2	18	1	0	.056
1965	MIL N	0	3	.000	2.82	61	0	0	83	81	40	54	0	0	3	6	6	1	0	.167
1966	BOS A	4	3	.571	3.61	44	1	0	67.1	68	28	44	0	3	3	2	6	2	0	.333
1967		3	1	.750	2.54	34	0	0	63.2	61	14	38	0	3	1	2	9	3	0	.333
1969	CHI A	5	5	.500	3.56	51	0	0	60.2	56	23	27	0	5	5	2	3	0	0	.000
1970	HOU N	0	1	.000	9.00	3	0	0	4	5	2	1	0	0	1	0	0	0	0	–
	8 yrs.	29	28	.509	3.34	324	21	5	590	556	264	400	2	23	21	18	98	12	0	.122

WORLD SERIES

		W	L	PCT	ERA	G	GS	CG	IP	H	BB	SO	ShO	W	L	SV	AB	H	HR	BA
1967	BOS A	0	0	–	6.75	2	0	0	1.1	2	0	0	0	0	0	0	0	0	0	–

Claude Osteen

OSTEEN, CLAUDE WILSON   BL TL 5'11"   160 lbs.
B. Aug. 9, 1939, Caney Springs, Tenn.

		W	L	PCT	ERA	G	GS	CG	IP	H	BB	SO	ShO	W	L	SV	AB	H	HR	BA
1957	CIN N	0	0	–	2.25	3	0	0	4	4	3	3	0	0	0	0	1	0	0	.000
1959		0	0	–	7.04	2	0	0	7.2	11	9	3	0	0	0	0	2	0	0	.000
1960		0	1	.000	5.03	20	3	0	48.1	53	30	15	0	0	0	0	12	1	0	.083

	W	L	PCT	ERA	G	GS	CG	IP	H	BB	SO	ShO	Relief Pitching W	L	SV	BATTING AB	H	HR	BA

Claude Osteen continued

	W	L	PCT	ERA	G	GS	CG	IP	H	BB	SO	ShO	W	L	SV	AB	H	HR	BA
1961 2 teams			CIN	N	(1G 0–0)		WAS	A	(3G 1–1)										
" total	1	1	.500	4.82	4	3	0	18.2	14	9	14	0	0	0	0	7	1	0	.143
1962 WAS A	8	13	.381	3.65	28	22	7	150.1	140	47	59	2	0	0	1	48	10	0	.208
1963	9	14	.391	3.35	40	29	8	212.1	222	60	109	2	1	1	0	70	12	1	.171
1964	15	13	.536	3.33	37	36	13	257	256	64	133	0	0	0	0	90	14	1	.156
1965 LA N	15	15	.500	2.79	40	40	9	287	253	78	162	1	0	0	0	99	12	0	.121
1966	17	14	.548	2.85	39	38	8	240.1	238	65	137	3	0	0	0	76	16	1	.211
1967	17	17	.500	3.22	39	39	14	288.1	298	52	152	5	0	0	0	101	18	2	.178
1968	12	18	.400	3.08	39	36	5	254	267	54	119	3	0	0	0	84	15	0	.179
1969	20	15	.571	2.66	41	41	16	321	293	74	183	7	0	0	0	111	24	1	.216
1970	16	14	.533	3.82	37	37	11	259	280	52	114	4	0	0	0	93	19	1	.204
1971	14	11	.560	3.51	38	38	11	259	262	63	109	4	0	0	0	86	16	0	.186
1972	20	11	.645	2.64	33	33	14	252	232	69	100	4	0	0	0	88	24	1	.273
1973	16	11	.593	3.31	33	33	12	236.2	227	61	86	3	0	0	0	78	12	0	.154
1974 2 teams			HOU	N	(23G 9–9)		STL	N	(8G 0–2)										
" total	9	11	.450	3.80	31	23	7	161	184	58	51	2	0	1	0	53	13	0	.245
1975 CHI A	7	16	.304	4.36	37	37	5	204.1	237	92	63	0	0	0	0	0	0	0	–
18 yrs.	196	195	.501	3.30	541	488	140	3461	3471	940	1612	40	1	2	1	1099	207	8	.188

WORLD SERIES

	W	L	PCT	ERA	G	GS	CG	IP	H	BB	SO	ShO	W	L	SV	AB	H	HR	BA
1965 LA N	1	1	.500	0.64	2	2	1	14	9	5	4	1	0	0	0	3	1	0	.333
1966	0	1	.000	1.29	1	1	0	7	3	1	3	0	0	0	0	2	0	0	.000
2 yrs.	1	2	.333	0.86	3	3	1	21	12	6	7	1	0	0	0	5	1	0	.200

Darrell Osteen

OSTEEN, MILTON DARRELL   BR TR 6'1"   170 lbs.
B. Feb. 14, 1943, Oklahoma City, Okla.

	W	L	PCT	ERA	G	GS	CG	IP	H	BB	SO	ShO	W	L	SV	AB	H	HR	BA
1965 CIN N	0	0	–	0.00	3	0	0	3	2	4	1	0	0	0	0	0	0	0	–
1966	0	2	.000	12.00	13	0	0	15	26	9	17	0	0	2	1	2	1	0	.500
1967	0	2	.000	6.28	10	0	0	14.1	10	13	13	0	0	2	2	1	0	0	.000
1970 OAK A	1	0	1.000	6.00	3	1	0	6	9	3	3	0	0	0	0	2	0	0	.000
4 yrs.	1	4	.200	7.98	29	1	0	38.1	47	29	34	0	0	4	3	5	1	0	.200

Fred Ostendorf

OSTENDORF, FREDERICK   BL TL 6'½"   169 lbs.
B. Aug. 5, 1890, Baltimore, Md.   D. Mar. 2, 1965, Kecoughtan, Va.

	W	L	PCT	ERA	G	GS	CG	IP	H	BB	SO	ShO	W	L	SV	AB	H	HR	BA
1914 IND F	0	0	–	22.50	1	0	0	2	5	2	0	0	0	0	0	1	0	0	.000

Bill Oster

OSTER, WILLIAM PETER   BL TL 6'3"   198 lbs.
B. Jan. 2, 1933, New York, N. Y.

	W	L	PCT	ERA	G	GS	CG	IP	H	BB	SO	ShO	W	L	SV	AB	H	HR	BA
1954 PHI A	0	1	.000	6.32	8	1	0	15.2	19	12	5	0	0	0	0	3	1	0	.333

Fritz Ostermueller

OSTERMUELLER, FREDERICK RAYMOND   BL TL 5'11"   175 lbs.
B. Sept. 15, 1907, Quincy, Ill.   D. Dec. 17, 1957, Quincy, Ill.

	W	L	PCT	ERA	G	GS	CG	IP	H	BB	SO	ShO	W	L	SV	AB	H	HR	BA
1934 BOS A	10	13	.435	3.49	33	24	10	198.2	200	99	75	0	4	0	3	78	13	0	.167
1935	7	8	.467	3.92	22	19	10	137.2	135	78	41	0	0	0	1	49	14	0	.286
1936	10	16	.385	4.87	43	23	7	181	210	84	90	1	2	4	2	64	15	0	.234
1937	3	7	.300	4.98	25	7	2	86.2	101	44	29	0	1	4	1	33	11	0	.333
1938	13	5	.722	4.58	31	18	10	176.2	199	58	46	1	3	1	2	74	16	0	.216
1939	11	7	.611	4.24	34	20	8	159.1	173	58	61	0	3	1	4	56	9	0	.161
1940	9	5	.357	4.95	31	16	5	143.2	166	70	80	0	1	2	0	54	17	0	.315
1941 STL A	0	3	.000	4.50	15	2	0	46	45	23	20	0	0	3	0	14	3	0	.214
1942	3	1	.750	3.71	10	4	2	43.2	46	17	21	0	0	0	0	16	3	0	.188
1943 2 teams			STL	A	(11G 0–2)		BKN	N	(7G 1–1)										
" total	1	3	.250	4.18	18	4	0	56	57	25	19	0	1	2	0	18	2	0	.111
1944 2 teams			BKN	N	(10G 1–1)		PIT	N	(28G 11–7)										
" total	13	8	.619	2.81	38	28	17	246.1	247	77	97	1	0	0	2	93	22	0	.237
1945 PIT N	5	4	.556	4.57	14	11	4	80.2	74	37	29	1	0	0	0	28	9	0	.321
1946	13	10	.565	2.84	27	25	16	193.1	193	56	57	2	0	0	0	64	21	0	.328
1947	12	10	.545	3.84	26	24	10	183	181	68	66	3	0	0	0	64	12	0	.188
1948	8	11	.421	4.42	23	22	10	134.1	143	41	43	2	0	0	0	44	8	0	.182
15 yrs.	114	115	.498	3.99	390	247	113	2067	2170	835	774	11	15	17	15	749	175	0	.234

Joe Ostrowski

OSTROWSKI, JOSEPH PAUL (Professor)   BL TL 6'   180 lbs.
B. Nov. 15, 1916, West Wyoming, Pa.

	W	L	PCT	ERA	G	GS	CG	IP	H	BB	SO	ShO	W	L	SV	AB	H	HR	BA
1948 STL A	4	6	.400	5.97	26	9	3	78.1	108	17	20	0	1	0	3	18	4	0	.222
1949	8	8	.500	4.79	40	13	4	141	185	27	34	0	2	2	2	37	7	0	.189
1950 2 teams			STL	A	(9G 2–4)		NY	A	(21G 1–1)										
" total	3	5	.375	3.65	30	11	3	101	107	22	30	0	1	0	3	27	5	0	.185
1951 NY A	6	4	.600	3.49	34	3	2	95.1	103	18	30	0	4	4	5	28	3	0	.107
1952	2	2	.500	5.63	20	1	0	40	56	14	17	0	2	2	2	8	0	0	.000
5 yrs.	23	25	.479	4.54	150	37	12	455.2	559	98	131	0	10	8	15	118	19	0	.161

WORLD SERIES

	W	L	PCT	ERA	G	GS	CG	IP	H	BB	SO	ShO	W	L	SV	AB	H	HR	BA
1951 NY A	0	0	–	0.00	1	0	0	2	1	0	1	0	0	0	0	0	0	0	–

Bill Otey

OTEY, WILLIAM TILFORD (Steamboat Bill)   BL TL 6'2½"   181 lbs.
B. Dec. 16, 1886, Dayton, Ohio   D. Apr. 23, 1931, Dayton, Ohio

	W	L	PCT	ERA	G	GS	CG	IP	H	BB	SO	ShO	W	L	SV	AB	H	HR	BA
1907 PIT N	0	1	.000	4.41	3	2	1	16.1	23	4	5	0	0	0	0	4	1	0	.250
1910 WAS A	0	1	.000	3.38	9	1	1	34.2	40	6	12	0	0	0	0	13	5	0	.385
1911	1	3	.250	6.34	12	2	0	49.2	68	15	16	0	1	2	0	17	1	0	.059
3 yrs.	1	5	.167	5.01	24	5	2	100.2	131	25	33	0	1	2	0	34	7	0	.206

Harry Otis

OTIS, HARRY GEORGE (Cannonball)   BR TL 6'   180 lbs.
B. Oct. 5, 1886, W. New York, N. J.   D. Jan. 29, 1976, Trenton, N. J.

	W	L	PCT	ERA	G	GS	CG	IP	H	BB	SO	ShO	W	L	SV	AB	H	HR	BA
1909 CLE A	2	2	.500	1.37	5	3	0	26.1	26	18	6	0	1	0	0	9	1	0	.111

	W	L	PCT	ERA	G	GS	CG	IP	H	BB	SO	ShO	Relief Pitching W	L	SV	BATTING AB	H	HR	BA

Denny O'Toole

O'TOOLE, DENNIS JOSEPH   BR TR 6'3"   195 lbs.
Brother of Jim O'Toole.
B. Mar. 13, 1949, Chicago, Ill.

	W	L	PCT	ERA	G	GS	CG	IP	H	BB	SO	ShO	W	L	SV	AB	H	HR	BA
1969 CHI A	0	0	—	6.75	2	0	0	4	5	2	4	0	0	0	0	0	0	0	—
1970	0	0	—	3.00	3	0	0	3	5	3	3	0	0	0	0	0	0	0	—
1971	0	0	—	0.00	1	0	0	2	0	1	2	0	0	0	0	0	0	0	—
1972	0	0	—	5.40	3	0	0	5	10	2	5	0	0	0	0	0	0	0	—
1973	0	0	—	5.63	6	0	0	16	23	3	8	0	0	0	0	0	0	0	—
5 yrs.	0	0	—	5.10	15	0	0	30	43	10	22	0	0	0	0	0	0	0	—

Jim O'Toole

O'TOOLE, JAMES JEROME   BB TL 6'   190 lbs.
Brother of Denny O'Toole.
B. Jan. 10, 1937, Chicago, Ill.

	W	L	PCT	ERA	G	GS	CG	IP	H	BB	SO	ShO	W	L	SV	AB	H	HR	BA
1958 CIN N	0	1	.000	1.29	1	1	0	7	4	5	4	0	0	0	0	2	0	0	.000
1959	5	8	.385	5.15	28	19	3	129.1	144	73	68	1	0	0	0	37	5	0	.135
1960	12	12	.500	3.80	34	31	7	196.1	198	66	124	2	0	0	1	66	7	0	.106
1961	19	9	.679	3.10	39	35	11	252.2	229	93	178	3	1	0	2	93	16	0	.172
1962	16	13	.552	3.50	36	34	11	251.2	222	87	170	3	2	0	0	91	10	0	.110
1963	17	14	.548	2.88	33	32	12	234.1	208	57	146	5	0	0	0	74	11	0	.149
1964	17	7	.708	2.66	30	30	9	220	194	51	145	3	0	0	0	70	7	0	.100
1965	3	10	.231	5.92	29	22	2	127.2	154	47	71	0	0	0	1	45	4	0	.089
1966	5	7	.417	3.55	25	24	2	142	139	49	96	0	0	0	0	47	6	0	.128
1967 CHI A	4	3	.571	2.82	15	10	1	54.1	53	18	37	1	0	0	0	13	1	0	.077
10 yrs.	98	84	.538	3.57	270	238	58	1615.1	1545	546	1039	18	3	0	4	538	67	0	.125

WORLD SERIES
	W	L	PCT	ERA	G	GS	CG	IP	H	BB	SO	ShO	W	L	SV	AB	H	HR	BA
1961 CIN N	0	2	.000	3.00	2	2	0	12	11	7	4	0	0	0	0	3	0	0	.000

Marty O'Toole

O'TOOLE, MARTIN JAMES   BR TR 5'11"   175 lbs.
B. Nov. 27, 1888, William Penn, Pa.   D. Feb. 18, 1949, Aberdeen, Wash.

	W	L	PCT	ERA	G	GS	CG	IP	H	BB	SO	ShO	W	L	SV	AB	H	HR	BA
1908 CIN N	1	0	1.000	2.40	3	2	1	15	15	7	5	0	0	0	0	5	1	0	.200
1911 PIT N	3	2	.600	2.37	5	5	3	38	28	20	34	0	0	0	0	14	5	0	.357
1912	15	17	.469	2.71	37	36	17	275.1	237	159	150	6	0	1	0	99	22	0	.222
1913	6	8	.429	3.30	26	15	7	144.2	148	55	58	0	0	2	1	53	7	0	.132
1914 2 teams		PIT	N	(19G 1–8)		NY	N	(10G 1–1)											
" total	2	9	.182	4.56	29	14	3	126.1	126	59	49	0	0	2	0	40	8	0	.200
5 yrs.	27	36	.429	3.21	100	72	31	599.1	554	300	296	6	0	5	1	211	43	0	.204

Jim Otten

OTTEN, JAMES EDWARD   BR TR 6'2"   195 lbs.
B. July 1, 1951, Lewiston, Mont.

	W	L	PCT	ERA	G	GS	CG	IP	H	BB	SO	ShO	W	L	SV	AB	H	HR	BA
1974 CHI A	0	1	.000	5.63	5	1	0	16	22	12	11	0	0	0	0	0	0	0	—
1975	0	0	—	6.75	2	0	0	5.1	4	7	3	0	0	0	0	0	0	0	—
1976	0	0	—	4.50	2	0	0	6	9	2	3	0	0	0	0	0	0	0	—
1980 STL N	0	5	.000	5.56	31	4	0	55	71	26	38	0	0	1	0	5	1	0	.200
1981	1	0	1.000	5.25	24	0	0	36	44	20	20	0	1	0	0	2	0	0	.000
5 yrs.	1	6	.143	5.48	64	5	0	118.1	150	67	75	0	1	1	0	7	1	0	.143

Orval Overall

OVERALL, ORVAL   BB TR 6'2"   214 lbs.
B. Feb. 2, 1881, Visalia, Calif.   D. July 14, 1947, Fresno, Calif.

	W	L	PCT	ERA	G	GS	CG	IP	H	BB	SO	ShO	W	L	SV	AB	H	HR	BA
1905 CIN N	17	22	.436	2.86	42	39	32	318	290	147	173	2	1	1	0	117	17	0	.145
1906 2 teams		CIN	N	(13G 3–5)		CHI	N	(18G 12–3)											
" total	15	8	.652	2.74	31	24	19	226.1	193	97	127	2	2	0	1	84	15	0	.179
1907 CHI N	23	8	.742	1.70	35	29	26	265.1	199	69	139	8	1	2	3	94	20	0	.213
1908	15	11	.577	1.92	37	27	16	225	165	78	167	4	3	0	2	70	9	0	.129
1909	20	11	.645	1.42	38	32	23	285	204	80	205	9	1	0	1	96	22	2	.229
1910	12	6	.667	2.68	23	21	11	144.2	106	54	92	4	0	1	1	41	5	0	.122
1913	4	5	.444	3.31	11	9	6	68	73	26	30	1	0	0	0	24	6	0	.250
7 yrs.	106	71	.599	2.24 8th	217	181	133	1532.1	1230	551	933	30	8	4	9	526	94	2	.179

WORLD SERIES
	W	L	PCT	ERA	G	GS	CG	IP	H	BB	SO	ShO	W	L	SV	AB	H	HR	BA
1906 CHI N	0	0	—	1.50	2	0	0	12	10	3	8	0	0	0	0	4	1	0	.250
1907	1	0	1.000	1.00	2	2	1	18	14	4	11	0	0	0	0	5	1	0	.200
1908	2	0	1.000	0.98	3	2	2	18.1	7	7	15	1	0	0	0	6	2	0	.333
1910	0	1	.000	9.00	1	1	0	3	6	1	1	0	0	0	0	1	0	0	.000
4 yrs.	3	1	.750	1.58	8	5	3	51.1	37	15	35	1	0	0	0	16	4	0	.250

Stubby Overmire

OVERMIRE, FRANK   BR TL 5'7"   170 lbs.
B. May 16, 1919, Moline, Mich.   D. Mar. 3, 1977, Lakeland, Fla.

	W	L	PCT	ERA	G	GS	CG	IP	H	BB	SO	ShO	W	L	SV	AB	H	HR	BA
1943 DET A	7	6	.538	3.18	29	18	8	147	135	38	48	3	0	0	1	42	7	0	.167
1944	11	11	.500	3.07	32	28	11	199.2	214	41	57	3	0	0	1	63	11	0	.175
1945	9	9	.500	3.88	31	22	9	162.1	189	42	36	0	0	0	4	53	10	0	.189
1946	5	7	.417	4.62	24	13	3	97.1	106	29	34	0	1	3	1	33	5	0	.152
1947	11	5	.688	3.77	28	17	7	140.2	142	44	33	3	0	0	0	47	7	0	.149
1948	3	4	.429	5.97	37	4	0	66.1	89	31	14	0	3	3	3	14	1	0	.071
1949	1	3	.250	9.87	14	1	0	17.1	29	9	3	0	1	2	0	3	1	0	.333
1950 STL A	9	12	.429	4.19	31	19	8	161	200	45	39	2	1	2	0	48	8	0	.167
1951 2 teams		STL	A	(8G 1–6)		NY	A	(15G 1–1)											
" total	2	7	.222	4.04	23	11	4	98	111	39	27	0	0	2	0	21	2	0	.095
1952 STL A	0	3	.000	3.73	17	4	0	41	44	7	10	0	0	0	0	11	2	0	.182
10 yrs.	58	67	.464	3.96	266	137	50	1130.2	1259	325	301	11	9	12	10	335	54	0	.161

WORLD SERIES
	W	L	PCT	ERA	G	GS	CG	IP	H	BB	SO	ShO	W	L	SV	AB	H	HR	BA
1945 DET A	0	1	.000	3.00	1	1	0	6	4	2	2	0	0	0	0	1	0	0	.000

Mike Overy

OVERY, HAROLD MICHAEL   BR TR 6'2"   190 lbs.
B. Jan. 27, 1951, Clinton, Ill.

	W	L	PCT	ERA	G	GS	CG	IP	H	BB	SO	ShO	W	L	SV	AB	H	HR	BA
1976 CAL A	0	2	.000	6.43	5	0	0	7	6	3	8	0	0	2	0	0	0	0	—

	W	L	PCT	ERA	G	GS	CG	IP	H	BB	SO	ShO	Relief Pitching W	L	SV	BATTING AB	H	HR	BA

Ernie Ovitz

OVITZ, ERNEST GAYHART   BR TR 5'8½" 156 lbs.
B. Oct. 7, 1885, Mineral Point, Wis.   D. Sept. 11, 1980, Green Bay, Wis.

	W	L	PCT	ERA	G	GS	CG	IP	H	BB	SO	ShO	W	L	SV	AB	H	HR	BA
1911 CHI N	0	0	—	4.50	1	0	0	2	3	3	0	0	0	0	0	0	0	0	—

Bob Owchinko

OWCHINKO, ROBERT DENNIS   BL TL 6'2" 190 lbs.
B. Jan. 1, 1955, Detroit, Mich.

	W	L	PCT	ERA	G	GS	CG	IP	H	BB	SO	ShO	W	L	SV	AB	H	HR	BA
1976 SD N	0	2	.000	16.62	2	2	0	4.1	11	3	4	0	0	0	0	1	0	0	.000
1977	9	12	.429	4.45	30	28	3	170	191	67	101	2	1	0	0	49	4	0	.082
1978	10	13	.435	3.56	36	33	4	202	198	78	94	1	0	0	0	63	11	0	.175
1979	6	12	.333	3.74	42	20	2	149	144	55	66	0	2	5	0	33	4	0	.121
1980 CLE A	2	9	.182	5.29	29	14	1	114	138	47	66	1	1	0	0	0	0	0	—
1981 OAK A	4	3	.571	3.23	29	0	0	39	34	19	26	0	4	3	2	0	0	0	—
1982	2	4	.333	5.21	54	0	0	102	111	52	67	0	2	4	3	0	0	0	—
1983 PIT N	0	0	—	∞	1	0	0		2	0	0	0	0	0	0	0	0	0	—
1984 CIN N	3	5	.375	4.12	49	4	0	94	91	39	60	0	2	3	2	12	2	0	.167
9 yrs.	36	60	.375	4.30	272	101	10	874.1	920	360	484	4	12	15	7	158	21	0	.133
LEAGUE CHAMPIONSHIP SERIES																			
1981 OAK A	0	0	—	5.40	1	0	0	1.2	3	0	0	0	0	0	0	0	0	0	—

Frank Owen

OWEN, FRANK MALCOLM (Yip)   TR
B. Dec. 23, 1879, Ypsilanti, Mich.   D. Nov. 24, 1942, Dearborn, Mich.

	W	L	PCT	ERA	G	GS	CG	IP	H	BB	SO	ShO	W	L	SV	AB	H	HR	BA
1901 DET A	1	3	.250	4.34	8	5	3	56	70	30	17	0	0	0	0	20	1	0	.050
1903 CHI A	8	12	.400	3.50	26	20	15	167.1	167	44	66	1	1	2	1	57	7	0	.123
1904	21	15	.583	1.94	37	36	34	315	243	61	103	4	0	0	1	107	23	2	.215
1905	21	13	.618	2.10	42	38	32	334	276	56	125	3	0	1	0	124	18	0	.145
1906	22	13	.629	2.33	42	36	27	293	289	54	66	7	3	1	2	103	14	0	.136
1907	2	3	.400	2.49	11	4	2	47	43	13	15	0	0	1	0	16	4	0	.250
1908	6	7	.462	3.41	25	14	5	140	142	37	48	1	2	0	0	50	9	0	.180
1909	1	1	.500	4.50	3	2	1	16	19	3	3	0	0	0	0	6	1	0	.167
8 yrs.	82	67	.550	2.55	194	155	119	1368.1	1249	298	443	16	6	5	4	483	77	2	.159
WORLD SERIES																			
1906 CHI A	0	0	—	3.00	1	0	0	6	6	3	2	0	0	0	0	2	0	0	.000

Jim Owens

OWENS, JAMES PHILIP (Bear)   BR TR 5'11" 180 lbs.
B. Jan. 16, 1934, Gifford, Pa.

	W	L	PCT	ERA	G	GS	CG	IP	H	BB	SO	ShO	W	L	SV	AB	H	HR	BA
1955 PHI N	0	2	.000	8.31	3	2	0	8.2	13	7	6	0	0	0	0	1	0	0	.000
1956	0	4	.000	7.28	10	5	0	29.2	35	22	22	0	0	1	0	6	1	0	.167
1958	1	0	1.000	2.57	1	1	0	7	4	5	3	0	0	0	0	2	0	0	.000
1959	12	12	.500	3.21	31	30	11	221.1	203	73	135	1	0	0	1	75	9	0	.120
1960	4	14	.222	5.04	31	22	6	150	182	64	83	0	0	1	0	44	3	0	.068
1961	5	10	.333	4.47	20	17	3	106.2	119	32	38	0	0	1	0	27	2	0	.074
1962	2	4	.333	6.33	23	12	1	69.2	90	33	21	0	0	0	0	14	2	0	.143
1963 CIN N	0	2	.000	5.31	19	3	0	42.1	42	24	29	0	0	1	4	8	1	0	.125
1964 HOU N	8	7	.533	3.28	48	11	0	118	115	32	88	0	6	2	6	29	3	0	.103
1965	6	5	.545	3.28	50	0	0	71.1	64	29	53	0	6	5	8	8	1	0	.125
1966	4	7	.364	4.68	40	0	0	50	53	17	32	0	4	7	2	4	0	0	.000
1967	0	1	.000	4.22	10	0	0	10.2	12	2	6	0	0	1	0	0	0	0	—
12 yrs.	42	68	.382	4.31	286	103	21	885.1	932	340	516	1	16	19	21	218	22	0	.101

Rick Ownbey

OWNBEY, RICHARD WAYNE   BR TR 6'3" 185 lbs.
B. Oct. 20, 1957, Corona, Calif.

	W	L	PCT	ERA	G	GS	CG	IP	H	BB	SO	ShO	W	L	SV	AB	H	HR	BA
1982 NY N	1	2	.333	3.75	8	8	2	50.1	44	43	28	0	0	0	0	15	3	0	.200
1983	1	3	.250	4.67	10	4	0	34.2	31	21	19	0	1	0	0	9	1	0	.111
1984 STL N	0	3	.000	4.74	4	4	0	19	23	8	11	0	0	0	0	4	0	0	.000
3 yrs.	2	8	.200	4.24	22	16	2	104	98	72	58	0	1	0	0	28	4	0	.143

Doc Ozmer

OZMER, HORACE ROBERT   BR TR 5'10½" 185 lbs.
B. May 25, 1901, Atlanta, Ga.   D. Dec. 28, 1970, Atlanta, Ga.

	W	L	PCT	ERA	G	GS	CG	IP	H	BB	SO	ShO	W	L	SV	AB	H	HR	BA
1923 PHI A	0	0	—	4.50	1	0	0	2	1	1	0	0	0	0	0	0	0	0	—

John Pacella

PACELLA, JOHN LEWIS   BR TR 6'3" 195 lbs.
B. Sept. 15, 1956, Brooklyn, N. Y.

	W	L	PCT	ERA	G	GS	CG	IP	H	BB	SO	ShO	W	L	SV	AB	H	HR	BA
1977 NY N	0	0	—	0.00	3	0	0	4	2	2	1	0	0	0	0	0	0	0	—
1979	0	2	.000	4.50	4	3	0	16	16	4	12	0	0	0	0	4	0	0	.000
1980	3	4	.429	5.14	32	15	0	84	89	59	68	0	0	0	0	20	2	0	.100
1982 2 teams				NY A (3G 0−1)				MIN A (21G 1−2)											
" total	1	3	.250	7.30	24	2	0	61.2	74	46	22	0	1	1	2	0	0	0	—
1984 BAL A	0	1	.000	6.75	6	1	0	14.2	15	9	8	0	0	1	0	0	0	0	—
5 yrs.	4	10	.286	5.84	69	21	0	180.1	196	120	111	0	1	2	2	24	2	0	.083

Gene Packard

PACKARD, EUGENE MILO   BL TL 5'10" 155 lbs.
B. July 13, 1887, Colorado Springs, Colo.   D. May 19, 1959, Riverside, Calif.

	W	L	PCT	ERA	G	GS	CG	IP	H	BB	SO	ShO	W	L	SV	AB	H	HR	BA
1912 CIN N	1	0	1.000	3.00	1	1	1	9	7	4	2	0	0	0	0	4	1	0	.250
1913	7	11	.389	2.97	39	21	9	190.2	208	64	73	2	1	2	0	61	11	0	.180
1914 KC F	21	13	.618	2.89	42	34	24	302	282	88	154	4	3	0	4	116	28	1	.241
1915	20	11	.645	2.68	42	31	21	281.2	250	74	108	5	2	2	2	95	22	1	.232
1916 CHI N	10	6	.625	2.78	37	15	5	155.1	154	38	36	2	4	1	5	54	7	0	.130
1917 2 teams				CHI N (2G 0−0)				STL N (34G 9−6)											
" total	9	6	.600	2.55	36	11	6	155	141	25	45	0	6	0	2	52	15	0	.288
1918 STL N	12	12	.500	3.50	30	23	10	182.1	184	33	46	1	3	1	2	69	12	0	.174
1919 PHI N	6	8	.429	4.15	21	16	10	134.1	167	30	24	1	0	1	1	51	7	0	.137
8 yrs.	86	67	.562	3.01	248	152	86	1410.1	1393	356	488	15	19	7	16	502	103	2	.205

	W	L	PCT	ERA	G	GS	CG	IP	H	BB	SO	ShO	Relief Pitching W	L	SV	AB	BATTING H	HR	BA

Joe Pactwa

PACTWA, JOSEPH MARTIN   BL TL 5'11"   185 lbs.
B. June 2, 1948, Hammond, Ind.

	W	L	PCT	ERA	G	GS	CG	IP	H	BB	SO	ShO	W	L	SV	AB	H	HR	BA
1975 CAL A	1	0	1.000	3.86	4	3	0	16.1	23	10	3	0	1	0	0	0	0	0	–

Dave Pagan

PAGAN, DAVID PERCY   BR TR 6'2"   175 lbs.
B. Sept. 15, 1950, Nipawin, Sask., Canada

	W	L	PCT	ERA	G	GS	CG	IP	H	BB	SO	ShO	W	L	SV	AB	H	HR	BA
1973 NY A	0	0	–	2.84	4	1	0	12.2	16	1	9	0	0	0	0	0	0	0	–
1974	1	3	.250	5.14	16	6	1	49	49	28	39	0	0	1	0	0	0	0	–
1975	0	0	–	4.06	13	0	0	31	30	13	18	0	0	0	1	0	0	0	–
1976 2 teams			NY A (7G 1–1)			BAL A (20G 1–4)													
" total	2	5	.286	4.73	27	7	1	70.1	72	27	47	0	0	3	1	0	0	0	–
1977 2 teams			SEA A (24G 1–1)			PIT N (1G 0–0)													
" total	1	1	.500	5.87	25	4	1	69	87	26	34	1	0	1	2	0	0	0	–
5 yrs.	4	9	.308	4.97	85	18	3	232	254	95	147	1	0	5	4	0	0	0	–

Joe Page

PAGE, JOSEPH FRANCIS (Fireman, The Gay Reliever)   BL TL 6'3"   200 lbs.
B. Oct. 28, 1917, Cherry Valley, Pa.   D. Apr. 21, 1980, Latrobe, Pa.

	W	L	PCT	ERA	G	GS	CG	IP	H	BB	SO	ShO	W	L	SV	AB	H	HR	BA
1944 NY A	5	7	.417	4.56	19	16	4	102.2	100	52	63	0	0	0	0	32	5	0	.156
1945	6	3	.667	2.82	20	9	4	102	95	46	50	0	2	0	0	36	9	0	.250
1946	9	8	.529	3.57	31	17	6	136	126	72	77	1	2	4	3	43	7	1	.163
1947	14	8	.636	2.48	56	2	0	141.1	105	72	116	0	14	7	17	46	10	1	.217
1948	7	8	.467	4.26	55	1	0	107.2	116	66	77	0	7	8	16	24	7	0	.292
1949	13	8	.619	2.59	60	0	0	135.1	103	75	99	0	13	8	27	40	7	0	.175
1950	3	7	.300	5.04	37	0	0	55.1	66	31	33	0	3	7	13	8	2	0	.250
1954 PIT N	0	0	–	11.17	7	0	0	9.2	16	7	4	0	0	0	0	0	0	0	–
8 yrs.	57	49	.538	3.53	285	45	14	790	727	421	519	1	41	34	76	229	47	2	.205
WORLD SERIES																			
1947 NY A	1	1	.500	4.15	4	0	0	13	12	2	7	0	1	1	1	4	0	0	.000
1949	1	0	1.000	2.00	3	0	0	9	6	3	8	0	1	0	1	4	0	0	.000
2 yrs.	2	1	.667	3.27	7	0	0	22	18	5	15	0	2	1	2	8	0	0	.000

                   2nd

Phil Page

PAGE, PHILIP RAUSAC   BR TL 6'2"   175 lbs.
B. Aug. 23, 1905, Springfield, Mass.   D. June 26, 1958, Springfield, Mass.

	W	L	PCT	ERA	G	GS	CG	IP	H	BB	SO	ShO	W	L	SV	AB	H	HR	BA
1928 DET A	2	0	1.000	2.45	3	2	2	22	21	10	3	0	0	0	0	9	2	0	.222
1929	0	2	.000	8.17	10	4	1	25.1	29	19	6	0	0	1	0	8	1	0	.125
1930	0	1	.000	9.75	12	0	0	12	23	9	2	0	0	1	0	0	0	0	–
1934 BKN N	1	0	1.000	5.40	6	0	0	10	13	6	4	0	1	0	0	1	0	0	.000
4 yrs.	3	3	.500	6.23	31	6	3	69.1	86	44	15	0	1	2	0	18	3	0	.167

Sam Page

PAGE, SAMUEL WALTER   BL TR 6'   172 lbs.
B. Feb. 11, 1916, Woodruff, S. C.

	W	L	PCT	ERA	G	GS	CG	IP	H	BB	SO	ShO	W	L	SV	AB	H	HR	BA
1939 PHI A	0	3	.000	6.95	4	3	1	22	34	15	11	0	0	1	0	7	3	0	.429

Vance Page

PAGE, VANCE LINWOOD   BR TR 6'   180 lbs.
B. Sept. 15, 1905, Elm City, N. C.   D. July 14, 1951, Wilson, N. C.

	W	L	PCT	ERA	G	GS	CG	IP	H	BB	SO	ShO	W	L	SV	AB	H	HR	BA
1938 CHI N	5	4	.556	3.84	13	9	3	68	90	13	18	0	0	0	1	26	4	0	.154
1939	7	7	.500	3.88	27	17	8	139.1	169	37	43	1	1	0	1	47	12	0	.255
1940	1	3	.250	4.42	30	1	0	59	65	26	22	0	1	3	2	13	4	0	.308
1941	2	2	.500	4.28	25	3	1	48.1	48	30	17	0	2	2	1	7	2	0	.286
4 yrs.	15	16	.484	4.03	95	30	12	314.2	372	106	100	1	4	5	5	93	22	0	.237
WORLD SERIES																			
1938 CHI N	0	0	–	13.50	1	0	0	1.1	2	0	0	0	0	0	0	0	0	0	–

Pat Paige

PAIGE, GEORGE LYNN   BR TR 5'10"   175 lbs.
B. May 5, 1883, Paw Paw, Mich.   D. June 8, 1939, Berlin, Wis.

	W	L	PCT	ERA	G	GS	CG	IP	H	BB	SO	ShO	W	L	SV	AB	H	HR	BA
1911 CLE A	1	0	1.000	4.50	2	1	1	16	21	7	6	0	0	0	0	7	1	0	.143

Satchel Paige

PAIGE, LEROY ROBERT   BR TR 6'3½"   180 lbs.
B. July 7, 1906, Mobile, Ala.   D. June 8, 1982, Kansas City, Mo.
Hall of Fame 1971.

	W	L	PCT	ERA	G	GS	CG	IP	H	BB	SO	ShO	W	L	SV	AB	H	HR	BA
1948 CLE A	6	1	.857	2.48	21	7	3	72.2	61	25	45	2	2	1	1	23	2	0	.087
1949	4	7	.364	3.04	31	5	1	83	70	33	54	0	3	4	5	16	1	0	.063
1951 STL A	3	4	.429	4.79	23	3	0	62	67	29	48	0	3	2	5	16	2	0	.125
1952	12	10	.545	3.07	46	6	3	138	116	57	91	2	8	8	10	39	5	0	.128
1953	3	9	.250	3.53	57	4	0	117.1	114	39	51	0	2	8	11	29	2	0	.069
1965 KC A	0	0	–	0.00	1	1	0	3	1	0	1	0	0	0	0	1	0	0	.000
6 yrs.	28	31	.475	3.29	179	26	7	476	429	183	290	4	18	23	32	124	12	0	.097
WORLD SERIES																			
1948 CLE A	0	0	–	0.00	1	0	0	.2	0	0	0	0	0	0	0	0	0	0	–

Phil Paine

PAINE, PHILLIPS STEERE (Flip)   BR TR 6'2"   180 lbs.
B. June 8, 1930, Chepachet, R. I.   D. Feb. 19, 1978, Lebanon, Pa.

	W	L	PCT	ERA	G	GS	CG	IP	H	BB	SO	ShO	W	L	SV	AB	H	HR	BA
1951 BOS N	2	0	1.000	3.06	21	0	0	35.1	36	20	17	0	2	0	0	4	0	0	.000
1954 MIL N	1	0	1.000	3.86	11	0	0	14	14	12	11	0	1	0	0	0	0	0	–
1955	2	0	1.000	2.49	15	0	0	25.1	20	14	26	0	2	0	0	3	1	0	.333
1956	0	0	–	∞	1	0	0	0	3	0	0	0	0	0	0	0	0	0	–
1957	0	0	–	0.00	1	0	0	2	1	3	2	0	0	0	0	0	0	0	–
1958 STL N	5	1	.833	3.56	46	0	0	73.1	70	31	45	0	5	1	1	7	2	0	.286
6 yrs.	10	1	.909	3.36	95	0	0	150	144	80	101	0	10	1	1	14	3	0	.214

Mike Palagyi

PALAGYI, MICHAEL RAYMOND   BR TR 6'2"   185 lbs.
B. July 4, 1917, Conneaut, Ohio

	W	L	PCT	ERA	G	GS	CG	IP	H	BB	SO	ShO	W	L	SV	AB	H	HR	BA
1939 WAS A	0	0	–	∞	1	0	0	0	3	0	0	0	0	0	0	0	0	0	–

	W	L	PCT	ERA	G	GS	CG	IP	H	BB	SO	ShO	Relief Pitching W	L	SV	BATTING AB	H	HR	BA

Erv Palica

PALICA, ERVIN MARTIN   BR TR 6'1½" 180 lbs.
Also known as Ervin Martin Pavliecivich.
B. Feb. 9, 1928, Lomita, Calif.   D. May 29, 1982, Huntington Beach, Calif.

	W	L	PCT	ERA	G	GS	CG	IP	H	BB	SO	ShO	W	L	SV	AB	H	HR	BA
1945 **BKN N**	0	0	–	0.00	0	0	0		0	0	0	0	0	0	0	0	0	0	–
1947	0	1	.000	3.00	3	0	0	3	2	2	1	0	0	1	0	0	0	0	–
1948	6	6	.500	4.45	41	10	3	125.1	111	58	74	0	3	3	3	39	5	0	.128
1949	8	9	.471	3.62	49	1	0	97	93	49	44	0	8	8	6	19	3	0	.158
1950	13	8	.619	3.58	43	19	10	201.1	176	98	131	2	2	2	1	68	15	1	.221
1951	2	6	.250	4.75	19	8	0	53	55	20	15	0	2	1	0	13	2	0	.154
1953	0	0	–	12.00	4	0	0	6	10	8	3	0	0	0	0	1	1	0	1.000
1954	3	3	.500	5.32	25	3	0	67.2	77	31	25	0	3	2	0	16	4	0	.250
1955 **BAL A**	5	11	.313	4.14	33	25	5	169.2	165	83	68	1	0	0	2	55	13	0	.236
1956	4	11	.267	4.49	29	14	2	116.1	117	50	62	0	2	3	0	32	5	0	.156
10 yrs.	41	55	.427	4.22	246	80	20	839.1	806	399	423	3	20	20	12	243	48	1	.198

WORLD SERIES

	W	L	PCT	ERA	G	GS	CG	IP	H	BB	SO	ShO	W	L	SV	AB	H	HR	BA
1949 **BKN N**	0	0	–	0.00	1	0	0	2	1	1	1	0	0	0	0	0	0	0	–

Mike Palm

PALM, RICHARD PAUL   BR TR 6'3½" 190 lbs.
B. Feb. 13, 1925, Boston, Mass.

	W	L	PCT	ERA	G	GS	CG	IP	H	BB	SO	ShO	W	L	SV	AB	H	HR	BA
1948 **BOS A**	0	0	–	6.00	3	0	0	3	6	5	1	0	0	0	0	3	0	0	.000

Palmer

PALMER,
B. St. Louis, Mo.   Deceased.

	W	L	PCT	ERA	G	GS	CG	IP	H	BB	SO	ShO	W	L	SV	AB	H	HR	BA
1885 **STL N**	0	4	.000	3.44	4	4	4	34	46	20	9	0	0	0	0	11	1	0	.091

Dave Palmer

PALMER, DAVID WILLIAM   BR TR 6'1" 195 lbs.
B. Oct. 19, 1957, Glens Falls, N. Y.

	W	L	PCT	ERA	G	GS	CG	IP	H	BB	SO	ShO	W	L	SV	AB	H	HR	BA
1978 **MON N**	0	1	.000	2.70	5	1	0	10	9	2	7	0	0	0	0	1	0	0	.000
1979	10	2	.833	2.63	36	11	2	123	110	30	72	1	1	0	2	31	1	0	.032
1980	8	6	.571	2.98	24	19	3	130	124	30	73	1	0	0	0	45	9	0	.200
1982	6	4	.600	3.18	13	13	1	73.2	60	36	46	0	0	0	0	24	1	0	.042
1984	7	3	.700	3.84	20	19	1	105.1	101	44	66	1	0	1	0	33	5	1	.152
5 yrs.	31	16	.660	3.12	98	63	7	442	404	142	264	3	1	1	2	134	16	1	.119

Jim Palmer

PALMER, JAMES ALVIN   BR TR 6'3" 190 lbs.
B. Oct. 15, 1945, New York, N. Y.

	W	L	PCT	ERA	G	GS	CG	IP	H	BB	SO	ShO	W	L	SV	AB	H	HR	BA
1965 **BAL A**	5	4	.556	3.72	27	6	0	92	75	56	75	0	4	2	1	26	5	1	.192
1966	15	10	.600	3.46	30	30	6	208.1	176	91	147	0	0	0	0	73	7	1	.096
1967	3	1	.750	2.94	9	9	2	49	34	20	23	1	0	0	0	13	1	0	.077
1969	16	4	**.800**	2.34	26	23	11	181	131	64	123	6	2	0	0	64	13	0	.203
1970	20	10	.667	2.71	39	39	17	**305**	263	100	199	5	0	0	0	113	17	1	.150
1971	20	9	.690	2.68	37	37	20	282	231	106	184	3	0	0	0	102	20	0	.196
1972	21	10	.677	2.07	36	36	18	274.1	219	70	184	3	0	0	0	98	22	0	.224
1973	22	9	.710	**2.40**	38	37	19	296	225	113	158	6	0	0	1	0	0	0	–
1974	7	12	.368	3.27	26	26	5	179	176	69	84	2	0	0	1	0	0	0	–
1975	**23**	11	.676	**2.09**	39	38	25	323	253	80	193	**10**	0	0	1	0	0	0	–
1976	**22**	13	.629	2.51	40	**40**	23	**315**	255	84	159	6	0	0	0	0	0	0	–
1977	**20**	11	.645	2.91	39	**39**	**22**	**319**	263	99	193	3	0	0	0	0	0	0	–
1978	21	12	.636	2.46	38	38	19	**296**	246	97	138	6	0	0	0	0	0	0	–
1979	10	6	.625	3.29	23	22	7	156	144	43	67	0	0	0	0	0	0	0	–
1980	16	10	.615	3.98	34	33	4	224	238	74	109	0	0	0	0	0	0	0	–
1981	7	8	.467	3.76	22	22	5	127	117	46	35	0	0	0	0	0	0	0	–
1982	15	5	**.750**	3.13	36	32	8	227	195	63	103	2	0	1	1	0	0	0	–
1983	5	4	.556	4.23	14	11	0	76.2	86	19	34	0	0	0	0	0	0	0	–
1984	0	3	.000	9.17	5	3	0	17.2	22	17	4	0	0	1	0	0	0	0	–
19 yrs.	268	152	.638	2.86	558	521	211	3948	3349	1311	2212	53	6	4	4	489	85	3	.174

LEAGUE CHAMPIONSHIP SERIES

	W	L	PCT	ERA	G	GS	CG	IP	H	BB	SO	ShO	W	L	SV	AB	H	HR	BA
1969 **BAL A**	1	0	1.000	2.00	1	1	1	9	10	2	4	0	0	0	0	5	0	0	.000
1970	1	0	1.000	1.00	1	1	1	9	7	3	12	0	0	0	0	4	1	0	.250
1971	1	0	1.000	3.00	1	1	1	9	7	3	8	0	0	0	0	5	1	0	.200
1973	1	0	1.000	1.84	3	2	1	14.2	11	8	15	1	0	0	0	0	0	0	–
1974	0	1	.000	1.00	1	1	1	9	4	1	4	0	0	0	0	0	0	0	–
1979	0	0	–	3.00	1	1	0	9	7	2	3	0	0	0	0	0	0	0	–
6 yrs.	4	1	.800	1.96	8	7	5	59.2	46	19	46	1	0	0	0	14	2	0	.143

WORLD SERIES

	W	L	PCT	ERA	G	GS	CG	IP	H	BB	SO	ShO	W	L	SV	AB	H	HR	BA
1966 **BAL A**	1	0	1.000	0.00	1	1	1	9	4	3	6	1	0	0	0	3	0	0	.000
1969	0	1	.000	6.00	1	1	0	6	5	4	5	0	0	0	0	2	0	0	.000
1970	1	0	1.000	4.60	2	2	0	15.2	11	9	9	0	0	0	0	7	1	0	.143
1971	1	0	1.000	2.65	2	2	0	17	15	9	15	0	0	0	0	4	0	0	.000
1979	0	1	.000	3.60	2	2	0	15	18	5	8	0	0	0	0	4	0	0	.000
1983	1	0	1.000	0.00	1	0	0	2	2	1	1	0	1	0	0	0	0	0	–
6 yrs.	4	2	.667	3.20	9	8	1	64.2	55	31	44	1	1	0	0	21	1	0	.048
						10th		9th	9th		4th								

Lowell Palmer

PALMER, LOWELL RAYMOND   BR TR 6'1" 190 lbs.
B. Aug. 18, 1947, Sacramento, Calif.

	W	L	PCT	ERA	G	GS	CG	IP	H	BB	SO	ShO	W	L	SV	AB	H	HR	BA
1969 **PHI N**	2	8	.200	5.20	26	9	1	90	91	47	68	1	0	0	0	22	3	1	.136
1970	1	2	.333	5.47	38	5	0	102	98	55	85	0	1	1	0	27	4	0	.148
1971	0	0	–	6.00	3	1	0	15	13	13	6	0	0	0	0	5	1	0	.200
1972 **2 teams**			**CLE A** (1G 0–0)			**STL N**	(16G 0–3)												
" total	0	3	.000	3.89	17	2	0	37	32	28	28	0	0	1	0	5	0	0	.000
1974 **SD N**	2	5	.286	5.67	22	8	1	73	68	59	52	0	1	2	0	23	2	0	.087
5 yrs.	5	18	.217	5.28	106	25	2	317	302	202	239	1	2	4	0	82	10	1	.122

	W	L	PCT	ERA	G	GS	CG	IP	H	BB	SO	ShO	Relief Pitching W	L	SV	BATTING AB	H	HR	BA

Emilio Palmero

PALMERO, EMILIO ANTONIO
B. June 13, 1895, Havana, Cuba
D. July 15, 1970, Toledo, Ohio

BB TL 5'11"   157 lbs.
BL 1928

	W	L	PCT	ERA	G	GS	CG	IP	H	BB	SO	ShO	W	L	SV	AB	H	HR	BA
1915 NY N	0	2	.000	3.09	3	2	1	11.2	10	9	8	0	0	0	0	4	1	0	.250
1916	0	3	.000	8.04	4	1	0	15.2	17	8	8	0	0	2	0	3	0	0	.000
1921 STL A	4	7	.364	5.00	24	9	4	90	109	49	26	0	2	1	0	37	8	0	.216
1926 WAS A	2	2	.500	4.76	7	3	0	17	22	15	6	0	1	0	0	3	1	0	.333
1928 BOS N	0	1	.000	5.40	3	1	0	6.2	14	2	0	0	0	0	0	1	0	0	.000
5 yrs.	6	15	.286	5.17	41	16	5	141	172	83	48	0	3	3	0	48	10	0	.208

Ed Palmquist

PALMQUIST, EDWIN LEE
B. June 10, 1933, Los Angeles, Calif.

BR TR 6'3"   195 lbs.

	W	L	PCT	ERA	G	GS	CG	IP	H	BB	SO	ShO	W	L	SV	AB	H	HR	BA
1960 LA N	1	0	.000	2.54	22	0	0	39	34	16	23	0	0	1	0	7	0	0	.000
1961 2 teams			LA	N (5G 0–1)		MIN	A	(9G 1–1)											
" total	1	2	.333	8.49	14	2	0	29.2	43	20	18	0	1	1	1	3	0	0	.000
2 yrs.	1	3	.250	5.11	36	2	0	68.2	77	36	41	0	1	2	1	10	0	0	.000

Jim Panther

PANTHER, JAMES EDWARD
B. Mar. 1, 1945, Burlington, Iowa

BR TR 6'1"   190 lbs.

	W	L	PCT	ERA	G	GS	CG	IP	H	BB	SO	ShO	W	L	SV	AB	H	HR	BA
1971 OAK A	0	1	.000	10.50	4	0	0	6	10	5	4	0	0	1	0	1	0	0	.000
1972 TEX A	5	9	.357	4.12	58	4	0	94	101	46	44	0	5	5	0	8	1	0	.125
1973 ATL N	2	3	.400	7.55	23	0	0	31	45	9	8	0	2	3	0	0	0	0	
3 yrs.	7	13	.350	5.22	85	4	0	131	156	60	56	0	7	9	0	9	1	0	.111

John Papa

PAPA, JOHN PAUL
B. Dec. 5, 1940, Bridgeport, Conn.

BR TR 5'11"   190 lbs.

	W	L	PCT	ERA	G	GS	CG	IP	H	BB	SO	ShO	W	L	SV	AB	H	HR	BA
1961 BAL A	0	0	–	18.00	2	0	0	1	2	3	3	0	0	0	0	0	0	0	–
1962	0	0	–	27.00	1	0	0	1	3	1	0	0	0	0	0	0	0	0	–
2 yrs.	0	0	–	22.50	3	0	0	2	5	4	3	0	0	0	0	0	0	0	–

Al Papai

PAPAI, ALFRED THOMAS
B. May 7, 1919, Divernon, Ill.

BR TR 6'3"   185 lbs.

	W	L	PCT	ERA	G	GS	CG	IP	H	BB	SO	ShO	W	L	SV	AB	H	HR	BA
1948 STL N	0	1	.000	5.06	10	0	0	16	14	7	8	0	0	1	0	2	0	0	.000
1949 STL A	4	11	.267	5.06	42	15	6	142.1	175	81	31	0	2	3	2	38	3	0	.079
1950 2 teams			BOS	A (16G 4–2)		STL	N	(13G 1–0)											
" total	5	2	.714	6.33	29	3	2	69.2	82	42	26	0	4	0	2	20	3	0	.150
1955 CHI A	0	0	–	3.86	7	0	0	11.2	10	8	5	0	0	0	0	2	0	0	.000
4 yrs.	9	14	.391	5.37	88	18	8	239.2	281	138	70	0	6	4	4	62	6	0	.097

Larry Pape

PAPE, LAURENCE ALBERT
B. July 21, 1883, Norwood, Ohio   D. July 21, 1918, Swissvale, Pa.

BR TR 6'   175 lbs.

	W	L	PCT	ERA	G	GS	CG	IP	H	BB	SO	ShO	W	L	SV	AB	H	HR	BA
1909 BOS A	2	0	1.000	2.01	11	3	2	58.1	46	12	18	1	0	0	2	21	3	0	.143
1911	10	8	.556	2.45	27	19	10	176.1	167	63	49	1	1	0	0	64	13	0	.203
1912	1	1	.500	4.99	13	2	1	48.2	74	16	17	0	1	0	1	17	4	0	.235
3 yrs.	13	9	.591	2.80	51	24	13	283.1	287	91	84	2	2	0	3	102	20	0	.196

Frank Papish

PAPISH, FRANK RICHARD (Pap)
B. Oct. 21, 1917, Pueblo, Colo.   D. Aug. 30, 1965, Pueblo, Colo.

BR TL 6'2"   192 lbs.

	W	L	PCT	ERA	G	GS	CG	IP	H	BB	SO	ShO	W	L	SV	AB	H	HR	BA
1945 CHI A	4	4	.500	3.74	19	5	3	84.1	75	40	45	0	4	4	1	26	6	0	.231
1946	7	5	.583	2.74	31	15	6	138	122	63	66	2	0	1	0	43	8	0	.186
1947	12	12	.500	3.26	38	26	6	199	185	98	79	1	2	0	3	58	5	0	.086
1948	2	8	.200	5.00	32	14	2	95.1	97	75	41	0	1	4	4	27	5	0	.185
1949 CLE A	1	0	1.000	3.19	25	3	1	62	54	39	23	0	1	0	1	8	1	0	.125
1950 PIT N	0	0	–	27.00	4	1	0	2.1	8	4	1	0	0	0	0	0	0	0	
6 yrs.	26	29	.473	3.58	149	64	18	581	541	319	255	3	7	6	9	162	25	0	.154

John Pappalau

PAPPALAU, JOHN JOSEPH
B. Apr. 3, 1875, Albany, N. Y.   D. May 12, 1944, Albany, N. Y.

BR TR 6'   175 lbs.

	W	L	PCT	ERA	G	GS	CG	IP	H	BB	SO	ShO	W	L	SV	AB	H	HR	BA
1897 CLE N	0	1	.000	10.50	2	1	1	12	22	6	3	0	0	0	0	5	0	0	.000

Milt Pappas

PAPPAS, MILTON STEVEN (Gimpy)
B. May 11, 1939, Detroit, Mich.

BR TR 6'3"   190 lbs.

	W	L	PCT	ERA	G	GS	CG	IP	H	BB	SO	ShO	W	L	SV	AB	H	HR	BA
1957 BAL A	0	0	–	1.00	4	0	0	9	6	3	3	0	0	0	0	1	0	0	.000
1958	10	10	.500	4.06	31	21	3	135.1	135	48	72	0	1	1	0	42	6	1	.143
1959	15	9	.625	3.27	33	27	15	209.1	175	75	120	4	1	0	3	79	11	0	.139
1960	15	11	.577	3.37	30	27	11	205.2	184	83	126	3	2	1	0	70	3	1	.043
1961	13	9	.591	3.04	26	23	11	177.2	134	78	89	4	1	0	1	66	9	3	.136
1962	12	10	.545	4.03	35	32	9	205.1	200	75	130	1	0	0	0	69	6	4	.087
1963	16	9	.640	3.03	34	32	11	216.2	186	69	120	4	0	0	0	71	9	2	.127
1964	16	7	.696	2.97	37	36	13	251.2	225	48	157	7	0	0	0	93	12	0	.129
1965	13	9	.591	2.60	34	34	9	221.1	192	52	127	3	0	0	0	70	5	0	.071
1966 CIN N	12	11	.522	4.29	33	32	6	209.2	224	39	133	2	0	1	0	75	8	1	.107
1967	16	13	.552	3.35	34	32	5	217.2	218	38	129	3	2	0	0	72	7	1	.097
1968 2 teams			CIN	N (15G 2–5)		ATL	N	(22G 10–8)											
" total	12	13	.480	3.47	37	30	3	184	181	32	118	1	0	1	0	53	7	1	.132
1969 ATL N	6	10	.375	3.63	26	24	1	144	149	44	72	0	0	0	0	45	7	2	.156
1970 2 teams			ATL	N (11G 2–2)		CHI	N	(22G 10–8)											
" total	12	10	.545	3.34	32	23	7	180.1	179	43	105	2	1	0	0	60	12	2	.200
1971 CHI N	17	14	.548	3.52	35	35	14	261	279	62	99	5	0	0	0	91	14	0	.154
1972	17	7	.708	2.77	29	28	10	195	187	29	80	3	0	0	0	68	13	1	.191
1973	7	12	.368	4.28	30	29	1	162	192	40	48	1	0	0	0	48	3	1	.063
17 yrs.	209	164	.560	3.40	520	465	129	3185.2	3046	858	1728	43	8	4	4	1073	132	20	.123

LEAGUE CHAMPIONSHIP SERIES

	W	L	PCT	ERA	G	GS	CG	IP	H	BB	SO	ShO	W	L	SV	AB	H	HR	BA
1969 ATL N	0	0	–	11.57	1	0	0	2.1	4	0	4	0	0	0	0	1	0	0	.000

	W	L	PCT	ERA	G	GS	CG	IP	H	BB	SO	ShO	Relief Pitching W	L	SV	BATTING AB	H	HR	BA

Jim Park

PARK, JAMES   BR TR 6'2"   175 lbs.
B. Nov. 10, 1892, Richmond, Ky.   D. Dec. 17, 1970, Lexington, Ky.

	W	L	PCT	ERA	G	GS	CG	IP	H	BB	SO	ShO	W	L	SV	AB	H	HR	BA
1915 STL A	2	0	1.000	1.19	3	3	1	22.2	18	9	5	0	0	0	0	10	4	0	.400
1916	1	4	.200	2.62	26	6	1	79	69	25	26	0	1	0	0	20	2	0	.100
1917	1	1	.500	6.64	13	0	0	20.1	27	12	9	0	1	1	0	2	0	0	.000
3 yrs.	4	5	.444	3.02	42	9	2	122	114	46	40	0	2	1	0	32	6	0	.188

Doc Parker

PARKER, HARLEY PARK   BR TR 6'2"   200 lbs.
Brother of Jay Parker.
B. June 14, 1874, Theresa, N. Y.   D. Mar. 3, 1941, Chicago, Ill.

	W	L	PCT	ERA	G	GS	CG	IP	H	BB	SO	ShO	W	L	SV	AB	H	HR	BA
1893 CHI N	0	0	–	13.50	1	0	0	2	5	1	0	0	0	0	1	1	0	0	.000
1895	4	2	.667	3.68	7	6	5	51.1	65	9	9	1	0	0	0	22	7	0	.318
1896	1	5	.167	6.16	9	7	7	73	100	27	15	0	0	0	0	36	10	0	.278
1901 CIN N	0	1	.000	15.75	1	1	1	8	26	2	0	0	0	0	0	3	0	0	.000
4 yrs.	5	8	.385	5.90	18	14	13	134.1	196	39	24	1	0	0	1	62	17	0	.274

Harry Parker

PARKER, HARRY WILLIAM   BR TR 6'3"   190 lbs.
B. Sept. 14, 1947, Highland, Ill.

	W	L	PCT	ERA	G	GS	CG	IP	H	BB	SO	ShO	W	L	SV	AB	H	HR	BA
1970 STL N	1	1	.500	3.27	7	4	0	22	24	15	9	0	1	1	0	8	2	0	.250
1971	0	0	–	7.20	4	0	0	5	6	2	2	0	0	0	0	0	0	0	–
1973 NY N	8	4	.667	3.35	38	9	0	96.2	79	36	63	0	4	2	5	23	4	0	.174
1974	4	12	.250	3.92	40	16	1	131	145	46	58	0	0	2	4	36	0	0	.000
1975 2 teams	NY	N	(18G 2–3)		STL	N	(14G 0–1)												
" total	4	8	.333	5.06	32	7	1	53.1	58	29	35	0	2	3	3	3	0	0	.000
1976 CLE A	0	0	–	0.00	3	0	0	7	3	0	5	0	0	0	0	0	0	0	–
6 yrs.	15	21	.417	3.86	124	30	1	315	315	128	172	0	7	8	12	70	6	0	.086

LEAGUE CHAMPIONSHIP SERIES																			
1973 NY N	0	1	.000	9.00	1	0	0	1	1	0	0	0	0	1	0	0	0	0	–

WORLD SERIES																			
1973 NY N	0	1	.000	0.00	3	0	0	3.1	2	2	2	0	0	1	0	0	0	0	–

Jay Parker

PARKER, JAY   BR TR 5'11"   185 lbs.
Brother of Doc Parker.
B. July 8, 1874, Theresa, N. Y.   D. June 8, 1935, Hartford, Mich.

	W	L	PCT	ERA	G	GS	CG	IP	H	BB	SO	ShO	W	L	SV	AB	H	HR	BA
1899 PIT N	0	0	–	∞	1	1	0	0	2	0	0	0	0	0	0	0	0	0	–

Roy Parker

PARKER, ROY W.   BR TR 6'2"   185 lbs.
B. 1897

	W	L	PCT	ERA	G	GS	CG	IP	H	BB	SO	ShO	W	L	SV	AB	H	HR	BA
1919 STL N	0	0	–	31.50	2	0	0	2	6	1	0	0	0	0	0	0	0	0	–

Slicker Parks

PARKS, VERNON HENRY   BR TR 5'10"   158 lbs.
B. Nov. 10, 1895, Dallas, Mich.   D. Feb. 21, 1978, Royal Oak, Mich.

	W	L	PCT	ERA	G	GS	CG	IP	H	BB	SO	ShO	W	L	SV	AB	H	HR	BA
1921 DET A	3	2	.600	5.68	10	1	0	25.1	33	16	10	0	3	2	0	9	1	0	.111

Roy Parmelee

PARMELEE, LeROY EARL (Bud)   BR TR 6'1"   190 lbs.
B. Apr. 25, 1907, Lambertville, Mich.   D. Aug. 31, 1981, Monroe, Mich.

	W	L	PCT	ERA	G	GS	CG	IP	H	BB	SO	ShO	W	L	SV	AB	H	HR	BA
1929 NY N	1	0	1.000	9.00	2	1	0	7	13	3	1	0	0	0	0	2	1	0	.500
1930	0	1	.000	9.43	11	1	0	21	18	26	19	0	0	0	0	4	1	0	.250
1931	2	2	.500	3.68	13	5	4	58.2	47	33	30	0	0	0	0	20	4	0	.200
1932	0	3	.000	3.91	8	3	0	25.1	25	14	23	0	0	0	0	5	2	0	.400
1933	13	8	.619	3.17	32	32	14	218.1	191	77	132	3	0	0	0	81	19	1	.235
1934	10	6	.625	3.42	22	20	7	152.2	134	60	83	3	0	0	0	55	11	2	.200
1935	14	10	.583	4.22	34	31	13	226	214	97	79	0	1	0	0	86	18	0	.209
1936 STL N	11	11	.500	4.56	37	28	9	221	226	107	79	0	0	1	2	76	15	0	.197
1937 CHI N	7	8	.467	5.13	33	18	8	145.2	165	79	55	0	0	1	0	52	9	2	.173
1939 PHI A	1	6	.143	6.45	14	5	0	44.2	42	35	13	0	1	2	1	15	2	0	.133
10 yrs.	59	55	.518	4.27	206	144	55	1120.1	1075	531	514	6	2	4	3	396	82	5	.207

Mel Parnell

PARNELL, MELVIN LLOYD (Dusty)   BL TL 6'   180 lbs.
B. June 13, 1922, New Orleans, La.

	W	L	PCT	ERA	G	GS	CG	IP	H	BB	SO	ShO	W	L	SV	AB	H	HR	BA
1947 BOS A	2	3	.400	6.39	15	5	1	50.2	60	27	23	0	1	1	0	18	1	0	.056
1948	15	8	.652	3.14	35	27	16	212	205	90	77	1	0	2	0	80	13	0	.163
1949	25	7	.781	2.77	39	33	27	295.1	258	134	122	4	1	1	2	114	29	0	.254
1950	18	10	.643	3.61	40	31	21	249	244	106	93	2	0	1	3	98	19	0	.194
1951	18	11	.621	3.26	36	29	11	221	229	77	77	3	2	0	2	81	25	0	.309
1952	12	12	.500	3.62	33	29	15	214	207	89	107	3	0	0	2	84	8	1	.095
1953	21	8	.724	3.06	38	34	12	241	217	116	136	5	1	0	0	94	21	0	.223
1954	3	7	.300	3.70	19	15	4	92.1	104	35	38	1	0	0	0	34	3	0	.088
1955	2	3	.400	7.83	13	9	0	46	62	25	18	0	0	0	1	19	6	0	.316
1956	7	6	.538	3.77	21	20	6	131.1	129	59	41	1	0	1	0	46	7	0	.152
10 yrs.	123	75	.621	3.50	289	232	113	1752.2	1715	758	732	20	5	6	10	668	132	1	.198

Rube Parnham

PARNHAM, JAMES ARTHUR   BR TR 6'3"   185 lbs.
B. Feb. 1, 1894, Heidelberg, Pa.   D. Nov. 25, 1963, McKeesport, Pa.

	W	L	PCT	ERA	G	GS	CG	IP	H	BB	SO	ShO	W	L	SV	AB	H	HR	BA
1916 PHI A	2	1	.667	0.36	4	3	2	24.2	27	13	8	0	0	0	0	11	3	0	.273
1917	0	1	.000	4.09	2	2	0	11	12	9	4	0	0	0	0	3	0	0	.000
2 yrs.	2	2	.500	1.51	6	5	2	35.2	39	22	12	0	0	0	0	14	3	0	.214

Mike Parrott

PARROTT, MICHAEL EVERETT   BR TR 6'4"   210 lbs.
B. Dec. 6, 1954, Camarillo, Calif.

	W	L	PCT	ERA	G	GS	CG	IP	H	BB	SO	ShO	W	L	SV	AB	H	HR	BA
1977 BAL A	0	0	–	2.25	3	0	0	4	4	2	2	0	0	0	0	0	0	0	–
1978 SEA A	1	5	.167	5.14	27	10	0	82.1	108	32	41	0	0	1	1	0	0	0	–
1979	14	12	.538	3.77	38	30	13	229	231	86	127	2	1	0	0	0	0	0	–
1980	1	16	.059	7.28	27	16	1	94	136	42	53	0	0	2	3	0	0	0	–
1981	3	6	.333	5.08	24	12	0	85	102	28	43	0	0	0	1	0	0	0	–
5 yrs.	19	39	.328	4.88	119	68	14	494.1	581	190	266	2	1	3	5	0	0	0	–

	W	L	PCT	ERA	G	GS	CG	IP	H	BB	SO	ShO	Relief Pitching W	L	SV	BATTING AB	H	HR	BA

Tom Parrott

PARROTT, THOMAS WILLIAM (Tacky Tom)   BR TR 6'2"   170 lbs.
Brother of Jiggs Parrott.
B. Apr. 10, 1868, Portland, Ore.   D. Jan. 1, 1932, Dundee, Ore.

	W	L	PCT	ERA	G	GS	CG	IP	H	BB	SO	ShO	W	L	SV	AB	H	HR	BA
1893 **2 teams**		CHI N (4G 0–3)		CIN N (22G 10–7)															
" total	10	10	.500	4.48	26	20	13	181	209	87	40	1	3	0	0	95	20	1	.211
1894 **CIN N**	17	19	.472	5.60	41	36	31	308.2	402	126	61	1	0	1	1	229	74	4	.323
1895	11	18	.379	5.47	41	31	23	263.1	382	76	57	0	3	1	3	201	69	3	.343
1896 **STL N**	1	1	.500	6.21	7	2	2	42	62	18	8	0	0	0	0	474	138	7	.291
4 yrs.	39	48	.448	5.33	115	89	69	795	1055	307	166	2	6	2	4	*			

Jiggs Parson

PARSON, WILLIAM EDWIN   BR TR 6'2"   180 lbs.
B. Dec. 27, 1885, Parker, S. D.   D. May 19, 1967, Los Angeles, Calif.

	W	L	PCT	ERA	G	GS	CG	IP	H	BB	SO	ShO	W	L	SV	AB	H	HR	BA
1910 **BOS N**	0	2	.000	3.82	10	4	0	35.1	35	26	7	0	0	1	0	12	1	0	.083
1911	0	1	.000	6.48	7	0	0	25	36	15	7	0	0	1	0	10	2	0	.200
2 yrs.	0	3	.000	4.92	17	4	0	60.1	71	41	14	0	0	2	0	22	3	0	.136

Bill Parsons

PARSONS, WILLIAM RAYMOND   BR TR 6'6"   195 lbs.
B. Aug. 17, 1948, Riverside, Calif.

	W	L	PCT	ERA	G	GS	CG	IP	H	BB	SO	ShO	W	L	SV	AB	H	HR	BA
1971 **MIL A**	13	17	.433	3.20	36	35	12	245	219	93	139	4	0	0	0	72	12	1	.167
1972	13	13	.500	3.91	33	30	10	214	194	68	111	2	0	0	0	67	11	0	.164
1973	3	6	.333	6.79	20	17	0	59.2	59	67	30	0	0	0	0	0	0	0	—
1974 **OAK A**	0	0	—	0.00	4	0	0	2	1	3	2	0	0	0	0	0	0	0	—
4 yrs.	29	36	.446	3.89	93	82	22	520.2	473	231	282	6	0	0	0	139	23	1	.165

Charlie Parsons

PARSONS, CHARLES JAMES   BL TL 5'10"   160 lbs.
B. July 18, 1863, Cherry Flats, Pa.   D. Mar. 24, 1936, Mansfield, Pa.

	W	L	PCT	ERA	G	GS	CG	IP	H	BB	SO	ShO	W	L	SV	AB	H	HR	BA
1886 **BOS N**	0	2	.000	3.94	2	2	2	16	20	4	5	0	0	0	0	8	3	0	.375
1887 **NY AA**	1	1	.500	4.50	4	4	4	34	51	6	5	0	0	0	0	15	3	0	.200
1890 **CLE N**	0	1	.000	6.00	2	1	0	9	12	6	2	0	0	0	0	4	3	0	.750
3 yrs.	1	4	.200	4.58	8	7	6	59	83	16	12	0	0	0	0	27	9	0	.333

Tom Parsons

PARSONS, THOMAS ANTHONY (Long Tom)   BR TR 6'7"   210 lbs.
B. Sept. 13, 1939, Lakeville, Conn.

	W	L	PCT	ERA	G	GS	CG	IP	H	BB	SO	ShO	W	L	SV	AB	H	HR	BA
1963 **PIT N**	0	1	.000	8.31	1	1	0	4.1	7	2	2	0	0	0	0	2	0	0	.000
1964 **NY N**	1	2	.333	4.19	4	2	1	19.1	20	6	10	0	1	0	0	7	0	0	.000
1965	1	10	.091	4.67	35	11	1	90.2	108	17	58	1	0	3	1	18	1	0	.056
3 yrs.	2	13	.133	4.72	40	14	2	114.1	135	25	70	1	1	3	1	27	1	0	.037

Stan Partenheimer

PARTENHEIMER, STANWOOD WENDELL (Party)   BB TL 5'11"   175 lbs.
Son of Steve Partenheimer.   BL 1944
B. Oct. 21, 1922, Chicopee Falls, Mass.

	W	L	PCT	ERA	G	GS	CG	IP	H	BB	SO	ShO	W	L	SV	AB	H	HR	BA
1944 **BOS A**	0	0	—	18.00	1	1	0	1	3	2	0	0	0	0	0	1	0	0	.000
1945 **STL N**	0	0	—	6.08	8	2	0	13.1	12	16	6	0	0	0	0	3	0	0	.000
2 yrs.	0	0	—	6.91	9	3	0	14.1	15	18	6	0	0	0	0	4	0	0	.000

Bill Paschall

PASCHALL, WILLIAM HERBERT   BR TR 6'   175 lbs.
B. Apr. 22, 1954, Norfolk, Va.

	W	L	PCT	ERA	G	GS	CG	IP	H	BB	SO	ShO	W	L	SV	AB	H	HR	BA
1978 **KC A**	0	1	.000	3.38	2	0	0	8	6	0	5	0	0	1	1	0	0	0	—
1979	0	1	.000	6.43	7	0	0	14	18	5	3	0	0	1	0	0	0	0	—
1981	0	0	—	4.50	2	0	0	2	2	0	1	0	0	0	0	0	0	0	—
3 yrs.	0	2	.000	5.25	11	0	0	24	26	5	9	0	0	2	1	0	0	0	—

Camilo Pascual

PASCUAL, CAMILO ALBERTO (Little Potato)   BR TR 5'11"   165 lbs.
Brother of Carlos Pascual.
B. Jan. 20, 1934, Havana, Cuba

	W	L	PCT	ERA	G	GS	CG	IP	H	BB	SO	ShO	W	L	SV	AB	H	HR	BA
1954 **WAS A**	4	7	.364	4.22	48	4	1	119.1	126	61	60	0	4	4	3	30	4	0	.133
1955	2	12	.143	6.14	43	16	1	129	158	70	82	0	0	4	3	32	7	0	.219
1956	6	18	.250	5.87	39	27	6	188.2	194	89	162	0	1	1	2	58	8	0	.138
1957	8	17	.320	4.10	29	26	8	175.2	168	76	113	2	0	3	0	50	7	0	.140
1958	8	12	.400	3.15	31	27	6	177.1	166	60	146	2	0	0	0	57	9	0	.158
1959	17	10	.630	2.64	32	30	17	238.2	202	69	185	6	0	0	0	86	26	0	.302
1960	12	8	.600	3.03	26	22	8	151.2	139	53	143	3	0	1	2	51	9	1	.176
1961 **MIN A**	15	16	.484	3.46	35	33	15	252.1	205	100	221	8	0	1	0	85	14	0	.165
1962	20	11	.645	3.32	34	33	18	257.2	236	59	206	5	0	0	0	97	26	2	.268
1963	21	9	.700	2.46	31	31	18	248.1	205	81	202	3	0	0	0	92	23	0	.250
1964	15	12	.556	3.30	36	36	14	267.1	245	98	213	1	0	0	0	94	17	0	.181
1965	9	3	.750	3.35	27	27	5	156	126	63	96	1	0	0	0	60	12	2	.200
1966	8	6	.571	4.89	21	19	2	103	113	30	56	0	0	0	0	37	8	0	.216
1967 **WAS A**	12	10	.545	3.28	28	27	5	164.2	147	43	106	1	0	0	0	51	9	0	.176
1968	13	12	.520	2.69	31	31	8	201	181	59	111	4	0	0	0	65	12	0	.185
1969 **2 teams**		WAS A (14G 2–5)		CIN N (5G 0–0)															
" total	2	5	.286	7.07	19	14	0	62.1	63	42	37	0	0	0	0	17	4	0	.235
1970 **LA N**	0	0	—	2.57	10	0	0	14	12	5	8	0	0	0	0	0	0	0	—
1971 **CLE A**	2	2	.500	3.13	9	1	0	23	17	11	20	0	2	1	0	5	3	0	.600
18 yrs.	174	170	.506	3.63	529	404	132	2930	2703	1069	2167	36	7	15	10	967	198	5	.205

WORLD SERIES
| 1965 **MIN A** | 0 | 1 | .000 | 5.40 | 1 | 1 | 0 | 5 | 8 | 1 | 0 | 0 | 0 | 0 | 0 | 1 | 0 | 0 | .000 |

Carlos Pascual

PASCUAL, CARLOS LUIS   BR TR 5'6½"   172 lbs.
Brother of Camilo Pascual.
B. Mar. 13, 1930, Havana, Cuba

	W	L	PCT	ERA	G	GS	CG	IP	H	BB	SO	ShO	W	L	SV	AB	H	HR	BA
1950 **WAS A**	1	1	.500	2.12	2	2	2	17	12	8	3	0	0	0	0	4	1	0	.250

Larry Pashnick

PASHNICK, LARRY J.   BR TR 6'3"   205 lbs.
B. Apr. 25, 1956, Lincoln Park, Mich.

	W	L	PCT	ERA	G	GS	CG	IP	H	BB	SO	ShO	W	L	SV	AB	H	HR	BA
1982 **DET A**	4	4	.500	4.01	28	13	1	94.1	110	25	19	0	1	0	0	0	0	0	—
1983	1	3	.250	5.26	12	6	0	37.2	48	18	17	0	1	0	0	0	0	0	—

	W	L	PCT	ERA	G	GS	CG	IP	H	BB	SO	ShO	Relief Pitching W	L	SV	BATTING AB	H	HR	BA

Harley Payne

PAYNE, HARLEY FENWICK (Lady)   TL 6'   160 lbs.
B. Jan. 9, 1866, Windsor, Ont., Canada   D. Dec. 29, 1935, Orwell, Ohio

	W	L	PCT	ERA	G	GS	CG	IP	H	BB	SO	ShO	W	L	SV	AB	H	HR	BA
1896 BKN N	14	16	.467	3.39	34	28	24	241.2	284	58	52	2	2	2	0	98	21	0	.214
1897	14	17	.452	4.63	40	38	30	280	350	71	86	1	0	0	0	110	26	0	.236
1898	1	0	1.000	4.00	1	1	1	9	11	3	2	0	0	0	0	4	3	0	.750
1899 PIT N	1	3	.250	3.76	5	5	2	26.1	33	4	8	0	0	0	0	10	1	0	.100
4 yrs.	30	36	.455	4.04	80	72	57	557	678	136	148	3	2	2	0	222	51	0	.230

Mike Payne

PAYNE, MICHAEL EARL   BR TR 5'11"   165 lbs.
B. Nov. 15, 1961, Woonsocket, R. I.

	W	L	PCT	ERA	G	GS	CG	IP	H	BB	SO	ShO	W	L	SV	AB	H	HR	BA
1984 ATL N	0	1	.000	6.35	3	1	0	5.2	7	3	3	0	0	0	0	1	0	0	.000

Mike Pazik

PAZIK, MICHAEL JOSEPH   BL TL 6'2"   195 lbs.
B. Jan. 26, 1950, Lynn, Mass.

	W	L	PCT	ERA	G	GS	CG	IP	H	BB	SO	ShO	W	L	SV	AB	H	HR	BA
1975 MIN A	0	4	.000	8.24	5	3	0	19.2	28	10	8	0	0	1	0	0	0	0	—
1976	0	0	—	7.00	5	0	0	9	13	4	6	0	0	0	0	0	0	0	—
1977	1	0	1.000	2.50	3	0	0	18	18	6	6	0	0	0	0	0	0	0	—
3 yrs.	1	4	.200	5.79	13	6	0	46.2	59	20	20	0	0	1	0	0	0	0	—

Frank Pearce

PEARCE, FRANK
B. Louisville, Ky.   Deceased.

	W	L	PCT	ERA	G	GS	CG	IP	H	BB	SO	ShO	W	L	SV	AB	H	HR	BA
1876 LOU N	0	0	—	4.50	1	0	0	4	5	1	1	0	0	0	0	2	0	0	.000

Frank Pearce

PEARCE, FRANKLIN THOMAS   BR TR 6'   170 lbs.
B. Aug. 31, 1905, Middletown, Ky.   D. Sept. 3, 1950, Van Buren, N. Y.

	W	L	PCT	ERA	G	GS	CG	IP	H	BB	SO	ShO	W	L	SV	AB	H	HR	BA
1933 PHI N	5	4	.556	3.62	20	7	3	82	78	29	18	1	2	2	0	26	5	0	.192
1934	0	2	.000	7.20	7	1	0	20	25	5	4	0	0	1	0	3	2	0	.667
1935	0	0	—	8.31	5	0	0	13	22	6	7	0	0	0	0	4	2	0	.500
3 yrs.	5	6	.455	4.77	32	8	3	115	125	40	29	1	2	3	0	33	9	0	.273

George Pearce

PEARCE, GEORGE THOMAS   BL TL 5'10½"   175 lbs.
B. Jan. 10, 1888, Aurora, Ill.   D. Oct. 11, 1935, Joliet, Ill.

	W	L	PCT	ERA	G	GS	CG	IP	H	BB	SO	ShO	W	L	SV	AB	H	HR	BA
1912 CHI N	0	0	—	5.52	3	2	0	14.2	15	12	9	0	0	0	0	6	1	0	.167
1913	13	5	.722	2.31	25	21	14	163.1	137	59	73	3	1	0	0	55	4	0	.073
1914	8	12	.400	3.51	30	16	4	141	122	65	78	0	2	3	1	45	4	0	.089
1915	13	9	.591	3.32	36	20	8	176	158	77	96	2	4	1	0	56	11	0	.196
1916	0	0	—	2.08	4	1	0	4.1	6	1	0	0	0	0	0	0	0	0	—
1917 STL N	1	1	.500	3.48	5	0	0	10.1	7	3	4	0	1	1	0	4	0	0	.000
6 yrs.	35	27	.565	3.11	103	60	26	509.2	445	217	260	5	8	5	1	166	20	0	.120

Jim Pearce

PEARCE, JAMES MADISON   BR TR 6'6"   180 lbs.
B. June 9, 1925, Zebulon, N. C.

	W	L	PCT	ERA	G	GS	CG	IP	H	BB	SO	ShO	W	L	SV	AB	H	HR	BA
1949 WAS A	0	1	.000	8.44	2	1	0	5.1	9	5	1	0	0	0	0	2	0	0	.000
1950	2	1	.667	6.04	20	3	1	56.2	58	37	18	0	1	1	0	13	2	0	.154
1953	0	1	.000	7.71	4	1	0	9.1	15	6	0	0	0	0	0	1	0	0	.000
1954 CIN N	1	0	1.000	2.45	2	1	1	11	7	5	3	0	0	0	0	3	0	0	.000
1955	0	1	.000	10.80	2	1	0	3.1	8	0	0	0	0	0	0	0	0	0	—
5 yrs.	3	4	.429	5.78	30	7	2	85.2	97	53	22	0	1	1	0	19	2	0	.105

Frank Pears

PEARS, FRANK H.
B. Aug. 30, 1866, Kentucky   D. Nov. 29, 1920, St. Louis, Mo.

	W	L	PCT	ERA	G	GS	CG	IP	H	BB	SO	ShO	W	L	SV	AB	H	HR	BA
1889 KC AA	0	2	.000	4.91	3	2	2	22	21	9	5	0	0	0	0	11	1	0	.091
1893 STL N	0	0	—	13.50	1	0	0	4	9	2	0	0	0	0	0	2	0	0	.000
2 yrs.	0	2	.000	6.23	4	2	2	26	30	11	5	0	0	0	0	13	1	0	.077

Alex Pearson

PEARSON, ALEXANDER FRANKLIN   BR TR 5'10½" 160 lbs.
B. Mar. 9, 1877, Greensboro, Pa.   D. Oct. 30, 1966, Rochester, Pa.

	W	L	PCT	ERA	G	GS	CG	IP	H	BB	SO	ShO	W	L	SV	AB	H	HR	BA
1902 STL N	2	6	.250	3.95	11	10	8	82	90	22	24	0	0	0	0	34	9	0	.265
1903 CLE A	1	2	.333	3.56	4	3	2	30.1	34	3	12	0	0	0	0	12	1	0	.083
2 yrs.	3	8	.273	3.85	15	13	10	112.1	124	25	36	0	0	0	0	46	10	0	.217

Dave Pearson

PEARSON, DAVID P.   BR TR 5'7"   142 lbs.
Born David P. Pierson.   Brother of Dick Pierson.
B. Aug. 20, 1855, Wilkes-Barre, Pa.   D. Nov. 11, 1922, Trenton, N. J.

	W	L	PCT	ERA	G	GS	CG	IP	H	BB	SO	ShO	W	L	SV	AB	H	HR	BA
1876 CIN N	0	1	.000	∞	1	1	0		2	0	0	0	0	0	0	*			

Ike Pearson

PEARSON, ISSAC OVERTON   BR TR 6'1"   180 lbs.
B. Mar. 1, 1917, Grenada, Miss.

	W	L	PCT	ERA	G	GS	CG	IP	H	BB	SO	ShO	W	L	SV	AB	H	HR	BA
1939 PHI N	2	13	.133	5.76	26	13	4	125	144	56	29	0	0	2	0	37	2	0	.054
1940	3	14	.176	5.45	29	20	5	145.1	160	57	43	1	0	1	1	44	9	0	.205
1941	4	14	.222	3.57	46	10	0	136	139	70	38	0	4	4	6	40	5	0	.125
1942	1	6	.143	4.54	35	7	0	85.1	87	50	21	0	1	1	0	23	1	0	.043
1946	1	0	1.000	3.77	5	2	1	14.1	19	8	6	1	0	0	0	5	1	1	.200
1948 CHI A	2	3	.400	4.92	23	2	0	53	62	27	12	0	1	2	1	10	2	0	.200
6 yrs.	13	50	.206	4.83	164	54	10	559	611	268	149	2	6	10	8	159	20	1	.126

Monte Pearson

PEARSON, MONTGOMERY MARCELLUS   BR TR 6'   175 lbs.
B. Sept. 2, 1909, Oakland, Calif.   D. Jan. 27, 1978, Fresno, Calif.

	W	L	PCT	ERA	G	GS	CG	IP	H	BB	SO	ShO	W	L	SV	AB	H	HR	BA
1932 CLE A	0	0	—	10.13	8	0	0	8	10	11	5	0	0	0	0	0	0	0	—
1933	10	5	.667	2.33	19	16	10	135.1	111	55	54	0	0	0	0	50	13	0	.260
1934	18	13	.581	4.52	39	33	19	254.2	257	130	140	0	2	1	2	92	25	1	.272
1935	8	13	.381	4.90	30	24	10	181.2	199	103	90	1	2	1	0	62	11	0	.177
1936 NY A	19	7	.731	3.71	33	31	15	223	191	135	118	1	1	0	1	91	23	1	.253
1937	9	3	.750	3.17	22	20	7	144.2	145	64	71	1	0	0	1	51	11	0	.216
1938	16	7	.696	3.97	28	27	17	202	198	113	98	1	0	0	0	76	13	0	.171
1939	12	5	.706	4.49	22	20	8	146.1	151	70	76	0	0	1	0	53	17	0	.321
1940	7	5	.583	3.69	16	16	7	109.2	108	44	43	1	0	0	0	33	4	0	.121

	W	L	PCT	ERA	G	GS	CG	IP	H	BB	SO	ShO	Relief Pitching W	L·	SV	BATTING AB	H	HR	BA

Monte Pearson continued

	W	L	PCT	ERA	G	GS	CG	IP	H	BB	SO	ShO	W	L	SV	AB	H	HR	BA
1941 CIN N	1	3	.250	5.18	7	4	1	24.1	22	15	8	0	0	0	0	5	0	0	.000
10 yrs.	100	61	.621	4.00	224	191	94	1429.2	1392	740	703	5	5	3	4	513	117	2	.228
WORLD SERIES																			
1936 NY A	1	0	1.000	2.00	1	1	1	9	7	2	7	0	0	0	0	4	2	0	.500
1937	1	0	1.000	1.04	1	1	0	8.2	5	2	4	0	0	0	0	3	0	0	.000
1938	1	0	1.000	1.00	1	1	1	9	5	2	9	0	0	0	0	3	1	0	.333
1939	1	0	1.000	0.00	1	1	1	9	2	1	8	1	0	0	0	2	0	0	.000
4 yrs.	4	0	1.000 1st	1.01 7th	4	4	3	35.2	19	7	28	1	0	0	0	12	3	0	.250

Marv Peasley

PEASLEY, MARVIN WARREN BL TL 6'1" 175 lbs.
B. July 16, 1889, Jonesport, Me. D. Dec. 27, 1948, San Francisco, Calif.

	W	L	PCT	ERA	G	GS	CG	IP	H	BB	SO	ShO	W	L	SV	AB	H	HR	BA
1910 DET A	0	1	.000	8.10	2	1	0	10	13	11	4	0	0	0	0	3	0	0	.000

George Pechiney

PECHINEY, GEORGE ADOLPHE BR TR 5'9" 184 lbs.
B. Sept. 20, 1861, Cincinnati, Ohio D. July 14, 1943, Cincinnati, Ohio

	W	L	PCT	ERA	G	GS	CG	IP	H	BB	SO	ShO	W	L	SV	AB	H	HR	BA
1885 CIN AA	7	4	.636	2.02	11	11	11	98	95	30	49	1	0	0	0	40	6	0	.150
1886	15	21	.417	4.14	40	40	35	330.1	355	133	110	2	0	0	0	144	30	1	.208
1887 CLE AA	1	9	.100	7.12	10	10	10	86	118	44	24	0	0	0	0	36	9	0	.250
3 yrs.	23	34	.404	4.23	61	61	56	514.1	568	207	183	3	0	0	0	220	45	1	.205

Steve Peek

PEEK, STEPHEN GEORGE BB TR 6'2" 195 lbs.
B. July 30, 1914, Springfield, Mass.

	W	L	PCT	ERA	G	GS	CG	IP	H	BB	SO	ShO	W	L	SV	AB	H	HR	BA
1941 NY A	4	2	.667	5.06	17	8	2	80	85	39	18	0	0	0	0	28	1	0	.036

Red Peery

PEERY, GEORGE A. BL TL 5'11" 160 lbs.
B. Aug. 15, 1906, Payson, Utah

	W	L	PCT	ERA	G	GS	CG	IP	H	BB	SO	ShO	W	L	SV	AB	H	HR	BA
1927 PIT N	0	0	—	0.00	1	0	0	1	0	1	0	0	0	0	0	0	0	0	—
1929 BOS N	0	1	.000	5.11	9	1	0	44	53	9	3	0	0	0	0	14	3	0	.214
2 yrs.	0	1	.000	5.00	10	1	0	45	53	10	3	0	0	0	0	14	3	0	.214

Heinie Peitz

PEITZ, HENRY CLEMENT BR TR 5'11" 165 lbs.
Brother of Joe Peitz.
B. Nov. 28, 1870, St. Louis, Mo. D. Oct. 23, 1943, Cincinnati, Ohio

	W	L	PCT	ERA	G	GS	CG	IP	H	BB	SO	ShO	W	L	SV	AB	H	HR	BA
1894 STL N	0	0	—	9.00	1	0	0	3	7	2	0	0	0	0	0	338	89	3	.263
1897 CIN N	0	1	.000	7.88	2	1	1	8	9	4	0	0	0	0	0	266	78	1	.293
1899	0	0	—	5.40	1	0	0	5	6	1	3	0	0	0	0	290	79	1	.272
3 yrs.	0	1	.000	7.31	4	1	1	16	22	7	3	0	0	0	0	*			

Barney Pelty

PELTY, BARNEY BR TR
B. Sept. 10, 1880, Farmington, Mo. D. May 24, 1939, Farmington, Mo.

	W	L	PCT	ERA	G	GS	CG	IP	H	BB	SO	ShO	W	L	SV	AB	H	HR	BA
1903 STL A	3	3	.500	2.40	7	6	5	48.2	49	15	20	0	0	0	1	20	3	0	.150
1904	15	18	.455	2.84	39	35	31	301	270	77	126	2	2	0	0	118	15	0	.127
1905	14	14	.500	2.75	31	28	26	258.2	222	68	114	1	1	0	0	98	15	0	.153
1906	16	11	.593	1.59	34	30	25	260.2	189	59	92	4	1	0	2	95	16	0	.168
1907	12	21	.364	2.57	36	31	29	273	234	64	85	5	0	3	1	95	16	0	.168
1908	7	4	.636	1.99	20	13	7	122	104	32	36	1	1	1	0	42	5	0	.119
1909	11	11	.500	2.30	27	23	17	199.1	158	53	88	5	0	2	0	91	15	0	.165
1910	5	11	.313	3.48	27	18	12	165.1	157	70	48	3	1	1	0	56	5	0	.089
1911	7	15	.318	2.83	28	22	18	207	197	69	59	1	0	2	0	65	9	0	.138
1912 2 teams		STL	A (6G 1-5)		WAS	A	(11G 1-4)												
" total	2	9	.182	4.37	17	10	3	82.1	83	25	25	0	1	2	0	21	2	0	.095
10 yrs.	92	117	.440	2.62	266	216	173	1918	1663	532	693	22	7	11	4	701	101	0	.144

Alejandro Pena

PENA, ALEJANDRO VASQUEZ BR TR 6'3" 200 lbs.
B. June 25, 1959, Cambiaso Puerto Plata, Dominican Republic

	W	L	PCT	ERA	G	GS	CG	IP	H	BB	SO	ShO	W	L	SV	AB	H	HR	BA
1981 LA N	1	1	.500	2.88	14	0	0	25	18	11	14	0	1	1	2	6	0	0	.000
1982	0	2	.000	4.79	29	0	0	35.2	37	21	20	0	0	2	0	0	0	0	—
1983	12	9	.571	2.75	34	26	4	177	152	51	120	3	2	1	1	60	6	1	.100
1984	12	6	.667	2.48	28	28	8	199.1	186	46	135	4	0	0	0	66	8	0	.121
4 yrs.	25	18	.581	2.80	105	54	12	437	393	129	289	7	3	4	3	132	14	1	.106
LEAGUE CHAMPIONSHIP SERIES																			
1981 LA N	0	0	—	0.00	2	0	0	2.1	1	0	0	0	0	0	0	0	0	0	—
1983	0	0	—	6.75	1	0	0	2.2	4	1	3	0	0	0	0	1	1	0	1.000
2 yrs.	0	0	—	3.60	3	0	0	5	5	1	3	0	0	0	0	1	1	0	1.000

Jose Pena

PENA, JOSE BR TR 6'2" 190 lbs.
B. Dec. 3, 1942, Ciudad Juarez, Mexico

	W	L	PCT	ERA	G	GS	CG	IP	H	BB	SO	ShO	W	L	SV	AB	H	HR	BA
1969 CIN N	1	1	.500	18.00	6	0	0	5	10	5	3	0	1	1	0	0	0	0	—
1970 LA N	4	3	.571	4.42	29	0	0	57	51	29	31	0	4	3	4	8	1	0	.125
1971	2	0	1.000	3.56	21	0	0	43	32	18	44	0	2	0	1	3	2	0	.667
1972	0	0	—	8.59	5	0	0	7.1	13	6	4	0	0	0	0	0	0	0	—
4 yrs.	7	4	.636	4.97	61	0	0	112.1	106	58	82	0	7	4	5	11	3	0	.273

Orlando Pena

PENA, ORLANDO GREGORY BR TR 5'11" 154 lbs.
B. Nov. 17, 1933, Victoria de las Tunas, Cuba

	W	L	PCT	ERA	G	GS	CG	IP	H	BB	SO	ShO	W	L	SV	AB	H	HR	BA
1958 CIN N	1	0	1.000	0.60	9	0	0	15	10	4	11	0	1	0	3	0	0	0	—
1959	5	9	.357	4.76	46	8	1	136	150	39	76	0	2	4	5	34	3	0	.088
1960	0	1	.000	2.89	4	0	0	9.1	8	3	9	0	0	1	0	1	0	0	.000
1962 KC A	6	4	.600	3.01	13	12	6	89.2	71	27	56	1	0	0	0	31	5	0	.161
1963	12	20	.375	3.69	35	33	9	217	218	53	128	3	1	0	0	62	9	1	.145
1964	12	14	.462	4.43	40	32	5	219.1	231	73	184	0	0	0	0	75	12	1	.160
1965 2 teams		KC	A (12G 0-6)		DET	A	(30G 4-6)												
" total	4	12	.250	4.18	42	5	0	92.2	96	33	79	0	4	7	4	17	3	0	.176

	W	L	PCT	ERA	G	GS	CG	IP	H	BB	SO	ShO	Relief Pitching W	L	SV	BATTING AB	H	HR	BA

Orlando Pena continued

	W	L	PCT	ERA	G	GS	CG	IP	H	BB	SO	ShO	W	L	SV	AB	H	HR	BA
1966 DET A	4	2	.667	3.08	54	0	0	108	105	35	79	0	4	2	7	18	2	0	.111
1967 2 teams		DET	A (2G 0–1)		CLE	A	(48G 0–3)												
" total	0	4	.000	3.59	50	1	0	90.1	72	22	74	0	0	3	8	8	0	0	.000
1970 PIT N	2	1	.667	4.74	23	0	0	38	38	7	25	0	2	1	2	6	0	0	.000
1971 BAL A	0	1	.000	3.00	5	0	0	15	16	5	4	0	0	1	0	3	0	0	.000
1973 2 teams		BAL	A (11G 1–1)		STL	N	(42G 4–4)												
" total	5	5	.500	2.94	53	2	0	107	96	22	61	0	5	5	7	7	1	0	.143
1974 2 teams		STL	N (42G 5–2)		CAL	A	(4G 0–0)												
" total	5	2	.714	2.21	46	0	0	53	51	21	28	0	5	2	4	2	1	0	.500
1975 CAL A	0	2	.000	2.13	7	0	0	12.2	13	8	4	0	0	2	0	0	0	0	–
14 yrs.	56	77	.421	3.70	427	93	21	1203	1175	352	818	4	24	28	40	264	36	2	.136

Russ Pence

PENCE, RUSSELL WILLIAM   BR TR 6'   185 lbs.
B. Mar. 11, 1900, Marine, Ill.   D. Aug. 11, 1971, Hot Springs, Ark.

	W	L	PCT	ERA	G	GS	CG	IP	H	BB	SO	ShO	W	L	SV	AB	H	HR	BA
1921 CHI A	0	0	–	8.44	4	0	0	5.1	6	7	2	0	0	0	0	1	0	0	.000

Ken Penner

PENNER, KENNETH WILLIAM   BL TR 5'11½" 170 lbs.
B. Apr. 24, 1896, Booneville, Ind.   D. May 28, 1959, Sacramento, Calif.

	W	L	PCT	ERA	G	GS	CG	IP	H	BB	SO	ShO	W	L	SV	AB	H	HR	BA
1916 CLE A	1	0	1.000	4.26	4	2	0	12.2	14	4	5	0	0	0	0	2	0	0	.000
1929 CHI N	0	1	.000	2.84	5	0	0	12.2	14	6	3	0	0	1	0	4	1	0	.250
2 yrs.	1	1	.500	3.55	9	2	0	25.1	28	10	8	0	0	1	0	6	1	0	.167

Kewpie Pennington

PENNINGTON, GEORGE LOUIS   BR TR 5'8½" 168 lbs.
B. Sept. 24, 1896, New York, N. Y.   D. May 3, 1953, Newark, N. J.

	W	L	PCT	ERA	G	GS	CG	IP	H	BB	SO	ShO	W	L	SV	AB	H	HR	BA
1917 STL A	0	0	–	0.00	1	0	0	1	1	0	0	0	0	0	0	0	0	0	–

Herb Pennock

PENNOCK, HERBERT JEFFERIS (The Knight of Kennett Square)   BB TL 6'   160 lbs.
B. Feb. 10, 1894, Kennett Square, Pa.   BL 1934
D. Jan. 30, 1948, New York, N. Y.
Hall of Fame 1948.

	W	L	PCT	ERA	G	GS	CG	IP	H	BB	SO	ShO	W	L	SV	AB	H	HR	BA
1912 PHI A	1	2	.333	4.50	17	2	1	50	48	30	38	0	1	1	2	15	2	0	.133
1913	2	1	.667	5.13	14	4	1	33.1	30	22	17	0	1	0	0	9	1	0	.111
1914	11	4	.733	2.79	28	14	8	151.2	136	65	90	3	2	2	3	56	12	0	.214
1915 2 teams		PHI	A (11G 3–6)		BOS	A	(5G 0–0)												
" total	3	6	.333	6.36	16	9	3	58	69	39	31	1	0	1	1	24	6	0	.250
1916 BOS A	0	2	.000	3.04	9	2	0	26.2	23	8	12	0	0	0	1	8	1	0	.125
1917	5	5	.500	3.31	24	5	4	100.2	90	23	35	1	2	3	1	24	4	0	.167
1919	16	8	.667	2.71	32	26	16	219	223	48	70	5	1	0	0	75	13	0	.173
1920	16	13	.552	3.68	37	31	19	242.1	244	61	68	4	3	0	2	77	20	0	.260
1921	12	14	.462	4.04	32	32	15	222.2	268	59	91	1	0	0	0	85	18	1	.212
1922	10	17	.370	4.32	32	26	15	202	230	74	59	1	1	1	1	65	9	0	.138
1923 NY A	19	6	.760	3.33	35	27	21	224.1	235	68	93	1	1	0	3	83	16	0	.193
1924	21	9	.700	2.83	40	34	25	286.1	302	64	101	4	1	0	3	101	16	2	.158
1925	16	17	.485	2.96	47	31	21	277	267	71	88	2	1	2	2	99	20	0	.202
1926	23	11	.676	3.62	40	33	19	266.1	294	43	78	1	2	1	2	85	18	0	.212
1927	19	8	.704	3.00	34	26	18	209.2	225	48	51	1	2	0	2	69	15	0	.217
1928	17	6	.739	2.56	28	24	19	211	215	40	53	5	0	0	3	74	15	0	.203
1929	9	11	.450	4.90	27	23	8	158	205	28	49	1	0	1	2	51	9	0	.176
1930	11	7	.611	4.32	25	19	11	156.1	194	20	46	1	1	1	0	60	11	0	.183
1931	11	6	.647	4.28	25	25	12	189.1	247	30	65	1	0	0	0	66	10	1	.152
1932	9	5	.643	4.60	22	21	9	146.2	191	38	54	1	0	1	0	53	8	0	.151
1933	7	4	.636	5.54	23	5	5	65	96	21	22	1	3	3	4	21	5	0	.238
1934 BOS A	2	0	1.000	3.05	30	2	1	62	68	16	16	0	1	0	1	14	3	0	.214
22 yrs.	240	162	.597	3.61	617	421	248	3558.1	3900	916	1227	35	23	17	33	1214	232	4	.191

WORLD SERIES

	W	L	PCT	ERA	G	GS	CG	IP	H	BB	SO	ShO	W	L	SV	AB	H	HR	BA
1914 PHI A	0	0	–	0.00	1	0	0	3	2	2	3	0	0	0	0	1	0	0	.000
1923 NY A	2	0	1.000	3.63	3	2	1	17.1	19	1	8	0	0	0	1	6	0	0	.000
1926	2	0	1.000	1.23	3	2	2	22	13	4	8	0	0	0	0	7	1	0	.143
1927	1	0	1.000	1.00	1	1	1	9	3	0	1	0	0	0	0	4	0	0	.000
1932	0	0	–	2.25	2	0	0	4	2	1	4	0	0	0	2	1	0	0	.000
5 yrs.	5	0	1.000	1.95	10	5	4	55.1	39	8	24	0	0	0	3	19	1	0	.053
	8th		1st												4th				

Paul Penson

PENSON, PAUL EUGENE   BR TR 6'1"   185 lbs.
B. July 12, 1931, Kansas City, Kans.

	W	L	PCT	ERA	G	GS	CG	IP	H	BB	SO	ShO	W	L	SV	AB	H	HR	BA
1954 PHI N	1	1	.500	4.50	5	3	0	16	14	14	3	0	0	0	0	7	0	0	.000

Gene Pentz

PENTZ, EUGENE DAVID   BR TR 6'1"   200 lbs.
B. June 21, 1953, Johnstown, Pa.

	W	L	PCT	ERA	G	GS	CG	IP	H	BB	SO	ShO	W	L	SV	AB	H	HR	BA
1975 DET A	0	4	.000	3.20	13	0	0	25.1	27	20	21	0	0	4	0	0	0	0	–
1976 HOU N	3	3	.500	2.95	40	0	0	64	62	31	36	0	3	3	5	5	1	0	.200
1977	5	2	.714	3.83	41	4	0	87	76	44	51	0	3	0	2	13	0	0	.000
1978	0	0	–	6.00	10	0	0	15	12	13	8	0	0	0	0	1	0	0	.000
4 yrs.	8	9	.471	3.62	104	4	0	191.1	177	108	116	0	6	7	7	19	1	0	.053

Jimmy Peoples

PEOPLES, JAMES ELSWORTH   TR   165 lbs.
B. Oct. 8, 1863, Big Beaver, Mich.   D. Aug. 29, 1920, Detroit, Mich.

	W	L	PCT	ERA	G	GS	CG	IP	H	BB	SO	ShO	W	L	SV	AB	H	HR	BA
1885 CIN AA	0	2	.000	12.00	2	2	1	15	30	2	4	0	0	0	0	*			

Bill Pepper

PEPPER, WILLIAM HARRISON
B. Sept., 1866, Ky.   D. Nov. 5, 1903, Webb City, Mo.

	W	L	PCT	ERA	G	GS	CG	IP	H	BB	SO	ShO	W	L	SV	AB	H	HR	BA
1894 LOU N	0	1	.000	6.75	2	1	0	8	10	4	0	0	0	0	0	4	0	0	.000

	W	L	PCT	ERA	G	GS	CG	IP	H	BB	SO	ShO	Relief Pitching W	L	SV	Batting AB	H	HR	BA

Bob Pepper

PEPPER, ROBERT ERNEST
B. May 3, 1895, Rosston, Pa. D. Apr. 8, 1968, Fort Cliff, Pa. BR TR 6'2" 178 lbs.

	W	L	PCT	ERA	G	GS	CG	IP	H	BB	SO	ShO	W	L	SV	AB	H	HR	BA
1915 PHI A	0	0	–	1.80	1	0	0	5	6	4	0	0	0	0	0	2	0	0	.000

Laurin Pepper

PEPPER, HUGH McLAURIN
B. Jan. 18, 1931, Vaughan, Miss. BR TR 5'11" 190 lbs.

	W	L	PCT	ERA	G	GS	CG	IP	H	BB	SO	ShO	W	L	SV	AB	H	HR	BA
1954 PIT N	1	5	.167	7.99	14	8	0	50.2	63	43	17	0	0	0	0	17	4	0	.235
1955	0	1	.000	10.35	14	1	0	20	30	25	7	0	0	0	0	2	0	0	.000
1956	1	1	.500	3.00	11	7	0	30	30	25	12	0	0	0	0	6	0	0	.000
1957	0	1	.000	8.00	5	1	0	9	11	5	4	0	0	1	0	0	0	0	–
4 yrs.	2	8	.200	7.06	44	17	0	109.2	134	98	40	0	0	1	0	25	4	0	.160

Luis Peraza

PERAZA, LUIS
B. June 17, 1943, Rio Piedras, Puerto Rico BR TR 5'11" 185 lbs.

	W	L	PCT	ERA	G	GS	CG	IP	H	BB	SO	ShO	W	L	SV	AB	H	HR	BA
1969 PHI N	0	0	–	6.00	8	0	0	9	12	2	7	0	0	0	0	1	0	0	.000

Hub Perdue

PERDUE, HERBERT RODNEY (The Gallatin Squash) BR TR 5'10½" 192 lbs.
B. June 7, 1882, Bethpage, Tenn. D. Oct. 31, 1968, Gallatin, Tenn.

	W	L	PCT	ERA	G	GS	CG	IP	H	BB	SO	ShO	W	L	SV	AB	H	HR	BA
1911 BOS N	6	10	.375	4.98	24	19	9	137.1	180	41	40	0	0	0	1	48	10	0	.208
1912	13	16	.448	3.80	37	30	20	249	295	54	101	1	0	2	3	87	12	0	.138
1913	16	13	.552	3.26	38	32	16	212.1	201	39	91	3	2	0	1	67	7	0	.104
1914 2 teams								BOS N (9G 2–5)		STL N (22G 8–8)									
" total	10	13	.435	3.57	31	28	14	204.1	220	46	56	0	0	0	1	62	9	0	.145
1915 STL N	6	12	.333	4.21	31	13	5	115.1	141	19	29	1	3	5	1	36	4	0	.111
5 yrs.	51	64	.443	3.85	161	122	64	918.1	1037	199	317	5	5	7	7	300	42	0	.140

George Perez

PEREZ, GEORGE THOMAS
B. Dec. 29, 1937, San Fernando, Calif. BR TR 6'2½" 200 lbs.

	W	L	PCT	ERA	G	GS	CG	IP	H	BB	SO	ShO	W	L	SV	AB	H	HR	BA
1958 PIT N	0	1	.000	5.40	4	0	0	8.1	9	4	2	0	0	1	1	2	0	0	.000

Pascual Perez

PEREZ, PASCUAL GROSS
B. May 17, 1957, Haina, Dominican Republic BR TR 6'2" 162 lbs.

	W	L	PCT	ERA	G	GS	CG	IP	H	BB	SO	ShO	W	L	SV	AB	H	HR	BA
1980 PIT N	0	1	.000	3.75	2	2	0	12	15	2	7	0	0	0	0	4	1	0	.250
1981	2	7	.222	3.98	17	13	2	86	92	34	46	0	0	1	0	22	3	0	.136
1982 ATL N	4	4	.500	3.06	16	11	0	79.1	85	17	29	0	2	0	0	18	3	0	.167
1983	15	8	.652	3.43	33	33	7	215.1	213	51	144	1	0	0	0	75	12	0	.160
1984	14	8	.636	3.74	30	30	4	211.2	208	51	145	1	0	0	0	66	5	0	.076
5 yrs.	35	28	.556	3.57	98	89	13	604.1	613	155	371	2	2	1	0	185	24	0	.130
LEAGUE CHAMPIONSHIP SERIES																			
1982 ATL N	0	1	.000	5.19	2	1	0	8.2	10	2	4	0	0	0	0	3	0	0	.000

Cecil Perkins

PERKINS, CECIL BOYCE
B. Dec. 1, 1940, Baltimore, Md. BR TR 6' 175 lbs.

	W	L	PCT	ERA	G	GS	CG	IP	H	BB	SO	ShO	W	L	SV	AB	H	HR	BA
1967 NY A	0	1	.000	9.00	2	1	0	6	6	2	1	0	0	0	0	1	0	0	.000

Charlie Perkins

PERKINS, CHARLES SULLIVAN (Lefty)
B. Sept. 9, 1905, Birmingham, Ala. BR TL 6' 175 lbs.

	W	L	PCT	ERA	G	GS	CG	IP	H	BB	SO	ShO	W	L	SV	AB	H	HR	BA
1930 PHI A	0	0	–	6.46	8	1	0	23.2	25	15	15	0	0	0	0	8	1	0	.125
1934 BKN N	0	3	.000	8.51	11	2	0	24.1	37	14	5	0	0	1	0	7	2	0	.286
2 yrs.	0	3	.000	7.50	19	3	0	48	62	29	20	0	0	1	0	15	3	0	.200

John Perkovich

PERKOVICH, JOHN JOSEPH
B. Mar. 10, 1924, Chicago, Ill. BR TR 5'11" 175 lbs.

	W	L	PCT	ERA	G	GS	CG	IP	H	BB	SO	ShO	W	L	SV	AB	H	HR	BA
1950 CHI A	0	0	–	7.20	1	0	0	5	7	1	3	0	0	0	0	1	0	0	.000

Harry Perkowski

PERKOWSKI, HARRY WALTER
B. Sept. 6, 1922, Dante, Va. BL TL 6'2½" 196 lbs.

	W	L	PCT	ERA	G	GS	CG	IP	H	BB	SO	ShO	W	L	SV	AB	H	HR	BA
1947 CIN N	0	0	–	3.68	3	1	0	7.1	12	3	2	0	0	0	0	1	0	0	.000
1949	1	1	.500	4.56	5	3	2	23.2	21	14	3	0	0	0	0	9	3	0	.333
1950	0	0	–	5.24	22	0	0	34.1	36	23	19	0	0	0	0	22	7	0	.318
1951	3	6	.333	2.82	35	7	1	102	96	46	56	0	0	2	1	25	1	0	.040
1952	12	10	.545	3.80	33	24	11	194	197	89	86	1	0	0	0	75	12	0	.160
1953	12	11	.522	4.52	33	25	9	193	204	62	70	2	2	0	2	69	14	0	.203
1954	2	8	.200	6.11	28	12	3	95.2	100	62	32	1	0	2	0	25	4	1	.160
1955 CHI N	3	4	.429	5.29	25	4	0	47.2	53	25	28	0	3	1	2	13	2	0	.154
8 yrs.	33	40	.452	4.37	184	76	24	697.2	719	324	296	4	5	7	5	239	43	1	.180

Len Perme

PERME, LEONARD JOHN
B. Nov. 25, 1917, Cleveland, Ohio BL TL 6' 170 lbs.

	W	L	PCT	ERA	G	GS	CG	IP	H	BB	SO	ShO	W	L	SV	AB	H	HR	BA
1942 CHI A	0	1	.000	1.38	4	1	1	13	5	4	4	0	0	0	0	3	1	0	.333
1946	0	0	–	8.31	4	0	0	4.1	6	7	2	0	0	0	0	0	0	0	–
2 yrs.	0	1	.000	3.12	8	1	1	17.1	11	11	6	0	0	0	0	3	1	0	.333

Hub Pernoll

PERNOLL, HENRY HUBBARD BR TL
B. Mar. 14, 1888, Grant's Pass, Ore. D. Feb. 18, 1944, Grant's Pass, Ore.

	W	L	PCT	ERA	G	GS	CG	IP	H	BB	SO	ShO	W	L	SV	AB	H	HR	BA
1910 DET A	4	3	.571	2.96	11	5	4	54.2	54	14	25	0	0	2	0	16	1	0	.063
1912	0	0	–	6.00	3	0	0	9	9	4	3	0	0	0	0	3	0	0	.000
2 yrs.	4	3	.571	3.39	14	5	4	63.2	63	18	28	0	0	2	0	19	1	0	.053

Ron Perranoski

PERRANOSKI, RONALD PETER
B. Apr. 1, 1936, Paterson, N. J. BL TL 6' 180 lbs.

	W	L	PCT	ERA	G	GS	CG	IP	H	BB	SO	ShO	W	L	SV	AB	H	HR	BA
1961 LA N	7	5	.583	2.65	53	1	0	91.2	82	41	56	0	7	5	6	12	1	0	.083
1962	6	6	.500	2.85	70	0	0	107.1	103	36	68	0	6	6	20	14	1	0	.071
1963	16	3	.842	1.67	69	0	0	129	112	43	75	0	16	3	21	24	3	0	.125
1964	5	7	.417	3.09	72	0	0	125.1	128	46	79	0	5	7	14	19	2	0	.105
1965	6	6	.500	2.24	59	0	0	104.2	85	40	53	0	6	6	17	19	3	0	.158

	W	L	PCT	ERA	G	GS	CG	IP	H	BB	SO	ShO	Relief Pitching W	L	SV	BATTING AB	H	HR	BA

Ron Perranoski continued

	W	L	PCT	ERA	G	GS	CG	IP	H	BB	SO	ShO	W	L	SV	AB	H	HR	BA
1966	6	7	.462	3.18	55	0	0	82	82	31	50	0	6	7	7	8	2	0	.250
1967	6	7	.462	2.45	70	0	0	110	97	45	75	0	6	7	16	10	1	0	.100
1968 MIN A	8	7	.533	3.10	66	0	0	87	86	38	65	0	8	7	6	7	0	0	.000
1969	9	10	.474	2.11	75	0	0	119.2	85	52	62	0	9	10	31	24	2	0	.083
1970	7	8	.467	2.43	67	0	0	111	108	42	55	0	7	8	34	24	1	0	.042
1971 2 teams		MIN	MIN A (36G 1–4)		DET	A (11G 0–1)													
" total	1	5	.167	5.49	47	0	0	60.2	76	31	29	0	1	5	7	5	0	0	.000
1972 2 teams		DET	DET A (17G 0–1)		LA	N (9G 2–0)													
" total	2	1	.667	5.30	26	0	0	35.2	42	16	15	0	2	1	0	1	0	0	.000
1973 CAL A	0	2	.000	4.09	8	0	0	11	11	7	5	0	0	2	0	0	0	0	–
13 yrs.	79	74	.516	2.79	737	1	0	1175	1097	468	687	0	79	74	179	167	16	0	.096
															10th				

LEAGUE CHAMPIONSHIP SERIES

	W	L	PCT	ERA	G	GS	CG	IP	H	BB	SO	ShO	W	L	SV	AB	H	HR	BA
1969 MIN A	0	1	.000	5.79	3	0	0	4.2	8	0	2	0	0	1	0	1	0	0	.000
1970	0	0	–	19.29	2	0	0	2.1	5	1	3	0	0	0	0	0	0	0	–
2 yrs.	0	1	.000	10.29	5	0	0	7	13	1	5	0	0	1	0	1	0	0	.000

WORLD SERIES

	W	L	PCT	ERA	G	GS	CG	IP	H	BB	SO	ShO	W	L	SV	AB	H	HR	BA
1963 LA N	0	0	–	0.00	1	0	0	.2	1	0	1	0	0	0	1	0	0	0	–
1965	0	0	–	7.36	2	0	0	3.2	3	4	1	0	0	0	0	0	0	0	–
1966	0	0	–	5.40	2	0	0	3.1	4	1	2	0	0	0	0	0	0	0	–
3 yrs.	0	0	–	5.87	5	0	0	7.2	8	5	4	0	0	0	1	0	0	0	–

Bill Perrin

PERRIN, WILLIAM JOSEPH (Lefty)   BR TL 5'11"   172 lbs.
B. June 23, 1911, New Orleans, La.   D. June 30, 1974, New Orleans, La.

	W	L	PCT	ERA	G	GS	CG	IP	H	BB	SO	ShO	W	L	SV	AB	H	HR	BA
1934 CLE A	0	1	.000	14.40	1	1	0	5	13	2	3	0	0	0	0	2	0	0	.000

George Perring

PERRING, GEORGE WILSON   BR TR 6'   190 lbs.
B. Aug. 13, 1884, Sharon, Wis.   D. Aug. 20, 1960, Beloit, Wis.

	W	L	PCT	ERA	G	GS	CG	IP	H	BB	SO	ShO	W	L	SV	AB	H	HR	BA
1914 KC F	0	0	–	13.50	1	0	0	.2	2	1	0	0	0	0	0	*			

Pol Perritt

PERRITT, WILLIAM DAYTON   BR TR 6'   175 lbs.
B. Aug. 30, 1892, Arcadia, La.   D. Oct. 15, 1947, Shreveport, La.

	W	L	PCT	ERA	G	GS	CG	IP	H	BB	SO	ShO	W	L	SV	AB	H	HR	BA
1912 STL N	1	1	.500	3.19	6	3	1	31	25	10	13	0	0	0	0	9	2	0	.222
1913	6	14	.300	5.25	36	21	8	175	205	64	64	0	3	0	0	59	12	0	.203
1914	16	13	.552	2.36	41	32	18	286	248	93	115	3	2	1	2	92	13	0	.141
1915 NY N	12	18	.400	2.66	35	30	16	220	226	59	91	4	1	1	0	68	11	0	.162
1916	18	11	.621	2.62	40	28	17	251	243	56	115	5	2	5	2	83	7	0	.084
1917	17	7	.708	1.88	35	26	14	215	186	45	72	5	2	3	1	70	11	0	.157
1918	18	13	.581	2.74	35	31	19	233	212	38	60	6	1	1	0	80	14	0	.175
1919	1	1	.500	7.11	11	3	0	19	27	12	2	0	1	0	1	4	0	0	.000
1920	0	0	–	1.80	8	0	0	15	9	4	3	0	0	0	2	4	0	0	.000
1921 2 teams		NY	NY N (5G 2–0)		DET	A (4G 1–0)													
" total	3	0	1.000	4.38	9	3	0	24.2	35	9	8	0	2	0	0	8	2	0	.250
10 yrs.	92	78	.541	2.89	256	177	93	1469.2	1416	390	543	23	14	11	8	477	72	0	.151

WORLD SERIES

	W	L	PCT	ERA	G	GS	CG	IP	H	BB	SO	ShO	W	L	SV	AB	H	HR	BA
1917 NY N	0	0	–	2.16	3	0	0	8.1	9	3	3	0	0	0	0	2	2	0	1.000

Gaylord Perry

PERRY, GAYLORD JACKSON   BR TR 6'4"   205 lbs.
Brother of Jim Perry.
B. Sept. 15, 1938, Williamston, N. C.

	W	L	PCT	ERA	G	GS	CG	IP	H	BB	SO	ShO	W	L	SV	AB	H	HR	BA
1962 SF N	3	1	.750	5.23	13	7	1	43	54	14	20	0	0	0	0	13	3	0	.231
1963	1	6	.143	4.03	31	4	0	76	84	29	52	0	1	5	2	18	4	0	.222
1964	12	11	.522	2.75	44	19	5	206.1	179	43	155	2	6	5	5	56	3	0	.054
1965	8	12	.400	4.19	47	26	6	195.2	194	70	170	0	1	1	1	64	10	0	.156
1966	21	8	.724	2.99	36	35	13	255.2	242	40	201	3	1	0	0	86	16	0	.186
1967	15	17	.469	2.61	39	37	18	293	231	84	230	3	0	1	1	91	13	0	.143
1968	16	15	.516	2.45	39	38	19	290.2	240	59	173	3	0	0	1	97	11	0	.113
1969	19	14	.576	2.49	40	39	26	325	290	91	233	3	0	0	0	117	14	1	.120
1970	23	13	.639	3.20	41	41	23	329	292	84	214	5	0	0	0	120	14	1	.117
1971	16	12	.571	2.76	37	37	14	280	255	67	158	2	0	0	0	98	10	1	.102
1972 CLE A	24	16	.600	1.92	41	40	29	343	253	82	234	5	0	0	1	110	17	1	.155
1973	19	19	.500	3.38	41	41	29	344	315	115	238	7	0	0	0	0	0	0	–
1974	21	13	.618	2.52	37	37	28	322	230	99	216	4	0	0	0	0	0	0	–
1975 2 teams		CLE	CLE A (15G 6–9)		TEX	A (22G 12–8)													
" total	18	17	.514	3.24	37	37	25	305.2	277	70	233	5	0	0	0	0	0	0	–
1976 TEX A	15	14	.517	3.24	32	32	21	250	232	52	143	2	0	0	0	0	0	0	–
1977	15	12	.556	3.37	34	34	13	238	239	56	177	4	0	0	0	0	0	0	–
1978 SD N	21	6	.778	2.72	37	37	5	261	241	66	154	2	0	0	0	87	8	0	.092
1979	12	11	.522	3.05	32	32	10	233	225	67	140	0	0	0	0	71	6	1	.085
1980 2 teams		TEX	TEX A (24G 6–9)		NY	A (10G 4–4)													
" total	10	13	.435	3.67	34	32	6	206	224	64	135	2	1	0	0	0	0	0	–
1981 ATL N	8	9	.471	3.93	23	23	3	151	182	24	60	0	0	0	0	48	12	1	.250
1982 SEA A	10	12	.455	4.40	32	32	6	216.2	245	54	116	0	0	0	0	0	0	0	–
1983 2 teams		SEA	SEA A (16G 3–10)		KC	A (14G 4–4)													
" total	7	14	.333	4.64	30	30	3	186.1	214	49	82	1	0	0	0	0	0	0	–
22 yrs.	314	265	.542	3.10	777	690	303	5351	4938	1379	3534	53	9	12	11	1076	141	6	.131
			4th				4th				3rd								

LEAGUE CHAMPIONSHIP SERIES

	W	L	PCT	ERA	G	GS	CG	IP	H	BB	SO	ShO	W	L	SV	AB	H	HR	BA
1971 SF N	1	1	.500	6.14	2	2	0	14.2	19	3	11	0	0	0	0	4	1	0	.250

Jim Perry

PERRY, JAMES EVAN   BB TR 6'4"   190 lbs.
Brother of Gaylord Perry.
B. Oct. 3, 1936, Williamston, N. C.

	W	L	PCT	ERA	G	GS	CG	IP	H	BB	SO	ShO	W	L	SV	AB	H	HR	BA
1959 CLE A	12	10	.545	2.65	44	13	8	153	122	55	79	2	5	4	4	50	15	0	.300
1960	18	10	.643	3.62	41	36	10	261.1	257	91	120	4	1	0	1	91	22	0	.242

	W	L	PCT	ERA	G	GS	CG	IP	H	BB	SO	ShO	Relief Pitching W	L	SV	BATTING AB	H	HR	BA

Jim Perry continued

	W	L	PCT	ERA	G	GS	CG	IP	H	BB	SO	ShO	W	L	SV	AB	H	HR	BA
1961	10	17	.370	4.71	35	35	6	223.2	238	87	90	1	0	0	0	73	12	0	.164
1962	12	12	.500	4.14	35	27	7	193.2	213	59	74	3	0	0	0	60	11	0	.183
1963 2 teams		CLE	A (5G 0–0)		MIN	A	(35G 9–9)												
" total	9	9	.500	3.83	40	25	5	178.2	179	59	72	1	0	1	1	53	11	0	.208
1964 MIN A	6	3	.667	3.44	42	1	0	65.1	61	23	55	0	6	2	2	13	2	0	.154
1965	12	7	.632	2.63	36	19	4	167.2	142	47	88	2	5	0	0	53	9	0	.170
1966	11	7	.611	2.54	33	25	8	184.1	149	53	122	1	0	0	0	59	13	1	.220
1967	8	7	.533	3.03	37	11	3	130.2	123	50	94	2	3	4	0	42	8	1	.190
1968	8	6	.571	2.27	32	18	3	139	113	26	69	2	1	0	1	42	6	2	.143
1969	20	6	.769	2.82	46	36	12	261.2	244	66	153	3	3	0	0	93	16	0	.172
1970	24	12	.667	3.03	40	40	13	279	258	57	168	4	0	0	0	97	24	1	.247
1971	17	17	.500	4.23	40	39	8	270	263	102	126	0	0	0	1	92	17	0	.185
1972	13	16	.448	3.34	35	35	5	218	191	60	85	2	0	0	0	71	11	0	.155
1973 DET A	14	13	.519	4.03	35	34	7	203	225	55	66	1	0	0	0	0	0	0	—
1974 CLE A	17	12	.586	2.96	36	36	8	252	242	64	71	3	0	0	0	0	0	0	—
1975 2 teams		CLE	A (8G 1–6)		OAK	A	(15G 3–4)												
" total	4	10	.286	5.38	23	17	2	105.1	107	44	44	1	0	1	0	0	0	0	—
17 yrs.	215	174	.553	3.45	630	447	109	3286.1	3127	998	1576	32	24	12	10	889	177	5	.199

LEAGUE CHAMPIONSHIP SERIES

	W	L	PCT	ERA	G	GS	CG	IP	H	BB	SO	ShO	W	L	SV	AB	H	HR	BA
1969 MIN A	0	0	—	3.38	1	1	0	8	6	3	3	0	0	0	0	3	0	0	.000
1970	0	1	.000	13.50	2	1	0	5.1	10	1	3	0	0	0	0	1	0	0	.000
2 yrs.	0	1	.000	7.43	3	2	0	13.1	16	4	6	0	0	0	0	4	0	0	.000

WORLD SERIES

	W	L	PCT	ERA	G	GS	CG	IP	H	BB	SO	ShO	W	L	SV	AB	H	HR	BA
1965 MIN A	0	0	—	4.50	2	0	0	4	5	2	4	0	0	0	0	0	0	0	—

Scott Perry

PERRY, HERBERT SCOTT   BL TR 6'1"   195 lbs.
B. Apr. 17, 1891, Dennison, Tex.   D. Oct. 27, 1959, Kansas City, Mo.

	W	L	PCT	ERA	G	GS	CG	IP	H	BB	SO	ShO	W	L	SV	AB	H	HR	BA
1915 STL A	0	0	—	13.50	1	1	0	2	5	1	0	0	0	0	0	0	0	0	—
1916 CHI N	2	1	.667	2.54	4	3	2	28.1	30	3	10	1	0	0	0	11	3	0	.273
1917 CIN N	0	0	—	6.75	4	1	0	13.1	17	8	4	0	0	0	0	5	0	0	.000
1918 PHI A	21	19	.525	1.98	44	36	30	332.1	295	111	81	4	4	2	1	112	15	0	.134
1919	4	17	.190	3.58	25	21	12	183.2	193	72	38	0	0	2	1	59	8	0	.136
1920	11	25	.306	3.62	42	34	20	263.2	310	65	79	1	1	2	1	83	13	1	.157
1921	3	6	.333	4.11	12	8	5	70	77	24	19	0	0	1	0	26	1	0	.038
7 yrs.	41	68	.376	3.07	132	104	69	893.1	927	284	231	6	5	7	4	296	40	1	.135

Parson Perryman

PERRYMAN, EMMETT KEY   BR TR 6'4½"   193 lbs.
B. Oct. 24, 1888, Everette Springs, Ga.   D. Sept. 12, 1966, Starke, Fla.

	W	L	PCT	ERA	G	GS	CG	IP	H	BB	SO	ShO	W	L	SV	AB	H	HR	BA
1915 STL A	2	4	.333	3.93	24	3	0	50.1	52	16	19	0	2	1	0	6	0	0	.000

Bill Pertica

PERTICA, WILLIAM ANDREW   BR TR 5'9"   165 lbs.
B. Mar. 5, 1897, Santa Barbara, Calif.   D. Dec. 28, 1967, Los Angeles, Calif.

	W	L	PCT	ERA	G	GS	CG	IP	H	BB	SO	ShO	W	L	SV	AB	H	HR	BA
1918 BOS A	0	0	—	3.00	1	0	0	3	3	0	1	0	0	0	0	1	0	0	.000
1921 STL A	14	10	.583	3.37	38	31	15	208.1	212	70	67	2	0	1	2	70	10	0	.143
1922	8	8	.500	5.91	34	14	2	117.1	153	65	30	0	4	2	0	33	6	0	.182
1923	0	0	—	3.86	1	1	0	2.1	2	3	0	0	0	0	0	1	0	0	.000
4 yrs.	22	18	.550	4.27	74	46	17	331	370	138	98	2	4	3	2	105	16	0	.152

Stan Perzanowski

PERZANOWSKI, STANLEY   BR TR 6'2"   170 lbs.
B. Aug. 25, 1950, East Chicago, Ind.

	W	L	PCT	ERA	G	GS	CG	IP	H	BB	SO	ShO	W	L	SV	AB	H	HR	BA
1971 CHI A	0	1	.000	12.00	5	0	0	6	14	3	5	0	0	1	1	2	0	0	.000
1974	0	0	—	22.50	2	1	0	2	8	2	2	0	0	0	0	0	0	0	—
1975 TEX A	3	3	.500	3.00	12	8	1	66	59	25	26	0	0	0	0	0	0	0	—
1976	0	0	—	9.75	5	0	0	12	20	4	6	0	0	0	0	0	0	0	—
1978 MIN A	2	7	.222	5.24	13	7	1	56.2	59	26	31	0	0	3	1	0	0	0	—
5 yrs.	5	11	.313	5.11	37	16	2	142.2	160	60	70	0	0	4	2	2	0	0	.000

Gary Peters

PETERS, GARY CHARLES   BL TL 6'2"   200 lbs.
B. Apr. 21, 1937, Grove City, Pa.

	W	L	PCT	ERA	G	GS	CG	IP	H	BB	SO	ShO	W	L	SV	AB	H	HR	BA
1959 CHI A	0	0	—	0.00	2	0	0	1	2	2	1	0	0	0	0	0	0	0	—
1960	0	0	—	2.70	2	0	0	3.1	4	1	4	0	0	0	0	0	0	0	—
1961	0	0	—	1.74	3	0	0	10.1	10	2	6	0	0	0	1	3	1	0	.333
1962	0	1	.000	5.68	5	0	0	6.1	8	1	4	0	0	1	0	0	0	0	—
1963	19	8	.704	2.33	41	30	13	243	192	68	189	4	0	2	1	81	21	3	.259
1964	20	8	.714	2.50	37	36	11	273.2	217	104	205	3	0	0	0	120	25	4	.208
1965	10	12	.455	3.62	33	30	1	176.1	181	63	95	0	0	0	0	72	13	1	.181
1966	12	10	.545	1.98	30	27	11	204.2	156	45	129	4	0	1	0	81	19	1	.235
1967	16	11	.593	2.28	38	36	11	260	187	91	215	3	0	0	0	99	21	2	.212
1968	4	13	.235	3.76	31	25	6	162.2	146	60	110	1	0	0	1	72	15	2	.208
1969	10	15	.400	4.53	36	32	7	218.2	238	78	140	3	0	0	0	71	12	2	.169
1970 BOS A	16	11	.593	4.05	34	34	10	222	221	83	155	4	0	0	0	82	20	1	.244
1971	14	11	.560	4.37	34	32	9	214	241	70	100	1	0	0	1	96	26	3	.271
1972	3	3	.500	4.34	33	4	0	85	91	38	67	0	2	1	1	30	6	0	.200
14 yrs.	124	103	.546	3.25	359	286	79	2081	1894	706	1420	23	2	5	5	*			

Johnny Peters

PETERS, JOHN PAUL   BR TR   180 lbs.
B. Apr. 8, 1850, Louisiana, Mo.   D. Jan. 4, 1924, St. Louis, Mo.

	W	L	PCT	ERA	G	GS	CG	IP	H	BB	SO	ShO	W	L	SV	AB	H	HR	BA
1876 CHI N	0	0	—	0.00	1	0	0	1	1	1	0	0	0	0	1	*			

Ray Peters

PETERS, RAYMOND JAMES   BR TR 6'5½"   210 lbs.
B. Aug. 27, 1946, Buffalo, N. Y.

	W	L	PCT	ERA	G	GS	CG	IP	H	BB	SO	ShO	W	L	SV	AB	H	HR	BA
1970 MIL A	0	2	.000	31.50	2	2	0	2	7	5	1	0	0	0	0	0	0	0	—

	W	L	PCT	ERA	G	GS	CG	IP	H	BB	SO	ShO	Relief Pitching W	L	SV	BATTING AB	H	HR	BA

Rube Peters
PETERS, OSCAR C. BR TR 6' 185 lbs.
B. Mar. 15, 1886, Grand Fork, Ill.

	W	L	PCT	ERA	G	GS	CG	IP	H	BB	SO	ShO	W	L	SV	AB	H	HR	BA
1912 CHI A	5	6	.455	4.14	28	11	4	108.2	134	33	39	0	1	1	0	31	6	0	.194
1914 BKN F	2	2	.500	3.82	11	3	1	37.2	52	16	13	0	1	0	0	11	1	0	.091
2 yrs.	7	8	.467	4.06	39	14	5	146.1	186	49	52	0	2	1	0	42	7	0	.167

Fritz Peterson
PETERSON, FRED INGELS BB TL 6' 185 lbs.
B. Feb. 8, 1942, Chicago, Ill.

	W	L	PCT	ERA	G	GS	CG	IP	H	BB	SO	ShO	W	L	SV	AB	H	HR	BA
1966 NY A	12	11	.522	3.31	34	32	11	215	96	40	96	2	0	0	0	67	15	0	.224
1967	8	14	.364	3.47	36	30	6	181.1	179	43	102	1	2	1	0	48	7	0	.146
1968	12	11	.522	2.63	36	27	6	212.1	187	29	115	2	1	1	0	63	5	0	.079
1969	17	16	.515	2.55	37	37	16	272	228	43	150	4	0	0	0	80	9	0	.113
1970	20	11	.645	2.91	39	37	8	260	247	40	127	2	1	0	0	90	20	2	.222
1971	15	13	.536	3.05	37	35	16	274	269	42	139	4	1	0	1	85	7	0	.082
1972	17	15	.531	3.24	35	35	12	250	270	44	100	3	0	0	0	82	19	0	.232
1973	8	15	.348	3.95	31	31	6	184.1	207	49	59	0	0	0	0	0	0	0	–
1974 2 teams		NY	A	(3G 0–0)		CLE	A	(29G 9–14)											
" total	9	14	.391	4.36	32	30	3	161	200	39	57	0	0	0	0	0	0	0	–
1975 CLE A	14	8	.636	3.94	25	25	6	146.1	154	40	47	2	0	0	0	0	0	0	–
1976 2 teams		CLE	A	(9G 0–3)		TEX	A	(4G 1–0)											
" total	1	3	.250	5.08	13	11	0	62	80	17	23	0	0	0	0	0	0	0	–
11 yrs.	133	131	.504	3.30	355	330	90	2218.1	2217	426	1015	20	5	2	1	515	82	2	.159

Jim Peterson
PETERSON, JAMES NIELS BR TR 6'½" 200 lbs.
B. Aug. 18, 1908, Philadelphia, Pa.   D. Apr. 8, 1975, Palm Beach, Fla.

	W	L	PCT	ERA	G	GS	CG	IP	H	BB	SO	ShO	W	L	SV	AB	H	HR	BA
1931 PHI A	0	1	.000	6.23	6	1	1	13	18	4	7	0	0	0	0	2	1	0	.500
1933	2	5	.286	4.96	32	5	0	90.2	114	36	18	0	2	3	0	27	4	0	.148
1937 BKN N	0	0	–	7.94	3	0	0	5.2	8	2	4	0	0	0	0	0	0	0	–
3 yrs.	2	6	.250	5.27	41	6	1	109.1	140	42	29	0	2	3	0	29	5	0	.172

Kent Peterson
PETERSON, KENT FRANKLIN BR TL 5'10" 170 lbs.
B. Dec. 21, 1925, Goshen, Utah

	W	L	PCT	ERA	G	GS	CG	IP	H	BB	SO	ShO	W	L	SV	AB	H	HR	BA
1944 CIN N	0	0	–	0.00	1	0	0	1	0	0	0	0	0	0	0	0	0	0	–
1947	6	13	.316	4.25	37	17	3	152.1	156	62	78	1	2	2	2	44	3	0	.068
1948	2	15	.118	4.60	43	17	2	137	146	59	64	0	0	3	1	36	5	0	.139
1949	4	5	.444	6.24	30	7	2	66.1	66	46	28	0	1	2	0	18	1	0	.056
1950	0	3	.000	7.20	9	2	0	20	25	17	6	0	0	1	0	3	1	0	.333
1951	1	1	.500	6.52	9	0	0	9.2	13	8	5	0	1	1	0	1	0	0	.000
1952 PHI N	0	0	–	0.00	3	0	0	7	2	2	7	0	0	0	2	1	0	0	.000
1953	0	1	.000	6.67	15	0	0	27	26	21	20	0	0	1	0	7	0	0	.000
8 yrs.	13	38	.255	4.95	147	43	7	420.1	434	215	208	1	4	10	5	110	10	0	.091

Sid Peterson
PETERSON, SIDNEY HERBERT BR TR 6'3" 200 lbs.
B. Jan. 31, 1918, Havelock, N. D.

	W	L	PCT	ERA	G	GS	CG	IP	H	BB	SO	ShO	W	L	SV	AB	H	HR	BA
1943 STL A	2	0	1.000	2.70	3	0	0	10	15	3	0	0	2	0	0	2	0	0	.000

Dan Petry
PETRY, DANIEL JOSEPH BR TR 6'4" 185 lbs.
B. Nov. 13, 1958, Palo Alto, Calif.

	W	L	PCT	ERA	G	GS	CG	IP	H	BB	SO	ShO	W	L	SV	AB	H	HR	BA
1979 DET A	6	5	.545	3.95	15	15	2	98	90	33	43	0	0	0	0	0	0	0	–
1980	10	9	.526	3.93	27	25	4	165	156	83	88	3	1	0	0	0	0	0	–
1981	10	9	.526	3.00	23	22	7	141	115	57	79	2	0	0	0	0	0	0	–
1982	15	9	.625	3.22	35	35	8	246	220	100	132	1	0	0	0	0	0	0	–
1983	19	11	.633	3.92	38	38	9	266.1	256	99	122	2	0	0	0	0	0	0	–
1984	18	8	.692	3.24	35	35	7	233.1	231	66	144	2	0	0	0	0	0	0	–
6 yrs.	78	51	.605	3.52	173	170	37	1149.2	1068	438	608	10	1	0	0	0	0	0	–
LEAGUE CHAMPIONSHIP SERIES																			
1984 DET A	0	0	–	2.57	1	1	0	7	4	1	4	0	0	0	0	0	0	0	–
WORLD SERIES																			
1984 DET A	0	1	.000	9.00	2	2	0	8	14	5	4	0	0	0	0	0	0	0	–

Jeff Pettibone
PETTIBONE, HARRY JAY BR TR 6'4" 185 lbs.
B. June 21, 1957, Mt. Clemons, Mich.

	W	L	PCT	ERA	G	GS	CG	IP	H	BB	SO	ShO	W	L	SV	AB	H	HR	BA
1983 MIN A	0	4	.000	5.33	4	4	1	27	28	8	10	0	0	0	0	0	0	0	–

Bob Pettit
PETTIT, ROBERT HENRY BL 5'9" 160 lbs.
B. July 19, 1861, Williamstown, Mass.   D. Nov. 1, 1910, Derby, Conn.

	W	L	PCT	ERA	G	GS	CG	IP	H	BB	SO	ShO	W	L	SV	AB	H	HR	BA
1887 CHI N	0	0	–	0.00	1	0	0	1	3	2	0	0	0	0	1	*			

Leon Pettit
PETTIT, LEON ARTHUR (Lefty) BL TL 5'10½" 165 lbs.
B. June 23, 1902, Waynesburg, Pa.   D. Nov. 11, 1974, Columbia, Tenn.

	W	L	PCT	ERA	G	GS	CG	IP	H	BB	SO	ShO	W	L	SV	AB	H	HR	BA
1935 WAS A	8	5	.615	4.95	41	7	1	109	129	58	45	0	6	3	3	25	2	0	.080
1937 PHI N	0	1	.000	11.25	3	1	0	4	6	4	0	0	0	0	0	0	0	0	–
2 yrs.	8	6	.571	5.18	44	8	1	113	135	62	45	0	6	3	3	25	2	0	.080

Paul Pettit
PETTIT, GEORGE WILLIAM PAUL (Lefty) BL TL 6'2" 195 lbs.
B. Nov. 29, 1931, Los Angeles, Calif.

	W	L	PCT	ERA	G	GS	CG	IP	H	BB	SO	ShO	W	L	SV	AB	H	HR	BA
1951 PIT N	0	0	–	3.38	2	0	0	2.2	2	1	0	0	0	0	0	1	0	0	.000
1953	1	2	.333	7.71	10	5	0	28	33	20	14	0	0	0	0	8	2	0	.250
2 yrs.	1	2	.333	7.34	12	5	0	30.2	35	21	14	0	0	0	0	9	2	0	.222

Charlie Petty
PETTY, CHARLES E. TR
B. June 28, 1866, Nashville, Tenn.   Deceased.

	W	L	PCT	ERA	G	GS	CG	IP	H	BB	SO	ShO	W	L	SV	AB	H	HR	BA
1889 CIN AA	2	3	.400	5.52	5	5	5	44	44	20	10	0	0	0	0	20	6	0	.300
1893 NY N	5	2	.714	3.33	9	6	4	54	66	28	12	0	2	0	0	22	7	1	.318
1894 2 teams		WAS	N	(16G 3–8)		CLE	N	(4G 0–2)											
" total	3	10	.231	6.23	20	15	10	130	198	46	18	0	0	0	0	53	9	0	.170
3 yrs.	10	15	.400	5.41	34	26	19	228	308	94	40	0	2	0	0	95	22	1	.232

	W	L	PCT	ERA	G	GS	CG	IP	H	BB	SO	ShO	Relief Pitching W	L	SV	AB	H	HR	BA

Jesse Petty

PETTY, JESSE LEE (The Silver Fox) BR TL 6' 195 lbs.
B. Nov. 23, 1894, Orr, Okla. D. Oct. 23, 1971, St Paul, Minn.

	W	L	PCT	ERA	G	GS	CG	IP	H	BB	SO	ShO	W	L	SV	AB	H	HR	BA
1921 CLE A	0	0	–	2.00	4	0	0	9	10	0	0	0	0	0	0	2	0	0	.000
1925 BKN N	9	9	.500	4.88	28	22	7	153	188	47	39	0	3	0	0	50	7	0	.140
1926	17	17	.500	2.84	38	33	23	275.2	246	79	101	1	2	1	1	97	17	0	.175
1927	13	18	.419	2.98	42	33	19	271.2	263	53	101	2	2	1	1	91	9	0	.099
1928	15	15	.500	4.04	40	31	15	234	264	56	74	2	1	2	1	81	9	0	.111
1929 PIT N	11	10	.524	3.71	36	25	12	184.1	197	42	58	1	1	0	0	67	7	0	.104
1930 2 teams		PIT	N (10G 1–6)		CHI	N (9G 1–3)													
" total	2	9	.182	5.69	19	10	0	80.2	118	19	34	0	1	1	1	25	4	0	.160
7 yrs.	67	78	.462	3.68	207	154	76	1208.1	1286	296	407	6	10	5	4	413	53	0	.128

Pretzels Pezzullo

PEZZULLO, JOHN BL TL 5'11½" 180 lbs.
B. Dec. 10, 1911, Bridgeport, Conn.

	W	L	PCT	ERA	G	GS	CG	IP	H	BB	SO	ShO	W	L	SV	AB	H	HR	BA
1935 PHI N	3	5	.375	6.40	41	7	2	84.1	115	45	24	0	1	1	1	24	6	0	.250
1936	0	0	–	4.50	1	0	0	2	1	6	0	0	0	0	0	0	0	0	–
2 yrs.	3	5	.375	6.36	42	7	2	86.1	116	51	24	0	1	1	1	24	6	0	.250

Big Jeff Pfeffer

PFEFFER, FRANCIS XAVIER BR TR
Brother of Jeff Pfeffer.
B. Mar. 31, 1882, Champaign, Ill. D. Dec. 19, 1954, Kankakee, Ill.

	W	L	PCT	ERA	G	GS	CG	IP	H	BB	SO	ShO	W	L	SV	AB	H	HR	BA
1905 CHI N	4	5	.444	2.50	15	11	9	101	84	36	56	0	0	0	0	40	8	0	.200
1906 BOS N	13	22	.371	2.95	35	35	33	302.1	270	114	158	4	0	0	0	158	31	1	.196
1907	6	8	.429	3.00	19	16	12	144	129	61	65	1	0	0	0	60	15	0	.250
1908	0	0	–	12.60	4	0	0	10	18	8	3	0	0	0	0	2	0	0	.000
1910 CHI N	1	0	1.000	3.27	13	1	1	41.1	43	16	11	0	0	0	0	17	3	0	.176
1911 BOS N	7	5	.583	4.73	26	6	4	97	116	57	24	1	4	2	2	46	9	1	.196
6 yrs.	31	40	.437	3.30	112	69	59	695.2	660	292	317	6	4	2	2	*			

Fred Pfeffer

PFEFFER, NATHANIEL FREDERICK (Dandelion) BR TR 5'10½" 168 lbs.
B. Mar. 17, 1860, Louisville, Ky. D. Apr. 10, 1932, Chicago, Ill.
Manager 1892.

	W	L	PCT	ERA	G	GS	CG	IP	H	BB	SO	ShO	W	L	SV	AB	H	HR	BA
1884 CHI N	0	0	–	9.00	1	0	0	1	3	1	0	0	0	0	0	467	135	25	.289
1885	2	1	.667	2.56	5	2	2	31.2	26	8	13	0	1	0	2	469	113	6	.241
1892 LOU N	0	0	–	1.80	1	0	0	5	4	5	0	0	0	0	0	470	121	2	.257
1894	0	0	–	2.57	1	0	0	7	8	6	0	0	0	0	0	409	126	5	.308
4 yrs.	2	1	.667	2.62	8	2	2	44.2	41	20	13	0	1	0	2	*			

Jeff Pfeffer

PFEFFER, EDWARD JOSEPH BR TR 6'3" 210 lbs.
Brother of Big Jeff Pfeffer.
B. Mar. 4, 1888, Seymour, Ill. D. Aug. 15, 1972, Chicago, Ill.

	W	L	PCT	ERA	G	GS	CG	IP	H	BB	SO	ShO	W	L	SV	AB	H	HR	BA
1911 STL A	0	0	–	7.20	2	0	0	10	11	4	4	0	0	0	0	4	0	0	.000
1913 BKN N	0	1	.000	3.33	5	2	1	24.1	28	13	13	0	0	0	0	7	0	0	.000
1914	23	12	.657	1.97	43	34	27	315	264	91	135	3	0	2	4	116	23	0	.198
1915	19	14	.576	2.10	40	34	26	291.2	243	76	84	6	1	2	3	106	27	0	.255
1916	25	11	.694	1.92	41	37	30	328.2	274	63	128	6	1	0	1	122	34	0	.279
1917	11	15	.423	2.23	30	30	24	266	225	66	115	3	0	0	0	100	13	0	.130
1918	1	0	1.000	0.00	1	1	1	9	2	3	1	1	0	0	0	4	1	0	.250
1919	17	13	.567	2.66	30	30	26	267	270	49	92	4	0	0	0	97	20	0	.206
1920	16	9	.640	3.01	30	28	20	215	225	45	80	2	1	0	0	74	18	0	.243
1921 2 teams		BKN	N (6G 1–5)		STL	N (18G 9–3)													
" total	10	8	.556	4.35	24	18	9	130.1	151	37	30	1	2	0	0	40	4	0	.100
1922 STL N	19	12	.613	3.58	44	32	19	261.1	286	58	83	1	3	1	2	98	24	0	.245
1923	8	9	.471	4.02	26	18	7	152.1	171	40	32	1	1	1	0	55	7	0	.127
1924 2 teams		STL	N (16G 4–5)		PIT	N (15G 5–3)													
" total	9	8	.529	4.35	31	16	4	136.2	170	47	39	0	4	3	0	51	9	0	.176
13 yrs.	158	112	.585	2.77	347	280	194	2407.1	2320	592	836	28	13	9	10	874	180	0	.206

WORLD SERIES

	W	L	PCT	ERA	G	GS	CG	IP	H	BB	SO	ShO	W	L	SV	AB	H	HR	BA
1916 BKN N	0	1	.000	2.53	3	1	0	10.2	7	4	5	0	0	0	1	4	1	0	.250
1920	0	0	–	3.00	1	0	0	3	4	2	1	0	0	0	0	1	0	0	.000
2 yrs.	0	1	.000	2.63	4	1	0	13.2	11	6	6	0	0	0	1	5	1	0	.200

Jack Pfiester

PFIESTER, JOHN ALBERT (Jack the Giant Killer) BR TL 5'11" 180 lbs.
Born John Albert Hagenbush.
B. May 24, 1878, Cincinnati, Ohio D. Sept. 3, 1953, Twightwee, Ohio

	W	L	PCT	ERA	G	GS	CG	IP	H	BB	SO	ShO	W	L	SV	AB	H	HR	BA
1903 PIT N	0	3	.000	6.16	3	3	2	19	26	10	15	0	0	0	0	6	0	0	.000
1904	1	1	.500	7.20	3	2	1	20	28	9	6	0	0	0	0	7	2	0	.286
1906 CHI N	20	8	.714	1.56	31	29	20	241.2	173	63	153	4	1	0	0	84	4	0	.048
1907	15	9	.625	1.15	30	22	13	195	143	48	90	3	2	1	0	64	6	0	.094
1908	12	10	.545	2.00	33	29	18	252	204	70	117	3	0	1	0	79	8	0	.101
1909	17	6	.739	2.43	29	25	13	196.2	179	49	73	5	0	0	0	65	11	0	.169
1910	6	3	.667	1.79	14	13	5	100.1	82	26	34	2	0	0	0	33	3	0	.091
1911	0	4	.000	4.01	6	5	3	33.2	34	18	15	0	0	0	0	11	2	0	.182
8 yrs.	71	44	.617	2.04	149	128	75	1058.1	869	293	503	17	4	2	0	349	36	0	.103

WORLD SERIES

	W	L	PCT	ERA	G	GS	CG	IP	H	BB	SO	ShO	W	L	SV	AB	H	HR	BA
1906 CHI N	0	2	.000	6.10	2	1	1	10.1	7	3	11	0	0	0	0	2	0	0	.000
1907	1	0	1.000	1.00	1	1	1	9	9	1	3	0	0	0	0	2	0	0	.000
1908	0	1	.000	7.88	1	1	0	8	10	3	1	0	0	0	0	2	0	0	.000
1910	0	0	–	0.00	1	0	0	6.2	9	1	1	0	0	0	0	2	0	0	.000
4 yrs.	1	3	.250	3.97	5	3	2	34	35	8	16	0	0	0	0	8	0	0	.000

Dan Pfister

PFISTER, DANIEL ALBIN BR TR 6' 187 lbs.
B. Dec. 20, 1936, Plainfield, N. J.

	W	L	PCT	ERA	G	GS	CG	IP	H	BB	SO	ShO	W	L	SV	AB	H	HR	BA
1961 KC A	0	0	–	15.43	2	0	0	2.1	5	4	3	0	0	0	0	0	0	0	–
1962	4	14	.222	4.54	41	25	2	196.1	175	106	123	0	0	1	1	65	12	0	.185
1963	1	0	1.000	1.93	3	1	0	9.1	8	3	9	0	0	0	0	3	0	0	.000

	W	L	PCT	ERA	G	GS	CG	IP	H	BB	SO	ShO	Relief Pitching W	L	SV	BATTING AB	H	HR	BA

Dan Pfister continued

	W	L	PCT	ERA	G	GS	CG	IP	H	BB	SO	ShO	W	L	SV	AB	H	HR	BA
1964	1	5	.167	6.53	19	3	0	41.1	50	29	21	0	1	3	0	6	0	0	.000
4 yrs.	6	19	.240	4.87	65	29	2	249.1	238	142	156	0	1	4	1	74	12	0	.162

Bill Pflann

PFLANN, WILLIAM F
B. Brooklyn, N. Y.   Deceased.   6'   205 lbs.

	W	L	PCT	ERA	G	GS	CG	IP	H	BB	SO	ShO	W	L	SV	AB	H	HR	BA
1894 CIN N	0	1	.000	27.00	1	1	0	3	10	4	0	0	0	0	0	1	0	0	.000

Lee Pfund

PFUND, LeROY HERBERT   BR TR 6'1"   185 lbs.
B. Oct. 10, 1919, Oak Park, Ill.

	W	L	PCT	ERA	G	GS	CG	IP	H	BB	SO	ShO	W	L	SV	AB	H	HR	BA
1945 BKN N	3	2	.600	5.20	15	10	2	62.1	69	35	27	0	0	0	0	22	4	0	.182

Bill Phebus

PHEBUS, RAYMOND WILLIAM   BR TR 5'9"   170 lbs.
B. Aug. 9, 1909, Cherryvale, Kans.

	W	L	PCT	ERA	G	GS	CG	IP	H	BB	SO	ShO	W	L	SV	AB	H	HR	BA
1936 WAS A	0	0	–	2.45	2	1	0	7.1	4	4	4	0	0	0	0	1	0	0	.000
1937	3	2	.600	2.21	6	5	4	40.2	33	24	12	1	0	0	1	8	0	0	.000
1938	0	0	–	11.37	5	0	0	6.1	9	7	2	0	0	0	1	1	0	0	.000
3 yrs.	3	2	.600	3.31	13	6	4	54.1	46	35	18	1	0	0	2	10	0	0	.000

Ray Phelps

PHELPS, RAYMOND CLIFFORD   BR TR 6'2"   200 lbs.
B. Dec. 11, 1903, Dunlap, Tenn.   D. July 7, 1971, Fort Pierce, Fla.

	W	L	PCT	ERA	G	GS	CG	IP	H	BB	SO	ShO	W	L	SV	AB	H	HR	BA
1930 BKN N	14	7	.667	4.11	36	24	11	179.2	198	52	64	2	2	1	0	68	10	1	.147
1931	7	9	.438	5.00	28	26	3	149.1	184	44	50	2	0	0	0	51	8	0	.157
1932	4	5	.444	5.90	20	8	4	79.1	101	27	21	1	1	3	0	23	2	0	.087
1935 CHI A	4	8	.333	4.82	27	17	4	125	126	55	38	0	0	1	1	41	5	0	.122
1936	4	6	.400	6.03	15	4	2	68.2	91	42	17	0	3	3	0	26	6	0	.231
5 yrs.	33	35	.485	4.93	126	79	24	602	700	220	190	5	6	8	1	209	31	1	.148

Deacon Phillippe

PHILLIPPE, CHARLES LOUIS   BR TR 6'½"   180 lbs.
B. May 23, 1872, Rural Retreat, Va.   D. Mar. 30, 1952, Avalon, Pa.

	W	L	PCT	ERA	G	GS	CG	IP	H	BB	SO	ShO	W	L	SV	AB	H	HR	BA
1899 LOU N	20	17	.541	3.17	42	38	33	321	331	64	68	2	3	0	1	128	26	0	.203
1900 PIT N	18	14	.563	2.84	38	33	29	279	274	42	75	1	2	1	0	105	19	0	.181
1901	22	12	.647	2.22	37	32	30	296	274	38	103	1	1	1	2	113	26	1	.230
1902	20	9	.690	2.05	31	30	29	272	265	26	122	5	0	0	2	113	25	1	.221
1903	24	7	.774	2.43	36	33	31	289.1	269	29	123	4	0	0	2	124	26	1	.210
1904	10	10	.500	3.24	21	19	17	166.2	183	26	82	3	1	0	1	65	8	0	.123
1905	22	13	.629	2.19	38	33	25	279	235	48	133	5	3	0	0	97	9	0	.093
1906	15	10	.600	2.47	33	24	19	218.2	216	26	90	3	2	1	0	82	20	0	.244
1907	13	11	.542	2.61	35	26	17	214	214	36	61	1	3	0	2	65	12	0	.185
1908	0	0	–	11.25	5	0	0	12	20	3	1	0	0	0	0	4	1	0	.250
1909	8	3	.727	2.32	22	12	7	131.2	121	14	38	1	2	0	0	42	3	0	.071
1910	14	2	.875	2.29	31	8	5	121.2	111	9	30	1	7	1	4	41	9	1	.220
1911	0	0	–	7.50	3	0	0	6	5	2	3	0	0	0	0	1	1	0	1.000
13 yrs.	186	108	.633	2.59	372	288	242	2607	2518	363	929	27	24	4	12	980	185	3	.189
WORLD SERIES																			
1903 PIT N	3	2	.600	3.27	5	5	5	44	38	3	20	0	0	0	0	18	4	0	.222
1909	0	0	–	0.00	2	0	0	6	2	1	2	0	0	0	0	1	0	0	.000
2 yrs.	3	2	.600	2.88	7	5	5	50	40	4	22	0	0	0	0	19	4	0	.211
						10th														

Bill Phillips

PHILLIPS, WILLIAM CORCORAN (Whoa Bill, Silver Bill)   BR TR 5'11"   180 lbs.
B. Nov. 9, 1868, Allenport, Pa.   D. Oct. 25, 1941, Charleroi, Pa.
Manager 1914-15.

	W	L	PCT	ERA	G	GS	CG	IP	H	BB	SO	ShO	W	L	SV	AB	H	HR	BA
1890 PIT N	1	9	.100	7.57	10	10	9	82	123	29	25	0	0	0	0	46	11	0	.239
1895 CIN N	6	7	.462	6.03	18	9	6	109	126	44	15	0	3	2	2	48	15	0	.313
1899	17	9	.654	3.32	33	27	18	227.2	234	71	43	1	2	1	1	92	12	0	.130
1900	9	11	.450	4.28	29	24	17	208.1	229	67	51	3	1	0	0	79	13	0	.165
1901	14	20	.412	4.64	37	36	29	281.1	364	67	109	1	0	0	0	109	22	0	.202
1902	16	15	.516	2.50	33	32	29	263	264	50	85	0	0	0	0	114	39	0	.342
1903	8	6	.571	3.35	16	13	11	118.1	134	30	46	1	0	0	0	57	10	0	.175
7 yrs.	71	77	.480	4.10	176	151	119	1289.2	1474	358	374	6	6	3	3	545	122	0	.224

Buz Phillips

PHILLIPS, ALBERT ABERNATHY   BR TR 5'11½" 185 lbs.
B. May 25, 1904, Newton, N. C.   D. Nov. 6, 1964, Baltimore, Md.

	W	L	PCT	ERA	G	GS	CG	IP	H	BB	SO	ShO	W	L	SV	AB	H	HR	BA
1930 PHI N	0	0	–	8.04	14	1	0	43.2	68	18	9	0	0	0	0	13	6	1	.462

Ed Phillips

PHILLIPS, NORMAN EDWIN   BR TR 6'1"   190 lbs.
B. Sept. 20, 1944, Ardmore, Okla.

	W	L	PCT	ERA	G	GS	CG	IP	H	BB	SO	ShO	W	L	SV	AB	H	HR	BA
1970 BOS A	0	2	.000	5.25	18	0	0	29	10	23	0	0	2	0	0	3	0	0	.000

Jack Phillips

PHILLIPS, JACK DORN (Stretch)   BR TR 6'4"   193 lbs.
B. Sept. 6, 1921, Clarence, N. Y.

	W	L	PCT	ERA	G	GS	CG	IP	H	BB	SO	ShO	W	L	SV	AB	H	HR	BA
1950 PIT N	0	0	–	7.20	1	0	0	5	7	1	2	0	0	0	0	*			

John Phillips

PHILLIPS, JOHN STEPHEN   BR TR 6'1"   185 lbs.
B. May 24, 1921, St. Louis, Mo.   D. June 9, 1958, St. Louis, Mo.

	W	L	PCT	ERA	G	GS	CG	IP	H	BB	SO	ShO	W	L	SV	AB	H	HR	BA
1945 NY N	0	0	–	10.38	1	0	0	4.1	5	4	0	0	0	0	0	2	1	0	.500

Red Phillips

PHILLIPS, CLARENCE LEMUEL   BR TR 6'3½" 195 lbs.
B. Nov. 3, 1908, Pauls Valley, Okla.

	W	L	PCT	ERA	G	GS	CG	IP	H	BB	SO	ShO	W	L	SV	AB	H	HR	BA
1934 DET A	2	0	1.000	6.17	7	1	1	23.1	31	16	3	0	1	0	1	12	3	0	.250
1936	2	4	.333	6.49	22	6	3	87.1	124	22	15	0	1	1	0	33	10	0	.303
2 yrs.	4	4	.500	6.42	29	7	4	110.2	155	38	18	0	2	1	1	45	13	0	.289

	W	L	PCT	ERA	G	GS	CG	IP	H	BB	SO	ShO	Relief Pitching W	L	SV	BATTING AB	H	HR	BA

Taylor Phillips

PHILLIPS, WILLIAM TAYLOR (Tay)
B. June 18, 1933, Atlanta, Ga.
BL TL 5'11" 185 lbs.

	W	L	PCT	ERA	G	GS	CG	IP	H	BB	SO	ShO	W	L	SV	AB	H	HR	BA
1956 MIL N	5	3	.625	2.26	23	6	3	87.2	69	33	36	0	2	1	2	21	0	0	.000
1957	3	2	.600	5.55	27	6	0	73	82	40	36	0	2	1	2	20	2	0	.100
1958 CHI N	7	10	.412	4.76	39	27	5	170.1	178	79	102	1	1	0	1	54	3	0	.056
1959 2 teams			CHI N (7G 0-2)			PHI N (32G 1-4)													
" total	1	6	.143	5.54	39	5	1	79.2	94	42	40	0	0	3	1	15	1	0	.067
1960 PHI N	0	1	.000	8.36	10	1	0	14	21	4	6	0	0	0	0	1	0	0	.000
1963 CHI A	0	0	–	10.29	9	0	0	14	16	13	13	0	0	0	0	2	0	0	.000
6 yrs.	16	22	.421	4.82	147	45	9	438.2	460	211	233	1	5	5	6	113	6	0	.053

Tom Phillips

PHILLIPS, THOMAS GERALD
B. Apr. 1, 1889, Philipsburg, Pa.   D. Apr. 12, 1929, Philipsburg, Pa.
BR TR 6'2" 190 lbs.

	W	L	PCT	ERA	G	GS	CG	IP	H	BB	SO	ShO	W	L	SV	AB	H	HR	BA
1915 STL A	1	3	.250	2.96	5	4	1	27.1	28	12	5	0	0	0	0	9	1	0	.111
1919 CLE A	3	2	.600	2.95	22	3	2	55	55	34	18	0	1	1	0	11	4	0	.364
1921 WAS A	1	0	1.000	2.00	1	1	1	9	9	3	2	0	0	0	0	3	0	0	.000
1922	3	7	.300	4.89	17	7	2	70	72	22	19	1	2	0	0	20	3	0	.150
4 yrs.	8	12	.400	3.74	45	15	6	161.1	164	71	44	1	3	1	0	43	8	0	.186

Tom Phoebus

PHOEBUS, THOMAS HAROLD
B. Apr. 7, 1942, Baltimore, Md.
BR TR 5'8" 185 lbs.

	W	L	PCT	ERA	G	GS	CG	IP	H	BB	SO	ShO	W	L	SV	AB	H	HR	BA
1966 BAL A	2	1	.667	1.23	3	3	2	22	16	6	17	2	0	0	0	6	1	0	.167
1967	14	9	.609	3.33	33	33	7	208	177	114	179	4	0	0	0	76	11	1	.145
1968	15	15	.500	2.62	36	36	9	240.2	186	105	193	3	0	0	0	82	15	1	.183
1969	14	7	.667	3.52	35	33	6	202	180	87	117	2	0	0	0	75	15	0	.200
1970	5	5	.500	3.07	27	21	3	135	106	62	72	0	0	0	0	43	7	0	.163
1971 SD N	3	11	.214	4.47	29	21	2	133	144	64	80	0	0	0	0	36	6	0	.167
1972 2 teams			SD N (1G 0-1)			CHI N (37G 3-3)													
" total	3	4	.429	4.04	38	2	0	89	79	51	67	0	3	2	6	17	2	0	.118
7 yrs.	56	52	.519	3.33	201	149	29	1029.2	888	489	725	11	3	2	6	335	57	2	.170
WORLD SERIES																			
1970 BAL A	1	0	1.000	0.00	1	0	0	1.2	1	0	0	0	1	0	0	0	0	0	–

Bill Phyle

PHYLE, WILLIAM JOSEPH
B. June 25, 1875, Duluth, Minn.   D. Aug. 7, 1953, Los Angeles, Calif.
TR

	W	L	PCT	ERA	G	GS	CG	IP	H	BB	SO	ShO	W	L	SV	AB	H	HR	BA
1898 CHI N	2	1	.667	0.78	3	3	3	23	24	6	4	2	0	0	0	9	1	0	.111
1899	1	8	.111	4.20	10	9	9	83.2	92	29	10	0	0	0	1	34	6	0	.176
1901 NY N	7	10	.412	4.27	24	19	16	168.2	208	54	62	0	0	0	1	66	12	0	.182
1906 STL N	0	0	–	0.00	0	0	0	0	0	0	0	0	0	0	0	73	13	0	.178
4 yrs.	10	19	.345	3.96	37	31	28	275.1	324	89	76	2	0	0	2	182	32	0	.176

Wiley Piatt

PIATT, WILEY HAROLD (Iron Man)
B. July 13, 1874, Blue Creek, Ohio   D. Sept. 20, 1946, Cincinnati, Ohio
BL TL 5'10" 175 lbs.

	W	L	PCT	ERA	G	GS	CG	IP	H	BB	SO	ShO	W	L	SV	AB	H	HR	BA
1898 PHI N	24	14	.632	3.18	39	37	33	306	285	97	121	6	1	0	0	122	32	0	.262
1899	23	15	.605	3.45	39	38	31	305	323	86	89	2	1	0	0	122	33	0	.270
1900	9	10	.474	4.65	22	20	16	160.2	194	71	47	1	0	1	0	68	17	0	.250
1901 2 teams			PHI A (18G 5-12)			CHI A (7G 4-2)													
" total	9	14	.391	4.13	25	22	19	191.2	218	74	64	1	1	1	1	75	15	0	.200
1902 CHI A	12	12	.500	3.51	32	30	22	246	263	66	96	2	0	0	0	85	17	0	.200
1903 BOS N	8	13	.381	3.18	25	23	18	181	198	61	100	0	0	1	0	71	16	0	.225
6 yrs.	85	78	.521	3.60	182	170	139	1390.1	1481	455	517	12	3	3	1	543	130	0	.239

Ron Piche

PICHE, RONALD JACQUES
B. May 22, 1935, Verdun, Que., Canada
BR TR 5'11" 165 lbs.

	W	L	PCT	ERA	G	GS	CG	IP	H	BB	SO	ShO	W	L	SV	AB	H	HR	BA
1960 MIL N	3	5	.375	3.56	37	0	0	48	48	23	38	0	3	5	9	7	0	0	.000
1961	2	2	.500	3.47	12	1	1	23.1	20	16	16	0	1	2	1	5	0	0	.000
1962	3	2	.600	4.85	14	8	2	52	54	29	28	0	0	0	0	18	1	0	.056
1963	1	1	.500	3.40	37	1	0	53	53	25	40	0	1	1	0	7	0	0	.000
1965 CAL A	0	3	.000	6.86	14	1	0	19.2	20	12	14	0	0	2	0	1	0	0	.000
1966 STL N	1	3	.250	4.26	20	0	0	25.1	21	18	21	0	1	3	2	4	0	0	.000
6 yrs.	10	16	.385	4.19	134	11	3	221.1	216	123	157	0	6	13	12	42	1	0	.024

Charlie Pickett

PICKETT, CHARLES ALBERT
B. Mar. 1, 1883, Delaware, Ohio   D. May 20, 1969, Springfield, Ohio
BR TR 6'1" 175 lbs.

	W	L	PCT	ERA	G	GS	CG	IP	H	BB	SO	ShO	W	L	SV	AB	H	HR	BA
1910 STL N	0	0	–	1.50	2	0	0	6	7	2	2	0	0	0	0	0	0	0	–

Clarence Pickrel

PICKREL, CLARENCE DOUGLAS
B. Mar. 28, 1911, Gretna, Va.   D. Dec. 9, 1983, Rocky Mount, Va.
BR TR 6'1" 180 lbs.

	W	L	PCT	ERA	G	GS	CG	IP	H	BB	SO	ShO	W	L	SV	AB	H	HR	BA
1933 PHI N	1	0	1.000	3.95	9	0	0	13.2	20	3	6	0	1	0	0	1	0	0	.000
1934 BOS N	0	0	–	5.06	10	1	0	16	24	7	9	0	0	0	0	2	0	0	.000
2 yrs.	1	0	1.000	4.55	19	1	0	29.2	44	10	15	0	1	0	0	3	0	0	.000

Mario Picone

PICONE, MARIO PETER (Babe)
B. July 5, 1926, Brooklyn, N. Y.
BR TR 5'11" 180 lbs.

	W	L	PCT	ERA	G	GS	CG	IP	H	BB	SO	ShO	W	L	SV	AB	H	HR	BA
1947 NY N	0	0	–	7.71	2	1	0	7	10	2	1	0	0	0	0	2	1	0	.500
1952	0	1	.000	7.00	2	1	0	9	11	5	3	0	0	0	0	2	0	0	.000
1954 2 teams			NY N (5G 0-0)			CIN N (4G 0-1)													
" total	0	1	.000	5.63	9	1	0	24	22	18	7	0	0	0	0	2	0	0	.000
3 yrs.	0	2	.000	6.30	13	3	0	40	43	25	11	0	0	0	0	6	1	0	.167

Al Piechota

PIECHOTA, ALOYSIUS EDWARD
B. Jan. 19, 1914, Chicago, Ill.
BR TR 6' 195 lbs.

	W	L	PCT	ERA	G	GS	CG	IP	H	BB	SO	ShO	W	L	SV	AB	H	HR	BA
1940 BOS N	2	5	.286	5.75	21	8	2	61	68	41	18	0	1	1	0	20	4	0	.200
1941	0	0	–	0.00	1	0	0	1	0	1	0	0	0	0	0	0	0	0	–
2 yrs.	2	5	.286	5.66	22	8	2	62	68	42	18	0	1	1	0	20	4	0	.200

	W	L	PCT	ERA	G	GS	CG	IP	H	BB	SO	ShO	Relief Pitching W	L	SV	BATTING AB	H	HR	BA

Cy Pieh

PIEH, EDWIN JOHN   BR TR 6'2"   190 lbs.
B. Sept. 29, 1886, Wannikee, Wis.   D. Sept. 12, 1945, Jacksonville, Fla.

	W	L	PCT	ERA	G	GS	CG	IP	H	BB	SO	ShO	W	L	SV	AB	H	HR	BA
1913 NY A	1	0	1.000	4.35	4	0	0	10.1	10	7	6	0	1	0	0	4	1	0	.250
1914	4	4	.500	5.05	18	4	1	62.1	68	29	24	0	3	2	0	17	2	0	.118
1915	4	5	.444	2.87	21	8	3	94	78	39	46	2	2	0	0	30	2	0	.067
3 yrs.	9	9	.500	3.78	43	12	4	166.2	156	75	76	2	6	2	0	51	5	0	.098

Billy Pierce

PIERCE, WALTER WILLIAM   BL TL 5'10"   160 lbs.
B. Apr. 2, 1927, Detroit, Mich.

	W	L	PCT	ERA	G	GS	CG	IP	H	BB	SO	ShO	W	L	SV	AB	H	HR	BA
1945 DET A	0	0	—	1.80	5	0	0	10	6	10	10	0	0	0	0	2	0	0	.000
1948	3	0	1.000	6.34	22	5	0	55.1	47	51	36	0	1	0	0	17	5	0	.294
1949 CHI A	7	15	.318	3.88	32	26	8	171.2	145	112	95	0	1	0	0	51	9	0	.176
1950	12	16	.429	3.98	33	29	15	219.1	189	137	118	1	1	0	1	77	20	0	.260
1951	15	14	.517	3.03	37	28	18	240.1	237	73	113	1	0	3	2	79	16	0	.203
1952	15	12	.556	2.57	33	32	14	255.1	144	79	144	4	0	0	1	91	17	0	.187
1953	18	12	.600	2.72	40	33	19	271.1	216	102	186	7	3	0	3	87	11	0	.126
1954	9	10	.474	3.48	36	26	12	188.2	179	86	148	4	0	0	3	57	11	0	.193
1955	15	10	.600	1.97	33	26	16	205.2	162	64	157	6	2	0	1	70	12	0	.171
1956	20	9	.690	3.32	35	33	21	276.1	261	100	192	1	0	1	1	102	16	0	.157
1957	20	12	.625	3.26	37	34	16	257	228	71	171	4	0	1	2	99	17	0	.172
1958	17	11	.607	2.68	35	32	19	245	204	66	144	3	0	0	2	83	17	0	.205
1959	14	15	.483	3.62	34	33	12	224	217	62	114	2	0	0	0	68	13	0	.191
1960	14	7	.667	3.62	32	30	8	196.1	201	46	108	1	1	0	0	67	12	0	.179
1961	10	9	.526	3.80	39	28	5	180	190	54	106	1	3	0	3	56	8	0	.143
1962 SF N	16	6	.727	3.49	30	23	7	162.1	147	35	76	2	0	0	1	56	12	0	.214
1963	3	11	.214	4.27	38	13	3	99	106	20	52	1	0	5	8	31	4	0	.129
1964	3	0	1.000	2.20	34	1	0	49	40	10	29	0	2	0	4	9	3	0	.333
18 yrs.	211	169	.555	3.27	585	432	193	3306.2	2989	1178	1999	38	14	10	32	1102	203	0	.184

WORLD SERIES

	W	L	PCT	ERA	G	GS	CG	IP	H	BB	SO	ShO	W	L	SV	AB	H	HR	BA
1959 CHI A	0	0	—	0.00	3	0	0	4	2	2	3	0	0	0	0	0	0	0	—
1962 SF N	1	1	.500	2.40	2	2	1	15	8	2	5	0	0	0	0	5	0	0	.000
2 yrs.	1	1	.500	1.89	5	2	1	19	10	4	8	0	0	0	0	5	0	0	.000

Ray Pierce

PIERCE, RAYMOND LESTER (Lefty)   BL TL 5'7"   156 lbs.
B. June 6, 1897, Emporia, Kans.   D. May 4, 1963, Denver, Colo.

	W	L	PCT	ERA	G	GS	CG	IP	H	BB	SO	ShO	W	L	SV	AB	H	HR	BA
1924 CHI N	0	0	—	7.36	6	0	0	7.1	7	4	2	0	0	0	0	0	0	0	—
1925 PHI N	5	4	.556	5.50	23	8	4	90	134	24	18	0	1	1	0	28	5	0	.179
1926	2	7	.222	5.63	37	7	1	84.2	128	35	18	0	2	2	0	24	3	0	.125
3 yrs.	7	11	.389	5.64	66	15	5	182	269	63	38	0	3	3	0	52	8	0	.154

Tony Pierce

PIERCE, TONY MICHAEL   BR TL 6'1"   190 lbs.
B. Jan. 29, 1946, Brunswick, Ga.

	W	L	PCT	ERA	G	GS	CG	IP	H	BB	SO	ShO	W	L	SV	AB	H	HR	BA
1967 KC A	3	4	.429	3.04	49	6	0	97.2	79	30	61	0	2	1	7	20	0	0	.000
1968 OAK A	1	2	.333	3.86	17	3	0	32.2	39	10	16	0	0	0	1	6	0	0	.000
2 yrs.	4	6	.400	3.25	66	9	0	130.1	118	40	77	0	2	1	8	26	0	0	.000

Bill Piercy

PIERCY, WILLIAM BENTON (Wild Bill)   BR TR 6'1½"   170 lbs.
B. May 2, 1896, El Monte, Calif.   D. Aug. 28, 1951, Long Beach, Calif.

	W	L	PCT	ERA	G	GS	CG	IP	H	BB	SO	ShO	W	L	SV	AB	H	HR	BA
1917 NY A	0	1	.000	3.00	1	1	1	9	9	2	4	0	0	0	0	2	0	0	.000
1921	5	4	.556	2.98	14	10	5	81.2	82	28	35	1	1	1	0	28	6	0	.214
1922 BOS A	3	9	.250	4.67	29	12	7	121.1	140	62	24	1	0	1	0	34	5	0	.147
1923	8	17	.320	3.41	30	24	11	187.1	193	73	51	0	0	4	0	53	7	0	.132
1924	5	7	.417	6.20	22	17	3	114.2	147	64	20	0	0	0	0	36	5	0	.139
1926 CHI N	6	5	.545	4.48	19	5	1	90.1	96	37	31	0	4	3	0	35	9	0	.257
6 yrs.	27	43	.386	4.29	115	69	28	604.1	667	266	165	2	5	9	0	188	32	0	.170

WORLD SERIES

	W	L	PCT	ERA	G	GS	CG	IP	H	BB	SO	ShO	W	L	SV	AB	H	HR	BA
1921 NY A	0	0	—	0.00	1	0	0	1	2	0	2	0	0	0	0	0	0	0	—

Marino Pieretti

PIERETTI, MARINO PAUL (Chick)   BR TR 5'7"   153 lbs.
B. Sept. 23, 1920, Lucca, Italy   D. Jan. 30, 1981, San Francisco, Calif.

	W	L	PCT	ERA	G	GS	CG	IP	H	BB	SO	ShO	W	L	SV	AB	H	HR	BA
1945 WAS A	14	13	.519	3.32	44	27	14	233.1	235	91	66	3	1	1	2	81	18	0	.222
1946	2	2	.500	5.95	30	2	1	62	70	40	20	0	1	1	0	14	3	0	.214
1947	2	4	.333	4.21	23	10	2	83.1	97	47	32	1	0	1	0	26	6	0	.231
1948 2 teams			WAS	A (8G 0–2)			CHI	A (21G 8–10)											
" total	8	12	.400	5.47	29	19	4	131.2	135	59	34	0	1	1	1	41	7	0	.171
1949 CHI A	4	6	.400	5.51	39	9	0	116	131	54	25	0	2	1	4	38	9	0	.237
1950 CLE A	0	1	.000	4.18	29	1	0	47.1	45	30	11	0	0	1	1	7	2	0	.286
6 yrs.	30	38	.441	4.53	194	68	21	673.2	713	321	188	4	5	6	8	207	45	0	.217

Al Pierotti

PIEROTTI, ALBERT FELIX   BR TR 5'10½"   195 lbs.
B. Oct. 24, 1895, Boston, Mass.   D. Feb. 12, 1964, Revere, Mass.

	W	L	PCT	ERA	G	GS	CG	IP	H	BB	SO	ShO	W	L	SV	AB	H	HR	BA
1920 BOS N	1	1	.500	2.88	6	2	2	25	23	9	12	0	0	0	0	8	2	0	.250
1921	0	1	.000	21.60	2	0	0	1.2	3	3	1	0	0	0	0	1	0	0	.000
2 yrs.	1	2	.333	4.05	8	2	2	26.2	26	12	13	0	0	0	0	9	2	0	.222

Bill Pierro

PIERRO, WILLIAM LEONARD (Wild Bill)   BR TR 6'1"   155 lbs.
B. Apr. 15, 1926, Brooklyn, N. Y.

	W	L	PCT	ERA	G	GS	CG	IP	H	BB	SO	ShO	W	L	SV	AB	H	HR	BA
1950 PIT N	0	2	.000	10.55	12	3	0	29	33	28	13	0	0	0	0	9	2	0	.222

Bill Pierson

PIERSON, WILLIAM MORRIS (Wild Bill)   BL TL 6'2"   180 lbs.
B. June 13, 1899, Atlantic City, N. J.   D. Feb. 20, 1959, Atlantic City, N. J.

	W	L	PCT	ERA	G	GS	CG	IP	H	BB	SO	ShO	W	L	SV	AB	H	HR	BA
1918 PHI A	0	1	.000	3.32	8	1	0	21.2	20	20	6	0	0	0	0	4	1	0	.250
1919	0	0	—	3.52	2	1	0	7.2	9	8	4	0	0	0	0	3	1	0	.333
1924	0	0	—	3.38	1	0	0	2.2	3	3	0	0	0	0	0	0	0	0	—
3 yrs.	0	1	.000	3.38	11	2	0	32	32	31	10	0	0	0	0	7	2	0	.286

	W	L	PCT	ERA	G	GS	CG	IP	H	BB	SO	ShO	Relief Pitching W	L	SV	BATTING AB	H	HR	BA

George Piktuzis

PIKTUZIS, GEORGE RICHARD
B. Jan. 3, 1932, Chicago, Ill.

BR TL 6'2" 200 lbs.

	W	L	PCT	ERA	G	GS	CG	IP	H	BB	SO	ShO	W	L	SV	AB	H	HR	BA
1956 CHI N	0	0	–	7.20	2	0	0	5	6	2	3	0	0	0	0	0	0	0	–

Duane Pillette

PILLETTE, DUANE XAVIER (Dee)
Son of Herman Pillette.
B. July 24, 1922, Detroit, Mich.

BR TR 6'3" 195 lbs.

	W	L	PCT	ERA	G	GS	CG	IP	H	BB	SO	ShO	W	L	SV	AB	H	HR	BA
1949 NY A	2	4	.333	4.34	12	3	2	37.1	43	19	9	0	1	2	0	11	0	0	.000
1950 2 teams			NY	A (4G 0–0)		STL	A (24G 3–5)												
" total	3	5	.375	6.58	28	7	1	80.2	113	47	22	0	1	4	2	22	3	0	.136
1951 STL A	6	14	.300	4.99	35	24	6	191	205	115	65	1	1	1	0	59	8	0	.136
1952	10	13	.435	3.59	30	30	9	205.1	222	55	62	1	0	0	0	66	12	0	.182
1953	7	13	.350	4.48	31	25	5	166.2	181	62	58	1	0	1	0	53	7	1	.132
1954 BAL A	10	14	.417	3.12	25	25	11	179	158	67	66	1	0	0	0	53	7	0	.132
1955	0	3	.000	6.53	7	5	0	20.2	31	14	13	0	0	0	0	6	1	0	.167
1956 PHI N	0	0	–	6.56	20	0	0	23.1	32	12	10	0	0	0	0	1	0	0	.000
8 yrs.	38	66	.365	4.40	188	119	34	904	985	391	305	4	3	8	2	271	38	1	.140

Herman Pillette

PILLETTE, HERMAN POLYCARP (Old Folks)
Father of Duane Pillette.
B. Dec. 26, 1895, St. Paul, Ore. D. Apr. 30, 1960, Sacramento, Calif.

BR TR 6'2" 190 lbs.

	W	L	PCT	ERA	G	GS	CG	IP	H	BB	SO	ShO	W	L	SV	AB	H	HR	BA
1917 CIN N	0	0	–	18.00	1	0	0	1	4	0	0	0	0	0	0	0	0	0	–
1922 DET A	19	12	.613	2.85	40	37	18	274.2	270	95	71	4	1	0	1	99	17	0	.172
1923	14	19	.424	3.85	47	37	14	250.1	280	83	64	0	3	2	1	85	21	0	.247
1924	1	1	.500	4.78	19	3	1	37.2	46	14	13	0	0	0	1	11	4	0	.364
4 yrs.	34	32	.515	3.45	107	77	33	563.2	600	192	148	4	4	2	3	195	42	0	.215

Squiz Pillion

PILLION, CECIL RANDOLPH
B. Apr. 13, 1894, Hartford, Conn. D. Sept. 30, 1962, Pittsburgh, Pa.

BL TL 6' 178 lbs.

	W	L	PCT	ERA	G	GS	CG	IP	H	BB	SO	ShO	W	L	SV	AB	H	HR	BA
1915 PHI A	0	0	–	6.75	2	0	0	5.1	10	2	0	0	0	0	0	1	0	0	.000

Horacio Pina

PINA, HORACIO GARCIA
B. Mar. 12, 1945, Coahuila, Mexico

BR TR 6'2" 177 lbs.

	W	L	PCT	ERA	G	GS	CG	IP	H	BB	SO	ShO	W	L	SV	AB	H	HR	BA
1968 CLE A	1	1	.500	1.72	12	3	0	31.1	24	15	24	0	0	0	2	6	0	0	.000
1969	4	2	.667	5.21	31	4	0	46.2	44	27	32	0	3	1	1	6	3	0	.500
1970 WAS A	5	3	.625	2.79	61	0	0	71	66	35	41	0	5	3	6	3	0	0	.000
1971	1	1	.500	3.57	56	0	0	58	47	31	38	0	1	1	2	1	0	0	.000
1972 TEX A	2	7	.222	3.20	60	0	0	76	61	43	60	0	2	7	15	5	1	0	.200
1973 OAK A	6	3	.667	2.76	47	0	0	88	58	34	41	0	6	3	8	0	0	0	
1974 2 teams			CHI	N (34G 3–4)		CAL	A (11G 1–2)												
" total	4	6	.400	3.66	45	0	0	59	58	31	38	0	4	6	4	5	1	0	.200
1978 PHI N	0	0	–	0.00	2	0	0	2	0	0	4	0	0	0	0	1	0	0	.000
8 yrs.	23	23	.500	3.25	314	7	0	432	358	216	278	0	21	21	38	27	5	0	.185
LEAGUE CHAMPIONSHIP SERIES																			
1973 OAK A	0	0	–	0.00	1	0	0	2	3	1	1	0	0	0	0	0	0	0	–
WORLD SERIES																			
1973 OAK A	0	0	–	0.00	2	0	0	3	6	2	0	0	0	0	0	0	0	0	–

George Pinckney

PINCKNEY, GEORGE BURTON
B. Jan. 11, 1862, Peoria, Ill. D. Nov. 9, 1926, Peoria, Ill.

BR TR

	W	L	PCT	ERA	G	GS	CG	IP	H	BB	SO	ShO	W	L	SV	AB	H	HR	BA
1886 BKN AA	0	0	–	4.50	1	0	0	2	2	0	0	0	0	0	0	*			

Ed Pinnance

PINNANCE, EDWARD D.
B. Oct. 22, 1879, Walpole Island, Ont., Canada D. Dec. 12, 1944, Walpole Island, Ont., Canada

TR

	W	L	PCT	ERA	G	GS	CG	IP	H	BB	SO	ShO	W	L	SV	AB	H	HR	BA
1903 PHI A	0	0	–	2.57	2	1	0	7	5	2	2	0	0	0	1	3	0	0	.000

Lerton Pinto

PINTO, WILLIAM LERTON
B. Apr. 8, 1899, Chillicothe, Ohio D. May 13, 1983, Oxnard, Calif.

BL TL 6' 190 lbs.

	W	L	PCT	ERA	G	GS	CG	IP	H	BB	SO	ShO	W	L	SV	AB	H	HR	BA
1922 PHI N	0	0	.000	5.11	9	0	0	24.2	31	14	4	0	0	1	0	9	1	0	.111
1924	0	0	–	9.00	3	0	0	4	7	0	1	0	0	0	0	1	0	0	.000
2 yrs.	0	1	.000	5.65	12	0	0	28.2	38	14	5	0	0	1	0	10	1	0	.100

Ed Pipgras

PIPGRAS, EDWARD JOHN
Brother of George Pipgras.
B. June 15, 1904, Schleswig, Iowa D. Apr. 13, 1964, Currie, Minn.

BR TR 6'2½" 175 lbs.

	W	L	PCT	ERA	G	GS	CG	IP	H	BB	SO	ShO	W	L	SV	AB	H	HR	BA
1932 BKN N	0	1	.000	5.40	5	1	0	10	16	6	5	0	0	1	0	2	0	0	.000

George Pipgras

PIPGRAS, GEORGE WILLIAM
Brother of Ed Pipgras.
B. Dec. 20, 1899, Ida Grove, Iowa

BR TR 6'1½" 185 lbs.

	W	L	PCT	ERA	G	GS	CG	IP	H	BB	SO	ShO	W	L	SV	AB	H	HR	BA
1923 NY A	1	3	.250	5.94	8	2	2	33.1	34	25	12	0	0	2	0	9	0	0	.000
1924	0	1	.000	9.98	9	1	0	15.1	20	18	4	0	0	0	1	3	1	0	.333
1927	10	3	.769	4.11	29	21	9	166.1	148	77	81	1	0	0	0	67	16	1	.239
1928	24	13	.649	3.38	46	38	22	300.2	314	103	139	4	0	1	3	115	18	0	.157
1929	18	12	.600	4.23	39	33	13	225.1	229	95	125	3	2	1	0	84	12	0	.143
1930	15	15	.500	4.11	44	30	15	221	230	70	111	3	1	2	4	80	12	1	.150
1931	7	6	.538	3.79	36	14	6	137.2	134	58	59	0	3	2	3	41	1	0	.024
1932	16	9	.640	4.19	32	27	14	219	235	87	111	2	1	2	0	82	18	0	.220
1933 2 teams			NY	A (4G 2–2)		BOS	A (22G 9–8)												
" total	11	10	.524	3.90	26	21	12	161.1	172	57	70	2	1	2	1	57	10	0	.175
1934 BOS A	0	0	–	8.10	2	1	0	3.1	4	3	0	0	0	0	0	1	0	0	.000
1935	0	1	.000	14.40	5	1	0	5	9	5	2	0	0	0	0	0	0	0	–
11 yrs.	102	73	.583	4.09	276	189	93	1488.1	1529	598	714	15	8	12	12	539	88	2	.163
WORLD SERIES																			
1927 NY A	1	0	1.000	2.00	1	1	1	9	7	1	2	0	0	0	0	3	1	0	.333

	W	L	PCT	ERA	G	GS	CG	IP	H	BB	SO	ShO	Relief Pitching W	L	SV	BATTING AB	H	HR	BA

George Pipgras continued

	W	L	PCT	ERA	G	GS	CG	IP	H	BB	SO	ShO	W	L	SV	AB	H	HR	BA
1928	1	0	1.000	2.00	1	1	1	9	4	4	8	0	0	0	0	2	0	0	.000
1932	1	0	1.000	4.50	1	1	0	8	9	3	1	0	0	0	0	5	0	0	.000
3 yrs.	3	0	1.000	2.77	3	3	2	26	20	8	11	0	0	0	0	10	1	0	.100
				1st															

Cotton Pippen

PIPPEN, HENRY HAROLD
B. Apr. 2, 1910, Cisco, Tex.   BR TR 6'2"   180 lbs.

	W	L	PCT	ERA	G	GS	CG	IP	H	BB	SO	ShO	W	L	SV	AB	H	HR	BA
1936 STL N	0	2	.000	7.71	6	3	0	21	37	8	8	0	0	0	0	6	1	0	.167
1939 2 teams			PHI	A	(25G	4–11)	DET	A	(3G	0–1)									
" total	4	12	.250	6.11	28	19	5	132.2	187	46	38	0	0	1	1	40	5	0	.125
1940 DET A	1	2	.333	6.75	4	3	0	21.1	29	10	9	0	0	0	0	8	0	0	.000
3 yrs.	5	16	.238	6.38	38	25	5	175	253	64	55	0	0	1	1	54	6	0	.111

Gerry Pirtle

PIRTLE, GERALD EUGENE
B. Dec. 3, 1947, Tulsa, Okla.   BR TR 6'1"   185 lbs.

	W	L	PCT	ERA	G	GS	CG	IP	H	BB	SO	ShO	W	L	SV	AB	H	HR	BA
1978 MON N	0	2	.000	5.88	19	0	0	26	33	23	14	0	0	2	0	0	0	0	–

Skip Pitlock

PITLOCK, LEE PATRICK
B. Nov. 6, 1947, Hillside, Ill.   BL TL 6'2"   180 lbs.

	W	L	PCT	ERA	G	GS	CG	IP	H	BB	SO	ShO	W	L	SV	AB	H	HR	BA
1970 SF N	5	5	.500	4.66	18	15	1	87	92	48	56	0	0	0	0	25	2	1	.080
1974 CHI A	3	3	.500	4.42	40	5	0	106	103	55	68	0	2	2	1	0	0	0	–
1975	0	0	–	0.00	1	0	0	1	0	0	0	0	0	0	0	0	0	0	–
3 yrs.	8	8	.500	4.52	59	20	1	193	196	103	124	0	2	2	1	25	2	1	.080

Togie Pittinger

PITTINGER, CHARLES RENO
B. 1871, Greencastle, Pa.   D. Jan. 14, 1909, Greencastle, Pa.   BL TR 6'2"

	W	L	PCT	ERA	G	GS	CG	IP	H	BB	SO	ShO	W	L	SV	AB	H	HR	BA
1900 BOS N	2	9	.182	5.13	18	13	8	114	135	54	27	0	0	0	0	46	6	0	.130
1901	13	16	.448	3.01	34	33	27	281.1	288	76	129	1	0	0	0	100	11	0	.110
1902	27	15	.643	2.52	46	40	36	389.1	360	128	174	7	2	3	0	147	20	0	.136
1903	19	23	.452	3.48	44	39	35	351.2	396	143	140	2	2	1	0	128	14	1	.109
1904	15	21	.417	2.66	38	38	35	335.1	298	144	146	5	0	0	0	121	13	0	.107
1905 PHI N	23	14	.622	3.10	46	37	29	337	311	104	136	4	3	2	2	122	19	0	.156
1906	8	10	.444	3.40	20	16	9	129.2	128	50	43	2	1	1	0	44	4	0	.091
1907	9	5	.643	3.00	16	12	8	102	101	35	37	1	2	0	0	36	5	0	.139
8 yrs.	116	113	.507	3.10	262	228	187	2040.1	2017	734	832	22	10	7	2	744	92	1	.124

Stan Pitula

PITULA, STANLEY
B. Mar. 23, 1931, Hackensack, N. J.   D. Aug. 15, 1965, Hackensack, N. J.   BR TR 5'10"   170 lbs.

	W	L	PCT	ERA	G	GS	CG	IP	H	BB	SO	ShO	W	L	SV	AB	H	HR	BA
1957 CLE A	2	2	.500	4.98	23	5	1	59.2	67	32	17	0	0	0	0	15	3	0	.200

Juan Pizarro

PIZARRO, JUAN CORDOVA
B. Feb. 7, 1938, Santurce, Puerto Rico   BL TL 5'11"   170 lbs.

	W	L	PCT	ERA	G	GS	CG	IP	H	BB	SO	ShO	W	L	SV	AB	H	HR	BA
1957 MIL N	5	6	.455	4.62	24	10	3	99.1	99	51	68	0	3	1	0	36	9	1	.250
1958	6	4	.600	2.70	16	10	7	96.2	75	47	84	1	1	1	1	32	8	0	.250
1959	6	2	.750	3.77	29	14	6	133.2	117	70	126	2	0	0	0	41	5	0	.122
1960	6	7	.462	4.55	21	17	3	114.2	105	72	88	0	1	1	0	40	11	0	.275
1961 CHI A	14	7	.667	3.05	39	25	12	194.2	164	89	188	1	0	0	2	69	17	0	.246
1962	12	14	.462	3.81	36	32	9	203.1	182	97	173	1	3	0	1	69	11	0	.159
1963	16	8	.667	2.39	32	28	10	214.2	177	63	163	3	2	0	1	73	13	2	.178
1964	19	9	.679	2.56	33	33	11	239	193	55	162	4	0	0	0	90	19	3	.211
1965	6	3	.667	3.43	18	18	2	97	96	37	65	1	0	0	0	34	8	1	.235
1966	8	6	.571	3.76	34	9	1	88.2	91	39	42	0	4	2	3	26	4	0	.154
1967 PIT N	8	10	.444	3.95	50	9	1	107	99	52	96	1	7	5	9	27	7	0	.259
1968 2 teams			PIT	N	(12G	1–1)	BOS	A	(19G	6–8)									
" total	7	9	.438	3.56	31	21	1	118.2	111	54	90	0	2	3	2	33	5	0	.152
1969 3 teams			BOS	A	(6G	0–1)	CLE	A	(48G	3–3)	OAK	A	(3G	1–1)					
" total	4	5	.444	3.35	57	4	1	99.1	84	58	52	0	3	5	7	20	5	0	.250
1970 CHI N	0	0	–	4.50	12	0	0	16	16	9	14	0	0	0	1	3	0	0	.000
1971	7	6	.538	3.48	16	14	6	101	78	40	67	3	0	0	0	34	6	1	.176
1972	4	5	.444	3.97	16	14	6	59	66	32	24	0	3	0	1	21	3	0	.143
1973 2 teams			CHI	N	(2G	0–1)	HOU	N	(15G	2–2)									
" total	2	3	.400	7.24	17	1	0	27.1	34	12	13	0	2	2	0	0	0	0	.000
1974 PIT N	1	1	.500	1.88	7	2	0	24	20	11	7	0	0	0	0	6	2	0	.333
18 yrs.	131	105	.555	3.43	488	245	79	2034	1807	888	1522	17	31	20	28	658	133	8	.202

LEAGUE CHAMPIONSHIP SERIES

	W	L	PCT	ERA	G	GS	CG	IP	H	BB	SO	ShO	W	L	SV	AB	H	HR	BA
1974 PIT N	0	0	–	0.00	1	0	0	.2	0	1	0	0	0	0	0	0	0	0	–

WORLD SERIES

	W	L	PCT	ERA	G	GS	CG	IP	H	BB	SO	ShO	W	L	SV	AB	H	HR	BA
1957 MIL N	0	0	–	10.80	1	0	0	1.2	3	2	1	0	0	0	0	1	0	0	.000
1958	0	0	–	5.40	1	0	0	1.2	2	1	3	0	0	0	0	0	0	0	–
2 yrs.	0	0	–	8.10	2	0	0	3.1	5	3	4	0	0	0	0	1	0	0	.000

Gordon Pladson

PLADSON, GORDON CECIL
B. July 31, 1956, New Westminster, B. C., Canada   BR TR 6'4"   210 lbs.

	W	L	PCT	ERA	G	GS	CG	IP	H	BB	SO	ShO	W	L	SV	AB	H	HR	BA
1979 HOU N	0	0	–	4.50	4	0	0	4	9	2	2	0	0	0	0	0	0	0	–
1980	0	4	.000	4.39	12	6	0	41	38	16	13	0	0	0	0	10	0	0	.000
1981	0	0	–	9.00	2	0	0	4	9	3	3	0	0	0	0	0	0	0	–
1982	0	0	–	54.00	2	0	0	1.1	10	2	0	0	0	0	0	0	0	0	–
4 yrs.	0	4	.000	6.08	20	6	0	50.1	66	23	18	0	0	0	0	10	0	0	.000

Emil Planeta

PLANETA, EMIL JOSEPH
B. Jan. 13, 1909, Higganum, Conn.   D. Feb. 2, 1963, Rocky Hill, Conn.   BR TR 6'   190 lbs.

	W	L	PCT	ERA	G	GS	CG	IP	H	BB	SO	ShO	W	L	SV	AB	H	HR	BA
1931 NY N	0	0	–	10.13	2	0	0	5.1	7	4	0	0	0	0	0	0	0	0	.000

	W	L	PCT	ERA	G	GS	CG	IP	H	BB	SO	ShO	Relief Pitching W	L	SV	BATTING AB	H	HR	BA

Eddie Plank

PLANK, EDWARD ARTHUR
B. Apr. 9, 1952, Chicago, Ill.
BR TR 6'1" 205 lbs.

	W	L	PCT	ERA	G	GS	CG	IP	H	BB	SO	ShO	W	L	SV	AB	H	HR	BA
1978 SF N	0	0	–	3.86	5	0	0	7	6	2	1	0	0	0	0	0	0	0	–
1979	0	0	–	6.75	4	0	0	4	9	2	1	0	0	0	0	0	0	0	–
2 yrs.	0	0	–	4.91	9	0	0	11	15	4	2	0	0	0	0	0	0	0	–

Eddie Plank

PLANK, EDWARD STEWART (Gettysburg Eddie)
B. Aug. 31, 1875, Gettysburg, Pa.   D. Feb. 24, 1926, Gettysburg, Pa.
Hall of Fame 1946.
BL TL 5'11½" 175 lbs.

	W	L	PCT	ERA	G	GS	CG	IP	H	BB	SO	ShO	W	L	SV	AB	H	HR	BA
1901 PHI A	17	13	.567	3.31	33	32	28	260.2	254	68	90	1	0	0	0	99	18	0	.182
1902	20	15	.571	3.30	36	32	31	300	319	61	107	1	2	1	0	120	35	0	.292
1903	23	16	.590	2.38	43	40	33	336	317	65	176	3	1	1	0	134	25	1	.187
1904	26	16	.619	2.14	43	43	37	357	309	86	201	7	0	0	0	129	31	0	.240
1905	25	12	.676	2.26	41	41	36	346.2	287	75	210	4	0	0	0	126	29	0	.230
1906	19	6	.760	2.25	26	25	21	211.2	173	51	108	5	0	1	0	73	17	0	.233
1907	24	16	.600	2.20	43	40	33	343.2	282	85	183	8	1	0	0	123	26	1	.211
1908	14	16	.467	2.17	34	28	21	244.2	202	46	135	4	2	2	1	89	16	0	.180
1909	19	10	.655	1.70	34	33	24	275.1	215	62	132	3	0	0	0	96	21	1	.219
1910	16	10	.615	2.01	38	32	22	250.1	218	55	123	1	0	0	2	86	11	0	.128
1911	23	8	.742	2.10	40	30	24	256.2	237	77	149	6	3	1	4	94	18	0	.191
1912	26	6	.813	2.22	37	30	24	259.2	234	83	110	5	5	0	2	90	24	0	.267
1913	18	10	.643	2.60	41	29	18	242.2	211	57	151	7	4	0	4	75	8	0	.107
1914	15	7	.682	2.87	34	22	12	185.1	178	42	110	4	4	1	3	60	9	0	.150
1915 STL F	21	11	.656	2.08	42	31	23	268.1	212	54	147	6	2	3	3	93	24	0	.258
1916 STL A	16	15	.516	2.33	37	26	17	235.2	203	67	88	3	3	3	3	81	15	0	.185
1917	5	6	.455	1.79	20	13	8	131	105	38	26	1	0	1	1	38	4	0	.105
17 yrs.	327	193	.629	2.34	622	527	412	4505.1	3956	1072	2246	69	27	14	23	1606	331	3	.206
	9th											5th							

WORLD SERIES

	W	L	PCT	ERA	G	GS	CG	IP	H	BB	SO	ShO	W	L	SV	AB	H	HR	BA
1905 PHI A	0	2	.000	1.59	2	2	2	17	14	4	11	0	0	0	0	6	1	0	.167
1911	1	1	.500	1.86	2	1	1	9.2	6	0	8	0	0	1	0	3	0	0	.000
1913	1	1	.500	0.95	2	2	2	19	9	3	7	0	0	0	0	7	1	0	.143
1914	0	1	.000	1.00	1	1	1	9	7	4	6	0	0	0	0	2	0	0	.000
4 yrs.	2	5	.286	1.32	7	6	6	54.2	36	11	32	0	0	1	0	18	2	0	.111
	2nd			10th			6th												

Bill Pleis

PLEIS, WILLIAM
B. Aug. 5, 1937, St. Louis, Mo.
BL TL 5'10" 170 lbs.

	W	L	PCT	ERA	G	GS	CG	IP	H	BB	SO	ShO	W	L	SV	AB	H	HR	BA
1961 MIN A	4	2	.667	4.95	37	0	0	56.1	59	34	32	0	4	2	2	9	1	0	.111
1962	2	5	.286	4.40	21	4	0	45	46	14	31	0	2	2	3	14	4	0	.286
1963	6	2	.750	4.37	36	4	1	68	67	16	37	0	4	1	0	16	2	0	.125
1964	4	1	.800	3.91	47	0	0	50.2	43	31	42	0	4	1	4	4	1	0	.250
1965	4	4	.500	2.98	41	2	0	51.1	49	27	33	0	4	2	4	7	0	0	.000
1966	1	2	.333	1.93	8	0	0	9.1	5	4	9	0	1	2	0	0	0	0	–
6 yrs.	21	16	.568	4.07	190	10	1	280.2	269	126	184	0	19	10	13	50	8	0	.160

WORLD SERIES

	W	L	PCT	ERA	G	GS	CG	IP	H	BB	SO	ShO	W	L	SV	AB	H	HR	BA
1965 MIN A	0	0	–	9.00	1	0	0	1	2	0	0	0	0	0	0	0	0	0	–

Norman Plitt

PLITT, NORMAN WILLIAM
B. Feb. 21, 1893, York, Pa.   D. Feb. 1, 1954, New York, N. Y.
BR TR 5'11" 170 lbs.

	W	L	PCT	ERA	G	GS	CG	IP	H	BB	SO	ShO	W	L	SV	AB	H	HR	BA
1918 BKN N	0	0	–	4.50	1	0	0	2	3	1	0	0	0	0	0	1	1	0	1.000
1927 2 teams		BKN	N (19G 2–6)		NY	N (3G 1–0)													
" total	3	6	.333	4.78	22	8	1	69.2	82	37	9	0	2	1	0	19	4	0	.211
2 yrs.	3	6	.333	4.77	23	8	1	71.2	85	38	9	0	2	1	0	20	5	0	.250

Tim Plodinec

PLODINEC, TIMOTHY ALFRED
B. Jan. 27, 1947, Aliquippa, Pa.
BR TR 6'4" 190 lbs.

	W	L	PCT	ERA	G	GS	CG	IP	H	BB	SO	ShO	W	L	SV	AB	H	HR	BA
1972 STL N	0	0	–	27.00	1	0	0	.1	3	0	0	0	0	0	0	0	0	0	–

Ray Poat

POAT, RAYMOND WILLIS
B. Dec. 19, 1917, Chicago, Ill.
BR TR 6'2" 200 lbs.

	W	L	PCT	ERA	G	GS	CG	IP	H	BB	SO	ShO	W	L	SV	AB	H	HR	BA
1942 CLE A	1	3	.250	5.40	4	4	1	18.1	24	9	8	1	0	0	0	5	0	0	.000
1943	2	5	.286	4.40	17	4	1	45	44	20	31	0	0	4	0	13	2	0	.154
1944	4	8	.333	5.13	36	6	1	80.2	82	37	40	0	3	4	1	17	0	0	.000
1947 NY N	4	3	.571	2.55	7	7	5	60	53	13	25	0	0	0	0	21	4	1	.190
1948	11	10	.524	4.34	39	24	7	157.2	162	67	57	3	2	3	0	56	7	0	.125
1949 2 teams		NY	N (2G 0–0)		PIT	N (11G 0–1)													
" total	0	1	.000	7.04	13	2	0	38.1	60	16	17	0	0	0	0	10	1	0	.100
6 yrs.	22	30	.423	4.55	116	47	15	400	425	162	178	4	5	11	1	122	14	1	.115

Bud Podbielan

PODBIELAN, CLARENCE ANTHONY
B. Mar. 6, 1924, Curlew, Wash.   D. Oct. 26, 1982, Syracuse, N. Y.
BR TR 6'1½" 170 lbs.

	W	L	PCT	ERA	G	GS	CG	IP	H	BB	SO	ShO	W	L	SV	AB	H	HR	BA
1949 BKN N	0	1	.000	3.65	7	1	0	12.1	9	9	5	0	0	1	0	3	0	0	.000
1950	5	4	.556	5.33	20	10	2	72.2	93	29	28	0	1	2	1	28	3	0	.107
1951	2	2	.500	3.50	27	5	1	79.2	67	36	26	0	2	1	0	23	7	0	.304
1952 2 teams		BKN	N (3G 0–0)		CIN	N (24G 4–5)													
" total	4	5	.444	3.15	27	7	4	88.2	82	29	23	1	1	1	1	25	4	0	.160
1953 CIN N	6	16	.273	4.73	36	24	8	186.1	214	67	74	1	1	1	1	56	7	0	.125
1954	7	10	.412	5.36	27	24	4	131	157	58	42	0	0	0	0	42	6	0	.143
1955	1	2	.333	3.21	17	2	0	42	36	11	26	0	1	0	0	5	2	0	.400
1957	0	1	.000	6.19	5	3	1	16	18	4	13	0	0	0	0	5	0	0	.000
1959 CLE A	0	1	.000	5.84	6	0	0	12.1	17	2	5	0	0	0	0	1	0	0	.000
9 yrs.	25	42	.373	4.49	172	76	20	641	693	245	242	2	6	7	3	188	29	0	.154

	W	L	PCT	ERA	G	GS	CG	IP	H	BB	SO	ShO	Relief Pitching W	L	SV	BATTING AB	H	HR	BA

Johnny Podgajny

PODGAJNY, JOHN SIGMUND (Specs)
B. June 10, 1920, Chester, Pa. D. Mar. 2, 1971, Chester, Pa. BR TR 6'2" 173 lbs.

	W	L	PCT	ERA	G	GS	CG	IP	H	BB	SO	ShO	W	L	SV	AB	H	HR	BA
1940 PHI N	1	3	.250	2.83	4	4	3	35	33	1	12	0	0	0	0	12	2	0	.167
1941	9	12	.429	4.62	34	24	8	181.1	191	70	53	0	1	0	0	62	8	0	.129
1942	6	14	.300	3.91	43	23	6	186.2	191	63	40	0	0	1	0	60	11	0	.183
1943 2 teams			PHI	N	(13G 4–4)		PIT	N	(15G 0–4)										
" total	4	8	.333	4.39	28	10	3	98.1	114	29	20	0	1	2	0	27	6	0	.222
1946 CLE A	0	0	–	5.00	6	0	0	9	13	2	4	0	0	0	0	0	0	0	–
5 yrs.	20	37	.351	4.20	115	61	20	510.1	542	165	129	0	2	3	0	161	27	0	.168

Johnny Podres

PODRES, JOHN JOSEPH
B. Sept. 30, 1932, Witherbee, N. Y. BL TL 5'11" 170 lbs.

	W	L	PCT	ERA	G	GS	CG	IP	H	BB	SO	ShO	W	L	SV	AB	H	HR	BA
1953 BKN N	9	4	.692	4.23	33	18	3	115	126	64	82	1	4	0	0	36	11	0	.306
1954	11	7	.611	4.27	29	21	6	151.2	147	53	79	2	1	0	0	60	17	0	.283
1955	9	10	.474	3.95	27	24	5	159.1	160	57	114	2	0	0	0	60	11	0	.183
1957	12	9	.571	**2.66**	31	27	10	196	168	44	109	6	1	0	3	72	15	0	.208
1958 LA N	13	15	.464	3.72	39	31	10	210.1	208	78	143	2	0	1	1	71	9	0	.127
1959	14	9	.609	4.11	34	29	6	195	192	74	145	2	1	0	0	65	16	0	.246
1960	14	12	.538	3.08	34	33	8	227.2	217	71	159	1	1	0	0	66	9	0	.136
1961	18	5	**.783**	3.74	32	29	6	182.2	192	51	124	1	2	0	0	69	16	0	.232
1962	15	13	.536	3.81	40	40	8	255	270	71	178	0	0	0	0	88	14	1	.159
1963	14	12	.538	3.54	37	34	10	198.1	196	64	134	5	0	0	1	64	9	1	.141
1964	0	2	.000	16.88	2	2	0	2.2	5	3	0	0	0	0	0	0	0	0	–
1965	7	6	.538	3.43	27	22	2	134	126	39	63	1	0	2	1	45	8	0	.178
1966 2 teams			LA	N	(1G 0–0)		DET	A	(36G 4–5)										
" total	4	5	.444	3.38	37	13	2	109.1	108	35	54	1	2	1	4	30	7	0	.233
1967 DET A	3	1	.750	3.84	21	8	0	63.1	58	11	34	0	1	0	1	20	2	0	.100
1969 SD N	5	6	.455	4.29	17	9	1	65	66	28	17	0	0	0	0	16	1	0	.063
15 yrs.	148	116	.561	3.67	440	340	77	2265.1	2239	743	1435	24	13	4	11	762	145	2	.190

WORLD SERIES

	W	L	PCT	ERA	G	GS	CG	IP	H	BB	SO	ShO	W	L	SV	AB	H	HR	BA
1953 BKN N	0	1	.000	3.38	1	1	0	2.2	1	2	0	0	0	0	0	1	1	0	1.000
1955	2	0	1.000	1.00	2	2	2	18	15	4	10	1	0	0	0	7	1	0	.143
1959 LA N	1	0	1.000	4.82	2	2	0	9.1	7	6	4	0	0	0	0	4	2	0	.500
1963	1	0	1.000	1.08	1	1	0	8.1	6	1	4	0	0	0	0	4	1	0	.250
4 yrs.	4	1	.800	2.11	6	6	2	38.1	29	13	18	1	0	0	0	16	5	0	.313

Joe Poetz

POETZ, JOSEPH FRANK
B. Nov. 30, 1895, St. Louis, Mo. D. Feb. 7, 1942, St. Louis, Mo. BR TR 5'10½" 185 lbs.

	W	L	PCT	ERA	G	GS	CG	IP	H	BB	SO	ShO	W	L	SV	AB	H	HR	BA
1926 NY N	0	1	.000	3.38	2	1	0	8	5	8	0	0	0	0	0	1	0	0	.000

Boots Poffenberger

POFFENBERGER, CLETUS ELWOOD
B. July 1, 1915, Williamsport, Md. BR TR 5'10" 178 lbs.

	W	L	PCT	ERA	G	GS	CG	IP	H	BB	SO	ShO	W	L	SV	AB	H	HR	BA
1937 DET A	10	5	.667	4.65	29	16	5	137.1	147	79	35	0	3	1	3	51	11	0	.216
1938	6	7	.462	4.82	25	15	8	125	147	66	28	0	0	2	1	44	8	0	.182
1939 BKN N	0	0	–	5.40	3	1	0	5	7	4	2	0	0	0	0	1	0	0	.000
3 yrs.	16	12	.571	4.75	57	32	13	267.1	301	149	65	0	3	3	4	96	19	0	.198

Tom Poholsky

POHOLSKY, THOMAS GEORGE
B. Aug. 26, 1929, Detroit, Mich. BR TR 6'3" 205 lbs.

	W	L	PCT	ERA	G	GS	CG	IP	H	BB	SO	ShO	W	L	SV	AB	H	HR	BA
1950 STL N	0	0	–	3.68	5	1	0	14.2	16	3	2	0	0	0	0	2	0	0	.000
1951	7	13	.350	4.43	38	26	10	195	204	68	70	1	1	2	1	67	14	0	.209
1954	5	7	.417	3.06	25	13	4	106	101	20	55	0	0	2	0	27	4	0	.148
1955	9	11	.450	3.81	30	24	8	151	143	35	66	2	0	0	0	44	8	0	.182
1956	9	14	.391	3.59	33	29	7	203	210	44	95	2	0	0	0	69	11	0	.159
1957 CHI N	1	7	.125	4.93	28	11	1	84	117	22	28	0	0	0	0	19	2	0	.105
6 yrs.	31	52	.373	3.93	159	104	30	753.2	791	192	316	5	1	4	1	228	39	0	.171

Jennings Poindexter

POINDEXTER, CHESTER JENNINGS (Jinx)
B. Sept. 30, 1910, Pauls Valley, Okla. D. Mar. 3, 1983, Norman, Okla. BL TL 5'10" 165 lbs.

	W	L	PCT	ERA	G	GS	CG	IP	H	BB	SO	ShO	W	L	SV	AB	H	HR	BA
1936 BOS A	0	2	.000	6.75	3	3	0	10.2	13	16	2	0	0	0	0	4	0	0	.000
1939 PHI N	0	0	–	4.15	11	1	0	30.1	29	15	12	0	0	0	0	10	2	0	.200
2 yrs.	0	2	.000	4.83	14	4	0	41	42	31	14	0	0	0	0	14	2	0	.143

Lou Polchow

POLCHOW, LOUIS WILLIAM
B. Mar. 14, 1881, Mankato, Minn. D. Aug. 15, 1912, Good Thunder, Minn. 5'9"

	W	L	PCT	ERA	G	GS	CG	IP	H	BB	SO	ShO	W	L	SV	AB	H	HR	BA
1902 CLE A	0	1	.000	5.63	1	1	1	8	9	4	2	0	0	0	0	4	0	0	.000

Dick Pole

POLE, RICHARD HENRY
B. Oct. 13, 1950, Trout Creek, Mich. BR TR 6'3" 200 lbs.

	W	L	PCT	ERA	G	GS	CG	IP	H	BB	SO	ShO	W	L	SV	AB	H	HR	BA
1973 BOS A	3	2	.600	5.56	12	7	0	55	70	18	24	0	0	0	0	0	0	0	–
1974	1	1	.500	4.20	15	2	0	45	55	13	32	0	1	0	1	0	0	0	–
1975	4	6	.400	4.42	18	11	2	89.2	102	32	42	1	1	0	0	0	0	0	–
1976	6	5	.545	4.31	31	15	1	121	131	48	49	0	0	1	0	1	0	0	.000
1977 SEA A	7	12	.368	5.16	25	24	3	122	127	57	51	0	0	0	0	0	0	0	–
1978	4	11	.267	6.48	21	18	2	98.2	122	41	41	0	0	1	0	0	0	0	–
6 yrs.	25	37	.403	5.05	122	77	8	531.1	607	209	239	1	2	2	1	1	0	0	.000

WORLD SERIES

	W	L	PCT	ERA	G	GS	CG	IP	H	BB	SO	ShO	W	L	SV	AB	H	HR	BA
1975 BOS A	0	0	–	∞	1	0	0	0	1	0	0	0	0	0	0	0	0	0	–

Ken Polivka

POLIVKA, KENNETH LYLE (Soup)
B. Jan. 21, 1921, Chicago, Ill. BL TL 5'10½" 183 lbs.

	W	L	PCT	ERA	G	GS	CG	IP	H	BB	SO	ShO	W	L	SV	AB	H	HR	BA
1947 CIN N	0	0	–	3.00	2	0	0	3	3	3	1	0	0	0	0	0	0	0	–

	W	L	PCT	ERA	G	GS	CG	IP	H	BB	SO	ShO	Relief Pitching W	L	SV	AB	H	HR	BA

Howie Pollet

POLLET, HOWARD JOSEPH
B. June 26, 1921, New Orleans, La.   D. Aug. 8, 1974, Houston, Tex.
BL TL 6'1½" 175 lbs.

Year	Team	W	L	PCT	ERA	G	GS	CG	IP	H	BB	SO	ShO	RW	RL	SV	AB	H	HR	BA
1941	STL N	5	2	.714	1.93	9	8	6	70	55	27	37	2	0	0	0	28	5	0	.179
1942		7	5	.583	2.88	27	13	5	109.1	102	39	42	2	0	1	0	31	7	0	.226
1943		8	4	.667	1.75	16	14	12	118.1	83	32	61	5	0	0	0	43	7	0	.163
1946		21	10	.677	2.10	40	32	22	266	228	86	107	4	0	0	5	87	14	0	.161
1947		9	11	.450	4.34	37	24	9	176.1	195	87	73	0	1	0	2	65	15	0	.231
1948		13	8	.619	4.54	36	26	11	186.1	216	67	80	0	2	0	0	68	8	0	.118
1949		20	9	.690	2.77	39	28	17	230.2	228	59	108	5	3	1	1	82	16	0	.195
1950		14	13	.519	3.29	37	30	14	232.1	228	68	117	2	1	1	2	84	12	0	.143
1951	2 teams			STL	N (6G 0–3)			PIT	N (21G 6–10)											
"	total	6	13	.316	4.98	27	23	4	141	151	59	57	1	0	2	1	37	5	0	.135
1952	PIT N	7	16	.304	4.12	31	30	9	214	217	71	90	1	0	0	0	68	13	0	.191
1953	2 teams			PIT	N (5G 1–1)			CHI	N (25G 5–6)											
"	total	6	7	.462	4.79	30	18	2	124	147	50	53	0	0	1	1	34	5	0	.147
1954	CHI N	8	10	.444	3.58	20	20	4	128.1	131	54	58	2	0	0	0	47	13	0	.277
1955		4	3	.571	5.61	24	7	1	61	62	27	27	1	3	0	5	15	6	0	.400
1956	2 teams			CHI	A (11G 3–1)			PIT	N (19G 0–4)											
"	total	3	5	.375	3.62	30	4	0	49.2	45	19	24	0	3	4	3	9	3	0	.333
	14 yrs.	131	116	.530	3.51	403	277	116	2107.1	2088	745	934	25	13	10	20	698	129	0	.185

WORLD SERIES

Year	Team	W	L	PCT	ERA	G	GS	CG	IP	H	BB	SO	ShO	RW	RL	SV	AB	H	HR	BA
1942	STL N	0	0	—	0.00	1	0	0	0	0	0	0	0	0	0	0	0	0	0	—
1946		0	1	.000	3.48	2	2	1	10.1	12	4	3	0	0	0	0	4	0	0	.000
	2 yrs.	0	1	.000	3.38	3	2	1	10.2	12	4	3	0	0	0	0	4	0	0	.000

Lou Polli

POLLI, LOUIS AMERICO (Crip)
B. July 9, 1901, Barre, Vt.
BR TR 5'10½" 165 lbs.

Year	Team	W	L	PCT	ERA	G	GS	CG	IP	H	BB	SO	ShO	RW	RL	SV	AB	H	HR	BA
1932	STL A	0	0	—	5.40	5	0	0	6.2	13	3	5	0	0	0	0	2	1	0	.500
1944	NY N	0	2	.000	4.54	19	0	0	35.2	42	20	6	0	0	2	3	6	0	0	.000
	2 yrs.	0	2	.000	4.68	24	0	0	42.1	55	23	11	0	0	2	3	8	1	0	.125

John Poloni

POLONI, JOHN PAUL
B. Feb. 28, 1954, Dearborn, Mich.
BL TL 6'5" 210 lbs.

Year	Team	W	L	PCT	ERA	G	GS	CG	IP	H	BB	SO	ShO	RW	RL	SV	AB	H	HR	BA
1977	TEX A	1	0	1.000	6.43	2	1	0	7	8	1	5	0	0	0	0	0	0	0	—

John Pomorski

POMORSKI, JOHN LEO
B. Dec. 30, 1905, Brooklyn, N. Y.   D. Dec. 6, 1977, Brampton, Ont., Canada
BR TR 6' 178 lbs.

Year	Team	W	L	PCT	ERA	G	GS	CG	IP	H	BB	SO	ShO	RW	RL	SV	AB	H	HR	BA
1934	CHI A	0	0	—	5.40	3	0	0	1.2	1	2	0	0	0	0	0	0	0	0	—

Arlie Pond

POND, ERASMUS ARLINGTON
B. Jan. 19, 1872, Rutland, Vt.   D. Sept. 19, 1930, Cebu, Philippines
BR TR 5'10" 160 lbs.

Year	Team	W	L	PCT	ERA	G	GS	CG	IP	H	BB	SO	ShO	RW	RL	SV	AB	H	HR	BA
1895	BAL N	0	1	.000	5.93	6	1	1	13.2	10	12	13	0	0	0	0	6	2	0	.333
1896		16	8	.667	3.49	28	26	21	214.1	232	57	80	2	1	0	0	81	19	0	.235
1897		18	9	.667	3.52	32	28	23	248	267	72	59	0	1	0	0	90	22	0	.244
1898		1	1	.500	0.45	3	2	1	20	8	9	4	1	0	0	0	7	2	0	.286
	4 yrs.	35	19	.648	3.45	69	57	46	496	517	150	156	3	2	0	2	184	45	0	.245

Elmer Ponder

PONDER, CHARLES ELMER
B. June 26, 1893, Reed, Okla.   D. Apr. 20, 1974, Albuquerque, N. M.
BR TR 6' 178 lbs.

Year	Team	W	L	PCT	ERA	G	GS	CG	IP	H	BB	SO	ShO	RW	RL	SV	AB	H	HR	BA
1917	PIT N	1	1	.500	1.69	3	2	1	21.1	12	6	11	1	0	0	0	7	0	0	.000
1919		0	5	.000	3.99	9	5	0	47.1	55	6	6	0	0	0	0	15	2	0	.133
1920		11	15	.423	2.62	33	23	13	196	182	40	62	2	3	3	0	59	7	0	.119
1921	2 teams			PIT	N (8G 2–0)			CHI	N (16G 3–6)											
"	total	5	6	.455	4.18	24	12	6	114	146	20	34	0	1	0	0	43	4	0	.093
	4 yrs.	17	27	.386	3.21	69	42	20	378.2	395	72	113	3	4	3	0	124	13	0	.105

Ed Poole

POOLE, EDWARD I.
B. Sept. 7, 1874, Canton, Ohio   D. Mar. 11, 1919, Malvern, Ohio
BR TR 5'10" 175 lbs.

Year	Team	W	L	PCT	ERA	G	GS	CG	IP	H	BB	SO	ShO	RW	RL	SV	AB	H	HR	BA
1900	PIT N	1	0	1.000	1.29	1	0	0	7	4	0	3	0	1	0	0	4	2	1	.500
1901		5	4	.556	3.60	12	10	8	80	78	30	26	1	0	0	0	78	16	1	.205
1902	2 teams			PIT	N (1G 0–0)			CIN	N (16G 12–4)											
"	total	12	4	.750	2.10	17	16	16	146	136	57	57	2	0	0	0	65	8	0	.123
1903	CIN N	8	13	.381	3.28	25	21	18	184	188	77	73	1	0	0	0	70	17	0	.243
1904	BKN N	8	13	.381	3.39	25	23	19	178	178	74	67	1	1	0	1	62	8	0	.129
	5 yrs.	34	34	.500	3.04	80	70	61	595	584	238	226	5	2	0	1	279	51	2	.183

Tom Poorman

POORMAN, THOMAS IVERSON
B. Oct. 14, 1857, Lock Haven, Pa.   D. Feb. 18, 1905, Lock Haven, Pa.
BL TR 5'10½" 170 lbs.

Year	Team	W	L	PCT	ERA	G	GS	CG	IP	H	BB	SO	ShO	RW	RL	SV	AB	H	HR	BA
1880	2 teams			BUF	N (11G 1–8)			CHI	N (2G 2–0)											
"	total	3	8	.273	3.87	13	10	9	100	129	27	13	0	1	0	1	95	16	0	.168
1884	TOL AA	0	0	1.000	3.00	1	1	1	9	13	2	0	0	0	0	0	382	89	0	.233
1887	PHI AA	0	0	—	40.50	1	0	0	.2	5	1	1	0	0	0	0	585	155	4	.265
	3 yrs.	3	9	.250	4.02	15	11	10	109.2	147	30	14	0	1	0	1	*			

Bill Popp

POPP, WILLIAM PETER
B. June 7, 1877, St. Louis, Mo.   D. Sept. 5, 1909, St. Louis, Mo.
TR

Year	Team	W	L	PCT	ERA	G	GS	CG	IP	H	BB	SO	ShO	RW	RL	SV	AB	H	HR	BA
1902	STL N	2	6	.250	4.92	9	7	5	60.1	87	26	20	1	0	0	0	21	1	0	.048

Ed Porray

PORRAY, EDMUND JOSEPH
B. Dec. 15, 1888, Brooklyn, N. Y.   D. July 13, 1954, Lackawaxen, Pa.

Year	Team	W	L	PCT	ERA	G	GS	CG	IP	H	BB	SO	ShO	RW	RL	SV	AB	H	HR	BA
1914	BUF F	1	1	.500	4.35	3	3	0	10.1	18	7	0	0	0	0	0	4	0	0	.000

Chuck Porter

PORTER, CHARLES WILLIAM
B. Jan. 12, 1956, Baltimore, Md.
BR TR 6'3" 188 lbs.

Year	Team	W	L	PCT	ERA	G	GS	CG	IP	H	BB	SO	ShO	RW	RL	SV	AB	H	HR	BA
1981	MIL A	0	0	—	4.50	3	0	0	4	6	1	1	0	0	0	0	0	0	0	—
1982		0	0	—	4.91	3	0	0	3.2	3	1	3	0	0	0	0	0	0	0	—
1983		7	9	.438	4.50	25	21	6	134	162	38	76	1	0	1	0	0	0	0	—

	W	L	PCT	ERA	G	GS	CG	IP	H	BB	SO	ShO	Relief Pitching W	L	SV	BATTING AB	H	HR	BA

Chuck Porter continued

	W	L	PCT	ERA	G	GS	CG	IP	H	BB	SO	ShO	W	L	SV	AB	H	HR	BA
1984	6	4	.600	3.87	17	12	1	81.1	92	12	48	0	0	0	0	0	0	0	–
4 yrs.	13	13	.500	4.28	48	33	7	223	263	52	128	1	0	1	0	0	0	0	–

Henry Porter

PORTER, HENRY   BR TR
B. 1861, Vergennes, Vt.   D. Dec. 30, 1906, Brockton, Mass.

	W	L	PCT	ERA	G	GS	CG	IP	H	BB	SO	ShO	W	L	SV	AB	H	HR	BA
1884 KC U	3	3	.500	3.00	6	6	6	51	32	9	71	1	0	0	0	52	12	0	.231
1885 BKN AA	33	21	.611	2.78	54	54	53	481.2	427	107	197	2	0	0	0	195	40	0	.205
1886	27	19	.587	3.42	48	48	48	424	439	120	163	1	0	0	0	184	33	0	.179
1887	15	24	.385	4.21	40	40	38	339.2	416	96	74	1	0	0	0	146	29	1	.199
1888 KC AA	18	37	.327	4.16	55	54	53	474	527	120	145	4	1	0	0	195	28	0	.144
1889	0	3	.000	12.52	4	4	3	23	52	14	9	0	0	0	0	10	1	0	.100
6 yrs.	96	107	.473	3.70	207	206	201	1793.1	1893	466	659	9	1	0	0	782	143	1	.183

Jim Porter

PORTER, ODIE OSCAR
B. July 24, 1877, Borden, Ind.   D. May 2, 1903, Borden, Ind.

	W	L	PCT	ERA	G	GS	CG	IP	H	BB	SO	ShO	W	L	SV	AB	H	HR	BA
1902 PHI A	0	1	.000	3.38	1	1	1	8	12	5	2	0	0	0	0	3	0	0	.000

Ned Porter

PORTER, NED SWINDELL   BR TR   6'   173 lbs.
B. May 6, 1905, Apalachicola, Fla.   D. June 30, 1968, Gainesville, Fla.

	W	L	PCT	ERA	G	GS	CG	IP	H	BB	SO	ShO	W	L	SV	AB	H	HR	BA
1926 NY N	0	0	–	4.50	2	0	0	2	2	0	1	0	0	0	0	0	0	0	–
1927	0	0	–	0.00	1	0	0	2	3	1	0	0	0	0	0	0	0	0	–
2 yrs.	0	0	–	2.25	3	0	0	4	5	1	1	0	0	0	0	0	0	0	–

Bob Porterfield

PORTERFIELD, ERWIN COOLIDGE   BR TR   6'   190 lbs.
B. Aug. 10, 1923, Newport, Va.   D. Apr. 28, 1980, Charlotte, N. C.

	W	L	PCT	ERA	G	GS	CG	IP	H	BB	SO	ShO	W	L	SV	AB	H	HR	BA
1948 NY A	5	3	.625	4.50	16	12	2	78	85	34	30	1	1	0	0	24	6	0	.250
1949	2	5	.286	4.06	12	8	3	57.2	53	29	25	0	0	2	0	19	1	0	.053
1950	1	1	.500	8.69	10	2	0	19.2	28	8	9	0	1	0	1	3	1	0	.333
1951 2 teams			NY	A	(2G 0–0)		WAS	A	(19G 9–8)										
" total	9	8	.529	3.50	21	19	10	136.1	114	57	55	3	0	0	0	46	6	0	.130
1952 WAS A	13	14	.481	2.72	31	29	15	231.1	222	85	80	3	1	0	0	79	15	0	.190
1953	22	10	.688	3.35	34	32	24	255	243	73	77	9	1	0	0	98	25	3	.255
1954	13	15	.464	3.32	32	31	21	244	249	77	82	2	1	0	0	88	9	1	.102
1955	10	17	.370	4.45	30	27	8	178	197	55	74	2	0	1	0	63	12	0	.190
1956 BOS A	3	12	.200	5.14	25	18	4	126	127	64	53	1	0	2	0	43	14	1	.326
1957	4	4	.500	4.05	28	9	3	102.1	107	30	28	1	1	0	1	29	5	0	.172
1958 2 teams			BOS	A	(2G 0–0)		PIT	N	(37G 4–6)										
" total	4	6	.400	3.34	39	6	2	91.2	81	19	40	1	2	3	5	20	1	1	.050
1959 2 teams			PIT	N	(36G 1–2)		CHI	N	(4G 0–0)										
" total	1	2	.333	5.29	40	0	0	47.2	65	22	19	0	1	1	1	4	0	0	.000
12 yrs.	87	97	.473	3.79	318	193	92	1567.2	1571	553	572	23	9	10	8	516	95	6	.184

Al Porto

PORTO, ALFRED (Lefty)   BL TL   5'11"   176 lbs.
B. June 27, 1926, Heilwood, Pa.

	W	L	PCT	ERA	G	GS	CG	IP	H	BB	SO	ShO	W	L	SV	AB	H	HR	BA
1948 PHI N	0	0	–	0.00	3	0	0	4	2	1	1	0	0	0	0	0	0	0	–

Arnie Portocarrero

PORTOCARRERO, ARNOLD MARIO   BR TR   6'3"   196 lbs.
B. July 5, 1931, New York, N. Y.

	W	L	PCT	ERA	G	GS	CG	IP	H	BB	SO	ShO	W	L	SV	AB	H	HR	BA
1954 PHI A	9	18	.333	4.06	34	33	16	248	233	114	132	1	0	0	0	75	8	1	.107
1955 KC A	5	9	.357	4.77	24	20	4	111.1	109	67	34	1	0	0	0	37	4	1	.108
1956	0	1	.000	10.13	3	1	0	8	9	7	2	0	0	0	0	1	0	0	.000
1957	4	9	.308	3.92	33	17	1	114.2	103	34	42	0	2	0	0	28	3	0	.107
1958 BAL A	15	11	.577	3.25	32	27	10	204.2	173	57	90	3	0	1	2	67	11	1	.164
1959	2	7	.222	6.80	27	14	1	90	107	32	23	0	0	0	0	21	0	0	.000
1960	3	2	.600	4.43	13	5	1	40.2	44	9	15	0	1	1	0	11	0	0	.000
7 yrs.	38	57	.400	4.32	166	117	33	817.1	778	320	338	5	3	2	2	240	26	3	.108

Bill Posedel

POSEDEL, WILLIAM JOHN (Sailor Bill)   BR TR   5'11"   175 lbs.
B. Aug. 2, 1906, San Francisco, Calif.

	W	L	PCT	ERA	G	GS	CG	IP	H	BB	SO	ShO	W	L	SV	AB	H	HR	BA
1938 BKN N	8	9	.471	5.66	33	17	6	140	178	46	49	1	0	3	1	44	10	0	.227
1939 BOS N	15	13	.536	3.92	33	29	18	220.2	221	78	73	5	1	0	3	73	8	0	.110
1940	12	17	.414	4.13	35	32	18	233	263	81	86	0	1	0	1	82	14	0	.171
1941	4	4	.500	4.87	18	9	3	57.1	40	30	10	0	1	0	0	25	8	0	.320
1946	2	0	1.000	6.99	19	0	0	28.1	34	13	9	0	2	0	4	3	0	0	.000
5 yrs.	41	43	.488	4.56	138	87	45	679.1	757	248	227	6	5	3	6	227	40	0	.176

Bob Poser

POSER, JOHN FALK   BL TR   6'   173 lbs.
B. Mar. 16, 1910, Columbus, Wis.

	W	L	PCT	ERA	G	GS	CG	IP	H	BB	SO	ShO	W	L	SV	AB	H	HR	BA
1932 CHI A	0	0	–	27.00	1	0	0	.2	3	2	1	0	0	0	0	3	0	0	.000
1935 STL A	1	1	.500	9.22	4	1	0	13.2	26	4	1	0	1	0	0	4	1	0	.250
2 yrs.	1	1	.500	10.05	5	1	0	14.1	29	6	2	0	1	0	0	7	1	0	.143

Lou Possehl

POSSEHL, LOUIS THOMAS   BR TR   6'2"   180 lbs.
B. Apr. 12, 1926, Chicago, Ill.

	W	L	PCT	ERA	G	GS	CG	IP	H	BB	SO	ShO	W	L	SV	AB	H	HR	BA
1946 PHI N	1	2	.333	5.93	4	4	0	13.2	19	10	4	0	0	0	0	3	0	0	.000
1947	0	0	–	4.15	2	0	0	4.1	5	0	1	0	0	0	0	0	0	0	–
1948	1	1	.500	4.91	3	2	1	14.2	17	4	7	0	0	0	0	4	1	0	.250
1951	0	1	.000	6.00	2	1	0	6	9	3	6	0	0	0	0	1	0	0	.000
1952	0	1	.000	4.97	4	1	0	12.2	12	7	4	0	0	0	0	2	0	0	.000
5 yrs.	2	5	.286	5.26	15	8	1	51.1	62	24	22	0	0	0	0	10	1	0	.100

Nellie Pott

POTT, NELSON ADOLPH (Lefty)   BL TL   6'   185 lbs.
B. July 16, 1899, Cincinnati, Ohio   D. Dec. 3, 1963, Cincinnati, Ohio

	W	L	PCT	ERA	G	GS	CG	IP	H	BB	SO	ShO	W	L	SV	AB	H	HR	BA
1922 CLE A	0	0	–	31.50	2	0	0	2	7	2	0	0	0	0	0	0	0	0	–

	W	L	PCT	ERA	G	GS	CG	IP	H	BB	SO	ShO	Relief Pitching W	L	SV	BATTING AB	H	HR	BA

Dykes Potter

POTTER, MARYLAND DYKES
Brother of Squire Potter.
B. Sept. 7, 1910, Ashland, Ky.

BR TR 6' 185 lbs.

	W	L	PCT	ERA	G	GS	CG	IP	H	BB	SO	ShO	RP W	L	SV	AB	H	HR	BA
1938 BKN N	0	0	—	4.50	2	0	0	2	4	0	1	0	0	0	0	0	0	0	—

Nels Potter

POTTER, NELSON THOMAS
B. Aug. 23, 1911, Mt. Morris, Ill.

BL TR 5'11" 180 lbs.

	W	L	PCT	ERA	G	GS	CG	IP	H	BB	SO	ShO	RP W	L	SV	AB	H	HR	BA
1936 STL N	0	0	—	0.00	1	0	0	1	0	0	0	0	0	0	0	0	0	0	—
1938 PHI A	2	12	.143	6.47	35	9	4	111.1	139	49	43	0	1	3	5	39	10	0	.256
1939	8	12	.400	6.60	41	25	9	196.1	258	88	60	0	0	2	2	67	12	0	.179
1940	9	14	.391	4.44	31	25	13	200.2	213	71	73	0	1	1	0	71	18	0	.254
1941 2 teams					PHI A (10G 1–1)					BOS A (10G 2–0)									
" total	3	1	.750	7.06	20	3	1	43.1	56	32	13	0	2	0	2	9	1	0	.111
1943 STL A	10	5	.667	2.78	33	13	8	168.1	146	54	80	0	2	0	1	55	8	0	.145
1944	19	7	.731	2.83	32	29	16	232	211	70	91	3	0	2	0	82	13	0	.159
1945	15	11	.577	2.47	32	32	21	255.1	212	68	129	3	0	0	0	92	28	0	.304
1946	8	9	.471	3.72	23	19	10	145	152	59	72	0	0	0	0	52	12	0	.231
1947	4	10	.286	4.04	32	10	3	122.2	130	44	65	0	2	2	2	35	9	0	.257
1948 3 teams					STL A (2G 1–1)					PHI A (8G 2–2)					BOS N (18G 5–2)				
" total	8	5	.615	2.86	28	9	3	113.1	105	17	64	0	3	2	3	37	14	0	.378
1949 BOS N	6	11	.353	4.19	41	3	1	96.2	99	30	57	0	5	11	7	23	3	0	.130
12 yrs.	92	97	.487	3.99	349	177	89	1686	1721	582	747	6	16	23	22	562	128	0	.228
WORLD SERIES																			
1944 STL A	0	1	.000	0.93	2	2	0	9.2	10	3	6	0	0	0	0	4	0	0	.000
1948 BOS N	0	0	—	8.44	2	1	0	5.1	6	2	1	0	0	0	0	2	1	0	.500
2 yrs.	0	1	.000	3.60	4	3	0	15	16	5	7	0	0	0	0	6	1	0	.167

Squire Potter

POTTER, ROBERT H.
Brother of Dykes Potter.
B. Mar. 18, 1902, Flatwoods, Ky.   D. Jan. 27, 1983, Ashland, Ky.

BR TR 6'1" 185 lbs.

	W	L	PCT	ERA	G	GS	CG	IP	H	BB	SO	ShO	RP W	L	SV	AB	H	HR	BA
1923 WAS A	0	0	—	21.00	1	0	0	3	11	4	1	0	0	0	0	0	0	0	—

Bill Pounds

POUNDS, JEARED WELLS
B. Mar. 11, 1878, Paterson, N. J.   D. July 7, 1936, Paterson, N. J.

	W	L	PCT	ERA	G	GS	CG	IP	H	BB	SO	ShO	RP W	L	SV	AB	H	HR	BA
1903 2 teams					CLE A (1G 0–0)					BKN N (1G 0–0)									
" total	0	0	—	8.18	2			11	16	2	4	0	0	0	0	5	3	0	.600

Abner Powell

POWELL, CHARLES ABNER
B. Dec. 15, 1860, Shenandoah, Pa.   D. Aug. 7, 1953, New Orleans, La.

BR TR 5'7" 160 lbs.

	W	L	PCT	ERA	G	GS	CG	IP	H	BB	SO	ShO	RP W	L	SV	AB	H	HR	BA
1884 WAS U	6	12	.333	3.43	18	17	14	134	135	19	78	1	1	0	0	191	54	0	.283
1886 2 teams					BAL AA (7G 2–5)					CIN AA (4G 0–1)									
" total	2	6	.250	5.02	11	8	8	75.1	82	35	19	0	0	0	0	113	24	0	.212
2 yrs.	8	18	.308	4.00	29	25	22	209.1	217	54	97	1	1	0	0	*			

Bill Powell

POWELL, WILLIAM BURRIS
B. May 8, 1885, Grafton, W. Va.   D. Sept. 28, 1967, East Liverpool, Ohio

BR TR 6'2½" 182 lbs.

	W	L	PCT	ERA	G	GS	CG	IP	H	BB	SO	ShO	RP W	L	SV	AB	H	HR	BA
1909 PIT N	0	1	.000	3.68	3	1	0	7.1	7	6	2	0	0	0	0	4	1	0	.250
1910	4	6	.400	2.40	12	9	4	75	65	34	23	2	1	0	0	23	6	0	.261
1912 CHI N	0	0	—	9.00	1	0	0	2	2	1	0	0	0	0	0	0	0	0	—
1913 CIN N	0	1	.000	54.00	1	1	0	.1	2	2	0	0	0	0	0	0	0	0	—
4 yrs.	4	8	.333	2.87	17	11	4	84.2	76	43	25	2	1	0	0	27	7	0	.259

Grover Powell

POWELL, GROVER DAVID
B. Oct. 10, 1940, Sayre, Pa.

BL TL 5'10" 175 lbs.

	W	L	PCT	ERA	G	GS	CG	IP	H	BB	SO	ShO	RP W	L	SV	AB	H	HR	BA
1963 NY N	1	1	.500	2.72	20	4	1	49.2	37	32	39	1	0	0	0	10	2	0	.200

Jack Powell

POWELL, JOHN JOSEPH
B. July 9, 1874, Bloomington, Ill.   D. Oct. 17, 1944, Chicago, Ill.

BR TR

	W	L	PCT	ERA	G	GS	CG	IP	H	BB	SO	ShO	RP W	L	SV	AB	H	HR	BA
1897 CLE N	15	9	.625	3.16	27	26	24	225	245	62	61	2	0	0	0	97	20	0	.206
1898	24	15	.615	3.00	42	41	36	342	328	112	93	6	0	1	0	136	18	0	.132
1899 STL N	23	21	.523	3.52	48	43	40	373	433	85	87	2	2	0	0	134	27	0	.201
1900	17	17	.500	4.44	38	37	28	287.2	325	77	77	3	1	0	0	109	31	1	.284
1901	19	19	.500	3.54	45	37	33	338.1	351	50	133	2	2	2	3	119	21	2	.176
1902 STL A	22	17	.564	3.21	42	39	36	328.1	320	93	137	3	1	0	2	127	26	1	.205
1903	15	19	.441	2.91	38	34	33	306.1	294	58	169	4	1	0	2	120	25	0	.208
1904 NY A	23	19	.548	2.44	47	45	38	390.1	340	92	202	3	1	0	0	146	26	0	.178
1905 2 teams					NY A (36G 8–13)					STL A (3G 2–1)									
" total	10	14	.417	3.29	39	26	16	230	236	62	96	1	2	3	1	75	13	1	.173
1906 STL A	13	14	.481	1.77	28	26	25	244	196	55	132	3	1	0	1	94	22	1	.234
1907	13	16	.448	2.68	32	31	27	255.2	229	62	96	4	0	0	1	91	12	0	.132
1908	16	13	.552	2.11	33	32	23	256	208	47	85	6	0	0	1	89	21	0	.236
1909	12	16	.429	2.11	34	27	18	239	221	42	82	4	2	0	3	78	14	0	.179
1910	7	11	.389	2.30	21	18	8	129.1	121	28	52	3	2	1	0	43	7	0	.163
1911	8	19	.296	3.29	31	27	18	207.2	224	44	52	1	0	2	1	73	12	0	.164
1912	9	16	.360	3.10	32	28	19	235.1	248	52	67	0	0	0	0	82	15	1	.183
16 yrs.	246	255	.491	2.97	577	517	422	4388	4319	1021	1621	47	15	9	15	1613	310	7	.192
		5th																	

Sam Powell

POWELL, SAMUEL
B. Unknown.

	W	L	PCT	ERA	G	GS	CG	IP	H	BB	SO	ShO	RP W	L	SV	AB	H	HR	BA
1913 STL A	0	0	—	0.00	2	0	0	2	1	2	0	0	0	0	0	0	0	0	—

Ted Power

POWER, TED HENRY
B. Jan. 31, 1955, Guthrie, Okla.

BR TR 6'4" 220 lbs.

	W	L	PCT	ERA	G	GS	CG	IP	H	BB	SO	ShO	RP W	L	SV	AB	H	HR	BA
1981 LA N	1	3	.250	3.21	5	2	0	14	16	7	7	0	1	1	0	3	0	0	.000
1982	1	1	.500	6.68	12	4	0	33.2	38	23	15	0	0	0	0	6	0	0	.000

	W	L	PCT	ERA	G	GS	CG	IP	H	BB	SO	ShO	Relief Pitching W	L	SV	BATTING AB	H	HR	BA

Jack Quinn continued

	W	L	PCT	ERA	G	GS	CG	IP	H	BB	SO	ShO	W	L	SV	AB	H	HR	BA
1926 PHI A	10	11	.476	3.41	31	21	8	163.2	191	36	58	3	1	2	1	46	8	0	.174
1927	15	10	.600	3.17	34	25	11	207.1	211	37	43	3	1	2	1	66	6	0	.091
1928	18	7	.720	2.90	31	28	18	211.1	239	34	43	4	0	0	1	79	13	0	.165
1929	11	9	.550	3.97	35	18	7	161	182	39	41	0	4	2	2	60	8	0	.133
1930	9	7	.563	4.42	35	7	0	89.2	109	22	28	0	8	3	6	34	9	1	.265
1931 BKN N	5	4	.556	2.66	39	1	0	64.1	65	24	25	0	5	3	15	15	3	0	.200
1932	3	7	.300	3.30	42	0	0	87.1	102	24	28	0	3	7	8	20	4	0	.200
1933 CIN N	0	1	.000	4.02	14	0	0	15.2	20	5	3	0	0	1	1	1	0	0	.000
23 yrs.	247	217	.532	3.27	755	443	242	3934.2	4234	859	1329	28	54	35	57	1348	248	8	.184
WORLD SERIES																			
1921 NY A	0	1	.000	9.82	1	0	0	3.2	8	2	2	0	0	1	0	2	0	0	.000
1929 PHI A	0	0	–	9.00	1	1	0	5	7	2	2	0	0	0	0	2	0	0	.000
1930	0	0	–	4.50	1	0	0	2	3	0	1	0	0	0	0	0	0	0	–
3 yrs.	0	1	.000	8.44	3	1	0	10.2	18	4	5	0	0	1	0	4	0	0	.000

Wimpy Quinn

QUINN, WELLINGTON HUNT BR TR 6'2" 187 lbs.
B. May 14, 1918, Birmingham, Ala. D. Sept. 1, 1954, Los Angeles, Calif.

	W	L	PCT	ERA	G	GS	CG	IP	H	BB	SO	ShO	W	L	SV	AB	H	HR	BA
1941 CHI N	0	0	–	7.20	3	0	0	5	3	3	2	0	0	0	0	2	1	0	.500

Luis Quintana

QUINTANA, LUIS JOAQUIN BL TL 6'2" 175 lbs.
Also known as Luis Joaquin Santos.
B. Nov. 25, 1951, Vega Baja, Puerto Rico

	W	L	PCT	ERA	G	GS	CG	IP	H	BB	SO	ShO	W	L	SV	AB	H	HR	BA
1974 CAL A	2	1	.667	4.15	18	0	0	13	17	14	11	0	2	1	0	0	0	0	–
1975	0	2	.000	6.43	4	0	0	7	13	6	5	0	0	2	0	0	0	0	–
2 yrs.	2	3	.400	4.95	22	0	0	20	30	20	16	0	2	3	0	0	0	0	–

Art Quirk

QUIRK, ARTHUR LINCOLN BR TL 5'11" 170 lbs.
B. Apr. 11, 1938, Providence, R. I.

	W	L	PCT	ERA	G	GS	CG	IP	H	BB	SO	ShO	W	L	SV	AB	H	HR	BA
1962 BAL A	2	2	.500	5.93	7	5	0	27.1	36	18	18	0	0	0	0	7	1	0	.143
1963 WAS A	1	0	1.000	4.29	7	3	0	21	23	8	12	0	0	0	0	4	1	0	.250
2 yrs.	3	2	.600	5.21	14	8	0	48.1	59	26	30	0	0	0	0	11	2	0	.182

Dan Quisenberry

QUISENBERRY, DANIEL RAYMOND BR TR 6'2" 170 lbs.
B. Feb. 7, 1953, Santa Monica, Calif.

	W	L	PCT	ERA	G	GS	CG	IP	H	BB	SO	ShO	W	L	SV	AB	H	HR	BA
1979 KC A	3	2	.600	3.15	32	0	0	40	42	7	13	0	3	2	5	0	0	0	–
1980	12	7	.632	3.09	75	0	0	128	129	27	37	0	12	7	33	0	0	0	–
1981	1	4	.200	1.74	40	0	0	62	59	15	20	0	1	4	18	0	0	0	–
1982	9	7	.563	2.57	72	0	0	136.2	126	12	46	0	9	7	35	0	0	0	–
1983	5	3	.625	1.94	69	0	0	139	118	11	48	0	5	3	45¹	0	0	0	–
1984	6	3	.667	2.64	72	0	0	129.1	121	12	41	0	6	3	44	0	0	0	–
6 yrs.	36	26	.581	2.51	360	0	0	635	595	84	205	0	36	26	180 8th	0	0	0	–
DIVISIONAL PLAYOFF SERIES																			
1981 KC A	0	0	–	0.00	1	0	0	1	1	0	0	0	0	0	0	0	0	0	–
LEAGUE CHAMPIONSHIP SERIES																			
1980 KC A	1	0	1.000	0.00	2	0	0	4.2	4	2	1	0	1	0	1	0	0	0	–
1984	0	1	.000	3.00	1	0	0	3	2	1	1	0	0	1	0	0	0	0	–
2 yrs.	1	1	.500	1.17	3	0	0	7.2	6	3	2	0	1	1	1	0	0	0	–
WORLD SERIES																			
1980 KC A	1	2	.333	5.23	6	0	0	10.1	10	3	0	0	1	2	1 2nd	0	0	0	–

Charlie Rabe

RABE, CHARLES HENRY BL TL 6'1" 180 lbs.
B. May 6, 1932, Boyce, Tex.

	W	L	PCT	ERA	G	GS	CG	IP	H	BB	SO	ShO	W	L	SV	AB	H	HR	BA
1957 CIN N	0	1	.000	2.16	2	1	0	8.1	5	0	6	0	0	0	0	2	0	0	.000
1958	0	3	.000	4.34	9	1	0	18.2	25	9	10	0	0	2	0	4	0	0	.000
2 yrs.	0	4	.000	3.67	11	2	0	27	30	9	16	0	0	2	0	6	0	0	.000

Steve Rachunok

RACHUNOK, STEPHEN STEPANOVICH BR TR 6'3½" 200 lbs.
B. Dec. 5, 1916, Rittman, Ohio

	W	L	PCT	ERA	G	GS	CG	IP	H	BB	SO	ShO	W	L	SV	AB	H	HR	BA
1940 BKN N	0	1	.000	4.50	2	1	1	10	9	5	10	0	0	0	0	2	0	0	.000

Dick Radatz

RADATZ, RICHARD RAYMOND (The Monster) BR TR 6'6" 230 lbs.
B. Apr. 2, 1937, Detroit, Mich.

	W	L	PCT	ERA	G	GS	CG	IP	H	BB	SO	ShO	W	L	SV	AB	H	HR	BA
1962 BOS A	9	6	.600	2.24	62	0	0	124.2	95	40	144	0	9	6	24	31	3	0	.097
1963	15	6	.714	1.97	66	0	0	132.1	94	51	162	0	15	6	25	29	2	0	.069
1964	16	9	.640	2.29	79	0	0	157	103	58	181	0	16	9	29	37	6	0	.162
1965	9	11	.450	3.91	63	0	0	124.1	104	53	121	0	9	11	22	27	5	1	.185
1966 2 teams			BOS A (16G 0–2)		CLE A (39G 0–3)														
" total	0	5	.000	4.64	55	0	0	75.2	73	45	68	0	0	5	14	11	1	0	.091
1967 2 teams			CLE A (3G 0–0)		CHI N (20G 1–0)														
" total	1	0	1.000	6.49	23	0	0	26.1	17	26	19	0	1	0	3	4	1	0	.250
1969 2 teams			DET A (11G 2–2)		MON N (22G 0–4)														
" total	2	6	.250	4.89	33	0	0	53.1	46	23	50	0	2	6	3	6	1	0	.167
7 yrs.	52	43	.547	3.13	381	0	0	693.2	532	296	745	0	52	43	122	145	19	1	.131

George Radbourn

RADBOURN, GEORGE B. (Dordy)
Brother of Old Hoss Radbourn.
B. Apr. 8, 1856, Bloomington, Ill. D. Jan. 1, 1904, Bloomington, Ill.

	W	L	PCT	ERA	G	GS	CG	IP	H	BB	SO	ShO	W	L	SV	AB	H	HR	BA
1883 DET N	1	2	.333	6.55	3	3	2	22	38	7	2	0	0	0	0	12	2	0	.167

	W	L	PCT	ERA	G	GS	CG	IP	H	BB	SO	ShO	Relief Pitching W	L	SV	BATTING AB	H	HR	BA

Old Hoss Radbourn

RADBOURN, CHARLES GARDNER
Brother of George Radbourn.
B. Dec. 11, 1854, Rochester, N.Y.   D. Feb. 5, 1897, Bloomington, Ill.
Hall of Fame 1939.
BR TR 5'9"   168 lbs.

	W	L	PCT	ERA	G	GS	CG	IP	H	BB	SO	ShO	RW	RL	RSV	AB	H	HR	BA
1880 BUF N	0	0	–	0.00	0	0	0		0	0	0	0	0	0	0	21	3	0	.143
1881 PRO N	25	11	.694	2.43	41	36	34	325.1	309	64	117	3	1	1	0	270	59	0	.219
1882	31	19	.620	2.09	55	52	51	474	429	51	201	6	1	0	0	326	78	1	.239
1883	49	25	.662	2.05	76	68	66	632.1	563	56	315	4	3	2	1	381	108	3	.283
1884	60	12	.833	1.38	75	73	73	678.2	528	98	441	11	1	0	1	361	83	1	.230
1885	26	20	.565	2.20	49	49	49	445.2	423	83	154	2	0	0	0	249	58	0	.233
1886 BOS N	27	30	.474	3.00	58	58	57	509.1	521	111	218	3	0	0	0	253	60	2	.237
1887	24	23	.511	4.55	50	50	48	425	505	133	87	1	0	0	0	175	40	1	.229
1888	7	16	.304	2.87	24	24	24	207	187	45	64	1	0	0	0	79	17	0	.215
1889	20	11	.645	3.63	33	31	28	277	282	72	99	1	1	0	0	122	23	1	.189
1890 BOS P	27	12	.692	3.31	41	38	36	343	352	100	80	1	1	1	0	154	39	0	.253
1891 CIN N	12	12	.500	4.25	26	24	23	218	236	62	54	2	0	1	0	96	17	0	.177
12 yrs.	308	191	.617	2.67	528	503	489	4535.1	4335	875	1830	35	8	5	2	*			
						7th													

Roy Radebaugh

RADEBAUGH, ROY
B. Feb. 22, 1884, Champaign, Ill.   D. Jan. 17, 1945, Cedar Rapids, Iowa
BR TR 5'7"   160 lbs.

	W	L	PCT	ERA	G	GS	CG	IP	H	BB	SO	ShO	RW	RL	RSV	AB	H	HR	BA
1911 STL N	0	0	–	2.70	2	1	0	10	6	4	1	0	0	0	0	3	0	0	.000

Drew Rader

RADER, DREW LEON (Lefty)
B. May 14, 1901, Elmira, N.Y.   D. June 5, 1975, Catskill, N.Y.
BR TL 6'   190 lbs.

	W	L	PCT	ERA	G	GS	CG	IP	H	BB	SO	ShO	RW	RL	RSV	AB	H	HR	BA
1921 PIT N	0	0	–	0.00	1	0	0	2	2	0	0	0	0	0	0	1	0	0	.000

Paul Radford

RADFORD, PAUL REVERE
B. Oct. 14, 1861, Roxbury, Mass.   D. Feb. 21, 1945, Boston, Mass.
BR TR 5'6"   148 lbs.

	W	L	PCT	ERA	G	GS	CG	IP	H	BB	SO	ShO	RW	RL	RSV	AB	H	HR	BA
1884 PRO N	0	2	.000	7.62	2	2	1	13	27	3	2	0	0	0	0	355	70	1	.197
1885	0	2	.000	7.85	3	2	2	18.1	34	8	3	0	0	0	0	371	90	0	.243
1887 NY AA	0	0	–	18.00	2	0	0	5	15	3	4	0	0	0	0	486	129	4	.265
1890 CLE P	0	0	–	3.60	1	0	0	5	7	1	3	0	0	0	0	466	136	2	.292
1891 BOS AA	0	0	–	0.00	1	0	0	1	0	0	0	0	0	0	0	456	118	0	.259
1893 WAS N	0	0	–	18.00	1	0	0	1	2	2	1	0	0	0	0	464	106	2	.228
6 yrs.	0	4	.000	8.52	10	4	3	43.1	85	17	13	0	0	0	0	*			

Hal Raether

RAETHER, HAROLD HERMAN (Bud)
B. Oct. 10, 1932, Lake Mills, Wis.
BR TR 6'1"   185 lbs.

	W	L	PCT	ERA	G	GS	CG	IP	H	BB	SO	ShO	RW	RL	RSV	AB	H	HR	BA
1954 PHI A	0	0	–	4.50	1	0	0	2	1	4	0	0	0	0	0	0	0	0	–
1957 KC A	0	0	–	9.00	1	0	0	2	2	0	0	0	0	0	0	0	0	0	–
2 yrs.	0	0	–	6.75	2	0	0	4	3	4	0	0	0	0	0	0	0	0	–

Ken Raffensberger

RAFFENSBERGER, KENNETH DAVID
B. Aug. 8, 1917, York, Pa.
BR TL 6'2"   185 lbs.

	W	L	PCT	ERA	G	GS	CG	IP	H	BB	SO	ShO	RW	RL	RSV	AB	H	HR	BA
1939 STL N	0	0	–	0.00	1	0	0	1	2	0	1	0	0	0	0	0	0	0	–
1940 CHI N	7	9	.438	3.38	43	10	3	114.2	120	29	55	0	4	4	3	30	5	0	.167
1941	0	1	.000	4.50	10	1	0	18	17	7	5	0	0	1	0	5	0	0	.000
1943 PHI N	0	1	.000	1.13	1	1	1	8	7	2	3	0	0	0	0	3	0	0	.000
1944	13	20	.394	3.06	37	31	18	258.2	257	45	136	3	1	2	0	80	11	0	.138
1945	0	3	.000	4.44	5	4	1	24.1	28	14	6	0	0	0	0	8	0	0	.000
1946	8	15	.348	3.63	39	23	14	196	203	39	73	2	0	0	6	60	10	0	.167
1947 2 teams			PHI	N (10G 2–6)		CIN	N	(19G 6–5)											
" total	8	11	.421	4.51	29	22	10	147.2	182	37	54	1	1	2	1	52	10	0	.192
1948 CIN N	11	12	.478	3.84	40	24	7	180.1	187	37	57	4	3	0	0	62	7	0	.113
1949	18	17	.514	3.39	41	38	20	284	289	80	103	5	1	1	0	90	16	1	.178
1950	14	19	.424	4.26	38	35	18	239	271	40	87	4	0	1	0	82	11	1	.134
1951	16	17	.485	3.44	42	33	14	248.2	232	38	81	5	2	2	5	82	10	0	.122
1952	17	13	.567	2.81	38	33	18	247	247	45	93	6	0	2	1	75	8	1	.107
1953	7	14	.333	3.93	26	26	9	174	200	33	47	1	0	0	0	57	8	1	.140
1954	0	2	.000	7.84	6	1	0	10.1	15	3	5	0	0	0	0	2	1	0	.500
15 yrs.	119	154	.436	3.60	396	282	133	2151.2	2257	449	806	31	12	16	16	688	97	4	.141

Al Raffo

RAFFO, ALBERT MARTIN
B. Nov. 27, 1941, San Francisco, Calif.
BR TR 6'5"   210 lbs.

	W	L	PCT	ERA	G	GS	CG	IP	H	BB	SO	ShO	RW	RL	RSV	AB	H	HR	BA
1969 PHI N	1	3	.250	4.13	45	0	0	72	81	25	38	0	1	3	1	6	1	0	.167

Pat Ragan

RAGAN, DON CARLOS PATRICK
B. Nov. 15, 1888, Blanchard, Iowa   D. Sept. 4, 1956, Los Angeles, Calif.
BR TR 5'10½" 185 lbs.

	W	L	PCT	ERA	G	GS	CG	IP	H	BB	SO	ShO	RW	RL	RSV	AB	H	HR	BA
1909 2 teams			CIN	N (2G 0–1)		CHI	N	(2G 0–0)											
" total	0	1	.000	3.09	4	0	0	11.2	11	5	4	0	0	1	0	4	1	0	.250
1911 BKN N	4	3	.571	2.11	22	7	5	93.2	81	31	39	2	0	1	1	29	4	0	.138
1912	7	18	.280	3.63	36	26	12	208	211	65	101	1	0	1	2	67	4	0	.060
1913	15	18	.455	3.77	44	32	14	264.2	284	64	109	0	3	3	0	91	15	0	.165
1914	10	15	.400	2.98	38	26	14	208.1	214	85	106	1	1	2	3	75	10	0	.133
1915 2 teams			BKN	N (5G 1–0)		BOS	N	(33G 15–12)											
" total	16	12	.571	2.34	38	26	13	246.2	219	67	88	3	4	1	0	86	13	0	.151
1916 BOS N	9	9	.500	2.08	28	23	14	182	143	47	94	3	0	0	0	60	13	0	.217
1917	6	9	.400	2.93	30	13	5	147.2	138	35	61	1	3	2	1	48	6	1	.125
1918	8	17	.320	3.23	30	25	15	206.1	212	44	68	2	0	2	0	71	13	0	.183
1919 3 teams			BOS	N (4G 0–2)		NY	N	(7G 1–0)		CHI	A	(1G 0–0)							
" total	1	2	.333	3.44	12	4	0	36.2	36	17	10	0	0	0	0	11	4	0	.364
1923 PHI N	0	0	–	6.00	1	0	0	3	6	0	0	0	0	0	0	2	1	0	.500
11 yrs.	76	104	.422	2.99	283	182	93	1608.2	1555	470	680	13	12	13	6	544	84	1	.154

	W	L	PCT	ERA	G	GS	CG	IP	H	BB	SO	ShO	Relief Pitching W	L	SV	BATTING AB	H	HR	BA

Pete Redfern

REDFERN, PETER IRVING
B. Aug. 25, 1954, Glendale, Calif.   BR TR 6'2"   195 lbs.

	W	L	PCT	ERA	G	GS	CG	IP	H	BB	SO	ShO	W	L	SV	AB	H	HR	BA
1976 MIN A	8	8	.500	3.51	23	23	1	118	105	63	74	1	0	0	0	0	0	0	–
1977	6	9	.400	5.19	30	28	1	137	164	66	73	0	0	0	0	0	0	0	–
1978	0	2	.000	6.52	3	2	0	9.2	10	6	4	0	0	0	0	0	0	0	–
1979	7	3	.700	3.50	40	6	0	108	106	35	85	0	4	3	1	0	0	0	–
1980	7	7	.500	4.54	23	16	2	105	117	33	73	0	1	1	2	0	0	0	–
1981	9	8	.529	4.06	24	23	3	142	140	52	77	0	0	0	0	0	0	0	–
1982	5	11	.313	6.58	27	13	2	94.1	122	51	40	0	2	3	0	0	0	0	–
7 yrs.	42	48	.467	4.54	170	111	9	714	764	306	426	1	7	7	3	0	0	0	–

Bob Reed

REED, ROBERT EDWARD
B. Jan. 12, 1945, Boston, Mass.   BR TR 5'10"   175 lbs.

	W	L	PCT	ERA	G	GS	CG	IP	H	BB	SO	ShO	W	L	SV	AB	H	HR	BA
1969 DET A	0	0	–	1.84	8	1	0	14.2	9	8	9	0	0	0	0	2	1	0	.500
1970	2	4	.333	4.89	16	4	0	46	54	14	26	0	1	2	2	12	1	0	.083
2 yrs.	2	4	.333	4.15	24	5	0	60.2	63	22	35	0	1	2	2	14	2	0	.143

Howie Reed

REED, HOWARD DEAN (Diz)
B. Dec. 21, 1936, Dallas, Tex.   D. Dec. 7, 1984, Corpus Christi, Tex.   BR TR 6'1"   195 lbs.

	W	L	PCT	ERA	G	GS	CG	IP	H	BB	SO	ShO	W	L	SV	AB	H	HR	BA
1958 KC A	1	0	1.000	0.87	3	1	1	10.1	5	4	5	0	0	0	0	2	0	0	.000
1959	0	3	.000	7.40	6	3	0	20.2	26	10	11	0	0	1	0	3	0	0	.000
1960	0	0	–	0.00	1	0	0	1.2	2	0	1	0	0	0	0	0	0	0	–
1964 LA N	3	4	.429	3.20	26	7	0	90	79	36	52	0	0	1	1	20	2	0	.100
1965	7	5	.583	3.12	38	5	0	78	73	27	47	0	6	3	1	12	0	0	.000
1966 2 teams			LA	N (1G 0–0)				CAL	A	(19G 0–1)									
" total	0	1	.000	2.82	20	1	0	44.2	40	15	17	0	0	0	1	7	0	0	.000
1967 HOU N	1	1	.500	3.44	4	2	0	18.1	19	2	9	0	1	0	0	4	0	0	.000
1969 MON N	6	7	.462	4.84	31	15	2	106	119	50	59	1	0	0	1	32	4	1	.125
1970	6	5	.545	3.13	57	1	0	89	81	40	42	0	6	4	5	10	0	0	.000
1971	2	3	.400	4.26	43	0	0	57	66	24	25	0	2	3	0	1	0	0	.000
10 yrs.	26	29	.473	3.72	229	35	3	515.2	510	208	268	1	15	12	9	91	6	1	.066

WORLD SERIES

	W	L	PCT	ERA	G	GS	CG	IP	H	BB	SO	ShO	W	L	SV	AB	H	HR	BA
1965 LA N	0	0	–	8.10	2	0	0	3.1	2	2	4	0	0	0	0	0	0	0	–

Jerry Reed

REED, JERRY MAXWELL
B. Oct. 8, 1955, Bryson City, N. C.   BR TR 6'1"   190 lbs.

	W	L	PCT	ERA	G	GS	CG	IP	H	BB	SO	ShO	W	L	SV	AB	H	HR	BA
1981 PHI N	0	1	.000	7.20	4	0	0	5	7	6	5	0	0	1	0	0	0	0	–
1982 2 teams			PHI	N (7G 1–0)				CLE	A	(6G 1–1)									
" total	2	1	.667	4.07	13	1	0	24.1	26	6	11	0	2	0	0	0	0	0	–
1983 CLE A	0	0	–	7.17	7	0	0	21.1	26	9	11	0	0	0	0	0	0	0	–
3 yrs.	2	2	.500	5.68	24	1	0	50.2	59	21	27	0	2	1	0	0	0	0	–

Ron Reed

REED, RONALD LEE
B. Nov. 2, 1942, La Porte, Ind.   BR TR 6'6"   215 lbs.

	W	L	PCT	ERA	G	GS	CG	IP	H	BB	SO	ShO	W	L	SV	AB	H	HR	BA
1966 ATL N	1	1	.500	2.16	2	2	0	8.1	7	4	6	0	0	0	0	2	0	0	.000
1967	1	1	.500	2.95	3	3	0	21.1	21	3	11	0	0	0	0	8	0	0	.000
1968	11	10	.524	3.35	35	28	6	201.2	189	49	111	1	0	0	0	62	10	0	.161
1969	18	10	.643	3.47	36	33	7	241	227	56	160	1	0	0	0	80	10	0	.125
1970	7	10	.412	4.40	21	18	6	135	140	39	68	0	0	1	0	44	4	0	.091
1971	13	14	.481	3.73	32	32	8	222	221	54	129	1	0	0	0	74	11	0	.149
1972	11	15	.423	3.93	31	30	11	213	222	60	111	1	0	0	0	73	13	0	.178
1973	4	11	.267	4.42	20	19	2	116	133	31	64	0	0	0	1	45	9	0	.200
1974	10	11	.476	3.39	28	28	6	186	171	41	78	2	0	0	0	57	6	0	.105
1975 2 teams			ATL	N (10G 4–5)				STL	N	(24G 9–8)									
" total	13	13	.500	3.52	34	34	8	250.1	274	53	139	2	0	0	0	82	15	0	.183
1976 PHI N	8	7	.533	2.46	59	4	1	128	88	32	96	0	6	6	14	24	4	0	.167
1977	7	5	.583	2.76	60	3	0	124	101	37	84	0	7	4	15	18	2	0	.111
1978	3	4	.429	2.23	66	0	0	109	87	23	85	0	3	4	17	6	0	0	.000
1979	13	8	.619	4.15	61	0	0	102	110	32	58	0	13	8	5	10	3	0	.300
1980	7	5	.583	4.05	55	0	0	91	88	30	54	0	7	5	9	10	3	0	.300
1981	5	3	.625	3.10	39	0	0	61	54	17	40	0	5	3	8	6	3	0	.500
1982	5	5	.500	2.66	57	2	0	98	85	24	57	0	4	4	14	12	4	0	.333
1983	9	1	.900	3.48	61	0	0	95.2	89	34	73	0	9	1	8	6	1	0	.167
1984 CHI A	0	6	.000	3.08	51	0	0	73	67	14	57	0	0	6	12	1	0	0	.000
19 yrs.	146	140	.510	3.46	751	236	55	2476.1	2374	633	1481	8	54	42	103	620	98	0	.158

DIVISIONAL PLAYOFF SERIES

	W	L	PCT	ERA	G	GS	CG	IP	H	BB	SO	ShO	W	L	SV	AB	H	HR	BA
1981 PHI N	0	0	–	3.00	4	0	0	6	5	3	4	0	0	0	0	0	0	0	–

LEAGUE CHAMPIONSHIP SERIES

	W	L	PCT	ERA	G	GS	CG	IP	H	BB	SO	ShO	W	L	SV	AB	H	HR	BA
1969 ATL N	0	1	.000	21.60	1	1	0	1.2	5	3	3	0	0	0	0	0	0	0	–
1976 PHI N	0	0	–	7.71	2	0	0	4.2	6	2	2	0	0	0	0	1	0	0	.000
1977	0	0	–	1.80	3	0	0	5	3	2	5	0	0	0	0	0	0	0	–
1978	0	0	–	2.25	3	0	0	4	6	0	2	0	0	0	0	0	0	0	–
1980	0	1	.000	18.00	3	0	0	2	3	1	1	0	0	1	0	0	0	0	–
1983	0	0	–	2.70	2	0	0	3.1	4	1	3	0	0	0	0	1	0	0	.000
6 yrs.	0	2	.000	6.53	13	1	0	20.2	27	9	16	0	0	1	0	1	0	0	.000

WORLD SERIES

	W	L	PCT	ERA	G	GS	CG	IP	H	BB	SO	ShO	W	L	SV	AB	H	HR	BA
1980 PHI N	0	0	–	0.00	2	0	0	2	2	0	2	0	0	0	1	0	0	0	–
1983	0	0	–	2.70	3	0	0	3.1	4	2	4	0	0	0	0	0	0	0	–
2 yrs.	0	0	–	1.69	5	0	0	5.1	6	2	6	0	0	0	1	0	0	0	–

Bill Reeder

REEDER, WILLIAM EDGAR
B. Feb. 20, 1922, Dike, Tex.   BR TR 6'5"   205 lbs.

	W	L	PCT	ERA	G	GS	CG	IP	H	BB	SO	ShO	W	L	SV	AB	H	HR	BA
1949 STL N	1	1	.500	5.08	21	1	0	33.2	33	30	21	0	1	0	0	3	0	0	.000

	W	L	PCT	ERA	G	GS	CG	IP	H	BB	SO	ShO	Relief Pitching W	L	SV	BATTING AB	H	HR	BA

Stan Reese

REESE, STANLEY MILTON
B. Feb. 23, 1899, Cynthiana, Ky.   D. Aug. 29, 1937, Lexington, Ky.   TR

	W	L	PCT	ERA	G	GS	CG	IP	H	BB	SO	ShO	W	L	SV	AB	H	HR	BA
1918 WAS A	1	0	1.000	0.00	2	0	0	2	3	4	1	0	1	0	0	0	0	0	—

Bobby Reeves

REEVES, ROBERT EDWIN (Gunner)
B. June 24, 1904, Hill City, Tenn.   BR TR 5'11" 170 lbs.

	W	L	PCT	ERA	G	GS	CG	IP	H	BB	SO	ShO	W	L	SV	AB	H	HR	BA
1931 BOS A	0	0	—	3.68	1	0	0	7.1	6	1	0	0	0	0	0		*		

Mike Regan

REGAN, MICHAEL JOHN
B. Nov. 19, 1887, Phoenix, N. Y.   D. May 22, 1961, Albany, N. Y.   BR TR 5'11" 165 lbs.

	W	L	PCT	ERA	G	GS	CG	IP	H	BB	SO	ShO	W	L	SV	AB	H	HR	BA
1917 CIN N	11	10	.524	2.71	32	26	16	216	228	41	50	1	0	0	0	75	15	0	.200
1918	5	5	.500	3.26	22	6	4	80	77	29	15	3	3	2	2	27	8	0	.296
1919	0	0	—	0.00	1	0	0	2.1	1	0	1	0	0	0	0	1	0	0	.000
3 yrs.	16	15	.516	2.84	55	32	20	298.1	306	70	66	4	3	2	2	103	23	0	.223

Phil Regan

REGAN, PHILIP RAYMOND (The Vulture)
B. Apr. 6, 1937, Otsego, Mich.   BR TR 6'3" 200 lbs.

	W	L	PCT	ERA	G	GS	CG	IP	H	BB	SO	ShO	W	L	SV	AB	H	HR	BA
1960 DET A	0	4	.000	4.50	17	7	0	68	70	25	38	0	0	0	1	17	1	0	.059
1961	10	7	.588	5.25	32	16	6	120	134	41	46	0	2	2	2	40	3	0	.075
1962	11	9	.550	4.04	35	23	6	171.1	169	64	87	0	1	2	0	63	13	0	.206
1963	15	9	.625	3.86	38	27	5	189	179	59	115	1	2	1	1	63	9	1	.143
1964	5	10	.333	5.03	32	21	2	146.2	162	49	91	0	1	0	1	41	13	0	.317
1965	1	5	.167	5.05	16	7	1	51.2	57	20	37	0	0	0	0	12	1	0	.083
1966 LA N	14	1	.933	1.62	65	0	0	116.2	85	24	88	0	14	1	21	21	3	0	.143
1967	6	9	.400	2.99	55	3	0	96.1	108	32	53	0	5	7	6	10	1	0	.100
1968 2 teams			LA	N (5G 2–0)		CHI	N	(68G 10–5)											
" total	12	5	.706	2.27	73	0	0	134.2	119	25	67	0	12	5	25	21	3	0	.143
1969 CHI N	12	6	.667	3.70	71	0	0	112	120	35	56	0	12	6	17	15	1	0	.067
1970	5	9	.357	4.74	54	0	0	76	81	32	31	0	5	9	12	9	0	0	.000
1971	5	5	.500	3.95	48	1	0	73	84	33	28	0	4	5	6	8	0	0	.000
1972 2 teams			CHI	N (5G 0–1)		CHI	A	(10G 0–1)											
" total	0	2	.000	3.63	15	0	0	17.1	24	8	6	0	0	2	0	1	1	0	1.000
13 yrs.	96	81	.542	3.84	551	105	20	1372.2	1392	447	743	1	58	40	92	321	49	1	.153
WORLD SERIES																			
1966 LA N	0	0	—	0.00	2	0	0	1.2	0	1	2	0	0	0	0	0	0	0	—

Earl Reid

REID, EARL PERCY
B. June 8, 1913, Bangor, Ala.   D. May 11, 1984, Cullman, Ala.   BL TR 6'3" 190 lbs.

	W	L	PCT	ERA	G	GS	CG	IP	H	BB	SO	ShO	W	L	SV	AB	H	HR	BA
1946 BOS N	1	0	1.000	3.00	2	0	0	3	4	3	2	0	1	0	0	0	0	0	—

Bill Reidy

REIDY, WILLIAM JOSEPH
B. Oct. 9, 1873, Cleveland, Ohio   D. Oct. 14, 1915, Cleveland, Ohio   TR 5'8" 155 lbs.

	W	L	PCT	ERA	G	GS	CG	IP	H	BB	SO	ShO	W	L	SV	AB	H	HR	BA
1896 NY N	0	1	.000	7.62	2	1	1	13	24	2	1	0	0	0	0	5	0	0	.000
1899 BKN N	1	0	1.000	2.57	2	1	1	7	9	2	2	0	0	0	1	3	0	0	.000
1901 MIL A	16	20	.444	4.21	37	33	28	301.1	364	62	50	2	2	2	0	112	16	0	.143
1902 STL A	3	4	.429	4.45	12	9	7	95	111	13	16	0	1	0	0	41	8	0	.195
1903 2 teams			STL	A (5G 1–4)		BKN	N	(15G 7–6)											
" total	8	10	.444	3.61	20	18	16	147	183	21	29	1	0	1	0	52	10	0	.192
1904 BKN N	0	4	.000	4.46	6	4	2	38.1	49	6	11	0	0	0	0	32	5	0	.156
6 yrs.	28	39	.418	4.17	79	66	55	601.2	740	106	109	3	2	4	2	245	39	0	.159

Art Reinhart

REINHART, ARTHUR CONRAD
B. May 29, 1899, Ackley, Iowa   D. Nov. 11, 1946, Houston, Tex.   BL TL 6'1" 170 lbs.

	W	L	PCT	ERA	G	GS	CG	IP	H	BB	SO	ShO	W	L	SV	AB	H	HR	BA
1919 STL N	0	0	—	0.00	1	0	0	0	0	0	0	0	0	0	0	0	0	0	—
1925	11	5	.688	3.05	20	16	15	144.2	149	47	26	1	0	0	0	67	22	0	.328
1926	10	5	.667	4.22	27	11	9	143	159	47	26	0	2	2	0	63	20	0	.317
1927	5	2	.714	4.19	21	9	4	81.2	82	36	15	2	0	0	1	32	10	0	.313
1928	4	6	.400	2.87	23	9	3	75.1	80	27	12	1	2	2	2	24	4	0	.167
5 yrs.	30	18	.625	3.60	92	45	31	444.2	470	157	79	4	4	4	3	186	56	0	.301
WORLD SERIES																			
1926 STL N	0	1	.000	∞	1	0	0		1	4	0	0	0	1	0	0	0	0	—

Bobby Reis

REIS, ROBERT JOSEPH THOMAS
B. Jan. 2, 1909, Woodside, N. Y.   D. May 1, 1973, St. Paul, Minn.   BR TR 6'1" 175 lbs.

	W	L	PCT	ERA	G	GS	CG	IP	H	BB	SO	ShO	W	L	SV	AB	H	HR	BA
1935 BKN N	3	2	.600	2.83	14	2	1	41.1	46	24	7	0	1	2	2	85	21	0	.247
1936 BOS N	6	5	.545	4.48	35	5	3	138.2	152	74	25	0	5	1	0	60	13	0	.217
1937	0	0	—	1.80	4	0	0	5	3	5	0	0	0	0	0	86	21	0	.244
1938	1	6	.143	4.99	16	2	1	57.2	61	41	20	0	1	4	0	49	9	0	.184
4 yrs.	10	13	.435	4.27	69	9	5	242.2	262	144	52	0	7	7	2	*			

Jack Reis

REIS, HARRIE CRANE
B. June 14, 1890, Cincinnati, Ohio   D. July 20, 1939, Cincinnati, Ohio   BR TR 5'10½" 160 lbs.

	W	L	PCT	ERA	G	GS	CG	IP	H	BB	SO	ShO	W	L	SV	AB	H	HR	BA
1911 STL N	0	0	—	0.96	3	0	0	9.1	5	8	4	0	0	0	0	2	0	0	.000

Laurie Reis

REIS, LAWRENCE P.
B. Nov. 20, 1858, Illinois   D. Jan. 24, 1921, Chicago, Ill.   BL TR 160 lbs.

	W	L	PCT	ERA	G	GS	CG	IP	H	BB	SO	ShO	W	L	SV	AB	H	HR	BA
1877 CHI N	3	1	.750	0.75	4	4	4	36	29	6	11	1	0	0	0	16	2	0	.125
1878	1	3	.250	3.25	4	4	4	36	55	4	8	0	0	0	0	20	3	0	.150
2 yrs.	4	4	.500	2.00	8	8	8	72	84	10	19	1	0	0	0	36	5	0	.139

Tommy Reis

REIS, THOMAS EDWARD
B. Aug. 6, 1914, Newport, Ky.   BR TR 6'2" 180 lbs.

	W	L	PCT	ERA	G	GS	CG	IP	H	BB	SO	ShO	W	L	SV	AB	H	HR	BA
1938 2 teams			PHI	N (4G 0–1)		BOS	N	(4G 0–0)											
" total	0	1	.000	12.27	8	0	0	11	16	9	6	0	0	1	0	2	0	0	.000

	W	L	PCT	ERA	G	GS	CG	IP	H	BB	SO	ShO	Relief Pitching W	L	SV	BATTING AB	H	HR	BA

Elmer Riddle

RIDDLE, ELMER RAY   BR TR 5'11½" 170 lbs.
Brother of Johnny Riddle.
B. July 31, 1914, Columbus, Ga.   D. May 14, 1984, Colombus, Ga.

	W	L	PCT	ERA	G	GS	CG	IP	H	BB	SO	ShO	W	L	SV	AB	H	HR	BA
1939 CIN N	0	0	–	0.00	1	0	0	2	1	0	0	0	0	0	0	0	0	0	.143
1940	1	2	.333	1.87	15	1	1	33.2	30	17	9	0	1	1	2	7	1	0	.143
1941	19	4	**.826**	**2.24**	33	22	15	216.2	180	59	80	4	3	0	1	71	16	0	.225
1942	7	11	.389	3.69	29	19	7	158.1	157	79	78	1	2	1	0	58	15	0	.259
1943	**21**	11	.656	2.63	36	33	19	260.1	235	107	69	5	0	0	3	93	18	0	.194
1944	2	2	.500	4.05	4	4	2	26.2	25	12	6	0	0	0	0	8	1	0	.125
1945	1	4	.200	8.19	12	3	0	29.2	39	27	5	0	1	0	0	11	3	0	.273
1947	1	0	1.000	8.31	16	3	0	30.1	42	31	8	0	0	0	0	5	0	0	.000
1948 PIT N	12	10	.545	3.49	28	27	12	191	184	81	63	3	0	0	1	64	12	1	.188
1949	1	8	.111	5.33	16	12	1	74.1	81	45	24	0	0	1	1	22	3	0	.136
10 yrs.	65	52	.556	3.40	190	124	57	1023	974	458	342	13	7	4	8	339	69	1	.204

WORLD SERIES
1940 CIN N	0	0	–	0.00	1	0	0	1	0	1	2	0	0	0	0	0	0	0	–

Denny Riddleberger

RIDDLEBERGER, DENNIS MICHAEL   BR TL 6'3" 195 lbs.
B. Nov. 22, 1945, Clifton Forge, Va.

	W	L	PCT	ERA	G	GS	CG	IP	H	BB	SO	ShO	W	L	SV	AB	H	HR	BA
1970 WAS A	0	0	–	1.00	8	0	0	9	7	2	5	0	0	0	0	0	0	0	–
1971	3	1	.750	3.21	57	0	0	70	67	32	56	0	3	1	1	4	0	0	.000
1972 CLE A	1	3	.250	2.50	38	0	0	54	45	22	34	0	1	3	0	4	0	0	.000
3 yrs.	4	4	.500	2.77	103	0	0	133	119	56	95	0	4	4	1	8	0	0	.000

Dorsey Riddlemoser

RIDDLEMOSER, DORSEY LEE   BR TR
B. Mar. 25, 1875, Frederick, Md.   D. May 11, 1954, Frederick, Md.

	W	L	PCT	ERA	G	GS	CG	IP	H	BB	SO	ShO	W	L	SV	AB	H	HR	BA
1899 WAS N	0	0	–	18.00	1	0	0	2	7	2	0	0	0	0	0	1	0	0	.000

Jack Ridgeway

RIDGEWAY, JOHN A.   BL TR 5'11" 174 lbs.
B. July 23, 1889, Philadelphia, Pa.   D. Feb. 23, 1928, Philadelphia, Pa.

	W	L	PCT	ERA	G	GS	CG	IP	H	BB	SO	ShO	W	L	SV	AB	H	HR	BA
1914 BAL F	0	0	–	11.00	4	1	0	9	20	3	2	0	0	0	0	1	0	0	.000

Steve Ridzik

RIDZIK, STEPHEN GEORGE   BR TR 5'11" 170 lbs.
B. Apr. 29, 1929, Yonkers, N. Y.

	W	L	PCT	ERA	G	GS	CG	IP	H	BB	SO	ShO	W	L	SV	AB	H	HR	BA
1950 PHI N	0	0	–	6.00	1	0	0	3	3	1	2	0	0	0	0	0	0	0	–
1952	4	2	.667	3.01	24	9	2	92.2	74	37	43	0	2	0	0	22	3	0	.136
1953	9	6	.600	3.77	42	12	1	124	119	48	53	0	7	1	0	36	7	1	.194
1954	4	5	.444	4.13	35	6	0	80.2	72	44	45	0	4	1	0	22	5	0	.227
1955 2 teams			PHI N	(3G 0–1)			CIN N	(13G 0–3)											
" total	0	4	.000	3.95	16	2	0	41	42	22	12	0	0	1	0	10	1	0	.100
1956 NY N	6	2	.750	3.80	41	5	1	92.1	80	65	53	1	3	1	0	28	7	0	.250
1957	0	2	.000	4.73	15	0	0	26.2	19	19	13	0	0	2	0	5	1	0	.200
1958 CLE A	0	2	.000	2.08	6	0	0	8.2	9	5	6	0	0	2	0	1	0	0	.000
1963 WAS A	5	6	.455	4.82	20	10	0	89.2	82	35	47	0	2	1	1	29	5	0	.172
1964	5	5	.500	2.89	49	3	0	112	96	31	60	0	5	3	2	27	6	0	.222
1965	6	4	.600	4.02	63	0	0	109.2	108	43	72	0	6	4	8	18	3	0	.167
1966 PHI N	0	0	–	7.71	2	0	0	2	5	1	0	0	0	0	0	0	0	0	–
12 yrs.	39	38	.506	3.79	314	48	4	782.2	709	351	406	1	29	17	11	198	38	1	.192

Elmer Rieger

RIEGER, ELMER JAY   BB TR 6' 175 lbs.
B. Feb. 25, 1889, Perris, Calif.   D. Oct. 21, 1959, Los Angeles, Calif.

	W	L	PCT	ERA	G	GS	CG	IP	H	BB	SO	ShO	W	L	SV	AB	H	HR	BA
1910 STL N	0	2	.000	5.48	13	2	0	21.1	26	7	9	0	0	1	0	3	0	0	.000

Dave Righetti

RIGHETTI, DAVID ALLAN   BL TL 6'2" 170 lbs.
B. Nov. 28, 1958, San Jose, Calif.

	W	L	PCT	ERA	G	GS	CG	IP	H	BB	SO	ShO	W	L	SV	AB	H	HR	BA
1979 NY A	0	1	.000	3.71	3	3	0	17	10	10	13	0	0	0	0	0	0	0	–
1981	8	4	.667	2.06	15	15	2	105	75	38	89	0	0	0	0	0	0	0	–
1982	11	10	.524	3.79	33	27	4	183	155	108	163	0	0	0	1	0	0	0	–
1983	14	8	.636	3.44	31	31	7	217	194	67	169	2	0	0	0	0	0	0	–
1984	5	6	.455	2.34	64	0	0	96.1	79	37	90	0	5	6	31	0	0	0	–
5 yrs.	38	29	.567	3.14	146	76	13	618.1	513	260	524	2	5	6	32	0	0	0	–

DIVISIONAL PLAYOFF SERIES
1981 NY A	2	0	1.000	1.00	2	1	0	9	8	3	13	0	1	0	0	0	0	0	–

LEAGUE CHAMPIONSHIP SERIES
1981 NY A	1	0	1.000	0.00	1	1	0	6	4	2	4	0	0	0	0	0	0	0	–

WORLD SERIES
1981 NY A	0	0	–	13.50	1	1	0	2	3	1	0	0	0	0	0	1	0	0	.000

Johnny Rigney

RIGNEY, JOHN DUNGAN   BR TR 6'2" 190 lbs.
B. Oct. 28, 1914, Oak Park, Ill.   D. Oct. 23, 1984, Chicago, Ill.

	W	L	PCT	ERA	G	GS	CG	IP	H	BB	SO	ShO	W	L	SV	AB	H	HR	BA
1937 CHI A	2	5	.286	4.96	22	4	1	90.2	107	46	38	1	2	2	1	30	5	0	.167
1938	9	9	.500	3.56	38	12	7	167	164	72	84	1	5	3	1	55	8	0	.145
1939	15	8	.652	3.70	35	29	11	218.2	208	84	119	2	0	0	0	80	16	0	.200
1940	14	18	.438	3.11	39	33	19	280.2	240	90	141	2	2	1	3	93	20	0	.215
1941	13	13	.500	3.84	30	29	18	237	224	92	119	3	0	0	0	84	17	0	.202
1942	3	3	.500	3.20	7	7	6	59	40	16	34	0	0	0	0	19	1	0	.053
1946	5	5	.500	4.03	15	11	3	82.2	76	35	51	2	0	1	0	26	4	0	.154
1947	2	3	.400	1.95	11	7	2	50.2	42	15	19	0	0	0	0	14	0	0	.000
8 yrs.	63	64	.496	3.59	197	132	67	1186.1	1101	450	605	11	9	7	5	401	71	0	.177

Jose Rijo

RIJO, JOSE ANTONIO   BR TR 6'1" 160 lbs.
B. May 13, 1965, San Cristobal, Dominican Republic

	W	L	PCT	ERA	G	GS	CG	IP	H	BB	SO	ShO	W	L	SV	AB	H	HR	BA
1984 NY A	2	8	.200	4.76	24	5	0	62.1	74	33	47	0	2	4	2	0	0	0	–

	W	L	PCT	ERA	G	GS	CG	IP	H	BB	SO	ShO	Relief Pitching W	L	SV	BATTING AB	H	HR	BA

George Riley

RILEY, GEORGE MICHAEL
B. Oct. 6, 1956, Philadelphia, Pa.   BL TL 6'2"   210 lbs.

	W	L	PCT	ERA	G	GS	CG	IP	H	BB	SO	ShO	W	L	SV	AB	H	HR	BA
1979 CHI N	0	1	.000	5.54	4	1	0	13	16	6	5	0	0	0	0	2	0	0	.000
1980	0	4	.000	5.75	22	0	0	36	41	20	18	0	0	4	0	1	0	0	.000
1984 SF N	1	0	1.000	3.99	5	4	0	29.1	39	7	12	0	0	0	0	10	1	0	.100
3 yrs.	1	5	.167	5.06	31	5	0	78.1	96	33	35	0	0	4	0	13	1	0	.077

Andy Rincon

RINCON, ANDREW JOHN
B. Mar. 5, 1959, Pico Rivera, Calif.   BR TR 6'3"   195 lbs.

	W	L	PCT	ERA	G	GS	CG	IP	H	BB	SO	ShO	W	L	SV	AB	H	HR	BA
1980 STL N	3	1	.750	2.61	4	4	1	31	23	7	22	0	0	0	0	12	3	0	.250
1981	3	1	.750	1.75	5	5	1	36	27	5	13	1	0	0	0	13	3	0	.231
1982	2	3	.400	4.73	11	6	1	40	35	25	11	0	1	0	0	10	1	0	.100
3 yrs.	8	5	.615	3.11	20	15	3	107	85	37	46	1	1	0	0	35	7	0	.200

Jeff Rineer

RINEER, JEFFREY ALAN
B. July 3, 1955, Lancaster, Pa.   BL TL 6'4"   205 lbs.

	W	L	PCT	ERA	G	GS	CG	IP	H	BB	SO	ShO	W	L	SV	AB	H	HR	BA
1979 BAL A	0	0	–	0.00	1	0	0	1	0	0	0	0	0	0	0	0	0	0	–

Jimmy Ring

RING, JAMES JOSEPH
B. Feb. 15, 1895, Brooklyn, N. Y.   D. July 6, 1965, New York, N. Y.   BR TR 6'1"   170 lbs.

	W	L	PCT	ERA	G	GS	CG	IP	H	BB	SO	ShO	W	L	SV	AB	H	HR	BA
1917 CIN N	3	7	.300	4.40	24	7	3	88	90	35	33	0	0	3	2	26	2	0	.077
1918	9	5	.643	2.85	21	18	13	142.1	130	48	26	4	0	0	0	50	6	0	.120
1919	10	9	.526	2.26	32	18	12	183	150	51	61	2	1	1	3	62	6	0	.097
1920	17	16	.515	3.23	42	33	18	292.2	268	92	73	1	2	1	1	96	19	0	.198
1921 PHI N	10	19	.345	4.24	34	30	21	246	258	88	88	0	1	1	1	83	12	0	.145
1922	12	18	.400	4.58	40	33	17	249.1	292	103	116	0	2	1	1	88	13	1	.148
1923	18	16	.529	3.76	39	36	23	313.1	336	115	112	0	1	2	0	113	12	1	.106
1924	10	12	.455	3.97	32	31	16	215.1	236	108	72	1	0	0	0	74	17	0	.230
1925	14	16	.467	4.37	38	37	21	270	325	119	93	1	0	0	0	101	11	2	.109
1926 NY N	11	10	.524	4.57	39	23	5	183.1	207	74	76	0	2	0	2	56	8	0	.143
1927 STL N	0	4	.000	6.55	13	3	1	33	39	17	13	0	0	2	0	8	3	0	.375
1928 PHI N	4	17	.190	6.40	35	25	4	173	214	103	72	0	0	1	1	60	11	0	.183
12 yrs.	118	149	.442	4.06	389	294	154	2389.1	2545	953	835	9	9	11	11	817	120	4	.147

WORLD SERIES

	W	L	PCT	ERA	G	GS	CG	IP	H	BB	SO	ShO	W	L	SV	AB	H	HR	BA
1919 CIN N	1	1	.500	0.64	2	1	1	14	7	6	4	1	0	0	0	5	0	0	.000

Allen Ripley

RIPLEY, ALLEN STEVENS
Son of Walt Ripley.
B. Oct. 18, 1952, Norwood, Mass.   BR TR 6'3"   190 lbs.

	W	L	PCT	ERA	G	GS	CG	IP	H	BB	SO	ShO	W	L	SV	AB	H	HR	BA
1978 BOS A	2	5	.286	5.55	15	11	1	73	92	22	26	0	0	0	0	0	0	0	–
1979	3	1	.750	5.12	16	3	0	65	77	25	34	0	2	0	1	0	0	0	–
1980 SF N	9	10	.474	4.14	23	20	2	113	119	36	65	0	1	1	0	40	6	0	.150
1981	4	4	.500	4.05	19	14	1	91	103	27	47	0	0	0	0	30	4	0	.133
1982 CHI N	5	7	.417	4.26	28	19	0	122.2	130	38	57	0	0	1	0	38	5	0	.132
5 yrs.	23	27	.460	4.51	101	67	4	464.2	521	148	229	0	3	2	1	108	15	0	.139

Walt Ripley

RIPLEY, WALTER FRANKLIN
Father of Allen Ripley.
B. Nov. 26, 1916, Worcester, Mass.   BR TR 6'   168 lbs.

	W	L	PCT	ERA	G	GS	CG	IP	H	BB	SO	ShO	W	L	SV	AB	H	HR	BA
1935 BOS A	0	0	–	9.00	2	0	0	4	7	3	0	0	0	0	0	0	0	0	–

Charlie Ripple

RIPPLE, CHARLES DAWSON
B. Dec. 1, 1921, Bolton, N. C.   D. May 6, 1979, Wilmington, N. C.   BL TL 6'2"   210 lbs.

	W	L	PCT	ERA	G	GS	CG	IP	H	BB	SO	ShO	W	L	SV	AB	H	HR	BA
1944 PHI N	0	0	–	15.43	1	1	0	2.1	6	4	2	0	0	0	0	1	1	0	1.000
1945	0	1	.000	7.04	4	0	0	7.2	7	10	5	0	0	1	0	1	0	0	.000
1946	1	0	1.000	10.80	6	0	0	3.1	5	6	3	0	1	0	0	0	0	0	–
3 yrs.	1	1	.500	9.45	11	1	0	13.1	18	20	10	0	1	1	0	2	1	0	.500

Ray Ripplemeyer

RIPPLEMEYER, RAYMOND ROY
B. July 9, 1933, Valmeyer, Ill.   BR TR 6'3"   200 lbs.

	W	L	PCT	ERA	G	GS	CG	IP	H	BB	SO	ShO	W	L	SV	AB	H	HR	BA
1962 WAS A	1	2	.333	5.49	18	1	0	39.1	47	17	17	0	1	1	0	6	3	1	.500

Jay Ritchie

RITCHIE, JAY SEAY
B. Nov. 20, 1936, Salisbury, N. C.   BR TR 6'4"   175 lbs.

	W	L	PCT	ERA	G	GS	CG	IP	H	BB	SO	ShO	W	L	SV	AB	H	HR	BA
1964 BOS A	1	1	.500	2.74	21	0	0	46	43	14	35	0	1	1	0	9	1	0	.111
1965	1	2	.333	3.17	44	0	0	71	83	26	55	0	1	2	2	5	1	0	.200
1966 ATL N	0	1	.000	4.08	22	0	0	35.1	32	12	33	0	0	1	4	4	2	0	.500
1967	4	6	.400	3.17	52	0	0	82.1	75	29	57	0	4	6	2	10	3	0	.300
1968 CIN N	2	3	.400	4.61	28	2	0	56.2	68	13	32	0	2	1	0	7	0	0	.000
5 yrs.	8	13	.381	3.49	167	2	0	291.1	301	94	212	0	8	11	8	35	7	0	.200

Hank Ritter

RITTER, WILLIAM HERBERT
B. Oct. 12, 1893, McCoysville, Pa.   D. Sept. 3, 1964, Akron, Ohio   BR TR 6'   180 lbs.

	W	L	PCT	ERA	G	GS	CG	IP	H	BB	SO	ShO	W	L	SV	AB	H	HR	BA
1912 PHI N	0	0	–	4.50	3	0	0	6	5	5	1	0	0	0	0	1	0	0	.000
1914 NY N	1	0	1.000	1.13	1	0	0	8	4	4	4	0	1	0	0	3	0	0	.000
1915	2	1	.667	4.63	22	2	0	58.1	66	15	35	0	1	0	1	16	2	0	.125
1916	1	0	1.000	0.00	3	0	0	5	3	0	3	0	1	0	0	0	0	0	–
4 yrs.	4	1	.800	3.96	29	2	0	77.1	78	24	43	0	3	0	1	20	2	0	.100

Jim Rittwage

RITTWAGE, JAMES MICHAEL
B. Oct. 23, 1945, Cleveland, Ohio   BR TR 6'3"   190 lbs.

	W	L	PCT	ERA	G	GS	CG	IP	H	BB	SO	ShO	W	L	SV	AB	H	HR	BA
1970 CLE A	1	1	.500	4.15	8	3	1	26	18	21	16	0	0	0	0	8	3	0	.375

	W	L	PCT	ERA	G	GS	CG	IP	H	BB	SO	ShO	Relief Pitching W	L	SV	BATTING AB	H	HR	BA

Dick Rudolph continued

	W	L	PCT	ERA	G	GS	CG	IP	H	BB	SO	ShO	W	L	SV	AB	H	HR	BA
1920	4	8	.333	4.04	18	12	3	89	104	24	24	0	2	1	0	27	5	0	.185
1922	0	2	.000	5.06	3	3	1	16	22	5	3	0	0	0	0	5	2	0	.400
1923	1	2	.333	3.72	4	4	1	19.1	27	10	3	1	0	0	0	7	0	0	.000
1927	0	0	—	0.00	1	0	0	1.1	1	1	1	0	0	0	0	0	0	0	—
13 yrs.	122	108	.530	2.66	280	241	172	2049	1971	402	786	26	7	8	8	698	131	2	.188
WORLD SERIES																			
1914 BOS N	2	0	1.000	0.50	2	2	2	18	12	4	15	0	0	0	0	6	2	0	.333

Don Rudolph

RUDOLPH, FREDERICK DONALD   BL TL 5'11''   195 lbs.
B. Aug. 16, 1931, Baltimore, Md.   D. Sept. 12, 1968, Granada Hills, Calif.

	W	L	PCT	ERA	G	GS	CG	IP	H	BB	SO	ShO	W	L	SV	AB	H	HR	BA
1957 CHI A	1	0	1.000	2.25	5	0	0	12	6	2	2	0	1	0	0	2	1	0	.500
1958	1	0	1.000	2.57	7	0	0	7	4	5	2	0	1	0	1	0	0	0	—
1959 2 teams			CHI A (4G 0–0)				CIN N (5G 0–0)												
" total	0	0	—	3.48	9	0	0	10.1	17	5	8	0	0	0	1	1	0	0	.000
1962 2 teams			CLE A (1G 0–0)				WAS A (37G 8–10)												
" total	8	10	.444	3.62	38	23	6	176.2	188	42	68	2	0	2	0	57	10	0	.175
1963 WAS A	7	19	.269	4.55	37	26	4	174	189	36	70	0	0	2	1	45	8	1	.178
1964	1	3	.250	4.09	28	8	0	70.1	81	12	32	0	0	0	0	15	1	0	.067
6 yrs.	18	32	.360	4.00	124	57	10	450.1	485	102	182	2	2	4	3	120	20	1	.167

Ernie Rudolph

RUDOLPH, ERNEST WILLIAM   BL TR 5'8''   165 lbs.
B. Feb. 13, 1910, Black River Falls, Wis.

	W	L	PCT	ERA	G	GS	CG	IP	H	BB	SO	ShO	W	L	SV	AB	H	HR	BA
1945 BKN N	1	0	1.000	5.19	7	0	0	8.2	12	7	3	0	1	0	0	0	0	0	—

Dutch Ruether

RUETHER, WALTER HENRY   BL TL 6'1½''   180 lbs.
B. Sept. 13, 1893, Alameda, Calif.   D. May 16, 1970, Phoenix, Ariz.

	W	L	PCT	ERA	G	GS	CG	IP	H	BB	SO	ShO	W	L	SV	AB	H	HR	BA
1917 2 teams			CHI N (10G 2–0)				CIN N (7G 1–2)												
" total	3	2	.600	3.00	17	8	2	72	80	26	35	1	0	0	0	68	17	0	.250
1918 CIN N	0	1	.000	2.70	2	2	1	10	10	3	10	0	0	0	0	3	0	0	.000
1919	19	6	.760	1.82	33	29	20	242.2	195	83	78	3	0	0	0	92	24	0	.261
1920	16	12	.571	2.47	37	33	23	265.2	235	96	99	5	0	1	3	104	20	0	.192
1921 BKN N	10	13	.435	4.26	36	27	12	211.1	247	67	78	1	0	0	2	97	34	2	.351
1922	21	12	.636	3.53	35	35	26	267.1	290	92	89	2	0	0	0	125	26	2	.208
1923	15	14	.517	4.22	34	34	20	275	308	86	87	0	0	0	0	117	32	0	.274
1924	8	13	.381	3.94	30	21	13	166.2	189	45	65	2	1	1	3	62	15	0	.242
1925 WAS A	18	7	.720	3.87	30	29	16	223.1	241	105	68	1	0	1	0	108	36	1	.333
1926 2 teams			WAS A (23G 12–6)				NY A (5G 2–3)												
" total	14	9	.609	4.60	28	28	10	205.1	246	84	56	0	0	0	0	113	25	1	.221
1927 NY A	13	6	.684	3.38	27	26	12	184	202	52	45	3	0	0	0	80	21	1	.263
11 yrs.	137	95	.591	3.50	309	272	155	2123.1	2243	739	710	18	1	3	8	*			
WORLD SERIES																			
1919 CIN N	1	0	1.000	2.57	2	2	1	14	12	4	1	0	0	0	0	6	4	0	.667
1926 NY A	0	1	.000	8.31	1	1	0	4.1	7	2	1	0	0	0	0	4	0	0	.000
2 yrs.	1	1	.500	3.93	3	3	1	18.1	19	6	2	0	0	0	0	11	4	0	.364

Red Ruffing

RUFFING, CHARLES HERBERT   BR TR 6'1½''   205 lbs.
B. May 3, 1904, Granville, Ill.
Hall of Fame 1967.

	W	L	PCT	ERA	G	GS	CG	IP	H	BB	SO	ShO	W	L	SV	AB	H	HR	BA
1924 BOS A	0	0	—	6.65	8	2	0	23	29	9	10	0	0	0	1	7	1	0	.143
1925	9	18	.333	5.01	37	27	13	217.1	253	75	64	3	1	1	1	79	17	0	.215
1926	6	15	.286	4.39	37	22	6	166	169	68	58	0	1	2	2	51	10	1	.196
1927	5	13	.278	4.66	26	18	10	158.1	160	87	77	0	1	1	2	55	14	0	.255
1928	10	25	.286	3.89	42	34	25	289.1	303	96	118	1	0	2	2	121	38	2	.314
1929	9	22	.290	4.86	35	30	18	244.1	280	118	109	2	0	3	1	114	35	2	.307
1930 2 teams			BOS A (4G 0–3)				NY A (34G 15–5)												
" total	15	8	.652	4.38	38	28	19	221.2	242	68	131	2	2	1	1	110	40	4	.364
1931 NY A	16	14	.533	4.41	37	30	19	237	240	87	132	1	1	2	2	109	36	3	.330
1932	18	7	.720	3.09	35	29	22	259	219	115	190	3	1	1	1	124	38	3	.306
1933	9	14	.391	3.91	35	28	18	235	230	93	122	0	1	0	3	115	29	2	.252
1934	19	11	.633	3.93	36	31	19	256.1	232	104	149	5	1	1	0	113	28	2	.248
1935	16	11	.593	3.12	30	29	19	222	201	76	81	2	0	1	0	109	37	2	.339
1936	20	12	.625	3.85	33	33	25	271	274	90	102	3	0	0	0	127	37	5	.291
1937	20	7	.741	2.98	31	31	22	256.1	242	68	131	5	0	0	0	129	26	1	.202
1938	21	7	.750	3.31	31	31	22	247.1	246	82	127	4	0	0	0	107	24	3	.224
1939	21	7	.750	2.93	28	28	22	233.1	211	75	95	5	0	0	0	114	35	1	.307
1940	15	12	.556	3.38	30	30	20	226	218	76	97	3	0	1	0	89	11	1	.124
1941	15	6	.714	3.54	23	23	13	185.2	177	54	60	2	0	0	0	89	27	2	.303
1942	14	7	.667	3.21	24	24	16	193.2	183	41	80	4	0	0	0	80	20	1	.250
1945	7	3	.700	2.89	11	11	8	87.1	85	20	24	1	0	0	0	46	10	1	.217
1946	5	1	.833	1.77	8	8	4	61	37	23	19	2	0	0	0	25	3	0	.120
1947 CHI A	3	5	.375	6.11	9	9	1	53	63	16	11	0	0	0	0	24	5	0	.208
22 yrs.	273	225	.548	3.80	624	536	335	4344	4294	1541	1987	48	9	15	16	*			
											8th								
WORLD SERIES																			
1932 NY A	1	0	1.000	4.00	1	1	1	9	10	6	10	0	0	0	0	4	0	0	.000
1936	1	0	1.000	4.50	2	2	0	14	16	5	12	0	0	0	0	5	0	0	.000
1937	1	0	1.000	1.00	1	1	1	9	7	3	8	0	0	0	0	4	2	0	.500
1938	2	0	1.000	1.50	2	2	2	18	17	2	11	0	0	0	0	6	1	0	.167
1939	1	0	1.000	1.00	1	1	1	9	4	1	4	0	0	0	0	3	1	0	.333
1941	1	0	1.000	1.00	1	1	1	9	6	3	5	0	0	0	0	3	0	0	.000
1942	1	1	.500	4.08	2	2	1	17.2	14	7	11	0	0	0	0	9	2	0	.222
7 yrs.	7	2	.778	2.63	10	10	7	85.2	74	27	61	0	0	0	0	34	6	0	.176
			2nd				4th 4th		3rd	4th	6th	4th							

	W	L	PCT	ERA	G	GS	CG	IP	H	BB	SO	ShO	Relief Pitching W	L	SV	BATTING AB	H	HR	BA

Vern Ruhle

RUHLE, VERNON GERALD
B. Jan. 25, 1951, Coleman, Mich. BR TR 6'1" 185 lbs.

	W	L	PCT	ERA	G	GS	CG	IP	H	BB	SO	ShO	W	L	SV	AB	H	HR	BA
1974 DET A	2	0	1.000	2.73	5	3	1	33	35	6	10	0	0	0	0	0	0	0	—
1975	11	12	.478	4.03	32	31	8	190	199	65	67	3	0	0	0	0	0	0	—
1976	9	12	.429	3.92	32	32	5	200	227	59	88	1	0	0	0	0	0	0	—
1977	3	5	.375	5.73	14	10	0	66	83	15	27	0	0	0	0	0	0	0	—
1978 HOU N	3	3	.500	2.12	13	10	2	68	57	20	27	2	0	1	0	18	1	0	.056
1979	2	6	.250	4.09	13	10	2	66	64	8	33	2	0	1	0	19	1	0	.053
1980	12	4	.750	2.38	28	22	6	159	148	29	55	2	0	0	0	49	12	0	.245
1981	4	6	.400	2.91	20	15	1	102	97	20	39	0	0	1	1	24	6	0	.250
1982	9	13	.409	3.93	31	21	3	149	169	24	56	2	3	0	1	41	4	0	.098
1983	8	5	.615	3.69	41	9	0	114.2	107	36	43	0	7	3	3	19	2	0	.105
1984	1	9	.100	4.58	40	6	0	90.1	112	29	60	0	0	5	2	12	1	0	.083
11 yrs.	64	75	.460	3.66	269	169	28	1238	1298	311	505	12	10	11	7	182	27	0	.148

DIVISIONAL PLAYOFF SERIES
| 1981 HOU N | 0 | 1 | .000 | 2.25 | 1 | 1 | 1 | 8 | 4 | 2 | 1 | 0 | 0 | 0 | 0 | 1 | 0 | 0 | .000 |

LEAGUE CHAMPIONSHIP SERIES
| 1980 HOU N | 0 | 0 | — | 3.86 | 1 | 1 | 0 | 7 | 8 | 1 | 3 | 0 | 0 | 0 | 0 | 3 | 0 | 0 | .000 |

Andy Rush

RUSH, JESS HOWARD
B. Dec. 26, 1889, Longton, Kans. D. Mar. 16, 1969, Fresno, Calif. BR TR 6'3" 180 lbs.

| 1925 BKN N | 0 | 1 | .000 | 9.31 | 4 | 2 | 0 | 9.2 | 16 | 5 | 4 | 0 | 0 | 0 | 0 | 3 | 0 | 0 | .000 |

Bob Rush

RUSH, ROBERT RANSOM
B. Dec. 21, 1925, Battle Creek, Mich. BR TR 6'4" 205 lbs.

1948 CHI N	5	11	.313	3.92	36	16	4	133.1	153	37	72	0	2	0	0	39	5	0	.128
1949	10	18	.357	4.07	35	27	9	201	197	79	80	1	2	0	4	63	2	0	.032
1950	13	20	.394	3.71	39	34	19	254.2	261	93	93	1	0	2	1	90	15	1	.167
1951	11	12	.478	3.83	37	29	12	211.1	219	68	129	2	2	0	2	68	13	0	.191
1952	17	13	.567	2.70	34	32	17	250.1	205	81	157	4	0	2	0	96	28	0	.292
1953	9	14	.391	4.54	29	28	8	166.2	177	66	84	1	0	0	0	54	6	0	.111
1954	13	15	.464	3.77	33	32	11	236.1	213	103	124	0	0	0	0	83	23	2	.277
1955	13	11	.542	3.50	33	33	14	234	204	73	130	3	0	0	0	82	9	1	.110
1956	13	10	.565	3.19	32	32	13	239.2	210	59	104	1	0	0	0	82	8	0	.098
1957	6	16	.273	4.38	31	29	5	205.1	211	66	103	0	0	0	0	69	14	0	.203
1958 MIL N	10	6	.625	3.42	28	20	5	147.1	142	31	84	2	3	1	0	45	9	0	.200
1959	5	6	.455	2.40	31	9	1	101.1	102	23	64	1	3	2	0	32	6	0	.188
1960 2 teams	MIL N	(10G 2–0)		CHI A		(9G 0–0)													
" total	2	0	1.000	4.91	19	2	0	29.1	40	10	20	0	2	0	1	4	2	0	.500
13 yrs.	127	152	.455	3.65	417	321	118	2410.2	2334	789	1244	16	14	7	8	807	140	4	.173

WORLD SERIES
| 1958 MIL N | 0 | 1 | .000 | 3.00 | 1 | 1 | 0 | 6 | 3 | 5 | 2 | 0 | 0 | 0 | 0 | 2 | 0 | 0 | .000 |

Amos Rusie

RUSIE, AMOS WILSON (The Hoosier Thunderbolt)
B. May 30, 1871, Mooresville, Ind. D. Dec. 6, 1942, Seattle, Wash. BR TR 6'1" 200 lbs.
Hall of Fame 1977.

1889 IND N	13	10	.565	5.32	33	22	19	225	246	128	113	1	2	0	0	103	18	0	.175
1890 NY N	29	30	.492	2.56	67	63	56	548.2	436	289	345	4	1	1	1	284	79	0	.278
1891	33	20	.623	2.55	61	57	52	500.1	391	262	337	6	2	1	1	220	54	0	.245
1892	32	28	.533	2.88	64	61	58	532	405	267	303	2	0	2	0	252	53	1	.210
1893	29	18	.617	3.23	56	52¹	50¹	482¹	451	218¹	208	4	0	0	1	212	57	3	.269
1894	36	13	.735	2.78	54	50	45	444	426	200	195	3	2	0	1	186	52	0	.280
1895	22	21	.512	3.73	49	47	42	393.1	384	159	201	4	1	1	0	179	44	1	.246
1897	29	8	.784	2.54	38	37	35	322.1	314	87	135	2	0	1	0	144	40	0	.278
1898	20	11	.645	3.03	37	36	33	300	288	103	114	4	0	0	1	138	29	0	.210
1901 CIN N	0	1	.000	8.59	3	2	2	22	43	3	6	0	0	0	0	8	1	0	.125
10 yrs.	243	160	.603	3.07	462	427	392	3769.2	3384	1716	1957	30	10	7	5	*			
										5th									

Allan Russell

RUSSELL, ALLAN E.
Brother of Lefty Russell.
B. July 31, 1893, Baltimore, Md. D. Oct. 20, 1972, Baltimore, Md. BR TR 5'11" 165 lbs.

1915 NY A	1	2	.333	2.67	5	3	1	27	21	21	21	0	0	0	0	8	2	0	.250
1916	6	10	.375	3.20	34	18	8	171.1	138	75	104	1	1	0	6	45	2	0	.044
1917	7	8	.467	2.24	25	10	6	104.1	89	39	55	0	4	2	2	31	10	0	.323
1918	7	11	.389	3.26	27	18	7	141	139	73	54	2	0	3	4	42	7	0	.167
1919 2 teams	NY A	(23G 5–5)		BOS A		(21G 10–4)													
" total	15	9	.625	2.94	44	20	13	211	194	71	113	2	1	1	5	71	12	0	.169
1920 BOS A	5	6	.455	3.01	16	10	7	107.2	100	38	53	0	1	1	1	41	5	0	.122
1921	7	11	.389	4.11	39	14	8	173	204	77	60	0	4	2	3	57	7	0	.123
1922	6	7	.462	5.01	34	11	1	125.2	152	57	34	0	3	2	2	38	3	0	.079
1923 WAS A	10	8	.556	3.03	52	6	3	181.1	177	77	67	0	9	7	9	50	10	0	.200
1924	5	1	.833	4.37	37	0	0	82.1	83	45	17	0	5	1	8	18	5	0	.278
1925	2	4	.333	5.77	32	2	0	68.2	85	37	25	0	2	3	4	14	2	0	.143
11 yrs.	71	77	.480	3.52	345	112	54	1393.1	1382	610	603	5	34	21	42	415	65	0	.157

WORLD SERIES
| 1924 WAS A | 0 | 0 | — | 3.00 | 1 | 0 | 0 | 3 | 4 | 0 | 0 | 0 | 0 | 0 | 0 | 0 | 0 | 0 | — |

Jack Russell

RUSSELL, JACK ERWIN
B. Oct. 24, 1905, Paris, Tex. BR TR 6'1½" 178 lbs.

1926 BOS A	0	5	.000	3.58	36	5	1	98	94	24	17	0	0	2	0	21	4	0	.190
1927	4	9	.308	4.10	34	15	4	147	172	40	25	1	1	1	0	48	6	0	.125
1928	11	14	.440	3.84	32	26	10	201.1	233	41	27	1	0	0	0	62	13	0	.210
1929	6	18	.250	3.94	35	32	13	226.1	263	40	37	0	0	0	0	70	9	0	.129
1930	9	20	.310	5.45	35	30	15	229.2	302	53	35	0	0	0	0	79	14	1	.177
1931	10	18	.357	5.16	36	31	13	232	298	65	45	0	0	1	0	82	16	0	.195

	W	L	PCT	ERA	G	GS	CG	IP	H	BB	SO	ShO	Relief Pitching W	L	SV	BATTING AB	H	HR	BA

Jack Russell continued

	W	L	PCT	ERA	G	GS	CG	IP	H	BB	SO	ShO	W	L	SV	AB	H	HR	BA
1932 2 teams	**BOS**	**A** (11G 1–7)			**CLE**	**A** (18G 5–7)										51	13	0	.255
" total	6	14	.300	5.25	29	17	7	152.2	207	42	34	0	0	3	1	34	5	0	.147
1933 WAS A	12	6	.667	2.69	50	3	2	124	119	32	28	0	11	4	13	44	7	0	.159
1934	5	10	.333	4.17	54	9	3	157.2	179	56	38	0	2	7	7	35	7	0	.200
1935	4	9	.308	5.71	43	7	2	126	170	37	30	0	4	5	3				
1936 2 teams		**WAS**	**A** (18G 3–2)		**BOS**	**A** (23G 0–3)										22	2	0	.091
" total	3	5	.375	6.02	41	7	1	89.2	123	41	15	0	1	4	3	7	0	0	.000
1937 DET A	2	5	.286	7.59	25	0	0	40.1	63	20	10	0	2	5	4	32	7	0	.219
1938 CHI N	6	1	.857	3.34	42	0	0	102.1	100	30	29	0	6	1	3	17	0	0	.000
1939	4	3	.571	3.67	39	0	0	68.2	78	24	32	0	4	3	3	13	0	0	.000
1940 STL N	3	4	.429	2.50	26	0	0	54	53	26	16	0	3	4	1				
15 yrs.	85	141	.376	4.47	557	182	71	2049.2	2454	571	418	3	35	40	38	617	103	1	.167
WORLD SERIES																			
1933 WAS A	0	1	.000	0.87	3	0	0	10.1	8	0	7	0	0	1	0	2	0	0	.000
1938 CHI N	0	0	–	0.00	2	0	0	1.2	1	1	0	0	0	0	0	0	0	0	–
2 yrs.	0	1	.000	0.75	5	0	0	12	9	1	7	0	0	1	0	2	0	0	.000

Jeff Russell

RUSSELL, JEFFREY LEE
B. Sept. 2, 1961, Cincinnati, Ohio
BR TR 6'4" 200 lbs.

	W	L	PCT	ERA	G	GS	CG	IP	H	BB	SO	ShO	W	L	SV	AB	H	HR	BA
1983 CIN N	4	5	.444	3.03	10	10	2	68.1	58	22	40	0	0	0	0	21	3	1	.143
1984	6	18	.250	4.26	33	30	4	181.2	186	65	101	2	0	0	0	57	8	0	.140
2 yrs.	10	23	.303	3.92	43	40	6	250	244	87	141	2	0	0	0	78	11	1	.141

John Russell

RUSSELL, JOHN ALBERT
B. Oct. 20, 1894, San Mateo, Calif.   D. Nov. 19, 1930, Ely, Nev.
BL TL 6'2" 195 lbs.

	W	L	PCT	ERA	G	GS	CG	IP	H	BB	SO	ShO	W	L	SV	AB	H	HR	BA
1917 BKN N	0	1	.000	4.50	5	1	1	16	12	6	1	0	0	0	0	4	1	0	.250
1918	0	0	–	18.00	1	0	0	1	2	1	0	0	0	0	0	0	0	0	–
1921 CHI A	2	5	.286	5.29	11	8	4	66.1	82	35	15	0	0	0	0	25	10	0	.400
1922	0	1	.000	6.75	4	1	0	6.2	7	4	3	0	0	0	1	1	0	0	.000
4 yrs.	2	7	.222	5.40	21	10	5	90	103	46	19	0	0	0	1	30	11	0	.367

Lefty Russell

RUSSELL, CLARENCE DIXON
Brother of Allan Russell.
B. July 8, 1890, Baltimore, Md.   D. Jan. 22, 1962, Baltimore, Md.
BL TL 6'1" 165 lbs.

	W	L	PCT	ERA	G	GS	CG	IP	H	BB	SO	ShO	W	L	SV	AB	H	HR	BA
1910 PHI A	1	0	1.000	0.00	1	1	1	9	8	2	5	1	0	0	0	3	0	0	.000
1911	0	3	.000	7.67	7	2	0	31.2	45	18	7	0	0	1	0	13	5	0	.385
1912	0	2	.000	7.27	5	2	2	17.1	18	14	9	0	0	1	0	4	0	0	.000
3 yrs.	1	5	.167	6.36	13	5	3	58	71	34	21	1	0	2	0	20	5	0	.250

Reb Russell

RUSSELL, EWELL ALBERT
B. Apr. 12, 1889, Jackson, Miss.   D. Sept. 30, 1973, Indianapolis, Ind.
BL TL 5'11" 185 lbs.

	W	L	PCT	ERA	G	GS	CG	IP	H	BB	SO	ShO	W	L	SV	AB	H	HR	BA
1913 CHI A	22	16	.579	1.91	51	36	26	316	249	79	122	8	3	1	4	106	20	0	.189
1914	8	12	.400	2.90	38	23	8	167.1	168	33	79	1	1	0	1	64	17	0	.266
1915	11	10	.524	2.59	41	25	10	229.1	215	47	90	3	1	1	2	86	21	0	.244
1916	18	11	.621	2.42	56	25	16	264.1	207	42	112	5	5	1	3	91	13	0	.143
1917	15	5	.750	1.95	35	24	11	189.1	170	32	54	5	2	1	3	68	19	0	.279
1918	7	5	.583	2.60	19	14	10	124.2	117	33	38	2	0	0	0	50	7	0	.140
1919	0	0	–	0.00	1	0	0	1	1	1	0	0	0	0	0	0	0	0	–
1922 PIT N	0	0	–	0.00	0	0	0	0	0	0	0	0	0	0	0	220	81	12	.368
1923	0	0	–	0.00	0	0	0	0	0	0	0	0	0	0	0	291	84	9	.289
9 yrs.	81	59	.579	2.34	241	147	81	1291	1127	267	495	24	12	4	13	*			
WORLD SERIES																			
1917 CHI A	0	0	–	∞	1	1	0		2	1	0	0	0	0	0	0	0	0	–

Marius Russo

RUSSO, MARIUS UGO (Lefty)
B. July 19, 1914, Brooklyn, N.Y.
BR TL 6'1" 190 lbs.

	W	L	PCT	ERA	G	GS	CG	IP	H	BB	SO	ShO	W	L	SV	AB	H	HR	BA
1939 NY A	8	3	.727	2.41	21	11	9	116	86	41	55	2	0	1	2	41	10	0	.244
1940	14	8	.636	3.28	30	24	15	189.1	181	55	87	0	0	0	1	64	12	0	.188
1941	14	10	.583	3.09	28	27	17	209.2	195	87	105	3	0	0	1	78	18	0	.231
1942	4	1	.800	2.78	9	5	2	45.1	41	14	15	0	1	0	0	17	4	0	.235
1943	5	10	.333	3.72	24	14	5	101.2	89	45	42	1	1	2	1	31	6	0	.194
1946	0	2	.000	4.34	8	3	0	18.2	26	11	7	0	0	0	0	4	0	0	.000
6 yrs.	45	34	.570	3.13	120	84	48	680.2	618	253	311	6	2	3	5	235	50	0	.213
WORLD SERIES																			
1941 NY A	1	0	1.000	1.00	1	1	1	9	4	2	5	0	0	0	0	4	0	0	.000
1943	1	0	1.000	0.00	1	1	1	9	7	1	2	0	0	0	0	3	2	0	.667
2 yrs.	2	0	1.000	0.50	2	2	2	18	11	3	7	0	0	0	0	7	2	0	.286

Rust

RUST,
B. Louisville, Ky.   Deceased.

	W	L	PCT	ERA	G	GS	CG	IP	H	BB	SO	ShO	W	L	SV	AB	H	HR	BA
1882 BAL AA	0	1	.000	7.20	1	1	0	5	10	1	0	0	0	0	0	3	1	0	.333

Dick Rusteck

RUSTECK, RICHARD FRANK
B. July 12, 1941, Chicago, Ill.
BR TL 6'1" 175 lbs.

	W	L	PCT	ERA	G	GS	CG	IP	H	BB	SO	ShO	W	L	SV	AB	H	HR	BA
1966 NY N	1	2	.333	3.00	8	3	1	24	24	8	9	1	0	0	0	5	0	0	.000

Babe Ruth

RUTH, GEORGE HERMAN (The Sultan of Swat, The Bambino)   BL TL 6'2"   215 lbs.
B. Feb. 6, 1895, Baltimore, Md.   D. Aug. 16, 1948, New York, N.Y.
Hall of Fame 1936.

	W	L	PCT	ERA	G	GS	CG	IP	H	BB	SO	ShO	W	L	SV	AB	H	HR	BA
1914 BOS A	2	1	.667	3.91	4	3	1	23	21	7	3	0	0	0	0	10	2	0	.200
1915	18	8	.692	2.44	32	28	16	217.2	166	85	112	1	0	0	0	92	29	4	.315
1916	23	12	.657	1.75	44	41	23	323.2	230	118	170	9	0	1	1	136	37	3	.272
1917	24	13	.649	2.01	41	38	35	326.1	244	108	128	6	0	0	2	123	40	2	.325
1918	13	7	.650	2.22	20	19	18	166.1	125	49	40	1	0	1	0	317	95	11	.300
1919	9	5	.643	2.97	17	15	12	133.1	148	58	30	0	1	0	1	432	139	29	.322

		W	L	PCT	ERA	G	GS	CG	IP	H	BB	SO	ShO	Relief Pitching W	L	SV	BATTING AB	H	HR	BA

Babe Ruth continued

		W	L	PCT	ERA	G	GS	CG	IP	H	BB	SO	ShO	W	L	SV	AB	H	HR	BA
1920	NY A	1	0	1.000	4.50	1	1	0	4	3	2	0	0	0	0	0	458	172	54	.376
1921		2	0	1.000	9.00	2	1	0	9	14	9	2	0	1	0	0	540	204	59	.378
1930		1	0	1.000	3.00	1	1	1	9	11	2	3	0	0	0	0	518	186	49	.359
1933		1	0	1.000	5.00	1	1	1	9	12	3	0	0	0	0	0	459	138	34	.301
10 yrs.		94	46	.671	2.28	163	148	107	1221.1	974	441	488	17	2	2	4	*			
WORLD SERIES																				
1916	BOS A	1	0	1.000	0.64	1	1	1	14	6	3	4	0	0	0	0	5	0	0	.000
1918		2	0	1.000	1.06	2	2	1	17	13	7	4	1	0	0	0	5	1	0	.200
2 yrs.		3	0	1.000	0.87	3	3	2	31	19	10	8	1	0	0	0	129	42	15	.326
				1st	3rd															

Johnny Rutherford

RUTHERFORD, JOHN WILLIAM (Doc)
B. May 5, 1925, Belleville, Ont., Canada   BL TR 5'10½" 170 lbs.

		W	L	PCT	ERA	G	GS	CG	IP	H	BB	SO	ShO	W	L	SV	AB	H	HR	BA
1952	BKN N	7	7	.500	4.25	22	11	4	97.1	97	29	29	0	2	2	2	31	9	0	.290
WORLD SERIES																				
1952	BKN N	0	0	–	9.00	1	0	0	1	1	1	1	0	0	0	0	0	0	0	–

Dick Ruthven

RUTHVEN, RICHARD DAVID
B. Mar. 27, 1951, Sacramento, Calif.   BR TR 6'3" 190 lbs.

		W	L	PCT	ERA	G	GS	CG	IP	H	BB	SO	ShO	W	L	SV	AB	H	HR	BA
1973	PHI N	6	9	.400	4.21	25	23	3	128.1	125	75	98	1	1	0	1	38	5	0	.132
1974		9	13	.409	4.01	35	35	6	213	182	116	153	0	1	0	0	68	13	0	.191
1975		2	2	.500	4.17	11	7	0	41	37	22	26	0	0	0	0	13	2	0	.154
1976	ATL N	14	17	.452	4.20	36	36	8	240	255	90	142	4	0	0	0	76	13	0	.171
1977		7	13	.350	4.23	25	23	6	151	158	62	84	2	0	0	0	45	12	1	.267
1978 2 teams	ATL N (13G 2–6)				PHI	N (20G 13–5)														
" total		15	11	.577	3.38	33	33	11	231.2	214	56	120	3	0	0	0	77	17	0	.221
1979	PHI N	7	5	.583	4.28	20	20	3	122	121	37	58	2	0	0	0	41	6	0	.146
1980		17	10	.630	3.55	33	33	6	223	241	74	86	1	0	0	0	68	16	0	.235
1981		12	7	.632	5.14	23	22	5	147	162	54	80	0	0	0	0	50	7	0	.140
1982		11	11	.500	3.79	33	31	8	204.1	189	59	115	2	0	0	0	64	7	0	.109
1983 2 teams	PHI N (7G 1–3)				CHI	N (25G 12–9)														
" total		13	12	.520	4.38	32	32	7	183	202	38	99	2	0	0	0	62	13	0	.210
1984	CHI N	6	10	.375	5.04	23	22	0	126.2	154	41	55	0	0	0	0	44	7	0	.159
12 yrs.		119	120	.498	4.12	329	317	61	2011	2040	724	1116	17	1	0	1	646	118	1	.183
DIVISIONAL PLAYOFF SERIES																				
1981	PHI N	0	1	.000	4.50	1	1	0	4	3	1	0	0	0	0	0	1	0	0	.000
LEAGUE CHAMPIONSHIP SERIES																				
1978	PHI N	0	1	.000	5.79	1	1	0	4.2	6	0	3	0	0	0	0	1	0	0	.000
1980		1	0	1.000	2.00	2	1	0	9	3	5	4	0	1	0	0	2	0	0	.000
2 yrs.		1	1	.500	3.29	3	2	0	13.2	9	5	7	0	1	0	0	3	0	0	.000
WORLD SERIES																				
1980	PHI N	0	0	–	3.00	1	0	0	9	9	0	7	0	0	0	0	0	0	0	–

Cyclone Ryan

RYAN, DANIEL R.
B. 1866, Capperwhite, Ireland   D. Jan. 30, 1917, Medfield, Mass.   6'

		W	L	PCT	ERA	G	GS	CG	IP	H	BB	SO	ShO	W	L	SV	AB	H	HR	BA
1887	NY AA	0	1	.000	23.14	2	1	0	2.1	5	6	0	0	0	0	0	32	7	0	.219
1891	BOS N	0	0	–	0.00	1	0	0	3	2	1	0	0	0	0	0	1	0	0	.000
2 yrs.		0	1	.000	10.13	3	1	0	5.1	7	7	0	0	0	0	0	*			

Jack Ryan

RYAN, JACK (Gulfport)
B. Sept. 19, 1884, Lawrenceville, Ill.   D. Oct. 16, 1949, Hondsboro, Miss.   TR

		W	L	PCT	ERA	G	GS	CG	IP	H	BB	SO	ShO	W	L	SV	AB	H	HR	BA
1908	CLE A	1	1	.500	2.27	8	1	1	35.2	27	2	7	0	0	1	1	11	1	0	.091
1909	BOS A	4	3	.571	3.23	13	8	2	61.1	65	20	24	0	1	0	0	19	4	0	.211
1911	BKN N	0	1	.000	3.00	3	1	0	6	9	4	1	0	0	0	0	1	0	0	.000
3 yrs.		5	5	.500	2.88	24	10	3	103	101	26	32	0	1	1	1	31	5	0	.161

Jimmy Ryan

RYAN, JAMES E.
B. Feb. 11, 1863, Clinton, Mass.   D. Oct. 26, 1923, Chicago, Ill.   BR TL 5'9" 162 lbs.

		W	L	PCT	ERA	G	GS	CG	IP	H	BB	SO	ShO	W	L	SV	AB	H	HR	BA
1886	CHI N	0	0	–	4.63	5	0	0	23.1	19	13	15	0	0	0	0	327	100	4	.306
1887		2	1	.667	4.20	8	3	2	45	53	17	14	0	1	0	1	508	145	11	.285
1888		4	0	1.000	3.05	8	2	1	38.1	47	12	11	0	3	0	0	549	182	16	.332
1891		0	0	–	1.59	2	0	0	5.2	11	2	2	0	0	0	1	505	145	9	.287
1893		0	0	–	0.00	1	0	0	4.2	3	0	1	0	0	0	0	341	102	3	.299
5 yrs.		6	1	.857	3.62	24	5	3	117	133	44	43	0	4	0	2	*			

John Ryan

RYAN, JOHN BERNARD (Jack)
B. Nov. 12, 1869, Haverhill, Mass.   D. Aug. 21, 1952, Boston, Mass.   BR TR 5'10½" 165 lbs.

		W	L	PCT	ERA	G	GS	CG	IP	H	BB	SO	ShO	W	L	SV	AB	H	HR	BA
1902	STL N	1	0	1.000	0.00	1	1	1	7	3	4	1	1	0	0	0	*			

John Ryan

RYAN, JOHN M.
B. Hamilton, Ohio   Deceased.

		W	L	PCT	ERA	G	GS	CG	IP	H	BB	SO	ShO	W	L	SV	AB	H	HR	BA
1884	BAL U	3	2	.600	3.35	6	6	5	51	61	16	33	0	0	0	0	25	2	0	.080

Johnny Ryan

RYAN, JOHN JOSEPH
B. Philadelphia, Pa.   D. Mar. 22, 1902, Philadelphia, Pa.   5'7½" 150 lbs.

		W	L	PCT	ERA	G	GS	CG	IP	H	BB	SO	ShO	W	L	SV	AB	H	HR	BA
1876	LOU N	0	0	–	5.63	1	0	0	8	22	0	1	0	0	0	0	*			

Nolan Ryan

RYAN, LYNN NOLAN
B. Jan. 31, 1947, Refugio, Tex.   BR TR 6'2" 170 lbs.

		W	L	PCT	ERA	G	GS	CG	IP	H	BB	SO	ShO	W	L	SV	AB	H	HR	BA
1966	NY N	0	1	.000	15.00	2	1	0	3	5	3	6	0	0	0	0	0	0	0	–
1968		6	9	.400	3.09	21	18	3	134	93	75	133	0	0	0	0	44	5	0	.114
1969		6	3	.667	3.53	25	10	2	89.1	60	53	92	0	3	0	1	29	3	0	.103
1970		7	11	.389	3.41	27	19	5	132	86	97	125	2	0	0	0	45	8	0	.178
1971		10	14	.417	3.97	30	26	3	152	125	116	137	0	1	0	0	47	6	0	.128

Nolan Ryan continued

	W	L	PCT	ERA	G	GS	CG	IP	H	BB	SO	ShO	Relief Pitching W	L	SV	AB	H	HR	BA
1972 CAL A	19	16	.543	2.28	39	39	20	284	166	157	329	9	0	0	0	96	13	0	.135
1973	21	16	.568	2.87	41	39	26	326	238	162	383[1]	4	0	0	1	0	0	0	—
1974	22	16	.579	2.89	42	41	26	333	221	202	367	3	1	0	0	0	0	0	—
1975	14	12	.538	3.45	28	28	10	198	152	132	186	5	0	0	0	0	0	0	—
1976	17	18	.486	3.36	39	39	21	284	193	183	327	7	0	0	0	0	0	0	—
1977	19	16	.543	2.77	37	37	22	299	198	204	341	4	0	0	0	0	0	0	—
1978	10	13	.435	3.71	31	31	14	235	183	148	260	3	0	0	0	0	0	0	—
1979	16	14	.533	3.59	34	34	17	223	169	114	223	5	0	0	0	70	6	1	.086
1980 HOU N	11	10	.524	3.35	35	35	4	234	205	98	200	2	0	0	0	51	11	0	.216
1981	11	5	.688	1.69	21	21	5	149	99	68	140	3	0	0	0	0	0	0	—
1982	16	12	.571	3.16	35	35	10	250.1	196	109	245	3	0	0	0	83	10	0	.120
1983	14	9	.609	2.98	29	29	5	196.1	134	101	183	2	0	0	0	69	5	0	.072
1984	12	11	.522	3.04	30	30	5	183.2	143	69	197	2	0	0	0	61	6	0	.098
18 yrs.	231	206	.529	3.10	546	512	198	3705.2	2666	2091 1st	3874 1st	54	5	0	3	595	73	1	.123

DIVISIONAL PLAYOFF SERIES
	W	L	PCT	ERA	G	GS	CG	IP	H	BB	SO	ShO	W	L	SV	AB	H	HR	BA
1981 HOU N	1	1	.500	1.80	2	2	1	15	6	3	14	0	0	0	0	4	1	0	.250

LEAGUE CHAMPIONSHIP SERIES
	W	L	PCT	ERA	G	GS	CG	IP	H	BB	SO	ShO	W	L	SV	AB	H	HR	BA
1969 NY N	1	0	1.000	2.57	1	0	0	7	3	2	7	0	1	0	0	4	2	0	.500
1979 CAL A	0	0	—	1.29	1	1	0	7	4	3	8	0	0	0	0	4	0	0	.000
1980 HOU N	0	0	—	5.40	2	2	0	13.1	16	3	14	0	0	0	0	0	0	0	—
3 yrs.	1	0	1.000	3.62	4	3	0	27.1	23	8	29	0	1	0	0	8	2	0	.250

WORLD SERIES
	W	L	PCT	ERA	G	GS	CG	IP	H	BB	SO	ShO	W	L	SV	AB	H	HR	BA
1969 NY N	0	0	—	0.00	1	0	0	2.1	1	2	3	0	0	0	1	0	0	0	—

Rosy Ryan

RYAN, WILFRED PATRICK
Also known as Dolan Ryan.
B. Mar. 15, 1898, Worcester, Mass.   D. Dec. 10, 1980, Scottsdale, Ariz.

BL TR 6'   185 lbs.

	W	L	PCT	ERA	G	GS	CG	IP	H	BB	SO	ShO	W	L	SV	AB	H	HR	BA
1919 NY N	1	2	.333	3.10	4	3	1	20.1	20	9	7	0	1	0	0	6	0	0	.000
1920	0	1	.000	1.76	3	1	1	15.1	14	4	5	0	0	0	0	5	0	0	.000
1921	7	10	.412	3.73	36	16	5	147.1	140	32	58	0	1	4	3	45	9	0	.200
1922	17	12	.586	3.01	46	20	12	191.2	194	74	75	1	7	3	3	62	12	0	.194
1923	16	5	.762	3.49	45	15	7	172.2	169	46	58	0	9	2	4	53	11	0	.208
1924	8	6	.571	4.26	37	9	2	124.2	137	37	36	0	6	2	5	36	5	0	.139
1925 BOS N	2	8	.200	6.31	37	7	1	122.2	152	52	48	0	2	5	2	39	11	1	.282
1926	0	2	.000	7.58	7	2	0	19	29	7	1	0	0	0	0	5	1	0	.200
1928 NY A	0	0	—	16.50	3	0	0	6	17	1	5	0	0	0	0	4	0	0	.000
1933 BKN N	1	1	.500	4.55	30	0	0	61.1	69	16	22	0	1	1	2	13	2	0	.154
10 yrs.	52	47	.525	4.14	248	73	29	881	941	278	315	1	27	17	19	268	51	1	.190

WORLD SERIES
	W	L	PCT	ERA	G	GS	CG	IP	H	BB	SO	ShO	W	L	SV	AB	H	HR	BA
1922 NY N	1	0	1.000	0.00	1	0	0	2	1	0	2	0	1	0	0	0	0	0	—
1923	1	0	1.000	0.96	3	0	0	9.1	11	3	3	0	1	0	0	2	0	0	.000
1924	1	0	1.000	3.18	2	0	0	5.2	7	4	3	0	1	0	0	2	1	1	.500
3 yrs.	3	0	1.000	1.59	6	0	0	17	19	7	8	0	3 1st	0	0	4	1	1	.250

Mike Ryba

RYBA, DOMINIC JOSEPH
B. June 9, 1903, DeLancey, Pa.   D. Dec. 13, 1971, Brookline Station, Mo.

BR TR 5'10½" 180 lbs.

	W	L	PCT	ERA	G	GS	CG	IP	H	BB	SO	ShO	W	L	SV	AB	H	HR	BA
1935 STL N	1	1	.500	3.38	2	1	1	16	15	1	6	0	1	0	0	5	2	0	.400
1936	5	1	.833	5.40	14	0	0	45	55	16	25	0	5	1	0	18	3	0	.167
1937	9	6	.600	4.13	38	8	5	135	152	40	57	0	6	3	0	48	15	0	.313
1938	1	1	.500	5.40	3	0	0	5	8	1	0	0	1	1	0	0	0	0	—
1941 BOS A	7	3	.700	4.46	40	0	0	121	143	42	54	0	6	2	6	37	8	0	.216
1942	3	3	.500	3.86	18	0	0	44.1	49	13	16	0	3	3	3	17	5	0	.294
1943	7	5	.583	3.26	40	8	4	143.2	142	57	50	1	4	4	2	43	8	0	.186
1944	12	7	.632	3.33	42	7	2	138	119	39	50	0	9	5	2	41	6	0	.146
1945	7	6	.538	2.49	34	9	4	123	122	33	44	1	4	2	2	36	9	0	.250
1946	0	1	.000	3.55	9	0	0	12.2	12	5	5	0	0	1	1	2	2	0	1.000
10 yrs.	52	34	.605	3.66	240	36	16	783.2	817	247	307	2	39	22	16	247	58	0	.235

WORLD SERIES
	W	L	PCT	ERA	G	GS	CG	IP	H	BB	SO	ShO	W	L	SV	AB	H	HR	BA
1946 BOS A	0	0	—	13.50	1	0	0	.2	2	1	0	0	0	0	0	0	0	0	—

Gary Ryerson

RYERSON, GARY LAWRENCE
B. June 17, 1948, Los Angeles, Calif.

BL TL 6'1"   175 lbs.

	W	L	PCT	ERA	G	GS	CG	IP	H	BB	SO	ShO	W	L	SV	AB	H	HR	BA
1972 MIL A	3	8	.273	3.62	20	14	4	102	119	21	45	1	0	0	0	24	1	0	.042
1973	0	1	.000	7.83	9	4	0	23	32	7	10	0	0	0	0	0	0	0	—
2 yrs.	3	9	.250	4.39	29	18	4	125	151	28	55	1	0	0	0	24	1	0	.042

Bret Saberhagen

SABERHAGEN, BRET WILLIAM
B. Apr. 13, 1964, Chicago, Ill.

BR TR 6'1"   160 lbs.

	W	L	PCT	ERA	G	GS	CG	IP	H	BB	SO	ShO	W	L	SV	AB	H	HR	BA
1984 KC A	10	11	.476	3.48	38	18	2	157.2	138	36	73	1	4	1	1	0	0	0	—

LEAGUE CHAMPIONSHIP SERIES
	W	L	PCT	ERA	G	GS	CG	IP	H	BB	SO	ShO	W	L	SV	AB	H	HR	BA
1984 KC A	0	0	—	2.25	1	1	0	8	6	1	5	0	0	0	0	0	0	0	—

Ray Sadecki

SADECKI, RAYMOND MICHAEL
B. Dec. 26, 1940, Kansas City, Kans.

BL TL 5'11"   180 lbs.

	W	L	PCT	ERA	G	GS	CG	IP	H	BB	SO	ShO	W	L	SV	AB	H	HR	BA
1960 STL N	9	9	.500	3.78	26	26	7	157.1	148	86	95	1	0	0	0	57	12	0	.211
1961	14	10	.583	3.72	31	31	13	222.2	196	102	114	0	0	0	0	87	22	0	.253
1962	6	8	.429	5.54	22	17	4	102.1	121	43	50	1	1	0	1	37	3	1	.081
1963	10	10	.500	4.10	36	28	4	193.1	198	78	136	1	1	0	1	75	12	0	.160
1964	20	11	.645	3.68	37	32	9	220	232	60	119	2	0	2	1	55	11	0	.200
1965	6	15	.286	5.21	36	28	4	172.2	192	64	122	0	0	0	0	55	11	0	.200

	W	L	PCT	ERA	G	GS	CG	IP	H	BB	SO	ShO	W	L	SV	AB	H	HR	BA
													Relief Pitching			BATTING			

Ray Sadecki *continued*

	W	L	PCT	ERA	G	GS	CG	IP	H	BB	SO	ShO	W	L	SV	AB	H	HR	BA
1966 2 teams			STL N (5G 2-1)		SF	N	(26G 3-7)												
" total	5	8	.385	4.80	31	22	4	129.1	141	48	83	1	0	0	0	41	14	3	.341
1967 SF N	12	6	.667	2.78	35	24	10	188	165	58	145	2	1	0	0	73	18	0	.247
1968	12	18	.400	2.91	38	36	13	253.2	225	70	206	6	0	0	0	85	8	0	.094
1969	5	8	.385	4.24	29	17	4	138	137	53	104	3	0	0	0	40	5	1	.125
1970 NY N	8	4	.667	3.88	28	19	4	139	134	52	89	0	0	0	0	39	8	0	.205
1971	7	7	.500	2.93	34	20	5	163	139	44	120	2	1	0	0	50	10	0	.200
1972	2	1	.667	3.09	34	2	0	75.2	73	31	38	0	1	0	0	13	2	0	.154
1973	5	4	.556	3.39	31	11	1	116.2	109	41	87	0	1	0	1	31	7	0	.226
1974	8	8	.500	3.48	34	10	3	101	107	35	46	1	4	3	0	27	7	0	.259
1975 3 teams			STL N (8G 1-0)		ATL	N	(25G 2-3)			KC	A	(5G 1-0)							
" total	4	3	.571	4.03	38	5	0	80.1	91	31	32	0	3	1	1	15	3	0	.200
1976 2 teams			KC A (3G 0-0)		MIL	A	(36G 2-0)												
" total	2	0	1.000	3.86	39	0	0	42	45	23	28	0	2	0	1	0	0	0	—
1977 NY N	0	0	.000	6.00	4	0	0	3	3	3	0	0	0	0	0	0	0	0	—
18 yrs.	135	131	.508	3.79	563	328	85	2498	2456	922	1614	20	15	7	7	789	151	5	.191

WORLD SERIES

	W	L	PCT	ERA	G	GS	CG	IP	H	BB	SO	ShO	W	L	SV	AB	H	HR	BA
1964 STL N	1	0	1.000	8.53	2	2	0	6.1	12	5	2	0	0	0	0	2	1	0	.500
1973 NY N	0	0	—	1.93	4	0	0	4.2	5	1	6	0	0	0	1	0	0	0	—
2 yrs.	1	0	1.000	5.73	6	2	0	11	17	6	8	0	0	0	1	2	1	0	.500

Bob Sadowski

SADOWSKI, ROBERT F.
Brother of Eddie Sadowski.   Brother of Ted Sadowski.
B. Feb. 19, 1938, Pittsburgh, Pa.   BR TR 6'2"   195 lbs.

	W	L	PCT	ERA	G	GS	CG	IP	H	BB	SO	ShO	W	L	SV	AB	H	HR	BA
1963 MIL N	5	7	.417	2.62	19	18	5	116.2	99	30	72	1	0	0	0	35	2	0	.057
1964	9	10	.474	4.10	51	18	5	166.2	159	56	96	0	3	2	5	52	8	0	.154
1965	5	9	.357	4.32	34	13	3	123	117	35	78	0	2	1	3	35	3	0	.086
1966 BOS A	1	1	.500	5.40	11	5	0	33.1	41	9	11	0	0	0	0	7	0	0	.000
4 yrs.	20	27	.426	3.87	115	54	13	439.2	416	130	257	1	5	3	8	129	13	0	.101

Jim Sadowski

SADOWSKI, JAMES MICHAEL
B. Aug. 7, 1951, Pittsburgh, Pa.   BR TR 6'3"   195 lbs.

	W	L	PCT	ERA	G	GS	CG	IP	H	BB	SO	ShO	W	L	SV	AB	H	HR	BA
1974 PIT N	0	1	.000	6.00	4	0	0	9	7	9	1	0	0	1	0	1	0	0	.000

Ted Sadowski

SADOWSKI, THEODORE
Brother of Eddie Sadowski.   Brother of Bob Sadowski.
B. Apr. 1, 1936, Pittsburgh, Pa.   BR TR 6'1½"   190 lbs.

	W	L	PCT	ERA	G	GS	CG	IP	H	BB	SO	ShO	W	L	SV	AB	H	HR	BA
1960 WAS A	1	0	1.000	5.19	9	1	0	17.1	17	9	12	0	1	0	1	3	0	0	.000
1961 MIN A	0	2	.000	6.82	15	1	0	33	49	11	12	0	0	1	0	6	0	0	.000
1962	1	1	.500	5.03	19	0	0	34	37	11	15	0	1	1	0	4	2	0	.500
3 yrs.	2	3	.400	5.76	43	2	0	84.1	103	31	39	0	2	2	1	13	2	0	.154

Johnny Sain

SAIN, JOHN FRANKLIN
B. Sept. 25, 1917, Havana, Ark.   BR TR 6'2"   185 lbs.

	W	L	PCT	ERA	G	GS	CG	IP	H	BB	SO	ShO	W	L	SV	AB	H	HR	BA
1942 BOS N	4	7	.364	3.90	40	3	0	97	79	63	68	0	3	6	6	27	2	0	.074
1946	20	14	.588	2.21	37	34	24	265	225	87	129	3	1	0	2	94	28	0	.298
1947	21	12	.636	3.52	38	35	22	266	265	79	132	3	0	0	1	107	37	0	.346
1948	24	15	.615	2.60	42	39	28	314.2	297	83	137	4	1	0	1	115	25	0	.217
1949	10	17	.370	4.81	37	36	16	243	285	75	73	1	0	0	0	97	20	0	.206
1950	20	13	.606	3.94	37	37	25	278.1	294	70	96	3	0	0	0	102	21	1	.206
1951 2 teams			BOS N (26G 5-13)		NY	A	(7G 2-1)												
" total	7	14	.333	4.20	33	26	7	197.1	236	53	84	1	0	0	2	66	15	1	.227
1952 NY A	11	6	.647	3.46	35	16	8	148.1	149	38	57	0	3	1	7	71	19	1	.268
1953	14	7	.667	3.00	40	19	10	189	189	45	84	1	4	1	9	68	17	0	.250
1954	6	6	.500	3.16	45	0	0	77	66	15	33	0	6	6	22	17	6	0	.353
1955 2 teams			NY A (3G 0-0)		KC	A	(25G 2-5)												
" total	2	5	.286	5.58	28	0	0	50	60	11	17	0	2	5	1	10	0	0	.000
11 yrs.	139	116	.545	3.49	412	245	140	2125.2	2145	619	910	16	20	19	51	774	190	3	.245

WORLD SERIES

	W	L	PCT	ERA	G	GS	CG	IP	H	BB	SO	ShO	W	L	SV	AB	H	HR	BA
1948 BOS N	1	1	.500	1.06	2	2	2	17	9	0	9	1	0	0	0	5	1	0	.200
1951 NY A	0	0	—	9.00	1	0	0	2	4	2	2	0	0	0	0	1	0	0	.000
1952	0	1	.000	3.00	1	0	0	6	6	3	3	0	0	1	0	3	0	0	.000
1953	1	0	1.000	4.76	2	0	0	5.2	8	1	1	0	1	0	0	2	1	0	.500
4 yrs.	2	2	.500	2.64	6	2	2	30.2	27	6	15	1	1	1	0	11	2	0	.182

Randy St. Claire

ST. CLAIRE, RANDY ANTHONY
Son of Ebba St. Claire.
B. Aug. 23, 1960, Glen Falls, N. Y.   BR TR 6'3"   180 lbs.

	W	L	PCT	ERA	G	GS	CG	IP	H	BB	SO	ShO	W	L	SV	AB	H	HR	BA
1984 MON N	0	0	—	4.50	4	0	0	8	11	2	4	0	0	0	0	0	0	0	—

Jim St. Vrain

ST. VRAIN, JAMES MARCELLIN
B. June 6, 1871, Ralls County, Mo.   D. June 12, 1937, Butte, Mont.   TL

	W	L	PCT	ERA	G	GS	CG	IP	H	BB	SO	ShO	W	L	SV	AB	H	HR	BA
1902 CHI N	4	6	.400	2.08	12	11	10	95	88	25	51	1	0	0	0	31	3	0	.097

Freddy Sale

SALE, FREDERICK LINK
B. May 2, 1902, Chester, S. C.   D. May 27, 1956, Hermosa Beach, Calif.   BR TR 5'9"   160 lbs.

	W	L	PCT	ERA	G	GS	CG	IP	H	BB	SO	ShO	W	L	SV	AB	H	HR	BA
1924 PIT N	0	0	—	0.00	1	0	0	2	0	0	0	0	0	0	0	0	0	0	—

Bill Salisbury

SALISBURY, WILLIAM A.
B. 1876, Iowa   5'8½"   165 lbs.

	W	L	PCT	ERA	G	GS	CG	IP	H	BB	SO	ShO	W	L	SV	AB	H	HR	BA
1902 PHI N	0	0	—	13.50	2	1	0	6	15	2	0	0	0	0	0	1	0	0	.000

	W	L	PCT	ERA	G	GS	CG	IP	H	BB	SO	ShO	Relief Pitching W	L	SV	BATTING AB	H	HR	BA

Harry Salisbury

SALISBURY, HENRY H.   BL
B. May 15, 1855, Providence, R. I.   D. Mar. 29, 1933, Chicago, Ill.

	W	L	PCT	ERA	G	GS	CG	IP	H	BB	SO	ShO	W	L	SV	AB	H	HR	BA
1879 TRO N	4	6	.400	2.22	10	10	9	89	103	11	31	0	0	0	0	36	2	0	.056
1882 PIT AA	20	18	.526	2.63	38	38	38	335	315	37	135	1	0	0	0	145	22	0	.152
2 yrs.	24	24	.500	2.55	48	48	47	424	418	48	166	1	0	0	0	181	24	0	.133

Slim Sallee

SALLEE, HARRY FRANKLIN   BL TL 6'3"   180 lbs.
B. Feb. 3, 1885, Higginsport, Ohio   D. Mar. 22, 1950, Higginsport, Ohio

	W	L	PCT	ERA	G	GS	CG	IP	H	BB	SO	ShO	W	L	SV	AB	H	HR	BA
1908 STL N	3	8	.273	3.15	25	12	7	128.2	144	36	39	1	1	0	0	41	2	0	.049
1909	10	11	.476	2.42	32	27	12	219	223	59	55	1	0	2	0	71	8	0	.113
1910	7	8	.467	2.97	18	13	9	115	112	24	46	1	1	1	2	37	4	0	.108
1911	15	9	.625	2.76	36	30	18	245	234	64	74	1	1	1	2	89	15	0	.169
1912	16	17	.485	2.60	48	32	20	294	289	72	108	3	4	3	6	103	14	0	.136
1913	18	15	.545	2.70	49	31	17	273	254	59	105	3	2	1	5	94	19	2	.202
1914	18	17	.514	2.10	46	30	18	282.1	252	72	105	3	2	5	6	91	21	0	.231
1915	13	17	.433	2.84	46	33	17	275.1	245	57	91	2	0	2	3	92	11	0	.120
1916 2 teams		STL	N	(16G 5–5)			NY	N	(15G 9–4)								53	12	0	.226
" total	14	9	.609	2.18	31	18	11	181.2	171	33	63	4	4	1	1	77	17	0	.221
1917 NY N	18	7	.720	2.17	34	24	18	215.2	199	34	54	1	2	3	4	41	5	0	.122
1918	8	8	.500	2.25	18	16	12	132	122	12	33	1	0	0	2	41	4	0	.189
1919 CIN N	21	7	.750	2.06	29	28	22	227.2	221	20	24	4	1	0	0	74	14	0	.189
1920 2 teams		CIN	N	(21G 5–6)			NY	N	(5G 1–0)								38	7	0	.184
" total	6	6	.500	3.11	26	13	7	133	145	16	15	0	0	1	2	22	8	0	.364
1921 NY N	6	4	.600	3.64	37	0	0	96.1	115	14	23	0	6	4	2	22	8	0	.364
14 yrs.	173	143	.547	2.56	475	307	188	2818.2	2726	572	835	25	24	24	35	923	157	2	.170

WORLD SERIES																			
1917 NY N	0	2	.000	4.70	2	2	1	15.1	20	4	4	0	0	0	0	6	1	0	.167
1919 CIN N	1	1	.500	1.35	2	2	1	13.1	19	1	2	0	0	0	0	4	0	0	.000
2 yrs.	1	3	.250	3.14	4	4	2	28.2	39	5	6	0	0	0	0	10	1	0	.100

Roger Salmon

SALMON, ROGER ELLIOTT   BL TL 6'2"   170 lbs.
B. May 11, 1891, Newark, N. J.   D. June 17, 1974, Belfast, Me.

	W	L	PCT	ERA	G	GS	CG	IP	H	BB	SO	ShO	W	L	SV	AB	H	HR	BA
1912 PHI A	1	0	1.000	9.00	2	1	0	5	7	4	5	0	0	0	0	1	0	0	.000

Gus Salve

SALVE, AUGUSTUS WILLIAM   BL TL 6'   190 lbs.
B. Dec. 29, 1885, Boston, Mass.   D. Mar. 29, 1971, Providence, R. I.

	W	L	PCT	ERA	G	GS	CG	IP	H	BB	SO	ShO	W	L	SV	AB	H	HR	BA
1908 PHI A	0	1	.000	1.93	1	1	1	9.1	9	8	5	0	0	0	0	4	0	0	.000

Jack Salveson

SALVESON, JOHN THEODORE   BR TR 6'½"   180 lbs.
B. Jan. 5, 1914, Fullerton, Calif.   D. Dec. 28, 1974, Norwalk, Calif.

	W	L	PCT	ERA	G	GS	CG	IP	H	BB	SO	ShO	W	L	SV	AB	H	HR	BA
1933 NY N	0	2	.000	3.82	8	2	2	30.2	30	14	8	0	0	0	0	9	1	0	.111
1934	3	1	.750	3.52	12	4	0	38.1	43	13	18	0	2	0	0	10	3	0	.300
1935 2 teams		PIT	N	(5G 0–1)			CHI	A	(20G 1–2)								22	6	1	.273
" total	1	3	.250	5.25	25	2	2	73.2	90	28	24	0	1	3	-1	26	6	1	.231
1943 CLE A	5	3	.625	3.35	23	11	4	86	87	26	24	3	1	1	3	10	4	1	.400
1945	0	0	–	3.68	19	0	0	44	52	6	11	0	0	0	0	0	0	0	–
5 yrs.	9	9	.500	3.99	87	19	8	272.2	302	87	85	3	4	4	4	77	20	3	.260

Manny Salvo

SALVO, MANUEL (Gyp)   BR TR 6'4"   210 lbs.
B. June 30, 1913, Sacramento, Calif.

	W	L	PCT	ERA	G	GS	CG	IP	H	BB	SO	ShO	W	L	SV	AB	H	HR	BA
1939 NY N	4	10	.286	4.63	32	18	4	136	150	76	69	0	1	0	1	41	4	1	.098
1940 BOS N	10	9	.526	3.08	21	20	14	160.2	151	43	60	5	0	0	0	58	6	0	.103
1941	7	16	.304	4.06	35	27	11	195	192	93	67	2	1	1	0	62	7	0	.113
1942	7	8	.467	3.03	25	14	6	130.2	129	41	25	1	2	1	0	41	5	0	.122
1943 3 teams		BOS	N	(1G 0–0)			PHI	N	(1G 0–0)			BOS	N	(20G 5–6)		30	8	0	.267
" total	5	7	.417	3.55	22	14	5	99	101	32	26	1	0	0	0	232	30	1	.129
5 yrs.	33	50	.398	3.69	135	93	40	721.2	723	285	247	9	4	2	1	232	30	1	.129

Joe Sambito

SAMBITO, JOSEPH CHARLES   BL TL 6'1"   185 lbs.
B. June 28, 1952, Brooklyn, N. Y.

	W	L	PCT	ERA	G	GS	CG	IP	H	BB	SO	ShO	W	L	SV	AB	H	HR	BA
1976 HOU N	3	2	.600	3.57	20	4	1	53	45	14	26	1	1	0	1	9	2	0	.222
1977	5	5	.500	2.33	54	1	0	89	77	24	67	0	5	5	7	13	2	0	.154
1978	4	9	.308	3.07	62	0	0	88	85	32	96	0	4	9	11	6	1	0	.167
1979	8	7	.533	1.78	63	0	0	91	80	23	83	0	8	7	22	7	2	0	.286
1980	8	4	.667	2.20	64	0	0	90	65	22	75	0	8	4	17	9	0	0	.000
1981	5	5	.500	1.83	49	0	0	64	43	22	41	0	5	5	10	5	0	0	.000
1982	0	0	–	0.71	9	0	0	12.2	7	2	7	0	0	0	4	1	0	0	.000
1984	0	0	–	3.02	32	0	0	47.2	39	16	26	0	0	0	0	2	0	0	.000
8 yrs.	33	32	.508	2.42	353	5	1	535.1	441	155	421	1	31	30	72	52	7	0	.135

DIVISIONAL PLAYOFF SERIES																			
1981 HOU N	1	0	1.000	16.20	2	0	0	1.2	5	2	2	0	1	0	0	0	0	0	–

LEAGUE CHAMPIONSHIP SERIES																			
1980 HOU N	0	1	.000	4.91	3	0	0	3.2	4	2	6	0	0	1	0	0	0	0	–

Joe Samuels

SAMUELS, JOSEPH JONAS (Skabotch)   BR TR 6'1½"   196 lbs.
B. Mar. 21, 1905, Scranton, Pa.

	W	L	PCT	ERA	G	GS	CG	IP	H	BB	SO	ShO	W	L	SV	AB	H	HR	BA
1930 DET A	0	0	–	16.50	2	0	0	6	10	6	1	0	0	0	0	1	0	0	.000

Luis Sanchez

SANCHEZ, LUIS MERCEDES   BR TR 6'2"   170 lbs.
B. Aug. 24, 1953, Cariaco, Sucre, Venezuela

	W	L	PCT	ERA	G	GS	CG	IP	H	BB	SO	ShO	W	L	SV	AB	H	HR	BA
1981 CAL A	0	2	.000	2.91	17	0	0	34	39	11	13	0	0	2	2	0	0	0	–
1982	7	4	.636	3.21	46	0	0	92.2	89	34	58	0	7	4	5	0	0	0	–
1983	10	8	.556	3.66	56	1	0	98.1	92	40	49	0	10	7	7	0	0	0	–
1984	9	7	.563	3.33	49	0	0	83.2	84	33	62	0	9	7	11	0	0	0	–
4 yrs.	26	21	.553	3.35	168	1	0	308.2	304	118	182	0	26	20	25	0	0	0	–

LEAGUE CHAMPIONSHIP SERIES																			
1982 CAL A	0	1	.000	6.75	2	0	0	2.2	4	1	1	0	0	1	0	0	0	0	–

	W	L	PCT	ERA	G	GS	CG	IP	H	BB	SO	ShO	Relief Pitching W	L	SV	BATTING AB	H	HR	BA

Raul Sanchez

SANCHEZ, RAUL GUADALUPE RODRIGUEZ
B. Dec. 12, 1930, Marianao, Cuba   BR TR 6'   150 lbs.

	W	L	PCT	ERA	G	GS	CG	IP	H	BB	SO	ShO	W	L	SV	AB	H	HR	BA
1952 WAS A	1	1	.500	3.55	3	2	1	12.2	13	7	6	1	0	0	0	5	0	0	.000
1957 CIN N	3	2	.600	4.76	38	0	0	62.1	61	25	37	0	3	2	5	7	2	0	.286
1960	1	0	1.000	4.91	8	0	0	14.2	12	11	5	0	1	0	0	2	1	0	.500
3 yrs.	5	3	.625	4.62	49	2	1	89.2	86	43	48	1	4	2	5	14	3	0	.214

Ben Sanders

SANDERS, ALEXANDER BENNETT
B. Feb. 16, 1865, Catharpin, Va.   D. Aug. 29, 1930, Memphis, Tenn.   BR TR 6'   210 lbs.

	W	L	PCT	ERA	G	GS	CG	IP	H	BB	SO	ShO	W	L	SV	AB	H	HR	BA
1888 PHI N	19	10	.655	1.90	31	29	28	275.1	240	33	121	4	0	1	0	236	58	1	.246
1889	19	18	.514	3.55	44	39	34	349.2	406	96	123	1	1	0	1	169	47	0	.278
1890 PHI P	20	17	.541	3.76	43	40	37	346.2	412	69	107	2	0	0	1	189	59	1	.312
1891 PHI AA	11	5	.688	3.79	19	18	15	145	157	37	40	0	0	0	0	156	39	1	.250
1892 LOU N	12	19	.387	3.22	31	31	30	268.1	281	62	77	3	0	0	0	198	54	3	.273
5 yrs.	81	69	.540	3.24	168	157	144	1385	1496	297	468	10	1	1	2	*			

Dee Sanders

SANDERS, DEE WILMA
B. Apr. 8, 1921, Quitman, Tex.   BR TR 6'3"   195 lbs.

	W	L	PCT	ERA	G	GS	CG	IP	H	BB	SO	ShO	W	L	SV	AB	H	HR	BA
1945 STL A	0	0	—	40.50	2	0	0	1.1	7	1	1	0	0	0	0	0	0	0	—

Ken Sanders

SANDERS, KENNETH GEORGE (Daffy)
B. July 8, 1941, St. Louis, Mo.   BR TR 5'11"   168 lbs.

	W	L	PCT	ERA	G	GS	CG	IP	H	BB	SO	ShO	W	L	SV	AB	H	HR	BA
1964 KC A	0	2	.000	3.67	21			27	23	17	18	0	0	2	1	0	0	0	—
1966 2 teams				BOS	A	(24G	3–6)	KC	A	(38G	3–4)								
" total	6	10	.375	3.75	62	1	0	112.2	95	76	74	0	6	10	3	14	2	0	.143
1968 OAK A	0	1	.000	3.38	7	0	0	10.2	8	8	6	0	0	1	0	0	0	0	—
1970 MIL A	5	2	.714	1.76	50	0	0	92	64	25	64	0	5	2	13	13	3	0	.231
1971	7	12	.368	1.92	83	0	0	136	111	34	80	0	7	12	31	14	0	0	.000
1972	2	9	.182	3.13	62	0	0	92	88	31	51	0	2	9	17	7	1	0	.143
1973 2 teams				MIN	A	(27G	2–4)	CLE	A	(15G	5–1)								
" total	7	5	.583	4.40	42	0	0	71.2	71	30	33	0	7	5	13	0	0	0	—
1974 2 teams				CLE	A	(9G	0–1)	CAL	A	(9G	0–0)								
" total	0	1	.000	6.53	18	0	0	20.2	31	8	8	0	0	1	2	0	0	0	—
1975 NY N	1	1	.500	2.30	29	0	0	43	31	14	8	0	1	1	5	2	0	0	.000
1976 2 teams				NY	N	(31G	1–2)	KC	A	(3G	0–0)								
" total	1	2	.333	2.70	34	0	0	50	42	15	18	0	1	2	1	2	0	0	.000
10 yrs.	29	45	.392	2.98	408	1	0	655.2	564	258	360	0	29	45	86	52	6	0	.115

Roy Sanders

SANDERS, ROY GARVIN (Butch, Pep)
B. Aug. 1, 1892, Stafford, Kans.   D. Jan. 17, 1950, Kansas City, Mo.   BR TR 6½"   195 lbs.

	W	L	PCT	ERA	G	GS	CG	IP	H	BB	SO	ShO	W	L	SV	AB	H	HR	BA
1917 CIN N	0	1	.000	4.50	2	2	1	14	12	16	3	0	0	0	0	6	0	0	.000
1918 PIT N	7	9	.438	2.60	28	14	6	156	135	52	55	1	3	3	1	53	8	0	.151
2 yrs.	7	10	.412	2.75	30	16	7	170	147	68	58	1	3	3	1	59	8	0	.136

Roy Sanders

SANDERS, ROY L. (Simon)
B. 1894   BR TR 6'   185 lbs.

	W	L	PCT	ERA	G	GS	CG	IP	H	BB	SO	ShO	W	L	SV	AB	H	HR	BA
1918 NY A	0	2	.000	4.21	6	2	0	25.2	28	16	8	0	0	0	0	7	0	0	.000
1920 STL A	1	1	.500	5.19	8	1	0	17.1	20	17	2	0	0	1	0	4	0	0	.000
2 yrs.	1	3	.250	4.60	14	3	0	43	48	33	10	0	0	1	0	11	0	0	.000

War Sanders

SANDERS, WARREN WILLIAMS
B. Aug. 2, 1877, Maynardville, Tenn.   D. Aug. 3, 1962, Chattanooga, Tenn.   BR TL 5'10"   160 lbs.

	W	L	PCT	ERA	G	GS	CG	IP	H	BB	SO	ShO	W	L	SV	AB	H	HR	BA
1903 STL N	1	5	.167	6.08	8	6	3	40	48	21	9	0	0	1	0	15	1	0	.067
1904	1	2	.333	4.74	4	3	1	19	25	1	11	0	0	0	0	6	0	0	—
2 yrs.	2	7	.222	5.64	12	9	4	59	73	22	20	0	0	1	0	21	1	0	.048

Scott Sanderson

SANDERSON, SCOTT DOUGLAS
B. July 22, 1956, Dearborn, Mich.   BR TR 6'5"   195 lbs.

	W	L	PCT	ERA	G	GS	CG	IP	H	BB	SO	ShO	W	L	SV	AB	H	HR	BA
1978 MON N	4	2	.667	2.51	10	9	1	61	52	21	50	1	0	0	0	19	2	0	.105
1979	9	8	.529	3.43	34	24	5	168	148	54	138	3	1	1	1	50	8	0	.160
1980	16	11	.593	3.11	33	33	7	211	206	56	125	3	0	0	0	64	5	0	.078
1981	9	7	.563	2.96	22	22	4	137	122	31	77	1	0	0	0	35	4	0	.114
1982	12	12	.500	3.46	32	32	7	224	212	58	158	0	0	0	0	57	8	1	.140
1983	6	7	.462	4.65	18	16	0	81.1	98	20	55	0	0	0	1	28	4	0	.143
1984 CHI N	8	5	.615	3.14	24	24	3	140.2	140	24	76	0	0	0	0	42	5	0	.119
7 yrs.	64	52	.552	3.31	173	160	27	1023	978	264	679	8	1	1	2	295	36	1	.122

DIVISIONAL PLAYOFF SERIES

	W	L	PCT	ERA	G	GS	CG	IP	H	BB	SO	ShO	W	L	SV	AB	H	HR	BA
1981 MON N	0	0	—	6.75	1	1	0	2.2	4	2	2	0	0	0	0	1	0	0	.000

LEAGUE CHAMPIONSHIP SERIES

	W	L	PCT	ERA	G	GS	CG	IP	H	BB	SO	ShO	W	L	SV	AB	H	HR	BA
1984 CHI N	0	0	—	5.79	1	1	0	4.2	6	1	2	0	0	0	0	2	0	0	.000

Fred Sanford

SANFORD, JOHN FREDERICK
B. Aug. 9, 1919, Garfield, Utah   BB TR 6'1"   200 lbs.   BR 1948

	W	L	PCT	ERA	G	GS	CG	IP	H	BB	SO	ShO	W	L	SV	AB	H	HR	BA
1943 STL A	0	0	—	1.93	3	0	0	9.1	7	4	2	0	0	0	0	0	0	0	—
1946	2	1	.667	2.05	3	3	2	22	19	9	8	2	0	0	0	7	2	0	.286
1947	7	16	.304	3.71	34	23	9	186.2	186	76	62	0	0	2	4	54	11	0	.204
1948	12	21	.364	4.64	42	33	9	227	250	91	79	1	2	2	3	73	11	1	.151
1949 NY A	7	3	.700	3.87	29	11	3	95.1	100	57	51	0	2	0	0	34	4	0	.118
1950	5	4	.556	4.55	26	12	2	112.2	103	79	54	0	1	2	2	35	8	0	.229
1951 3 teams				NY	A	(11G	0–3)	WAS	A	(7G	2–3)	STL	A	(9G	2–4)			
" total	4	10	.286	6.82	27	16	1	91	103	75	29	0	0	0	0	26	3	0	.115
7 yrs.	37	55	.402	4.45	164	98	26	744	768	391	285	3	5	6	6	229	39	1	.170

	W	L	PCT	ERA	G	GS	CG	IP	H	BB	SO	ShO	Relief Pitching W	L	SV	BATTING AB	H	HR	BA

John Scheneberg

SCHENEBERG, JOHN BLUFORD
B. Nov. 20, 1887, Guyandotte, W. Va.   D. Sept. 7, 1950, Huntington, W. Va.

BB TR 6'1"   180 lbs.

	W	L	PCT	ERA	G	GS	CG	IP	H	BB	SO	ShO	W	L	SV	AB	H	HR	BA
1913 PIT N	0	1	.000	6.00	1	1	0	6	10	2	1	0	0	0	0	2	1	0	.500
1920 STL A	0	0	–	27.00	1	0	0	2	7	1	0	0	0	0	0	0	0	0	
2 yrs.	0	1	.000	11.25	2	1	0	8	17	3	1	0	0	0	0	2	1	0	.500

Fred Scherman

SCHERMAN, FREDERICK JOHN
B. July 25, 1944, Dayton, Ohio

BL TL 6'1"   195 lbs.

	W	L	PCT	ERA	G	GS	CG	IP	H	BB	SO	ShO	W	L	SV	AB	H	HR	BA
1969 DET A	1	0	1.000	6.75	4	0	0	4	6	0	3	0	1	0	0	0	0	0	
1970	4	4	.500	3.21	48	0	0	70	61	28	58	0	4	4	1	12	2	0	.167
1971	11	6	.647	2.71	69	1	1	113	91	49	46	0	10	6	20	24	5	0	.208
1972	7	3	.700	3.64	57	3	0	94	91	53	53	0	7	1	12	22	2	0	.091
1973	2	2	.500	4.21	34	0	0	62	59	30	28	0	2	2	1	0	0	0	
1974 HOU N	2	5	.286	4.13	53	0	0	61	67	26	35	0	2	5	4	3	0	0	.000
1975 2 teams			HOU	N (16G 0–1)	MON	N	(34G 4–3)												
" total	4	4	.500	3.79	50	7	0	92.2	105	45	56	0	4	1	0	17	1	0	.059
1976 MON N	2	2	.500	4.95	31	0	0	40	42	14	18	0	2	2	1	4	1	0	.250
8 yrs.	33	26	.559	3.66	346	11	1	536.2	522	245	297	0	32	21	39	82	11	0	.134

LEAGUE CHAMPIONSHIP SERIES
| 1972 DET A | 0 | 0 | – | 0.00 | 1 | 0 | 0 | .2 | 1 | 0 | 1 | 0 | 0 | 0 | 0 | 0 | 0 | 0 | |

Bill Scherrer

SCHERRER, WILLIAM JOSEPH
B. Jan. 20, 1958, Tonawanda, N. Y.

BL TL 6'4"   180 lbs.

	W	L	PCT	ERA	G	GS	CG	IP	H	BB	SO	ShO	W	L	SV	AB	H	HR	BA
1982 CIN N	0	1	.000	2.60	5	2	0	17.1	17	0	7	0	0	0	0	2	1	0	.500
1983	2	3	.400	2.74	73	0	0	92	73	33	57	0	2	3	10	11	1	0	.091
1984 2 teams			CIN	N (36G 1–0)	DET	A	(18G 1–0)												
" total	2	1	.667	4.16	54	0	0	71.1	78	23	51	0	2	1	1	3	0	0	.000
3 yrs.	4	5	.444	3.29	132	2	0	180.2	168	56	115	0	4	4	11	16	2	0	.125

WORLD SERIES
| 1984 DET A | 0 | 0 | – | 3.00 | 3 | 0 | 0 | 3 | 5 | 0 | 0 | 0 | 0 | 0 | 0 | 0 | 0 | 0 | – |

Dutch Schesler

SCHESLER, CHARLES
B. June 1, 1900, Frankfurt, Germany   D. Nov. 19, 1953, Harrisburg, Pa.

BR TR 6'2"   180 lbs.

	W	L	PCT	ERA	G	GS	CG	IP	H	BB	SO	ShO	W	L	SV	AB	H	HR	BA
1931 PHI N	0	0	–	7.28	17	0	0	38.1	65	18	14	0	0	0	0	9	1	0	.111

Lou Schettler

SCHETTLER, LOUIS MARTIN
B. June 12, 1886, Pittsburgh, Pa.   D. May 1, 1960, Youngstown, Ohio

TR

	W	L	PCT	ERA	G	GS	CG	IP	H	BB	SO	ShO	W	L	SV	AB	H	HR	BA
1910 PHI N	2	6	.250	3.20	27	7	3	107	96	51	62	0	1	2	1	41	7	0	.171

Red Schillings

SCHILLINGS, ELBERT ISAIAH
B. Mar. 29, 1900, Deport, Tex.   D. Jan. 7, 1954, Oklahoma City, Okla.

BR TR 5'10"   180 lbs.

	W	L	PCT	ERA	G	GS	CG	IP	H	BB	SO	ShO	W	L	SV	AB	H	HR	BA
1922 PHI A	0	0	–	6.75	4	0	0	8	10	11	4	0	0	0	0	2	0	0	.000

Calvin Schiraldi

SCHIRALDI, CALVIN DREW
B. June 16, 1962, Houston, Tex.

BR TR 6'4"   200 lbs.

	W	L	PCT	ERA	G	GS	CG	IP	H	BB	SO	ShO	W	L	SV	AB	H	HR	BA
1984 NY N	0	2	.000	5.71	5	3	0	17.1	20	10	16	0	0	0	0	3	0	0	.000

Biff Schlitzer

SCHLITZER, VICTOR JOSEPH
B. Dec. 4, 1884, Rochester, N. Y.   D. Jan. 4, 1948, Wellesley Hills, Mass.

BR TR 5'11"   175 lbs.

	W	L	PCT	ERA	G	GS	CG	IP	H	BB	SO	ShO	W	L	SV	AB	H	HR	BA
1908 PHI A	6	8	.429	3.16	24	18	11	131	110	45	57	2	0	0	0	46	9	0	.196
1909 2 teams			PHI	A (4G 0–3)	BOS	A	(13G 4–4)												
" total	4	7	.364	3.54	17	11	5	89	94	26	30	0	1	1	1	33	6	0	.182
1914 BUF F	0	0	–	16.20	3	0	0	3.1	7	2	1	0	0	0	0	1	1	0	1.000
3 yrs.	10	15	.400	3.51	44	29	16	223.1	211	73	88	2	1	1	1	80	16	0	.200

George Schmees

SCHMEES, GEORGE EDWARD (Rocky)
B. Sept. 6, 1924, Cincinnati, Ohio

BL TL 6'   190 lbs.

	W	L	PCT	ERA	G	GS	CG	IP	H	BB	SO	ShO	W	L	SV	AB	H	HR	BA
1952 BOS A	0	0	–	3.00	2	1	0	6	9	2	2	0	0	0	0	*			

Al Schmelz

SCHMELZ, ALAN GEORGE
B. Nov. 12, 1943, Whittier, Calif.

BR TR 6'4"   210 lbs.

	W	L	PCT	ERA	G	GS	CG	IP	H	BB	SO	ShO	W	L	SV	AB	H	HR	BA
1967 NY N	0	0	–	3.00	2	0	0	3	4	1	2	0	0	0	0	0	0	0	–

Butch Schmidt

SCHMIDT, CHARLES JOHN
B. July 19, 1887, Baltimore, Md.   D. Sept. 4, 1952, Baltimore, Md.

BL TL 6'1½"   200 lbs.

	W	L	PCT	ERA	G	GS	CG	IP	H	BB	SO	ShO	W	L	SV	AB	H	HR	BA
1909 NY A	0	0	–	7.20	1	0	0	5	5	1	2	0	0	0	0	*			

Dave Schmidt

SCHMIDT, DAVID JOSEPH
B. Apr. 22, 1957, Niles, Mich.

BR TR 6'1"   185 lbs.

	W	L	PCT	ERA	G	GS	CG	IP	H	BB	SO	ShO	W	L	SV	AB	H	HR	BA
1981 TEX A	0	1	.000	3.09	14	1	0	32	31	11	13	0	0	0	1	0	0	0	–
1982	4	6	.400	3.20	33	8	0	109.2	118	25	69	0	3	1	6	0	0	0	–
1983	3	3	.500	3.88	31	0	0	46.1	42	14	29	0	3	3	2	0	0	0	–
1984	6	6	.500	2.56	43	0	0	70.1	69	20	46	0	6	6	12	0	0	0	–
4 yrs.	13	16	.448	3.14	121	9	0	258.1	260	70	157	0	12	10	21	0	0	0	–

Freddy Schmidt

SCHMIDT, FREDERICK ALBERT
B. Feb. 9, 1916, Hartford, Conn.

BR TR 6'1"   185 lbs.

	W	L	PCT	ERA	G	GS	CG	IP	H	BB	SO	ShO	W	L	SV	AB	H	HR	BA
1944 STL N	7	3	.700	3.15	37	9	3	114.1	94	58	58	2	3	0	5	34	7	0	.206
1946	1	0	1.000	3.29	16	0	0	27.1	27	15	14	0	1	0	0	1	0	0	.000
1947 3 teams			STL	N (2G 0–0)	PHI	N	(29G 5–8)	CHI	N (1G 0–0)										
" total	5	8	.385	4.73	32	6	0	83.2	85	49	26	0	5	4	0	22	1	0	.045
3 yrs.	13	11	.542	3.75	85	15	3	225.1	206	122	98	2	9	4	5	57	8	0	.140

WORLD SERIES
| 1944 STL N | 0 | 0 | – | 0.00 | 1 | 0 | 0 | 3.1 | 1 | 1 | 1 | 0 | 0 | 0 | 0 | 1 | 0 | 0 | .000 |

	W	L	PCT	ERA	G	GS	CG	IP	H	BB	SO	ShO	W	L	SV	AB	H	HR	BA

Henry Schmidt

SCHMIDT, HENRY MARTIN   BR TR 5'11"   170 lbs.
B. June 26, 1873, Brownsville, Tex.   D. Apr. 23, 1926, Nashville, Tenn.

	W	L	PCT	ERA	G	GS	CG	IP	H	BB	SO	ShO	W	L	SV	AB	H	HR	BA
1903 BKN N	21	13	.618	3.83	40	36	29	301	321	120	96	5	1	0	2	107	21	1	.196

Pete Schmidt

SCHMIDT, HERMAN   BR TR 5'11"   175 lbs.
B. July 23, 1890, Lowden, Iowa   D. Mar. 11, 1973, Pembroke, Ont., Canada

	W	L	PCT	ERA	G	GS	CG	IP	H	BB	SO	ShO	W	L	SV	AB	H	HR	BA
1913 STL A	0	0	–	4.50	1	0	0	2	3	2	0	0	0	0	1	0	0	0	–

Willard Schmidt

SCHMIDT, WILLARD RAYMOND   BR TR 6'1"   187 lbs.
B. May 29, 1928, Hays, Kans.

	W	L	PCT	ERA	G	GS	CG	IP	H	BB	SO	ShO	W	L	SV	AB	H	HR	BA
1952 STL N	2	3	.400	5.19	18	3	0	34.2	36	18	30	0	1	1	1	8	1	0	.125
1953	0	2	.000	9.17	6	2	0	17.2	21	13	11	0	0	0	0	4	0	0	.000
1955	7	6	.538	2.78	20	15	8	129.2	89	57	86	1	0	0	0	42	5	0	.119
1956	6	8	.429	3.84	33	21	2	147.2	131	78	52	0	0	0	1	43	10	0	.233
1957	10	3	.769	4.78	40	8	1	116.2	146	49	63	0	5	3	0	33	7	0	.212
1958 CIN N	3	5	.375	2.86	41	2	0	69.1	60	33	41	0	3	5	0	11	1	0	.091
1959	3	2	.600	3.95	36	4	0	70.2	80	30	40	0	2	0	0	12	1	0	.083
7 yrs.	31	29	.517	3.93	194	55	11	586.1	563	278	323	1	11	9	2	153	25	0	.163

Crazy Schmit

SCHMIT, FREDERIC M. (Germany)   BL TL 5'10½" 165 lbs.
B. Feb. 13, 1866, Chicago, Ill.   D. Oct. 5, 1940, Chicago, Ill.

	W	L	PCT	ERA	G	GS	CG	IP	H	BB	SO	ShO	W	L	SV	AB	H	HR	BA
1890 PIT N	1	9	.100	5.83	11	10	9	83.1	108	42	35	1	0	1	0	33	2	0	.061
1892 BAL N	1	4	.200	3.23	6	6	6	47.1	37	26	17	0	0	0	0	19	2	0	.105
1893 2 teams		BAL	N	(9G 3–2)		NY	N	(4G 0–2)											
" total	3	4	.429	6.85	13	10	5	69.2	97	39	15	0	0	0	0	30	9	0	.300
1899 CLE N	2	17	.105	5.86	20	19	16	138.1	197	62	24	0	0	0	0	70	11	0	.157
1901 BAL A	0	2	.000	1.99	4	3	1	22.2	25	16	2	0	0	0	0	9	2	0	.222
5 yrs.	7	36	.163	5.45	54	48	37	361.1	464	185	93	1	0	1	0	161	26	0	.161

Johnny Schmitz

SCHMITZ, JOHN ALBERT (Bear Tracks)   BR TL 6'   170 lbs.
B. Nov. 27, 1920, Wausau, Wis.

	W	L	PCT	ERA	G	GS	CG	IP	H	BB	SO	ShO	W	L	SV	AB	H	HR	BA
1941 CHI N	2	0	1.000	1.31	5	3	1	20.2	12	9	11	0	1	0	0	7	4	0	.571
1942	3	7	.300	3.43	23	10	1	86.2	70	45	51	0	0	1	0	26	4	0	.154
1946	11	11	.500	2.61	41	31	14	224.1	184	94	135	3	1	1	2	70	9	1	.129
1947	13	18	.419	3.22	38	28	10	207	209	80	97	3	1	3	4	68	9	0	.132
1948	18	13	.581	2.64	34	30	18	242	186	97	100	2	3	0	1	84	11	0	.131
1949	11	13	.458	4.35	36	31	9	207	227	92	75	3	1	1	3	70	10	0	.143
1950	10	16	.385	4.99	39	27	8	193	217	91	75	3	1	1	0	67	8	0	.119
1951 2 teams		CHI	N	(8G 1–2)		BKN	N	(16G 1–4)											
" total	2	6	.250	5.99	24	9	0	73.2	77	43	26	0	0	2	0	24	5	1	.208
1952 3 teams		BKN	N	(10G 1–1)		NY	A	(5G 1–1)		CIN	N	(3G 1–0)							
" total	3	2	.600	3.71	18	5	2	53.1	47	30	17	0	1	1	1	13	4	0	.308
1953 2 teams		NY	A	(3G 0–0)		WAS	A	(24G 2–7)											
" total	2	7	.222	3.62	27	13	5	112	120	40	39	0	1	1	4	34	2	0	.059
1954 WAS A	11	8	.579	2.91	29	23	12	185.1	176	64	56	2	0	1	1	60	7	0	.117
1955	7	10	.412	3.71	32	21	6	165	187	54	49	1	0	0	1	54	10	0	.185
1956 2 teams		BOS	A	(2G 0–0)		BAL	N	(18G 0–3)											
" total	0	3	.000	3.59	20	3	0	42.2	54	18	15	0	0	0	1	10	0	0	.000
13 yrs.	93	114	.449	3.55	366	235	86	1812.2	1766	757	746	17	10	13	19	587	83	2	.141

Charlie Schmutz

SCHMUTZ, CHARLES OTTO   BR TR 6'3"   195 lbs.
B. Jan. 1, 1890, San Diego, Calif.   D. June 27, 1962, Seattle, Wash.

	W	L	PCT	ERA	G	GS	CG	IP	H	BB	SO	ShO	W	L	SV	AB	H	HR	BA
1914 BKN N	1	3	.250	3.30	18	5	1	57.1	57	13	21	0	1	0	0	16	3	0	.188
1915	0	0	–	6.75	1	0	0	4	7	1	1	0	0	0	0	1	0	0	.000
2 yrs.	1	3	.250	3.52	19	5	1	61.1	64	14	22	0	1	0	0	17	3	0	.176

Frank Schneiberg

SCHNEIBERG, FRANK FREDERICK
B. Mar. 12, 1882, Milwaukee, Wis.   D. May 18, 1948, Milwaukee, Wis.

	W	L	PCT	ERA	G	GS	CG	IP	H	BB	SO	ShO	W	L	SV	AB	H	HR	BA
1910 BKN N	0	0	–	63.00	1	0	0	1	5	4	0	0	0	0	0	0	0	0	–

Dan Schneider

SCHNEIDER, DANIEL LOUIS   BL TL 6'3"   170 lbs.
B. Aug. 29, 1942, Evansville, Ind.

	W	L	PCT	ERA	G	GS	CG	IP	H	BB	SO	ShO	W	L	SV	AB	H	HR	BA
1963 MIL N	1	0	1.000	3.09	30	3	0	43.2	36	20	19	0	1	0	0	7	0	0	.000
1964	1	2	.333	5.45	13	0	0	36.1	38	13	14	0	1	1	0	8	0	0	.000
1966 ATL N	0	0	–	3.42	14	0	0	26.1	35	5	11	0	0	0	0	8	4	0	.500
1967 HOU N	0	2	.000	4.96	54	0	0	52.2	60	27	39	0	0	2	2	5	1	0	.200
1969	0	1	.000	14.14	6	0	0	7	16	5	3	0	0	1	0	1	0	0	.000
5 yrs.	2	5	.286	4.72	117	8	0	166	185	70	86	0	1	4	2	29	5	0	.172

Jeff Schneider

SCHNEIDER, JEFFREY THEODORE   BB TL 6'3"   195 lbs.
B. Dec. 6, 1952, Bremerton, Wash.

	W	L	PCT	ERA	G	GS	CG	IP	H	BB	SO	ShO	W	L	SV	AB	H	HR	BA
1981 BAL A	0	0	–	4.88	11	0	0	24	27	12	17	0	0	0	1	0	0	0	–

Pete Schneider

SCHNEIDER, PETER JOSEPH   BR TR 6'1"   194 lbs.
B. Aug. 20, 1895, Los Angeles, Calif.   D. June 1, 1957, Los Angeles, Calif.

	W	L	PCT	ERA	G	GS	CG	IP	H	BB	SO	ShO	W	L	SV	AB	H	HR	BA
1914 CIN N	5	13	.278	2.81	29	20	11	144.1	143	56	62	1	1	3	1	45	8	1	.178
1915	13	19	.406	2.48	48	35	19	275.2	254	104	108	5	1	3	1	94	23	2	.245
1916	10	19	.345	2.69	44	31	16	274.1	259	82	117	3	2	0	1	89	21	0	.236
1917	20	19	.513	1.98	46	42	25	341.2	316	119	142	0	1	0	0	114	19	1	.167
1918	10	15	.400	3.51	33	30	17	217.2	213	117	51	2	0	0	0	83	24	1	.289
1919 NY A	0	1	.000	3.41	7	4	0	29	19	22	11	0	0	0	0	9	1	0	.111
6 yrs.	58	86	.403	2.62	207	162	85	1282.2	1204	500	491	11	6	5	4	434	96	5	.221

Karl Schnell

SCHNELL, KARL OTTO   BR TR 6'1"   176 lbs.
B. Sept. 20, 1899, Los Angeles, Calif.

	W	L	PCT	ERA	G	GS	CG	IP	H	BB	SO	ShO	W	L	SV	AB	H	HR	BA
1922 CIN N	0	0	–	2.70	10	0	0	20	21	18	5	0	0	0	0	4	1	0	.250

	W	L	PCT	ERA	G	GS	CG	IP	H	BB	SO	ShO	Relief Pitching W	L	SV	BATTING AB	H	HR	BA

Karl Schnell continued

	W	L	PCT	ERA	G	GS	CG	IP	H	BB	SO	ShO	W	L	SV	AB	H	HR	BA
1923	0	0	–	36.00	1	0	0	1	2	2	0	0	0	0	0	0	0	0	–
2 yrs.	0	0	–	4.29	11	0	0	21	23	20	5	0	0	0	0	4	1	0	.250

Gerry Schoen

SCHOEN, GERALD THOMAS   BR TR 6'3"   215 lbs.
B. Jan. 15, 1947, New Orleans, La.

	W	L	PCT	ERA	G	GS	CG	IP	H	BB	SO	ShO	W	L	SV	AB	H	HR	BA
1968 WAS A	0	1	.000	7.36	1	1	0	3.2	6	1	1	0	0	0	0	1	0	0	.000

Jumbo Schoeneck

SCHOENECK, LEWIS N.   BR TR   235 lbs.
B. Mar. 3, 1862, Chicago, Ill.   D. Jan. 20, 1930, Chicago, Ill.

	W	L	PCT	ERA	G	GS	CG	IP	H	BB	SO	ShO	W	L	SV	AB	H	HR	BA
1888 IND N	0	0	–	0.00	2	0	0	4.1	5	1	1	0	0	0	0	*			

Ed Schorr

SCHORR, EDWARD WALTER   BR TR 6'2½"   180 lbs.
B. Feb. 16, 1891, Bremen, Ohio   D. Sept. 12, 1969, Atlantic City, N. J.

	W	L	PCT	ERA	G	GS	CG	IP	H	BB	SO	ShO	W	L	SV	AB	H	HR	BA
1915 CHI N	0	0	–	7.50	2	0	0	6	9	5	3	0	0	0	0	2	1	0	.500

Gene Schott

SCHOTT, ARTHUR EUGENE   BR TR 6'2"   185 lbs.
B. July 14, 1913, Batavia, Ohio

	W	L	PCT	ERA	G	GS	CG	IP	H	BB	SO	ShO	W	L	SV	AB	H	HR	BA
1935 CIN N	8	11	.421	3.91	33	19	9	159	153	64	49	1	0	1	0	60	12	0	.200
1936	11	11	.500	3.80	31	22	8	180	184	73	65	0	3	1	1	60	18	1	.300
1937	4	13	.235	2.97	37	17	7	154.1	150	48	56	2	0	3	1	49	7	0	.143
1938	5	5	.500	4.45	31	4	0	83	89	32	21	0	4	3	2	24	3	0	.125
1939 PHI N	0	1	.000	4.91	4	0	0	11	14	5	1	0	0	1	0	6	2	0	.333
5 yrs.	28	41	.406	3.72	136	62	24	587.1	590	222	192	3	7	9	4	199	42	1	.211

Barney Schreiber

SCHREIBER, DAVID HENRY   BL TL 6'   185 lbs.
B. May 8, 1882, Waverly, Ohio   D. Oct. 6, 1964, Chillicothe, Ohio

	W	L	PCT	ERA	G	GS	CG	IP	H	BB	SO	ShO	W	L	SV	AB	H	HR	BA
1911 CIN N	0	0	–	5.40	3	0	0	10	19	2	5	0	0	0	0	3	0	0	.000

Paul Schreiber

SCHREIBER, PAUL FREDERICK (Von)   BR TR 6'2"   180 lbs.
B. Oct. 8, 1902, Jacksonville, Fla.   D. Jan. 28, 1982, Sarasota, Fla.

	W	L	PCT	ERA	G	GS	CG	IP	H	BB	SO	ShO	W	L	SV	AB	H	HR	BA
1922 BKN N	0	0	–	0.00	1	0	0	1	2	0	0	0	0	0	0	0	0	0	–
1923	0	0	–	4.20	9	0	0	15	16	8	4	0	0	0	1	2	0	0	.000
1945 NY A	0	0	–	4.15	2	0	0	4.1	4	2	1	0	0	0	0	1	0	0	.000
3 yrs.	0	0	–	3.98	12	0	0	20.1	22	10	5	0	0	0	1	3	0	0	.000

Al Schroll

SCHROLL, ALBERT BRINGHURST (Bull)   BR TR 6'2"   210 lbs.
B. Mar. 22, 1933, New Orleans, La.

	W	L	PCT	ERA	G	GS	CG	IP	H	BB	SO	ShO	W	L	SV	AB	H	HR	BA
1958 BOS A	0	0	–	4.50	5	0	0	10	6	4	7	0	0	0	0	1	1	0	1.000
1959 2 teams			PHI N	(3G 1–1)		BOS A	(14G 1–4)												
" total	2	5	.286	5.37	17	5	1	55.1	59	28	30	0	1	2	0	13	2	0	.154
1960 CHI N	0	0	–	10.13	2	0	0	2.2	3	5	2	0	0	0	0	1	1	0	1.000
1961 MIN A	4	4	.500	5.22	11	8	2	50	53	27	24	0	1	0	0	18	5	1	.278
4 yrs.	6	9	.400	5.34	35	13	3	118	121	64	63	0	2	2	0	33	9	1	.273

Ken Schrom

SCHROM, KENNETH MARVIN   BR TR 6'2"   195 lbs.
B. Nov. 23, 1954, Grangeville, Ida.

	W	L	PCT	ERA	G	GS	CG	IP	H	BB	SO	ShO	W	L	SV	AB	H	HR	BA
1980 TOR A	1	0	1.000	5.23	17	0	0	31	32	19	13	0	1	0	1	0	0	0	–
1982	1	0	1.000	5.87	6	0	0	15.1	13	15	8	0	1	0	0	0	0	0	–
1983 MIN A	15	8	.652	3.71	33	28	6	196.1	196	80	80	1	1	0	0	0	0	0	–
1984	5	11	.313	4.47	25	21	3	137	156	41	49	0	0	0	0	0	0	0	–
4 yrs.	22	19	.537	4.20	81	49	9	379.2	397	155	150	1	3	0	1	0	0	0	–

Ron Schueler

SCHUELER, RONALD RICHARD   BR TR 6'4"   205 lbs.
B. Apr. 18, 1948, Hays, Kans.

	W	L	PCT	ERA	G	GS	CG	IP	H	BB	SO	ShO	W	L	SV	AB	H	HR	BA
1972 ATL N	5	8	.385	3.66	37	18	3	145	122	60	96	0	3	0	2	42	8	0	.190
1973	8	7	.533	3.86	39	20	4	186.1	179	66	124	2	2	3	2	62	11	0	.177
1974 PHI N	11	16	.407	3.72	44	27	5	203	202	98	109	0	2	1	1	51	6	0	.118
1975	4	4	.500	5.23	46	6	1	93	88	40	69	0	2	1	0	13	2	0	.154
1976	1	0	1.000	4.20	35	0	0	49.2	44	16	43	0	1	0	3	2	0	0	.000
1977 MIN A	8	7	.533	4.40	52	7	0	135	131	61	77	0	7	6	3	0	0	0	–
1978 CHI A	3	5	.375	4.30	30	7	0	81.2	76	39	39	0	1	1	0	0	0	0	–
1979	0	1	.000	7.20	8	1	0	20	19	13	6	0	0	1	0	0	0	0	–
8 yrs.	40	48	.455	4.08	291	86	13	913.2	861	393	563	2	18	13	11	170	27	0	.159

Dave Schuler

SCHULER, DAVID PAUL   BR TL 6'4"   210 lbs.
B. Oct. 4, 1953, Framingham, Mass.

	W	L	PCT	ERA	G	GS	CG	IP	H	BB	SO	ShO	W	L	SV	AB	H	HR	BA
1979 CAL A	0	0	–	9.00	1	0	0	2	2	0	0	0	0	0	0	0	0	0	–
1980	0	1	.000	3.46	8	0	0	13	13	2	7	0	0	1	0	0	0	0	–
2 yrs.	0	1	.000	4.20	9	0	0	15	15	2	7	0	0	1	0	0	0	0	–

Barney Schultz

SCHULTZ, GEORGE WARREN   BR TR 6'2"   200 lbs.
B. Aug. 15, 1926, Beverly, N. J.

	W	L	PCT	ERA	G	GS	CG	IP	H	BB	SO	ShO	W	L	SV	AB	H	HR	BA
1955 STL N	1	2	.333	7.89	19	0	0	29.2	28	15	19	0	1	2	4	4	0	0	.000
1959 DET A	1	2	.333	4.42	13	0	0	18.1	17	14	17	0	1	2	0	2	2	0	1.000
1961 CHI N	7	6	.538	2.70	41	0	0	66.2	57	25	59	0	7	6	7	10	1	0	.100
1962	5	5	.500	3.82	51	0	0	77.2	66	23	58	0	5	5	5	5	0	0	.000
1963 2 teams			CHI N	(15G 1–0)		STL N	(24G 2–0)												
" total	3	0	1.000	3.59	39	0	0	62.2	61	17	44	0	3	0	3	4	0	0	.000
1964 STL N	1	3	.250	1.64	30	0	0	49.1	35	11	29	0	1	3	14	6	1	0	.167
1965	2	2	.500	3.83	34	0	0	42.1	39	11	38	0	2	2	2	2	0	0	.000
7 yrs.	20	20	.500	3.63	227	0	0	346.2	303	116	264	0	20	20	35	33	4	0	.121
WORLD SERIES																			
1964 STL N	0	1	.000	18.00	4	0	0	4	9	3	1	0	0	1	1	1	0	0	.000

	W	L	PCT	ERA	G	GS	CG	IP	H	BB	SO	ShO	Relief Pitching W	L	SV	BATTING AB	H	HR	BA

Bob Schultz

SCHULTZ, ROBERT DUFFY (Bill)   BR TL 6'3"   200 lbs.
B. Nov. 27, 1923, Louisville, Ky.   D. Mar. 31, 1979, Nashville, Tenn.

	W	L	PCT	ERA	G	GS	CG	IP	H	BB	SO	ShO	W	L	SV	AB	H	HR	BA
1951 CHI N	3	6	.333	5.24	17	10	2	77.1	75	51	27	0	1	0	0	29	4	0	.138
1952	6	3	.667	4.01	29	5	1	74	63	51	31	0	4	0	0	18	4	0	.222
1953 2 teams			CHI N	(7G 0–2)		PIT N		(11G 0–2)											
" total	0	4	.000	7.12	18	4	0	30.1	39	21	9	0	0	1	0	5	0	0	.000
1955 DET A	0	0	—	20.25	1	0	0	1.1	2	2	0	0	0	0	0	0	0	0	—
4 yrs.	9	13	.409	5.16	65	19	3	183	179	125	67	0	5	1	0	52	8	0	.154

Buddy Schultz

SCHULTZ, CHARLES BUDD   BR TL 6'   170 lbs.
B. Sept. 19, 1950, Cleveland, Ohio

	W	L	PCT	ERA	G	GS	CG	IP	H	BB	SO	ShO	W	L	SV	AB	H	HR	BA
1975 CHI N	2	0	1.000	6.00	6	0	0	6	11	5	4	0	2	0	0	0	0	0	
1976	1	1	.500	6.00	29	0	0	24	37	9	15	0	1	1	2	4	0	0	.000
1977 STL N	6	1	.857	2.33	40	0	0	85	76	24	66	0	4	1	1	12	2	0	.167
1978	2	4	.333	3.80	62	0	0	83	68	36	70	0	2	4	6	5	1	0	.200
1979	4	3	.571	4.50	31	0	0	42	40	14	38	0	4	3	3	4	0	0	.000
5 yrs.	15	9	.625	3.68	168	0	0	240	232	88	193	0	13	9	12	25	3	0	.120

Mike Schultz

SCHULTZ, WILLIAM MICHAEL   BL TL 6'1"   175 lbs.
B. Dec. 17, 1920, Syracuse, N. Y.

	W	L	PCT	ERA	G	GS	CG	IP	H	BB	SO	ShO	W	L	SV	AB	H	HR	BA
1947 CIN N	0	0	—	4.50	1	0	0	2	4	2	0	0	0	0	0	0	0	0	—

Webb Schultz

SCHULTZ, WEBB CARL   BR TR 5'11"   172 lbs.
B. Jan. 31, 1898, Wautoma, Wis.

	W	L	PCT	ERA	G	GS	CG	IP	H	BB	SO	ShO	W	L	SV	AB	H	HR	BA
1924 CHI A	0	0	—	9.00	1	0	0	1	1	1	0	0	0	0	0	0	0	0	—

John Schultze

SCHULTZE, JOHN F.   6'½"   165 lbs.
B. Burlington, N. J.   Deceased.

	W	L	PCT	ERA	G	GS	CG	IP	H	BB	SO	ShO	W	L	SV	AB	H	HR	BA
1891 PHI N	0	1	.000	6.60	6	0	0	15	18	11	4	0	0	0	0	6	1	0	.167

Al Schulz

SCHULZ, ALBERT CHRISTOPHER (Lefty)   BR TL 6'   182 lbs.
B. May 12, 1889, Toledo, Ohio   D. Dec. 13, 1931, Gallipolis, Ohio

	W	L	PCT	ERA	G	GS	CG	IP	H	BB	SO	ShO	W	L	SV	AB	H	HR	BA
1912 NY A	1	1	.500	2.20	3	1	1	16.1	11	11	8	0	1	0	0	5	0	0	.000
1913	7	13	.350	3.73	38	22	9	193	197	69	77	0	1	0	0	63	11	0	.175
1914 2 teams			NY A	(6G 1–3)		BUF F		(27G 10–11)											
" total	11	14	.440	3.57	33	27	11	199.1	187	87	105	0	3	0	1	63	10	1	.159
1915 BUF F	21	14	.600	3.08	42	38	25	309.2	264	149	160	5	0	0	0	109	18	0	.165
1916 CIN N	8	19	.296	3.14	44	22	10	215	208	93	95	0	4	4	2	64	8	0	.125
5 yrs.	48	61	.440	3.32	160	110	56	933.1	867	409	445	5	9	4	3	304	47	1	.155

Walt Schulz

SCHULZ, WALTER FREDERICK   BR TR 6'   170 lbs.
B. Apr. 16, 1900, St. Louis, Mo.   D. Feb. 27, 1928, Prescott, Ariz.

	W	L	PCT	ERA	G	GS	CG	IP	H	BB	SO	ShO	W	L	SV	AB	H	HR	BA
1920 STL N	0	0	—	6.00	2	0	0	6	10	2	0	0	0	0	0	2	0	0	.000

Don Schulze

SCHULZE, DONALD ARTHUR   BR TR 6'3"   215 lbs.
B. Sept. 27, 1962, Roselle, Ill.

	W	L	PCT	ERA	G	GS	CG	IP	H	BB	SO	ShO	W	L	SV	AB	H	HR	BA
1983 CHI N	0	1	.000	7.07	4	3	0	14	19	7	8	0	0	0	0	1	0	0	.000
1984 2 teams			CHI N	(1G 0–0)		CLE A		(19G 3–6)											
" total	3	6	.333	5.08	20	15	2	88.2	113	28	41	0	0	0	0	0	0	0	—
2 yrs.	3	7	.300	5.35	24	18	2	102.2	132	35	49	0	0	0	0	1	0	0	.000

Hal Schumacher

SCHUMACHER, HAROLD HENRY (Prince Hal)   BR TR 6'   190 lbs.
B. Nov. 23, 1910, Hinckley, N. Y.

	W	L	PCT	ERA	G	GS	CG	IP	H	BB	SO	ShO	W	L	SV	AB	H	HR	BA
1931 NY N	1	0	1.000	10.80	8	2	1	18.1	31	14	11	0	0	0	1	7	1	0	.143
1932	5	6	.455	3.55	27	13	2	101.1	119	39	38	1	0	1	0	31	7	0	.226
1933	19	12	.613	2.16	35	33	21	258.2	199	84	96	7	0	1	1	98	21	0	.214
1934	23	10	.697	3.18	41	36	18	297	299	89	112	2	2	2	0	117	28	6	.239
1935	19	9	.679	2.89	33	33	19	261.2	235	70	79	3	0	0	0	107	21	2	.196
1936	11	13	.458	3.49	35	30	9	214.1	234	69	75	3	0	0	0	74	16	1	.216
1937	13	12	.520	3.60	38	29	10	217.2	222	89	100	1	2	1	1	81	18	2	.222
1938	13	8	.619	3.50	28	28	12	185	178	50	54	4	0	0	0	67	16	2	.239
1939	13	10	.565	4.81	29	27	8	181.2	199	89	58	1	0	0	0	69	14	0	.203
1940	13	13	.500	3.25	34	30	12	227	218	96	123	1	1	0	1	78	15	1	.192
1941	12	10	.545	3.36	30	26	12	206	187	79	63	3	1	1	1	66	10	0	.152
1942	12	13	.480	3.04	29	29	12	216	208	82	49	3	0	0	0	75	13	1	.173
1946	4	4	.500	3.91	24	13	2	96.2	95	52	48	0	1	0	1	26	1	0	.038
13 yrs.	158	120	.568	3.36	391	329	138	2481.1	2424	902	906	29	6	6	7	896	181	15	.202
WORLD SERIES																			
1933 NY N	1	0	1.000	2.45	2	2	1	14.2	13	5	3	0	0	0	0	7	2	0	.286
1936	1	1	.500	5.25	2	2	1	12	13	10	11	0	0	0	0	4	0	0	.000
1937	0	1	.000	6.00	1	1	0	6	9	4	3	0	0	0	0	1	0	0	.000
3 yrs.	2	2	.500	4.13	5	5	2	32.2	35	19	17	0	0	0	0	12	2	0	.167

Hack Schumann

SCHUMANN, CARL J.   TR 6'2"   230 lbs.
B. Aug. 13, 1884, Buffalo, N. Y.   D. Apr. 25, 1946, Millgrove, N. Y.

	W	L	PCT	ERA	G	GS	CG	IP	H	BB	SO	ShO	W	L	SV	AB	H	HR	BA
1906 PHI A	0	2	—	4.00	4	2	1	18	21	8	9	0	0	0	0	6	0	0	.000

Ferdie Schupp

SCHUPP, FERDINAND MAURICE   BR TL 5'10"   150 lbs.
B. Jan. 16, 1891, Louisville, Ky.   D. Dec. 16, 1971, Los Angeles, Calif.

	W	L	PCT	ERA	G	GS	CG	IP	H	BB	SO	ShO	W	L	SV	AB	H	HR	BA
1913 NY N	0	0	—	0.75	5	1	0	12	10	3	2	0	0	0	0	3	1	0	.333
1914	0	0	—	5.82	8	0	0	17	19	9	9	0	0	0	1	2	0	0	.000
1915	1	0	1.000	5.10	23	1	0	54.2	57	29	28	0	1	0	0	10	2	0	.200
1916	9	3	.750	0.90	30	11	8	140.1	79	37	86	4	2	1	1	41	4	0	.098
1917	21	7	**.750**	1.95	36	32	25	272	202	70	147	6	0	1	1	93	15	0	.161
1918	0	1	.000	7.56	10	2	1	33.1	42	27	22	0	0	0	0	9	1	0	.111

	W	L	PCT	ERA	G	GS	CG	IP	H	BB	SO	ShO	Relief Pitching W	L	SV	BATTING AB	H	HR	BA

Al Smith

SMITH, ALFRED JOHN
B. Oct. 12, 1907, Belleville, Ill.   D. Apr. 28, 1977, Brownsville, Tex.   BL TL 5'11"   180 lbs.

	W	L	PCT	ERA	G	GS	CG	IP	H	BB	SO	ShO	W	L	SV	AB	H	HR	BA
1934 NY N	3	5	.375	4.32	30	5	0	66.2	70	21	27	0	3	1	5	14	4	0	.286
1935	10	8	.556	3.41	40	10	4	124	125	32	44	1	5	4	5	34	4	1	.118
1936	14	13	.519	3.78	43	30	9	209.1	217	69	89	4	4	1	2	73	10	0	.137
1937	5	4	.556	4.20	33	9	2	85.2	91	30	41	0	3	2	0	25	3	0	.120
1938 PHI N	1	4	.200	6.28	37	1	0	86	115	40	46	0	0	4	1	21	0	0	.000
1939	0	0	—	4.00	5	0	0	9	11	5	2	0	0	0	0	2	0	0	.000
1940 CLE A	15	7	.682	3.44	31	24	11	183	187	55	46	1	1	1	2	62	19	0	.306
1941	12	13	.480	3.83	29	27	13	206.2	204	75	76	2	0	0	0	71	11	1	.155
1942	10	15	.400	3.96	30	24	7	168.1	163	71	66	1	2	2	0	60	15	0	.250
1943	17	7	.708	2.55	29	27	14	208.1	186	72	72	3	0	0	1	68	14	0	.206
1944	7	13	.350	3.42	28	26	7	181.2	197	69	44	1	1	1	0	64	10	0	.156
1945	5	12	.294	3.84	21	19	8	133.2	141	48	34	3	0	0	1	41	12	0	.293
12 yrs.	99	101	.495	3.72	356	202	75	1662.1	1707	587	587	16	19	16	17	535	102	2	.191

WORLD SERIES

	W	L	PCT	ERA	G	GS	CG	IP	H	BB	SO	ShO	W	L	SV	AB	H	HR	BA
1936 NY N	0	0	—	81.00	1	0	0	.1	2	1	0	0	0	0	0	0	0	0	—
1937	0	0	—	3.00	2	0	0	3	2	0	1	0	0	0	0	0	0	0	—
2 yrs.	0	0	—	10.80	3	0	0	3.1	4	1	1	0	0	0	0	0	0	0	—

Al Smith

SMITH, ALFRED KENDRICKS
B. Dec. 13, 1903, Norristown, Pa.   BR TR 6'   170 lbs.

	W	L	PCT	ERA	G	GS	CG	IP	H	BB	SO	ShO	W	L	SV	AB	H	HR	BA
1926 NY N	0	0	—	9.00	1	0	0	2	4	2	0	0	0	0	0	0	0	0	—

Art Smith

SMITH, ARTHUR LAIRD
B. June 21, 1906, Boston, Mass.   BR TR 6'   175 lbs.

	W	L	PCT	ERA	G	GS	CG	IP	H	BB	SO	ShO	W	L	SV	AB	H	HR	BA
1932 CHI A	0	1	.000	11.57	3	2	0	7	17	4	1	0	0	0	0	1	0	0	.000

Bill Smith

SMITH, WILLIAM
D. Oct. 28, 1897, Guelph, Ont., Canada   151 lbs.

	W	L	PCT	ERA	G	GS	CG	IP	H	BB	SO	ShO	W	L	SV	AB	H	HR	BA
1886 DET N	5	4	.556	4.09	9	9	9	77	81	30	36	0	0	0	0	38	7	0	.184

Bill Smith

SMITH, WILLIAM GARLAND
B. June 8, 1934, Washington, D. C.   BL TL 6'   190 lbs.

	W	L	PCT	ERA	G	GS	CG	IP	H	BB	SO	ShO	W	L	SV	AB	H	HR	BA
1958 STL N	0	1	.000	6.52	2	1	0	9.2	12	4	4	0	0	0	0	2	0	0	.000
1959	0	0	—	1.08	6	0	0	8.1	11	3	4	0	0	0	1	1	0	0	.000
1962 PHI N	1	5	.167	4.29	24	5	0	50.1	59	10	26	0	1	1	0	11	2	0	.182
3 yrs.	1	6	.143	4.21	32	6	0	68.1	82	17	34	0	1	1	1	14	2	0	.143

Billy Smith

SMITH, BILLY LAVERN
B. Sept. 13, 1956, LaMarque, Tex.   BR TR 6'7"   200 lbs.

	W	L	PCT	ERA	G	GS	CG	IP	H	BB	SO	ShO	W	L	SV	AB	H	HR	BA
1981 HOU N	1	1	.500	3.00	10	1	0	21	20	3	3	0	0	1	1	2	0	0	.000

DIVISIONAL PLAYOFF SERIES

	W	L	PCT	ERA	G	GS	CG	IP	H	BB	SO	ShO	W	L	SV	AB	H	HR	BA
1981 HOU N	0	0	—	0.00	1	0	0	.1	0	0	0	0	0	0	0	0	0	0	—

Bob Smith

SMITH, ROBERT ASHLEY
B. July 19, 1890, Hardwick, Vt.   BR TR 5'11"   160 lbs.

	W	L	PCT	ERA	G	GS	CG	IP	H	BB	SO	ShO	W	L	SV	AB	H	HR	BA
1913 CHI A	0	0	—	13.50	1	0	0	2	3	3	1	0	0	0	0	0	0	0	—
1915 BUF F	0	0	—	18.00	1	0	0	1	1	2	0	0	0	0	0	0	0	0	—
2 yrs.	0	0	—	15.00	2	0	0	3	4	5	1	0	0	0	0	0	0	0	—

Bob Smith

SMITH, ROBERT ELDRIDGE
B. Apr. 22, 1898, Rogersville, Tenn.   BR TR 5'10"   175 lbs.

	W	L	PCT	ERA	G	GS	CG	IP	H	BB	SO	ShO	W	L	SV	AB	H	HR	BA
1923 BOS N	0	0	—	0.00	0	0	0	0	0	0	0	0	0	0	0	375	94	0	.251
1924	0	0	—	0.00	0	0	0	0	0	0	0	0	0	0	0	347	79	2	.228
1925	5	3	.625	4.47	13	10	6	92.2	110	36	19	0	0	1	0	174	49	0	.282
1926	10	13	.435	3.91	33	23	14	193.1	199	75	44	4	2	0	1	84	25	0	.298
1927	10	18	.357	3.76	41	32	16	260.2	297	75	81	1	2	2	3	109	27	1	.248
1928	13	17	.433	3.87	38	25	14	244.1	274	74	59	0	2	2	2	92	23	1	.250
1929	11	17	.393	4.68	34	29	19	231	256	71	65	1	0	1	3	99	17	1	.172
1930	10	14	.417	4.26	38	24	14	219.2	247	85	84	2	2	0	5	81	19	0	.235
1931 CHI N	15	12	.556	3.22	36	29	18	240.1	239	62	63	2	0	0	2	87	19	0	.218
1932	4	3	.571	4.61	34	11	4	119	148	36	35	1	0	1	2	42	10	0	.238
1933 2 teams			CIN	N	(16G	4–4)		BOS	N	(14G	4–3)									
" total	8	7	.533	2.65	30	10	7	132.1	143	18	34	1	3	2	1	45	9	0	.200
1934 BOS N	6	9	.400	4.66	39	5	3	121.2	133	36	26	0	4	6	5	36	9	0	.250
1935	8	18	.308	3.94	46	20	8	203.1	232	61	58	2	3	3	5	63	17	0	.270
1936	6	7	.462	3.77	35	11	5	136	142	35	36	2	2	1	8	45	10	0	.222
1937	0	1	.000	4.09	18	0	0	44	52	6	14	0	1	1	3	10	2	0	.200
15 yrs.	106	139	.433	3.95	435	229	128	2238.1	2472	670	618	16	20	20	40	*			

WORLD SERIES

	W	L	PCT	ERA	G	GS	CG	IP	H	BB	SO	ShO	W	L	SV	AB	H	HR	BA
1932 CHI N	0	0	—	9.00	1	0	0	1	2	0	1	0	0	0	0	0	0	0	—

Bob Smith

SMITH, ROBERT GILCHRIST
B. Feb. 1, 1931, Woodsville, N. H.   BR TL 6'1½"   190 lbs.

	W	L	PCT	ERA	G	GS	CG	IP	H	BB	SO	ShO	W	L	SV	AB	H	HR	BA
1955 BOS A	0	0	—	0.00	1	0	0	1.2	1	1	1	0	0	0	0	0	0	0	—
1957 2 teams		STL	N	(6G	0–0)		PIT	N	(20G	2–4)										
" total	2	4	.333	3.34	26	4	2	64.2	60	31	46	0	0	3	1	15	1	0	.067
1958 PIT N	2	2	.500	4.43	35	4	0	61	61	31	24	0	2	0	1	11	1	0	.091
1959 2 teams		PIT	N	(20G	0–0)		DET	A	(9G	0–3)										
" total	0	3	.000	4.81	29	0	0	39.1	52	20	22	0	0	3	0	3	0	0	.000
4 yrs.	4	9	.308	4.05	91	8	2	166.2	174	83	93	0	2	6	2	29	2	0	.069

Bryn Smith

SMITH, BRYN NELSON   BR TR 6'2" 200 lbs.
B. Aug. 11, 1955, Marietta, Ga.

Year	Team		W	L	PCT	ERA	G	GS	CG	IP	H	BB	SO	ShO	W	L	SV	AB	H	HR	BA
1981	MON	N	1	0	1.000	2.77	7	0	0	13	14	3	9	0	1	0	0	1	0	0	.000
1982			2	4	.333	4.20	47	1	0	79.1	81	23	50	0	2	3	3	8	0	0	.000
1983			6	11	.353	2.49	49	12	5	155.1	142	43	101	3	1	4	3	30	5	0	.167
1984			12	13	.480	3.32	28	28	4	179	178	51	101	2	0	0	0	53	7	0	.132
4 yrs.			21	28	.429	3.16	131	41	9	426.2	415	120	261	5	4	7	6	92	12	0	.130

Charlie Smith

SMITH, CHARLES EDWIN   BR TR
Brother of Fred Smith.
B. Apr. 20, 1880, Cleveland, Ohio   D. Jan. 3, 1929, Wickliffe, Ohio

Year	Team		W	L	PCT	ERA	G	GS	CG	IP	H	BB	SO	ShO	W	L	SV	AB	H	HR	BA
1902	CLE	A	2	1	.667	4.05	3	3	2	20	23	5	5	1	0	0	0	8	1	0	.125
1906	WAS	A	9	16	.360	2.91	33	22	17	235.1	250	75	105	2	3	2	0	87	16	1	.184
1907			10	20	.333	2.61	36	31	21	258.2	254	51	119	3	0	3	0	84	12	0	.143
1908			9	13	.409	2.40	26	22	13	184	166	60	83	1	0	1	1	65	8	0	.123
1909	2 teams				WAS	A	(23G	3–12)		BOS	A	(3G	3–0)								
"	total		6	12	.333	3.11	26	18	9	170.2	163	39	83	1	0	2	0	55	10	0	.182
1910	BOS	A	11	6	.647	2.30	24	18	11	156.1	141	35	53	0	1	1	1	44	5	0	.114
1911	2 teams				BOS	A	(1G	0–0)		CHI	N	(7G	3–2)								
"	total		3	2	.600	1.80	8	6	3	40	33	8	11	1	0	0	0	13	1	0	.077
1912	CHI	N	7	4	.636	4.21	21	5	1	94	92	31	47	0	6	1	1	35	9	0	.257
1913			7	9	.438	2.55	20	17	8	137.2	138	34	47	1	1	0	0	45	4	0	.089
1914			2	4	.333	3.86	16	5	1	53.2	49	15	17	0	1	0	0	11	1	0	.091
10 yrs.			66	87	.431	2.81	213	147	86	1350.1	1309	353	570	10	12	10	3	447	67	1	.150

Chick Smith

SMITH, JOHN WILLIAM   BL TL 5'8" 165 lbs.
B. Dec. 2, 1892, Dayton, Ky.   D. Oct. 11, 1935, Dayton, Ky.

Year	Team		W	L	PCT	ERA	G	GS	CG	IP	H	BB	SO	ShO	W	L	SV	AB	H	HR	BA
1913	CIN	N	0	1	.000	3.57	5	1	0	17.2	15	11	11	0	0	0	0	4	0	0	.000

Clay Smith

SMITH, CLAY JAMIESON   BR TR 6'2" 190 lbs.
B. Sept. 11, 1914, Cambridge, Kans.

Year	Team		W	L	PCT	ERA	G	GS	CG	IP	H	BB	SO	ShO	W	L	SV	AB	H	HR	BA
1938	CLE	A	0	0	—	6.55	4	0	0	11	18	2	3	0	0	0	0	4	0	0	.000
1940	DET	A	1	1	.500	5.08	14	1	0	28.1	32	13	14	0	1	0	0	7	0	0	.000
2 yrs.			1	1	.500	5.49	18	1	0	39.1	50	15	17	0	1	0	0	11	0	0	.000

WORLD SERIES

Year	Team		W	L	PCT	ERA	G	GS	CG	IP	H	BB	SO	ShO	W	L	SV	AB	H	HR	BA
1940	DET	A	0	0	—	2.25	1	0	0	4	1	3	1	0	0	0	0	1	0	0	.000

Dave Smith

SMITH, DAVID MERWIN   BR TR 5'10" 170 lbs.
B. Dec. 17, 1914, Sellers, S. C.

Year	Team		W	L	PCT	ERA	G	GS	CG	IP	H	BB	SO	ShO	W	L	SV	AB	H	HR	BA
1938	PHI	A	2	1	.667	5.08	21	0	0	44.1	50	28	13	0	2	1	0	12	0	0	.000
1939			0	0	—	0.00	1	0	0	1	1	2	0	0	0	0	0	0	0	0	—
2 yrs.			2	1	.667	5.08	22	0	0	44.1	51	30	13	0	2	1	0	12	0	0	.000

Dave Smith

SMITH, DAVID S., JR.   BR TR 6'1" 195 lbs.
B. Jan. 21, 1955, San Francisco, Calif.

Year	Team		W	L	PCT	ERA	G	GS	CG	IP	H	BB	SO	ShO	W	L	SV	AB	H	HR	BA
1980	HOU	N	7	5	.583	1.92	57	0	0	103	90	32	85	0	7	5	10	12	0	0	.000
1981			5	3	.625	2.76	42	0	0	75	54	23	52	0	5	3	8	8	2	0	.250
1982			5	4	.556	3.84	49	1	0	63.1	69	31	28	0	5	4	11	2	0	0	.000
1983			3	1	.750	3.10	42	0	0	72.2	72	36	41	0	3	1	6	5	0	0	.000
1984			5	4	.556	2.21	53	0	0	77.1	60	20	45	0	5	4	5	4	0	0	.000
5 yrs.			25	17	.595	2.67	243	1	0	391.1	345	142	251	0	25	17	40	31	2	0	.065

DIVISIONAL PLAYOFF SERIES

Year	Team		W	L	PCT	ERA	G	GS	CG	IP	H	BB	SO	ShO	W	L	SV	AB	H	HR	BA
1981	HOU	N	0	0	—	3.86	2	0	0	2.1	2	0	4	0	0	0	0	0	0	0	—

LEAGUE CHAMPIONSHIP SERIES

Year	Team		W	L	PCT	ERA	G	GS	CG	IP	H	BB	SO	ShO	W	L	SV	AB	H	HR	BA
1980	HOU	N	1	0	1.000	3.86	3	0	0	2.1	4	2	4	0	1	0	0	0	0	0	—

Dave Smith

SMITH, DAVID WAYNE   BR TR 6'1" 190 lbs.
B. Aug. 30, 1957, Tomball, Tex.

Year	Team		W	L	PCT	ERA	G	GS	CG	IP	H	BB	SO	ShO	W	L	SV	AB	H	HR	BA
1984	CAL	A	0	0	—	18.00	1	0	0	1	4	0	0	0	0	0	0	0	0	0	—

Doug Smith

SMITH, DOUGLAS WELDON   BL TL 5'10" 168 lbs.
B. May 25, 1893, Miller's Falls, Mass.   D. Sept. 18, 1973, Greenfield, Mass.

Year	Team		W	L	PCT	ERA	G	GS	CG	IP	H	BB	SO	ShO	W	L	SV	AB	H	HR	BA
1912	BOS	A	0	0	—	3.00	1	0	0	3	4	0	1	0	0	0	0	0	0	0	—

Ed Smith

SMITH, RHESA EDWARD   BR TR 5'11" 170 lbs.
B. Feb. 21, 1879, Mentone, Ind.   D. Mar. 20, 1955, Tarpon Springs, Fla.

Year	Team		W	L	PCT	ERA	G	GS	CG	IP	H	BB	SO	ShO	W	L	SV	AB	H	HR	BA
1906	STL	A	8	11	.421	3.72	19	18	13	154.2	153	53	45	0	1	0	0	54	11	0	.204

Eddie Smith

SMITH, EDGAR   BB TL 5'10" 174 lbs.
B. Dec. 14, 1913, Columbus, N. J.

Year	Team		W	L	PCT	ERA	G	GS	CG	IP	H	BB	SO	ShO	W	L	SV	AB	H	HR	BA
1936	PHI	A	1	1	.500	1.89	2	2	2	19	22	8	7	0	0	0	0	8	1	0	.125
1937			4	17	.190	3.94	38	23	14	196.2	178	90	79	1	0	1	5	73	17	0	.233
1938			3	10	.231	5.92	43	7	0	130.2	151	76	78	0	0	5	4	42	12	0	.286
1939	2 teams				PHI	A	(3G	1–0)		CHI	A	(29G	9–11)								
"	total		10	11	.476	3.79	32	22	7	180.1	168	92	70	1	2	0	0	52	6	0	.115
1940	CHI	A	14	9	.609	3.21	32	28	12	207.1	179	95	119	0	0	1	0	69	15	0	.217
1941			13	17	.433	3.18	34	33	21	263.1	243	114	111	1	0	0	1	88	19	0	.216
1942			7	20	.259	3.98	29	28	18	215	223	86	78	2	0	0	0	73	9	0	.123
1943			11	11	.500	3.69	25	25	14	187.2	197	76	66	2	0	0	0	69	11	1	.159
1946			8	11	.421	2.85	24	21	3	145.1	135	60	59	1	1	0	0	45	8	0	.178
1947	2 teams				CHI	A	(15G	1–3)		BOS	A	(8G	1–3)								
"	total		2	6	.250	7.33	23	8	0	50.1	58	42	27	0	0	1	0	12	2	0	.167
10 yrs.			73	113	.392	3.82	282	197	91	1595.2	1554	739	694	8	3	8	12	531	100	1	.188

	W	L	PCT	ERA	G	GS	CG	IP	H	BB	SO	ShO	Relief Pitching W	L	SV	BATTING AB	H	HR	BA

Edgar Smith

SMITH, EDGAR EUGENE   BR TR 5'10"   160 lbs.
B. June 12, 1862, Providence, R. I.   D. Nov. 3, 1892, Providence, R. I.

	W	L	PCT	ERA	G	GS	CG	IP	H	BB	SO	ShO	W	L	SV	AB	H	HR	BA
1883 PHI N	0	1	.000	15.43	1	1	0	7	18	3	2	0	0	0	0	13	5	0	.385
1884 WAS AA	0	2	.000	4.91	3	2	2	22	27	5	4	0	0	0	0	57	5	0	.088
1885 PRO N	1	0	1.000	1.00	1	1	1	9	9	0	1	0	0	0	0	4	1	0	.250
1890 CLE N	1	4	.200	4.30	6	6	5	44	42	10	11	0	0	0	0	24	7	0	.292
4 yrs.	2	7	.222	5.05	11	10	8	82	96	18	18	0	0	0	0	*			

Elmer Smith

SMITH, ELMER ELLSWORTH   BL TL 5'11"   178 lbs.
B. Mar. 23, 1868, Pittsburgh, Pa.   D. Nov. 3, 1945, Pittsburgh, Pa.

	W	L	PCT	ERA	G	GS	CG	IP	H	BB	SO	ShO	W	L	SV	AB	H	HR	BA
1886 CIN AA	4	5	.444	3.75	10	10	9	81.2	65	54	41	0	0	0	0	32	9	0	.281
1887	33	18	.647	2.94	52	52	49	447.1	400	126	176	3	0	0	0	186	47	0	.253
1888	22	17	.564	2.74	40	40	37	348.1	309	89	154	5	0	0	0	129	29	0	.225
1889	9	12	.429	4.88	29	22	16	203	253	101	104	0	2	0	0	83	23	2	.277
1892 PIT N	6	7	.462	3.63	17	13	12	134	140	58	51	1	0	1	0	511	140	4	.274
1894	0	0	–	4.50	1	0	0	4	6	1	0	0	0	0	0	489	174	6	.356
1898 CIN N	0	0	–	18.00	1	0	0	1	2	3	0	0	0	0	0	486	166	3	.342
7 yrs.	74	59	.556	3.35	150	137	123	1219.1	1175	432	526	9	2	1	0	*			

Frank Smith

SMITH, FRANK ELMER (Piano Mover)   BR TR 5'10½"   194 lbs.
Also known as Frank Elmer Schmidt.
B. Oct. 28, 1879, Pittsburgh, Pa.   D. Nov. 3, 1952, Pittsburgh, Pa.

	W	L	PCT	ERA	G	GS	CG	IP	H	BB	SO	ShO	W	L	SV	AB	H	HR	BA
1904 CHI A	16	9	.640	2.09	26	23	22	202.1	157	58	107	4	2	0	0	72	18	0	.250
1905	19	13	.594	2.13	39	31	27	291.2	215	107	171	4	2	1	0	106	24	1	.226
1906	5	5	.500	3.39	20	13	8	122	124	37	53	1	0	0	1	41	12	0	.293
1907	23	10	.697	2.47	41	37	29	310	280	111	139	3	0	0	1	92	18	0	.196
1908	16	17	.485	2.03	41	35	24	297.2	213	73	129	3	1	1	1	106	20	0	.189
1909	25	17	.595	1.80	51	41	37	365	278	70	177	7	3	2	1	127	22	0	.173
1910 2 teams			CHI	A	(19G	4–9)		BOS	A	(4G	1–2)									
" total	5	11	.313	2.53	23	18	11	156.2	113	51	58	3	0	0	0	52	9	0	.173
1911 2 teams			BOS	A	(1G	0–0)		CIN	N	(34G	10–14)									
" total	10	14	.417	4.13	35	19	10	178.2	204	58	68	0	4	5	1	56	12	0	.214
1912 CIN N	1	1	.500	6.35	7	3	1	22.2	34	15	5	0	1	0	0	6	0	0	.000
1914 BAL F	9	8	.529	2.99	39	22	9	174.2	180	47	83	1	1	2	2	59	12	0	.203
1915 2 teams			BAL	F	(17G	4–4)		BKN	F	(15G	5–2)									
" total	9	6	.600	4.04	32	14	6	151.2	177	49	61	1	3	0	0	49	9	1	.184
11 yrs.	138	111	.554	2.59	354	256	184	2273	1975	676	1051	27	17	11	6	766	156	2	.204

Frank Smith

SMITH, FRANK THOMAS   BR TR 6'3"   195 lbs.
B. Apr. 4, 1928, Pierrepont Manor, N. Y.

	W	L	PCT	ERA	G	GS	CG	IP	H	BB	SO	ShO	W	L	SV	AB	H	HR	BA
1950 CIN N	2	7	.222	3.87	38	4	0	90.2	73	39	55	0	2	4	3	21	2	0	.095
1951	5	5	.500	3.20	50	0	0	76	65	22	34	0	5	5	11	10	0	0	.000
1952	12	11	.522	3.75	53	2	1	122.1	109	41	77	0	12	9	7	29	5	0	.172
1953	8	1	.889	5.49	50	1	0	83.2	89	25	42	0	8	1	2	13	2	0	.154
1954	5	8	.385	2.67	50	0	0	81	60	29	51	0	5	8	20	10	1	0	.100
1955 STL N	3	1	.750	3.23	28	0	0	39	27	23	17	0	3	1	1	4	0	0	.000
1956 CIN N	0	0	–	12.00	2	0	0	3	3	2	1	0	0	0	0	0	0	0	–
7 yrs.	35	33	.515	3.81	271	7	1	495.2	426	181	277	0	35	28	44	87	10	0	.115

Fred Smith

SMITH, FREDERICK C.   BL TR 5'11"   156 lbs.
B. Mar. 25, 1863, Greene, N. Y.   D. Jan. 9, 1941, Syracuse, N. Y.

	W	L	PCT	ERA	G	GS	CG	IP	H	BB	SO	ShO	W	L	SV	AB	H	HR	BA
1890 TOL AA	19	13	.594	3.27	35	34	31	286	273	90	116	2	0	0	0	126	21	0	.167

Fred Smith

SMITH, FREDERICK C.   BR TR 6'   186 lbs.
B. Nov. 24, 1879, New Diggins, Wis.   D. Feb. 4, 1964, Los Angeles, Calif.

	W	L	PCT	ERA	G	GS	CG	IP	H	BB	SO	ShO	W	L	SV	AB	H	HR	BA
1907 CIN N	2	7	.222	2.85	18	9	5	85.1	90	24	19	0	0	3	1	28	3	0	.107

George Smith

SMITH, GEORGE ALLEN (Columbia George)   BR TR 6'2"   163 lbs.
B. May 31, 1892, Byram, Conn.   D. Jan. 7, 1965, Greenwich, Conn.

	W	L	PCT	ERA	G	GS	CG	IP	H	BB	SO	ShO	W	L	SV	AB	H	HR	BA
1916 NY N	1	0	1.000	2.61	9	1	0	20.2	14	6	9	0	0	0	0	2	0	0	.000
1917	0	3	.000	2.84	14	1	1	38	38	11	16	0	0	2	0	9	0	0	.000
1918 3 teams			CIN	N	(10G	2–3)		NY	N	(5G	2–3)		BKN	N	(8G	4–1)				
" total	8	7	.533	3.41	23	13	9	132	140	22	41	1	2	1	0	40	5	0	.125
1919 2 teams			NY	N	(3G	0–2)		PHI	N	(31G	5–11)									
" total	5	13	.278	3.36	34	22	11	195.2	212	50	42	1	1	1	0	63	8	0	.127
1920 PHI N	13	18	.419	3.45	43	28	10	250.2	265	51	51	2	3	5	2	72	7	0	.097
1921	4	20	.167	4.76	39	28	12	221.1	303	52	45	1	1	1	1	71	4	0	.056
1922	5	14	.263	4.78	42	18	6	194	250	35	44	1	1	3	0	66	5	0	.076
1923 BKN N	3	6	.333	3.66	25	7	3	91	99	28	15	0	0	3	1	26	5	0	.192
8 yrs.	39	81	.325	3.89	229	118	52	1143.1	1321	255	263	6	8	16	4	349	34	0	.097

George Smith

SMITH, GEORGE SELBY   BR TR 6'1"   175 lbs.
B. Oct. 27, 1901, Louisville, Ky.   D. May 26, 1981, Richmond, Va.

	W	L	PCT	ERA	G	GS	CG	IP	H	BB	SO	ShO	W	L	SV	AB	H	HR	BA
1926 DET A	1	2	.333	6.95	23	1	0	44	55	33	15	0	1	1	0	5	0	0	.000
1927	4	1	.800	3.91	29	0	0	71.1	62	50	32	0	4	1	0	19	7	2	.368
1928	1	1	.500	4.42	39	2	0	106	103	50	54	0	1	1	3	27	3	0	.111
1929	3	2	.600	5.80	14	2	1	35.2	42	36	13	0	2	2	0	12	5	0	.417
1930 BOS A	1	2	.333	6.84	27	2	0	73.2	92	49	21	0	1	2	0	24	8	0	.333
5 yrs.	10	8	.556	5.33	132	7	1	330.2	354	218	135	0	8	7	3	87	23	2	.264

Germany Smith

SMITH, GEORGE J.   BR TR 6'   175 lbs.
B. Apr. 21, 1863, Pittsburgh, Pa.   D. Dec. 1, 1927, Altoona, Pa.

	W	L	PCT	ERA	G	GS	CG	IP	H	BB	SO	ShO	W	L	SV	AB	H	HR	BA
1884 ALT U	0	0	–	9.00	1	0	0	1	3	0	1	0	0	0	0	*			

	W	L	PCT	ERA	G	GS	CG	IP	H	BB	SO	ShO	W	L	SV	AB	H	HR	BA
													Relief Pitching			**BATTING**			

Hal Smith
SMITH, HAROLD LAVERN
B. June 30, 1902, Creston, Iowa — BR TR 6'3" 195 lbs.

	W	L	PCT	ERA	G	GS	CG	IP	H	BB	SO	ShO	W	L	SV	AB	H	HR	BA
1932 PIT N	1	0	1.000	0.75	2	1	1	12	9	2	4	1	0	0	0	3	0	0	.000
1933	8	7	.533	2.86	28	19	8	145	149	31	40	2	1	0	1	47	6	0	.128
1934	3	4	.429	7.20	20	5	1	50	72	18	15	0	1	2	0	17	1	0	.059
1935	0	0	–	3.00	1	0	0	3	2	1	0	0	0	0	0	0	0	0	
4 yrs.	12	11	.522	3.77	51	25	10	210	232	52	59	3	2	2	1	67	7	0	.104

Harry Smith
SMITH, HARRISON M.
B. Aug. 15, 1889, Avoca, Neb. D. July 26, 1964, Dunbar, Neb. — BR TR 5'9" 160 lbs.

	W	L	PCT	ERA	G	GS	CG	IP	H	BB	SO	ShO	W	L	SV	AB	H	HR	BA
1912 CHI A	1	0	1.000	1.80	1	1	0	5	6	0	1	0	0	0	0	1	0	0	.000

Heinie Smith
SMITH, GEORGE HENRY
B. Oct. 24, 1871, Pittsburgh, Pa. D. June 25, 1939, Buffalo, N. Y. — BR TR 5'9½" 160 lbs.
Manager 1902.

	W	L	PCT	ERA	G	GS	CG	IP	H	BB	SO	ShO	W	L	SV	AB	H	HR	BA
1901 NY N	0	1	.000	8.10	2	1	1	13.1	24	5	5	0	0	0	0	*			

Jack Smith
SMITH, JACK HATFIELD
B. Nov. 15, 1935, Pikeville, Ky. — BR TR 6' 185 lbs.

	W	L	PCT	ERA	G	GS	CG	IP	H	BB	SO	ShO	W	L	SV	AB	H	HR	BA
1962 LA N	0	0	–	4.50	8	0	0	10	10	4	7	0	0	0	1	1	0	0	.000
1963	0	0	–	7.56	4	0	0	8.1	10	2	5	0	0	0	0	2	0	0	.000
1964 MIL N	2	2	.500	3.77	22	0	0	31	28	11	19	0	2	2	0	3	1	0	.333
3 yrs.	2	2	.500	4.56	34	0	0	49.1	48	17	31	0	2	2	1	6	1	0	.167

Jake Smith
SMITH, JACOB G.
B. Dubois, Pa.

	W	L	PCT	ERA	G	GS	CG	IP	H	BB	SO	ShO	W	L	SV	AB	H	HR	BA
1911 PHI N	0	0	–	0.00	2	0	0	5	3	2	1	0	0	0	0	3	0	0	.000

Lee Smith
SMITH, LEE ARTHUR JR.
B. Dec. 4, 1957, Jamestown, La. — BR TR 6'5" 220 lbs.

	W	L	PCT	ERA	G	GS	CG	IP	H	BB	SO	ShO	W	L	SV	AB	H	HR	BA
1980 CHI N	2	0	1.000	2.86	18	0	0	22	21	14	17	0	2	0	0	0	0	0	–
1981	3	6	.333	3.49	40	1	0	67	57	31	50	0	3	5	1	9	0	0	.000
1982	2	5	.286	2.69	72	5	0	117	105	37	99	0	2	1	17	16	1	1	.063
1983	4	10	.286	1.65	66	0	0	103.1	70	41	91	0	4	10	29	9	1	0	.111
1984	9	7	.563	3.65	69	0	0	101	98	35	86	0	9	7	33	13	1	0	.077
5 yrs.	20	28	.417	2.81	265	6	0	410.1	351	158	343	0	20	23	80	47	3	1	.064

LEAGUE CHAMPIONSHIP SERIES

	W	L	PCT	ERA	G	GS	CG	IP	H	BB	SO	ShO	W	L	SV	AB	H	HR	BA
1984 CHI N	0	1	.000	9.00	2	0	0	2	3	0	3	0	0	1	1	0	0	0	–

Mark Smith
SMITH, MARK CHRISTOPHER
B. Nov. 23, 1955, Alexandria, Va. — BL TR 6'2" 215 lbs.

	W	L	PCT	ERA	G	GS	CG	IP	H	BB	SO	ShO	W	L	SV	AB	H	HR	BA
1983 OAK A	1	0	1.000	6.75	8	1	0	14.2	24	6	10	0	1	0	0	0	0	0	–

Mike Smith
SMITH, MICHAEL ANTHONY
B. Feb. 23, 1961, Jackson, Miss. — BB TR 6'1" 195 lbs.

	W	L	PCT	ERA	G	GS	CG	IP	H	BB	SO	ShO	W	L	SV	AB	H	HR	BA
1984 CIN N	1	0	1.000	5.23	8	0	0	10.1	12	5	7	0	1	0	0	0	0	0	–

Pete Smith
SMITH, PETER LUKE
B. Mar. 19, 1940, Natick, Mass. — BR TR 6'2" 190 lbs.

	W	L	PCT	ERA	G	GS	CG	IP	H	BB	SO	ShO	W	L	SV	AB	H	HR	BA
1962 BOS A	0	1	.000	19.64	1	1	0	3.2	7	2	1	0	0	0	0	1	0	0	.000
1963	0	0	–	3.60	6	1	0	15	11	6	6	0	0	0	0	2	0	0	.000
2 yrs.	0	1	.000	6.75	7	2	0	18.2	18	8	7	0	0	0	0	3	0	0	.000

Phenomenal Smith
SMITH, JOHN FRANCIS
Born John Francis Gammon.
B. Dec. 12, 1864, Philadelphia, Pa. D. Apr. 3, 1952, Manchester, N. H. — BL TL 5'6½" 161 lbs.

	W	L	PCT	ERA	G	GS	CG	IP	H	BB	SO	ShO	W	L	SV	AB	H	HR	BA
1884 3 teams	BAL U (10G 3–4)				PHI AA (1G 0–1)			PIT AA (1G 0–1)											
" total	3	6	.333	4.45	12	11	7	85	123	22	22	0	0	0	0	47	7	0	.149
1885 2 teams	BKN AA (1G 0–1)				PHI AA (1G 0–1)														
" total	0	2	.000	11.25	2	2	1	12	19	10	9	0	0	0	0	5	1	0	.200
1886 DET N	1	1	.500	2.16	3	3	3	25	16	8	15	0	0	0	0	9	1	0	.111
1887 BAL AA	25	30	.455	3.79	58	55	54	491.1	526	176	206	1	0	2	0	205	48	1	.234
1888 2 teams	BAL AA (35G 14–19)				PHI AA (3G 2–1)														
" total	16	20	.444	3.55	38	35	34	314	270	147	171	0	1	0	0	118	30	1	.254
1889 PHI AA	2	3	.400	4.40	5	5	4	43	53	25	12	0	0	0	0	16	3	0	.188
1890 2 teams	PHI N (24G 8–12)				PIT N (5G 1–3)														
" total	9	15	.375	4.06	29	25	24	248	248	102	96	1	1	0	0	103	31	0	.301
1891 PHI N	1	1	.500	4.26	3	2	0	19	20	8	3	0	0	0	0	8	3	0	.375
8 yrs.	57	78	.422	3.90	150	138	128	1237.1	1275	498	534	2	2	2	0	511	124	2	.243

Pop Smith
SMITH, CHARLES MARVIN
B. Oct. 12, 1856, Digby, N. S., Canada D. Apr. 18, 1927, Boston, Mass. — BR TR 5'11" 170 lbs.

	W	L	PCT	ERA	G	GS	CG	IP	H	BB	SO	ShO	W	L	SV	AB	H	HR	BA
1883 COL AA	0	0	–	6.35	3	0	0	5.2	10	0	0	0	0	0	0	*			

Pop Boy Smith
SMITH, CLARENCE OSSIE
B. May 23, 1892, Newport, Tenn. D. Feb. 16, 1924, Sweetwater, Tex. — BR TR 6'1" 176 lbs.

	W	L	PCT	ERA	G	GS	CG	IP	H	BB	SO	ShO	W	L	SV	AB	H	HR	BA
1913 CHI A	0	1	.000	3.38	15	2	0	32	31	11	13	0	0	0	0	5	0	0	.000
1916 CLE A	1	2	.333	3.86	5	3	0	25.2	25	11	4	0	0	1	1	7	2	0	.286
1917	0	1	.000	8.31	6	0	0	8.2	14	4	3	0	0	0	0	1	0	0	.000
3 yrs.	1	4	.200	4.21	26	5	0	66.1	70	26	20	0	0	2	1	13	2	0	.154

Reggie Smith
SMITH, REGINALD
B. Louisville, Ky. Deceased.

	W	L	PCT	ERA	G	GS	CG	IP	H	BB	SO	ShO	W	L	SV	AB	H	HR	BA
1886 PHI AA	0	1	.000	7.00	1	1	1	9	15	5	4	0	0	0	0	4	0	0	.000

	W	L	PCT	ERA	G	GS	CG	IP	H	BB	SO	ShO	Relief Pitching W	L	SV	BATTING AB	H	HR	BA

Riverboat Smith

SMITH, ROBERT WALKUP
B. May 13, 1928, Clarence, Mo.
BL TL 6'　185 lbs.
BB 1959

	W	L	PCT	ERA	G	GS	CG	IP	H	BB	SO	ShO	W	L	SV	AB	H	HR	BA
1958 BOS A	4	3	.571	3.78	17	7	1	66.2	61	45	43	0	1	1	0	19	2	0	.105
1959 2 teams			CHI N (1G 0–0)				CLE A (12G 0–1)												
" total	0	1	.000	6.90	13	3	0	30	36	14	17	0	0	0	0	6	0	0	.000
2 yrs.	4	4	.500	4.75	30	10	1	96.2	97	59	60	0	1	1	0	25	2	0	.080

Roy Smith

SMITH, LEROY PURDY III
B. Sept. 6, 1961, Mt. Vernon, N. Y.
BR TR 6'3"　205 lbs.

	W	L	PCT	ERA	G	GS	CG	IP	H	BB	SO	ShO	W	L	SV	AB	H	HR	BA
1984 CLE A	5	5	.500	4.59	22	14	0	86.1	91	40	55	0	0	0	0	0	0	0	–

Rufus Smith

SMITH, RUFUS FRAZIER
B. Jan. 24, 1905, Guilford College, N. C.
BR TL 5'8"　165 lbs.

	W	L	PCT	ERA	G	GS	CG	IP	H	BB	SO	ShO	W	L	SV	AB	H	HR	BA
1927 DET A	0	0	–	3.38	1	1	0	8	8	3	2	0	0	0	0	3	0	0	.000

Sherry Smith

SMITH, SHERROD MALONE
B. Feb. 18, 1891, Monticello, Ga.　D. Sept. 12, 1949, Reidsville, Ga.
BL TL 6'1"　170 lbs.

	W	L	PCT	ERA	G	GS	CG	IP	H	BB	SO	ShO	W	L	SV	AB	H	HR	BA
1911 PIT N	0	0	–	54.00	1	0	0	.2	4	1	0	0	0	0	0	0	0	0	–
1912	0	0	–	6.75	3	0	0	4	6	1	3	0	0	0	0	0	0	0	–
1915 BKN N	14	8	.636	2.59	29	20	11	173.2	169	42	52	2	3	1	2	57	14	0	.246
1916	14	10	.583	2.34	36	23	15	219	193	45	67	4	2	4	1	77	21	0	.273
1917	12	12	.500	3.32	38	23	15	211.1	210	51	58	0	2	1	3	77	15	0	.195
1919	7	12	.368	2.24	30	19	13	173	181	29	40	2	0	1	1	54	8	0	.148
1920	11	9	.550	1.85	33	12	6	136.1	134	27	33	2	6	3	3	43	10	0	.233
1921	7	11	.389	3.90	35	17	9	175.1	232	34	36	0	1	2	4	57	13	1	.228
1922 2 teams			BKN	N (28G 4–8)				CLE	A (2G 1–0)										
" total	5	8	.385	4.42	30	11	4	124.1	146	38	19	1	2	3	2	41	11	1	.268
1923 CLE A	9	6	.600	3.27	30	16	10	124	129	37	23	1	1	0	1	45	11	1	.244
1924	12	14	.462	3.02	39	27	20	247.2	267	42	34	2	2	0	1	89	18	1	.202
1925	11	14	.440	4.86	31	30	22	237	296	48	30	1	0	0	1	92	28	1	.304
1926	11	10	.524	3.73	27	24	16	188.1	214	31	25	2	1	0	0	65	14	1	.215
1927	1	4	.200	5.45	11	2	1	38	53	14	8	0	1	2	1	12	2	0	.167
14 yrs.	114	118	.491	3.32	373	224	142	2052.2	2234	440	428	17	21	17	20	709	165	6	.233

WORLD SERIES

	W	L	PCT	ERA	G	GS	CG	IP	H	BB	SO	ShO	W	L	SV	AB	H	HR	BA
1916 BKN N	0	1	.000	1.35	1	1	1	13.1	7	6	2	0	0	0	0	5	1	0	.200
1920	1	1	.500	0.53	2	2	2	17	10	3	3	0	0	0	0	6	0	0	.000
2 yrs.	1	2	.333	0.89	3	3	3	30.1	17	9	5	0	0	0	0	11	1	0	.091
				4th															

Tom Smith

SMITH, THOMAS E.
B. Dec. 5, 1871, Boston, Mass.　D. Mar. 2, 1929, Dorchester, Mass.

	W	L	PCT	ERA	G	GS	CG	IP	H	BB	SO	ShO	W	L	SV	AB	H	HR	BA
1894 BOS N	0	0	–	15.00	2	0	0	6	8	6	2	0	0	0	1	2	0	0	.000
1895 PHI N	2	3	.400	6.88	11	7	4	68	76	53	21	0	0	0	0	33	8	0	.242
1896 LOU N	2	3	.400	5.40	11	5	4	55	73	25	14	0	1	0	0	39	8	0	.205
1898 STL N	0	1	.000	2.00	1	1	1	9	9	5	1	0	0	0	0	2	1	0	.500
4 yrs.	4	7	.364	6.33	25	13	9	138	166	89	38	0	1	0	1	76	17	0	.224

Willie Smith

SMITH, WILLIE (Wonderful Willie)
B. Feb. 11, 1939, Anniston, Ala.
BL TL 6'　182 lbs.

	W	L	PCT	ERA	G	GS	CG	IP	H	BB	SO	ShO	W	L	SV	AB	H	HR	BA
1963 DET A	1	0	1.000	4.57	11	2	0	21.2	24	13	16	0	1	0	2	8	1	0	.125
1964 LA A	1	4	.200	2.84	15	1	0	31.2	34	10	20	0	1	4	0	359	108	11	.301
1968 2 teams			CLE A (2G 0–0)				CHI N (1G 0–0)												
" total	0	0	–	0.00	3	0	0	7.2	2	1	3	0	0	0	0	184	45	5	.245
3 yrs.	2	4	.333	3.10	29	3	0	61	60	24	39	0	2	4	2	*			

Zane Smith

SMITH, ZANE
B. Dec. 28, 1960, Madison, Wis.
BL TL 6'2"　195 lbs.

	W	L	PCT	ERA	G	GS	CG	IP	H	BB	SO	ShO	W	L	SV	AB	H	HR	BA
1984 ATL N	1	0	1.000	2.25	3	3	0	20	16	13	16	0	0	0	0	9	5	0	.556

Mike Smithson

SMITHSON, BILLY MIKE
B. Jan. 21, 1955, Centerville, Tenn.
BL TR 6'8"　200 lbs.

	W	L	PCT	ERA	G	GS	CG	IP	H	BB	SO	ShO	W	L	SV	AB	H	HR	BA
1982 TEX A	3	4	.429	5.01	8	8	3	46.2	51	13	24	0	0	0	0	0	0	0	–
1983	10	10	.417	3.91	33	33	10	223.1	233	71	135	0	0	0	0	0	0	0	–
1984 MIN A	15	13	.536	3.68	36	36	10	252	246	54	144	1	0	0	0	0	0	0	–
3 yrs.	28	31	.475	3.90	77	77	23	522	530	138	303	1	0	0	0	0	0	0	–

Lefty Smoll

SMOLL, CLYDE HETRICK
B. Apr. 17, 1914, Quakertown, Pa.
BB TL 5'10"　175 lbs.

	W	L	PCT	ERA	G	GS	CG	IP	H	BB	SO	ShO	W	L	SV	AB	H	HR	BA
1940 PHI N	2	8	.200	5.37	33	9	0	109	145	36	31	0	2	0	0	31	5	0	.161

Harry Smythe

SMYTHE, WILLIAM HENRY
B. Oct. 24, 1904, Augusta, Ga.　D. Aug. 28, 1980, Augusta, Ga.
BL TL 5'10½"　179 lbs.

	W	L	PCT	ERA	G	GS	CG	IP	H	BB	SO	ShO	W	L	SV	AB	H	HR	BA
1929 PHI N	4	6	.400	5.24	19	7	2	68.2	94	15	12	0	4	1	1	26	5	0	.192
1930	0	3	.000	7.79	25	3	0	49.2	84	31	9	0	0	1	2	14	4	0	.286
1934 2 teams			NY	A (8G 0–2)				BKN	N (8G 1–1)										
" total	1	3	.250	6.69	16	0	0	36.1	54	16	12	0	1	3	1	14	4	0	.286
3 yrs.	5	12	.294	6.40	60	10	2	154.2	232	62	33	0	5	5	4	54	13	0	.241

Nat Snell

SNELL, NATHANIEL
B. Sept. 2, 1955, Orangeburg, S. C.
BR TR 6'4"　190 lbs.

	W	L	PCT	ERA	G	GS	CG	IP	H	BB	SO	ShO	W	L	SV	AB	H	HR	BA
1984 BAL A	1	1	.500	2.35	5	0	0	7.2	8	1	7	0	1	1	0	0	0	0	–

Frank Snook

SNOOK, FRANK WALTER JR.
B. Mar. 28, 1949, Somerville, N. J.
BR TL 6'2"　180 lbs.

	W	L	PCT	ERA	G	GS	CG	IP	H	BB	SO	ShO	W	L	SV	AB	H	HR	BA
1973 SD N	0	2	.000	3.62	18	0	0	27.1	19	18	13	0	0	2	1	2	0	0	.000

	W	L	PCT	ERA	G	GS	CG	IP	H	BB	SO	ShO	Relief Pitching W	L	SV	AB	H	HR	BA

Colonel Snover

SNOVER, COLONEL LESTER (Bosco)
B. May 16, 1895, Hallstead, Pa.   D. Apr. 30, 1969, Rochester, N. Y.   BL TL 6'½" 200 lbs.

	W	L	PCT	ERA	G	GS	CG	IP	H	BB	SO	ShO	RP W	L	SV	AB	H	HR	BA
1919 NY N	0	1	.000	1.00	2	1	0	9	7	3	4	0	0	1	0	2	0	0	.000

Bill Snyder

SNYDER, WILLIAM NICHOLAS
B. Jan. 28, 1898, Mansfield, Ohio   D. Oct. 8, 1934, Vicksburg, Mich.   BR TR

	W	L	PCT	ERA	G	GS	CG	IP	H	BB	SO	ShO	RP W	L	SV	AB	H	HR	BA
1919 WAS A	0	1	.000	1.13	2	1	0	8	6	3	5	0	0	0	0	2	0	0	.000
1920	2	1	.667	4.17	16	4	1	54	59	28	17	0	1	1	1	19	6	0	.316
2 yrs.	2	2	.500	3.77	18	5	1	62	65	31	22	0	1	1	1	21	6	0	.286

Gene Snyder

SNYDER, GENE WALTER
B. Mar. 31, 1931, York, Pa.   BR TL 5'11" 175 lbs.

	W	L	PCT	ERA	G	GS	CG	IP	H	BB	SO	ShO	RP W	L	SV	AB	H	HR	BA
1959 LA N	1	1	.500	5.47	11	2	0	26.1	32	20	20	0	1	0	0	6	0	0	.000

George Snyder

SNYDER, GEORGE T.
B. 1849, Philadelphia, Pa.   D. Aug. 2, 1895, Philadelphia, Pa.

	W	L	PCT	ERA	G	GS	CG	IP	H	BB	SO	ShO	RP W	L	SV	AB	H	HR	BA
1882 PHI AA	1	0	1.000	0.00	1	1	1	9	4	2	0	0	0	0	0	3	1	0	.333

Julio Solano

SOLANO, JULIO CESAR
B. Jan. 8, 1960, Aqua Blanca, Dominican Republic   BR TR 6'1" 157 lbs.

	W	L	PCT	ERA	G	GS	CG	IP	H	BB	SO	ShO	RP W	L	SV	AB	H	HR	BA
1983 HOU N	0	2	.000	6.00	4	0	0	6	5	4	3	0	0	2	0	0	0	0	–
1984	1	3	.250	1.95	31	0	0	50.2	31	18	33	0	1	3	0	3	1	0	.333
2 yrs.	1	5	.167	2.38	35	0	0	56.2	36	22	36	0	1	5	0	3	1	0	.333

Marcelino Solis

SOLIS, MARCELINO
B. July 19, 1930, San Luis Potosi, Mexico   BL TL 6'1" 185 lbs.

	W	L	PCT	ERA	G	GS	CG	IP	H	BB	SO	ShO	RP W	L	SV	AB	H	HR	BA
1958 CHI N	3	3	.500	6.06	15	4	0	52	74	20	15	0	3	1	0	20	5	0	.250

Eddie Solomon

SOLOMON, EDDIE JR (Buddy)
B. Feb. 9, 1951, Perry, Ga.   BR TR 6'3½" 198 lbs.

	W	L	PCT	ERA	G	GS	CG	IP	H	BB	SO	ShO	RP W	L	SV	AB	H	HR	BA
1973 LA N	0	0	–	7.11	4	0	0	6.1	10	4	6	0	0	0	0	1	0	0	.000
1974	0	0	–	1.35	4	0	0	6.2	5	2	2	0	0	0	1	0	0	0	–
1975 CHI N	0	0	–	1.29	6	0	0	7	7	6	3	0	0	0	0	0	0	0	–
1976 STL N	1	1	.500	4.86	26	2	0	37	45	16	19	0	0	1	0	5	2	0	.400
1977 ATL N	6	6	.500	4.55	18	16	0	89	110	34	54	0	0	0	0	31	4	0	.129
1978	4	6	.400	4.08	37	8	0	106	98	50	64	0	1	3	2	29	4	0	.138
1979	7	14	.333	4.21	31	30	4	186	184	51	96	0	0	0	0	64	13	0	.203
1980 PIT N	7	3	.700	2.70	26	12	2	100	96	37	35	0	2	0	0	32	7	0	.219
1981	8	6	.571	3.12	22	17	2	127	133	27	38	0	1	1	1	43	7	0	.163
1982 2 teams		PIT N (11G 2–6)			CHI	A (6G 1–0)													
" total	3	6	.333	6.33	17	10	0	54	76	20	20	0	2	0	0	15	2	0	.133
10 yrs.	36	42	.462	3.99	191	95	8	719	764	247	337	0	6	5	4	220	39	0	.177

LEAGUE CHAMPIONSHIP SERIES

	W	L	PCT	ERA	G	GS	CG	IP	H	BB	SO	ShO	RP W	L	SV	AB	H	HR	BA
1974 LA N	0	0	–	0.00	1	0	0	2	2	1	1	0	0	0	0	0	0	0	–

Joe Sommer

SOMMER, JOSEPH JOHN
B. Nov. 20, 1858, Covington, Ky.   D. Jan. 16, 1938, Cincinnati, Ohio   BR TR

	W	L	PCT	ERA	G	GS	CG	IP	H	BB	SO	ShO	RP W	L	SV	AB	H	HR	BA
1883 CIN AA	0	0	–	5.40	1	0	0	5	9	1	2	0	0	0	0	413	115	3	.278
1885 BAL AA	0	0	–	9.00	2	0	0	3	6	0	0	0	0	0	1	471	118	1	.251
1886	0	0	–	18.00	1	0	0	4	14	3	1	0	0	0	0	560	117	1	.209
1887	0	0	–	9.00	1	0	0	1	2	1	0	0	0	0	0	463	123	0	.266
1890 CLE N	0	0	–	0.00	1	0	0	1	2	2	0	0	0	0	0	164	41	0	.250
5 yrs.	0	0	–	9.64	6	0	0	14	33	7	3	0	0	0	1	*			

Rudy Sommers

SOMMERS, RUDOLPH
B. Oct. 30, 1888, Cincinnati, Ohio   D. Mar. 18, 1949, Louisville, Ky.   BL TL 5'11" 170 lbs.

	W	L	PCT	ERA	G	GS	CG	IP	H	BB	SO	ShO	RP W	L	SV	AB	H	HR	BA
1912 CHI N	0	1	.000	3.00	1	0	0	3	4	2	2	0	0	1	0	0	0	0	–
1914 BKN F	4	7	.364	4.06	23	8	2	82	88	34	40	0	3	0	0	24	6	0	.250
1926 BOS A	0	0	–	13.50	2	0	0	2	3	3	0	0	0	0	0	0	0	0	–
1927	0	0	–	8.36	7	0	0	14	18	14	2	0	0	0	1	2	1	0	.500
4 yrs.	4	8	.333	4.81	33	8	2	101	113	53	44	0	3	1	0	26	7	0	.269

Andy Sommerville

SOMMERVILLE, ANDREW HENRY
Born Henry Travers Summersgill.
B. Feb. 6, 1876, Brooklyn, N. Y.   D. June 16, 1931, Richmond Hill, N. Y.

	W	L	PCT	ERA	G	GS	CG	IP	H	BB	SO	ShO	RP W	L	SV	AB	H	HR	BA
1894 BKN N	0	1	.000	162.00	1	1	0	.1	1	5	0	0	0	0	0	0	0	0	–

Don Songer

SONGER, DON
B. Jan. 31, 1899, Walnut, Kans.   D. Oct. 3, 1962, Kansas City, Mo.   BL TL 6' 165 lbs.

	W	L	PCT	ERA	G	GS	CG	IP	H	BB	SO	ShO	RP W	L	SV	AB	H	HR	BA
1924 PIT N	0	0	–	6.75	4	1	0	9.1	14	3	3	0	0	0	1	2	0	0	.000
1925	0	1	.000	2.31	8	0	0	11.2	14	8	4	0	0	1	0	2	0	0	.000
1926	7	8	.467	3.13	35	15	5	126.1	118	52	27	1	0	2	2	38	4	0	.105
1927 2 teams		PIT N (2G 0–0)			NY	N (22G 3–5)													
" total	3	5	.375	3.60	24	1	0	55	58	35	10	0	3	4	1	11	3	0	.273
4 yrs.	10	14	.417	3.38	71	17	5	202.1	204	98	44	1	3	7	4	53	7	0	.132

Lary Sorensen

SORENSEN, LARY ALAN
B. Oct. 4, 1955, Detroit, Mich.   BR TR 6'2" 200 lbs.

	W	L	PCT	ERA	G	GS	CG	IP	H	BB	SO	ShO	RP W	L	SV	AB	H	HR	BA
1977 MIL A	7	10	.412	4.37	23	20	9	142	147	36	57	0	0	1	0	0	0	0	–
1978	18	12	.600	3.21	37	36	17	280.2	277	50	78	3	0	0	1	0	0	0	–
1979	15	14	.517	3.98	34	34	16	235	250	42	63	2	0	0	0	0	0	0	–
1980	12	10	.545	3.67	35	29	8	196	242	45	54	2	0	1	1	0	0	0	–
1981 STL N	7	7	.500	3.28	23	23	3	140	149	26	52	1	0	0	0	46	3	0	.065
1982 CLE A	10	15	.400	5.61	32	30	6	189.1	251	55	62	1	0	0	0	0	0	0	–
1983	12	11	.522	4.24	36	34	8	222.2	238	65	76	1	0	0	0	0	0	0	–

	W	L	PCT	ERA	G	GS	CG	IP	H	BB	SO	ShO	Relief Pitching			BATTING			BA
													W	L	SV	AB	H	HR	

Lary Sorensen continued

	W	L	PCT	ERA	G	GS	CG	IP	H	BB	SO	ShO	W	L	SV	AB	H	HR	BA
1984 OAK A	6	13	.316	4.91	46	21	2	183.1	240	44	63	0	1	2	1	0	0	0	–
8 yrs.	87	92	.486	4.12	266	227	69	1589	1794	363	505	10	1	4	3	46	3	0	.065

Vic Sorrell

SORRELL, VICTOR GARLAND   BR TR 5'10" 180 lbs.
B. Apr. 9, 1901, Morrisville, N. C.   D. May 4, 1972, Raleigh, N. C.

	W	L	PCT	ERA	G	GS	CG	IP	H	BB	SO	ShO	W	L	SV	AB	H	HR	BA
1928 DET A	8	11	.421	4.79	29	23	8	171	182	83	67	0	0	0	0	55	6	0	.109
1929	14	15	.483	5.18	36	31	13	226	270	106	81	1	2	0	1	83	12	0	.145
1930	16	11	.593	3.86	35	30	14	233.1	245	106	97	2	2	1	1	80	15	0	.188
1931	13	14	.481	4.12	35	32	19	247	267	114	99	1	0	0	1	88	14	0	.159
1932	14	14	.500	4.03	32	31	13	234.1	234	77	84	1	1	0	0	76	9	0	.118
1933	11	15	.423	3.79	36	28	13	232.2	233	78	75	2	2	1	1	74	11	0	.149
1934	6	9	.400	4.79	28	19	6	129.2	146	45	46	0	0	2	2	37	4	0	.108
1935	4	3	.571	4.03	12	6	4	51.1	65	25	22	0	0	2	0	18	0	0	.000
1936	6	7	.462	5.28	30	14	5	131.1	153	64	37	1	2	3	3	39	6	0	.154
1937	0	2	.000	9.00	7	2	0	17	25	8	11	0	0	0	0	3	0	0	.000
10 yrs.	92	101	.477	4.43	280	216	95	1673.2	1820	706	619	8	9	9	10	553	77	0	.139

Elias Sosa

SOSA, ELIAS MARTINEZ   BR TR 6'2" 186 lbs.
B. June 10, 1950, La Vega, Dominican Republic

	W	L	PCT	ERA	G	GS	CG	IP	H	BB	SO	ShO	W	L	SV	AB	H	HR	BA
1972 SF N	0	1	.000	2.25	8	0	0	16	10	12	10	0	0	1	3	4	0	0	.000
1973	10	4	.714	3.28	71	1	0	107	95	41	70	0	10	3	18	14	1	0	.071
1974	9	7	.563	3.48	68	0	0	101	94	45	48	0	9	7	6	15	1	0	.067
1975 2 teams			STL	N	(14G 0–3)		ATL	N	(43G 2–2)										
" total	2	5	.286	4.32	57	1	0	89.2	92	43	46	0	2	4	2	15	2	0	.133
1976 2 teams			ATL	N	(21G 4–4)		LA	N	(24G 2–4)										
" total	6	8	.429	4.43	45	0	0	69	71	25	52	0	6	8	4	7	1	0	.143
1977 LA N	2	2	.500	1.97	44	0	0	64	42	12	47	0	2	2	1	4	1	0	.250
1978 OAK A	8	2	.800	2.64	68	0	0	109	106	44	61	0	8	2	14	0	0	0	–
1979 MON N	8	7	.533	1.95	62	0	0	97	77	37	59	0	8	7	18	13	2	0	.154
1980	9	6	.600	3.06	67	0	0	94	104	19	58	0	9	6	9	11	1	0	.091
1981	1	2	.333	3.69	32	0	0	39	46	8	18	0	1	2	3	2	2	0	1.000
1982 DET A	3	3	.500	4.43	38	0	0	61	64	18	24	0	3	3	4	0	0	0	–
1983 SD N	1	4	.200	4.35	41	1	0	72.1	72	30	45	0	1	4	1	7	1	0	.143
12 yrs.	59	51	.536	3.32	601	3	0	919	873	334	538	0	59	49	83	92	12	0	.130

DIVISIONAL PLAYOFF SERIES

	W	L	PCT	ERA	G	GS	CG	IP	H	BB	SO	ShO	W	L	SV	AB	H	HR	BA
1981 MON N	0	0	–	3.00	2	0	0	3	4	0	1	0	0	0	0	0	0	0	–

LEAGUE CHAMPIONSHIP SERIES

	W	L	PCT	ERA	G	GS	CG	IP	H	BB	SO	ShO	W	L	SV	AB	H	HR	BA
1977 LA N	0	1	.000	10.13	2	0	0	2.2	5	0	0	0	0	1	0	1	0	0	.000
1981 MON N	0	0	–	0.00	1	0	0	.1	1	1	0	0	0	0	0	0	0	0	–
2 yrs.	0	1	.000	9.00	3	0	0	3	6	1	0	0	0	1	0	1	0	0	.000

WORLD SERIES

	W	L	PCT	ERA	G	GS	CG	IP	H	BB	SO	ShO	W	L	SV	AB	H	HR	BA
1977 LA N	0	0	–	11.57	2	0	0	2.1	3	1	1	0	0	0	0	0	0	0	–

Jose Sosa

SOSA, JOSE YNOCENCIO   BR TR 5'11" 158 lbs.
B. Dec. 28, 1952, Santo Domingo, Dominican Republic

	W	L	PCT	ERA	G	GS	CG	IP	H	BB	SO	ShO	W	L	SV	AB	H	HR	BA
1975 HOU N	1	3	.250	4.02	25	2	0	47	51	23	31	0	1	3	1	9	3	1	.333
1976	0	0	–	6.75	9	0	0	12	16	6	5	0	0	0	0	0	0	0	–
2 yrs.	1	3	.250	4.58	34	2	0	59	67	29	36	0	1	3	1	9	3	1	.333

Allen Sothoron

SOTHORON, ALLEN SUTTON   BB TR 5'11" 182 lbs.
B. Apr. 29, 1893, Laura, Ohio   BR 1924-26
D. June 17, 1939, St. Louis, Mo.
Manager 1933.

	W	L	PCT	ERA	G	GS	CG	IP	H	BB	SO	ShO	W	L	SV	AB	H	HR	BA
1914 STL A	0	0	–	6.00	1	0	0	6	6	4	3	0	0	0	0	2	0	0	.000
1915	0	1	.000	7.36	3	1	0	3.2	8	5	2	0	0	0	0	1	0	0	.000
1917	14	19	.424	2.83	48	33	17	276.2	259	96	85	3	2	3	4	91	19	0	.209
1918	12	12	.500	1.94	29	24	14	209	152	67	71	2	0	1	0	63	10	0	.159
1919	20	13	.606	2.20	40	30	21	270	256	87	106	3	5	0	3	97	17	0	.175
1920	8	15	.348	4.70	36	26	12	218.1	263	89	81	1	0	1	2	72	16	0	.222
1921 3 teams			STL	A	(5G 1–2)		BOS	A	(2G 0–2)		CLE	A	(22G 12–4)						
" total	13	8	.619	3.89	29	22	11	178.1	194	71	72	2	2	0	0	69	18	0	.261
1922 CLE A	1	3	.250	6.39	6	4	2	25.1	26	14	8	0	0	1	0	9	4	0	.444
1924 STL N	10	16	.385	3.57	29	28	16	196.2	209	84	62	4	0	1	0	72	14	0	.194
1925	10	10	.500	4.05	28	23	8	155.2	173	63	67	2	1	1	0	56	11	0	.196
1926	3	3	.500	4.22	15	4	1	42.2	37	16	19	0	2	2	0	13	3	0	.231
11 yrs.	91	100	.476	3.31	264	195	102	1582.1	1583	596	576	17	12	10	9	545	112	0	.206

Mario Soto

SOTO, MARIO MELVIN   BR TR 6' 174 lbs.
B. July 12, 1956, Bani, Dominican Republic

	W	L	PCT	ERA	G	GS	CG	IP	H	BB	SO	ShO	W	L	SV	AB	H	HR	BA
1977 CIN N	2	6	.250	5.31	12	10	2	61	60	26	44	1	0	0	0	13	1	0	.077
1978	1	0	1.000	2.50	5	1	0	18	13	13	13	0	1	0	0	2	0	0	.000
1979	3	2	.600	5.35	25	0	0	37	33	30	32	0	3	2	0	7	4	0	.571
1980	10	8	.556	3.08	53	12	3	190	126	84	182	1	3	8	4	46	2	0	.043
1981	12	9	.571	3.29	25	25	10	175	142	61	151	3	0	0	0	59	4	0	.068
1982	14	13	.519	2.79	35	34	13	257.2	202	71	274	2	1	0	0	84	14	0	.167
1983	17	13	.567	2.70	34	34	18	273.2	207	95	242	3	0	0	0	88	11	0	.125
1984	18	7	.720	3.53	33	33	13	237.1	181	87	185	0	0	0	0	87	18	0	.207
8 yrs.	77	58	.570	3.22	222	149	59	1249.2	964	467	1123	10	8	10	4	386	54	1	.140

LEAGUE CHAMPIONSHIP SERIES

	W	L	PCT	ERA	G	GS	CG	IP	H	BB	SO	ShO	W	L	SV	AB	H	HR	BA
1979 CIN N	0	0	–	0.00	1	0	0	2	0	1	1	0	0	0	0	0	0	0	–

Mark Souza

SOUZA, KENNETH MARK
B. Feb. 1, 1955, Redwood City, Calif.
BL TL 6' 180 lbs.

	W	L	PCT	ERA	G	GS	CG	IP	H	BB	SO	ShO	Relief W	Relief L	Relief SV	AB	H	HR	BA
1980 OAK A	0	0	—	7.71	5	0	0	7	9	5	2	0	0	0	0	0	0	0	—

Bill Sowders

SOWDERS, WILLIAM JEFFERSON
Brother of Len Sowders.   Brother of John Sowders.
B. Nov. 29, 1864, Louisville, Ky.   D. Feb. 2, 1951, Indianapolis, Ind.
BR TR 6'

	W	L	PCT	ERA	G	GS	CG	IP	H	BB	SO	ShO	Relief W	Relief L	Relief SV	AB	H	HR	BA
1888 BOS N	19	15	.559	2.07	36	35	34	317	278	73	132	2	0	0	0	122	18	0	.148
1889 2 teams			BOS	N (7G 2-2)			PIT	N (13G 6-5)											
" total	8	7	.533	6.37	20	15	12	94.2	147	52	43	0	2	0	2	65	17	0	.262
1890 PIT N	3	8	.273	4.42	15	11	9	106	117	24	30	0	1	1	0	50	9	0	.180
3 yrs.	30	30	.500	3.34	71	61	55	517.2	542	149	205	2	3	1	2	237	44	0	.186

John Sowders

SOWDERS, JOHN
Brother of Len Sowders.   Brother of Bill Sowders.
B. Dec. 10, 1866, Louisville, Ky.   D. July 29, 1908, Indianapolis, Ind.
BR TL

	W	L	PCT	ERA	G	GS	CG	IP	H	BB	SO	ShO	Relief W	Relief L	Relief SV	AB	H	HR	BA
1887 IND N	0	0	—	21.00	1	0	0	3	11	5	0	0	0	0	0	2	0	0	.000
1889 KC AA	6	16	.273	4.82	25	23	20	185	204	105	104	0	0	0	1	87	19	0	.218
1890 BKN P	19	16	.543	3.82	39	37	28	309	358	161	91	1	0	0	0	132	25	0	.189
3 yrs.	25	32	.439	4.29	65	60	48	497	573	271	195	1	0	0	1	221	44	1	.199

Bob Spade

SPADE, ROBERT
B. Jan. 4, 1877, Akron, Ohio   D. Sept. 7, 1924, Cincinnati, Ohio
BR TR 5'10" 190 lbs.

	W	L	PCT	ERA	G	GS	CG	IP	H	BB	SO	ShO	Relief W	Relief L	Relief SV	AB	H	HR	BA
1907 CIN N	1	2	.333	1.00	3	3	3	27	21	9	7	1	0	0	0	7	2	0	.286
1908	17	12	.586	2.74	35	28	22	249.1	230	85	74	2	1	1	1	87	17	0	.195
1909	5	5	.500	2.85	14	13	8	98	91	39	31	0	1	0	0	34	10	0	.294
1910 2 teams			CIN	N (3G 1-2)			STL	A (7G 1-3)											
" total	2	5	.286	5.19	10	8	3	52	69	26	9	1	0	0	0	16	3	0	.188
4 yrs.	25	24	.510	2.96	62	52	36	426.1	411	159	121	4	2	1	1	144	32	0	.222

Warren Spahn

SPAHN, WARREN EDWARD
B. Apr. 23, 1921, Buffalo, N.Y.
Hall of Fame 1973.
BL TL 6' 172 lbs.

	W	L	PCT	ERA	G	GS	CG	IP	H	BB	SO	ShO	Relief W	Relief L	Relief SV	AB	H	HR	BA
1942 BOS N	0	0	—	5.74	4	2	1	15.2	25	11	7	0	0	0	0	6	1	0	.167
1946	8	5	.615	2.94	24	16	8	125.2	107	36	67	0	0	0	1	43	7	0	.163
1947	21	10	.677	2.33	40	35	22	289.2	245	84	123	7	0	0	3	98	16	0	.163
1948	15	12	.556	3.71	36	35	16	257	237	77	114	3	0	0	1	90	15	1	.167
1949	21	14	.600	3.07	38	38	25	302.1	283	86	151	4	0	0	0	111	18	2	.162
1950	21	17	.553	3.16	41	39	25	293	248	111	191	1	0	1	1	106	23	1	.217
1951	22	14	.611	2.98	39	36	26	310.2	278	109	164	7	0	3	0	116	22	1	.190
1952	14	19	.424	2.98	40	35	19	290	263	73	183	5	0	1	3	112	18	2	.161
1953 MIL N	23	7	.767	2.10	35	32	24	265.2	211	70	148	5	0	0	3	105	23	2	.219
1954	21	12	.636	3.14	39	34	23	283.1	262	86	136	1	1	1	3	101	21	1	.208
1955	17	14	.548	3.26	39	32	16	245.2	249	65	110	1	0	3	1	81	17	4	.210
1956	20	11	.645	2.78	39	35	20	281.1	249	52	128	3	0	0	3	105	22	3	.210
1957	21	11	.656	2.69	39	35	18	271	241	78	111	4	1	0	3	94	13	2	.138
1958	22	11	.667	3.07	38	36	23	290	257	76	150	2	0	0	1	108	36	2	.333
1959	21	15	.583	2.96	40	36	21	292	282	70	143	4	0	3	0	104	24	2	.231
1960	21	10	.677	3.50	40	33	18	267.2	254	74	154	4	2	2	2	95	14	3	.147
1961	21	13	.618	3.02	38	34	21	262.2	236	64	115	4	1	3	0	94	21	4	.223
1962	18	14	.563	3.04	34	34	22	269.1	248	55	118	0	0	0	0	98	18	2	.184
1963	23	7	.767	2.60	33	33	22	259.2	241	49	102	7	0	0	0	90	16	2	.178
1964	6	13	.316	5.29	38	25	4	173.2	204	52	78	1	0	0	4	90	16	1	.186
1965 2 teams			NY	N (20G 4-12)			SF	N (16G 3-4)											
" total	7	16	.304	4.01	36	30	8	197.2	210	56	90	0	0	0	0	56	7	0	.125
21 yrs.	363	245	.597	3.09	750	665	382	5243.2	4830	1434	2583	63	5	18	29	1872	363	35	.194
	5th	7th						5th				6th							

WORLD SERIES

	W	L	PCT	ERA	G	GS	CG	IP	H	BB	SO	ShO	Relief W	Relief L	Relief SV	AB	H	HR	BA
1948 BOS N	1	1	.500	3.00	3	1	0	12	10	3	12	0	1	0	0	4	0	0	.000
1957 MIL N	1	1	.500	4.70	2	2	1	15.1	18	2	2	0	0	0	0	4	0	0	.000
1958	2	1	.667	2.20	3	3	2	28.2	19	8	18	1	0	0	0	12	4	0	.333
3 yrs.	4	3	.571	3.05	8	6	3	56	47	13	32	1	1	0	0	20	4	0	.200

Al Spalding

SPALDING, ALBERT GOODWILL
B. Sept. 2, 1850, Byron, Ill.   D. Sept. 9, 1915, Point Loma, Calif.
Manager 1876-77.
Hall of Fame 1939.
BR TR 6'1" 170 lbs.

	W	L	PCT	ERA	G	GS	CG	IP	H	BB	SO	ShO	Relief W	Relief L	Relief SV	AB	H	HR	BA
1876 CHI N	47	13	.783	1.75	61	60	53	528.2	542	26	39	8	0	0	0	292	91	0	.312
1877	1	0	1.000	3.27	4	1	0	11	17	0	2	0	1	0	1	254	65	0	.256
1878	0	0	—	0.00	0	0	0	0	0	0	0	0	0	0	0	4	2	0	.500
3 yrs.	48	13	.787	1.78	65	61	53	539.2	559	26	41	8	1	0	1	*			

Bill Spanswick

SPANSWICK, WILLIAM HENRY
B. July 8, 1938, Springfield, Mass.
BL TL 6'3" 195 lbs.

	W	L	PCT	ERA	G	GS	CG	IP	H	BB	SO	ShO	Relief W	Relief L	Relief SV	AB	H	HR	BA
1964 BOS A	2	3	.400	6.89	29	7	0	65.1	75	44	55	0	1	0	0	14	4	0	.286

Tully Sparks

SPARKS, THOMAS FRANK
B. Dec. 12, 1874, Aetna, Ga.   D. July 15, 1937, Anniston, Ala.
BR TR

	W	L	PCT	ERA	G	GS	CG	IP	H	BB	SO	ShO	Relief W	Relief L	Relief SV	AB	H	HR	BA
1897 PHI N	0	1	.000	10.13	1	1	1	8	12	4	0	0	0	0	0	3	0	0	.000
1899 PIT N	8	6	.571	3.86	28	17	8	170	180	82	53	0	2	1	0	62	8	0	.129
1901 MIL A	7	16	.304	3.51	29	26	18	210	228	93	62	0	1	0	0	71	12	0	.169
1902 2 teams			NY	N (15G 4-10)			BOS	A (17G 7-9)											
" total	11	19	.367	3.60	32	28	26	257.2	274	80	77	1	1	1	1	89	13	0	.146
1903 PHI N	11	15	.423	2.72	28	28	27	248	248	56	88	0	0	0	0	92	10	0	.109
1904	7	18	.280	2.65	26	25	19	200.2	208	43	67	3	1	0	0	76	8	0	.105
1905	14	11	.560	2.18	34	26	20	260	217	73	98	3	1	1	1	94	12	0	.128
1906	19	16	.543	2.16	42	37	29	316.2	244	62	114	6	1	0	0	104	16	0	.154

	W	L	PCT	ERA	G	GS	CG	IP	H	BB	SO	ShO	Relief Pitching W	L	SV	BATTING AB	H	HR	BA

Tully Sparks continued

	W	L	PCT	ERA	G	GS	CG	IP	H	BB	SO	ShO	W	L	SV	AB	H	HR	BA
1907	22	8	.733	2.00	33	31	24	265	221	51	90	3	1	0	1	89	3	0	.034
1908	16	15	.516	2.60	33	31	24	263.1	251	51	85	2	0	0	2	77	4	0	.052
1909	6	11	.353	2.96	24	16	6	121.2	126	32	40	1	2	0	0	36	5	0	.139
1910	0	2	.000	6.00	3	3	0	15	22	2	4	0	0	0	0	5	0	0	.000
12 yrs.	121	138	.467	2.79	313	269	202	2336	2231	629	778	19	8	4	8	798	91	0	.114

Joe Sparma

SPARMA, JOSEPH BLASE BR TR 6'1" 190 lbs.
B. Feb. 4, 1942, Massillon, Ohio

	W	L	PCT	ERA	G	GS	CG	IP	H	BB	SO	ShO	W	L	SV	AB	H	HR	BA
1964 DET A	5	6	.455	3.00	21	11	3	84	62	45	71	2	1	1	0	25	4	0	.160
1965	13	8	.619	3.18	30	28	6	167	142	75	127	0	1	0	0	52	7	0	.135
1966	2	7	.222	5.30	29	13	0	91.2	103	52	61	0	0	0	0	23	5	0	.217
1967	16	9	.640	3.76	37	37	11	217.2	186	85	153	5	0	0	0	74	4	0	.054
1968	10	10	.500	3.70	34	31	7	182.1	169	77	110	1	1	0	0	60	8	0	.133
1969	6	8	.429	4.76	23	16	3	92.2	78	77	41	2	0	1	0	29	4	0	.138
1970 MON N	0	4	.000	7.14	9	6	1	29	34	25	23	0	0	0	0	6	0	0	.000
7 yrs.	52	52	.500	3.95	183	142	31	864.1	774	436	586	10	3	2	0	269	32	0	.119

WORLD SERIES

	W	L	PCT	ERA	G	GS	CG	IP	H	BB	SO	ShO	W	L	SV	AB	H	HR	BA
1968 DET A	0	0	-	54.00	1	0	0	.1	2	0	0	0	0	0	0	0	0	0	-

Tris Speaker

SPEAKER, TRISTRAM E (The Grey Eagle, Spoke) BL TL 5'11½" 193 lbs.
B. Apr. 4, 1888, Hubbard, Tex.   D. Dec. 8, 1958, Lake Whitney, Tex.
Manager 1919-26.
Hall of Fame 1937.

	W	L	PCT	ERA	G	GS	CG	IP	H	BB	SO	ShO	W	L	SV	AB	H	HR	BA
1914 BOS A	0	0	-	9.00	1	0	0	1	2	0	0	0	0	0	0	*			

Byron Speece

SPEECE, BYRON FRANKLIN BR TR 5'11" 170 lbs.
B. Jan. 6, 1897, West Baden, Ind.   D. Sept. 29, 1974, Elgin, Ore.

	W	L	PCT	ERA	G	GS	CG	IP	H	BB	SO	ShO	W	L	SV	AB	H	HR	BA
1924 WAS A	2	1	.667	2.65	21	1	0	54.1	60	27	15	0	2	0	0	20	3	0	.150
1925 CLE A	3	5	.375	4.28	28	3	3	90.1	106	28	26	0	2	3	1	31	5	0	.161
1926	0	0	-	0.00	2	0	0	3	1	2	1	0	0	0	0	0	0	0	-
1930 PHI N	0	0	-	13.27	11	0	0	19.2	41	4	9	0	0	0	0	3	1	0	.333
4 yrs.	5	6	.455	4.73	62	4	3	167.1	208	61	51	0	4	3	1	54	9	0	.167

WORLD SERIES

	W	L	PCT	ERA	G	GS	CG	IP	H	BB	SO	ShO	W	L	SV	AB	H	HR	BA
1924 WAS A	0	0	-	9.00	1	0	0	1	3	0	0	0	0	0	0	0	0	0	-

Floyd Speer

SPEER, VERNIE FLOYD BR TR 6' 180 lbs.
B. Jan. 27, 1913, Booneville, Ark.   D. Mar. 22, 1969, Little Rock, Ark.

	W	L	PCT	ERA	G	GS	CG	IP	H	BB	SO	ShO	W	L	SV	AB	H	HR	BA
1943 CHI A	0	0	-	9.00	1	0	0	1	1	2	1	0	0	0	0	0	0	0	-
1944	0	0	-	9.00	2	0	0	2	4	0	1	0	0	0	0	0	0	0	-
2 yrs.	0	0	-	9.00	3	0	0	3	5	2	2	0	0	0	0	0	0	0	-

Kid Speer

SPEER, GEORGE NATHAN BL TL
B. June 16, 1886, Corning Mo.   D. Jan. 13, 1946, Edmonton, Alta., Canada

	W	L	PCT	ERA	G	GS	CG	IP	H	BB	SO	ShO	W	L	SV	AB	H	HR	BA
1909 DET A	4	4	.500	2.83	12	8	4	76.1	88	13	12	0	1	1	1	25	3	0	.120

Fred Spencer

SPENCER, FRED CALVIN BR TR 5'8" 170 lbs.
B. Apr. 25, 1885, St. Cloud, Minn.   D. Feb. 5, 1969, Minneapolis, Minn.

	W	L	PCT	ERA	G	GS	CG	IP	H	BB	SO	ShO	W	L	SV	AB	H	HR	BA
1912 STL A	0	0	-	0.00	1	0	0	1.2	0	1	0	0	0	0	0	0	0	0	-

George Spencer

SPENCER, GEORGE ELWELL BR TR 6'1" 215 lbs.
B. July 7, 1926, Columbus, Ohio

	W	L	PCT	ERA	G	GS	CG	IP	H	BB	SO	ShO	W	L	SV	AB	H	HR	BA
1950 NY N	1	0	1.000	2.49	10	1	1	25.1	12	7	5	0	0	0	0	4	0	0	.000
1951	10	4	.714	3.75	57	4	2	132	125	56	36	0	8	2	6	32	4	0	.125
1952	3	5	.375	5.55	35	4	0	60	57	21	27	0	3	4	3	10	2	0	.200
1953	0	0	-	7.71	1	0	0	2.1	3	2	1	0	0	0	0	0	0	0	-
1954	1	0	1.000	3.65	6	0	0	12.1	9	8	4	0	1	0	0	3	0	0	.000
1955	0	0	-	5.40	1	0	0	1.2	1	3	0	0	0	0	0	0	0	0	-
1958 DET A	1	0	1.000	2.70	7	0	0	10	11	4	5	0	1	0	0	1	0	0	-
1960	0	1	.000	3.52	5	0	0	7.2	10	5	4	0	0	1	0	1	0	0	.000
8 yrs.	16	10	.615	4.05	122	9	3	251.1	228	106	82	0	13	7	9	50	6	0	.120

WORLD SERIES

	W	L	PCT	ERA	G	GS	CG	IP	H	BB	SO	ShO	W	L	SV	AB	H	HR	BA
1951 NY N	0	0	-	18.90	2	0	0	3.1	6	3	4	0	0	0	0	0	0	0	-

Glenn Spencer

SPENCER, GLENN EDWARD BR TR 5'11" 155 lbs.
B. Sept. 11, 1905, Corning, N.Y.   D. Dec. 30, 1958, Binghamton, N.Y.

	W	L	PCT	ERA	G	GS	CG	IP	H	BB	SO	ShO	W	L	SV	AB	H	HR	BA
1928 PIT N	0	0	-	1.59	4	0	0	5.2	4	3	2	0	0	0	0	1	0	0	.000
1930	8	9	.471	5.40	41	10	5	156.2	185	63	60	0	3	5	4	53	6	0	.113
1931	11	12	.478	3.42	38	18	11	186.2	180	65	51	1	3	3	3	52	5	0	.096
1932	4	8	.333	4.97	39	13	5	137.2	167	44	35	1	2	1	1	37	6	0	.162
1933 NY N	0	2	.000	5.13	17	3	1	47.1	52	26	14	0	0	0	0	12	2	0	.167
5 yrs.	23	31	.426	4.53	139	44	22	534	588	201	162	2	8	9	8	155	19	0	.123

Bob Spicer

SPICER, ROBERT OBERTON BL TR 5'10" 173 lbs.
B. Apr. 11, 1925, Richmond, Va.

	W	L	PCT	ERA	G	GS	CG	IP	H	BB	SO	ShO	W	L	SV	AB	H	HR	BA
1955 KC A	0	0	-	33.75	2	0	0	2.2	9	4	2	0	0	0	0	1	0	0	.000
1956	0	0	-	19.29	2	0	0	2.1	6	1	0	0	0	0	0	0	0	0	-
2 yrs.	0	0	-	27.00	4	0	0	5	15	5	2	0	0	0	0	1	0	0	.000

Dan Spillner

SPILLNER, DANIEL RAY BR TR 6'1" 190 lbs.
B. Nov. 27, 1951, Casper, Wyo.

	W	L	PCT	ERA	G	GS	CG	IP	H	BB	SO	ShO	W	L	SV	AB	H	HR	BA
1974 SD N	9	11	.450	4.01	30	25	5	148	153	70	95	2	1	0	0	43	1	0	.023
1975	5	13	.278	4.26	37	25	3	167	194	63	104	0	0	0	1	45	6	0	.133
1976	2	11	.154	5.06	32	14	0	106.2	120	55	57	0	1	1	0	25	1	0	.040

	W	L	PCT	ERA	G	GS	CG	IP	H	BB	SO	ShO	Relief Pitching W	L	SV	BATTING AB	H	HR	BA

Dan Spillner continued

	W	L	PCT	ERA	G	GS	CG	IP	H	BB	SO	ShO	W	L	SV	AB	H	HR	BA
1977	7	6	.538	3.73	76	0	0	123	130	60	74	0	7	6	6	17	2	0	.118
1978 2 teams					SD	N (17G 1–0)		CLE	A (36G 3–1)										
" total	4	1	.800	3.94	53	0	0	82.1	86	28	64	0	4	1	3	0	0	0	—
1979 CLE A	9	5	.643	4.61	49	13	3	158	153	64	97	0	3	3	1	0	0	0	—
1980	16	11	.593	5.29	34	30	7	194	225	74	100	1	1	0	0	0	0	0	—
1981	4	4	.500	3.15	32	5	1	97	86	39	59	0	3	0	7	0	0	0	—
1982	12	10	.545	2.49	65	0	0	133.2	117	45	90	0	12	10	21	0	0	0	—
1983	2	9	.182	5.07	60	0	0	92.1	117	38	48	0	2	9	8	0	0	0	—
1984 2 teams					CLE	A (14G 0–5)		CHI	A (22G 1–0)										
" total	1	5	.167	4.89	36	0	0	99.1	121	36	49	0	1	0	2	0	0	0	—
11 yrs.	71	86	.452	4.26	504	120	19	1401.1	1502	572	837	3	35	30	49	130	10	0	.077

Scipio Spinks

SPINKS, SCIPIO RONALD
B. July 12, 1947, Chicago, Ill.
BR TR 6'1" 183 lbs.

	W	L	PCT	ERA	G	GS	CG	IP	H	BB	SO	ShO	W	L	SV	AB	H	HR	BA
1969 HOU N	0	0	—	0.00	1	0	0	2	1	1	4	0	0	0	0	0	0	0	—
1970	0	1	.000	9.64	5	2	0	14	17	9	6	0	0	0	0	0	0	0	—
1971	1	0	1.000	3.72	5	3	1	29	22	13	26	0	0	0	0	3	0	0	.000
1972 STL N	5	5	.500	2.67	16	16	6	118	96	59	93	0	0	0	0	9	2	0	.222
1973	1	5	.167	4.89	8	8	0	38.2	39	25	25	0	0	0	0	42	7	0	.167
5 yrs.	7	11	.389	3.70	35	29	7	201.2	175	107	154	0	0	0	0	65	11	1	.169

Paul Splittorff

SPLITTORFF, PAUL WILLIAM JR
B. Oct. 8, 1946, Evansville, Ind.
BL TL 6'3" 205 lbs.

	W	L	PCT	ERA	G	GS	CG	IP	H	BB	SO	ShO	W	L	SV	AB	H	HR	BA
1970 KC A	0	1	.000	7.00	2	1	0	9	16	5	10	0	0	0	0	2	1	0	.500
1971	8	9	.471	2.69	22	22	6	144	129	35	80	3	0	0	0	48	5	0	.104
1972	12	12	.500	3.12	35	33	12	216.1	189	67	140	2	0	0	0	71	16	0	.225
1973	20	11	.645	3.99	38	38	12	261.2	279	78	110	3	0	0	0	0	0	0	—
1974	13	19	.406	4.10	36	36	8	226	252	75	90	1	0	0	0	0	0	0	—
1975	9	10	.474	3.17	35	23	6	159	156	56	76	3	1	0	1	0	0	0	—
1976	11	8	.579	3.96	26	23	5	159	169	59	59	1	0	0	0	0	0	0	—
1977	16	6	.727	3.69	37	37	6	229	243	83	99	2	0	0	0	0	0	0	—
1978	19	13	.594	3.40	39	38	13	262	244	60	76	2	0	0	0	0	0	0	—
1979	15	17	.469	4.24	36	35	11	240	248	77	77	0	0	0	0	0	0	0	—
1980	14	11	.560	4.15	34	33	4	204	236	43	53	0	0	0	0	0	0	0	—
1981	5	5	.500	4.36	21	15	1	99	111	23	48	1	0	1	0	0	0	0	—
1982	10	10	.500	4.28	29	28	0	162	166	57	74	0	0	0	0	0	0	0	—
1983	13	8	.619	3.63	27	27	4	156	159	52	61	0	0	0	0	0	0	0	—
1984	1	3	.250	7.71	12	3	0	28	47	10	4	0	1	0	0	0	0	0	—
15 yrs.	166	143	.537	3.81	429	392	88	2555	2644	780	1057	17	3	0	1	121	22	0	.182

LEAGUE CHAMPIONSHIP SERIES

	W	L	PCT	ERA	G	GS	CG	IP	H	BB	SO	ShO	W	L	SV	AB	H	HR	BA
1976 KC A	1	0	1.000	1.93	2	0	0	9.1	7	5	2	0	1	0	0	0	0	0	—
1977	1	0	1.000	2.40	2	2	0	15	14	3	4	0	0	0	0	0	0	0	—
1978	0	0	—	4.91	1	1	0	7.1	9	0	2	0	0	0	0	0	0	0	—
1980	0	0	—	1.69	1	1	0	5.1	5	2	3	0	0	0	0	0	0	0	—
4 yrs.	2	0	1.000	2.68	6	4	0	37	35	10	11	0	1	0	0	0	0	0	—

WORLD SERIES

	W	L	PCT	ERA	G	GS	CG	IP	H	BB	SO	ShO	W	L	SV	AB	H	HR	BA
1980 KC A	0	0	—	5.40	1	0	0	1.2	4	0	0	0	0	0	0	0	0	0	—

Carl Spongburg

SPONGBURG, CARL GUSTAVE
B. May 21, 1884, Idaho Falls, Ida.   D. July 21, 1938, Los Angeles, Calif.
BR TR

	W	L	PCT	ERA	G	GS	CG	IP	H	BB	SO	ShO	W	L	SV	AB	H	HR	BA
1908 CHI N	0	0	—	9.00	1	0	0	7	9	6	4	0	0	0	0	3	2	0	.667

Karl Spooner

SPOONER, KARL BENJAMIN
B. June 23, 1931, Oriskany Falls, N. Y.   D. Apr. 10, 1984, Vero Beach, Fla.
BR TL 6' 185 lbs.

	W	L	PCT	ERA	G	GS	CG	IP	H	BB	SO	ShO	W	L	SV	AB	H	HR	BA
1954 BKN N	2	0	1.000	0.00	2	2	2	18	7	6	27	2	0	0	0	6	1	0	.167
1955	8	6	.571	3.65	29	14	2	98.2	79	41	78	1	5	1	2	28	8	0	.286
2 yrs.	10	6	.625	3.09	31	16	4	116.2	86	47	105	3	5	1	2	34	9	0	.265

WORLD SERIES

	W	L	PCT	ERA	G	GS	CG	IP	H	BB	SO	ShO	W	L	SV	AB	H	HR	BA
1955 BKN N	0	1	.000	13.50	2	1	0	3.1	4	3	6	0	0	0	0	0	0	0	—

Homer Spragins

SPRAGINS, HOMER FRANKLIN
B. Nov. 9, 1920, Grenada, Miss.
BR TR 6'1" 190 lbs.

	W	L	PCT	ERA	G	GS	CG	IP	H	BB	SO	ShO	W	L	SV	AB	H	HR	BA
1947 PHI N	0	0	—	6.75	4	0	0	5.1	3	3	3	0	0	0	0	0	0	0	—

Charlie Sprague

SPRAGUE, CHARLES WELLINGTON
B. Oct. 10, 1864, Cleveland, Ohio   D. Dec. 31, 1912, Des Moines, Iowa
BL TL 5'11" 150 lbs.

	W	L	PCT	ERA	G	GS	CG	IP	H	BB	SO	ShO	W	L	SV	AB	H	HR	BA
1887 CHI N	1	0	1.000	4.91	3	3	2	22	24	13	9	0	0	0	0	13	2	0	.154
1889 CLE N	0	2	.000	8.47	2	2	2	17	27	10	8	0	0	0	0	7	1	0	.143
1890 TOL AA	9	5	.643	3.89	19	12	9	122.2	111	78	59	0	1	2	0	199	47	1	.236
3 yrs.	10	7	.588	4.51	24	17	13	161.2	162	101	76	0	1	2	0	*			

Ed Sprague

SPRAGUE, EDWARD NELSON
B. Sept. 16, 1945, Boston, Mass.
BR TR 6'4" 195 lbs.

	W	L	PCT	ERA	G	GS	CG	IP	H	BB	SO	ShO	W	L	SV	AB	H	HR	BA
1968 OAK A	3	4	.429	3.28	47	1	0	68.2	51	34	34	0	3	3	4	7	0	0	.000
1969	1	1	.500	4.47	27	0	0	46.1	47	31	20	0	1	1	2	5	1	0	.200
1971 CIN N	1	0	1.000	0.00	7	0	0	11	8	1	7	0	1	0	0	1	0	0	.000
1972	3	3	.500	4.13	33	0	0	56.2	55	26	25	0	2	3	0	7	0	0	.000
1973 3 teams					CIN	N (28G 1–3)		STL	N (8G 0–0)		MIL	A (7G 0–1)							
" total	1	4	.200	5.43	43	0	0	56.1	56	40	24	0	1	4	2	2	0	0	.000
1974 MIL A	7	2	.778	2.39	20	10	3	94	94	31	57	0	0	0	0	0	0	0	—
1975	1	7	.125	4.68	18	11	0	67.1	81	40	21	0	0	2	1	0	0	0	—
1976	0	2	.000	6.75	3	1	0	8	14	3	0	0	0	2	0	0	0	0	—
8 yrs.	17	23	.425	3.84	198	23	3	408.1	406	206	188	0	8	15	9	22	1	0	.045

	W	L	PCT	ERA	G	GS	CG	IP	H	BB	SO	ShO	W	L	SV	AB	H	HR	BA

Ed Stein continued

	W	L	PCT	ERA	G	GS	CG	IP	H	BB	SO	ShO	W	L	SV	AB	H	HR	BA
1898	0	2	.000	5.48	3	2	2	23	39	9	6	0	0	0	0	10	4	0	.400
8 yrs.	110	78	.585	3.96	216	184	159	1665	1697	733	535	12	11	2	3	663	150	2	.226

Irv Stein

STEIN, IRVIN MICHAEL
B. May 21, 1911, Madisonville, La.   D. Jan. 7, 1981, Covington, La.
BR TR 6'2"   170 lbs.

	W	L	PCT	ERA	G	GS	CG	IP	H	BB	SO	ShO	W	L	SV	AB	H	HR	BA
1932 PHI A	0	0	–	12.00	1	0	0	3	7	1	0	0	0	0	0	1	0	0	.000

Randy Stein

STEIN, WILLIAM RANDOLPH
B. Mar. 7, 1953, Pomona, Calif.
BR TR 6'4"   210 lbs.

	W	L	PCT	ERA	G	GS	CG	IP	H	BB	SO	ShO	W	L	SV	AB	H	HR	BA
1978 MIL A	3	2	.600	5.33	31	1	0	72.2	78	39	42	0	3	1	1	0	0	0	–
1979 SEA A	2	3	.400	5.93	23	1	0	41	48	27	39	0	2	2	0	0	0	0	–
1981	0	1	.000	11.00	5	0	0	9	18	8	6	0	0	1	0	0	0	0	–
1982 CHI N	0	0	–	3.48	6	0	0	10.1	7	7	6	0	0	0	0	0	0	0	–
4 yrs.	5	6	.455	5.75	65	2	0	133	151	81	93	0	5	4	1	0	0	0	–

Ray Steineder

STEINEDER, RAYMOND
B. Nov. 13, 1895, Salem, N. J.   D. Aug. 25, 1982, Vineland, N. J.
BR TR 6'½"   160 lbs.

	W	L	PCT	ERA	G	GS	CG	IP	H	BB	SO	ShO	W	L	SV	AB	H	HR	BA
1923 PIT N	2	0	1.000	4.75	15	2	1	55	58	18	23	0	1	0	0	15	7	0	.467
1924 2 teams			PIT N (5G 0–1)					PHI N (9G 1–1)											
" total	1	2	.333	5.17	14	0	0	31.1	37	21	11	0	1	2	0	10	3	0	.300
2 yrs.	3	2	.600	4.90	29	2	1	86.1	95	39	34	0	2	2	0	25	10	0	.400

Ricky Steirer

STEIRER, RICKY FRANCIS
B. Aug. 27, 1956, Balso, Md.
BR TR 6'4"   200 lbs.

	W	L	PCT	ERA	G	GS	CG	IP	H	BB	SO	ShO	W	L	SV	AB	H	HR	BA
1982 CAL A	1	0	1.000	3.76	10	1	0	26.1	25	11	14	0	1	0	0	0	0	0	–
1983	3	2	.600	4.82	19	5	0	61.2	77	18	25	0	2	1	0	0	0	0	–
1984	0	1	.000	16.88	1	1	0	2.2	6	2	2	0	0	0	0	0	0	0	–
3 yrs.	4	3	.571	4.86	30	7	0	90.2	108	31	41	0	3	1	0	0	0	0	–

Bill Stellberger

STELLBERGER, WILLIAM F.
B. Apr. 22, 1865, Detroit, Mich.   D. Nov. 9, 1936, Detroit, Mich.

	W	L	PCT	ERA	G	GS	CG	IP	H	BB	SO	ShO	W	L	SV	AB	H	HR	BA
1885 PRO N	0	1	.000	7.88	1	1	1	8	14	4	0	0	0	0	0	4	0	0	.000

Jeff Stember

STEMBER, JEFFREY ALAN
B. Mar. 2, 1958, Elizabeth, N. J.
BR TR 6'5"   220 lbs.

	W	L	PCT	ERA	G	GS	CG	IP	H	BB	SO	ShO	W	L	SV	AB	H	HR	BA
1980 SF N	0	0	–	3.00	1	1	0	3	2	2	0	0	0	0	0	1	0	0	.000

Bill Stemmyer

STEMMYER, WILLIAM (Cannon Ball Bill)
B. May 6, 1865, Cleveland, Ohio   D. May 3, 1945, Cleveland, Ohio
BR TR 6'2"   190 lbs.

	W	L	PCT	ERA	G	GS	CG	IP	H	BB	SO	ShO	W	L	SV	AB	H	HR	BA
1885 BOS N	1	1	.500	0.00	2	2	2	11	7	11	8	1	0	0	0	7	3	0	.429
1886	22	18	.550	3.02	41	41	41	348.2	300	144	239	0	0	0	0	148	41	0	.277
1887	6	8	.429	5.20	15	14	14	119.1	138	41	41	0	0	0	1	47	12	1	.255
1888 CLE AA	0	2	.000	9.00	2	2	2	16	37	9	7	0	0	0	0	10	4	0	.400
4 yrs.	29	29	.500	3.67	60	59	59	495	482	205	295	1	0	0	1	212	60	1	.283

Dave Stenhouse

STENHOUSE, DAVID ROTCHFORD
B. Sept. 12, 1933, Westerly, R. I.
BR TR 6'   195 lbs.

	W	L	PCT	ERA	G	GS	CG	IP	H	BB	SO	ShO	W	L	SV	AB	H	HR	BA
1962 WAS A	11	12	.478	3.65	34	26	9	197	169	90	123	2	0	1	0	58	3	0	.052
1963	3	9	.250	4.55	16	16	2	87	90	45	47	1	0	0	0	25	2	0	.080
1964	2	7	.222	4.81	26	14	1	88	80	39	44	0	0	1	1	20	6	0	.300
3 yrs.	16	28	.364	4.14	76	56	12	372	339	174	214	3	0	2	1	103	11	0	.107

Buzz Stephen

STEPHEN, LOUIS ROBERTS
B. July 13, 1944, Porterville, Calif.
BR TR 6'4"   205 lbs.

	W	L	PCT	ERA	G	GS	CG	IP	H	BB	SO	ShO	W	L	SV	AB	H	HR	BA
1968 MIN A	1	1	.500	4.76	2	2	0	11.1	11	7	4	0	0	0	0	3	0	0	.000

Bryan Stephens

STEPHENS, BRYAN MARIS
B. July 14, 1920, Fayetteville, Ark.
BR TR 6'4"   175 lbs.

	W	L	PCT	ERA	G	GS	CG	IP	H	BB	SO	ShO	W	L	SV	AB	H	HR	BA
1947 CLE A	5	10	.333	4.01	31	5	1	92	79	39	34	0	4	6	1	27	3	0	.111
1948 STL A	3	6	.333	6.02	43	12	2	122.2	141	67	35	0	2	1	3	32	4	0	.125
2 yrs.	8	16	.333	5.16	74	17	3	214.2	220	106	69	0	6	7	4	59	7	0	.119

Clarence Stephens

STEPHENS, CLARENCE WRIGHT
B. Aug. 19, 1863, Cincinnati, Ohio   D. Feb. 28, 1945, Cincinnati, Ohio
TR

	W	L	PCT	ERA	G	GS	CG	IP	H	BB	SO	ShO	W	L	SV	AB	H	HR	BA
1886 CIN AA	1	0	1.000	5.63	1	1	1	8	9	5	6	0	0	0	0	5	3	0	.600
1891 CIN N	0	1	.000	7.88	1	1	1	8	9	3	3	0	0	0	0	3	0	0	.000
1892	0	1	.000	1.29	1	1	0	7	12	4	1	0	0	0	0	2	0	0	.000
3 yrs.	1	2	.333	5.09	3	3	2	23	30	12	10	0	0	0	0	10	3	0	.300

George Stephens

STEPHENS, GEORGE BENJAMIN
B. Sept. 28, 1867, Romeo, Mich.   D. Aug. 5, 1896, Armada, Mich.
5'10½"   170 lbs.

	W	L	PCT	ERA	G	GS	CG	IP	H	BB	SO	ShO	W	L	SV	AB	H	HR	BA
1892 BAL N	1	1	.500	2.79	5	2	2	29	37	9	7	0	0	0	1	13	0	0	.000
1893 WAS N	0	6	.000	5.80	9	6	6	63.2	83	31	14	0	0	0	0	29	3	0	.103
1894	0	1	.000	4.91	3	2	1	11	19	8	1	1	0	0	0	4	1	0	.250
3 yrs.	1	8	.111	4.86	17	10	9	103.2	139	48	22	1	0	0	1	46	4	0	.087

Earl Stephenson

STEPHENSON, CHESTER EARL
B. July 31, 1947, Benson, N. C.
BL TL 6'3"   175 lbs.

	W	L	PCT	ERA	G	GS	CG	IP	H	BB	SO	ShO	W	L	SV	AB	H	HR	BA
1971 CHI N	1	0	1.000	4.50	16	0	0	20	24	11	11	0	1	1	1	2	0	0	.000
1972 MIL A	3	5	.375	3.26	35	8	1	80	79	33	33	0	1	0	0	18	0	0	.000
1977 BAL A	0	0	–	9.00	1	0	0	3	5	0	2	0	0	0	0	0	0	0	–
1978	0	0	–	2.79	2	0	0	9.2	10	5	4	0	0	0	0	0	0	0	–
4 yrs.	4	5	.444	3.59	54	8	1	112.2	118	49	50	0	2	1	1	20	0	0	.000

	W	L	PCT	ERA	G	GS	CG	IP	H	BB	SO	ShO	Relief Pitching W	L	SV	BATTING AB	H	HR	BA

Jerry Stephenson

STEPHENSON, JERRY JOSEPH
Son of Joe Stephenson.
B. Oct. 6, 1943, Detroit, Mich. — BL TR 6'2" 185 lbs.

	W	L	PCT	ERA	G	GS	CG	IP	H	BB	SO	ShO	W	L	SV	AB	H	HR	BA
1963 BOS A	0	0	–	7.71	1	1	0	2.1	5	2	3	0	0	0	0	1	0	0	.000
1965	1	5	.167	6.23	15	8	0	52	62	33	49	0	0	0	0	13	3	0	.231
1966	2	5	.286	5.83	15	11	1	66.1	68	44	50	0	0	0	0	17	2	0	.118
1967	3	1	.750	3.86	8	6	0	39.2	32	16	24	0	0	0	1	16	4	0	.250
1968	2	8	.200	5.64	23	7	2	68.2	81	42	51	0	0	3	0	17	6	0	.353
1969 SEA A	0	0	–	10.13	2	0	0	2.2	6	3	1	0	0	0	0	0	0	0	–
1970 LA N	0	0	–	9.00	3	0	0	7	11	5	6	0	0	0	0	1	0	0	.000
7 yrs.	8	19	.296	5.69	67	33	3	238.2	265	145	184	0	0	3	1	65	15	0	.231
WORLD SERIES																			
1967 BOS A	0	0	–	9.00	1	0	0	2	3	1	0	0	0	0	0	0	0	0	–

John Sterling

STERLING, JOHN A.
B. Philadelphia, Pa. Deceased.

	W	L	PCT	ERA	G	GS	CG	IP	H	BB	SO	ShO	W	L	SV	AB	H	HR	BA
1890 PHI AA	0	1	.000	21.60	1	1	1	5	16	4	1	0	0	0	0	2	0	0	.000

Randy Sterling

STERLING, RANDALL WAYNE
B. Apr. 21, 1951, Key West, Fla. — BR TR 6'2" 195 lbs.

	W	L	PCT	ERA	G	GS	CG	IP	H	BB	SO	ShO	W	L	SV	AB	H	HR	BA
1974 NY N	1	1	.500	5.00	3	2	0	9	13	3	2	0	0	0	0	2	0	0	.000

Jim Stevens

STEVENS, JAMES ARTHUR (Harry)
B. Aug. 25, 1889, Williamsburg, Md. D. Sept. 25, 1966, Baltimore, Md. — BR TR 5'11" 180 lbs.

	W	L	PCT	ERA	G	GS	CG	IP	H	BB	SO	ShO	W	L	SV	AB	H	HR	BA
1914 WAS A	0	0	–	9.00	2	0	0	3	4	2	0	0	0	0	0	1	0	0	.000

Bunky Stewart

STEWART, VESTON GOFF
B. Jan. 7, 1931, Jasper, N. C. — BL TL 6' 154 lbs.

	W	L	PCT	ERA	G	GS	CG	IP	H	BB	SO	ShO	W	L	SV	AB	H	HR	BA
1952 WAS A	0	0	–	18.00	1	0	0	1	2	1	1	0	0	0	0	0	0	0	–
1953	0	2	.000	4.70	2	2	1	15.1	17	11	3	0	0	0	0	5	1	0	.200
1954	0	2	.000	7.64	29	2	0	50.2	67	27	27	0	0	1	1	3	0	0	.000
1955	0	0	–	4.11	7	1	0	15.1	18	6	10	0	0	0	0	2	0	0	.000
1956	5	7	.417	5.57	33	9	1	105	111	82	36	0	4	2	2	28	7	0	.250
5 yrs.	5	11	.313	6.01	72	14	2	187.1	215	127	77	0	4	3	3	38	8	0	.211

Dave Stewart

STEWART, DAVID KEITH
B. Feb. 19, 1957, Oakland, Calif. — BR TR 6'2" 200 lbs.

	W	L	PCT	ERA	G	GS	CG	IP	H	BB	SO	ShO	W	L	SV	AB	H	HR	BA
1978 LA N	0	0	–	0.00	1	0	0	2	1	0	1	0	0	0	0	0	0	0	–
1981	4	3	.571	2.51	32	0	0	43	40	14	29	0	4	3	6	5	2	0	.400
1982	9	8	.529	3.81	45	14	0	146.1	137	49	80	0	6	3	1	39	7	0	.179
1983 2 teams					LA N (46G 5–2)			TEX A (8G 5–2)											
" total	10	4	.714	2.60	54	9	2	135	117	50	78	0	5	2	8	7	1	0	.143
1984 TEX A	7	14	.333	4.73	32	27	3	192.1	193	87	119	0	0	1	0	0	0	0	–
5 yrs.	30	29	.508	3.71	164	50	5	518.2	488	200	307	0	15	9	15	51	10	0	.196
DIVISIONAL PLAYOFF SERIES																			
1981 LA N	0	2	.000	40.50	2	0	0	.2	4	0	1	0	0	2	0	0	0	0	–
WORLD SERIES																			
1981 LA N	0	0	–	0.00	2	0	0	1.2	1	1	2	1	0	0	0	0	0	0	–

Frank Stewart

STEWART, FRANK
B. Sept. 8, 1906, Minneapolis, Minn. — BR TR 6'½" 178 lbs.

	W	L	PCT	ERA	G	GS	CG	IP	H	BB	SO	ShO	W	L	SV	AB	H	HR	BA
1927 CHI A	0	1	.000	9.00	1	1	0	4	5	4	0	0	0	0	0	1	0	0	.000

Joe Stewart

STEWART, JOSEPH LAWRENCE
B. Mar. 11, 1879, Monroe, N. C. D. Feb. 10, 1913, Youngstown, Ohio — 5'11" 175 lbs.

	W	L	PCT	ERA	G	GS	CG	IP	H	BB	SO	ShO	W	L	SV	AB	H	HR	BA
1904 BOS N	0	0	–	9.64	2	0	0	9.1	12	4	1	0	0	0	0	5	1	0	.200

Lefty Stewart

STEWART, WALTER CLEVELAND
B. Sept. 23, 1900, Sparta, Tenn. D. Sept. 26, 1974, Knoxville, Tenn. — BR TL 5'10" 160 lbs.

	W	L	PCT	ERA	G	GS	CG	IP	H	BB	SO	ShO	W	L	SV	AB	H	HR	BA
1921 DET A	0	0	–	12.00	5	0	0	9	20	5	4	0	0	0	1	1	0	0	.000
1927 STL A	8	11	.421	4.28	27	19	11	155.2	187	43	43	0	0	1	1	49	15	0	.306
1928	7	9	.438	4.67	29	17	7	142.2	173	32	25	1	2	0	3	45	14	0	.275
1929	9	6	.600	3.25	29	18	8	149.1	137	49	47	1	1	1	0	51	6	0	.118
1930	20	12	.625	3.45	35	33	23	271	281	70	79	1	1	1	0	90	22	0	.244
1931	14	17	.452	4.40	36	33	20	258	287	85	89	1	1	1	0	88	22	0	.250
1932	14	19	.424	4.61	41	32	18	259.2	269	99	86	2	0	3	1	82	12	0	.146
1933 WAS A	15	6	.714	3.82	34	31	11	230.2	227	60	69	1	0	0	0	77	11	0	.143
1934	7	11	.389	4.03	24	22	7	152	184	36	36	1	0	1	0	45	7	0	.156
1935 2 teams					WAS A (1G 0–1)			CLE A (24G 6–6)											
" total	6	7	.462	5.67	25	11	2	93.2	130	19	25	1	2	2	2	31	6	0	.194
10 yrs.	100	98	.505	4.19	279	216	107	1721.2	1895	498	503	9	7	10	8	565	115	0	.204
WORLD SERIES																			
1933 WAS A	0	1	.000	9.00	1	1	0	2	6	0	0	0	0	0	0	1	0	0	.000

Mack Stewart

STEWART, WILLIAM MACKLIN
B. Sept. 23, 1914, Stevenson, Ala. D. Mar. 21, 1960, Macon, Ga. — BR TR 6' 167 lbs.

	W	L	PCT	ERA	G	GS	CG	IP	H	BB	SO	ShO	W	L	SV	AB	H	HR	BA
1944 CHI N	0	0	–	1.46	8	0	0	12.1	11	4	3	0	0	0	0	1	0	0	.000
1945	0	1	.000	4.76	16	1	0	28.1	37	14	9	0	0	0	0	3	1	0	.333
2 yrs.	0	1	.000	3.76	24	1	0	40.2	48	18	12	0	0	0	0	4	1	0	.250

Sammy Stewart

STEWART, SAMUEL LEE
B. Oct. 28, 1954, Asheville, N. C. — BR TR 6'3" 200 lbs.

	W	L	PCT	ERA	G	GS	CG	IP	H	BB	SO	ShO	W	L	SV	AB	H	HR	BA
1978 BAL A	1	1	.500	3.18	2	2	0	11.1	10	3	11	0	0	0	0	0	0	0	–
1979	8	5	.615	3.51	31	3	1	118	96	71	71	0	6	4	1	0	0	0	–
1980	7	7	.500	3.55	33	3	2	119	103	60	78	0	6	6	3	0	0	0	–

	W	L	PCT	ERA	G	GS	CG	IP	H	BB	SO	ShO	Relief Pitching W	L	SV	BATTING AB	H	HR	BA

Sammy Stewart continued

	W	L	PCT	ERA	G	GS	CG	IP	H	BB	SO	ShO	W	L	SV	AB	H	HR	BA
1981	4	8	.333	2.33	29	3	0	112	89	57	57	0	4	5	4	0	0	0	–
1982	10	9	.526	4.14	38	12	1	139	140	62	69	1	7	4	5	0	0	0	–
1983	9	4	.692	3.62	58	1	0	144.1	138	67	95	0	9	3	7	0	0	0	–
1984	7	4	.636	3.29	60	0	0	93	81	47	56	0	7	4	13	0	0	0	–
7 yrs.	46	38	.548	3.45	251	24	4	736.2	657	367	437	1	39	26	33	0	0	0	–

LEAGUE CHAMPIONSHIP SERIES

	W	L	PCT	ERA	G	GS	CG	IP	H	BB	SO	ShO	W	L	SV	AB	H	HR	BA
1983 BAL A	0	0	–	0.00	1	0	0	4.1	2	1	2	0	0	0	1	0	0	0	–

WORLD SERIES

	W	L	PCT	ERA	G	GS	CG	IP	H	BB	SO	ShO	W	L	SV	AB	H	HR	BA
1979 BAL A	0	0	–	0.00	1	0	0	2.2	4	1	0	0	0	0	0	1	0	0	.000
1983	0	0	–	0.00	3	0	0	5	2	2	6	0	0	0	0	2	0	0	.000
2 yrs.	0	0	–	0.00	4	0	0	7.2	6	3	6	0	0	0	0	3	0	0	.000

Dave Stieb

STIEB, DAVID ANDREW   BR TR 6'   185 lbs.
B. July 22, 1957, Santa Ana, Calif.

	W	L	PCT	ERA	G	GS	CG	IP	H	BB	SO	ShO	W	L	SV	AB	H	HR	BA
1979 TOR A	8	8	.500	4.33	18	18	7	129	139	48	52	1	0	0	0	0	0	0	–
1980	12	15	.444	3.70	34	32	14	243	232	83	108	4	0	0	0	1	0	0	.000
1981	11	10	.524	3.18	25	25	11	184	148	61	89	2	0	0	0	0	0	0	–
1982	17	14	.548	3.25	38	38	19	288.1	271	75	141	5	0	0	0	0	0	0	–
1983	17	12	.586	3.04	36	36	14	278	223	93	187	4	0	0	0	0	0	0	–
1984	16	8	.667	2.83	35	35	11	267	215	88	198	2	0	0	0	1	0	0	.000
6 yrs.	81	67	.547	3.30	186	184	76	1389.1	1228	448	775	18	0	0	0	0	0	0	–

Fred Stiely

STIELY, FRED WARREN   BB TL 5'8"   170 lbs.
B. June 1, 1901, Pillow, Pa.   D. Jan. 6, 1981, Valley View, Pa.

	W	L	PCT	ERA	G	GS	CG	IP	H	BB	SO	ShO	W	L	SV	AB	H	HR	BA
1929 STL A	1	0	1.000	0.00	1	1	1	9	11	3	2	0	0	0	0	3	2	0	.667
1930	0	1	.000	8.53	4	2	1	19	27	8	5	0	0	0	0	7	3	0	.429
1931	0	0	–	6.75	4	0	0	6.2	7	3	2	0	0	0	0	0	0	0	–
3 yrs.	1	1	.500	5.97	9	3	2	34.2	45	14	9	0	0	0	0	10	5	0	.500

Dick Stigman

STIGMAN, RICHARD LEWIS   BR TL 6'3"   200 lbs.
B. Jan. 24, 1936, Nimrod, Minn.

	W	L	PCT	ERA	G	GS	CG	IP	H	BB	SO	ShO	W	L	SV	AB	H	HR	BA
1960 CLE A	5	11	.313	4.51	41	18	3	133.2	118	87	104	0	2	3	9	36	8	0	.222
1961	2	5	.286	4.62	22	6	0	64.1	65	25	48	0	1	1	0	16	2	0	.125
1962 MIN A	12	5	.706	3.66	40	15	6	142.2	122	64	116	0	3	2	3	45	2	0	.044
1963	15	15	.500	3.25	33	33	15	241	210	81	193	3	0	0	0	84	9	0	.107
1964	6	15	.286	4.03	32	29	5	190	160	70	159	1	1	0	0	69	7	0	.101
1965	4	2	.667	4.37	33	8	0	70	59	33	70	0	4	2	4	15	2	0	.133
1966 BOS A	2	1	.667	5.44	34	10	1	81	85	46	65	1	1	0	0	17	2	0	.118
7 yrs.	46	54	.460	4.03	235	119	30	922.2	819	406	755	5	12	8	16	282	32	0	.113

Rollie Stiles

STILES, ROLLAND MAYS   BR TR 6'1½"   180 lbs.
B. Nov. 17, 1906, Ratcliff, Ark.

	W	L	PCT	ERA	G	GS	CG	IP	H	BB	SO	ShO	W	L	SV	AB	H	HR	BA
1930 STL A	3	6	.333	5.89	20	7	3	102.1	136	41	25	0	1	3	0	37	10	0	.270
1931	3	1	.750	7.22	34	2	0	81	112	60	32	0	2	0	0	22	1	0	.045
1933	3	7	.300	5.01	31	9	6	115	154	47	29	1	1	3	1	33	2	0	.061
3 yrs.	9	14	.391	5.91	85	18	9	298.1	402	148	86	1	4	6	1	92	13	0	.141

Archie Stimmel

STIMMEL, ARCHIBALD MAY (Lumbago)   BR TR 6'   175 lbs.
B. May 30, 1873, Woodsboro, Md.   D. Aug. 18, 1958, Frederick, Md.

	W	L	PCT	ERA	G	GS	CG	IP	H	BB	SO	ShO	W	L	SV	AB	H	HR	BA
1900 CIN N	1	1	.500	6.92	2	1	1	13	18	4	2	0	1	0	0	5	1	0	.200
1901	4	14	.222	4.11	20	18	14	153.1	170	44	55	1	0	0	0	62	5	0	.081
1902	0	4	.000	3.46	4	3	3	26	37	12	7	0	0	0	0	10	2	0	.200
3 yrs.	5	19	.208	4.21	26	22	18	192.1	225	60	64	1	1	0	0	77	8	0	.104

Carl Stimson

STIMSON, CARL REMUS   BR TR 6'5"   190 lbs.
B. July 18, 1894, Hamburg, Iowa   D. Nov. 9, 1936, Omaha, Neb.

	W	L	PCT	ERA	G	GS	CG	IP	H	BB	SO	ShO	W	L	SV	AB	H	HR	BA
1923 BOS A	0	0	–	22.50	2	0	0	4	12	5	1	0	0	0	0	2	0	0	.000

Harry Stine

STINE, HARRY C.   5'6"   150 lbs.
B. Feb. 20, 1864, Shenandoah, Pa.   D. June 5, 1924, Niagara Falls, N. Y.

	W	L	PCT	ERA	G	GS	CG	IP	H	BB	SO	ShO	W	L	SV	AB	H	HR	BA
1890 PHI AA	0	1	.000	9.00	1	1	1	8	17	4	1	0	0	0	0	3	0	0	.000

Lee Stine

STINE, LEE ELBERT   BR TR 5'11"   185 lbs.
B. Nov. 17, 1913, Stillwater, Okla.

	W	L	PCT	ERA	G	GS	CG	IP	H	BB	SO	ShO	W	L	SV	AB	H	HR	BA
1934 CHI A	0	0	–	8.18	4	0	0	11	11	10	8	0	0	0	0	1	0	0	.000
1935	0	0	–	9.00	1	0	0	2	2	3	1	0	0	0	0	0	0	0	–
1936 CIN N	3	8	.273	5.03	40	13	5	121.2	157	41	26	1	0	1	2	27	8	0	.296
1938 NY A	0	0	–	1.04	4	0	0	8.2	9	1	4	0	0	0	0	2	1	0	.500
4 yrs.	3	8	.273	5.09	49	13	5	143.1	179	55	39	1	0	1	2	30	9	0	.300

Jack Stivetts

STIVETTS, JOHN ELMER (Happy Jack)   BR TR 6'2"   185 lbs.
B. Mar. 31, 1868, Ashland, Pa.   D. Apr. 18, 1930, Ashland, Pa.

	W	L	PCT	ERA	G	GS	CG	IP	H	BB	SO	ShO	W	L	SV	AB	H	HR	BA
1889 STL AA	13	7	.650	2.25	26	20	18	191.2	153	68	143	2	3	1	1	79	18	0	.228
1890	29	20	.592	3.52	54	46	41	419.1	399	179	289	3	3	2	0	226	65	7	.288
1891	33	22	.600	2.86	64	56	40	440	357	232	259	3	4	1	1	302	92	7	.305
1892 BOS N	35	16	.686	3.04	53	48	45	414.2	346	171	180	3	2	1	1	240	71	3	.296
1893	19	13	.594	4.41	37	33	29	283.2	315	115	61	1	2	0	1	172	51	3	.297
1894	28	13	.683	4.90	45	39	30	338	429	127	76	0	3	1	0	244	80	8	.328
1895	17	17	.500	4.64	38	34	30	291	341	89	111	0	1	0	0	158	30	0	.190
1896	21	13	.618	4.10	42	36	31	329	353	99	71	2	1	0	0	221	76	3	.344
1897	12	5	.706	3.41	18	15	15	129.1	147	43	27	0	1	0	0	111	28	2	.252
1898	1	0	1.000	8.25	2	1	1	12	17	7	1	0	0	0	0	39	8	0	.205
1899 CLE N	0	4	.000	5.68	7	4	3	38	48	25	5	0	0	0	0	*			
11 yrs.	207	131	.612	3.74	386	332	278	2886.2	2905	1155	1223	14	19	7	4				

	W	L	PCT	ERA	G	GS	CG	IP	H	BB	SO	ShO	Relief Pitching W	L	SV	BATTING AB	H	HR	BA

Chuck Stobbs

STOBBS, CHARLES KLEIN
B. July 2, 1929, Wheeling, W. Va.   BL TL 6'1"   185 lbs.

Year/Team	W	L	PCT	ERA	G	GS	CG	IP	H	BB	SO	ShO	W	L	SV	AB	H	HR	BA
1947 BOS A	0	1	.000	6.00	4	1	0	9	10	10	5	0	0	0	0	1	0	0	.000
1948	0	0	–	6.43	6	0	0	7	9	7	4	0	0	0	0	1	0	0	.000
1949	11	6	.647	4.03	26	19	10	152	145	75	70	0	0	2	0	53	11	0	.208
1950	12	7	.632	5.10	32	21	6	169.1	158	88	78	0	1	1	1	57	14	0	.246
1951	10	9	.526	4.76	34	25	6	170	180	74	75	0	0	0	0	61	11	0	.180
1952 CHI A	7	12	.368	3.13	38	17	2	135	118	72	73	0	3	1	1	38	3	0	.079
1953 WAS A	11	8	.579	3.29	27	20	8	153	146	44	67	0	0	0	0	44	10	0	.227
1954	11	11	.500	4.10	31	24	10	182	189	67	67	3	1	0	0	51	7	0	.137
1955	4	14	.222	5.00	41	16	2	140.1	169	57	60	0	3	3	3	35	6	0	.171
1956	15	15	.500	3.60	37	33	15	240	264	54	97	1	1	0	1	84	15	0	.179
1957	8	20	.286	5.36	42	31	5	211.2	235	80	114	2	1	2	1	76	16	0	.211
1958 2 teams		WAS	A	(19G 2–6)		STL	N	(17G 1–3)											
" total	3	9	.250	5.04	36	8	0	96.1	127	30	48	0	2	3	1	16	1	0	.063
1959 WAS A	1	8	.111	2.98	41	7	0	90.2	82	24	50	0	0	3	7	19	2	0	.105
1960	12	7	.632	3.32	40	13	1	119.1	115	38	72	1	6	2	2	34	3	0	.088
1961 MIN A	2	3	.400	7.46	24	3	0	44.2	56	15	17	0	2	1	2	8	3	0	.375
15 yrs.	107	130	.451	4.29	459	238	65	1920.1	2003	735	897	7	20	18	19	578	102	0	.176

Wes Stock

STOCK, WESLEY GAY
B. Apr. 10, 1934, Longview, Wash.   BR TR 6'2"   188 lbs.

Year/Team	W	L	PCT	ERA	G	GS	CG	IP	H	BB	SO	ShO	W	L	SV	AB	H	HR	BA
1959 BAL A	0	0	–	3.55	7	0	0	12.2	16	2	8	0	0	0	1	2	0	0	.000
1960	2	2	.500	2.88	17	0	0	34.1	26	14	23	0	2	2	2	6	0	0	.000
1961	5	0	1.000	3.01	35	1	0	71.2	58	27	47	0	5	0	3	11	0	0	.000
1962	3	2	.600	4.43	53	0	0	65	50	36	34	0	3	2	3	3	0	0	.000
1963	7	0	1.000	3.94	47	0	0	75.1	69	31	55	0	7	0	1	10	0	0	.000
1964 2 teams		BAL	A	(14G 2–0)		KC	A	(50G 6–3)											
" total	8	3	.727	2.30	64	0	0	113.2	86	42	115	0	8	3	5	19	3	0	.158
1965 KC A	0	4	.000	5.24	62	2	0	99.2	96	40	52	0	0	3	4	6	0	0	.000
1966	2	2	.500	2.66	35	0	0	44	30	21	31	0	2	2	3	2	0	0	.000
1967	0	0	–	18.00	1	0	0	1	3	2	0	0	0	0	0	0	0	0	–
9 yrs.	27	13	.675	3.60	321	3	0	517.1	434	215	365	0	27	12	22	59	3	0	.051

Otis Stockdale

STOCKDALE, OTIS HINKLEY
B. Aug. 7, 1871, Carroll County, Md.   D. Mar. 15, 1933, Pennsville, N. J.   5'10½" 180 lbs.

Year/Team	W	L	PCT	ERA	G	GS	CG	IP	H	BB	SO	ShO	W	L	SV	AB	H	HR	BA
1893 WAS N	2	8	.200	8.22	11	11	7	69	111	32	12	0	0	0	0	40	12	0	.300
1894	5	9	.357	5.06	18	14	11	117.1	176	42	10	0	0	1	0	71	23	0	.324
1895 2 teams		WAS	N	(20G 6–11)		BOS	N	(4G 2–2)											
" total	8	13	.381	6.06	24	21	12	159	230	60	25	0	0	0	1	89	27	0	.303
1896 BAL N	0	1	.000	16.20	1	0	0	1.2	4	2	1	0	0	1	0	3	1	0	.333
4 yrs.	15	31	.326	6.20	54	46	30	347	521	136	48	0	0	2	1	203	63	0	.310

Bob Stoddard

STODDARD, ROBERT LYLE
B. Mar. 8, 1957, Morgan Hill, Calif.   BR TR 6'1"   190 lbs.

Year/Team	W	L	PCT	ERA	G	GS	CG	IP	H	BB	SO	ShO	W	L	SV	AB	H	HR	BA
1981 SEA A	2	1	.667	2.57	5	5	1	35	35	9	22	0	0	0	0	0	0	0	–
1982	3	3	.500	2.41	9	9	2	67.1	48	18	24	1	0	0	0	0	0	0	–
1983	9	17	.346	4.41	35	23	2	175.2	182	58	87	1	1	4	0	0	0	0	–
1984	2	3	.400	5.13	27	6	0	79	86	37	39	0	2	1	0	0	0	0	–
4 yrs.	16	24	.400	4.01	76	43	5	357	351	122	172	2	3	5	0	0	0	0	–

Tim Stoddard

STODDARD, TIMOTHY PAUL
B. Jan. 24, 1953, East Chicago, Ind.   BR TR 6'7"   230 lbs.

Year/Team	W	L	PCT	ERA	G	GS	CG	IP	H	BB	SO	ShO	W	L	SV	AB	H	HR	BA
1975 CHI A	0	0	–	9.00	1	0	0	1	2	0	0	0	0	0	0	0	0	0	–
1978 BAL A	0	1	.000	6.00	8	0	0	18	22	8	14	0	0	1	0	0	0	0	–
1979	3	1	.750	1.71	29	0	0	58	44	19	47	0	3	1	3	0	0	0	–
1980	5	3	.625	2.51	64	0	0	86	72	38	64	0	5	3	26	0	0	0	–
1981	4	2	.667	3.89	31	0	0	37	38	18	32	0	4	2	7	0	0	0	–
1982	3	4	.429	4.02	50	0	0	56	53	29	42	0	3	4	12	0	0	0	–
1983	4	3	.571	6.09	47	0	0	57.2	65	29	50	0	4	3	9	0	0	0	–
1984 CHI N	10	6	.625	3.82	58	0	0	92	77	57	87	0	10	6	7	11	1	0	.091
8 yrs.	29	20	.592	3.71	288	0	0	405.2	373	198	336	0	29	20	64	11	1	0	.091

LEAGUE CHAMPIONSHIP SERIES

Year/Team	W	L	PCT	ERA	G	GS	CG	IP	H	BB	SO	ShO	W	L	SV	AB	H	HR	BA
1984 CHI N	0	0	–	4.50	2	0	0	2	1	2	2	0	0	0	0	0	0	0	–

WORLD SERIES

Year/Team	W	L	PCT	ERA	G	GS	CG	IP	H	BB	SO	ShO	W	L	SV	AB	H	HR	BA
1979 BAL A	1	0	1.000	5.40	4	0	0	5	6	1	3	0	1	0	0	1	1	0	1.000

Art Stokes

STOKES, ARTHUR MILTON
B. Sept. 13, 1896, Emmitsburg, Md.   D. June 3, 1962, Titusville, Pa.   BR TR 5'10½" 155 lbs.

Year/Team	W	L	PCT	ERA	G	GS	CG	IP	H	BB	SO	ShO	W	L	SV	AB	H	HR	BA
1925 PHI A	1	1	.500	4.07	12	0	0	24.1	24	10	7	0	1	1	0	4	0	0	.000

Arnie Stone

STONE, EDWIN ARNOLD
B. Dec. 19, 1892, North Creek, N. Y.   D. July 29, 1948, Hudson Falls, N. Y.   BR TL 6'   180 lbs.

Year/Team	W	L	PCT	ERA	G	GS	CG	IP	H	BB	SO	ShO	W	L	SV	AB	H	HR	BA
1923 PIT N	0	1	.000	8.03	9	0	0	12.1	19	4	2	0	0	1	0	1	0	0	.000
1924	4	2	.667	2.95	26	2	1	64	57	15	7	0	3	1	0	15	2	0	.133
2 yrs.	4	3	.571	3.77	35	2	1	76.1	76	19	9	0	3	2	0	16	2	0	.125

Dean Stone

STONE, DARRAH DEAN
B. Sept. 1, 1930, Moline, Ill.   BL TL 6'4"   205 lbs.

Year/Team	W	L	PCT	ERA	G	GS	CG	IP	H	BB	SO	ShO	W	L	SV	AB	H	HR	BA
1953 WAS A	0	1	.000	8.31	3	1	0	8.2	13	5	5	0	0	0	0	2	0	0	.000
1954	12	10	.545	3.22	31	23	10	178.2	161	69	87	2	1	0	0	52.	5	1	.096
1955	6	13	.316	4.15	43	24	5	180	180	114	84	1	0	2	1	46	2	0	.043
1956	5	7	.417	6.27	41	21	2	132	148	93	86	0	0	1	3	34	3	0	.088
1957 2 teams		WAS	A	(3G 0–0)		BOS	A	(17G 1–3)											
" total	1	3	.250	5.27	20	8	0	54.2	61	37	35	0	0	0	1	14	0	0	.000
1959 STL N	0	1	.000	4.20	18	1	0	30	30	16	17	0	0	0	1	4	0	0	.000

	W	L	PCT	ERA	G	GS	CG	IP	H	BB	SO	ShO	Relief Pitching W	L	SV	AB	H	HR	BA

Mike Sullivan continued

	W	L	PCT	ERA	G	GS	CG	IP	H	BB	SO	ShO	W	L	SV	AB	H	HR	BA
1899	1	0	1.000	5.00	1	1	1	9	10	4	1	0	0	0	0	3	1	0	.333
11 yrs.	54	66	.450	5.11	163	121	99	1123.1	1311	577	286	1	9	5	4	494	97	2	.196

Pat Sullivan

SULLIVAN, PATRICK B.
B. Dec. 22, 1862, Milwaukee, Wis.   D. Mar. 29, 1886
TR 5'11" 165 lbs.

	W	L	PCT	ERA	G	GS	CG	IP	H	BB	SO	ShO	W	L	SV	AB	H	HR	BA
1884 KC U	0	1	.000	11.57	1	1	0	7	15	5	1	0	0	0	0	*			

Sleeper Sullivan

SULLIVAN, THOMAS JEFFERSON
B. St. Louis, Mo.   D. Sept. 25, 1899, Camden, N. J.
BR 175 lbs.

	W	L	PCT	ERA	G	GS	CG	IP	H	BB	SO	ShO	W	L	SV	AB	H	HR	BA
1882 STL AA	0	1	.000	8.00	1	1	1	9	15	1	0	0	0	0	0	188	34	0	.181
1884 STL U	1	0	1.000	4.50	1	1	0	6	10	0	3	0	0	0	0	9	1	0	.111
2 yrs.	1	1	.500	6.60	2	2	1	15	25	1	3	0	0	0	0	*			

Suter Sullivan

SULLIVAN, SUTER G.
B. Oct. 14, 1872, Baltimore, Md.   D. Apr. 19, 1925, Baltimore, Md.

	W	L	PCT	ERA	G	GS	CG	IP	H	BB	SO	ShO	W	L	SV	AB	H	HR	BA
1898 STL N	0	0	—	1.50	1	0	0	6	10	4	3	0	0	0	0	*			

Tom Sullivan

SULLIVAN, THOMAS AUGUST
B. Oct. 18, 1897, Boston, Mass.   D. Sept. 23, 1962, Boston, Mass.
BL TL 5'11" 178 lbs.

	W	L	PCT	ERA	G	GS	CG	IP	H	BB	SO	ShO	W	L	SV	AB	H	HR	BA
1922 PHI N	0	0	—	11.25	3	0	0	8	16	5	2	0	0	0	0	4	1	1	.250

Tom Sullivan

SULLIVAN, THOMAS AUGUSTIN
B. Mar. 1, 1860, New York, N. Y.   D. Apr. 12, 1947, Cincinnati, Ohio

	W	L	PCT	ERA	G	GS	CG	IP	H	BB	SO	ShO	W	L	SV	AB	H	HR	BA
1884 COL AA	2	2	.500	4.06	4	4	4	31	42	3	12	0	0	0	0	11	1	0	.091
1886 LOU AA	2	7	.222	3.96	9	9	8	75	94	33	27	0	0	0	0	27	3	0	.111
1888 KC AA	8	16	.333	3.40	24	24	24	214.2	227	68	84	0	0	0	0	92	10	0	.109
1889	2	8	.200	5.67	10	10	10	87.1	111	48	24	0	0	0	0	33	5	0	.152
4 yrs.	14	33	.298	4.04	47	47	46	408	474	152	147	0	0	0	0	163	19	0	.117

Ed Summers

SUMMERS, ORON EDGAR (Kickapoo)
B. Dec. 5, 1884, Ladoga, Ind.   D. May 12, 1953, Indianapolis, Ind.
BB TR 6'2" 180 lbs.

	W	L	PCT	ERA	G	GS	CG	IP	H	BB	SO	ShO	W	L	SV	AB	H	HR	BA
1908 DET A	24	12	.667	1.64	40	32	24	301	271	55	103	5	5	0	1	113	14	0	.124
1909	19	9	.679	2.24	35	32	24	281.2	243	52	107	3	3	0	0	94	10	0	.106
1910	13	12	.520	2.53	30	25	18	220.1	211	60	82	1	1	1	0	76	14	2	.184
1911	11	11	.500	3.66	30	20	13	179.1	189	51	65	0	0	2	1	63	16	0	.254
1912	1	1	.500	4.86	3	3	1	16.2	16	3	5	0	0	0	0	6	3	0	.500
5 yrs.	68	45	.602	2.42	138	112	80	999	930	221	362	9	9	3	3	352	57	2	.162

WORLD SERIES

	W	L	PCT	ERA	G	GS	CG	IP	H	BB	SO	ShO	W	L	SV	AB	H	HR	BA
1908 DET A	0	2	.000	4.30	2	1	0	14.2	18	4	7	0	0	1	0	5	1	0	.200
1909	0	2	.000	8.59	2	2	0	7.1	13	4	4	0	0	0	0	3	0	0	.000
2 yrs. 7th	0	4	.000	5.73	4	3	0	22	31	8	11	0	0	1	0	8	1	0	.125

Billy Sunday

SUNDAY, WILLIAM ASHLEY (The Evangelist)
B. Nov. 19, 1862, Ames, Iowa   D. Nov. 6, 1935, Chicago, Ill.
BL TR 5'10" 160 lbs.

	W	L	PCT	ERA	G	GS	CG	IP	H	BB	SO	ShO	W	L	SV	AB	H	HR	BA
1890 PHI N	0	0	—	∞	1	0	0			2	0	0	0	0	0	*			

Gordie Sundin

SUNDIN, GORDON VINCENT
B. Oct. 10, 1937, Minneapolis, Minn.
BR TR 6'4" 215 lbs.

	W	L	PCT	ERA	G	GS	CG	IP	H	BB	SO	ShO	W	L	SV	AB	H	HR	BA
1956 BAL A	0	0	—	∞	1	0	0		0	2	0	0	0	0	0	0	0	0	—

Steve Sundra

SUNDRA, STEPHEN RICHARD (Smokey)
B. Mar. 27, 1910, Luxor, Pa.
D. Mar. 23, 1952, Cleveland, Ohio
BB TR 6'1" 185 lbs.
BR 1941-43

	W	L	PCT	ERA	G	GS	CG	IP	H	BB	SO	ShO	W	L	SV	AB	H	HR	BA
1936 NY A	0	0	—	0.00	1	0	0	2	2	2	1	0	0	0	0	1	0	0	.000
1938	6	4	.600	4.80	25	8	3	93.2	107	43	33	0	3	2	0	33	6	0	.182
1939	11	1	.917	2.76	24	11	8	120.2	110	56	27	1	3	0	0	49	13	0	.265
1940	4	6	.400	5.53	27	8	2	99.1	121	42	26	0	2	2	2	29	4	0	.138
1941 WAS A	9	13	.409	5.29	28	23	11	168.1	203	61	50	0	0	0	0	60	13	0	.217
1942 2 teams		WAS	A (6G 1–3)		STL	A	(20G 8–3)												
" total	9	6	.600	4.24	26	17	8	144.1	165	44	31	0	1	0	0	52	11	1	.212
1943 STL A	15	11	.577	3.25	32	29	13	208	212	66	44	3	0	1	0	73	16	0	.219
1944	2	0	1.000	1.42	3	3	2	19	15	4	1	0	0	0	0	5	0	0	.000
1946	0	0	—	11.25	2	0	0	4	9	3	1	0	0	0	0	0	0	0	—
9 yrs.	56	41	.577	4.17	168	99	47	859.1	944	321	214	4	9	5	2	302	63	2	.209

WORLD SERIES

	W	L	PCT	ERA	G	GS	CG	IP	H	BB	SO	ShO	W	L	SV	AB	H	HR	BA
1939 NY A	0	0	—	0.00	1	0	0	2.2	4	1	2	0	0	0	0	0	0	0	—

Tom Sunkel

SUNKEL, THOMAS JACOB (Lefty)
B. Aug. 9, 1912, Paris, Ill.
BL TL 6'1" 190 lbs.

	W	L	PCT	ERA	G	GS	CG	IP	H	BB	SO	ShO	W	L	SV	AB	H	HR	BA
1937 STL N	0	0	—	2.06	9	1	0	39.1	24	11	9	0	0	0	1	9	1	0	.111
1939	4	4	.500	4.22	20	11	2	85.1	79	56	54	1	0	0	0	28	9	0	.321
1941 NY N	1	1	.500	2.93	2	2	1	15.1	7	12	14	1	0	0	0	6	2	0	.333
1942	3	6	.333	4.81	19	11	3	63.2	65	41	29	0	0	0	0	19	2	0	.105
1943	0	1	.000	10.13	1	0	0	2.2	4	3	0	0	0	0	0	0	0	0	—
1944 BKN N	1	3	.250	7.50	12	3	0	24	39	10	6	0	1	1	1	4	0	0	.000
6 yrs.	9	15	.375	4.34	63	29	6	230.1	218	133	112	2	1	1	2	66	14	0	.212

Max Surkont

SURKONT, MATTHEW CONSTANTINE
B. June 16, 1922, Central Falls, R. I.
BR TR 6'1" 195 lbs.

	W	L	PCT	ERA	G	GS	CG	IP	H	BB	SO	ShO	W	L	SV	AB	H	HR	BA
1949 CHI A	3	5	.375	4.78	44	2	0	96	92	60	38	0	3	4	4	22	1	0	.045
1950 BOS N	5	2	.714	3.23	9	6	2	55.2	63	20	21	0	2	0	0	23	10	1	.435
1951	12	16	.429	3.99	37	33	11	237	230	89	110	2	1	0	1	73	11	0	.151
1952	12	13	.480	3.77	31	29	12	215	201	76	125	1	0	0	0	63	7	0	.111

	W	L	PCT	ERA	G	GS	CG	IP	H	BB	SO	ShO	Relief Pitching W	L	SV	BATTING AB	H	HR	BA

Max Surkont continued

	W	L	PCT	ERA	G	GS	CG	IP	H	BB	SO	ShO	W	L	SV	AB	H	HR	BA
1953 MIL N	11	5	.688	4.18	28	24	11	170	168	64	83	2	0	0	0	56	16	0	.286
1954 PIT N	9	18	.333	4.41	33	29	11	208.1	216	78	78	0	1	0	0	60	10	0	.167
1955	7	14	.333	5.57	35	22	5	166.1	194	78	84	0	1	1	2	50	7	0	.140
1956 3 teams			PIT N	(1G 0–0)		STL N	(5G 0–0)		NY	N	(8G 2–2)								
" total	2	2	.500	5.45	14	4	1	39.2	36	14	24	0	0	1	0	10	1	0	.100
1957 NY N	0	1	.000	9.95	5	0	0	6.1	9	2	8	0	0	1	0	0	0	0	—
9 yrs.	61	76	.445	4.38	236	149	53	1194.1	1209	481	571	7	8	6	8	357	63	1	.176

George Susce

SUSCE, GEORGE DANIEL
Son of George Susce.
B. Sept. 13, 1931, Pittsburgh, Pa. BR TR 6'1" 180 lbs.

	W	L	PCT	ERA	G	GS	CG	IP	H	BB	SO	ShO	W	L	SV	AB	H	HR	BA
1955 BOS A	9	7	.563	3.06	29	15	6	144.1	123	49	60	1	2	1	1	49	7	0	.143
1956	2	4	.333	6.20	21	6	0	69.2	71	44	26	0	2	1	0	18	4	0	.222
1957	3	2	.700	4.28	29	5	0	88.1	93	41	40	0	1	1	1	25	3	0	.120
1958 2 teams			BOS	A	(2G 0–0)		DET	A	(27G 4–3)										
" total	4	3	.571	3.98	29	10	2	92.2	96	27	42	0	3	2	1	24	3	0	.125
1959 DET A	0	0	—	12.89	9	0	0	14.2	24	9	9	0	0	0	0	1	0	0	.000
5 yrs.	22	17	.564	4.42	117	36	8	409.2	407	170	177	1	13	5	3	117	17	0	.145

Rick Sutcliffe

SUTCLIFFE, RICHARD LEE
B. June 21, 1956, Independence, Mo. BL TR 6'7" 215 lbs.

	W	L	PCT	ERA	G	GS	CG	IP	H	BB	SO	ShO	W	L	SV	AB	H	HR	BA
1976 LA N	0	0	—	0.00	1	1	0	5	2	1	3	0	0	0	0	1	0	0	.000
1978	0	0	—	0.00	2	0	0	2	2	1	0	0	0	0	0	0	0	0	—
1979	17	10	.630	3.46	39	30	5	242	217	97	117	1	1	2	0	85	21	1	.247
1980	3	9	.250	5.56	42	10	1	110	122	55	59	1	2	5	5	27	4	0	.148
1981	2	2	.500	4.02	14	6	0	47	41	20	16	0	0	0	0	11	2	0	.182
1982 CLE A	14	8	.636	**2.96**	34	27	6	216	174	98	142	1	2	1	1	0	0	0	—
1983	17	11	.607	4.29	36	35	10	243.1	251	102	160	2	1	0	0	0	0	0	—
1984 2 teams			CLE	A	(15G 4–5)		CHI	N	(20G 16–1)										
" total	20	6	.769	3.64	35	35	9	244.2	234	85	213	3	0	0	0	56	14	0	.250
8 yrs.	73	46	.613	3.79	203	144	31	1110	1043	459	710	8	6	8	6	180	41	1	.228

LEAGUE CHAMPIONSHIP SERIES

| 1984 CHI N | 1 | 1 | .500 | 3.38 | 2 | 2 | 0 | 13.1 | 9 | 8 | 10 | 0 | 0 | 0 | 0 | 6 | 3 | 1 | .500 |

Rube Suter

SUTER, HARRY RICHARD
B. Sept. 15, 1887, Independence, Mo. D. July 24, 1971, Topeka, Kans. TL

	W	L	PCT	ERA	G	GS	CG	IP	H	BB	SO	ShO	W	L	SV	AB	H	HR	BA
1909 CHI A	2	3	.400	2.47	18	6	3	87.1	72	28	53	1	0	0	1	32	3	0	.094

Darrell Sutherland

SUTHERLAND, DARRELL WAYNE
Brother of Gary Sutherland.
B. Nov. 14, 1941, Glendale, Calif. BR TR 6'4" 169 lbs.

	W	L	PCT	ERA	G	GS	CG	IP	H	BB	SO	ShO	W	L	SV	AB	H	HR	BA
1964 NY N	0	3	.000	7.76	10	4	0	26.2	32	12	9	0	0	0	0	5	1	0	.200
1965	3	1	.750	2.81	18	2	0	48	33	17	16	0	3	0	0	13	2	0	.154
1966	2	0	1.000	4.87	31	0	0	44.1	60	25	23	0	2	0	1	3	2	0	.667
1968 CLE A	0	0	—	8.10	3	0	0	3.1	6	4	2	0	0	0	0	0	0	0	—
4 yrs.	5	4	.556	4.78	62	6	0	122.1	131	58	50	0	5	0	1	21	5	0	.238

Dizzy Sutherland

SUTHERLAND, HOWARD ALVIN
B. Apr. 9, 1923, Washington, D. C. D. Aug. 21, 1979, Washington, D. C. BL TL 6' 200 lbs.

	W	L	PCT	ERA	G	GS	CG	IP	H	BB	SO	ShO	W	L	SV	AB	H	HR	BA
1949 WAS A	0	1	.000	45.00	1	1	0	2	6	0	0	0	0	0	0	0	0	0	—

Suds Sutherland

SUTHERLAND, HARVEY SCOTT
B. Feb. 20, 1894, Coburg, Ore. D. May 11, 1972, Portland, Ore. BR TR 6' 180 lbs.

	W	L	PCT	ERA	G	GS	CG	IP	H	BB	SO	ShO	W	L	SV	AB	H	HR	BA
1921 DET A	6	2	.750	4.97	13	8	3	58	80	18	18	0	2	2	0	27	11	0	.407

Bruce Sutter

SUTTER, HOWARD BRUCE
B. Jan. 8, 1953, Lancaster, Pa. BR TR 6'2" 190 lbs.

	W	L	PCT	ERA	G	GS	CG	IP	H	BB	SO	ShO	W	L	SV	AB	H	HR	BA
1976 CHI N	6	3	.667	2.71	52	0	0	83	63	26	73	0	6	3	10	8	0	0	.000
1977	7	3	.700	1.35	62	0	0	107	69	23	129	0	7	3	31	20	3	0	.150
1978	8	10	.444	3.18	64	0	0	99	82	34	106	0	8	10	27	13	1	0	.077
1979	6	6	.500	2.23	62	0	0	101	67	32	110	0	6	6	37	12	3	0	.250
1980	5	8	.385	2.65	60	0	0	102	90	34	76	0	5	8	28	9	1	0	.111
1981 STL N	3	5	.375	2.63	48	0	0	82	64	24	57	0	3	5	25	9	0	0	.000
1982	9	8	.529	2.90	70	0	0	102.1	88	34	61	0	9	8	36	8	1	0	.125
1983	9	10	.474	4.23	60	0	0	89.1	90	30	64	0	9	10	21	7	0	0	.000
1984	5	7	.417	1.54	71	0	0	122.2	109	23	77	0	5	7	45[1]	10	0	0	.000
9 yrs.	58	60	.492	2.54	549	0	0	888.1	722	260	753	0	58	60	260 2nd	96	9	0	.094

LEAGUE CHAMPIONSHIP SERIES

| 1982 STL N | 1 | 0 | 1.000 | 0.00 | 2 | 0 | 0 | 4.1 | 0 | 1 | 1 | 0 | 1 | 0 | 1 | 1 | 0 | 0 | .000 |

WORLD SERIES

| 1982 STL N | 1 | 0 | 1.000 | 4.70 | 4 | 0 | 0 | 7.2 | 6 | 3 | 6 | 0 | 1 | 0 | 2 | 0 | 0 | 0 | — |

Jack Sutthoff

SUTTHOFF, JOHN GERHARD (Sunny Jack)
B. June 29, 1873, Cincinnati, Ohio D. Aug. 3, 1942, Cincinnati, Ohio BR TR 5'9" 175 lbs.

	W	L	PCT	ERA	G	GS	CG	IP	H	BB	SO	ShO	W	L	SV	AB	H	HR	BA
1898 WAS N	0	0	—	12.96	2	1	0	8.1	16	8	3	0	0	0	0	3	1	0	.333
1899 STL N	1	1	.500	10.38	2	2	1	13	19	10	4	0	0	0	0	6	0	0	.000
1901 CIN N	1	3	.250	5.50	10	4	4	70.1	82	39	12	0	0	0	0	28	3	0	.107
1903	16	10	.615	2.80	30	27	21	224.2	207	79	76	3	0	0	0	84	12	0	.143
1904 2 teams			CIN	N	(12G 5–6)		PHI	N	(19G 6–13)										
" total	11	19	.367	3.19	31	28	25	253.2	255	114	73	1	2	1	0	94	16	0	.170
1905 PHI N	3	4	.429	3.81	13	6	4	78	82	36	26	1	0	1	0	25	2	0	.080
6 yrs.	32	37	.464	3.65	88	68	55	648	661	286	194	4	2	2	0	240	34	0	.142

	W	L	PCT	ERA	G	GS	CG	IP	H	BB	SO	ShO	Relief W	L	SV	AB	H	HR	BA

Josh Swindell

SWINDELL, JOSHUA ERNEST
B. July 5, 1883, Rose Hill, Kans.   D. Mar. 19, 1969, Fruita, Colo.
BR TR 6'   180 lbs.

	W	L	PCT	ERA	G	GS	CG	IP	H	BB	SO	ShO	W	L	SV	AB	H	HR	BA
1911 CLE A	0	1	.000	2.08	4	1	1	17.1	19	4	6	0	0	0	0	4	1	0	.250
1913	0	0	—	0.00	0	0	0		0	0	0	0	0	0	0	0	0	0	—
2 yrs.	0	1	.000	2.08	4	1	1	17.1	19	4	6	0	0	0	0	4	1	0	.250

Len Swormstedt

SWORMSTEDT, LEONARD B.
B. Oct. 6, 1878, Cincinnati, Ohio   D. July 19, 1964, Salem, Mass.
BR TR 5'11½" 165 lbs.

	W	L	PCT	ERA	G	GS	CG	IP	H	BB	SO	ShO	W	L	SV	AB	H	HR	BA
1901 CIN N	2	1	.667	1.73	3	3	3	26	19	5	13	0	0	0	0	9	0	0	.000
1902	0	2	.000	4.00	2	2	2	18	22	5	3	0	0	0	0	6	0	0	.000
1906 BOS N	1	1	.500	1.29	3	2	2	21	17	0	6	0	0	0	0	8	1	0	.125
3 yrs.	3	4	.429	2.22	8	7	7	65	58	10	22	0	0	0	0	23	1	0	.043

Bob Sykes

SYKES, ROBERT JOSEPH
B. Dec. 11, 1954, Neptune, N. J.
BB TL 6'1"   195 lbs.

	W	L	PCT	ERA	G	GS	CG	IP	H	BB	SO	ShO	W	L	SV	AB	H	HR	BA
1977 DET A	5	7	.417	4.40	32	20	3	133	141	50	58	0	0	1	0	0	0	0	—
1978	6	6	.500	3.94	22	10	3	93.2	99	34	58	2	3	1	2	0	0	0	—
1979 STL N	4	3	.571	6.18	13	11	0	67	86	34	35	0	0	0	0	21	2	0	.095
1980	6	10	.375	4.64	27	19	4	126	134	54	50	3	0	3	0	39	4	0	.103
1981	2	0	1.000	4.62	22	1	0	37	37	18	14	0	2	0	0	2	0	0	.000
5 yrs.	23	26	.469	4.65	116	61	10	456.2	497	190	215	5	5	5	2	62	6	0	.097

Lou Sylvester

SYLVESTER, LOUIS J.
B. Feb. 14, 1855, Springfield, Ill.   Deceased.
BR TR 5'3"   165 lbs.

	W	L	PCT	ERA	G	GS	CG	IP	H	BB	SO	ShO	W	L	SV	AB	H	HR	BA
1884 CIN U	0	1	.000	3.58	6	1	1	32.2	32	6	7	0	0	0	1	*			

John Taber

TABER, JOHN PARDON
B. June 28, 1868, Acushnet, Mass.   D. Feb. 21, 1940, Boston, Mass.
BR TR 5'3"   165 lbs.

	W	L	PCT	ERA	G	GS	CG	IP	H	BB	SO	ShO	W	L	SV	AB	H	HR	BA
1890 BOS N	0	1	.000	4.15	2	1	1	13	11	8	3	0	0	0	1	6	0	0	.000

Lefty Taber

TABER, EDWARD TIMOTHY
B. Jan. 11, 1900, Rock Island, Ill.   D. Nov. 5, 1983, Lincoln, Neb.
BL TL 6'   180 lbs.

	W	L	PCT	ERA	G	GS	CG	IP	H	BB	SO	ShO	W	L	SV	AB	H	HR	BA
1926 PHI N	0	0	—	7.56	6	0	0	8.1	8	5	0	0	0	0	0	1	0	0	.000
1927	0	1	.000	18.90	3	1	0	3.1	8	5	0	0	0	0	0	1	0	0	.000
2 yrs.	0	1	.000	10.80	9	1	0	11.2	16	10	0	0	0	0	0	2	0	0	.000

John Taff

TAFF, JOHN GALLATIN
B. June 3, 1890, Austin, Tex.   D. May 15, 1961, Houston, Tex.
BR TR 6'   170 lbs.

	W	L	PCT	ERA	G	GS	CG	IP	H	BB	SO	ShO	W	L	SV	AB	H	HR	BA
1913 PHI A	0	1	.000	6.62	7	1	0	17.2	22	5	9	0	0	0	1	5	1	0	.200

Doug Taitt

TAITT, DOUGLAS JOHN (Poco)
B. Aug. 3, 1902, Bay City, Mich.   D. Dec. 12, 1970, Portland, Ore.
BL TR 6'   176 lbs.

	W	L	PCT	ERA	G	GS	CG	IP	H	BB	SO	ShO	W	L	SV	AB	H	HR	BA
1928 BOS A	0	0	—	27.00	1	0	0	1	2	2	1	0	0	0	0	*			

Fred Talbot

TALBOT, FRED LEALAND (Bubby)
B. June 28, 1941, Washington, D. C.
BR TR 6'2"   195 lbs.

	W	L	PCT	ERA	G	GS	CG	IP	H	BB	SO	ShO	W	L	SV	AB	H	HR	BA
1963 CHI A	0	0	—	3.00	1	0	0	3	2	4	2	0	0	0	0	1	0	0	.000
1964	4	5	.444	3.70	17	12	3	75.1	83	20	34	2	1	1	0	19	5	0	.263
1965 KC A	10	12	.455	4.14	39	33	2	198	188	86	117	1	0	1	0	70	14	0	.200
1966 2 teams	KC	A	(11G 4–4)		NY	A	(23G 7–7)												
" total	11	11	.500	4.36	34	30	3	192	188	73	85	0	0	0	0	55	8	0	.145
1967 NY A	6	8	.429	4.22	29	22	2	138.2	132	54	61	0	1	1	0	38	6	1	.158
1968	1	9	.100	3.36	29	11	1	99	89	42	67	0	0	0	0	17	2	1	.118
1969 3 teams	NY	A	(8G 0–0)		SEA	A	(25G 5–8)		OAK	A	(12G 1–2)								
" total	6	10	.375	4.38	45	18	1	146	160	54	83	1	2	2	1	41	7	2	.171
1970 OAK A	0	1	.000	9.00	1	0	0	2	2	1	0	0	0	1	0	0	0	0	—
8 yrs.	38	56	.404	4.12	195	126	12	854	844	334	449	4	5	7	1	241	42	4	.174

Roy Talcott

TALCOTT, LeROY EVERETT
B. Jan. 16, 1921, Boston, Mass.
BR TR 6'1½" 180 lbs.

	W	L	PCT	ERA	G	GS	CG	IP	H	BB	SO	ShO	W	L	SV	AB	H	HR	BA
1943 BOS N	0	0	—	27.00	1	0	0	.2	1	2	0	0	0	0	0	0	0	0	—

Vito Tamulis

TAMULIS, VITAUTIS CASIMIRUS
B. July 11, 1911, Cambridge, Mass.   D. May 5, 1974, Nashville, Tenn.
BL TL 5'9"   170 lbs.

	W	L	PCT	ERA	G	GS	CG	IP	H	BB	SO	ShO	W	L	SV	AB	H	HR	BA
1934 NY A	1	0	1.000	0.00	1	1	1	9	7	1	5	1	0	0	0	4	1	0	.250
1935	10	5	.667	4.09	30	19	9	160.2	178	55	57	3	2	0	1	57	14	1	.246
1938 2 teams	STL	A	(3G 0–3)		BKN	N	(38G 12–6)												
" total	12	9	.571	4.17	41	20	9	175	207	50	81	0	3	3	2	60	9	0	.150
1939 BKN N	9	8	.529	4.37	39	17	8	158.2	177	45	83	1	1	1	4	55	10	0	.182
1940	8	5	.615	3.09	41	12	4	154.1	147	34	55	1	3	5	2	46	6	0	.130
1941 2 teams	PHI	N	(6G 0–1)		BKN	N	(12G 0–0)												
" total	0	1	.000	5.56	18	1	0	34	42	17	13	0	0	0	1	7	0	0	.000
6 yrs.	40	28	.588	3.97	170	70	31	691.2	758	202	294	6	9	9	10	229	40	1	.175

Frank Tanana

TANANA, FRANK DARRYL
B. July 3, 1953, Detroit, Mich.
BL TL 6'2"   180 lbs.

	W	L	PCT	ERA	G	GS	CG	IP	H	BB	SO	ShO	W	L	SV	AB	H	HR	BA
1973 CAL A	2	2	.500	3.08	4	4	2	26.1	20	8	22	1	0	0	0	0	0	0	—
1974	14	19	.424	3.11	39	35	12	269	262	77	180	4	2	0	0	0	0	0	—
1975	16	9	.640	2.62	34	33	16	257.1	211	73	269	5	0	0	0	0	0	0	—
1976	19	10	.655	2.44	34	34	23	288	212	73	261	2	0	0	0	0	0	0	—
1977	15	9	.625	2.54	31	31	20	241.1	201	61	205	7	0	0	0	0	0	0	—
1978	18	12	.600	3.65	33	33	10	239	239	60	137	4	0	0	0	0	0	0	—
1979	7	5	.583	3.90	18	17	2	90	93	25	46	1	0	0	0	0	0	0	—
1980	11	12	.478	4.15	32	31	7	204	223	45	113	0	0	0	0	0	0	0	—
1981 BOS A	4	10	.286	4.02	24	23	5	141	142	43	78	2	0	0	0	0	0	0	—
1982 TEX A	7	18	.280	4.21	30	30	7	194.1	199	55	87	0	1	0	0	0	0	0	—
1983	7	9	.438	3.16	29	22	3	159.1	144	49	108	0	0	0	0	0	0	0	—

	W	L	PCT	ERA	G	GS	CG	IP	H	BB	SO	ShO	Relief Pitching			BATTING			
													W	L	SV	AB	H	HR	BA

Frank Tanana continued

	W	L	PCT	ERA	G	GS	CG	IP	H	BB	SO	ShO	W	L	SV	AB	H	HR	BA
1984	15	15	.500	3.25	35	35	9	246.1	234	81	141	1	0	0	0	0	0	0	—
12 yrs.	135	130	.509	3.25	343	328	116	2356	2180	650	1647	27	3	0	0	0	0	0	—

LEAGUE CHAMPIONSHIP SERIES

| 1979 CAL A | 0 | 0 | — | 3.60 | 1 | 1 | 0 | 5 | 6 | 2 | 3 | 0 | 0 | 0 | 0 | 0 | 0 | 0 | — |

Jesse Tannehill

TANNEHILL, JESSE NILES
Brother of Lee Tannehill.
B. July 14, 1874, Dayton, Ky.   D. Sept. 22, 1956, Dayton, Ky.

BB TL 5'8"   150 lbs.
BL 1903

	W	L	PCT	ERA	G	GS	CG	IP	H	BB	SO	ShO	W	L	SV	AB	H	HR	BA
1894 CIN N	1	0	1.000	7.14	5	1	1	29	37	16	7	0	0	0	0	11	0	0	.000
1897 PIT N	9	9	.500	4.25	21	16	11	142	172	24	40	1	1	2	1	184	49	0	.266
1898	25	13	.658	2.95	43	38	34	326.2	338	63	93	5	1	0	2	152	44	1	.289
1899	24	14	.632	2.57	41	35	32	333	367	52	64	3	3	1	1	132	34	0	.258
1900	20	6	.769	2.88	29	27	23	234	247	43	50	2	0	0	0	110	37	0	.336
1901	18	10	.643	2.18	32	30	25	252.1	240	36	118	4	0	0	1	135	33	1	.244
1902	20	6	.769	1.95	26	24	23	231	203	25	100	2	2	0	0	148	43	1	.291
1903 NY N	15	15	.500	3.27	32	31	22	239.2	258	34	106	2	0	0	0	111	26	1	.234
1904 BOS A	21	11	.656	2.04	33	31	30	281.2	256	33	116	4	2	0	0	122	24	0	.197
1905	22	9	.710	2.48	37	31	27	271.2	238	59	113	6	3	1	0	93	21	1	.226
1906	13	11	.542	3.16	27	26	18	196.1	207	39	82	2	0	0	0	79	22	0	.278
1907	6	7	.462	2.47	18	16	10	131	131	20	29	2	0	0	1	51	10	0	.196
1908 2 teams			BOS	A (1G 0–0)				WAS	A (10G 2–4)										
" total	2	4	.333	3.76	11	10	5	76.2	81	26	16	0	0	0	0	45	12	0	.267
1909 WAS A	1	1	.500	3.43	3	2	2	21	19	5	8	1	0	0	0	36	6	0	.167
1911 CIN N	0	0	—	6.23	1	0	0	4.1	6	3	1	0	0	0	0	1	0	0	.000
15 yrs.	197	116	.629	2.77	359	318	263	2770.1	2800	478	943	34	12	4	7	*			

Al Tate

TATE, WALTER ALVIN
B. July 1, 1918, Coleman, Okla.

BR TR 6'   180 lbs.

1946 PIT N	0	1	.000	5.00	2	1	1	9	8	7	2	0	0	0	0	3	1	0	.333

Randy Tate

TATE, RANDALL LEE
B. Oct. 23, 1952, Florence, Ala.

BR TR 6'3"   190 lbs.

1975 NY N	5	13	.278	4.43	26	23	2	138	121	86	99	0	0	0	0	41	0	0	.000

Ken Tatum

TATUM, KENNETH RAY
B. Apr. 25, 1944, Alexandria, La.

BR TR 6'2"   205 lbs.

	W	L	PCT	ERA	G	GS	CG	IP	H	BB	SO	ShO	W	L	SV	AB	H	HR	BA
1969 CAL A	7	2	.778	1.36	45	0	0	86.1	51	39	65	0	7	2	22	21	6	2	.286
1970	7	4	.636	2.93	62	0	0	89	68	26	50	0	7	4	17	11	2	1	.182
1971 BOS A	2	4	.333	4.17	36	1	0	54	50	25	21	0	2	3	9	10	3	1	.300
1972	0	2	.000	3.10	22	0	0	29	32	15	15	0	0	2	4	2	0	0	.000
1973	0	0	—	9.00	1	0	0	4	6	3	0	0	0	0	0	0	0	0	—
1974 CHI A	0	0	—	4.71	10	0	0	21	23	9	5	0	0	0	0	1	0	0	.000
6 yrs.	16	12	.571	2.92	176	2	0	283.1	230	117	156	0	16	11	52	45	11	4	.244

Walt Tauscher

TAUSCHER, WALTER EDWARD
B. Nov. 22, 1901, LaSalle, Ind.

BR TR 6'1"   186 lbs.

	W	L	PCT	ERA	G	GS	CG	IP	H	BB	SO	ShO	W	L	SV	AB	H	HR	BA
1928 PIT N	0	0	—	4.91	17	0	0	29.1	28	12	7	0	0	0	1	6	1	0	.167
1931 WAS A	1	0	1.000	7.50	6	0	0	12	24	4	5	0	1	0	0	0	0	0	—
2 yrs.	1	0	1.000	5.66	23	0	0	41.1	52	16	12	0	1	0	1	6	1	0	.167

Arlas Taylor

TAYLOR, ARLAS WALTER (Lefty, Foxy)
B. Mar. 16, 1896, Warick County, Ind.   D. Sept. 10, 1968, Dade City, Fla.

BR TL 5'11"

1921 PHI A	0	1	.000	22.50	1	1	0	2	7	2	0	0	0	0	0	0	0	0	—

Ben Taylor

TAYLOR, BENJAMIN HARRISON
B. Apr. 2, 1889, Paoli, Ind.   D. Nov. 3, 1946, Martin County, Ind.

TR 5'11"   163 lbs.

1912 CIN N	0	0	—	3.18	2	0	0	5.2	9	3	2	0	0	0	0	2	0	0	.000

Billy Taylor

TAYLOR, WILLIAM HENRY (Bollicky)
B. 1855, Washington, D.C.   D. May 14, 1900, Jacksonville, Fla.

BR TR 5'11½" 204 lbs.

	W	L	PCT	ERA	G	GS	CG	IP	H	BB	SO	ShO	W	L	SV	AB	H	HR	BA
1881 2 teams			WOR	N (1G 0–1)				CLE	N (1G 0–0)										
" total	0	1	.000	5.73	2	1	1	11	15	7	2	0	0	0	0	135	30	0	.222
1882 PIT AA	0	1	.000	16.20	1	0	0	5	11	4	1	0	0	1	0	299	84	4	.281
1883	4	7	.364	5.39	19	9	8	127	166	34	41	0	1	1	0	369	96	2	.260
1884 2 teams			STL	U (33G 25–4)				PHI	AA (30G 18–12)										
" total	43	16	.729	2.10	63	59	59	523	454	84	284	3	0	0	4	297	96	3	.323
1885 PHI AA	1	5	.167	3.27	6	6	6	52.1	68	9	11	0	0	0	0	21	4	0	.190
1886 BAL AA	1	6	.143	5.72	8	8	8	72.1	87	20	37	0	0	0	0	39	12	0	.308
1887 PHI AA	1	0	1.000	3.00	1	1	1	9	10	7	0	0	0	0	0	4	1	0	.250
7 yrs.	50	36	.581	3.17	100	84	83	799.2	811	165	376	3	1	2	4	*			

Bruce Taylor

TAYLOR, BRUCE BELL
B. Apr. 16, 1953, Holden, Mass.

BR TR 6'   178 lbs.

	W	L	PCT	ERA	G	GS	CG	IP	H	BB	SO	ShO	W	L	SV	AB	H	HR	BA
1977 DET A	1	0	1.000	3.41	19	0	0	29	23	10	19	0	1	0	2	0	0	0	—
1978	0	0	—	0.00	1	0	0	1	0	0	0	0	0	0	0	0	0	0	—
1979	1	2	.333	4.74	10	0	0	19	16	7	8	0	1	2	0	0	0	0	—
3 yrs.	2	2	.500	3.86	30	0	0	49	39	17	27	0	2	2	2	0	0	0	—

Chuck Taylor

TAYLOR, CHARLES GILBERT
B. Apr. 18, 1942, Murfreesboro, Tenn.

BR TR 6'2"   195 lbs.

	W	L	PCT	ERA	G	GS	CG	IP	H	BB	SO	ShO	W	L	SV	AB	H	HR	BA
1969 STL N	7	5	.583	2.55	27	13	5	127	108	30	62	1	0	0	0	39	7	0	.179
1970	6	7	.462	3.12	56	7	1	124	116	31	64	1	3	5	8	26	3	0	.115
1971	3	1	.750	3.55	43	1	0	71	72	25	46	0	3	2	3	12	2	0	.167

	W	L	PCT	ERA	G	GS	CG	IP	H	BB	SO	ShO	Relief W	L	SV	Bat AB	H	HR	BA

Chuck Taylor continued

Year/Team	W	L	PCT	ERA	G	GS	CG	IP	H	BB	SO	ShO	W	L	SV	AB	H	HR	BA
1972 2 teams			NY N (20G 0–0)		MIL A (5G 0–0)														
" total	0	0	–	4.40	25	0	0	43	52	12	14	0	0	0	3	5	1	0	.200
1973 MON N	2	0	1.000	1.77	8	0	0	20.1	17	2	10	0	2	0	0	4	0	0	.000
1974	6	2	.750	2.17	61	0	0	108	101	25	43	0	6	2	11	10	3	0	.300
1975	2	2	.500	3.53	54	0	0	74	72	24	29	0	2	2	6	2	0	0	.000
1976	2	3	.400	4.50	31	0	0	40	38	13	14	0	2	3	0	3	0	0	.000
8 yrs.	28	20	.583	3.07	305	21	6	607.1	576	162	282	2	18	14	31	101	16	0	.158

Dummy Taylor

TAYLOR, LUTHER HADEN   BR TR 6'1"   160 lbs.
B. Feb. 21, 1875, Oskaloosa, Kans.   D. Aug. 22, 1958, Jacksonville, Ill.

Year/Team	W	L	PCT	ERA	G	GS	CG	IP	H	BB	SO	ShO	W	L	SV	AB	H	HR	BA
1900 NY N	4	3	.571	2.45	11	7	6	62.1	74	24	16	0	0	0	0	22	3	0	.136
1901	18	27	.400	3.18	45	43	37	353.1	377	112	136	4	1	1	0	136	18	0	.132
1902 2 teams			CLE A (4G 1–3)		NY N (26G 7–15)														
" total	8	18	.308	2.19	30	29	22	234.2	231	63	95	1	0	0	0	75	7	0	.093
1903 NY N	13	13	.500	4.23	33	31	18	244.2	306	89	94	1	0	1	0	82	12	0	.146
1904	21	15	.583	2.34	37	36	29	296.1	231	75	138	5	0	1	0	102	16	0	.157
1905	15	9	.625	2.66	32	28	18	213	200	51	91	4	0	0	0	69	9	0	.130
1906	17	9	.654	2.20	31	27	13	213	186	57	91	0	0	2	0	76	14	0	.184
1907	11	7	.611	2.42	28	21	11	171	145	46	56	3	2	0	1	48	6	0	.125
1908	8	5	.615	2.33	27	15	6	127.2	127	34	50	1	2	0	2	35	8	0	.229
9 yrs.	115	106	.520	2.75	274	237	160	1916	1877	551	767	21	5	5	3	645	93	0	.144

Gary Taylor

TAYLOR, GARY WILLIAM   BR TR 6'2"   190 lbs.
B. Oct. 19, 1945, Detroit, Mich.

Year/Team	W	L	PCT	ERA	G	GS	CG	IP	H	BB	SO	ShO	W	L	SV	AB	H	HR	BA
1969 DET A	0	1	.000	5.23	7	0	0	10.1	10	6	3	0	0	0	0	1	0	0	.000

Harry Taylor

TAYLOR, HARRY EVANS   BR TR 6'   185 lbs.
B. Dec. 2, 1935, San Angelo, Tex.

Year/Team	W	L	PCT	ERA	G	GS	CG	IP	H	BB	SO	ShO	W	L	SV	AB	H	HR	BA
1957 KC A	0	0	–	3.12	2	0	0	8.2	11	4	4	0	0	0	0	4	1	0	.250

Harry Taylor

TAYLOR, JAMES HARRY   BR TR 6'1"   175 lbs.
B. May 20, 1919, East Glenn, Ind.

Year/Team	W	L	PCT	ERA	G	GS	CG	IP	H	BB	SO	ShO	W	L	SV	AB	H	HR	BA
1946 BKN N	0	0	–	3.86	4	0	0	4.2	5	1	6	0	0	0	1	0	0	0	–
1947	10	5	.667	3.11	33	20	10	162	130	83	58	2	0	0	1	62	8	0	.129
1948	2	7	.222	5.36	17	13	2	80.2	90	61	32	0	0	1	0	22	6	0	.273
1950 BOS A	2	0	1.000	1.42	3	2	2	19	13	8	8	1	0	0	0	7	2	0	.286
1951	4	9	.308	5.75	31	8	1	81.1	100	42	22	0	2	5	2	29	3	0	.103
1952	1	0	1.000	1.80	2	1	1	10	6	6	1	0	0	0	0	4	1	0	.250
6 yrs.	19	21	.475	4.10	90	44	16	357.2	344	201	127	3	2	6	4	124	20	0	.161

WORLD SERIES

Year/Team	W	L	PCT	ERA	G	GS	CG	IP	H	BB	SO	ShO	W	L	SV	AB	H	HR	BA
1947 BKN N	0	0	–	0.00	1	1	0	2	1	0	0	0	0	0	0	0	0	0	–

Jack Taylor

TAYLOR, JOHN B. (Brewery Jack)   BR TR 6'1"   190 lbs.
B. May 23, 1873, Staten Island, N.Y.   D. Feb. 7, 1900, Staten Island, N.Y.

Year/Team	W	L	PCT	ERA	G	GS	CG	IP	H	BB	SO	ShO	W	L	SV	AB	H	HR	BA
1891 NY N	0	1	.000	1.13	1	1	1	8	4	3	3	0	0	0	0	2	0	0	.000
1892 PHI N	1	0	1.000	1.38	3	3	2	26	28	10	7	0	0	0	0	12	2	0	.167
1893	10	9	.526	4.24	25	16	14	170	189	77	41	0	3	2	1	93	20	0	.215
1894	23	13	.639	4.08	41	34	31	298	347	96	76	1	1	2	1	144	48	0	.333
1895	26	14	.650	4.49	41	37	33	335	403	83	93	1	1	2	0	155	45	3	.290
1896	20	21	.488	4.79	45	41	35	359	459	112	97	1	0	1	1	157	29	0	.185
1897	16	20	.444	4.23	40	37	35	317.1	376	76	88	2	0	1	2	139	35	1	.252
1898 STL N	15	29	.341	3.90	50	47	42	397.1	465	83	89	0	0	0	1	157	38	1	.242
1899 CIN N	9	10	.474	4.12	24	18	15	168.1	197	41	34	2	1	1	2	68	17	0	.250
9 yrs.	120	117	.506	4.23	270	234	208	2079	2468	581	528	7	6	9	9	927	234	5	.252

Jack Taylor

TAYLOR, JOHN W.   BR TR 5'10"   170 lbs.
B. Jan. 14, 1874, Straightville, Ohio   D. Mar. 4, 1938, Columbus, Ohio

Year/Team	W	L	PCT	ERA	G	GS	CG	IP	H	BB	SO	ShO	W	L	SV	AB	H	HR	BA
1898 CHI N	5	0	1.000	2.20	5	5	5	41	32	10	11	0	0	0	0	15	3	0	.200
1899	18	21	.462	3.76	41	39	39	354.2	380	84	67	1	1	0	0	139	37	0	.266
1900	10	17	.370	2.55	28	26	25	222.1	226	58	57	2	1	0	0	81	19	1	.235
1901	13	19	.406	3.36	33	31	30	275.2	341	44	68	0	1	0	0	106	23	0	.217
1902	22	11	.667	1.33	36	33	33	324.2	271	43	83	8	1	0	1	186	44	0	.237
1903	21	14	.600	2.45	37	33	33	312.1	277	57	83	1	1	1	1	126	28	0	.222
1904 STL N	21	19	.525	2.22	41	39	39	352	297	82	103	2	0	1	1	133	28	1	.211
1905	15	21	.417	3.44	37	34	34	309	302	85	102	3	1	1	1	121	23	0	.190
1906 2 teams			STL N (17G 8–9)		CHI N (17G 12–3)														
" total	20	12	.625	1.99	34	33	32	302.1	249	86	61	3	0	0	0	106	22	0	.208
1907 CHI N	6	5	.545	3.29	18	13	8	123	127	33	22	0	1	0	0	47	9	0	.191
10 yrs.	151	139	.521	2.66	310	286	278	2617	2502	582	657	20	7	2	5	*			

Pete Taylor

TAYLOR, VERNON CHARLES   BR TR 6'1"   170 lbs.
B. Nov. 26, 1927, Severn, Md.

Year/Team	W	L	PCT	ERA	G	GS	CG	IP	H	BB	SO	ShO	W	L	SV	AB	H	HR	BA
1952 STL A	0	0	–	13.50	1	0	0	2	4	3	0	0	0	0	0	0	0	0	–

Ron Taylor

TAYLOR, RONALD WESLEY   BR TR 6'1"   195 lbs.
B. Dec. 13, 1937, Toronto, Ont., Canada

Year/Team	W	L	PCT	ERA	G	GS	CG	IP	H	BB	SO	ShO	W	L	SV	AB	H	HR	BA
1962 CLE A	2	2	.500	5.94	8	4	1	33.1	36	13	15	0	1	0	0	11	3	0	.273
1963 STL N	9	7	.563	2.84	54	9	2	133.1	119	30	91	0	7	3	11	32	1	0	.031
1964	8	4	.667	4.62	63	2	0	101.1	109	33	69	0	8	2	7	15	2	0	.133
1965 2 teams			STL N (25G 2–1)		HOU N (32G 1–5)														
" total	3	6	.333	5.60	57	1	0	101.1	111	31	63	0	2	1	5	18	2	0	.111
1966 HOU N	2	3	.400	5.71	36	1	0	64.2	89	10	29	0	2	3	0	12	2	0	.167
1967 NY N	4	6	.400	2.34	50	0	0	73	60	23	46	0	4	6	8	7	0	0	.000
1968	1	5	.167	2.70	58	0	0	76.2	64	18	49	0	1	5	13	9	0	0	.000
1969	9	4	.692	2.72	59	0	0	76	61	24	42	0	9	4	13	4	1	0	.250

	W	L	PCT	ERA	G	GS	CG	IP	H	BB	SO	ShO	Relief Pitching W	L	SV	Batting AB	H	HR	BA

Ron Taylor continued

	W	L	PCT	ERA	G	GS	CG	IP	H	BB	SO	ShO	W	L	SV	AB	H	HR	BA
1970	5	4	.556	3.95	57	0	0	66	65	16	28	0	5	4	13	4	0	0	.000
1971	2	2	.500	3.65	45	0	0	69	71	11	32	0	2	2	2	4	1	0	.250
1972 SD N	0	0	—	12.60	4	0	0	5	9	0	0	0	0	0	0	0	0	0	
11 yrs.	45	43	.511	3.93	491	17	3	799.2	794	209	464	0	41	30	72	116	12	0	.103
LEAGUE CHAMPIONSHIP SERIES
1969 NY N	1	0	1.000	0.00	2	0	0	3.1	3	0	4	0	1	0	1	0	0	0	—
WORLD SERIES
1964 STL N	0	0	—	0.00	2	0	0	4.2	0	1	2	0	0	0	1	1	0	0	.000
1969 NY N	0	0	—	0.00	2	0	0	2.1	0	1	3	0	0	0	1	0	0	0	
2 yrs.	0	0	—	0.00	4	0	0	7	0	2	5	0	0	0	2	1	0	0	.000

Rube Taylor

TAYLOR, EDGAR REUBEN
B. Mar. 23, 1877, Palestine, Tex.   D. Jan. 30, 1912, Dallas, Tex.

	W	L	PCT	ERA	G	GS	CG	IP	H	BB	SO	ShO	W	L	SV	AB	H	HR	BA
1903 STL N	0	0	—	0.00	1	0	0	3	0	0	1	0	0	0	0	1	0	0	.000

Wiley Taylor

TAYLOR, PHILIP WILEY   BR TR 6'1" 175 lbs.
B. Mar. 18, 1888, Wamego, Kans.   D. July 8, 1954, Westmoreland, Kans.

	W	L	PCT	ERA	G	GS	CG	IP	H	BB	SO	ShO	W	L	SV	AB	H	HR	BA
1911 DET A	0	2	.000	3.79	3	2	1	19	18	10	9	0	0	0	0	6	0	0	.000
1912 CHI A	0	1	.000	4.95	3	3	0	20	21	14	4	0	0	0	0	5	0	0	.000
1913 STL A	0	2	.000	4.83	5	4	1	31.2	33	16	12	0	0	0	0	10	0	0	.000
1914	2	5	.286	3.42	16	8	2	50	41	25	20	1	0	1	0	12	2	0	.167
4 yrs.	2	10	.167	4.10	27	17	4	120.2	113	65	45	1	0	1	0	33	2	0	.061

Bud Teachout

TEACHOUT, ARTHUR JOHN   BR TL 6'2" 183 lbs.
B. Feb. 27, 1904, Los Angeles, Calif.

	W	L	PCT	ERA	G	GS	CG	IP	H	BB	SO	ShO	W	L	SV	AB	H	HR	BA
1930 CHI N	11	4	.733	4.06	40	16	6	153	178	48	59	0	4	1	0	63	17	0	.270
1931	1	2	.333	5.72	27	3	1	61.1	79	28	14	0	1	0	0	21	5	0	.238
1932 STL N	0	0	—	0.00	1	0	0	1	2	0	0	0	0	0	0	0	0	0	—
3 yrs.	12	6	.667	4.51	68	19	7	215.1	259	76	73	0	5	1	0	84	22	0	.262

Patsy Tebeau

TEBEAU, OLIVER WENDELL   BR TR
Brother of White Wings Tebeau.
B. Dec. 5, 1864, St. Louis, Mo.   D. May 15, 1918, St. Louis, Mo.
Manager 1890-1900.

	W	L	PCT	ERA	G	GS	CG	IP	H	BB	SO	ShO	W	L	SV	AB	H	HR	BA
1896 CLE N	0	0	—	0.00	1	0	0	1	1	0	0	0	0	0	0	*			

White Wings Tebeau

TEBEAU, GEORGE E. (Hard Call)   BR TR 5'9" 175 lbs.
Brother of Patsy Tebeau.
B. Dec. 26, 1862, St. Louis, Mo.   D. Feb. 4, 1923, Denver, Colo.

	W	L	PCT	ERA	G	GS	CG	IP	H	BB	SO	ShO	W	L	SV	AB	H	HR	BA
1887 CIN AA	0	1	.000	13.50	1	1	1	8	21	3	1	0	0	0	0	318	94	4	.296
1890 TOL AA	0	0	—	9.00	1	0	0	5	9	5	0	0	0	0	0	381	102	1	.268
2 yrs.	0	1	.000	11.77	2	1	1	13	30	8	1	0	0	0	0	*			

Al Tedrow

TEDROW, ALLEN SEYMOUR   BR TL 6' 180 lbs.
B. Dec. 14, 1891, Westerville, Ohio   D. Jan. 23, 1958, Westerville, Ohio

	W	L	PCT	ERA	G	GS	CG	IP	H	BB	SO	ShO	W	L	SV	AB	H	HR	BA
1914 CLE A	1	2	.333	1.21	4	3	1	22.1	19	14	4	0	0	0	0	6	1	0	.167

Kent Tekulve

TEKULVE, KENTON CHARLES   BR TR 6'4" 180 lbs.
B. Mar. 5, 1947, Cincinnati, Ohio

	W	L	PCT	ERA	G	GS	CG	IP	H	BB	SO	ShO	W	L	SV	AB	H	HR	BA
1974 PIT N	1	1	.500	6.00	8	0	0	9	12	5	6	0	1	1	0	0	0	0	—
1975	1	2	.333	2.25	34	0	0	56	43	23	28	0	1	2	5	11	1	0	.091
1976	5	3	.625	2.45	64	0	0	102.2	91	25	68	0	5	3	9	9	0	0	.000
1977	10	1	.909	3.06	72	0	0	103	89	33	59	0	10	1	7	12	3	0	.250
1978	8	7	.533	2.33	91	0	0	135	115	55	77	0	8	7	31	21	2	0	.095
1979	10	8	.556	2.75	94	0	0	134	109	49	75	0	10	8	31	15	2	0	.133
1980	8	12	.400	3.39	78	0	0	93	96	40	47	0	8	12	21	9	0	0	.000
1981	5	5	.500	2.49	45	0	0	65	61	17	34	0	5	5	3	2	0	0	.000
1982	12	8	.600	2.87	85	0	0	128.2	113	46	66	0	12	8	20	14	1	0	.071
1983	7	5	.583	1.64	76	0	0	99	78	36	52	0	7	5	18	8	0	0	.000
1984	3	9	.250	2.66	72	0	0	88	86	33	36	0	3	9	13	7	0	0	.000
11 yrs.	70	61	.534	2.64	719	0	0	1013.1	893	362	548	0	70	61	158	108	9	0	.083
LEAGUE CHAMPIONSHIP SERIES
1975 PIT N	0	0	—	6.75	2	0	0	1.1	3	1	2	0	0	0	0	0	0	0	—
1979	0	0	—	3.00	2	0	0	3	2	2	2	0	0	0	0	1	0	0	.000
2 yrs.	0	0	—	4.15	4	0	0	4.1	5	3	4	0	0	0	0	1	0	0	.000
WORLD SERIES
1979 PIT N	0	1	.000	2.89	5	0	0	9.1	4	3	10	0	0	1	3	2	0	0	.000
															4th				

Tom Tellmann

TELLMANN, THOMAS JOHN   BR TR 6'3" 195 lbs.
B. Mar. 29, 1954, Warren, Pa.

	W	L	PCT	ERA	G	GS	CG	IP	H	BB	SO	ShO	W	L	SV	AB	H	HR	BA
1979 SD N	0	0	—	15.00	1	0	0	3	7	0	1	0	0	0	0	1	0	0	.000
1980	3	0	1.000	1.64	6	2	2	22	23	8	9	0	1	0	1	8	1	0	.125
1983 MIL A	9	4	.692	2.80	44	0	0	99.2	95	35	48	0	9	4	8	0	0	0	—
1984	6	3	.667	2.78	50	0	0	81	82	31	28	0	6	3	4	0	0	0	—
4 yrs.	18	7	.720	2.84	101	2	2	205.2	207	74	86	0	16	7	13	9	1	0	.111

Chuck Templeton

TEMPLETON, CHARLES SHERMAN   BR TL 6'3" 210 lbs.
B. June 1, 1932, Detroit, Mich.

	W	L	PCT	ERA	G	GS	CG	IP	H	BB	SO	ShO	W	L	SV	AB	H	HR	BA
1955 BKN N	0	1	.000	11.57	4	0	0	4.2	5	5	3	0	0	1	0	0	0	0	—
1956	0	1	.000	6.61	6	2	0	16.1	20	10	8	0	0	0	0	3	0	0	.000
2 yrs.	0	2	.000	7.71	10	2	0	21	25	15	11	0	0	1	0	3	0	0	.000

	W	L	PCT	ERA	G	GS	CG	IP	H	BB	SO	ShO	Relief Pitching W	L	SV	BATTING AB	H	HR	BA

Hal Toenes

TOENES, WILLIAM HARREL
B. Oct. 8, 1917, Mobile, Ala.   BR TR 5'11½" 175 lbs.

	W	L	PCT	ERA	G	GS	CG	IP	H	BB	SO	ShO	W	L	SV	AB	H	HR	BA
1947 WAS A	0	1	.000	6.75	3	1	0	6.2	11	2	5	0	0	0	0	1	0	0	.000

Freddie Toliver

TOLIVER, FREDDIE LEE
B. Feb. 3, 1961, Natchez, Miss.   BR TR 6'1" 170 lbs.

	W	L	PCT	ERA	G	GS	CG	IP	H	BB	SO	ShO	W	L	SV	AB	H	HR	BA
1984 CIN N	0	0	—	0.90	3	1	0	10	7	7	4	0	0	0	0	1	0	0	.000

Dick Tomanek

TOMANEK, RICHARD CARL (Bones)
B. Jan. 6, 1931, Avon Lake, Ohio   BL TL 6'1" 175 lbs.

	W	L	PCT	ERA	G	GS	CG	IP	H	BB	SO	ShO	W	L	SV	AB	H	HR	BA
1953 CLE A	1	0	1.000	2.00	1	1	1	9	6	6	6	0	0	0	0	5	0	0	.000
1954	0	0	—	5.40	1	0	0	1.2	1	1	0	0	0	0	0	0	0	0	—
1957	2	1	.667	5.68	34	2	0	69.2	67	37	55	0	2	1	0	13	3	0	.231
1958 2 teams			CLE	A (18G 2–3)		KC	A	(36G 5–5)											
" total	7	8	.467	4.50	54	8	3	130	130	56	92	0	6	5	5	30	5	1	.167
1959 KC A	0	1	.000	6.53	16	0	0	20.2	27	12	13	0	0	1	2	2	1	0	.500
5 yrs.	10	10	.500	4.95	106	11	4	231	231	112	166	0	8	7	7	50	9	1	.180

Andy Tomasic

TOMASIC, ANDREW JOHN
B. Dec. 10, 1919, Hokendauqua, Pa.   BR TR 6' 175 lbs.

	W	L	PCT	ERA	G	GS	CG	IP	H	BB	SO	ShO	W	L	SV	AB	H	HR	BA
1949 NY N	0	1	.000	18.00	2	0	0	5	9	5	2	0	0	1	0	1	0	0	.000

Dave Tomlin

TOMLIN, DAVID ALLEN
B. June 22, 1949, Maysville, Ky.   BL TL 6'2" 180 lbs.

	W	L	PCT	ERA	G	GS	CG	IP	H	BB	SO	ShO	W	L	SV	AB	H	HR	BA
1972 CIN N	0	0	—	9.00	3	0	0	4	7	1	2	0	0	0	0	0	0	0	—
1973	1	2	.333	4.88	16	0	0	27.2	24	15	20	0	1	2	1	3	0	0	.000
1974 SD N	2	0	1.000	4.34	47	0	0	58	59	30	29	0	2	0	2	4	0	0	.000
1975	4	2	.667	3.25	67	0	0	83	87	31	48	0	4	2	1	5	1	0	.200
1976	0	1	.000	2.84	49	1	0	73	62	20	43	0	0	0	0	8	0	0	.000
1977	4	4	.500	3.00	76	0	0	102	98	32	55	0	4	4	3	7	2	0	.286
1978 CIN N	9	1	.900	5.81	57	0	0	62	88	30	32	0	9	1	4	5	1	0	.200
1979	2	2	.500	2.64	53	0	0	58	59	18	30	0	2	2	1	2	1	0	.500
1980	3	0	1.000	5.54	27	0	0	26	38	11	6	0	3	0	0	0	0	0	—
1982 MON N	0	0	—	4.50	1	0	0	2	1	1	2	0	0	0	0	0	0	0	—
1983 PIT N	0	0	—	6.75	5	0	0	4	6	1	5	0	0	0	0	0	0	0	—
11 yrs.	25	12	.676	3.80	401	1	0	499.2	529	190	272	0	25	11	12	34	5	0	.147

LEAGUE CHAMPIONSHIP SERIES

	W	L	PCT	ERA	G	GS	CG	IP	H	BB	SO	ShO	W	L	SV	AB	H	HR	BA
1973 CIN N	0	0	—	16.20	1	0	0	1.2	5	1	1	0	0	0	0	0	0	0	—
1979	0	0	—	0.00	3	0	0	3	3	2	3	0	0	0	0	0	0	0	—
2 yrs.	0	0	—	5.79	4	0	0	4.2	8	3	4	0	0	0	0	0	0	0	—

Chuck Tompkins

TOMPKINS, CHARLES HERBERT
B. Sept. 1, 1889, Prescott, Ark.   D. Sept. 20, 1975, Prescott, Ark.   BR TR 6' 185 lbs.

	W	L	PCT	ERA	G	GS	CG	IP	H	BB	SO	ShO	W	L	SV	AB	H	HR	BA
1912 CIN N	0	0	—	0.00	1	0	0	3	5	0	1	0	0	0	0	1	1	0	1.000

Ron Tompkins

TOMPKINS, RONALD EVERETT (Stretch)
B. Nov. 27, 1944, San Diego, Calif.   BR TR 6'4" 198 lbs.

	W	L	PCT	ERA	G	GS	CG	IP	H	BB	SO	ShO	W	L	SV	AB	H	HR	BA
1965 KC A	0	0	—	3.48	5	1	0	10.1	9	3	4	0	0	0	0	1	0	0	.000
1971 CHI N	0	2	.000	4.05	35	0	0	40	31	21	20	0	0	2	3	0	0	0	—
2 yrs.	0	2	.000	3.93	40	1	0	50.1	40	24	24	0	0	2	3	1	0	0	.000

Tommy Toms

TOMS, THOMAS HOWARD
B. Oct. 15, 1951, Charlottesville, Va.   BR TR 6'4" 195 lbs.

	W	L	PCT	ERA	G	GS	CG	IP	H	BB	SO	ShO	W	L	SV	AB	H	HR	BA
1975 SF N	0	1	.000	6.30	7	0	0	10	13	6	6	0	0	1	0	0	0	0	—
1976	0	1	.000	6.23	7	0	0	8.2	13	1	4	0	0	1	1	0	0	0	—
1977	0	1	.000	2.25	4	0	0	4	7	2	2	0	0	1	0	0	0	0	—
3 yrs.	0	3	.000	5.56	18	0	0	22.2	33	9	12	0	0	3	1	0	0	0	—

Fred Toney

TONEY, FRED ALEXANDRA
B. Dec. 11, 1888, Nashville, Tenn.   D. Mar. 11, 1953, Nashville, Tenn.   BR TR 6'6" 245 lbs.

	W	L	PCT	ERA	G	GS	CG	IP	H	BB	SO	ShO	W	L	SV	AB	H	HR	BA
1911 CHI N	1	1	.500	2.42	18	4	1	67	55	35	27	0	0	0	0	18	2	0	.111
1912	1	2	.333	5.25	9	2	0	24	21	11	9	0	1	0	0	5	0	0	.000
1913	2	2	.500	6.00	7	5	2	39	52	22	12	0	0	0	0	12	3	0	.250
1915 CIN N	15	6	.714	1.58	36	23	18	222.2	160	73	108	6	1	1	2	74	7	0	.095
1916	14	17	.452	2.28	41	38	21	300	247	78	146	3	0	0	1	99	12	0	.121
1917	24	16	.600	2.20	43	42	31	339.2	300	77	123	7	0	0	1	116	13	0	.112
1918 2 teams			CIN	N (21G 6–10)		NY	N	(11G 6–2)											
" total	12	12	.500	2.43	32	28	16	222	203	38	51	2	0	0	3	74	15	0	.203
1919 NY N	13	6	.684	1.84	24	20	14	181	157	35	40	4	0	1	1	66	15	0	.227
1920	21	11	.656	2.65	42	37	17	278.1	266	57	81	4	2	0	1	96	23	0	.240
1921	18	11	.621	3.61	42	32	16	249.1	274	65	63	1	3	0	3	86	18	3	.209
1922	5	6	.455	4.17	13	12	6	86.1	91	31	10	0	0	0	0	30	2	0	.067
1923 STL N	11	12	.478	3.84	29	28	16	196.2	211	61	48	1	0	0	0	69	8	0	.116
12 yrs.	137	102	.573	2.69	336	271	158	2206	2037	583	718	28	7	2	12	745	118	3	.158

WORLD SERIES

	W	L	PCT	ERA	G	GS	CG	IP	H	BB	SO	ShO	W	L	SV	AB	H	HR	BA
1921 NY N	0	0	—	23.63	2	2	0	2.2	7	3	1	0	0	0	0	0	0	0	—

Doc Tonkin

TONKIN, HARRY GLENVILLE
B. Aug. 11, 1881, Concord, N. H.   D. May 30, 1959, Miami, Fla.   BL TL

	W	L	PCT	ERA	G	GS	CG	IP	H	BB	SO	ShO	W	L	SV	AB	H	HR	BA
1907 WAS A	0	0	—	6.75	1	0	0	2.2	6	5	0	0	0	0	0	2	2	0	1.000

Steve Toole

TOOLE, STEPHEN JOHN
B. Apr. 9, 1859, New Orleans, La.   D. Mar. 28, 1919, Pittsburgh, Pa.   BL TL 6' 170 lbs.

	W	L	PCT	ERA	G	GS	CG	IP	H	BB	SO	ShO	W	L	SV	AB	H	HR	BA
1886 BKN AA	6	6	.500	4.41	13	12	11	104	100	64	48	0	0	0	0	57	20	0	.351
1887	14	10	.583	4.31	24	24	22	194	186	106	48	1	0	0	0	103	24	1	.233
1888 KC AA	5	6	.455	6.68	12	10	10	91.2	124	50	35	0	1	0	0	48	10	0	.208

	W	L	PCT	ERA	G	GS	CG	IP	H	BB	SO	ShO	Relief Pitching W	L	SV	BATTING AB	H	HR	BA

Steve Toole continued

	W	L	PCT	ERA	G	GS	CG	IP	H	BB	SO	ShO	W	L	SV	AB	H	HR	BA
1890 **B-B** AA	2	4	.333	4.05	6	6	6	53.1	47	39	10	0	0	0	0	20	6	0	.300
4 yrs.	27	26	.509	4.79	55	52	49	443	457	259	141	1	1	0	0	228	60	1	.263

Rupe Toppin

TOPPIN, RUPERTO
B. Dec. 7, 1941, Panama City, Panama

BR TR 6'1" 185 lbs.

	W	L	PCT	ERA	G	GS	CG	IP	H	BB	SO	ShO	W	L	SV	AB	H	HR	BA
1962 **KC** A	0	0	–	13.50	2	0	0	2	1	5	1	0	0	0	0	1	1	0	1.000

Red Torkelson

TORKELSON, CHESTER LeROY
B. Mar. 19, 1894, Chicago, Ill.   D. Sept. 22, 1964, Chicago, Ill.

BR TR 6' 175 lbs.

	W	L	PCT	ERA	G	GS	CG	IP	H	BB	SO	ShO	W	L	SV	AB	H	HR	BA
1917 **CLE** A	2	1	.667	7.66	4	3	0	22.1	33	13	10	0	0	0	0	9	2	0	.222

Pablo Torrealba

TORREALBA, PABLO ARNOLDO
B. Apr. 28, 1949, Barouisimento, Venezuela

BL TL 5'10" 173 lbs.

	W	L	PCT	ERA	G	GS	CG	IP	H	BB	SO	ShO	W	L	SV	AB	H	HR	BA
1975 **ATL** N	0	1	.000	1.29	6	0	0	7	7	3	5	0	0	1	0	1	1	0	1.000
1976	0	2	.000	3.57	36	0	0	53	67	22	33	0	0	2	2	4	0	0	.000
1977 **OAK** A	4	6	.400	2.62	41	10	3	117	127	38	51	0	3	1	2	0	0	0	–
1978 **CHI** A	2	4	.333	4.71	25	3	1	57.1	69	39	23	1	1	3	1	0	0	0	–
1979	0	0	–	1.50	3	0	0	6	5	2	1	0	0	0	0	0	0	0	–
5 yrs.	6	13	.316	3.26	111	13	4	240.1	275	104	113	1	4	7	5	5	1	0	.200

Angel Torres

TORRES, ANGEL RAFAEL
Also known as Angel Rafael Ruiz.
B. Oct. 24, 1952, Azua, Dominican Republic

BL TL 5'11" 168 lbs.

	W	L	PCT	ERA	G	GS	CG	IP	H	BB	SO	ShO	W	L	SV	AB	H	HR	BA
1977 **CIN** N	0	0	–	2.25	5	0	0	8	7	8	8	0	0	0	0	0	0	0	–

Gil Torres

TORRES, DON GILBERTO NUNEZ
Son of Ricardo Torres.
B. Aug. 23, 1915, Regla, Cuba   D. Jan. 11, 1983, Regla, Cuba

BR TR 6' 155 lbs.

	W	L	PCT	ERA	G	GS	CG	IP	H	BB	SO	ShO	W	L	SV	AB	H	HR	BA
1940 **WAS** A	0	0	–	0.00	2	0	0	2.2	3	0	1	0	0	0	0	0	0	0	–
1946	0	0	–	7.71	3	0	0	7	9	3	2	0	0	0	1	185	47	0	.254
2 yrs.	0	0	–	5.59	5	0	0	9.2	12	3	3	0	0	0	1	*			

Hector Torres

TORRES, HECTOR EPITACIO
B. Sept. 16, 1945, Monterrey, Mexico

BR TR 6' 175 lbs.

	W	L	PCT	ERA	G	GS	CG	IP	H	BB	SO	ShO	W	L	SV	AB	H	HR	BA
1972 **MON** N	0	0	–	27.00	1	0	0	.2	1	0	0	0	0	0	0	*			

Mike Torrez

TORREZ, MICHAEL AUGUSTINE
B. Aug. 28, 1946, Topeka, Kans.

BR TR 6'5" 220 lbs.

	W	L	PCT	ERA	G	GS	CG	IP	H	BB	SO	ShO	W	L	SV	AB	H	HR	BA
1967 **STL** N	0	1	.000	3.18	3	1	0	5.2	5	1	5	0	0	1	0	1	0	0	.000
1968	2	1	.667	2.84	5	2	0	19	20	12	6	0	1	0	0	7	2	0	.286
1969	10	4	.714	3.58	24	15	3	108	96	62	61	0	0	0	0	41	3	0	.073
1970	8	10	.444	4.22	30	28	5	179	168	103	100	1	0	0	0	63	17	0	.270
1971 2 teams	STL	N (9G 1–2)		MON	N (1G 0–0)														
" total	1	2	.333	5.54	10	6	0	39	45	31	10	0	0	0	0	7	1	0	.143
1972 **MON** N	16	12	.571	3.33	34	33	13	243.1	215	103	112	0	0	0	0	85	15	0	.176
1973	9	12	.429	4.46	35	34	3	208	207	115	90	1	0	0	0	69	12	0	.174
1974	15	8	.652	3.58	32	30	6	186	184	84	92	1	0	0	0	64	8	0	.125
1975 **BAL** A	20	9	**.690**	3.06	36	36	16	270.2	238	133	119	2	0	0	0	0	0	0	–
1976 **OAK** A	16	12	.571	2.50	39	39	13	266	231	87	115	4	0	0	0	0	0	0	–
1977 2 teams	OAK	A (4G 3–1)		NY	A (31G 14–12)														
" total	17	13	.567	3.92	35	35	17	243.1	235	86	102	2	0	0	0	0	0	0	–
1978 **BOS** A	16	13	.552	3.96	36	36	15	250	272	99	120	2	0	0	0	0	0	0	–
1979	16	13	.552	4.50	36	36	12	252	254	121	125	1	0	0	0	0	0	0	–
1980	9	16	.360	5.09	36	32	6	207	256	75	97	1	0	2	0	0	0	0	–
1981	10	3	.769	3.69	22	22	2	127	130	51	54	0	0	0	0	0	0	0	–
1982	9	9	.500	5.23	31	31	1	175.2	196	74	84	0	0	0	0	0	0	0	–
1983 **NY** N	10	17	.370	4.37	39	34	5	222.1	227	113	94	0	0	0	0	65	3	0	.046
1984 2 teams	NY	N (9G 1–5)		OAK	A (2G 0–0)														
" total	1	5	.167	6.30	11	8	0	40	64	21	18	0	0	0	0	10	3	0	.300
18 yrs.	185	160	.536	3.97	494	458	117	3042	3043	1371	1404	15	1	3	0	412	64	0	.155

LEAGUE CHAMPIONSHIP SERIES

	W	L	PCT	ERA	G	GS	CG	IP	H	BB	SO	ShO	W	L	SV	AB	H	HR	BA
1977 **NY** A	0	1	.000	4.09	2	1	0	11	11	5	5	0	0	0	0	0	0	0	–

WORLD SERIES

	W	L	PCT	ERA	G	GS	CG	IP	H	BB	SO	ShO	W	L	SV	AB	H	HR	BA
1977 **NY** A	2	0	1.000	2.50	2	2	2	18	16	5	15	0	0	0	0	6	0	0	.000

Lou Tost

TOST, LOUIS EUGENE
B. June 1, 1911, Cumberland, Wash.   D. Feb. 22, 1967, Santa Clara, Calif.

BL TL 6' 175 lbs.

	W	L	PCT	ERA	G	GS	CG	IP	H	BB	SO	ShO	W	L	SV	AB	H	HR	BA
1942 **BOS** N	10	10	.500	3.53	35	22	5	147.2	146	52	43	1	3	2	0	51	9	0	.176
1943	0	1	.000	5.40	3	1	0	6.2	10	4	3	0	0	0	0	1	0	0	.000
1947 **PIT** N	0	0	–	9.00	1	0	0	1	3	0	0	0	0	0	0	0	0	0	–
3 yrs.	10	11	.476	3.65	39	23	5	155.1	159	56	46	1	3	2	0	52	9	0	.173

Paul Toth

TOTH, PAUL LOUIS
B. June 30, 1935, McRoberts, Ky.

BR TR 6'1" 175 lbs.

	W	L	PCT	ERA	G	GS	CG	IP	H	BB	SO	ShO	W	L	SV	AB	H	HR	BA
1962 2 teams	STL	N (6G 1–0)		CHI	N (6G 3–1)														
" total	4	1	.800	4.62	12	5	2	50.2	47	14	16	0	0	0	0	16	4	0	.250
1963 **CHI** N	5	9	.357	3.10	27	14	3	130.2	115	35	66	2	1	3	0	39	1	0	.026
1964	0	2	.000	8.44	4	2	0	10.2	15	5	0	0	0	0	0	3	1	0	.333
3 yrs.	9	12	.429	3.80	43	21	5	192	177	54	82	2	1	3	0	58	6	0	.103

Clay Touchstone

TOUCHSTONE, CLAYTON MAFFITT
B. Jan. 24, 1903, Moore, Pa.   D. Apr. 28, 1949, Beaumont, Tex.

BR TR 5'11½" 175 lbs.

	W	L	PCT	ERA	G	GS	CG	IP	H	BB	SO	ShO	W	L	SV	AB	H	HR	BA
1928 **BOS** N	0	0	–	4.50	5	0	0	8	15	2	1	0	0	0	0	2	0	0	.000
1929	0	0	–	16.88	1	0	0	2.2	6	1	0	0	0	0	0	1	1	0	1.000

	W	L	PCT	ERA	G	GS	CG	IP	H	BB	SO	ShO	Relief Pitching W	L	SV	BATTING AB	H	HR	BA

Bucky Walters continued

	W	L	PCT	ERA	G	GS	CG	IP	H	BB	SO	ShO	W	L	SV	AB	H	HR	BA
1932	0	0	—	0.00	0	0	0	0	0	0	0	0	0	0	0	75	14	0	.187
1933 BOS A	0	0	—	0.00	0	0	0		0	0	0	0	0	0	0	195	50	4	.256
1934 PHI N	0	0	—	1.29	2	1	0	7	8	2	7	0	0	0	0	388	97	8	.250
1935	9	9	.500	4.17	24	22	8	151	168	68	40	2	0	1	0	96	24	0	.250
1936	11	21	.344	4.26	40	33	15	258	284	115	66	4	1	1	0	121	29	1	.240
1937	14	15	.483	4.75	37	34	15	246.1	292	86	87	3	0	1	0	137	38	1	.277
1938 2 teams			PHI	N	(12G	4–8)		CIN	N	(27G	11–6)								
" total	15	14	.517	4.20	39	34	20	251	259	108	93	3	1	0	1	99	19	1	.192
1939 CIN N	27	11	.711	2.29	39	36	31	319	250	109	137	2	0	3	0	120	39	1	.325
1940	22	10	.688	2.48	36	36	29	305	241	92	115	3	0	0	0	117	24	1	.205
1941	19	15	.559	2.83	37	35	27	302	292	88	129	5	0	0	2	106	20	0	.189
1942	15	14	.517	2.66	34	32	21	253.2	223	73	109	2	0	1	0	99	24	2	.242
1943	15	15	.500	3.54	34	34	21	246.1	244	109	80	5	0	0	0	90	24	1	.267
1944	23	8	.742	2.40	34	32	27	285	233	87	77	6	1	0	1	107	30	0	.280
1945	10	10	.500	2.68	22	22	12	168	166	51	45	3	0	0	0	61	14	3	.230
1946	10	7	.588	2.56	22	22	10	151.1	146	64	60	2	0	0	0	55	7	0	.127
1947	8	8	.500	5.75	20	20	5	122	137	49	43	2	0	0	0	45	12	0	.267
1948	0	3	.000	4.63	7	5	1	35	42	18	19	0	0	0	0	15	4	0	.267
1950 BOS N	0	0	—	4.50	1	0	0	4	5	2	0	0	0	0	0	2	0	0	.000
19 yrs.	198	160	.553	3.30	428	398	242	3104.2	2990	1121	1107	42	3	7	4	*			

WORLD SERIES																			
1939 CIN N	0	2	.000	4.91	2	1	1	11	13	1	6	0	0	0	0	3	0	0	.000
1940	2	0	1.000	1.50	2	2	2	18	8	6	6	1	0	0	0	7	2	1	.286
2 yrs.	2	2	.500	2.79	4	3	3	29	21	7	12	1	0	0	0	10	2	1	.200

Charley Walters

WALTERS, CHARLES LEONARD   BR TR 6'4"   190 lbs.
B. Feb. 21, 1947, Minneapolis, Minn.

	W	L	PCT	ERA	G	GS	CG	IP	H	BB	SO	ShO	W	L	SV	AB	H	HR	BA
1969 MIN A	0	0	—	5.40	6	0	0	6.2	6	3	2	0	0	0	0	0	0	0	—

Mike Walters

WALTERS, MICHAEL CHARLES   BR TR 6'5"   195 lbs.
B. Oct. 18, 1957, St. Louis, Mo.

	W	L	PCT	ERA	G	GS	CG	IP	H	BB	SO	ShO	W	L	SV	AB	H	HR	BA
1983 MIN A	1	1	.500	4.12	23	0	0	59	52	20	21	0	1	1	2	0	0	0	—
1984	0	3	.000	3.72	23	0	0	29	31	14	10	0	0	3	2	0	0	0	—
2 yrs.	1	4	.200	3.99	46	0	0	88	83	34	31	0	1	4	4	0	0	0	—

Dick Wantz

WANTZ, RICHARD CARTER   BR TR 6'5"   175 lbs.
B. Apr. 11, 1940, South Gate, Calif.   D. May 14, 1965, Inglewood, Calif.

	W	L	PCT	ERA	G	GS	CG	IP	H	BB	SO	ShO	W	L	SV	AB	H	HR	BA
1965 CAL A	0	0	—	18.00	1	0	0	1	3	0	2	0	0	0	0	0	0	0	—

Ward

WARD,
B. St. Louis, Mo.   Deceased.

	W	L	PCT	ERA	G	GS	CG	IP	H	BB	SO	ShO	W	L	SV	AB	H	HR	BA
1885 PRO N	0	1	.000	4.50	1	1	1	8	10	1	3	0	0	0	0	3	0	0	.000

Dick Ward

WARD, RICHARD (Ole)   BR TR 6'1"   198 lbs.
B. May 21, 1909, Herrick, S. D.   D. May 31, 1966, Freeland, Wash.

	W	L	PCT	ERA	G	GS	CG	IP	H	BB	SO	ShO	W	L	SV	AB	H	HR	BA
1934 CHI N	0	0	—	3.18	3	0	0	5.2	9	2	1	0	0	0	0	1	0	0	.000
1935 STL N	0	0	—	0.00	1	0	0	0	0	1	0	0	0	0	0	0	0	0	—
2 yrs.	0	0	—	3.18	4	0	0	5.2	9	3	1	0	0	0	0	1	0	0	.000

Monte Ward

WARD, JOHN MONTGOMERY   BL TR 5'9"   165 lbs.
B. Mar. 3, 1860, Bellefonte, Pa.   BB 1888
D. Mar. 4, 1925, Augusta, Ga.
Manager 1884, 1890-94.
Hall of Fame 1964.

	W	L	PCT	ERA	G	GS	CG	IP	H	BB	SO	ShO	W	L	SV	AB	H	HR	BA
1878 PRO N	22	13	.629	1.51	37	37	37	334	308	34	116	6	0	0	0	138	27	1	.196
1879	47	17	.734	2.15	70	60	58	587	571	36	239	2	5	1	1	364	104	2	.286
1880	40	23	.635	1.74	70	67	59	595	501	45	230	9	1	1	1	356	81	0	.228
1881	18	18	.500	2.13	39	35	32	330	326	53	119	3	1	1	0	357	87	0	.244
1882	19	13	.594	2.59	33	32	29	278	261	36	72	4	0	0	1	355	87	0	.245
1883 NY N	12	14	.462	2.70	33	25	24	277	278	31	121	1	4	1	0	380	97	7	.255
1884	3	3	.500	3.41	9	5	5	60.2	72	18	23	0	0	1	0	482	122	2	.253
7 yrs.	161	101	.615	2.10	291	261	244	2461.2	2317	253	920	25	11	5	3	*			
				4th															

Jon Warden

WARDEN, JONATHAN EDGAR (Warbler)   BB TL 6'   205 lbs.
B. Oct. 1, 1946, Columbus, Ohio

	W	L	PCT	ERA	G	GS	CG	IP	H	BB	SO	ShO	W	L	SV	AB	H	HR	BA
1968 DET A	4	1	.800	3.62	28	0	0	37.1	30	15	25	0	4	1	3	2	0	0	.000

Curt Wardle

WARDLE, CURTIS   BL TL 6'5"   220 lbs.
B. Nov. 16, 1960, Downey, Calif.

	W	L	PCT	ERA	G	GS	CG	IP	H	BB	SO	ShO	W	L	SV	AB	H	HR	BA
1984 MIN A	0	0	—	4.50	2	0	0	4	3	1	5	0	0	0	0	0	0	0	—

Jack Warhop

WARHOP, JOHN MILTON (Crab, Chief)   BR TR 5'9½"   168 lbs.
Born John Milton Wauhop.
B. July 4, 1884, Hinton, W. Va.   D. Oct. 4, 1960, Freeport, Ill.

	W	L	PCT	ERA	G	GS	CG	IP	H	BB	SO	ShO	W	L	SV	AB	H	HR	BA
1908 NY A	1	2	.333	4.46	5	4	3	36.1	40	8	11	0	0	0	0	16	1	0	.063
1909	13	15	.464	2.40	36	23	21	243.1	197	81	95	3	4	2	2	86	11	0	.128
1910	14	14	.500	2.87	37	27	20	254	219	79	75	0	3	2	2	79	14	0	.177
1911	12	13	.480	4.16	31	25	17	209.2	239	44	71	1	1	2	0	77	12	0	.156
1912	10	19	.345	2.86	39	22	16	258	256	59	110	0	4	3	3	92	19	0	.207
1913	4	6	.400	3.75	15	7	1	62.1	69	33	11	0	0	3	0	23	3	0	.130
1914	8	15	.348	2.37	37	23	15	216.2	182	44	56	0	0	3	0	71	10	0	.141

	W	L	PCT	ERA	G	GS	CG	IP	H	BB	SO	ShO	Relief Pitching W	L	SV	AB	H	HR	BA

Jack Warhop continued

	W	L	PCT	ERA	G	GS	CG	IP	H	BB	SO	ShO	W	L	SV	AB	H	HR	BA
1915	7	9	.438	3.96	21	19	12	143.1	164	52	34	0	1	0	0	51	7	0	.137
8 yrs.	69	93	.426	3.09	221	150	105	1423.2	1366	400	463	4	13	15	7	495	77	0	.156

Cy Warmoth

WARMOTH, WALLACE WALTER   BL TL 5'11"   158 lbs.
B. Feb. 2, 1893, Bone Gap, Ill.   D. June 20, 1957, Mt. Carmel, Ill.

	W	L	PCT	ERA	G	GS	CG	IP	H	BB	SO	ShO	W	L	SV	AB	H	HR	BA
1916 STL N	0	0	–	14.40	3	0	0	5	12	4	1	0	0	0	0	2	0	0	.000
1922 WAS A	1	0	1.000	1.42	5	1	1	19	15	9	8	0	1	0	0	7	1	0	.143
1923	7	4	.636	4.29	21	13	4	105	103	76	45	0	1	0	0	36	8	0	.222
3 yrs.	8	4	.667	4.26	29	14	5	129	130	89	54	0	2	0	0	45	9	0	.200

Lon Warneke

WARNEKE, LONNIE (The Arkansas Humming Bird)   BR TR 6'2"   185 lbs.
B. Mar. 28, 1909, Mt. Ida, Ark.   D. June 23, 1976, Hot Springs, Ark.

	W	L	PCT	ERA	G	GS	CG	IP	H	BB	SO	ShO	W	L	SV	AB	H	HR	BA
1930 CHI N	0	0	–	33.75	1	0	0	1.1	2	5	0	0	0	0	0	0	0	0	
1931	2	4	.333	3.22	20	7	3	64.1	67	37	27	0	0	1	0	19	5	0	.263
1932	22	6	.786	2.37	35	32	25	277	247	64	106	4	0	0	0	99	19	0	.192
1933	18	13	.581	2.00	36	34	26	287.1	262	75	133	4	0	0	1	100	30	2	.300
1934	22	10	.688	3.21	43	35	23	291.1	273	66	143	3	2	1	3	113	22	0	.195
1935	20	13	.606	3.06	42	30	20	261.2	257	50	120	1	4	3	4	91	20	0	.220
1936	16	13	.552	3.44	40	29	13	240.2	246	76	113	4	1	5	1	84	17	1	.202
1937 STL N	18	11	.621	4.53	36	33	18	238.2	280	69	87	2	0	0	0	80	21	0	.263
1938	13	8	.619	3.97	31	26	12	197	199	64	89	4	2	0	0	71	23	0	.324
1939	13	7	.650	3.78	34	21	6	162	160	49	59	3	3	1	2	52	10	0	.192
1940	16	10	.615	3.14	33	31	17	232	235	47	85	1	0	0	0	86	18	1	.209
1941	17	9	.654	3.15	37	30	12	246	227	82	83	4	3	1	0	77	9	0	.117
1942 2 teams		STL	N (12G 6–4)		CHI	N (15G 5–7)													
" total	11	11	.500	2.73	27	24	13	181	173	36	59	1	0	0	2	62	16	0	.258
1943 CHI N	4	5	.444	3.16	21	10	4	88.1	82	18	30	0	1	0	0	26	5	0	.192
1945	1	1	.500	3.86	9	1	0	14	16	1	6	0	1	0	0	2	0	0	.000
15 yrs.	193	121	.615	3.18	445	343	192	2782.2	2726	739	1140	31	17	12	13	962	215	4	.223
WORLD SERIES																			
1932 CHI N	0	1	.000	5.91	2	1	1	10.2	15	5	8	0	0	0	0	4	0	0	.000
1935	2	0	1.000	0.54	3	2	1	16.2	9	4	5	1	0	0	0	5	1	0	.200
2 yrs.	2	1	.667	2.63	5	3	2	27.1	24	9	13	1	0	0	0	9	1	0	.111

Ed Warner

WARNER, EDWARD EMORY   BR TL 5'10½" 165 lbs.
B. June 20, 1889, Fitchburg, Mass.   D. Feb. 2, 1954, Fitchburg, Mass.

	W	L	PCT	ERA	G	GS	CG	IP	H	BB	SO	ShO	W	L	SV	AB	H	HR	BA
1912 PIT N	1	1	.500	3.60	11	3	1	45	40	18	13	1	0	0	0	15	2	0	.133

Jack Warner

WARNER, JACK DYER   BR TR 5'11"   190 lbs.
B. July 12, 1940, Brandywine, W. Va.

	W	L	PCT	ERA	G	GS	CG	IP	H	BB	SO	ShO	W	L	SV	AB	H	HR	BA
1962 CHI N	0	0	–	7.71	7	0	0	7	9	3	0	0	0	0	0	0	0	0	–
1963	0	1	.000	2.78	8	0	0	22.2	21	8	7	0	0	1	0	4	1	0	.250
1964	0	0	–	2.89	7	0	0	9.1	12	4	6	0	0	0	0	0	0	0	–
1965	0	1	.000	8.62	11	0	0	15.2	22	9	7	0	0	1	0	1	0	0	.000
4 yrs.	0	2	.000	5.10	33	0	0	54.2	64	21	23	0	0	2	0	5	1	0	.200

Mike Warren

WARREN, MICHAEL BURCE   BR TR 6'1"   175 lbs.
B. Mar. 26, 1961, Inglewood, Calif.

	W	L	PCT	ERA	G	GS	CG	IP	H	BB	SO	ShO	W	L	SV	AB	H	HR	BA
1983 OAK A	5	3	.625	4.11	12	9	3	65.2	51	18	30	1	0	1	0	0	0	0	–
1984	3	6	.333	4.90	24	12	0	90	104	44	61	0	0	0	0	0	0	0	–
2 yrs.	8	9	.471	4.57	36	21	3	155.2	155	62	91	1	0	1	0	0	0	0	–

Tommy Warren

WARREN, THOMAS GENTRY   BL TR 6'1"   180 lbs.
B. July 5, 1917, Tulsa, Okla.   D. Jan. 2, 1968, Tulsa, Okla.

	W	L	PCT	ERA	G	GS	CG	IP	H	BB	SO	ShO	W	L	SV	AB	H	HR	BA
1944 BKN N	1	4	.200	4.98	22	4	2	68.2	74	40	18	0	0	1	0	43	11	0	.256

Dan Warthen

WARTHEN, DANIEL DEAN   BR TL 6'   200 lbs.
B. Dec. 1, 1952, Omaha, Neb.

	W	L	PCT	ERA	G	GS	CG	IP	H	BB	SO	ShO	W	L	SV	AB	H	HR	BA
1975 MON N	8	6	.571	3.11	40	18	2	168	130	87	128	0	4	2	3	51	6	0	.118
1976	2	10	.167	5.30	23	16	2	90	76	66	67	1	0	0	0	27	0	0	.000
1977 2 teams		MON	N (12G 2–3)		PHI	N (3G 0–1)													
" total	2	4	.333	7.22	15	6	1	38.2	37	43	27	0	1	1	0	9	1	0	.111
1978 HOU N	0	1	.000	4.09	5	1	0	11	10	2	2	0	0	0	0	2	0	0	.000
4 yrs.	12	21	.364	4.30	83	41	5	307.2	253	198	224	1	5	3	3	89	7	0	.079

George Washburn

WASHBURN, GEORGE EDWARD   BL TR 6'1"   175 lbs.
B. Oct. 6, 1914, Solon, Me.   D. Jan. 5, 1979, Baton Rouge, La.

	W	L	PCT	ERA	G	GS	CG	IP	H	BB	SO	ShO	W	L	SV	AB	H	HR	BA
1941 NY A	0	1	.000	13.50	1	1	0	2	2	5	1	0	0	0	0	1	0	0	.000

Greg Washburn

WASHBURN, GREGORY JAMES   BR TR 6'   190 lbs.
B. Dec. 3, 1946, Joliet, Ill.

	W	L	PCT	ERA	G	GS	CG	IP	H	BB	SO	ShO	W	L	SV	AB	H	HR	BA
1969 CAL A	0	2	.000	7.94	8	2	0	11.1	21	5	4	0	0	0	0	0	0	0	–

Libe Washburn

WASHBURN, LIBE   BB TL
B. June 16, 1874, Lyme, N. H.   D. Mar. 22, 1940, Malone, N. Y.

	W	L	PCT	ERA	G	GS	CG	IP	H	BB	SO	ShO	W	L	SV	AB	H	HR	BA
1903 PHI N	0	4	.000	4.37	4	4	4	35	44	11	9	0	0	0	0	*			

Ray Washburn

WASHBURN, RAY CLARK   BR TR 6'1"   205 lbs.
B. May 31, 1938, Pasco, Wash.

	W	L	PCT	ERA	G	GS	CG	IP	H	BB	SO	ShO	W	L	SV	AB	H	HR	BA
1961 STL N	1	1	.500	1.77	3	2	1	20.1	10	7	12	0	0	0	0	8	1	0	.125
1962	12	9	.571	4.10	34	25	2	175.2	187	58	109	1	1	0	2	56	10	0	.179
1963	5	3	.625	3.08	19	11	4	64.1	50	14	47	2	0	0	0	19	1	0	.053
1964	3	4	.429	4.05	15	10	0	60	60	17	28	0	0	0	2	15	2	0	.133
1965	9	11	.450	3.62	28	16	1	119.1	114	28	67	1	5	0	2	33	5	0	.152

	W	L	PCT	ERA	G	GS	CG	IP	H	BB	SO	ShO	Relief Pitching W	L	SV	BATTING AB	H	HR	BA

Ray Washburn continued

	W	L	PCT	ERA	G	GS	CG	IP	H	BB	SO	ShO	W	L	SV	AB	H	HR	BA
1966	11	9	.550	3.76	27	26	4	170	183	44	98	1	0	0	0	54	5	1	.093
1967	10	7	.588	3.53	27	27	3	186.1	190	42	98	1	0	0	0	66	6	0	.091
1968	14	8	.636	2.26	31	30	8	215.1	191	47	124	4	1	0	0	60	5	0	.083
1969	3	8	.273	3.07	28	16	2	132	133	49	80	0	0	0	1	37	3	0	.081
1970 CIN N	4	4	.500	6.95	35	3	0	66	90	48	37	0	4	2	0	13	0	0	.000
10 yrs.	72	64	.529	3.54	239	166	25	1209.1	1208	354	700	10	11	4	5	361	38	1	.105

WORLD SERIES

	W	L	PCT	ERA	G	GS	CG	IP	H	BB	SO	ShO	W	L	SV	AB	H	HR	BA
1967 STL N	0	0	—	0.00	2	0	0	2.1	1	1	2	0	0	0	0	0	0	0	—
1968	1	1	.500	9.82	2	2	0	7.1	7	7	6	0	0	0	0	3	0	0	.000
1970 CIN N	0	0	—	13.50	1	0	0	1.1	2	2	0	0	0	0	0	0	0	0	—
3 yrs.	1	1	.500	8.18	5	2	0	11	10	10	8	0	0	0	0	3	0	0	.000

Buck Washer

WASHER, WILLIAM   TR 5'10" 175 lbs.
B. Oct. 11, 1882, Akron, Ohio   D. Dec. 8, 1955, Akron, Ohio

	W	L	PCT	ERA	G	GS	CG	IP	H	BB	SO	ShO	W	L	SV	AB	H	HR	BA
1905 PHI N	0	0	—	6.00	1	0	0	3	4	5	0	0	0	0	0	1	0	0	.000

Gary Waslewski

WASLEWSKI, GARY LEE   BR TR 6'4" 190 lbs.
B. July 21, 1941, Meriden, Conn.

	W	L	PCT	ERA	G	GS	CG	IP	H	BB	SO	ShO	W	L	SV	AB	H	HR	BA
1967 BOS A	2	2	.500	3.21	12	8	0	42	34	20	20	0	0	0	0	11	1	0	.091
1968	4	7	.364	3.67	34	11	2	105.1	108	40	59	0	1	1	2	26	1	0	.038
1969 2 teams		STL N	(12G 0–2)		MON	N	(30G 3–7)												
" total	3	9	.250	3.39	42	14	3	130	121	71	79	1	0	2	2	31	1	0	.032
1970 2 teams		MON	N	(6G 0–2)	NY	A	(26G 2–2)												
" total	2	4	.333	3.71	32	9	0	80	65	42	46	0	1	0	0	16	1	0	.063
1971 NY A	0	1	.000	3.25	24	0	0	36	28	16	17	0	0	1	1	1	0	0	.000
1972 OAK A	0	3	.000	2.00	8	0	0	18	12	8	8	0	0	3	0	3	0	0	.000
6 yrs.	11	26	.297	3.44	152	42	5	411.1	368	197	229	1	2	7	5	88	4	0	.045

WORLD SERIES

	W	L	PCT	ERA	G	GS	CG	IP	H	BB	SO	ShO	W	L	SV	AB	H	HR	BA
1967 BOS A	0	0	—	2.16	2	1	0	8.1	4	2	7	0	0	0	0	1	0	0	.000

Steve Waterbury

WATERBURY, STEVEN CRAIG   BR TR 6'5" 190 lbs.
B. Apr. 6, 1952, Marion, Ill.

	W	L	PCT	ERA	G	GS	CG	IP	H	BB	SO	ShO	W	L	SV	AB	H	HR	BA
1976 STL N	0	0	—	6.00	5	0	0	6	7	3	4	0	0	0	0	0	0	0	—

Fred Waters

WATERS, FRED WARREN   BL TL 5'11" 185 lbs.
B. Feb. 2, 1927, Benton, Miss.

	W	L	PCT	ERA	G	GS	CG	IP	H	BB	SO	ShO	W	L	SV	AB	H	HR	BA
1955 PIT N	0	0	—	3.60	2	0	0	5	7	2	0	0	0	0	0	1	0	0	.000
1956	2	2	.500	2.82	23	5	1	51	48	30	14	0	0	1	0	20	1	0	.050
2 yrs.	2	2	.500	2.89	25	5	1	56	55	32	14	0	0	1	0	21	1	0	.048

Bob Watkins

WATKINS, ROBERT CECIL   BR TR 6'1" 170 lbs.
B. Mar. 12, 1948, San Francisco, Calif.

	W	L	PCT	ERA	G	GS	CG	IP	H	BB	SO	ShO	W	L	SV	AB	H	HR	BA
1969 HOU N	0	0	—	5.06	5	0	0	16	13	13	11	0	0	0	0	2	0	0	.000

Doc Watson

WATSON, CHARLES JOHN   BR TL 5'10½" 170 lbs.
B. Jan. 30, 1885, Kensington, Ohio   D. Dec. 30, 1949, San Diego, Calif.

	W	L	PCT	ERA	G	GS	CG	IP	H	BB	SO	ShO	W	L	SV	AB	H	HR	BA
1913 CHI N	1	0	1.000	1.00	1	1	1	9	8	6	1	0	0	0	0	2	0	0	.000
1914 2 teams		CHI	F	(26G 9–11)	STL	F	(9G 3–4)												
" total	12	15	.444	2.01	35	25	14	228	186	73	87	5	1	3	1	70	7	0	.100
1915 STL F	7	10	.412	3.98	33	20	6	135.2	132	58	45	0	2	0	0	40	5	0	.125
3 yrs.	20	25	.444	2.70	69	46	21	372.2	326	137	133	5	3	3	1	112	12	0	.107

Milt Watson

WATSON, MILTON WILSON (Mule)   BR TR 6'1" 180 lbs.
B. Jan. 10, 1890, Floville, Ga.   D. Apr. 10, 1962, Pine Bluff, Ark.

	W	L	PCT	ERA	G	GS	CG	IP	H	BB	SO	ShO	W	L	SV	AB	H	HR	BA
1916 STL N	4	6	.400	3.06	18	13	5	103	109	33	27	2	0	0	0	32	7	0	.219
1917	10	13	.435	3.51	41	20	5	161.1	149	51	45	3	3	3	0	51	5	0	.098
1918 PHI N	5	7	.417	3.43	23	11	6	112.2	126	36	29	0	2	1	0	40	3	0	.075
1919	2	4	.333	5.17	8	4	3	47	51	19	12	0	1	1	0	16	1	0	.063
4 yrs.	21	30	.412	3.57	90	48	19	424	435	139	113	5	6	5	0	139	16	0	.115

Mother Watson

WATSON, WALTER L.   5'9" 145 lbs.
B. Jan. 27, 1865, Middleport, Ohio   D. Nov. 23, 1898, Middleport, Ohio

	W	L	PCT	ERA	G	GS	CG	IP	H	BB	SO	ShO	W	L	SV	AB	H	HR	BA
1887 CIN AA	0	1	.000	5.79	2	2	1	14	22	6	1	0	0	0	0	8	1	0	.125

Mule Watson

WATSON, JOHN REEVES   BR TR 6'1½" 185 lbs.
B. Oct. 15, 1896, Homer, La.   D. Aug. 25, 1949, Shreveport, La.

	W	L	PCT	ERA	G	GS	CG	IP	H	BB	SO	ShO	W	L	SV	AB	H	HR	BA
1918 PHI A	7	10	.412	3.37	21	19	11	141.2	139	44	30	3	0	0	0	52	7	0	.135
1919	0	1	.000	6.91	4	2	0	14.1	17	7	6	0	0	0	0	6	0	0	.000
1920 2 teams		BOS	N	(13G 5–4)	PIT	N	(5G 0–0)												
" total	5	4	.556	4.29	18	10	4	86	94	24	17	2	0	1	0	27	3	0	.111
1921 BOS N	14	13	.519	3.85	44	31	15	259.1	269	57	48	1	2	1	2	87	12	0	.138
1922	8	14	.364	4.70	41	29	8	201	262	59	53	1	1	0	1	66	13	0	.197
1923 2 teams		BOS	N	(11G 1–2)	NY	N	(17G 8–5)												
" total	9	7	.563	3.84	28	19	9	138.1	159	41	36	0	1	0	1	54	10	0	.185
1924 NY N	7	4	.636	3.79	22	16	6	99.2	122	24	18	1	1	0	0	35	9	2	.257
7 yrs.	50	53	.485	4.04	178	126	53	940.1	1062	256	208	8	5	2	4	327	54	2	.165

WORLD SERIES

	W	L	PCT	ERA	G	GS	CG	IP	H	BB	SO	ShO	W	L	SV	AB	H	HR	BA
1923 NY N	0	0	—	13.50	1	1	0	2	4	1	1	0	0	0	0	0	0	0	—
1924	0	0	—	0.00	1	0	0	.2	0	0	0	0	0	0	1	0	0	0	—
2 yrs.	0	0	—	10.13	2	1	0	2.2	4	1	1	0	0	0	1	0	0	0	—

	W	L	PCT	ERA	G	GS	CG	IP	H	BB	SO	ShO	Relief Pitching			BATTING			BA
													W	L	SV	AB	H	HR	

Eddie Watt

WATT, EDWARD DEAN
B. Apr. 4, 1942, Lamonie, Iowa BR TR 5'10" 183 lbs.

	W	L	PCT	ERA	G	GS	CG	IP	H	BB	SO	ShO	W	L	SV	AB	H	HR	BA
1966 BAL A	9	7	.563	3.83	43	13	1	145.2	123	44	102	0	7	2	4	46	14	2	.304
1967	3	5	.375	2.26	49	0	0	103.2	67	37	93	0	3	5	8	22	4	1	.182
1968	5	5	.500	2.27	59	0	0	83.1	63	35	72	0	5	5	11	8	0	0	.000
1969	5	2	.714	1.65	56	0	0	71	49	26	46	0	5	2	16	8	0	0	.000
1970	7	7	.500	3.27	53	0	0	55	44	29	33	0	7	7	12	8	1	0	.125
1971	3	1	.750	1.80	35	0	0	40	39	8	26	0	3	1	11	5	0	0	.000
1972	2	3	.400	2.15	38	0	0	46	30	20	23	0	2	3	7	2	0	0	.000
1973	3	4	.429	3.30	30	0	0	71	62	21	38	0	3	4	5	0	0	0	—
1974 PHI N	1	1	.500	4.03	42	0	0	38	39	26	23	0	1	1	6	1	0	0	.000
1975 CHI N	0	1	.000	13.50	6	0	0	6	14	8	6	0	0	1	0	0	0	0	—
10 yrs.	38	36	.514	2.91	411	13	1	659.2	530	254	462	0	36	31	80	100	19	3	.190
LEAGUE CHAMPIONSHIP SERIES																			
1969 BAL A	0	0	—	0.00	1	0	0	2	0	0	2	0	0	0	0	0	0	0	—
1971	0	0	—	0.00	1	0	0	2	2	0	1	0	0	0	1	0	0	0	—
1973	0	0	—	0.00	1	0	0	.1	0	0	0	0	0	0	0	0	0	0	—
3 yrs.	0	0	—	0.00	3	0	0	4.1	2	0	3	0	0	0	1	0	0	0	—
WORLD SERIES																			
1969 BAL A	0	1	.000	3.00	2	0	0	3	4	0	3	0	0	1	0	0	0	0	—
1970	0	1	.000	9.00	1	0	0	1	2	1	3	0	0	1	0	0	0	0	—
1971	0	1	.000	3.86	2	0	0	2.1	4	0	2	0	0	0	0	0	0	0	—
3 yrs.	0	3	.000	4.26	5	0	0	6.1	10	1	8	0	0	2	0	0	0	0	—
														2nd					

Frank Watt

WATT, FRANK MARION (Kilo)
Brother of Bob Watson.
B. Dec. 15, 1902, Washington, D. C. D. Aug. 31, 1956, Washington, D. C. BR TR 6'1" 205 lbs.

	W	L	PCT	ERA	G	GS	CG	IP	H	BB	SO	ShO	W	L	SV	AB	H	HR	BA
1931 PHI N	5	5	.500	4.84	38	12	5	122.2	147	49	25	0	1	0	2	39	8	0	.205

Jim Waugh

WAUGH, JAMES ELDEN
B. Nov. 25, 1933, Lancaster, Ohio BR TR 6'3" 185 lbs.

	W	L	PCT	ERA	G	GS	CG	IP	H	BB	SO	ShO	W	L	SV	AB	H	HR	BA
1952 PIT N	1	6	.143	6.36	17	7	1	52.1	61	32	18	0	0	1	0	10	1	0	.100
1953	4	5	.444	6.48	29	11	1	90.1	108	56	23	0	0	0	0	22	5	0	.227
2 yrs.	5	11	.313	6.43	46	18	2	142.2	169	88	41	0	0	1	0	32	6	0	.188

Frank Wayenberg

WAYENBERG, FRANK
B. Aug. 27, 1899, Fleming, Kans. D. Apr. 16, 1975, Zanesville, Ohio BR TR 6'½" 172 lbs.

	W	L	PCT	ERA	G	GS	CG	IP	H	BB	SO	ShO	W	L	SV	AB	H	HR	BA
1924 CLE A	0	0	—	5.40	2	1	0	6.2	7	5	3	0	0	0	0	2	1	0	.500

Hal Weafer

WEAFER, KENNETH ALBERT (Al)
B. Feb. 6, 1914, Woburn, Mass. BR TR 6'½" 183 lbs.

	W	L	PCT	ERA	G	GS	CG	IP	H	BB	SO	ShO	W	L	SV	AB	H	HR	BA
1936 BOS N	0	0	—	12.00	1	0	0	3	6	3	0	0	0	0	0	1	0	0	.000

Floyd Weaver

WEAVER, DAVID FLOYD
B. May 12, 1941, Ben Franklin, Tex. BR TR 6'4" 195 lbs.

	W	L	PCT	ERA	G	GS	CG	IP	H	BB	SO	ShO	W	L	SV	AB	H	HR	BA
1962 CLE A	1	0	1.000	1.80	1	1	0	5	3	0	8	0	0	0	0	2	1	0	.500
1965	2	2	.500	5.43	32	1	0	61.1	61	24	37	0	2	2	1	11	1	0	.091
1970 CHI A	1	2	.333	4.35	31	3	0	62	52	31	51	0	1	2	0	7	0	0	.000
1971 MIL A	0	1	.000	7.33	21	0	0	27	33	18	12	0	0	1	0	0	0	0	—
4 yrs.	4	5	.444	5.21	85	5	0	155.1	149	73	108	0	3	5	1	20	2	0	.100

Harry Weaver

WEAVER, HARRY
B. Feb. 26, 1892, Clarendon, Pa. D. May 30, 1983, Rochester, N. Y. BR TR 5'11" 160 lbs.

	W	L	PCT	ERA	G	GS	CG	IP	H	BB	SO	ShO	W	L	SV	AB	H	HR	BA
1915 PHI N	0	2	.000	3.00	2	2	2	18	18	10	1	0	0	0	0	6	1	0	.167
1916	0	0	—	10.13	3	0	0	8	14	5	2	0	0	0	0	2	1	0	.500
1917 CHI N	1	1	.500	2.75	4	2	1	19.2	17	7	8	0	0	0	0	5	1	0	.200
1918	2	2	.500	2.20	8	3	1	32.2	27	7	9	1	1	0	1	8	2	0	.250
1919	0	1	.000	10.80	2	1	0	3.1	6	2	1	0	0	0	0	1	0	0	.000
5 yrs.	3	6	.333	3.64	19	8	4	81.2	82	31	21	1	1	0	1	22	5	0	.227

Jim Weaver

WEAVER, JAMES BRIAN (Fluss)
B. Feb. 19, 1939, Lancaster, Pa. BL TL 6' 178 lbs.

	W	L	PCT	ERA	G	GS	CG	IP	H	BB	SO	ShO	W	L	SV	AB	H	HR	BA
1967 CAL A	3	0	1.000	2.67	13	2	0	30.1	26	9	20	0	1	0	1	6	0	0	.000
1968	0	1	.000	2.38	14	0	0	22.2	22	10	8	0	0	1	0	1	0	0	.000
2 yrs.	3	1	.750	2.55	27	2	0	53	48	19	28	0	1	1	1	7	0	0	.000

Jim Weaver

WEAVER, JAMES DEMENT (Big Jim)
B. Nov. 25, 1903, Fulton, Ky. D. Feb. 16, 1984, Lakeland, Fla. BR TR 6'6" 230 lbs.

	W	L	PCT	ERA	G	GS	CG	IP	H	BB	SO	ShO	W	L	SV	AB	H	HR	BA
1928 WAS A	0	0	—	1.50	3	0	0	6	2	6	2	0	0	0	0	1	0	0	.000
1931 NY A	2	1	.667	5.31	17	5	2	57.2	66	29	28	0	0	1	0	20	1	0	.050
1934 2 teams		STL	A	(5G 2-0)	CHI	N	(27G 11-9)												
" total	13	9	.591	4.18	32	25	10	178.2	180	74	109	1	2	0	0	59	4	0	.068
1935 PIT N	14	8	.636	3.42	33	22	11	176.1	177	58	87	4	2	0	0	56	4	0	.071
1936	14	8	.636	4.31	38	31	11	225.2	239	74	108	1	0	0	0	79	8	0	.101
1937	8	5	.615	3.20	32	9	2	109.2	106	31	44	1	5	4	0	27	4	0	.148
1938 2 teams		STL	A	(1G 0-1)	CIN	N	(30G 6-4)												
" total	6	5	.545	3.43	31	16	2	136.1	118	63	68	0	1	1	3	46	9	0	.196
1939 CIN N	0	0	—	3.00	3	0	0	3	3	1	3	0	0	0	0	1	0	0	.000
8 yrs.	57	36	.613	3.88	189	108	38	893.1	891	336	449	7	10	5	3	289	30	0	.104

Monte Weaver

WEAVER, MONTGOMERY MORTON (Prof)
B. June 15, 1906, Hilton, N. C. BL TR 6' 170 lbs.

	W	L	PCT	ERA	G	GS	CG	IP	H	BB	SO	ShO	W	L	SV	AB	H	HR	BA
1931 WAS A	1	0	1.000	4.50	3	1	1	10	11	6	6	0	0	0	0	3	0	0	.000
1932	22	10	.688	4.08	43	30	13	234	236	112	83	1	2	2	2	94	27	0	.287
1933	10	5	.667	3.25	23	21	12	152.1	147	53	45	1	0	0	0	56	7	0	.125

	W	L	PCT	ERA	G	GS	CG	IP	H	BB	SO	ShO	Relief Pitching W	L	SV	BATTING AB	H	HR	BA

Doc White

WHITE, GUY HARRIS
B. Apr. 9, 1879, Washington, D. C.   D. Feb. 19, 1969, Silver Springs, Md.   BL TL 6'1"   150 lbs.

	W	L	PCT	ERA	G	GS	CG	IP	H	BB	SO	ShO	W	L	SV	AB	H	HR	BA
1901 PHI N	14	13	.519	3.19	31	27	22	236.2	241	56	132	0	1	1	0	95	26	1	.274
1902	16	20	.444	2.53	36	35	34	306	277	72	185	3	0	0	1	179	47	1	.263
1903 CHI A	17	16	.515	2.13	37	36	29	300	258	69	114	3	0	0	0	99	20	0	.202
1904	16	12	.571	1.78	30	30	23	228	201	68	115	7	0	0	0	76	12	0	.158
1905	18	14	.563	1.76	36	33	25	260.1	204	58	120	4	1	0	0	86	14	0	.163
1906	18	6	.750	1.52	28	24	20	219.1	160	38	95	7	2	1	0	65	12	0	.185
1907	27	13	.675	2.26	46	35	24	291	270	38	141	7	5	1	1	90	20	0	.222
1908	18	13	.581	2.55	41	37	24	296	267	69	126	5	0	0	0	109	25	0	.229
1909	11	9	.550	1.72	24	21	14	177.2	149	31	77	3	1	0	0	192	45	0	.234
1910	15	13	.536	2.56	33	29	20	245.2	219	50	111	2	1	0	1	126	25	0	.198
1911	10	14	.417	2.98	34	29	16	214.1	219	35	72	4	1	0	2	78	20	0	.256
1912	8	10	.444	3.24	32	19	9	172	172	47	57	1	2	2	0	56	7	0	.125
1913	2	4	.333	3.50	19	8	2	103	106	39	39	0	0	1	0	25	3	0	.120
13 yrs.	190	157	.548	2.38	427	363	262	3050	2743	670	1384	46	14	6	5	*			

WORLD SERIES

| 1906 CHI A | 1 | 1 | .500 | 1.80 | 3 | 2 | 1 | 15 | 12 | 7 | 4 | 0 | 0 | 0 | 1 | 3 | 0 | 0 | .000 |

Ernie White

WHITE, ERNEST DANIEL
B. Sept. 5, 1916, Pacolet Mills, S. C.   D. May 22, 1974, Augusta, Ga.   BR TL 5'11½" 175 lbs.

	W	L	PCT	ERA	G	GS	CG	IP	H	BB	SO	ShO	W	L	SV	AB	H	HR	BA
1940 STL N	1	1	.500	4.15	8	1	0	21.2	29	14	15	0	1	0	0	7	3	0	.429
1941	17	7	.708	2.40	32	25	12	210	169	70	117	3	3	0	2	79	15	0	.190
1942	7	5	.583	2.52	26	19	7	128.1	113	41	67	1	1	0	2	41	8	0	.195
1943	5	5	.500	3.78	14	10	5	78.2	78	33	28	1	1	0	1	28	6	0	.214
1946 BOS N	0	1	.000	4.18	12	1	0	23.2	22	12	8	0	0	1	0	4	1	0	.250
1947	0	0	—	0.00	1	1	0	4	1	1	1	0	0	0	0	1	1	0	1.000
1948	0	2	.000	1.96	15	0	0	23	13	17	8	0	0	2	2	3	0	0	.000
7 yrs.	30	21	.588	2.78	108	57	24	489.1	425	188	244	5	5	3	6	163	34	0	.209

WORLD SERIES

| 1942 STL N | 1 | 0 | 1.000 | 0.00 | 1 | 1 | 1 | 9 | 6 | 0 | 6 | 1 | 0 | 0 | 0 | 2 | 0 | 0 | .000 |

Hal White

WHITE, HAROLD GEORGE
B. Mar. 18, 1919, Utica, N. Y.   BL TR 5'10" 165 lbs.

	W	L	PCT	ERA	G	GS	CG	IP	H	BB	SO	ShO	W	L	SV	AB	H	HR	BA
1941 DET A	0	0	—	6.00	4	0	0	9	11	6	2	0	0	0	0	2	0	0	.000
1942	12	12	.500	2.91	34	25	12	216.2	212	82	93	4	1	3	1	77	13	0	.169
1943	7	12	.368	3.39	32	24	7	177.2	150	71	58	2	0	2	2	57	8	0	.140
1946	1	1	.500	5.60	11	1	1	27.1	34	15	12	0	0	1	0	7	0	0	.000
1947	4	5	.444	3.61	35	5	0	84.2	91	47	33	0	4	2	2	18	3	0	.167
1948	2	1	.667	6.12	27	0	0	42.2	46	26	17	0	2	1	1	13	2	0	.154
1949	1	0	1.000	0.00	9	0	0	12	5	4	4	0	1	0	2	3	1	0	.333
1950	9	6	.600	4.54	42	8	3	111	96	65	53	1	6	3	1	33	4	0	.121
1951	3	4	.429	4.74	38	4	0	76	74	49	23	0	2	1	4	16	4	0	.250
1952	1	8	.111	3.69	41	0	0	63.1	53	39	18	0	1	8	5	11	2	0	.182
1953 2 teams			STL N (10G 0–0)				STL N (49G 6–5)												
" total	6	5	.545	2.94	59	0	0	95	92	42	34	0	6	5	7	17	0	0	.000
1954 STL N	0	0	—	19.80	4	0	0	5	11	4	2	0	0	0	0	1	0	0	.000
12 yrs.	46	54	.460	3.78	336	67	23	920.1	875	450	349	7	23	26	25	255	37	0	.145

Kirby White

WHITE, OLIVER KIRBY (Redbuck Buck)
B. Jan. 3, 1884, Hillsboro, Ohio   D. Apr. 22, 1943, Hillsboro, Ohio   BL TR 6'   190 lbs.

	W	L	PCT	ERA	G	GS	CG	IP	H	BB	SO	ShO	W	L	SV	AB	H	HR	BA
1909 BOS N	6	13	.316	3.22	23	19	11	148.1	134	80	53	0	1	0	0	50	8	0	.160
1910 2 teams			BOS N (3G 1–2)				PIT N (30G 10–9)												
" total	11	11	.500	3.16	33	24	10	179.1	157	87	48	3	2	1	2	52	14	0	.269
1911 PIT N	0	1	.000	9.00	2	1	0	3	3	1	1	0	0	0	0	1	0	0	.000
3 yrs.	17	25	.405	3.24	58	44	21	330.2	294	168	102	3	3	1	2	103	22	0	.214

Larry White

WHITE, LARRY DAVID
B. Sept. 25, 1958, San Fernando, Calif.   BR TR 6'4" 185 lbs.

	W	L	PCT	ERA	G	GS	CG	IP	H	BB	SO	ShO	W	L	SV	AB	H	HR	BA
1983 LA N	0	0	—	1.29	4	0	0	7	4	3	5	0	0	0	0	0	0	0	—
1984	0	1	.000	3.00	7	1	0	12	9	6	10	0	0	1	0	1	0	0	.000
2 yrs.	0	1	.000	2.37	11	1	0	19	13	9	15	0	0	1	0	1	0	0	.000

Steve White

WHITE, STEPHEN VINCENT
B. Dec. 21, 1884, Dorchester, Mass.   D. Jan. 29, 1975, Braintree, Mass.   BR TR 5'10" 160 lbs.

	W	L	PCT	ERA	G	GS	CG	IP	H	BB	SO	ShO	W	L	SV	AB	H	HR	BA
1912 2 teams			WAS A (1G 0–0)				BOS N (3G 0–0)												
" total	0	0	—	5.40	4	0	0	6.2	11	5	3	0	0	0	0	3	0	0	.000

Will White

WHITE, WILLIAM HENRY (Whoop-La)
Brother of Deacon White.
B. Oct. 11, 1854, Caton, N. Y.   D. Aug. 31, 1911, Port Carling, Ont., Canada   BB TR 5'9½" 175 lbs.
Manager 1884.

	W	L	PCT	ERA	G	GS	CG	IP	H	BB	SO	ShO	W	L	SV	AB	H	HR	BA
1877 BOS N	2	1	.667	3.00	3	3	3	27	27	2	7	1	0	0	0	15	3	0	.200
1878 CIN N	30	21	.588	1.79	52	52	52	468	477	45	169	5	0	0	0	197	28	0	.142
1879	43	31	.581	1.99	76	75	75	680	676	68	232	4	0	0	0	294	40	0	.136
1880	18	42	.300	2.14	62	62	58	517.1	550	56	161	3	0	0	0	207	35	0	.169
1881 DET N	0	2	.000	5.00	2	2	2	18	24	2	5	0	0	0	0	7	0	0	.000
1882 CIN AA	40	12	.769	1.54	54	54	52	480	411	71	122	8	0	0	0	207	55	0	.266
1883	43	22	.662	2.09	65	64	64	577	473	104	141	6	0	1	0	240	54	0	.225
1884	34	18	.654	3.32	52	52	52	456	479	74	118	7	0	0	0	184	35	1	.190
1885	18	15	.545	3.53	34	34	33	293.1	295	64	80	2	0	0	0	118	20	0	.169
1886	1	2	.333	4.15	3	3	3	26	28	10	6	0	0	0	0	9	1	0	.111
10 yrs.	229	166	.580	2.28	403	401	394	3542.2	3440	496	1041	36	0	1	0	1478	271	1	.183
				10th															

	W	L	PCT	ERA	G	GS	CG	IP	H	BB	SO	ShO	Relief Pitching W	L	SV	BATTING AB	H	HR	BA

John Whitehead

WHITEHEAD, JOHN HENDERSON (Silent John) BR TR 6'2" 195 lbs.
B. Apr. 27, 1909, Coleman, Tex. D. Oct. 20, 1964, Bonham, Tex.

	W	L	PCT	ERA	G	GS	CG	IP	H	BB	SO	ShO	W	L	SV	AB	H	HR	BA
1935 CHI A	13	13	.500	3.72	28	27	18	222.1	209	101	72	1	0	0	0	82	12	0	.146
1936	13	13	.500	4.64	34	32	15	230.2	254	98	70	1	0	0	0	87	21	0	.241
1937	11	8	.579	4.07	26	24	8	165.2	191	56	45	1	0	0	1	58	13	0	.224
1938	10	11	.476	4.76	32	24	10	183.1	218	80	38	2	1	0	2	60	6	0	.100
1939 2 teams			CHI A	(7G 0–3)			STL A	(26G 1–3)											
" total	1	6	.143	6.61	33	8	0	98	148	22	18	0	1	1	1	26	1	0	.038
1940 STL A	1	3	.250	5.40	15	4	1	40	46	14	11	1	0	2	0	12	2	0	.167
1942	0	0	–	6.75	4	0	0	4	8	1	0	0	0	0	0	0	0	0	–
7 yrs.	49	54	.476	4.60	172	119	52	944	1074	372	254	9	2	3	4	325	55	0	.169

Milt Whitehead

WHITEHEAD, MILTON P.
B. 1862, Canada D. Aug. 15, 1901, Highland, Calif.

	W	L	PCT	ERA	G	GS	CG	IP	H	BB	SO	ShO	W	L	SV	AB	H	HR	BA
1884 STL U	0	1	.000	9.00	1	1	1	8	14	2	2	0	0	0	0	*			

Earl Whitehill

WHITEHILL, EARL OLIVER BL TL 5'9½" 174 lbs.
B. Feb. 7, 1899, Cedar Rapids, Iowa D. Oct. 22, 1954, Omaha, Neb.

	W	L	PCT	ERA	G	GS	CG	IP	H	BB	SO	ShO	W	L	SV	AB	H	HR	BA
1923 DET A	2	0	1.000	2.73	8	3	2	33	22	15	19	1	2	0	0	11	4	0	.364
1924	17	9	.654	3.86	35	32	16	233	260	79	65	2	0	2	0	89	19	0	.213
1925	11	11	.500	4.66	35	33	15	239.1	267	88	83	1	0	0	2	87	19	0	.218
1926	16	13	.552	3.99	36	34	13	252.1	271	79	109	0	2	0	0	91	23	0	.253
1927	16	14	.533	3.36	41	31	17	236	238	105	95	3	3	1	3	78	16	0	.205
1928	11	16	.407	4.31	31	30	12	196.1	214	78	93	1	1	0	0	67	13	0	.194
1929	14	15	.483	4.62	38	28	18	245.1	267	96	103	1	4	1	1	90	23	3	.256
1930	17	13	.567	4.24	34	31	16	220.2	248	80	109	0	0	1	1	83	16	0	.193
1931	13	16	.448	4.06	34	34	22	272.1	287	118	81	0	0	0	0	97	15	0	.155
1932	16	12	.571	4.54	33	31	17	244	255	93	81	3	1	0	0	90	22	0	.244
1933 WAS A	22	8	.733	3.33	39	37	19	270	271	100	96	2	0	0	1	108	24	0	.222
1934	14	11	.560	4.52	32	31	15	235	269	94	96	0	0	0	0	85	17	1	.200
1935	14	13	.519	4.29	34	34	19	279.1	318	104	102	1	0	0	0	104	19	0	.183
1936	14	11	.560	4.87	28	28	14	212.1	252	89	63	0	0	0	0	77	13	0	.169
1937 CLE A	8	8	.500	6.49	33	22	6	147	189	80	53	1	0	0	2	49	11	0	.224
1938	9	8	.529	5.56	26	23	4	160.1	187	83	60	0	1	0	0	56	7	0	.125
1939 CHI N	4	7	.364	5.14	24	11	2	89.1	102	50	42	1	0	1	1	29	3	0	.103
17 yrs.	218	185	.541	4.36	541	473	227	3565.2	3917	1431	1350	17	14	6	11	1291	264	4	.204

WORLD SERIES

	W	L	PCT	ERA	G	GS	CG	IP	H	BB	SO	ShO	W	L	SV	AB	H	HR	BA
1933 WAS A	1	0	1.000	0.00	1	1	1	9	5	2	5	1	0	0	0	3	0	0	.000

Charlie Whitehouse

WHITEHOUSE, CHARLES EVIS (Lefty) BB TL 6' 152 lbs.
B. Jan. 25, 1894, Charleston, Ill. D. July 19, 1960, Indianapolis, Ind.

	W	L	PCT	ERA	G	GS	CG	IP	H	BB	SO	ShO	W	L	SV	AB	H	HR	BA
1914 IND F	2	0	1.000	4.85	8	2	2	26	34	5	10	0	0	0	0	8	0	0	.000
1915 NWK F	2	2	.500	4.31	11	3	1	39.2	46	17	18	0	1	0	0	10	0	0	.000
1919 WAS A	0	1	.000	4.50	6	1	0	12	13	6	5	0	0	0	0	1	0	0	.000
3 yrs.	4	3	.571	4.52	25	6	3	77.2	93	28	33	0	1	0	0	19	0	0	.000

Gil Whitehouse

WHITEHOUSE, GILBERT ARTHUR BB TR 5'10½" 170 lbs.
B. Oct. 15, 1893, Somerville, Mass. D. Feb. 14, 1926, Brewer, Me.

	W	L	PCT	ERA	G	GS	CG	IP	H	BB	SO	ShO	W	L	SV	AB	H	HR	BA
1915 NWK F	0	0	–	0.00	1	0	0	1	0	1	0	0	0	0	0	*			

Len Whitehouse

WHITEHOUSE, LEONARD JOSEPH BL TL 5'11" 175 lbs.
B. Sept. 10, 1957, Burlington, Vt.

	W	L	PCT	ERA	G	GS	CG	IP	H	BB	SO	ShO	W	L	SV	AB	H	HR	BA
1981 TEX A	0	1	.000	18.00	2	1	0	3	8	2	2	0	0	0	0	0	0	0	–
1983 MIN A	7	1	.875	4.15	60	0	0	73.2	70	44	44	0	7	1	2	0	0	0	–
1984	2	2	.500	3.16	30	0	0	31.1	29	17	18	0	2	2	1	0	0	0	–
3 yrs.	9	4	.692	4.25	92	1	0	108	107	63	64	0	9	3	3	0	0	0	–

Jesse Whiting

WHITING, JESSE W.
B. May 30, 1879, Philadelphia, Pa. D. Oct. 28, 1937, Philadelphia, Pa.

	W	L	PCT	ERA	G	GS	CG	IP	H	BB	SO	ShO	W	L	SV	AB	H	HR	BA
1902 PHI N	0	1	.000	5.00	1	1	1	9	13	6	0	0	0	0	0	3	1	0	.333
1906 BKN N	1	1	.500	2.92	3	2	2	24.2	26	6	7	1	0	0	0	10	3	0	.300
1907	0	0	–	12.00	1	0	0	3	3	3	2	0	0	0	0	2	0	0	.000
3 yrs.	1	2	.333	4.17	5	3	3	36.2	42	15	9	1	0	0	0	15	4	0	.267

Art Whitney

WHITNEY, ARTHUR WILSON BR TR
Brother of Frank Whitney.
B. Jan. 16, 1858, Brockton, Mass. D. Aug. 17, 1943, Lowell, Mass.

	W	L	PCT	ERA	G	GS	CG	IP	H	BB	SO	ShO	W	L	SV	AB	H	HR	BA
1882 DET N	0	1	.000	6.00	3	2	1	18	31	8	11	0	0	0	0	155	24	0	.155
1886 PIT AA	0	0	–	3.00	1	0	0	6	7	3	2	0	0	0	0	511	122	0	.239
1889 NY N	0	1	.000	3.00	1	0	0	6	7	3	3	0	0	0	0	473	103	1	.218
3 yrs.	0	2	.000	4.80	5	2	1	30	45	14	16	0	0	0	0	*			

Jim Whitney

WHITNEY, JAMES E. (Grasshopper, Grasshopper Jim) BL TR 6'2"
B. Nov. 10, 1857, Conklin, N.Y. D. May 21, 1891, Binghamton, N.Y.

	W	L	PCT	ERA	G	GS	CG	IP	H	BB	SO	ShO	W	L	SV	AB	H	HR	BA
1881 BOS N	31	33	.484	2.48	66	63	57	552.1	548	90	162	6	0	1	0	282	72	0	.255
1882	24	21	.533	2.64	49	48	46	420	404	41	180	3	0	0	0	251	81	5	.323
1883	37	21	.638	2.24	62	56	54	514	492	35	345	1	3	0	2	409	115	5	.281
1884	24	17	.585	2.09	41	40	35	336	272	27	270	6	0	1	0	270	70	3	.259
1885	18	32	.360	2.98	51	50	50	441.1	503	37	200	0	0	0	0	290	68	0	.234
1886 KC N	12	32	.273	4.49	46	44	42	393	465	55	167	3	0	0	0	247	59	2	.239
1887 WAS N	24	21	.533	3.22	47	47	46	404.2	430	42	146	3	0	0	0	201	53	2	.264
1888	18	21	.462	3.05	39	39	37	325	317	54	79	2	0	0	0	141	24	1	.170
1889 IND N	2	7	.222	6.81	9	8	7	70	106	19	16	0	0	0	0	32	12	0	.375
1890 PHI AA	2	2	.500	5.18	6	4	3	40	61	11	6	0	0	1	0	21	5	0	.238
10 yrs.	192	207	.481	2.97	416	399	377	3496.1	3598	411	1571	26	3	3	2	*			

	W	L	PCT	ERA	G	GS	CG	IP	H	BB	SO	ShO	Relief Pitching W	L	SV	BATTING AB	H	HR	BA

Carl Willis

WILLIS, CARL BLAKE   BL TR 6'3"   210 lbs.
B. Dec. 28, 1960, Danville, Va.

	W	L	PCT	ERA	G	GS	CG	IP	H	BB	SO	ShO	W	L	SV	AB	H	HR	BA
1984 2 teams DET A (10G 0–2) CIN N (7G 0–1)																			
" total	0	3	.000	5.96	17			25.2	33	7	7	0	0	2	1	0	0	0	–

Dale Willis

WILLIS, DALE JEROME   BR TR 5'11"   165 lbs.
B. May 29, 1938, Calhoun, Ga.

	W	L	PCT	ERA	G	GS	CG	IP	H	BB	SO	ShO	W	L	SV	AB	H	HR	BA
1963 KC A	0	2	.000	5.04	25	0	0	44.2	46	25	47	0	0	2	1	6	1	0	.167

Jim Willis

WILLIS, JAMES GLADDEN   BL TR 6'3"   175 lbs.
B. Mar. 20, 1927, Doyline, La.

	W	L	PCT	ERA	G	GS	CG	IP	H	BB	SO	ShO	W	L	SV	AB	H	HR	BA
1953 CHI N	2	1	.667	3.12	13	3	2	43.1	37	17	15	0	0	0	0	9	0	0	.000
1954	0	1	.000	3.91	14	1	0	23	22	18	5	0	0	0	0	5	0	0	.000
2 yrs.	2	2	.500	3.39	27	4	2	66.1	59	35	20	0	0	0	0	14	0	0	.000

Joe Willis

WILLIS, JOSEPH DENK (Big Joe)   BR TL 6'1"   185 lbs.
B. Apr. 9, 1890, Coal Grove, Ohio   D. Dec. 3, 1966, Ironton, Ohio

	W	L	PCT	ERA	G	GS	CG	IP	H	BB	SO	ShO	W	L	SV	AB	H	HR	BA
1911 2 teams STL A (1G 0–1) STL N (2G 0–1)																			
" total	0	2	.000	4.50	3	3	1	22	21	7	5	0	0	0	0	7	0	0	.000
1912 STL N	4	9	.308	4.44	31	17	4	129.2	143	62	55	0	1	2	2	38	6	0	.158
1913	0	0	–	7.45	7	0	0	9.2	9	11	6	0	0	0	1	3	0	0	.000
3 yrs.	4	11	.267	4.63	41	20	5	161.1	173	80	66	0	1	2	3	48	6	0	.125

Lefty Willis

WILLIS, CHARLES WILLIAM   BL TL 6'1"   175 lbs.
B. Nov. 4, 1905, Leetown, W. Va.   BR 1925
D. May 10, 1962, Bethesda, Md.

	W	L	PCT	ERA	G	GS	CG	IP	H	BB	SO	ShO	W	L	SV	AB	H	HR	BA
1925 PHI A	0	0	–	10.80	1	1	0	5	9	2	3	0	0	0	0	3	0	0	.000
1926	0	0	–	1.39	13	1	0	32.1	31	12	13	0	0	0	1	9	2	0	.222
1927	3	1	.750	5.67	15	2	1	27	32	11	7	0	2	0	0	6	0	0	.000
3 yrs.	3	1	.750	3.92	29	4	1	64.1	72	25	23	0	2	0	1	18	2	0	.111

Les Willis

WILLIS, LESTER EVANS (Lefty, Wimpy)   BL TL 5'9½"   195 lbs.
B. Jan. 17, 1908, Nacogdoches, Tex.   D. Jan. 22, 1982, Jasper, Tex.

	W	L	PCT	ERA	G	GS	CG	IP	H	BB	SO	ShO	W	L	SV	AB	H	HR	BA
1947 CLE A	0	2	.000	3.48	22	2	0	44	58	24	10	0	0	1	1	11	1	0	.091

Mike Willis

WILLIS, MICHAEL HENRY   BL TL 6'2"   205 lbs.
B. Dec. 26, 1950, Oklahoma City, Okla.

	W	L	PCT	ERA	G	GS	CG	IP	H	BB	SO	ShO	W	L	SV	AB	H	HR	BA
1977 TOR A	2	6	.250	3.95	43	3	0	107	105	38	59	0	2	5	5	0	0	0	–
1978	3	7	.300	4.56	44	2	1	100.2	104	39	52	0	2	6	7	0	0	0	–
1979	0	3	.000	8.33	17	1	0	27	35	16	8	0	0	2	0	0	0	0	–
1980	2	1	.667	1.73	20	0	0	26	25	11	14	0	2	1	3	0	0	0	–
1981	0	4	.000	5.91	20	0	0	35	43	20	16	0	0	4	0	0	0	0	–
5 yrs.	7	21	.250	4.60	144	6	1	295.2	312	124	149	0	6	18	15	0	0	0	–

Ron Willis

WILLIS, RONALD EARL   BR TR 6'2"   185 lbs.
B. July 12, 1943, Willisville, Tenn.   D. Nov. 21, 1977, Memphis, Tenn.

	W	L	PCT	ERA	G	GS	CG	IP	H	BB	SO	ShO	W	L	SV	AB	H	HR	BA
1966 STL N	0	0	–	0.00	4	0	0	3	1	1	2	0	0	0	1	0	0	0	–
1967	6	5	.545	2.67	65	0	0	81	76	43	42	0	6	5	10	8	3	0	.375
1968	2	3	.400	3.39	48	0	0	63.2	50	28	39	0	2	3	4	11	0	0	.000
1969 2 teams STL N (26G 1–2) HOU N (3G 0–0)																			
" total	1	2	.333	3.89	29	0	0	34.2	29	19	25	0	1	2	0	1	1	0	1.000
1970 SD N	2	2	.500	4.02	42	0	0	56	53	28	20	0	2	2	4	5	0	0	.000
5 yrs.	11	12	.478	3.32	188	0	0	238.1	209	119	128	0	11	12	19	25	4	0	.160
WORLD SERIES																			
1967 STL N	0	0	–	27.00	3	0	0	1	2	4	1	0	0	0	0	0	0	0	–
1968	0	0	–	8.31	3	0	0	4.1	2	4	3	0	0	0	0	0	0	0	–
2 yrs.	0	0	–	11.81	6	0	0	5.1	4	8	4	0	0	0	0	0	0	0	–

Vic Willis

WILLIS, VICTOR GAZAWAY   BR TR 6'2"   185 lbs.
B. Apr. 12, 1876, Wilmington, Del.   D. Aug. 3, 1947, Elkton, Md.

	W	L	PCT	ERA	G	GS	CG	IP	H	BB	SO	ShO	W	L	SV	AB	H	HR	BA
1898 BOS N	24	13	.649	2.84	41	38	29	311	264	148	160	1	1	1	0	117	17	0	.145
1899	27	10	.730	2.50	41	38	35	342.2	277	117	120	5	0	0	2	134	29	0	.216
1900	10	17	.370	4.19	32	29	22	236	258	106	53	2	1	0	0	88	12	0	.136
1901	20	17	.541	2.36	38	35	33	305.1	262	78	133	6	2	0	0	107	20	1	.187
1902	27	19	.587	2.20	51	46	45	410	372	101	225	4	1	1	3	150	23	0	.153
1903	12	18	.400	2.98	33	32	29	278	256	88	125	2	0	0	0	128	24	0	.188
1904	18	25	.419	2.85	43	43	39	350	357	109	196	2	0	0	0	148	27	0	.182
1905	11	29	.275	3.21	41	41	36	342	340	107	149	4	0	0	0	131	20	0	.153
1906 PIT N	22	13	.629	1.73	41	36	32	322	295	76	124	6	1	0	1	115	20	0	.174
1907	22	11	.667	2.34	39	37	27	292.2	234	69	107	6	1	0	1	103	14	0	.136
1908	23	11	.676	2.07	41	38	25	304.2	239	69	97	7	1	0	0	103	17	0	.165
1909	22	11	.667	2.24	39	35	24	289.2	243	83	95	4	2	1	0	103	14	0	.136
1910 STL N	9	12	.429	3.35	33	23	12	212	224	61	67	1	3	0	3	66	11	0	.167
13 yrs.	247	206	.545	2.63	513	471	388	3996	3621	1212	1651	50	13	3	10	1493	248	1	.166
WORLD SERIES																			
1909 PIT N	0	1	.000	4.76	2	1	0	11.1	10	8	3	0	0	0	0	4	0	0	.000

Claude Willoughby

WILLOUGHBY, CLAUDE WILLIAM (Weeping Willie)   BR TR 5'9½"   165 lbs.
B. Nov. 14, 1898, Fredonia, Kans.   D. Aug. 14, 1973, McPherson, Kans.

	W	L	PCT	ERA	G	GS	CG	IP	H	BB	SO	ShO	W	L	SV	AB	H	HR	BA
1925 PHI N	2	1	.667	1.96	3	3	1	23	26	11	6	0	0	0	0	8	0	0	.000
1926	8	12	.400	5.95	47	18	6	168	218	71	37	0	4	1	1	52	11	0	.212
1927	3	7	.300	6.54	35	6	1	97.2	126	53	14	1	2	3	2	26	2	0	.077
1928	6	5	.545	5.30	35	13	5	130.2	180	83	26	1	1	2	1	40	6	0	.150
1929	15	14	.517	4.99	49	34	14	243.1	288	108	50	1	0	2	4	91	13	0	.143
1930	4	17	.190	7.59	41	24	5	153	241	68	38	1	1	1	1	48	5	0	.104

	W	L	PCT	ERA	G	GS	CG	IP	H	BB	SO	ShO	Relief Pitching W	L	SV	BATTING AB	H	HR	BA

Claude Willoughby continued

	W	L	PCT	ERA	G	GS	CG	IP	H	BB	SO	ShO	W	L	SV	AB	H	HR	BA
1931 PIT N	0	2	.000	6.31	9	2	1	25.2	32	12	4	0	0	1	0	7	2	0	.286
7 yrs.	38	58	.396	5.84	219	100	33	841.1	1111	406	175	4	8	9	9	272	39	0	.143

Jim Willoughby

WILLOUGHBY, JAMES ARTHUR
B. Jan. 31, 1949, Salinas, Calif.   BR TR 6'2" 185 lbs.

	W	L	PCT	ERA	G	GS	CG	IP	H	BB	SO	ShO	W	L	SV	AB	H	HR	BA
1971 SF N	0	1	.000	9.00	2	1	0	4	8	1	3	0	0	0	0	1	0	0	.000
1972	6	4	.600	2.35	11	11	7	88	72	14	40	0	0	0	0	27	5	0	.185
1973	4	5	.444	4.70	39	12	1	122.2	138	37	60	1	1	2	1	28	4	1	.143
1974	1	4	.200	4.61	18	4	0	41	51	9	12	0	1	1	0	10	1	0	.100
1975 BOS A	5	2	.714	3.54	24	0	0	48.1	46	16	29	0	5	2	8	0	0	0	—
1976	3	12	.200	2.82	54	0	0	99	94	31	37	0	3	12	10	1	0	0	.000
1977	6	2	.750	4.94	31	0	0	54.2	54	18	33	0	6	2	2	0	0	0	—
1978 CHI A	1	6	.143	3.86	59	0	0	93.1	95	19	36	0	1	6	13	0	0	0	—
8 yrs.	26	36	.419	3.79	238	28	8	551	558	145	250	1	16	25	34	67	10	1	.149
WORLD SERIES																			
1975 BOS A	0	1	.000	0.00	3	0	0	6.1	3	0	2	0	0	1	0	0	0	0	—

Frank Wills

WILLS, FRANK LEE JR.
B. Oct. 26, 1958, New Orleans, La.   BR TR 6'2" 200 lbs.

	W	L	PCT	ERA	G	GS	CG	IP	H	BB	SO	ShO	W	L	SV	AB	H	HR	BA
1983 KC A	2	1	.667	4.15	6	4	0	34.2	35	15	23	0	0	0	0	0	0	0	—
1984	2	3	.400	5.11	10	5	0	37	39	13	21	0	1	0	0	0	0	0	—
2 yrs.	4	4	.500	4.65	16	9	0	71.2	74	28	44	0	1	0	0	0	0	0	—

Ted Wills

WILLS, THEODORE CARL
B. Feb. 9, 1934, Fresno, Calif.   BL TL 6'2" 200 lbs.

	W	L	PCT	ERA	G	GS	CG	IP	H	BB	SO	ShO	W	L	SV	AB	H	HR	BA
1959 BOS A	2	6	.250	5.27	9	8	2	56.1	68	24	24	0	0	0	0	16	4	0	.250
1960	1	1	.500	7.42	15	0	0	30.1	38	16	28	0	1	1	1	8	2	0	.250
1961	3	2	.600	5.95	17	0	0	19.2	24	19	11	0	3	2	1	2	0	0	.000
1962 2 teams			BOS	A (1G 0–0)			CIN	N	(26G 0–2)										
" total	2	0	.000	5.46	27	5	0	61	63	24	58	0	0	1	3	16	5	0	.313
1965 CHI A	2	0	1.000	2.84	15	0	0	19	17	14	12	0	2	0	1	2	0	0	.000
5 yrs.	8	11	.421	5.51	83	13	2	186.1	210	97	133	0	6	4	5	44	11	0	.250

Whitey Wilshere

WILSHERE, VERNON SPRAGUE
B. Aug. 3, 1912, Poplar Ridge, N. Y.   BL TL 6' 180 lbs.

	W	L	PCT	ERA	G	GS	CG	IP	H	BB	SO	ShO	W	L	SV	AB	H	HR	BA
1934 PHI A	0	1	.000	12.05	9	2	0	21.2	39	15	19	0	0	0	0	3	0	0	.000
1935	9	9	.500	4.05	27	18	7	142.1	136	78	80	3	2	1	1	43	4	0	.093
1936	1	2	.333	6.87	5	3	0	18.1	21	19	4	0	0	0	0	4	0	0	.000
3 yrs.	10	12	.455	5.28	41	23	7	182.1	196	112	103	3	2	1	1	50	4	0	.080

Terry Wilshusen

WILSHUSEN, TERRY WAYNE
B. Mar. 22, 1949, Atascadero, Calif.   BR TR 6'2" 210 lbs.

	W	L	PCT	ERA	G	GS	CG	IP	H	BB	SO	ShO	W	L	SV	AB	H	HR	BA
1973 CAL A	0	0	—	81.00	1	0	0	.1	0	2	0	0	0	0	0	0	0	0	—

Bill Wilson

WILSON, WILLIAM DONALD
B. Nov. 6, 1928, Central City, Neb.   BR TR 6'2" 200 lbs.

	W	L	PCT	ERA	G	GS	CG	IP	H	BB	SO	ShO	W	L	SV	AB	H	HR	BA
1955 KC A	0	0	—	0.00	1	0	0	1	1	1	1	0	0	0	0	*			

Bill Wilson

WILSON, WILLIAM HARLAN
B. Sept. 21, 1942, Pomeroy, Ohio   BR TR 6'2" 195 lbs.

	W	L	PCT	ERA	G	GS	CG	IP	H	BB	SO	ShO	W	L	SV	AB	H	HR	BA
1969 PHI N	2	5	.286	3.34	37	0	0	62	53	36	48	0	2	5	6	6	0	0	.000
1970	1	0	1.000	4.81	37	0	0	58	57	33	41	0	1	0	0	4	1	0	.250
1971	4	6	.400	3.05	38	0	0	59	39	22	40	0	4	6	7	10	1	0	.100
1972	1	1	.500	3.30	23	0	0	30	26	11	18	0	1	1	0	0	0	0	—
1973	1	3	.250	6.66	44	0	0	48.2	54	29	24	0	1	3	4	4	0	0	.000
5 yrs.	9	15	.375	4.23	179	0	0	257.2	229	131	171	0	9	15	17	24	2	0	.083

Chink Wilson

WILSON, HOWARD WILLIAM
B. Unknown.   BR TR

	W	L	PCT	ERA	G	GS	CG	IP	H	BB	SO	ShO	W	L	SV	AB	H	HR	BA
1906 WAS A	0	1	.000	2.57	1	1	1	7	3	2	1	0	0	0	0	2	0	0	.000

Don Wilson

WILSON, DONALD EDWARD
B. Feb. 12, 1945, Monroe, La.   D. Jan. 5, 1975, Houston, Tex.   BR TR 6'2½" 195 lbs.

	W	L	PCT	ERA	G	GS	CG	IP	H	BB	SO	ShO	W	L	SV	AB	H	HR	BA
1966 HOU N	1	0	1.000	3.00	1	0	0	6	5	1	7	0	1	0	0	2	1	0	.500
1967	10	9	.526	2.79	31	28	7	184	141	69	159	3	0	0	0	66	6	0	.091
1968	13	16	.448	3.28	33	30	9	208.2	187	70	175	3	0	2	0	70	15	1	.214
1969	16	12	.571	4.00	34	34	13	225	210	97	235	1	0	0	0	81	8	0	.099
1970	11	6	.647	3.91	29	27	3	184	188	66	94	0	0	0	0	69	8	0	.116
1971	16	10	.615	2.45	35	34	18	268	195	79	180	3	0	0	0	91	14	0	.154
1972	15	10	.600	2.68	33	33	13	228.1	196	66	172	3	0	0	0	76	8	0	.105
1973	11	16	.407	3.20	37	32	10	239.1	187	92	149	3	1	0	2	79	14	0	.177
1974	11	13	.458	3.07	33	27	5	205	170	100	112	4	1	0	0	63	13	0	.206
9 yrs.	104	92	.531	3.15	266	245	78	1748.1	1479	640	1283	20	3	4	2	597	87	1	.146

Duane Wilson

WILSON, DUANE LEWIS
B. June 29, 1934, Wichita, Kans.   BL TL 6'1" 185 lbs.

	W	L	PCT	ERA	G	GS	CG	IP	H	BB	SO	ShO	W	L	SV	AB	H	HR	BA
1958 BOS A	0	0	—	5.68	2	2	0	6.1	10	7	3	0	0	0	0	1	0	0	.000

Earl Wilson

WILSON, EARL LAWRENCE
B. Oct. 2, 1934, Ponchatoula, La.   BR TR 6'3" 216 lbs.

	W	L	PCT	ERA	G	GS	CG	IP	H	BB	SO	ShO	W	L	SV	AB	H	HR	BA
1959 BOS A	1	1	.500	6.08	9	4	0	23.2	21	31	17	0	1	0	0	8	4	0	.500
1960	3	2	.600	4.71	13	9	2	65	61	48	40	0	0	0	0	23	4	0	.174
1962	12	8	.600	3.90	31	28	4	191.1	163	111	137	1	0	0	0	69	12	3	.174
1963	11	16	.407	3.76	37	34	6	210.2	184	105	123	3	0	0	0	72	15	1	.208

	W	L	PCT	ERA	G	GS	CG	IP	H	BB	SO	ShO	Relief Pitching W	L	SV	BATTING AB	H	HR	BA

Mike Witt

WITT, MICHAEL ATWATER
B. July 20, 1960, Fullerton, Calif.
BR TR 6'7" 185 lbs.

	W	L	PCT	ERA	G	GS	CG	IP	H	BB	SO	ShO	W	L	SV	AB	H	HR	BA
1981 CAL A	8	9	.471	3.28	22	21	7	129	123	47	75	1	0	1	0	0	0	0	—
1982	8	6	.571	3.51	33	26	5	179.2	177	47	85	1	0	1	0	0	0	0	—
1983	7	14	.333	4.91	43	19	2	154	173	75	77	0	3	3	5	0	0	0	—
1984	15	11	.577	3.47	34	34	9	246.2	227	84	196	2	0	0	0	0	0	0	—
4 yrs.	38	40	.487	3.76	132	100	23	709.1	700	253	433	4	3	5	5	0	0	0	—

LEAGUE CHAMPIONSHIP SERIES
| 1982 CAL A | 0 | 0 | — | 6.00 | 1 | 0 | 0 | 3 | 2 | 2 | 3 | 0 | 0 | 0 | 0 | 0 | 0 | 0 | — |

Johnnie Wittig

WITTIG, JOHN CARL (Hans)
B. June 16, 1914, Baltimore, Md.
BR TR 6' 180 lbs.

	W	L	PCT	ERA	G	GS	CG	IP	H	BB	SO	ShO	W	L	SV	AB	H	HR	BA
1938 NY N	2	3	.400	4.81	13	6	2	39.1	41	26	14	0	1	0	0	10	0	0	.000
1939	0	2	.000	7.56	5	2	1	16.2	18	14	4	0	0	0	0	5	0	0	.000
1941	3	5	.375	5.59	25	9	0	85.1	111	45	47	0	1	1	0	25	5	0	.200
1943	5	15	.250	4.23	40	22	4	164	77	76	56	1	0	1	4	51	5	0	.098
1949 BOS A	0	0	—	9.00	1	0	0	2	2	2	0	0	0	0	0	0	0	0	—
5 yrs.	10	25	.286	4.89	84	39	7	307.1	249	163	121	1	2	2	4	91	10	0	.110

Pete Wojey

WOJEY, PETER PAUL
B. Dec. 1, 1919, Stowe, Pa.
BR TR 5'11" 185 lbs.

	W	L	PCT	ERA	G	GS	CG	IP	H	BB	SO	ShO	W	L	SV	AB	H	HR	BA
1954 BKN N	1	1	.500	3.25	14	1	0	27.2	24	14	21	0	0	0	1	3	0	0	.000
1956 DET A	0	0	—	2.25	2	0	0	4	2	1	1	0	0	0	0	0	0	0	—
1957	0	0	—	0.00	2	0	0	1.1	1	0	0	0	0	0	0	0	0	0	—
3 yrs.	1	1	.500	3.00	18	1	0	33	27	15	22	0	0	0	1	3	0	0	.000

Chicken Wolf

WOLF, WILLIAM VAN WINKLE
B. May 12, 1862, Louisville, Ky.   D. May 16, 1903, Louisville, Ky.
Manager 1889.
BR TR 5'9" 190 lbs.

	W	L	PCT	ERA	G	GS	CG	IP	H	BB	SO	ShO	W	L	SV	AB	H	HR	BA
1882 LOU AA	0	0	—	9.00	1	0	0	6	11	3	1	0	0	0	0	318	95	0	.299
1885	0	0	—	9.00	1	0	0	1	1	0	1	0	0	0	0	483	141	1	.292
1886	0	0	—	15.00	1	0	0	3	7	0	0	0	0	0	0	545	148	3	.272
3 yrs.	0	0	—	10.80	3	0	0	10	19	3	2	0	0	0	0	*			

Ernie Wolf

WOLF, ERNEST ADOLPH
B. Feb. 2, 1889, Newark, N. J.   D. May 23, 1964, Atlantic Highlands, N. J.
BR TR 5'11" 174 lbs.

	W	L	PCT	ERA	G	GS	CG	IP	H	BB	SO	ShO	W	L	SV	AB	H	HR	BA
1912 CLE A	0	0	—	6.35	1	0	0	5.2	8	4	1	0	0	0	0	2	0	0	.000

Lefty Wolf

WOLF, WALTER FRANCIS
B. June 10, 1900, Hartford, Conn.   D. Sept. 25, 1971, New Orleans, La.
BR TL 5'10" 163 lbs.

	W	L	PCT	ERA	G	GS	CG	IP	H	BB	SO	ShO	W	L	SV	AB	H	HR	BA
1921 PHI A	0	0	—	7.20	8	0	0	15	15	16	12	0	0	0	0	4	1	0	.250

Wally Wolf

WOLF, WALTER BECK
B. Jan. 5, 1942, Los Angeles, Calif.
BR TR 6'½" 191 lbs.

	W	L	PCT	ERA	G	GS	CG	IP	H	BB	SO	ShO	W	L	SV	AB	H	HR	BA
1969 CAL A	0	0	—	11.57	2	0	0	2.1	3	3	2	0	0	0	0	0	0	0	—
1970	0	0	—	5.40	4	0	0	5	3	4	5	0	0	0	0	0	0	0	—
2 yrs.	0	0	—	7.36	6	0	0	7.1	6	7	7	0	0	0	0	0	0	0	—

Bill Wolfe

WOLFE, WILBERT OTTO (Barney)
B. Jan. 9, 1876, Independence, Pa.   D. Feb. 27, 1953, Belle Vernon, Pa.
BR TR 6'1"

	W	L	PCT	ERA	G	GS	CG	IP	H	BB	SO	ShO	W	L	SV	AB	H	HR	BA
1903 NY A	6	9	.400	2.97	20	16	12	148.1	143	26	48	1	0	1	0	53	4	0	.075
1904 2 teams				NY A (7G 0-3)				WAS A (17G 6-9)											
" total	6	12	.333	3.26	24	19	15	160.1	162	26	52	2	0	1	0	52	5	0	.096
1905 WAS A	8	14	.364	2.57	28	24	17	182	162	37	52	1	1	0	2	60	8	1	.133
1906	0	3	.000	4.05	4	3	2	20	17	10	8	0	0	0	0	7	2	0	.286
4 yrs.	20	38	.345	2.96	76	62	46	510.2	484	99	160	4	1	2	2	172	19	1	.110

Bill Wolfe

WOLFE, WILLIAM
B. Jersey City, N. J.

	W	L	PCT	ERA	G	GS	CG	IP	H	BB	SO	ShO	W	L	SV	AB	H	HR	BA
1902 PHI N	0	1	.000	4.00	1	1	1	9	11	4	3	0	0	0	0	3	1	0	.333

Chuck Wolfe

WOLFE, CHARLES HUNT
B. Feb. 15, 1897, Wolfsburg, Pa.   D. Nov. 27, 1957, Schellsburg, Pa.
BL TR 5'7" 175 lbs.

	W	L	PCT	ERA	G	GS	CG	IP	H	BB	SO	ShO	W	L	SV	AB	H	HR	BA
1923 PHI A	0	0	—	3.72	3	0	0	9.2	6	8	1	0	0	0	0	3	1	0	.333

Ed Wolfe

WOLFE, EEDWARD ANTHONY
B. Jan. 2, 1929, Los Angeles, Calif.
BR TR 6'3" 185 lbs.

	W	L	PCT	ERA	G	GS	CG	IP	H	BB	SO	ShO	W	L	SV	AB	H	HR	BA
1952 PIT N	0	0	—	7.36	3	0	0	3.2	7	5	1	0	0	0	0	0	0	0	—

Roger Wolff

WOLFF, ROGER FRANCIS
B. Apr. 10, 1911, Evansville, Ill.
BR TR 6'1½" 208 lbs.

	W	L	PCT	ERA	G	GS	CG	IP	H	BB	SO	ShO	W	L	SV	AB	H	HR	BA
1941 PHI A	0	2	.000	3.18	2	2	2	17	15	4	2	0	0	0	0	5	1	0	.200
1942	12	15	.444	3.32	32	25	15	214.1	206	69	94	2	2	3	3	68	6	0	.088
1943	10	15	.400	3.54	41	26	13	221	232	72	91	2	2	2	6	74	9	0	.122
1944 WAS A	4	15	.211	4.99	33	21	5	155	186	60	73	0	1	2	2	55	12	0	.218
1945	20	10	.667	2.12	33	29	21	250	200	53	108	4	0	2	2	84	9	0	.107
1946	5	8	.385	2.58	21	17	6	122	115	30	50	0	1	2	0	39	4	0	.103
1947 2 teams				CLE A (7G 0-0)				PIT N (13G 1-4)											
" total	1	4	.200	7.04	20	8	1	46	64	28	12	0	1	0	0	12	0	0	.000
7 yrs.	52	69	.430	3.41	182	128	63	1025.1	1018	316	430	8	6	11	13	337	41	0	.122

Mellie Wolfgang

WOLFGANG, MELDON JOHN
B. Mar. 20, 1890, Albany, N. Y.   D. June 30, 1947, Albany, N. Y.
BR TR 5'9" 160 lbs.

	W	L	PCT	ERA	G	GS	CG	IP	H	BB	SO	ShO	W	L	SV	AB	H	HR	BA
1914 CHI A	9	5	.643	1.89	24	11	9	119.1	96	32	50	2	4	0	0	40	7	0	.175
1915	2	2	.500	1.84	17	2	0	53.2	39	12	21	0	2	1	0	17	2	0	.118
1916	4	6	.400	1.98	27	14	6	127	103	42	36	1	0	2	0	40	9	0	.225

	W	L	PCT	ERA	G	GS	CG	IP	H	BB	SO	ShO	Relief Pitching W	L	SV	BATTING AB	H	HR	BA

Mellie Wolfgang continued

	W	L	PCT	ERA	G	GS	CG	IP	H	BB	SO	ShO	W	L	SV	AB	H	HR	BA
1917	0	0	–	5.09	5	0	0	17.2	18	6	3	0	0	0	0	4	0	0	.000
1918	0	1	.000	5.40	4	0	0	8.1	12	3	1	0	0	1	0	2	1	0	.500
5 yrs.	15	14	.517	2.18	77	27	15	326	268	95	111	3	6	4	0	103	19	0	.184

Harry Wolter

WOLTER, HARRY MEIGS BL TL 5'10" 175 lbs.
B. July 11, 1884, Monterey, Calif. D. July 7, 1970, Palo Alto, Calif.

	W	L	PCT	ERA	G	GS	CG	IP	H	BB	SO	ShO	W	L	SV	AB	H	HR	BA
1907 2 teams				STL N (3G 1–2)				PIT N (1G 0–0)											
" total	1	2	.333	4.32	4	3	1	25	30	20	8	0	0	0	0	63	18	0	.286
1909 BOS A	4	4	.500	3.91	10	6	0	53	53	28	20	0	1	1	0	119	29	2	.244
2 yrs.	5	6	.455	4.04	14	9	1	78	83	48	28	0	1	1	0	*			

Dooley Womack

WOMACK, HORACE GUY BL TR 6' 170 lbs.
B. Aug. 25, 1939, Columbia, S. C.

	W	L	PCT	ERA	G	GS	CG	IP	H	BB	SO	ShO	W	L	SV	AB	H	HR	BA
1966 NY A	7	3	.700	2.64	42	1	0	75	52	23	50	0	7	2	4	5	1	0	.200
1967	5	6	.455	2.41	65	0	0	97	80	35	57	0	5	6	18	14	4	0	.286
1968	3	7	.300	3.21	45	0	0	61.2	53	29	27	0	3	7	2	5	1	0	.200
1969 2 teams				HOU N (30G 2–1)				SEA A (9G 2–1)											
" total	4	2	.667	3.31	39	0	0	65.1	64	23	40	0	4	2	0	7	1	0	.143
1970 OAK A	0	0	–	15.00	2	0	0	3	4	1	3	0	0	0	0	0	0	0	–
5 yrs.	19	18	.514	2.95	193	1	0	302	253	111	177	0	19	17	24	31	7	0	.226

George Wood

WOOD, GEORGE A. (Dandy) BL TR 5'10½" 175 lbs.
B. Nov. 9, 1858, Boston, Mass. D. Apr. 4, 1924, Harrisburg, Pa.
Manager 1891.

	W	L	PCT	ERA	G	GS	CG	IP	H	BB	SO	ShO	W	L	SV	AB	H	HR	BA
1883 DET N	0	0	–	7.20	1	0	0	5	8	3	0	0	0	0	0	441	133	5	.302
1885	0	0	–	0.00	1	0	0	4	5	1	1	0	0	0	0	362	105	5	.290
1888 PHI N	0	0	–	4.50	2	0	0	2	3	1	0	0	0	0	2	433	99	6	.229
1889	0	0	–	18.00	1	0	0	1	2	0	2	0	0	0	0	432	108	5	.250
4 yrs.	0	0	–	5.25	5	0	0	12	18	5	3	0	0	0	2	*			

Joe Wood

WOOD, JOE (Smoky Joe) BR TR 5'11" 180 lbs.
Father of Joe Wood.
B. Oct. 25, 1889, Kansas City, Mo.

	W	L	PCT	ERA	G	GS	CG	IP	H	BB	SO	ShO	W	L	SV	AB	H	HR	BA
1908 BOS A	1	1	.500	2.38	6	2	1	22.2	14	16	11	1	0	0	0	7	0	0	.000
1909	11	7	.611	2.21	24	19	13	158.2	121	43	88	4	2	0	0	55	9	0	.164
1910	12	13	.480	1.68	35	17	14	197.2	155	56	145	3	6	3	0	69	18	1	.261
1911	23	17	.575	2.02	44	33	25	276.2	226	76	231	5	6	2	3	88	23	2	.261
1912	34	5	.872	1.91	43	38	35	344	267	82	258	10	1	0	1	124	36	1	.290
1913	11	5	.688	2.29	23	18	12	145.2	120	61	123	1	1	1	2	56	15	0	.268
1914	9	3	.750	2.62	18	14	11	113.1	94	34	67	1	0	1	2	43	6	0	.140
1915	15	5	.750	1.49	25	16	10	157.1	120	44	63	3	3	2	2	54	14	1	.259
1917 CLE A	0	1	.000	3.45	5	1	0	15.2	17	7	2	0	0	0	1	6	0	0	.000
1919	0	0	–	0.00	1	0	0	.2	0	0	0	0	0	0	1	192	49	1	.255
1920	0	0	–	22.50	1	0	0	2	4	2	1	0	0	0	0	137	37	1	.270
11 yrs.	116	57	.671	2.03	225	158	121	1434.1	1138	421	989	28	19	8	11	*			

WORLD SERIES

	W	L	PCT	ERA	G	GS	CG	IP	H	BB	SO	ShO	W	L	SV	AB	H	HR	BA
1912 BOS A	3	1	.750	3.68	4	3	2	22	27	3	21	0	1	0	0	7	2	0	.286

Joe Wood

WOOD, JOE FRANK BR TR 6' 190 lbs.
Son of Joe Wood.
B. May 20, 1916, Shohola, Pa.

	W	L	PCT	ERA	G	GS	CG	IP	H	BB	SO	ShO	W	L	SV	AB	H	HR	BA
1944 BOS A	0	1	.000	6.52	3	1	0	9.2	13	3	5	0	0	0	0	2	0	0	.000

John Wood

WOOD, JOHN B. 5'7" 142 lbs.
Deceased.

	W	L	PCT	ERA	G	GS	CG	IP	H	BB	SO	ShO	W	L	SV	AB	H	HR	BA
1896 STL N	0	0	–	∞	1	0	0	1	2	0	0	0	0	0	0	0	0	0	–

Pete Wood

WOOD, PETER BURKE 5'7" 185 lbs.
Brother of Fred Wood.
B. Feb. 1, 1867, Hamilton, Ont., Canada D. Mar. 15, 1923, Chicago, Ill.

	W	L	PCT	ERA	G	GS	CG	IP	H	BB	SO	ShO	W	L	SV	AB	H	HR	BA
1885 BUF N	8	15	.348	4.44	24	22	21	198.2	235	66	38	0	0	1	0	104	23	0	.221
1889 PHI N	1	1	.500	5.21	3	2	2	19	28	3	8	0	0	0	0	8	0	0	.000
2 yrs.	9	16	.360	4.51	27	24	23	217.2	263	69	46	0	0	1	0	112	23	0	.205

Spades Wood

WOOD, CHARLES ASHER BL TL 5'10½" 150 lbs.
B. Jan. 13, 1909, Spartanburg, S. C.

	W	L	PCT	ERA	G	GS	CG	IP	H	BB	SO	ShO	W	L	SV	AB	H	HR	BA
1930 PIT N	4	3	.571	5.12	9	7	4	58	61	32	23	2	0	1	0	20	5	0	.250
1931	2	6	.250	6.05	15	10	2	64	69	46	33	0	0	0	0	22	5	0	.227
2 yrs.	6	9	.400	5.61	24	17	6	122	130	78	56	2	0	1	0	42	10	0	.238

Wilbur Wood

WOOD, WILBUR FORRESTER BR TL 6' 180 lbs.
B. Oct. 22, 1941, Cambridge, Mass.

	W	L	PCT	ERA	G	GS	CG	IP	H	BB	SO	ShO	W	L	SV	AB	H	HR	BA
1961 BOS A	0	0	–	5.54	6	1	0	13	14	7	7	0	0	0	0	3	0	0	.000
1962	0	0	–	3.52	1	1	0	7.2	6	3	3	0	0	0	0	3	0	0	.000
1963	0	5	.000	3.76	25	1	0	64.2	67	13	28	0	0	1	0	12	0	0	.000
1964 2 teams				BOS A (4G 0–0)				PIT N (3G 0–2)											
" total	0	2	.000	7.04	7	2	1	23	29	14	12	0	0	0	0	6	0	0	.000
1965 PIT N	1	1	.500	3.16	34	1	0	51.1	44	16	29	0	1	0	0	6	0	0	.000
1967 CHI A	4	2	.667	2.45	51	0	0	95.1	95	28	47	0	0	0	4	16	1	0	.063
1968	13	12	.520	1.87	88	2	0	159	127	33	74	0	12	11	16	22	2	0	.091
1969	10	11	.476	3.01	76	0	0	119.2	113	40	73	0	10	11	15	15	0	0	.000
1970	9	13	.409	2.80	77	0	0	122	118	36	85	0	9	13	21	18	2	0	.111
1971	22	13	.629	1.91	44	42	22	334	272	62	210	7	0	0	1	96	5	0	.052
1972	24	17	.585	2.51	49	49	20	376.2	325	74	193	8	0	0	0	125	17	0	.136
1973	24	20	.545	3.46	49	48	21	359.1	381	91	199	4	1	0	0	0	0	0	–

	W	L	PCT	ERA	G	GS	CG	IP	H	BB	SO	ShO	Relief Pitching W	L	SV	BATTING AB	H	HR	BA

Wilbur Wood continued

	W	L	PCT	ERA	G	GS	CG	IP	H	BB	SO	ShO	W	L	SV	AB	H	HR	BA
1974	20	19	.513	3.60	42	**42**	22	320	305	80	169	1	0	0	0	0	0	0	–
1975	16	20	.444	4.11	43	**43**	14	291.1	309	92	140	2	0	0	0	0	0	0	–
1976	4	3	.571	2.25	7	7	5	56	51	11	31	1	0	0	0	0	0	0	–
1977	7	8	.467	4.98	24	18	5	123	139	50	42	1	0	0	0	0	0	0	–
1978	10	10	.500	5.20	28	27	4	168	187	74	69	0	0	0	0	0	0	0	–
17 yrs.	164	156	.513	3.24	651	297	114	2684	2582	724	1411	24	33	36	57	322	27	0	.084

Gene Woodburn

WOODBURN, EUGENE STEWART　　BR TR 6'　175 lbs.
B. Aug. 20, 1886, Bellaire, Ohio.　D. Jan. 18, 1961, Sandusky, Ohio.

	W	L	PCT	ERA	G	GS	CG	IP	H	BB	SO	ShO	W	L	SV	AB	H	HR	BA
1911 STL N	1	5	.167	5.40	11	6	1	38.1	22	40	23	0	0	1	0	6	1	0	.167
1912	1	4	.200	5.59	20	5	1	48.1	60	42	25	0	1	0	0	13	0	0	.000
2 yrs.	2	9	.182	5.50	31	11	2	86.2	82	82	48	0	1	1	0	19	1	0	.053

Fred Woodcock

WOODCOCK, FRED WEYLAND　　TL
B. May 17, 1868, Winchendon, Mass.　D. Aug. 11, 1943, Ashburnham, Mass.

	W	L	PCT	ERA	G	GS	CG	IP	H	BB	SO	ShO	W	L	SV	AB	H	HR	BA
1892 PIT N	1	2	.333	3.55	5	4	3	33	42	17	8	0	0	0	0	15	3	0	.200

George Woodend

WOODEND, GEORGE ANTHONY　　BR TR 6'　200 lbs.
B. Dec. 9, 1917, Hartford, Conn.　D. Feb. 6, 1980, Hartford, Conn.

	W	L	PCT	ERA	G	GS	CG	IP	H	BB	SO	ShO	W	L	SV	AB	H	HR	BA
1944 BOS N	0	0	–	13.50	3	0	0	2	5	5	0	0	0	0	0	0	0	0	–

Hal Woodeshick

WOODESHICK, HAROLD JOSEPH　　BR TL 6'3"　200 lbs.
B. Aug. 24, 1932, Wilkes-Barre, Pa.

	W	L	PCT	ERA	G	GS	CG	IP	H	BB	SO	ShO	W	L	SV	AB	H	HR	BA
1956 DET A	0	2	.000	13.50	2	2	0	5.1	12	3	1	0	0	0	0	0	0	0	–
1958 CLE A	6	6	.500	3.64	14	9	3	71.2	71	25	27	0	3	0	0	24	4	0	.167
1959 WAS A	2	4	.333	3.69	31	3	0	61	58	36	30	0	2	1	0	8	0	0	.000
1960	4	5	.444	4.70	41	14	1	115	131	60	46	0	2	1	4	29	2	0	.069
1961 2 teams					WAS	A (7G 3-2)			DET	A (12G 1-1)										
" total	4	3	.571	5.22	19	8	1	58.2	63	41	37	0	1	0	0	20	2	0	.100
1962 HOU N	5	16	.238	4.39	31	26	2	139.1	161	54	82	1	0	1	0	37	3	0	.081
1963	11	9	.550	1.97	55	0	0	114	75	42	94	0	11	9	10	23	3	0	.130
1964	2	9	.182	2.76	61	0	0	78.1	73	32	58	0	2	9	23	10	0	0	.000
1965 2 teams					HOU	N (27G 3-4)			STL	N (51G 3-2)										
" total	6	6	.500	2.25	78	0	0	92	74	45	59	0	6	6	18	14	1	0	.071
1966 STL N	2	1	.667	1.92	59	0	0	70.1	57	23	30	0	2	1	2	5	1	0	.200
1967	2	1	.667	5.18	36	0	0	41.2	41	28	20	0	2	1	2	4	0	0	.000
11 yrs.	44	62	.415	3.56	427	62	7	847.1	816	389	484	1	31	29	61	174	16	0	.092
WORLD SERIES																			
1967 STL N	0	0	–	0.00	1	0	0	1	1	1	0	0	0	0	0	0	0	0	–

Dan Woodman

WOODMAN, DANIEL COURTENAY (Cocoa)　　BR TR 5'8"　160 lbs.
B. July 8, 1893, Danvers, Mass.　D. Dec. 14, 1962, Danvers, Mass.

	W	L	PCT	ERA	G	GS	CG	IP	H	BB	SO	ShO	W	L	SV	AB	H	HR	BA
1914 BUF F	0	0	–	2.41	13	0	0	33.2	30	11	13	0	0	0	1	7	1	0	.143
1915	0	0	–	4.11	5	1	0	15.1	14	9	1	0	0	0	0	4	1	0	.250
2 yrs.	0	0	–	2.94	18	1	0	49	44	20	14	0	0	0	1	11	2	0	.182

Clarence Woods

WOODS, CLARENCE COFIELD　　6'5½"　230 lbs.
B. June 11, 1892, Ohio County, Ind.　D. July 2, 1969, Rising Sun, Ind.

	W	L	PCT	ERA	G	GS	CG	IP	H	BB	SO	ShO	W	L	SV	AB	H	HR	BA
1914 IND F	0	0	–	4.50	2	0	0	2	1	2	1	0	0	0	1	0	0	0	–

John Woods

WOODS, JOHN FULTON　　BR TR 5'11"　150 lbs.
B. Jan. 18, 1898, Princeton, W. Va.　D. Oct. 4, 1946, Norfolk, Va.

	W	L	PCT	ERA	G	GS	CG	IP	H	BB	SO	ShO	W	L	SV	AB	H	HR	BA
1924 BOS A	0	0	–	0.00	1	0	0	1	0	3	0	0	0	0	0	0	0	0	–

Pinky Woods

WOODS, GEORGE ROWLAND　　BR TR 6'5"　225 lbs.
B. May 22, 1915, Waterbury, Conn.　D. Oct. 30, 1982, Los Angeles, Calif.

	W	L	PCT	ERA	G	GS	CG	IP	H	BB	SO	ShO	W	L	SV	AB	H	HR	BA
1943 BOS A	5	6	.455	4.92	23	12	2	100.2	109	55	32	0	2	0	1	36	8	0	.222
1944	4	8	.333	3.27	38	20	5	170.2	171	88	56	1	0	1	0	48	7	0	.146
1945	4	7	.364	4.19	24	12	3	107.1	108	63	36	0	1	1	2	42	9	0	.214
3 yrs.	13	21	.382	3.97	85	44	10	378.2	388	206	124	1	3	2	3	126	24	0	.190

Walt Woods

WOODS, WALTER SYDNEY　　5'9½"　165 lbs.
B. Apr. 28, 1875, Rye, N. H.　D. Oct. 30, 1951, Portsmouth, N. H.

	W	L	PCT	ERA	G	GS	CG	IP	H	BB	SO	ShO	W	L	SV	AB	H	HR	BA
1898 CHI N	9	13	.409	3.14	27	22	18	215	224	59	26	3	0	1	0	154	27	0	.175
1899 LOU N	9	13	.409	3.28	26	21	17	186.1	216	37	21	0	2	1	0	126	19	1	.151
1900 PIT N	0	0	–	21.00	1	0	0	3	9	1	1	0	0	0	0	1	0	0	.000
3 yrs.	18	26	.409	3.34	54	43	35	404.1	449	97	48	3	2	2	0	*			

Dick Woodson

WOODSON, RICHARD LEE　　BR TR 6'5"　205 lbs.
B. Mar. 30, 1945, Oelwein, Iowa.

	W	L	PCT	ERA	G	GS	CG	IP	H	BB	SO	ShO	W	L	SV	AB	H	HR	BA
1969 MIN A	7	5	.583	3.67	44	10	2	110.1	99	49	66	0	3	2	1	27	2	0	.074
1970	1	2	.333	3.77	21	0	0	31	29	19	22	0	1	2	1	2	0	0	.000
1972	14	14	.500	2.71	36	36	9	252	193	101	150	3	0	0	0	88	7	0	.080
1973	10	8	.556	3.95	23	23	4	141.1	137	68	53	2	0	0	0	0	0	0	–
1974 2 teams					MIN	A (5G 1-1)			NY	A (8G 1-2)										
" total	2	3	.400	5.07	13	7	0	55	64	16	24	0	1	0	0	0	0	0	–
5 yrs.	34	32	.515	3.46	137	76	15	589.2	522	253	315	5	5	4	2	117	9	0	.077
LEAGUE CHAMPIONSHIP SERIES																			
1969 MIN A	0	0	–	10.80	1	0	0	1.2	3	3	2	0	0	0	0	1	1	0	1.000
1970	0	0	–	9.00	1	0	0	1	2	1	0	0	0	0	0	0	0	0	–
2 yrs.	0	0	–	10.13	2	0	0	2.2	5	4	2	0	0	0	0	1	1	0	1.000

	W	L	PCT	ERA	G	GS	CG	IP	H	BB	SO	ShO	Relief Pitching W	L	SV	Batting AB	H	HR	BA

Frank Woodward

WOODWARD, FRANK RUSSELL
B. May 17, 1894, New Haven, Conn.   D. June 11, 1961, New Haven, Conn.   BR TR 5'10"   175 lbs.

	W	L	PCT	ERA	G	GS	CG	IP	H	BB	SO	ShO	RW	RL	SV	AB	H	HR	BA
1918 PHI N	0	0	–	6.00	2	0	0	6	6	4	4	0	0	0	0	3	1	0	.333
1919 2 teams			PHI	N (17G 6–9)		STL	N (17G 3–5)												
" total	9	14	.391	3.86	34	19	8	172.2	174	63	45	0	3	2	1	50	7	0	.140
1921 WAS A	0	0	–	5.91	3	1	0	10.2	11	3	4	0	0	0	0	3	1	0	.333
1922	0	0	–	11.57	1	0	0	2.1	3	3	2	0	0	0	0	1	0	0	.000
1923 CHI A	0	1	.000	13.50	2	1	0	2	5	1	0	0	0	0	0	0	0	0	–
5 yrs.	9	15	.375	4.23	42	21	8	193.2	199	74	55	0	3	2	1	57	9	0	.158

Floyd Wooldridge

WOOLDRIDGE, FLOYD LEWIS
B. Aug. 25, 1928, Jerico Springs, Mo.   BR TR 6'1"   185 lbs.

	W	L	PCT	ERA	G	GS	CG	IP	H	BB	SO	ShO	RW	RL	SV	AB	H	HR	BA
1955 STL N	2	4	.333	4.84	18	8	2	57.2	64	27	14	0	0	1	0	18	4	0	.222

Earl Wooten

WOOTEN, EARL HAZWELL (Junior)
B. Jan. 16, 1924, Pelzer, S. C.   BR TL 5'11"   160 lbs.

	W	L	PCT	ERA	G	GS	CG	IP	H	BB	SO	ShO	RW	RL	SV	AB	H	HR	BA
1948 WAS A	0	0	–	9.00	1	0	0	2	2	2	1	0	0	0	0	*			

Fred Worden

WORDEN, FRED B.
B. Sept. 4, 1894, St. Louis, Mo.   D. Nov. 9, 1941, St. Louis, Mo.   BR TR

	W	L	PCT	ERA	G	GS	CG	IP	H	BB	SO	ShO	RW	RL	SV	AB	H	HR	BA
1914 PHI A	0	0	–	18.00	1	0	0	2	8	0	1	0	0	0	0	1	0	0	.000

Hoge Workman

WORKMAN, HARRY HALL
B. Sept. 25, 1899, Huntington, W. Va.   D. May 20, 1972, Fort Myers, Fla.   BR TR 5'11"   170 lbs.

	W	L	PCT	ERA	G	GS	CG	IP	H	BB	SO	ShO	RW	RL	SV	AB	H	HR	BA
1924 BOS A	0	0	–	8.50	11	0	0	18	25	11	7	0	0	0	0	2	0	0	.000

Ralph Works

WORKS, RALPH TALMADGE (Judge)
B. Mar. 16, 1888, Payson, Ill.   D. Aug. 8, 1941, Pasadena, Calif.   BL TR 6'2½"   185 lbs.

	W	L	PCT	ERA	G	GS	CG	IP	H	BB	SO	ShO	RW	RL	SV	AB	H	HR	BA
1909 DET A	4	1	.800	1.97	16	4	4	64	62	17	31	0	1	0	2	17	1	0	.059
1910	3	6	.333	3.57	18	10	5	85.2	73	39	36	0	0	1	1	30	8	0	.267
1911	11	5	.688	3.87	30	15	9	167.1	173	67	68	3	4	0	1	61	9	0	.148
1912 2 teams	6	11	.353		DET	A (27G 5–10)		CIN	N (3G 1–1)										
" total	6	11	.353	4.16	30	18	10	166.2	189	71	69	1	1	1	1	61	9	0	.148
1913 CIN N	0	1	.000	7.80	5	2	0	15	15	8	4	0	0	0	0	6	1	0	.167
5 yrs.	24	24	.500	3.79	99	49	28	498.2	512	202	208	4	6	2	5	175	28	0	.160

WORLD SERIES

	W	L	PCT	ERA	G	GS	CG	IP	H	BB	SO	ShO	RW	RL	SV	AB	H	HR	BA
1909 DET A	0	0	–	9.00	1	0	0	2	4	1	2	0	0	0	0	0	0	0	–

Rich Wortham

WORTHAM, RICHARD COOPER
B. Oct. 22, 1953, Odessa, Tex.   BR TL 6'   185 lbs.

	W	L	PCT	ERA	G	GS	CG	IP	H	BB	SO	ShO	RW	RL	SV	AB	H	HR	BA
1978 CHI A	3	2	.600	3.05	8	8	2	59	59	23	25	0	0	0	0	0	0	0	–
1979	14	14	.500	4.90	34	33	5	204	195	100	119	0	0	0	0	0	0	0	–
1980	4	7	.364	5.97	41	10	0	92	102	58	45	0	2	2	1	0	0	0	–
1983 OAK A	0	0	–	∞	1	0	0	3	3	1	0	0	0	0	0	0	0	0	–
4 yrs.	21	23	.477	4.89	84	51	7	355	359	182	189	0	2	2	1	0	0	0	–

Al Worthington

WORTHINGTON, ALLAN FULTON (Red)
B. Feb. 5, 1929, Birmingham, Ala.   BR TR 6'2"   195 lbs.

	W	L	PCT	ERA	G	GS	CG	IP	H	BB	SO	ShO	RW	RL	SV	AB	H	HR	BA
1953 NY N	4	8	.333	3.44	20	17	5	102	103	54	52	2	0	1	0	31	2	0	.065
1954	0	2	.000	3.50	10	1	0	18	21	15	8	0	0	0	0	4	0	0	.000
1956	7	14	.333	3.97	28	24	4	165.2	158	74	95	0	0	1	0	51	12	1	.235
1957	8	11	.421	4.22	55	12	1	157.2	140	56	90	1	7	5	4	40	4	0	.100
1958 SF N	11	7	.611	3.63	54	12	1	151.1	152	57	76	0	3	4	6	44	8	0	.182
1959	2	3	.400	3.68	42	3	0	73.1	68	37	45	0	1	2	2	13	1	0	.077
1960 2 teams			BOS	A (6G 0–1)		CHI	A (4G 1–1)												
" total	1	2	.333	6.35	10	0	0	17	20	15	8	0	1	2	0	3	2	0	.667
1963 CIN N	4	4	.500	2.99	50	0	0	81.1	75	31	55	0	4	4	10	12	1	0	.083
1964 2 teams			CIN	N (6G 1–0)		MIN	A (41G 5–6)												
" total	6	6	.500	2.16	47	0	0	79.1	61	30	65	0	6	6	14	16	1	0	.063
1965 MIN A	10	7	.588	2.13	62	0	0	80.1	57	41	59	0	10	7	21	10	1	0	.100
1966	6	3	.667	2.46	65	0	0	91.1	66	27	93	0	6	3	16	11	3	0	.273
1967	8	9	.471	2.84	59	0	0	92	77	38	80	0	8	9	16	8	0	0	.000
1968	4	5	.444	2.71	54	0	0	76.1	67	32	57	0	4	5	18	7	0	0	.000
1969	4	1	.800	4.57	46	0	0	61	65	20	51	0	4	1	3	5	0	0	.000
14 yrs.	75	82	.478	3.39	602	69	11	1246.2	1130	527	834	3	54	50	110	255	35	1	.137

LEAGUE CHAMPIONSHIP SERIES

	W	L	PCT	ERA	G	GS	CG	IP	H	BB	SO	ShO	RW	RL	SV	AB	H	HR	BA
1969 MIN A	0	0	–	6.75	1	0	0	1.1	3	1	1	0	0	0	0	0	0	0	–

WORLD SERIES

	W	L	PCT	ERA	G	GS	CG	IP	H	BB	SO	ShO	RW	RL	SV	AB	H	HR	BA
1965 MIN A	0	0	–	0.00	2	0	0	4	2	2	2	0	0	0	0	0	0	0	–

Bob Wright

WRIGHT, ROBERT CASSIUS
B. Dec. 13, 1891, Greensburg, Ind.   BR TR 6'1½"   175 lbs.

	W	L	PCT	ERA	G	GS	CG	IP	H	BB	SO	ShO	RW	RL	SV	AB	H	HR	BA
1915 CHI N	0	0	–	2.25	2	0	0	4	6	0	3	0	0	0	0	0	0	0	–

Clarence Wright

WRIGHT, CLARENCE EUGENE
B. Dec. 11, 1878, Cleveland, Ohio   D. Oct. 29, 1930, Barberton, Ohio   BR TR 6'2½"   190 lbs.

	W	L	PCT	ERA	G	GS	CG	IP	H	BB	SO	ShO	RW	RL	SV	AB	H	HR	BA
1901 BKN N	1	0	1.000	1.00	1	1	1	9	6	1	6	0	0	0	0	3	1	0	.333
1902 CLE A	7	11	.389	3.95	21	18	15	148	150	75	52	1	0	0	0	70	10	1	.143
1903 2 teams			CLE	A (15G 3–9)		STL	A (8G 3–5)												
" total	6	14	.300	4.98	23	20	15	162.2	195	74	79	1	0	1	1	64	12	0	.188
1904 STL A	0	1	.000	13.50	1	1	0	4	10	2	3	0	0	0	0	1	0	0	.000
4 yrs.	14	26	.350	4.50	46	40	31	323.2	361	152	140	2	0	2	1	138	23	1	.167

	W	L	PCT	ERA	G	GS	CG	IP	H	BB	SO	ShO	Relief Pitching W	L	SV	BATTING AB	H	HR	BA

Clyde Wright

WRIGHT, CLYDE
B. Feb. 20, 1941, Jefferson City, Tenn.   BR TL 6'1"   180 lbs.

	W	L	PCT	ERA	G	GS	CG	IP	H	BB	SO	ShO	W	L	SV	AB	H	HR	BA
1966 CAL A	4	7	.364	3.74	20	13	3	91.1	92	25	37	1	1	1	0	29	3	0	.103
1967	5	5	.500	3.26	20	11	1	77.1	76	24	35	0	1	0	0	22	6	0	.273
1968	10	6	.625	3.94	41	13	2	125.2	123	44	71	1	6	0	3	37	8	0	.216
1969	1	8	.111	4.10	37	5	0	63.2	66	30	31	0	1	3	0	11	2	0	.182
1970	22	12	.647	2.83	39	39	7	261	226	88	110	2	0	0	0	105	18	2	.171
1971	16	17	.485	2.99	37	37	10	277	225	82	135	2	0	0	0	91	14	0	.154
1972	18	11	.621	2.98	35	35	15	251	229	80	87	2	0	0	0	83	18	2	.217
1973	11	19	.367	3.68	37	36	13	257	273	76	65	1	0	0	0	0	0	0	–
1974 MIL A	9	20	.310	4.42	38	32	15	232	264	54	64	0	1	1	0	0	0	0	–
1975 TEX A	4	6	.400	4.44	25	14	1	93.1	105	47	32	0	1	0	0	0	0	0	–
10 yrs.	100	111	.474	3.50	329	235	67	1729.1	1679	550	667	9	11	5	3	378	69	4	.183

Dave Wright

WRIGHT, DAVID WILLIAM
B. Aug. 27, 1875, Dennison, Ohio   D. Jan. 18, 1946, Dennison, Ohio   BR TR 5'10"   148 lbs.

	W	L	PCT	ERA	G	GS	CG	IP	H	BB	SO	ShO	W	L	SV	AB	H	HR	BA
1895 PIT N	0	0	–	27.00	1	0	0	2	6	1	0	0	0	0	0	1	0	0	.000
1897 CHI N	1	0	1.000	15.43	1	1	1	7	17	2	4	0	0	0	0	3	1	0	.333
2 yrs.	1	0	1.000	18.00	2	1	1	9	23	3	4	0	0	0	0	4	1	0	.250

Ed Wright

WRIGHT, HENDERSON EDWARD
B. May 15, 1919, Dyersburg, Tenn.   BR TR 6'1"   180 lbs.

	W	L	PCT	ERA	G	GS	CG	IP	H	BB	SO	ShO	W	L	SV	AB	H	HR	BA
1945 BOS N	8	3	.727	2.51	15	12	7	111.1	104	33	24	1	0	0	0	39	5	0	.128
1946	12	9	.571	3.52	36	21	9	176.1	164	71	44	2	2	0	0	59	18	0	.305
1947	3	3	.500	6.40	23	6	1	64.2	80	35	14	0	1	0	0	23	3	0	.130
1948	0	0	–	1.93	3	0	0	4.2	9	2	2	0	0	0	0	0	0	0	–
1952 PHI A	2	1	.667	6.53	24	0	0	41.1	55	20	9	0	2	1	1	7	1	0	.143
5 yrs.	25	16	.610	4.00	101	39	17	398.1	412	161	93	3	5	1	1	128	27	0	.211

George Wright

WRIGHT, GEORGE
Brother of Harry Wright.   Brother of Sam Wright.
B. Jan. 28, 1847, Yonkers, N. Y.   D. Aug. 21, 1937, Boston, Mass.
Manager 1879.
Hall of Fame 1937.   BR TR 5'9½"   150 lbs.

	W	L	PCT	ERA	G	GS	CG	IP	H	BB	SO	ShO	W	L	SV	AB	H	HR	BA
1876 BOS N	0	0	–	0.00	1	0	0	1	1	0	1	0	0	0	0	*			

Jim Wright

WRIGHT, JAMES
B. Sept. 19, 1900, Hyde, England   D. Apr. 10, 1963, Oakland, Calif.   BR TR 6'4"   195 lbs.

	W	L	PCT	ERA	G	GS	CG	IP	H	BB	SO	ShO	W	L	SV	AB	H	HR	BA
1927 STL A	1	0	1.000	4.50	2	1	1	12	8	4	4	0	0	0	0	4	0	0	.000
1928	0	0	–	13.50	2	0	0	2	3	2	2	0	0	0	0	0	0	0	–
2 yrs.	1	0	1.000	5.79	4	1	1	14	11	6	6	0	0	0	0	4	0	0	.000

Jim Wright

WRIGHT, JAMES CLIFTON
B. Dec. 21, 1950, Reed City, Mich.   BR TR 6'5"   205 lbs.

	W	L	PCT	ERA	G	GS	CG	IP	H	BB	SO	ShO	W	L	SV	AB	H	HR	BA
1978 BOS A	8	4	.667	3.57	24	16	5	116	122	24	56	3	0	0	0	0	0	0	–
1979	1	0	1.000	5.09	11	1	0	23	19	7	15	0	0	0	0	0	0	0	–
2 yrs.	9	4	.692	3.82	35	17	5	139	141	31	71	3	0	0	0	0	0	0	–

Jim Wright

WRIGHT, JAMES LEON JR.
B. Mar. 3, 1955, St. Joseph, Mo.   BR TR 6'5"   205 lbs.

	W	L	PCT	ERA	G	GS	CG	IP	H	BB	SO	ShO	W	L	SV	AB	H	HR	BA
1981 KC A	2	3	.400	3.46	17	4	0	52	57	21	27	0	1	1	0	0	0	0	–
1982	0	0	–	5.32	7	0	0	23.2	32	6	9	0	0	0	0	0	0	0	–
2 yrs.	2	3	.400	4.04	24	4	0	75.2	89	27	36	0	1	1	0	0	0	0	–

Ken Wright

WRIGHT, KENNETH WARREN
B. Sept. 4, 1946, Pensacola, Fla.   BR TR 6'2"   210 lbs.

	W	L	PCT	ERA	G	GS	CG	IP	H	BB	SO	ShO	W	L	SV	AB	H	HR	BA
1970 KC A	1	2	.333	5.26	47	0	0	53	49	29	30	0	1	2	3	4	0	0	.000
1971	3	6	.333	3.69	21	12	1	78	66	47	56	0	0	1	1	22	2	0	.091
1972	1	2	.333	5.00	17	0	0	18	15	15	18	0	1	2	4	2	0	0	.000
1973	6	5	.545	4.89	25	12	1	81	60	82	75	0	1	0	0	0	0	0	–
1974 NY A	0	0	–	3.00	3	0	0	6	5	7	2	0	0	0	0	0	0	0	–
5 yrs.	11	15	.423	4.54	113	24	2	236	195	180	181	0	3	4	8	28	2	0	.071

Lucky Wright

WRIGHT, WILLIAM SIMMONS (William The Red, Deacon)
B. Feb. 21, 1880, Tontogany, Ohio   D. July 8, 1941, Tontogany, Ohio   BR TR 6'   178 lbs.

	W	L	PCT	ERA	G	GS	CG	IP	H	BB	SO	ShO	W	L	SV	AB	H	HR	BA
1909 CLE A	0	4	.000	3.97	5	4	3	22.2	20	8	6	0	0	0	0	7	0	0	.000

Mel Wright

WRIGHT, MELVIN JAMES
B. May 11, 1928, Manila, Ark.   D. May 16, 1983, Houston, Tex.   BR TR 6'3"   210 lbs.

	W	L	PCT	ERA	G	GS	CG	IP	H	BB	SO	ShO	W	L	SV	AB	H	HR	BA
1954 STL N	0	0	–	10.45	9	0	0	10.1	16	11	4	0	0	0	0	1	0	0	.000
1955	2	2	.500	6.19	29	0	0	36.1	44	9	18	0	2	2	1	6	0	0	.000
1960 CHI N	0	1	.000	4.96	9	0	0	16.1	17	3	8	0	0	1	2	2	0	0	.000
1961	0	1	.000	10.71	11	0	0	21	42	4	6	0	0	1	0	2	0	0	.000
4 yrs.	2	4	.333	7.61	58	0	0	84	119	27	36	0	2	4	3	11	0	0	.000

Rasty Wright

WRIGHT, WAYNE BROMLEY
B. Nov. 5, 1895, Ceredo, W. Va.   D. June 12, 1948, Columbus, Ohio   BR TR 5'11"   160 lbs.

	W	L	PCT	ERA	G	GS	CG	IP	H	BB	SO	ShO	W	L	SV	AB	H	HR	BA
1917 STL A	0	1	.000	5.45	16	1	0	39.2	48	10	5	0	0	0	0	10	2	0	.200
1918	8	2	.800	2.51	18	13	6	111.1	99	18	25	1	0	0	0	34	10	0	.294
1919	0	5	.000	5.54	24	5	2	63.1	79	20	14	0	0	0	0	12	1	0	.083
1922	9	7	.563	2.92	31	16	5	154	148	50	44	0	3	2	5	50	7	0	.140
1923	7	4	.636	6.42	20	8	4	82.2	107	34	26	0	4	1	0	27	6	0	.222
5 yrs.	24	19	.558	4.05	109	43	17	451	481	132	114	1	7	3	5	133	26	0	.195

	W	L	PCT	ERA	G	GS	CG	IP	H	BB	SO	ShO	Relief Pitching W	L	SV	BATTING AB	H	HR	BA

Ricky Wright

WRIGHT, JAMES RICHARD B. Nov. 22, 1958, Paris, Tex.   BL TL 6'3" 175 lbs.

	W	L	PCT	ERA	G	GS	CG	IP	H	BB	SO	ShO	W	L	SV	AB	H	HR	BA
1982 LA N	2	1	.667	3.03	14	5	0	32.2	28	20	24	0	1	1	0	8	1	0	.125
1983 2 teams					LA	N (6G 0-0)		TEX	A (1G 0-0)										
" total	0	0	–	2.16	7	0	0	8.1	5	3	7	0	0	0	0	0	0	0	–
1984 TEX A	0	2	.000	6.14	8	1	0	14.2	20	11	6	0	0	2	0	0	0	0	–
3 yrs.	2	3	.400	3.72	29	6	0	55.2	53	34	37	0	1	3	0	8	1	0	.125

Roy Wright

WRIGHT, ROY EARL B. Sept. 26, 1933, Buchtel, Ohio   BR TR 6'2" 170 lbs.

	W	L	PCT	ERA	G	GS	CG	IP	H	BB	SO	ShO	W	L	SV	AB	H	HR	BA
1956 NY N	0	1	.000	16.88	1	1	0	2.2	8	2	0	0	0	0	0	1	0	0	.000

Frank Wurm

WURM, FRANK JAMES B. Apr. 27, 1924, Cambridge, N. Y.   BB TL 6'1" 175 lbs.

	W	L	PCT	ERA	G	GS	CG	IP	H	BB	SO	ShO	W	L	SV	AB	H	HR	BA
1944 BKN N	0	0	–	108.00	1	1	0	.1	1	5	1	0	0	0	0	0	0	0	–

John Wyatt

WYATT, JOHN THOMAS B. Apr. 19, 1935, Chicago, Ill.   BR TR 5'11½" 200 lbs.

	W	L	PCT	ERA	G	GS	CG	IP	H	BB	SO	ShO	W	L	SV	AB	H	HR	BA
1961 KC A	0	0	–	2.45	5	0	0	7.1	8	4	6	0	0	0	1	0	0	0	–
1962	10	7	.588	4.46	59	9	0	125	121	80	106	0	7	4	11	29	3	0	.103
1963	6	4	.600	3.13	63	0	0	92	83	43	81	0	6	4	21	9	0	0	.000
1964	9	8	.529	3.59	81	0	0	128	111	52	74	0	9	8	20	14	0	0	.000
1965	2	6	.250	3.25	65	0	0	88.2	78	53	70	0	2	6	18	4	0	0	.000
1966 2 teams					KC	A (19G 0-3)		BOS	A (42G 3-4)										
" total	3	7	.300	3.68	61	0	0	95.1	78	43	88	0	3	7	10	11	0	0	.000
1967 BOS A	10	7	.588	2.60	60	0	0	93.1	71	39	68	0	10	7	20	12	1	0	.083
1968 3 teams					BOS A (8G 1-2)	NY A (7G 0-2)		DET	A (22G 1-0)										
" total	2	4	.333	2.74	37	0	0	49.1	42	26	42	0	2	4	2	3	0	0	.000
1969 OAK A	0	1	.000	5.40	4	0	0	8.1	8	6	5	0	0	1	0	1	0	0	.000
9 yrs.	42	44	.488	3.47	435	9	0	687.1	600	346	540	0	39	41	103	83	4	0	.048

WORLD SERIES

	W	L	PCT	ERA	G	GS	CG	IP	H	BB	SO	ShO	W	L	SV	AB	H	HR	BA
1967 BOS A	1	0	1.000	4.91	2	0	0	3.2	1	3	1	0	1	0	0	0	0	0	–

Whit Wyatt

WYATT, JOHN WHITLOW B. Sept. 27, 1907, Kensington, Ga.   BR TR 6'1" 185 lbs.

	W	L	PCT	ERA	G	GS	CG	IP	H	BB	SO	ShO	W	L	SV	AB	H	HR	BA
1929 DET A	0	1	.000	6.75	4	4	1	25.1	30	18	14	0	0	0	0	10	1	0	.100
1930	4	5	.444	3.57	21	7	3	85.2	76	35	68	0	3	2	2	34	12	1	.353
1931	0	2	.000	8.44	4	1	1	21.1	30	12	8	0	0	1	0	7	2	0	.286
1932	9	13	.409	5.03	43	22	10	205.2	228	102	82	0	3	1	1	78	15	2	.192
1933 2 teams					DET	A (10G 0-1)		CHI	A (26G 3-4)										
" total	3	5	.375	4.56	36	7	2	104.2	111	54	40	0	1	2	1	30	6	0	.200
1934 CHI A	4	11	.267	7.18	23	6	2	67.2	83	37	36	0	3	6	2	26	6	0	.231
1935	4	3	.571	6.75	30	1	0	52	65	25	22	0	4	3	5	13	3	0	.231
1936	0	0	–	0.00	3	0	0	3	3	0	0	0	0	0	1	0	0	0	–
1937 CLE A	2	3	.400	4.44	29	4	2	73	67	40	52	0	2	2	0	18	7	0	.389
1939 BKN N	8	3	.727	2.31	16	14	6	109	88	39	52	2	2	0	0	36	6	0	.167
1940	15	14	.517	3.46	37	34	16	239.1	233	62	124	5	1	1	0	80	14	1	.175
1941	22	10	.688	2.34	38	35	23	288.1	223	82	176	7	0	1	1	109	26	3	.239
1942	19	7	.731	2.73	31	30	16	217.1	185	63	104	0	1	0	0	77	14	0	.182
1943	14	5	.737	2.49	26	26	13	180.2	139	43	80	3	0	0	0	60	17	0	.283
1944	2	6	.250	7.17	9	9	1	37.2	51	16	4	0	0	0	0	13	2	0	.154
1945 PHI N	0	7	.000	5.26	10	10	2	51.1	72	14	10	0	0	0	0	16	2	0	.125
16 yrs.	106	95	.527	3.78	360	210	97	1762	1684	642	872	17	20	19	13	607	133	7	.219

WORLD SERIES

	W	L	PCT	ERA	G	GS	CG	IP	H	BB	SO	ShO	W	L	SV	AB	H	HR	BA
1941 BKN N	1	1	.500	2.50	2	2	2	18	15	10	14	0	0	0	0	6	1	0	.167

John Wyckoff

WYCKOFF, JOHN WELDON B. Feb. 19, 1892, Williamsport, Pa.   D. May 8, 1961, Sheboygan Falls, Wis.   BR TR 6'1" 175 lbs.

	W	L	PCT	ERA	G	GS	CG	IP	H	BB	SO	ShO	W	L	SV	AB	H	HR	BA
1913 PHI A	2	4	.333	4.38	17	7	3	61.2	56	46	31	0	0	1	0	21	4	0	.190
1914	11	7	.611	3.02	32	20	11	185	153	103	86	0	1	1	2	75	11	1	.147
1915	10	22	.313	3.52	43	34	20	276	238	165	157	1	1	1	0	96	12	0	.125
1916 2 teams					PHI	A (7G 0-1)		BOS	A (8G 0-0)										
" total	0	1	.000	5.11	15	2	1	44	39	38	22	0	0	0	1	14	4	0	.286
1917 BOS A	0	0	–	1.80	1	0	0	5	4	4	1	0	0	0	0	1	0	0	.000
1918	0	0	–	0.00	1	0	0	2	4	1	2	0	0	0	0	1	0	0	.000
6 yrs.	23	34	.404	3.55	109	63	35	573.2	494	357	299	1	2	3	3	208	31	1	.149

WORLD SERIES

	W	L	PCT	ERA	G	GS	CG	IP	H	BB	SO	ShO	W	L	SV	AB	H	HR	BA
1914 PHI A	0	0	–	2.45	1	0	0	3.2	3	1	2	0	0	0	0	1	1	0	1.000

Frank Wyman

WYMAN, FRANK C. B. May 10, 1862, Haverhill, Mass.   D. Feb. 4, 1916, Everett, Mass.

	W	L	PCT	ERA	G	GS	CG	IP	H	BB	SO	ShO	W	L	SV	AB	H	HR	BA
1884 KC U	0	1	.000	6.86	3	1	1	21	37	3	9	0	0	0	0	*			

Early Wynn

WYNN, EARLY (Gus) B. Jan. 6, 1920, Hartford, Ala.   Hall of Fame 1971.   BB TR 6' 190 lbs.   BR 1939-44

	W	L	PCT	ERA	G	GS	CG	IP	H	BB	SO	ShO	W	L	SV	AB	H	HR	BA
1939 WAS A	0	2	.000	5.75	3	3	1	20.1	26	10	1	0	0	0	0	6	1	0	.167
1941	3	1	.750	1.58	5	5	4	40	35	10	15	0	0	0	0	15	2	0	.133
1942	10	16	.385	5.12	30	28	10	190	246	73	58	1	0	2	0	69	15	0	.217
1943	18	12	.600	2.91	37	33	12	256.2	232	83	89	3	2	0	0	98	29	1	.296
1944	8	17	.320	3.38	33	25	19	207.2	221	67	65	2	0	2	2	92	19	1	.207
1946	8	5	.615	3.11	17	12	9	107	112	33	36	0	1	0	0	47	15	1	.319
1947	7	15	.318	3.64	33	31	22	247	251	90	73	0	1	0	0	120	33	2	.275
1948	8	19	.296	5.82	33	31	15	198	236	94	49	1	0	0	0	106	23	0	.217
1949 CLE A	11	7	.611	4.15	26	23	6	164.2	186	57	62	1	0	0	0	70	10	1	.143
1950	18	8	.692	3.20	32	28	14	213.2	166	101	143	2	1	2	0	77	18	2	.234

	W	L	PCT	ERA	G	GS	CG	IP	H	BB	SO	ShO	Relief Pitching W	L	SV	BATTING AB	H	HR	BA

Early Wynn continued

	W	L	PCT	ERA	G	GS	CG	IP	H	BB	SO	ShO	W	L	SV	AB	H	HR	BA
1951	20	13	.606	3.02	37	34	21	274.1	227	107	133	3	1	0	1	108	20	1	.185
1952	23	12	.657	2.90	42	33	19	285.2	239	132	153	4	3	1	3	99	22	0	.222
1953	17	12	.586	3.93	36	34	16	251.2	234	107	138	1	2	0	0	91	25	3	.275
1954	23	11	.676	2.73	40	36	20	270.2	225	83	155	3	0	1	2	93	17	0	.183
1955	17	11	.607	2.82	32	31	16	230	207	80	122	6	0	0	0	84	15	1	.179
1956	20	9	.690	2.72	38	35	18	277.2	233	91	158	1	0	0	2	101	23	1	.228
1957	14	17	.452	4.31	40	37	13	263	270	104	184	1	0	1	1	86	10	0	.116
1958 CHI A	14	16	.467	4.13	40	34	11	239.2	214	104	179	4	0	2	2	75	15	0	.200
1959	22	10	.688	3.17	37	37	14	255.2	202	119	179	5	0	0	0	90	22	2	.244
1960	13	12	.520	3.49	36	35	13	237.1	220	112	158	4	0	0	1	75	15	1	.200
1961	8	2	.800	3.51	17	16	5	110.1	88	47	64	0	0	0	0	37	6	0	.162
1962	7	15	.318	4.46	27	26	11	167.2	171	56	91	3	0	0	0	54	7	0	.130
1963 CLE A	1	2	.333	2.28	20	5	1	55.1	50	15	29	0	0	1	1	11	3	0	.273
23 yrs.	300 9th	244	.551	3.54	691	612	290	4564	4291	1775	2334 2nd	49	11	12	15	*			

WORLD SERIES																			
1954 CLE A	0	1	.000	3.86	1	1	0	7	4	2	5	0	0	0	0	2	1	0	.500
1959 CHI A	1	1	.500	5.54	3	3	0	13	19	4	10	0	0	0	0	5	1	0	.200
2 yrs.	1	2	.333	4.95	4	4	0	20	23	6	15	0	0	0	0	7	2	0	.286

Bill Wynne

WYNNE, WILLIAM ANDREW   BR TR 6'3"
B. Mar. 27, 1869, Neuse, N. C.   D. Aug. 7, 1951, Raleigh, N. C.

	W	L	PCT	ERA	G	GS	CG	IP	H	BB	SO	ShO	W	L	SV	AB	H	HR	BA
1894 WAS N	0	1	.000	6.75	1	1	1	8	10	8	2	0	0	0	0	3	0	0	.000

Billy Wynne

WYNNE, BILLY VERNON   BR TR 6'3" 205 lbs. BB 1967
B. July 31, 1943, Williamston, N. C.

	W	L	PCT	ERA	G	GS	CG	IP	H	BB	SO	ShO	W	L	SV	AB	H	HR	BA
1967 NY N	0	0	–	3.12	6	1	0	8.2	12	2	4	0	0	0	0	1	0	0	.000
1968 CHI A	0	0	–	4.50	1	0	0	2	2	2	1	0	0	0	0	0	0	0	–
1969	7	7	.500	4.06	20	20	6	128.2	143	50	67	1	0	0	0	41	5	0	.122
1970	1	4	.200	5.32	12	9	0	44	54	22	19	0	0	0	0	13	1	0	.077
1971 CAL A	0	0	–	4.50	3	0	0	4	6	2	6	0	0	0	0	0	0	0	–
5 yrs.	8	11	.421	4.32	42	30	6	187.1	217	78	97	1	0	0	0	55	6	0	.109

Hank Wyse

WYSE, HENRY WASHINGTON (Hooks)   BR TR 5'11½" 185 lbs.
B. Mar. 1, 1918, Lunsford, Ark.

	W	L	PCT	ERA	G	GS	CG	IP	H	BB	SO	ShO	W	L	SV	AB	H	HR	BA
1942 CHI N	2	1	.667	1.93	4	4	1	28	33	6	8	1	0	0	0	8	1	0	.125
1943	9	7	.563	2.94	38	15	8	156	160	34	45	2	1	2	5	50	4	0	.080
1944	16	15	.516	3.15	41	34	14	257.1	277	57	86	3	2	1	1	90	16	0	.178
1945	22	10	.688	2.68	38	34	23	278.1	272	55	77	2	1	0	0	101	17	0	.168
1946	14	12	.538	2.68	40	27	12	201.1	206	52	52	2	0	0	1	74	18	0	.243
1947	6	9	.400	4.31	37	19	5	142	158	64	53	1	1	0	1	45	5	0	.111
1950 PHI A	9	14	.391	5.85	41	24	4	170.2	192	87	33	0	1	4	0	59	9	0	.153
1951 2 teams					PHI A (9G 1–2)				WAS A (3G 0–0)										
" total	1	2	.333	8.63	12	3	0	24	41	18	8	0	1	0	0	8	1	0	.125
8 yrs.	79	70	.530	3.52	251	159	67	1257.2	1339	373	362	11	7	8	8	435	71	0	.163

WORLD SERIES																			
1945 CHI N	0	1	.000	7.04	3	1	0	7.2	8	4	1	0	0	0	0	3	0	0	.000

Biff Wysong

WYSONG, HARLIN   BL TL 6'3" 195 lbs.
B. Apr. 13, 1905, Clarksville, Ohio   D. Aug. 8, 1951, Xenia, Ohio

	W	L	PCT	ERA	G	GS	CG	IP	H	BB	SO	ShO	W	L	SV	AB	H	HR	BA
1930 CIN N	0	1	.000	19.29	1	1	0	2.1	6	3	1	0	0	0	0	0	0	0	–
1931	0	2	.000	7.89	12	2	0	21.2	25	23	5	0	0	0	0	4	1	0	.250
1932	1	0	1.000	3.65	7	0	0	12.1	13	8	5	0	1	0	0	2	0	0	.000
3 yrs.	1	3	.250	7.18	20	3	0	36.1	44	34	11	0	1	0	0	6	1	0	.167

Rusty Yarnall

YARNALL, WALDO WARD   BR TR 6' 175 lbs.
B. Oct. 22, 1902, Chicago, Ill.

	W	L	PCT	ERA	G	GS	CG	IP	H	BB	SO	ShO	W	L	SV	AB	H	HR	BA
1926 PHI N	0	1	.000	18.00	1	0	0	3	3	1	0	0	0	1	0	1	0	0	.000

Rube Yarrison

YARRISON, BYRON WARDSWORTH   BR TR 5'11" 165 lbs.
B. Mar. 9, 1896, Montgomery, Pa.   D. Apr. 22, 1977, Williamsport, Pa.

	W	L	PCT	ERA	G	GS	CG	IP	H	BB	SO	ShO	W	L	SV	AB	H	HR	BA
1922 PHI A	1	2	.333	8.29	18	1	0	33.2	50	12	10	0	1	1	0	6	1	0	.167
1924 BKN N	0	2	.000	6.55	3	2	0	11	12	3	2	0	0	0	0	2	0	0	.000
2 yrs.	1	4	.200	7.86	21	3	0	44.2	62	15	12	0	1	1	0	8	1	0	.125

Emil Yde

YDE, EMIL OGDEN   BB TL 5'11" 165 lbs. BL 1925
B. Jan. 28, 1900, Great Lakes, Ill.
D. Dec. 5, 1968, Leesburg, Fla.

	W	L	PCT	ERA	G	GS	CG	IP	H	BB	SO	ShO	W	L	SV	AB	H	HR	BA
1924 PIT N	16	3	.842	2.83	33	22	14	194	171	62	53	4	1	0	0	88	21	1	.239
1925	17	9	.654	4.13	33	28	13	207	254	75	41	0	2	0	0	89	17	0	.191
1926	8	7	.533	3.65	37	22	12	187.1	181	81	34	1	0	0	0	74	17	0	.230
1927	1	3	.250	9.71	9	2	0	29.2	45	15	9	0	1	0	1	18	3	0	.167
1929 DET A	7	3	.700	5.30	29	6	4	86.2	100	63	23	1	3	1	0	48	16	0	.333
5 yrs.	49	25	.662	4.02	141	80	43	704.2	751	296	160	6	7	2	0	*			

WORLD SERIES																			
1925 PIT N	0	1	.000	11.57	1	1	0	2.1	5	3	1	0	0	0	0	1	0	0	.000

Joe Yeager

YEAGER, JOSEPH F. (Little Joe)   TR
B. Aug. 28, 1875, Philadelphia, Pa.   D. July 2, 1937, Detroit, Mich.

	W	L	PCT	ERA	G	GS	CG	IP	H	BB	SO	ShO	W	L	SV	AB	H	HR	BA
1898 BKN N	12	22	.353	3.65	36	33	32	291.1	333	80	70	0	1	2	0	134	23	0	.172
1899	2	2	.500	4.72	10	4	2	47.2	56	16	6	1	1	1	1	47	9	0	.191
1900	1	1	.500	6.88	2	2	2	17	21	5	2	0	0	0	0	9	3	0	.333
1901 DET A	12	11	.522	2.61	26	25	22	199.2	209	46	38	3	0	0	0	125	37	2	.296
1902	6	12	.333	4.82	19	15	14	140	171	41	28	0	1	2	0	161	39	1	.242

	W	L	PCT	ERA	G	GS	CG	IP	H	BB	SO	ShO	Relief Pitching W	L	SV	BATTING AB	H	HR	BA

Joe Yeager continued

	W	L	PCT	ERA	G	GS	CG	IP	H	BB	SO	ShO	W	L	SV	AB	H	HR	BA
1903	0	1	.000	4.00	1	1	1	9	15	0	1	0	0	0	0	402	103	0	.256
6 yrs.	33	49	.402	3.74	94	80	73	704.2	805	188	145	4	3	5	2	*			

Jim Yeargin

YEARGIN, JAMES ALMOND (Grapefruit) BR TR 5'11" 170 lbs.
B. Oct. 16, 1902, Mauldin, S. C.   D. May 8, 1937, Greenville, S. C.

	W	L	PCT	ERA	G	GS	CG	IP	H	BB	SO	ShO	W	L	SV	AB	H	HR	BA
1922 BOS N	0	1	.000	1.29	1	1	1	7	5	2	1	0	0	0	0	3	0	0	.000
1924	1	11	.083	5.09	32	12	6	141.1	162	42	34	0	0	1	0	42	6	0	.143
2 yrs.	1	12	.077	4.91	33	13	7	148.1	167	44	35	0	0	1	0	45	6	0	.133

Larry Yellen

YELLEN, LAWRENCE ALAN BR TR 5'11" 190 lbs.
B. Jan. 4, 1943, Brooklyn, N. Y.

	W	L	PCT	ERA	G	GS	CG	IP	H	BB	SO	ShO	W	L	SV	AB	H	HR	BA
1963 HOU N	0	0	–	3.60	1	1	0	5	7	1	3	0	0	0	0	2	0	0	.000
1964	0	0	–	6.86	13	1	0	21	27	10	9	0	0	0	0	3	0	0	.000
2 yrs.	0	0	–	6.23	14	2	0	26	34	11	12	0	0	0	0	5	0	0	.000

Chief Yellowhorse

YELLOWHORSE, MOSES J. BR TR 5'10" 180 lbs.
B. Jan. 28, 1898, Pawnee, Okla.   D. Apr. 10, 1964, Pawnee, Okla.

	W	L	PCT	ERA	G	GS	CG	IP	H	BB	SO	ShO	W	L	SV	AB	H	HR	BA
1921 PIT N	5	3	.625	2.98	10	4	1	48.1	45	13	19	0	3	0	1	17	0	0	.000
1922	3	1	.750	4.52	28	5	2	77.2	92	20	24	0	2	0	0	19	6	0	.316
2 yrs.	8	4	.667	3.93	38	9	3	126	137	33	43	0	5	0	1	36	6	0	.167

Carroll Yerkes

YERKES, CHARLES CARROLL (Lefty) BR TL 5'11" 162 lbs.
B. June 13, 1903, McSherrystown, Pa.   D. Dec. 20, 1950, Oakland, Calif.

	W	L	PCT	ERA	G	GS	CG	IP	H	BB	SO	ShO	W	L	SV	AB	H	HR	BA
1927 PHI A	0	0	–	0.00	1	0	0	1	0	1	0	0	0	0	0	0	0	0	–
1928	0	1	.000	2.08	2	1	1	8.2	7	2	1	0	0	0	0	3	0	0	.000
1929	1	0	1.000	4.58	19	2	0	37.1	47	13	11	0	1	0	1	10	0	0	.000
1932 CHI N	0	0	–	3.00	2	0	0	9	5	3	4	0	0	0	0	3	1	0	.333
1933	0	0	–	4.50	1	0	0	2	2	1	0	0	0	0	0	0	0	0	–
5 yrs.	1	1	.500	3.88	25	3	1	58	61	20	16	0	1	0	1	16	1	0	.063

Stan Yerkes

YERKES, STANLEY LEWIS 5'10"
B. Nov. 28, 1874, Cheltonham, Pa.   D. July 28, 1940, Boston, Mass.

	W	L	PCT	ERA	G	GS	CG	IP	H	BB	SO	ShO	W	L	SV	AB	H	HR	BA
1901 2 teams	BAL A (1G 0–1)				STL N (4G 3–1)														
" total	3	2	.600	3.86	5	5	5	42	47	8	19	0	0	0	0	15	2	0	.133
1902 STL N	11	20	.355	3.66	39	37	27	272.2	341	79	81	0	0	0	0	91	12	0	.132
1903	0	1	.000	1.80	1	1	0	5	8	0	3	0	0	0	0	2	0	0	.000
3 yrs.	14	23	.378	3.66	45	43	32	319.2	396	87	103	1	0	0	0	108	14	0	.130

Earl Yingling

YINGLING, EARL HERSHEY (Chink) BL TL 5'11½" 180 lbs.
B. Oct. 29, 1888, Chillicothe, Ohio   D. Oct. 2, 1962, Columbus, Ohio

	W	L	PCT	ERA	G	GS	CG	IP	H	BB	SO	ShO	W	L	SV	AB	H	HR	BA
1911 CLE A	1	0	1.000	4.43	4	3	1	22.1	30	9	6	0	0	0	0	11	3	0	.273
1912 BKN N	6	11	.353	3.59	25	16	12	163	186	56	51	0	1	3	0	64	16	0	.250
1913	8	8	.500	2.58	26	13	8	146.2	158	10	40	0	3	3	0	60	23	0	.383
1914 CIN N	8	13	.381	3.45	34	27	8	198	207	54	80	3	0	0	0	120	23	1	.192
1918 WAS A	1	2	.333	2.13	5	2	2	38	30	12	15	0	1	0	0	15	7	0	.467
5 yrs.	24	34	.414	3.22	94	61	31	568	611	141	192	5	5	6	0	*			

Joe Yingling

YINGLING, JOSEPH GRANVILLE BR TL 5'7" 145 lbs.
B. July 26, 1866, Westminster, Md.   D. Oct. 24, 1946, Manchester, Md.

	W	L	PCT	ERA	G	GS	CG	IP	H	BB	SO	ShO	W	L	SV	AB	H	HR	BA
1886 WAS N	0	0	–	12.00	1	0	0	3	7	1	1	0	0	0	0	2	0	0	.000

Len Yochim

YOCHIM, LEONARD JOSEPH BL TL 6'2" 200 lbs.
Brother of Ray Yochim.
B. Oct. 16, 1928, New Orleans, La.

	W	L	PCT	ERA	G	GS	CG	IP	H	BB	SO	ShO	W	L	SV	AB	H	HR	BA
1951 PIT N	1	1	.500	8.31	2	2	0	8.2	10	11	5	0	0	0	0	3	0	0	.000
1954	0	1	.000	7.32	10	1	0	19.2	30	8	7	0	0	0	0	2	1	0	.500
2 yrs.	1	2	.333	7.62	12	3	0	28.1	40	19	12	0	0	0	0	5	1	0	.200

Ray Yochim

YOCHIM, RAYMOND AUSTIN ALOYSIUS BR TR 6'1" 170 lbs.
Brother of Len Yochim.
B. July 19, 1922, New Orleans, La.

	W	L	PCT	ERA	G	GS	CG	IP	H	BB	SO	ShO	W	L	SV	AB	H	HR	BA
1948 STL N	0	0	–	0.00	1	0	0	1	0	3	1	0	0	0	0	0	0	0	–
1949	0	0	–	15.43	3	0	0	2.1	3	4	3	0	0	0	0	0	0	0	–
2 yrs.	0	0	–	10.80	4	0	0	3.1	3	7	4	0	0	0	0	0	0	0	–

Jim York

YORK, JAMES HARLAN BR TR 6'3" 200 lbs.
B. Aug. 27, 1947, Maywood, Calif.

	W	L	PCT	ERA	G	GS	CG	IP	H	BB	SO	ShO	W	L	SV	AB	H	HR	BA
1970 KC A	1	1	.500	3.38	4	2	0	8	5	2	6	0	1	1	0	2	0	0	.000
1971	5	5	.500	2.90	53	0	0	93	70	44	103	0	5	5	3	17	2	1	.118
1972 HOU N	0	1	.000	5.25	26	0	0	36	45	18	25	0	0	1	0	1	0	0	.000
1973	3	4	.429	4.42	41	0	0	53	65	20	22	0	3	4	6	5	0	0	.000
1974	2	2	.500	3.32	28	0	0	38	48	19	15	0	2	2	1	4	0	0	.000
1975	4	4	.500	3.83	19	4	0	47	43	25	17	0	1	3	0	11	1	0	.091
1976 NY A	1	0	1.000	5.59	3	0	0	9.2	14	4	6	0	1	0	0	0	0	0	–
7 yrs.	16	17	.485	3.79	174	4	0	284.2	290	132	194	0	13	16	10	40	3	1	.075

Lefty York

YORK, JAMES EDWARD BL TL 5'10" 185 lbs.
B. Nov. 1, 1892, West Fork, Ark.   D. Apr. 9, 1961, York, Pa.

	W	L	PCT	ERA	G	GS	CG	IP	H	BB	SO	ShO	W	L	SV	AB	H	HR	BA
1919 PHI A	0	2	.000	24.92	2	2	0	4.1	13	5	2	0	0	0	0	1	0	0	.000
1921 CHI N	5	9	.357	4.73	40	10	4	139	170	63	57	1	4	0	1	39	5	0	.128
2 yrs.	5	11	.313	5.34	42	12	4	143.1	183	68	59	1	4	0	1	40	5	0	.125

	W	L	PCT	ERA	G	GS	CG	IP	H	BB	SO	ShO	Relief Pitching W	L	SV	BATTING AB	H	HR	BA

Gus Yost

YOST, GUS
B. Toronto, Ont., Canada   D. Oct. 16, 1895, Toronto, Ont., Canada

	W	L	PCT	ERA	G	GS	CG	IP	H	BB	SO	ShO	W	L	SV	AB	H	HR	BA
1893 CHI N	0	1	.000	13.50	1	1	0	2.2	3	8	1	0	0	0	0	1	0	0	.000

Charlie Young

YOUNG, CHARLES (Cy)   BR TR 5'10½" 180 lbs.
B. Jan. 12, 1893, Philadelphia, Pa.   D. May 12, 1952, Riverside, N. J.

	W	L	PCT	ERA	G	GS	CG	IP	H	BB	SO	ShO	W	L	SV	AB	H	HR	BA
1915 BAL F	1	3	.250	5.91	9	5	1	35	39	21	13	0	0	0	0	9	2	0	.222

Curt Young

YOUNG, CURTIS   BR TL 6'   175 lbs.
B. Apr. 16, 1960, Saginaw, Mich.

	W	L	PCT	ERA	G	GS	CG	IP	H	BB	SO	ShO	W	L	SV	AB	H	HR	BA
1983 OAK A	0	1	.000	16.00	8	2	0	9	17	5	5	0	0	0	0	0	0	0	–
1984	9	4	.692	4.06	20	17	2	108.2	118	31	41	1	0	0	0	0	0	0	–
2 yrs.	9	5	.643	4.97	28	19	2	117.2	135	36	46	1	0	0	0	0	0	0	–

Cy Young

YOUNG, DENTON TRUE   BR TR 6'2"   210 lbs.
B. Mar. 29, 1867, Gilmore, Ohio   D. Nov. 4, 1955, Peoli, Ohio
Manager 1907.
Hall of Fame 1937.

	W	L	PCT	ERA	G	GS	CG	IP	H	BB	SO	ShO	W	L	SV	AB	H	HR	BA
1890 CLE N	9	7	.563	3.47	17	16	16	147.2	145	30	36	0	0	0	0	65	8	0	.123
1891	27	20	.574	2.85	55	46	44	423.2	431	140	147	0	1	3	2	174	29	1	.167
1892	36	11	.766	1.93	53	49	48	453	363	118	167	9	1	1	0	196	31	1	.158
1893	32	16	.667	3.36	53	46	42	422.2	442	103	102	1	4	1	1	187	44	1	.235
1894	25	22	.532	3.94	52	47	44	408.2	488	106	101	2	1	1	1	186	40	2	.215
1895	35	10	.778	3.24	47	40	40	369.2	363	75	121	4	7	0	0	140	30	1	.214
1896	29	16	.644	3.24	51	46	42	414.1	477	62	137	5	0	1	3	180	52	3	.289
1897	21	18	.538	3.79	46	38	35	335	391	49	87	2	1	4	0	153	34	0	.222
1898	25	14	.641	2.53	46	41	40	377.2	387	41	107	1	0	1	0	154	39	2	.253
1899 STL N	26	15	.634	2.58	44	42	40	369.1	368	44	111	4	0	1	1	148	32	1	.216
1900	20	18	.526	3.00	41	35	32	321.1	337	36	119	4	2	2	0	124	22	1	.177
1901 BOS A	33	10	.767	1.62	43	41	38	371.1	324	37	158	5	2	0	0	153	32	0	.209
1902	32	11	.744	2.15	45	43	41	384.2	350	53	160	3	0	0	0	148	34	1	.230
1903	28	9	.757	2.08	40	35	34	341.2	294	37	176	7	2	1	2	137	44	1	.321
1904	26	16	.619	1.97	43	41	40	380	327	29	203	10	1	0	1	148	33	1	.223
1905	18	19	.486	1.82	38	33	32	320.2	248	30	208	4	5	0	0	120	18	2	.150
1906	13	21	.382	3.19	39	34	28	287.2	288	25	140	0	0	1	2	104	16	0	.154
1907	22	15	.595	1.99	43	37	33	343.1	286	51	147	6	3	0	1	125	27	1	.216
1908	21	11	.656	1.26	36	33	30	299	230	37	150	3	0	2	0	115	26	0	.226
1909 CLE A	19	15	.559	2.26	35	34	30	295	267	59	109	3	0	1	0	107	21	0	.196
1910	7	10	.412	2.53	21	20	14	163.1	149	27	58	1	0	0	0	55	8	0	.145
1911 2 teams			CLE A (7G 3–4)		**BOS N**		(11G 4–5)												
" total	7	9	.438	3.78	18	18	12	126.1	137	28	55	2	0	0	0	41	3	0	.073
22 yrs.	511	313	.620	2.63	906	815	751	7356	7092	1217	2799	76	30	18	16	2960	623	18	.210
	1st	1st				3rd	1st	1st				4th							

WORLD SERIES

	W	L	PCT	ERA	G	GS	CG	IP	H	BB	SO	ShO	W	L	SV	AB	H	HR	BA
1903 BOS A	2	1	.667	1.59	4	3	3	34	31	4	17	0	0	0	0	15	2	0	.133

Harley Young

YOUNG, HARLAN EDWARD (Cy The Third)   BR TR 6'2"
B. Sept. 28, 1883, Portland, Ind.   D. Mar. 26, 1975, Jacksonville, Fla.

	W	L	PCT	ERA	G	GS	CG	IP	H	BB	SO	ShO	W	L	SV	AB	H	HR	BA
1908 2 teams			PIT N (8G 0–2)		**BOS N**		(6G 0–1)												
" total	0	3	.000	2.62	14	5	1	75.2	69	14	29	0	0	0	0	22	3	0	.136

Irv Young

YOUNG, IRVING MELROSE (Young Cy, Cy the Second)   BL TL 5'10"   185 lbs.
B. July 21, 1877, Columbia Falls, Me.   D. Jan. 14, 1935, Brewer, Me.

	W	L	PCT	ERA	G	GS	CG	IP	H	BB	SO	ShO	W	L	SV	AB	H	HR	BA
1905 BOS N	20	21	.488	2.90	43	42	41	378	337	71	156	7	0	0	0	136	14	0	.103
1906	16	25	.390	2.91	43	41	37	358.1	349	83	151	4	0	1	0	125	12	0	.096
1907	10	23	.303	3.96	40	32	22	245.1	287	58	86	3	2	1	1	80	13	0	.163
1908 2 teams			BOS N (16G 4–8)		**PIT**		N (16G 4–3)												
" total	8	11	.421	2.42	32	18	10	174.2	167	40	63	2	1	2	1	62	11	0	.177
1910 CHI A	4	8	.333	2.72	27	17	7	135.2	122	39	64	4	0	0	0	44	5	0	.114
1911	5	6	.455	4.37	24	11	3	92.2	99	25	40	1	2	0	2	28	5	0	.179
6 yrs.	63	94	.401	3.11	209	161	120	1384.2	1361	316	560	21	5	4	4	475	60	0	.126

J. D. Young

YOUNG, J. D.
B. Mt. Carmel, Pa.   Deceased.

	W	L	PCT	ERA	G	GS	CG	IP	H	BB	SO	ShO	W	L	SV	AB	H	HR	BA
1892 STL N	0	0	–	22.50	1	0	0	2	9	2	1	0	0	0	0	1	0	0	.000

Kip Young

YOUNG, KIP LANE   BR TR 5'11"   175 lbs.
B. Oct. 29, 1954, Georgetown, Ohio

	W	L	PCT	ERA	G	GS	CG	IP	H	BB	SO	ShO	W	L	SV	AB	H	HR	BA
1978 DET A	6	7	.462	2.81	14	13	7	105.2	94	30	49	0	0	1	0	0	0	0	–
1979	2	2	.500	6.34	13	7	0	44	60	11	22	0	0	1	0	0	0	0	–
2 yrs.	8	9	.471	3.85	27	20	7	149.2	154	41	71	0	0	2	0	0	0	0	–

Matt Young

YOUNG, MATTHEW JOHN   BL TL 6'3"   205 lbs.
B. Aug. 9, 1958, Pasadena, Calif.

	W	L	PCT	ERA	G	GS	CG	IP	H	BB	SO	ShO	W	L	SV	AB	H	HR	BA
1983 SEA A	11	15	.423	3.27	33	32	5	203.2	178	79	130	2	0	0	0	0	0	0	–
1984	6	8	.429	5.72	22	22	1	113.1	141	57	73	0	0	0	0	0	0	0	–
2 yrs.	17	23	.425	4.15	55	54	6	317	319	136	203	2	0	0	0	0	0	0	–

Chief Youngblood

YOUNGBLOOD, ARTHUR CLYDE   BR TR 6'3"   202 lbs.
B. June 13, 1900, Hillsboro, Tex.   D. July 6, 1968, Amarillo, Tex.

	W	L	PCT	ERA	G	GS	CG	IP	H	BB	SO	ShO	W	L	SV	AB	H	HR	BA
1922 WAS A	0	0	–	14.54	2	0	0	4.1	9	7	0	0	0	0	0	2	0	0	.000

	W	L	PCT	ERA	G	GS	CG	IP	H	BB	SO	ShO	Relief Pitching W	L	SV	AB	H	HR	BA

Ducky Yount

YOUNT, HERBERT MACON (Hub)
B. Dec. 7, 1885, Iredell County, N. C.   D. May 7, 1970, Winston-Salem, N. C.
BR TR 6'5"   190 lbs.

	W	L	PCT	ERA	G	GS	CG	IP	H	BB	SO	ShO	W	L	SV	AB	H	HR	BA
1914 BAL F	1	3	.250	4.14	13	1	1	41.1	44	19	19	0	1	2	0	12	1	0	.083

Larry Yount

YOUNT, LAWRENCE KING
Brother of Robin Yount.
B. Feb. 15, 1950, Houston, Tex.
BR TR 6'2"   185 lbs.

	W	L	PCT	ERA	G	GS	CG	IP	H	BB	SO	ShO	W	L	SV	AB	H	HR	BA
1971 HOU N	0	0	–	0.00	1	0	0	0	0	0	0	0	0	0	0	0	0	0	–

Carl Yowell

YOWELL, CARL COLUMBUS (Sundown)
B. Dec. 20, 1902, Madison, Va.
BL TL 6'4"   180 lbs.

	W	L	PCT	ERA	G	GS	CG	IP	H	BB	SO	ShO	W	L	SV	AB	H	HR	BA
1924 CLE A	1	1	.500	6.67	4	2	2	27	37	13	8	0	0	0	0	11	2	0	.182
1925	2	3	.400	4.46	12	4	1	36.1	40	17	12	0	1	0	0	8	1	0	.125
2 yrs.	3	4	.429	5.40	16	6	3	63.1	77	30	20	0	1	0	0	19	3	0	.158

Eddie Yuhas

YUHAS, JOHN EDWARD
B. Aug. 5, 1924, Youngstown, Ohio
BR TR 6'1"   180 lbs.

	W	L	PCT	ERA	G	GS	CG	IP	H	BB	SO	ShO	W	L	SV	AB	H	HR	BA
1952 STL N	12	2	.857	2.72	54	2	0	99.1	90	35	39	0	11	1	6	21	4	0	.190
1953	0	0	–	18.00	2	0	0	1	3	0	0	0	0	0	0	0	0	0	–
2 yrs.	12	2	.857	2.87	56	2	0	100.1	93	35	39	0	11	1	6	21	4	0	.190

Adrian Zabala

ZABALA, ADRIAN RODRIGUEZ
B. Aug. 26, 1916, San Antonio de los Banos, Cuba
BL TL 5'11"   165 lbs.

	W	L	PCT	ERA	G	GS	CG	IP	H	BB	SO	ShO	W	L	SV	AB	H	HR	BA
1945 NY N	2	4	.333	4.78	11	5	1	43.1	46	20	14	0	1	1	0	13	3	0	.231
1949	2	3	.400	5.27	15	4	2	41	44	10	13	1	0	2	1	13	1	0	.077
2 yrs.	4	7	.364	5.02	26	9	3	84.1	90	30	27	1	1	3	1	26	4	0	.154

Zip Zabel

ZABEL, GEORGE WASHINGTON
B. Feb. 18, 1891, Wetmore, Kans.   D. May 31, 1970, Beloit, Wis.
BR TR 6'1½"   185 lbs.

	W	L	PCT	ERA	G	GS	CG	IP	H	BB	SO	ShO	W	L	SV	AB	H	HR	BA
1913 CHI N	1	0	1.000	0.00	1	1	0	5	3	1	0	0	0	0	0	2	0	0	.000
1914	4	4	.500	2.18	29	7	2	128	104	45	50	0	2	0	1	38	7	0	.184
1915	7	10	.412	3.20	36	17	8	163	124	84	60	3	2	2	0	54	4	0	.074
3 yrs.	12	14	.462	2.71	66	25	10	296	231	130	110	3	4	2	1	94	11	0	.117

Chink Zachary

ZACHARY, ALBERT MYRON
B. Oct. 19, 1917, Brooklyn, N. Y.
BR TR 5'11"   182 lbs.

	W	L	PCT	ERA	G	GS	CG	IP	H	BB	SO	ShO	W	L	SV	AB	H	HR	BA
1944 BKN N	0	2	.000	9.58	4	2	0	10.1	10	7	3	0	0	2	0	3	0	0	.000

Chris Zachary

ZACHARY, WILLIAM CHRIS
B. Feb. 19, 1944, Knoxville, Tenn.
BL TR 6'2"   200 lbs.

	W	L	PCT	ERA	G	GS	CG	IP	H	BB	SO	ShO	W	L	SV	AB	H	HR	BA
1963 HOU N	2	2	.500	4.89	22	7	0	57	62	22	42	0	0	0	0	13	0	0	.000
1964	0	1	.000	9.00	1	1	0	4	6	1	2	0	0	0	0	1	0	0	.000
1965	0	2	.000	4.22	4	2	0	10.2	12	6	4	0	0	0	0	2	0	0	.000
1966	3	5	.375	3.44	10	8	0	55	44	32	37	0	0	1	0	18	4	0	.222
1967	1	6	.143	5.70	9	7	0	36.1	42	12	18	0	0	0	0	10	1	0	.100
1969 KC A	0	1	.000	7.85	8	2	0	18.1	27	7	6	0	0	0	0	2	1	0	.500
1971 STL N	3	10	.231	5.30	23	12	1	90	114	26	48	1	1	2	0	33	8	0	.242
1972 DET A	1	1	.500	1.42	25	1	0	38	27	15	21	0	1	0	1	2	1	0	.500
1973 PIT N	0	1	.000	3.00	6	0	0	12	10	1	6	0	0	1	1	2	0	0	.000
9 yrs.	10	29	.256	4.57	108	40	1	321.1	344	122	184	1	2	4	2	83	15	0	.181

LEAGUE CHAMPIONSHIP SERIES

	W	L	PCT	ERA	G	GS	CG	IP	H	BB	SO	ShO	W	L	SV	AB	H	HR	BA
1972 DET A	0	0	–	∞	1	0	0	0	1	0	0	0	0	0	0	0	0	0	–

Tom Zachary

ZACHARY, JONATHAN THOMPSON WALTON
Played as Zach Walton 1918.
B. May 7, 1896, Graham, N. C.   D. Jan. 24, 1969, Burlington, N. C.
BL TL 6'1"   187 lbs.

	W	L	PCT	ERA	G	GS	CG	IP	H	BB	SO	ShO	W	L	SV	AB	H	HR	BA
1918 PHI A	2	0	1.000	5.63	2	2	0	8	9	7	1	0	0	0	0	4	2	0	.500
1919 WAS A	1	5	.167	2.92	17	7	0	61.2	68	20	9	0	0	1	0	15	5	0	.333
1920	15	16	.484	3.77	44	30	18	262.2	289	78	53	3	3	0	2	111	29	0	.261
1921	18	16	.529	3.96	39	31	17	250	314	59	53	2	3	3	1	90	23	0	.256
1922	15	10	.600	3.12	32	25	13	184.2	190	43	37	1	1	1	1	71	21	1	.296
1923	10	16	.385	4.49	35	29	10	204.1	270	63	40	0	1	2	0	78	15	0	.192
1924	15	9	.625	2.75	33	27	13	202.2	198	53	45	1	1	0	2	72	22	0	.306
1925	12	15	.444	3.85	38	33	11	217.2	247	74	58	1	1	2	2	69	12	1	.174
1926 STL A	14	15	.483	3.60	34	31	18	247.1	264	97	53	3	0	0	0	86	23	1	.267
1927 2 teams	STL	(13G 4–6)		WAS	A	(15G 4–7)													
" total	8	13	.381	3.96	28	26	11	188.2	236	57	26	1	1	2	0	64	8	0	.125
1928 2 teams	WAS	(20G 6–9)		NY	A	(7G 3–3)													
" total	9	12	.429	4.98	27	20	8	148.1	184	55	26	1	1	1	1	48	12	1	.250
1929 NY A	12	0	1.000	2.48	26	11	7	119.2	131	30	35	2	3	0	2	42	10	0	.238
1930 2 teams	NY	A	(3G 1–1)		BOS	N	(24G 11–5)												
" total	12	6	.667	4.77	27	25	10	168	210	59	58	1	1	0	0	62	15	2	.242
1931 BOS N	11	15	.423	3.10	33	28	16	229	243	53	64	3	0	3	2	84	14	0	.167
1932	12	11	.522	3.10	32	24	12	212	231	55	67	4	2	1	0	77	21	0	.273
1933	7	9	.438	3.53	26	20	6	125	134	35	22	2	0	0	2	42	5	0	.119
1934 2 teams	BOS	N	(5G 1–2)		BKN	N	(22G 5–6)												
" total	6	8	.429	4.23	27	16	6	125.2	149	29	32	1	1	1	2	46	7	0	.152
1935 BKN N	7	12	.368	3.53	27	16	8	158	193	35	33	1	5	0	4	52	7	0	.135
1936 2 teams	BKN	N	(1G 0–0)		PHI	N	(7G 0–3)												
" total	0	3	.000	8.71	8	2	0	20.2	30	12	8	0	0	0	1	9	3	0	.333
19 yrs.	186	191	.493	3.72	533	408	185	3134	3590	914	720	24	17	20	22	1122	254	6	.226

WORLD SERIES

	W	L	PCT	ERA	G	GS	CG	IP	H	BB	SO	ShO	W	L	SV	AB	H	HR	BA
1924 WAS A	2	0	1.000	2.04	2	2	1	17.2	13	3	3	0	0	0	0	5	0	0	.000
1925	0	0	–	10.80	1	0	0	1.2	3	1	0	0	0	0	0	0	0	0	–
1928 NY A	1	0	1.000	3.00	1	1	1	9	9	1	7	0	0	0	0	4	0	0	.000
3 yrs.	3	0	1.000	2.86	4	3	2	28.1	25	5	10	0	0	0	0	9	0	0	.000
			1st																

	W	L	PCT	ERA	G	GS	CG	IP	H	BB	SO	ShO	Relief Pitching W	L	SV	BATTING AB	H	HR	BA

Pat Zachry

ZACHRY, PATRICK PAUL
B. Apr. 24, 1952, Richmond, Tex.   BR TR 6'5" 180 lbs.

	W	L	PCT	ERA	G	GS	CG	IP	H	BB	SO	ShO	W	L	SV	AB	H	HR	BA
1976 CIN N	14	7	.667	2.74	38	28	6	204	170	83	143	1	2	0	0	62	7	0	.113
1977 2 teams	CIN N	(12G 3–7)			NY	N	(19G 7–6)												
" total	10	13	.435	4.25	31	31	5	194.2	207	77	99	2	0	0	0	64	9	0	.141
1978 NY N	10	6	.625	3.33	21	21	5	138	120	60	78	2	0	0	0	43	3	0	.070
1979	5	1	.833	3.56	7	7	1	43	44	21	17	0	0	0	0	16	2	0	.125
1980	6	10	.375	3.00	28	26	7	165	145	58	88	3	0	0	0	46	2	0	.043
1981	7	14	.333	4.14	24	24	3	139	151	56	76	0	0	0	0	38	6	0	.158
1982	6	9	.400	4.05	36	16	2	137.2	149	57	69	0	2	3	1	38	3	0	.079
1983 LA N	6	1	.857	2.49	40	1	0	61.1	63	21	36	0	5	1	0	4	2	0	.500
1984	5	6	.455	3.81	58	0	0	82.2	84	51	55	0	5	6	2	6	2	0	.333
9 yrs.	69	67	.507	3.51	283	154	29	1165.1	1133	484	661	8	14	11	3	317	36	0	.114
LEAGUE CHAMPIONSHIP SERIES																			
1976 CIN N	1	0	1.000	3.60	1	1	0	5	6	3	3	0	0	0	0	1	0	0	.000
1983 LA N	0	0	–	2.25	2	0	0	4	4	2	2	0	0	0	0	0	0	0	–
2 yrs.	1	0	1.000	3.00	3	1	0	9	10	5	5	0	0	0	0	1	0	0	.000
WORLD SERIES																			
1976 CIN N	1	0	1.000	2.70	1	1	0	6.2	6	5	6	0	0	0	0	0	0	0	–

George Zackert

ZACKERT, GEORGE CARL
B. Dec. 24, 1884, St. Joseph, Mo.   D. Feb. 18, 1977, Burlington, Iowa   BL TL 6' 177 lbs.

	W	L	PCT	ERA	G	GS	CG	IP	H	BB	SO	ShO	W	L	SV	AB	H	HR	BA
1911 STL N	0	2	.000	11.05	4	1	0	7.1	17	6	6	0	0	1	0	1	0	0	.000
1912	0	0	–	18.00	1	0	0	1	2	1	0	0	0	0	0	1	0	0	.000
2 yrs.	0	2	.000	11.88	5	1	0	8.1	19	7	6	0	0	1	0	2	0	0	.000

Geoff Zahn

ZAHN, GEOFFREY CLAYTON
B. Dec. 19, 1946, Baltimore, Md.   BL TL 6'1" 180 lbs.

	W	L	PCT	ERA	G	GS	CG	IP	H	BB	SO	ShO	W	L	SV	AB	H	HR	BA
1973 LA N	1	0	1.000	1.35	6	1	0	13.1	5	2	9	0	0	0	0	2	0	0	.000
1974	3	5	.375	2.03	21	10	1	80	78	16	33	0	0	1	0	23	4	0	.174
1975 2 teams	LA	N	(2G 0–1)		CHI	N	(16G 2–7)												
" total	2	8	.200	4.66	18	10	0	65.2	69	31	22	0	2	1	1	15	2	0	.133
1976 CHI N	0	1	.000	11.25	3	2	0	8	16	2	4	0	0	0	0	3	0	0	.000
1977 MIN A	12	14	.462	4.68	34	32	7	198	234	66	88	1	0	0	0	0	0	0	–
1978	14	14	.500	3.03	35	35	12	252.1	260	81	106	1	0	0	0	0	0	0	–
1979	13	7	.650	3.57	26	24	4	169	181	41	58	0	0	0	0	0	0	0	–
1980	14	18	.438	4.40	38	35	13	233	273	66	96	5	0	0	0	0	0	0	–
1981 CAL A	10	11	.476	4.42	25	25	9	161	181	43	52	0	0	0	0	0	0	0	–
1982	18	8	.692	3.73	34	34	12	229.1	225	65	81	4	0	0	0	0	0	0	–
1983	9	11	.450	3.33	29	28	11	203	212	51	81	3	0	0	0	0	0	0	–
1984	13	10	.565	3.12	28	27	9	199.1	200	48	61	5	0	0	0	43	6	0	.140
12 yrs.	109	107	.505	3.73	297	263	78	1812	1934	512	691	19	2	3	1	43	6	0	.140
LEAGUE CHAMPIONSHIP SERIES																			
1982 CAL A	0	1	.000	7.36	1	1	0	3.2	4	1	2	0	0	0	0	0	0	0	–

Paul Zahniser

ZAHNISER, PAUL VERNON
B. Sept. 6, 1896, Sal City, Iowa   D. Sept. 26, 1964, Klamath Falls, Ore.   BR TR 5'10½" 170 lbs.

	W	L	PCT	ERA	G	GS	CG	IP	H	BB	SO	ShO	W	L	SV	AB	H	HR	BA
1923 WAS A	9	10	.474	3.86	33	21	10	177	201	76	52	1	2	2	0	52	5	0	.096
1924	5	7	.417	4.40	24	14	5	92	98	49	28	1	1	0	0	30	4	0	.133
1925 BOS A	5	12	.294	5.15	37	21	7	176.2	232	89	30	1	1	0	1	58	8	0	.138
1926	6	18	.250	4.97	30	24	7	172	213	69	35	1	0	2	0	49	8	0	.163
1929 CIN N	0	0	–	27.00	1	0	0	1	2	1	0	0	0	0	0	0	0	0	–
5 yrs.	25	47	.347	4.66	125	80	29	618.2	746	284	145	4	4	4	1	189	25	0	.132

Carl Zamloch

ZAMLOCH, CARL EUGENE
B. Oct. 6, 1889, Oakland, Calif.   D. Aug. 19, 1963, Santa Barbara, Calif.   BR TR 6'1" 176 lbs.

	W	L	PCT	ERA	G	GS	CG	IP	H	BB	SO	ShO	W	L	SV	AB	H	HR	BA
1913 DET A	1	6	.143	2.45	17	5	3	69.2	66	23	28	0	1	2	1	22	4	0	.182

Oscar Zamora

ZAMORA, OSCAR JOSE
B. Sept. 23, 1944, Camaguey, Cuba   BR TR 5'10" 178 lbs.

	W	L	PCT	ERA	G	GS	CG	IP	H	BB	SO	ShO	W	L	SV	AB	H	HR	BA
1974 CHI N	3	9	.250	3.11	56	0	0	84	82	19	38	0	3	9	10	11	2	0	.182
1975	5	2	.714	5.07	52	0	0	71	84	15	28	0	5	2	10	6	1	0	.167
1976	5	3	.625	5.24	40	2	0	55	70	17	27	0	5	2	3	9	0	0	.000
1978 HOU N	0	0	–	7.20	10	0	0	15	20	7	6	0	0	0	0	2	0	0	.000
4 yrs.	13	14	.481	4.52	158	2	0	225	256	58	99	0	13	13	23	28	3	0	.107

Dom Zanni

ZANNI, DOMINICK THOMAS
B. Mar. 1, 1932, Bronx, N.Y.   BR TR 5'11" 180 lbs.

	W	L	PCT	ERA	G	GS	CG	IP	H	BB	SO	ShO	W	L	SV	AB	H	HR	BA
1958 SF N	1	0	1.000	2.25	1	0	0	4	7	1	3	0	1	0	0	2	0	0	.000
1959	0	0	–	6.55	9	0	0	11	12	8	11	0	0	0	0	0	0	0	–
1961	1	0	1.000	3.95	8	0	0	13.2	13	12	11	0	1	0	0	0	0	0	–
1962 CHI A	6	5	.545	3.75	44	2	0	86.1	67	31	66	0	6	3	5	18	5	0	.278
1963 2 teams	CHI	A	(5G 0–0)		CIN	N	(31G 1–1)												
" total	1	1	.500	4.56	36	1	0	47.1	44	25	42	0	1	1	5	3	1	0	.333
1965 CIN N	0	0	–	1.35	8	0	0	13.1	7	5	10	0	0	0	0	1	0	0	.000
1966	0	0	–	0.00	5	0	0	7.1	5	3	5	0	0	0	0	1	1	0	1.000
7 yrs.	9	6	.600	3.79	111	3	0	183	155	85	148	0	9	4	10	25	7	0	.280

Jeff Zaske

ZASKE, LLOYD JEFFREY
B. Oct. 6, 1960, Seattle, Wash.   BR TR 6'5" 180 lbs.

	W	L	PCT	ERA	G	GS	CG	IP	H	BB	SO	ShO	W	L	SV	AB	H	HR	BA
1984 PIT N	0	0	–	0.00	3	0	0	5	4	1	2	0	0	0	0	0	0	0	–

Zay

ZAY,
Deceased.

	W	L	PCT	ERA	G	GS	CG	IP	H	BB	SO	ShO	W	L	SV	AB	H	HR	BA
1886 BAL AA	0	1	.000	9.00	1	1	0	2	4	4	2	0	0	0	0	1	0	0	.000

	W	L	PCT	ERA	G	GS	CG	IP	H	BB	SO	ShO	Relief Pitching W	L	SV	BATTING AB	H	HR	BA

Matt Zeiser

ZEISER, MATTHEW J.
B. Sept. 25, 1888, Chicago, Ill.   D. June 10, 1942, Norwood Park, Ill.
BR TR 5'10" 170 lbs.

	W	L	PCT	ERA	G	GS	CG	IP	H	BB	SO	ShO	W	L	SV	AB	H	HR	BA
1914 BOS A	0	0	–	1.80	2	0	0	10	9	8	0	0	0	0	0	3	0	0	.000

Bill Zepp

ZEPP, WILLIAM CLINTON
B. July 22, 1946, Detroit, Mich.
BR TR 6'2" 185 lbs.

	W	L	PCT	ERA	G	GS	CG	IP	H	BB	SO	ShO	W	L	SV	AB	H	HR	BA
1969 MIN A	0	0	–	6.75	4	0	0	5.1	6	4	2	0	0	0	0	1	0	0	.000
1970	9	4	.692	3.22	43	20	0	151	154	51	64	1	3	0	2	44	6	0	.136
1971 DET A	1	1	.500	5.06	16	4	0	32	41	17	15	0	0	1	2	4	0	0	.000
3 yrs.	10	5	.667	3.63	63	24	1	188.1	201	72	81	1	3	1	4	49	6	0	.122
LEAGUE CHAMPIONSHIP SERIES																			
1970 MIN A	0	0	–	6.75	2	0	0	1.1	2	2	2	0	0	0	0	0	0	0	–

George Zettlein

ZETTLEIN, GEORGE (The Charmer)
B. July 18, 1844, Brooklyn, N.Y.   D. May 23, 1905, Patchogue, N.Y.
BR TR 5'9" 162 lbs.

	W	L	PCT	ERA	G	GS	CG	IP	H	BB	SO	ShO	W	L	SV	AB	H	HR	BA
1876 PHI N	4	20	.167	3.88	28	25	23	234	358	6	10	1	0	0	2	128	27	0	.211

Bob Zick

ZICK, ROBERT GEORGE
B. Apr. 26, 1927, Chicago, Ill.
BL TR 6' 168 lbs.

	W	L	PCT	ERA	G	GS	CG	IP	H	BB	SO	ShO	W	L	SV	AB	H	HR	BA
1954 CHI N	0	0	–	8.27	8	0	0	16.1	23	7	9	0	0	0	0	4	1	0	.250

George Ziegler

ZIEGLER, GEORGE J.
B. 1872, Chicago, Ill.   D. July 22, 1916, Kankakee, Ill.

	W	L	PCT	ERA	G	GS	CG	IP	H	BB	SO	ShO	W	L	SV	AB	H	HR	BA
1890 PIT N	0	1	.000	10.50	1	1	0	6	12	0	1	0	0	0	0	2	0	0	.000

Walt Zink

ZINK, WALTER NOBLE
B. Nov. 21, 1899, Pittsfield, Mass.   D. June 12, 1964, Quincy, Mass.
BR TR 6' 165 lbs.

	W	L	PCT	ERA	G	GS	CG	IP	H	BB	SO	ShO	W	L	SV	AB	H	HR	BA
1921 NY N	0	0	–	2.25	2	0	0	4	4	3	1	0	0	0	0	1	0	0	.000

Jimmy Zinn

ZINN, JAMES EDWARD
B. Jan. 31, 1895, Benton, Ark.
BL TR 6'1½" 195 lbs.
BR 1929

	W	L	PCT	ERA	G	GS	CG	IP	H	BB	SO	ShO	W	L	SV	AB	H	HR	BA
1919 PHI A	1	3	.250	6.31	5	3	2	25.2	38	10	9	0	0	0	0	13	4	1	.308
1920 PIT N	1	1	.500	3.48	6	3	2	31	32	5	18	0	0	0	0	15	3	0	.200
1921	7	6	.538	3.68	32	9	5	127.1	159	30	49	1	3	1	4	49	11	0	.224
1922	0	0	–	1.86	5	0	0	9.2	11	2	3	0	0	0	1	1	0	0	.000
1929 CLE A	4	6	.400	5.04	18	11	6	105.1	150	33	29	1	0	1	2	42	16	1	.381
5 yrs.	13	16	.448	4.30	66	26	15	299	390	80	108	2	3	3	7	120	34	2	.283

Bill Zinser

ZINSER, WILLIAM FREDERICK
B. Jan. 6, 1918, Astoria, N.Y.
BR TR 6'1" 185 lbs.

	W	L	PCT	ERA	G	GS	CG	IP	H	BB	SO	ShO	W	L	SV	AB	H	HR	BA
1944 WAS A	0	0	–	27.00	2	0	0	.2	1	5	1	0	0	0	0	0	0	0	–

Ed Zmich

ZMICH, EDWARD ALBERT (Ike)
B. Oct. 1, 1884, Cleveland, Ohio   D. Aug. 20, 1950, Cleveland, Ohio
BL TL 6' 180 lbs.

	W	L	PCT	ERA	G	GS	CG	IP	H	BB	SO	ShO	W	L	SV	AB	H	HR	BA
1910 STL N	0	5	.000	6.25	9	6	2	36	38	29	19	0	0	0	0	13	1	0	.077
1911	1	0	1.000	2.13	4	0	0	12.2	8	8	4	0	1	0	0	4	0	0	.000
2 yrs.	1	5	.167	5.18	13	6	2	48.2	46	37	23	0	1	0	0	17	1	0	.059

Sam Zoldak

ZOLDAK, SAMUEL WALTER (Sad Sam)
B. Dec. 8, 1918, Brooklyn, N.Y.   D. Aug. 25, 1966, New Hyde Park, N.Y.
BL TL 5'11½" 185 lbs.

	W	L	PCT	ERA	G	GS	CG	IP	H	BB	SO	ShO	W	L	SV	AB	H	HR	BA
1944 STL A	0	0	–	3.72	18	0	0	38.2	49	19	15	0	0	0	0	6	2	0	.333
1945	3	2	.600	3.36	26	1	1	69.2	74	18	19	0	2	2	0	20	1	0	.050
1946	9	11	.450	3.43	35	21	9	170.1	166	57	51	2	1	1	2	52	9	0	.173
1947	9	10	.474	3.47	35	19	6	171	162	76	36	1	2	1	1	58	10	0	.172
1948 2 teams	STL	A (11G 2–4)		CLE	A (23G 9–6)														
" total	11	10	.524	3.44	34	21	4	159.2	168	43	30	1	4	2	0	58	11	0	.190
1949 CLE A	1	2	.333	4.25	27	0	0	53	60	18	11	0	1	2	0	8	3	0	.375
1950	4	2	.667	3.96	33	3	0	63.2	64	21	15	0	4	0	4	16	3	0	.188
1951 PHI A	6	10	.375	3.16	26	18	8	128	127	24	18	1	0	1	0	45	7	0	.156
1952	0	6	.000	4.06	16	10	2	75.1	86	25	12	0	0	1	0	23	4	0	.174
9 yrs.	43	53	.448	3.54	250	93	30	929.1	956	301	207	5	14	9	8	286	50	0	.175

Bill Zuber

ZUBER, WILLIAM HENRY (Goober)
B. Mar. 26, 1913, Middle Amana, Iowa   D. Nov. 2, 1982, Cedar Rapids, Iowa
BR TR 6'2" 195 lbs.

	W	L	PCT	ERA	G	GS	CG	IP	H	BB	SO	ShO	W	L	SV	AB	H	HR	BA
1936 CLE A	1	1	.500	6.59	2	2	1	13.2	14	15	5	0	0	0	0	5	1	0	.200
1938	0	3	.000	5.02	15	0	0	28.2	33	20	14	0	0	3	1	7	0	0	.000
1939	2	0	1.000	5.97	16	1	0	31.2	41	19	16	0	2	0	0	5	1	0	.200
1940	1	1	.500	5.63	17	0	0	24	25	14	12	0	1	1	0	3	1	0	.333
1941 WAS A	6	4	.600	5.42	36	7	1	96.1	110	61	51	0	1	2	2	26	0	0	.000
1942	9	9	.500	3.84	37	7	3	126.2	115	82	64	1	7	5	1	39	6	0	.154
1943 NY A	8	4	.667	3.89	20	13	7	118	100	74	57	0	1	1	1	38	7	0	.184
1944	5	7	.417	4.21	22	13	2	107	101	54	59	1	1	1	0	31	4	0	.129
1945	5	11	.313	3.19	21	14	7	127	121	56	50	1	2	0	1	42	7	0	.167
1946 2 teams	NY	A (3G 0–1)		BOS	A (15G 5–1)														
" total	5	2	.714	3.47	18	7	2	62.1	47	42	32	1	1	1	0	20	2	0	.100
1947 BOS A	1	0	1.000	5.33	20	1	0	50.2	60	31	23	0	1	0	0	13	2	0	.154
11 yrs.	43	42	.506	4.28	224	65	23	786	767	468	383	3	17	14	6	229	31	0	.135
WORLD SERIES																			
1946 BOS A	0	0	–	4.50	1	0	0	2	3	1	1	0	0	0	0	0	0	0	–

George Zuverink

ZUVERINK, GEORGE
B. Aug. 20, 1924, Holland, Mich.
BR TR 6'4" 195 lbs.

	W	L	PCT	ERA	G	GS	CG	IP	H	BB	SO	ShO	W	L	SV	AB	H	HR	BA
1951 CLE A	0	0	–	5.33	16	0	0	25.1	24	13	14	0	0	0	0	0	0	0	–
1952	0	0	–	0.00	2	0	0	1.1	1	0	1	0	0	0	0	0	0	0	–
1954 2 teams	CIN	N (2G 0–0)		DET	A (35G 9–13)														
" total	9	13	.409	3.75	37	25	9	209	211	63	72	2	0	0	4	66	9	0	.136

	W	L	PCT	ERA	G	GS	CG	IP	H	BB	SO	ShO	Relief Pitching W	L	SV	BATTING AB	H	HR	BA

George Zuverink continued

	W	L	PCT	ERA	G	GS	CG	IP	H	BB	SO	ShO	W	L	SV	AB	H	HR	BA
1955 **2 teams**			**DET**	**A**	(14G	0–5)		**BAL**	**A**	(28G	4–3)								
" total	4	8	.333	3.38	42	6	0	114.2	118	31	44	0	3	6	4	27	5	0	.185
1956 **BAL A**	7	6	.538	4.16	62	0	0	97.1	112	34	33	0	7	6	16	17	2	0	.118
1957	10	6	.625	2.48	56	0	0	112.2	105	39	36	0	10	6	9	23	3	0	.130
1958	2	2	.500	3.39	45	0	0	69	74	17	22	0	2	2	7	9	2	0	.222
1959	0	1	.000	4.15	6	0	0	13	15	6	1	0	0	1	0	0	0	0	–
8 yrs.	32	36	.471	3.54	265	31	9	642.1	660	203	223	2	22	21	40	142	21	0	.148

DATE	TRADED TO		TRADED WITH	TRADED BY		IN EXCHANGE FOR

Hank Aaron

DATE	TRADED TO		TRADED WITH	TRADED BY		IN EXCHANGE FOR
Nov 2, 1974	MIL	A	————	ATL	N	Dave May minor league P Roger Alexander

Don Aase

DATE	TRADED TO		TRADED WITH	TRADED BY		IN EXCHANGE FOR
Dec 8, 1977	CAL	A	cash	BOS	A	Jerry Remy
Dec 13, 1984	BAL	A	————	CAL	A	No compensation (free agent signing)

Ed Abbaticchio

DATE	TRADED TO		TRADED WITH	TRADED BY		IN EXCHANGE FOR
Dec 1906	PIT	N	————	BOS	N	Ginger Beaumont Claude Ritchey Patsy Flaherty
May 1910	BOS	N	————	PIT	N	Cash

Glenn Abbott

DATE	TRADED TO		TRADED WITH	TRADED BY		IN EXCHANGE FOR
Aug 23, 1983	DET	A	————	SEA	A	$100,000.

Al Aber

DATE	TRADED TO		TRADED WITH	TRADED BY		IN EXCHANGE FOR
June 15, 1953	DET	A	*See Ray Boone*	CLE	A	————
Aug 27, 1957	KC	A	————	DET	A	Waiver price

Ted Abernathy

DATE	TRADED TO		TRADED WITH	TRADED BY		IN EXCHANGE FOR
April 14, 1965	CHI	N	————	CLE	A	Cash
May 28, 1966	ATL	N	————	CHI	N	Lee Thomas
Jan 9, 1969	CHI	N	————	CIN	N	Bill Plummer Clarence Jones minor league P Ken Myette
May 29, 1970	STL	N	————	CHI	N	Phil Gagliano
July 1, 1970	KC	A	————	STL	N	Chris Zachary

Cal Abrams

DATE	TRADED TO		TRADED WITH	TRADED BY		IN EXCHANGE FOR
June 9, 1952	CIN	N	————	BKN	N	Rudy Rufer and cash
Oct 14, 1952	PIT	N	Joe Rossi Gail Henley	CIN	N	Gus Bell
May 25, 1954	BAL	A	————	PIT	N	Dick Littlefield
Oct 18, 1955	CHI	A	————	BAL	A	Bobby Adams

Bill Abstein

DATE	TRADED TO		TRADED WITH	TRADED BY		IN EXCHANGE FOR
Jan 1910	STL	A	————	PIT	N	Cash

Tom Acker

DATE	TRADED TO		TRADED WITH	TRADED BY		IN EXCHANGE FOR
Nov 21, 1959	KC	A	————	CIN	N	Frank House

Fritz Ackley

DATE	TRADED TO		TRADED WITH	TRADED BY		IN EXCHANGE FOR
Nov 24, 1964	STL	N	————	CHI	A	Cash

Cy Acosta

DATE	TRADED TO		TRADED WITH	TRADED BY		IN EXCHANGE FOR
March 17, 1975	PHI	N	————	CHI	A	Cash

Ed Acosta

DATE	TRADED TO		TRADED WITH	TRADED BY		IN EXCHANGE FOR
Aug 10, 1971	SD	N	John Jeter	PIT	N	Bob Miller

DATE	TRADED TO		TRADED WITH	TRADED BY		IN EXCHANGE FOR

Jose Acosta

| Jan 10, 1922 | PHI | A | Bing Miller | WAS | A | Joe Dugan |

(Part of three-team trade involving Boston, Philadelphia, and Washington.)

| Feb 4, 1922 | CHI | A | ———— | PHI | A | Cash |

Merito Acosta

| May 25, 1918 | PHI | A | ———— | WAS | A | Cash |

Jerry Adair

| June 12, 1966 | CHI | A | minor league OF Johnny Riddle | BAL | A | Eddie Fisher |
| June 3, 1967 | BOS | A | ———— | CHI | A | Don McMahon minor league P Bob Snow |

Babe Adams

| Oct 1907 | PIT | N | ———— | STL | N | Cash |

Bert Adams

| Jan 1915 | PHI | N | Al Demaree Milt Stock | NY | N | Hans Lobert |

Bob Adams

| March 29, 1971 | MIN | A | minor league P Art Clifford | DET | A | Bill Zepp |

Bobby Adams

| July 26, 1955 | CHI | A | ———— | CIN | N | Cash |
| Oct 18, 1955 | BAL | A | ———— | CHI | A | Cal Abrams |

Buster Adams

June 1, 1943	PHI	N	Coaker Triplett Dain Clay	STL	N	Danny Litwhiler Earl Naylor
May 8, 1945	STL	N	————	PHI	N	John Antonelli Glenn Crawford
March 21, 1947	PHI	N	————	STL	N	Cash

Glenn Adams

| Dec 6, 1976 | MIN | A | ———— | SF | N | Cash |

Herb Adams

| Sept 11, 1950 | CLE | A | ———— | CHI | A | Waiver price |

Mike Adams

| April 1, 1978 | OAK | A | ———— | CHI | N | Cash |

Sparky Adams

Nov 28, 1927	PIT	N	Pete Scott	CHI	N	Kiki Cuyler
Nov 1929	STL	N	————	PIT	N	Cash
May 7, 1933	CIN	N	Paul Derringer Allyn Stout	STL	N	Leo Durocher Dutch Henry Jack Ogden

Spencer Adams

| Jan 20, 1926 | NY | A | ———— | WAS | A | Cash |

DATE	TRADED TO		TRADED WITH	TRADED BY		IN EXCHANGE FOR

Joe Adcock

Feb 16, 1953	MIL	N	————	CIN	N	Rocky Bridges and cash

(Part of four-team trade involving Milwaukee Braves, Philadelphia Phillies, Brooklyn, and Cincinnati.)

Nov 27, 1962	CLE	A	Jack Curtis	MIL	N	Ty Cline Don Dillard Frank Funk
Dec 2, 1963	LA	A	Barry Latman	CLE	A	Leon Wagner

Bob Addis

Oct 11, 1951	CHI	N	————	BOS	N	Jack Cusick
June 4, 1953	PIT	N	————	CHI	N	*See Ralph Kiner*

Jim Adduci

Oct 3, 1984	MIL	A	Paul Householder	STL	N	Minor leaguers P Rich Buonantony C Jim Koontz IF Ron Koenigsfeld

Dave Adlesh

Oct 11, 1968	STL	N	Dave Giusti	HOU	N	Johnny Edwards minor league C Tommy Smith
March 25, 1969	ATL	N	————	STL	N	Bob Johnson

Tommie Agee

Jan 20, 1965	CHI	A	Tommy John Johnny Romano	CLE	A	Rocky Colavito Cam Carreon

(Part of three-team trade involving Kansas City, Cleveland, and Chicago White Sox.)

Dec 15, 1967	NY	N	Al Weis	CHI	A	Tommy Davis Jack Fisher Billy Wynne Buddy Booker
Nov 27, 1972	HOU	N	————	NY	N	Rich Chiles Buddy Harris
Aug 18, 1973	STL	N	————	HOU	N	Dave Campbell and cash
Dec 5, 1973	LA	N	————	STL	N	Pete Richert

Joe Agler

May 1915	BAL	F	————	BUF	F	Cash

Sam Agnew

Dec 1915	BOS	A	————	STL	A	Cash
Jan 1919	WAS	A	————	BOS	A	Cash

Hank Aguirre

Feb 18, 1958	DET	A	Jim Hegan	CLE	A	Hal Woodeshick J. W. Porter
April 3, 1968	LA	N	————	DET	A	Minor league IF Fred Moulder

Willie Aikens

Dec 6, 1979	KC	A	Rance Mulliniks	CAL	A	Al Cowens Todd Cruz Craig Eaton
Dec 20, 1983	TOR	A	————	KC	A	Jorge Orta

DATE	TRADED TO		TRADED WITH	TRADED BY		IN EXCHANGE FOR

Eddie Ainsmith

| Jan 17, 1919 | BOS | A | George Dumont | WAS | A | Hal Janvrin and cash |
| Jan 17, 1919 | DET | A | Chick Shorten Slim Love | BOS | A | Ossie Vitt |

Jack Aker

May 20, 1969	NY	A	————	SEA	A	Fred Talbot
Jan 20, 1972	CHI	N	————	NY	A	Johnny Callison
June 14, 1974	NY	N	————	ATL	N	Cash

Butch Alberts

| Dec 8, 1977 | TOR | A | Dale Kelly | CAL | A | Ron Fairly |

Santo Alcala

| May 21, 1977 | MON | N | ———— | CIN | N | Shane Rawley Angel Torres |
| March 23, 1978 | SEA | A | ———— | MON | N | Cash |

(Alcala was returned to Montreal before the start of the 1979 season.)

Luis Alcaraz

| March 24, 1971 | CHI | A | cash | KC | A | Bobby Knoop |

Vic Aldridge

Oct 27, 1924	PIT	N	George Grantham Al Niehaus	CHI	N	Charlie Grimm Rabbit Maranville Wilbur Cooper
Feb 11, 1928	NY	N	————	PIT	N	Burleigh Grimes
Dec 9, 1928	BKN	N	————	NY	N	Waiver price

(Aldridge refused to report and retired.)

Dale Alexander

| June 12, 1932 | BOS | A | Roy Johnson | DET | A | Earl Webb |

Doyle Alexander

Dec 2, 1971	BAL	A	Bob O'Brien Sergio Robles Royle Stillman	LA	N	Frank Robinson Pete Richert
June 15, 1976	NY	A	————	BAL	A	*See Tippy Martinez*
Nov 23, 1976	TEX	A	————	NY	A	No compensation (free agent signing)
Dec 6, 1979	ATL	N	Larvell Blanks and $50,000.	TEX	A	Adrian Devine Pepe Frias
Dec 12, 1980	SF	N	————	ATL	N	John Montefusco minor league OF Craig Landis
March 30, 1982	NY	A	————	SF	N	Andy McGaffigan Ted Wilborn

Gary Alexander

| March 15, 1978 | OAK | A | Gary Thomasson Dave Heaverlo Alan Wirth John Henry Johnson Phil Huffman Mario Guerrero and $390,000. | SF | N | Vida Blue |
| June 15, 1978 | CLE | A | ———— | OAK | A | Joe Wallis |

DATE	TRADED TO		TRADED WITH	TRADED BY		IN EXCHANGE FOR

Ruben Amaro continued

| Nov 6, 1968 | CAL | A | ———— | NY | A | Cash |

Red Ames

May 22, 1913	CIN	N	Heinie Groh Josh Devore and $20,000.	NY	N	Art Fromme Eddie Grant
July 24, 1915	STL	N	————	CIN	N	Cash
Sept 5, 1919	PHI	N	————	STL	N	Cash

(Ames was returned to St. Louis in October.)

Sandy Amoros

| May 7, 1960 | DET | A | ———— | LA | N | Gail Harris |

Larry Andersen

Dec 21, 1979	PIT	N	————	CLE	A	Larry Littleton and minor league P John Burden
April 1, 1980	SEA	A	cash	PIT	N	Odell Jones
July 29, 1983	PHI	N	————	SEA	A	Cash

Bob Anderson

| Nov 28, 1962 | DET | A | ———— | CHI | N | Steve Boros |
| Nov 18, 1963 | KC | A | *See Rocky Colavito* | DET | A | ———— |

Bud Anderson

| Dec 6, 1979 | CLE | A | Rafael Vasquez
and minor league
P Bob Pietroburgo | SEA | A | Ted Cox |

Dwain Anderson

| May 15, 1972 | STL | N | ———— | OAK | A | Don Shaw |
| June 7, 1973 | SD | N | ———— | STL | N | Dave Campbell |

Fred Anderson

| Feb 10, 1916 | NY | N | ———— | BUF | F | Cash |

Harry Anderson

| June 15, 1960 | CIN | N | Wally Post
minor league
1B Fred Hopke | PHI | N | Tony Gonzalez
Lee Walls |

Jim Anderson

| Aug 29, 1979 | SEA | A | ———— | CAL | A | John Montague |

John Anderson

| May 7, 1962 | HOU | N | Carl Warwick | STL | N | Bobby Shantz |

John Anderson

Oct 26, 1903	NY	A	————	STL	A	Jack O'Connor
June 3, 1905	WAS	A	————	NY	A	Waiver price
Jan 1908	CHI	A	————	WAS	A	Cash

Larry Anderson

| Oct 21, 1976 | CHI | A | ———— | TOR | A | Phil Roof |
| Aug 18, 1977 | CHI | N | cash | CHI | A | Steve Renko |

DATE	TRADED TO		TRADED WITH	TRADED BY		IN EXCHANGE FOR

Larry Anderson continued

| Aug 6, 1978 | PHI | N | ——— | CHI | N | Davy Johnson |

Mike Anderson

| Dec 9, 1975 | STL | N | ——— | PHI | N | Ron Reed |

Rick Anderson

| Nov 1, 1979 | SEA | A | *See Jim Beattie* | NY | A | ——— |

Sparky Anderson

| Dec 23, 1958 | PHI | N | ——— | LA | N | Rip Repulski
Jim Golden
Gene Snyder |

Fred Andrews

| March 24, 1978 | NY | N | cash | PHI | N | Bud Harrelson |

Ivy Andrews

June 5, 1932	BOS	A	Hank Johnson and $50,000.	NY	A	Danny MacFayden
Dec 14, 1933	STL	A	Smead Jolley and cash	BOS	A	Carl Reynolds
Jan 17, 1937	CLE	A	Lyn Lary Moose Solters	STL	A	Bill Knickerbocker Joe Vosmik Oral Hildebrand
Aug 14, 1937	NY	A	———	CLE	A	$7,500.

John Andrews

| Dec 6, 1973 | CAL | A | ——— | STL | N | Jeff Torborg |

Mike Andrews

| Dec 1, 1970 | CHI | A | Luis Alvarado | BOS | A | Luis Aparicio |

Nate Andrews

Sept 25, 1939	STL	A	———	STL	N	Cash
June 10, 1940	CLE	A	———	STL	A	Cash
Dec 4, 1942	BOS	N	Eddie Joost and $25,000.	CIN	N	Eddie Miller
Aug 22, 1945	CIN	N	———	BOS	N	Cash

Rob Andrews

| Dec 3, 1974 | HOU | N | Enos Cabell | BAL | A | Lee May
Jay Schlueter |
| March 26, 1977 | SF | N | cash | HOU | N | Willie Crawford
Rob Sperring |

Joaquin Andujar

| Oct 24, 1975 | HOU | N | ——— | CIN | N | Luis Sanchez
minor league
P Carlos Alfonso |
| June 7, 1981 | STL | N | ——— | HOU | N | Tony Scott |

Norm Angelini

| June 30, 1975 | ATL | N | Bruce Dal Canton
Al Autry | KC | A | Ray Sadecki
and cash |

(Atlanta received Angelini and Autry on September 4.)

DATE	TRADED TO		TRADED WITH	TRADED BY		IN EXCHANGE FOR

Gene Bearden continued

| Feb 14, 1952 | STL | A | Bob Cain
Dick Kryhoski | DET | A | Dick Littlefield
Ben Taylor
Cliff Mapes |
| March 18, 1953 | CHI | A | ————— | STL | A | Waiver price |

Gary Beare

| March 28, 1979 | PHI | N | ————— | MIL | A | Danny Boitano |

Jim Beattie

| Nov 1, 1979 | SEA | A | Rick Anderson
Juan Beniquez
Jerry Narron | NY | A | Ruppert Jones
Jim Lewis |

Jim Beauchamp

Feb 17, 1964	HOU	N	Chuck Taylor	STL	N	Carl Warwick
May 13, 1965	MIL	N	Ken Johnson	HOU	N	Lee Maye
Oct 10, 1967	CIN	N	Mack Jones Jay Ritchie	ATL	N	Deron Johnson
June 13, 1970	STL	N	Leon McFadden	HOU	N	George Culver
Oct 18, 1971	NY	N	—————	STL	N	*See Jim Bibby*

Ginger Beaumont

| Dec 1906 | BOS | N | Claude Ritchey
Patsy Flaherty | PIT | N | Ed Abbaticchio |
| Feb 1910 | CHI | N | ————— | BOS | N | Fred Liese |

Johnny Beazley

| April 18, 1947 | BOS | N | | STL | N | Cash |

Clyde Beck

| Jan 1931 | CIN | N | ————— | CHI | N | Waiver price |

Fred Beck

| March 1911 | CIN | N | ————— | BOS | N | Cash |
| July 15, 1911 | PHI | N | Bill Burns | CIN | N | Bert Humphries |

Heinie Beckendorf

| April 1910 | WAS | A | ————— | DET | A | Cash |

Beals Becker

June 1908	BOS	N	—————	PIT	N	Cash
Dec 1909	NY	N	—————	BOS	N	Buck Herzog
June 5, 1913	PHI	N	Josh Devore	CIN	N	John Dodge Red Nelson

Heinz Becker

| May 1946 | CLE | A | ————— | CHI | N | Mickey Rocco |

Glenn Beckert

| Nov 7, 1973 | SD | N | Bobby Fenwick | CHI | N | Jerry Morales |

Jake Beckley

| Feb 1904 | STL | N | ————— | CIN | N | Cash |

DATE	TRADED TO		TRADED WITH	TRADED BY		IN EXCHANGE FOR

Joe Beckwith

| Dec 7, 1983 | KC | A | ———— | LA | N | Minor leaguers
C Joe Szekeley
P Jose Torres and
P John Serritella |

Fred Beebe

July 1, 1906	STL	N	Pete Noonan and cash	CHI	N	Jack Taylor
Feb 1910	CIN	N	Alan Storke	STL	N	Miller Huggins Rebel Oakes Frank Corridon
Feb 1911	PHI	N	*See Dode Paskert*	CIN	N	————

Fred Beene

| Dec 1, 1970 | SD | N | ———— | BAL | A | *See Pat Dobson* |
| April 27, 1974 | CLE | A | ———— | NY | A | *See Chris Chambliss* |

Joe Beggs

| Jan 4, 1940 | CIN | N | ———— | NY | A | Lee Grissom |
| June 7, 1947 | NY | N | ———— | CIN | N | Babe Young |

Rick Behenna

| Aug 28, 1983 | CLE | A | Brett Butler
Brook Jacoby
and $150,000. | ATL | N | Len Barker |

(Butler and Jacoby were sent to Cleveland at the end of the season.)

Mel Behney

| March 27, 1973 | BOS | A | ———— | CIN | N | Phil Gagliano
Andy Kosco |

Hank Behrman

May 3, 1947	PIT	N	Kirby Higbe Cal McLish Gene Mauch Dixie Howell	BKN	N	Al Gionfriddo and $100,000.
June 14, 1947	BKN	N	————	PIT	N	Cash
Feb 26, 1949	NY	N	————	BKN	N	Cash

Mark Belanger

| Dec 11, 1981 | LA | N | ———— | BAL | A | No compensation
(free agent signing) |

Wayne Belardi

June 9, 1954	DET	A	————	BKN	N	Charlie Kress Johnny Bucha Ernie Nevel and cash
Dec 5, 1956	KC	A	*See Ned Garver*	DET	A	————
Feb 19, 1957	NY	A	————	KC	A	*See Billy Hunter*

Bo Belinsky

| Dec 3, 1964 | PHI | N | ———— | LA | A | Costen Shockley
Rudy May |

DATE	TRADED TO		TRADED WITH	TRADED BY		IN EXCHANGE FOR

Beau Bell

| May 13, 1939 | DET | A | Bobo Newsom
Red Kress
Jim Walkup | STL | A | Vern Kennedy
Bob Harris
George Gill
Roxie Lawson
Chet Laabs
Mark Christman |
| Jan 20, 1940 | CLE | A | ——————— | DET | A | Bruce Campbell |

Buddy Bell

| Dec 8, 1978 | TEX | A | ——————— | CLE | A | Toby Harrah |

Gary Bell

| June 4, 1967 | BOS | A | ——————— | CLE | A | Tony Horton
Don Demeter |
| June 8, 1969 | CHI | A | ——————— | SEA | A | Bob Locker |

Gus Bell

Oct 14, 1952	CIN	N	———————	PIT	N	Cal Abrams Joe Rossi Gail Henley
Nov 28, 1961	MIL	N	cash	NY	N	Frank Thomas
			(Milwaukee received Bell on May 21, 1962.)			

Kevin Bell

| March 27, 1981 | OAK | A | Tony Phillips
minor league
P Eric Mustard | SD | N | Bob Lacey
minor league
P Ray Moretti |

Les Bell

| March 25, 1928 | BOS | N | ——————— | STL | N | Andy High
and $25,000. |
| Oct 29, 1929 | CHI | N | ——————— | BOS | N | Waiver price |

Zeke Bella

| Aug 22, 1958 | KC | A | cash | NY | A | Murry Dickson |

Bob Belloir

| June 7, 1975 | ATL | N | Blue Moon Odom | CLE | A | Roric Harrison |

Chief Bender

| Feb 10, 1916 | PHI | N | ——————— | BAL | F | Cash |

Ray Benge

Dec 15, 1932	BKN	N	$15,000.	PHI	N	Cy Moore Mickey Finn Jack Warner
Dec 12, 1935	BOS	N	Tony Cuccinello Al Lopez Bobby Reis	BKN	N	Ed Brandt Randy Moore
Aug 4, 1936	PHI	N	———————	BOS	N	Fabian Kowalik

Juan Beniquez

Nov 17, 1975	TEX	A	Steve Barr Craig Skok	BOS	A	Ferguson Jenkins
Nov 10, 1978	NY	A	*See Dave Righetti*	TEX	A	———————
Nov 1, 1979	SEA	A	Jim Beattie Rick Anderson Jerry Narron	NY	A	Ruppert Jones Jim Lewis

DATE	TRADED TO		TRADED WITH	TRADED BY		IN EXCHANGE FOR

Juan Beniquez continued

DATE	TRADED TO		TRADED WITH	TRADED BY		IN EXCHANGE FOR
Dec 29, 1980	CAL	A	————	SEA	A	No compensation (free agent signing)

Dennis Bennett

| Nov 29, 1964 | BOS | A | ———— | PHI | N | Dick Stuart |
| June 24, 1967 | NY | N | ———— | BOS | A | Al Yates and cash |

Joe Bennett

| May 1921 | STL | A | ———— | CHI | A | Cash |

Jack Bentley

| Dec 30, 1925 | PHI | N | Wayland Dean | NY | N | Jimmy Ring |
| Sept 15, 1926 | NY | N | ———— | PHI | N | Waiver price |

Al Benton

| Jan 1938 | DET | A | ———— | PHI | A | Cash |
| April 20, 1949 | CLE | A | ———— | DET | A | Cash |

Butch Benton

| April 6, 1981 | CHI | N | ———— | NY | N | Cash |

Larry Benton

| July 30, 1922 | BOS | N | Fred Toney and $100,000. | NY | N | Hugh McQuillan |

(Toney refused to report and remained Giants' property.)

| June 12, 1927 | NY | N | Zack Taylor Herb Thomas | BOS | N | Hugh McQuillan Kent Greenfield Doc Farrell |
| May 21, 1930 | CIN | N | ———— | NY | N | Hughie Critz |

Rube Benton

| Aug 19, 1915 | NY | N | ———— | CIN | N | $3,000. |
| July 30, 1922 | CIN | N | ———— | NY | N | Cash |

Johnny Berardino

| Nov 22, 1947 | WAS | A | ———— | STL | A | Gerry Priddy |

(Berardino announced his retirement to go into movies. Commissioner Chandler cancelled the trade. Berardino then unretired.)

| Dec 9, 1947 | CLE | A | ———— | STL | A | Catfish Metkovich and $50,000. |

(Metkovich was returned to Cleveland because of a broken finger and the St. Louis Browns received another $15,000 to complete the trade.)

| Aug 18, 1952 | PIT | N | minor league P Charlie Sipple and $50,000. | CLE | A | George Strickland Ted Wilks |

Lou Berberet

Feb 8, 1956	WAS	A	*See Whitey Herzog*	NY	A	————
May 1, 1958	BOS	A	————	WAS	A	Ken Aspromonte
Dec 2, 1958	DET	A	————	BOS	A	Herb Moford

Juan Berenguer

| March 31, 1981 | KC | A | ———— | NY | N | Marvell Wynne minor league P John Skinner |
| Aug 8, 1981 | TOR | A | ———— | KC | A | Cash |

DATE	TRADED TO		TRADED WITH	TRADED BY		IN EXCHANGE FOR

Bruce Berenyi

DATE	TRADED TO		TRADED WITH	TRADED BY		IN EXCHANGE FOR
June 15, 1984	NY	N	———	CIN	N	Jay Tibbs minor leaguers 3B Eddie Williams and P Matt Bullinger

Moe Berg

DATE	TRADED TO		TRADED WITH	TRADED BY		IN EXCHANGE FOR
Aug 1925	CHI	A	———	BKN	N	Cash
April 2, 1931	CLE	A	———	CHI	A	Waiver price

Bill Bergen

DATE	TRADED TO		TRADED WITH	TRADED BY		IN EXCHANGE FOR
Feb 1904	BKN	N	———	CIN	N	Cash

Boze Berger

DATE	TRADED TO		TRADED WITH	TRADED BY		IN EXCHANGE FOR
April 1937	CHI	A	———	CLE	A	Cash
Dec 21, 1938	BOS	A	———	CHI	A	Eric McNair
Dec 26, 1939	BKN	N	———	BOS	A	Waiver price

Wally Berger

DATE	TRADED TO		TRADED WITH	TRADED BY		IN EXCHANGE FOR
June 15, 1937	NY	N	———	BOS	N	Frank Gabler and $35,000.
June 6, 1938	CIN	N	———	NY	N	Alex Kampouris

Dave Bergman

DATE	TRADED TO		TRADED WITH	TRADED BY		IN EXCHANGE FOR
June 15, 1977	HOU	N	Randy Niemann Mike Fischlin	NY	A	Cliff Johnson
			(Houston received Bergman on November 23.)			
April 20, 1981	SF	N	Jeff Leonard	HOU	N	Mike Ivie
March 24, 1984	PHI	N	———	SF	N	Alejandro Sanchez
March 24, 1984	DET	A	Willie Hernandez	PHI	N	John Wockenfuss Glenn Wilson

Dwight Bernard

DATE	TRADED TO		TRADED WITH	TRADED BY		IN EXCHANGE FOR
Oct 26, 1979	MIL	A	———	NY	N	Mark Bomback

Tony Bernazard

DATE	TRADED TO		TRADED WITH	TRADED BY		IN EXCHANGE FOR
Dec 12, 1980	CHI	A	———	MON	N	Rich Wortham
June 15, 1983	SEA	A	———	CHI	A	Julio Cruz
Dec 7, 1983	CLE	A	———	SEA	A	Gorman Thomas Jack Perconte

Bill Bernhard

DATE	TRADED TO		TRADED WITH	TRADED BY		IN EXCHANGE FOR
June 1902	CLE	A	———	PHI	A	Ossee Schreckengost Frank Bonner

Juan Bernhardt

DATE	TRADED TO		TRADED WITH	TRADED BY		IN EXCHANGE FOR
July 6, 1979	CHI	A	———	SEA	A	Rich Hinton

Dale Berra

DATE	TRADED TO		TRADED WITH	TRADED BY		IN EXCHANGE FOR
Dec 20, 1984	NY	A	minor league P Jay Buhner	PIT	N	Steve Kemp Tim Foli and $400,000.

Ray Berres

DATE	TRADED TO		TRADED WITH	TRADED BY		IN EXCHANGE FOR
June 14, 1940	BOS	N	$40,000.	PIT	N	Al Lopez
Feb 6, 1942	NY	N	———	BOS	N	Cash

DATE	TRADED TO		TRADED WITH	TRADED BY		IN EXCHANGE FOR

Charlie Berry

DATE	TRADED TO		TRADED WITH	TRADED BY		IN EXCHANGE FOR
April 29, 1932	CHI	A	————	BOS	A	Bennie Tate Smead Jolley Cliff Watwood
Dec 12, 1933	PHI	A	$20,000.	CHI	A	George Earnshaw Johnny Pasek

Joe Berry

DATE	TRADED TO		TRADED WITH	TRADED BY		IN EXCHANGE FOR
May 1946	CLE	A	————	PHI	A	Cash

Ken Berry

DATE	TRADED TO		TRADED WITH	TRADED BY		IN EXCHANGE FOR
Nov 30, 1970	CAL	A	Syd O'Brien Billy Wynne	CHI	A	Jay Johnstone Tom Egan Tom Bradley
Oct 22, 1973	MIL	A	Clyde Wright Steve Barber Art Kusnyer and cash	CAL	A	Ellie Rodriguez Skip Lockwood Gary Ryerson Ollie Brown Joe Lahoud

Neil Berry

DATE	TRADED TO		TRADED WITH	TRADED BY		IN EXCHANGE FOR
Oct 27, 1952	STL	A	Cliff Mapes and $25,000.	DET	A	Rufus Crawford
Sept 1, 1953	CHI	A	————	STL	A	Waiver price
Feb 5, 1954	BAL	A	Sam Mele	CHI	A	Johnny Groth Johnny Lipon

Frank Bertaina

DATE	TRADED TO		TRADED WITH	TRADED BY		IN EXCHANGE FOR
May 29, 1967	WAS	A	Mike Epstein	BAL	A	Pete Richert
June 16, 1969	BAL	A	————	WAS	A	Minor league P Paul Campbell
Aug 14, 1970	STL	N	————	BAL	A	Cash

Dick Bertell

DATE	TRADED TO		TRADED WITH	TRADED BY		IN EXCHANGE FOR
May 29, 1965	SF	N	Len Gabrielson	CHI	N	Harvey Kuenn Ed Bailey Bob Hendley

Reno Bertoia

DATE	TRADED TO		TRADED WITH	TRADED BY		IN EXCHANGE FOR
Dec 6, 1958	WAS	A	————	DET	A	*See Eddie Yost*
June 1, 1961	KC	A	Paul Giel	MIN	A	Bill Tuttle
			(Giel was returned to Minnesota for a cash payment.)			
Aug 2, 1961	DET	A	Gerry Staley	KC	A	Ozzie Virgil Bill Fischer

Bob Bescher

DATE	TRADED TO		TRADED WITH	TRADED BY		IN EXCHANGE FOR
Dec 12, 1913	NY	N	————	CIN	N	Buck Herzog Grover Hartley
			(Hartley jumped to the Federal League and Herzog was made Cincinnati manager.)			

Kurt Bevacqua

DATE	TRADED TO		TRADED WITH	TRADED BY		IN EXCHANGE FOR
May 8, 1971	CLE	A	————	CIN	N	Buddy Bradford
Nov 2, 1972	KC	A	————	CLE	A	Mike Hedlund
Dec 4, 1973	PIT	N	Ed Kirkpatrick minor league 1B Winston Cole	KC	A	Nellie Briles Fernando Gonzalez
July 8, 1974	KC	A	————	PIT	N	Minor league IF Cal Meier and cash

DATE	TRADED TO		TRADED WITH	TRADED BY		IN EXCHANGE FOR

Kurt Bevacqua continued

DATE	TRADED TO		TRADED WITH	TRADED BY		IN EXCHANGE FOR
March 6, 1975	MIL	A	————	KC	A	Cash
Oct 22, 1976	SEA	A	————	MIL	A	Cash
Oct 25, 1978	SD	N	Mike Hargrove Bill Fahey	TEX	A	Oscar Gamble Dave Roberts and $300,000.
Aug 5, 1980	PIT	N	Mark Lee	SD	N	Rick Lancellotti Luis Salazar

Hal Bevan

DATE	TRADED TO		TRADED WITH	TRADED BY		IN EXCHANGE FOR
May 3, 1952	PHI	A	————	BOS	A	Waiver price

Bill Bevens

DATE	TRADED TO		TRADED WITH	TRADED BY		IN EXCHANGE FOR
Jan 17, 1949	CHI	A	————	NY	A	Cash

(Bevens was returned to New York Yankees on March 28, 1949.)

Monte Beville

DATE	TRADED TO		TRADED WITH	TRADED BY		IN EXCHANGE FOR
July 25, 1904	DET	A	————	NY	A	Frank McManus

Jim Bibby

DATE	TRADED TO		TRADED WITH	TRADED BY		IN EXCHANGE FOR
Oct 18, 1971	STL	N	Art Shamsky Rich Folkers Charles Hudson	NY	N	Jim Beauchamp Chuck Taylor Harry Parker Tom Coulter
June 6, 1973	TEX	A	————	STL	N	Mike Nagy John Wockenfuss
June 13, 1975	CLE	A	Jackie Brown Rick Waits and $100,000.	TEX	A	Gaylord Perry
March 15, 1978	PIT	N	————	CLE	A	No compensation (free agent signing)
Feb 7, 1984	TEX	A	————	PIT	N	No compensation (free agent signing)

Vern Bickford

DATE	TRADED TO		TRADED WITH	TRADED BY		IN EXCHANGE FOR
Feb 10, 1954	BAL	A	————	MIL	N	Charlie White and $10,000.

Elliott Bigelow

DATE	TRADED TO		TRADED WITH	TRADED BY		IN EXCHANGE FOR
Dec 15, 1928	BOS	A	Milt Gaston Hod Lisenbee Bobby Reeves Grant Gillis	WAS	A	Buddy Myer

Larry Biittner

DATE	TRADED TO		TRADED WITH	TRADED BY		IN EXCHANGE FOR
Dec 20, 1973	MON	N	————	TEX	A	Pat Jarvis
May 17, 1976	CHI	N	Steve Renko	MON	N	Andre Thornton
Jan 8, 1981	CIN	N	————	CHI	N	No compensation (free agent signing)

Steve Bilko

DATE	TRADED TO		TRADED WITH	TRADED BY		IN EXCHANGE FOR
April 30, 1954	CHI	N	————	STL	N	$12,500.
June 15, 1958	LA	N	Johnny Klippstein	CIN	N	Don Newcombe

DATE	TRADED TO		TRADED WITH	TRADED BY		IN EXCHANGE FOR

Jack Billingham

| Jan 22, 1969 | HOU | N | Jesus Alou
Donn Clendenon
Skip Guinn
and $100,000. | MON | N | Rusty Staub |

(Clendenon refused to report, and Houston was sent Billingham, Guinn, and cash on April 8, 1969.)

Nov 29, 1971	CIN	N	*See Joe Morgan*	HOU	N	——————
March 6, 1978	DET	A	——————	CIN	N	George Cappuzzello minor league OF John Valle
May 12, 1980	BOS	A	——————	DET	A	Cash

Dick Billings

| Aug 12, 1974 | STL | N | —————— | TEX | A | Cash |

Josh Billings

| March 1919 | STL | A | —————— | CLE | A | Les Nunamaker |

George Binks

| Feb 14, 1947 | PHI | A | —————— | WAS | A | Lou Knerr |
| June 4, 1948 | STL | A | $20,000. | PHI | A | Ray Coleman |

Doug Bird

April 3, 1979	PHI	N	——————	KC	A	Todd Cruz
June 12, 1981	CHI	N	Mike Griffin and $400,000.	NY	A	Rick Reuschel
Dec 10, 1982	BOS	A	——————	CHI	N	Chuck Rainey

Ralph Birkofer

| Dec 4, 1936 | BKN | N | Cookie Lavagetto | PIT | N | Ed Brandt |

Babe Birrer

| April 5, 1956 | BAL | A | —————— | DET | A | Waiver price |

John Bischoff

| July 11, 1925 | BOS | A | —————— | CHI | A | Cash |

Max Bishop

| Dec 12, 1933 | BOS | A | Lefty Grove
Rube Walberg | PHI | A | Bob Kline
Rabbit Warstler
and $125,000. |

Rivington Bisland

| March 1913 | STL | A | —————— | PIT | N | Waiver price |

Hi Bithorn

| Jan 25, 1947 | PIT | N | —————— | CHI | N | Cash |
| March 22, 1947 | CHI | A | —————— | PIT | N | Waiver price |

George Bjorkman

| March 16, 1983 | HOU | N | —————— | STL | N | Minor league
P Jeff Meadows |

Bill Black

| Aug 14, 1952 | DET | A | —————— | STL | A | *See Vic Wertz* |

DATE	TRADED TO		TRADED WITH	TRADED BY		IN EXCHANGE FOR

Bud Black
| Oct 23, 1981 | KC | A | ——— | SEA | A | Manny Castillo |

Don Black
| Oct 2, 1945 | CLE | A | ——— | PHI | A | Cash |

Joe Black
| June 9, 1955 | CIN | N | ——— | BKN | N | Bob Borkowski and cash |

Earl Blackburn
| June 1912 | CIN | N | ——— | PIT | N | Cash |

Lena Blackburne
| Feb 1919 | BOS | N | ——— | CIN | N | Wally Rehg |
| July 9, 1919 | PHI | N | ——— | BOS | N | Cash |

Ewell Blackwell
| Aug 28, 1952 | NY | A | ——— | CIN | N | Jim Greengrass Johnny Schmitz Ernie Nevel Bob Marquis and $35,000. |
| March 30, 1955 | KC | A | Dick Kryhoski Tom Gorman | NY | A | $50,000. |

Tim Blackwell
April 19, 1976	PHI	N	———	BOS	A	Cash
June 15, 1977	MON	N	Wayne Twitchell	PHI	N	Barry Foote Dan Warthen
Jan 14, 1982	MON	N	———	CHI	N	No compensation (free agent signing)

Rick Bladt
| Jan 20, 1977 | BAL | A | Elliott Maddox | NY | A | Paul Blair |

George Blaeholder
| May 21, 1935 | PHI | A | ——— | STL | A | Ed Coleman Sugar Cain |
| Jan 27, 1936 | CLE | A | ——— | PHI | A | Waiver price |

Dennis Blair
| July 14, 1977 | BAL | A | ——— | MON | N | Fred Holdsworth |

Paul Blair
| Jan 20, 1977 | NY | A | ——— | BAL | A | Elliott Maddox Rick Bladt |

Sheriff Blake
| July 27, 1931 | PHI | N | ——— | CHI | N | Waiver price |

Johnny Blanchard
| May 3, 1965 | KC | A | Rollie Sheldon | NY | A | Doc Edwards |
| Sept 9, 1965 | MIL | N | ——— | KC | A | Cash |

Gil Blanco
| June 10, 1966 | KC | A | Roger Repoz Bill Stafford | NY | A | Fred Talbot Billy Bryan |

DATE	TRADED TO		TRADED WITH	TRADED BY		IN EXCHANGE FOR

Ossie Blanco

Nov 30, 1970	CHI	N	Jose Ortiz	CHI	A	Pat Jacquez
						Dave Lemonds
						Roe Skidmore

Larvell Blanks

Dec 12, 1975	CHI	A	Ralph Garr	ATL	N	Ken Henderson
						Dick Ruthven
						Danny Osborn
Dec 12, 1975	CLE	A	————	CHI	A	Jack Brohamer
Oct 3, 1978	TEX	A	Jim Kern	CLE	A	Bobby Bonds
						Len Barker
Dec 6, 1979	ATL	N	Doyle Alexander	TEX	A	Adrian Devine
			and $50,000.			Pepe Frias

Don Blasingame

Dec 15, 1959	SF	N	————	STL	N	Daryl Spencer
						Leon Wagner
April 27, 1961	CIN	N	Bob Schmidt	SF	N	Ed Bailey
			Sherman Jones			
July 1, 1963	WAS	A	————	CIN	N	Cash
Aug 22, 1966	KC	A	————	WAS	A	Cash

Wade Blasingame

| June 15, 1967 | HOU | N | ———— | ATL | N | Claude Raymond |
| June 6, 1972 | NY | A | ———— | HOU | N | Cash |

Steve Blateric

| Sept 16, 1972 | NY | A | ———— | CIN | N | Cash |

Johnny Blatnik

| April 27, 1950 | STL | N | ———— | PHI | N | Ken Johnson |

Gary Blaylock

| July 26, 1959 | NY | A | ———— | STL | N | Waiver price |

Curt Blefary

Dec 4, 1968	HOU	N	minor leaguer	BAL	A	Mike Cuellar
			John Mason			Enzo Hernandez
						and minor league
						IF Elijah Johnson
Dec 4, 1969	NY	A	————	HOU	N	Joe Pepitone
May 26, 1971	OAK	A	————	NY	A	Rob Gardner
May 17, 1972	SD	N	Mike Kilkenny	OAK	A	Ollie Brown
			minor league			
			OF Greg Schubert			

Ron Blomberg

| Nov 17, 1977 | CHI | A | ———— | NY | A | No compensation |
| | | | | | | (free agent signing) |

Jimmy Bloodworth

Dec 12, 1941	DET	A	Doc Cramer	WAS	A	Frank Croucher
						Bruce Campbell
Dec 12, 1946	PIT	N	————	DET	A	Cash
May 10, 1950	PHI	N	————	CIN	N	Cash

DATE	TRADED TO		TRADED WITH	TRADED BY		IN EXCHANGE FOR

Bert Blue

| July 1908 | PHI | A | ———— | STL | A | Syd Smith |

Lu Blue

| Dec 2, 1927 | STL | A | Heinie Manush | DET | A | Chick Galloway
Elam Vangilder
Harry Rice |
| April 3, 1931 | CHI | A | ———— | STL | A | $15,000. |

Vida Blue

| March 15, 1978 | SF | N | ———— | OAK | A | Gary Alexander
Gary Thomasson
Dave Heaverlo
Alan Wirth
John Henry Johnson
Phil Huffman
Mario Guerrero
and $390,000. |
| March 30, 1982 | KC | A | Bob Tufts | SF | N | Renie Martin
Craig Chamberlain
Atlee Hammaker
Brad Wellman |

Otto Bluege

| Dec 20, 1933 | PHI | N | Irv Jeffries | CIN | N | Mark Koenig |

Jim Bluejacket

| Feb 10, 1916 | CIN | N | ———— | BKN | F | Cash |

Bert Blyleven

| June 1, 1976 | TEX | A | Danny Thompson | MIN | A | Bill Singer
Roy Smalley
Mike Cubbage
Jim Gideon
and $250,000. |
| Dec 8, 1977 | PIT | N | John Milner | TEX | A | Al Oliver
Nelson Norman |

(Part of four-team trade involving Texas, New York Mets, Pittsburgh, and Atlanta.)

| Dec 9, 1980 | CLE | A | Manny Sanguillen | PIT | N | Gary Alexander
Victor Cruz
Rafael Vasquez
Bob Owchinko |

Mike Blyzka

| Dec 1, 1954 | NY | A | *See Dick Kryhoski* | BAL | A | ———— |

Randy Bobb

| March 29, 1970 | NY | N | ———— | CHI | N | J. C. Martin |

John Boccabella

| April 1, 1974 | SF | N | ———— | MON | N | Don Carrithers |

Bruce Bochte

| May 11, 1977 | CLE | A | Sid Monge
and $250,000. | CAL | A | Dave LaRoche
Dave Schuler |
| Dec 20, 1977 | SEA | A | ———— | CLE | A | No compensation
(free agent signing) |

DATE	TRADED TO		TRADED WITH	TRADED BY		IN EXCHANGE FOR

Bruce Bochy
| Feb 11, 1981 | NY | N | ———— | HOU | N | Minor leaguers C Stan Hough and IF Randy Rogers |

Eddie Bockman
| Oct 19, 1946 | CLE | A | Joe Gordon | NY | A | Allie Reynolds |
| Jan 16, 1948 | PIT | N | ———— | CLE | A | Cash |

Ping Bodie
| March 8, 1918 | NY | A | | PHI | A | George Burns |

Tony Boeckel
| June 12, 1919 | BOS | N | ———— | PIT | N | Waiver price |

Joe Boehling
| Aug 18, 1916 | CLE | A | Danny Moeller | WAS | A | Elmer Smith Joe Leonard |

Len Boehmer
| Sept 18, 1967 | NY | A | ———— | CIN | N | Bill Henry |

Tommy Boggs
| Dec 8, 1977 | ATL | N | Adrian Devine Eddie Miller | TEX | A | Willie Montanez |

(Part of four-team trade involving Texas, Atlanta, Pittsburgh, and New York Mets.)

Pat Bohen
| Jan 1914 | PIT | N | ———— | PHI | A | Waiver price |

Sammy Bohne
| June 15, 1926 | BKN | N | ———— | CIN | N | Cash |

Danny Boitano
March 28, 1979	MIL	A	————	PHI	N	Gary Beare
April 5, 1981	NY	N	————	MIL	A	Cash
Dec 11, 1981	TEX	A	Doug Flynn	NY	N	Jim Kern
Feb 4, 1984	CLE	A	Otis Nixon minor league P Guy Elston	NY	A	Toby Harrah minor league P Rick Brown

Bob Boken
| May 12, 1934 | CHI | A | ———— | WAS | A | Red Kress |

Joe Boley
| June 6, 1932 | CLE | A | ———— | PHI | A | Cash |

Jim Bolger
Oct 1, 1954	CHI	N	Ted Tappe Harry Perkowski	CIN	N	Johnny Klippstein Jim Willis
Jan 23, 1959	CLE	A	Johnny Briggs	CHI	N	Earl Averill
June 6, 1959	PHI	N	cash	CLE	A	Willie Jones
Nov 30, 1962	HOU	N	Connie Grob	MIL	N	Norm Larker

Bobby Bolin
| Dec 12, 1969 | SEA | A | ———— | SF | N | Steve Whitaker Dick Simpson |

DATE	TRADED TO		TRADED WITH	TRADED BY		IN EXCHANGE FOR

Bobby Bolin continued

DATE	TRADED TO		TRADED WITH	TRADED BY		IN EXCHANGE FOR
Sept 10, 1970	BOS	A	——————	MIL	A	Cash

Frank Bolling

Dec 7, 1960	MIL	N	Neil Chrisley	DET	A	Bill Bruton Terry Fox Dick Brown Chuck Cottier

Milt Bolling

April 29, 1957	WAS	A	Russ Kemmerer Faye Throneberry	BOS	A	Dean Stone Bob Chakales
Feb 25, 1958	CLE	A	——————	WAS	A	Minor league P Pete Mesa
March 27, 1958	DET	A	Vito Valentinetti	CLE	A	Pete Wojey and $20,000.

Don Bollweg

May 14, 1951	NY	A	$15,000.	STL	N	Billy Johnson
Dec 16, 1953	PHI	A	——————	NY	A	*See Harry Byrd*

Cliff Bolton

June 10, 1937	DET	A	——————	WAS	A	Waiver price

Mark Bomback

Oct 26, 1979	NY	N	——————	MIL	A	Dwight Bernard
April 6, 1981	TOR	A	——————	NY	N	Charlie Puleo and cash

Bobby Bonds

Oct 22, 1974	NY	A	——————	SF	N	Bobby Murcer
Dec 11, 1975	CAL	A	——————	NY	A	Mickey Rivers Ed Figueroa
Dec 5, 1977	CHI	A	Thad Bosley Rich Dotson	CAL	A	Brian Downing Chris Knapp Dave Frost
May 16, 1978	TEX	A	——————	CHI	A	Claudell Washington Rusty Torres
Oct 3, 1978	CLE	A	Len Barker	TEX	A	Jim Kern Larvell Blanks
Dec 7, 1979	STL	N	——————	CLE	A	Jerry Mumphrey John Denny
June 4, 1981	CHI	N	——————	TEX	A	Cash

Bill Bonham

Oct 31, 1977	CIN	N	——————	CHI	N	Woodie Fryman Bill Caudill

Ernie Bonham

Oct 21, 1946	PIT	N	——————	NY	A	Cookie Cuccurullo

Juan Bonilla

April 1, 1981	SD	N	——————	CLE	A	Bob Lacey

Barry Bonnell

May 7, 1975	ATL	N	Jim Essian and cash	PHI	N	Richie Allen Johnny Oates
Dec 5, 1979	TOR	A	Pat Rockett Joey McLaughlin	ATL	N	Chris Chambliss Luis Gomez

DATE	TRADED TO		TRADED WITH	TRADED BY		IN EXCHANGE FOR

Barry Bonnell continued

| Dec 8, 1983 | SEA | A | ———— | TOR | A | Bryan Clark |

Frank Bonner

| June 1902 | PHI | A | Ossee Schreckengost | CLE | A | Bill Bernhard |

Zeke Bonura

March 18, 1938	WAS	A	————	CHI	A	Joe Kuhel
Dec 11, 1938	NY	N	————	WAS	A	Jim Carlin Tom Baker and $20,000.
April 26, 1940	WAS	A	————	NY	N	$20,000.
July 22, 1940	CHI	N	————	WAS	A	Cash

Everett Booe

| June 1914 | BUF | F | ———— | IND | F | Cash |

Buddy Booker

| Dec 15, 1967 | CHI | A | ———— | NY | N | *See Tommie Agee* |

Al Bool

| Nov 12, 1930 | BOS | N | ———— | PIT | N | Waiver price |

Bob Boone

| Dec 6, 1981 | CAL | A | ———— | PHI | N | Cash |

Danny Boone

| June 8, 1982 | HOU | N | ———— | SD | N | Joe Pittman |

Danny Boone

| Jan 7, 1924 | BOS | A | Steve O'Neill
Joe Connolly
Bill Wambsganss | CLE | A | George Burns
Roxy Walters
Chick Fewster |

Ray Boone

June 15, 1953	DET	A	Al Aber Steve Gromek Dick Weik	CLE	A	Art Houtteman Owen Friend Bill Wight Joe Ginsberg
June 15, 1958	CHI	A	Bob Shaw	DET	A	Bill Fischer Tito Francona
May 2, 1959	KC	A	————	CHI	A	Harry Simpson
Aug 20, 1959	MIL	N	————	KC	A	Waiver price
May 17, 1960	BOS	A	————	MIL	N	Ron Jackson

Pedro Borbon

| Nov 25, 1969 | CIN | N | Jim McGlothlin
Vern Geishert | CAL | A | Alex Johnson
Chico Ruiz |
| June 28, 1979 | SF | N | ———— | CIN | N | Hector Cruz |

Frenchy Bordagaray

Dec 3, 1936	STL	N	Dutch Leonard Jimmy Jordan	BKN	N	Tom Winsett
Dec 8, 1938	CIN	N	————	STL	N	Dusty Cooke
April 4, 1942	BOS	N	————	NY	A	Cash

Rich Bordi

| Dec 9, 1981 | SEA | A | ———— | OAK | A | Dan Meyer |

DATE	TRADED TO		TRADED WITH	TRADED BY		IN EXCHANGE FOR
Rich Bordi continued						
Dec 9, 1982	CHI	N	————	SEA	A	Steve Henderson
Dec 4, 1984	NY	A	Henry Cotto Ron Hassey Porfirio Altamirano	CHI	N	Ray Fontenot Brian Dayett
Glenn Borgmann						
Jan 29, 1980	CHI	A	————	MIN	A	No compensation (free agent signing)
March 24, 1981	CLE	A	————	CHI	A	No compensation (free agent signing)
Paul Boris						
April 10, 1982	MIN	A	Ron Davis Greg Gagne	NY	A	Roy Smalley
Bob Borkowski						
Oct 4, 1951	CIN	N	Smoky Burgess	CHI	N	Johnny Pramesa Bob Usher
June 9, 1955	BKN	N	cash	CIN	N	Joe Black
Tom Borland						
March 24, 1962	HOU	N	————	BOS	A	Dave Philley
Steve Boros						
Nov 28, 1962	CHI	N	————	DET	A	Bob Anderson
Hank Borowy						
July 27, 1945	CHI	N	————	NY	A	$97,000.
Dec 14, 1948	PHI	N	Eddie Waitkus	CHI	N	Monk Dubiel Dutch Leonard
June 12, 1950	PIT	N	————	PHI	N	$10,000.
Aug 3, 1950	DET	A	————	PIT	N	$15,000.
Babe Borton						
June 1, 1913	NY	A	Rollie Zeider	CHI	A	Hal Chase
Feb 10, 1916	STL	A	*See Eddie Plank*	STL	F	————
Don Bosch						
Dec 6, 1966	NY	N	Don Cardwell	PIT	N	Dennis Ribant Gary Kolb
Oct 16, 1968	MON	N	————	NY	N	Cash
Rick Bosetti						
June 15, 1977	STL	N	Tom Underwood Dane Iorg	PHI	N	Bake McBride Steve Waterbury
March 15, 1978	TOR	A	————	STL	N	Cash
June 10, 1981	OAK	A	————	TOR	A	Cash
Thad Bosley						
Dec 5, 1977	CHI	A	————	CAL	A	*See Brian Downing*
April 1, 1981	MIL	A	————	CHI	A	John Poff
March 5, 1982	SEA	A	————	MIL	A	Mike Parrott
March 30, 1983	CHI	N	————	OAK	A	Cash
Dick Bosman						
May 10, 1973	CLE	A	Ted Ford	TEX	A	Steve Dunning

DATE	TRADED TO		TRADED WITH	TRADED BY		IN EXCHANGE FOR

Dick Bosman continued

| May 20, 1975 | OAK | A | Jim Perry | CLE | A | Blue Moon Odom and cash |

Harley Boss

| Dec 15, 1932 | CLE | A | ——— | WAS | A | Jack Russell
Bruce Connatser |

Lyman Bostock

| Nov 21, 1976 | CAL | A | ——— | MIN | A | No compensation (free agent signing) |

Ken Boswell

| Oct 29, 1974 | HOU | N | ——— | NY | N | Bob Gallagher |

Dick Botelho

| Feb 23, 1979 | CHI | N | Barry Foote
Ted Sizemore
Jerry Martin
minor league
P Henry Mack | PHI | N | Manny Trillo
Dave Rader
Greg Gross |
| March 30, 1984 | CHI | N | | KC | A | Alan Hargesheimer |

Jim Bottomley

| Dec 17, 1932 | CIN | N | ——— | STL | N | Estel Crabtree
Ownie Carroll |
| March 21, 1936 | STL | A | ——— | CIN | N | Johnny Burnett |

Ed Bouchee

| May 13, 1960 | CHI | N | Don Cardwell | PHI | N | Tony Taylor
Cal Neeman |

Medric Boucher

| Aug 1914 | PIT | F | ——— | BAL | F | Doc Kerr |

Carl Bouldin

| July 13, 1964 | CHI | A | Bill Skowron | WAS | A | Joe Cunningham
Frank Kreutzer |

Chris Bourjos

| Dec 8, 1980 | HOU | N | Bob Knepper | SF | N | Enos Cabell |
| April 1, 1981 | BAL | A | cash | HOU | N | Kiko Garcia |

Pat Bourque

Aug 29, 1973	OAK	A	———	CHI	N	Gonzalo Marquez
Aug 19, 1974	MIN	A	———	OAK	A	Jim Holt
Oct 23, 1974	OAK	A	———	MIN	A	Dan Ford minor league P Denny Myers

Jim Bouton

| Oct 21, 1968 | SEA | A | ——— | NY | A | Cash |
| Aug 24, 1969 | HOU | N | ——— | SEA | A | Dooley Womack
Roric Harrison |

Larry Bowa

| Jan 27, 1982 | CHI | N | Ryne Sandberg | PHI | N | Ivan DeJesus |

DATE	TRADED TO		TRADED WITH	TRADED BY		IN EXCHANGE FOR

Sam Bowens
| Nov 28, 1967 | WAS | A | ———— | BAL | A | Cash |

Frank Bowerman
| Feb 1900 | NY | N | ———— | PIT | N | Cash |
| Dec 3, 1907 | BOS | N | ———— | NY | N | *See Fred Tenney* |

Bob Bowman
| Dec 5, 1940 | NY | N | ———— | STL | N | Cash |
| Dec 4, 1941 | CHI | N | ———— | NY | N | Hank Leiber |

Ernie Bowman
| Dec 3, 1963 | MIL | N | *See Felipe Alou* | SF | N | |

Joe Bowman
| Dec 13, 1934 | PHI | N | ———— | NY | N | Kiddo Davis |
| April 16, 1937 | PIT | N | ———— | PHI | N | Earl Browne |

Roger Bowman
| May 12, 1953 | PIT | N | ———— | NY | N | Waiver price |

Ted Bowsfield
June 13, 1960	CLE	A	Marty Keough	BOS	A	Russ Nixon
						Carroll Hardy
July 23, 1962	KC	A	Gordie Windhorn	LA	A	Dan Osinski
			(Kansas City received Bowsfield on November 30.)			

Bob Boyd
| Jan 24, 1961 | KC | A | ———— | BAL | A | *See Russ Snyder* |
| June 10, 1961 | MIL | N | ———— | KC | A | Cash |

Clete Boyer
Feb 19, 1957	NY	A	Art Ditmar	KC	A	Billy Hunter
			Bobby Shantz			Rip Coleman
			Jack McMahan			Tom Morgan
			Wayne Belardi			Mickey McDermott
			Curt Roberts			Milt Graff
						Irv Noren
			(New York received Roberts on April 4, and Boyer on June 4, 1957.)			
Nov 29, 1966	ATL	N	————	NY	A	Bill Robinson
						Chi Chi Olivo

Ken Boyer
Oct 20, 1965	NY	N	————	STL	N	Charley Smith
						Al Jackson
July 22, 1967	CHI	A	————	NY	N	J. C. Martin
						Bill Southworth

Dorian Boyland
| Dec 11, 1981 | SF | N | ———— | PIT | N | Tom Griffin |

Gene Brabender
| March 31, 1969 | SEA | A | Gordon Lund | BAL | A | Chico Salmon |
| Jan 28, 1971 | CAL | A | ———— | MIL | A | Bill Voss |

Gib Brack
| July 11, 1938 | PHI | N | ———— | BKN | N | Tuck Stainback |

DATE	TRADED TO		TRADED WITH	TRADED BY		IN EXCHANGE FOR

Buddy Bradford

June 15, 1970	CLE	A	————	CHI	A	Barry Moore Bob Miller
May 8, 1971	CIN	N	————	CLE	A	Kurt Bevacqua
June 30, 1975	STL	N	———	CHI	A	Bill Parsons and cash
Dec 12, 1975	CHI	A	Greg Terlecky	STL	N	Lee Richard

Bert Bradley

| Dec 8, 1984 | NY | A | *See Rickey Henderson* | OAK | A | |

Fred Bradley

| Feb 24, 1948 | CHI | A | Aaron Robinson
Bill Wight | NY | A | Ed Lopat |

Hugh Bradley

| Feb 1915 | NWK | F | Larry Pratt
Tom Seaton | BKN | F | Cy Falkenberg |

Mark Bradley

| March 29, 1983 | NY | N | ———— | LA | N | Minor league
Ps Steve Walker
Jody Johnston
and cash |

Tom Bradley

| Nov 30, 1970 | CHI | A | ———— | CAL | A | *See Ken Berry* |
| Nov 28, 1972 | SF | N | ——— | CHI | A | Ken Henderson
Steve Stone |

Charlie Brady

| Oct 1906 | PIT | N | ——— | PHI | N | Cash |

Bobby Bragan

| March 24, 1943 | BKN | N | ———— | PHI | N | Tex Kraus
and cash |

Dave Brain

July 4, 1905	PIT	N	————	STL	N	George McBride
Dec 15, 1905	BOS	N	Del Howard Vive Lindaman	PIT	N	Vic Willis
Feb 1908	CIN	N	————	BOS	N	Cash
July 1908	NY	N	————	CIN	N	Cash

Ralph Branca

| July 10, 1953 | DET | A | ———— | BKN | N | Waiver price |

Harvey Branch

| Sept 1, 1962 | STL | N | ———— | CHI | N | Paul Toth |

Darrell Brandon

| Sept 14, 1965 | BOS | A | ———— | HOU | N | Jack Lamabe |
| July 8, 1969 | MIN | A | ———— | SEA | A | Cash |

DATE	TRADED TO		TRADED WITH	TRADED BY		IN EXCHANGE FOR

Ed Brandt

Dec 12, 1935	BKN	N	Randy Moore	BOS	N	Tony Cuccinello Al Lopez Ray Benge Bobby Reis
Dec 4, 1936	PIT	N	————	BKN	N	Cookie Lavagetto Ralph Birkofer

Jackie Brandt

June 14, 1956	NY	N	Red Schoendienst Bobby Stephenson Dick Littlefield Bill Sarni	STL	N	Alvin Dark Ray Katt Don Liddle Whitey Lockman
Nov 30, 1959	BAL	A	Gordon Jones Roger McCardell	SF	N	Billy O'Dell Billy Loes
Dec 6, 1965	PHI	N	Darold Knowles	BAL	A	Jack Baldschun
June 3, 1967	HOU	N	————	PHI	N	Cash

Kitty Bransfield

Dec 20, 1904	PHI	N	Otto Krueger Moose McCormick	PIT	N	Del Howard
Aug 9, 1911	CHI	N	————	PHI	N	Cash

Marshall Brant

April 1, 1980	NY	A	————	NY	N	Cash
June 15, 1983	OAK	A	Ben Callahan and cash	NY	A	Matt Keough

Steve Braun

June 1, 1978	KC	A	————	SEA	A	Jim Colborn

Angel Bravo

Dec 15, 1969	CIN	N	————	CHI	A	Jerry Arrigo
May 13, 1971	SD	N	————	CIN	N	Al Ferrara

Garland Braxton

Aug 27, 1926	WAS	A	Nick Cullop	NY	A	Dutch Ruether

(New York sent Braxton and Cullop to Washington on October 19, 1926.)

June 16, 1930	CHI	A	Bennie Tate	WAS	A	Art Shires
July 13, 1931	STL	A	————	CHI	A	Waiver price

Danny Breeden

Dec 3, 1968	SD	N	Ed Spiezio Ron Davis minor league P Phil Knuckles	STL	N	Dave Giusti
June 30, 1969	CIN	N	————	SD	N	Cash
Nov 30, 1970	CHI	N	————	CIN	N	Willie Smith
Nov 18, 1974	STL	N	Ed Brinkman	SD	N	Alan Foster Rich Folkers Sonny Siebert

(Part of three-team trade involving San Diego, Detroit, and St. Louis Cardinals.)

Hal Breeden

Nov 30, 1970	CHI	N	————	ATL	N	Hoyt Wilhelm
April 7, 1972	MON	N	Hector Torres	CHI	N	Dan McGinn

DATE	TRADED TO		TRADED WITH	TRADED BY		IN EXCHANGE FOR

Marv Breeding

| Dec 5, 1962 | WAS | A | Barry Shetrone and minor league P Art Quick | BAL | A | Bob Johnson Pete Burnside |
| July 20, 1963 | LA | N | ———— | WAS | A | Ed Roebuck |

Fred Breining

| June 28, 1979 | SF | N | ———— | PIT | N | *See Bill Madlock* |
| Feb 27, 1984 | MON | N | Max Venable Andy McGaffigan | SF | N | Al Oliver |

(San Francisco sent McGaffigan to Montreal on April 1, 1984, after Breining reported to the Expos with a sore arm.)

Ad Brennan

| Jan 20, 1910 | PHI | N | ———— | CIN | N | Harry Coveleski |
| June 1918 | CLE | A | ———— | WAS | A | Cash |

Tom Brennan

| Jan 21, 1984 | CHI | A | ———— | CLE | A | Player to be named later |

Roger Bresnahan

| Dec 12, 1908 | STL | N | ———— | NY | N | Admiral Schlei Bugs Raymond Red Murray |
| June 8, 1913 | CHI | N | ———— | STL | N | Cash |

Rube Bressler

| March 13, 1928 | BKN | N | ———— | CIN | N | Waiver price |
| June 28, 1932 | STL | N | ———— | PHI | N | Waiver price |

Ed Bressoud

Nov 26, 1961	BOS	A	————	HOU	N	Don Buddin
Nov 30, 1965	NY	N	————	BOS	A	Joe Christopher
April 1, 1967	STL	N	Danny Napoleon and cash	NY	N	Jerry Buchek Art Mahaffey Tony Martinez

Ken Brett

Oct 11, 1971	MIL	A	*See George Scott*	BOS	A	————
Oct 31, 1972	PHI	N	————	MIL	A	*See Don Money*
Oct 18, 1973	PIT	N	————	PHI	N	Dave Cash
Dec 11, 1975	NY	A	Willie Randolph Dock Ellis	PIT	N	Doc Medich
May 18, 1976	CHI	A	Rich Coggins	NY	A	Carlos May
June 15, 1977	CAL	A	————	CHI	A	Don Kirkwood John Verhoeven John Flannery

Jim Brewer

| Dec 13, 1963 | LA | N | Cuno Barragan | CHI | N | Dick Scott |
| July 15, 1975 | CAL | A | ———— | LA | N | Cash |

Charlie Brewster

| June 6, 1943 | PHI | N | ———— | CIN | N | Dain Clay |

Fred Brickell

| Aug 7, 1930 | PHI | N | ———— | PIT | N | Denny Sothern |

DATE	TRADED TO		TRADED WITH	TRADED BY		IN EXCHANGE FOR

Fritzie Brickell

| April 4, 1961 | LA | A | ———— | NY | A | Duke Maas |

Jim Brideweser

May 11, 1954	BAL	A	————	NY	A	Waiver price
Dec 6, 1954	CHI	A	*See Clint Courtney*	BAL	A	————
May 15, 1956	DET	A	Harry Byrd Bob Kennedy	CHI	A	Fred Hatfield Jim Delsing
Feb 8, 1957	BAL	A	————	DET	A	Cash
Oct 14, 1958	STL	N	Art Ceccarelli	BAL	A	Jim Finigan

Marshall Bridges

| Aug 2, 1960 | CIN | N | ———— | STL | N | Waiver price |
| Nov 27, 1963 | WAS | A | ———— | NY | A | Cash |

Rocky Bridges

| Feb 16, 1953 | MIL | N | Jim Pendleton | BKN | N | Russ Meyer |

(Part of four-team trade involving Milwaukee, Philadelphia Phillies, Brooklyn, and Cincinnati.)

| Feb 16, 1953 | CIN | N | cash | MIL | N | Joe Adcock |

(Part of four-team trade involving Milwaukee Braves, Philadelphia Phillies, Brooklyn, and Cincinnati.)

May 20, 1957	WAS	A	————	CIN	N	Waiver price
Dec 6, 1958	DET	A	Eddie Yost Neil Chrisley	WAS	A	Reno Bertoia Ron Samford Jim Delsing
July 26, 1960	CLE	A	Red Wilson	DET	A	Hank Foiles
Sept 2, 1960	STL	N	————	CLE	A	Cash

Al Bridwell

March 1906	BOS	N	————	CIN	N	Jim Delahanty Chick Fraser
Dec 3, 1907	NY	N	Fred Tenney Tom Needham	BOS	N	Dan McGann Frank Bowerman Bill Dahlen George Browne George Ferguson
July 22, 1911	BOS	N	Hank Gowdy	NY	N	Buck Herzog
Nov 1912	CHI	N	————	BOS	N	Cash

Buttons Briggs

| Dec 30, 1905 | BKN | N | Billy Maloney
Jack McCarthy
Doc Casey
and $2,000. | CHI | N | Jimmy Sheckard |

Dan Briggs

March 30, 1979	SD	N	————	CLE	A	Mike Champion
Nov 27, 1979	MON	N	Bill Almon	SD	N	Dave Cash
March 16, 1982	CHI	N	————	MON	N	Mike Griffin

John Briggs

| April 22, 1971 | MIL | A | ———— | PHI | N | Ray Peters
Pete Koegel |
| June 14, 1975 | MIN | A | ———— | MIL | A | Bobby Darwin |

Johnny Briggs

| Jan 23, 1959 | CLE | A | Jim Bolger | CHI | N | Earl Averill |

DATE	TRADED TO		TRADED WITH	TRADED BY		IN EXCHANGE FOR

Johnny Briggs continued

| July 30, 1960 | KC | A | ———— | CLE | A | Cash |
| Jan 25, 1961 | CIN | N | John Tsitouris | KC | A | Joe Nuxhall |

Harry Bright

Dec 16, 1960	WAS	A	Bennie Daniels R C Stevens	PIT	N	Bobby Shantz
Nov 24, 1962	CIN	N	————	WAS	A	Rogelio Alvarez
April 21, 1963	NY	A	————	CIN	N	Cash

Nellie Briles

Jan 29, 1971	PIT	N	Vic Davalillo	STL	N	Matty Alou George Brunet
Dec 4, 1973	KC	A	Fernando Gonzalez	PIT	N	Ed Kirkpatrick Kurt Bevacqua minor league 1B Winston Cole
Nov 12, 1975	TEX	A	————	KC	A	Dave Nelson
Sept 19, 1977	BAL	A	————	TEX	A	Cash

Chuck Brinkman

| July 11, 1974 | PIT | N | ———— | CHI | A | Cash |

Ed Brinkman

| Oct 9, 1970 | DET | A | Joe Coleman
Aurelio Rodriguez
Jim Hannan | WAS | A | Denny McLain
Don Wert
Norm McRae
Elliott Maddox |
| Nov 18, 1974 | SD | N | Bob Strampe
Dick Sharon | DET | A | Nate Colbert |

(Part of three-team trade involving San Diego, Detroit, and St. Louis Cardinals.)

| Nov 18, 1974 | STL | N | Danny Breeden | SD | N | Alan Foster
Rich Folkers
Sonny Siebert |

(Part of three-team trade involving San Diego, Detroit, and St. Louis Cardinals.)

| June 4, 1975 | TEX | A | Tommy Moore | STL | N | Willie Davis |
| June 13, 1975 | NY | A | ———— | TEX | A | Cash |

Lou Brissie

| April 30, 1951 | CLE | A | ———— | PHI | A | Sam Zoldak
Ray Murray
Minnie Minoso |

(Part of three-team trade involving Cleveland, Philadelphia A's, and Chicago White Sox.)

Jim Britton

| Dec 2, 1969 | MON | N | minor league
C Don Johnson | ATL | N | Larry Jaster |

Johnny Broaca

| Nov 1938 | CLE | A | ———— | NY | A | Waiver price |

Pete Broberg

Dec 5, 1974	MIL	A	————	TEX	A	Clyde Wright
April 20, 1977	CHI	N	————	SEA	A	Jim Todd
March 29, 1978	OAK	A	————	CHI	N	Rodney Scott and cash

DATE	TRADED TO		TRADED WITH	TRADED BY		IN EXCHANGE FOR

Jim Busby continued

DATE	TRADED TO		TRADED WITH	TRADED BY		IN EXCHANGE FOR
June 13, 1957	BAL	A	————	CLE	A	Dick Williams
Dec 15, 1958	BOS	A	————	BAL	A	Billy Klaus

Donie Bush

DATE	TRADED TO		TRADED WITH	TRADED BY		IN EXCHANGE FOR
Aug 20, 1921	WAS	A	————	DET	A	Waiver price

Guy Bush

DATE	TRADED TO		TRADED WITH	TRADED BY		IN EXCHANGE FOR
Nov 22, 1934	PIT	N	Jim Weaver Babe Herman	CHI	N	Larry French Freddie Lindstrom
Feb 2, 1938	STL	N	————	BOS	N	Cash

Joe Bush

DATE	TRADED TO		TRADED WITH	TRADED BY		IN EXCHANGE FOR
Dec 14, 1917	BOS	A	Amos Strunk Wally Schang	PHI	A	Vean Gregg Merlin Kopp Pinch Thomas and $60,000.
Dec 20, 1921	NY	A	Everett Scott Sad Sam Jones	BOS	A	Roger Peckinpaugh Jack Quinn Rip Collins Bill Piercy
Dec 17, 1924	STL	A	Milt Gaston Joe Giard	NY	A	Urban Shocker
Feb 1926	WAS	A	Jack Tobin	STL	A	Tom Zachary Win Ballou
July 1, 1926	PIT	N	————	WAS	A	Cash

Mike Buskey

DATE	TRADED TO		TRADED WITH	TRADED BY		IN EXCHANGE FOR
Dec 10, 1975	PHI	N	Jim Kaat	CHI	A	Dick Ruthven Roy Thomas Alan Bannister
Sept 11, 1978	HOU	N	————	PHI	N	Cash

Tom Buskey

DATE	TRADED TO		TRADED WITH	TRADED BY		IN EXCHANGE FOR
April 27, 1974	CLE	A	————	NY	A	*See Chris Chambliss*
Feb 28, 1978	TEX	A	John Lowenstein	CLE	A	Willie Horton David Clyde

Ray Busse

DATE	TRADED TO		TRADED WITH	TRADED BY		IN EXCHANGE FOR
Nov 28, 1972	STL	N	Bobby Fenwick	HOU	N	Skip Jutze Milt Ramirez
June 8, 1973	HOU	N	————	STL	N	Stan Papi

John Butcher

DATE	TRADED TO		TRADED WITH	TRADED BY		IN EXCHANGE FOR
Dec 7, 1983	MIN	A	Mike Smithson minor league C Sam Sorce	TEX	A	Gary Ward

Max Butcher

DATE	TRADED TO		TRADED WITH	TRADED BY		IN EXCHANGE FOR
Aug 8, 1938	PHI	N	————	BKN	N	Wayne LaMaster
July 28, 1939	PIT	N	————	PHI	N	Gus Suhr

Sal Butera

DATE	TRADED TO		TRADED WITH	TRADED BY		IN EXCHANGE FOR
March 25, 1983	DET	A	————	MIN	A	Minor league C Stine Poole and cash

Art Butler

DATE	TRADED TO		TRADED WITH	TRADED BY		IN EXCHANGE FOR
Jan 1912	PIT	N	————	BOS	N	Cash

DATE	TRADED TO		TRADED WITH	TRADED BY		IN EXCHANGE FOR

Art Butler continued

| Dec 12, 1913 | STL | N | ———— | PIT | N | *See Ed Konetchy* |

Bill Butler

| July 11, 1972 | CLE | A | ———— | KC | A | Cash |

Brett Butler

| Aug 28, 1983 | CLE | A | Rick Behenna
Brook Jacoby
and $150,000. | ATL | N | Len Barker |

(Butler and Jacoby were sent to Cleveland at the end of the season.)

Johnny Butler

| Dec 1927 | CHI | N | ———— | BKN | N | Howard Freigau |

John Buzhardt

Jan 11, 1960	PHI	N	Alvin Dark Jim Woods	CHI	N	Richie Ashburn
Nov 28, 1961	CHI	A	Charley Smith	PHI	N	Roy Sievers
Aug 21, 1967	BAL	A	————	CHI	A	Cash
Sept 23, 1967	HOU	N	————	BAL	A	Cash

Bud Byerly

| June 15, 1952 | BKN | N | cash | CIN | N | Bud Podbielan |
| June 24, 1958 | BOS | A | ———— | WAS | A | Jack Spring |

Harry Byrd

Dec 16, 1953	NY	A	Eddie Robinson Tom Hamilton Carmen Mauro Loren Babe	PHI	A	Don Bollweg John Gray Jim Robertson Jim Finigan Vic Power Bill Renna
Nov 18, 1954	BAL	A	————	NY	A	*See Bob Turley*
June 15, 1955	CHI	A	————	BAL	A	Waiver price
May 15, 1956	DET	A	Jim Brideweser Bob Kennedy	CHI	A	Fred Hatfield Jim Delsing

Sammy Byrd

| Dec 19, 1934 | CIN | N | ———— | NY | A | Cash |

Bobby Byrne

Aug 19, 1909	PIT	N	————	STL	N	Jap Barbeau Alan Storke
Aug 20, 1913	PHI	N	Howie Camnitz	PIT	N	Cozy Dolan and cash
Sept 1917	CHI	A	————	PHI	N	Waiver price

Tommy Byrne

June 15, 1951	STL	A	$25,000.	NY	A	Stubby Overmire
Oct 16, 1952	CHI	A	Joe DeMaestri	STL	A	Willie Miranda Hank Edwards
June 11, 1953	WAS	A	————	CHI	A	Cash

Marty Bystrom

| June 30, 1984 | NY | A | minor league
OF Keith Hughes | PHI | N | Shane Rawley |

DATE	TRADED TO		TRADED WITH	TRADED BY		IN EXCHANGE FOR

Enos Cabell

DATE	TRADED TO		TRADED WITH	TRADED BY		IN EXCHANGE FOR
Dec 3, 1974	HOU	N	Rob Andrews	BAL	A	Lee May Jay Schlueter
Dec 8, 1980	SF	N	————	HOU	N	Bob Knepper Chris Bourjos
March 4, 1982	DET	A	cash	SF	N	Champ Summers
Feb 14, 1984	HOU	N	————	DET	A	No compensation (free agent signing)

Craig Cacek

DATE	TRADED TO		TRADED WITH	TRADED BY		IN EXCHANGE FOR
Dec 17, 1981	CAL	A	————	PIT	N	Cash

Leon Cadore

DATE	TRADED TO		TRADED WITH	TRADED BY		IN EXCHANGE FOR
July 6, 1923	CHI	A	————	BKN	N	Waiver price

Hick Cady

DATE	TRADED TO		TRADED WITH	TRADED BY		IN EXCHANGE FOR
Jan 10, 1918	PHI	A	Larry Gardner Tilly Walker	BOS	A	Stuffy McInnis

Wayne Cage

DATE	TRADED TO		TRADED WITH	TRADED BY		IN EXCHANGE FOR
March 26, 1981	SEA	A	————	CLE	A	Rodney Craig

Bob Cain

DATE	TRADED TO		TRADED WITH	TRADED BY		IN EXCHANGE FOR
May 15, 1951	DET	A	————	CHI	A	Saul Rogovin
Feb 14, 1952	STL	A	Gene Bearden Dick Kryhoski	DET	A	Dick Littlefield Ben Taylor Cliff Mapes
Dec 17, 1953	PHI	A	————	BAL	A	Frank Fanovich Joe Coleman

Sugar Cain

DATE	TRADED TO		TRADED WITH	TRADED BY		IN EXCHANGE FOR
May 21, 1935	STL	A	Ed Coleman	PHI	A	George Blaeholder
May 5, 1936	CHI	A	————	STL	A	Les Tietje

Sammy Calderone

DATE	TRADED TO		TRADED WITH	TRADED BY		IN EXCHANGE FOR
Feb 1, 1954	MIL	N	————	NY	N	*See Johnny Antonelli*

Mike Caldwell

DATE	TRADED TO		TRADED WITH	TRADED BY		IN EXCHANGE FOR
Oct 25, 1973	SF	N	————	SD	N	Willie McCovey Bernie Williams
Oct 20, 1976	STL	N	John D'Acquisto Dave Rader	SF	N	Willie Crawford Vic Harris John Curtis
March 29, 1977	CIN	N	————	STL	N	Pat Darcy
June 15, 1977	MIL	A	————	CIN	N	Minor leaguers P Dick O'Keefe and IF Garry Pyka

Ray Caldwell

DATE	TRADED TO		TRADED WITH	TRADED BY		IN EXCHANGE FOR
Dec 18, 1918	BOS	A	Frank Gilhooley Slim Love Roxy Walters and $15,000.	NY	A	Ernie Shore Duffy Lewis Dutch Leonard

Ben Callahan

DATE	TRADED TO		TRADED WITH	TRADED BY		IN EXCHANGE FOR
June 15, 1983	OAK	A	Marshall Brant and cash	NY	A	Matt Keough

DATE	TRADED TO		TRADED WITH	TRADED BY		IN EXCHANGE FOR

Johnny Callison

Dec 9, 1959	PHI	N	————	CHI	A	Gene Freese
Nov 17, 1969	CHI	N	————	PHI	N	Dick Selma Oscar Gamble
Jan 20, 1972	NY	A	————	CHI	N	Jack Aker

Paul Calvert

| Feb 15, 1950 | DET | A | ———— | WAS | A | Waiver price |

Ernie Camacho

April 6, 1981	PIT	N	cash	OAK	A	Bob Owchinko
March 21, 1982	CHI	A	Vance Law	PIT	N	Ross Baumgarten Butch Edge
June 6, 1983	CLE	A	Gorman Thomas Jamie Easterly	MIL	A	Rick Manning Rick Waits

Hank Camelli

| Sept 30, 1946 | BOS | N | Bob Elliott | PIT | N | Billy Herman
Elmer Singleton
Stan Wentzel
Whitey Wietelmann |

Dolf Camilli

June 11, 1934	PHI	N	————	CHI	N	Don Hurst
March 6, 1938	BKN	N	————	PHI	N	Eddie Morgan and $45,000.
July 31, 1943	NY	N	Johnny Allen	BKN	N	Bill Lohrman Bill Sayles Joe Orengo

(Camilli refused to report to New York and retired.)

Doug Camilli

| Nov 30, 1964 | WAS | A | ———— | LA | N | Cash |

Howie Camnitz

| Aug 20, 1913 | PHI | N | Bobby Byrne | PIT | N | Cozy Dolan
and cash |

Bert Campaneris

| Nov 17, 1976 | TEX | A | ———— | OAK | A | No compensation
(free agent signing) |
| May 4, 1979 | CAL | A | ———— | TEX | A | Dave Chalk |

Jim Campanis

| Dec 15, 1968 | KC | A | ———— | LA | N | Two minor leaguers |
| Dec 2, 1970 | PIT | N | ———— | KC | A | *See Freddie Patek* |

Bill Campbell

Nov 6, 1976	BOS	A	————	MIN	A	No compensation (free agent signing)
Dec 8, 1981	CHI	N	————	BOS	A	No compensation (free agent signing)
March 26, 1984	PHI	N	Mike Diaz	CHI	N	Gary Matthews Bob Dernier Porfirio Altamirano

Bruce Campbell

| April 27, 1932 | STL | A | Bump Hadley | CHI | A | Red Kress |

DATE	TRADED TO		TRADED WITH	TRADED BY		IN EXCHANGE FOR

Bruce Campbell continued

Nov 20, 1934	CLE	A	————	STL	A	Johnny Burnett Bob Weiland and cash
Jan 20, 1940	DET	A	————	CLE	A	Beau Bell
Dec 12, 1941	WAS	A	Frank Croucher	DET	A	Jimmy Bloodworth Doc Cramer

Dave Campbell

March 31, 1979	MON	N	————	ATL	N	Pepe Frias

Dave Campbell

Dec 4, 1969	SD	N	Pat Dobson	DET	A	Joe Niekro
June 7, 1973	STL	N	————	SD	N	Dwain Anderson
Aug 18, 1973	HOU	N	cash	STL	N	Tommie Agee

Jim Campbell

Oct 9, 1963	CIN	N	————	HOU	N	Cash

Jim Campbell

Oct 21, 1970	BOS	A	————	STL	N	Dick Schofield

Ron Campbell

Jan 15, 1969	PIT	N	Chuck Hartenstein	CHI	N	Manny Jimenez

Vin Campbell

Jan 1910	PIT	N	————	CHI	N	Cash
Feb 1912	BOS	N	————	PIT	N	Mike Donlin

Card Camper

May 28, 1976	CLE	A	————	STL	N	Cash

Sal Campisi

Oct 20, 1970	MIN	A	Jim Kennedy	STL	N	Herman Hill minor league OF Charlie Wissler

Milo Candini

Jan 29, 1943	WAS	A	Gerry Priddy	NY	A	Bill Zuber and cash

Chris Cannizzaro

Dec 7, 1966	NY	A	————	NY	N	Cash
Dec 19, 1966	DET	A	————	NY	A	Cash
Nov 29, 1967	PIT	N	————	DET	A	Cash
March 28, 1969	SD	N	Tommie Sisk	PIT	N	Ron Davis Bobby Klaus
May 19, 1971	CHI	N	————	SD	N	Garry Jestadt
Dec 17, 1971	LA	N	————	CHI	N	Cash

Joe Cannon

Nov 27, 1978	TOR	A	Pedro Hernandez Mark Lemongello	HOU	N	Alan Ashby

Ben Cantwell

June 15, 1928	BOS	N	Al Spohrer Bill Clarkson Virgil Barnes	NY	N	Joe Genewich

DATE	TRADED TO		TRADED WITH	TRADED BY		IN EXCHANGE FOR
Ben Cantwell continued						
Jan 27, 1937	NY	N	Hal Lee	BOS	N	Cash
Aug 9, 1937	BKN	N	————	NY	N	Cash
Doug Capilla						
June 15, 1977	CIN	N	————	STL	N	Rawley Eastwick
May 3, 1979	CHI	N	————	CIN	N	Minor league P Mark Gilbert
Dec 7, 1981	SF	N	————	CHI	N	Allen Ripley
George Cappuzzello						
March 6, 1978	CIN	N	minor league OF John Valle	DET	A	Jack Billingham
Buzz Capra						
March 26, 1974	ATL	N	————	NY	N	Cash
Ralph Capron						
Jan 1913	PHI	N	————	PIT	N	Cash
Bernie Carbo						
May 19, 1972	STL	N	————	CIN	N	Joe Hague
Oct 26, 1973	BOS	A	Rick Wise	STL	N	Reggie Smith Ken Tatum
June 3, 1976	MIL	A	————	BOS	A	Tom Murphy Bobby Darwin
Dec 6, 1976	BOS	A	George Scott	MIL	A	Cecil Cooper
June 15, 1978	CLE	A	————	BOS	A	Cash
March 10, 1979	STL	N	————	CLE	A	No compensation (free agent signing)
Jose Cardenal						
Nov 21, 1964	LA	A	————	SF	N	Jack Hiatt
Nov 29, 1967	CLE	A	————	CAL	A	Chuck Hinton
Nov 21, 1969	STL	N	————	CLE	A	Vada Pinson
July 29, 1971	MIL	A	Dick Schofield Bob Reynolds	STL	N	Ted Kubiak minor league P Charlie Loseth
Dec 3, 1971	CHI	N	————	MIL	A	Brock Davis Jim Colborn Earl Stephenson
Oct 25, 1977	PHI	N	————	CHI	N	Minor league P Manny Seaone
Aug 2, 1979	NY	N	————	PHI	N	Cash
Leo Cardenas						
Nov 21, 1968	MIN	A	————	CIN	N	Jim Merritt
Nov 30, 1971	CAL	A	————	MIN	A	Dave LaRoche
April 2, 1973	CLE	A	————	CAL	A	Tom McCraw and minor league 2B Bob Marcano
Feb 12, 1974	TEX	A	————	CLE	A	Ken Suarez
Don Cardwell						
May 13, 1960	CHI	N	Ed Bouchee	PHI	N	Tony Taylor Cal Neeman

DATE	TRADED TO		TRADED WITH	TRADED BY		IN EXCHANGE FOR

Darrel Chaney
| Dec 12, 1975 | ATL | N | ———— | CIN | N | Mike Lum |

Charlie Chant
| Oct 28, 1975 | STL | N | ———— | OAK | A | Larry Lintz |

Tiny Chaplin
| Jan 17, 1936 | BOS | N | ———— | NY | N | Cash |

Ben Chapman
June 14, 1936	WAS	A	————	NY	A	Jake Powell
June 11, 1937	BOS	A	Bobo Newsom	WAS	A	Wes Ferrell Rick Ferrell Mel Almada
Dec 15, 1938	CLE	A	————	BOS	A	Denny Galehouse Tommy Irwin
Dec 24, 1940	WAS	A	————	CLE	A	Joe Krakauskas
June 15, 1945	PHI	N	————	BKN	N	Johnny Peacock

Harry Chapman
| Dec 15, 1912 | CIN | N | *See Joe Tinker* | CHI | N | ———— |
| Feb 10, 1916 | STL | A | *See Eddie Plank* | STL | F | ———— |

Sam Chapman
| May 10, 1951 | CLE | A | ———— | PHI | A | Allie Clark
Lou Klein |

Larry Chappell
| Aug 21, 1915 | CLE | A | Braggo Roth
Ed Klepfer
and $31,500. | CHI | A | Joe Jackson |
| May 1916 | BOS | N | ———— | CLE | A | Cash |

Bill Chappelle
| May 24, 1909 | CIN | N | ———— | BOS | N | Cash |

Chappy Charles
| Aug 22, 1909 | CIN | N | ———— | STL | N | Mike Mowrey |

Ed Charles
| Dec 15, 1961 | KC | A | Joe Azcue
Manny Jimenez | MIL | N | Bob Shaw
Lou Klimchock |
| May 10, 1967 | NY | N | ———— | KC | A | Larry Elliot
and $50,000. |

Mike Chartak
| June 7, 1942 | STL | A | Steve Sundra | WAS | A | Roy Cullenbine
Bill Trotter |

Hal Chase
| June 1, 1913 | CHI | A | ———— | NY | A | Rollie Zeider
Babe Borton |
| Feb 2, 1919 | NY | N | ———— | CIN | N | Bill Rariden |

Ken Chase
| Dec 13, 1941 | BOS | A | Johnny Welaj | WAS | A | Stan Spence
Jack Wilson |

DATE	TRADED TO		TRADED WITH	TRADED BY		IN EXCHANGE FOR

Ossie Chavarria

| Dec 5, 1969 | NY | A | Danny Cater | OAK | A | Al Downing
Frank Fernandez |

Dave Cheadle

| June 7, 1973 | ATL | N | Frank Tepedino
Wayne Nordhagen
Al Closter | NY | A | Pat Dobson |

Charlie Chech

| Feb 18, 1909 | BOS | A | Jack Ryan
and $12,500. | CLE | A | Cy Young |

Larry Cheney

Aug 1915	BKN	N	———	CHI	N	Joe Schultz and $3,000.
June 1919	BOS	N	———	BKN	N	Waiver price
Aug 1919	PHI	N	———	BOS	N	Waiver price

Tom Cheney

| Dec 21, 1959 | PIT | N | Gino Cimoli | STL | N | Ron Kline |
| June 29, 1961 | WAS | A | ——— | PIT | N | Tom Sturdivant |

Jack Chesbro

| Jan 1900 | LOU | N | ——— | PIT | N | *See Honus Wagner* |
| Sept 11, 1909 | BOS | A | ——— | NY | A | Waiver price |

Floyd Chiffer

| Dec 7, 1984 | MIN | A | ——— | SD | N | Ray Smith |

Cupid Childs

| Jan 1900 | CHI | N | ——— | STL | N | Cash |

Rich Chiles

| Nov 27, 1972 | NY | N | Buddy Harris | HOU | N | Tommie Agee |

Lou Chiozza

| Dec 8, 1936 | NY | N | ——— | PHI | N | George Scharein
and cash |

Bob Chipman

| June 6, 1944 | CHI | N | ——— | BKN | N | Eddie Stanky |
| April 18, 1950 | BOS | N | ——— | CHI | N | Cash |

Tom Chism

| Dec 7, 1979 | MIN | A | ——— | BAL | A | Dan Graham |

Harry Chiti

July 26, 1960	DET	A	———	KC	A	Cash
Nov 16, 1961	CLE	A	Ray Barker and minor leaguer Art Kay	BAL	A	Johnny Temple
April 26, 1962	NY	N	———	CLE	A	Cash

Nels Chittum

| March 15, 1959 | BOS | A | ——— | STL | N | Dean Stone |
| May 6, 1960 | LA | N | ——— | BOS | A | Rip Repulski |

DATE	TRADED TO		TRADED WITH	TRADED BY		IN EXCHANGE FOR

Bob Chlupsa
| June 20, 1972 | SD | N | Mike Fiore | STL | N | Rafael Robles |

(Fiore was returned to St. Louis on July 3.)

Don Choate
| March 25, 1959 | SF | N | Sam Jones | STL | N | Bill White
Ray Jablonski |

Mike Chris
| Dec 9, 1981 | SF | N | Dan Schatzeder | DET | A | Larry Herndon |
| Sept 30, 1983 | CHI | N | —————— | SF | N | Cash |

Neil Chrisley
Nov 8, 1955	WAS	A	——————	BOS	A	*See Mickey Vernon*
Dec 6, 1958	DET	A	*See Eddie Yost*	WAS	A	——————
Dec 7, 1960	MIL	N	——————	DET	A	*See Bill Bruton*
Oct 16, 1961	NY	N	——————	MIL	N	Cash

Bob Christian
| Sept 30, 1968 | CHI | A | —————— | DET | A | Cash |

Mark Christman
| May 13, 1939 | STL | A | —————— | DET | A | *See Beau Bell* |
| April 9, 1947 | WAS | A | —————— | STL | A | Cash |

Steve Christmas
| Nov 21, 1983 | CHI | A | —————— | CIN | N | Fran Mullins |

Joe Christopher
| Nov 30, 1965 | BOS | A | —————— | NY | N | Ed Bressoud |
| June 14, 1966 | DET | A | Earl Wilson | BOS | A | Julio Navarro
Don Demeter |

Russ Christopher
| April 3, 1948 | CLE | A | —————— | PHI | A | Cash |

Bubba Church
| May 23, 1952 | CIN | N | —————— | PHI | N | Johnny Wyrostek
Kent Peterson |
| June 12, 1953 | CHI | N | —————— | CIN | N | Fred Baczewski
Bob Kelly |

Chuck Churn
| March 26, 1958 | CLE | A | —————— | BOS | A | Waiver price |

Al Cicotte
May 14, 1958	WAS	A	——————	NY	A	Cash
June 23, 1958	DET	A	——————	WAS	A	Vito Valentinetti
Nov 20, 1958	CLE	A	Billy Martin	DET	A	Don Mossi Ray Narleski Ossie Alvarez
Jan 26, 1961	STL	N	——————	LA	A	Leon Wagner Cal Browning Ellis Burton and cash
Oct 13, 1961	HOU	N	——————	STL	N	Cash

DATE	TRADED TO		TRADED WITH	TRADED BY		IN EXCHANGE FOR

Eddie Cicotte

| July 22, 1912 | CHI | A | ——— | BOS | A | Cash |

Pete Cimino

| Dec 2, 1966 | CAL | A | ——— | MIN | A | *See Dean Chance* |

Gino Cimoli

Dec 4, 1958	STL	N	———	LA	N	Wally Moon Phil Paine
Dec 21, 1959	PIT	N	Tom Cheney	STL	N	Ron Kline
June 15, 1961	MIL	N	———	PIT	N	Johnny Logan

Galen Cisco

| Sept 7, 1962 | NY | N | | BOS | A | Waiver price |

Bill Cissell

April 24, 1932	CLE	A	Jim Moore	CHI	A	Johnny Hodapp Bob Seeds
Oct 12, 1933	BOS	A	———	CLE	A	Lloyd Brown
March 1938	NY	N	———	PHI	A	Cash

Doug Clarey

| March 30, 1977 | NY | N | ——— | STL | N | Benny Ayala |

Allie Clark

Oct 10, 1947	CLE	A	———	NY	A	Red Embree
May 10, 1951	PHI	A	Lou Klein	CLE	A	Sam Chapman
May 12, 1953	CHI	A	———	PHI	A	Waiver price

Bobby Clark

| Dec 20, 1983 | MIL | A | ——— | CAL | A | Jim Slaton |

Bryan Clark

| Dec 8, 1983 | TOR | A | ——— | SEA | A | Barry Bonnell |

Cap Clark

| Dec 8, 1937 | PHI | N | ——— | STL | A | Earl Grace |

Danny Clark

| Oct 30, 1922 | BOS | A | Carl Holling
Howard Ehmke
Babe Herman
and $25,000. | DET | A | Del Pratt
Rip Collins |

Jim Clark

| July 10, 1972 | KC | A | ——— | CLE | A | Tom Hilgendorf |

Rickey Clark

| Jan 29, 1973 | PHI | N | ——— | CAL | A | Cash |

Ron Clark

Jan 15, 1970	OAK	A	*See Don Mincher*	MIL	A	———
June 20, 1972	MIL	A	———	OAK	A	Bill Voss
July 28, 1972	CAL	A	Paul Ratliff	MIL	A	Syd O'Brien Joe Azcue

DATE	TRADED TO		TRADED WITH	TRADED BY		IN EXCHANGE FOR

Watty Clark
| June 16, 1933 | NY | N | Lefty O'Doul | BKN | N | Sam Leslie |

Fred Clarke
| Jan 1900 | PIT | N | *See Honus Wagner* | LOU | N | ———— |

Horace Clarke
| May 31, 1974 | SD | N | ———— | NY | A | Cash |

Nig Clarke
Aug 1, 1905	DET	A	————	CLE	A	Cash
Aug 11, 1905	CLE	A	————	DET	A	Cash
Oct 1910	STL	A	————	CLE	A	Art Griggs
Nov 1919	PIT	N	————	PHI	N	Waiver price

Tommy Clarke
| April 28, 1918 | NY | A | ———— | CIN | N | Lee Magee |

Bill Clarkson
| June 15, 1928 | BOS | N | Ben Cantwell
Al Spohrer
Virgil Barnes | NY | N | Joe Genewich |

Walter Clarkson
| May 16, 1907 | CLE | A | ———— | NY | A | Earl Moore |

Ellis Clary
| Aug 18, 1943 | STL | A | Ox Miller
and cash | WAS | A | Harlond Clift
Johnny Niggeling |

Dain Clay
| June 1, 1943 | PHI | N | Buster Adams
Coaker Triplett | STL | N | Danny Litwhiler
Earl Naylor |
| June 6, 1943 | CIN | N | ———— | PHI | N | Charlie Brewster |

Ken Clay
| Aug 14, 1980 | TEX | A | minor league
OF Marvin Thompson | NY | A | Gaylord Perry |
| Dec 12, 1980 | SEA | A | ———— | TEX | A | *See Rick Honeycutt* |

Mark Clear
| Dec 10, 1980 | BOS | A | Carney Lansford
Rick Miller | CAL | A | Rick Burleson
Butch Hobson |

Clem Clemens
| Feb 10, 1916 | CHI | N | *See Three Finger Brown* | CHI | F | ———— |

Doug Clemens
| June 15, 1964 | CHI | N | ———— | STL | N | *See Lou Brock* |
| Jan 10, 1966 | PHI | N | ———— | CHI | N | Wes Covington |

Jack Clements
| Jan 1900 | BOS | N | ———— | CLE | N | Cash |

Lance Clemons
| Dec 2, 1971 | HOU | N | Jim York | KC | A | John Mayberry
minor league
IF Dave Grangaard |

DATE	TRADED TO		TRADED WITH	TRADED BY		IN EXCHANGE FOR

Lance Clemons continued

DATE	TRADED TO		TRADED WITH	TRADED BY		IN EXCHANGE FOR
April 15, 1972	STL	N	Scipio Spinks	HOU	N	Jerry Reuss
Jan 24, 1973	BOS	A	———————	STL	N	Mike Nagy

Donn Clendenon

DATE	TRADED TO		TRADED WITH	TRADED BY		IN EXCHANGE FOR
Jan 22, 1969	HOU	N	Jesus Alou Jack Billingham Skip Guinn and $100,000.	MON	N	Rusty Staub

(Clendenon refused to report, and Houston was sent Billingham, Guinn, and cash on April 8, 1969.)

DATE	TRADED TO		TRADED WITH	TRADED BY		IN EXCHANGE FOR
June 15, 1969	NY	N	———————	MON	N	Steve Renko Kevin Collins minor league Ps Bill Carden and Dave Colon

Reggie Cleveland

DATE	TRADED TO		TRADED WITH	TRADED BY		IN EXCHANGE FOR
Dec 7, 1973	BOS	A	Diego Segui Terry Hughes	STL	N	Lynn McGlothen John Curtis Mike Garman
April 18, 1978	TEX	A	———————	BOS	A	Cash
Dec 15, 1978	MIL	A	———————	TEX	A	Ed Farmer Gary Holle and cash

Tex Clevenger

DATE	TRADED TO		TRADED WITH	TRADED BY		IN EXCHANGE FOR
Nov 8, 1955	WAS	A	———————	BOS	A	*See Mickey Vernon*
May 8, 1961	NY	A	Bob Cerv	LA	A	Lee Thomas Ryne Duren Johnny James

Harlond Clift

DATE	TRADED TO		TRADED WITH	TRADED BY		IN EXCHANGE FOR
Aug 18, 1943	WAS	A	Johnny Niggeling	STL	A	Ellis Clary Ox Miller and cash

Ty Cline

DATE	TRADED TO		TRADED WITH	TRADED BY		IN EXCHANGE FOR
Nov 27, 1962	MIL	N	Don Dillard Frank Funk	CLE	A	Joe Adcock Jack Curtis
May 31, 1967	SF	N	———————	ATL	N	Cash
June 15, 1970	CIN	N	———————	MON	N	Clyde Mashore

Gene Clines

DATE	TRADED TO		TRADED WITH	TRADED BY		IN EXCHANGE FOR
Oct 22, 1974	NY	N	———————	PIT	N	Duffy Dyer
Dec 12, 1975	TEX	A	———————	NY	N	Joe Lovitto
Feb 5, 1977	CHI	N	cash	TEX	A	Darold Knowles

Billy Clingman

DATE	TRADED TO		TRADED WITH	TRADED BY		IN EXCHANGE FOR
Jan 1900	CHI	N	———————	WAS	N	Cash

Lu Clinton

DATE	TRADED TO		TRADED WITH	TRADED BY		IN EXCHANGE FOR
June 4, 1964	LA	A	———————	BOS	A	Lee Thomas
Sept 9, 1965	CLE	A	———————	CAL	A	Waiver price

(Clinton was claimed on waivers by Kansas City and played one game for them before Cleveland's claim was upheld.)

DATE	TRADED TO		TRADED WITH	TRADED BY		IN EXCHANGE FOR
Jan 14, 1966	NY	A	———————	CLE	A	Doc Edwards

DATE	TRADED TO		TRADED WITH	TRADED BY		IN EXCHANGE FOR

Tony Cloninger

DATE	TRADED TO		TRADED WITH	TRADED BY		IN EXCHANGE FOR
June 11, 1968	CIN	N	Woody Woodward Clay Carroll	ATL	N	Milt Pappas Ted Davidson Bob Johnson
March 24, 1972	STL	N	————	CIN	N	Julian Javier

Al Closter

DATE	TRADED TO		TRADED WITH	TRADED BY		IN EXCHANGE FOR
April 5, 1966	WAS	A	————	CLE	A	Cash
May 3, 1966	NY	A	————	WAS	A	Cash
June 7, 1973	ATL	N	Frank Tepedino Wayne Nordhagen Dave Cheadle	NY	A	Pat Dobson

David Clyde

DATE	TRADED TO		TRADED WITH	TRADED BY		IN EXCHANGE FOR
Feb 28, 1978	CLE	A	Willie Horton	TEX	A	Tom Buskey John Lowenstein
Jan 4, 1980	TEX	A	Jim Norris	CLE	A	Larry McCall Gary Gray minor league 3B-OF Mike Bucci

Otis Clymer

DATE	TRADED TO		TRADED WITH	TRADED BY		IN EXCHANGE FOR
June 26, 1907	WAS	A	————	PIT	N	Cash
July 1913	BOS	N	————	CHI	N	Cash

Andy Coakley

DATE	TRADED TO		TRADED WITH	TRADED BY		IN EXCHANGE FOR
Sept 1908	CHI	N	————	CIN	N	Cash

Gil Coan

DATE	TRADED TO		TRADED WITH	TRADED BY		IN EXCHANGE FOR
Feb 18, 1954	BAL	A	————	WAS	A	Roy Sievers
July 17, 1955	CHI	A	————	BAL	A	Waiver price
Aug 26, 1955	NY	N	————	CHI	A	Waiver price

Jim Coates

DATE	TRADED TO		TRADED WITH	TRADED BY		IN EXCHANGE FOR
April 21, 1963	WAS	A	————	NY	A	Steve Hamilton

Mickey Cochrane

DATE	TRADED TO		TRADED WITH	TRADED BY		IN EXCHANGE FOR
Dec 12, 1933	DET	A	————	PHI	A	Johnny Pasek and $100,000.

Jack Coffey

DATE	TRADED TO		TRADED WITH	TRADED BY		IN EXCHANGE FOR
July 1918	BOS	A	————	DET	A	Cash

Dick Coffman

DATE	TRADED TO		TRADED WITH	TRADED BY		IN EXCHANGE FOR
Oct 19, 1927	STL	A	Earl McNeely	WAS	A	Milt Gaston
June 9, 1932	WAS	A	————	STL	A	Carl Fischer
Dec 13, 1932	STL	A	————	WAS	A	Carl Fischer
Nov 14, 1935	NY	N	————	STL	A	Cash

Slick Coffman

DATE	TRADED TO		TRADED WITH	TRADED BY		IN EXCHANGE FOR
Dec 9, 1939	PHI	A	Benny McCoy	DET	A	Wally Moses

(Commissioner Landis ruled that Detroit had kept McCoy covered up in the minors and declared him a free agent, cancelling the deal. McCoy then signed with Philadelphia for a $10,000 bonus.)

DATE	TRADED TO		TRADED WITH	TRADED BY		IN EXCHANGE FOR
Jan 30, 1940	STL	A	————	DET	A	Billy Sullivan

DATE	TRADED TO		TRADED WITH	TRADED BY		IN EXCHANGE FOR

Frank Coggins

| April 4, 1970 | CLE | A | Roy Foster and cash | MIL | A | Max Alvis Russ Snyder |

Rich Coggins

Dec 4, 1974	MON	N	Dave McNally minor league P Bill Kirkpatrick	BAL	A	Ken Singleton Mike Torrez
June 20, 1975	NY	A	——————	MON	N	Cash
May 18, 1976	CHI	A	Ken Brett	NY	A	Carlos May
July 14, 1976	PHI	N	——————	CHI	A	Wayne Nordhagen

Jimmie Coker

Nov 21, 1962	BAL	A	——————	PHI	N	Cash
Dec 15, 1962	SF	N	——————	BAL	A	*See Mike McCormick*
Oct 1, 1963	STL	N	——————	SF	N	Ken MacKenzie
April 9, 1964	MIL	N	Gary Kolb	STL	N	Bob Uecker

Rocky Colavito

April 17, 1960	DET	A	——————	CLE	A	Harvey Kuenn
Nov 18, 1963	KC	A	Bob Anderson and $50,000.	DET	A	Jerry Lumpe Ed Rakow Dave Wickersham
Jan 20, 1965	CHI	A	——————	KC	A	Jim Landis Mike Hershberger Fred Talbot

(Part of three-team trade involving Kansas City, Cleveland, and the Chicago White Sox.)

| Jan 20, 1965 | CLE | A | Cam Carreon | CHI | A | Tommy John Tommie Agee Johnny Romano |

(Part of three-team trade involving Kansas City, Cleveland, and Chicago White Sox.)

| July 29, 1967 | CHI | A | —————— | CLE | A | Jim King Marv Staehle |
| March 26, 1968 | LA | N | —————— | CHI | A | Cash |

Nate Colbert

| Nov 18, 1974 | DET | A | —————— | SD | N | Ed Brinkman Bob Strampe Dick Sharon |

(Part of three-team trade involving San Diego, Detroit, and St. Louis Cardinals.)

| June 15, 1975 | MON | N | —————— | DET | A | Cash |

Vince Colbert

| Nov 30, 1972 | TEX | A | —————— | CLE | A | Tom Ragland |
| March 8, 1973 | CLE | A | Rich Hinton | TEX | A | Alex Johnson |

Jim Colborn

Dec 3, 1971	MIL	A	Brock Davis Earl Stephenson	CHI	N	Jose Cardenal
Dec 6, 1976	KC	A	Darrell Porter	MIL	A	Jim Wohlford Jamie Quirk Bob McClure
June 1, 1978	SEA	A	——————	KC	A	Steve Braun

Bert Cole

| July 1925 | CLE | A | —————— | DET | A | Cash |

DATE	TRADED TO		TRADED WITH	TRADED BY		IN EXCHANGE FOR

Dave Cole

| March 20, 1954 | CHI | N | cash | MIL | N | Roy Smalley |
| March 19, 1955 | PHI | N | ———— | CHI | N | Cash |

Dick Cole

| June 15, 1951 | PIT | N | *See Joe Garagiola* | STL | N | ———— |
| April 3, 1957 | MIL | N | ———— | PIT | N | Jim Pendleton |

Ed Cole

| Feb 10, 1938 | STL | A | Roy Hughes
Billy Sullivan | CLE | A | Rollie Hemsley |

King Cole

| June 22, 1912 | PIT | N | Solly Hofman | CHI | N | Tommy Leach
Lefty Leifield |

Dave Coleman

| Feb 3, 1979 | MIN | A | ———— | BOS | A | Larry Wolfe |

Ed Coleman

| May 21, 1935 | STL | A | Sugar Cain | PHI | A | George Blaeholder |

Gordy Coleman

| Dec 15, 1959 | CIN | N | Cal McLish
Billy Martin | CLE | A | Johnny Temple |

Joe Coleman

Oct 9, 1970	DET	A	Ed Brinkman Aurelio Rodriguez Jim Hannan	WAS	A	Denny McLain Don Wert Norm McRae Elliott Maddox
June 8, 1976	CHI	N	————	DET	A	Cash
March 15, 1977	OAK	A	————	CHI	N	Jim Todd
May 22, 1978	TOR	A	————	OAK	A	Cash

Joe Coleman

| Dec 17, 1953 | BAL | A | Frank Fanovich | PHI | A | Bob Cain |

Ray Coleman

June 4, 1948	PHI	A	————	STL	A	George Binks and $20,000.
Dec 13, 1949	STL	A	Frankie Gustine Billy DeMars minor league OF Ray Ippolito and $100,000.	PHI	A	Bob Dillinger Paul Lehner
July 31, 1951	CHI	A	————	STL	A	Waiver price
July 28, 1952	STL	A	J. W. Porter	CHI	A	Jim Rivera Darrell Johnson
Oct 14, 1952	BKN	N	Bob Mahoney Stan Rojek and $90,000.	STL	A	Billy Hunter

Rip Coleman

| Feb 19, 1957 | KC | A | *See Billy Hunter* | NY | A | ———— |
| Sept 6, 1959 | BAL | A | ———— | KC | A | Waiver price |

DATE	TRADED TO		TRADED WITH	TRADED BY		IN EXCHANGE FOR

Chris Coletta

Aug 15, 1972	CAL	A	————	BOS	A	Andy Kosco
Aug 14, 1973	PHI	N	Aurelio Monteagudo Billy Grabarkewitz	CAL	A	Denny Doyle

Bill Collins

June 10, 1911	CHI	N	————	BOS	N	*See Johnny Kling*

Dave Collins

Dec 9, 1977	CIN	N	————	SEA	A	Shane Rawley
Dec 23, 1981	NY	A	————	CIN	N	No compensation (free agent signing)
Dec 9, 1982	TOR	A	Mike Morgan minor league 1B Fred McGriff and $400,000.	NY	A	Dale Murray minor league OF Tom Dodd
Dec 8, 1984	OAK	A	Alfredo Griffin and cash	TOR	A	Bill Caudill

Don Collins

Feb 15, 1980	CLE	A	————	ATL	N	Minor league P Gary Melson

Eddie Collins

Dec 8, 1914	CHI	A	————	PHI	A	$50,000.

Jimmy Collins

June 7, 1907	PHI	A	————	BOS	A	Jack Knight

Joe Collins

March 20, 1958	PHI	N	———— (Collins refused to report and retired.)	NY	A	Cash

Kevin Collins

June 15, 1969	MON	N	Steve Renko minor league Ps Bill Carden and Dave Colon	NY	N	Donn Clendenon
June 15, 1973	CLE	A	Tom Timmerman	DET	A	Ed Farmer

Pat Collins

Dec 13, 1928	BOS	N	————	NY	A	$7,500.

Phil Collins

May 18, 1935	STL	N	————	PHI	N	Cash

Rip Collins

Dec 20, 1921	BOS	A	Roger Peckinpaugh Jack Quinn Bill Piercy	NY	A	Everett Scott Joe Bush Sad Sam Jones
Oct 30, 1922	DET	A	Del Pratt	BOS	A	Carl Holling Howard Ehmke Danny Clark Babe Herman and $25,000.

Ripper Collins

Oct 8, 1936	CHI	N	Roy Parmelee	STL	N	Lon Warneke

DATE	TRADED TO		TRADED WITH	TRADED BY		IN EXCHANGE FOR

Shano Collins

| March 4, 1921 | BOS | A | Nemo Leibold | CHI | A | Harry Hooper |

Zip Collins

| Sept 3, 1915 | BOS | N | ———— | PIT | N | Cash |

Jackie Collum

May 23, 1953	CIN	N	————	STL	N	Eddie Erautt
Jan 31, 1956	STL	N	————	CIN	N	Brooks Lawrence Sonny Senerchia
Dec 11, 1956	CHI	N	*See Tom Poholsky*	STL	N	————
May 23, 1957	BKN	N	————	CHI	N	Don Elston Vito Valentinetti
Aug 20, 1962	CLE	A	Georges Maranda and cash	MIN	A	Ruben Gomez

Bob Coluccio

May 8, 1975	CHI	A	————	MIL	A	Bill Sharp
June 8, 1978	STL	N	————	HOU	N	Frank Riccelli
Oct 2, 1978	NY	N	————	STL	N	Paul Siebert

Merrill Combs

| May 8, 1950 | WAS | A | Tommy O'Brien | BOS | A | Clyde Vollmer |
| April 1, 1951 | CLE | A | Snuffy Stirnweiss | STL | A | Freddie Marsh
and $35,000. |

Wayne Comer

| March 23, 1963 | DET | A | ———— | WAS | A | Bobo Osborne |
| May 11, 1970 | WAS | A | ———— | MIL | A | Hank Allen
Ron Theobald |

Adam Comorosky

| Nov 17, 1933 | CIN | N | Tony Piet | PIT | N | Red Lucas
Wally Roettger |

Pete Compton

| June 1916 | PIT | N | ———— | BOS | N | Cash |

(Pittsburgh returned Compton to Boston ten days later.)

Bunk Congalton

| May 20, 1907 | BOS | A | ———— | CLE | A | Cash |

Billy Conigliaro

| Oct 11, 1971 | MIL | A | *See George Scott* | BOS | A | ———— |
| Feb 14, 1973 | OAK | A | ———— | MIL | A | Cash |

Tony Conigliaro

| Oct 11, 1970 | CAL | A | Ray Jarvis
Gerry Moses | BOS | A | Ken Tatum
Jarvis Tatum
Doug Griffin |

Gene Conley

| March 31, 1959 | PHI | N | Joe Koppe
Harry Hanebrink | MIL | N | Stan Lopata
Ted Kazanski
Johnny O'Brien |
| Dec 15, 1960 | BOS | A | ———— | PHI | N | Frank Sullivan |

DATE	TRADED TO		TRADED WITH	TRADED BY		IN EXCHANGE FOR

Fritzie Connally

| Dec 7, 1983 | SD | N | Carmelo Martinez
Craig Lefferts | CHI | N | Scott Sanderson |

(Part of three-team trade involving Chicago Cubs, San Diego, and Montreal.)

Bruce Connatser

| Dec 15, 1932 | WAS | A | Jack Russell | CLE | A | Harley Boss |

Joe Connolly

| April 10, 1913 | BOS | N | —————— | WAS | A | Cash |

Joe Connolly

| Jan 7, 1924 | BOS | A | *See Bill Wambsganss* | CLE | A | —————— |

Joe Connor

| June 1901 | CLE | A | —————— | MIL | A | Cash |

Bill Connors

| Aug 20, 1967 | NY | N | —————— | CHI | N | Cash |

Chuck Connors

| Oct 10, 1950 | CHI | N | Dee Fondy | BKN | N | Hank Edwards
and cash |

Billy Consolo

| June 11, 1959 | WAS | A | Murray Wall | BOS | A | Dick Hyde
Herb Plews |

(Hyde was returned to Washington and Wall was returned to Boston.)

June 1, 1961	MIL	N	——————	MIN	A	Billy Martin
May 8, 1962	LA	A	——————	PHI	N	Cash
June 26, 1962	KC	A	——————	LA	A	Cash

Jim Constable

| June 7, 1958 | CLE | A | —————— | SF | N | Waiver price |
| July 12, 1958 | WAS | A | —————— | CLE | A | Waiver price |

Sandy Consuegra

May 12, 1953	CHI	A	——————	WAS	A	Cash
May 14, 1956	BAL	A	——————	CHI	A	Cash
May 14, 1957	NY	N	——————	BAL	A	Waiver price

Jack Conway

| Jan 16, 1948 | NY | N | —————— | CLE | A | Cash |

Cliff Cook

| May 7, 1962 | NY | N | Bob Miller | CIN | N | Don Zimmer |

Dusty Cooke

| Dec 8, 1938 | STL | N | —————— | CIN | N | Frenchy Bordagaray |

Duff Cooley

Feb 1900	PIT	N	——————	PHI	N	Tully Sparks Heinie Reitz
May 1901	BOS	N	——————	PIT	N	Cash
Oct 1904	DET	A	——————	BOS	N	Waiver price

DATE	TRADED TO		TRADED WITH	TRADED BY		IN EXCHANGE FOR

Danny Coombs
| Oct 22, 1969 | SD | N | ———— | HOU | N | Cash |

Jimmy Cooney
Dec 11, 1925	CHI	N	————	STL	N	Vic Keen
June 7, 1927	PHI	N	Tony Kaufmann	CHI	N	Hal Carlson
Dec 13, 1927	STL	N	Johnny Mokan Bubber Jonnard	PHI	N	Johnny Schulte Jimmy Ring
Feb 3, 1928	BOS	N	————	STL	N	Waiver price

Johnny Cooney
| Oct 4, 1937 | STL | N | Jim Bucher
Joe Stripp
Roy Henshaw | BKN | N | Leo Durocher |

Cecil Cooper
| Dec 6, 1976 | MIL | A | ———— | BOS | A | George Scott
Bernie Carbo |

Claude Cooper
| Feb 10, 1916 | PHI | N | ———— | BKN | F | Cash |

Don Cooper
| Dec 10, 1982 | TOR | A | ———— | MIN | A | Dave Baker |

Guy Cooper
| May 27, 1914 | BOS | A | ———— | NY | A | Cash |

Mort Cooper
| May 23, 1945 | BOS | N | ———— | STL | N | Red Barrett
and $60,000. |
| June 13, 1947 | NY | N | ———— | BOS | N | Bill Voiselle
and cash |

Walker Cooper
Jan 5, 1946	NY	N	————	STL	N	$175,000.
June 13, 1949	CIN	N	————	NY	N	Ray Mueller
May 10, 1950	BOS	N	————	CIN	N	Connie Ryan
May 19, 1954	CHI	N	————	PIT	N	Waiver price

Wilbur Cooper
| Oct 27, 1924 | CHI | N | Charlie Grimm,
Rabbit Maranville | PIT | N | Vic Aldridge
George Grantham
Al Niehaus |
| June 7, 1926 | DET | A | ———— | CHI | N | Waiver price |

Doug Corbett
| May 12, 1982 | CAL | A | Rob Wilfong | MIN | A | Tom Brunansky
Mike Walters
and $400,000. |

Claude Corbitt
| March 18, 1946 | CIN | N | ———— | BKN | N | Cash |

Tim Corcoran
| Aug 23, 1981 | MIN | A | ———— | DET | A | Ron Jackson |

DATE	TRADED TO		TRADED WITH	TRADED BY		IN EXCHANGE FOR

Mardie Cornejo

| March 13, 1979 | DET | A | ———— | NY | N | Ed Glynn |

Pat Corrales

Oct 27, 1965	STL	N	Art Mahaffey Alex Johnson	PHI	N	Bill White Dick Groat Bob Uecker
Feb 8, 1968	CIN	N	minor league IF Jimmy Williams	STL	N	Johnny Edwards
June 11, 1972	SD	N	————	CIN	N	Bob Barton

Vic Correll

| March 26, 1974 | ATL | N | | BOS | A | Chuck Goggin |

Red Corriden

| Nov 16, 1912 | CIN | N | ———— | DET | A | Cash |
| Dec 15, 1912 | CHI | N | ———— | CIN | N | *See Joe Tinker* |

Frank Corridon

July 20, 1904	PHI	N	Jack Sutthoff	CHI	N	Shad Barry
Jan 20, 1910	CIN	N	————	PHI	N	Bob Ewing
Feb 1910	STL	N	Miller Huggins Rebel Oakes	CIN	N	Fred Beebe Alan Storke

Pete Coscarart

| Dec 12, 1941 | PIT | N | Luke Hamlin
Babe Phelps
Jimmy Wasdell | BKN | N | Arky Vaughan |

Dan Costello

| Jan 1914 | PIT | N | ———— | NY | A | Waiver price |

Dick Cotter

| Oct 1911 | CHI | N | ———— | PHI | N | Peaches Graham |

Chuck Cottier

Dec 7, 1960	DET	A	Bill Bruton Terry Fox Dick Brown	MIL	N	Frank Bolling Neil Chrisley
June 5, 1961	WAS	A	————	DET	A	Hal Woodeshick
Feb 16, 1967	CAL	A	————	WAS	A	Cash

Henry Cotto

| Dec 4, 1984 | NY | A | Ron Hassey
Rich Bordi
Porfirio Altamirano | CHI | N | Ray Fontenot
Brian Dayett |

Ensign Cottrell

| Jan 1912 | CHI | N | ———— | PIT | N | Cash |
| April 18, 1915 | NY | A | ———— | BOS | N | Cash |

Johnny Couch

| Aug 2, 1923 | PHI | N | ———— | CIN | N | Waiver price |

Bill Coughlin

| Aug 10, 1904 | DET | A | Lew Drill | WAS | A | $7,500. |

DATE	TRADED TO		TRADED WITH	TRADED BY		IN EXCHANGE FOR

General Crowder

DATE	TRADED TO		TRADED WITH	TRADED BY		IN EXCHANGE FOR
July 7, 1927	STL	A	——————	WAS	A	Tom Zachary
June 13, 1930	WAS	A	Heinie Manush	STL	A	Goose Goslin
Aug 4, 1934	DET	A	——————	WAS	A	Waiver price

George Crowe

| April 9, 1956 | CIN | N | —————— | MIL | N | Bob Hazle
Corky Valentine |
| Oct 3, 1958 | STL | N | Alex Kellner
Alex Grammas | CIN | N | Bob Mabe
Eddie Kasko
Del Ennis |

Terry Crowley

Dec 6, 1973	TEX	A	——————	BAL	A	Cash
March 19, 1974	CIN	N	——————	TEX	A	Cash
April 7, 1976	ATL	N	——————	CIN	N	Mike Thompson

Walt Cruise

| May 1919 | BOS | N | —————— | STL | N | Cash |

Hector Cruz

Dec 8, 1977	CHI	N	Dave Rader	STL	N	Jerry Morales Steve Swisher and cash
June 15, 1978	SF	N	——————	CHI	N	Lynn McGlothen
June 28, 1979	CIN	N	——————	SF	N	Pedro Borbon
Dec 12, 1980	CHI	N	——————	CIN	N	Mike Vail

Henry Cruz

| Sept 2, 1977 | CHI | A | —————— | LA | N | Cash |

Jose Cruz

| Oct 24, 1974 | HOU | N | —————— | STL | N | Cash |

Julio Cruz

| June 15, 1983 | CHI | A | —————— | SEA | A | Tony Bernazard |

Todd Cruz

April 3, 1979	KC	A	——————	PHI	N	Doug Bird
Dec 6, 1979	CAL	A	Al Cowens Craig Eaton	KC	A	Rance Mulliniks Willie Aikens
June 12, 1980	CHI	A	——————	CAL	A	Randy Scarbery
Dec 11, 1981	SEA	A	Jim Essian Rod Allen	CHI	A	Tom Paciorek
June 30, 1983	BAL	A	——————	SEA	A	Cash

Tommy Cruz

| Oct 26, 1973 | TEX | A | cash | STL | N | Sonny Siebert |
| Dec 12, 1977 | NY | A | Jim Spencer
minor league
P Bob Polinsky | CHI | A | Stan Thomas
minor league
P Ed Ricks |

Victor Cruz

| Dec 6, 1977 | TOR | A | Tom Underwood | STL | N | Pete Vuckovich
John Scott |

DATE	TRADED TO		TRADED WITH	TRADED BY		IN EXCHANGE FOR

Victor Cruz continued

| Dec 5, 1978 | CLE | A | ———— | TOR | A | Alfredo Griffin minor league 3B Phil Lansford |
| Dec 9, 1980 | PIT | N | Gary Alexander Rafael Vasquez Bob Owchinko | CLE | A | Bert Blyleven Manny Sanguillen |

Mike Cubbage

| June 1, 1976 | MIN | A | *See Roy Smalley* | TEX | A | ———— |
| Dec 19, 1980 | NY | N | ———— | MIN | A | No compensation (free agent signing) |

Tony Cuccinello

March 14, 1932	BKN	N	Joe Stripp Clyde Sukeforth	CIN	N	Babe Herman Wally Gilbert Ernie Lombardi
Dec 12, 1935	BOS	N	Al Lopez Ray Benge Bobby Reis	BKN	N	Ed Brandt Randy Moore
June 15, 1940	NY	N	————	BOS	N	Manny Salvo Al Glossop

Cookie Cuccurullo

| Oct 21, 1946 | NY | A | ———— | PIT | N | Ernie Bonham |

Bobby Cuellar

| Aug 31, 1978 | CLE | A | minor league OF Dave Rivera | TEX | A | Johnny Grubb |

Mike Cuellar

| June 15, 1965 | HOU | N | Ron Taylor | STL | N | Hal Woodeshick Chuck Taylor |
| Dec 4, 1968 | BAL | A | Enzo Hernandez and minor league IF Elijah Johnson | HOU | N | Curt Blefary and minor leaguer John Mason |

Leon Culberson

| Dec 10, 1947 | WAS | A | Al Kozar | BOS | A | Stan Spence |
| May 13, 1948 | NY | A | $15,000. | WAS | A | Bud Stewart |

Jack Cullen

| April 3, 1967 | LA | N | John Miller and $25,000. | NY | A | John Kennedy |

Tim Cullen

| Feb 13, 1968 | CHI | A | Buster Narum Bob Priddy | WAS | A | Dennis Higgins Steve Jones Ron Hansen |
| Aug 2, 1968 | WAS | A | ———— | CHI | A | Ron Hansen |

Roy Cullenbine

May 27, 1940	STL	A	————	BKN	N	Joe Gallagher
June 7, 1942	WAS	A	Bill Trotter	STL	A	Mike Chartak Steve Sundra
Aug 31, 1942	NY	A	————	WAS	A	Waiver price
Dec 17, 1942	CLE	A	Buddy Rosar	NY	A	Roy Weatherly Oscar Grimes

DATE	TRADED TO		TRADED WITH	TRADED BY		IN EXCHANGE FOR

Jerry DaVanon continued

DATE	TRADED TO		TRADED WITH	TRADED BY		IN EXCHANGE FOR
Nov 23, 1976	STL	N	Larry Dierker	HOU	N	Joe Ferguson Bob Detherage

Mike Davey

| Feb 23, 1979 | SEA | A | ———— | ATL | N | Cash |

Ted Davidson

| June 11, 1968 | ATL | N | *See Milt Pappas* | CIN | N | ———— |

Bill Davis

| Oct 21, 1968 | SD | N | ———— | CLE | A | Zoilo Versalles |
| May 22, 1969 | STL | N | Jerry DaVanon | SD | N | John Sipin
John Ruberto |

Brock Davis

| Dec 3, 1971 | MIL | A | Jim Colborn
Earl Stephenson | CHI | N | Jose Cardenal |
| Feb 25, 1975 | CLE | A | Dave LaRoche | CHI | N | Milt Wilcox |

Curt Davis

May 21, 1936	CHI	N	Ethan Allen	PHI	N	Chuck Klein Fabian Kowalik
April 16, 1938	STL	N	Clyde Shoun Tuck Stainback and $185,000.	CHI	N	Dizzy Dean
June 12, 1940	BKN	N	Joe Medwick	STL	N	Ernie Koy Carl Doyle Sam Nahem Bert Haas and $125,000.

Dick Davis

March 1, 1981	PHI	N	————	MIL	A	Randy Lerch
June 15, 1982	TOR	A	————	PHI	N	Wayne Nordhagen
June 22, 1982	PIT	N	————	TOR	A	Wayne Nordhagen

Dixie Davis

| Jan 21, 1919 | STL | N | Milt Stock
Pickles Dillhoefer | PHI | N | Doug Baird
Stuffy Stewart
Gene Packard |

George Davis

| Dec 1912 | BOS | N | Guy Zinn | NY | A | Cash |

Jacke Davis

Dec 11, 1962	LA	A	————	PHI	N	Earl Averill
March 29, 1963	SF	N	————	LA	A	Charlie Dees
July 29, 1963	STL	N	cash	NY	N	Duke Carmel

Jim Davis

| Dec 11, 1956 | STL | N | ———— | CHI | N | *See Tom Poholsky* |
| June 4, 1957 | NY | N | ———— | STL | N | Waiver price |

Kiddo Davis

| Dec 12, 1932 | NY | N | ———— | PHI | N | Gus Dugas
Chick Fullis |

(Part of three-team trade involving New York, Philadelphia, and Pittsburgh.)

DATE	TRADED TO		TRADED WITH	TRADED BY		IN EXCHANGE FOR

Kiddo Davis continued

DATE	TRADED TO		TRADED WITH	TRADED BY		IN EXCHANGE FOR
Feb 1934	STL	N	————	NY	N	George Watkins
June 15, 1934	PHI	N	————	STL	N	Chick Fullis
Dec 13, 1934	NY	N	————	PHI	N	Joe Bowman
Aug 4, 1937	CIN	N	————	NY	N	Cash

Lefty Davis

DATE	TRADED TO		TRADED WITH	TRADED BY		IN EXCHANGE FOR
May 1901	PIT	N	————	BKN	N	Tom McCreery

Mark Davis

DATE	TRADED TO		TRADED WITH	TRADED BY		IN EXCHANGE FOR
Dec 14, 1982	SF	N	Mike Krukow minor league OF Charles Penigar	PHI	N	Joe Morgan Al Holland

Peaches Davis

DATE	TRADED TO		TRADED WITH	TRADED BY		IN EXCHANGE FOR
Aug 19, 1939	PHI	N	————	CIN	N	Cash

Ron Davis

DATE	TRADED TO		TRADED WITH	TRADED BY		IN EXCHANGE FOR
June 15, 1968	STL	N	————	HOU	N	Dick Simpson Hal Gilson
Dec 3, 1968	SD	N	Danny Breeden Ed Spiezio minor league P Phil Knuckles	STL	N	Dave Giusti
March 28, 1969	PIT	N	Bobby Klaus	SD	N	Chris Cannizzaro Tommie Sisk

Ron Davis

DATE	TRADED TO		TRADED WITH	TRADED BY		IN EXCHANGE FOR
June 10, 1978	NY	A	————	CHI	N	Ken Holtzman
April 10, 1982	MIN	A	Paul Boris Greg Gagne	NY	A	Roy Smalley

Spud Davis

DATE	TRADED TO		TRADED WITH	TRADED BY		IN EXCHANGE FOR
May 11, 1928	PHI	N	Homer Peel	STL	N	Jimmie Wilson
Nov 15, 1933	STL	N	Eddie Delker (Wilson was named manager of the Phillies.)	PHI	N	Jimmie Wilson
Dec 2, 1936	CIN	N	————	STL	N	Cash
June 13, 1938	PHI	N	Al Hollingsworth and $50,000.	CIN	N	Bucky Walters
Oct 27, 1939	PIT	N	————	PHI	N	Cash

Tommy Davis

DATE	TRADED TO		TRADED WITH	TRADED BY		IN EXCHANGE FOR
Nov 29, 1966	NY	N	Derrell Griffith	LA	N	Ron Hunt Jim Hickman
Dec 15, 1967	CHI	A	Jack Fisher Billy Wynne Buddy Booker	NY	N	Tommie Agee Al Weis
Aug 30, 1969	HOU	N	————	SEA	A	Danny Walton Sandy Valdespino
June 22, 1970	OAK	A	————	HOU	N	Cash
Sept 16, 1970	CHI	N	————	OAK	A	Cash
Aug 18, 1972	BAL	A	————	CHI	N	Ellie Hendricks
Sept 20, 1976	KC	A	————	CAL	A	Cash

Willie Davis

DATE	TRADED TO		TRADED WITH	TRADED BY		IN EXCHANGE FOR
Dec 5, 1973	MON	N	————	LA	N	Mike Marshall

DATE	TRADED TO		TRADED WITH	TRADED BY		IN EXCHANGE FOR

Larry Dierker
| Nov 23, 1976 | STL | N | Jerry DaVanon | HOU | N | Joe Ferguson
Bob Detherage |

Bill Dietrich
| July 1, 1936 | WAS | A | ———— | PHI | A | Waiver price |
| July 20, 1936 | CHI | A | ———— | WAS | A | Waiver price |

Dick Dietz
| April 14, 1972 | LA | N | ———— | SF | N | Cash |
| March 27, 1973 | ATL | N | ———— | LA | N | Cash |

Dutch Dietz
| Aug 1940 | PIT | N | ———— | CIN | N | Cash |
| June 15, 1943 | PHI | N | ———— | PIT | N | Johnny Podgajny |

Don Dillard
| Nov 27, 1962 | MIL | N | Ty Cline
Frank Funk | CLE | A | Joe Adcock
Jack Curtis |

Steve Dillard
| Jan 30, 1978 | DET | A | ———— | BOS | A | Minor league
Ps Mike Burns
and Frank Harris
and cash |
| March 20, 1979 | CHI | N | ———— | DET | A | Ed Putman |

Pickles Dillhoefer
| Dec 11, 1917 | PHI | N | Mike Prendergast
and $55,000. | CHI | N | Grover Alexander
Bill Killefer |
| Jan 21, 1919 | STL | N | Milt Stock
Dixie Davis | PHI | N | Doug Baird
Stuffy Stewart
Gene Packard |

Bob Dillinger
Dec 13, 1949	PHI	A	Paul Lehner	STL	A	Ray Coleman Frankie Gustine Billy DeMars minor league OF Ray Ippolito and $100,000.
July 20, 1950	PIT	N	————	PHI	A	$35,000.
May 16, 1951	CHI	A	————	PIT	N	Cash

Bill Dillman
| Dec 5, 1969 | STL | N | ———— | BAL | A | Cash |

Pop Dillon
| Jan 1901 | DET | A | ———— | PIT | N | Cash |
| July 1902 | BAL | A | ———— | DET | A | Cash |

Miguel Dilone
April 4, 1978	OAK	A	Elias Sosa Mike Edwards	PIT	N	Manny Sanguillen
July 4, 1979	CHI	N	————	OAK	A	Cash
May 7, 1980	CLE	A	————	CHI	N	Cash
Aug 25, 1983	CHI	A	————	CLE	A	Rich Barnes

DATE	TRADED TO		TRADED WITH	TRADED BY		IN EXCHANGE FOR

Miguel Dilone continued

DATE	TRADED TO		TRADED WITH	TRADED BY		IN EXCHANGE FOR
Sept 7, 1983	PIT	N	minor league P Mike Maitland	CHI	A	Randy Niemann
Jan 19, 1984	MON	N	————	PIT	N	No compensation (free agent signing)

Vince DiMaggio

Aug 10, 1938	CIN	N	Tommy Reis Johnny Babich Gil English Johnny Riddle and cash	BOS	N	Eddie Miller
May 8, 1940	PIT	N	————	CIN	N	Johnny Rizzo
March 31, 1945	PHI	N	————	PIT	N	Al Gerheauser
May 1, 1946	NY	N	————	PHI	N	Clyde Kluttz

Kerry Dineen

March 26, 1977	PHI	N	————	NY	A	Sergio Ferrer

Bill Dinneen

Jan 10, 1900	BOS	N	Kirtley Baker Shad Barry	WAS	N	Cash
June 22, 1907	STL	A	————	BOS	A	Beany Jacobson and $1,000.

Frank DiPino

Aug 30, 1982	HOU	N	Kevin Bass Mike Madden and cash	MIL	A	Don Sutton

Art Ditmar

Feb 19, 1957	NY	A	Bobby Shantz Jack McMahan Wayne Belardi Curt Roberts Clete Boyer	KC	A	Billy Hunter Rip Coleman Tom Morgan Mickey McDermott Milt Graff Irv Noren

(New York received Roberts on April 4, and Boyer on June 4, 1957.)

June 14, 1961	KC	A	Deron Johnson	NY	A	Buddy Daley

Jack Dittmer

Feb 12, 1957	DET	A	————	MIL	N	Charlie King Cash

Sonny Dixon

June 11, 1954	CHI	A	————	WAS	A	Gus Keriazakos
June 11, 1954	PHI	A	Al Sima Bill Wilson and $20,000.	CHI	A	Ed McGhee Morrie Martin
May 11, 1955	NY	A	cash	KC	A	Johnny Sain Enos Slaughter

Bill Doak

June 13, 1924	BKN	N	————	STL	N	Leo Dickerman

Dan Dobbek

Jan 30, 1962	CIN	N	————	MIN	A	Jerry Zimmerman

John Dobbs

July 1902	CHI	N	————	CIN	N	Cash

DATE	TRADED TO		TRADED WITH	TRADED BY		IN EXCHANGE FOR

John Dobbs continued

DATE	TRADED TO		TRADED WITH	TRADED BY		IN EXCHANGE FOR
May 1903	BKN	N	————	CHI	N	Cash

Joe Dobson

DATE	TRADED TO		TRADED WITH	TRADED BY		IN EXCHANGE FOR
Dec 12, 1940	BOS	A	Frankie Pytlak Odell Hale	CLE	A	Gene Desautels Jim Bagby Gee Walker
Dec 10, 1950	CHI	A	Dick Littlefield Al Zarilla	BOS	A	Ray Scarborough Bill Wight

Pat Dobson

DATE	TRADED TO		TRADED WITH	TRADED BY		IN EXCHANGE FOR
Dec 4, 1969	SD	N	Dave Campbell	DET	A	Joe Niekro
Dec 1, 1970	BAL	A	Tom Dukes	SD	N	Tom Phoebus Al Severinsen Fred Beene Enzo Hernandez
Nov 30, 1972	ATL	N	Roric Harrison Davy Johnson Johnny Oates	BAL	A	Earl Williams Taylor Duncan
June 7, 1973	NY	A	————	ATL	N	Frank Tepedino Wayne Nordhagen Al Closter Dave Cheadle
Nov 22, 1975	CLE	A	————	NY	A	Oscar Gamble

Larry Doby

DATE	TRADED TO		TRADED WITH	TRADED BY		IN EXCHANGE FOR
Oct 25, 1955	CHI	A	————	CLE	A	Jim Busby Chico Carrasquel
Dec 3, 1957	BAL	A	Jack Harshman Russ Heman Jim Marshall	CHI	A	Tito Francona Ray Moore Billy Goodman
April 1, 1958	CLE	A	Don Ferrarese	BAL	A	Buddy Daley Dick Williams Gene Woodling
March 21, 1959	DET	A	————	CLE	A	Tito Francona
May 13, 1959	CHI	A	————	DET	A	$30,000.

John Dodge

DATE	TRADED TO		TRADED WITH	TRADED BY		IN EXCHANGE FOR
June 5, 1913	CIN	N	Red Nelson	PHI	N	Josh Devore Beals Becker

Ed Doheny

DATE	TRADED TO		TRADED WITH	TRADED BY		IN EXCHANGE FOR
June 1901	PIT	N	————	NY	N	Heinie Smith

Cozy Dolan

DATE	TRADED TO		TRADED WITH	TRADED BY		IN EXCHANGE FOR
May 1912	PHI	N	————	NY	A	Cash
Aug 20, 1913	PIT	N	cash	PHI	N	Bobby Byrne Howie Camnitz
Dec 12, 1913	STL	N	————	PIT	N	*See Ed Konetchy*

Cozy Dolan

DATE	TRADED TO		TRADED WITH	TRADED BY		IN EXCHANGE FOR
June 1901	BKN	N	————	CHI	N	Cash
June 9, 1903	CIN	N	Tom Daly	CHI	A	George Magoon
June 6, 1905	BOS	N	————	CIN	N	Cash

Joe Dolan

DATE	TRADED TO		TRADED WITH	TRADED BY		IN EXCHANGE FOR
May 1901	PHI	A	————	PHI	N	Cash

DATE	TRADED TO		TRADED WITH	TRADED BY		IN EXCHANGE FOR

Jiggs Donahue

DATE	TRADED TO		TRADED WITH	TRADED BY		IN EXCHANGE FOR
April 1901	MIL	A	————	PIT	N	Cash
May 16, 1909	WAS	A	Nick Altrock Gavvy Cravath	CHI	A	Bill Burns

Pat Donahue

DATE	TRADED TO		TRADED WITH	TRADED BY		IN EXCHANGE FOR
May 1910	PHI	A	————	BOS	A	Cash
Sept 1910	CLE	A	————	PHI	A	Cash

Red Donahue

DATE	TRADED TO		TRADED WITH	TRADED BY		IN EXCHANGE FOR
June 1903	CLE	A	————	STL	A	Completes Charlie Hemphill May, 1902.
Dec 1905	DET	A	————	CLE	A	Cash

John Donaldson

DATE	TRADED TO		TRADED WITH	TRADED BY		IN EXCHANGE FOR
June 14, 1969	SEA	A	————	OAK	A	Larry Haney
May 18, 1970	OAK	A	————	MIL	A	Roberto Pena
May 22, 1971	DET	A	————	OAK	A	Daryl Patterson

Mike Donlin

DATE	TRADED TO		TRADED WITH	TRADED BY		IN EXCHANGE FOR
July 3, 1904	NY	N	————	CIN	N	Moose McCormick
Aug 1, 1911	BOS	N	————	NY	N	Cash
Feb 1912	PIT	N	————	BOS	N	Vin Campbell
Dec 1912	PHI	N	————	PIT	N	Waiver price

(Donlin refused to report and announced his retirement.)

Blix Donnelly

DATE	TRADED TO		TRADED WITH	TRADED BY		IN EXCHANGE FOR
July 6, 1946	PHI	N	————	STL	N	Cash
April 16, 1951	BOS	N	————	PHI	N	Waiver price

Jim Donohue

DATE	TRADED TO		TRADED WITH	TRADED BY		IN EXCHANGE FOR
June 15, 1960	LA	N	————	STL	N	John Glenn
June 7, 1961	LA	A	————	DET	A	Jerry Casale
May 29, 1962	MIN	A	————	LA	A	Don Lee

Pete Donohue

DATE	TRADED TO		TRADED WITH	TRADED BY		IN EXCHANGE FOR
May 27, 1930	NY	N	Ethan Allen	CIN	N	Pat Crawford

Dick Donovan

DATE	TRADED TO		TRADED WITH	TRADED BY		IN EXCHANGE FOR
Oct 5, 1961	CLE	A	Gene Green Jim Mahoney	WAS	A	Jimmy Piersall

Mike Donovan

DATE	TRADED TO		TRADED WITH	TRADED BY		IN EXCHANGE FOR
Jan 1908	NY	A	————	CLE	A	Cash

Patsy Donovan

DATE	TRADED TO		TRADED WITH	TRADED BY		IN EXCHANGE FOR
Jan 1900	STL	N	————	PIT	N	$1,000.

Red Dooin

DATE	TRADED TO		TRADED WITH	TRADED BY		IN EXCHANGE FOR
Nov 1914	CIN	N	————	PHI	N	Bert Niehoff
July 6, 1915	NY	N	————	CIN	N	Waiver price

Mickey Doolan

DATE	TRADED TO		TRADED WITH	TRADED BY		IN EXCHANGE FOR
Feb 10, 1916	CHI	N	*See Three Finger Brown*	CHI	F	————

DATE	TRADED TO		TRADED WITH	TRADED BY		IN EXCHANGE FOR

Mickey Doolan continued

Aug 28, 1916	NY	N	Heinie Zimmerman	CHI	N	Larry Doyle
						Herb Hunter
						Merwin Jacobson

Tom Doran

May 18, 1905	DET	A	———————	BOS	A	Waiver price

Harry Dorish

May 9, 1950	STL	A	———————	BOS	A	Cash
June 6, 1955	BAL	A	———————	CHI	A	Les Moss
June 25, 1956	BOS	A	———————	BAL	A	Cash

Gus Dorner

May 13, 1906	BOS	N	———————	CIN	N	Cash

Jim Dorsey

Jan 23, 1981	BOS	A	Frank Tanana	CAL	A	Fred Lynn
			Joe Rudi			Steve Renko

Jack Doscher

June 1903	BKN	N	———————	CHI	N	Cash

Rich Dotson

Dec 5, 1977	CHI	A	Bobby Bonds	CAL	A	Brian Downing
			Thad Bosley			Chris Knapp
						Dave Frost

Patsy Dougherty

June 18, 1904	NY	A	———————	BOS	A	Bob Unglaub
June 6, 1906	CHI	A	———————	NY	A	Cash

Phil Douglas

June 13, 1915	BKN	N	———————	CIN	N	Cash
Sept 8, 1915	CHI	N	———————	BKN	N	Cash
July 25, 1919	NY	N	———————	CHI	N	Dave Robertson

Whammy Douglas

Jan 30, 1959	CIN	N	———————	PIT	N	*See Harvey Haddix*

Taylor Douthit

June 15, 1931	CIN	N	———————	STL	N	Wally Roettger
April 29, 1933	CHI	N	———————	CIN	N	Waiver price

Snooks Dowd

April 1919	PHI	A	———————	DET	A	Cash

Dave Dowling

May 11, 1965	CHI	N	———————	STL	N	Waiver price
April 22, 1968	STL	N	Pete Mikkelsen	CHI	N	Jack Lamabe
						Ron Piche

Pete Dowling

May 1901	CLE	A	———————	MIL	A	Cash

Tom Downey

Jan 18, 1909	CIN	N	Kid Durbin	CHI	N	Johnny Kane

DATE	TRADED TO		TRADED WITH	TRADED BY		IN EXCHANGE FOR

Tom Downey continued

| Aug 1912 | CHI | N | ———— | PHI | N | Cash |

Al Downing

Dec 5, 1969	OAK	A	Frank Fernandez	NY	A	Danny Cater Ossie Chavarria
June 11, 1970	MIL	A	Tito Francona	OAK	A	Steve Hovley
Feb 10, 1971	LA	N	————	MIL	A	Andy Kosco

Brian Downing

| Dec 5, 1977 | CAL | A | Chris Knapp
Dave Frost | CHI | A | Bobby Bonds
Thad Bosley
Rich Dotson |

Red Downs

| May 1912 | CHI | N | ———— | BKN | N | Cash |

Brian Doyle

| Feb 17, 1977 | NY | A | Greg Pryor
and cash | TEX | A | Sandy Alomar |
| Nov 3, 1980 | OAK | A | Fred Stanley | NY | A | Mike Morgan |

Carl Doyle

| June 12, 1940 | STL | N | Ernie Koy
Sam Nahem
Bert Haas
and $125,000. | BKN | N | Joe Medwick
Curt Davis |

Conny Doyle

| Jan 1900 | PIT | N | *See Honus Wagner* | LOU | N | ———— |

Denny Doyle

| Aug 14, 1973 | CAL | A | ———— | PHI | N | Aurelio Monteagudo
Chris Coletta
Billy Grabarkewitz |
| June 14, 1975 | BOS | A | ———— | CAL | A | Cash |

(California also received minor league P Chuck Ross on March 5, 1976.)

Jack Doyle

Feb 1901	CHI	N	————	NY	N	Sammy Strang
Feb 1902	NY	N	Jim Delahanty	CHI	N	Cash
Jan 30, 1903	BKN	N	————	WAS	A	Cash
April 30, 1904	PHI	N	Deacon Van Buren	BKN	N	Cash

Larry Doyle

Aug 28, 1916	CHI	N	Herb Hunter Merwin Jacobson	NY	N	Heinie Zimmerman Mickey Doolan
Jan 4, 1918	BOS	N	Art Wilson and $15,000.	CHI	N	Lefty Tyler
Jan 8, 1918	NY	N	Jesse Barnes	BOS	N	Buck Herzog

Paul Doyle

| Nov 27, 1969 | CAL | A | ———— | ATL | N | Cash |
| Aug 25, 1970 | SD | N | ———— | CAL | A | Cash |

Slow Joe Doyle

| May 1910 | CIN | N | ———— | NY | A | Cash |

DATE	TRADED TO		TRADED WITH	TRADED BY		IN EXCHANGE FOR

Moe Drabowsky

March 31, 1961	MIL	N	Seth Morehead	CHI	N	Andre Rodgers Daryl Robertson
Aug 13, 1962	KC	A	—————	CIN	N	Cash
June 15, 1970	BAL	A	—————	KC	A	Bobby Floyd
Nov 30, 1970	STL	N	—————	BAL	A	Jerry DaVanon

Dick Drago

Oct 24, 1973	BOS	A	—————	KC	A	Marty Pattin
March 3, 1976	CAL	A	—————	BOS	A	John Balaz Dick Sharon Dave Machemer
June 13, 1977	BAL	A	—————	CAL	A	Dyar Miller
April 8, 1981	SEA	A	—————	BOS	A	Manny Sarmiento

Solly Drake

| June 9, 1959 | PHI | N | ————— | LA | N | Waiver price |

Clem Dreisewerd

| Nov 18, 1947 | STL | A | ————— | BOS | A | *See Ellis Kinder* |

Rob Dressler

| July 18, 1978 | STL | N | ————— | SF | N | John Tamargo |
| June 7, 1979 | SEA | A | ————— | STL | N | Cash |

Karl Drews

| Aug 9, 1948 | STL | A | ————— | NY | A | Cash |
| June 15, 1954 | CIN | N | ————— | PHI | N | Cash |

Dan Driessen

| July 26, 1984 | MON | N | ————— | CIN | N | Andy McGaffigan
minor league
P Jim Jefferson |

Lew Drill

| Sept 1902 | WAS | A | ————— | BAL | A | Cash |
| Aug 10, 1904 | DET | A | Bill Coughlin | WAS | A | $7,500. |

Walt Dropo

June 3, 1952	DET	A	Bill Wight Fred Hatfield Johnny Pesky Don Lenhardt	BOS	A	Dizzy Trout George Kell Johnny Lipon Hoot Evers
Dec 6, 1954	CHI	A	Ted Gray Bob Nieman	DET	A	Leo Cristante Ferris Fain Jack Phillips
June 24, 1958	CIN	N	—————	CHI	A	Waiver price
June 23, 1959	BAL	A	—————	CIN	N	Whitey Lockman

Carl Druhot

| July 25, 1906 | STL | N | Shad Barry | CIN | N | Homer Smoot |

Keith Drumright

| April 27, 1979 | KC | A | ————— | HOU | N | George Throop |
| Dec 11, 1980 | OAK | A | Cliff Johnson | CHI | N | Minor league
P Mike King |

DATE	TRADED TO		TRADED WITH	TRADED BY		IN EXCHANGE FOR

Monk Dubiel

DATE	TRADED TO		TRADED WITH	TRADED BY		IN EXCHANGE FOR
Dec 14, 1948	CHI	N	Dutch Leonard	PHI	N	Hank Borowy Eddie Waitkus
Dec 20, 1952	BOS	N	——————	CHI	N	Sheldon Jones

Jim Duckworth

DATE	TRADED TO		TRADED WITH	TRADED BY		IN EXCHANGE FOR
June 23, 1966	KC	A	——————	WAS	A	Ken Harrelson
July 30, 1966	WAS	A	——————	KC	A	Diego Segui

Clise Dudley

DATE	TRADED TO		TRADED WITH	TRADED BY		IN EXCHANGE FOR
Oct 14, 1930	PHI	N	Jumbo Elliott Hal Lee and cash	BKN	N	Lefty O'Doul Fresco Thompson

Jim Duffalo

DATE	TRADED TO		TRADED WITH	TRADED BY		IN EXCHANGE FOR
May 4, 1965	CIN	N	——————	SF	N	Bill Henry

Frank Duffy

DATE	TRADED TO		TRADED WITH	TRADED BY		IN EXCHANGE FOR
May 29, 1971	SF	N	Vern Geishert	CIN	N	George Foster
Nov 29, 1971	CLE	A	Gaylord Perry	SF	N	Sam McDowell
March 24, 1978	BOS	A	——————	CLE	A	Rick Kreuger

Joe Dugan

DATE	TRADED TO		TRADED WITH	TRADED BY		IN EXCHANGE FOR
Jan 10, 1922	WAS	A	——————	PHI	A	Jose Acosta Bing Miller

(Part of three-team trade involving Boston, Philadelphia, and Washington.)

DATE	TRADED TO		TRADED WITH	TRADED BY		IN EXCHANGE FOR
Jan 10, 1922	BOS	A	Frank O'Rourke	WAS	A	Roger Peckinpaugh

(Part of three-team trade involving Boston, Philadelphia, and Washington.)

DATE	TRADED TO		TRADED WITH	TRADED BY		IN EXCHANGE FOR
July 23, 1922	NY	A	Elmer Smith	BOS	A	Chick Fewster Elmer Miller Johnny Mitchell Lefty O'Doul and $50,000.
Dec 29, 1928	BOS	N	——————	NY	A	Waiver price

Gus Dugas

DATE	TRADED TO		TRADED WITH	TRADED BY		IN EXCHANGE FOR
Dec 12, 1932	NY	N	Glenn Spencer	PIT	N	Freddie Lindstrom

(Part of three-team trade involving New York, Philadelphia, and Pittsburgh.)

DATE	TRADED TO		TRADED WITH	TRADED BY		IN EXCHANGE FOR
Dec 12, 1932	PHI	N	Chick Fullis	NY	N	Kiddo Davis

(Part of three-team trade involving New York, Philadelphia, and Pittsburgh.)

Oscar Dugey

DATE	TRADED TO		TRADED WITH	TRADED BY		IN EXCHANGE FOR
Feb 10, 1915	PHI	N	Possum Whitted	BOS	N	Cash

Bill Duggleby

DATE	TRADED TO		TRADED WITH	TRADED BY		IN EXCHANGE FOR
July 15, 1907	PIT	N	——————	PHI	N	Cash

Tom Dukes

DATE	TRADED TO		TRADED WITH	TRADED BY		IN EXCHANGE FOR
Oct 13, 1966	HOU	N	Dan Schneider Lee Bales	ATL	N	Gene Ratliff John Hoffman minor league IF Ed Pacheco
Dec 1, 1970	BAL	A	*See Pat Dobson*	SD	N	——————

DATE	TRADED TO		TRADED WITH	TRADED BY		IN EXCHANGE FOR

George Dumont

| Jan 17, 1919 | BOS | A | Eddie Ainsmith | WAS | A | Hal Janvrin and cash |

Dave Duncan

March 24, 1973	CLE	A	George Hendrick	OAK	A	Ray Fosse Jack Heidemann
Feb 25, 1975	BAL	A	minor league OF Al McGrew	CLE	A	Boog Powell Don Hood
Nov 18, 1976	CHI	A	———————	BAL	A	Pat Kelly

Pat Duncan

| Oct 1924 | WAS | A | ——————— | CIN | N | Waiver price |

Taylor Duncan

| Nov 30, 1972 | BAL | A | *See Earl Williams* | ATL | N | ——————— |
| Sept 7, 1977 | STL | N | ——————— | BAL | A | Cash |

Davey Dunkle

| June 1903 | WAS | A | | CHI | A | Ducky Holmes |

Jack Dunn

| June 1900 | PHI | N | ——————— | BKN | N | Cash |

Steve Dunning

May 10, 1973	TEX	A	———————	CLE	A	Dick Bosman Ted Ford
Feb 25, 1975	CHI	A	———————	TEX	A	Stan Perzanowski
Dec 11, 1975	CAL	A	Bill Melton	CHI	A	Jim Spencer Morris Nettles
Nov 6, 1976	STL	N	Pat Scanlon Tony Scott	MON	N	Bill Greif Angel Torres Sam Mejias
Aug 12, 1977	OAK	A	———————	STL	N	Randy Scarbery

Kid Durbin

| Jan 18, 1909 | CIN | N | Tom Downey | CHI | N | Johnny Kane |
| May 28, 1909 | PIT | N | ——————— | CIN | N | Ward Miller and cash |

Ryne Duren

Oct 11, 1956	KC	A	Jim Pisoni	BAL	A	Art Ceccarelli Al Pilarcik
June 15, 1957	NY	A	Jim Pisoni Milt Graff Harry Simpson	KC	A	Billy Martin Woodie Held Ralph Terry Bob Martyn
May 8, 1961	LA	A	Lee Thomas Johnny James	NY	A	Tex Clevenger Bob Cerv
March 14, 1963	PHI	N	———————	LA	A	Cash
May 13, 1964	CIN	N	———————	PHI	N	Cash

Don Durham

| July 16, 1973 | TEX | A | ——————— | STL | N | Jim Kremmel |

DATE	TRADED TO		TRADED WITH	TRADED BY		IN EXCHANGE FOR

Ed Durham

| Dec 15, 1932 | CHI | A | Hal Rhyne | BOS | A | Johnny Hodapp
Greg Mulleavy
Bob Fothergill
Bob Seeds |

Leon Durham

| Dec 9, 1980 | CHI | N | Ken Reitz
Ty Waller | STL | N | Bruce Sutter |

Leo Durocher

Feb 2, 1930	CIN	N	————	NY	A	Waiver price
May 7, 1933	STL	N	Dutch Henry Jack Ogden	CIN	N	Paul Derringer Sparky Adams Allyn Stout
Oct 4, 1937	BKN	N	————	STL	N	Johnny Cooney Jim Bucher Joe Stripp Roy Henshaw

Cedric Durst

| Feb 8, 1927 | NY | A | Joe Giard | STL | A | Sad Sam Jones |
| May 6, 1930 | BOS | A | $50,000. | NY | A | Red Ruffing |

Erv Dusak

| May 17, 1951 | PIT | N | Rocky Nelson | STL | N | Stan Rojek |

Jim Dwyer

July 25, 1975	MON	N	————	STL	N	Larry Lintz
July 21, 1976	NY	N	Pepe Mangual	MON	N	Del Unser Wayne Garrett
Dec 8, 1976	CHI	N	————	NY	N	Sheldon Mallory
			(Part of three-team trade involving Chicago Cubs, New York Mets, and Kansas City.)			
Oct 25, 1977	SF	N	————	STL	N	Frank Riccelli
			(San Francisco received Dwyer on June 15, 1978.)			
March 15, 1979	BOS	A	————	SF	N	Cash
Dec 23, 1980	BAL	A	————	BOS	A	No compensation (free agent signing)

Jerry Dybzinski

| April 1, 1983 | CHI | A | ———— | CLE | A | Pat Tabler |

Jim Dyck

April 17, 1954	CLE	A	————	BAL	A	Bob Kennedy
July 16, 1955	BAL	A	————	CLE	A	Cash
May 11, 1956	CIN	N	————	BAL	A	$25,000.

Duffy Dyer

Oct 22, 1974	PIT	N	————	NY	N	Gene Clines
Nov 28, 1978	MON	N	————	PIT	N	No compensation (free agent signing)
March 15, 1980	DET	A	————	MON	N	Jerry Manuel

Jimmy Dykes

| Sept 28, 1932 | CHI | A | Al Simmons
Mule Haas | PHI | A | $100,000. |
| Aug 10, 1960 | CLE | A | ———— | DET | A | Joe Gordon |

DATE	TRADED TO		TRADED WITH	TRADED BY		IN EXCHANGE FOR

Arnie Earley
Dec 15, 1965	MIL	N	Lee Thomas Jay Ritchie	BOS	A	Bob Sadowski Dan Osinski

Jake Early
Dec 16, 1946	STL	A	————	WAS	A	Frank Mancuso
March 26, 1948	WAS	A	————	STL	A	Cash

George Earnshaw
Dec 12, 1933	CHI	A	Johnny Pasek	PHI	A	Charlie Berry and $20,000.
May 16, 1935	BKN	N	————	CHI	A	Cash
July 1936	STL	N	————	BKN	N	Cash

Mike Easler
Sept 30, 1975	STL	N	————	HOU	N	Mike Barlow
Sept 3, 1976	CAL	A	————	STL	N	Minor league IF Ron Farkas
April 4, 1977	PIT	N	————	CAL	A	Minor league P Randy Sealy
Oct 27, 1978	BOS	A	————	PIT	N	Cash
March 15, 1979	PIT	N	————	BOS	A	Minor league OF George Hill and P Martin Rivas and cash
Dec 6, 1983	BOS	A	————	PIT	N	John Tudor

Mal Eason
April 1902	BOS	N	————	CHI	N	Cash

Jamie Easterly
Oct 19, 1979	MON	N	————	ATL	N	Cash
Sept 22, 1980	MIL	A	————	MON	N	Cash
June 6, 1983	CLE	A	Gorman Thomas Ernie Camacho	MIL	A	Rick Manning Rick Waits

Ted Easterly
Jan 1912	CHI	A	————	CLE	A	Cash

Rawley Eastwick
June 15, 1977	STL	N	————	CIN	N	Doug Capilla
Dec 12, 1977	NY	A	————	STL	N	No compensation (free agent signing)
June 14, 1978	PHI	N	————	NY	A	Jay Johnstone Bobby Brown

Craig Eaton
Dec 6, 1979	CAL	A	Al Cowens Todd Cruz	KC	A	Rance Mulliniks Willie Aikens

Eddie Eayrs
Aug 31, 1921	BKN	N	————	BOS	N	Cash

Dennis Eckersley
March 30, 1978	BOS	A	Fred Kendall	CLE	A	Bo Diaz Rick Wise Mike Paxton Ted Cox

DATE	TRADED TO		TRADED WITH	TRADED BY		IN EXCHANGE FOR

Dennis Eckersley continued

May 25, 1984	CHI	N	——————	BOS	A	Bill Buckner minor league OF Mike Brumley

Don Eddy

July 9, 1972	SD	N	cash	CHI	A	Ed Spiezio

Joe Edelen

Sept 10, 1981	CIN	N	Neil Fiala	STL	N	Doug Bair

Mike Eden

June 13, 1976	ATL	N	——————	SF	N	*See Darrell Evans*

Butch Edge

March 21, 1982	PIT	N	Ross Baumgarten	CHI	A	Vance Law Ernie Camacho

Bill Edgerton

Feb 15, 1965	CLE	A	——————	KC	A	Waiver price
April 9, 1965	KC	A	——————	CLE	A	Waiver price

Bruce Edwards

June 15, 1951	CHI	N	——————	BKN	N	*See Andy Pafko*

Dave Edwards

Dec 8, 1980	SD	N	——————	MIN	A	Chuck Baker

Doc Edwards

May 25, 1963	KC	A	$100,000.	CLE	A	Joe Azcue Dick Howser
May 3, 1965	NY	A	——————	KC	A	Johnny Blanchard Rollie Sheldon
Jan 14, 1966	CLE	A	——————	NY	A	Lu Clinton
Jan 4, 1967	HOU	N	Jim Landis Jim Weaver	CLE	A	Lee Maye Ken Retzer

Hank Edwards

May 7, 1949	CHI	N	——————	CLE	A	Waiver price
Oct 10, 1950	BKN	N	cash	CHI	N	Chuck Connors Dee Fondy
July 21, 1951	CIN	N	——————	BKN	N	Waiver price
Sept 1, 1952	CHI	A	——————	CIN	N	Howie Judson
			(Cincinnati received Judson on December 9.)			
Oct 16, 1952	STL	A	Willie Miranda	CHI	A	Joe DeMaestri Tommy Byrne

Jim Joe Edwards

July 1925	CHI	A	——————	CLE	A	Cash

Johnny Edwards

Feb 8, 1968	STL	N	——————	CIN	N	Pat Corrales minor league IF Jimmy Williams
Oct 11, 1968	HOU	N	minor league C Tommy Smith	STL	N	Dave Giusti Dave Adlesh

DATE	TRADED TO		TRADED WITH	TRADED BY		IN EXCHANGE FOR

Mike Edwards
| April 4, 1978 | OAK | A | Miguel Dilone
Elias Sosa | PIT | N | Manny Sanguillen |

Ben Egan
| Aug 20, 1914 | CLE | A | Adam Johnson
Fritz Coumbe | BOS | A | Vean Gregg |

Dick Egan
| Dec 1913 | CIN | N | $6,500. | BKN | N | Joe Tinker |

(Tinker demanded $2,000 of the purchase price; when this was refused, he jumped to the Federal League and the deal was cancelled.)

| April 1914 | BKN | N | ———— | CIN | N | Herbie Moran
Earl Yingling |
| April 23, 1915 | BOS | N | ———— | BKN | N | Cash |

Dick Egan
| May 27, 1966 | LA | N | minor league
IF John Butler | CAL | A | Howie Reed |

Tom Egan
| Nov 30, 1970 | CHI | A | ———— | CAL | A | *See Ken Berry* |

Howard Ehmke
Feb 10, 1916	DET	A	Jack Dalton	BUF	F	Cash
Oct 30, 1922	BOS	A	Carl Holling Danny Clark Babe Herman and $25,000.	DET	A	Del Pratt Rip Collins
June 15, 1926	PHI	A	Tom Jenkins	BOS	A	Fred Heimach Slim Harriss Baby Doll Jacobson

Rube Ehrhardt
| April 18, 1929 | CIN | N | Johnny Gooch | BKN | N | Val Picinich |

Juan Eichelberger
| Nov 18, 1982 | CLE | A | Broderick Perkins | SD | N | Ed Whitson |

Dave Eilers
| Aug 18, 1965 | NY | N | ———— | MIL | N | Cash |

Harry Eisenstat
| June 14, 1939 | CLE | A | cash | DET | A | Earl Averill |

Kid Elberfeld
| June 10, 1903 | NY | A | ———— | DET | A | Herman Long
Ernie Courtney |
| Dec 16, 1909 | WAS | A | ———— | NY | A | $5,000. |

Lee Elia
| Dec 1, 1964 | CHI | A | Danny Cater | PHI | N | Ray Herbert
Jeoff Long |
| April 19, 1969 | NY | A | ———— | CHI | N | Nate Oliver |

Frank Ellerbe
| May 31, 1921 | STL | A | ———— | WAS | A | Earl Smith |
| June 3, 1924 | CLE | A | ———— | STL | A | Cash |

DATE	TRADED TO		TRADED WITH		TRADED BY		IN EXCHANGE FOR

Bruce Ellingsen

| April 3, 1974 | CLE | A | ———— | | LA | N | Pedro Guerrero |

Larry Elliot

| May 10, 1967 | KC | A | $50,000. | | NY | N | Ed Charles |

Bob Elliott

Sept 30, 1946	BOS	N	Hank Camelli		PIT	N	Billy Herman Elmer Singleton Stan Wentzel Whitey Wietelmann
April 8, 1952	NY	N	————		BOS	N	Sheldon Jones and $50,000.
June 13, 1953	CHI	A	Virgil Trucks		STL	A	Darrell Johnson Lou Kretlow and $75,000.

Claude Elliott

| Aug 1904 | NY | N | ———— | | CIN | N | Cash |

Jumbo Elliott

| Oct 14, 1930 | PHI | N | Clise Dudley
Hal Lee
and cash | | BKN | N | Lefty O'Doul
Fresco Thompson |
| May 16, 1934 | BOS | N | ———— | | PHI | N | Cash |

Dock Ellis

Dec 11, 1975	NY	A	Willie Randolph Ken Brett		PIT	N	Doc Medich
April 27, 1977	OAK	A	Marty Perez Larry Murray		NY	A	Mike Torrez
June 15, 1977	TEX	A	————		OAK	A	Cash
June 15, 1979	NY	N	————		TEX	A	Bob Myrick Mike Bruhert
Sept 21, 1979	PIT	N	————		NY	N	Cash

Jim Ellis

| April 23, 1968 | LA | N | Ted Savage | | CHI | N | Jim Hickman
Phil Regan |
| Oct 20, 1970 | MIL | A | Carl Taylor | | STL | N | Jerry McNertney
George Lauzerique
minor league
P Jesse Higgins |

John Ellis

| Nov 27, 1972 | CLE | A | Jerry Kenney
Charlie Spikes
Rusty Torres | | NY | A | Graig Nettles
Gerry Moses |
| Dec 9, 1975 | TEX | A | ———— | | CLE | A | Stan Thomas
Ron Pruitt |

Sammy Ellis

Nov 29, 1967	CAL	A	————		CIN	N	Bill Kelso Jorge Rubio
Jan 20, 1969	CHI	A	————		CAL	A	Bill Voss minor league P Andy Rubicotta
June 13, 1969	CLE	A	————		CHI	A	Jack Hamilton

DATE	TRADED TO		TRADED WITH	TRADED BY		IN EXCHANGE FOR

Dick Ellsworth

DATE	TRADED TO		TRADED WITH	TRADED BY		IN EXCHANGE FOR
Dec 7, 1966	PHI	N	————	CHI	N	Ray Culp and cash
Dec 15, 1967	BOS	A	Gene Oliver	PHI	N	Mike Ryan and cash
April 19, 1969	CLE	A	*See Ken Harrelson*	BOS	A	————
Aug 7, 1970	MIL	A	————	CLE	A	Cash

Don Elston

DATE	TRADED TO		TRADED WITH	TRADED BY		IN EXCHANGE FOR
Dec 9, 1955	BKN	N	Randy Jackson	CHI	N	Don Hoak Russ Meyer Walt Moryn
May 23, 1957	CHI	N	Vito Valentinetti	BKN	N	Jackie Collum

Red Embree

DATE	TRADED TO		TRADED WITH	TRADED BY		IN EXCHANGE FOR
Oct 10, 1947	NY	A	————	CLE	A	Allie Clark
Dec 13, 1948	STL	A	Sherm Lollar Dick Starr and $100,000.	NY	A	Fred Sanford Roy Partee

Clyde Engle

DATE	TRADED TO		TRADED WITH	TRADED BY		IN EXCHANGE FOR
May 10, 1910	BOS	A	————	NY	A	Harry Wolter
Feb 10, 1916	CLE	A	————	BUF	F	Cash

Dave Engle

DATE	TRADED TO		TRADED WITH	TRADED BY		IN EXCHANGE FOR
Feb 3, 1979	MIN	A	Ken Landreaux Paul Hartzell Brad Havens	CAL	A	Rod Carew

Gil English

DATE	TRADED TO		TRADED WITH	TRADED BY		IN EXCHANGE FOR
June 1937	BOS	N	————	DET	A	Cash
Aug 10, 1938	CIN	N	Tommy Reis Johnny Babich Johnny Riddle Vince DiMaggio and cash	BOS	N	Eddie Miller

Woody English

DATE	TRADED TO		TRADED WITH	TRADED BY		IN EXCHANGE FOR
Dec 5, 1936	BKN	N	Roy Henshaw	CHI	N	Lonny Frey
July 8, 1938	CIN	N	————	BKN	N	Cash

Del Ennis

DATE	TRADED TO		TRADED WITH	TRADED BY		IN EXCHANGE FOR
Nov 19, 1956	STL	N	————	PHI	N	Bobby Morgan Rip Repulski
Oct 3, 1958	CIN	N	Bob Mabe Eddie Kasko	STL	N	George Crowe Alex Kellner Alex Grammas
May 1, 1959	CHI	A	————	CIN	N	Don Rudolph Lou Skizas

Johnny Enzmann

DATE	TRADED TO		TRADED WITH	TRADED BY		IN EXCHANGE FOR
Dec 1919	PHI	N	————	CLE	A	Cash

Mike Epstein

DATE	TRADED TO		TRADED WITH	TRADED BY		IN EXCHANGE FOR
May 29, 1967	WAS	A	Frank Bertaina	BAL	A	Pete Richert

DATE	TRADED TO		TRADED WITH	TRADED BY		IN EXCHANGE FOR

Mike Epstein continued

DATE	TRADED TO		TRADED WITH	TRADED BY		IN EXCHANGE FOR
May 8, 1971	OAK	A	Darold Knowles	WAS	A	Frank Fernandez Don Mincher Paul Lindblad and cash
Nov 30, 1972	TEX	A	————	OAK	A	Horacio Pina
May 20, 1973	CAL	A	Rich Hand Rick Stelmaszek	TEX	A	Jim Spencer Lloyd Allen

Eddie Erautt

DATE	TRADED TO		TRADED WITH	TRADED BY		IN EXCHANGE FOR
May 23, 1953	STL	N	————	CIN	N	Jackie Collum

Eric Erickson

DATE	TRADED TO		TRADED WITH	TRADED BY		IN EXCHANGE FOR
July 5, 1919	WAS	A	————	DET	A	Doc Ayers

Paul Erickson

DATE	TRADED TO		TRADED WITH	TRADED BY		IN EXCHANGE FOR
May 20, 1948	PHI	N	————	CHI	N	Waiver price
July 1, 1948	NY	N	————	PHI	N	Waiver price
July 30, 1948	PIT	N	————	NY	N	Cash

Roger Erickson

DATE	TRADED TO		TRADED WITH	TRADED BY		IN EXCHANGE FOR
May 12, 1982	NY	A	Butch Wynegar	MIN	A	John Pacella Larry Milbourne Pete Filson and cash
Dec 7, 1983	KC	A	Steve Balboni	NY	A	Mike Armstrong minor league C Duane Dewey

Tex Erwin

DATE	TRADED TO		TRADED WITH	TRADED BY		IN EXCHANGE FOR
June 1914	CIN	N	————	BKN	N	Cash

Juan Espino

DATE	TRADED TO		TRADED WITH	TRADED BY		IN EXCHANGE FOR
April 1, 1984	CLE	A	————	NY	A	Cash

Nino Espinosa

DATE	TRADED TO		TRADED WITH	TRADED BY		IN EXCHANGE FOR
March 27, 1979	PHI	N	————	NY	N	Richie Hebner Jose Moreno

Cecil Espy

DATE	TRADED TO		TRADED WITH	TRADED BY		IN EXCHANGE FOR
March 30, 1982	LA	N	Minor league P Bert Geiger	CHI	A	Rudy Law

Chuck Essegian

DATE	TRADED TO		TRADED WITH	TRADED BY		IN EXCHANGE FOR
Dec 3, 1958	STL	N	————	PHI	N	Ruben Amaro
June 15, 1959	LA	N	Lloyd Merritt	STL	N	Dick Gray
April 12, 1961	KC	A	Jerry Walker	BAL	A	Dick Hall Dick Williams
May 3, 1961	CLE	A	————	KC	A	Cash
Feb 27, 1963	KC	A	————	CLE	A	Jerry Walker

Jim Essian

DATE	TRADED TO		TRADED WITH	TRADED BY		IN EXCHANGE FOR
Dec 3, 1974	CHI	A	cash (Chicago received Essian on May 15, 1975.)	ATL	N	Richie Allen
May 7, 1975	ATL	N	Barry Bonnell and cash	PHI	N	Richie Allen Johnny Oates
March 30, 1978	OAK	A	Steve Renko	CHI	A	Pablo Torrealba

DATE	TRADED TO		TRADED WITH		TRADED BY		IN EXCHANGE FOR

Jim Essian continued

Nov 20, 1980	CHI	A	————		OAK	A	No compensation (free agent signing)
Dec 11, 1981	SEA	A	Todd Cruz Rod Allen		CHI	A	Tom Paciorek
Jan 21, 1983	CLE	A	————		SEA	A	Cash
Dec 6, 1983	OAK	A	————		CLE	A	Luis Quinones

Bobby Estalella

Sept 10, 1941	WAS	A	————		STL	A	George Archie
March 21, 1943	PHI	A	cash		WAS	A	Bob Johnson

Francisco Estrada

Dec 10, 1971	CAL	A	Nolan Ryan Don Rose Leroy Stanton		NY	N	Jim Fregosi
June 12, 1972	BAL	A	————		CAL	A	Cash
Oct 27, 1972	CHI	N	————		BAL	A	Ellie Hendricks

Andy Etchebarren

June 15, 1975	CAL	A	————		BAL	A	Cash
Dec 15, 1977	MIL	A	————		CAL	A	Cash

Bobby Etheridge

Dec 5, 1969	SD	N	Bob Barton Ron Herbel		SF	N	Frank Reberger

Nick Etten

Jan 22, 1943	NY	A	Al Gettel		PHI	N	Tom Padden Al Gerheauser Ed Levy and $10,000.

Al Evans

Feb 5, 1951	BOS	A	————		WAS	A	Waiver price

Barry Evans

Feb 22, 1982	NY	A	————		SD	N	Cash

Darrell Evans

June 13, 1976	SF	N	Marty Perez		ATL	N	Willie Montanez Craig Robinson Mike Eden Jake Brown
Dec 19, 1983	DET	A	————		SF	N	No compensation (free agent signing)

Joe Evans

Jan 8, 1923	WAS	A	————		CLE	A	Frank Brower
Jan 1924	STL	A	————		WAS	A	Cash

Roy Evans

July 1902	BKN	N	Joe Wall		NY	N	Cash
July 1903	STL	A	————		BKN	N	Cash

Steve Evans

June 1915	BAL	F	————		BKN	F	Frank Smith

DATE	TRADED TO		TRADED WITH	TRADED BY		IN EXCHANGE FOR

Leon Everitt

| April 17, 1969 | SD | N | Tommy Dean | LA | N | Al McBean |

Hoot Evers

June 3, 1952	BOS	A	Dizzy Trout George Kell Johnny Lipon	DET	A	Walt Dropo Bill Wight Fred Hatfield Johnny Pesky Don Lenhardt
May 18, 1954	NY	N	————	BOS	A	Waiver price
July 29, 1954	DET	A	————	NY	N	Waiver price
Jan 3, 1955	BAL	A	————	DET	A	Cash
July 13, 1955	CLE	A	————	BAL	A	Bill Wight
May 13, 1956	BAL	A	————	CLE	A	Dave Pope

Johnny Evers

| Feb 1914 | BOS | N | ———— | CHI | N | Bill Sweeney
and cash |
| July 12, 1917 | PHI | N | ———— | BOS | N | Waiver price |

Bob Ewing

| Jan 20, 1910 | PHI | N | ———— | CIN | N | Frank Corridon |

Homer Ezzell

| Dec 1923 | BOS | A | ———— | STL | A | Norm McMillan |
| Dec 9, 1925 | DET | A | Tex Vache | BOS | A | Fred Haney |

Roy Face

| Aug 31, 1968 | DET | A | ———— | PIT | N | Cash |

Bill Fahey

| Oct 25, 1978 | SD | N | Mike Hargrove
Kurt Bevacqua | TEX | A | Oscar Gamble
Dave Roberts
and $300,000. |
| March 24, 1981 | DET | A | ———— | SD | N | Cash |

Ferris Fain

| Jan 27, 1953 | CHI | A | minor league
2B Bob Wilson | PHI | A | Joe DeMaestri
Eddie Robinson
Ed McGhee |
| Dec 6, 1954 | DET | A | Leo Cristante
Jack Phillips | CHI | A | Walt Dropo
Ted Gray
Bob Nieman |

Ron Fairly

June 11, 1969	MON	N	Paul Popovich	LA	N	Maury Wills Manny Mota
Dec 6, 1974	STL	N	————	MON	N	Minor leaguers IF Rudy Kinard and 1B Ed Kurpiel
Sept 14, 1976	OAK	A	————	STL	N	Cash
Feb 24, 1977	TOR	A	————	OAK	A	Minor league IF Mike Weathers and cash
Dec 8, 1977	CAL	A	————	TOR	A	Dale Kelly Butch Alberts

DATE	TRADED TO		TRADED WITH	TRADED BY		IN EXCHANGE FOR

Pete Falcone

Date	To		With	By		For
Dec 8, 1975	STL	N	————	SF	N	Ken Reitz
Dec 5, 1978	NY	N	————	STL	N	Tom Grieve Kim Seaman
Jan 25, 1983	ATL	N		NY	N	No compensation (free agent signing)

Bibb Falk

Date	To		With	By		For
Feb 28, 1929	CLE	A	————	CHI	A	Martin Autry

Cy Falkenberg

Date	To		With	By		For
Aug 1908	CLE	A	Dave Altizer	WAS	A	Cash
Feb 1915	BKN	F	————	NWK	F	Hugh Bradley Larry Pratt Tom Seaton

Frank Fanovich

Date	To		With	By		For
Dec 17, 1953	BAL	A	Joe Coleman	PHI	A	Bob Cain

Carmen Fanzone

Date	To		With	By		For
Dec 3, 1970	CHI	N	————	BOS	A	Phil Gagliano

Bob Farley

Date	To		With	By		For
Nov 30, 1961	CHI	A	————	SF	N	*See Billy Pierce*
June 25, 1962	DET	A	————	CHI	A	Charlie Maxwell

Ed Farmer

Date	To		With	By		For
June 15, 1973	DET	A	————	CLE	A	Tom Timmerman Kevin Collins
March 19, 1974	NY	A	Rick Sawyer Walt Williams	DET	A	Gerry Moses

(Part of three-team trade involving Detroit, New York Yankees, and Cleveland.)

Date	To		With	By		For
March 21, 1974	PHI	N	————	NY	A	Cash
Dec 3, 1974	MIL	A	————	PHI	N	Minor league IF Steve McCartney
Dec 15, 1978	TEX	A	Gary Holle and cash	MIL	A	Reggie Cleveland
June 15, 1979	CHI	A	Gary Holle	TEX	A	Eric Soderholm
Jan 28, 1982	PHI	N	————	CHI	A	Free agent signing

(Chicago selected Joel Skinner of Pittsburgh from the compensation pool.)

Dick Farrell

Date	To		With	By		For
May 4, 1961	LA	N	Joe Koppe	PHI	N	Don Demeter Charley Smith
May 8, 1967	PHI	N	————	HOU	N	Cash

Doc Farrell

Date	To		With	By		For
June 12, 1927	BOS	N	Hugh McQuillan Kent Greenfield	NY	N	Zack Taylor Larry Benton Herb Thomas
June 14, 1929	NY	N	————	BOS	N	Jimmy Welsh
April 10, 1930	STL	N	Showboat Fisher	NY	N	Wally Roettger
June 29, 1930	CHI	N	————	STL	N	Waiver price

Bill Faul

Date	To		With	By		For
March 27, 1965	CHI	N	————	DET	A	Cash

DATE	TRADED TO		TRADED WITH	TRADED BY		IN EXCHANGE FOR

Ernie Fazio

| June 4, 1965 | KC | A | Jess Hickman and $100,000. | HOU | N | Jim Gentile |

(Kansas City received Fazio on October 15.)

Gus Felix

| Oct 7, 1925 | BKN | N | Jesse Barnes Mickey O'Neil | BOS | N | Zack Taylor Jimmy Johnston Eddie Brown |

Bobby Fenwick

| Nov 28, 1972 | STL | N | Ray Busse | HOU | N | Skip Jutze Milt Ramirez |
| Nov 7, 1973 | SD | N | Glenn Beckert | CHI | N | Jerry Morales |

Alex Ferguson

Feb 24, 1922	BOS	A	————	NY	A	Waiver price
May 5, 1925	NY	A	Bobby Veach	BOS	A	Ray Francis and $9,000.
Aug 19, 1925	WAS	A	————	NY	A	Cash
Oct 1926	PHI	N	————	WAS	A	Cash
May 14, 1929	BKN	N	————	PHI	N	Cash

George Ferguson

| Dec 3, 1907 | BOS | N | ———— | NY | N | *See Fred Tenney* |

Joe Ferguson

June 15, 1976	STL	N	Bob Detherage minor league IF Fred Tisdale	LA	N	Reggie Smith
Nov 23, 1976	HOU	N	Bob Detherage	STL	N	Larry Dierker Jerry DaVanon
July 1, 1978	LA	N	cash	HOU	N	Rafael Landestoy Jeff Leonard

Chico Fernandez

April 5, 1957	PHI	N	————	BKN	N	Ron Negray Tim Harkness Elmer Valo Ben Flowers minor league SS Mel Geho
Dec 5, 1959	DET	A	Ray Semproch	PHI	N	Ken Walters Ted Lepcio minor league P Alex Cosmidis
May 8, 1963	MIL	N	————	DET	A	Lou Johnson and cash
May 8, 1963	NY	N	————	MIL	N	Larry Foss
April 23, 1964	CHI	A	minor league C Bobby Catton and cash	NY	N	Charley Smith

Frank Fernandez

Dec 5, 1969	OAK	A	Al Downing	NY	A	Danny Cater Ossie Chavarria
May 8, 1971	WAS	A	Don Mincher Paul Lindblad and cash	OAK	A	Mike Epstein Darold Knowles
June 23, 1971	OAK	A	————	WAS	A	Cash

DATE	TRADED TO		TRADED WITH	TRADED BY		IN EXCHANGE FOR

Frank Fernandez continued

Aug 31, 1971	CHI	N	Bill McNulty	OAK	A	Adrian Garrett

Sid Fernandez

Dec 8, 1983	NY	N	Ross Jones	LA	N	Carlos Diaz Bob Bailor

Al Ferrara

May 13, 1971	CIN	N	————	SD	N	Angel Bravo

Don Ferrarese

Dec 6, 1954	BAL	A	————	CHI	A	*See Clint Courtney*
April 1, 1958	CLE	A	Larry Doby	BAL	A	Buddy Daley Dick Williams Gene Woodling
Dec 6, 1959	CHI	A	————	CLE	A	*See Norm Cash*
April 28, 1962	STL	N	————	PHI	N	Larry Locke and cash

Mike Ferraro

April 30, 1969	BAL	A	Gerry Schoen	SEA	A	John O'Donoghue Tom Fisher and minor league P Lloyd Fourroux
March 27, 1973	MIN	A	————	MIL	A	Ken Reynolds

Rick Ferrell

May 9, 1933	BOS	A	Lloyd Brown	STL	A	Merv Shea and cash
June 11, 1937	WAS	A	Wes Ferrell Mel Almada	BOS	A	Ben Chapman Bobo Newsom
May 15, 1941	STL	A	————	WAS	A	Vern Kennedy
March 1, 1944	WAS	A	————	STL	A	Tony Giuliani Gene Moore and cash

(Giuliani announced his retirement, and St. Louis received Moore to complete the trade.)

Wes Ferrell

May 25, 1934	BOS	A	Dick Porter	CLE	A	Bob Weiland Bob Seeds and $25,000.
June 11, 1937	WAS	A	Rick Ferrell Mel Almada	BOS	A	Ben Chapman Bobo Newsom

Sergio Ferrer

Oct 24, 1975	PHI	N	————	MIN	A	Larry Cox
March 26, 1977	NY	A	————	PHI	N	Kerry Dineen
Dec 9, 1977	NY	N	————	NY	A	Roy Staiger

Tom Ferrick

Sept 22, 1941	CLE	A	————	PHI	A	Waiver price
June 24, 1946	STL	A	————	CLE	A	Cash
Jan 14, 1947	WAS	A	————	STL	A	Cash
Oct 4, 1948	STL	A	John Sullivan and $25,000.	WAS	A	Sam Dente

DATE	TRADED TO		TRADED WITH	TRADED BY		IN EXCHANGE FOR

Tom Ferrick continued

| June 15, 1950 | NY | A | Joe Ostrowski
Leo Thomas
Sid Schacht | STL | A | Jim Delsing
Don Johnson
Duane Pillette
Snuffy Stirnweiss
and $50,000. |
| June 15, 1951 | WAS | A | Fred Sanford
Bob Porterfield | NY | A | Bob Kuzava |

Hobe Ferris

| Oct 1907 | NY | A | ———— | BOS | A | Cash |
| Feb 1908 | STL | A | Jimmy Williams
Danny Hoffman | NY | A | Fred Glade
Charlie Hemphill |

Lou Fette

| July 1940 | BKN | N | ———— | BOS | N | Cash |

Chick Fewster

July 23, 1922	BOS	A	Elmer Miller Johnny Mitchell Lefty O'Doul and $50,000.	NY	A	Joe Dugan Elmer Smith
Jan 7, 1924	CLE	A	————	BOS	A	*See Bill Wambsganss*
Jan 1926	BKN	N	————	CLE	A	Cash

Neil Fiala

| Sept 10, 1981 | CIN | N | Joe Edelen | STL | N | Doug Bair |

Dan Fife

| March 27, 1973 | MIN | A | cash | DET | A | Jim Perry |

Ed Figueroa

| Dec 11, 1975 | NY | A | Mickey Rivers | CAL | A | Bobby Bonds |
| July 28, 1980 | TEX | A | ———— | NY | A | Cash |

Jesus Figueroa

| Dec 12, 1980 | SF | N | Jerry Martin
minor league
IF Mike Turgeon | CHI | N | Joe Strain
Phil Nastu |

Tom Filer

| April 27, 1981 | CHI | N | cash | NY | A | Barry Foote |

Pete Filson

| May 12, 1982 | MIN | A | John Pacella
Larry Milbourne
and cash | NY | A | Butch Wynegar
Roger Erickson |

Jack Fimple

| Dec 9, 1981 | LA | N | Jorge Orta
Larry White | CLE | A | Rick Sutcliffe
Jack Perconte |

Steve Finch

| Dec 12, 1980 | SEA | A | ———— | TEX | A | *See Rick Honeycutt* |

Rollie Fingers

| Dec 14, 1976 | SD | N | ———— | OAK | A | No compensation
(free agent signing) |

DATE	TRADED TO		TRADED WITH	TRADED BY		IN EXCHANGE FOR

Rollie Fingers continued

| Dec 8, 1980 | STL | N | Bob Shirley
Gene Tenace
minor league
C Bob Geren | SD | N | Terry Kennedy
Steve Swisher
Mike Phillips
John Littlefield
John Urrea
Kim Seaman
Alan Olmsted |
| Dec 12, 1980 | MIL | A | Pete Vuckovich
Ted Simmons | STL | N | Sixto Lezcano
David Green
Lary Sorensen
Dave LaPoint |

Jim Finigan

Dec 16, 1953	PHI	A	Don Bollweg John Gray Jim Robertson Vic Power Bill Renna	NY	A	Harry Byrd Eddie Robinson Tom Hamilton Carmen Mauro Loren Babe
Dec 5, 1956	DET	A	Jack Crimian Bill Harrington Eddie Robinson	KC	A	Ned Garver Gene Host Virgil Trucks Wayne Belardi and $20,000.
Jan 28, 1958	SF	N	$25,000.	DET	A	Gail Harris Ozzie Virgil
Oct 14, 1958	BAL	A	————	STL	N	Jim Brideweser Art Ceccarelli

Mickey Finn

| Dec 15, 1932 | PHI | N | Cy Moore
Jack Warner | BKN | N | Ray Benge
and $15,000. |

Happy Finneran

| May 1918 | NY | A | ———— | DET | A | Cash |

Lou Finney

| May 8, 1939 | BOS | A | ———— | PHI | A | Cash |
| July 27, 1945 | STL | A | ———— | BOS | A | Cash |

Mike Fiore

May 28, 1970	BOS	A	————	KC	A	Tommy Matchick
March 20, 1972	STL	N	————	BOS	A	Bob Burda
June 20, 1972	SD	N	Bob Chlupsa	STL	N	Rafael Robles

(Fiore was returned to St. Louis on July 3.)

Steve Fireovid

| Aug 31, 1983 | PHI | N | Sixto Lezcano | SD | N | Marty Decker
minor league
Ps Ed Wojna
Darren Burroughs
and
Lance McCullers |

Bill Fischer

| Feb 10, 1916 | CHI | N | *See Three Finger Brown* | CHI | F | ———— |
| July 29, 1916 | PIT | N | Wildfire Schulte | CHI | N | Art Wilson
Otto Knabe |

DATE	TRADED TO		TRADED WITH	TRADED BY		IN EXCHANGE FOR

Bill Fischer

June 15, 1958	DET	A	Tito Francona	CHI	A	Ray Boone Bob Shaw
Sept 11, 1958	WAS	A	————	DET	A	Waiver price
July 22, 1960	DET	A	————	WAS	A	Tom Morgan
Aug 2, 1961	KC	A	Ozzie Virgil	DET	A	Gerry Staley Reno Bertoia

Carl Fischer

June 9, 1932	STL	A		WAS	A	Dick Coffman
Dec 13, 1932	WAS	A		STL	A	Dick Coffman
Dec 14, 1932	DET	A	Firpo Marberry	WAS	A	Earl Whitehill
May 17, 1935	CHI	A	————	DET	A	Cash
May 1937	WAS	A	————	CLE	A	Cash

Hank Fischer

| June 15, 1966 | CIN | N | ———— | ATL | N | Joey Jay |
| Aug 15, 1966 | BOS | A | ———— | CIN | N | Dick Stigman
Rollie Sheldon |

(Cincinnati received Stigman and Sheldon on December 15, 1966.)

Mike Fischlin

| June 15, 1977 | HOU | N | Randy Niemann
Dave Bergman | NY | A | Cliff Johnson |

(Houston received Bergman on November 23.)

| April 3, 1981 | CLE | A | ———— | HOU | N | Jim Lentine
and cash |

Bob Fisher

| Jan 1916 | CIN | N | ———— | CHI | N | Cash |

Chauncey Fisher

| May 1901 | STL | N | ———— | NY | N | Bill Magee |

Eddie Fisher

Nov 30, 1961	CHI	A	Dom Zanni Verle Tiefenthaler Bob Farley	SF	N	Billy Pierce Don Larsen
June 12, 1966	BAL	A	————	CHI	A	Jerry Adair and minor league OF Johnny Riddle
Nov 28, 1967	CLE	A	minor leaguers P Bob Scott and IF John Scruggs	BAL	A	John O'Donoghue Gordon Lund
Oct 8, 1968	CAL	A	————	CLE	A	Jack Hamilton
Aug 17, 1972	CHI	A	————	CAL	A	Bruce Miller Bruce Kimm
Aug 29, 1973	STL	N	————	CHI	A	Cash

Gus Fisher

| March 1912 | NY | A | | CLE | A | Waiver price |

Jack Fisher

| Dec 15, 1962 | SF | N | Jimmie Coker
Billy Hoeft | BAL | A | Mike McCormick
Stu Miller
John Orsino |
| Oct 10, 1963 | NY | N | ———— | SF | N | $30,000. |

DATE	TRADED TO		TRADED WITH	TRADED BY		IN EXCHANGE FOR

Doug Flynn

DATE	TRADED TO		TRADED WITH	TRADED BY		IN EXCHANGE FOR
June 15, 1977	NY	N	Pat Zachry Steve Henderson Dan Norman	CIN	N	Tom Seaver
Dec 11, 1981	TEX	A	Danny Boitano	NY	N	Jim Kern
Aug 2, 1982	MON	N	————	TEX	A	Cash

John Flynn

Feb 1912	WAS	A	————	PIT	N	Waiver price

Lee Fohl

Oct 1903	CIN	N	————	PIT	N	Waiver price

Hank Foiles

May 3, 1953	CLE	A	————	CIN	N	Cash
May 15, 1956	PIT	N	————	CLE	A	Preston Ward
Dec 15, 1959	KC	A	————	PIT	N	Cash
June 1, 1960	PIT	N	Cash	KC	A	Danny Kravitz
June 2, 1960	CLE	A	————	PIT	N	Johnny Powers
July 26, 1960	DET	A	————	CLE	A	Rocky Bridges Red Wilson
April 20, 1962	CIN	N	————	BAL	A	Cash

Tim Foli

April 5, 1972	MON	N	Ken Singleton Mike Jorgensen	NY	N	Rusty Staub
April 27, 1977	SF	N	————	MON	N	Chris Speier
Dec 7, 1977	NY	N	————	SF	N	Cash
April 19, 1979	PIT	N	minor league P Greg Field	NY	N	Frank Taveras
Dec 11, 1981	CAL	A	————	PIT	N	Brian Harper
Dec 7, 1983	NY	A	————	CAL	A	Curt Kaufman and cash
Dec 20, 1984	PIT	N	Steve Kemp and $400,000.	NY	A	Dale Berra minor league P Jay Buhner

Rich Folkers

Oct 18, 1971	STL	N	*See Jim Bibby*	NY	N	————
Nov 18, 1974	SD	N	Alan Foster Sonny Siebert	STL	N	Ed Brinkman Danny Breeden

(Part of three-team trade involving San Diego, Detroit, and St. Louis Cardinals.)

March 23, 1977	MIL	A	————	SD	N	Cash
Dec 9, 1977	DET	A	Jim Slaton	MIL	A	Ben Oglivie

Dee Fondy

Oct 10, 1950	CHI	N	Chuck Connors	BKN	N	Hank Edwards and cash
May 1, 1957	PIT	N	Gene Baker	CHI	N	Dale Long Lee Walls
Dec 28, 1957	CIN	N	————	PIT	N	Ted Kluszewski

Lew Fonseca

March 30, 1925	PHI	N	————	CIN	N	Cash
May 17, 1931	CHI	A	————	CLE	A	Willie Kamm

DATE	TRADED TO		TRADED WITH	TRADED BY		IN EXCHANGE FOR

Ray Fontenot

DATE	TRADED TO		TRADED WITH	TRADED BY		IN EXCHANGE FOR
Aug 1, 1979	NY	A	Oscar Gamble Gene Nelson minor league 3B Amos Lewis	TEX	A	Mickey Rivers minor league Ps Bob Polinsky Neil Mersch and Mark Softy
Dec 4, 1984	CHI	N	Brian Dayett	NY	A	Henry Cotto Ron Hassey Rich Bordi Porfirio Altamirano

Jim Foor

DATE	TRADED TO		TRADED WITH	TRADED BY		IN EXCHANGE FOR
Nov 30, 1972	PIT	N	Norm McRae	DET	A	Dick Sharon
March 28, 1974	KC	A	——————	PIT	N	Wayne Simpson

Barry Foote

DATE	TRADED TO		TRADED WITH	TRADED BY		IN EXCHANGE FOR
June 15, 1977	PHI	N	Dan Warthen	MON	N	Wayne Twitchell Tim Blackwell
Feb 23, 1979	CHI	N	Ted Sizemore Jerry Martin Dick Botelho minor league P Henry Mack	PHI	N	Manny Trillo Dave Rader Greg Gross
April 27, 1981	NY	A	——————	CHI	N	Tom Filer and cash

Dan Ford

DATE	TRADED TO		TRADED WITH	TRADED BY		IN EXCHANGE FOR
Oct 23, 1974	MIN	A	minor league P Denny Myers	OAK	A	Pat Bourque
Dec 4, 1978	CAL	A	——————	MIN	A	Ron Jackson Danny Goodwin
Jan 28, 1982	BAL	A	——————	CAL	A	Doug DeCinces Jeff Schneider

Hod Ford

DATE	TRADED TO		TRADED WITH	TRADED BY		IN EXCHANGE FOR
Dec 15, 1923	PHI	N	Ray Powell	BOS	N	Cotton Tierney

(Powell announced his intention to retire after the 1924 season. He remained with Boston, and Philadelphia received cash instead.)

DATE	TRADED TO		TRADED WITH	TRADED BY		IN EXCHANGE FOR
May 16, 1925	BKN	N	——————	PHI	N	Waiver price
Jan 26, 1932	STL	N	——————	CIN	N	Cash

Ted Ford

DATE	TRADED TO		TRADED WITH	TRADED BY		IN EXCHANGE FOR
April 3, 1972	TEX	A	——————	CLE	A	Roy Foster Tom McCraw
May 10, 1973	CLE	A	Dick Bosman	TEX	A	Steve Dunning

Frank Foreman

DATE	TRADED TO		TRADED WITH	TRADED BY		IN EXCHANGE FOR
April 1901	BAL	A	——————	BOS	A	Cash

Mike Fornieles

DATE	TRADED TO		TRADED WITH	TRADED BY		IN EXCHANGE FOR
Dec 10, 1952	CHI	A	——————	WAS	A	Chuck Stobbs
May 21, 1956	BAL	A	Bob Nieman Connie Johnson George Kell	CHI	A	Jim Wilson Dave Philley
June 14, 1957	BOS	A	——————	BAL	A	Billy Goodman
June 14, 1963	MIN	A	——————	BOS	A	Cash

Ken Forsch

DATE	TRADED TO		TRADED WITH	TRADED BY		IN EXCHANGE FOR
April 1, 1981	CAL	A	——————	HOU	N	Dickie Thon

DATE	TRADED TO		TRADED WITH	TRADED BY		IN EXCHANGE FOR

Terry Forster

Dec 10, 1976	PIT	N	Goose Gossage	CHI	A	Richie Zisk Silvio Martinez
Nov 22, 1977	LA	N	—————	PIT	N	No compensation (free agent signing)
Dec 1, 1982	ATL	N	—————	LA	N	No compensation (free agent signing)

Larry Foss

| Sept 6, 1962 | NY | N | ————— | PIT | N | Waiver price |
| May 8, 1963 | MIL | N | ————— | NY | N | Chico Fernandez |

Ray Fosse

March 24, 1973	OAK	A	Jack Heidemann	CLE	A	George Hendrick Dave Duncan
Dec 9, 1975	CLE	A	—————	OAK	A	Cash
Sept 9, 1977	SEA	A	—————	CLE	A	Bill Laxton and cash

Alan Foster

Dec 11, 1970	CLE	A	Ray Lamb	LA	N	Duke Sims
Oct 5, 1971	CAL	A	—————	CLE	A	*See Alex Johnson*
April 5, 1973	STL	N	—————	CAL	A	Cash
Nov 18, 1974	SD	N	Rich Folkers Sonny Siebert	STL	N	Ed Brinkman Danny Breeden

(Part of three-team trade involving San Diego, Detroit, and St. Louis Cardinals.)

Eddie Foster

| Jan 20, 1920 | BOS | A | Mike Menosky
Harry Harper | WAS | A | Braggo Roth
Red Shannon |
| Aug 15, 1922 | STL | A | ————— | BOS | A | Waiver price |

George Foster

| May 29, 1971 | CIN | N | ————— | SF | N | Frank Duffy
Vern Geishert |
| Feb 10, 1982 | NY | N | ————— | CIN | N | Alex Trevino
Jim Kern
Greg Harris |

Leo Foster

| March 29, 1978 | BOS | A | ————— | NY | N | Jim Burton |

Pop Foster

| Sept 1901 | CHI | A | ————— | WAS | A | Cash |

Roy Foster

April 4, 1970	CLE	A	Frank Coggins and cash	MIL	A	Max Alvis Russ Snyder
Dec 2, 1971	TEX	A	—————	CLE	A	*See Del Unser*
April 3, 1972	CLE	A	Tom McCraw	TEX	A	Ted Ford

Rube Foster

| April 1918 | CIN | N | ————— | BOS | A | Dave Shean |

(Foster refused to report to Cincinnati; Cincinnati received cash instead.)

Bob Fothergill

| July 18, 1930 | CHI | A | ————— | DET | A | Waiver price |

DATE	TRADED TO		TRADED WITH	TRADED BY		IN EXCHANGE FOR

Bob Fothergill continued

DATE	TRADED TO		TRADED WITH	TRADED BY		IN EXCHANGE FOR
Dec 15, 1932	BOS	A	Johnny Hodapp Greg Mulleavy Bob Seeds	CHI	A	Ed Durham Hal Rhyne

Steve Foucault

DATE	TRADED TO		TRADED WITH	TRADED BY		IN EXCHANGE FOR
April 12, 1977	DET	A	————	TEX	A	Willie Horton
Aug 16, 1978	KC	A	————	DET	A	Cash

Jack Fournier

DATE	TRADED TO		TRADED WITH	TRADED BY		IN EXCHANGE FOR
May 8, 1912	CHI	A	————	BOS	A	Cash
Feb 15, 1923	BKN	N	————	STL	N	Hy Myers Ray Schmandt
Nov 5, 1926	BOS	N	————	BKN	N	Cash

Howie Fox

DATE	TRADED TO		TRADED WITH	TRADED BY		IN EXCHANGE FOR
Dec 10, 1951	PHI	N	*See Smoky Burgess*	CIN	N	————

Nellie Fox

DATE	TRADED TO		TRADED WITH	TRADED BY		IN EXCHANGE FOR
Oct 19, 1949	CHI	A	————	PHI	A	Joe Tipton
Dec 10, 1963	HOU	N	————	CHI	A	Jim Golden Danny Murphy and cash

Paddy Fox

DATE	TRADED TO		TRADED WITH	TRADED BY		IN EXCHANGE FOR
Jan 1900	LOU	N	————	PIT	N	*See Honus Wagner*

Pete Fox

DATE	TRADED TO		TRADED WITH	TRADED BY		IN EXCHANGE FOR
Dec 12, 1940	BOS	A	————	DET	A	Cash

Terry Fox

DATE	TRADED TO		TRADED WITH	TRADED BY		IN EXCHANGE FOR
Dec 7, 1960	DET	A	*See Bill Bruton*	MIL	N	————
May 10, 1966	PHI	N	————	DET	A	Cash

Bill Foxen

DATE	TRADED TO		TRADED WITH	TRADED BY		IN EXCHANGE FOR
July 1910	CHI	N	————	PHI	N	Fred Luderus

Jimmie Foxx

DATE	TRADED TO		TRADED WITH	TRADED BY		IN EXCHANGE FOR
Dec 10, 1935	BOS	A	Johnny Marcum	PHI	A	Gordon Rhodes minor league C George Savino and $150,000.
June 1, 1942	CHI	N	————	BOS	A	Waiver price

Joe Foy

DATE	TRADED TO		TRADED WITH	TRADED BY		IN EXCHANGE FOR
Dec 3, 1969	NY	N	————	KC	A	Amos Otis Bob Johnson

Paul Foytack

DATE	TRADED TO		TRADED WITH	TRADED BY		IN EXCHANGE FOR
June 15, 1963	LA	A	Frank Kostro	DET	A	George Thomas and cash

Ken Frailing

DATE	TRADED TO		TRADED WITH	TRADED BY		IN EXCHANGE FOR
Dec 11, 1973	CHI	N	Steve Stone Steve Swisher Jim Kremmel	CHI	A	Ron Santo

Ray Francis

DATE	TRADED TO		TRADED WITH	TRADED BY		IN EXCHANGE FOR
Nov 24, 1922	DET	A	————	WAS	A	Chick Gagnon

DATE	TRADED TO		TRADED WITH	TRADED BY		IN EXCHANGE FOR

Ray Francis continued

DATE	TRADED TO		TRADED WITH	TRADED BY		IN EXCHANGE FOR
May 5, 1925	BOS	A	$9,000.	NY	A	Bobby Veach Alex Ferguson

John Franco

| May 9, 1983 | CIN | N | minor league
P Brett Wise | LA | N | Rafael Landestoy |

Julio Franco

| Dec 9, 1982 | CLE | A | Manny Trillo
George Vukovich
Jay Baller
Jerry Willard | PHI | N | Von Hayes |

Tito Francona

Dec 3, 1957	CHI	A	Ray Moore Billy Goodman	BAL	A	Jack Harshman Russ Heman Jim Marshall Larry Doby
June 15, 1958	DET	A	Bill Fischer	CHI	A	Ray Boone Bob Shaw
March 21, 1959	CLE	A	—————	DET	A	Larry Doby
Dec 15, 1964	STL	N	—————	CLE	A	Cash
April 10, 1967	PHI	N	—————	STL	N	Cash
June 12, 1967	ATL	N	—————	PHI	N	Cash
Aug 22, 1969	OAK	A	—————	ATL	N	Cash
June 11, 1970	MIL	A	Al Downing	OAK	A	Steve Hovley

Fred Frankhouse

June 16, 1930	BOS	N	Bill Sherdel	STL	N	Burleigh Grimes
Feb 6, 1936	BKN	N	—————	BOS	N	Johnny Babich Gene Moore
Dec 13, 1938	BOS	N	—————	BKN	N	Joe Stripp

Herman Franks

| Feb 6, 1940 | BKN | N | ————— | STL | N | Cash |

Chick Fraser

Dec 20, 1904	BOS	N	Harry Wolverton	PHI	N	Togie Pittinger
March 1906	CIN	N	Jim Delahanty	BOS	N	Al Bridwell
Oct 1906	CHI	N	—————	CIN	N	Jack Harper

George Frazier

Dec 8, 1977	STL	N	—————	MIL	A	Buck Martinez
June 7, 1981	NY	A	—————	STL	N	Cash
June 13, 1984	CHI	N	Rick Sutcliffe Ron Hassey	CLE	A	Mel Hall Joe Carter minor league P Darryl Banks

Joe Frazier

Nov 20, 1947	STL	A	Dick Kokos Bryan Stephens and $25,000.	CLE	A	Bob Muncrief Walt Judnich
May 16, 1956	CIN	N	Alex Grammas	STL	N	Chuck Harmon
June 26, 1956	BAL	A	—————	CIN	N	Cash

DATE	TRADED TO		TRADED WITH	TRADED BY		IN EXCHANGE FOR
Vic Frazier						
June 2, 1933	DET	A	——————	CHI	A	Whit Wyatt
Roger Freed						
Dec 16, 1970	PHI	N	——————	BAL	A	Grant Jackson Jim Hutto Sam Parrilla
Nov 30, 1972	CLE	A	Oscar Gamble	PHI	N	Del Unser minor league IF Terry Wedgewood
Hersh Freeman						
May 10, 1955	CIN	N	——————	BOS	A	Cash
May 8, 1958	CHI	N	——————	CIN	N	Turk Lown
Jimmy Freeman						
April 17, 1975	BAL	A	$75,000.	ATL	N	Earl Williams
June 15, 1976	NY	A	——————	BAL	A	*See Tippy Martinez*
Mark Freeman						
April 8, 1959	KC	A	——————	NY	A	Jack Urban
			(Freeman was returned to the Yankees on May 8, 1959.)			
May 19, 1960	CHI	N	——————	NY	A	Art Ceccarelli minor league IF Ray Bellino
Gene Freese						
June 15, 1958	STL	N	Johnny O'Brien	PIT	N	Dick Schofield and cash
Sept 29, 1958	PHI	N	——————	STL	N	Solly Hemus
			(Hemus was named St. Louis manager.)			
Dec 9, 1959	CHI	A	——————	PHI	N	Johnny Callison
Dec 15, 1960	CIN	N	——————	CHI	A	Juan Pizarro Cal McLish
Nov 26, 1963	PIT	N	——————	CIN	N	Cash
Aug 25, 1965	CHI	A	——————	PIT	N	Cash
July 20, 1966	HOU	N	——————	CHI	A	Jim Mahoney and cash
George Freese						
April 7, 1953	DET	A	——————	STL	A	Cash
June 4, 1953	PIT	N	——————	CHI	N	*See Ralph Kiner*
Jim Fregosi						
Dec 10, 1971	NY	N	——————	CAL	A	Nolan Ryan Don Rose Leroy Stanton Francisco Estrada
July 11, 1973	TEX	A	——————	NY	N	Cash
June 15, 1977	PIT	N	——————	TEX	A	Ed Kirkpatrick
Howard Freigau						
May 23, 1925	CHI	N	Mike Gonzalez	STL	N	Bob O'Farrell
Dec 1927	BKN	N	——————	CHI	N	Johnny Butler
June 23, 1928	BOS	N	——————	BKN	N	Cash

DATE	TRADED TO		TRADED WITH	TRADED BY		IN EXCHANGE FOR

Dave Freisleben

DATE	TRADED TO		TRADED WITH	TRADED BY		IN EXCHANGE FOR
June 22, 1978	CLE	A	————	SD	N	Bill Laxton
Nov 3, 1978	TOR	A	————	CLE	A	Sheldon Mallory

Tony Freitas

Dec 1933	CIN	N	————	PHI	A	Cash

Charlie French

May 1910	CHI	A	————	BOS	A	Cash

Larry French

Nov 22, 1934	CHI	N	Freddie Lindstrom	PIT	N	Guy Bush Jim Weaver Babe Herman
Aug 20, 1941	BKN	N	————	CHI	N	Waiver price

Benny Frey

April 11, 1932	STL	N	Harvey Hendrick and cash	CIN	N	Chick Hafey
May 10, 1932	CIN	N	————	STL	N	Cash

Lonny Frey

Dec 5, 1936	CHI	N	————	BKN	N	Roy Henshaw Woody English
Feb 4, 1938	CIN	N	————	CHI	N	Cash
April 16, 1947	CHI	N	————	CIN	N	Cash
June 25, 1947	NY	A	————	CHI	N	Cash

Pepe Frias

March 31, 1979	ATL	N	————	MON	N	Dave Campbell
Dec 6, 1979	TEX	A	Adrian Devine	ATL	N	Doyle Alexander Larvell Blanks and $50,000.
Sept 13, 1980	LA	N	————	TEX	A	Dennis Lewallyn

Barney Friberg

June 15, 1925	PHI	N	————	CHI	N	Waiver price
Jan 7, 1933	BOS	A	————	PHI	N	Waiver price

Jim Fridley

April 6, 1953	STL	A	————	CLE	A	Waiver price
Dec 1, 1954	NY	A	*See Dick Kryhoski*	BAL	A	————

Bob Friend

Dec 10, 1965	NY	A	————	PIT	N	Pete Mikkelsen and cash
June 15, 1966	NY	N	————	NY	A	Cash

Owen Friend

Dec 4, 1952	DET	A	————	STL	A	*See Virgil Trucks*
June 15, 1953	CLE	A	————	DET	A	*See Ray Boone*

John Frill

Jan 1912	CIN	N	————	STL	A	Waiver price

DATE	TRADED TO		TRADED WITH	TRADED BY		IN EXCHANGE FOR

Charlie Frisbee

| Feb 17, 1900 | NY | N | ———— | BOS | N | Cash |

Frankie Frisch

| Dec 20, 1926 | STL | N | Jimmy Ring | NY | N | Rogers Hornsby |

Danny Frisella

Nov 2, 1972	ATL	N	Gary Gentry	NY	N	Felix Millan George Stone
Nov 8, 1974	SD	N	————	ATL	N	Clarence Gaston
April 8, 1976	STL	N	————	SD	N	Ken Reynolds and minor leaguer Bob Stewart
June 7, 1976	MIL	A	————	STL	N	Sam Mejias

Sam Frock

| June 1, 1910 | BOS | N | ———— | PIT | N | Kirby White |

Art Fromme

| Dec 12, 1908 | CIN | N | Ed Karger | STL | N | Admiral Schlei |
| May 22, 1913 | NY | N | Eddie Grant | CIN | N | Red Ames
Heinie Groh
Josh Devore
and $20,000. |

Dave Frost

| Dec 5, 1977 | CAL | A | *See Brian Downing* | CHI | A | ———— |
| Feb 3, 1982 | KC | A | ———— | CAL | A | No compensation
(free agent signing) |

Woodie Fryman

Dec 15, 1967	PHI	N	Don Money Bill Laxton minor league P Hal Clem	PIT	N	Jim Bunning
Aug 2, 1972	DET	A	————	PHI	N	Cash
Dec 4, 1974	MON	N	————	DET	A	Tom Walker Terry Humphrey
Dec 16, 1976	CIN	N	Dale Murray	MON	N	Tony Perez Will McEnaney
Oct 31, 1977	CHI	N	Bill Caudill	CIN	N	Bill Bonham
June 9, 1978	MON	N	————	CHI	N	Jerry White

Tito Fuentes

Dec 6, 1974	SD	N	Butch Metzger	SF	N	Derrel Thomas
Feb 23, 1977	DET	A	————	SD	N	No compensation (free agent signing)
Jan 30, 1978	MON	N	————	DET	A	Cash

Chick Fullis

| Dec 12, 1932 | PHI | N | Gus Dugas | NY | N | Kiddo Davis |

(Part of three-team trade involving New York, Philadelphia, and Pittsburgh.)

| June 15, 1934 | STL | N | ———— | PHI | N | Kiddo Davis |

Dave Fultz

| March 1903 | NY | A | ———— | PHI | A | Cash |

DATE	TRADED TO		TRADED WITH	TRADED BY		IN EXCHANGE FOR

Frank Funk
Nov 27, 1962	MIL	N	Ty Cline Don Dillard	CLE	A	Joe Adcock Jack Curtis

Fred Fussell
Dec 1927	PIT	N	————	CHI	N	Mike Cvengros

Frank Gabler
June 15, 1937	BOS	N	$35,000.	NY	N	Wally Berger
May 2, 1938	CHI	A	————	BOS	N	Cash

Len Gabrielson
June 3, 1964	CHI	N	————	MIL	N	Merritt Ranew and $40,000.
May 29, 1965	SF	N	Dick Bertell	CHI	N	Harvey Kuenn Ed Bailey Bob Hendley
Dec 14, 1966	CAL	A	————	SF	N	Norm Siebern
May 10, 1967	LA	N	————	CAL	A	Johnny Werhas

Phil Gagliano
May 29, 1970	CHI	N	————	STL	N	Ted Abernathy
Dec 3, 1970	BOS	A	————	CHI	N	Carmen Fanzone
March 27, 1973	CIN	N	Andy Kosco	BOS	A	Mel Behney

Greg Gagne
April 10, 1982	MIN	A	Ron Davis Paul Boris	NY	A	Roy Smalley

Ed Gagnier
July 1915	BUF	F	Ed Lafitte	BKN	F	Fred Smith

Chick Gagnon
Nov 24, 1922	WAS	A	————	DET	A	Ray Francis

Joe Gaines
Dec 15, 1962	BAL	A	————	CIN	N	Dick Luebke minor league IF Willard Oplinger
June 15, 1964	HOU	N	————	BAL	A	Johnny Weekly and cash

Del Gainor
June 2, 1914	BOS	A	————	DET	A	Waiver price

Augie Galan
Dec 4, 1946	CIN	N	————	BKN	N	Ed Heusser

Rich Gale
Dec 11, 1981	SF	N	Bill Laskey	KC	A	Jerry Martin
Jan 5, 1983	CIN	N	————	SF	N	Mike Vail

Denny Galehouse
Dec 15, 1938	BOS	A	Tommy Irwin	CLE	A	Ben Chapman
Dec 3, 1940	STL	A	————	BOS	A	Cash
June 20, 1947	BOS	A	————	STL	A	Cash

DATE	TRADED TO		TRADED WITH	TRADED BY		IN EXCHANGE FOR

Alan Gallagher
| April 14, 1973 | CAL | A | ——— | SF | N | Bruce Miller |

Bob Gallagher
| Oct 29, 1974 | NY | N | ——— | HOU | N | Ken Boswell |

Joe Gallagher
| June 13, 1939 | STL | A | ——— | NY | A | Roy Hughes and cash |
| May 27, 1940 | BKN | N | ——— | STL | A | Roy Cullenbine |

Bert Gallia
| Dec 15, 1917 | STL | A | $15,000. | WAS | A | Burt Shotton Doc Lavan |
| April 1920 | PHI | N | ——— | STL | A | Cash |

Chick Galloway
| Dec 2, 1927 | STL | A | ——— | PHI | A | Cash |
| Dec 2, 1927 | DET | A | Elam Vangilder Harry Rice | STL | A | Heinie Manush Lu Blue |

Oscar Gamble
Nov 17, 1969	PHI	N	Dick Selma	CHI	N	Johnny Callison
Nov 30, 1972	CLE	A	Roger Freed	PHI	N	Del Unser minor league IF Terry Wedgewood
Nov 22, 1975	NY	A	———	CLE	A	Pat Dobson
April 5, 1977	CHI	A	LaMarr Hoyt minor league P Bob Polinsky and $200,000.	NY	A	Bucky Dent
Nov 29, 1977	SD	N	———	CHI	A	No compensation (free agent signing)
Oct 25, 1978	TEX	A	Dave Roberts and $300,000.	SD	N	Mike Hargrove Kurt Bevacqua Bill Fahey
Aug 1, 1979	NY	A	Ray Fontenot Gene Nelson minor league 3B Amos Lewis	TEX	A	Mickey Rivers minor league Ps Bob Polinsky Neil Mersch and Mark Softy

Chick Gandil
| Feb 15, 1916 | CLE | A | ——— | WAS | A | $7,500. |
| Feb 25, 1917 | CHI | A | ——— | CLE | A | $3,500. |

Bob Ganley
| Feb 1907 | WAS | A | ——— | PIT | N | Cash |
| May 1909 | PHI | A | ——— | WAS | A | Cash |

John Ganzel
| Feb 1901 | NY | N | ——— | CHI | N | Cash |

Joe Garagiola
| June 15, 1951 | PIT | N | Bill Howerton Howie Pollet Ted Wilks Dick Cole | STL | N | Cliff Chambers Wally Westlake |

DATE	TRADED TO		TRADED WITH	TRADED BY		IN EXCHANGE FOR

Joe Garagiola continued

DATE	TRADED TO		TRADED WITH	TRADED BY		IN EXCHANGE FOR
June 4, 1953	CHI	N	Ralph Kiner Howie Pollet Catfish Metkovich	PIT	N	Toby Atwell Bob Schultz Preston Ward George Freese Bob Addis Gene Hermanski $150,000.
Sept 8, 1954	NY	N	————	CHI	N	Waiver price

Gene Garber

DATE	TRADED TO		TRADED WITH	TRADED BY		IN EXCHANGE FOR
Oct 25, 1972	KC	A	————	PIT	N	Jim Rooker
June 15, 1978	ATL	N	————	PHI	N	Dick Ruthven

Damaso Garcia

DATE	TRADED TO		TRADED WITH	TRADED BY		IN EXCHANGE FOR
Nov 1, 1979	TOR	A	Chris Chambliss Paul Mirabella	NY	A	Tom Underwood Rick Cerone Ted Wilborn

Kiko Garcia

DATE	TRADED TO		TRADED WITH	TRADED BY		IN EXCHANGE FOR
April 1, 1981	HOU	N	————	BAL	A	Chris Bourjos and cash

Pedro Garcia

DATE	TRADED TO		TRADED WITH	TRADED BY		IN EXCHANGE FOR
June 10, 1976	DET	A	————	MIL	A	Gary Sutherland

Billy Gardner

DATE	TRADED TO		TRADED WITH	TRADED BY		IN EXCHANGE FOR
April 21, 1956	BAL	A	————	NY	N	$20,000.
April 3, 1960	WAS	A	————	BAL	A	Clint Courtney Ron Samford
June 14, 1961	NY	A	————	MIN	A	Danny McDevitt
June 12, 1962	BOS	A	————	NY	A	Tommy Umphlett and cash

Larry Gardner

DATE	TRADED TO		TRADED WITH	TRADED BY		IN EXCHANGE FOR
Jan 10, 1918	PHI	A	Tilly Walker Hick Cady	BOS	A	Stuffy McInnis
March 1, 1919	CLE	A	Elmer Myers Charlie Jamieson	PHI	A	Braggo Roth

Rob Gardner

DATE	TRADED TO		TRADED WITH	TRADED BY		IN EXCHANGE FOR
June 12, 1967	CHI	N	Johnny Stephenson	NY	N	Bob Hendley
March 30, 1968	CLE	A	————	CHI	N	Bobby Tiefenauer
April 9, 1971	OAK	A	Ron Klimkowski	NY	A	Felipe Alou
May 26, 1971	NY	A	————	OAK	A	Curt Blefary
Nov 24, 1972	OAK	A	Rich McKinney	NY	A	Matty Alou
May 31, 1973	MIL	A	————	OAK	A	Cash

(Deal was cancelled and Gardner was returned to Oakland on July 16.)

Wayne Garland

DATE	TRADED TO		TRADED WITH	TRADED BY		IN EXCHANGE FOR
Nov 19, 1976	CLE	A	————	BAL	A	No compensation (free agent signing)

Mike Garman

DATE	TRADED TO		TRADED WITH	TRADED BY		IN EXCHANGE FOR
Dec 7, 1973	STL	N	Lynn McGlothen John Curtis	BOS	A	Reggie Cleveland Diego Segui Terry Hughes
Oct 28, 1975	CHI	N	minor league IF Bobby Hrapmann	STL	N	Don Kessinger

DATE	TRADED TO		TRADED WITH	TRADED BY		IN EXCHANGE FOR

Mike Garman continued

| Jan 11, 1977 | LA | N | Rick Monday | CHI | N | Bill Buckner
Ivan DeJesus
minor league
P Jeff Albert |
| May 20, 1978 | MON | N | ———— | LA | N | Larry Landreth
Gerry Hannahs |

Debs Garms

| March 3, 1940 | PIT | N | ———— | BOS | N | Cash |

Phil Garner

| March 15, 1977 | PIT | N | Tommy Helms
Chris Batton | OAK | A | Dave Giusti
Doc Medich
Doug Bair
Rick Langford
Tony Armas
Mitchell Page |
| Aug 31, 1981 | HOU | N | ———— | PIT | N | Johnny Ray
Randy Niemann
minor league
OF Kevin Houston |

Ralph Garr

| Dec 12, 1975 | CHI | A | Larvell Blanks | ATL | N | Ken Henderson
Dick Ruthven
Danny Osborn |
| Sept 20, 1979 | CAL | A | ———— | CHI | A | Cash |

Adrian Garrett

May 8, 1964	MIL	N	Jay Hook	NY	N	Roy McMillan
Aug 31, 1971	OAK	A	————	CHI	N	Frank Fernandez Bill McNulty
July 31, 1975	CAL	A	————	CHI	N	Cash

Greg Garrett

| Dec 15, 1970 | CIN | N | ———— | CAL | A | Jim Maloney |

Wayne Garrett

| July 21, 1976 | MON | N | Del Unser | NY | N | Jim Dwyer
Pepe Mangual |
| July 21, 1978 | STL | N | ———— | MON | N | Cash |

Gil Garrido

| May 16, 1966 | ATL | N | ———— | SF | N | Cash |
| Dec 4, 1973 | PHI | N | ———— | ATL | N | Bob Beall |

Ford Garrison

| May 7, 1944 | PHI | A | ———— | BOS | A | Hal Wagner |

Ned Garver

| Aug 14, 1952 | DET | A | Jim Delsing
Dave Madison
Bill Black | STL | A | Dick Littlefield
Marlin Stuart
Don Lenhardt
Vic Wertz |
| Dec 5, 1956 | KC | A | Gene Host
Virgil Trucks
Wayne Belardi
and $20,000. | DET | A | Jim Finigan
Jack Crimian
Bill Harrington
Eddie Robinson |

DATE	TRADED TO		TRADED WITH	TRADED BY		IN EXCHANGE FOR

Steve Garvey

| Dec 21, 1982 | SD | N | ———— | LA | N | No compensation (free agent signing) |

Jerry Garvin

| Jan 18, 1983 | STL | N | ———— | TOR | A | Cash |

Ned Garvin

| Sept 1904 | NY | A | ———— | BKN | N | Waiver price |

Rod Gaspar

| Sept 1, 1970 | SD | N | ———— | NY | N | Ron Herbel |

(San Diego received Gaspar on October 20.)

Clarence Gaston

| Nov 8, 1974 | ATL | N | ———— | SD | N | Danny Frisella |
| Sept 22, 1978 | PIT | N | ———— | ATL | N | Cash |

Milt Gaston

Dec 17, 1924	STL	A	Joe Bush Joe Giard	NY	A	Urban Shocker
Oct 19, 1927	WAS	A	————	STL	A	Dick Coffman Earl McNeely
Dec 15, 1928	BOS	A	Hod Lisenbee Bobby Reeves Grant Gillis Elliott Bigelow	WAS	A	Buddy Myer
Dec 2, 1931	CHI	A	————	BOS	A	Bob Weiland

Doc Gautreau

| July 1, 1925 | BOS | N | ———— | PHI | A | Cash |

Dinty Gearin

| June 5, 1924 | BOS | N | ———— | NY | N | Cash |

Joe Gedeon

| Jan 22, 1918 | STL | A | Les Nunamaker
Fritz Maisel
Nick Cullop
Urban Shocker | NY | A | Eddie Plank
Del Pratt
and $15,000. |

Johnny Gee

| June 12, 1944 | NY | N | ———— | PIT | N | Cash |

Phil Geier

| June 1901 | MIL | A | ———— | PHI | A | Tom Leahy |

Gary Geiger

| Dec 2, 1958 | BOS | A | Vic Wertz | CLE | A | Jimmy Piersall |

Dave Geisel

| Dec 28, 1981 | TOR | A | ———— | CHI | N | Paul Mirabella |

Vern Geishert

| Nov 25, 1969 | CIN | N | Pedro Borbon
Jim McGlothlin | CAL | A | Alex Johnson
Chico Ruiz |
| May 29, 1971 | SF | N | Frank Duffy | CIN | N | George Foster |

DATE	TRADED TO		TRADED WITH		TRADED BY		IN EXCHANGE FOR

Charley Gelbert

Dec 2, 1936	CIN	N	———		STL	N	Cash
July 9, 1937	DET	A	———		CIN	N	Waiver price
Aug 30, 1940	BOS	A	———		WAS	A	Waiver price

John Gelnar

Oct 18, 1968	KC	A	———		PIT	N	Cash
April 1, 1969	SEA	A	Steve Whitaker		KC	A	Lou Piniella
May 11, 1971	DET	A	Jose Herrera		MIL	A	Jim Hannan

Joe Genewich

June 15, 1928	NY	N	———		BOS	N	Ben Cantwell
							Al Spohrer
							Bill Clarkson
							Virgil Barnes

Jim Gentile

Nov 27, 1963	KC	A	cash		BAL	A	Norm Siebern
June 4, 1965	HOU	N	———		KC	A	Jess Hickman
							Ernie Fazio
							and $100,000.

(Kansas City received Fazio on October 15.)

| July 19, 1966 | CLE | A | ——— | | HOU | N | Tony Curry |

Gary Gentry

| Nov 2, 1972 | ATL | N | Danny Frisella | | NY | N | Felix Millan |
| | | | | | | | George Stone |

Lefty George

| Jan 1912 | CLE | A | ——— | | STL | A | George Stovall |

Jug Gerard

March 28, 1963	HOU	N	Danny Murphy		CHI	N	Merritt Ranew
							Hal Haydel
							Dick LeMay

Wally Gerber

| April 25, 1928 | BOS | A | ——— | | STL | A | Hal Wiltse |

Al Gerheauser

Jan 22, 1943	PHI	N	Tom Padden		NY	A	Nick Etten
			Ed Levy				Al Gettel
			and $10,000.				
March 31, 1945	PIT	N	———		PHI	N	Vince DiMaggio
Dec 5, 1946	BKN	N	———		PIT	N	Eddie Basinski

Dick Gernert

Nov 21, 1959	CHI	N	———		BOS	A	Dave Hillman
							Jim Marshall
Aug 31, 1960	DET	A	———		CHI	N	Cash
May 10, 1961	CIN	N	———		DET	A	Jim Baumer

Cesar Geronimo

Nov 29, 1971	CIN	N	Joe Morgan		HOU	N	Lee May
			Denis Menke				Tommy Helms
			Jack Billingham				Jimmy Stewart
			Ed Armbrister				

DATE	TRADED TO		TRADED WITH	TRADED BY		IN EXCHANGE FOR

Cesar Geronimo continued

| Jan 21, 1981 | KC | A | ———— | CIN | N | German Barranca |

Doc Gessler

| May 8, 1906 | CHI | N | ———— | BKN | N | Cash |
| Sept 1909 | WAS | A | ———— | BOS | A | Charlie Smith |

Al Gettel

Jan 22, 1943	NY	A	Nick Etten	PHI	N	Tom Padden Al Gerheauser Ed Levy and $10,000.
Dec 20, 1946	CLE	A	Hal Peck Gene Bearden	NY	A	Sherm Lollar Ray Mack
June 2, 1948	CHI	A	Pat Seerey	CLE	A	Bob Kennedy
July 12, 1949	WAS	A	————	CHI	A	Cash

Gus Getz

| June 1918 | PIT | N | ———— | CLE | A | Waiver price |

Joe Giard

| Dec 17, 1924 | STL | A | Joe Bush
Milt Gaston | NY | A | Urban Shocker |
| Feb 8, 1927 | NY | A | Cedric Durst | STL | A | Sad Sam Jones |

Joe Gibbon

| Oct 1, 1965 | SF | N | Ozzie Virgil | PIT | N | Matty Alou |
| June 10, 1969 | PIT | N | ———— | SF | N | Ron Kline |

Frank Gibson

| Dec 15, 1927 | STL | N | ———— | BOS | N | Cash |

George Gibson

| Aug 5, 1916 | NY | N | ———— | PIT | N | Waiver price |

Russ Gibson

| April 4, 1970 | SF | N | ———— | BOS | A | Cash |

Jim Gideon

| June 1, 1976 | MIN | A | *See Roy Smalley* | TEX | A | ———— |

Paul Giel

| April 13, 1959 | PIT | N | ———— | SF | N | Waiver price |
| June 1, 1961 | KC | A | Reno Bertoia | MIN | A | Bill Tuttle |

(Giel was returned to Minnesota for a cash payment.)

Bob Giggie

| May 11, 1960 | KC | A | ———— | MIL | N | George Brunet |

Gus Gil

| Oct 15, 1966 | CLE | A | ———— | CIN | N | Cash |

Charlie Gilbert

| May 6, 1941 | CHI | N | Johnny Hudson
and $65,000. | BKN | N | Billy Herman |
| June 15, 1946 | PHI | N | ———— | CHI | N | Cash |

DATE	TRADED TO		TRADED WITH	TRADED BY		IN EXCHANGE FOR

Wally Gilbert

| March 14, 1932 | CIN | N | Babe Herman
Ernie Lombardi | BKN | N | Tony Cuccinello
Joe Stripp
Clyde Sukeforth |

Bill Gilbreth

| Sept 6, 1972 | CAL | A | ———— | DET | A | Cash |
| Sept 12, 1974 | CLE | A | ———— | CAL | A | Charles Hudson |

Frank Gilhooley

| Aug 25, 1913 | NY | A | ———— | STL | N | Cash |
| Dec 18, 1918 | BOS | A | ———— | NY | A | *See Duffy Lewis* |

George Gill

| May 13, 1939 | STL | A | ———— | DET | A | *See Beau Bell* |

Grant Gillis

| Dec 15, 1928 | BOS | A | Milt Gaston
Hod Lisenbee
Bobby Reeves
Elliott Bigelow | WAS | A | Buddy Myer |

Hal Gilson

| June 15, 1968 | HOU | N | Dick Simpson | STL | N | Ron Davis |

Joe Ginsberg

| June 15, 1953 | CLE | A | ———— | DET | A | *See Ray Boone* |
| Aug 17, 1956 | BAL | A | ———— | KC | A | Hal Smith |

Al Gionfriddo

| May 3, 1947 | BKN | N | $100,000. | PIT | N | Kirby Higbe
Hank Behrman
Cal McLish
Gene Mauch
Dixie Howell |

Tony Giuliani

| March 24, 1938 | WAS | A | ———— | STL | A | Cash |
| March 1, 1944 | STL | A | Gene Moore
and cash | WAS | A | Rick Ferrell |

(Giuliani announced his retirement, and St. Louis received Moore to complete the trade.)

Dave Giusti

Oct 11, 1968	STL	N	Dave Adlesh	HOU	N	Johnny Edwards minor league C Tommy Smith
Dec 3, 1968	STL	N	————	SD	N	Danny Breeden Ed Spiezio Ron Davis minor league P Phil Knuckles
Oct 21, 1969	PIT	N	Dave Ricketts	STL	N	Carl Taylor minor league OF Frank Vanzin
March 15, 1977	OAK	A	————	PIT	N	*See Phil Garner*
Aug 5, 1977	CHI	N	————	OAK	A	Cash

Fred Gladding

| Aug 17, 1967 | HOU | N | cash | DET | A | Eddie Mathews |

DATE	TRADED TO		TRADED WITH	TRADED BY		IN EXCHANGE FOR

Fred Glade

| Feb 1908 | NY | A | Charlie Hemphill | STL | A | Jimmy Williams
Hobe Ferris
Danny Hoffman |

Tommy Glaviano

| Sept 30, 1952 | PHI | N | ————— | STL | N | Waiver price |

Whitey Glazner

| May 22, 1923 | PHI | N | Cotton Tierney
and $50,000. | PIT | N | Lee Meadows
Johnny Rawlings |

Jerry Gleaton

| Dec 12, 1980 | SEA | A | ————— | TEX | A | *See Rick Honeycutt* |
| June 29, 1984 | CHI | A | Gene Nelson | SEA | A | Salome Barojas |

Jim Gleeson

| Jan 24, 1939 | CHI | N | ————— | NY | A | $25,000. |
| Dec 4, 1940 | CIN | N | Bobby Mattick | CHI | N | Billy Myers |

Joe Glenn

| Oct 26, 1938 | STL | A | Myril Hoag | NY | A | Oral Hildebrand
Buster Mills |

John Glenn

| June 15, 1960 | STL | N | ————— | LA | N | Jim Donohue |

Al Glossop

June 15, 1940	BOS	N	Manny Salvo	NY	N	Tony Cuccinello
March 9, 1943	BKN	N	Lloyd Waner	PHI	N	Babe Dahlgren
Sept 28, 1943	CHI	N	—————	BKN	N	Cash

Ed Glynn

March 13, 1979	NY	N	—————	DET	A	Mardie Cornejo
April 6, 1981	CLE	A	—————	NY	N	Minor league P Dominick Bullinger
June 24, 1984	NY	N	—————	CLE	A	Minor league P Rich Miles
Nov 9, 1984	BOS	A	—————	NY	N	Cash

Danny Godby

| March 29, 1975 | BOS | A | ————— | STL | N | Danny Cater |

Ed Goebel

| Feb 10, 1923 | BOS | A | Val Picinich
Howard Shanks | WAS | A | Muddy Ruel
Allan Russell |

Chuck Goggin

| May 24, 1973 | ATL | N | ————— | PIT | N | Cash |
| March 26, 1974 | BOS | A | ————— | ATL | N | Vic Correll |

Bill Gogolewski

| March 23, 1974 | CLE | A | ————— | TEX | A | Steve Hargan |

Jim Golden

| Dec 23, 1958 | LA | N | Rip Repulski
Gene Snyder | PHI | N | Sparky Anderson |

DATE	TRADED TO		TRADED WITH	TRADED BY		IN EXCHANGE FOR

Jim Golden continued

| Dec 10, 1963 | CHI | A | Danny Murphy and cash | HOU | N | Nellie Fox |

Gordon Goldsberry

| Nov 27, 1951 | STL | A | ———— | CHI | A | *See Sherm Lollar* |

Mike Goliat

| Sept 12, 1951 | STL | A | ———— | PHI | N | Waiver price |

Dave Goltz

| Nov 15, 1979 | LA | N | ———— | MIN | A | No compensation (free agent signing) |

Lefty Gomez

| Jan 25, 1943 | BOS | N | ———— | NY | A | Cash |

Luis Gomez

| Dec 5, 1979 | ATL | N | Chris Chambliss | TOR | A | Barry Bonnell Pat Rockett Joey McLaughlin |

Ruben Gomez

| Dec 3, 1958 | PHI | N | Valmy Thomas | SF | N | Jack Sanford |
| Aug 20, 1962 | MIN | A | ———— | CLE | A | Georges Maranda Jackie Collum and cash |

Jesse Gonder

| July 1, 1963 | NY | N | ———— | CIN | N | Charlie Neal Sammy Taylor |
| July 21, 1965 | MIL | N | ———— | NY | N | Gary Kolb |

Fernando Gonzalez

Dec 4, 1973	KC	A	Nellie Briles	PIT	N	Ed Kirkpatrick Kurt Bevacqua minor league 1B Winston Cole
May 5, 1974	NY	A	————	KC	A	Cash
June 5, 1978	SD	N	————	PIT	N	Cash

Julio Gonzalez

| Dec 8, 1976 | HOU | N | ———— | CHI | N | Greg Gross |

Mike Gonzalez

April 8, 1915	STL	N	————	CIN	N	Ivy Wingo
May 1919	NY	N	————	STL	N	Waiver price
Dec 6, 1921	CIN	N	George Burns and $150,000.	NY	N	Heinie Groh
April 27, 1924	STL	N	————	BKN	N	Milt Stock
May 23, 1925	CHI	N	Howard Freigau	STL	N	Bob O'Farrell

Orlando Gonzalez

| July 25, 1980 | OAK | A | ———— | PHI | N | Cash |

Pedro Gonzalez

| May 10, 1965 | CLE | A | ———— | NY | A | Ray Barker |

DATE	TRADED TO		TRADED WITH	TRADED BY		IN EXCHANGE FOR

Ted Gray
Dec 6, 1954	CHI	A	Walt Dropo Bob Nieman	DET	A	Leo Cristante Ferris Fain Jack Phillips

Dallas Green
April 11, 1965	WAS	A	——————	PHI	N	Cash

(Green was returned to Philadelphia on May 11.)

David Green
Dec 12, 1980	STL	N	Sixto Lezcano Lary Sorensen Dave LaPoint	MIL	A	Pete Vuckovich Rollie Fingers Ted Simmons

Freddie Green
Sept 25, 1961	WAS	A	——————	PIT	N	Waiver price

Gene Green
Dec 2, 1959	BAL	A	minor league C Charles Staniland	STL	N	Bob Nieman
Oct 5, 1961	CLE	A	Dick Donovan Jim Mahoney	WAS	A	Jimmy Piersall
Aug 1, 1963	CIN	N	——————	CLE	A	Sammy Taylor

Lenny Green
May 26, 1959	WAS	A	——————	BAL	A	Albie Pearson
June 11, 1964	LA	A	Vic Power	MIN	A	Jerry Kindall Frank Kostro

(Part of three-team trade involving Los Angeles Angels, Minnesota, and Cleveland.)

Sept 5, 1964	BAL	A	——————	LA	A	Cash

Pumpsie Green
Dec 11, 1962	NY	N	Tracy Stallard Al Moran	BOS	A	Felix Mantilla

Hank Greenberg
Jan 18, 1947	PIT	N	——————	DET	A	$75,000.

Al Greene
June 2, 1980	STL	N	John Martin	DET	A	Jim Lentine

Kent Greenfield
June 12, 1927	BOS	N	Hugh McQuillan Doc Farrell	NY	N	Zack Taylor Larry Benton Herb Thomas
July 4, 1929	BKN	N	——————	BOS	N	Cash

Jim Greengrass
Aug 28, 1952	CIN	N	Johnny Schmitz Ernie Nevel Bob Marquis and $35,000.	NY	A	Ewell Blackwell
April 30, 1955	PHI	N	*See Andy Seminick*	CIN	N	——————

Hal Gregg
Dec 8, 1947	PIT	N	Dixie Walker Vic Lombardi	BKN	N	Preacher Roe Billy Cox Gene Mauch

DATE	TRADED TO		TRADED WITH	TRADED BY		IN EXCHANGE FOR
Vean Gregg						
Aug 20, 1914	BOS	A	————	CLE	A	Adam Johnson Fritz Coumbe Ben Egan
Dec 14, 1917	PHI	A	Merlin Kopp Pinch Thomas and $60,000.	BOS	A	Amos Strunk Joe Bush Wally Schang
Bill Greif						
Dec 3, 1971	SD	N	Derrel Thomas Mark Schaeffer	HOU	N	Dave Roberts
May 19, 1976	STL	N	————	SD	N	Luis Melendez
Nov 6, 1976	MON	N	Angel Torres Sam Mejias	STL	N	Steve Dunning Pat Scanlon Tony Scott
Ed Gremminger						
July 24, 1904	DET	A	————	BOS	N	Cash
Bobby Grich						
Nov 24, 1976	CAL	A	————	BAL	A	No compensation (free agent signing)
Tom Grieve						
Dec 8, 1977	NY	N	Willie Montanez Ken Henderson	TEX	A	Jon Matlack John Milner
			(Part of four-team trade involving Texas, New York Mets, Pittsburgh, and Atlanta.)			
Dec 5, 1978	STL	N	Kim Seaman	NY	N	Pete Falcone
Ken Griffey						
Nov 4, 1981	NY	A	————	CIN	N	Freddie Toliver minor league P Bryan Ryder
Alfredo Griffin						
Dec 5, 1978	TOR	A	minor league 3B Phil Lansford	CLE	A	Victor Cruz
Dec 8, 1984	OAK	A	Dave Collins and cash	TOR	A	Bill Caudill
Doug Griffin						
Oct 11, 1970	BOS	A	————	CAL	A	*See Tony Conigliaro*
Hank Griffin						
June 10, 1911	BOS	N	*See Johnny Kling*	CHI	N	————
Mike Griffin						
Nov 10, 1978	NY	A	*See Dave Righetti*	TEX	A	————
June 12, 1981	CHI	N	Doug Bird and $400,000.	NY	A	Rick Reuschel
March 16, 1982	MON	N	————	CHI	N	Dan Briggs
June 8, 1982	SD	N	————	MON	N	Jerry Manuel
Tom Griffin						
Aug 3, 1976	SD	N	————	HOU	N	Cash
Dec 11, 1981	PIT	N	————	SF	N	Dorian Boyland

DATE	TRADED TO		TRADED WITH	TRADED BY		IN EXCHANGE FOR

Wayne Gross
Dec 8, 1983	BAL	A	————	OAK	A	Tim Stoddard

Jerry Grote
Oct 19, 1965	NY	N	————	HOU	N	Tom Parsons and cash
Aug 31, 1977	LA	N	————	NY	N	Minor leaguers P Dan Smith and IF Randy Rogers
Feb 5, 1981	KC	A	————	LA	N	No compensation (free agent signing)

Ernie Groth
Dec 2, 1948	CHI	A	Bob Kuzava	CLE	A	Frank Papish

Johnny Groth
Dec 4, 1952	STL	A	Virgil Trucks Hal White	DET	A	Owen Friend Bob Nieman J. W. Porter
Feb 5, 1954	CHI	A	Johnny Lipon	BAL	A	Neil Berry Sam Mele
June 7, 1955	WAS	A	Bob Chakales Clint Courtney	CHI	A	Jim Busby
April 16, 1956	KC	A	————	WAS	A	Cash
Aug 1, 1957	DET	A	————	KC	A	Cash

Lefty Grove
Dec 12, 1933	BOS	A	Rube Walberg Max Bishop	PHI	A	Bob Kline Rabbit Warstler and $125,000.

Roy Grover
June 1919	WAS	A	————	PHI	A	Cash

Johnny Grubb
Dec 8, 1976	CLE	A	Fred Kendall Hector Torres	SD	N	George Hendrick
Aug 31, 1978	TEX	A	————	CLE	A	Bobby Cuellar minor league OF Dave Rivera
March 24, 1983	DET	A	————	TEX	A	Dave Tobik

Frank Grube
Dec 15, 1933	STL	A	————	CHI	A	Cash
Sept 20, 1935	CHI	A	————	STL	A	Cash

Joe Grzenda
Aug 14, 1967	NY	N	————	KC	A	Cash
Nov 29, 1967	MIN	A	————	NY	N	Cash
March 21, 1970	WAS	A	Charley Walters	MIN	A	Brant Alyea
Nov 3, 1971	STL	N	————	TEX	A	Ted Kubiak

Mike Guerra
Dec 2, 1946	PHI	A	————	WAS	A	Cash
Dec 13, 1950	BOS	A	————	PHI	A	Cash
May 7, 1951	WAS	A	————	BOS	A	Cash

DATE	TRADED TO		TRADED WITH	TRADED BY		IN EXCHANGE FOR

Mario Guerrero

DATE	TRADED TO		TRADED WITH	TRADED BY		IN EXCHANGE FOR
April 4, 1975	STL	N	————	BOS	A	Jim Willoughby
May 29, 1976	CAL	A	————	STL	N	Minor leaguers C Ed Jordan and 1B Ed Kurpiel
March 15, 1978	OAK	A	————	SF	N	*See Vida Blue*
Dec 8, 1980	SEA	A	————	OAK	A	Cash

Pedro Guerrero

DATE	TRADED TO		TRADED WITH	TRADED BY		IN EXCHANGE FOR
April 3, 1974	LA	N	————	CLE	A	Bruce Ellingsen

Skip Guinn

DATE	TRADED TO		TRADED WITH	TRADED BY		IN EXCHANGE FOR
Jan 22, 1969	HOU	N	Jesus Alou Donn Clendenon Jack Billingham and $100,000.	MON	N	Rusty Staub

(Clendenon refused to report, and Houston was sent Billingham, Guinn, and cash on April 8, 1969.)

Brad Gulden

DATE	TRADED TO		TRADED WITH	TRADED BY		IN EXCHANGE FOR
Feb 15, 1979	NY	A	————	LA	N	Gary Thomasson
Nov 18, 1980	SEA	A	$150,000.	NY	A	Larry Milbourne
April 5, 1982	MON	N	————	NY	A	Bobby Ramos
Oct 26, 1982	NY	A	————	MON	N	Cash

Don Gullett

DATE	TRADED TO		TRADED WITH	TRADED BY		IN EXCHANGE FOR
Nov 18, 1976	NY	A	————	CIN	N	No compensation (free agent signing)

Glenn Gulliver

DATE	TRADED TO		TRADED WITH	TRADED BY		IN EXCHANGE FOR
July 5, 1984	STL	N	————	BAL	A	A player to be named later

Harry Gumbert

DATE	TRADED TO		TRADED WITH	TRADED BY		IN EXCHANGE FOR
May 14, 1941	STL	N	Paul Dean and cash	NY	N	Bill McGee
June 15, 1944	CIN	N	————	STL	N	Cash
July 27, 1949	PIT	N	————	CIN	N	Waiver price

Randy Gumpert

DATE	TRADED TO		TRADED WITH	TRADED BY		IN EXCHANGE FOR
July 28, 1948	CHI	A	————	NY	A	Cash
Nov 13, 1951	BOS	A	Don Lenhardt	CHI	A	Mel Hoderlein Chuck Stobbs
June 10, 1952	WAS	A	Walt Masterson	BOS	A	Sid Hudson

Larry Gura

DATE	TRADED TO		TRADED WITH	TRADED BY		IN EXCHANGE FOR
Aug 31, 1973	TEX	A	————	CHI	N	Mike Paul
May 8, 1974	NY	A	cash	TEX	A	Duke Sims
May 16, 1976	KC	A	————	NY	A	Fran Healy

Frankie Gustine

DATE	TRADED TO		TRADED WITH	TRADED BY		IN EXCHANGE FOR
Dec 8, 1948	CHI	N	Cal McLish	PIT	N	Clyde McCullough Cliff Chambers
Sept 14, 1949	PHI	A	————	CHI	N	Waiver price

DATE	TRADED TO		TRADED WITH	TRADED BY		IN EXCHANGE FOR

Frankie Gustine continued

| Dec 13, 1949 | STL | A | Ray Coleman
Billy DeMars
minor league
OF Ray Ippolito
and $100,000. | PHI | A | Bob Dillinger
Paul Lehner |

Cesar Gutierrez

| Sept 2, 1969 | DET | A | ———— | SF | N | Cash |
| March 24, 1972 | MON | N | ———— | DET | A | Cash |

Don Gutteridge

| March 26, 1948 | PIT | N | ———— | BOS | A | Cash |

Bert Haas

| June 12, 1940 | STL | N | Ernie Koy
Carl Doyle
Sam Nahem
and $125,000. | BKN | N | Joe Medwick
Curt Davis |
| Dec 11, 1947 | PHI | N | ———— | CIN | N | Tommy Hughes |

Eddie Haas

| Dec 5, 1957 | MIL | N | Don Kaiser
Bob Rush | CHI | N | Taylor Phillips
Sammy Taylor |

Mule Haas

| Sept 28, 1932 | CHI | A | Al Simmons
Jimmy Dykes | PHI | A | $100,000. |

Bob Habenicht

| Oct 1, 1952 | STL | A | ———— | STL | N | Waiver price |

Rich Hacker

| March 31, 1971 | MON | N | Ron Swoboda | NY | N | Don Hahn |

Warren Hacker

| Nov 13, 1956 | CIN | N | Don Hoak
Pete Whisenant | CHI | N | Elmer Singleton
Ray Jablonski |
| June 26, 1957 | PHI | N | ———— | CIN | N | Waiver price |

Harvey Haddix

May 11, 1956	PHI	N	Ben Flowers Stu Miller	STL	N	Murry Dickson Herm Wehmeier
Dec 16, 1957	CIN	N	————	PHI	N	Wally Post
Jan 30, 1959	PIT	N	Smoky Burgess Don Hoak	CIN	N	Whammy Douglas Jim Pendleton Frank Thomas Johnny Powers
Dec 14, 1963	BAL	A	————	PIT	N	Minor league SS Dick Yencha and cash

Bump Hadley

Dec 4, 1931	CHI	A	Jackie Hayes Sad Sam Jones	WAS	A	Carl Reynolds John Kerr
April 27, 1932	STL	A	Bruce Campbell	CHI	A	Red Kress
Jan 22, 1935	WAS	A	————	STL	A	Luke Sewell
Jan 17, 1936	NY	A	Roy Johnson	WAS	A	Jimmie DeShong Jesse Hill

DATE	TRADED TO		TRADED WITH	TRADED BY		IN EXCHANGE FOR

Bump Hadley continued

Jan 2, 1941	NY	N	————	NY	A	Cash
May 29, 1941	PHI	A	————	NY	N	Cash

Kent Hadley

Nov 20, 1957	KC	A	————	DET	A	*See Billy Martin*
Dec 11, 1959	NY	A	*See Roger Maris*	KC	A	————

Mickey Haefner

July 21, 1949	CHI	A	————	WAS	A	Cash
Aug 8, 1950	BOS	N	————	CHI	A	Cash

Bud Hafey

Aug 5, 1939	PHI	N	————	CIN	N	Cash

Chick Hafey

April 11, 1932	CIN	N	————	STL	N	Harvey Hendrick Benny Frey and cash

Casey Hageman

June 1914	BKN	N	————	STL	N	Joe Riggert
June 1914	CHI	N	————	BKN	N	Cash

Joe Hague

May 19, 1972	CIN	N	————	STL	N	Bernie Carbo

Don Hahn

March 31, 1971	NY	N	————	MON	N	Ron Swoboda Rich Hacker
Dec 3, 1974	PHI	N	Tug McGraw Dave Schneck	NY	N	Del Unser John Stearns Mac Scarce
June 24, 1975	SD	N	————	STL	N	Cash

Ed Hahn

May 9, 1906	CHI	A	————	NY	A	Cash

Noodles Hahn

April 1906	NY	A	————	CIN	N	Waiver price

Hal Haid

Jan 1931	BOS	N	————	STL	N	Waiver price

Jerry Hairston

June 13, 1977	PIT	N	————	CHI	A	Cash

Bob Hale

July 26, 1961	NY	A	————	CLE	A	Cash

John Hale

Sept 2, 1977	TOR	A	————	LA	N	Cash
Sept 14, 1977	SEA	A	————	TOR	A	Cash

Odell Hale

Dec 12, 1940	BOS	A	Frankie Pytlak Joe Dobson	CLE	A	Gene Desautels Jim Bagby Gee Walker

DATE	TRADED TO		TRADED WITH	TRADED BY		IN EXCHANGE FOR

Odell Hale continued
| June 19, 1941 | NY | N | ——— | BOS | A | Waiver price |

Sammy Hale
| Dec 11, 1929 | STL | A | ——— | PHI | A | Wally Schang |

Ray Haley
| Sept 2, 1916 | PHI | A | ——— | BOS | A | Jimmy Walsh |

Ed Halicki
| June 20, 1980 | CAL | A | ——— | SF | N | Cash |

Bob Hall
| April 1905 | BKN | N | ——— | NY | N | Cash |

Dick Hall
Dec 15, 1959	KC	A	Ken Hamlin	PIT	N	Hal Smith
April 12, 1961	BAL	A	Dick Williams	KC	A	Jerry Walker Chuck Essegian
Dec 15, 1966	PHI	N	———	BAL	A	John Morris

Jimmie Hall
Dec 2, 1966	CAL	A	Don Mincher Pete Cimino	MIN	A	Dean Chance Jackie Hernandez
June 15, 1968	CLE	A	———	CAL	A	Vic Davalillo
April 14, 1969	NY	A	———	CLE	A	Cash
Sept 11, 1969	CHI	N	———	NY	A	Minor league P Terry Bongiovanni and cash
June 29, 1970	ATL	N	———	CHI	N	Cash

Mel Hall
| June 13, 1984 | CLE | A | Joe Carter
minor league
P Darryl Banks | CHI | N | Rick Sutcliffe
George Frazier
Ron Hassey |

Tom Hall
Dec 3, 1971	CIN	N	———	MIN	A	Wayne Granger
April 15, 1975	NY	N	———	CIN	N	Mac Scarce
May 7, 1976	KC	A	———	NY	N	Minor league IF Bryan Jones and cash

Bill Hallahan
| May 31, 1936 | CIN | N | ——— | STL | N | Cash |

Tom Haller
Feb 13, 1968	LA	N	minor league P Frank Kasmeta	SF	N	Ron Hunt Nate Oliver
Dec 2, 1971	DET	A	———	LA	N	Minor league P Bernie Beckman and cash
Oct 25, 1972	PHI	N	Don Leshnock	DET	A	Cash

Jack Hallett
| Dec 9, 1941 | PHI | A | Mike Kreevich | CHI | A | Wally Moses |

DATE	TRADED TO		TRADED WITH	TRADED BY		IN EXCHANGE FOR

Dave Hamilton

DATE	TRADED TO		TRADED WITH	TRADED BY		IN EXCHANGE FOR
June 15, 1975	CHI	A	Chet Lemon	OAK	A	Stan Bahnsen Skip Pitlock
Aug 31, 1977	STL	N	Nyls Nyman Silvio Martinez	CHI	A	Clay Carroll
May 28, 1978	PIT	N	————	STL	N	Cash

Earl Hamilton

DATE	TRADED TO		TRADED WITH	TRADED BY		IN EXCHANGE FOR
May 30, 1916	DET	A	————	STL	A	Cash
June 22, 1916	STL	A	————	DET	A	Waiver price
Unknown	PIT	N	————	STL	A	Cash
Dec 1923	PHI	N	————	PIT	N	Waiver price

Jack Hamilton

DATE	TRADED TO		TRADED WITH	TRADED BY		IN EXCHANGE FOR
Dec 4, 1963	DET	A	Don Demeter	PHI	N	Jim Bunning Gus Triandos
Oct 14, 1965	NY	N	————	DET	A	Cash
June 10, 1967	CAL	A	————	NY	N	Nick Willhite
Oct 8, 1968	CLE	A	————	CAL	A	Eddie Fisher
June 13, 1969	CHI	A	————	CLE	A	Sammy Ellis

Steve Hamilton

DATE	TRADED TO		TRADED WITH	TRADED BY		IN EXCHANGE FOR
May 3, 1962	WAS	A	Don Rudolph	CLE	A	Willie Tasby
April 21, 1963	NY	A	————	WAS	A	Jim Coates
Sept 9, 1970	CHI	A	————	NY	A	Cash
March 23, 1971	SF	N	————	CHI	A	Steve Huntz

Tom Hamilton

DATE	TRADED TO		TRADED WITH	TRADED BY		IN EXCHANGE FOR
Dec 16, 1953	NY	A	*See Harry Byrd*	PHI	A	————

Ken Hamlin

DATE	TRADED TO		TRADED WITH	TRADED BY		IN EXCHANGE FOR
Dec 15, 1959	KC	A	Dick Hall	PIT	N	Hal Smith

Luke Hamlin

DATE	TRADED TO		TRADED WITH	TRADED BY		IN EXCHANGE FOR
Dec 12, 1941	PIT	N	Pete Coscarart Babe Phelps Jimmy Wasdell	BKN	N	Arky Vaughan

Pete Hamm

DATE	TRADED TO		TRADED WITH	TRADED BY		IN EXCHANGE FOR
Feb 5, 1972	CHI	A	————	MIN	A	Cash

Atlee Hammaker

DATE	TRADED TO		TRADED WITH	TRADED BY		IN EXCHANGE FOR
March 30, 1982	SF	N	Renie Martin Craig Chamberlain Brad Wellman	KC	A	Vida Blue Bob Tufts

Jack Hammond

DATE	TRADED TO		TRADED WITH	TRADED BY		IN EXCHANGE FOR
May 13, 1922	PIT	N	————	CLE	A	Cash

Steve Hammond

DATE	TRADED TO		TRADED WITH	TRADED BY		IN EXCHANGE FOR
April 28, 1982	KC	A	————	ATL	N	Cash

Granny Hamner

DATE	TRADED TO		TRADED WITH	TRADED BY		IN EXCHANGE FOR
May 16, 1959	CLE	A	————	PHI	N	Humberto Robinson

Ike Hampton

DATE	TRADED TO		TRADED WITH	TRADED BY		IN EXCHANGE FOR
March 22, 1975	CAL	A	————	NY	N	Ken Sanders

DATE	TRADED TO		TRADED WITH	TRADED BY		IN EXCHANGE FOR

Garry Hancock

DATE	TRADED TO		TRADED WITH	TRADED BY		IN EXCHANGE FOR
Dec 9, 1977	BOS	A	——————	CLE	A	Jack Baker
Dec 6, 1982	OAK	A	Carney Lansford minor league P Jerry King	BOS	A	Tony Armas Jeff Newman

Rich Hand

DATE	TRADED TO		TRADED WITH	TRADED BY		IN EXCHANGE FOR
Dec 2, 1971	TEX	A	Roy Foster Ken Suarez Mike Paul	CLE	A	Del Unser Denny Riddleberger Gary Jones minor league P Terry Ley
May 20, 1973	CAL	A	Mike Epstein Rick Stelmaszek	TEX	A	Jim Spencer Lloyd Allen
Sept 5, 1974	STL	N	——————	CAL	A	Orlando Pena
	(St. Louis received Hand on October 15.)					

Bill Hands

DATE	TRADED TO		TRADED WITH	TRADED BY		IN EXCHANGE FOR
Dec 2, 1965	CHI	N	Randy Hundley	SF	N	Lindy McDaniel Don Landrum Jim Rittwage
Nov 30, 1972	MIN	A	Joe Decker minor league P Bob Maneely	CHI	N	Dave LaRoche
Sept 9, 1974	TEX	A	——————	MIN	A	Cash
Feb 24, 1976	NY	N	——————	TEX	A	George Stone

Harry Hanebrink

DATE	TRADED TO		TRADED WITH	TRADED BY		IN EXCHANGE FOR
March 31, 1959	PHI	N	Gene Conley Joe Koppe	MIL	N	Stan Lopata Ted Kazanski Johnny O'Brien

Fred Haney

DATE	TRADED TO		TRADED WITH	TRADED BY		IN EXCHANGE FOR
Dec 9, 1925	BOS	A	——————	DET	A	Tex Vache Homer Ezzell
July 12, 1927	CHI	N	——————	BOS	A	Cash

Larry Haney

DATE	TRADED TO		TRADED WITH	TRADED BY		IN EXCHANGE FOR
June 14, 1969	OAK	A	——————	SEA	A	John Donaldson
Sept 6, 1972	OAK	A	——————	SD	N	Cash
Sept 1, 1973	STL	N	Lew Krausse	OAK	A	Cash
March 26, 1974	OAK	A	——————	STL	N	Cash
Dec 6, 1976	MIL	A	——————	OAK	A	Cash

Gerry Hannahs

DATE	TRADED TO		TRADED WITH	TRADED BY		IN EXCHANGE FOR
May 20, 1978	LA	N	Larry Landreth	MON	N	Mike Garman

Jim Hannan

DATE	TRADED TO		TRADED WITH	TRADED BY		IN EXCHANGE FOR
Oct 9, 1970	DET	A	——————	WAS	A	*See Denny McLain*
May 11, 1971	MIL	A	——————	DET	A	John Gelnar Jose Herrera

Jack Hannifin

DATE	TRADED TO		TRADED WITH	TRADED BY		IN EXCHANGE FOR
June 1906	NY	N	——————	PHI	A	Waiver price
April 1908	BOS	N	——————	NY	N	Cash

DATE	TRADED TO		TRADED WITH	TRADED BY		IN EXCHANGE FOR

Andy Hansen

Jan 13, 1954	PIT	N	Lucky Lohrke and $70,000.	PHI	N	Murry Dickson

Ron Hansen

Jan 14, 1963	CHI	A	Hoyt Wilhelm Pete Ward Dave Nicholson	BAL	A	Luis Aparicio Al Smith
Feb 13, 1968	WAS	A	Dennis Higgins Steve Jones	CHI	A	Tim Cullen Buster Narum Bob Priddy
Aug 2, 1968	CHI	A	————	WAS	A	Tim Cullen
Feb 28, 1970	NY	A	————	CHI	A	Cash

Snipe Hansen

June 22, 1935	STL	A	————	PHI	N	Cash

Jim Hardin

May 28, 1971	NY	A	————	BAL	A	Bill Burbach

Carroll Hardy

June 13, 1960	BOS	A	Russ Nixon	CLE	A	Marty Keough Ted Bowsfield
Dec 10, 1962	HOU	N	————	BOS	A	Dick Williams

Larry Hardy

Dec 11, 1975	HOU	N	Joe McIntosh	SD	N	Doug Rader

Steve Hargan

March 23, 1974	TEX	A	————	CLE	A	Bill Gogolewski
May 9, 1977	TEX	A	Jim Mason and $200,000.	TOR	A	Roy Howell
June 15, 1977	ATL	N	————	TEX	A	Cash

Alan Hargesheimer

Oct 15, 1982	CHI	N	————	SF	N	Herman Segelke
March 30, 1984	KC	A	————	CHI	N	Dick Botelho

Pinky Hargrave

June 8, 1925	STL	A	George Mogridge	WAS	A	Hank Severeid
Jan 15, 1927	DET	A	Marty McManus Bobby LaMotte	STL	A	Lefty Stewart Frank O'Rourke Billy Mullen Otto Miller
Sept 10, 1930	WAS	A	————	DET	A	Cash
Dec 1931	BOS	N	————	WAS	A	Waiver price

Charlie Hargreaves

June 8, 1928	PIT	N	————	BKN	N	Joe Harris Johnny Gooch

Mike Hargrove

Oct 25, 1978	SD	N	Kurt Bevacqua Bill Fahey	TEX	A	Oscar Gamble Dave Roberts and $300,000.
June 14, 1979	CLE	A	————	SD	N	Paul Dade

DATE	TRADED TO		TRADED WITH	TRADED BY		IN EXCHANGE FOR

Tim Harkness

DATE	TRADED TO		TRADED WITH	TRADED BY		IN EXCHANGE FOR
April 5, 1957	BKN	N	Ron Negray Elmer Valo Ben Flowers minor league SS Mel Geho	PHI	N	Chico Fernandez
Nov 30, 1962	NY	N	Larry Burright	LA	N	Bob Miller

Dick Harley

DATE	TRADED TO		TRADED WITH	TRADED BY		IN EXCHANGE FOR
April 1900	CIN	N	————	CLE	N	Cash

Larry Harlow

DATE	TRADED TO		TRADED WITH	TRADED BY		IN EXCHANGE FOR
June 5, 1979	CAL	A	————	BAL	A	Floyd Rayford and cash

Bob Harmon

DATE	TRADED TO		TRADED WITH	TRADED BY		IN EXCHANGE FOR
Dec 12, 1913	PIT	N	Ed Konetchy Mike Mowrey	STL	N	Art Butler Dots Miller Cozy Dolan Owen Wilson Hank Robinson

Chuck Harmon

DATE	TRADED TO		TRADED WITH	TRADED BY		IN EXCHANGE FOR
May 16, 1956	STL	N	————	CIN	N	Joe Frazier Alex Grammas
May 10, 1957	PHI	N	————	STL	N	Glen Gorbous

Brian Harper

DATE	TRADED TO		TRADED WITH	TRADED BY		IN EXCHANGE FOR
Dec 11, 1981	PIT	N	————	CAL	A	Tim Foli
Dec 12, 1984	STL	N	John Tudor	PIT	N	George Hendrick minor league C Steve Barnard

George Harper

DATE	TRADED TO		TRADED WITH	TRADED BY		IN EXCHANGE FOR
May 30, 1924	PHI	N	————	CIN	N	Curt Walker
Jan 9, 1927	NY	N	Butch Henline	PHI	N	Jack Scott Fresco Thompson
			(Part of three-team trade involving Philadelphia, New York, and Brooklyn.)			
May 1, 1928	STL	N	————	NY	N	Bob O'Farrell
Dec 8, 1928	BOS	N	————	STL	N	Cash

Harry Harper

DATE	TRADED TO		TRADED WITH	TRADED BY		IN EXCHANGE FOR
Jan 20, 1920	BOS	A	Mike Menosky Eddie Foster	WAS	A	Braggo Roth Red Shannon
Dec 15, 1920	NY	A	*See Waite Hoyt*	BOS	A	————

Jack Harper

DATE	TRADED TO		TRADED WITH	TRADED BY		IN EXCHANGE FOR
Jan 1900	STL	N	Otto Krueger Joe Quinn Jim Hughey	CLE	N	Cash
Oct 1906	CIN	N	————	CHI	N	Chick Fraser

Tommy Harper

DATE	TRADED TO		TRADED WITH	TRADED BY		IN EXCHANGE FOR
Nov 21, 1967	CLE	A	————	CIN	N	George Culver Fred Whitfield Bob Raudman

DATE	TRADED TO		TRADED WITH	TRADED BY		IN EXCHANGE FOR

Tommy Harper continued

Oct 11, 1971	BOS	A	Marty Pattin Lew Krausse Pat Skrable	MIL	A	Billy Conigliaro Joe Lahoud Jim Lonborg Ken Brett George Scott Don Pavletich
Dec 2, 1974	CAL	A	————	BOS	A	Bob Heise
Aug 13, 1975	OAK	A	————	CAL	A	Cash

Toby Harrah

| Dec 8, 1978 | CLE | A | ———— | TEX | A | Buddy Bell |
| Feb 4, 1984 | NY | A | minor league
P Rick Brown | CLE | A | Danny Boitano
Otis Nixon
minor league
P Guy Elston |

Billy Harrell

| Feb 2, 1959 | STL | N | ———— | CLE | A | Waiver price |

Ray Harrell

Dec 8, 1938	CHI	N	————	STL	N	Cash
May 29, 1939	PHI	N	Joe Marty Kirby Higbe	CHI	N	Claude Passeau
Jan 22, 1940	PIT	N	————	PHI	N	Waiver price

Bill Harrelson

| Jan 14, 1970 | CIN | N | minor league
IF Dan Loomer | CAL | A | Jack Fisher |

Bud Harrelson

| March 24, 1978 | PHI | N | ———— | NY | N | Fred Andrews
and cash |

Ken Harrelson

June 23, 1966	WAS	A	————	KC	A	Jim Duckworth
June 9, 1967	KC	A	————	WAS	A	Cash
April 19, 1969	CLE	A	Juan Pizarro Dick Ellsworth	BOS	A	Sonny Siebert Joe Azcue Vicente Romo

Bill Harrington

| Dec 5, 1956 | DET | A | ———— | KC | A | *See Ned Garver* |

Bob Harris

| May 13, 1939 | STL | A | ———— | DET | A | *See Beau Bell* |
| June 1, 1942 | PHI | A | Bob Swift | STL | A | Frankie Hayes |

Bucky Harris

| Dec 19, 1928 | DET | A | ———— | WAS | A | Jack Warner |
| | | | (Harris was named Detroit manager.) | | | |

Buddy Harris

| Nov 27, 1972 | NY | N | Rich Chiles | HOU | N | Tommie Agee |

Charlie Harris

| May 2, 1951 | CLE | A | ———— | PHI | A | Cash |

DATE	TRADED TO		TRADED WITH	TRADED BY		IN EXCHANGE FOR

Dave Harris
| June 13, 1930 | WAS | A | ——— | CHI | A | Red Barnes |

Gail Harris
| Jan 28, 1958 | DET | A | Ozzie Virgil | SF | N | Jim Finigan and $25,000. |
| May 7, 1960 | LA | N | ——— | DET | A | Sandy Amoros |

Greg Harris
| Feb 10, 1982 | CIN | N | Alex Trevino Jim Kern | NY | N | George Foster |
| Sept 27, 1983 | MON | N | ——— | CIN | N | Cash |

Joe Harris
Dec 24, 1921	BOS	A	George Burns Elmer Smith	CLE	A	Stuffy McInnis
April 26, 1925	WAS	A	———	BOS	A	Paul Zahniser Roy Carlyle
Feb 4, 1927	PIT	N	———	WAS	A	Waiver price
June 8, 1928	BKN	N	Johnny Gooch	PIT	N	Charlie Hargreaves

John Harris
| Jan 10, 1983 | CIN | N | ——— | CAL | A | Mike O'Berry |

Lum Harris
| Feb 14, 1947 | WAS | A | ——— | PHI | A | Waiver price |

Mickey Harris
| June 13, 1949 | WAS | A | Sam Mele | BOS | A | Walt Masterson |
| April 22, 1952 | CLE | A | ——— | WAS | A | Waiver price |

Vic Harris
July 20, 1972	TEX	A	Marty Martinez Steve Lawson	OAK	A	Don Mincher Ted Kubiak
Oct 25, 1973	CHI	N	Bill Madlock	TEX	A	Ferguson Jenkins
Dec 22, 1975	STL	N	———	CHI	N	Mick Kelleher
Oct 20, 1976	SF	N	———	STL	N	*See Mike Caldwell*

Chuck Harrison
| Oct 8, 1967 | ATL | N | Sonny Jackson | HOU | N | Denny Lemaster Denis Menke |
| Oct 17, 1968 | KC | A | ——— | HOU | N | Cash |

Roric Harrison
Aug 24, 1969	SEA	A	Dooley Womack	HOU	N	Jim Bouton
April 5, 1971	BAL	A	minor leaguer Marion Jackson	MIL	A	Marcelino Lopez
Nov 30, 1972	ATL	N	———	BAL	A	*See Earl Williams*
June 7, 1975	CLE	A	———	ATL	N	Blue Moon Odom Bob Belloir
April 7, 1976	STL	N	———	CLE	A	Harry Parker

Slim Harriss
| June 15, 1926 | BOS | A | Fred Heimach Baby Doll Jacobson | PHI | A | Tom Jenkins Howard Ehmke |

DATE	TRADED TO		TRADED WITH	TRADED BY		IN EXCHANGE FOR

Earl Harrist

DATE	TRADED TO		TRADED WITH	TRADED BY		IN EXCHANGE FOR
June 9, 1948	WAS	A	————	CHI	A	Marino Pieretti
March 7, 1953	CHI	A	————	STL	A	Cash
May 23, 1953	DET	A	————	CHI	A	Waiver price

Jack Harshman

DATE	TRADED TO		TRADED WITH	TRADED BY		IN EXCHANGE FOR
Dec 3, 1957	BAL	A	*See Larry Doby*	CHI	A	————
June 15, 1959	BOS	A	————	BAL	A	Billy Hoeft
July 30, 1959	CLE	A	————	BOS	A	Waiver price

Jim Ray Hart

DATE	TRADED TO		TRADED WITH	TRADED BY		IN EXCHANGE FOR
April 17, 1973	NY	A	————	SF	N	Cash

Mike Hart

DATE	TRADED TO		TRADED WITH	TRADED BY		IN EXCHANGE FOR
Dec 8, 1978	TEX	A	————	MON	N	Jim Mason

Chuck Hartenstein

DATE	TRADED TO		TRADED WITH	TRADED BY		IN EXCHANGE FOR
Jan 15, 1969	PIT	N	Ron Campbell	CHI	N	Manny Jimenez
June 22, 1970	STL	N	————	PIT	N	Cash
Nov 5, 1976	TOR	A	————	SD	N	Cash

Grover Hartley

DATE	TRADED TO		TRADED WITH	TRADED BY		IN EXCHANGE FOR
Dec 12, 1913	CIN	N	Buck Herzog	NY	N	Bob Bescher
			(Hartley jumped to the Federal League and Herzog was made Cincinnati manager.)			
Feb 10, 1916	STL	A	*See Eddie Plank*	STL	F	————
Dec 1927	CLE	A	————	BOS	A	Waiver price

Bob Hartman

DATE	TRADED TO		TRADED WITH	TRADED BY		IN EXCHANGE FOR
June 24, 1962	CLE	A	————	MIL	N	Ken Aspromonte and cash

Topsy Hartsel

DATE	TRADED TO		TRADED WITH	TRADED BY		IN EXCHANGE FOR
April 1901	CHI	N	Mike Kahoe	CIN	N	Cash

Roy Hartsfield

DATE	TRADED TO		TRADED WITH	TRADED BY		IN EXCHANGE FOR
Jan 17, 1953	BKN	N	$50,000.	MIL	N	Andy Pafko

Paul Hartzell

DATE	TRADED TO		TRADED WITH	TRADED BY		IN EXCHANGE FOR
Feb 3, 1979	MIN	A	Ken Landreaux Dave Engle Brad Havens	CAL	A	Rod Carew

Roy Hartzell

DATE	TRADED TO		TRADED WITH	TRADED BY		IN EXCHANGE FOR
Jan 1911	NY	A	————	STL	A	Jimmy Austin Frank LaPorte

Erwin Harvey

DATE	TRADED TO		TRADED WITH	TRADED BY		IN EXCHANGE FOR
May 1901	CLE	A	————	CHI	A	Cash

Mickey Haslin

DATE	TRADED TO		TRADED WITH	TRADED BY		IN EXCHANGE FOR
April 30, 1936	BOS	N	————	PHI	N	Pinky Whitney
Dec 4, 1936	NY	N	————	BOS	N	Eddie Mayo

Buddy Hassett

DATE	TRADED TO		TRADED WITH	TRADED BY		IN EXCHANGE FOR
Jan 1936	BKN	N	————	NY	A	Cash

DATE	TRADED TO		TRADED WITH	TRADED BY		IN EXCHANGE FOR

Buddy Hassett continued

DATE	TRADED TO		TRADED WITH	TRADED BY		IN EXCHANGE FOR
Dec 13, 1938	BOS	N	Jimmy Outlaw	BKN	N	Gene Moore Ira Hutchinson
Feb 5, 1942	NY	A	Gene Moore	BOS	N	Tommy Holmes

Ron Hassey

June 13, 1984	CHI	N	Rick Sutcliffe George Frazier	CLE	A	Mel Hall Joe Carter minor league P Darryl Banks
Dec 4, 1984	NY	A	Henry Cotto Rich Bordi Porfirio Altamirano	CHI	N	Ray Fontenot Brian Dayett

Andy Hassler

July 5, 1976	KC	A	————	CAL	A	Cash
July 24, 1978	BOS	A	————	KC	A	Cash
June 15, 1979	NY	N	————	BOS	A	Cash
Nov 19, 1979	PIT	N	————	NY	N	No compensation (free agent signing)
June 10, 1980	CAL	A	————	PIT	N	Cash

Mickey Hatcher

March 30, 1981	MIN	A	minor leaguers P Matt Reeves and 1B Kelly Snider	LA	N	Ken Landreaux

Fred Hatfield

June 3, 1952	DET	A	————	BOS	A	*See George Kell*
May 15, 1956	CHI	A	Jim Delsing	DET	A	Jim Brideweser Harry Byrd Bob Kennedy
Dec 4, 1957	CLE	A	Minnie Minoso	CHI	A	Early Wynn Al Smith
April 23, 1958	CIN	N	————	CLE	A	Bob Kelly

Joe Hatten

June 15, 1951	CHI	N	Bruce Edwards Eddie Miksis Gene Hermanski	BKN	N	Johnny Schmitz Rube Walker Andy Pafko Wayne Terwilliger

Grady Hatton

April 18, 1954	CHI	A	————	CIN	N	Johnny Lipon
May 23, 1954	BOS	A	$100,000.	CHI	A	George Kell
May 11, 1956	STL	N	————	BOS	A	Cash
Aug 1, 1956	BAL	A	————	STL	N	Cash

Phil Haugstad

May 25, 1952	CIN	N	————	BKN	N	Waiver price

Joe Hauser

June 7, 1929	CLE	A	————	PHI	A	Waiver price

Tom Hausman

Nov 21, 1977	NY	N	————	MIL	A	No compensation (free agent signing)
Sept 10, 1982	ATL	N	————	NY	N	Carlos Diaz

DATE	TRADED TO		TRADED WITH	TRADED BY		IN EXCHANGE FOR

Brad Havens

| Feb 3, 1979 | MIN | A | Ken Landreaux
Dave Engle
Paul Hartzell | CAL | A | Rod Carew |

Wynn Hawkins

| Nov 27, 1962 | NY | N | ———— | CLE | A | Cash |

Pink Hawley

| Feb 27, 1900 | NY | N | ———— | CIN | N | Cash |

Hal Haydel

| March 28, 1963 | CHI | N | Merritt Ranew
Dick LeMay | HOU | N | Jug Gerard
Danny Murphy |

Frankie Hayes

June 1, 1942	STL	A	————	PHI	A	Bob Harris Bob Swift
Feb 17, 1944	PHI	A	————	STL	A	Sam Zoldak and minor league OF Barney Lutz
May 29, 1945	CLE	A	————	PHI	A	Buddy Rosar
June 1946	CHI	A	————	CLE	A	Tom Jordan

Jackie Hayes

| Dec 4, 1931 | CHI | A | Bump Hadley
Sad Sam Jones | WAS | A | Carl Reynolds
John Kerr |

Von Hayes

| Dec 9, 1982 | PHI | N | ———— | CLE | A | Manny Trillo
George Vukovich
Jay Baller
Julio Franco
Jerry Willard |

Joe Haynes

Jan 4, 1941	CHI	A	————	WAS	A	Cash
Nov 22, 1948	CLE	A	————	CHI	A	Joe Tipton
Dec 14, 1948	WAS	A	Eddie Klieman Eddie Robinson	CLE	A	Mickey Vernon Early Wynn

Ray Hayworth

| Sept 14, 1938 | BKN | N | ———— | DET | A | Waiver price |
| Aug 23, 1939 | NY | N | ———— | BKN | N | Jimmy Ripple |

Bob Hazle

| April 9, 1956 | MIL | N | Corky Valentine | CIN | N | George Crowe |
| May 24, 1958 | DET | A | ———— | MIL | N | Cash |

Fran Healy

| April 2, 1973 | KC | A | ———— | SF | N | Greg Minton |
| May 16, 1976 | NY | A | ———— | KC | A | Larry Gura |

Francis Healy

| May 4, 1934 | STL | N | ———— | NY | N | Cash |

Jim Hearn

| July 10, 1950 | NY | N | ———— | STL | N | Cash |

DATE	TRADED TO		TRADED WITH	TRADED BY		IN EXCHANGE FOR

Jess Hickman

| June 4, 1965 | KC | A | Ernie Fazio and $100,000. | HOU | N | Jim Gentile |

(Kansas City received Fazio on October 15.)

Jim Hickman

| Feb 10, 1916 | BKN | N | ———— | BAL | F | Cash |

Jim Hickman

Nov 29, 1966	LA	N	Ron Hunt	NY	N	Tommy Davis Derrell Griffith
April 23, 1968	CHI	N	Phil Regan	LA	N	Ted Savage Jim Ellis
March 23, 1974	STL	N	————	CHI	N	Scipio Spinks

Piano Legs Hickman

Feb 17, 1900	NY	N	————	BOS	N	Cash
May 30, 1902	CLE	A	————	BOS	A	Candy LaChance
Aug 7, 1904	DET	A	————	CLE	A	Charlie Carr Fritz Buelow
July 6, 1905	WAS	A	————	DET	A	Cash
Aug 1, 1907	CHI	A	————	WAS	A	Cash
Nov 1907	CLE	A	————	CHI	A	Cash

Jim Hicks

| Oct 13, 1967 | STL | N | ———— | CHI | N | Cash |
| May 30, 1969 | CAL | A | ———— | STL | N | Vic Davalillo |

Kirby Higbe

May 29, 1939	PHI	N	Joe Marty Ray Harrell	CHI	N	Claude Passeau
Nov 11, 1940	BKN	N	————	PHI	N	Vito Tamulis Bill Crouch Mickey Livingston and $100,000.
May 3, 1947	PIT	N	Hank Behrman Cal McLish Gene Mauch Dixie Howell	BKN	N	Al Gionfriddo and $100,000.
June 6, 1949	NY	N	————	PIT	N	Ray Poat Bobby Rhawn

Dennis Higgins

Feb 13, 1968	WAS	A	*See Ron Hansen*	CHI	A	————
Dec 5, 1969	CLE	A	Barry Moore	WAS	A	Dave Nelson Horacio Pina Ron Law
July 15, 1971	STL	N	————	CLE	A	Cash
Sept 1, 1972	SD	N	————	STL	N	Cash

Pinky Higgins

Dec 9, 1936	BOS	A	————	PHI	A	Bill Werber
Dec 15, 1938	DET	A	Archie McKain	BOS	A	Eldon Auker Jake Wade Chet Morgan
May 19, 1946	BOS	A	————	DET	A	Cash

DATE	TRADED TO		TRADED WITH	TRADED BY		IN EXCHANGE FOR

Andy High

July 25, 1925	BOS	N	——————	BKN	N	Waiver price
March 25, 1928	STL	N	$25,000.	BOS	N	Les Bell
Dec 2, 1931	CIN	N	——————	STL	N	Nick Cullop and cash

Hugh High

Jan 7, 1915	NY	A	——————	DET	A	Waiver price

Oral Hildebrand

Jan 17, 1937	STL	A	Bill Knickerbocker Joe Vosmik	CLE	A	Ivy Andrews Lyn Lary Moose Solters
Oct 26, 1938	NY	A	Buster Mills	STL	A	Joe Glenn Myril Hoag

Tom Hilgendorf

July 10, 1972	CLE	A	——————	KC	A	Jim Clark
March 6, 1975	PHI	N	——————	CLE	A	Minor league OF Nelson Garcia

Carmen Hill

Aug 28, 1929	STL	N	——————	PIT	N	Waiver price

Herman Hill

Oct 20, 1970	STL	N	minor league OF Charlie Wissler	MIN	A	Sal Campisi Jim Kennedy

Hunter Hill

July 14, 1904	WAS	A	Frank Huelsman (Huelsmann went to Washington on loan.)	STL	A	Charlie Moran

Jesse Hill

Jan 17, 1936	WAS	A	Jimmie DeShong	NY	A	Bump Hadley Roy Johnson
July 13, 1937	PHI	A	——————	WAS	A	Cash

Marc Hill

Oct 14, 1974	SF	N	——————	STL	N	Elias Sosa Ken Rudolph
June 20, 1980	SEA	A	——————	SF	N	Cash
Feb 12, 1981	CHI	A	——————	SEA	A	No compensation (free agent signing)

Chuck Hiller

May 12, 1965	NY	N	——————	SF	N	Cash
July 11, 1967	PHI	N	——————	NY	N	Phil Linz

Frank Hiller

Jan 3, 1952	CIN	N	——————	CHI	N	Willie Ramsdell
Oct 13, 1952	NY	N	——————	CIN	N	Gail Henley

Dave Hillman

Nov 21, 1959	BOS	A	Jim Marshall	CHI	N	Dick Gernert

Dave Hilton

Nov 22, 1976	TOR	A	Dave Roberts John Scott	SD	N	Cash

DATE	TRADED TO		TRADED WITH	TRADED BY		IN EXCHANGE FOR

Rick Honeycutt continued

| Dec 12, 1980 | TEX | A | Mario Mendoza
Larry Cox
Leon Roberts
Willie Horton | SEA | A | Richie Zisk
Rick Auerbach
Ken Clay
Jerry Gleaton
Brian Allard
Steve Finch |
| Aug 19, 1983 | LA | N | ——————— | TEX | A | Dave Stewart
Ricky Wright
and $200,000. |

Don Hood

Feb 25, 1975	CLE	A	Boog Powell	BAL	A	Dave Duncan and minor league OF Al McGrew
June 15, 1979	NY	A	———————	CLE	A	Cliff Johnson
March 13, 1980	STL	N	———————	NY	A	No compensation (free agent signing)

Wally Hood

| July 1920 | PIT | N | ——————— | BKN | N | Cash |

Jay Hook

| May 8, 1964 | MIL | N | Adrian Garrett | NY | N | Roy McMillan |

Bob Hooper

| Dec 19, 1952 | CLE | A | ——————— | PHI | A | Dick Rozek
minor league
2B Bob Wilson |
| April 13, 1955 | CIN | N | ——————— | CLE | A | Cash |

Harry Hooper

| March 4, 1921 | CHI | A | ——————— | BOS | A | Shano Collins
Nemo Leibold |

Burt Hooton

| May 2, 1975 | LA | N | ——————— | CHI | N | Geoff Zahn
Eddie Solomon |
| Dec 20, 1984 | TEX | A | ——————— | LA | N | No compensation
(free agent signing) |

Don Hopkins

| March 26, 1975 | OAK | A | ——————— | MON | N | Cash |

Gail Hopkins

| Oct 13, 1970 | KC | A | John Matias | CHI | A | Pat Kelly
Don O'Riley |
| July 11, 1974 | LA | N | ——————— | SD | N | Cash |

Marty Hopkins

| June 27, 1934 | CHI | A | ——————— | PHI | N | Waiver price |

Paul Hopkins

| June 26, 1929 | STL | A | ——————— | WAS | A | Cash |

Johnny Hopp

| Feb 5, 1946 | BOS | N | ——————— | STL | N | Eddie Joost
and $40,000. |

DATE	TRADED TO		TRADED WITH	TRADED BY		IN EXCHANGE FOR

Johnny Hopp continued

DATE	TRADED TO		TRADED WITH	TRADED BY		IN EXCHANGE FOR
Nov 18, 1947	PIT	N	Danny Murtaugh	BOS	N	Jim Russell Bill Salkeld Al Lyons
May 18, 1949	BKN	N	$25,000. (Trade was cancelled on June 7, 1949.)	PIT	N	Marv Rackley
Sept 5, 1950	NY	A	————	PIT	N	Cash

Rogers Hornsby

DATE	TRADED TO		TRADED WITH	TRADED BY		IN EXCHANGE FOR
Dec 20, 1926	NY	N	————	STL	N	Frankie Frisch Jimmy Ring
Jan 10, 1928	BOS	N	————	NY	N	Shanty Hogan Jimmy Welsh
Nov 7, 1928	CHI	N	————	BOS	N	Socks Seibold Percy Jones Lou Legett Freddie Maguire Bruce Cunningham and $200,000.

Tony Horton

DATE	TRADED TO		TRADED WITH	TRADED BY		IN EXCHANGE FOR
June 4, 1967	CLE	A	Don Demeter	BOS	A	Gary Bell

Willie Horton

DATE	TRADED TO		TRADED WITH	TRADED BY		IN EXCHANGE FOR
April 12, 1977	TEX	A	————	DET	A	Steve Foucault
Feb 28, 1978	CLE	A	David Clyde	TEX	A	Tom Buskey John Lowenstein
Aug 15, 1978	TOR	A	Phil Huffman	OAK	A	Rico Carty
Jan 27, 1979	SEA	A	————	TOR	A	No compensation (free agent signing)
Dec 12, 1980	TEX	A	Rick Honeycutt Mario Mendoza Larry Cox Leon Roberts	SEA	A	Richie Zisk Rick Auerbach Ken Clay Jerry Gleaton Brian Allard Steve Finch

Tim Hosley

DATE	TRADED TO		TRADED WITH	TRADED BY		IN EXCHANGE FOR
April 19, 1976	OAK	A	————	CHI	N	Cash

Gene Host

DATE	TRADED TO		TRADED WITH	TRADED BY		IN EXCHANGE FOR
Dec 5, 1956	KC	A	*See Ned Garver*	DET	A	————

Dave Hostetler

DATE	TRADED TO		TRADED WITH	TRADED BY		IN EXCHANGE FOR
March 31, 1982	TEX	A	Larry Parrish	MON	N	Al Oliver
Nov 8, 1984	MON	N	————	TEX	A	Chris Welsh

Charlie Hough

DATE	TRADED TO		TRADED WITH	TRADED BY		IN EXCHANGE FOR
July 11, 1980	TEX	A	————	LA	N	Cash

Frank House

DATE	TRADED TO		TRADED WITH	TRADED BY		IN EXCHANGE FOR
Nov 20, 1957	KC	A	————	DET	A	*See Billy Martin*
Nov 21, 1959	CIN	N	————	KC	A	Tom Acker

Tom House

DATE	TRADED TO		TRADED WITH	TRADED BY		IN EXCHANGE FOR
Dec 12, 1975	BOS	A	————	ATL	N	Roger Moret
May 28, 1977	SEA	A	————	BOS	A	Cash

DATE	TRADED TO		TRADED WITH	TRADED BY		IN EXCHANGE FOR

Mike Ivie

DATE	TRADED TO		TRADED WITH	TRADED BY		IN EXCHANGE FOR
Feb 28, 1978	SF	N	———	SD	N	Derrel Thomas
April 20, 1981	HOU	N	———	SF	N	Dave Bergman Jeff Leonard

Ray Jablonski

DATE	TRADED TO		TRADED WITH	TRADED BY		IN EXCHANGE FOR
Dec 8, 1954	CIN	N	Gerry Staley	STL	N	Frank Smith
Nov 13, 1956	CHI	N	Elmer Singleton	CIN	N	Don Hoak Warren Hacker Pete Whisenant
April 16, 1957	NY	N	Ray Katt	CHI	N	Dick Littlefield Bob Lennon
March 25, 1959	STL	N	Bill White	SF	N	Sam Jones Don Choate
Aug 20, 1959	KC	A	———	STL	N	Waiver price

Fred Jacklitsch

DATE	TRADED TO		TRADED WITH	TRADED BY		IN EXCHANGE FOR
Feb 1903	BKN	N	———	PHI	N	Cash

Al Jackson

DATE	TRADED TO		TRADED WITH	TRADED BY		IN EXCHANGE FOR
Oct 20, 1965	STL	N	Charley Smith	NY	N	Ken Boyer
July 16, 1967	NY	N	———	STL	N	Jack Lamabe
June 13, 1969	CIN	N	———	NY	N	Cash

Grant Jackson

DATE	TRADED TO		TRADED WITH	TRADED BY		IN EXCHANGE FOR
Dec 16, 1970	BAL	A	Jim Hutto Sam Parrilla	PHI	N	Roger Freed
June 15, 1976	NY	A	———	BAL	A	*See Tippy Martinez*
Dec 7, 1976	PIT	N	———	SEA	A	Craig Reynolds Jimmy Sexton
Sept 1, 1981	MON	N	———	PIT	N	$50,000.
Jan 19, 1982	KC	A	———	MON	N	Ken Phelps

Joe Jackson

DATE	TRADED TO		TRADED WITH	TRADED BY		IN EXCHANGE FOR
July 25, 1910	CLE	A	———	PHI	A	Bris Lord
Aug 21, 1915	CHI	A	———	CLE	A	Braggo Roth Larry Chappell Ed Klepfer and $31,500.

Larry Jackson

DATE	TRADED TO		TRADED WITH	TRADED BY		IN EXCHANGE FOR
Oct 17, 1962	CHI	N	Jimmie Schaffer Lindy McDaniel	STL	N	George Altman Don Cardwell Moe Thacker
April 21, 1966	PHI	N	Bob Buhl	CHI	N	Adolfo Phillips John Herrnstein Ferguson Jenkins

Lou Jackson

DATE	TRADED TO		TRADED WITH	TRADED BY		IN EXCHANGE FOR
Dec 6, 1959	CIN	N	Bill Henry Lee Walls	CHI	N	Frank Thomas

Mike Jackson

DATE	TRADED TO		TRADED WITH	TRADED BY		IN EXCHANGE FOR
Sept 6, 1969	PHI	N	———	BOS	A	Gary Wagner
Sept 13, 1971	STL	N	———	KC	A	Cash

DATE	TRADED TO		TRADED WITH	TRADED BY		IN EXCHANGE FOR

Randy Jackson

Dec 9, 1955	BKN	N	Don Elston	CHI	N	Don Hoak Russ Meyer Walt Moryn
Aug 4, 1958	CLE	A	————	LA	N	Cash
May 4, 1959	CHI	N	————	CLE	A	Riverboat Smith

Reggie Jackson

April 2, 1976	BAL	A	Ken Holtzman minor leaguer Bill Van Bommell	OAK	A	Don Baylor Mike Torrez Paul Mitchell
Nov 29, 1976	NY	A	————	BAL	A	No compensation (free agent signing)
Jan 22, 1982	CAL	A	————	NY	A	No compensation (free agent signing)

Ron Jackson

| Nov 3, 1959 | BOS | A | ———— | CHI | A | Frank Baumann |
| May 17, 1960 | MIL | N | ———— | BOS | A | Ray Boone |

Ron Jackson

Dec 4, 1978	MIN	A	Danny Goodwin	CAL	A	Dan Ford
Aug 23, 1981	DET	A	————	MIN	A	Tim Corcoran
April 11, 1982	CAL	A	————	DET	A	No compensation (free agent signing)

Roy Lee Jackson

| Dec 12, 1980 | TOR | A | ———— | NY | N | Bob Bailor |

Sonny Jackson

| Oct 8, 1967 | ATL | N | Chuck Harrison | HOU | N | Denny Lemaster
Denis Menke |

Elmer Jacobs

Dec 1915	PIT	N	————	PHI	N	Cash
July 1, 1918	PHI	N	————	PIT	N	Erskine Mayer
July 14, 1919	STL	N	Frank Woodward Doug Baird	PHI	N	Lee Meadows Gene Paulette

Spook Jacobs

| June 23, 1956 | PIT | N | ———— | KC | A | Jack McMahan |

Baby Doll Jacobson

Aug 18, 1915	STL	A	————	DET	A	Bill James Grover Lowdermilk
June 15, 1926	PHI	A	————	STL	A	Bing Miller
June 15, 1926	BOS	A	Fred Heimach Slim Harriss	PHI	A	Tom Jenkins Howard Ehmke
June 12, 1927	CLE	A	————	BOS	A	Cash
Aug 5, 1927	PHI	A	————	CLE	A	Waiver price

Beany Jacobson

| Dec 1905 | STL | A | ———— | WAS | A | Willie Sudhoff |
| June 22, 1907 | BOS | A | $1,000. | STL | A | Bill Dinneen |

DATE	TRADED TO		TRADED WITH	TRADED BY		IN EXCHANGE FOR

Merwin Jacobson

| Aug 28, 1916 | CHI | N | Larry Doyle
Herb Hunter | NY | N | Heinie Zimmerman
Mickey Doolan |

Brook Jacoby

| Aug 28, 1983 | CLE | A | Rick Behenna
Brett Butler
and $150,000. | ATL | N | Len Barker |

(Butler and Jacoby were sent to Cleveland at the end of the season.)

Pat Jacquez

| Nov 30, 1970 | CHI | A | Dave Lemonds
Roe Skidmore | CHI | N | Jose Ortiz
Ossie Blanco |
| Nov 28, 1972 | STL | N | ———— | CIN | N | Bill Voss |

Art Jahn

| May 29, 1928 | PHI | N | ———— | NY | N | Russ Wrightstone |

Bill James

Aug 18, 1915	DET	A	Grover Lowdermilk	STL	A	Baby Doll Jacobson
Aug 1919	BOS	A	————	DET	A	Cash
Aug 1919	CHI	A	————	BOS	A	Cash

Bob James

| May 4, 1983 | MON | N | ———— | DET | A | Cash |
| Dec 7, 1984 | CHI | A | Bryan Little | MON | N | Vance Law
Bert Roberge |

Charlie James

| Dec 14, 1964 | CIN | N | Roger Craig | STL | N | Bob Purkey |

Johnny James

| May 8, 1961 | LA | A | Lee Thomas
Ryne Duren | NY | A | Tex Clevenger
Bob Cerv |

Skip James

| March 27, 1979 | MIL | A | ———— | SF | N | Cash |

Charlie Jamieson

| July 17, 1917 | PHI | A | ———— | WAS | A | Waiver price |
| March 1, 1919 | CLE | A | Larry Gardner
Elmer Myers | PHI | A | Braggo Roth |

Gerry Janeski

| Dec 13, 1969 | CHI | A | Syd O'Brien
minor league
P Billy Farmer | BOS | A | Don Pavletich
Gary Peters |

(Janeski replaced Farmer, who retired.)

| Feb 9, 1971 | WAS | A | ———— | CHI | A | Rick Reichardt |

Hal Janvrin

Jan 17, 1919	WAS	A	cash	BOS	A	Eddie Ainsmith George Dumont
Sept 10, 1919	STL	N	————	WAS	A	Waiver price
June 18, 1921	BKN	N	Ferdie Schupp	STL	N	Jeff Pfeffer

Pat Jarvis

| Feb 28, 1973 | MON | N | ———— | ATL | N | Carl Morton |

DATE	TRADED TO		TRADED WITH	TRADED BY		IN EXCHANGE FOR

Pat Jarvis continued

| Dec 20, 1973 | TEX | A | ——— | MON | N | Larry Biittner |

Ray Jarvis

| Oct 11, 1970 | CAL | A | *See Tony Conigliaro* | BOS | A | ——— |

Larry Jaster

| Dec 2, 1969 | ATL | N | ——— | MON | N | Jim Britton
minor league
C Don Johnson |

Julian Javier

| May 28, 1960 | STL | N | Ed Bauta | PIT | N | Vinegar Bend Mizell
Dick Gray |
| March 24, 1972 | CIN | N | ——— | STL | N | Tony Cloninger |

Stan Javier

| Dec 8, 1984 | OAK | A | ——— | NY | A | *See Rickey Henderson* |

Joey Jay

| Dec 15, 1960 | CIN | N | Juan Pizarro | MIL | N | Roy McMillan |
| June 15, 1966 | ATL | N | ——— | CIN | N | Hank Fischer |

Hal Jeffcoat

| Nov 28, 1955 | CIN | N | ——— | CHI | N | Hobie Landrith |
| June 8, 1959 | STL | N | ——— | CIN | N | Jim Brosnan |

Jesse Jefferson

June 15, 1975	CHI	A	———	BAL	A	Tony Muser
Sept 11, 1980	PIT	N	———	TOR	A	Cash
Jan 23, 1981	CAL	A	———	PIT	N	No compensation (free agent signing)
Feb 19, 1982	BAL	A	———	CAL	A	No compensation (free agent signing)

Irv Jeffries

| Dec 20, 1933 | PHI | N | Otto Bluege | CIN | N | Mark Koenig |

Ferguson Jenkins

April 21, 1966	CHI	N	Adolfo Phillips John Herrnstein	PHI	N	Larry Jackson Bob Buhl
Oct 25, 1973	TEX	A	———	CHI	N	Bill Madlock Vic Harris
Nov 17, 1975	BOS	A	———	TEX	A	Juan Beniquez Steve Barr Craig Skok
Dec 14, 1977	TEX	A	———	BOS	A	John Poloni and cash
Dec 8, 1981	CHI	N	———	TEX	A	No compensation (free agent signing)

Jack Jenkins

| Sept 1, 1969 | LA | N | ——— | WAS | A | Cash |

Tom Jenkins

| June 15, 1926 | PHI | A | Howard Ehmke | BOS | A | Fred Heimach
Slim Harriss
Baby Doll Jacobson |

DATE	TRADED TO		TRADED WITH	TRADED BY		IN EXCHANGE FOR

Syl Johnson

Jan 11, 1934	CIN	N	Bob O'Farrell	STL	N	Glenn Spencer
			(O'Farrell was named Cincinnati manager.)			
May 16, 1934	PHI	N	Johnny Moore	CIN	N	Ted Kleinhans
						Wes Schulmerich
						Art Ruble

Tim Johnson

April 24, 1973	MIL	A	————	LA	N	Cash
April 29, 1978	TOR	A	————	MIL	A	Tim Nordbrook

Vic Johnson

Dec 12, 1945	CLE	A	cash	BOS	A	Jim Bagby

Wallace Johnson

May 25, 1983	SF	N	————	MON	N	Mike Vail

Doc Johnston

Feb 22, 1915	PIT	N	————	CLE	A	$7,500.
Feb 16, 1922	PHI	A	————	CLE	A	Cash

Greg Johnston

April 3, 1980	MIN	A	————	SF	N	Cash

Jimmy Johnston

Oct 7, 1925	BOS	N	Zack Taylor	BKN	N	Jesse Barnes
			Eddie Brown			Mickey O'Neil
						Gus Felix
July 1926	NY	N	————	BOS	N	Waiver price

Jay Johnstone

Nov 30, 1970	CHI	A	Tom Egan	CAL	A	Ken Berry
			Tom Bradley			Syd O'Brien
						Billy Wynne
Jan 9, 1974	STL	N	————	OAK	A	Cash
June 14, 1978	NY	A	Bobby Brown	PHI	N	Rawley Eastwick
June 15, 1979	SD	N	————	NY	A	Dave Wehrmeister
Dec 4, 1979	LA	N	————	SD	N	No compensation
						(free agent signing)

Stan Jok

May 10, 1954	CHI	A	————	PHI	N	Waiver price

Smead Jolley

April 29, 1932	BOS	A	Bennie Tate	CHI	A	Charlie Berry
			Cliff Watwood			
Dec 14, 1933	STL	A	Ivy Andrews	BOS	A	Carl Reynolds
			and cash			

Dave Jolly

Oct 15, 1957	NY	N	————	MIL	N	Waiver price

Charlie Jones

Oct 5, 1907	STL	A	————	WAS	A	Ollie Pickering

DATE	TRADED TO		TRADED WITH	TRADED BY		IN EXCHANGE FOR

Clarence Jones

| Jan 9, 1969 | CIN | N | Bill Plummer
minor league
P Ken Myette | CHI | N | Ted Abernathy |

Dalton Jones

| Dec 13, 1969 | DET | A | ———— | BOS | A | Tommy Matchick |
| May 30, 1972 | TEX | A | ———— | DET | A | Norm McRae |

Davy Jones

| Dec 1912 | CHI | A | ———— | DET | A | Cash |

Gary Jones

| Dec 2, 1971 | TEX | A | minor league
P Terry Ley | NY | A | Bernie Allen |
| Dec 2, 1971 | CLE | A | Del Unser
Denny Riddleberger
minor league
P Terry Ley | TEX | A | Roy Foster
Ken Suarez
Mike Paul
Rich Hand |

Gordon Jones

| Oct 1, 1956 | NY | N | ———— | STL | N | Cash |
| Nov 30, 1959 | BAL | A | Jackie Brandt
Roger McCardell | SF | N | Billy O'Dell
Billy Loes |

Jake Jones

| June 14, 1947 | BOS | A | ———— | CHI | A | Rudy York |

Johnny Jones

| Aug 15, 1919 | BOS | N | Joe Oeschger
Red Causey
Mickey O'Neil
and $55,000. | NY | N | Art Nehf |

Mack Jones

| Oct 10, 1967 | CIN | N | Jim Beauchamp
Jay Ritchie | ATL | N | Deron Johnson |

Odell Jones

| Dec 5, 1978 | SEA | A | Rafael Vasquez
Mario Mendoza | PIT | N | Enrique Romo
Rick Jones
Tommy McMillan |
| April 1, 1980 | PIT | N | ———— | SEA | A | Larry Andersen
and cash |

Percy Jones

| Nov 7, 1928 | BOS | N | Socks Seibold
Lou Legett
Freddie Maguire
Bruce Cunningham
and $200,000. | CHI | N | Rogers Hornsby |
| April 9, 1930 | PIT | N | cash | BOS | N | Burleigh Grimes |

Randy Jones

| Dec 15, 1980 | NY | N | ———— | SD | N | John Pacella
Jose Moreno |

Rick Jones

| Dec 5, 1978 | PIT | N | ———— | SEA | A | *See Mario Mendoza* |

DATE	TRADED TO		TRADED WITH	TRADED BY		IN EXCHANGE FOR

Ross Jones
| Dec 8, 1983 | NY | N | Sid Fernandez | LA | N | Carlos Diaz
Bob Bailor |

Ruppert Jones
| Nov 1, 1979 | NY | A | Jim Lewis | SEA | A | Jim Beattie
Rick Anderson
Juan Beniquez
Jerry Narron |
| April 1, 1981 | SD | N | Joe Lefebvre
Tim Lollar
Chris Welsh | NY | A | Jerry Mumphrey
John Pacella |

Sad Sam Jones
April 12, 1916	BOS	A	Fred Thomas and $55,000.	CLE	A	Tris Speaker
Dec 20, 1921	NY	A	Everett Scott Joe Bush	BOS	A	Roger Peckinpaugh Jack Quinn Rip Collins Bill Piercy
Feb 8, 1927	STL	A	————	NY	A	Cedric Durst Joe Giard
Sept 28, 1927	WAS	A	————	STL	A	Waiver price
Dec 4, 1931	CHI	A	Jackie Hayes Bump Hadley	WAS	A	Carl Reynolds John Kerr

Sam Jones
Nov 16, 1954	CHI	N	Gale Wade and $60,000.	CLE	A	Ralph Kiner
Dec 11, 1956	STL	N	Hobie Landrith Jim Davis Eddie Miksis	CHI	N	Tom Poholsky Jackie Collum Ray Katt minor league P Wally Lammers
March 25, 1959	SF	N	Don Choate	STL	N	Bill White Ray Jablonski
Dec 1, 1961	DET	A	————	HOU	N	Bob Bruce Manny Montejo

Sheldon Jones
| April 8, 1952 | BOS | N | $50,000. | NY | N | Bob Elliott |
| Dec 20, 1952 | CHI | N | ———— | BOS | N | Monk Dubiel |

Sherman Jones
| April 27, 1961 | CIN | N | Bob Schmidt
Don Blasingame | SF | N | Ed Bailey |

Steve Jones
| Feb 13, 1968 | WAS | A | *See Ron Hansen* | CHI | A | ———— |

Tim Jones
| March 29, 1978 | MON | N | ———— | PIT | N | Will McEnaney |

Tom Jones
| Aug 20, 1909 | DET | A | ———— | STL | A | Claude Rossman |

Willie Jones
| June 6, 1959 | CLE | A | ———— | PHI | N | Jim Bolger
and cash |
| July 1, 1959 | CIN | N | ———— | CLE | A | Cash |

DATE	TRADED TO		TRADED WITH	TRADED BY		IN EXCHANGE FOR

Bubber Jonnard

DATE	TRADED TO		TRADED WITH	TRADED BY		IN EXCHANGE FOR
Dec 13, 1927	STL	N	Johnny Mokan Jimmy Cooney	PHI	N	Johnny Schulte Jimmy Ring

Eddie Joost

Dec 4, 1942	BOS	N	Nate Andrews and $25,000.	CIN	N	Eddie Miller
Feb 5, 1946	STL	N	$40,000.	BOS	N	Johnny Hopp

Buck Jordan

May 12, 1937	CIN	N	—————	BOS	N	Cash
June 10, 1938	PHI	N	—————	CIN	N	Justin Stein

Jimmy Jordan

Dec 3, 1936	STL	N	Frenchy Bordagaray Dutch Leonard	BKN	N	Tom Winsett

Niles Jordan

Dec 10, 1951	CIN	N	—————	PHI	N	*See Smoky Burgess*

Tim Jordan

May 1901	BAL	A	—————	WAS	A	Cash

Tom Jordan

June 1946	CLE	A	—————	CHI	A	Frankie Hayes

Mike Jorgensen

April 5, 1972	MON	N	Tim Foli Ken Singleton	NY	N	Rusty Staub
May 22, 1977	OAK	A	—————	MON	N	Stan Bahnsen
Jan 21, 1978	TEX	A	—————	OAK	A	No compensation (free agent signing)
Aug 12, 1979	NY	N	Ed Lynch	TEX	A	Willie Montanez
June 15, 1983	ATL	N	—————	NY	N	$75,000.
June 15, 1984	STL	N	Ken Dayley	ATL	N	Ken Oberkfell

Duane Josephson

March 31, 1971	BOS	A	Danny Murphy	CHI	A	Vicente Romo Tony Muser

Von Joshua

Jan 29, 1975	SF	N	—————	LA	N	Cash
June 2, 1976	MIL	A	—————	SF	N	Cash
Dec 3, 1979	SD	N	—————	LA	N	Cash

Mike Joyce

March 31, 1964	NY	N	—————	CHI	A	Cash

Oscar Judd

May 31, 1945	PHI	N	—————	BOS	A	Waiver price

Ralph Judd

May 15, 1930	STL	N	—————	NY	N	Clarence Mitchell

Walt Judnich

Jan 30, 1940	STL	A	—————	NY	A	Cash

DATE	TRADED TO		TRADED WITH	TRADED BY		IN EXCHANGE FOR

Walt Judnich continued

DATE	TRADED TO		TRADED WITH	TRADED BY		IN EXCHANGE FOR
Nov 20, 1947	CLE	A	Bob Muncrief	STL	A	Dick Kokos Bryan Stephens Joe Frazier and $25,000.
Feb 9, 1949	PIT	N	————	CLE	A	Waiver price

Howie Judson

Sept 1, 1952	CIN	N	————	CHI	A	Hank Edwards
			(Cincinnati received Judson on December 9.)			

Bill Jurges

Dec 6, 1938	NY	N	Frank Demaree Ken O'Dea	CHI	N	Dick Bartell Hank Leiber Gus Mancuso

Al Jurisich

Feb 5, 1946	PHI	N	————	STL	N	Cash

Skip Jutze

Nov 28, 1972	HOU	N	Milt Ramirez	STL	N	Ray Busse Bobby Fenwick
Jan 12, 1977	SEA	A	————	HOU	N	Minor league P Alan Griffin and cash

Jim Kaat

Aug 15, 1973	CHI	A	————	MIN	A	Cash
Dec 10, 1975	PHI	N	Mike Buskey	CHI	A	Dick Ruthven Roy Thomas Alan Bannister
May 11, 1979	NY	A	————	PHI	N	Cash
April 30, 1980	STL	N	————	NY	A	Cash

Mike Kahoe

April 1901	CHI	N	Topsy Hartsel	CIN	N	Cash
March 1905	PHI	N	————	STL	A	Cash
June 27, 1907	WAS	A	————	CHI	N	Cash

Al Kaiser

June 10, 1911	BOS	N	*See Johnny Kling*	CHI	N	————

Don Kaiser

Dec 5, 1957	MIL	N	Eddie Haas Bob Rush	CHI	N	Taylor Phillips Sammy Taylor
Oct 15, 1959	DET	A	Mike Roarke Casey Wise	MIL	N	Charlie Lau Don Lee

Willie Kamm

May 17, 1931	CLE	A	————	CHI	A	Lew Fonseca

Alex Kampouris

June 6, 1938	NY	N	————	CIN	N	Wally Berger
May 20, 1943	WAS	A	————	BKN	N	Cash

Johnny Kane

Jan 18, 1909	CHI	N	————	CIN	N	Kid Durbin Tom Downey

DATE	TRADED TO		TRADED WITH	TRADED BY		IN EXCHANGE FOR

Erv Kantlehner
| Sept 2, 1916 | PHI | N | ————— | PIT | N | Cash |

Ed Karger
June 3, 1906	STL	N	—————	PIT	N	Cash
Dec 12, 1908	CIN	N	Art Fromme	STL	N	Admiral Schlei
June 1909	BOS	A	—————	CIN	N	Waiver price

Andy Karl
| March 27, 1947 | BOS | N | ————— | PHI | N | Don Padgett |

Eddie Kasko
Oct 3, 1958	CIN	N	Bob Mabe Del Ennis	STL	N	George Crowe Alex Kellner Alex Grammas
Jan 20, 1964	HOU	N	—————	CIN	N	Jim Dickson Wally Wolf and cash
April 3, 1966	BOS	A	—————	HOU	N	Felix Mantilla

John Katoll
| May 5, 1902 | BAL | A | Herm McFarland | CHI | A | Cash |

Ray Katt
June 14, 1956	STL	N	—————	NY	N	*See Red Schoendienst*
Dec 11, 1956	CHI	N	*See Tom Poholsky*	STL	N	—————
April 16, 1957	NY	N	Ray Jablonski	CHI	N	Dick Littlefield Bob Lennon
April 2, 1958	STL	N	—————	SF	N	Jim King

Benny Kauff
| Dec 23, 1915 | NY | N | ————— | BKN | F | $35,000. |

Curt Kaufman
| Dec 7, 1983 | CAL | A | cash | NY | A | Tim Foli |

Tony Kaufmann
| June 7, 1927 | PHI | N | Jimmy Cooney | CHI | N | Hal Carlson |
| Sept 10, 1927 | STL | N | ————— | PHI | N | Cash |

Marty Kavanagh
May 1916	CLE	A	—————	DET	A	Cash
June 1918	STL	N	—————	CLE	A	Cash
Aug 1918	DET	A	—————	STL	N	Cash

Eddie Kazak
| May 13, 1952 | CIN | N | Wally Westlake | STL | N | Dick Sisler
Virgil Stallcup |

Ted Kazanski
| March 31, 1959 | MIL | N | Stan Lopata
Johnny O'Brien | PHI | N | Gene Conley
Joe Koppe
Harry Hanebrink |

Steve Kealey
| March 15, 1971 | CHI | A | ————— | CAL | A | Cash |
| Aug 29, 1973 | CIN | N | ————— | CHI | A | Jim McGlothlin |

DATE	TRADED TO		TRADED WITH	TRADED BY		IN EXCHANGE FOR

Doc Kerr
| Aug 1914 | BAL | F | ——— | PIT | F | Medric Boucher |

John Kerr
| Dec 4, 1931 | WAS | A | Carl Reynolds | CHI | A | Jackie Hayes
Bump Hadley
Sad Sam Jones |

Joe Kerrigan
| Dec 7, 1977 | BAL | A | Don Stanhouse
Gary Roenicke | MON | N | Rudy May
Randy Miller
Bryn Smith |

Don Kessinger
| Oct 28, 1975 | STL | N | ——— | CHI | N | Mike Garman
minor league
IF Bobby Hrapmann |
| Aug 20, 1977 | CHI | A | ——— | STL | N | Minor league
P Steve Staniland |

Leo Kiely
| Jan 8, 1960 | CLE | A | ——— | BOS | A | Ray Webster |
| April 5, 1960 | KC | A | ——— | CLE | A | Bob Grim |

Pete Kilduff
| July 31, 1917 | CHI | N | ——— | NY | N | Al Demaree |
| June 2, 1919 | BKN | N | ——— | CHI | N | Lee Magee |

Mike Kilkenny
May 9, 1972	OAK	A	———	DET	A	Reggie Sanders
May 17, 1972	SD	N	Curt Blefary minor league OF Greg Schubert	OAK	A	Ollie Brown
June 11, 1972	CLE	A	———	SD	N	Fred Stanley

Bill Killefer
| Dec 11, 1917 | CHI | N | Grover Alexander | PHI | N | Mike Prendergast
Pickles Dillhoefer
and $55,000. |

Red Killefer
| Aug 13, 1909 | WAS | A | Germany Schaefer | DET | A | Jim Delahanty |
| July 20, 1916 | NY | N | Buck Herzog | CIN | N | Christy Mathewson
Edd Roush
Bill McKechnie |

Frank Killen
| 1900 | CHI | N | ——— | BOS | N | Cash |

Ed Killian
| Jan 1904 | DET | A | Jesse Stovall | CLE | A | Billy Lush |

Newt Kimball
Dec 8, 1939	BKN	N	Gus Mancuso	CHI	N	Al Todd
Sept 1940	STL	N	———	BKN	N	Cash
			(Sale was cancelled by Commissioner Landis.)			
May 20, 1943	PHI	N	———	BKN	N	Cash

DATE	TRADED TO		TRADED WITH	TRADED BY		IN EXCHANGE FOR

Bruce Kimm

| Aug 17, 1972 | CAL | A | Bruce Miller | CHI | A | Eddie Fisher |
| Aug 30, 1979 | CHI | N | ———— | DET | A | Cash |

Chad Kimsey

| Sept 9, 1932 | CHI | A | ———— | STL | A | Cash |

Jerry Kindall

| Nov 27, 1961 | CLE | A | ———— | CHI | N | Larry Locke |
| June 11, 1964 | LA | A | ———— | CLE | A | Billy Moran |

(Part of three-team trade involving Los Angeles Angels, Cleveland, and Minnesota.)

| June 11, 1964 | MIN | A | Frank Kostro | LA | A | Lenny Green
Vic Power |

(Part of three-team trade involving Los Angeles Angels, Minnesota, and Cleveland.)

Ellis Kinder

Nov 18, 1947	BOS	A	Billy Hitchcock	STL	A	Sam Dente Clem Dreisewerd Bill Sommers and $65,000.
Dec 4, 1955	STL	N	————	BOS	A	Waiver price
July 11, 1956	CHI	A	————	STL	N	Waiver price

Ralph Kiner

| June 4, 1953 | CHI | N | Joe Garagiola
Howie Pollet
Catfish Metkovich | PIT | N | Toby Atwell
Bob Schultz
Preston Ward
George Freese
Bob Addis
Gene Hermanski
$150,000. |
| Nov 16, 1954 | CLE | A | ———— | CHI | N | Sam Jones
Gale Wade
and $60,000. |

Charlie King

Feb 12, 1957	MIL	N	Cash	DET	A	Jack Dittmer
Nov 10, 1957	CHI	N	Ben Johnson minor league OF Len Williams	MIL	N	Casey Wise
May 19, 1959	STL	N	————	CHI	N	Irv Noren

Clyde King

| Oct 10, 1952 | CIN | N | ———— | BKN | N | Cash |

Hal King

| Dec 2, 1971 | TEX | A | ———— | ATL | N | Paul Casanova |

Jim King

April 20, 1957	STL	N	————	CHI	N	Ed Mayer Bobby Del Greco
April 2, 1958	SF	N	————	STL	N	Ray Katt
June 15, 1967	CHI	A	————	WAS	A	Ed Stroud
July 29, 1967	CLE	A	Marv Staehle	CHI	A	Rocky Colavito

Lee King

| Jan 1919 | NY | N | ———— | PIT | N | Cash |

DATE	TRADED TO		TRADED WITH	TRADED BY		IN EXCHANGE FOR

Rick Langford
| March 15, 1977 | OAK | A | ——— | PIT | N | *See Phil Garner* |

Hal Lanier
| Feb 2, 1972 | NY | A | ——— | SF | N | Cash |

Max Lanier
| Dec 11, 1951 | NY | N | Chuck Diering | STL | N | Eddie Stanky |
| | | | (Stanky was named St. Louis manager.) | | | |

Johnny Lanning
| Dec 6, 1939 | PIT | N | ——— | BOS | N | Jim Tobin and cash |

Carney Lansford
| Dec 10, 1980 | BOS | A | Rick Miller Mark Clear | CAL | A | Rick Burleson Butch Hobson |
| Dec 6, 1982 | OAK | A | Garry Hancock minor league P Jerry King | BOS | A | Tony Armas Jeff Newman |

Paul LaPalme
Jan 11, 1955	STL	N	———	PIT	N	Ben Wade and cash
May 1, 1956	CIN	N	———	STL	N	Milt Smith
June 22, 1956	CHI	A	———	CIN	N	Waiver price

Dave LaPoint
| Dec 12, 1980 | STL | N | Sixto Lezcano David Green Lary Sorensen | MIL | A | Pete Vuckovich Rollie Fingers Ted Simmons |

Ralph LaPointe
| April 7, 1948 | STL | N | $30,000. | PHI | N | Dick Sisler |

Frank LaPorte
Dec 1907	BOS	A	———	NY	A	Cash
Aug 17, 1908	NY	A	———	BOS	A	Harry Niles
Jan 1911	STL	A	Jimmy Austin	NY	A	Roy Hartzell
July 1912	WAS	A	———	STL	A	Cash

Jack Lapp
| Jan 7, 1916 | CHI | A | | PHI | A | Cash |

Norm Larker
| Nov 30, 1962 | MIL | N | ——— | HOU | N | Connie Grob Jim Bolger |
| Aug 8, 1963 | SF | N | ——— | MIL | N | Cash |

Dave LaRoche
Nov 30, 1971	MIN	A	———	CAL	A	Leo Cardenas
Nov 30, 1972	CHI	N	———	MIN	A	Bill Hands Joe Decker minor league P Bob Maneely
Feb 25, 1975	CLE	A	Brock Davis	CHI	N	Milt Wilcox

DATE	TRADED TO		TRADED WITH	TRADED BY		IN EXCHANGE FOR

Dave LaRoche continued

DATE	TRADED TO		TRADED WITH	TRADED BY		IN EXCHANGE FOR
May 11, 1977	CAL	A	Dave Schuler	CLE	A	Bruce Bochte Sid Monge and $250,000.

Don Larsen

DATE	TRADED TO		TRADED WITH	TRADED BY		IN EXCHANGE FOR
Nov 18, 1954	NY	A	Bob Turley Billy Hunter	BAL	A	Harry Byrd Jim McDonald Hal Smith Gus Triandos Gene Woodling Willie Miranda

(First part of 18-player trade completed on December 1, 1954; see Dick Kryhoski.)

DATE	TRADED TO		TRADED WITH	TRADED BY		IN EXCHANGE FOR
Dec 11, 1959	KC	A	Hank Bauer Norm Siebern Marv Throneberry	NY	A	Roger Maris Joe DeMaestri Kent Hadley
June 10, 1961	CHI	A	Ray Herbert Andy Carey Al Pilarcik	KC	A	Wes Covington Bob Shaw Gerry Staley Stan Johnson
Nov 30, 1961	SF	N	Billy Pierce	CHI	A	Eddie Fisher Dom Zanni Verle Tiefenthaler Bob Farley
May 20, 1964	HOU	N	————	SF	N	Cash
April 24, 1965	BAL	A	————	HOU	N	Bob Saverine and cash

Dan Larson

DATE	TRADED TO		TRADED WITH	TRADED BY		IN EXCHANGE FOR
Aug 15, 1974	HOU	N	Minor league P Ron Selak	STL	N	Claude Osteen
Dec 8, 1981	CHI	N	Keith Moreland Dickie Noles	PHI	N	Mike Krukow and cash

Tony LaRussa

DATE	TRADED TO		TRADED WITH	TRADED BY		IN EXCHANGE FOR
Aug 14, 1971	ATL	N	————	OAK	A	Cash
Oct 20, 1972	CHI	N	————	ATL	N	Tom Phoebus

Frank Lary

DATE	TRADED TO		TRADED WITH	TRADED BY		IN EXCHANGE FOR
May 30, 1964	NY	N	————	DET	A	Cash
Aug 8, 1964	MIL	N	————	NY	N	Dennis Ribant and cash
March 20, 1965	NY	N	————	MIL	N	Cash
July 8, 1965	CHI	A	————	NY	N	Jimmie Schaffer

Lyn Lary

DATE	TRADED TO		TRADED WITH	TRADED BY		IN EXCHANGE FOR
May 15, 1934	BOS	A	————	NY	A	Freddie Muller and $20,000.
Oct 26, 1934	WAS	A	$225,000.	BOS	A	Joe Cronin
June 29, 1935	STL	A	————	WAS	A	Alan Strange
Jan 17, 1937	CLE	A	Ivy Andrews Moose Solters	STL	A	Bill Knickerbocker Joe Vosmik Oral Hildebrand
May 3, 1939	BKN	N	————	CLE	A	Cash
Aug 14, 1939	STL	N	————	BKN	N	Waiver price

DATE	TRADED TO		TRADED WITH	TRADED BY		IN EXCHANGE FOR

Fred Lasher

| May 22, 1970 | CLE | A | ———— | DET | A | Rusty Nagelson Billy Rohr |

Bill Laskey

| Dec 11, 1981 | SF | N | Rich Gale | KC | A | Jerry Martin |

Tacks Latimer

| Jan 1900 | PIT | N | *See Honus Wagner* | LOU | N | ———— |

Barry Latman

April 18, 1960	CLE	A	————	CHI	A	Herb Score
Dec 2, 1963	LA	A	Joe Adcock	CLE	A	Leon Wagner
Dec 15, 1965	HOU	N	————	CAL	A	Minor league C Ed Pacheco and cash

Charlie Lau

Oct 15, 1959	MIL	N	Don Lee	DET	A	Don Kaiser Mike Roarke Casey Wise
July 1, 1963	KC	A	————	BAL	A	Cash
June 15, 1964	BAL	A	————	KC	A	Wes Stock
May 31, 1967	ATL	N	————	BAL	A	Cash

George Lauzerique

| Dec 7, 1969 | SEA | A | Ted Kubiak | OAK | A | Diego Segui Ray Oyler |
| Oct 20, 1970 | STL | N | Jerry McNertney minor league P Jesse Higgins | MIL | A | Carl Taylor Jim Ellis |

Cookie Lavagetto

| Dec 4, 1936 | BKN | N | Ralph Birkofer | PIT | N | Ed Brandt |

Doc Lavan

Aug 24, 1913	PHI	A	————	STL	A	Cash
Feb 5, 1914	STL	A	————	PHI	A	Cash
Dec 15, 1917	WAS	A	Burt Shotton	STL	A	Bert Gallia and $15,000.
Jan 1919	STL	N	————	WAS	A	Cash

Jimmy Lavender

| Jan 16, 1917 | PHI | N | $5,000. | CHI | N | Al Demaree |

Ron Law

| Dec 5, 1969 | WAS | A | Dave Nelson Horacio Pina | CLE | A | Dennis Higgins Barry Moore |

Rudy Law

| March 30, 1982 | CHI | A | ———— | LA | N | Minor league P Bert Geiger Cecil Espy |

Vance Law

| March 21, 1982 | CHI | A | Ernie Camacho | PIT | N | Ross Baumgarten Butch Edge |

DATE	TRADED TO		TRADED WITH	TRADED BY		IN EXCHANGE FOR

Vance Law continued

| Dec 7, 1984 | MON | N | Bert Roberge | CHI | A | Bob James
Bryan Little |

Tom Lawless

| Aug 16, 1984 | MON | N | ——————
(Rose was named Cincinnati manager.) | CIN | N | Pete Rose |

Brooks Lawrence

| Jan 31, 1956 | CIN | N | Sonny Senerchia | STL | N | Jackie Collum |

Roxie Lawson

| May 13, 1939 | STL | A | —————— | DET | A | *See Beau Bell* |

Steve Lawson

| July 20, 1972 | TEX | A | Marty Martinez
Vic Harris | OAK | A | Don Mincher
Ted Kubiak |

Bill Laxton

Dec 15, 1967	PHI	N	Don Money Woodie Fryman minor league P Hal Clem	PIT	N	Jim Bunning
Dec 12, 1975	DET	A	Rusty Staub	NY	N	Mickey Lolich Bobby Baldwin
Sept 9, 1977	CLE	A	cash	SEA	A	Ray Fosse
June 22, 1978	SD	N	——————	CLE	A	Dave Freisleben

Pete Layden

| Nov 17, 1947 | STL | A | —————— | BOS | A | *See Vern Stephens* |

Freddy Leach

| Oct 29, 1928 | NY | N | —————— | PHI | N | Lefty O'Doul
and cash |
| March 19, 1932 | BOS | N | —————— | NY | N | $10,000. |

Terry Leach

| April 9, 1984 | ATL | N | —————— | CHI | N | Ron Meridith |

Tommy Leach

| Jan 1900 | PIT | N | *See Honus Wagner* | LOU | N | —————— |
| June 22, 1912 | CHI | N | Lefty Leifield | PIT | N | King Cole
Solly Hofman |

Tom Leahy

| June 1901 | PHI | A | —————— | MIL | A | Phil Geier |

Fred Lear

| Feb 1920 | NY | N | —————— | CHI | N | Cash |

Bevo LeBourveau

| Feb 8, 1923 | PHI | A | —————— | PHI | N | Cash |

Bill Lee

| Aug 5, 1943 | PHI | N | —————— | CHI | N | Mickey Livingston |
| July 14, 1945 | BOS | N | —————— | PHI | N | Cash |

DATE	TRADED TO		TRADED WITH	TRADED BY		IN EXCHANGE FOR

Bill Lee
| Dec 7, 1978 | MON | N | ———— | BOS | A | Stan Papi |

Bob Lee
| Dec 15, 1966 | LA | N | ———— | CAL | A | Nick Willhite |
| May 31, 1967 | CIN | N | ———— | LA | N | Cash |

Cliff Lee
| May 1921 | PHI | N | ———— | PIT | N | Waiver price |
| June 20, 1924 | CIN | N | ———— | PHI | N | Cash |

Don Lee
Oct 15, 1959	MIL	N	Charlie Lau	DET	A	Don Kaiser Mike Roarke Casey Wise
May 29, 1962	LA	A	————	MIN	A	Jim Donohue
June 1, 1965	HOU	N	————	CAL	A	Al Spangler

Hal Lee
Oct 14, 1930	PHI	N	Clise Dudley Jumbo Elliott and cash	BKN	N	Lefty O'Doul Fresco Thompson
June 17, 1933	BOS	N	Pinky Whitney	PHI	N	Fritz Knothe Wes Schulmerich and cash
Jan 27, 1937	NY	N	Ben Cantwell	BOS	N	Cash

Leron Lee
| June 11, 1971 | SD | N | Fred Norman | STL | N | Al Santorini |
| March 28, 1974 | CLE | A | ———— | SD | N | Cash |

Mark Lee
| Aug 5, 1980 | PIT | N | Kurt Bevacqua | SD | N | Rick Lancellotti
Luis Salazar |

Mike Lee
| May 10, 1961 | STL | N | Joe Morgan
and cash | CLE | A | Bob Nieman |

(St. Louis received Lee on September 25.)

Thornton Lee
| Dec 10, 1936 | CHI | A | ———— | CLE | A | Jack Salveson |

(Part of three-team trade involving Chicago, Cleveland, and Washington.)

Joe Lefebvre
| April 1, 1981 | SD | N | Ruppert Jones
Tim Lollar
Chris Welsh | NY | A | Jerry Mumphrey
John Pacella |
| May 22, 1983 | PHI | N | ———— | SD | N | Sid Monge |

Craig Lefferts
| Dec 7, 1983 | SD | N | Carmelo Martinez
Fritzie Connally | CHI | N | Scott Sanderson |

(Part of three-team trade involving Chicago Cubs, San Diego, and Montreal.)

Ron LeFlore
| Dec 7, 1979 | MON | N | ———— | DET | A | Dan Schatzeder |

DATE	TRADED TO		TRADED WITH	TRADED BY		IN EXCHANGE FOR

Ron LeFlore continued

| Dec 6, 1980 | CHI | A | ———— | MON | N | No compensation (free agent signing) |

Lou Legett

| Nov 7, 1928 | BOS | N | Socks Seibold Percy Jones Freddie Maguire Bruce Cunningham and $200,000. | CHI | N | Rogers Hornsby |

Ken Lehman

June 4, 1957	BAL	A	————	BKN	N	$30,000.
Oct 2, 1958	PHI	N	————	BAL	A	Waiver price
March 20, 1962	CLE	A	Tony Curry	PHI	N	Mel Roach

Paul Lehner

| Dec 13, 1949 | PHI | A | Bob Dillinger | STL | A | Ray Coleman Frankie Gustine Billy DeMars minor league OF Ray Ippolito and $100,000. |
| April 30, 1951 | CHI | A | Minnie Minoso | PHI | A | Gus Zernial Dave Philley |

(Part of three-team trade involving Chicago White Sox, Philadelphia A's, and Cleveland.)

June 4, 1951	STL	A	Kermit Wahl and cash	CHI	A	Don Lenhardt
July 19, 1951	CLE	A	————	STL	A	Waiver price
June 25, 1952	BOS	A	————	CLE	A	Waiver price

Hank Leiber

| Dec 6, 1938 | CHI | N | Dick Bartell Gus Mancuso | NY | N | Frank Demaree Bill Jurges Ken O'Dea |
| Dec 4, 1941 | NY | N | ———— | CHI | N | Bob Bowman |

Nemo Leibold

July 7, 1915	CHI	A	————	CLE	A	Waiver price
March 4, 1921	BOS	A	Shano Collins	CHI	A	Harry Hooper
May 26, 1923	WAS	A	————	BOS	A	Waiver price

Lefty Leifield

| June 22, 1912 | CHI | N | Tommy Leach | PIT | N | King Cole Solly Hofman |

Ed Leip

| April 1940 | PIT | N | ———— | WAS | A | Cash |

Dummy Leitner

| May 1902 | CHI | A | ———— | CLE | A | Cash |

Frank Leja

| March 30, 1962 | LA | A | ———— | STL | N | Cash |

DATE	TRADED TO		TRADED WITH	TRADED BY		IN EXCHANGE FOR

John Mayberry continued

| May 5, 1982 | NY | A | ——— | TOR | A | Dave Revering
minor league
3B Jeff Reynolds |

Lee Maye

May 13, 1965	HOU	N	———	MIL	N	Ken Johnson Jim Beauchamp
Jan 4, 1967	CLE	A	Ken Retzer	HOU	N	Jim Landis Jim Weaver Doc Edwards
June 20, 1969	WAS	A	———	CLE	A	Bill Denehy and cash
Sept 10, 1970	CHI	A	———	WAS	A	Cash

Ed Mayer

| April 20, 1957 | CHI | N | Bobby Del Greco | STL | N | Jim King |

Erskine Mayer

| July 1, 1918 | PIT | N | ——— | PHI | N | Elmer Jacobs |
| Aug 1919 | CHI | A | ——— | PIT | N | Waiver price |

Eddie Mayo

| Dec 4, 1936 | BOS | N | ——— | NY | N | Mickey Haslin |

Carl Mays

| July 29, 1919 | NY | A | ——— | BOS | A | Allan Russell
Bob McGraw
and $40,000. |
| Dec 11, 1923 | CIN | N | ——— | NY | A | Cash |

Willie Mays

| May 11, 1972 | NY | N | ——— | SF | N | Charlie Williams
and $50,000. |

Lee Mazzilli

April 1, 1982	TEX	A	———	NY	N	Ron Darling Walt Terrell
Aug 8, 1982	NY	A	———	TEX	A	Bucky Dent
Dec 22, 1982	PIT	N	———	NY	A	Four minor leaguers: P John Holland P Tim Burke 1B Jose Rivera OF Don Aubin

Bill McAfee

| Oct 14, 1930 | BOS | N | Wes Schulmerich | CHI | N | Bob Smith
Jimmy Welsh |
| Dec 1933 | STL | A | ——— | WAS | A | Cash |

Sport McAllister

| Sept 1902 | BAL | A | ——— | DET | A | Cash |

(Baltimore returned McAllister to Detroit later in September.)

Jim McAnany

| April 1, 1961 | CHI | N | ——— | LA | A | Lou Johnson |

Jim McAndrew

| Dec 20, 1973 | SD | N | ——— | NY | N | Steve Simpson |

DATE	TRADED TO		TRADED WITH	TRADED BY		IN EXCHANGE FOR

Ike McAuley
| May 24, 1917 | STL | N | ———— | PIT | N | Waiver price |

Dick McAuliffe
| Oct 23, 1973 | BOS | A | ———— | DET | A | Ben Oglivie |

Al McBean
| April 17, 1969 | LA | N | ———— | SD | N | Tommy Dean |
| | | | | | | Leon Everitt |

Algie McBride
| May 30, 1901 | NY | N | ———— | CIN | N | Cash |

Bake McBride
June 15, 1977	PHI	N	Steve Waterbury	STL	N	Tom Underwood
						Dane Iorg
						Rick Bosetti
Feb 16, 1982	CLE	A	————	PHI	N	Sid Monge

George McBride
| July 4, 1905 | STL | N | ———— | PIT | N | Dave Brain |

Tom McBride
| May 14, 1947 | WAS | A | ———— | BOS | A | Cash |

Bill McCabe
| May 1920 | BKN | N | ———— | CHI | N | Cash |

Joe McCabe
| Oct 15, 1964 | WAS | A | ———— | MIN | A | Ken Retzer |

Larry McCall
Sept 16, 1974	CAL	A	————	BAL	A	Cash
Nov 10, 1978	TEX	A	————	NY	A	*See Dave Righetti*
Jan 4, 1980	CLE	A	Gary Gray	TEX	A	David Clyde
			minor league			Jim Norris
			3B-OF Mike Bucci			

Roger McCardell
| Nov 30, 1959 | BAL | A | Jackie Brandt | SF | N | Billy O'Dell |
| | | | Gordon Jones | | | Billy Loes |

Alex McCarthy
| Sept 5, 1915 | CHI | N | ———— | PIT | N | Cash |
| July 1916 | PIT | N | ———— | CHI | N | Cash |

Jack McCarthy
Feb 10, 1900	CHI	N	————	PIT	N	$2,000.
Dec 30, 1905	BKN	N	Billy Maloney	CHI	N	Jimmy Sheckard
			Doc Casey			
			Buttons Briggs			
			and $2,000.			

Johnny McCarthy
Jan 1936	NY	N	————	BKN	N	$40,000.
Dec 11, 1941	STL	N	Ken O'Dea	NY	N	Johnny Mize
			Bill Lohrman			
			and $50,000.			

DATE	TRADED TO		TRADED WITH	TRADED BY		IN EXCHANGE FOR

Cal McLish continued

| Dec 15, 1961 | PHI | N | Frank Barnes
Andy Carey | CHI | A | Bob Sadowski
Taylor Phillips
minor league
IF Lou Vassie |

(Carey refused to report, and the Phillies received McLish in exchange
for Vassie to complete the trade on March 24, 1962.)

Jack McMahan

| June 23, 1956 | KC | A | ———— | PIT | N | Spook Jacobs |
| Feb 19, 1957 | NY | A | ———— | KC | A | *See Billy Hunter* |

Don McMahon

May 9, 1962	HOU	N	————	MIL	N	Cash
Sept 30, 1963	CLE	A	————	HOU	N	Cash
June 2, 1966	BOS	A	Lee Stange	CLE	A	Dick Radatz
June 3, 1967	CHI	A	minor league P Bob Snow	BOS	A	Jerry Adair
July 21, 1968	DET	A	————	CHI	A	Dennis Ribant
Aug 9, 1969	SF	N	————	DET	A	Cash

Frank McManus

| July 25, 1904 | NY | A | ———— | DET | A | Monte Beville |

Jim McManus

| Nov 20, 1957 | KC | A | ———— | DET | A | *See Billy Martin* |

Marty McManus

| Jan 15, 1927 | DET | A | Bobby LaMotte
Pinky Hargrave | STL | A | Lefty Stewart
Frank O'Rourke
Billy Mullen
Otto Miller |
| Aug 31, 1931 | BOS | A | ———— | DET | A | Muddy Ruel |

Norm McMillan

| Jan 30, 1923 | BOS | A | Camp Skinner
George Murray
and $50,000. | NY | A | Herb Pennock |
| Dec 1923 | STL | A | ———— | BOS | A | Homer Ezzell |

Roy McMillan

| Dec 15, 1960 | MIL | N | ———— | CIN | N | Joey Jay
Juan Pizarro |
| May 8, 1964 | NY | N | ———— | MIL | N | Jay Hook
Adrian Garrett |

Tommy McMillan

| Dec 5, 1978 | PIT | N | ———— | SEA | A | *See Mario Mendoza* |

Tommy McMillan

| May 1910 | CIN | N | ———— | BKN | N | Cash |

Ken McMullen

| Dec 4, 1964 | WAS | A | Frank Howard
Phil Ortega
Pete Richert
Dick Nen | LA | N | Claude Osteen
John Kennedy
and $100,000. |
| April 27, 1970 | CAL | A | ———— | WAS | A | Aurelio Rodriguez
Rick Reichardt |

DATE	TRADED TO		TRADED WITH	TRADED BY		IN EXCHANGE FOR

Ken McMullen continued

Nov 28, 1972	LA	N	Andy Messersmith	CAL	A	Frank Robinson
						Bill Singer
						Mike Strahler
						Billy Grabarkewitz
						Bobby Valentine
Feb 25, 1977	MIL	A	————	OAK	A	Cash

Eric McNair

Jan 4, 1936	BOS	A	Doc Cramer	PHI	A	Hank Johnson
						Al Niemiec
						and $75,000.
Dec 21, 1938	CHI	A	————	BOS	A	Boze Berger
Dec 18, 1940	DET	A	————	CHI	A	Waiver price
July 17, 1942	WAS	A	————	DET	A	Jack Wilson
			(McNair refused to report.)			
July 25, 1942	PHI	A	————	DET	A	Cash

Dave McNally

Dec 4, 1974	MON	N	Rich Coggins	BAL	A	Ken Singleton
			minor league			Mike Torrez
			P Bill Kirkpatrick			

Mike McNally

Dec 15, 1920	NY	A	*See Waite Hoyt*	BOS	A	————
Dec 10, 1924	BOS	A	————	NY	A	Howard Shanks
Dec 11, 1924	WAS	A	————	BOS	A	Doc Prothro

Tim McNamara

| April 17, 1925 | NY | N | ———— | BOS | N | Rosy Ryan |

Rusty McNealy

Dec 9, 1981	OAK	A	minor league	SEA	A	Roy Thomas
			P Tim Hallgren			
Dec 7, 1983	MON	N	cash	OAK	A	Ray Burris

Earl McNeely

| Oct 19, 1927 | STL | A | Dick Coffman | WAS | A | Milt Gaston |

Jerry McNertney

Oct 20, 1970	STL	N	George Lauzerique	MIL	A	Carl Taylor
			minor league			Jim Ellis
			P Jesse Higgins			
May 4, 1973	PIT	N	————	OAK	A	Cash

Bill McNulty

Aug 31, 1971	CHI	N	Frank Fernandez	OAK	A	Adrian Garrett
Oct 30, 1972	TEX	A	Brant Alyea	OAK	A	Paul Lindblad
March 28, 1973	NY	N	————	TEX	A	Bill Sudakis

George McQuillan

Feb 1911	CIN	N	Johnny Bates	PHI	N	Fred Beebe
			Eddie Grant			Jack Rowan
			Lew Moren			Dode Paskert
						Hans Lobert
Feb 14, 1915	PHI	N	————	PIT	N	Waiver price

DATE	TRADED TO		TRADED WITH	TRADED BY		IN EXCHANGE FOR

Hugh McQuillan

| July 30, 1922 | NY | N | ———— | BOS | N | Fred Toney Larry Benton and $100,000. |

(Toney refused to report and remained Giants' property.)

| June 12, 1927 | BOS | N | Kent Greenfield Doc Farrell | NY | N | Zack Taylor Larry Benton Herb Thomas |

George McQuinn

| Oct 16, 1945 | PHI | A | ———— | STL | A | Dick Siebert |

Hal McRae

| Nov 30, 1972 | KC | A | Wayne Simpson | CIN | N | Roger Nelson Richie Scheinblum |

Norm McRae

Oct 9, 1970	WAS	A	*See Denny McLain*	DET	A	————
May 30, 1972	DET	A	————	TEX	A	Dalton Jones
Nov 30, 1972	PIT	N	Jim Foor	DET	A	Dick Sharon

Doug McWeeny

| Feb 1930 | CIN | N | ———— | BKN | N | Dolf Luque |

Larry McWilliams

| June 30, 1982 | PIT | N | ———— | ATL | N | Pascual Perez minor league SS Carlos Rios |

Lee Meadows

| July 14, 1919 | PHI | N | Gene Paulette | STL | N | Elmer Jacobs Frank Woodward Doug Baird |
| May 22, 1923 | PIT | N | Johnny Rawlings | PHI | N | Whitey Glazner Cotton Tierney and $50,000. |

Doc Medich

Dec 11, 1975	PIT	N	————	NY	A	Willie Randolph Ken Brett Dock Ellis
March 15, 1977	OAK	A	Dave Giusti Doug Bair Rick Langford Tony Armas Mitchell Page	PIT	N	Phil Garner Tommy Helms Chris Batton
Sept 13, 1977	SEA	A	————	OAK	A	Cash
Sept 26, 1977	NY	N	————	SEA	A	Cash
Nov 11, 1977	TEX	A	————	NY	N	No compensation (free agent signing)
Aug 11, 1982	MIL	A	————	TEX	A	Cash

Joe Medwick

June 12, 1940	BKN	N	Curt Davis	STL	N	Ernie Koy Carl Doyle Sam Nahem Bert Haas and $125,000.
July 6, 1943	NY	N	————	BKN	N	Cash
June 16, 1945	BOS	N	Ewald Pyle	NY	N	Clyde Kluttz

DATE	TRADED TO		TRADED WITH	TRADED BY		IN EXCHANGE FOR
Jouett Meekin						
Jan 1900	PIT	N	————	BOS	N	Cash
Roman Mejias						
Nov 26, 1962	BOS	A	————	HOU	N	Pete Runnels
Sam Mejias						
June 7, 1976	STL	N	————	MIL	A	Danny Frisella
Nov 6, 1976	MON	N	Bill Greif Angel Torres	STL	N	Steve Dunning Pat Scanlon Tony Scott
Dec 14, 1978	CHI	N	————	MON	N	Rodney Scott Jerry White
July 4, 1979	CIN	N	————	CHI	N	Cash
Sam Mele						
June 13, 1949	WAS	A	Mickey Harris	BOS	A	Walt Masterson
May 3, 1952	CHI	A	————	WAS	A	Jim Busby Mel Hoderlein
Feb 5, 1954	BAL	A	Neil Berry	CHI	A	Johnny Groth Johnny Lipon
July 29, 1954	BOS	A	————	BAL	A	Waiver price
June 23, 1955	CIN	N	————	BOS	A	Cash
Luis Melendez						
May 19, 1976	SD	N	————	STL	N	Bill Greif
Oscar Melillo						
May 21, 1935	BOS	A	————	STL	A	Moose Solters and cash
Paul Meloan						
April 1911	STL	A	————	CHI	A	Cash
Bill Melton						
Dec 11, 1975	CAL	A	Steve Dunning	CHI	A	Jim Spencer Morris Nettles
Dec 3, 1976	CLE	A	————	CAL	A	Stan Perzanowski and cash
Rube Melton						
Dec 12, 1942	BKN	N	————	PHI	N	Johnny Allen and $30,000.
Mario Mendoza						
Dec 5, 1978	SEA	A	Odell Jones Rafael Vasquez	PIT	N	Enrique Romo Rick Jones Tommy McMillan
Dec 12, 1980	TEX	A	*See Rick Honeycutt*	SEA	A	————
Denis Menke						
Oct 8, 1967	HOU	N	Denny Lemaster	ATL	N	Sonny Jackson Chuck Harrison
Nov 29, 1971	CIN	N	*See Joe Morgan*	HOU	N	————
Feb 18, 1974	HOU	N	————	CIN	N	Pat Darcy and cash

DATE	TRADED TO		TRADED WITH	TRADED BY		IN EXCHANGE FOR

Mike Menosky

DATE	TRADED TO		TRADED WITH	TRADED BY		IN EXCHANGE FOR
Feb 10, 1916	WAS	A	————	PIT	F	Cash
Jan 20, 1920	BOS	A	Harry Harper Eddie Foster	WAS	A	Braggo Roth Red Shannon

Mike Meola

DATE	TRADED TO		TRADED WITH	TRADED BY		IN EXCHANGE FOR
July 1936	BOS	A	————	STL	A	Cash

Rudi Meoli

DATE	TRADED TO		TRADED WITH	TRADED BY		IN EXCHANGE FOR
Sept 17, 1975	SD	N	Bobby Valentine	CAL	A	Gary Ross
April 5, 1976	CIN	N	cash	SD	N	Merv Rettenmund

Win Mercer

DATE	TRADED TO		TRADED WITH	TRADED BY		IN EXCHANGE FOR
Feb 9, 1900	NY	N	————	WAS	N	Cash

Spike Merena

DATE	TRADED TO		TRADED WITH	TRADED BY		IN EXCHANGE FOR
Sept 24, 1934	DET	A	————	BOS	A	Cash

Ron Meridith

DATE	TRADED TO		TRADED WITH	TRADED BY		IN EXCHANGE FOR
Feb 14, 1984	ATL	N	————	HOU	N	Jose Alvarez
April 9, 1984	CHI	N	————	ATL	N	Terry Leach

Fred Merkle

DATE	TRADED TO		TRADED WITH	TRADED BY		IN EXCHANGE FOR
Aug 20, 1916	BKN	N	————	NY	N	Lew McCarty
Aug 16, 1917	CHI	N	————	BKN	N	$3,500.

Lloyd Merriman

DATE	TRADED TO		TRADED WITH	TRADED BY		IN EXCHANGE FOR
Feb 10, 1955	CHI	A	————	CIN	N	Cash
April 16, 1955	CHI	N	————	CHI	A	Cash

Jim Merritt

DATE	TRADED TO		TRADED WITH	TRADED BY		IN EXCHANGE FOR
Nov 21, 1968	CIN	N	————	MIN	A	Leo Cardenas

Lloyd Merritt

DATE	TRADED TO		TRADED WITH	TRADED BY		IN EXCHANGE FOR
June 15, 1959	LA	N	Chuck Essegian	STL	N	Dick Gray

Sam Mertes

DATE	TRADED TO		TRADED WITH	TRADED BY		IN EXCHANGE FOR
July 13, 1906	STL	N	Doc Marshall	NY	N	Spike Shannon

Steve Mesner

DATE	TRADED TO		TRADED WITH	TRADED BY		IN EXCHANGE FOR
Dec 27, 1939	STL	N	Gene Lillard and cash	CHI	N	Ken Raffensberger
Feb 1, 1943	BKN	N	————	CIN	N	Waiver price

(Landis voided the sale because Mesner had already been drafted at the time of the deal.)

Andy Messersmith

DATE	TRADED TO		TRADED WITH	TRADED BY		IN EXCHANGE FOR
Nov 28, 1972	LA	N	Ken McMullen	CAL	A	Frank Robinson Bill Singer Mike Strahler Billy Grabarkewitz Bobby Valentine
April 10, 1976	ATL	N	————	LA	N	No compensation (free agent signing)
Dec 7, 1977	NY	A	————	ATL	N	Cash

Catfish Metkovich

DATE	TRADED TO		TRADED WITH	TRADED BY		IN EXCHANGE FOR
April 2, 1947	CLE	A	————	BOS	A	Cash

DATE	TRADED TO		TRADED WITH	TRADED BY		IN EXCHANGE FOR

Catfish Metkovich continued

| Dec 9, 1947 | STL | A | $50,000. | CLE | A | Johnny Berardino |

(Metkovich was returned to Cleveland because of a broken finger and the St. Louis Browns received another $15,000 to complete the trade.)

| June 4, 1953 | CHI | N | Ralph Kiner
Joe Garagiola
Howie Pollet | PIT | N | Toby Atwell
Bob Schultz
Preston Ward
George Freese
Bob Addis
Gene Hermanski
$150,000. |
| Dec 7, 1953 | MIL | N | ———— | CHI | N | Cash |

Charlie Metro

| Aug 13, 1944 | PHI | A | ———— | DET | A | Cash |

Butch Metzger

Dec 6, 1974	SD	N	Tito Fuentes	SF	N	Derrel Thomas
May 17, 1977	STL	N	————	SD	N	John D'Acquisto Pat Scanlon
April 5, 1978	NY	N	————	STL	N	Cash
July 4, 1978	PHI	N	————	NY	N	Cash

Roger Metzger

| Oct 12, 1970 | HOU | N | ———— | CHI | N | Hector Torres |
| June 15, 1978 | SF | N | ———— | HOU | N | Cash |

Alex Metzler

| July 21, 1930 | STL | A | ———— | CHI | A | Cash |

Bob Meusel

| Oct 16, 1929 | CIN | N | ———— | NY | A | Waiver price |

Irish Meusel

| July 25, 1921 | NY | N | ———— | PHI | N | Curt Walker
Butch Henline
Jesse Winters
and $30,000. |

Benny Meyer

| May 1914 | BUF | F | ———— | PIT | F | Cash |

Bob Meyer

June 12, 1964	LA	A	————	NY	A	Cash
July 29, 1964	KC	A	————	LA	A	Cash
Aug 29, 1969	SEA	A	Pete Koegel	OAK	A	Fred Talbot

Dan Meyer

| Dec 9, 1981 | OAK | A | ———— | SEA | A | Rich Bordi |

Dutch Meyer

| April 27, 1945 | CLE | A | Don Ross | DET | A | Roy Cullenbine |

Russ Meyer

| Oct 11, 1948 | PHI | N | ———— | CHI | N | Cash |
| Feb 16, 1953 | MIL | N | cash | PHI | N | Earl Torgeson |

(Part of four-team trade involving Milwaukee Braves, Philadelphia Phillies, Brooklyn, and Cincinnati.)

DATE	TRADED TO		TRADED WITH	TRADED BY		IN EXCHANGE FOR

John Milner continued

| Aug 20, 1981 | MON | N | ———— | PIT | N | Willie Montanez |

Don Mincher

April 4, 1960	WAS	A	Earl Battey and $150,000.	CHI	A	Roy Sievers
Dec 2, 1966	CAL	A	Jimmie Hall Pete Cimino	MIN	A	Dean Chance Jackie Hernandez
Jan 15, 1970	OAK	A	Ron Clark	MIL	A	Mike Hershberger Lew Krausse Phil Roof Ken Sanders
May 8, 1971	WAS	A	Frank Fernandez Paul Lindblad and cash	OAK	A	Mike Epstein Darold Knowles
July 20, 1972	OAK	A	Ted Kubiak	TEX	A	Marty Martinez Vic Harris Steve Lawson

Craig Minetto

| Feb 24, 1982 | BAL | A | ———— | OAK | A | Minor league P Allen Edwards |
| Dec 21, 1983 | HOU | N | ———— | BAL | A | Bobby Sprowl |

Paul Minner

| Oct 14, 1949 | CHI | N | Preston Ward | BKN | N | $100,000. |

Minnie Minoso

| April 30, 1951 | PHI | A | Sam Zoldak Ray Murray | CLE | A | Lou Brissie |

(Part of three-team trade involving Cleveland, Philadelphia A's, and Chicago White Sox.)

| April 30, 1951 | CHI | A | Paul Lehner | PHI | A | Gus Zernial Dave Philley |

(Part of three-team trade involving Chicago White Sox, Philadelphia A's, and Cleveland.)

Dec 4, 1957	CLE	A	Fred Hatfield	CHI	A	Early Wynn Al Smith
Dec 6, 1959	CHI	A	Dick Brown Don Ferrarese Jake Striker	CLE	A	Johnny Romano Bubba Phillips Norm Cash
Nov 27, 1961	STL	N	————	CHI	A	Joe Cunningham
April 2, 1963	WAS	A	————	STL	N	Cash and minor league player to be named later

Jim Minshall

| Oct 15, 1976 | SEA | A | ———— | PIT | N | Cash |

Greg Minton

| April 2, 1973 | SF | N | ———— | KC | A | Fran Healy |

Paul Mirabella

Nov 10, 1978	NY	A	*See Dave Righetti*	TEX	A	————
Nov 1, 1979	TOR	A	*See Chris Chambliss*	NY	A	————
Dec 28, 1981	CHI	N	————	TOR	A	Dave Geisel

DATE	TRADED TO		TRADED WITH	TRADED BY		IN EXCHANGE FOR

Paul Mirabella continued

| March 26, 1982 | TEX | A | minor league P Paul Semall and cash | CHI | N | Bump Wills |

Willie Miranda

Oct 24, 1951	CHI	A	————	WAS	A	Floyd Baker
June 15, 1952	STL	A	Al Zarilla	CHI	A	Tom Wright Leo Thomas
June 28, 1952	CHI	A	————	STL	A	Waiver price
Oct 16, 1952	STL	A	Hank Edwards	CHI	A	Joe DeMaestri Tommy Byrne
June 12, 1953	NY	A	————	STL	A	Cash
Nov 18, 1954	BAL	A	————	NY	A	*See Bob Turley*

Bobby Mitchell

| Jan 6, 1982 | MIN | A | Bobby Castillo | LA | N | Minor leaguers P Paul Voigt and C Scotti Madison |

Bobby Mitchell

| June 7, 1971 | MIL | A | Frank Tepedino | NY | A | Danny Walton |

Clarence Mitchell

Oct 16, 1917	BKN	N	————	CIN	N	Waiver price
Feb 11, 1923	PHI	N	————	BKN	N	George Smith
May 15, 1930	NY	N	————	STL	N	Ralph Judd

Dale Mitchell

| July 29, 1956 | BKN | N | ———— | CLE | A | Cash |

Fred Mitchell

April 1902	PHI	A	————	BOS	A	Cash
Aug 18, 1904	BKN	N	————	PHI	N	Cash
Dec 14, 1916	CHI	N	————	BOS	N	Joe Kelly

Johnny Mitchell

| July 23, 1922 | BOS | A | Chick Fewster Elmer Miller Lefty O'Doul and $50,000. | NY | A | Joe Dugan Elmer Smith |
| Nov 1923 | BKN | N | ———— | BOS | A | Cash |

Mike Mitchell

Dec 15, 1912	CHI	N	Bert Humphries Red Corriden Pete Knisely Art Phelan	CIN	N	Joe Tinker Grover Lowdermilk Harry Chapman
July 29, 1913	PIT	N	————	CHI	N	Waiver price
July 20, 1914	WAS	A	————	PIT	N	Waiver price

Paul Mitchell

April 2, 1976	OAK	A	————	BAL	A	*See Reggie Jackson*
Aug 4, 1977	SEA	A	————	OAK	A	Cash
June 7, 1979	MIL	A	————	SEA	A	Randy Stein

DATE	TRADED TO		TRADED WITH	TRADED BY		IN EXCHANGE FOR

Joe Morgan

June 23, 1960	PHI	N	————	MIL	N	Alvin Dark
Aug 9, 1960	CLE	A	————	PHI	N	Cash
May 10, 1961	STL	N	Mike Lee and cash	CLE	A	Bob Nieman

(St. Louis received Lee on September 25.)

Mike Morgan

Nov 3, 1980	NY	A	————	OAK	A	Fred Stanley Brian Doyle
Dec 9, 1982	TOR	A	Dave Collins minor league 1B Fred McGriff and $400,000.	NY	A	Dale Murray minor league OF Tom Dodd

Tom Morgan

Feb 19, 1957	KC	A	*See Billy Hunter*	NY	A	————
Nov 20, 1957	DET	A	*See Billy Martin*	KC	A	————
July 22, 1960	WAS	A	————	DET	A	Bill Fischer
Jan 31, 1961	LA	A	————	WAS	A	Cash

George Moriarty

Jan 1909	DET	A	————	NY	A	Cash

Dan Morogiello

Feb 1, 1982	STL	N	————	ATL	N	Donnie Moore

John Morris

Dec 15, 1966	BAL	A	————	PHI	N	Dick Hall

Jim Morrison

April 13, 1979	CHI	A	————	PHI	N	Jack Kucek
June 14, 1982	PIT	N	————	CHI	A	Eddie Solomon

Bubba Morton

May 4, 1963	MIL	N	————	DET	A	Cash
June 15, 1965	CAL	A	cash	CLE	A	Phil Roof

(California received Morton on September 15, 1965.)

Carl Morton

Feb 28, 1973	ATL	N	————	MON	N	Pat Jarvis
Dec 9, 1976	TEX	A	Ken Henderson Dave May Roger Moret Adrian Devine and $250,000.	ATL	N	Jeff Burroughs

Walt Moryn

Dec 9, 1955	CHI	N	Don Hoak Russ Meyer	BKN	N	Randy Jackson Don Elston
June 15, 1960	STL	N	————	CHI	N	Jim McKnight
June 15, 1961	PIT	N	————	STL	N	Cash

Earl Moseley

Dec 23, 1915	CIN	N	————	NWK	F	$5,000.

Walter Moser

June 1911	STL	A	————	BOS	A	Cash

DATE	TRADED TO		TRADED WITH	TRADED BY		IN EXCHANGE FOR

Gerry Moses

DATE	TRADED TO		TRADED WITH	TRADED BY		IN EXCHANGE FOR
Oct 11, 1970	CAL	A	*See Tony Conigliaro*	BOS	A	————
Oct 5, 1971	CLE	A	*See Alex Johnson*	CAL	A	————
Nov 27, 1972	NY	A	*See Graig Nettles*	CLE	A	————
March 19, 1974	DET	A	————	NY	A	Rick Sawyer Walt Williams Ed Farmer

(Part of three-team trade involving Detroit, New York Yankees, and Cleveland.)

DATE	TRADED TO		TRADED WITH	TRADED BY		IN EXCHANGE FOR
Jan 30, 1975	NY	N	————	DET	A	Cash
April 28, 1975	SD	N	————	CHI	A	Cash
July 18, 1975	CHI	A	————	SD	N	Cash

Wally Moses

DATE	TRADED TO		TRADED WITH	TRADED BY		IN EXCHANGE FOR
Dec 9, 1939	DET	A	————	PHI	A	Benny McCoy Slick Coffman

(Commissioner Landis ruled that Detroit had kept McCoy covered up in the minors and declared him a free agent, cancelling the deal. McCoy then signed with Philadelphia for a $10,000 bonus.)

DATE	TRADED TO		TRADED WITH	TRADED BY		IN EXCHANGE FOR
Dec 9, 1941	CHI	A	————	PHI	A	Mike Kreevich Jack Hallett
July 23, 1946	BOS	A	————	CHI	A	Cash

Paul Moskau

DATE	TRADED TO		TRADED WITH	TRADED BY		IN EXCHANGE FOR
Feb 9, 1982	BAL	A	————	CIN	N	Wayne Krenchicki
April 3, 1982	PIT	N	————	BAL	A	Cash

Les Moss

DATE	TRADED TO		TRADED WITH	TRADED BY		IN EXCHANGE FOR
May 17, 1951	BOS	A	————	STL	A	Matt Batts Jim Suchecki Jim McDonald and $100,000.
Nov 28, 1951	STL	A	Tom Wright	BOS	A	Ken Wood Gus Niarhos
June 6, 1955	CHI	A	————	BAL	A	Harry Dorish

Ray Moss

DATE	TRADED TO		TRADED WITH	TRADED BY		IN EXCHANGE FOR
May 28, 1931	BOS	N	————	BKN	N	Cash

Don Mossi

DATE	TRADED TO		TRADED WITH	TRADED BY		IN EXCHANGE FOR
Nov 20, 1958	DET	A	Ray Narleski Ossie Alvarez	CLE	A	Billy Martin Al Cicotte
March 18, 1964	CHI	A	————	DET	A	Cash

Manny Mota

DATE	TRADED TO		TRADED WITH	TRADED BY		IN EXCHANGE FOR
Nov 30, 1962	HOU	N	Dick LeMay	SF	N	Joey Amalfitano
April 4, 1963	PIT	N	————	HOU	N	Howie Goss and cash
June 11, 1969	LA	N	Maury Wills	MON	N	Ron Fairly Paul Popovich

Curt Motton

DATE	TRADED TO		TRADED WITH	TRADED BY		IN EXCHANGE FOR
Dec 9, 1971	MIL	A	————	BAL	A	Bob Reynolds and cash

Glen Moulder

DATE	TRADED TO		TRADED WITH	TRADED BY		IN EXCHANGE FOR
April 6, 1948	CHI	A	————	STL	A	Cash

DATE	TRADED TO		TRADED WITH	TRADED BY		IN EXCHANGE FOR

Mike Mowrey

DATE	TRADED TO		TRADED WITH	TRADED BY		IN EXCHANGE FOR
Oct 1908	CIN	N	————	PHI	N	Cash
Aug 22, 1909	STL	N	————	CIN	N	Chappy Charles
Dec 12, 1913	PIT	N	Ed Konetchy Bob Harmon	STL	N	Art Butler Dots Miller Cozy Dolan Owen Wilson Hank Robinson
Feb 10, 1916	BKN	N	————	PIT	F	Cash

Don Mueller

DATE	TRADED TO		TRADED WITH	TRADED BY		IN EXCHANGE FOR
March 21, 1958	CHI	A	————	SF	N	Cash

Heinie Mueller

DATE	TRADED TO		TRADED WITH	TRADED BY		IN EXCHANGE FOR
June 14, 1926	NY	N	————	STL	N	Billy Southworth

Ray Mueller

DATE	TRADED TO		TRADED WITH	TRADED BY		IN EXCHANGE FOR
Dec 16, 1938	PIT	N	————	BOS	N	Al Todd Johnny Dickshot and cash
June 13, 1949	NY	N	————	CIN	N	Walker Cooper
May 17, 1950	PIT	N	————	NY	N	Cash

Billy Muffett

DATE	TRADED TO		TRADED WITH	TRADED BY		IN EXCHANGE FOR
Oct 8, 1958	SF	N	Hobie Landrith Benny Valenzuela	STL	N	Ernie Broglio Marv Grissom

Hugh Mulcahy

DATE	TRADED TO		TRADED WITH	TRADED BY		IN EXCHANGE FOR
Jan 1947	PIT	N	————	PHI	N	Cash

Greg Mulleavy

DATE	TRADED TO		TRADED WITH	TRADED BY		IN EXCHANGE FOR
Dec 15, 1932	BOS	A	Johnny Hodapp Bob Fothergill Bob Seeds	CHI	A	Ed Durham Hal Rhyne

Billy Mullen

DATE	TRADED TO		TRADED WITH	TRADED BY		IN EXCHANGE FOR
Jan 15, 1927	STL	A	————	DET	A	*See Marty McManus*

Freddie Muller

DATE	TRADED TO		TRADED WITH	TRADED BY		IN EXCHANGE FOR
May 15, 1934	NY	A	$20,000.	BOS	A	Lyn Lary

George Mullin

DATE	TRADED TO		TRADED WITH	TRADED BY		IN EXCHANGE FOR
May 17, 1913	WAS	A	————	DET	A	Waiver price

Jim Mullin

DATE	TRADED TO		TRADED WITH	TRADED BY		IN EXCHANGE FOR
Aug 31, 1904	WAS	A	————	PHI	A	Cash

Rance Mulliniks

DATE	TRADED TO		TRADED WITH	TRADED BY		IN EXCHANGE FOR
Dec 6, 1979	KC	A	Willie Aikens	CAL	A	Al Cowens Todd Cruz Craig Eaton
March 25, 1982	TOR	A	————	KC	A	Phil Huffman

Fran Mullins

DATE	TRADED TO		TRADED WITH	TRADED BY		IN EXCHANGE FOR
Nov 21, 1983	CIN	N	————	CHI	A	Steve Christmas

Jerry Mumphrey

DATE	TRADED TO		TRADED WITH	TRADED BY		IN EXCHANGE FOR
Dec 7, 1979	CLE	A	John Denny	STL	N	Bobby Bonds

DATE	TRADED TO		TRADED WITH	TRADED BY		IN EXCHANGE FOR

Jerry Mumphrey continued

DATE	TRADED TO		TRADED WITH	TRADED BY		IN EXCHANGE FOR
Feb 15, 1980	SD	N	————	CLE	A	Bob Owchinko Jim Wilhelm
April 1, 1981	NY	A	John Pacella	SD	N	Ruppert Jones Joe Lefebvre Tim Lollar Chris Welsh
Aug 10, 1983	HOU	N	————	NY	A	Omar Moreno

Bob Muncrief

Nov 20, 1947	CLE	A	Walt Judnich	STL	A	Dick Kokos Bryan Stephens Joe Frazier and $25,000.
Nov 20, 1948	PIT	N	————	CLE	A	$20,000.
June 6, 1949	CHI	N	————	PIT	N	Waiver price

George Munger

May 3, 1952	PIT	N	————	STL	N	Bill Werle

Scott Munninghoff

Nov 20, 1981	CLE	A	Lonnie Smith	PHI	N	Bo Diaz

(Part of three-team trade involving Cleveland, Philadelphia, and St. Louis.)

Steve Mura

Dec 10, 1981	STL	N	Ozzie Smith Alan Olmsted	SD	N	Sixto Lezcano Garry Templeton Luis DeLeon

(Templeton and Smith were exchanged on February 11, 1982; Olmsted and DeLeon were exchanged on February 19.)

Jan 26, 1983	CHI	A	————	STL	N	

(Claimed in compensation draft after Chicago lost free agent OF Steve Kemp to Yankees.)

Bobby Murcer

Oct 22, 1974	SF	N	————	NY	A	Bobby Bonds
Feb 11, 1977	CHI	N	Steve Ontiveros minor league P Andy Muhlstock	SF	N	Bill Madlock Rob Sperring
June 26, 1979	NY	A	————	CHI	N	Minor league P Pete Semall

Danny Murphy

March 28, 1963	HOU	N	Jug Gerard	CHI	N	Merritt Ranew Hal Haydel Dick LeMay
Dec 10, 1963	CHI	A	Jim Golden and cash	HOU	N	Nellie Fox
March 31, 1971	BOS	A	Duane Josephson	CHI	A	Vicente Romo Tony Muser

Eddie Murphy

July 15, 1915	CHI	A	————	PHI	A	$13,500.

Frank Murphy

July 1901	NY	N	————	BOS	N	Cash

Tom Murphy

May 5, 1972	KC	A	————	CAL	A	Bob Oliver

DATE	TRADED TO		TRADED WITH	TRADED BY		IN EXCHANGE FOR

Tom Murphy continued

DATE	TRADED TO		TRADED WITH	TRADED BY		IN EXCHANGE FOR
May 8, 1973	STL	N	————	KC	A	Al Santorini
Dec 8, 1973	MIL	A	————	STL	N	Bob Heise
June 3, 1976	BOS	A	Bobby Darwin	MIL	A	Bernie Carbo
July 27, 1977	TOR	A	————	BOS	A	Cash

Dale Murray

DATE	TRADED TO		TRADED WITH	TRADED BY		IN EXCHANGE FOR
Dec 16, 1976	CIN	N	Woodie Fryman	MON	N	Tony Perez Will McEnaney
May 19, 1978	NY	N	————	CIN	N	Ken Henderson
Aug 30, 1979	MON	N	————	NY	N	Cash
Dec 9, 1982	NY	A	minor league OF Tom Dodd	TOR	A	Dave Collins Mike Morgan minor league 1B Fred McGriff and $400,000.

George Murray

DATE	TRADED TO		TRADED WITH	TRADED BY		IN EXCHANGE FOR
Jan 30, 1923	BOS	A	Camp Skinner Norm McMillan and $50,000.	NY	A	Herb Pennock

Larry Murray

DATE	TRADED TO		TRADED WITH	TRADED BY		IN EXCHANGE FOR
April 27, 1977	OAK	A	Dock Ellis Marty Perez	NY	A	Mike Torrez

Ray Murray

DATE	TRADED TO		TRADED WITH	TRADED BY		IN EXCHANGE FOR
April 30, 1951	PHI	A	Sam Zoldak Minnie Minoso	CLE	A	Lou Brissie

(Part of three-team trade involving Cleveland, Philadelphia A's, and Chicago White Sox.)

DATE	TRADED TO		TRADED WITH	TRADED BY		IN EXCHANGE FOR
March 28, 1954	BAL	A	————	PHI	A	$25,000.

Red Murray

DATE	TRADED TO		TRADED WITH	TRADED BY		IN EXCHANGE FOR
Dec 12, 1908	NY	N	Admiral Schlei Bugs Raymond	STL	N	Roger Bresnahan

Ivan Murrell

DATE	TRADED TO		TRADED WITH	TRADED BY		IN EXCHANGE FOR
April 1, 1974	ATL	N	————	SD	N	Cash

Danny Murtaugh

DATE	TRADED TO		TRADED WITH	TRADED BY		IN EXCHANGE FOR
Nov 18, 1947	PIT	N	Johnny Hopp	BOS	N	Jim Russell Bill Salkeld Al Lyons

Tony Muser

DATE	TRADED TO		TRADED WITH	TRADED BY		IN EXCHANGE FOR
March 31, 1971	CHI	A	Vicente Romo	BOS	A	Duane Josephson Danny Murphy
June 15, 1975	BAL	A	————	CHI	A	Jesse Jefferson

Ron Musselman

DATE	TRADED TO		TRADED WITH	TRADED BY		IN EXCHANGE FOR
Dec 21, 1982	TEX	A	————	SEA	A	Pat Putnam

Buddy Myer

DATE	TRADED TO		TRADED WITH	TRADED BY		IN EXCHANGE FOR
May 2, 1927	BOS	A	————	WAS	A	Topper Rigney

DATE	TRADED TO		TRADED WITH	TRADED BY		IN EXCHANGE FOR

Buddy Myer continued

| Dec 15, 1928 | WAS | A | ———— | BOS | A | Milt Gaston
Hod Lisenbee
Bobby Reeves
Grant Gillis
Elliott Bigelow |

Billy Myers

| Dec 14, 1934 | CIN | N | cash | NY | N | Mark Koenig
Allyn Stout |
| Dec 4, 1940 | CHI | N | ———— | CIN | N | Jim Gleeson
Bobby Mattick |

Elmer Myers

| March 1, 1919 | CLE | A | Larry Gardner
Charlie Jamieson | PHI | A | Braggo Roth |
| June 1920 | BOS | A | ———— | CLE | A | Waiver price |

Hap Myers

| May 1911 | BOS | A | ———— | STL | A | Cash |

Hy Myers

Feb 15, 1923	STL	N	Ray Schmandt	BKN	N	Jack Fournier
April 22, 1925	CIN	N	————	STL	N	Cash
May 4, 1925	STL	N	————	CIN	N	Cash

Bob Myrick

| June 15, 1979 | TEX | A | Mike Bruhert | NY | N | Dock Ellis |

Bill Nagel

| March 21, 1941 | PHI | N | ———— | PHI | A | Cash |

Rusty Nagelson

| May 22, 1970 | DET | A | Billy Rohr | CLE | A | Fred Lasher |

Judge Nagle

| June 21, 1911 | BOS | A | ———— | PIT | N | Cash |

Mike Nagy

Jan 24, 1973	STL	N	————	BOS	A	Lance Clemons
Feb 1, 1973	TEX	A	Charles Hudson	STL	N	Mike Thompson
			(Thompson and Nagy were exchanged on March 31.)			
June 6, 1973	STL	N	John Wockenfuss	TEX	A	Jim Bibby

Sam Nahem

| June 12, 1940 | STL | N | Ernie Koy
Carl Doyle
Bert Haas
and $125,000. | BKN | N | Joe Medwick
Curt Davis |

Bill Nahorodny

| Sept 8, 1977 | CHI | A | ———— | PHI | N | Cash |
| Dec 3, 1979 | ATL | N | ———— | CHI | A | Minor league
P Rick Wieters |

Danny Napoleon

| April 1, 1967 | STL | N | Ed Bressoud
and cash | NY | N | Jerry Buchek
Art Mahaffey
Tony Martinez |

DATE	TRADED TO		TRADED WITH	TRADED BY		IN EXCHANGE FOR

Hal Naragon
| May 25, 1959 | WAS | A | Hal Woodeshick | CLE | A | Ed Fitz Gerald |

Ray Narleski
| Nov 20, 1958 | DET | A | Don Mossi
Ossie Alvarez | CLE | A | Billy Martin
Al Cicotte |

Jerry Narron
| Nov 1, 1979 | SEA | A | *See Jim Beattie* | NY | A | ——————— |

Buster Narum
| March 31, 1964 | WAS | A | ——————— | BAL | A | Lou Piniella |
| Feb 13, 1968 | CHI | A | ——————— | WAS | A | *See Ron Hansen* |

Cotton Nash
| May 6, 1967 | CHI | A | cash | CAL | A | Bill Skowron |

Jim Nash
| Dec 3, 1969 | ATL | N | ——————— | OAK | A | Felipe Alou |
| June 15, 1972 | PHI | N | Gary Neibauer | ATL | N | Joe Hoerner
Andre Thornton |

Phil Nastu
| Dec 12, 1980 | CHI | N | Joe Strain | SF | N | Jerry Martin
Jesus Figueroa
minor league
IF Mike Turgeon |

Julio Navarro
| April 28, 1964 | DET | A | ——————— | LA | A | Willie Smith |
| June 14, 1966 | BOS | A | Don Demeter | DET | A | Earl Wilson
Joe Christopher |

Earl Naylor
| June 1, 1943 | STL | N | Danny Litwhiler | PHI | N | Buster Adams
Coaker Triplett
Dain Clay |

Charlie Neal
| Dec 15, 1961 | NY | N | ——————— | LA | N | Lee Walls
and $100,000. |
| July 1, 1963 | CIN | N | Sammy Taylor | NY | N | Jesse Gonder |

Greasy Neale
| Feb 22, 1921 | PHI | N | Jimmy Ring | CIN | N | Eppa Rixey |
| June 2, 1921 | CIN | N | ——————— | PHI | N | Waiver price |

Tom Needham
| Dec 3, 1907 | NY | N | *See Fred Tenney* | BOS | N | ——————— |
| Dec 1908 | CHI | N | ——————— | NY | N | Cash |

Cal Neeman
| May 13, 1960 | PHI | N | Tony Taylor | CHI | N | Ed Bouchee
Don Cardwell |

Ron Negray
| April 5, 1957 | BKN | N | ——————— | PHI | N | *See Chico Fernandez* |

DATE	TRADED TO		TRADED WITH	TRADED BY		IN EXCHANGE FOR

Art Nehf

Aug 15, 1919	NY	N	————	BOS	N	Joe Oeschger Red Causey Johnny Jones Mickey O'Neil and $55,000.
May 11, 1926	CIN	N	————	NY	N	Cash
Sept 4, 1927	CHI	N	————	CIN	N	Cash

Gary Neibauer

June 15, 1972	PHI	N	Jim Nash	ATL	N	Joe Hoerner Andre Thornton

Bernie Neis

Feb 4, 1925	BOS	N	————	BKN	N	Cotton Tierney
June 15, 1927	CHI	A	————	CLE	A	Cash

Dave Nelson

Dec 5, 1969	WAS	A	Horacio Pina Ron Law	CLE	A	Dennis Higgins Barry Moore
Nov 12, 1975	KC	A	————	TEX	A	Nellie Briles

Gene Nelson

Aug 1, 1979	NY	A	Oscar Gamble Ray Fontenot minor league 3B Amos Lewis	TEX	A	Mickey Rivers minor league Ps Bob Polinsky Neil Mersch and Mark Softy
April 1, 1982	SEA	A	Bill Caudill Bobby Brown	NY	A	Shane Rawley
June 29, 1984	CHI	A	Jerry Gleaton	SEA	A	Salome Barojas

Jamie Nelson

Dec 7, 1984	CHI	N	————	MIL	A	Cash

Lynn Nelson

Feb 23, 1940	DET	A	————	PHI	A	Waiver price

Red Nelson

Aug 1912	PHI	N	————	STL	A	Cash
June 5, 1913	CIN	N	John Dodge	PHI	N	Josh Devore Beals Becker

Rocky Nelson

May 17, 1951	PIT	N	Erv Dusak	STL	N	Stan Rojek
Sept 20, 1951	CHI	A	————	PIT	N	Waiver price
July 30, 1956	STL	N	————	BKN	N	Waiver price

Roger Nelson

Nov 29, 1967	BAL	A	————	CHI	A	*See Luis Aparicio*
Nov 30, 1972	CIN	N	Richie Scheinblum	KC	A	Hal McRae Wayne Simpson
Oct 25, 1974	CHI	A	————	CIN	N	Cash

Dick Nen

Dec 4, 1964	WAS	A	*See Frank Howard*	LA	N	————
April 3, 1968	CHI	N	————	WAS	A	Cash
Oct 1, 1968	WAS	A	————	CHI	N	Cash

DATE	TRADED TO		TRADED WITH	TRADED BY		IN EXCHANGE FOR

Graig Nettles

DATE	TRADED TO		TRADED WITH	TRADED BY		IN EXCHANGE FOR
Dec 10, 1969	CLE	A	Dean Chance Bob Miller Ted Uhlaender	MIN	A	Luis Tiant Stan Williams
Nov 27, 1972	NY	A	Gerry Moses	CLE	A	John Ellis Jerry Kenney Charlie Spikes Rusty Torres
March 30, 1984	SD	N	————	NY	A	Dennis Rasmussen minor league P Darin Cloninger

Morris Nettles

DATE	TRADED TO		TRADED WITH	TRADED BY		IN EXCHANGE FOR
Dec 11, 1975	CHI	A	Jim Spencer	CAL	A	Bill Melton Steve Dunning

Dan Neumeier

DATE	TRADED TO		TRADED WITH	TRADED BY		IN EXCHANGE FOR
Oct 23, 1973	HOU	N	————	CHI	A	Hector Torres

Ernie Nevel

DATE	TRADED TO		TRADED WITH	TRADED BY		IN EXCHANGE FOR
Aug 28, 1952	CIN	N	————	NY	A	*See Ewell Blackwell*
June 9, 1954	BKN	N	Charlie Kress Johnny Bucha and cash	DET	A	Wayne Belardi

Don Newcombe

DATE	TRADED TO		TRADED WITH	TRADED BY		IN EXCHANGE FOR
June 15, 1958	CIN	N	————	LA	N	Steve Bilko Johnny Klippstein
July 29, 1960	CLE	A	————	CIN	N	Cash

Jeff Newman

DATE	TRADED TO		TRADED WITH	TRADED BY		IN EXCHANGE FOR
Dec 6, 1982	BOS	A	Tony Armas	OAK	A	Carney Lansford Garry Hancock minor league P Jerry King

Ray Newman

DATE	TRADED TO		TRADED WITH	TRADED BY		IN EXCHANGE FOR
Dec 6, 1973	DET	A	————	MIL	A	Mike Strahler

Bobo Newsom

DATE	TRADED TO		TRADED WITH	TRADED BY		IN EXCHANGE FOR
May 21, 1935	WAS	A	————	STL	A	$40,000.
June 11, 1937	BOS	A	Ben Chapman	WAS	A	Wes Ferrell Rick Ferrell Mel Almada
Dec 2, 1937	STL	A	Red Kress Buster Mills	BOS	A	Joe Vosmik
May 13, 1939	DET	A	Beau Bell Red Kress Jim Walkup	STL	A	Vern Kennedy Bob Harris George Gill Roxie Lawson Chet Laabs Mark Christman
March 31, 1942	WAS	A	————	DET	A	$40,000.
Aug 30, 1942	BKN	N	————	WAS	A	$25,000.
July 15, 1943	STL	A	————	BKN	N	Fritz Ostermueller Archie McKain
Aug 31, 1943	WAS	A	————	STL	A	Cash
Dec 13, 1943	PHI	A	————	WAS	A	Roger Wolff
July 11, 1947	NY	A	————	WAS	A	Waiver price

DATE	TRADED TO		TRADED WITH	TRADED BY		IN EXCHANGE FOR

Skeeter Newsome
| Dec 12, 1945 | PHI | N | ———— | BOS | A | Cash |

Doc Newton
| July 1901 | BKN | N | ———— | CIN | N | Cash |

Gus Niarhos
June 27, 1950	CHI	A	————	NY	A	$10,000.
Nov 27, 1951	STL	A	————	CHI	A	*See Sherm Lollar*
Nov 28, 1951	BOS	A	Ken Wood	STL	A	Les Moss Tom Wright

Kid Nichols
| July 16, 1905 | PHI | N | ———— | STL | N | Waiver price |

Bill Nicholson
| Oct 4, 1948 | PHI | N | ———— | CHI | N | Harry Walker |

Dave Nicholson
Jan 14, 1963	CHI	A	Hoyt Wilhelm Pete Ward Ron Hansen	BAL	A	Luis Aparicio Al Smith
Dec 1, 1965	HOU	N	Bill Heath	CHI	A	Jack Lamabe minor league P Ray Cordeiro and cash
Dec 31, 1966	ATL	N	Bob Bruce	HOU	N	Sandy Alomar Eddie Mathews Arnie Umbach

Fred Nicholson
| June 30, 1919 | PIT | N | ———— | DET | A | Waiver price |
| Feb 23, 1921 | BOS | N | Billy Southworth
Walter Barbare
and $15,000. | PIT | N | Rabbit Maranville |

Steve Nicosia
| Aug 19, 1983 | SF | N | ———— | PIT | N | Milt May
and cash |

Al Niehaus
| Oct 27, 1924 | PIT | N | Vic Aldridge
George Grantham | CHI | N | Charlie Grimm
Rabbit Maranville
Wilbur Cooper |
| May 20, 1925 | CIN | N | ———— | PIT | N | Tom Sheehan |

Bert Niehoff
Nov 1914	PHI	N	————	CIN	N	Red Dooin
April 4, 1918	STL	N	$500.	PHI	N	Milt Watson
May 18, 1918	NY	N	————	STL	N	Waiver price

Joe Niekro
April 25, 1969	SD	N	Gary Ross Francisco Libran	CHI	N	Dick Selma
Dec 4, 1969	DET	A	————	SD	N	Pat Dobson Dave Campbell
Aug 7, 1973	ATL	N	————	DET	A	Cash
April 6, 1975	HOU	N	————	ATL	N	$35,000.

DATE	TRADED TO		TRADED WITH		TRADED BY		IN EXCHANGE FOR

Phil Niekro

| Jan 6, 1984 | NY | A | ————— | | ATL | N | No compensation (free agent signing) |

Bob Nieman

Dec 4, 1952	DET	A	Owen Friend J. W. Porter		STL	A	Virgil Trucks Hal White Johnny Groth
Dec 6, 1954	CHI	A	Walt Dropo Ted Gray		DET	A	Leo Cristante Ferris Fain Jack Phillips
May 21, 1956	BAL	A	Mike Fornieles Connie Johnson George Kell		CHI	A	Jim Wilson Dave Philley
Dec 2, 1959	STL	N	—————		BAL	A	Gene Green minor league C Charles Staniland
May 10, 1961	CLE	A	—————		STL	N	Joe Morgan Mike Lee and cash

(St. Louis received Lee on September 25.)

| April 29, 1962 | SF | N | ————— | | CLE | A | Cash |

Randy Niemann

| June 15, 1977 | HOU | N | Mike Fischlin Dave Bergman | | NY | A | Cliff Johnson |

(Houston received Bergman on November 23.)

| Aug 31, 1981 | PIT | N | Johnny Ray minor league OF Kevin Houston | | HOU | N | Phil Garner |
| Sept 7, 1983 | CHI | A | ————— | | PIT | N | Miguel Dilone minor league P Mike Maitland |

Al Niemiec

| Jan 4, 1936 | PHI | A | Hank Johnson and $75,000. | | BOS | A | Doc Cramer Eric McNair |

Johnny Niggeling

| Jan 4, 1940 | STL | A | ————— | | CIN | N | Waiver price |
| Aug 18, 1943 | WAS | A | Harlond Clift | | STL | A | Ellis Clary Ox Miller and cash |

Harry Niles

Nov 1907	NY	A	—————		STL	A	Cash
Aug 17, 1908	BOS	A	—————		NY	A	Frank LaPorte
May 1910	CLE	A	—————		BOS	A	Cash

Rabbit Nill

| Aug 11, 1907 | CLE | A | ————— | | WAS | A | Pete O'Brien Howard Wakefield |

Ron Nischwitz

| Nov 27, 1962 | CLE | A | Gordon Seyfried | | DET | A | Bubba Phillips |

Otis Nixon

| Feb 4, 1984 | CLE | A | Danny Boitano minor league P Guy Elston | | NY | A | Toby Harrah minor league P Rick Brown |

DATE	TRADED TO		TRADED WITH	TRADED BY		IN EXCHANGE FOR

Russ Nixon

| March 16, 1960 | BOS | A | ———— | CLE | A | Sammy White
Jim Marshall |

(Trade was cancelled when White decided to retire.)

| June 13, 1960 | BOS | A | Carroll Hardy | CLE | A | Marty Keough
Ted Bowsfield |
| April 6, 1966 | MIN | A | Chuck Schilling | BOS | A | Dick Stigman
and minor league
1B Jose Calero |

Gary Nolan

| June 15, 1977 | CAL | A | ———— | CIN | N | Minor league
IF Craig Henderson |

Joe Nolan

| March 26, 1982 | BAL | A | ———— | CIN | N | Dallas Williams
minor league
P Brooks Carey |

Dickie Noles

| Dec 8, 1981 | CHI | N | Keith Moreland
Dan Larson | PHI | N | Mike Krukow
and cash |
| July 1, 1984 | TEX | A | ———— | CHI | N | Dwayne Henry
minor league
IF Jorge Gomez |

(The Cubs received Henry and Gomez on December 22.)

Pete Noonan

| July 1, 1906 | STL | N | Fred Beebe
and cash | CHI | N | Jack Taylor |

Jerry Nops

| Jan 1900 | BKN | N | Jimmy Sheckard
Broadway Aleck Smith
Frank Kitson
Harry Howell
Joe McGinnity | BAL | N | Cash |

Tim Nordbrook

Sept 9, 1976	CAL	A	————	BAL	A	Cash
Aug 30, 1977	TOR	A	————	CHI	A	Cash
April 29, 1978	MIL	A	————	TOR	A	Tim Johnson

Wayne Nordhagen

June 7, 1973	ATL	N	Frank Tepedino Al Closter Dave Cheadle	NY	A	Pat Dobson
May 28, 1975	STL	N	Ron Reed	ATL	N	Elias Sosa Ray Sadecki
July 14, 1976	CHI	A	————	PHI	N	Rich Coggins
April 2, 1982	TOR	A	————	CHI	A	Aurelio Rodriguez
June 15, 1982	PHI	N	————	TOR	A	Dick Davis
June 15, 1982	PIT	N	————	PHI	N	Bill Robinson
June 22, 1982	TOR	A	————	PIT	N	Dick Davis
Dec 10, 1982	CHI	N	————	TOR	A	No compensation (free agent signing)

DATE	TRADED TO		TRADED WITH	TRADED BY		IN EXCHANGE FOR

Irv Noren

DATE	TRADED TO		TRADED WITH	TRADED BY		IN EXCHANGE FOR
May 3, 1952	NY	A	Tom Upton	WAS	A	Jackie Jensen Spec Shea Jerry Snyder Archie Wilson
Feb 19, 1957	KC	A	*See Billy Hunter*	NY	A	——————
Aug 31, 1957	STL	N	——————	KC	A	Waiver price
May 19, 1959	CHI	N	——————	STL	N	Charlie King

Dan Norman

DATE	TRADED TO		TRADED WITH	TRADED BY		IN EXCHANGE FOR
June 15, 1977	NY	N	Pat Zachry Doug Flynn Steve Henderson	CIN	N	Tom Seaver
May 29, 1981	MON	N	Jeff Reardon	NY	N	Ellis Valentine

Fred Norman

DATE	TRADED TO		TRADED WITH	TRADED BY		IN EXCHANGE FOR
Dec 15, 1963	CHI	N	——————	KC	A	Nelson Mathews
Sept 28, 1970	STL	N	——————	LA	N	Cash
June 11, 1971	SD	N	Leron Lee	STL	N	Al Santorini
June 12, 1973	CIN	N	——————	SD	N	Gene Locklear Mike Johnson and cash

Nelson Norman

DATE	TRADED TO		TRADED WITH	TRADED BY		IN EXCHANGE FOR
Dec 8, 1977	TEX	A	Al Oliver	PIT	N	Bert Blyleven John Milner

(Part of four-team trade involving Texas, New York Mets, Pittsburgh, and Atlanta.)

Jim Norris

DATE	TRADED TO		TRADED WITH	TRADED BY		IN EXCHANGE FOR
Jan 4, 1980	TEX	A	David Clyde	CLE	A	Larry McCall Gary Gray minor league 3B-OF Mike Bucci

Billy North

DATE	TRADED TO		TRADED WITH	TRADED BY		IN EXCHANGE FOR
Nov 21, 1972	OAK	A	——————	CHI	N	Bob Locker
May 17, 1978	LA	N	——————	OAK	A	Glenn Burke

Lou North

DATE	TRADED TO		TRADED WITH	TRADED BY		IN EXCHANGE FOR
June 17, 1924	BOS	N	——————	STL	N	Cash

Hub Northen

DATE	TRADED TO		TRADED WITH	TRADED BY		IN EXCHANGE FOR
April 1911	BKN	N	——————	CIN	N	Cash

Ron Northey

DATE	TRADED TO		TRADED WITH	TRADED BY		IN EXCHANGE FOR
May 3, 1947	STL	N	——————	PHI	N	Harry Walker Freddy Schmidt
Dec 14, 1949	CIN	N	Lou Klein	STL	N	Harry Walker
June 7, 1950	CHI	N	——————	CIN	N	Bob Scheffing

Jim Northrup

DATE	TRADED TO		TRADED WITH	TRADED BY		IN EXCHANGE FOR
Aug 7, 1974	MON	N	——————	DET	A	Cash
Sept 16, 1974	BAL	A	——————	MON	N	Cash

Willie Norwood

DATE	TRADED TO		TRADED WITH	TRADED BY		IN EXCHANGE FOR
Dec 12, 1980	SEA	A	——————	MIN	A	Byron McLaughlin

DATE	TRADED TO		TRADED WITH	TRADED BY		IN EXCHANGE FOR

Joe Nossek

May 11, 1966	KC	A	—————	MIN	A	Cash
July 12, 1969	STL	N	—————	OAK	A	Bob Johnson

Don Nottebart

Nov 30, 1962	HOU	N	—————	MIL	N	Cash
April 27, 1969	CHI	N	—————	CIN	N	Minor league IF Jim Armstrong and cash

Wynn Noyes

Aug 1919	CHI	A	—————	PHI	A	Cash

Les Nunamaker

May 13, 1914	NY	A	—————	BOS	A	Cash
Jan 22, 1918	STL	A	—————	NY	A	*See Eddie Plank*
March 1919	CLE	A	—————	STL	A	Josh Billings

Howie Nunn

Dec 21, 1961	NY	N	—————	CIN	N	Cash

(Nunn was returned to Cincinnati on April 2, 1962.)

Joe Nuxhall

Jan 25, 1961	KC	A		CIN	N	John Tsitouris Johnny Briggs

Rich Nye

Dec 4, 1969	STL	N	—————	CHI	N	Boots Day
May 15, 1970	MON	N	—————	STL	N	Cash

Jerry Nyman

March 30, 1970	SD	N	—————	CHI	A	Tommie Sisk

Nyls Nyman

Aug 31, 1977	STL	N	Dave Hamilton Silvio Martinez	CHI	A	Clay Carroll

Rebel Oakes

Feb 1910	STL	N	Miller Huggins Frank Corridon	CIN	N	Fred Beebe Alan Storke

Johnny Oates

Nov 30, 1972	ATL	N	—————	BAL	A	*See Earl Williams*
May 7, 1975	PHI	N	Richie Allen	ATL	N	Jim Essian Barry Bonnell and cash
Dec 20, 1976	LA	N	minor league P Quincy Hill	PHI	N	Ted Sizemore

Ken Oberkfell

June 15, 1984	ATL	N		STL	N	Mike Jorgensen Ken Dayley

Frank Oberlin

Aug 11, 1907	WAS	A	—————	BOS	A	Cash

Mike O'Berry

Aug 17, 1979	CHI	N	cash	BOS	A	Ted Sizemore

DATE	TRADED TO		TRADED WITH	TRADED BY		IN EXCHANGE FOR

Mike O'Berry continued

Oct 17, 1980	CIN	N	————	CHI	N	Jay Howell
Jan 10, 1983	CAL	A	————	CIN	N	John Harris
Dec 8, 1983	NY	A	————	CAL	A	No compensation (free agent signing)

Bob O'Brien

| Dec 2, 1971 | BAL | A | ———— | LA | N | *See Frank Robinson* |

Buck O'Brien

| July 1913 | CHI | A | ———— | BOS | A | Cash |

Dan O'Brien

| Nov 9, 1979 | SEA | A | ———— | STL | N | Cash |

Jack O'Brien

| May 1901 | CLE | A | ———— | WAS | A | Cash |

John O'Brien

| Jan 1900 | LOU | N | ———— | PIT | N | *See Honus Wagner* |

Johnny O'Brien

| June 15, 1958 | STL | N | Gene Freese | PIT | N | Dick Schofield and cash |
| March 31, 1959 | MIL | N | Stan Lopata Ted Kazanski | PHI | N | Gene Conley Joe Koppe Harry Hanebrink |

Pete O'Brien

| Dec 1906 | CLE | A | ———— | STL | A | Fritz Buelow |
| Aug 11, 1907 | WAS | A | Howard Wakefield | CLE | A | Rabbit Nill |

Syd O'Brien

Dec 13, 1969	CHI	A	minor league P Billy Farmer Gerry Janeski (Janeski replaced Farmer, who retired.)	BOS	A	Don Pavletich Gary Peters
Nov 30, 1970	CAL	A	*See Ken Berry*	CHI	A	————
July 28, 1972	MIL	A	Joe Azcue	CAL	A	Paul Ratliff Ron Clark

Tom O'Brien

| Feb 1900 | PIT | N | ———— | NY | N | Cash |

Tommy O'Brien

| May 8, 1950 | WAS | A | Merrill Combs | BOS | A | Clyde Vollmer |

Danny O'Connell

| Dec 26, 1953 | MIL | N | ———— | PIT | N | Sid Gordon Max Surkont Sam Jethroe Curt Raydon Fred Walters minor league P Larry Lasalle |
| June 15, 1957 | NY | N | Ray Crone Bobby Thomson | MIL | N | Red Schoendienst |

DATE	TRADED TO		TRADED WITH	TRADED BY		IN EXCHANGE FOR

Jack O'Connor

DATE	TRADED TO		TRADED WITH	TRADED BY		IN EXCHANGE FOR
May 10, 1900	PIT	N	————	STL	N	Cash
Oct 26, 1903	STL	A	————	NY	A	John Anderson

Ken O'Dea

DATE	TRADED TO		TRADED WITH	TRADED BY		IN EXCHANGE FOR
Oct 26, 1934	CHI	N	————	STL	N	Pat Malone
Dec 6, 1938	NY	N	Frank Demaree Bill Jurges	CHI	N	Dick Bartell Hank Leiber Gus Mancuso
Dec 11, 1941	STL	N	Bill Lohrman Johnny McCarthy and $50,000.	NY	N	Johnny Mize
July 8, 1946	BOS	N	————	STL	N	Cash

Billy O'Dell

DATE	TRADED TO		TRADED WITH	TRADED BY		IN EXCHANGE FOR
Nov 30, 1959	SF	N	Billy Loes	BAL	A	Jackie Brandt Gordon Jones Roger McCardell
Feb 1, 1965	MIL	N	————	SF	N	Ed Bailey
June 15, 1966	PIT	N	————	ATL	N	Don Schwall

Blue Moon Odom

DATE	TRADED TO		TRADED WITH	TRADED BY		IN EXCHANGE FOR
May 20, 1975	CLE	A	cash	OAK	A	Dick Bosman Jim Perry
June 7, 1975	ATL	N	Bob Belloir	CLE	A	Roric Harrison
June 15, 1976	CHI	A	————	ATL	N	Pete Varney

John O'Donoghue

DATE	TRADED TO		TRADED WITH	TRADED BY		IN EXCHANGE FOR
April 6, 1966	CLE	A	————	KC	A	Ralph Terry and cash
Nov 28, 1967	BAL	A	Gordon Lund	CLE	A	Eddie Fisher minor leaguers P Bob Scott and IF John Scruggs
April 30, 1969	SEA	A	Tom Fisher and minor league P Lloyd Fourroux	BAL	A	Gerry Schoen Mike Ferraro
June 15, 1970	MON	N	————	MIL	A	Cash

Lefty O'Doul

DATE	TRADED TO		TRADED WITH	TRADED BY		IN EXCHANGE FOR
July 23, 1922	BOS	A	Chick Fewster Elmer Miller Johnny Mitchell and $50,000.	NY	A	Joe Dugan Elmer Smith
Oct 29, 1928	PHI	N	cash	NY	N	Freddy Leach
Oct 14, 1930	BKN	N	Fresco Thompson	PHI	N	Clise Dudley Jumbo Elliott Hal Lee and cash
June 16, 1933	NY	N	Watty Clark	BKN	N	Sam Leslie

Joe Oeschger

DATE	TRADED TO		TRADED WITH	TRADED BY		IN EXCHANGE FOR
May 27, 1919	NY	N	————	PHI	N	George Smith
Aug 15, 1919	BOS	N	Red Causey Johnny Jones Mickey O'Neil and $55,000.	NY	N	Art Nehf

DATE	TRADED TO		TRADED WITH	TRADED BY		IN EXCHANGE FOR

Tiny Osborne
| May 16, 1924 | BKN | N | ———— | CHI | N | Cash |

Dan Osinski
| July 23, 1962 | LA | A | ———— | KC | A | Gordie Windhorn
Ted Bowsfield |

(Kansas City received Bowsfield on November 30.)

| Oct 14, 1964 | MIL | N | ———— | LA | A | Phil Roof
Ron Piche |
| Dec 15, 1965 | BOS | A | Bob Sadowski | MIL | N | Lee Thomas
Arnie Earley
Jay Ritchie |

Champ Osteen
| Jan 1904 | NY | A | ———— | WAS | A | Cash |

Claude Osteen
Sept 16, 1961	WAS	A	————	CIN	N	Dave Sisler and cash
Dec 4, 1964	LA	N	John Kennedy and $100,000.	WAS	A	Frank Howard Phil Ortega Pete Richert Dick Nen Ken McMullen
Dec 6, 1973	HOU	N	minor league P Dave Culpepper	LA	N	Jimmy Wynn
Aug 15, 1974	STL	N	————	HOU	N	Minor league P Ron Selak Dan Larson

Darrell Osteen
| Oct 20, 1967 | KC | A | Floyd Robinson | CIN | N | Ron Tompkins |

Fritz Ostermueller
| Dec 3, 1940 | STL | A | ———— | BOS | A | Cash |
| July 15, 1943 | BKN | N | Archie McKain | STL | A | Bobo Newsom |

Joe Ostrowski
| Nov 17, 1947 | STL | A | ———— | BOS | A | *See Vern Stephens* |
| June 15, 1950 | NY | A | ———— | STL | A | *See Snuffy Stirnweiss* |

John Ostrowski
| May 31, 1950 | WAS | A | ———— | CHI | A | *See Eddie Robinson* |

Amos Otis
| Dec 3, 1969 | KC | A | Bob Johnson | NY | N | Joe Foy |
| Dec 19, 1983 | PIT | N | ———— | KC | A | No compensation
(free agent signing) |

Denny O'Toole
| Oct 26, 1973 | STL | N | ———— | CHI | A | Jim Kremmel |

Jim O'Toole
| Dec 15, 1966 | CHI | A | ———— | CIN | N | Floyd Robinson |

Marty O'Toole
| Aug 14, 1914 | NY | N | ———— | PIT | N | Cash |

DATE	TRADED TO		TRADED WITH	TRADED BY		IN EXCHANGE FOR

Ed Ott

| April 1, 1981 | CAL | A | Mickey Mahler | PIT | N | Jason Thompson |

Jimmy Outlaw

| Dec 13, 1938 | BKN | N | ———— | CIN | N | Lew Krausse and cash |
| Dec 13, 1938 | BOS | N | Buddy Hassett | BKN | N | Gene Moore Ira Hutchinson |

Orval Overall

| June 2, 1906 | CHI | N | ———— | CIN | N | Bob Wicker and $2,000. |

Stubby Overmire

Dec 1, 1949	STL	A	————	DET	A	Waiver price
June 15, 1951	NY	A	————	STL	A	Tommy Byrne and $25,000.
May 13, 1952	STL	A	————	NY	A	Waiver price

Bob Owchinko

Feb 15, 1980	CLE	A	Jim Wilhelm	SD	N	Jerry Mumphrey
Dec 9, 1980	PIT	N	————	CLE	A	*See Bert Blyleven*
April 6, 1981	OAK	A	————	PIT	N	Ernie Camacho and cash
Nov 12, 1983	CIN	N	————	PIT	N	Cash

Marv Owen

| Dec 2, 1937 | CHI | A | Mike Tresh Gee Walker | DET | A | Vern Kennedy Tony Piet Dixie Walker |
| Dec 8, 1939 | BOS | A | ———— | CHI | A | Cash |

Mickey Owen

| Dec 4, 1940 | BKN | N | ———— | STL | N | Gus Mancuso Minor league P John Pintar and $65,000. |

Jim Owens

| Nov 27, 1962 | CIN | N | ———— | PHI | N | Cookie Rojas |

Rick Ownbey

| June 15, 1983 | STL | N | Neil Allen | NY | N | Keith Hernandez |

Ray Oyler

| Dec 7, 1969 | OAK | A | Diego Segui | SEA | A | Ted Kubiak George Lauzerique |
| April 17, 1970 | CAL | A | ———— | OAK | A | Cash |

John Pacella

Dec 15, 1980	SD	N	Jose Moreno	NY	N	Randy Jones
April 1, 1981	NY	A	Jerry Mumphrey	SD	N	Ruppert Jones Joe Lefebvre Tim Lollar Chris Welsh
May 12, 1982	MIN	A	Larry Milbourne Pete Filson and cash	NY	A	Butch Wynegar Roger Erickson
Nov 1, 1982	TEX	A	————	MIN	A	Len Whitehouse

DATE	TRADED TO		TRADED WITH	TRADED BY		IN EXCHANGE FOR

Tom Paciorek

DATE	TRADED TO		TRADED WITH	TRADED BY		IN EXCHANGE FOR
Nov 17, 1975	ATL	N	Jimmy Wynn Lee Lacy Jerry Royster	LA	N	Dusty Baker Ed Goodson
Dec 11, 1981	CHI	A	————	SEA	A	Todd Cruz Jim Essian Rod Allen

Gene Packard

DATE	TRADED TO		TRADED WITH	TRADED BY		IN EXCHANGE FOR
Feb 10, 1916	CHI	N	Charlie Pechous	KC	F	Cash
April 1917	STL	N	————	CHI	N	Cash
Jan 21, 1919	PHI	N	Doug Baird Stuffy Stewart	STL	N	Milt Stock Pickles Dillhoefer Dixie Davis

Tom Padden

DATE	TRADED TO		TRADED WITH	TRADED BY		IN EXCHANGE FOR
Oct 1937	STL	N	minor leaguer Bernie Cobb	PIT	N	Johnny Rizzo
Jan 22, 1943	PHI	N	Al Gerheauser Ed Levy and $10,000.	NY	A	Nick Etten Al Gettel

Del Paddock

DATE	TRADED TO		TRADED WITH	TRADED BY		IN EXCHANGE FOR
Jan 1912	NY	A	————	CHI	A	Cash

Don Padgett

DATE	TRADED TO		TRADED WITH	TRADED BY		IN EXCHANGE FOR
Dec 10, 1941	BKN	N	————	STL	N	$30,000.
June 12, 1946	BOS	N	————	BKN	N	Cash
March 27, 1947	PHI	N	————	BOS	N	Andy Karl

Ernie Padgett

DATE	TRADED TO		TRADED WITH	TRADED BY		IN EXCHANGE FOR
Feb 1926	CLE	A	————	BOS	N	Cash

Dennis Paepke

DATE	TRADED TO		TRADED WITH	TRADED BY		IN EXCHANGE FOR
Dec 12, 1968	KC	A	Ed Kirkpatrick	CAL	A	Hoyt Wilhelm

Andy Pafko

DATE	TRADED TO		TRADED WITH	TRADED BY		IN EXCHANGE FOR
June 15, 1951	BKN	N	Johnny Schmitz Rube Walker Wayne Terwilliger	CHI	N	Bruce Edwards Joe Hatten Eddie Miksis Gene Hermanski
Jan 17, 1953	MIL	N	————	BKN	N	Roy Hartsfield and $50,000.

Dave Pagan

DATE	TRADED TO		TRADED WITH	TRADED BY		IN EXCHANGE FOR
June 15, 1976	BAL	A	*See Tippy Martinez*	NY	A	————
July 27, 1977	PIT	N	————	SEA	A	Rick Honeycutt

Jose Pagan

DATE	TRADED TO		TRADED WITH	TRADED BY		IN EXCHANGE FOR
May 22, 1965	PIT	N	————	SF	N	Dick Schofield

Mitchell Page

DATE	TRADED TO		TRADED WITH	TRADED BY		IN EXCHANGE FOR
March 15, 1977	OAK	A	————	PIT	N	*See Phil Garner*

Karl Pagel

DATE	TRADED TO		TRADED WITH	TRADED BY		IN EXCHANGE FOR
June 23, 1980	CLE	A	cash	CHI	N	Cliff Johnson

DATE	TRADED TO		TRADED WITH	TRADED BY		IN EXCHANGE FOR
Jim Pagliaroni						
Nov 20, 1962	PIT	N	Don Schwall	BOS	A	Jack Lamabe Dick Stuart
Dec 3, 1967	OAK	A	———	PIT	N	Cash
May 27, 1969	SEA	A	———	OAK	A	Cash
Phil Paine						
April 19, 1958	STL	N	———	MIL	N	Waiver price
Dec 4, 1958	LA	N	Wally Moon	STL	N	Gino Cimoli
Erv Palica						
March 17, 1955	BAL	A	———	BKN	N	Frank Kellert and cash
Lowell Palmer						
Sept 18, 1972	CLE	A	———	STL	N	Cash
June 12, 1973	NY	A	———	CLE	A	Mike Kekich
May 31, 1974	SD	N	———	NY	A	Cash
Stan Palys						
April 30, 1955	CIN	N	———	PHI	N	*See Andy Seminick*
April 3, 1958	DET	A	———	CIN	N	Waiver price
Jim Panther						
March 4, 1972	TEX	A	Don Stanhouse	OAK	A	Denny McLain
Oct 27, 1972	ATL	N	———	TEX	A	Rico Carty
Al Papai						
May 4, 1949	STL	A	———	STL	N	Waiver price
Dec 1, 1949	BOS	A	———	STL	A	Waiver price
Stan Papi						
June 8, 1973	STL	N	———	HOU	N	Ray Busse
Dec 7, 1978	BOS	A	———	MON	N	Bill Lee
March 30, 1980	PHI	N	cash	BOS	A	Dave Rader
May 29, 1980	DET	A	———	PHI	N	Cash
Frank Papish						
Dec 2, 1948	CLE	A	———	CHI	A	Bob Kuzava Ernie Groth
Dec 14, 1949	PIT	N	———	CLE	A	Cash
Milt Pappas						
Dec 9, 1965	CIN	N	Jack Baldschun Dick Simpson	BAL	A	Frank Robinson
June 11, 1968	ATL	N	Ted Davidson Bob Johnson	CIN	N	Woody Woodward Clay Carroll Tony Cloninger
June 23, 1970	CHI	N	———	ATL	N	Cash
Freddy Parent						
April 1908	CHI	A	———	BOS	A	Cash
Kelly Paris						
March 31, 1983	CIN	N	———	STL	N	Minor league P Jim Strichek

DATE	TRADED TO		TRADED WITH	TRADED BY		IN EXCHANGE FOR

Ken Raffensberger continued

| June 14, 1947 | CIN | N | Hugh Poland | PHI | N | Al Lakeman |

Pat Ragan

May 20, 1909	CHI	N	————	CIN	N	Cash
April 28, 1915	BOS	N	————	BKN	N	Cash
May 21, 1919	NY	N	————	BOS	N	Jim Thorpe
Sept 1919	CHI	A	————	NY	N	Waiver price

Tom Ragland

| Nov 30, 1972 | CLE | A | ———— | TEX | A | Vince Colbert |

Chuck Rainey

| Dec 10, 1982 | CHI | N | ———— | BOS | A | Doug Bird |
| July 15, 1984 | OAK | A | ———— | CHI | N | Davey Lopes |

(The Cubs received Lopes on August 31.)

Dave Rajsich

| Nov 10, 1978 | TEX | A | ———— | NY | A | *See Dave Righetti* |
| Oct 20, 1981 | PHI | N | ———— | TEX | A | Ramon Aviles |

Gary Rajsich

| April 3, 1981 | NY | N | ———— | HOU | N | Minor league OF John Csefalvay |
| April 4, 1984 | STL | N | ———— | NY | N | Cash |

Ed Rakow

| March 30, 1961 | KC | A | ———— | LA | N | Howie Reed and cash |
| Nov 18, 1963 | DET | A | ———— | KC | A | *See Rocky Colavito* |

Bob Ramazzotti

| May 16, 1949 | CHI | N | ———— | BKN | N | Hank Schenz |

Milt Ramirez

| Nov 28, 1972 | HOU | N | Skip Jutze | STL | N | Ray Busse Bobby Fenwick |

Bobby Ramos

| April 5, 1982 | NY | A | ———— | MON | N | Brad Gulden |
| Nov 3, 1982 | MON | N | ———— | NY | A | Cash |

Domingo Ramos

| Nov 10, 1978 | TEX | A | ———— | NY | A | *See Dave Righetti* |
| Nov 5, 1979 | TOR | A | ———— | TEX | A | Cash |

Pedro Ramos

April 2, 1962	CLE	A	————	MIN	A	Dick Stigman Vic Power
Sept 5, 1964	NY	A	————	CLE	A	Ralph Terry Buddy Daley and $75,000.
Dec 14, 1966	PHI	N	————	NY	A	Joe Verbanic and cash

Willie Ramsdell

| May 10, 1950 | CIN | N | ———— | BKN | N | Cash |

DATE	TRADED TO		TRADED WITH	TRADED BY		IN EXCHANGE FOR
Willie Ramsdell continued						
Jan 3, 1952	CHI	N	————	CIN	N	Frank Hiller
Mike Ramsey						
July 1, 1984	MON	N	————	STL	N	Chris Speier
Newt Randall						
June 24, 1907	BOS	N	Bill Sweeney	CHI	N	Del Howard
Lenny Randle						
April 26, 1977	NY	N	————	TEX	A	Rick Auerbach and cash
June 28, 1979	PIT	N	*See Bill Madlock*	SF	N	————
Aug 2, 1979	NY	A	————	PIT	N	Cash
March 8, 1980	SEA	A	————	NY	N	No compensation (free agent signing)
April 2, 1980	CHI	N	————	SEA	A	Cash
April 6, 1981	SEA	A	————	CHI	N	No compensation (free agent signing)
Willie Randolph						
Dec 11, 1975	NY	A	Ken Brett Dock Ellis	PIT	N	Doc Medich
Merritt Ranew						
March 28, 1963	CHI	N	Hal Haydel Dick LeMay	HOU	N	Jug Gerard Danny Murphy
June 3, 1964	MIL	N	$40,000.	CHI	N	Len Gabrielson
Earl Rapp						
Sept 1, 1951	STL	A	————	NY	N	Waiver price
June 10, 1952	WAS	A	————	STL	A	Freddie Marsh
Goldie Rapp						
July 1, 1921	PHI	N	Lee King Lance Richbourg	NY	N	Casey Stengel Johnny Rawlings Red Causey
Vern Rapp						
May 7, 1949	CHI	A	————	DET	A	Don Kolloway
Bill Rariden						
Dec 23, 1915	NY	N	Bill McKechnie	NWK	F	Cash
Feb 2, 1919	CIN	N	————	NY	N	Hal Chase
Vic Raschi						
Feb 23, 1954	STL	N	————	NY	A	$85,000.
Dennis Rasmussen						
Aug 31, 1982	NY	A	————	CAL	A	Tommy John
Aug 26, 1983	SD	N	Eduardo Rodriguez and $200,000.	NY	A	John Montefusco
March 30, 1984	NY	A	minor league P Darin Cloninger	SD	N	Graig Nettles
Eric Rasmussen						
May 26, 1978	SD	N	————	STL	N	George Hendrick

DATE	TRADED TO		TRADED WITH	TRADED BY		IN EXCHANGE FOR

Eddie Robinson continued

Dec 16, 1953	NY	A	Harry Byrd Tom Hamilton Carmen Mauro Loren Babe	PHI	A	Don Bollweg John Gray Jim Robertson Jim Finigan Vic Power Bill Renna
June 14, 1956	KC	A	Lou Skizas	NY	A	Moe Burtschy Bill Renna and cash
Dec 5, 1956	DET	A	Jim Finigan Jack Crimian Bill Harrington	KC	A	Ned Garver Gene Host Virgil Trucks Wayne Belardi and $20,000.

Floyd Robinson

Dec 15, 1966	CIN	N	———————	CHI	A	Jim O'Toole
Oct 20, 1967	KC	A	Darrell Osteen	CIN	N	Ron Tompkins
July 31, 1968	BOS	A	———————	OAK	A	Cash

Frank Robinson

Dec 9, 1965	BAL	A	———————	CIN	N	Milt Pappas Jack Baldschun Dick Simpson
Dec 2, 1971	LA	N	Pete Richert	BAL	A	Doyle Alexander Bob O'Brien Sergio Robles Royle Stillman
Nov 28, 1972	CAL	A	Bill Singer Mike Strahler Billy Grabarkewitz Bobby Valentine	LA	N	Andy Messersmith Ken McMullen
Sept 12, 1974	CLE	A	———————	CAL	A	Ken Suarez Rusty Torres and cash

Hank Robinson

| Dec 12, 1913 | STL | N | ——————— | PIT | N | *See Ed Konetchy* |
| June 20, 1918 | NY | A | ——————— | STL | N | Cash |

Humberto Robinson

| April 11, 1959 | CLE | A | ——————— | MIL | N | Mickey Vernon |
| May 16, 1959 | PHI | N | ——————— | CLE | A | Granny Hamner |

Jackie Robinson

| Dec 13, 1956 | NY | N | ——————— | BKN | N | Dick Littlefield
and $30,000. |

(Trade was cancelled when Robinson retired.)

Wilbert Robinson

| Feb 11, 1900 | STL | N | John McGraw
Bill Keister | BAL | N | Cash |

Rafael Robles

| June 20, 1972 | STL | N | ——————— | SD | N | Mike Fiore
Bob Chlupsa |

(Fiore was returned to St. Louis on July 3.)

DATE	TRADED TO		TRADED WITH	TRADED BY		IN EXCHANGE FOR

Sergio Robles

Dec 2, 1971	BAL	A	———	LA	N	*See Frank Robinson*

Mickey Rocco

May 1946	CHI	N	———	CLE	A	Heinz Becker

Pat Rockett

Dec 5, 1979	TOR	A	Barry Bonnell Joey McLaughlin	ATL	N	Chris Chambliss Luis Gomez

Andre Rodgers

Oct 31, 1960	MIL	N	———	SF	N	Alvin Dark
March 31, 1961	CHI	N	Daryl Robertson	MIL	N	Moe Drabowsky Seth Morehead
Dec 9, 1964	PIT	N	———	CHI	N	Roberto Pena and cash

Bill Rodgers

May 1915	BOS	A	———	CLE	A	Cash
June 1915	CIN	N	———	BOS	A	Cash

Aurelio Rodriguez

April 27, 1970	WAS	A	Rick Reichardt	CAL	A	Ken McMullen
Oct 9, 1970	DET	A	Joe Coleman Ed Brinkman Jim Hannan	WAS	A	Denny McLain Don Wert Norm McRae Elliott Maddox
Dec 7, 1979	SD	N	———	DET	A	$200,000.
Aug 4, 1980	NY	A	———	SD	N	Cash
Nov 17, 1981	TOR	A	———	NY	A	Minor league C Mike Lebo
April 2, 1982	CHI	A	———	TOR	A	Wayne Nordhagen
Feb 7, 1983	BAL	A	———	CHI	A	No compensation (free agent signing)

Ed Rodriguez

Feb 26, 1979	KC	A	———	MIL	A	Cash

Eduardo Rodriguez

Aug 26, 1983	SD	N	Dennis Rasmussen and $200,000.	NY	A	John Montefusco

Ellie Rodriguez

Feb 2, 1971	MIL	A	———	KC	A	Carl Taylor
Oct 22, 1973	CAL	A	———	MIL	A	*See Clyde Wright*
March 21, 1976	LA	N	———	CAL	A	Jesus Alvarez and cash

Freddy Rodriguez

Dec 10, 1957	CHI	N	———	NY	N	Tom Poholsky

Roberto Rodriguez

May 26, 1970	SD	N	———	OAK	A	Cash
June 23, 1970	CHI	N	———	SD	N	Cash

DATE	TRADED TO		TRADED WITH	TRADED BY		IN EXCHANGE FOR

Preacher Roe

DATE	TRADED TO		TRADED WITH	TRADED BY		IN EXCHANGE FOR
Dec 8, 1947	BKN	N	Billy Cox Gene Mauch	PIT	N	Dixie Walker Hal Gregg Vic Lombardi
Dec 13, 1954	BAL	A	Billy Cox	BKN	N	Minor leaguers John Jancse and Harry Schwegeman and $50,000.

(Roe retired; Erv Palica trade of March 17, 1955 was additional compensation.)

Ed Roebuck

DATE	TRADED TO		TRADED WITH	TRADED BY		IN EXCHANGE FOR
July 20, 1963	WAS	A	————	LA	N	Marv Breeding
April 21, 1964	PHI	N	————	WAS	A	Cash

Gary Roenicke

DATE	TRADED TO		TRADED WITH	TRADED BY		IN EXCHANGE FOR
Dec 7, 1977	BAL	A	Don Stanhouse Joe Kerrigan	MON	N	Rudy May Randy Miller Bryn Smith

Wally Roettger

DATE	TRADED TO		TRADED WITH	TRADED BY		IN EXCHANGE FOR
April 10, 1930	NY	N	————	STL	N	Showboat Fisher Doc Farrell
Oct 29, 1930	CIN	N	————	NY	N	Cash
June 15, 1931	STL	N	————	CIN	N	Taylor Douthit
Dec 1931	CIN	N	————	STL	N	Cash
Nov 17, 1933	PIT	N	Red Lucas	CIN	N	Adam Comorosky Tony Piet

Billy Rogell

DATE	TRADED TO		TRADED WITH	TRADED BY		IN EXCHANGE FOR
Dec 6, 1939	CHI	N	————	DET	A	Dick Bartell

Tom Rogers

DATE	TRADED TO		TRADED WITH	TRADED BY		IN EXCHANGE FOR
April 1919	PHI	A	————	STL	A	Cash

Garry Roggenburk

DATE	TRADED TO		TRADED WITH	TRADED BY		IN EXCHANGE FOR
Sept 7, 1966	BOS	A	————	MIN	A	Cash
June 23, 1969	SEA	A	————	BOS	A	Cash

Saul Rogovin

DATE	TRADED TO		TRADED WITH	TRADED BY		IN EXCHANGE FOR
May 15, 1951	CHI	A	————	DET	A	Bob Cain
Dec 10, 1953	CIN	N	Connie Ryan Rocky Krsnich	CHI	A	Willard Marshall

Billy Rohr

DATE	TRADED TO		TRADED WITH	TRADED BY		IN EXCHANGE FOR
May 22, 1970	DET	A	Rusty Nagelson	CLE	A	Fred Lasher

Cookie Rojas

DATE	TRADED TO		TRADED WITH	TRADED BY		IN EXCHANGE FOR
Nov 27, 1962	PHI	N	————	CIN	N	Jim Owens
Oct 7, 1969	STL	N	————	PHI	N	*See Curt Flood*
June 13, 1970	KC	A	————	STL	N	Fred Rico

Stan Rojek

DATE	TRADED TO		TRADED WITH	TRADED BY		IN EXCHANGE FOR
Nov 14, 1947	PIT	N	————	BKN	N	Cash
May 17, 1951	STL	N	————	PIT	N	Erv Dusak Rocky Nelson
Jan 24, 1952	STL	A	————	STL	N	Waiver price

DATE	TRADED TO		TRADED WITH	TRADED BY		IN EXCHANGE FOR

Stan Rojek continued
| Oct 14, 1952 | BKN | N | Bob Mahoney
Ray Coleman
and $90,000. | STL | A | Billy Hunter |

Jim Roland
Feb 24, 1969	OAK	A	————	MIN	A	Cash
April 28, 1972	NY	A	————	OAK	A	Cash
Aug 30, 1972	TEX	A	————	NY	A	Casey Cox

Johnny Romano
| Dec 6, 1959 | CLE | A | Bubba Phillips
Norm Cash | CHI | A | Dick Brown
Don Ferrarese
Jake Striker
Minnie Minoso |
| Jan 20, 1965 | CHI | A | Tommy John
Tommie Agee | CLE | A | Rocky Colavito
Cam Carreon |

(Part of three-team trade involving Kansas City, Cleveland, and Chicago White Sox.)

| Dec 14, 1966 | STL | N | minor league
P Lee White | CHI | A | Walt Williams
Don Dennis |

Enrique Romo
| Dec 5, 1978 | PIT | N | Rick Jones
Tommy McMillan | SEA | A | Odell Jones
Rafael Vasquez
Mario Mendoza |

Vicente Romo
April 19, 1969	BOS	A	————	CLE	A	*See Ken Harrelson*
March 31, 1971	CHI	A	Tony Muser	BOS	A	Duane Josephson Danny Murphy
Oct 28, 1972	SD	N	————	CHI	A	John Jeter

Gene Roof
| Sept 16, 1983 | MON | N | ———— | STL | N | Cash |

Phil Roof
| Oct 14, 1964 | LA | A | Ron Piche | MIL | N | Dan Osinski |
| June 15, 1965 | CLE | A | ———— | CAL | A | Bubba Morton
and cash |

(California received Morton on September 15, 1965.)

Dec 1, 1965	KC	A	Joe Rudi	CLE	A	Jim Landis Jim Rittwage
Jan 15, 1970	MIL	A	Mike Hershberger Lew Krausse Ken Sanders	OAK	A	Don Mincher Ron Clark
Oct 21, 1976	TOR	A	————	CHI	A	Larry Anderson

Jim Rooker
| Sept 30, 1968 | NY | A | ———— | DET | A | Cash |
| Oct 25, 1972 | PIT | N | ———— | KC | A | Gene Garber |

Pat Rooney
| Dec 20, 1983 | NY | A | ———— | MON | N | Minor league
P Tim Burke |

Jorge Roque
| Nov 6, 1972 | MON | N | ———— | STL | N | Tim McCarver |

DATE	TRADED TO		TRADED WITH	TRADED BY		IN EXCHANGE FOR

Buddy Rosar

DATE	TRADED TO		TRADED WITH	TRADED BY		IN EXCHANGE FOR
Dec 17, 1942	CLE	A	Roy Cullenbine	NY	A	Roy Weatherly Oscar Grimes
May 29, 1945	PHI	A	————	CLE	A	Frankie Hayes
Oct 8, 1949	BOS	A	————	PHI	A	Billy Hitchcock

Don Rose

DATE	TRADED TO		TRADED WITH	TRADED BY		IN EXCHANGE FOR
Dec 10, 1971	CAL	A	Nolan Ryan Leroy Stanton Francisco Estrada	NY	N	Jim Fregosi

Pete Rose

DATE	TRADED TO		TRADED WITH	TRADED BY		IN EXCHANGE FOR
Dec 5, 1978	PHI	N	————	CIN	N	No compensation (free agent signing)
Jan 20, 1984	MON	N	————	PHI	N	No compensation (free agent signing)
Aug 16, 1984	CIN	N	————	MON	N	Tom Lawless
			(Rose was named Cincinnati manager.)			

Johnny Roseboro

DATE	TRADED TO		TRADED WITH	TRADED BY		IN EXCHANGE FOR
Nov 28, 1967	MIN	A	Ron Perranoski Bob Miller	LA	N	Mudcat Grant Zoilo Versalles

Dave Rosello

DATE	TRADED TO		TRADED WITH	TRADED BY		IN EXCHANGE FOR
Dec 5, 1977	CLE	A	————	CHI	N	Minor leaguers P Norm Churchill and OF Bruce Compton

Goody Rosen

DATE	TRADED TO		TRADED WITH	TRADED BY		IN EXCHANGE FOR
April 27, 1946	NY	N	————	BKN	N	Cash

Larry Rosenthal

DATE	TRADED TO		TRADED WITH	TRADED BY		IN EXCHANGE FOR
May 29, 1941	CLE	A	————	CHI	A	Cash
July 6, 1944	PHI	A	————	NY	A	Cash

Buck Ross

DATE	TRADED TO		TRADED WITH	TRADED BY		IN EXCHANGE FOR
April 30, 1941	CHI	A	————	PHI	A	Cash

Don Ross

DATE	TRADED TO		TRADED WITH	TRADED BY		IN EXCHANGE FOR
Sept 14, 1938	BKN	N	————	DET	A	Cash
April 27, 1945	CLE	A	Dutch Meyer	DET	A	Roy Cullenbine

Gary Ross

DATE	TRADED TO		TRADED WITH	TRADED BY		IN EXCHANGE FOR
April 25, 1969	SD	N	Joe Niekro Francisco Libran	CHI	N	Dick Selma
Sept 17, 1975	CAL	A	————	SD	N	Bobby Valentine Rudi Meoli

Joe Rossi

DATE	TRADED TO		TRADED WITH	TRADED BY		IN EXCHANGE FOR
Oct 14, 1952	PIT	N	Cal Abrams Gail Henley	CIN	N	Gus Bell

Claude Rossman

DATE	TRADED TO		TRADED WITH	TRADED BY		IN EXCHANGE FOR
Dec 1906	DET	A	————	CLE	A	Cash
Aug 20, 1909	STL	A	————	DET	A	Tom Jones

DATE	TRADED TO		TRADED WITH	TRADED BY		IN EXCHANGE FOR
Braggo Roth						
Aug 21, 1915	CLE	A	Larry Chappell Ed Klepfer and $31,500.	CHI	A	Joe Jackson
March 1, 1919	PHI	A	————	CLE	A	Larry Gardner Elmer Myers Charlie Jamieson
June 27, 1919	BOS	A	Red Shannon	PHI	A	Amos Strunk Jack Barry
			(Barry refused to report, and retired.)			
Jan 20, 1920	WAS	A	Red Shannon	BOS	A	Mike Menosky Harry Harper Eddie Foster
Jan 20, 1921	NY	A	————	WAS	A	Duffy Lewis George Mogridge
Frank Roth						
Feb 1905	CHI	A	————	STL	A	Branch Rickey
Jack Rothrock						
April 30, 1932	CHI	A	————	BOS	A	Cash
Edd Roush						
Dec 23, 1915	NY	N	————	NWK	F	$7,500.
July 20, 1916	CIN	N	Christy Mathewson Bill McKechnie	NY	N	Buck Herzog Red Killefer
Feb 9, 1927	NY	N	————	CIN	N	George Kelly and cash
Jack Rowan						
Feb 1911	PHI	N	*See Dode Paskert*	CIN	N	————
Aug 1911	CHI	N	————	PHI	N	Cliff Curtis
Wade Rowdon						
Aug 23, 1982	CIN	N	minor league OF Leo Garcia	CHI	A	Jim Kern
Ken Rowe						
Sept 10, 1964	BAL	A	————	LA	N	Cash
Schoolboy Rowe						
April 30, 1942	BKN	N	————	DET	A	Cash
March 24, 1943	PHI	N	————	BKN	N	Cash
Bama Rowell						
March 6, 1948	BKN	N	Ray Sanders and $40,000.	BOS	N	Eddie Stanky
April 15, 1948	PHI	N	————	BKN	N	Waiver price
Luther Roy						
July 24, 1929	BKN	N	————	PHI	N	Lou Koupal
Jerry Royster						
Nov 17, 1975	ATL	N	Jimmy Wynn Tom Paciorek Lee Lacy	LA	N	Dusty Baker Ed Goodson

DATE	TRADED TO		TRADED WITH	TRADED BY		IN EXCHANGE FOR

Dick Rozek

| Dec 19, 1952 | PHI | A | minor league 2B Bob Wilson | CLE | A | Bob Hooper |

Dave Rozema

| Dec 27, 1984 | TEX | A | ———— | DET | A | No compensation (free agent signing) |

Vic Roznovsky

| March 30, 1966 | BAL | A | ———— | CHI | N | Carl Warwick |

John Ruberto

| May 22, 1969 | SD | N | John Sipin | STL | N | Bill Davis Jerry DaVanon |

Jorge Rubio

| Nov 29, 1967 | CIN | N | Bill Kelso | CAL | A | Sammy Ellis |

Art Ruble

| May 16, 1934 | CIN | N | Ted Kleinhans Wes Schulmerich | PHI | N | Syl Johnson Johnny Moore |

Dave Rucker

| June 22, 1983 | STL | N | ———— | DET | A | Doug Bair |

Joe Rudi

Dec 1, 1965	KC	A	Phil Roof	CLE	A	Jim Landis Jim Rittwage
Nov 17, 1976	CAL	A	————	OAK	A	No compensation (free agent signing)
Jan 23, 1981	BOS	A	Frank Tanana Jim Dorsey	CAL	A	Fred Lynn Steve Renko
Dec 4, 1981	OAK	A	————	BOS	A	No compensation (free agent signing)

Don Rudolph

| May 1, 1959 | CIN | N | Lou Skizas | CHI | A | Del Ennis |
| May 3, 1962 | WAS | A | Steve Hamilton | CLE | A | Willie Tasby |

Ken Rudolph

March 19, 1974	SF	N	————	CHI	N	Willie Prall
Oct 14, 1974	STL	N	Elias Sosa	SF	N	Marc Hill
March 31, 1977	SF	N	————	STL	N	Cash
July 27, 1977	BAL	A	————	SF	N	Cash

Muddy Ruel

Aug 21, 1917	NY	A	————	STL	A	Cash
Dec 15, 1920	BOS	A	Del Pratt Sammy Vick Hank Thormahlen	NY	A	Waite Hoyt Harry Harper Wally Schang Mike McNally
Feb 10, 1923	WAS	A	Allan Russell	BOS	A	Val Picinich Howard Shanks Ed Goebel
Dec 15, 1930	BOS	A	————	WAS	A	Cash
Aug 31, 1931	DET	A	————	BOS	A	Marty McManus
Dec 1932	STL	A	————	DET	A	Waiver price

DATE	TRADED TO		TRADED WITH	TRADED BY		IN EXCHANGE FOR

Dutch Ruether

DATE	TRADED TO		TRADED WITH	TRADED BY		IN EXCHANGE FOR
July 17, 1917	CIN	N	————	CHI	N	Waiver price
Dec 15, 1920	BKN	N	————	CIN	N	Rube Marquard
Dec 17, 1924	WAS	A	————	BKN	N	Cash
Aug 27, 1926	NY	A	————	WAS	A	Garland Braxton Nick Cullop

(New York sent Braxton and Cullop to Washington on October 19, 1926.)

Rudy Rufer

DATE	TRADED TO		TRADED WITH	TRADED BY		IN EXCHANGE FOR
June 9, 1952	BKN	N	cash	CIN	N	Cal Abrams

Red Ruffing

DATE	TRADED TO		TRADED WITH	TRADED BY		IN EXCHANGE FOR
May 6, 1930	NY	A	————	BOS	A	Cedric Durst and $50,000.

Vern Ruhle

DATE	TRADED TO		TRADED WITH	TRADED BY		IN EXCHANGE FOR
Dec 20, 1984	CLE	A	————	HOU	N	No compensation (free agent signing)

Chico Ruiz

DATE	TRADED TO		TRADED WITH	TRADED BY		IN EXCHANGE FOR
Nov 25, 1969	CAL	A	Alex Johnson	CIN	N	Pedro Borbon Jim McGlothlin Vern Geishert

Pete Runnels

DATE	TRADED TO		TRADED WITH	TRADED BY		IN EXCHANGE FOR
Jan 23, 1958	BOS	A	————	WAS	A	Albie Pearson Norm Zauchin
Nov 26, 1962	HOU	N	————	BOS	A	Roman Mejias

Bob Rush

DATE	TRADED TO		TRADED WITH	TRADED BY		IN EXCHANGE FOR
Dec 5, 1957	MIL	N	Eddie Haas Don Kaiser	CHI	N	Taylor Phillips Sammy Taylor
June 11, 1960	CHI	A	————	MIL	N	Cash

Amos Rusie

DATE	TRADED TO		TRADED WITH	TRADED BY		IN EXCHANGE FOR
Dec 15, 1900	CIN	N	————	NY	N	Christy Mathewson

Allan Russell

DATE	TRADED TO		TRADED WITH	TRADED BY		IN EXCHANGE FOR
July 29, 1919	BOS	A	Bob McGraw and $40,000.	NY	A	Carl Mays
Feb 10, 1923	WAS	A	Muddy Ruel	BOS	A	Val Picinich Howard Shanks Ed Goebel

Jack Russell

DATE	TRADED TO		TRADED WITH	TRADED BY		IN EXCHANGE FOR
June 10, 1932	CLE	A	————	BOS	A	Pete Appleton
Dec 15, 1932	WAS	A	Bruce Connatser	CLE	A	Harley Boss
June 13, 1936	BOS	A	————	WAS	A	Joe Cascarella

Jim Russell

DATE	TRADED TO		TRADED WITH	TRADED BY		IN EXCHANGE FOR
Nov 18, 1947	BOS	N	Bill Salkeld Al Lyons	PIT	N	Johnny Hopp Danny Murtaugh
Dec 24, 1949	BKN	N	Ed Sauer and cash	BOS	N	Luis Olmo

DATE	TRADED TO		TRADED WITH	TRADED BY		IN EXCHANGE FOR

Babe Ruth
Jan 3, 1920	NY	A	————	BOS	A	$125,000 and a $300,000 loan to Boston owner Harry Frazee

Dick Ruthven
Dec 10, 1975	CHI	A	Roy Thomas Alan Bannister	PHI	N	Jim Kaat Mike Buskey
Dec 12, 1975	ATL	N	Ken Henderson Danny Osborn	CHI	A	Ralph Garr Larvell Blanks
June 15, 1978	PHI	N	————	ATL	N	Gene Garber
May 22, 1983	CHI	N	Bill Johnson	PHI	N	Willie Hernandez

Blondy Ryan
Nov 1, 1934	PHI	N	Pretzels Pezzullo Johnny Vergez George Watkins and cash	NY	N	Dick Bartell
Aug 6, 1935	NY	A	————	PHI	N	Cash

Connie Ryan
April 27, 1943	BOS	N	Hugh Poland	NY	N	Ernie Lombardi
May 10, 1950	CIN	N	————	BOS	N	Walker Cooper
Dec 10, 1951	PHI	N	Smoky Burgess Howie Fox	CIN	N	Andy Seminick Eddie Pellagrini Dick Sisler Niles Jordan
Aug 25, 1953	CHI	A	————	PHI	N	Waiver price
Dec 10, 1953	CIN	N	Saul Rogovin Rocky Krsnich	CHI	A	Willard Marshall

Jack Ryan
Feb 18, 1909	BOS	A	Charlie Chech and $12,500.	CLE	A	Cy Young

Mike Ryan
Dec 15, 1967	PHI	N	cash	BOS	A	Dick Ellsworth Gene Oliver
Jan 31, 1974	PIT	N	————	PHI	N	Jackie Hernandez

Nolan Ryan
Dec 10, 1971	CAL	A	Don Rose Leroy Stanton Francisco Estrada	NY	N	Jim Fregosi
Nov 19, 1979	HOU	N	————	CAL	A	No compensation (free agent signing)

Rosy Ryan
April 17, 1925	BOS	N	————	NY	N	Tim McNamara

Gary Ryerson
Oct 22, 1973	CAL	A	————	MIL	A	*See Clyde Wright*

Ray Sadecki
May 8, 1966	SF	N	————	STL	N	Orlando Cepeda
Dec 12, 1969	NY	N	Dave Marshall	SF	N	Bob Heise Jim Gosger
Oct 13, 1974	STL	N	Tommy Moore	NY	N	Joe Torre

DATE	TRADED TO		TRADED WITH	TRADED BY		IN EXCHANGE FOR

Ray Sadecki continued

| May 28, 1975 | ATL | N | Elias Sosa | STL | N | Ron Reed
Wayne Nordhagen |
| June 30, 1975 | KC | A | cash | ATL | N | Bruce Dal Canton
Norm Angelini
Al Autry |

(Atlanta received Angelini and Autry on September 4.)

Bob Sadowski

| June 15, 1963 | MIL | N | Gene Oliver | STL | N | Lew Burdette |
| Dec 15, 1965 | BOS | A | Dan Osinski | MIL | N | Lee Thomas
Arnie Earley
Jay Ritchie |

Bob Sadowski

| Dec 15, 1961 | CHI | A | Taylor Phillips
minor league
IF Lou Vassie | PHI | N | Frank Barnes
Andy Carey
Cal McLish |

(Carey refused to report, and the Phillies received McLish in exchange
for Vassie to complete the trade on March 24, 1962.)

Jim Sadowski

| Nov 6, 1976 | CIN | N | ——— | PIT | N | Tom Carroll |

Tom Saffell

| Sept 14, 1955 | KC | A | ——— | PIT | N | Waiver price |
| April 16, 1956 | BKN | N | Lee Wheat
and cash | KC | A | Tim Thompson |

Johnny Sain

| Aug 30, 1951 | NY | A | ——— | BOS | N | Lew Burdette
and $50,000. |
| May 11, 1955 | KC | A | Enos Slaughter | NY | A | Sonny Dixon
and cash |

Ebba St. Claire

| Feb 1, 1954 | NY | N | *See Johnny Antonelli* | MIL | N | ——— |

Lenn Sakata

| Dec 6, 1979 | BAL | A | ——— | MIL | A | John Flinn |

Argenis Salazar

| Jan 24, 1985 | STL | N | ——— | MON | N | |

(Claimed in compensation draft after St. Louis lost free agent P Bruce
Sutter to Atlanta.)

Luis Salazar

| Aug 5, 1980 | SD | N | Rick Lancellotti | PIT | N | Kurt Bevacqua
Mark Lee |
| Dec 6, 1984 | CHI | A | Tim Lollar
minor leaguers
SS Ozzie Guillen and
P Bill Long | SD | N | LaMarr Hoyt
minor leaguers
P Todd Simmons and
P Kevin Kristan |

Bill Salkeld

| Nov 18, 1947 | BOS | N | Jim Russell
Al Lyons | PIT | N | Johnny Hopp
Danny Murtaugh |
| Sept 26, 1949 | CHI | A | ——— | BOS | N | Cash |

DATE	TRADED TO		TRADED WITH	TRADED BY		IN EXCHANGE FOR

Slim Sallee

July 23, 1916	NY	N	————	STL	N	$10,000.
March 8, 1919	CIN	N	————	NY	N	Waiver price
Sept 5, 1920	NY	N	————	CIN	N	Waiver price

Chico Salmon

| April 1, 1964 | CLE | A | ———— | MIL | N | Mike de la Hoz |
| March 31, 1969 | BAL | A | ———— | SEA | A | Gene Brabender
Gordon Lund |

Jack Salveson

Dec 11, 1934	PIT	N	————	NY	N	Waiver price
June 16, 1935	CHI	A	————	PIT	N	Cash
Dec 10, 1936	CLE	A	————	CHI	A	Thornton Lee
			(Part of three-team trade involving Chicago, Cleveland, and Washington.)			
Dec 10, 1936	WAS	A	————	CLE	A	Earl Whitehill
			(Part of three-team trade involving Chicago, Cleveland, and Washington.)			

Manny Salvo

| June 15, 1940 | BOS | N | Al Glossop | NY | N | Tony Cuccinello |
| May 12, 1943 | PHI | N | ———— | BOS | N | Cash |

Ron Samford

April 8, 1955	DET	A	————	NY	N	Waiver price
Dec 6, 1958	WAS	A	————	DET	A	*See Eddie Yost*
April 3, 1960	BAL	A	Clint Courtney	WAS	A	Billy Gardner

Amado Samuel

| Oct 15, 1963 | NY | N | ———— | MIL | N | Cash |

Alejandro Sanchez

| March 24, 1984 | SF | N | ———— | PHI | N | Dave Bergman |

Luis Sanchez

| Oct 24, 1975 | CIN | N | minor league
P Carlos Alfonso | HOU | N | Joaquin Andujar |

Orlando Sanchez

| May 17, 1984 | BAL | A | ———— | KC | A | Cash |

Heinie Sand

| Dec 13, 1928 | STL | N | $10,000. | PHI | N | Tommy Thevenow |

Ryne Sandberg

| Jan 27, 1982 | CHI | N | Larry Bowa | PHI | N | Ivan DeJesus |

Ken Sanders

June 13, 1966	KC	A	Jim Gosger Guido Grilli	BOS	A	John Wyatt Rollie Sheldon Jose Tartabull
Jan 15, 1970	MIL	A	————	OAK	A	*See Don Mincher*
Oct 31, 1972	PHI	N	————	MIL	A	*See Don Money*
Nov 30, 1972	MIN	A	Ken Reynolds Joe Lis	PHI	N	Cesar Tovar
Aug 3, 1973	CLE	A	————	MIN	A	Cash

DATE	TRADED TO		TRADED WITH	TRADED BY		IN EXCHANGE FOR

Ken Sanders continued

DATE	TRADED TO		TRADED WITH	TRADED BY		IN EXCHANGE FOR
March 22, 1975	NY	N	———————	CAL	A	Ike Hampton
Sept 17, 1976	KC	A	———————	NY	N	Cash

Ray Sanders

DATE	TRADED TO		TRADED WITH	TRADED BY		IN EXCHANGE FOR
April 15, 1946	BOS	N	———————	STL	N	$25,000.
March 6, 1948	BKN	N	Bama Rowell and $40,000.	BOS	N	Eddie Stanky
April 19, 1948	BOS	N	———————	BKN	N	$60,000.

Reggie Sanders

DATE	TRADED TO		TRADED WITH	TRADED BY		IN EXCHANGE FOR
May 9, 1972	DET	A	———————	OAK	A	Mike Kilkenny
March 29, 1975	ATL	N	———————	DET	A	Jack Pierce

Scott Sanderson

DATE	TRADED TO		TRADED WITH	TRADED BY		IN EXCHANGE FOR
Dec 7, 1983	SD	N	———————	MON	N	Gary Lucas
Dec 7, 1983	CHI	N	———————	SD	N	Carmelo Martinez Craig Lefferts Fritzie Connally

(Part of three-team trade involving Chicago Cubs, San Diego, and Montreal.)

Mike Sandlock

DATE	TRADED TO		TRADED WITH	TRADED BY		IN EXCHANGE FOR
Dec 19, 1953	PHI	N	———————	PIT	N	Cash

Charlie Sands

DATE	TRADED TO		TRADED WITH	TRADED BY		IN EXCHANGE FOR
April 2, 1973	DET	A	———————	PIT	N	Chris Zachary

Tom Sandt

DATE	TRADED TO		TRADED WITH	TRADED BY		IN EXCHANGE FOR
March 25, 1977	STL	N	———————	OAK	A	Cash

Fred Sanford

DATE	TRADED TO		TRADED WITH	TRADED BY		IN EXCHANGE FOR
Dec 13, 1948	NY	A	Roy Partee	STL	A	Sherm Lollar Red Embree Dick Starr and $100,000.
June 15, 1951	WAS	A	Tom Ferrick Bob Porterfield	NY	A	Bob Kuzava
July 30, 1951	STL	A	———————	WAS	A	Dick Starr

Jack Sanford

DATE	TRADED TO		TRADED WITH	TRADED BY		IN EXCHANGE FOR
Dec 3, 1958	SF	N	———————	PHI	N	Valmy Thomas Ruben Gomez
Aug 18, 1965	CAL	A	———————	SF	N	Cash
June 15, 1967	KC	A	Jackie Warner	CAL	A	Roger Repoz

Manny Sanguillen

DATE	TRADED TO		TRADED WITH	TRADED BY		IN EXCHANGE FOR
Nov 5, 1976	OAK	A	$100,000.	PIT	N	Chuck Tanner
April 4, 1978	PIT	N	———————	OAK	A	Miguel Dilone Elias Sosa Mike Edwards
Dec 9, 1980	CLE	A	Bert Blyleven	PIT	N	Gary Alexander Victor Cruz Rafael Vasquez Bob Owchinko

Rafael Santana

DATE	TRADED TO		TRADED WITH	TRADED BY		IN EXCHANGE FOR
Feb 16, 1981	STL	N	———————	NY	A	Cash

DATE	TRADED TO		TRADED WITH	TRADED BY		IN EXCHANGE FOR

Joel Skinner

Feb 2, 1982	CHI	A	———	PIT	N	

(Claimed in compensation draft after Chicago lost free agent P Ed Farmer to Philadelphia.)

Lou Skizas

June 14, 1956	KC	A	Eddie Robinson	NY	A	Moe Burtschy Bill Renna and cash
Nov 20, 1957	DET	A	*See Billy Martin*	KC	A	———
May 1, 1959	CIN	N	Don Rudolph	CHI	A	Del Ennis

Craig Skok

Nov 17, 1975	TEX	A	Juan Beniquez Steve Barr	BOS	A	Ferguson Jenkins

Bill Skowron

Nov 26, 1962	LA	N	———	NY	A	Stan Williams
Dec 6, 1963	WAS	A	———	LA	N	Cash
July 13, 1964	CHI	A	Carl Bouldin	WAS	A	Joe Cunningham Frank Kreutzer
May 6, 1967	CAL	A	———	CHI	A	Cotton Nash and cash

Pat Skrable

Oct 11, 1971	BOS	A	———	MIL	A	*See George Scott*

Gordon Slade

Feb 1933	STL	N	Dazzy Vance	BKN	N	Jake Flowers Ownie Carroll
Dec 1933	CIN	N	———	STL	N	Waiver price

Jimmy Slagle

Jan 1900	PHI	N	———	WAS	N	Cash
June 1901	BOS	N	———	PHI	N	Shad Barry

Jim Slaton

Dec 9, 1977	DET	A	Rich Folkers	MIL	A	Ben Oglivie
Nov 29, 1978	MIL	A	———	DET	A	No compensation (free agent signing)
Dec 20, 1983	CAL	A	———	MIL	A	Bobby Clark

Jack Slattery

April 1903	CHI	A	———	CLE	A	Cash

Enos Slaughter

April 11, 1954	NY	A	———	STL	N	Bill Virdon Mel Wright minor league OF Emil Tellinger
May 11, 1955	KC	A	Johnny Sain	NY	A	Sonny Dixon and cash
Aug 25, 1956	NY	A	———	KC	A	Waiver price
Sept 12, 1959	MIL	N	———	NY	A	Waiver price

DATE	TRADED TO		TRADED WITH	TRADED BY		IN EXCHANGE FOR

Lou Sleater

July 31, 1951	NY	A	Bobby Hogue Kermit Wahl Tom Upton	STL	A	Cliff Mapes
May 12, 1952	WAS	A	Freddie Marsh	STL	A	Cass Michaels
April 28, 1955	KC	A	——————	NY	A	Cash
June 2, 1958	BAL	A	——————	DET	A	Waiver price

Jim Small

| Nov 20, 1957 | KC | A | —————— | DET | A | *See Billy Martin* |

Roy Smalley

| March 20, 1954 | MIL | N | —————— | CHI | N | Dave Cole
and cash |
| April 30, 1955 | PHI | N | —————— | MIL | N | Cash |

Roy Smalley

June 1, 1976	MIN	A	Bill Singer Mike Cubbage Jim Gideon and $250,000.	TEX	A	Bert Blyleven Danny Thompson
April 10, 1982	NY	A	——————	MIN	A	Ron Davis Paul Boris Greg Gagne
July 17, 1984	CHI	A	——————	NY	A	Kevin Hickey minor league P Doug Drabek

Al Smith

| Dec 20, 1937 | STL | N | —————— | NY | N | Cash |
| Dec 29, 1937 | PHI | N | —————— | STL | N | Waiver price |

Al Smith

Dec 4, 1957	CHI	A	Early Wynn	CLE	A	Fred Hatfield Minnie Minoso
Jan 14, 1963	BAL	A	Luis Aparicio	CHI	A	Hoyt Wilhelm Pete Ward Ron Hansen Dave Nicholson
Dec 4, 1963	CLE	A	$25,000.	BAL	A	Willie Kirkland

Bill Smith

| Dec 4, 1959 | PHI | N | Bobby Gene Smith | STL | N | Carl Sawatski |

Bob Smith

Oct 14, 1930	CHI	N	Jimmy Welsh	BOS	N	Bill McAfee Wes Schulmerich
Nov 30, 1932	CIN	N	Rollie Hemsley Johnny Moore Lance Richbourg	CHI	N	Babe Herman
Aug 2, 1933	BOS	N	——————	CIN	N	Waiver price

Bob Smith

| May 14, 1957 | PIT | N | —————— | STL | N | Cash |
| June 13, 1959 | DET | A | —————— | PIT | N | Waiver price |

Bobby Gene Smith

| Dec 4, 1959 | PHI | N | Bill Smith | STL | N | Carl Sawatski |

DATE	TRADED TO		TRADED WITH	TRADED BY		IN EXCHANGE FOR

Bobby Gene Smith continued

| April 26, 1962 | CHI | N | ———— | NY | N | Sammy Taylor |
| June 5, 1962 | STL | N | Daryl Robertson | CHI | N | Don Landrum
Alex Grammas |

Broadway Aleck Smith

| Jan 1900 | BKN | N | Jimmy Sheckard
Jerry Nops
Frank Kitson
Harry Howell
Joe McGinnity | BAL | N | Cash |

Bryn Smith

| Dec 7, 1977 | MON | N | Rudy May
Randy Miller | BAL | A | Don Stanhouse
Joe Kerrigan
Gary Roenicke |

Carr Smith

| Dec 12, 1924 | CLE | A | Byron Speece | WAS | A | Stan Coveleski |

Charley Smith

May 4, 1961	PHI	N	Don Demeter	LA	N	Dick Farrell Joe Koppe
Nov 28, 1961	CHI	A	John Buzhardt	PHI	N	Roy Sievers
April 23, 1964	NY	N	————	CHI	A	Chico Fernandez minor league C Bobby Catton and cash
Oct 20, 1965	STL	N	Al Jackson	NY	N	Ken Boyer
Dec 8, 1966	NY	A	————	STL	N	Roger Maris
Dec 6, 1968	SF	N	————	NY	A	Nate Oliver
March 28, 1969	CHI	N	————	SF	N	Cash

Charlie Smith

| Sept 1909 | BOS | A | ———— | WAS | A | Doc Gessler |
| April 1911 | CHI | N | ———— | BOS | A | Cash |

Chris Smith

| March 31, 1980 | MON | N | LaRue Washington | TEX | A | Rusty Staub |
| Feb 2, 1983 | SF | N | ———— | MON | N | Jim Wohlford |

Dick Smith

| Oct 11, 1962 | NY | N | ———— | LA | N | Cash |
| Oct 15, 1964 | LA | N | ———— | NY | N | Larry Miller |

Earl Smith

| May 31, 1921 | WAS | A | ———— | STL | A | Frank Ellerbe |

Earl Smith

June 7, 1923	BOS	N	Jesse Barnes	NY	N	Hank Gowdy Mule Watson
July 6, 1924	PIT	N	————	BOS	N	Cash
July 10, 1928	STL	N	————	PIT	N	Cash

Eddie Smith

| April 27, 1939 | CHI | A | ———— | PHI | A | Waiver price |

DATE	TRADED TO		TRADED WITH	TRADED BY		IN EXCHANGE FOR

Elmer Smith
Aug 8, 1900	NY	N	————	CIN	N	Cash
Jan 1901	PIT	N	————	NY	N	Cash
May 1901	BOS	N	————	PIT	N	Cash

Elmer Smith
Aug 18, 1916	WAS	A	Joe Leonard	CLE	A	Joe Boehling Danny Moeller
June 13, 1917	CLE	A	————	WAS	A	$4,000.
Dec 24, 1921	BOS	A	George Burns Joe Harris	CLE	A	Stuffy McInnis
July 23, 1922	NY	A	Joe Dugan	BOS	A	Chick Fewster Elmer Miller Johnny Mitchell Lefty O'Doul and $50,000.

Frank Smith
Aug 9, 1910	BOS	A	Billy Purtell	CHI	A	Harry Lord Amby McConnell
May 11, 1911	CIN	N	————	BOS	A	$5,000.
June 1915	BKN	F	————	BAL	F	Steve Evans

Frank Smith
| Dec 8, 1954 | STL | N | ———— | CIN | N | Ray Jablonski Gerry Staley |
| April 10, 1956 | CIN | N | ———— | STL | N | Waiver price |

Fred Smith
| July 1915 | BKN | F | ———— | BUF | F | Ed Gagnier Ed Lafitte |

George Smith
June 20, 1918	NY	N	————	CIN	N	Cash
July 15, 1918	BKN	N	————	NY	N	Cash
Oct 1918	NY	N	————	BKN	N	Cash
May 27, 1919	PHI	N	————	NY	N	Joe Oeschger
Feb 11, 1923	BKN	N	————	PHI	N	Clarence Mitchell

George Smith
| Oct 4, 1965 | BOS | A | George Thomas | DET | A | Bill Monbouquette |

Hal Smith
Nov 18, 1954	BAL	A	————	NY	A	*See Bob Turley*
Aug 17, 1956	KC	A	————	BAL	A	Joe Ginsberg
Dec 15, 1959	PIT	N	————	KC	A	Ken Hamlin Dick Hall

Harry Smith
| Jan 1908 | BOS | N | ———— | PIT | N | Cash |

Heinie Smith
| June 1901 | NY | N | ———— | PIT | N | Ed Doheny |

Jack Smith
| April 19, 1926 | BOS | N | ———— | STL | N | Cash |

DATE	TRADED TO		TRADED WITH	TRADED BY		IN EXCHANGE FOR

Chris Speier

DATE	TRADED TO		TRADED WITH	TRADED BY		IN EXCHANGE FOR
April 27, 1977	MON	N	————	SF	N	Tim Foli
July 1, 1984	STL	N	————	MON	N	Mike Ramsey
Aug 19, 1984	MIN	A	————	STL	N	Cash and a player to be named later

Stan Spence

DATE	TRADED TO		TRADED WITH	TRADED BY		IN EXCHANGE FOR
Dec 13, 1941	WAS	A	Jack Wilson	BOS	A	Ken Chase Johnny Welaj
Dec 10, 1947	BOS	A	————	WAS	A	Leon Culberson Al Kozar
May 8, 1949	STL	A	cash	BOS	A	Al Zarilla

Daryl Spencer

DATE	TRADED TO		TRADED WITH	TRADED BY		IN EXCHANGE FOR
Dec 15, 1959	STL	N	Leon Wagner	SF	N	Don Blasingame
May 30, 1961	LA	N	————	STL	N	Bob Lillis Carl Warwick

Glenn Spencer

DATE	TRADED TO		TRADED WITH	TRADED BY		IN EXCHANGE FOR
Dec 12, 1932	NY	N	Gus Dugas	PIT	N	Freddie Lindstrom

(Part of three-team trade involving New York, Philadelphia, and Pittsburgh.)

DATE	TRADED TO		TRADED WITH	TRADED BY		IN EXCHANGE FOR
Nov 15, 1933	CIN	N	————	NY	N	George Grantham
Jan 11, 1934	STL	N	————	CIN	N	Bob O'Farrell Syl Johnson

(O'Farrell was named Cincinnati manager.)

Jim Spencer

DATE	TRADED TO		TRADED WITH	TRADED BY		IN EXCHANGE FOR
May 20, 1973	TEX	A	Lloyd Allen	CAL	A	Mike Epstein Rich Hand Rick Stelmaszek
Dec 10, 1975	CAL	A	$100,000.	TEX	A	Bill Singer
Dec 11, 1975	CHI	A	Morris Nettles	CAL	A	Bill Melton Steve Dunning
Dec 12, 1977	NY	A	Tommy Cruz minor league P Bob Polinsky	CHI	A	Stan Thomas minor league P Ed Ricks
May 20, 1981	OAK	A	Tom Underwood	NY	A	Dave Revering Mike Patterson minor league P Chuck Dougherty

Roy Spencer

DATE	TRADED TO		TRADED WITH	TRADED BY		IN EXCHANGE FOR
Jan 7, 1933	CLE	A	————	WAS	A	Luke Sewell

Tom Spencer

DATE	TRADED TO		TRADED WITH	TRADED BY		IN EXCHANGE FOR
Nov 6, 1976	CHI	A	————	CIN	N	Hugh Yancy

Tubby Spencer

DATE	TRADED TO		TRADED WITH	TRADED BY		IN EXCHANGE FOR
Dec 12, 1908	BOS	A	————	STL	A	Lou Criger

Rob Sperring

DATE	TRADED TO		TRADED WITH	TRADED BY		IN EXCHANGE FOR
Feb 11, 1977	SF	N	Bill Madlock	CHI	N	Bobby Murcer Steve Ontiveros minor league P Andy Muhlstock
March 26, 1977	HOU	N	Willie Crawford	SF	N	Rob Andrews and cash

DATE	TRADED TO		TRADED WITH	TRADED BY		IN EXCHANGE FOR

Ed Spiezio

DATE	TRADED TO		TRADED WITH	TRADED BY		IN EXCHANGE FOR
Dec 3, 1968	SD	N	Danny Breeden Ron Davis minor league P Phil Knuckles	STL	N	Dave Giusti
July 9, 1972	CHI	A	————	SD	N	Don Eddy and cash

Charlie Spikes

Nov 27, 1972	CLE	A	————	NY	A	*See Graig Nettles*
Dec 9, 1977	DET	A	————	CLE	A	Tom Veryzer

Dan Spillner

June 14, 1978	CLE	A	————	SD	N	Dennis Kinney
June 21, 1984	CHI	A	————	CLE	A	Jim Siwy

Harry Spilman

June 8, 1981	HOU	N	————	CIN	N	Rafael Landestoy

Scipio Spinks

April 15, 1972	STL	N	Lance Clemons	HOU	N	Jerry Reuss
March 23, 1974	CHI	N	————	STL	N	Jim Hickman

Al Spohrer

June 15, 1928	BOS	N	Ben Cantwell Bill Clarkson Virgil Barnes	NY	N	Joe Genewich

Ed Sprague

Oct 20, 1970	CIN	N	————	OAK	A	Cash
July 27, 1973	STL	N	Roe Skidmore	CIN	N	Ed Crosby minor league C Gene Dusan
Sept 4, 1973	MIL	A	————	STL	N	Cash

George Spriggs

March 15, 1971	NY	N	————	KC	A	Cash

Jack Spring

June 24, 1958	WAS	A	————	BOS	A	Bud Byerly
May 15, 1964	CHI	N	————	LA	A	Cash
June 15, 1964	STL	N	*See Lou Brock*	CHI	N	————

Bobby Sprowl

June 13, 1979	HOU	N	Pete Ladd and cash	BOS	A	Bob Watson
Dec 21, 1983	BAL	A	————	HOU	N	Craig Minetto

Eddie Stack

Dec 1911	BKN	N	————	PHI	N	Cash
July 1913	CHI	N	cash	BKN	N	Ed Reulbach

Marv Staehle

July 29, 1967	CLE	A	Jim King	CHI	A	Rocky Colavito
Sept 13, 1969	MON	N	————	SEA	A	Cash

DATE	TRADED TO		TRADED WITH	TRADED BY		IN EXCHANGE FOR

Ray Starr continued

| June 23, 1945 | CHI | N | ———— | PIT | N | Waiver price |

Jigger Statz

| July 1920 | BOS | A | ———— | NY | N | Cash |

Rusty Staub

| Jan 22, 1969 | MON | N | ———— | HOU | N | Jesus Alou
Donn Clendenon
Jack Billingham
Skip Guinn
and $100,000. |

(Clendenon refused to report, and Houston was sent Billingham, Guinn, and cash on April 8, 1969.)

April 5, 1972	NY	N	————	MON	N	Tim Foli Ken Singleton Mike Jorgensen
Dec 12, 1975	DET	A	Bill Laxton	NY	N	Mickey Lolich Bobby Baldwin
July 20, 1979	MON	N	————	DET	A	Minor league C Randy Schafer and cash
March 31, 1980	TEX	A	————	MON	N	LaRue Washington Chris Smith
Dec 16, 1980	NY	N	————	TEX	A	No compensation (free agent signing)

John Stearns

| Dec 3, 1974 | NY | N | Del Unser
Mac Scarce | PHI | N | Tug McGraw
Don Hahn
Dave Schneck |

Bill Steele

| July 1914 | BKN | N | ———— | STL | N | Cash |

Bob Steele

| June 14, 1917 | PIT | N | ———— | STL | N | Doug Baird |
| June 1918 | NY | N | ———— | PIT | N | Cash |

Elmer Steele

| Feb 1910 | PIT | N | ———— | BOS | A | Waiver price |
| Sept 16, 1911 | BKN | N | ———— | PIT | N | Cash |

Farmer Steelman

| Jan 1900 | BKN | N | ———— | LOU | N | Cash |
| April 1901 | PHI | A | ———— | BKN | N | Cash |

Bill Steen

| June 1915 | DET | A | ———— | CLE | A | Cash |

Dave Stegman

| Dec 12, 1980 | SD | N | ———— | DET | A | Dennis Kinney |

Bill Stein

| Dec 19, 1980 | TEX | A | ———— | SEA | A | No compensation
(free agent signing) |

Justin Stein

| June 10, 1938 | CIN | N | ———— | PHI | N | Buck Jordan |

DATE	TRADED TO		TRADED WITH	TRADED BY		IN EXCHANGE FOR

Randy Stein
| June 7, 1979 | SEA | A | ———— | MIL | A | Paul Mitchell |

Ray Steineder
| May 25, 1924 | PHI | N | ———— | PIT | N | Cash |

Harry Steinfeldt
| March 1906 | CHI | N | ———— | CIN | N | Hans Lobert
Jake Weimer |
| March 1911 | BOS | N | ———— | CHI | N | Cash |

Rick Stelmaszek
| May 20, 1973 | CAL | A | *See Mike Epstein* | TEX | A | ———— |
| July 28, 1974 | CHI | N | ———— | CAL | A | Horacio Pina |

Casey Stengel
Jan 9, 1918	PIT	N	George Cutshaw	BKN	N	Chuck Ward Burleigh Grimes Al Mamaux
Aug 1919	PHI	N	————	PIT	N	Possum Whitted
July 1, 1921	NY	N	Johnny Rawlings Red Causey	PHI	N	Goldie Rapp Lee King Lance Richbourg
Nov 12, 1923	BOS	N	Dave Bancroft Bill Cunningham (Bancroft was named Boston manager.)	NY	N	Billy Southworth Joe Oeschger

Dave Stenhouse
| Dec 15, 1961 | WAS | A | Bob Schmidt | CIN | N | Johnny Klippstein
Marty Keough |

Rennie Stennett
| Dec 12, 1979 | SF | N | ———— | PIT | N | No compensation
(free agent signing) |

Buzz Stephen
| June 15, 1970 | BAL | A | Dick Baney | MIL | A | Dave May |

Bryan Stephens
| Nov 20, 1947 | STL | A | Dick Kokos
Joe Frazier
and $25,000. | CLE | A | Bob Muncrief
Walt Judnich |

Gene Stephens
| June 9, 1960 | BAL | A | ———— | BOS | A | Willie Tasby |
| June 8, 1961 | KC | A | ———— | BAL | A | Marv Throneberry |

Vern Stephens
Nov 17, 1947	BOS	A	Jack Kramer	STL	A	Roy Partee Jim Wilson Al Widmar Eddie Pellagrini Pete Layden Joe Ostrowski and $310,000.
Feb 9, 1953	CHI	A	————	BOS	A	Hal Brown Marv Grissom Bill Kennedy
July 20, 1953	STL	A	————	CHI	A	Waiver price

DATE	TRADED TO		TRADED WITH	TRADED BY		IN EXCHANGE FOR

Bobby Stephenson
| June 14, 1956 | NY | N | *See Red Schoendienst* | STL | N | ———— |

Earl Stephenson
| Dec 3, 1971 | MIL | A | Brock Davis
Jim Colborn | CHI | N | Jose Cardenal |
| Oct 31, 1972 | PHI | N | ———— | MIL | A | *See Don Money* |

Johnny Stephenson
| June 12, 1967 | CHI | N | Rob Gardner | NY | N | Bob Hendley |

Ed Stevens
| Nov 14, 1947 | PIT | N | ———— | BKN | N | Cash |

R C Stevens
| Dec 16, 1960 | WAS | A | Bennie Daniels
Harry Bright | PIT | N | Bobby Shantz |

Bud Stewart
| May 13, 1948 | WAS | A | ———— | NY | A | Leon Culberson
and $15,000. |
| Dec 11, 1950 | CHI | A | ———— | WAS | A | Mike McCormick |

Dave Stewart
| Aug 19, 1983 | TEX | A | Ricky Wright
and $200,000. | LA | N | Rick Honeycutt |

Jimmy Stewart
| May 22, 1967 | CHI | A | ———— | CHI | N | Cash |
| Nov 29, 1971 | HOU | N | ———— | CIN | N | *See Joe Morgan* |

Lefty Stewart
Jan 15, 1927	STL	A	Frank O'Rourke Billy Mullen Otto Miller	DET	A	Marty McManus Bobby LaMotte Pinky Hargrave
Dec 14, 1932	WAS	A	Goose Goslin Fred Schulte	STL	A	Sammy West Carl Reynolds Lloyd Brown and $20,000.
May 14, 1935	CLE	A	————	WAS	A	Belve Bean

Stuffy Stewart
| Jan 21, 1919 | PHI | N | Doug Baird
Gene Packard | STL | N | Milt Stock
Pickles Dillhoefer
Dixie Davis |

Dick Stigman
April 2, 1962	MIN	A	Vic Power	CLE	A	Pedro Ramos
April 6, 1966	BOS	A	minor league 1B Jose Calero	MIN	A	Russ Nixon Chuck Schilling
Aug 15, 1966	CIN	N	Rollie Sheldon	BOS	A	Hank Fischer
			(Cincinnati received Stigman and Sheldon on December 15, 1966.)			

Royle Stillman
| Dec 2, 1971 | BAL | A | ———— | LA | N | *See Frank Robinson* |

Craig Stimac
| Jan 27, 1982 | CLE | A | ———— | SD | N | Cash |

DATE	TRADED TO		TRADED WITH	TRADED BY		IN EXCHANGE FOR

Bob Stinson

DATE	TRADED TO		TRADED WITH	TRADED BY		IN EXCHANGE FOR
Oct 5, 1970	STL	N	Ted Sizemore	LA	N	Richie Allen
Nov 3, 1971	HOU	N	——————	STL	N	Marty Martinez
March 28, 1973	MON	N	——————	HOU	N	Cash
March 31, 1975	KC	A	——————	MON	N	Cash

Snuffy Stirnweiss

DATE	TRADED TO		TRADED WITH	TRADED BY		IN EXCHANGE FOR
June 15, 1950	STL	A	Jim Delsing Don Johnson Duane Pillette and $50,000.	NY	A	Tom Ferrick Joe Ostrowski Leo Thomas Sid Schacht
April 1, 1951	CLE	A	Merrill Combs	STL	A	Freddie Marsh and $35,000.

Chuck Stobbs

DATE	TRADED TO		TRADED WITH	TRADED BY		IN EXCHANGE FOR
Nov 13, 1951	CHI	A	Mel Hoderlein	BOS	A	Randy Gumpert Don Lenhardt
Dec 10, 1952	WAS	A	——————	CHI	A	Mike Fornieles
July 9, 1958	STL	N	——————	WAS	A	Waiver price

Milt Stock

DATE	TRADED TO		TRADED WITH	TRADED BY		IN EXCHANGE FOR
Jan 1915	PHI	N	Al Demaree Bert Adams	NY	N	Hans Lobert
Jan 21, 1919	STL	N	Pickles Dillhoefer Dixie Davis	PHI	N	Doug Baird Stuffy Stewart Gene Packard
April 27, 1924	BKN	N	——————	STL	N	Mike Gonzalez

Wes Stock

DATE	TRADED TO		TRADED WITH	TRADED BY		IN EXCHANGE FOR
June 15, 1964	KC	A	——————	BAL	A	Charlie Lau

Tim Stoddard

DATE	TRADED TO		TRADED WITH	TRADED BY		IN EXCHANGE FOR
Dec 8, 1983	OAK	A	——————	BAL	A	Wayne Gross
March 26, 1984	CHI	N	——————	OAK	A	Minor leaguers P Stan Kyles and OF Stan Boderick

Dean Stone

DATE	TRADED TO		TRADED WITH	TRADED BY		IN EXCHANGE FOR
April 29, 1957	BOS	A	Bob Chakales	WAS	A	Milt Bolling Russ Kemmerer Faye Throneberry
March 15, 1959	STL	N	——————	BOS	A	Nels Chittum
June 22, 1962	CHI	A	——————	HOU	N	Russ Kemmerer

George Stone

DATE	TRADED TO		TRADED WITH	TRADED BY		IN EXCHANGE FOR
Nov 2, 1972	NY	N	Felix Millan	ATL	N	Gary Gentry Danny Frisella
Feb 24, 1976	TEX	A	——————	NY	N	Bill Hands

George Stone

DATE	TRADED TO		TRADED WITH	TRADED BY		IN EXCHANGE FOR
Jan 16, 1904	WAS	A	——————	BOS	A	Cash
Jan 16, 1905	BOS	A	——————	WAS	A	Cash
Jan 16, 1905	STL	A	——————	BOS	A	Jesse Burkett

John Stone

DATE	TRADED TO		TRADED WITH	TRADED BY		IN EXCHANGE FOR
Dec 20, 1933	WAS	A	——————	DET	A	Goose Goslin

DATE	TRADED TO		TRADED WITH	TRADED BY		IN EXCHANGE FOR

Ron Stone
| Jan 20, 1969 | PHI | N | ———— | BAL | A | Clay Dalrymple |

Steve Stone
Nov 28, 1972	CHI	A	Ken Henderson	SF	N	Tom Bradley
Dec 11, 1973	CHI	N	Ken Frailing Steve Swisher Jim Kremmel	CHI	A	Ron Santo
Nov 24, 1976	CHI	A	————	CHI	N	No compensation (free agent signing)
Nov 29, 1978	BAL	A	————	CHI	A	No compensation (free agent signing)

Bill Stoneman
| April 4, 1974 | CAL | A | ———— | MON | N | Cash |

Alan Storke
| Aug 19, 1909 | STL | N | Jap Barbeau | PIT | N | Bobby Byrne |
| Feb 1910 | CIN | N | Fred Beebe | STL | N | Miller Huggins Rebel Oakes Frank Corridon |

Allyn Stout
| May 7, 1933 | CIN | N | ———— | STL | N | *See Leo Durocher* |
| Dec 14, 1934 | NY | N | Mark Koenig | CIN | N | Billy Myers and cash |

George Stovall
| Jan 1912 | STL | A | ———— | CLE | A | Lefty George |

Jesse Stovall
| Jan 1904 | DET | A | Ed Killian | CLE | A | Billy Lush |

Mike Strahler
| Nov 28, 1972 | CAL | A | ———— | LA | N | *See Andy Messersmith* |
| Dec 6, 1973 | MIL | A | ———— | DET | A | Ray Newman |

Joe Strain
| Dec 12, 1980 | CHI | N | Phil Nastu | SF | N | Jerry Martin Jesus Figueroa minor league IF Mike Turgeon |

Bob Strampe
| Nov 18, 1974 | SD | N | Ed Brinkman Dick Sharon | DET | A | Nate Colbert |

(Part of three-team trade involving San Diego, Detroit, and St. Louis Cardinals.)

Sammy Strang
Feb 1901	NY	N	————	CHI	N	Jack Doyle
March 1903	BKN	N	————	CHI	N	Cash
Feb 1905	NY	N	————	BKN	N	Cash

Alan Strange
| June 29, 1935 | WAS | A | ———— | STL | A | Lyn Lary |

DATE	TRADED TO		TRADED WITH	TRADED BY		IN EXCHANGE FOR

Gabby Street

June 6, 1905	BOS	N	—————	CIN	N	Cash
July 30, 1905	CIN	N	—————	BOS	N	Cash
Dec 1911	NY	A	Jack Lelivelt	WAS	A	John Knight Roxy Roach

George Strickland

| Aug 18, 1952 | CLE | A | Ted Wilks | PIT | N | Johnny Berardino
minor league
P Charlie Sipple
and $50,000. |

Jake Striker

| Dec 6, 1959 | CHI | A | ————— | CLE | A | *See Norm Cash* |

Nick Strincevich

| May 7, 1941 | PIT | N | ————— | BOS | N | Lloyd Waner |
| May 15, 1948 | PHI | N | ————— | PIT | N | Cash |

Joe Stripp

March 14, 1932	BKN	N	Tony Cuccinello Clyde Sukeforth	CIN	N	Babe Herman Wally Gilbert Ernie Lombardi
Oct 4, 1937	STL	N	Johnny Cooney Jim Bucher Roy Henshaw	BKN	N	Leo Durocher
Aug 1, 1938	BOS	N	—————	STL	N	Cash
Dec 13, 1938	BKN	N	—————	BOS	N	Fred Frankhouse

John Strohmayer

| July 16, 1973 | NY | N | ————— | MON | N | Cash |

Brent Strom

| Nov 27, 1972 | CLE | A | Bob Rauch | NY | N | Phil Hennigan |
| June 15, 1974 | SD | N | minor league
P Jerry Lee | CLE | A | Steve Arlin |

Ed Stroud

| June 15, 1967 | WAS | A | ————— | CHI | A | Jim King |
| March 29, 1971 | CHI | A | ————— | WAS | A | Tom McCraw |

Steve Stroughter

| Dec 19, 1980 | MIN | A | ————— | SEA | A | Mike Bacsik |

Amos Strunk

Dec 14, 1917	BOS	A	Joe Bush Wally Schang	PHI	A	Vean Gregg Merlin Kopp Pinch Thomas and $60,000.
June 27, 1919	PHI	A	Jack Barry	BOS	A	Braggo Roth Red Shannon
			(Barry refused to report, and retired.)			
July 23, 1920	CHI	A	—————	PHI	A	Waiver price
Aug 1924	PHI	A	—————	CHI	A	Waiver price

Dick Stuart

| Nov 20, 1962 | BOS | A | Jack Lamabe | PIT | N | Jim Pagliaroni
Don Schwall |

DATE	TRADED TO		TRADED WITH	TRADED BY		IN EXCHANGE FOR

Dick Stuart continued

DATE	TRADED TO		TRADED WITH	TRADED BY		IN EXCHANGE FOR
Nov 29, 1964	PHI	N	————	BOS	A	Dennis Bennett
Feb 22, 1966	NY	N	————	PHI	N	Jimmie Schaffer Bobby Klaus Wayne Graham

Marlin Stuart

DATE	TRADED TO		TRADED WITH	TRADED BY		IN EXCHANGE FOR
Aug 14, 1952	STL	A	*See Vic Wertz*	DET	A	————
July 4, 1954	NY	A	————	BAL	A	Waiver price

Bill Stumpf

DATE	TRADED TO		TRADED WITH	TRADED BY		IN EXCHANGE FOR
May 20, 1913	CLE	A	Jack Lelivelt	NY	A	Roger Peckinpaugh

John Stuper

DATE	TRADED TO		TRADED WITH	TRADED BY		IN EXCHANGE FOR
Sept 10, 1984	CIN	N	————	STL	N	Paul Householder

Tom Sturdivant

DATE	TRADED TO		TRADED WITH	TRADED BY		IN EXCHANGE FOR
May 26, 1959	KC	A	Johnny Kucks Jerry Lumpe	NY	A	Hector Lopez Ralph Terry
Dec 3, 1959	BOS	A	————	KC	A	Pete Daley
June 29, 1961	PIT	N	————	WAS	A	Tom Cheney
May 4, 1963	DET	A	————	PIT	N	Cash
July 23, 1963	KC	A	————	DET	A	Cash

Bobby Sturgeon

DATE	TRADED TO		TRADED WITH	TRADED BY		IN EXCHANGE FOR
March 1, 1948	BOS	N	————	CHI	N	Dick Culler

Ken Suarez

DATE	TRADED TO		TRADED WITH	TRADED BY		IN EXCHANGE FOR
Dec 2, 1971	TEX	A	————	CLE	A	*See Del Unser*
Feb 12, 1974	CLE	A	————	TEX	A	Leo Cardenas
Sept 12, 1974	CAL	A	Rusty Torres and cash	CLE	A	Frank Robinson

Jim Suchecki

DATE	TRADED TO		TRADED WITH	TRADED BY		IN EXCHANGE FOR
May 17, 1951	STL	A	Matt Batts Jim McDonald and $100,000.	BOS	A	Les Moss
March 4, 1952	PIT	N	————	STL	A	Cash
May 5, 1952	CHI	A	————	PIT	N	Waiver price

Bill Sudakis

DATE	TRADED TO		TRADED WITH	TRADED BY		IN EXCHANGE FOR
March 27, 1972	NY	N	————	LA	N	Cash
March 28, 1973	TEX	A	————	NY	N	Bill McNulty
Dec 7, 1973	NY	A	————	TEX	A	Cash
Dec 3, 1974	CAL	A	————	NY	A	Skip Lockwood

Willie Sudhoff

DATE	TRADED TO		TRADED WITH	TRADED BY		IN EXCHANGE FOR
Dec 1905	WAS	A	————	STL	A	Beany Jacobson

Joe Sugden

DATE	TRADED TO		TRADED WITH	TRADED BY		IN EXCHANGE FOR
Feb 1902	STL	A	————	CHI	A	Cash

Gus Suhr

DATE	TRADED TO		TRADED WITH	TRADED BY		IN EXCHANGE FOR
July 28, 1939	PHI	N	————	PIT	N	Max Butcher

DATE	TRADED TO		TRADED WITH	TRADED BY		IN EXCHANGE FOR

Clyde Sukeforth

March 14, 1932	BKN	N	Tony Cuccinello Joe Stripp	CIN	N	Babe Herman Wally Gilbert Ernie Lombardi

Billy Sullivan

Jan 29, 1936	CLE	A	———————	CIN	N	Cash
Feb 10, 1938	STL	A	Ed Cole Roy Hughes	CLE	A	Rollie Hemsley
Jan 30, 1940	DET	A	———————	STL	A	Slick Coffman
March 13, 1942	BKN	N	———————	DET	A	Cash

Denny Sullivan

Sept 1908	CLE	A	———————	BOS	A	Cash

Frank Sullivan

Dec 15, 1960	PHI	N	———————	BOS	A	Gene Conley

Haywood Sullivan

Dec 29, 1960	KC	A	———————	WAS	A	Marty Kutyna and cash

Joe Sullivan

June 20, 1941	PIT	N	———————	BOS	N	Cash

John Sullivan

May 11, 1921	CHI	N	———————	BOS	N	Cash

John Sullivan

Oct 4, 1948	STL	A	Tom Ferrick and $25,000.	WAS	A	Sam Dente

Homer Summa

Jan 5, 1929	PHI	A	———————	CLE	A	Cash

Champ Summers

April 6, 1975	CHI	N	cash	OAK	A	Jim Todd
Feb 16, 1977	CIN	N	———————	CHI	N	Dave Schneck
May 25, 1979	DET	A	———————	CIN	N	Sheldon Burnside
March 4, 1982	SF	N	———————	DET	A	Enos Cabell and cash
Dec 6, 1983	SD	N	———————	SF	N	Joe Pittman minor league OF Tommy Francis

Jim Sundberg

Dec 8, 1983	MIL	A	———————	TEX	A	Ned Yost minor league P Dan Scarpetta

Steve Sundra

Dec 11, 1935	NY	A	Monte Pearson	CLE	A	Johnny Allen
March 27, 1941	WAS	A	———————	NY	A	Cash
June 7, 1942	STL	A	Mike Chartak	WAS	A	Roy Cullenbine Bill Trotter

DATE	TRADED TO		TRADED WITH	TRADED BY		IN EXCHANGE FOR

Ron Taylor

DATE	TRADED TO		TRADED WITH	TRADED BY		IN EXCHANGE FOR
Dec 15, 1962	STL	N	Jack Kubiszyn	CLE	A	Fred Whitfield
June 15, 1965	HOU	N	Mike Cuellar	STL	N	Hal Woodeshick Chuck Taylor
Feb 10, 1967	NY	N	————	HOU	N	Cash
Oct 20, 1971	MON	N	————	NY	N	Cash

Sammy Taylor

DATE	TRADED TO		TRADED WITH	TRADED BY		IN EXCHANGE FOR
Dec 5, 1957	CHI	N	Taylor Phillips	MIL	N	Eddie Haas Don Kaiser Bob Rush
April 26, 1962	NY	N	————	CHI	N	Bobby Gene Smith
July 1, 1963	CIN	N	Charlie Neal	NY	N	Jesse Gonder
Aug 1, 1963	CLE	A	————	CIN	N	Gene Green

Tony Taylor

DATE	TRADED TO		TRADED WITH	TRADED BY		IN EXCHANGE FOR
May 13, 1960	PHI	N	Cal Neeman	CHI	N	Ed Bouchee Don Cardwell
June 12, 1971	DET	A	————	PHI	N	Minor league Ps Mike Fremuth and Carl Cavanaugh

Zack Taylor

DATE	TRADED TO		TRADED WITH	TRADED BY		IN EXCHANGE FOR
Oct 7, 1925	BOS	N	Jimmy Johnston Eddie Brown	BKN	N	Jesse Barnes Mickey O'Neil Gus Felix
June 12, 1927	NY	N	Larry Benton Herb Thomas	BOS	N	Hugh McQuillan Kent Greenfield Doc Farrell
Feb 1928	BOS	N	————	NY	N	Cash
July 6, 1929	CHI	N	————	BOS	N	Waiver price

Bud Teachout

DATE	TRADED TO		TRADED WITH	TRADED BY		IN EXCHANGE FOR
Dec 1931	STL	N	Hack Wilson	CHI	N	Burleigh Grimes

Birdie Tebbetts

DATE	TRADED TO		TRADED WITH	TRADED BY		IN EXCHANGE FOR
May 20, 1947	BOS	A	————	DET	A	Hal Wagner
Dec 13, 1950	CLE	A	————	BOS	A	Cash

Tom Tellmann

DATE	TRADED TO		TRADED WITH	TRADED BY		IN EXCHANGE FOR
Oct 15, 1982	MIL	A	————	SD	N	Minor league Ps Weldon Swift and Tim Cook

Johnny Temple

DATE	TRADED TO		TRADED WITH	TRADED BY		IN EXCHANGE FOR
Dec 15, 1959	CLE	A	————	CIN	N	Cal McLish Billy Martin Gordy Coleman
Nov 16, 1961	BAL	A	————	CLE	A	Ray Barker Harry Chiti and minor leaguer Art Kay
Aug 11, 1962	HOU	N	————	BAL	A	Cash

DATE	TRADED TO		TRADED WITH	TRADED BY		IN EXCHANGE FOR

Garry Templeton

| Dec 10, 1981 | SD | N | Sixto Lezcano
Luis DeLeon | STL | N | Ozzie Smith
Steve Mura
Alan Olmsted |

(Templeton and Smith were exchanged on February 11, 1982; Olmsted and DeLeon were exchanged on February 19.)

Gene Tenace

Dec 14, 1976	SD	N	————	OAK	A	No compensation (free agent signing)
Dec 8, 1980	STL	N	Rollie Fingers Bob Shirley minor league C Bob Geren	SD	N	Terry Kennedy Steve Swisher Mike Phillips John Littlefield John Urrea Kim Seaman Alan Olmsted
Dec 1, 1982	PIT	N	————	STL	N	No compensation (free agent signing)

Fred Tenney

| Dec 3, 1907 | NY | N | Al Bridwell
Tom Needham | BOS | N | Dan McGann
Frank Bowerman
Bill Dahlen
George Browne
George Ferguson |

Frank Tepedino

| June 7, 1971 | MIL | A | Bobby Mitchell | NY | A | Danny Walton |
| June 7, 1973 | ATL | N | Wayne Nordhagen
Al Closter
Dave Cheadle | NY | A | Pat Dobson |

Greg Terlecky

| Dec 12, 1975 | CHI | A | Buddy Bradford | STL | N | Lee Richard |

Jeff Terpko

| Nov 3, 1970 | PHI | N | Greg Goossen
Gene Martin | WAS | A | Curt Flood |
| March 15, 1977 | MON | N | ———— | TEX | A | Rodney Scott |

Walt Terrell

| April 1, 1982 | NY | N | Ron Darling | TEX | A | Lee Mazzilli |
| Dec 7, 1984 | DET | A | ———— | NY | N | Howard Johnson |

Ralph Terry

June 15, 1957	KC	A	Billy Martin Woodie Held Bob Martyn	NY	A	Ryne Duren Jim Pisoni Milt Graff Harry Simpson
May 26, 1959	NY	A	Hector Lopez	KC	A	Johnny Kucks Tom Sturdivant Jerry Lumpe
Sept 5, 1964	CLE	A	Buddy Daley and $75,000.	NY	A	Pedro Ramos
April 6, 1966	KC	A	cash	CLE	A	John O'Donoghue
Aug 6, 1966	NY	N	————	KC	A	Cash

Zeb Terry

| Jan 1920 | CHI | N | ———— | PIT | N | Cash |

DATE	TRADED TO		TRADED WITH	TRADED BY		IN EXCHANGE FOR

Faye Throneberry
| April 29, 1957 | WAS | A | Milt Bolling
Russ Kemmerer | BOS | A | Dean Stone
Bob Chakales |

Marv Throneberry
Dec 11, 1959	KC	A	Hank Bauer Don Larsen Norm Siebern	NY	A	Roger Maris Joe DeMaestri Kent Hadley
June 8, 1961	BAL	A	————	KC	A	Gene Stephens
May 9, 1962	NY	N	————	BAL	A	Hobie Landrith and cash

George Throop
| April 27, 1979 | HOU | N | ———— | KC | A | Keith Drumright |

Sloppy Thurston
| May 12, 1923 | CHI | A | ———— | STL | A | Cash |
| Jan 15, 1927 | WAS | A | Leo Mangum | CHI | A | Roger Peckinpaugh |

Luis Tiant
| Dec 10, 1969 | MIN | A | Stan Williams | CLE | A | Dean Chance
Bob Miller
Graig Nettles
Ted Uhlaender |
| Nov 13, 1978 | NY | A | ———— | BOS | A | No compensation
(free agent signing) |

Jay Tibbs
| June 15, 1984 | CIN | N | minor leaguers
3B Eddie Williams and
P Matt Bullinger | NY | N | Bruce Berenyi |

Dick Tidrow
April 27, 1974	NY	A	Chris Chambliss Cecil Upshaw	CLE	A	Fritz Peterson Steve Kline Fred Beene Tom Buskey
May 23, 1979	CHI	N	————	NY	A	Ray Burris
Jan 25, 1983	CHI	A	Scott Fletcher Pat Tabler Randy Martz	CHI	N	Steve Trout Warren Brusstar
Jan 27, 1984	NY	N	————	CHI	A	No compensation (free agent signing)

Bobby Tiefenauer
| Sept 8, 1955 | DET | A | ———— | STL | N | Ben Flowers |
| March 30, 1968 | CHI | N | ———— | CLE | A | Rob Gardner |

Verle Tiefenthaler
| Nov 30, 1961 | CHI | A | ———— | SF | N | *See Billy Pierce* |

Cotton Tierney
| May 22, 1923 | PHI | N | Whitey Glazner
and $50,000. | PIT | N | Lee Meadows
Johnny Rawlings |
| Dec 15, 1923 | BOS | N | ———— | PHI | N | Hod Ford
Ray Powell |

(Powell announced his intention to retire after the 1924 season. He remained with Boston, and Philadelphia received cash instead.)

| Feb 4, 1925 | BKN | N | ———— | BOS | N | Bernie Neis |

DATE	TRADED TO		TRADED WITH	TRADED BY		IN EXCHANGE FOR

Les Tietje

| May 5, 1936 | STL | A | —————— | CHI | A | Sugar Cain |

Bob Tillman

Aug 8, 1967	NY	A	——————	BOS	A	Cash
Dec 7, 1967	ATL	N	Dale Roberts	NY	A	Bobby Cox
Dec 2, 1970	MIL	A	——————	ATL	N	Hank Allen minor leaguers P Paul Click and IF John Ryan

Thad Tillotson

| Sept 10, 1966 | NY | A | cash | LA | N | Dick Schofield |

Tom Timmerman

| June 15, 1973 | CLE | A | Kevin Collins | DET | A | Ed Farmer |

Joe Tinker

| Dec 15, 1912 | CIN | N | Grover Lowdermilk Harry Chapman | CHI | N | Bert Humphries Red Corriden Pete Knisely Art Phelan Mike Mitchell |
| Dec 1913 | BKN | N | —————— | CIN | N | Dick Egan and $6,500. |

(Tinker demanded $2,000 of the purchase price; when this was refused, he jumped to the Federal League and the deal was cancelled.)

| Feb 10, 1916 | CHI | N | *See Three Finger Brown* | CHI | F | —————— |

Bud Tinning

| Nov 21, 1934 | STL | N | Dick Ward and cash | CHI | N | Tex Carleton |

Joe Tipton

Nov 22, 1948	CHI	A	——————	CLE	A	Joe Haynes
Oct 19, 1949	PHI	A	——————	CHI	A	Nellie Fox
June 23, 1952	CLE	A	——————	PHI	A	Waiver price
Jan 20, 1954	WAS	A	——————	CLE	A	Mickey Grasso

John Titus

| July 1, 1912 | BOS | N | —————— | PHI | N | Doc Miller |

Dave Tobik

| March 24, 1983 | TEX | A | —————— | DET | A | Johnny Grubb |

Jack Tobin

| Feb 1926 | WAS | A | Joe Bush | STL | A | Tom Zachary Win Ballou |
| July 31, 1926 | BOS | A | —————— | WAS | A | Cash |

Jim Tobin

| Dec 6, 1939 | BOS | N | cash | PIT | N | Johnny Lanning |
| Aug 1945 | DET | A | —————— | BOS | N | Cash |

Johnny Tobin

| Feb 10, 1916 | STL | A | *See Eddie Plank* | STL | F | —————— |